T0413323

2020
Harris
California
Manufacturers Register

Exclusive Provider of
Dun & Bradstreet Library Solutions

 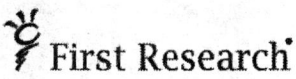 

Published January 2020 next update January 2021

Publisher

Mergent Inc.
444 Madison Ave
New York, NY 10022

©Mergent Inc All Rights Reserved
2020 Mergent Business Press
ISSN 1080-2614
ISBN 978-1-64141-594-1

MERGENT
BUSINESS PRESS
by FTSE Russell

TABLE OF CONTENTS

SUMMARY OF CONTENTS

Number of Companies 24,702

Number of Decision Makers 64,170

Minimum Number of Employees 10

EXPLANATORY NOTES

How to Cross-Reference in This Directory

This directory includes manufacturing establishments and corporate offices of manufacturing establishments. All of these firms are listed under Standard Industrial Classifications (SIC codes) 1011-1499 and 2011 through 3999. In addition, Prepackaged Software (SIC 7372), Tire Retreading & Repair Shops (SIC 7534), Welding Repair (SIC 7692), and Armature Rewinding Shops (SIC 7694) are also included in this directory because they frequently provide value-added services that can be considered a manufacturing process.

Source Suggestions Welcome

Although all known sources were used to compile this directory, it is possible that companies were inadvertently omitted. Your assistance in calling attention to such omissions would be greatly appreciated. A special form on the facing page will help you in the reporting process.

Analysis

Every effort has been made to contact all firms to verify their information. The one exception to this rule is the annual sales figure, which is considered by many companies to be confidential information. Therefore, estimated sales have been calculated by multiplying the nationwide average sales per employee for the firm's major SIC code by the firm's number of employees. Nationwide averages for sales per employee by 4-digit SIC code are provided by the U.S. Department of Commerce and are updated annually. All sales—sales (est)—have been estimated by this method. The exceptions are parent companies (PA), division headquarters (DH) and headquarter locations (HQ) which may include an actual corporate sales figure—sales (corporate-wide) if available.

Types of Companies

Descriptive and statistical data are included for companies in the entire state. These comprise manufacturers, machine shops, fabricators, assemblers, and printers. Also identified are corporate offices in the state.

Employment Data

This directory contains companies with 10 or more employees. The employment figure shown in the Products & Services Section includes male and female employees and embraces all levels of the company: administrative, clerical, sales and maintenance. This figure is for the facility listed and does not include other plants or offices. It should be recognized that these figures represent an approximate year-round average. These employment figures are broken into codes A through F and used in the Alphabetic and Geographic Sections to further help you in qualifying a company. Be sure to check the footnotes on the bottom right hand pages for the code breakdowns.

Standard Industrial Classification (SIC)

The Standard Industrial Classification (SIC) system used in this directory was developed by the federal government for use in classifying establishments by the type of activity they are engaged in. The SIC classifications used in this directory are from the 1987 edition published by the U.S. Government's Office of Management and Budget. The SIC system separates all activities into broad industrial divisions (e.g., manufacturing, mining, retail trade). It further subdivides each division. The range of manufacturing industry classes extends from two-digit codes (major industry group) to four-digit codes (product).

For example:

Industry Breakdown	Code	Industry, Product, etc.
*Major industry group	20	Food and kindred products
Industry group	203	Canned and frozen foods
*Industry	2033	Fruits and vegetables, etc.

*Classifications used in this directory

Only two-digit and four-digit codes are used in this directory.

Arrangement

1. The **Product & Services Section** contains complete in-depth corporate data. This section lists companies under their primary SIC. SIC codes are in numerical order with companies listed alphabetically under each code. A numerical and alphabetical index precedes this section.

> IMPORTANT NOTICE: It is a violation of both federal and state law to transmit an unsolicited advertisement to a facsimile machine. Any user of this product that violates such laws may be subject to civil and criminal penalties, which may exceed $500 for each transmission of an unsolicited facsimile. Mergent Inc. provides fax numbers for lawful purposes only and expressly forbids the use of these numbers in any unlawful manner.

3. The **Alphabetic Section** lists all companies with their full physical or mailing addresses and telephone number.

4. The **Geographic Section** is sorted by cities listed in alphabetic order and companies listed alphabetically within each city.

Selectory® Online Business Database

Get unlimited online access to the most accurate, up-to-date company profiles for ALL companies in the U.S., Mexico and Canada, as well as 200 countries worldwide. Build targeted lists and find new opportunities for sales in minutes! Register for your free trial at **mergentprivateonline.com**.

USER'S GUIDE TO LISTINGS

PRODUCT & SERVICES SECTION

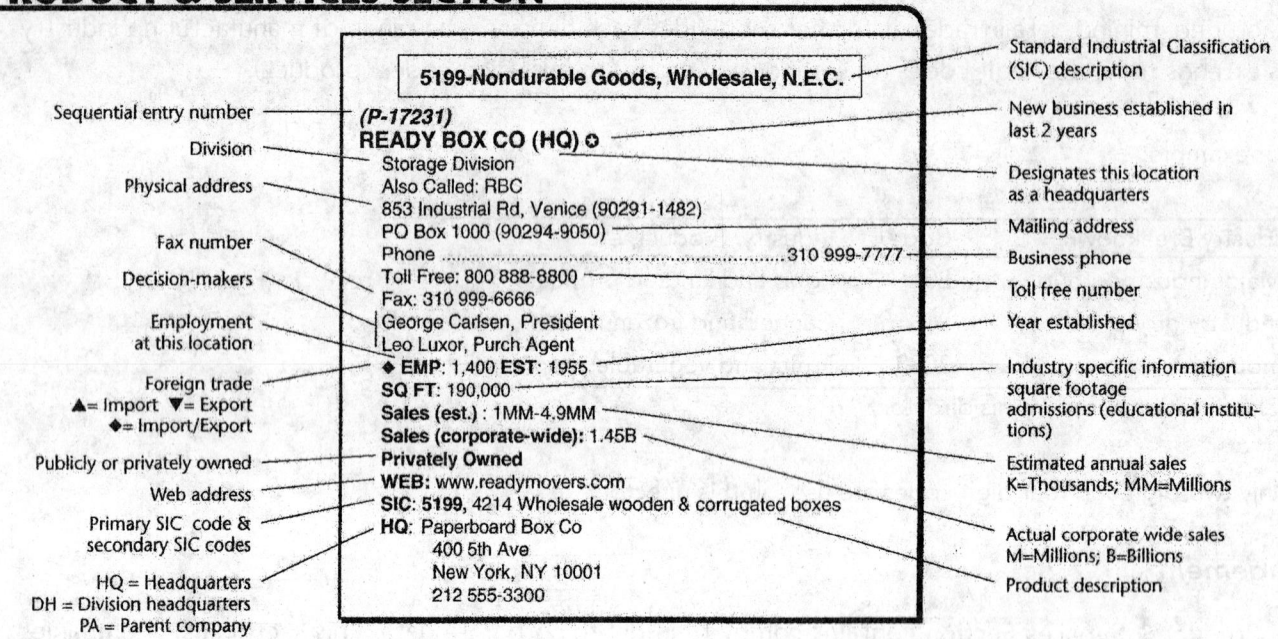

Sequential entry number
Division
Physical address
Fax number
Decision-makers
Employment at this location
Foreign trade ▲= Import ▼= Export ◆= Import/Export
Publicly or privately owned
Web address
Primary SIC code & secondary SIC codes
HQ = Headquarters DH = Division headquarters PA = Parent company

5199-Nondurable Goods, Wholesale, N.E.C.

(P-17231)
READY BOX CO (HQ) ✪
Storage Division
Also Called: RBC
853 Industrial Rd, Venice (90291-1482)
PO Box 1000 (90294-9050)
Phone 310 999-7777
Toll Free: 800 888-8800
Fax: 310 999-6666
George Carlsen, President
Leo Luxor, Purch Agent
◆ **EMP:** 1,400 **EST:** 1955
SQ FT: 190,000
Sales (est.) : 1MM-4.9MM
Sales (corporate-wide): 1.45B
Privately Owned
WEB: www.readymovers.com
SIC: 5199, 4214 Wholesale wooden & corrugated boxes
HQ: Paperboard Box Co
400 5th Ave
New York, NY 10001
212 555-3300

Standard Industrial Classification (SIC) description
New business established in last 2 years
Designates this location as a headquarters
Mailing address
Business phone
Toll free number
Year established
Industry specific information square footage admissions (educational institutions)
Estimated annual sales K=Thousands; MM=Millions
Actual corporate wide sales M=Millions; B=Billions
Product description

ALPHABETIC SECTION

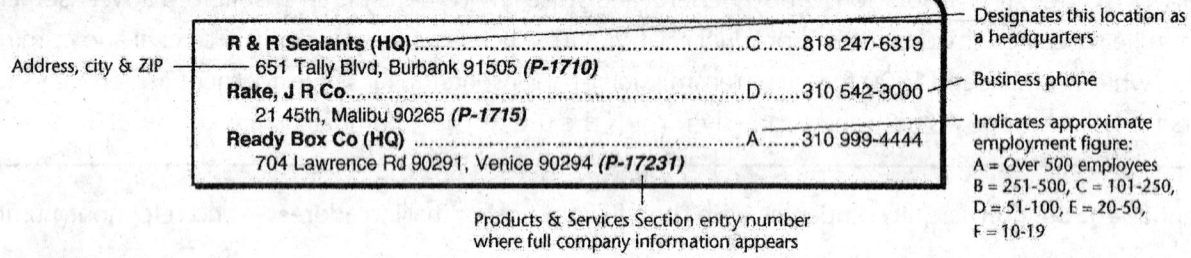

Address, city & ZIP

R & R Sealants (HQ) ....C......818 247-6319
651 Tally Blvd, Burbank 91505 **(P-1710)**
Rake, J R Co ....D......310 542-3000
21 45th, Malibu 90265 **(P-1715)**
Ready Box Co (HQ) ....A......310 999-4444
704 Lawrence Rd 90291, Venice 90294 **(P-17231)**

Designates this location as a headquarters
Business phone
Indicates approximate employment figure:
A = Over 500 employees
B = 251-500, C = 101-250,
D = 51-100, E = 20-50,
F = 10-19

Products & Services Section entry number where full company information appears

GEOGRAPHIC SECTION

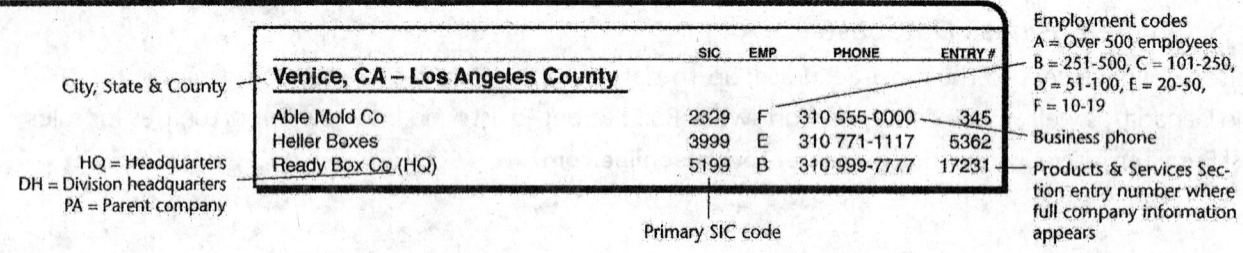

City, State & County

HQ = Headquarters
DH = Division headquarters
PA = Parent company

	SIC	EMP	PHONE	ENTRY #
Venice, CA – Los Angeles County				
Able Mold Co	2329	F	310 555-0000	345
Heller Boxes	3999	E	310 771-1117	5362
Ready Box Co (HQ)	5199	B	310 999-7777	17231

Employment codes
A = Over 500 employees
B = 251-500, C = 101-250,
D = 51-100, E = 20-50,
F = 10-19
Business phone
Products & Services Section entry number where full company information appears

Primary SIC code

6

NUMERICAL INDEX of SIC DESCRIPTIONS
ALPHABETICAL INDEX of SIC DESCRIPTIONS

PRODUCTS & SERVICES SECTION
Companies listed alphabetically under thier primary SIC
In-depth company data listed

ALPHABETIC SECTION
Company listings in alphabetical order

GEOGRAPHIC INDEX
Companies sorted by city in alphabetical order

SIC INDEX

PRDTS & SVCS

ALPHABETIC

GEOGRAPHIC

California
County Map

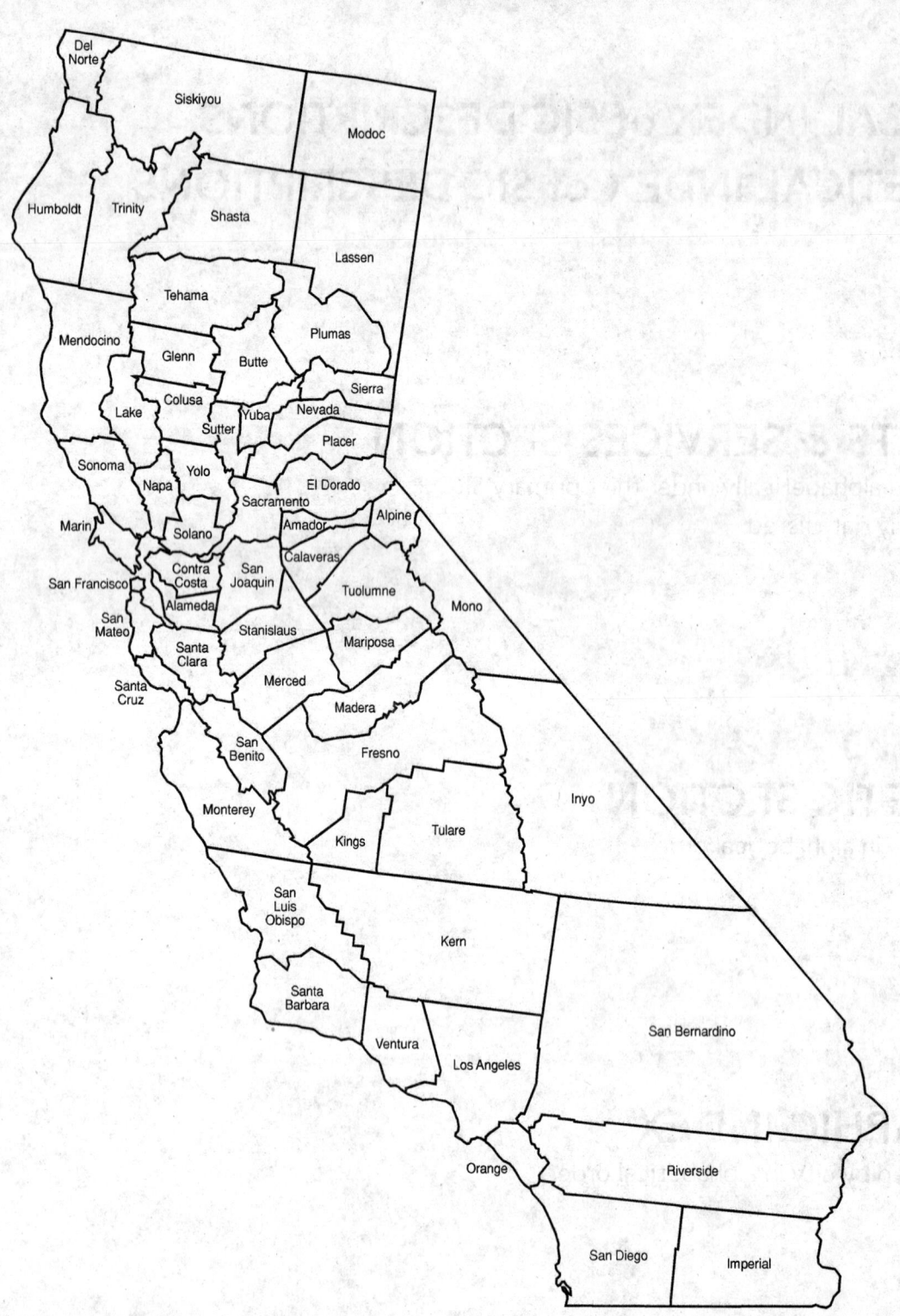

SIC INDEX

Standard Industrial Classification Numerical Index

SIC NO	PRODUCT

10 metal mining
1031 Lead & Zinc Ores
1041 Gold Ores
1044 Silver Ores
1081 Metal Mining Svcs
1099 Metal Ores, NEC

12 coal mining
1221 Bituminous Coal & Lignite: Surface Mining
1241 Coal Mining Svcs

13 oil and gas extraction
1311 Crude Petroleum & Natural Gas
1321 Natural Gas Liquids
1381 Drilling Oil & Gas Wells
1382 Oil & Gas Field Exploration Svcs
1389 Oil & Gas Field Svcs, NEC

14 mining and quarrying of nonmetallic minerals, except fuels
1411 Dimension Stone
1422 Crushed & Broken Limestone
1423 Crushed & Broken Granite
1429 Crushed & Broken Stone, NEC
1442 Construction Sand & Gravel
1446 Industrial Sand
1455 Kaolin & Ball Clay
1459 Clay, Ceramic & Refractory Minerals, NEC
1479 Chemical & Fertilizer Mining
1481 Nonmetallic Minerals Svcs, Except Fuels
1499 Miscellaneous Nonmetallic Mining

20 food and kindred products
2011 Meat Packing Plants
2013 Sausages & Meat Prdts
2015 Poultry Slaughtering, Dressing & Processing
2021 Butter
2022 Cheese
2023 Milk, Condensed & Evaporated
2024 Ice Cream
2026 Milk
2032 Canned Specialties
2033 Canned Fruits, Vegetables & Preserves
2034 Dried Fruits, Vegetables & Soup
2035 Pickled Fruits, Vegetables, Sauces & Dressings
2037 Frozen Fruits, Juices & Vegetables
2038 Frozen Specialties
2041 Flour, Grain Milling
2043 Cereal Breakfast Foods
2044 Rice Milling
2045 Flour, Blended & Prepared
2046 Wet Corn Milling
2047 Dog & Cat Food
2048 Prepared Feeds For Animals & Fowls
2051 Bread, Bakery Prdts Exc Cookies & Crackers
2052 Cookies & Crackers
2053 Frozen Bakery Prdts
2061 Sugar, Cane
2062 Sugar, Cane Refining
2063 Sugar, Beet
2064 Candy & Confectionery Prdts
2066 Chocolate & Cocoa Prdts
2067 Chewing Gum
2068 Salted & Roasted Nuts & Seeds
2074 Cottonseed Oil Mills
2075 Soybean Oil Mills
2076 Vegetable Oil Mills
2077 Animal, Marine Fats & Oils
2079 Shortening, Oils & Margarine
2082 Malt Beverages
2084 Wine & Brandy
2085 Liquors, Distilled, Rectified & Blended
2086 Soft Drinks
2087 Flavoring Extracts & Syrups
2091 Fish & Seafoods, Canned & Cured
2092 Fish & Seafoods, Fresh & Frozen
2095 Coffee
2096 Potato Chips & Similar Prdts
2097 Ice
2098 Macaroni, Spaghetti & Noodles
2099 Food Preparations, NEC

21 tobacco products
2111 Cigarettes
2121 Cigars
2131 Tobacco, Chewing & Snuff

22 textile mill products
2211 Cotton, Woven Fabric
2221 Silk & Man-Made Fiber
2231 Wool, Woven Fabric
2241 Fabric Mills, Cotton, Wool, Silk & Man-Made
2251 Hosiery, Women's Full & Knee Length
2252 Hosiery, Except Women's
2253 Knit Outerwear Mills
2254 Knit Underwear Mills
2257 Circular Knit Fabric Mills
2258 Lace & Warp Knit Fabric Mills
2259 Knitting Mills, NEC
2261 Cotton Fabric Finishers
2262 Silk & Man-Made Fabric Finishers
2269 Textile Finishers, NEC
2273 Carpets & Rugs
2281 Yarn Spinning Mills
2282 Yarn Texturizing, Throwing, Twisting & Winding Mills
2284 Thread Mills
2295 Fabrics Coated Not Rubberized
2296 Tire Cord & Fabric
2297 Fabrics, Nonwoven
2298 Cordage & Twine
2299 Textile Goods, NEC

23 apparel and other finished products made from fabrics and similar material
2311 Men's & Boys' Suits, Coats & Overcoats
2321 Men's & Boys' Shirts
2322 Men's & Boys' Underwear & Nightwear
2323 Men's & Boys' Neckwear
2325 Men's & Boys' Separate Trousers & Casual Slacks
2326 Men's & Boys' Work Clothing
2329 Men's & Boys' Clothing, NEC
2331 Women's & Misses' Blouses
2335 Women's & Misses' Dresses
2337 Women's & Misses' Suits, Coats & Skirts
2339 Women's & Misses' Outerwear, NEC
2341 Women's, Misses' & Children's Underwear & Nightwear
2342 Brassieres, Girdles & Garments
2353 Hats, Caps & Millinery
2361 Children's & Infants' Dresses & Blouses
2369 Girls' & Infants' Outerwear, NEC
2371 Fur Goods
2381 Dress & Work Gloves
2384 Robes & Dressing Gowns
2385 Waterproof Outerwear
2386 Leather & Sheep Lined Clothing
2387 Apparel Belts
2389 Apparel & Accessories, NEC
2391 Curtains & Draperies
2392 House furnishings: Textile
2393 Textile Bags
2394 Canvas Prdts
2395 Pleating & Stitching For The Trade
2396 Automotive Trimmings, Apparel Findings, Related Prdts
2397 Schiffli Machine Embroideries
2399 Fabricated Textile Prdts, NEC

24 lumber and wood products, except furniture
2411 Logging
2421 Saw & Planing Mills
2426 Hardwood Dimension & Flooring Mills
2429 Special Prdt Sawmills, NEC
2431 Millwork
2434 Wood Kitchen Cabinets
2435 Hardwood Veneer & Plywood
2436 Softwood Veneer & Plywood
2439 Structural Wood Members, NEC
2441 Wood Boxes
2448 Wood Pallets & Skids
2449 Wood Containers, NEC
2451 Mobile Homes
2452 Prefabricated Wood Buildings & Cmpnts
2491 Wood Preserving
2493 Reconstituted Wood Prdts
2499 Wood Prdts, NEC

25 furniture and fixtures
2511 Wood Household Furniture
2512 Wood Household Furniture, Upholstered
2514 Metal Household Furniture
2515 Mattresses & Bedsprings
2517 Wood T V, Radio, Phono & Sewing Cabinets
2519 Household Furniture, NEC
2521 Wood Office Furniture
2522 Office Furniture, Except Wood
2531 Public Building & Related Furniture
2541 Wood, Office & Store Fixtures
2542 Partitions & Fixtures, Except Wood
2591 Drapery Hardware, Window Blinds & Shades
2599 Furniture & Fixtures, NEC

26 paper and allied products
2611 Pulp Mills
2621 Paper Mills
2631 Paperboard Mills
2652 Set-Up Paperboard Boxes
2653 Corrugated & Solid Fiber Boxes
2655 Fiber Cans, Tubes & Drums
2656 Sanitary Food Containers
2657 Folding Paperboard Boxes
2671 Paper Coating & Laminating for Packaging
2672 Paper Coating & Laminating, Exc for Packaging
2673 Bags: Plastics, Laminated & Coated
2674 Bags: Uncoated Paper & Multiwall
2675 Die-Cut Paper & Board
2676 Sanitary Paper Prdts
2677 Envelopes
2678 Stationery Prdts
2679 Converted Paper Prdts, NEC

27 printing, publishing, and allied industries
2711 Newspapers: Publishing & Printing
2721 Periodicals: Publishing & Printing
2731 Books: Publishing & Printing
2732 Book Printing, Not Publishing
2741 Misc Publishing
2752 Commercial Printing: Lithographic
2754 Commercial Printing: Gravure
2759 Commercial Printing
2761 Manifold Business Forms
2771 Greeting Card Publishing
2782 Blankbooks & Looseleaf Binders
2789 Bookbinding
2791 Typesetting
2796 Platemaking & Related Svcs

28 chemicals and allied products
2812 Alkalies & Chlorine
2813 Industrial Gases
2816 Inorganic Pigments
2819 Indl Inorganic Chemicals, NEC
2821 Plastics, Mtrls & Nonvulcanizable Elastomers
2822 Synthetic Rubber (Vulcanizable Elastomers)
2823 Cellulosic Man-Made Fibers
2824 Synthetic Organic Fibers, Exc Cellulosic
2833 Medicinal Chemicals & Botanical Prdts
2834 Pharmaceuticals
2835 Diagnostic Substances
2836 Biological Prdts, Exc Diagnostic Substances
2841 Soap & Detergents
2842 Spec Cleaning, Polishing & Sanitation Preparations
2843 Surface Active & Finishing Agents, Sulfonated Oils
2844 Perfumes, Cosmetics & Toilet Preparations
2851 Paints, Varnishes, Lacquers, Enamels
2861 Gum & Wood Chemicals
2865 Cyclic-Crudes, Intermediates, Dyes & Org Pigments
2869 Industrial Organic Chemicals, NEC
2873 Nitrogenous Fertilizers
2874 Phosphatic Fertilizers
2875 Fertilizers, Mixing Only
2879 Pesticides & Agricultural Chemicals, NEC
2891 Adhesives & Sealants
2892 Explosives
2893 Printing Ink
2895 Carbon Black
2899 Chemical Preparations, NEC

29 petroleum refining and related industries
2911 Petroleum Refining

SIC NO	PRODUCT
2951	Paving Mixtures & Blocks
2952	Asphalt Felts & Coatings
2992	Lubricating Oils & Greases
2999	Products Of Petroleum & Coal, NEC

30 rubber and miscellaneous plastics products

SIC NO	PRODUCT
3011	Tires & Inner Tubes
3021	Rubber & Plastic Footwear
3052	Rubber & Plastic Hose & Belting
3053	Gaskets, Packing & Sealing Devices
3061	Molded, Extruded & Lathe-Cut Rubber Mechanical Goods
3069	Fabricated Rubber Prdts, NEC
3081	Plastic Unsupported Sheet & Film
3082	Plastic Unsupported Profile Shapes
3083	Plastic Laminated Plate & Sheet
3084	Plastic Pipe
3085	Plastic Bottles
3086	Plastic Foam Prdts
3087	Custom Compounding Of Purchased Plastic Resins
3088	Plastic Plumbing Fixtures
3089	Plastic Prdts

31 leather and leather products

SIC NO	PRODUCT
3111	Leather Tanning & Finishing
3131	Boot & Shoe Cut Stock & Findings
3142	House Slippers
3143	Men's Footwear, Exc Athletic
3144	Women's Footwear, Exc Athletic
3149	Footwear, NEC
3151	Leather Gloves & Mittens
3161	Luggage
3171	Handbags & Purses
3172	Personal Leather Goods
3199	Leather Goods, NEC

32 stone, clay, glass, and concrete products

SIC NO	PRODUCT
3211	Flat Glass
3221	Glass Containers
3229	Pressed & Blown Glassware, NEC
3231	Glass Prdts Made Of Purchased Glass
3241	Cement, Hydraulic
3251	Brick & Structural Clay Tile
3253	Ceramic Tile
3255	Clay Refractories
3259	Structural Clay Prdts, NEC
3261	China Plumbing Fixtures & Fittings
3262	China, Table & Kitchen Articles
3263	Earthenware, Whiteware, Table & Kitchen Articles
3264	Porcelain Electrical Splys
3269	Pottery Prdts, NEC
3271	Concrete Block & Brick
3272	Concrete Prdts
3273	Ready-Mixed Concrete
3274	Lime
3275	Gypsum Prdts
3281	Cut Stone Prdts
3291	Abrasive Prdts
3292	Asbestos products
3295	Minerals & Earths: Ground Or Treated
3296	Mineral Wool
3297	Nonclay Refractories
3299	Nonmetallic Mineral Prdts, NEC

33 primary metal industries

SIC NO	PRODUCT
3312	Blast Furnaces, Coke Ovens, Steel & Rolling Mills
3313	Electrometallurgical Prdts
3315	Steel Wire Drawing & Nails & Spikes
3316	Cold Rolled Steel Sheet, Strip & Bars
3317	Steel Pipe & Tubes
3321	Gray Iron Foundries
3322	Malleable Iron Foundries
3324	Steel Investment Foundries
3325	Steel Foundries, NEC
3331	Primary Smelting & Refining Of Copper
3334	Primary Production Of Aluminum
3339	Primary Nonferrous Metals, NEC
3341	Secondary Smelting & Refining Of Nonferrous Metals
3351	Rolling, Drawing & Extruding Of Copper
3353	Aluminum Sheet, Plate & Foil
3354	Aluminum Extruded Prdts
3355	Aluminum Rolling & Drawing, NEC
3356	Rolling, Drawing-Extruding Of Nonferrous Metals
3357	Nonferrous Wire Drawing
3363	Aluminum Die Castings
3364	Nonferrous Die Castings, Exc Aluminum
3365	Aluminum Foundries
3366	Copper Foundries
3369	Nonferrous Foundries: Castings, NEC
3398	Metal Heat Treating

SIC NO	PRODUCT
3399	Primary Metal Prdts, NEC

34 fabricated metal products, except machinery and transportation equipment

SIC NO	PRODUCT
3411	Metal Cans
3412	Metal Barrels, Drums, Kegs & Pails
3421	Cutlery
3423	Hand & Edge Tools
3425	Hand Saws & Saw Blades
3429	Hardware, NEC
3431	Enameled Iron & Metal Sanitary Ware
3432	Plumbing Fixture Fittings & Trim, Brass
3433	Heating Eqpt
3441	Fabricated Structural Steel
3442	Metal Doors, Sash, Frames, Molding & Trim
3443	Fabricated Plate Work
3444	Sheet Metal Work
3446	Architectural & Ornamental Metal Work
3448	Prefabricated Metal Buildings & Cmpnts
3449	Misc Structural Metal Work
3451	Screw Machine Prdts
3452	Bolts, Nuts, Screws, Rivets & Washers
3462	Iron & Steel Forgings
3463	Nonferrous Forgings
3465	Automotive Stampings
3466	Crowns & Closures
3469	Metal Stampings, NEC
3471	Electroplating, Plating, Polishing, Anodizing & Coloring
3479	Coating & Engraving, NEC
3482	Small Arms Ammunition
3483	Ammunition, Large
3484	Small Arms
3489	Ordnance & Access, NEC
3491	Industrial Valves
3492	Fluid Power Valves & Hose Fittings
3493	Steel Springs, Except Wire
3494	Valves & Pipe Fittings, NEC
3495	Wire Springs
3496	Misc Fabricated Wire Prdts
3497	Metal Foil & Leaf
3498	Fabricated Pipe & Pipe Fittings
3499	Fabricated Metal Prdts, NEC

35 industrial and commercial machinery and computer equipment

SIC NO	PRODUCT
3511	Steam, Gas & Hydraulic Turbines & Engines
3519	Internal Combustion Engines, NEC
3523	Farm Machinery & Eqpt
3524	Garden, Lawn Tractors & Eqpt
3531	Construction Machinery & Eqpt
3532	Mining Machinery & Eqpt
3533	Oil Field Machinery & Eqpt
3534	Elevators & Moving Stairways
3535	Conveyors & Eqpt
3536	Hoists, Cranes & Monorails
3537	Indl Trucks, Tractors, Trailers & Stackers
3541	Machine Tools: Cutting
3542	Machine Tools: Forming
3543	Industrial Patterns
3544	Dies, Tools, Jigs, Fixtures & Indl Molds
3545	Machine Tool Access
3546	Power Hand Tools
3547	Rolling Mill Machinery & Eqpt
3548	Welding Apparatus
3549	Metalworking Machinery, NEC
3552	Textile Machinery
3553	Woodworking Machinery
3554	Paper Inds Machinery
3555	Printing Trades Machinery & Eqpt
3556	Food Prdts Machinery
3559	Special Ind Machinery, NEC
3561	Pumps & Pumping Eqpt
3562	Ball & Roller Bearings
3563	Air & Gas Compressors
3564	Blowers & Fans
3565	Packaging Machinery
3566	Speed Changers, Drives & Gears
3567	Indl Process Furnaces & Ovens
3568	Mechanical Power Transmission Eqpt, NEC
3569	Indl Machinery & Eqpt, NEC
3571	Electronic Computers
3572	Computer Storage Devices
3575	Computer Terminals
3577	Computer Peripheral Eqpt, NEC
3578	Calculating & Accounting Eqpt
3579	Office Machines, NEC
3581	Automatic Vending Machines
3582	Commercial Laundry, Dry Clean & Pressing Mchs
3585	Air Conditioning & Heating Eqpt
3586	Measuring & Dispensing Pumps

SIC NO	PRODUCT
3589	Service Ind Machines, NEC
3592	Carburetors, Pistons, Rings & Valves
3593	Fluid Power Cylinders & Actuators
3594	Fluid Power Pumps & Motors
3596	Scales & Balances, Exc Laboratory
3599	Machinery & Eqpt, Indl & Commercial, NEC

36 electronic and other electrical equipment and components, except computer

SIC NO	PRODUCT
3612	Power, Distribution & Specialty Transformers
3613	Switchgear & Switchboard Apparatus
3621	Motors & Generators
3624	Carbon & Graphite Prdts
3625	Relays & Indl Controls
3629	Electrical Indl Apparatus, NEC
3631	Household Cooking Eqpt
3632	Household Refrigerators & Freezers
3634	Electric Household Appliances
3635	Household Vacuum Cleaners
3639	Household Appliances, NEC
3641	Electric Lamps
3643	Current-Carrying Wiring Devices
3644	Noncurrent-Carrying Wiring Devices
3645	Residential Lighting Fixtures
3646	Commercial, Indl & Institutional Lighting Fixtures
3647	Vehicular Lighting Eqpt
3648	Lighting Eqpt, NEC
3651	Household Audio & Video Eqpt
3652	Phonograph Records & Magnetic Tape
3661	Telephone & Telegraph Apparatus
3663	Radio & T V Communications, Systs & Eqpt, Broadcast/Studio
3669	Communications Eqpt, NEC
3671	Radio & T V Receiving Electron Tubes
3672	Printed Circuit Boards
3674	Semiconductors
3675	Electronic Capacitors
3676	Electronic Resistors
3677	Electronic Coils & Transformers
3678	Electronic Connectors
3679	Electronic Components, NEC
3691	Storage Batteries
3692	Primary Batteries: Dry & Wet
3694	Electrical Eqpt For Internal Combustion Engines
3695	Recording Media
3699	Electrical Machinery, Eqpt & Splys, NEC

37 transportation equipment

SIC NO	PRODUCT
3711	Motor Vehicles & Car Bodies
3713	Truck & Bus Bodies
3714	Motor Vehicle Parts & Access
3715	Truck Trailers
3716	Motor Homes
3721	Aircraft
3724	Aircraft Engines & Engine Parts
3728	Aircraft Parts & Eqpt, NEC
3731	Shipbuilding & Repairing
3732	Boat Building & Repairing
3743	Railroad Eqpt
3751	Motorcycles, Bicycles & Parts
3761	Guided Missiles & Space Vehicles
3764	Guided Missile/Space Vehicle Propulsion Units & parts
3769	Guided Missile/Space Vehicle Parts & Eqpt, NEC
3792	Travel Trailers & Campers
3795	Tanks & Tank Components
3799	Transportation Eqpt, NEC

38 measuring, analyzing and controlling instruments; photographic, medical an

SIC NO	PRODUCT
3812	Search, Detection, Navigation & Guidance Systs & Instrs
3821	Laboratory Apparatus & Furniture
3822	Automatic Temperature Controls
3823	Indl Instruments For Meas, Display & Control
3824	Fluid Meters & Counters
3825	Instrs For Measuring & Testing Electricity
3826	Analytical Instruments
3827	Optical Instruments
3829	Measuring & Controlling Devices, NEC
3841	Surgical & Medical Instrs & Apparatus
3842	Orthopedic, Prosthetic & Surgical Appliances/Splys
3843	Dental Eqpt & Splys
3844	X-ray Apparatus & Tubes
3845	Electromedical & Electrotherapeutic Apparatus
3851	Ophthalmic Goods
3861	Photographic Eqpt & Splys
3873	Watch & Clock Devices & Parts

39 miscellaneous manufacturing industries

SIC NO	PRODUCT
3911	Jewelry: Precious Metal
3914	Silverware, Plated & Stainless Steel Ware

SIC

SIC INDEX

SIC NO	PRODUCT

A

3291 Abrasive Prdts
2891 Adhesives & Sealants
3563 Air & Gas Compressors
3585 Air Conditioning & Heating Eqpt
3721 Aircraft
3724 Aircraft Engines & Engine Parts
3728 Aircraft Parts & Eqpt, NEC
2812 Alkalies & Chlorine
3363 Aluminum Die Castings
3354 Aluminum Extruded Prdts
3365 Aluminum Foundries
3355 Aluminum Rolling & Drawing, NEC
3353 Aluminum Sheet, Plate & Foil
3483 Ammunition, Large
3826 Analytical Instruments
2077 Animal, Marine Fats & Oils
2389 Apparel & Accessories, NEC
2387 Apparel Belts
3446 Architectural & Ornamental Metal Work
7694 Armature Rewinding Shops
3292 Asbestos products
2952 Asphalt Felts & Coatings
3822 Automatic Temperature Controls
3581 Automatic Vending Machines
3465 Automotive Stampings
2396 Automotive Trimmings, Apparel Findings, Related Prdts

B

2673 Bags: Plastics, Laminated & Coated
2674 Bags: Uncoated Paper & Multiwall
3562 Ball & Roller Bearings
2836 Biological Prdts, Exc Diagnostic Substances
1221 Bituminous Coal & Lignite: Surface Mining
2782 Blankbooks & Looseleaf Binders
3312 Blast Furnaces, Coke Ovens, Steel & Rolling Mills
3564 Blowers & Fans
3732 Boat Building & Repairing
3452 Bolts, Nuts, Screws, Rivets & Washers
2732 Book Printing, Not Publishing
2789 Bookbinding
2731 Books: Publishing & Printing
3131 Boot & Shoe Cut Stock & Findings
2342 Brassieres, Girdles & Garments
2051 Bread, Bakery Prdts Exc Cookies & Crackers
3251 Brick & Structural Clay Tile
3991 Brooms & Brushes
3995 Burial Caskets
2021 Butter

C

3578 Calculating & Accounting Eqpt
2064 Candy & Confectionery Prdts
2033 Canned Fruits, Vegetables & Preserves
2032 Canned Specialties
2394 Canvas Prdts
3624 Carbon & Graphite Prdts
2895 Carbon Black
3955 Carbon Paper & Inked Ribbons
3592 Carburetors, Pistons, Rings & Valves
2273 Carpets & Rugs
2823 Cellulosic Man-Made Fibers
3241 Cement, Hydraulic
3253 Ceramic Tile
2043 Cereal Breakfast Foods
2022 Cheese
1479 Chemical & Fertilizer Mining
2899 Chemical Preparations, NEC
2067 Chewing Gum
2361 Children's & Infants' Dresses & Blouses
3261 China Plumbing Fixtures & Fittings
3262 China, Table & Kitchen Articles
2066 Chocolate & Cocoa Prdts
2111 Cigarettes
2121 Cigars
2257 Circular Knit Fabric Mills
3255 Clay Refractories
1459 Clay, Ceramic & Refractory Minerals, NEC
1241 Coal Mining Svcs
3479 Coating & Engraving, NEC
2095 Coffee
3316 Cold Rolled Steel Sheet, Strip & Bars
3582 Commercial Laundry, Dry Clean & Pressing Mchs
2759 Commercial Printing
2754 Commercial Printing: Gravure
2752 Commercial Printing: Lithographic

3646 Commercial, Indl & Institutional Lighting Fixtures
3669 Communications Eqpt, NEC
3577 Computer Peripheral Eqpt, NEC
3572 Computer Storage Devices
3575 Computer Terminals
3271 Concrete Block & Brick
3272 Concrete Prdts
3531 Construction Machinery & Eqpt
1442 Construction Sand & Gravel
2679 Converted Paper Prdts, NEC
3535 Conveyors & Eqpt
2052 Cookies & Crackers
3366 Copper Foundries
2298 Cordage & Twine
2653 Corrugated & Solid Fiber Boxes
3961 Costume Jewelry & Novelties
2261 Cotton Fabric Finishers
2211 Cotton, Woven Fabric
2074 Cottonseed Oil Mills
3466 Crowns & Closures
1311 Crude Petroleum & Natural Gas
1423 Crushed & Broken Granite
1422 Crushed & Broken Limestone
1429 Crushed & Broken Stone, NEC
3643 Current-Carrying Wiring Devices
2391 Curtains & Draperies
3087 Custom Compounding Of Purchased Plastic Resins
3281 Cut Stone Prdts
3421 Cutlery
2865 Cyclic-Crudes, Intermediates, Dyes & Org Pigments

D

3843 Dental Eqpt & Splys
2835 Diagnostic Substances
2675 Die-Cut Paper & Board
3544 Dies, Tools, Jigs, Fixtures & Indl Molds
1411 Dimension Stone
2047 Dog & Cat Food
3942 Dolls & Stuffed Toys
2591 Drapery Hardware, Window Blinds & Shades
2381 Dress & Work Gloves
2034 Dried Fruits, Vegetables & Soup
1381 Drilling Oil & Gas Wells

E

3263 Earthenware, Whiteware, Table & Kitchen Articles
3634 Electric Household Appliances
3641 Electric Lamps
3694 Electrical Eqpt For Internal Combustion Engines
3629 Electrical Indl Apparatus, NEC
3699 Electrical Machinery, Eqpt & Splys, NEC
3845 Electromedical & Electrotherapeutic Apparatus
3313 Electrometallurgical Prdts
3675 Electronic Capacitors
3677 Electronic Coils & Transformers
3679 Electronic Components, NEC
3571 Electronic Computers
3678 Electronic Connectors
3676 Electronic Resistors
3471 Electroplating, Plating, Polishing, Anodizing & Coloring
3534 Elevators & Moving Stairways
3431 Enameled Iron & Metal Sanitary Ware
2677 Envelopes
2892 Explosives

F

2241 Fabric Mills, Cotton, Wool, Silk & Man-Made
3499 Fabricated Metal Prdts, NEC
3498 Fabricated Pipe & Pipe Fittings
3443 Fabricated Plate Work
3069 Fabricated Rubber Prdts, NEC
3441 Fabricated Structural Steel
2399 Fabricated Textile Prdts, NEC
2295 Fabrics Coated Not Rubberized
2297 Fabrics, Nonwoven
3523 Farm Machinery & Eqpt
3965 Fasteners, Buttons, Needles & Pins
2875 Fertilizers, Mixing Only
2655 Fiber Cans, Tubes & Drums
2091 Fish & Seafoods, Canned & Cured
2092 Fish & Seafoods, Fresh & Frozen
3211 Flat Glass
2087 Flavoring Extracts & Syrups
2045 Flour, Blended & Prepared
2041 Flour, Grain Milling
3824 Fluid Meters & Counters

3593 Fluid Power Cylinders & Actuators
3594 Fluid Power Pumps & Motors
3492 Fluid Power Valves & Hose Fittings
2657 Folding Paperboard Boxes
3556 Food Prdts Machinery
2099 Food Preparations, NEC
3149 Footwear, NEC
2053 Frozen Bakery Prdts
2037 Frozen Fruits, Juices & Vegetables
2038 Frozen Specialties
2371 Fur Goods
2599 Furniture & Fixtures, NEC

G

3944 Games, Toys & Children's Vehicles
3524 Garden, Lawn Tractors & Eqpt
3053 Gaskets, Packing & Sealing Devices
2369 Girls' & Infants' Outerwear, NEC
3221 Glass Containers
3231 Glass Prdts Made Of Purchased Glass
1041 Gold Ores
3321 Gray Iron Foundries
2771 Greeting Card Publishing
3769 Guided Missile/Space Vehicle Parts & Eqpt, NEC
3764 Guided Missile/Space Vehicle Propulsion Units & parts
3761 Guided Missiles & Space Vehicles
2861 Gum & Wood Chemicals
3275 Gypsum Prdts

H

3423 Hand & Edge Tools
3425 Hand Saws & Saw Blades
3171 Handbags & Purses
3429 Hardware, NEC
2426 Hardwood Dimension & Flooring Mills
2435 Hardwood Veneer & Plywood
2353 Hats, Caps & Millinery
3433 Heating Eqpt
3536 Hoists, Cranes & Monorails
2252 Hosiery, Except Women's
2251 Hosiery, Women's Full & Knee Length
2392 House furnishings: Textile
3142 House Slippers
3639 Household Appliances, NEC
3651 Household Audio & Video Eqpt
3631 Household Cooking Eqpt
2519 Household Furniture, NEC
3632 Household Refrigerators & Freezers
3635 Household Vacuum Cleaners

I

2097 Ice
2024 Ice Cream
2819 Indl Inorganic Chemicals, NEC
3823 Indl Instruments For Meas, Display & Control
3569 Indl Machinery & Eqpt, NEC
3567 Indl Process Furnaces & Ovens
3537 Indl Trucks, Tractors, Trailers & Stackers
2813 Industrial Gases
2869 Industrial Organic Chemicals, NEC
3543 Industrial Patterns
1446 Industrial Sand
3491 Industrial Valves
2816 Inorganic Pigments
3825 Instrs For Measuring & Testing Electricity
3519 Internal Combustion Engines, NEC
3462 Iron & Steel Forgings

J

3915 Jewelers Findings & Lapidary Work
3911 Jewelry: Precious Metal

K

1455 Kaolin & Ball Clay
2253 Knit Outerwear Mills
2254 Knit Underwear Mills
2259 Knitting Mills, NEC

L

3821 Laboratory Apparatus & Furniture
2258 Lace & Warp Knit Fabric Mills
1031 Lead & Zinc Ores
3952 Lead Pencils, Crayons & Artist's Mtrls
2386 Leather & Sheep Lined Clothing
3151 Leather Gloves & Mittens
3199 Leather Goods, NEC
3111 Leather Tanning & Finishing

S
I
C

SIC NO	PRODUCT	SIC NO	PRODUCT	SIC NO	PRODUCT

3648 Lighting Eqpt, NEC
3274 Lime
3996 Linoleum & Hard Surface Floor Coverings, NEC
2085 Liquors, Distilled, Rectified & Blended
2411 Logging
2992 Lubricating Oils & Greases
3161 Luggage

M

2098 Macaroni, Spaghetti & Noodles
3545 Machine Tool Access
3541 Machine Tools: Cutting
3542 Machine Tools: Forming
3599 Machinery & Eqpt, Indl & Commercial, NEC
3322 Malleable Iron Foundries
2082 Malt Beverages
2761 Manifold Business Forms
3999 Manufacturing Industries, NEC
3953 Marking Devices
2515 Mattresses & Bedsprings
3829 Measuring & Controlling Devices, NEC
3586 Measuring & Dispensing Pumps
2011 Meat Packing Plants
3568 Mechanical Power Transmission Eqpt, NEC
2833 Medicinal Chemicals & Botanical Prdts
2329 Men's & Boys' Clothing, NEC
2323 Men's & Boys' Neckwear
2325 Men's & Boys' Separate Trousers & Casual Slacks
2321 Men's & Boys' Shirts
2311 Men's & Boys' Suits, Coats & Overcoats
2322 Men's & Boys' Underwear & Nightwear
2326 Men's & Boys' Work Clothing
3143 Men's Footwear, Exc Athletic
3412 Metal Barrels, Drums, Kegs & Pails
3411 Metal Cans
3442 Metal Doors, Sash, Frames, Molding & Trim
3497 Metal Foil & Leaf
3398 Metal Heat Treating
2514 Metal Household Furniture
1081 Metal Mining Svcs
1099 Metal Ores, NEC
3469 Metal Stampings, NEC
3549 Metalworking Machinery, NEC
2026 Milk
2023 Milk, Condensed & Evaporated
2431 Millwork
3296 Mineral Wool
3295 Minerals & Earths: Ground Or Treated
3532 Mining Machinery & Eqpt
3496 Misc Fabricated Wire Prdts
2741 Misc Publishing
3449 Misc Structural Metal Work
1499 Miscellaneous Nonmetallic Mining
2451 Mobile Homes
3061 Molded, Extruded & Lathe-Cut Rubber Mechanical Goods
3716 Motor Homes
3714 Motor Vehicle Parts & Access
3711 Motor Vehicles & Car Bodies
3751 Motorcycles, Bicycles & Parts
3621 Motors & Generators
3931 Musical Instruments

N

1321 Natural Gas Liquids
2711 Newspapers: Publishing & Printing
2873 Nitrogenous Fertilizers
3297 Nonclay Refractories
3644 Noncurrent-Carrying Wiring Devices
3364 Nonferrous Die Castings, Exc Aluminum
3463 Nonferrous Forgings
3369 Nonferrous Foundries: Castings, NEC
3357 Nonferrous Wire Drawing
3299 Nonmetallic Mineral Prdts, NEC
1481 Nonmetallic Minerals Svcs, Except Fuels

O

2522 Office Furniture, Except Wood
3579 Office Machines, NEC
1382 Oil & Gas Field Exploration Svcs
1389 Oil & Gas Field Svcs, NEC
3533 Oil Field Machinery & Eqpt
3851 Ophthalmic Goods
3827 Optical Instruments
3489 Ordnance & Access, NEC
3842 Orthopedic, Prosthetic & Surgical Appliances/Splys

P

3565 Packaging Machinery
2851 Paints, Varnishes, Lacquers, Enamels

2671 Paper Coating & Laminating for Packaging
2672 Paper Coating & Laminating, Exc for Packaging
3554 Paper Inds Machinery
2621 Paper Mills
2631 Paperboard Mills
2542 Partitions & Fixtures, Except Wood
2951 Paving Mixtures & Blocks
3951 Pens & Mechanical Pencils
2844 Perfumes, Cosmetics & Toilet Preparations
2721 Periodicals: Publishing & Printing
3172 Personal Leather Goods
2879 Pesticides & Agricultural Chemicals, NEC
2911 Petroleum Refining
2834 Pharmaceuticals
3652 Phonograph Records & Magnetic Tape
2874 Phosphatic Fertilizers
3861 Photographic Eqpt & Splys
2035 Pickled Fruits, Vegetables, Sauces & Dressings
3085 Plastic Bottles
3086 Plastic Foam Prdts
3083 Plastic Laminated Plate & Sheet
3084 Plastic Pipe
3088 Plastic Plumbing Fixtures
3089 Plastic Prdts
3082 Plastic Unsupported Profile Shapes
3081 Plastic Unsupported Sheet & Film
2821 Plastics, Mtrls & Nonvulcanizable Elastomers
2796 Platemaking & Related Svcs
2395 Pleating & Stitching For The Trade
3432 Plumbing Fixture Fittings & Trim, Brass
3264 Porcelain Electrical Splys
2096 Potato Chips & Similar Prdts
3269 Pottery Prdts, NEC
2015 Poultry Slaughtering, Dressing & Processing
3546 Power Hand Tools
3612 Power, Distribution & Specialty Transformers
3448 Prefabricated Metal Buildings & Cmpnts
2452 Prefabricated Wood Buildings & Cmpnts
7372 Prepackaged Software
2048 Prepared Feeds For Animals & Fowls
3229 Pressed & Blown Glassware, NEC
3692 Primary Batteries: Dry & Wet
3399 Primary Metal Prdts, NEC
3339 Primary Nonferrous Metals, NEC
3334 Primary Production Of Aluminum
3331 Primary Smelting & Refining Of Copper
3672 Printed Circuit Boards
2893 Printing Ink
3555 Printing Trades Machinery & Eqpt
2999 Products Of Petroleum & Coal, NEC
2531 Public Building & Related Furniture
2611 Pulp Mills
3561 Pumps & Pumping Eqpt

R

3663 Radio & T V Communications, Systs & Eqpt, Broadcast/Studio
3671 Radio & T V Receiving Electron Tubes
3743 Railroad Eqpt
3273 Ready-Mixed Concrete
2493 Reconstituted Wood Prdts
3695 Recording Media
3625 Relays & Indl Controls
3645 Residential Lighting Fixtures
2044 Rice Milling
2384 Robes & Dressing Gowns
3547 Rolling Mill Machinery & Eqpt
3351 Rolling, Drawing & Extruding Of Copper
3356 Rolling, Drawing-Extruding Of Nonferrous Metals
3021 Rubber & Plastic Footwear
3052 Rubber & Plastic Hose & Belting

S

2068 Salted & Roasted Nuts & Seeds
2656 Sanitary Food Containers
2676 Sanitary Paper Prdts
2013 Sausages & Meat Prdts
2421 Saw & Planing Mills
3596 Scales & Balances, Exc Laboratory
2397 Schiffli Machine Embroideries
3451 Screw Machine Prdts
3812 Search, Detection, Navigation & Guidance Systs & Instrs
3341 Secondary Smelting & Refining Of Nonferrous Metals
3674 Semiconductors
3589 Service Ind Machines, NEC
2652 Set-Up Paperboard Boxes
3444 Sheet Metal Work
3731 Shipbuilding & Repairing
2079 Shortening, Oils & Margarine
3993 Signs & Advertising Displays

2262 Silk & Man-Made Fabric Finishers
2221 Silk & Man-Made Fiber
1044 Silver Ores
3914 Silverware, Plated & Stainless Steel Ware
3484 Small Arms
3482 Small Arms Ammunition
2841 Soap & Detergents
2086 Soft Drinks
2436 Softwood Veneer & Plywood
2075 Soybean Oil Mills
2842 Spec Cleaning, Polishing & Sanitation Preparations
3559 Special Ind Machinery, NEC
2429 Special Prdt Sawmills, NEC
3566 Speed Changers, Drives & Gears
3949 Sporting & Athletic Goods, NEC
2678 Stationery Prdts
3511 Steam, Gas & Hydraulic Turbines & Engines
3325 Steel Foundries, NEC
3324 Steel Investment Foundries
3317 Steel Pipe & Tubes
3493 Steel Springs, Except Wire
3315 Steel Wire Drawing & Nails & Spikes
3691 Storage Batteries
3259 Structural Clay Prdts, NEC
2439 Structural Wood Members, NEC
2063 Sugar, Beet
2061 Sugar, Cane
2062 Sugar, Cane Refining
2843 Surface Active & Finishing Agents, Sulfonated Oils
3841 Surgical & Medical Instrs & Apparatus
3613 Switchgear & Switchboard Apparatus
2824 Synthetic Organic Fibers, Exc Cellulosic
2822 Synthetic Rubber (Vulcanizable Elastomers)

T

3795 Tanks & Tank Components
3661 Telephone & Telegraph Apparatus
2393 Textile Bags
2269 Textile Finishers, NEC
2299 Textile Goods, NEC
3552 Textile Machinery
2284 Thread Mills
2296 Tire Cord & Fabric
3011 Tires & Inner Tubes
2131 Tobacco, Chewing & Snuff
3799 Transportation Eqpt, NEC
3792 Travel Trailers & Campers
3713 Truck & Bus Bodies
3715 Truck Trailers
2791 Typesetting

V

3494 Valves & Pipe Fittings, NEC
2076 Vegetable Oil Mills
3647 Vehicular Lighting Eqpt

W

3873 Watch & Clock Devices & Parts
2385 Waterproof Outerwear
3548 Welding Apparatus
7692 Welding Repair
2046 Wet Corn Milling
2084 Wine & Brandy
3495 Wire Springs
2331 Women's & Misses' Blouses
2335 Women's & Misses' Dresses
2339 Women's & Misses' Outerwear, NEC
2337 Women's & Misses' Suits, Coats & Skirts
3144 Women's Footwear, Exc Athletic
2341 Women's, Misses' & Children's Underwear & Nightwear
2441 Wood Boxes
2449 Wood Containers, NEC
2511 Wood Household Furniture
2512 Wood Household Furniture, Upholstered
2434 Wood Kitchen Cabinets
2521 Wood Office Furniture
2448 Wood Pallets & Skids
2499 Wood Prdts, NEC
2491 Wood Preserving
2517 Wood T V, Radio, Phono & Sewing Cabinets
2541 Wood, Office & Store Fixtures
3553 Woodworking Machinery
2231 Wool, Woven Fabric

X

3844 X-ray Apparatus & Tubes

Y

2281 Yarn Spinning Mills
2282 Yarn Texturizing, Throwing, Twisting & Winding Mills

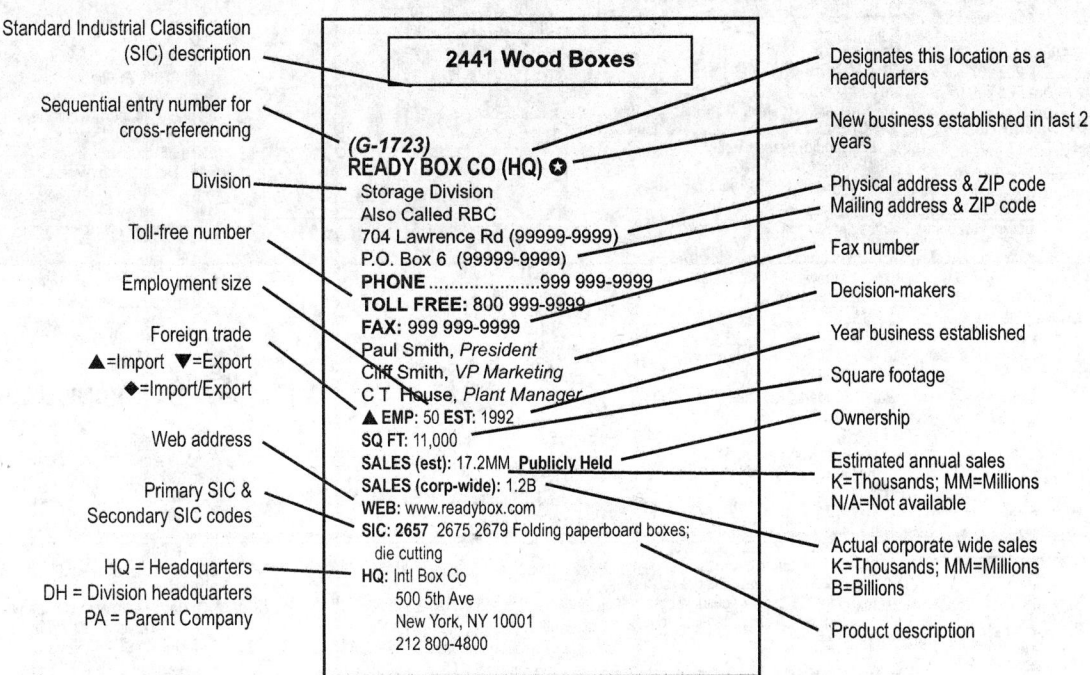

Standard Industrial Classification (SIC) description — 2441 Wood Boxes

Sequential entry number for cross-referencing — (G-1723)

Division — Storage Division

Toll-free number — TOLL FREE: 800 999-9999

Employment size — EMP: 50

Foreign trade ▲=Import ▼=Export ◆=Import/Export

Web address — WEB: www.readybox.com

Primary SIC & Secondary SIC codes

HQ = Headquarters DH = Division headquarters PA = Parent Company

Designates this location as a headquarters

New business established in last 2 years

Physical address & ZIP code / Mailing address & ZIP code

Fax number

Decision-makers

Year business established

Square footage

Ownership

Estimated annual sales K=Thousands; MM=Millions N/A=Not available

Actual corporate wide sales K=Thousands; MM=Millions B=Billions

Product description

READY BOX CO (HQ) ✪
Storage Division
Also Called RBC
704 Lawrence Rd (99999-9999)
P.O. Box 6 (99999-9999)
PHONE 999 999-9999
TOLL FREE: 800 999-9999
FAX: 999 999-9999
Paul Smith, *President*
Cliff Smith, *VP Marketing*
C T House, *Plant Manager*
▲ EMP: 50 EST: 1992
SQ FT: 11,000
SALES (est): 17.2MM **Publicly Held**
SALES (corp-wide): 1.2B
WEB: www.readybox.com
SIC: 2657 2675 2679 Folding paperboard boxes;
  die cutting
HQ: Intl Box Co
  500 5th Ave
  New York, NY 10001
  212 800-4800

- Companies in this section are listed numerically under their primary SIC Companies are in alphabetical order under each code.

- A numerical and alphabetcal index precedes this section.

- **Sequential Entry Numbers.** Each establishment in this section is numbered sequentially. The number assigned to each establishment's Entry Number. To make cross-referencing easier, each listing in the Product's & Services, Alphabetic and Geographical Section includes the establishment's entry number. To facilitate locating an entry in this section, the entry numbers for the first listing on the left page and the last listing on the right page are printed at the top of the page next to the Standard Industrial Classification (SIC) description.

- Further information can be found in the Explanatory Notes starting on page 5.

- See the footnotes for symbols and abbreviations.

IMPORTANT NOTICE: It is a violation of both federal and state law to transmit an unsolicited advertisement to a facsimile machine. Any user of this product that violates such laws may be subject to civil and criminal penalties which may exceed $500 for each transmission of an unsolicited facsimile. Harris InfoSource provides fax numbers for lawful purposes only and expressly forbids the use of these numbers in any unlawful manner.

1041 Gold Ores

(P-1)
BARRICK GOLD CORPORATION
Also Called: Mc Laughlin Mine
26775 Morgan Valley Rd, Lower Lake
(95457-9411)
PHONE...................................707 995-6070
Pat Purtell, *Branch Mgr*
EMP: 100
SALES (est): 11.8MM
SALES (corp-wide): 7.2B **Privately Held**
WEB: www.barrick.com
SIC: 1041 Gold ores
PA: Barrick Gold Corporation
  161 Bay St Suite 3700
  Toronto ON M5J 2
  416 861-9911

(P-2)
CRYSTAL MINING CORPORATION
20380 Stevens Creek Blvd, Cupertino
(95014-2299)
PHONE...................................386 479-5823
Sylvestre Ygay IV, *CEO*
EMP: 15
SALES (est): 760.7K **Privately Held**
SIC: 1041 Gold ores processing

(P-3)
FIRST GOLD CORP
3108 Ponte Morino Dr # 210, Cameron
Park (95682-7453)
PHONE...................................530 677-5974
Stephen Akerfeldt, *CEO*
James W Kluber, *CFO*
EMP: 10
SALES (est): 577.1K **Privately Held**
SIC: 1041 Gold ores mining

(P-4)
GOLDEN QUEEN MINING CO LLC
2818 Silver Queen Rd, Mojave
(93501-7021)
P.O. Box 1030 (93502-1030)
PHONE...................................661 824-4300
Thomas Clay, *Ch of Bd*
Andree St-Germain, *CFO*
Joe Balas, *Opers Staff*
EMP: 180
SQ FT: 2,500
SALES (est): 63MM **Privately Held**
SIC: 1041 Gold ores mining

(P-5)
LITTLE DIGGER MINING & SUP LLC
3524 Maine Ave, Baldwin Park
(91706-5153)
PHONE...................................626 856-3366

Curtis Timmons,
EMP: 40
SALES (est): 3.1MM **Privately Held**
SIC: 1041 Open pit gold mining

(P-6)
LOST DUTCHMANS MININGS ASSN (DH)
43445 Bus Pk Dr Ste 113, Temecula
(92590-3671)
P.O. Box 891509 (92589-1509)
PHONE...................................951 699-4749
Perry Massie, *President*
Tom Massie, *Admin Sec*
▲ EMP: 30
SQ FT: 3,200
SALES (est): 2.3MM
SALES (corp-wide): 122.8MM **Privately Held**
SIC: 1041 Gold ores
HQ: Outdoor Channel Holdings, Inc.
  1000 Chopper Cir
  Denver CO 80204
  951 699-6991

(P-7)
MERIDIAN GOLD INC
Also Called: Royal Mountain King
4461 Rock Creek Rd, Copperopolis
(95228)
PHONE...................................209 785-3222
Edgar Smith, *Branch Mgr*

EMP: 160
SALES (corp-wide): 1.8B **Privately Held**
SIC: 1041 Gold ores
HQ: Meridian Gold Inc.
  4635 Longley Ln Ste 110
  Reno NV 89502

(P-8)
STAVATTI INDUSTRIES LTD
1443 S Gage St, San Bernardino
(92408-2835)
P.O. Box 211258, Eagan MN (55121-2658)
PHONE...................................651 238-5369
Christopher R Beskar, *Branch Mgr*
Christopher Beskar, *CEO*
EMP: 60
SALES (corp-wide): 2MM **Privately Held**
SIC: 1041 1081 3511 3533 Gold ores
  mining; metal mining exploration & devel-
  opment services; turbines & turbine gen-
  erator set units, complete; oil & gas field
  machinery; truck trailers
PA: Stavatti Industries Ltd
  1061 Tiffany Dr
  Eagan MN 55123
  651 238-5369

(P-9)
USECB JOINT VENTURE INC
Also Called: Sutter Gold Mining Company
11500 String Bean Aly, Sutter Creek
(95685)
P.O. Box 1689 (95685-1689)
PHONE..................................209 267-5594
Stacy Rhodes, *President*
EMP: 14
SALES (est): 1.1MM **Privately Held**
SIC: 1041 Gold ores

1044 Silver Ores

(P-10)
**MAGELLAN GOLD
CORPORATION**
2010a Harbison Dr 312, Vacaville
(95687-3900)
PHONE..................................707 884-3766
David E Drips, *President*
Frank A Pastorino, *COO*
Michael P Martinez, *Officer*
EMP: 38
SALES: 123.9K **Privately Held**
SIC: 1044 1031 Silver ores; lead & zinc
ores

1081 Metal Mining Svcs

(P-11)
NATIONAL EWP INC
1961 Meeker Ave, Richmond (94804-6405)
PHONE..................................510 236-6282
Chris Tatum, *Branch Mgr*
EMP: 15
SALES (corp-wide): 97.5MM **Privately
Held**
SIC: 1081 Metal mining exploration & de-
velopment services
PA: National Ewp, Inc.
1200 W San Pedro St
Gilbert AZ 85233
530 419-2117

(P-12)
NATIONAL EWP INC
Also Called: National Explrtion Wells Pumps
5566 Arrow Hwy, Montclair (91763-1606)
PHONE..................................909 931-4014
Tom Moreland, *Branch Mgr*
EMP: 26
SALES (corp-wide): 97.5MM **Privately
Held**
SIC: 1081 Metal mining exploration & de-
velopment services
PA: National Ewp, Inc.
1200 W San Pedro St
Gilbert AZ 85233
530 419-2117

(P-13)
UNICO INCORPORATED
8880 Rio San Diego Dr # 8, San Diego
(92108-1634)
PHONE..................................619 209-6124
Mark A Lopez, *President*
Kenneth Wiedrich, *CFO*
Charles M Madsen, *Exec VP*
C Wayne Hartle, *Admin Sec*
EMP: 16
SALES (est): 1.1MM **Privately Held**
SIC: 1081 Metal mining exploration & de-
velopment services

1099 Metal Ores, NEC

(P-14)
**US-VN-MYNMAR RARE ERTH
MTLS GR**
4000 Barranca Pkwy # 250, Irvine
(92604-4710)
PHONE..................................949 262-3673
Robert Quang Lam, *Principal*
Anh Tran, *Principal*
Huong Truong, *Principal*
EMP: 10
SALES (est): 220.2K **Privately Held**
SIC: 1099 Rare-earth ores mining

1221 Bituminous Coal & Lignite: Surface Mining

(P-15)
CHEVRON MINING INC
Moly
67750 Bailey Rd, Mountain Pass (92366)
PHONE..................................760 856-7625
Allen Randle, *Branch Mgr*
EMP: 400
SALES (corp-wide): 166.3B **Publicly
Held**
SIC: 1221 Surface mining, bituminous
HQ: Chevron Mining Inc.
116 Invrneco Dr E Ste 207
Englewood CO 80112
303 930-3600

(P-16)
**CUSTOM CRUSHING
INDUSTRIES**
2409 E Oberlin Rd, Yreka (96097-9577)
P.O. Box 357, Grenada (96038-0357)
PHONE..................................530 842-5544
Clara Goodwin, *Treasurer*
Paul Goodwin, *President*
EMP: 11
SALES (est): 5.5MM **Privately Held**
SIC: 1221 3295 3281 1499 Strip mining,
bituminous; minerals, ground or treated;
stone, quarrying & processing of own
stone products; peat mining & processing;
excavation & grading, building construc-
tion; highway & street construction

(P-17)
**KENNEDY HILLS ENTERPRISES
LLC**
Also Called: Kennedy Hills Materials
19486 Woodlands Dr, Huntington Beach
(92648-5570)
PHONE..................................714 596-7444
EMP: 10
SALES: 3MM **Privately Held**
SIC: 1221

1241 Coal Mining Svcs

(P-18)
GREKA INC
1791 Sinton Rd, Santa Maria (93458-9708)
P.O. Box 5489 (93456-5489)
PHONE..................................805 347-8700
Andy Devegvar, *President*
Randeep Grewal, *CEO*
EMP: 150
SQ FT: 3,000
SALES: 40MM **Privately Held**
SIC: 1241 1081 Coal mining services;
metal mining services

(P-19)
RIO TINTO MINERALS INC
Also Called: Reno Tenco
14486 Borax Rd, Boron (93516-2017)
PHONE..................................760 762-7121
Xiaoling Liu, *CEO*
Preston Chiaro, *President*
Hugo Bague, *Principal*
Trevor Plote, *Engineer*
Shalaine Fink, *Analyst*
▼ **EMP:** 150
SALES (est): 17.1MM
SALES (corp-wide): 40.5B **Privately Held**
SIC: 1241 Coal mining services
HQ: U.S. Borax Inc.
8051 E Maplewood Ave # 100
Greenwood Village CO 80111
303 713-5000

(P-20)
TAFT PRODUCTION COMPANY
950 Petroleum Club Rd, Taft (93268-9748)
P.O. Box 1277 (93268-1277)
PHONE..................................661 765-7194
Daniel S Jaffee, *President*
EMP: 95

SALES (est): 8.3MM
SALES (corp-wide): 277MM **Publicly
Held**
WEB: www.oildri.com
SIC: 1241 1081 Coal mining services;
metal mining services
PA: Oil-Dri Corporation Of America
410 N Michigan Ave Fl 4
Chicago IL 60611
312 321-1515

1311 Crude Petroleum & Natural Gas

(P-21)
ANDEAVOR
Also Called: Tesoro
2350 E 223rd St, Carson (90810-1615)
PHONE..................................310 847-5705
EMP: 11 **Publicly Held**
SIC: 1311 Crude petroleum production
HQ: Andeavor Llc
19100 Ridgewood Pkwy
San Antonio TX 78259
210 626-6000

(P-22)
**ARMSTRONG PETROLEUM
CORP (PA)**
1080 W 17th St, Costa Mesa (92627-4503)
P.O. Box 1547, Newport Beach (92659-
0547)
PHONE..................................949 650-4000
William Armstrong, *President*
Margaret Armstrong, *Admin Sec*
▲ **EMP:** 31
SQ FT: 2,000
SALES (est): 2.3MM **Privately Held**
SIC: 1311 1389 Crude petroleum produc-
tion; servicing oil & gas wells

(P-23)
BENTLEY-SIMONSON INC
1746 S Victoria Ave Ste F, Ventura
(93003-6190)
PHONE..................................805 650-2794
James Bentley, *Ch of Bd*
Theodore Bentley, *Ch of Bd*
Clifton O Simonson, *President*
Petter Romming, *Vice Pres*
EMP: 100
SQ FT: 1,000
SALES (est): 4.1MM **Privately Held**
SIC: 1311 Crude petroleum & natural gas
production

(P-24)
**BERRY PETROLEUM COMPANY
LLC**
25121 Sierra Hwy, Newhall (91321-2007)
PHONE..................................661 255-6066
Eddie Azevedo, *Manager*
EMP: 13
SALES (corp-wide): 586.5MM **Publicly
Held**
WEB: www.bry.com
SIC: 1311 Crude petroleum production;
natural gas production
HQ: Berry Petroleum Company, Llc
5201 Truxtun Ave Ste 100
Bakersfield CA 93309
661 616-3900

(P-25)
**BERRY PETROLEUM COMPANY
LLC**
28700 Hovey Hills Rd, Taft (93268)
P.O. Box 925 (93268-0925)
PHONE..................................661 769-8820
Tom Cruise, *Manager*
EMP: 37
SALES (corp-wide): 586.5MM **Publicly
Held**
WEB: www.bry.com
SIC: 1311 Crude petroleum production
HQ: Berry Petroleum Company, Llc
5201 Truxtun Ave Ste 100
Bakersfield CA 93309
661 616-3900

(P-26)
**BERRY PETROLEUM COMPANY
LLC (HQ)**
5201 Truxtun Ave Ste 100, Bakersfield
(93309-0422)
PHONE..................................661 616-3900
Trem Smith, *President*
Stephen Burke, *Director*
Stephen Cropper, *Director*
Michael Reddin, *Director*
EMP: 65
SALES (est): 506.4MM
SALES (corp-wide): 586.5MM **Publicly
Held**
WEB: www.bry.com
SIC: 1311 Crude petroleum production;
natural gas production
PA: Berry Petroleum Corporation
16000 Dallas Pkwy Ste 500
Dallas TX 75248
661 616-3900

(P-27)
**BERRY PETROLEUM COMPANY
LLC**
Coastal Division
5713 W Gonzales Rd, Oxnard
(93036-2739)
PHONE..................................805 984-0053
Fax: 805 985-8362
EMP: 12
SQ FT: 685
SALES (corp-wide): 4.9B **Publicly Held**
SIC: 1311
HQ: Berry Petroleum Company, Llc
600 Travis St Ste 4900
Houston TX 93309
281 840-4000

(P-28)
BEVERLY HILLCREST OIL CORP
27241 Burbank, El Toro (92610-2500)
PHONE..................................949 598-7300
Morris Hodges, *President*
Katherine Hodges, *Vice Pres*
EMP: 15
SALES (est): 1.2MM **Privately Held**
SIC: 1311 1321 Crude petroleum produc-
tion; natural gas liquids production

(P-29)
**BP WEST COAST PRODUCTS
LLC**
22600 Wilmington Ave, Carson
(90745-4307)
PHONE..................................310 816-8787
EMP: 310
SALES (corp-wide): 298.7B **Privately
Held**
SIC: 1311 Crude petroleum & natural gas
HQ: Bp West Coast Products Llc
4519 Grandview Rd
Blaine WA 98230
310 549-6204

(P-30)
**BP WEST COAST PRODUCTS
LLC**
1306 Canal Blvd, Richmond (94804-3556)
PHONE..................................510 231-4724
Fred Glueck, *Vice Pres*
EMP: 310
SQ FT: 4,550
SALES (corp-wide): 298.7B **Privately
Held**
SIC: 1311 Crude petroleum production
HQ: Bp West Coast Products Llc
4519 Grandview Rd
Blaine WA 98230
310 549-6204

(P-31)
BREA CANON OIL CO INC
23903 Normandie Ave, Harbor City
(90710-1400)
PHONE..................................310 326-4002
Andrew Barkler, *President*
Ray Javier, *Vice Pres*
Rod Benny, *Manager*
EMP: 17
SALES (est): 745.6K **Privately Held**
SIC: 1311 Crude petroleum production

SALES (corp-wide): 4.5MM **Privately
Held**
WEB: www.aaproduction.com
SIC: **1381** Drilling oil & gas wells
PA: Aa Production Services, Inc.
433 2nd St Ste 103
Woodland CA 95695
530 668-7525

(P-82)
AERA ENERGY LLC (HQ)
10000 Ming Ave, Bakersfield (93311-1301)
P.O. Box 11164 (93389-1164)
PHONE..............................661 665-5000
Christina S Sistrunk, *President*
Andrew Hoyer, *Chief Mktg Ofcr*
Bill Hanson, *Exec VP*
Robert C Alberstadt, *Senior VP*
Brent D Carnahan, *Senior VP*
EMP: 800
SALES (est): 2.1B
SALES (corp-wide): 388.3B **Privately
Held**
WEB: www.aeraenergy.com
SIC: **1381** Directional drilling oil & gas
wells
PA: Royal Dutch Shell Plc
Shell Centre
London SE1 7
207 934-1234

(P-83)
AERA ENERGY LLC
Also Called: Security Front Desk
59231 Main Camp Rd, Mc Kittrick
(93251-9740)
PHONE..............................661 665-4400
Mike Brown, *Principal*
EMP: 47
SALES (corp-wide): 388.3B **Privately
Held**
WEB: www.aeraenergy.com
SIC: **1381** Directional drilling oil & gas
wells
HQ: Aera Energy Llc
10000 Ming Ave
Bakersfield CA 93311
661 665-5000

(P-84)
AERA ENERGY LLC
Also Called: Aera Energy South Midway
29235 Highway 33, Maricopa
(93252-9793)
PHONE..............................661 665-3200
Andy Anderson, *Manager*
Bob Alberstadt, *Vice Pres*
Sandeep Brar, *Administration*
Jay Licata, *Production*
EMP: 60
SALES (corp-wide): 388.3B **Privately
Held**
WEB: www.aeraenergy.com
SIC: **1381** Directional drilling oil & gas
wells
HQ: Aera Energy Llc
10000 Ming Ave
Bakersfield CA 93311
661 665-5000

(P-85)
ALUMATEC INC
18411 Sherman Way, Reseda
(91335-4319)
PHONE..............................818 609-7460
Francesco Chinaglia, *President*
Yazmin Ibarlucea, *Treasurer*
Laura Chinaglia, *Admin Sec*
EMP: 80
SALES (est): 2.8MM **Privately Held**
WEB: www.alumatec.com
SIC: **1381** Drilling oil & gas wells

(P-86)
AMS DRILLING
120 Tustin Ave Ste C, Newport Beach
(92663-4729)
PHONE............................949 232-1149
Adrienne Marie Salyer, *President*
John Clark, *Partner*
EMP: 10
SALES (est): 457.7K **Privately Held**
SIC: **1381** Drilling oil & gas wells

(P-87)
ASTA CONSTRUCTION CO INC (PA)
1090 Saint Francis Way, Rio Vista
(94571-1200)
P.O. Box 758 (94571-0758)
PHONE.......................707 374-6472
Walt Koenig, *CEO*
Christien Koenig, *President*
Joan Brown, *Treasurer*
Schmitt V Scott, *Vice Pres*
Lisa Ramsey, *Office Mgr*
▲ EMP: 32
SQ FT: 1,200
SALES (est): 11.8MM **Privately Held**
WEB: www.astaconstruction.com
SIC: **1381** 1611 5032 Drilling oil & gas
wells; general contractor, highway &
street construction; sand, construction;
gravel

(P-88)
BAKERSFIELD WELL CASING LLC
17876 Zerker Rd, Bakersfield
(93308-9221)
P.O. Box 82575 (93380-2575)
PHONE..............................661 399-2976
James S Camp, *Mng Member*
Richard C Camp,
Jane Camp-Micks,
Candi Glen,
Don M Hart,
EMP: 10
SQ FT: 10,000
SALES (est): 1MM **Privately Held**
SIC: **1381** Drilling water intake wells

(P-89)
BLE INC
Also Called: Beryl Lockhart Enterprises
11360 Goss St, Sun Valley (91352-3205)
PHONE..............................818 504-9577
Beryl P Lockhart, *CEO*
EMP: 15
SQ FT: 2,200
SALES (est): 2.7MM **Privately Held**
SIC: **1381** Drilling oil & gas wells

(P-90)
DICK BROWN TECHNICAL SERVICES
Also Called: Aera Energy
553 Airport Rd Ste B, Rio Vista
(94571-1293)
P.O. Box 1035 (94571-3035)
PHONE.......................707 374-2133
Richard Brown, *President*
EMP: 18
SALES (est): 2.1MM **Privately Held**
SIC: **1381** Drilling oil & gas wells

(P-91)
ELYSIUM JENNINGS LLC
1600 Norris Rd, Bakersfield (93308-2234)
PHONE..............................661 679-1700
Steve Layton,
EMP: 200
SALES (est): 8.7MM **Privately Held**
SIC: **1381** Drilling oil & gas wells
PA: E & B Natural Resources Management
Corporation
1600 Norris Rd
Bakersfield CA 93308

(P-92)
EXCALIBUR WELL SERVICES CORP (PA)
22034 Rosedale Hwy, Bakersfield
(93314-9704)
PHONE..............................661 589-5338
Stephen Layton, *President*
Frachsco Galesi, *President*
Gordon Isbel, *Vice Pres*
Mary Telupessy, *Business Mgr*
EMP: 78
SALES (est): 40.3MM **Privately Held**
SIC: **1381** 1389 Drilling oil & gas wells;
fishing for tools, oil & gas field

(P-93)
GOLDEN STATE DRILLING INC
3500 Fruitvale Ave, Bakersfield
(93308-5106)
PHONE..............................661 589-0730
Philip F Phelps, *President*
James Phelps, *Treasurer*
Velma Phelps, *Vice Pres*
Mike McCutcheon, *Manager*
EMP: 75
SALES (est): 14.1MM **Privately Held**
WEB: www.gsdrilling.com
SIC: **1381** Directional drilling oil & gas
wells

(P-94)
HOWELL DICK HOLE DRILLING SVC
Also Called: Howell Drilling
2579 E 67th St, Long Beach (90805-1701)
PHONE..............................562 633-9898
Richard Howell Jr, *President*
Patty Howell, *Treasurer*
Paul Howell, *Vice Pres*
EMP: 12 EST: 1971
SALES (est): 1.6MM **Privately Held**
SIC: **1381** 1629 1741 Drilling oil & gas
wells; blasting contractor, except building
demolition; foundation building

(P-95)
J & H DRILLING CO INC
7431 Walnut Ave, Buena Park
(90620-1761)
PHONE..............................714 994-0402
Brian Hoien, *President*
Stephen Jones, *Corp Secy*
William Jones, *Vice Pres*
EMP: 13
SQ FT: 5,000
SALES (est): 4MM **Privately Held**
SIC: **1381** 8748 Directional drilling oil &
gas wells; environmental consultant

(P-96)
JA WOUTERS INC
2305 Iron Stone Loop, Templeton
(93465-8396)
PHONE.......................805 221-5333
Justin Wouters, *CEO*
Julie Anderson, *President*
EMP: 10
SALES (est): 2.9MM **Privately Held**
SIC: **1381** Directional drilling oil & gas
wells

(P-97)
KUSTER CO OIL WELL SERVICES
Also Called: Kuster Company
2900 E 29th St, Long Beach (90806-2398)
PHONE..............................562 595-0661
John Davidson, *CEO*
▲ EMP: 23
SALES (est): 8MM **Privately Held**
WEB: www.kusterco.com
SIC: **1381** Drilling oil & gas wells
PA: Probe Holdings, Inc.
1132 Everman Pkwy Ste 100
Fort Worth TX 76140

(P-98)
LEGEND PUMP & WELL SERVICE INC
1324 W Rialto Ave, San Bernardino
(92410-1611)
PHONE..............................909 384-1000
Keith Collier, *President*
EMP: 20 EST: 2010
SALES (est): 4.6MM **Privately Held**
SIC: **1381** 1781 Service well drilling; water
well servicing

(P-99)
LEON KROUS DRILLING INC
9300 Borden Ave, Sun Valley (91352-2006)
PHONE..............................818 833-4654
Leon Krus, *President*
EMP: 25
SQ FT: 1,000
SALES (est): 12.1MM **Privately Held**
SIC: **1381** Directional drilling oil & gas
wells

(P-100)
NATIONAL OILWELL VARCO INC
743 N Eckhoff St, Orange (92868-1005)
PHONE..............................714 456-1244
Greg Renfro, *Branch Mgr*
Darlene Brown, *Administration*
Lisa Provencio, *Technology*
Stan Curlee, *Electrical Engi*
Laura Acocella, *Engineer*
EMP: 12
SALES (corp-wide): 8.4B **Publicly Held**
SIC: **1381** Drilling oil & gas wells
PA: National Oilwell Varco, Inc.
7909 Parkwood Circle Dr
Houston TX 77036
713 346-7500

(P-101)
PACIFIC OPERATORS INC
205 E Carrillo St Ste 200, Santa Barbara
(93101-7181)
PHONE..............................805 899-3144
Richard L Carone, *President*
Robert P Carone, *Vice Pres*
EMP: 30
SQ FT: 3,100
SALES (est): 3.2MM **Privately Held**
SIC: **1381** Drilling oil & gas wells

(P-102)
PAUL GRAHAM DRILLING & SVC CO
2500 Airport Rd, Rio Vista (94571-1034)
P.O. Box 669 (94571-0669)
PHONE..............................707 374-5123
Kevin P Graham, *President*
Jill Graham, *CFO*
Clarence Santos, *Vice Pres*
Eddie Woodruff, *General Mgr*
Ted Coffey, *Sales Mgr*
EMP: 170
SQ FT: 30,000
SALES (est): 30MM **Privately Held**
SIC: **1381** 7389 7359 Drilling oil & gas
wells; crane & aerial lift service; industrial
truck rental

(P-103)
PETRO-LUD INC
12625 Jomani Dr Ste 104, Bakersfield
(93312-3445)
PHONE..............................661 747-4779
Clayton Ludington, *Principal*
EMP: 12
SALES (est): 3.2MM **Privately Held**
SIC: **1381** Drilling oil & gas wells

(P-104)
PRIMEBORE DIRECTIONAL BORING
10822 Vernon Ave, Ontario (91762-4041)
PHONE..............................909 821-4643
Jess B Basave, *CEO*
EMP: 13 EST: 2003
SALES (est): 847K **Privately Held**
SIC: **1381** Directional drilling oil & gas
wells

(P-105)
SCIENTIFIC DRILLING INTL INC
31101 Coberly Rd, Shafter (93263-9702)
PHONE..............................661 831-0636
Joe Williams, *Manager*
EMP: 20
SALES (corp-wide): 20.8MM **Privately
Held**
SIC: **1381** Directional drilling oil & gas
wells
PA: Scientific Drilling International, Inc.
16071 Greenspoint Park
Houston TX 77060
281 443-3300

(P-106)
T & D SERVICES INC
Also Called: T&D Trenchless
42363 Guava St, Murrieta (92562-7271)
P.O. Box 609 (92564-0609)
PHONE..............................951 304-1190
Donald Van Dyke, *President*
Dawn Van Dyke, *Treasurer*
EMP: 13
SQ FT: 1,200

SALES (est): 6.2MM **Privately Held**
SIC: 1381 Directional drilling oil & gas wells

(P-107)
WEST AMERICAN ENERGY CORP
4949 Buckley Way Ste 207, Bakersfield (93309-4882)
P.O. Box 22016 (93390-2016)
PHONE..................661 747-7732
Howard Caywood, *President*
EMP: 12
SQ FT: 640
SALES (est): 1.2MM **Privately Held**
SIC: 1381 Drilling oil & gas wells

(P-108)
WOODWARD DRILLING COMPANY
550 River Rd, Rio Vista (94571-1216)
P.O. Box 336 (94571-0336)
PHONE..................707 374-4300
Concing Woodward, *President*
Wayne G Woodward, *Ch of Bd*
EMP: 28
SQ FT: 40,000
SALES (est): 9.8MM **Privately Held**
WEB: www.woodwarddrilling.com
SIC: 1381 1781 Service well drilling; water well drilling

1382 Oil & Gas Field Exploration Svcs

(P-109)
ARGUELLO INC
17100 Clle Mariposa Reina, Goleta (93117-9737)
PHONE..................805 567-1632
James C Flores, *President*
Winston Taldert, *CFO*
Doss Dourgeois, *Exec VP*
John F Wombwell, *Exec VP*
EMP: 25
SALES (est): 1.7MM
SALES (corp-wide): 18.6B **Publicly Held**
WEB: www.arguello.com
SIC: 1382 Oil & gas exploration services
HQ: Freeport-Mcmoran Oil & Gas Llc
700 Milam St Ste 3100
Houston TX 77002
713 579-6000

(P-110)
BNK PETROLEUM (US) INC
760 Paseo Camarillo # 350, Camarillo (93010-6000)
PHONE..................805 484-3613
Wolf E Regener, *President*
Ray W Payne, *Vice Pres*
Steven M Warshauer, *Executive*
Jason Byl, *Exploration*
Derrick Schneider, *Engineer*
EMP: 25
SQ FT: 3,000
SALES (est): 9.4MM **Privately Held**
SIC: 1382 Oil & gas exploration services

(P-111)
CALIFORNIA HEAVY OIL INC
10889 Wilshire Blvd, Los Angeles (90024-4201)
PHONE..................888 848-4754
Todd A Stevens, *CEO*
EMP: 39
SALES (est): 938.9K
SALES (corp-wide): 3B **Publicly Held**
SIC: 1382 Oil & gas exploration services
PA: California Resources Corporation
27200 Tourney Rd Ste 200
Santa Clarita CA 91355
888 848-4754

(P-112)
CALIFORNIA RESOURCES CORP
900 Old River Rd, Bakersfield (93311-9501)
PHONE..................661 412-5222
Karen Plotts, *Branch Mgr*
EMP: 12

SALES (corp-wide): 3B **Publicly Held**
SIC: 1382 Oil & gas exploration services
PA: California Resources Corporation
27200 Tourney Rd Ste 200
Santa Clarita CA 91355
888 848-4754

(P-113)
CALIFORNIA RESOURCES CORP
2692 Amerada Rd, Rio Vista (94571-1121)
PHONE..................707 374-4109
EMP: 19
SALES (corp-wide): 3B **Publicly Held**
SIC: 1382 Oil & gas exploration services
PA: California Resources Corporation
27200 Tourney Rd Ste 200
Santa Clarita CA 91355
888 848-4754

(P-114)
CALIFORNIA RESOURCES CORP
3055 Pacific Coast Hwy, Ventura (93001-9742)
PHONE..................805 641-5566
Paul Roden, *Manager*
EMP: 13
SALES (corp-wide): 3B **Publicly Held**
WEB: www.vintagetul.com
SIC: 1382 Oil & gas exploration services
PA: California Resources Corporation
27200 Tourney Rd Ste 200
Santa Clarita CA 91355
888 848-4754

(P-115)
CALIFRNIA RSRCES ELK HILLS LLC
900 Old River Rd, Bakersfield (93311-9501)
P.O. Box 1001, Tupman (93276-1001)
PHONE..................661 412-5000
Karen Plotts,
Michael L Preston,
Marshall D Smith,
EMP: 400 EST: 1997
SALES (est): 35.7MM
SALES (corp-wide): 3B **Publicly Held**
WEB: www.oxy.com
SIC: 1382 Oil & gas exploration services
PA: California Resources Corporation
27200 Tourney Rd Ste 200
Santa Clarita CA 91355
888 848-4754

(P-116)
CONSOLIDATED GEOSCIENCE INC
Also Called: R M A Geoscience
14738 Central Ave, Chino (91710-9502)
PHONE..................909 393-9700
EMP: 11 EST: 2004
SALES (est): 950K **Privately Held**
SIC: 1382 8999

(P-117)
DCOR LLC (PA)
290 Maple Ct Ste 290 # 290, Ventura (93003-9144)
P.O. Box 3401 (93006-3401)
PHONE..................805 535-2000
Bill Templeton,
Alan C Templeton, *CFO*
Greg Cavette, *Vice Pres*
Dennis Conley, *Vice Pres*
Bob Garcia, *Vice Pres*
EMP: 76
SALES (est): 154.1MM **Privately Held**
WEB: www.dcor.com
SIC: 1382 Oil & gas exploration services

(P-118)
DELCO OPERATING CO LP
Also Called: Delco Oheb Energy
1999 Avenue Of The Stars, Los Angeles (90067-6022)
PHONE..................310 525-3535
Aziz Delrahim, *Partner*
Bianca Delrahim, *Partner*
Shahram Delrahim, *Partner*
Shawn Delrahim, *Partner*
EMP: 16

SALES (est): 1MM **Privately Held**
WEB: www.delcopetroleum.com
SIC: 1382 Oil & gas exploration services

(P-119)
DEMENNO KERDOON
2000 N Alameda St, Compton (90222-2799)
PHONE..................310 537-7100
Shane Bamelin, *Principal*
Jim Tice, *Principal*
Jim Ennis, *Director*
EMP: 125
SQ FT: 11,614
SALES (est): 25.6MM **Privately Held**
WEB: www.demennokerdoon.com
SIC: 1382 Oil & gas exploration services

(P-120)
E & B NTRAL RESOURCES MGT CORP
1848 Perkins Rd, New Cuyama (93254)
P.O. Box 179 (93254-0179)
PHONE..................661 766-2501
Edward Fetterman, *Branch Mgr*
EMP: 30 **Privately Held**
SIC: 1382 Oil & gas exploration services
PA: E & B Natural Resources Management Corporation
1600 Norris Rd
Bakersfield CA 93308

(P-121)
E AND B NATURAL RESOURCES
1600 Norris Rd, Bakersfield (93308-2234)
PHONE..................661 679-1700
Francesco Galesi, *CEO*
Melissa Ysaguirre, *Supervisor*
EMP: 52
SALES (est): 9.4MM **Privately Held**
SIC: 1382 Oil & gas exploration services

(P-122)
EAGLE DOMINION ENERGY CORP
Also Called: Eagle Dominion Trust
200 N Hayes Ave, Oxnard (93030-5420)
PHONE..................805 272-9557
Roger H Shears, *President*
Nancy Davis, *Vice Pres*
EMP: 36
SQ FT: 1,500
SALES (est): 1.4MM **Privately Held**
SIC: 1382 Oil & gas exploration services

(P-123)
FREEPORT-MCMORAN OIL & GAS LLC
760 W Hueneme Rd, Oxnard (93033-9013)
PHONE..................805 567-1601
Eric Vang, *Branch Mgr*
EMP: 27
SALES (corp-wide): 18.6B **Publicly Held**
SIC: 1382 Oil & gas exploration services
HQ: Freeport-Mcmoran Oil & Gas Llc
700 Milam St Ste 3100
Houston TX 77002
713 579-6000

(P-124)
FREEPORT-MCMORAN OIL & GAS LLC
1821 Price Canyon Rd, San Luis Obispo (93401-8405)
PHONE..................805 547-8969
Larry Norton, *Branch Mgr*
Paul De Lorenzo, *Manager*
EMP: 10
SQ FT: 2,691
SALES (corp-wide): 18.6B **Publicly Held**
SIC: 1382 Oil & gas exploration services
HQ: Freeport-Mcmoran Oil & Gas Llc
700 Milam St Ste 3100
Houston TX 77002
713 579-6000

(P-125)
GREKA INTEGRATED INC (PA)
1700 Sinton Rd, Santa Maria (93458-9708)
P.O. Box 5489 (93456-5489)
PHONE..................805 347-8700
Randeep S Grewal, *CEO*
Ken Miller, *CFO*
Susan Whalen, *Vice Pres*

▲ **EMP:** 145
SALES (est): 32MM **Privately Held**
WEB: www.grekaenergy.com
SIC: 1382 Oil & gas exploration services

(P-126)
GRENFIELD CONSULTING
1801 Century Park E Fl 23, Los Angeles (90067-2325)
PHONE..................310 286-0200
EMP: 26
SALES (est): 1MM **Privately Held**
SIC: 1382 8742

(P-127)
KERN RIVER HOLDING INC
7700 Downing Ave, Bakersfield (93308-5012)
PHONE..................661 589-2507
J Don Collier, *Principal*
EMP: 13
SALES (est): 780.4K
SALES (corp-wide): 12.7MM **Privately Held**
SIC: 1382 Oil & gas exploration services
PA: All American Oil & Gas Incorporated
250 Greenwich St Fl 29
New York NY

(P-128)
LUCA INTERNATIONAL GROUP LLC (PA)
39650 Liberty St Ste 490, Fremont (94538-2261)
PHONE..................510 498-8829
Bing Yang, *President*
James Diaz, *Officer*
Lily Lei, *Vice Pres*
Angie Yip,
▲ **EMP:** 17
SALES (est): 3.4MM **Privately Held**
SIC: 1382 Oil & gas exploration services

(P-129)
MACPHERSON OIL COMPANY
24118 Round Mountain Rd, Bakersfield (93308-9115)
P.O. Box 5368 (93388-5368)
PHONE..................661 556-6096
Wes Duncan, *Manager*
Clare Pagnini, *Human Res Mgr*
Cameron Francis, *Maintence Staff*
Tim Lovley, *Manager*
EMP: 12
SALES (corp-wide): 17.7MM **Privately Held**
WEB: www.macphersonoil.com
SIC: 1382 1311 Oil & gas exploration services; crude petroleum & natural gas production
HQ: Macpherson Oil Company
100 Wilshire Blvd Ste 800
Santa Monica CA 90401
310 452-3880

(P-130)
MAGNETRON POWER INVENTIONS INC
2226 W 232nd St, Torrance (90501-5720)
PHONE..................310 462-6970
Ninan N Johnson, *CEO*
EMP: 15
SQ FT: 2,500
SALES: 5MM **Privately Held**
SIC: 1382 Oil & gas exploration services

(P-131)
NATIONS PETROLEUM CAL LLC
9600 Ming Ave Ste 300, Bakersfield (93311-1365)
PHONE..................661 387-6402
Phil Sorvet,
EMP: 60
SALES (est): 4MM
SALES (corp-wide): 2.1MM **Privately Held**
SIC: 1382 Oil & gas exploration services
PA: Nations Petroleum Company Ltd
255 5 Ave Sw Suite 750
Calgary AB T2P 3
403 206-1420

(P-132)
NEWPORT ENERGY LLC
19200 Von Karman Ave # 400, Irvine
(92612-8553)
PHONE....................................408 230-7545
Nyle Khan, *CEO*
Gordon Burk, *COO*
EMP: 25 EST: 2012
SQ FT: 5,000
SALES (est): 953.6K **Privately Held**
SIC: 1382 Oil & gas exploration services

(P-133)
PAULSSON INC
16543 Arminta St, Van Nuys (91406-1745)
PHONE....................................310 780-2219
Bjorn Paulsson, *President*
Phillip Oseas, *CFO*
EMP: 11
SALES (est): 3.5MM **Privately Held**
SIC: 1382 7382 Oil & gas exploration
services; security systems services

(P-134)
QRE OPERATING LLC
707 Wilshire Blvd # 4600, Los Angeles
(90017-3501)
PHONE....................................213 225-5900
Alan L Smith, *Mng Member*
EMP: 208
SALES (est): 708K **Privately Held**
SIC: 1382 Oil & gas exploration services
PA: Qr Energy, Lp
    707 Wilshire Blvd # 4600
    Los Angeles CA 90017

(P-135)
QUANTUM ENERGY LLC
Also Called: Quaneco
22801 Ventura Blvd # 200, Woodland Hills
(91364-1222)
PHONE....................................800 950-3519
Harrison Schumacher, *Branch Mgr*
EMP: 20
SALES (corp-wide): 3.4MM **Privately
Held**
SIC: 1382 Oil & gas exploration services
PA: Quantum Energy Llc
    10405 Locust Grove Dr
    Chardon OH 44024
    440 285-7381

(P-136)
**R W LYALL & COMPANY INC
(DH)**
2665 Research Dr, Corona (92882-6918)
P.O. Box 2259 (92878-2259)
PHONE....................................951 270-1500
Jeffrey W Lyall, *President*
Jennifer Fritchle, *COO*
Bruce Lange, *COO*
Tony Mauer, *CFO*
Andrew Babcock, *Opers Mgr*
▲ EMP: 168
SQ FT: 70,000
SALES (est): 152.4MM
SALES (corp-wide): 4.4B **Publicly Held**
WEB: www.rwlyall.com
SIC: 1382 Oil & gas exploration services

(P-137)
**ROYALE ENERGY FUNDS INC
(HQ)**
1870 Cordell Ct Ste 210, El Cajon
(92020-0916)
PHONE....................................619 383-6600
Donald H Hosmer, *President*
Stephen M Hosmer, *President*
Jennie Steingraber, *Executive Asst*
Ronald Lipnick, *VP Finance*
EMP: 11
SALES: 1MM
SALES (corp-wide): 5.4MM **Publicly Held**
WEB: www.royl.com
SIC: 1382 Oil & gas exploration services
PA: Royale Energy, Inc.
    1870 Cordell Ct Ste 210
    El Cajon CA 92020
    619 383-6600

(P-138)
**SANTA MARIA ENRGY
HOLDINGS LLC**
2811 Airpark Dr, Santa Maria (93455-1417)
P.O. Box 7202 (93456-7202)
PHONE....................................805 938-3320
David Pratt, *CEO*
EMP: 20
SALES (est): 2.9MM **Privately Held**
SIC: 1382 Oil & gas exploration services

(P-139)
SEISMIC RESERVOIR 2020 INC
3 Pointe Dr Ste 212, Brea (92821-7624)
PHONE....................................562 697-9711
EMP: 21
SALES: 4MM **Privately Held**
SIC: 1382

(P-140)
**SHARPE ENERGY SERVICES
INC**
5094 Northlawn Dr, San Jose
(95130-1835)
PHONE....................................408 489-3581
Kelly Sharpe, *President*
David Koshiyama, *Vice Pres*
Terry Sharpe, *Vice Pres*
Steven Sharpe, *General Mgr*
EMP: 15
SALES (est): 907.7K **Privately Held**
SIC: 1382 Oil & gas exploration services

(P-141)
SIGNAL HILL PETROLEUM INC
2633 Cherry Ave, Signal Hill (90755-2008)
PHONE....................................562 595-6440
Jerrel Barto, *Ch of Bd*
Craig C Barto, *President*
Parra Diane, *Executive Asst*
Floyd Leeson, *Engineer*
Michael Kuzmits, *VP Finance*
EMP: 49
SALES (est): 19.4MM **Privately Held**
WEB: www.shpi.net
SIC: 1382 Geological exploration, oil & gas
field

(P-142)
SOLIMAR ENERGY LLC
121 N Fir St Ste H, Ventura (93001-2094)
PHONE....................................805 643-4100
Frank Petruzzeli, *Mng Member*
EMP: 10
SALES (est): 802.2K **Privately Held**
SIC: 1382 Oil & gas exploration services

(P-143)
U S WEATHERFORD L P
19608 Broken Ct, Shafter (93263-9583)
PHONE....................................661 746-3415
EMP: 27 **Privately Held**
SIC: 1382
HQ: U S Weatherford L P
    2000 Saint James Pl
    Houston TX 70395
    713 693-4000

(P-144)
UNIVERSAL DYNAMICS INC
5313 3rd St, Irwindale (91706-2085)
PHONE....................................626 480-0035
Issa Alasker, *President*
Sahak Sahakian, *Accounting Mgr*
EMP: 12
SQ FT: 15,000
SALES (est): 1.2MM **Privately Held**
SIC: 1382 7382 Oil & gas exploration
services; security systems services

(P-145)
VACA ENERGY LLC
4407 Sturgis Rd, Oxnard (93030)
PHONE....................................310 385-3684
Clint Walker, *Mng Member*
EMP: 14
SALES (est): 1.2MM **Privately Held**
SIC: 1382 Oil & gas exploration services

(P-146)
**WEP TRANSPORT HOLDINGS
LLC**
16909 Via De Santa Fe, Rancho Santa Fe
(92067-9519)
P.O. Box 7068 (92067-7068)
PHONE....................................858 756-1010
Steven Marshall, *President*
EMP: 14
SALES (est): 675.3K **Privately Held**
SIC: 1382 Oil & gas exploration services

(P-147)
**WESTERN ENERGY
PRODUCTION LLC**
16909 Via De Santa Fe, Rancho Santa Fe
(92067-9519)
P.O. Box 7068 (92067-7068)
PHONE....................................858 756-1010
Steven Marshall, *President*
EMP: 10
SALES (est): 940K **Privately Held**
SIC: 1382 Geological exploration, oil & gas
field

(P-148)
WICKLAND PIPELINES LLC (PA)
8950 Cal Center Dr # 125, Sacramento
(95826-3262)
PHONE....................................916 978-2432
Roy L Wickland, *Principal*
EMP: 13 EST: 2010
SALES (est): 3.5MM **Privately Held**
SIC: 1382 Oil & gas exploration services

1389 Oil & Gas Field Svcs, NEC

(P-149)
**260 RESOURCE MANAGEMENT
LLC**
100 Bayview Cir Ste 505, Newport Beach
(92660-2984)
P.O. Box 112, Lawndale (90260-0112)
PHONE....................................866 700-1031
Kevin Williams, *Mng Member*
EMP: 12
SQ FT: 4,000
SALES (est): 378.6K **Privately Held**
SIC: 1389 Gas field services

(P-150)
**AA PRODUCTION SERVICES
INC (PA)**
433 2nd St Ste 103, Woodland
(95695-4065)
PHONE....................................530 668-7525
John Adams, *President*
Elden D Hinkle, *Vice Pres*
Daniel Miantre, *Vice Pres*
EMP: 35
SQ FT: 3,500
SALES (est): 4.5MM **Privately Held**
WEB: www.aaproduction.com
SIC: 1389 Oil & gas wells: building, repair-
ing & dismantling

(P-151)
AC PUMPING UNIT REPAIR INC
2625 Dawson Ave, Signal Hill
(90755-2019)
PHONE....................................562 492-1300
Michael Quike, *CEO*
Micheal Quirke, *Vice Pres*
Alfonso Campas, *CEO*
EMP: 25
SALES (est): 3MM **Privately Held**
SIC: 1389 Oil & gas wells: building, repair-
ing & dismantling

(P-152)
ALLY ENTERPRISES
5001 E Commercecenter Dr # 260, Bakers-
field (93309-1663)
P.O. Box 20580 (93390-0580)
PHONE....................................661 412-9933
Rick Noland, *President*
EMP: 20
SALES (est): 462.7K **Privately Held**
SIC: 1389 Oil field services

(P-153)
**AMERICAN TRUCK
DISMANTLING**
15303 Arrow Blvd, Fontana (92335-1213)
PHONE....................................909 429-2166
Vrej Mairman, *Owner*
EMP: 18 EST: 1998
SQ FT: 4,000
SALES (est): 1.5MM **Privately Held**
WEB: www.amtrkdism.com
SIC: 1389 3714 Construction, repair & dis-
mantling services; motor vehicle parts &
accessories

(P-154)
ANATESCO INC
128 Bedford Way, Bakersfield
(93308-1702)
P.O. Box 5694 (93388-5694)
PHONE....................................661 399-6990
Douglas Paul Denesha, *President*
Jean Denesha, *Vice Pres*
EMP: 15
SQ FT: 3,000
SALES (est): 1.2MM **Privately Held**
WEB: www.anatesco.com
SIC: 1389 Testing, measuring, surveying &
analysis services

(P-155)
ARCHROCK INC
3333 Gibson St, Bakersfield (93308-5255)
PHONE....................................661 321-0271
Gerald Quinn, *Manager*
EMP: 16 **Publicly Held**
WEB: www.exterran.com
SIC: 1389 5084 Gas compressing (natural
gas) at the fields; compressors, except air
conditioning
PA: Archrock Inc.
    9807 Katy Fwy Ste 100
    Houston TX 77024

(P-156)
B & L CASING SERVICE LLC
Also Called: United Wealth Control
21054 Kratzmeyer Rd, Bakersfield
(93314-9482)
P.O. Box 22260 (93390-2260)
PHONE....................................661 589-9080
Larry Jenkins, *Mng Member*
Brian Jenkins, *Vice Pres*
Rod Ledesma, *Vice Pres*
Stuart Feliz, *District Mgr*
Stacy Lopez, *Admin Asst*
EMP: 13
SALES (est): 3.3MM **Privately Held**
SIC: 1389 Oil field services

(P-157)
**BAKER HGHES OLFLD
OPRTIONS LLC**
Also Called: Baker Atlas
4730 Armstrong Rd, Bakersfield
(93313-2115)
P.O. Box 956, Taft (93268-0956)
PHONE....................................661 831-5200
Steve Tipton, *Manager*
EMP: 10
SALES (corp-wide): 22.8B **Privately Held**
WEB: www.bakeratlas.com
SIC: 1389 Oil field services
HQ: Baker Hughes Oilfield Operations Llc
    17021 Aldine Westfield Rd
    Houston TX 77073
    713 879-1000

(P-158)
**BAKER HGHES OLFLD
OPRTIONS LLC**
5421 Argosy Ave, Huntington Beach
(92649-1038)
PHONE....................................714 893-8511
EMP: 55
SALES (corp-wide): 22.8B **Privately Held**
WEB: www.bot.bhi-net.com
SIC: 1389 Oil field services
HQ: Baker Hughes Oilfield Operations Llc
    17021 Aldine Westfield Rd
    Houston TX 77073
    713 879-1000

(P-159)
BAKER HGHES OLFLD OPRTIONS LLC
Also Called: Baker Oil Tools
15421 Assembly Ln, Huntington Beach
(92649-1329)
PHONE.....................714 891-8544
Steve Cook, *Manager*
EMP: 17
SQ FT: 10,000
SALES (corp-wide): 22.8B **Privately Held**
WEB: www.bot.bhi-net.com
SIC: **1389** Oil field services
HQ: Baker Hughes Oilfield Operations Llc
　　17021 Aldine Westfield Rd
　　Houston TX 77073
　　713 879-1000

(P-160)
BAKER HGHES OLFLD OPRTIONS LLC
5700 Doolittle Ave, Shafter (93263-4035)
PHONE.....................661 834-9654
Bob Ledet, *Manager*
EMP: 50
SALES (corp-wide): 22.8B **Privately Held**
WEB: www.bot.bhi-net.com
SIC: **1389** 7353 5084 Oil field services; oil
　　field equipment, rental or leasing; drilling
　　bits
HQ: Baker Hughes Oilfield Operations Llc
　　17021 Aldine Westfield Rd
　　Houston TX 77073
　　713 879-1000

(P-161)
BAKER HUGHES A GE COMPANY LLC
5421 Argosy Ave, Huntington Beach
(92649-1038)
PHONE.....................714 893-8511
David A Patti, *Manager*
Robert Dempsey, *District Mgr*
EMP: 84
SALES (corp-wide): 22.8B **Privately Held**
SIC: **1389** Oil field services
PA: Baker Hughes, A Ge Company Llc
　　17021 Aldine Westfield Rd
　　Houston TX 77073
　　713 439-8600

(P-162)
BAKER HUGHES A GE COMPANY LLC
3901 Fanucchi Way, Shafter (93263-9539)
PHONE.....................661 834-9654
Rebecca Garnett, *Manager*
Kristin Carter-Matheson, *Technical Staff*
David Escobar, *Opers Staff*
EMP: 41
SALES (corp-wide): 22.8B **Privately Held**
SIC: **1389** Oil field services
PA: Baker Hughes, A Ge Company Llc
　　17021 Aldine Westfield Rd
　　Houston TX 77073
　　713 439-8600

(P-163)
BAKER HUGHES A GE COMPANY LLC
1127 Carrier Parkway Ave, Bakersfield
(93308-9666)
PHONE.....................661 387-1010
Charles Laymance, *Branch Mgr*
Chris Long, *Opers Mgr*
EMP: 87
SALES (corp-wide): 22.8B **Privately Held**
SIC: **1389** Oil field services
PA: Baker Hughes, A Ge Company Llc
　　17021 Aldine Westfield Rd
　　Houston TX 77073
　　713 439-8600

(P-164)
BAKER HUGHES A GE COMPANY LLC
5145 Boylan St, Bakersfield (93308-4511)
PHONE.....................800 229-7447
Lori Robinson, *Manager*
EMP: 87
SALES (corp-wide): 22.8B **Privately Held**
WEB: www.bakerhughes.com
SIC: **1389** Oil field services

PA: Baker Hughes, A Ge Company Llc
　　17021 Aldine Westfield Rd
　　Houston TX 77073
　　713 439-8600

(P-165)
BAKER HUGHES A GE COMPANY LLC
Also Called: Unichem
19433 Colombo St, Bakersfield
(93308-9517)
PHONE.....................661 391-0794
Rusty Davis, *Branch Mgr*
EMP: 12
SALES (corp-wide): 22.8B **Privately Held**
WEB: www.bjservices.com
SIC: **1389** Acidizing wells
PA: Baker Hughes, A Ge Company Llc
　　17021 Aldine Westfield Rd
　　Houston TX 77073
　　713 439-8600

(P-166)
BAKER PETROLITE LLC
2280 Bates Ave Ste A, Concord
(94520-1235)
PHONE.....................925 682-3313
Joe Rund, *Manager*
EMP: 11
SALES (corp-wide): 22.8B **Privately Held**
WEB: www.bakerpetrolite.com
SIC: **1389** Oil field services
HQ: Baker Petrolite Llc
　　12645 W Airport Blvd
　　Sugar Land TX 77478
　　281 276-5400

(P-167)
BAKER PETROLITE LLC
5125 Boylan St, Bakersfield (93308-4511)
PHONE.....................661 325-4138
Doug Thomas, *Manager*
EMP: 60
SALES (corp-wide): 22.8B **Privately Held**
WEB: www.bakerpetrolite.com
SIC: **1389** Oil field services
HQ: Baker Petrolite Llc
　　12645 W Airport Blvd
　　Sugar Land TX 77478
　　281 276-5400

(P-168)
BAKER PETROLITE LLC
11808 Bloomfield Ave, Santa Fe Springs
(90670-4610)
PHONE.....................562 406-7090
Bob Whitton, *Manager*
EMP: 12
SALES (corp-wide): 22.8B **Privately Held**
WEB: www.bakerpetrolite.com
SIC: **1389** Oil field services
HQ: Baker Petrolite Llc
　　12645 W Airport Blvd
　　Sugar Land TX 77478
　　281 276-5400

(P-169)
BAKER PETROLITE LLC
Also Called: Baker Hughes
265 Quail Ct, Santa Paula (93060-9653)
PHONE.....................805 525-4404
Brad Porchuk, *Manager*
EMP: 20
SALES (corp-wide): 22.8B **Privately Held**
SIC: **1389** Oil field services
HQ: Baker Petrolite Llc
　　12645 W Airport Blvd
　　Sugar Land TX 77478
　　281 276-5400

(P-170)
BASIC ENERGY SERVICES INC
12891 Nelson St, Garden Grove
(92840-5018)
PHONE.....................714 530-0855
Roe T M Patterson, *Manager*
EMP: 34
SALES (corp-wide): 964.7MM **Publicly Held**
SIC: **1389** Construction, repair & dismantling services; oil field services
PA: Basic Energy Services, Inc.
　　801 Cherry St Unit 2
　　Fort Worth TX 76102
　　817 334-4100

(P-171)
BASIC ENERGY SERVICES INC
6710 Stewart Way, Bakersfield (93308)
PHONE.....................661 588-3800
EMP: 34
SALES (corp-wide): 547.5MM **Publicly Held**
SIC: **1389**
PA: Basic Energy Services, Inc.
　　801 Cherry St Unit 2
　　Fort Worth TX 76102
　　817 334-4100

(P-172)
BLACK GOLD PUMP & SUPPLY INC
2459 Lewis Ave, Signal Hill (90755-3427)
PHONE.....................323 298-0077
Michael L Bair, *CEO*
James L Hurd, *President*
Thomas E Casec, *Corp Secy*
Steve Bollweg, *Vice Pres*
Erin Meehan, *Executive Asst*
▲ EMP: 17
SALES (est): 3.3MM **Privately Held**
SIC: **1389** Oil field services

(P-173)
BLOWOUT TOOLS INC
19484 Broken Ct, Shafter (93263-3146)
PHONE.....................661 746-1700
EMP: 14 **Publicly Held**
SIC: **1389** Oil field services
HQ: Blowout Tools, Inc.
　　2202 Oil Center Ct
　　Houston TX 77073
　　405 671-3800

(P-174)
C & H TESTING SERVICE INC (PA)
6224 Price Way, Bakersfield (93308-5117)
P.O. Box 9907 (93389-1907)
PHONE.....................661 589-4030
Donald T Hoover, *President*
Karen K Hoover, *Corp Secy*
EMP: 31 EST: 1981
SQ FT: 1,500
SALES (est): 7.7MM **Privately Held**
SIC: **1389** Oil field services

(P-175)
C CASE COMPANY INC
Also Called: Case's Oil
7010 W Cerini Ave, Riverdale
(93656-9622)
PHONE.....................559 867-3912
Coofas Wayne Case Jr, *President*
Rodney Craig Case, *Vice Pres*
Sarah Dewey, *Admin Sec*
EMP: 33
SALES (est): 5MM **Privately Held**
SIC: **1389** 1311 Oil & gas wells: building,
　　repairing & dismantling; crude petroleum
　　production

(P-176)
CAL COAST ACIDIZING CO
Also Called: Cal Coast Acidizing Service
6226 Dominion Rd, Santa Maria (93454)
P.O. Box 2050, Orcutt (93457-2050)
PHONE.....................805 934-2411
Bruce Edward Conway, *CEO*
EMP: 18
SQ FT: 2,000
SALES (est): 2.3MM **Privately Held**
SIC: **1389** Oil field services

(P-177)
CAL QUAKE CONSTRUCTION INC
636 N Formosa Ave, Los Angeles
(90036-1943)
PHONE.....................323 931-2969
Sheldon Perluss, *President*
John Taferner, *Vice Pres*
Seth Taferner, *Office Mgr*
Isael Duarte, *Director*
EMP: 20
SALES (est): 1.2MM **Privately Held**
WEB: www.cal-quake.com
SIC: **1389** Construction, repair & dismantling services

(P-178)
CALIFRNIA RSRUCES LONG BCH INC
111 W Ocean Blvd Ste 800, Long Beach
(90802-7930)
PHONE.....................562 624-3204
Frank Komin, *CEO*
EMP: 116
SALES (est): 1.6MM
SALES (corp-wide): 3B **Publicly Held**
SIC: **1389** Oil field services
PA: California Resources Corporation
　　27200 Tourney Rd Ste 200
　　Santa Clarita CA 91355
　　888 848-4754

(P-179)
CALPI INC
7141 Downing Ave, Bakersfield
(93308-5815)
P.O. Box 81795 (93380-1795)
PHONE.....................661 589-5648
Robert Larkie Barnett, *President*
Jeff Barnett, *Vice Pres*
Brian Martin, *Plant Engr*
EMP: 11 EST: 1981
SQ FT: 5,032
SALES (est): 1MM **Privately Held**
WEB: www.calpi.net
SIC: **1389** 4959 Cleaning wells; toxic or
　　hazardous waste cleanup

(P-180)
CAMERON INTERNATIONAL CORP
Also Called: Camserv
1282 Bayview Farm Rd, Pinole (94564)
PHONE.....................510 928-1480
EMP: 56 **Publicly Held**
SIC: **1389** Oil field services
HQ: Cameron International Corporation
　　4646 W Sam Houston Pkwy N
　　Houston TX 77041

(P-181)
CARRERA CONSTRUCTION INC
Also Called: S&J Carrera Constructions
1961 Main St Ste 261, Watsonville
(95076-3027)
PHONE.....................831 728-3299
Steven Carrera, *President*
EMP: 10
SALES: 1.8MM **Privately Held**
SIC: **1389** Construction, repair & dismantling services

(P-182)
CENTRAL CALIFORNIA CNSTR INC
7221 Downing Ave, Bakersfield
(93308-5817)
PHONE.....................661 978-8230
Dereke Gerecke, *Principal*
Tammie K Rankin-Gerecke, *Principal*
EMP: 11
SALES (est): 1.2MM **Privately Held**
SIC: **1389** Construction, repair & dismantling services

(P-183)
CJD CONSTRUCTION SERVICES INC
416 S Vermont Ave, Glendora
(91741-6256)
PHONE.....................626 335-1116
Diego A Debenedetto, *President*
Diego Dibenedetto, *President*
EMP: 40
SALES (est): 3.9MM **Privately Held**
SIC: **1389** Construction, repair & dismantling services

(P-184)
CL KNOX INC
Also Called: Advanced Industrial Services
34933 Imperial St, Bakersfield (93308)
PHONE.....................661 837-0477
Leslie Knox, *President*
Chris Knox, *Corp Secy*
Stephanie Smith, *Manager*
Will Taylor, *Manager*
EMP: 80

2020 California
Manufacturers Register
▲ = Import ▼=Export
◆ =Import/Export

SALES (est): 10.6MM **Privately Held**
SIC: **1389** 8742 Oil field services; industrial consultant

(P-185)
COLT SERVICES LP
Also Called: Colt Group
1399 E Burnett St, Signal Hill (90755-3511)
PHONE..................................562 988-2658
David Balster, *Branch Mgr*
EMP: 12
SALES (corp-wide): 10.5MM **Privately Held**
SIC: **1389** 7699 Construction, repair & dismantling services; boiler & heating repair services
PA: Colt Services, L.P.
    626 N 16th St
    La Porte TX 77571
    281 471-9099

(P-186)
CORE LABORATORIES LP
3437 Landco Dr, Bakersfield (93308-6187)
PHONE..................................661 325-5657
Bryon Bell, *Partner*
EMP: 20
SALES (corp-wide): 700.8MM **Privately Held**
SIC: **1389** Oil field services
HQ: Core Laboratories Lp
    6316 Windfern Rd
    Houston TX 77040
    -

(P-187)
CUMMINGS VACUUM SERVICE INC
Also Called: Cummings Transportation
19605 Broken Ct, Shafter (93263-9583)
PHONE..................................661 746-1786
Pam Cummings, *President*
Ted Cummings, *Vice Pres*
Dave Stitt, *Maint Spvr*
EMP: 60
SQ FT: 3,000
SALES (est): 7.6MM **Privately Held**
SIC: **1389** Oil field services

(P-188)
DAWSON ENTERPRISES
Also Called: Cavins Oil Well Tools
815 Main St, Taft (93268-3118)
P.O. Box 695 (93268-0695)
PHONE..................................661 765-2181
Charles Palmer, *Manager*
EMP: 11
SALES (corp-wide): 9.7MM **Privately Held**
WEB: www.cavins.com
SIC: **1389** Well logging
PA: Dawson Enterprises
    2853 Cherry Ave
    Signal Hill CA 90755
    562 424-8564

(P-189)
DE VRIES INTERNATIONAL INC (PA)
17671 Armstrong Ave, Irvine (92614-5727)
PHONE..................................949 252-1212
Don Devries, *President*
David Kazmierski, *QC Mgr*
▲ EMP: 44
SALES (est): 22.8MM **Privately Held**
WEB: www.devriesintl.com
SIC: **1389** Lease tanks, oil field: erecting, cleaning & repairing

(P-190)
DTE STOCKTON LLC
2526 W Washington St, Stockton (95203-2952)
PHONE..................................209 467-3838
Nelson Nail, *Mng Member*
EMP: 34
SALES (est): 4.2MM **Publicly Held**
SIC: **1389** Construction, repair & dismantling services
HQ: Dte Energy Services, Inc.
    414 S Main St Ste 600
    Ann Arbor MI 48104

(P-191)
DWAYNES ENGINEERING & CNSTR
3655 Addie Ave, Mc Kittrick (93251)
P.O. Box 116 (93251-0116)
PHONE..................................661 762-7261
Dwayne Emfinger, *President*
EMP: 78
SALES (est): 7.8MM **Privately Held**
WEB: www.dwayneseng.com
SIC: **1389** Construction, repair & dismantling services

(P-192)
ENGEL & GRAY INC
745 W Betteravia Rd Ste A, Santa Maria (93455-1298)
P.O. Box 5020 (93456-5020)
PHONE..................................805 925-2771
Carl W Engel Jr, *President*
Robert Engel, *Vice Pres*
EMP: 35 EST: 1946
SQ FT: 3,000
SALES (est): 7.1MM **Privately Held**
WEB: www.recycleaward.com
SIC: **1389** 1623 7389 2875 Construction, repair & dismantling services; haulage, oil field; pipeline construction; crane & aerial lift service; compost

(P-193)
ENGINEERED WELL SVC INTL INC
3120 Standard St, Bakersfield (93308-6241)
PHONE..................................866 913-6283
Paul Sturgeon, *CEO*
John E Powell Jr, *Principal*
EMP: 125 EST: 2009
SALES (est): 44MM **Privately Held**
SIC: **1389** Oil field services

(P-194)
ETHOSENERGY FIELD SERVICES LLC
2485 Courage Dr Ste 100, Fairfield (94533-6740)
PHONE..................................707 399-0420
Ed Moore, *Branch Mgr*
EMP: 14
SALES (corp-wide): 10B **Privately Held**
SIC: **1389** Oil consultants
HQ: Field Ethosenergy Services Llc
    10455 Slusher Dr Bldg 12
    Santa Fe Springs CA 90670

(P-195)
ETHOSENERGY FIELD SERVICES LLC (DH)
Also Called: Wg
10455 Slusher Dr Bldg 12, Santa Fe Springs (90670-3750)
PHONE..................................310 639-3523
Rob Duby, *President*
Patricia Lelito, *CFO*
Mike Fieldhouse, *Vice Pres*
Mary Ros, *General Mgr*
EMP: 75
SALES (est): 29.9MM
SALES (corp-wide): 10B **Privately Held**
WEB: www.woodgroupgts.com
SIC: **1389** 8711 3462 Oil consultants; industrial engineers; pump, compressor & turbine forgings

(P-196)
ETHOSENERGY PWR PLANT SVCS LLC
3215 47th Ave, Sacramento (95824-2400)
PHONE..................................916 391-2993
EMP: 32
SALES (corp-wide): 10B **Privately Held**
WEB: www.wgpo.com
SIC: **1389** Cementing oil & gas well casings
HQ: Ethosenergy Power Plant Services, Llc
    12600 Drfeld Pkwy Ste 315
    Alpharetta GA 30004
    678 393-7800

(P-197)
FIELD FOUNDATION
15306 Carmenita Rd, Santa Fe Springs (90670-5606)
P.O. Box 4236, Cerritos (90703-4236)
PHONE..................................562 921-3567
Irwin Field, *Owner*
EMP: 50
SALES (est): 24.3K **Privately Held**
SIC: **1389** Oil sampling service for oil companies

(P-198)
FIRST ENERGY SERVICES INC
1031 Carrier Parkway Ave, Bakersfield (93308-9670)
P.O. Box 80844 (93380-0844)
PHONE..................................661 387-1972
Richard Chase, *President*
Charlotte Maddon, *Treasurer*
Jack Chase, *Vice Pres*
EMP: 20
SQ FT: 7,000
SALES (est): 3.2MM **Privately Held**
SIC: **1389** Servicing oil & gas wells

(P-199)
GAINES WELL SERVICE INC (PA)
10063 Colony Rd, Wilton (95693-9506)
P.O. Box 369 (95693-0369)
PHONE..................................916 687-6751
Joseph Gaines, *President*
Reba Gaines, *Treasurer*
Michael Gaines, *Vice Pres*
Gregory Gaines, *Admin Sec*
EMP: 20
SALES (est): 1.6MM **Privately Held**
SIC: **1389** Servicing oil & gas wells

(P-200)
GAS RECOVERY SYSTEMS LLC
20662 Newport Coast Dr, Irvine (92612)
PHONE..................................949 718-1430
Tom Holter, *Manager*
EMP: 16
SALES (corp-wide): 198.8MM **Privately Held**
SIC: **1389** Removal of condensate gasoline from field (gathering) lines
HQ: Gas Recovery Systems, Llc
    1 N Lexington Ave Ste 620
    White Plains NY 10601
    914 421-4903

(P-201)
GENE WATSON CONSTRUCTION A CA
801 Kern St, Taft (93268-2734)
PHONE..................................661 763-5254
Gene Watson, *Ltd Ptnr*
Patricia Watson, *Ltd Ptnr*
EMP: 530
SALES (est): 11.2MM **Privately Held**
WEB: www.gwc-ltd.com
SIC: **1389** 1382 Oil field services; oil & gas exploration services

(P-202)
GRAYSON SERVICE INC
1845 Greeley Rd, Bakersfield (93314-9547)
PHONE..................................661 589-5444
Carol A Grayson, *President*
Cheryl Grayson, *Vice Pres*
EMP: 150
SALES (est): 5.7MM **Privately Held**
SIC: **1389** Servicing oil & gas wells

(P-203)
GROUNDMETRICS INC
Also Called: GMI
3954 Murphy Canyon Rd D207, San Diego (92123-4420)
PHONE..................................619 786-8023
George A Eiskamp, *CEO*
Jeffrey Symington, *CFO*
Jessie Kaffai, *Vice Pres*
Carlos Heredia, *Admin Sec*
Devin Charters, *Information Mgr*
EMP: 15
SALES (est): 2.7MM **Privately Held**
SIC: **1389** 3829 Oil field services; surveying instruments & accessories

(P-204)
HALLIBURTON COMPANY
34722 7th Standard Rd, Bakersfield (93314-9435)
PHONE..................................661 393-8111
Dennis Lovett, *Branch Mgr*
Mark Hansen, *Technical Staff*
Richard Noffke, *Engineer*
David Self, *Manager*
EMP: 87 **Publicly Held**
SIC: **1389** Oil field services
PA: Halliburton Company
    3000 N Sam Houston Pkwy E
    Houston TX 77032

(P-205)
HARBISON-FISCHER INC
116 E Main St, Taft (93268-9727)
P.O. Box 1015 (93268-1015)
PHONE..................................661 765-7792
Robin Carter, *Principal*
EMP: 31
SALES (corp-wide): 1.2B **Publicly Held**
SIC: **1389** Oil field services
HQ: Harbison-Fischer, Inc.
    901 N Crowley Rd
    Crowley TX 76036
    817 297-2211

(P-206)
HAZE BERT AND ASSOSSIATES
3188 Airway Ave Ste K1, Costa Mesa (92626-4652)
PHONE..................................714 557-1567
Bert Haze, *Owner*
EMP: 14
SQ FT: 2,000
SALES: 300K **Privately Held**
WEB: www.berthaze.com
SIC: **1389** Testing, measuring, surveying & analysis services

(P-207)
HILLS WLDG & ENGRG CONTR INC
Also Called: Hwe Mechanical
22038 Stockdale Hwy, Bakersfield (93314-8889)
PHONE..................................661 746-5400
Debora M Hill, *Vice Pres*
Robert Hill, *Shareholder*
EMP: 92
SALES (est): 7.1MM **Privately Held**
SIC: **1389** Testing, measuring, surveying & analysis services

(P-208)
HIRSH INC
Also Called: Better Mens Clothes
860 S Los Angeles St # 900, Los Angeles (90014-3311)
PHONE..................................213 622-9441
Mistie Banks, *General Mgr*
Stanley Hirsh, *President*
EMP: 50
SALES (est): 1MM **Privately Held**
SIC: **1389** Lease tanks, oil field: erecting, cleaning & repairing

(P-209)
HORIZON WELL LOGGING INC
711 Saint Andrews Way, Lompoc (93436-1326)
PHONE..................................805 733-0972
Doug Milham, *President*
James Eastes, *Opers Staff*
William Gilmore, *Director*
▲ EMP: 16
SALES (est): 1.3MM **Privately Held**
WEB: www.horizon-well-logging.com
SIC: **1389** Oil field services

(P-210)
HUNTING ENERGY SERVICES INC
Also Called: Hunting-Vinson
4900 California Ave 100a, Bakersfield (93309-7024)
PHONE..................................661 633-4272
Bobby Ford, *Branch Mgr*
EMP: 76

SALES (corp-wide): 911.4MM **Privately
Held**
WEB: www.hunting-inc.com
SIC: **1389** Oil field services
HQ: Hunting Energy Services, Inc.
　16825 Northchase Dr # 600
　Houston TX 77060

(P-211)
HVI CAT CANYON INC
Also Called: Greka Oil & Gas
2617 E Clark Ave, Santa Maria
(93455-5815)
P.O. Box 5489 (93456-5489)
PHONE....................................805 621-5800
Alex G Dimitrijevic, *President*
Randeep S Grewal, *President*
Ken Miller, *CFO*
Susan Whalen, *Vice Pres*
EMP: 125
SALES (est): 11MM **Privately Held**
SIC: **1389** Oil field services

(P-212)
INNOVATIVE RV TECHNOLOGIES
Also Called: Hydralift
205 Via Morada, San Clemente
(92673-3504)
PHONE....................................949 559-5372
Brad Christian, *President*
▲ EMP: 40
SALES (est): 1.1MM **Privately Held**
SIC: **1389** Hydraulic fracturing wells

(P-213)
JERRY MELTON & SONS CNSTR
Also Called: Jerry Melton & Sons Cnstr
100 Jamison Ln, Taft (93268-4329)
PHONE....................................661 765-5546
Jerry W Melton, *President*
Karen Melton, *Treasurer*
Judy Melton, *Vice Pres*
Steven Melton, *Admin Sec*
EMP: 85
SALES (est): 11.6MM **Privately Held**
WEB: www.jerrymelton.com
SIC: **1389** Oil & gas wells: building, repair-
ing & dismantling; grading oil & gas well
foundations

(P-214)
JIM GRAHAM INC
4 Hill Ct, Rio Vista (94571-1400)
PHONE....................................707 374-5114
Jim Graham, *President*
Dorothy Graham, *Treasurer*
Robert Graham, *Vice Pres*
Edwina Messina, *Controller*
EMP: 28
SALES: 750K **Privately Held**
WEB: www.adamgraham.com
SIC: **1389** 7359 Servicing oil & gas wells;
tool rental

(P-215)
JOHN M PHILLIPS LLC
Also Called: John M Phillips Oil Field Eqp
2800 Gibson St, Bakersfield (93308-6106)
PHONE....................................661 327-3118
Melody Shamaker, *Office Mgr*
EMP: 11
SALES (est): 380.7K
SALES (corp-wide): 8.1MM **Privately
Held**
SIC: **1389** Oil field services
PA: John M. Phillips, Llc
　2755 Dawson Ave
　Signal Hill CA 90755
　562 595-7363

(P-216)
KATERRA INC (PA)
2494 Sand Hill Rd Ste 100, Menlo Park
(94025-6981)
PHONE....................................650 422-3572
Michael Marks, *CEO*
Paal Kibsgaard, *COO*
Matthew Marsh, *CFO*
Joanne Solomon, *CFO*
Winnie Geng, *Vice Pres*
EMP: 100 EST: 2015

SALES (est): 151.2MM **Privately Held**
SIC: **1389** 8741 8711 Construction, repair
& dismantling services; construction management; construction & civil engineering

(P-217)
KBA LTD OF KERN COUNTY LLP
2152 Mohawk St, Bakersfield (93308)
P.O. Box 1200 (93302-1200)
PHONE....................................661 323-0487
Brad Orear, *Partner*
Brad O'Rear, *Partner*
EMP: 15
SQ FT: 3,000
SALES (est): 613.5K **Privately Held**
SIC: **1389** Construction, repair & disman-
tling services

(P-218)
KEY ENERGY SERVICES INC
5080 California Ave # 150, Bakersfield
(93309-1697)
PHONE....................................661 334-8100
Lori Hatfield, *Manager*
Brenda Brown, *Administration*
EMP: 46
SALES (corp-wide): 521.7MM **Publicly
Held**
WEB: www.keyenergy.com
SIC: **1389** Oil field services
PA: Key Energy Services, Inc.
　1301 Mckinney St Ste 1800
　Houston TX 77010
　713 651-4300

(P-219)
KEY ENERGY SERVICES INC
3587 N Ventura Ave, Ventura (93001-1230)
PHONE....................................805 653-1300
Bob Wentz, *Branch Mgr*
EMP: 46
SALES (corp-wide): 521.7MM **Publicly
Held**
SIC: **1389** Oil field services
PA: Key Energy Services, Inc.
　1301 Mckinney St Ste 1800
　Houston TX 77010
　713 651-4300

(P-220)
M-I LLC
4400 Fanucchi Way, Shafter (93263-9552)
PHONE....................................661 321-5400
Forest Purpiance, *Branch Mgr*
EMP: 31 **Publicly Held**
SIC: **1389** Mud service, oil field drilling; oil
field services
HQ: M-I L.L.C.
　5950 N Course Dr
　Houston TX 77072
　281 561-1300

(P-221)
MARK SHEFFIELD CONSTRUCTION
9105 Langley Rd, Bakersfield
(93312-2156)
PHONE....................................661 589-8520
Mark Sheffield, *President*
Linda Sheffield, *Treasurer*
Steven Sheffield, *Vice Pres*
EMP: 20
SALES: 2MM **Privately Held**
SIC: **1389** 7389 Oil field services; crane &
aerial lift service

(P-222)
MIC LABS
7643 Corrinne Pl, San Ramon
(94583-4010)
PHONE....................................925 822-2847
Michael J Knudtson, *Owner*
EMP: 10
SQ FT: 1,690
SALES: 70K **Privately Held**
SIC: **1389** Gas field services

(P-223)
MID OHIO FIELD SERVICES LLC
4686 Ontario Mills Pkwy, Ontario
(91764-5104)
PHONE....................................614 755-5067
EMP: 10
SALES (est): 610K **Privately Held**
SIC: **1389**

(P-224)
MMI SERVICES INC
4042 Patton Way, Bakersfield
(93308-5030)
PHONE....................................661 589-9366
Steve McGowan, *President*
Mel McGowan, *CEO*
Eric Olson, *Vice Pres*
Roxanne Campbell, *Info Tech Dir*
Erick Olson, *Human Res Dir*
EMP: 250
SQ FT: 4,500
SALES (est): 51.3MM **Privately Held**
WEB: www.mmi-services.com
SIC: **1389** Oil field services

(P-225)
MR T TRANSPORT
15535 Garfield Ave, Paramount
(90723-4033)
PHONE....................................562 602-5536
Telesoro Torres, *CEO*
Erica Torres, *CFO*
Oscar Torres, *Director*
EMP: 17
SQ FT: 9,426
SALES (est): 1.7MM **Privately Held**
SIC: **1389** 4212 7629 Servicing oil & gas
wells; local trucking, without storage;
telecommunication equipment repair (ex-
cept telephones)

(P-226)
MTS STIMULATION SERVICES INC (PA)
Also Called: M T S
7131 Charity Ave, Bakersfield
(93308-5870)
PHONE....................................661 589-5804
Tommy T Reed, *President*
Polly Clark, *Shareholder*
Gary Starling, *Shareholder*
Craig Barto, *Ch of Bd*
Don Blurton, *Admin Sec*
EMP: 40
SQ FT: 1,400
SALES (est): 8.4MM **Privately Held**
WEB: www.mts-stim.com
SIC: **1389** Oil field services

(P-227)
NABORS WELL SERVICES CO
2567 N Ventura Ave C, Ventura
(93001-1201)
PHONE....................................805 648-2731
Paul Smith, *Manager*
Charles Marshall, *Vice Pres*
James Bentley, *Branch Mgr*
Jim Brady, *Branch Mgr*
Dean Sherrill, *General Mgr*
EMP: 90 **Privately Held**
SIC: **1389** Oil field services
HQ: Nabors Well Services Co.
　515 W Greens Rd Ste 1000
　Houston TX 77067
　281 874-0035

(P-228)
NABORS WELL SERVICES CO
1025 Earthmover Ct, Bakersfield
(93314-9529)
PHONE....................................661 588-6140
Tom Jaquez, *Manager*
EMP: 160 **Privately Held**
SIC: **1389** Oil field services
HQ: Nabors Well Services Co.
　515 W Greens Rd Ste 1000
　Houston TX 77067
　281 874-0035

(P-229)
NABORS WELL SERVICES CO
7515 Rosedale Hwy, Bakersfield
(93308-5727)
PHONE....................................661 589-3970
Alan Pounds, *Sales Executive*
Jerry Fernandez, *Area Mgr*
Melanie Mendoza, *Maintence Staff*
Ron C Cleveland, *Manager*
Joe Deford, *Manager*
EMP: 270 **Privately Held**
SIC: **1389** 1382 Servicing oil & gas wells;
oil & gas exploration services

HQ: Nabors Well Services Co.
　515 W Greens Rd Ste 1000
　Houston TX 77067
　281 874-0035

(P-230)
NABORS WELL SERVICES CO
19431 S Santa Fe Ave, Compton
(90221-5912)
PHONE....................................310 639-7074
Bernie Fish, *Manager*
Juan Landron, *Technology*
Gary Kaufman, *Human Res Mgr*
EMP: 230 **Privately Held**
SIC: **1389** Gas field services; oil field serv-
ices
HQ: Nabors Well Services Co.
　515 W Greens Rd Ste 1000
　Houston TX 77067
　281 874-0035

(P-231)
NABORS WELL SERVICES CO
1954 James Rd, Bakersfield (93308-9749)
PHONE....................................661 392-7668
Dave Warner, *District Mgr*
EMP: 76 **Privately Held**
SIC: **1389** Oil field services
HQ: Nabors Well Services Co.
　515 W Greens Rd Ste 1000
　Houston TX 77067
　281 874-0035

(P-232)
NASCO PETROLEUM LLC
20532 El Toro Rd Ste 102, Mission Viejo
(92692-5309)
PHONE....................................949 461-5212
EMP: 10 EST: 2013
SQ FT: 800
SALES (est): 530K **Privately Held**
SIC: **1389** 5172

(P-233)
NATIONAL CNSTR RENTALS INC
1045 S Greenwood Ave, Montebello
(90640-6001)
PHONE....................................323 838-1800
Glen Green, *Manager*
EMP: 13
SALES (corp-wide): 123.3MM **Privately
Held**
WEB: www.rentnational.com
SIC: **1389** Construction, repair & disman-
tling services
HQ: National Construction Rentals, Inc.
　15319 Chatsworth St
　Mission Hills CA 91345
　818 221-6000

(P-234)
NATIONAL OILWELL VARCO INC
Also Called: R & M Energy System
1320 E Los Angeles Ave, Shafter
(93263-9631)
PHONE....................................661 387-9316
Darryll May, *Branch Mgr*
Lonnie White, *Branch Mgr*
EMP: 15
SALES (corp-wide): 8.4B **Publicly Held**
WEB: www.rmenergy.com
SIC: **1389** Oil field services
PA: National Oilwell Varco, Inc.
　7909 Parkwood Circle Dr
　Houston TX 77036
　713 346-7500

(P-235)
NATIONAL OILWELL VARCO INC
Also Called: Pacific Inspection
1438b Ohm Rd, Arbuckle (95912)
PHONE....................................530 682-0571
EMP: 10
SALES (corp-wide): 20B **Publicly Held**
SIC: **1389**
PA: National Oilwell Varco, Inc.
　7909 Parkwood Circle Dr
　Houston TX 77036
　713 346-7500

(P-236)
NOBLE METHANE INC
104 Matmor Rd, Woodland (95776-6006)
PHONE....................................530 668-7961

▲ = Import ▼=Export
◆ =Import/Export

Brent Noble, *President*
Tiana Noble, *Admin Sec*
EMP: 10
SALES: 150K **Privately Held**
SIC: 1389 Servicing oil & gas wells

(P-237)
NORMAN WIRELINE SERVICE INC
1301 James Rd, Bakersfield (93308-9844)
PHONE..................................661 399-5697
James Norman, *President*
EMP: 13
SALES: 600K **Privately Held**
SIC: 1389 Construction, repair & dismantling services; oil field services

(P-238)
OIL WELL SERVICE COMPANY (PA)
10840 Norwalk Blvd, Santa Fe Springs (90670-3826)
PHONE..................................562 612-0600
Jack Frost, *President*
Connie Laws, *Treasurer*
Matthew Hensley, *Exec VP*
Richard Laws, *Vice Pres*
Matt Hensley, *Admin Sec*
EMP: 105
SQ FT: 9,000
SALES (est): 54.4MM **Privately Held**
WEB: www.ows1.com
SIC: 1389 Oil field services

(P-239)
OIL WELL SERVICE COMPANY
10255 Enos Ln, Shafter (93263-9572)
PHONE..................................661 746-4809
Rick Hobbs, *Office Mgr*
EMP: 45
SALES (corp-wide): 54.4MM **Privately Held**
WEB: www.ows1.com
SIC: 1389 Swabbing wells
PA: Oil Well Service Company
10840 Norwalk Blvd
Santa Fe Springs CA 90670
562 612-0600

(P-240)
OIL WELL SERVICE COMPANY
1015 Mission Rock Rd, Santa Paula (93060-9730)
PHONE..................................805 525-2103
Harvey Himinell, *Manager*
EMP: 21
SALES (corp-wide): 54.4MM **Privately Held**
WEB: www.ows1.com
SIC: 1389 Oil field services
PA: Oil Well Service Company
10840 Norwalk Blvd
Santa Fe Springs CA 90670
562 612-0600

(P-241)
PACHUNGA GAS STATION
45000 Pechanga Pkwy, Temecula (92592-5810)
PHONE..................................951 506-4575
Butch Murphy, *CEO*
EMP: 10
SALES (est): 453.4K **Privately Held**
SIC: 1389 Gas field services

(P-242)
PACIFIC PERFORATING INC
25090 Highway 33, Fellows (93224-9777)
PHONE..................................661 768-9224
Troy Ducharme, *President*
Perry Parker, *Vice Pres*
▼ **EMP:** 35 **EST:** 1969
SQ FT: 4,000
SALES (est): 4.6MM **Privately Held**
WEB: www.pacificperforating.com
SIC: 1389 Oil field services

(P-243)
PACIFIC PROCESS SYSTEMS INC (PA)
7401 Rosedale Hwy, Bakersfield (93308-5736)
PHONE..................................661 321-9681
Jerry Wise, *CEO*
Robert Peterson, *CFO*

Alan George, *Corp Secy*
Curt Avis, *Opers Mgr*
Anthony Munoz, *Supervisor*
▼ **EMP:** 90
SQ FT: 7,000
SALES (est): 262.1MM **Privately Held**
WEB: www.pps-equipment.com
SIC: 1389 7353 5082 Testing, measuring, surveying & analysis services; oil field equipment, rental or leasing; oil field equipment

(P-244)
PALMER TANK & CONSTRUCTION INC
2464 S Union Ave, Bakersfield (93307-5007)
PHONE..................................661 834-1110
Jerry Palmer, *President*
EMP: 20
SQ FT: 1,200
SALES (est): 2.2MM **Privately Held**
SIC: 1389 5731 Oil & gas wells: building, repairing & dismantling; antennas

(P-245)
PC MECHANICAL INC
2803 Industrial Pkwy, Santa Maria (93455-1811)
PHONE..................................805 925-2888
Lew Parker, *President*
Brandon Burginger, *COO*
Mary Parker, *Exec VP*
Mitch Caron, *Vice Pres*
EMP: 50
SQ FT: 67,000
SALES (est): 11.3MM **Privately Held**
WEB: www.pcmechanical.com
SIC: 1389 Oil field services

(P-246)
PETROLEUM SOLIDS CONTROL INC (PA)
1320 E Hill St, Signal Hill (90755-3526)
PHONE..................................562 424-0254
Michael Vignovich, *President*
Debbie Vignovich, *Treasurer*
Derek Vignovich, *Vice Pres*
Martin Vignovich, *Vice Pres*
Lan Nguyen, *Admin Sec*
EMP: 12
SQ FT: 2,450
SALES (est): 3MM **Privately Held**
WEB: www.petroleumsolids.com
SIC: 1389 Oil field services

(P-247)
PIXLEY CONSTRUCTION INC
27607 Industrial Blvd, Hayward (94545-4044)
P.O. Box 185 (94557-0185)
PHONE..................................510 783-3020
Chuck Pixley, *President*
EMP: 13 **EST:** 2013
SALES (est): 1.1MM **Privately Held**
SIC: 1389 Construction, repair & dismantling services

(P-248)
PRIME COMPLIANCE SOLUTIONS
4010 Watson Plaza Dr # 245, Lakewood (90712-4044)
PHONE..................................310 748-8103
Daniel Peterson, *President*
EMP: 12 **EST:** 2016
SALES (est): 855K **Privately Held**
SIC: 1389 Cementing oil & gas well casings

(P-249)
PRO VAC
26857 Henry Rd, Fellows (93224-9794)
P.O. Box 153, Taft (93268-8153)
PHONE..................................661 765-7298
Dennis Hill, *Owner*
EMP: 15
SALES (est): 1.6MM **Privately Held**
SIC: 1389 Oil field services

(P-250)
PRODUCTION DATA INC
1210 33rd St, Bakersfield (93301-2124)
P.O. Box 3266 (93385-3266)
PHONE..................................661 327-4776

Gerald Tonnelli, *President*
EMP: 19
SQ FT: 1,800
SALES (est): 2.6MM **Privately Held**
WEB: www.productiondatainc.com
SIC: 1389 Oil field services

(P-251)
PROS INCORPORATED
3400 Patton Way, Bakersfield (93308-5722)
P.O. Box 20996 (93390-0996)
PHONE..................................661 589-5400
Robert Lewis, *President*
Randy Dubois, *Exploration*
Jack Turner, *Sales Staff*
EMP: 58
SALES (est): 19.7MM **Privately Held**
SIC: 1389 Oil field services

(P-252)
PSC INDUSTRIAL OUTSOURCING LP
Also Called: Hydrochempsc
200 Old Yard Dr, Bakersfield (93307-4268)
PHONE..................................661 833-9991
Peter Burger, *Principal*
EMP: 18
SALES (corp-wide): 607.5MM **Privately Held**
WEB: www.tscnow.com
SIC: 1389 Oil field services
PA: Psc Industrial Outsourcing, Lp
900 Georgia Ave
Deer Park TX 77536
713 393-5600

(P-253)
RESOURCE CEMENTING LLC
2500 Airport Rd, Rio Vista (94571-1034)
P.O. Box 1027 (94571-3027)
PHONE..................................707 374-3350
Kevin P Graham, *Mng Member*
EMP: 15 **EST:** 2014
SALES (est): 183.3K **Privately Held**
SIC: 1389 1781 Cementing oil & gas well casings; geothermal drilling

(P-254)
RICHARD YARBROUGH
Also Called: R & R Pumping Unit Repr & Svc
2493 N Ventura Ave, Ventura (93001-1314)
PHONE..................................805 643-1021
Richard Yarbrough, *Owner*
EMP: 33
SALES (est): 1.8MM **Privately Held**
SIC: 1389 Oil & gas wells: building, repairing & dismantling; pumping of oil & gas wells

(P-255)
ROBERT HEELY CONSTRUCTION LP (PA)
Also Called: Robert Heely Construction
5401 Woodmere Dr, Bakersfield (93313-2777)
PHONE..................................661 617-1400
Robert Heely, *Chairman*
Craig Bonna, *President*
Robert Hopkins, *Engineer*
Hopkins Robert, *Engineer*
Chrystal Abbott, *Human Res Mgr*
EMP: 350
SQ FT: 7,000
SALES (est): 57.6MM **Privately Held**
WEB: www.robertheely.com
SIC: 1389 Oil field services

(P-256)
RPC INC
9457 Adlai Ter, Lakeside (92040-4830)
PHONE..................................619 647-9911
Roger Ramos, *Principal*
EMP: 10
SALES (est): 947.5K **Privately Held**
SIC: 1389 Oil field services

(P-257)
S D DRILLING
24660 E Old Julian Hwy, Ramona (92065-6760)
P.O. Box 1818 (92065-0915)
PHONE..................................760 789-5658
Ruth Torres, *Partner*
Ruben Levezma, *Partner*
EMP: 10

SALES (est): 1.1MM **Privately Held**
WEB: www.sddrilling.com
SIC: 1389 1381 Building oil & gas well foundations on site; grading oil & gas well foundations; drilling oil & gas wells

(P-258)
SAYBOLT LP
21730 S Wilmington Ave # 203, Carson (90810-1640)
PHONE..................................310 518-4400
Ken Nabi, *Manager*
EMP: 17
SALES (corp-wide): 700.8MM **Privately Held**
WEB: www.corelab.com
SIC: 1389 Testing, measuring, surveying & analysis services
HQ: Saybolt Lp
6316 Windfern Rd
Houston TX 77040
713 328-2673

(P-259)
SCHLUMBERGER TECHNOLOGY CORP
Also Called: Schlumberger Oilfield Services
1710 Callens Rd, Ventura (93003-5611)
PHONE..................................805 642-8230
Ken Gade, *Manager*
EMP: 25 **Publicly Held**
SIC: 1389 Oil field services
HQ: Schlumberger Technology Corp
300 Schlumberger Dr
Sugar Land TX 77478
281 285-8500

(P-260)
SCHLUMBERGER TECHNOLOGY CORP
Also Called: Schlumberger Well Services
2841 Pegasus Dr, Bakersfield (93308-6896)
PHONE..................................661 864-4750
Fax: 661 642-2065
EMP: 70 **Privately Held**
SIC: 1389 1382
HQ: Schlumberger Technology Corp
100 Gillingham Ln
Sugar Land TX 77478
281 285-8500

(P-261)
SCHLUMBERGER TECHNOLOGY CORP
Schlumberger, Well Completions
12131 Industry St, Garden Grove (92841-2813)
PHONE..................................714 379-7332
Gene Barnett, *Systems Mgr*
EMP: 51 **Publicly Held**
SIC: 1389 3561 Oil & gas wells: building, repairing & dismantling; pumps & pumping equipment
HQ: Schlumberger Technology Corp
300 Schlumberger Dr
Sugar Land TX 77478
281 285-8500

(P-262)
SCHLUMBERGER TECHNOLOGY CORP
Also Called: Schlumberger Well Services
3530 Arundell Cir, Ventura (93003-4922)
PHONE..................................805 644-8325
Steve Emerick, *Manager*
EMP: 10 **Publicly Held**
SIC: 1389 Oil field services
HQ: Schlumberger Technology Corp
300 Schlumberger Dr
Sugar Land TX 77478
281 285-8500

(P-263)
SIERRA ASSET SERVICING LLC
10232 Donner Pass Rd # 4, Truckee (96161-2337)
PHONE..................................530 582-7300
Kevin Crosby, *Principal*
EMP: 10
SALES (est): 977.4K **Privately Held**
SIC: 1389 Roustabout service

P R O D U C T S & S V C S

(P-264)
SMITH INTERNATIONAL INC
Also Called: Omni Seals, Inc.
11031 Jersey Blvd Ste A, Rancho Cuca-
monga (91730-5150)
PHONE..........................909 906-7900
Monte Russell, *Managing Dir*
EMP: 130 **Publicly Held**
SIC: 1389 Oil field services
HQ: Smith International, Inc.
　　1310 Rankin Rd
　　Houston TX 77073
　　281 443-3370

(P-265)
SMITH INTERNATIONAL INC
Smith Services
3101 Steam Ct, Bakersfield (93308-5725)
PHONE..........................661 589-8304
EMP: 10
SALES (corp-wide): 190.3K **Privately
Held**
SIC: 1389
HQ: Smith International, Inc.
　　1310 Rankin Rd
　　Houston TX 77073
　　281 443-3370

(P-266)
SOLI-BOND INC
4230 Foster Ave, Bakersfield (93308-4559)
PHONE..........................661 631-1633
Dwight Hartley, *President*
EMP: 50
SALES (corp-wide): 34.8MM **Privately
Held**
SIC: 1389 Oil field services
PA: Soli-Bond, Inc.
　　2377 2 Mile Rd
　　Bay City MI 48706
　　989 684-9611

(P-267)
STEELCLAD INC
2664 Saturn St Ste A, Brea (92821-6789)
PHONE..........................714 529-0277
Caren Hallam, *President*
EMP: 25
SQ FT: 4,000
SALES (est): 2.3MM **Privately Held**
WEB: www.steelcladinc.com
SIC: 1389 0782 Oil field services; land-
scape contractors

(P-268)
TEAM CASING
5073 Arboga Rd, Marysville (95901)
P.O. Box 1723 (95901-0050)
PHONE..........................530 743-5424
William W Cates, *President*
William Scheiber, *Treasurer*
Sandra Cates, *Admin Sec*
EMP: 16
SQ FT: 700
SALES (est): 1.4MM **Privately Held**
SIC: 1389 Running, cutting & pulling cas-
ings, tubes & rods

(P-269)
**TIGER CASED HOLE SERVICES
INC**
2828 Junipero Ave, Signal Hill
(90755-2112)
PHONE..........................562 426-4044
Joseph Baxter, *Principal*
EMP: 10
SALES (est): 929.7K **Privately Held**
SIC: 1389 Oil field services

(P-270)
TITAN OILFIELD SERVICES INC
21535 Kratzmeyer Rd, Bakersfield
(93314-9482)
PHONE..........................661 861-1630
Terry Hibbitts, *President*
Tim Barman, *Vice Pres*
Tony Palacpac, *Admin Sec*
EMP: 13
SALES (est): 1.8MM **Privately Held**
SIC: 1389 Oil field services

(P-271)
TOMS SIERRA COMPANY INC
Also Called: Sierra Energy
4710 Marshall Rd, Garden Valley
(95633-9472)
PHONE..........................530 333-4620
Don Saldey, *Manager*
EMP: 10
SQ FT: 3,080
SALES (corp-wide): 96.7MM **Privately
Held**
WEB: www.sierraenergy.net
SIC: 1389 Gas field services
PA: Toms Sierra Company, Inc.
　　1020 Winding Creek Rd
　　Roseville CA 95678
　　916 218-1600

(P-272)
TOTAL-WESTERN INC (HQ)
8049 Somerset Blvd, Paramount
(90723-4396)
PHONE..........................562 220-1450
Paul F Conrad, *CEO*
Mary A Pool, *CFO*
Earl Grebing, *Vice Pres*
Dora Maldonado, *Personnel*
Jerry Balos, *Director*
EMP: 50
SQ FT: 13,000
SALES (est): 166.5MM
SALES (corp-wide): 381.4MM **Privately
Held**
WEB: www.total-western.com
SIC: 1389 Oil field services; construction,
repair & dismantling services; excavating
slush pits & cellars; grading oil & gas well
foundations
PA: Bragg Investment Company, Inc.
　　6251 N Paramount Blvd
　　Long Beach CA 90805
　　562 984-2400

(P-273)
TRINGEN CORPORATION
Also Called: Allied Engrg & Consulting
238 E Norris Rd, Bakersfield (93308-3572)
PHONE..........................661 393-3039
Fax: 661 393-0799
EMP: 10
SQ FT: 1,000
SALES (est): 1.1MM **Privately Held**
WEB: www.tringen.com
SIC: 1389

(P-274)
TRYAD SERVICE CORPORATION
5900 E Lerdo Hwy, Shafter (93263-4023)
PHONE..........................661 391-1524
James Varner, *President*
Estate of Burl G Varner, *Shareholder*
Danny Seely, *Vice Pres*
▲ **EMP:** 90
SALES (est): 9.7MM **Privately Held**
SIC: 1389 Oil & gas wells: building, repair-
ing & dismantling

(P-275)
**TUBOSCOPE PIPELINE SVCS
INC**
Also Called: Tuboscope Nat Oilwell Varco
4621 Burr St, Bakersfield (93308-6143)
PHONE..........................661 321-3400
Bill Grahm, *Manager*
EMP: 35
SALES (corp-wide): 8.4B **Publicly Held**
SIC: 1389 Pipe testing, oil field service
HQ: Tuboscope Pipeline Services Inc.
　　2835 Holmes Rd
　　Houston TX 77051

(P-276)
U S WEATHERFORD L P
2815 Fruitvale Ave, Bakersfield
(93308-5907)
PHONE..........................661 589-9483
Rick Benton, *Branch Mgr*
EMP: 100 **Privately Held**
WEB: www.gaslift.com
SIC: 1389 Oil field services
HQ: U S Weatherford L P
　　179 Weatherford Dr
　　Schriever LA 70395
　　985 493-6100

(P-277)
ULTRAMAR INC
Also Called: Valero
961 S La Paloma Ave, Wilmington
(90744-6420)
PHONE..........................310 834-7254
Mark Phair, *Manager*
EMP: 40
SALES (corp-wide): 117B **Publicly Held**
WEB: www.divi.com
SIC: 1389 Gas field services
HQ: Ultramar Inc.
　　1 Valero Way
　　San Antonio TX 78249
　　210 345-2000

(P-278)
**VALLEY WATER MANAGEMENT
CO**
7500 Meany Ave, Bakersfield (93308-5178)
PHONE..........................661 410-7500
John Gatlin, *President*
EMP: 12 **EST:** 1932
SQ FT: 23,522
SALES: 7.9MM **Privately Held**
SIC: 1389 Oil field services

(P-279)
VAQUERO ENERGY INC
5060 California Ave, Bakersfield
(93309-0728)
P.O. Box 13550 (93389-3550)
PHONE..........................661 616-0600
Kenneth H Hunter, *CEO*
Seth Hunter, *Vice Pres*
Cary Nikkel, *Admin Sec*
Wendy Hall, *Accountant*
Wyatt Shipley, *Opers Mgr*
EMP: 21
SALES (est): 3.8MM **Privately Held**
WEB: www.vaqueroenergy.com
SIC: 1389 Testing, measuring, surveying &
analysis services

(P-280)
WATSON ME INC (PA)
801 Kern St, Taft (93268-2734)
PHONE..........................661 763-5254
Gene Watson, *CEO*
Pat Watson, *Vice Pres*
Joe Weninger, *Manager*
EMP: 12
SQ FT: 6,000
SALES (est): 51.7MM **Privately Held**
SIC: 1389 Oil field services

(P-281)
WEATHERFORD ARTIFICIA
21728 Rosedale Hwy, Bakersfield
(93314-9787)
PHONE..........................661 654-8120
EMP: 32 **Privately Held**
SIC: 1389 Oil field services
HQ: Weatherford Artificial Lift Systems, Llc
　　2000 Saint James Pl
　　Houston TX 77056
　　713 836-4000

(P-282)
**WEATHERFORD COMPLETION
SYSTEMS**
Also Called: Peric Oil Tool
19468 Creek Rd, Bakersfield (93314-8451)
PHONE..........................661 746-1391
Dennis Church, *District Mgr*
▲ **EMP:** 29
SALES (est): 1.7MM **Privately Held**
SIC: 1389 Oil field services

(P-283)
**WEATHERFORD
INTERNATIONAL LLC**
201 Hallock Dr, Santa Paula (93060-9647)
P.O. Box 31 (93061-0031)
PHONE..........................805 933-0242
Larry Brixey, *Manager*
EMP: 32 **Privately Held**
WEB: www.weatherford.com
SIC: 1389 Oil field services
HQ: Weatherford International, Llc
　　2000 Saint James Pl
　　Houston TX 77056
　　713 693-4000

(P-284)
**WEATHERFORD
INTERNATIONAL LLC**
1880 Santa Barbara Ave # 220, San Luis
Obispo (93401-4481)
PHONE..........................805 781-3580
Chris Smith, *Branch Mgr*
Kevin Rowley, *Manager*
EMP: 73 **Privately Held**
SIC: 1389 Oil field services
HQ: Weatherford International, Llc
　　2000 Saint James Pl
　　Houston TX 77056
　　713 693-4000

(P-285)
**WEATHERFORD
INTERNATIONAL LLC**
Also Called: Coroc
21728 Rosedale Hwy, Bakersfield
(93314-9787)
PHONE..........................661 587-9753
Mark Sarcen, *Branch Mgr*
Michael Winterberg, *Sr Software Eng*
Gregg Hurst, *Sales Staff*
Jason Truitt, *Advisor*
Daniel Adame, *Supervisor*
EMP: 60 **Privately Held**
WEB: www.weatherford.com
SIC: 1389 Oil field services
HQ: Weatherford International, Llc
　　2000 Saint James Pl
　　Houston TX 77056
　　713 693-4000

(P-286)
**WEATHERFORD
INTERNATIONAL LLC**
3701 Enterprise St, Shafter (93263-2212)
PHONE..........................661 589-2146
Daniel Erbs, *Branch Mgr*
EMP: 40 **Privately Held**
SIC: 1389 Oil field services
HQ: Weatherford International, Llc
　　2000 Saint James Pl
　　Houston TX 77056
　　713 693-4000

(P-287)
**WEATHERFORD
INTERNATIONAL LLC**
250 W Stanley Ave, Ventura (93001-1305)
P.O. Box 1668 (93002-1668)
PHONE..........................805 643-1279
Scott Antosen, *Branch Mgr*
Jason Ng, *Engineer*
EMP: 14 **Privately Held**
WEB: www.weatherford.com
SIC: 1389 Oil field services
HQ: Weatherford International, Llc
　　2000 Saint James Pl
　　Houston TX 77056
　　713 693-4000

1411 Dimension Stone

(P-288)
ARCHWOOD MFG GROUP INC
15058 Delano St, Van Nuys (91411-2016)
PHONE..........................818 781-7673
Carlos E Subero, *Principal*
EMP: 11
SALES (est): 918.6K **Privately Held**
SIC: 1411 Marble, dimension-quarrying

(P-289)
BO DEAN CO INC (PA)
1060 N Dutton Ave, Santa Rosa
(95401-5011)
PHONE..........................707 576-8205
Dean N Soiland, *CEO*
Belinda Soiland, *Vice Pres*
Charlie Young, *Project Mgr*
Heather Hammerich, *Manager*
Damon Weatherly, *Manager*
EMP: 30
SQ FT: 5,000
SALES (est): 16.3MM **Privately Held**
WEB: www.bodeancompany.com
SIC: 1411 2951 Greenstone, dimension-
quarrying; concrete, asphaltic (not from
refineries)

▲ = Import ▼=Export
◆ =Import/Export

(P-290)
CHANDLER AGGREGATES INC (PA)
24867 Maitri Rd, Corona (92883-5136)
P.O. Box 78450 (92877-0148)
PHONE..........................951 277-1341
Larry Werner, *President*
EMP: 20
SALES (est): 6.7MM **Privately Held**
SIC: 1411 1422 Dimension stone; crushed & broken limestone

(P-291)
COSA MARBLE CO
13040 San Fernando Rd A, Sylmar (91342-3692)
PHONE..................◆........818 364-8800
Halie Cieollo, *Office Mgr*
◆ EMP: 13
SALES (est): 655.5K **Privately Held**
SIC: 1411 Marble, dimension-quarrying

(P-292)
MINESTONE
17739 Valley Vista Blvd, Encino (91316-3746)
PHONE..........................818 775-5999
Richard McDonald, *Principal*
Arbi Torossian, *Manager*
▲ EMP: 10
SALES (est): 854.3K **Privately Held**
SIC: 1411 Limestone & marble dimension stone

(P-293)
REGIONAL MTLS RECOVERY INC
Also Called: Wyroc Materials
2142 Industrial Ct Ste D, Vista (92081-7960)
P.O. Box 1239 (92085-1239)
PHONE..........................760 727-0878
EMP: 20 EST: 1995
SALES: 950K **Privately Held**
SIC: 1411

(P-294)
SPARK STONE LLC
2300 E Winston Rd, Anaheim (92806-5529)
PHONE..........................714 772-7575
Jacek G Chyczewski,
EMP: 15
SALES (est): 1.6MM **Privately Held**
SIC: 1411 Granite dimension stone

(P-295)
TAKE IT FOR GRANITE INC
345 Phelan Ave, San Jose (95112-4104)
PHONE..........................408 790-2812
Jason Krulee, *President*
▲ EMP: 20 EST: 1997
SQ FT: 32,000
SALES (est): 6.1MM **Privately Held**
WEB: www.tifgranite.com
SIC: 1411 Dimension stone

(P-296)
WYROC INC (PA)
2142 Industrial Ct Ste D, Vista (92081-7960)
P.O. Box 1239 (92085-1239)
PHONE..........................760 727-0878
William Halloran, *President*
Dorothy Leckband, *Asst Treas*
EMP: 12
SQ FT: 2,500
SALES (est): 1.4MM **Privately Held**
WEB: www.wyroc.com
SIC: 1411 1423 Sandstone, dimension-quarrying; crushed & broken granite

---

1422 Crushed & Broken Limestone

(P-297)
AZUSA ROCK LLC (DH)
3901 Fish Canyon Rd, Azusa (91702)
PHONE..........................858 530-9444
Ron McAbee, *President*
Ed Kelly, *Senior VP*
Jeff McOrmick, *Vice Pres*
Ronnie Walker, *Vice Pres*

Paul Stanford, *Admin Sec*
EMP: 10
SQ FT: 40,000
SALES (est): 17.8MM **Publicly Held**
SIC: 1422 3273 2951 1442 Cement rock, crushed & broken-quarrying; ready-mixed concrete; asphalt paving mixtures & blocks; construction sand & gravel
HQ: Legacy Vulcan, Llc
1200 Urban Center Dr
Vestavia AL 35242
205 298-3000

(P-298)
AZUSA ROCK INC
3605 Dehesa Rd, El Cajon (92019-2903)
PHONE..........................619 440-2363
Tom Nelson, *Manager*
EMP: 13 **Publicly Held**
SIC: 1422 Crushed & broken limestone
HQ: Azusa Rock, Llc
3901 Fish Canyon Rd
Azusa CA 91702
858 530-9444

(P-299)
CALMAT CO
16101 Hwy 156, Maricopa (93252)
P.O. Box 22800, Bakersfield (93390-2800)
PHONE..........................661 858-2673
Angela Bailey, *Manager*
EMP: 35 **Publicly Held**
SIC: 1422 Crushed & broken limestone
HQ: Calmat Co.
500 N Brand Blvd Ste 500 # 500
Glendale CA 91203
818 553-8821

(P-300)
LEGACY VULCAN LLC
Parkridge & Quarry Sts, Corona (92877)
P.O. Box 1058 (92878-1058)
PHONE..........................714 737-2922
Donald Purcell, *Branch Mgr*
George Hanny, *President*
EMP: 45 **Publicly Held**
WEB: www.vulcanmaterials.com
SIC: 1422 Crushed & broken limestone
HQ: Legacy Vulcan, Llc
1200 Urban Center Dr
Vestavia AL 35242
205 298-3000

(P-301)
LEGACY VULCAN LLC
Also Called: Western Division
655 W Tehachapi Blvd, Tehachapi (93561-1685)
PHONE..........................661 822-4158
Gunner Hildeberandt, *Manager*
EMP: 26 **Publicly Held**
WEB: www.vulcanmaterials.com
SIC: 1422 Crushed & broken limestone
HQ: Legacy Vulcan, Llc
1200 Urban Center Dr
Vestavia AL 35242
205 298-3000

(P-302)
LEGACY VULCAN LLC
3195 Andreasen Dr, Lafayette (94549-4801)
P.O. Box 2472, Richmond (94802)
PHONE..........................925 284-4686
Larry P Boland, *President*
Tabitha Jones, *HR Admin*
Larry Clemons, *Purchasing*
Mary Carlisle, *Manager*
EMP: 15 **Publicly Held**
WEB: www.vulcanmaterials.com
SIC: 1422 Crushed & broken limestone
HQ: Legacy Vulcan, Llc
1200 Urban Center Dr
Vestavia AL 35242
205 298-3000

(P-303)
LEGACY VULCAN LLC
Also Called: Rock & Sand Plant
7220 Trade St Ste 200, San Diego (92121-2326)
P.O. Box 3098 (92163-3098)
PHONE..........................858 566-2730
Dave Becker, *Branch Mgr*
EMP: 20 **Publicly Held**
WEB: www.vulcanmaterials.com

SIC: 1422 Crushed & broken limestone
HQ: Legacy Vulcan, Llc
1200 Urban Center Dr
Vestavia AL 35242
205 298-3000

(P-304)
SPECIALTY MINERALS INC
Minerals Technology
6565 Meridian Rd, Lucerne Valley (92356-8602)
P.O. Box 558 (92356-0558)
PHONE..........................760 248-5300
Doug Mayger, *Branch Mgr*
EMP: 150 **Publicly Held**
WEB: www.specialtyminerals.com
SIC: 1422 Crushed & broken limestone
HQ: Specialty Minerals Inc.
622 3rd Ave Fl 38
New York NY 10017
212 878-1800

(P-305)
SYAR INDUSTRIES INC
885 Lake Herman Rd, Vallejo (94591-8324)
P.O. Box 2540, NAPA (94558-0524)
PHONE..........................707 643-3261
Mike Burneson, *Manager*
EMP: 100
SALES (corp-wide): 100.2MM **Privately Held**
WEB: www.syar.com
SIC: 1422 5211 Crushed & broken limestone; cement
PA: Syar Industries, Inc.
2301 Napa Vallejo Hwy
Napa CA 94558
707 252-8711

(P-306)
VULCAN MATERIALS COMPANY
3605 Dehesa Rd, El Cajon (92019-2903)
PHONE..........................619 440-2363
Tom Nelson, *Branch Mgr*
EMP: 17 **Publicly Held**
SIC: 1422 Crushed & broken limestone
PA: Vulcan Materials Company
1200 Urban Center Dr
Vestavia AL 35242

(P-307)
VULCAN MATERIALS COMPANY
Also Called: Table Mountain Quarry
2216 Table Mountain Blvd, Oroville (95965-9109)
PHONE..........................530 534-4517
Jim Cusick, *Manager*
EMP: 14 **Publicly Held**
WEB: www.martinmarietta.com
SIC: 1422 Crushed & broken limestone
PA: Vulcan Materials Company
1200 Urban Center Dr
Vestavia AL 35242

1423 Crushed & Broken Granite

(P-308)
C W MCGRATH INC
13080 Highway 8 Business, El Cajon (92021-1845)
P.O. Box 2488 (92021-0488)
PHONE..........................619 443-3811
Michael P McGrath, *President*
June C McGrath, *Corp Secy*
Kelly McGrath, *Vice Pres*
Laurie McGrath, *Vice Pres*
▲ EMP: 14 EST: 1937
SQ FT: 2,000
SALES: 3.5MM **Privately Held**
WEB: www.cwmcgrath.com
SIC: 1423 Crushed & broken granite

(P-309)
KIEWIT CORPORATION
Also Called: Aggregate - Red Hill Quarry
Hwy 395 And Cinder Rd, Little Lake (93542)
P.O. Box 18 (93542-0018)
PHONE..........................760 377-3117
Benton Boyd, *Branch Mgr*

EMP: 20
SALES (corp-wide): 16.1B **Privately Held**
SIC: 1423 Crushed & broken granite
HQ: Kiewit Corporation
3555 Farnam St Ste 1000
Omaha NE 68131
402 342-2052

(P-310)
MARTIN MARIETTA MATERIALS INC
1500 Rubidoux Blvd, Riverside (92509-1840)
PHONE..........................951 682-0918
Marietta Martin, *CEO*
EMP: 21 **Publicly Held**
SIC: 1423 Crushed & broken granite
PA: Martin Marietta Materials Inc
2710 Wycliff Rd
Raleigh NC 27607

1429 Crushed & Broken Stone, NEC

(P-311)
AGGREGATE PRODUCTS INC (PA)
100 Brawley Ave, Thermal (92274-8420)
PHONE..........................760 395-5312
John Corcoran, *President*
Maria E Corcoran, *Vice Pres*
EMP: 12
SQ FT: 1,000
SALES (est): 8.1MM **Privately Held**
SIC: 1429 Igneous rock, crushed & broken-quarrying

(P-312)
BOHAN CNLIS - ASTIN CREEK RDYM
Also Called: Austn Creek Materials
1528 Copperhill Pkwy F, Santa Rosa (95403-8200)
P.O. Box 317, Cazadero (95421-0317)
PHONE..........................707 632-5296
Timothy Canelis, *President*
Homer Canelis, *Treasurer*
EMP: 15 EST: 1946
SQ FT: 800
SALES: 2MM **Privately Held**
WEB: www.bohancanelis.com
SIC: 1429 Basalt, crushed & broken-quarrying

(P-313)
CHILI BAR LLC
Also Called: Chili Bar Slate
11380 State Highway 193, Placerville (95667-9601)
PHONE..........................530 622-3325
Jacob Montazeri, *Principal*
EMP: 20 EST: 2012
SALES (est): 2.7MM **Privately Held**
SIC: 1429 Slate, crushed & broken-quarrying

(P-314)
GM MARBLE & GRANITE INC
Also Called: Granite Kitchen Countertops
1375 Franquette Ave Ste F, Concord (94520-7932)
PHONE..........................925 676-8385
Gregory Markiel, *CEO*
EMP: 11
SQ FT: 3,000
SALES: 900K **Privately Held**
SIC: 1429 Marble, crushed & broken-quarrying

(P-315)
LANGLEY HILL QUARRY
12 Langley Hill Rd, Woodside (94062-4829)
P.O. Box 620626 (94062-0626)
PHONE..........................650 851-0179
Michael Dempsey, *Partner*
Patrick Dempsey, *Partner*
EMP: 15
SALES: 1.9MM **Privately Held**
SIC: 1429 Igneous rock, crushed & broken-quarrying

PRODUCTS & SVCS

(P-316)
NORBERG CRUSHING INC
592 Tyrone St, El Cajon (92020-2233)
PHONE..................619 390-4200
Stephen Norberg, *President*
Heidi Spicer, *CFO*
Dana Farrell, *Vice Pres*
EMP: 15
SQ FT: 3,500
SALES (est): 2.7MM **Privately Held**
SIC: 1429 Igneous rock, crushed & bro-
ken-quarrying

(P-317)
OLIVER DE SILVA INC (PA)
Also Called: Gallagher & Burk
11555 Dublin Blvd, Dublin (94568-2854)
P.O. Box 2922 (94568-0922)
PHONE..................925 829-9220
Edwin O De Silva, *Chairman*
Richard B Gates, *President*
David De Silva, *Exec VP*
J Scott Archibald, *Vice Pres*
Ernest Lampkin, *Vice Pres*
EMP: 20
SQ FT: 60,000
SALES (est): 83.8MM **Privately Held**
SIC: 1429 Igneous rock, crushed & bro-
ken-quarrying

(P-318)
**PAUL HUBBS CONSTRUCTION
INC (PA)**
542 W C St, Colton (92324-2140)
PHONE..................951 360-3990
Jay P Hubbs, *President*
Lucile M Hubbs, *Treasurer*
John L Hubbs, *Vice Pres*
Pat Hubbs, *Admin Sec*
EMP: 18
SQ FT: 4,000
SALES (est): 2.6MM **Privately Held**
SIC: 1429 Riprap quarrying

(P-319)
**SAN RAFAEL ROCK QUARRY
INC (HQ)**
Also Called: Dutra Materials
2350 Kerner Blvd Ste 200, San Rafael
(94901-5595)
PHONE..................415 459-7740
Bill Toney Dutra, *CEO*
EMP: 70
SALES (est): 65.2MM
SALES (corp-wide): 145.1MM **Privately
Held**
SIC: 1429 1629 Basalt, crushed & broken-
quarrying; marine construction
PA: The Dutra Group
    2350 Kerner Blvd Ste 200
    San Rafael CA 94901
    415 258-6876

(P-320)
**TRIANGLE ROCK PRODUCTS
LLC**
500 N Brand Blvd Ste 500 # 500, Glendale
(91203-3319)
PHONE..................818 553-8820
Stanley G Bass, *President*
Annie Hovanessian,
EMP: 30
SQ FT: 20,000
SALES (est): 1.5MM **Publicly Held**
SIC: 1429 1442 2951 3273 Igneous rock,
crushed & broken-quarrying; construction
sand & gravel; asphalt paving mixtures &
blocks; ready-mixed concrete; nonresi-
dential building operators
HQ: Calmat Co.
    500 N Brand Blvd Ste 500 # 500
    Glendale CA 91203
    818 553-8821

| 1442 Construction Sand & |
| Gravel |

(P-321)
A TEICHERT & SON INC
Also Called: Teichert Aggregates
13879 Butterfield Dr, Truckee
(96161-3331)
P.O. Box 447 (96160-0447)
PHONE..................530 587-3811
Ed Herrnberger, *Plant Mgr*
EMP: 40
SALES (corp-wide): 784MM **Privately
Held**
SIC: 1442 Construction sand & gravel
HQ: A. Teichert & Son, Inc.
    3500 American River Dr
    Sacramento CA 95864

(P-322)
A TEICHERT & SON INC
Also Called: Teichert Aggregates
36314 S Bird Rd, Tracy (95304-8678)
PHONE..................209 832-4150
Jerry Hansen, *Plant Mgr*
EMP: 40
SALES (corp-wide): 784MM **Privately
Held**
SIC: 1442 Construction sand & gravel
HQ: A. Teichert & Son, Inc.
    3500 American River Dr
    Sacramento CA 95864

(P-323)
A TEICHERT & SON INC
Also Called: Teichert Aggregates
35030 County Road 20, Woodland
(95695-9251)
PHONE..................530 661-4290
Brandon Stauffer, *Plant Mgr*
Angie Felix, *Clerk*
EMP: 30
SALES (corp-wide): 784MM **Privately
Held**
SIC: 1442 Construction sand & gravel
HQ: A. Teichert & Son, Inc.
    3500 American River Dr
    Sacramento CA 95864

(P-324)
A TEICHERT & SON INC
Also Called: Teichert Aggregates
2601 State Highway 49, Cool
(95614-9528)
P.O. Box 280 (95614-0280)
PHONE..................530 885-4244
Ed Herrnberger, *Plant Mgr*
EMP: 15
SALES (corp-wide): 784MM **Privately
Held**
SIC: 1442 Construction sand & gravel
HQ: A. Teichert & Son, Inc.
    3500 American River Dr
    Sacramento CA 95864

(P-325)
A TEICHERT & SON INC
Also Called: Teichert Aggregates
3331 Walnut Ave, Marysville (95901-9421)
PHONE..................530 749-1230
Brandon Stauffer, *Plant Mgr*
EMP: 40
SALES (corp-wide): 784MM **Privately
Held**
SIC: 1442 Construction sand & gravel
HQ: A. Teichert & Son, Inc.
    3500 American River Dr
    Sacramento CA 95864

(P-326)
A TEICHERT & SON INC
Also Called: Teichert Aggregates
4249 Hmmnton Smrtville Rd, Marysville
(95901)
PHONE..................530 743-6111
Brandon Stauffer, *Plant Mgr*
EMP: 40

SALES (corp-wide): 784MM **Privately
Held**
SIC: 1442 Construction sand & gravel
HQ: A. Teichert & Son, Inc.
    3500 American River Dr
    Sacramento CA 95864
-

(P-327)
A TEICHERT & SON INC
Also Called: Teichert Aggregates
3417 Grant Line Rd, Rancho Cordova
(95742-7000)
P.O. Box 981, Folsom (95763-0981)
PHONE..................916 351-0123
Mike Cunningham, *Plant Mgr*
EMP: 40
SALES (corp-wide): 784MM **Privately
Held**
SIC: 1442 Construction sand & gravel
HQ: A. Teichert & Son, Inc.
    3500 American River Dr
    Sacramento CA 95864

(P-328)
A TEICHERT & SON INC
Also Called: Teichert Aggregates
8760 Kiefer Blvd, Sacramento
(95826-3917)
P.O. Box 15002 (95851-0002)
PHONE..................916 386-6900
Mike Cunningham, *Plant Mgr*
EMP: 40
SALES (corp-wide): 784MM **Privately
Held**
SIC: 1442 Construction sand & gravel
HQ: A. Teichert & Son, Inc.
    3500 American River Dr
    Sacramento CA 95864

(P-329)
**ALAMEDA CONSTRUCTION
SVCS INC**
2528 E 125th St, Compton (90222-1502)
PHONE..................310 635-3277
Kevin Ramsey, *CEO*
Tracey Watson, *Vice Pres*
Tiffany Ramsey, *Manager*
April Hawley, *Fellow*
Ray Coronado, *Superintendent*
EMP: 20
SQ FT: 8,000
SALES (est): 6MM **Privately Held**
SIC: 1442 Construction sand & gravel

(P-330)
BAY AREA DRILLING INC
1860 Loveridge Rd, Pittsburg (94565-4111)
PHONE..................925 427-7574
Mark Lucido, *CEO*
EMP: 15
SALES (est): 2.7MM **Privately Held**
SIC: 1442 Construction sand & gravel

(P-331)
BUTTE SAND AND GRAVEL
10373 S Butte Rd, Sutter (95982-9316)
P.O. Box 749 (95982-0749)
PHONE..................530 755-0225
Darren Morehead, *President*
Martin Morehead, *CFO*
Joseph Morehead II, *Vice Pres*
EMP: 20
SQ FT: 1,000
SALES (est): 4.3MM **Privately Held**
WEB: www.buttesand.com
SIC: 1442 5211 Gravel mining; sand &
gravel

(P-332)
CALPORTLAND
2025 E Financial Way, Glendora
(91741-4692)
P.O. Box 567, Thousand Palms (92276-
0567)
PHONE..................760 343-3403
Terri Stelter, *President*
Debra Rubenzer, *Corp Secy*
Diane Sarauer, *Vice Pres*
Claude Jaynes, *Technical Staff*
Leanne Condon, *Purchasing*
EMP: 15
SQ FT: 480

SALES (est): 2.5MM **Privately Held**
WEB: www.a-1aggregates.com
SIC: 1442 Gravel mining; construction
sand mining

(P-333)
CALPORTLAND
72200 Vista Chino, Thousand Palms
(92276-2605)
P.O. Box 567 (92276-0567)
PHONE..................760 343-3126
Terri Stelter, *President*
EMP: 15 **Privately Held**
SIC: 1442 Construction sand & gravel
HQ: Calportland
    20601 Ne Marine Dr
    Fairview OR 97024

(P-334)
CANYON ROCK CO INC
Also Called: River Ready Mix
7525 Hwy 116, Forestville (95436-9227)
P.O. Box 639 (95436-0639)
PHONE..................707 887-2207
Wendell Trappe, *President*
Gwen Trappe, *Vice Pres*
EMP: 20
SQ FT: 3,000
SALES (est): 11.8MM **Privately Held**
SIC: 1442 3273 Construction sand &
gravel; ready-mixed concrete

(P-335)
**COLOR MARBLE PROJECT
GROUP INC**
20521 Earlgate St, Walnut (91789-2909)
PHONE..................909 595-8858
TSE Min Jemmy You, *President*
▲ **EMP:** 10
SALES (est): 1.2MM **Privately Held**
SIC: 1442 Construction sand & gravel

(P-336)
CONSTRUCTION ON TIME INC
5657 Meridian Ave, San Jose (95118-3436)
PHONE..................408 209-1799
Peter Luckiewicz, *President*
EMP: 10
SALES: 200K **Privately Held**
SIC: 1442 Construction sand & gravel

(P-337)
DAN COPP CRUSHING CORP
22765 Savi Ranch Pkwy E, Yorba Linda
(92887-4620)
PHONE..................714 777-6400
Karen Ayres, *Admin Sec*
Jason Ayres, *President*
Robert Virgil, *Vice Pres*
EMP: 38 **EST:** 1978
SALES (est): 8MM **Privately Held**
SIC: 1442 Construction sand & gravel

(P-338)
ENNISS INC
12535 Vigilante Rd, Lakeside (92040-1167)
P.O. Box 1769 (92040-0917)
PHONE..................619 561-1101
David Von Bhren, *President*
D Lois Miller, *Admin Sec*
EMP: 40
SQ FT: 4,700
SALES (est): 7.9MM **Privately Held**
SIC: 1442 4212 3271 4953 Sand mining;
local trucking, without storage; architec-
tural concrete: block, split, fluted, screen,
etc.; recycling, waste materials; iron work,
structural

(P-339)
FISHER SAND & GRAVEL CO
24560 Cooperstown Rd, Oakdale (95361)
PHONE..................602 619-0325
Derek Schoonover, *Branch Mgr*
EMP: 10
SALES (corp-wide): 314MM **Privately
Held**
SIC: 1442 Construction sand mining
PA: Fisher Sand & Gravel Co.
    3020 Energy Dr
    Dickinson ND 58601
    701 456-9184

▲ = Import ▼=Export
◆ =Import/Export

(P-340)
GAIL MATERIALS INC
10060 Dawson Canyon Rd, Corona
(92883-2112)
PHONE....................951 667-6106
Nick Leinen, *CEO*
Mitch Leinen, *President*
Kurt Hutcheson, *Opers Mgr*
Gordon-Ross John, *Opers Mgr*
Dave Dzwilewski, *Sales Mgr*
EMP: 30
SQ FT: 5,000
SALES (est): 4.7MM **Privately Held**
SIC: 1442 Construction sand & gravel

(P-341)
GRANITE ROCK CO (PA)
350 Technology Dr, Watsonville
(95076-2488)
P.O. Box 50001 (95077-5001)
PHONE....................831 768-2000
Thomas H Squeri, *CEO*
Bruce G Woolpert, *Vice Chairman*
Mary E Woolpert, *Chairman*
Todd Barreras, *Officer*
Greg Diehl, *Vice Pres*
EMP: 100
SQ FT: 10,000
SALES (est): 992MM **Privately Held**
WEB: www.graniterock.com
SIC: 1442 3273 5032 2951 Gravel mining; construction sand mining; readymixed concrete; sand; construction; stone, crushed or broken; asphalt & asphaltic paving mixtures (not from refineries); highway & street paving contractor; concrete block & brick

(P-342)
GRANITE ROCK CO
Also Called: AR Wilson Quarry
Quarry Rd, Aromas (95004)
P.O. Box 699 (95004-0699)
PHONE....................831 768-2300
Bruce Wollepert, *President*
EMP: 100
SALES (corp-wide): 992MM **Privately Held**
WEB: www.graniterock.com
SIC: 1442 2951 Gravel mining; asphalt paving mixtures & blocks
PA: Granite Rock Co.
350 Technology Dr
Watsonville CA 95076
831 768-2000

(P-343)
HANSEN BROS ENTERPRISES (PA)
Also Called: Hbe Rental
11727 La Barr Meadows Rd, Grass Valley
(95949-7722)
P.O. Box 1599 (95945-1599)
PHONE....................530 273-3100
Orson Hansen, *President*
Frank Bennallack, *Treasurer*
Craig Arthur, *Vice Pres*
Helen Hansen, *Vice Pres*
Sue Peterson, *Vice Pres*
EMP: 90
SQ FT: 20,000
SALES (est): 36.2MM **Privately Held**
WEB: www.gohbe.com
SIC: 1442 3273 1794 7359 Gravel mining; ready-mixed concrete; excavation work; equipment rental & leasing

(P-344)
HANSON AGGREGATES LLC
24001 Stevens Creek Blvd, Cupertino
(95014-5659)
PHONE....................408 996-4000
Steve Tarantino, *Branch Mgr*
Denis Curran, *Partner*
Eric Powell, *Safety Mgr*
Pattie Lovell, *Warehouse Mgr*
EMP: 28
SALES (corp-wide): 20.6B **Privately Held**
WEB: www.hansonind.com
SIC: 1442 Construction sand & gravel
HQ: Hanson Aggregates Llc
8505 Freport Pkwy Ste 500
Irving TX 75063
469 417-1200

(P-345)
HANSON AGGREGATES LLC
13550 Live Oak Ln, Baldwin Park
(91706-1318)
PHONE....................626 856-6700
Michael Rogers, *Manager*
EMP: 40
SALES (est): 20.6B **Privately Held**
WEB: www.hansonind.com
SIC: 1442 Construction sand & gravel
HQ: Hanson Aggregates Llc
8505 Freport Pkwy Ste 500
Irving TX 75063
469 417-1200

(P-346)
HANSON AGGREGATES LLC
5325 Foxen Canyon Rd, Santa Maria
(93454-9550)
PHONE....................805 934-4931
Rick Sanford, *Manager*
EMP: 12
SALES (corp-wide): 20.6B **Privately Held**
WEB: www.hansonind.com
SIC: 1442 Common sand mining
HQ: Hanson Aggregates Llc
8505 Freport Pkwy Ste 500
Irving TX 75063
469 417-1200

(P-347)
HANSON AGGREGATES LLC
131 Suburban Rd, San Luis Obispo
(93401-7506)
P.O. Box 71 (93406-0071)
PHONE....................805 543-8100
Dave Grummitt, *Branch Mgr*
EMP: 22
SALES (corp-wide): 20.6B **Privately Held**
WEB: www.hansonind.com
SIC: 1442 Common sand mining
HQ: Hanson Aggregates Llc
8505 Freport Pkwy Ste 500
Irving TX 75063
469 417-1200

(P-348)
LEGACY VULCAN LLC
San Bernardino Division
2400 W Highland Ave, San Bernardino
(92407-6408)
PHONE....................909 875-1150
Darryl Charleson, *Sales/Mktg Dir*
Allyson Noah, *Manager*
EMP: 50 **Publicly Held**
WEB: www.vulcanmaterials.com
SIC: 1442 3273 Sand mining; ready-mixed concrete
HQ: Legacy Vulcan, Llc
1200 Urban Center Dr
Vestavia AL 35242
205 298-3000

(P-349)
LEGACY VULCAN LLC
6232 Santos Diaz St, Irwindale
(91702-3267)
PHONE....................626 856-6153
Jack Perkins, *Branch Mgr*
EMP: 12 **Publicly Held**
WEB: www.vulcanmaterials.com
SIC: 1442 Construction sand & gravel
HQ: Legacy Vulcan, Llc
1200 Urban Center Dr
Vestavia AL 35242
205 298-3000

(P-350)
LEGACY VULCAN LLC
11447 Tuxford St, Sun Valley (91352-2639)
PHONE....................818 983-1323
Joe Ellison, *Manager*
EMP: 22 **Publicly Held**
WEB: www.vulcanmaterials.com
SIC: 1442 Construction sand & gravel
HQ: Legacy Vulcan, Llc
1200 Urban Center Dr
Vestavia AL 35242
205 298-3000

(P-351)
LEGACY VULCAN LLC
Also Called: Reliance Rock
16001 E Foothill Blvd, Irwindale
(91702-2813)
PHONE....................626 856-6143

Donnie McDuffie, *Manager*
EMP: 30 **Publicly Held**
WEB: www.vulcanmaterials.com
SIC: 1442 Construction sand & gravel
HQ: Legacy Vulcan, Llc
1200 Urban Center Dr
Vestavia AL 35242
205 298-3000

(P-352)
MAGORIAN MINE SERVICES (PA)
10310 Sierra Hills Ln, Auburn
(95602-9402)
P.O. Box 8015 (95604-8015)
PHONE....................530 269-1960
Don Magorian, *Owner*
EMP: 12
SALES (est): 2.8MM **Privately Held**
WEB: www.magmineserv.com
SIC: 1442 Gravel & pebble mining

(P-353)
NEVOCAL ENTERPRISES INC
Also Called: Kh Construction
5320 N Barcus Ave, Fresno (93722-5050)
PHONE....................559 277-0700
Frank Cornell, *President*
EMP: 75
SQ FT: 4,575
SALES (est): 4.2MM **Privately Held**
SIC: 1442 Construction sand & gravel

(P-354)
NORTH COUNTY SAND AND GRAV INC
26227 Sherman Rd, Sun City
(92585-9223)
PHONE....................951 928-2881
M J La Paglia III, *President*
Michael J La Paglia III, *President*
Tracy Paglia, *CFO*
EMP: 18
SALES (est): 5.5MM **Privately Held**
SIC: 1442 5032 Construction sand & gravel; sand, construction; gravel

(P-355)
NORTHERN AGGREGATES INC
500 Cropley Ln, Willits (95490-4140)
P.O. Box 1566 (95490-1566)
PHONE....................707 459-3929
Frank Dutra, *President*
Randy Lucchetti, *Vice Pres*
Pat Allen, *Info Tech Mgr*
EMP: 25
SQ FT: 10,000
SALES (est): 5MM **Privately Held**
SIC: 1442 Construction sand & gravel

(P-356)
PECK ROAD GRAVEL PIT
128 Live Oak Ave, Monrovia (91016-5050)
P.O. Box 1286 (91017-1286)
PHONE....................626 574-7570
Steve Bubalo, *President*
Louise Bubalo, *Treasurer*
Stephanie Bubalo Becerra, *Vice Pres*
Juan Yanez, *Executive*
EMP: 30
SALES (est): 3.7MM **Privately Held**
SIC: 1442 Construction sand & gravel

(P-357)
PERRAULT CORPORATION
30640 N River Rd, Bonsall (92003-7123)
P.O. Box 578 (92003-0578)
PHONE....................760 466-1024
Charles Perrault, *CEO*
EMP: 10
SALES (est): 2.4MM **Privately Held**
SIC: 1442 Construction sand & gravel

(P-358)
SANTA FE AGGREGATES INC (HQ)
11650 Shaffer Rd, Winton (95388-9604)
PHONE....................209 358-3303
Ron C Turcotte, *President*
EMP: 18 **EST:** 1938
SALES (est): 3.4MM
SALES (corp-wide): 784MM **Privately Held**
SIC: 1442 Construction sand & gravel

PA: Teichert, Inc.
3500 American River Dr
Sacramento CA 95864
916 484-3011

(P-359)
SIERRA CASCADE AGGREGATE & ASP
6600 Old Ski Rd, Chester (96020)
P.O. Box 1193 (96020-1193)
PHONE....................530 258-4555
Kacie Holland, *President*
Caleb Holland, *Treasurer*
EMP: 15
SALES (est): 3.8MM **Privately Held**
SIC: 1442 Construction sand & gravel

(P-360)
SPECIALTY ROCK INC
5405 Alton Pkwy Irvine, Irvine (92604)
PHONE....................909 334-2265
Michael Holcomb, *CEO*
Richard Newman, *Treasurer*
▼ **EMP:** 13
SQ FT: 4,100
SALES: 4.5MM **Privately Held**
SIC: 1442 Construction sand & gravel

(P-361)
STONE VALLEY MATERIALS LLC
3500b Pyrite St, Riverside (92509-1123)
PHONE....................951 681-7830
Brady Kooiman,
Chris Van Veldhuizen,
Stephen Vanderhart,
EMP: 10 **EST:** 2010
SALES (est): 637.7K **Privately Held**
WEB: www.stonevalleymaterials.com
SIC: 1442 Construction sand & gravel

(P-362)
STONY POINT ROCK QUARRY INC (PA)
7171 Stony Point Rd, Cotati (94931-9724)
PHONE....................707 795-1775
Marvin Soiland, *President*
Marlene Berney, *Vice Pres*
EMP: 18
SQ FT: 1,600
SALES (est): 3.3MM **Privately Held**
WEB: www.sprqinc.com
SIC: 1442 Gravel mining

(P-363)
SWA MOUNTAIN GATE
20285 Radcliffe, Redding (96003)
P.O. Box 492335 (96049-2335)
PHONE....................530 221-3406
Corkey Harmon, *Manager*
Wayne Clay, *Marketing Staff*
EMP: 15
SQ FT: 800
SALES (est): 1.1MM **Privately Held**
SIC: 1442 Construction sand & gravel

(P-364)
THOMES CREEK ROCK CO INC
6069 99w, Corning (96021-9130)
PHONE....................530 824-0191
Mary Belle Coulter, *President*
EMP: 12
SQ FT: 1,000
SALES (est): 1.6MM **Privately Held**
SIC: 1442 Gravel & pebble mining

(P-365)
VULCAN AGGREGATES COMPANY LLC
Also Called: Lexington Quarry
18500 Limekiln Canyon Rd, Los Gatos
(95033-8629)
PHONE....................408 354-7904
EMP: 14 **Publicly Held**
SIC: 1442 Construction sand & gravel
HQ: Vulcan Aggregates Company, Llc
2215 Olan Mills Dr Ste A
Chattanooga TN 37421
423 510-2605

(P-366)
VULCAN CONSTRUCTION MTLS LLC
346 Mathew St, Santa Clara (95050-3114)
PHONE....................408 213-4270
EMP: 16 **Publicly Held**

SIC: 1442 Construction sand mining
HQ: Vulcan Construction Materials, Llc
1200 Urban Center Dr
Vestavia AL 35242
205 298-3000

(P-367)
WAYNE J SAND & GRAVEL INC
9455 Buena Vista St, Moorpark (93021)
PHONE.....................805 529-1323
Brett Jones, *President*
EMP: 14
SALES (est): 1.7MM **Privately Held**
SIC: 1442 Construction sand mining;
gravel mining

(P-368)
WEST COAST AGGREGATE SUPPLY
Also Called: Aggregate West Coast
92500 Airport Blvd, Thermal (92274)
P.O. Box 790 (92274-0790)
PHONE.....................760 342-7598
Marvin Struiksma, *President*
EMP: 50
SALES (est): 5.4MM **Privately Held**
SIC: 1442 Common sand mining

(P-369)
WEST COAST SAND GRAVEL
7715 Avenue 296, Visalia (93291-9540)
PHONE.....................559 625-9426
Dan Reynebeld, *CEO*
EMP: 20
SALES (est): 1.8MM **Privately Held**
SIC: 1442 Construction sand & gravel

(P-370)
WM J CLARK TRUCKING SVC INC
Also Called: Arroyo Seco Rock
319 Division St, King City (93930-3005)
P.O. Box 682 (93930-0682)
PHONE.....................831 385-4000
Sonama Clark, *President*
Sonoma Clark, *President*
William Clark, *Treasurer*
Emmy Clark, *Admin Sec*
EMP: 13
SQ FT: 800
SALES (est): 1.3MM **Privately Held**
SIC: 1442 4212 Construction sand &
gravel; local trucking, without storage

1446 Industrial Sand

(P-371)
BCJ SAND AND ROCK INC
3388 Regional Pkwy Ste A, Santa Rosa
(95403-8219)
P.O. Box 440, Fulton (95439-0440)
PHONE.....................707 544-0303
J Brad Slender, *President*
EMP: 16
SALES (est): 2.8MM **Privately Held**
SIC: 1446 Industrial sand

(P-372)
COVIA HOLDINGS CORPORATION
1300 Camino Diablo Rd, Byron (94514)
P.O. Box 216 (94514-0216)
PHONE.....................925 634-3575
Massoud Keshari, *Manager*
EMP: 30
SALES (corp-wide): 142.6MM **Publicly Held**
WEB: www.unimin.com
SIC: 1446 Silica mining
HQ: Covia Holdings Corporation
3 Summit Park Dr Ste 700
Independence OH 44131
440 214-3284

(P-373)
PIONEER SANDS LLC
9952 Enos Ln, Bakersfield (93314)
PHONE.....................661 746-5789
Donna Bartlett, *Branch Mgr*
EMP: 22
SALES (corp-wide): 9.4B **Publicly Held**
SIC: 1446 Silica mining

HQ: Pioneer Sands Llc
5205 N O Connor Blvd # 200
Irving TX 75039
972 444-9001

(P-374)
PIONEER SANDS LLC
31302 Ortega Hwy, San Juan Capistrano
(92675)
PHONE.....................949 728-0171
Mike Miclette, *Branch Mgr*
EMP: 53
SALES (corp-wide): 9.4B **Publicly Held**
SIC: 1446 Silica sand mining
HQ: Pioneer Sands Llc
5205 N O Connor Blvd # 200
Irving TX 75039
972 444-9001

(P-375)
PW GILLIBRAND CO INC (PA)
4537 Ish Dr, Simi Valley (93063-7667)
P.O. Box 1019 (93062-1019)
PHONE.....................805 526-2195
Celine Gillibrand, *CEO*
Richard Valencia, *President*
Jim Costello, *Corp Secy*
EMP: 72
SQ FT: 11,000
SALES (est): 30.9MM **Privately Held**
WEB: www.pwgcoinc.com
SIC: 1446 Grinding sand mining

1455 Kaolin & Ball Clay

(P-376)
IMERYS CLAYS INC
2500 Miguelito Rd, Lompoc (93436-9743)
PHONE.....................805 737-2445
EMP: 10
SALES (corp-wide): 3MM **Privately Held**
SIC: 1455 Kaolin mining
HQ: Imerys Clays, Inc.
100 Mansell Ct E Ste 300
Roswell GA 30076
770 594-0660

1459 Clay, Ceramic & Refractory Minerals, NEC

(P-377)
BLUE SKY HOME & ACC INC
1360 E Locust St, Ontario (91761-4567)
PHONE.....................909 930-6200
Henry Wang, *Controller*
▲ **EMP:** 25
SALES (est): 1.6MM **Privately Held**
SIC: 1459 Clay & related minerals

(P-378)
ELEMENTIS SPECIALTIES INC
31763 Mountain View Rd, Newberry
Springs (92365-9763)
PHONE.....................760 257-9112
Mike McGath, *Manager*
Steve Miller, *Safety Mgr*
Joyce Fitzgerald, *Manager*
Angela Harrell, *Manager*
EMP: 39
SALES (corp-wide): 822.2MM **Privately Held**
WEB: www.elementis-specialties.com
SIC: 1459 Clays, except kaolin & ball
HQ: Elementis Specialties, Inc.
469 Old Trenton Rd
East Windsor NJ 08512
609 443-2000

1479 Chemical & Fertilizer Mining

(P-379)
MORTON SALT INC
1050 Pier F Ave, Long Beach
(90802-6215)
P.O. Box 2289 (90801-2289)
PHONE.....................562 437-0071
Ken Dobson, *Branch Mgr*
EMP: 14
SALES (corp-wide): 4.6B **Privately Held**
SIC: 1479 Salt & sulfur mining

HQ: Morton Salt, Inc.
444 W Lake St Ste 3000
Chicago IL 60606
-

(P-380)
SEARLES VALLEY MINERALS INC
80201 Trona Rd, Trona (93562)
PHONE.....................760 372-2259
Burnell Blanchard, *Vice Pres*
EMP: 600
SALES (corp-wide): 873MM **Privately Held**
SIC: 1479 Salt & sulfur mining
HQ: Searles Valley Minerals Inc.
9401 Indn Crk Pkwy # 1000
Overland Park KS 66210
913 344-9500

1481 Nonmetallic Minerals Svcs, Except Fuels

(P-381)
DEMETRIUS POHL
2179 W 20th St, Los Angeles (90018-1407)
PHONE.....................323 735-1027
Demetrius Pohl, *Owner*
Cris Carlson, *Director*
EMP: 12
SALES (est): 398.1K **Privately Held**
SIC: 1481 Nonmetallic mineral services

(P-382)
IMERYS MINERALS CALIFORNIA INC
Also Called: Imerys Filtration Minerals
2500 Miguelito Canyon Rd, Lompoc
(93436)
PHONE.....................805 736-1221
Kenneth Schweibert, *Manager*
Jeff Taniguchi, *Manager*
EMP: 346
SALES (corp-wide): 3MM **Privately Held**
SIC: 1481 3295 Nonmetallic mineral serv-
ices; minerals, ground or treated
HQ: Imerys Minerals California, Inc.
2500 San Miguelito Rd
Lompoc CA 93436

(P-383)
MP MINE OPERATIONS LLC
67750 Bailey Rd, Mountain Pass (92366)
PHONE.....................702 277-0848
Michael Rosethal, *Mng Member*
James H Litinsky, *CEO*
EMP: 108
SALES (est): 220.2K **Privately Held**
SIC: 1481 Mine exploration, nonmetallic
minerals

1499 Miscellaneous Nonmetallic Mining

(P-384)
CELITE CORPORATION
2500 San Miguelito Rd, Lompoc
(93436-9743)
PHONE.....................805 736-1221
EMP: 10
SALES (est): 845K **Privately Held**
SIC: 1499 Miscellaneous nonmetallic min-
erals

(P-385)
DAKOTAHOUSE INDUSTRIES INC
5262 Cartwright Ave Apt 4, North Hollywood
(91601-5437)
PHONE.....................310 596-1100
Joshua Gbelawoe, *Principal*
EMP: 12
SALES (est): 514.7K **Privately Held**
SIC: 1499 6082 1041 Diamond mining,
industrial; foreign trade & international
banking institutions; open pit gold mining

(P-386)
DICAPERL CORPORATION (DH)
Also Called: Grefco Dicaperl
23705 Crenshaw Blvd, Torrance
(90505-5236)
PHONE.....................610 667-6640
Ray Perelman, *CEO*
Glenn Jones, *President*
Mike Cull, *Treasurer*
Barry Katz, *Senior VP*
▼ **EMP:** 90
SQ FT: 5,000
SALES (est): 9.5MM **Privately Held**
SIC: 1499 3677 Perlite mining; filtration
devices, electronic
HQ: Grefco Minerals Inc.
1 Bala Ave Ste 310
Bala Cynwyd PA 19004
610 660-8820

(P-387)
FEATHEROCK INC (PA)
20219 Bahama St, Chatsworth
(91311-6204)
PHONE.....................818 882-3888
Eric Anderson, *President*
Bob Campagna, *Controller*
Olivia Nicholson, *Sales Staff*
EMP: 15
SQ FT: 20,000
SALES: 1.7MM **Privately Held**
SIC: 1499 Pumice mining

(P-388)
GLOBAL PUMICE LLC
19968 Bear Valley Rd C, Apple Valley
(92308-5105)
P.O. Box 174 (92307-0003)
PHONE.....................760 240-3544
Thomas Hrubik,
EMP: 11
SALES: 1.5MM **Privately Held**
SIC: 1499 Pumice mining

(P-389)
H LIMA COMPANY INC
704 E Yosemite Ave, Manteca
(95336-5827)
PHONE.....................209 239-6787
Michael Lima, *President*
Frank Lima, *Owner*
Debbie Enos, *Treasurer*
Henry Frank Lima Jr, *Vice Pres*
Mark Lima, *Vice Pres*
EMP: 26
SQ FT: 1,300
SALES (est): 5.6MM **Privately Held**
SIC: 1499 Gypsum mining

(P-390)
IMERYS FILTRATION MINERALS INC (DH)
1732 N 1st St Ste 450, San Jose
(95112-4579)
PHONE.....................805 562-0200
Douglas A Smith, *CEO*
Leslie Zimmer, *CFO*
Fred Weber, *Treasurer*
Paul Woodberry, *Vice Ch Bd*
Daniel Moncino, *Vice Pres*
◆ **EMP:** 50
SQ FT: 11,600
SALES (est): 1.2B
SALES (corp-wide): 3MM **Privately Held**
SIC: 1499 Diatomaceous earth mining
HQ: Imerys Usa, Inc.
100 Mansell Ct E Ste 300
Roswell GA 30076
770 645-3300

(P-391)
IMERYS MINERALS CALIFORNIA INC (DH)
2500 San Miguelito Rd, Lompoc
(93436-9743)
P.O. Box 519 (93438-0519)
PHONE.....................805 736-1221
Douglas A Smith, *President*
John Oskam, *CEO*
John Leichty, *CFO*
Bruno Van Herpen, *Vice Pres*
Ken Rasmussen, *General Mgr*
▼ **EMP:** 70
SQ FT: 11,600

SALES (est): 1B
SALES (corp-wide): 3MM **Privately Held**
SIC: 1499 3295 Diatomaceous earth mining; minerals, ground or treated

(P-392)
MONARCHY DIAMOND INC
550 S Hill St Ste 1088, Los Angeles
(90013-2417)
PHONE..................................213 924-1161
Rajnikumar Patel, *President*
EMP: 425
SALES (est): 12.3MM **Privately Held**
SIC: 1499 Gem stones (natural) mining

(P-393)
ORGANICSORB LLC
Also Called: Save-Sorb
630 S Los Angeles St, Los Angeles
(90014-2178)
PHONE..................................310 795-4011
Chase Ahders,
Elma Salari, *CFO*
Ronnie Ebanks, *Sales Mgr*
Brie Gennusa,
Fatina Johnston,
EMP: 15
SALES (est): 1.2MM **Privately Held**
SIC: 1499 Miscellaneous nonmetallic minerals

(P-394)
UNITED STATES PUMICE COMPANY (PA)
Also Called: Featherrock
20219 Bahama St, Chatsworth
(91311-6287)
PHONE..................................818 882-0300
Eric L Anderson, *President*
Robert Campagna, *CFO*
▲ EMP: 12 EST: 1942
SQ FT: 2,000
SALES (est): 4.1MM **Privately Held**
WEB: www.uspumice.com
SIC: 1499 3291 Pumice mining; abrasive buffs, bricks, cloth, paper, stones, etc.

2011 Meat Packing Plants

(P-395)
ASIA FOOD INC
566 Monterey Pass Rd, Monterey Park
(91754-2417)
PHONE..................................626 284-1328
Bingham Lee, *CEO*
Chui Lee, *President*
EMP: 15
SQ FT: 15,000
SALES (est): 2.5MM **Privately Held**
SIC: 2011 2032 2092 2037 Meat packing plants; Chinese foods: packaged in cans, jars, etc.; fresh or frozen packaged fish; frozen fruits & vegetables; frozen specialties; fruit (fresh) packing services; vegetable packing services

(P-396)
BURNETT & SON MEAT CO INC
Also Called: Burnett Fine Foods
1420 S Myrtle Ave, Monrovia (91016-4153)
PHONE..................................626 357-2165
Donald L Burnett, *President*
▲ EMP: 80 EST: 1978
SQ FT: 20,000
SALES (est): 17.1MM **Privately Held**
WEB: www.burnettandson.com
SIC: 2011 Meat by-products from meat slaughtered on site; beef products from beef slaughtered on site

(P-397)
CALPERF INC (PA)
1810 Richard Ave, Santa Clara
(95050-2818)
PHONE..................................408 829-7779
Saswata Bhattacharya, *President*
Lali Dasgupta, *Director*
EMP: 10
SALES: 4.9MM **Privately Held**
SIC: 2011 5147 5144 Lamb products from lamb slaughtered on site; meats & meat products; poultry products

(P-398)
CARGILL MEAT SOLUTIONS CORP
2350 Academy Ave, Sanger (93657-9559)
PHONE..................................559 875-2232
Robert Case, *Branch Mgr*
EMP: 198
SALES (corp-wide): 114.7B **Privately Held**
SIC: 2011 Meat packing plants
HQ: Cargill Meat Solutions Corp
151 N Main St Ste 900
Wichita KS 67202
316 291-2500

(P-399)
CARGILL MEAT SOLUTIONS CORP
Cargill Food Distribution
10602 N Trademark Pkwy # 500, Rancho Cucamonga (91730-5937)
PHONE..................................909 476-3120
Guy Milam, *General Mgr*
EMP: 42
SALES (corp-wide): 114.7B **Privately Held**
SIC: 2011 Meat by-products from meat slaughtered on site
HQ: Cargill Meat Solutions Corp
151 N Main St Ste 900
Wichita KS 67202
316 291-2500

(P-400)
CARGILL MEAT SOLUTIONS CORP
3115 S Fig Ave, Fresno (93706-5647)
P.O. Box 12503 (93778-2503)
PHONE..................................559 268-5586
Tod Ventura, *Manager*
EMP: 200
SALES (corp-wide): 114.7B **Privately Held**
SIC: 2011 Beef products from beef slaughtered on site
HQ: Cargill Meat Solutions Corp
151 N Main St Ste 900
Wichita KS 67202
316 291-2500

(P-401)
CENTRAL VALLEY MEAT CO INC (PA)
10431 8 3/4 Ave, Hanford (93230-9248)
PHONE..................................559 583-9624
Brian Coelho, *CEO*
Lawrence Coelho, *President*
Bruce Hunt, *CFO*
Steve Coelho, *Vice Pres*
Brain Cohen, *Vice Pres*
▲ EMP: 200
SQ FT: 30,000
SALES (est): 168.8MM **Privately Held**
WEB: www.centralvalleymeat.com
SIC: 2011 Meat packing plants

(P-402)
CERTIFIED MEAT PRODUCTS INC
4586 E Commerce Ave, Fresno
(93725-2203)
P.O. Box 12051 (93776-2051)
PHONE..................................559 256-1433
Cassi Maxery, *CEO*
Matthew Lloyd, *Prdtn Mgr*
EMP: 45
SALES: 81.7MM **Privately Held**
WEB: www.certifiedmeatproducts.com
SIC: 2011 Meat packing plants

(P-403)
CLAUSEN MEAT COMPANY INC
19455 W Clausen Rd, Turlock (95380)
P.O. Box 1826 (95381-1826)
PHONE..................................209 667-8690
Ping Lau, *CEO*
Ying Hung Vinh, *CFO*
Kenneth Khoo, *Vice Pres*
George Chandler, *Principal*
Jean Johnson, *Principal*
▲ EMP: 40
SQ FT: 15,000
SALES (est): 6.2MM **Privately Held**
SIC: 2011 Meat packing plants

(P-404)
CLOUGHERTY PACKING LLC (DH)
Also Called: Smithfield Foods
3049 E Vernon Ave, Vernon (90058-1800)
P.O. Box 58870, Los Angeles (90058-0870)
PHONE..................................323 583-4621
Kenneth J Baptist, *President*
Martin Chen, *Vice Pres*
Lidwina Van Kooten, *Vice Pres*
Mandeep Saini, *Research*
Xung Dang, *Engineer*
EMP: 300
SQ FT: 1,000,000
SALES (est): 269MM **Privately Held**
WEB: www.farmerjohn.com
SIC: 2011 2013 Meat packing plants; sausages & other prepared meats
HQ: Smithfield Foods, Inc.
200 Commerce St
Smithfield VA 23430
757 365-3000

(P-405)
COLUMBUS FOODS LLC
30977 San Antonio St, Hayward
(94544-7109)
PHONE..................................510 921-3400
Ralph Denisco, *CEO*
John Piccetti, *Ch of Bd*
Adam Ferrif, *CFO*
Jeannea Enriquez, *Cust Mgr*
▲ EMP: 345
SALES (est): 63.5MM **Privately Held**
SIC: 2011 5143 5147 Luncheon meat from meat slaughtered on site; cheese; meats & meat products

(P-406)
ELLENSBURG LAMB COMPANY INC
Also Called: Superior Packing Co
7390 Rio Dixon Rd, Dixon (95620-9665)
P.O. Box 940 (95620-0940)
PHONE..................................707 678-3091
Martin Ducken, *Manager*
EMP: 150 **Privately Held**
SIC: 2011 Meat packing plants
HQ: Ellensburg Lamb Company, Inc.
2530 River Plaza Dr # 200
Sacramento CA 95833

(P-407)
ELLENSBURG LAMB COMPANY INC (HQ)
Also Called: Superior Farms
2530 River Plaza Dr # 200, Sacramento
(95833-3675)
PHONE..................................530 758-3091
Les Oestereich, *President*
Jeff Evanson, *CFO*
Gary Pfeiffer, *Exec VP*
Rebecca Adkins, *Executive*
Rachel Jensen, *General Mgr*
▼ EMP: 18
SQ FT: 7,500
SALES (est): 33.3MM **Privately Held**
SIC: 2011 Lamb products from lamb slaughtered on site

(P-408)
FIRSTCLASS FOODS - TROJAN INC
Also Called: First Class Foods
12500 Inglewood Ave, Hawthorne
(90250-4217)
P.O. Box 2397 (90251-2397)
PHONE..................................310 676-2500
Salomon Benzimra, *President*
Lucy Benzimra, *CFO*
Albert Benzimra, *Corp Secy*
Felix Benzimra, *VP Sales*
EMP: 135
SQ FT: 45,000
SALES (est): 23.6MM **Publicly Held**
WEB: www.firstclassfoods.com
SIC: 2011 5147 Meat packing plants; meats & meat products
HQ: Us Foods, Inc.
9399 W Higgins Rd # 100
Rosemont IL 60018

(P-409)
FLANAGAN-GORHAM INC (PA)
Also Called: Real Meat Company, The
2029 Verdugo Blvd Ste 311, Montrose
(91020-1626)
PHONE..................................818 279-2473
EMP: 13
SALES (est): 3.2MM **Privately Held**
SIC: 2011 Canned meats (except baby food), meat slaughtered on site

(P-410)
GAYLORDS HRI MEATS
Also Called: Gaylord's Meat Co
1100 E Ash Ave Ste C, Fullerton
(92831-5004)
PHONE..................................714 526-2278
Michael Smith, *Ch of Bd*
Vance Dixon, *President*
EMP: 18 EST: 1975
SQ FT: 10,000
SALES (est): 2.4MM **Privately Held**
SIC: 2011 5147 5144 Meat packing plants; meats & meat products; poultry & poultry products

(P-411)
GOLDEN VALLEY INDUSTRIES INC
960 Lone Palm Ave, Modesto
(95351-1533)
PHONE..................................209 939-3370
Mike Sullivan, *President*
Matt Ridjaneck, *Vice Pres*
EMP: 40
SQ FT: 40,000
SALES (est): 10.8MM **Privately Held**
WEB: www.goldenvalleyindustries.com
SIC: 2011 Meat packing plants

(P-412)
GOLDEN WEST FOOD GROUP INC (PA)
4401 S Downey Rd, Vernon (90058-2518)
PHONE..................................888 807-3663
Erik Litmanovich, *CEO*
Michael Bean, *Vice Pres*
EMP: 36 EST: 2011
SALES (est): 18.8MM **Privately Held**
SIC: 2011 2013 2015 Meat packing plants; sausages & other prepared meats; poultry, slaughtered & dressed

(P-413)
HARRIS RANCH BEEF COMPANY
16277 S Mccall Ave, Selma (93662-9458)
P.O. Box 220 (93662-0220)
PHONE..................................559 896-3081
John Harris, *Ch of Bd*
▼ EMP: 700
SALES (est): 168.8MM **Privately Held**
WEB: www.harrisranchbeef.com
SIC: 2011 2013 Meat packing plants; sausages & other prepared meats
PA: Central Valley Meat Co., Inc.
10431 8 3/4 Ave
Hanford CA 93230
559 583-9624

(P-414)
JOBBERS MEAT PACKING CO INC
3336 Fruitland Ave, Vernon (90058-3714)
P.O. Box 58368, Los Angeles (90058-0368)
PHONE..................................323 585-6328
Martin Evanson, *CEO*
Steig Osberg, *Vice Pres*
EMP: 12 EST: 1978
SQ FT: 19,000
SALES (est): 4MM **Privately Held**
WEB: www.jobbersmeat.com
SIC: 2011 Beef products from beef slaughtered on site

(P-415)
K & M PACKING CO INC
Also Called: K & M Meat Co
2443 E 27th St, Vernon (90058-1219)
PHONE..................................323 585-5318
Felix Goldberg, *President*
Roz White, *Executive*
EMP: 150
SQ FT: 30,000

SALES (est): 18.1MM **Privately Held**
SIC: 2011 Meat packing plants

(P-416)
LOS BANOS ABATTOIR CO INC
1312 W Pacheco Blvd, Los Banos
(93635-7807)
P.O. Box 949 (93635-0949)
PHONE...................................209 826-2212
Steven La Salvia, *President*
Laura La Salvia, *Vice Pres*
EMP: 35
SQ FT: 7,500
SALES (est): 5.9MM **Privately Held**
SIC: 2011 5147 Beef products from beef
slaughtered on site; veal from meat
slaughtered on site; meats & meat prod-
ucts

(P-417)
MANNINGS BEEF LLC
9531 Beverly Rd, Pico Rivera
(90660-2134)
P.O. Box 1156 (90660-1156)
PHONE...................................562 908-1089
Anthony Di Maria, *Mng Member*
Andrew D Broberg,
Lloyd Manning,
EMP: 79
SQ FT: 75,000
SALES (est): 16.1MM **Privately Held**
SIC: 2011 Meat packing plants

(P-418)
MOHAWK LAND & CATTLE CO INC
1660 Old Bayshore Hwy, San Jose
(95112-4304)
P.O. Box 601 (95106-0601)
PHONE...................................408 436-1800
Steve Tognoli, *President*
▼ EMP: 64 EST: 1957
SQ FT: 50,000
SALES (est): 6.3MM **Privately Held**
SIC: 2011 Meat packing plants
HQ: Smithfield Packaged Meats Corp.
805 E Kemper Rd
Cincinnati OH 45246
513 782-3800

(P-419)
NAGLES VEAL INC
1411 E Base Line St, San Bernardino
(92410-4113)
PHONE...................................909 383-7075
Michael Lemler, *President*
Timothy Haggard, *General Mgr*
Cathy Martin,
▲ EMP: 50
SQ FT: 12,500
SALES (est): 8.1MM **Privately Held**
SIC: 2011 Veal from meat slaughtered on
site; beef products from beef slaughtered
on site; lamb products from lamb slaugh-
tered on site

(P-420)
OLLI SALUMERIA AMERICANA LLC
1301 Rocky Point Dr, Oceanside
(92056-5864)
PHONE...................................804 427-7866
Oliviero Colmignoll,
EMP: 15
SALES (corp-wide): 4.2MM **Privately Held**
SIC: 2011 Meat packing plants
PA: Olli Salumeria Americana, Llc
8505 Bell Creek Rd Ste H
Mechanicsville VA 23116
804 427-7866

(P-421)
R B R MEAT COMPANY INC
Also Called: Rightway
5151 Alcoa Ave, Vernon (90058-3715)
P.O. Box 58225, Los Angeles (90058-0225)
PHONE...................................323 973-4868
Irwin Miller, *President*
Larry Vanden Bos, *Vice Pres*
James Craig, *Vice Pres*
EMP: 75 EST: 1951
SQ FT: 65,000
SALES (est): 12MM **Privately Held**
SIC: 2011 Meat packing plants

(P-422)
RAMAR INTERNATIONAL CORP
Also Called: Orientex
539 Garcia Ave Ste E, Pittsburg
(94565-7403)
PHONE...................................925 432-4267
Tito Sanchez, *Manager*
EMP: 30
SALES (corp-wide): 25.4MM **Privately Held**
SIC: 2011 Sausages from meat slaugh-
tered on site
PA: Ramar International Corp
1101 Railroad Ave
Pittsburg CA 94565
925 439-9009

(P-423)
RICHWOOD MEAT COMPANY INC
2751 N Santa Fe Ave, Merced
(95348-4109)
P.O. Box 2599 (95344-0599)
PHONE...................................209 722-8171
Michael J Wood, *President*
Carol J Wood, *Shareholder*
Hellen Diane Inks-Fragie, *CFO*
Steve Wood, *Vice Pres*
Steven J Wood, *Vice Pres*
EMP: 100
SQ FT: 43,000
SALES: 57.7MM **Privately Held**
WEB: www.richwoodmeat.com
SIC: 2011 5147 5421 Meat packing
plants; meats, fresh; meats, cured or
smoked; meat & fish markets

(P-424)
SERV-RITE MEAT COMPANY INC
Also Called: Packers Bar M
2515 N San Fernando Rd, Los Angeles
(90065-1325)
P.O. Box 65026 (90065-0026)
PHONE...................................323 227-1911
Gary Marks, *CEO*
Mark Pierce, *CFO*
Norman Marks, *Vice Pres*
Phil Tanico, *Regional Mgr*
Norma Marks, *Admin Sec*
EMP: 55
SQ FT: 55,000
SALES (est): 14.3MM **Privately Held**
SIC: 2011 Meat packing plants

(P-425)
SMITHFIELD PACKAGED MEATS CORP
Mohawk Packing
1660 Old Bayshore Hwy, San Jose
(95112-4304)
PHONE...................................408 392-0442
Kevin Connor, *Manager*
Pablo Pineda, *Human Res Mgr*
Larry Scicluna, *Safety Mgr*
Chuck Carlson, *Manager*
EMP: 130
SQ FT: 32,942 **Privately Held**
WEB: www.johnmorrell.com
SIC: 2011 Meat packing plants
HQ: Smithfield Packaged Meats Corp.
805 E Kemper Rd
Cincinnati OH 45246
513 782-3800

(P-426)
TRANSHUMANCE HOLDING CO INC
Also Called: Superior Farms
7390 Rio Dixon Rd, Dixon (95620-9665)
P.O. Box 940 (95620-0940)
PHONE...................................707 693-2303
Julie Angel, *Manager*
Anders Hemphill, *Vice Pres*
Lynn Fox, *Maintence Staff*
Ray Bodine, *Director*
EMP: 200 **Privately Held**
WEB: www.superiorfarms.com
SIC: 2011 Lamb products from lamb
slaughtered on site
PA: Transhumance Holding Company, Inc.
2530 River Plaza Dr # 200
Sacramento CA 95833

(P-427)
TYSON FRESH MEATS INC
Also Called: I B P Service Center
500 S Kraemer Blvd # 380, Brea
(92821-6728)
PHONE...................................714 528-5543
Brian Holeman, *Manager*
John Duane, *Sales Staff*
EMP: 15
SALES (corp-wide): 42.4B **Publicly Held**
SIC: 2011 Meat packing plants
HQ: Tyson Fresh Meats, Inc.
800 Stevens Port Dr
Dakota Dunes SD 57049
605 235-2061

(P-428)
V J PROVISION INC
Also Called: Jacobellis
410 S Varney St, Burbank (91502-2124)
PHONE...................................818 843-3945
Sam Jacobellis, *President*
George Jacobellis, *Treasurer*
Vito Jacobellis, *Vice Pres*
Tony Jacobellis, *Admin Sec*
EMP: 18
SQ FT: 11,300
SALES: 5MM **Privately Held**
WEB: www.jacobellis.com
SIC: 2011 Meat packing plants

(P-429)
VENUS FOODS INC
770 S Stimson Ave, City of Industry
(91745-1638)
PHONE...................................626 369-5188
Gin Shen Wu, *Ch of Bd*
Robert Y Tsai, *President*
Shih-Ai Meng, *Treasurer*
T K Chow, *Vice Pres*
▲ EMP: 20 EST: 1980
SQ FT: 20,000
SALES (est): 3.7MM **Privately Held**
WEB: www.venusfoods.com
SIC: 2011 2099 Meat packing plants; food
preparations

(P-430)
VIZ CATTLE CORPORATION
Also Called: Sukarne
17890 Castleton St # 350, City of Industry
(91748-5793)
PHONE...................................310 884-5260
Edwin Botero, *President*
Aofonso Marco, *CFO*
Arturo Villarrel, *Vice Pres*
Anna Vizcarra, *Vice Pres*
▲ EMP: 24
SALES: 700MM **Privately Held**
SIC: 2011 5154 Meat packing plants; cat-
tle
PA: Grupo Viz, S.A. De C.V.
Av. Diana Tang No. 59-A
Culiacan SIN. 80300

(P-431)
WEST LAKE FOOD CORPORATION
Also Called: Tay Ho
2430 Cape Cod Way, Santa Ana
(92703-3540)
PHONE...................................714 973-2286
Chieu Nguyen, *CEO*
Chuong Nguyen, *Vice Pres*
Jayce Yenson, *Admin Sec*
◆ EMP: 75
SQ FT: 11,238
SALES (est): 12MM **Privately Held**
SIC: 2011 Meat packing plants

(P-432)
WHOLESOME HARVEST BAKING INC
Also Called: Maple Consumer Foods
7840 Madison Ave Ste 135, Fair Oaks
(95628-3591)
PHONE...................................916 967-1633
EMP: 10
SALES (corp-wide): 4.2B **Privately Held**
SIC: 2011
HQ: Wholesome Harvest Baking, Inc.
1011 E Touhy Ave Ste 500
Des Plaines IL 60631
847 655-8100

(P-433)
YOSEMITE VLY BEEF PKG CO INC
970 E Sandy Mush Rd, Merced
(95341-7903)
P.O. Box 1828, Duarte (91009-4828)
PHONE...................................626 435-0170
Michael Ban, *President*
E K Ban, *Controller*
Wesley Jones, *QC Mgr*
Ek Ban, *Manager*
EMP: 28
SQ FT: 5,000
SALES (est): 4.8MM **Privately Held**
SIC: 2011 Meat packing plants

2013 Sausages & Meat Prdts

(P-434)
AIDELLS SAUSAGE COMPANY INC
2411 Baumann Ave, San Lorenzo
(94580-1801)
PHONE...................................510 614-5450
Ernie Gabiati, *President*
Yvette Abreu, *Office Mgr*
Tony Kwan, *Controller*
Cristina Montemayor, *Human Res Mgr*
Edwin Bell, *Plant Mgr*
EMP: 900
SQ FT: 15,000
SALES (est): 186.3MM
SALES (corp-wide): 42.4B **Publicly Held**
WEB: www.aidells.com
SIC: 2013 5147 Sausages from pur-
chased meat; meats & meat products
HQ: The Hillshire Brands Company
400 S Jefferson St Fl 1
Chicago IL 60607
312 614-6000

(P-435)
ALPENA SAUSAGE INC
5329 Craner Ave, North Hollywood
(91601-3313)
PHONE...................................818 505-9482
Frederick Thaller, *President*
EMP: 15
SQ FT: 6,000
SALES: 2.5MM **Privately Held**
SIC: 2013 Sausages from purchased meat

(P-436)
ALPINE MEATS INC
9850 Lower Sacramento Rd, Stockton
(95210-3915)
PHONE...................................209 477-2691
Rick Martin, *CEO*
Bill Kraljev, *Controller*
Robby Jaynes, *Manager*
Dean Wickett, *Manager*
EMP: 50
SALES (est): 8.1MM **Privately Held**
SIC: 2013 Smoked meats from purchased
meat

(P-437)
AMERICAN CUSTOM MEATS LLC
4276 N Tracy Blvd, Tracy (95304-1501)
PHONE...................................209 839-8800
Neil Kinney, *President*
EMP: 88
SQ FT: 75,000
SALES: 39.3MM **Privately Held**
SIC: 2013 2015 2032 Prepared beef
products from purchased meat; roast beef
from purchased meat; prepared pork
products from purchased pork; poultry
slaughtering & processing; puddings, ex-
cept meat: packaged in cans, jars, etc.

(P-438)
ARMONA FROZEN FOOD LOCKERS
Also Called: Raven's Deli
10870 14th Ave, Armona (93202)
P.O. Box 367 (93202-0367)
PHONE...................................559 584-3948
William M Raven, *Owner*
Marlene Raven, *Co-Owner*
EMP: 10
SQ FT: 13,000

SALES (est): 884.8K **Privately Held**
SIC: **2013** 5411 5421 Beef, dried: from purchased meat; delicatessens; meat markets, including freezer provisioners

(P-439)
BAR-S FOODS CO
392 Railroad Ct, Milpitas (95035-4339)
PHONE..................................408 941-9958
Olga Vasquez, *Manager*
EMP: 346 **Privately Held**
SIC: **2013** Sausages & other prepared meats
HQ: Bar-S Foods Co.
5090 N 40th St Ste 300
Phoenix AZ 85018
602 264-7272

(P-440)
BAR-S FOODS CO
Also Called: Bar-S Foods Co. Los Angeles
4919 Alcoa Ave, Vernon (90058-3022)
PHONE..................................323 589-3600
EMP: 290 **Privately Held**
SIC: **2013** Sausages & other prepared meats
HQ: Bar-S Foods Co.
5090 N 40th St Ste 300
Phoenix AZ 85018
602 264-7272

(P-441)
BEFORE BUTCHER INC
2550 Britannia Blvd, San Diego
(92154-7404)
PHONE..................................858 265-9511
Abel Olivera, *CEO*
Ernest De Los Reyes, *Controller*
EMP: 10
SALES (est): 283.4K **Privately Held**
SIC: **2013** Sausages & other prepared meats

(P-442)
BOYD SPECIALTIES LLC
1016 E Cooley Dr Ste N, Colton
(92324-3962)
PHONE..................................909 219-5120
Jae Boyd,
Sue Boyd, *Manager*
▲ EMP: 52
SQ FT: 10,000
SALES (est): 6MM **Privately Held**
WEB: www.carnivorecandy.com
SIC: **2013** Snack sticks, including jerky: from purchased meat

(P-443)
BUMBLE BEE HOLDINGS INC (HQ)
280 10th Ave, San Diego (92101-7406)
P.O. Box 85362 (92186-5362)
PHONE..................................858 715-4000
Robert P Kirby, *Ch of Bd*
Kent McNeil, *CFO*
Richard J Sosnoski, *CFO*
David J Carmany, *Treasurer*
Peter D Lemahieu, *Senior VP*
◆ EMP: 420 EST: 1926
SQ FT: 275,000
SALES (est): 177.1MM **Privately Held**
WEB: www.castleberrys.com
SIC: **2013** 2032 2033 Beef stew from purchased meat; canned meats (except baby food) from purchased meat; frozen meats from purchased meat; chili with or without meat: packaged in cans, jars, etc.; vegetables & vegetable products in cans, jars, etc.

(P-444)
BUSSETO FOODS INC (PA)
1351 N Crystal Ave, Fresno (93728-1142)
P.O. Box 12403 (93777-2403)
PHONE..................................559 485-9882
G Michael Grazier, *President*
Randy Hergenroeder, *CFO*
Ed Fanucchi, *Admin Sec*
James Freeny, *Purchasing*
▲ EMP: 155
SQ FT: 40,000
SALES (est): 39.2MM **Privately Held**
WEB: www.busseto.com
SIC: **2013** Sausages from purchased meat

(P-445)
C R W DISTRIBUTORS INC
1223 Wilshire Blvd, Santa Monica
(90403-5406)
PHONE..................................310 463-4577
Brian Wrye, *President*
EMP: 21
SQ FT: 7,000
SALES: 2.7MM **Privately Held**
SIC: **2013** Prepared beef products from purchased beef

(P-446)
CATTANEO BROS INC
769 Caudill St, San Luis Obispo
(93401-5729)
PHONE..................................805 543-7188
Mike Kaney, *President*
Jayne Kaney, *Corp Secy*
William Cattaneo Sr, *Founder*
Ken Castro, *Opers Staff*
Heidi Heller, *Sales Mgr*
EMP: 20
SQ FT: 5,500
SALES: 1.2MM **Privately Held**
WEB: www.cattaneobros.com
SIC: **2013** 5961 Beef, dried: from purchased meat; sausages from purchased meat; food, mail order

(P-447)
CHOICE FOOD PRODUCTS INC
Also Called: Saladino Sausage Company
1822 W Hedges Ave, Fresno (93728-1140)
PHONE..................................559 266-1674
Ty Kenny, *President*
Marlese Kinney, *Treasurer*
EMP: 15
SQ FT: 3,048
SALES (est): 2.4MM **Privately Held**
WEB: www.saladinosausage.com
SIC: **2013** Sausages & other prepared meats

(P-448)
CLOUGHERTY PACKING LLC
3922 Avenue 120, Corcoran (93212-9532)
P.O. Box 247 (93212-0247)
PHONE..................................559 992-8421
Don Davidson, *Manager*
EMP: 10 **Privately Held**
WEB: www.farmerjohn.com
SIC: **2013** Sausages & other prepared meats
HQ: Clougherty Packing, Llc
3049 E Vernon Ave
Vernon CA 90058
323 583-4621

(P-449)
COLUMBUS MANUFACTURING INC (HQ)
30977 San Antonio St, Hayward
(94544-7109)
PHONE..................................510 921-3423
Joe Ennen, *CEO*
Randy Sieve, *CFO*
▲ EMP: 100
SQ FT: 121,000
SALES (corp-wide): 9.5B **Publicly Held**
SIC: **2013** Sausages & related products, from purchased meat; roast beef from purchased meat
PA: Hormel Foods Corporation
1 Hormel Pl
Austin MN 55912
507 437-5611

(P-450)
CORRALITOS MARKET & SAUSAGE CO
569 Corralitos Rd, Watsonville
(95076-0596)
PHONE..................................831 722-2633
Dave Peterson, *President*
Ken Wong, *Vice Pres*
Jo Ellen Tartala, *Admin Sec*
EMP: 19
SQ FT: 5,000
SALES (est): 2.8MM **Privately Held**
SIC: **2013** 5411 Sausages & other prepared meats; grocery stores

(P-451)
COURAGE PRODUCTION LLC
2475 Courage Dr, Fairfield (94533-6723)
PHONE..................................707 422-6300
Philip Gatto, *Mng Member*
EMP: 100
SALES (est): 23.1MM **Privately Held**
SIC: **2013** Sausages from purchased meat

(P-452)
DEMES GOURMET CORPORATION
Also Called: Master Link Sausage
327 N State College Blvd, Fullerton
(92831-4205)
PHONE..................................714 870-6040
Randy Martin, *President*
Mary Martin, *Vice Pres*
EMP: 22
SQ FT: 17,600
SALES (est): 3.6MM **Privately Held**
SIC: **2013** Sausages & other prepared meats

(P-453)
DEREK AND CONSTANCE LEE CORP (PA)
Also Called: Great River Food
19355 San Jose Ave, City of Industry
(91748-1420)
PHONE..................................909 595-8831
Derek E Lee, *President*
▲ EMP: 95
SQ FT: 50,000
SALES (est): 20.5MM **Privately Held**
SIC: **2013** 1541 Sausages & other prepared meats; food products manufacturing or packing plant construction

(P-454)
E G MEAT AND PROVISION INC (PA)
4350 Alcoa Ave, Vernon (90058-2410)
PHONE..................................323 588-5333
Encarnacion Gutierrez, *CEO*
EMP: 14 EST: 2007
SALES (est): 2.5MM **Privately Held**
SIC: **2013** 5146 Roast beef from purchased meat; pork, smoked: from purchased meat; fish & seafoods

(P-455)
EVERGOOD SAUSAGE CO
Also Called: Evergood Fine Foods
1932 Van Dyke Ave, San Francisco
(94124)
PHONE..................................415 822-4660
Harlan Miller Sr, *President*
Donald Miller, *Vice Pres*
Harlan J Miller Jr, *Vice Pres*
Kevin Bentley, *Plant Mgr*
Ron Delucchi, *Sales Staff*
EMP: 98
SQ FT: 30,000
SALES (est): 17.7MM **Privately Held**
WEB: www.evergoodfoods.com
SIC: **2013** Sausages from purchased meat

(P-456)
FORMOSA MEAT COMPANY INC
Also Called: Universal Meat Company
10646 Fulton Ct, Rancho Cucamonga
(91730-4848)
PHONE..................................909 987-0470
Cheng-Ting Shih, *Vice Pres*
Hsiu-Ō Kan, *Treasurer*
Micki Jack, *Vice Pres*
Marcy Venegas, *Purchasing*
▲ EMP: 40
SQ FT: 23,000
SALES (est): 6.6MM **Privately Held**
SIC: **2013** Snack sticks, including jerky: from purchased meat

(P-457)
FRA MANI LLC
Also Called: Fra' Mani Handcrafted Salumi
1311 8th St, Berkeley (94710-1453)
PHONE..................................510 526-7000
Paul Bertolli, *General Ptnr*
Thomas Garrity, *General Counsel*
Linda Bertolli, *Manager*
EMP: 12
SQ FT: 10,000

SALES (est): 2.7MM **Privately Held**
SIC: **2013** Sausages & related products, from purchased meat

(P-458)
FULLFILLMENT SYSTEMS INC
Also Called: D'Ambrosio Bros
1228 Reamwood Ave, Sunnyvale
(94089-2225)
PHONE..................................408 745-7675
Pasquale Vitonti, *Manager*
Pasquale Bitonti, *Opers Mgr*
EMP: 75
SALES (corp-wide): 77.8MM **Privately Held**
WEB: www.nicolinosgardencafe.com
SIC: **2013** 2011 Sausages from purchased meat; sausages from meat slaughtered on site
PA: Fullfillment Systems, Inc.
1228 Reamwood Ave
Sunnyvale CA 94089
408 745-7675

(P-459)
GLENOAKS FOOD INC
11030 Randall St, Sun Valley (91352-2621)
PHONE..................................818 768-9091
John J Fallon III, *President*
Marvin Caeser, *Shareholder*
Katty Majailovic, *Shareholder*
EMP: 25
SQ FT: 30,000
SALES (est): 3.2MM **Privately Held**
WEB: www.glenoaksfood.com
SIC: **2013** 2015 Beef, dried: from purchased meat; poultry slaughtering & processing

(P-460)
GOLDEN ISLAND JERKY CO INC (DH)
10646 Fulton Ct, Rancho Cucamonga
(91730-4848)
PHONE..................................844 362-3222
Cheng Shih, *President*
▲ EMP: 31 EST: 2012
SALES (est): 10MM
SALES (corp-wide): 42.4B **Publicly Held**
SIC: **2013** Snack sticks, including jerky: from purchased meat
HQ: The Hillshire Brands Company
400 S Jefferson St Fl 1
Chicago IL 60607
312 614-6000

(P-461)
GOLDEN ISLAND JERKY CO INC
9955 6th St, Rancho Cucamonga
(91730-5752)
PHONE..................................844 362-3222
EMP: 11
SALES (corp-wide): 42.4B **Publicly Held**
SIC: **2013** Snack sticks, including jerky: from purchased meat
HQ: Golden Island Jerky Company, Inc.
10646 Fulton Ct
Rancho Cucamonga CA 91730
844 362-3222

(P-462)
GREEN DINING TABLE
625 S Palm Ave, Alhambra (91803-1424)
PHONE..................................626 782-7916
▲ EMP: 10
SALES (est): 1.1MM **Privately Held**
SIC: **2013** Frozen meats from purchased meat

(P-463)
HAWA CORPORATION
Also Called: Beef Jerky Factory
125 E Laurel St, Colton (92324-2462)
PHONE..................................909 825-8882
Waleed Saab, *Vice Pres*
EMP: 20
SQ FT: 34,500
SALES (est): 1.6MM **Privately Held**
SIC: **2013** Beef, dried: from purchased meat

(P-464)
HILLSHIRE BRANDS COMPANY
9357 Richmond Pl Ste 101, Rancho Cucamonga (91730-6032)
PHONE..................................909 481-0760

PRODUCTS & SVCS

Jerry Newham, *Branch Mgr*
EMP: 322
SALES (corp-wide): 42.4B **Publicly Held**
SIC: 2013 2053 2051 Sausages & other prepared meats; frozen bakery products, except bread; bread, cake & related products
HQ: The Hillshire Brands Company
400 S Jefferson St Fl 1
Chicago IL 60607
312 614-6000

(P-465)
HILLSHIRE BRANDS COMPANY
Also Called: Sara Lee
2411 Baumann Ave, San Lorenzo (94580-1801)
PHONE....................510 276-1300
Alfred Yu, *Branch Mgr*
Linda Saxton, *MIS Mgr*
Bill Sereni, *Maintence Staff*
William Sereni, *Manager*
EMP: 400
SQ FT: 20,000
SALES (corp-wide): 42.4B **Publicly Held**
SIC: 2013 Sausages & other prepared meats
HQ: The Hillshire Brands Company
400 S Jefferson St Fl 1
Chicago IL 60607
312 614-6000

(P-466)
HILLSHIRE BRANDS COMPANY
Also Called: Superior Coffee & Foods
10715 Springdale Ave # 5, Santa Fe Springs (90670-3858)
PHONE....................562 903-9260
Kevin Mc Klavende, *Branch Mgr*
EMP: 50
SALES (corp-wide): 42.4B **Publicly Held**
SIC: 2013 Sausages & other prepared meats
HQ: The Hillshire Brands Company
400 S Jefferson St Fl 1
Chicago IL 60607
312 614-6000

(P-467)
HORMEL FOODS CORP SVCS LLC
2 Venture Ste 250, Irvine (92618-7408)
PHONE....................949 753-5350
Randy Kemmipz, *Manager*
Randal S Kemnitz, *Director*
EMP: 40
SALES (corp-wide): 9.5B **Publicly Held**
SIC: 2013 Canned meats (except baby food); beef stew from purchased meat; corned beef from purchased meat; spreads, sandwich: meat from purchased meat
HQ: Hormel Foods Corporate Services, Llc
1 Hormel Pl
Austin MN 55912
507 437-5611

(P-468)
HSIN TUNG YANG FOODS COMPANY
Also Called: New Horizon
405 S Airport Blvd, South San Francisco (94080-6909)
PHONE....................650 589-7689
Kaiyen MAI, *CEO*
Su Wuan MAI, *Ch of Bd*
▲ **EMP:** 11
SQ FT: 86,000
SALES (est): 2.2MM **Privately Held**
WEB: www.htyusa.com
SIC: 2013 5149 2051 Sausages & other prepared meats; canned goods: fruit, vegetables, seafood, meats, etc.; bread, cake & related products

(P-469)
JENSEN MEAT COMPANY INC
2550 Britannia Blvd # 101, San Diego (92154-7404)
PHONE....................619 754-6400
Abel Olivera, *CEO*
Jeff Hamann, *Co-Owner*
Sam Acuna, *CFO*
EMP: 95
SQ FT: 25,000

SALES (est): 44MM **Privately Held**
SIC: 2013 Sausages & other prepared meats

(P-470)
JODY MARONIS ITALIAN
2011 Ocean Front Walk, Venice (90291-4118)
PHONE....................310 822-5639
Jordan A Monkarsh, *President*
Richard Leivenberg, *Vice Pres*
EMP: 20
SQ FT: 2,200
SALES (est): 1.6MM **Privately Held**
SIC: 2013 5812 Sausages & other prepared meats; eating places

(P-471)
KADI ENTERPRISES INC
802 N Victory Blvd, Burbank (91502-1630)
P.O. Box 3148 (91508-3148)
PHONE....................818 556-3400
Sami El Kadi, *President*
Richard Freeman, *Exec VP*
John Stenmo, *Division Mgr*
EMP: 11
SQ FT: 2,000
SALES (est): 2.4MM **Privately Held**
WEB: www.kadienterprise.com
SIC: 2013 Snack sticks, including jerky: from purchased meat

(P-472)
KITCHEN CUTS LLC
6045 District Blvd, Maywood (90270)
PHONE....................323 560-7415
Raul Tapia Sr, *CEO*
EMP: 49
SALES (est): 3.2MM
SALES (corp-wide): 266.4MM **Privately Held**
SIC: 2013 Beef stew from purchased meat
PA: Tapia Enterprises Inc.
6067 District Blvd
Maywood CA 90270
323 560-7415

(P-473)
KMB FOODS INC (PA)
1010 S Sierra Way, San Bernardino (92408-2124)
PHONE....................626 447-0545
Scott Biedermann, *President*
Sam Mangiaterra, *COO*
Becky Benham, *Administration*
▲ **EMP:** 20 **EST:** 1998
SQ FT: 6,000
SALES (est): 9MM **Privately Held**
SIC: 2013 2099 Prepared beef products from purchased beef; food preparations

(P-474)
KRAVE PURE FOODS INC
Also Called: Krave Jerky
117 W Napa St Ste A, Sonoma (95476-6691)
PHONE....................707 939-9176
Jonathan A Sebastiani, *CEO*
Philippe Barnoud, *Vice Pres*
Katie Tessitore, *Executive*
Brian Link, *Regional Mgr*
Robert Daniels, *Finance Mgr*
EMP: 58
SALES (est): 23.9MM
SALES (corp-wide): 7.7B **Publicly Held**
SIC: 2013 5147 Snack sticks, including jerky: from purchased meat; meats & meat products
PA: Hershey Company
19 E Chocolate Ave
Hershey PA 17033
717 534-4200

(P-475)
KRUSE AND SON INC
235 Kruse Ave, Monrovia (91016-4899)
P.O. Box 945 (91017-0945)
PHONE....................626 358-4536
David R Kruse, *CEO*
EMP: 25
SQ FT: 20,000
SALES (est): 4.5MM **Privately Held**
SIC: 2013 Ham, smoked: from purchased meat; bacon, side & sliced: from purchased meat

(P-476)
LA ESPANOLA MEATS INC
25020 Doble Ave, Harbor City (90710-3155)
PHONE....................310 539-0455
Alex Motamedi, *CEO*
Juana Faraone, *President*
Frank Faraone, *Treasurer*
◆ **EMP:** 25
SQ FT: 8,800
SALES (est): 5MM **Privately Held**
WEB: www.laespanolameats.com
SIC: 2013 5421 Sausages & related products, from purchased meat; meat markets, including freezer provisioners

(P-477)
MARISA FOODS LLC
1401 Santa Fe Ave, Long Beach (90813-1236)
PHONE....................562 437-7775
Vincent Passanisi,
Liana Passanisi,
EMP: 11
SALES (est): 1.7MM **Privately Held**
SIC: 2013 Sausages & other prepared meats

(P-478)
MARTIN PUREFOODS CORPORATION
1713 W 2nd St, Pomona (91766-1253)
PHONE....................909 865-4440
Rick Martin, *President*
▲ **EMP:** 10
SQ FT: 7,700
SALES (est): 1.2MM **Privately Held**
WEB: www.martinpurefoods.com
SIC: 2013 2011 Sausages & other prepared meats; sausages from meat slaughtered on site

(P-479)
MEADOW FARMS SAUSAGE CO INC
6215 S Western Ave, Los Angeles (90047-1441)
PHONE....................323 752-2300
Joe Toia, *President*
EMP: 10
SQ FT: 8,000
SALES (est): 1MM **Privately Held**
SIC: 2013 Sausages from purchased meat

(P-480)
MIKAILIAN MEAT PRODUCT INC
25310 Avenue Stanford, Santa Clarita (91355-1214)
PHONE....................661 257-1055
Gebril Mikailian, *President*
Swedlanan Mikailian, *Vice Pres*
EMP: 10
SQ FT: 14,000
SALES (est): 3MM **Privately Held**
SIC: 2013 Ham, roasted: from purchased meat; bologna from purchased meat; sausages from purchased meat

(P-481)
MILLER PACKING COMPANY
Also Called: Miller Hot Dogs
1122 Industrial Way, Lodi (95240-3119)
P.O. Box 1390 (95241-1390)
PHONE....................209 339-2310
Michael A De Benedetti, *President*
Staige P Debenedetti, *CEO*
EMP: 50
SQ FT: 40,000
SALES (est): 7.2MM **Privately Held**
WEB: www.millerhotdogs.com
SIC: 2013 Sausages & other prepared meats

(P-482)
MONDELEZ GLOBAL LLC
Also Called: Kraft Foods
6201 Knott Ave, Buena Park (90620-1010)
PHONE....................714 690-7428
Jeferey Orchard, *Branch Mgr*
Cory Mead, *Manager*
EMP: 562 **Publicly Held**
WEB: www.kraftfoods.com
SIC: 2013 Sausages & other prepared meats

HQ: Mondelez Global Llc
3 N Pkwy Ste 300
Deerfield IL 60015
847 943-4000

(P-483)
OHANYANS INC (PA)
Also Called: Ohanyan's Deli
3296 W Sussex Way, Fresno (93722-4929)
PHONE....................559 225-4290
Jerry Hancer, *President*
Robert Hancer, *Treasurer*
Markos Garabetyan, *Vice Pres*
Hayik Garabetyan, *Admin Sec*
EMP: 10
SQ FT: 9,000
SALES: 3MM **Privately Held**
SIC: 2013 5411 Beef, dried: from purchased meat; sausages from purchased meat; delicatessens

(P-484)
ONE WORLD MEAT COMPANY LLC
6363 Knott Ave, Buena Park (90620-1021)
PHONE....................800 782-1670
Eric Brandt, *CEO*
EMP: 15
SALES (est): 528.5K **Privately Held**
SIC: 2013 Prepared beef products from purchased beef

(P-485)
P G MOLINARI & SONS INC
Also Called: Molinari Salami Co
1401 Yosemite Ave, San Francisco (94124-3321)
PHONE....................415 822-5555
Frank P Giorgi, *President*
Gloria Giorgi, *Vice Pres*
▲ **EMP:** 23
SQ FT: 48,000
SALES (est): 5.5MM **Privately Held**
WEB: www.molinarisalame.com
SIC: 2013 Sausages from purchased meat; spiced meats from purchased meat

(P-486)
PAMPANGA FOODS COMPANY INC
1835 N Orngthrp Park A, Anaheim (92801-1143)
PHONE....................714 773-0537
Ray Reyes, *President*
Coni Reyes, *Vice Pres*
EMP: 15
SQ FT: 11,000
SALES (est): 2.7MM **Privately Held**
WEB: www.pampangafoods.com
SIC: 2013 5812 8742 2011 Sausages & other prepared meats; eating places; food & beverage consultant; sausages from meat slaughtered on site

(P-487)
PAPA CANTELLAS INCORPORATED
Also Called: Papa Cantella's Sausage Plant
3341 E 50th St, Vernon (90058-3003)
PHONE....................323 584-7272
Thomas P Cantella, *CEO*
Chris Stafford, *Vice Pres*
Roche Sanchez, *Purch Mgr*
Silvana Burd, *QC Mgr*
Emily Mraule, *Manager*
EMP: 60
SQ FT: 13,000
SALES (est): 15.4MM **Privately Held**
WEB: www.papacantella.com
SIC: 2013 Sausages from purchased meat

(P-488)
PEOPLES SAUSAGE COMPANY
1132 E Pico Blvd, Los Angeles (90021-2224)
PHONE....................213 627-8633
Mark Bianchetti, *President*
EMP: 16
SQ FT: 5,500
SALES (est): 2.4MM **Privately Held**
WEB: www.peopleschoicebeefjerky.com
SIC: 2013 5147 Beef, dried: from purchased meat; meats, fresh

(P-489)
POCINO FOODS COMPANY
14250 Lomitas Ave, City of Industry
(91746-3014)
P.O. Box 2219, La Puente (91746-0219)
PHONE.............................626 968-8000
Frank J Pocino, *President*
Ravi Sheshadri, *CFO*
Frank G Pocino, *Vice Pres*
David Sanchez, *Purch Agent*
Cruz Casas, *Plant Mgr*
▲ EMP: 100
SQ FT: 70,000
SALES (est): 28.7MM **Privately Held**
WEB: www.pocinofoods.com
SIC: 2013 Sausages from purchased
meat; roast beef from purchased meat

(P-490)
PROVENA FOODS INC
Swiss-American Sausage
251 Darcy Pkwy, Lathrop (95330-8756)
PHONE.............................209 858-5555
Theodore Arena, *Branch Mgr*
EMP: 45
SQ FT: 49,000
SALES (corp-wide): 9.5B **Publicly Held**
SIC: 2013 Sausages & other prepared
meats
HQ: Provena Foods Inc.
5010 Eucalyptus Ave
Chino CA 91710
909 627-1082

(P-491)
RAEMICA INC
Also Called: Far West Meats
7759 Victoria Ave, Highland (92346-5637)
P.O. Box 248 (92346-0248)
PHONE.............................909 864-1990
Thomas R Serrato, *CEO*
Michael Serrato, *Corp Secy*
Wade Snyder, *Vice Pres*
EMP: 41
SQ FT: 35,000
SALES (est): 7.6MM **Privately Held**
SIC: 2013 5421 Cured meats from pur-
chased meat; meat markets, including
freezer provisioners

(P-492)
RICE FIELD CORPORATION
14500 Valley Blvd, City of Industry
(91746-2918)
PHONE.............................626 968-6917
Derek Lee, *Principal*
▲ EMP: 120
SQ FT: 100,000
SALES (est): 18.8MM **Privately Held**
SIC: 2013 Sausages & other prepared
meats

(P-493)
S & S FOODS LLC
1120 W Foothill Blvd, Azusa (91702-2818)
PHONE.............................626 633-1609
Kirk Smith,
Randy Shuman, *President*
Robert Horowitz, *CEO*
Horst Sieben, *CFO*
Pam Cardinale, *Finance Dir*
▲ EMP: 220
SQ FT: 115,000
SALES (est): 46.4MM
SALES (corp-wide): 67.9MM **Privately
Held**
SIC: 2013 Cooked meats from purchased
meat; frozen meats from purchased meat;
sausages & related products, from pur-
chased meat
HQ: Cti Foods Holding Co., Llc
3405 E Overland Rd # 360
Meridian ID 83642

(P-494)
SAAB ENTERPRISES INC
Also Called: Enjoy Food
1433 Miller Dr, Colton (92324-2456)
PHONE.............................909 823-2228
Waleed Saab, *President*
Walleb Saab, *President*
Saadi Kabab, *Vice Pres*
EMP: 70
SQ FT: 38,000

SALES (est): 10.4MM **Privately Held**
WEB: www.enjoybeefjerky.com
SIC: 2013 Beef, dried: from purchased
meat

(P-495)
SAAGS PRODUCTS LLC
1799 Factor Ave, San Leandro
(94577-5617)
P.O. Box 2078 (94577-0207)
PHONE.............................510 678-3412
Jim Mosle, *CEO*
Timothy Dam, *President*
Peter Turcotte, *Technology*
▲ EMP: 85
SQ FT: 40,000
SALES (est): 19.6MM
SALES (corp-wide): 9.5B **Publicly Held**
WEB: www.saags.com
SIC: 2013 Sausages from purchased
meat; spiced meats from purchased meat
PA: Hormel Foods Corporation
1 Hormel Pl
Austin MN 55912
507 437-5611

(P-496)
SAPAR USA INC (PA)
Also Called: Fabrique Delices
1610 Delta Ct Ste 1, Hayward
(94544-7043)
PHONE.............................510 441-9500
Marc Poinsignon, *President*
Antonio Pinheiro, *Vice Pres*
Vanessa Sanchez, *Office Mgr*
EMP: 27
SQ FT: 20,000
SALES (est): 4.6MM **Privately Held**
WEB: www.fabriquedelices.com
SIC: 2013 Spreads, sandwich: meat from
purchased meat

(P-497)
**SAVORY CREATIONS
INTERNATIONAL**
32611 Central Ave, Union City
(94587-2008)
PHONE.............................510 477-0395
Douglas Eakiewa, *Owner*
EMP: 20 EST: 2011
SALES (est): 2.8MM **Privately Held**
SIC: 2013 Sausages & other prepared
meats

(P-498)
SETTLERS JERKY INC
307 Paseo Sonrisa, Walnut (91789-2721)
PHONE.............................909 444-3999
Cherron L Hart, *CEO*
Aaron J Anderson, *CEO*
Carrie M Anderson, *Principal*
EMP: 27
SQ FT: 20,000
SALES: 5MM **Privately Held**
SIC: 2013 Snack sticks, including jerky:
from purchased meat

(P-499)
SPAR SAUSAGE CO
Also Called: Caspers
688 Williams St, San Leandro
(94577-2624)
PHONE.............................510 614-8100
Jack Dorian, *Manager*
EMP: 13
SQ FT: 9,750
SALES (est): 2MM
SALES (corp-wide): 1.9MM **Privately
Held**
SIC: 2013 Sausages from purchased meat
PA: Spar Sausage Co
3508 Mt Diablo Blvd Ste J
Lafayette CA 94549
925 283-6877

(P-500)
SQUARE H BRANDS INC
Also Called: Hoffy
2731 S Soto St, Vernon (90058-8026)
PHONE.............................323 267-4600
Henry Haskell, *CEO*
William Hannigan, *CFO*
◆ EMP: 150
SQ FT: 100,000

SALES (est): 41.9MM **Privately Held**
WEB: www.squarehbrands.com
SIC: 2013 Sausages from purchased meat

(P-501)
**SUNNYVALLEY SMOKED MEATS
INC**
2475 W Yosemite Ave, Manteca
(95337-9641)
P.O. Box 2158 (95336-1159)
PHONE.............................209 825-0288
William Andreetta, *President*
Stacey Wellwood, *CFO*
Treva Andreetta, *Vice Pres*
Heather Grandstaff, *Human Res Dir*
Debi Hawkes, *QC Mgr*
▲ EMP: 110
SQ FT: 41,000
SALES (est): 39.8MM **Privately Held**
WEB: www.sunnyvalleysmokedmeats.com
SIC: 2013 Ham, smoked: from purchased
meat

(P-502)
SWIFT BEEF COMPANY
Also Called: Jbs Case Ready
15555 Meridian Pkwy, Riverside
(92518-3046)
PHONE.............................951 571-2237
Andre Nogueira, *CEO*
EMP: 200
SALES (est): 306.8K **Publicly Held**
SIC: 2013 Beef, dried: from purchased
meat
HQ: Jbs Usa Food Company
1770 Promontory Cir
Greeley CO 80634
970 506-8000

(P-503)
T&J SAUSAGE KITCHEN INC
Also Called: T & J Sausage Kitchen
2831 E Miraloma Ave, Anaheim
(92806-1804)
PHONE.............................714 632-8350
Tom Drozdowski, *CEO*
David Armendariz, *Vice Pres*
Walter Wolpert, *General Mgr*
Julie Granger, *Sales Staff*
Mike Aranda, *Manager*
EMP: 45
SQ FT: 20,000
SALES (est): 7.7MM **Privately Held**
WEB: www.tandjsausage.com
SIC: 2013 Sausages & other prepared
meats

(P-504)
**TRANSHUMANCE HOLDING CO
INC**
Also Called: Superior Farms
2851 E 44th St, Vernon (90058-2401)
P.O. Box 58106, Los Angeles (90058-0106)
PHONE.............................323 583-5503
Joey Garraird, *Manager*
EMP: 10 **Privately Held**
WEB: www.superiorfarms.com
SIC: 2013 5147 2011 Sausages & other
prepared meats; meats & meat products;
lamb products from lamb slaughtered on
site
PA: Transhumance Holding Company, Inc.
2530 River Plaza Dr # 200
Sacramento CA 95833

(P-505)
VALLEY PROTEIN LLC
1828 E Hedges Ave, Fresno (93703-3633)
PHONE.............................559 498-7115
Robert Coyle, *Mng Member*
Angela Sanchez, *Controller*
EMP: 95 EST: 2010
SALES (est): 22.4MM **Privately Held**
SIC: 2013 Prepared beef products from
purchased beef

(P-506)
VIET HUNG PARIS INC
Also Called: V H Paris Co
1975 Chota Rd, La Habra Heights
(90631-8403)
PHONE.............................562 944-4919
Vinh P Pham, *President*
EMP: 15
SQ FT: 6,000

SALES (est): 1.8MM **Privately Held**
SIC: 2013 Sausages from purchased meat

(P-507)
WYCEN FOODS INC (PA)
560 Estabrook St, San Leandro
(94577-3512)
PHONE.............................510 351-1987
Arthur Leong, *President*
Nancy Leong, *Treasurer*
▲ EMP: 17
SQ FT: 25,000
SALES (est): 2.1MM **Privately Held**
SIC: 2013 2038 Sausages from pur-
chased meat; ethnic foods, frozen

(P-508)
YONEKYU USA INC
3615 E Vernon Ave, Vernon (90058-1815)
PHONE.............................323 581-4194
Osamu Saito, *President*
Kenji Ikeda, *CEO*
Arihito Tanaka, *CFO*
Don Ferris, *Exec VP*
Hiroyuki Tashiro, *Prdtn Mgr*
▼ EMP: 52
SQ FT: 31,000
SALES (est): 18.5MM **Privately Held**
SIC: 2013 Sausages from purchased meat
HQ: Yonekyu Corporation
1259, Terabayashi, Okanomiya
Numazu SZO 410-0

**2015 Poultry Slaughtering,
Dressing & Processing**

(P-509)
EGGS WEST LLC
14460 Palm Ave, Wasco (93280-9551)
PHONE.............................661 758-9700
Scott Simpkins, *Mng Member*
David Demler, *Mng Member*
▲ EMP: 26
SALES (est): 2.1MM **Privately Held**
SIC: 2015 Egg processing

(P-510)
**FIELD TO FAMILY NATURAL
FOODS**
224 Weller St Ste C, Petaluma
(94952-3136)
P.O. Box 2917 (94953-2917)
PHONE.............................707 765-6756
Wayne Dufond, *President*
Amy Dufond, *Vice Pres*
EMP: 10
SALES (est): 843.7K **Privately Held**
SIC: 2015 Chicken, processed: fresh

(P-511)
FOSTER POULTRY FARMS (PA)
Also Called: Foster Farms
1000 Davis St, Livingston (95334-1526)
P.O. Box 457 (95334-0457)
PHONE.............................209 394-6914
Dan Huber, *CEO*
Ron M Foster, *President*
Donald Jackson, *President*
Leslie Cardoso, *COO*
Caryn Doyle, *CFO*
◆ EMP: 250
SQ FT: 40,000
SALES (est): 3B **Privately Held**
WEB: www.fosterfarms.com
SIC: 2015 Poultry slaughtering & process-
ing

(P-512)
FOSTER POULTRY FARMS
Also Called: Foster Farms
1307 Ellenwood Rd, Waterford
(95386-8702)
PHONE.............................209 394-7901
Jay Husman, *Manager*
Janice Cardoza, *Supervisor*
EMP: 50
SQ FT: 68,316
SALES (corp-wide): 3B **Privately Held**
WEB: www.fosterfarms.com
SIC: 2015 Poultry slaughtering & process-
ing

PA: Foster Poultry Farms
1000 Davis St
Livingston CA 95334
209 394-6914

(P-513)
FOSTER POULTRY FARMS
Also Called: Foster Farms
1333 Swan St, Livingston (95334-1559)
P.O. Box 457 (95334-0457)
PHONE..........................209 394-7901
Brent Allen, *Branch Mgr*
Jonathan Foster, *Vice Pres*
Brian Kellert, *Vice Pres*
Donna Machado, *Creative Dir*
Jeremy Handy, *Programmer Anys*
EMP: 125
SALES (corp-wide): 3B Privately Held
WEB: www.fosterfarms.com
SIC: 2015 Poultry slaughtering & process-ing
PA: Foster Poultry Farms
1000 Davis St
Livingston CA 95334
209 394-6914

(P-514)
FOSTER POULTRY FARMS
Also Called: Foster Turkey Live Haul
1033 S Center St, Turlock (95380-5568)
PHONE..........................209 668-5922
Steve Page, *Manager*
EMP: 100
SALES (corp-wide): 3B Privately Held
WEB: www.fosterfarms.com
SIC: 2015 Poultry slaughtering & process-ing
PA: Foster Poultry Farms
1000 Davis St
Livingston CA 95334
209 394-6914

(P-515)
FOSTER POULTRY FARMS
900 W Belgravia Ave, Fresno (93706-3909)
PHONE..........................559 265-2000
Jessi Amezcua, *Branch Mgr*
Andy Rutherford, *Foreman/Supr*
Eric Baker, *Marketing Staff*
EMP: 567
SALES (corp-wide): 3B Privately Held
WEB: www.fosterfarms.com
SIC: 2015 5812 0173 5191 Chicken slaughtering & processing; turkey pro-cessing & slaughtering; chicken restau-rant; almond grove; animal feeds; local trucking, without storage; chicken hatch-ery
PA: Foster Poultry Farms
1000 Davis St
Livingston CA 95334
209 394-6914

(P-516)
FOSTER POULTRY FARMS
770 N Plano St, Porterville (93257-6329)
PHONE..........................559 793-5501
Paul Bravinder, *Manager*
EMP: 400
SALES (corp-wide): 3B Privately Held
WEB: www.fosterfarms.com
SIC: 2015 5421 Chicken, processed: fresh; meat & fish markets
PA: Foster Poultry Farms
1000 Davis St
Livingston CA 95334
209 394-6914

(P-517)
FOSTER POULTRY FARMS
1805 N Santa Fe Ave, Compton (90221-1009)
PHONE..........................310 223-1499
Ronald Altman, *Branch Mgr*
Arselia Guerrero, *Human Res Mgr*
Norma Bustamante, *Director*
EMP: 257
SALES (corp-wide): 3B Privately Held
WEB: www.conagra.com
SIC: 2015 Poultry slaughtering & process-ing
PA: Foster Poultry Farms
1000 Davis St
Livingston CA 95334
209 394-6914

(P-518)
GRIMAUD FARMS CALIFORNIA INC (DH)
1320 S Aurora St Ste A, Stockton (95206-1616)
PHONE..........................209 466-3200
Rheal Cayer, *President*
Fricrick Grimaud, *Ch of Bd*
▲ EMP: 20
SQ FT: 42,000
SALES (est): 14MM
SALES (corp-wide): 355.8K Privately Held
WEB: www.grimaud.com
SIC: 2015 Poultry slaughtering & process-ing
HQ: Groupe Grimaud La Corbiere Grimaud
Saint-Macaire-En-Mauges 49450
964 435-509

(P-519)
INGENUE INC
Also Called: Q C Poultry
6114 Scott Way, Commerce (90040-3518)
P.O. Box 17238, Anaheim (92817-7238)
PHONE..........................323 726-8084
Nick Macis, *President*
Michelle Macis, *Admin Sec*
Angelique Macis, *Assistant*
EMP: 100
SQ FT: 10,000
SALES (est): 26.6MM Privately Held
SIC: 2015 Poultry slaughtering & process-ing

(P-520)
KIFUKI USA CO INC (HQ)
15547 1st St, Irwindale (91706-6201)
PHONE..........................626 334-8090
Kuniaki Ishikaiwa, *President*
▲ EMP: 90
SQ FT: 52,000
SALES (est): 77.6MM Privately Held
SIC: 2015 2013 2035 Eggs, processed: dehydrated; poultry, processed; beef, dried: from purchased meat; seasonings & sauces, except tomato & dry; dress-ings, salad: raw & cooked (except dry mixes); mayonnaise

(P-521)
LOS ANGELES POULTRY CO INC
4816 Long Beach Ave, Los Angeles (90058-1915)
P.O. Box 58328 (90058-0328)
PHONE..........................323 232-1619
David Dahan, *President*
Dror Dahan, *Vice Pres*
Jamie Kidder, *Info Tech Mgr*
Manuel Ramos, *Manager*
EMP: 88
SQ FT: 32,000
SALES (est): 14.4MM Privately Held
WEB: www.lapoultry.com
SIC: 2015 Poultry slaughtering & process-ing

(P-522)
LUUS FAMILY CORP
302 S San Joaquin St, Stockton (95203-3536)
PHONE..........................209 466-1952
Doc Luu, *President*
Ming Lou, *Manager*
EMP: 40
SALES (est): 6MM Privately Held
WEB: www.luufamily.net
SIC: 2015 Chicken slaughtering & process-ing

(P-523)
OLIVERA EGG RANCH LLC
Also Called: Olivera Foods
3315 Sierra Rd, San Jose (95132-3099)
P.O. Box 32126 (95152-2126)
PHONE..........................408 258-8074
Edward F Olivera,
▲ EMP: 60
SQ FT: 35,000
SALES (est): 17.6MM Privately Held
SIC: 2015 5143 5142 5144 Egg process-ing; cheese; butter; packaged frozen goods; eggs

(P-524)
PHU HUONG FOODS CO INC
9008 Garvey Ave Ste I, Rosemead (91770-3361)
PHONE..........................626 280-8607
Long Nguyen, *President*
EMP: 14
SQ FT: 4,000
SALES (est): 1.3MM Privately Held
SIC: 2015 Poultry slaughtering & process-ing

(P-525)
PLEASANT VALLEY FARMS (PA)
Also Called: Jenkins Poultry Farms
30636 E Carter Rd, Farmington (95230-9633)
P.O. Box 752, Ripon (95366-0752)
PHONE..........................209 886-1000
Richard Jenkins, *Mng Member*
John Dendulk,
Jerry Jenkins,
EMP: 70
SALES (est): 32MM Privately Held
SIC: 2015 Poultry slaughtering & process-ing

(P-526)
RICH CHICKS LLC
13771 Gramercy Pl, Gardena (90249-2470)
PHONE..........................209 879-4104
Charlie Brust, *Vice Pres*
EMP: 20 Privately Held
SIC: 2015 Chicken, processed: frozen
PA: Rich Chicks, Llc
4276 N Tracy Blvd
Tracy CA 95304

(P-527)
RICH CHICKS LLC (PA)
Also Called: Rich Chicks, Rich In Nutrition
4276 N Tracy Blvd, Tracy (95304-1501)
PHONE..........................209 879-4104
Neil Kinney, *Managing Prtnr*
Paul Byrd, *General Mgr*
EMP: 34
SALES: 5MM Privately Held
SIC: 2015 Chicken, processed: frozen

(P-528)
TWENTY-NINERS PROVISIONS INC
Also Called: Twenty Niners Club
1784 E Vernon Ave, Vernon (90058-1526)
PHONE..........................323 233-7864
Seiichi Shibata, *President*
EMP: 35
SALES (est): 2.8MM Privately Held
WEB: www.macsei.com
SIC: 2015 2013 Poultry slaughtering & processing; sausages & other prepared meats

(P-529)
VALLEY FRESH INC (HQ)
1404 S Fresno Ave, Stockton (95206-1174)
PHONE..........................209 943-5411
Ronald W Fielding, *CEO*
Eugene Carney, *Vice Pres*
EMP: 50
SQ FT: 120,000
SALES (est): 47.2MM
SALES (corp-wide): 9.5B Publicly Held
WEB: www.valleyfresh.com
SIC: 2015 Poultry, processed: canned; poultry, processed: frozen
PA: Hormel Foods Corporation
1 Hormel Pl
Austin MN 55912
507 437-5611

(P-530)
VUE-TEMP INC (PA)
618 S Kilroy Rd, Turlock (95380-9531)
PHONE..........................209 634-2914
Anthony Volks, *President*
▲ EMP: 60
SQ FT: 66,981
SALES (est): 7.6MM Privately Held
WEB: www.volkenterprises.com
SIC: 2015 5084 3089 Chicken slaughter-ing & processing; machine tools & metal-working machinery; plastic processing

(P-531)
WESTERN SUPREME INC
Also Called: California Poultry
865 Produce Ct, Los Angeles (90021-1831)
PHONE..........................213 627-3861
Frank Fogarty, *President*
Marlene Fogarty, *Corp Secy*
EMP: 125
SQ FT: 10,000
SALES (est): 12.7MM Privately Held
SIC: 2015 Chicken slaughtering & process-ing

(P-532)
WIN FAT FOOD LLC
700 Monterey Pass Rd A, Monterey Park (91754-3618)
PHONE..........................323 261-1869
MEI Lan Liang,
Jun Yuan Liang,
EMP: 50
SALES (est): 3.2MM Privately Held
SIC: 2015 Poultry slaughtering & process-ing

(P-533)
ZACKY & SONS POULTRY LLC
Also Called: Turkey Processing Plant
2222 S East Ave, Fresno (93721-3405)
P.O. Box 12556 (93778-2556)
PHONE..........................559 443-2750
EMP: 400
SALES (corp-wide): 213.6MM Privately Held
SIC: 2015 Poultry, processed
PA: Zacky & Sons Poultry Llc
2020 S East Ave
Fresno CA 93721
559 443-2700

(P-534)
ZACKY & SONS POULTRY LLC (PA)
Also Called: Zacky Farms
2020 S East Ave, Fresno (93721-3328)
P.O. Box 12556 (93778-2556)
PHONE..........................559 443-2700
Lillian Zacky,
Kirk Vandergeest, *CFO*
EMP: 207 EST: 2013
SALES (est): 213.6MM Privately Held
SIC: 2015 Poultry slaughtering & process-ing

(P-535)
ZACKY & SONS POULTRY LLC
1111 Navy Dr, Stockton (95206-1125)
PHONE..........................209 948-0129
John Ross, *Manager*
EMP: 400
SALES (corp-wide): 213.6MM Privately Held
SIC: 2015 Chicken slaughtering & process-ing
PA: Zacky & Sons Poultry Llc
2020 S East Ave
Fresno CA 93721
559 443-2700

2021 Butter

(P-536)
BONELLI FINE FOOD INC
3525 Del Mar Heights Rd, San Diego (92130-2199)
PHONE..........................650 906-9896
Ali Tabatabaei, *President*
▼ EMP: 10
SALES (est): 837.3K Privately Held
SIC: 2021 2035 Creamery butter; spreads, garlic

(P-537)
CALIFORNIA DAIRIES INC
Also Called: San Joaquin Valley Dairymen
475 S Tegner Rd, Turlock (95380-9406)
PHONE..........................209 656-1942
Tamara Staggs, *Branch Mgr*
EMP: 80

SALES (corp-wide): 253.1MM **Privately Held**
WEB: www.californiadairies.com
SIC: 2023 2026 Creamery butter; dry, condensed, evaporated dairy products; fluid milk
PA: California Dairies, Inc.
2000 N Plaza Dr
Visalia CA 93291
559 625-2200

(P-538)
MIYOKOS KITCHEN
2086 Marina Ave, Petaluma (94954-6714)
PHONE..................................415 521-5313
Miyoko Schinner, *CEO*
Shonn Tom, *CFO*
Dan Rauch, *Research*
Conny Soares, *Purchasing*
Julie Brewer, *Marketing Staff*
◆ EMP: 100
SQ FT: 30,000
SALES (est): 10.5MM **Privately Held**
SIC: 2021 2022 Creamery butter; cheese, natural & processed; cheese spreads, dips, pastes & other cheese products

(P-539)
STRAUS FAMILY CREAMERY INC
1105 Industrial Ave # 200, Petaluma (94952-1141)
PHONE..................................707 776-2887
Albert Straus, *CEO*
Deborah Parrish, *CFO*
EMP: 64
SQ FT: 40,000
SALES (est): 14.9MM **Privately Held**
SIC: 2021 2023 2026 Creamery butter; ice cream mix, unfrozen: liquid or dry; yogurt

(P-540)
VENTURA FOODS LLC
Also Called: Saffola Quality Foods
2900 Jurupa St, Ontario (91761-2915)
PHONE..................................323 262-9157
Tom Bospic, *Manager*
EMP: 148 **Privately Held**
WEB: www.venturafoods.com
SIC: 2021 2035 5199 2079 Creamery butter; dressings, salad: raw & cooked (except dry mixes); oils, animal or vegetable; edible fats & oils
PA: Ventura Foods, Llc
40 Pointe Dr
Brea CA 92821

2022 Cheese

(P-541)
ARIZA CHEESE CO INC
7602 Jackson St, Paramount (90723-4912)
PHONE..................................562 630-4144
Fatima Cristina Ariza, *CEO*
Ausencio Ariza, *President*
EMP: 40
SQ FT: 8,000
SALES (est): 6.8MM **Privately Held**
SIC: 2022 Cheese, natural & processed

(P-542)
CACIQUE INC (PA)
Also Called: Cacique Cheese
800 Royal Oaks Dr Ste 200, Monrovia (91016-6364)
P.O. Box 1047 (91017-1047)
PHONE..................................626 961-3399
Ana De Cardenas-Raptis, *CEO*
Francoise Mattice, *CFO*
Jennie De Cardenas, *Exec VP*
Bob Cashen, *Vice Pres*
Gilbert B De Cardenas, *Vice Pres*
EMP: 230 EST: 1976
SQ FT: 82,000
SALES (est): 100.8MM **Privately Held**
WEB: www.caciqueusa.com
SIC: 2022 Natural cheese

(P-543)
CASTLE IMPORTING INC
14550 Miller Ave, Fontana (92336-1696)
PHONE..................................909 428-9200

Vito Borruso, *President*
Giancomo Borruso, *CFO*
Josephine Borruso, *Admin Sec*
▲ EMP: 17
SQ FT: 68,000
SALES (est): 4.1MM **Privately Held**
WEB: www.castleimporting.com
SIC: 2022 5812 Processed cheese; eating places

(P-544)
CHEESE ADMINISTRATIVE CORP INC
429 H St, Los Banos (93635-4113)
PHONE..................................209 826-3744
Frank Peluso, *CEO*
EMP: 35
SQ FT: 3,000
SALES (est): 5.7MM **Privately Held**
SIC: 2022 Natural cheese

(P-545)
CYPRESS GROVE CHEVRE INC
1330 Q St, Arcata (95521-5740)
PHONE..................................707 825-1100
Pamela Dressler, *President*
▲ EMP: 52
SQ FT: 12,500
SALES (est): 9.2MM
SALES (corp-wide): 251.6MM **Privately Held**
WEB: www.cypressgrovechevre.com
SIC: 2022 Natural cheese
HQ: Emmi Ag
Landenbergstrasse 1
Luzern LU 6005
582 272-727

(P-546)
DAIRY FARMERS AMERICA INC
600 Trade Way, Turlock (95380-9433)
PHONE..................................209 667-9627
Thomas Baker, *Manager*
Tom Baker, *Plant Mgr*
Sara Santos, *Marketing Staff*
EMP: 93
SQ FT: 63,976
SALES (corp-wide): 13.6B **Privately Held**
WEB: www.dfamilk.com
SIC: 2022 2026 Cheese, natural & processed; fluid milk
PA: Dairy Farmers Of America, Inc.
1405 N 98th St
Kansas City KS 66111
816 801-6455

(P-547)
EINSTEIN NOAH REST GROUP INC
Also Called: Noah's New York Bagels
16304 Beach Blvd, Westminster (92683-7857)
PHONE..................................714 847-4609
Fransico Valdez, *Manager*
EMP: 15
SALES (corp-wide): 2.4B **Privately Held**
WEB: www.noahs.com
SIC: 2022 5812 Spreads, cheese; cafe
HQ: Einstein Noah Restaurant Group, Inc.
555 Zang St Ste 300
Lakewood CO 80228

(P-548)
EINSTEIN NOAH REST GROUP INC
Also Called: Noah's
15996 Los Gatos Blvd, Los Gatos (95032-3424)
PHONE..................................408 358-5895
Susan Asef, *Manager*
EMP: 13
SALES (corp-wide): 2.4B **Privately Held**
WEB: www.noahs.com
SIC: 2022 5812 Spreads, cheese; cafe
HQ: Einstein Noah Restaurant Group, Inc.
555 Zang St Ste 300
Lakewood CO 80228

(P-549)
ESTATE CHEESE GROUP LLC (PA)
670 W Napa St Ste G, Sonoma (95476-6437)
PHONE..................................707 996-1000
John Crean,
Lou Biaggi,
David Viviani,
▼ EMP: 10
SALES (est): 16.5MM **Privately Held**
SIC: 2022 Natural cheese

(P-550)
EXCELPRO INC (PA)
1630 Amapola Ave, Torrance (90501-3101)
PHONE..................................323 415-8544
Peter Ernster, *President*
Gregg Rowland, *CFO*
John H Ernster Jr, *Admin Sec*
EMP: 16 EST: 1973
SQ FT: 36,000
SALES (est): 1.7MM **Privately Held**
SIC: 2022 2023 Processed cheese; dietary supplements, dairy & non-dairy based

(P-551)
GALLO GLOBAL NUTRITION LLC
Also Called: Joseph Farms
10561 Highway 140, Atwater (95301-9309)
P.O. Box 775 (95301-0775)
PHONE..................................209 394-7984
Michael Gallo, *CEO*
Musa Mustafa, *Vice Pres*
Tod Gerhardt, *Info Tech Mgr*
Jenny Cargill, *Human Res Dir*
Kenneth Jelacich, *Manager*
EMP: 105 EST: 2003
SQ FT: 5,000
SALES (est): 15.7MM **Privately Held**
SIC: 2022 8099 0241 Cheese spreads, dips, pastes & other cheese products; nutrition services; dairy farms

(P-552)
GOLDEN VALLEY DAIRY PRODUCTS
1025 E Bardsley Ave, Tulare (93274-5752)
PHONE..................................559 687-1188
John Prince, *CEO*
EMP: 125
SALES (est): 11.5MM
SALES (corp-wide): 6.8B **Privately Held**
WEB: www.realcheese.com
SIC: 2022 Cheese, natural & processed
PA: Land O'lakes, Inc.
4001 Lexington Ave N
Arden Hills MN 55126
651 375-2222

(P-553)
GREEN VALLEY FOODS PRODUCT
25684 Community Blvd, Barstow (92311-9671)
PHONE..................................760 964-1105
Hector Huerta, *President*
EMP: 15
SQ FT: 10,000
SALES (est): 2.5MM **Privately Held**
SIC: 2022 Cheese, natural & processed

(P-554)
HILMAR CHEESE COMPANY INC
3600 W Canal Dr, Turlock (95380-8507)
P.O. Box 910, Hilmar (95324-0910)
PHONE..................................209 667-6076
David Ahlem, *CEO*
EMP: 54
SALES (corp-wide): 328.9MM **Privately Held**
SIC: 2022 Natural cheese
PA: Hilmar Cheese Company, Inc.
8901 Lander Ave
Hilmar CA 95324
209 667-6076

(P-555)
HILMAR CHEESE COMPANY INC (PA)
Also Called: Hilmar Ingredients
8901 Lander Ave, Hilmar (95324-9327)
P.O. Box 910 (95324-0910)
PHONE..................................209 667-6076
John J Jeter, *President*
Donald Jay Hicks, *CFO*
James Shriver, *Sales Mgr*
Jeanne Amongol, *Sales Staff*
Josh Foster, *Manager*
◆ EMP: 277
SALES (est): 328.9MM **Privately Held**
WEB: www.hilmarcheese.com
SIC: 2022 Natural cheese

(P-556)
IDB HOLDINGS INC (DH)
601 S Rockefeller Ave, Ontario (91761-7871)
PHONE..................................909 390-5624
Jim Dekeyser, *CEO*
Peter Dolan, *Corp Secy*
Daniel O'Connell, *Asst Sec*
◆ EMP: 15
SQ FT: 4,000
SALES (est): 116MM
SALES (corp-wide): 1.8B **Privately Held**
SIC: 2022 5143 Processed cheese; cheese
HQ: Ornua Foods Uk Limited
Sunnyhills Road Barnfields Industrial Estate
Leek STAFFS ST13
153 839-9111

(P-557)
KAROUN DAIRIES INC
5117 Santa Monica Blvd, Los Angeles (90029-2413)
PHONE..................................323 666-6222
EMP: 10
SALES (corp-wide): 13.2MM **Privately Held**
SIC: 2022 5143
PA: Karoun Dairies, Inc.
13023 Arroyo St
San Fernando CA 91340
818 365-3333

(P-558)
KAROUN DAIRIES INC (PA)
Also Called: Karoun Cheese
13023 Arroyo St, San Fernando (91340-1540)
PHONE..................................818 767-7000
Anto Baghdassarian, *President*
Rostom Baghdassarian, *COO*
Tsolak Khatcherian, *CFO*
Ohan Baghdassarian, *Vice Pres*
Seta Baghdassarian, *Admin Sec*
▲ EMP: 70
SQ FT: 70,000
SALES (est): 14.2MM **Privately Held**
WEB: www.karoundairies.com
SIC: 2022 5143 Natural cheese; cheese

(P-559)
KRAFT HEINZ FOODS COMPANY
3735 Imperial Way, Stockton (95215-9691)
PHONE..................................209 942-0102
EMP: 213
SALES (corp-wide): 26.2B **Publicly Held**
SIC: 2022 Processed cheese
HQ: Kraft Heinz Foods Company
1 Ppg Pl Fl 34
Pittsburgh PA 15222
412 456-5700

(P-560)
LAND OLAKES INC
400 S M St, Tulare (93274-5431)
PHONE..................................559 687-8287
Jack Gherty, *CEO*
EMP: 96
SALES (corp-wide): 6.8B **Privately Held**
WEB: www.landolakes.com
SIC: 2022 Cheese, natural & processed
PA: Land O'lakes, Inc.
4001 Lexington Ave N
Arden Hills MN 55126
651 375-2222

P R O D U C T S & S V C S

(P-561)
LAND OLAKES INC
3601 County Road C, Orland (95963-9117)
PHONE..................................530 865-7626
Carolyn Macon, *CEO*
EMP: 29
SALES (corp-wide): 6.8B **Privately Held**
WEB: www.landolakes.com
SIC: 2022 Cheese, natural & processed
PA: Land O'lakes, Inc.
　　4001 Lexington Ave N
　　Arden Hills MN 55126
　　651 375-2222

(P-562)
LAURA CHENELS CHEVRE INC
Also Called: Parent Is Sas Ltries H Trbllat
22085 Carneros Vinyrd Way, Sonoma
(95476-2826)
PHONE..................................707 996-4477
Hugues Triballat, *CEO*
Pierre Girier, *COO*
Sylvie Forero, *CFO*
▲EMP: 68
SALES (est): 15.6MM
SALES (corp-wide): 4.4MM **Privately Held**
WEB: www.laurachenel.com
SIC: 2022 Cheese spreads, dips, pastes &
　other cheese products
HQ: Laiteries H. Triballat

　　Rians 18220
　　248 662-200

(P-563)
LEPRINO FOODS COMPANY
2401 N Macarthur Dr, Tracy (95376-2095)
PHONE..................................209 835-8340
Joel Crane, *General Mgr*
Andy Gault, *Technical Staff*
Lisa Miller, *Controller*
Ed Ellingen, *Mfg Spvr*
Lisa Melo, *Plant Engr*
EMP: 300
SALES (corp-wide): 1.7B **Privately Held**
WEB: www.leprinofoods.com
SIC: 2022 Processed cheese
PA: Leprino Foods Company
　　1830 W 38th Ave
　　Denver CO 80211
　　303 480-2600

(P-564)
LEPRINO FOODS COMPANY
490 F St, Lemoore (93245-2661)
PHONE..................................559 924-7722
Dave Direking, *Branch Mgr*
Brad Bernhardt, *Manager*
Pat Gomez, *Supervisor*
EMP: 275
SALES (corp-wide): 1.7B **Privately Held**
WEB: www.leprinofoods.com
SIC: 2022 Natural cheese; whey, raw or
　liquid
PA: Leprino Foods Company
　　1830 W 38th Ave
　　Denver CO 80211
　　303 480-2600

(P-565)
LEPRINO FOODS COMPANY
351 Belle Haven Dr, Lemoore
(93245-9247)
PHONE..................................559 924-7939
James Leprino, *President*
Thomas Robinson, *Technician*
Ben Schlegelmilch, *Maintence Staff*
EMP: 200
SALES (corp-wide): 1.7B **Privately Held**
WEB: www.leprinofoods.com
SIC: 2022 Natural cheese
PA: Leprino Foods Company
　　1830 W 38th Ave
　　Denver CO 80211
　　303 480-2600

(P-566)
LIFELINE FOOD CO INC
118 Cypress Lakes Ct, Marina
(93933-2521)
PHONE..................................831 899-5040
Jone Chappell, *President*
EMP: 10
SQ FT: 2,750

SALES (est): 1MM **Privately Held**
WEB: www.lifetimefatfree.com
SIC: 2022 5143 Natural cheese; cheese

(P-567)
LOLETA CHEESE COMPANY INC
252 Loleta Dr, Loleta (95551)
PHONE..................................707 733-5470
Robert E Laffranchi, *President*
Robert Laffranchi, *Executive*
EMP: 11
SALES (est): 1.1MM **Privately Held**
SIC: 2022 Cheese, natural & processed

(P-568)
MARIN FRENCH CHEESE COMPANY
Also Called: Rouge & Noir
7500 Red Hill Rd, Petaluma (94952-9438)
PHONE..................................707 762-6001
Hugues Triballat, *CEO*
Luis Romo, *Manager*
EMP: 12 EST: 1865
SQ FT: 10,000
SALES (est): 1.9MM
SALES (corp-wide): 4.4MM **Privately Held**
WEB: www.marinfrenchcheese.com
SIC: 2022 Natural cheese
HQ: Laiteries H. Triballat

　　Rians 18220
　　248 662-200

(P-569)
OAKDALE CHEESE & SPECIALTIES
10040 State Highway 120, Oakdale
(95361-8718)
PHONE..................................209 848-3139
Walter Bulk, *Owner*
John Bulk, *Co-Owner*
Leneka Bulk, *Co-Owner*
EMP: 10
SALES (est): 946.1K **Privately Held**
WEB: www.oakdalecheese.com
SIC: 2022 5143 Natural cheese; cheese

(P-570)
RIZO-LOPEZ FOODS INC
Also Called: Don Francisco Cheese
201 S Mcclure Rd, Modesto (95357-0519)
P.O. Box 1689, Empire (95319-1689)
PHONE..................................800 626-5587
Edwin Rizo, *President*
Ivan Rizo, *CEO*
Sergio Vaca, *Controller*
Juan Luis De La Torre, *Plant Mgr*
▲EMP: 178
SQ FT: 3,800
SALES (est): 40.1MM **Privately Held**
SIC: 2022 5143 2023 5141 Natural
　cheese; whey, raw or liquid; processed
　cheese; dairy products, except dried or
　canned; dry, condensed, evaporated dairy
　products; yogurt mix; groceries, general
　line

(P-571)
RUMIANO CHEESE CO (PA)
1629 County Road E, Willows
(95988-9642)
P.O. Box 863 (95988-0863)
PHONE..................................530 934-5438
Baird Rumiano, *President*
John F Rumiano, *Vice Pres*
Raymond Rumiano, *Prdtn Mgr*
▲EMP: 106
SQ FT: 30,000
SALES (est): 32MM **Privately Held**
SIC: 2022 Natural cheese

(P-572)
RUMIANO CHEESE CO
511 9th St, Crescent City (95531-3408)
P.O. Box 305 (95531-0305)
PHONE..................................707 465-1535
Baird Rumiano, *Manager*
EMP: 30
SALES (corp-wide): 32MM **Privately Held**
SIC: 2022 Cheese, natural & processed
PA: Rumiano Cheese Co.
　　1629 County Road E
　　Willows CA 95988
　　530 934-5438

(P-573)
SAPUTO CHEESE USA INC
800 E Paige Ave, Tulare (93274-6863)
PHONE..................................559 687-8411
Steven Tomasetti, *Manager*
EMP: 300
SALES (est): 3.7B **Privately Held**
SIC: 2022 Cheese spreads, dips, pastes &
　other cheese products
HQ: Saputo Cheese Usa Inc.
　　1 Overlook Pt Ste 300
　　Lincolnshire IL 60069
　　-

(P-574)
SAPUTO CHEESE USA INC
Also Called: Stella Cheese
901 E Levin Ave, Tulare (93274-6525)
PHONE..................................559 687-9999
Bob Timmons, *Manager*
EMP: 150
SALES (corp-wide): 3.7B **Privately Held**
SIC: 2022 Natural cheese
HQ: Saputo Cheese Usa Inc.
　　1 Overlook Pt Ste 300
　　Lincolnshire IL 60069

(P-575)
SAPUTO CHEESE USA INC
Stell Foods
5611 Imperial Hwy, South Gate
(90280-7419)
PHONE..................................562 862-7686
Rick McKenney, *Manager*
EMP: 200
SALES (corp-wide): 3.7B **Privately Held**
SIC: 2022 5143 Natural cheese; cheese
HQ: Saputo Cheese Usa Inc.
　　1 Overlook Pt Ste 300
　　Lincolnshire IL 60069

(P-576)
SCHREIBER FOODS INC
1901 Via Burton, Fullerton (92831-5341)
PHONE..................................714 490-7360
EMP: 181
SALES (corp-wide): 2.2B **Privately Held**
SIC: 2022 Processed cheese; natural
　cheese
PA: Schreiber Foods, Inc.
　　400 N Washington St
　　Green Bay WI 54301
　　920 437-7601

(P-577)
SIERRA NEVADA CHEESE CO INC
6505 County Road 39, Willows
(95988-9709)
PHONE..................................530 934-8660
Ben Gregersen, *President*
John Dundon, *Vice Pres*
Meghan Curry, *Mktg Coord*
Racheloriana Schraeder, *Director*
EMP: 58
SQ FT: 27,000
SALES (est): 14.3MM **Privately Held**
WEB: www.sierranevadacheese.com
SIC: 2022 Natural cheese

(P-578)
TOP BRANDS DISTRIBUTION INC
9675 Distribution Ave, San Diego
(92121-2307)
PHONE..................................858 578-0319
Steve Kwon, *CEO*
EMP: 15
SALES (est): 3.7MM **Privately Held**
SIC: 2022 Cheese spreads, dips, pastes &
　other cheese products

2023 Milk, Condensed & Evaporated

(P-579)
BETTER BAR MANUFACTURING LLC
6975 Arlington Ave, Riverside
(92503-1537)
PHONE..................................951 525-3111

Tariq Kelker,
EMP: 20 EST: 2018
SALES (est): 940K **Privately Held**
SIC: 2023 Dietary supplements, dairy &
　non-dairy based

(P-580)
BETTER NUTRITIONALS LLC
17120 S Figueroa St Ste B, Gardena
(90248-3024)
PHONE..................................310 502-2277
Sharon Hoffman, *Mng Member*
▼EMP: 100
SQ FT: 100,000
SALES: 5MM **Privately Held**
SIC: 2023 Dietary supplements, dairy &
　non-dairy based

(P-581)
BF SUMA PHARMACEUTICALS INC
5077 Walnut Grove Ave, San Gabriel
(91776-2023)
PHONE..................................626 285-8366
Chak Yeung Chan, *President*
Wendy Cheung, *Office Mgr*
Yanbing Chen, *QA Dir*
Annie Cheng, *Controller*
▲EMP: 13
SQ FT: 10,000
SALES (est): 1.8MM **Privately Held**
SIC: 2023 Dietary supplements, dairy &
　non-dairy based

(P-582)
BIO-NUTRITIONAL RES GROUP INC (PA)
Also Called: Bnrg
6 Morgan Ste 100, Irvine (92618-1920)
P.O. Box 3669, Torrance (90510-3669)
PHONE..................................714 427-6990
Kevin Lawrence, *CEO*
Curtis Steinhaus, *COO*
Karen L Stensby, *Treasurer*
Jack Thomas, *Vice Pres*
Jennifer Pera, *Controller*
EMP: 67 EST: 1991
SQ FT: 3,000
SALES (est): 63.9MM **Privately Held**
WEB: www.bnrg.com
SIC: 2023 Dietary supplements, dairy &
　non-dairy based

(P-583)
CAPS & TABS INC
3111 Camino Del Rio N # 400, San Diego
(92108-5720)
PHONE..................................619 285-5400
Jeffery S Grossman, *President*
EMP: 42
SALES (est): 4.3MM **Privately Held**
WEB: www.capsandtabs.com
SIC: 2023 Dietary supplements, dairy &
　non-dairy based

(P-584)
CYVEX NUTRITION INC
8141 E Kaiser Blvd # 180, Anaheim
(92808-2258)
PHONE..................................949 622-9030
Joe Vidal, *President*
Bret Scholtes, *CEO*
Quang La, *Opers Staff*
▲EMP: 10
SALES (est): 1.3MM
SALES (corp-wide): 268.6MM **Privately Held**
WEB: www.cyvex.com
SIC: 2023 8742 Dietary supplements,
　dairy & non-dairy based; marketing con-
　sulting services
HQ: Omega Protein Corporation
　　610 Menhaden Rd
　　Reedville VA 22539
　　804 453-6262

(P-585)
DO WELL LABORATORIES INC
14791 Myford Rd, Tustin (92780-7228)
PHONE..................................949 252-0001
Houn Simon Hsia, *President*
▲EMP: 15
SALES (est): 1.8MM **Privately Held**
SIC: 2023 Dietary supplements, dairy &
　non-dairy based

▲ = Import ▼=Export
◆ =Import/Export

(P-586)
ESPERER WEBSTORES LLC
Also Called: Diatomaceous Earth.com
3820 State St Ste B, Santa Barbara
(93105-3182)
PHONE..................................805 880-1900
David Stephen Sorensen, *Mng Member*
EMP: 19
SALES (est): 643.7K Privately Held
SIC: 2023 5499 Dietary supplements,
dairy & non-dairy based; vitamin food
stores

(P-587)
FEIHE INTERNATIONAL INC (PA)
2275 Huntington Dr # 278, San Marino
(91108-2640)
PHONE..................................626 757-8885
You B Leng, *President*
Hua Liu, *Vice Pres*
Paul Ryan,
EMP: 1932
SALES (est): 341.7MM Privately Held
SIC: 2023 Dry, condensed, evaporated
dairy products

(P-588)
FIVE FLAVORS HERBS
344 40th St, Oakland (94609-2609)
PHONE..................................510 923-0178
Benjamin Zappin, *Partner*
EMP: 10
SALES (est): 737K Privately Held
SIC: 2023 Dietary supplements, dairy &
non-dairy based

(P-589)
FORM FACTORY INC
2917 Santa Monica Blvd, Santa Monica
(90404-2413)
PHONE..................................937 572-6126
Tony Bash, *CEO*
EMP: 55
SALES (est): 1.5MM Privately Held
SIC: 2023 Dried & powdered milk & milk
products

(P-590)
FOSTER DAIRY FARMS
572 State Highway 1, Fortuna
(95540-9705)
PHONE..................................707 725-6182
Rich Gilladuci, *Manager*
EMP: 115
**SALES (corp-wide): 397.9MM Privately
Held**
SIC: 2023 Powdered milk
PA: Foster Dairy Farms
529 Kansas Ave
Modesto CA 95351
209 576-3400

(P-591)
FREAL FOODS LLC
6121 Hollis St Ste 500, Emeryville
(94608-2078)
PHONE..................................800 483-3218
Dinsh Guzdar, *President*
John Diemer, *Engineer*
Jennifer Balenzuela, *Opers Staff*
Martin Fogle, *Opers Staff*
Diane Garvin, *Opers Staff*
◆ EMP: 100
SALES (est): 21.3MM
SALES (corp-wide): 3.8B Privately Held
WEB: www.frealfoods.com
SIC: 2023 Milkshake mix
PA: Rich Products Corporation
1 Robert Rich Way
Buffalo NY 14213
716 878-8000

(P-592)
FUSION DIET SYSTEMS INC
(PA)
620 Nwport Ctr Dr Ste 350, Newport Beach
(92660)
PHONE..................................801 783-1194
Yin Yan, *President*
EMP: 10
SALES: 300K Privately Held
SIC: 2023 Dietary supplements, dairy &
non-dairy based; powdered whey

(P-593)
GSL TECH INC
3134 Maxson Rd, El Monte (91732-3102)
PHONE..................................626 572-9617
▲ EMP: 16
SALES (est): 1.8MM Privately Held
SIC: 2023 5499 2834

(P-594)
**HERBS YEH MANUFACTURING
CO**
Also Called: Natural Medicine Intl
195 N 2nd Ave, Upland (91786-6019)
PHONE..................................909 946-0794
Pearl Weh, *President*
Timothy Yeh, *Vice Pres*
EMP: 10
SALES (est): 760.8K Privately Held
SIC: 2023 Dietary supplements, dairy &
non-dairy based

(P-595)
**HERITAGE DISTRIBUTING
COMPANY**
Also Called: Ninth Avenue Foods
425 S 9th Ave, City of Industry
(91746-3314)
PHONE..................................626 333-9526
Ted De Groot, *Branch Mgr*
EMP: 22 Privately Held
SIC: 2023 Dry, condensed, evapo-
rated dairy products; fluid milk
PA: Heritage Distributing Company
5743 Smithway St Ste 105
Commerce CA 90040

(P-596)
**HILMAR WHEY PROTEIN INC
(PA)**
9001 Lander Ave, Hilmar (95324-8320)
P.O. Box 910 (95324-0910)
PHONE..................................209 667-6076
John J Jeter, *President*
EMP: 400 EST: 1991
SALES (est): 46.9MM Privately Held
SIC: 2023 Concentrated whey

(P-597)
HILMAR WHEY PROTEIN INC
8901 Lander Ave, Hilmar (95324-9327)
P.O. Box 910 (95324-0910)
PHONE..................................209 667-6076
EMP: 76
**SALES (corp-wide): 46.9MM Privately
Held**
SIC: 2023 Concentrated whey
PA: Hilmar Whey Protein Inc
9001 Lander Ave
Hilmar CA 95324
209 667-6076

(P-598)
**K-MAX HEALTH PRODUCTS
INTERNAT**
1468 E Mission Blvd, Pomona
(91766-2229)
PHONE..................................909 455-0158
Angela Ye, *CEO*
▲ EMP: 14
SALES (est): 2MM Privately Held
SIC: 2023 Dietary supplements, dairy &
non-dairy based

(P-599)
KAGED MUSCLE LLC
101 Main St Ste 360, Huntington Beach
(92648-8107)
PHONE..................................844 445-2433
Justin White, *President*
Rod Davis, *Controller*
◆ EMP: 20 EST: 2016
SQ FT: 2,000
SALES (est): 1.7MM Privately Held
SIC: 2023 Dietary supplements, dairy &
non-dairy based

(P-600)
KERRY INC
64405 Lincoln St, Mecca (92254-6501)
P.O. Box 398 (92254-0398)
PHONE..................................760 396-2116
Darren Worden, *President*
EMP: 65 Privately Held

SIC: 2023 Dry, condensed, evaporated
dairy products
HQ: Kerry Inc.
3400 Millington Rd
Beloit WI 53511
608 363-1200

(P-601)
LEANER CREAMER LLC
9107 Wilshire Blvd # 450, Beverly Hills
(90210-5531)
PHONE..................................818 621-5274
Jonathan Kashani,
Jacqueline Martinez, *Internal Med*
EMP: 10
SALES (est): 987.1K Privately Held
SIC: 2023 Powdered cream

(P-602)
LONIX PHARMACEUTICAL INC
5001 Earle Ave, Rosemead (91770-1169)
PHONE..................................626 287-4700
Chak Yeung Chan, *President*
Wendy Cheung, *Office Mgr*
EMP: 18
SQ FT: 5,000
SALES: 500K Privately Held
SIC: 2023 Dietary supplements, dairy &
non-dairy based

(P-603)
MATTHIAS RATH INC (HQ)
1260 Memorex Dr, Santa Clara
(95050-2812)
PHONE..................................408 567-5000
Matthias Rath, *President*
Aleksandra Niedzwiecki, *Vice Pres*
EMP: 10
SQ FT: 4,000
SALES (est): 2.8MM
**SALES (corp-wide): 48.4MM Privately
Held**
WEB: www.matthiasrath.com
SIC: 2023 Dietary supplements, dairy &
non-dairy based
PA: Matthias Rath Holding B.V.
Tesla 2
Heerlen 6422
457 111-100

(P-604)
MIRACLE GREENS INC
8477 Steller Dr, Culver City (90232-2424)
PHONE..................................800 521-5867
Michael G Dave, *President*
EMP: 120
SALES (est): 9.7MM Privately Held
SIC: 2023 Dietary supplements, dairy &
non-dairy based

(P-605)
MISSION AG RESOURCES LLC
Also Called: Sierra Feeds
6801 Avenue 430 Unit A, Reedley
(93654-9002)
PHONE..................................559 591-3333
Al Cumin, *Mng Member*
Therald Benevedo, *Mng Member*
Michelle Bonce, *Assistant*
EMP: 20
SALES (est): 3.8MM Privately Held
SIC: 2023 Dietary supplements, dairy &
non-dairy based

(P-606)
**MUSCLEPHARM CORPORATION
(PA)**
4400 W Vanowen St, Burbank
(91505-1134)
PHONE..................................303 396-6100
Ryan Drexler, *Ch of Bd*
Alberto Andrade, *COO*
Brian Casutto, *Exec VP*
EMP: 56
SQ FT: 30,302
SALES: 102.1MM Publicly Held
SIC: 2023 Dietary supplements, dairy &
non-dairy based

(P-607)
MYOSCI TECHNOLOGIES INC
Also Called: True Protein
1211 Liberty Way Ste B, Vista
(92081-8307)
PHONE..................................760 433-5376
Douglas A Smith, *CEO*

Brian Trudel, *Vice Pres*
EMP: 13
SQ FT: 5,000
SALES (est): 1.5MM Privately Held
WEB: www.trueprotein.com
SIC: 2023 Dietary supplements, dairy &
non-dairy based

(P-608)
NATURALIFE ECO VITE LABS
Also Called: Paragon Laboratories
20433 Earl St, Torrance (90503-2414)
PHONE..................................310 370-1563
Jay Kaufman, *CEO*
Steven Billis, *CFO*
Richard Kaufman, *Exec VP*
Claire Kaufman, *Admin Sec*
Vicky Hembree, *Purchasing*
▲ EMP: 100
SQ FT: 25,000
SALES (est): 24.5MM Privately Held
WEB: www.paragonlabsusa.com
SIC: 2023 2844 2834 5122 Dietary sup-
plements, dairy & non-dairy based; toilet
preparations; suppositories; vitamins &
minerals

(P-609)
NESTLE USA INC
Also Called: Nestle Dsd
4065 E Therese Ave, Fresno (93725-8920)
PHONE..................................559 834-2554
Miguel Alvarez, *Branch Mgr*
EMP: 18
SALES (corp-wide): 92B Privately Held
SIC: 2023 Evaporated milk
HQ: Nestle Usa, Inc.
1812 N Moore St Ste 118
Rosslyn VA 22209
818 549-6000

(P-610)
NESTLE USA INC
Also Called: Nestle Confections Factory
736 Garner Rd, Modesto (95357-0515)
PHONE..................................209 574-2000
Stephanie Hart, *Branch Mgr*
EMP: 85
SALES (corp-wide): 92B Privately Held
WEB: www.nestleusa.com
SIC: 2023 2033 2064 2099 Evaporated
milk; canned milk, whole; cream substitutes; fruits: packaged in cans, jars, etc.;
tomato paste: packaged in cans, jars,
etc.; tomato sauce: packaged in cans,
jars, etc.; candy & other confectionery
products; breakfast bars; pasta, uncooked: packaged with other ingredients
HQ: Nestle Usa, Inc.
1812 N Moore St Ste 118
Rosslyn VA 22209
818 549-6000

(P-611)
**NEUROHACKER COLLECTIVE
LLC**
5938 Priestly Dr Ste 200, Carlsbad
(92008-8847)
PHONE..................................855 281-2328
James Schmachtenberge,
Shawn Ramer, *Senior VP*
Robert Greenhall,
Daniel Schmachtenberger,
EMP: 18
SALES (est): 1.1MM Privately Held
SIC: 2023 Dietary supplements, dairy &
non-dairy based

(P-612)
NUTRI GRANULATIONS INC
16024 Phoebe Ave, La Mirada
(90638-5606)
PHONE..................................714 994-7855
Gene E Alley, *CEO*
Patrick Marantette, *President*
▲ EMP: 70
SQ FT: 45,000
SALES (est): 8.5MM
**SALES (corp-wide): 319MM Privately
Held**
WEB: www.nutrigran.com
SIC: 2023 Dietary supplements, dairy &
non-dairy based

PA: E. T. Horn Company
16050 Canary Ave
La Mirada CA 90638
714 523-8050

(P-613)
OMANA GROUP LLC
11562 Knott St Ste 5, Garden Grove
(92841-1823)
PHONE..............................714 891-9488
Than Nguyen, *Principal*
Harrison Phan, *Managing Dir*
EMP: 10
SQ FT: 2,000
SALES (est): 943.7K **Privately Held**
WEB: www.eomana.com
SIC: 2023 5122 Dietary supplements,
dairy & non-dairy based; drugs, propri-
etaries & sundries

(P-614)
PHARMACHEM LABORATORIES LLC
2929 E White Star Ave, Anaheim
(92806-2628)
PHONE..............................714 630-6000
George Joseph, *Vice Pres*
EMP: 16
SALES (corp-wide): 3.7B **Publicly Held**
SIC: 2023 Dietary supplements, dairy &
non-dairy based
HQ: Pharmachem Laboratories, Llc
265 Harrison Tpke
Kearny NJ 07032
201 246-1000

(P-615)
PHYTO ANIMAL HEALTH LLC
550 W C St Ste 2040, San Diego
(92101-3565)
PHONE..............................888 871-4505
Stuart Titus, *CEO*
Ian Quinn, *CEO*
EMP: 20
SQ FT: 15,000
SALES (est): 671.8K **Privately Held**
SIC: 2023 Dietary supplements, dairy &
non-dairy based

(P-616)
PREMIUM HERBAL USA LLC
Also Called: Dr. J'S Natural
10517 Garden Grove Blvd, Garden Grove
(92843-1128)
PHONE..............................800 567-7878
Jacqueline Nguyen, *CEO*
EMP: 10
SALES (est): 342.9K **Privately Held**
SIC: 2023 Dietary supplements, dairy &
non-dairy based

(P-617)
PROLACTA BIOSCIENCE INC
1800 Highland Ave, Duarte (91010-2837)
PHONE..............................626 599-9260
Scott A Elster, *CEO*
EMP: 304
SALES (corp-wide): 45.4MM **Privately
Held**
SIC: 2023 Dried & powdered milk & milk
products
PA: Prolacta Bioscience, Inc.
757 Baldwin Park Blvd
City Of Industry CA 91746
626 599-9260

(P-618)
SANTINI FOODS INC
Also Called: Santini Fine Wines
16505 Worthley Dr, San Lorenzo
(94580-1811)
PHONE..............................510 317-8888
Bruce Liu, *President*
Alyssia Smith, *Admin Asst*
Punit Dave, *Research*
Lisa Medina, *Finance Mgr*
Phil Mosca, *Safety Mgr*
◆ **EMP:** 133
SQ FT: 105,000

SALES (est): 39.4MM **Privately Held**
WEB: www.santinifoods.com
SIC: 2023 2026 2032 2087 Condensed,
concentrated & evaporated milk products;
milk processing (pasteurizing, homogenizing, bottling); ethnic foods: canned,
jarred, etc.; beverage bases, concentrates, syrups, powders & mixes

(P-619)
SELECT SUPPLEMENTS INC
2390 Oak Ridge Way, Vista (92081-8345)
PHONE..............................760 431-7509
Hector A Gudino, *Exec VP*
Julie Chavez, *Technology*
Joel Imaizumi, *Controller*
▲ **EMP:** 10
SALES (est): 1.6MM **Privately Held**
WEB: www.select-ssi.com
SIC: 2023 2087 Dry, condensed, evapo-
rated dairy products; powders, drink
HQ: Kyowa Hakko U. S. A., Inc.
600 3rd Ave Fl 19
New York NY 10016
212 319-5353

(P-620)
SOURCE OF HEALTH INC
1055 Bay Blvd Ste A, Chula Vista
(91911-1628)
PHONE..............................619 409-9500
Oskar Thorvaldsson, *President*
▲ **EMP:** 21 **EST:** 2000
SALES (est): 2.7MM **Privately Held**
SIC: 2023 Dietary supplements, dairy &
non-dairy based

(P-621)
SOURCE SUPERFOODS LLC
15615 Vista Vicente Dr # 200, Ramona
(92065-4372)
PHONE..............................760 884-6575
Nancy Delaney,
EMP: 12
SALES (est): 438.8K **Privately Held**
SIC: 2023 Dietary supplements, dairy &
non-dairy based

(P-622)
TROPICAL FUNCTIONAL LABS LLC
Also Called: Tahiti Trading Company
7111 Arlington Ave Ste F, Riverside
(92503-1522)
PHONE..............................951 688-2619
Lawrence Logsdon, *President*
▲ **EMP:** 11
SALES (est): 1.8MM **Privately Held**
SIC: 2023 Dietary supplements, dairy &
non-dairy based

(P-623)
ULTRA H2 LP
1601 Dove St Ste 126, Newport Beach
(92660-1419)
PHONE..............................657 999-5188
Yisheng Lin, *Principal*
EMP: 10
SALES (est): 200K **Privately Held**
SIC: 2023 Dietary supplements, dairy &
non-dairy based

(P-624)
VITAMIN FRIENDS LLC
17120 S Figueroa St Ste B, Gardena
(90248-3024)
PHONE..............................310 356-9018
Sharon Hoffman,
▲ **EMP:** 50
SQ FT: 5,000
SALES (est): 5.6MM **Privately Held**
SIC: 2023 Dietary supplements, dairy &
non-dairy based

(P-625)
WAKUNAGA OF AMERICA CO LTD (HQ)
Also Called: KYOLIC
23501 Madero, Mission Viejo (92691-2744)
PHONE..............................949 855-2776
Kazuhiko Nomura, *President*
Hiyoshi Sakai, *Vice Pres*
Kathy Comstock, *Admin Asst*
Alexandra Hansen, *Administration*
Rene King, *Info Tech Mgr*
◆ **EMP:** 64

SQ FT: 36,000
SALES: 31MM **Privately Held**
WEB: www.kyolic.com
SIC: 2023 Dietary supplements, dairy &
non-dairy based

(P-626)
XHALE DISTRIBUTORS
464 E 4th St, Los Angeles (90013-1604)
PHONE..............................888 942-5355
Zara Hbaiu, *Co-Owner*
Alex Hbaiu, *Owner*
EMP: 11 **EST:** 2008
SQ FT: 6,000
SALES: 3.8MM **Privately Held**
SIC: 2023 Dietary supplements, dairy &
non-dairy based

(P-627)
YBCC INC
17800 Castleton St # 386, City of Industry
(91748-1791)
PHONE..............................626 213-3945
Xiuhua Song, *President*
EMP: 38
SALES: 2.2MM **Privately Held**
SIC: 2023 Dietary supplements, dairy &
non-dairy based

2024 Ice Cream

(P-628)
AMPERSAND ICE CREAM LLC
1940 N Echo Ave, Fresno (93704-6004)
PHONE..............................559 264-8000
Amelia Bennett,
Jeffrey Bennett,
EMP: 12
SQ FT: 1,640
SALES: 500K **Privately Held**
SIC: 2024 Ice cream & frozen desserts

(P-629)
ARCTIC ZERO INC
1345 Broadway, El Cajon (92021-5811)
PHONE..............................619 342-1423
Amit Pandhi, *CEO*
Greg Holtman, *COO*
Deanna Spooner, *CFO*
Christopher Calano, *Vice Pres*
Jason Paine, *Vice Pres*
EMP: 31
SALES: 22.7MM **Privately Held**
SIC: 2024 5143 5142 Dairy based frozen
desserts; non-dairy based frozen
desserts; frozen dairy desserts; packaged
frozen goods

(P-630)
BERENICE 2 AM CORP
Also Called: Bobboi Natural Gelato
8008 Girard Ave Ste 150, La Jolla
(92037-4159)
PHONE..............................858 255-8693
Andrea Racca, *Officer*
EMP: 10
SQ FT: 900
SALES: 1.2MM **Privately Held**
SIC: 2024 Ice cream & frozen desserts

(P-631)
BERT & ROCKYS CREAM CO INC
242 Yale Ave, Claremont (91711-4724)
PHONE..............................909 625-1852
Sherry Hunter, *Manager*
EMP: 10
SALES (est): 547.8K
SALES (corp-wide): 1.4MM **Privately
Held**
WEB: www.bertandrockys.com
SIC: 2024 5143 5812 Ice cream & frozen
desserts; ice cream & ices; ice cream,
soft drink & soda fountain stands
PA: Bert & Rockys Cream Co Inc
555 N Benson Ave Ste K
Upland CA 91786
909 946-6805

(P-632)
BLITZERS PREMIUM FROZEN YOGURT
29101 Newport Rd, Menifee (92584-5110)
PHONE..............................951 679-7709

Roger Copp, *Principal*
EMP: 10
SALES: 456K **Privately Held**
SIC: 2024 Yogurt desserts, frozen

(P-633)
BROTHERS INTL DESSERTS
2727 S Susan St, Santa Ana (92704-5817)
PHONE..............................949 655-0080
Gary M Winkler, *CEO*
▲ **EMP:** 120 **EST:** 1974
SQ FT: 30,000
SALES (est): 33.3MM **Privately Held**
WEB: www.brothersdesserts.com
SIC: 2024 Ice cream, bulk; ices, flavored
(frozen dessert)

(P-634)
CHANTILLY
Also Called: Chantilly Ice Cream
202 Park Ave, Laguna Beach (92651-2142)
PHONE..............................949 494-7702
Robert Sarhaddar, *Owner*
A Sauveur Ghozland, *Treasurer*
EMP: 30
SQ FT: 1,300
SALES (est): 2.6MM **Privately Held**
WEB: www.chantilly.com
SIC: 2024 5461 Ice cream & frozen
desserts; bread

(P-635)
CHILL SPOT INC
11706 Moorpark St, Studio City
(91604-2111)
PHONE..............................818 762-0041
Yevgeniy Shneyder, *Principal*
EMP: 10
SALES (est): 775.9K **Privately Held**
SIC: 2024 Yogurt desserts, frozen

(P-636)
COLDSTONE CREAMERY 256
25395 Madison Ave 106d, Murrieta
(92562-9093)
PHONE..............................951 304-9777
Maureen Kaczarski, *Owner*
John Kaczarski, *Co-Owner*
EMP: 17
SALES (est): 1.6MM **Privately Held**
SIC: 2024 Ice cream, bulk

(P-637)
COLDSTONE MIRA MESA 114
10716 Westview Pkwy, San Diego
(92126-2962)
PHONE..............................858 695-9771
Doug Ducey, *President*
EMP: 14
SALES (est): 1.6MM **Privately Held**
SIC: 2024 2999 Ice cream, bulk; coke

(P-638)
DANONE US LLC
3500 Barranca Pkwy # 240, Irvine
(92606-8226)
PHONE..............................949 474-9670
John Mastrotaolo, *Director*
EMP: 390
SALES (corp-wide): 762.4MM **Privately
Held**
SIC: 2024 Ice cream & frozen desserts
HQ: Danone Us, Llc
1 Maple Ave
White Plains NY 10605
914 872-8400

(P-639)
DOLCE DOLCI LLC
Also Called: Villa Dolce Gelato
16745 Saticoy St Ste 112, Van Nuys
(91406-2710)
PHONE..............................818 343-8400
Wes Schertz,
EMP: 19
SALES (corp-wide): 16MM **Privately
Held**
SIC: 2024 Ice cream & ice milk
PA: Dolce Dolci, Llc
6900 Canby Ave Ste 106
Reseda CA 91335
818 343-8400

(P-640)
EDEN CREAMERY LLC (PA)
Also Called: Halo Top
4470 W Sunset Blvd # 90182, Los Angeles
(90027-6302)
PHONE..................................855 425-6867
Doug Bouton, *Mng Member*
Rich Franzosa, *Financial Analy*
Erin Conners, *Opers Mgr*
Justin Ball, *VP Sales*
Lily Dang, *Marketing Staff*
EMP: 10
SALES (est): 5.8MM **Privately Held**
SIC: 2024 Ice cream, bulk

(P-641)
EL PARAISO NO 2
1760 E Florence Ave, Los Angeles
(90001-2550)
PHONE..................................323 587-2073
Ramon Romero, *Owner*
EMP: 29
SQ FT: 2,760
SALES (est): 1.6MM **Privately Held**
SIC: 2024 Ice cream & ice milk

(P-642)
FARCHITECTURE BB LLC
Also Called: Coolhaus
8588 Washington Blvd, Culver City
(90232-7463)
PHONE..................................917 701-2777
Natasha Case, *Mng Member*
Daniel Fishman, *President*
Teena Ngyuen, *General Mgr*
Jake Vita, *Store Mgr*
Jarett Margolis, *Sales Mgr*
EMP: 30
SALES (est): 707.7K **Privately Held**
SIC: 2024 Ice cream, packaged: molded,
on sticks, etc.

(P-643)
FIORELLOS ITALIAN ICE CREAM
3100 Kerner Blvd Ste Hh, San Rafael
(94901-5445)
PHONE..................................415 459-8004
Anthony Bonviso, *Owner*
EMP: 11
SQ FT: 716
SALES (est): 1.1MM **Privately Held**
SIC: 2024 5143 Ice cream, bulk; ice
cream & ices

(P-644)
FLOR DE CALIFORNIA
1930 S Bon View Ave # 18, Ontario
(91761-5532)
PHONE..................................909 673-1968
Jose Vertiz, *Owner*
EMP: 20
SQ FT: 1,381
SALES (est): 1.1MM **Privately Held**
SIC: 2024 Ice cream & frozen desserts

(P-645)
FONO UNLIMITED INC (PA)
Also Called: Bravo Fono
99 Stanford Shopping Ctr, Palo Alto
(94304-1424)
PHONE..................................650 322-4664
Paulette Fono, *President*
Laslo Fono, *Vice Pres*
EMP: 30
SALES: 3MM **Privately Held**
SIC: 2024 5812 5813 Ice cream, bulk;
Italian restaurant; drinking places

(P-646)
FRUITI POPS INC
15418 Cornet St, Santa Fe Springs
(90670-5534)
PHONE..................................562 404-2568
Rodolpho Aguado, *Partner*
Jaqueline Aguado, *Partner*
EMP: 12
SQ FT: 13,000
SALES (est): 1.8MM **Privately Held**
WEB: www.fruitipops.net
SIC: 2024 Fruit pops, frozen

(P-647)
**GUNTHERS QUALITY ICE
CREAM**
2801 Franklin Blvd, Sacramento
(95818-2719)
PHONE..................................916 457-3339
Richard D Klopp, *Partner*
Marlena Klopp, *Partner*
EMP: 13
SQ FT: 4,800
SALES: 830K **Privately Held**
SIC: 2024 5143 5812 Ice cream, bulk; ice
cream & ices; ice cream stands or dairy
bars

(P-648)
**HALO TOP INTERNATIONAL LLC
(PA)**
Also Called: Halo Top Creamery
1348 N Sierra Bonita Ave # 107, West Hol-
lywood (90046-8528)
PHONE..................................434 409-2057
Doug Bouton, *Mng Member*
Justin Woolverton,
EMP: 50
SALES (est): 323.5K
SALES (corp-wide): 18.5MM **Privately
Held**
SIC: 2024 Ice cream & frozen desserts

(P-649)
HARRISON BEVERAGE INC
Also Called: Harrison Group
726 Arabian Ln, Walnut (91789-1297)
PHONE..................................626 757-1159
Diana Tsai, *President*
▲ **EMP:** 15
SQ FT: 72,000
SALES: 3MM **Privately Held**
SIC: 2024 Ices, flavored (frozen dessert)

(P-650)
HELADOS LA TAPATIA INC
4495 W Shaw Ave, Fresno (93722-6206)
PHONE..................................559 441-1105
Emilio Sandoval, *Principal*
Sergio Sandoval, *CFO*
EMP: 40
SQ FT: 8,800
SALES (est): 9.3MM **Privately Held**
SIC: 2024 5143 Ice cream & frozen
desserts; ice cream & ices

(P-651)
HELADOS VALLARTA INC
1418 G St, Fresno (93706)
PHONE..................................559 709-1177
Emilio Sandoval, *President*
David Valdivia, *Vice Pres*
EMP: 10
SQ FT: 5,000
SALES: 482K **Privately Held**
WEB: www.icesations.com
SIC: 2024 5143 Ice cream & frozen
desserts; ice cream & ices

(P-652)
K-CAL GROUP INC
117 W Garvey Ave, Monterey Park
(91754-2807)
PHONE..................................626 922-1103
Zhuqi Zhang, *Principal*
EMP: 14
SALES (corp-wide): 1.5MM **Privately
Held**
SIC: 2024 Ice cream & ice milk
PA: K-Cal Group Inc
7171 Talasi Dr Corona
Eastvale CA 92880
626 922-1103

(P-653)
LOCO VENTURES INC
Also Called: Loard's Ice Cream and Candies
2000 Wayne Ave, San Leandro
(94571-3333)
PHONE..................................510 351-0405
Steven Cohen, *President*
Scott Cohen, *Vice Pres*
EMP: 25
SQ FT: 16,000

SALES (est): 3.5MM **Privately Held**
SIC: 2024 2064 5812 5441 Ice cream,
bulk; candy & other confectionery products; ice cream stands or dairy bars;
candy

(P-654)
LONG BEACH CREAMERY LLC
4141 Long Beach Blvd, Long Beach
(90807-2651)
PHONE..................................562 252-2730
Dina Amadril, *Mng Member*
EMP: 13
SALES: 273K **Privately Held**
SIC: 2024 5143 5451 Ice cream & frozen
desserts; ice cream & ices; ice cream
(packaged)

(P-655)
**MACKIE INTERNATIONAL INC
(PA)**
Also Called: Sun Ice USA
7344 Magnolia Ave Ste 205, Riverside
(92504-3819)
PHONE..................................951 346-0530
Ernesto U Dacay Jr, *President*
Danica Dacay, *Sales Staff*
Cruz Coronado, *Clerk*
▲ **EMP:** 40
SQ FT: 70,000
SALES: 3MM **Privately Held**
WEB: www.mackieinternational.net
SIC: 2024 2086 5199 Ices, flavored
(frozen dessert); fruit pops, frozen; gelatin
pops, frozen; fruit drinks (less than 100%
juice): packaged in cans, etc.; baskets

(P-656)
MARIANNES ICE CREAM LLC
218 State Park Dr, Aptos (95003-4324)
PHONE..................................831 713-4746
Charles Wilcox, *Mng Member*
EMP: 40 **Privately Held**
SIC: 2024 Custard, frozen
PA: Marianne's Ice Cream, Llc
2100 Delaware Ave Ste B
Santa Cruz CA 95060

(P-657)
**MARIANNES ICE CREAM LLC
(PA)**
2100 Delaware Ave Ste B, Santa Cruz
(95060-6362)
PHONE..................................831 457-1447
Charles Wilcox, *Mng Member*
Kelly Dillon,
▲ **EMP:** 10
SALES (est): 4.3MM **Privately Held**
SIC: 2024 5812 Ice cream & frozen
desserts; ice cream stands or dairy bars

(P-658)
MATTERHORN ICE CREAM INC
1221 66th St, Sacramento (95819-4323)
PHONE..................................208 287-8916
Thomas Nist, *President*
Todd Wilson, *CFO*
EMP: 85
SQ FT: 24,000
SALES (est): 9.4MM **Privately Held**
SIC: 2024 Ice cream & ice milk

(P-659)
MAVENS CREAMERY LLC
1701 N 7th St Ste 7, San Jose
(95112-6000)
PHONE..................................408 216-9270
Kim Lam, *Mng Member*
Christine Nguyen, *Opers Mgr*
Tony Lam, *Mng Member*
EMP: 30
SQ FT: 5,000
SALES (est): 2.9MM **Privately Held**
SIC: 2024 Ice cream & frozen desserts

(P-660)
NADOLIFE INC
Also Called: Moo Time
2709 Newton Ave, San Diego
(92113-3713)
P.O. Box 182225, Coronado (92178-2225)
PHONE..................................619 522-6890
David Spatafore, *CEO*
Leroy Mossell, *Vice Pres*
Jennifer Spatafore, *Principal*

EMP: 60
SALES (est): 10.1MM **Privately Held**
WEB: www.mootime.com
SIC: 2024 Ice cream, bulk

(P-661)
NAIA INC
Also Called: Gelateria Naia
736 Alfred Nobel Dr, Hercules
(94547-1805)
PHONE..................................510 724-2479
Christopher C Tan, *Principal*
Jesse Porter, *Opers Mgr*
EMP: 34
SALES (est): 6.2MM **Privately Held**
SIC: 2024 Ice cream, bulk

(P-662)
**NESTLE DREYERS ICE CREAM
CO**
Also Called: Dreyer's Grand Ice Cream
7301 District Blvd, Bakersfield
(93313-2042)
PHONE..................................661 398-5448
Mark McLenithan, *Manager*
James Yako, *Research*
EMP: 10
SALES (corp-wide): 92B **Privately Held**
WEB: www.dreyersinc.com
SIC: 2024 Ice cream, packaged: molded,
on sticks, etc.
HQ: Nestle Dreyer's Ice Cream Company
5929 College Ave
Oakland CA 94618
-

(P-663)
**NESTLE DREYERS ICE CREAM
CO**
Also Called: Dreyer's Grand Ice Cream
4065 E Therese Ave, Fresno (93725-8920)
PHONE..................................559 834-2554
Miguel Alvarez, *Manager*
EMP: 10
SALES (corp-wide): 92B **Privately Held**
WEB: www.dreyersinc.com
SIC: 2024 Ice cream & frozen desserts
HQ: Nestle Dreyer's Ice Cream Company
5929 College Ave
Oakland CA 94618
-

(P-664)
**RAMAR INTERNATIONAL CORP
(PA)**
Also Called: Orientex Foods
1101 Railroad Ave, Pittsburg (94565-2641)
P.O. Box 111 (94565-0011)
PHONE..................................925 439-9009
Primo Quesada, *President*
Grace Cruz, *Office Mgr*
Rommel Catanghal, *Engineer*
Racqui Levy, *Accounts Mgr*
◆ **EMP:** 40 **EST:** 1968
SALES (est): 25.4MM **Privately Held**
SIC: 2024 2013 5141 Ice cream & frozen
desserts; sausages & other prepared
meats; groceries, general line

(P-665)
RITAS FELICITA
1875 S Centre City Pkwy, Escondido
(92025-6585)
PHONE..................................760 975-3302
Chris Uhles, *Owner*
EMP: 18
SALES (est): 1MM **Privately Held**
SIC: 2024 5812 Ice cream & frozen
desserts; caterers

(P-666)
**ROSA BROTHERS MILK CO INC
(PA)**
10090 2nd Ave, Hanford (93230-9370)
PHONE..................................559 582-8825
Noel M Rosa, *President*
Rolland Rosa, *Vice Pres*
EMP: 35
SALES (est): 2.9MM **Privately Held**
SIC: 2024 2026 Ice cream & frozen
desserts; half & half

PRODUCTS & SVCS

(P-667)
SCREAMIN MIMIS INC
6902 Sebastopol Ave, Sebastopol (95472-3411)
PHONE.........................707 823-5902
Maraline Olson, *President*
EMP: 18
SALES (est): 1.8MM **Privately Held**
WEB: www.screaminmisicecream.com
SIC: 2024 5812 Ice cream, bulk; ice cream, soft drink & soda fountain stands

(P-668)
STREMICKS HERITAGE FOODS LLC
11503 Pierce St, Riverside (92505-3350)
PHONE.........................951 352-1344
Andy Holm, *Branch Mgr*
EMP: 70
SALES (corp-wide): 13.6B **Privately Held**
WEB: www.stremicksheritagefoods.com
SIC: 2024 Ice cream & frozen desserts
HQ: Stremicks Heritage Foods, Llc
4002 Westminster Ave
Santa Ana CA 92703
714 775-5000

(P-669)
SUPER STORE INDUSTRIES
Also Called: Mid Valley Dairy
2600 Spengler Way, Turlock (95380-8591)
PHONE.........................209 668-2100
Joe Mc Gill, *Manager*
Yancy Hopper, *Engineer*
Mark Hujdic, *Manager*
EMP: 100
SALES (corp-wide): 293.7MM **Privately Held**
SIC: 2024 5143 Ice cream & frozen desserts; ice cream & ices
PA: Super Store Industries
16888 Mckinley Ave
Lathrop CA 95330
209 858-3365

(P-670)
SUPERIOR DAIRY PRODUCTS CO
325 N Douty St, Hanford (93230-3993)
PHONE.........................559 582-0481
Susan Wing, *President*
Tim Jones, *Vice Pres*
James Wing, *Supervisor*
EMP: 34
SQ FT: 7,500
SALES: 825K **Privately Held**
WEB: www.superiordairy.com
SIC: 2024 Ice cream & ice milk

(P-671)
SWEETY NOVELTY INC
633 Monterey Pass Rd, Monterey Park (91754-2418)
PHONE.........................310 533-6010
Traci Lee, *President*
Stephen Lee, *Vice Pres*
Patty Lee, *Manager*
▲ **EMP:** 13
SQ FT: 11,680
SALES (est): 2MM **Privately Held**
SIC: 2024 Ice cream & frozen desserts

(P-672)
THREE TWINS ORGANIC INC (PA)
Also Called: Three Twins Organic Ice Cream
419 1st St, Petaluma (94952-4226)
PHONE.........................707 763-8946
Neal H Gottlieb, *CEO*
Nathan Reynolds, *Manager*
Edith Jimenez, *Assistant*
EMP: 21
SALES (est): 3.3MM **Privately Held**
SIC: 2024 5199 5812 Ice cream, bulk; ice, manufactured or natural; ice cream stands or dairy bars

(P-673)
THRIFTY CORPORATION
9200 Telstar Ave, El Monte (91731-2814)
PHONE.........................818 571-0122
Larry Crosby, *Director*
EMP: 13
SQ FT: 50,000

SALES (corp-wide): 21.6B **Publicly Held**
SIC: 2024 Ice cream, bulk
HQ: Thrifty Corporation
30 Hunter Ln
Camp Hill PA 17011
717 761-2633

(P-674)
TROPICALE FOODS INC
1237 W State St, Ontario (91762-4015)
P.O. Box 2224, Chino (91708-2224)
PHONE.........................909 635-0390
Ruben Gutierrez, *President*
Lupe Gutierrez, *Admin Sec*
Luis Huapaya, *Controller*
Ericca Ruic, *Human Res Mgr*
John Sommerville, *Sales Staff*
▲ **EMP:** 49
SALES (est): 22.5MM **Privately Held**
WEB: www.tropicalefoods.com
SIC: 2024 Ice milk, packaged: molded, on sticks, etc.

(P-675)
VAMPIRE PENGUIN LLC (PA)
907 K St, Sacramento (95814-3511)
PHONE.........................916 553-4197
Leo Alejandro San Luis, *Mng Member*
EMP: 13
SALES (est): 1.9MM **Privately Held**
SIC: 2024 Ice cream, bulk

(P-676)
VENTURE CAPITAL ENTPS LLC
Also Called: Twist Frozen Yogurt
10669 Wellworth Ave, Los Angeles (90024-5011)
PHONE.........................914 275-7305
Abdelmajid Sabour, *Mng Member*
EMP: 10 **EST:** 2012
SALES: 1.5MM **Privately Held**
SIC: 2024 Yogurt desserts, frozen

(P-677)
VON HOPPEN ICE CREAM (HQ)
Also Called: Frutstix Company
1525 State St Ste 203, Santa Barbara (93101-6512)
PHONE.........................805 965-2009
William McKinley, *President*
Mariam Schroeder, *Admin Sec*
▲ **EMP:** 10
SALES (est): 3.6MM
SALES (corp-wide): 14.8MM **Privately Held**
WEB: www.frutstix.com
SIC: 2024 Juice pops, frozen
PA: The Lafayette Corporation
1525 State St Ste 203
Santa Barbara CA 93101
805 965-2009

(P-678)
VON HOPPEN ICE CREAM
Also Called: Frutstix Company
8221 Arjons Dr Ste A, San Diego (92126-6319)
PHONE.........................858 695-9111
Jim Elwel, *Manager*
Thomas Triffo, *Opers Dir*
EMP: 15
SALES (corp-wide): 14.8MM **Privately Held**
WEB: www.frutstix.com
SIC: 2024 Ice cream, bulk
HQ: Von Hoppen Ice Cream
1525 State St Ste 203
Santa Barbara CA 93101
805 965-2009

(P-679)
WE THE PIE PEOPLE LLC
Also Called: Jc's Pie Pops
9909 Topanga Canyon Blvd # 159, Chatsworth (91311-3602)
PHONE.........................818 349-1880
Jennifer Constantine, *Mng Member*
Thomas Spler, *General Mgr*
▲ **EMP:** 50
SALES (est): 5.4MM **Privately Held**
SIC: 2024 Non-dairy based frozen desserts

(P-680)
WHOLESOME YO CURD
19755 Colima Rd, Rowland Heights (91748-3206)
PHONE.........................909 859-8758
Charanjit Jaujhar, *Owner*
EMP: 10
SALES (est): 405.9K **Privately Held**
SIC: 2024 Yogurt desserts, frozen

(P-681)
ZIEGENFELDER COMPANY
12290 Colony Ave, Chino (91710-2095)
PHONE.........................909 590-0493
Allan Hawthorne, *Branch Mgr*
EMP: 40
SALES (corp-wide): 21MM **Privately Held**
SIC: 2024 Ice cream, packaged: molded, on sticks, etc.
PA: The Ziegenfelder Company
87 18th St
Wheeling WV 26003
304 232-6360

2026 Milk

(P-682)
ALBERT GOYENETCHE DAIRY
6041 Brandt Rd, Buttonwillow (93206-9547)
PHONE.........................661 764-6176
Albert Goyenetche, *Owner*
EMP: 12
SALES (est): 1.2MM **Privately Held**
SIC: 2026 5541 Milk processing (pasteurizing, homogenizing, bottling); gasoline service stations

(P-683)
ALTA-DENA CERTIFIED DAIRY LLC
123 Aero Camino, Goleta (93117-3177)
PHONE.........................805 685-8328
EMP: 134 **Publicly Held**
SIC: 2026
HQ: Alta-Dena Certified Dairy, Llc
17637 E Valley Blvd
City Of Industry CA 91744
626 964-6401

(P-684)
ALTA-DENA CERTIFIED DAIRY LLC
17851 Railroad St, City of Industry (91748-1118)
PHONE.........................800 395-7004
Michael Greenwald, *Manager*
EMP: 134
SALES (corp-wide): 941.7MM **Privately Held**
SIC: 2026 Cottage cheese
HQ: Alta-Dena Certified Dairy, Llc
17637 E Valley Blvd
City Of Industry CA 91744
626 964-6401

(P-685)
ALTA-DENA CERTIFIED DAIRY LLC (DH)
17637 E Valley Blvd, City of Industry (91744-5731)
PHONE.........................626 964-6401
John Keith,
Jack Tewers, *CFO*
Bob Pettigrew, *Vice Pres*
Steve Schaffer, *General Mgr*
Carl Reynolds, *Purch Mgr*
EMP: 370 **EST:** 1945
SQ FT: 100,000
SALES (est): 164.9MM
SALES (corp-wide): 941.7MM **Privately Held**
WEB: www.altadenadairy.com
SIC: 2026 Milk & cream, except fermented, cultured & flavored

(P-686)
BERKELEY FARMS LLC
7444 Reese Rd, Sacramento (95828-3706)
PHONE.........................916 689-7613
Richard Hunter, *Branch Mgr*
EMP: 30

SALES (corp-wide): 941.7MM **Privately Held**
WEB: www.berkeleyfarms.com
SIC: 2026 Fluid milk
HQ: Berkeley Farms, Llc
25500 Clawiter Rd
Hayward CA 94545
510 265-8600

(P-687)
BERKELEY FARMS LLC (DH)
Also Called: Buds Ice Cream San Francisco
25500 Clawiter Rd, Hayward (94545-2739)
P.O. Box 4616 (94540-4616)
PHONE.........................510 265-8600
Terry Dana,
David Smydra, *Maintence Staff*
▲ **EMP:** 300
SQ FT: 220,000
SALES (est): 57.1MM
SALES (corp-wide): 941.7MM **Privately Held**
WEB: www.berkeleyfarms.com
SIC: 2026 0241 5143 Fluid milk; dairy farms; butter

(P-688)
CALIFORNIA DAIRIES INC (PA)
2000 N Plaza Dr, Visalia (93291-9358)
PHONE.........................559 625-2200
Andrei Mikhalevsky, *CEO*
John Azevedo, *Ch of Bd*
Dave Bush, *COO*
Phil Girard, *CFO*
Joe L Heffington, *Senior VP*
◆ **EMP:** 80 **EST:** 1938
SALES (est): 253.1MM **Privately Held**
WEB: www.californiadairies.com
SIC: 2026 2021 2023 Fluid milk; creamery butter; dry, condensed, evaporated dairy products

(P-689)
CALIFORNIA DAIRIES INC
755 F St, Fresno (93706-3416)
P.O. Box 11865 (93775-1865)
PHONE.........................559 233-5154
Robert Ray, *Branch Mgr*
Bill Twist, *Branch Mgr*
EMP: 100
SALES (corp-wide): 253.1MM **Privately Held**
WEB: www.californiadairies.com
SIC: 2026 2021 2023 Fluid milk; creamery butter; dried milk
PA: California Dairies, Inc.
2000 N Plaza Dr
Visalia CA 93291
559 625-2200

(P-690)
CALIFORNIA DAIRIES INC
11709 Artesia Blvd, Artesia (90701-3803)
PHONE.........................562 809-2595
Joe Heffington, *Branch Mgr*
John C Rocha, *Bd of Directors*
Pete Cassinerio, *Vice Pres*
EMP: 65
SALES (corp-wide): 253.1MM **Privately Held**
WEB: www.californiadairies.com
SIC: 2026 Milk processing (pasteurizing, homogenizing, bottling)
PA: California Dairies, Inc.
2000 N Plaza Dr
Visalia CA 93291
559 625-2200

(P-691)
CREST BEVERAGE LLC
8870 Liquid Ct, San Diego (92121-2234)
PHONE.........................858 452-2300
Steven S Sourapas, *Mng Member*
Randy Treadway, *District Mgr*
Dean McMillan, *General Mgr*
Tricia Barclay, *Admin Sec*
Alan Estrada, *Sales Staff*
▲ **EMP:** 400
SQ FT: 200,000
SALES (est): 48.4MM **Privately Held**
SIC: 2026 2082 Beer & other fermented malt liquors

▲ = Import ▼=Export
◆ =Import/Export

(P-692)
CRYSTAL CREAM & BUTTER CO (HQ)
8340 Belvedere Ave, Sacramento (95826-5902)
PHONE.................................916 444-7200
Donald K Hansen, *Chairman*
Michael J Newell, *President*
Dan Kosewski, *Vice Pres*
EMP: 100
SQ FT: 100,000
SALES (est): 53.3MM
SALES (corp-wide): 2.2B **Privately Held**
WEB: www.crystal-milk.com
SIC: 2026 2021 2024 Milk processing (pasteurizing, homogenizing, bottling); cottage cheese; yogurt; creamery butter; ice cream & ice milk
PA: Hp Hood Llc
    6 Kimball Ln Ste 400
    Lynnfield MA 01940
    617 887-8441

(P-693)
DAIRY FARMERS AMERICA INC
170 N Maple St Ste 106, Corona (92880-1781)
PHONE.................................951 493-4900
EMP: 15
SALES (corp-wide): 13.6B **Privately Held**
WEB: www.dfamilk.com
SIC: 2026 Fluid milk
PA: Dairy Farmers Of America, Inc.
    1405 N 98th St
    Kansas City KS 66111
    816 801-6455

(P-694)
DAIRY FARMERS AMERICA INC
4375 N Ventura Ave, Ventura (93001-1124)
PHONE.................................805 653-0042
Kevin Clark, *Manager*
EMP: 90
SALES (corp-wide): 13.6B **Privately Held**
WEB: www.dfamilk.com
SIC: 2026 2022 2021 2023 Milk processing (pasteurizing, homogenizing, bottling); natural cheese; creamery butter; condensed milk; ice cream & ice milk; roasted coffee
PA: Dairy Farmers Of America, Inc.
    1405 N 98th St
    Kansas City KS 66111
    816 801-6455

(P-695)
DEAN FOODS COMPANY
605 N J St, Tulare (93274-2845)
PHONE.................................559 687-1927
Buck Buchanan, *Branch Mgr*
EMP: 19 **Publicly Held**
SIC: 2026 Fluid milk
PA: Dean Foods Company
    2711 N Haskell Ave # 340
    Dallas TX 75204

(P-696)
DEAN FOODS COMPANY CAL INC
6408 Regio Ave, Buena Park (90620-1017)
PHONE.................................714 684-2160
Joe Scalo, *President*
Ralph Hughes, *Manager*
EMP: 40
SQ FT: 44,000
SALES (est): 5.4MM **Publicly Held**
SIC: 2026 Fluid milk
HQ: Dean Holding Company
    2711 N Haskell Ave # 340
    Dallas TX 75204
    214 303-3400

(P-697)
DEAN SOCAL LLC
Also Called: Swiss Dairy
17637 E Valley Blvd, City of Industry (91744-5731)
PHONE.................................951 734-3950
EMP: 140
SQ FT: 25,000
SALES (est): 21.1MM **Publicly Held**
WEB: www.deanfoods.com
SIC: 2026 Fluid milk

PA: Dean Foods Company
    2711 N Haskell Ave # 340
    Dallas TX 75204
    -

(P-698)
FARMDALE CREAMERY INC
1049 W Base Line St, San Bernardino (92411-2310)
PHONE.................................909 888-4938
Norman R Shotts III, *CEO*
Michael Shotts, *President*
Scott Hofferber, *CFO*
Nicholas J Sibilio, *Vice Pres*
Nicholas Sibilio, *Vice Pres*
▲ EMP: 100
SQ FT: 110,000
SALES (est): 23.7MM **Privately Held**
WEB: www.farmdale.net
SIC: 2026 2022 Buttermilk, cultured; natural cheese

(P-699)
FROGLANDERS LA JOLLA
915 Pearl St Ste A, La Jolla (92037-5073)
PHONE.................................858 459-3764
Esther Thompson, *Owner*
EMP: 12
SALES (est): 635.7K **Privately Held**
SIC: 2026 5812 5451 Fluid milk; eating places; dairy products stores

(P-700)
GENERAL MILLS INC
1055 Sandhill Ave, Carson (90746-1312)
P.O. Box 4589 (90749-4589)
PHONE.................................310 605-6108
Jeff Crandle, *Manager*
EMP: 20
SQ FT: 62,497
SALES (corp-wide): 16.8B **Publicly Held**
WEB: www.generalmills.com
SIC: 2026 2041 Yogurt; flour mixes
PA: General Mills, Inc.
    1 General Mills Blvd
    Minneapolis MN 55426
    763 764-7600

(P-701)
GOLDEN STATE MIXING INC
415 D St, Turlock (95380-5452)
P.O. Box 3046 (95381-3046)
PHONE.................................209 632-3656
Tim D Brewster, *President*
Brant Enoch, *Vice Pres*
EMP: 25 EST: 2009
SALES (est): 5MM **Privately Held**
SIC: 2026 Fluid milk

(P-702)
HERITAGE DISTRIBUTING COMPANY (PA)
Also Called: Rex Creamery
5743 Smithway St Ste 105, Commerce (90040-1548)
P.O. Box 668, Downey (90241-0668)
PHONE.................................323 838-1225
Ted S Degroot, *President*
Gary Ericks, *Accounts Mgr*
EMP: 43
SALES (est): 11MM **Privately Held**
SIC: 2026 Milk processing (pasteurizing, homogenizing, bottling)

(P-703)
HP HOOD LLC
8340 Belvedere Ave, Sacramento (95826-5902)
PHONE.................................916 379-9266
Gary Saavedra, *Branch Mgr*
EMP: 296
SALES (corp-wide): 2.2B **Privately Held**
SIC: 2026 Fluid milk
PA: Hp Hood Llc
    6 Kimball Ln Ste 400
    Lynnfield MA 01940
    617 887-8441

(P-704)
JACKSON-MITCHELL INC (PA)
Also Called: Meyenburg Goat Milk Products
1240 South Ave, Turlock (95380-5113)
P.O. Box 934 (95381-0934)
PHONE.................................209 667-0786
Robert Jackson, *Ch of Bd*
Doug Buehrle, *CFO*

Carol Jackson, *Treasurer*
Frank Fillman, *Executive*
Jonathan Mitchell, *Admin Sec*
EMP: 22
SQ FT: 11,200
SALES (est): 5.9MM **Privately Held**
WEB: www.jackson-mitchell.com
SIC: 2026 Milk, ultra-high temperature (longlife); evaporated milk; powdered milk

(P-705)
MID VALLEY MILK CO
10786 Avenue 144, Tipton (93272-9526)
PHONE.................................661 721-8419
Myron Schotanus, *Owner*
EMP: 15
SALES (est): 1.3MM **Privately Held**
SIC: 2026 Fluid milk

(P-706)
PAC FILL INC
Also Called: Sun Dairy
5471 W San Fernando Rd, Los Angeles (90039-1014)
PHONE.................................818 409-0117
Vahik Sarkissian, *CEO*
Edward Sarkissian, *Vice Pres*
Jerry Nicoghosian, *Admin Sec*
Ed Sarkissian, *Director*
EMP: 25
SQ FT: 22,000
SALES (est): 5.6MM **Privately Held**
SIC: 2026 2086 Yogurt; carbonated soft drinks, bottled & canned

(P-707)
PARAMOUNT DAIRY INC (PA)
17801 Cartwright Rd, Irvine (92614-6216)
PHONE.................................949 265-8077
Adiel Gorel Mana, *CEO*
Phillip Chang, *Branch Mgr*
▲ EMP: 28
SALES (est): 9.3MM **Privately Held**
SIC: 2026 Yogurt

(P-708)
PARAMOUNT DAIRY INC
15255 Texaco Ave, Paramount (90723-3917)
PHONE.................................562 361-1800
Phillip C Chang, *Branch Mgr*
EMP: 42
SALES (corp-wide): 9.3MM **Privately Held**
SIC: 2026 Yogurt
PA: Paramount Dairy, Inc.
    17801 Cartwright Rd
    Irvine CA 92614
    949 265-8077

(P-709)
SAPUTO DAIRY FOODS USA LLC
Also Called: Morningstar Foods
299 5th Ave, Gustine (95322-1202)
PHONE.................................209 854-6461
Richard Rosemire, *Manager*
Lisa Crist, *Human Res Mgr*
EMP: 175
SQ FT: 5,000
SALES (corp-wide): 3.7B **Privately Held**
WEB: www.morningstarfoods.com
SIC: 2026 Cream, whipped
HQ: Saputo Dairy Foods Usa, Llc
    2711 N Haske Ave Ste 3700
    Dallas TX 75204
    214 863-2300

(P-710)
SAPUTO DAIRY FOODS USA LLC
1901 Via Burton, Fullerton (92831-5341)
PHONE.................................714 772-8861
Klein Ron, *Branch Mgr*
Craig Murphy, *Manager*
EMP: 125
SALES (corp-wide): 3.7B **Privately Held**
SIC: 2026 Cream, whipped
HQ: Saputo Dairy Foods Usa, Llc
    2711 N Haske Ave Ste 3700
    Dallas TX 75204
    214 863-2300

(P-711)
STREMICKS HERITAGE FOODS LLC (HQ)
4002 Westminster Ave, Santa Ana (92703-1310)
PHONE.................................714 775-5000
Louis J Stremick, *Mng Member*
Mike Malone, *CFO*
Rob Ball, *Vice Pres*
▼ EMP: 300
SALES (est): 419.4MM
SALES (corp-wide): 13.6B **Privately Held**
WEB: www.stremicksheritagefoods.com
SIC: 2026 Cream, sour
PA: Dairy Farmers Of America, Inc.
    1405 N 98th St
    Kansas City KS 66111
    816 801-6455

(P-712)
VITAFOODS AMERICA LLC
Also Called: Dr. Shica's Healthy Surprises
680 E Colo Blvd Ste 180, Pasadena (91101)
PHONE.................................800 695-4750
Washica Little,
Ladale Jackson,
EMP: 10 **EST: 2014**
SQ FT: 900
SALES: 10MM **Privately Held**
SIC: 2026 Whipped topping, except frozen or dry mix

(P-713)
WIN SOON INC
Also Called: Epoca Yocool
4569 Firestone Blvd, South Gate (90280-3343)
PHONE.................................323 564-5070
Jun Sang Lee, *President*
Bk Yoo, *CFO*
Brian Ju, *General Mgr*
▲ EMP: 25
SQ FT: 7,000
SALES (est): 5.3MM **Privately Held**
WEB: www.winsoon.com
SIC: 2026 5149 Yogurt; soft drinks

(P-714)
WWF OPERATING COMPANY
Also Called: White Wave Foods
18275 Arenth Ave Bldg 1, City of Industry (91748-1225)
PHONE.................................626 810-1775
Bob King, *Manager*
EMP: 235
SALES (corp-wide): 762.4MM **Privately Held**
WEB: www.morningstarfoods.com
SIC: 2026 Milk processing (pasteurizing, homogenizing, bottling)
HQ: Wwf Operating Company
    12002 Airport Way
    Broomfield CO 80021
    214 303-3400

(P-715)
YOPLAIT U S A INC
1055 Sandhill Ave, Carson (90746-1332)
PHONE.................................310 632-9502
Terry Lennon, *Principal*
Doug Edman, *Director*
EMP: 20
SALES (est): 3.5MM **Privately Held**
SIC: 2026 Yogurt

2032 Canned Specialties

(P-716)
ADESA INTERNATIONAL LLC
1440 S Vineyard Ave, Ontario (91761-8042)
PHONE.................................909 321-8240
Alberto Santiago,
EMP: 24
SQ FT: 1,500
SALES (est): 2.4MM **Privately Held**
SIC: 2032 Mexican foods: packaged in cans, jars, etc.

PRODUCTS & SVCS

(P-717)
AFP ADVANCED FOOD PRODUCTS LLC
1211 E Noble Ave, Visalia (93292-3040)
P.O. Box 1551 (93279-1551)
PHONE.................................559 627-2070
Barry Ritchard, *Branch Mgr*
EMP: 130
SALES (corp-wide): 6.3B **Privately Held**
WEB: www.afpllc.com
SIC: 2032 2022 2026 Puddings, except meat: packaged in cans, jars, etc.; soups, except seafood: packaged in cans, jars, etc.; cheese spreads, dips, pastes & other cheese products; spreads, cheese; pastes, cheese; fluid milk
HQ: Afp Advanced Food Products Llc
   402 S Custer Ave
   New Holland PA 17557
   717 355-8667

(P-718)
BASTAN CORPORATION
2260 Main St Ste 17, Chula Vista (91911-3956)
PHONE.................................619 424-3416
Teresa Delenne, *President*
Alonso Anciza, *Vice Pres*
EMP: 16
SALES (est): 2MM **Privately Held**
SIC: 2032 5812 Mexican foods: packaged in cans, jars, etc.; Mexican restaurant

(P-719)
BIEN PADRE FOODS INC
1459 Railroad St, Eureka (95501-2147)
P.O. Box 3748 (95502-3748)
PHONE.................................707 442-4585
Benito Lim, *President*
Rosita Lim, *Treasurer*
Bob McCall, *Vice Pres*
Domingo Bernardo Jr, *Admin Sec*
▲ EMP: 28
SQ FT: 14,000
SALES (est): 5.4MM **Privately Held**
WEB: www.bienpadre.com
SIC: 2032 5149 2099 2096 Ethnic foods: canned, jarred, etc.; canned goods: fruit, vegetables, seafood, meats, etc.; spices & seasonings; tortillas, fresh or refrigerated; potato chips & similar snacks

(P-720)
BOBBY SLZARS MXCAN FD PDTS INC (PA)
Also Called: Bobby Salazar Corporate
2810 San Antonio Dr, Fowler (93625-9799)
PHONE.................................559 834-4787
Robert Salazar, *CEO*
Bobby Salazar, *President*
Charles Gamoian, *Vice Pres*
Charlie Lopez, *Sales Executive*
Shiela Martinez, *Sales Staff*
EMP: 25
SQ FT: 16,375
SALES: 5MM **Privately Held**
SIC: 2032 5812 Mexican foods: packaged in cans, jars, etc.; Mexican restaurant

(P-721)
CAER INC
Also Called: Yumi
129 N Laurel Ave, Los Angeles (90048-3511)
PHONE.................................415 879-9864
Angela Sutherland, *CEO*
Evelyn Rusli, *President*
▲ EMP: 27
SALES (est): 2.5MM **Privately Held**
SIC: 2032 7389 Baby foods, including meats: packaged in cans, jars, etc.;

(P-722)
CG FINANCIAL LLC
Also Called: SD Fresh Products
7020 Alamitos Ave Ste B, San Diego (92154-4710)
P.O. Box 212996, Chula Vista (91921-2996)
PHONE.................................619 656-2919
Gustavo Gonzalez Jr, *Mng Member*
Catherine Gonzalez, *President*
EMP: 15

SALES: 3.4MM **Privately Held**
SIC: 2032 Mexican foods: packaged in cans, jars, etc.

(P-723)
CORN MAIDEN FOODS INC
24201 Frampton Ave, Harbor City (90710-2105)
PHONE.................................310 784-0400
Pascal Dropsy, *President*
EMP: 65
SQ FT: 40,000
SALES (est): 12.2MM **Privately Held**
WEB: www.cornmaidenfoods.com
SIC: 2032 Canned specialties

(P-724)
DEMAIZ INC
77 S 28th St, San Jose (95116-2315)
PHONE.................................650 518-6268
Alejandro Arreola, *CEO*
Celia Madrid, *Vice Pres*
EMP: 13
SQ FT: 7,200
SALES (est): 469.1K **Privately Held**
SIC: 2032 Tamales: packaged in cans, jars, etc.

(P-725)
DOLORES CANNING COINC
1020 N Eastern Ave, Los Angeles (90063-3214)
P.O. Box 63187 (90063-0187)
PHONE.................................323 263-9155
Steve A Munoz, *CEO*
Frank T Munoz, *President*
Bert Munoz, *Sales Mgr*
EMP: 25 EST: 1956
SQ FT: 5,000
SALES (est): 1.6MM **Privately Held**
WEB: www.dolorescanning.com
SIC: 2032 2011 Mexican foods: packaged in cans, jars, etc.; meat packing plants

(P-726)
EDS WRAP AND ROLL FOODS LLC
2545 Barrington Ct, Hayward (94545-1167)
PHONE.................................510 266-0888
Chan Fan Ho, *Owner*
Ide Ng, *Co-Owner*
EMP: 20
SALES: 1.2MM **Privately Held**
SIC: 2032 Chinese foods: packaged in cans, jars, etc.

(P-727)
FRESH PACKING CORPORATION
4333 S Maywood Ave, Vernon (90058-2521)
P.O. Box 3009, Alhambra (91803-0009)
PHONE.................................213 612-0136
Monica Zambada Lopez, *CEO*
EMP: 20
SALES (est): 4.2MM **Privately Held**
SIC: 2032 Chili with or without meat: packaged in cans, jars, etc.

(P-728)
HOMESTEAD RAVIOLI COMPANY INC
Also Called: Homestead Fine Foods
315 S Maple Ave Ste 106, South San Francisco (94080-6335)
PHONE.................................650 615-0750
Terry Hall, *President*
Charles Osborne, *Treasurer*
Christopher Osborne, *Admin Sec*
EMP: 20 EST: 1904
SQ FT: 19,000
SALES (est): 2.1MM **Privately Held**
WEB: www.homesteadpasta.com
SIC: 2032 2038 5149 2098 Ravioli: packaged in cans, jars, etc.; frozen specialties; sauces; macaroni & spaghetti; pickles, sauces & salad dressings

(P-729)
IF COPACK LLC
Also Called: Initiative Foods
1912 Industrial Way, Sanger (93657-9508)
PHONE.................................559 875-3354
John Ypma, *President*
Jeff Jankovic, *CFO*

EMP: 42
SQ FT: 51,348
SALES (est): 1.2MM **Privately Held**
SIC: 2032 Baby foods, including meats: packaged in cans, jars, etc.

(P-730)
INITIATIVE FOODS LLC
1912 Industrial Way, Sanger (93657-9508)
PHONE.................................559 875-3354
John Ypma,
Richard Turner,
EMP: 130
SALES (est): 21.9MM **Privately Held**
SIC: 2032 Baby foods, including meats: packaged in cans, jars, etc.
PA: If Holding, Inc.
   1912 Industrial Way
   Sanger CA 93657
   559 875-3354

(P-731)
JIMENEZ MEXICAN FOODS INC
11010 Wells Ave, Riverside (92505-2751)
PHONE.................................951 351-0102
Roberto Jimenez, *CEO*
Veronica Jimenez, *CFO*
EMP: 20
SALES (est): 83K **Privately Held**
SIC: 2032 Mexican foods: packaged in cans, jars, etc.

(P-732)
JUANITAS FOODS
Also Called: Pico Pica Foods
645 Eubank Ave, Wilmington (90744-6055)
P.O. Box 847 (90748-0847)
PHONE.................................310 834-5339
Aaron De La Torre, *CEO*
James Steveson, *CFO*
Mark De La Torre, *Chairman*
Sam Aguilar, *Network Mgr*
Werblin Richard, *Finance Mgr*
EMP: 125
SQ FT: 85,000
SALES (est): 36.4MM **Privately Held**
WEB: www.juanitasfoods.com
SIC: 2032 Mexican foods: packaged in cans, jars, etc.

(P-733)
KINGS ASIAN GOURMET INC
683 Brannan St Unit 304, San Francisco (94107-1592)
PHONE.................................415 222-6100
Inja Wang, *President*
Jane Park, *Financial Exec*
Walter Wang, *Manager*
▲ EMP: 37
SQ FT: 25,000
SALES (est): 2.9MM **Privately Held**
WEB: www.kingsasian.com
SIC: 2032 Ethnic foods: canned, jarred, etc.

(P-734)
KRAFT HEINZ FOODS COMPANY
57 Stonebridge Ct, Tracy (95376)
PHONE.................................209 832-4269
James Brimgham, *Manager*
EMP: 50
SALES (corp-wide): 26.2B **Publicly Held**
SIC: 2032 Canned specialties
HQ: Kraft Heinz Foods Company
   1 Ppg Pl Fl 34
   Pittsburgh PA 15222
   412 456-5700

(P-735)
KRAFT HEINZ FOODS COMPANY
2450 White Rd, Irvine (92614-6250)
PHONE.................................949 250-4080
Dan Foss, *Manager*
EMP: 220
SALES (corp-wide): 26.2B **Publicly Held**
SIC: 2032 2035 Soups, except seafood: packaged in cans, jars, etc.; seasonings & sauces, except tomato & dry; dressings, salad: raw & cooked (except dry mixes)
HQ: Kraft Heinz Foods Company
   1 Ppg Pl Fl 34
   Pittsburgh PA 15222
   412 456-5700

(P-736)
LA CASCADA INC
1940 Union St Ste 10, Oakland (94607-2352)
PHONE.................................510 452-3663
Mohammad Bahrani, *President*
Mohsen Bahrani, *CFO*
Asad Bahrani, *Admin Sec*
EMP: 19
SQ FT: 2,500
SALES (est): 886.7K **Privately Held**
SIC: 2032 Mexican foods: packaged in cans, jars, etc.

(P-737)
LA INDIANA TAMALES INC
15268 Proctor Ave, City of Industry (91745-1036)
PHONE.................................323 262-4682
Raul Ramos, *President*
EMP: 32 EST: 1999
SQ FT: 8,000
SALES (est): 4.3MM **Privately Held**
WEB: www.laindianatamales.com
SIC: 2032 Tamales: packaged in cans, jars, etc.

(P-738)
MARIN FOOD SPECIALTIES INC
14800 Byron Hwy, Byron (94514)
P.O. Box 609 (94514-0609)
PHONE.................................925 634-6126
Fred J Vuylsteke, *President*
Larry Brucia, *Corp Secy*
▲ EMP: 35
SQ FT: 27,000
SALES (est): 6.4MM **Privately Held**
SIC: 2032 Canned specialties

(P-739)
MICHAEL BS LLC
22625 S Western Ave, Torrance (90501-4950)
PHONE.................................310 320-0141
Michael Boden,
EMP: 30
SALES (est): 2.4MM **Privately Held**
SIC: 2032 Canned specialties

(P-740)
NATIVE KJALII FOODS INC
1474 29th Ave, San Francisco (94122-3234)
P.O. Box 471030 (94147-1030)
PHONE.................................415 592-8670
Julie Jeremy, *CEO*
Bret Jeremy, *Shareholder*
Fred Levinson, *Vice Pres*
Sophia Rosensteel, *Manager*
EMP: 25
SQ FT: 1,000
SALES (est): 2.9MM **Privately Held**
WEB: www.sfsalsa.com
SIC: 2032 Canned specialties

(P-741)
NATURAS FOODS CALIFORNIA INC
334 Paseo Sonrisa, Walnut (91789-2720)
PHONE.................................909 594-7838
Ariel Espinoza, *President*
EMP: 15
SQ FT: 4,500
SALES (est): 1.3MM **Privately Held**
SIC: 2032 Mexican foods: packaged in cans, jars, etc.

(P-742)
PANORAMA INTL CL CO INC
200 Toland St, San Francisco (94124-1120)
PHONE.................................415 891-8478
EMP: 11
SALES (corp-wide): 8MM **Privately Held**
SIC: 2032 Italian foods: packaged in cans, jars, etc.
PA: Panorama International Clothing Company, Inc.
   0 Meadowood Dr
   Larkspur CA 94939
   415 891-8478

(P-743)
RAMONAS FOOD GROUP LLC
13633 S Western Ave, Gardena
(90249-2597)
PHONE..................................310 323-1950
Robert Banuelos-Medina, *Mng Member*
Teresa Cordova, *Plant Mgr*
Ricardo Sanchez, *Opers Staff*
Edward Medina,
EMP: 160
SQ FT: 55,000
SALES (est): 8MM **Privately Held**
SIC: 2032 Mexican foods: packaged in
cans, jars, etc.

(P-744)
REYNALDOS MEXICAN FOOD
CO LLC (PA)
3301 E Vernon Ave, Vernon (90058-1809)
PHONE..................................562 803-3188
Douglas Reed, *CFO*
Gilbert D Cardenas, *Principal*
Lonnie Cope, *Sales Dir*
Marisol Scrugham,
Al Soto, *Mng Member*
EMP: 160
SALES (est): 30.2MM **Privately Held**
WEB: www.rmfood.com
SIC: 2032 Mexican foods: packaged in
cans, jars, etc.

(P-745)
SHINE FOOD INC (PA)
19216 Normandie Ave, Torrance
(90502-1011)
PHONE..................................310 329-3829
Stephen Y S Lee, *CEO*
Tracy Lee, *Vice Pres*
▲ **EMP:** 50 **EST:** 1986
SQ FT: 30,000
SALES (est): 14.6MM **Privately Held**
WEB: www.shinefood.com
SIC: 2032 Canned specialties

(P-746)
SONOMA VALLEY FOODS INC
3645 Standish Ave, Santa Rosa
(95407-8142)
PHONE..................................707 585-2200
Rene Valencia, *CEO*
Lilly Ramos, *Marketing Mgr*
Adrian Rodriguez, *Sales Mgr*
EMP: 22
SALES (est): 4MM **Privately Held**
SIC: 2032 5411 Tortillas: packaged in
cans, jars etc.; supermarkets

(P-747)
T & T FOODS INC
Also Called: Colonel Lee's Enterprises
3080 E 50th St, Vernon (90058-2918)
PHONE..................................323 588-2158
Michelle MA, *CEO*
David MA, *Vice Pres*
EMP: 50
SQ FT: 19,000
SALES (est): 9.2MM **Privately Held**
SIC: 2032 2099 Ethnic foods: canned,
jarred, etc.; food preparations

(P-748)
TAY HO FOOD CORPORATION
2430 Cape Cod Way, Santa Ana
(92703-3540)
PHONE..................................714 973-2286
Jayce Yenson, *CEO*
Chuong Nguyen, *Vice Pres*
MAI Nguyen, *Admin Sec*
EMP: 35
SQ FT: 27,000
SALES (est): 3.7MM **Privately Held**
WEB: www.tayho.com
SIC: 2032 Ethnic foods: canned, jarred,
etc.

(P-749)
TEASDALE FOODS INC (PA)
Also Called: Teasdale Latin Foods
901 Packers St, Atwater (95301-4614)
P.O. Box 814 (95301-0814)
PHONE..................................209 358-5616
Chris Kiser, *CEO*
Russell Kenerly, *CFO*
Paula Demuria, *Ch Credit Ofcr*
Cale Nelson, *Chief Mktg Ofcr*
Jerry Cook, *Exec VP*

▼ **EMP:** 277
SQ FT: 250,000
SALES (est): 285.9MM **Privately Held**
SIC: 2032 2034 Beans, baked without
meat: packaged in cans, jars, etc.; chili
with or without meat: packaged in cans,
jars, etc.; Mexican foods: packaged in
cans, jars, etc.; dehydrated fruits, vegetables, soups

(P-750)
WEI LABORATORIES INC
3002 Scott Blvd, Santa Clara (95054-3323)
PHONE..................................408 970-8700
Jeffery WEI, *CEO*
Jeffrey Horan, *President*
Sarah LI, *Vice Pres*
Craig Condiff, *Purch Mgr*
EMP: 25
SALES (est): 3.5MM **Privately Held**
WEB: www.weilab.com
SIC: 2032 Chinese foods: packaged in
cans, jars, etc.

(P-751)
WELLINGTON FOODS INC
1930 California Ave, Corona (92881-6491)
PHONE..................................562 989-0111
Anthony H Harnack Sr, *Chairman*
Jim Melvani, *CFO*
Jim Mulvaney, *CFO*
Jose Sanchez, *Controller*
Richard Phillips, *Warehouse Mgr*
▲ **EMP:** 50 **EST:** 1974
SQ FT: 50,000
SALES (est): 13.3MM **Privately Held**
SIC: 2032 Canned specialties

(P-752)
YUCATAN FOODS LLC
9841 Arprt Blvd Ste 1578, Los Angeles
(90045)
PHONE..................................310 342-5363
Ardeshir Haerizadeh, *CEO*
Michael Modjeski, *VP Sales*
Jessica Brown, *Marketing Staff*
◆ **EMP:** 15
SALES (est): 6.1MM
SALES (corp-wide): 557.5MM **Publicly**
Held
WEB: www.avocado.com
SIC: 2032 5149 Mexican foods: packaged
in cans, jars, etc.; specialty food items
HQ: Curation Foods, Inc.
2811 Airpark Dr
Santa Maria CA 93455
800 454-1355

```
┌─────────────────────────┐
│   2033 Canned Fruits,   │
│  Vegetables & Preserves │
└─────────────────────────┘
```

(P-753)
ABSINTHE GROUP INC
2043 Airpark Ct Ste 30, Auburn
(95602-9009)
PHONE..................................530 823-8527
Kim Sullivan, *Director*
EMP: 20
SALES (corp-wide): 6.4MM **Privately**
Held
WEB: www.absinthe.com
SIC: 2033 2099 8742 2035 Barbecue
sauce: packaged in cans, jars, etc.; food
preparations; food & beverage consultant;
pickles, sauces & salad dressings
PA: The Absinthe Group Inc
368 Hayes St
San Francisco CA 94102
415 864-2693

(P-754)
AMAZON PRSRVATION
PARTNERS INC
Also Called: Zola Acai
1501a Vermont St, San Francisco
(94107-3250)
PHONE..................................415 775-6355
Chris Cuvelier, *CEO*
Devin Cardoza, *Sales Staff*
Ben Winter, *Director*
▲ **EMP:** 24
SQ FT: 1,500

SALES (est): 6.9MM **Privately Held**
WEB: www.zolaacai.com
SIC: 2033 Fruit juices: fresh

(P-755)
BEAUMONT JUICE INC
Also Called: Perricone Juices
550 B St, Beaumont (92223-2672)
PHONE..................................951 769-7171
Robert Paul Rovzar, *CEO*
Joe Perricone, *CFO*
Paul Golub, *Treasurer*
Thomas M Carmody, *Principal*
Jose Grajeda, *Maintence Staff*
▲ **EMP:** 98
SQ FT: 30,000
SALES (est): 29.6MM
SALES (corp-wide): 5.3MM **Privately**
Held
SIC: 2033 Fruit juices: fresh
PA: G B & P Citrus Co Inc
1601 E Olympic Blvd # 111
Los Angeles CA 90021
213 312-1380

(P-756)
BELL-CARTER FOODS INC
Also Called: Bell-Carter Packaging
4207 Finch Rd, Modesto (95357-4101)
PHONE..................................209 549-5939
Bill Floyd, *Manager*
Michael Mitchell, *Plant Mgr*
Kathleen Creech, *Manager*
Rosemary Rando, *Manager*
EMP: 20
SALES (corp-wide): 145.3MM **Privately**
Held
WEB: www.bellcarter.com
SIC: 2033 Olives: packaged in cans, jars,
etc.
PA: Bell-Carter Foods, Llc
590 Ygnacio Valley Rd # 300
Walnut Creek CA 94596
209 549-5939

(P-757)
BELL-CARTER FOODS LLC (PA)
Also Called: Bell-Carter Olive Company
590 Ygnacio Valley Rd # 300, Walnut Creek
(94596-3807)
PHONE..................................209 549-5939
Timothy T Carter, *CEO*
John Toth, *CFO*
Paul Adcock, *Exec VP*
Doug Reifsteck, *Exec VP*
Paul McGinty, *Vice Pres*
◆ **EMP:** 277 **EST:** 1912
SQ FT: 9,000
SALES (est): 145.3MM **Privately Held**
WEB: www.bellcarter.com
SIC: 2033 Olives: packaged in cans, jars,
etc.

(P-758)
BIG HEART PET BRANDS
Also Called: Del Monte Foods 48
18284 S Harlan Rd, Lathrop (95330-8757)
PHONE..................................209 547-7200
Glenn Lewis, *Manager*
Ken Shamp, *Finance Mgr*
EMP: 15
SALES (corp-wide): 7.8B **Publicly Held**
SIC: 2033 5149 Fruits & fruit products in
cans, jars, etc.; canned goods: fruit, veg-
etables, seafood, meats, etc.
HQ: Big Heart Pet Brands, Inc.
1 Maritime Plz Fl 2
San Francisco CA 94111
415 247-3000

(P-759)
BIG HEART PET BRANDS
Also Called: Star-Kist
24700 Main St, Carson (90745-6321)
PHONE..................................310 519-3791
EMP: 190
SALES (corp-wide): 5.6B **Publicly Held**
SIC: 2033
HQ: Big Heart Pet Brands
1 Maritime Plz Fl 2
San Francisco CA 94111
415 247-3000

(P-760)
CALIFORNIA TREATS INC
Also Called: Betty Clark's Confections
2131 Tyler Ave, El Monte (91733-2754)
PHONE..................................626 454-4099
Steve Nelson, *President*
EMP: 60
SQ FT: 25,818
SALES (est): 4.7MM **Privately Held**
WEB: www.caltreats.com
SIC: 2033 2034 2035 2099 Jellies, edi-
ble, including imitation: in cans, jars, etc.;
soup mixes; seasonings, meat sauces
(except tomato & dry); food preparations;
potato chips & similar snacks; popcorn
balls or other treated popcorn products

(P-761)
DEL MAR FOOD PRODUCTS
CORP
1720 Beach Rd, Watsonville (95076-9536)
P.O. Box 891 (95077-0891)
PHONE..................................831 722-3516
P J Mecozzi, *CEO*
Wayne Jordan, *CFO*
Paul Wendt, *CFO*
Carolyn Mecozzi, *Treasurer*
Roger Wyant, *Vice Pres*
◆ **EMP:** 500
SQ FT: 53,408
SALES (est): 113.6MM **Privately Held**
WEB: www.delmarfoods.com
SIC: 2033 2099 Canned fruits & special-
ties; food preparations

(P-762)
DEL MONTE FOODS INC
1509 Draper St Ste A, Kingsburg
(93631-1950)
PHONE..................................559 419-9214
Brian Okland, *Manager*
EMP: 85
SQ FT: 111,920 **Privately Held**
SIC: 2033 Fruits: packaged in cans, jars,
etc.; vegetables: packaged in cans, jars,
etc.; preserves, including imitation: in
cans, jars, etc.; jams, including imitation:
packaged in cans, jars, etc.
HQ: Del Monte Foods, Inc.
3003 Oak Rd Ste 600
Walnut Creek CA 94597
925 949-2772

(P-763)
DEL MONTE FOODS INC
10652 Jackson Ave, Hanford (93230-9552)
PHONE..................................559 639-6160
Ted Leaman, *Manager*
Phil McNabb, *Warehouse Mgr*
Ryan Fischer, *Maintence Staff*
EMP: 104 **Privately Held**
SIC: 2033 2035 Tomato paste: packaged
in cans, jars, etc.; tomato purees: pack-
aged in cans, jars, etc.; tomato sauce:
packaged in cans, jars, etc.; pickles,
sauces & salad dressings
HQ: Del Monte Foods, Inc.
3003 Oak Rd Ste 600
Walnut Creek CA 94597
925 949-2772

(P-764)
DEL MONTE FOODS INC
4000 Yosemite Blvd, Modesto
(95357-1580)
P.O. Box 576008 (95357-6008)
PHONE..................................209 548-5509
Jim Fullmer, *Manager*
Ron Collins, *Engineer*
Jacob Gaston, *Engineer*
Robin McConnell, *Purch Mgr*
Scott Nielsen, *Manager*
EMP: 280
SQ FT: 5,000 **Privately Held**
SIC: 2033 Tomato purees: packaged in
cans, jars, etc.
HQ: Del Monte Foods, Inc.
3003 Oak Rd Ste 600
Walnut Creek CA 94597
925 949-2772

(P-765)
DEL MONTE FOODS INC (HQ)
3003 Oak Rd Ste 600, Walnut Creek
(94597-4501)
PHONE..................................925 949-2772

P
R
O
D
U
C
T
S

&

S
V
C
S

Nils Lommerin, *CEO*
Paul Miller, *CFO*
Alfred Artis, *Treasurer*
Bibie Wu, *Chief Mktg Ofcr*
Robert Long, *Vice Pres*
◆ **EMP:** 125 **EST:** 2013
SALES (est): 1B **Privately Held**
SIC: 2033 5149 Canned fruits & specialties; groceries & related products

(P-766)
EARTH & VINE PROVISIONS INC
160 Flocchini Cir, Lincoln (95648-1700)
P.O. Box 1637, Loomis (95650-1637)
PHONE......................916 434-8399
Tressa Cooper, *President*
Ron Cooper, *CFO*
EMP: 10 **EST:** 1997
SQ FT: 5,000
SALES (est): 1MM **Privately Held**
SIC: 2033 2099 5149 Jams, jellies & preserves: packaged in cans, jars, etc.; sauces: gravy, dressing & dip mixes; sauces

(P-767)
EL BURRITO MXICAN FD PDTS CORP
14944 Don Julian Rd, City of Industry (91746-3111)
P.O. Box 90125 (91715-0125)
PHONE......................626 369-7828
Tatsumi Yamaguchi, *CEO*
Shigeru Natake, *President*
Shige Harukoga, *CFO*
Catalina Castillo, *Manager*
EMP: 16
SALES (est): 2.6MM
SALES (corp-wide): 1.9MM **Privately Held**
SIC: 2033 2099 Canned fruits & specialties; food preparations
PA: House Foods Holding Usa Inc.
14944 Don Julian Rd
City Of Industry CA 91746
626 369-7828

(P-768)
FRUIT FILLINGS INC
2531 E Edgar Ave, Fresno (93706-5410)
PHONE......................559 237-4715
Sg Norcross, *CEO*
Stephen Norcross, *President*
Keith Siemens, *Treasurer*
Everett Norcross III, *Admin Sec*
▼ **EMP:** 25
SQ FT: 3,600
SALES (est): 9.1MM **Privately Held**
WEB: www.fruitfillings.com
SIC: 2033 Fruit pie mixes & fillings: packaged in cans, jars, etc.

(P-769)
FRUSELVA USA LLC
4440 Von Karman Ave, Newport Beach (92660-2088)
PHONE......................949 798-0061
Javi Hernandez, *Mng Member*
◆ **EMP:** 10
SALES (est): 227.8K **Privately Held**
SIC: 2033 Fruits: packaged in cans, jars, etc.

(P-770)
G L MEZZETTA INC
105 Mezzetta Ct, American Canyon (94503-9604)
PHONE......................707 648-1050
Jeffery Mezzetta, *CEO*
Ronald J Mezzetta, *President*
◆ **EMP:** 80
SQ FT: 35,000
SALES (est): 32.1MM **Privately Held**
SIC: 2033 Pizza sauce: packaged in cans, jars, etc.; spaghetti & other pasta sauce: packaged in cans, jars, etc.

(P-771)
GEORGE DELALLO COMPANY INC
Also Called: Delallo Italian Foods
1800 Idora St, Oroville (95966-6767)
PHONE......................530 533-3303
George Hoag, *Manager*
Jose Gonzales, *Executive*
EMP: 20

SQ FT: 48,750
SALES (corp-wide): 183.1MM **Privately Held**
SIC: 2033 Olives: packaged in cans, jars, etc.
PA: George Delallo Company, Inc.
1 Delallo Way
Mount Pleasant PA 15666
724 925-2222

(P-772)
HAPPY GIRL KITCHEN CO
173 Central Ave, Pacific Grove (93950-3015)
PHONE......................831 373-4475
Todd Champagne, *Owner*
Jessica J Champagne, *Co-Owner*
EMP: 10
SQ FT: 2,700
SALES: 300K **Privately Held**
SIC: 2033 Preserves, including imitation: in cans, jars, etc.

(P-773)
HEIDENS INC
Also Called: Heiden's Foods
2900 E Blue Star St, Anaheim (92806-2509)
PHONE......................714 525-3414
Robert E Heiden, *President*
Dawne Walker, *Corp Secy*
Derek Walker, *Vice Pres*
Valerie Uribe, *Manager*
EMP: 12
SQ FT: 10,000
SALES (est): 1.9MM **Privately Held**
WEB: www.heidensfoods.com
SIC: 2033 2032 Barbecue sauce: packaged in cans, jars, etc.; soups, except seafood: packaged in cans, jars, etc.

(P-774)
HIGHLAND WHOLESALE FOODS INC
1604 Tillie Lewis Dr, Stockton (95206-1159)
PHONE......................209 933-0580
T Gregory Stagnitto, *President*
Bill Burch, *COO*
Tommy Sodaro, *Senior VP*
Melissa Hobbie, *Director*
▼ **EMP:** 49
SQ FT: 140,000
SALES (est): 20.2MM **Privately Held**
SIC: 2033 Canned fruits & specialties

(P-775)
HK CANNING INC (PA)
130 N Garden St, Ventura (93001-2529)
PHONE......................805 652-1392
Henry Knaust, *President*
Carol Knaust, *Vice Pres*
EMP: 21
SQ FT: 91,552
SALES: 4MM **Privately Held**
SIC: 2033 Vegetables: packaged in cans, jars, etc.

(P-776)
HUY FONG FOODS INC
4800 Azusa Canyon Rd, Irwindale (91706-1938)
PHONE......................626 286-8328
David Tran, *President*
Ada Tran, *CFO*
Donna Lam, *Admin Sec*
Tiffany Lam, *IT/INT Sup*
◆ **EMP:** 20 **EST:** 1980
SQ FT: 68,000
SALES (est): 6.1MM **Privately Held**
SIC: 2033 Chili sauce, tomato: packaged in cans, jars, etc.

(P-777)
INGOMAR PACKING COMPANY LLC (PA)
9950 S Ingomar Grade, Los Banos (93635)
P.O. Box 1448 (93635-1448)
PHONE......................209 826-9494
Gregory Pruett, *President*
Dan Green, *CFO*
William B Cahill Jr, *Vice Pres*
John F Bennett,
◆ **EMP:** 100
SQ FT: 10,000

SALES (est): 70.7MM **Privately Held**
WEB: www.ingomarpacking.com
SIC: 2033 Tomato paste: packaged in cans, jars, etc.

(P-778)
J M SMUCKER COMPANY
800 Commercial Ave, Oxnard (93030-7234)
P.O. Box 5161 (93031-5161)
PHONE......................805 487-5483
Al Yamamoto, *Manager*
Daniel Cabrera, *Engineer*
Linda Vaccani, *Manager*
EMP: 25
SQ FT: 20,000
SALES (corp-wide): 7.8B **Publicly Held**
WEB: www.smuckers.com
SIC: 2033 Canned fruits & specialties
PA: The J M Smucker Company
1 Strawberry Ln
Orrville OH 44667
330 682-3000

(P-779)
JG BOSWELL TOMATO - KERN LLC
36889 Hwy 58, Buttonwillow (93206)
PHONE......................661 764-9000
Sherm Railsback,
James W Boswell, *Principal*
Joel Molina, *Accounting Mgr*
◆ **EMP:** 33
SQ FT: 1,080
SALES (est): 11.6MM **Privately Held**
WEB: www.riobravotomato.com
SIC: 2033 Tomato products: packaged in cans, jars, etc.

(P-780)
JUICE HEADS INC
Also Called: Lorton's Fresh Squeezed Juices
735 E Base Line St, San Bernardino (92410-3912)
PHONE......................909 386-7933
Fax: 909 884-6297
EMP: 10
SQ FT: 10,000
SALES (est): 561.8K
SALES (corp-wide): 1.3B **Privately Held**
SIC: 2033 4212
HQ: Sunopta Global Organic Ingredients Inc.
100 Enterprise Way Ste B1
Scotts Valley CA 95066

(P-781)
KADBANOU LLC
1951 Gardena Ave, Glendale (91204-2910)
PHONE......................818 409-0118
Vahik Sarkissian, *Mng Member*
EMP: 10
SALES (est): 821.6K **Privately Held**
SIC: 2033 Fruits & fruit products in cans, jars, etc.; vegetables & vegetable products in cans, jars, etc.

(P-782)
KAGOME INC (HQ)
333 Johnson Rd, Los Banos (93635-9768)
PHONE......................209 826-8850
Luis De Oliviera, *President*
Pete Watanabe, *CFO*
Ann Hall, *Vice Pres*
Molly Miller, *Vice Pres*
Cynthia Fritz, *Technician*
◆ **EMP:** 194
SQ FT: 175,000
SALES (est): 72.2MM **Privately Held**
WEB: www.kagomeusa.com
SIC: 2033 Tomato products: packaged in cans, jars, etc.

(P-783)
KOZLOWSKI FARMS A CORPORATION
5566 Hwy 116, Forestville (95436-9697)
PHONE......................707 887-1587
Cindy Kozlowski Hayworth, *CEO*
Carol Kozlowski Every, *Vice Pres*
EMP: 20 **EST:** 1949
SQ FT: 8,000

SALES (est): 3.6MM **Privately Held**
WEB: www.kozlowskifarms.com
SIC: 2033 5149 2035 2099 Jams, jellies & preserves: packaged in cans, jars, etc.; fruit butters: packaged in cans, jars, etc.; condiments; sauces; pickles, sauces & salad dressings; vinegar

(P-784)
KRAFT HEINZ FOODS COMPANY
Also Called: Kraft Foods
3971 E Airport Dr, Ontario (91761-1538)
PHONE......................909 605-7201
Tony Iannello, *Manager*
EMP: 10
SALES (corp-wide): 26.2B **Publicly Held**
WEB: www.kraftfoods.com
SIC: 2033 Canned fruits & specialties
HQ: Kraft Heinz Foods Company
1 Ppg Pl Fl 34
Pittsburgh PA 15222
412 456-5700

(P-785)
KRAFT HEINZ FOODS COMPANY
Also Called: Kraft Foods
2494 S Orange Ave, Fresno (93725-1328)
PHONE......................559 441-8515
Mark Librizzi, *Branch Mgr*
Ben Farias, *Opers Staff*
EMP: 400
SQ FT: 167,590
SALES (corp-wide): 26.2B **Publicly Held**
WEB: www.kraftfoods.com
SIC: 2033 Fruit juices: packaged in cans, jars, etc.
HQ: Kraft Heinz Foods Company
1 Ppg Pl Fl 34
Pittsburgh PA 15222
412 456-5700

(P-786)
KRAFT HEINZ FOODS COMPANY
2603 Camino Ramon Ste 180, San Ramon (94583-9127)
PHONE......................925 242-4504
EMP: 15
SALES (corp-wide): 18.3B **Publicly Held**
SIC: 2033
HQ: Heinz Kraft Foods Company
1 Ppg Pl Ste 3200
Pittsburgh PA 15222
412 456-5700

(P-787)
KRAFT HEINZ FOODS COMPANY
1905 Mchenry Ave, Escalon (95320-9601)
PHONE......................209 552-6021
Scott Adrian, *Branch Mgr*
EMP: 300
SALES (corp-wide): 26.2B **Publicly Held**
SIC: 2033 Canned fruits & specialties
HQ: Kraft Heinz Foods Company
1 Ppg Pl Fl 34
Pittsburgh PA 15222
412 456-5700

(P-788)
LANDEC CORPORATION (PA)
5201 Great America Pkwy # 232, Santa Clara (95054-1126)
PHONE......................650 306-1650
Albert D Bolles, *President*
Andrew Powell, *Ch of Bd*
Ronald L Midyett, *COO*
Gregory S Skinner, *CFO*
Matt Glover, *Officer*
EMP: 96
SQ FT: 3,657
SALES: 557.5MM **Publicly Held**
WEB: www.landec.com
SIC: 2033 5148 5999 Fruits: packaged in cans, jars, etc.; vegetables: packaged in cans, jars, etc.; fresh fruits & vegetables; medical apparatus & supplies

(P-789)
LIDESTRI FOODS INC
Also Called: International Co-Packing Co
568 S Temperance Ave, Fresno (93727-6601)
PHONE......................559 251-1000
Willie Bynum, *Branch Mgr*
EMP: 100

SALES (corp-wide): 247.9MM **Privately Held**
WEB: www.francescorinaldi.com
SIC: **2033** Spaghetti & other pasta sauce: packaged in cans, jars, etc.; tomato products: packaged in cans, jars, etc.
PA: Lidestri Foods, Inc.
815 Whitney Rd W
Fairport NY 14450
585 377-7700

(P-790)
LLC LYONS MAGNUS (PA)
3158 E Hamilton Ave, Fresno
(93702-4163)
PHONE.................559 268-5966
Ed Carolan, *CEO*
Ian Yrigollen, *Business Anlyst*
Osvaldo Velazquez, *Human Resources*
Connor Monroe, *Sales Staff*
Tom Moore, *Senior Mgr*
◆ EMP: 285 EST: 1967
SQ FT: 63,000
SALES (est): 234.2MM **Privately Held**
WEB: www.lyonsmagnus.com
SIC: **2033** 2026 2087 Jams, including imitation: packaged in cans, jars, etc.; jellies, edible, including imitation: in cans, jars, etc.; preserves, including imitation: in cans, jars, etc.; fruit pie mixes & fillings: packaged in cans, jars, etc.; yogurt; syrups, flavoring (except drink); extracts, flavoring

(P-791)
LOS GATOS TOMATO PRODUCTS LLC (PA)
7041 N Van Ness Blvd, Fresno
(93711-7169)
P.O. Box 429, Huron (93234-0429)
PHONE.................559 945-2700
Reuben Peterson, *Mng Member*
Beatriz Mota, *Controller*
Brandon Clement, *Manager*
◆ EMP: 20
SQ FT: 35,000
SALES (est): 5.1MM **Privately Held**
WEB: www.losgatostomato.com
SIC: **2033** Tomato paste: packaged in cans, jars, etc.

(P-792)
LOS OLIVOS PACKAGING INC (PA)
929 Ridgecrest St, Monterey Park
(91754-4622)
PHONE.................323 261-2218
Fax: 323 261-1026
▲ EMP: 105 EST: 1925
SQ FT: 22,000
SALES (est): 9.3MM **Privately Held**
SIC: **2033**

(P-793)
LYONS MAGNUS INC
1636 S 2nd St, Fresno (93702-4143)
PHONE.................559 268-5966
Robert E Smittcamp, *Branch Mgr*
Rich Connor, *President*
Jim Davis, *Executive*
Ken Atkins, *Maintenance Dir*
EMP: 30
SALES (corp-wide): 234.2MM **Privately Held**
SIC: **2033** 2026 2087 Jams, including imitation: packaged in cans, jars, etc.; jellies, edible, including imitation: in cans, jars, etc.; preserves, including imitation: in cans, jars, etc.; fruit pie mixes & fillings: packaged in cans, jars, etc.; yogurt; syrups, flavoring (except drink); extracts, flavoring
PA: Lyons Magnus, Llc
3158 E Hamilton Ave
Fresno CA 93702
559 268-5966

(P-794)
MANGIA INC
1 Marconi Ste F, Irvine (92618-2560)
PHONE.................949 581-1274
Matt A Maslowski, *President*
Joe Wirth, *Accountant*
Lisa Malilay, *Director*
Rachel Zimmerman, *Director*
▲ EMP: 12

SALES (est): 2.6MM **Privately Held**
WEB: www.mangiainc.com
SIC: **2033** Canned fruits & specialties

(P-795)
MANZANA PRODUCTS CO INC
9141 Green Valley Rd, Sebastopol
(95472-2245)
P.O. Box 209 (95473-0209)
PHONE.................707 823-5313
Jean-Jacques Ducom, *CEO*
Suzanne C Kaido, *President*
Richard H Norton, *Treasurer*
Ralph E Sandborn, *Vice Pres*
Edith Norton, *Admin Sec*
◆ EMP: 40 EST: 1920
SQ FT: 91,000
SALES (est): 12MM **Privately Held**
SIC: **2033** 2099 Apple sauce: packaged in cans, jars, etc.; fruit juices: packaged in cans, jars, etc.; vinegar

(P-796)
MONTEREY BAY BEVERAGE CO INC
14535 Benefit St Unit 4, Sherman Oaks
(91403-3741)
PHONE.................818 784-4885
EMP: 25
SQ FT: 5,500
SALES (est): 2.1MM **Privately Held**
SIC: **2033** 5921

(P-797)
MORNING STAR COMPANY
Also Called: Morning Star Packing
13448 Volta Rd, Los Banos (93635-9785)
PHONE.................209 827-2724
Chris Rufer, *President*
EMP: 60
SALES (corp-wide): 49.2MM **Privately Held**
SIC: **2033** Tomato paste: packaged in cans, jars, etc.
PA: The Morning Star Company
724 Main St Ste 202
Woodland CA 95695
530 666-6600

(P-798)
MORNING STAR PACKING CO LP
12045 Ingomar Grade, Los Banos
(93635-9796)
PHONE.................209 826-8000
Greg Wuttke, *Marketing Staff*
EMP: 45
SALES (corp-wide): 28.7MM **Privately Held**
SIC: **2033** Tomato paste: packaged in cans, jars, etc.
PA: The Morning Star Packing Company LP
13448 Volta Rd
Los Banos CA 93635
209 826-8000

(P-799)
MORNING STAR PACKING CO LP
2211 Old Highway 99, Williams (95987)
PHONE.................530 473-3642
Rich Rostomily, *Branch Mgr*
EMP: 30
SALES (corp-wide): 28.7MM **Privately Held**
SIC: **2033** Tomato paste: packaged in cans, jars, etc.
PA: The Morning Star Packing Company LP
13448 Volta Rd
Los Banos CA 93635
209 826-8000

(P-800)
MOTU GLOBAL LLC
924 W 9th St, Upland (91786-4576)
PHONE.................801 471-7800
EMP: 25
SQ FT: 8,200
SALES: 10K **Privately Held**
SIC: **2033**

(P-801)
NASCO GOURMET FOODS INC
Also Called: Platinum Distribution
22720 Savi Ranch Pkwy, Yorba Linda
(92887-4608)
PHONE.................714 279-2100
Burhan Nasser, *President*
Mary Beth Nasser, *Corp Secy*
Jerry Pascoe, *Vice Pres*
EMP: 65
SQ FT: 42,000
SALES (est): 17.6MM
SALES (corp-wide): 133.7MM **Privately Held**
WEB: www.platinum-distribution.com
SIC: **2033** Seasonings, tomato: packaged in cans, jars, etc.
PA: Nasser Company, Inc.
22720 Savi Ranch Pkwy
Yorba Linda CA 92887
714 279-2100

(P-802)
NEIL JONES FOOD COMPANY
San Benito Foods
711 Sally St, Hollister (95023-3934)
P.O. Box 100 (95024-0100)
PHONE.................831 637-0573
Steven Arnoldy, *Manager*
George Micha, *IT/INT Sup*
Carlos Flores, *Plant Mgr*
Luis Solorio, *Prdtn Mgr*
Ronnie Leyva, *Production*
EMP: 80
SALES (corp-wide): 40.8MM **Privately Held**
SIC: **2033** Canned fruits & specialties
PA: The Neil Jones Food Company
1701 W 16th St
Vancouver WA 98660
360 696-4356

(P-803)
NEIL JONES FOOD COMPANY
Also Called: Toma Tek
2502 N St, Firebaugh (93622-2456)
P.O. Box 8 (93622-0008)
PHONE.................559 659-5100
Steve Arnoldy, *Vice Pres*
EMP: 25
SALES (corp-wide): 40.8MM **Privately Held**
WEB: www.neiljonesfoodcompany.com
SIC: **2033** Tomato products: packaged in cans, jars, etc.
PA: The Neil Jones Food Company
1701 W 16th St
Vancouver WA 98660
360 696-4356

(P-804)
NU-HEALTH CALIFORNIA LLC
16910 Cherie Pl, Carson (90746-1305)
P.O. Box 12376, Marina Del Rey (90295-3376)
PHONE.................800 806-0519
Dmitriy Sharin,
Sabrina Jaramillo, *Executive*
EMP: 15 EST: 2015
SALES: 800K **Privately Held**
SIC: **2033** Canned fruits & specialties

(P-805)
OASIS FOODS INC
10881 Toews Ave, Le Grand (95333-9754)
PHONE.................209 382-0263
Eric Stephen Bocks, *President*
Lorraine Bocks, *Corp Secy*
EMP: 50 EST: 1975
SQ FT: 3,367
SALES (est): 5.5MM **Privately Held**
WEB: www.oasisfoodsinc.com
SIC: **2033** Fruits & fruit products in cans, jars, etc.

(P-806)
ODWALLA INC
700 Isis Ave, Inglewood (90301-2913)
PHONE.................310 342-3920
Doug Kinsey, *Manager*
EMP: 30
SALES (corp-wide): 31.8B **Publicly Held**
WEB: www.odwalla.com
SIC: **2033** Fruit juices: packaged in cans, jars, etc.; vegetable juices: packaged in cans, jars, etc.

HQ: Odwalla, Inc.
1 Coca Cola Plz Nw
Atlanta GA 30313
479 721-6260

(P-807)
ODWALLA INC
1805 Las Plumas Ave, San Jose
(95133-1706)
PHONE.................408 254-5800
Ron Kennedy, *Principal*
EMP: 20
SALES (corp-wide): 31.8B **Publicly Held**
WEB: www.odwalla.com
SIC: **2033** Fruit juices: packaged in cans, jars, etc.; vegetable juices: packaged in cans, jars, etc.
HQ: Odwalla, Inc.
1 Coca Cola Plz Nw
Atlanta GA 30313
479 721-6260

(P-808)
OH JUICE INC
5631 Palmer Way Ste A, Carlsbad
(92010-7243)
PHONE.................619 318-0207
Hanna Gregor, *CEO*
Michael Mendoza, *Shareholder*
EMP: 15 EST: 2013
SALES (est): 581.4K **Privately Held**
SIC: **2033** Fruit juices: packaged in cans, jars, etc.; vegetable juices: packaged in cans, jars, etc.

(P-809)
OLAM TOMATO PROCESSORS INC
1175 S 19th Ave, Lemoore (93245)
PHONE.................559 447-1390
EMP: 13
SALES (corp-wide): 22.2B **Privately Held**
SIC: **2033** Tomato sauce: packaged in cans, jars, etc.
HQ: Olam Tomato Processors, Inc.
205 E River Park Cir # 310
Fresno CA 93720
-

(P-810)
OLAM TOMATO PROCESSORS INC (DH)
205 E River Park Cir # 310, Fresno
(93720-1571)
P.O. Box 160, Lemoore (93245-0160)
PHONE.................559 447-1390
Sunny Verghese, *CEO*
Greg Estep, *President*
John Gibbons, *Principal*
◆ EMP: 56
SALES (est): 71.5K
SALES (corp-wide): 22.2B **Privately Held**
SIC: **2033** 0723 Tomato sauce: packaged in cans, jars, etc.; crop preparation services for market
HQ: Olam Americas Inc
25 Union Pl Ste 3
Fresno CA 93720
559 447-1390

(P-811)
OLAM WEST COAST INC
Also Called: Olam Spices and Vegetables
1400 Churchill Downs Ave, Woodland
(95776-6113)
PHONE.................530 473-4290
Rich Freidas, *Branch Mgr*
EMP: 800
SALES (corp-wide): 22.2B **Privately Held**
SIC: **2033** Tomato products: packaged in cans, jars, etc.
HQ: Olam West Coast, Inc.
205 E Rver Pk Pl Ste 3
Fresno CA 93720
559 447-1390

(P-812)
OLIVE MUSCO PRODUCTS INC (PA)
Also Called: Musco Family Olive Co
17950 Via Nicolo, Tracy (95377-9767)
PHONE.................209 836-4600
Nicholas Musco, *CEO*
Felix Musco, *CEO*
Scott Hamilton, *CFO*

John Hamliton, *CFO*
Bill McFarland, *Vice Pres*
▲ **EMP:** 300
SQ FT: 350,000
SALES (est): 95.7MM **Privately Held**
SIC: 2033 2035 Canned fruits & specialties; olives, brined: bulk

(P-813)
PACIFIC COAST PRODUCERS
741 S Stockton St, Lodi (95240-4809)
P.O. Box 880 (95241-0880)
PHONE......................209 334-3352
Mike Van Gundy, *Branch Mgr*
Sotheara Ong, *Production*
EMP: 60
SALES (corp-wide): 806.2MM **Privately Held**
SIC: 2033 Vegetables: packaged in cans, jars, etc.; fruits: packaged in cans, jars, etc.
PA: Pacific Coast Producers
　631 N Cluff Ave
　Lodi CA 95240
　209 367-8800

(P-814)
PACIFIC COAST PRODUCERS (PA)
631 N Cluff Ave, Lodi (95240-0756)
P.O. Box 1600 (95241-1600)
PHONE......................209 367-8800
Daniel L Vincent, *CEO*
Dale Waldschmitt, *COO*
Matthew Strong, *CFO*
Zeb Rocha, *Treasurer*
Andrew K Russick, *Vice Pres*
◆ **EMP:** 300
SQ FT: 20,000
SALES: 806.2MM **Privately Held**
WEB: www.pcoastp.com
SIC: 2033 Fruits: packaged in cans, jars, etc.; vegetables: packaged in cans, jars, etc.

(P-815)
PACIFIC COAST PRODUCERS
1601 Mitchell Ave, Oroville (95965-5863)
P.O. Box 311 (95965-0311)
PHONE......................530 533-4311
Niraj Raj, *Principal*
Kim Bryson, *Vice Pres*
Tom Deel, *Supervisor*
EMP: 140
SQ FT: 60,000
SALES (corp-wide): 806.2MM **Privately Held**
SIC: 2033 Fruits: packaged in cans, jars, etc.; vegetables: packaged in cans, jars, etc.
PA: Pacific Coast Producers
　631 N Cluff Ave
　Lodi CA 95240
　209 367-8800

(P-816)
PACIFIC COAST PRODUCERS
Also Called: Contadina Foods
1376 Lemen Ave, Woodland (95776-3369)
PHONE......................530 662-8661
Craig Powell, *Branch Mgr*
EMP: 400
SALES (corp-wide): 806.2MM **Privately Held**
SIC: 2033 Canned fruits & specialties
PA: Pacific Coast Producers
　631 N Cluff Ave
　Lodi CA 95240
　209 367-8800

(P-817)
PRESS BROTHERS JUICERY LLC
2551 Beverly Blvd Ste A, Los Angeles (90057-1020)
P.O. Box 27699 (90027-0699)
PHONE......................213 389-3645
Jack David Jones,
EMP: 20
SALES: 800K **Privately Held**
SIC: 2033 5499 Fruit juices: fresh; juices, fruit or vegetable

(P-818)
PURITY ORGANICS INC
14900 W Belmont Ave, Kerman (93630-9602)
PHONE......................559 842-5600
Nick Koretoff, *CEO*
Greg Holzman, *President*
Todd Fenton, *Vice Pres*
Kayte Mooney, *Regional Mgr*
Liza Bennett, *Controller*
EMP: 25
SQ FT: 10,000
SALES (est): 7.5MM **Privately Held**
WEB: www.purityorganic.com
SIC: 2033 Fruit juices: fresh

(P-819)
PURVEYORS KITCHEN
2043 Airpark Ct Ste 30, Auburn (95602-9009)
PHONE......................530 823-8527
Karen Foley, *CEO*
John Foley, *Principal*
EMP: 20
SALES (est): 5MM
SALES (corp-wide): 6.4MM **Privately Held**
SIC: 2033 2099 8742 2035 Barbecue sauce: packaged in cans, jars, etc.; food preparations; food & beverage consultant; pickles, sauces & salad dressings
PA: The Absinthe Group Inc
　368 Hayes St
　San Francisco CA 94102
　415 864-2693

(P-820)
RIO PLUMA COMPANY LLC (HQ)
1900 Highway 99, Gridley (95948-9401)
P.O. Box 948 (95948-0948)
PHONE......................530 846-5200
Brad Stapleton, *President*
Eric Heitman,
Gavin Heitman,
◆ **EMP:** 32
SQ FT: 100,000
SALES (est): 5.2MM
SALES (corp-wide): 58.9MM **Privately Held**
SIC: 2033 2034 2068 0723 Fruits & fruit products in cans, jars, etc.; dried & dehydrated fruits; nuts: dried, dehydrated, salted or roasted; fruit crops market preparation services
PA: Stapleton - Spence Packing Co.
　1900 State Highway 99
　Gridley CA 95948
　408 297-8815

(P-821)
ROBEKS CORPORATION
Also Called: Robeks Juice
3891 Overland Ave, Culver City (90232-3306)
PHONE......................310 838-2332
Cesar Torres, *Manager*
EMP: 11 **Privately Held**
SIC: 2033 5149 Fruit juices: fresh; juices
PA: Robeks Corporation
　5220 Pacific Concourse Dr
　Los Angeles CA 90045

(P-822)
SAN JOAQUIN TOMATO GROWERS INC
22001 E St, Crows Landing (95313)
P.O. Box 578 (95313-0578)
PHONE......................209 837-4721
Thomas Perez, *President*
Earl Perez, *Vice Pres*
EMP: 10
SALES (est): 9MM **Privately Held**
SIC: 2033 Tomato products: packaged in cans, jars, etc.

(P-823)
SFFI COMPANY INC (PA)
Also Called: Simply Fresh Fruit
4383 Exchange Ave, Vernon (90058-2619)
PHONE......................323 586-0000
William T Sander, *President*
Bruce Spiro, *Vice Pres*
Jaxon Potter, *General Mgr*
Dominic Marlia, *Purchasing*
Rafael Raya, *Purchasing*

▲ **EMP:** 58
SQ FT: 65,000
SALES (est): 26.8MM **Privately Held**
SIC: 2033 Canned fruits & specialties

(P-824)
SPECIALTY CO PACK LLC
1651 Fremont Ct, Ontario (91761-8309)
PHONE......................909 673-0439
Giacomino Drago,
EMP: 11
SALES (est): 1.4MM **Privately Held**
SIC: 2033 Canned fruits & specialties

(P-825)
STANISLAUS FOOD PRODUCTS CO (PA)
1202 D St, Modesto (95354-2407)
P.O. Box 3951 (95352-3951)
PHONE......................209 548-3537
Thomas A Cortopassi, *CEO*
William D Butler, *Exec VP*
Rick Serpa, *Senior VP*
Mark Kimmel, *Vice Pres*
▼ **EMP:** 105
SQ FT: 50,000
SALES (est): 25.6MM **Privately Held**
SIC: 2033 Tomato paste: packaged in cans, jars, etc.; tomato purees: packaged in cans, jars, etc.; tomato sauce: packaged in cans, jars, etc.; tomato juice: packaged in cans, jars, etc.

(P-826)
SUNDOWN FOODS USA INC
10891 Business Dr, Fontana (92337-8235)
PHONE......................909 606-6797
Jeff Wartell, *President*
Diane Boese, *QC Mgr*
Khosrow Farhad, *Manager*
▲ **EMP:** 30
SALES (est): 5.7MM **Privately Held**
WEB: www.sundownfoods.com
SIC: 2033 Vegetables & vegetable products in cans, jars, etc.

(P-827)
SUNNY DELIGHT BEVERAGES CO
1230 N Tustin Ave, Anaheim (92807-1617)
PHONE......................714 630-6251
J C Oswalt, *Branch Mgr*
Mike Eigenbrod, *Engineer*
Elaine Sanchez, *Human Resources*
Tim Branson, *Plant Engr*
EMP: 120
SALES (corp-wide): 1.2B **Privately Held**
SIC: 2033 3085 Fruit juices: packaged in cans, jars, etc.; plastics bottles
HQ: Sunny Delight Beverage Co
　10300 Alliance Rd Ste 500
　Blue Ash OH 45242
　513 483-3300

(P-828)
SUNNYGEM LLC
500 N F St, Wasco (93280-1435)
PHONE......................661 758-0491
Charles R Bye,
Susan Huseman, *Controller*
Buck Moore, *Plant Mgr*
Lisa Lamborn, *QC Mgr*
John Vidovich Rick,
◆ **EMP:** 300
SQ FT: 270,000
SALES (est): 83.4MM **Privately Held**
SIC: 2033 3556 Fruit juices: fresh; juice extractors, fruit & vegetable: commercial type

(P-829)
TAPATIO FOODS LLC
Also Called: Tapatio Hot Sauce
4685 District Blvd, Vernon (90058-2731)
PHONE......................323 587-8933
Jose L Saavedra, *Mng Member*
Dolores McCoy,
EMP: 16
SQ FT: 30,000
SALES: 4.1MM **Privately Held**
WEB: www.tapatiohotsauce.com
SIC: 2033 Canned fruits & specialties

(P-830)
TREE TOP INC
1250 E 3rd St, Oxnard (93030-6107)
P.O. Box 248, Selah WA (98942-0248)
PHONE......................509 697-7251
Keith Gomes, *Branch Mgr*
Tom Stokes, *CEO*
EMP: 236
SALES (corp-wide): 399.9MM **Privately Held**
SIC: 2033 Fruit juices: packaged in cans, jars, etc.
PA: Tree Top, Inc.
　220 E 2nd Ave
　Selah WA 98942
　509 697-7251

(P-831)
TROPICAL PRESERVING CO INC
1711 E 15th St, Los Angeles (90021-2715)
PHONE......................213 748-5108
Ronald Randall, *President*
Joe Davis, *Consultant*
EMP: 23 **EST:** 1928
SQ FT: 25,000
SALES (est): 4.2MM **Privately Held**
WEB: www.tropicalpreserving.com
SIC: 2033 Jams, jellies & preserves: packaged in cans, jars, etc.

(P-832)
TROPICANA PRODUCTS INC
240 N Orange Ave, City of Industry (91744-3433)
PHONE......................626 968-1299
Kevin Frebert, *Plant Mgr*
Lilian Mayor, *IT/INT Sup*
Julie Goodenough, *Accounting Mgr*
Dave Perry, *Finance Mgr*
Paul Ahnberg, *Corp Comm Staff*
EMP: 150
SQ FT: 1,512
SALES (corp-wide): 64.6B **Publicly Held**
WEB: www.tropicana.com/biz
SIC: 2033 Fruit juices: fresh
HQ: Tropicana Products, Inc.
　1001 13th Ave E
　Bradenton FL 34208
　941 747-4461

(P-833)
VALLEY VIEW FOODS INC
7547 Sawtelle Ave, Yuba City (95991-9514)
PHONE......................530 673-7356
Jaswant Bains, *President*
Satwant Bains, *Admin Sec*
Anneke Amiga, *Administration*
EMP: 70
SQ FT: 80,000
SALES: 10MM **Privately Held**
SIC: 2033 Fruit juices: fresh

(P-834)
VANNELLI BRANDS LLC
4031 Alvis Ct, Rocklin (95677-4011)
PHONE......................916 824-1717
Chuck Eaton, *President*
Jerry Moore, *Director*
EMP: 12
SQ FT: 25,000
SALES: 5.5MM **Privately Held**
SIC: 2033 Spaghetti & other pasta sauce: packaged in cans, jars, etc.

(P-835)
VIE-DEL COMPANY (PA)
11903 S Chestnut Ave, Fresno (93725-9618)
P.O. Box 2908 (93745-2908)
PHONE......................559 834-2525
Dianne S Nury, *President*
Richard D Watson, *Treasurer*
Janice Terry, *Executive Asst*
Massud S Nury, *Admin Sec*
Richard Watson, *Controller*
▲ **EMP:** 75
SQ FT: 500,000
SALES (est): 12.8MM **Privately Held**
SIC: 2033 2084 Fruit juices: concentrated, hot pack; brandy

(P-836)
VITA-PAKT CITRUS PRODUCTS CO (PA)
203 E Badillo St, Covina (91723-2116)
P.O. Box 309 (91723-0309)
PHONE.................................626 332-1101
James R Boyles, *CEO*
Lloyd Shimizu, *CFO*
Linda Bernal, *Controller*
Lily Hernandez, *HR Admin*
◆ **EMP:** 50
SQ FT: 70,000
SALES (est): 28.3MM **Privately Held**
WEB: www.vita-pakt.com
SIC: 2033 2037 Apple sauce: packaged in cans, jars, etc.; fruit juices: fresh; fruit juices, frozen

(P-837)
WALKER FOODS INC
Also Called: La Flora Del Sur
237 N Mission Rd, Los Angeles
(90033-2103)
PHONE.................................323 268-5191
Robert L Walker Jr, *President*
Denise Walker, *Admin Sec*
Gloria Michel, *Manager*
EMP: 65
SQ FT: 150,000
SALES (est): 13.9MM **Privately Held**
WEB: www.walkerfoods.com
SIC: 2033 2032 2099 Canned fruits & specialties; canned specialties; ready-to-eat meals, salads & sandwiches

(P-838)
WARD E WALDO & SON INC
Also Called: Ward E Waldo & Son Marmalades
273 E Highland Ave, Sierra Madre
(91024-2014)
P.O. Box 266 (91025-0266)
PHONE.................................626 355-1218
Richard H Ward, *President*
Jeffrey Ward, *Vice Pres*
EMP: 12
SQ FT: 10,000
SALES (est): 1.8MM **Privately Held**
WEB: www.waldoward.com
SIC: 2033 Preserves, including imitation: in cans, jars, etc.; jellies, edible, including imitation: in cans, jars, etc.; fruits: packaged in cans, jars, etc.

(P-839)
WILDBRINE LLC (PA)
322 Bellevue Ave, Santa Rosa
(95407-7711)
PHONE.................................707 657-7607
Chris Glab, *Mng Member*
Richard Goldberg,
EMP: 40 **EST:** 2012
SQ FT: 9,000
SALES (est): 3.3MM **Privately Held**
SIC: 2033 5149 Sauerkraut: packaged in cans, jars, etc.; beverages, except coffee & tea

---

**2034 Dried Fruits,
Vegetables & Soup**

(P-840)
AGUSA
1055 S 19th Ave, Lemoore (93245-9747)
PHONE.................................559 924-4785
Joel Delira, *CEO*
Inigo Martinez, *COO*
Javier Souchard, *CFO*
Joel De Lira, *General Mgr*
Danny Serrano, *Finance Mgr*
◆ **EMP:** 36
SQ FT: 28,000
SALES (est): 8.2MM **Privately Held**
WEB: www.agusa.net
SIC: 2034 Dried & dehydrated fruits

(P-841)
AMERICAN FOOD INGREDIENTS INC
4021 Avenida Plata 501, Oceanside
(92056)
PHONE.................................760 967-6287
Karen Koppenhaver, *CEO*

▲ **EMP:** 30
SQ FT: 2,000
SALES (est): 7.5MM **Privately Held**
SIC: 2034 Dried & dehydrated vegetables

(P-842)
B & R FARMS LLC
Also Called: Four Oaks Farming
5280 Fairview Rd, Hollister (95023-9009)
PHONE.................................831 637-9168
Jim Rossey, *Principal*
Mari Rossey, *Principal*
Brian Rossi, *Manager*
▲ **EMP:** 34
SALES (est): 5.1MM **Privately Held**
SIC: 2034 0191 Dried & dehydrated fruits; general farms, primarily crop

(P-843)
BASIC AMERICAN INC (PA)
Also Called: Basic American Foods
2999 Oak Rd Ste 800, Walnut Creek
(94597-2054)
PHONE.................................925 472-4438
Bryan Reese, *President*
James Collins, *CFO*
Stacy Williams, *Regional Mgr*
John Barnecut, *Admin Sec*
Brenda Auten, *Admin Asst*
◆ **EMP:** 60
SALES (est): 440.1MM **Privately Held**
WEB: www.baf.com
SIC: 2034 2099 Potato products, dried & dehydrated; vegetables, dried or dehydrated (except freeze-dried); potatoes, peeled for the trade

(P-844)
BATTH DEHYDRATOR LLC
4624 W Nebraska Ave, Caruthers
(93609-9566)
P.O. Box 309 (93609-0309)
PHONE.................................559 864-3501
Charanjit S Batth,
Kanwarjit S Batth,
▲ **EMP:** 40
SQ FT: 217,800
SALES (est): 5.5MM **Privately Held**
SIC: 2034 Raisins

(P-845)
CALIFORNIA DRIED FRUIT INC
Also Called: Midway Farms
9145 W Herndon Ave, Fresno
(93723-9302)
P.O. Box 11187 (93772-1187)
PHONE.................................559 233-0970
Christopher Cubre, *Principal*
Jennifer Dart, *Office Mgr*
EMP: 22
SQ FT: 1,200
SALES (est): 3.4MM **Privately Held**
SIC: 2034 Dried & dehydrated fruits

(P-846)
CARO NUT COMPANY
2885 S Cherry Ave, Fresno (93706-5406)
PHONE.................................559 439-2365
David Mahaffy, *CEO*
Germanjit Chhina, *Maint Spvr*
▲ **EMP:** 50 **EST:** 2008
SALES (est): 26.6MM
SALES (corp-wide): 48.4MM **Privately Held**
SIC: 2034 Dried & dehydrated fruits
PA: Candor-Ags, Inc.
2885 S Cherry Ave
Fresno CA 93706
559 439-2365

(P-847)
CARUTHERS RAISIN PKG CO INC (PA)
12797 S Elm Ave, Caruthers (93609-9711)
PHONE.................................559 864-9448
Donald Kizirian, *President*
Don Kizirian, *President*
Gina Elsea, *CFO*
Dennis Housepian, *Exec VP*
Gregg Weaver, *Regional Mgr*
◆ **EMP:** 70
SQ FT: 4,000
SALES (est): 17.9MM **Privately Held**
WEB: www.caruthersraisin.com
SIC: 2034 Dehydrated fruits, vegetables, soups

(P-848)
CULINARY FARMS INC
1244 E Beamer St, Woodland
(95776-6002)
PHONE.................................916 375-3000
Kirk Bewley, *President*
▲ **EMP:** 50
SALES (est): 14.9MM **Privately Held**
WEB: www.culinaryfarms.com
SIC: 2034 Dried & dehydrated vegetables

(P-849)
DEL REY ENTERPRISES INC
8898 E Central Ave, Del Rey (93616)
PHONE.................................559 233-4452
Robert E Naugle, *President*
Michael Graves, *Treasurer*
Aaron Avedian, *Vice Pres*
Mark Avedian, *Vice Pres*
EMP: 12
SQ FT: 20,000
SALES (est): 1.5MM **Privately Held**
SIC: 2034 Dried & dehydrated fruits; raisins

(P-850)
INLAND EMPIRE FOODS INC (PA)
5425 Wilson St, Riverside (92509-2434)
PHONE.................................951 682-8222
Mark H Sterner, *President*
Paul Stiritz, *Vice Pres*
Dave Macias, *Sales Mgr*
▼ **EMP:** 35
SQ FT: 85,000
SALES (est): 13.6MM **Privately Held**
WEB: www.inlandempirefoods.com
SIC: 2034 Vegetables, dried or dehydrated (except freeze-dried)

(P-851)
LA VIENA RANCH
9408 Road 23, Madera (93637-9358)
P.O. Box 457 (93639-0457)
PHONE.................................559 674-6725
Carrie Besuner, *President*
EMP: 50
SALES (est): 4MM **Privately Held**
SIC: 2034 Dried & dehydrated fruits

(P-852)
LION RAISINS INC (PA)
Also Called: Lion Packing Co
9500 S De Wolf Ave, Selma (93662-9534)
P.O. Box 1350 (93662-1350)
PHONE.................................559 834-6677
Alfred Lion Jr, *President*
Bruce Lion, *Vice Pres*
Isabel Lion, *Principal*
Larry Lion, *Principal*
Carol North, *Technician*
◆ **EMP:** 400
SQ FT: 130,000
SALES (est): 106.1MM **Privately Held**
WEB: www.lionraisins.com
SIC: 2034 Raisins

(P-853)
MARIANI PACKING CO INC
Also Called: Mariani Bros
9281 Highway 70, Marysville (95901-3064)
PHONE.................................530 749-6565
Mark Kettmann, *Manager*
EMP: 20
SALES (corp-wide): 120.1MM **Privately Held**
WEB: www.marianifruit.com
SIC: 2034 Prunes, dried
PA: Mariani Packing Co., Inc.
500 Crocker Dr
Vacaville CA 95688
707 452-2800

(P-854)
MELKONIAN ENTERPRISES INC
Also Called: California Fruit Basket
2730 S De Wolf Ave, Sanger (93657-9770)
PHONE.................................559 485-6191
Mark Melkonian, *CEO*
Dennis Melkonian, *Vice Pres*
Douglas Melkonian, *Vice Pres*
EMP: 20
SQ FT: 160,000

SALES (est): 3.7MM **Privately Held**
WEB: www.californiafruitbasket.com
SIC: 2034 0172 5431 Raisins; fruits, dried or dehydrated, except freeze-dried; grapes; fruit stands or markets

(P-855)
MERCER FOODS LLC
1836 Lapham Dr, Modesto (95354-3900)
PHONE.................................209 529-0150
David A Noland, *CEO*
Clark Driftmier, *Exec VP*
Mike Alaga, *Vice Pres*
Stephen Kaufman, *Vice Pres*
Tim Lacombe, *Vice Pres*
▲ **EMP:** 16
SQ FT: 160,000
SALES (est): 19.6MM
SALES (corp-wide): 256.5MM **Privately Held**
WEB: www.mercerfoods.com
SIC: 2034 Dehydrated fruits, vegetables, soups
PA: Graham Partners, Inc.
3811 West Chester Pike # 200
Newtown Square PA 19073
610 408-0500

(P-856)
MOLES FARM
9503 S Hughes Ave, Fresno (93706-9731)
PHONE.................................559 444-0324
Ray Moles, *President*
EMP: 65
SALES (est): 2.9MM **Privately Held**
SIC: 2034 Raisins

(P-857)
PROFOOD TROPICAL FRUITS INC
33288 Alvarado Niles Rd, Union City
(94587-3156)
PHONE.................................510 890-0070
Allan Lee, *Mng Member*
EMP: 11
SQ FT: 20,000
SALES: 20MM **Privately Held**
SIC: 2034 Dehydrated fruits, vegetables, soups

(P-858)
RAISIN VALLEY FARMS LLC
3678 N Modoc Ave, Kerman (93630-9517)
PHONE.................................559 846-8138
Marvin Horne, *Mng Member*
Laura Horne,
▲ **EMP:** 14
SALES (est): 2.1MM **Privately Held**
SIC: 2034 0172 Raisins; grapes

(P-859)
RAISIN VALLEY FARMS DISTRG INC
2267 N Lassen Ave, Kerman (93630-9511)
PHONE.................................559 846-8138
Marvin Horne, *CEO*
Jack Blehm, *President*
Sheryl Miller, *Manager*
EMP: 10
SALES (est): 480.8K **Privately Held**
SIC: 2034 Dried & dehydrated fruits

(P-860)
SALWASSER INC
4087 N Howard Ave, Kerman (93630-9674)
P.O. Box 296, Biola (93606-0296)
PHONE.................................559 843-2882
George J Salwasser, *President*
George Salwasser, *President*
Charlotte Salwasser, *Vice Pres*
EMP: 56 **EST:** 1977
SQ FT: 50,000
SALES: 4MM **Privately Held**
SIC: 2034 Raisins

(P-861)
SENSIENT NTRAL INGREDIENTS LLC
7474 Cressey Way, Livingston (95334)
PHONE.................................209 394-7979
Kris Van Elsywk, *Principal*
Terrence Alexis, *Human Res Dir*
Felipe Aguilar, *Director*
Robby Force, *Director*
Robert Leguillou, *Manager*

PRODUCTS & SVCS

EMP: 13
SALES (corp-wide): 1.3B **Publicly Held**
SIC: 2034 Dehydrated fruits, vegetables, soups
HQ: Sensient Natural Ingredients Llc
151 S Walnut Rd
Turlock CA 95380
209 667-2777

(P-862)
SENSIENT NTRAL INGREDIENTS LLC (HQ)
Also Called: Sensient Dehydrated Flavors
151 S Walnut Rd, Turlock (95380-5127)
P.O. Box 1524 (95381-1524)
PHONE.............................209 667-2777
Paul Manning, *President*
Mike Hagood, *Plant Mgr*
Jim Shank, *Maintence Staff*
EMP: 84
SALES (est): 51.9MM
SALES (corp-wide): 1.3B **Publicly Held**
SIC: 2034 Vegetables, dried or dehydrated (except freeze-dried)
PA: Sensient Technologies Corporation
777 E Wisconsin Ave # 1100
Milwaukee WI 53202
414 271-6755

(P-863)
SIMONE FRUIT CO INC
8008 W Shields Ave, Fresno (93723-9657)
PHONE.............................559 275-1368
Mauro Simone, *President*
Margaret Simone, *Admin Sec*
▼ **EMP:** 10
SQ FT: 2,400
SALES (est): 1.4MM **Privately Held**
SIC: 2034 Dehydrated fruits, vegetables, soups

(P-864)
STUTZ PACKING COMPANY
82689 Avenue 45, Indio (92201-2386)
PHONE.............................760 342-1666
Jack Stutz, *President*
Patty Stutz, *Admin Sec*
EMP: 13
SALES (est): 6.3MM **Privately Held**
SIC: 2034 Dehydrated fruits, vegetables, soups

(P-865)
SUN VLLEY RSINS INC A CAL CORP
9595 S Hughes Ave, Fresno (93706-9731)
PHONE.............................559 233-8070
Ermel Ray Moles, *President*
Debra Moles, *Vice Pres*
Cortney Moles, *Manager*
▼ **EMP:** 15
SQ FT: 18,000
SALES (est): 4.6MM **Privately Held**
SIC: 2034 Raisins

(P-866)
SUNRISE FRESH LLC
Also Called: Sunrise Fresh Dried Fruit Co
2716 E Miner Ave, Stockton (95205-4705)
P.O. Box 128, Linden (95236-0128)
PHONE.............................209 932-0192
Jane Samuel,
Jake Samuel, *Opers Staff*
James Samuel,
EMP: 30
SQ FT: 42,000
SALES: 2.8MM **Privately Held**
SIC: 2034 Dehydrated fruits, vegetables, soups

(P-867)
SUNSWEET DRYERS
23760 Loleta Ave, Corning (96021-9699)
P.O. Box 201 (96021-0201)
PHONE.............................530 824-5854
Dan Lima, *Manager*
EMP: 12
SALES (corp-wide): 244.8MM **Privately Held**
SIC: 2034 Prunes, dried
HQ: Sunsweet Dryers
901 N Walton Ave
Yuba City CA 95993
530 846-5578

(P-868)
SUNSWEET DRYERS
26 E Evans Reimer Rd, Gridley (95948-9544)
PHONE.............................530 846-5578
Jeff Wilson, *Manager*
EMP: 60
SALES (corp-wide): 244.8MM **Privately Held**
SIC: 2034 Prunes, dried
HQ: Sunsweet Dryers
901 N Walton Ave
Yuba City CA 95993
530 846-5578

(P-869)
SUNSWEET DRYERS INC
28390 Avenue 12, Madera (93637-9102)
P.O. Box 607 (93639-0607)
PHONE.............................559 673-4140
Javier Celerda, *Office Mgr*
Dan Lima, *Plant Mgr*
Pat Brogdon, *Manager*
Javier Delacerda, *Manager*
Mike Russell, *Superintendent*
EMP: 17
SALES (est): 1.8MM **Privately Held**
SIC: 2034 Dried & dehydrated fruits

(P-870)
SUNSWEET GROWERS INC (PA)
901 N Walton Ave, Yuba City (95993-9370)
PHONE.............................800 417-2253
Dane Lance, *President*
Brendon S Flynn, *Ch of Bd*
Ana Klein, *CEO*
Don Wood, *CFO*
Sharon Braun, *Vice Pres*
◆ **EMP:** 600 **EST:** 1917
SQ FT: 1,200,000
SALES: 244.8MM **Privately Held**
WEB: www.sunsweet.com
SIC: 2034 2037 2086 Dried & dehydrated fruits; fruit juices; fruit drinks (less than 100% juice): packaged in cans, etc.

(P-871)
TRUE LEAF FARMS LLC
1275 San Justo Rd, San Juan Bautista (95045-9733)
P.O. Box 509, Salinas (93902-0509)
PHONE.............................831 623-4667
Rio Farms, *Mng Member*
Pradeep Hadavale, *Vice Pres*
EMP: 500
SALES (est): 126.1MM **Privately Held**
WEB: www.trueleaffarms.com
SIC: 2034 Vegetables, dried or dehydrated (except freeze-dried)

(P-872)
VACAVILLE FRUIT CO INC
2055 Cessna Dr, Vacaville (95688-8838)
P.O. Box 1537 (95696-1537)
PHONE.............................707 448-5292
Nicole Ciarabellini, *Principal*
Sonia Nunez, *Accountant*
Mary Quinonez, *Sales Dir*
◆ **EMP:** 40
SQ FT: 15,000
SALES (est): 8.1MM **Privately Held**
WEB: www.vacavillefruit.com
SIC: 2034 Prunes, dried; fruits, dried or dehydrated, except freeze-dried

(P-873)
VALLEY VIEW PACKING CO INC
1764 The Alameda, San Jose (95126-1729)
P.O. Box 5699 (95150-5699)
PHONE.............................408 289-8300
Salvadore Rubino, *CEO*
Patricia Rubino, *Treasurer*
◆ **EMP:** 50
SQ FT: 9,000
SALES (est): 5.5MM **Privately Held**
WEB: www.valleyviewpacking.com
SIC: 2034 2033 Fruits, dried or dehydrated, except freeze-dried; prunes, dried; fruit juices: packaged in cans, jars, etc.; fruit juices: concentrated, hot pack

(P-874)
VICTOR PACKING INC
11687 Road 27 1/2, Madera (93637-9440)
PHONE.............................559 673-5908
Victor Sahatdjian, *President*
Margaret Sahatdjian, *Vice Pres*
Jennifer Williams, *Accountant*
Kristina Sahatjian, *VP Sales*
Matt Pestorich, *Sales Staff*
▼ **EMP:** 50 **EST:** 1963
SQ FT: 150,000
SALES (est): 11.7MM **Privately Held**
WEB: www.victorpacking.com
SIC: 2034 Raisins

(P-875)
VSP PRODUCTS INC
3324 Orestimba Rd, Newman (95360-9628)
PHONE.............................209 862-1200
Chris J Rufer, *President*
Robert Benech, *President*
▲ **EMP:** 53
SQ FT: 27,000
SALES (est): 7MM
SALES (corp-wide): 53.7MM **Privately Held**
SIC: 2034 Dehydrated fruits, vegetables, soups
PA: The Morning Star Company
724 Main St Ste 202
Woodland CA 95695
530 666-6600

(P-876)
WEST COAST GROWERS INC
1849 N Helm Ave Ste 110, Fresno (93727-1624)
PHONE.............................559 843-2294
Charlotte E Salwasser, *President*
George Sousa, *President*
Mark Mariani, *CEO*
Janice Husnagl, *CFO*
Charlotte Salwasser, *Principal*
▼ **EMP:** 40
SQ FT: 50,000
SALES (est): 8.9MM
SALES (corp-wide): 120.1MM **Privately Held**
WEB: www.marianifruit.com
SIC: 2034 Raisins; fruits, dried
PA: Mariani Packing Co., Inc.
500 Crocker Dr
Vacaville CA 95688
707 452-2800

(P-877)
WILL PAK FOODS INC
Also Called: Taste Adventure
4471 Santa Ana St Ste C, Ontario (91761-8110)
PHONE.............................800 874-0883
Gary L Morris, *President*
EMP: 10
SQ FT: 10,000
SALES (est): 1MM **Privately Held**
WEB: www.tasteadventure.com
SIC: 2034 Dehydrated fruits, vegetables, soups

2035 Pickled Fruits, Vegetables, Sauces & Dressings

(P-878)
A-1 ESTRN-HOME-MADE PICKLE INC
1832 Johnston St, Los Angeles (90031-3447)
PHONE.............................323 223-1141
Martin Morhar, *President*
Murray Berger, *Vice Pres*
EMP: 29
SQ FT: 40,000
SALES (est): 5.4MM **Privately Held**
SIC: 2035 Pickled fruits & vegetables

(P-879)
BELL-CARTER FOODS INC
Also Called: Bell-Carterolive Company
1012 2nd St, Corning (96021-3248)
PHONE.............................530 528-4820
Steve Henderson, *Branch Mgr*
Patty Beth, *Accounting Mgr*
Lori Rindahl, *Buyer*
Bra Gravitt, *Safety Dir*
Bob Asmus, *Plant Engr*

EMP: 300
SALES (corp-wide): 145.3MM **Privately Held**
WEB: www.bellcarter.com
SIC: 2035 2033 Olives, brined: bulk; canned fruits & specialties
PA: Bell-Carter Foods, Llc
590 Ygnacio Valley Rd # 300
Walnut Creek CA 94596
209 549-5939

(P-880)
CALCHEF FOODS LLC
4221 E Mariposa Rd Ste B, Stockton (95215-8139)
PHONE.............................888 638-7083
Dan Costa,
EMP: 28
SALES (est): 283.7K
SALES (corp-wide): 35.8MM **Privately Held**
SIC: 2035 2032 5142 Pickles, sauces & salad dressings; ethnic foods: canned, jarred, etc.; dinners, frozen
PA: Noble Rider, Llc
4300 Spyres Way
Modesto CA 95356
209 566-7800

(P-881)
GARLIC VALLEY FARMS INC
624 Ruberta Ave, Glendale (91201-2335)
PHONE.............................818 247-9600
William Anderson, *President*
Sonja Anderson, *Corp Secy*
Bill Brock, *Research*
Jared Valenzuela, *Natl Sales Mgr*
EMP: 11
SQ FT: 11,250
SALES (est): 1.3MM **Privately Held**
WEB: www.garlicvalleyfarms.com
SIC: 2035 5812 Seasonings & sauces, except tomato & dry; eating places

(P-882)
GFF INC
Also Called: Girard Food Service
145 Willow Ave, City of Industry (91746-2047)
PHONE.............................323 232-6255
Jack Tucey, *Chairman*
Bill Perry, *President*
William Perry, *President*
Farrell Hirsch, *CEO*
Sandra Velasquez, *Executive Asst*
▲ **EMP:** 89
SQ FT: 92,000
SALES (est): 34.7MM
SALES (corp-wide): 455.1MM **Privately Held**
WEB: www.girardsdressings.com
SIC: 2035 Pickles, sauces & salad dressings
PA: Haco Holding Ag
Worbstrasse 262
Muri Bei Bern BE 3074
319 501-111

(P-883)
GINGER GOLDEN PRODUCTS INC
5860 Bandini Blvd, Commerce (90040-2925)
PHONE.............................323 838-1070
Koichi Takeuchi, *President*
Yoshiji Kono, *Vice Pres*
▲ **EMP:** 27
SQ FT: 15,000
SALES (est): 3.8MM **Privately Held**
SIC: 2035 2099 Pickled fruits & vegetables; food preparations

(P-884)
H V FOOD PRODUCTS COMPANY
1221 Broadway, Oakland (94612-1837)
PHONE.............................510 271-7612
George C Roeth, *President*
Pamela Fletcher, *Vice Pres*
EMP: 200
SQ FT: 218,000
SALES (est): 16.7MM
SALES (corp-wide): 6.2B **Publicly Held**
WEB: www.kingsford.com
SIC: 2035 Pickles, sauces & salad dressings

HQ: The Kingsford Products Company Llc
1221 Broadway Ste 1300
Oakland CA 94612
510 271-7000

(P-885)
JUST INC
2000 Folsom St, San Francisco
(94110-1318)
PHONE...................................844 423-6637
Joshua Tetrick, *CEO*
Beth Lawrence, *Partner*
Alexandra Dallago, *President*
Lee Chae, *Vice Pres*
Caroline Love, *Vice Pres*
EMP: 249 EST: 2011
SQ FT: 2,300
SALES (est): 86.1MM **Privately Held**
SIC: 2035 2052 Mayonnaise; cookies

(P-886)
KRINOS FOODS LLC
Also Called: Santa Barbara Olives Co
1105 E Foster Rd Ste E, Santa Maria
(93455-6438)
PHONE...................................805 922-6700
Lourdez Clayton, *Manager*
EMP: 17
SALES (corp-wide): 57.7MM **Privately Held**
SIC: 2035 Olives, brined: bulk
PA: Krinos Foods Llc
1750 Bathgate Ave
Bronx NY 10457
718 729-9000

(P-887)
KRUGER FOODS INC
18362 E Highway 4, Stockton
(95215-9433)
P.O. Box 220, Farmington (95230-0220)
PHONE...................................209 941-8518
Kara Kruger, *CEO*
Leslie Kruger, *COO*
Eric Kruger, *VP Opers*
▼ EMP: 155
SQ FT: 80,000
SALES (est): 47.4MM **Privately Held**
WEB: www.krugerfoods.com
SIC: 2035 Pickles, vinegar; vegetables, pickled

(P-888)
LEE BROTHERS INC
Also Called: Four In One Company
1011 Timothy Dr, San Jose (95133-1043)
PHONE...................................650 964-9650
Gene Lee, *President*
Jay Lee, *Corp Secy*
Jim Lee, *Vice Pres*
EMP: 30
SQ FT: 46,000
SALES: 23MM **Privately Held**
SIC: 2035 Dressings, salad: raw & cooked (except dry mixes); soy sauce

(P-889)
MAJESTIC GARLIC INC
2222 Foothill Blvd Ste E, La Canada
(91011-1485)
PHONE...................................951 677-0555
Lucie Sabounjian, *Owner*
EMP: 15
SALES: 500K **Privately Held**
SIC: 2035 Spreads, garlic

(P-890)
MOREHOUSE FOODS INC
760 Epperson Dr, City of Industry
(91748-1336)
PHONE...................................626 854-1655
David L Latter Sr, *Chairman*
David L Latter Jr, *President*
Paul Latter, *Manager*
Mike Paulus, *Manager*
Angel Rodriguez, *Manager*
▲ EMP: 50
SQ FT: 65,000
SALES (est): 11MM **Privately Held**
WEB: www.morehousefoods.com
SIC: 2035 5149 Mustard, prepared (wet); horseradish, prepared; seasonings, sauces & extracts

(P-891)
NOR CAL FOOD SOLUTIONS LLC
Also Called: Mad Will's Food Company
2043 Airpark Ct, Auburn (95602-9009)
PHONE...................................530 823-8527
Scott Bartosh, *Mng Member*
Tonya Gregerson, *Bookkeeper*
▼ EMP: 14
SALES: 3MM **Privately Held**
SIC: 2035 2099 Pickles, sauces & salad dressings; sauces: gravy, dressing & dip mixes

(P-892)
OLIVE MUSCO PRODUCTS INC
Swift & 5th St # 5, Orland (95963)
P.O. Box 368 (95963-0368)
PHONE...................................530 865-4111
Dennis Burreson, *Plant Mgr*
EMP: 30
SALES (corp-wide): 95.7MM **Privately Held**
SIC: 2035 2033 Pickles, sauces & salad dressings; olives: packaged in cans, jars, etc.
PA: Olive Musco Products Inc
17950 Via Nicolo
Tracy CA 95377
209 836-4600

(P-893)
ORGANIC HORSERADISH CO
7890 County Road 120, Tulelake
(96134-8228)
PHONE...................................530 664-3862
David Krizo, *Partner*
Jacqueline Krizo, *Partner*
EMP: 30
SALES (est): 2.2MM **Privately Held**
SIC: 2035 Horseradish, prepared

(P-894)
PACIFIC CHOICE BRANDS INC (PA)
4667 E Date Ave, Fresno (93725-2101)
PHONE...................................559 892-5365
Allan R Andrews, *CEO*
◆ EMP: 275 EST: 1930
SQ FT: 225,000
SALES (est): 65.3MM **Privately Held**
WEB: www.pacificchoicebrands.com
SIC: 2035 Pickled fruits & vegetables

(P-895)
PACIFIC PICKLE WORKS INC
718 Union Ave Snta Brbara Santa Barbara,
Santa Barbara (93103)
PHONE...................................805 765-1779
Bradley Bennett, *CEO*
EMP: 13 EST: 2010
SALES (est): 1.6MM **Privately Held**
SIC: 2035 2087 Pickled fruits & vegetables; cocktail mixes, nonalcoholic

(P-896)
Q & B FOODS INC (DH)
15547 1st St, Irwindale (91706-6201)
PHONE...................................626 334-8090
Kuniaki Ishikaiwa, *President*
Akio Okumura, *CEO*
Jerry Shepherd, *Exec VP*
Paul Yun, *Sales Mgr*
Fernando Moreno, *Supervisor*
◆ EMP: 69
SQ FT: 52,000
SALES (est): 16.9MM **Privately Held**
WEB: www.qbfoods.com
SIC: 2035 Dressings, salad: raw & cooked (except dry mixes); mayonnaise
HQ: Kifuki U.S.A. Co., Inc.
15547 1st St
Irwindale CA 91706
626 334-8090

(P-897)
RED SHELL FOODS INC
825 Baldwin Park Blvd, City of Industry
(91746-1205)
P.O. Box 91744 (91715-1744)
PHONE...................................626 937-6501
Hiro Watanabe, *President*
EMP: 10
SQ FT: 2,400

SALES: 125.6K **Privately Held**
WEB: www.redshell.com
SIC: 2035 Dressings, salad: raw & cooked (except dry mixes)

(P-898)
S M S BRINERS INC
17750 E Highway 4, Stockton
(95215-9721)
PHONE...................................209 941-8515
Kara Kruger, *CEO*
Frances Sousa, *President*
Laurie Flatter, *Corp Secy*
Arnold Sousa, *Vice Pres*
EMP: 15
SQ FT: 5,000
SALES (est): 3.3MM **Privately Held**
SIC: 2035 Vegetables, brined

(P-899)
SCOTTS FOOD PRODUCTS INC
7331 Alondra Blvd, Paramount
(90723-4013)
P.O. Box 17 (90723-0017)
PHONE...................................562 630-8448
Tony Lobue, *Owner*
▼ EMP: 10
SALES (est): 1MM **Privately Held**
WEB: www.scottsfoodproducts.com
SIC: 2035 Pickles, sauces & salad dressings

(P-900)
SONOMA GOURMET INC
Also Called: Pometta's
21684 8th St E Ste 100, Sonoma
(95476-2816)
PHONE...................................707 939-3700
William K Weber, *President*
EMP: 25
SQ FT: 50,000
SALES (est): 4.3MM **Privately Held**
WEB: www.sonomagourmet.com
SIC: 2035 Pickles, sauces & salad dressings

(P-901)
SUNOPTA GLBAL ORGNIC ING INC (DH)
Also Called: Sunopta Food Solutions
100 Enterprise Way Ste B1, Scotts Valley
(95066-3248)
PHONE...................................831 685-6506
Joseph Stern, *President*
▲ EMP: 20
SQ FT: 2,800
SALES (est): 8MM
SALES (corp-wide): 1.2B **Privately Held**
WEB: www.organic-ingredients.com
SIC: 2035 2033 Relishes, vinegar; fruit nectars: packaged in cans, jars, etc.; fruit purees: packaged in cans, jars, etc.; fruit juices: concentrated, hot pack; vegetable purees: packaged in cans, jars, etc.

(P-902)
TMARZETTI COMPANY
Also Called: Marzetti West
876 Yosemite Dr, Milpitas (95035-5437)
PHONE...................................408 263-7540
John Herlihy, *Manager*
EMP: 140
SQ FT: 50,000
SALES (corp-wide): 1.2B **Publicly Held**
SIC: 2035 Dressings, salad: raw & cooked (except dry mixes)
HQ: T.Marzetti Company
380 Polaris Pkwy Ste 400
Westerville OH 43082
614 846-2232

(P-903)
U S ENTERPRISE CORPORATION
Also Called: Wing Nien Company
30560 San Antonio St, Hayward
(94544-7102)
PHONE...................................510 487-8877
David H Hall, *President*
Ken Jue MD, *Vice Pres*
Gregory Hall, *Admin Sec*
▲ EMP: 30
SQ FT: 40,000

SALES (est): 5.1MM **Privately Held**
WEB: www.wnfoods.com
SIC: 2035 5141 Seasonings & sauces, except tomato & dry; groceries, general line

(P-904)
VALLEY GARLIC INC
500 Enterprise Pkwy, Coalinga
(93210-9513)
PHONE...................................559 934-1763
Gary Caneza, *President*
EMP: 20
SALES (est): 3.6MM **Privately Held**
SIC: 2035 Spreads, garlic

2037 Frozen Fruits, Juices & Vegetables

(P-905)
CALIFORNIA CONCENTRATE COMPANY
Also Called: Kimberley Wine Vinegars
18678 N Highway 99, Acampo
(95220-9557)
PHONE...................................209 334-9112
Dennis Alexander, *President*
Kim Roberts, *CFO*
Andy Alexander, *Vice Pres*
Thomas P Alexander, *Vice Pres*
◆ EMP: 20 EST: 1969
SQ FT: 17,000
SALES (est): 4.2MM **Privately Held**
WEB: www.californiaconcentrate.com
SIC: 2037 2082 Fruit juice concentrates, frozen; malt extract

(P-906)
CANADAS FINEST FOODS INC
Also Called: Reliant Foodservice
26090 Ynez Rd, Temecula (92591-6000)
PHONE...................................951 296-1040
David Canada, *President*
Joe Demeter, *Opers Mgr*
Christian Staff, *VP Sales*
Sandie Mullins, *Sales Staff*
McKenna Adrid, *Cust Mgr*
▲ EMP: 70
SQ FT: 102,000
SALES: 520MM **Privately Held**
SIC: 2037 2024 Fruit juices; dairy based frozen desserts

(P-907)
CHIQUITA BRANDS INTL INC
3586 Arden Rd, Hayward (94545-3921)
PHONE...................................510 732-9500
Dan Clay, *Branch Mgr*
EMP: 18
SALES (corp-wide): 3B **Privately Held**
WEB: www.chiquita.com
SIC: 2037 Fruit juices
HQ: Chiquita Brands International, Inc.
1855 Griffin Rd Ste C436
Dania FL 33004
954 924-5700

(P-908)
CROWN CITRUS COMPANY INC
551 W Main St, Brawley (92227-2262)
PHONE...................................760 344-1930
Mark McBroom, *President*
EMP: 10
SALES (est): 1.5MM **Privately Held**
SIC: 2037 Citrus pulp, dried

(P-909)
DEL REY JUICE CO
Also Called: Paramount Food Processing
5286 S Del Rey Ave, Del Rey (93616)
PHONE...................................559 888-8533
EMP: 99
SALES (est): 8.1MM **Privately Held**
SIC: 2037

(P-910)
DOLE PACKAGED FOODS LLC (HQ)
Also Called: Glacier Foods Division
3059 Townsgate Rd Ste 400, Westlake Village (91361-3190)
P.O. Box 5132 (91359-5132)
PHONE...................................805 601-5500
David A Delorenzo, *Mng Member*
Bob Barnhouse, *Vice Pres*

PRODUCTS & SVCS

Jon Rodacy, *Vice Pres*
Jim Kelley, *Business Mgr*
Carolyn Leach, *Marketing Staff*
◆ **EMP:** 550
SALES (est): 214.2MM **Privately Held**
WEB: www.jrwood.com
SIC: 2037 Fruits, quick frozen & cold pack (frozen); vegetables, quick frozen & cold pack, excl. potato products

(P-911)
DOLE PACKAGED FOODS LLC
Also Called: Glacier Foods Division
1117 K St, Sanger (93657-3200)
PHONE..................................559 875-3354
Alvin Mc Avoy, *Manager*
Teri Thomas, *Executive Asst*
Sylvia Lopez, *Administration*
Kevin Miguel, *Finance*
Maureen Brennan, *Human Res Mgr*
EMP: 180 **Privately Held**
WEB: www.jrwood.com
SIC: 2037 2033 2095 2032 Fruits, quick frozen & cold pack (frozen); canned fruits & specialties; roasted coffee; canned specialties; frozen specialties
HQ: Dole Packaged Foods, Llc
  3059 Townsgate Rd Ste 400
  Westlake Village CA 91361
  805 601-5500

(P-912)
FORAGER PROJECT LLC
235 Montgomery St Ste 730, San Francisco (94104-2917)
PHONE..................................855 729-5253
Stephen Williamson, *Mng Member*
Christopher Michell, *Controller*
Susan Kirmayer, *Human Resources*
EMP: 55
SALES (est): 6MM **Privately Held**
SIC: 2037 Fruit juices

(P-913)
HAYWARD ENTERPRISES INC
2700 Napa Valley Corp Dr, NAPA (94558)
PHONE..................................707 261-5100
Tracy Collier Hayward, *President*
Jose Osuch, *CFO*
Sharon Bahr, *Vice Pres*
Kevin Zeigler, *Controller*
Jerry Benjamin, *Human Res Mgr*
▼ **EMP:** 15
SQ FT: 8,166
SALES (est): 1.9MM **Privately Held**
WEB: www.perfectpuree.com
SIC: 2037 Frozen fruits & vegetables

(P-914)
HUSKS UNLIMITED (PA)
1616 Silvas St, Chula Vista (91911-4622)
PHONE..................................619 476-8301
Luis Duenas, *CEO*
Eric Brenk, *President*
EMP: 23
SQ FT: 15,000
SALES (est): 5MM **Privately Held**
SIC: 2037 Frozen fruits & vegetables

(P-915)
IMPERIAL VALLEY FOODS INC
1961 Buchanan Ave, Calexico (92231-4306)
P.O. Box 233 Paulin Ave (92231)
PHONE..................................760 203-1896
Gustavo Cabellero Jr, *President*
Edna Cabellero, *Treasurer*
▲ **EMP:** 300
SALES (est): 38.7MM **Privately Held**
SIC: 2037 Frozen fruits & vegetables

(P-916)
J HELLMAN FROZEN FOODS INC (PA)
1601 E Olympic Blvd # 200, Los Angeles (90021-1941)
P.O. Box 86267 (90086-0267)
PHONE..................................213 243-9105
Tracy Hellman, *CEO*
Bryce Hellman, *President*
EMP: 50
SQ FT: 21,000
SALES (est): 9MM **Privately Held**
SIC: 2037 Frozen fruits & vegetables

(P-917)
JR SIMPLOT COMPANY
12688 S Colorado Ave, Fresno (93729)
P.O. Box 28955 (93729-8955)
PHONE..................................559 439-3900
EMP: 54
SALES (corp-wide): 4.8B **Privately Held**
SIC: 2037 Potato products, quick frozen & cold pack
PA: J.R. Simplot Company
  1099 W Front St
  Boise ID 83702
  208 780-3287

(P-918)
JUMP START JUICE BAR
Also Called: Jumpstart Juice
8001 Irvine Center Dr # 40, Irvine (92618-2938)
PHONE..................................949 754-3120
EMP: 15
SALES (est): 630K **Privately Held**
SIC: 2037

(P-919)
L & H INDUSTRIES
925 E Arlee Pl, Anaheim (92805-5645)
PHONE..................................714 635-1555
Kevin Heenan, *Partner*
Randy Ricketts, *Partner*
EMP: 11 **EST:** 1961
SQ FT: 5,000
SALES: 1MM **Privately Held**
SIC: 2037 Fruits, quick frozen & cold pack (frozen)

(P-920)
LA ALOE LLC
2301 E 7th St Ste A152, Los Angeles (90023-1044)
PHONE..................................888 968-2563
Dino Sarti,
Manuel Campos,
Daniel Stepper,
▲ **EMP:** 21
SQ FT: 47,000
SALES: 4MM **Privately Held**
SIC: 2037 Fruit juices

(P-921)
OXNARD LEMON COMPANY
2001 Sunkist Cir, Oxnard (93033-3902)
P.O. Box 2240 (93034-2240)
PHONE..................................805 483-1173
Sam Mayhew, *General Mgr*
Nancy Low, *Office Mgr*
Tom Mayhew, *Superintendent*
Juan Vancini, *Supervisor*
EMP: 15
SALES (est): 3.5MM **Privately Held**
WEB: www.oxnardlemon.com
SIC: 2037 0723 5148 Frozen fruits & vegetables; crop preparation services for market; fresh fruits & vegetables

(P-922)
PACKERS FOOD PRODUCTS INC
Also Called: Gems of Fruit Co
701 W Kimberly Ave # 210, Placentia (92870-6342)
PHONE..................................913 262-6200
Ed Haft, *President*
Ivan Veselic, *Vice Pres*
▲ **EMP:** 47
SQ FT: 2,500
SALES (est): 6MM **Privately Held**
WEB: www.gemsoffruit.com
SIC: 2037 Fruits, quick frozen & cold pack (frozen); fruit juice concentrates, frozen

(P-923)
PATTERSON FROZEN FOODS INC
10 S 3rd St, Patterson (95363-2509)
P.O. Box 487 (95363-0487)
PHONE..................................209 892-5060
Angelo Ielmini, *President*
Susan Scheuber, *CFO*
◆ **EMP:** 11
SQ FT: 600,000

SALES (est): 1.8MM **Privately Held**
WEB: www.pattersonfrozenfoods.com
SIC: 2037 Fruits, quick frozen & cold pack (frozen); vegetables, quick frozen & cold pack, excl. potato products

(P-924)
PERFECT PUREE OF NAPA VLY LLC
2700 Napa Valley Corp Dr, NAPA (94558)
PHONE..................................707 261-5100
Kevin Zeigler, *President*
Becky Walker, *Human Res Dir*
Montia Garcia, *Marketing Staff*
Dawn Wachsning, *Sales Staff*
▲ **EMP:** 19
SALES (est): 7.5MM **Privately Held**
SIC: 2037 Frozen fruits & vegetables

(P-925)
PURITY ORGANIC LLC
405 14th St Ste 1000, Oakland (94612-2706)
PHONE..................................415 440-7777
Greg Holzman, *Mng Member*
EMP: 25
SALES (est): 121.5K **Privately Held**
SIC: 2037 Fruit juices

(P-926)
QUALITY PRODUCED LLC
Also Called: Pulp Story
987 N Enterprise St, Orange (92867-5448)
PHONE..................................310 592-8834
EMP: 15
SALES (corp-wide): 1MM **Privately Held**
SIC: 2037 Fruit juices
PA: Quality Produced Llc
  11693 San Vicente Blvd
  Los Angeles CA 90049
  310 592-8834

(P-927)
SMOOTHIE OPERATOR INC
8690 Sierra College Blvd, Roseville (95661-5961)
PHONE..................................916 773-9541
Ritchie Labate, *Principal*
Leslie Sue Broadland, *Principal*
EMP: 16
SALES (est): 215.3K **Privately Held**
SIC: 2037 Frozen fruits & vegetables

(P-928)
SONOMA BEVERAGE COMPANY LLC (PA)
2710 Giffen Ave, Santa Rosa (95407-7331)
PHONE..................................707 431-1099
David Langer, *Mng Member*
Tim Snowden, *General Mgr*
Bruce Langer,
▲ **EMP:** 20
SALES (est): 3.9MM **Privately Held**
SIC: 2037 Fruit juices

(P-929)
SUN TROPICS INC
2420 Camino Ramon Ste 101, San Ramon (94583-4207)
P.O. Box 407 (94583-0407)
PHONE..................................925 202-2221
Ashley Lao, *CEO*
Sharon Sy, *Vice Pres*
◆ **EMP:** 16
SALES (est): 4MM **Privately Held**
WEB: www.suntropics.com
SIC: 2037 Fruit juices

(P-930)
SUNSATION INC
100 S Cambridge Ave, Claremont (91711-4842)
PHONE..................................909 542-0280
Perry Eichor, *President*
David Bryant, *CFO*
EMP: 25
SQ FT: 30,000
SALES (est): 6.1MM **Privately Held**
SIC: 2037 Fruit juices

(P-931)
TITAN FROZEN FRUIT LLC (PA)
585 Auto Center Dr Ste A, Watsonville (95076-3764)
PHONE..................................831 540-4110

Jonathan V Larsen,
Pablo Rodriguez, *Manager*
EMP: 22
SALES (est): 6.9MM **Privately Held**
SIC: 2037 Frozen fruits & vegetables

(P-932)
VENTURA COASTAL LLC (PA)
2325 Vista Del Mar Dr, Ventura (93001-3751)
P.O. Box 69 (93002-0069)
PHONE..................................805 653-7000
William M Borgers,
Bill Borgers, *CEO*
Will Borgers, *Financial Analy*
Donald Dames,
Rolph Scherer,
◆ **EMP:** 80
SQ FT: 25,000
SALES (est): 18.6MM **Privately Held**
WEB: www.vcoastal.com
SIC: 2037 Fruit juice concentrates, frozen

(P-933)
VENTURA COASTAL LLC
12310 Avenue 368, Visalia (93291-9500)
PHONE..................................559 737-9836
Gene Keck, *Branch Mgr*
EMP: 14
SALES (est): 1.9MM
SALES (corp-wide): 18.6MM **Privately Held**
WEB: www.vcoastal.com
SIC: 2037 2087 2033 Fruit juices; flavoring extracts & syrups; canned fruits & specialties
PA: Ventura Coastal, Llc
  2325 Vista Del Mar Dr
  Ventura CA 93001
  805 653-7000

(P-934)
WAWONA FROZEN FOODS (PA)
100 W Alluvial Ave, Clovis (93611-9176)
PHONE..................................559 299-2901
William Smittcamp, *President*
Earl Smittcamp, *Ch of Bd*
Muriel Smittcamp, *Corp Secy*
Kristi Losson, *Executive Asst*
Galen Destefano, *IT/INT Sup*
▲ **EMP:** 2200
SQ FT: 125,000
SALES (est): 228.8MM **Privately Held**
SIC: 2037 Fruits, quick frozen & cold pack (frozen)

(P-935)
YOUNGSTOWN GRAPE DISTRS INC
1625 G St, Reedley (93654-3435)
P.O. Box 271 (93654-0271)
PHONE..................................559 638-2271
Michael J Forrest, *CEO*
Brian Forrest, *Sales Mgr*
▲ **EMP:** 206
SQ FT: 100,000
SALES (est): 59.5MM **Privately Held**
SIC: 2037 Fruit juice concentrates, frozen

2038 Frozen Specialties

(P-936)
AJINOMOTO FOODS NORTH AMER INC
Also Called: Windsor Foods
2395 American Ave, Hayward (94545-1807)
PHONE..................................510 293-1838
Venita Darien, *Branch Mgr*
Janet Zhou, *Accountant*
EMP: 17 **Privately Held**
SIC: 2038 2037 Frozen specialties; frozen fruits & vegetables
HQ: Ajinomoto Foods North America, Inc.
  4200 Concours Ste 100
  Ontario CA 91764
  -

(P-937)
AJINOMOTO FOODS NORTH AMER INC
Also Called: Windsor Foods
4200 Concours Ste 100, Ontario (91764-4982)
PHONE..................909 477-4700
Steve Charles, *Manager*
EMP: 244 **Privately Held**
SIC: 2038 5142 Frozen specialties; packaged frozen goods
HQ: Ajinomoto Foods North America, Inc.
4200 Concours Ste 100
Ontario CA 91764

(P-938)
AJINOMOTO FOODS NORTH AMER INC (DH)
4200 Concours Ste 100, Ontario (91764-4982)
PHONE..................909 477-4700
Bernard Kreilmann, *President*
Fon Wong, *CFO*
Haruo Kurata, *Chairman*
John Gordon, *Treasurer*
George Jurkovich, *Exec VP*
▲ EMP: 100
SQ FT: 100,000
SALES (est): 302.8MM **Privately Held**
WEB: www.ajichem.com
SIC: 2038 2037 Frozen specialties; frozen fruits & vegetables
HQ: Ajinomoto North America Holdings, Inc.
7124 N Marine Dr
Portland OR 97203
503 505-5783

(P-939)
AJINOMOTO WINDSOR INC
Also Called: Golden Tiger
6711 S Alameda St, Los Angeles (90001-2123)
PHONE..................323 277-7000
EMP: 250 **Privately Held**
SIC: 2038 Ethnic foods, frozen
HQ: Ajinomoto Foods North America, Inc.
4200 Concours Ste 100
Ontario CA 91764

(P-940)
AMYS KITCHEN INC
1650 Corp Cir Ste 200, Petaluma (94954)
P.O. Box 449 (94953-0449)
PHONE..................707 568-4500
Shayne Young, *Branch Mgr*
Mark Rudolph, *CFO*
Andy Kopral, *Treasurer*
Bret Mohar, *Exec VP*
Michael Resch, *Exec VP*
EMP: 27
SALES (corp-wide): 278.7MM **Privately Held**
WEB: www.amyskitchen.com
SIC: 2038 2053 Dinners, frozen & packaged; frozen bakery products, except bread
PA: Amy's Kitchen, Inc.
2330 Northpoint Pkwy
Santa Rosa CA 95407
707 578-7188

(P-941)
AMYS KITCHEN INC (PA)
2330 Northpoint Pkwy, Santa Rosa (95407-5004)
P.O. Box 4759, Petaluma (94955-4759)
PHONE..................707 578-7188
Andy Berliner, *CEO*
Cindy L Gillespie, *Executive*
Ana Jesus, *Surgery Dir*
Luis Mendoza, *General Mgr*
Dennis Bee, *Planning*
▲ EMP: 800
SQ FT: 100,000
SALES (est): 278.7MM **Privately Held**
WEB: www.amyskitchen.com
SIC: 2038 2053 Dinners, frozen & packaged; frozen bakery products, except bread

(P-942)
ARISTA FOODS CORPORATION
1240 N Barsten Way, Anaheim (92806-1822)
PHONE..................714 666-1001
Fax: 714 666-8488
EMP: 11
SQ FT: 11,989
SALES (est): 680K **Privately Held**
SIC: 2038

(P-943)
ARMANINO FOODS DISTINCTION INC
30588 San Antonio St, Hayward (94544-7102)
PHONE..................510 441-9300
Edmond J Pera, *CEO*
Georgianne Stephen, *COO*
Edgar Estonina, *CFO*
Jeff Goshorn, *Vice Pres*
Deborah Armanino, *Sales Staff*
▼ EMP: 41
SQ FT: 31,783
SALES (est): 8.8MM **Privately Held**
WEB: www.armanino.biz
SIC: 2038 2099 Frozen specialties; sauces: gravy, dressing & dip mixes

(P-944)
ASTROCHEF LLC
Also Called: Pegasus Foods
1111 Mateo St, Los Angeles (90021-1717)
P.O. Box 86404 (90086-0404)
PHONE..................213 627-9860
Jim Zaferis, *CEO*
Evangelos Ambatielos, *President*
Stephen Castanedo, *General Mgr*
Mark Hamilton, *Purch Mgr*
Vanessa Thanos, *VP Sales*
EMP: 55
SQ FT: 60,000
SALES (est): 25.1MM **Privately Held**
SIC: 2038 Frozen specialties

(P-945)
BABA FOODS SLO LLC
Also Called: Baba Small Batch
3889 Long St Ste 100, San Luis Obispo (93401-7581)
P.O. Box 507, Avila Beach (93424-0507)
PHONE..................805 439-2250
Moez Bensalem,
Cecilia Boettcher, *General Mgr*
Cecilia Voettcher, *General Mgr*
EMP: 16
SQ FT: 4,000
SALES: 900K **Privately Held**
SIC: 2038 Ethnic foods, frozen

(P-946)
BENS ALTERNATIVE FOODS
2712 Marina Blvd Ste 36, San Leandro (94577-4056)
PHONE..................510 614-6745
Benjamin Meshack, *Owner*
▼ EMP: 15
SALES (est): 673.2K **Privately Held**
SIC: 2038 Ethnic foods, frozen

(P-947)
BEYOND MEAT INC (PA)
119 Standard St, El Segundo (90245-3833)
PHONE..................866 756-4112
Ethan Brown, *President*
Seth Goldman, *Ch of Bd*
Sanjay Shah, *COO*
Mark J Nelson, *CFO*
Stuart Kronauge, *Chief Mktg Ofcr*
▲ EMP: 20
SALES: 87.9MM **Publicly Held**
SIC: 2038 2013 Frozen specialties; frozen meats from purchased meat

(P-948)
BEYOND MEAT INC
1325 E El Segundo Blvd, El Segundo (90245-4303)
PHONE..................310 567-3323
Aaron Hicks, *Branch Mgr*
Will Schafer, *VP Mktg*
EMP: 26
SALES (corp-wide): 87.9MM **Publicly Held**
SIC: 2038 Frozen specialties

PA: Beyond Meat, Inc.
119 Standard St
El Segundo CA 90245
866 756-4112

(P-949)
CAMINO REAL FOODS INC (PA)
Also Called: Camino Real Kitchens
2638 E Vernon Ave, Vernon (90058-1825)
P.O. Box 30729, Los Angeles (90030-0729)
PHONE..................323 585-6599
Rob Cross, *President*
Richard Lunsford, *CFO*
Chris Perry, *CFO*
Yessica Carrillo, *Admin Asst*
Chip Diep, *Info Tech Mgr*
EMP: 150
SALES (est): 87.7MM **Privately Held**
WEB: www.crfoods.com
SIC: 2038 Frozen specialties

(P-950)
CAULIPOWER LLC
16200 Ventura Blvd # 400, Encino (91436-4918)
PHONE..................844 422-8544
Gail Becker, *CEO*
Cassie Abrams, *CFO*
EMP: 32
SQ FT: 500
SALES: 45MM **Privately Held**
SIC: 2038 Pizza, frozen

(P-951)
CEDARLANE NATURAL FOODS INC
717 E Artesia Blvd, Carson (90746-1200)
PHONE..................310 527-7833
EMP: 617
SALES (corp-wide): 87.6MM **Privately Held**
SIC: 2038 Dinners, frozen & packaged
PA: Cedarlane Natural Foods, Inc.
1135 E Artesia Blvd
Carson CA 90746
310 886-7720

(P-952)
CRAVE FOODS INC
2043 Imperial St, Los Angeles (90021-3203)
PHONE..................562 900-7272
Shaheda Sayed, *President*
Riaz A Surti, *Senior VP*
▲ EMP: 40 EST: 1992
SQ FT: 20,000
SALES (est): 3MM **Privately Held**
SIC: 2038 Frozen specialties

(P-953)
CULINARY BRANDS INC (PA)
3280 E 44th St, Vernon (90058-2426)
PHONE..................626 289-3000
Frank Calma, *President*
Mohsen Ganeian, *Principal*
EMP: 94 EST: 2011
SQ FT: 2,000
SALES (est): 37.2MM **Privately Held**
SIC: 2038 Frozen specialties

(P-954)
DEL REAL LLC (PA)
Also Called: Del Real Foods
11041 Inland Ave, Jurupa Valley (91752-1155)
PHONE..................951 681-0395
Michael Axelrod, *CEO*
Jesus Cardenas, *Mng Member*
EMP: 120
SQ FT: 175,000
SALES (est): 38.2MM **Privately Held**
WEB: www.delrealfoods.com
SIC: 2038 Ethnic foods, frozen

(P-955)
DON MIGUEL MEXICAN FOODS INC (HQ)
Also Called: Don Miguel Foods
333 S Anita Dr Ste 1000, Orange (92868-3318)
PHONE..................714 385-4500
Jeff Frank, *CEO*
Saralyn Brown, *Vice Pres*
Michael Chaignot, *VP Finance*
Michelle Ojeda, *Senior Buyer*
Donald Goglia, *VP Mfg*

▲ EMP: 45 EST: 1908
SQ FT: 80,000
SALES (est): 187MM **Privately Held**
WEB: www.donmiguel.com
SIC: 2038 Frozen specialties

(P-956)
DUBON & SONS INC
2852 E 11th St, Los Angeles (90023-3406)
P.O. Box 15282 (90015-0282)
PHONE..................213 923-1182
David Dubon Jr, *CEO*
▲ EMP: 16
SQ FT: 140,000
SALES: 53.5MM **Privately Held**
SIC: 2038 2086 5145 5149 Snacks, including onion rings, cheese sticks, etc.; carbonated beverages, nonalcoholic: bottled & canned; snack foods; beverages, except coffee & tea

(P-957)
EXCELLINE FOOD PRODUCTS LLC
833 N Hollywood Way, Burbank (91505-2814)
PHONE..................818 701-7710
Carlos Angulo, *CEO*
EMP: 116
SQ FT: 23,000
SALES: 30MM **Privately Held**
WEB: www.excellinefoods.com
SIC: 2038 Ethnic foods, frozen

(P-958)
EXCELLINE FOODS INC
833 N Hollywood Way, Burbank (91505-2814)
PHONE..................818 701-7710
EMP: 15 EST: 2012
SALES (est): 3.2MM **Privately Held**
SIC: 2038 Ethnic foods, frozen

(P-959)
FIVE STAR GOURMET FOODS INC
3880 Ebony St, Ontario (91761-1500)
PHONE..................909 390-0032
Tal Shoshan, *CEO*
Masha Simonian, *CFO*
Michelle Eoff, *Exec VP*
Phil Abreo, *Vice Pres*
Mark Baida, *Vice Pres*
EMP: 750
SQ FT: 130,000
SALES (est): 93.2MM **Privately Held**
SIC: 2038 2099 Frozen specialties; ready-to-eat meals, salads & sandwiches; salads, fresh or refrigerated

(P-960)
GOLDEN STATE FOODS CORP
640 S 6th Ave, City of Industry (91746-3086)
PHONE..................626 465-7500
Chad Buechel, *Branch Mgr*
Frank Listi, *President*
Larry Jacobsen, *Vice Pres*
Sonya Gomez, *Human Res Mgr*
Alan Knowles, *Purch Mgr*
EMP: 350
SALES (corp-wide): 1.3B **Privately Held**
WEB: www.goldenstatefoods.com
SIC: 2038 2087 2026 2051 Frozen specialties; flavoring extracts & syrups; fluid milk; bread, cake & related products
PA: Golden State Foods Corp.
18301 Von Karman Ave # 1100
Irvine CA 92612
949 247-8000

(P-961)
HARVEST FARMS INC
45000 Yucca Ave, Lancaster (93534-2526)
PHONE..................661 945-3636
Craig Shugert, *CEO*
Eric Shiring, *CFO*
Joe Hughes, *General Mgr*
▲ EMP: 100
SQ FT: 18,000
SALES (est): 27MM
SALES (corp-wide): 431MM **Privately Held**
SIC: 2038 5144 Lunches, frozen & packaged; poultry & poultry products

P
R
O
D
U
C
T
S

&

S
V
C
S

HQ: Good Source Solutions, Inc.
3115 Melrose Dr Ste 160
Carlsbad CA 92010
858 455-4800

(P-962)
ICEE COMPANY (HQ)
1205 S Dupont Ave, Ontario (91761-1536)
PHONE..................................800 426-4233
Gerald B Shreiber, *President*
Dan Fachner, *President*
Kent Galloway, *CFO*
Rod Sexton, *Vice Pres*
Rodney N Sexton, *Vice Pres*
▲ EMP: 80
SQ FT: 30,000
SALES (est): 306.3MM
SALES (corp-wide): 1.1B **Publicly Held**
WEB: www.theiceecompany.com
SIC: 2038 5145 3559 2087 Frozen spe-
cialties; popcorn & supplies; plastics
working machinery; flavoring extracts &
syrups
PA: J & J Snack Foods Corp.
6000 Central Hwy
Pennsauken NJ 08109
856 665-9533

(P-963)
ICEE COMPANY
4250 E Lowell St, Ontario (91761-1529)
PHONE..................................909 974-3518
Dan Fachner, *Branch Mgr*
EMP: 33
SALES (corp-wide): 1.1B **Publicly Held**
SIC: 2038 Frozen specialties
HQ: The Icee Company
1205 S Dupont Ave
Ontario CA 91761
800 426-4233

(P-964)
LA MEXICANA LLC
10615 Ruchti Rd, South Gate
(90280-7427)
PHONE..................................323 277-3660
Angelo Fraggos, *CEO*
EMP: 40
SQ FT: 45,000
SALES: 16MM
SALES (corp-wide): 488.2MM **Privately
Held**
SIC: 2038 Ethnic foods, frozen
PA: Blue Point Capital Partners Llc
127 Public Sq Ste 5100
Cleveland OH 44114
216 535-4700

(P-965)
LA MOUSSE
11150 La Grange Ave, Los Angeles
(90025-5632)
PHONE..................................310 478-6051
Nadine Korman, *President*
EMP: 60
SQ FT: 11,000
SALES (est): 9MM **Privately Held**
WEB: www.lamoussedesserts.com
SIC: 2038 Frozen specialties

(P-966)
NATES FINE FOODS LLC
8880 Industrial Ave # 100, Roseville
(95678-5946)
PHONE..................................310 897-2690
Nathan Barker, *COO*
EMP: 39
SQ FT: 50,000
SALES (est): 638.7K **Privately Held**
SIC: 2038 Ethnic foods, frozen; lunches,
frozen & packaged

(P-967)
NESTLE PIZZA COMPANY INC
Also Called: Kraft Foods
2530 E 11th St, Oakland (94601-1425)
PHONE..................................510 261-8001
John McCormick, *Branch Mgr*
EMP: 19
SALES (corp-wide): 92B **Privately Held**
SIC: 2038 Pizza, frozen
HQ: Nestle Pizza Company, Inc.
1 Kraft Ct
Glenview IL 60025
847 646-2000

(P-968)
NESTLE USA INC
Also Called: Nestle Dist Ctr & Logistics
3450 Dulles Dr, Jurupa Valley
(91752-3242)
PHONE..................................951 360-7200
Dean Ingram, *Branch Mgr*
EMP: 18
SALES (corp-wide): 92B **Privately Held**
WEB: www.nestleusa.com
SIC: 2038 Frozen specialties
HQ: Nestle Usa, Inc.
1812 N Moore St Ste 118
Rosslyn VA 22209
818 549-6000

(P-969)
NIPPON INDUSTRIES INC
2430 S Watney Way, Fairfield
(94533-6730)
PHONE..................................707 427-3127
Eric D Wong, *President*
◆ EMP: 31 EST: 1999
SQ FT: 30,000
SALES (est): 9.9MM **Privately Held**
SIC: 2038 Dinners, frozen & packaged

(P-970)
OTTOS PIZZA STIX INC
9040 Sunland Blvd, Sun Valley
(91352-2049)
P.O. Box 337 (91353-0337)
PHONE..................................562 519-5304
Otto Rafael Penarredonda, *CEO*
EMP: 10
SALES (est): 395.8K **Privately Held**
SIC: 2038 Pizza, frozen

(P-971)
OVERHILL FARMS INC
431 Isis Ave, Inglewood (90301-2009)
P.O. Box 58806, Los Angeles (90058-0806)
PHONE..................................323 587-5985
James Rudis, *President*
EMP: 250 **Privately Held**
WEB: www.overhillfarms.com
SIC: 2038 2015 8734 2099 Frozen spe-
cialties; poultry slaughtering & process-
ing; testing laboratories; food
preparations
HQ: Overhill Farms, Inc.
2727 E Vernon Ave
Vernon CA 90058
323 582-9977

(P-972)
OVERHILL FARMS INC (DH)
Also Called: Chicago Brothers
2727 E Vernon Ave, Vernon (90058-1822)
P.O. Box 58806 (90058-0806)
PHONE..................................323 582-9977
James Rudis, *President*
Rick Alvarez, *President*
Denise Ouellette, *President*
Robert C Bruning, *CFO*
Robert A Olivarez, *Vice Pres*
EMP: 43
SQ FT: 170,000
SALES (est): 174.3MM **Privately Held**
WEB: www.overhillfarms.com
SIC: 2038 Frozen specialties
HQ: Bellisio Foods, Inc.
1201 Harmon Pl Ste 302
Minneapolis MN 55403
218 723-5555

(P-973)
OVERHILL FARMS INC
3055 E 44th St, Vernon (90058-2439)
P.O. Box 806, Los Angeles (90078-0806)
PHONE..................................323 584-4375
Cruz Quirod, *Superintendent*
EMP: 214
SQ FT: 3,000 **Privately Held**
WEB: www.overhillfarms.com
SIC: 2038 2013 2015 Frozen specialties;
sausages & other prepared meats; poul-
try, processed: frozen
HQ: Overhill Farms, Inc.
2727 E Vernon Ave
Vernon CA 90058
323 582-9977

(P-974)
**PAMPANGA FOODS
INCORPORATED**
1835 N Orngthrp Park A, Anaheim
(92801-1143)
PHONE..................................714 331-7206
Rey Reyes, *President*
Coni Reyes, *Admin Sec*
Janet Ferinejal, *Controller*
▲ EMP: 40
SQ FT: 10,000
SALES (est): 8.2MM **Privately Held**
SIC: 2038 2099 2098 8742 Ethnic foods,
frozen; food preparations; noodles (e.g.
egg, plain & water), dry; food & beverage
consultant; meat packing plants

(P-975)
**PASCO CORPORATION OF
AMERICA**
19191 S Vt Ave Ste 420, Torrance
(90502-1051)
PHONE..................................503 289-6500
Hiroyuki Horie, *CEO*
▼ EMP: 50
SALES (est): 10.4MM **Privately Held**
WEB: www.pascoamerica.com
SIC: 2038 Ethnic foods, frozen
PA: Pasco Shikishima Corporation
5-3, Shirakabe, Higashi-Ku
Nagoya AIC 461-0

(P-976)
PICTSWEET COMPANY
732 Hanson Way, Santa Maria
(93458-9710)
P.O. Box 5878 (93456-5878)
PHONE..................................805 928-4414
Thomas Kerulas, *Branch Mgr*
EMP: 300
SALES (corp-wide): 421.8MM **Privately
Held**
WEB: www.pictsweet.com
SIC: 2038 2099 Frozen specialties; food
preparations
PA: The Pictsweet Company
10 Pictsweet Dr
Bells TN 38006
731 663-7600

(P-977)
RICHANDRE INC
Also Called: Ardella's
1170 Sandhill Ave, Carson (90746-1315)
PHONE..................................310 762-1560
Andre Oviedo, *President*
Hap Frank, *CFO*
Richard Shanz, *Admin Sec*
Frank Oviedo, *VP Opers*
Claudia Hutcherson, *Plant Mgr*
EMP: 12
SQ FT: 25,000
SALES: 10MM **Privately Held**
SIC: 2038 Frozen specialties

(P-978)
**RUIZ FOOD PRODUCTS INC
(PA)**
501 S Alta Ave, Dinuba (93618-2100)
P.O. Box 37 (93618-0037)
PHONE..................................559 591-5510
Rachel Cullen, *President*
Kim R Beck, *Ch of Bd*
Forrest Chandler, *CFO*
Matthew Ruiz, *Bd of Directors*
Olga Balderama, *Vice Pres*
EMP: 1884 EST: 1965
SQ FT: 200,000
SALES (est): 519.7MM **Privately Held**
WEB: www.elmonterey.com
SIC: 2038 2099 Ethnic foods, frozen; food
preparations

(P-979)
SAN FRANCISCO FOODS INC
14054 Catalina St, San Leandro
(94577-5508)
PHONE..................................510 357-7343
Hamad M Malak, *CEO*
Robert F Steel, *President*
Charley Luckhardt, *General Mgr*
John Sims, *Engineer*
Richard Earle, *Mfg Staff*
▲ EMP: 55

SQ FT: 12,000
SALES (est): 11.8MM **Privately Held**
SIC: 2038 Pizza, frozen

(P-980)
SHINE FOOD INC
Jesse Lord
21100 S Western Ave, Torrance
(90501-1700)
PHONE..................................310 533-6010
John Freschi, *Manager*
EMP: 20
SALES (corp-wide): 14.6MM **Privately
Held**
WEB: www.shinefood.com
SIC: 2038 2053 2052 2051 Frozen spe-
cialties; frozen bakery products, except
bread; cookies & crackers; bread, cake &
related products
PA: Shine Food, Inc.
19216 Normandie Ave
Torrance CA 90502
310 329-3829

(P-981)
STIR FOODS LLC
1820 E Walnut Ave, Fullerton (92831-4844)
PHONE..................................714 871-9231
Phil Decarion, *CEO*
EMP: 25
SALES (corp-wide): 1.4B **Privately Held**
SIC: 2038 2099 Frozen specialties; food
preparations
HQ: Stir Foods, Llc
1581 N Main St
Orange CA 92867
714 637-6050

(P-982)
STIR FOODS LLC (HQ)
1581 N Main St, Orange (92867-3439)
PHONE..................................714 637-6050
Milton Liu, *CEO*
Pablo Gallo Llorente, *CFO*
Zef Delgadillo, *Vice Pres*
Bill Happy, *Vice Pres*
Marco Velarde, *QA Dir*
EMP: 110
SQ FT: 40,000
SALES (est): 31.3MM
SALES (corp-wide): 1.4B **Privately Held**
WEB: www.stirfoods.com
SIC: 2038 2099 Frozen specialties; food
preparations
PA: Wind Point Partners, L.P.
676 N Michigan Ave # 3700
Chicago IL 60611
312 255-4800

(P-983)
**WESTECH INV ADVISORS LLC
(PA)**
104 La Mesa Dr 102, Portola Valley
(94028-7510)
PHONE..................................650 234-4300
Jay Cohan,
Ronald W Swenson, *Ch of Bd*
EMP: 34
SQ FT: 1,500
SALES (est): 4.7MM **Privately Held**
SIC: 2038 7359 6141 Frozen specialties;
equipment rental & leasing; personal
credit institutions

(P-984)
WHITTIER ENTERPRISE LLC
Also Called: Popkoff's
18901 Railroad St, City of Industry
(91748-1322)
PHONE..................................844 767-5633
Igor Cherdak, *Mng Member*
▲ EMP: 20 EST: 2010
SQ FT: 50,000
SALES: 5.2MM **Privately Held**
SIC: 2038 Frozen specialties

(P-985)
**WINDSOR QUALITY FOOD CO
LTD**
Also Called: Windsor Foods
4200 Concours Ste 100, Ontario
(91764-4982)
PHONE..................................713 843-5200
Orry Boscia, *President*
EMP: 3300

▲ = Import ▼=Export
◆ =Import/Export

SALES (est): 142.2K **Privately Held**
SIC: 2038 Frozen specialties

(P-986)
ZEN MONKEY LLC
655 N Central Ave Fl 1700, Glendale
(91203-1439)
PHONE....................................310 504-2899
Eric Glandian, *Mng Member*
EMP: 10 **EST:** 2013
SALES (est): 1.1MM **Privately Held**
SIC: 2038 Breakfasts, frozen & packaged

2041 Flour, Grain Milling

(P-987)
ADM MILLING CO
1603 Old Hwy 99 W, Arbuckle (95912)
PHONE....................................530 476-2662
Johnny Barnette, *Branch Mgr*
EMP: 76
SALES (corp-wide): 64.3B **Publicly Held**
WEB: www.admmilling.com
SIC: 2041 Grain mills (except rice)
HQ: Adm Milling Co.
8000 W 110th St Ste 300
Overland Park KS 66210
913 491-9400

(P-988)
ANDREW LLC
Also Called: Sanluisina
1710 S Grove Ave Ste A&B, Ontario
(91761-4545)
PHONE....................................909 270-9356
Miriam Navarro, *Mng Member*
EMP: 18
SALES: 1.5MM **Privately Held**
SIC: 2041 Corn meal

(P-989)
ARCHER-DANIELS-MIDLAND COMPANY
Also Called: ADM
455 N 6th St, Colton (92324-2988)
PHONE....................................909 783-7574
Stephen Brooks, *General Mgr*
EMP: 12
SALES (corp-wide): 64.3B **Publicly Held**
WEB: www.admworld.com
SIC: 2041 Flour & other grain mill products
PA: Archer-Daniels-Midland Company
77 W Wacker Dr Ste 4600
Chicago IL 60601
312 634-8100

(P-990)
ARCHER-DANIELS-MIDLAND COMPANY
Also Called: ADM
1543 Calada St, Los Angeles (90023-3210)
PHONE....................................323 266-2750
John Vanpleabe, *Manager*
EMP: 50
SALES (corp-wide): 64.3B **Publicly Held**
WEB: www.admworld.com
SIC: 2041 Flour & other grain mill products
PA: Archer-Daniels-Midland Company
77 W Wacker Dr Ste 4600
Chicago IL 60601
312 634-8100

(P-991)
ARCHER-DANIELS-MIDLAND COMPANY
ADM
2282 Davis Ct, Hayward (94545-1114)
PHONE....................................510 346-3309
Mike Alo, *Branch Mgr*
EMP: 112
SALES (corp-wide): 64.3B **Publicly Held**
WEB: www.admworld.com
SIC: 2041 Flour & other grain mill products
PA: Archer-Daniels-Midland Company
77 W Wacker Dr Ste 4600
Chicago IL 60601
312 634-8100

(P-992)
ARCHER-DANIELS-MIDLAND COMPANY
Also Called: ADM
3691 Noakes St, Los Angeles
(90023-3244)
PHONE....................................323 269-8175
Dan Munoz, *Manager*
EMP: 15
SQ FT: 20,264
SALES (corp-wide): 64.3B **Publicly Held**
WEB: www.admworld.com
SIC: 2041 Flour & other grain mill products
PA: Archer-Daniels-Midland Company
77 W Wacker Dr Ste 4600
Chicago IL 60601
312 634-8100

(P-993)
ARCHER-DANIELS-MIDLAND COMPANY
Also Called: ADM
350 N Guild Ave, Lodi (95240-0803)
P.O. Box 2675 (95241-2675)
PHONE....................................209 339-1252
EMP: 135
SALES (corp-wide): 64.3B **Publicly Held**
SIC: 2041 Flour & other grain mill products
PA: Archer-Daniels-Midland Company
77 W Wacker Dr Ste 4600
Chicago IL 60601
312 634-8100

(P-994)
ARDENT MILLS LLC
2020 E Steel Rd, Colton (92324-4008)
PHONE....................................951 201-1170
Brad Beckwith, *Branch Mgr*
EMP: 33
SALES (corp-wide): 473.4MM **Privately Held**
WEB: www.conagra.com
SIC: 2041 Flour & other grain mill products
PA: Ardent Mills, Llc
1875 Lawrence St Ste 1400
Denver CO 80202
800 851-9618

(P-995)
ARDENT MILLS LLC
5471 Ferguson Dr, Commerce
(90022-5118)
PHONE....................................323 725-0771
Dagoberto Castillo, *Branch Mgr*
EMP: 10
SALES (corp-wide): 473.4MM **Privately Held**
WEB: www.horizonmilling.com
SIC: 2041 Flour & other grain mill products
PA: Ardent Mills, Llc
1875 Lawrence St Ste 1400
Denver CO 80202
800 851-9618

(P-996)
ARDENT MILLS LLC
Also Called: Cargill Flour Milling Division
19684 Cajon Blvd, San Bernardino
(92407-1813)
PHONE....................................909 887-3407
Nelson Selmer, *Branch Mgr*
Gabe Lopez, *Safety Mgr*
EMP: 27
SQ FT: 26,180
SALES (corp-wide): 473.4MM **Privately Held**
WEB: www.horizonmilling.com
SIC: 2041 Flour mills, cereal (except rice)
PA: Ardent Mills, Llc
1875 Lawrence St Ste 1400
Denver CO 80202
800 851-9618

(P-997)
BAKAKERS SPECIALTY FOODS INC
Also Called: Martha's All Natural
2619 Lycoming St Ste 200, Stockton
(95206-4902)
PHONE....................................209 234-5935
Roylene F Brown, *President*
▼ **EMP:** 15
SQ FT: 9,000

SALES (est): 3.2MM **Privately Held**
SIC: 2041 2066 2099 Flour & other grain mill products; chocolate & cocoa products; food preparations

(P-998)
CENTRAL VALLEY AG GRINDING INC (PA)
Also Called: Cvag
5509 Langworth Rd, Oakdale
(95361-7909)
PHONE....................................209 869-1721
Michael Barry, *President*
Ryan Hogan, *CFO*
EMP: 29
SQ FT: 80,000
SALES (est): 24.5MM **Privately Held**
SIC: 2041 0723 Flour & other grain mill products; grain milling, custom services

(P-999)
D & D GOLD PRODUCT CORP
11608 Quartz Ave Fl 2, Fountain Valley
(92708-2532)
PHONE....................................714 550-0372
Trong Nguyen, *President*
Lang Nguyen, *Treasurer*
Hung Nguyen, *Admin Sec*
▲ **EMP:** 19
SQ FT: 12,000
SALES (est): 2.5MM **Privately Held**
SIC: 2041 2099 Flour & other grain mill products; spices, including grinding

(P-1000)
GENERAL MILLS INC
4309 Fruitland Ave, Vernon (90058-3176)
PHONE....................................323 584-3433
Jeff Shapiro, *Branch Mgr*
EMP: 40
SQ FT: 81,186
SALES (corp-wide): 16.8B **Publicly Held**
WEB: www.generalmills.com
SIC: 2041 Flour mills, cereal (except rice)
PA: General Mills, Inc.
1 General Mills Blvd
Minneapolis MN 55426
763 764-7600

(P-1001)
GIUSTOS SPECIALTY FOODS LLC (PA)
344 Littlefield Ave, South San Francisco
(94080-6103)
PHONE....................................650 873-6566
Craig A Moore, *Mng Member*
Jarjeet Bahia, *COO*
Ann Moore, *CFO*
▲ **EMP:** 43
SQ FT: 5,000
SALES: 24MM **Privately Held**
SIC: 2041 Flour mills, cereal (except rice); grain mills (except rice)

(P-1002)
GIUSTOS SPECIALTY FOODS LLC
241 E Harris Ave, South San Francisco
(94080-6807)
PHONE....................................650 873-6566
Craig A Moore, *Branch Mgr*
EMP: 37
SALES (est): 3MM
SALES (corp-wide): 24MM **Privately Held**
SIC: 2041 Flour & other grain mill products
PA: Giusto's Specialty Foods, Llc
344 Littlefield Ave
South San Francisco CA 94080
650 873-6566

(P-1003)
GK FOODS INC
Also Called: San Marcos Trading Company
133 Mata Way Ste 101, San Marcos
(92069-2937)
PHONE....................................760 752-5230
Laurence James Hickerson, *CEO*
John Bartelt, *Admin Sec*
Armando Ramos, *Prdtn Mgr*
EMP: 20
SQ FT: 15,000

SALES (est): 7.1MM **Privately Held**
WEB: www.globalkaizen.com
SIC: 2041 7389 5149 Flour & other grain mill products; packaging & labeling services; organic & diet foods

(P-1004)
GRAIN CRAFT INC
Also Called: California Milling Co
1861 E 55th St, Los Angeles (90058-3836)
PHONE....................................323 585-0131
Kurt Gallehugh, *Branch Mgr*
Johana Barajas, *Cust Mgr*
EMP: 45
SALES (corp-wide): 288.5MM **Privately Held**
WEB: www.cerealfood.com
SIC: 2041 Flour mills, cereal (except rice)
PA: Grain Craft, Inc.
201 W Main St Ste 203
Chattanooga TN 37408
423 265-2313

(P-1005)
LACEY MILLING COMPANY INC
217 W 5th St Ste 231, Hanford
(93230-5034)
P.O. Box 1193 (93232-1193)
PHONE....................................559 584-6634
Charles Lendrum, *President*
Karen Lacey, *Shareholder*
Tim Lacey, *Shareholder*
Scott Lendrum, *Treasurer*
Holly Caldera, *Admin Sec*
EMP: 15 **EST:** 1887
SQ FT: 40,000
SALES (est): 2.3MM **Privately Held**
SIC: 2041 Flour

(P-1006)
LT FOODS AMERICAS INC (HQ)
11130 Warland Dr, Cypress (90630-5032)
PHONE....................................562 340-4040
Abhinav Arora, *CEO*
Ankush Kukreja, *QC Mgr*
Kelly Orita, *Marketing Staff*
◆ **EMP:** 30
SQ FT: 30,000
SALES (est): 9MM
SALES (corp-wide): 330.5MM **Privately Held**
SIC: 2041 5149 Flour & other grain mill products; pasta & rice
PA: Lt Foods Limited
4th Floor, Mvl-I Park, Sector 15
Gurgaon HR 12200
124 305-5100

(P-1007)
MILLER MILLING COMPANY LLC
2908 S Maple Ave, Fresno (93725-2220)
PHONE....................................559 441-8133
Damon Sidles, *Manager*
Bonnie Kiehl, *IT/INT Sup*
Alisha Ruiz, *Buyer*
John Renteria, *Facilities Mgr*
EMP: 25 **Privately Held**
WEB: www.millermillingca.com
SIC: 2041 2045 Flour; prepared flour mixes & doughs
HQ: Miller Milling Company, Llc
7808 Creekridge Cir # 100
Minneapolis MN 55439
952 826-6331

(P-1008)
PILLSBURY COMPANY LLC
220 S Kenwood St Ste 202, Glendale
(91205-1671)
PHONE....................................818 522-3952
Linda Goodman, *Branch Mgr*
Linda Pillsbury, *Social Worker*
EMP: 55
SALES (corp-wide): 16.8B **Publicly Held**
SIC: 2041 Doughs & batters
HQ: The Pillsbury Company Llc
1 General Mills Blvd
Minneapolis MN 55426

(P-1009)
PRESTALE USA LP
3255 Saco St, Vernon (90058-1445)
PHONE....................................818 818-0976
Alen Navasargian, *CEO*

EMP: 50
SALES (est): 3MM **Privately Held**
SIC: 2041 Bread & bread-type roll mixes

(P-1010)
ROAN MILLS LLC
11069 Penrose St, Sun Valley
(91352-2722)
PHONE..............................818 249-4686
Robert P Dedlow, *Principal*
EMP: 10
SALES (est): 1MM **Privately Held**
SIC: 2041 Flour & other grain mill products

(P-1011)
VALLEY FINE FOODS COMPANY INC (PA)
Also Called: Pasta Prima
3909 Park Rd Ste H, Benicia (94510-1167)
PHONE..............................707 746-6888
Todd Nettleton, *CEO*
Ryan Tu, *Ch of Bd*
Mike Defabio, *President*
Wayne Tu, *COO*
David Weber, *CFO*
▲ **EMP:** 100
SQ FT: 83,598
SALES (est): 103.2MM **Privately Held**
WEB: www.valleyfinefoods.com
SIC: 2041 2038 Doughs, frozen or refrigerated; frozen specialties; snacks, including onion rings, cheese sticks, etc.

(P-1012)
VICOLO WHOLESALE (PA)
Also Called: Vicolo Pizza
31112 San Clemente St, Hayward
(94544-7802)
PHONE..............................510 475-6019
Eric Mount, *Partner*
Richard Sander, *Partner*
EMP: 29
SQ FT: 1,400
SALES (est): 8.2MM **Privately Held**
WEB: www.vicolopizza.com
SIC: 2041 Flour & other grain mill products

(P-1013)
WESTERN FOODS LLC (PA)
420 N Pioneer Ave, Woodland
(95776-6122)
P.O. Box 115 (95776-0115)
PHONE..............................530 601-5991
Miguel Reyna, *Mng Member*
Colin Garner, *Sales Staff*
Matthew Labriola,
▲ **EMP:** 50 **EST:** 2010
SALES (est): 15.4MM **Privately Held**
WEB: www.westernfoodsco.com
SIC: 2041 Flour

2043 Cereal Breakfast Foods

(P-1014)
AGRA-FARM FOODS INC
Also Called: Sincere Food Co
2223 Seaman Ave, El Monte (91733-2630)
PHONE..............................626 443-2335
Wen Yian Ling, *President*
EMP: 19
SQ FT: 11,000
SALES (est): 2.2MM **Privately Held**
SIC: 2043 Soy: prepared as cereal breakfast food

(P-1015)
ANNONA COMPANY LLC
Also Called: Earnest Eats
444 S Cedros Ave Ste 175, Solana Beach
(92075-1974)
PHONE..............................858 299-4238
Andrew Aussie, *Mng Member*
Adrianne Paegel, *Finance Mgr*
Tanya Beszeditz, *Sales Staff*
Mark Oliver, *Mng Member*
EMP: 10 **EST:** 2006
SQ FT: 5,000
SALES: 4MM **Privately Held**
SIC: 2043 2064 Cereal breakfast foods; breakfast bars

(P-1016)
CARIBBEAN COFFEE COMPANY INC
495 Pine Ave Ste A, Goleta (93117-3709)
PHONE..............................805 692-2200
John O Goerke, *CEO*
EMP: 16
SALES (est): 3.5MM **Privately Held**
SIC: 2043 2095 Coffee substitutes, made from grain; roasted coffee

(P-1017)
CHEERPAK
7778 Varna Ave, North Hollywood
(91605-1739)
PHONE..............................818 922-5451
Sargis Danielyan, *Principal*
EMP: 12
SALES (est): 438.8K **Privately Held**
SIC: 2043 Cereal breakfast foods

(P-1018)
EAST WEST TEA COMPANY LLC
Also Called: Golden Temple
1616 Preuss Rd, Los Angeles
(90035-4212)
PHONE..............................310 275-9891
Gurudhan S Khalsa, *Manager*
K Khalsa, *Vice Pres*
EMP: 16
SALES (corp-wide): 56.3MM **Privately Held**
WEB: www.peacecereal.com
SIC: 2043 2099 2064 8721 Cereal breakfast foods; tea blending; candy & other confectionery products; billing & bookkeeping service
PA: East West Tea Company, Llc
1325 Westec Dr
Eugene OR 97402
541 461-2160

(P-1019)
ELLEN LARK FARM
Also Called: Grainless Goodness
420 Bryant Cir Ste B, Ojai (93023-4209)
PHONE..............................805 272-8448
Kelley D'Angelo, *President*
Rachel Townley, *Purch Mgr*
EMP: 11 **EST:** 2015
SQ FT: 2,500
SALES: 1MM **Privately Held**
SIC: 2043 Cereal breakfast foods

(P-1020)
GENERAL MILLS INC
2000 W Turner Rd, Lodi (95242-2239)
P.O. Box 3002 (95241-1906)
PHONE..............................209 334-7061
Fax: 209 333-2949
EMP: 50
SALES (corp-wide): 17.6B **Publicly Held**
SIC: 2043 2045
PA: General Mills, Inc.
1 General Mills Blvd
Minneapolis MN 55426
763 764-7600

(P-1021)
GENERAL MILLS INC
620 N Kenwood St, Glendale (91206-2323)
PHONE..............................818 553-6777
EMP: 58
SALES (corp-wide): 16.8B **Publicly Held**
SIC: 2043 Wheat flakes: prepared as cereal breakfast food
PA: General Mills, Inc.
1 General Mills Blvd
Minneapolis MN 55426
763 764-7600

(P-1022)
GENERAL MILLS INC
11618 Mulberry Ave, Fontana
(92337-7618)
PHONE..............................951 685-7030
Gary M Roth, *Manager*
EMP: 100

SALES (corp-wide): 16.8B **Publicly Held**
WEB: www.generalmills.com
SIC: 2043 2041 2045 2099 Wheat flakes: prepared as cereal breakfast food; oats, rolled: prepared as cereal breakfast food; corn flakes: prepared as cereal breakfast food; rice: prepared as cereal breakfast food; flour; flour mixes; prepared flour mixes & doughs; cake mixes, prepared: from purchased flour; biscuit mixes, prepared: from purchased flour; dessert mixes & fillings; frosting mixes, dry: for cakes, cookies, etc.; potatoes, dried: packaged with other ingredients; pasta, uncooked: packaged with other ingredients; fruit & fruit peel confections; granola & muesli, bars & clusters; corn chips & other corn-based snacks
PA: General Mills, Inc.
1 General Mills Blvd
Minneapolis MN 55426
763 764-7600

(P-1023)
INGENUITY FOODS INC
Also Called: Ingenuity Brands
1564 Rollins Rd Ste 4, Burlingame
(94010-2311)
PHONE..............................650 562-7483
Mark Brooks, *President*
Jonathan Wolfson, *CEO*
EMP: 13 **EST:** 2017
SALES (est): 1MM **Privately Held**
SIC: 2043 Infants' foods, cereal type

(P-1024)
INTELLIGENT BLENDS LP
5330 Eastgate Mall, San Diego
(92121-2804)
PHONE..............................858 888-7937
Michael Ishayik, *President*
Ken Roy, *Creative Dir*
Patricia Tjong, *Manager*
▲ **EMP:** 38
SALES (est): 8.6MM **Privately Held**
SIC: 2043 Cereal breakfast foods

(P-1025)
KELLOGG COMPANY
2001 N Main St Ste 450, Walnut Creek
(94596-7268)
PHONE..............................925 952-8423
EMP: 385
SALES (corp-wide): 13.5B **Publicly Held**
SIC: 2043 Cereal breakfast foods
PA: Kellogg Company
1 Kellogg Sq
Battle Creek MI 49017
269 961-2000

(P-1026)
KELLOGG COMPANY
475 Eggo Way, San Jose (95116-1016)
PHONE..............................408 295-8656
Virgil Thomas, *Branch Mgr*
Curt Kruse, *Executive*
Kristin Gilmore, *Director*
EMP: 207
SALES (corp-wide): 13.5B **Publicly Held**
WEB: www.kelloggs.com
SIC: 2043 Cereal breakfast foods
PA: Kellogg Company
1 Kellogg Sq
Battle Creek MI 49017
269 961-2000

(P-1027)
KELLOGG SALES COMPANY
300 Harding Blvd Ste 215, Roseville
(95678-2474)
PHONE..............................916 787-0414
Shawn Snyder, *Principal*
EMP: 50
SALES (corp-wide): 13.5B **Publicly Held**
WEB: www.kellogg.com
SIC: 2043 Cereal breakfast foods
HQ: Kellogg Sales Company
1 Kellogg Sq
Battle Creek MI 49017
269 961-2000

(P-1028)
LADERA FOODS INC
20 Coquito Ct, Portola Valley (94028-7402)
PHONE..............................650 823-7186
Brian Tetrud, *CEO*

Daniel Imperiale-Hagerman, *VP Mktg*
EMP: 14 **EST:** 2013
SALES (est): 1.1MM **Privately Held**
SIC: 2043 Granola & muesli, except bars & clusters

(P-1029)
LE BARBOCCE INC
Also Called: Cafe Fanny
1328 6th St Frnt Frnt, Berkeley
(94710-1460)
PHONE..............................510 526-7664
James Maser, *President*
Alice Waters, *Vice Pres*
EMP: 20
SQ FT: 3,400
SALES (est): 2.6MM **Privately Held**
WEB: www.cafefanny.com
SIC: 2043 5812 Cereal breakfast foods; cafe

(P-1030)
NORTHERN QUINOA PROD CORP
Also Called: Tiny Hero
200 Kansas St Ste 215, San Francisco
(94103-5146)
PHONE..............................806 535-8118
Nick Kelley, *CEO*
William Hauser, *CFO*
EMP: 40
SQ FT: 10,000
SALES: 10MM **Privately Held**
SIC: 2043 Oats, rolled: prepared as cereal breakfast food

(P-1031)
ORGANIC MILLING INC
505 W Allen Ave, San Dimas (91773-1487)
PHONE..............................800 638-8686
Wolfgang Buehler, *Principal*
Lupe Martinez, *Vice Pres*
Connie Monk, *Controller*
EMP: 89
SALES (est): 18.1MM **Privately Held**
SIC: 2043 Cereal breakfast foods

(P-1032)
ORGANIC MILLING CORPORATION (PA)
505 W Allen Ave, San Dimas (91773-1487)
PHONE..............................909 599-0961
Bruce Olsen, *President*
Norm Bowers, *Vice Pres*
John Duenas, *Principal*
Chris Wadden, *General Mgr*
Michael Lopez, *IT/INT Sup*
▲ **EMP:** 108
SQ FT: 43,000
SALES (est): 30.7MM **Privately Held**
WEB: www.organicmilling.com
SIC: 2043 Granola & muesli, except bars & clusters

(P-1033)
ORGANIC MILLING CORPORATION
305 S Acacia St Ste A, San Dimas
(91773-2928)
PHONE..............................909 305-0185
Lupe Martinez, *Branch Mgr*
EMP: 17
SALES (corp-wide): 30.7MM **Privately Held**
WEB: www.organicmilling.com
SIC: 2043 Granola & muesli, except bars & clusters
PA: Organic Milling Corporation
505 W Allen Ave
San Dimas CA 91773
909 599-0961

2044 Rice Milling

(P-1034)
AMERICAN RICE INC
Comet Rice Division
1 Comet Ln, Maxwell (95955)
PHONE..............................530 438-2265
Jonn Burrnet, *Manager*
EMP: 60 **Privately Held**
WEB: www.amrice.com
SIC: 2044 Rice milling

HQ: American Rice Inc.
10700 North Fwy Ste 800
Houston TX 77037
281 272-8800

(P-1035)
BUNGE NORTH AMERICA INC
Also Called: Pacific Intl Rice Mills
845 Kentucky Ave, Woodland
(95695-2744)
P.O. Box 652 (95776-0652)
PHONE..................................530 666-1691
Melveryn Anderson, *President*
EMP: 100 **Privately Held**
SIC: 2044 Rice milling
HQ: Bunge North America, Inc.
1391 Tmberlake Manor Pkwy
Chesterfield MO 63017
314 292-2000

(P-1036)
CALIFORNIA FAMILY FOODS LLC
6550 Struckmeyer Rd, Arbuckle (95912)
PHONE..................................530 476-3326
David Myers, *President*
Perry Charter,
Tom Charter, *Mng Member*
Bruce Meyers, *Mng Member*
Laura Cobb, *Manager*
▼ EMP: 75
SQ FT: 75,000
SALES (est): 18.2MM **Privately Held**
SIC: 2044 0723 Rice milling; rice drying services

(P-1037)
CALIFORNIA HERITAGE MILLS INC
1 Comet Ln, Maxwell (95955)
P.O. Box 152 (95955-0152)
PHONE..................................530 438-2100
Paul Richter, *President*
Steven Sutter, *CEO*
Alyssa Ramirez, *Technician*
Patrick Brandon, *Marketing Staff*
◆ EMP: 30 EST: 2011
SALES: 6.8MM **Privately Held**
SIC: 2044 Rice milling

(P-1038)
CALIFRNIA PCF RICE MIL A CA LP
194 W Main St, Woodland (95695-2999)
P.O. Box 8729 (95776-8729)
PHONE..................................530 661-1923
Grant F Chappell, *Partner*
Joe Westover, *Partner*
EMP: 102
SQ FT: 10,000
SALES (est): 7.1MM **Privately Held**
SIC: 2044 Rice milling

(P-1039)
FAR WEST RICE INC
3455 Nelson Rd, Nelson (95958)
P.O. Box 370, Durham (95938-0370)
PHONE..................................530 891-1339
C W Johnson, *CEO*
Gregory Johnson, *President*
Charles Schwab, *Treasurer*
◆ EMP: 35
SQ FT: 3,000
SALES (est): 12.2MM **Privately Held**
WEB: www.farwestrice.com
SIC: 2044 5141 2099 Rice milling; groceries, general line; food preparations

(P-1040)
FARMERS RICE COOPERATIVE (PA)
Also Called: Frc
2566 River Plaza Dr, Sacramento
(95833-3673)
P.O. Box 15223 (95851-0223)
PHONE..................................916 923-5100
Frank Bragg, *CEO*
Bill Tanimoto, *CFO*
H Kirk Messick, *Senior VP*
Keith Hargrove, *Vice Pres*
Rob Paschoal, *Vice Pres*
◆ EMP: 35
SQ FT: 12,000

SALES (est): 98.6MM **Privately Held**
WEB: www.farmersrice.com
SIC: 2044 Rice milling

(P-1041)
FARMERS RICE COOPERATIVE
1800 Terminal Rd, Sacramento (95820)
PHONE..................................916 373-5549
Karen Martinelli, *Branch Mgr*
EMP: 50
SALES (corp-wide): 98.6MM **Privately Held**
WEB: www.farmersrice.com
SIC: 2044 Rice milling
PA: Farmers Rice Cooperative
2566 River Plaza Dr
Sacramento CA 95833
916 923-5100

(P-1042)
FARMERS RICE COOPERATIVE
2224 Industrial Blvd, West Sacramento
(95691-3429)
P.O. Box 15223, Sacramento (95851-0223)
PHONE..................................916 373-5500
Keith Hargrove, *Manager*
EMP: 125
SALES (corp-wide): 98.6MM **Privately Held**
WEB: www.farmersrice.com
SIC: 2044 Rice milling
PA: Farmers Rice Cooperative
2566 River Plaza Dr
Sacramento CA 95833
916 923-5100

(P-1043)
FARMERS RICE COOPERATIVE
2224 Industrial Blvd, West Sacramento
(95691-3429)
PHONE..................................916 373-5500
EMP: 150
SALES (corp-wide): 98.6MM **Privately Held**
WEB: www.farmersrice.com
SIC: 2044 Rice milling
PA: Farmers Rice Cooperative
2566 River Plaza Dr
Sacramento CA 95833
916 923-5100

(P-1044)
GOLD RIVER MILLS LLC (PA)
1620 E Kentucky Ave, Woodland
(95776-6110)
P.O. Box 8729 (95776-8729)
PHONE..................................530 661-1923
Thomas S Atkinson II,
Tom Atkinson,
Timothy R Magil,
John Perry,
▲ EMP: 51
SALES (est): 7.6MM **Privately Held**
WEB: www.goldrivermills.com
SIC: 2044 Rice milling

(P-1045)
I AMIRA GRAND FOODS INC (PA)
1 Park Plz Ste 600, Irvine (92614-5987)
PHONE..................................949 852-4468
Karan A Chanana, *Chairman*
◆ EMP: 15
SALES (est): 4.6MM **Privately Held**
SIC: 2044 Brown rice

(P-1046)
KODA FARMS INC
22540 Russell Ave, South Dos Palos
(93665)
P.O. Box 10 (93665-0010)
PHONE..................................209 392-2191
Edward K Koda, *President*
Laura Koda, *Vice Pres*
Robin Koda, *Vice Pres*
Ross Koda, *Vice Pres*
Tama T Koda, *Vice Pres*
▲ EMP: 50 EST: 1946
SQ FT: 20,000
SALES (est): 8.3MM **Privately Held**
WEB: www.kodafarms.com
SIC: 2044 0112 Rice milling; rice

(P-1047)
KODA FARMS MILLING INC
22540 Russell Ave, South Dos Palos
(93665)
P.O. Box 10 (93665-0010)
PHONE..................................209 392-2191
Ross K Koda, *CEO*
Karen Crutcher, *Admin Sec*
EMP: 25
SALES (est): 7.8MM **Privately Held**
SIC: 2044 2099 Rice milling; rice, uncooked: packaged with other ingredients

(P-1048)
MARS FOOD US LLC
Also Called: Uncle Ben's
6875 Pacific View Dr, Los Angeles
(90068-1831)
PHONE..................................562 616-7347
EMP: 350
SALES (corp-wide): 37.6B **Privately Held**
SIC: 2044 Rice milling
HQ: Mars Food Us, Llc
2001 E Cashdan St Ste 201
Rancho Dominguez CA 90220
310 933-0670

(P-1049)
POLIT FARMS INC
4334 Old Hwy 99w 99 W, Maxwell (95955)
PHONE..................................530 438-2759
Mike Polit, *President*
Sherry Polit, *Vice Pres*
▼ EMP: 10
SQ FT: 6,000
SALES (est): 1.7MM **Privately Held**
SIC: 2044 Milled rice

(P-1050)
RIVERBEND RICE MILL INC
234 Main St, Colusa (95932)
P.O. Box 830 (95932-0830)
PHONE..................................530 458-8561
Fax: 530 458-8569
EMP: 17
SALES (est): 2.2MM **Privately Held**
SIC: 2044

(P-1051)
SUN VALLEY RICE COMPANY LLC
7050 Eddy Rd, Arbuckle (95912-9789)
P.O. Box 8, Dunnigan (95937-0008)
PHONE..................................530 476-3000
Kenneth M Lagrande, *Mng Member*
Chris Fantl, *Administration*
Brett Lagrande, *Accountant*
Joan Quinlan, *Controller*
Marta Stegall, *Human Res Dir*
◆ EMP: 98
SQ FT: 20,000
SALES (est): 19.2MM **Privately Held**
WEB: www.sunvalleyrice.com
SIC: 2044 Rice milling

(P-1052)
SUNFOODS LLC
194 W Main St Ste 200, Woodland
(95695-2999)
P.O. Box 8729 (95776-8729)
PHONE..................................530 661-1923
Matt Alonso, *CEO*
EMP: 10 **Privately Held**
SIC: 2044 Rice milling
HQ: Sunfoods, Llc
1620 E Kentucky Ave
Woodland CA 95776

(P-1053)
TAMAKI RICE CORPORATION
1701 Abel Rd, Williams (95987-5156)
PHONE..................................530 473-2862
Masami Kitagawa, *President*
Kurt Barrett, *General Mgr*
▲ EMP: 20
SQ FT: 14,000
SALES (est): 2.8MM **Privately Held**
WEB: www.tamakimai.com
SIC: 2044 Rice milling
PA: Hombo Shoten Co.,Ltd.
8-56, Kinkocho
Kagoshima KGM 892-0

(P-1054)
WEHAH FARM INC
Also Called: Lundberg Family Farms
5311 Midway, Richvale (95974)
P.O. Box 369 (95974-0369)
PHONE..................................530 538-3500
Grant Lundberg, *CEO*
Mike Denny, *Vice Pres*
Jessica Wilhite, *Planning*
Anders Lundberg, *Technician*
Janice Willadsen, *Engineer*
EMP: 255
SALES (est): 69.5MM **Privately Held**
SIC: 2044 Rice milling

> ## 2045 Flour, Blended & Prepared

(P-1055)
BAKEMARK USA LLC (PA)
7351 Crider Ave, Pico Rivera (90660-3705)
PHONE..................................562 949-1054
Jim Parker, *President*
Gary Schmidt, *President*
Refugio Reynoso, *CFO*
John Kupniewski, *Vice Pres*
Steve Scales, *Vice Pres*
◆ EMP: 300
SQ FT: 275,000
SALES (est): 538.9MM **Privately Held**
WEB: www.yourbakemark.com
SIC: 2045 5149 3556 2099 Flours & flour mixes, from purchased flour; bakery products; food products machinery; food preparations

(P-1056)
BRIDGFORD FOODS CORPORATION (HQ)
1308 N Patt St, Anaheim (92801-2551)
P.O. Box 3773 (92803-3773)
PHONE..................................714 526-5533
John V Simmons, *President*
William L Bridgford, *Ch of Bd*
Raymond F Lancy, *CFO*
Allan L Bridgford, *Vice Pres*
Hugh Wm Bridgford, *Vice Pres*
EMP: 277
SQ FT: 100,000
SALES: 174.2MM **Publicly Held**
WEB: www.bridgford.com
SIC: 2045 2099 2015 2013 Biscuit dough, prepared: from purchased flour; doughs, frozen or refrigerated: from purchased flour; sandwiches, assembled & packaged: for wholesale market; salads, fresh or refrigerated; poultry sausage, luncheon meats & other poultry products; snack sticks, including jerky: from purchased meat; cheese, natural & processed; dips, cheese-based; frozen specialties
PA: Bridgford Industries Incorporated
1601 S Good Latimer Expy
Dallas TX 75226
214 428-1535

(P-1057)
KWEEN FOODS LLC
429 S Sierra Ave Unit 130, Solana Beach
(92075-2203)
PHONE..................................805 895-0003
Eric Myles Katz, *Mng Member*
Alexandra Bonar,
EMP: 15
SALES (est): 1.1MM **Privately Held**
SIC: 2045 Bread & bread type roll mixes: from purchased flour

(P-1058)
LANGLOIS COMPANY
Also Called: Langlois Flour Company
10810 San Sevaine Way, Jurupa Valley
(91752-1116)
PHONE..................................951 360-3900
Richard W Langlois, *President*
Lynn Langlois Nye, *Treasurer*
Jeff Langlois, *Vice Pres*
Sally Langlois, *Vice Pres*
Teresa Cisneros, *Administration*
▼ EMP: 50
SQ FT: 48,000

PRODUCTS & SVCS

SALES (est): 17MM **Privately Held**
WEB: www.langloiscompany.com
SIC: 2045 2035 2079 2099 Blended flour: from purchased flour; mayonnaise; dressings, salad: raw & cooked (except dry mixes); vegetable refined oils (except corn oil); gelatin dessert preparations; flavoring extracts & syrups

(P-1059)
POPLA INTERNATIONAL INC
1740 S Sacramento Ave, Ontario (91761-7744)
PHONE....................909 923-6899
Mike Shinozaki, *President*
Ashley Shinozaki, *Admin Sec*
▲ **EMP:** 20
SQ FT: 8,000
SALES (est): 3.7MM **Privately Held**
WEB: www.popla.com
SIC: 2045 Prepared flour mixes & doughs

2046 Wet Corn Milling

(P-1060)
CORN PRODUCTS DEVELOPMENT INC (HQ)
1021 Industrial Dr, Stockton (95206-3928)
P.O. Box 6129 (95206-0129)
PHONE....................209 982-1920
Samuel Scott, *Principal*
EMP: 12
SALES (est): 8.9MM
SALES (corp-wide): 5.8B **Publicly Held**
SIC: 2046 Wet corn milling
PA: Ingredion Incorporated
5 Westbrook Corporate Ctr # 500
Westchester IL 60154
708 551-2600

(P-1061)
INGREDION INCORPORATED
Also Called: Corn Products-Stockton Plant
1021 Industrial Dr, Stockton (95206-3928)
P.O. Box 6129 (95206-0129)
PHONE....................209 982-1920
Mark Madsen, *Manager*
Enrique Casillas, *Engineer*
Michael Levy,
Roger Hoffdahl, *Manager*
EMP: 76
SALES (corp-wide): 5.8B **Publicly Held**
WEB: www.cornproducts.com
SIC: 2046 Corn sugars & syrups
PA: Ingredion Incorporated
5 Westbrook Corporate Ctr # 500
Westchester IL 60154
708 551-2600

(P-1062)
SIN MA IMPORTS COMPANY
Also Called: Lucky Foods
1425 Minnesota St, San Francisco (94107-3519)
PHONE....................415 285-9369
Fred S Pang, *Owner*
Steven Pang, *Office Mgr*
▲ **EMP:** 10 **EST:** 1973
SQ FT: 7,500
SALES (est): 857.9K **Privately Held**
SIC: 2046 2075 2074 Corn oil, refined; soybean oil mills; cottonseed oil mills

(P-1063)
SMART FOODS LLC
3398 Leonis Blvd Vernon, Vernon (90058)
PHONE....................818 660-2238
Keyvan Khalifian,
◆ **EMP:** 25
SALES (est): 979.1K **Privately Held**
SIC: 2046 2076 Corn oil, refined; vegetable oil mills; coconut oil

(P-1064)
TAPIOCA EXPRESS
81 Curtner Ave, San Jose (95125-1064)
PHONE....................408 999-0128
Vivian Nguyen, *Owner*
EMP: 15
SALES (est): 1.2MM **Privately Held**
SIC: 2046 Tapioca

(P-1065)
TAPIOCA EXPRESS
6145 El Cajon Blvd Ste G, San Diego (92115-3923)
PHONE....................619 286-0484
Nip Lee, *Owner*
EMP: 11 **EST:** 2010
SALES (est): 92.7K **Privately Held**
SIC: 2046 Tapioca

2047 Dog & Cat Food

(P-1066)
ARCHEYY & FRIENDS LLC
3630 Andrews Dr Apt 114, Pleasanton (94588-3015)
PHONE....................703 579-7649
Sean Marler,
EMP: 20
SALES (est): 671.8K **Privately Held**
SIC: 2047 0752 Dog food; animal boarding services; showing services, pet & animal specialties; grooming services, pet & animal specialties

(P-1067)
ARIES PREPARED BEEF COMPANY
11850 Sheldon St, Sun Valley (91352-1507)
PHONE....................818 771-0181
Zelco Majstorich, *Branch Mgr*
EMP: 45
SALES (corp-wide): 11MM **Privately Held**
SIC: 2047 Dog food
PA: Aries Prepared Beef Company
17 W Magnolia Blvd
Burbank CA 91502
818 526-4855

(P-1068)
ARTHUR DOGSWELL LLC (PA)
11301 W Olympic Blvd, Los Angeles (90064-1653)
PHONE....................888 559-8833
Brad Casper, *Mng Member*
Berenice Officer, *Vice Pres*
Regina Miller, *Controller*
Rodrigo Ayres, *Opers Mgr*
Sam Schein, *Natl Sales Mgr*
▲ **EMP:** 33
SQ FT: 2,000
SALES (est): 24.5MM **Privately Held**
SIC: 2047 5149 Dog food; pet foods

(P-1069)
BIG HEART PET BRANDS INC (HQ)
1 Maritime Plz Fl 2, San Francisco (94111-3407)
P.O. Box 193575 (94119-3575)
PHONE....................415 247-3000
Richard K Smucker, *CEO*
David J West, *President*
Mark R Belgya, *CFO*
Barry C Dunaway, *Senior VP*
Jill Penrose, *Vice Pres*
◆ **EMP:** 300
SALES (est): 1.6B
SALES (corp-wide): 7.8B **Publicly Held**
WEB: www.delmontefoods.com
SIC: 2047 Dog & cat food
PA: The J M Smucker Company
1 Strawberry Ln
Orrville OH 44667
330 682-3000

(P-1070)
CANIDAE CORPORATION
Also Called: Canidae Pet Foods
1975 Tandem, Norco (92860-3608)
P.O. Box 3610, San Luis Obispo (93403-3610)
PHONE....................909 599-5190
John Gordon, *President*
Scott Whipple, *CFO*
Ryan Hon, *Administration*
Brittney Robinson, *Administration*
Michael Garcia, *Controller*
EMP: 10 **EST:** 1963
SALES (est): 2.1MM **Privately Held**
WEB: www.canidae.com
SIC: 2047 Dog & cat food

(P-1071)
CANINE CAVIAR PET FOODS DE INC
4131 Tigris Way, Riverside (92503-4844)
PHONE....................714 223-1800
Jeff A Baker, *Principal*
EMP: 18
SALES (est): 615.3K **Privately Held**
SIC: 2047 Dog & cat food

(P-1072)
DEXTERS DELI
2508 El Cmino Real Ste B2, Carlsbad (92008)
PHONE....................760 720-7507
Rosay Tori, *Owner*
EMP: 30
SALES (corp-wide): 1.8MM **Privately Held**
SIC: 2047 Dog & cat food
PA: Dexters Deli
1229 Camino Del Mar
Del Mar CA 92014
858 792-3707

(P-1073)
DIAMOND PET FOOD PROCESSORS O
250 Roth Rd, Lathrop (95330-9724)
PHONE....................209 983-4900
Michael Kampeter, *Mng Member*
Richard Kampeter,
Gary Schell,
Mark Schell,
◆ **EMP:** 45 **EST:** 1998
SALES (est): 5.8MM **Privately Held**
SIC: 2047 Dog & cat food

(P-1074)
GENTLE GIANTS PRODUCTS INC
4867 Pedley Ave, Norco (92860-1646)
PHONE....................951 818-2512
Tracy Posner Ward, *CEO*
Burt Ward, *President*
EMP: 10 **EST:** 2005
SQ FT: 15,000
SALES (est): 1.9MM **Privately Held**
SIC: 2047 Dog & cat food

(P-1075)
INABA FOODS (USA) INC
19301 Pcf Gtwy Dr Ste 120, Torrance (90502)
PHONE....................310 818-2270
Atsuhiro Inaba, *CEO*
▲ **EMP:** 10
SALES (est): 1MM **Privately Held**
SIC: 2047 Dog & cat food

(P-1076)
J & R TAYLOR BROS ASSOC INC
Also Called: Premium Pet Foods
16321 Arrow Hwy, Irwindale (91706-2018)
PHONE....................626 334-9301
Rick Taylor, *President*
◆ **EMP:** 58
SALES (est): 6.8MM
SALES (corp-wide): 2B **Publicly Held**
WEB: www.breeders-choice.com
SIC: 2047 Dog food; prepared feeds
PA: Central Garden & Pet Company
1340 Treat Blvd Ste 600
Walnut Creek CA 94597
925 948-4000

(P-1077)
MARS PETCARE US INC
2765 Lexington Way, San Bernardino (92407-1842)
PHONE....................909 887-8131
Ed Skokan, *Manager*
EMP: 50
SQ FT: 76,000
SALES (corp-wide): 37.6B **Privately Held**
SIC: 2047 2048 Dog food; prepared feeds
HQ: Mars Petcare Us, Inc.
2013 Ovation Pkwy
Franklin TN 37067
615 807-4626

(P-1078)
MARS PETCARE US INC
13243 Nutro Way, Victorville (92395-7789)
PHONE....................760 261-7900

EMP: 50
SALES (corp-wide): 37.6B **Privately Held**
SIC: 2047 Cat food; dog food
HQ: Mars Petcare Us, Inc.
2013 Ovation Pkwy
Franklin TN 37067
615 807-4626

(P-1079)
NESTLE PURINA PETCARE COMPANY
800 N Brand Blvd Fl 5, Glendale (91203-4281)
PHONE....................314 982-1000
EMP: 125
SALES (corp-wide): 92B **Privately Held**
WEB: www.purina.com
SIC: 2047 Dog & cat food
HQ: Nestle Purina Petcare Company
1 Checkerboard Sq
Saint Louis MO 63164
314 982-1000

(P-1080)
PERFECTION PET FOODS LLC (DH)
Also Called: Perfection Pet Brands
1111 N Miller Park Ct, Visalia (93291-9454)
PHONE....................559 302-4880
Kevin Kruse, *CEO*
Jeremy Wilhelm, *President*
Brian Ubegin, *CFO*
Mike Gagene, *Vice Pres*
Rob Haynes, *Vice Pres*
EMP: 25
SALES (est): 13MM
SALES (corp-wide): 553.7MM **Privately Held**
SIC: 2047 Dog food
HQ: Western Milling, Llc
31120 West St
Goshen CA 93227
559 302-1000

(P-1081)
PET CAROUSEL INC
2350 Academy Ave, Sanger (93657-9559)
PHONE....................316 291-2500
Gary D Becker, *CEO*
Siegfried W Habild, *President*
EMP: 28
SQ FT: 36,000
SALES (est): 4.4MM **Privately Held**
SIC: 2047 Dog & cat food

(P-1082)
PRIMAL PET FOODS INC
535 Watt Dr Ste B, Fairfield (94534-1790)
PHONE....................415 642-7400
Matthew Koss, *CEO*
Sarah Quinn, *Accounting Mgr*
Matthew Pirz, *VP Sales*
Megan Pearson, *Regl Sales Mgr*
Stephanie Real, *Sales Mgr*
▲ **EMP:** 12
SQ FT: 5,000
SALES (est): 1.8MM **Privately Held**
WEB: www.primalpetfoods.com
SIC: 2047 Dog & cat food

(P-1083)
SCHELL & KAMPETER INC
250 Roth Rd, Lathrop (95330-9724)
PHONE....................209 983-4900
Gary Schell, *Branch Mgr*
Jon Lowe, *Warehouse Mgr*
EMP: 45
SALES (corp-wide): 68.2K **Privately Held**
SIC: 2047 Dog food
PA: Schell & Kampeter, Inc.
103 N Olive St
Meta MO 65058
573 229-4203

2048 Prepared Feeds For Animals & Fowls

(P-1084)
ARTEMIS PET FOOD COMPANY INC
18010 S Figueroa St, Gardena (90248-4213)
PHONE....................818 771-0700

▲ = Import ▼=Export
◆ =Import/Export

Ken Park, *President*
Alex Kim, *Exec VP*
Alex J Kim, *Vice Pres*
▲ **EMP:** 10
SQ FT: 10,000
SALES (est): 1.5MM **Privately Held**
SIC: 2048 Canned pet food (except dog & cat); dry pet food (except dog & cat); frozen pet food (except dog & cat)

(P-1085)
BORIS BS FRMS VTRNARY SVCS INC
9245 Laguna Springs Dr, Elk Grove (95758-7987)
PHONE......................916 730-4225
Boris Baidoo, *CEO*
Nana OSI Akumia, *CFO*
Edwin Korankye, *Admin Sec*
EMP: 64
SALES: 6MM
SALES (corp-wide): 831.4MM **Privately Held**
SIC: 2048 Poultry feeds
PA: Boris B's Farms & Veterinary Supplies
Ghana Limited
Opposite Presbyterian Church, Plot 9, Block 5 North Suntreso Ma
Kumasi
322 033-800

(P-1086)
BROOKHURST MILL
3315 Van Buren Blvd, Riverside (92503-5697)
PHONE......................951 688-3511
Bradley C Pope, *CEO*
Bradley Pope, *President*
Gail Morrison, *Corp Secy*
Kevin Pope, *Office Mgr*
▼ **EMP:** 14
SQ FT: 10,800
SALES (est): 2.6MM **Privately Held**
SIC: 2048 Poultry feeds; livestock feeds

(P-1087)
CALVA PRODUCTS CO INC
4351 E Winery Rd, Acampo (95220-9506)
P.O. Box 126 (95220-0126)
PHONE......................209 339-1516
Jim Cook Sr, *CEO*
Bill Cook, *Vice Pres*
◆ **EMP:** 39 **EST:** 1975
SQ FT: 62,000
SALES (est): 13.1MM
SALES (corp-wide): 6.8B **Privately Held**
WEB: www.calvaproducts.com
SIC: 2048 Prepared feeds
HQ: Purina Animal Nutrition Llc
100 Danforth Dr
Gray Summit MO 63039

(P-1088)
CANINE CAVIAR PET FOODS INC
4131 Tigris Way, Riverside (92503-4844)
P.O. Box 5872, Norco (92860-8029)
PHONE......................714 223-1800
Jeff Baker, *President*
Gary Ward, *Vice Pres*
Jamie Carper, *Sales Staff*
Dawn Barraco, *Pub Rel Staff*
◆ **EMP:** 30
SQ FT: 6,000
SALES (est): 7.2MM **Privately Held**
WEB: www.caninecaviar.com
SIC: 2048 Canned pet food (except dog & cat)

(P-1089)
DAIRYMENS FEED & SUP COOP ASSN
323 E Washington St, Petaluma (94952-3120)
PHONE......................707 763-1585
Jerry Renner, *President*
Arnold Riebli, *CEO*
Bob McClure, *Vice Pres*
EMP: 14
SQ FT: 50,000
SALES (est): 5.5MM **Privately Held**
WEB: www.dairymensfeed.com
SIC: 2048 Livestock feeds

(P-1090)
DEXT COMPANY OF MARYLAND (DH)
Also Called: Reconserve of Maryland
2811 Wilshire Blvd # 410, Santa Monica (90403-4803)
P.O. Box 2211 (90407-2211)
PHONE......................310 458-1574
Meyer Luskin, *Ch of Bd*
Robert McMullen, *President*
Rida Hamed, *Vice Pres*
Gerald Truelove, *Vice Pres*
EMP: 20
SQ FT: 4,000
SALES: 70MM
SALES (corp-wide): 203.7MM **Privately Held**
SIC: 2048 Prepared feeds
HQ: Reconserve, Inc.
2811 Wilshire Blvd # 410
Santa Monica CA 90403
310 458-1574

(P-1091)
ECONOMY STOCK FEED COMPANY
10508 E Central Ave, Del Rey (93616-9711)
PHONE......................559 888-2187
Rod Kramer, *President*
Judy Kramer, *Vice Pres*
EMP: 15
SQ FT: 1,200
SALES (est): 1.9MM **Privately Held**
SIC: 2048 Prepared feeds

(P-1092)
ELK GROVE MILLING INC
8320 Eschinger Rd, Elk Grove (95757-9739)
PHONE......................916 684-2056
Robert Lent, *President*
Simone Keyawa, *Admin Asst*
Steven Ruiz, *Opers Mgr*
Sherri Lafoon, *Sales Mgr*
Brian Lent, *Maint Spvr*
▲ **EMP:** 25
SQ FT: 400,000
SALES (est): 5.5MM **Privately Held**
WEB: www.elkgrovemilling.com
SIC: 2048 3541 5191 Livestock feeds; shell crushing, for feed; machine tools, metal cutting type; animal feeds

(P-1093)
FEEDSTUFFS PROCESSING CO
112 Lark Ct, Alamo (94507-1800)
PHONE......................925 820-5454
Craig Zellmer, *President*
Vernon Johnson, *Shareholder*
Barbara Corneille, *Treasurer*
Pat Conklin, *Admin Sec*
▼ **EMP:** 15 **EST:** 1943
SQ FT: 50,000
SALES: 5.5MM **Privately Held**
SIC: 2048 Feed supplements

(P-1094)
FOSTER COMMODITIES
Also Called: Foster Farms
1900 Kern St, Kingsburg (93631-9687)
P.O. Box 457, Livingston (95334-0457)
PHONE......................559 897-1081
Todd Elrod, *Manager*
Doug Kooren, *CFO*
Brian Tavernas, *Controller*
John Rocha, *Opers Mgr*
Melissa Springer, *Plant Mgr*
EMP: 25
SALES (est): 3.1MM **Privately Held**
SIC: 2048 Prepared feeds

(P-1095)
FOSTER FARMS LLC
1900 Kern St, Kingsburg (93631-9687)
PHONE......................559 897-1081
Donald Jones, *Branch Mgr*
EMP: 28
SALES (corp-wide): 1.4B **Privately Held**
WEB: www.fosterfarms.com
SIC: 2048 Poultry feeds
PA: Foster Farms, Llc
1000 Davis St
Livingston CA 95334
209 394-7901

(P-1096)
FOSTER POULTRY FARMS
221 Stefani Ave, Livingston (95334-1543)
PHONE......................209 394-7950
Jeremiah Nord, *Manager*
Janet Dewey, *Purch Mgr*
EMP: 25
SALES (corp-wide): 3B **Privately Held**
WEB: www.fosterfarms.com
SIC: 2048 Poultry feeds
PA: Foster Poultry Farms
1000 Davis St
Livingston CA 95334
209 394-6914

(P-1097)
FRONTIER AG CO INC (PA)
46735 County Road 32b, Davis (95618-9501)
PHONE......................530 297-1020
John Pereira, *President*
Matthew S Labriola, *Shareholder*
Mathew Labriola, *Admin Sec*
EMP: 50
SALES (est): 13MM **Privately Held**
WEB: www.frontieragco.com
SIC: 2048 0723 Livestock feeds; rice drying services

(P-1098)
GEORGE VERHOEVEN GRAIN INC (PA)
5355 E Airport Dr, Ontario (91761-8604)
PHONE......................909 605-1531
Randall Verhoeven, *President*
Robert Verhoeven, *Vice Pres*
EMP: 15
SQ FT: 2,100
SALES (est): 3.5MM **Privately Held**
SIC: 2048 5153 Livestock feeds; grain elevators

(P-1099)
HARBOR GREEN GRAIN LP
13181 Crssroads Pkwy N, City of Industry (91746)
PHONE......................310 991-8089
Shing Lo, *President*
Zach Xu, *CEO*
◆ **EMP:** 45
SALES (est): 12.2MM **Privately Held**
SIC: 2048 Alfalfa, cubed

(P-1100)
HRK PET FOOD PRODUCTS INC
12924 Pierce St, Pacoima (91331-2526)
PHONE......................818 897-2521
Joey Herrick, *President*
Lynnda Herrick, *Vice Pres*
▲ **EMP:** 19
SQ FT: 30,000
SALES (est): 1.9MM **Privately Held**
SIC: 2048 Canned pet food (except dog & cat)

(P-1101)
INTERNATIONAL PROCESSING CORP (DH)
233 Wilshire Blvd Ste 310, Santa Monica (90401-1206)
P.O. Box 2211 (90407-2211)
PHONE......................310 458-1574
Bob McMullen, *President*
EMP: 25
SALES (est): 24.9MM
SALES (corp-wide): 203.7MM **Privately Held**
SIC: 2048 Prepared feeds
HQ: Reconserve, Inc.
2811 Wilshire Blvd # 410
Santa Monica CA 90403
310 458-1574

(P-1102)
J D HEISKELL HOLDINGS LLC
11518 Road 120, Pixley (93256-9727)
P.O. Box 1379, Tulare (93275-1379)
PHONE......................559 757-3135
Robert Hodgen, *Manager*
EMP: 80
SALES (corp-wide): 745.3MM **Privately Held**
SIC: 2048 5191 Prepared feeds; animal feeds

PA: J. D. Heiskell Holdings, Llc
1939 Hillman St
Tulare CA 93274
559 685-6100

(P-1103)
J S WEST MILLING CO INC
501 9th St, Modesto (95354-3420)
PHONE......................209 529-4232
D Gary West, *President*
Robert J Benson, *Ch of Bd*
Bob Metz, *CFO*
Eric Benson, *Vice Pres*
Jill Benson, *Vice Pres*
EMP: 26
SQ FT: 1,692
SALES (est): 4.5MM **Privately Held**
SIC: 2048 0252 5999 5191 Livestock feeds; started pullet farm; pets & pet supplies; animal feeds

(P-1104)
JIMINYS LLC
2855 Mandela Pkwy Ste 11, Oakland (94608-4051)
PHONE......................415 939-6314
Anne Carlson, *Mng Member*
EMP: 10
SQ FT: 3,000
SALES (est): 50K **Privately Held**
SIC: 2048 Dry pet food (except dog & cat)

(P-1105)
KOCH FEEDS INC
10916 Amsterdam Rd, Winton (95388-9749)
PHONE......................209 725-8253
Rochelle Koch, *President*
EMP: 20 **EST:** 2000
SALES (est): 1.7MM **Privately Held**
SIC: 2048 Feed supplements

(P-1106)
KOIS & PONDS INC
4460 Brooks St Ste B, Montclair (91763-4135)
PHONE......................800 936-3638
Michael Hernandez, *CEO*
Michelle Swanson, *Principal*
EMP: 10
SQ FT: 1,300
SALES: 128.4K **Privately Held**
SIC: 2048 Fish food

(P-1107)
LAWLEYS INC
4554 Qantas Ln, Stockton (95206-4919)
P.O. Box 31447 (95213-1447)
PHONE......................209 572-1700
Kenneth Lawley, *President*
Donna Enoch, *Corp Secy*
Ron Lawley, *Vice Pres*
EMP: 19
SQ FT: 4,200
SALES (est): 4.3MM **Privately Held**
WEB: www.lawleys.com
SIC: 2048 Feed premixes

(P-1108)
LIND MARINE INC (PA)
100 E D St, Petaluma (94952-3109)
PHONE......................707 762-7251
Mike Lind, *President*
Bill Butler, *Vice Pres*
Aaron Lind, *Vice Pres*
Christian Lind, *Vice Pres*
Chris Lind, *General Mgr*
EMP: 40 **EST:** 1920
SQ FT: 18,500
SALES (est): 8.3MM **Privately Held**
WEB: www.jericoproducts.com
SIC: 2048 1629 Oyster shells, ground: prepared as animal feed; dredging contractor

(P-1109)
MANCHESTER FEEDS INC (PA)
Also Called: Manchester Feeds San Marcos
1520 E Barham Dr, San Marcos (92078-4505)
P.O. Box 1987, Perris (92572-1987)
PHONE......................714 637-7062
William Richard Cramer, *President*
Bertrum Bonner, *Treasurer*
EMP: 19 **EST:** 1962
SQ FT: 7,542

PRODUCTS & SVCS

SALES (est): 1.7MM **Privately Held**
SIC: 2048 Chicken feeds, prepared

(P-1110)
MANNA PRO PRODUCTS LLC
Also Called: Manna Pro Feeds
2962 S Cedar Ave, Fresno (93725-2301)
P.O. Box 1027, Goshen (93227-1027)
PHONE....................................559 486-1810
Richard Beral, *Manager*
EMP: 20
SALES (corp-wide): 85MM **Privately Held**
SIC: 2048 5191 Prepared feeds; animal feeds
PA: Manna Pro Products, Llc
707 Spirit 40 Park Dr # 150
Chesterfield MO 63005
636 681-1700

(P-1111)
MARYBELLE FARMS INC
Also Called: Ross Hay
3761 Nicolaus Rd, Lincoln (95648-9531)
PHONE....................................916 645-8568
Gary Ross, *President*
EMP: 20
SALES (est): 2.4MM **Privately Held**
WEB: www.marybellefarms.com
SIC: 2048 0139 Cereal-, grain-, & seed-based feeds; hay farm; alfalfa farm

(P-1112)
MENEZES HAY CO
5030 Dwight Way, Livingston (95334-9604)
PHONE....................................209 394-3111
Jeremy Menezes, *President*
EMP: 12
SALES (est): 1.6MM **Privately Held**
SIC: 2048 Hay, cubed

(P-1113)
NATURAL BALANCE PET FOODS INC (DH)
100 N First St Ste 200, Burbank (91502-1845)
P.O. Box 397, Upland (91785-0397)
PHONE....................................800 829-4493
Joseph Herrick, *President*
David J West, *CEO*
Lynnda Herrick, *Corp Secy*
Lee Kunkler, *District Mgr*
James Matthews, *District Mgr*
▲ **EMP:** 25
SQ FT: 55,000
SALES (est): 19.9MM
SALES (corp-wide): 7.8B **Publicly Held**
WEB: www.naturalbalanceinc.com
SIC: 2048 5199 Prepared feeds; pet supplies
HQ: Big Heart Pet Brands, Inc.
1 Maritime Plz Fl 2
San Francisco CA 94111
415 247-3000

(P-1114)
NUTRA BLEND LLC
Also Called: Thomas Products
2140 W Industrial Ave, Madera (93637-5210)
PHONE....................................559 661-6161
Mike Osborne, *Branch Mgr*
EMP: 70
SALES (corp-wide): 6.8B **Privately Held**
SIC: 2048 5191 Pulverized oats, prepared as animal feed; animal feeds
HQ: Nutra-Blend, L.L.C.
3200 2nd St
Neosho MO 64850
417 451-6111

(P-1115)
NUTRIUS LLC
39494 Clarkson Dr, Kingsburg (93631-9100)
PHONE....................................559 897-5862
Jim Hansen,
▲ **EMP:** 45
SALES (est): 12.5MM **Privately Held**
SIC: 2048 Prepared feeds

(P-1116)
NUWEST MILLING LLC
4636 Geer Rd, Hughson (95326-9403)
P.O. Box 1031 (95326-1031)
PHONE....................................209 883-1163

Gary West, *Mng Member*
Eric H Benson,
Barbara Abeloe, *Manager*
◆ **EMP:** 16
SQ FT: 1,250
SALES (est): 4.5MM **Privately Held**
SIC: 2048 Prepared feeds

(P-1117)
PACIFIC CATCH INC
770 Tamalpais Dr Ste 400, Corte Madera (94925-1739)
PHONE....................................415 504-6905
Keith M Cox, *President*
Mary Christensen, *Marketing Mgr*
EMP: 21
SALES (est): 3.5MM **Privately Held**
SIC: 2048 Prepared feeds

(P-1118)
PITMAN FAMILY FARMS
10365 Iona Ave, Hanford (93230-9553)
PHONE....................................559 585-3330
Al Ward, *Plant Mgr*
EMP: 55
SALES (corp-wide): 41MM **Privately Held**
WEB: www.cargill.com
SIC: 2048 Livestock feeds
PA: Pitman Family Farms
1075 North Ave
Sanger CA 93657
559 875-9300

(P-1119)
PURINA ANIMAL NUTRITION LLC
1125 Paulson Rd, Turlock (95380-5542)
PHONE....................................209 634-9101
Dan McNutt, *Manager*
EMP: 35
SALES (corp-wide): 6.8B **Privately Held**
SIC: 2048 Prepared feeds
HQ: Purina Animal Nutrition Llc
100 Danforth Dr
Gray Summit MO 63039

(P-1120)
RECONSERVE INC (HQ)
Also Called: Dext Company
2811 Wilshire Blvd # 410, Santa Monica (90403-4803)
P.O. Box 2211 (90407-2211)
PHONE....................................310 458-1574
Meyer Luskin, *CEO*
David Luskin, *COO*
Bryan Bergquist, *Vice Pres*
Joe Douglas, *Vice Pres*
Kevin Shore, *Vice Pres*
EMP: 25 **EST:** 1966
SQ FT: 5,000
SALES: 264.6MM
SALES (corp-wide): 203.7MM **Privately Held**
SIC: 2048 Livestock feeds
PA: Scope Industries
2811 Wilshire Blvd # 410
Santa Monica CA 90403
310 458-1574

(P-1121)
REED MARICULTURE INC
Also Called: Instant Algae
900 E Hamilton Ave # 100, Campbell (95008-0664)
P.O. Box 1049, Freedom (95019-1049)
PHONE....................................408 377-1065
Timothy Allen Reed, *CEO*
Lyn Reed, *COO*
Shawn Neverve, *Vice Pres*
Edwin Reed, *Admin Sec*
▲ **EMP:** 18
SQ FT: 217,800
SALES (est): 3.4MM **Privately Held**
WEB: www.reedmariculture.com
SIC: 2048 Fish food

(P-1122)
RIPON MILLING LLC
30636 E Carter Rd, Farmington (95230-9633)
PHONE....................................209 599-4269
George E Jenkins,
Arie E Den Dulk III, *Vice Pres*
Walter Den Dulk, *Vice Pres*
Ronald Den Dulk,

Mark Devries, *Manager*
EMP: 25
SQ FT: 8,000
SALES (est): 4.9MM **Privately Held**
SIC: 2048 Poultry feeds

(P-1123)
ROBINSON FARMS FEED COMPANY
7000 S Inland Dr, Stockton (95206-9688)
PHONE....................................209 466-7915
Michael S Robinson, *President*
Dale L Drury, *Corp Secy*
Jerry N Robinson, *Vice Pres*
EMP: 17
SQ FT: 10,000
SALES (est): 2.4MM **Privately Held**
WEB: www.championhorses.com
SIC: 2048 0139 0119 0115 Feed premixes; stock feeds, dry; alfalfa or alfalfa meal, prepared as animal feed; alfalfa farm; safflower farm; corn; wheat

(P-1124)
ROUDYBUSH INC (PA)
340 Hanson Way, Woodland (95776-6212)
PHONE....................................530 668-6196
Thomas Roudybush, *President*
Mark Felipe, *Opers Mgr*
▼ **EMP:** 13
SQ FT: 32,000
SALES (est): 2.1MM **Privately Held**
WEB: www.roudybush.com
SIC: 2048 Cereal-, grain-, & seed-based feeds

(P-1125)
SAN FRANCISCO BAY BRAND INC (PA)
8239 Enterprise Dr, Newark (94560-3305)
PHONE....................................510 792-7200
Andreas Schmidt, *President*
Anthony Schmidt, *Exec VP*
Dave Fedde, *Vice Pres*
Yana Dutt-Singkh, *Research*
Kearny Wong, *Controller*
◆ **EMP:** 35
SQ FT: 30,000
SALES (est): 6.7MM **Privately Held**
WEB: www.sfbb.com
SIC: 2048 Fish food

(P-1126)
SEED FACTORY NORTHWEST INC (PA)
4319 Jessup Rd, Ceres (95307-9604)
P.O. Box 245 (95307-0245)
PHONE....................................209 634-8522
Randall Steele, *President*
Lynda Blakemore, *Admin Sec*
▲ **EMP:** 20
SQ FT: 30,000
SALES (est): 2.9MM **Privately Held**
WEB: www.seedfactory.com
SIC: 2048 Bird food, prepared

(P-1127)
SMOOTH RUN EQUINE INC
11590 W Bernardo Ct # 110, San Diego (92127-1624)
PHONE....................................760 751-8988
EMP: 12
SALES (est): 1.5MM **Privately Held**
SIC: 2048

(P-1128)
SOUTHWEST PROCESSORS INC
Also Called: Southwest Treatment Systems
4120 Bandini Blvd, Vernon (90058-4294)
PHONE....................................323 269-9876
Richard T Jerome, *President*
Donna Jerome, *Treasurer*
Susan Alfonso, *Admin Sec*
Richard Jerome, *VP Opers*
Jeffery Jerome, *Manager*
EMP: 12
SQ FT: 2,000
SALES (est): 2MM **Privately Held**
SIC: 2048 Feeds, specialty: mice, guinea pig, etc.

(P-1129)
STAR MILLING CO
24067 Water Ave, Perris (92570-7395)
P.O. Box 1987 (92572-1987)
PHONE....................................951 657-3143
William R Cramer Jr, *President*
Jane Anderson, *Admin Sec*
Gerrit Van Leeuwen, *Purch Mgr*
Robin Hoeflinger, *Sales Staff*
Sandy Caldwell, *Supervisor*
◆ **EMP:** 123 **EST:** 1970
SQ FT: 25,000
SALES (est): 44.5MM **Privately Held**
WEB: www.starmilling.com
SIC: 2048 Poultry feeds

(P-1130)
SUN-GRO COMMODITIES INC (PA)
34575 Famoso Rd, Bakersfield (93308-9769)
PHONE....................................661 393-2612
Donald G Smith, *CEO*
Lori Melendez, *Treasurer*
Scott Smith, *Vice Pres*
Wendy Smith, *Admin Sec*
EMP: 25
SQ FT: 1,400
SALES (est): 4.7MM **Privately Held**
SIC: 2048 4212 Livestock feeds; local trucking, without storage

(P-1131)
VIRTUS NUTRITION LLC
520 Industrial Ave, Corcoran (93212-9629)
PHONE....................................559 992-5033
Jim Hyer, *Mng Member*
Matt Swanson,
EMP: 10
SALES (est): 2.1MM
SALES (corp-wide): 99.9MM **Privately Held**
SIC: 2048 Prepared feeds
PA: Associated Feed & Supply Co.
5213 W Main St
Turlock CA 95380
209 667-2708

(P-1132)
WESTWAY FEED PRODUCTS LLC
Also Called: Cargill Molasses
2130 W Washington St, Stockton (95203-2932)
PHONE....................................209 466-4391
Joe Marchado, *Branch Mgr*
Andy Fagundes, *District Mgr*
EMP: 13
SALES (corp-wide): 8.1B **Privately Held**
WEB: www.westway.com
SIC: 2048 Feed supplements
HQ: Westway Feed Products Llc
365 Canal St Ste 2929
New Orleans LA 70130
504 934-1850

2051 Bread, Bakery Prdts Exc Cookies & Crackers

(P-1133)
A TASTE OF DENMARK
3401 Telegraph Ave, Oakland (94609-3002)
PHONE....................................510 420-8889
Mark Davis, *President*
Carmen Luna, *Treasurer*
Michael Kang, *Vice Pres*
Cathy Caulkett, *General Mgr*
Edward Yoo, *Admin Sec*
EMP: 27
SQ FT: 10,000
SALES (est): 2.8MM **Privately Held**
SIC: 2051 Cakes, bakery: except frozen

(P-1134)
ACME BREAD CO
362 E Grand Ave, South San Francisco (94080-6210)
PHONE....................................650 938-2978
Drew Wescott, *Principal*
EMP: 85

SALES (est): 8.8MM **Privately Held**
WEB: www.acmebread.com
SIC: **2051** Bakery: wholesale or whole-
sale/retail combined

(P-1135)
ANDRE-BOUDIN BAKERIES INC
67 Broadwalk Ln, Walnut Creek (94596)
PHONE...........................925 935-4375
Andrew Friedman, *Manager*
EMP: 15 **Privately Held**
WEB: www.boudinbakery.com
SIC: **2051** 5812 Bread, cake & related
products; cafe
HQ: Andre-Boudin Bakeries, Inc.
50 Francisco St Ste 200
San Francisco CA 94133
415 882-1849

(P-1136)
ANDRE-BOUDIN BAKERIES INC
Also Called: Boudin Souerdough BAKery&
Cafe
2855 Stevens Crk 2451, San Jose (95128)
PHONE...........................408 249-4101
Doug Wheelar, *Manager*
EMP: 15 **Privately Held**
WEB: www.boudinbakery.com
SIC: **2051** Bread, cake & related products
HQ: Andre-Boudin Bakeries, Inc.
50 Francisco St Ste 200
San Francisco CA 94133
415 882-1849

(P-1137)
ANNIES BAKING LLC (DH)
1610 5th St, Berkeley (94710-1715)
PHONE...........................510 558-7500
John Foraker, *Mng Member*
EMP: 32 **EST: 2014**
SALES (est): 18.4MM
SALES (corp-wide): 16.8B **Publicly Held**
SIC: **2051** 2052 5149 Bakery: wholesale
or wholesale/retail combined; bakery
products, dry; bakery products

(P-1138)
ARTISAN CRUST
754 E Florence Ave, Los Angeles
(90001-2322)
PHONE...........................323 759-7000
Maziar Mansori, *Mng Member*
EMP: 25
SALES (est): 1.8MM **Privately Held**
SIC: **2051** Bakery: wholesale or whole-
sale/retail combined

(P-1139)
BAGELRY INC (PA)
320 Cedar St Ste A, Santa Cruz
(95060-4362)
PHONE...........................831 429-8049
John Hamstra, *President*
Laurie Rivin, *Vice Pres*
EMP: 35
SQ FT: 3,000
SALES: 1.9MM **Privately Held**
SIC: **2051** 5812 2052 Bakery: wholesale
or wholesale/retail combined; eating
places; cookies & crackers

(P-1140)
BAKE R US INC
Also Called: Dave's Donuts & Baking Co
13400 S Western Ave, Gardena
(90249-1928)
P.O. Box 3160, Santa Monica (90408-
3160)
PHONE...........................310 630-5873
Fairy Aframian, *CEO*
Mike Aframian, *President*
EMP: 14
SALES (est): 180.1K **Privately Held**
WEB: www.bakerus.com
SIC: **2051** Doughnuts, except frozen

(P-1141)
BAKERY DEPOT INC
4489 Bandini Blvd, Vernon (90058-4309)
PHONE...........................323 261-8388
Wilton Thinh Thai, *CEO*
◆ EMP: 15 **EST: 2005**
SALES (est): 5.2MM **Privately Held**
SIC: **2051** Bakery: wholesale or whole-
sale/retail combined

(P-1142)
BANH MI & CHE CALI
13838 Brookhurst St, Garden Grove
(92843-3121)
PHONE...........................714 534-6987
Boyce Nguyen Jr, *Owner*
EMP: 28
SALES (est): 2.2MM **Privately Held**
SIC: **2051** Bread, cake & related products

(P-1143)
BAY CITIES ITALIAN BAKERY INC
1120 W Mahalo Pl, Compton (90220-5443)
PHONE...........................310 608-1881
Linda Ferrera, *President*
Mario Ferrera, *CEO*
EMP: 13
SQ FT: 7,200
SALES (est): 650K **Privately Held**
SIC: **2051** 5461 Bakery: wholesale or
wholesale/retail combined; bakeries

(P-1144)
BECKMANNS OLD WORLD BAKERY LTD
104 Bronson St Ste 6, Santa Cruz
(95062-3487)
PHONE...........................831 423-9242
Beth Holland, *CEO*
Peter Beckmann, *President*
Sharon May, *Vice Pres*
▲ EMP: 150
SQ FT: 17,000
SALES (est): 24.4MM **Privately Held**
WEB: www.beckmannsbakery.com
SIC: **2051** 5461 Bakery: wholesale or
wholesale/retail combined; bakeries

(P-1145)
BEST EXPRESS FOODS INC
1742 Sabre St, Hayward (94545-1016)
PHONE...........................510 782-5338
Jesus Mendoza, *President*
Daniel Mendoza, *Vice Pres*
EMP: 270
SQ FT: 35,000
SALES: 45MM **Privately Held**
SIC: **2051** Breads, rolls & buns

(P-1146)
BIMBO BAKERIES USA INC
1749 Reliance St, Modesto (95358-5708)
PHONE...........................209 538-6170
Gary Harris, *Manager*
EMP: 15 **Privately Held**
SIC: **2051** Bread, cake & related products
HQ: Bimbo Bakeries Usa, Inc
255 Business Center Dr # 200
Horsham PA 19044
215 347-5500

(P-1147)
BIMBO BAKERIES USA INC
3580 Sueldo St, San Luis Obispo
(93401-7338)
PHONE...........................805 544-7687
Carol Rounsaville, *Principal*
EMP: 80 **Privately Held**
SIC: **2051** Bread, all types (white, wheat,
rye, etc): fresh or frozen
HQ: Bimbo Bakeries Usa, Inc
255 Business Center Dr # 200
Horsham PA 19044
215 347-5500

(P-1148)
BIMBO BAKERIES USA INC
385 N Sherman Ave, Corona (92882-1890)
PHONE...........................951 280-9044
EMP: 18 **Privately Held**
SIC: **2051** Cakes, bakery: except frozen
HQ: Bimbo Bakeries Usa, Inc
255 Business Center Dr # 200
Horsham PA 19044
215 347-5500

(P-1149)
BIMBO BAKERIES USA INC
Also Called: Bimbo Bakeries U.S.A.
480 S Vale Ave, Montebello (90640)
PHONE...........................323 720-6099
Edgar Jaramillo, *Director*
EMP: 18 **Privately Held**

SIC: **2051** Bread, all types (white, wheat,
rye, etc): fresh or frozen
HQ: Bimbo Bakeries Usa, Inc
255 Business Center Dr # 200
Horsham PA 19044
215 347-5500

(P-1150)
BIMBO BAKERIES USA INC
Also Called: Sara Lee Bakery Group
3495 Swetzer Rd, Loomis (95650-9581)
P.O. Box 5387, Sacramento (95817-0387)
PHONE...........................916 456-3863
Fred Grinder, *Branch Mgr*
EMP: 15
SQ FT: 1,159 **Privately Held**
SIC: **2051** Bakery: wholesale or whole-
sale/retail combined
HQ: Bimbo Bakeries Usa, Inc
255 Business Center Dr # 200
Horsham PA 19044
215 347-5500

(P-1151)
BIMBO BAKERIES USA INC
7601 Wilbur Way, Sacramento
(95828-4927)
PHONE...........................916 681-8069
EMP: 24 **Privately Held**
SIC: **2051** Bakery: wholesale or whole-
sale/retail combined
HQ: Bimbo Bakeries Usa, Inc
255 Business Center Dr # 200
Horsham PA 19044
215 347-5500

(P-1152)
BIMBO BAKERIES USA INC
3231 6th Ave, Sacramento (95817-3276)
P.O. Box 5387 (95817-0387)
PHONE...........................916 732-4733
Belsrida Plunk, *Branch Mgr*
EMP: 700 **Privately Held**
SIC: **2051** Bread, all types (white, wheat,
rye, etc): fresh or frozen
HQ: Bimbo Bakeries Usa, Inc
255 Business Center Dr # 200
Horsham PA 19044
215 347-5500

(P-1153)
BIMBO BAKERIES USA INC
2069 Aldergrove Ave, Escondido
(92029-1902)
PHONE...........................760 737-7700
Eduardo Aiza, *Principal*
EMP: 18 **Privately Held**
SIC: **2051** Bread, cake & related products
HQ: Bimbo Bakeries Usa, Inc
255 Business Center Dr # 200
Horsham PA 19044
215 347-5500

(P-1154)
BIMBO BAKERIES USA INC
Also Called: Oroweat Foods
4000 Ruffin Rd Ste B, San Diego
(92123-1866)
PHONE...........................858 677-0573
Mark Edwards, *Principal*
EMP: 80 **Privately Held**
WEB: www.englishmuffin.com
SIC: **2051** Bakery: wholesale or whole-
sale/retail combined
HQ: Bimbo Bakeries Usa, Inc
255 Business Center Dr # 200
Horsham PA 19044
215 347-5500

(P-1155)
BIMBO BAKERIES USA INC
1836 G St, Fresno (93706-1617)
PHONE...........................559 498-3632
EMP: 18
SALES (corp-wide): 13.7B **Privately Held**
SIC: **2051**
HQ: Bimbo Bakeries Usa, Inc
255 Business Center Dr # 200
Horsham PA 19044
215 347-5500

(P-1156)
BIMBO BAKERIES USA INC
14388 Washington Ave, San Leandro
(94578-3419)
PHONE...........................510 614-4500

Juan Muldoon, *Principal*
EMP: 18
SQ FT: 9,320 **Privately Held**
SIC: **2051** Bread, cake & related products
HQ: Bimbo Bakeries Usa, Inc
255 Business Center Dr # 200
Horsham PA 19044
215 347-5500

(P-1157)
BIMBO BAKERIES USA INC
264 S Spruce Ave, South San Francisco
(94080-4550)
PHONE...........................650 583-5828
Laura Thompson, *Branch Mgr*
EMP: 20 **Privately Held**
SIC: **2051** Bread, cake & related products
HQ: Bimbo Bakeries Usa, Inc
255 Business Center Dr # 200
Horsham PA 19044
215 347-5500

(P-1158)
BIMBO BAKERIES USA INC
Also Called: Oroweat Foods
1220 Howell St, Anaheim (92805)
PHONE...........................714 634-8068
Mike Prichard, *General Mgr*
EMP: 60 **Privately Held**
WEB: www.englishmuffin.com
SIC: **2051** Bread, cake & related products
HQ: Bimbo Bakeries Usa, Inc
255 Business Center Dr # 200
Horsham PA 19044
215 347-5500

(P-1159)
BIMBO BAKERIES USA INC
116 Ponderosa Dr, Sonora (95370-4818)
PHONE...........................209 532-5185
Sandy Wynne, *Branch Mgr*
EMP: 76 **Privately Held**
SIC: **2051** Bakery: wholesale or whole-
sale/retail combined
HQ: Bimbo Bakeries Usa, Inc
255 Business Center Dr # 200
Horsham PA 19044
215 347-5500

(P-1160)
BIMBO BAKERIES USA INC
Also Called: Mrs Baird's Bakeries
1771 Blake Ave, Los Angeles (90031-1006)
PHONE...........................323 913-7214
Joe Dangelmaier, *Vice Pres*
EMP: 50 **Privately Held**
WEB: www.mrsbairds.com
SIC: **2051** Bakery: wholesale or whole-
sale/retail combined
HQ: Bimbo Bakeries Usa, Inc
255 Business Center Dr # 200
Horsham PA 19044
215 347-5500

(P-1161)
BIMBO BAKERIES USA INC
Also Called: Old Country Bakery
475 S Canal St, South San Francisco
(94080-4607)
PHONE...........................650 583-3259
Dan Hobson, *Manager*
EMP: 40 **Privately Held**
WEB: www.englishmuffin.com
SIC: **2051** Bread, cake & related products
HQ: Bimbo Bakeries Usa, Inc
255 Business Center Dr # 200
Horsham PA 19044
215 347-5500

(P-1162)
BIMBO BAKERIES USA INC
333 Dawson Dr Ste A, Camarillo
(93012-8093)
PHONE...........................805 384-1059
Robert Hernandez, *Manager*
EMP: 15 **Privately Held**
SIC: **2051** Bakery: wholesale or whole-
sale/retail combined
HQ: Bimbo Bakeries Usa, Inc
255 Business Center Dr # 200
Horsham PA 19044
215 347-5500

PRODUCTS & SVCS

(P-1163)
BIMBO BAKERIES USA INC
2740 Soquel Ave, Santa Cruz
(95062-1409)
PHONE..........................831 465-1214
Rick Roberts, *Manager*
EMP: 12 **Privately Held**
SIC: 2051 Bread, cake & related products
HQ: Bimbo Bakeries Usa, Inc
255 Business Center Dr # 200
Horsham PA 19044
215 347-5500

(P-1164)
BIMBO BAKERIES USA INC
Also Called: Oroweat
1201 El Camino Ave, Sacramento
(95815-2615)
PHONE..........................916 922-1307
Michael Smith, *Manager*
EMP: 20 **Privately Held**
WEB: www.englishmuffin.com
SIC: 2051 Bread, cake & related products
HQ: Bimbo Bakeries Usa, Inc
255 Business Center Dr # 200
Horsham PA 19044
215 347-5500

(P-1165)
BIMBO BAKERIES USA INC
3525 Arden Rd Ste 300, Hayward
(94545-3909)
PHONE..........................510 436-5350
Bob Thompson, *Branch Mgr*
EMP: 250 **Privately Held**
SIC: 2051 Bread, all types (white, wheat,
rye, etc): fresh or frozen; buns, bread
type: fresh or frozen; rolls, bread type:
fresh or frozen
HQ: Bimbo Bakeries Usa, Inc
255 Business Center Dr # 200
Horsham PA 19044
215 347-5500

(P-1166)
BIMBO BAKERIES USA INC
2380 N Clovis Ave, Fresno (93727-1213)
PHONE..........................650 291-3213
Allen Petersen, *Manager*
EMP: 30 **Privately Held**
SIC: 2051 Bakery: wholesale or whole-
sale/retail combined
HQ: Bimbo Bakeries Usa, Inc
255 Business Center Dr # 200
Horsham PA 19044
215 347-5500

(P-1167)
BIMBO BAKERIES USA INC
Rainbo Bread
3292 S Willow Ave Ste 101, Fresno
(93725-9906)
P.O. Box 132 (93707-0132)
PHONE..........................559 489-0980
Chuck Linthicum, *Branch Mgr*
EMP: 175
SQ FT: 110,000 **Privately Held**
SIC: 2051 Bakery: wholesale or whole-
sale/retail combined
HQ: Bimbo Bakeries Usa, Inc
255 Business Center Dr # 200
Horsham PA 19044
215 347-5500

(P-1168)
BON APPETIT DANISH INC
Also Called: Bon Appetit Bakery
4525 District Blvd, Vernon (90058-2711)
PHONE..........................323 584-9500
Mahasti Mashhoon, *President*
Bob Matwiczak, *Vice Pres*
Sonny Cutwright, *General Mgr*
Carlos Flores, *Chief Engr*
Jack Avunjian, *Accountant*
EMP: 100
SQ FT: 19,727
SALES (est): 37.9MM **Privately Held**
WEB: www.bonappetitbakery.com
SIC: 2051 Bread, cake & related products

(P-1169)
BORDENAVES MARIN BAKING
Also Called: Bordenaves
1512 4th St, San Rafael (94901-2713)
P.O. Box 150505 (94915-0505)
PHONE..........................415 453-2957

Fred Radwan,
EMP: 53
SQ FT: 24,000
SALES (est): 11MM **Privately Held**
SIC: 2051 Bread, all types (white, wheat,
rye, etc): fresh or frozen

(P-1170)
BROOKS STREET COMPANIES
Also Called: Brooks Street Baking Company
5560 Brooks St, Montclair (91763-4522)
P.O. Box 1667, Ontario (91762-0667)
PHONE..........................909 983-6090
Fred Scalzo, *President*
Fred Sealzo, *President*
EMP: 125
SQ FT: 22,000
SALES (est): 14MM **Privately Held**
WEB: www.brooksstreetbakery.com
SIC: 2051 Bakery: wholesale or whole-
sale/retail combined

(P-1171)
CAKE CAFE BAR LLC
131 Mill St Ste 1, Grass Valley
(95945-4717)
PHONE..........................530 615-4126
Christine Cain,
EMP: 15
SALES (est): 528.5K **Privately Held**
SIC: 2051 Bakery: wholesale or whole-
sale/retail combined

(P-1172)
CALIFORNIA CHURROS
CORPORATION
751 Via Lata, Colton (92324-3930)
PHONE..........................909 370-4777
Jorge D Martinez, *CEO*
Jorge D Martinez Sr, *President*
Frank Ruvalcaba, *Vice Pres*
Eva A Martinez, *Admin Sec*
EMP: 130
SQ FT: 54,800
SALES (est): 22.8MM
SALES (corp-wide): 1B **Publicly Held**
WEB: www.churros.com
SIC: 2051 Pastries, e.g. danish: except
frozen
HQ: J & J Snack Foods Corp. Of California
5353 S Downey Rd
Vernon CA 90058
323 581-0171

(P-1173)
CALIFORNIA SMART FOODS
2565 3rd St Ste 342, San Francisco
(94107-3159)
PHONE..........................415 826-0449
Rudy Melnitzer, *Owner*
Helaine Melnitzer, *Co-Owner*
EMP: 22
SALES: 5.3MM **Privately Held**
SIC: 2051 Bread, cake & related products

(P-1174)
CARAVAN BAKERY INC
33300 Western Ave, Union City
(94587-2211)
PHONE..........................510 487-2600
Joseph Maroun Sr, *President*
EMP: 26
SALES (est): 7.3MM **Privately Held**
SIC: 2051 Bakery: wholesale or whole-
sale/retail combined

(P-1175)
CARAVAN TRADING COMPANY
Also Called: Sterling Foods
33300 Western Ave, Union City
(94587-2211)
PHONE..........................510 487-8090
John Likovich, *President*
Steve Reesing, *CFO*
Ira Hermann, *Vice Pres*
Carmen Maroun, *Vice Pres*
Lucia Bendezu, *Planning*
EMP: 85
SQ FT: 100,000
SALES (est): 20.9MM **Privately Held**
WEB: www.caravantrd.com
SIC: 2051 Bagels, fresh or frozen
HQ: Sterling Foods, Llc
1075 Arion Pkwy
San Antonio TX 78216
210 490-1669

(P-1176)
CHANTILLY BAKERY INC
12714 Chandon Ct, San Diego
(92130-2794)
PHONE..........................858 693-3300
Christina L Manly, *CEO*
Christina Manly, *Owner*
EMP: 18
SALES: 1MM **Privately Held**
SIC: 2051 Bakery: wholesale or whole-
sale/retail combined

(P-1177)
CHEESE CAKE CITY INC
1225 4th St, Berkeley (94710-1302)
PHONE..........................510 524-9404
Steve Zwetsch, *President*
Lori Hughes, *Admin Sec*
EMP: 10
SQ FT: 3,700
SALES (est): 900.3K **Privately Held**
WEB: www.cheesecakecity.com
SIC: 2051 5961 2053 2024 Cakes, bak-
ery: except frozen; food, mail order;
frozen bakery products, except bread; ice
cream & frozen desserts

(P-1178)
CHEESECAKE FACTORY
BAKERY INC (HQ)
26950 Agoura Rd, Agoura Hills
(91301-5335)
PHONE..........................818 880-9323
David Overton, *Ch of Bd*
Keith T Carango, *President*
Max Byfuglin, *Exec VP*
▲ EMP: 350
SQ FT: 60,000
SALES (est): 91.8MM **Publicly Held**
SIC: 2051 5812 Cakes, bakery: except
frozen; eating places

(P-1179)
CHEF BRAND FOODS
Also Called: Chef Brands
8637 W Doe Ave, Visalia (93291-8938)
PHONE..........................559 651-1696
J L Logan, *Owner*
EMP: 20
SALES (est): 1.7MM **Privately Held**
SIC: 2051 Pastries, e.g. danish: except
frozen

(P-1180)
CITY BAKING COMPANY
1373 Lowrie Ave, South San Francisco
(94080-6403)
PHONE..........................650 589-8128
Alex Bulazo, *President*
Judie Gee, *Cust Mgr*
EMP: 55 EST: 1991
SALES (est): 9.9MM **Privately Held**
WEB: www.citybaking.com
SIC: 2051 Bread, cake & related products

(P-1181)
CORBIN-HILL INC
Also Called: Corbin Foods
2961 W Macarthur Blvd, Santa Ana
(92704-6913)
P.O. Box 28139 (92799-8139)
PHONE..........................714 966-6695
Jl Corbin, *Ch of Bd*
A Moreno, *President*
R W Carlyle, *CFO*
Karen Kelley, *Admin Sec*
EMP: 100
SQ FT: 20,000
SALES (est): 9MM **Privately Held**
WEB: www.edibowls.com
SIC: 2051 Bread, cake & related products

(P-1182)
CREATIVE INTL PASTRIES
950 Illinois St, San Francisco (94107-3136)
PHONE..........................415 255-1128
Gerhard Michler, *President*
Mary Michler, *Vice Pres*
Alex Leong, *Human Res Mgr*
EMP: 25
SQ FT: 3,000
SALES: 400K **Privately Held**
WEB: www.gerhardmichler.com
SIC: 2051 2052 Cakes, pies & pastries;
cookies

(P-1183)
CUCINA HOLDINGS INC
4 Embarcadero Ctr Lbby 4 # 4, San Fran-
cisco (94111-4112)
PHONE..........................415 986-8688
Patrick Dougherty, *Manager*
EMP: 10 **Privately Held**
WEB: www.javacity.com
SIC: 2051 5812 Bread, all types (white,
wheat, rye, etc): fresh or frozen; cafe
HQ: Cucina Holdings, Inc.
1300 Del Paso Rd
Sacramento CA 95834
916 565-5500

(P-1184)
D GOLDENWEST INC
2700 Pacific Coast Hwy # 2, Torrance
(90505-7061)
PHONE..........................310 564-2641
Dan Almquist, *President*
Robert Jonas, *Vice Pres*
EMP: 50
SQ FT: 5,000
SALES (est): 3.2MM **Privately Held**
SIC: 2051 Sponge goods, bakery: except
frozen

(P-1185)
DAWN FOOD PRODUCTS INC
Also Called: Dawn Bakery Service Center
2845 Faber St, Union City (94587-1203)
PHONE..........................510 487-9007
Paul Lawrence, *Branch Mgr*
Cindy Kwan, *Sales Staff*
John Jackson, *Manager*
EMP: 30
SALES (corp-wide): 1.6B **Privately Held**
WEB: www.dawnfoods.com
SIC: 2051 2045 5046 Bread, cake & re-
lated products; prepared flour mixes &
doughs; bakery equipment & supplies
HQ: Dawn Food Products, Inc.
3333 Sargent Rd
Jackson MI 49201

(P-1186)
DESSERTS ON US INC
57 Belle Falor Ct, Arcata (95521-9234)
PHONE..........................707 822-0160
Emran Essa, *CEO*
Kathleen Essa, *Admin Sec*
▲ EMP: 15
SQ FT: 20,000
SALES (est): 3.7MM **Privately Held**
WEB: www.dessertsonus.com
SIC: 2051 2099 2052 Pastries, e.g. dan-
ish: except frozen; dessert mixes & fill-
ings; cookies

(P-1187)
DIMUFIDRA USA INC
Also Called: Melrose Bakery
7356 Melrose Ave, Los Angeles
(90046-7527)
PHONE..........................323 651-3822
Kevin Chapchin, *President*
EMP: 80
SQ FT: 10,000
SALES (est): 17MM **Privately Held**
WEB: www.viennacafe.com
SIC: 2051 Bakery: wholesale or whole-
sale/retail combined

(P-1188)
DISTINCT INDULGENCE INC
Also Called: Mrs Appletree's Bakery
5018 Lante St, Baldwin Park (91706-1839)
PHONE..........................818 546-1700
Robert W Gray, *President*
Suzanne Gray, *Corp Secy*
▲ EMP: 38
SQ FT: 10,000
SALES (est): 6.6MM **Privately Held**
SIC: 2051 5499 Bakery: wholesale or
wholesale/retail combined; health & di-
etetic food stores

(P-1189)
DO-NUT WHEEL INC
10250 N De Anza Blvd, Cupertino
(95014-2219)
PHONE..........................408 252-8193
Daniel Taing, *President*
EMP: 10

▲ = Import ▼ =Export
◆ =Import/Export

SALES (est): 550K **Privately Held**
SIC: 2051 Doughnuts, except frozen

(P-1190)
DOUCE DE FRANCE
686 Brdwy St, Redwood City (94063)
PHONE..................................650 369-9644
Mauro Ferreira, *Manager*
EMP: 14
SALES (est): 1.4MM
SALES (corp-wide): 586.9K **Privately Held**
WEB: www.doucefrancebakery.com
SIC: 2051 Bread, cake & related products
PA: Douce De France
104 Town And Country Vlg
Palo Alto CA 94301
650 322-3601

(P-1191)
DOUGHTRONICS INC (PA)
Also Called: Acme Bread Company
1601 San Pablo Ave, Berkeley
(94702-1317)
PHONE..................................510 524-1327
Steven Sullivan, *President*
Susan Sullivan, *Vice Pres*
Doug Volkmer, *Vice Pres*
EMP: 30
SALES (est): 15.7MM **Privately Held**
SIC: 2051 5461 Bakery: wholesale or
wholesale/retail combined; bread

(P-1192)
DOUGHTRONICS INC
Also Called: Acme Bread Co Div II
2730 9th St, Berkeley (94710-2633)
PHONE..................................510 843-2978
Rick Kirkby, *Manager*
EMP: 50
SQ FT: 4,372
SALES (corp-wide): 15.7MM **Privately Held**
SIC: 2051 Bakery: wholesale or whole-
sale/retail combined
PA: Doughtronics, Inc.
1601 San Pablo Ave
Berkeley CA 94702
510 524-1327

(P-1193)
DOUGHTRONICS INC
1 Ferry Building Ste 15, San Francisco
(94111-4228)
PHONE..................................415 288-2978
Drew Westcott, *Branch Mgr*
EMP: 30
SALES (corp-wide): 15.7MM **Privately Held**
SIC: 2051 Bread, cake & related products
PA: Doughtronics, Inc.
1601 San Pablo Ave
Berkeley CA 94702
510 524-1327

(P-1194)
DTBM INC
Also Called: Fortune Bakery
1825 Durfee Ave Ste C, South El Monte
(91733-3742)
PHONE..................................626 579-7033
Terry C Peng, *President*
▲ **EMP:** 13
SQ FT: 5,000
SALES: 600K **Privately Held**
WEB: www.dtbm.com
SIC: 2051 5461 Pastries, e.g. danish: ex-
cept frozen; bakeries

(P-1195)
E D D INVESTMENT CO
Also Called: Polly's Tasty Foods & Pies
2025 N Tustin St, Orange (92865-3901)
PHONE..................................714 637-3040
Arlene Larochelle, *Manager*
EMP: 50
SQ FT: 5,000
SALES (corp-wide): 29.2MM **Privately Held**
SIC: 2051 Cakes, pies & pastries
PA: E D D Investment Co
14325 Iseli Rd
Santa Fe Springs CA

(P-1196)
EDNAS INC
390 Buckley Rd Ste F, San Luis Obispo
(93401-8164)
P.O. Box 4610 (93403-4610)
PHONE..................................805 541-3563
Edna Ryzebol, *President*
EMP: 15
SQ FT: 10,000
SALES (est): 1.6MM **Privately Held**
SIC: 2051 Cakes, pies & pastries

(P-1197)
EDNER CORPORATION
Also Called: Wayfarers
528 Oakshire Pl, Alamo (94507-2325)
PHONE..................................925 831-1248
Ehud L Kirshner, *President*
EMP: 30
SQ FT: 21,408
SALES (est): 3.6MM **Privately Held**
SIC: 2051 5149 Bread, cake & related
products; groceries & related products

(P-1198)
EL METATE FOODS INC
Also Called: El Metate Mercado
125n Rancho Santiago Blvd, Orange
(92869-3501)
PHONE..................................714 542-3913
Mike Mercado, *Branch Mgr*
EMP: 10
SALES (corp-wide): 36.6MM **Privately Held**
WEB: www.elmetate.com
SIC: 2051 2052 2099 5812 Breads, rolls
& buns; cakes, pies & pastries; cookies;
tortillas, fresh or refrigerated; Mexican
restaurant
PA: El Metate Foods Inc.
838 E 1st St
Santa Ana CA 92701
714 542-3913

(P-1199)
EL METATE FOODS INC
Also Called: El Metate Market
817 W 19th St, Costa Mesa (92627-3518)
PHONE..................................949 646-9362
Brian Murrieta, *Branch Mgr*
EMP: 50
SALES (corp-wide): 36.6MM **Privately Held**
WEB: www.elmetate.com
SIC: 2051 2052 2099 5812 Breads, rolls
& buns; cakes, pies & pastries; cookies;
tortillas, fresh or refrigerated; Mexican
restaurant
PA: El Metate Foods Inc.
838 E 1st St
Santa Ana CA 92701
714 542-3913

(P-1200)
EL SEGUNDO BREAD BAR LLC
701 E El Segundo Blvd, El Segundo
(90245-4108)
PHONE..................................310 615-9898
Myrna Al-Midani, *CEO*
Ali Chalabi, *President*
▲ **EMP:** 32
SQ FT: 8,000
SALES (est): 2.7MM **Privately Held**
SIC: 2051 5149 Bread, all types (white,
wheat, rye, etc): fresh or frozen; bakery
products

(P-1201)
FARGO CHOICE FOODS LLC
2885 Adeline St, Oakland (94608-4409)
P.O. Box 220, San Ramon (94583-0220)
PHONE..................................510 774-0064
Daniel Mendoza, *President*
Jesus Mendoza, *Vice Pres*
EMP: 48
SQ FT: 24,000
SALES: 3.7MM **Privately Held**
SIC: 2051 Breads, rolls & buns

(P-1202)
FEEMSTER CO INC
Also Called: Some Crust Bakery
119 Yale Ave, Claremont (91711-4723)
PHONE..................................909 621-9772
Larry Feemster, *President*
Sandra Feemster, *Officer*

Tasha Cockrell, *Business Mgr*
Scott Feemster, *Manager*
Katrina Murillo, *Manager*
EMP: 30 **EST:** 1997
SQ FT: 3,000
SALES (est): 3.6MM **Privately Held**
WEB: www.somecrust.com
SIC: 2051 5461 Bread, cake & related
products; bakeries

(P-1203)
FIESTA MEXICAN FOODS INC
979 G St, Brawley (92227-2615)
PHONE..................................760 344-3580
Raymond Armenta, *President*
EMP: 30 **EST:** 1956
SQ FT: 4,000
SALES (est): 3.2MM **Privately Held**
SIC: 2051 2099 Pastries, e.g. danish: ex-
cept frozen; tortillas, fresh or refrigerated

(P-1204)
FLOUR FUSION
133 N Main St, Lake Elsinore
(92530-4105)
PHONE..................................951 245-1166
EMP: 12
SALES (est): 774.2K **Privately Held**
SIC: 2051 5812

(P-1205)
FLOWERS BAKING CO MODESTO LLC
736 Mariposa Rd, Modesto (95354-4133)
PHONE..................................209 857-4600
Paul Holshouser,
EMP: 99
SQ FT: 250,000
SALES (est): 14.7MM
SALES (corp-wide): 3.9B **Publicly Held**
SIC: 2051 Breads, rolls & buns
PA: Flowers Foods, Inc.
1919 Flowers Cir
Thomasville GA 31757
229 226-9110

(P-1206)
FREEPORT BAKERY INC
2966 Freeport Blvd, Sacramento
(95818-3855)
PHONE..................................916 442-4256
Marlene Goetzeler, *President*
Walter Goetzeler, *Principal*
EMP: 45
SALES (est): 6.3MM **Privately Held**
WEB: www.freeportbakery.com
SIC: 2051 5461 5812 Bread, cake & re-
lated products; bakeries; eating places

(P-1207)
FRESNO FRENCH BREAD BAKERY INC
Also Called: Basque French Bakery
2625 Inyo St, Fresno (93721-2732)
PHONE..................................559 268-7088
Al Lewis, *President*
Rita Ingmire, *Vice Pres*
EMP: 34 **EST:** 1963
SQ FT: 32,000
SALES (est): 5.2MM **Privately Held**
SIC: 2051 Bread, all types (white, wheat,
rye, etc): fresh or frozen

(P-1208)
FRISCO BAKING COMPANY INC
621 W Avenue 26, Los Angeles
(90065-1095)
PHONE..................................323 225-6111
Aldo Pricco Jr, *CEO*
James Pricco, *President*
Ronald Perata, *Treasurer*
Mary Anne Fetter, *Vice Pres*
John Pricco, *Vice Pres*
EMP: 115 **EST:** 1938
SQ FT: 18,000
SALES (est): 29.1MM **Privately Held**
WEB: www.buonaforchetta.com
SIC: 2051 Bread, all types (white, wheat,
rye, etc): fresh or frozen

(P-1209)
FULLBLOOM BAKING COMPANY INC
6500 Overlake Pl, Newark (94560-1083)
PHONE..................................510 456-3638

Karen Trilevsky, *CEO*
Mike Larue, *Engineer*
Leo Carpio, *Manager*
▲ **EMP:** 286
SQ FT: 95,000
SALES (est): 55.5MM
SALES (corp-wide): 3.9B **Privately Held**
SIC: 2051 Bread, cake & related products
HQ: Aryzta Llc
6080 Center Dr Ste 900
Los Angeles CA 90045
310 417-4700

(P-1210)
FUN O CAKE
2324 4th Ave Apt 201, Los Angeles
(90018-4901)
PHONE..................................323 213-8684
Rashaad Lassiter, *Principal*
EMP: 10
SALES (est): 342.9K **Privately Held**
SIC: 2051 Bakery: wholesale or whole-
sale/retail combined

(P-1211)
FUSION FOOD FACTORY
Also Called: La Jolla Baking Co
9350 Trade Pl Ste A, San Diego
(92126-6334)
PHONE..................................858 578-8001
Steve Kwon, *President*
Jose Ramirez, *General Mgr*
EMP: 45
SQ FT: 8,000
SALES (est): 7.3MM **Privately Held**
SIC: 2051 Bread, cake & related products

(P-1212)
FUTURE FINE FOODS
2615 De La Vina St Ste 1, Santa Barbara
(93105-4144)
PHONE..................................805 682-9421
Peter Zadeh, *Owner*
EMP: 12 **EST:** 1998
SALES (est): 1.1MM **Privately Held**
WEB: www.futurefinefoods.com
SIC: 2051 Bread, cake & related products

(P-1213)
GALDAZA FOOD CORPORATION
Also Called: D'Lido Bakery
1147 W Washington Blvd, Los Angeles
(90015-3315)
PHONE..................................213 747-4025
Luis Galdamez, *President*
Anna Galdamez, *Vice Pres*
EMP: 25
SQ FT: 11,500
SALES (est): 2.2MM **Privately Held**
SIC: 2051 Bakery: wholesale or whole-
sale/retail combined

(P-1214)
GANPAC DISTRIBUTION LLC
7727 Formula Pl, San Diego (92121-2419)
PHONE..................................858 586-1868
Stanley Smiedt,
Julian Josephson,
Rick Ronald,
EMP: 24
SALES (est): 1.9MM **Privately Held**
SIC: 2051 Bagels, fresh or frozen

(P-1215)
GFORCE CORPORATION
1144 N Grove St, Anaheim (92806-2109)
PHONE..................................714 630-0909
Farren Mataele, *President*
▲ **EMP:** 16
SALES (est): 2MM **Privately Held**
SIC: 2051 Bakery: wholesale or whole-
sale/retail combined

(P-1216)
GHS CHAMPION INC
1090 Martin Ave, Santa Clara
(95050-2609)
PHONE..................................650 326-8485
Henry Chan, *President*
Sophia Chan, *Treasurer*
Garland Chan, *Vice Pres*
EMP: 24
SALES (est): 2.6MM **Privately Held**
SIC: 2051 Bakery: wholesale or whole-
sale/retail combined

P
R
O
D
U
C
T
S

&

S
V
C
S

(P-1217)
GIULIANO-PAGANO CORPORATION
Also Called: Giuliano's Bakery
1264 E Walnut St, Carson (90746-1319)
PHONE..................310 537-7700
Nancy Ritmire Giuliano, *Ch of Bd*
Gregory Ritmire, *President*
EMP: 100
SQ FT: 40,000
SALES (est): 24.2MM **Privately Held**
SIC: 2051 Bakery: wholesale or whole-sale/retail combined

(P-1218)
GOLD COAST BAKING COMPANY INC (PA)
Also Called: Gold Coast Bakeries
1590 E Saint Gertrude Pl, Santa Ana
(92705-5310)
PHONE..................714 545-2253
Rick Anderson, *CEO*
Mark Press, *President*
Paul Cannon, *COO*
Terrilynn Vu, *Controller*
Dan Cuellar, *VP Sales*
EMP: 97
SQ FT: 60,000
SALES (est): 65.7MM **Privately Held**
SIC: 2051 Bakery: wholesale or whole-sale/retail combined

(P-1219)
GOLDEN OCTAGON INC
Also Called: San Francisco Fine Bakery
2537 Middlefield Rd, Redwood City
(94063-2825)
P.O. Box 610145 (94061-0145)
PHONE..................650 369-8573
Greg Endom, *Business Mgr*
Daniel Huang, *CEO*
Bob Pham, *Purch Mgr*
EMP: 75
SALES (est): 7.3MM **Privately Held**
SIC: 2051 Bakery: wholesale or whole-sale/retail combined

(P-1220)
GOLDEN SHEAF BREAD CO INC
125 Hangar Way Ste 230, Watsonville
(95076-2493)
PHONE..................831 722-0179
Joe Platin, *CEO*
EMP: 30
SQ FT: 7,500
SALES (est): 4.2MM **Privately Held**
SIC: 2051 Bakery: wholesale or whole-sale/retail combined

(P-1221)
GOLDILOCKS CORP CALIFORNIA (PA)
Also Called: Goldilocks Bakeshop and Rest
10329 Painter Ave, Santa Fe Springs
(90670-3427)
PHONE..................562 946-9995
Mendrei Leelin, *President*
Menard Leelin, *President*
Cecilia Leelin, *Treasurer*
EMP: 50
SQ FT: 12,000
SALES (est): 9.4MM **Privately Held**
SIC: 2051 Bread, cake & related products

(P-1222)
GRAND CASINO ON MAIN INC
3826 Main St, Culver City (90232-2620)
PHONE..................310 253-9066
Linda Boyle, *President*
Frank Lamanna, *Vice Pres*
▲ **EMP:** 25
SALES (est): 1.5MM **Privately Held**
SIC: 2051 Bread, cake & related products

(P-1223)
HANNAHMAX BAKING INC
14601 S Main St, Gardena (90248-1916)
PHONE..................310 380-6778
Joanne Adirim, *CEO*
Stuart Scwartz, *President*
Ericka Gettman Kamer, *Vice Pres*
EMP: 145
SQ FT: 15,000

SALES (est): 14.5MM **Privately Held**
WEB: www.hannahmax.com
SIC: 2051 Bakery: wholesale or whole-sale/retail combined

(P-1224)
HEALTH BREADS INC
Also Called: Oasis Breads
155 Mata Way Ste 112, San Marcos
(92069-2983)
PHONE..................760 747-7390
Jim Pickell, *President*
Dennis Walsh, *President*
EMP: 25
SQ FT: 9,500
SALES (est): 4.8MM **Privately Held**
WEB: www.oasisbreads.com
SIC: 2051 Bakery: wholesale or whole-sale/retail combined

(P-1225)
HOLSUM BAKERY INC
21540 Blythe St, Canoga Park
(91304-4910)
PHONE..................818 884-6562
EMP: 45
SALES (corp-wide): 3.9B **Publicly Held**
SIC: 2051 Bakery: wholesale or whole-sale/retail combined
HQ: Holsum Bakery, Inc.
2322 W Lincoln St
Phoenix AZ 85009
602 252-2351

(P-1226)
HOUSE OF BAGELS INC (PA)
1007 Washington St, San Carlos
(94070-5318)
PHONE..................650 595-4700
Larry Chassy, *President*
EMP: 15
SALES (est): 6.3MM **Privately Held**
SIC: 2051 5461 Bread, cake & related products; bakeries

(P-1227)
JEANNINES BKG CO SANTA BARBARA (PA)
Also Called: Jeannine's Bakery
15 E Figueroa St, Santa Barbara
(93101-2781)
PHONE..................805 966-1717
Gordon W Hardey, *CEO*
Eleanor Hardey, *President*
EMP: 18
SQ FT: 1,800
SALES: 1.5MM **Privately Held**
SIC: 2051 5812 Bread, cake & related products; American restaurant

(P-1228)
LA BOULANGERIE FRENCH BKY CAFE
730 W Shaw Ave, Fresno (93704-2301)
PHONE..................559 222-0555
Patrick Bourrel, *Owner*
EMP: 14
SALES (est): 2.3MM **Privately Held**
SIC: 2051 Bagels, fresh or frozen

(P-1229)
LAS CUATROS MILPAS
856 N Mount Vernon Ave, San Bernardino
(92411-2753)
P.O. Box 7555 (92411-0555)
PHONE..................909 885-3344
Henry Mata, *Owner*
EMP: 12 **EST:** 1971
SALES (est): 635.3K **Privately Held**
WEB: www.korkyt.net
SIC: 2051 2099 Bread, cake & related products; tortillas, fresh or refrigerated

(P-1230)
LAURAS FRENCH BAKING CO INC
722 S Oxford Ave Apt 107, Los Angeles
(90005-2996)
PHONE..................323 585-5144
Laura Kim, *President*
Mike Ji, *Vice Pres*
Sterling Kim, *Vice Pres*
EMP: 23
SQ FT: 18,600

SALES (est): 3.9MM **Privately Held**
WEB: www.labakery.com
SIC: 2051 Bakery: wholesale or whole-sale/retail combined

(P-1231)
LAURAS ORIGINAL BOSTON
Also Called: Bhu Food
1022 W Morena Blvd, San Diego
(92110-3919)
PHONE..................619 855-3258
Laura Katleman, *CEO*
EMP: 18
SQ FT: 4,000
SALES (est): 1.6MM **Privately Held**
SIC: 2051 2052 Bread, cake & related products; cookies & crackers

(P-1232)
LAVASH CORPORATION
Also Called: Old Fashion Lavash
2835 Newell St, Los Angeles (90039-3817)
PHONE..................323 663-5249
Edmond Hartounin, *President*
EMP: 25 **EST:** 1980
SQ FT: 10,000
SALES (est): 4.6MM **Privately Held**
SIC: 2051 Bread, cake & related products

(P-1233)
LEY GRAND FOODS CORPORATION
287 S 6th Ave, La Puente (91746-2916)
PHONE..................626 336-2244
Frank Chen, *President*
Chien Chen, *Vice Pres*
J J Chen, *Admin Sec*
▲ **EMP:** 23
SQ FT: 4,000
SALES (est): 3.6MM **Privately Held**
SIC: 2051 Bread, cake & related products

(P-1234)
LEYVAS MEXICAN FOOD
4032 Tyler Ave, El Monte (91731-2040)
PHONE..................626 350-6328
Octaviano Leyva, *Partner*
EMP: 20
SALES (est): 1.7MM **Privately Held**
SIC: 2051 Bakery: wholesale or whole-sale/retail combined

(P-1235)
LIBERTY CAFE
410 Cortland Ave, San Francisco
(94110-5538)
PHONE..................415 695-8777
Vega Freeman, *Owner*
EMP: 28
SALES (est): 2.2MM **Privately Held**
SIC: 2051 5812 Bakery: wholesale or wholesale/retail combined; American restaurant

(P-1236)
LITTLE BROTHERS BAKERY LLC
320 W Alondra Blvd, Gardena
(90248-2423)
PHONE..................310 225-3790
Paul C Giuliano,
Anthony S Giuliano,
Joann Giuliano,
Paul G Giuliano Jr,
Arve Johansson, *Manager*
▲ **EMP:** 65
SQ FT: 15,000
SALES (est): 13.2MM **Privately Held**
WEB: www.littlebrothersbakery.com
SIC: 2051 5149 Bakery: wholesale or wholesale/retail combined; bakery products

(P-1237)
LUPITAS BAKERY INC (PA)
1848 W Florence Ave, Los Angeles
(90047-2123)
PHONE..................323 752-2391
Able Diaz, *President*
Martha Diaz, *Admin Sec*
EMP: 18
SQ FT: 8,000
SALES (est): 1.7MM **Privately Held**
SIC: 2051 5461 Bread, all types (white, wheat, rye, etc): fresh or frozen; bread

(P-1238)
LY BROTHERS CORPORATION (PA)
Also Called: Sugar Bowl Bakery
1963 Sabre St, Hayward (94545-1021)
PHONE..................510 782-2118
Andrew A Ly, *President*
Tom Ly, *Chairman*
Paul Ly, *Treasurer*
Sam Ly, *Exec VP*
Binh Ly, *Vice Pres*
▲ **EMP:** 41
SQ FT: 100,000
SALES (est): 79.3MM **Privately Held**
WEB: www.sugarbowlbakery.com
SIC: 2051 Bakery: wholesale or whole-sale/retail combined

(P-1239)
LY BROTHERS CORPORATION
Also Called: Sugar Bowl Bakery
20389 Corsair Blvd, Hayward
(94545-1026)
PHONE..................510 782-2118
Andrew A Ly, *President*
EMP: 206
SALES (corp-wide): 79.3MM **Privately Held**
SIC: 2051 Bakery: wholesale or whole-sale/retail combined
PA: Ly Brothers Corporation
1963 Sabre St
Hayward CA 94545
510 782-2118

(P-1240)
MARY ANNS BAKING CO INC
8371 Carbide Ct, Sacramento
(95828-5636)
PHONE..................916 681-7444
George A Demas, *President*
Robert Burzinski, *CFO*
Mark Deushane, *Vice Pres*
John Demas, *Admin Sec*
Lori Hoffelt, *Opers Staff*
EMP: 200
SQ FT: 75,000
SALES: 33MM **Privately Held**
WEB: www.maryannsbaking.com
SIC: 2051 Doughnuts, except frozen; rolls, sweet: except frozen; rolls, bread type: fresh or frozen

(P-1241)
MIDDLE EAST BAKING CO
1380 Marsten Rd, Burlingame
(94010-2406)
PHONE..................650 348-7200
Isaac Cohen, *Owner*
▲ **EMP:** 20
SALES (est): 2.6MM **Privately Held**
SIC: 2051 Bakery: wholesale or whole-sale/retail combined

(P-1242)
MILKY MAMA LLC
10722 Arrow Rte Ste 104, Rancho Cuca-monga (91730-4809)
PHONE..................877 886-4559
Krystal Duhaney, *Mng Member*
EMP: 14 **EST:** 2016
SALES (est): 1.7MM **Privately Held**
SIC: 2051 Bakery products, partially cooked (except frozen)

(P-1243)
MILTONS BAKING COMPANY LLC
5875 Avenida Encinas, Carlsbad
(92008-4457)
PHONE..................858 350-9696
John Reaves, *Mng Member*
Michael Cox, *Vice Pres*
Chris Mamos, *Vice Pres*
Christin Fraser, *Marketing Staff*
Lisa Garrucho, *Manager*
EMP: 36
SQ FT: 6,700
SALES: 100MM **Privately Held**
SIC: 2051 Bakery: wholesale or whole-sale/retail combined

▲ = Import ▼=Export
◆ =Import/Export

(P-1244)
MOCHI ICE CREAM COMPANY (PA)
Also Called: Mikawaya
5563 Alcoa Ave, Vernon (90058-3730)
PHONE..........................323 587-5504
Jerry Bucan, *CEO*
Tom Bulowski, *Vice Pres*
Michael Cheng, *Info Tech Dir*
Hernan Pazmino, *Research*
Joel Freeman, *Manager*
◆ **EMP:** 30 **EST:** 1910
SQ FT: 10,000
SALES (est): 17.8MM **Privately Held**
WEB: www.mikawayausa.com
SIC: 2051 2024 5451 Cakes, pies & pastries; ice cream & frozen desserts; ice cream (packaged)

(P-1245)
MONDELEZ GLOBAL LLC
Also Called: Kraft Foods
1220 Howell St, Anaheim (92805)
PHONE..........................714 634-2773
Harry Irwin, *Branch Mgr*
EMP: 22 **Publicly Held**
SIC: 2051 Bakery: wholesale or wholesale/retail combined
HQ: Mondelez Global Llc
3 N Pkwy Ste 300
Deerfield IL 60015
847 943-4000

(P-1246)
MRS REDDS PIE CO INC
150 S La Cadena Dr, Colton (92324-3416)
P.O. Box 555 (92324-0555)
PHONE..........................909 825-4800
Tom P Telliard, *President*
Nick Telliard, *Vice Pres*
EMP: 20
SQ FT: 76,030
SALES (est): 3.6MM **Privately Held**
SIC: 2051 Cakes, bakery: except frozen; pies, bakery: except frozen; yeast goods, sweet: except frozen

(P-1247)
NABOLOM BAKERY
2708 Russell St, Berkeley (94705-2318)
PHONE..........................510 845-2253
Bruce Russell, *President*
EMP: 11
SALES (est): 1.1MM **Privately Held**
WEB: www.nabolom.com
SIC: 2051 Bakery: wholesale or wholesale/retail combined

(P-1248)
NEW YORK FROZEN FOODS INC
Mamma Bella Foods
5100 Rivergrade Rd, Baldwin Park (91706-1406)
PHONE..........................626 338-3000
Bob Willist, *Branch Mgr*
EMP: 50
SALES (corp-wide): 1.2B **Publicly Held**
WEB: www.lancaster.com
SIC: 2051 Buns, bread type: fresh or frozen
HQ: New York Frozen Foods, Inc.
25900 Fargo Ave
Bedford OH 44146
216 292-5655

(P-1249)
NORMANDIE COUNTRY BAKERY INC (PA)
3022 S Cochran Ave, Los Angeles (90016-3706)
PHONE..........................323 939-5528
Josette Leblond, *President*
▲ **EMP:** 21
SQ FT: 12,000
SALES (est): 3.3MM **Privately Held**
SIC: 2051 2011 Bakery: wholesale or wholesale/retail combined; sausages from meat slaughtered on site

(P-1250)
NORTHS BAKERY CALIFORNIA INC
5430 Satsuma Ave, North Hollywood (91601-2837)
PHONE..........................818 761-2892
Graham North, *CEO*
Karl North, *Treasurer*
Sally Walheim, *Manager*
EMP: 35
SQ FT: 35,000
SALES (est): 6.2MM **Privately Held**
SIC: 2051 Bakery: wholesale or wholesale/retail combined

(P-1251)
NOUSHIG INC
Also Called: Amoretti
451 Lombard St, Oxnard (93030-5143)
PHONE..........................805 983-2903
Jack Barsoumian, *CEO*
Hayop L Barsoumian, *President*
Maral Barsoumian, *Corp Secy*
▲ **EMP:** 50
SQ FT: 10,000
SALES (est): 10.4MM **Privately Held**
WEB: www.capriccio.com
SIC: 2051 5149 Bread, cake & related products; soft drinks

(P-1252)
OAKHURST INDUSTRIES INC (PA)
Also Called: Freund Baking
2050 S Tubeway Ave, Commerce (90040-1624)
P.O. Box 911457, Los Angeles (90091-1238)
PHONE..........................323 724-3000
James Freund, *President*
Jonathan Freund, *Vice Pres*
Ronald Martin, *Vice Pres*
Linda F Freund, *Admin Sec*
Will Gallardo, *Safety Mgr*
EMP: 140
SQ FT: 81,000
SALES (est): 88.4MM **Privately Held**
WEB: www.oakhurstproperties.com
SIC: 2051 5149 Buns, bread type: fresh or frozen; groceries & related products

(P-1253)
OC BAKING COMPANY
1960 N Glassell St, Orange (92865-4314)
PHONE..........................714 998-2253
Dean Kim, *President*
EMP: 80
SALES (est): 11.8MM **Privately Held**
SIC: 2051 Bakery: wholesale or wholesale/retail combined

(P-1254)
OLD NEW YORK BAGEL & DELI CO (PA)
Also Called: Old New York Deli & Bagel Co
4972 Verdugo Way, Camarillo (93012-8632)
P.O. Box 1288, Somis (93066-1288)
PHONE..........................805 484-3354
Michael J Raimondo, *President*
Julie Raimondo, *Vice Pres*
EMP: 17
SQ FT: 2,400
SALES (est): 2.7MM **Privately Held**
WEB: www.oldnewyork.com
SIC: 2051 5812 Bakery: wholesale or wholesale/retail combined; coffee shop

(P-1255)
OVEN FRESH BAKERY INCORPORATED
23188 Foley St, Hayward (94545-1602)
PHONE..........................650 366-9201
Juanita Casillas, *President*
Jorge A Alfonso, *Treasurer*
EMP: 15
SQ FT: 18,000
SALES (est): 1.9MM **Privately Held**
SIC: 2051 2053 Bakery: wholesale or wholesale/retail combined; frozen bakery products, except bread

(P-1256)
PAMELAS PRODUCTS INCORPORATED
1 Carousel Ln Ste D, Ukiah (95482-9509)
PHONE..........................707 462-6605
Pamela L Giusto, *CEO*
Lene Vinding, *Manager*
EMP: 85
SALES (est): 20.2MM **Privately Held**
WEB: www.pamelasproducts.com
SIC: 2051 2052 Bakery products, partially cooked (except frozen); cookies & crackers

(P-1257)
PAN-O-RAMA BAKING INC
500 Florida St, San Francisco (94110-1415)
PHONE..........................415 522-5500
Bill Upson, *President*
Bob Mannion, *Sales Executive*
EMP: 40
SALES (est): 4.7MM **Privately Held**
WEB: www.panoramabaking.com
SIC: 2051 Bakery: wholesale or wholesale/retail combined

(P-1258)
PANCHOS BAKERY
1759 E Florence Ave, Los Angeles (90001-2523)
PHONE..........................323 582-9109
Francisco Cedillo, *Owner*
EMP: 20 **EST:** 1973
SQ FT: 5,000
SALES (est): 1.3MM **Privately Held**
SIC: 2051 5461 Bakery: wholesale or wholesale/retail combined; bakeries

(P-1259)
PASTRIES BY EDIE INC
7226 Topanga Canyon Blvd, Canoga Park (91303-1239)
PHONE..........................818 340-0203
Edie Gour, *President*
Michele Gour, *Vice Pres*
Jason Gour, *Admin Sec*
EMP: 35
SALES (est): 4.8MM **Privately Held**
WEB: www.pastriesbyedie.com
SIC: 2051 Bread, cake & related products

(P-1260)
PEDRO PALLAN
Also Called: San Antonio Bakery
344 W Rosecrans Ave, Compton (90222-4055)
PHONE..........................310 638-1763
Salvador Martinez, *President*
EMP: 18
SQ FT: 2,400
SALES (est): 1.4MM **Privately Held**
SIC: 2051 2052 5149 5461 Sponge goods, bakery: except frozen; cookies; bakery products; cookies; bread

(P-1261)
PETITS PAINS & CO LP
1730 Gilbreth Rd, Burlingame (94010-1305)
PHONE..........................650 692-6000
Alain Bourgade, *Principal*
EMP: 18
SALES (est): 3.4MM **Privately Held**
SIC: 2051 Bakery: wholesale or wholesale/retail combined

(P-1262)
PIN HSIAO & ASSOCIATES LLC
Also Called: Antonina's Bakery
1316 Dupont Ct, Manteca (95336-6004)
P.O. Box 40177, Bellevue WA (98015-4177)
PHONE..........................209 665-4176
Todd Wetherell, *Plant Mgr*
EMP: 40
SALES (corp-wide): 20MM **Privately Held**
SIC: 2051 Bakery: wholesale or wholesale/retail combined
PA: Pin Hsiao & Associates L.L.C.
5501 West Valley Hwy E A101
Sumner WA 98390
425 637-3357

(P-1263)
PORTOS FOOD PRODUCT INC
2085 Garfield Ave, Commerce (90040-1803)
PHONE..........................323 480-8400
Raul Porto, *Owner*
▲ **EMP:** 92
SALES (est): 8.4MM **Privately Held**
SIC: 2051 Bakery: wholesale or wholesale/retail combined

(P-1264)
PRINCESS BRANDY CORP (PA)
Also Called: Incredible Cheesecake
3161 Adams Ave, San Diego (92116-1638)
PHONE..........................619 563-9722
Michelle Satren, *President*
Scott Satren, *Vice Pres*
EMP: 10
SQ FT: 3,300
SALES (est): 957.8K **Privately Held**
WEB: www.incrediblecheesecake.net
SIC: 2051 5461 Cakes, bakery: except frozen; cakes

(P-1265)
PURITAN BAKERY INC
1624 E Carson St, Carson (90745-2599)
PHONE..........................310 830-5451
Matthew R Grimes, *President*
John G Markulis, *Corp Secy*
John John Markulis, *Vice Pres*
Casey Muldoon, *Sales Staff*
Manuel Rodriguez, *Manager*
EMP: 200
SQ FT: 60,000
SALES (est): 65.1MM **Privately Held**
SIC: 2051 Bakery products, partially cooked (except frozen)

(P-1266)
PYRENEES FRENCH BAKERY INC
717 E 21st St, Bakersfield (93305-5240)
P.O. Box 3626 (93385-3626)
PHONE..........................661 322-7159
Marianne Laxague, *President*
Juanita Laxague, *Corp Secy*
EMP: 26
SQ FT: 33,750
SALES (est): 2.6MM **Privately Held**
WEB: www.pyreneesbakery.com
SIC: 2051 5461 Bakery: wholesale or wholesale/retail combined; bread, all types (white, wheat, rye, etc): fresh or frozen; bakeries

(P-1267)
ROLLING DOUGH CORPORATION
624 E Holt Blvd, Ontario (91761-1708)
PHONE..........................714 884-2801
Christian A Niteo, *Owner*
Cesar Herrera, *President*
EMP: 10 **EST:** 2017
SALES (est): 1MM **Privately Held**
SIC: 2051 Bakery products, partially cooked (except frozen)

(P-1268)
ROMA BAKERY INC
655 S Almaden Ave, San Jose (95110-2999)
P.O. Box 348 (95103-0348)
PHONE..........................408 294-0123
Robert Pera, *President*
Mario Pera II, *Vice Pres*
Steven Pera, *Admin Sec*
EMP: 60
SQ FT: 15,000
SALES (est): 9.2MM **Privately Held**
SIC: 2051 Bread, all types (white, wheat, rye, etc): fresh or frozen; rolls, bread type: fresh or frozen

(P-1269)
ROSETTIS FINE FOODS INC
Also Called: Biscotti House
3 Railroad Ave, Clovis (93612-1219)
PHONE..........................559 323-6450
Diane Rosetti, *Principal*
Matt Rosetti, *Manager*
EMP: 13
SQ FT: 3,135

P R O D U C T S & S V C S

SALES (est): 1.9MM **Privately Held**
WEB: www.rosettis.com
SIC: 2051 Bakery: wholesale or whole-sale/retail combined

(P-1270)
ROSSMOOR PASTRIES MGT INC
2325 Redondo Ave, Signal Hill
(90755-4019)
PHONE..................562 498-2253
Charles Feder, *CEO*
Janice Ahlgren, *Partner*
EMP: 80 EST: 2000
SALES (est): 11.1MM **Privately Held**
WEB: www.rossmoorpastries.com
SIC: 2051 Bread, cake & related products

(P-1271)
SACRAMENTO BAKING CO INC
9221 Beatty Dr, Sacramento (95826-9702)
PHONE..................916 361-2000
Samir Elajou, *CEO*
Juma Al Ajon, *President*
Juma Elajou, *President*
Samira Al Ajon, *CEO*
EMP: 30
SQ FT: 10,000
SALES (est): 5.3MM **Privately Held**
SIC: 2051 5812 Bread, all types (white, wheat, rye, etc): fresh or frozen; pastries, e.g. danish: except frozen; cafe

(P-1272)
SARA LEE FRESH INC
5200 S Alameda St, Vernon (90058-3420)
PHONE..................215 347-5500
Alfred Penny, *President*
Ed Penny, *President*
Barry Horner, *Info Tech Dir*
▲ EMP: 607
SQ FT: 120,000
SALES (est): 48.8K **Privately Held**
SIC: 2051 Bread, all types (white, wheat, rye, etc): fresh or frozen; rolls, bread type: fresh or frozen; bagels, fresh or frozen
HQ: Bimbo Bakeries Usa, Inc
255 Business Center Dr # 200
Horsham PA 19044
215 347-5500

(P-1273)
SCIAMBR-PASSINI FRENCH BKY INC
Also Called: Sciambra French Bakery
685 S Freeway Dr, NAPA (94558-6057)
PHONE..................707 252-3072
Micheal Sciambra, *President*
Patricia Spears, *Treasurer*
EMP: 30
SQ FT: 8,000
SALES (est): 4.5MM **Privately Held**
SIC: 2051 Breads, rolls & buns

(P-1274)
SCONE HENGE INC
2787 Shattuck Ave, Berkeley (94705-1036)
PHONE..................510 845-5168
June Lee, *President*
Yong Lee, *Vice Pres*
EMP: 15 EST: 1998
SALES (est): 1.4MM **Privately Held**
SIC: 2051 Bread, cake & related products

(P-1275)
SGB BETTER BAKING CO LLC
14528 Blythe St, Van Nuys (91402-6006)
PHONE..................818 787-9992
Chris Botticella, *CEO*
Ash Aghasi, *COO*
EMP: 57
SALES: 4.6MM
SALES (corp-wide): 40.6MM **Privately Held**
SIC: 2051 5149 Bakery: wholesale or wholesale/retail combined; bakery products
PA: Surge Global Bakeries Holdings Llc
13336 Paxton St
Pacoima CA 91331
818 896-0525

(P-1276)
SGB BUBBLES BAKING CO LLC
15215 Keswick St, Van Nuys (91405-1014)
PHONE..................818 786-1700
Tom Beauchamp,

Blanca Izaguirre, *Accountant*
Lewis Sharp,
EMP: 100
SQ FT: 50,000
SALES: 100K **Privately Held**
SIC: 2051 5461 Bread, cake & related products; biscuits, baked: baking powder & raised; bakeries

(P-1277)
SHENG-KEE BAKERY
201 S Hill Dr, Brisbane (94005-1204)
PHONE..................415 468-3800
Mark KAO, *Owner*
▲ EMP: 61
SALES (est): 1.3MM **Privately Held**
SIC: 2051 Bakery: wholesale or whole-sale/retail combined

(P-1278)
SLJ WHOLESALE LLC
Also Called: Sweet Lady Jane
13850 Del Sur St, San Fernando (91340-3440)
PHONE..................323 662-8900
Sabrina Sin, *Principal*
Oscar Gomez, *Opers Staff*
EMP: 20
SQ FT: 7,000
SALES (est): 2.1MM **Privately Held**
SIC: 2051 2053 Cakes, bakery: except frozen; pies, bakery: except frozen; cakes, bakery: frozen; pies, bakery: frozen

(P-1279)
SUGAR FOODS CORPORATION
6190 E Slauson Ave, Commerce (90040-3010)
PHONE..................323 727-8290
Harland Gray, *Manager*
Sherry De Keyser, *Human Resources*
EMP: 100
SALES (corp-wide): 286.3MM **Privately Held**
WEB: www.sugarfoods.com
SIC: 2051 2052 2099 Bread, cake & related products; cookies & crackers; food preparations
PA: Sugar Foods Corporation
950 3rd Ave Fl 21
New York NY 10022
212 753-6900

(P-1280)
SUNRISE BAKERY
Also Called: Sunrise Bakery and Cafe
1561 Geer Rd, Turlock (95380-3200)
PHONE..................209 632-9400
Filameh Givargis, *Owner*
Shargon Eddy, *Opers Mgr*
EMP: 12
SQ FT: 2,400
SALES (est): 986.3K **Privately Held**
SIC: 2051 Bakery: wholesale or whole-sale/retail combined

(P-1281)
SWEETIE PIES LLC
520 Main St, NAPA (94559-3353)
PHONE..................707 257-7280
Toni M Chiappetta,
EMP: 19
SQ FT: 600
SALES (est): 3.3MM **Privately Held**
WEB: www.sweetiepies.com
SIC: 2051 5812 Bakery: wholesale or wholesale/retail combined; eating places

(P-1282)
TABLE DE FRANCE INC
2020 S Haven Ave, Ontario (91761-0735)
PHONE..................909 923-5205
Herve Le Bayon, *President*
Philip L Bayon, *CFO*
Philip Le Bayon, *CFO*
EMP: 12
SQ FT: 30,000
SALES (est): 1.9MM **Privately Held**
SIC: 2051 Bakery: wholesale or whole-sale/retail combined

(P-1283)
TAHOE HOUSE INC
625 W Lake Blvd, Tahoe City (96145)
P.O. Box 1899 (96145-1899)
PHONE..................530 583-1377
Barbara Vogt, *President*
Caroline Vogt, *Treasurer*
Helen Vogt, *Vice Pres*
▲ EMP: 12
SQ FT: 6,800
SALES: 1MM **Privately Held**
WEB: www.tahoe-house.com
SIC: 2051 Bakery: wholesale or whole-sale/retail combined

(P-1284)
TANBIL BAKERY INC
Also Called: Tanbit Bakery
8150 Garvey Ave Ste 104, Rosemead (91770-2473)
PHONE..................626 280-2638
Chia Fu Fang, *President*
Wang A Hsueh Fang, *Admin Sec*
▲ EMP: 11
SALES (est): 780.5K **Privately Held**
SIC: 2051 Bakery: wholesale or whole-sale/retail combined

(P-1285)
TARTINE LP
Also Called: Tartine Bakery & Cafe
600 Guerrero St, San Francisco (94110-1528)
PHONE..................415 487-2600
Frederic Soulies, *CEO*
Elisabeth Prueitt, *Principal*
Chad Robertson, *Principal*
Robin Rodriguez, *General Mgr*
Josh Drew, *Director*
EMP: 45
SALES (est): 5.2MM **Privately Held**
SIC: 2051 5812 5921 Breads, rolls & buns; cakes, pies & pastries; cafe; wine & beer

(P-1286)
THE FRENCH PATISSERIE INC
Also Called: Looka Patisserie
1080 Palmetto Ave, Pacifica (94044-2216)
PHONE..................650 738-4990
Marta Spasic, *President*
Frank Spasic, *Vice Pres*
Joann Leong, *Technology*
◆ EMP: 90
SQ FT: 34,000
SALES (est): 19.6MM **Privately Held**
WEB: www.frenchpatisserie.com
SIC: 2051 Bread, cake & related products

(P-1287)
TOUFIC INC
Also Called: La Boulangerie
2324 Grand Canal Blvd # 1, Stockton (95207-8214)
PHONE..................209 478-4780
Raymond Bitar, *President*
John Bitar, *Corp Secy*
Allen Bitar, *Officer*
EMP: 14
SQ FT: 3,000
SALES (est): 1.7MM **Privately Held**
WEB: www.toufic.com
SIC: 2051 5812 Bread, all types (white, wheat, rye, etc): fresh or frozen; eating places

(P-1288)
UNITED BAKERY INC
727 S Flower St, Burbank (91502-2014)
PHONE..................818 843-1892
Daniel Sanchez, *President*
Mark Sanchez, *Treasurer*
EMP: 35
SQ FT: 20,000
SALES (est): 2.3MM **Privately Held**
WEB: www.unitedbakery.com
SIC: 2051 Bakery: wholesale or whole-sale/retail combined

(P-1289)
VALLEY LAHVOSH BAKING CO INC
502 M St, Fresno (93721-3013)
PHONE..................559 485-2700
Janet F Saghatelian, *President*
Agnes Wilson, *Vice Pres*

Rebecca Cline, *Administration*
Danny Giosa, *Opers Mgr*
▲ EMP: 30
SQ FT: 27,000
SALES (est): 7.6MM **Privately Held**
WEB: www.valleylahvosh.com
SIC: 2051 5461 Bread, all types (white, wheat, rye, etc): fresh or frozen; breads, rolls & buns; bread

(P-1290)
VENICE BAKING CO
134 Main St, El Segundo (90245-3801)
PHONE..................310 322-7357
James N Desisto, *CEO*
Larry De Sisto, *President*
Brian Khoddam, *COO*
Phil Alva, *Purch Mgr*
Miguel Gomez, *Director*
EMP: 40
SQ FT: 35,000
SALES (est): 7.6MM **Privately Held**
SIC: 2051 5149 Bread, all types (white, wheat, rye, etc): fresh or frozen; baking supplies; pizza supplies

(P-1291)
VITAL VITTLES BAKERY INC
Also Called: Schwin and Tran Mill & Bakery
2810 San Pablo Ave, Berkeley (94702-2204)
PHONE..................510 644-2022
Binh Tran, *President*
EMP: 18
SQ FT: 2,424
SALES (est): 1.2MM **Privately Held**
SIC: 2051 2052 5461 Bakery: wholesale or wholesale/retail combined; cookies & crackers; bakeries

(P-1292)
WESTERN BAGEL BAKING CORP (PA)
7814 Sepulveda Blvd, Van Nuys (91405-1062)
PHONE..................818 786-5847
Steven Ustin, *President*
Mark Weisner, *Info Tech Mgr*
David Beltran, *Controller*
Jeff Ustin, *VP Prdtn*
Corie Ustin, *Mktg Dir*
▼ EMP: 225
SQ FT: 23,500
SALES: 56.6MM **Privately Held**
WEB: www.westernbagel.com
SIC: 2051 5461 Bagels, fresh or frozen; bagels

(P-1293)
WESTERN BAGEL BAKING CORP
21749 Ventura Blvd, Woodland Hills (91364-1835)
PHONE..................818 887-5451
Tim Brennen, *Principal*
EMP: 35
SALES (corp-wide): 56.6MM **Privately Held**
WEB: www.westernbagel.com
SIC: 2051 5461 Bagels, fresh or frozen; bagels
PA: Western Bagel Baking Corp
7814 Sepulveda Blvd
Van Nuys CA 91405
818 786-5847

(P-1294)
WESTERN BAGEL BAKING CORP
Also Called: Western Bagel Too
11628 Santa Monica Blvd # 12, Los Angeles (90025-2950)
PHONE..................310 479-4823
Fax: 310 826-2383
EMP: 20
SALES (corp-wide): 39.6MM **Privately Held**
SIC: 2051
PA: Western Bagel Baking Corp
7814 Sepulveda Blvd
Van Nuys CA 91405
818 786-5847

▲ = Import ▼=Export
◆ =Import/Export

(P-1295)
WESTLAKE BAKERY INC
Also Called: Bread Basket
7099 Mission St, Daly City (94014-2253)
PHONE..................................650 994-7741
Jaime Cavan, *President*
Nelly Cavan, *Vice Pres*
EMP: 15
SQ FT: 5,000
SALES (est): 1.8MM Privately Held
SIC: 2051 5461 Bakery: wholesale or wholesale/retail combined; bakeries

(P-1296)
WHOLESOME HARVEST BAKING LLC
Also Called: Maple Leaf Bakery
3200 Regatta Blvd Ste G, Richmond (94804-6401)
PHONE..................................510 231-7200
Kevin Kamkar, *Branch Mgr*
EMP: 200 Privately Held
SIC: 2051 Bakery: wholesale or whole-sale/retail combined
HQ: Wholesome Harvest Baking, Llc
8550 W Bryn Mawr Ave # 10
Chicago IL 60631
800 550-6810

(P-1297)
WHOLESOME HARVEST BAKING LLC
Also Called: Pioneer French Bakery
2701 Statham Blvd, Oxnard (93033-3920)
PHONE..................................805 487-5191
Donald Hall, *Plant Mgr*
EMP: 150 Privately Held
WEB: www.mapleleaffoodsusa.com
SIC: 2051 Breads, rolls & buns; bread, all types (white, wheat, rye, etc): fresh or frozen
HQ: Wholesome Harvest Baking, Llc
8550 W Bryn Mawr Ave # 10
Chicago IL 60631
800 550-6810

(P-1298)
WINDMILL CORPORATION
Also Called: Wedemeyer Bakery
314 Harbor Way, South San Francisco (94080-6900)
PHONE..................................650 873-1000
Larry Strain, *President*
EMP: 25 EST: 2004
SALES (est): 4.3MM Privately Held
SIC: 2051 5461 5149 Bread, all types (white, wheat, rye, etc): fresh or frozen; rolls, bread type: fresh or frozen; bakeries; groceries & related products

(P-1299)
YOU ARE LOVED FOODS LLC
1282 Newbury Rd, Newbury Park (91320-3606)
PHONE..................................818 578-8288
Jonathan Heine, *Mng Member*
EMP: 10
SALES (est): 1.2MM Privately Held
SIC: 2051 Bread, cake & related products

2052 Cookies & Crackers

(P-1300)
AMAYS BAKERY & NOODLE CO INC (PA)
837 E Commercial St, Los Angeles (90012-3413)
PHONE..................................213 626-2713
Kee Hom, *CEO*
▲ EMP: 63 EST: 1968
SQ FT: 20,000
SALES (est): 12.1MM Privately Held
WEB: www.amaysbakery.com
SIC: 2052 2098 Cookies; noodles (e.g. egg, plain & water), dry

(P-1301)
ARBO INC
Also Called: Joy of Cookies
1205 Stanford Ave, Oakland (94608-2621)
P.O. Box 8688 (94662-0688)
PHONE..................................510 658-3700
Adele Connor, *President*

Joe Connor, *Vice Pres*
EMP: 21
SQ FT: 5,400
SALES (est): 2.5MM Privately Held
WEB: www.suncakes.net
SIC: 2052 Cookies

(P-1302)
ARYZTA HOLDINGS IV LLC (HQ)
6080 Center Dr Ste 900, Los Angeles (90045-9226)
PHONE..................................310 417-4700
John Yamin, *CEO*
Sean Masterson, *Account Dir*
▼ EMP: 235
SALES: 1.7B
SALES (corp-wide): 3.9B Privately Held
SIC: 2052 2053 2045 2051 Cookies & crackers; cookies; frozen bakery products, except bread; bread & bread type roll mixes: from purchased flour; breads, rolls & buns
PA: Aryzta Ag
Ifangstrasse 9
Schlieren ZH 8952
445 834-200

(P-1303)
ARYZTA LLC
Also Called: Fresh Start Bakeries
1220 S Baker Ave, Ontario (91761-7739)
P.O. Box 1283, Alhambra (91802-1283)
PHONE..................................909 472-3500
Rob Crawford, *General Mgr*
Curtis Smith, *Director*
EMP: 197
SALES (corp-wide): 3.9B Privately Held
WEB: www.fsbglobal.net
SIC: 2052 Cookies
HQ: Aryzta Llc
6080 Center Dr Ste 900
Los Angeles CA 90045
310 417-4700

(P-1304)
ARYZTA LLC
2350 Pullman St, Santa Ana (92705-5507)
PHONE..................................949 261-7400
Zac Morris, *Branch Mgr*
Nancy Kirksey, *Vice Pres*
EMP: 115
SALES (corp-wide): 3.9B Privately Held
SIC: 2052 Cookies
HQ: Aryzta Llc
6080 Center Dr Ste 900
Los Angeles CA 90045
310 417-4700

(P-1305)
ARYZTA LLC (DH)
6080 Center Dr Ste 900, Los Angeles (90045-9226)
PHONE..................................310 417-4700
Dave Johnson, *Officer*
Suzanne Wooley, *President*
Andrew Brimacombe, *Officer*
Culbert Lu, *Officer*
John Malone, *Officer*
◆ EMP: 235 EST: 1977
SQ FT: 90,000
SALES: 1.6B
SALES (corp-wide): 3.9B Privately Held
SIC: 2052 2053 2051 Cookies; frozen bakery products, except bread; cakes, pies & pastries; breads, rolls & buns
WEB: www.spunkmeyer.com

(P-1306)
ARYZTA US HOLDINGS I CORP
14490 Catalina St, San Leandro (94577-5516)
PHONE..................................800 938-1900
John Yamin, *CEO*
Brian Younglove, *President*
Ronan Minahan, *COO*
Robin Jones, *CFO*
Jon Davis, *Vice Pres*
EMP: 9500
SALES (est): 228.8MM
SALES (corp-wide): 3.9B Privately Held
SIC: 2052 2053 2051 Cookies; frozen bakery products, except bread; cakes, pies & pastries

PA: Aryzta Ag
Ifangstrasse 9
Schlieren ZH 8952
445 834-200

(P-1307)
BISCOMERICA CORP
565 W Slover Ave, Rialto (92377)
P.O. Box 1070 (92377-1070)
PHONE..................................909 877-5997
Nadi Soltan, *Ch of Bd*
Ayad Fargo, *President*
Angelica Lopez, *Traffic Mgr*
Jean Novak, *VP Sales*
Norma Serrano, *Transportation*
▲ EMP: 250
SQ FT: 250,000
SALES (est): 65.7MM Privately Held
WEB: www.biscomerica.com
SIC: 2052 2064 Cookies & crackers; candy & other confectionery products

(P-1308)
BLOOMFIELD BAKERS
10711 Bloomfield St, Los Alamitos (90720-2503)
PHONE..................................626 610-2253
William R Ross, *General Ptnr*
Maggie Acquisition Corp, *General Ptnr*
Aiko Acquisition Corp, *Partner*
Gary Marx, *Branch Mgr*
▼ EMP: 600
SQ FT: 75,000
SALES (est): 130.4MM
SALES (corp-wide): 5.8B Publicly Held
SIC: 2052 2064 Cookies; candy & other confectionery products
HQ: Treehouse Private Brands, Inc.
2021 Spring Rd Ste 600
Oak Brook IL 60523

(P-1309)
BREAD LOS ANGELES
1527 Beach St, Montebello (90640-5431)
PHONE..................................323 201-3953
Vachik M Elchibegian,
Melecio Espain, *Opers Mgr*
Beatrice M Elchibegian,
▲ EMP: 40
SALES (est): 8.2MM Privately Held
SIC: 2052 2051 Cookies & crackers; bread, cake & related products

(P-1310)
BROWNIE BAKER INC
4870 W Jacquelyn Ave, Fresno (93722-5027)
PHONE..................................559 277-7070
Dennis Perkins, *CEO*
Janea Marks, *Human Res Dir*
Ken Morgan, *Sales Staff*
▲ EMP: 70 EST: 1979
SQ FT: 30,000
SALES (est): 14.3MM Privately Held
WEB: www.browniebaker.com
SIC: 2052 2051 Cookies; bread, cake & related products

(P-1311)
D F STAUFFER BISCUIT CO INC
Laguna Cookie Company
4041 W Garry Ave, Santa Ana (92704-6315)
PHONE..................................714 546-6855
Albert Ovalle, *Manager*
EMP: 50 Privately Held
WEB: www.stauffers.net
SIC: 2052 Cookies
HQ: D F Stauffer Biscuit Co Inc
360 S Belmont St
York PA 17403
717 815-4600

(P-1312)
DAWN FOOD PRODUCTS INC
2455 Tenaya Dr, Modesto (95354-3918)
PHONE..................................517 789-4400
Ty Hackman, *Manager*
Jessica Shepard, *Project Mgr*
Steve Zylstra, *Project Engr*
Lena Boyovich, *Buyer*
Cathy Wunderink, *Safety Mgr*
EMP: 15

SALES (corp-wide): 1.6B Privately Held
WEB: www.dawnfoods.com
SIC: 2052 Bakery products, dry
HQ: Dawn Food Products, Inc.
3333 Sargent Rd
Jackson MI 49201

(P-1313)
DEEP FOODS INC
4000 Whipple Rd, Union City (94587-1506)
PHONE..................................510 475-1900
Archit Amin, *Branch Mgr*
EMP: 11
SALES (corp-wide): 48.3MM Privately Held
WEB: www.deepfoods.com
SIC: 2052 Bakery products, dry; crackers, dry
PA: Deep Foods Inc
1090 Springfield Rd Ste 1
Union NJ 07083
908 810-7500

(P-1314)
ELEMENTS FOOD GROUP INC
5560 Brooks St, Montclair (91763-4522)
P.O. Box 4020, Newport Beach (92661-4020)
PHONE..................................909 983-2011
Wayne Sorensen, *President*
EMP: 60
SQ FT: 23,000
SALES (est): 12.5MM Privately Held
SIC: 2052 Bakery products, dry; breakfasts, frozen & packaged; dinners, frozen & packaged; lunches, frozen & packaged

(P-1315)
FOWLIE ENTERPRISES INC
Also Called: Pretzelmaker
1143 Fern Oaks Dr, Santa Paula (93060-1203)
PHONE..................................805 583-2800
EMP: 25
SALES (est): 1.6MM Privately Held
SIC: 2052 2096

(P-1316)
J & J SNACK FOODS CORP CAL (HQ)
5353 S Downey Rd, Vernon (90058-3725)
PHONE..................................323 581-0171
Gerald B Shreiber, *CEO*
Dennis Moore, *Vice Pres*
Robyn Shreiber, *Vice Pres*
Leong Tan, *Executive*
Mitzi Moreno, *Research*
▲ EMP: 204
SQ FT: 132,000
SALES (est): 114.9MM
SALES (corp-wide): 1.1B Publicly Held
WEB: www.jjsnack.com
SIC: 2052 5149 Pretzels; cookies
PA: J & J Snack Foods Corp.
6000 Central Hwy
Pennsauken NJ 08109
856 665-9533

(P-1317)
JUST OFF MELROSE INC
1196 Montalvo Way, Palm Springs (92262-5441)
PHONE..................................714 533-4566
Brandon Tesmer, *President*
David Parker, *Executive*
EMP: 40
SQ FT: 12,000
SALES (est): 6.2MM Privately Held
WEB: www.justoffmelrose.com
SIC: 2052 2051 Crackers, dry; cookies; bakery products, dry; bread, cake & related products

(P-1318)
KEEBLER COMPANY
14000 183rd St, La Palma (90623-1010)
PHONE..................................714 228-1555
EMP: 60
SALES (corp-wide): 12.9B Publicly Held
SIC: 2052 2051
HQ: Keebler Company
1 Kellogg Sq
Battle Creek MI 49017
269 961-2000

PRODUCTS & SVCS

(P-1319)
LAGUNA COOKIE COMPANY INC
4041 W Garry Ave, Santa Ana
(92704-6315)
PHONE....................714 546-6855
Takeshi Izumi, *CEO*
Rod Sanchez, *Manager*
EMP: 100
SQ FT: 55,000
SALES (est): 17.9MM **Privately Held**
WEB: www.stauffers.net
SIC: 2052 Cookies & crackers
HQ: D F Stauffer Biscuit Co Inc
360 S Belmont St
York PA 17403
717 815-4600

(P-1320)
MARTHA OLSONS GREAT FOODS INC
Also Called: Martha's All Natural
4407 Giannecchini Ln, Stockton
(95206-3954)
PHONE....................209 234-5935
Michael Brown, *CEO*
Roylene Brown, *CFO*
EMP: 10
SQ FT: 7,250
SALES (est): 1.4MM **Privately Held**
WEB: www.marthasallnatural.com
SIC: 2052 2034 2035 Bakery products,
dry; soup mixes; pickles, sauces & salad
dressings

(P-1321)
MICROBIOTIC HEALTH FOODS INC
Also Called: Nana's Cookie Company
4901 Morena Blvd Ste 403, San Diego
(92117-7305)
PHONE....................858 273-5775
Miriam Diamond, *President*
Janet Nager, *VP Sales*
EMP: 14
SQ FT: 3,000
SALES (est): 1.9MM **Privately Held**
SIC: 2052 Cookies

(P-1322)
MURRAY BISCUIT COMPANY LLC
Also Called: Famous Amos Chclat Chip
Cookie
5250 Claremont Ave, Stockton
(95207-5700)
PHONE....................209 472-3718
Chris Lopes, *Branch Mgr*
EMP: 23
SALES (corp-wide): 13.5B **Publicly Held**
WEB: www.littlebrownie.com
SIC: 2052 Cookies
HQ: Murray Biscuit Company, L.L.C.
1550 Marvin Griffin Rd
Augusta GA 30906
706 798-8600

(P-1323)
PADERIA LLC
18279 Brookhurst St Ste 1, Fountain Valley
(92708-6750)
PHONE....................949 478-5273
Nathan Vuong,
EMP: 14
SALES (est): 993.8K **Privately Held**
SIC: 2052 Cookies & crackers

(P-1324)
PAK GROUP LLC
Also Called: Dellarise
236 N Chester Ave Ste 200, Pasadena
(91106-5166)
PHONE....................626 316-6555
Walter Postelwait, *President*
Khosrow Pakravan,
▲ EMP: 21
SQ FT: 6,200
SALES (est): 3.2MM
SALES (corp-wide): 538.2K **Privately Held**
SIC: 2052 2099 5149 Bakery products,
dry; food preparations; yeast
PA: Tech Us Corp
236 N Chester Ave Ste 200
Pasadena CA 91106
626 316-6555

(P-1325)
PRESIDENT GLOBAL CORPORATION (HQ)
6965 Aragon Cir, Buena Park (90620-1118)
PHONE....................714 994-2990
Ping Chih Wu, *President*
▲ EMP: 10
SQ FT: 37,000
SALES (est): 34.2MM **Privately Held**
SIC: 2052 5149 2099 Cookies & crack-
ers; groceries & related products; food
preparations

(P-1326)
RENAISSANCE FOOD INC
Also Called: Renaissance Pastry
14540 Friar St, Van Nuys (91411-2308)
PHONE....................818 778-6230
Eric Khayam, *President*
EMP: 11
SALES (est): 1.1MM **Privately Held**
WEB: www.renaissancefood.com
SIC: 2052 Cookies

(P-1327)
SANTA BRBARA ESSNTIAL FODS LLC
233 E Gutierrez St, Santa Barbara
(93101-1704)
PHONE....................805 965-1948
Peter Kayfetz-Gaum, *CEO*
Janet Kayfetz-Gaum,
EMP: 35
SQ FT: 2,000
SALES (est): 6.4MM **Privately Held**
SIC: 2052 Pretzels

(P-1328)
SHENG-KEE OF CALIFORNIA INC
Also Called: Wawa
10961 N Wolfe Rd, Cupertino
(95014-0617)
PHONE....................408 865-6000
Hsaio Y KAO, *Manager*
EMP: 20
SALES (corp-wide): 25.8MM **Privately Held**
WEB: www.shengkee.com
SIC: 2052 Bakery products, dry; cones; ice
cream; biscuits, dry
PA: Sheng-Kee Of California, Inc.
1941 Irving St
San Francisco CA 94122
415 564-4800

(P-1329)
SONORA MILLS FOODS INC (PA)
Also Called: Pop Chips
3064 E Maria St, E Rncho Dmngz
(90221-5804)
PHONE....................310 639-5333
Patrick Turpin, *CEO*
Martin Basch, *Vice Pres*
▲ EMP: 75
SQ FT: 80,000
SALES (est): 66.6MM **Privately Held**
WEB: www.sonoramills.com
SIC: 2052 Rice cakes

(P-1330)
SOOJIANS INC
Also Called: AK Mak Bakeries Division
89 Academy Ave, Sanger (93657-2104)
PHONE....................559 875-5511
Manoog Soojian, *President*
Hagop Soojian, *Vice Pres*
EMP: 30
SQ FT: 8,000
SALES (est): 4.8MM **Privately Held**
SIC: 2052 5046 Crackers, dry; bakery
equipment & supplies

(P-1331)
SOUTH COAST BAKING LLC (HQ)
Also Called: South Coast Baking Co.
1722 Kettering, Irvine (92614-5616)
PHONE....................949 851-9654
Kent Hayden, *CEO*
James Bergeson, *Partner*
Rick Ptak, *COO*
Carole Ann Sushkoff, *Controller*

◆ EMP: 55
SQ FT: 22,500
SALES (est): 110.3MM
SALES (corp-wide): 171.5MM **Privately Held**
SIC: 2052 5149 Cookies; cookies
PA: Le Petit Pain Holdings, Llc
676 N Michigan Ave
Chicago IL 60611
312 981-3770

(P-1332)
TIMKEV INTERNATIONAL INC
9050 Rosecrans Ave, Bellflower
(90706-2038)
PHONE....................562 232-1691
Jeong Hwan RHO, *CEO*
▲ EMP: 10 EST: 2011
SALES (est): 1.1MM **Privately Held**
SIC: 2052 Cookies & crackers

(P-1333)
TRADITIONAL BAKING INC
2575 S Willow Ave, Bloomington
(92316-3256)
PHONE....................909 877-8471
Kathleen V Cunningham, *President*
▲ EMP: 75
SQ FT: 60,000
SALES (est): 19.2MM **Privately Held**
WEB: www.traditionalbaking.com
SIC: 2052 Cookies

(P-1334)
TRIPLE C FOODS INC
Also Called: Golden Phoenix Bakery
1465 Factor Ave, San Leandro
(94577-5615)
PHONE....................510 357-8880
Tom Chua, *President*
Kim Chua, *Vice Pres*
Aaron Chua, *Office Mgr*
EMP: 80
SQ FT: 65,000
SALES (est): 9.7MM **Privately Held**
SIC: 2052 Cookies

(P-1335)
UMEYA INC
Also Called: Umeya Rice Cake Co
414 Crocker St, Los Angeles (90013-2115)
P.O. Box 1071, Glendale (91209-1071)
PHONE....................213 626-8341
Tak Hamano, *President*
Bunji Hayata, *Corp Secy*
▲ EMP: 30 EST: 1938
SQ FT: 16,000
SALES (est): 3.9MM **Privately Held**
WEB: www.umeyaricecake.com
SIC: 2052 Cookies; crackers, dry

(P-1336)
UTBBB INC
10711 Bloomfield St, Los Alamitos
(90720-2503)
PHONE....................562 594-4411
Gary Marks, *CEO*
William R Ross, *President*
Gene Kester, *Principal*
◆ EMP: 200
SQ FT: 1,000
SALES (est): 16.3MM
SALES (corp-wide): 5.8B **Publicly Held**
WEB: www.bloomfieldbakers.com
SIC: 2052 5141 Cookies & crackers; food
brokers
HQ: Treehouse Private Brands, Inc.
2021 Spring Rd Ste 600
Oak Brook IL 60523

(P-1337)
WETZELS PRETZELS LLC (HQ)
35 Hugus Aly Ste 300, Pasadena
(91103-3648)
PHONE....................626 432-6900
Jennifer Schuler, *CEO*
Doug Flaig, *Vice Pres*
Vincent Montanelli, *Vice Pres*
Don Braxton, *Regional Mgr*
Michael Olivares, *Regional Mgr*
▼ EMP: 10
SQ FT: 4,000
SALES (est): 16.4MM **Privately Held**
SIC: 2052 5461 6794 Pretzels; pretzels;
franchises, selling or licensing

PA: Centeroak Partners Llc
100 Crescent Ct Ste 1700
Dallas TX 75201
214 301-4201

2053 Frozen Bakery Prdts

(P-1338)
BENNETTS BAKING COMPANY
Also Called: Bennett's Bakery
2530 Tesla Way, Sacramento (95825-1912)
PHONE....................916 481-3349
Michael Bennett, *President*
EMP: 15
SQ FT: 3,000
SALES: 2MM **Privately Held**
SIC: 2053 Frozen bakery products, except
bread

(P-1339)
CHRISTINE MILNE
Also Called: Upper Crust
1133 Francisco Blvd E H, San Rafael
(94901-5426)
PHONE....................415 485-5658
Christine Milne, *Owner*
EMP: 10
SQ FT: 3,800
SALES (est): 860.6K **Privately Held**
WEB: www.christinespies.com
SIC: 2053 2051 Pies, bakery: frozen;
bread, cake & related products

(P-1340)
DEBBIES DELIGHTS INC
233 E Gutierrez St, Santa Barbara
(93101-1704)
PHONE....................805 966-3504
Peter Gaum, *CEO*
EMP: 20
SQ FT: 2,500
SALES: 1.2MM **Privately Held**
SIC: 2053 Buns, sweet: frozen

(P-1341)
GALAXY DESSERTS
1100 Marina Way S Ste D, Richmond
(94804-3727)
PHONE....................510 439-3160
Paul Levitan, *CEO*
Jean-Yves Charon, *Vice Pres*
Rohana Stone Rice, *Controller*
Seck Rokhaya, *Purchasing*
▲ EMP: 160
SQ FT: 56,000
SALES (est): 43.6MM
SALES (corp-wide): 6.2MM **Privately Held**
WEB: www.galaxydesserts.com
SIC: 2053 Frozen bakery products, except
bread
HQ: Brioche Pasquier Cerqueux
Pitch
Les Cerqueux 49360
241 637-541

(P-1342)
HC BRILL
Also Called: Telco Food
2111 W Valley Blvd, Colton (92324-1814)
PHONE....................909 825-7343
Michelle Stirling, *Principal*
EMP: 500
SALES (corp-wide): 962.9K **Privately Held**
WEB: www.bestbrandscorp.com
SIC: 2053 2051 Pies, bakery: frozen;
bread, cake & related products
PA: H.C. Brill
2003 S Bibb Dr
Tucker GA
770 723-3449

(P-1343)
HORIZON SNACK FOODS INC
Also Called: Cutie Pie Snack Pies
197 Darcy Pkwy, Lathrop (95330-9222)
PHONE....................925 373-7700
William D Reynolds, *President*
Andrew Kunkler, *CFO*
Lee Rucker, *CFO*
Betty Blakely, *Manager*
EMP: 62
SQ FT: 9,000

SALES (est): 14.9MM
SALES (corp-wide): 84.4MM **Privately Held**
WEB: www.cutiepie.com
SIC: 2053 Pies, bakery: frozen
PA: Horizon Holdings Llc
1 Bush St Ste 650
San Francisco CA 94104
415 788-2000

(P-1344)
INTERNATIONALLY DELICIOUS INC (PA)
Also Called: Masterpiece Cookies
174 Lawrence Dr Ste J, Livermore
(94551-5150)
PHONE...............925 426-6155
Steven Wechler, *President*
Alan Brooks, *Treasurer*
Renee Stocks, *Admin Sec*
EMP: 10 **EST:** 1996
SALES (est): 1.9MM **Privately Held**
SIC: 2053 Frozen bakery products, except bread

(P-1345)
MARYS COUNTRY KITCHEN
Also Called: Malibu Kitchen
3900 Cross Creek Rd Ste 3, Malibu
(90265-4962)
PHONE...............310 456-7845
William Miller, *Owner*
Blake Pomeroy, *Marketing Staff*
EMP: 15
SALES (est): 1.6MM **Privately Held**
SIC: 2053 Pies, bakery: frozen

(P-1346)
NATURAL DECADENCE LLC
3750 Harris St, Eureka (95503-4854)
PHONE...............707 444-2629
Milia Lando, *Principal*
Rosa Dixon,
Melanie Barnett, *Manager*
EMP: 12
SALES (est): 1.1MM **Privately Held**
SIC: 2053 2052 Pies, bakery: frozen; cookies

(P-1347)
OPERA PATISSERIE FINES INC
8480 Redwood Creek Ln, San Diego
(92126-1067)
PHONE...............858 536-5800
Diane Anderson, *Principal*
Vincent Garcia, *Admin Sec*
Lauren Gehrke, *Technology*
Elena Rodriguez, *Technology*
Dalil Kabbage, *Sales Staff*
EMP: 45
SQ FT: 9,000
SALES: 3.5MM **Privately Held**
WEB: www.operapatisserie.com
SIC: 2053 5812 Pastries (danish): frozen; cafe

2061 Sugar, Cane

(P-1348)
AZUMEX CORP
9295 Siempre Viva Rd A, San Diego
(92154-7648)
PHONE...............619 710-8855
Fabian Gomez-Ibarra, *CEO*
Azumex Sugar, *Marketing Mgr*
Rodrigo Alonzo, *Sales Mgr*
EMP: 28
SQ FT: 10,000
SALES: 20MM **Privately Held**
SIC: 2061 Granulated cane sugar; clarified cane sugar

2062 Sugar, Cane Refining

(P-1349)
AMERICAN SUGAR REFINING INC
Also Called: C&H Sugar Company
830 Loring Ave, Crockett (94525-1104)
PHONE...............510 787-6763
Charles Nelson, *Branch Mgr*
Jim Koeppen, *Controller*

Eric Myles, *Safety Mgr*
Kevin Williams, *Manager*
EMP: 400
SALES (corp-wide): 2B **Privately Held**
WEB:
www.dominospecialtyingredients.com
SIC: 2062 Granulated cane sugar from purchased raw sugar or syrup
HQ: American Sugar Refining, Inc.
1 N Clematis St Ste 200
West Palm Beach FL 33401
561 366-5100

2063 Sugar, Beet

(P-1350)
C&H SUGAR COMPANY INC
Also Called: C&H Sugar
830 Loring Ave, Crockett (94525-1104)
PHONE...............510 787-2121
Antonio L Contreras, *CEO*
Luis J Fernandez, *President*
Gregory H Smith, *CFO*
Gregory A Maitner, *Treasurer*
Antonio Contreras, *Co-President*
▲ **EMP:** 550
SQ FT: 385,000
SALES (est): 113.9MM
SALES (corp-wide): 2B **Privately Held**
WEB: www.chsugar.com
SIC: 2063 Beet sugar
HQ: American Sugar Refining, Inc.
1 N Clematis St Ste 200
West Palm Beach FL 33401
561 366-5100

(P-1351)
IMPERIAL SUGAR COMPANY
Also Called: Spreckels Sugar
395 W Keystone Rd, Brawley
(92227-9739)
P.O. Box 581 (92227-0581)
PHONE...............760 344-3110
Bill Stewart, *Opers-Prdtn-Mfg*
Ernest Garcia, *Purchasing*
EMP: 130
SALES (corp-wide): 37.6B **Privately Held**
SIC: 2063 2062 Beet sugar from beet sugar refinery; cane sugar refining
HQ: Imperial Sugar Company
3 Sugar Creek Center Blvd # 500
Sugar Land TX 77478
281 491-9181

(P-1352)
SPRECKELS SUGAR COMPANY INC
395 W Keystone Rd, Brawley
(92227-9739)
P.O. Box 581 (92227-0581)
PHONE...............760 344-3110
John A Richmond, *President*
Neil Rudeen, *Ch of Bd*
Jeff Plathe, *CEO*
Jay Creiglow, *Engineer*
Sergio Bastidas, *Accountant*
▲ **EMP:** 260 **EST:** 1905
SALES (est): 58MM
SALES (corp-wide): 465.2MM **Privately Held**
WEB: www.smbsc.com
SIC: 2063 Beet sugar from beet sugar refinery
PA: Southern Minnesota Beet Sugar Cooperative
83550 County Road 21
Renville MN 56284
320 329-8305

2064 Candy & Confectionery Prdts

(P-1353)
18 RABBITS INC (PA)
995 Market St Fl 2, San Francisco
(94103-1732)
P.O. Box 411142 (94141-1142)
PHONE...............415 922-6006
Alison Vercruysse, *CEO*
Josephine Nguyen, *Opers Mgr*
Craig Vercruysse, *Director*
EMP: 19

SALES (est): 3.3MM **Privately Held**
SIC: 2064 Granola & muesli, bars & clusters

(P-1354)
ADAMS AND BROOKS INC
4345 Hallmark Pkwy, San Bernardino
(92407-1829)
PHONE...............213 392-8700
EMP: 90
SALES (corp-wide): 23MM **Privately Held**
SIC: 2064
PA: Adams And Brooks, Inc.
4345 Hallmark Pkwy
San Bernardino CA 92407
909 880-2305

(P-1355)
AMERICAN LICORICE COMPANY
2477 Liston Way, Union City (94587-1979)
P.O. Box 826 (94587-0826)
PHONE...............510 487-5500
John Sullivan, *Principal*
James Kretchmer, *President*
Suresh Kumar, *CIO*
Joaquin Almaguer, *Prdtn Mgr*
EMP: 350
SALES (corp-wide): 112.3MM **Privately Held**
WEB: www.redvines.com
SIC: 2064 Licorice candy
PA: American Licorice Company
1900 Whirlpool Dr S
La Porte IN 46350
510 487-5500

(P-1356)
ANNABELLE CANDY INC
27211 Industrial Blvd, Hayward
(94545-3392)
P.O. Box 3665 (94540-3665)
PHONE...............510 783-2900
Susan Gamson Karl, *CEO*
Annabelle Altschuler Block, *Ch of Bd*
Shelley Craft, *Vice Pres*
Victor Moreno, *Safety Mgr*
Luna Andrea, *Mktg Dir*
EMP: 75
SQ FT: 60,000
SALES (est): 15.4MM **Privately Held**
WEB: www.annabelle-candy.com
SIC: 2064 Candy bars, including chocolate covered bars; chocolate candy, except solid chocolate

(P-1357)
BLOMMER CHOCOLATE COMPANY
1515 Pacific St, Union City (94587-2041)
P.O. Box 797 (94587-0797)
PHONE...............510 471-3401
Henry Blommer, *Principal*
Neal Murphy, *Vice Pres*
Lori Smith, *Research*
Thomas Bruguier, *Engineer*
Howard Chu, *Engineer*
EMP: 25 **Privately Held**
SIC: 2064 Candy & other confectionery products
HQ: The Blommer Chocolate Company
1101 Blommer Dr
East Greenville PA 18041
800 825-8181

(P-1358)
CALIFORNIA SNACK FOODS INC
Also Called: California Candy
2131 Tyler Ave, South El Monte
(91733-2754)
PHONE...............626 444-4508
Murl W Nelson, *CEO*
Steve Nelson, *President*
Paul Mullen, *Vice Pres*
Mary Nelson, *Admin Sec*
EMP: 45
SQ FT: 30,000
SALES (est): 6.8MM **Privately Held**
WEB: www.cal-snacks.com
SIC: 2064 2024 2099 2051 Fruits: candied, crystallized, or glazed; juice pops, frozen; popcorn, packaged: except already popped; cakes, pies & pastries; dried & dehydrated soup mixes; novelties & specialties, metal

(P-1359)
CANDIES TOLTECA
2139 N Pleasant Ave, Fresno
(93705-4730)
P.O. Box 4729 (93744-4729)
PHONE...............559 266-9193
Aaron Ordaz, *CEO*
EMP: 35
SQ FT: 5,000
SALES (est): 6MM **Privately Held**
SIC: 2064 Candy & other confectionery products

(P-1360)
CHIODO CANDY CO
2923 Adeline St, Oakland (94608-4422)
P.O. Box 8155 (94662-0155)
PHONE...............510 464-2977
Louis J Chiodo, *President*
EMP: 65
SALES (est): 6MM **Privately Held**
SIC: 2064 Candy & other confectionery products

(P-1361)
CJS TOFFEE & TOPPINGS LLC
Also Called: Toffee Tops
2269 Chestnut St 298, San Francisco
(94123-2600)
PHONE...............415 929-7852
Catherine J Hughes, *Principal*
EMP: 10
SALES: 200K **Privately Held**
SIC: 2064 Candy & other confectionery products

(P-1362)
COUNTRY HOUSE
Also Called: Seloah Gourmet Food
2852 Walnut Ave Ste C1, Tustin
(92780-7033)
PHONE...............714 505-8988
Monica Ching, *Owner*
Monica Diggan, *Manager*
◆ **EMP:** 18 **EST:** 1994
SQ FT: 9,400
SALES (est): 630.5K **Privately Held**
WEB: www.countryhouse.com
SIC: 2064 Candy & other confectionery products

(P-1363)
DIVINE FOODS INC
Also Called: Rise Bar
16752 Millikan Ave, Irvine (92606-5010)
PHONE...............800 440-6476
Peter Spenuzza, *President*
Philipson Katie, *Mktg Coord*
▲ **EMP:** 20
SQ FT: 15,000
SALES (est): 4.1MM **Privately Held**
SIC: 2064 Breakfast bars

(P-1364)
EL CHAVITO INC
6020 Progressive Ave # 600, San Diego
(92154-6638)
PHONE...............844 424-2848
Bashar Ballo, *CEO*
Hugo Farias, *Opers Staff*
EMP: 14 **EST:** 2017
SQ FT: 13,000
SALES (est): 876.5K **Privately Held**
SIC: 2064 Candy & other confectionery products

(P-1365)
EL SUPER LEON PNCHIN SNCKS INC
2545 Britannia Blvd Ste A, San Diego
(92154-7427)
PHONE...............619 426-2968
Alfonso Guerrero, *President*
EMP: 21 **Privately Held**
SIC: 2064 Candy & other confectionery products
PA: El Super Leon Ponchin Snacks, Inc.
2545 Britannia Blvd
San Diego CA 92154

(P-1366)
EZAKI GLICO USA CORP
18022 Cowan Ste 110, Irvine (92614-6805)
PHONE...............949 251-0144

PRODUCTS & SVCS

Akitoshi Oku, *President*
George Iwashita, *Marketing Staff*
Marie Pumilia, *Marketing Staff*
▲ **EMP:** 19
SALES (est): 4.1MM **Privately Held**
WEB: www.glico.co.jp
SIC: 2064 8111 Candy & other confectionery products; general practice attorney, lawyer
PA: Ezaki Glico Co.,Ltd.
4-6-5, Utajima, Nishiyodogawa-Ku
Osaka OSK 555-0
-

(P-1367)
FOOD TECHNOLOGY AND DESIGN LLC
Also Called: Food Pharma
10012 Painter Ave, Santa Fe Springs (90670-3016)
PHONE....................562 944-7821
Glen Marinelli, *Mng Member*
Jerry Jacobs, *CFO*
Fidel Medina, *IT/INT Sup*
Tommy Gardea, *Accountant*
Regina Medina, *Safety Mgr*
EMP: 40
SQ FT: 20,000
SALES (est): 9MM **Privately Held**
WEB: www.foodpharma.com
SIC: 2064 Candy & other confectionery products

(P-1368)
GENESIS FOODS CORPORATION (DH)
Also Called: Garvey Nut & Candy
8825 Mercury Ln, Pico Rivera (90660-6707)
PHONE....................323 890-5890
Steven R Corri, *President*
▲ **EMP:** 60
SQ FT: 35,000
SALES (est): 11.8MM
SALES (corp-wide): 1.6MM **Privately Held**
SIC: 2064 5149 Candy & other confectionery products; cookies

(P-1369)
GOLD RUSH KETTLE KORN LLC
Also Called: Kettle Pop
4690 E 2nd St Ste 9, Benicia (94510-1008)
PHONE....................707 747-6773
Jeff Schletewitz, *Mng Member*
William Baker Jr,
Aaron Reimer, *Manager*
▲ **EMP:** 20
SQ FT: 1,596
SALES (est): 3.4MM **Privately Held**
SIC: 2064 Popcorn balls or other treated popcorn products

(P-1370)
HAWAIIAN HOST CANDIES LA INC
15601 S Avalon Blvd, Gardena (90248-2371)
PHONE....................310 532-0543
Keith Sakamoto, *President*
◆ **EMP:** 60
SQ FT: 100,000
SALES (est): 12.4MM
SALES (corp-wide): 88.1MM **Privately Held**
WEB: www.hawaiianhost.com
SIC: 2064 Candy & other confectionery products
PA: Hawaiian Host, Inc.
500 Alakawa St Rm 111
Honolulu HI 96817
808 848-0500

(P-1371)
HGC HOLDINGS INC
3303 Mrtn Lthr King Jr Bl, Lynwood (90262-1905)
PHONE....................323 567-2226
Robert I Hadgraft, *CEO*
David Worth, *CEO*
Robert Worth, *Admin Sec*
EMP: 120
SQ FT: 90,000

SALES (est): 16.6MM **Privately Held**
SIC: 2064 5441 Chocolate candy, except solid chocolate; candy

(P-1372)
HOTLIX (PA)
Also Called: Hotlix Candy
966 Griffin St, Grover Beach (93433-3019)
P.O. Box 447 (93483-0447)
PHONE....................805 473-0596
Larry Peterman, *President*
Richard Lara, *Data Proc Staff*
Kathy Mitchell, *Accounts Mgr*
▼ **EMP:** 50
SQ FT: 1,500
SALES (est): 5.8MM **Privately Held**
WEB: www.hotlix.com
SIC: 2064 Lollipops & other hard candy

(P-1373)
HOTLIX
179 Pomeroy Ave, Pismo Beach (93449-2639)
PHONE....................805 773-1942
Larry Peterman, *Manager*
EMP: 11
SQ FT: 2,133
SALES (est): 1.4MM
SALES (corp-wide): 5.8MM **Privately Held**
WEB: www.hotlix.com
SIC: 2064 Candy & other confectionery products
PA: Hotlix
966 Griffin St
Grover Beach CA 93433
805 473-0596

(P-1374)
INSIGNIA SC HOLDINGS LLC (HQ)
1333 N Calif Blvd Ste 520, Walnut Creek (94596-4534)
PHONE....................925 399-8900
Dave Lowe, *Ch of Bd*
EMP: 814
SALES (est): 177.6MM **Privately Held**
SIC: 2064 5145 Nuts, candy covered; nuts, salted or roasted
PA: Insignia Capital Partners, L.P.
1333 N Calif Blvd Ste 520
Walnut Creek CA 94596
925 399-8900

(P-1375)
ISLAND SNACKS INC
Also Called: Island Products
7650 Stage Rd, Buena Park (90621-1226)
PHONE....................714 994-1228
Alin Barak, *President*
◆ **EMP:** 20 **EST:** 1980
SQ FT: 6,600
SALES (est): 12.6MM **Privately Held**
WEB: www.islandsnacks.com
SIC: 2064 Candy & other confectionery products

(P-1376)
JELLY BELLY CANDY COMPANY (PA)
1 Jelly Belly Ln, Fairfield (94533-6741)
PHONE....................707 428-2800
Robert M Simpson Jr, *CEO*
Herman G Rowland Sr, *Ch of Bd*
Robert Simpson, *President*
Lisa Brasher, *Corp Secy*
William Kelley, *Vice Ch Bd*
◆ **EMP:** 400 **EST:** 1900
SQ FT: 350,000
SALES (est): 210.6MM **Privately Held**
WEB: www.jellybelly.com
SIC: 2064 Candy & other confectionery products

(P-1377)
JELLY BELLY CANDY COMPANY
2400 N Watney Way, Fairfield (94533-6734)
PHONE....................707 428-2800
Albert Larson, *Vice Pres*
Jeff Brown, *Director*
EMP: 40

SALES (corp-wide): 210.6MM **Privately Held**
WEB: www.jellybelly.com
SIC: 2064 Candy & other confectionery products
PA: Jelly Belly Candy Company
1 Jelly Belly Ln
Fairfield CA 94533
707 428-2800

(P-1378)
JEWEL DATE COMPANY INC
84675 60th Ave, Thermal (92274-8780)
PHONE....................760 399-4474
Gregory Raumin, *President*
◆ **EMP:** 20
SALES (est): 4.5MM **Privately Held**
SIC: 2064 Sugared dates

(P-1379)
JOSE MARTINEZ
Also Called: Jose Martinez Candy
1281 S Hicks Ave, Los Angeles (90023-3238)
PHONE....................323 263-6230
Jose Martinez, *Owner*
▼ **EMP:** 10
SQ FT: 3,000
SALES (est): 1.3MM **Privately Held**
SIC: 2064 5145 Candy & other confectionery products; candy

(P-1380)
KONA BAR LLC
2601 Ocean Park Blvd # 310, Santa Monica (90405-5270)
PHONE....................808 927-1934
Christian Zenger, *CEO*
EMP: 15
SQ FT: 10,000
SALES (est): 1MM **Privately Held**
SIC: 2064 Candy bars, including chocolate covered bars

(P-1381)
LA ZAMORANA CANDY
7100 Wilson Ave, Los Angeles (90001-2249)
PHONE....................323 583-7100
Vicente Mendez, *President*
Carmen Artiaga, *Co-Owner*
EMP: 12
SALES (est): 737.9K **Privately Held**
SIC: 2064 5145 Candy & other confectionery products; candy

(P-1382)
LDVC INC
Also Called: Lasdos Victorias Candy Company
9606 Valley Blvd, Rosemead (91770-1510)
PHONE....................626 448-4611
Jenny Lee, *President*
David Lee, *CFO*
EMP: 20
SQ FT: 8,000
SALES (est): 2.3MM **Privately Held**
SIC: 2064 Candy & other confectionery products

(P-1383)
LE BELGE CHOCOLATIER INC
761 Skyway Ct, NAPA (94558-7510)
PHONE....................707 258-9200
David Grunhut, *CEO*
Debby Kelly, *Vice Pres*
◆ **EMP:** 25
SQ FT: 15,000
SALES (est): 5.4MM
SALES (corp-wide): 97.2MM **Privately Held**
WEB: www.lebelgechocolatier.com
SIC: 2064 2066 Chocolate candy, except solid chocolate; chocolate candy, solid
PA: Astor Chocolate Corp.
651 New Hampshire Ave
Lakewood NJ 08701
732 901-1000

(P-1384)
LOCHIRCO FRUIT AND PRODUCE INC
Also Called: Happy Apple
41899 Road 120, Orosi (93647-9452)
PHONE....................559 528-4194
John Myer, *Manager*

EMP: 25
SALES (corp-wide): 7.7MM **Privately Held**
WEB: www.happyapples.com
SIC: 2064 Fruits: candied, crystallized, or glazed
PA: Lochirco Fruit And Produce, Inc.
527 Commercial Dr
Union MO 63084
636 583-5000

(P-1385)
MAGIC GUMBALL INTERNATIONAL
9310 Mason Ave, Chatsworth (91311-5201)
PHONE....................818 716-1888
Don Hart, *President*
Guy Hart, *Vice Pres*
▼ **EMP:** 30
SALES (est): 5.8MM **Privately Held**
WEB: www.magicgumball.com
SIC: 2064 3581 2067 Candy & other confectionery products; automatic vending machines; chewing gum

(P-1386)
MARICH CONFECTIONERY CO INC
2101 Bert Dr, Hollister (95023-2562)
PHONE....................831 634-4700
Bradley M Van Dam, *President*
Von Packard, *Shareholder*
Steve Mangelsen, *CFO*
Ronald B Packard, *Chairman*
Troy Van Dam, *Exec VP*
▲ **EMP:** 150
SQ FT: 60,000
SALES (est): 33.3MM **Privately Held**
WEB: www.marich.com
SIC: 2064 2099 2068 Candy & other confectionery products; food preparations; salted & roasted nuts & seeds

(P-1387)
MARIMIX COMPANY INC
987 N Enterprise St, Orange (92867-5448)
PHONE....................714 633-7300
Mari Fassett, *President*
EMP: 10
SQ FT: 11,000
SALES (est): 1.2MM **Privately Held**
WEB: www.marimix.com
SIC: 2064 Candy & other confectionery products

(P-1388)
MAVE ENTERPRISES INC
Also Called: It's Delish
11555 Cantara St Ste B-E, North Hollywood (91605-1652)
P.O. Box 480620, Los Angeles (90048-1620)
PHONE....................818 767-4533
Amy Grawitzky, *CEO*
Moshe Grawitzky, *Vice Pres*
Rochell Legarreta, *Admin Sec*
Roberto Munoz, *Manager*
▲ **EMP:** 35
SQ FT: 35,000
SALES (est): 6MM **Privately Held**
WEB: www.itsdelish.com
SIC: 2064 2099 2033 2068 Candy & other confectionery products; seasonings & spices; canned fruits & specialties; salted & roasted nuts & seeds

(P-1389)
MCKEEVER DANLEE CONFECTIONARY
760 N Mckeever Ave, Azusa (91702-2349)
PHONE....................626 334-8964
Gerald Morris, *President*
David A Pistole, *CFO*
Brian Halpert, *Corp Secy*
EMP: 20
SQ FT: 10,000
SALES (est): 1.7MM
SALES (corp-wide): 143.3MM **Privately Held**
WEB: www.specialtimesgifts.com
SIC: 2064 Candy & other confectionery products

▲ = Import ▼=Export
◆ =Import/Export

HQ: Morris National, Inc.
760 N Mckeever Ave
Azusa CA 91702
626 385-2000

(P-1390)
NELLSON NUTRACEUTICAL INC (PA)
5115 E La Palma Ave, Anaheim (92807-2018)
PHONE..................................626 812-6522
Scott Greenwood, *CEO*
Ben Muhlenkamp, *President*
Jeff Moran, *CEO*
Paul Hanson, *Senior VP*
Bart Child, *Vice Pres*
▲ EMP: 297
SQ FT: 100,000
SALES (est): 44.8MM **Privately Held**
SIC: 2064 Candy bars, including chocolate covered bars

(P-1391)
NELLSON NUTRACEUTICAL LLC (PA)
5115 E La Palma Ave, Anaheim (92807-2018)
PHONE..................................714 765-7000
James Better, *CEO*
Jean Filion, *COO*
Manuel Martinez, *CFO*
Bart Child, *Vice Pres*
Raymond Collins, *Vice Pres*
EMP: 277
SALES (est): 322.6MM **Privately Held**
SIC: 2064 Candy bars, including chocolate covered bars

(P-1392)
ROBERTS FERRY NUT COMPANY INC
20493 Yosemite Blvd, Waterford (95386-9506)
PHONE..................................209 874-3247
Nic West, *President*
Kim West, *Treasurer*
Brad Humble, *Vice Pres*
Stacey Humble, *Admin Sec*
EMP: 12
SQ FT: 10,000
SALES (est): 2.2MM **Privately Held**
WEB: www.robertsferrynuts.com
SIC: 2064 5145 Nuts, candy covered; nuts, salted or roasted

(P-1393)
S & C FOODS INC
Also Called: Garvey Nut and Candy
6094 Malburg Way, Vernon (90058)
PHONE..................................323 205-6887
Steve Corri, *President*
EMP: 20
SALES (corp-wide): 1.6MM **Privately Held**
SIC: 2064 Candy & other confectionery products
HQ: Genesis Foods Corporation
8825 Mercury Ln
Pico Rivera CA 90660
323 890-5890

(P-1394)
SANDERS CANDY FACTORY INC
5051 Calmview Ave, Baldwin Park (91706-1802)
PHONE..................................626 814-2038
Timothy Sanders, *CEO*
Steven L Peralez, *Treasurer*
Mark Sanders, *Vice Pres*
Charlie Profilet, *General Mgr*
EMP: 20
SQ FT: 40,000
SALES (est): 5.3MM **Privately Held**
SIC: 2064 Candy & other confectionery products

(P-1395)
SCONZA CANDY COMPANY
1 Sconza Candy Ln, Oakdale (95361-7899)
PHONE..................................209 845-3700
James R Sconza, *President*
Ronald J Sconza, *Vice Pres*
Alan Cotich, *Engineer*

Patricia Cruise, *Credit Mgr*
Jesse Hodges, *Purchasing*
▲ EMP: 100 EST: 1939
SQ FT: 40,000
SALES (est): 34.8MM **Privately Held**
WEB: www.sconzacandy.com
SIC: 2064 Lollipops & other hard candy

(P-1396)
SEES CANDIES INC (DH)
210 El Camino Real, South San Francisco (94080-5998)
PHONE..................................650 761-2490
Warren E Buffett, *Ch of Bd*
Ken Scott, *CFO*
Eileen Duag, *Vice Pres*
George Duckworth, *Store Mgr*
Casey Khor, *Technician*
▲ EMP: 500
SQ FT: 250,000
SALES (est): 702.6MM
SALES (corp-wide): 225.3B **Publicly Held**
WEB: www.seescandies.com
SIC: 2064 5441 Candy & other confectionery products; candy
HQ: See's Candy Shops, Incorporated
210 El Camino Real
South San Francisco CA 94080
650 761-2490

(P-1397)
SEES CANDY SHOPS INCORPORATED (HQ)
Also Called: See's Candies
210 El Camino Real, South San Francisco (94080-5968)
PHONE..................................650 761-2490
Warren E Buffet, *Ch of Bd*
Daryl Wollenburg, *Treasurer*
Bernie Bishop, *Vice Pres*
Nancy Hoffer, *MIS Staff*
Sean Carlin, *IT/INT Sup*
▲ EMP: 40
SQ FT: 250,000
SALES (est): 702.6MM
SALES (corp-wide): 225.3B **Publicly Held**
WEB: www.sees.com
SIC: 2064 5441 Candy & other confectionery products; candy; confectionery
PA: Berkshire Hathaway Inc.
3555 Farnam St Ste 1140
Omaha NE 68131
402 346-1400

(P-1398)
SEES CANDY SHOPS INCORPORATED
9839 Paramount Blvd, Downey (90240-3803)
PHONE..................................562 928-2912
Gayle Hill, *Manager*
EMP: 10
SQ FT: 1,317
SALES (corp-wide): 225.3B **Publicly Held**
WEB: www.sees.com
SIC: 2064 5441 Candy & other confectionery products; candy; confectionery
HQ: See's Candy Shops, Incorporated
210 El Camino Real
South San Francisco CA 94080
650 761-2490

(P-1399)
SEES CANDY SHOPS INCORPORATED
Also Called: See's Candies
3423 S La Cienega Blvd, Los Angeles (90016-4401)
PHONE..................................310 559-4919
Greg Ward, *Director*
Richard Doren, *Vice Pres*
Iris Eshoo, *Vice Pres*
Jack Larson, *Safety Mgr*
Debbie Tapia, *Opers Mgr*
EMP: 200
SQ FT: 170,396
SALES (corp-wide): 225.3B **Publicly Held**
WEB: www.sees.com
SIC: 2064 2066 Candy & other confectionery products; chocolate & cocoa products

HQ: See's Candy Shops, Incorporated
210 El Camino Real
South San Francisco CA 94080
650 761-2490

(P-1400)
SENCHA NATURALS INC
104 N Union Ave, Los Angeles (90026-5408)
PHONE..................................213 353-9908
David Kerdoon, *President*
▲ EMP: 15
SALES (est): 680K **Privately Held**
SIC: 2064 Candy & other confectionery products

(P-1401)
SENOR SNACKS MANUFACTURING LTD
2325 Raymer Ave, Fullerton (92833-2514)
PHONE..................................714 739-1073
Jose V Mazon, *Partner*
EMP: 60
SALES (est): 5MM **Privately Held**
SIC: 2064 Candy & other confectionery products

(P-1402)
SIERRA FOOTHILLS FUDGE FACTORY
Also Called: Fudge Factory Farm
2860 High Hill Rd, Placerville (95667-5102)
PHONE..................................530 644-3492
Jean Reinders, *Owner*
EMP: 6
SQ FT: 600
SALES: 200K **Privately Held**
SIC: 2064 5441 0175 Chocolate candy, except solid chocolate; candy, nut & confectionery stores; apple orchard

(P-1403)
SUNSHINE RAISIN CORPORATION (PA)
Also Called: National Raisin Company
626 S 5th St, Fowler (93625-9745)
P.O. Box 219 (93625-0219)
PHONE..................................559 834-5981
Lindakay Abdulian, *President*
May Firkus, *CFO*
Paul Bedrosian, *Admin Sec*
Jeanette Pereira, *CIO*
Raul Martinez, *Info Tech Mgr*
◆ EMP: 249 EST: 1968
SQ FT: 400,000
SALES (est): 140.5MM **Privately Held**
SIC: 2064 0723 Candy & other confectionery products; crop preparation services for market

(P-1404)
THATS IT NUTRITION LLC
834 S Broadway Ste 800, Los Angeles (90014-3525)
PHONE..................................818 782-1701
Miriam Lewensztain, *Mng Member*
Lior Lewensztein,
EMP: 11
SQ FT: 8,000
SALES: 20MM **Privately Held**
SIC: 2064 Granola & muesli, bars & clusters

(P-1405)
TOM CLARK CONFECTIONS
Also Called: Popcorn Tree
1193 Nicole Ct, Glendora (91740-5387)
PHONE..................................909 599-4700
Timothy D Clark, *CEO*
Beverly Clark, *Corp Secy*
Tim Clark, *Vice Pres*
▼ EMP: 32
SQ FT: 18,500
SALES (est): 10.9MM **Privately Held**
SIC: 2064 Popcorn balls or other treated popcorn products

2066 Chocolate & Cocoa Prdts

(P-1406)
BARRY CALLEBAUT USA LLC
1175 Commerce Blvd Ste D, American Canyon (94503-9626)
PHONE..................................707 642-8200
Peter Dell,
EMP: 18
SALES (corp-wide): 45.7MM **Privately Held**
SIC: 2066 Chocolate
HQ: Barry Callebaut U.S.A. Llc
600 W Chicago Ave Ste 860
Chicago IL 60654

(P-1407)
BLOMMER CHOCOLATE CO CAL INC
1515 Pacific St, Union City (94587-2041)
PHONE..................................510 471-4300
Henry J Blommer Jr, *CEO*
Joseph W Blommer, *President*
Peter W Blommer, *Vice Pres*
Martin Krueger, *Vice Pres*
Jack S Larsen, *Vice Pres*
◆ EMP: 200
SQ FT: 142,000
SALES (est): 33.2MM **Privately Held**
WEB: www.blommer.com
SIC: 2066 Chocolate coatings & syrup; powdered cocoa; cocoa butter
HQ: The Blommer Chocolate Company
1101 Blommer Dr
East Greenville PA 18041
800 825-8181

(P-1408)
CALIFORNIA GOLD BARS INC (PA)
1041 Folger Ave, Berkeley (94710-2819)
PHONE..................................510 848-9292
Daniel Hood, *CEO*
Jonathan Schwartz, *Director*
EMP: 10 EST: 2014
SALES: 500K **Privately Held**
SIC: 2066 5149 Chocolate & cocoa products; chocolate

(P-1409)
COCO DELICE
1555 Park Ave Ste A, Emeryville (94608-3586)
PHONE..................................510 601-1394
EMP: 10
SALES (est): 1.3MM **Privately Held**
SIC: 2066

(P-1410)
ECLIPSE CHOCOLATE BAR & BISTRO
2145 Fern St, San Diego (92104-5517)
PHONE..................................619 578-2984
William Gustwiller, *Owner*
EMP: 11
SALES (est): 1MM **Privately Held**
SIC: 2066 Chocolate

(P-1411)
GUITTARD CHOCOLATE CO
10 Guittard Rd, Burlingame (94010-2203)
P.O. Box 4308 (94011-4308)
PHONE..................................650 697-4427
Gary W Guittard, *President*
Brad Newcombe, *Executive*
Ed Fong, *Info Tech Dir*
Alvin Oey, *Personnel*
Bob Carpenter, *Purch Mgr*
◆ EMP: 240 EST: 1868
SALES (est): 80.5MM **Privately Held**
WEB: www.guittard.com
SIC: 2066 2064 Chocolate; cocoa & cocoa products; candy & other confectionery products

(P-1412)
NAYLOR CORP
Spc 112 Pier 39, San Francisco (94133)
PHONE..................................415 421-1789
Robert Lee, *Office Mgr*
John Naylor, *President*

EMP: 28
SALES (est): 2.7MM Privately Held
SIC: 2066 Chocolate

(P-1413)
SSI G DEBBAS CHOCOLATIER LLC
2794 N Larkin Ave, Fresno (93727-1315)
PHONE...................559 294-2071
Bret Lorenc, *President*
EMP: 37
SALES (est): 4.1MM Privately Held
SIC: 2066 Chocolate & cocoa products

(P-1414)
TCHO VENTURES INC
1900 Powell St Ste 600, Emeryville
(94608-1885)
PHONE...................415 981-0189
Marcel Bens, *CEO*
EMP: 11 Privately Held
SIC: 2066 Chocolate
HQ: Tcho Ventures, Inc.
3100 San Pablo Ave
Berkeley CA 94702

(P-1415)
TCHO VENTURES INC (HQ)
3100 San Pablo Ave, Berkeley
(94702-2498)
PHONE...................510 210-8445
Marcel Bens, *CEO*
Catherine Liu, *Manager*
▲ **EMP: 46**
SQ FT: 29,734
SALES (est): 8.2MM Privately Held
SIC: 2066 Chocolate & cocoa products

(P-1416)
TRC COCOA LLC
3721 Douglas Blvd Ste 375, Roseville
(95661-4255)
PHONE...................916 847-2390
Jay Kaeila, *President*
Xavier Verspieren, *CFO*
EMP: 12 EST: 2017
SQ FT: 6,000
SALES (est): 25MM Privately Held
SIC: 2066 Cocoa & cocoa products
HQ: Trc Trading Corporation
3721 Douglas Blvd Ste 375
Roseville CA 95661

(P-1417)
VERY SPECIAL CHOCOLATS INC
760 N Mckeever Ave, Azusa (91702-2349)
PHONE...................626 334-7838
Gerry Morris Zubatoff, *CEO*
Gerald Morris, *President*
David Pistole, *CFO*
Bram Morris, *Admin Sec*
▲ **EMP: 150**
SQ FT: 40,000
SALES: 8.5MM
SALES (corp-wide): 143.3MM Privately Held
WEB: www.morrisnational.com
SIC: 2066 Chocolate & cocoa products
HQ: Morris National, Inc.
760 N Mckeever Ave
Azusa CA 91702
626 385-2000

2068 Salted & Roasted Nuts & Seeds

(P-1418)
180 SNACKS (PA)
Also Called: Mareblu Naturals
1173 N Armando St, Anaheim
(92806-2609)
PHONE...................714 238-1192
Michael Kim, *President*
Katherine Kim, *Vice Pres*
Eugene Kim, *QA Dir*
Tim Kim, *Opers Staff*
Mike Runion, *Opers Staff*
◆ **EMP: 47**
SQ FT: 10,000

SALES: 16MM Privately Held
SIC: 2068 2034 Salted & roasted nuts & seeds; dried & dehydrated fruits

(P-1419)
ALMOND COMPANY
22782 Road 9, Chowchilla (93610-8967)
PHONE...................559 665-4405
Russell Harris, *President*
▼ **EMP: 80**
SALES (est): 12.6MM Privately Held
SIC: 2068 Nuts: dried, dehydrated, salted or roasted

(P-1420)
ALMOND VALLEY NUT CO
11255 E Whitmore Ave, Denair
(95316-9741)
P.O. Box 68, Hickman (95323-0068)
PHONE...................209 480-7300
Brent Zehrung, *Partner*
EMP: 22
SALES (est): 1.4MM Privately Held
SIC: 2068 Nuts: dried, dehydrated, salted or roasted

(P-1421)
ASSALI HULLING & SHELLING
8618 E Whitmore Ave, Hughson
(95326-9446)
P.O. Box 69 (95326-0069)
PHONE...................209 883-4263
Frank Assali, *President*
EMP: 10 EST: 1970
SALES (est): 1.1MM Privately Held
WEB: www.assalihullingandshelling.com
SIC: 2068 Nuts: dried, dehydrated, salted or roasted

(P-1422)
BLUE DIAMOND GROWERS
10840 E Mckinley Ave, Sanger
(93657-9480)
PHONE...................559 251-4044
EMP: 143
SALES (corp-wide): 1.6B Privately Held
SIC: 2068 Nuts: dried, dehydrated, salted or roasted
PA: Diamond Blue Growers
1802 C St
Sacramento CA 95811
916 442-0771

(P-1423)
CAL TRADERS
Also Called: Farmers International
1260 Muir Ave, Chico (95973-8644)
PHONE...................530 566-1405
Monish Seth, *Administration*
Versha Seth, *Admin Sec*
Mohnish Seth, *Administration*
EMP: 10
SALES (est): 743.1K Privately Held
SIC: 2068 Nuts: dried, dehydrated, salted or roasted

(P-1424)
DIAMOND FOODS LLC (PA)
Also Called: Diamond of California
1050 Diamond St, Stockton (95205-7020)
PHONE...................209 467-6000
Craig Hope, *CEO*
Lloyd J Johnson, *President*
David Colo, *COO*
Ray Silcock, *CFO*
Isobel Jones, *Exec VP*
◆ **EMP: 575 EST: 2015**
SALES (est): 536MM Privately Held
WEB: www.diamondfoods.com
SIC: 2068 2096 Salted & roasted nuts & seeds; potato chips & similar snacks

(P-1425)
DIAMOND FOODS LLC
600 Montgomery St Fl 17, San Francisco
(94111-2719)
PHONE...................209 467-6000
Carter Dunlap, *Manager*
Pat Marnell, *Opers Staff*
Victor Figueroa, *Production*
Julie Lutz-Lenosky, *Manager*
EMP: 11
SALES (corp-wide): 536MM Privately Held
SIC: 2068 Salted & roasted nuts & seeds

PA: Diamond Foods, Llc
1050 Diamond St
Stockton CA 95205
209 467-6000

(P-1426)
G & P GROUP INC
Also Called: Mr. Nature
13842 Bettencourt St, Cerritos
(90703-1010)
PHONE...................323 268-2686
George Barraza, *Managing Dir*
Philip Borup, *Managing Dir*
▼ **EMP: 13**
SALES (est): 1.9MM Privately Held
SIC: 2068 0723 Salted & roasted nuts & seeds; fruit (farm-dried) packing services

(P-1427)
HUGHSON NUT INC (HQ)
1825 Verduga Rd, Hughson (95326-9675)
P.O. Box 1150 (95326-1150)
PHONE...................209 883-0403
Martin Pohl, *President*
◆ **EMP: 100**
SQ FT: 40,000
SALES (est): 72.4MM
SALES (corp-wide): 22.2B Privately Held
SIC: 2068 Salted & roasted nuts & seeds
PA: Olam International Limited
7 Straits View
Singapore 01893
633 941-00

(P-1428)
JOHN B SANFILIPPO & SON INC
29241 Cottonwood Rd, Gustine
(95322-9574)
PHONE...................209 854-2455
Isidro Cortez, *Manager*
EMP: 400
SQ FT: 1,286
SALES (corp-wide): 876.2MM Publicly Held
WEB: www.jbssinc.com
SIC: 2068 Nuts: dried, dehydrated, salted or roasted
PA: John B. Sanfilippo & Son, Inc.
1703 N Randall Rd
Elgin IL 60123
847 289-1800

(P-1429)
KLEIN BROS HOLDINGS LTD
Also Called: Klein Bros Snacks
1515 S Fresno Ave, Stockton (95206-1179)
PHONE...................209 465-5033
Thomas B Klein, *Ch of Bd*
Robert J Corkern, *CEO*
EMP: 35
SQ FT: 130,000
SALES (est): 6.2MM Privately Held
WEB: www.jumbosnacks.net
SIC: 2068 4783 5141 Seeds: dried, dehydrated, salted or roasted; nuts: dried, dehydrated, salted or roasted; packing & crating; groceries, general line

(P-1430)
KRAFT HEINZ FOODS COMPANY
Also Called: Heinz Seeds
6755 C E Dixon St, Stockton (95206-4947)
PHONE...................209 932-5700
Ross Siragusa, *Director*
Matthew Leinfelder, *Regl Sales Mgr*
EMP: 35
SALES (corp-wide): 26.2B Publicly Held
SIC: 2068 3999 Seeds: dried, dehydrated, salted or roasted; seeds, coated or treated, from purchased seeds
HQ: Kraft Heinz Foods Company
1 Ppg Pl Fl 34
Pittsburgh PA 15222
412 456-5700

(P-1431)
KRAFT HEINZ FOODS COMPANY
Also Called: Cornnuts Division of Planters
4343 E Florence Ave, Fresno (93725-1151)
PHONE...................559 237-9206
F Chavez, *Opers-Prdtn-Mfg*
EMP: 70
SQ FT: 55,200

SALES (corp-wide): 26.2B Publicly Held
WEB: www.kraftfoods.com
SIC: 2068 2096 Nuts: dried, dehydrated, salted or roasted; potato chips & similar snacks
HQ: Kraft Heinz Foods Company
1 Ppg Pl Fl 34
Pittsburgh PA 15222
412 456-5700

(P-1432)
LAKE COUNTY WALNUT INC
4545 Loasa Dr, Kelseyville (95451)
P.O. Box 308 (95451-0308)
PHONE...................707 279-1200
Ray Snyder, *President*
Mark Snyder, *Vice Pres*
EMP: 18
SALES (est): 1.9MM Privately Held
WEB: www.lcwalnut.com
SIC: 2068 Salted & roasted nuts & seeds

(P-1433)
MELLACE FAMILY BRANDS INC
6195 El Camino Real, Carlsbad
(92009-1602)
P.O. Box 22831, San Diego (92192-2831)
PHONE...................760 448-1940
Michael Mellace, *President*
▲ **EMP: 125**
SQ FT: 45,000
SALES (est): 16.1MM Privately Held
SIC: 2068 Nuts: dried, dehydrated, salted or roasted

(P-1434)
MIXED NUTS INC
7909 Crossway Dr, Pico Rivera
(90660-4449)
PHONE...................323 587-6887
Vanik Hartounian, *President*
◆ **EMP: 25**
SALES (est): 6.3MM Privately Held
WEB: www.mixednutsinc.com
SIC: 2068 5145 Nuts: dried, dehydrated, salted or roasted; nuts, salted or roasted

(P-1435)
NICHOLS PISTACHIO
Also Called: Nichols Farms
13762 1st Ave, Hanford (93230-9316)
PHONE...................559 584-6811
Chuck Nichols, *Principal*
Susan Nichols, *Treasurer*
Kari Arnett, *Sales Staff*
April McDaniel, *Manager*
◆ **EMP: 200**
SQ FT: 110,000
SALES (est): 54.9MM Privately Held
SIC: 2068 Salted & roasted nuts & seeds

(P-1436)
PADDACK ENTERPRISES
Also Called: Paddack Almond Hlling Shelling
27052 State Highway 120, Escalon
(95320-9502)
PHONE...................209 838-1536
Vernon Paddack, *President*
Pauline Paddack, *Treasurer*
EMP: 25
SQ FT: 3,000
SALES (est): 1.3MM Privately Held
WEB: www.pad-enterprises.com
SIC: 2068 Nuts: dried, dehydrated, salted or roasted

(P-1437)
PRIMEX FARMS LLC (PA)
16070 Wildwood Rd, Wasco (93280-9210)
PHONE...................661 758-7790
Ali Amin, *President*
Andrik Sarkasian, *Human Res Dir*
Christina Vanworth, *QC Mgr*
Allen Reaves, *Maintence Staff*
Gerardo Godina, *Manager*
EMP: 30
SQ FT: 136,837
SALES: 116.5MM Privately Held
WEB: www.primexfarms.com
SIC: 2068 Nuts: dried, dehydrated, salted or roasted

▲ = Import ▼=Export
◆ =Import/Export

(P-1438)
SNAK CLUB LLC
Also Called: New Century Snacks
5560 E Slauson Ave, Commerce
(90040-2921)
PHONE..............................323 278-9578
Farhad Morshed, *President*
Nader Morovati, *Vice Pres*
Bob Riley, *Sales Staff*
EMP: 25
SALES (corp-wide): 177.6MM **Privately Held**
SIC: 2068 2099 Salted & roasted nuts & seeds; food preparations
HQ: Snak Club, Llc
607 N Nash St
El Segundo CA 90245
310 322-4400

(P-1439)
STEWART & JASPER MARKETING INC (PA)
Also Called: Stewart & Jasper Orchards
3500 Shiells Rd, Newman (95360-9798)
PHONE..............................209 862-9600
Jim Jasper, *President*
Susan Dompe, *Corp Secy*
Jason Jasper, *Vice Pres*
Donna Corgiat, *Relations*
Frankie Silveria, *Relations*
◆ EMP: 175
SQ FT: 225,000
SALES (est): 52.8MM **Privately Held**
WEB: www.stewartandjasper.com
SIC: 2068 0723 0173 5148 Nuts: dried, dehydrated, salted or roasted; crop preparation services for market; almond hulling & shelling services; tree nuts; fresh fruits & vegetables; food preparations

(P-1440)
SUNDIAL ORCHRDS HULLING DRYING
1500 Kirk Rd, Gridley (95948-9417)
PHONE..............................530 846-6155
Brad Barrow, *Principal*
EMP: 20
SALES (est): 1.9MM **Privately Held**
SIC: 2068 Nuts: dried, dehydrated, salted or roasted

(P-1441)
WIZARD MANUFACTURING INC
2244 Ivy St, Chico (95928-7172)
PHONE..............................530 342-1861
Alan Reiff, *CEO*
Justin McCurdy, *Engineer*
EMP: 19
SALES (est): 3.5MM **Privately Held**
SIC: 2068 Nuts: dried, dehydrated, salted or roasted

(P-1442)
WONDERFUL PSTCHIOS ALMONDS LLC (HQ)
Also Called: Paramount Farms
11444 W Olympic Blvd, Los Angeles
(90064-1549)
P.O. Box 200937, Dallas TX (75320-0937)
PHONE..............................310 966-4650
Stewart Resnick, *President*
Bill Phillimore, *Exec VP*
Craig B Cooper, *Senior VP*
James Kfouri, *Admin Sec*
Zoraida Condoretti, *Controller*
◆ EMP: 25
SQ FT: 15,000
SALES (est): 394.2MM
SALES (corp-wide): 1.5B **Privately Held**
WEB: www.almondaccents.com
SIC: 2068 Salted & roasted nuts & seeds
PA: The Wonderful Company Llc
11444 W Olympic Blvd # 210
Los Angeles CA 90064
310 966-5700

2075 Soybean Oil Mills

(P-1443)
GOLDEN GATE TOFU INCORPORATED
1265 Griffith St, San Francisco
(94124-3408)
PHONE..............................415 822-5613
Robert Chen, *President*
▲ EMP: 14
SALES (est): 1.7MM **Privately Held**
SIC: 2075 Soybean protein concentrates & isolates

(P-1444)
MIYAKO ORIENTAL FOODS INC
4287 Puente Ave, Baldwin Park
(91706-3420)
PHONE..............................626 962-9633
Noritoshi Kanai, *President*
Teruo Shimizu, *Vice Pres*
▲ EMP: 14
SQ FT: 18,000
SALES (est): 2.9MM **Privately Held**
WEB: www.coldmountainmiso.com
SIC: 2075 Soybean oil, cake or meal
HQ: Mutual Trading Co., Inc.
431 Crocker St
Los Angeles CA 90013
213 626-9458

(P-1445)
MLINE TRANSPORTATION COMPANY
6621 Clear Creek Ct, Citrus Heights
(95610-4609)
P.O. Box 643 (95611-0643)
PHONE..............................916 729-1053
Mary Jo Rablin, *President*
EMP: 29
SALES (est): 3MM **Privately Held**
SIC: 2075 4731 Soybean oil mills; truck transportation brokers

(P-1446)
SOYFOODS OF AMERICA
1091 Hamilton Rd, Duarte (91010-2743)
PHONE..............................626 358-3836
Ka Nin Lee, *President*
EMP: 27
SQ FT: 15,000
SALES (est): 4.9MM **Privately Held**
WEB: www.soyfoods.com
SIC: 2075 Soybean oil mills

(P-1447)
VISOY FOOD PRODUCTS & MFG INC
111 W Elmyra St, Los Angeles
(90012-1818)
PHONE..............................323 221-4079
Wayne Wong, *President*
Lap T Kwan, *Vice Pres*
EMP: 10
SQ FT: 2,500
SALES (est): 848.1K
SALES (corp-wide): 975.1K **Privately Held**
SIC: 2075 Soybean oil mills
PA: Zhuhai Bocom Pharmacy Co., Ltd.
Xiaolin Hongdengwei,Hongqi
Town,Jinwang District
Zhuhai 51909
756 399-2888

2076 Vegetable Oil Mills

(P-1448)
BUNGE OILS INC
Also Called: Bunge North America
436 S Mcclure Rd, Modesto (95357-0519)
PHONE..............................209 574-9981
Dale Casky, *Manager*
EMP: 72
SQ FT: 76,824 **Privately Held**
WEB: www.bungeoils.com
SIC: 2076 Vegetable oil mills
HQ: Bunge Oils, Inc.
1391 Tmbarlake Manor Pkwy
Chesterfield MO 63017
314 292-2000

(P-1449)
PEARL CROP INC
Also Called: Turkhan Nuts
17641 French Camp Rd, Ripon
(95366-9799)
PHONE..............................209 982-9933
EMP: 25
SALES (corp-wide): 140MM **Privately Held**
SIC: 2076 Walnut oil; tung oil
PA: Pearl Crop, Inc.
1550 Industrial Dr
Stockton CA 95206
209 808-7575

(P-1450)
WILMAR OILS FATS STOCKTON LLC
2008 Port Road B, Stockton (95203-2923)
PHONE..............................925 627-1600
Thomas Lim, *Mng Member*
SNG Miow Ching,
Mike Fargas,
▲ EMP: 25
SALES: 136MM **Privately Held**
SIC: 2076 Palm kernel oil

2077 Animal, Marine Fats & Oils

(P-1451)
ARTISAN MOSS LLC
3450 Palmer Dr Ste 4, Cameron Park
(95682-8274)
PHONE..............................833 667-7278
Erin Kinsey,
EMP: 15 EST: 2016
SALES (est): 1.3MM **Privately Held**
SIC: 2077 Animal & marine fats & oils

(P-1452)
BAKER COMMODITIES INC (PA)
4020 Bandini Blvd, Vernon (90058-4274)
PHONE..............................323 268-2801
James M Andreoli, *President*
Denis Luckey, *Exec VP*
Mitchell Ebright, *Vice Pres*
Jason Whittaker, *Info Tech Mgr*
James Pairsh, *Plant Mgr*
▼ EMP: 150
SQ FT: 12,000
SALES (est): 153.6MM **Privately Held**
WEB: www.bakercommodities.com
SIC: 2077 2048 Tallow rendering, inedible; poultry feeds

(P-1453)
BAKER COMMODITIES INC
16801 W Jensen Ave, Kerman
(93630-9194)
P.O. Box 416 (93630-0416)
PHONE..............................559 237-4320
Manuel Ponte, *Director*
EMP: 30
SQ FT: 28,690
SALES (corp-wide): 153.6MM **Privately Held**
WEB: www.bakercommodities.com
SIC: 2077 Tallow rendering, inedible
PA: Baker Commodities, Inc.
4020 Bandini Blvd
Vernon CA 90058
323 268-2801

(P-1454)
BAKER COMMODITIES INC
7480 Hanford Armona Rd, Hanford
(93230-9343)
P.O. Box 1286 (93232-1286)
PHONE..............................559 686-4797
Doug Fletcher, *Manager*
EMP: 26
SALES (corp-wide): 153.6MM **Privately Held**
WEB: www.bakercommodities.com
SIC: 2077 2048 Tallow rendering, inedible; prepared feeds
PA: Baker Commodities, Inc.
4020 Bandini Blvd
Vernon CA 90058
323 268-2801

(P-1455)
BAKER COMMODITIES INC
3001 Sierra Pine Ave, Vernon
(90058-4120)
PHONE..............................323 318-8260
EMP: 38
SALES (corp-wide): 153.6MM **Privately Held**
SIC: 2077 Animal & marine fats & oils
PA: Baker Commodities, Inc.
4020 Bandini Blvd
Vernon CA 90058
323 268-2801

(P-1456)
DARLING INGREDIENTS INC
429 Amador St Pier 92, San Francisco
(94124-1232)
P.O. Box 880006 (94188-0006)
PHONE..............................415 647-4890
Gene Hanson, *General Mgr*
Mike Hudlow, *Exec VP*
Ashley Gosney, *Admin Sec*
Greg Hensley, *Plant Mgr*
Greg Grossheim, *Manager*
EMP: 55
SALES (corp-wide): 3.3B **Publicly Held**
WEB: www.darlingii.com
SIC: 2077 2048 5172 Grease rendering, inedible; tallow rendering, inedible; bone meal, except as animal feed; meat meal & tankage, except as animal feed; prepared feeds; lubricating oils & greases
PA: Darling Ingredients Inc.
5601 N Macarthur Blvd
Irving TX 75038
972 717-0300

(P-1457)
DARLING INGREDIENTS INC
795 W Belgravia Ave, Fresno (93706)
P.O. Box 11445 (93773-1445)
PHONE..............................559 268-5325
Edward H Jenkins, *Manager*
EMP: 30
SQ FT: 10,500
SALES (corp-wide): 3.3B **Publicly Held**
WEB: www.darlingii.com
SIC: 2077 2048 Animal & marine fats & oils; prepared feeds
PA: Darling Ingredients Inc.
5601 N Macarthur Blvd
Irving TX 75038
972 717-0300

(P-1458)
DARLING INGREDIENTS INC
2626 E 25th St, Los Angeles (90058-1212)
P.O. Box 58725 (90058-0725)
PHONE..............................323 583-6311
Thomas Nunley, *General Mgr*
Adam Roth, *Manager*
EMP: 77
SALES (corp-wide): 3.3B **Publicly Held**
WEB: www.darlingii.com
SIC: 2077 2048 Animal & marine fats & oils; prepared feeds
PA: Darling Ingredients Inc.
5601 N Macarthur Blvd
Irving TX 75038
972 717-0300

(P-1459)
DARLING INGREDIENTS INC
407 S Tegner Rd, Turlock (95380-9406)
PHONE..............................209 620-7267
Myra Pena, *Branch Mgr*
EMP: 10
SALES (corp-wide): 3.3B **Publicly Held**
SIC: 2077 Animal & marine fats & oils; grease rendering, inedible; tallow rendering, inedible; bone meal, except as animal feed
PA: Darling Ingredients Inc.
5601 N Macarthur Blvd
Irving TX 75038
972 717-0300

(P-1460)
DARLING INTERNATIONAL INC
11946 Carpenter Rd, Crows Landing
(95313-9749)
P.O. Box 1608, Turlock (95381-1608)
PHONE..............................209 667-9153
Dick Labuga, *General Mgr*
Richard Searcy, *Plant Mgr*

EMP: 35
SQ FT: 43,498
SALES (corp-wide): 3.3B **Publicly Held**
WEB: www.darlingii.com
SIC: 2077 2048 Grease rendering, inedible; tallow rendering, inedible; bone meal, except as animal feed; meat meal & tankage, except as animal feed; prepared feeds
PA: Darling Ingredients Inc.
5601 N Macarthur Blvd
Irving TX 75038
972 717-0300

(P-1461)
JR GREASE SERVICES
5900 S Eastrn Ave Ste 104, Commerce (90040)
P.O. Box 226894, Los Angeles (90022-0594)
PHONE..................................323 318-2096
Jesse Rodriguez, *Principal*
EMP: 20
SALES (est): 2MM **Privately Held**
SIC: 2077 Grease rendering, inedible

(P-1462)
NORDIC NATURALS INC (PA)
Also Called: Westport Scandinavia
111 Jennings Way, Watsonville (95076-2054)
PHONE..................................800 662-2544
Joar A Opheim, *CEO*
Michele Opheim, *Vice Pres*
Cecile Lariviere, *Comms Dir*
Jenni Baca, *Executive Asst*
Geri Zerbini, *Administration*
▲ EMP: 118
SALES (est): 28.8MM **Privately Held**
WEB: www.nordicnaturals.com
SIC: 2077 Fish oil

(P-1463)
NORTH STATE RENDERING CO INC
15 Shippee Rd, Oroville (95965-9297)
P.O. Box 239, Durham (95938-0239)
PHONE..................................530 343-6076
Chris Ottone, *President*
Patrick Ottone, *Vice Pres*
William Ottone, *Admin Sec*
EMP: 23
SQ FT: 15,000
SALES (est): 3.7MM **Privately Held**
SIC: 2077 Tallow rendering, inedible

(P-1464)
PARK WEST ENTERPRISES
Also Called: Co-West Commodities
2586 Shenandoah Way, San Bernardino (92407-1845)
PHONE..................................909 383-8341
Sergio Perez, *CEO*
Freddie Peterson, *CFO*
EMP: 30
SALES (est): 7MM **Privately Held**
SIC: 2077 Animal & marine fats & oils

(P-1465)
SALINAS TALLOW CO INC
1 Work Cir, Salinas (93901-4349)
PHONE..................................831 422-6436
William Ottone, *President*
Philip Ottone, *Vice Pres*
EMP: 20
SALES (est): 3.4MM **Privately Held**
SIC: 2077 2079 Tallow rendering, inedible; cooking oils, except corn: vegetable refined

(P-1466)
SRC MILLING CO LLC
Also Called: Sacramento Rendering Co
11350 Kiefer Blvd, Sacramento (95830-9405)
PHONE..................................916 363-4821
Jim Walsh, *Mng Member*
A Michael Koewler,
Michael Patrick Koewler,
Timothy D Koewler,
Richard Wilbur,
▲ EMP: 20 EST: 1996
SALES (est): 2.9MM **Privately Held**
WEB: www.srccompanies.com
SIC: 2077 Rendering

2079 Shortening, Oils & Margarine

(P-1467)
CALIFORNIA OLIVE AND VINE LLC
Also Called: Sutter Buttes Olive Oil
1670 Poole Blvd, Yuba City (95993-2610)
PHONE..................................530 763-7921
Alka Kumar, *President*
Arek Kazimierczak, *Manager*
EMP: 15
SQ FT: 10,000
SALES (est): 3MM **Privately Held**
SIC: 2079 5921 Olive oil; liquor stores

(P-1468)
CALIFORNIA OLIVE RANCH INC (PA)
1367 E Lassen Ave Ste A1, Chico (95973-7881)
PHONE..................................530 846-8000
Gregory B Kelly, *CEO*
Pedro Olabrria, *Ch of Bd*
Mike Forbes, *Vice Pres*
Jim Lipman, *Vice Pres*
Antonio Valla, *Vice Pres*
◆ EMP: 43
SALES (est): 63.3MM **Privately Held**
WEB: www.californiaoliveranch.com
SIC: 2079 Olive oil

(P-1469)
CARGILL INCORPORATED
566 N Gilbert St, Fullerton (92833-2549)
PHONE..................................323 588-2274
EMP: 50
SQ FT: 28,410
SALES (corp-wide): 134.8B **Privately Held**
SIC: 2079 2046 2013 2011
PA: Cargill, Incorporated
15407 Mcginty Rd W
Wayzata MN 55391
952 742-7575

(P-1470)
CIUTI INTERNATIONAL INC
Also Called: Cuiti International
8790 Rochester Ave Ste A, Rancho Cucamonga (91730-4925)
PHONE..................................909 484-1414
Marcello Trincale, *CEO*
Eric Trincale, *President*
Jason Watkins, *Sales Dir*
▲ EMP: 15
SQ FT: 20,000
SALES: 18MM **Privately Held**
SIC: 2079 5149 Olive oil; groceries & related products

(P-1471)
DECAMILLA BROTHERS LLC
Also Called: West Coast Products
717 Tehama St, Orland (95963-1248)
PHONE..................................530 865-3379
Mark J De Camilla, *Mng Member*
▲ EMP: 12
SALES (est): 1.4MM **Privately Held**
SIC: 2079 Olive oil

(P-1472)
GEMSA ENTERPRISES LLC
Also Called: Gemsa Oils
14370 Gannet St, La Mirada (90638-5221)
P.O. Box 1447 (90637-1447)
PHONE..................................714 521-1736
Emilio Viscomi,
Angela Verrico Viscomi,
▲ EMP: 20
SQ FT: 60,000
SALES (est): 7.8MM **Privately Held**
SIC: 2079 Olive oil

(P-1473)
IL FIORELLO OLIVE OIL CO
2625 Mankas Corner Rd, Fairfield (94534-3137)
PHONE..................................707 864-1529
Mark Sievers, *Owner*
Ann Sievers, *Co-Owner*
Stephanie Oriarte, *Manager*
▲ EMP: 50

SQ FT: 5,000
SALES (est): 3.7MM **Privately Held**
SIC: 2079 2084 Olive oil; wines

(P-1474)
LIBERTY VEGETABLE OIL COMPANY
15306 Carmenita Rd, Santa Fe Springs (90670-5606)
P.O. Box 4207, Cerritos (90703-4207)
PHONE..................................562 921-3567
Irwin Field, *President*
Ronald Field, *Admin Sec*
◆ EMP: 40 EST: 1948
SQ FT: 30,000
SALES (est): 10MM **Privately Held**
SIC: 2079 Olive oil

(P-1475)
MCEVOY OF MARIN LLC
Also Called: McEvoy Ranch
5935 Red Hill Rd, Petaluma (94952-9437)
P.O. Box 341 (94953-0341)
PHONE..................................707 778-2307
Nion McEvoy,
Ria Aversa, *Opers Staff*
Nan Tucker McEvoy,
Joseph Ternes, *Director*
◆ EMP: 100
SALES (est): 17.3MM **Privately Held**
SIC: 2079 Olive oil

(P-1476)
MILL AT KINGS RIVER LLC
15111 E Goodfellow Ave, Sanger (93657-8881)
PHONE..................................559 875-7800
John M Mesrobian, *Mng Member*
EMP: 23 EST: 2015
SALES (est): 3.9MM **Privately Held**
SIC: 2079 Olive oil

(P-1477)
MY FRUITY FACES LLC
2400 Lincoln Ave, Altadena (91001-5436)
PHONE..................................877 358-9210
Bob D Ntoya, *Mng Member*
Brian Jones, *COO*
Kevin Cammarata,
Adam Gerber,
Jason Gerber,
EMP: 10
SALES: 1MM **Privately Held**
SIC: 2079 2899 Edible fats & oils; gelatin: edible, technical, photographic or pharmaceutical
PA: 3becom, Inc.
2400 Lincoln Ave Ste 216
Altadena CA 91001

(P-1478)
NICK SCIABICA & SONS A CORP
Also Called: Sciabica's
2150 Yosemite Blvd, Modesto (95354-3931)
PHONE..................................209 577-5067
Gemma Sciabica, *CEO*
Joseph N Sciabica, *President*
Daniel R Sciabica, *Corp Secy*
Verna Smith, *Office Mgr*
Craig Hilliker, *Project Mgr*
▲ EMP: 20 EST: 1925
SQ FT: 68,728
SALES (est): 4.7MM **Privately Held**
WEB: www.sciabica.com
SIC: 2079 5149 Olive oil; cooking oils

(P-1479)
OLIVE BARI OIL COMPANY
40063 Road 56, Dinuba (93618-9708)
PHONE..................................559 595-9260
Kyle Sawatzky, *CEO*
Ryan Sawatzky, *COO*
Breann Janes, *Sales Mgr*
Breann Borges, *Accounts Mgr*
EMP: 12
SQ FT: 20,000
SALES: 500K **Privately Held**
SIC: 2079 Olive oil

(P-1480)
OLIVE BARIANI OIL LLC
1330 Waller St, San Francisco (94117-2921)
PHONE..................................415 864-1917

Emmanuel Bariani, *Principal*
EMP: 19
SALES (corp-wide): 569.7K **Privately Held**
SIC: 2079 Olive oil
PA: Olive Bariani Oil Llc
9460 Bar Du Ln
Sacramento CA 95829
530 666-1563

(P-1481)
OLIVE CORTO L P
10201 Live Oak Rd, Stockton (95212-9319)
P.O. Box 1706, Lodi (95241-1706)
PHONE..................................209 888-8100
Brady Whitlow, *President*
▲ EMP: 15
SALES (est): 4MM **Privately Held**
WEB: www.corto-olive.com
SIC: 2079 Olive oil

(P-1482)
OLIVE PRESS LLC (PA)
24724 Arnold Dr, Sonoma (95476-2814)
PHONE..................................707 939-8900
Ed Stolman,
Eve Priestly, *Controller*
◆ EMP: 12
SALES (est): 28.5MM **Privately Held**
WEB: www.theolivepress.com
SIC: 2079 5199 Olive oil; oils, animal or vegetable

(P-1483)
SPECTRUM ORGANIC PRODUCTS LLC
Also Called: Spectrum Naturals
2201 S Mcdowell Blvd Ext, Petaluma (94954-7624)
PHONE..................................888 343-6637
Neil G Blomquist, *President*
Jethren P Phillips, *Ch of Bd*
Randall H Sias, *Vice Pres*
Nils Michael Langenborg, *VP Mktg*
▲ EMP: 66 EST: 1980
SQ FT: 18,600
SALES (est): 13.4MM **Publicly Held**
WEB: www.spectrumorganics.com
SIC: 2079 2035 2099 2834 Edible fats & oils; dressings, salad: raw & cooked (except dry mixes); mayonnaise; vinegar; vitamin, nutrient & hematinic preparations for human use
PA: The Hain Celestial Group Inc
1111 Marcus Ave Ste 100
New Hyde Park NY 11042

(P-1484)
VENTURA FOODS LLC
2900 Jurupa St, Ontario (91761-2915)
PHONE..................................714 257-3700
Wayne Kess, *Manager*
EMP: 164 **Privately Held**
WEB: www.venturafoods.com
SIC: 2079 2035 Vegetable shortenings (except corn oil); cooking oils, except corn: vegetable refined; pickles, sauces & salad dressings
PA: Ventura Foods, Llc
40 Pointe Dr
Brea CA 92821

(P-1485)
VENTURA FOODS LLC (PA)
Also Called: Lou Ana Foods
40 Pointe Dr, Brea (92821-3652)
PHONE..................................714 257-3700
Christopher Furman, *President*
Erika Noonburg-Morgan, *CFO*
Andy Euser, *Officer*
Alan Blake, *Exec VP*
John Buckles, *Exec VP*
◆ EMP: 200
SALES (est): 188.6MM **Privately Held**
WEB: www.venturafoods.com
SIC: 2079 2035 Vegetable shortenings (except corn oil); cooking oils, except corn: vegetable refined; pickles, sauces & salad dressings

---

(P-1486)
VERONICA FOODS COMPANY
1991 Dennison St, Oakland (94606-5225)
P.O. Box 2225 (94621-0125)
PHONE.................................510 535-6833
Michael Bradley, *President*
Gregg Niemuth, *CFO*
Veronica Bradley, *Vice Pres*
◆ **EMP:** 50 **EST:** 1940
SALES (est): 11.1MM **Privately Held**
WEB: www.evoliveoil.com
SIC: 2079 5149 Cooking oils, except corn;
vegetable refined; olive oil; salad oils, except corn: vegetable refined; cooking oils
& shortenings; dried or canned foods

(P-1487)
WILSEY FOODS INC
40 Pointe Dr, Brea (92821-3652)
PHONE.................................714 257-3700
Takashi Fukunaga, *CEO*
Steve Takagi, *President*
Hiro Matsumura, *Vice Pres*
◆ **EMP:** 2100
SQ FT: 103,378
SALES (est): 210MM **Privately Held**
SIC: 2079 5149 Cooking oils, except corn;
vegetable refined; vegetable shortenings
(except corn oil); shortening, vegetable
PA: Mitsui & Co., Ltd.
1-1-3, Marunouchi
Chiyoda-Ku TKY 100-0
-

2082 Malt Beverages

(P-1488)
23 BOTTLES OF BEER LLC
Also Called: Russian River Brewing Co
725 4th St, Santa Rosa (95404-4407)
PHONE.................................707 545-2337
Vinnie Cilurzo, *Mng Member*
Natalie Cilurzo,
▲ **EMP:** 40
SALES (est): 7.7MM **Privately Held**
WEB: www.russianriverbrewing.com
SIC: 2082 Beer (alcoholic beverage)

(P-1489)
ABSOLUTION BREWING
COMPANY (PA)
2878 Columbia St, Torrance (90503-3808)
PHONE.................................310 787-9563
Nigel Heath, *CEO*
Steve Farguson, *Vice Pres*
▲ **EMP:** 10 **EST:** 2013
SQ FT: 7,000
SALES (est): 1.5MM **Privately Held**
SIC: 2082 Malt liquors

(P-1490)
ANDERSON VALLEY BREWING
INC
Also Called: Anderson Valley Brewing Co
17700 Hwy 253, Boonville (95415)
P.O. Box 505 (95415-0505)
PHONE.................................707 895-2337
Kenneth D Allen, *President*
Todd Hamrick, *Area Mgr*
Mike Halligan, *Sales Staff*
Ryan Niebuhr, *Sales Staff*
Brian Jette, *Cust Mgr*
◆ **EMP:** 45
SQ FT: 5,000
SALES (est): 8.6MM **Privately Held**
SIC: 2082 5812 Ale (alcoholic beverage);
porter (alcoholic beverage); stout (alcoholic beverage); cafe

(P-1491)
ANHEUSER-BUSCH LLC
15800 Roscoe Blvd, Van Nuys
(91406-1379)
PHONE.................................818 989-5300
Gary P Lee, *Manager*
Aida Miller, *Treasurer*
Bruce Borst, *General Mgr*
Luis Cayo, *General Mgr*
Jeff Bower, *Planning*
EMP: 162
SALES (corp-wide): 1.5B **Privately Held**
WEB: www.hispanicbud.com
SIC: 2082 Beer (alcoholic beverage)

HQ: Anheuser-Busch, Llc
1 Busch Pl
Saint Louis MO 63118
800 342-5283

(P-1492)
ANHEUSER-BUSCH LLC
5959 Santa Fe St, San Diego
(92109-1623)
P.O. Box 80758 (92138-0758)
PHONE.................................858 581-7000
Denise Cooper, *General Mgr*
Ed Cebula, *Regl Sales Mgr*
EMP: 200
SALES (corp-wide): 1.5B **Privately Held**
WEB: www.hispanicbud.com
SIC: 2082 Beer (alcoholic beverage)
HQ: Anheuser-Busch, Llc
1 Busch Pl
Saint Louis MO 63118
800 342-5283

(P-1493)
ANHEUSER-BUSCH LLC
2800 S Reservoir St, Pomona
(91766-6525)
PHONE.................................800 622-2667
Dan Partelow, *General Mgr*
EMP: 162
SQ FT: 105,471
SALES (corp-wide): 1.5B **Privately Held**
WEB: www.hispanicbud.com
SIC: 2082 Beer (alcoholic beverage)
HQ: Anheuser-Busch, Llc
1 Busch Pl
Saint Louis MO 63118
800 342-5283

(P-1494)
ARTISAN BREWERS LLC
Also Called: Drake's Brewing Company
1933 Davis St Ste 177, San Leandro
(94577-1256)
PHONE.................................510 567-4926
John Martin,
Roy Kirkorian,
◆ **EMP:** 44
SALES (est): 5.9MM **Privately Held**
SIC: 2082 Beer (alcoholic beverage)

(P-1495)
ASSOCIATED
MICROBREWERIES INC
9675 Scranton Rd, San Diego
(92121-1761)
PHONE.................................858 587-2739
Bryan King, *Branch Mgr*
EMP: 93
SALES (corp-wide): 72.1MM **Privately Held**
SIC: 2082 Beer (alcoholic beverage)
PA: Associated Microbreweries, Inc.
5985 Santa Fe St
San Diego CA 92109
858 273-2739

(P-1496)
ASSOCIATED
MICROBREWERIES INC
901 S Coast Dr Ste A, Costa Mesa
(92626-7790)
PHONE.................................714 546-2739
David Sadeler, *Manager*
EMP: 70
SALES (corp-wide): 72.1MM **Privately Held**
SIC: 2082 Beer (alcoholic beverage)
PA: Associated Microbreweries, Inc.
5985 Santa Fe St
San Diego CA 92109
858 273-2739

(P-1497)
ASSOCIATED
MICROBREWERIES INC (PA)
Also Called: Karl Strauss Brewery Garden
5985 Santa Fe St, San Diego
(92109-1623)
PHONE.................................858 273-2739
Christopher W Cramer, *President*
Matthew H Rattner, *CFO*
EMP: 50
SQ FT: 2,000

SALES (est): 72.1MM **Privately Held**
WEB: www.karlstrauss.com
SIC: 2082 5812 Beer (alcoholic beverage); eating places

(P-1498)
ASSOCIATED
MICROBREWERIES INC
Also Called: Karl Strauss Brewery & Rest
1157 Columbia St, San Diego
(92101-3511)
PHONE.................................619 234-2739
Shawn Phaby, *Manager*
EMP: 105
SALES (corp-wide): 72.1MM **Privately Held**
WEB: www.karlstrauss.com
SIC: 2082 5812 Beer (alcoholic beverage); eating places
PA: Associated Microbreweries, Inc.
5985 Santa Fe St
San Diego CA 92109
858 273-2739

(P-1499)
BALLAST POINT SPIRITS LLC
Also Called: Ballast Point Brewing
9045 Carroll Way, San Diego (92121-2405)
PHONE.................................858 695-2739
Jack R White, *Principal*
Maddie Tomey, *Buyer*
◆ **EMP:** 148
SALES: 26.6MM
SALES (corp-wide): 8.1B **Publicly Held**
SIC: 2082 Malt beverages
HQ: Home Brew Mart, Inc.
9045 Carroll Way
San Diego CA 92121

(P-1500)
BAREBOTTLE BREWING
COMPANY INC
1525 Cortland Ave # 6, San Francisco
(94110-5714)
PHONE.................................415 926-8617
Michael Seitz, *CEO*
Ben Sterling, *Principal*
Lester Koga, *Admin Sec*
EMP: 19
SQ FT: 17,000
SALES: 550K **Privately Held**
SIC: 2082 Ale (alcoholic beverage)

(P-1501)
BEAR REPUBLIC BREWING CO
INC (PA)
110 Sandholm Ln Ste 10, Cloverdale
(95425-4439)
PHONE.................................707 894-2722
Richard R Norgrove, *President*
Peter Kruger, *COO*
Tammy Hucke-Norgrove, *CFO*
Tami Norgrove, *CFO*
Sandra D Norgrove, *Admin Sec*
EMP: 152
SQ FT: 6,500
SALES (est): 30.1MM **Privately Held**
WEB: www.bearrepublic.com
SIC: 2082 5812 5813 Beer (alcoholic beverage); eating places; drinking places

(P-1502)
BEAR REPUBLIC BREWING CO
INC
345 Healdsburg Ave, Healdsburg
(95448-4105)
PHONE.................................707 433-2337
Richard Norgrove, *Branch Mgr*
EMP: 10
SALES (est): 926.8K **Privately Held**
SIC: 2082 Beer (alcoholic beverage)
PA: Bear Republic Brewing Co Inc
110 Sandholm Ln Ste 10
Cloverdale CA 95425

(P-1503)
BLANCO BASURA BEVERAGE
INC
Also Called: Bruvado Imports
5776 Stoneridge Mall Rd # 338, Pleasanton
(94588-2832)
PHONE.................................888 705-7225
Scott D Gold, *CEO*

Chad Blair, *President*
Pete Noto, *President*
Karen Watts, *CFO*
EMP: 150
SALES (est): 5.9MM **Privately Held**
SIC: 2082 Beer (alcoholic beverage)

(P-1504)
BLINKING OWL DISTILLERY
210 N Bush St, Santa Ana (92701-5361)
PHONE.................................949 370-4688
Thomas A Zeigler, *Principal*
▲ **EMP:** 10
SALES (est): 619.9K **Privately Held**
SIC: 2082 Beer (alcoholic beverage)

(P-1505)
BREW4U LLC
935 Washington St, San Carlos
(94070-5316)
PHONE.................................415 516-8211
Christopher Garrett, *Mng Member*
EMP: 15
SALES (est): 1.3MM **Privately Held**
SIC: 2082 2812 Beer (alcoholic beverage); soda ash, sodium carbonate (anhydrous)

(P-1506)
BREWMASTER INC
Also Called: Speakeasy Ales & Lagers
1195 Evans Ave, San Francisco
(94124-1704)
P.O. Box 882724 (94188-2724)
PHONE.................................415 642-3371
Thomas E Baird, *CEO*
Forest Gray, *President*
Sam Cappione, *Vice Pres*
Raman Sharma, *Finance*
Kathleen Allen, *Opers Staff*
▲ **EMP:** 33
SQ FT: 11,000
SALES (est): 7.3MM **Privately Held**
WEB: www.goodbeer.com
SIC: 2082 Beer (alcoholic beverage)
PA: Hunters Point Brewery, Llc
8380 Pardee Dr
Oakland CA
-

(P-1507)
BU LLC
9073 Pulsar Ct Ste A, Corona
(92883-7357)
PHONE.................................951 277-7470
Ryan Mason, *Mng Member*
Andres Kummen, *Officer*
EMP: 15
SQ FT: 1,500
SALES: 2MM **Privately Held**
SIC: 2082 Malt beverages

(P-1508)
BURNING BEARD BREWING
COMPANY
785 Vernon Way, El Cajon (92020-1938)
PHONE.................................619 456-9185
Jeff Wiedekehr, *Co-Owner*
Shannon Lynette, *Principal*
Mike Maass, *Marketing Staff*
EMP: 12 **EST:** 2016
SALES (est): 1.4MM **Privately Held**
SIC: 2082 Beer (alcoholic beverage)

(P-1509)
BUZZWORKS INC
365 11th St, San Francisco (94103-4313)
PHONE.................................415 863-5964
Vladimir Cood, *CEO*
EMP: 15
SALES (est): 1.2MM **Privately Held**
SIC: 2082 5813 Beer (alcoholic beverage); tavern (drinking places)

(P-1510)
CASA AGRIA
701 Del Norte Blvd, Oxnard (93030-7909)
PHONE.................................805 485-1454
Ryan Exline, *Principal*
EMP: 10
SALES (est): 1MM **Privately Held**
SIC: 2082 Malt beverages

(P-1511)
CHARLIES BEER COMPANY USA LLC
9581 Bus Ctr Dr Ste G, Rancho Cucamonga (91730)
PHONE...................................909 980-0436
Lamont Jefferies,
▲ EMP: 13
SQ FT: 1,800
SALES (est): 1.5MM **Privately Held**
SIC: 2082 Beer (alcoholic beverage)

(P-1512)
CLEOPHUS QUEALY BEER COMPANY
448 Hester St, San Leandro (94577-1024)
PHONE...................................510 463-4534
Peter Henderson Baker, *CEO*
EMP: 10
SALES (est): 811.5K **Privately Held**
SIC: 2082 Beer (alcoholic beverage)

(P-1513)
COMEBACK BREWING II INC
Also Called: Trumer Brauerei
1404 4th St, Berkeley (94710-1323)
PHONE...................................510 526-1160
Carlos Alverez, *President*
Lars Larson, *Master*
EMP: 15
SALES (est): 2.2MM
SALES (corp-wide): 8.6MM **Privately Held**
WEB: www.gambrinus.com
SIC: 2082 Beer (alcoholic beverage)
PA: Comeback Brewing Ii, Inc.
14800 San Pedro Ave Fl 3
San Antonio TX 78232
210 490-9128

(P-1514)
COORS BREWING COMPANY
3001 Douglas Blvd Ste 200, Roseville (95661-3809)
PHONE...................................916 786-2666
Fax: 916 786-9396
EMP: 20
SALES (corp-wide): 3.5B **Publicly Held**
SIC: 2082 5181
HQ: Coors Brewing Company
17735 W 32nd Ave
Golden CO 80401
303 279-6565

(P-1515)
CRISPINIAN INC
Also Called: Crispin Cider Works, The
1213 S Auburn St Ste A, Colfax (95713-9800)
PHONE...................................530 346-8411
Scott Whitley, *CEO*
Trevor John Heron, *CEO*
Lesley Anne Heron, *Admin Sec*
▲ EMP: 22
SALES (est): 5.1MM **Privately Held**
SIC: 2082 5999 Ale (alcoholic beverage);
alcoholic beverage making equipment & supplies

(P-1516)
CWS BEVERAGE
2732 Danley Ct Ste 101, Paso Robles (93446-7020)
P.O. Box 457 (93447-0457)
PHONE...................................805 286-2735
EMP: 12
SALES (est): 1.3MM **Privately Held**
SIC: 2082

(P-1517)
CYDEA INC
Also Called: Beveragefactory.com
8510 Miralani Dr, San Diego (92126-4351)
PHONE...................................800 710-9939
Craig Costanzo, *President*
Michael Costanzo, *CFO*
Barbara Costanzo, *Admin Sec*
Carey Correia, *Sales Staff*
Christian Johnston, *Director*
◆ EMP: 20
SQ FT: 12,000
SALES (est): 6.7MM **Privately Held**
SIC: 2082 2084 5046 Beer (alcoholic beverage); wines, brandy & brandy spirits;
coffee brewing equipment & supplies

(P-1518)
D&S BREWING SOLUTIONS INC
6148 E Oakbrook St, Long Beach (90815-2228)
PHONE...................................650 207-4524
Dylan Mobley, *President*
EMP: 49 EST: 2014
SALES (est): 1.9MM **Privately Held**
SIC: 2082 Malt beverages

(P-1519)
DELTA COAST BEER LLC
2034 E Lincoln Ave, Anaheim (92806-4101)
PHONE...................................213 604-2428
Daniel Wheeler, *CEO*
Wing Lam, *COO*
EMP: 10
SALES (est): 342.9K **Privately Held**
SIC: 2082 5182 7389 Beer (alcoholic beverage); liquor;

(P-1520)
DESERT BROTHERS CRAFT
Also Called: Angry Horse Brewing
603 W Whittier Blvd, Montebello (90640-5235)
PHONE...................................323 530-0015
Nathan McCusker, *President*
EMP: 10 EST: 2014
SALES (est): 336.4K **Privately Held**
SIC: 2082 Malt beverages

(P-1521)
DSB ENTERPRISES INC
Also Called: Oggi's Pizza & Brewing Co
425 S Melrose Dr, Vista (92081-6619)
PHONE...................................760 295-3500
Dan Borshell, *Owner*
▲ EMP: 46
SALES (est): 1.5MM **Privately Held**
SIC: 2082 5812 Malt beverages; pizza restaurants

(P-1522)
DUDES BREWING COMPANY
1840 W 208th St, Somis (93066)
P.O. Box 276 (93066-0276)
PHONE...................................424 271-2915
Toby Humes, *Owner*
EMP: 22
SALES (est): 2.4MM **Privately Held**
SIC: 2082 5921 Beer (alcoholic beverage); beer (packaged)

(P-1523)
ENCINITAS OGGIS INC
305 Encinitas Blvd, Encinitas (92024-3724)
PHONE...................................760 579-3211
Charidy Mann Alcoser, *Principal*
EMP: 10
SALES (est): 924.4K **Privately Held**
SIC: 2082 Malt beverages

(P-1524)
ENGLISH ALES BREWERS INC
223 Reindollar Ave Ste A, Marina (93933-3851)
PHONE...................................831 883-3000
Peter Blackwell, *President*
EMP: 11
SALES (est): 1.4MM **Privately Held**
WEB: www.englishalesbrewery.com
SIC: 2082 Beer (alcoholic beverage)

(P-1525)
EPIDEMIC ALES
150 Mason Cir, Concord (94520-8551)
PHONE...................................925 566-8850
▲ EMP: 12
SALES (est): 1.6MM **Privately Held**
SIC: 2082 Malt beverages

(P-1526)
FERMENTED SCIENCES INC
Also Called: Flying Embers
910 E Aliso St, Ojai (93023-2909)
PHONE...................................805 798-2790
William Castagna, *President*
EMP: 10
SALES (est): 827.5K **Privately Held**
SIC: 2082 Malt beverage products

(P-1527)
FIRESTONE WALKER INC
Also Called: Firestone Walker Brewing Co
620 Mcmurray Rd, Buellton (93427-2511)
PHONE...................................805 254-4205
Patrick McAlary, *General Mgr*
EMP: 21
SALES (corp-wide): 151.3MM **Privately Held**
WEB: www.firestonewalker.com
SIC: 2082 Beer (alcoholic beverage)
PA: Firestone Walker, Inc.
1400 Ramada Dr
Paso Robles CA 93446
805 225-5911

(P-1528)
FIRESTONE WALKER INC (PA)
Also Called: Firestone Walker Brewing Co
1400 Ramada Dr, Paso Robles (93446-3993)
PHONE...................................805 225-5911
David Walker, *CEO*
Andy Wickstrom, *Creative Dir*
Adam Firestone, *Principal*
Matt Brynildson, *Mfg Mgr*
Jamie Smith, *Marketing Mgr*
▲ EMP: 225
SALES (est): 151.3MM **Privately Held**
WEB: www.firestonewalker.com
SIC: 2082 Beer (alcoholic beverage)

(P-1529)
FIRESTONE WALKER LLC
Also Called: Firestone Walker Brewing Co
10130 Commercial Ave, Penn Valley (95946-9466)
PHONE...................................805 225-5911
David Walker, *CEO*
EMP: 64
SALES (corp-wide): 151.3MM **Privately Held**
SIC: 2082 Beer (alcoholic beverage)
PA: Firestone Walker, Inc.
1400 Ramada Dr
Paso Robles CA 93446
805 225-5911

(P-1530)
FISH ON RICE LLC
Also Called: Kamikaze 7 Sushi Joint
3250 Grey Hawk Ct, Carlsbad (92010-6651)
PHONE...................................619 696-6262
Kevin T Roberts, *Mng Member*
EMP: 10
SALES (est): 972.7K **Privately Held**
SIC: 2082 Beer (alcoholic beverage)

(P-1531)
GFBC INC
Also Called: Green Flash Brewing
6550 Mira Mesa Blvd, San Diego (92121-4100)
PHONE...................................858 622-0085
Michael Hinkley, *CEO*
Steve Goodger, *CFO*
Elena Bolino, *District Mgr*
Brian Udvardi, *District Mgr*
Katie Wolbrink, *Accountant*
EMP: 15
SALES (est): 3.6MM **Privately Held**
SIC: 2082 Beer (alcoholic beverage)

(P-1532)
GLACIER DESIGN SYSTEMS INC (PA)
5405 Production Dr, Huntington Beach (92649-1524)
PHONE...................................714 897-2337
Robert Asahi, *VP Opers*
▲ EMP: 15
SQ FT: 8,500
SALES (est): 3.4MM **Privately Held**
WEB: www.glacier-design.com
SIC: 2082 5078 Beer (alcoholic beverage); refrigerated beverage dispensers

(P-1533)
GORDON BIERSCH BREWING COMPANY
357 E Taylor St, San Jose (95112-3105)
PHONE...................................408 792-1546
William Bullard, *Manager*
Steven Soucy, *Training Spec*

EMP: 93
SALES (corp-wide): 98.8MM **Privately Held**
SIC: 2082 Malt beverages
PA: Gordon Biersch Brewing Company
10801 W Charleston Blvd # 600
Las Vegas NV 89135

(P-1534)
GRAMIC ENTERPRISES INC
21770 Deveron Cv, Yorba Linda (92887-2662)
PHONE...................................714 329-8627
Michael Sy, *President*
▲ EMP: 15
SALES (est): 1.4MM **Privately Held**
SIC: 2082 Malt beverages

(P-1535)
HOLLISTER BREWING COMPANY LLC
6980 Market Place Dr, Goleta (93117-2997)
PHONE...................................805 968-2810
Marshall A Rose,
Larry Kreider,
Eric Rose,
Jennifer Rose, *Manager*
EMP: 45
SALES (est): 5.8MM **Privately Held**
WEB: www.hollisterbrewco.com
SIC: 2082 Beer (alcoholic beverage)

(P-1536)
HOME BREW MART INC
9045 Carroll Way, San Diego (92121-2405)
PHONE...................................858 695-2739
Aaron Justin, *Branch Mgr*
EMP: 20
SALES (corp-wide): 8.1B **Publicly Held**
WEB: www.homebrewmart.com
SIC: 2082 5999 Ale (alcoholic beverage); alcoholic beverage making equipment & supplies
HQ: Home Brew Mart, Inc.
9045 Carroll Way
San Diego CA 92121

(P-1537)
HOME BREW MART INC (HQ)
Also Called: Ballast Pt Brewing & Spirits
9045 Carroll Way, San Diego (92121-2405)
PHONE...................................858 790-6900
Jim Buechler, *CEO*
Jack White, *CEO*
Yuseff Cherney, *COO*
Rick Morgan, *CFO*
Julie Buechler, *Admin Sec*
▲ EMP: 200
SQ FT: 107,000
SALES (est): 180.3MM
SALES (corp-wide): 8.1B **Publicly Held**
WEB: www.homebrewmart.com
SIC: 2082 5999 Ale (alcoholic beverage); alcoholic beverage making equipment & supplies
PA: Constellation Brands, Inc.
207 High Point Dr # 100
Victor NY 14564
585 678-7100

(P-1538)
INDIAN WELLS COMPANIES
Also Called: Indian Wells Brewery
2565 State Highway 14, Inyokern (93527-2700)
PHONE...................................760 377-4290
Greg Antonaros, *Partner*
Rick Lovett, *Partner*
Pete Mitchell, *VP Mktg*
▲ EMP: 20
SALES: 960K **Privately Held**
SIC: 2082 2086 Beer (alcoholic beverage); pasteurized & mineral waters, bottled & canned

(P-1539)
ISLAND BREWING CO
5049 6th St, Carpinteria (93013-2001)
PHONE...................................805 745-8272
Paul Wright, *President*
EMP: 16

▲ = Import ▼=Export
◆ =Import/Export

SALES (est): 2.1MM **Privately Held**
WEB: www.islandbrewingcompany.com
SIC: 2082 Malt beverages

(P-1540)
**KARL STRAUSS BREWING
COMPANY (PA)**
5985 Santa Fe St, San Diego
(92109-1623)
P.O. Box 5965 (92165-5965)
PHONE..............................858 273-2739
Chris Cramer, *CEO*
Matt Rattner, *Principal*
Michael Kochka, *Recruiter*
Jessica Charles, *Sales Staff*
Kristine Petrini, *Manager*
EMP: 80
SALES (est): 15.9MM **Privately Held**
SIC: 2082 Beer (alcoholic beverage)

(P-1541)
**LAGUNITAS BREWING
COMPANY (DH)**
1280 N Mcdowell Blvd, Petaluma
(94954-1113)
PHONE..............................707 322-4651
Tony Magee, *President*
▲ EMP: 200
SQ FT: 17,500
SALES (est): 73.7MM
SALES (corp-wide): 12.5MM **Privately
Held**
WEB: www.lagunitas.com
SIC: 2082 Beer (alcoholic beverage)

(P-1542)
**LEFT COAST BREWING
COMPANY**
1245 Puerta Del Sol, San Clemente
(92673-6310)
PHONE..............................949 218-3961
George Hadjis, *President*
Dora Hadjis, *CFO*
Jack Shaw, *Officer*
Tommy Hadjis, *General Mgr*
Pete Lacava, *General Mgr*
EMP: 15 EST: 2004
SQ FT: 7,500
SALES (est): 1.4MM **Privately Held**
SIC: 2082 Beer (alcoholic beverage)

(P-1543)
**LENGTHWISE BREWING
COMPANY**
7700 District Blvd, Bakersfield
(93313-4861)
PHONE..............................661 836-2537
Jeffery James Williams, *CEO*
Darin Schwicker, *Vice Pres*
EMP: 48
SQ FT: 6,000
SALES (est): 6.1MM **Privately Held**
WEB: www.lengthwise.com
SIC: 2082 Beer (alcoholic beverage)

(P-1544)
**LORD LEVIASON ENTERPRISES
LLC**
Also Called: Sweeneys Ale House
17337 Ventura Blvd Ste 10, Encino
(91316-3903)
PHONE..............................818 453-8245
Jackson Fox, *General Mgr*
EMP: 30 EST: 2015
SALES (est): 1.4MM **Privately Held**
SIC: 2082 Ale (alcoholic beverage)

(P-1545)
**LOS ANGELES ALE WORKS
LLC**
12918 Cerise Ave, Hawthorne
(90250-5521)
PHONE..............................213 422-6569
Kristofor Barnes, *Mng Member*
John Rockwell, *Principal*
Kandice TSE, *Controller*
Andrew Fowler,
Jeff Szafarski,
EMP: 12
SALES (est): 1.4MM **Privately Held**
SIC: 2082 Beer (alcoholic beverage)

(P-1546)
**LUCKY LUKE BREWING
COMPANY**
610 W Avenue O Ste 104, Palmdale
(93551-3661)
PHONE..............................661 270-5588
Samantha Schmitz, *Mng Member*
EMP: 13
SALES: 750K **Privately Held**
SIC: 2082 Beer (alcoholic beverage)

(P-1547)
MCLEAN BREWERY INC
Also Called: Magnolia Pub & Brewery
1398 Haight St, San Francisco
(94117-2909)
PHONE..............................415 864-7468
David McLean, *President*
▲ EMP: 24
SQ FT: 4,000
SALES (est): 3.3MM **Privately Held**
WEB: www.magnoliapub.com
SIC: 2082 Malt beverages

(P-1548)
**MENDOCINO BREWING
COMPANY INC**
Also Called: Hopland Brewery
13351 S Highway 101, Hopland (95449)
PHONE..............................707 744-1015
Leeq Q Whitman, *Manager*
EMP: 50 **Publicly Held**
SIC: 2082 Malt beverages
HQ: Mendocino Brewing Company Inc
1601 Airport Rd
Ukiah CA 95482
-

(P-1549)
MILLERCOORS LLC
15801 1st St, Irwindale (91706-6202)
PHONE..............................626 969-6811
Edward Beers, *Branch Mgr*
EMP: 75
SQ FT: 800,000
SALES (corp-wide): 10.7B **Publicly Held**
SIC: 2082 Beer (alcoholic beverage)
HQ: Millercoors Llc
250 S Wacker Dr Ste 800
Chicago IL 60606
312 496-2700

(P-1550)
**NORTH COAST BREWING CO
INC (PA)**
Also Called: Brew Building
455 N Main St, Fort Bragg (95437-3215)
PHONE..............................707 964-2739
Sam Kraynek, *CEO*
Mark E Ruedrich, *President*
Tom Allen, *Vice Pres*
Sheila Martins, *Vice Pres*
▲ EMP: 75
SQ FT: 3,000
SALES (est): 16.4MM **Privately Held**
WEB: www.northcoastbrewing.com
SIC: 2082 5812 5813 Beer (alcoholic bev-
erage); eating places; bars & lounges

(P-1551)
**NUTRACEUTICAL BREWS FOR
LF INC**
Also Called: Dr. Jekyll's
825 Cambridge Ct, Pasadena
(91107-1977)
PHONE..............................310 273-8339
Thomas Costa, *CEO*
Gene Lim, *COO*
EMP: 10
SALES: 300K **Privately Held**
SIC: 2082 7389 Beer (alcoholic bever-
age);

(P-1552)
OCEAN AVENUE BREWING CO
Also Called: Ocean Brewing Company
237 Ocean Ave, Laguna Beach
(92651-2106)
PHONE..............................949 497-3381
Jonathan Thomas, *President*
EMP: 25
SQ FT: 3,500

SALES (est): 3MM **Privately Held**
WEB: www.oceanbrewing.com
SIC: 2082 5812 Beer (alcoholic bever-
age); eating places

(P-1553)
OGGIS PIZZA & BREWING CO
Also Called: HEI
12840 Carmel Country Rd, San Diego
(92130-2155)
PHONE..............................858 481-7883
George Hadjis, *President*
Dora Hadjis, *Vice Pres*
John Hadjis, *Vice Pres*
EMP: 45
SQ FT: 3,200
SALES (est): 5.6MM **Privately Held**
SIC: 2082 5813 5812 Beer (alcoholic bev-
erage); bar (drinking places); pizza
restaurants

(P-1554)
ORIGINAL PATTERN INC
Also Called: Original Pattern Beer
292 4th St, Oakland (94607-4332)
PHONE..............................510 844-4833
Max Silverstein, *CEO*
Ryan Frank, *Administration*
EMP: 12
SALES (est): 1.8MM **Privately Held**
SIC: 2082 Malt beverages

(P-1555)
OTTANO INC
11555 Los Osos Valley Rd # 201, San Luis
Obispo (93405-6472)
PHONE..............................805 547-2088
Nipool Patel, *President*
EMP: 12
SALES (est): 1.6MM **Privately Held**
SIC: 2082 Beer (alcoholic beverage)

(P-1556)
OUTLAW BEVERAGE INC
405 14th St Ste 1000, Oakland
(94612-2706)
P.O. Box 3478, La Habra (90632-3478)
PHONE..............................310 424-5077
Douglas Weekes, *CEO*
Lance Collins, *Founder*
Julia Weekes, *Director*
EMP: 18
SALES (est): 2.1MM **Privately Held**
SIC: 2082 Malt beverages

(P-1557)
**PABST BREWING COMPANY
LLC (PA)**
10635 Santa Monica Blvd, Los Angeles
(90025-8300)
PHONE..............................310 470-0962
Eugene Kashper, *CEO*
Dan McHugh, *Chief Mktg Ofcr*
Robert Urband, *Officer*
Mark S Beatty, *Vice Pres*
Tim McGettigan, *Vice Pres*
▼ EMP: 280
SQ FT: 12,500
SALES (est): 228.8MM **Privately Held**
SIC: 2082 Beer (alcoholic beverage)

(P-1558)
**PLEASANTON MAIN ST
BREWRY INC**
830 Main St Ste Frnt, Pleasanton
(94566-6076)
PHONE..............................925 462-8218
Matt Billings, *Partner*
Sharon Billings, *Partner*
EMP: 10
SALES (est): 1MM **Privately Held**
SIC: 2082 5812 Malt beverages; eating
places

(P-1559)
PORT BREWING LLC
155 Mata Way Ste 104, San Marcos
(92069-2983)
PHONE..............................800 918-6816
Vince Marsaglia, *Mng Member*
Jim Comstock, *CFO*
Tomme Arthur, *Mng Member*
▲ EMP: 37
SALES (est): 7.6MM **Privately Held**
SIC: 2082 Beer (alcoholic beverage)

(P-1560)
**POWER BRANDS CONSULTING
LLC**
5805 Sepulveda Blvd # 501, Van Nuys
(91411-2551)
PHONE..............................818 989-9646
Darin Ezra,
Michelle Mallilin, *Accounting Mgr*
EMP: 40
SQ FT: 5,000
SALES: 6.8MM **Privately Held**
SIC: 2082 8742 Malt beverage products;
food & beverage consultant

(P-1561)
PROHIBITION BREWING CO INC
2004 E Vista Way, Vista (92084-3321)
PHONE..............................760 295-3525
Ronald Adams, *CEO*
Kathy Adams, *Manager*
EMP: 26
SALES (est): 4.2MM **Privately Held**
SIC: 2082 Malt beverages

(P-1562)
**SANTA CLARA VALLEY
BREWING INC**
101 E Alma Ave, San Jose (95112-5944)
PHONE..............................408 288-5181
Craig B Rashkis, *Administration*
EMP: 16
SALES (est): 1.9MM **Privately Held**
SIC: 2082 Malt beverages

(P-1563)
**SIERRA NEVADA BREWING CO
(PA)**
1075 E 20th St, Chico (95928-6722)
PHONE..............................530 893-3520
Jeff White, *CEO*
Kenneth Grossman, *President*
Paul Janicki, *CFO*
Chad McRae, *Social Dir*
Scott Cargile, *Area Mgr*
◆ EMP: 475
SALES: 300MM **Privately Held**
WEB: www.sierranevada.com
SIC: 2082 5812 Beer (alcoholic bever-
age); eating places

(P-1564)
SILVERADO BREWING CO L L C
4104 Saint Helena Hwy, Calistoga
(94515-9629)
PHONE..............................707 341-3089
Michael Fradelizio,
Debbie Fradelizio,
Ken Mee,
EMP: 20
SALES (est): 2.1MM **Privately Held**
WEB: www.silveradobrewery.com
SIC: 2082 5812 Malt beverages; American
restaurant

(P-1565)
SINGHA NORTH AMERICA INC
303 Twin Dolphin Dr # 600, Redwood City
(94065-1422)
PHONE..............................714 206-5097
Palit Bbhakdi, *CEO*
Soravij B Bhakdi, *President*
Mario Ylanan, *Treasurer*
Mithlesh Singh, *Sr Software Eng*
▲ EMP: 17
SALES (est): 2.1MM **Privately Held**
SIC: 2082 Beer (alcoholic beverage)
PA: Boonrawd Brewery Company Limited
999 Samsen Road
Dusit 10300

(P-1566)
**STEINBECK BREWING
COMPANY**
Also Called: Buffalo Bills Brewery
1082 B St, Hayward (94541-4108)
PHONE..............................510 888-0695
Geoffrey A Harries, *President*
Jim Crudo, *Director*
EMP: 84
SQ FT: 4,000
SALES (est): 13.7MM **Privately Held**
WEB: www.buffalobillsbrewery.com
SIC: 2082 5812 Beer (alcoholic bever-
age); eating places

(P-1567)
STRAUSS KARL BREWERY AND REST
1044 Wall St Ste C, La Jolla (92037-4437)
PHONE.............................858 551-2739
Chris Cramer, *President*
EMP: 40
SALES (est): 3.8MM **Privately Held**
SIC: 2082 Beer (alcoholic beverage)

(P-1568)
TABLE BLUFF BREWING INC (PA)
Also Called: Lost Coast Brewery & Cafe
617 4th St, Eureka (95501-1013)
PHONE.............................707 445-4480
Barbara Groom, *CEO*
Wendy Pound, *Corp Secy*
Kurt Kovacs, *Vice Pres*
◆ **EMP:** 30
SALES (est): 8.6MM **Privately Held**
WEB: www.lostcoast.com
SIC: 2082 5812 5813 Beer (alcoholic beverage); eating places; bar (drinking places)

(P-1569)
TEMBLOR BREWING LLC
3200 Buck Owens Blvd, Bakersfield (93308-6318)
PHONE.............................661 489-4855
Donald Bynum, *CEO*
EMP: 49
SQ FT: 19,000
SALES (est): 7.5MM **Privately Held**
SIC: 2082 5813 Ale (alcoholic beverage); bars & lounges

(P-1570)
THIRSTY BEAR BREWING CO LLC
661 Howard St, San Francisco (94105-3915)
PHONE.............................415 974-0905
Ragnhild Lorentzen,
Brenden Brewer, *Manager*
Gregg Buczowski, *Manager*
Aleksandra Grozdanic, *Manager*
EMP: 100
SQ FT: 18,000
SALES (est): 14.3MM **Privately Held**
WEB: www.thirstybear.com
SIC: 2082 5812 7299 Beer (alcoholic beverage); eating places; banquet hall facilities

(P-1571)
TOWNE PARK BREW INC
1566 W Lincoln Ave, Anaheim (92801-5850)
PHONE.............................714 844-2492
Brett Lawrence, *President*
EMP: 25
SQ FT: 20,000
SALES: 250K **Privately Held**
SIC: 2082 5149 Beer (alcoholic beverage); beverages, except coffee & tea

(P-1572)
UKIAH BREWING CO LLC
551 Cypress Ave, Ukiah (95482-3923)
PHONE.............................707 468-5898
Bret Cooperrider,
Sid Cooperrider,
Bret Cooperrider,
EMP: 30
SQ FT: 5,000
SALES (est): 600K **Privately Held**
WEB: www.ukiahbrewingco.com
SIC: 2082 5812 Beer (alcoholic beverage); cafe

2084 Wine & Brandy

(P-1573)
3 BADGE BEVERAGE CORPORATION
32 Patten St, Sonoma (95476-6727)
PHONE.............................707 343-1167
Richard Zeller, *President*
August David Sebastiani, *CEO*
Keith Casale, *COO*
Jennifer Klein, *Analyst*

Alice Castorena, *Controller*
EMP: 15
SALES (est): 3MM **Privately Held**
SIC: 2084 Wine cellars, bonded: engaged in blending wines; bottling wines & liquors

(P-1574)
55 DEGREE WINE
3111 Glendale Blvd Ste 2, Los Angeles (90039-1841)
PHONE.............................323 662-5556
Andy Hasroun, *President*
EMP: 10 **EST:** 2008
SALES (est): 685.9K **Privately Held**
SIC: 2084 2082 Wines, brandy & brandy spirits; beer (alcoholic beverage)

(P-1575)
7 & 8 LLC
Also Called: Vineyard 7 & 8
4028 Spring Mountain Rd, Saint Helena (94574-9773)
PHONE.............................707 963-9425
John L Steffens,
James Imbach, *Sales Dir*
Alissa Menchaca, *Director*
Julia Sanchez, *Director*
EMP: 11 **EST:** 2002
SALES (est): 1.4MM **Privately Held**
SIC: 2084 Wines

(P-1576)
ADVANCED VITICULTURE INC
930 Shiloh Rd Bldg 44-E, Windsor (95492-9664)
P.O. Box 2236 (95492-2236)
PHONE.............................707 838-3805
Mark Greenspan, *President*
Linda Greenspan, *Vice Pres*
EMP: 12
SALES (est): 656.9K **Privately Held**
SIC: 2084 0762 0172 0721 Wines; vineyard management & maintenance services; grapes; orchard tree & vine services; scientific consulting

(P-1577)
AGUA DULCE VINEYARDS LLC
9640 Sierra Hwy, Agua Dulce (91390-4622)
PHONE.............................661 268-7402
Raymond A Watt,
Steve Wizan, *General Mgr*
EMP: 20
SALES (est): 3.4MM **Privately Held**
WEB: www.aguadulcevineyards.com
SIC: 2084 5921 Wines; wine

(P-1578)
AH WINES INC
Also Called: Winery Direct Distributors
27 E Vine St, Lodi (95240-4854)
PHONE.............................209 625-8170
Jeffery W Hansen, *President*
Richard Gerlach, *CFO*
Lita Castor, *Associate*
◆ **EMP:** 17
SQ FT: 5,000
SALES (est): 5MM **Privately Held**
SIC: 2084 5182 Wines; wine

(P-1579)
ALFRED DOMAINE
7525 Orcutt Rd, San Luis Obispo (93401-8341)
PHONE.............................805 541-9463
Terry Speizer, *President*
▲ **EMP:** 12
SQ FT: 3,000
SALES (est): 1MM **Privately Held**
WEB: www.domainealfred.com
SIC: 2084 Wines

(P-1580)
ALMA ROSA WINERY VINEYARDS LLC (PA)
181 Industrial Way Ste C, Buellton (93427-9680)
PHONE.............................805 688-9090
J Richard Sanford,
Richard Sanford, *Prdtn Mgr*
EMP: 12
SALES (est): 1.6MM **Privately Held**
SIC: 2084 Wines

(P-1581)
ALPHA OMEGA WINERY LLC
Also Called: Ao Winery
1155 Mee Ln, Saint Helena (94574-9792)
P.O. Box 822, Rutherford (94573-0822)
PHONE.............................707 963-9999
Kenneth Robin Baggett, *Mng Member*
Jeff Knowles, *COO*
Jean Hoefliger, *General Mgr*
Sara Hitchcock, *Business Mgr*
Layla Kajer, *Business Mgr*
▲ **EMP:** 10
SALES (est): 2.2MM **Privately Held**
WEB: www.alphaomegawinery.com
SIC: 2084 Wines

(P-1582)
ANCHOR DISTILLING COMPANY
1705 Mariposa St, San Francisco (94107-2334)
PHONE.............................415 863-8350
Charles Keith Greggor, *President*
Dennis Carr, *Vice Pres*
Lynn Lackey, *VP Mktg*
Ameena Gill, *Director*
Carolyn Stewart, *Director*
◆ **EMP:** 26 **EST:** 1988
SALES (est): 4MM **Privately Held**
SIC: 2084 Wine cellars, bonded: engaged in blending wines

(P-1583)
ANTINORI CALIFORNIA
Also Called: Antica NAPA Valley
3149 Soda Canyon Rd, NAPA (94558-9448)
PHONE.............................707 265-8866
Marchese P Antinori, *President*
▲ **EMP:** 22
SALES (est): 3.5MM **Privately Held**
SIC: 2084 5921 Wines; wine

(P-1584)
ARCHANGEL INVESTMENTS LLC
Also Called: Baldacci Family Vineyard
6236 Silverado Trl, NAPA (94558-9414)
PHONE.............................707 944-9261
Michael Baldacci, *President*
Kellie Duckhorn, *General Mgr*
Elizabeth Burchard, *Director*
EMP: 10
SALES (est): 606.7K **Privately Held**
SIC: 2084 Wines

(P-1585)
ASV WINES INC (PA)
1998 Road 152, Delano (93215-9437)
PHONE.............................661 792-3159
Marko B Zaninovich, *President*
Kent Stephens, *CFO*
Sherry Delay, *Admin Asst*
Andrew Beckwith, *Manager*
▲ **EMP:** 25 **EST:** 1981
SQ FT: 4,000
SALES (est): 4.9MM **Privately Held**
SIC: 2084 Wines

(P-1586)
AVV WINERY CO LLC
Also Called: Alexander Valley Vineyards
8644 Highway 128, Healdsburg (95448-9021)
P.O. Box 175 (95448-0175)
PHONE.............................707 433-7209
Harry H Wetzel III, *Mng Member*
Linda Wetzel, *COO*
Kevin Hall, *Lab Dir*
Hank Wetzel, *Software Engr*
Kara Beaman, *Asst Controller*
▲ **EMP:** 25
SQ FT: 32,000
SALES (est): 5MM **Privately Held**
WEB: www.avvwine.com
SIC: 2084 Wines

(P-1587)
AWG LTD INC
Also Called: Andretti Winery
4162 Big Ranch Rd, NAPA (94558-1405)
PHONE.............................707 259-6777
Mike O' Connell, *President*
Joseph Antonini, *President*
Joe Antonini, *Chairman*
▲ **EMP:** 12

SALES (est): 2MM **Privately Held**
WEB: www.andrettiwinery.com
SIC: 2084 Wines

(P-1588)
B & R VINYARDS INC
4350 Monterey Rd, Gilroy (95020-8029)
P.O. Box 247 (95021-0247)
PHONE.............................408 842-5649
John Rapazzini, *President*
Zondra Rapazzini, *Vice Pres*
EMP: 15
SQ FT: 12,000
SALES (est): 1.1MM **Privately Held**
SIC: 2084 5182 5411 2035 Wines; wine; delicatessens; pickles, sauces & salad dressings

(P-1589)
BAILEY ESSEL WILLIAM JR
Also Called: Knights Bridge Winery
1373 Lincoln Ave, Calistoga (94515-1701)
PHONE.............................707 341-3391
Essel W Bailey, *Owner*
Debi Cali, *General Mgr*
EMP: 10 **EST:** 2015
SALES (est): 301.1K **Privately Held**
SIC: 2084 Wines

(P-1590)
BARBOUR VINEYARDS LLC
104 Camino Dorado, NAPA (94558-6212)
PHONE.............................707 257-1829
Jim Barbour, *Mng Member*
EMP: 90
SALES (est): 13.9MM **Privately Held**
SIC: 2084 Wines

(P-1591)
BARREL TEN QARTER CIR LAND INC (HQ)
6342 Bystrum Rd, Ceres (95307-6652)
P.O. Box 3400, NAPA (94558-0551)
PHONE.............................707 258-0550
Fred T Franzia, *President*
▲ **EMP:** 21
SALES (est): 3.4MM
SALES (corp-wide): 196.9MM **Privately Held**
SIC: 2084 Wines
PA: Bronco Wine Company
6342 Bystrum Rd
Ceres CA 95307
209 538-3131

(P-1592)
BAYWOOD CELLARS INC
Also Called: Hook or Crook Cellars
5573 W Woodbridge Rd, Lodi (95242-9497)
PHONE.............................415 606-4640
William Stokes, *CEO*
John Healy, *Partner*
Allen Lambardi, *Partner*
EMP: 30
SALES: 30MM **Privately Held**
SIC: 2084 Wines

(P-1593)
BEDFORD WINERY
448 Bell St, Los Alamos (93440)
PHONE.............................805 344-2107
Stephan Bedford, *Owner*
EMP: 10
SALES (est): 719.3K **Privately Held**
WEB: www.bedfordthompsonwinery.com
SIC: 2084 Wines

(P-1594)
BELLA VINEYARDS LLC
9711 W Dry Creek Rd, Healdsburg (95448-8113)
PHONE.............................707 473-9171
Scott Adams,
EMP: 10
SALES (est): 1.1MM **Privately Held**
WEB: www.bellawinery.com
SIC: 2084 Wines

(P-1595)
BERNARDO WINERY INC (PA)
13330 Pseo Del Vrano Nrte, San Diego (92128)
PHONE.............................858 487-1866
Ross Rizzo, *President*
Selena Roberts, *General Mgr*

▲ = Import ▼=Export
◆ =Import/Export

Sam Pewitt, *Director*
Veronica Hall-Rizzo, *Manager*
Terry Lowrey, *Manager*
EMP: 20 **EST:** 1932
SALES (est): 1.6MM **Privately Held**
WEB: www.bernardowinery.com
SIC: 2084 5921 7941 Wines; wine; sports field or stadium operator, promoting sports events

(P-1596)
BERNARDUS LLC (PA)
Also Called: Bernardus Winery
5 W Carmel Valley Rd, Carmel Valley (93924)
P.O. Box 1800 (93924-1800)
PHONE..........................831 659-1900
Bernardus Pon, *Mng Member*
Mark Chesebro,
▲ **EMP:** 26
SQ FT: 5,000
SALES (est): 5.3MM **Privately Held**
WEB: www.bernardus.com
SIC: 2084 0172 Wines; grapes

(P-1597)
BERTAGNA ORCHARDS INC
3329 Hegan Ln, Chico (95928-9589)
PHONE..........................530 343-8014
Ben N Bertagna, *President*
Mary Jane Bertagna, *Vice Pres*
EMP: 12
SALES (est): 3MM **Privately Held**
SIC: 2084 Wines

(P-1598)
BFW ASSOCIATES LLC (HQ)
Also Called: Benziger Family Winery
1883 London Ranch Rd, Glen Ellen (95442-9728)
PHONE..........................707 935-3000
David Mackesey, *President*
Stephanie Harland, *Graphic Designe*
Brian Reeves, *VP Sales*
Gerard N Benziger,
Lisa Amaroli, *Director*
▲ **EMP:** 30
SQ FT: 6,000
SALES (est): 6.5MM
SALES (corp-wide): 148.2MM **Privately Held**
WEB: www.benziger.com
SIC: 2084 0172 Wines; grapes
PA: The Wine Group Llc
4596 S Tracy Blvd
Tracy CA 95377
415 986-8700

(P-1599)
BIALE ESTATE
Also Called: Robert Biale Vineyards
4038 Big Ranch Rd, NAPA (94558-1405)
PHONE..........................707 257-7555
Robert A Biale, *Owner*
Chris Dearden, *COO*
Jeannie Coleman, *Administration*
Maggie Pramuk, *Manager*
▲ **EMP:** 10
SALES (est): 1.2MM **Privately Held**
SIC: 2084 Wines

(P-1600)
BLACK STALLION WINERY LLC
4089 Silverado Trl, NAPA (94558-1113)
PHONE..........................707 253-1400
Terrance J Maglich,
Michael G Maglich,
▲ **EMP:** 11
SALES (est): 1MM **Privately Held**
SIC: 2084 Wines

(P-1601)
BOEGER WINERY INC
1709 Carson Rd, Placerville (95667-5195)
PHONE..........................530 622-8094
Greg Boeger, *President*
Susan Boeger, *Treasurer*
EMP: 50
SQ FT: 8,000
SALES (est): 6.9MM **Privately Held**
WEB: www.boegerwinery.com
SIC: 2084 0172 Wines; grapes

(P-1602)
BONNEAU WINES LLC
Also Called: Egret
75 Bonneau Rd, Sonoma (95476-9229)
PHONE..........................707 996-0420
John Bambury, *Mng Member*
Barbara Church, *Administration*
Salman Rehman, *Director*
EMP: 15
SALES (est): 600.1K **Privately Held**
SIC: 2084 Wines

(P-1603)
BONNY DOON VINEYARD (PA)
328 Ingalls St, Santa Cruz (95060-5882)
PHONE..........................831 425-3625
Lisa Kohrf, *Owner*
Sara Rossini, *Executive Asst*
Ed Moya, *Opers Mgr*
Alex Krause, *Sales Executive*
Lindsey Sonu, *Manager*
EMP: 16
SALES (est): 2MM **Privately Held**
SIC: 2084 Wines

(P-1604)
BONNY DOON WINERY INC
328 Ingalls St, Santa Cruz (95060-5882)
PHONE..........................831 425-3625
Randall Grahm, *President*
Lisa Kohrs, *CFO*
Gregory Brady, *General Mgr*
Barbara Smith, *Natl Sales Mgr*
▲ **EMP:** 60
SQ FT: 20,000
SALES (est): 6.5MM **Privately Held**
WEB: www.bonnydoonwinery.com
SIC: 2084 Wines

(P-1605)
BOUCHAINE VINEYARDS INC
Also Called: Bouchaine Wineary
1075 Buchli Station Rd, NAPA (94559-9716)
PHONE..........................707 252-9065
Tatiana Copeland, *President*
Gerret Copeland, *Chairman*
Annie Trimpe, *Office Mgr*
Jennifer Brooks, *Sales Staff*
Chris Kajani, *Manager*
EMP: 18
SQ FT: 35,000
SALES: 3MM **Privately Held**
WEB: www.bouchaine.com
SIC: 2084 5812 Wines; eating places

(P-1606)
BRIDLEWOOD WINERY
Also Called: E and J Gallo
3555 Roblar Ave, Santa Ynez (93460-9724)
PHONE..........................805 688-9000
Ej Gallo, *President*
EMP: 22
SQ FT: 28,000
SALES (est): 2.5MM **Privately Held**
WEB: www.bridlewoodwinery.com
SIC: 2084 5182 Wines; wine

(P-1607)
BROKEN EARTH WINERY
5625 E Highway 46, Paso Robles (93446-6301)
P.O. Box 1498 (93447-1498)
PHONE..........................805 239-2562
Chris Cameron, *Vice Pres*
EMP: 11 **EST:** 2011
SALES (est): 1.3MM **Privately Held**
SIC: 2084 Wines

(P-1608)
BROWN ESTATE VINEYARD LLC
3233 Sage Canyon Rd, Saint Helena (94574-9642)
PHONE..........................707 963-2435
David Brown,
Susan Terracciano, *Sales Mgr*
Coral Brown,
Deann Brown,
Rachael Buckingham, *Supervisor*
EMP: 12
SALES (est): 1.6MM **Privately Held**
WEB: www.brownestate.com
SIC: 2084 Wines

(P-1609)
BRUTOCAO CELLARS (PA)
1400 Highway 175, Hopland (95449-9754)
P.O. Box 780 (95449-0780)
PHONE..........................707 744-1066
Steve Brutocao, *Partner*
Leonard Brutocao, *Partner*
◆ **EMP:** 12
SALES (est): 2.2MM **Privately Held**
WEB: www.brutocaocellars.com
SIC: 2084 Wine cellars, bonded: engaged in blending wines; wines

(P-1610)
BRUTOCAO VINEYARDS
Also Called: Brutocaosellers.com
1400 Highway 175, Hopland (95449-9754)
PHONE..........................707 744-1320
Leonard Brutocao Jr, *Partner*
Daniel Brutocao, *Partner*
David Brutocao, *Partner*
Steven Brutocao, *Partner*
Renee Ortiz, *Partner*
EMP: 20
SQ FT: 5,000
SALES (est): 3MM **Privately Held**
WEB: www.blissvineyard.com
SIC: 2084 Wines

(P-1611)
BURGESS CELLARS INC
1108 Deer Park Rd, Saint Helena (94574-9728)
P.O. Box 282 (94574-0282)
PHONE..........................707 963-4766
Thomas E Burgess, *President*
Charlotte Ryan, *Marketing Staff*
Jim Callahan, *Manager*
EMP: 14
SQ FT: 20,000
SALES (est): 2.4MM **Privately Held**
WEB: www.burgesscellars.com
SIC: 2084 0172 Wines; grapes

(P-1612)
BUTTONWOOD FARM WINERY INC
1500 Alamo Pintado Rd, Solvang (93463-9756)
P.O. Box 1007 (93464-1007)
PHONE..........................805 688-3032
Bret C Davenport, *President*
Elizabeth Williams, *Corp Secy*
Seyburn Zorthian, *Vice Pres*
EMP: 12
SALES (est): 1.9MM **Privately Held**
SIC: 2084 Wines

(P-1613)
C MONDAVI & FAMILY (PA)
Also Called: Charles Krug Winery
2800 Main St, Saint Helena (94574-9502)
P.O. Box 191 (94574-0191)
PHONE..........................707 967-2200
John Lennon, *President*
Peter Mondavi Jr, *Treasurer*
Mark Mondavi, *Admin Sec*
▲ **EMP:** 85 **EST:** 1866
SQ FT: 175,000
SALES (est): 20.7MM **Privately Held**
WEB: www.charleskrug.com
SIC: 2084 0172 Wine cellars, bonded: engaged in blending wines; grapes

(P-1614)
CACCIATORE FINE WNS & OLV OIL (PA)
1875 S Elm St, Pixley (93256-9524)
P.O. Box 923 (93256-0923)
PHONE..........................559 757-9463
Vincent Cacciatore, *President*
EMP: 10
SALES (est): 2.6MM **Privately Held**
WEB: www.cwocorp.com
SIC: 2084 0172 Wines; grapes

(P-1615)
CAIN CELLARS INC
Also Called: Cain Vineyard & Winery
3800 Langtry Rd, Saint Helena (94574-9772)
PHONE..........................707 963-1616
Nancy Medlock, *President*
Shari Coloumbe, *CFO*
James Medlock, *CFO*
William Medlock, *Vice Pres*
Ashley Anderson, *Human Res Mgr*
▲ **EMP:** 20
SQ FT: 30,000
SALES (est): 3.5MM **Privately Held**
WEB: www.cainfive.com
SIC: 2084 5921 Wines; wine

(P-1616)
CAKEBREAD CELLARS
Also Called: Cakebread Cellar Vineyards
8300 Saint Helena Hwy, Rutherford (94573)
P.O. Box 216 (94573-0216)
PHONE..........................707 963-5221
Jack E Cakebread, *CEO*
Bruce Cakebread, *President*
Josef Wally, *CFO*
Dolores Cakebread, *Senior VP*
Dennis Cakebread, *Vice Pres*
▲ **EMP:** 60
SQ FT: 100,000
SALES (est): 11.3MM **Privately Held**
WEB: www.cakebread.com
SIC: 2084 Wines

(P-1617)
CALIPASO WINERY LLC
4230 Buena Vista Dr, Paso Robles (93446-9533)
PHONE..........................805 226-9296
Alan Kinne, *Mng Member*
Sherry Degner, *Office Mgr*
Trevor Iba, *Finance*
Jamee Freitas, *Manager*
EMP: 21
SALES (est): 3.5MM **Privately Held**
SIC: 2084 Wines

(P-1618)
CALLAWAY VINEYARD & WINERY
32720 Rancho Cal Rd, Temecula (92591-4925)
P.O. Box 9014 (92589-9014)
PHONE..........................951 676-4001
Mike Jellison, *President*
Donna Craig, *Sales Staff*
▲ **EMP:** 70 **EST:** 1969
SALES (est): 8.1MM **Privately Held**
SIC: 2084 Wine cellars, bonded: engaged in blending wines; wines

(P-1619)
CANANDAIGUA WINE COMPANY INC
12667 Road 24, Madera (93637-9020)
PHONE..........................559 673-7071
Marvin Sands, *Ch of Bd*
Richard Sands, *President*
Thomas Howe, *Treasurer*
Lynn K Fetterman, *Vice Pres*
James P Finkle, *Vice Pres*
◆ **EMP:** 700
SALES (est): 66.1MM
SALES (corp-wide): 8.1B **Publicly Held**
WEB: www.cbrands.com
SIC: 2084 Wines, brandy & brandy spirits
PA: Constellation Brands, Inc.
207 High Point Dr # 100
Victor NY 14564
585 678-7100

(P-1620)
CARNEROS RANCHING INC
1134 Dealy Ln, NAPA (94559-9706)
PHONE..........................707 253-9464
Francis Mahoney, *President*
EMP: 10
SALES (est): 857.6K **Privately Held**
SIC: 2084 Wines

(P-1621)
CARVALHO FAMILY WINERY LLC
35265 Willow Ave, Clarksburg (95612)
P.O. Box 278 (95612-0278)
PHONE..........................916 744-1615
John Carvalho, *Principal*
Marnie Stiles, *Director*
EMP: 11
SALES (est): 1.4MM **Privately Held**
SIC: 2084 Wines

PRODUCTS & SVCS

(P-1622)
CASTORO CELLARS (PA)
1315 N Bethel Rd, Templeton
(93465-9403)
P.O. Box 954 (93465-0954)
PHONE...................................805 467-2002
Neils Udsen, *President*
Ryan McGuire, *Manager*
▼ **EMP:** 25
SALES (est): 2.7MM **Privately Held**
WEB: www.castorobottling.com
SIC: 2084 Wines

(P-1623)
CEDAR MOUNTAIN WINERY INC
Also Called: Brushy Peak Winery
10843 Reuss Rd, Livermore (94550-9734)
PHONE...................................925 373-6636
Linda Ault, *CEO*
Earl Ault, *Principal*
EMP: 12
SQ FT: 2,500
SALES (est): 1.4MM **Privately Held**
SIC: 2084 Wines

(P-1624)
CELEBRATION CELLARS LLC
Also Called: Miramonte Winery
33410 Rancho Cal Rd, Temecula
(92591-4928)
PHONE...................................951 506-5500
Cane Vanederhoof,
Dawn Zuniga, *Asst Controller*
Jason Bozlak, *Controller*
Sandra Williams,
Michelle Herrera, *Manager*
EMP: 10
SQ FT: 63,000
SALES (est): 2MM **Privately Held**
WEB: www.miramontewinery.com
SIC: 2084 Wines

(P-1625)
CENTRAL COAST WINE WAREHOUSE (PA)
Also Called: Central Coast Wine Services
2717 Aviation Way Ste 101, Santa Maria
(93455-1506)
PHONE...................................805 928-9210
Jim Lunt, *Ltd Ptnr*
Jeff Maiken, *Ltd Ptnr*
▲ **EMP:** 30
SQ FT: 35,000
SALES (est): 5.1MM **Privately Held**
WEB: www.centralcoastwineservices.com
SIC: 2084 5182 7389 Wines; bottling
    wines & liquors; field warehousing

(P-1626)
CHAMBERS & CHAMBERS INC
Also Called: Chambers Chmbers Wine Mr-
chants
14011 Ventura Blvd 210e, Sherman Oaks
(91423-5215)
PHONE...................................818 995-6961
Glen Grisham, *Director*
EMP: 11
SALES (corp-wide): 27MM **Privately
Held**
SIC: 2084 5182 Wines; wine
PA: Chambers & Chambers, Inc.
    2140 Palou Ave
    San Francisco CA 94124
    415 642-5500

(P-1627)
CHAMISAL VINEYARDS LLC
7525 Orcutt Rd, San Luis Obispo
(93401-8341)
PHONE...................................866 808-9463
Andrea De Palo, *Principal*
Norman L Goss, *Principal*
▲ **EMP:** 15
SALES (est): 43.3K
SALES (corp-wide): 67.7MM **Publicly
Held**
SIC: 2084 0172 Wines; grapes
PA: Crimson Wine Group, Ltd.
    2700 Napa Vly Corp Dr B
    Napa CA 94558
    800 486-0503

(P-1628)
CHAPPELLET VINEYARD
1581 Sage Canyon Rd, Saint Helena
(94574-9628)
PHONE...................................707 286-4219
Donn Chappellet,
Andrew Opatz,
EMP: 50
SALES (est): 4.2MM **Privately Held**
SIC: 2084 Wines

(P-1629)
CHAPPELLET WINERY INC (PA)
1581 Sage Canyon Rd, Saint Helena
(94574-9628)
PHONE...................................707 286-4268
Cyril Donn Chappellet, *CEO*
Devonna Smith, *CFO*
David Francke, *Managing Dir*
Erica Alfaro-Lopez, *Executive Asst*
Mary Alice Chappellet, *Admin Sec*
▲ **EMP:** 35
SQ FT: 22,472
SALES (est): 4.2MM **Privately Held**
WEB: www.chappellet.com
SIC: 2084 Wines

(P-1630)
CHATEAU DIANA LLC (PA)
6195 Dry Creek Rd, Healdsburg
(95448-8100)
P.O. Box 1013 (95448-1013)
PHONE...................................707 433-6992
Corey Manning, *Mng Member*
Danna Gibson, *CFO*
Ed Hajeian,
Krystle Lindberg,
Donna Manning,
▲ **EMP:** 15 **EST:** 1978
SQ FT: 8,000
SALES (est): 3.4MM **Privately Held**
WEB: www.chateaud.com
SIC: 2084 Wines

(P-1631)
CHATEAU MASSON LLC
Also Called: Mountain Winery
14831 Pierce Rd, Saratoga (95070-9724)
PHONE...................................408 741-7002
William Hirschman,
Stuart Ferguson,
Jay Campbell, *Director*
Raihni Vaughn, *Director*
EMP: 25
SQ FT: 1,500
SALES (est): 6.2MM **Privately Held**
WEB: www.mountainwinery.com
SIC: 2084 Wines

(P-1632)
CHATEAU MONTELENA WINERY
1429 Tubbs Ln, Calistoga (94515-9726)
PHONE...................................707 942-5105
James L Barrett, *General Ptnr*
Phil Calinda, *Sales Staff*
Bo Barrett,
Matt Crafton,
Cameron Parry,
◆ **EMP:** 30
SQ FT: 22,000
SALES (est): 6.5MM **Privately Held**
WEB: www.chateaumontelena.net
SIC: 2084 0172 Wines; grapes

(P-1633)
CHATEAU POTELLE INC
528 Coombs St, NAPA (94559-3340)
PHONE...................................707 255-9440
Jean Fourmeaux, *President*
Marketta Fourmeaux, *Admin Sec*
▲ **EMP:** 20
SQ FT: 5,000
SALES (est): 2.4MM **Privately Held**
WEB: www.chateaupotelle.com
SIC: 2084 0172 Wines; grapes

(P-1634)
CHATEAU POTELLE HOLDINGS LLC
1200 Dowdell Ln, Saint Helena
(94574-1407)
PHONE...................................707 255-9440
Jean-Noel Fourmeaux, *Principal*
EMP: 13
SALES (est): 1.8MM **Privately Held**
SIC: 2084 Wines

(P-1635)
CLENDENEN LINDQUIST VINTNERS
4665 Santa Maria Mesa Rd, Santa Maria
(93454-9638)
P.O. Box 998 (93456-0998)
PHONE...................................805 937-9801
Jim Clendenen, *President*
Michael Meluskey, *CFO*
EMP: 10
SALES (est): 910.1K **Privately Held**
SIC: 2084 Wines

(P-1636)
CLIFF VINE WINERY INC
7400 Silverado Trl, NAPA (94558-9425)
PHONE...................................707 944-2388
Nell Sweeney, *President*
Tara Valle, *Executive*
EMP: 12
SQ FT: 5,000
SALES (est): 910K **Privately Held**
WEB: www.vinecliff.com
SIC: 2084 5812 Wines; eating places

(P-1637)
CLOS DE LA TECH LLC
575 Eastview Way, Woodside
(94062-4009)
PHONE...................................650 722-3038
Thurman J Rodgers, *Mng Member*
Valeta Massey, *Mng Member*
EMP: 14
SALES (est): 2.7MM **Privately Held**
WEB: www.closdelatech.com
SIC: 2084 Wines

(P-1638)
CLOS DU BOIS WINES INC
Also Called: Constlltion Brnds US Oprations
19410 Geyserville Ave, Geyserville
(95441-9603)
PHONE...................................707 857-1651
Eric Olsen, *President*
Jon Moramarco, *President*
Tom Hobart, *Vice Pres*
Mike Jellison, *Vice Pres*
▲ **EMP:** 35
SALES (est): 5MM **Privately Held**
WEB: www.closdubois.com
SIC: 2084 Wines
HQ: Beam Suntory Inc.
    222 Merchandise Mart Plz # 1600
    Chicago IL 60654
    312 964-6999

(P-1639)
CLOS DU VAL WINE COMPANY LTD
Also Called: Golet Wine Estates
5330 Silverado Trl, NAPA (94558-9410)
PHONE...................................707 259-2200
Bernard Portet, *Chairman*
Jon-Mark Chappellet, *President*
Adam Torpy, *CEO*
Stacy Spring, *Human Res Mgr*
Raquel Royers, *Marketing Mgr*
◆ **EMP:** 50
SQ FT: 32,000
SALES (est): 11.1MM **Privately Held**
WEB: www.closduval.com
SIC: 2084 Wines

(P-1640)
CLOS LA CHANCE WINES INC
1 Hummingbird Ln, San Martin
(95046-9473)
PHONE...................................408 686-1050
Bill Murphy, *Ch of Bd*
Bob Dunnett, *Corp Secy*
Clos Lachance, *VP Sales*
▲ **EMP:** 45
SQ FT: 25,000
SALES (est): 7.1MM **Privately Held**
WEB: www.closlachance.com
SIC: 2084 Wine cellars, bonded: engaged
    in blending wines; wines

(P-1641)
CLOS PEGASE WINERY INC
1060 Dunaweal Ln, Calistoga
(94515-9642)
P.O. Box 305 (94515-0305)
PHONE...................................707 942-4981
Jan Isaac Shrem, *President*

Richard Sowalsky, *Principal*
▲ **EMP:** 30
SALES (est): 6.3MM **Privately Held**
WEB: www.clospegase.com
SIC: 2084 Wines

(P-1642)
COASTAL VINEYARD SERVICES LLC
120 Callie Ct, Arroyo Grande (93420-2939)
PHONE...................................805 441-4465
Kevin Wilkinson, *Principal*
EMP: 11
SALES (est): 1.6MM **Privately Held**
SIC: 2084 Wines

(P-1643)
CODORNIU NAPA INC
Also Called: Artesa Winery
1345 Henry Rd, NAPA (94559-9705)
PHONE...................................707 254-2148
Xavier Pages, *CEO*
Tim O'Leary, *CFO*
Michael Kenton, *Principal*
Susan Sueiro, *General Mgr*
David Gilbreath, *Admin Sec*
▲ **EMP:** 89
SQ FT: 120,000
SALES (est): 14.8MM **Privately Held**
WEB: www.artesawinery.com
SIC: 2084 Wines
HQ: Codorniu Sa
    Avenida Jaume De Codorniu, S/N
    Sant Sadurni D Anoia 08770
    935 051-551

(P-1644)
CONETECH CUSTOM SERVICES LLC
Also Called: Martini Prati Winery
2191 Laguna Rd, Santa Rosa
(95401-3705)
PHONE...................................707 823-2404
Wayne Salk, *Principal*
EMP: 15
SQ FT: 1,280
SALES (est): 1.5MM **Privately Held**
SIC: 2084 Wines

(P-1645)
CONSTELLATION BRANDS INC
1255 Battery St, San Francisco
(94111-1166)
PHONE...................................415 912-3880
Anushil Kumar, *Vice Pres*
Dale Stratton, *Vice Pres*
Michael Walker, *Vice Pres*
Reggie Carey, *Engineer*
Ben Duemler, *VP Finance*
EMP: 38
SALES (corp-wide): 8.1B **Publicly Held**
SIC: 2084 Wines
PA: Constellation Brands, Inc.
    207 High Point Dr # 100
    Victor NY 14564
    585 678-7100

(P-1646)
CONSTELLATION BRANDS INC
Also Called: Dunnewood Vineyards
2399 N State St, Ukiah (95482-3129)
P.O. Box 268 (95482-0268)
PHONE...................................707 467-4840
George Phelan, *Opers-Prdtn-Mfg*
EMP: 20
SALES (corp-wide): 8.1B **Publicly Held**
WEB: www.cbrands.com
SIC: 2084 0172 Wines; grapes
PA: Constellation Brands, Inc.
    207 High Point Dr # 100
    Victor NY 14564
    585 678-7100

(P-1647)
CONSTELLATION BRANDS US OPRS
Also Called: Mission Bell Winery
12667 Road 24, Madera (93637-9020)
PHONE...................................559 485-0141
Michael Othites, *Branch Mgr*
Leticia Motz, *Buyer*
John Prado, *Plant Engr*
EMP: 773
SALES (corp-wide): 8.1B **Publicly Held**
SIC: 2084 Wines

▲ = Import ▼=Export
◆ =Import/Export

HQ: Constellation Brands U.S. Operations, Inc.
235 N Bloomfield Rd
Canandaigua NY 14424
585 396-7600

(P-1648)
CONSTELLATION BRANDS US OPRS
Also Called: Beam Wine Estates
349 Healdsburg Ave, Healdsburg (95448-4137)
PHONE...................707 433-8268
EMP: 773
SALES (corp-wide): 8.1B **Publicly Held**
SIC: 2084 0172 Wines; grapes
HQ: Constellation Brands U.S. Operations, Inc.
235 N Bloomfield Rd
Canandaigua NY 14424
585 396-7600

(P-1649)
COPAIN WINE CELLARS LLC
Also Called: Copain Wine Sellers
7800 Eastside Rd, Healdsburg (95448-9375)
PHONE...................707 836-8822
Clifford J Thomson, *Mng Member*
Wells Guthrie,
EMP: 6
SALES (est): 1.9MM **Privately Held**
SIC: 2084 Wines

(P-1650)
CORBETT CANYON VINEYARDS
2195 Corbett Canyon Rd, Arroyo Grande (93420-4974)
P.O. Box 3159, San Luis Obispo (93403-3159)
PHONE...................805 782-9463
Arthur Ciocca, *President*
Paul Flowers, *Vice Pres*
EMP: 15
SALES (est): 200.1K
SALES (corp-wide): 148.2MM **Privately Held**
WEB: www.corbettcanyon.com
SIC: 2084 Wines
HQ: The Wine Group Inc
17000 E State Highway 120
Ripon CA 95366
209 599-4111

(P-1651)
COSENTINO SIGNATURE WINERIES
Also Called: Cosentino Winery
7415 St Helena Hwy, Yountville (94599)
P.O. Box 2818 (94599-2818)
PHONE...................707 921-2809
Mitch Cosentino, *President*
Larry J Soldinger, *Ch of Bd*
EMP: 22
SQ FT: 7,000
SALES (est): 1.8MM **Privately Held**
WEB: www.cosentinowinery.com
SIC: 2084 Wines

(P-1652)
COURTSIDE CELLARS LLC
2425 Mission St, San Miguel (93451-9556)
PHONE...................805 467-2882
David McHenry, *General Mgr*
EMP: 30
SALES (corp-wide): 5.5MM **Privately Held**
WEB: www.tolosawinery.com
SIC: 2084 Wine cellars, bonded: engaged in blending wines; wines
PA: Courtside Cellars, Llc
4910 Edna Rd
San Luis Obispo CA 93401
805 782-0500

(P-1653)
COURTSIDE CELLARS LLC (PA)
Also Called: Tolosa Winery
4910 Edna Rd, San Luis Obispo (93401-7938)
PHONE...................805 782-0500
Bob Schiebelhut,
Carla Wiley, *CFO*
June McIvor, *General Mgr*
Cathe Lincoln, *Admin Asst*
John Shakley, *Administration*

▲ EMP: 30
SQ FT: 70,000
SALES (est): 5.5MM **Privately Held**
WEB: www.tolosawinery.com
SIC: 2084 Wines

(P-1654)
CREW WINE COMPANY LLC
12300 County Rd 92b, Zamora (95698)
P.O. Box 493 (95698-0493)
PHONE...................530 662-1032
Lane Giguiere,
John Giguiere,
▲ EMP: 10
SALES (est): 1.7MM
SALES (corp-wide): 8.1B **Publicly Held**
SIC: 2084 Wines
PA: Constellation Brands, Inc.
207 High Point Dr # 100
Victor NY 14564
585 678-7100

(P-1655)
DANZA DEL SOL WINERY INC
39050 De Portola Rd, Temecula (92592-8833)
P.O. Box 892889 (92589-2889)
PHONE...................951 302-6363
Robert Olson, *President*
Kelly Hefely, *Merchandise Mgr*
Sean Miller, *Director*
Candice Crawford, *Manager*
Tiffany Smith, *Manager*
EMP: 11
SALES (est): 147K **Privately Held**
SIC: 2084 Wines

(P-1656)
DARIOUSH KHALEDI WINERY LLC
4240 Silverado Trl, NAPA (94558-1117)
PHONE...................707 257-2345
Darioush Khaledi, *Mng Member*
Jessica Hague, *Vice Pres*
Yvette Sherer, *Executive Asst*
Viktoriya Kobzar, *Accounting Mgr*
Edgar Chadez, *Opers Staff*
▲ EMP: 21
SALES (est): 4.3MM **Privately Held**
SIC: 2084 Wines

(P-1657)
DAVID BRUCE WINERY INC
21439 Bear Creek Rd, Los Gatos (95033-9429)
PHONE...................408 354-4214
David Bruce, *Ch of Bd*
EMP: 15
SQ FT: 12,000
SALES (est): 3MM **Privately Held**
WEB: www.davidbrucewinery.com
SIC: 2084 0172 Wines; grapes

(P-1658)
DEERFIELD RANCH WINERY LLC
1310 Warm Springs Rd, Glen Ellen (95442-9709)
PHONE...................707 833-5215
Robert W Rex,
Paulette Rex, *Managing Prtnr*
Robert Rex,
▲ EMP: 10
SQ FT: 4,000
SALES (est): 1.7MM **Privately Held**
WEB: www.deerfieldranch.com
SIC: 2084 Wines

(P-1659)
DELICATO VINEYARDS (PA)
Also Called: Costal Brands
12001 S Highway 99, Manteca (95336-8499)
PHONE...................209 824-3600
Christopher Indelicato, *CEO*
Jolene Yee, *Vice Pres*
Marie Indelicato Mathews, *Admin Sec*
Melissa Graham, *HR Admin*
Alexis Traverso, *Marketing Staff*
◆ EMP: 150
SQ FT: 12,000
SALES (est): 56.2MM **Privately Held**
WEB: www.winequest.com
SIC: 2084 Wines

(P-1660)
DELICATO VINEYARDS
455 Devlin Rd Ste 201, NAPA (94558-7562)
PHONE...................707 265-1700
Chris Indelicato, *Manager*
David De Boer, *Vice Pres*
Randy Wexler, *Regional Mgr*
Greg McKinley, *Administration*
Elizabeth Rice, *Opers Dir*
EMP: 42
SALES (corp-wide): 56.2MM **Privately Held**
WEB: www.winequest.com
SIC: 2084 Wines
PA: Delicato Vineyards
12001 S Highway 99
Manteca CA 95336
209 824-3600

(P-1661)
DELICATO VINEYARDS
4089 Silverado Trl, NAPA (94558-1113)
PHONE...................707 253-1400
Ana Simoes, *Manager*
EMP: 20
SALES (corp-wide): 56.2MM **Privately Held**
SIC: 2084 Wines
PA: Delicato Vineyards
12001 S Highway 99
Manteca CA 95336
209 824-3600

(P-1662)
DELICATO VINEYARDS
Also Called: Cypress Ridge Winery
51955 Oasis Rd, King City (93930-9778)
PHONE...................831 385-7587
Jim Thompson, *Manager*
EMP: 13
SALES (corp-wide): 56.2MM **Privately Held**
WEB: www.winequest.com
SIC: 2084 Wines
PA: Delicato Vineyards
12001 S Highway 99
Manteca CA 95336
209 824-3600

(P-1663)
DEVOTO-WADE LLC
Also Called: Golden State Cider
655 Gold Ridge Rd, Sebastopol (95472-3931)
P.O. Box 117 (95473-0117)
PHONE...................415 265-4461
Chris Lacey, *CEO*
Jolie Devoto-Wade, *Principal*
Hunter Wade, *Principal*
EMP: 11
SALES (est): 1.8MM **Privately Held**
SIC: 2084 Wines, brandy & brandy spirits

(P-1664)
DIAGEO NORTH AMERICA INC
Also Called: Glen Ellen Carneros Winery
21468 8th St E Ste 1, Sonoma (95476-9782)
P.O. Box 1636 (95476-1636)
PHONE...................707 939-6200
Fax: 707 938-2592
EMP: 75
SALES (corp-wide): 16.6B **Privately Held**
SIC: 2084 0172
HQ: Diageo North America Inc.
801 Main Ave
Norwalk CT 06851
203 229-2100

(P-1665)
DIAGEO NORTH AMERICA INC
Also Called: United Distlrs Vintners N Amer
1160 Battery St Ste 30, San Francisco (94111-1215)
PHONE...................415 835-7300
Karen Cass, *Branch Mgr*
EMP: 96
SALES (corp-wide): 16.3B **Privately Held**
SIC: 2084 2082 Wines, brandy & brandy spirits; malt beverages
HQ: Diageo North America Inc.
801 Main Ave
Norwalk CT 06851
203 229-2100

(P-1666)
DIAGEO NORTH AMERICA INC
Also Called: Diageno Chateau & Estate Wines
555 Gateway Dr, NAPA (94558-6291)
PHONE...................707 299-2600
Ray Chadwick, *General Mgr*
Jennifer Morris, *Director*
EMP: 80
SALES (corp-wide): 16.3B **Privately Held**
SIC: 2084 Wines, brandy & brandy spirits
HQ: Diageo North America Inc.
801 Main Ave
Norwalk CT 06851
203 229-2100

(P-1667)
DIAMOND CREEK VINEYARD
1500 Diamond Mountain Rd, Calistoga (94515-9669)
PHONE...................707 942-6926
Adelle Brounstein, *Owner*
Caren Fischer, *Controller*
▲ EMP: 12
SQ FT: 1,799
SALES (est): 1.8MM **Privately Held**
WEB: www.diamondcreekvineyards.com
SIC: 2084 0172 Wines; grapes

(P-1668)
DOGPATCH WINEWORKS
170 Henry St, San Francisco (94114-1217)
PHONE...................415 525-4440
Lynne Carmichael, *Principal*
EMP: 14 EST: 2011
SALES (est): 1.6MM **Privately Held**
SIC: 2084 Wines

(P-1669)
DOMAINE CHANDON INC (DH)
1 California Dr, Yountville (94599-1426)
PHONE...................707 944-8844
Matthew Wood, *CEO*
Greg Godchaux, *Vice Pres*
Lisa Meyer, *Executive*
Remi Foucaud, *Human Res Dir*
Michael Stedman, *Mktg Dir*
▲ EMP: 100 EST: 1973
SQ FT: 240,000
SALES (est): 38MM
SALES (corp-wide): 361.7MM **Privately Held**
WEB: www.chandon.com
SIC: 2084 5812 0762 5813 Wines; eating places; vineyard management & maintenance services; drinking places
HQ: Moet Hennessy Usa, Inc.
85 10th Ave Fl 2
New York NY 10011
212 888-7575

(P-1670)
DOMAINE DE LA TERRE ROUGE
Also Called: Terre Rouge Winery
10801 Dickson Rd, Plymouth (95669)
P.O. Box 41, Fiddletown (95629-0041)
PHONE...................209 245-4277
Bill Easton, *President*
EMP: 10
SALES (est): 1.1MM **Privately Held**
SIC: 2084 5182 Wines; brandy & brandy spirits

(P-1671)
DOMINUS ESTATE CORPORATION
2570 Napa Nook Rd, Yountville (94599-1455)
PHONE...................707 944-8954
Christian Moueix, *President*
Kassidy Harris, *Marketing Mgr*
Julie Levitan, *Director*
▲ EMP: 18
SQ FT: 4,000
SALES (est): 2.4MM **Privately Held**
WEB: www.dominusestate.com
SIC: 2084 Wines

(P-1672)
DRY CREEK VINEYARD INC
3770 Lambert Bridge Rd, Healdsburg (95448-9713)
P.O. Box T (95448-0107)
PHONE...................707 433-1000
Don Wallace,
Joe Czesnakowicz, *General Mgr*

Jerry Smith, *General Mgr*
Laura Levin, *Technician*
Sally Kerstetter, *Human Resources*
▲ **EMP:** 35
SQ FT: 11,000
SALES (est): 7.6MM **Privately Held**
WEB: www.drycreekvineyard.com
SIC: 2084 0172 Wines; grapes

(P-1673)
DUCKHORN WINE COMPANY
14100 Mountain House Rd, Hopland
(95449-9782)
PHONE........................707 744-2800
Daniel J Duckhorn, *President*
Neil Bernardi, *Vice Pres*
EMP: 27
SALES (corp-wide): 33.3MM **Privately
Held**
SIC: 2084 0172 Wines; grapes
HQ: Duckhorn Wine Company
1000 Lodi Ln
Saint Helena CA 94574
707 963-7108

(P-1674)
DUCKHORN WINE COMPANY (HQ)
Also Called: Goldeneye
1000 Lodi Ln, Saint Helena (94574-9410)
PHONE........................707 963-7108
Alex Ryan, *Officer*
Lori Beaudoin, *CFO*
Ashley O'Leary, *Vice Pres*
Caitlin Hartwigsen, *District Mgr*
Scott Miller, *District Mgr*
▲ **EMP:** 40
SALES (est): 11.9MM
SALES (corp-wide): 33.3MM **Privately
Held**
WEB: www.goldeneyewinery.com
SIC: 2084 0172 Wines; grapes
PA: Tsg Consumer Partners, Llc
600 Montgomery St # 2900
San Francisco CA 94111
415 217-2300

(P-1675)
DUCKHORN WINE COMPANY
Also Called: Goldeneye Winery
9200 Highway 128, Philo (95466-9516)
P.O. Box 137 (95466-0137)
PHONE........................707 895-3202
Bob Nye, *Manager*
EMP: 13
SALES (corp-wide): 33.3MM **Privately
Held**
WEB: www.goldeneyewinery.com
SIC: 2084 Wines
HQ: Duckhorn Wine Company
1000 Lodi Ln
Saint Helena CA 94574
707 963-7108

(P-1676)
DUFF BEVILL VINEYARD MANAGMENT
4724 Dry Creek Rd, Healdsburg
(95448-9714)
PHONE........................707 433-6691
Duffern P Bevill, *Owner*
EMP: 35
SALES (est): 2MM **Privately Held**
SIC: 2084 Wines

(P-1677)
DURNEY WINERY CORPORATION
Also Called: Heller State
18820 Cachagua Rd, Carmel Valley
(93924-9393)
P.O. Box 999 (93924-0999)
PHONE........................831 659-2690
Rich Tanguay, *Manager*
EMP: 10
SALES (corp-wide): 853.3K **Privately
Held**
WEB: www.durneywines.com
SIC: 2084 Wines
PA: Durney Winery Corporation
69 W Carmel Valley Rd
Carmel Valley CA 93924
831 659-6220

(P-1678)
E & J GALLO WINERY (PA)
Also Called: California Natural Color
600 Yosemite Blvd, Modesto (95354-2760)
P.O. Box 1130 (95353-1130)
PHONE........................209 341-3111
Joseph E Gallo, *CEO*
Chris Kalabokes, *Vice Pres*
Tom Odonnell, *Principal*
Allissa Curtis, *Executive Asst*
Valentin Khoubiar, *Planning*
◆ **EMP:** 2500
SALES (est): 2.3B **Privately Held**
WEB: www.gallo.com
SIC: 2084 0172 Wines; grapes

(P-1679)
E & J GALLO WINERY
5610 E Olive Ave, Fresno (93727-2707)
P.O. Box 1081 (93714-1081)
PHONE........................559 458-0807
Joe Rossi, *Branch Mgr*
Craig Trzepkowski, *Software Engr*
Phillip Moore, *Engineer*
Jenna Cervantez, *Training Spec*
Kent Johnson, *Buyer*
EMP: 140
SALES (corp-wide): 2.3B **Privately Held**
WEB: www.gallo.com
SIC: 2084 0172 Wines; grapes
PA: E. & J. Gallo Winery
600 Yosemite Blvd
Modesto CA 95354
209 341-3111

(P-1680)
E & J GALLO WINERY
Also Called: San Joaquin Vly Concentrates
5631 E Olive Ave, Fresno (93727-2708)
PHONE........................559 458-2500
Gary Schmidt, *Principal*
Phillip Prull, *Business Anlyst*
Kai Loo, *QC Mgr*
Thomas Lampe, *Sales Mgr*
EMP: 57
SALES (corp-wide): 2.3B **Privately Held**
WEB: www.gallo.com
SIC: 2084 Wines
PA: E. & J. Gallo Winery
600 Yosemite Blvd
Modesto CA 95354
209 341-3111

(P-1681)
E & J GALLO WINERY
Also Called: Gallo Os Sonoma
3387 Dry Creek Rd, Healdsburg
(95448-9740)
PHONE........................707 431-1946
Wayne Van Wagner, *Director*
Christine Hansen, *Engineer*
Gary Vanderwerff, *Engineer*
Dan Michael, *Mktg Dir*
EMP: 20
SQ FT: 2,700
SALES (corp-wide): 2.3B **Privately Held**
WEB: www.gallo.com
SIC: 2084 0172 Wines; grapes
PA: E. & J. Gallo Winery
600 Yosemite Blvd
Modesto CA 95354
209 341-3111

(P-1682)
E & J GALLO WINERY
2101 Yosemite Blvd, Modesto
(95354-3024)
PHONE........................209 341-3111
Joseph E Gallo, *CEO*
William McMorran, *Vice Pres*
Mark Barry, *Managing Dir*
Brant Scott, *Regional Mgr*
Corona Mary Slan, *General Mgr*
EMP: 19
SALES (corp-wide): 2.3B **Privately Held**
SIC: 2084 Wines
PA: E. & J. Gallo Winery
600 Yosemite Blvd
Modesto CA 95354
209 341-3111

(P-1683)
E & J GALLO WINERY
Also Called: Lerexa Winery
18000 River Rd, Livingston (95334-9514)
PHONE........................209 394-6215

Kent Mann, *Manager*
Jonathan Lockhart, *Technician*
Justin Ferreria, *Engineer*
James Mulhearn, *Engineer*
Isaac Ochoa, *Train & Dev Mgr*
EMP: 250
SALES (est): 2.3B **Privately Held**
WEB: www.gallo.com
SIC: 2084 0172 Wines; grapes
PA: E. & J. Gallo Winery
600 Yosemite Blvd
Modesto CA 95354
209 341-3111

(P-1684)
E & J GALLO WINERY
Also Called: Edna Valley Vineyard
2585 Biddle Ranch Rd, San Luis Obispo
(93401-8319)
PHONE........................805 544-5855
Josh Baker, *Branch Mgr*
Ariana Tway, *Associate*
EMP: 209
SALES (corp-wide): 2.3B **Privately Held**
SIC: 2084 Wines
PA: E. & J. Gallo Winery
600 Yosemite Blvd
Modesto CA 95354
209 341-3111

(P-1685)
E & J GALLO WINERY
2650 Commerce Way, Commerce
(90040-1413)
PHONE........................323 720-6400
Bob Gillespie, *Opers Mgr*
Candice Mosley, *Sales Staff*
EMP: 300
SALES (corp-wide): 2.3B **Privately Held**
SIC: 2084 Wines
PA: E. & J. Gallo Winery
600 Yosemite Blvd
Modesto CA 95354
209 341-3111

(P-1686)
E & J GALLO WINERY
Also Called: Louis M. Martini Winery
254 Saint Helena Hwy S, Saint Helena
(94574-2203)
PHONE........................707 963-2736
Ernest Gallo, *Ch of Bd*
EMP: 50
SALES (corp-wide): 2.3B **Privately Held**
WEB: www.gallo.com
SIC: 2084 0172 Wines; grapes
PA: E. & J. Gallo Winery
600 Yosemite Blvd
Modesto CA 95354
209 341-3111

(P-1687)
E & J GALLO WINERY
Also Called: Gallo Advertising
200 E Sandy Blvd, Modesto (95354)
P.O. Box 1348 (95353-1348)
PHONE........................209 341-7862
Pat Broughton, *Principal*
Sarah Bar, *Project Mgr*
Dante Stovall, *Engineer*
EMP: 13
SALES (corp-wide): 2.3B **Privately Held**
WEB: www.gallo.com
SIC: 2084 Wines
PA: E. & J. Gallo Winery
600 Yosemite Blvd
Modesto CA 95354
209 341-3111

(P-1688)
ELLISTON VINEYARDS INC
463 Kilkare Rd, Sunol (94586-9415)
PHONE........................925 862-2377
Donna Flavetta, *President*
EMP: 55
SQ FT: 1,000
SALES (est): 5.9MM **Privately Held**
WEB: www.elliston.com
SIC: 2084 Wines; wine cellars, bonded:
engaged in blending wines

(P-1689)
ENVY WINES LLC
1170 Tubbs Ln, Calistoga (94515-1054)
PHONE........................707 942-4670

Mark J Carter, *Mng Member*
Nils Venge,
▲ **EMP:** 11
SALES (est): 1.7MM **Privately Held**
SIC: 2084 Wines

(P-1690)
EOS ESTATE WINERY
2300 Airport Rd, Paso Robles
(93446-8549)
PHONE........................805 239-2562
Frank Arciero, *Partner*
Phil Arciero, *Partner*
Fern Underwood, *Partner*
▲ **EMP:** 47
SALES (est): 5.9MM **Privately Held**
WEB: www.eosvintage.com
SIC: 2084 0172 3172 Wines; grapes; per-
sonal leather goods

(P-1691)
ESCALERA-BOULET LLC
Also Called: Consilience Converge
2923 Grand Ave, Los Olivos (93441-4403)
P.O. Box 529 (93441-0529)
PHONE........................805 691-1020
William Sanger, *Mng Member*
Jodie Boulet Daughters, *Administration*
EMP: 10
SALES (est): 690.4K **Privately Held**
SIC: 2084 Wines

(P-1692)
ESTANCIA ESTATES
980 Bryant Cyn, Soledad (93960-2830)
PHONE........................707 431-1975
Richard Sands, *President*
▲ **EMP:** 72
SALES (est): 5.2MM **Privately Held**
WEB: www.estanciaestates.com
SIC: 2084 Wines

(P-1693)
ETUDE WINES INC
1250 Cuttings Wharf Rd, NAPA
(94559-9738)
P.O. Box 3382 (94558-0338)
PHONE........................707 257-5300
Jon Priest, *Manager*
David Cone, *Sales Staff*
Tammy White, *Sales Staff*
Melanie Edwards, *Manager*
EMP: 16
SQ FT: 6,000
SALES (est): 2MM **Privately Held**
WEB: www.etudewines.com
SIC: 2084 Wines

(P-1694)
F KORBEL & BROS (PA)
Also Called: Korbel Champagne Cellers
13250 River Rd, Guerneville (95446-9593)
PHONE........................707 824-7000
Gary B Heck, *President*
David Faris, *Treasurer*
Brian McClusky, *Treasurer*
Andrew Matthias, *Officer*
Dan Baker, *Exec VP*
▲ **EMP:** 300
SQ FT: 66,000
SALES (est): 98.2MM **Privately Held**
WEB: www.korbel.com
SIC: 2084 0172 Wines; grapes

(P-1695)
F KORBEL & BROS
Also Called: Heck Cellars
15401 Bear Mtn Winery Rd, Di Giorgio
(93203-9743)
PHONE........................661 854-6120
Guy Ruhland, *Opers-Prdtn-Mfg*
Bryan Walsh, *Manager*
EMP: 36
SQ FT: 250,000
SALES (corp-wide): 98.2MM **Privately
Held**
WEB: www.korbel.com
SIC: 2084 0172 Wines; grapes
PA: F. Korbel & Bros.
13250 River Rd
Guerneville CA 95446
707 824-7000

▲ = Import ▼=Export
◆ =Import/Export

(P-1696)
FALKNER WINERY INC
40620 Calle Contento, Temecula
(92591-5041)
PHONE..................................951 676-6741
Ray Falkner, *CEO*
Loretta Falkner, *Principal*
Holly Estrema, *Manager*
Teri Lee, *Manager*
EMP: 65
SALES (est): 10.1MM **Privately Held**
WEB: www.falknerwinery.com
SIC: 2084 7299 Wines; banquet hall facilities

(P-1697)
FANUCCICHARTER OAK WINERY
831 Charter Oak Ave, Saint Helena
(94574-1311)
PHONE..................................707 963-2298
Robert M Fanucci, *Principal*
▲ EMP: 10 EST: 2010
SALES (est): 724.3K **Privately Held**
SIC: 2084 Wines

(P-1698)
FAR NIENTE WINERY INC
Also Called: Far Niente Wine Estates
1350 Acacia Dr, Oakville (94562)
P.O. Box 327 (94562-0327)
PHONE..................................707 944-2861
Larry Maguire, *CEO*
Erik Nickel, *Partner*
Jeremy Nickel, *Partner*
Laura Harwood, *CFO*
Mary Grace, *Vice Pres*
▲ EMP: 100
SQ FT: 30,000
SALES (est): 24.1MM **Privately Held**
WEB: www.farniente.com
SIC: 2084 Wines

(P-1699)
FERRAR-CRANO VNYRDS WINERY LLC (PA)
Also Called: Prevail Wines
8761 Dry Creek Rd, Healdsburg
(95448-9133)
P.O. Box 1549 (95448-1549)
PHONE..................................707 433-6700
Donald L Carano, *Mng Member*
Jim Boswell, *Manager*
Teri Rolleri, *Manager*
Melissa Rush, *Manager*
▲ EMP: 110
SQ FT: 46,000
SALES (est): 22.5MM **Privately Held**
WEB: www.fcwinery.com
SIC: 2084 0172 Wines; grapes

(P-1700)
FETZER VINEYARDS (HQ)
12901 Old River Rd, Hopland
(95449-9813)
P.O. Box 611 (95449-0611)
PHONE..................................707 744-1250
Eduardo Guilisasti Gana, *CEO*
Wade Grote, *President*
Sid Goldstein, *Vice Pres*
Penny Kosut, *Vice Pres*
Dennis Martin, *Vice Pres*
◆ EMP: 242
SALES (est): 66.8MM **Privately Held**
WEB: www.earlytimes.com
SIC: 2084 Wines

(P-1701)
FETZER VINEYARDS
Also Called: Fetzer Production Facility
8998 N River Rd, Paso Robles
(93446-6334)
PHONE..................................805 467-0192
Will Roddick, *Branch Mgr*
EMP: 19 **Privately Held**
WEB: www.earlytimes.com
SIC: 2084 Wines
HQ: Fetzer Vineyards
12901 Old River Rd
Hopland CA 95449
707 744-1250

(P-1702)
FIELD STONE WINERY & VINEYARD
10075 Highway 128, Healdsburg
(95448-9025)
PHONE..................................707 433-7266
John C Staten, *President*
Ben Staten, *Corp Secy*
Staten Katrina J, *Vice Pres*
Katrina J Staten, *Vice Pres*
EMP: 12
SQ FT: 4,000
SALES (est): 1.7MM **Privately Held**
WEB: www.fieldstonewinery.com
SIC: 2084 5921 Wines; wine

(P-1703)
FIRESTONE VINEYARD LP
Also Called: Curtis Winery
5000 Zaca Station Rd, Los Olivos
(93441-4566)
P.O. Box 244 (93441-0244)
PHONE..................................805 688-3940
Michael L Gravelle, *Partner*
Adam Firestone, *Partner*
Alan Kuper, *Sales Mgr*
▲ EMP: 85
SQ FT: 45,000
SALES (est): 9.4MM
SALES (corp-wide): 109.6MM **Privately Held**
WEB: www.firestonewine.com
SIC: 2084 0172 Wines; grapes
HQ: Foley Family Wines, Inc.
200 Concourse Blvd
Paso Robles CA 93446

(P-1704)
FLOOD RANCH COMPANY
Also Called: Rancho Sisquoc Winery
6600 Foxen Canyon Rd, Santa Maria
(93454-9656)
PHONE..................................805 937-3616
Ed A Holt, *Manager*
Becki Rodriguez, *Manager*
EMP: 15
SALES (est): 2.7MM
SALES (corp-wide): 2.6MM **Privately Held**
SIC: 2084 Wines
PA: Flood Ranch Company
870 Market St Ste 1100
San Francisco CA 94102
415 982-5645

(P-1705)
FLORA SPRINGS WINE COMPANY
1978 Zinfandel Ln, Saint Helena
(94574-1611)
PHONE..................................707 963-5711
John Komes, *President*
Martha Komes, *Manager*
Julie Garvey, *Vice Pres*
Patrick Garvey, *Vice Pres*
Elisa Sherburne, *Vice Pres*
▲ EMP: 19
SQ FT: 16,000
SALES (est): 3.5MM **Privately Held**
SIC: 2084 Wines

(P-1706)
FLOWERS VINEYARD & WINERY LLC
28500 Seaview Rd, Cazadero
(95421-9767)
PHONE..................................707 847-3661
Jason Jardine, *President*
Christina Zapel, *Production*
▲ EMP: 15
SALES (est): 2.6MM **Privately Held**
WEB: www.flowerswinery.com
SIC: 2084 Wines

(P-1707)
FOLEY FAMILY WINES INC (HQ)
Also Called: Foley Wine Group
200 Concourse Blvd, Paso Robles (93446)
PHONE..................................707 708-7600
William Patrick Foley II, *CEO*
Shawn Schiffer, *President*
Melanie Sandoval, *Executive Asst*
Torrence Reed, *Administration*
Brittany Carte, *Accountant*

◆ EMP: 58
SALES (est): 109.6MM **Privately Held**
SIC: 2084 0172 Wines; grapes
PA: Foley Family Wines Holdings, Inc.
200 Concourse Blvd
Santa Rosa CA 95403
805 688-3940

(P-1708)
FOX BARREL CIDER COMPANY INC
1213 S Auburn St Ste A, Colfax
(95713-9800)
P.O. Box 753 (95713-0753)
PHONE..................................530 346-9699
Bruce Nissen, *President*
Sean Deorsey, *CFO*
EMP: 50
SALES (est): 5.1MM
SALES (corp-wide): 10.7B **Publicly Held**
WEB: www.foxbarrel.com
SIC: 2084 Wines
HQ: Crispin Cider Company
3939 W Highland Blvd
Milwaukee WI 53208
530 346-9699

(P-1709)
FRANCIS FORD CPPOLA PRSNTS LLC
Also Called: Francis Ford Coppola Winery
300 Via Archimedes, Geyserville
(95441-9325)
PHONE..................................707 251-3200
Francis Coppola, *Mng Member*
Wendy Putman,
◆ EMP: 20
SALES: 6.4MM **Privately Held**
SIC: 2084 Wines

(P-1710)
FRANCISCAN VINEYARDS INC
Also Called: Ravenswood Winery
18701 Gehricke Rd, Sonoma (95476-4710)
PHONE..................................707 933-2332
Joel Peterson, *Branch Mgr*
William Skowronski, *CFO*
Sara Tarango, *Marketing Mgr*
Cathleen Francisco, *Manager*
EMP: 188
SALES (corp-wide): 8.1B **Publicly Held**
WEB: www.ravenswood-wine.com
SIC: 2084 5921 Wines; wine
HQ: Franciscan Vineyards Inc.
1178 Galleron Rd
Saint Helena CA 94574
707 963-7111

(P-1711)
FRANCISCAN VINEYARDS INC
Also Called: Woodbridge Winery
5950 E Woodbridge Rd, Acampo
(95220-9429)
P.O. Box 1260, Woodbridge (95258-1260)
PHONE..................................209 369-5861
Mark Garbrielli, *Manager*
EMP: 300
SQ FT: 2,450
SALES (corp-wide): 8.1B **Publicly Held**
WEB: www.robertmondaviwinery.com
SIC: 2084 Wines
HQ: Franciscan Vineyards Inc.
1178 Galleron Rd
Saint Helena CA 94574
707 963-7111

(P-1712)
FRANCISCAN VINEYARDS INC (HQ)
1178 Galleron Rd, Saint Helena
(94574-9790)
PHONE..................................707 963-7111
Agustin Francisco Huneeus, *President*
Bill Skowronski, *CFO*
▲ EMP: 75
SQ FT: 110,000
SALES (est): 51.1MM
SALES (corp-wide): 8.1B **Publicly Held**
WEB: www.ravenswood-wine.com
SIC: 2084 Wines
PA: Constellation Brands, Inc.
207 High Point Dr # 100
Victor NY 14564
585 678-7100

(P-1713)
FRANCISCAN VINYARDS INC
Also Called: Simi Winery
16275 Healdsburg Ave, Healdsburg
(95448-9075)
P.O. Box 698 (95448-0698)
PHONE..................................707 433-6981
Hustin Huneeus, *President*
▲ EMP: 75
SALES (est): 6.8MM
SALES (corp-wide): 8.1B **Publicly Held**
WEB: www.simiwinery.com
SIC: 2084 0172 5812 Wines; grapes; eating places
PA: Constellation Brands, Inc.
207 High Point Dr # 100
Victor NY 14564
585 678-7100

(P-1714)
FRANZIA/SANGER WINERY
Also Called: Franzia Winery
17000 E State Highway 120, Ripon
(95366-9412)
PHONE..................................209 599-4111
Arthur Ciocca, *Partner*
F Lynn Bates, *Partner*
Craig Calders, *Sales Staff*
▲ EMP: 200 EST: 1933
SQ FT: 160,000
SALES (est): 38.2MM **Privately Held**
SIC: 2084 Wines

(P-1715)
FREEMARK ABBEY WNERY LTD PRTNR
3022 Saint Helena Hwy N, Saint Helena
(94574-9652)
P.O. Box 410 (94574-0410)
PHONE..................................707 963-9694
John Bryan,
Reed Kimberly, *Director*
Barry Dodds, *Manager*
Russell Flood, *Supervisor*
Clint Smith, *Supervisor*
EMP: 20
SQ FT: 4,500
SALES (est): 1.9MM **Privately Held**
SIC: 2084 0172 Wines; grapes

(P-1716)
FREIXENET SONOMA CAVES INC
Also Called: Gloria Ferrer Winery
23555 Arnold Dr, Sonoma (95476-9285)
P.O. Box 1949 (95476-1949)
PHONE..................................707 996-4981
Jose M Ferrer, *CEO*
Diego Jimenez, *President*
▲ EMP: 40
SQ FT: 4,000
SALES (est): 8.8MM
SALES (corp-wide): 242.4MM **Privately Held**
SIC: 2084 5812 Wines; eating places
PA: Freixenet Sa
Plaza Joan Sala 2
Sant Sadurni D Anoia 08770
938 917-000

(P-1717)
FROGS LEAP WINERY
8815 Conn Creek Rd, Rutherford (94573)
P.O. Box 189 (94573-0189)
PHONE..................................707 963-4704
John T Williams, *President*
Leah S White, *Executive Asst*
Kristy Byrd, *Sales Mgr*
Carolyn Dallara, *Sales Associate*
Pablo Polanco, *Master*
◆ EMP: 36
SQ FT: 8,000
SALES (est): 6.1MM **Privately Held**
WEB: www.frogsleap.com
SIC: 2084 Wines

(P-1718)
GALLEANO ENTERPRISES INC
4231 Wineville Ave, Jurupa Valley
(91752-1412)
PHONE..................................951 685-5376
Donald Galleano, *President*
Charlene Galleano, *Vice Pres*
EMP: 100

SALES (est): 7.2MM **Privately Held**
SIC: 2084 Wines

(P-1719)
GANDONA INC A CALIFORNIA CORP
1535 Sage Canyon Rd, Saint Helena (94574-9628)
PHONE..................................707 967-5550
Manuel Pires, *President*
EMP: 10
SALES (est): 876.9K **Privately Held**
SIC: 2084 Wines

(P-1720)
GEKKEIKAN SAKE USAINC
1136 Sibley St, Folsom (95630-3223)
PHONE..................................916 985-3111
Masahiro Namise, *CEO*
Yu Hyodo, *Admin Sec*
◆ **EMP:** 25
SQ FT: 390,000
SALES (est): 7.4MM **Privately Held**
WEB: www.gekkeikan-sake.com
SIC: 2084 Wines
PA: Gekkeikan Sake Company,Ltd.
    247, Minamihamacho, Fushimi-Ku
    Kyoto KYO 612-8
    -

(P-1721)
GEORIS WINERY
4 Pilot Rd, Carmel Valley (93924-9515)
PHONE..................................831 659-1050
Walter Georgis, *Owner*
▲ **EMP:** 10
SALES (est): 1.3MM **Privately Held**
WEB: www.georiswine.com
SIC: 2084 Wines

(P-1722)
GEYSER PEAK WINERY
Also Called: Canyon Road Winery
2306 Magnolia Dr, Healdsburg (95448-9406)
PHONE..................................707 857-9463
Stephen Brower, *President*
Tim Matz, *Director*
▲ **EMP:** 45
SALES (est): 7.1MM **Privately Held**
SIC: 2084 Wines

(P-1723)
GIBSON WINE COMPANY
1720 Academy Ave, Sanger (93657-3704)
PHONE..................................559 875-2505
Wayne Albrecht, *CEO*
Donald Weber, *Treasurer*
Kim Spruance, *Admin Sec*
EMP: 25 **EST:** 1939
SQ FT: 2,000
SALES (est): 6.7MM
SALES (corp-wide): 196.9MM **Privately Held**
SIC: 2084 Wines
PA: Bronco Wine Company
    6342 Bystrum Rd
    Ceres CA 95307
    209 538-3131

(P-1724)
GIMELLI VINEYARDS
403 Grass Valley Rd, Hollister (95023-9621)
PHONE..................................831 637-5445
Ken Gimelli, *Owner*
EMP: 12
SQ FT: 500
SALES (est): 1.1MM **Privately Held**
SIC: 2084 Wines

(P-1725)
GNEKOW FAMILY WINERY LLC
17347 E Gawne Rd, Stockton (95215-9646)
PHONE..................................209 463-0697
Sean Gnekow,
Rudy Gnekow,
EMP: 14
SQ FT: 18,000
SALES (est): 2.3MM **Privately Held**
SIC: 2084 Wines

(P-1726)
GOLDEN STATE VINTNERS (PA)
4596 S Tracy Blvd, Tracy (95377-8106)
PHONE..................................707 254-4900
Brian Jay Vos, *CEO*
John Oliver Sutton, *CFO*
▼ **EMP:** 15
SQ FT: 8,000
SALES (est): 49.7MM **Privately Held**
SIC: 2084 Wines; brandy

(P-1727)
GOLDEN STATE VINTNERS
1075 Golden Gate Dr, NAPA (94558-6187)
PHONE..................................707 254-1985
Mike Blom,
EMP: 49
SALES (corp-wide): 49.7MM **Privately Held**
SIC: 2084 Wine cellars, bonded: engaged in blending wines
PA: Golden State Vintners
    4596 S Tracy Blvd
    Tracy CA 95377
    707 254-4900

(P-1728)
GOLDEN STATE VINTNERS
1777 Metz Rd, Soledad (93960-2805)
PHONE..................................831 678-3991
Jay Clark, *Manager*
EMP: 34
SALES (corp-wide): 49.7MM **Privately Held**
SIC: 2084 0172 Wines; grapes
PA: Golden State Vintners
    4596 S Tracy Blvd
    Tracy CA 95377
    707 254-4900

(P-1729)
GOLDEN STATE VINTNERS
1175 Commmerce Blvd, Vallejo (94503)
PHONE..................................707 553-6480
Jeff Neil, *Branch Mgr*
EMP: 27
SALES (corp-wide): 49.7MM **Privately Held**
SIC: 2084 Wines; brandy & brandy spirits
PA: Golden State Vintners
    4596 S Tracy Blvd
    Tracy CA 95377
    707 254-4900

(P-1730)
GOLDEN VLY GRAPE JICE WINE LLC (PA)
11770 Road 27 1/2, Madera (93637-9108)
PHONE..................................559 661-4657
Gerard Pantaleo, *Mng Member*
Rodger Williams, *Sales Staff*
Frank Pantaleo,
Jerry Pantaleo,
Nicholas Pantaleo,
▲ **EMP:** 40
SALES (est): 19.9MM **Privately Held**
SIC: 2084 Wines

(P-1731)
GOLDSTONE LAND COMPANY LLC
Also Called: Bear Creek Winery
11900 Furry Rd, Lodi (95240-7201)
PHONE..................................209 368-3113
Joan M Kautz, *Mng Member*
Craig Rous, *Opers Staff*
Tom Rappe, *Sales Executive*
Stan Hall, *Maintence Staff*
Stephen J Kautz, *Mng Member*
◆ **EMP:** 30
SALES (est): 6.6MM **Privately Held**
SIC: 2084 Wines

(P-1732)
GOOSECROSS CELLARS A CAL CORP
1119 State Ln, Yountville (94599-9407)
PHONE..................................707 944-1986
David Topper, *CEO*
Geoffrey Gorsuch, *Vice Pres*
EMP: 14
SALES (est): 1.8MM **Privately Held**
SIC: 2084 Wine cellars, bonded: engaged in blending wines; wines

(P-1733)
GOOSECROSS CELLARS COORSTEK
1119 State Ln, Yountville (94599-9407)
PHONE..................................707 944-1986
Christi Coors Ficeli, *CEO*
EMP: 14
SALES (est): 25.3K **Privately Held**
WEB: www.goosecross.com
SIC: 2084 5921 Wines; wine

(P-1734)
GRAPE LINKS INC
Also Called: Barefoot Cellars
420 Aviation Blvd Ste 106, Santa Rosa (95403-1039)
P.O. Box 1130, Modesto (95353-1130)
PHONE..................................707 524-8000
Michael C Houlihan, *President*
Martin A Jones, *Exec VP*
Bonnie Harvey, *Vice Pres*
Jennifer Wall, *Admin Sec*
Aaron J Fein, *Sales Staff*
EMP: 17
SQ FT: 4,200
SALES (est): 1.8MM
SALES (corp-wide): 2.3B **Privately Held**
WEB: www.barefootcellars.com
SIC: 2084 Wines
PA: E. & J. Gallo Winery
    600 Yosemite Blvd
    Modesto CA 95354
    209 341-3111

(P-1735)
GREAT AMERICAN WINERIES INC
2511 Garden Rd Ste B100, Monterey (93940-5344)
P.O. Box 444, New York NY (10272-0444)
PHONE..................................831 920-4736
Robert S Brower Sr, *President*
Robert S Brower, *President*
Patricia Brower, *Vice Pres*
EMP: 20 **EST:** 1982
SQ FT: 14,000
SALES (est): 3.3MM **Privately Held**
SIC: 2084 5182 Wines; wine

(P-1736)
GREGORY GRAZIANO
Also Called: Domaine Saint Gregory
1170 Bel Arbres Dr, Redwood Valley (95470-9695)
PHONE..................................707 485-9463
Gregory Graziano, *Owner*
EMP: 10
SQ FT: 35,000
SALES (est): 852.8K **Privately Held**
SIC: 2084 Wines

(P-1737)
GRGICH HILLS CELLAR
Also Called: G and H Vineyards
1829 St Helena Hwy, Rutherford (94573)
P.O. Box 450 (94573-0450)
PHONE..................................707 963-2784
Miljenko Mike Grgich, *President*
Austin E Hills, *Shareholder*
Violet Grgich, *Corp Secy*
Ivo Jeramaz, *Vice Pres*
Shannon Willison, *Accounting Mgr*
▲ **EMP:** 35
SQ FT: 43,000
SALES (est): 7.4MM **Privately Held**
WEB: www.grgich.com
SIC: 2084 5812 0172 Wines; eating places; grapes

(P-1738)
GROSKOPF WAREHOUSE & LOGISTICS
20580 8th St E, Sonoma (95476-9590)
P.O. Box 128, Vineburg (95487-0128)
PHONE..................................707 939-3100
Alec Merriam, *Owner*
Shelly Levin, *Human Res Dir*
Todd Finch, *Manager*
▲ **EMP:** 41 **EST:** 2001
SALES (est): 16MM **Privately Held**
WEB: www.groskopf.com
SIC: 2084 Wines

(P-1739)
GROWEST INC (PA)
Also Called: Growest Development
10490 Dawson Canyon Rd, Corona (92883-4139)
PHONE..................................951 638-1000
John Bremer, *President*
Chandra Sanjay, *Director*
EMP: 15
SQ FT: 10,000
SALES (est): 11.4MM **Privately Held**
SIC: 2084 5193 Wines; nursery stock

(P-1740)
GUENOC WINERY INC
Also Called: Langtry Estates and Vineyards
200 Concourse Blvd, Santa Rosa (95403-8210)
PHONE..................................707 987-2385
Easton Manson, *President*
Michael Schochet, *CFO*
EMP: 32
SALES (est): 5MM **Privately Held**
WEB: www.guenoc.com
SIC: 2084 Wine cellars, bonded: engaged in blending wines; wines

(P-1741)
HAGAFEN CELLARS INC
4160 Silverado Trl, NAPA (94558-1118)
PHONE..................................707 252-0781
Ernie Weir, *President*
Irit Weir, *Vice Pres*
▲ **EMP:** 12
SQ FT: 6,000
SALES (est): 1.8MM **Privately Held**
WEB: www.hagafen.com
SIC: 2084 Wines

(P-1742)
HAHN ESTATE
Also Called: Smith & Hook Winery Inc
37700 Foothill Rd, Soledad (93960-9620)
P.O. Box C (93960-0167)
PHONE..................................831 678-2132
Philip Hahn, *CEO*
Nicolaus Hahn, *Ch of Bd*
Gabrielle Hahn, *Admin Sec*
Ashley Hagewood, *Administration*
Brandon Allen, *Mktg Coord*
▲ **EMP:** 55
SQ FT: 25,000
SALES (est): 9.4MM
SALES (corp-wide): 19.7MM **Privately Held**
SIC: 2084 0172 Wines; grapes
PA: Kvl Holdings, Inc.
    37700 Foothill Rd
    Soledad CA 93960
    831 678-2132

(P-1743)
HALL WINES LLC
401 Saint Helena Hwy S, Saint Helena (94574-2200)
P.O. Box 25, Rutherford (94573-0025)
PHONE..................................707 967-2626
Mike Reynolds,
Whitney Jacobson, *Vice Pres*
Wayne Wright, *Vice Pres*
Amy Taylor, *Executive Asst*
Tierney Deal, *Information Mgr*
▲ **EMP:** 50
SQ FT: 20,000
SALES (est): 13.8MM **Privately Held**
SIC: 2084 Wines

(P-1744)
HALTER WINERY LLC
8910 Adelaida Rd, Paso Robles (93446-8798)
PHONE..................................805 226-9455
Mitchell S Wyss,
Hansjorg Wyss,
EMP: 25
SALES (est): 2.2MM **Privately Held**
SIC: 2084 Wines

(P-1745)
HANDLEY CELLARS LTD
Also Called: Handley Cellars Winery
3151 Highway 128, Philo (95466-9468)
P.O. Box 66 (95466-0066)
PHONE..................................707 895-3876
Milla Handley, *General Ptnr*
Raymond Handley, *Partner*

▲ = Import ▼=Export
◆ =Import/Export

EMP: 18
SQ FT: 10,000
SALES: 1.2MM **Privately Held**
WEB: www.handleycellars.com
SIC: 2084 Wines

(P-1746)
HANNA WINERY INC (PA)
9280 Highway 128, Healdsburg
(95448-8028)
PHONE..................................707 431-4310
Christine Hanna, *President*
Shelley Witten, *Office Mgr*
Tami Rojes, *Asst Controller*
Leslie Bottorff, *Sales Executive*
Noel Hanna, *Sales Staff*
▲ **EMP:** 15
SQ FT: 3,000
SALES (est): 3MM **Privately Held**
WEB: www.hannawinery.com
SIC: 2084 Wines

(P-1747)
HANZELL VINEYARDS
18596 Lomita Ave, Sonoma (95476-4619)
PHONE..................................707 996-3860
Jean L Arnold, *President*
Lynda Hanson, *Director*
EMP: 15
SALES (est): 2MM **Privately Held**
WEB: www.hanzell.com
SIC: 2084 Wines

(P-1748)
HARMONY CELLARS
3255 Harmony Valley Rd, Harmony
(93435-5000)
PHONE..................................805 927-1625
Kimberly Mulligan, *Partner*
Charles Mulligan, *Partner*
EMP: 13
SALES (est): 1.8MM **Privately Held**
WEB: www.harmonycellars.com
SIC: 2084 5813 5921 Wine cellars,
bonded: engaged in blending wines; wine
bar; wine

(P-1749)
HARTFORD JACKSON LLC
Also Called: Hartford Family Winery
8075 Martinelli Rd, Forestville
(95436-9255)
P.O. Box 1459 (95436-1459)
PHONE..................................707 887-1756
Don Hartford,
EMP: 15
SQ FT: 40,000
SALES (est): 1.9MM **Privately Held**
WEB: www.hartfordwines.com
SIC: 2084 Wines

(P-1750)
HDD LLC
Also Called: Vml Winery
4035 Westside Rd, Healdsburg
(95448-9456)
P.O. Box 1532 (95448-1532)
PHONE..................................707 433-9545
EMP: 15
SALES (corp-wide): 6.4MM **Publicly Held**
SIC: 2084 Wines
HQ: H.D.D. Llc
125 Foss Creek Cir
Healdsburg CA 95448
707 395-0289

(P-1751)
HEDGESIDE VINTNERS
Also Called: Del Dotto
540 Technology Way, NAPA (94558-7513)
PHONE..................................707 963-2134
Dave Del Dotto, *Owner*
Michelle Aldous, *Admin Asst*
Michelle Clark, *Sales Mgr*
▲ **EMP:** 22
SALES (est): 2.8MM **Privately Held**
SIC: 2084 Wines

(P-1752)
HESS COLLECTION WINERY (DH)
Also Called: Hess Collection Import Co
4411 Redwood Rd, NAPA (94558-9708)
P.O. Box 4140 (94558-0565)
PHONE..................................707 255-1144
Timothy Persson, *CEO*

Clement J Firko, *President*
Tom Selfridge, *President*
John Grant, *COO*
Randle Johnson, *COO*
◆ **EMP:** 25
SQ FT: 100,000
SALES (est): 25MM **Privately Held**
WEB: www.hesscollection.com
SIC: 2084 Wines
HQ: Colome Holding Ag
Hohle Gasse 4
Liebefeld BE
319 703-131

(P-1753)
HOLMAN RANCH CORPORATION
19 E Carmel Valley Rd C, Carmel Valley
(93924-9703)
P.O. Box 149 (93924-0149)
PHONE..................................831 659-2640
Dorothy Mc Ewen, *President*
EMP: 10
SALES (est): 1.9MM **Privately Held**
SIC: 2084 Wines

(P-1754)
HOMEWOOD WINERY
23120 Burndale Rd, Sonoma (95476-9722)
PHONE..................................707 996-6353
Dave Homewood, *Owner*
▲ **EMP:** 10
SALES (est): 620K **Privately Held**
WEB: www.homewoodwinery.com
SIC: 2084 Wines

(P-1755)
HOPE FAMILY WINES (PA)
1585 Live Oak Rd, Paso Robles
(93446-9637)
P.O. Box 3260 (93447-3260)
PHONE..................................805 238-4112
Austin Hope, *President*
EMP: 22
SALES (est): 3.3MM **Privately Held**
SIC: 2084 Wines

(P-1756)
HTR LLC
Also Called: Hill Top Winery
30803 Hilltop View Ct, Valley Center
(92082-6793)
P.O. Box 2570 (92082-2570)
PHONE..................................760 297-4402
Michael Schimpf, *Mng Member*
Liz Kasten, *Project Mgr*
EMP: 12
SALES (est): 995.1K **Privately Held**
SIC: 2084 7389 Wines; packaging & label-
ing services

(P-1757)
HUNEEUS VINTNERS LLC (PA)
Also Called: Quintessa Vinyards
1040 Main St Ste 204, NAPA (94559-2605)
P.O. Box 505, Rutherford (94573-0505)
PHONE..................................707 286-2724
Agustin Huneeus, *Mng Member*
▲ **EMP:** 25
SQ FT: 40,000
SALES (est): 4MM **Privately Held**
SIC: 2084 Wines

(P-1758)
HUSCH VINEYARDS INC (PA)
4400 Highway 128, Philo (95466-9476)
P.O. Box 189, Talmage (95481-0189)
PHONE..................................707 895-3216
Zac Robinson, *President*
Richard Robinson, *President*
Amanda Robinson, *CFO*
Al White, *Finance Mgr*
Brad Holstine, *Mfg Dir*
EMP: 30
SALES (est): 3.6MM **Privately Held**
WEB: www.huschvineyards.com
SIC: 2084 0172 Wines; grapes

(P-1759)
INGLENOOK
1991 St Helena Hwy, Rutherford (94573)
PHONE..................................707 968-1100
Francis Ford Coppola, *Principal*
Norma Villegas, *Human Res Mgr*
▲ **EMP:** 11

SALES (est): 1.1MM **Privately Held**
SIC: 2084 Wines

(P-1760)
J LOHR WINERY CORPORATION (PA)
Also Called: J Lohr Viney
1000 Lenzen Ave, San Jose (95126-2739)
PHONE..................................408 288-5057
Steven W Lohr, *CEO*
Jerome J Lohr, *President*
Bruce Arkley, *Vice Pres*
Cindy Paup, *Vice Pres*
James Schuett, *Vice Pres*
▲ **EMP:** 50
SQ FT: 47,000
SALES (est): 21.1MM **Privately Held**
WEB: www.jlohr.com
SIC: 2084 Wines

(P-1761)
J PEDRONCELLI WINERY
1220 Canyon Rd, Geyserville
(95441-9639)
PHONE..................................707 857-3531
John A Pedroncelli, *President*
James A Pedroncelli, *Treasurer*
EMP: 20
SQ FT: 25,000
SALES: 4MM **Privately Held**
WEB: www.pedroncelli.com
SIC: 2084 0172 Wine cellars, bonded: en-
gaged in blending wines; grapes

(P-1762)
JACKSON FAMILY FARMS LLC (PA)
425 Aviation Blvd, Santa Rosa
(95403-1069)
PHONE..................................707 837-1000
Don Hartford,
Kathy Reddick, *Training Dir*
EMP: 34 **EST:** 1999
SALES (est): 12.9MM **Privately Held**
SIC: 2084 Wines

(P-1763)
JACKSON FAMILY FARMS LLC
5660 Skylane Blvd, Santa Rosa
(95403-1086)
PHONE..................................707 836-2047
Jeff Jackson, *Manager*
EMP: 34
SALES (corp-wide): 12.9MM **Privately
Held**
SIC: 2084 Wines
PA: Jackson Family Farms Llc
425 Aviation Blvd
Santa Rosa CA 95403
707 837-1000

(P-1764)
JACKSON FAMILY WINES INC
Also Called: Card Nale Tasting Room,
7600 Saint Helena Hwy, Oakville (94562)
P.O. Box 328 (94562-0328)
PHONE..................................707 948-2643
Ed Farver, *Manager*
EMP: 40
SALES (corp-wide): 329.7MM **Privately
Held**
WEB: www.cambriawines.com
SIC: 2084 Wines
PA: Jackson Family Wines, Inc.
421 And 425 Aviation Blvd
Santa Rosa CA 95403
707 544-4000

(P-1765)
JACKSON FAMILY WINES INC
Also Called: La Crema Winery
3690 Laughlin Rd, Windsor (95492-8241)
PHONE..................................707 528-6278
Richard Bonatati, *General Mgr*
EMP: 30
SQ FT: 400,000
SALES (corp-wide): 329.7MM **Privately
Held**
WEB: www.cambriawines.com
SIC: 2084 Wines
PA: Jackson Family Wines, Inc.
421 And 425 Aviation Blvd
Santa Rosa CA 95403
707 544-4000

(P-1766)
JACKSON FAMILY WINES INC (PA)
Also Called: Vineyards of Monterey
421 And 425 Aviation Blvd, Santa Rosa
(95403)
PHONE..................................707 544-4000
Barbara Banke, *Director*
Matt Conneely, *Division VP*
Rick Tigner, *Exec VP*
Gayle Bartscherer, *Senior VP*
David K Bowman, *Senior VP*
◆ **EMP:** 100
SQ FT: 25,000
SALES (est): 329.7MM **Privately Held**
WEB: www.cambriawines.com
SIC: 2084 0172 5813 Wines; grapes;
wine bar

(P-1767)
JACKSON FAMILY WINES INC
Also Called: Cambria Winery
5475 Chardonnay Ln, Santa Maria
(93454-9600)
PHONE..................................805 938-7300
Bill Hammond, *Branch Mgr*
Tara Machin, *Manager*
EMP: 30
SALES (corp-wide): 329.7MM **Privately
Held**
WEB: www.cambriawines.com
SIC: 2084 Wines
PA: Jackson Family Wines, Inc.
421 And 425 Aviation Blvd
Santa Rosa CA 95403
707 544-4000

(P-1768)
JACKSON FAMILY WINES INC
Stonestreet Winery
7111 Highway 128, Healdsburg
(95448-8090)
PHONE..................................707 433-9463
Robert Carroll, *General Mgr*
EMP: 20
SALES (corp-wide): 329.7MM **Privately
Held**
WEB: www.cambriawines.com
SIC: 2084 0172 Wines; grapes
PA: Jackson Family Wines, Inc.
421 And 425 Aviation Blvd
Santa Rosa CA 95403
707 544-4000

(P-1769)
JACUZZI FAMILY VINEYARDS LLC
24724 Arnold Dr, Sonoma (95476-2814)
PHONE..................................707 931-7500
Frederick T Cline,
Chris Merino, *Planning*
Nancy J Cline,
Teresa Hernando, *Director*
Mariangela Gatto, *Manager*
▲ **EMP:** 15
SALES (est): 2.1MM **Privately Held**
SIC: 2084 Wines

(P-1770)
JAMES FRASINETTI & SONS
Also Called: Frasinettis Winery & Rest
7395 Frasinetti Rd, Sacramento
(95828-3718)
P.O. Box 292368 (95829-2368)
PHONE..................................916 383-2447
Howard Frasinetti, *Partner*
Gary Frasinetti, *Partner*
EMP: 36
SQ FT: 15,000
SALES: 2MM **Privately Held**
WEB: www.frasinetti.com
SIC: 2084 5812 5921 Wines; American
restaurant; wine

(P-1771)
JAMES TOBIN CELLARS INC
8950 Union Rd, Paso Robles (93446-9356)
PHONE..................................805 239-2204
Tobin J Shumrick, *President*
Monica Martin, *General Mgr*
Lance Silver, *Manager*
EMP: 30
SQ FT: 10,000

SALES (est): 5.6MM **Privately Held**
WEB: www.tobinjames.com
SIC: 2084 Wine cellars, bonded: engaged in blending wines

(P-1772)
JARVIS
Also Called: Jarvis Winery
2970 Monticello Rd, NAPA (94558-9615)
PHONE.....................707 255-5280
William R Jarvis, *President*
William E Jarvis, *Ch of Bd*
Deanna Martinez, *CFO*
Leticia Jarvis, *Vice Pres*
EMP: 30
SQ FT: 45,000
SALES: 6.7MM **Privately Held**
WEB: www.jarvisnapa.com
SIC: 2084 Wines

(P-1773)
JESSIES GROVE WINERY
1973 W Turner Rd, Lodi (95242-9677)
P.O. Box 1406, Woodbridge (95258-1406)
PHONE.....................209 368-0880
Greg Burns, *President*
Wanda Bechthold, *Vice Pres*
Lisa Brand, *Manager*
Sarah Williams, *Manager*
EMP: 15
SALES (est): 2.4MM **Privately Held**
WEB: www.jgwinery.com
SIC: 2084 Wines

(P-1774)
JIM BEAUREGARD
1661 Pine Flat Rd, Santa Cruz
(95060-9713)
PHONE.....................831 423-9453
Jim Beauregard, *Owner*
EMP: 100
SALES (est): 4.4MM **Privately Held**
SIC: 2084 Wines

(P-1775)
JOHN PINA JR & SONS
Also Called: Pina Cellars
7960 Silverado Trl, NAPA (94558-9433)
P.O. Box 373, Oakville (94562-0373)
PHONE.....................707 944-2229
David Pina, *Partner*
John C Pina, *Partner*
John White, *Partner*
▲ EMP: 50
SALES (est): 4.1MM **Privately Held**
SIC: 2084 Wines

(P-1776)
JORDAN VINEYARD & WINERY LP
1474 Alexander Valley Rd, Healdsburg
(95448-9003)
PHONE.....................707 431-5250
Jordan John, *President*
Angela Smith, *Director*
▲ EMP: 28
SALES (est): 4.7MM **Privately Held**
SIC: 2084 Wines

(P-1777)
JUSTIN VINEYARDS & WINERY LLC (DH)
11680 Chimney Rock Rd, Paso Robles
(93446-9792)
PHONE.....................805 238-6932
David Ricanati, *President*
Deborah Baldwin, *Vice Pres*
Will Torres, *Executive*
Danny Hanson, *Human Res Mgr*
Craig B Cooper,
◆ EMP: 50
SQ FT: 60,000
SALES (est): 10.8MM
SALES (corp-wide): 1.5B **Privately Held**
WEB: www.justinwine.com
SIC: 2084 Wines
HQ: Fiji Water Company, Llc
11444 W Olympic Blvd # 250
Los Angeles CA 90064
310 966-5700

(P-1778)
JVW CORPORATION
Also Called: Jordan Vineyard & Winery
1474 Alexander Valley Rd, Healdsburg
(95448-9003)
P.O. Box 878 (95448-0878)
PHONE.....................707 431-5250
John Jordan, *CEO*
Thomas N Jordan Jr, *President*
◆ EMP: 75
SQ FT: 50,000
SALES (est): 18.5MM **Privately Held**
WEB: www.jordanwinery.com
SIC: 2084 0172 Wines; grapes

(P-1779)
KB WINES LLC
Also Called: Kosta Browne
220 Morris St, Sebastopol (95472-3801)
P.O. Box 1959 (95473-1959)
PHONE.....................707 823-7430
Chris Costello,
Michael Brown,
Casey Castello,
Daniel Kosta,
Damon Wong, *Director*
▼ EMP: 28
SALES (est): 2.5MM **Privately Held**
SIC: 2084 Wines

(P-1780)
KEITH NICHOLS
Also Called: Nichols Winery & Cellars
8180 Manitoba St Apt 356, Playa Del Rey
(90293-8653)
PHONE.....................310 305-0397
Keith Nichols, *Owner*
▲ EMP: 25
SQ FT: 1,700
SALES: 1MM **Privately Held**
WEB: www.nicholswinery.com
SIC: 2084 0172 Wines; grapes

(P-1781)
KELSEY SEE CANYON VINEYARDS
1945 See Canyon Rd, San Luis Obispo
(93405-8023)
PHONE.....................805 595-9700
Delores Kelsey, *Owner*
Dick Kelsey, *Co-Owner*
Kelsey Canyon, *Director*
EMP: 10
SALES (est): 1.2MM **Privately Held**
WEB: www.kelseywine.com
SIC: 2084 Wines

(P-1782)
KENDALL-JACKSON WINE ESTATES (HQ)
425 Aviation Blvd, Santa Rosa
(95403-1069)
PHONE.....................707 544-4000
Edward Pitlik, *CEO*
Jonathan Hollister, *President*
Jess Jackson, *President*
Jill Bartley, *CEO*
Tyler Comstock, *Treasurer*
EMP: 275
SQ FT: 10,000
SALES (est): 89.9MM
SALES (corp-wide): 329.7MM **Privately Held**
SIC: 2084 Wines
PA: Jackson Family Wines, Inc.
421 And 425 Aviation Blvd
Santa Rosa CA 95403
707 544-4000

(P-1783)
KOSTA BROWNE WINES LLC
Also Called: Kosta Browne Winery
220 Morris St, Sebastopol (95472-3801)
P.O. Box 1959 (95473-1959)
PHONE.....................707 823-7430
Kosta Browne,
▲ EMP: 29
SALES (est): 2.5MM **Privately Held**
SIC: 2084 Wines

(P-1784)
KRUPP BROTHERS LLC
1345 Hestia Way, NAPA (94558-2105)
PHONE.....................707 226-2215
Jan Krupp, *Mng Member*

Brian Thompson, *Vice Pres*
Cathy Stern, *Opers Mgr*
Marcus Krupp, *VP Mktg*
Bart Krurpp,
▲ EMP: 10
SALES (est): 1.1MM **Privately Held**
WEB: www.veraison.net
SIC: 2084 0172 Wines; grapes

(P-1785)
KULETO VILLA LLC
Also Called: Kuleto Estate
200 Concourse Blvd, Santa Rosa
(95403-8210)
PHONE.....................707 967-8577
Pat Kuleto, *Mng Member*
Ken Hearnsberger, *CFO*
▲ EMP: 20 EST: 1998
SALES (est): 2.5MM **Privately Held**
WEB: www.kuletoestate.com
SIC: 2084 Wines

(P-1786)
KUNDE ENTERPRISES INC
Also Called: Kunde Estate Winery
9825 Sonoma Hwy, Kenwood (95452)
P.O. Box 639 (95452-0639)
PHONE.....................707 833-5501
Don Chase, *President*
▲ EMP: 60
SQ FT: 15,000
SALES (est): 10MM **Privately Held**
SIC: 2084 Wine cellars, bonded: engaged in blending wines

(P-1787)
KUNIN WINES LLC
28 Anacapa St Ste A, Santa Barbara
(93101-1882)
PHONE.....................805 963-9633
Seth H Kunin,
Magan Engan, *Manager*
EMP: 11 EST: 1998
SALES (est): 1.4MM **Privately Held**
SIC: 2084 Wines

(P-1788)
L FOPPIANO WINE CO
Also Called: Foppiano Vineyards
12707 Old Redwood Hwy, Healdsburg
(95448-9241)
P.O. Box 606 (95448-0606)
PHONE.....................707 433-2736
Louis J Foppiano, *President*
Paul Foppiano, *Executive*
Joseph Naujokas, *Executive*
Bill Regan, *Opers Staff*
Rob McNeill, *Consultant*
EMP: 20
SQ FT: 140,000
SALES (est): 4.2MM **Privately Held**
WEB: www.foppiano.com
SIC: 2084 Wines

(P-1789)
LAETITIA VINEYARD & WINERY INC
Also Called: Laetitia Winery
453 Laetitia Vineyard Dr, Arroyo Grande
(93420-9701)
PHONE.....................805 481-1772
Selim K Zilkha, *President*
Lino Bozzano, *Bd of Directors*
Wnedell Cottle, *Manager*
Dave Hickey, *Manager*
Robbie Melero, *Supervisor*
▲ EMP: 65
SALES (est): 12.1MM **Privately Held**
WEB: www.laetitiawine.com
SIC: 2084 Wines

(P-1790)
LAFOND VINEYARD INC
Also Called: Santa Ynez Vineyards
114 E Haley St Ste M, Santa Barbara
(93101-5323)
PHONE.....................805 962-9303
Pierre Lafond, *President*
Marty Poole, *CFO*
EMP: 15
SQ FT: 1,400
SALES: 400K **Privately Held**
WEB: www.lafondwinery.com
SIC: 2084 Wines

(P-1791)
LAGUNA OAKS VNYARDS WINERY INC
Also Called: Balletto Vineyards
5700 Occidental Rd, Santa Rosa
(95401-5533)
P.O. Box 2579, Sebastopol (95473-2579)
PHONE.....................707 568-2455
John G Balleto, *President*
Teresa M Balleto, *Vice Pres*
Jacqueline Balletto, *Manager*
▲ EMP: 12
SQ FT: 9,600
SALES (est): 1.9MM **Privately Held**
SIC: 2084 Wines

(P-1792)
LAIRD FAMILY ESTATE LLC (PA)
5055 Solano Ave, NAPA (94558-1326)
PHONE.....................707 257-0360
Rebecca A Laird, *Mng Member*
Sandra Delgado, *Lab Dir*
Rebecca Laird, *General Mgr*
Gail Laird,
Ken Laird, *Mng Member*
▲ EMP: 42
SQ FT: 64,000
SALES (est): 7.8MM **Privately Held**
WEB: www.lairdfamilyestate.com
SIC: 2084 Wines

(P-1793)
LAMBERT BRIDGE WINERY INC
4085 W Dry Creek Rd, Healdsburg
(95448-9117)
PHONE.....................707 431-9600
Patricia A Chambers, *President*
EMP: 14
SQ FT: 13,000
SALES (est): 2MM **Privately Held**
WEB: www.lambertbridge.com
SIC: 2084 Wines

(P-1794)
LANCASTER VINEYARDS INC
Also Called: Lancaster Estate
200 Concourse Blvd, Santa Rosa
(95403-8210)
PHONE.....................707 433-8178
Theodore Simpkins, *President*
Nicole Simpkins, *Manager*
EMP: 10 EST: 1953
SALES (est): 1MM **Privately Held**
WEB: www.lancasterestate.com
SIC: 2084 Wines

(P-1795)
LANE BENNETT WINERY
3340 State Highway 128, Calistoga
(94515-9727)
PHONE.....................707 942-6684
Randy Lynch, *Owner*
▲ EMP: 10
SALES (est): 1.4MM **Privately Held**
SIC: 2084 Wines

(P-1796)
LANGETWINS WINE COMPANY INC
Also Called: Langetwins Winery & Vineyards
1525 E Jahant Rd, Acampo (95220-9187)
PHONE.....................209 334-9780
Marissa Lange, *President*
Kendra Altnow, *Vice Pres*
Philip Lange, *Admin Sec*
Joseph Lange, *Asst Sec*
EMP: 22
SALES: 20MM **Privately Held**
SIC: 2084 Wines

(P-1797)
LARSON FAMILY WINERY INC
Also Called: Sonoma Creek Winery
23355 Millerick Rd, Sonoma (95476-9282)
PHONE.....................707 938-3031
Tom Larson, *President*
Thomas C Larson, *Vice Pres*
▲ EMP: 10
SQ FT: 5,500
SALES (est): 1.2MM **Privately Held**
WEB: www.larsonfamilywinery.com
SIC: 2084 Wines

(P-1798)
LATCHAM GRANITE INC
Also Called: Latcham Vineyards
2860 Omo Ranch Rd, Somerset
(95684-9204)
P.O. Box 80, Mount Aukum (95656-0080)
PHONE...................................530 620-6642
Franklin C Latcham, *President*
Patricia Latcham, *Corp Secy*
Jonathon Latcham, *Senior VP*
Margaret Latcham, *Senior VP*
EMP: 14
SQ FT: 6,000
SALES (est): 1.3MM **Privately Held**
WEB: www.latcham.com
SIC: 2084 0172 5921 5182 Wines;
 grapes; wine; wine & distilled beverages

(P-1799)
LAVA SPRINGS INC
Also Called: Lava Cap Winery
2221 Fruitridge Rd, Placerville
(95667-3700)
PHONE...................................530 621-0175
Thomas D Jones, *President*
Jeanne H Jones, *Chairman*
Kevin Jones, *Marketing Staff*
Danny Mantle, *Sales Staff*
Charlie Jones, *Manager*
▲ EMP: 30
SQ FT: 18,000
SALES (est): 4.4MM **Privately Held**
WEB: www.lavacap.com
SIC: 2084 Wines

(P-1800)
LEONESSE CELLARS LLC
38311 De Portola Rd, Temecula
(92592-8923)
P.O. Box 1371 (92593-1371)
PHONE...................................951 302-7601
Gary Winder, *Mng Member*
Rebaux Steyn, *General Mgr*
Michael Rennie,
Joel Reese, *Director*
Krystal Aponte, *Manager*
▲ EMP: 25
SQ FT: 6,000
SALES (est): 5.7MM **Privately Held**
WEB: www.leonessecellars.com
SIC: 2084 Wines

(P-1801)
LEVECKE LLC
10810 Inland Ave, Jurupa Valley
(91752-3235)
PHONE...................................951 681-8600
Tim Levecke, *Mng Member*
Brad Gilreath, *Vice Pres*
Gustavo Iglesias, *Executive*
Martin Rezac, *Production*
Neil Levecke, *Mng Member*
EMP: 70
SQ FT: 150,000
SALES (est): 5.5MM **Privately Held**
SIC: 2084 Wines, brandy & brandy spirits

(P-1802)
LINDQUIST ROBERT N & ASSOC
(PA)
4665 Santa Maria Mesa Rd, Santa Maria
(93454-9638)
PHONE...................................805 937-9801
Robert Lindquist, *President*
EMP: 10
SALES (est): 1.1MM **Privately Held**
SIC: 2084 Wines

(P-1803)
LOCKWOOD VINEYARD (PA)
9777 Blue Larkspur Ln # 101, Monterey
(93940-6554)
PHONE...................................831 642-9566
R Paul Toeppen, *Partner*
Philip Johnson, *Partner*
W B Lindley, *Partner*
◆ EMP: 10
SALES (est): 1.9MM **Privately Held**
WEB: www.lockwoodwine.com
SIC: 2084 8741 0172 Wines; manage-
 ment services; grapes

(P-1804)
LOTUS BEVERAGES
Also Called: Mendias Imports
2542 San Gabriel Blvd, Rosemead
(91770-3252)
PHONE...................................213 216-1434
Scott Mendias, *Owner*
EMP: 10
SALES: 900K **Privately Held**
SIC: 2084 Wines, brandy & brandy spirits

(P-1805)
LOUIDAR LLC
Also Called: Mount Palomar Winery
33820 Rancho Cal Rd, Temecula
(92591-4930)
P.O. Box 891510 (92589-1510)
PHONE...................................951 676-5047
Peter Poole, *Principal*
Carol Darwish, *General Mgr*
Louis Darwish, *Mng Member*
EMP: 30
SQ FT: 4,000
SALES (est): 3.6MM **Privately Held**
SIC: 2084 Wines

(P-1806)
LUNA VINEYARDS INC
2921 Silverado Trl, NAPA (94558-2016)
PHONE...................................707 255-2474
Andre Crisp, *President*
Mary Ann Tsai, *President*
E Michael Moone, *Co-COB*
George A Vare, *Co-COB*
Janel Sizelove, *Corp Secy*
▲ EMP: 20
SALES (est): 4.5MM **Privately Held**
WEB: www.lunawine.com
SIC: 2084 5182 5921 Wines; wine; wine

(P-1807)
MACCHIA INC
7099 E Peltier Rd, Acampo (95220-9605)
PHONE...................................209 333-2600
Tim Holdener, *President*
EMP: 15
SALES (est): 1.6MM **Privately Held**
SIC: 2084 Wines

(P-1808)
MADRIGAL VINEYARD
MANAGEMENT
Also Called: Madrigal Vineyards
3718 Saint Helena Hwy, Calistoga
(94515-9651)
P.O. Box 937 (94515-0937)
PHONE...................................707 942-8691
Jesus Madrigal, *Owner*
Chris Madrigal, *CEO*
Justin Ovard, *CFO*
EMP: 50
SALES (est): 5.1MM **Privately Held**
WEB: www.madrigalvineyards.com
SIC: 2084 Wines

(P-1809)
MAGITO & COMPANY LLC
1446 Industrial Ave, Sebastopol
(95472-4848)
PHONE...................................707 567-1521
Tom Meadowcroft,
▼ EMP: 10
SALES (est): 1MM **Privately Held**
SIC: 2084 Wines

(P-1810)
MARIETTA CELLARS
INCORPORATED
Also Called: Marietta Marketing
22295 Chianti Rd, Geyserville
(95441-9702)
P.O. Box 800 (95441-0800)
PHONE...................................707 433-2747
Chris Bilbro, *President*
Barry Ackerman, *Controller*
Jason Johnson, *Sales Staff*
Tais Tillman, *Manager*
▲ EMP: 15
SALES (est): 2.5MM **Privately Held**
WEB: www.mariettacellars.com
SIC: 2084 Wines

(P-1811)
MARIMAR TORRES ESTATE
CORP
Also Called: Caliame
11400 Graton Rd, Sebastopol
(95472-8901)
PHONE...................................707 823-4365
Marimar Torres, *President*
▲ EMP: 10
SQ FT: 1,040
SALES (est): 1.3MM **Privately Held**
WEB: www.marimarestate.com
SIC: 2084 5812 Wine cellars, bonded: en-
 gaged in blending wines; eating places

(P-1812)
MARTELLOTTO INC
Also Called: One Vine Wines
12934 Francine Ter, Poway (92064-4114)
PHONE...................................619 567-9244
Greg Martellotto, *President*
▲ EMP: 10
SQ FT: 2,500
SALES (est): 828.8K **Privately Held**
SIC: 2084 Wines

(P-1813)
MATANZAS CREEK WINERY
6097 Bennett Valley Rd, Santa Rosa
(95404-8570)
PHONE...................................707 528-6464
Jeff Jackson, *President*
▲ EMP: 35
SQ FT: 20,000
SALES (est): 3.8MM **Privately Held**
WEB: www.matanzascreek.com
SIC: 2084 0172 Wine cellars, bonded: en-
 gaged in blending wines; grapes

(P-1814)
MAURICE CARRIE WINERY
34225 Rancho Cal Rd, Temecula
(92591-5054)
PHONE...................................951 676-1711
Buddy Linn, *President*
Cheri Linn, *Vice Pres*
EMP: 30
SQ FT: 14,000
SALES: 1MM **Privately Held**
WEB: www.mauricecarriewinery.com
SIC: 2084 5921 0172 Wines; wine;
 grapes

(P-1815)
MCNAB RIDGE WINERY LLC
2350 Mcnab Ranch Rd, Ukiah
(95482-9350)
PHONE...................................707 462-2423
John A Parducci, *Mng Member*
Willard A Carle,
Richard M Lawson,
EMP: 11
SALES (est): 920K **Privately Held**
SIC: 2084 Wines

(P-1816)
MELVILLE WINERY LLC
5185 E Highway 246, Lompoc
(93436-9613)
PHONE...................................805 735-7030
Ronald Melville, *President*
Marina Brennan, *Admin Asst*
Brent Melville,
Chad Melville,
EMP: 12
SALES (est): 1.4MM **Privately Held**
SIC: 2084 Wines

(P-1817)
MERRYVALE VINEYARDS LLC
Also Called: Starmont Winery
1000 Main St, Saint Helena (94574-2011)
PHONE...................................707 963-2225
Rene Schlatter, *President*
Mark Evans, *COO*
Glenn Ochsner, *CPA*
Clos Bois, *Mktg Dir*
▲ EMP: 40
SQ FT: 30,850
SALES (est): 13.2MM **Privately Held**
WEB: www.merryvale.com
SIC: 2084 0172 Wines; grapes

(P-1818)
MICHEL-SCHLMBERGER
PARTNERS LP
Also Called: Michel-Schlumberger Fine Wine
4155 Wine Creek Rd, Healdsburg
(95448-9112)
PHONE...................................707 433-7427
Jacques Schlumberger, *General Ptnr*
Simone Popov, *Business Dir*
Barbara Fitzgerald, *Director*
▲ EMP: 20
SQ FT: 20,000
SALES: 2MM **Privately Held**
WEB: www.michelschlumberger.com
SIC: 2084 Wines

(P-1819)
MILDARA BLASS INC
Also Called: Windsor Vineyards
205 Concourse Blvd, Santa Rosa
(95403-8258)
P.O. Box 368, Windsor (95492-0368)
PHONE...................................707 836-5000
Kate Langford, *President*
▲ EMP: 160
SALES (est): 21.5MM **Privately Held**
SIC: 2084 5182 Wines; brandy & brandy
 spirits
PA: Vintage Wine Estates, Inc.
 205 Concourse Blvd
 Santa Rosa CA 95403
 -

(P-1820)
MILL CREEK VNEYARDS
WINERY INC
1401 Westside Rd, Healdsburg
(95448-9462)
P.O. Box 925 (95448-0925)
PHONE...................................707 433-4788
William C Kreck, *President*
Sherrie Mazzanti, *Office Mgr*
EMP: 15
SQ FT: 1,500
SALES (est): 1.8MM **Privately Held**
SIC: 2084 5921 Wines; wine

(P-1821)
MONT ST JOHN CELLARS INC
5400 Old Sonoma Rd, NAPA (94559-9708)
PHONE...................................707 255-8864
Andrea Bartolucci, *President*
EMP: 10 EST: 1977
SQ FT: 14,000
SALES (est): 1.2MM **Privately Held**
WEB: www.madonnaestate.com
SIC: 2084 Wines

(P-1822)
MONTE DE ORO WINERY
35820 Rancho Cal Rd, Temecula
(92591-5126)
PHONE...................................951 491-6551
Kenneth Zignorski, *Principal*
Ken Zignorski, *Managing Prtnr*
Kelley O'Neill, *Admin Asst*
Betty Muro, *Controller*
Jordan Laliotis, *Opers Mgr*
EMP: 12
SALES (est): 1.7MM **Privately Held**
SIC: 2084 Wines

(P-1823)
MONTERY WINE COMPANY LLC
1010 Industrial Way, King City
(93930-2506)
PHONE...................................831 386-1100
Steven McIntyre,
Shannon Valladarez, *Finance*
EMP: 19
SALES (est): 5.9MM **Privately Held**
WEB: www.montereywinecompany.com
SIC: 2084 Wines

(P-1824)
MONTICELLO CELLARS INC
4242 Big Ranch Rd, NAPA (94558-1396)
P.O. Box 2486 (94558-0248)
PHONE...................................707 253-2802
John Kevin Corley, *President*
EMP: 15
SQ FT: 25,000

SALES (est): 2.1MM
SALES (corp-wide): 2.7MM **Privately Held**
WEB: www.monticellovineyards.com
SIC: 2084 Wines
PA: Monticello Vineyards
4242 Big Ranch Rd
Napa CA
707 253-2802

(P-1825)
MORGAN WINERY INC (PA)
590 Brunken Ave Ste C, Salinas
(93901-4355)
PHONE.....................831 751-7777
Daniel Lee, *President*
Donna Lee, *Vice Pres*
Jim McAllister, *Sales Staff*
Deborah Canepa, *Manager*
Marc Cutino, *Manager*
◆ **EMP:** 10
SALES (est): 1.4MM **Privately Held**
WEB: www.morganwinery.com
SIC: 2084 Wines

(P-1826)
MOSAIC VINEYARDS & WINERY INC
2001 Highway 128, Geyserville
(95441-9489)
PHONE.....................707 857-2000
Tom Fuchs, *President*
Bill Mc Cardell, *Corp Secy*
EMP: 15
SQ FT: 2,113
SALES (est): 1MM **Privately Held**
SIC: 2084 Wine cellars, bonded: engaged in blending wines

(P-1827)
MPL BRANDS INC (PA)
71 Liberty Ship Way, Sausalito
(94965-1731)
PHONE.....................888 513-3022
Michael Patane, *CEO*
EMP: 40
SQ FT: 5,000
SALES: 50MM **Privately Held**
SIC: 2084 Wines, brandy & brandy spirits

(P-1828)
MPL BRANDS INC
2280 Union St, San Francisco
(94123-3902)
PHONE.....................415 515-3536
Michael Patane, *CEO*
EMP: 10
SALES (corp-wide): 50MM **Privately Held**
SIC: 2084 Wines, brandy & brandy spirits
PA: Mpl Brands, Inc.
71 Liberty Ship Way
Sausalito CA 94965
888 513-3022

(P-1829)
MUNSELLE VINEYARDS LLC
3660 Highway 128, Geyserville
(95441-9432)
P.O. Box 617 (95441-0617)
PHONE.....................707 857-9988
Reta Munselle, *Mng Member*
EMP: 15
SALES (est): 805.2K **Privately Held**
SIC: 2084 Wines

(P-1830)
MUSCARDINI CELLARS LLC
9380 Sonoma Hwy, Kenwood
(95452-9032)
PHONE.....................707 933-9305
Michael Muscardini, *Principal*
Alice Schimm, *Office Mgr*
Natalie Owdom, *Sales Staff*
Jennifer Kosko, *Manager*
Meghan Letters, *Manager*
EMP: 11
SALES (est): 1.5MM **Privately Held**
SIC: 2084 Wines

(P-1831)
MUTT LYNCH WINERY INC
3451 Airway Dr Ste C, Santa Rosa
(95403-2054)
P.O. Box 511, Healdsburg (95448-0511)
PHONE.....................707 473-8080

Christopher C Lynch, *President*
Brenda Lynch, *Principal*
EMP: 16
SALES (est): 1.9MM **Privately Held**
SIC: 2084 Wines

(P-1832)
N C W G INC
Also Called: Nevada City Winery
321 Spring St, Nevada City (95959-2420)
PHONE.....................530 265-9463
John Chase, *General Mgr*
Wyn Spiller, *CEO*
EMP: 10
SQ FT: 7,500
SALES: 858.1K **Privately Held**
WEB: www.ncwinery.com
SIC: 2084 Wines

(P-1833)
NAGGIAR VINEYARDS LLC
18125 Rosemary Ln, Grass Valley
(95949-7820)
PHONE.....................530 268-9059
Michel Naggiar,
Shawn Naggiar,
Anthony Tibshirani,
EMP: 15
SQ FT: 3,100
SALES (est): 2MM **Privately Held**
SIC: 2084 Wines

(P-1834)
NAPA BEAUCANON ESTATE
1006 Monticello Rd, NAPA (94558-2032)
PHONE.....................707 254-1460
Louis De Coninck, *President*
Chantal De Coninck, *Vice Pres*
▲ **EMP:** 11
SQ FT: 18,000
SALES (est): 1.2MM **Privately Held**
WEB: www.beaucanon.com
SIC: 2084 Wines

(P-1835)
NAPA WINE COMPANY LLC
7830 St Helena Hwy 40, Oakville
(94562-9200)
P.O. Box 434 (94562-0434)
PHONE.....................707 944-8669
Rob Lawson,
Andy Hoxsey,
▲ **EMP:** 35
SQ FT: 100,000
SALES (est): 5.7MM **Privately Held**
WEB: www.napawineco.com
SIC: 2084 Wines; wine cellars, bonded: engaged in blending wines

(P-1836)
NAVARRO WINERY
Also Called: Navarro Vineyard
5601 Highway 128, Philo (95466-9513)
P.O. Box 47 (95466-0047)
PHONE.....................707 895-3686
Edward T Bennett, *Partner*
Deborah S Cahn, *Partner*
▲ **EMP:** 75 **EST:** 1974
SQ FT: 10,000
SALES: 10.4MM **Privately Held**
WEB: www.navarrowine.com
SIC: 2084 0172 5921 Wine cellars, bonded: engaged in blending wines; grapes; wine

(P-1837)
NEAL FAMILY VINEYARDS LLC
716 Liparita Ave, Angwin (94508-9693)
PHONE.....................707 965-2800
Mark Neal,
▲ **EMP:** 10 **EST:** 2000
SQ FT: 3,096
SALES (est): 1.1MM **Privately Held**
WEB: www.nealvineyards.com
SIC: 2084 Wines

(P-1838)
NELSON & SONS INC
Also Called: Nelson Family Vineyard
550 Nelson Ranch Rd, Ukiah (95482-9316)
PHONE.....................707 462-3755
Gregory Nelson, *President*
Christopher Nelson, *Vice Pres*
Tyler Nelson, *Vice Pres*
EMP: 20

SALES (est): 3.3MM **Privately Held**
WEB: www.nelsonfamilyvineyard.com
SIC: 2084 0172 Wines; grapes

(P-1839)
NEWTON VINEYARD LLC (DH)
2555 Madrona Ave, Saint Helena
(94574-2300)
PHONE.....................707 963-9000
Peter L Newton,
Russell J Bollman,
Dr Su Hua Newton,
Robert Mann, *Director*
Mario Dussurget, *Manager*
◆ **EMP:** 40
SQ FT: 2,500
SALES (est): 21.4MM
SALES (corp-wide): 361.7MM **Privately Held**
WEB: www.newtonvineyard.com
SIC: 2084 0172 Wines; grapes
HQ: Moet Hennessy
Moet Hennessy Estates Wines Moet Henne
Paris 8e Arrondissement 75008
144 132-222

(P-1840)
NICHOLSON RANCH LLC
4200 Napa Rd, Sonoma (95476-2800)
PHONE.....................707 938-8822
Ramona Nicholson,
Valentino Pecak, *Opers Staff*
Deepak Gulrajani,
EMP: 20
SALES (est): 3MM **Privately Held**
WEB: www.nicholsonranch.com
SIC: 2084 Wines

(P-1841)
NIEBAM-CPPOLA ESTATE WINERY LP
Also Called: Cafe Niebaum Coppola
916 Kearny St, San Francisco
(94133-5107)
PHONE.....................415 291-1700
Krista Voisin, *Manager*
EMP: 20 **Privately Held**
SIC: 2084 Wines
PA: Niebaum-Coppola Estate Winery, L.P.
1991 St Helena Hwy
Rutherford CA 94573

(P-1842)
NIEBAM-CPPOLA ESTATE WINERY LP (PA)
1991 St Helena Hwy, Rutherford (94573)
P.O. Box 208 (94573-0208)
PHONE.....................707 968-1100
Gordon Wang, *CFO*
Niebaum-Coppola Estate Winery, *General Ptnr*
The Coppola Family Trust, *Ltd Ptnr*
American Zoetrope, *Ltd Ptnr*
Earl Martin, *President*
▲ **EMP:** 150
SALES (est): 26.1MM **Privately Held**
SIC: 2084 Wines

(P-1843)
NINER WINE ESTATES LLC
2400 W Highway 46, Paso Robles
(93446-8602)
PHONE.....................805 239-2233
Richard T Niner,
Rebecca Ogrady, *CFO*
Sue Underwood, *Vice Pres*
Bricklyn Brown, *Technician*
Tom Bower, *Engineer*
▲ **EMP:** 12
SALES (est): 1.9MM **Privately Held**
SIC: 2084 Wines

(P-1844)
OAK RIDGE WINERY LLC
6100 E Hwy 12 Victor Rd, Lodi (95240)
PHONE.....................209 369-4768
Rudy Maggio,
Chad Kosina, *Regional Mgr*
Bob Strohn, *Area Mgr*
Denise Stanley, *District Mgr*
Keith Auerbach, *Division Mgr*
▲ **EMP:** 50

SALES (est): 10.6MM **Privately Held**
WEB: www.oakridgewinery.com
SIC: 2084 Wines

(P-1845)
OLD CREEK RANCH WINERY INC
10024 Creek Rd, Oak View (93022-9728)
P.O. Box 173 (93022-0173)
PHONE.....................805 649-4132
Andrew Holguin, *President*
EMP: 12 **EST:** 1981
SQ FT: 600
SALES (est): 124.4K **Privately Held**
WEB: www.oldcreekranch.com
SIC: 2084 Wines

(P-1846)
OPAL MOON WINERY LLC
21660 8th St E Ste A, Sonoma
(95476-2828)
PHONE.....................707 996-0420
John Bambury,
EMP: 15 **EST:** 2011
SQ FT: 30,000
SALES (est): 1MM **Privately Held**
SIC: 2084 Wines

(P-1847)
OPOLO VINEYARDS INC (PA)
7110 Vineyard Dr, Paso Robles
(93446-7684)
PHONE.....................805 238-9593
Richard Lawrence Quinn, *CEO*
Scott Welcher, *General Mgr*
Sandy Montgomery, *Manager*
EMP: 27
SALES (est): 5.4MM **Privately Held**
SIC: 2084 Wines

(P-1848)
OPOLO VINEYARDS INC
2801 Townsgate Rd Ste 123, Westlake Village (91361-3033)
P.O. Box 277, Paso Robles (93447-0277)
PHONE.....................805 238-9593
Jeff Faber, *Sales Staff*
EMP: 12
SALES (corp-wide): 5.4MM **Privately Held**
WEB: www.opolo.com
SIC: 2084 Wines
PA: Opolo Vineyards, Inc.
7110 Vineyard Dr
Paso Robles CA 93446
805 238-9593

(P-1849)
OPUS ONE WINERY LLC (PA)
7900 St Helena Hwy, Oakville (94562)
P.O. Box 6 (94562-0006)
PHONE.....................707 944-9442
David Pearson, *CEO*
Robert Fowles, *CFO*
Roger Asleson, *Vice Pres*
Robert Ruex, *Vice Pres*
Michael Silacci, *Vice Pres*
◆ **EMP:** 75
SQ FT: 85,000
SALES (est): 18.6MM **Privately Held**
WEB: www.opusonewinery.com
SIC: 2084 Wines

(P-1850)
ORFILA VINEYARDS INC (PA)
Also Called: Orfila Vineyards & Winery
13455 San Pasqual Rd, Escondido
(92025-7833)
PHONE.....................760 738-6500
Alejandro Orfila, *President*
Danica Gvozden, *CFO*
Justin Mund, *Vice Pres*
Helga Orfila, *Vice Pres*
▲ **EMP:** 31
SQ FT: 12,000
SALES (est): 2.7MM **Privately Held**
WEB: www.orfila.com
SIC: 2084 0172 7299 Wines; grapes; wedding chapel, privately operated

▲ = Import ▼=Export
◆ =Import/Export

(P-1851)
OVERLOOK VINEYARDS LLC (DH)
Also Called: Landmark Vineyards
101 Adobe Canyon Rd, Kenwood
(95452-9045)
P.O. Box 340 (95452-0340)
PHONE..................707 833-0053
Mike Colhoun,
Margaret Benelli,
Mary Colhoun,
Kim Pasquali, *Senior Mgr*
Donna Carroll, *Manager*
▲ **EMP:** 27
SQ FT: 10,000
SALES (est): 2.2MM
SALES (corp-wide): 1.5B **Privately Held**
WEB: www.landmarkwine.com
SIC: 2084 0172 Wines; grapes
HQ: Fiji Water Company, Llc
11444 W Olympic Blvd # 250
Los Angeles CA 90064
310 966-5700

(P-1852)
OVERLOOK VINEYARDS LLC
Also Called: Hop Kiln Winery, The
58 W North St Ste 101, Healdsburg
(95448-4843)
PHONE..................707 433-6491
EMP: 10
SALES (corp-wide): 1.5B **Privately Held**
SIC: 2084 Wines
HQ: Overlook Vineyards Llc
101 Adobe Canyon Rd
Kenwood CA 95452
707 833-0053

(P-1853)
OZEKI SAKE U S A INC (HQ)
249 Hillcrest Rd, Hollister (95023-4921)
PHONE..................831 637-9217
Bunjiro Osabe, *Ch of Bd*
Norio Sumomogi, *Treasurer*
Masaru Ogihara, *Vice Pres*
Ruth Reid, *Office Mgr*
Toshio Kuriyama, *Marketing Mgr*
▲ **EMP:** 25
SQ FT: 22,000
SALES (est): 4.3MM **Privately Held**
WEB: www.ozekisake.com
SIC: 2084 Wines

(P-1854)
PAN MAGNA GROUP
Also Called: Domaine St George Winery
1141 Grant Ave, Healdsburg (95448-9570)
P.O. Box 548 (95448-0548)
PHONE..................707 433-5508
Somchai Likitprakong, *Principal*
EMP: 22
SQ FT: 1,237
SALES (corp-wide): 9.5MM **Privately Held**
WEB: www.domainesaintgeorge.com
SIC: 2084 0172 Wines; grapes
PA: Pan Magna Group
350 Sansome St Ste 1010
San Francisco CA
415 394-7244

(P-1855)
PARADIGM WINERY
683 Dwyer Rd, Oakville (94562)
P.O. Box 323 (94562-0323)
PHONE..................707 944-1683
Marilyn Harris, *Partner*
Ren Harris, *Partner*
▲ **EMP:** 15
SALES: 700K **Privately Held**
WEB: www.paradigmwinery.com
SIC: 2084 5182 5921 Wines; wine; wine

(P-1856)
PARADISE RIDGE WINERY
4545 Thomas Lk Harris Dr, Santa Rosa
(95403-0108)
PHONE..................707 528-9463
Walter Byck, *Owner*
▲ **EMP:** 10
SALES (est): 1.1MM **Privately Held**
WEB: www.prwinery.com
SIC: 2084 Wines

(P-1857)
PARDUCCI WINE ESTATES LLC
Also Called: Mendicino Wine Company
501 Parducci Rd, Ukiah (95482-3015)
PHONE..................707 463-5350
Carl Thoma,
Tom Thornhill, *Managing Prtnr*
Jennifer Gulbrandsen, *Executive*
Michele King, *Accounting Mgr*
Mike Hizengia, *Analyst*
▲ **EMP:** 35
SALES (est): 5.4MM **Privately Held**
WEB: www.parducci.com
SIC: 2084 Wines

(P-1858)
PAUL HOBBS WINERY LP
3355 Gravenstein Hwy N, Sebastopol
(95472-2327)
PHONE..................707 824-9879
Paul Hobbs, *Partner*
Joan Maxwell, *CFO*
Jenifer Freebairn, *Vice Pres*
Megan Baccitich, *Director*
Scott Zapotocky, *Director*
▲ **EMP:** 10
SQ FT: 1,995
SALES (est): 1.8MM **Privately Held**
WEB: www.paulhobbs.com
SIC: 2084 Wines

(P-1859)
PEAR VALLEY VINEYARD INC
Also Called: Pear Valley Vineyard & Winery
4900 Union Rd, Paso Robles (93446-9345)
P.O. Box 5120 (93447-5120)
PHONE..................805 237-2861
Kathleen Maas, *President*
Frederick Thomas Maas Jr, *Vice Pres*
EMP: 10
SALES (est): 1.7MM **Privately Held**
SIC: 2084 Wines

(P-1860)
PEAY VINEYARDS LLC
207a N Cloverdale Blvd, Cloverdale
(95425-3318)
PHONE..................707 894-8720
Nicholas Peay, *Mng Member*
Gordon A Peay,
EMP: 12
SALES (est): 1.8MM **Privately Held**
SIC: 2084 Wines

(P-1861)
PELLEGRINI RANCHES
Also Called: Pellegrine Wine Company
4055 W Olivet Rd, Santa Rosa
(95401-3839)
PHONE..................707 545-8680
Robert V Pellegrini, *CEO*
Fred Reno, *President*
EMP: 10
SQ FT: 4,000
SALES (est): 924.2K **Privately Held**
SIC: 2084 Wines

(P-1862)
PERNOD RICARD USA LLC
Also Called: Kenwood Vineyards
9592 Sonoma Hwy, Kenwood
(95452-8028)
P.O. Box 669 (95452-0669)
PHONE..................707 833-5891
Elyse Kirkhoff, *Technician*
Marcus Black, *VP Finance*
EMP: 75
SQ FT: 1,414
SALES (corp-wide): 182.4MM **Privately Held**
WEB: www.korbel.com
SIC: 2084 0172 Wines; grapes
HQ: Pernod Ricard Usa, Llc
250 Park Ave Ste 17a
New York NY 10177
212 372-5400

(P-1863)
PERNOD RICARD USA LLC
Also Called: Mumm NAPA Valley
8445 Silverado Trl, Rutherford (94573)
PHONE..................707 967-7770
Samuel Bronfman II, *Branch Mgr*
EMP: 65

SALES (corp-wide): 182.4MM **Privately Held**
WEB: www.adw-academy.com
SIC: 2084 Wines
HQ: Pernod Ricard Usa, Llc
250 Park Ave Ste 17a
New York NY 10177
212 372-5400

(P-1864)
PERRY CREEK WINERY
7400 Perry Creek Rd, Somerset
(95684-9207)
PHONE..................530 620-5175
Peter Juergens, *Owner*
▲ **EMP:** 11
SALES (est): 1.2MM **Privately Held**
SIC: 2084 Wines

(P-1865)
PETALUMAIDENCE OPCO LLC
Also Called: Vineyard Post Acute
101 Monroe St, Petaluma (94954-2328)
PHONE..................707 763-4109
Jason Murray, *Principal*
Mark Hancock, *Principal*
EMP: 124
SALES (est): 10.8MM **Privately Held**
SIC: 2084 8051 Wines; skilled nursing
care facilities

(P-1866)
PINE RIDGE WINERY LLC
Also Called: Pine Ridge Vineyards
5901 Silverado Trl, NAPA (94558-9417)
P.O. Box 2508, Yountville (94599-2508)
PHONE..................707 253-7500
Michael Beaulac,
Winnie St John, *Controller*
Hunt Patterson, *Sales Mgr*
Ian M Cumming,
Joseph A Orlando,
▲ **EMP:** 100
SQ FT: 17,000
SALES (est): 18.6MM
SALES (corp-wide): 67.7MM **Publicly Held**
SIC: 2084 5812 0172 Wines; eating
places; grapes
PA: Crimson Wine Group, Ltd.
2700 Napa Vly Corp Dr B
Napa CA 94558
800 486-0503

(P-1867)
PJK WINERY LLC
Also Called: Quivira Vineyards
4900 W Dry Creek Rd, Healdsburg
(95448-9721)
PHONE..................707 431-8333
Pete Kight, *Mng Member*
EMP: 25
SQ FT: 5,400
SALES (est): 1.8MM **Privately Held**
WEB: www.quivirawine.com
SIC: 2084 Wines

(P-1868)
PLC LLC
Also Called: McNab Ridge Winery
2350 Mcnab Ranch Rd, Ukiah
(95482-9350)
PHONE..................707 462-2423
John Parducci, *Mng Member*
Bill Carle,
EMP: 11
SQ FT: 30,000
SALES (est): 1.7MM **Privately Held**
WEB: www.mcnabridge.com
SIC: 2084 Wines

(P-1869)
POMAR JUNCTION CELLARS LLC
5036 S El Pomar Rd, Templeton
(93465-8673)
P.O. Box 789 (93465-0789)
PHONE..................805 238-9940
Dana Merrill, *General Mgr*
Marcia Merrill,
Matthew Merrill,
Nicole Merrill,
EMP: 20
SQ FT: 1,600
SALES (est): 1.2MM **Privately Held**
SIC: 2084 5182 Wines; wine

(P-1870)
PRESQUILE WINERY
5391 Presquile Dr, Santa Maria
(93455-5811)
PHONE..................805 937-8110
Robert Madison Murphy II, *President*
Anna Murphy, *Vice Pres*
Jonathan Murphy, *Admin Sec*
Janeen Garcia, *Accountant*
Brian Evans, *Manager*
EMP: 10
SALES (est): 1.2MM **Privately Held**
SIC: 2084 Wines

(P-1871)
PRESTON VINEYARDS INC
Also Called: Preston Vineyards & Winery
9282 W Dry Creek Rd, Healdsburg
(95448-9134)
PHONE..................707 433-3372
Louis Preston, *President*
Susan Preston, *Vice Pres*
Ken Blair, *Sales Dir*
Matthew Wells, *Sales Staff*
EMP: 15 **EST:** 1973
SALES (est): 1.7MM **Privately Held**
WEB: www.prestonvineyards.com
SIC: 2084 5812 5182 Wines; eating
places; wine

(P-1872)
PROVENANCE VINEYARDS
1695 Saint Helena Hwy S, Saint Helena
(94574-9777)
P.O. Box 688, Rutherford (94573-0688)
PHONE..................707 968-3633
Tom Rinaldi, *Owner*
▲ **EMP:** 14
SALES (est): 1.3MM **Privately Held**
WEB: www.provenancevineyards.com
SIC: 2084 Wines
HQ: Treasury Wine Estates Americas Company
555 Gateway Dr
Napa CA 94558
707 259-4500

(P-1873)
PURPLE WINE COMPANY LLC
9119 Graton Rd, Graton (95444-9373)
P.O. Box 390 (95444-0390)
PHONE..................707 829-6100
Derek Benham, *Mng Member*
Joe Joffe, *COO*
Ron Janowczyk, *Senior VP*
Lisa Ehrlich, *Vice Pres*
Michael Mestas, *Vice Pres*
▲ **EMP:** 28
SALES: 2MM **Privately Held**
SIC: 2084 Wines

(P-1874)
PYRAMIDS WINERY INC
5875 Lakeville Hwy, Petaluma
(94954-9263)
PHONE..................707 765-2768
Arturo Keller, *President*
▲ **EMP:** 40
SALES (est): 3MM **Privately Held**
WEB: www.kellerestate.com
SIC: 2084 Wines

(P-1875)
QUADY LLC (PA)
13181 Road 24, Madera (93637-9087)
P.O. Box 728 (93639-0728)
PHONE..................559 673-8068
Andrew Quady, *CEO*
Laurel Quady, *CFO*
EMP: 46
SQ FT: 16,000
SALES (est): 2.9MM **Privately Held**
SIC: 2084 Wines

(P-1876)
QUADY WINERY INC
13181 Road 24, Madera (93637-9087)
P.O. Box 728 (93639-0728)
PHONE..................559 673-8068
Andrew K Quady, *President*
Laurel Quady, *Vice Pres*
David Glover, *Technology*
Marnee Coushman, *Bookkeeper*
Jim Fricke, *Sales Staff*
EMP: 16 **EST:** 1979
SQ FT: 16,000

SALES (est): 3.3MM **Privately Held**
WEB: www.quadywinery.com
SIC: 2084 Wines

(P-1877)
RAMS GATE WINERY LLC
28700 Arnold Dr, Sonoma (95476-9700)
PHONE.....................................707 721-8700
Jeffrey O'Neill, *Mng Member*
Michael J John,
Peter Mullin,
Paul Violich,
Valerie Valente, *Manager*
▲ EMP: 38
SALES (est): 8MM **Privately Held**
SIC: 2084 Wines

(P-1878)
RANCHO DE SOLIS WINERY INC
3920 Hecker Pass Rd, Gilroy (95020-8805)
PHONE.....................................408 847-6306
David Vanni, *President*
EMP: 10
SALES (est): 915.1K **Privately Held**
WEB: www.soliswinery.com
SIC: 2084 Wines

(P-1879)
RANCHO GUEJITO CORPORATION
17224 San Pasqual Vly Rd, Escondido
(92027-7007)
PHONE.....................................800 519-4441
Theodate Coates, *President*
Cheryl Barnett, *Admin Sec*
Hank Rupp, *General Counsel*
EMP: 10 EST: 2010
SALES (est): 1.2MM **Privately Held**
SIC: 2084 Wines

(P-1880)
RANG DONG JOINT STOCK COMPANY
Also Called: Rang Dong Winery
3 Executive Way, NAPA (94558-6271)
PHONE.....................................707 259-9446
Mailynh Phan, *General Mgr*
EMP: 14
SQ FT: 47,900
SALES (est): 845.9K
SALES (corp-wide): 61MM **Privately Held**
SIC: 2084 Wines
PA: Rang Dong Joint Stock Company
J45 Ton Duc Thang Street,
Phan Thiet
252 382-2301

(P-1881)
RB WINE ASSOCIATES LLC
Also Called: Rack & Riddle
499 Moore Ln, Healdsburg (95448-4825)
P.O. Box 2400 (95448-2400)
PHONE.....................................707 433-8400
Bruce Lundquist,
Kathy Dogali, *Admin Asst*
Stan Jennings, *Facilities Mgr*
Rebecca Faust,
Ray Brammeier, *Manager*
EMP: 80
SQ FT: 100,000
SALES: 11MM **Privately Held**
SIC: 2084 Wines

(P-1882)
RBZ VINEYARDS LLC
Also Called: Sextant Wines
2324 W Highway 46, Paso Robles
(93446-8602)
P.O. Box 391 (93447-0391)
PHONE.....................................805 542-0133
Craig Stoller, *Principal*
Amy Griffith, *Director*
EMP: 30
SALES: 5.3MM **Privately Held**
SIC: 2084 Wines

(P-1883)
REGAL III LLC
Also Called: Regal Wine Co
1190 Kittyhawk Blvd, Windsor (95492)
PHONE.....................................707 836-2100
Donald M Hartford Jr, *Mng Member*
Brent Bolding, *Vice Pres*
Melinda Arnold, *Executive*
Jenna Perry, *Executive*

Chris Cooke, *District Mgr*
◆ EMP: 63
SQ FT: 8,000
SALES: 100K **Privately Held**
SIC: 2084 Wines

(P-1884)
REGUSCI VINEYARD MGT INC
Also Called: Regusci Winery
5584 Silverado Trl, NAPA (94558-9411)
PHONE.....................................707 254-0403
James Regusci, *President*
Diana Regusci, *Vice Pres*
Jason Lauritsen, *Director*
EMP: 30
SALES (est): 6.6MM **Privately Held**
WEB: www.regusciwinery.com
SIC: 2084 0762 Wines; vineyard manage-
ment & maintenance services

(P-1885)
REN ACQUISITION INC
12225 Steiner Rd, Plymouth (95669-9502)
PHONE.....................................209 245-6979
Robert I Smerling, *Chairman*
▲ EMP: 11
SALES (est): 1.3MM **Privately Held**
SIC: 2084 Wines

(P-1886)
REVERIE ON DIAMOND MTN LLC
Also Called: Reverie Winery
4410 Lake County Hwy, Calistoga
(94515-9706)
PHONE.....................................707 942-6800
Norman Kiken,
Evelyn Kiken,
▲ EMP: 10
SALES (est): 780K **Privately Held**
WEB: www.reveriewine.com
SIC: 2084 Wines

(P-1887)
RHYS VINEYARDS LLC
11715 Skyline Blvd, Los Gatos
(95033-9588)
PHONE.....................................650 419-2050
Kevin Harvey,
Javier Meza,
▲ EMP: 19
SALES (est): 3.4MM **Privately Held**
SIC: 2084 Wines

(P-1888)
RIDEAU VINEYARD LLC
1562 Alamo Pintado Rd, Solvang
(93463-9756)
PHONE.....................................805 688-0717
Iris Rideau,
Jennifer Iverson,
Caren Rideau,
▲ EMP: 10
SALES (est): 1.5MM **Privately Held**
WEB: www.rideauvineyard.com
SIC: 2084 Wines

(P-1889)
RIOS-LOVELL ESTATE WINERY
Also Called: Rios-Lovell Winery
6500 Tesla Rd, Livermore (94550-9123)
PHONE.....................................925 443-0434
Max Rios, *Partner*
Katie Lovell, *Partner*
EMP: 20
SALES (est): 2.2MM **Privately Held**
WEB: www.rioslovellwinery.com
SIC: 2084 Wines

(P-1890)
RIVER BENCH VINEYARDS
137 Anacapa St, Santa Barbara
(93101-1848)
PHONE.....................................805 324-4100
Laura Booras, *Branch Mgr*
EMP: 18 **Privately Held**
SIC: 2084 0172 Wines; grapes
PA: River Bench Llc
6020 Foxen Canyon Rd
Santa Maria CA 93454

(P-1891)
ROBERT MONDAVI CORPORATION (HQ)
166 Gateway Rd E, NAPA (94558-7576)
P.O. Box 106, Oakville (94562-0106)
PHONE.....................................707 967-2100
Gregory Evans, *President*
Gregory M Evans, *President*
Henry J Salvo Jr, *CFO*
Timothy J Mondavi, *Vice Ch Bd*
▲ EMP: 75 EST: 1966
SQ FT: 5,000
SALES (est): 65.7MM
SALES (corp-wide): 8.1B **Publicly Held**
WEB: www.rmcoastalwines.com
SIC: 2084 Wines
PA: Constellation Brands, Inc.
207 High Point Dr # 100
Victor NY 14564
585 678-7100

(P-1892)
ROBERT MONDAVI CORPORATION
770 N Guild Ave, Lodi (95240-0861)
PHONE.....................................209 365-2995
Rick Anderson, *Manager*
EMP: 30
SALES (corp-wide): 8.1B **Publicly Held**
WEB: www.rmcoastalwines.com
SIC: 2084 Wines
HQ: The Robert Mondavi Corporation
166 Gateway Rd E
Napa CA 94558
707 967-2100

(P-1893)
ROBINSON FAMILY WINERY
5880 Silverado Trl, NAPA (94558-9418)
PHONE.....................................707 287-8428
Thomas Butler, *President*
EMP: 10
SALES (est): 432.8K **Privately Held**
SIC: 2084 Wines

(P-1894)
ROCK WALL WINE COMPANY INC
2301 Monarch St, Alameda (94501-7554)
PHONE.....................................510 522-5700
Kent Rosenblum, *CEO*
EMP: 20
SQ FT: 200
SALES (est): 3.4MM **Privately Held**
SIC: 2084 Wines

(P-1895)
ROMBAUER VINEYARDS INC
Also Called: Renwood Winery
851 Napa Vly Corp Way I, NAPA (94558)
PHONE.....................................209 245-6979
Jason Robinson, *Manager*
Wendy Worthington, *Technology*
EMP: 10
SALES (corp-wide): 18.7MM **Privately Held**
SIC: 2084 0172 Wines; grapes
PA: Rombauer Vineyards, Inc.
3522 Silverado Trl N
Saint Helena CA 94574
707 963-5170

(P-1896)
ROMBAUER VINEYARDS INC (PA)
3522 Silverado Trl N, Saint Helena
(94574-9663)
PHONE.....................................707 963-5170
Koerner Rombauer, *President*
Matthew Owings, *CFO*
Kendall Tompioner, *Executive Asst*
Sheana Rombauer, *Info Tech Dir*
Jane Ashley, *Accountant*
▲ EMP: 52
SQ FT: 25,000
SALES (est): 18.7MM **Privately Held**
WEB: www.rombauer.com
SIC: 2084 Wines

(P-1897)
ROTARY CLUB OF AJAI WEST
1129 Maricopa Hwy, Ojai (93023-3126)
PHONE.....................................805 646-3794
Michael Caldwell, *President*
Laurie Johnson, *Admin Sec*

EMP: 50
SALES (est): 2.9MM **Privately Held**
SIC: 2084 7991 Wines; athletic club &
gymnasiums, membership

(P-1898)
ROTTA WINERY INC
250 Winery Rd, Templeton (93465-9597)
PHONE.....................................805 237-0510
Michael D Giubbini, *President*
Mike Giubbini, *President*
Pete Gaidis, *CFO*
Steve Pasetti, *Vice Pres*
EMP: 10
SALES (est): 665.7K **Privately Held**
WEB: www.rottawinery.com
SIC: 2084 Wines

(P-1899)
ROUND HILL CELLARS
Also Called: Rutherford Wine Company
1680 Silverado Trl S, Saint Helena
(94574-9542)
P.O. Box 387, Rutherford (94573-0387)
PHONE.....................................707 968-3200
Marko B Zaninovich, *President*
Theo Zaninovich, *Principal*
Sierra Macintyre, *Marketing Staff*
Armando Padilla, *Manager*
▼ EMP: 55
SQ FT: 31,000
SALES (est): 10.5MM **Privately Held**
WEB: www.rutherfordranch.com
SIC: 2084 Wines

(P-1900)
ROYAL WINE CORPORATION
Also Called: Herzog Wine Cellars
3201 Camino Del Sol, Oxnard
(93030-8915)
PHONE.....................................805 983-1560
Joseph Herzog, *General Mgr*
Jacy Basile, *Controller*
Jenny Guy, *Marketing Staff*
Baruch Boyko, *Manager*
Donna Leary, *Manager*
EMP: 25
SALES (corp-wide): 44MM **Privately Held**
SIC: 2084 5182 Wines; wine; liquor
PA: Royal Wine Corporation
63 Lefante Dr
Bayonne NJ 07002
718 384-2400

(P-1901)
RUDD WINES INC (PA)
Also Called: Rudd Winery
500 Oakville Xrd, Oakville (94562)
P.O. Box 105 (94562-0105)
PHONE.....................................707 944-8577
Leslei Rudd, *President*
▲ EMP: 20
SALES (est): 2.2MM **Privately Held**
WEB: www.ruddwines.com
SIC: 2084 Wines

(P-1902)
RUSSIAN RIVER WINERY INC
2191 Laguna Rd, Santa Rosa
(95401-3705)
PHONE.....................................707 824-2005
Courtney M Benham, *CEO*
EMP: 39
SQ FT: 76,000
SALES: 5.1MM **Privately Held**
SIC: 2084 Wines

(P-1903)
S L CELLARS
9380 Sonoma Hwy, Kenwood
(95452-9032)
PHONE.....................................707 833-5070
J Bruce Jacobs, *President*
EMP: 12
SQ FT: 4,000
SALES (est): 603.3K
SALES (corp-wide): 1.9MM **Privately Held**
WEB: www.slcellars.com
SIC: 2084 Wines
PA: Simon Levi Company, Ltd.
9380 Sonoma Hwy
Kenwood CA
707 833-4455

▲ = Import ▼=Export
◆ =Import/Export

(P-1904)
S&B VINEYARD LLC
200 Rutherford Hill Rd, Rutherford (94573)
P.O. Box 427 (94573-0427)
PHONE....................707 963-7194
Anthony J Terlato, *Mng Member*
EMP: 45 **EST:** 1996
SALES (est): 4.8MM
SALES (corp-wide): 124.3MM **Privately Held**
WEB: www.rutherfordhills.com
SIC: 2084 Wines
PA: Terlato Wine Group, Ltd.
900 Armour Dr
Lake Bluff IL 60044
847 604-8900

(P-1905)
SAINTSBURY LLC
1500 Los Carneros Ave, NAPA (94559-9742)
PHONE....................707 252-0592
Richard Ward, *General Mgr*
Virginia Rogstad, *Administration*
Heather Vance, *Accountant*
Lisa Stuijvenberg, *Controller*
Lisa Van Stuijvenberg, *Controller*
EMP: 18
SQ FT: 32,500
SALES (est): 3MM **Privately Held**
WEB: www.saintsbury.com
SIC: 2084 Wines

(P-1906)
SAN ANTONIO WINERY INC (PA)
Also Called: San Antonio Gift Shop
737 Lamar St, Los Angeles (90031-2591)
PHONE....................323 223-1401
Santo Riboli, *CEO*
Maddelena Riboli, *Corp Secy*
Elise Keeling, *Store Mgr*
Cathey Riboli, *Asst Treas*
Dominic Menton, *Opers Mgr*
◆ **EMP:** 101 **EST:** 1917
SQ FT: 310,000
SALES (est): 24.1MM **Privately Held**
WEB: www.sanantoniowinery.com
SIC: 2084 5182 5812 Wines; wine; eating places

(P-1907)
SAVANNAH CHANELLE VINEYARDS
Also Called: Mariani Winery
23600 Big Basin Way, Saratoga (95070-9755)
PHONE....................408 741-2934
Michael Ballard, *President*
EMP: 22
SALES (est): 2.5MM **Privately Held**
WEB: www.savannahchanelle.com
SIC: 2084 5812 0172 Wines; eating places; grapes

(P-1908)
SBRAGIA FAMILY VINEYARDS LLC
9990 Dry Creek Rd, Geyserville (95441-9686)
PHONE....................707 473-2992
Edward Sbragia, *Mng Member*
EMP: 23
SALES (est): 4.3MM **Privately Held**
SIC: 2084 Wines

(P-1909)
SEAVEY VINEYARD LTD PARTNR
1310 Conn Valley Rd, Saint Helena (94574-9610)
PHONE....................707 963-8339
Dorothy Seavey, *CFO*
Arthur Seavey, *General Mgr*
EMP: 10
SALES (est): 376.2K **Privately Held**
SIC: 2084 Wines

(P-1910)
SEBASTIANI VINEYARDS INC
Also Called: Sebastiani Vineyards & Winery
389 4th St E, Sonoma (95476-5790)
PHONE....................707 933-3200
Mary Ann Sebastiani Cuneo, *CEO*
Richard Cuneo, *Ch of Bd*
Emma Swain, *COO*
Paul Bergena, *Exec VP*

◆ **EMP:** 100
SQ FT: 2,000
SALES (est): 14.9MM
SALES (corp-wide): 109.6MM **Privately Held**
WEB: www.sebastiani.com
SIC: 2084 Wines
HQ: Foley Family Wines, Inc.
200 Concourse Blvd
Paso Robles CA 93446

(P-1911)
SEGHESIO WINERIES INC
Also Called: Seghesio Winery
700 Grove St, Healdsburg (95448-4753)
PHONE....................707 433-3579
Eugene Peter Seghesio, *CEO*
Amy Seghesio, *Treasurer*
Raymond Seghesio, *Vice Pres*
Edward H Seghesio Jr, *Admin Sec*
Shane Hastings, *Production*
▼ **EMP:** 20
SQ FT: 6,000
SALES (est): 3.4MM **Privately Held**
WEB: www.seghesio.com
SIC: 2084 0172 Wines; grapes

(P-1912)
SELBY INC
Also Called: Selby Winery
498 Moore Ln Ste A, Healdsburg (95448-4840)
PHONE....................707 431-1703
Susie Selby, *President*
EMP: 10
SALES (est): 990K **Privately Held**
WEB: www.selbywinery.com
SIC: 2084 Wines

(P-1913)
SHAFER VINEYARDS
6154 Silverado Trl, NAPA (94558-9748)
PHONE....................707 944-2877
John Shafer, *Chairman*
Elizabeth S Cafaro, *Shareholder*
Bradford J Shafer, *Shareholder*
Douglas S Shafer, *President*
Matthew Sharp, *Sales Staff*
▲ **EMP:** 17
SQ FT: 2,000
SALES (est): 2.6MM **Privately Held**
WEB: www.shafervineyards.com
SIC: 2084 Wines

(P-1914)
SHANNON RIDGE INC
13888 Point Lakeview Rd, Lower Lake (95457-9617)
P.O. Box 676 (95457-0676)
PHONE....................707 994-9656
Clay Shannon, *President*
Mark Altrecht, *CFO*
Sheila Lapoint, *Controller*
Margarita Shannon, *Controller*
Angie Bigham, *Natl Sales Mgr*
EMP: 20 **EST:** 2003
SALES (est): 14MM **Privately Held**
SIC: 2084 5921 Wines; wine

(P-1915)
SHORELINE CELLARS INC
Also Called: Waters Edge Winery - Long Bch
217 Pine Ave, Long Beach (90802-3043)
PHONE....................909 322-6816
Mark Mitzenmacher, *Director*
Stephan Demartimprey, *Director*
Collin Mitzenmacher, *Director*
Wesley Wegner, *Director*
EMP: 12
SALES (est): 576.8K **Privately Held**
SIC: 2084 Wines

(P-1916)
SIERRA SUNRISE VINEYARD INC
Also Called: Montevina Winery
20680 Shenandoah Schl Rd, Plymouth (95669-9511)
P.O. Box 248, Saint Helena (94574-0248)
PHONE....................209 245-6942
Louis Trinchero, *Ch of Bd*
Robery Tortelson, *President*
Roger Trinchero, *CEO*
Jeff Meyers, *Vice Pres*
Vera Trinchero Torres, *Admin Sec*
EMP: 26

SQ FT: 52,000
SALES (est): 3.3MM
SALES (corp-wide): 184.6MM **Privately Held**
WEB: www.frewines.com
SIC: 2084 0172 Wines; grapes
PA: Sutter Home Winery, Inc.
100 Saint Helena Hwy S
Saint Helena CA 94574
707 963-3104

(P-1917)
SILENUS VINTNERS
5225 Solano Ave, NAPA (94558-1019)
PHONE....................707 299-3930
Bob Williamson, *Owner*
▲ **EMP:** 10
SALES (est): 1.3MM
SALES (corp-wide): 1.4MM **Privately Held**
SIC: 2084 Wines
HQ: Henan Meijing Group Co., Ltd.
Room 1601, Torch Building B, Hi-Tech Industrial Development Area
Zhengzhou 45004
371 569-9516

(P-1918)
SILVER HORSE VINEYARDS INC
Also Called: Silver Ranch and Winery
1205 Beaver Creek Ln, Paso Robles (93446-4942)
P.O. Box 2010 (93447-2010)
PHONE....................805 467-9463
Jim Kroener, *President*
EMP: 18
SALES (est): 1.6MM **Privately Held**
WEB: www.silverhorsevineyards.com
SIC: 2084 Wines

(P-1919)
SILVER OAK WINE CELLARS LP (PA)
915 Oakville Cross Rd, Oakville (94562)
P.O. Box 414 (94562-0414)
PHONE....................707 942-7022
David R Duncan, *Partner*
Raymond Duncan, *Partner*
Veronica Jauregui, *Human Res Dir*
Vivien Gay, *Sales Mgr*
Scott Bothof, *Sales Staff*
EMP: 15
SALES (est): 12.8MM **Privately Held**
SIC: 2084 Wines

(P-1920)
SOCIETE BREWING COMPANY LLC
8262 Clairemont Mesa Blvd, Del Mar (92014)
PHONE....................858 598-5415
EMP: 15
SALES (est): 1MM **Privately Held**
SIC: 2084

(P-1921)
SONOMA WINE COMPANY LLC
9119 Graton Rd, Graton (95444-9373)
P.O. Box 390 (95444-0390)
PHONE....................707 829-6100
Derek Benham, *Mng Member*
Dan Johnson, *Planning*
Robin Nehasil, *Controller*
Jim Bragg, *Maintence Staff*
Craig McCormick, *Maintence Staff*
▲ **EMP:** 160
SALES (est): 27.6MM **Privately Held**
SIC: 2084 Wine cellars, bonded: engaged in blending wines; wines

(P-1922)
SONOMA WINE HARDWARE INC
360 Swift Ave Ste 34, South San Francisco (94080-6220)
PHONE....................650 866-3020
James Mackey, *President*
EMP: 20
SALES (est): 118.4K **Privately Held**
SIC: 2084 Wines, brandy & brandy spirits

(P-1923)
SOUTH COAST WINERY INC
Also Called: South Coast Winery Resort Spa
34843 Rancho Cal Rd, Temecula (92591-4006)
PHONE....................951 587-9463

James A Carter, *President*
Stephanie Espinoza, *Director*
▲ **EMP:** 32
SALES (est): 8.3MM
SALES (corp-wide): 11.4MM **Privately Held**
SIC: 2084 7011 7991 Wines; resort hotel; spas
PA: Grove Spruce Inc
3719 S Plaza Dr
Santa Ana CA 92704
714 546-4255

(P-1924)
SPANISH CASTLE INC
Also Called: Union Wine Company
22201 Camay Ct, Calabasas (91302-6116)
PHONE....................818 222-4496
Steve Ventrello, *President*
Steve Stump, *Vice Pres*
EMP: 14
SALES (est): 1.2MM **Privately Held**
WEB: www.spanishcastle.com
SIC: 2084 Wines

(P-1925)
SPRING MOUNTAIN VINEYARDS INC
2805 Spring Mountain Rd, Saint Helena (94574-1775)
P.O. Box 991 (94574-0491)
PHONE....................707 967-4188
Don Yannias, *President*
Jean-Pierre Boustany, *Vice Pres*
George Peterson, *General Mgr*
Valli Ferrell, *Director*
EMP: 42
SQ FT: 16,000
SALES: 8MM **Privately Held**
WEB: www.springmtn.com
SIC: 2084 0762 Wines; vineyard management & maintenance services

(P-1926)
ST GEORGE SPIRITS INC
2601 Monarch St, Alameda (94501-7541)
PHONE....................510 769-1601
Jorg Rupf, *Principal*
Lance Winters, *President*
Meysa Budzinski, *Admin Asst*
James Lee, *Production*
Steven Ciavola, *VP Sales*
◆ **EMP:** 25
SQ FT: 65,000
SALES (est): 4.8MM **Privately Held**
WEB: www.stgeorgespirits.com
SIC: 2084 2085 Brandy spirits; distilled & blended liquors

(P-1927)
ST SUPERY INC (DH)
Also Called: Skalli Vineyards
8440 St Helena Hwy, Rutherford (94573)
P.O. Box 38 (94573-0038)
PHONE....................707 963-4507
Emma Swain, *CEO*
◆ **EMP:** 50
SQ FT: 20,000
SALES (est): 8.1MM **Privately Held**
SIC: 2084 Wines
HQ: Chanel, Inc.
9 W 57th St Bsmt 2b
New York NY 10019
212 688-5055

(P-1928)
STAGS LEAP WINE CELLARS
Also Called: Hawk Crest
5766 Silverado Trl, NAPA (94558-9413)
PHONE....................707 944-2020
Warren Winiarski, *Principal*
Brian Jones, *COO*
Sara Martinez, *Treasurer*
Bertha Rodriguez, *Executive*
Timothy Rowe, *Technician*
▲ **EMP:** 110
SQ FT: 40,000
SALES (est): 17.3MM **Privately Held**
WEB: www.cask23.com
SIC: 2084 Wines

(P-1929)
STEELE WINES INC
4350 Thomas Dr, Kelseyville (95451)
P.O. Box 190 (95451-0190)
PHONE....................707 279-9475

PRODUCTS & SVCS

Jedediah T Steele, *President*
Naomi Key, *Admin Sec*
Pam Prisco, *Manager*
EMP: 25
SALES (est): 2.6MM **Privately Held**
WEB: www.steelewines.com
SIC: 2084 Wines

(P-1930)
STERLING VINEYARDS INC (PA)
1111 Dunaweal Ln, Calistoga (94515-9799)
P.O. Box 365 (94515-0365)
PHONE..................................707 942-3300
Samuel Bronfman II, *Ch of Bd*
Ron Lilly, *Vice Pres*
Mike Westrick, *Vice Pres*
▲ **EMP:** 50
SQ FT: 80,000
SALES (est): 25MM **Privately Held**
WEB: www.sterlingvineyards.com
SIC: 2084 0172 Wine cellars, bonded: engaged in blending wines; grapes

(P-1931)
STERLING VINEYARDS INC
1105 Oak Knoll Ave, NAPA (94558-1304)
P.O. Box 365, Calistoga (94515-0365)
PHONE..................................707 252-7410
Vincent Vinnodo, *Manager*
EMP: 30
SALES (est): 2MM
SALES (corp-wide): 25MM **Privately Held**
WEB: www.sterlingvineyards.com
SIC: 2084 0172 Wines; grapes
PA: Sterling Vineyards, Inc.
    1111 Dunaweal Ln
    Calistoga CA 94515
    707 942-3300

(P-1932)
STERLING VINEYARDS INC
3690 Santa Lina Hwy, Calistoga (94515)
PHONE..................................707 942-9602
Jim Munk, *Principal*
EMP: 10
SALES (corp-wide): 25MM **Privately Held**
WEB: www.sterlingvineyards.com
SIC: 2084 Wine cellars, bonded: engaged in blending wines
PA: Sterling Vineyards, Inc.
    1111 Dunaweal Ln
    Calistoga CA 94515
    707 942-3300

(P-1933)
STEVEN KENT LLC
Also Called: La- Rochelle
5443 Tesla Rd, Livermore (94550-9621)
PHONE..................................925 243-6442
Steven Mirassou, *Mng Member*
Michael Ghielnitti,
▲ **EMP:** 29 EST: 2001
SALES (est): 3.3MM **Privately Held**
WEB: www.stevenkent.com
SIC: 2084 Wines

(P-1934)
STOLPMAN VINEYARDS LLC (PA)
2434 Alamo Pintado Rd, Los Olivos (93441-4500)
PHONE..................................805 736-5000
Thomas Stolpman, *Mng Member*
Marilyn Stolpman, *Mng Member*
EMP: 14
SALES (est): 5.6MM **Privately Held**
SIC: 2084 Wines

(P-1935)
STOLPMAN VINEYARDS LLC
1700 Industrial Way B, Lompoc (93436-4947)
P.O. Box B, Los Olivos (93441)
PHONE..................................805 736-5000
Tom Stolpman, *Branch Mgr*
EMP: 47
SALES (corp-wide): 5.6MM **Privately Held**
SIC: 2084 Wines
PA: Stolpman Vineyards Llc
    2434 Alamo Pintado Rd
    Los Olivos CA 93441
    805 736-5000

(P-1936)
STONE BRIDGE CELLARS INC (PA)
Also Called: Joseph Phelps Vineyards
200 Taplin Rd, Saint Helena (94574-9544)
P.O. Box 1031 (94574-0531)
PHONE..................................707 963-2745
Joseph Phelps, *Ch of Bd*
Robert Boyd, *President*
Clarice Turner, *President*
William H Phelps, *CEO*
AMI Iadarola, *CFO*
▲ **EMP:** 100
SQ FT: 50,000
SALES (est): 16.1MM **Privately Held**
WEB: www.jpvwines.com
SIC: 2084 Wines

(P-1937)
STONE EDGE WINERY LLC
Also Called: Stone Edge Farm
19330 Carriger Rd, Sonoma (95476-6229)
P.O. Box 487 (95476-0487)
PHONE..................................707 935-6520
John A McQuown,
Kim Bandel, *Opers Mgr*
Whitney Reese, *Director*
EMP: 12
SQ FT: 1,500
SALES (est): 1.3MM **Privately Held**
SIC: 2084 Wines

(P-1938)
STONECUSHION INC (PA)
Also Called: Wilson Artisan Wineries
1400 Lytton Springs Rd, Healdsburg (95448-9695)
P.O. Box 487, Geyserville (95441-0487)
PHONE..................................707 433-1911
Kenneth C Wilson, *President*
EMP: 25
SALES (est): 4.2MM **Privately Held**
SIC: 2084 Wines

(P-1939)
STUART CELLARS LLC
41006 Simi Ct, Temecula (92591-4988)
PHONE..................................951 676-6414
Marshall Stuart,
▲ **EMP:** 17 EST: 1996
SQ FT: 2,240
SALES (est): 1.6MM **Privately Held**
SIC: 2084 Wines

(P-1940)
SUGARLOAF FARMING CORPORATION
Also Called: Peter Michael Winery
12400 Ida Clayton Rd, Calistoga (94515-9507)
PHONE..................................707 942-4459
Scott Rodde, *CEO*
Bill Vyenielo, *Vice Pres*
▼ **EMP:** 25
SQ FT: 1,000
SALES (est): 5.3MM
SALES (corp-wide): 45.6MM **Privately Held**
WEB: www.petermichaelwinery.com
SIC: 2084 Wines
PA: Stockford Limited
    Sheet Street
    Windsor BERKS SL4 1

(P-1941)
SUTTER HOME WINERY INC (PA)
Also Called: Trinchero Family Estates
100 Saint Helena Hwy S, Saint Helena (94574-2204)
P.O. Box 248 (94574-0248)
PHONE..................................707 963-3104
Roger J Trinchero, *CEO*
Louis Trinchero, *CEO*
Anthony R Torres, *Vice Pres*
Randy Hecklinski, *VP Sales*
Lorie Bruneman, *Senior Mgr*
◆ **EMP:** 200
SQ FT: 17,000
SALES (est): 184.6MM **Privately Held**
WEB: www.frewines.com
SIC: 2084 0172 Wines; grapes

(P-1942)
SUTTER HOME WINERY INC
Also Called: Trinchero Family Estates
18655 Jacob Brack Rd, Lodi (95242-9185)
PHONE..................................707 963-5928
EMP: 139
SALES (corp-wide): 184.6MM **Privately Held**
SIC: 2084 Brandy
PA: Sutter Home Winery, Inc.
    100 Saint Helena Hwy S
    Saint Helena CA 94574
    707 963-3104

(P-1943)
SUTTER HOME WINERY INC
560 Gateway Dr, NAPA (94558-7517)
PHONE..................................707 963-3104
EMP: 49
SALES (corp-wide): 184.6MM **Privately Held**
SIC: 2084 Wines
PA: Sutter Home Winery, Inc.
    100 Saint Helena Hwy S
    Saint Helena CA 94574
    707 963-3104

(P-1944)
SVP WINERY LLC
Also Called: Tarrica Wine Cellars
111 Clark Rd, Shandon (93461)
P.O. Box 195 (93461-0195)
PHONE..................................805 237-8693
Sam Balakian, *Mng Member*
EMP: 15 EST: 1999
SQ FT: 1,624
SALES (est): 1.9MM **Privately Held**
WEB: www.tarricawinecellars.com
SIC: 2084 Wines

(P-1945)
SYLVESTER WINERY INC
5115 Buena Vista Dr, Paso Robles (93446-8558)
PHONE..................................805 227-4000
Syliva Phillini, *President*
Scott Keller, *CFO*
Zina Miakinkova, *Marketing Mgr*
Savannah Romero, *Manager*
EMP: 38
SALES (est): 2.4MM **Privately Held**
WEB: www.sylvesterwinery.com
SIC: 2084 Wines

(P-1946)
TABLAS CREEK VINEYARD LLC
9339 Adelaida Rd, Paso Robles (93446-9785)
PHONE..................................805 237-1231
Bob Haas, *Partner*
Heather Hildenbrand, *Asst Controller*
Darren Delmore, *Natl Sales Mgr*
Jason Haas, *Mktg Dir*
Lauren Cross, *Mktg Coord*
▲ **EMP:** 18
SQ FT: 40,000
SALES (est): 3.6MM **Privately Held**
WEB: www.tablascreek.com
SIC: 2084 Wines

(P-1947)
TAFT STREET INC
Also Called: Taft Street Winery
2030 Barlow Ln, Sebastopol (95472-2555)
PHONE..................................707 823-2049
Michael Tierney, *President*
Mike Martini, *CFO*
Martin Tierney Jr, *Vice Pres*
Laurie Keith, *Sales Mgr*
Bruce Walker, *Sales Staff*
EMP: 20
SQ FT: 30,000
SALES (est): 3.5MM **Privately Held**
WEB: www.taftstreetwinery.com
SIC: 2084 Wines

(P-1948)
TANDEM WINES LLC
Also Called: La Follette Wines
4900 W Dry Creek Rd, Healdsburg (95448-9721)
PHONE..................................707 395-3902
Peter J Kight, *Mng Member*
Dave Lese,
EMP: 12

(P-1949)
TEMECULA VALLEY WINERY MGT LLC
Also Called: Leonesse Cellars
27495 Diaz Rd, Temecula (92590-3414)
PHONE..................................951 699-8896
Willem Rebaux Steyn,
Tim Kramer, *COO*
Angela Murphy, *Executive*
Catherine Pruhsmeier, *Accounting Mgr*
Ashleigh Prose, *Human Res Mgr*
EMP: 56 EST: 2008
SQ FT: 40,000
SALES (est): 10.4MM **Privately Held**
SIC: 2084 Wines

(P-1950)
TERRAVANT WINE COMPANY LLC (PA)
70 Industrial Way, Buellton (93427-9567)
PHONE..................................805 688-4245
Lew Eisaguirre, *President*
Eric J Guerra, *Senior VP*
Joyce Soares, *Vice Pres*
Matt Valine, *Creative Dir*
Marcie Casillas, *Human Res Mgr*
▲ **EMP:** 45
SQ FT: 25,000
SALES (est): 19.3MM **Privately Held**
WEB: www.terravant.com
SIC: 2084 Wines

(P-1951)
TESLA VINEYARDS LP
Also Called: Concannon Vineyard
4590 Tesla Rd, Livermore (94550-9002)
PHONE..................................925 456-2500
Eric Wente, *Partner*
Edward Lanphier, *Partner*
Henry Wilder, *Partner*
Dennis Wood, *Partner*
Michael Wood, *Partner*
▲ **EMP:** 15
SALES (est): 2.5MM **Privately Held**
WEB: www.concannonvineyard.com
SIC: 2084 0721 Wines; vines, cultivation of

(P-1952)
TESTAROSSA VINEYARDS LLC
300 College Ave Ste A, Los Gatos (95030-7066)
P.O. Box 969 (95031-0969)
PHONE..................................408 354-6150
Diana Jensen,
Lanee Powell, *Human Res Mgr*
Julie Scopazzi, *Marketing Mgr*
Robert Jensen,
Greg Pussehl, *Regional*
▲ **EMP:** 25
SQ FT: 10,000
SALES (est): 5.4MM **Privately Held**
WEB: www.testarossa.com
SIC: 2084 Wines

(P-1953)
THOMAS DEHLINGER
Also Called: Dehlinger Winery
4101 Ginehill Rd, Sebastopol (95472)
PHONE..................................707 823-2378
Thomas Dehlinger, *Owner*
Carmen Dehlinger, *Sales Staff*
EMP: 12
SQ FT: 18,000
SALES (est): 1.2MM **Privately Held**
SIC: 2084 0172 Wines; grapes

(P-1954)
THOMAS FOGARTY WINERY LLC (PA)
3130 Alpine Rd, Portola Valley (94028-7549)
PHONE..................................650 851-6777
Thomas J Fogarty MD,
Michael Martella, *Manager*
Nathan W Kandler, *Associate*
▲ **EMP:** 25
SQ FT: 4,000

SALES (est): 1.1MM **Privately Held**
SIC: 2084 Wine cellars, bonded: engaged in blending wines

SALES: 1.2MM **Privately Held**
WEB: www.fogartywinery.com
SIC: **2084** 0172 7299 Wines; grapes; facility rental & party planning services

(P-1955)
THOMAS LEONARDINI
Also Called: Whitehall Lane Winery
1563 Saint Helena Hwy S, Saint Helena (94574-9775)
PHONE..................707 963-9454
Thomas Leonardini, *Owner*
▲ EMP: 15
SQ FT: 24,000
SALES (est): 2MM **Privately Held**
WEB: www.bennettlane.com
SIC: **2084** 0172 Wines; grapes

(P-1956)
THORNTON WINERY
Also Called: Cafe Champagne
32575 Rancho Cal Rd, Temecula (92591-4935)
P.O. Box 9008 (92589-9008)
PHONE..................951 699-0099
John M Thornton, *Ch of Bd*
Steve Thornton, *President*
EMP: 98
SQ FT: 41,000
SALES (est): 15.5MM **Privately Held**
WEB: www.thorntonwine.com
SIC: **2084** 5812 5947 Wine cellars, bonded: engaged in blending wines; eating places; gift shop

(P-1957)
THREE STICKS WINES LLC
21692 8th St E Ste 280, Sonoma (95476-2804)
P.O. Box 1869 (95476-1869)
PHONE..................707 996-3328
Bill Price, *Owner*
EMP: 21
SALES (est): 1.7MM **Privately Held**
SIC: **2084** Wines

(P-1958)
TMR WINE COMPANY
Also Called: Continuum Estate
1677 Sage Canyon Rd, Saint Helena (94574-9809)
PHONE..................707 944-8100
Tim Mondalvi, *Owner*
Marcia Mandalvi, *Principal*
EMP: 11
SALES (est): 1.2MM **Privately Held**
SIC: **2084** Wines

(P-1959)
TOAD HOLLOW VINEYARDS INC
4024 Westside Rd, Healdsburg (95448-9356)
P.O. Box 876 (95448-0876)
PHONE..................707 431-1441
Robert Todd Williams, *President*
Bill Zuur, *Technician*
Cherie Zouzounis, *Mfg Mgr*
▲ EMP: 14
SQ FT: 3,000
SALES (est): 2.8MM **Privately Held**
WEB: www.toadhollow.com
SIC: **2084** Wines

(P-1960)
TOP IT OFF BOTTLING LLC
2747 Napa Valley Corp Dr, NAPA (94558)
PHONE..................707 252-0331
Michael Glavin,
Bill Crawford, *Opers Staff*
Randall Ramos,
EMP: 10
SALES (est): 1.6MM **Privately Held**
SIC: **2084** Wines

(P-1961)
TREANA WINERY LLC
Also Called: Liberty School
4280 Second Wind Way, Paso Robles (93446-6309)
P.O. Box 3260 (93447-3260)
PHONE..................805 237-2932
Charles Hope,
Charles Wagner,
Abigail Rapp, *Manager*
▲ EMP: 30 EST: 1996

SALES (est): 5.9MM **Privately Held**
WEB: www.treana.com
SIC: **2084** Wines

(P-1962)
TREASURY CHATEAU & ESTATES
Also Called: Carmenet Vineyards
1700 Moon Mountain Rd, Sonoma (95476-3022)
PHONE..................707 996-5870
EMP: 13
SQ FT: 1,232
SALES (corp-wide): 16.6B **Privately Held**
SIC: **2084**
HQ: Treasury Chateau & Estates
10300 Chalk Hill Rd
Healdsburg CA 95448
707 299-2600

(P-1963)
TREASURY WINE ESTATES AMERICAS (HQ)
555 Gateway Dr, NAPA (94558-6291)
PHONE..................707 259-4500
Michael Clarke, *CEO*
Robert Foye, *President*
Don McCall, *President*
Bob Spooner, *President*
Noel Meehan, *CFO*
◆ EMP: 400 EST: 1973
SQ FT: 26,000
SALES (est): 412.5MM **Privately Held**
WEB: www.stclement.com
SIC: **2084** Wines

(P-1964)
TREASURY WINE ESTATES AMERICAS
600 Airpark Rd, NAPA (94558-7516)
PHONE..................707 259-4500
Deborah Dubois, *Branch Mgr*
Seth Hynes, *Vice Pres*
Warwick Every-Burns, *Exec Dir*
Scott Bowden, *District Mgr*
Terry Dicarlo, *General Mgr*
EMP: 121 **Privately Held**
SIC: **2084** Wines
HQ: Treasury Wine Estates Americas Company
555 Gateway Dr
Napa CA 94558
707 259-4500

(P-1965)
TREASURY WINE ESTATES AMERICAS
Also Called: Beringer Vineyards
2000 Main St, Saint Helena (94574-9500)
P.O. Box 111 (94574-0111)
PHONE..................707 963-7115
Brenda Wand, *Manager*
Ed Broshears, *Manager*
Nancy Mena, *Manager*
Claire Wilkins, *Manager*
EMP: 81 **Privately Held**
WEB: www.stclement.com
SIC: **2084** Wines
HQ: Treasury Wine Estates Americas Company
555 Gateway Dr
Napa CA 94558
707 259-4500

(P-1966)
TREASURY WINE ESTATES AMERICAS
Also Called: Beringer Vinyards
1000 Pratt Ave, Saint Helena (94574-1020)
P.O. Box 111 (94574-0111)
PHONE..................707 963-4812
Walter Klenz, *Manager*
EMP: 300 **Privately Held**
WEB: www.stclement.com
SIC: **2084** 5182 5921 Wines; wine; liquor stores
HQ: Treasury Wine Estates Americas Company
555 Gateway Dr
Napa CA 94558
707 259-4500

(P-1967)
TREASURY WINE ESTATES AMERICAS
Also Called: Chateau St Jean
8555 Sonoma Hwy, Kenwood (95452-9026)
P.O. Box 293 (95452-0293)
PHONE..................707 833-4134
Lisa Saroni, *Principal*
EMP: 20 **Privately Held**
WEB: www.stclement.com
SIC: **2084** 0172 Wines; grapes
HQ: Treasury Wine Estates Americas Company
555 Gateway Dr
Napa CA 94558
707 259-4500

(P-1968)
TREASURY WINE ESTATES AMERICAS
Also Called: Asti Winery
26150 Asti Rd, Cloverdale (95425-7003)
PHONE..................707 894-2541
Lou Toninato, *Director*
EMP: 35 **Privately Held**
WEB: www.stclement.com
SIC: **2084** Wines
HQ: Treasury Wine Estates Americas Company
555 Gateway Dr
Napa CA 94558
707 259-4500

(P-1969)
TREASURY WINE ESTATES AMERICAS
2000 Saint Helena Hwy N, Saint Helena (94574)
PHONE..................707 963-7115
Sally Buchanan, *General Mgr*
EMP: 81 **Privately Held**
WEB: www.stclement.com
SIC: **2084** Wines
HQ: Treasury Wine Estates Americas Company
555 Gateway Dr
Napa CA 94558
707 259-4500

(P-1970)
TREFETHEN VINEYARDS WINERY INC
Also Called: Trefethen Family Vineyards
1160 Oak Knoll Ave, NAPA (94558-1398)
P.O. Box 2460 (94558-0291)
PHONE..................707 255-7700
Jon Ruel, *President*
Carla Trefethen, *Shareholder*
Loren Trefethen, *Exec VP*
David Whitehouse, *Vice Pres*
Betty Calvin, *Executive*
▲ EMP: 50
SQ FT: 4,000
SALES (est): 10.2MM **Privately Held**
WEB: www.trefethen.com
SIC: **2084** 5921 Wines; wine

(P-1971)
TRINCHERO FAMILY ESTATES INC
Also Called: Folie A Deux Winery
3070 Saint Helena Hwy N, Saint Helena (94574-9656)
PHONE..................707 963-1160
Richard Peterson, *Branch Mgr*
EMP: 10
SALES (corp-wide): 184.6MM **Privately Held**
WEB: www.frewines.com
SIC: **2084** 0172 Wines; grapes
PA: Sutter Home Winery, Inc.
100 Saint Helena Hwy S
Saint Helena CA 94574
707 963-3104

(P-1972)
TRUETT-HURST INC (PA)
125 Foss Creek Cir, Healdsburg (95448-4288)
P.O. Box 1532 (95448-1532)
PHONE..................707 431-4423
Philip L Hurst, *Ch of Bd*
Karen Weaver, *CFO*
Jason Strobbe, *Exec VP*

Marcus Benedetti, *Director*
Daniel Carroll, *Director*
▲ EMP: 27 EST: 2007
SQ FT: 2,500
SALES: 6.4MM **Publicly Held**
SIC: **2084** Wine cellars, bonded: engaged in blending wines

(P-1973)
TULOCAY WINERY
1426 Coombsville Rd, NAPA (94558-3907)
PHONE..................707 255-4064
William C Cadman, *Owner*
EMP: 10
SALES: 148K **Privately Held**
WEB: www.tulocay.com
SIC: **2084** Wines

(P-1974)
TURLEY WINE CELLARS
2900 Vineyard Dr, Templeton (93465-9417)
PHONE..................805 434-1030
Larry Turley, *President*
Rich Ardson, *General Mgr*
Lynn Stiefeling, *Controller*
Malanie Anderson, *Opers Mgr*
Valeri Crane, *Opers-Prdtn-Mfg*
EMP: 12 EST: 1928
SQ FT: 3,500
SALES (est): 1.2MM **Privately Held**
WEB: www.turleywinecellars.com
SIC: **2084** Wines

(P-1975)
TURLEY WINE CELLARS INC
Also Called: Pesenti Winery
3358 Saint Helena Hwy N, Saint Helena (94574-9660)
PHONE..................707 968-2700
Larry Turley, *President*
EMP: 11
SALES (est): 2MM **Privately Held**
SIC: **2084** Wines

(P-1976)
TURNBULL WINE CELLARS
8210 St Helena Hwy, Oakville (94562)
P.O. Box 29 (94562-0029)
PHONE..................707 963-5839
Patrick O'Dell, *President*
Laura Meltzer, *Administration*
Peter Heitz, *Opers Mgr*
Tyler Neiburger, *Manager*
▲ EMP: 10 EST: 1977
SQ FT: 1,600
SALES (est): 1.3MM
SALES (corp-wide): 9.8MM **Privately Held**
SIC: **2084** Wines
PA: Humboldt Group
180 S Fortuna Blvd
Fortuna CA
707 725-6661

(P-1977)
TWIN PEAKS WINERY INC
1473 Yountville Cross Rd, Yountville (94599-9471)
PHONE..................707 945-0855
Cliff Lede, *Principal*
EMP: 13
SALES (est): 1.9MM **Privately Held**
SIC: **2084** Wines

(P-1978)
TWISTED OAK WINERY LLC (PA)
4280 Red Hill Rd, Vallecito (95251)
P.O. Box 2385, Murphys (95247-2385)
PHONE..................209 728-3000
Jeffrey Stai,
EMP: 20
SQ FT: 1,000
SALES (est): 2.7MM **Privately Held**
SIC: **2084** Wine cellars, bonded: engaged in blending wines; wines

(P-1979)
TWO BLIND MICE LLC
Also Called: Maestro Cellars
5016 E Crescent Dr, Anaheim (92807-3631)
PHONE..................714 279-0600
Kevin Crampton, *Mng Member*
EMP: 11
SALES: 1.3MM **Privately Held**
SIC: **2084** Wines

(P-1980)
VALLEY OF MOON WINERY
777 Madrone Rd, Glen Ellen (95442-9522)
P.O. Box 1951 (95442-1951)
PHONE..............................707 939-4500
Gary Heck, *President*
◆ EMP: 25
SQ FT: 10,000
SALES (est): 2.6MM
SALES (corp-wide): 98.2MM **Privately Held**
WEB: www.vomwinery.com
SIC: 2084 0172 Wines; grapes
PA: F. Korbel & Bros.
13250 River Rd
Guerneville CA 95446
707 824-7000

(P-1981)
VIADER VINEYARDS
Also Called: Viader Vineyard & Winery
1120 Deer Park Rd, Deer Park
(94576-9715)
P.O. Box 280 (94576-0280)
PHONE..............................707 963-3816
Delia Viader, *CEO*
Chip Fey,
▲ EMP: 10
SQ FT: 5,000
SALES (est): 1.3MM **Privately Held**
WEB: www.viader.com
SIC: 2084 Wines

(P-1982)
VIE-DEL COMPANY
13363 S Indianola Ave, Kingsburg
(93631-9268)
PHONE..............................559 896-3065
Richard Watson, *Principal*
EMP: 20
SALES (corp-wide): 12.8MM **Privately Held**
SIC: 2084 2037 Brandy; wines; frozen
fruits & vegetables
PA: Vie-Del Company
11903 S Chestnut Ave
Fresno CA 93725
559 834-2525

(P-1983)
VIGNETTE WINERY LLC
Also Called: Wine Foundry
45 Enterprise Ct Ste 3, NAPA
(94558-7586)
PHONE..............................707 637-8821
Aaron Hayos, *Principal*
EMP: 11
SALES (corp-wide): 2.6MM **Privately Held**
SIC: 2084 Wines
PA: Vignette Winery, Llc
45 Enterprise Ct
Napa CA 94558
707 637-8821

(P-1984)
VILLA AMOROSA
Also Called: Castello Diamorosa
4045 Saint Helena Hwy, Calistoga
(94515-9609)
PHONE..............................707 942-8200
Georg Falzner, *President*
▲ EMP: 100
SALES (est): 15MM **Privately Held**
SIC: 2084 Wines

(P-1985)
VILLA ENCINAL PARTNERS LP
Also Called: Plumjack Winery
620 Oakville Cross Rd, NAPA
(94558-9740)
PHONE..............................707 945-1220
Gavin Newsom, *General Ptnr*
▲ EMP: 10
SALES (est): 682.6K **Privately Held**
SIC: 2084 5812 Wine cellars, bonded: en-
gaged in blending wines; eating places

(P-1986)
VILLA TOSCANO WINERY
10600 Shenandoah Rd, Plymouth
(95669-9513)
P.O. Box 1029 (95669-1029)
PHONE..............................209 245-3800
Jerry Wright, *Owner*
▲ EMP: 27

SQ FT: 18,000
SALES (est): 2.3MM **Privately Held**
WEB: www.villatoscano.com
SIC: 2084 Wines

(P-1987)
VINEBURG WINE COMPANY INC
(PA)
Also Called: Bartholomew Park Winery
2000 Denmark St, Sonoma (95476-9615)
P.O. Box 1, Vineburg (95487-0001)
PHONE..............................707 938-5277
Jim Bundschu, *CEO*
Nancy Bundschu, *President*
Lisa Dencklau, *Executive*
Jennifer Sahouria-Pangle, *Asst Controller*
Leila Pearson, *Sales Staff*
▲ EMP: 25
SQ FT: 4,000
SALES (est): 5.8MM **Privately Held**
WEB: www.gunbun.com
SIC: 2084 0172 Wines; grapes

(P-1988)
VINEYARD 29 LLC
2929 Saint Helena Hwy N, Saint Helena
(94574-9701)
P.O. Box 93 (94574-0093)
PHONE..............................707 963-9292
Chuck McMinn, *Owner*
▲ EMP: 10
SQ FT: 1,464
SALES (est): 1.3MM **Privately Held**
SIC: 2084 Wines

(P-1989)
VINTAGE POINT LLC
564 Broadway, Sonoma (95476-6602)
PHONE..............................707 939-6766
David H Biggar,
Teresa M Sullivan,
Tabitha Alger, *Manager*
Sara Andrews, *Manager*
▲ EMP: 25
SQ FT: 2,400
SALES (est): 3.1MM **Privately Held**
SIC: 2084 Wines

(P-1990)
VINTAGE WINE ESTATES INC
1060 Dunaweal Ln, Calistoga
(94515-9798)
PHONE..............................707 942-4981
Patrick Roney, *President*
EMP: 12 **Privately Held**
SIC: 2084 Wines
PA: Vintage Wine Estates, Inc.
205 Concourse Blvd
Santa Rosa CA 95403

(P-1991)
VINTAGE WINE ESTATES INC
Also Called: B.R. Cohn
15000 Hwy 12, Glen Ellen (95442-9454)
PHONE..............................707 933-9675
Paula Horosco, *Executive*
EMP: 35 **Privately Held**
SIC: 2084 0172 5921 Wines; grapes;
wine
PA: Vintage Wine Estates, Inc.
205 Concourse Blvd
Santa Rosa CA 95403
-

(P-1992)
VINTAGE WINE ESTATES INC
(PA)
205 Concourse Blvd, Santa Rosa
(95403-8258)
PHONE..............................877 289-9463
Patrick Roney, *CEO*
Terry Wheatley, *President*
Jeff Nicholson, *COO*
Karen L Diepholz, *CFO*
▲ EMP: 162
SALES (est): 99.4MM **Privately Held**
SIC: 2084 Wines

(P-1993)
WATERS EDGE WINERIES INC
Also Called: Waters Edge Winery
8560 Vineyard Ave Ste 408, Rancho Cuca-
monga (91730-4351)
PHONE..............................909 468-9463
Ken Lineberger, *Principal*

EMP: 15
SALES (est): 2.3MM **Privately Held**
SIC: 2084 6794 Wines; franchises, selling
or licensing

(P-1994)
WEIBEL INCORPORATED
Also Called: Weibel Champagne Vineyards
1 Winemaster Way Ste D, Lodi
(95240-0860)
P.O. Box 87, Woodbridge (95258-0087)
PHONE..............................209 365-9463
Fred E Weibel Jr, *President*
Suzanne Cruz-Y-Corro, *Treasurer*
Gary Habluetzel, *Vice Pres*
Doug Richards, *Vice Pres*
Jim Cimarusti, *Manager*
▲ EMP: 35
SALES (est): 7MM **Privately Held**
WEB: www.weibel.com
SIC: 2084 Wines

(P-1995)
WENTE BROS (PA)
Also Called: Wente Vineyards
5565 Tesla Rd, Livermore (94550-9149)
PHONE..............................925 456-2300
Eric P Wente, *CEO*
Philip Wente, *Vice Chairman*
Carolyn Wente, *President*
Jean Wente, *Chairman*
Brendan Finley, *Exec VP*
▼ EMP: 100
SQ FT: 168,000
SALES (est): 113.3MM **Privately Held**
WEB: www.wentevineyards.com
SIC: 2084 8742 Wines; restaurant & food
services consultants

(P-1996)
WENTE BROS
Also Called: Wente Brothers Winery
37995 Elm Ave, Greenfield (93927-9710)
PHONE..............................831 674-5642
Keith Roberts, *Manager*
Kristian Jelm, *Regl Sales Mgr*
EMP: 25
SALES (corp-wide): 113.3MM **Privately Held**
WEB: www.wentevineyards.com
SIC: 2084 Wines
PA: Wente Bros.
5565 Tesla Rd
Livermore CA 94550
925 456-2300

(P-1997)
WG BEST WEINKELLEREI INC
Also Called: Montesquieu Winery
8929 Aero Dr Ste C, San Diego
(92123-2231)
PHONE..............................858 627-1747
Fonda Hopkins, *CEO*
Frank Kryger, *Admin Sec*
▲ EMP: 18
SQ FT: 29,000
SALES (est): 3.4MM **Privately Held**
SIC: 2084 5182 5921 Wine cellars,
bonded: engaged in blending wines; wine;
wine

(P-1998)
WHEELER WINERY INC
849 Zinfandel Ln, Saint Helena
(94574-1645)
PHONE..............................415 979-0630
Jean Boisset, *President*
Alain Leonnet, *Vice Pres*
EMP: 35
SQ FT: 50,000
SALES (est): 5.1MM
SALES (corp-wide): 3.5MM **Privately Held**
WEB: www.boissetamerica.com
SIC: 2084 Wines
HQ: Jean-Claude Boisset Wines U.S.A.,
Inc.
849 Zinfandel Ln
Saint Helena CA 94574
707 967-7667

(P-1999)
WHISPERKOOL CORPORATION
Also Called: Whisperkoll
1738 E Alpine Ave, Stockton (95205-2505)
PHONE..............................800 343-9463

Thomas R Schneider, *CEO*
Doug Smith, *Sales Dir*
EMP: 14
SQ FT: 32,000
SALES: 12MM **Privately Held**
SIC: 2084 Wine coolers (beverages)

(P-2000)
WIENS CELLARS LLC
35055 Via Del Ponte, Temecula
(92592-8022)
PHONE..............................951 694-9892
George M Wiens,
Jeff Wiens, *General Mgr*
David Owthwaite, *Sales Staff*
Jaime Purinton, *Sales Staff*
Tim Conti, *Manager*
EMP: 24 EST: 2001
SALES (est): 3.7MM **Privately Held**
SIC: 2084 Wines

(P-2001)
WILLIAMS & SELYEM WINERY
Also Called: Williams Selyem
7227 Westside Rd, Healdsburg
(95448-8357)
PHONE..............................707 433-6425
John Dyson,
Eric Grams, *Officer*
Jana Church, *Social Dir*
Kelly O'Brien, *Office Mgr*
Jessica Gilmore, *Opers Mgr*
▼ EMP: 12
SQ FT: 18,000
SALES (est): 2.7MM **Privately Held**
SIC: 2084 Wines

(P-2002)
WILSON CREEK WNERY
VNYARDS INC
35960 Rancho Cal Rd, Temecula
(92591-5088)
PHONE..............................951 699-9463
Gerald R Wilson, *CEO*
William J Wilson, *CEO*
Michael Wilson, *Vice Pres*
Rosemary Wilson, *Vice Pres*
Michelle Glover, *Regional Mgr*
EMP: 110
SQ FT: 6,000
SALES (est): 21.8MM **Privately Held**
WEB: www.wilsoncreekwinery.com
SIC: 2084 8999 Wines; personal services

(P-2003)
WINC INC
5340 Alla Rd Ste 105, Los Angeles
(90066-7049)
PHONE..............................855 282-5829
Matt Thelen, *Vice Pres*
Arianna Mesbahi, *Accounting Mgr*
Erica Nussen, *Sales Mgr*
Sarah McDonald, *Marketing Staff*
Brooke Matthias, *Director*
EMP: 12 EST: 2007
SALES (est): 1.3MM **Privately Held**
SIC: 2084 Wines, brandy & brandy spirits

(P-2004)
WINDSOR OAKS VINEYARDS
LLP
10810 Hillview Rd, Windsor (95492-7519)
P.O. Box 883 (95492-0883)
PHONE..............................707 433-4050
Windsor Oaks, *Partner*
Doug Lumgair, *Manager*
◆ EMP: 20
SALES (est): 3MM **Privately Held**
WEB: www.windsoroaks.com
SIC: 2084 Wines

(P-2005)
WINE CELLAR IMPRESSIONS
INC
2013 Stone Ave, San Jose (95125-1447)
PHONE..............................408 277-0100
Thang Hoang Nguyen, *President*
▲ EMP: 15
SALES (est): 1.4MM **Privately Held**
WEB: www.wcimpression.com
SIC: 2084 Wine cellars, bonded: engaged
in blending wines

(P-2006)
WINE COMPANY OF SAN FRANCISCO
Also Called: Gomberg Fredrikson & Assoc
231 Ware Rd Ste 823, Woodside
(94062-4538)
PHONE..................................650 851-0965
John Fredrikson, *President*
EMP: 10
SALES (est): 30.5K **Privately Held**
SIC: 2084 Wines

(P-2007)
WINE GROUP INC (HQ)
Also Called: Mogan David Wine
17000 E State Highway 120, Ripon
(95366-9412)
PHONE..................................209 599-4111
Brian Jay Vos, *CEO*
Arthur Ciocca, *Ch of Bd*
Morris Ball, *Vice Pres*
Stephen Hughes, *Vice Pres*
Louis Quaccia, *Vice Pres*
◆ **EMP:** 200
SQ FT: 3,000
SALES (est): 141.6MM
SALES (corp-wide): 148.2MM **Privately Held**
SIC: 2084 Wines
PA: The Wine Group Llc
    4596 S Tracy Blvd
    Tracy CA 95377
    415 986-8700

(P-2008)
ZARIF COMPANIES
4187 Carpinteria Ave # 3, Carpinteria
(93013-3300)
PHONE..................................805 318-1800
EMP: 11
SALES (est): 1.3MM **Privately Held**
SIC: 2084 Wines

2085 Liquors, Distilled, Rectified & Blended

(P-2009)
BAR NONE INC
1302 Santa Fe Dr, Tustin (92780-6495)
PHONE..................................714 259-8450
John Underwood, *President*
Elizabeth Underwood, *Corp Secy*
EMP: 18
SQ FT: 20,000
SALES (est): 3.4MM
SALES (corp-wide): 604.2MM **Privately Held**
WEB: www.barnone.net
SIC: 2085 2087 3565 Cocktails, alcoholic; cordials & premixed alcoholic cocktails; beverage bases, concentrates, syrups, powders & mixes; bottling machinery: filling, capping, labeling
HQ: First Advantage Corporation
    1 Concrse Pkwy Ne Ste 200
    Atlanta GA 30328
    800 888-5773

(P-2010)
BOOCHERY INC
Also Called: Boochcraft
684 Anita St Ste F, Chula Vista
(91911-7170)
PHONE..................................619 738-1008
Adam Hiner, *President*
Michael Kent, *Corp Secy*
Andrew Clark, *Vice Pres*
EMP: 17
SQ FT: 5,000
SALES (est): 1.4MM **Privately Held**
SIC: 2085 Distilled & blended liquors

(P-2011)
BOUDOIR SPIRITS INC
Also Called: Boudoir Vodka
7197 Boulder Ave Ste 12, Highland
(92346-3498)
PHONE..................................909 714-6644
Adam Ames, *CEO*
EMP: 10
SQ FT: 1,500
SALES: 90K **Privately Held**
SIC: 2085 Distilled & blended liquors

(P-2012)
BRANDED SPIRITS USA LTD
500 Sansome St Ste 600, San Francisco
(94111-3222)
PHONE..................................415 813-5045
George Chen, *CEO*
Britt Bachner, *COO*
EMP: 10
SALES (est): 799.8K **Privately Held**
SIC: 2085 5921 Distilled & blended liquors; hard liquor

(P-2013)
DIAGEO NORTH AMERICA INC
Also Called: Beaulieu Vineyard
1960 Saint Helena Hwy, Rutherford
(94573)
P.O. Box 219 (94573-0219)
PHONE..................................707 967-5200
Armond Rist, *Dir Ops-Prd-Mfg*
EMP: 100
SALES (corp-wide): 16.3B **Privately Held**
SIC: 2085 2084 0172 Distilled & blended liquors; wines, brandy & brandy spirits; grapes
HQ: Diageo North America Inc.
    801 Main Ave
    Norwalk CT 06851
    203 229-2100

(P-2014)
JIM BEAM BRANDS CO
Also Called: Beam Suntory
17901 Von Karman Ave # 920, Irvine
(92614-5251)
PHONE..................................949 200-7200
Susan Morris Sr, *Manager*
EMP: 10 **Privately Held**
WEB: www.jbbworldwide.com
SIC: 2085 Distillers' dried grains & solubles & alcohol
HQ: Jim Beam Brands Co.
    510 Lake Cook Rd Ste 200
    Deerfield IL 60015
    847 948-8903

(P-2015)
LIN FRANK DISTILLERS
2455 Huntington Dr, Fairfield (94533-9734)
PHONE..................................707 437-1092
Frank Lin, *Principal*
EMP: 16 **EST:** 2010
SALES (est): 3.5MM **Privately Held**
SIC: 2085 Distilled & blended liquors

(P-2016)
POINT BLANKS INC
43 S Olive St, Ventura (93001-2501)
PHONE..................................805 643-8616
Yvon Chouinard, *President*
▲ **EMP:** 15
SQ FT: 1,200
SALES (est): 1.3MM **Privately Held**
WEB: www.pointblanks.com
SIC: 2085 Scotch whiskey

(P-2017)
RARE BREED DISTILLING LLC (DH)
Also Called: Wild Turkey Distillery
55 Francisco St Ste 100, San Francisco
(94133-2136)
PHONE..................................415 315-8060
Francesca Mazzoleni, *Principal*
▼ **EMP:** 28
SALES (est): 9.4MM
SALES (corp-wide): 177.9K **Privately Held**
SIC: 2085 Distilled & blended liquors
HQ: Davide Campari Milano Spa
    Via Franco Sacchetti 20
    Sesto San Giovanni MI 20099
    026 225-1

(P-2018)
SAZERAC COMPANY INC
2202 E Del Amo Blvd, Carson (90749)
P.O. Box 6263 (90749-6263)
PHONE..................................310 604-8717
Michael Dominick, *Manager*
EMP: 45
SALES (corp-wide): 306.3MM **Privately Held**
WEB: www.bartoninc.com
SIC: 2085 Distilled & blended liquors

PA: Sazerac Company, Inc.
    3850 N Causeway Blvd # 1695
    Metairie LA 70002
    504 831-9450

(P-2019)
SUPERNOVA SPIRITS INC
10288 Richwood Dr, Cupertino
(95014-3361)
PHONE..................................415 819-3154
Vijay Caveripakkam, *President*
Ward Karson, *COO*
▲ **EMP:** 25
SALES: 3MM **Privately Held**
SIC: 2085 Vodka (alcoholic beverage)

(P-2020)
TAKARA SAKE USA INC (DH)
Also Called: Numano Sake Company
708 Addison St, Berkeley (94710-1925)
PHONE..................................510 540-8250
Yoshihiro Naka, *CEO*
Yoichiro Miyakuni, *President*
Atsushi Himeno, *General Mgr*
Michiyo Ihara, *Purchasing*
Masa Takano, *Marketing Staff*
◆ **EMP:** 32
SQ FT: 15,000
SALES (est): 7MM **Privately Held**
WEB: www.takarasake.com
SIC: 2085 5182 Grain alcohol for beverage purposes; wine

(P-2021)
TEQUILAS PREMIUM INC
470 Columbus Ave Ste 210, San Francisco
(94133-3930)
PHONE..................................415 399-0496
Juan Sanchez, *President*
Patrick Carney, *CFO*
▲ **EMP:** 17
SALES (est): 1.4MM **Privately Held**
SIC: 2085 Distilled & blended liquors

2086 Soft Drinks

(P-2022)
ADVANCED REFRESHMENT LLC (HQ)
Also Called: Advanced H2o
2560 E Philadelphia St, Ontario
(91761-7768)
PHONE..................................425 746-8100
Robert Abramowitz,
EMP: 15
SQ FT: 270,000
SALES (est): 12.9MM
SALES (corp-wide): 316.8MM **Privately Held**
WEB: www.advanced-h2o.com
SIC: 2086 Mineral water, carbonated: packaged in cans, bottles, etc.
PA: Niagara Bottling, Llc
    1440 Bridgegate Dr
    Diamond Bar CA 91765
    909 230-5000

(P-2023)
AMCAN BEVERAGES INC
Also Called: Pokka Beverages
1201 Commerce Blvd, American Canyon
(94503-9611)
PHONE..................................707 557-0500
Don Soetaert, *President*
EMP: 125
SQ FT: 250,000
SALES (est): 14MM
SALES (corp-wide): 31.8B **Publicly Held**
SIC: 2086 Iced tea & fruit drinks, bottled & canned; fruit drinks (less than 100% juice): packaged in cans, etc.
PA: The Coca-Cola Company
    1 Coca Cola Plz Nw
    Atlanta GA 30313
    404 676-2121

(P-2024)
AMERICAN BOTTLING COMPANY
Also Called: Dr Pepper Snapple Group
1188 Mt Vernon Ave, Riverside
(92507-1829)
PHONE..................................951 341-7500
Vince Spurgeon, *Sales/Mktg Mgr*

EMP: 175 **Publicly Held**
WEB: www.cs-americas.com
SIC: 2086 5149 Bottled & canned soft drinks; soft drinks
HQ: The American Bottling Company
    5301 Legacy Dr
    Plano TX 75024

(P-2025)
AMERICAN BOTTLING COMPANY
Also Called: Seven-Up Bottling
2210 S Mcdowell Blvd Ext, Petaluma
(94954-5659)
PHONE..................................707 766-9750
Ray Gutendorf, *Manager*
EMP: 30
SQ FT: 1,600 **Publicly Held**
WEB: www.7upcal.com
SIC: 2086 Bottled & canned soft drinks
HQ: The American Bottling Company
    5301 Legacy Dr
    Plano TX 75024

(P-2026)
AMERICAN BOTTLING COMPANY
Also Called: Seven-Up Bottling
100 Wabash Ave, Ukiah (95482-6313)
PHONE..................................707 462-8871
Allen Brown, *Manager*
EMP: 16 **Publicly Held**
WEB: www.7upcal.com
SIC: 2086 Bottled & canned soft drinks
HQ: The American Bottling Company
    5301 Legacy Dr
    Plano TX 75024

(P-2027)
AMERICAN BOTTLING COMPANY
230 E 18th St, Bakersfield (93305-5609)
PHONE..................................661 323-7921
Brian Sutton, *Manager*
EMP: 37 **Publicly Held**
WEB: www.cs-americas.com
SIC: 2086 5149 Bottled & canned soft drinks; soft drinks
HQ: The American Bottling Company
    5301 Legacy Dr
    Plano TX 75024

(P-2028)
AMERICAN BOTTLING COMPANY
2012 S Pearl St, Fresno (93721-3312)
PHONE..................................559 442-1553
Mariel Guardado, *Manager*
EMP: 60
SQ FT: 25,000 **Publicly Held**
WEB: www.cs-americas.com
SIC: 2086 Soft drinks: packaged in cans, bottles, etc.
HQ: The American Bottling Company
    5301 Legacy Dr
    Plano TX 75024

(P-2029)
AMERICAN BOTTLING COMPANY
1555 Heartwood Dr, McKinleyville
(95519-3989)
PHONE..................................707 840-9727
Ron Ellis, *General Mgr*
EMP: 11 **Publicly Held**
WEB: www.7upcal.com
SIC: 2086 Bottled & canned soft drinks
HQ: The American Bottling Company
    5301 Legacy Dr
    Plano TX 75024

(P-2030)
AMERICAN BOTTLING COMPANY
1981 N Broadway Ste 215, Walnut Creek
(94596-3872)
PHONE..................................925 938-8777
Linda Orcy, *Branch Mgr*
EMP: 70 **Publicly Held**

(PA)=Parent Co (HQ)=Headquarters (DH)=Div Headquarters
✪ = New Business established in last 2 years

WEB: www.7upcal.com
SIC: 2086 Soft drinks: packaged in cans, bottles, etc.
HQ: The American Bottling Company
5301 Legacy Dr
Plano TX 75024

(P-2031)
AMERICAN BOTTLING COMPANY
1166 Arroyo St, San Fernando (91340-1824)
PHONE......................818 898-1471
Ed Nemecek, *Branch Mgr*
EMP: 200 **Publicly Held**
WEB: www.cs-americas.com
SIC: 2086 5149 Soft drinks: packaged in cans, bottles, etc.; soft drinks
HQ: The American Bottling Company
5301 Legacy Dr
Plano TX 75024

(P-2032)
AMERICAN BOTTLING COMPANY
618 Hanson Way, Santa Maria (93458-9734)
PHONE......................805 928-1001
Richard Roese, *Branch Mgr*
EMP: 31 **Publicly Held**
WEB: www.cs-americas.com
SIC: 2086 Soft drinks: packaged in cans, bottles, etc.
HQ: The American Bottling Company
5301 Legacy Dr
Plano TX 75024

(P-2033)
AMERICAN BOTTLING COMPANY
Also Called: 7 Up / R C Bottling Co
3220 E 26th St, Vernon (90058-0008)
PHONE......................323 268-7779
Russ Wolfe, *Controller*
EMP: 500 **Publicly Held**
WEB: www.cs-americas.com
SIC: 2086 5149 Soft drinks: packaged in cans, bottles, etc.; groceries & related products
HQ: The American Bottling Company
5301 Legacy Dr
Plano TX 75024

(P-2034)
AMERICAN BOTTLING COMPANY
Also Called: Seven-Up Btlg Co Marysville
2720 Land Ave, Sacramento (95815-1834)
PHONE......................916 929-3575
Jim Hough, *Manager*
EMP: 13 **Publicly Held**
WEB: www.7upcal.com
SIC: 2086 Bottled & canned soft drinks
HQ: The American Bottling Company
5301 Legacy Dr
Plano TX 75024

(P-2035)
AMERICAN BOTTLING COMPANY
2670 Land Ave, Sacramento (95815-2380)
PHONE......................916 929-7777
EMP: 70 **Publicly Held**
SIC: 2086 Soft drinks: packaged in cans, bottles, etc.
HQ: The American Bottling Company
5301 Legacy Dr
Plano TX 75024

(P-2036)
AMERICAN BOTTLING COMPANY
11205 Commercial Pkwy, Castroville (95012-3205)
PHONE......................831 632-0777
EMP: 70 **Publicly Held**
SIC: 2086 Soft drinks: packaged in cans, bottles, etc.

HQ: The American Bottling Company
5301 Legacy Dr
Plano TX 75024

(P-2037)
AMERICAN BOTTLING COMPANY
6160 Stoneridge Mall Rd # 280, Pleasanton (94588-3285)
PHONE......................925 251-3001
EMP: 70 **Publicly Held**
SIC: 2086 Soft drinks: packaged in cans, bottles, etc.
HQ: The American Bottling Company
5301 Legacy Dr
Plano TX 75024

(P-2038)
AMERIPEC INC
6965 Aragon Cir, Buena Park (90620-1118)
PHONE......................714 690-9191
Ping C Wu, *CEO*
Ed Muratori, *General Mgr*
Mathew Bamberger, *Purchasing*
Cynthia Medina, *Warehouse Mgr*
EMP: 150
SQ FT: 215,000
SALES (est): 34.2MM **Privately Held**
WEB: www.ameripecinc.com
SIC: 2086 Carbonated soft drinks, bottled & canned
HQ: President Global Corporation
6965 Aragon Cir
Buena Park CA 90620
714 994-2990

(P-2039)
AQUAHYDRATE INC
5870 W Jefferson Blvd D, Los Angeles (90016-3159)
PHONE......................310 559-5058
John Cochran, *CEO*
Joe Gleason, *President*
Mark Loeffler, *Corp Secy*
Ericka Pittman, *Chief Mktg Ofcr*
Al Hermsen, *Vice Pres*
◆ EMP: 68
SALES (est): 24.9MM **Privately Held**
SIC: 2086 Mineral water, carbonated: packaged in cans, bottles, etc.

(P-2040)
ASEPTIC SLTONS USA VNTURES LLC
Also Called: Aseptic Solutions USA-Corona
484 Alcoa Cir, Corona (92880-9323)
PHONE......................951 736-9230
Alan Morris,
Bob Danko, *Vice Pres*
Aaron Harris, *Vice Pres*
Jim Parr, *Engineer*
Xiaomei Shi, *Accountant*
▲ EMP: 117
SQ FT: 67,000
SALES (est): 26.5MM **Privately Held**
WEB: www.asepticusa.com
SIC: 2086 Carbonated beverages, nonalcoholic: bottled & canned
PA: Glanbia Public Limited Company
Glanbia House
Kilkenny

(P-2041)
AT MOBILE BOTTLING LINE LLC
413 Saint Andrews Dr, NAPA (94558-1534)
PHONE......................707 257-3757
John W Davis, *Principal*
EMP: 14 EST: 2007
SALES (est): 2MM **Privately Held**
SIC: 2086 Bottled & canned soft drinks

(P-2042)
AVITA BEVERAGE COMPANY INC (PA)
18401 Burbank Blvd # 121, Tarzana (91356-2822)
PHONE......................213 477-1979
Clinton Stokes III, *CEO*
Kenneth Mayeaux, *COO*
Jamie Mayeaux, *CFO*
EMP: 10
SQ FT: 3,000

SALES: 879K **Privately Held**
SIC: 2086 Water, pasteurized: packaged in cans, bottles, etc.

(P-2043)
BLUE CAN WATER (PA)
8309 Laurel Cny Blvd 219, Sun Valley (91352)
PHONE......................818 450-3290
Rick Eye, *CEO*
James Skylar, *CFO*
EMP: 11
SALES: 1MM **Privately Held**
SIC: 2086 Mineral water, carbonated: packaged in cans, bottles, etc.

(P-2044)
BOTTLERS UNLIMITED INC
753 Jefferson St, NAPA (94559-0421)
PHONE......................707 255-0595
Carole R Kelly, *President*
Sharon Puffer, *Vice Pres*
EMP: 45
SALES: 800K **Privately Held**
SIC: 2086 Bottled & canned soft drinks

(P-2045)
BOTTLING GROUP LLC
1150 E North Ave, Fresno (93725-1929)
PHONE......................559 485-5050
EMP: 14
SALES (corp-wide): 64.6B **Publicly Held**
SIC: 2086 Bottled & canned soft drinks
HQ: Bottling Group, Llc
1111 Westchester Ave
White Plains NY 10604
914 253-2000

(P-2046)
BOTTLING GROUP LLC
Also Called: Pepsico
6659 Sycamore Canyon Blvd, Riverside (92507-0733)
PHONE......................951 697-3200
Jon Hess, *Principal*
Donna Fontana, *Admin Asst*
Greg Sawyer, *Purch Mgr*
Becky Banda, *QC Mgr*
Jesse Anderson, *Marketing Staff*
EMP: 31
SALES (est): 8MM **Privately Held**
SIC: 2086 Carbonated soft drinks, bottled & canned

(P-2047)
BULLETPROOF BRANDS CO INC
1704 Halifax Way, El Dorado Hills (95762-5834)
PHONE......................916 635-3718
EMP: 11
SQ FT: 3,200
SALES (est): 1.2MM **Privately Held**
SIC: 2086

(P-2048)
CALIFIA FARMS LLC
33374 Lerdo Hwy, Bakersfield (93308-9782)
PHONE......................661 679-1000
Greg Stelpenpoho, *CEO*
Dan Mader, *Vice Pres*
JC McConnell, *Vice Pres*
Kim McCabe, *Director*
EMP: 36
SALES (corp-wide): 100MM **Privately Held**
SIC: 2086 Fruit drinks (less than 100% juice): packaged in cans, etc.
PA: Califia Farms, Llc
1321 Palmetto St
Los Angeles CA 90013
213 694-4667

(P-2049)
CALIFORNIA BOTTLING COMPANY
Also Called: High Country Water
8250 Industrial Ave, Roseville (95678-5900)
PHONE......................916 772-1000
Robert Wikse, *President*
Christopher Crain, *Vice Pres*
L Douglas McKenzie, *Vice Pres*
EMP: 50
SQ FT: 50,000

SALES (est): 10.2MM **Privately Held**
WEB: www.cbcwater.com
SIC: 2086 Water, pasteurized: packaged in cans, bottles, etc.

(P-2050)
CALIFORNIA HOT SPRINGS WATER
42231 Hot Springs Dr, Calif Hot Spg (93207-9715)
P.O. Box 146 (93207-0146)
PHONE......................661 548-6582
Ronald Gilbert, *Owner*
EMP: 10
SQ FT: 25,000
SALES (est): 900K **Privately Held**
WEB: www.cahsrealty.com
SIC: 2086 Water, pasteurized: packaged in cans, bottles, etc.

(P-2051)
CAPITOL BEVERAGE PACKERS
Also Called: Seven Up Bottling
2670 Land Ave, Sacramento (95815-2380)
PHONE......................916 929-7777
Millard C Tonkin, *President*
Millard Tonkin, *Shareholder*
▲ EMP: 96
SQ FT: 110,360
SALES (est): 11.5MM **Privately Held**
SIC: 2086 5078 Bottled & canned soft drinks; refrigerated beverage dispensers

(P-2052)
CCBCC OPERATIONS LLC
Also Called: Coca-Cola
1123 W Avenue L14, Lancaster (93534-7061)
PHONE......................661 723-0714
Robert Macias, *Branch Mgr*
EMP: 112
SQ FT: 15,895
SALES (corp-wide): 4.6B **Publicly Held**
SIC: 2086 Bottled & canned soft drinks
HQ: Ccbcc Operations, Llc
4100 Coca Cola Plz
Charlotte NC 28211
704 364-8728

(P-2053)
CG ROXANE LLC
Also Called: Cg Roxane Shasta
1400 Marys Dr, Weed (96094-9643)
P.O. Box 560 (96094-0560)
PHONE......................530 225-1260
Rick Moore, *Manager*
EMP: 80
SALES (corp-wide): 178.4MM **Privately Held**
WEB: www.cgroxane.com
SIC: 2086 Water, pasteurized: packaged in cans, bottles, etc.
PA: Cg Roxane Llc
1210 State Hwy 395
Olancha CA 93549
760 764-2885

(P-2054)
CG ROXANE LLC (PA)
Also Called: Crystal Geyser Alpine Spring W
1210 State Hwy 395, Olancha (93549)
P.O. Box A (93549-0903)
PHONE......................760 764-2885
Ronan Papillaud, *President*
Page Beykpour, *COO*
Patrice Marquet, *Senior VP*
Veronique Belgum, *Vice Pres*
Fabien Pottier, *Maintence Staff*
▲ EMP: 100
SQ FT: 75,000
SALES (est): 178.4MM **Privately Held**
WEB: www.cgroxane.com
SIC: 2086 Water, pasteurized: packaged in cans, bottles, etc.

(P-2055)
CHAMELEON BEVERAGE COMPANY INC (PA)
6444 E 26th St, Commerce (90040-3214)
PHONE......................323 724-8223
Derek Reineman, *President*
Erin Zheo, *CFO*
Morgan Reed, *General Mgr*
Lok Man Chiu, *Technology*
Araceli Ramirez, *QC Mgr*
▲ EMP: 70

SQ FT: 100,000
SALES (est): 14.6MM **Privately Held**
WEB: www.chameleonbeverage.com
SIC: **2086** 5149 Water, pasteurized: packaged in cans, bottles, etc.; soft drinks

(P-2056)
CL-ONE CORPORATION
29582 Spotted Bull Ln, San Juan Capistrano (92675-1034)
P.O. Box 458, Placentia (92871-0458)
PHONE..........................949 364-2895
Les Gilmer, *CEO*
Marcus Franco, *Vice Pres*
EMP: 100
SQ FT: 18,000
SALES (est): 5.4MM **Privately Held**
SIC: **2086** Carbonated beverages, nonalcoholic: bottled & canned

(P-2057)
COASTAL COCKTAILS INC (PA)
Also Called: Modern Gourmet Foods
18011 Mitchell S Ste B, Irvine (92614-6863)
PHONE.............:..............949 250-3129
Nadeem Mumal, *CEO*
Jason Hoffman, *Vice Pres*
Jian Qiu,
▲ EMP: 40
SALES: 48MM **Privately Held**
SIC: **2086** Bottled & canned soft drinks

(P-2058)
COCA COLA BTLG OF EUREKA CAL
Also Called: Coca-Cola
1335 Albee St, Eureka (95501-2224)
PHONE..........................707 443-2796
Dave Hallagan, *Manager*
Jim Slade, *Manager*
EMP: 15 EST: 1962
SALES (est): 1.6MM **Privately Held**
SIC: **2086** Bottled & canned soft drinks

(P-2059)
COCA-COLA COMPANY
1650 S Vintage Ave, Ontario (91761-3656)
PHONE..........................909 975-5200
Melvin Robinson, *Manager*
EMP: 103
SALES (corp-wide): 31.8B **Publicly Held**
SIC: **2086** Bottled & canned soft drinks
PA: The Coca-Cola Company
1 Coca Cola Plz Nw
Atlanta GA 30313
404 676-2121

(P-2060)
COCA-COLA COMPANY
13255 Amar Rd, City of Industry (91746-1203)
PHONE..........................626 855-4440
Kimberly Curtis, *Branch Mgr*
EMP: 50
SALES (corp-wide): 31.8B **Publicly Held**
SIC: **2086** Bottled & canned soft drinks
WEB: www.cocacola.com
PA: The Coca-Cola Company
1 Coca Cola Plz Nw
Atlanta GA 30313
404 676-2121

(P-2061)
COCA-COLA COMPANY
3 Park Plz Ste 600, Irvine (92614-2575)
PHONE..........................949 250-5961
Dan Manning, *Manager*
EMP: 125
SALES (corp-wide): 31.8B **Publicly Held**
WEB: www.cocacola.com
SIC: **2086** Bottled & canned soft drinks
PA: The Coca-Cola Company
1 Coca Cola Plz Nw
Atlanta GA 30313
404 676-2121

(P-2062)
COCA-COLA COMPANY
2121 E Winston Rd, Anaheim (92806-5535)
PHONE..........................714 991-7031
Linda Martin, *Branch Mgr*
EMP: 28

SALES (corp-wide): 31.8B **Publicly Held**
WEB: www.cocacola.com
SIC: **2086** Bottled & canned soft drinks
PA: The Coca-Cola Company
1 Coca Cola Plz Nw
Atlanta GA 30313
404 676-2121

(P-2063)
COCA-COLA COMPANY
2025 Pike Ave, San Leandro (94577-6708)
PHONE..........................510 476-7048
EMP: 116
SALES (corp-wide): 31.8B **Publicly Held**
SIC: **2086** Bottled & canned soft drinks
PA: The Coca-Cola Company
1 Coca Cola Plz Nw
Atlanta GA 30313
404 676-2121

(P-2064)
COCA-COLA REFRESHMENTS USA INC
5335 Walker St, Ventura (93003-7499)
PHONE..........................805 644-2211
EMP: 116
SALES (corp-wide): 31.8B **Publicly Held**
SIC: **2086** Bottled & canned soft drinks
HQ: Coca-Cola Refreshments Usa, Inc.
2500 Windy Ridge Pkwy Se
Atlanta GA 30339
770 989-3000

(P-2065)
COCA-COLA REFRESHMENTS USA INC
3900 Ocean Ranch Blvd, Oceanside (92056-2692)
PHONE..........................760 435-7111
Coca Refreshments, *Branch Mgr*
EMP: 57
SALES (corp-wide): 31.8B **Publicly Held**
WEB: www.cokecce.com
SIC: **2086** Bottled & canned soft drinks
HQ: Coca-Cola Refreshments Usa, Inc.
2500 Windy Ridge Pkwy Se
Atlanta GA 30339
770 989-3000

(P-2066)
CRYSTAL BOTTLING COMPANY INC
Also Called: Crystal Mountain Springwater
8631 Younger Creek Dr, Sacramento (95828-1028)
PHONE..........................916 568-3300
Hayes Johnson, *CEO*
EMP: 80
SQ FT: 12,000
SALES (est): 7.7MM **Privately Held**
WEB: www.crystalwater.com
SIC: **2086** 5963 Pasteurized & mineral waters, bottled & canned; bottled water delivery

(P-2067)
CRYSTAL GEYSER WATER COMPANY
5001 Fermi Dr, Fairfield (94534-6894)
PHONE..........................707 647-4410
Ernesto Olivarez, *Branch Mgr*
EMP: 30 **Privately Held**
WEB: www.crystalgeyserasw.com
SIC: **2086** Water, pasteurized: packaged in cans, bottles, etc.
HQ: Crystal Geyser Water Company
501 Washington St
Calistoga CA 94515
707 265-3900

(P-2068)
CRYSTAL GEYSER WATER COMPANY
1233 E California Ave, Bakersfield (93307-1205)
PHONE..........................661 323-6296
Gerhard Gaugel, *Branch Mgr*
Carmen Maib, *Plant Mgr*
EMP: 30 **Privately Held**
WEB: www.crystalgeyserasw.com

SIC: **2086** 5141 2099 2033 Mineral water, carbonated: packaged in cans, bottles, etc.; carbonated beverages, nonalcoholic: bottled & canned; groceries, general line; food preparations; canned fruits & specialties; bottled water delivery
HQ: Crystal Geyser Water Company
501 Washington St
Calistoga CA 94515
707 265-3900

(P-2069)
CRYSTAL GEYSER WATER COMPANY
2351 E Brundage Ln Ste A, Bakersfield (93307-3063)
PHONE..........................661 321-0896
Robert Hofferd, *Manager*
Kevin Moloughney, *Vice Pres*
EMP: 15 **Privately Held**
WEB: www.crystalgeyserasw.com
SIC: **2086** Mineral water, carbonated: packaged in cans, bottles, etc.
HQ: Crystal Geyser Water Company
501 Washington St
Calistoga CA 94515
707 265-3900

(P-2070)
CUSTOM LABELING & BTLG CORP
15005 Concord Cir, Morgan Hill (95037-5417)
PHONE..........................408 371-6171
Tillie Pacheco, *President*
Tom Wilkenson, *Vice Pres*
EMP: 15
SQ FT: 120,000
SALES (est): 2.5MM **Privately Held**
SIC: **2086** Bottled & canned soft drinks

(P-2071)
DESIGNER DRINKS
Also Called: New Generation Sourcing
5050 Avenida Encinas, Carlsbad (92008-4381)
PHONE..........................760 444-2355
David Jenkins, *Owner*
EMP: 25
SALES (est): 1.5MM **Privately Held**
SIC: **2086** Water, pasteurized: packaged in cans, bottles, etc.

(P-2072)
DR PEPPER/SEVEN UP INC
1901 Russell Ave, Santa Rosa (95403-2646)
PHONE..........................707 545-7797
Ray Gutendorf, *Principal*
EMP: 68 **Publicly Held**
SIC: **2086** Soft drinks: packaged in cans, bottles, etc.
HQ: Dr Pepper/Seven Up, Inc.
5301 Legacy Dr Fl 1
Plano TX 75024
972 673-7000

(P-2073)
DS SERVICES OF AMERICA INC
Also Called: Sparkletts Water
1449 N Avenue 46, Los Angeles (90041-3410)
PHONE..........................323 551-5724
Reggie Doster, *Manager*
EMP: 55
SALES (corp-wide): 2.2B **Privately Held**
SIC: **2086** 5499 Bottled & canned soft drinks; beverage stores
HQ: Ds Services Of America, Inc.
2300 Windy Ridge Pkwy Se 500n
Atlanta GA 30339
770 933-1400

(P-2074)
ESSENCE WATER INC
12802 Knott St, Garden Grove (92841-3906)
PHONE..........................855 738-7426
Joel Gabriel, *CEO*
Jaci Conrad, *CFO*
EMP: 12
SQ FT: 20,000
SALES: 2.4MM **Privately Held**
SIC: **2086** Water, pasteurized: packaged in cans, bottles, etc.

(P-2075)
FIRE MOUNTAIN BEVERAGE
27240 Turnberry Ln # 200, Valencia (91355-1029)
PHONE..........................661 362-0716
Anthony Miller, *CEO*
EMP: 50
SALES (est): 2.8MM **Privately Held**
SIC: **2086** Water, pasteurized: packaged in cans, bottles, etc.

(P-2076)
FORTUNE DRINK INC
19925 Stevens Creek Blvd # 100, Cupertino (95014-2300)
PHONE..........................408 805-9526
Robert Chen, *President*
EMP: 10
SALES (est): 283.4K **Privately Held**
SIC: **2086** 2087 Bottled & canned soft drinks; flavoring extracts & syrups

(P-2077)
GENIUS PRODUCTS NT INC
6960 S Centinela Ave, Culver City (90230-6305)
PHONE..........................510 671-0219
Chris Clifford, *CEO*
EMP: 110
SALES (est): 2.7MM **Privately Held**
SIC: **2086** Carbonated beverages, nonalcoholic: bottled & canned

(P-2078)
GREEN SPOT PACKAGING INC
100 S Cambridge Ave, Claremont (91711-4842)
PHONE..........................909 625-8771
John Tsu, *CEO*
Dana Staal, *COO*
Terry Hughes, *Vice Pres*
Stephanie Rodriguez, *Manager*
EMP: 20
SQ FT: 100,000
SALES (est): 4.6MM **Privately Held**
WEB: www.greenspotusa.com
SIC: **2086** Fruit drinks (less than 100% juice): packaged in cans, etc.
PA: Green Spot International
C/O Grand Pavilion Main Entrance
West Bay GR CAYMAN

(P-2079)
GTS LIVING FOODS LLC
Also Called: Synergy Beverages
4415 Bandini Blvd, Vernon (90058-4309)
P.O. Box 2352, Beverly Hills (90213-2352)
PHONE..........................323 581-7787
George Thomas Dave,
EMP: 700
SALES (est): 48.5MM **Privately Held**
SIC: **2086** Bottled & canned soft drinks

(P-2080)
H A RIDER & SONS
2482 Freedom Blvd, Watsonville (95076-1099)
PHONE..........................831 722-3882
George C Rider, *Partner*
Thomas Rider, *Partner*
Stephen Rider, *Technology*
Tom Rider, *Human Res Mgr*
George Rider, *Safety Mgr*
▲ EMP: 45
SQ FT: 168,000
SALES (est): 9.3MM **Privately Held**
WEB: www.hariderandsons.com
SIC: **2086** Soft drinks: packaged in cans, bottles, etc.

(P-2081)
HINT INC
2124 Union St Ste D, San Francisco (94123-4044)
P.O. Box 29078 (94129-0078)
PHONE..........................415 513-4051
Kara Goldin, *CEO*
Theo Goldin, *COO*
Theodore Goldin, *COO*
Stephanie Russo, *Creative Dir*
Lance Cohen, *Area Mgr*
EMP: 44

SALES (est): 17.2MM **Privately Held**
WEB: www.drinkhint.com
SIC: 2086 Mineral water, carbonated: packaged in cans, bottles, etc.; fruit drinks (less than 100% juice): packaged in cans, etc.; carbonated beverages, nonalcoholic: bottled & canned

(P-2082)
JOHN FITZPATRICK & SONS
Also Called: Pepsico
1480 Beltline Rd, Redding (96003-1410)
PHONE.................................530 241-3216
John Fitzpatrick Jr, *CEO*
Jerome Fitzpatrick, *Vice Pres*
EMP: 17 **EST:** 1958
SQ FT: 2,000
SALES (est): 2.7MM **Privately Held**
SIC: 2086 Carbonated soft drinks, bottled & canned

(P-2083)
KEURIG DR PEPPER INC
1188 Mt Vernon Ave, Riverside (92507-1829)
PHONE.................................951 341-7500
EMP: 94 **Publicly Held**
SIC: 2086 Soft drinks: packaged in cans, bottles, etc.
PA: Keurig Dr Pepper Inc.
53 South Ave
Burlington MA 01803

(P-2084)
KEURIG DR PEPPER INC
306 Otterson Dr, Chico (95928-8250)
PHONE.................................530 893-4501
Barry Thompson, *Principal*
EMP: 34 **Publicly Held**
WEB: www.7upbottling.com
SIC: 2086 Soft drinks: packaged in cans, bottles, etc.
PA: Keurig Dr Pepper Inc.
53 South Ave
Burlington MA 01803

(P-2085)
KEURIG DR PEPPER INC
1981 N Broadway, Walnut Creek (94596-3852)
PHONE.................................925 938-8777
James Fox, *Branch Mgr*
Debby Steele, *Executive*
EMP: 99 **Publicly Held**
SIC: 2086 Soft drinks: packaged in cans, bottles, etc.
PA: Keurig Dr Pepper Inc.
53 South Ave
Burlington MA 01803

(P-2086)
KEVITA INC (HQ)
2220 Celsius Ave Ste A, Oxnard (93030-5181)
PHONE.................................805 200-2250
Andrea Theodore, *CEO*
Ada Cheng, *CFO*
Cynthia Nastanski, *Admin Sec*
EMP: 60
SQ FT: 17,000
SALES: 60MM
SALES (corp-wide): 64.6B **Publicly Held**
SIC: 2086 Bottled & canned soft drinks
PA: Pepsico, Inc.
700 Anderson Hill Rd
Purchase NY 10577
914 253-2000

(P-2087)
KUANTUM BRANDS LLC
1747 Hancock St Ste A, San Diego (92101-1130)
PHONE.................................760 412-2432
Will Righeimer, *President*
Lorena Aguirre, *CFO*
EMP: 200 **EST:** 2015
SALES: 50MM **Privately Held**
SIC: 2086 Carbonated beverages, nonalcoholic: bottled & canned

(P-2088)
LA BOTTLEWORKS INC
1605 Beach St, Montebello (90640-5432)
PHONE.................................323 724-4076
Ryan Marsh, *CEO*
Matthew Marsh, *Vice Pres*
EMP: 20
SALES (est): 4.6MM **Privately Held**
SIC: 2086 Bottled & canned soft drinks

(P-2089)
LIFEAID BEVERAGE COMPANY LLC
2833 Mission St, Santa Cruz (95060-5755)
PHONE.................................888 558-1113
Orion Melehan,
EMP: 67
SALES (est): 1.8MM **Privately Held**
SIC: 2086 Bottled & canned soft drinks

(P-2090)
LIVING APOTHECARY LLC
770 National Ct, Richmond (94804-2008)
PHONE.................................917 951-2810
Shari Stein,
Traci L Hunt,
EMP: 10
SALES (est): 1.1MM **Privately Held**
SIC: 2086 Bottled & canned soft drinks

(P-2091)
MC CLELLAN BOTTLING GROUP
4712 Mountain Lakes Blvd, Redding (96003-1475)
PHONE.................................530 241-2600
Christina Holden, *Principal*
EMP: 14
SALES (est): 2.1MM **Privately Held**
SIC: 2086 Carbonated soft drinks, bottled & canned

(P-2092)
MEC CORONA SUMMIT III LLC
1 Monster Way, Corona (92879-7101)
PHONE.................................951 739-6200
EMP: 140
SALES (est): 4.2MM
SALES (corp-wide): 3.8B **Publicly Held**
SIC: 2086 Soft drinks: packaged in cans, bottles, etc.; carbonated beverages, nonalcoholic: bottled & canned; iced tea & fruit drinks, bottled & canned
PA: Monster Beverage Corporation
1 Monster Way
Corona CA 92879
951 739-6200

(P-2093)
MONSTER BEVERAGE COMPANY
1990 Pomona Rd, Corona (92880-6955)
PHONE.................................866 322-4466
Mark Hall, *Principal*
Ben Ashlin, *Marketing Staff*
Brent Hamilton, *Marketing Staff*
Ash Hodges, *Marketing Staff*
Robert Asmo, *Sales Staff*
EMP: 699
SALES (est): 45.7MM
SALES (corp-wide): 3.8B **Publicly Held**
SIC: 2086 Soft drinks: packaged in cans, bottles, etc.
PA: Monster Beverage Corporation
1 Monster Way
Corona CA 92879
951 739-6200

(P-2094)
MONSTER BEVERAGE CORPORATION (PA)
1 Monster Way, Corona (92879-7101)
PHONE.................................951 739-6200
Rodney C Sacks, *Ch of Bd*
Guy P Carling, *President*
Hilton H Schlosberg, *President*
Emelie C Tirre, *President*
Roger Pondel, *Officer*
EMP: 65
SQ FT: 141,000
SALES: 3.8B **Publicly Held**
SIC: 2086 Carbonated beverages, nonalcoholic: bottled & canned

(P-2095)
MT SHASTA BTLG DISTRG CO INC
Also Called: Pepsi-Cola Btlg Co Mt Shasta
302 Chestnut St, Mount Shasta (96067-2213)
PHONE.................................530 926-3121
Jean Ferl, *President*
Helen Chiment, *Vice Pres*
Robert Ferl, *General Mgr*
EMP: 19
SQ FT: 10,000
SALES: 3.5MM **Privately Held**
SIC: 2086 5181 Carbonated soft drinks, bottled & canned; beer & ale

(P-2096)
NIAGARA BOTTLING LLC
1401 Alder Ave, Rialto (92376-3005)
PHONE.................................909 230-5000
EMP: 12
SALES (corp-wide): 316.8MM **Privately Held**
SIC: 2086 Bottled & canned soft drinks
PA: Niagara Bottling, Llc
1440 Bridgegate Dr
Diamond Bar CA 91765
909 230-5000

(P-2097)
NIAGARA BOTTLING LLC
811 Zephyr St, Stockton (95206-4206)
PHONE.................................209 983-8436
EMP: 11
SALES (corp-wide): 316.8MM **Privately Held**
SIC: 2086 Bottled & canned soft drinks
PA: Niagara Bottling, Llc
1440 Bridgegate Dr
Diamond Bar CA 91765
909 230-5000

(P-2098)
NIAGARA BOTTLING LLC (PA)
Also Called: Niagara Drinking Water
1440 Bridgegate Dr, Diamond Bar (91765-3932)
PHONE.................................909 230-5000
Andy Peykoff II, *Mng Member*
Rali Sanderson, *Exec VP*
Michelle Kishon, *Executive Asst*
Dhiraj Mehta, *Info Tech Dir*
Peter Blenkiron, *MIS Mgr*
◆ **EMP:** 14
SALES (est): 316.8MM **Privately Held**
WEB: www.niagarawater.com
SIC: 2086 Water, pasteurized: packaged in cans, bottles, etc.

(P-2099)
NOAHS BOTTLED WATER
416 Hosmer Ave, Modesto (95351-3920)
PHONE.................................209 526-2945
John Varty, *President*
EMP: 50
SALES (est): 4.1MM **Privately Held**
SIC: 2086 Water, pasteurized: packaged in cans, bottles, etc.

(P-2100)
NOR-CAL BEVERAGE CO INC
1375 Terminal St, West Sacramento (95691-3514)
PHONE.................................916 372-1700
Larry Buban, *Manager*
EMP: 30
SALES (corp-wide): 248.5MM **Privately Held**
SIC: 2086 5181 Carbonated beverages, nonalcoholic: bottled & canned; soft drinks: packaged in cans, bottles, etc.; beer & ale
PA: Nor-Cal Beverage Co., Inc.
2150 Stone Blvd
West Sacramento CA 95691
916 372-0600

(P-2101)
OMENKAUSA LLC
Also Called: Omenkastore.com
720 N La Brea Ave, Inglewood (90302-2204)
P.O. Box 1966, Hawthorne (90251-1966)
PHONE.................................877 415-6590
Paulinus Ndibe, *Mng Member*
EMP: 10

SALES (est): 283.4K **Privately Held**
SIC: 2086 2096 5149 5145 Bottled & canned soft drinks; potato chips & similar snacks; canned goods: fruit, vegetables, seafood, meats, etc.; snack foods; snacks, direct sales; beverage stores

(P-2102)
ONE WORLD ENTERPRISES LLC
Also Called: One Natural Experience
1333 S Mayflower Ave # 100, Monrovia (91016-5265)
PHONE.................................310 802-4220
Rodrigo Veloso, *CEO*
▲ **EMP:** 30
SALES (est): 3.9MM **Privately Held**
SIC: 2086 Water, pasteurized: packaged in cans, bottles, etc.

(P-2103)
ORANGE BANG INC
13115 Telfair Ave, Sylmar (91342-3574)
PHONE.................................818 833-1000
David Fox, *President*
EMP: 40
SQ FT: 33,000
SALES (est): 6.5MM **Privately Held**
SIC: 2086 Soft drinks: packaged in cans, bottles, etc.

(P-2104)
ORGAIN INC
16631 Millikan Ave, Irvine (92606-5028)
P.O. Box 4918 (92616-4918)
PHONE.................................949 930-0039
Andrew Abraham, *CEO*
Carter Elenz, *President*
Stephen Hennessy, *Vice Pres*
Ron Osborne, *Vice Pres*
Slava Khabovets, *Opers Staff*
EMP: 10
SALES: 155MM **Privately Held**
SIC: 2086 Fruit drinks (less than 100% juice): packaged in cans, etc.

(P-2105)
P-AMERICAS LLC
Also Called: Pepsico
3586 Arden Rd, Hayward (94545-3921)
PHONE.................................510 732-9500
EMP: 25
SALES (corp-wide): 64.6B **Publicly Held**
SIC: 2086 Carbonated soft drinks, bottled & canned
HQ: P-Americas Llc
1 Pepsi Way
Somers NY 10589
336 896-5740

(P-2106)
P-AMERICAS LLC
Also Called: Pepsico
4375 N Ventura Ave, Ventura (93001-1124)
P.O. Box 25070 (93002-5070)
PHONE.................................805 641-4200
Daniel Sassen, *Branch Mgr*
Timothy Omdahl, *Admin Sec*
EMP: 107
SALES (corp-wide): 64.6B **Publicly Held**
SIC: 2086 Carbonated soft drinks, bottled & canned
HQ: P-Americas Llc
1 Pepsi Way
Somers NY 10589
336 896-5740

(P-2107)
PEPSI BOTTLING GROUP
Also Called: Pepsico
6230 Descanso Ave, Buena Park (90620-1013)
PHONE.................................714 522-9742
EMP: 10 **EST:** 2017
SALES (est): 812K **Privately Held**
SIC: 2086 Carbonated soft drinks, bottled & canned

(P-2108)
PEPSI COLA BTLG OF BKERSFIELD
215 E 21st St, Bakersfield (93305-5186)
PHONE.................................661 327-9992
James B Lindsey Jr, *President*
Fay W Penney, *Corp Secy*
Marjorie Lindsey, *Vice Pres*

EMP: 200
SQ FT: 30,000
SALES (est): 12.3MM Privately Held
SIC: 2086 Soft drinks: packaged in cans, bottles, etc.

(P-2109)
PEPSI-COLA BOTTLING GROUP
Also Called: Pepsico
215 E 21st St, Bakersfield (93305-5186)
PHONE.............................661 635-1100
Steve Longfield, *Branch Mgr*
Conception Andrew, *Sales Staff*
Benjamin Peace, *Sales Staff*
Scott Hawkins, *Manager*
EMP: 150
SALES (corp-wide): 64.6B Publicly Held
SIC: 2086 Carbonated soft drinks, bottled & canned
HQ: Pepsi-Cola Bottling Group
1111 Westchester Ave
White Plains NY 10604
914 767-6000

(P-2110)
PEPSI-COLA METRO BTLG CO INC
Also Called: Pepsico
2345 Thompson Way, Santa Maria (93455-1050)
PHONE.............................805 739-2160
Joe Pearson, *Branch Mgr*
EMP: 60
SALES (corp-wide): 64.6B Publicly Held
WEB: www.pbg.com
SIC: 2086 Carbonated soft drinks, bottled & canned
HQ: Pepsi-Cola Metropolitan Bottling Company, Inc.
1111 Westchester Ave
White Plains NY 10604
914 767-6000

(P-2111)
PEPSI-COLA METRO BTLG CO INC
6261 Caballero Blvd, Buena Park (90620-1191)
PHONE.............................714 522-9635
Margaret Gramann, *Manager*
Jim E Williams, *Business Mgr*
Migel Huertas, *Purch Mgr*
Lars Christesen, *Manager*
Belen Otero, *Manager*
EMP: 500
SALES (corp-wide): 64.6B Publicly Held
WEB: www.joy-of-cola.com
SIC: 2086 5149 Carbonated soft drinks, bottled & canned; soft drinks
HQ: Pepsi-Cola Metropolitan Bottling Company, Inc.
1111 Westchester Ave
White Plains NY 10604
914 767-6000

(P-2112)
PEPSI-COLA METRO BTLG CO INC
4699 Old Ironsides Dr # 150, Santa Clara (95054-1824)
PHONE.............................408 617-2200
Jerry Titwell, *Branch Mgr*
EMP: 200
SALES (corp-wide): 64.6B Publicly Held
WEB: www.joy-of-cola.com
SIC: 2086 Carbonated soft drinks, bottled & canned
HQ: Pepsi-Cola Metropolitan Bottling Company, Inc.
1111 Westchester Ave
White Plains NY 10604
914 767-6000

(P-2113)
PEPSI-COLA METRO BTLG CO INC
19700 Figueroa St, Carson (90745-1098)
PHONE.............................310 327-4222
Stefan Freeman, *Manager*
Lauren Turnbull, *Surgery Dir*
Taylor Harrity, *Mfg Staff*
Carol Clodius, *Production*
EMP: 700

SALES (corp-wide): 64.6B Publicly Held
WEB: www.joy-of-cola.com
SIC: 2086 5149 Carbonated soft drinks, bottled & canned; soft drinks
HQ: Pepsi-Cola Metropolitan Bottling Company, Inc.
1111 Westchester Ave
White Plains NY 10604
914 767-6000

(P-2114)
PEPSI-COLA METRO BTLG CO INC
7550 Reese Rd, Sacramento (95828-3707)
PHONE.............................916 423-1000
Randy Kieser, *Manager*
Michael Hassel, *Technical Staff*
Laura Thayer, *Maintence Staff*
EMP: 400
SALES (corp-wide): 64.6B Publicly Held
WEB: www.joy-of-cola.com
SIC: 2086 5962 Soft drinks: packaged in cans, bottles, etc.; merchandising machine operators
HQ: Pepsi-Cola Metropolitan Bottling Company, Inc.
1111 Westchester Ave
White Plains NY 10604
914 767-6000

(P-2115)
PEPSI-COLA METRO BTLG CO INC
Also Called: Pepsico
4225 Pepsi Pl, Stockton (95215-2316)
PHONE.............................209 367-7140
Sydney Van Vusan, *Principal*
EMP: 50
SALES (corp-wide): 64.6B Publicly Held
WEB: www.pbg.com
SIC: 2086 Carbonated soft drinks, bottled & canned
HQ: Pepsi-Cola Metropolitan Bottling Company, Inc.
1111 Westchester Ave
White Plains NY 10604
914 767-6000

(P-2116)
PEPSI-COLA METRO BTLG CO INC
6659 Sycamore Canyon Blvd, Riverside (92507-0733)
PHONE.............................909 885-0741
Eli Bernard, *Manager*
EMP: 300
SALES (corp-wide): 64.6B Publicly Held
SIC: 2086 Soft drinks: packaged in cans, bottles, etc.
HQ: Pepsi-Cola Metropolitan Bottling Company, Inc.
1111 Westchester Ave
White Plains NY 10604
914 767-6000

(P-2117)
PEPSI-COLA METRO BTLG CO INC
4701 Park Rd, Benicia (94510-1125)
PHONE.............................707 746-5404
Neal Sturrock, *Owner*
EMP: 125
SQ FT: 5,000
SALES (corp-wide): 64.6B Publicly Held
WEB: www.joy-of-cola.com
SIC: 2086 5149 Carbonated soft drinks, bottled & canned; groceries & related products
HQ: Pepsi-Cola Metropolitan Bottling Company, Inc.
1111 Westchester Ave
White Plains NY 10604
914 767-6000

(P-2118)
PEPSI-COLA METRO BTLG CO INC
Also Called: Pepsico
7995 Armour St, San Diego (92111-3780)
PHONE.............................858 560-6735
Art Brennan, *Branch Mgr*
Brandon Hall, *Sales Staff*
Sachary Naranjo, *Senior Mgr*
EMP: 400

SALES (corp-wide): 64.6B Publicly Held
WEB: www.pbg.com
SIC: 2086 Carbonated soft drinks, bottled & canned
HQ: Pepsi-Cola Metropolitan Bottling Company, Inc.
1111 Westchester Ave
White Plains NY 10604
914 767-6000

(P-2119)
PEPSI-COLA METRO BTLG CO INC
135 Martella St, Salinas (93901-2894)
PHONE.............................831 796-2000
Oscar Broyer, *Manager*
Robert Davis, *Opers Mgr*
EMP: 120
SALES (corp-wide): 64.6B Publicly Held
WEB: www.joy-of-cola.com
SIC: 2086 5149 Soft drinks: packaged in cans, bottles, etc.; groceries & related products
HQ: Pepsi-Cola Metropolitan Bottling Company, Inc.
1111 Westchester Ave
White Plains NY 10604
914 767-6000

(P-2120)
PEPSI-COLA METRO BTLG CO INC
4416 Azusa Canyon Rd, Baldwin Park (91706-2797)
PHONE.............................626 338-5531
Terry Dana, *Manager*
EMP: 200
SQ FT: 65,113
SALES (corp-wide): 64.6B Publicly Held
WEB: www.joy-of-cola.com
SIC: 2086 Carbonated soft drinks, bottled & canned
HQ: Pepsi-Cola Metropolitan Bottling Company, Inc.
1111 Westchester Ave
White Plains NY 10604
914 767-6000

(P-2121)
PEPSI-COLA METRO BTLG CO INC
1200 Arroyo St, San Fernando (91340-1545)
PHONE.............................818 898-3829
Bob Simpson, *Branch Mgr*
Chris Bozzo, *Manager*
Paul Cachay, *Manager*
EMP: 207
SALES (corp-wide): 64.6B Publicly Held
WEB: www.joy-of-cola.com
SIC: 2086 Carbonated soft drinks, bottled & canned
HQ: Pepsi-Cola Metropolitan Bottling Company, Inc.
1111 Westchester Ave
White Plains NY 10604
914 767-6000

(P-2122)
PEPSI-COLA METRO BTLG CO INC
200 Jennings St, San Francisco (94124-1723)
PHONE.............................415 206-7400
Dan Atkins, *Branch Mgr*
EMP: 95
SALES (corp-wide): 64.6B Publicly Held
WEB: www.joy-of-cola.com
SIC: 2086 5142 Carbonated soft drinks, bottled & canned; packaged frozen goods
HQ: Pepsi-Cola Metropolitan Bottling Company, Inc.
1111 Westchester Ave
White Plains NY 10604
914 767-6000

(P-2123)
PEPSI-COLA METRO BTLG CO INC
2471 Nadeau St, Mojave (93501-1507)
PHONE.............................661 824-2051
Blaine Sherritt, *Manager*
Kyra W Gilbert, *Senior Mgr*
EMP: 75

SALES (corp-wide): 64.6B Publicly Held
WEB: www.joy-of-cola.com
SIC: 2086 5149 Bottled & canned soft drinks; soft drinks
HQ: Pepsi-Cola Metropolitan Bottling Company, Inc.
1111 Westchester Ave
White Plains NY 10604
914 767-6000

(P-2124)
PEPSI-COLA METRO BTLG CO INC
83801 Citrus Ave, Indio (92201-3458)
PHONE.............................760 775-2660
Rick Valenti, *Manager*
EMP: 10
SALES (corp-wide): 64.6B Publicly Held
WEB: www.joy-of-cola.com
SIC: 2086 Carbonated soft drinks, bottled & canned
HQ: Pepsi-Cola Metropolitan Bottling Company, Inc.
1111 Westchester Ave
White Plains NY 10604
914 767-6000

(P-2125)
PEPSI-COLA METRO BTLG CO INC
29000 Hesperian Blvd, Hayward (94545-5014)
PHONE.............................510 781-3600
Toll Free:.............................877 -
Greg Knabe, *Manager*
Kristin Mohs, *Manager*
EMP: 350
SALES (corp-wide): 64.6B Publicly Held
WEB: www.joy-of-cola.com
SIC: 2086 Carbonated soft drinks, bottled & canned
HQ: Pepsi-Cola Metropolitan Bottling Company, Inc.
1111 Westchester Ave
White Plains NY 10604
914 767-6000

(P-2126)
PEPSI-COLA METRO BTLG CO INC
Also Called: Pepsico
27717 Aliso Creek Rd, Aliso Viejo (92656-3804)
PHONE.............................949 643-5700
Natolie Daniel, *Manager*
Naqeeb Hasan, *Finance*
Tracy Nord, *Manager*
EMP: 200
SALES (corp-wide): 64.6B Publicly Held
WEB: www.pbg.com
SIC: 2086 Carbonated soft drinks, bottled & canned
HQ: Pepsi-Cola Metropolitan Bottling Company, Inc.
1111 Westchester Ave
White Plains NY 10604
914 767-6000

(P-2127)
PEPSICO INC
4416 Azusa Canyon Rd, Baldwin Park (91706-2740)
PHONE.............................626 338-5531
Kip Zaughan, *Manager*
Claire Padmore, *Admin Mgr*
Ryan Windley, *Research*
Fidel Morales, *Financial Analy*
Craig McFarland, *Sales Staff*
EMP: 200
SALES (corp-wide): 64.6B Publicly Held
WEB: www.pepsico.com
SIC: 2086 Carbonated soft drinks, bottled & canned; carbonated beverages, nonalcoholic: bottled & canned
PA: Pepsico, Inc.
700 Anderson Hill Rd
Purchase NY 10577
914 253-2000

(P-2128)
PEREGRINE MOBILE BOTTLING LLC
20590 Pueblo Ave, Sonoma (95476-7956)
PHONE.............................707 637-7584
Thomas Jordan, *Principal*

PRODUCTS & SVCS

Justin Cude, *Opers Mgr*
Tom Deegan, *Regl Sales Mgr*
EMP: 14
SALES (est): 2.1MM **Privately Held**
SIC: 2086 Bottled & canned soft drinks

(P-2129)
PURE-FLO WATER CO (PA)
Also Called: Pure Flo Water
7737 Mission Gorge Rd, Santee
(92071-3306)
P.O. Box 660579, Dallas TX (75266-0579)
PHONE......................619 596-4130
Braian Grant, *CEO*
Marian Grant, *Corp Secy*
Heather Schoeneman, *Controller*
Art Ortega, *Manager*
EMP: 75
SQ FT: 9,000
SALES (est): 11.4MM **Privately Held**
SIC: 2086 Water, pasteurized: packaged in cans, bottles, etc.; pasteurized & mineral waters, bottled & canned

(P-2130)
RAINBOW ORCHARDS
2569 Larsen Dr, Camino (95709-9704)
PHONE......................530 644-1594
Tom Heflin, *Partner*
Christa Campbell, *Partner*
EMP: 11
SALES (est): 1.5MM **Privately Held**
SIC: 2086 0175 Fruit drinks (less than 100% juice): packaged in cans, etc.; apple orchard

(P-2131)
RED BULL NORTH AMERICA INC
1630 Stewart St Ste A, Santa Monica
(90404-4020)
PHONE......................310 393-4647
Jennifer Barney, *Branch Mgr*
EMP: 54
SALES (corp-wide): 3.9B **Privately Held**
SIC: 2086 Carbonated beverages, nonalcoholic: bottled & canned
HQ: Red Bull North America, Inc.
1740 Stewart St
Santa Monica CA 90404

(P-2132)
REFRESCO BEVERAGES US INC
631 S Waterman Ave, San Bernardino
(92408-2329)
PHONE......................909 915-1400
Armando Martinez, *Branch Mgr*
EMP: 92
SALES (corp-wide): 3.3B **Privately Held**
SIC: 2086 Carbonated beverages, nonalcoholic: bottled & canned
HQ: Refresco Beverages Us Inc.
8112 Woodland Center Blvd
Tampa FL 33614
813 313-1800

(P-2133)
REFRESCO BEVERAGES US INC
Also Called: San Bernardino Canning Co.
499 E Mill St, San Bernardino
(92408-1523)
PHONE......................909 915-1430
Ed Williams, *Manager*
EMP: 35
SQ FT: 76,180
SALES (corp-wide): 3.3B **Privately Held**
SIC: 2086 5149 Carbonated beverages, nonalcoholic: bottled & canned; soft drinks
HQ: Refresco Beverages Us Inc.
8112 Woodland Center Blvd
Tampa FL 33614
813 313-1800

(P-2134)
REYES COCA-COLA BOTTLING LLC (PA)
3 Park Plz Ste 600, Irvine (92614-2575)
PHONE......................213 744-8616
James Quincy, *CEO*
Nehal Desai, *CFO*
Angelo Lombardo, *Vice Pres*
Quinton Martin, *Vice Pres*
Dan Manning, *Manager*
◆ **EMP:** 300

SQ FT: 80,000
SALES (est): 785.2MM **Privately Held**
SIC: 2086 Bottled & canned soft drinks

(P-2135)
REYES COCA-COLA BOTTLING LLC
4320 Ride St, Bakersfield (93313-4831)
PHONE......................661 324-6531
Ed Shell, *Manager*
Tyvonne Glenn, *Admin Sec*
Donna Sowell, *Admin Asst*
Charlie Gwynn, *Sales Staff*
Eddie Griffin, *Director*
EMP: 100
SALES (corp-wide): 785.2MM **Privately Held**
SIC: 2086 Bottled & canned soft drinks
PA: Reyes Coca-Cola Bottling, L.L.C.
3 Park Plz Ste 600
Irvine CA 92614
213 744-8616

(P-2136)
REYES COCA-COLA BOTTLING LLC
1555 Old Bayshore Hwy, San Jose
(95112-4303)
PHONE......................408 436-3700
Larry Loeffer, *Manager*
EMP: 100
SALES (corp-wide): 785.2MM **Privately Held**
SIC: 2086 Bottled & canned soft drinks
PA: Reyes Coca-Cola Bottling, L.L.C.
3 Park Plz Ste 600
Irvine CA 92614
213 744-8616

(P-2137)
REYES COCA-COLA BOTTLING LLC
8729 Cleta St, Downey (90241-5202)
PHONE......................562 803-8100
Kim Curtis, *Manager*
EMP: 90
SQ FT: 76,395
SALES (corp-wide): 785.2MM **Privately Held**
SIC: 2086 5149 Bottled & canned soft drinks; groceries & related products
PA: Reyes Coca-Cola Bottling, L.L.C.
3 Park Plz Ste 600
Irvine CA 92614
213 744-8616

(P-2138)
REYES COCA-COLA BOTTLING LLC
1551 Atlantic St, Union City (94587-2005)
PHONE......................510 476-7000
Andy Darren, *Branch Mgr*
EMP: 80
SALES (corp-wide): 785.2MM **Privately Held**
SIC: 2086 5149 Bottled & canned soft drinks; groceries & related products
PA: Reyes Coca-Cola Bottling, L.L.C.
3 Park Plz Ste 600
Irvine CA 92614
213 744-8616

(P-2139)
REYES COCA-COLA BOTTLING LLC
14655 Wicks Blvd, San Leandro
(94577-6715)
PHONE......................510 667-6300
Ron King, *Branch Mgr*
EMP: 110
SALES (corp-wide): 785.2MM **Privately Held**
SIC: 2086 2087 2037 2095 Bottled & canned soft drinks; syrups, drink; fruit juice concentrates, frozen; roasted coffee; tea blending; wines
PA: Reyes Coca-Cola Bottling, L.L.C.
3 Park Plz Ste 600
Irvine CA 92614
213 744-8616

(P-2140)
REYES COCA-COLA BOTTLING LLC
3220 E Malaga Ave, Fresno (93725-9353)
PHONE......................559 264-4631
Mike Lozier, *Branch Mgr*
EMP: 95
SQ FT: 62,365
SALES (corp-wide): 785.2MM **Privately Held**
SIC: 2086 Bottled & canned soft drinks
PA: Reyes Coca-Cola Bottling, L.L.C.
3 Park Plz Ste 600
Irvine CA 92614
213 744-8616

(P-2141)
REYES COCA-COLA BOTTLING LLC
5335 Walker St, Ventura (93003-7406)
PHONE......................805 644-2211
Jim Donelson, *Manager*
EMP: 100
SALES (corp-wide): 785.2MM **Privately Held**
SIC: 2086 5149 Bottled & canned soft drinks; groceries & related products
PA: Reyes Coca-Cola Bottling, L.L.C.
3 Park Plz Ste 600
Irvine CA 92614
213 744-8616

(P-2142)
REYES COCA-COLA BOTTLING LLC
1467 El Pinal Dr, Stockton (95205-2672)
PHONE......................209 466-9501
Clay Frenzel, *Manager*
EMP: 45
SALES (corp-wide): 785.2MM **Privately Held**
SIC: 2086 Bottled & canned soft drinks
PA: Reyes Coca-Cola Bottling, L.L.C.
3 Park Plz Ste 600
Irvine CA 92614
213 744-8616

(P-2143)
REYES COCA-COLA BOTTLING LLC
86375 Industrial Way, Coachella
(92236-2729)
PHONE......................760 396-4500
Andrell Gritley, *General Mgr*
EMP: 67
SALES (corp-wide): 785.2MM **Privately Held**
SIC: 2086 Bottled & canned soft drinks
PA: Reyes Coca-Cola Bottling, L.L.C.
3 Park Plz Ste 600
Irvine CA 92614
213 744-8616

(P-2144)
REYES COCA-COLA BOTTLING LLC
120 E Jones St, Santa Maria (93454-5101)
PHONE......................805 925-2629
Dan Suchecki, *Manager*
EMP: 35
SQ FT: 50
SALES (corp-wide): 785.2MM **Privately Held**
SIC: 2086 Bottled & canned soft drinks
PA: Reyes Coca-Cola Bottling, L.L.C.
3 Park Plz Ste 600
Irvine CA 92614
213 744-8616

(P-2145)
REYES COCA-COLA BOTTLING LLC
715 Vandenberg St, Salinas (93905-3355)
PHONE......................831 755-8300
Bill Neighbors, *Branch Mgr*
EMP: 55
SALES (corp-wide): 785.2MM **Privately Held**
SIC: 2086 Bottled & canned soft drinks
PA: Reyes Coca-Cola Bottling, L.L.C.
3 Park Plz Ste 600
Irvine CA 92614
213 744-8616

(P-2146)
REYES COCA-COLA BOTTLING LLC
10670 6th St, Rancho Cucamonga
(91730-5912)
PHONE......................909 980-3121
Sid Campa, *Manager*
EMP: 115
SALES (corp-wide): 785.2MM **Privately Held**
SIC: 2086 5149 Bottled & canned soft drinks; groceries & related products
PA: Reyes Coca-Cola Bottling, L.L.C.
3 Park Plz Ste 600
Irvine CA 92614
213 744-8616

(P-2147)
REYES COCA-COLA BOTTLING LLC
1000 Fairway Dr, Santa Maria
(93455-1512)
PHONE......................805 614-3702
Dan Suchecki, *Manager*
EMP: 75
SALES (corp-wide): 785.2MM **Privately Held**
SIC: 2086 Bottled & canned soft drinks
PA: Reyes Coca-Cola Bottling, L.L.C.
3 Park Plz Ste 600
Irvine CA 92614
213 744-8616

(P-2148)
REYES COCA-COLA BOTTLING LLC
1580 Beltline Rd, Redding (96003-1408)
PHONE......................530 241-4315
David Hallagan, *Manager*
EMP: 25
SQ FT: 75,000
SALES (corp-wide): 785.2MM **Privately Held**
SIC: 2086 Bottled & canned soft drinks
PA: Reyes Coca-Cola Bottling, L.L.C.
3 Park Plz Ste 600
Irvine CA 92614
213 744-8616

(P-2149)
REYES COCA-COLA BOTTLING LLC
1348 47th St, San Diego (92102-2510)
PHONE......................619 266-6300
Randy Cleveland, *Manager*
EMP: 35
SQ FT: 20,000
SALES (corp-wide): 785.2MM **Privately Held**
SIC: 2086 5149 Bottled & canned soft drinks; groceries & related products
PA: Reyes Coca-Cola Bottling, L.L.C.
3 Park Plz Ste 600
Irvine CA 92614
213 744-8616

(P-2150)
REYES COCA-COLA BOTTLING LLC
666 Union St, Montebello (90640-6624)
PHONE......................323 278-2600
Gary Drees, *Manager*
EMP: 100
SQ FT: 127,556
SALES (corp-wide): 785.2MM **Privately Held**
SIC: 2086 Bottled & canned soft drinks
PA: Reyes Coca-Cola Bottling, L.L.C.
3 Park Plz Ste 600
Irvine CA 92614
213 744-8616

(P-2151)
REYES COCA-COLA BOTTLING LLC
1430 Melody Rd, Marysville (95901)
PHONE......................530 743-6533
Tom Quilty, *Manager*
EMP: 20
SALES (corp-wide): 785.2MM **Privately Held**
SIC: 2086 Bottled & canned soft drinks

▲ = Import ▼=Export
◆ =Import/Export

PA: Reyes Coca-Cola Bottling, L.L.C.
3 Park Plz Ste 600
Irvine CA 92614
213 744-8616

(P-2152)
REYES COCA-COLA BOTTLING LLC
700 W Grove Ave, Orange (92865-3214)
PHONE.....................714 974-1901
Thomas Murphy, *Branch Mgr*
EMP: 118
SQ FT: 7,043
SALES (corp-wide): 785.2MM **Privately Held**
SIC: 2086 Bottled & canned soft drinks
PA: Reyes Coca-Cola Bottling, L.L.C.
3 Park Plz Ste 600
Irvine CA 92614
213 744-8616

(P-2153)
REYES COCA-COLA BOTTLING LLC
530 Getty Ct, Benicia (94510-1139)
PHONE.....................707 747-2000
Gerold Henderickson, *Manager*
EMP: 120
SALES (corp-wide): 785.2MM **Privately Held**
SIC: 2086 Bottled & canned soft drinks
PA: Reyes Coca-Cola Bottling, L.L.C.
3 Park Plz Ste 600
Irvine CA 92614
213 744-8616

(P-2154)
REYES COCA-COLA BOTTLING LLC
1338 E 14th St, Los Angeles (90021)
PHONE.....................213 744-8659
Perry Fitch, *General Mgr*
EMP: 50
SALES (corp-wide): 785.2MM **Privately Held**
SIC: 2086 Bottled & canned soft drinks
PA: Reyes Coca-Cola Bottling, L.L.C.
3 Park Plz Ste 600
Irvine CA 92614
213 744-8616

(P-2155)
REYES COCA-COLA BOTTLING LLC
2603 Camino Ramon Ste 550, San Ramon (94583-9131)
PHONE.....................925 830-6500
Jim Hegenbart, *Manager*
EMP: 90
SALES (corp-wide): 785.2MM **Privately Held**
SIC: 2086 Bottled & canned soft drinks
PA: Reyes Coca-Cola Bottling, L.L.C.
3 Park Plz Ste 600
Irvine CA 92614
213 744-8616

(P-2156)
REYES COCA-COLA BOTTLING LLC
19875 Pacific Gateway Dr, Torrance (90502-1118)
PHONE.....................310 965-2653
David Carey, *Manager*
EMP: 175
SQ FT: 65,998
SALES (corp-wide): 785.2MM **Privately Held**
SIC: 2086 Bottled & canned soft drinks
PA: Reyes Coca-Cola Bottling, L.L.C.
3 Park Plz Ste 600
Irvine CA 92614
213 744-8616

(P-2157)
REYES COCA-COLA BOTTLING LLC
15346 Anacapa Rd, Victorville (92392-2448)
PHONE.....................760 241-2653
Rose Wols, *Manager*
EMP: 50
SALES (corp-wide): 785.2MM **Privately Held**
SIC: 2086 Bottled & canned soft drinks

PA: Reyes Coca-Cola Bottling, L.L.C.
3 Park Plz Ste 600
Irvine CA 92614
213 744-8616

(P-2158)
REYES COCA-COLA BOTTLING LLC
126 S 3rd St, El Centro (92243-2542)
PHONE.....................760 352-1561
Jose Chaira, *Manager*
EMP: 27
SALES (corp-wide): 785.2MM **Privately Held**
SIC: 2086 Bottled & canned soft drinks
PA: Reyes Coca-Cola Bottling, L.L.C.
3 Park Plz Ste 600
Irvine CA 92614
213 744-8616

(P-2159)
RISING BEVERAGE COMPANY LLC
10351 Santa Monica Blvd, Los Angeles (90025-6908)
PHONE.....................310 556-4500
Anders D Eisner, *Chairman*
Reza Mirza, *President*
Craig Berger, *CFO*
Burke H Eiteljorg, *Co-Founder*
EMP: 55
SALES (est): 7.2MM **Privately Held**
SIC: 2086 Fruit drinks (less than 100% juice): packaged in cans, etc.; lemonade: packaged in cans, bottles, etc.; mineral water, carbonated: packaged in cans, bottles, etc.

(P-2160)
RIVIERA BEVERAGES LLC
12782 Monarch St, Garden Grove (92841-3928)
PHONE.....................714 895-5169
Ken Klentz,
Chris Solberg, *Engineer*
Wilfredo Orozco, *Mfg Staff*
Kevin Clark,
Francisco Antillon, *Manager*
EMP: 40 EST: 2009
SALES (est): 5.5MM **Privately Held**
SIC: 2086 Water, pasteurized: packaged in cans, bottles, etc.

(P-2161)
ROCKSTAR INC
Also Called: Rockstar Energy Drink
8530 Wilshire Blvd Fl 3, Beverly Hills (90211-3114)
PHONE.....................323 785-2820
Taylor Liptak, *Marketing Mgr*
EMP: 149
SALES (corp-wide): 96.3MM **Privately Held**
SIC: 2086 Carbonated beverages, nonalcoholic: bottled & canned
PA: Rockstar, Inc.
101 Convention Center Dr # 777
Las Vegas NV 89109
702 939-5535

(P-2162)
ROGER ENRICO
Also Called: Pepsi-Cola
1150 E North Ave, Fresno (93725-1929)
PHONE.....................559 485-5050
Eric Foss, *CEO*
Craig Weatherup, *Ch of Bd*
Robert King, *President*
Terri Scherer, *Analyst*
Corinne Rogers, *Human Res Dir*
EMP: 500 EST: 1900
SQ FT: 250,000
SALES (est): 29.8K **Privately Held**
SIC: 2086 Soft drinks: packaged in cans, bottles, etc.; carbonated beverages, nonalcoholic: bottled & canned

(P-2163)
SACRAMENTO COCA-COLA BTLG INC (HQ)
4101 Gateway Park Blvd, Sacramento (95834-1951)
PHONE.....................916 928-2300
Steven A Cahillane, *CEO*
David Etheridge, *President*

EMP: 365
SQ FT: 260,000
SALES (est): 53.5MM
SALES (corp-wide): 785.2MM **Privately Held**
WEB: www.saccoke.com
SIC: 2086 Bottled & canned soft drinks
PA: Reyes Coca-Cola Bottling, L.L.C.
3 Park Plz Ste 600
Irvine CA 92614
213 744-8616

(P-2164)
SACRAMENTO COCA-COLA BTLG INC
1733 Morgan Rd Ste 200, Modesto (95358-5841)
PHONE.....................209 541-3200
Rex McGowen, *Principal*
EMP: 50
SALES (corp-wide): 785.2MM **Privately Held**
SIC: 2086 Bottled & canned soft drinks
HQ: Sacramento Coca-Cola Bottling Co., Inc.
4101 Gateway Park Blvd
Sacramento CA 95834
916 928-2300

(P-2165)
SBM DAIRIES INC (HQ)
Also Called: Heartland Farms
17851 Railroad St, City of Industry (91748-1118)
PHONE.....................626 923-3000
▼ EMP: 59
SQ FT: 250,000
SALES (est): 50.8MM **Publicly Held**
SIC: 2086 2026 2033 Fruit drinks (less than 100% juice): packaged in cans, etc.; fluid milk; milk processing (pasteurizing, homogenizing, bottling); buttermilk, cultured; canned fruits & specialties

(P-2166)
SEQUOIA PURE WATER INC
1640 W 134th St, Compton (90222-1624)
PHONE.....................310 637-8500
Dae Young Lee, *President*
EMP: 20
SQ FT: 80,000
SALES (est): 1.5MM **Privately Held**
SIC: 2086 Pasteurized & mineral waters, bottled & canned

(P-2167)
SEVEN UP BTLG CO SAN FRANCISCO (HQ)
Also Called: Seven-Up Bottling
2875 Prune Ave, Fremont (94539-6731)
PHONE.....................925 938-8777
Roger Easley, *Ch of Bd*
Linda Orsi, *Vice Pres*
EMP: 175
SALES (est): 68.3MM **Publicly Held**
WEB: www.7upcal.com
SIC: 2086 5149 4225 Bottled & canned soft drinks; groceries & related products; general warehousing & storage

(P-2168)
SEVEN UP BTLG CO SAN FRANCISCO
Also Called: Seven-Up Bottling
11205 Commercial Pkwy, Castroville (95012-3205)
PHONE.....................831 632-0777
Frank Reyes, *General Mgr*
EMP: 45 **Publicly Held**
WEB: www.7upcal.com
SIC: 2086 Bottled & canned soft drinks
HQ: Seven Up Bottling Company Of San Francisco
2875 Prune Ave
Fremont CA 94539
925 938-8777

(P-2169)
SEVEN UP BTLG CO SAN FRANCISCO
Also Called: Seven-Up Bottling
2670 Land Ave, Sacramento (95815-2380)
P.O. Box 15820 (95852-0820)
PHONE.....................916 929-7777
Tom Tontes, *Manager*

Wayne Buffington, *Production*
EMP: 96 **Publicly Held**
WEB: www.7upcal.com
SIC: 2086 5078 Soft drinks: packaged in cans, bottles, etc.; refrigerated beverage dispensers
HQ: Seven Up Bottling Company Of San Francisco
2875 Prune Ave
Fremont CA 94539
925 938-8777

(P-2170)
SEVEN-UP RC OF CHICO
306 Otterson Dr Ste 10, Chico (95928-8250)
P.O. Box 3610 (95927-3610)
PHONE.....................530 893-4501
Edward Frazer, *President*
EMP: 22 EST: 1930
SQ FT: 23,000
SALES (est): 3.2MM **Privately Held**
WEB: www.7uprcofchico.com
SIC: 2086 Bottled & canned soft drinks

(P-2171)
SHASTA BEVERAGES INC (DH)
Also Called: National Bevpak
26901 Indl Blvd, Hayward (94545)
PHONE.....................954 581-0922
Joseph G Caporella, *CEO*
John Minton, *President*
Dean McCoy, *Vice Pres*
Nick Caporella, *Principal*
Jerry House, *Plant Supt*
◆ EMP: 80
SQ FT: 156,000
SALES (est): 141.7MM
SALES (corp-wide): 1B **Publicly Held**
SIC: 2086 Soft drinks: packaged in cans, bottles, etc.; carbonated beverages, non-alcoholic: bottled & canned

(P-2172)
SHASTA BEVERAGES INC
14405 Artesia Blvd, La Mirada (90638-5886)
PHONE.....................714 523-2280
Bruce McDowell, *Opers-Prdtn-Mfg*
Randy Terry, *Plant Mgr*
EMP: 100
SALES (corp-wide): 1B **Publicly Held**
SIC: 2086 5149 Soft drinks: packaged in cans, bottles, etc.; soft drinks
HQ: Shasta Beverages, Inc.
26901 Indl Blvd
Hayward CA 94545
954 581-0922

(P-2173)
SMUCKER NATURAL FOODS INC (HQ)
37 Speedway Ave, Chico (95928-9554)
PHONE.....................530 899-5000
Richard K Smucker, *CEO*
Timothy P Smucker, *President*
Julia Sabin, *Vice Pres*
Darlene Weber, *Administration*
Kim Dietz, *Human Res Dir*
◆ EMP: 130
SQ FT: 85,000
SALES (est): 375.8MM
SALES (corp-wide): 7.8B **Publicly Held**
WEB: www.knudsenjuices.com
SIC: 2086 2033 2087 Iced tea & fruit drinks, bottled & canned; carbonated beverages, nonalcoholic: bottled & canned; canned fruits & specialties; syrups, drink
PA: The J M Smucker Company
1 Strawberry Ln
Orrville OH 44667
330 682-3000

(P-2174)
SOLANO COUNTY WATER AGENCY
810 Vaca Valley Pkwy # 203, Vacaville (95688-8835)
P.O. Box 349, Elmira (95625-0349)
PHONE.....................707 455-1105
David Okita, *Manager*
Thomas Tate, *Principal*
EMP: 10

P
R
O
D
U
C
T
S

&

S
V
C
S

SALES (est): 980K **Privately Held**
WEB: www.scwa2.com
SIC: 2086 Pasteurized & mineral waters,
bottled & canned

(P-2175)
SVC MFG INC A CORP
Also Called: Pepsi Co
5625 International Blvd, Oakland
(94621-4403)
PHONE..........................510 261-5800
David Chu, *Principal*
Nemesio Dumlao, *Manager*
▲ EMP: 11
SALES (est): 2.4MM **Privately Held**
SIC: 2086 Carbonated soft drinks, bottled
& canned

(P-2176)
**TOGNAZZINI BEVERAGE
SERVICE**
Also Called: Coca-Cola
241 Roemer Way, Santa Maria
(93454-1129)
PHONE..........................805 928-1144
Jim Tognazzini, *Owner*
Meck Tognazzini, *Co-Owner*
EMP: 12
SQ FT: 18,000
SALES (est): 3.5MM **Privately Held**
WEB: www.togbev.com
SIC: 2086 7699 Bottled & canned soft
drinks; fountain repair

(P-2177)
**TRENT BEVERAGE COMPANY
LLC**
Also Called: Trent Beverages
47230 Golden Bush Ct, Palm Desert
(92260-6079)
PHONE..........................310 384-6776
Bruce Trent, *Mng Member*
EMP: 12
SALES (est): 800K **Privately Held**
SIC: 2086 Carbonated beverages, nonal-
coholic: bottled & canned

(P-2178)
UNIX PACKAGING INC
Also Called: Mammoth Water
9 Minson Way, Montebello (90640-6744)
PHONE..........................213 627-5050
Bobby Melamed, *CEO*
Kourosh Melamed, *CFO*
Shawn Arianpour, *Vice Pres*
▲ EMP: 120
SQ FT: 125,000
SALES (est): 40MM **Privately Held**
SIC: 2086 Pasteurized & mineral waters,
bottled & canned

(P-2179)
USIWATER LLC
1433 W San Bernardino Rd, Covina
(91722-3471)
PHONE..........................626 600-5156
Wen Chen Guan, *Mng Member*
EMP: 10
SALES (est): 758.4K **Privately Held**
SIC: 2086 Mineral water, carbonated:
packaged in cans, bottles, etc.

(P-2180)
**VARNI BROTHERS
CORPORATION (PA)**
Also Called: Stanislaus Distributing Co
400 Hosmer Ave, Modesto (95351-3920)
PHONE..........................209 521-1777
John Varni, *President*
Fred Varni, *Corp Secy*
John Salzman, *Maintence Staff*
◆ EMP: 80
SQ FT: 80,000
SALES (est): 73.7MM **Privately Held**
WEB: www.noahs7up.com
SIC: 2086 5182 5181 Bottled & canned
soft drinks; wine; beer & other fermented
malt liquors

(P-2181)
**VARNI BROTHERS
CORPORATION**
Also Called: 7 Up
1109 W Anderson St, Stockton
(95206-1158)
PHONE..........................209 464-7778
Larry Varni, *Manager*
EMP: 20
SALES (corp-wide): 73.7MM **Privately
Held**
WEB: www.noahs7up.com
SIC: 2086 Bottled & canned soft drinks
PA: Varni Brothers Corporation
400 Hosmer Ave
Modesto CA 95351
209 521-1777

(P-2182)
WAIAKEA INC
Also Called: Wiakea Springs
5800 Hannum Ave Ste A135, Culver City
(90230-6685)
PHONE..........................855 924-2532
Ryan Emmons, *CEO*
Matthew Meyer, *COO*
Robert Emmons, *Treasurer*
Alexandra Alegria, *Manager*
EMP: 10 EST: 2012
SQ FT: 2,000
SALES (est): 1.2MM
SALES (corp-wide): 1.8MM **Privately
Held**
SIC: 2086 Water, pasteurized: packaged in
cans, bottles, etc.
PA: Waiakea Investments Llc
736 Cima Linda Ln
Santa Barbara CA 93108
805 450-0981

(P-2183)
**WAIAKEA INVESTMENTS LLC
(PA)**
736 Cima Linda Ln, Santa Barbara
(93108-1813)
PHONE..........................805 450-0981
Robert Emmons, *Principal*
Ryan Emmons,
Matthew Meyer,
EMP: 10
SALES (est): 1.8MM **Privately Held**
SIC: 2086 Water, pasteurized: packaged in
cans, bottles, etc.

(P-2184)
WIT GROUP
1822 Buenaventura Blvd # 101, Redding
(96001-6313)
PHONE..........................530 243-4447
Paul A Kassis, *President*
James Akers, *Vice Pres*
▼ EMP: 35
SQ FT: 1,100
SALES (est): 6.1MM **Privately Held**
SIC: 2086 Water, pasteurized: packaged in
cans, bottles, etc.

(P-2185)
ZEVIA LLC
15821 Ventura Blvd # 145, Encino
(91436-5201)
PHONE..........................310 202-7000
Padraic Spence, *Mng Member*
Robert J Gay, *Vice Pres*
Natalie Gershon, *Vice Pres*
Kenneth Panitz, *Vice Pres*
Jonathan Prince, *Vice Pres*
EMP: 75
SQ FT: 5,000
SALES (est): 29.5MM **Privately Held**
WEB: www.zevia.com
SIC: 2086 Carbonated soft drinks, bottled
& canned

(P-2186)
ZICO BEVERAGES LLC (HQ)
2101 E El Segundo Blvd # 403, El Segundo
(90245-4518)
PHONE..........................866 729-9426
Ronald J Lewis, *Mng Member*
Marie D Quintero-Johnson, *Mng Member*
▲ EMP: 38
SQ FT: 10,000

SALES (est): 7.4MM
SALES (corp-wide): 31.8B **Publicly Held**
SIC: 2086 Bottled & canned soft drinks
PA: The Coca-Cola Company
1 Coca Cola Plz Nw
Atlanta GA 30313
404 676-2121

**2087 Flavoring Extracts &
Syrups**

(P-2187)
**AA LABORATORY EGGS INC
(PA)**
Also Called: Balut Pateros
15075 Weststate St, Westminster
(92683-6526)
PHONE..........................714 893-5675
Thomas Dam, *President*
EMP: 15
SQ FT: 2,000
SALES (est): 2.5MM **Privately Held**
WEB: www.egglab.com
SIC: 2087 0252 5499 Concentrates,
drink; chicken eggs; eggs & poultry

(P-2188)
ADINA FOR LIFE INC
660 York St Ste 205, San Francisco
(94110-2102)
PHONE..........................415 285-9300
Norman E Snyder, *President*
Sherbrook Capital, *Shareholder*
Bradmer Foods, *Shareholder*
Social Enterprise Expansion Fu,
Shareholder
Seraph LLC, *Shareholder*
EMP: 26
SALES (est): 3.2MM **Privately Held**
WEB: www.adinaworld.com
SIC: 2087 5149 Beverage bases, concen-
trates, syrups, powders & mixes; bever-
ages, except coffee & tea

(P-2189)
**AMERICAN FRUITS & FLAVORS
LLC (HQ)**
Also Called: Juice Division
10725 Sutter Ave, Pacoima (91331-2553)
P.O. Box 331060 (91333-1060)
PHONE..........................818 899-9574
William Haddad, *President*
Sara Tapia, *CFO*
Bill Haddad, *Vice Pres*
Jack Haddad, *Vice Pres*
Laurie Katalbas, *Executive Asst*
◆ EMP: 125
SQ FT: 10,000
SALES (est): 106.2MM
SALES (corp-wide): 3.8B **Publicly Held**
WEB: www.americanfruit.com
SIC: 2087 Concentrates, drink; powders,
drink; syrups, drink
PA: Monster Beverage Corporation
1 Monster Way
Corona CA 92879
951 739-6200

(P-2190)
**AMERICAN FRUITS & FLAVORS
LLC**
Also Called: Flavors Division
1547 Knowles Ave, Los Angeles
(90063-1606)
PHONE..........................323 264-7791
Stacy West, *Branch Mgr*
Stacey West, *Opers Mgr*
EMP: 20
SALES (corp-wide): 3.8B **Publicly Held**
WEB: www.americanfruit.com
SIC: 2087 Extracts, flavoring
HQ: American Fruits And Flavors, Llc
10725 Sutter Ave
Pacoima CA 91331
818 899-9574

(P-2191)
BERRI PRO INC
929 Colorado Ave, Santa Monica
(90401-2716)
PHONE..........................781 929-8288
Jerome Joseph TSE, *CEO*
EMP: 19

SALES (est): 1MM **Privately Held**
SIC: 2087 Concentrates, drink

(P-2192)
BETTER BEVERAGES INC (PA)
Also Called: Chem-Mark of Orange County
10624 Midway Ave, Cerritos (90703-1581)
P.O. Box 1399, Bellflower (90707-1399)
PHONE..........................562 924-8321
H Ronald Harris, *CEO*
Tricia Harris, *Corp Secy*
Patrick Dickson, *Vice Pres*
William Kendig, *Vice Pres*
Kerrie Hernandez, *Human Res Mgr*
▲ EMP: 40
SQ FT: 15,000
SALES (est): 11.6MM **Privately Held**
WEB: www.betbev.com
SIC: 2087 7359 5169 Beverage bases;
syrups, drink; equipment rental & leasing;
industrial gases

(P-2193)
BI NUTRACEUTICALS INC (HQ)
2384 E Pacifica Pl, Rancho Dominguez
(90220-6214)
PHONE..........................310 669-2100
George Pontiakos, *President*
Christoph Kirchner, *CFO*
Bob Harvey, *Vice Pres*
Corey Leon, *Vice Pres*
Andrea Allen, *Buyer*
◆ EMP: 30
SQ FT: 7,600
SALES (est): 23MM **Privately Held**
WEB: www.botanicals.com
SIC: 2087 2833 5122 5149 Flavoring ex-
tracts & syrups; medicinals & botanicals;
vitamins & minerals; pharmaceuticals;
medicinals & botanicals; seasonings,
sauces & extracts; spices & seasonings;
flavourings & fragrances
PA: Mb Capital Investments, Inc.
300 Harmon Meadow Blvd
Secaucus NJ 07094
201 659-3100

(P-2194)
BLOSSOM VALLEY FOODS INC
Also Called: Pepper Plant, The
20 Casey Ln, Gilroy (95020-4539)
PHONE..........................408 848-5520
Robert M Wagner, *President*
EMP: 25
SQ FT: 27,000
SALES (est): 5.1MM **Privately Held**
WEB: www.blossomvalleyfoods.com
SIC: 2087 2099 Cocktail mixes, nonalco-
holic; food preparations

(P-2195)
**BLUE PCF FLVORS
FRAGRANCES INC**
1354 Marion Ct, City of Industry
(91745-2418)
PHONE..........................626 934-0099
Donald F Wilkes, *President*
▲ EMP: 20
SQ FT: 40,000
SALES (est): 4.9MM **Privately Held**
SIC: 2087 2869 Extracts, flavoring; per-
fumes, flavorings & food additives

(P-2196)
BYRNES & KIEFER CO
501 Airpark Dr, Fullerton (92833-2501)
PHONE..........................714 554-4000
EMP: 55
SALES (est): 5MM **Privately Held**
SIC: 2087 Colorings, confectioners'

(P-2197)
CALIFORNIA COCKTAILS INC
Also Called: Lataz Product
345 Oak Pl, Brea (92821-4122)
P.O. Box 459 (92822-0459)
PHONE..........................714 990-0982
Larry Casey, *President*
▲ EMP: 13
SQ FT: 18,000
SALES (est): 963.3K **Privately Held**
SIC: 2087 2099 Cocktail mixes, nonalco-
holic; food preparations

▲ = Import ▼=Export
◆ =Import/Export

(P-2198)
CALIFORNIA CUSTOM FRUITS (PA)
Also Called: California Cstm Frt & Flavors
15800 Tapia St, Irwindale (91706-2178)
PHONE..................................626 736-4130
Mike Mulhausen, *President*
Nicole Banuelos, *President*
James Fragnoli, *CFO*
Daniel Birshan, *Research*
Catherine White, *Human Res Mgr*
◆ EMP: 76
SALES (est): 21MM **Privately Held**
SIC: 2087 2033 2099 5083 Extracts, flavoring; fruits: packaged in cans, jars, etc.; food preparations; dairy machinery & equipment

(P-2199)
CARMI FLVR & FRAGRANCE CO INC (PA)
Also Called: Carmi Flavors
6030 Scott Way, Commerce (90040-3516)
PHONE..................................323 888-9240
Eliot Carmi, *President*
Janine Bell, *Office Mgr*
Sarah Foster, *Office Mgr*
Nastasha Winniczuk, *Business Mgr*
Lauren Contreras, *Marketing Staff*
▲ EMP: 40
SQ FT: 35,000
SALES: 16MM **Privately Held**
SIC: 2087 2844 Extracts, flavoring; toilet preparations

(P-2200)
COCA-COLA COMPANY
1650 S Vintage Ave, Ontario (91761-3656)
PHONE..................................909 975-5200
EMP: 100
SALES (corp-wide): 44.2B **Publicly Held**
SIC: 2087 5149
PA: The Coca-Cola Company
1 Coca Cola Plz Nw
Atlanta GA 30313
404 676-2121

(P-2201)
CREATIVE CONCEPTS HOLDINGS LLC (HQ)
580 Garcia Ave, Pittsburg (94565-4901)
PHONE..................................949 705-6584
EMP: 11
SALES (est): 2.4MM
SALES (corp-wide): 10.2MM **Privately Held**
WEB: www.creativeflavorconcepts.com
SIC: 2087 Extracts, flavoring
PA: Flavor Producers, Llc
8521 Fllbrook Ave Ste 380
West Hills CA 91304
818 307-4062

(P-2202)
DELANO GROWERS GRAPE PRODUCTS
32351 Bassett Ave, Delano (93215-9699)
PHONE..................................661 725-3255
Jim Cesare, *President*
Daniel Lord, *Plant Mgr*
▲ EMP: 55 EST: 1940
SQ FT: 40,000
SALES (est): 29.1MM **Privately Held**
WEB: www.delanocc.com
SIC: 2087 Concentrates, drink

(P-2203)
DISTRIBUTORS PROCESSING INC
Also Called: D P I
17656 Avenue 168, Porterville (93257-9263)
PHONE.....................................559 781-0297
Randy Walker, *President*
Gary Jacinto, *Ch of Bd*
William Blatnick, *Corp Secy*
Marcia Pierce, *Admin Sec*
Mike Rincker, *Research*
▼ EMP: 17
SQ FT: 23,050
SALES (est): 3.1MM **Privately Held**
WEB: www.dpiglobal.com
SIC: 2087 Extracts, flavoring

(P-2204)
DR SMOOTHIE BRANDS INC
1730 Raymer Ave, Fullerton (92833-2530)
PHONE..................................714 449-9787
Sam Lteif, *CEO*
Wes Lanier, *Plant Engr*
Ron Garrett, *Mktg Dir*
Susy Sandoval, *Sales Staff*
Robb Anderson, *Director*
▼ EMP: 33
SQ FT: 30,000
SALES (est): 5.4MM
SALES (corp-wide): 50.8MM **Privately Held**
SIC: 2087 Beverage bases, concentrates, syrups, powders & mixes
PA: Juice Tyme, Inc.
4401 S Oakley Ave
Chicago IL 60609
773 579-1291

(P-2205)
DR SMOOTHIE ENTERPRISES
1730 Raymer Ave, Fullerton (92833-2530)
PHONE..................................714 449-9787
Bill Haugh, *President*
William P Haugh, *Principal*
Mike Finch, *Buyer*
▼ EMP: 21
SQ FT: 30,000
SALES (est): 4.4MM **Privately Held**
WEB: www.drsmoothie.com
SIC: 2087 Beverage bases, concentrates, syrups, powders & mixes

(P-2206)
DRY CREEK NUTRITION INC
600 Yosemite Blvd, Modesto (95354-2760)
PHONE..................................209 341-5696
Robert J Gallo, *Ch of Bd*
Peter Kovacs, *President*
EMP: 15 EST: 2000
SALES (est): 1.2MM **Privately Held**
WEB: www.activin.com
SIC: 2087 Extracts, flavoring

(P-2207)
FELBRO FOOD PRODUCTS INC
5700 W Adams Blvd, Los Angeles (90016-2402)
PHONE..................................323 936-5266
Michael Feldmar, *CEO*
Barton Feldman, *President*
Barton J Feldmar, *CEO*
Raul Juarez, *Purch Mgr*
Rebecca Gelston, *Manager*
EMP: 49 EST: 1946
SQ FT: 35,000
SALES (est): 27MM **Privately Held**
WEB: www.felbro.com
SIC: 2087 Syrups, drink

(P-2208)
FISCHLER INVESTMENTS INC (DH)
Also Called: Affinity Flavors
2026 Cecilia Cir, Corona (92881-3389)
PHONE..................................951 479-4682
Tom Damiano, *CEO*
EMP: 10 EST: 1998
SQ FT: 38,000
SALES (est): 2.1MM **Privately Held**
WEB: www.affinityflavors.com
SIC: 2087 Extracts, flavoring
HQ: T. Hasegawa U.S.A. Inc.
14017 183rd St
Cerritos CA 90703
714 522-1900

(P-2209)
FLAVOR HOUSE INC
16378 Koala Rd, Adelanto (92301-3916)
PHONE..................................760 246-9131
Richard Staley, *President*
◆ EMP: 40 EST: 1977
SQ FT: 23,600
SALES (est): 7.6MM **Privately Held**
WEB: www.flavorhouse.com
SIC: 2087 Flavoring extracts & syrups

(P-2210)
FLAVORCHEM CORPORATION
271 Calle Pintoresco, San Clemente (92672-7506)
PHONE..................................949 369-7900
Baron Zachary, *Branch Mgr*

Philip Chapoulie, *Sales Staff*
Rae L Velker, *Manager*
EMP: 30
SALES (corp-wide): 31.7MM **Privately Held**
WEB: www.flavorchem.com
SIC: 2087 Extracts, flavoring
PA: Flavorchem Corporation
1525 Brook Dr
Downers Grove IL 60515
630 932-8100

(P-2211)
FPG OC INC
24855 Corbit Pl Ste B, Yorba Linda (92887-5543)
PHONE..................................714 692-2950
Joshua Cua, *CEO*
Priscilla Latter, *President*
Julie Hodson, *Vice Pres*
▲ EMP: 53
SQ FT: 74,300
SALES (est): 6.1MM **Privately Held**
SIC: 2087 Extracts, flavoring

(P-2212)
FROZEN BEAN INC
9238 Bally Ct, Rancho Cucamonga (91730-5313)
PHONE..................................855 837-6936
John Bae, *CEO*
Thuy Dang, *Director*
Tammy Le, *Manager*
David Spry, *Manager*
Sharon Kang, *Assistant*
▼ EMP: 30 EST: 2011
SALES (est): 5.6MM **Privately Held**
SIC: 2087 Beverage bases, concentrates, syrups, powders & mixes

(P-2213)
FRUTAROM
790 E Harrison St, Corona (92879-1348)
PHONE..................................951 734-6620
Imtiaz Syed, *Branch Mgr*
Richard Davidson, *Branch Mgr*
Jay Harris, *Info Tech Mgr*
EMP: 19
SALES (corp-wide): 387.6MM **Privately Held**
SIC: 2087 Extracts, flavoring
PA: Frutarom Industries Ltd
2 Hamanofim, Entrance
Herzliya 46725
747 177-126

(P-2214)
GOLDEN STATE FOODS CORP (PA)
18301 Von Karman Ave # 1100, Irvine (92612-1009)
PHONE..................................949 247-8000
Mark Wetterau, *Ch of Bd*
Mike Waitukaitis, *Vice Chairman*
Ryan Hammer, *President*
Wayne Morgan, *President*
Scott Thomas, *Bd of Directors*
◆ EMP: 35
SALES (est): 1.3B **Privately Held**
WEB: www.goldenstatefoods.com
SIC: 2087 5142 5148 5149 Syrups, drink; packaged frozen goods; vegetables; vegetables, fresh; condiments; meats, cured or smoked

(P-2215)
HERBALIFE MANUFACTURING LLC
20481 Crescent Bay Dr, Lake Forest (92630-8817)
PHONE..................................949 457-0951
Gerry Holly, *Senior VP*
Michael Crombie, *Production*
◆ EMP: 75
SQ FT: 145,000
SALES (est): 23.8MM **Privately Held**
SIC: 2087 2023 Beverage bases, concentrates, syrups, powders & mixes; dietary supplements, dairy & non-dairy based
HQ: Herbalife International, Inc.
800 W Olympic Blvd # 406
Los Angeles CA 90015
310 410-9600

(P-2216)
ICEE COMPANY
6800 Sierra Ct Ste M, Dublin (94568-2644)
PHONE..................................925 828-5807
Mike Fehely, *Manager*
EMP: 13
SALES (corp-wide): 1B **Publicly Held**
WEB: www.theiceecompany.com
SIC: 2087 Beverage bases, concentrates, syrups, powders & mixes
HQ: The Icee Company
1205 S Dupont Ave
Ontario CA 91761
800 426-4233

(P-2217)
J & J PROCESSING INC
Also Called: Custom Foods
14715 Anson Ave, Santa Fe Springs (90670-5305)
PHONE..................................562 926-2333
James B Nelson, *CEO*
Paul Nelson, *COO*
Andrea Goettman, *Office Mgr*
Lisa Goldstein, *Research*
Chris Conners, *Purchasing*
▲ EMP: 50
SQ FT: 44,000
SALES (est): 15.7MM **Privately Held**
SIC: 2087 2041 2099 Beverage bases; flour & other grain mill products; seasonings: dry mixes; spices, including grinding

(P-2218)
JAVO BEVERAGE COMPANY INC
1311 Specialty Dr, Vista (92081-8521)
PHONE..................................760 560-5286
Dennis Riley, *President*
Chris Johnson, *Exec VP*
David Estes, *Regional Mgr*
Larry Gilbert, *Regional Mgr*
Dan Paraboschi, *Regional Mgr*
▲ EMP: 55
SQ FT: 39,000
SALES (est): 15.4MM **Privately Held**
WEB: www.javobeverage.com
SIC: 2087 Extracts, flavoring

(P-2219)
LA PAZ PRODUCTS INC
345 Oak Pl, Brea (92821-4122)
P.O. Box 459 (92822-0459)
PHONE..................................714 990-0982
Suanne Casey, *CEO*
Roy Farhi, *Sales Dir*
▼ EMP: 18
SQ FT: 18,000
SALES (est): 3.6MM **Privately Held**
WEB: www.lapazproducts.com
SIC: 2087 Cocktail mixes, nonalcoholic

(P-2220)
MASTERTASTE INC
Also Called: Kerry Ingredients and Flavours
1916 S Tubeway Ave, Commerce (90040-1612)
PHONE..................................323 727-2100
Chris Long, *General Mgr*
EMP: 74 **Privately Held**
WEB: www.mastertaste.com
SIC: 2087 Flavoring extracts & syrups
HQ: Mastertaste Inc.
160 Terminal Ave
Clark NJ 07066
732 882-0202

(P-2221)
MISSION FLAVORS FRAGRANCES INC
25882 Wright, El Toro (92610-3503)
PHONE..................................949 461-3344
Patrick S Imburgia, *CEO*
EMP: 15
SALES (est): 3.7MM **Privately Held**
WEB: www.missionflavors.com
SIC: 2087 Extracts, flavoring; syrups, flavoring (except drink)

(P-2222)
NEWPORT FLAVORS & FRAGRANCES
Also Called: Nature's Flavors
833 N Elm St, Orange (92867-7909)
PHONE..................................714 771-2200

William R Sabo, *CEO*
Jeanne A Rossman, *Admin Sec*
Ben Moreno, *QC Mgr*
Lane Melland, *Director*
▲ EMP: 30
SALES (est): 5.6MM **Privately Held**
WEB: www.newportflavours.com
SIC: 2087 Extracts, flavoring

(P-2223)
PACIFIC COAST PRODUCTS LLC (PA)
Also Called: Perfumer's Apprentice
170 Technology Cir, Scotts Valley
(95066-3520)
PHONE..................................831 316-7137
Linda Andrews, *Mng Member*
Travis McIntosh, *Opers Mgr*
David Hertzberg, *Prdtn Mgr*
EMP: 15
SQ FT: 50,000
SALES: 23.3MM **Privately Held**
SIC: 2087 5141 8741 Extracts, flavoring;
food brokers; administrative management

(P-2224)
PACIFIC COAST PRODUCTS LLC
Also Called: Perfumer's Apprentice
200 Technology Cir, Scotts Valley
(95066-3500)
PHONE..................................831 316-7137
David Hertzberg, *Prdtn Mgr*
EMP: 32
SQ FT: 26,000
SALES (corp-wide): 23.3MM **Privately Held**
SIC: 2087 2844 Extracts, flavoring; concentrates, perfume
PA: Pacific Coast Products Llc
170 Technology Cir
Scotts Valley CA 95066
831 316-7137

(P-2225)
PRIMAL ESSENCE INC
1351 Maulhardt Ave, Oxnard (93030-7963)
PHONE..................................805 981-2409
Preman Brady, *President*
Dr Mark Smythe, *CFO*
Susan Smythe, *Treasurer*
Carolyn Brenthel, *Vice Pres*
▲ EMP: 10
SQ FT: 12,780
SALES: 1.9MM **Privately Held**
WEB: www.primalessence.com
SIC: 2087 Flavoring extracts & syrups

(P-2226)
QUAKER OATS COMPANY
5625 International Blvd, Oakland
(94621-4403)
PHONE..................................510 261-5800
Joan Parrott Sheffer, *Branch Mgr*
EMP: 120
SALES (corp-wide): 64.6B **Publicly Held**
WEB: www.quakeroats.com
SIC: 2087 2086 Beverage bases, concentrates, syrups, powders & mixes; bottled & canned soft drinks
HQ: The Quaker Oats Company
555 W Monroe St Fl 1
Chicago IL 60661
312 821-1000

(P-2227)
R TORRE & COMPANY INC (PA)
Also Called: Torani Syrups & Flavors
233 E Harris Ave, South San Francisco
(94080-6807)
PHONE..................................800 775-1925
Melanie Dulbecco, *CEO*
Doug Reifsteck, *COO*
Julie Garlikov, *Vice Pres*
Lisa Lucheta, *Principal*
Paul Lucheta, *Principal*
◆ EMP: 160 EST: 1925
SQ FT: 110,000
SALES (est): 39.8MM **Privately Held**
WEB: www.torani.com
SIC: 2087 Syrups, drink

(P-2228)
R TORRE & COMPANY INC
400 Littlefield Ave, South San Francisco
(94080-6105)
PHONE..................................650 624-2830

Steve Schultz, *Surgery Dir*
EMP: 35
SALES (est): 39.8MM **Privately Held**
SIC: 2087 Syrups, drink
PA: R. Torre & Company, Inc.
233 E Harris Ave
South San Francisco CA 94080
800 775-1925

(P-2229)
SCISOREK & SON FLAVORS INC
Also Called: S&S Flavours
2951 Enterprise St, Brea (92821-6212)
PHONE..................................714 524-0550
Mark Tuerffs, *President*
Dan Hart, *Vice Pres*
Curtis Krystek, *Plant Mgr*
EMP: 50
SQ FT: 33,000
SALES (est): 4.5MM **Privately Held**
WEB: www.ssflavors.com
SIC: 2087 Extracts, flavoring

(P-2230)
SEELECT INC
833 N Elm St, Orange (92867-7909)
PHONE..................................714 744-3700
William R Sabo, *CEO*
Bill Sabo, *President*
EMP: 17 EST: 1935
SALES (est): 2.2MM **Privately Held**
WEB: www.seelecttea.com
SIC: 2087 Flavoring extracts & syrups

(P-2231)
SYMRISE INC
332 Forest Ave, Laguna Beach
(92651-2117)
PHONE..................................949 276-4600
Steve Koehr, *Branch Mgr*
EMP: 11
SALES (corp-wide): 3.6B **Privately Held**
WEB: www.flavorinfusion.com
SIC: 2087 Syrups, drink
HQ: Symrise Inc.
891 Busse Rd
Elk Grove Village IL 60007
201 288-3200

(P-2232)
T HASEGAWA USA INC (HQ)
14017 183rd St, Cerritos (90703-7000)
PHONE..................................714 522-1900
Tom Damiano, *CEO*
Tokujiro Hasegawa, *President*
Dan Freimuth, *Vice Pres*
Laura Gibbons, *Executive Asst*
Jennifer Wade, *Executive Asst*
▲ EMP: 50
SQ FT: 56,000
SALES (est): 16.1MM **Privately Held**
WEB: www.thasegawa.com
SIC: 2087 Extracts, flavoring

(P-2233)
UNION FLAVORS INC
14145 Proctor Ave Ste 15, City of Industry
(91746-2841)
PHONE..................................626 333-1612
Nam Duck Kim, *President*
▼ EMP: 10
SQ FT: 4,500
SALES: 5MM **Privately Held**
SIC: 2087 Extracts, flavoring

(P-2234)
UNITED BRANDS COMPANY INC
5930 Cornerstone Ct W # 170, San Diego
(92121-3772)
PHONE..................................619 461-5220
Michael Michail, *President*
EMP: 43
SQ FT: 1,800
SALES (est): 13.1MM **Privately Held**
SIC: 2087 2082 Beverage bases; ale (alcoholic beverage)

(P-2235)
WEIDER HEALTH AND FITNESS
21100 Erwin St, Woodland Hills
(91367-3772)
PHONE..................................818 884-6800
Eric Weider, *President*
Tonja Fuller, *Treasurer*

Lian Katz, *Treasurer*
George Lengvari, *Vice Ch Bd*
Peggy Sukawaty, *Executive Asst*
EMP: 466
SQ FT: 6,000
SALES (est): 47.2MM **Privately Held**
WEB: www.weider.com
SIC: 2087 7991 7999 Beverage bases, concentrates, syrups, powders & mixes; physical fitness facilities; physical fitness instruction

┌─────────────────────────┐
│ **2091 Fish & Seafoods,** │
│ **Canned & Cured** │
└─────────────────────────┘

(P-2236)
AQUAMAR INC
10888 7th St, Rancho Cucamonga
(91730-5421)
PHONE..................................909 481-4700
Hugo Yamakawa, *Principal*
Taka Iwasaki, *Vice Pres*
Arlene Coste, *Human Res Mgr*
Saemi Cheon, *Opers Staff*
Francisco Jaimes, *Manager*
◆ EMP: 150
SQ FT: 42,000
SALES (est): 37.8MM **Privately Held**
WEB: www.aquamar.net
SIC: 2091 2092 Shellfish, canned & cured; fresh or frozen packaged fish

(P-2237)
BUMBLE BEE CAPITAL CORP
280 10th Ave, San Diego (92101-7406)
PHONE..................................858 715-4000
Christopher Lischew, *Principal*
EMP: 123
SALES (est): 8MM **Privately Held**
SIC: 2091 Tuna fish: packaged in cans, jars, etc.
HQ: Bee Bumble Foods Llc
280 10th Ave
San Diego CA 92101
858 715-4000

(P-2238)
BUMBLE BEE FOODS LLC (DH)
Also Called: Bumble Bee
280 10th Ave, San Diego (92101-7406)
P.O. Box 85362 (92186-5362)
PHONE..................................858 715-4000
Jan Tharp, *CEO*
Ron Schindler, *Senior VP*
Joe Berry, *Vice Pres*
Brett Butler, *Vice Pres*
Jeff Conyers, *Vice Pres*
◆ EMP: 277
SALES (est): 172.2MM **Privately Held**
SIC: 2091 Tuna fish: packaged in cans, jars, etc.
HQ: Bee Bumble Holdings Inc
280 10th Ave
San Diego CA 92101
858 715-4000

(P-2239)
BUMBLE BEE SEAFOODS LP
280 10th Ave, San Diego (92101-7406)
P.O. Box 85362 (92186-5362)
PHONE..................................858 715-4000
Christopher Lischewsky, *Partner*
James Badet, *Vice Pres*
Tony Costa, *Vice Pres*
Robert Dorsey, *Vice Pres*
Steven Dudal, *Vice Pres*
▼ EMP: 78
SALES (est): 47.6MM **Privately Held**
SIC: 2091 2047 Tuna fish: packaged in cans, jars, etc.; dog & cat food

(P-2240)
BUMBLE BEE SEAFOODS INC
280 10th Ave, San Diego (92101-7406)
PHONE..................................858 715-4000
Gabriela Silva, *CEO*
Teresa Karp, *Vice Pres*
Patty Chavez, *Executive Asst*
Patricia Curran, *Prgrmr*
Rich Ennis, *Project Mgr*
◆ EMP: 21
SALES (est): 3.2MM **Privately Held**
SIC: 2091 Tuna fish: packaged in cans, jars, etc.

(P-2241)
BUMBLE BEE SEAFOODS INC
280 10th Ave, San Diego (92101-7406)
P.O. Box 85362 (92186-5362)
PHONE..................................858 715-4068
◆ EMP: 3000
SALES (est): 308.8MM **Privately Held**
SIC: 2091 2047

(P-2242)
BUMBLE BEE SEAFOODS LLC
13100 Arctic Cir, Santa Fe Springs
(90670-5508)
PHONE..................................562 483-7474
Sheri Glazebrook, *CEO*
John Frenzley, *Info Tech Mgr*
Ricky Vazquez, *Network Enginr*
EMP: 20
SALES (est): 3MM **Privately Held**
SIC: 2091 Canned & cured fish & seafoods

(P-2243)
COAST SEAFOODS COMPANY
25 Waterfront Dr, Eureka (95501-0370)
PHONE..................................707 442-2947
Greg Dale, *Manager*
EMP: 30
SALES (corp-wide): 70.7MM **Privately Held**
WEB: www.coastseafoods.com
SIC: 2091 0913 2092 Oysters: packaged in cans, jars, etc.; oyster beds; fresh or frozen packaged fish
HQ: Coast Seafoods Company
1200 Robert Bush Dr
Bellevue WA 98007

(P-2244)
GLOBAL OCEAN TRADING LLC
430 S Grfield Ave Ste 405, Alhambra
(91801)
PHONE..................................626 281-0800
Makoto Kikuchi, *Manager*
▼ EMP: 10
SALES: 1.1MM **Privately Held**
SIC: 2091 Canned & cured fish & seafoods

(P-2245)
KEYSOURCE FOODS LLC
2263 W 190th St, Torrance (90504-6001)
PHONE..................................310 879-4888
Roger Lin, *Mng Member*
▲ EMP: 23
SALES (est): 4.3MM **Privately Held**
SIC: 2091 Seafood products: packaged in cans, jars, etc.

(P-2246)
OCEAN BEAUTY SEAFOODS LLC
Three Star Smoked Fish Co
629 S Central Ave, Los Angeles
(90021-1050)
PHONE..................................213 624-2101
Mark Palmer, *President*
EMP: 200
SQ FT: 68,000
SALES (corp-wide): 438.8MM **Privately Held**
WEB: www.oceanbeauty.com
SIC: 2091 5149 Fish, smoked; fish, cured; chocolate
PA: Ocean Beauty Seafoods Llc
1100 W Ewing St
Seattle WA 98119
206 285-6800

(P-2247)
OCEAN FRESH LLC (PA)
Also Called: Ocean Fresh Seafood Products
350 N Main St, Fort Bragg (95437-3406)
PHONE..................................707 964-1389
Robert S Juntz, *Mng Member*
Susan Juntz
▲ EMP: 41
SQ FT: 5,000
SALES: 4.7MM **Privately Held**
SIC: 2091 Fish, canned & cured

(P-2248)
PACIFIC PLAZA IMPORTS INC
Also Called: Plaze De Caviar
3018 Willow Pass Rd # 102, Concord
(94519-2543)
PHONE..........................925 349-4000
Mark Bolourchi, *President*
Ali Bolourchi, *Vice Pres*
Sharon Bolourchi, *Vice Pres*
▲ EMP: 18 EST: 1985
SQ FT: 24,000
SALES (est): 15MM **Privately Held**
WEB: www.pacificplaza.net
SIC: 2091 Caviar: packaged in cans, jars, etc.

(P-2249)
RLT SEAFOOD SUPERMARKET INC
Also Called: SM Asian Market
333 S E St, San Bernardino (92401-2010)
PHONE..........................909 888-6520
Ronald Loca Tsu, *CEO*
EMP: 10
SALES (est): 974.4K **Privately Held**
SIC: 2091 Seafood products: packaged in cans, jars, etc.

(P-2250)
SAFE CATCH INC
85 Liberty Ship Way, Sausalito
(94965-3316)
PHONE..........................415 944-4442
Bryan Boches, *CEO*
Sean Wittenberg, *President*
Kevin McCay, *COO*
Craig Cuffney, *Opers Staff*
◆ EMP: 12
SQ FT: 4,000
SALES (est): 1.1MM **Privately Held**
SIC: 2091 Tuna fish: packaged in cans, jars, etc.

(P-2251)
SANTA MONICA SEAFOOD COMPANY (PA)
18531 S Broadwick St, Rancho Dominguez
(90220-6440)
PHONE..........................310 886-7900
Toll Free:..........................888 -
Roger O'Brien, *CEO*
Michael Cigliano II, *Treasurer*
Cindy Duncan, *Vice Pres*
Richard Neligan, *Vice Pres*
Jim Sawyer, *Vice Pres*
▲ EMP: 100
SQ FT: 65,000
SALES (est): 129.2MM **Privately Held**
WEB: www.smseafood.com
SIC: 2091 Bouillon, clam: packaged in cans, jars, etc.

(P-2252)
SOUTH PACIFIC TUNA CORPORATION
501 W Broadway, San Diego (92101-3536)
PHONE..........................619 233-2060
Max Chou, *President*
Annette Schlife, *CFO*
Capt Bobby Virissimo, *Vice Pres*
Capt B Virissimo, *Vice Pres*
Robert Virissimo, *Vice Pres*
EMP: 12 EST: 2007
SALES (est): 1.4MM **Privately Held**
SIC: 2091 Tuna fish, preserved & cured

(P-2253)
TAOKAENOI USA INC
Also Called: Gim Factory
13767 Milroy Pl, Santa Fe Springs
(90670-5130)
PHONE..........................562 404-9888
Itthipat Peeradechapan, *CEO*
Grace Kim, *Manager*
EMP: 13
SQ FT: 27,000
SALES (est): 1.1MM **Privately Held**
SIC: 2091 Canned & cured fish & seafoods

(P-2254)
THAI UNION NORTH AMERICA INC (HQ)
9330 Scranton Rd Ste 500, El Segundo
(90245)
PHONE..........................424 397-8556
Thiraphong Chansiri, *CEO*
Ignatius Dharma, *Vice Pres*
Christi Reed, *Vice Pres*
◆ EMP: 12
SALES (est): 63.4MM **Privately Held**
SIC: 2091 Tuna fish: packaged in cans, jars, etc.; salmon: packaged in cans, jars, etc.

(P-2255)
YAMASA ENTERPRISES
Also Called: Yamasa Fish Cake
515 Stanford Ave, Los Angeles
(90013-2189)
PHONE..........................213 626-2211
Frank Kawana, *President*
Yuji Kawana, *Vice Pres*
Sachie Kawana, *Admin Sec*
Doug Watanabe, *Sales Mgr*
▲ EMP: 27
SQ FT: 20,000
SALES (est): 4.1MM **Privately Held**
SIC: 2091 Fish & seafood cakes: packaged in cans, jars, etc.

2092 Fish & Seafoods, Fresh & Frozen

(P-2256)
AZUMA FOODS INTL INC USA (HQ)
Also Called: Azuma Foods Internatl
20201 Mack St, Hayward (94545-1224)
PHONE..........................510 782-1112
Toshinobu Azuma, *Chairman*
Takahiro Tamura, *President*
Toshie Azuma, *CFO*
Kimiyuki Inamura, *Officer*
◆ EMP: 70
SQ FT: 70,000
SALES (est): 13.6MM **Privately Held**
WEB: www.azumafoods.com
SIC: 2092 5146 Fresh or frozen packaged fish; seafoods

(P-2257)
CALIFORNIA SHELLFISH CO INC (PA)
818 E Broadway C, San Gabriel
(91776-1902)
P.O. Box 2028, San Francisco (94126-2028)
PHONE..........................415 923-7400
Robin Yuan, *Principal*
Dave Zeller, *CFO*
EMP: 15
SQ FT: 6,000
SALES (est): 105.4MM **Privately Held**
WEB: www.dfeh.ca.gov
SIC: 2092 Fresh or frozen packaged fish

(P-2258)
DEL MAR SEAFOODS INC (PA)
331 Ford St, Watsonville (95076-4108)
PHONE..........................831 763-3000
Joe Cappuccio, *President*
Joe Roggio, *CFO*
Kevin Cappuccio, *Vice Pres*
Roseanne Cappuccio, *Vice Pres*
Randy Roberts, *Opers Staff*
◆ EMP: 200
SQ FT: 40,000
SALES (est): 38.3MM **Privately Held**
WEB: www.delmarseafoods.com
SIC: 2092 Seafoods, fresh: prepared

(P-2259)
FISH HOUSE FOODS INC
1263 Linda Vista Dr, San Marcos
(92078-3827)
PHONE..........................760 597-1270
Ron Butler, *President*
Ronald J Butler, *CEO*
Rex Butler, *Vice Pres*
Karen Butler, *Admin Sec*
EMP: 430
SQ FT: 52,000
SALES (est): 31.2MM
SALES (corp-wide): 29.5MM **Privately Held**
WEB: www.fishhousefoods.com
SIC: 2092 5149 Seafoods, fresh: prepared; groceries & related products

PA: The Fish House Vera Cruz Inc
3585 Main St Ste 212
Riverside CA 92501
760 744-8000

(P-2260)
FISHERMANS PRIDE PRCESSORS INC
Also Called: Neptune Foods
4510 S Alameda St, Vernon (90058-2011)
PHONE..........................323 232-1980
Howard Choi, *CEO*
Hector Poon, *COO*
Charlene Lau, *Technology*
Martin Tsai, *Controller*
Carmen Aguila, *Human Res Mgr*
◆ EMP: 300
SQ FT: 125,000
SALES (est): 91MM **Privately Held**
WEB: www.neptunefoods.com
SIC: 2092 Fresh or frozen packaged fish

(P-2261)
J DELUCA FISH COMPANY INC (PA)
Also Called: Nautilus Seafood
2194 Signal Pl, San Pedro (90731-7225)
PHONE..........................310 684-5180
John Deluca, *President*
◆ EMP: 40
SQ FT: 60,000
SALES (est): 11.8MM **Privately Held**
SIC: 2092 Seafoods, frozen: prepared

(P-2262)
LONG BEACH ENTERPRISE INC (PA)
Also Called: Sea One Seafood
12319 Florence Ave, Santa Fe Springs
(90670-3807)
P.O. Box 3048 (90670-0048)
PHONE..........................562 944-8945
Tai Van Tran, *President*
Thanh Thu Nguyen, *Corp Secy*
Norman N EXT, *Sales Staff*
▲ EMP: 27 EST: 1978
SQ FT: 6,000
SALES (est): 3.5MM **Privately Held**
WEB: www.seaoneseafoods.com
SIC: 2092 Seafoods, frozen: prepared

(P-2263)
LONG BEACH SEAFOODS CO
4643 Hackett Ave, Lakewood (90713-2632)
PHONE..........................562 432-7300
Tony Delucia, *President*
Star Delucia, *Vice Pres*
EMP: 38
SQ FT: 50,000
SALES (est): 5.5MM **Privately Held**
WEB: www.longbeachseafood.com
SIC: 2092 5146 Fresh or frozen packaged fish; fish & seafoods

(P-2264)
MARUHIDE MARINE PRODUCTS INC
Also Called: M M P
2145 W 17th St, Long Beach (90813-1013)
PHONE..........................562 435-6509
Hideo Kawamura, *President*
EMP: 60
SQ FT: 14,352
SALES (est): 7.3MM **Privately Held**
WEB: www.maruhide.us
SIC: 2092 Shellfish, frozen: prepared

(P-2265)
MS INTERTRADE INC (PA)
Also Called: Sonoma Foods
2221 Bluebell Dr Ste A, Santa Rosa
(95403-2545)
P.O. Box 6083 (95406-0083)
PHONE..........................707 837-8057
Matthew J Mariani, *CEO*
Scott A Gray, *President*
Charles Hansen, *Vice Pres*
EMP: 44
SQ FT: 8,000
SALES (est): 5.1MM **Privately Held**
SIC: 2092 Fresh or frozen fish or seafood chowders, soups & stews

(P-2266)
NIKKO ENTERPRISE CORPORATION
Also Called: Hanna Fuji Sushi
13168 Sandoval St, Santa Fe Springs
(90670-6600)
PHONE..........................562 941-6080
Tlang T Mawii, *CEO*
Sein Myint, *Shareholder*
Robby Sharma, *Vice Pres*
Miho Arao, *Manager*
EMP: 23 EST: 1995
SQ FT: 5,000
SALES (est): 4.4MM **Privately Held**
WEB: www.necsushi.com
SIC: 2092 Fresh or frozen fish or seafood chowders, soups & stews

(P-2267)
OCEAN DIRECT LLC (PA)
Also Called: Boardwalk Solutions
13771 Gramercy Pl, Gardena
(90249-2470)
PHONE..........................424 266-9300
Neil Kinney,
Matthew Hamel, *Info Tech Mgr*
John Bagley, *Controller*
Michael Schodorf, *Opers Staff*
▼ EMP: 47
SQ FT: 20,000
SALES (est): 13MM **Privately Held**
WEB: www.oceandirect.com
SIC: 2092 2022 2037 2033 Fresh or frozen fish or seafood chowders, soups & stews; prepared fish or other seafood cakes & sticks; natural cheese; frozen fruits & vegetables; vegetables & vegetable products in cans, jars, etc.; groceries, general line

(P-2268)
RICH PRODUCTS CORPORATION
320 O St, Fresno (93721-3086)
P.O. Box 631 (93709-0631)
PHONE..........................559 486-7380
Gary Rogers, *Finance Other*
Clay Ory, *Manager*
EMP: 152
SQ FT: 64,413
SALES (corp-wide): 3.8B **Privately Held**
WEB: www.richs.com
SIC: 2092 2045 2038 Fresh or frozen packaged fish; prepared flour mixes & doughs; frozen specialties
PA: Rich Products Corporation
1 Robert Rich Way
Buffalo NY 14213
716 878-8000

(P-2269)
SEA SNACK FOODS INC (PA)
914 E 11th St, Los Angeles (90021-2091)
P.O. Box 21467 (90021-0467)
PHONE..........................213 622-2204
Fred W Ockrim, *CEO*
Barbara Kahn, *Treasurer*
Jeffrey Kahn, *Vice Pres*
Sheri Ockrim, *Admin Sec*
◆ EMP: 50
SQ FT: 2,000
SALES (est): 9.2MM **Privately Held**
SIC: 2092 Fish, frozen: prepared

(P-2270)
SIMPLY FRESH LLC
Also Called: Rojo's
11215 Knott Ave Ste A, Cypress
(90630-5495)
PHONE..........................714 562-5000
Dale Jabour, *CEO*
Chris Boyd, *Vice Pres*
▼ EMP: 160
SQ FT: 20,000
SALES (est): 40MM
SALES (corp-wide): 103.2MM **Privately Held**
WEB: www.spcap.com
SIC: 2092 Fresh or frozen packaged fish
PA: Lakeview Farms, Llc
1600 Gressel Dr
Delphos OH 45833
419 695-9925

(P-2271)
SUN COAST CALAMARI INC
928 E 3rd St, Oxnard (93030-6119)
P.O. Box 151 (93032-0151)
PHONE........................805 385-0056
John Borman, *President*
Jeff Reichle, *Vice Pres*
Wayne Reichle, *Vice Pres*
EMP: 150
SQ FT: 15,000
SALES (est): 20.7MM **Privately Held**
SIC: 2092 Fresh or frozen packaged fish

(P-2272)
SUSAN ZADI
Also Called: Revolutionario
4220 Beverly Blvd, Los Angeles
(90004-4430)
PHONE........................424 223-3526
Susan Zadi, *Owner*
EMP: 11
SQ FT: 1,000
SALES (est): 724.5K **Privately Held**
SIC: 2092 Eating places

(P-2273)
TARDIO ENTERPRISES INC
Also Called: Newport Fish
457 S Canal St, South San Francisco
(94080-4607)
PHONE........................650 877-7200
Andrew Tardio, *President*
EMP: 25
SALES (est): 4.6MM **Privately Held**
SIC: 2092 5421 Fresh or frozen packaged fish; fish & seafood markets

2095 Coffee

(P-2274)
AMERICAS BEST BEVERAGE INC
600 50th Ave, Oakland (94601-5004)
PHONE........................800 723-8808
Hovik Azadkhanian, *CEO*
EMP: 25
SQ FT: 25,000
SALES: 10MM **Privately Held**
SIC: 2095 2086 Roasted coffee; tea, iced: packaged in cans, bottles, etc.

(P-2275)
APFFELS COFFEE INC
12115 Pacific St, Santa Fe Springs
(90670-2989)
P.O. Box 2506 (90670-0506)
PHONE........................562 309-0400
Darryl Blunk, *CEO*
Alvin Apffel, *President*
Mike Rogers, *Exec VP*
Edward Apffel, *Vice Pres*
Louie Romero, *Accountant*
◆ **EMP:** 25
SQ FT: 100,000
SALES (est): 5.4MM **Privately Held**
WEB: www.apffels.com
SIC: 2095 5149 Coffee roasting (except by wholesale grocers); coffee, ground: mixed with grain or chicory; coffee, green or roasted; tea

(P-2276)
BAY AREA COFFEE INC
4201 Industrial Way, Benicia (94510-1228)
PHONE........................707 745-1320
Thomas Waterman, *CEO*
Reed Waterman, *Plant Mgr*
David Wride, *Plant Mgr*
Michael Daugherty, *Manager*
Joseph Lin, *Accounts Mgr*
EMP: 50
SALES (est): 8.4MM **Privately Held**
SIC: 2095 Coffee roasting (except by wholesale grocers)

(P-2277)
BORESHA INTERNATIONAL INC
7041 Koll Center Pkwy # 100, Pleasanton
(94566-3192)
PHONE........................925 676-1400
Tony Drexel Smith, *President*
George Najjar, *President*
EMP: 30

SALES (est): 5.3MM **Privately Held**
SIC: 2095 Coffee extracts

(P-2278)
BRAD BARRY COMPANY LTD
Also Called: Caffe D'Vita
14020 Central Ave Ste 580, Chino
(91710-5524)
PHONE........................909 591-9493
Robert S Greene, *President*
Jerome Greener, *CFO*
Maggie Lopez, *Accountant*
April Higbee, *Opers Mgr*
Alan Dossey, *Natl Sales Mgr*
◆ **EMP:** 30
SQ FT: 39,600
SALES (est): 11.5MM **Privately Held**
WEB: www.caffedvita.com
SIC: 2095 Roasted coffee

(P-2279)
CAFE VIRTUOSO LLC
1622 National Ave, San Diego
(92113-1009)
PHONE........................619 550-1830
Laurie Britton, *CEO*
Greg Luli, *General Mgr*
Savannah Britton, *Training Spec*
EMP: 14
SQ FT: 5,500
SALES (est): 931.7K **Privately Held**
SIC: 2095 5812 Coffee roasting (except by wholesale grocers); coffee shop

(P-2280)
CAFECITO ORGANICO OC LLC
2916 Heathercliff Rd, Malibu (90265)
PHONE........................213 537-8367
Jose A Orozco, *Principal*
EMP: 14
SALES (corp-wide): 4.8MM **Privately Held**
SIC: 2095 Roasted coffee
PA: Cafecito Organico Oc, Llc
    710 N Heliotrope Dr
    Los Angeles CA 90029
    213 537-8367

(P-2281)
CAFFE CARDINALE COF ROASTING
246 The Crossroads Blvd, Carmel
(93923-8651)
P.O. Box 7222 (93921-7222)
PHONE........................831 626-2095
Gaspher Cardinale, *Partner*
Carmella Cardinale, *Partner*
Rocco Cardinale, *Partner*
EMP: 10 **EST:** 1992
SQ FT: 2,000
SALES (est): 801.3K **Privately Held**
WEB: www.carmelcoffee.com
SIC: 2095 5812 Coffee roasting (except by wholesale grocers); cafe

(P-2282)
CAFFE CLABRIA COF ROASTERS LLC
3933 30th St, San Diego (92104-3004)
PHONE........................619 683-7787
Arne Holt,
Susan Holt,
▲ **EMP:** 40 **EST:** 2000
SALES (est): 4.3MM **Privately Held**
SIC: 2095 Roasted coffee

(P-2283)
CAFFE CLASSICO FOODS INC
2500 Annalisa Dr, Concord (94520-1178)
PHONE........................925 602-5400
Tom Heffernan, *President*
▲ **EMP:** 18
SALES (est): 3MM **Privately Held**
WEB: www.caffeclassicofoods.com
SIC: 2095 Roasted coffee

(P-2284)
COFFEE GUYS INC (PA)
Also Called: Calistoga Roastery, The
975 Silverado Trl, Calistoga (94515-1128)
P.O. Box 666 (94515-0666)
PHONE........................707 942-5747
Terry Rich, *President*
Clive Richardson, *Ch of Bd*
EMP: 21
SQ FT: 1,200

SALES (est): 2.5MM **Privately Held**
WEB: www.calistogaroastery.com
SIC: 2095 5812 5149 5499 Coffee roasting (except by wholesale grocers); coffee shop; caterers; coffee, green or roasted; coffee; food, mail order

(P-2285)
COFFEE WORKS INC
3418 Folsom Blvd, Sacramento
(95816-5312)
PHONE........................916 452-1086
John Shahabian, *Owner*
Edwin Alagozian, *General Mgr*
EMP: 18
SQ FT: 4,000
SALES (est): 2.2MM **Privately Held**
WEB: www.coffeeworks.com
SIC: 2095 5499 Coffee roasting (except by wholesale grocers); coffee

(P-2286)
DAILY OFFRNGS COF ROASTERY LLC
Also Called: Roastery, The
475 W Agua Caliente Rd, Sonoma
(95476-3305)
PHONE........................805 423-7410
Kristy Kotze,
EMP: 10
SALES (est): 18.6K **Privately Held**
SIC: 2095 5812 Roasted coffee; coffee shop

(P-2287)
DAYMAR CORPORATION
Also Called: Daymar Select Fine Coffees
460 Cypress Ln Ste B, El Cajon
(92020-1647)
PHONE........................619 444-1155
Ricardo L Granados, *President*
Robert Salazar, *Shareholder*
Rogeolio Gallegos, *COO*
Enrique Lizarraga Osuna, *CFO*
Leonardo Rico, *Admin Sec*
EMP: 10
SQ FT: 6,000
SALES (est): 1.2MM **Privately Held**
WEB: www.daymar.net
SIC: 2095 5149 Roasted coffee; coffee, green or roasted

(P-2288)
F GAVINA & SONS INC
Also Called: Gavia
2700 Fruitland Ave, Vernon (90058-2893)
PHONE........................323 582-0671
Pedro Gavina, *President*
Jose Gavina, *Treasurer*
Leonor Gavi A-Valls, *Vice Pres*
Lois Colburn, *Vice Pres*
Francisco M Gavina, *Vice Pres*
▲ **EMP:** 295
SQ FT: 239,000
SALES (est): 72.6MM **Privately Held**
WEB: www.gavina.com
SIC: 2095 Coffee roasting (except by wholesale grocers)

(P-2289)
FARMER BROS CO
7855 Ostrow St Ste A, San Diego
(92111-3634)
PHONE........................858 292-7578
Albert Moya, *General Mgr*
Mark Bailey, *Branch Mgr*
EMP: 20
SQ FT: 19,036
SALES (corp-wide): 595.9MM **Publicly Held**
WEB: www.farmerbros.com
SIC: 2095 5149 Coffee roasting (except by wholesale grocers); coffee, green or roasted
PA: Farmer Bros. Co.
    1912 Farmer Brothers Dr
    Northlake TX 76262
    888 998-2468

(P-2290)
FARMER BROS CO
Also Called: Farmers Brothers Coffee
20671 Corsair Blvd, Hayward
(94545-1007)
PHONE........................510 638-1660
Dustin Clark, *Branch Mgr*

Joe Gonzales, *Sales Staff*
EMP: 17
SALES (corp-wide): 595.9MM **Publicly Held**
WEB: www.farmerbros.com
SIC: 2095 7389 5149 Coffee roasting (except by wholesale grocers); coffee service; coffee, green or roasted
PA: Farmer Bros. Co.
    1912 Farmer Brothers Dr
    Northlake TX 76262
    888 998-2468

(P-2291)
FARMER BROS CO
8802 Swigert Ct, Bakersfield (93311-9647)
PHONE........................661 663-9908
Mike Ward, *Manager*
EMP: 10
SALES (corp-wide): 595.9MM **Publicly Held**
WEB: www.farmerbros.com
SIC: 2095 5149 Coffee roasting (except by wholesale grocers); coffee, green or roasted
PA: Farmer Bros. Co.
    1912 Farmer Brothers Dr
    Northlake TX 76262
    888 998-2468

(P-2292)
FARMER BROS CO
480 Ryan Ave Ste 100, Chico
(95973-8899)
PHONE........................530 343-3165
Tom Santos, *Manager*
EMP: 10
SALES (corp-wide): 595.9MM **Publicly Held**
WEB: www.farmerbros.com
SIC: 2095 5149 Coffee roasting (except by wholesale grocers); coffee, green or roasted
PA: Farmer Bros. Co.
    1912 Farmer Brothers Dr
    Northlake TX 76262
    888 998-2468

(P-2293)
FARMER BROS CO
Also Called: Farmers Brothers Coffee
4243 Arch Rd, Stockton (95215-8325)
PHONE........................209 466-0203
Wade Selpy, *Manager*
EMP: 20
SALES (corp-wide): 595.9MM **Publicly Held**
WEB: www.farmerbros.com
SIC: 2095 7389 5149 5046 Coffee roasting (except by wholesale grocers); coffee service; coffee, green or roasted; coffee brewing equipment & supplies
PA: Farmer Bros. Co.
    1912 Farmer Brothers Dr
    Northlake TX 76262
    888 998-2468

(P-2294)
FUTURE WAVE TECHNOLOGIES INC
Also Called: Caffe Del Mar
1343 Camino Teresa, Solana Beach
(92075-1635)
PHONE........................858 481-1112
Fax: 858 794-4033
▲ **EMP:** 30
SQ FT: 20,000
SALES (est): 3.1MM **Privately Held**
WEB: www.caffedelmar.com
SIC: 2095 2086

(P-2295)
GOURMET COFFEE WAREHOUSE INC
Also Called: Groundwork Coffee Company
11275 Chandler Blvd, North Hollywood
(91601-2708)
PHONE........................818 423-2626
EMP: 55 **Privately Held**
SIC: 2095 Roasted coffee
PA: Gourmet Coffee Warehouse, Inc.
    920 N Formosa Ave
    Los Angeles CA 90046

▲ = Import ▼=Export
◆ =Import/Export

(P-2296)
GOURMET COFFEE
WAREHOUSE INC (PA)
Also Called: Groundwork Coffee Company
920 N Formosa Ave, Los Angeles
(90046-6702)
PHONE..................323 871-8930
Richard Karno, *President*
EMP: 20
SQ FT: 10,000
SALES (est): 8.9MM **Privately Held**
SIC: 2095 5149 5499 Coffee roasting (except by wholesale grocers); coffee & tea; coffee

(P-2297)
GROUNDWORK COFFEE
ROASTERS LLC
5457 Cleon Ave, North Hollywood
(91601-2834)
PHONE..................818 506-6020
Steven Levan, *Partner*
Jeffrey Chean, *Partner*
Samantha Mitchell, *Project Mgr*
Kim Schultz, *Human Resources*
Evan Dohrmann, *VP Opers*
EMP: 160
SQ FT: 4,650
SALES: 9MM **Privately Held**
SIC: 2095 5812 5149 Roasted coffee; contract food services; coffee, green or roasted

(P-2298)
HERITAGE MISSIONAL
COMMUNITY
Also Called: Heritage Roasting Company
4302 Shasta Dam Blvd, Shasta Lake
(96019-9420)
PHONE..................530 605-1990
Stuart Sutherland, *Director*
EMP: 10
SALES (est): 192.5K **Privately Held**
SIC: 2095 5812 5499 Roasted coffee; coffee shop; coffee

(P-2299)
HOT CAN INC
10620 Treena St Ste 230, San Diego
(92131-1140)
PHONE..................707 601-6013
James Scudder, *President*
▲ EMP: 50
SQ FT: 1,160
SALES: 2MM **Privately Held**
WEB: www.hot-can.com
SIC: 2095 Coffee roasting (except by wholesale grocers)

(P-2300)
INTERCONTINENTAL COF TRDG
LLC
Also Called: Intercontinental Coffee Trdg
110 W A St Ste 110 # 110, San Diego
(92101-3702)
PHONE..................619 338-8335
Lisa Colon, *CEO*
▲ EMP: 11
SQ FT: 3,800
SALES (est): 14.7MM **Privately Held**
SIC: 2095 Roasted coffee

(P-2301)
JEREMIAHS PICK COFFEE
COMPANY
1495 Evans Ave, San Francisco
(94124-1706)
PHONE..................415 206-9900
Jeremiah Pick, *President*
Mike Ahmadi, *Shareholder*
Krislyn Asagra, *Webmaster*
Ronnie Crabtree, *Human Res Mgr*
▲ EMP: 19
SQ FT: 11,000
SALES (est): 3.4MM **Privately Held**
WEB: www.jeremiahspick.com
SIC: 2095 5149 Coffee roasting (except by wholesale grocers); coffee, green or roasted

(P-2302)
KAV AMERICA AG INC
422 Commercial Rd, San Bernardino
(92408-3706)
PHONE..................855 528-8721
Tak Lam, *CEO*
▲ EMP: 28
SALES (est): 4.8MM **Privately Held**
SIC: 2095 Coffee extracts

(P-2303)
KEYSTONE COFFEE COMPANY
2230 Will Wool Dr Ste 100, San Jose
(95112-2605)
PHONE..................408 998-2221
Tim Wright, *President*
Marlena Wright, *Corp Secy*
EMP: 17
SQ FT: 22,000
SALES (est): 1.8MM **Privately Held**
WEB: www.keystonecoffee.com
SIC: 2095 Coffee roasting (except by wholesale grocers)

(P-2304)
KLATCH COFFEE INC (PA)
Also Called: Coffee Klatch
8767 Onyx Ave, Rancho Cucamonga
(91730-4533)
PHONE..................909 981-4031
Mike Perry, *CEO*
Heather Perry, *Vice Pres*
Cindy Perry, *Admin Sec*
Helene Ingstrom, *Business Mgr*
EMP: 21
SQ FT: 2,400
SALES: 3.5MM **Privately Held**
SIC: 2095 Roasted coffee

(P-2305)
NAPA VALLEY COFFEE
ROASTING CO (PA)
948 Main St, NAPA (94559-3045)
PHONE..................707 224-2233
Denise Fox, *President*
Leon Sange, *Corp Secy*
EMP: 11
SALES (est): 1.7MM **Privately Held**
WEB: www.napavalleycoffeeroasting.com
SIC: 2095 5499 Coffee roasting (except by wholesale grocers); coffee

(P-2306)
NUZEE INC
2865 Scott St Ste 107, Vista (92081-8555)
PHONE..................760 295-2408
Masa Higashida, *Ch of Bd*
Travis Gorney, *President*
Shanoop Kothari, *CFO*
EMP: 23
SALES: 1.3MM **Privately Held**
SIC: 2095 5499 Roasted coffee; coffee extracts; instant coffee; coffee

(P-2307)
PEERLESS COFFEE COMPANY
INC
Also Called: Peerles Coffee and Tea
260 Oak St, Oakland (94607-4512)
PHONE..................510 763-1763
George J Vukasin Jr, *CEO*
Mike Pine, *CFO*
Kristina V Brouhard, *Exec VP*
John Ziglar, *Vice Pres*
Aaron Markel, *Purch Mgr*
EMP: 85
SQ FT: 65,000
SALES (est): 17.6MM **Privately Held**
WEB: www.peerlesscoffee.com
SIC: 2095 5149 Coffee roasting (except by wholesale grocers); tea; spices & seasonings

(P-2308)
PEETS COFFEE & TEA LLC (HQ)
1400 Park Ave, Emeryville (94608-3520)
PHONE..................510 594-2100
David Burwick, *CEO*
Paul Clayton, *President*
Shawn Conway, *Vice Pres*
▲ EMP: 277 EST: 1971
SQ FT: 60,000

SALES (est): 1.5B
SALES (corp-wide): 2.4B **Privately Held**
SIC: 2095 5149 Roasted coffee; coffee, green or roasted
PA: Krispy Kreme Holdco, Inc.
1701 Penn Ave Nw Ste 801
Washington DC 20006
202 602-1301

(P-2309)
SANTA BARBARA COFFEE LLC
Also Called: Red Star Coffee
6489 Calle Real Ste G, Goleta
(93117-1538)
PHONE..................805 683-2555
Daniel M Randall, *Mng Member*
Werner Diaz,
Kevin C Donnelly,
EMP: 15
SQ FT: 1,645
SALES (est): 2.6MM **Privately Held**
SIC: 2095 5499 Coffee roasting (except by wholesale grocers); coffee

(P-2310)
SANTA CRUZ COFFEE
ROASTING CO
Also Called: Aptos Coffee Roasting Co
19 Rancho Del Mar Ste A, Aptos
(95003-3988)
P.O. Box 2427, Watsonville (95077-2427)
PHONE..................831 685-0100
Roxanna Medeiros, *Manager*
EMP: 20
SALES (corp-wide): 1.5MM **Privately Held**
SIC: 2095 Roasted coffee
PA: Santa Cruz Coffee Roasting Co, The
1330 Pacific Ave
Santa Cruz CA 95060
831 459-0100

(P-2311)
TAYLOR MAID FARMS LLC
6790 Mckinley Ave, Sebastopol
(95472-3496)
PHONE..................707 824-9110
Christ Martin,
Michael Presley,
EMP: 30 EST: 2000
SALES: 3.5MM **Privately Held**
SIC: 2095 Roasted coffee

(P-2312)
TULLYS COFFEE CO INC (HQ)
2455 Fillmore St, San Francisco
(94115-1814)
PHONE..................415 929-8808
Tom O' Keefe, *President*
Steve Griffin, *CFO*
James Kingsbury, *Manager*
EMP: 25
SQ FT: 8,000
SALES (est): 8.1MM **Privately Held**
SIC: 2095 5149 5499 5812 Coffee, ground: mixed with grain or chicory; coffee, green or roasted; coffee; coffee shop

(P-2313)
TULLYS COFFEE CO INC
1509 Sloat Blvd, San Francisco
(94132-1222)
PHONE..................415 213-8791
Jen Wong, *Manager*
EMP: 10 **Privately Held**
SIC: 2095 5499 Coffee roasting (except by wholesale grocers); coffee
HQ: Tully's Coffee Co Inc
2455 Fillmore St
San Francisco CA 94115
415 929-8808

2096 Potato Chips & Similar Prdts

(P-2314)
4505 MEATS INC
548 Market St, San Francisco
(94104-5401)
PHONE..................415 255-3094
Ryan Farr, *CEO*
EMP: 20
SALES: 394K **Privately Held**
SIC: 2096 Pork rinds

(P-2315)
ACAPULCO MEXICAN DELI INC
929 S Kern Ave, Los Angeles (90022-3013)
PHONE..................323 266-0267
Rubin Ibarra, *President*
Saul Casillas, *Vice Pres*
Acapulco Enrique, *Manager*
EMP: 34
SALES (est): 2.3MM **Privately Held**
SIC: 2096 2032 Tortilla chips; Mexican foods: packaged in cans, jars, etc.

(P-2316)
ALIVE & RADIANT FOODS INC
2921 Adeline St, Emeryville (94608-4422)
PHONE..................510 238-0128
Nicholas Taylor Kelley, *President*
Nicholas Kelley, *CEO*
▲ EMP: 25
SALES (est): 5.9MM **Privately Held**
SIC: 2096 Potato chips & similar snacks

(P-2317)
ANITAS MEXICAN FOODS CORP
(PA)
3454 N Mike Daley Dr, San Bernardino
(92407-1890)
PHONE..................909 884-8706
Ricardo Alvarez, *President*
Ricardo Robles, *COO*
Rene Robles, *COO*
Jacqueline Robles, *Admin Sec*
Paul Omness, *Finance*
▲ EMP: 126 EST: 1936
SQ FT: 330,000
SALES: 50MM **Privately Held**
SIC: 2096 Potato chips & similar snacks

(P-2318)
BOT N BOT INC
13005 Los Nietos Rd, Santa Fe Springs
(90670-3013)
PHONE..................562 906-4873
Francis E Llado, *President*
Carmencita J Llado, *Med Doctor*
EMP: 10
SQ FT: 6,353
SALES (est): 1.1MM **Privately Held**
SIC: 2096 Pork rinds

(P-2319)
CALIFORNIA NUGGETS INC
23073 S Frederick Rd, Ripon (95366-9616)
PHONE..................209 599-7131
Steve Gikas, *CEO*
Richard Piercefield, *CFO*
Barbara Bain, *Corp Secy*
Lori Gikas, *Vice Pres*
Chris Ben Groningen, *Controller*
◆ EMP: 40
SQ FT: 50,000
SALES (est): 6.7MM **Privately Held**
WEB: www.californianuggets.com
SIC: 2096 2068 Potato chips & similar snacks; nuts: dried, dehydrated, salted or roasted

(P-2320)
CORAZONAS FOODS INC
3780 Kilroy Airport Way # 430, Long Beach
(90806-2457)
PHONE..................800 388-8998
Ramona Cappello, *CEO*
Robert Crumby, *CFO*
▲ EMP: 11
SALES (est): 1.9MM **Privately Held**
WEB: www.corazonas.com
SIC: 2096 Tortilla chips

(P-2321)
EVANS FOOD WEST INC (PA)
1920 S Augusta Ave, Ontario (91761-5701)
PHONE..................909 947-3001
Alan F Sussna, *President*
EMP: 10
SALES (est): 1.5MM **Privately Held**
SIC: 2096 Potato chips & similar snacks

(P-2322)
FANTE INC (PA)
Also Called: Casa Sanchez Foods
2898 W Winton Ave, Hayward
(94545-1122)
P.O. Box 12582, San Francisco (94112-0582)
PHONE.................................650 697-7525
Robert C Sanchez, *President*
Robert Sanchez, *President*
Linda Renteria, *Manager*
▲ **EMP:** 30
SALES (est): 16.1MM **Privately Held**
WEB: www.fante.com
SIC: 2096 2099 Tortilla chips; dips, except
cheese & sour cream based

(P-2323)
FRITO-LAY NORTH AMERICA INC
9535 Archibald Ave, Rancho Cucamonga
(91730-5737)
PHONE.................................909 941-6214
Brian Birrell, *Manager*
Bob Biacsi, *Manager*
EMP: 500
SALES (corp-wide): 64.6B **Publicly Held**
WEB: www.fritolay.com
SIC: 2096 Potato chips & similar snacks
HQ: Frito-Lay North America, Inc.
7701 Legacy Dr
Plano TX 75024

(P-2324)
FRITO-LAY NORTH AMERICA INC
16701 Trojan Way, La Mirada
(90638-5906)
PHONE.................................714 562-7260
Jino Lerena, *Principal*
Barbara Sierra, *Manager*
EMP: 164
SALES (corp-wide): 64.6B **Publicly Held**
SIC: 2096 Potato chips & similar snacks
HQ: Frito-Lay North America, Inc.
7701 Legacy Dr
Plano TX 75024

(P-2325)
FRITO-LAY NORTH AMERICA INC
1190 Spreckels Rd, Manteca (95336-8962)
PHONE.................................209 824-3700
Keith Prather, *Manager*
EMP: 20
SALES (corp-wide): 64.6B **Publicly Held**
WEB: www.fritolay.com
SIC: 2096 5145 Potato chips & similar
snacks; confectionery
HQ: Frito-Lay North America, Inc.
7701 Legacy Dr
Plano TX 75024

(P-2326)
FRITO-LAY NORTH AMERICA INC
5045 Forni Dr, Concord (94520-1224)
PHONE.................................925 689-4260
Andy Glavich, *Manager*
EMP: 50
SQ FT: 10,792
SALES (corp-wide): 64.6B **Publicly Held**
WEB: www.fritolay.com
SIC: 2096 Potato chips & similar snacks
HQ: Frito-Lay North America, Inc.
7701 Legacy Dr
Plano TX 75024

(P-2327)
FRITO-LAY NORTH AMERICA INC
4535 Dupont Ct, Ventura (93003-7735)
PHONE.................................805 658-1668
Terri Livingston, *Manager*
EMP: 45
SALES (corp-wide): 64.6B **Publicly Held**
WEB: www.fritolay.com
SIC: 2096 Corn chips & other corn-based
snacks

HQ: Frito-Lay North America, Inc.
7701 Legacy Dr
Plano TX 75024

(P-2328)
FRITO-LAY NORTH AMERICA INC
4953 Paramount Dr, San Diego
(92123-1446)
PHONE.................................858 576-3300
Pete Rojas, *Manager*
EMP: 12
SQ FT: 75,896
SALES (corp-wide): 64.6B **Publicly Held**
WEB: www.fritolay.com
SIC: 2096 Potato chips & similar snacks
HQ: Frito-Lay North America, Inc.
7701 Legacy Dr
Plano TX 75024

(P-2329)
FRITO-LAY NORTH AMERICA INC
635 W Valley Blvd, Bloomington
(92316-2200)
PHONE.................................909 877-0902
Fred Schmidt, *Branch Mgr*
EMP: 100
SQ FT: 18,220
SALES (corp-wide): 64.6B **Publicly Held**
WEB: www.fritolay.com
SIC: 2096 5145 5149 4226 Potato chips
& similar snacks; confectionery; groceries
& related products; special warehousing
& storage
HQ: Frito-Lay North America, Inc.
7701 Legacy Dr
Plano TX 75024

(P-2330)
FRITO-LAY NORTH AMERICA INC
600 Garner Rd, Modesto (95357-0514)
PHONE.................................209 544-5400
Bob Schreck, *Manager*
Lee Hughes, *Manager*
EMP: 450
SALES (corp-wide): 64.6B **Publicly Held**
WEB: www.fritolay.com
SIC: 2096 2099 Potato chips & similar
snacks; food preparations
HQ: Frito-Lay North America, Inc.
7701 Legacy Dr
Plano TX 75024

(P-2331)
FRITO-LAY NORTH AMERICA INC
28801 Highway 58, Bakersfield
(93314-9000)
PHONE.................................661 328-6000
Jerry Matthews, *Manager*
Chris Casten, *Human Res Mgr*
Saul Esqueda, *Sales Staff*
EMP: 800
SALES (corp-wide): 64.6B **Publicly Held**
WEB: www.fritolay.com
SIC: 2096 2099 Potato chips & similar
snacks; food preparations
HQ: Frito-Lay North America, Inc.
7701 Legacy Dr
Plano TX 75024

(P-2332)
GRUMA CORPORATION
Also Called: Mission Foods Dc60
12316 World Trade Dr # 104, San Diego
(92128-3795)
PHONE.................................858 673-5780
Armando Romero, *Manager*
EMP: 10 **Privately Held**
WEB: www.missionfoods.com
SIC: 2096 Tortilla chips
HQ: Gruma Corporation
5601 Executive Dr Ste 800
Irving TX 75038
972 232-5000

(P-2333)
GRUMA CORPORATION
Also Called: Mission Foods
2849 E Edgar Ave, Fresno (93706-5454)
PHONE.................................559 498-7820
Kathy Trout, *Plant Mgr*
EMP: 99 **Privately Held**
WEB: www.missionfoods.com
SIC: 2096 Tortilla chips
HQ: Gruma Corporation
5601 Executive Dr Ste 800
Irving TX 75038
972 232-5000

(P-2334)
GRUMA CORPORATION
Also Called: Mission Foods
11559 Jersey Blvd Ste A, Rancho Cuca-
monga (91730-4924)
PHONE.................................909 980-3566
Victor Cervantes, *Manager*
EMP: 206 **Privately Held**
WEB: www.missionfoods.com
SIC: 2096 Tortilla chips
HQ: Gruma Corporation
5601 Executive Dr Ste 800
Irving TX 75038
972 232-5000

(P-2335)
KING HENRYS INC
29124 Hancock Pkwy 1, Valencia
(91355-1066)
PHONE.................................661 295-5566
Trina Davidian, *CEO*
◆ **EMP:** 45
SQ FT: 44,000
SALES: 19MM **Privately Held**
WEB: www.kinghenrys.com
SIC: 2096 2064 Cheese curls & puffs;
breakfast bars

(P-2336)
LAURA SCUDDERS COMPANY LLC
1537 E Mcfadden Ave Ste B, Santa Ana
(92705-4317)
PHONE.................................714 444-3700
Micheal Gallegos, *Mng Member*
▼ **EMP:** 25
SALES (est): 3.7MM **Privately Held**
SIC: 2096 Potato chips & similar snacks

(P-2337)
LOOKOUT ENTERPRISES INC
Also Called: Alto Rey
11468 Dona Teresa Dr, North Hollywood
(91604-4271)
PHONE.................................323 969-0178
David Ufberg, *President*
Kelly Hurley, *Vice Pres*
EMP: 15
SALES (est): 1.7MM **Privately Held**
WEB: www.altorey.com
SIC: 2096 Potato chips & similar snacks

(P-2338)
MARQUEZ MARQUEZ INC
Also Called: Marquez & Marquez Food PR
11821 Industrial Ave, South Gate
(90280-7914)
PHONE.................................562 408-0960
Elias Marquez, *President*
Adriana Marquez, *VP Sales*
EMP: 29
SALES (est): 5.6MM **Privately Held**
SIC: 2096 2041 Corn chips & other corn-
based snacks; flour

(P-2339)
POPSALOT LLC
Also Called: Popsalot Gourmet Popcorn
7723 Somerset Blvd, Paramount
(90723-4104)
P.O. Box 7040, Beverly Hills (90212-7040)
PHONE.................................213 761-0156
Victoria Ho, *Principal*
▼ **EMP:** 20
SQ FT: 8,400
SALES (est): 1.5MM **Privately Held**
SIC: 2096 Popcorn, already popped (ex-
cept candy covered)

(P-2340)
PURE NATURE FOODS LLC
700 Santa Anita Dr, Woodland
(95776-6102)
P.O. Box 2387 (95776-2387)
PHONE.................................530 723-5269
Miguel Reyna, *President*
Shan Staka, *CFO*
Matt Brabazon, *Vice Pres*
EMP: 25
SQ FT: 60,000
SALES (est): 1MM **Privately Held**
SIC: 2096 Rice chips

(P-2341)
RODRIGUEZ ISMAEL
Also Called: Lompoc Tortilla Shop
138 N D St, Lompoc (93436-6912)
PHONE.................................805 736-7362
Ismael Rodriguez, *Owner*
Juanita Rodriguez, *Co-Owner*
EMP: 10
SALES: 629K **Privately Held**
SIC: 2096 Tortilla chips

(P-2342)
RUDOLPH FOODS COMPANY INC
920 W Fourth St, Beaumont (92223-2675)
PHONE.................................909 388-2202
Fransico Quirarte, *Manager*
Greg Stanton, *Vice Pres*
EMP: 75
SALES (corp-wide): 138.3MM **Privately
Held**
SIC: 2096 Pork rinds
PA: Rudolph Foods Company, Inc.
6575 Bellefontaine Rd
Lima OH 45804
909 383-7463

(P-2343)
RUHE CORPORATION (PA)
901 S Leslie St, La Habra (90631-6841)
PHONE.................................714 777-8321
Thomas A Ruhe, *President*
Connie Ruhe, *Treasurer*
Scott Ruhe, *Vice Pres*
EMP: 173
SALES (est): 16.8MM **Privately Held**
SIC: 2096 Tortilla chips

(P-2344)
SENOR SNACKS INC
Also Called: Senor Snacks Holdings
2325 Raymer Ave, Fullerton (92833-2514)
PHONE.................................714 739-1073
EMP: 15
SQ FT: 16,264
SALES (est): 2.4MM **Privately Held**
WEB: www.senorsnacks.com
SIC: 2096

(P-2345)
SNACK IT FORWARD LLC
Also Called: World Peas Brand
6080 Center Dr Ste 600, Los Angeles
(90045-1540)
PHONE.................................310 242-5517
Nick Desai, *CEO*
Jason Webb, *Vice Pres*
EMP: 23
SQ FT: 500
SALES (est): 5.2MM **Privately Held**
SIC: 2096 Cheese curls & puffs

(P-2346)
TACO WORKS INC
3424 Sacramento Dr, San Luis Obispo
(93401-7128)
PHONE.................................805 541-1556
Roy D Bayly, *President*
Theresa Bayly, *Admin Sec*
EMP: 20
SQ FT: 9,900
SALES (est): 3.6MM **Privately Held**
SIC: 2096 5145 Tortilla chips; snack foods

(P-2347)
TACUPETO CHIPS & SALSA INC
1330 Distribution Way A, Vista
(92081-8837)
PHONE.................................760 597-9400
Gilberto Pablo Fajardo, *President*
Gilberto Ramon Fajardo, *Vice Pres*

EMP: 18
SALES (est): 25K **Privately Held**
SIC: 2096 Corn chips & other corn-based snacks

(P-2348)
WARNOCK FOOD PRODUCTS INC
20237 Masa St, Madera (93638-9457)
PHONE..................559 661-4845
Donald Warnock, *Principal*
Cathryn Warnock, *Admin Sec*
Maegan Nazaroff, *Controller*
Gary Long, *Plant Mgr*
Kristi Massetti, *Mktg Dir*
▲ EMP: 98
SQ FT: 25,000
SALES (est): 35.9MM **Privately Held**
WEB: www.warnockfoods.com
SIC: 2096 2099 2033 Tortilla chips; food preparations; canned fruits & specialties

---

2097 Ice

(P-2349)
ARCTIC GLACIER CALIFORNIA INC
Also Called: Jack Frost Ice Service
1440 Coldwell Ave, Modesto (95350-5704)
PHONE..................209 524-3128
Stephen Ward, *Regional Mgr*
EMP: 85
SALES: 950K **Privately Held**
SIC: 2097 Manufactured ice

(P-2350)
ARCTIC GLACIER USA INC
17011 Central Ave, Carson (90746-1303)
PHONE..................310 638-0321
Sharon Cooper, *Manager*
EMP: 200
SALES (corp-wide): 159.7MM **Privately Held**
SIC: 2097 Manufactured ice
HQ: Arctic Glacier U.S.A., Inc.
1654 Marthaler Ln
Saint Paul MN 55118
204 784-5873

(P-2351)
CHINO ICE SERVICE LLC
3640 Francis Ave, Chino (91710-1512)
PHONE..................909 628-2105
Gerald Ades,
EMP: 27
SQ FT: 6,000
SALES (est): 3.2MM **Privately Held**
WEB: www.chinoice.com
SIC: 2097 Block ice

(P-2352)
COACHELLE VALLEY ICE CO
83796 Date Ave, Indio (92201-4738)
P.O. Box 1256 (92202-1256)
PHONE..................760 347-3529
Hugh Mason, *President*
EMP: 20
SQ FT: 22,000
SALES (est): 1.8MM **Privately Held**
SIC: 2097 Manufactured ice

(P-2353)
CV ICE COMPANY INC
83796 Date Ave, Indio (92201-4738)
P.O. Box 1256 (92202-1256)
PHONE..................760 347-3529
Kevin Mason, *President*
EMP: 29
SALES (est): 3.5MM **Privately Held**
SIC: 2097 Manufactured ice

(P-2354)
FRESH INNOVATIONS LLC
Also Called: Terminal Freezers
908 E 3rd St, Oxnard (93030-6119)
P.O. Box 472 (93032-0472)
PHONE..................805 483-2265
John Brashear, *Manager*
EMP: 45
SALES (corp-wide): 10.1MM **Privately Held**
WEB: www.terminalfreezers.com
SIC: 2097 4222 Manufactured ice; refrigerated warehousing & storage

PA: Fresh Innovations, Llc
1135 Mountain View Ave
Oxnard CA 93030
805 201-2331

(P-2355)
GLACIER VALLEY ICE COMPANY LP (PA)
Also Called: Glacier Ice Company
8580 Laguna Station Rd, Elk Grove (95758-9550)
PHONE..................916 394-2939
Sarah Demartini, *Principal*
Angela Aistrup, *Systems Mgr*
Karen Anderson, *Human Resources*
Bob Sikes, *Sales Executive*
EMP: 40
SQ FT: 72,000
SALES (est): 3.8MM **Privately Held**
SIC: 2097 5199 Manufactured ice; ice, manufactured or natural

(P-2356)
GROWERS ICE CO
1124 Abbott St, Salinas (93901-4502)
P.O. Box 298 (93902-0298)
PHONE..................831 424-5781
Susan Merrill, *Ch of Bd*
Kathy Bullene, *Human Res Dir*
Scott Jackson, *Plant Mgr*
EMP: 36
SQ FT: 200,000
SALES (est): 12MM **Privately Held**
WEB: www.growersice.com
SIC: 2097 4222 7623 6512 Manufactured ice; warehousing, cold storage or refrigerated; ice making machinery repair service; commercial & industrial building operation

(P-2357)
ICE MAN INC
8710 Park St, Bellflower (90706-5527)
PHONE..................562 633-4423
Jim Mueller, *President*
Jeff Hendershot, *Corp Secy*
Diane Mueller, *Vice Pres*
EMP: 15
SQ FT: 5,000
SALES (est): 2.3MM **Privately Held**
WEB: www.iceman.com
SIC: 2097 Block ice; ice cubes

(P-2358)
KAR ICE SERVICE INC (PA)
2521 Solar Way, Barstow (92311-3616)
P.O. Box 1197 (92312-1197)
PHONE..................760 256-2648
Tom Lewis, *President*
Micheal Lewis, *CFO*
Carol Lewis, *Corp Secy*
EMP: 18
SQ FT: 14,400
SALES (est): 1.2MM **Privately Held**
WEB: www.karice.com
SIC: 2097 Ice cubes

(P-2359)
PARTY TIME ICE INC
983 N Pacific Ave, San Pedro (90731-1633)
PHONE..................310 833-0187
Ambrose Marchant III, *Ch of Bd*
Marea Marchant, *CFO*
Douglas N Marchant,
EMP: 15
SQ FT: 5,000
SALES (est): 2.3MM **Privately Held**
WEB: www.partytimeice.com
SIC: 2097 Manufactured ice

(P-2360)
PELTON-SHEPHERD INDUSTRIES INC (PA)
812 W Luce St Ste B, Stockton (95203-4937)
P.O. Box 30218 (95213-0218)
PHONE..................209 460-0893
Alicia M Shepherd, *President*
▲ EMP: 35 EST: 1950
SQ FT: 30,000
SALES (est): 14.4MM **Privately Held**
WEB: www.peltonshepherd.com
SIC: 2097 Manufactured ice

(P-2361)
R&JS BUSINESS GROUP INC
Also Called: Carving Ice
900 S Placentia Ave Ste B, Placentia (92870-8002)
PHONE..................714 224-1455
Roland Hernandez, *CEO*
David Sosnowski, *President*
Janice Hernandez, *CFO*
EMP: 17
SQ FT: 12,000
SALES: 1.2MM **Privately Held**
SIC: 2097 Manufactured ice

(P-2362)
REDDY ICE CORPORATION
462 N 8th St, Brawley (92227-1605)
PHONE..................760 344-0535
Robert Whitted, *CEO*
EMP: 22
SALES (corp-wide): 1.6B **Privately Held**
SIC: 2097 Manufactured ice
HQ: Reddy Ice Corporation
5720 Lyndon B Johnson Fwy # 200
Dallas TX 75240
214 526-6740

(P-2363)
SOUTHERN CALIFORNIA ICE CO
Also Called: Arrowhead Ice
22921 Lockness Ave, Torrance (90501-5118)
PHONE..................310 325-1040
Sharon Corbin, *President*
EMP: 13 EST: 1935
SQ FT: 11,000
SALES (est): 2.7MM **Privately Held**
WEB: www.sccu.edu
SIC: 2097 Ice cubes

(P-2364)
UNION ICE COMPANY
2970 E 50th St, Vernon (90058-2920)
PHONE..................323 277-1000
Richard L Burke, *Principal*
EMP: 14
SALES (est): 1.2MM **Privately Held**
SIC: 2097 Manufactured ice

(P-2365)
UNITED STATES COLD STORAGE INC
Also Called: U S Cold Storage
4701 Stine Rd, Bakersfield (93313-2342)
PHONE..................661 834-2371
Bob West, *Sales/Mktg Mgr*
EMP: 21
SALES (corp-wide): 13.5B **Privately Held**
WEB: www.uscold.com
SIC: 2097 Manufactured ice
HQ: United States Cold Storage, Inc.
2 Aquarium Dr Ste 400
Camden NJ 08103
856 354-8181

(P-2366)
YALDO ENTERPRISES INC
Also Called: Perkins Market
24680 Viejas Grade Rd B, Descanso (91916-9815)
P.O. Box 262 (91916-0262)
PHONE..................619 445-2578
Steve Yaldo, *President*
Sean Yaldo, *Vice Pres*
EMP: 12
SQ FT: 4,000
SALES (est): 1.4MM **Privately Held**
SIC: 2097 5199 Manufactured ice; ice, manufactured or natural

---

2098 Macaroni, Spaghetti & Noodles

(P-2367)
C NC NOODLE CO
1787 Sabre St, Hayward (94545-1015)
PHONE..................510 732-1318
Betty Lim, *Principal*
▲ EMP: 12
SALES (est): 1.6MM **Privately Held**
SIC: 2098 Noodles (e.g. egg, plain & water), dry

(P-2368)
FLORENCE MACARONI COMPANY
1312 W 2nd St, San Pedro (90732-3210)
PHONE..................310 548-5942
Beatrice Esposito, *President*
Pat Peterson, *Treasurer*
Joseph Esposito, *Vice Pres*
EMP: 13
SQ FT: 8,000
SALES (est): 885.5K **Privately Held**
SIC: 2098 Macaroni products (e.g. alphabets, rings & shells), dry; spaghetti, dry

(P-2369)
FUNGS VILLAGE INC
5339 E Washington Blvd, Commerce (90040-2111)
PHONE..................323 881-1600
Albert Lee, *President*
▲ EMP: 20
SQ FT: 18,000
SALES (est): 3MM **Privately Held**
SIC: 2098 Noodles (e.g. egg, plain & water), dry

(P-2370)
HERSHEY COMPANY
2704 S Maple Ave, Fresno (93725-2109)
P.O. Box 12146 (93776-2146)
PHONE..................559 485-8110
Thomas Martens, *Branch Mgr*
EMP: 125
SQ FT: 135,000
SALES (corp-wide): 7.7B **Publicly Held**
WEB: www.hersheys.com
SIC: 2098 Macaroni products (e.g. alphabets, rings & shells), dry
PA: Hershey Company
19 E Chocolate Ave
Hershey PA 17033
717 534-4200

(P-2371)
MARUCHAN INC
1902 Deere Ave, Irvine (92606-4819)
PHONE..................949 789-2300
Shino Saki, *Manager*
Jo Kaneko, *Accounting Mgr*
EMP: 250 **Privately Held**
WEB: www.maruchaninc.com
SIC: 2098 5146 Noodles (e.g. egg, plain & water), dry; fish, cured; fish, fresh; fish, frozen, unpackaged
HQ: Maruchan, Inc.
15800 Laguna Canyon Rd
Irvine CA 92618
949 789-2300

(P-2372)
MYOJO USA INC
6220 Prescott Ct, Chino (91710-7111)
PHONE..................909 464-1411
Yoshie Nakamura, *President*
Takuro Okada, *CFO*
▲ EMP: 16
SQ FT: 20,759
SALES (est): 3.6MM **Privately Held**
SIC: 2098 Noodles (e.g. egg, plain & water), dry
PA: Nissin Foods Holdings Co.,Ltd.
6-28-1, Shinjuku
Shinjuku-Ku TKY 160-0

(P-2373)
NANKA SEIMEN CO
3030 Leonis Blvd, Vernon (90058-2914)
PHONE..................323 585-9967
Shoichi Sayano, *President*
Kanji Sayano, *Shareholder*
Reigo Sayano, *Shareholder*
Fusako Yoshida, *Treasurer*
Toshiaki Yoshida, *Vice Pres*
▲ EMP: 18 EST: 1905
SQ FT: 20,000
SALES (est): 3.8MM **Privately Held**
SIC: 2098 Noodles (e.g. egg, plain & water), dry

(P-2374)
NESTLE REFRIGERATED FOOD CO
800 N Brand Blvd Fl 5, Glendale (91203-4281)
PHONE..................................818 549-6000
Fax: 818 549-6399
EMP: 500
SALES (est): 63.7MM
SALES (corp-wide): 94.6B Privately Held
SIC: 2098 2033
HQ: Nestle Usa, Inc.
800 N Brand Blvd
Glendale CA 22209
818 549-6000

(P-2375)
NEW HONG KONG NOODLE CO INC
360 Swift Ave Ste 22, South San Francisco (94080-6220)
PHONE..................................650 588-6425
Steven Lum, President
Wai-Kui England Lum, Treasurer
Richard Lum, Vice Pres
Lam Wai Lum, Admin Sec
◆ EMP: 40
SQ FT: 26,000
SALES (est): 8MM Privately Held
WEB: www.nhknoodle.com
SIC: 2098 Noodles (e.g. egg, plain & water), dry

(P-2376)
NISSIN FOODS USA COMPANY INC (HQ)
2001 W Rosecrans Ave, Gardena (90249-2994)
PHONE..................................310 327-8478
Hiroyuki Yoshida, CEO
Evelyn Jareno, President
Takahiro Enomoto, Vice Pres
Khin Leong, Vice Pres
Fumiko Carney, Admin Asst
◆ EMP: 200
SQ FT: 200,000
SALES (est): 120.1MM Privately Held
WEB: www.nissinfoods.com
SIC: 2098 2038 Noodles (e.g. egg, plain & water), dry; ethnic foods, frozen

(P-2377)
NOODLE THEORY
6099 Claremont Ave, Oakland (94618-1222)
PHONE..................................510 595-6988
Louis KAO, President
EMP: 12
SALES (est): 1.3MM Privately Held
SIC: 2098 Noodles (e.g. egg, plain & water), dry

(P-2378)
PASTA SONOMA LLC
640 Martin Ave Ste 1, Rohnert Park (94928-7994)
PHONE..................................707 584-0800
Don Luber,
▲ EMP: 17
SQ FT: 6,500
SALES: 2MM Privately Held
WEB: www.pastasonoma.com
SIC: 2098 5812 Macaroni & spaghetti; eating places

(P-2379)
PEKING NOODLE CO INC
1514 N San Fernando Rd, Los Angeles (90065-1282)
PHONE..................................323 223-0897
Frank Tong, President
Stephen Tong, President
Donna Tong, Corp Secy
Derek Tat, General Mgr
▲ EMP: 40 EST: 1928
SQ FT: 40,000
SALES (est): 9.1MM Privately Held
SIC: 2098 2052 Noodles (e.g. egg, plain & water), dry; cookies & crackers

(P-2380)
SAKURA NOODLE INC
620 E 7th St, Los Angeles (90021-1461)
PHONE..................................213 623-2396
Shohachi Suzuki, President

Taketoshi Inagaki, Admin Sec
▲ EMP: 14 EST: 1978
SQ FT: 9,000
SALES (est): 2.1MM Privately Held
SIC: 2098 2099 Noodles (e.g. egg, plain & water), dry; food preparations

(P-2381)
SAMYANG USA INC
3810 Wilshire Blvd # 1212, Los Angeles (90010-3204)
PHONE..................................562 946-9977
Mun K Chun, President
John Ha, Admin Sec
◆ EMP: 10
SQ FT: 195,580
SALES: 12MM Privately Held
WEB: www.samyang.com
SIC: 2098 Noodles (e.g. egg, plain & water), dry

(P-2382)
SANYO FOODS CORP AMERICA (HQ)
Also Called: Yorba Linda Country Club
11955 Monarch St, Garden Grove (92841-2194)
PHONE..................................714 891-3671
Junichiro Ida, CEO
Hiroaki Obuchi, Admin Sec
▲ EMP: 30 EST: 1978
SQ FT: 130,000
SALES: 20MM Privately Held
SIC: 2098 7997 Noodles (e.g. egg, plain & water), dry; golf club, membership

(P-2383)
SENG CHEANG MONG CO
Also Called: Seng Cheang Mong Food
2661 Merced Ave, El Monte (91733-1905)
PHONE..................................626 442-2899
Chay Ling, Owner
EMP: 10
SALES (est): 932.5K Privately Held
SIC: 2098 Macaroni & spaghetti

(P-2384)
TM NOODLE
4110 Manzanita Ave, Carmichael (95608-1726)
PHONE..................................916 486-2579
Minh Pham, Principal
EMP: 13
SALES (est): 670K Privately Held
SIC: 2098 Noodles (e.g. egg, plain & water), dry

(P-2385)
WAH FUNG NOODLES INC
4443 Rowland Ave, El Monte (91731-1121)
PHONE..................................626 442-0588
Zexiong Liang, President
▲ EMP: 13
SALES (est): 1.7MM Privately Held
SIC: 2098 Noodles (e.g. egg, plain & water), dry

(P-2386)
YONG KEE RICE NOODLE CO
Also Called: Young Kee
946 Stockton St Apt 10c, San Francisco (94108-1643)
PHONE..................................415 986-3759
Kwok Wong, Partner
Ying Wong, Partner
EMP: 15 EST: 1952
SQ FT: 1,500
SALES (est): 880K Privately Held
SIC: 2098 5411 Noodles (e.g. egg, plain & water), dry; grocery stores

---

2099 Food Preparations, NEC

(P-2387)
AB MAURI FOOD INC
Also Called: Fleis Chmanns Vinegar
12604 Hiddencreek Way A, Cerritos (90703-2137)
PHONE..................................562 483-4619
Dave Billings, President
EMP: 12

SALES (corp-wide): 19.8B Privately Held
WEB: www.breadworld.com
SIC: 2099 2087 Vinegar; flavoring extracts & syrups
HQ: Ab Mauri Food Inc.
4240 Duncan Ave Ste 150
Saint Louis MO 63110
314 392-0800

(P-2388)
ADELANTO ELEMENTARY SCHOOL DST
Also Called: Desert Trils Prpratory Academy
14350 Bellflower St, Adelanto (92301-4246)
P.O. Box 400880, Hesperia (92340-0880)
PHONE..................................760 530-7680
Mandy Plantz, Principal
EMP: 42
SALES (corp-wide): 105.7MM Privately Held
SIC: 2099 Food preparations
PA: Adelanto Elementary School District
11824 Air Expy
Adelanto CA 92301
760 246-8691

(P-2389)
ALEXANDER VALLEY GOURMET LLC
140 Grove Ct B, Healdsburg (95448-4780)
PHONE..................................707 473-0116
David Ehreth,
EMP: 20
SALES (est): 2.5MM Privately Held
SIC: 2099 Food preparations

(P-2390)
AMERICAN NATURALS COMPANY LLC
3737 Longridge Ave, Sherman Oaks (91423-4919)
PHONE..................................323 201-6891
Carlo Brandon, CEO
EMP: 22
SALES (est): 3.3MM Privately Held
SIC: 2099 Bouillon cubes

(P-2391)
AMERICAN YEAST CORPORATION
5455 District Blvd, Bakersfield (93313-2123)
PHONE..................................661 834-1050
Lloyd Fry, Executive
EMP: 30
SALES (corp-wide): 34.5MM Privately Held
SIC: 2099 Yeast
HQ: American Yeast Corporation
8215 Beachwood Rd
Baltimore MD 21222
410 477-3700

(P-2392)
AMZART INC
Also Called: MARGEAUX AND LINDA'S VEGAN KIT
3260 Casitas Ave, Los Angeles (90039-2206)
PHONE..................................323 404-9372
Aram Zadikian, President
Margaux Zadikian, Vice Pres
EMP: 10
SQ FT: 3,000
SALES: 604.3K Privately Held
SIC: 2099 Ready-to-eat meals, salads & sandwiches

(P-2393)
ANNIES INC (HQ)
Also Called: Homegrown Naturals
1610 5th St, Berkeley (94710-1715)
PHONE..................................510 558-7500
John Foraker, CEO
Molly F Ashby, Ch of Bd
Kelly J Kennedy, CFO
Bettina Whyte, Bd of Directors
Sarah Bird, Officer
EMP: 80
SQ FT: 33,500
SALES (est): 68.4MM
SALES (corp-wide): 16.8B Publicly Held
WEB: www.annies.com
SIC: 2099 Food preparations

PA: General Mills, Inc.
1 General Mills Blvd
Minneapolis MN 55426
763 764-7600

(P-2394)
ARANDAS TORTILLA COMPANY INC
1318 E Scotts Ave, Stockton (95205-6152)
PHONE..................................209 464-8675
Victor Aranda, CEO
Javier Aranda, Treasurer
Vicent Aranda, Vice Pres
EMP: 48
SQ FT: 20,000
SALES (est): 8.8MM Privately Held
SIC: 2099 Tortillas, fresh or refrigerated

(P-2395)
AREVALO TORTILLERIA INC
3033 Supply Ave, Commerce (90040-2709)
P.O. Box 788, Los Angeles (90078-0788)
PHONE..................................323 888-1711
Edward Arello, Manager
EMP: 30
SALES (est): 2MM
SALES (corp-wide): 23.9MM Privately Held
SIC: 2099 Tortillas, fresh or refrigerated
PA: Arevalo Tortilleria, Inc.
1537 W Mines Ave
Montebello CA 90640
323 888-1711

(P-2396)
AREVALO TORTILLERIA INC (PA)
1537 W Mines Ave, Montebello (90640-5414)
P.O. Box 788 (90640-0788)
PHONE..................................323 888-1711
Jose Luis Arevalo, CEO
Emilia Arevalo, Admin Sec
Luis Arevalo, Manager
▲ EMP: 112
SQ FT: 20,000
SALES (est): 23.9MM Privately Held
SIC: 2099 Food preparations

(P-2397)
ASIANA CUISINE ENTERPRISES INC
Also Called: Ace Sushi
22771 S Wstn Ave Ste 100, Torrance (90501)
PHONE..................................310 327-2223
Harlan Chin, President
Gary Chin, CFO
▲ EMP: 560
SQ FT: 6,000
SALES (est): 48.6MM Privately Held
WEB: www.acesushi.com
SIC: 2099 5812 8741 Ready-to-eat meals, salads & sandwiches; fast food restaurants & stands; management services

(P-2398)
BAKEMARK USA LLC
32621 Central Ave, Union City (94587-2008)
PHONE..................................510 487-8188
Dean Chavez, Manager
EMP: 50
SALES (corp-wide): 538.9MM Privately Held
SIC: 2099 Food preparations
PA: Bakemark Usa Llc
7351 Crider Ave
Pico Rivera CA 90660
562 949-1054

(P-2399)
BARNEY & CO CALIFORNIA LLC
2925 S Elm Ave Ste 101, Fresno (93706-5465)
PHONE..................................559 442-1752
Dawn Kelley, President
Steve Kelley, COO
Tiffany Nguyen, Accountant
Dale Killen, Plant Mgr
Kate Whitney, Marketing Staff
EMP: 18 EST: 2006
SQ FT: 37,000

▲ = Import ▼=Export
◆ =Import/Export

SALES (est): 6.9MM **Privately Held**
SIC: 2099 Almond pastes

(P-2400)
BAY LEAF SPICE COMPANY
21c Orinda Way 363, Orinda (94563-2534)
PHONE..................................925 330-1918
Mike Lewis, *President*
EMP: 20
SALES: 5MM **Privately Held**
SIC: 2099 Seasonings & spices

(P-2401)
BDS NATURAL PRODUCTS INC (PA)
Also Called: Npms Natural Products Mil Svcs
14824 S Main St, Gardena (90248-1919)
PHONE..................................310 518-2227
Steven G Brenneis, *CEO*
David Solomon, *Vice Pres*
Sonia Moir, *Controller*
John Kapski, *Opers Staff*
Ashley Myres, *Representative*
▲ EMP: 65
SQ FT: 80,000
SALES (est): 12.2MM **Privately Held**
WEB: www.bdsnatural.com
SIC: 2099 5149 Seasonings & spices; tea blending; natural & organic foods

(P-2402)
BERBER FOOD MANUFACTURING INC
Also Called: MI Rancho Tortilla Factory
425 Hester St, San Leandro (94577-1025)
PHONE..................................510 553-0444
Manuel Berber, *President*
Robert Berber Jr, *Corp Secy*
▼ EMP: 150
SQ FT: 85,000
SALES (est): 28.6MM **Privately Held**
SIC: 2099 Tortillas, fresh or refrigerated

(P-2403)
BEST FORMULATIONS INC
17758 Rowland St, City of Industry (91748-1148)
PHONE..................................626 912-9998
Charles Ung, *Chairman*
Jeffrey Goh, *President*
Eugene Ung, *CEO*
Robin C Koon, *Exec VP*
Nighat Ansari, *Vice Pres*
◆ EMP: 200
SQ FT: 50,000
SALES (est): 80.4MM **Privately Held**
WEB: www.bestformulations.com
SIC: 2099 8748 5149 2834 Food preparations; business consulting; health foods; pharmaceutical preparations

(P-2404)
BIMBO BAKERIES USA INC
38960 Trade Center Dr A, Palmdale (93551-3662)
PHONE..................................661 274-8458
Nenette Bertell, *Manager*
EMP: 16 **Privately Held**
SIC: 2099 Tortillas, fresh or refrigerated
HQ: Bimbo Bakeries Usa, Inc
255 Business Center Dr # 200
Horsham PA 19044
215 347-5500

(P-2405)
BIMBO BAKERIES USA INC
1215 Alek St, Anaheim (92805)
PHONE..................................714 533-9436
Jesse Delgado, *Manager*
EMP: 50 **Privately Held**
SIC: 2099 Tortillas, fresh or refrigerated
HQ: Bimbo Bakeries Usa, Inc
255 Business Center Dr # 200
Horsham PA 19044
215 347-5500

(P-2406)
BITCHIN INC
Also Called: Bitchin Sauce
6211 Yarrow Dr Ste C, Carlsbad (92011-1539)
PHONE..................................760 224-7447
Starr Edwards, *CEO*
Harrison Edwards, *Chief Mktg Ofcr*
EMP: 26 EST: 2012

SALES (est): 345.4K **Privately Held**
SIC: 2099 Sauces: gravy, dressing & dip mixes

(P-2407)
BLUE DIAMOND GROWERS
1701 C St, Sacramento (95811-1029)
PHONE..................................916 446-8464
EMP: 191
SALES (corp-wide): 1.6B **Privately Held**
SIC: 2099 Food preparations
PA: Diamond Blue Growers
1802 C St
Sacramento CA 95811
916 442-0771

(P-2408)
BLUE DIAMOND GROWERS
Also Called: Blue Diamond
1300 N Washington Rd, Turlock (95380-9506)
PHONE..................................209 604-1501
EMP: 100
SALES (corp-wide): 1.6B **Privately Held**
SIC: 2099 Food preparations
PA: Diamond Blue Growers
1802 C St
Sacramento CA 95811
916 442-0771

(P-2409)
BOTANAS MEXICO INC
11122 Rush St, South El Monte (91733)
PHONE..................................626 279-1512
Carlos Aleman, *President*
Miriam Aleman, *Vice Pres*
◆ EMP: 16
SALES (est): 2.6MM **Privately Held**
SIC: 2099 5499 Seasonings & spices; spices, including grinding; spices & herbs

(P-2410)
BRICKSTONE GROUP INC
15425 Antioch St Unit 304, Pacific Palisades (90272-4372)
PHONE..................................310 991-4747
Isaac Kaplan, *President*
EMP: 11
SALES: 800K **Privately Held**
SIC: 2099 Food preparations

(P-2411)
BRIGHT PEOPLE FOODS INC (PA)
Also Called: Dr McDougall's Right Foods
1640 Tide Ct, Woodland (95776-6210)
P.O. Box 2205 (95776-2205)
PHONE..................................530 669-6870
Michael L Vinnicombe, *President*
Carolyn Vinnicombe, *Vice Pres*
▼ EMP: 25
SQ FT: 30,000
SALES (est): 6.4MM **Privately Held**
SIC: 2099 Spices, including grinding

(P-2412)
C & F FOODS INC (PA)
15620 E Valley Blvd, City of Industry (91744-3926)
PHONE..................................626 723-1000
Manuel G Fernandez, *Ch of Bd*
Luis Faura, *President*
Alex Tran, *CFO*
Gloria Riesgo, *Executive Asst*
Jeanny Avila, *Admin Asst*
▲ EMP: 100
SQ FT: 165,000
SALES (est): 255.7MM **Privately Held**
WEB: www.cnf-foods.com
SIC: 2099 Food preparations

(P-2413)
C&S GLOBAL FOODS INC
Also Called: Ojo De Agua Produce
20110 State Highway 33, Dos Palos (93620-9701)
P.O. Box 1209, Los Banos (93635-1209)
PHONE..................................209 392-2223
Reuben Castaneda, *Owner*
EMP: 13
SALES (est): 1.8MM **Privately Held**
SIC: 2099 4789 Food preparations; freight car loading & unloading

(P-2414)
CACHE CREEK FOODS LLC
411 N Pioneer Ave, Woodland (95776-6122)
P.O. Box 180 (95776-0180)
PHONE..................................530 662-1764
Matthew Morehart,
Connie Stephens, *Office Mgr*
▲ EMP: 19
SQ FT: 40,000
SALES (est): 5MM **Privately Held**
WEB: www.cachecreek.com
SIC: 2099 2064 Almond pastes; nuts, glace

(P-2415)
CADENCE GOURMET LLC
Also Called: Cadence Gourmet Involve Foods
155 Klug Cir, Corona (92880-5424)
PHONE..................................951 272-5949
Brian J Wynn, *CEO*
David Wells, *President*
▲ EMP: 30
SQ FT: 12,000
SALES (est): 9.7MM **Privately Held**
SIC: 2099 Food preparations

(P-2416)
CALAVO GROWERS INC (PA)
1141 Cummings Rd Ste A, Santa Paula (93060-9118)
PHONE..................................805 525-1245
Lecil E Cole, *Ch of Bd*
James E Gibson, *President*
B John Lindeman, *CFO*
Marc Brown, *Bd of Directors*
Ronald A Araiza, *Vice Pres*
EMP: 277 EST: 1924
SALES: 1B **Publicly Held**
WEB: www.calavo.com
SIC: 2099 5148 Salads, fresh or refrigerated; fruits; fruits, fresh

(P-2417)
CALIF FRUT AND TMTO KTCHN LLC
1785 Ashby Rd, Merced (95348-4302)
PHONE..................................530 666-6600
Chris Rufer, *Mng Member*
Tim Cruise,
▼ EMP: 10 EST: 1946
SQ FT: 252,212
SALES (est): 1.3MM **Privately Held**
WEB: www.calfruittom.com
SIC: 2099 Food preparations

(P-2418)
CALIFORNIA NATURAL PRODUCTS
Also Called: Power Automation Systems
1250 Lathrop Rd, Lathrop (95330-9709)
P.O. Box 1219 (95330-1219)
PHONE..................................209 858-2525
Eric Beringause, *CEO*
Timothy Preuninger, *CFO*
John Ashby, *General Mgr*
David Stott, *Admin Sec*
David Tigerino, *Administration*
▲ EMP: 230 EST: 1976
SQ FT: 220,000
SALES (est): 88.6MM
SALES (corp-wide): 350.6MM **Privately Held**
SIC: 2099 7389 Food preparations; packaging & labeling services
HQ: Gf Assets Holdings Corporation
N116w15970 Main St
Germantown WI 53022
262 251-8572

(P-2419)
CALIFORNIA NEW FOODS LLC
11165 Commercial Pkwy, Castroville (95012-3207)
PHONE..................................831 444-1872
Peter Uli,
EMP: 25
SALES (est): 979.1K **Privately Held**
SIC: 2099 Food preparations

(P-2420)
CEDARLANE NATURAL FOODS INC (PA)
1135 E Artesia Blvd, Carson (90746-1602)
PHONE..................................310 886-7720

Robert Atallah, *CEO*
Neil Holmes, *CFO*
Kristin Harper, *Vice Pres*
Celia Gonzalez, *Executive*
Maly Sea, *Research*
▲ EMP: 100
SQ FT: 270,000
SALES (est): 87.6MM **Privately Held**
WEB: www.cedarlanefoods.com
SIC: 2099 Food preparations

(P-2421)
CEDARLANE NATURAL FOODS NORTH
Also Called: Cedar Lane North
150 Airport Blvd, South San Francisco (94080-4739)
PHONE..................................650 742-0444
EMP: 25
SALES (est): 4.1MM **Privately Held**
SIC: 2099

(P-2422)
CFARMS INC
1244 E Beamer St, Woodland (95776-6002)
PHONE..................................916 375-3000
Baljit Pattar, *Branch Mgr*
EMP: 28
SALES (corp-wide): 4.6MM **Privately Held**
SIC: 2099 5149 Food preparations; flavourings & fragrances
PA: Cfarms, Inc.
1330 N Dutton Ave Ste 100
Santa Rosa CA 95401
916 375-3000

(P-2423)
CHEF MERITO INC (PA)
Also Called: Merito.com
7915 Sepulveda Blvd, Van Nuys (91405-1032)
PHONE..................................818 787-0100
Jose J Corugedo, *CEO*
Plinio J Garcia Sr, *Shareholder*
Jose Corugedo, *CFO*
Natt Hasson, *Admin Sec*
Gus Hixson, *Info Tech Mgr*
▲ EMP: 84
SQ FT: 30,000
SALES (est): 13.4MM **Privately Held**
WEB: www.chefmerito.com
SIC: 2099 2033 2032 2044 Spices, including grinding; jellies, edible, including imitation: in cans, jars, etc.; soups, except seafood: packaged in cans, jars, etc.; enriched rice (vitamin & mineral fortified); sausages & other prepared meats

(P-2424)
CHEFMASTER
501 Airpark Dr, Fullerton (92833-2501)
PHONE..................................714 554-4000
Aaron G Byrnes, *President*
▲ EMP: 35
SALES: 1.3MM **Privately Held**
SIC: 2099 Sugar powdered from purchased ingredients

(P-2425)
CHH LP
Also Called: Rosa's Cafe & Tortilla Factory
28134 Jefferson Ave, Temecula (92590-6604)
PHONE..................................951 506-5800
Dale Hackbarth, *Managing Prtnr*
Bobby Cox, *Partner*
Edward Hackbarth, *Partner*
EMP: 35
SQ FT: 5,000
SALES (est): 4.1MM **Privately Held**
SIC: 2099 5812 Tortillas, fresh or refrigerated; caterers

(P-2426)
CJ FOODS MANUFACTURING CORP
500 S State College Blvd, Fullerton (92831-5114)
PHONE..................................714 888-3500
Joo Hong Shin, *President*
▲ EMP: 23 EST: 2012
SALES (est): 6.9MM **Privately Held**
SIC: 2099 Seasonings & spices

(P-2427)
CLARMIL MANUFACTURING CORP (PA)
Also Called: Goldilocks
30865 San Clemente St, Hayward (94544-7136)
PHONE................510 476-0700
Mary-Ann Yee Ortiz-Luis, President
Mary Ann Yee Ortiz Luis, President
Freddie L Go Jr, COO
Mannette Roxas, Treasurer
Yee Rob, General Mgr
▲ EMP: 98
SQ FT: 57,000
SALES (est): 21.5MM Privately Held
WEB: www.clarmil.com
SIC: 2099 5149 2051 Food preparations; bakery products; bread, cake & related products

(P-2428)
CLASSIC SALADS LLC
100 Harrington Rd, Royal Oaks (95076-5604)
P.O. Box 3800, Salinas (93912-3800)
PHONE................928 726-6196
Lance Batistich, Mng Member
Richard Urbach, Plant Mgr
Dale Chase, Sales Staff
Christina Batistich,
Rachelle Morales, Manager
▲ EMP: 44
SALES (est): 15.4MM Privately Held
WEB: www.classicsalads.com
SIC: 2099 Salads, fresh or refrigerated

(P-2429)
CLASSIC WINE VINEGAR CO INC
Also Called: Classic Vinegar
4110 Brew Master Dr, Ceres (95307-7583)
PHONE................209 538-7600
Walter Nicolau,
Donna Nicolau, Partner
EMP: 12
SQ FT: 15,000
SALES (est): 2.5MM Privately Held
WEB: www.classicwinevinegar.com
SIC: 2099 Vinegar

(P-2430)
CLW FOODS LLC (PA)
8765 E 3rd St, Hanford (93230-9605)
P.O. Box 11069, Los Angeles (90011-0069)
PHONE................559 639-6661
Todd Waldman,
Jeff Sterling, Vice Pres
Dayle Kanemaki, Info Tech Mgr
Josh Bornemane, Controller
Jay Wiviott,
EMP: 20
SQ FT: 60,000
SALES (est): 7.3MM Privately Held
SIC: 2099 Dessert mixes & fillings

(P-2431)
CNC NOODLE CORPORATION
325 Fallon St, Oakland (94607-4611)
PHONE................510 835-2269
Betty Lim, President
▲ EMP: 15
SQ FT: 12,000
SALES (est): 2.6MM Privately Held
SIC: 2099 Noodles, fried (Chinese)

(P-2432)
CONAGRA BRANDS INC
554 S Yosemite Ave, Oakdale (95361-4037)
PHONE................209 847-0321
Earl Ehret, Branch Mgr
EMP: 1145
SQ FT: 40,000
SALES (corp-wide): 9.5B Publicly Held
WEB: www.conagra.com
SIC: 2099 Food preparations
PA: Conagra Brands, Inc.
222 Mdse Mart Plz
Chicago IL 60654
312 549-5000

(P-2433)
COSMOS FOOD CO INC
16015 Phoenix Dr, City of Industry (91745-1624)
PHONE................323 221-9142
David Kim, President
EMP: 45
SQ FT: 85,000
SALES (est): 8.2MM Privately Held
WEB: www.cosmosfood.com
SIC: 2099 5149 Tortillas, fresh or refrigerated; groceries & related products

(P-2434)
CREATIVE FOODS LLC
12622 Poway Rd A, Poway (92064-4451)
PHONE................858 748-0070
Frank Interlandi, Principal
EMP: 25
SALES (est): 946.9K Privately Held
SIC: 2099 5812 Food preparations; eating places

(P-2435)
CUAHUTEMOC TORTILLERIA
3455 E 1st St, Los Angeles (90063-2945)
PHONE................323 262-0410
Maria Vasques, Owner
EMP: 20
SQ FT: 2,500
SALES (est): 1.2MM Privately Held
SIC: 2099 Tortillas, fresh or refrigerated

(P-2436)
CULINARY INTERNATIONAL LLC (PA)
3280 E 44th St, Vernon (90058-2426)
PHONE................626 289-3000
Cesar Rodarte,
EMP: 25
SALES (est): 57MM Privately Held
SIC: 2099 2038 5149 Food preparations; ethnic foods, frozen; natural & organic foods; specialty food items

(P-2437)
CULINARY SPECIALTIES INC
1231 Linda Vista Dr, San Marcos (92078-3809)
PHONE................760 744-8220
Chris Schragner, President
Patrick O Farrell, Vice Pres
Patrick Ofarrell, Vice Pres
Vishka Rosenblum, Natl Sales Mgr
Adela Beltran, Sales Staff
EMP: 53 EST: 1997
SQ FT: 6,400
SALES (est): 8.9MM Privately Held
SIC: 2099 2038 Emulsifiers, food; frozen specialties

(P-2438)
CURATION FOODS INC (HQ)
2811 Airpark Dr, Santa Maria (93455-1417)
P.O. Box 727, Guadalupe (93434-0727)
PHONE................800 454-1355
Bill Richardville, CEO
Tim Nykoluk, President
Debra Vanhorsen, President
Ann Baker, Vice Pres
Tim Kwan, Vice Pres
◆ EMP: 80
SQ FT: 200,000
SALES (est): 470.5MM
SALES (corp-wide): 557.5MM Publicly Held
WEB: www.apioinc.com
SIC: 2099 0723 Food preparations; vegetable packing services
PA: Landec Corporation
5201 Great America Pkwy # 232
Santa Clara CA 95054
650 306-1650

(P-2439)
CURATION FOODS INC
Also Called: O Olive Oil & Vinegar
1997 S Mcdwell Blvd Ste A, Petaluma (94954-7623)
PHONE................707 766-7511
Mario Aranda, Vice Pres
EMP: 12
SALES (corp-wide): 557.5MM Publicly Held
SIC: 2099 Food preparations

HQ: Curation Foods, Inc.
2811 Airpark Dr
Santa Maria CA 93455
800 454-1355

(P-2440)
DEAN DISTRIBUTORS INC
5015 Hallmark Pkwy, San Bernardino (92407-1871)
PHONE................323 587-8147
John D Garinger, Branch Mgr
Jay Brown, General Mgr
EMP: 20
SALES (corp-wide): 3.8MM Privately Held
WEB: www.cambridgedietusa.com
SIC: 2099 2087 2834 Sauces: dry mixes; syrups, flavoring (except drink); pharmaceutical preparations
PA: Dean Distributors, Inc.
800 Airport Blvd Ste 312
Burlingame CA 94010
800 792-0816

(P-2441)
DEL CASTILLO FOODS INC
Also Called: La Campana Tortilla Factory
2346 Maggio Cir, Lodi (95240-8812)
PHONE................209 369-2877
Marciano Del Castillo, President
Rosario Del Castillo, Treasurer
Bertha Del Castillo, Vice Pres
EMP: 40
SQ FT: 16,200
SALES (est): 5.2MM Privately Held
SIC: 2099 5461 5411 2096 Tortillas, fresh or refrigerated; bakeries; grocery stores; potato chips & similar snacks

(P-2442)
DELIVERY ZONE LLC
120 S Anderson St, Los Angeles (90033-3220)
PHONE................323 780-0888
Carl Ferro,
Elias Montero, Executive
Reyna Ceballos, Mng Officer
John Stewart,
EMP: 80
SQ FT: 4,700
SALES (est): 9.2MM Privately Held
WEB: www.sunfare.com
SIC: 2099 4215 Ready-to-eat meals, salads & sandwiches; courier services, except by air

(P-2443)
DELORI PRODUCTS INC
Also Called: Delori Foods
17043 Green Dr, City of Industry (91745-1812)
P.O. Box 92668 (91715-2668)
PHONE................626 965-3006
Jaime Brown, CEO
Blanca Brown, Treasurer
▲ EMP: 32
SALES (est): 6.8MM Privately Held
WEB: www.deloriproducts.com
SIC: 2099 Jelly, corncob (gelatin)

(P-2444)
DIAMOND CRYSTAL BRANDS INC
Also Called: Diamond Crystal Brands-Hormel
8700 W Doe Ave, Visalia (93291-8900)
PHONE................559 651-7782
Robert Elderdice, Branch Mgr
Terry Seifert, Plant Mgr
EMP: 40
SALES (corp-wide): 237.7MM Privately Held
SIC: 2099 Food preparations
PA: Diamond Crystal Brands, Inc
3000 Tremont Rd
Savannah GA 31405
912 651-5112

(P-2445)
DIANAS MEXICAN FOOD PDTS INC (PA)
Also Called: La Bonita
16330 Pioneer Blvd, Norwalk (90650-7042)
P.O. Box 369 (90651-0369)
PHONE................562 926-5802
Samuel Magana, CEO
Elmer Guzman, Chief Mktg Ofcr

Hortensia Magana, Vice Pres
Rosario Zavanero, Executive
Lydia Rodriguez, Purch Mgr
EMP: 50
SQ FT: 4,068
SALES (est): 76.4MM Privately Held
WEB: www.dianas.net
SIC: 2099 5812 Tortillas, fresh or refrigerated; ethnic food restaurants

(P-2446)
DIANAS MEXICAN FOOD PDTS INC
2905 Durfee Ave, El Monte (91732-3517)
PHONE................626 444-0555
Samuel Magana, Owner
EMP: 40
SQ FT: 13,530
SALES (corp-wide): 76.4MM Privately Held
WEB: www.dianas.net
SIC: 2099 5812 Tortillas, fresh or refrigerated; Mexican restaurant
PA: Diana's Mexican Food Products, Inc.
16330 Pioneer Blvd
Norwalk CA 90650
562 926-5802

(P-2447)
DIVINE PASTA COMPANY
140 W Providencia Ave, Burbank (91502-2121)
PHONE................213 542-3300
Alexander Palermo, President
Maureen Moore, Purchasing
Todd Ramsey, Opers Mgr
EMP: 49
SQ FT: 30,000
SALES: 26.8MM Privately Held
WEB: www.divinepasta.com
SIC: 2099 Packaged combination products: pasta, rice & potato

(P-2448)
DOLE FRESH VEGETABLES INC (HQ)
2959 Salinas Hwy, Monterey (93940-6400)
P.O. Box 2018 (93942-2018)
PHONE................831 422-8871
Howard Roeder, CEO
David H Murdock, President
Ray Riggi, President
Michael H Solomon, President
Roger Billingsly, Exec VP
◆ EMP: 150
SQ FT: 15,000
SALES: 125.2MM
SALES (corp-wide): 1.1B Privately Held
SIC: 2099 0723 Food preparations; fruit (fresh) packing services
PA: Dole Food Company, Inc.
1 Dole Dr
Westlake Village CA 91362
818 874-4000

(P-2449)
EARTHRISE NUTRITIONALS LLC
113 E Hoober Rd, Calipatria (92233-9703)
P.O. Box 270 (92233-0270)
PHONE................760 348-5027
Jose Perez, Manager
Lilibeth Flores, Accountant
EMP: 16 Privately Held
SIC: 2099 Chicory root, dried
HQ: Earthrise Nutritionals Llc
2151 Michelson Dr Ste 258
Irvine CA 92612
949 623-0980

(P-2450)
EL GALLITO MARKET INC
12242 Valley Blvd, El Monte (91732-3108)
PHONE................626 442-1190
Sandra Veisaga, President
Mario Rodriguez, Treasurer
EMP: 35
SQ FT: 1,200
SALES (est): 4.7MM Privately Held
SIC: 2099 5421 5411 Tortillas, fresh or refrigerated; meat & fish markets; grocery stores

▲ = Import ▼=Export
◆ =Import/Export

(P-2451)
EL INDIO TORTILLERIA
Also Called: El Indio Tortillas Fctry
1502 W 5th St, Santa Ana (92703-2902)
PHONE..................................714 542-3114
Humberto Sanchez, *President*
Graciela Sanchez, *Treasurer*
EMP: 12
SQ FT: 4,500
SALES: 850K **Privately Held**
WEB: www.elindiotortilleria.com
SIC: 2099 Tortillas, fresh or refrigerated

(P-2452)
ESPERANZAS TORTILLERIA INC
750 Rock Springs Rd, Escondido
(92025-1625)
PHONE..................................760 743-5908
Victor Martinez, *President*
Teresa Martinez, *Treasurer*
Hugo Martinez, *Vice Pres*
Leonor Batista, *Office Mgr*
EMP: 46
SALES (est): 7.7MM **Privately Held**
SIC: 2099 Tortillas, fresh or refrigerated

(P-2453)
EVERSON SPICE COMPANY INC
2667 Gundry Ave, Long Beach
(90755-1808)
PHONE..................................562 595-4785
Kim Everson, *CEO*
Ken Hopkins, *President*
Jim Ennis, *CFO*
Jerry Keifer, *Info Tech Mgr*
Robyn Eckardt, *IT/INT Sup*
▲ **EMP:** 35
SQ FT: 35,000
SALES (est): 8.9MM **Privately Held**
WEB: www.eversonspice.com
SIC: 2099 Spices, including grinding

(P-2454)
F I O IMPORTS INC
Also Called: Contessa Premium Foods
5980 Alcoa Ave, Vernon (90058-3925)
PHONE..................................323 263-5100
Dirk Leuenberger, *President*
Bob Nielsen, *CFO*
Tom Jedrzejewicz, *Info Tech Mgr*
Robert Santich, *Info Tech Mgr*
Rosslyn Banayat, *Human Res Dir*
EMP: 180
SALES (est): 22.8MM
SALES (corp-wide): 275.9MM **Privately Held**
SIC: 2099 Food preparations
PA: Aqua Star (Usa), Corp.
   2025 1st Ave Ste 200
   Seattle WA 98121
   206 448-5400

(P-2455)
FAMILY LOOMPYA CORPORATION
2626 Southport Way Ste F, National City
(91950-8753)
PHONE..................................619 477-2125
Alen Enriquez, *President*
Allen Enriquez, *Branch Mgr*
▲ **EMP:** 25
SQ FT: 10,000
SALES (est): 4.3MM **Privately Held**
WEB: www.lumpia.com
SIC: 2099 5149 Food preparations; specialty food items

(P-2456)
FAYES FOODS INC
Also Called: Fay's Foods
10650 Burbank Blvd, North Hollywood
(91601-2511)
PHONE..................................818 508-8392
EMP: 37
SQ FT: 15,000
SALES: 5MM **Privately Held**
SIC: 2099 5812 5149 5141

(P-2457)
FINEST FOOD INC
6491 Weathers Pl Ste A, San Diego
(92121-2935)
PHONE..................................858 699-4746
Jose Aldo Enrique Landman, *President*
Sylvia Landman, *CFO*
Guillermo Ayan Helmholt, *Vice Pres*

EMP: 12
SQ FT: 18,000
SALES: 200K **Privately Held**
WEB: www.panini.fr
SIC: 2099 Food preparations

(P-2458)
FIORE DI PASTA INC
4776 E Jensen Ave, Fresno (93725-1704)
PHONE..................................559 457-0431
Bernadetta Primavera, *President*
Anthony Primavera, *CFO*
Giacomo Ciabattini, *Research*
Ana Miller, *Controller*
Anna Dicicco, *Sales Staff*
▲ **EMP:** 67
SQ FT: 59,000
SALES: 16MM **Privately Held**
SIC: 2099 Pasta, uncooked: packaged with other ingredients

(P-2459)
FISHER NUT COMPANY
137 N Hart Rd, Modesto (95358-9537)
PHONE..................................209 527-0108
Ronald Fisher, *President*
▼ **EMP:** 15
SALES (est): 3.6MM **Privately Held**
WEB: www.fishernut.com
SIC: 2099 Food preparations

(P-2460)
FLORES BROTHERS INC
Also Called: Durango Foods
7777 Scout Ave, Bell (90201-4941)
PHONE..................................562 806-9128
David Flores, *President*
Armando Flores, *Vice Pres*
EMP: 20
SALES (est): 2.9MM **Privately Held**
SIC: 2099 Emulsifiers, food

(P-2461)
FOOD-O-MEX CORPORATION
Also Called: El Dorado Mexican Food Pdts
2928 N Main St, Los Angeles (90031-3325)
PHONE..................................323 225-1737
Eleanor Lopez, *President*
Elenore Lopez, *President*
Philip Manly, *Vice Pres*
EMP: 60
SQ FT: 18,000
SALES (est): 8.3MM **Privately Held**
WEB: www.eldoradotortillas.com
SIC: 2099 Tortillas, fresh or refrigerated

(P-2462)
FOREVER YOUNG
Also Called: Supernutrition
208 Palmetto Ave, Pacifica (94044-1374)
PHONE..................................650 355-5481
EMP: 24
SQ FT: 12,000
SALES (est): 2.9MM **Privately Held**
SIC: 2099 2834

(P-2463)
FORTUNA TORTILLA FACTORY
1425 C St, Livingston (95334-1416)
PHONE..................................209 394-3028
Joe Soto, *Owner*
EMP: 18
SQ FT: 7,200
SALES (est): 820K **Privately Held**
SIC: 2099 5411 Tortillas, fresh or refrigerated; grocery stores, independent

(P-2464)
FRESH & READY FOODS LLC
1145 Arroyo St Ste B, San Fernando
(91340-1842)
PHONE..................................818 837-7600
Art Sezgin, *President*
John Saladino, *Vice Pres*
EMP: 99
SALES (est): 4.5MM **Privately Held**
SIC: 2099 Salads, fresh or refrigerated

(P-2465)
FRESH EXPRESS INCORPORATED
950 E Blanco Rd, Salinas (93901-4487)
P.O. Box 80599 (93912-0599)
PHONE..................................831 424-2921
Mark Drever, *Branch Mgr*
Erik Teixeira, *Engineer*

Rocio Lozano, *Controller*
Michelle Mahi, *Human Res Mgr*
EMP: 20
SALES (corp-wide): 3B **Privately Held**
WEB: www.freshexpress.com
SIC: 2099 Food preparations
HQ: Fresh Express Incorporated
   4757 The Grove Dr Ste 260
   Windermere FL 34786
   407 612-5000

(P-2466)
FUJI NATURAL FOODS INC (HQ)
13500 S Hamner Ave, Ontario
(91761-2605)
P.O. Box 3728 (91761-0973)
PHONE..................................909 947-1008
Katsushiro Nakagawa, *CEO*
Ikuzo Sugiyama, *President*
◆ **EMP:** 72
SQ FT: 65,000
SALES (est): 8.7MM **Privately Held**
SIC: 2099 Food preparations

(P-2467)
GH FOODS CA LLC (DH)
8425 Carbide Ct, Sacramento
(95828-5609)
PHONE..................................916 844-1140
Jim Gibson,
EMP: 330
SQ FT: 60,000
SALES (est): 72.1MM
SALES (corp-wide): 1B **Publicly Held**
SIC: 2099 Salads, fresh or refrigerated
HQ: Renaissance Food Group, Llc
   11020 White Rock Rd Ste 1
   Rancho Cordova CA 95670
   916 638-8825

(P-2468)
GHIRINGHLLI SPCIALTY FOODS INC
101 Benicia Rd, Vallejo (94590-7003)
PHONE..................................707 561-7670
Mike Ghiringhelli, *President*
Ed Ferrero, *Vice Pres*
EMP: 145
SQ FT: 55,000
SALES (est): 41.2MM **Privately Held**
WEB: www.gfoods.net
SIC: 2099 Ready-to-eat meals, salads & sandwiches; salads, fresh or refrigerated

(P-2469)
GLUTEN FREE FOODS MFG LLC (PA)
5010 Eucalyptus Ave, Chino (91710-9216)
PHONE..................................909 823-8230
Luis Faura, *Mng Member*
EMP: 16
SALES (est): 3.3MM **Privately Held**
SIC: 2099 Pasta, uncooked: packaged with other ingredients

(P-2470)
GOBBLE INC
170 University St, San Francisco (94134)
PHONE..................................888 405-7481
Ooshma Garg, *CEO*
Will Medford, *Buyer*
EMP: 170
SALES (est): 592.2K **Privately Held**
SIC: 2099 Food preparations

(P-2471)
GOLD COAST INGREDIENTS INC
2429 Yates Ave, Commerce (90040-1917)
PHONE..................................323 724-8935
Clarence H Brasher, *CEO*
James A Sgro, *President*
Kenneth Chu, *Vice Pres*
Laurie Goddard, *Vice Pres*
Jon Wellwood, *General Mgr*
◆ **EMP:** 53
SQ FT: 50,000
SALES (est): 21.8MM **Privately Held**
WEB: www.goldcoastinc.com
SIC: 2099 Almond pastes

(P-2472)
GOLDEN SPECIALTY FOODS LLC
14605 Best Ave, Norwalk (90650-5258)
PHONE..................................562 802-2537

Philip Pisciotta, *CEO*
Jeff Chan, *President*
Deryk Howard, *CFO*
◆ **EMP:** 25
SQ FT: 31,000
SALES (est): 6.8MM **Privately Held**
WEB: www.goldenspecialtyfoods.com
SIC: 2099 2032 Food preparations; canned specialties

(P-2473)
GOOD VIEW FUTURE GROUP INC
277 S B St, San Mateo (94401-4017)
PHONE..................................408 834-5698
William Jiang, *CEO*
EMP: 18
SALES (est): 615.3K **Privately Held**
SIC: 2099 Desserts, ready-to-mix

(P-2474)
GOODMAN FOOD PRODUCTS INC (PA)
Also Called: Don Lee Farms
200 E Beach Ave Fl 1, Inglewood
(90302-3404)
PHONE..................................310 674-3180
Donald Goodman, *CEO*
Jean Harris, *Senior VP*
Suzanne Bootross, *Technology*
Marcos Lopez, *Accountant*
Joan Mockenhaupt, *Controller*
▲ **EMP:** 250 **EST:** 1982
SQ FT: 55,000
SALES (est): 71.1MM **Privately Held**
WEB: www.donleefarms.com
SIC: 2099 Food preparations

(P-2475)
GPDE SLVA SPCES INCRPORATION
Also Called: Peterson's Spices
8531 Loch Lomond Dr, Pico Rivera
(90660-2509)
PHONE..................................562 407-2643
Ravi De Silva, *President*
Rupa De Silva, *Vice Pres*
Binuka De Silva, *Sales Mgr*
▲ **EMP:** 60
SQ FT: 60,000
SALES: 60MM **Privately Held**
SIC: 2099 5149 Chili pepper or powder; spices, including grinding; spices & seasonings

(P-2476)
HAIGS DELICACIES LLC
25673 Nickel Pl, Hayward (94545-3221)
PHONE..................................510 782-6285
Rita Takvorian, *Mng Member*
Mark Takvorian, *COO*
Nadine Takvorian,
EMP: 20
SQ FT: 1,200
SALES (est): 4.1MM **Privately Held**
WEB: www.haigsdelicacies.com
SIC: 2099 Dips, except cheese & sour cream based

(P-2477)
HARMLESS HARVEST INC (PA)
712 Sansome St, San Francisco
(94111-1704)
PHONE..................................347 688-6286
Giannella Alvarez, *CEO*
Justin Guilbert, *President*
Brad Paris, *COO*
Warren Dewar, *CFO*
Blair Cornish, *Officer*
▲ **EMP:** 30
SALES (est): 6.8MM **Privately Held**
SIC: 2099 Coconut, desiccated & shredded

(P-2478)
HEALTHY TIMES
Also Called: Healty Times Natural Products
225 Broadway Ste 450, San Diego
(92101-5027)
PHONE..................................858 513-1550
Rondi Prescott, *CEO*
Richard Prescott, *President*
Jenn Goodrum, *Marketing Mgr*
EMP: 15
SQ FT: 2,800

SALES (est): 2.6MM **Privately Held**
WEB: www.healthytimes.com
SIC: 2099 2844 Food preparations; cosmetic preparations

(P-2479)
HESPERIA UNIFIED SCHOOL DST
Also Called: Hesperia Usd Food Service
11176 G Ave, Hesperia (92345-8315)
PHONE.................................760 948-1051
Janet Clesceri, *Branch Mgr*
EMP: 10
SALES (corp-wide): 263.4MM **Privately Held**
SIC: 2099 8322 8299 Box lunches, for sale off premises; geriatric social service; arts & crafts schools
PA: Hesperia Unified School District
15576 Main St
Hesperia CA 92345
760 244-4411

(P-2480)
HONEY BENNETTS FARM INC
Also Called: Bennett's Honey Farm
3176 Honey Ln, Fillmore (93015-2026)
PHONE.................................805 521-1375
Gilebert Vannoy, *President*
Ann Lindsay Bennett, *Principal*
EMP: 25
SQ FT: 20,000
SALES (est): 4MM **Privately Held**
SIC: 2099 5191 0279 Honey, strained & bottled; farm supplies; apiary (bee & honey farm)

(P-2481)
HOUSE FOODS AMERICA CORP (HQ)
Also Called: Hinoichi Tofu
7351 Orangewood Ave, Garden Grove (92841-1411)
PHONE.................................714 901-4350
Tatsumi Yamaguchi, *President*
Tadashi Okamoto, *CFO*
▲ EMP: 195
SQ FT: 30,000
SALES (est): 38.9MM **Privately Held**
WEB: www.house-foods.com
SIC: 2099 Food preparations

(P-2482)
IL PASTAIO FOODS INC
Also Called: IL Pastaio Fresh Pasta Company
1266 E Julian St, San Jose (95116-1009)
PHONE.................................408 753-9220
Francisco Avela, *President*
EMP: 10
SALES (est): 1MM **Privately Held**
SIC: 2099 Pasta, uncooked: packaged with other ingredients

(P-2483)
IMPOSSIBLE FOODS INC (PA)
400 Saginaw Dr, Redwood City (94063-4749)
PHONE.................................650 461-4385
Patrick Brown, *CEO*
Dennis Woodside, *President*
Dana Wagner,
Nick Halla, *Officer*
Dan Greene, *Senior VP*
▲ EMP: 60
SALES (est): 20MM **Privately Held**
SIC: 2099 Food preparations

(P-2484)
INGREDIENTS BY NATURE LLC
5555 Brooks St, Montclair (91763-4547)
PHONE.................................909 230-6200
Matt Outz, *President*
EMP: 27 EST: 2010
SALES (est): 5MM **Privately Held**
SIC: 2099 Molasses, mixed or blended: from purchased ingredients

(P-2485)
J W FLOOR COVERING INC
3401 Enterprise Ave, Hayward (94545-3201)
PHONE.................................858 444-1214
Decklan Donohue, *Manager*
EMP: 59

SALES (corp-wide): 43.6MM **Privately Held**
WEB: www.jwfloors.com
SIC: 2099 Food preparations
PA: J. W. Floor Covering, Inc.
9881 Carroll Centre Rd
San Diego CA 92126
858 536-8565

(P-2486)
JAYONE FOODS INC
7212 Alondra Blvd, Paramount (90723-3902)
PHONE.................................562 633-7400
Seung Hoon Lee, *President*
Chil Park, *Vice Pres*
Elizabeth Yoo, *Info Tech Mgr*
Chris Kim Jayone, *Purch Mgr*
Ik T Kim, *Opers Staff*
◆ EMP: 50
SQ FT: 28,000
SALES (est): 10.2MM **Privately Held**
WEB: www.jayone.com
SIC: 2099 Food preparations

(P-2487)
JBR INC (PA)
Also Called: Jbr Gourmet Foods
1731 Aviation Blvd, Lincoln (95648-9317)
PHONE.................................916 258-8000
Peter Rogers, *CEO*
Barbara Rogers, *Vice Pres*
Gina Lim, *Manager*
◆ EMP: 224 EST: 1979
SQ FT: 400,000
SALES (est): 71.6MM **Privately Held**
WEB: www.o-coffee.com
SIC: 2099 2095 Tea blending; coffee roasting (except by wholesale grocers)

(P-2488)
JESUS CABEZAS
Also Called: J C Kitchen
145 Utah Ave, South San Francisco (94080-6712)
PHONE.................................650 583-0469
Jesus Cabezas, *Owner*
EMP: 17
SALES (est): 1.9MM **Privately Held**
WEB: www.jesuscabezas.com
SIC: 2099 Vegetables, peeled for the trade

(P-2489)
JIMENES FOOD INC
7046 Jackson St, Paramount (90723-4835)
PHONE.................................562 602-2505
Reyna Jimenez, *President*
Juan Jimenez, *Vice Pres*
EMP: 30
SQ FT: 11,000
SALES (est): 6.1MM **Privately Held**
SIC: 2099 Tortillas, fresh or refrigerated

(P-2490)
JOHNS INCREDIBLE PIZZA CO
14766 Bear Valley Rd, Victorville (92395-9610)
PHONE.................................760 951-1111
John Parlet, *President*
Betty Parlet, *Treasurer*
EMP: 100
SQ FT: 16,000
SALES (est): 7.8MM **Privately Held**
SIC: 2099 5812 7993 Salads, fresh or refrigerated; pizza restaurants; Italian restaurant; video game arcade

(P-2491)
JOY PROCESSED FOODS INC
1330 Seabright Ave, Long Beach (90813-1189)
PHONE.................................562 435-1106
Alvin Clawson, *President*
EMP: 30 EST: 1966
SQ FT: 5,000
SALES (est): 3.3MM **Privately Held**
SIC: 2099 Vegetables, peeled for the trade

(P-2492)
JR SIMPLOT COMPANY
12688 S Colorado Ave, Helm (93627)
P.O. Box 128 (93627-0128)
PHONE.................................559 866-5681
Frank Gaufin, *Manager*
Keith Gaines, *Engineer*
Chris Ware, *Safety Mgr*

Matt Frank, *Prdtn Mgr*
EMP: 34
SQ FT: 2,000
SALES (corp-wide): 4.8B **Privately Held**
WEB: www.simplot.com
SIC: 2099 Food preparations
PA: J.R. Simplot Company
1099 W Front St
Boise ID 83702
208 780-3287

(P-2493)
JSL FOODS INC (PA)
3550 Pasadena Ave, Los Angeles (90031-1946)
PHONE.................................323 223-2484
Teiji Kawana, *President*
Koji Kawana, *Exec VP*
Darren Tristano, *Vice Pres*
Edwardo Rivas, *Info Tech Mgr*
Miguil Villanueva, *Research*
▲ EMP: 120
SALES (est): 26.4MM **Privately Held**
WEB: www.jslfoods.com
SIC: 2099 5142 2052 Pasta, uncooked: packaged with other ingredients; packaged frozen goods; cookies

(P-2494)
JSL FOODS INC
2222 1/2 Davie Ave, Commerce (90040-1708)
PHONE.................................323 727-9999
Teiji Kawana, *President*
EMP: 60
SALES (corp-wide): 26.4MM **Privately Held**
WEB: www.jslfoods.com
SIC: 2099 2052 Pasta, uncooked: packaged with other ingredients; cookies
PA: Jsl Foods, Inc.
3550 Pasadena Ave
Los Angeles CA 90031
323 223-2484

(P-2495)
JUNESHINE INC
3052 El Cajon Blvd, San Diego (92104-1618)
PHONE.................................619 501-8311
Greg Serrao, *CEO*
EMP: 12 EST: 2017
SALES (est): 2.4MM **Privately Held**
SIC: 2099 Tea blending

(P-2496)
KATE FARMS INC
101 Innovation Pl, Santa Barbara (93108-2268)
P.O. Box 50840 (93150-0840)
PHONE.................................805 845-2446
Richard Laver, *President*
Tom Beecher, *CFO*
John Hommeyer, *Exec VP*
Michelle Laver, *Vice Pres*
Corey Riley, *Sales Staff*
EMP: 123
SALES: 1.8MM **Privately Held**
SIC: 2099 Ready-to-eat meals, salads & sandwiches

(P-2497)
KDS INGREDIENTS LLC
3460 Mrron Rd Ste 103-229, Oceanside (92056)
PHONE.................................760 310-5245
Keri Ross, *CEO*
EMP: 20
SALES (corp-wide): 2.1MM **Privately Held**
SIC: 2099 Molasses, mixed or blended: from purchased ingredients
PA: Kds Ingredients Llc
15890 Bass Ln
San Diego CA 92127
608 469-0866

(P-2498)
KHYBER FOODS INCORPORATED
Also Called: Sun Glo Foods
500 S Acacia Ave, Fullerton (92831-5102)
P.O. Box 4324 (92834-4324)
PHONE.................................714 879-0900
A R Ghafoori, *President*
Larry Ballard, *Corp Secy*

▲ EMP: 25 EST: 1964
SQ FT: 55,000
SALES (est): 2MM **Privately Held**
SIC: 2099 Food preparations

(P-2499)
KNOTTS BERRY FARM LLC (HQ)
Also Called: Knott's Berry Farm
8039 Beach Blvd, Buena Park (90620-3225)
P.O. Box 5002 (90622-5002)
PHONE.................................714 827-1776
Jack Falfas, *Partner*
Larry Daniel, *Vice Pres*
Jeff Gahagan, *Vice Pres*
Raffi Kaprelyan, *Vice Pres*
Kent Maulsby, *Vice Pres*
▲ EMP: 500 EST: 1920
SQ FT: 5,000
SALES (est): 109.6MM
SALES (corp-wide): 1.3B **Publicly Held**
WEB: www.knotts.com
SIC: 2099 Syrups
PA: Cedar Fair, L.P.
1 Cedar Point Dr
Sandusky OH 44870
419 626-0830

(P-2500)
KOZY SHACK ENTERPRISES LLC
Also Called: Land O'Lakes
600 S Tegner Rd, Turlock (95380-9475)
PHONE.................................209 634-2131
EMP: 100
SALES (corp-wide): 6.8B **Privately Held**
WEB: www.kozyshack.com
SIC: 2099 Desserts, ready-to-mix; gelatin dessert preparations
HQ: Kozy Shack Enterprises, Llc
83 Ludy St
Hicksville NY 11801
516 870-3000

(P-2501)
KRAFT HEINZ FOODS COMPANY
Also Called: Kraft Foods
1500 E Walnut Ave, Fullerton (92831-4731)
PHONE.................................714 870-8235
Robert Pech, *Branch Mgr*
EMP: 500
SQ FT: 2,878
SALES (corp-wide): 26.2B **Publicly Held**
WEB: www.kraftfoods.com
SIC: 2099 Food preparations
HQ: Kraft Heinz Foods Company
1 Ppg Pl Fl 34
Pittsburgh PA 15222
412 456-5700

(P-2502)
KTS KITCHENS INC
1065 E Walnut St Ste C, Carson (90746-1384)
PHONE.................................310 764-0850
Kathleen D Taggares, *CEO*
Joan Paris, *Corp Secy*
EMP: 250
SALES (est): 62.4MM **Privately Held**
WEB: www.ktskitchens.com
SIC: 2099 2035 Pizza, refrigerated: except frozen; dressings, salad: raw & cooked (except dry mixes)

(P-2503)
LA BARCA TORTILLERIA INC
3047 Whittier Blvd, Los Angeles (90023-1651)
P.O. Box 23548 (90023-0548)
PHONE.................................323 268-1744
Jose Luis Arevalo, *CEO*
Antonio Arevalo, *President*
Al Arevalo, *Treasurer*
Alexander Arevalo, *Corp Secy*
EMP: 50
SQ FT: 6,000
SALES (est): 9.8MM **Privately Held**
SIC: 2099 Tortillas, fresh or refrigerated

(P-2504)
LA CARRETA FOOD PRODUCTS
Also Called: La Carreta Mexican Foods
302 S La Cadena Dr, Colton (92324-3420)
PHONE.................................909 825-0737
Celia Cervantes, *Owner*
EMP: 10 EST: 1945

▲ = Import ▼=Export
◆ =Import/Export

SQ FT: 2,500
SALES (est): 708K **Privately Held**
SIC: 2099 Tortillas, fresh or refrigerated

(P-2505)
LA CHAPALITA INC (PA)
1724 Chico Ave, El Monte (91733-2942)
PHONE..................................626 443-8556
Luis E Moya Jr, *President*
Claudia Moya, *Officer*
EMP: 20 **EST:** 1981
SQ FT: 15,000
SALES (est): 3.7MM **Privately Held**
WEB: www.lachapalita.com
SIC: 2099 Tortillas, fresh or refrigerated

(P-2506)
LA COLONIAL TORTILLA PDTS INC
Also Called: La Colonial Mexican Foods
543 Monterey Pass Rd, Monterey Park (91754-2416)
PHONE..................................626 289-3647
Daniel Robles, *President*
Adrian Robles, *Vice Pres*
Hector Robles, *Human Res Dir*
EMP: 185 **EST:** 1950
SQ FT: 27,000
SALES (est): 40MM **Privately Held**
WEB: www.lacolonial.com
SIC: 2099 Tortillas, fresh or refrigerated

(P-2507)
LA ESTRELLITA TIZAPAN MERCADO
Also Called: La Estrellita Market & Deli
2387 University Ave, East Palo Alto (94303-1620)
PHONE..................................650 328-0799
Hector Cornelio, *Branch Mgr*
EMP: 11
SALES (corp-wide): 2.2MM **Privately Held**
SIC: 2099 5411 5812 Tortillas, fresh or refrigerated; grocery stores, independent; Mexican restaurant
PA: La Estrellita Tizapan Mercado
2205 Middlefield Rd
Redwood City CA 94063
650 369-3877

(P-2508)
LA FORTALEZA INC
525 N Ford Blvd, Los Angeles (90022-1104)
PHONE..................................323 261-1211
Hermila Josefina Ortiz, *CEO*
David Ortiz, *Vice Pres*
Ramiro Ortiz Jr, *Vice Pres*
Mila Vargas, *Executive*
Tony Cassillia, *General Mgr*
EMP: 98
SQ FT: 40,000
SALES (est): 14.3MM **Privately Held**
WEB: www.lafortaleza.net
SIC: 2099 2096 Tortillas, fresh or refrigerated; potato chips & similar snacks

(P-2509)
LA GLORIA FOODS CORP (PA)
Also Called: La Gloria Tortilleria
3455 E 1st St, Los Angeles (90063-2945)
PHONE..................................323 262-0410
Maria De La Luz Vera, *CEO*
Luz V De La, *Agent*
▼ **EMP:** 100 **EST:** 1954
SQ FT: 8,000
SALES (est): 7MM **Privately Held**
SIC: 2099 5461 5812 Tortillas, fresh or refrigerated; bread; Mexican restaurant

(P-2510)
LA GLORIA FOODS CORP
Also Called: La Gloria Flour Tortillas
3285 E Cesar E Chavez Ave, Los Angeles (90063-2853)
PHONE..................................323 263-6755
Daniel Torrez, *Manager*
EMP: 60
SALES (corp-wide): 7MM **Privately Held**
SIC: 2099 5461 Tortillas, fresh or refrigerated; bakeries
PA: La Gloria Foods Corp.
3455 E 1st St
Los Angeles CA 90063
323 262-0410

(P-2511)
LA MANO TORTILLERIA
9529 Garvey Ave, South El Monte (91733-1015)
PHONE..................................626 350-4229
Vincente Cortez, *Owner*
EMP: 15
SQ FT: 1,755
SALES (est): 1.2MM **Privately Held**
SIC: 2099 Tortillas, fresh or refrigerated

(P-2512)
LA PRINCESITA TORTILLERIA (PA)
Also Called: Abalquiga
3432 E Cesar E Chavez Ave, Los Angeles (90063-4146)
PHONE..................................323 267-0673
Francisco Ramirez, *President*
EMP: 20
SQ FT: 2,195
SALES (est): 3.2MM **Privately Held**
SIC: 2099 Tortillas, fresh or refrigerated

(P-2513)
LA TAPATIA - NORCAL INC
23423 Cabot Blvd, Hayward (94545-1665)
PHONE..................................510 783-2045
Antonio Chavez, *President*
EMP: 150
SQ FT: 35,000
SALES (est): 16MM **Privately Held**
SIC: 2099 2096 Tortillas, fresh or refrigerated; tortilla chips

(P-2514)
LA TAPATIA TORTILLERIA INC
104 E Belmont Ave, Fresno (93701-1403)
PHONE..................................559 441-1030
Helen Chavez-Hansen, *Principal*
John Hansen, *Senior VP*
EMP: 170
SQ FT: 40,000
SALES (est): 31.4MM **Privately Held**
WEB: www.tortillas4u.com
SIC: 2099 Tortillas, fresh or refrigerated

(P-2515)
LA TERRA FINA USA INC
1300 Atlantic St, Union City (94587-2004)
PHONE..................................510 404-5888
Peter Molloy, *President*
Stephen Cottrell, *CFO*
Nalini Sudana, *Info Tech Mgr*
PHI Tran, *Financial Analy*
Scott Byrnes, *Controller*
EMP: 70
SQ FT: 24,000
SALES (est): 30.4MM **Privately Held**
SIC: 2099 Seasonings & spices

(P-2516)
LA TORTILLA FACTORY INC
3645 Standish Ave, Santa Rosa (95407-8142)
PHONE..................................707 586-4000
Carlos Tamayo, *President*
Sheryl Garcia, *Purch Mgr*
Nathan Wilson, *QC Mgr*
Lito De Guzman, *Maint Spvr*
EMP: 47
SALES (corp-wide): 157.8MM **Privately Held**
WEB: www.latortillafactory.com
SIC: 2099 Tortillas, fresh or refrigerated
PA: La Tortilla Factory Inc.
3300 Westwind Blvd
Santa Rosa CA 95403
707 586-4000

(P-2517)
LAM ENTERPRISES INC
824 S Center St, Stockton (95206-1308)
P.O. Box 640, MI Wuk Village (95346-0640)
PHONE..................................209 586-2217
Glenn Miller, *President*
Lucia Miller, *Corp Secy*
EMP: 10 **EST:** 1982
SQ FT: 30,000
SALES (est): 1.2MM **Privately Held**
SIC: 2099 5149 Spices, including grinding; spices & seasonings

(P-2518)
LAMORENITA TORTILLERA & MT MKT
1876 Fremont Blvd, Seaside (93955-3611)
PHONE..................................831 394-3770
Juventino Ibarra Magana, *Partner*
Antonio Moreno, *Partner*
EMP: 17
SALES (est): 2.1MM **Privately Held**
SIC: 2099 Tortillas, fresh or refrigerated

(P-2519)
LANTY INC
9660 Flair Dr, El Monte (91731-3017)
PHONE..................................626 582-8001
Dongmei LI, *CEO*
EMP: 181
SALES (est): 4.2MM **Privately Held**
SIC: 2099 Vegetables, peeled for the trade

(P-2520)
LAPERLA SPICE CO INC
Also Called: Laperla Del Mayab
555 N Fairview St, Santa Ana (92703-1806)
PHONE..................................714 543-5533
Wilbert Marrufo, *President*
EMP: 10
SQ FT: 5,000
SALES (est): 1MM **Privately Held**
WEB: www.delmayab.com
SIC: 2099 5149 Spices, including grinding; spices & seasonings

(P-2521)
LAROSA TORTILLA FACTORY
26 Menker St, Watsonville (95076-4915)
PHONE..................................831 728-5332
Alfonso Solorio, *Owner*
EMP: 98 **Privately Held**
WEB: www.larosatortillafactory.com
SIC: 2099 Tortillas, fresh or refrigerated
PA: Larosa Tortilla Factory
142 2nd St
Watsonville CA 95076
-

(P-2522)
LASELVA BEACH SPICE CO INC
453 Mcquaide Dr, Watsonville (95076-1908)
PHONE..................................831 724-4500
Floyd W Brady, *CEO*
EMP: 18
SALES (est): 2.5MM **Privately Held**
SIC: 2099 Seasonings & spices

(P-2523)
LASSONDE PAPPAS AND CO INC
1755 E Acacia St, Ontario (91761-7702)
PHONE..................................909 923-4041
Rick Jochums, *Manager*
EMP: 85
SALES (corp-wide): 402MM **Privately Held**
WEB: www.clementpappas.com
SIC: 2099 Food preparations
HQ: Lassonde Pappas And Company, Inc.
1 Collins Dr Ste 200
Carneys Point NJ 08069
856 455-1000

(P-2524)
LAURENT CULINARY SERVICE
Also Called: Jessie A Laurent
1945 Francisco Blvd E # 44, San Rafael (94901-5525)
PHONE..................................415 485-1122
Jessie Laurent Boucher, *Partner*
EMP: 13
SALES (est): 1.5MM **Privately Held**
SIC: 2099 5812 Ready-to-eat meals, salads & sandwiches; eating places

(P-2525)
LEE KUM KEE (USA) FOODS INC
14455 Don Julian Rd, City of Industry (91746-3102)
PHONE..................................626 709-1888
Simon Wu, *President*
Alan Lui, *CFO*
Dickson Chan, *Treasurer*
Ken Low, *Info Tech Mgr*
Johnny Mark, *Manager*

EMP: 99
SQ FT: 54,000
SALES (est): 3.6MM **Privately Held**
SIC: 2099 Sauces: gravy, dressing & dip mixes

(P-2526)
LEHMAN FOODS INC
Also Called: Fresh & Ready
1145 Arroyo St Ste B, San Fernando (91340-1842)
PHONE..................................818 837-7600
Charles Lehman, *CEO*
Art Sezgin, *President*
Harry Iknadosian, *Vice Pres*
Grace Sun, *Mktg Coord*
Cameron Childs, *Director*
EMP: 25
SQ FT: 15,000
SALES (est): 9.7MM **Privately Held**
WEB: www.freshandreadyfoods.com
SIC: 2099 Salads, fresh or refrigerated; sandwiches, assembled & packaged: for wholesale market

(P-2527)
LEQUIOS JAPAN CO LTD
14241 Firestone Blvd, La Mirada (90638-5530)
PHONE..................................410 629-8694
Ichiro Miyamoto, *CEO*
EMP: 12
SALES (est): 524.6K **Privately Held**
SIC: 2099 Food preparations

(P-2528)
LETS DO LUNCH
Also Called: Integrated Food Service
310 W Alondra Blvd, Gardena (90248-2423)
PHONE..................................310 523-3664
Paul G Giuliano, *President*
Jon Sugimoto, *Vice Pres*
David Watzke, *Director*
Pisey Kor, *Manager*
▲ **EMP:** 80
SQ FT: 57,000
SALES (est): 32MM **Privately Held**
WEB: www.integratedfoodservice.com
SIC: 2099 Sandwiches, assembled & packaged: for wholesale market

(P-2529)
LILLY TORTILLERIA
4271 University Ave, San Diego (92105-1536)
PHONE..................................619 281-2890
Delia Amezquita, *Owner*
EMP: 24
SALES (est): 2.4MM **Privately Held**
SIC: 2099 5411 Tortillas, fresh or refrigerated; grocery stores

(P-2530)
LIVING TREE COMMUNITY FOODS
1455 5th St, Berkeley (94710-1337)
P.O. Box 10082 (94709-5082)
PHONE..................................510 526-7106
Jesse Schwartz, *Owner*
EMP: 20
SQ FT: 600
SALES (est): 2.5MM **Privately Held**
WEB: www.livingtreecommunity.com
SIC: 2099 Food preparations

(P-2531)
LIVING WELLNESS PARTNERS LLC (PA)
Also Called: Buddha Teas
3305 Tyler St, Carlsbad (92008-3056)
PHONE..................................800 642-3754
John Boyd, *CEO*
Nicholas Narier,
Matt Deberry, *Manager*
EMP: 30
SQ FT: 10,000
SALES (est): 1MM **Privately Held**
SIC: 2099 Tea blending

(P-2532)
LOS PERICOS FOOD PRODUCTS LLC
2301 Valley Blvd, Pomona (91768-1105)
PHONE..................................909 623-5625

Marcelino Ortega, *Partner*
Guadalupe Ortega, *Partner*
Luis Ortega, *Partner*
EMP: 46
SQ FT: 20,000
SALES (est): 6.8MM **Privately Held**
WEB: www.lospericosfood.com
SIC: 2099 Tortillas, fresh or refrigerated

(P-2533)
LOUIE FOODS INTERNATIONAL
471 S Teilman Ave, Fresno (93706-1315)
PHONE..........................559 264-2745
Jay Louie, *President*
Stephanie Louie, *Admin Sec*
EMP: 15
SALES: 835K **Privately Held**
SIC: 2099 0182 5199 Noodles, fried (Chinese); tofu, except frozen desserts; bean sprouts grown under cover; packaging materials

(P-2534)
LUCERNE FOODS INC
5918 Stoneridge Mall Rd, Pleasanton (94588-3229)
PHONE..........................925 951-4724
Kenneth Gott, *President*
Peggy Han, *Senior VP*
▼ **EMP:** 40
SALES (est): 5.9MM
SALES (corp-wide): 60.5B **Privately Held**
SIC: 2099 Food preparations
HQ: Safeway Inc.
    5918 Stoneridge Mall Rd
    Pleasanton CA 94588
    925 226-5000

(P-2535)
LYRICAL FOODS INC
Also Called: Kite Hill
3180 Corporate Pl, Hayward (94545-3916)
PHONE..........................510 784-0955
John Haugen, *CEO*
Jean Prebot, *COO*
Jean Prevot, *COO*
David Bauer, *Vice Pres*
John Murphy, *Vice Pres*
▲ **EMP:** 108 **EST:** 2012
SQ FT: 20,000
SALES (est): 19.8MM **Privately Held**
SIC: 2099 Food preparations

(P-2536)
M C I FOODS INC
Also Called: Los Cabos Mexican Foods
13013 Molette St, Santa Fe Springs (90670-5521)
PHONE..........................562 977-4000
Alberta Southard, *Ch of Bd*
Daniel Southard, *President*
John M Southard, *Vice Pres*
Cathy Wong, *Research*
Manuel Avelar, *Business Mgr*
EMP: 140 **EST:** 1970
SQ FT: 15,000
SALES (est): 31.7MM **Privately Held**
WEB: www.mcifoods.com
SIC: 2099 Food preparations

(P-2537)
M R S FOODS INC (PA)
Also Called: La Rancherita Tortilla
4408 W 5th St, Santa Ana (92703-3224)
PHONE..........................714 554-2791
Laura Perez, *President*
Roxana Perez, *Treasurer*
Shirley Serna, *Admin Sec*
▲ **EMP:** 40
SQ FT: 4,000
SALES (est): 4.6MM **Privately Held**
SIC: 2099 5812 Tortillas, fresh or refrigerated; fast-food restaurant, independent

(P-2538)
MAMMA LINAS INCORPORATED
Also Called: Mamma Lina Ravioli Co
10741 Roselle St, San Diego (92121-1507)
PHONE..........................858 535-0620
Checchino Massullo, *Ch of Bd*
Emily Massullo, *CEO*
Lina Massullo, *Director*
EMP: 14
SALES: 1MM **Privately Held**
SIC: 2099 Pasta, uncooked: packaged with other ingredients

(P-2539)
MAN FON INC
421 S California St Ste C, San Gabriel (91762-2528)
PHONE..........................626 287-6043
Jimmy Chang, *President*
▲ **EMP:** 11
SQ FT: 1,500
SALES (est): 1.5MM **Privately Held**
WEB: www.manfon.com
SIC: 2099 Food preparations

(P-2540)
MAPLEGROVE GLUTEN FREE FOODS
5010 Eucalyptus Ave, Chino (91710-9216)
PHONE..........................909 334-7828
Raj Sukul, *President*
EMP: 37
SALES (est): 7MM **Privately Held**
SIC: 2099 Food preparations

(P-2541)
MARINPAK
Also Called: MPK Sonoma
21684 8th St E Ste 100, Sonoma (95476-2816)
PHONE..........................707 996-3931
Fax: 707 996-3999
▲ **EMP:** 14
SQ FT: 23,000
SALES (est): 1.1MM **Privately Held**
WEB: www.mpksonoma.com
SIC: 2099

(P-2542)
MARS FOOD US LLC (HQ)
2001 E Cashdan St Ste 201, Rancho Dominguez (90220-6438)
PHONE..........................310 933-0670
Vincent Howell, *Mng Member*
Stephanie Oliver, *Manager*
◆ **EMP:** 500
SALES (est): 131.2MM
SALES (corp-wide): 37.6B **Privately Held**
WEB: www.kalkan.com
SIC: 2099 Food preparations
PA: Mars, Incorporated
    6885 Elm St Ste 1
    Mc Lean VA 22101
    703 821-4900

(P-2543)
MARUCHAN INC (HQ)
15800 Laguna Canyon Rd, Irvine (92618-3103)
PHONE..........................949 789-2300
Noritaka Sumimoto, *CEO*
Sarah Otaki, *Administration*
Mark Horikawa, *Telecom Exec*
Takashi Ueno, *Info Tech Dir*
Gary Leeper, *Info Tech Mgr*
◆ **EMP:** 450
SQ FT: 300,000
SALES (est): 243MM **Privately Held**
WEB: www.maruchaninc.com
SIC: 2099 Food preparations

(P-2544)
MARUKAN VINEGAR U S A INC (HQ)
16203 Vermont Ave, Paramount (90723-5042)
PHONE..........................562 630-6060
Yasuo Sasada, *Ch of Bd*
Toshio Takeuchi, *President*
Denzaemon Sasada, *CEO*
Yoshi Tsumura, *CFO*
Junichi Oyama, *Exec VP*
◆ **EMP:** 105
SQ FT: 20,000
SALES (est): 21.6MM **Privately Held**
WEB: www.marukan-usa.com
SIC: 2099 Vinegar

(P-2545)
MARUKOME USA INC
17132 Pullman St, Irvine (92614-5524)
PHONE..........................949 863-0110
Shigeru Shirasaka, *President*
Toshio Abe, *Corp Secy*
Yuji Teranishi, *Sales Mgr*
Kazuhiko Fushimi, *Marketing Staff*
Sang Kim, *Sales Staff*
▲ **EMP:** 17

SQ FT: 134,172
SALES (est): 4.4MM **Privately Held**
WEB: www.marukomeusa.com
SIC: 2099 Seasonings & spices
PA: Marukome Co.,Ltd.
    883, Amori
    Nagano NAG 380-0

(P-2546)
MCCORMICK & COMPANY INC
180 N Riverview Dr, Anaheim (92808-1241)
PHONE..........................714 685-0934
EMP: 95
SALES (corp-wide): 5.4B **Publicly Held**
SIC: 2099 Spices, including grinding
PA: Mccormick & Company Incorporated
    24 Schilling Rd Ste 1
    Hunt Valley MD 21031
    410 771-7301

(P-2547)
MCCORMICK & COMPANY INC
340 El Cam Ste 20, Salinas (93901)
PHONE..........................831 775-3350
David Sasaki, *Branch Mgr*
EMP: 69
SALES (corp-wide): 5.4B **Publicly Held**
WEB: www.mccormick.com
SIC: 2099 Spices, including grinding
PA: Mccormick & Company Incorporated
    24 Schilling Rd Ste 1
    Hunt Valley MD 21031
    410 771-7301

(P-2548)
MCCORMICK & COMPANY INC
340 El Camino Real S # 20, Salinas (93901-4553)
P.O. Box 81311 (93912)
PHONE..........................831 758-2411
Fax: 831 755-0230
EMP: 200
SALES (corp-wide): 4.2B **Publicly Held**
SIC: 2099
PA: Mccormick & Company Incorporated
    18 Loveton Cir
    Sparks MD 21031
    410 771-7301

(P-2549)
MCCORMICK FRESH HERBS LLC
1575 W Walnut Pkwy, Compton (90220-5022)
PHONE..........................323 278-9750
EMP: 75
SALES (est): 5.8MM
SALES (corp-wide): 4.2B **Publicly Held**
SIC: 2099
PA: Mccormick & Company Incorporated
    18 Loveton Cir
    Sparks MD 21031
    410 771-7301

(P-2550)
MI RANCHO TORTILLA INC
801 Purvis Ave, Clovis (93612-2892)
PHONE..........................559 299-3183
Criss K Cruz, *CEO*
Dorothy Cruz, *President*
EMP: 56
SQ FT: 6,000
SALES (est): 11.4MM **Privately Held**
SIC: 2099 Tortillas, fresh or refrigerated

(P-2551)
MILLERS AMERICAN HONEY INC
Also Called: Superior Honey Company
1455 Riverview Dr, San Bernardino (92408-2931)
P.O. Box 500, Colton (92324-0500)
PHONE..........................909 825-1722
George T Murdock, *CEO*
Steve Smith, *Vice Pres*
◆ **EMP:** 34
SQ FT: 33,000
SALES (est): 5.6MM **Privately Held**
WEB: www.millershoney.com
SIC: 2099 Honey, strained & bottled

(P-2552)
MINSLEY INC
989 S Monterey Ave, Ontario (91761-3463)
PHONE..........................909 458-1100
Song Tae Jin, *CEO*
Jeff Kim, *General Mgr*
Brian Jung, *Manager*
▲ **EMP:** 40
SQ FT: 42,000
SALES (est): 8.2MM **Privately Held**
WEB: www.minsley.com
SIC: 2099 Packaged combination products: pasta, rice & potato

(P-2553)
MIZKAN AMERICAS INC
46 Walker St, Watsonville (95076-4925)
PHONE..........................831 728-2061
David Shields, *Manager*
Kevin Culver, *Vice Pres*
EMP: 15 **Privately Held**
SIC: 2099 Vinegar
HQ: Mizkan America, Inc.
    1661 Feehanville Dr # 200
    Mount Prospect IL 60056
    847 590-0059

(P-2554)
MIZKAN AMERICAS INC
Also Called: Indian Summer
10037 8th St, Rancho Cucamonga (91730-5210)
PHONE..........................909 484-8743
Pete Marsing, *Branch Mgr*
EMP: 45
SQ FT: 58,500 **Privately Held**
SIC: 2099 Vinegar
HQ: Mizkan America, Inc.
    1661 Feehanville Dr # 200
    Mount Prospect IL 60056
    847 590-0059

(P-2555)
MOJAVE FOODS CORPORATION
6200 E Slauson Ave, Commerce (90040-3012)
PHONE..........................323 890-8900
Richard D Lipka, *CEO*
Craig M Berger, *CFO*
◆ **EMP:** 200
SQ FT: 110,000
SALES (est): 43.2MM
SALES (corp-wide): 5.4B **Publicly Held**
WEB: www.mccormick.com
SIC: 2099 Butter, renovated & processed
PA: Mccormick & Company Incorporated
    24 Schilling Rd Ste 1
    Hunt Valley MD 21031
    410 771-7301

(P-2556)
MOORE FARMS INC
916 S Derby St, Arvin (93203-2312)
P.O. Box 698 (93203-0698)
PHONE..........................661 854-5588
John Moore, *President*
EMP: 15
SQ FT: 2,000
SALES: 970K **Privately Held**
SIC: 2099 0134 Potatoes, peeled for the trade; Irish potatoes

(P-2557)
MORINAGA NUTRITIONAL FOODS INC
3838 Del Amo Blvd Ste 201, Torrance (90503-7709)
P.O. Box 7969 (90504-9369)
PHONE..........................310 787-0200
Hiroyuki Imanishi, *President*
Tetsuhisa Tato, *Vice Pres*
Susan Buch R, *Mktg Dir*
▼ **EMP:** 19
SQ FT: 2,782
SALES (est): 4.3MM **Privately Held**
WEB: www.morinu.com
SIC: 2099 Food preparations
PA: Morinaga Milk Industry Co., Ltd.
    5-33-1, Shiba
    Minato-Ku TKY 108-0

(P-2558)
MORRIS KITCHEN INC
2525 Kenilworth Ave, Los Angeles
(90039-2637)
PHONE..................................646 413-5186
Kari Morris, *Owner*
EMP: 14
SALES (est): 1.9MM **Privately Held**
SIC: 2099 2032 2033 Food preparations;
chicken soup: packaged in cans, jars,
etc.; tomato products: packaged in cans,
jars, etc.

(P-2559)
MR TORTILLA INC
1112 Arroyo St, San Fernando
(91340-1850)
PHONE..................................818 307-7414
Douglas Brown, *CEO*
Tony Alcazar, *CEO*
Ronald Alcazar, *Opers Staff*
EMP: 14
SALES (est): 2MM **Privately Held**
SIC: 2099 Tortillas, fresh or refrigerated

(P-2560)
NANCYS SPECIALTY FOODS
2400 Olympic Blvd Ste 8, Walnut Creek
(94595-1500)
PHONE..................................510 494-1100
Adam Ferrif, *COO*
Nancy S Mueller, *President*
R Larry Booth, *Vice Pres*
David M Joiner, *Vice Pres*
EMP: 375
SQ FT: 86,000
SALES (est): 32.4MM
SALES (corp-wide): 26.2B **Publicly Held**
SIC: 2099 Food preparations
HQ: Kraft Heinz Foods Company
1 Ppg Pl Fl 34
Pittsburgh PA 15222
412 456-5700

(P-2561)
NANCYS TORTILLERIA & MINI MKT
348 S Towne Ave, Pomona (91766-2036)
PHONE..................................909 629-5889
Jose Vergara, *Owner*
Teresa Vergara, *Owner*
EMP: 34
SQ FT: 6,000
SALES (est): 3.2MM **Privately Held**
SIC: 2099 Tortillas, fresh or refrigerated

(P-2562)
NAPA VALLEY KITCHENS INC
Also Called: Consorzio
1610 5th St, Berkeley (94710-1715)
PHONE..................................510 558-7500
John Foraker, *CEO*
Sarah Bird, *Vice Pres*
Stephen Palmer, *Admin Sec*
EMP: 75
SQ FT: 10,000
SALES: 10MM
SALES (corp-wide): 16.8B **Publicly Held**
WEB: www.annies.com
SIC: 2099 Vinegar
HQ: Annie's, Inc.
1610 5th St
Berkeley CA 94710

(P-2563)
NATIONAL STABILIZERS INC
611 S Duggan Ave, Azusa (91702-5139)
PHONE..................................626 969-5700
Lorraine Mancilla, *Administration*
Robert Burger, *President*
EMP: 10 **EST:** 1975
SQ FT: 7,000
SALES (est): 1.3MM **Privately Held**
SIC: 2099 Food preparations

(P-2564)
NATREN INC
3105 Willow Ln, Thousand Oaks
(91361-4919)
PHONE..................................805 371-4737
Yordan Trenev, *CEO*
Natasha Trenev, *President*
Carol Green, *Executive Asst*
Odessa Braza, *Admin Sec*
Michael Chapovsky, *Info Tech Dir*

EMP: 60
SQ FT: 22,000
SALES (est): 12.3MM **Privately Held**
SIC: 2099 8011 Food preparations; offices
& clinics of medical doctors

(P-2565)
NECTAVE INC
6700 Caballero Blvd, Buena Park
(90620-1134)
PHONE..................................714 393-0144
Richard Ellinghausen, *President*
Annalisa Chavez, *CFO*
EMP: 15 **EST:** 2011
SQ FT: 30,000
SALES (est): 693.4K **Privately Held**
SIC: 2099 Sorghum syrups: for sweetening

(P-2566)
NEW GLOBAL FOOD
13577 Larwin Cir, Santa Fe Springs
(90670-5032)
PHONE..................................562 404-9953
Duk Kiml, *Principal*
EMP: 12
SALES (est): 1.3MM **Privately Held**
SIC: 2099 Food preparations

(P-2567)
NEW HORIZON FOODS INC
33440 Western Ave, Union City
(94587-3202)
PHONE..................................510 489-8600
Kenneth L Crawford, *President*
Elieser Pedroza, *Prdtn Mgr*
Harry Dizon, *QC Mgr*
EMP: 20
SQ FT: 20,000
SALES (est): 3.9MM
SALES (corp-wide): 14.4MM **Privately Held**
SIC: 2099 Food preparations
PA: Tova Industries, Llc
2902 Blankenbaker Rd
Louisville KY 40299
502 267-7333

(P-2568)
NEWLY WEDS FOODS INC
Also Called: Heller Seasoning
437 S Mcclure Rd, Modesto (95357-0519)
PHONE..................................209 491-7777
Allen Holzmen, *Manager*
Alan Holzman, *Plant Mgr*
Sonya Wong, *Sales Dir*
Dave Best, *Maintence Staff*
EMP: 50
SALES (corp-wide): 128.2MM **Privately Held**
WEB: www.newlywedsfoods.com
SIC: 2099 Spices, including grinding
PA: Newly Weds Foods, Inc.
4140 W Fullerton Ave
Chicago IL 60639
773 489-7000

(P-2569)
NINA MIA INC
Also Called: Pasta Mia
826 Enterprise Way, Fullerton
(92831-5015)
PHONE..................................714 773-5588
Diego Mazza, *President*
Jessica Mazza, *Vice Pres*
▲ **EMP:** 80
SQ FT: 32,000
SALES (est): 17.8MM **Privately Held**
WEB: www.pastamiacorp.com
SIC: 2099 Pasta, uncooked: packaged with
other ingredients

(P-2570)
NINAS MEXICAN FOODS INC
20631 Valley Blvd Ste A, Walnut
(91789-2751)
PHONE..................................909 468-5888
Ruben Vasquez, *President*
▲ **EMP:** 40
SQ FT: 14,000
SALES (est): 12.3MM **Privately Held**
SIC: 2099 Tortillas, fresh or refrigerated

(P-2571)
NIPPON TRENDS FOOD SERVICE INC
Also Called: Yamachan Ramen
631 Giguere Ct Ste A1, San Jose
(95133-1745)
PHONE..................................408 214-0511
Hideyuki Yamashita, *President*
Tomoko Yamashita, *Vice Pres*
▲ **EMP:** 60
SQ FT: 5,000
SALES (est): 3MM **Privately Held**
SIC: 2099 Noodles, uncooked: packaged
with other ingredients

(P-2572)
NUTIVA
213 W Cutting Blvd, Richmond
(94804-2015)
PHONE..................................510 255-2700
John Roulac, *CEO*
Pam Zahedani, *Executive Asst*
Caroline Hersom, *Planning*
Dave Ringot, *Info Tech Mgr*
Felipe Torres, *Prdtn Mgr*
◆ **EMP:** 91
SQ FT: 1,300
SALES (est): 26.3MM **Privately Held**
SIC: 2099 Vegetables, peeled for the trade

(P-2573)
NYDR HOLDINGS INC
Also Called: Genesis Natural Products
9525 Cozycroft Ave Ste M, Chatsworth
(91311-0712)
PHONE..................................818 626-8174
Helena Belmes, *CEO*
Eli Belmes, *Vice Pres*
▲ **EMP:** 10
SQ FT: 10,000
SALES: 5MM **Privately Held**
SIC: 2099 Food preparations

(P-2574)
OASIS DATE GARDEN INC
59111 Grapefruit Blvd, Thermal
(92274-8813)
P.O. Box 757 (92274-0757)
PHONE..................................760 399-5665
James Freimuth, *President*
Dana Emery, *Vice Pres*
Chris Nelsen, *Vice Pres*
Maribel Aguilar, *Personnel*
▲ **EMP:** 45
SQ FT: 14,000
SALES (est): 11.1MM **Privately Held**
WEB: www.oasisdategardens.com
SIC: 2099 5431 5148 0179 Food prepa-
rations; fruit stands or markets; fruits;
date orchard

(P-2575)
OLD PUEBLO RANCH INC
Also Called: La Reina
316 N Ford Blvd, Los Angeles
(90022-1121)
PHONE..................................323 268-2791
Mauro Robles, *Vice Pres*
Ricardo Robles, *President*
Marisela Robles, *Admin Sec*
EMP: 150 **EST:** 1958
SQ FT: 90,000
SALES (est): 47.7MM **Privately Held**
WEB: www.lareinainc.com
SIC: 2099 Tortillas, fresh or refrigerated

(P-2576)
OOGLOW
17250 Margaret Dr, Jamestown
(95327-9746)
PHONE..................................530 899-9927
Michael J Epperson, *President*
Michael Epperson, *President*
EMP: 13
SALES (est): 1.5MM **Privately Held**
SIC: 2099 Food preparations

(P-2577)
ORGANIC SPICES (PA)
4180 Business Center Dr, Fremont
(94538-6354)
PHONE..................................510 440-1044
Clara Bonner, *CEO*
Bijan Chansari, *CFO*
Marina Gonzales, *Opers Staff*
Jimmy Evans, *Account Dir*

Al Sandoval, *Accounts Exec*
▲ **EMP:** 30
SQ FT: 27,000
SALES (est): 3.5MM **Privately Held**
SIC: 2099 Chicory root, dried

(P-2578)
ORGANICGIRL LLC
900 Work St, Salinas (93901-4386)
P.O. Box 5999 (93915-5999)
PHONE..................................831 758-7800
Mark Drever,
Juan Cardenas, *CFO*
Tom Browning, *Vice Pres*
Steve Taylor,
Julie Vanacker, *Director*
EMP: 650
SQ FT: 125,000
SALES (est): 228.8MM **Privately Held**
SIC: 2099 5148 Ready-to-eat meals, sal-
ads & sandwiches; fresh fruits & vegeta-
bles

(P-2579)
OTSUKA AMERICA FOODS INC (HQ)
1 Embarcadero Ctr # 2020, San Francisco
(94111-3750)
PHONE..................................424 219-9425
Bradley Paris, *President*
Osamu Aizawa, *CFO*
EMP: 10
SQ FT: 5,000
SALES (est): 1MM **Privately Held**
SIC: 2099 Food preparations

(P-2580)
PACIFIC SPICE COMPANY INC
Also Called: Pacific Natural Spices
6430 E Slauson Ave, Commerce
(90040-3108)
PHONE..................................323 726-9190
Gershon D Schlussel, *CEO*
Akiba E Schlussel, *President*
Sharon Schlussel, *Admin Sec*
Jason Yasumi, *Technical Mgr*
Dahlia Bristol, *Finance Mgr*
◆ **EMP:** 82 **EST:** 1966
SQ FT: 150,000
SALES (est): 23.4MM **Privately Held**
WEB: www.pacspice.com
SIC: 2099 5149 Spices, including grinding;
spices & seasonings

(P-2581)
PAPPYS MEAT COMPANY INC
Also Called: Pappy's Fine Foods
5663 E Fountain Way, Fresno
(93727-7813)
P.O. Box 5257 (93755-5257)
PHONE..................................559 291-0218
Marie Papulias, *President*
Edward Papulias, *CEO*
Patricia Papulias, *Corp Secy*
EMP: 23
SQ FT: 10,000
SALES (est): 3.4MM **Privately Held**
WEB: www.pappyschoice.com
SIC: 2099 Seasonings & spices; season-
ings: dry mixes

(P-2582)
PASSPORT FOOD GROUP LLC (PA)
Also Called: Wing Hing Noodle Company
2539 E Philadelphia St, Ontario
(91761-7774)
PHONE..................................909 627-7312
▲ **EMP:** 150
SQ FT: 103,000
SALES (est): 41.7MM **Privately Held**
WEB: www.winghing.com
SIC: 2099 Packaged combination prod-
ucts: pasta, rice & potato

(P-2583)
PEARL CROP INC
Also Called: Linden Nut
8452 Demartini Ln, Linden (95236-9446)
PHONE..................................209 887-3731
Halil Ulas Turkhan, *President*
EMP: 50
SALES (corp-wide): 140MM **Privately Held**
SIC: 2099 2068 Food preparations; salted
& roasted nuts & seeds

PRODUCTS & SVCS

PA: Pearl Crop, Inc.
1550 Industrial Dr
Stockton CA 95206
209 808-7575

(P-2584)
PETIT POT INC
4221 Horton St, Emeryville (94608-3533)
PHONE..................650 488-7432
Maxime Pouvreau, CEO
Anne Lesgourgues, Director
EMP: 20
SQ FT: 20,000
SALES (est): 1.2MM **Privately Held**
SIC: 2099 Dessert mixes & fillings

(P-2585)
PGP INTERNATIONAL INC (DH)
351 Hanson Way, Woodland (95776-6224)
P.O. Box 2060 (95776-2060)
PHONE..................530 662-5056
Nicolas J Hanson, CEO
Carmen Sciackitano, Admin Sec
Rebecca Bolton, Controller
◆ **EMP:** 180
SALES (est): 70.3MM
SALES (corp-wide): 19.8B **Privately Held**
WEB: www.protient.com
SIC: 2099 Almond pastes

(P-2586)
PHAT N JICY BURGERS BRANDS LLC
Also Called: Phat N Juicy Brands
25876 The Old Rd 305, Stevenson Ranch (91381-1711)
PHONE..................310 420-7983
Christopher Champion,
Kenya Champion,
EMP: 30
SALES (est): 2.7MM **Privately Held**
SIC: 2099 Food preparations

(P-2587)
PRE-PEELED POTATO CO INC
1585 S Union St, Stockton (95206-2269)
P.O. Box 111 (95201-0111)
PHONE..................209 469-6911
Bart Birt, President
EMP: 19
SQ FT: 10,000
SALES: 3MM **Privately Held**
SIC: 2099 Potatoes, peeled for the trade; vegetables, peeled for the trade

(P-2588)
PRESTIGE CHINESE TEAS CO
Also Called: P C Teas
882 Mahler Rd, Burlingame (94010-1604)
PHONE..................650 697-8989
Sunny Wong, Owner
▲ **EMP:** 10
SQ FT: 3,300
SALES (est): 670K **Privately Held**
SIC: 2099 5149 5499 Tea blending; tea; spices & herbs

(P-2589)
PRO FOOD INC
19431 Bus Center Dr # 35, Northridge (91324-3507)
PHONE..................818 341-4040
Laurent Caraco, President
EMP: 10
SQ FT: 3,000
SALES: 1MM **Privately Held**
SIC: 2099 Food preparations

(P-2590)
PRODUCE WORLD INC
30611 San Antonio St, Hayward (94544-7103)
PHONE..................510 441-1449
Joseph Fereira, President
Dennis Dahlin, Vice Pres
EMP: 75
SQ FT: 20,000
SALES (est): 11.3MM **Privately Held**
SIC: 2099 Vegetables, peeled for the trade

(P-2591)
PSW INC
Also Called: Taste Nirvana International
149 Via Trevizio, Corona (92879-1773)
PHONE..................951 371-7100
Jack Wattanaporn, President

▲ **EMP:** 15
SQ FT: 23,667
SALES (est): 2.4MM **Privately Held**
WEB: www.psw.com
SIC: 2099 2095 5141 Tea blending; roasted coffee; groceries, general line

(P-2592)
PULMUONE WILDWOOD INC
5755 Rossi Ln, Gilroy (95020-7063)
PHONE..................714 361-0806
▲ **EMP:** 12
SALES (est): 2.1MM **Privately Held**
SIC: 2099 Food preparations

(P-2593)
QST INGREDIENTS AND PACKG INC
9734-40 6th St Rch, Rancho Cucamonga (91730)
PHONE..................909 989-4343
Chris Topps, President
Ramon Castillo, Director
▲ **EMP:** 15
SALES (est): 4.4MM **Privately Held**
SIC: 2099 5046 Seasonings & spices; commercial cooking & food service equipment

(P-2594)
QUEST NUTRITION LLC
2221 Park Pl, El Segundo (90245-4909)
PHONE..................562 446-3321
EMP: 28
SALES (est): 10MM **Privately Held**
SIC: 2099

(P-2595)
RAMA FOOD MANUFACTURE CORP (PA)
1486 E Cedar St, Ontario (91761-8300)
P.O. Box 4045 (91761-1002)
PHONE..................909 923-5305
Karen Trang Ving, CEO
▲ **EMP:** 40
SQ FT: 25,000
SALES (est): 5.8MM **Privately Held**
SIC: 2099 Noodles, fried (Chinese)

(P-2596)
READY PAC FOODS INC (HQ)
4401 Foxdale St, Irwindale (91706-2161)
PHONE..................626 856-8686
Mary Thompson, CEO
Dan Redfern, CFO
Scott Wilkerson, Vice Pres
Oscar Antunez, Technology
Kellie Dubois, Sales Staff
◆ **EMP:** 2000
SQ FT: 135,000
SALES (est): 973.1MM
SALES (corp-wide): 2.6MM **Privately Held**
SIC: 2099 5148 Salads, fresh or refrigerated; vegetables, fresh
PA: Bonduelle
Rue De La Woestyne
Renescure 59173
328 498-280

(P-2597)
RELS FOODS INC (PA)
1814 Franklin St Ste 310, Oakland (94612-3426)
P.O. Box 22851 (94609-5851)
PHONE..................510 652-2747
P Scott Sorensen, CEO
Soren Peder Sorensen, President
Peder Scott Sorensen, Treasurer
Dick Welch, Principal
EMP: 72
SQ FT: 4,000
SALES (est): 11MM **Privately Held**
WEB: www.relsfoods.com
SIC: 2099 5142 Sandwiches, assembled & packaged: for wholesale market; packaged frozen goods

(P-2598)
RENAISSANCE FOOD GROUP LLC (HQ)
Also Called: Garden Highway
11020 White Rock Rd Ste 1, Rancho Cordova (95670-6402)
PHONE..................916 638-8825

James S Catchot, President
Donald Ochoa, President
Jim Gibson, COO
Ken Catchot, CFO
Mark Lodge, Exec VP
▲ **EMP:** 48
SQ FT: 12,000
SALES (est): 92.2MM
SALES (corp-wide): 1B **Publicly Held**
SIC: 2099 Salads, fresh or refrigerated
PA: Calavo Growers, Inc.
1141 Cummings Rd Ste A
Santa Paula CA 93060
805 525-1245

(P-2599)
RISVOLDS INC
1234 W El Segundo Blvd, Gardena (90247-1593)
PHONE..................323 770-2674
Tim Brandon, CEO
Ed Scoullar, President
Jenifer Peterson, Purch Mgr
EMP: 65
SQ FT: 30,000
SALES: 12MM **Privately Held**
WEB: www.risvolds.com
SIC: 2099 Salads, fresh or refrigerated

(P-2600)
RITAS FINE FOOD
Also Called: Da Vinci Fine Food
8900 Grossmont Blvd Ste 5, La Mesa (91941-4047)
PHONE..................619 698-3925
Faris Auro, President
Basma Shammas, Vice Pres
Raad Shammas, Vice Pres
EMP: 12
SQ FT: 2,100
SALES: 650K **Privately Held**
SIC: 2099 Salads, fresh or refrigerated; sandwiches, assembled & packaged: for wholesale market

(P-2601)
ROBEKS CORPORATION
Also Called: Robeks Juice
8905 S Sepulveda Blvd, Los Angeles (90045-3603)
PHONE..................310 642-7800
Antje Frei, Manager
EMP: 15 **Privately Held**
SIC: 2099 5812 Ready-to-eat meals, salads & sandwiches; soft drink stand
PA: Robeks Corporation
5220 Pacific Concourse Dr
Los Angeles CA 90045

(P-2602)
ROBLES BROS INC (PA)
Also Called: La Colonial
1700 Rogers Ave, San Jose (95112-1107)
PHONE..................408 436-5551
George Robles, President
Claudia Robles, Corp Secy
Hector Robles, Vice Pres
EMP: 35
SQ FT: 7,000
SALES (est): 5.3MM **Privately Held**
SIC: 2099 Tortillas, fresh or refrigerated

(P-2603)
ROMEROS FOOD PRODUCTS INC (PA)
15155 Valley View Ave, Santa Fe Springs (90670-5323)
PHONE..................562 802-1858
Richard Scandalito, CEO
Leon Romero Sr, President
Leon S Romero, CEO
Raul Romero Sr, Vice Pres
Al Valcarcel, Opers Mgr
EMP: 100 **EST:** 1971
SQ FT: 20,000
SALES: 28MM **Privately Held**
WEB: www.romerosfood.com
SIC: 2099 2096 5461 Tortillas, fresh or refrigerated; tortilla chips; bakeries

(P-2604)
ROMEROS FOOD PRODUCTS INC
Also Called: Distribution Center
993 S Waterman Ave, San Bernardino (92408-2304)
PHONE..................909 884-5531
David Hernandez, Branch Mgr
Samuel Valenzuela, Branch Mgr
EMP: 10
SQ FT: 1,260
SALES (corp-wide): 28MM **Privately Held**
WEB: www.romerosfood.com
SIC: 2099 Tortillas, fresh or refrigerated
PA: Romero's Food Products, Incorporated
15155 Valley View Ave
Santa Fe Springs CA 90670
562 802-1858

(P-2605)
ROYAL ANGELUS MACARONI COMPANY
2539 E Philadelphia St, Ontario (91761-7774)
PHONE..................909 627-7312
▲ **EMP:** 130 **EST:** 2008
SALES (est): 150.3K
SALES (corp-wide): 41.7MM **Privately Held**
SIC: 2099 Pasta, uncooked: packaged with other ingredients
PA: Passport Food Group, Llc
2539 E Philadelphia St
Ontario CA 91761
909 627-7312

(P-2606)
RUIZ MEXICAN FOODS INC (PA)
Also Called: Ruiz Flour Tortillas
1200 Marlborough Ave A, Riverside (92507-2158)
PHONE..................909 947-7811
Dolores C Ruiz, CEO
Jonathan Elguea, Info Tech Mgr
Dana Warren, Accountant
Steve Hernandez, Controller
Ed Ruiz, Director
▼ **EMP:** 140 **EST:** 1976
SQ FT: 38,000
SALES (est): 28.8MM **Privately Held**
SIC: 2099 3556 Tortillas, fresh or refrigerated; food products machinery

(P-2607)
S MARTINELLI & COMPANY (PA)
735 W Beach St, Watsonville (95076-5141)
P.O. Box 1868 (95077-1868)
PHONE..................831 724-1126
Stephen C Martinelli, Chairman
Stephen John Martinelli, President
Gun Ruder, CFO
Doris M Brown, Vice Pres
Eliseo Mandlhate, Engineer
◆ **EMP:** 195
SALES (est): 63.2MM **Privately Held**
WEB: www.martinellis.com
SIC: 2099 Cider, nonalcoholic

(P-2608)
SAUER BRANDS INC
184 Suburban Rd, San Luis Obispo (93401-7502)
PHONE..................805 597-8900
William W Lovette, CEO
EMP: 65
SALES (corp-wide): 74.9MM **Privately Held**
SIC: 2099 Seasonings & spices
PA: Sauer Brands, Inc.
2000 W Broad St
Richmond VA 23220
804 359-5786

(P-2609)
SD DESSERTS LLC
1608 India St Ste 104, San Diego (92101-2564)
P.O. Box 2146, Rancho Santa Fe (92067-2146)
PHONE..................702 480-9083
Celine Maury,
Jean-Philippe Maury,
EMP: 10

SALES: 800K **Privately Held**
SIC: 2099 7389 Desserts, ready-to-mix;

(P-2610)
SENSIENT TECHNOLOGIES CORP
9984 W Walnut Ave, Livingston (95334)
P.O. Box 485 (95334-0485)
PHONE..................................209 394-7971
Joe Martins, *Branch Mgr*
EMP: 10
SALES (corp-wide): 1.3B **Publicly Held**
WEB: www.sensient-tech.com
SIC: 2099 2034 2087 Yeast; seasonings & spices; chili pepper or powder; seasonings: dry mixes; dehydrated fruits, vegetables, soups; beverage bases
PA: Sensient Technologies Corporation
   777 E Wisconsin Ave # 1100
   Milwaukee WI 53202
   414 271-6755

(P-2611)
SILAO TORTILLERIA INC
250 N California Ave, City of Industry (91744-4323)
PHONE..................................626 961-0761
Leandro Espinosa, *President*
Leandro Espinosa Jr, *Vice Pres*
EMP: 44
SALES (est): 6.1MM **Privately Held**
SIC: 2099 Tortillas, fresh or refrigerated

(P-2612)
SINBAD FOODS LLC
2401 W Almond Ave, Madera (93637-4807)
PHONE..................................559 674-4445
Mike Bizik,
EMP: 44
SALES (est): 2MM **Privately Held**
SIC: 2099 Food preparations

(P-2613)
SINCERE ORIENT COMMERCIAL CORP
Also Called: Sincere Orient Food Company
15222 Valley Blvd, City of Industry (91746-3323)
PHONE..................................626 333-8882
Andy Khun, *President*
▲ EMP: 70
SQ FT: 12,000
SALES (est): 6.7MM **Privately Held**
WEB: www.sincereorient.com
SIC: 2099 Packaged combination products: pasta, rice & potato

(P-2614)
SOUP BASES LOADED INC
2355 E Francis St, Ontario (91761-7727)
PHONE..................................909 230-6890
Alan Portney, *President*
Rosemary Ovalle, *General Mgr*
Minh Dao, *Research*
Laura Harlow, *Technical Staff*
Ryan Bish, *Sales Staff*
EMP: 45
SQ FT: 27,000
SALES (est): 9.8MM **Privately Held**
WEB: www.soupbasesloaded.com
SIC: 2099 2034 Seasonings: dry mixes; dried & dehydrated soup mixes

(P-2615)
SOUTHWEST PRODUCTS LLC
Also Called: Tortilla Land
8411 Siempre Viva Rd, San Diego (92154-6299)
PHONE..................................619 263-8000
Zeno Santache, *Mng Member*
Eric Brenk,
▲ EMP: 250 EST: 2013
SQ FT: 160,000
SALES (est): 53.9MM **Privately Held**
SIC: 2099 Tortillas, fresh or refrigerated
HQ: Ajinomoto Foods North America, Inc.
   4200 Concours Ste 100
   Ontario CA 91764

(P-2616)
SPICES UNLIMITED INC
2339 Tech Pkwy Ste J, Hollister (95023)
PHONE..................................831 636-3596
Dennis Voechting, *President*
Garron Billick, *Vice Pres*

Connie Voechting, *Admin Sec*
◆ EMP: 12 EST: 1948
SQ FT: 4,000
SALES: 500K **Privately Held**
SIC: 2099 Seasonings: dry mixes

(P-2617)
STANESS JONEKOS ENTPS INC
Also Called: Eat Like A Woman
4000 W Magnolia Blvd D, Burbank (91505-2827)
PHONE..................................818 606-2710
Staness Jonekos, *Owner*
EMP: 27
SALES: 3.1MM **Privately Held**
SIC: 2099 Food preparations

(P-2618)
SUN BASKET INC
1 Clarence Pl Unit 14, San Francisco (94107-2577)
PHONE..................................408 669-4418
Antonio Curren, *Opers Spvr*
EMP: 60
SALES (corp-wide): 76MM **Privately Held**
SIC: 2099 Almond pastes
PA: Sun Basket, Inc.
   1170 Olinder Ct
   San Jose CA 95122
   408 669-4418

(P-2619)
SUN RICH FOODS INTL CORP
1240 N Barsten Way, Anaheim (92806-1822)
PHONE..................................714 632-7577
Walid A Barakat, *President*
Shirley Barakat, *CFO*
Alex Barakat, *Vice Pres*
EMP: 17
SQ FT: 6,500
SALES (est): 3.2MM **Privately Held**
SIC: 2099 Food preparations

(P-2620)
SUNOPTA GRAINS AND FOODS INC
12128 Center St, South Gate (90280-8046)
PHONE..................................323 774-6000
EMP: 62
SALES (corp-wide): 1.2B **Privately Held**
SIC: 2099 Food preparations
HQ: Sunopta Grains And Foods Inc.
   7301 Ohms Ln Ste 600
   Minneapolis MN 55439

(P-2621)
SWEET EARTH INC
Also Called: Sweet Earth Natural Foods
3080 Hilltop Rd, Moss Landing (95039-9692)
PHONE..................................831 375-8673
Kelly Swette, *President*
Brian Swette, *President*
Rob Beitscher, *Finance*
EMP: 80
SQ FT: 30,000
SALES (est): 11MM
SALES (corp-wide): 92B **Privately Held**
SIC: 2099 Food preparations
PA: Nestle S.A.
   Avenue Nestle 55
   Vevey VD 1800
   219 242-111

(P-2622)
TAMPICO SPICE CO INCORPORATED
Also Called: Tampico Spice Company
5901 S Central Ave 5941, Los Angeles (90001-1128)
P.O. Box 1229 (90001-0229)
PHONE..................................323 235-3154
George Martinez, *CEO*
Baudelia Martinez, *Treasurer*
Delia Navarro, *Treasurer*
Mario Jaimes, *General Mgr*
Noe Ramos, *Administration*
▲ EMP: 40
SQ FT: 150,000
SALES (est): 8MM **Privately Held**
WEB: www.tampico.com
SIC: 2099 Spices, including grinding; seasonings: dry mixes

(P-2623)
TARAZI SPECIALTY FOODS LLC
13727 Seminole Dr, Chino (91710-5515)
PHONE..................................909 628-3601
Alexandra Vorbeck, *Mng Member*
▲ EMP: 13
SALES (est): 1.8MM **Privately Held**
SIC: 2099 Seasonings: dry mixes

(P-2624)
TEST LABORATORIES INC (PA)
Also Called: Brewster Foods
7121 Canby Ave, Reseda (91335-4304)
PHONE..................................818 881-4251
Gregory L Brewster, *President*
Andrew Waldrip, *CFO*
Karen G Brewster, *Corp Secy*
▲ EMP: 11
SQ FT: 5,000
SALES (est): 2.2MM **Privately Held**
WEB: www.testlabinc.com
SIC: 2099 Food preparations

(P-2625)
TEVA FOODS INC
4401 S Downey Rd, Vernon (90058-2518)
P.O. Box 58128, Los Angeles (90058-0128)
PHONE..................................323 267-8110
Erik Litmanovich, *President*
EMP: 30
SALES (est): 5.7MM **Privately Held**
SIC: 2099 Salads, fresh or refrigerated

(P-2626)
TOFU SHOP SPECIALTY FOODS INC
65 Frank Martin Ct, Arcata (95521-8930)
PHONE..................................707 822-7401
Matthew Schmit, *President*
Pam Olson, *Data Proc Dir*
EMP: 20
SQ FT: 4,400
SALES (est): 642.2K **Privately Held**
SIC: 2099 Tofu, except frozen desserts

(P-2627)
TOM HARRIS INC
Also Called: Uncle Bum's Gourmet Sauces
5821 Wilderness Ave, Riverside (92504-1004)
PHONE..................................951 352-5700
Tom Harris, *President*
Richard Harris, *Vice Pres*
Dave Smyth, *Vice Pres*
Jag Rajwan, *Director*
EMP: 60
SQ FT: 140,000
SALES (est): 3.9MM **Privately Held**
WEB: www.il.nacdnet.net
SIC: 2099 2035 Food preparations; pickles, sauces & salad dressings

(P-2628)
TOPNOTCH FOODS INC
1988 E 57th St, Vernon (90058-3464)
PHONE..................................323 586-2007
Meyer Luskin, *President*
Anna Arroyo, *Vice Pres*
Anna M Arroyo, *General Mgr*
Joe Giustra, *Manager*
EMP: 11
SQ FT: 20,000
SALES (est): 1.6MM
SALES (corp-wide): 203.7MM **Privately Held**
SIC: 2099 Bread crumbs, not made in bakeries
HQ: Reconserve, Inc.
   2811 Wilshire Blvd # 410
   Santa Monica CA 90403
   310 458-1574

(P-2629)
TORN RANCH INC (PA)
2198 S Mcdowell Blvd Ext, Petaluma (94954-6902)
PHONE..................................415 506-3000
Su Morrow, *CEO*
Dean Morrow, *President*
Kimberly Delasantos, *Controller*
Michelle Chodor, *Natl Sales Mgr*
Rich Shaffer, *Marketing Mgr*
◆ EMP: 80
SALES (est): 14.4MM **Privately Held**
WEB: www.tornranch.com
SIC: 2099 Food preparations

(P-2630)
TORTILLERIA LA CALIFORNIA INC
2241 Cypress Ave, Los Angeles (90065-1214)
PHONE..................................323 221-8940
Sergio Sanchez, *President*
EMP: 22 EST: 1972
SQ FT: 20,000
SALES (est): 3.3MM **Privately Held**
SIC: 2099 Tortillas, fresh or refrigerated

(P-2631)
TORTILLERIA LA MEJOR
Also Called: La Mejor Restaurant
684 S Farmersville Blvd, Farmersville (93223-2042)
P.O. Box 657 (93223-0657)
PHONE..................................559 747-0739
Rafael Vasquez, *Owner*
Octaviana Vasquez, *Co-Owner*
EMP: 55
SALES (est): 4.9MM **Privately Held**
SIC: 2099 5411 Tortillas, fresh or refrigerated; grocery stores, independent

(P-2632)
TORTILLERIA SAN MARCOS
Also Called: San Marco's Tortilla & Market
1927 E 1st St, Los Angeles (90033-3412)
PHONE..................................323 263-0208
Gregorio Garcia, *President*
Amparo Garcia, *Vice Pres*
EMP: 27
SQ FT: 8,750
SALES (est): 750K **Privately Held**
SIC: 2099 Tortillas, fresh or refrigerated

(P-2633)
TORTILLERIA SANTA FE
387 Zenith St, Chula Vista (91911-5751)
PHONE..................................619 585-0350
Guillermo Estrada, *Owner*
EMP: 28
SALES (est): 4.4MM **Privately Held**
WEB: www.tortillaflats.net
SIC: 2099 Tortillas, fresh or refrigerated

(P-2634)
TORTILLERIA TEMECULA
28780 Old Town Front St A7, Temecula (92590-2847)
PHONE..................................951 676-5272
Victor Castillo, *President*
Elizabeth Gonzales, *Controller*
EMP: 14
SALES: 1MM **Privately Held**
WEB: www.temeculainformation.com
SIC: 2099 Tortillas, fresh or refrigerated

(P-2635)
TRADITIONAL MEDICINALS INC (PA)
4515 Ross Rd, Sebastopol (95472-2250)
P.O. Box 239, Cotati (94931-0239)
PHONE..................................707 823-8911
Drake Sadler, *Principal*
Emily Davydov, *Partner*
Blair Kellison, *CEO*
Teal Tasso, *COO*
Jane C Howard, *CFO*
▲ EMP: 150
SQ FT: 20,000
SALES (est): 31.8MM **Privately Held**
WEB: www.traditionalmedicinals.com
SIC: 2099 Tea blending

(P-2636)
TRINIDAD BENHAM HOLDING CO
Also Called: Westlam Foods
5177 Chino Ave, Chino (91710-5110)
PHONE..................................909 627-7535
Gary Fash, *MIS Dir*
Dennis Liptak, *Controller*
EMP: 30
SQ FT: 47,719
SALES (corp-wide): 558.7MM **Privately Held**
WEB: www.trinidadbenham.com
SIC: 2099 2032 Popcorn, packaged: except already popped; beans, without meat: packaged in cans, jars, etc.

PA: Trinidad Benham Holding Company
3650 S Yosemite St # 300
Denver CO 80237
303 220-1400

(P-2637)
TRIPLE H FOOD PROCESSORS LLC
5821 Wilderness Ave, Riverside
(92504-1004)
PHONE...................951 352-5700
Tom Harris Jr,
Richard J Harris,
▲ **EMP:** 60
SQ FT: 120,000
SALES (est): 17.6MM **Privately Held**
WEB: www.triplehfoods.com
SIC: 2099 2035 2033 Food preparations; pickles, sauces & salad dressings; jams, jellies & preserves: packaged in cans, jars, etc.

(P-2638)
TRUROOTS INC (HQ)
Also Called: Enray Inc.
6999 Southfront Rd, Livermore
(94551-8221)
PHONE...................925 218-2205
Nimesh Ray, *CEO*
Esha Ray, *President*
▲ **EMP:** 25
SQ FT: 20,000
SALES (est): 2.1MM
SALES (corp-wide): 7.8B **Publicly Held**
SIC: 2099 Rice, uncooked: packaged with other ingredients
PA: The J M Smucker Company
1 Strawberry Ln
Orrville OH 44667
330 682-3000

(P-2639)
TRUROOTS INC
37 Speedway Ave, Chico (95928-9554)
PHONE...................925 218-2205
Emily Douglass, *Branch Mgr*
EMP: 17
SALES (corp-wide): 7.8B **Publicly Held**
SIC: 2099 Rice, uncooked: packaged with other ingredients
HQ: Truroots, Inc.
6999 Southfront Rd
Livermore CA 94551
925 218-2205

(P-2640)
TULKOFF FOOD PRODUCTS WEST INC
705 Bliss Ave, Pittsburg (94565-5005)
PHONE...................925 427-5157
Philip J Tulkoff, *CEO*
Paul Rostkowski, *CFO*
Alec Tulkoff, *Vice Pres*
EMP: 27
SQ FT: 40,000
SALES (est): 4.1MM
SALES (corp-wide): 20.1MM **Privately Held**
WEB: www.tulkoff.com
SIC: 2099 Food preparations
PA: Tulkoff Food Products, Inc.
2229 Van Deman St
Baltimore MD 21224
410 864-0526

(P-2641)
UNCLE LEES TEA INC
Also Called: Ten Fu Company Limited
11020 Rush St, El Monte (91733-3547)
PHONE...................626 350-3309
Kuo-Lin Lee, *President*
▲ **EMP:** 30
SQ FT: 7,772
SALES (est): 4.7MM **Privately Held**
WEB: www.unclelee.com
SIC: 2099 Tea blending

(P-2642)
UNITED FOODS INTL USA INC (HQ)
23447 Cabot Blvd, Hayward (94545-1665)
PHONE...................510 264-5850
Takeo Shimura, *President*
Kenji Maruta, *General Mgr*
Hana Otsuka, *Human Res Mgr*

Tadashi Isahai, *Sales Staff*
Miki Kakutani, *Manager*
▲ **EMP:** 49
SQ FT: 24,000
SALES (est): 13.1MM **Privately Held**
WEB: www.senbausa.com
SIC: 2099 Seasonings: dry mixes

(P-2643)
UPPER CRUST ENTERPRISES INC
411 Center St, Los Angeles (90012-3435)
PHONE...................213 625-0038
Gary Kawaguchi, *CEO*
Edward Shelley, *CFO*
Ken Kawaguchi, *Vice Pres*
Yaneth Cardinaux, *Natl Sales Mgr*
Jonathan Kawaguchi, *Sales Staff*
◆ **EMP:** 50
SQ FT: 45,000
SALES: 2.5K **Privately Held**
WEB: www.uppercrustent.com
SIC: 2099 Bread crumbs, not made in bakeries

(P-2644)
VALLEY FINE FOODS COMPANY INC
300 Epley Dr, Yuba City (95991-7221)
PHONE...................530 671-7200
EMP: 98 **Privately Held**
SIC: 2099 Food preparations
PA: Valley Fine Foods Company, Inc.
3909 Park Rd Ste H
Benicia CA 94510

(P-2645)
VIRGINIA PARK LLC
Also Called: Virginia Park Foods
2225 Via Cerro Ste A, Riverside
(92509-2440)
P.O. Box 1567, New York NY (10159-1567)
PHONE...................816 592-0776
Manoj Venugopal, *Mng Member*
Brian Rudolf,
Scott Rudolph,
EMP: 15
SQ FT: 35,000
SALES: 1MM
SALES (corp-wide): 4.2MM **Privately Held**
SIC: 2099 Pasta, uncooked: packaged with other ingredients
PA: Banza Llc
1570 Woodward Ave Fl 3
Detroit MI 48226
914 338-8009

(P-2646)
WHITE LABS INC (PA)
9495 Candida St, San Diego (92126-4541)
PHONE...................858 693-3441
Chris White, *President*
Chris Mueller, *Vice Pres*
EMP: 15
SQ FT: 5,000
SALES (est): 11.3MM **Privately Held**
WEB: www.whitelabs.com
SIC: 2099 Yeast

(P-2647)
WHOLESOME VALLEY FOODS (PA)
Also Called: Barnana
1746 Berkeley St Unit B, Santa Monica
(90404-4105)
PHONE...................858 480-1543
Caue Suplicy, *CEO*
Matt Clifford, *COO*
Nicholas Ingersoll, *Chief Mktg Ofcr*
Francesca Schechter, *Finance*
EMP: 13
SALES (est): 2.2MM **Privately Held**
SIC: 2099 Food preparations

(P-2648)
WOOLERY ENTERPRISES INC
Also Called: Will's Fresh Foods
1991 Republic Ave, San Leandro
(94577-4220)
PHONE...................510 357-5700
Daniel C Woolery, *CEO*
Susan Woolery, *Admin Sec*
EMP: 43

SQ FT: 23,000
SALES (est): 8.2MM **Privately Held**
SIC: 2099 Salads, fresh or refrigerated

(P-2649)
WORLDWIDE SPECIALTIES INC
Also Called: California Specialty Farms
2420 Modoc St, Los Angeles (90021-2916)
PHONE...................323 587-2200
Mady Joes, *Manager*
EMP: 120 **Privately Held**
SIC: 2099 Almond pastes
PA: Worldwide Specialties, Inc
2421 E 16th St
Los Angeles CA 90021

(P-2650)
YBP HOLDINGS LLC
Also Called: Yagi Brothers Produce LLC
5614 Lincoln Blvd, Livingston
(95334-9642)
PHONE...................209 394-7311
EMP: 45
SALES (est): 1.3MM **Privately Held**
SIC: 2099 Potatoes, dried: packaged with other ingredients

2111 Cigarettes

(P-2651)
COSMIC FOG VAPORS
3115 Airway Ave, Costa Mesa
(92626-4609)
PHONE...................949 266-1730
Robert Crofsey, *Mng Member*
Brant Peto, *Mng Member*
Dale Kampfer, *Accounts Exec*
EMP: 60 **EST:** 2016
SALES: 19.5MM **Privately Held**
SIC: 2111 Cigarettes

(P-2652)
DYNAMIC E-MARKETS LLC
Also Called: Sandi Duty Free
2335 Roll Dr Ste 5, San Diego
(92154-7274)
PHONE...................619 327-4777
Michael McVevin,
EMP: 10
SALES (est): 2.4MM **Privately Held**
SIC: 2111 5194 Cigarettes; tobacco & tobacco products

(P-2653)
HOOK IT UP
1513 S Grand Ave, Santa Ana
(92705-4410)
PHONE...................714 600-0100
Zack Zakari, *CEO*
EMP: 135
SQ FT: 5,000
SALES (est): 7.3MM **Privately Held**
SIC: 2111 Cigarettes

(P-2654)
PHILIP MORRIS USA INC
185 Technology Dr, Irvine (92618-2412)
PHONE...................949 453-3500
EMP: 69
SALES (corp-wide): 25.4B **Publicly Held**
SIC: 2111
HQ: Philip Morris Usa Inc.
6601 W Brd St
Richmond VA 23230
804 274-2000

(P-2655)
R J REYNOLDS TOBACCO COMPANY
8380 Miramar Mall Ste 117, San Diego
(92121-2549)
PHONE...................858 625-8453
Ken Stevens, *Principal*
EMP: 226
SALES (corp-wide): 31.4B **Privately Held**
WEB: www.carolinagroup.com
SIC: 2111 Cigarettes
HQ: R. J. Reynolds Tobacco Company
401 N Main St
Winston Salem NC 27101
336 741-5000

(P-2656)
SPACE JAM JUICE LLC
1041 Calle Trepadora, San Clemente
(92673-6204)
PHONE...................714 660-7467
Daniel Peykoff, *CEO*
Michael Crawford, *President*
Jessica Chae, *Accountant*
Ryan Battaglia, *Sales Staff*
▲ **EMP:** 60
SQ FT: 25,000
SALES: 20MM **Privately Held**
SIC: 2111 Cigarettes

(P-2657)
USA SALES INC
Also Called: Statewide Distributors
1560 S Archibald Ave, Ontario
(91761-7629)
PHONE...................909 390-9606
Kabiruddin Ali, *CEO*
EMP: 20
SALES (est): 4.6MM **Privately Held**
SIC: 2111 2121 Cigarettes; cigars

(P-2658)
VITACIG INC
433 N Camden Dr Fl 6, Beverly Hills
(90210-4416)
PHONE...................310 402-6937
Paul Rosenberg, *CEO*
Mike Hawkins, *CFO*
EMP: 64
SALES (est): 84.3K
SALES (corp-wide): 7MM **Publicly Held**
SIC: 2111 Cigarettes
PA: Mcig, Inc.
2901 S Highland Dr 13b
Las Vegas NV 89109
570 778-6459

2121 Cigars

(P-2659)
BJC
1356 Lomita Blvd Apt 1, Harbor City
(90710-2125)
PHONE...................310 977-6068
Brian Buenaventura, *Owner*
EMP: 10
SALES (est): 1MM **Privately Held**
SIC: 2121 Cigars

2131 Tobacco, Chewing & Snuff

(P-2660)
FANTASIA DISTRIBUTION INC
Also Called: Fantasia Hookah Tobacco
1566 W Embassy St, Anaheim
(92802-1016)
PHONE...................714 817-8300
Randy Jacob Bahbah, *CEO*
Issa Bahbah, *CFO*
◆ **EMP:** 24
SALES (est): 7.2MM **Privately Held**
SIC: 2131 Smoking tobacco

(P-2661)
LA EJUICE LLC
Also Called: Five Star Juice
22871 Lockness Ave, Torrance (90501)
PHONE...................310 531-3888
Robert Hummer, *Mng Member*
Dan Corbei, *Managing Prtnr*
Dan Cordei,
Fili Moala,
EMP: 27
SQ FT: 10,000
SALES (est): 1.7MM **Privately Held**
SIC: 2131 5194 Chewing & smoking tobacco; tobacco & tobacco products

---

2211 Cotton, Woven Fabric

(P-2662)
2016 MONTGOMERY INC
Also Called: People For Peace
755 E 14th Pl, Los Angeles (90021-2117)
PHONE...................323 316-6886

▲ = Import ▼=Export
◆ =Import/Export

▲ **EMP:** 10
SQ FT: 4,500
SALES (est): 730K **Privately Held**
SIC: 2211

(P-2663)
A ALPHA WAVE GUIDE CO (PA)
Also Called: A Alpha Waveguide Tube Co
1217 E El Segundo Blvd, El Segundo
(90245-4203)
PHONE....................................310 322-3487
James Kelley Jr, *Owner*
Jim J Joseph, *Manager*
▲ **EMP:** 12
SQ FT: 2,500
SALES: 3.5MM **Privately Held**
WEB: www.a-alphawaveguide.com
SIC: 2211 Tubing, seamless: cotton

(P-2664)
AIRCRAFT COVERS INC
Also Called: Bruce's Custom Covers
18850 Adams Ct, Morgan Hill
(95037-2816)
PHONE....................................408 738-3959
Bruce Perlitch, *President*
Heather Perlitch, *Vice Pres*
Javier Uranga, *General Mgr*
Sylvie Windeshausen, *Office Mgr*
Ivan Uranga, *Human Resources*
EMP: 65
SQ FT: 21,909
SALES (corp-wide): 10.2MM **Privately Held**
SIC: 2211 Canvas
PA: Aircraft Covers, Inc.
18850 Adams Ct
Morgan Hill CA 95037
408 738-3959

(P-2665)
ALSTYLE APPAREL LLC
1501 E Cerritos Ave, Anaheim
(92805-6400)
PHONE....................................714 765-0400
EMP: 3765 **EST:** 2014
SALES (est): 94.8K
SALES (corp-wide): 2.9B **Privately Held**
SIC: 2211 Apparel & outerwear fabrics, cotton
HQ: Alstyle Apparel & Activewear Management Co.
1501 E Cerritos Ave
Anaheim CA 92805
714 765-0400

(P-2666)
AMERICAN APPAREL RETAIL INC (DH)
747 Warehouse St, Los Angeles
(90021-1106)
P.O. Box 5129, Brandon MS (39047-5129)
PHONE....................................213 488-0226
Paula Schneider, *CEO*
Son Nguyen, *Planning*
◆ **EMP:** 29
SALES (est): 5.1MM
SALES (corp-wide): 2.9B **Privately Held**
SIC: 2211 Apparel & outerwear fabrics, cotton
HQ: App Winddown, Llc
747 Warehouse St
Los Angeles CA 90021
213 488-0226

(P-2667)
APPLIED SEWING RESOURCES INC
Also Called: Kiva Designs
6440 Goodyear Rd, Benicia (94510-1219)
PHONE....................................707 748-1614
EMP: 25
SALES: 3MM **Privately Held**
SIC: 2211 2393

(P-2668)
APTAN CORP
2000 S Main St, Los Angeles (90007-1420)
PHONE....................................213 748-5271
Ronald Tanzman, *President*
EMP: 12 **EST:** 1972
SQ FT: 10,000
SALES (est): 2.5MM **Privately Held**
WEB: www.aptancorp.com
SIC: 2211 2396 Linings & interlinings, cotton; pads, shoulder: for coats, suits, etc.

(P-2669)
B & M UPHOLSTERY
Also Called: Belmar Company
2525 16th St Ste 201, San Francisco
(94103-4246)
PHONE....................................415 621-7447
Markus Melitsky, *Owner*
Bella Miretsky, *President*
Markus Miretsky, *Vice Pres*
EMP: 19
SQ FT: 11,000
SALES (est): 1.9MM **Privately Held**
SIC: 2211 7641 Upholstery, tapestry & wall coverings: cotton; antique furniture repair & restoration

(P-2670)
BELAGIO ENTERPRISES INC
4801 W Jefferson Blvd, Los Angeles
(90016-3920)
PHONE....................................323 731-6934
Ruben Melamed, *CEO*
▲ **EMP:** 20
SALES: 9MM **Privately Held**
SIC: 2211 2269 Decorative trim & specialty fabrics, including twist weave; decorative finishing of narrow fabrics

(P-2671)
BONDED FIBERLOFT INC
2748 Tanager Ave, Commerce
(90040-2721)
PHONE....................................323 726-7820
Mark Bidner, *CEO*
Mike Wood, *CFO*
EMP: 350
SQ FT: 96,000
SALES (est): 22.5MM **Privately Held**
SIC: 2211 2823 2299 Broadwoven fabric mills, cotton; cellulosic manmade fibers; batts & batting: cotton mill waste & related material
PA: Western Synthetic Fiber Inc
2 Atlantic Ave Fl 4
Boston MA

(P-2672)
BRONCS INC
Also Called: Wct
12691 Pala Dr Ste A, Garden Grove
(92841-3936)
PHONE....................................714 705-4377
EMP: 165
SQ FT: 140,000
SALES (est): 5.3MM **Privately Held**
SIC: 2211 7389 Broadwoven fabric mills, cotton; textile & apparel services

(P-2673)
BUILDERS DRAPERY SERVICE INC
1494 Gladding Ct, Milpitas (95035-6831)
PHONE....................................408 263-3300
John A Garden Jr, *CEO*
Lottie Garden, *President*
▲ **EMP:** 35
SQ FT: 6,000
SALES (est): 5MM **Privately Held**
SIC: 2211 2591 Draperies & drapery fabrics, cotton; window blinds

(P-2674)
CABO INTERNATIONAL INC
Also Called: Cabo Gear
3512 Celinda Dr, Carlsbad (92008-2768)
PHONE....................................760 597-9199
Jacquelyn Stuart, *President*
Jim Stuart, *CFO*
James Stuart, *Vice Pres*
EMP: 15
SALES: 1.4MM **Privately Held**
WEB: www.cabogear.net
SIC: 2211 Apparel & outerwear fabrics, cotton

(P-2675)
CALIFORNIA COAST CLOTHING LLC
Also Called: Rd Jean
3690 S Santa Fe Ave, Vernon
(90058-1413)
PHONE....................................323 923-3870
Ralph Davis,
David S Ryan,

▲ **EMP:** 11 **EST:** 2007
SQ FT: 10,000
SALES (est): 1.5MM **Privately Held**
SIC: 2211 5131 5699 Denims; trimmings, apparel; caps & gowns (academic vestments)

(P-2676)
COLORMAX INDUSTRIES INC (PA)
1627 Paloma St, Los Angeles
(90021-3013)
PHONE....................................213 748-6600
Gholamreza Amighi, *President*
Goodarz Haydarzadeh, *CEO*
EMP: 25
SQ FT: 64,000
SALES (est): 4MM **Privately Held**
SIC: 2211 2269 2261 2254 Broadwoven fabric mills, cotton; finishing plants; finishing plants, cotton; dyeing & finishing knit underwear

(P-2677)
CONTEMPO WINDOW FASHIONS
5721 Newcastle Ave, Encino (91316-1054)
PHONE....................................818 768-1773
Kathleen Bryan, *Owner*
EMP: 10
SQ FT: 1,400
SALES (est): 500K **Privately Held**
SIC: 2211 5023 5714 Draperies & drapery fabrics, cotton; draperies; draperies

(P-2678)
COTTYON INC
Also Called: Cotty On
2202 E Anderson St, Vernon (90058-3451)
PHONE....................................323 589-1563
EMP: 20
SALES (est): 1.9MM **Privately Held**
SIC: 2211

(P-2679)
CREATIVE COSTUMING DESIGNS INC
15402 Electronic Ln, Huntington Beach
(92649-1334)
PHONE....................................714 895-0982
Noreen Roberts, *President*
Kevin Roberts, *CFO*
EMP: 35
SQ FT: 5,300
SALES (est): 4.2MM **Privately Held**
SIC: 2211 Apparel & outerwear fabrics, cotton

(P-2680)
DEAR JOHN DENIM INC
Also Called: Dear John American Classic
12318 Lower Azusa Rd, Arcadia
(91006-5872)
PHONE....................................626 350-5100
Chiu Yeung, *CEO*
Chelsay Adams, *Manager*
▲ **EMP:** 10
SALES (est): 738.5K **Privately Held**
SIC: 2211 Denims

(P-2681)
DEODAR BRANDS LLC
Also Called: Mek Denim
4715 S Alameda St, Vernon (90058-2014)
PHONE....................................323 235-7303
Eric C Choi, *Mng Member*
Soohan Kim, *CFO*
Young S Cho, *Admin Sec*
Khiem Nguyen, *Director*
▲ **EMP:** 25
SALES: 5MM **Privately Held**
SIC: 2211 Apparel & outerwear fabrics, cotton

(P-2682)
DESTINEY GROUP INC
Also Called: Unitex International
4800 District Blvd, Vernon (90058-2727)
P.O. Box 58127, Los Angeles (90058-0127)
PHONE....................................323 581-4477
Raymond Mashian, *President*
Shahriar Hebroni, *Vice Pres*
▲ **EMP:** 16
SQ FT: 18,000
SALES (est): 3.2MM **Privately Held**
SIC: 2211 Broadwoven fabric mills, cotton

(P-2683)
DOS FASHIONS
2633 Troy Ave, El Monte (91733-1429)
PHONE....................................626 454-4558
Do M Lam, *Owner*
EMP: 40
SALES (est): 2.2MM **Privately Held**
SIC: 2211 Apparel & outerwear fabrics, cotton

(P-2684)
DRAPERY PRODUCTIONS INC
33 E 4th Ave, San Mateo (94401-4001)
PHONE....................................650 340-8555
Gary Smith, *President*
Gary Schmidt, *Vice Pres*
Shirley Show, *Office Mgr*
EMP: 10
SALES (est): 743K **Privately Held**
SIC: 2211 5023 Draperies & drapery fabrics, cotton; draperies

(P-2685)
EAST SHORE GARMENT COMPANY LLC
2015 E 48th St, Vernon (90058-2021)
PHONE....................................323 923-4454
Michael Don Hutchinson,
EMP: 20
SALES: 77.1K
SALES (corp-wide): 58MM **Privately Held**
SIC: 2211 Broadwoven fabric mills, cotton
PA: Lakeshirts, Inc.
750 Randolph Rd
Detroit Lakes MN 56501
218 847-2171

(P-2686)
EXOTIC SILKS INC
Also Called: Thai Silks
1959 Leghorn St Ste B, Mountain View
(94043-1797)
PHONE....................................650 948-8611
Rosi Valqui, *Manager*
EMP: 12
SALES (corp-wide): 8.1MM **Privately Held**
WEB: www.exoticsilks.com
SIC: 2211 5949 Apparel & outerwear fabrics, cotton; fabric stores piece goods
PA: Exotic Silks, Inc.
1959 Leghorn St Ste B
Mountain View CA 94043
650 965-7760

(P-2687)
FACTORY ONE STUDIO INC
6700 Avalon Blvd Ste 101, Los Angeles
(90003-1920)
PHONE....................................323 752-1670
Steve C Rhee, *CEO*
EMP: 52
SALES: 10MM **Privately Held**
SIC: 2211 Denims

(P-2688)
FIRST FINISH INC
11126 Wright Rd, Lynwood (90262-3122)
PHONE....................................310 631-6717
Keyomars Fard, *President*
▲ **EMP:** 25
SQ FT: 10,000
SALES (est): 3.1MM **Privately Held**
WEB: www.firstfinish.com
SIC: 2211 Jean fabrics

(P-2689)
GOLDEN TEXTILE INC
2922 S Main St, Los Angeles (90007-3336)
PHONE....................................323 620-2612
Bruce Lee, *President*
▲ **EMP:** 15
SQ FT: 7,000
SALES: 900K **Privately Held**
SIC: 2211 Apparel & outerwear fabrics, cotton

(P-2690)
GREY STUDIO INC
629 S Clarence St, Los Angeles
(90023-1107)
PHONE....................................323 780-8111
Kendrick D Kim, *President*
EMP: 50

P R O D U C T S & S V C S

(PA)=Parent Co (HQ)=Headquarters (DH)=Div Headquarters
♻ = New Business established in last 2 years

SALES (est): 7MM **Privately Held**
SIC: 2211 Denims

(P-2691)
HIDDEN JEANS INC (PA)
Also Called: Cello Jeans
1001 Towne Ave Ste 103, Los Angeles
(90021-2088)
PHONE..................213 746-4223
Kenny Jin Park, *CEO*
Adam Lee, *Vice Pres*
▲ **EMP:** 11 **EST:** 2007
SQ FT: 4,000
SALES (est): 4.5MM **Privately Held**
SIC: 2211 Denims

(P-2692)
HUGE USA INC
1100 S San Pedro St J02, Los Angeles
(90015-2328)
PHONE..................213 741-1707
Jin Ser Park, *CEO*
Theo Soares, *Planning*
EMP: 11 **EST:** 2012
SALES (est): 370.7K **Privately Held**
SIC: 2211 Denims

(P-2693)
INDIE SEMICONDUCTOR
32 Journey Ste 100, Aliso Viejo
(92656-5329)
PHONE..................949 608-0854
Donald McClymont, *CEO*
Lionel Federspiel, *Vice Pres*
Paul Hollingworth, *Vice Pres*
Scott Kee, *Principal*
Laura Manjo, *Director*
EMP: 100
SALES (est): 108.6K **Privately Held**
SIC: 2211 5013 Automotive fabrics, cotton; testing equipment, electrical: automotive

(P-2694)
INTEGRATED MARKETING GROUP LLC
528 W Briardale Ave, Orange
(92865-4208)
PHONE..................714 771-2401
Gregory Dahlstrom, *Mng Member*
Colleen Anderson, *VP Sales*
Shane Webber, *Sales Staff*
Denise Hook,
Greg Dahlstrom, *Mng Member*
▲ **EMP:** 19
SALES (est): 3.1MM **Privately Held**
SIC: 2211 Apparel & outerwear fabrics, cotton

(P-2695)
J BRAND INC
Also Called: J Brand Jeans
1318 E 7th St Ste 260, Los Angeles
(90021-1131)
PHONE..................213 749-3500
Jeffrey Rudes, *President*
Roshanna Sabaratnam, *Vice Pres*
Aimee Poynor, *Technical Staff*
Tracy Kim, *Graphic Designe*
Alberto Valmeo, *Accounting Mgr*
◆ **EMP:** 60
SALES (est): 15.2MM **Privately Held**
SIC: 2211 Denims
PA: Fast Retailing Co., Ltd.
9-7-1, Akasaka
Minato-Ku TKY 107-0

(P-2696)
J MILLER CANVAS LLC
2429 S Birch St, Santa Ana (92707-3406)
PHONE..................714 641-0052
Daniel Neill,
Bryan Presby,
EMP: 22
SALES (est): 2.6MM **Privately Held**
SIC: 2211 Canvas

(P-2697)
JADE SPEC LLC
Also Called: Jadespec
15932 Downey Ave Ste A, Paramount
(90723-5140)
PHONE..................310 933-4338
Dylan Rodriguez, *Mng Member*
Steven Weiss,

EMP: 15
SALES (est): 268.1K **Privately Held**
SIC: 2211 2591 5021 Draperies & drapery fabrics, cotton; drapery hardware & blinds & shades; shade, curtain & drapery hardware; curtain & drapery rods, poles & fixtures; beds & bedding

(P-2698)
JC USA TRADING INC
Also Called: Jaba USA
159 N Sunset Ave, City of Industry
(91744-1850)
PHONE..................626 333-9990
Suhua Chen, *CEO*
EMP: 10
SQ FT: 30,000
SALES (est): 1.4MM **Privately Held**
SIC: 2211 5021 2392 5719 Sheets, bedding & table cloths: cotton; beds & bedding; blankets, comforters & beddings; bedding (sheets, blankets, spreads & pillows)

(P-2699)
JENTEX CO LTD
1103 Bramford Ct, Diamond Bar
(91765-4353)
PHONE..................909 273-1088
Jenny Yang, *President*
▲ **EMP:** 10
SALES (est): 825K
SALES (corp-wide): 5.4MM **Privately Held**
SIC: 2211 Diaper fabrics
PA: Shanghai Jentex Bag Manufacture Co., Ltd
No.1, 358 Lane, Zhuting Road, Yexie Town, Songjian G District
Shanghai 20003
216 443-4406

(P-2700)
JML TEXTILE INC
Also Called: W & M Textile
5801 S 2nd St, Vernon (90058-3403)
PHONE..................323 584-2323
Seung Choon Lim, *CEO*
Seung Hoon Lim, *President*
▲ **EMP:** 60
SQ FT: 350,000
SALES (est): 8.8MM **Privately Held**
WEB: www.wimatex.com
SIC: 2211 Apparel & outerwear fabrics, cotton

(P-2701)
KATHRYN M IRELAND INC (PA)
5285 W Washington Blvd, Los Angeles
(90016-1340)
PHONE..................323 965-9888
Kathryn Ireland, *President*
▲ **EMP:** 20 **EST:** 1998
SQ FT: 1,500
SALES (est): 1.5MM **Privately Held**
WEB: www.kathrynireland.com
SIC: 2211 7389 Broadwoven fabric mills, cotton; interior design services

(P-2702)
LOS ANGELES MILLS INC
2331 E 8th St, Los Angeles (90021-1732)
PHONE..................424 307-0075
William G Meyer, *President*
▲ **EMP:** 33 **EST:** 1963
SALES: 40MM **Privately Held**
SIC: 2211 2299 2281 2221 Cotton broad woven goods; yarns, specialty & novelty; yarn spinning mills; broadwoven fabric mills, manmade; throwing & winding mills

(P-2703)
MASTERPIECE ARTIST CANVAS LLC
Also Called: Canvas Concepts
1401 Air Wing Rd, San Diego
(92154-7705)
PHONE..................619 710-2500
John M Sooklaris, *President*
Donna Wilson, *Sales Staff*
Aracely Falciola, *Manager*
John Michael, *Agent*
▲ **EMP:** 50
SQ FT: 1,000

SALES (est): 479.7K **Privately Held**
WEB: www.masterpiecearts.com
SIC: 2211 Canvas

(P-2704)
MSP GROUP INC
206 W 140th St, Los Angeles (90061-1006)
PHONE..................310 660-0022
Jong H Lim, *President*
▲ **EMP:** 35
SQ FT: 1,000
SALES: 7MM **Privately Held**
SIC: 2211 Apparel & outerwear fabrics, cotton

(P-2705)
NOT ONLY JEANS INC
3004 S Main St, Los Angeles (90007-3825)
PHONE..................213 765-9725
EMP: 20
SALES (est): 2.2MM **Privately Held**
SIC: 2211

(P-2706)
NUTRADE INC
Also Called: Dreamworks Knitting
2808 Willis St, Santa Ana (92705-5714)
PHONE..................949 477-2300
Alan Hashemian, *CEO*
▲ **EMP:** 25 **EST:** 1998
SALES: 3.6MM **Privately Held**
WEB: www.nutrade.com
SIC: 2211 Apparel & outerwear fabrics, cotton

(P-2707)
PACIFIC WEAVING CORPORATION
1068 American St, San Carlos
(94070-5304)
PHONE..................650 592-9434
Andrew Sommer, *President*
EMP: 20
SALES (est): 1.6MM **Privately Held**
SIC: 2211 2221 Draperies & drapery fabrics, cotton; draperies & drapery fabrics, manmade fiber & silk

(P-2708)
PETUNIA PICKLE BOTTOM CORP
3567 Old Conejo Rd, Newbury Park
(91320-2122)
PHONE..................805 643-6697
Yann Boulbain, *CEO*
Denai Jones, *President*
Korie Fergeson, *Vice Pres*
Korie Conant, *Mktg Coord*
▲ **EMP:** 10
SQ FT: 26,000
SALES (est): 1.4MM **Privately Held**
WEB: www.petuniapicklebottom.com
SIC: 2211 Bags & bagging, cotton

(P-2709)
PJY INC
Also Called: Intimo Industry
3251 Leonis Blvd, Vernon (90058-3018)
PHONE..................323 583-7737
Paul Yang, *President*
Jorge Vigil, *Production*
Nicole Weaver, *Marketing Staff*
▲ **EMP:** 40
SALES (est): 6.6MM **Privately Held**
WEB: www.intimoindustry.com
SIC: 2211 Long cloth, cotton

(P-2710)
RNK INDUSTRIES CO
2816 E 11th St, Los Angeles (90023-3406)
PHONE..................323 446-0777
Rachel Lo, *President*
▲ **EMP:** 10
SALES (est): 1.5MM **Privately Held**
SIC: 2211 Twills, drills, denims & other ribbed fabrics: cotton

(P-2711)
SKY JEANS INC
6600 Avalon Blvd Ste 102, Los Angeles
(90003-1960)
PHONE..................323 778-2065
EMP: 20
SALES (est): 1.1MM **Privately Held**
SIC: 2211

(P-2712)
SLEEPOW LTD
11706 Darlington Ave, Los Angeles
(90049-5517)
PHONE..................646 688-0808
EMP: 40
SQ FT: 600
SALES (est): 2.9MM **Privately Held**
SIC: 2211

(P-2713)
STANZINO INC
17937 Santa Rita St, Encino (91316-3602)
PHONE..................818 602-5171
David Ghods, *Branch Mgr*
EMP: 133
SALES (corp-wide): 4MM **Privately Held**
SIC: 2211 Apparel & outerwear fabrics, cotton
PA: Stanzino, Inc.
16325 S Avalon Blvd
Gardena CA 90248
213 746-8822

(P-2714)
STANZINO INC (PA)
Also Called: Apparel House USA
16325 S Avalon Blvd, Gardena
(90248-2909)
PHONE..................213 746-8822
David Ghods, *CEO*
EMP: 12
SALES: 4MM **Privately Held**
SIC: 2211 Apparel & outerwear fabrics, cotton

(P-2715)
TUA FASHION INC (PA)
Also Called: Tua USA
8936 Appian Way, Los Angeles
(90046-7737)
PHONE..................213 422-2384
Yum Cho, *President*
Mark Cho, *COO*
Andrew Cho, *Principal*
Duck J Cho, *Principal*
EMP: 14
SQ FT: 22,000
SALES (est): 1.9MM **Privately Held**
WEB: www.tuausa.com
SIC: 2211 Apparel & outerwear fabrics, cotton

(P-2716)
UPHOLSTERY BY WAYNE STOEC
3316 E Annadale Ave, Fresno
(93725-1904)
PHONE..................559 233-1960
Wayne Stoec, *Owner*
EMP: 11
SALES: 900K **Privately Held**
SIC: 2211 Upholstery, tapestry & wall coverings: cotton

(P-2717)
VETERAN ENTERPRISE INC
Also Called: Veteran Company
620 Gladys Ave, Los Angeles
(90021-1004)
PHONE..................323 937-2233
Abraham Tashdjian, *CEO*
Harry Tashdjian, *Manager*
◆ **EMP:** 14
SALES: 8.5MM **Privately Held**
SIC: 2211 2221 Upholstery, tapestry & wall coverings: cotton; upholstery, tapestry & wall covering fabrics

(P-2718)
WOLFSON KNITTING MILLS INC
2124 Sacramento St, Los Angeles
(90021-1722)
PHONE..................213 627-8746
Stephanie Wolfson, *President*
EMP: 10
SQ FT: 12,500
SALES (est): 1.5MM **Privately Held**
SIC: 2211 Decorative trim & specialty fabrics, including twist weave

2020 California
Manufacturers Register

▲ = Import ▼=Export
◆ =Import/Export

(P-2719)
XCVI LLC (PA)
2311 S Santa Fe Ave, Los Angeles
(90058-1154)
PHONE..................................213 749-2661
Alon Zeltzer,
Daniela Zeltzer, *Exec VP*
Mordechia Zelter,
Gita Zeltzer,
▲ EMP: 120
SQ FT: 60,000
SALES (est): 21.9MM **Privately Held**
WEB: www.xcviwearables.com
SIC: 2211 Apparel & outerwear fabrics,
cotton; sheets, bedding & table cloths:
cotton

2221 Silk & Man-Made Fiber

(P-2720)
3 INK PRODUCTIONS INC
4790 W Jacquelyn Ave, Fresno
(93722-6406)
PHONE..................................559 275-4565
Craig Stidham, *President*
Dianne Stidham, *Partner*
EMP: 14
SALES (est): 1.1MM **Privately Held**
SIC: 2221 5023 Textile warping, on a con-
tract basis; sheets, textile

(P-2721)
**AGRICULTURE BAG MFG USA
INC (PA)**
Also Called: Agriculture Bag Manufacturing,
960 98th Ave, Oakland (94603-2347)
PHONE..................................510 632-5637
Jeff C Kuo, *CEO*
▲ EMP: 44
SALES (est): 6.8MM **Privately Held**
WEB: www.agriculturebag.com
SIC: 2221 2673 2393 Polypropylene
broadwoven fabrics; plastic & pliofilm
bags; textile bags

(P-2722)
**AMERICAN GARMENT
FINISHING**
17941 Lost Canyon Rd # 6, Canyon Coun-
try (91387-8266)
PHONE..................................310 962-1929
Michelle Vital, *President*
EMP: 33
SQ FT: 2,000
SALES: 7.5MM **Privately Held**
WEB: www.finishag.com
SIC: 2221 Textile mills, broadwoven: silk &
manmade, also glass

(P-2723)
BELLA NOTTE LINENS INC
60 Galli Dr Ste 2, Novato (94949-5713)
PHONE..................................415 883-3434
Kathleen McCoy, *President*
Bob Gunnell, *Corp Secy*
Mitchell Gately, *Vice Pres*
▲ EMP: 38
SQ FT: 13,000
SALES (est): 5.3MM **Privately Held**
WEB: www.bellanottelinens.com
SIC: 2221 Bedding, manmade or silk fabric

(P-2724)
DAE SHIN USA INC
610 N Gilbert St, Fullerton (92833-2555)
PHONE..................................714 578-8900
Jae Weon Lee, *CEO*
▲ EMP: 100
SQ FT: 10,000
SALES: 11MM **Privately Held**
SIC: 2221 Textile mills, broadwoven: silk &
manmade, also glass
PA: Daeshin Textile Co.,Ltd.
Choji-Dong
Ansan 15614

(P-2725)
DOOL FNA INC
Also Called: Grand Textile
16220 Manning Way, Cerritos
(90703-2223)
PHONE..................................562 483-4100
Jae Weon Lee, *CEO*

Jaeweon Lee, *Vice Pres*
Justine Lee, *Principal*
▲ EMP: 120
SQ FT: 100,000
SALES (est): 18.2MM **Privately Held**
SIC: 2221 Textile mills, broadwoven: silk &
manmade, also glass

(P-2726)
FABRITEX INC
2301 E 7th St Ste D102, Los Angeles
(90023-1041)
PHONE..................................213 747-1417
Kourosh Dayan, *President*
Norick Minisians, *CFO*
▲ EMP: 14
SQ FT: 30,000
SALES: 5.7MM **Privately Held**
WEB: www.fabritex.com
SIC: 2221 5131 Linings, rayon or silk;
piece goods & other fabrics

(P-2727)
FABTEX INC
Also Called: Ft Textiles
1202 W Struck Ave, Orange (92867-3532)
PHONE..................................714 538-0877
William P Friese, *Branch Mgr*
EMP: 105
SALES (corp-wide): 109.6MM **Privately
Held**
WEB: www.fabtex.com
SIC: 2221 2515 2392 2391 Draperies &
drapery fabrics, manmade fiber & silk;
bedding, manmade or silk fabric; mat-
tresses & bedsprings; household furnish-
ings; curtains & draperies
PA: Fabtex, Inc.
29 Woodbine Ln
Danville PA 17821
570 275-7500

(P-2728)
IMAGINARY FIBER GLASS INC
Also Called: Imaginery Fiberglass
15740 El Prado Rd, Chino (91710-9105)
PHONE..................................909 597-4110
Reinier Hoogenraad, *President*
Danny Hoogenraad, *Admin Sec*
Meila Hoogenraad, *Admin Sec*
▲ EMP: 15
SQ FT: 9,500
SALES (est): 1.5MM **Privately Held**
SIC: 2221 Fiberglass fabrics

(P-2729)
JUICY COUTURE INC
12723 Wentworth St, Arleta (91331-4330)
PHONE..................................888 824-8826
Pamela Levy, *CEO*
Ellen Rodriguez, *Senior VP*
Lisa Rodericks, *Admin Sec*
▲ EMP: 160
SALES (est): 61.9K
SALES (corp-wide): 6B **Publicly Held**
WEB: www.juicycouture.com
SIC: 2221 Broadwoven fabric mills, man-
made
HQ: Kate Spade Holdings Llc
2 Park Ave Fl 8
New York NY 10016
212 354-4900

(P-2730)
MEMORY THREADS
Also Called: West Trend
506 E Washington Ave A, Santa Ana
(92701-3841)
PHONE..................................818 837-7070
Julliette Slaybaugh, *CEO*
Russell Slaybaugh, *Vice Pres*
EMP: 12 EST: 2016
SALES: 1.5MM **Privately Held**
SIC: 2221 Apparel & outerwear fabric,
manmade fiber or silk

(P-2731)
POP 82 INC
8211 Orangethorpe Ave, Buena Park
(90621-3811)
PHONE..................................714 523-8500
Steven North, *CEO*
Marisela Ramos, *Admin Sec*
EMP: 15
SQ FT: 15,000

SALES: 1.2MM **Privately Held**
SIC: 2221 7389 Acrylic broadwoven fabrics; printing broker

(P-2732)
**S&B DEVELOPMENT GROUP
LLC**
1901 Avenue Of The Stars # 200, Los An-
geles (90067-6015)
PHONE..................................213 446-2818
Nathalio Ortez, *CEO*
Bijan Israel, *Mng Member*
EMP: 48
SQ FT: 50,000
SALES (est): 1.5MM **Privately Held**
SIC: 2221 5023 Broadwoven fabric mills,
manmade; sheets, textile

(P-2733)
SCRIMCO INC
2377 S Orange Ave, Fresno (93725-1021)
PHONE..................................559 237-7442
Todd J Stevens, *President*
Jasen Newton, *Maintence Staff*
▲ EMP: 10
SQ FT: 54,000
SALES (est): 2.4MM **Privately Held**
WEB: www.scrimco.com
SIC: 2221 Polyester broadwoven fabrics;
fiberglass fabrics

(P-2734)
SPD MANUFACTURING INC
1101 E Truslow Ave, Fullerton
(92831-4625)
PHONE..................................985 302-1902
Debra Macaluso, *CEO*
EMP: 19
SALES (est): 182.1K **Privately Held**
SIC: 2221 Apparel & outerwear fabric,
manmade fiber or silk

(P-2735)
SURPRISESILKCOM
628 Madre St, Pasadena (91107-5661)
PHONE..................................626 568-9889
EMP: 10
SALES (est): 400K **Privately Held**
SIC: 2221

(P-2736)
TEXTILE PRODUCTS INC
2512-2520 W Woodland Dr, Anaheim
(92801)
PHONE..................................714 761-0401
Piyush A Shah, *CEO*
Kevin Gearin, *Vice Pres*
Richard Murillo, *Plant Mgr*
Brenda Golanoski, *Sales Staff*
▲ EMP: 26
SQ FT: 16,000
SALES (est): 7.7MM
SALES (corp-wide): 3B **Privately Held**
WEB: www.textileproducts.com
SIC: 2221 Manmade & synthetic broadwo-
ven fabrics
HQ: Kordsa Teknik Tekstil Anonim Sirketi
No:90 Alikahya Fatih Mahallesi
Kocaeli 41310
262 316-7000

(P-2737)
TOMASINI INC
1001 E 60th St, Los Angeles (90001-1018)
PHONE..................................323 231-2349
Angela Brown, *President*
EMP: 20
SQ FT: 5,500
SALES (est): 1.9MM **Privately Held**
WEB: www.tomasini.com
SIC: 2221 5719 Bedding, manmade or silk
fabric; comforters & quilts, manmade fiber
& silk; bedding (sheets, blankets, spreads
& pillows)

(P-2738)
VALLEY DRAPERY INC
Also Called: Valley Drapery and Upholstery
16616 Schoenborn St, North Hills
(91343-6106)
PHONE..................................818 892-7744
Norman Sewitz, *President*
Michael Sewitz, *Vice Pres*
Francine Levin, *General Mgr*
David Sewitz, *Admin Sec*
▲ EMP: 62 EST: 1977

SQ FT: 15,000
WEB: www.valleydrapery.com
SIC: 2221 Draperies & drapery fabrics,
manmade fiber & silk

(P-2739)
VICTORY SPORTSWEAR INC
2381 Buena Vista St, Duarte (91010-3301)
PHONE..................................626 359-5400
Victor Ju, *CEO*
Xiao Can Zhang, *CFO*
▲ EMP: 22
SQ FT: 22,000
SALES: 11MM **Privately Held**
SIC: 2221 5199 5949 Spandex broadwo-
ven fabrics; fabrics, yarns & knit goods;
cotton yarns; leather goods, except
footwear, gloves, luggage, belting; knitting
goods & supplies

(P-2740)
WIND & SHADE SCREENS INC
1223 Linda Vista Dr, San Marcos
(92078-3809)
PHONE..................................760 761-4994
Paul Leathem, *President*
Patricia Somerville, *Vice Pres*
EMP: 10
SQ FT: 2,500
SALES: 650K **Privately Held**
SIC: 2221 2399 Polypropylene broadwo-
ven fabrics; banners, made from fabric

2231 Wool, Woven Fabric

(P-2741)
A AND G INC
Also Called: Alstyle Dyeing & Finishing
1501 E Cerritos Ave, Anaheim
(92805-6400)
PHONE..................................714 756-0400
Jim Gordon, *Manager*
EMP: 131
SALES (corp-wide): 2.9B **Privately Held**
WEB: www.murina.com
SIC: 2231 Dyeing & finishing: wool or simi-
lar fibers
HQ: A And G, Inc.
11296 Harrel St
Jurupa Valley CA 91752
714 765-0400

(P-2742)
**AMERICAN AP DYG & FINSHG
INC**
747 Warehouse St, Los Angeles
(90021-1106)
P.O. Box 5129, Brandon MS (39047-5129)
PHONE..................................310 644-4001
Sang Ho Lim, *President*
Joe Yi, *Office Mgr*
▲ EMP: 70
SALES (est): 7.1MM
SALES (corp-wide): 2.9B **Privately Held**
WEB: www.americanapparel.net
SIC: 2231 Dyeing & finishing: wool or simi-
lar fibers
HQ: App Winddown, Llc
747 Warehouse St
Los Angeles CA 90021
213 488-0226

(P-2743)
**CALIFORNIA INDUSTRIAL
FABRICS**
2325 Marconi Ct, San Diego (92154-7241)
PHONE..................................619 661-7166
Michael Lindsey, *CEO*
Erin McNamara, *CFO*
Patrick Dickey, *Vice Pres*
◆ EMP: 30
SQ FT: 24,000
SALES (est): 2.5MM **Privately Held**
WEB: www.ci-fabrics.com
SIC: 2231 Broadwoven fabric mills, wool

(P-2744)
COMFORT INDUSTRIES INC
12266 Rooks Rd, Whittier (90601-1613)
PHONE..................................562 692-8288
Kevin Do, *CEO*
Ken Quach, *Vice Pres*
Kevin Deal, *Admin Sec*

P R O D U C T S & S V C S

◆ **EMP:** 35
SQ FT: 18,000
SALES (est): 5.3MM **Privately Held**
SIC: 2231 Upholstery fabrics, wool

(P-2745)
ICON APPAREL GROUP LLC
2989 Promenade St Ste 100, West Sacramento (95691-6419)
PHONE.................................916 372-4266
Juan Carlos Ceja, *Mng Member*
Alberto Rivera, *Controller*
Ronald Leavitt, *Sales Executive*
Jerrad Fiore,
Ronnie Leavitt,
EMP: 35
SQ FT: 10,000
SALES (est): 2.1MM **Privately Held**
WEB: www.iconapparel.com
SIC: 2231 7389 2759 Apparel & outerwear broadwoven fabrics; apparel designers, commercial; screen printing

(P-2746)
LEKOS DYE & FINISHING INC
3131 E Harcourt St, Compton (90221-5505)
PHONE.................................310 763-0900
Ilgun Lee, *President*
Daniel Lee, *Executive*
▲ **EMP:** 65
SQ FT: 72,000
SALES (est): 10.2MM **Privately Held**
SIC: 2231 Dyeing & finishing: wool or similar fibers

(P-2747)
PACIFIC DRY GOODS INC
1085 Essex Ave, Richmond (94801-2112)
P.O. Box 3879, San Leandro (94578-0879)
PHONE.................................925 288-2929
Brian W Hudsono, *President*
Phillip Brown, *Treasurer*
▲ **EMP:** 10
SQ FT: 20,000
SALES (est): 1.3MM **Privately Held**
WEB: www.pacificdrygoods.com
SIC: 2231 3291 Sponging cloth: wool, mohair or similar fabric; cloth, abrasive: garnet, emery, aluminum oxide coated

(P-2748)
TRI-STAR DYEING & FINSHG INC
15125 Marquardt Ave, Santa Fe Springs (90670-5705)
PHONE.................................562 483-0123
Jang You, *Principal*
◆ **EMP:** 63
SQ FT: 60,000
SALES (est): 22.3MM **Privately Held**
SIC: 2231 Dyeing & finishing: wool or similar fibers
PA: Jangyou Co., Ltd.
Rm 12b-22
Ansan 15436

2241 Fabric Mills, Cotton, Wool, Silk & Man-Made

(P-2749)
ALL AMERICAN LABEL
Also Called: Label Gallery
1700 Wall St, Los Angeles (90015-3719)
PHONE.................................213 622-2222
Steve Firouz, *President*
EMP: 22
SALES (est): 246.1K **Privately Held**
SIC: 2241 Labels, woven

(P-2750)
AX II INC
Also Called: Gin'l Fabrics
13921 S Figueroa St, Los Angeles (90061-1027)
PHONE.................................310 292-6523
Anthony Xepolis, *President*
Ginny Xepolis, *Vice Pres*
EMP: 26
SALES (est): 2.8MM **Privately Held**
SIC: 2241 2396 Narrow fabric mills; automotive & apparel trimmings

(P-2751)
CHUA & SONS INC
Also Called: Reliable Tape Products
3300 E 50th St, Vernon (90058-3004)
P.O. Box 58261, Los Angeles (90058-0261)
PHONE.................................323 588-8044
Shirley Chua, *President*
▲ **EMP:** 23
SQ FT: 67,000
SALES (est): 3.6MM **Privately Held**
SIC: 2241 Fabric tapes

(P-2752)
FAIRWAY TRADING INC
5717 Ferguson Dr, Commerce (90022-5101)
PHONE.................................323 582-8111
Sam Farmanara, *President*
▲ **EMP:** 10
SALES (est): 2MM **Privately Held**
WEB: www.fairwaytrading.com
SIC: 2241 Trimmings, textile

(P-2753)
HANAH SILK INC
5155 Myrtle Ave, Eureka (95503-9506)
PHONE.................................707 442-0886
Brooke Exley, *President*
▲ **EMP:** 10
SALES (est): 905.4K **Privately Held**
SIC: 2241 Ribbons

(P-2754)
HORVATH HOLDINGS INC
Also Called: Clayborn Lab
40173 Truckee Airport Rd, Truckee (96161-4115)
PHONE.................................530 587-4700
Justin Horvath, *President*
Amy Horvath, *CFO*
EMP: 15
SQ FT: 4,500
SALES: 3MM **Privately Held**
SIC: 2241 Electric insulating tapes & braids, except plastic

(P-2755)
INDUSTRIAL WIPER & SUPPLY INC
1025 98th Ave A, Oakland (94603-2356)
PHONE.................................408 286-4752
Mitchell Tobin, *CEO*
Robert Tobin, *President*
▲ **EMP:** 29
SQ FT: 10,000
SALES (est): 4.8MM **Privately Held**
WEB: www.industrialwiper.com
SIC: 2241 Narrow fabric mills

(P-2756)
MAKO INC
736 Monterey Pass Rd, Monterey Park (91754-3607)
PHONE.................................323 262-2168
John Chaing, *President*
Jenney Tsung, *Vice Pres*
▲ **EMP:** 50
SALES (est): 4.3MM **Privately Held**
SIC: 2241 Trimmings, textile

(P-2757)
MAXSTRAPS INC
925 Gravenstein Ave, Sebastopol (95472-4573)
P.O. Box 63 (95473-0063)
PHONE.................................707 829-3000
Steven Williams, *President*
Elaine Williams, *Vice Pres*
EMP: 68
SALES (est): 5.8MM **Privately Held**
WEB: www.maxstraps.com
SIC: 2241 5013 Strapping webs; automotive supplies & parts

(P-2758)
RIVERA YARN PRODUCTS INC
1690 Cactus Rd, San Diego (92154-8101)
PHONE.................................619 661-6306
EMP: 20
SQ FT: 8,000
SALES (est): 2.3MM **Privately Held**
SIC: 2241 2298

(P-2759)
ROCKY LABEL MILLS INC
1930 Doreen Ave, South El Monte (91733-3332)
PHONE.................................323 278-0080
Frank Lin, *President*
▲ **EMP:** 23
SALES (est): 1.6MM **Privately Held**
SIC: 2241 Labels, woven

(P-2760)
SANTA FE TEXTILES INC
17370 Mount Herrmann St, Fountain Valley (92708-4104)
PHONE.................................949 251-1960
Fax: 949 251-9006
EMP: 18
SQ FT: 25,000
SALES (est): 1.4MM **Privately Held**
SIC: 2241 3496

(P-2761)
SILVER TEXTILE INCORPORATED
Also Called: Olympia Trading
2101 S Flower St, Los Angeles (90007-2051)
PHONE.................................213 747-2221
Sam Tehrani, *CEO*
Susan Tehrani, *Treasurer*
Shiva Tehrani, *Admin Sec*
▲ **EMP:** 12
SQ FT: 4,000
SALES (est): 2.1MM **Privately Held**
SIC: 2241 2221 5131 Narrow fabric mills; broadwoven fabric mills, manmade; silk piece goods, woven

(P-2762)
TRIMKNIT INC
7542 San Fernando Rd, Sun Valley (91352-4344)
PHONE.................................818 768-7878
Peter Krausz, *President*
EMP: 21
SQ FT: 12,000
SALES (est): 2.1MM **Privately Held**
SIC: 2241 Trimmings, textile

(P-2763)
VEGA TEXTILE INC
2751 S Alameda St, Los Angeles (90058-1311)
PHONE.................................323 923-0600
Linchun Liu, *President*
Zengle Wang, *Admin Sec*
▲ **EMP:** 10
SALES (est): 990K **Privately Held**
SIC: 2241 Bindings, textile

2251 Hosiery, Women's Full & Knee Length

(P-2764)
CALISON INC
2447 Leef Ave, South El Monte (91733)
PHONE.................................626 448-3328
Tina Wu, *Vice Pres*
EMP: 25
SQ FT: 7,000
SALES: 800K **Privately Held**
SIC: 2251 Women's hosiery, except socks

2252 Hosiery, Except Women's

(P-2765)
DRYMAX TECHNOLOGIES INC
9900 El Camino Real, Atascadero (93422-5573)
P.O. Box 2500 (93423-2500)
PHONE.................................805 239-2555
William Blythe, *CEO*
Robert Macgillivray, *Principal*
EMP: 15 **EST:** 2014
SALES (est): 1.8MM **Privately Held**
SIC: 2252 Socks

(P-2766)
GOLDEN GATE HOSIERY INC
14095 Laurelwood Pl, Chino (91710-5495)
PHONE.................................909 464-0805
Sang Hoon Moon, *President*
SAE Yang Chang, *Corp Secy*
▲ **EMP:** 25
SQ FT: 13,000
SALES (est): 3.3MM **Privately Held**
SIC: 2252 Socks

(P-2767)
SOCKSMITH DESIGN INC (PA)
1515 Pacific Ave, Santa Cruz (95060-3911)
PHONE.................................831 426-6416
Eric W Gil, *President*
▲ **EMP:** 24
SQ FT: 10,000
SALES (est): 3.3MM **Privately Held**
SIC: 2252 Socks

(P-2768)
THIRTY THREE THREADS INC
1330 Park Center Dr, Vista (92081-8300)
PHONE.................................877 486-3769
Joe Patterson, *CEO*
▲ **EMP:** 35 **EST:** 2009
SALES (est): 5.8MM **Privately Held**
SIC: 2252 Socks

(P-2769)
UNIVERSAL HOSIERY INC
28337 Constellation Rd, Valencia (91355-5048)
PHONE.................................661 702-8444
Johnathan Ekizian, *President*
▲ **EMP:** 75
SQ FT: 44,000
SALES (est): 45MM **Privately Held**
SIC: 2252 Socks

(P-2770)
VM PROVIDER INC (PA)
1135 1/2 N Berendo St, Los Angeles (90029-1705)
PHONE.................................800 674-3233
Vahe Mkhitaryan, *President*
EMP: 10
SALES (est): 871.9K **Privately Held**
SIC: 2252 Socks

2253 Knit Outerwear Mills

(P-2771)
ALSTYLE AP & ACTIVEWEAR MGT CO
Also Called: Alstyle Dyeing & Finishing
1501 E Cerritos Ave, Anaheim (92805-6400)
PHONE.................................714 765-0400
Rauf Gajiani, *Manager*
EMP: 10
SALES (corp-wide): 2.9B **Privately Held**
WEB: www.alstyle.com
SIC: 2253 T-shirts & tops, knit
HQ: Alstyle Apparel & Activewear Management Co.
1501 E Cerritos Ave
Anaheim CA 92805
714 765-0400

(P-2772)
BALBOA MANUFACTURING CO LLC (PA)
Also Called: Bobster Eyewear
9401 Waples St Ste 120, San Diego (92121-3909)
PHONE.................................858 715-0060
John Smaller, *Mng Member*
Mike Maxwell, *Admin Mgr*
Gina Lozano, *Admin Asst*
Scott McVay, *Marketing Staff*
Stacey Cox, *Manager*
▲ **EMP:** 42
SQ FT: 40,000
SALES: 3.9MM **Privately Held**
WEB: www.balboawholesale.com
SIC: 2253 2211 Hats & headwear, knit; apparel & outerwear fabrics, cotton

---

▲ = Import ▼=Export
◆ =Import/Export

(P-2773)
BALL OF COTTON INC
6400 E Washington Blvd, Commerce
(90040-1820)
PHONE.........................323 888-9448
Eddy Park, *President*
Elizabeth Park, *Vice Pres*
EMP: 45
SQ FT: 7,000
SALES: 5MM **Privately Held**
WEB: www.ballofcotton.com
SIC: 2253 Sweaters & sweater coats, knit

(P-2774)
**BROADWAY KNITTING MILLS
CORP**
1766 N Helm Ave Ste 101, Fresno
(93727-1627)
PHONE.........................559 456-0955
Jan Mattlin, *Manager*
EMP: 30
SALES (corp-wide): 2.2MM **Privately
Held**
WEB: www.broadwayalbion.com
SIC: 2253 Knit outerwear mills
PA: Broadway Knitting Mills Corp
2152 Sacramento St
Los Angeles CA
213 680-9694

(P-2775)
BYER CALIFORNIA
Alfred Paquette Division
1201 Rio Vista Ave, Los Angeles
(90023-2609)
PHONE.........................323 780-7615
Jan Shostak, *Manager*
Dan Shostak, *Prdtn Mgr*
EMP: 380
SQ FT: 10,000
SALES (corp-wide): 347.6MM **Privately
Held**
WEB: www.byer.com
SIC: 2253 2339 2335 Dresses, knit;
women's & misses' outerwear; women's,
juniors' & misses' dresses
PA: Byer California
66 Potrero Ave
San Francisco CA 94103
415 626-7844

(P-2776)
C A N ENTERPRISES
Also Called: C M Sport
291 Kinross Dr, Walnut Creek
(94598-2105)
PHONE.........................925 939-9736
Chereen Makhlouf, *Owner*
Hania Makhlouf, *Co-Owner*
▲ EMP: 70
SALES (est): 3MM **Privately Held**
WEB: www.canenterprises.com
SIC: 2253 Knit outerwear mills

(P-2777)
CARE TEX INDUSTRIES INC (PA)
4583 Firestone Blvd, South Gate
(90280-3343)
PHONE.........................323 567-5074
Richard Kang, *President*
Charles Kang, *CEO*
Dan Kang, *Admin Sec*
EMP: 60
SQ FT: 27,000
SALES (est): 7.4MM **Privately Held**
SIC: 2253 Dyeing & finishing knit outer-
wear, excl. hosiery & glove

(P-2778)
CASMARI INC
9035 Eton Ave Ste C, Canoga Park
(91304-6521)
PHONE.........................818 727-1856
Maria Carter, *CEO*
Rita Ragusa, *CFO*
EMP: 10
SALES (est): 1.1MM **Privately Held**
SIC: 2253 Sweaters & sweater coats, knit

(P-2779)
COLOR IMAGE APPAREL INC
Also Called: Bellacanvas
860 S Los Angeles St, Los Angeles
(90014-3311)
PHONE.........................855 793-3100
Daniel Harris, *Owner*

Nicholas Blanchard, *Business Anlyst*
EMP: 23 **Privately Held**
SIC: 2253 2396 T-shirts & tops, knit;
screen printing on fabric articles
PA: Color Image Apparel, Inc.
6670 Flotilla St
Commerce CA 90040

(P-2780)
COMPLETE GARMENT INC
2101 E 38th St, Vernon (90058-1616)
PHONE.........................323 846-3731
Steven Shaul, *CEO*
EMP: 33
SQ FT: 40,000
SALES (est): 4MM **Privately Held**
SIC: 2253 Dyeing & finishing knit outer-
wear, excl. hosiery & glove

(P-2781)
**DELTA PACIFIC ACTIVEWEAR
INC**
331 S Hale Ave, Fullerton (92831-4805)
PHONE.........................714 871-9281
Imran Parekh, *President*
▲ EMP: 80
SALES (est): 15.6MM **Privately Held**
SIC: 2253 2331 2321 T-shirts & tops, knit;
women's & misses' blouses & shirts;
men's & boys' furnishings

(P-2782)
DM COLLECTIVE INC
4536 District Blvd, Vernon (90058-2712)
PHONE.........................323 923-2400
Daniel S Lee, *CEO*
Monica Lee, *CFO*
▲ EMP: 30
SALES (est): 5.6MM **Privately Held**
SIC: 2253 5131 Warm weather knit outer-
wear, including beachwear; knit fabrics

(P-2783)
EMA TEXTILES INC
Also Called: Sworn Virgins
2947 E 44th St, Vernon (90058-2429)
PHONE.........................323 589-9800
EMP: 12
SQ FT: 10,000
SALES (est): 1.7MM **Privately Held**
WEB: www.ematex.com
SIC: 2253

(P-2784)
**FANTASY ACTIVEWEAR INC
(PA)**
Also Called: Fantasy Manufacturing
5383 Alcoa Ave, Vernon (90058-3734)
PHONE.........................213 705-4111
Anwar Gajiani, *CEO*
Yassmin Gajiani, *Vice Pres*
▲ EMP: 45
SQ FT: 20,000
SALES (est): 36.1MM **Privately Held**
WEB: www.fantasyincgroup.com
SIC: 2253 2331 2321 T-shirts & tops, knit;
women's & misses' blouses & shirts;
men's & boys' furnishings

(P-2785)
**FANTASY DYEING & FINISHING
INC**
5383 Alcoa Ave, Vernon (90058-3734)
PHONE.........................323 983-9988
Anwar M Gajiani, *CEO*
EMP: 100
SALES (est): 15MM **Privately Held**
SIC: 2253 Dyeing & finishing knit outer-
wear, excl. hosiery & glove

(P-2786)
FORTUNE SWIMWEAR LLC (HQ)
Also Called: Palisades Beach Club
2340 E Olympic Blvd Ste A, Los Angeles
(90021-2544)
PHONE.........................310 733-2130
Fred Kayne, *Mng Member*
Adeline Kevorkian, *Controller*
Stephen Soller,
◆ EMP: 30
SQ FT: 10,000

SALES (est): 6.9MM **Privately Held**
WEB: www.fortuneswimwear.com
SIC: 2253 2335 Bathing suits & swimwear,
knit; women's, juniors' & misses' dresses

(P-2787)
**FRESH PEACHES
INCORPORATED (PA)**
Also Called: Fresh Peaches Swimwear
8423 Rochester Ave # 103, Rancho Cuca-
monga (91730-3995)
PHONE.........................909 980-0172
Jeanette M Love, *President*
James M Love Jr, *Treasurer*
Lannette Love, *Admin Sec*
▲ EMP: 24
SQ FT: 6,650
SALES (est): 3MM **Privately Held**
WEB: www.fresh-peaches.com
SIC: 2253 5699 5632 Bathing suits &
swimwear, knit; body stockings, knit;
bathing suits; dancewear

(P-2788)
GARDENA TEXTILE INC
245 W 135th St, Los Angeles (90061-1625)
PHONE.........................310 327-5060
EMP: 18
SQ FT: 22,000
SALES (est): 106K **Privately Held**
SIC: 2253

(P-2789)
GRAND WEST INC (PA)
Also Called: Crown Fashion
1441 E Adams Blvd, Los Angeles
(90011-1819)
PHONE.........................323 235-2700
Dae Hyun Kim, *President*
EMP: 10
SQ FT: 52,000
SALES (est): 1.3MM **Privately Held**
WEB: www.grandwest.com
SIC: 2253 Jerseys, knit

(P-2790)
HIGH-END KNITWEAR INC
Also Called: T Q M Apparel Group
1100 S Hope St Ph 202, Los Angeles
(90015-2197)
PHONE.........................323 582-6061
EMP: 35
SQ FT: 30,000
SALES (est): 3.9MM **Privately Held**
SIC: 2253

(P-2791)
ISIQALO LLC
Also Called: Spectra USA
5521 Schaefer Ave, Chino (91710-9070)
PHONE.........................714 683-2820
Thomas Fenchel,
Nick Agakanian,
EMP: 350 EST: 2012
SQ FT: 350,000
SALES: 75MM **Privately Held**
SIC: 2253 5136 5137 2321 T-shirts &
tops, knit; men's & boys' clothing;
women's & children's clothing; sport
shirts, men's & boys': from purchased
materials; T-shirts & tops, women's: made
from purchased materials

(P-2792)
JBS PRIVATE LABEL INC
Also Called: J B'S Private Label
4383 Irvine Ave, Studio City (91604-2705)
PHONE.........................818 762-3736
Jackie Bender, *President*
EMP: 28
SQ FT: 2,500
SALES: 700K **Privately Held**
SIC: 2253 5199 2339 2337 Warm
weather knit outerwear, including beach-
wear; dresses & skirts; blouses, shirts,
pants & suits; knit goods; women's &
misses' outerwear; women's & misses'
suits & coats

(P-2793)
KOAM KNITECH INC
18118 S Broadway, Gardena (90248-3536)
PHONE.........................310 515-1121
James Park, *President*
▲ EMP: 49 EST: 1998
SQ FT: 20,000

SALES (est): 5MM **Privately Held**
SIC: 2253 2339 Sweaters & sweater
coats, knit; women's & misses' outerwear

(P-2794)
LIALEE INC
Also Called: Two Hands
525 E 87th Pl, Los Angeles (90003-3501)
PHONE.........................213 765-7788
Lia Seungeun Lee, *CEO*
Seung Eun Lee, *President*
▲ EMP: 15
SQ FT: 4,310
SALES (est): 3.2MM **Privately Held**
SIC: 2253 T-shirts & tops, knit

(P-2795)
**M & M SPORTSWEAR
MANUFACTURING**
18267 4th Ave, Jamestown (95327-9760)
P.O. Box 1429 (95327-1429)
PHONE.........................209 984-5632
Denny Minners, *President*
EMP: 10
SQ FT: 4,800
SALES (est): 620K **Privately Held**
WEB: www.mmsportswear.com
SIC: 2253 7336 2339 Jerseys, knit; com-
mercial art & graphic design; women's &
misses' outerwear

(P-2796)
MAXIT DESIGNS INC
4044 Wayside Ln Ste A, Carmichael
(95608-1756)
P.O. Box 1052 (95609-1052)
PHONE.........................916 489-1023
Gail Ellison, *President*
Mike Ellison, *Vice Pres*
EMP: 10
SQ FT: 6,500
SALES (est): 1.1MM **Privately Held**
WEB: www.headgator.com
SIC: 2253 Knit outerwear mills

(P-2797)
MILL 42 INC
3711 Long Beach Blvd # 500, Long Beach
(90807-3319)
PHONE.........................714 979-4200
Kevin Dunlap, *CEO*
Mike Dunlap, *CFO*
Brad Bleick, *VP Sales*
◆ EMP: 11
SALES (est): 4.5MM **Privately Held**
SIC: 2253 T-shirts & tops, knit

(P-2798)
MJ BLANKS INC
Also Called: Blanks Plus
1155 S Grand Ave Apt 614, Los Angeles
(90015-2780)
PHONE.........................213 629-0006
Sung Ho Hong, *President*
EMP: 30
SQ FT: 12,000
SALES (est): 3MM **Privately Held**
SIC: 2253 T-shirts & tops, knit

(P-2799)
MJCK CORPORATION
Also Called: Xzavier
3222 E Washington Blvd, Vernon
(90058-8022)
PHONE.........................888 992-8437
Tae Y Choi, *President*
EMP: 30 EST: 2010
SALES (est): 2.9MM **Privately Held**
SIC: 2253 2361 T-shirts & tops, knit; t-
shirts & tops: girls', children's & infants'

(P-2800)
PRO TAG CORP
8122 Maie Ave Unit C, Los Angeles
(90001-3855)
PHONE.........................213 272-9606
Sujung Choi, *President*
Jae S Park, *CEO*
Charlie Choi, *Vice Pres*
EMP: 20
SALES (est): 989.9K **Privately Held**
SIC: 2253 Shirts (outerwear), knit

(P-2801)
SNOWFLAKE DESIGNS
2893 Larkin Ave, Clovis (93612-3908)
PHONE........................559 291-6234
Ladonna Snow, *Co-Owner*
Richard L Snow, *Co-Owner*
EMP: 22
SQ FT: 7,100
SALES (est): 1.2MM **Privately Held**
WEB: www.snowleotards.com
SIC: 2253 5632 Leotards, knit; dancewear

(P-2802)
ST JOHN KNITS INTL INC
17622 Armstrong Ave, Irvine (92614-5728)
PHONE........................949 399-8200
Philip Miller, *CEO*
EMP: 439
SALES (corp-wide): 507.1MM **Privately Held**
WEB: www.stjohnknits.com
SIC: 2253 2339 2335 3961 Dresses, knit; skirts, knit; pants, slacks or trousers, knit; T-shirts & tops, knit; sportswear, women's; scarves, hoods, headbands, etc.: women's; jackets, untailored: women's, misses' & juniors'; slacks: women's, misses' & juniors'; women's, juniors' & misses' dresses; bridal & formal gowns; costume jewelry; apparel belts
HQ: St. John Knits International, Incorporated
17522 Armstrong Ave
Irvine CA 92614
949 863-1171

(P-2803)
STUDIO9D8 INC
9743 Alesia St, South El Monte (91733-3008)
PHONE........................626 350-0832
Ann Lem, *CEO*
EMP: 30 EST: 2011
SALES (est): 1.5MM **Privately Held**
SIC: 2253 2515 T-shirts & tops, knit; studio couches

(P-2804)
STYLE KNITS INC
1745 Chapin Rd, Montebello (90640-6609)
PHONE........................323 890-9080
Patrick Quinn, *President*
EMP: 60
SALES (est): 3MM **Privately Held**
SIC: 2253 Knit outerwear mills

(P-2805)
SUN DYEING AND FINISHING CO
15621 Broadway Center St, Gardena (90248-2138)
PHONE........................310 329-0844
Ronald Nam, *President*
Nam Chul Kim, *Director*
EMP: 15
SQ FT: 23,000
SALES (est): 1.7MM **Privately Held**
SIC: 2253 Dyeing & finishing knit outerwear, excl. hosiery & glove

(P-2806)
SUN TRADE GROUP INC (PA)
Also Called: Sun Dog International
1251 Burton St, Fullerton (92831-5211)
PHONE........................714 525-4888
Lori Gulsvig, *President*
Stuart Nichols, *COO*
EMP: 15
SQ FT: 45,000
SALES (est): 7MM **Privately Held**
WEB: www.sundoginternational.com
SIC: 2253 T-shirts & tops, knit

(P-2807)
THIENES APPAREL INC
1811 Floradale Ave, South El Monte (91733-3605)
PHONE........................626 575-2818
Chao Wen Chang, *Principal*
▲ EMP: 130
SQ FT: 17,500
SALES (est): 13.1MM **Privately Held**
SIC: 2253 Blouses, knit

(P-2808)
TIEN-HU KNITTING CO (US) INC
18935 Sydney Cir, Castro Valley (94546-2753)
PHONE........................510 268-8833
Tim Shing Chan, *President*
Jane Wm Chan, *Vice Pres*
▲ EMP: 80
SALES (est): 5.9MM **Privately Held**
SIC: 2253 2339 Sweaters & sweater coats, knit; women's & misses' outerwear

(P-2809)
YOUNG KNITTING MILLS
3499 E 15th St, Los Angeles (90023-3833)
PHONE........................323 980-8677
Fax: 323 980-5198
EMP: 21
SQ FT: 25,000
SALES (est): 961.3K **Privately Held**
SIC: 2253

2254 Knit Underwear Mills

(P-2810)
VAN TISSE INC
2565 3rd St Ste 319, San Francisco (94107-3155)
PHONE........................415 543-2404
Andres Van Dam, *President*
Diane Lee Van Dam, *Corp Secy*
EMP: 15
SQ FT: 12,000
SALES: 1MM **Privately Held**
SIC: 2254 2339 2322 2341 Nightwear (nightgowns, negligees, pajamas), knit; women's & misses' outerwear; women's & misses' athletic clothing & sportswear; men's & boys' underwear & nightwear; women's & children's underwear

---

2257 Circular Knit Fabric Mills

(P-2811)
MATCHMASTER DYG & FINSHG INC
Antex Knitting Mills
3750 Broadway Pl, Los Angeles (90007-4400)
PHONE........................323 232-2061
EMP: 65
SALES (corp-wide): 123.1MM **Privately Held**
SIC: 2257 5199
PA: Matchmaster Dyeing & Finishing, Inc.
3750 S Broadway
Los Angeles CA 90007
323 232-2061

(P-2812)
SHARA-TEX INC
3338 E Slauson Ave, Vernon (90058-3915)
PHONE........................323 587-7200
Shahram Fahimian, *Ch of Bd*
S Tony Souferian, *President*
▲ EMP: 45
SQ FT: 55,000
SALES (est): 9.6MM **Privately Held**
WEB: www.shara-tex.com
SIC: 2257 Weft knit fabric mills

(P-2813)
TENENBLATT CORPORATION
Also Called: Antex Knitting Mills
3750 Broadway Pl, Los Angeles (90007-4400)
PHONE........................323 232-2061
William Tenenblatt, *President*
Anna Tenenblatt, *Vice Pres*
◆ EMP: 200
SQ FT: 60,000
SALES (est): 18.3MM
SALES (corp-wide): 59.2MM **Privately Held**
WEB: www.antexknitting.com
SIC: 2257 Dyeing & finishing circular knit fabrics
PA: Matchmaster Dyeing & Finishing, Inc.
3750 S Broadway
Los Angeles CA 90007
323 232-2061

2258 Lace & Warp Knit Fabric Mills

(P-2814)
PRIME ALLIANCE LLC
360 W Victoria St, Compton (90220-6061)
PHONE........................310 764-1000
EMP: 50
SQ FT: 60,000
SALES: 7.2MM **Privately Held**
SIC: 2258

(P-2815)
TUBE RAGS
4382 Bandini Blvd, Vernon (90058-4323)
PHONE........................323 264-7770
AVI Mor, *CEO*
◆ EMP: 10
SALES (est): 68.7K **Privately Held**
SIC: 2258 Dyeing & finishing lace goods & warp knit fabric

2259 Knitting Mills, NEC

(P-2816)
AZITEX TRADING CORP
Also Called: Azitex Knitting Mills
1850 E 15th St, Los Angeles (90021-2820)
PHONE........................213 745-7072
Michael Azizi, *President*
Andrew Azizi, *Corp Secy*
Mozie Azizi, *Vice Pres*
▲ EMP: 60
SQ FT: 50,000
SALES (est): 13.3MM **Privately Held**
SIC: 2259 2253 Convertors, knit goods; knit outerwear mills

(P-2817)
COTTON KNITS TRADING
3097 E Ana St, Compton (90221-5604)
PHONE........................310 884-9600
Ali Farid, *President*
Hadi E Farid, *Vice Pres*
▲ EMP: 35
SQ FT: 110,000
SALES (est): 4.8MM **Privately Held**
WEB: www.natureusa.net
SIC: 2259 Bags & bagging, knit

(P-2818)
MIDTHRUST IMPORTS INC
830 E 14th Pl, Los Angeles (90021-2120)
PHONE........................213 749-6651
Kamran Noman, *CEO*
▲ EMP: 20
SALES (est): 4.1MM **Privately Held**
WEB: www.midthrust.com
SIC: 2259 Convertors, knit goods

(P-2819)
SAS TEXTILES INC
3100 E 44th St, Vernon (90058-2406)
PHONE........................323 277-5555
Sohrab Sassounian, *President*
Albert Sassounian, *Treasurer*
Soheil Sassounian, *Vice Pres*
Miriam Galeon, *Asst Controller*
▲ EMP: 70
SQ FT: 40,000
SALES (est): 13.4MM **Privately Held**
SIC: 2259 2257 7389 Convertors, knit goods; weft knit fabric mills; textile & apparel services

(P-2820)
SW SAFETY SOLUTIONS INC
33278 Central Ave Ste 102, Union City (94587-2016)
PHONE........................510 429-8692
Belle Chou, *CEO*
Tom Draskovics, *Chief Mktg Ofcr*
Bob Gaither, *Officer*
Mike Kimberley, *Regional Mgr*
Tammy Metz, *Regional Mgr*
EMP: 26
SALES: 9.5MM **Privately Held**
SIC: 2259 Gloves & mittens, knit

2261 Cotton Fabric Finishers

(P-2821)
AS MATCH DYEING CO INC
Also Called: National Dyeing
2522 E 37th St, Vernon (90058-1725)
PHONE........................323 277-0470
Geun Jo Cha, *President*
Young C Kim, *Admin Sec*
▲ EMP: 109
SQ FT: 60,000
SALES (est): 16.4MM **Privately Held**
SIC: 2261 2262 2269 Finishing plants, cotton; finishing plants, manmade fiber & silk fabrics; finishing plants

(P-2822)
BIG STUDIO INC
1247 E Hill St, Long Beach (90755-3523)
PHONE........................562 989-2444
Mitchell Kron, *President*
Chris Carder, *Assistant*
EMP: 15
SQ FT: 11,424
SALES (est): 1.7MM **Privately Held**
WEB: www.bigstudio.com
SIC: 2261 Screen printing of cotton broadwoven fabrics

(P-2823)
CAITAC GARMENT PROCESSING INC
14725 S Broadway, Gardena (90248-1813)
PHONE........................310 217-9888
Muneyuki Ishii, *CEO*
Azusa Sahara, *CFO*
Daisy Rodriguez, *Admin Asst*
Hiroyuki Shigenai, *CIO*
Isaac Norris, *Info Tech Mgr*
▲ EMP: 270
SQ FT: 200,000
SALES (est): 40.7MM **Privately Held**
WEB: www.caitacgarment.com
SIC: 2261 2339 2325 5651 Screen printing of cotton broadwoven fabrics; women's & misses' outerwear; men's & boys' trousers & slacks; jeans stores; embroidery kits
PA: Caitac Holdings Corp.
3-12, Showacho, Kita-Ku
Okayama OKA 700-0

(P-2824)
ESTEPHANIAN ORIGINALS INC
1550 E Mountain St, Pasadena (91104-3909)
PHONE........................626 358-7265
Mark Derestephanian, *President*
EMP: 30
SQ FT: 11,000
SALES (est): 2.8MM **Privately Held**
WEB: www.eodye.com
SIC: 2261 Screen printing of cotton broadwoven fabrics

(P-2825)
FULCRUM INTERNATIONAL INC
993 S Firefly Dr, Anaheim (92808-1504)
PHONE........................310 763-6823
Marcus J Reza, *President*
EMP: 48
SQ FT: 12,080
SALES (est): 4.2MM **Privately Held**
SIC: 2261 Dyeing cotton broadwoven fabrics

(P-2826)
HARRYS DYE AND WASH INC
1015 E Orangethorpe Ave, Anaheim (92801-1135)
PHONE........................714 446-0300
Harry Choung, *President*
Kang Ho Lee, *Vice Pres*
EMP: 30
SQ FT: 20,000
SALES (est): 3MM **Privately Held**
SIC: 2261 2269 Finishing plants, cotton; finishing plants

▲ = Import ▼=Export
◆ =Import/Export

(P-2827)
L A AIR LINE INC
3844 S Santa Fe Ave, Vernon
(90058-1713)
PHONE......................323 585-1088
Dennis Maroney, *President*
Sandy Maroney, *Treasurer*
EMP: 27
SQ FT: 20,600
SALES (est): 3.3MM **Privately Held**
WEB: www.laairline.com
SIC: 2261 2396 2269 Dyeing cotton broadwoven fabrics; printing & embossing on plastics fabric articles; screen printing on fabric articles; finishing plants

(P-2828)
LORBER INDUSTRIES CALIFORNIA
Also Called: Lorber Industries of Claif
823 N Roxbury Dr, Beverly Hills
(90210-3017)
PHONE......................310 275-1568
Tom Lorber, *President*
John Robertson, *CFO*
Michael Gruener, *Vice Pres*
Greg Lorber, *Vice Pres*
Michael Painter, *Vice Pres*
EMP: 435
SALES (est): 28MM **Privately Held**
SIC: 2261 2262 2253 2257 Screen printing of cotton broadwoven fabrics; bleaching cotton broadwoven fabrics; shrinking cotton cloth; napping of cotton broadwoven fabrics; screen printing: manmade fiber & silk broadwoven fabrics; bleaching: manmade fiber & silk broadwoven fabrics; shrinking: manmade fiber & silk cloth; napping: manmade fiber & silk broadwoven fabrics; knit outerwear mills; weft knit fabric mills

(P-2829)
MAD ENGINE LLC (PA)
6740 Cobra Way Ste 100, San Diego
(92121-4102)
PHONE......................858 558-5270
Danish Gajiani, *CEO*
Bill Bussiere, *CFO*
◆ **EMP:** 50
SQ FT: 50,000
SALES (est): 173MM **Privately Held**
WEB: www.madengine.com
SIC: 2261 Screen printing of cotton broadwoven fabrics

(P-2830)
MANDEGO INC
Also Called: Mandego Apparel
2300 Tech Pkwy Ste 2, Hollister (95023)
PHONE......................831 637-5241
Dean Machado, *President*
Kelly Machado, *Admin Sec*
EMP: 17
SQ FT: 4,000
SALES (est): 1.2MM **Privately Held**
WEB: www.mandego.com
SIC: 2261 Screen printing of cotton broadwoven fabrics

(P-2831)
PACIFIC CONTNTL TEXTILES INC
Pacific Contntl Dyne & Finshg
2880 E Ana St, E Rncho Dmngz
(90221-5602)
PHONE......................310 639-1500
Thomas MA, *Manager*
Edmund Kim, *CEO*
John Yi, *Opers Mgr*
EMP: 10
SQ FT: 80,850
SALES (corp-wide): 34.3MM **Privately Held**
SIC: 2261 2262 2269 2759 Dyeing cotton broadwoven fabrics; dyeing: manmade fiber & silk broadwoven fabrics; printing of narrow fabrics; dyeing: raw stock yarn & narrow fabrics; textile printing rolls: engraving
HQ: Pacific Continental Textiles, Inc.
2880 E Ana St
Compton CA 90221
310 604-1100

(P-2832)
PACIFIC IMPRESSIONS INC
3494 Edward Ave, Santa Clara
(95054-2130)
PHONE......................408 727-4200
John Kaveny, *President*
Diane Kaveny, *Corp Secy*
EMP: 10
SQ FT: 12,000
SALES (est): 500K **Privately Held**
WEB: www.pacimp.com
SIC: 2261 2759 2395 Screen printing of cotton broadwoven fabrics; screen printing; embroidery products, except schiffli machine

(P-2833)
PADILLA REMBERTO
Also Called: High Fidelity Textiles
3524 Union Pacific Ave, Los Angeles
(90023-3922)
PHONE......................323 268-1111
Remberto Padilla, *Owner*
EMP: 14
SQ FT: 7,000
SALES (est): 1.1MM **Privately Held**
SIC: 2261 Dyeing cotton broadwoven fabrics

(P-2834)
PRIMA-TEX INDUSTRIES CAL INC
6237 Descanso Cir, Buena Park
(90620-1018)
PHONE......................714 521-6104
Pienita S Tio, *President*
Josie Inouye, *CFO*
Richard Greer, *Vice Pres*
▲ **EMP:** 59
SQ FT: 40,000
SALES (est): 8.9MM **Privately Held**
SIC: 2261 2396 2299 2331 Printing of cotton broadwoven fabrics; automotive & apparel trimmings; textile mill waste & remnant processing; women's & misses' blouses & shirts

(P-2835)
RAINBOW NOVELTY CREATIONS CO
3431 E Olympic Blvd, Los Angeles
(90023-3030)
PHONE......................323 855-9464
Ja Yun, *Owner*
EMP: 25
SALES (est): 1.2MM **Privately Held**
SIC: 2261 Screen printing of cotton broadwoven fabrics

(P-2836)
RAOULS PRINTWORKS
110 Los Aguajes Ave, Santa Barbara
(93101-3818)
PHONE......................805 965-1694
Sally Mc Quillan, *Owner*
EMP: 10
SALES (est): 640.9K **Privately Held**
WEB: www.textile.com
SIC: 2261 Screen printing of cotton broadwoven fabrics

(P-2837)
SILK SCREEN SHIRTS INC
Also Called: SSS
6185 El Camino Real, Carlsbad
(92009-1602)
PHONE......................760 233-3900
Stephen H Taylor, *President*
William Regan, *CEO*
Laura D Wile, *Vice Pres*
Chad Taylor, *Prdtn Mgr*
◆ **EMP:** 30 **EST:** 1969
SQ FT: 20,000
SALES (est): 7.7MM **Privately Held**
WEB: www.silkscreenshirtsinc.com
SIC: 2261 2396 Screen printing of cotton broadwoven fabrics; automotive & apparel trimmings

(P-2838)
SRL APPAREL INC
Also Called: Printed Image, The
2209 Park Ave, Chico (95928-6704)
PHONE......................530 898-9525
Scott Laursen, *President*

Marie Halvorsen, *Shareholder*
David Bryant, *Accounts Exec*
EMP: 26
SQ FT: 14,130
SALES (est): 4.7MM **Privately Held**
WEB: www.smokeybearproducts.com
SIC: 2261 5137 5136 2396 Screen printing of cotton broadwoven fabrics; women's & children's sportswear & swimsuits; men's & boys' sportswear & work clothing; automotive & apparel trimmings

(P-2839)
SUNSET ISLANDWEAR
Also Called: Just For Kids
601 Mary Ann Dr, Redondo Beach
(90278-5306)
PHONE......................310 372-7960
David Faolridia, *President*
Miriam Ayala, *Office Mgr*
EMP: 18
SALES (est): 1.7MM **Privately Held**
SIC: 2261 2759 Screen printing of cotton broadwoven fabrics; screen printing

(P-2840)
TOMORROWS LOOK INC
Also Called: Dimensions In Screen Printing
17462 Von Karman Ave, Irvine
(92614-6206)
PHONE......................949 596-8400
Steven E Mellgren, *CEO*
Torrey Mellgren, *Admin Sec*
EMP: 70
SQ FT: 36,000
SALES (est): 8MM **Privately Held**
SIC: 2261 Screen printing of cotton broadwoven fabrics

(P-2841)
WASHINGTON GARMENT DYEING
1332 E 18th St, Los Angeles (90021-3027)
PHONE......................213 747-1111
Pradip Shah, *Manager*
EMP: 23
SALES (corp-wide): 6.9MM **Privately Held**
WEB: www.washingtongarments.com
SIC: 2261 2262 Finishing plants, cotton; finishing plants, manmade fiber & silk fabrics
PA: Washington Garment Dyeing & Finishing, Inc.
1341 E Washington Blvd
Los Angeles CA 90021
213 747-1111

2262 Silk & Man-Made Fabric Finishers

(P-2842)
ALVAREZ REFINISHING INC
23 W Romneya Dr, Anaheim (92801)
PHONE......................714 780-0171
Juan Rivera, *President*
EMP: 25 **EST:** 1998
SALES (est): 1.6MM **Privately Held**
SIC: 2262 Refinishing: manmade fiber & silk broadwoven fabrics

(P-2843)
CALIFORNIA SWATCH DYERS INC
776 E Washington Blvd, Los Angeles
(90021-3042)
PHONE......................213 748-8425
Delia Pineda, *President*
EMP: 30
SALES (est): 3.2MM **Privately Held**
SIC: 2262 Dyeing: manmade fiber & silk broadwoven fabrics

(P-2844)
FINAL FINISH INC
10910 Norwalk Blvd, Santa Fe Springs
(90670-3828)
PHONE......................562 777-7774
Luis Ibarria, *President*
EMP: 25
SQ FT: 20,000

SALES: 3.7MM **Privately Held**
WEB: www.finalfinish.com
SIC: 2262 Preshrinking: manmade fiber & silk broadwoven fabrics; dyeing: manmade fiber & silk broadwoven fabrics

(P-2845)
INX PRINTS INC
1802 Kettering, Irvine (92614-5618)
PHONE......................949 660-9190
Harold A Haase Jr, *CEO*
David Van Steenhuyse, *Owner*
Don Moos, *IT Executive*
▼ **EMP:** 100
SQ FT: 26,000
SALES (est): 17.7MM **Privately Held**
SIC: 2262 Screen printing: manmade fiber & silk broadwoven fabrics

(P-2846)
REID & CLARK SCREEN ARTS CO
722 33rd St, San Diego (92102-3338)
PHONE......................619 233-7541
Alejandro Melero, *President*
EMP: 12
SQ FT: 17,500
SALES (est): 1.8MM **Privately Held**
SIC: 2262 Screen printing: manmade fiber & silk broadwoven fabrics

(P-2847)
SPREADCO INC
803 Us Highway 78, Brawley (92227-9514)
P.O. Box 1400 (92227-1320)
PHONE......................760 351-0747
Mario Valenzuela, *President*
Roque Valenzuela, *Admin Sec*
EMP: 20
SALES (est): 2.8MM **Privately Held**
SIC: 2262 Chemical coating or treating: manmade broadwoven fabrics

(P-2848)
UNIVERSAL DYEING & PRINTING
2303 E 11th St, Los Angeles (90021-2846)
PHONE......................213 746-0818
Kee Sung Hwang, *President*
Betty Hwang, *Admin Sec*
▲ **EMP:** 100
SQ FT: 95,000
SALES (est): 7.1MM **Privately Held**
SIC: 2262 Printing: manmade fiber & silk broadwoven fabrics

(P-2849)
WASHINGTON GARMENT DYEING (PA)
1341 E Washington Blvd, Los Angeles
(90021-3037)
PHONE......................213 747-1111
Vijay Shah, *President*
Melissa Harman, *Bd of Directors*
EMP: 60
SQ FT: 20,000
SALES (est): 6.9MM **Privately Held**
WEB: www.washingtongarments.com
SIC: 2262 2261 2269 Dyeing: manmade fiber & silk broadwoven fabrics; dyeing cotton broadwoven fabrics; finishing plants

---

2269 Textile Finishers, NEC

(P-2850)
ALMORE DYE HOUSE INC
6850 Tujunga Ave, North Hollywood
(91605-6324)
PHONE......................818 506-5444
Jeffery Teichner, *President*
Don Kishner, *COO*
Donald Teichner, *Vice Pres*
Stuart Teichner, *Admin Sec*
Joel Romero, *Technology*
EMP: 45
SQ FT: 20,000
SALES (est): 6.6MM **Privately Held**
SIC: 2269 Dyeing: raw stock yarn & narrow fabrics

(P-2851)
CAL PACIFIC DYEING & FINISHING
233 E Gardena Blvd, Gardena (90248-2800)
PHONE.....................310 327-3792
Russell Cole Shoemaker, *President*
Price Shoemaker, *CFO*
EMP: 64
SQ FT: 100,000
SALES: 4.2MM **Privately Held**
SIC: 2269 Dyeing: raw stock yarn & narrow fabrics; finishing: raw stock, yarn & narrow fabrics

(P-2852)
DP PRINT SERVICES INC
2331 Walling Ave, La Habra (90631-4267)
PHONE.....................310 600-5250
David Ponzio, *President*
EMP: 15
SALES: 6MM **Privately Held**
SIC: 2269 Labels, cotton: printed

(P-2853)
EXPO DYEING & FINISHING INC
1365 N Knollwood Cir, Anaheim (92801-1312)
PHONE.....................714 220-9583
Eduardo J Kim, *President*
▲ EMP: 170
SQ FT: 86,000
SALES (est): 25.9MM **Privately Held**
SIC: 2269 Dyeing: raw stock yarn & narrow fabrics

(P-2854)
FREEDOM WOOD FINISHING INC
Also Called: Freedom Finishing
600 Wilshire Blvd # 1200, Los Angeles (90017-3212)
PHONE.....................213 534-6620
Dean Schlaufman, *CFO*
Richard Pack, *Partner*
Maya Jackson, *Vice Pres*
EMP: 88
SQ FT: 10,000
SALES: 5.4MM **Privately Held**
SIC: 2269 Finishing plants

(P-2855)
GREEN MATTRESS INC
6827 Mckinley Ave, Los Angeles (90001-1525)
PHONE.....................323 752-2026
Luis Ponce, *CEO*
Raquel Vizcarra, *Vice Pres*
EMP: 15
SQ FT: 28,000
SALES: 10MM **Privately Held**
SIC: 2269 Finishing: raw stock, yarn & narrow fabrics

(P-2856)
MATCHMASTER DYG & FINSHG INC (PA)
Also Called: Antex Knitting Mills
3750 S Broadway, Los Angeles (90007-4436)
PHONE.....................323 232-2061
William Tenenblatt, *President*
◆ EMP: 250
SQ FT: 66,000
SALES (est): 59.2MM **Privately Held**
SIC: 2269 Dyeing: raw stock yarn & narrow fabrics

(P-2857)
PACIFIC COAST BACH LABEL CO
3015 S Grand Ave, Los Angeles (90007-3814)
PHONE.....................213 612-0314
Dan Finnegan, *President*
▲ EMP: 23
SALES (est): 3.3MM **Privately Held**
WEB: www.bachlabel.net
SIC: 2269 2679 Labels, cotton: printed; labels, paper: made from purchased material

(P-2858)
PACIFIC CONTNTL TEXTILES INC (HQ)
Also Called: Pct
2880 E Ana St, Compton (90221-5602)
PHONE.....................310 604-1100
Edmund Kim, *CEO*
Matt Nasab, *Director*
◆ EMP: 43
SALES (est): 32.6MM
SALES (corp-wide): 34.3MM **Privately Held**
SIC: 2269 2329 Finishing plants; men's & boys' sportswear & athletic clothing
PA: Edmund Kim International, Inc.
2880 E Ana St
Compton CA 90221
310 604-1100

(P-2859)
REZEX CORPORATION
Also Called: Geltman Industries
1930 E 51st St, Vernon (90058-2804)
PHONE.....................213 622-2015
Shari Rezai, *President*
Amir R Rezai, *Vice Pres*
Mary Bejines, *Finance Mgr*
EMP: 25
SALES (est): 3.4MM **Privately Held**
WEB: www.geltman.com
SIC: 2269 Finishing plants

(P-2860)
STARR DESIGN FABRICS INC
440 Pig Aly, Etna (96027)
PHONE.....................530 467-5121
Kathleen Starr, *President*
Shelly Starr, *Vice Pres*
EMP: 14
SQ FT: 3,500
SALES: 600K **Privately Held**
WEB: www.starrfabrics.com
SIC: 2269 Linen fabrics: dyeing, finishing & printing

(P-2861)
TAG-IT PACIFIC INC
21900 Burbank Blvd # 270, Woodland Hills (91367-7461)
PHONE.....................818 444-4100
Colin Dyne, *CEO*
Steven Forte, *CEO*
Melodie Ross, *Vice Pres*
Cornelia Boylston, *Info Tech Dir*
▲ EMP: 50
SALES (est): 7MM **Publicly Held**
WEB: www.tag-it.com
SIC: 2269 Labels, cotton: printed
PA: Talon International, Inc.
21900 Burbank Blvd # 270
Woodland Hills CA 91367

(P-2862)
VALERIE TRADING INC
870 E 59th St, Los Angeles (90001-1006)
PHONE.....................323 231-4255
Josefina Perez, *President*
▼ EMP: 32
SALES (est): 2.2MM **Privately Held**
SIC: 2269 5651 Cloth mending, for the trade; unisex clothing stores

(P-2863)
WATTS LIQUIDATION CORPORATION
555 Van Ness Ave, Torrance (90501-1424)
PHONE.....................310 328-5999
Kenneth E Watts, *CEO*
Jindas Shah, *Ch of Bd*
▲ EMP: 17
SQ FT: 36,000
SALES (est): 3.8MM
SALES (corp-wide): 11.2MM **Privately Held**
WEB: www.coatedfabrics.com
SIC: 2269 Finishing plants
HQ: Coated Fabrics Company
12658 Cisneros Ln
Santa Fe Springs CA 90670

(P-2864)
WESTERN YARN DYEING INC
2011 Raymer Ave, Fullerton (92833-2664)
PHONE.....................714 578-9500
Chong Kim, *President*
Byeng C Ahn, *Admin Sec*
▲ EMP: 42
SQ FT: 60,000
SALES (est): 5MM **Privately Held**
SIC: 2269 Dyeing: raw stock yarn & narrow fabrics

2273 Carpets & Rugs

(P-2865)
ATLAS CARPET MILLS INC
3201 S Susan St, Santa Ana (92704-6838)
P.O. Box 11467, Mobile AL (36671-0467)
PHONE.....................323 724-7930
James Horwich, *President*
Ada Horwich, *Vice Pres*
Markos Varpas, *Vice Pres*
Stan Dunford, *Executive*
Mark Hesther, *Executive*
▲ EMP: 229
SALES (est): 1.2MM
SALES (corp-wide): 405MM **Publicly Held**
WEB: www.atlascarpetmills.com
SIC: 2273 Rugs, tufted
HQ: Tdg Operations, Llc
716 Bill Myles Dr
Saraland AL 36571
251 675-9080

(P-2866)
BENTLEY MILLS INC
315 S 7th Ave, City of Industry (91746-3117)
PHONE.....................800 423-4709
Maria Gonzalez, *Manager*
Tom Mee, *President*
Nadine Peralez, *Executive Asst*
Tim Sellers, *Database Admin*
Noelle Novak, *Marketing Staff*
EMP: 10
SALES (corp-wide): 222.2MM **Privately Held**
SIC: 2273 Carpets & rugs
PA: Bentley Mills, Inc.
14641 Don Julian Rd
City Of Industry CA 91746
626 333-4585

(P-2867)
BENTLEY MILLS INC (PA)
14641 Don Julian Rd, City of Industry (91746-3106)
PHONE.....................626 333-4585
Ralph Grogan, *President*
Jim Harley, *COO*
Hector Roman, *COO*
Eric Petty, *CFO*
Aimee Alfonso, *Vice Pres*
◆ EMP: 250
SQ FT: 390,000
SALES (est): 222.2MM **Privately Held**
SIC: 2273 2299 Carpets, textile fiber; batting, wadding, padding & fillings

(P-2868)
CATALINA CARPET MILLS INC (PA)
Also Called: Catalina Home
14418 Best Ave, Santa Fe Springs (90670-5133)
PHONE.....................562 926-5811
Duane Jensen, *President*
Jack Heinrich, *Vice Pres*
Catherine Vivo, *Marketing Staff*
Kyle Burnette, *Manager*
▲ EMP: 58
SQ FT: 60,000
SALES (est): 11.8MM **Privately Held**
WEB: www.catalinahome.com
SIC: 2273 5023 Finishers of tufted carpets & rugs; floor coverings

(P-2869)
FABRICA INTERNATIONAL INC
Also Called: Fabrica Fine Carpet
3201 S Susan St, Santa Ana (92704-6838)
PHONE.....................949 261-7181
Greg Uttecht, *President*

Jon A Faulkner, *CEO*
Santa Mendoza, *Accountant*
Gil Gastelo, *Human Res Mgr*
Cary Taylor, *Sales Staff*
▲ EMP: 167
SQ FT: 107,000
SALES (est): 41MM
SALES (corp-wide): 405MM **Publicly Held**
SIC: 2273 Carpets, hand & machine made; rugs, braided & hooked
PA: The Dixie Group Inc
475 Reed Rd
Dalton GA 30720
706 876-5800

(P-2870)
HOLLAND & SHERRY INC
8550 Melrose Ave, West Hollywood (90069-5112)
PHONE.....................310 657-8550
Elizabeth Eakins, *Branch Mgr*
EMP: 18
SALES (corp-wide): 1.9MM **Privately Held**
SIC: 2273 Carpets & rugs
PA: Holland & Sherry, Inc.
5 Taft St
Norwalk CT 06854
212 628-1950

(P-2871)
LAND N TOP CLEANING SERVICES
20953 Sioux Rd, Apple Valley (92308-4232)
PHONE.....................760 624-8845
Nichole Duran, *Principal*
EMP: 25
SALES (est): 1.4MM **Privately Held**
SIC: 2273 Axminster carpets

(P-2872)
MARSPRING CORPORATION (PA)
Also Called: Marflex
4920 S Boyle Ave, Vernon (90058-3017)
P.O. Box 58643 (90058-0643)
PHONE.....................323 589-5637
Ronald J Greitzer, *President*
Stan Greitzer, *Vice Pres*
Stanley Greitzer, *Vice Pres*
Angie Rosales, *Human Res Mgr*
▲ EMP: 34
SQ FT: 54,008
SALES (est): 10.3MM **Privately Held**
WEB: www.marflex.com
SIC: 2273 Carpets, textile fiber

(P-2873)
MAT CACTUS MFG CO
930 W 10th St, Azusa (91702-1936)
PHONE.....................626 969-0444
Debra Hartranft-Dering, *President*
Cailey Dering, *Treasurer*
Micheal Armstrong, *Info Tech Mgr*
Debbie Dering, *Train & Dev Mgr*
▲ EMP: 20 EST: 1934
SQ FT: 35,000
SALES (est): 4.2MM **Privately Held**
WEB: www.cactusmat.com
SIC: 2273 5023 3069 Carpets & rugs; floor coverings; mats or matting, rubber

(P-2874)
MOHAWK INDUSTRIES INC
9687 Transportation Way, Fontana (92335-2604)
PHONE.....................909 357-1064
Lisa Gomez, *Branch Mgr*
EMP: 80
SALES (corp-wide): 9.9B **Publicly Held**
SIC: 2273 3253 Finishers of tufted carpets & rugs; smyrna carpets & rugs, machine woven; ceramic wall & floor tile
PA: Mohawk Industries, Inc.
160 S Industrial Blvd
Calhoun GA 30701
706 629-7721

(P-2875)
MOHAWK INDUSTRIES INC
41490 Boyce Rd, Fremont (94538-3113)
PHONE.....................510 440-8790
Don Cruz, *Branch Mgr*
EMP: 140

▲ = Import ▼=Export
◆ =Import/Export

SALES (corp-wide): 9.9B **Publicly Held**
SIC: 2273 Finishers of tufted carpets & rugs
PA: Mohawk Industries, Inc.
160 S Industrial Blvd
Calhoun GA 30701
706 629-7721

(P-2876)
NEXT SYSTEM INC
20605 Soledad Canyon Rd # 222, Canyon Country (91351-2438)
PHONE..............................661 257-1600
Daniel Pharo, *President*
Alex Hembree, *Vice Pres*
EMP: 26
SQ FT: 8,600
SALES (est): 3.3MM **Privately Held**
WEB: www.nextsystem.net
SIC: 2273 Mats & matting

(P-2877)
OHNO AMERICA INC
Also Called: Soho Carpet & Rugs
18781 Winnwood Ln, Santa Ana (92705-1215)
PHONE..............................770 773-3820
▲ EMP: 20
SQ FT: 36,000
SALES (est): 1.6MM
SALES (corp-wide): 47.9MM **Privately Held**
SIC: 2273
PA: Ohno Inc.
5-15-1, Harayamadai, Minami-Ku
Sakai OSK 590-0
722 970-566

(P-2878)
SAVNIK & COMPANY INC
601 Mcclary Ave, Oakland (94621-1915)
PHONE..............................510 568-4628
Berry Savnik, *General Mgr*
Kathryn Savnik, *Treasurer*
Kurt Savnik, *Manager*
EMP: 11
SQ FT: 15,000
SALES: 400K **Privately Held**
SIC: 2273 Carpets, hand & machine made; rugs, tufted

(P-2879)
SHAW INDUSTRIES GROUP INC
11411 Valley View St, Cypress (90630-5368)
PHONE..............................562 430-4445
Stan Diehl, *Manager*
Nick Peters, *Vice Pres*
Nancy Landeros, *Supervisor*
EMP: 140
SALES (corp-wide): 225.3B **Publicly Held**
SIC: 2273 5713 5023 Finishers of tufted carpets & rugs; floor covering stores; home furnishings
HQ: Shaw Industries Group, Inc.
616 E Walnut Ave
Dalton GA 30721
800 446-9332

(P-2880)
STANTON CARPET CORP
Also Called: Hibernia Woolen Mills
2209 Pine Ave, Manhattan Beach (90266-2832)
PHONE..............................562 945-8711
Debbie Dearo, *Manager*
EMP: 49
SALES (corp-wide): 60.4MM **Privately Held**
WEB: www.hiberniawoolenmills.com
SIC: 2273 Carpets & rugs
PA: Stanton Carpet Corp.
100 Sunnyside Blvd # 100
Woodbury NY 11797
516 822-5878

(P-2881)
STUDENT SPORTS
23954 Madison St, Torrance (90505-6011)
PHONE..............................310 791-1142
Andy Bark, *Principal*
Brian Stumpf, *Vice Pres*
EMP: 10
SALES (est): 1MM **Privately Held**
SIC: 2273 Carpets & rugs

(P-2882)
TDG OPERATIONS LLC
340 S Avenue 17, Los Angeles (90031-2505)
PHONE..............................323 724-9000
Charles Jones, *Manager*
EMP: 52
SALES (corp-wide): 405MM **Publicly Held**
WEB: www.atlascarpetmills.com
SIC: 2273 Rugs, tufted
HQ: Tdg Operations, Llc
716 Bill Myles Dr
Saraland AL 36571
251 675-9080

(P-2883)
TDG OPERATIONS LLC
6433 Gayhart St, Commerce (90040-2505)
PHONE..............................323 724-9000
Pancha Vega, *Manager*
EMP: 15
SALES (corp-wide): 405MM **Publicly Held**
WEB: www.atlascarpetmills.com
SIC: 2273 Rugs, tufted
HQ: Tdg Operations, Llc
716 Bill Myles Dr
Saraland AL 36571
251 675-9080

2281 Yarn Spinning Mills

(P-2884)
PHARR-PALOMAR INC
6781 8th St, Buena Park (90620-1097)
P.O. Box 1939, Mc Adenville NC (28101-1939)
PHONE..............................714 522-4811
H W Gosney, *Principal*
Jim Howard, *Corp Secy*
Walt Davenport, *Vice Pres*
EMP: 1600
SQ FT: 52,000
SALES (est): 115.1MM
SALES (corp-wide): 12MM **Privately Held**
WEB: www.pharryarns.com
SIC: 2281 2282 Yarn spinning mills; carpet yarn: twisting, winding or spooling
HQ: Pharr Yarns, Llc
100 Main St
Mc Adenville NC 28101
704 824-3551

(P-2885)
TDG OPERATIONS LLC
Also Called: Candlewick-Porterville
600 S E St, Porterville (93257-5318)
PHONE..............................559 781-4116
Dennis Johnson, *Branch Mgr*
Darryl Tamashiro, *Technology*
Harry Gloth, *Marketing Staff*
EMP: 60
SQ FT: 144,964
SALES (corp-wide): 405MM **Publicly Held**
WEB: www.royaltycarpetmills.com
SIC: 2281 2221 Yarn spinning mills; broadwoven fabric mills, manmade
HQ: Tdg Operations, Llc
475 Reed Rd
Dalton GA 30720
706 876-5851

(P-2886)
WINDSOR TEXTILE CORPORATION
13122 S Normandie Ave, Gardena (90249-2128)
PHONE..............................310 323-3997
EMP: 12
SALES: 1MM **Privately Held**
SIC: 2281

2282 Yarn Texturizing, Throwing, Twisting & Winding Mills

(P-2887)
C S AMERICA INC (HQ)
13365 Estelle St, Corona (92879-1881)
PHONE..............................323 583-7627
SOO Bong Joo, *President*
◆ EMP: 45
SQ FT: 50,000
SALES (est): 11MM
SALES (corp-wide): 33.8MM **Privately Held**
SIC: 2282 Throwing & winding mills
PA: Cs Fibertech Co., Ltd.
80 Busong 1-Gil, Jiksan-Eup, Seobuk-Gu
Cheonan 31038
824 155-7621

(P-2888)
MUSTANG HILLS LLC
16409 K St, Mojave (93501)
PHONE..............................661 888-5810
James Spencer, *CEO*
Andrew Golembeski, *COO*
Charlie Williams, *CFO*
Christopher Shears, *Exec VP*
Kevin Sheen, *Vice Pres*
EMP: 24
SALES (est): 1.5MM
SALES (corp-wide): 352.2K **Privately Held**
SIC: 2282 Throwing & winding mills
HQ: Everpower Wind Holdings, Inc.
1251 Waterfront Pl Fl 3
Pittsburgh PA 15222

2284 Thread Mills

(P-2889)
AMERICAN & EFIRD LLC
6098 Rickenbacker Rd, Commerce (90040-3030)
PHONE..............................323 724-6884
Juan Anbric, *Manager*
Kevin Boye, *Accounts Mgr*
EMP: 93
SALES (corp-wide): 1B **Privately Held**
SIC: 2284 Thread mills
HQ: American & Efird Llc
22 American St
Mount Holly NC 28120
704 827-4311

(P-2890)
G R J FASHIONS
6750 Foster Bridge Blvd B, Bell Gardens (90201-2052)
PHONE..............................323 537-5814
Gabriel Carranza, *Partner*
Ricardo Hernandez, *Partner*
EMP: 14
SALES (est): 1.3MM **Privately Held**
SIC: 2284 Embroidery thread

(P-2891)
INSTATHREADS LLC
238 Lakeview Dr, Palmdale (93551-7933)
PHONE..............................661 470-7841
Pamela Foster, *President*
EMP: 10
SALES (est): 631.3K **Privately Held**
SIC: 2284 Needle & handicraft thread

(P-2892)
MEDRANO RAYMUNDO
Also Called: Best Ink and Thread
1752 S Bon View Ave, Ontario (91761-4411)
PHONE..............................909 947-5507
Raymundo Medrano, *Owner*
EMP: 20
SALES: 500K **Privately Held**
SIC: 2284 2759 Embroidery thread; screen printing

(P-2893)
POLYTEX MANUFACTURING INC (PA)
1140 S Hope St, Los Angeles (90015-2119)
PHONE..............................323 726-0140
Men Tao, *President*
▲ EMP: 15
SQ FT: 8,000
SALES (est): 19.6MM **Privately Held**
SIC: 2284 Thread mills

2295 Fabrics Coated Not Rubberized

(P-2894)
AOC LLC
Also Called: AOC California Plant
19991 Seaton Ave, Perris (92570-8724)
PHONE..............................951 657-5161
John Mulrine, *Manager*
Irwin Morfe, *Engineer*
EMP: 100
SALES (corp-wide): 242.1K **Privately Held**
WEB: www.aoc-resins.com
SIC: 2295 2821 5169 Resin or plastic coated fabrics; plastics materials & resins; synthetic resins, rubber & plastic materials
HQ: Aoc, Llc
955 Highway 57
Collierville TN 38017

(P-2895)
CALIFORNIA COMBINING CORP
5607 S Santa Fe Ave, Vernon (90058-3525)
PHONE..............................323 589-5727
Charlette Heller, *CEO*
Vincent Rosato, *President*
Kathy Diaz, *Corp Secy*
▲ EMP: 37
SQ FT: 68,000
SALES (est): 6.3MM **Privately Held**
SIC: 2295 Coated fabrics, not rubberized

(P-2896)
CYTEC AEROSPACE MTLS CA INC
Also Called: Cytec Engineered Materials
851 W 18th St, Costa Mesa (92627-4410)
PHONE..............................714 899-0400
David Drillock, *CEO*
Hisham Alameddine, *President*
Chris Jouppi, *President*
Jim Davis, *CEO*
Guillaume Gignac, *Vice Pres*
▲ EMP: 140
SQ FT: 51,300
SALES (est): 20.1MM
SALES (corp-wide): 12.8MM **Privately Held**
WEB: www.jdlincoln.com
SIC: 2295 2891 Coated fabrics, not rubberized; adhesives & sealants
HQ: Cytec Industries Inc.
4500 Mcginnis Ferry Rd
Alpharetta GA 30005

(P-2897)
FLEXFIRM HOLDINGS LLC
2300 Chico Ave, El Monte (91733-1611)
PHONE..............................323 283-1173
Barry Eichorn, *President*
EMP: 15
SQ FT: 10,000
SALES (est): 2.4MM **Privately Held**
WEB: www.flexfirmproducts.com
SIC: 2295 Resin or plastic coated fabrics

(P-2898)
SHERWIN-WILLIAMS COMPANY
5501 E Slauson Ave, Commerce (90040-2920)
PHONE..............................323 726-7272
Eric Westerman, *Branch Mgr*
EMP: 30
SALES (corp-wide): 17.5B **Publicly Held**
SIC: 2295 Resin or plastic coated fabrics

PA: The Sherwin-Williams Company
101 W Prospect Ave # 1020
Cleveland OH 44115
216 566-2000

(P-2899)
SOLECTA INC (PA)
4113 Avenida De La Plata, Oceanside
(92056-6002)
PHONE...................................760 630-9643
Michael Ahearn, *CEO*
▲ EMP: 36 EST: 2014
SALES (est): 10.6MM **Privately Held**
SIC: 2295 Chemically coated & treated
fabrics

(P-2900)
SPECILTY MTALS FABRICATION INC
11222 Woodside Ave N, Santee
(92071-4716)
PHONE...................................619 937-6100
Richard Buxton, *President*
Tom Buxton, *CFO*
Larry Hendry, *Admin Sec*
Sandy Fousek, *Manager*
EMP: 16
SALES (est): 1.9MM **Privately Held**
SIC: 2295 Metallizing of fabrics

2296 Tire Cord & Fabric

(P-2901)
BEBOP SENSORS INC
970 Miller Ave, Berkeley (94708-1406)
PHONE...................................510 848-3231
Keith A McMillen, *CEO*
Michelle Cook, *Admin Sec*
Ksenia Petrova, *Engineer*
EMP: 24
SALES (est): 797.6K **Privately Held**
SIC: 2296 Tire cord & fabrics

2297 Fabrics, Nonwoven

(P-2902)
APPARELWAY INC
4516 Loma Vista Ave, Vernon
(90058-2602)
PHONE...................................323 581-5888
Don X Ho, *CEO*
▲ EMP: 15
SALES (est): 2.2MM **Privately Held**
WEB: www.apparelway.com
SIC: 2297 Nonwoven fabrics

(P-2903)
IOU INTERNATIONAL INC
2624 Geraldine St, Los Angeles
(90011-1829)
PHONE...................................323 846-0056
Hee Ja Cha, *President*
EMP: 25 EST: 2009
SALES (est): 3.7MM **Privately Held**
SIC: 2297 Nonwoven fabrics

(P-2904)
TEXOLLINI INC
2575 E El Presidio St, Long Beach
(90810-1114)
PHONE...................................310 537-3400
Daniel Kadisha, *President*
▲ EMP: 250
SQ FT: 200,000
SALES (est): 45.1MM **Privately Held**
WEB: www.texollini.com
SIC: 2297 2262 2269 2221 Nonwoven
fabrics; dyeing: manmade fiber & silk
broadwoven fabrics; finishing plants;
broadwoven fabric mills, manmade

2298 Cordage & Twine

(P-2905)
ASSOCIATED WIRE ROPE & RIGGING
910 Mahar Ave, Wilmington (90744-3829)
PHONE...................................310 448-5444
Scott Fishfader, *President*
▲ EMP: 30

SALES (est): 5.2MM **Privately Held**
SIC: 2298 3315 5051 3536 Wire rope
centers; wire, steel: insulated or armored;
rope, wire (not insulated); hoists, cranes
& monorails; miscellaneous fabricated
wire products; industrial machinery &
equipment

(P-2906)
BAY ASSOCIATES WIRE TECH CORP (DH)
46840 Lakeview Blvd, Fremont
(94538-6543)
PHONE...................................510 988-3800
Harry Avonti, *CEO*
Jack Sanford, *Treasurer*
Mark Rotner, *Admin Sec*
Ernie Drinkman, *Info Tech Dir*
Martin Fish, *Info Tech Dir*
▲ EMP: 69
SQ FT: 45,000
SALES (est): 63MM
SALES (corp-wide): 75MM **Privately Held**
WEB: www.newenglandwire.com
SIC: 2298 3351 3357 Cable, fiber; copper
rolling & drawing; nonferrous wiredrawing
& insulating
HQ: New England Wire Technologies Cor-
poration
130 N Main St
Lisbon NH 03585
603 838-6624

(P-2907)
CABLE BUILDERS INC
846 Robert Ln, Encinitas (92024-5639)
P.O. Box 230872 (92023-0872)
PHONE...................................760 308-0042
Cliff Robert Renison, *President*
▲ EMP: 12
SALES (est): 1.1MM **Privately Held**
SIC: 2298 Ropes & fiber cables

(P-2908)
CABLE MANUFACTURING TECH
Also Called: Cmt
2455 Bates Ave Ste E, Concord
(94520-8520)
P.O. Box 2556, Rocklin (95677-8461)
PHONE...................................925 687-3700
Andrew Enriquez, *Owner*
▲ EMP: 12
SQ FT: 3,500
SALES (est): 885.7K **Privately Held**
WEB: www.cmtcables.com
SIC: 2298 Blasting mats, rope

(P-2909)
CABLECO
13100 Firestone Blvd, Santa Fe Springs
(90670-5517)
PHONE...................................562 942-8076
Greg Bailey, *Principal*
JP Pezina, *Sales Staff*
▲ EMP: 23
SALES (est): 4.9MM **Privately Held**
SIC: 2298 Cable, fiber

(P-2910)
COORDNTED WIRE ROPE RGGING INC
Also Called: Coordinated Wire Rope No. Ca.
790 139th Ave Ste 1, San Leandro
(94578-3214)
PHONE...................................510 569-6911
Ron Kutzman, *Branch Mgr*
EMP: 13
SALES (corp-wide): 2.2MM **Privately Held**
SIC: 2298 5251 Wire rope centers; hard-
ware
HQ: Coordinated Wire Rope & Rigging, Inc.
1707 E Anaheim St
Wilmington CA 90744
310 834-8535

(P-2911)
DYNAMEX CORPORATION
155 E Albertoni St, Carson (90746-1405)
PHONE...................................310 329-0399
Ben Bravin, *President*
◆ EMP: 20
SALES (est): 3.3MM **Privately Held**
WEB: www.dynamexcorp.com
SIC: 2298 Cable, fiber

(P-2912)
PACIFIC FIBRE & ROPE CO INC
903 Flint Ave 927, Wilmington
(90744-3740)
PHONE...................................310 834-4567
Mark Goldman, *President*
Allen Goldman, *President*
Michael Goldman, *Treasurer*
Ronald Goldman, *Vice Pres*
EMP: 15
SQ FT: 45,000
SALES: 1.5MM **Privately Held**
WEB: www.pacificfibre.com
SIC: 2298 0139 Cordage: abaca, sisal,
henequen, hemp, jute or other fiber; rope,
except wire rope

(P-2913)
PELICAN ROPE WORKS
1600 E Mcfadden Ave, Santa Ana
(92705-4310)
PHONE...................................714 545-0116
Gaylord C Whipple, *President*
Terry Walker, *Financial Exec*
Paul Ottone, *Opers Staff*
Malena Michota, *Sales Associate*
Michael Gardosik, *Director*
▲ EMP: 15
SQ FT: 20,000
SALES (est): 2.5MM **Privately Held**
WEB: www.pelicanrope.com
SIC: 2298 Ropes & fiber cables

(P-2914)
RIP-TIE INC
883 San Leandro Blvd, San Leandro
(94577-1530)
P.O. Box 549 (94577-0549)
PHONE...................................510 577-0200
Michael Paul Fennell, *President*
Bin MEI, *CFO*
▲ EMP: 18
SQ FT: 45,000
SALES (est): 1.8MM **Privately Held**
WEB: www.riptie.com
SIC: 2298 Cordage & twine

(P-2915)
RJ MFG
1201 S Blaker Rd, Turlock (95380-8305)
PHONE...................................209 632-9708
Richard Jones, *President*
▲ EMP: 10
SQ FT: 10,000
SALES: 1MM **Privately Held**
WEB: www.rjmanufacturing.com
SIC: 2298 Ropes & fiber cables; rope, ex-
cept asbestos & wire

(P-2916)
STRAND PRODUCTS INC
721 E Yanonali St, Santa Barbara
(93103-3235)
P.O. Box 4610 (93140-4610)
PHONE...................................805 568-0304
Kelly Allin, *Branch Mgr*
EMP: 20
SALES (corp-wide): 4MM **Privately Held**
WEB: www.strandproducts.com
SIC: 2298 Wire rope centers
PA: Strand Products Inc.
725 E Yanonali St
Santa Barbara CA 93103
805 568-0304

(P-2917)
TNT ASSEMBLY LLC
Also Called: TNT Cable Industries
1331 Specialty Dr, Vista (92081-8521)
PHONE...................................760 410-1750
Carlos Navarro, *Mng Member*
Chris Rutman, *COO*
EMP: 42
SQ FT: 7,000
SALES: 5MM **Privately Held**
SIC: 2298 3355 3357 Ropes & fiber ca-
bles; aluminum wire & cable; automotive
wire & cable, except ignition sets: nonfer-
rous

(P-2918)
TRADE MARKER INTERNATIONAL
Also Called: TMI
445 Ryan Dr Ste 101, San Marcos
(92078-4072)
PHONE...................................760 602-4864
Peter Nyari, *President*
Klara Nyari, *CFO*
▲ EMP: 10
SALES: 3.5MM **Privately Held**
SIC: 2298 0139 Cordage: abaca, sisal,
henequen, hemp, jute or other fiber; hard
fiber cordage & twine; soft fiber cordage &
twine; twine, cord & cordage;

(P-2919)
TSF CONSTRUCTION SERVICES INC
Also Called: Dvbe Supply
4805 Mercury St Ste E, San Diego
(92111-2110)
PHONE...................................619 202-7615
Theodore Foster, *President*
EMP: 11
SALES (est): 466.6K **Privately Held**
SIC: 2298 5099 3845 7359 Ropes & fiber
cables; lifesaving & survival equipment
(non-medical); respiratory analysis equip-
ment, electromedical; work zone traffic
equipment (flags, cones, barrels, etc.)

2299 Textile Goods, NEC

(P-2920)
AGRIBAG INC
3925 Alameda Ave, Oakland (94601-3931)
PHONE...................................510 533-2388
Hsieh Liang, *President*
Wen-Ping Liang, *Vice Pres*
Annie Chang, *General Mgr*
Belle Chang, *Graphic Designe*
Robert Clark, *Sales Staff*
▲ EMP: 25
SQ FT: 20,000
SALES (est): 3.9MM **Privately Held**
SIC: 2299 2673 Bagging, jute; bags: plas-
tic, laminated & coated

(P-2921)
ALMAC FIXTURE & SUPPLY CO
Also Called: Almac Felt Co
12932 Jolette Ave, Granada Hills
(91344-1068)
PHONE...................................818 360-1706
Al K Friedman, *President*
EMP: 20 EST: 1965
SQ FT: 55,000
SALES (est): 2.1MM **Privately Held**
WEB: www.almacfelt.com
SIC: 2299 2824 Garnetting of textile waste
& rags; organic fibers, noncellulosic

(P-2922)
AMERICAN DAWN INC (PA)
Also Called: ADI
401 W Artesia Blvd, Compton
(90220-5518)
PHONE...................................310 223-2000
Adnan Rawjee, *President*
Mahmud G Rawjee, *Ch of Bd*
Lillian Huang, *CFO*
Steve Berg, *Vice Pres*
Kenny Cohen, *Vice Pres*
◆ EMP: 60 EST: 1980
SQ FT: 212,000
SALES (est): 27.9MM **Privately Held**
WEB: www.americandawn.com
SIC: 2299 5023 5131 2393 Linen fabrics;
linens & towels; textiles, woven; cushions,
except spring & carpet: purchased materi-
als; pillows, bed: made from purchased
materials

(P-2923)
AMERICAN FOAM FIBER & SUPS INC
Also Called: Foam Depot
255 S 7th Ave Ste A, City of Industry
(91746-3256)
PHONE...................................626 969-7268
Jack Hung, *President*
Irene Hung, *Vice Pres*

▲ = Import ▼=Export
◆ =Import/Export

▲ **EMP:** 75
SALES (est): 11.7MM **Privately Held**
SIC: 2299 Hair, curled: for upholstery, pillow & quilt filling

(P-2924)
AMRAPUR OVERSEAS INCORPORATED (PA)
Also Called: Colonial Home Textiles
1560 E 6th St Ste 101, Corona
(92879-1712)
PHONE..............................714 893-8808
Chandru H Wadhwani, *CEO*
Dawn Fields, *Vice Pres*
Laxmi Wadhwani, *Admin Sec*
Ann Varallo, *Planning*
Tyler Fox, *Sales Executive*
▲ **EMP:** 25
SQ FT: 130,000
SALES (est): 5.4MM **Privately Held**
WEB: www.amrapur.com
SIC: 2299 2269 5023 Linen fabrics; linen fabrics: dyeing, finishing & printing; linens & towels

(P-2925)
ASHFORD TEXTILES LLC
1535 W 139th St, Gardena (90249-2603)
PHONE..............................310 327-4670
Jack Burns,
Emily Huang, *Project Mgr*
Allen Guo,
▲ **EMP:** 40
SQ FT: 32,000
SALES (est): 5.2MM **Privately Held**
WEB: www.ashfordtextiles.com
SIC: 2299 Hemp yarn, thread, roving & textiles

(P-2926)
B&F FEDELINI INC (PA)
1301 S Main St Ste 226, Los Angeles
(90015-2452)
PHONE..............................213 628-3901
Farhad Sadian, *President*
EMP: 24
SQ FT: 15,000
SALES: 50MM **Privately Held**
SIC: 2299 Apparel filling: cotton waste, kapok & related material

(P-2927)
B&F FEDELINI INC
305 E 9th St, Los Angeles (90015-1850)
PHONE..............................213 628-3901
Ben Aronoff, *Branch Mgr*
EMP: 24
SALES (corp-wide): 50MM **Privately Held**
SIC: 2299 Apparel filling: cotton waste, kapok & related material
PA: B&F Fedelini Inc.
1301 S Main St Ste 226
Los Angeles CA 90015
213 628-3901

(P-2928)
BRK GROUP LLC
8357 Loch Lomond Dr, Pico Rivera
(90660-2507)
PHONE..............................562 949-4394
Vy Nguyen, *Mng Member*
Carter Bucklin, *Sales Staff*
Jeff Miller, *Mng Member*
Tobe Kramer, *Manager*
▲ **EMP:** 36 **EST:** 2004
SALES (est): 6.9MM **Privately Held**
SIC: 2299 Textile mill waste & remnant processing

(P-2929)
CAL FIBER INC
1360 S Beverly Glen Blvd # 401, Los Angeles (90024-5254)
PHONE..............................323 268-0191
Peter S Kahn III, *President*
EMP: 10
SQ FT: 30,000
SALES (est): 940K **Privately Held**
SIC: 2299 Pillow fillings: curled hair, cotton waste, moss, hemp tow

(P-2930)
CALIFORNIA WEBBING MILLS INC
6920 Stanford Ave, Los Angeles
(90001-1544)
PHONE..............................323 753-0260
Albert Bakhshizaeeh, *President*
▲ **EMP:** 16
SALES (est): 2.3MM **Privately Held**
WEB: www.calwebmills.com
SIC: 2299 Acoustic felts

(P-2931)
DECCOFELT CORPORATION
555 S Vermont Ave, Glendora
(91741-6206)
P.O. Box 156 (91740-0156)
PHONE..............................626 963-8511
Gerald L Heinrich, *CEO*
Kathy Smith, *Executive*
Art Jones, *Technology*
Ashley Strader, *Purchasing*
Gary Smith, *Manager*
▲ **EMP:** 24
SQ FT: 33,000
SALES (est): 4.7MM **Privately Held**
WEB: www.deccofelt.com
SIC: 2299 Felts & felt products

(P-2932)
EVEREST GROUP USA INC
1885 S Vineyard Ave Ste 3, Ontario
(91761-7760)
PHONE..............................909 923-1818
Peter Ho, *CEO*
Niko Peng, *President*
◆ **EMP:** 20
SALES (est): 6.1MM **Privately Held**
WEB: www.everestgroupusa.com
SIC: 2299 Broadwoven fabrics: linen, jute, hemp & ramie

(P-2933)
F R INDUSTRIES INC
Also Called: Villa Firenze
3157 Dona Susana Dr, Studio City
(91604-4357)
PHONE..............................818 503-9143
Florence Keller, *President*
▲ **EMP:** 18
SQ FT: 8,900
SALES (est): 2MM **Privately Held**
WEB: www.frindustries.com
SIC: 2299 Upholstery filling, textile

(P-2934)
FASHION CAMP
2477 Park Ave, Tustin (92782-2705)
PHONE..............................714 259-0946
Erin Blanchi, *Owner*
EMP: 20
SALES (est): 262.5K **Privately Held**
SIC: 2299 Textile goods

(P-2935)
GANAR INDUSTRIES INC
13721 Harvard Pl, Gardena (90249-2594)
PHONE..............................310 515-5683
Gary Balbach, *President*
EMP: 10
SQ FT: 11,000
SALES (est): 1.1MM **Privately Held**
SIC: 2299 Fabrics: linen, jute, hemp, ramie

(P-2936)
INFINITY TEXTILE
10638 Painter Ave Ste C, Santa Fe Springs
(90670-6655)
PHONE..............................562 777-9770
Steve Kim, *Owner*
EMP: 15
SALES (est): 660K **Privately Held**
SIC: 2299 Linen fabrics

(P-2937)
IQ TEXTILE IND INC
3003 S Hill St, Los Angeles (90007-3824)
PHONE..............................213 745-2290
Zia Abhari, *President*
Fathima Gharibdoost, *Vice Pres*
Steve Song, *Vice Pres*
▲ **EMP:** 10
SQ FT: 20,000
SALES (est): 8MM **Privately Held**
SIC: 2299 Fabrics: linen, jute, hemp, ramie

(P-2938)
J H TEXTILES INC
2301 E 55th St, Vernon (90058-3435)
PHONE..............................323 585-4124
Jong Soon Hur, *CEO*
▲ **EMP:** 25
SQ FT: 80,000
SALES (est): 10.2MM **Privately Held**
SIC: 2299 Textile mill waste & remnant processing

(P-2939)
LASANI-FELT CO
830 E 59th St, Los Angeles (90001-1086)
PHONE..............................323 233-5278
Melvyn Goodman, *President*
Lynn Goodman, *Treasurer*
John Cioffi, *Vice Pres*
EMP: 40 **EST:** 1969
SQ FT: 55,000
SALES (est): 5.5MM **Privately Held**
SIC: 2299 2282 Batts & batting: cotton mill waste & related material; polypropylene filament yarn: twisting, winding, etc.

(P-2940)
LAVINDER INC
Also Called: Thomas Lavin
8687 Melrose Ave Ste B310, West Hollywood (90069-5724)
PHONE..............................310 278-2456
Thomas Patrick Lavin, *CEO*
EMP: 14
SALES (est): 1.9MM **Privately Held**
SIC: 2299 Linen fabrics

(P-2941)
LAWRENCE O LAWRENCE LTD
Also Called: Lawrence of La Brea
8104 Beverly Blvd, Los Angeles
(90048-4508)
PHONE..............................323 935-1100
David Nourasshan, *Branch Mgr*
EMP: 10
SALES (corp-wide): 1MM **Privately Held**
SIC: 2299 Scouring & carbonizing of textile fibers
PA: Lawrence O Lawrence Ltd
1408 Montana Ave
Santa Monica CA

(P-2942)
LAYNE LABORATORIES INC
Also Called: Patina Products
4303 Huasna Rd, Arroyo Grande
(93420-6175)
P.O. Box 1259 (93421-1259)
PHONE..............................805 242-7918
John Waterman, *CEO*
Patricia Moffitt, *President*
Krys Wood, *Prdtn Mgr*
▲ **EMP:** 19
SQ FT: 40,000
SALES: 3MM **Privately Held**
WEB: www.laynelabs.com
SIC: 2299 Batting, wadding, padding & fillings

(P-2943)
LF VISUALS INC
Also Called: Little Folk Visuals
39620 Entrepreneur Ln, Palm Desert
(92211-0400)
P.O. Box 14243 (92255-4243)
PHONE..............................760 345-5571
Michael Firman, *President*
▲ **EMP:** 15
SQ FT: 7,300
SALES (est): 1.4MM **Privately Held**
WEB: www.littlefolkvisuals.com
SIC: 2299 Felts & felt products

(P-2944)
LINENS EXCHANGE INC
Also Called: Coachella Valley Rag Company
3148 Martin Luther King, Lynwood
(90262-1858)
PHONE..............................310 638-5507
Cenk Mesta, *President*
Estella Navarro, *General Mgr*
EMP: 12 **EST:** 1991
SQ FT: 80,000
SALES (est): 1.4MM **Privately Held**
SIC: 2299 Carbonized rags

(P-2945)
MFB WORLDWIDE INC (PA)
4901 Patata St 201-204, Cudahy
(90201-5942)
PHONE..............................323 562-2339
Daniel Holmes, *CEO*
Pedro Garcia, *COO*
Robert Harrison, *Chief Mktg Ofcr*
EMP: 15
SQ FT: 20,000
SALES: 2.9MM **Privately Held**
SIC: 2299 Fabrics: linen, jute, hemp, ramie

(P-2946)
NEW HAVEN COMPANIES INC
13571 Vaughn St Unit E, San Fernando
(91340-3006)
PHONE..............................213 749-8181
James P Levine, *CEO*
EMP: 55
SALES (corp-wide): 59.8MM **Privately Held**
SIC: 2299 3537 2298 2273 Batting, wadding, padding & fillings; industrial trucks & tractors; cordage & twine; nets, seines, slings & insulator pads; cargo nets; carpets & rugs
PA: The New Haven Companies Inc
4820 Suthpoint Dr Ste 102
Fredericksburg VA 22407
540 898-2354

(P-2947)
NEXTRADE INC (PA)
Also Called: NEXTEX INTERNATIONAL
12411 Industrial Ave, South Gate
(90280-8221)
PHONE..............................562 944-9950
Jang R Cho, *President*
▲ **EMP:** 25
SQ FT: 40,000
SALES: 10.2MM **Privately Held**
SIC: 2299 Batting, wadding, padding & fillings

(P-2948)
PACESETTER FABRICS LLC (HQ)
11450 Sheldon St, Sun Valley
(91352-1121)
PHONE..............................213 741-9999
Ramin Namvar,
Sean Namvar,
◆ **EMP:** 17
SQ FT: 36,000
SALES (est): 2.6MM **Privately Held**
SIC: 2299 Tops & top processing, man-made or other fiber

(P-2949)
PACIFIC SHORE STONES BAKERSFIE
Also Called: Pacific Stones
3775 Buck Owens Blvd, Bakersfield
(93308-4940)
PHONE..............................661 335-0100
Andre Ogorodnik, *Mng Member*
Donald Ceri,
Marco Pieria,
EMP: 18
SQ FT: 6,000
SALES (est): 3.8MM **Privately Held**
SIC: 2299 Slubs & nubs

(P-2950)
PD PRODUCTS LLC
Also Called: Pipe Dream Products
21350 Lassen St, Chatsworth
(91311-4254)
PHONE..............................818 772-0100
Olga Kalinina, *Controller*
EMP: 11
SALES (est): 1.6MM
SALES (corp-wide): 29.6MM **Privately Held**
SIC: 2299 5092 Yarns, specialty & novelty; toys
PA: Diamond Products, Llc
21350 Lassen St
Chatsworth CA 91311
818 772-0100

P
R
O
D
U
C
T
S

&

S
V
C
S

(P-2951)
PROGRESSIVE PRODUCTS INC
1650 7th St, Riverside (92507-4455)
PHONE..................................951 784-9930
Todd Schmidt, *President*
Jacqueline Schmidt, *Vice Pres*
Todd M Schmidt, *Admin Sec*
Roy Riggs, *Research*
Izlem Ustunel, *Technology*
▲ EMP: 13
SQ FT: 30,000
SALES (est): 2.4MM **Privately Held**
WEB: www.progressiveproduct.com
SIC: 2299 Fabrics: linen, jute, hemp, ramie; padding & wadding, textile

(P-2952)
REDWOOD WELLNESS LLC
11814 Jefferson Blvd, Culver City
(90230-6310)
PHONE..................................323 843-2676
Robert Rosenheck, *CEO*
EMP: 38
SALES (est): 1MM **Privately Held**
SIC: 2299 Hemp yarn, thread, roving & textiles

(P-2953)
**RELIANCE UPHOLSTERY
SUPPLY INC**
Also Called: Reliance Carpet Cushion
4920 S Boyle Ave, Vernon (90058-3017)
PHONE..................................800 522-5252
Ronald J Greitzer, *President*
Doug Williams, *Vice Pres*
EMP: 10
SALES (est): 1.3MM **Privately Held**
SIC: 2299 Carpet cushions, felt

(P-2954)
S J STERILIZED WIPING RAGS
201 San Jose Ave, San Jose (95125-1009)
P.O. Box 5486 (95150-5486)
PHONE..................................408 287-2512
Richard Veccio, *Owner*
EMP: 17
SALES (est): 1.3MM **Privately Held**
SIC: 2299 Textile mill waste & remnant processing

(P-2955)
WELMARK TEXTILE INC
14824 S Main St, Gardena (90248-1919)
PHONE..................................310 516-7289
Min-Yu Hung, *President*
Irene Hung, *Vice Pres*
▲ EMP: 13
SALES (est): 1.1MM **Privately Held**
SIC: 2299 7389 Padding & wadding, textile; textile & apparel services

(P-2956)
WILDFLOWER LINEN INC (PA)
2655 Napa Valley Corp Dr, NAPA (94558)
PHONE..................................714 522-2777
Young Martin, *President*
▲ EMP: 36
SALES (est): 5MM **Privately Held**
SIC: 2299 Linen fabrics

(P-2957)
**ZOO ZOO WHAM WHAMS BLIP
BLOPS**
645 W Rosecrans Ave, Compton
(90222-3945)
PHONE..................................213 248-9591
Bernard Miller,
EMP: 10
SALES (est): 200K **Privately Held**
SIC: 2299 Batting, wadding, padding & fillings

**2311 Men's & Boys' Suits,
Coats & Overcoats**

(P-2958)
2BB UNLIMITED INC
Also Called: Mimo
724 E 1st St Ste 300, Los Angeles
(90012-4349)
PHONE..................................213 253-9810
K Y Lee, *President*
▲ EMP: 20

SQ FT: 6,000
SALES (est): 1.3MM **Privately Held**
SIC: 2311 Men's & boys' suits & coats

(P-2959)
ANGELS YOUNG INC
Also Called: Young Angels Children's Wear
514 S Broadway, Los Angeles
(90013-2302)
PHONE..................................213 614-0742
Blanca Duran, *President*
Sandor Duran, *Vice Pres*
EMP: 20
SQ FT: 3,500
SALES (est): 2.1MM **Privately Held**
SIC: 2311 2335 Tuxedos: made from purchased materials; bridal & formal gowns

(P-2960)
BARCO UNIFORMS INC
350 W Rosecrans Ave, Gardena
(90248-1728)
PHONE..................................310 323-7315
Michael Kenneth Donner, *CEO*
Danny Robertson, *President*
David Ayers, *CFO*
David Aquino, *Exec VP*
Edward Mitzel, *Senior VP*
◆ EMP: 150 EST: 1929
SQ FT: 74,000
SALES (est): 36.8MM **Privately Held**
WEB: www.barcouniforms.com
SIC: 2311 2326 2337 Men's & boys' uniforms; men's & boys' work clothing; uniforms, except athletic: women's, misses' & juniors'

(P-2961)
BLUE SPHERE INC
Also Called: Lucky-13 Apparel
10869 Portal Dr, Los Alamitos
(90720-2508)
PHONE..................................714 953-7555
Robert Kloetzly, *President*
▲ EMP: 45
SALES (est): 5.3MM **Privately Held**
SIC: 2311 2331 2369 Men's & boys' suits & coats; women's & misses' blouses & shirts; girls' & children's outerwear

(P-2962)
CROSSPORT MOCEAN
1611 Babcock St, Newport Beach
(92663-2805)
PHONE..................................949 646-1701
Bill Levitt, *President*
Pamela Green, *Treasurer*
Tim Hindman, *Admin Sec*
▲ EMP: 18
SQ FT: 3,000
SALES (est): 2.5MM **Privately Held**
WEB: www.mocean.net
SIC: 2311 Policemen's uniforms: made from purchased materials

(P-2963)
DESIGNS BY BATYA INC
1200 Santee St Ste 208, Los Angeles
(90015-2553)
PHONE..................................213 746-7844
Victoria Haiavy, *President*
EMP: 11
SQ FT: 2,000
SALES (est): 1MM **Privately Held**
SIC: 2311 2331 2321 2337 Men's & boys' suits & coats; women's & misses' blouses & shirts; men's & boys' furnishings; women's & misses' suits & coats; leather & sheep-lined coats & hats

(P-2964)
FIRST TACTICAL LLC
4300 Spyres Way, Modesto (95356-9259)
PHONE..................................855 665-3410
Dan J Costa,
Denise L Costa,
EMP: 901 EST: 2015
SALES (est): 47.5MM **Privately Held**
SIC: 2311 Military uniforms, men's & youths': purchased materials

(P-2965)
HUGO BOSS USA INC
395 Santa Monica Pl # 162, Santa Monica
(90401-3478)
PHONE..................................310 260-0109

Patrick Maini, *Branch Mgr*
EMP: 238
SALES (corp-wide): 3.2B **Privately Held**
SIC: 2311 Men's & boys' suits & coats
HQ: Hugo Boss Usa, Inc.
55 Water St Fl 48
New York NY 10041
212 940-0600

(P-2966)
J R U D E S HOLDINGS LLC
9200 W Sunset Blvd Ph 2, West Hollywood
(90069-3607)
PHONE..................................310 281-0800
Jeffrey Rudesk, *Mng Member*
Ruth Inouye, *Executive Asst*
EMP: 19 EST: 2014
SALES: 4MM **Privately Held**
SIC: 2311 Men's & boys' suits & coats

(P-2967)
LANSHON INC
Also Called: IL Canto
12995 Los Nietos Rd, Santa Fe Springs
(90670-3011)
PHONE..................................562 777-1688
Howey Chiang, *President*
▲ EMP: 20 EST: 1973
SQ FT: 2,200
SALES (est): 1.2MM **Privately Held**
WEB: www.ilcanto.com
SIC: 2311 2337 Suits, men's & boys': made from purchased materials; suits: women's, misses' & juniors'

(P-2968)
LITO CHILDRENS WEAR INC
3730 Union Pacific Ave, Los Angeles
(90023-3773)
PHONE..................................323 260-4692
Tom Lee, *Chairman*
▼ EMP: 42 EST: 1974
SQ FT: 13,000
SALES (est): 3.8MM **Privately Held**
WEB: www.litoonline.com
SIC: 2311 2361 2369 Suits, men's & boys': made from purchased materials; dresses: girls', children's & infants'; girls' & children's outerwear

(P-2969)
MARSHA VICKI ORIGINALS INC
Also Called: Vicki Marsha Uniforms
5292 Production Dr, Huntington Beach
(92649-1521)
PHONE..................................714 895-6371
Diane Cologne, *President*
Timothy Cologne, *Vice Pres*
Joan Gerlach, *Manager*
EMP: 45 EST: 1947
SQ FT: 14,500
SALES (est): 5.8MM **Privately Held**
SIC: 2311 Men's & boys' uniforms

(P-2970)
MEDELITA LLC
23456 S Pointe Dr Ste A, Laguna Hills
(92653-1587)
PHONE..................................949 542-4100
Lara Manchik,
Dan Stepchew, *Chief Mktg Ofcr*
Lauren Reinzuch, *Design Engr*
Dean Valerio, *Accounting Mgr*
Ryan Sabia, *Opers Staff*
▲ EMP: 10 EST: 2008
SALES (est): 1.5MM **Privately Held**
SIC: 2311 Topcoats, men's & boys': made from purchased materials

(P-2971)
NEW CHEF FASHION INC
3223 E 46th St, Vernon (90058-2407)
PHONE..................................323 581-0300
G Lucien Salama, *President*
Chantal Salama, *Vice Pres*
◆ EMP: 89
SALES: 21MM **Privately Held**
WEB: www.newchef.com
SIC: 2311 2339 2326 5137 Men's & boys' uniforms; women's & misses' outerwear; men's & boys' work clothing; uniforms, women's & children's

(P-2972)
NO SECOND THOUGHTS INC
Also Called: Nst
1333 30th St Ste D, San Diego
(92154-3487)
PHONE..................................619 428-5992
Audrey Swirsky, *President*
Onnie Ramos, *General Mgr*
EMP: 52 EST: 1999
SALES: 1.2MM **Privately Held**
SIC: 2311 2329 2326 Men's & boys' uniforms; men's & boys' sportswear & athletic clothing; medical & hospital uniforms, men's

(P-2973)
ORIGINAL WATERMEN INC
1198 Joshua Way, Vista (92081-7836)
PHONE..................................760 599-0990
Ken Miller, *CEO*
Jennifer Miller, *President*
▲ EMP: 10
SQ FT: 10,000
SALES: 2.5MM **Privately Held**
WEB: www.originalwatermen.com
SIC: 2311 Men's & boys' uniforms

(P-2974)
RDD ENTERPRISES INC
Also Called: Americawear
4638 E Washinton Blvd, Commerce
(90040)
PHONE..................................213 746-0020
Tony Lomeli, *Branch Mgr*
Golan Friedman, *Manager*
EMP: 15
SALES (corp-wide): 5MM **Privately Held**
SIC: 2311 Military uniforms, men's & youths': purchased materials
PA: R.D.D. Enterprises, Inc.
4638 E Washington Blvd
Commerce CA
213 742-0666

(P-2975)
ROBERT TALBOTT INC (PA)
Also Called: Talbott Ties
24560 Silver Cloud Ct, Monterey
(93940-6560)
PHONE..................................831 649-6000
Robert J Corliss, *CEO*
Robert Corliss II, *President*
Shelby Corliss, *Vice Pres*
Shelby Godfrey, *Vice Pres*
Joann Chinn, *Credit Mgr*
▲ EMP: 28
SQ FT: 77,000
SALES (est): 29.9MM **Privately Held**
WEB: www.talbottvineyards.com
SIC: 2311 2321 2322 2323 Men's & boys' suits & coats; men's & boys' furnishings; men's & boys' underwear & nightwear; men's & boys' neckwear; men's & boys' trousers & slacks; men's & boys' work clothing

(P-2976)
ROBINSON TEXTILES INC
24532 Woodward Ave, Lomita
(90717-1110)
PHONE..................................310 527-8110
Gary Lovemark, *President*
◆ EMP: 20
SALES (est): 2.7MM **Privately Held**
WEB: www.robinsontextiles.com
SIC: 2311 Men's & boys' uniforms

(P-2977)
SAMS TAILORING
18120 Brookhurst St, Fountain Valley
(92708-6727)
PHONE..................................714 963-6776
Charles Young, *Network Enginr*
EMP: 13
SALES (est): 1.3MM **Privately Held**
SIC: 2311 5949 Coats, tailored, men's & boys': from purchased materials; sewing supplies

(P-2978)
**SANTANA FORMAL
ACCESSORIES INC**
707 Arroyo St Ste B, San Fernando
(91340-1855)
P.O. Box 2248, Agoura Hills (91376-2248)
PHONE..................................818 898-3677

Delores Tennant, *President*
Doug Freed, *CFO*
EMP: 107
SQ FT: 18,000
SALES (est): 8.2MM **Privately Held**
WEB: www.santanaapparel.com
SIC: 2311 2339 2323 2389 Vests: made from purchased materials; women's & misses' outerwear; bow ties, men's & boys': made from purchased materials; cummerbunds

(P-2979)
TRUMAKER INC
Also Called: Trumaker & Co.
228 Grant Ave Fl 2, San Francisco (94108-4647)
PHONE..................................415 662-3836
Mark Lovas, *CEO*
Michael Zhang, *President*
Adam Sidney, *Vice Pres*
Lourdes Ramos, *Marketing Staff*
Kerriann Forester, *Director*
▲ **EMP:** 50
SALES (est): 5.2MM **Privately Held**
SIC: 2311 2321 2325 Men's & boys' suits & coats; men's & boys' furnishings; men's & boys' trousers & slacks

(P-2980)
TYLER TRAFFICANTE INC (PA)
Also Called: Richard Tyler
700 S Palm Ave, Alhambra (91803-1528)
PHONE..................................323 869-9299
Lisa Trafficante, *President*
Richard Tyler, *Vice Pres*
EMP: 54
SQ FT: 30,000
SALES: 9MM **Privately Held**
SIC: 2311 2335 5611 5621 Tailored suits & formal jackets; gowns, formal; suits, men's; dress shops; women's & misses' outerwear

(P-2981)
UNIVERSAL MERCHANDISE INC
Also Called: Mds
5422 Aura Ave, Tarzana (91356-3004)
P.O. Box 572152 (91357-2152)
PHONE..................................818 344-2044
Itender Singh, *President*
Jasbir Singh, *Vice Pres*
▲ **EMP:** 16 **EST:** 1994
SQ FT: 4,000
SALES (est): 1.1MM **Privately Held**
SIC: 2311 5049 2339 5136 Men's & boys' uniforms; religious supplies; uniforms, athletic: women's, misses' & juniors'; uniforms, men's & boys'; uniforms, women's & children's

(P-2982)
WARRENS DEPARTMENT STORE INC
Also Called: House of Uniforms
9800 De Soto Ave, Chatsworth (91311-4411)
PHONE..................................888 577-2735
Warren F Ackerman, *Chairman*
Cheryl Clough, *President*
Fred Kemmerling, *Vice Pres*
EMP: 47
SALES (est): 3MM **Privately Held**
SIC: 2311 2337 Men's & boys' uniforms; uniforms, except athletic: women's, misses' & juniors'

2321 Men's & Boys' Shirts

(P-2983)
101 APPAREL INC
1802 N Glassell St, Orange (92865-4312)
PHONE..................................714 454-8988
Eric Crandell, *Owner*
EMP: 19
SALES (est): 1.9MM **Privately Held**
SIC: 2321 2353 Sport shirts, men's & boys': from purchased materials; hats & caps

(P-2984)
ALLIED DVBE INC
Also Called: Allied Dvbe Supply
260 Bonita Glen Dr Apt V3, Chula Vista (91910-3178)
P.O. Box 182091, Coronado (92178-2091)
PHONE..................................619 690-4900
Steve Deorlow, *President*
EMP: 15
SALES (est): 440.1K **Privately Held**
SIC: 2321 Polo shirts, men's & boys': made from purchased materials

(P-2985)
BENIGNA
4630 Floral Dr, Los Angeles (90022-1244)
PHONE..................................323 262-2484
Al Rangel, *Owner*
EMP: 10 **EST:** 1971
SQ FT: 10,000
SALES (est): 390K **Privately Held**
SIC: 2321 Men's & boys' dress shirts

(P-2986)
BPS TACTICAL INC
2165 E Colton Ave, Mentone (92359-9657)
P.O. Box 868 (92359-0868)
PHONE..................................909 794-2435
William F Blankenship Jr, *President*
EMP: 13 **EST:** 1975
SQ FT: 1,800
SALES (est): 424.1K **Privately Held**
WEB: www.policemag.com
SIC: 2321 5699 Uniform shirts: made from purchased materials; uniforms

(P-2987)
CREATIVE DESIGN INDUSTRIES
2587 Otay Center Dr, San Diego (92154-7612)
PHONE..................................619 710-2525
Sylvia Habchi, *Partner*
Elie Habchi, *Partner*
▲ **EMP:** 125
SQ FT: 15,000
SALES (est): 9.4MM **Privately Held**
SIC: 2321 5137 Men's & boys' furnishings; sportswear, women's & children's

(P-2988)
EI-LO INC
2102 Alton Pkwy Ste B, Irvine (92606-4947)
PHONE..................................949 200-6626
Edward Chavez, *CEO*
EMP: 14
SALES (est): 1.5MM **Privately Held**
SIC: 2321 Sport shirts, men's & boys': from purchased materials

(P-2989)
FRESH JIVE MANUFACTURING INC
Also Called: Gonz's
1317 S Olive St, Los Angeles (90015-3018)
P.O. Box 7847, Northridge (91327-7847)
PHONE..................................213 748-0129
Richard Klotz, *President*
▲ **EMP:** 20
SQ FT: 10,000
SALES (est): 2.3MM **Privately Held**
WEB: www.freshjive.net
SIC: 2321 2311 2325 Men's & boys' furnishings; coats, overcoats & vests; shorts (outerwear): men's, youths' & boys'

(P-2990)
GINO CORPORATION
Also Called: Shaka Wear
555 E Jefferson Blvd, Los Angeles (90011-2430)
PHONE..................................323 234-7979
Sung Uk Park, *CEO*
▲ **EMP:** 18
SALES (est): 2.9MM **Privately Held**
SIC: 2321 5136 Men's & boys' dress shirts; shirts, men's & boys'

(P-2991)
JL DESIGN ENTERPRISES INC
Also Called: Jl Racing.com
1451 Edinger Ave Ste C, Tustin (92780-6250)
PHONE..................................714 479-0240

Jolene Sparza, *President*
Kenneth Mills, *Vice Pres*
▲ **EMP:** 63
SALES (est): 6.6MM **Privately Held**
WEB: www.jlracing.com
SIC: 2321 Sport shirts, men's & boys': from purchased materials

(P-2992)
JUST FOR FUN
Also Called: Jff Uniforms
557 Van Ness Ave, Torrance (90501-1424)
PHONE..................................310 320-1327
Corinne Stolz, *President*
Gary Stolz, *Vice Pres*
▲ **EMP:** 24 **EST:** 1975
SQ FT: 11,000
SALES (est): 2.6MM **Privately Held**
WEB: www.jffuniforms.com
SIC: 2321 2337 2339 2326 Uniform shirts: made from purchased materials; uniforms, except athletic: women's, misses' & juniors'; women's & misses' outerwear; men's & boys' work clothing

(P-2993)
SEAMAID MANUFACTURING CORP
960 Mission St, San Francisco (94103-2911)
PHONE..................................415 777-9978
Freda Lau, *President*
Jian Xiu Zhen, *Vice Pres*
▲ **EMP:** 50
SQ FT: 11,000
SALES (est): 2.5MM **Privately Held**
SIC: 2321 2325 2331 2335 Men's & boys' furnishings; men's & boys' trousers & slacks; women's & misses' blouses & shirts; women's, juniors' & misses' dresses; women's & misses' suits & coats; women's & misses' outerwear

(P-2994)
STARLION INC
Also Called: Star Lion
706 E 32nd St, Los Angeles (90011-2406)
PHONE..................................323 233-8823
Mike Lim, *President*
Moon Lim, *Principal*
EMP: 22
SQ FT: 11,000
SALES (est): 750K **Privately Held**
WEB: www.starlion.com
SIC: 2321 2331 Men's & boys' dress shirts; women's & misses' blouses & shirts

(P-2995)
TOP HEAVY CLOTHING COMPANY INC (PA)
28381 Vincent Moraga Dr, Temecula (92590-3653)
PHONE..................................951 442-8839
Tadd D Chilcott, *President*
Douglas Lo, *Vice Pres*
▲ **EMP:** 167
SQ FT: 40,000
SALES (est): 11.5MM **Privately Held**
WEB: www.topheavyclothing.com
SIC: 2321 Men's & boys' dress shirts; men's & boys' sports & polo shirts

(P-2996)
UNITED UNIFORM MFRS INC
1096 W Rialto Ave, San Bernardino (92410-2376)
P.O. Box 7298 (92411-0298)
PHONE..................................909 381-2682
Kambiz Zinati, *CEO*
James Russell, *President*
Winnie Chen, *CFO*
▲ **EMP:** 14
SQ FT: 45,000
SALES (est): 1.7MM **Privately Held**
WEB: www.uumfg.com
SIC: 2321 Uniform shirts: made from purchased materials
PA: Amwear International Group, Inc
250 Benjamin Dr Ste B
Corona CA 92879

(P-2997)
VAN HEUSEN FACTORY OUTLET
17600 Collier Ave D134, Lake Elsinore (92530-2633)
PHONE..................................951 674-1190
Tina Hoel, *Manager*
EMP: 10
SALES (est): 554.6K **Privately Held**
SIC: 2321 Men's & boys' dress shirts

(P-2998)
VERTICAL COLLECTIVE LLC
116 S Catalina Ave # 119, Redondo Beach (90277-3631)
PHONE..................................310 567-6200
Katherine Zabloudil, *Mng Member*
Morgane McGee, *Mng Member*
EMP: 11 **EST:** 2016
SALES: 8.5MM **Privately Held**
SIC: 2321 2331 8742 Men's & boys' dress shirts; T-shirts & tops, women's: made from purchased materials; new products & services consultants

2322 Men's & Boys' Underwear & Nightwear

(P-2999)
MAKERS USA INC
Also Called: Mu Gallery Makers
5000 District Blvd, Vernon (90058-2720)
PHONE..................................323 582-1800
Sangwoo Samuel Kim, *President*
EMP: 16
SQ FT: 130,000
SALES (est): 1.3MM **Privately Held**
WEB: www.makersusa.com
SIC: 2322 2389 Men's & boys' underwear & nightwear; men's miscellaneous accessories

(P-3000)
STATESIDE MERCHANTS LLC
Also Called: Pair of Thieves
5813 Washington Blvd, Culver City (90232-7330)
PHONE..................................424 251-5190
David Ehrenberg, *Mng Member*
Alan Stuart,
Cash Warren,
◆ **EMP:** 15
SQ FT: 3,000
SALES: 10MM **Privately Held**
SIC: 2322 2341 Men's & boys' underwear & nightwear; women's & children's undergarments

2323 Men's & Boys' Neckwear

(P-3001)
PVH NECKWEAR INC (HQ)
1735 S Santa Fe Ave, Los Angeles (90021-2904)
PHONE..................................213 688-7970
Marc Schneider, *CEO*
Patricia Winkler, *Human Res Dir*
◆ **EMP:** 520 **EST:** 1873
SQ FT: 210,000
SALES (est): 99.2MM
SALES (corp-wide): 9.6B **Publicly Held**
WEB: www.superba.com
SIC: 2323 Men's & boys' neckwear
PA: Pvh Corp.
200 Madison Ave Bsmt 1
New York NY 10016
212 381-3500

2325 Men's & Boys' Separate Trousers & Casual Slacks

(P-3002)
CORDOVAN & GREY LTD
4826 Gregg Rd, Pico Rivera (90660-2107)
PHONE..................................562 699-8300
Fax: 213 699-9910
EMP: 22

SALES (est): 1.3MM **Privately Held**
SIC: 2325

(P-3003)
DRY AGED DENIM LLC (PA)
Also Called: James Jeans
1545 Rio Vista Ave, Los Angeles
(90023-2619)
P.O. Box 76019 (90076-0019)
PHONE.....................323 780-6206
Seun Lim,
Michelle Ro, *Graphic Designe*
Michael Chung,
▲ EMP: 10
SALES (est): 3.7MM **Privately Held**
SIC: 2325 2369 5651 Jeans: men's, youths' & boys'; leggings: girls', children's & infants'; jeans stores

(P-3004)
GUESS INC (PA)
1444 S Alameda St, Los Angeles
(90021-2433)
PHONE.....................213 765-3100
Carlos Alberini, *CEO*
Maurice Marciano, *Ch of Bd*
Sandeep Reddy, *CFO*
Paul Marciano, *Ch Credit Ofcr*
Fabrice Benarouche, *Vice Pres*
◆ EMP: 700
SQ FT: 341,700
SALES: 2.6B **Publicly Held**
WEB: www.guess.com
SIC: 2325 2339 5611 5621 Men's & boys' jeans & dungarees; women's & misses' outerwear; clothing, sportswear, men's & boys'; women's sportswear; children's & infants' wear stores

(P-3005)
GUESS INC
358 Plaza Dr, West Covina (91790-2848)
PHONE.....................626 856-5555
EMP: 25
SALES (corp-wide): 2.6B **Publicly Held**
SIC: 2325 Men's & boys' jeans & dungarees
PA: Guess , Inc.
1444 S Alameda St
Los Angeles CA 90021
213 765-3100

(P-3006)
GUESS INC
Also Called: G By Guess
820 State St, Santa Barbara (93101-3256)
PHONE.....................805 963-9490
EMP: 10
SALES (corp-wide): 2.2B **Publicly Held**
SIC: 2325
PA: Guess , Inc.
1444 S Alameda St
Los Angeles CA 90021
213 765-3100

(P-3007)
GUESS INC
1 Mills Cir Ste 313, Ontario (91764-5209)
PHONE.....................909 987-7776
Yesenia Rodriguez, *Manager*
EMP: 25
SALES (corp-wide): 2.6B **Publicly Held**
WEB: www.guess.com
SIC: 2325 Men's & boys' jeans & dungarees
PA: Guess , Inc.
1444 S Alameda St
Los Angeles CA 90021
213 765-3100

(P-3008)
INDU FASHIONS
220 W 25th St Ste B, National City
(91950-6680)
PHONE.....................619 336-4638
Shashi Pal, *Owner*
▲ EMP: 30
SQ FT: 7,000
SALES: 1.2MM **Privately Held**
WEB: www.indufashions.com
SIC: 2325 Shorts (outerwear): men's, youths' & boys'

(P-3009)
J & C APPAREL
757 Towne Ave Unit B, Los Angeles
(90021-1419)
PHONE.....................323 490-8260
Cipriano Serrano, *President*
EMP: 40
SALES (est): 906.5K **Privately Held**
SIC: 2325 Men's & boys' trousers & slacks

(P-3010)
JAMES WEST INC (PA)
13344 S Main St Ste B, Los Angeles
(90061-1638)
PHONE.....................310 380-1510
James Ahn, *President*
Bobby Ahn, *Vice Pres*
Youn OK Ahn, *Vice Pres*
EMP: 10
SQ FT: 2,500
SALES: 295.9K **Privately Held**
SIC: 2325 2339 7389 Men's & boys' trousers & slacks; slacks: women's, misses' & juniors'; sewing contractor

(P-3011)
JB BRITCHES INC
2279 Ward Ave, Simi Valley (93065-1863)
PHONE.....................818 898-4046
Asdghik Bedrosian, *President*
Ohannes Bedrosian, *Vice Pres*
▲ EMP: 100 EST: 1978
SQ FT: 42,000
SALES (est): 17.8MM **Privately Held**
WEB: www.jbbritches.com
SIC: 2325 2321 2311 5611 Men's & boys' trousers & slacks; men's & boys' dress shirts; men's & boys' sports & polo shirts; men's & boys' suits & coats; tailored suits & formal jackets; suits, men's

(P-3012)
LEVI STRAUSS & CO (PA)
1155 Battery St, San Francisco
(94111-1264)
PHONE.....................415 501-6000
Charles V Bergh, *President*
Stephen C Neal, *Ch of Bd*
Roy Bagattini, *President*
Seth M Ellison, *President*
David Love, *President*
◆ EMP: 1600
SALES: 5.5B **Publicly Held**
WEB: www.levistrauss.com
SIC: 2325 2339 2321 2331 Jeans: men's, youths' & boys'; slacks, dress: men's, youths' & boys'; jeans: women's, misses' & juniors'; slacks: women's, misses' & juniors'; athletic clothing: women's, misses' & juniors'; men's & boys' furnishings; shirts, women's & juniors': made from purchased materials; T-shirts & tops, women's: made from purchased materials; skirts, separate: women's, misses' & juniors'; jackets (suede, leatherette, etc.), sport: men's & boys'; athletic (warmup, sweat & jogging) suits: men's & boys'

(P-3013)
LEVI STRAUSS & CO
316 N Beverly Dr, Beverly Hills
(90210-4701)
PHONE.....................310 246-9044
EMP: 13
SALES (corp-wide): 4.4B **Privately Held**
SIC: 2325
PA: Levi Strauss & Co.
1155 Battery St
San Francisco CA 94111
415 501-6000

(P-3014)
LEVI STRAUSS & CO
17600 Collier Ave, Lake Elsinore
(92530-2633)
PHONE.....................951 674-2694
Leslie Gollihar, *Manager*
EMP: 19
SALES (corp-wide): 5.5B **Publicly Held**
SIC: 2325 Jeans: men's, youths' & boys'
PA: Levi Strauss & Co.
1155 Battery St
San Francisco CA 94111
415 501-6000

(P-3015)
LUCKY BRAND DUNGAREES LLC (PA)
Also Called: Lucky Brand Jeans
540 S Santa Fe Ave, Los Angeles
(90013-2233)
PHONE.....................213 443-5700
Carlos Alberini,
Vernell Dixon, *Store Mgr*
Teresa Ordonez, *Store Mgr*
Jennifer Bonadio, *Business Anlyst*
Victor Lopez, *Technology*
◆ EMP: 67
SQ FT: 21,000
SALES (est): 300.8MM **Privately Held**
SIC: 2325 2339 Dungarees: men's, youths' & boys'; jeans: men's, youths' & boys'; jeans: women's, misses' & juniors'

(P-3016)
NEW RISE BRAND HOLDINGS LLC
801 S Figueroa St # 1000, Los Angeles
(90017-5508)
PHONE.....................323 233-9005
John Inn, *President*
Ryan Crenshaw, *Vice Pres*
Kevin Kok Leong Yap,
▲ EMP: 20
SALES (est): 4.3MM **Privately Held**
SIC: 2325 Men's & boys' trousers & slacks

(P-3017)
RED ENGINE INC
Also Called: Red Engine Jeans
1850 E 15th St, Los Angeles (90021-2820)
PHONE.....................213 742-8858
James Boldes, *President*
▲ EMP: 11
SQ FT: 10,000
SALES (est): 1.3MM **Privately Held**
WEB: www.redenginejeans.com
SIC: 2325 Jeans: men's, youths' & boys'

(P-3018)
ROB INC (PA)
Also Called: Robin's Jeans
6760 Foster Bridge Blvd, Bell Gardens
(90201-2030)
PHONE.....................562 806-5589
Robert Chretien, *CEO*
Gilberto Jimenez, *Vice Pres*
▲ EMP: 70
SQ FT: 26,000
SALES (est): 14MM **Privately Held**
WEB: www.rob.com
SIC: 2325 2339 2369 Jeans: men's, youths' & boys'; men's & boys' dress slacks & shorts; trousers, dress (separate): men's, youths' & boys'; women's & misses' culottes, knickers & shorts; knickers: women's, misses' & juniors'; jeans: women's, misses' & juniors'; shorts (outerwear): girls' & children's; jackets: girls', children's & infants'; jeans: girls', children's & infants'

(P-3019)
SEMORE INC
Also Called: Nubile
1437 Santee St Ste 201, Los Angeles
(90015-2590)
PHONE.....................213 746-4122
Fax: 213 746-2426
▲ EMP: 18
SQ FT: 10,000
SALES (est): 1.6MM **Privately Held**
WEB: www.solosemore.com
SIC: 2325 2321 2331

(P-3020)
TRUE RELIGION APPAREL INC (HQ)
Also Called: True Religion Brand Jeans
1888 Rosecrans Ave # 1000, Manhattan Beach (90266-3795)
PHONE.....................323 266-3072
Farla Efros, *CEO*
Lynne Koplin, *President*
Eric Bauer, *CFO*
Peter F Collins, *CFO*
David Chiovetti, *Senior VP*
▲ EMP: 300
SQ FT: 119,000

SALES (est): 636.5MM
SALES (corp-wide): 350MM **Privately Held**
WEB: www.truereligionbrandjeans.com
SIC: 2325 2339 2369 Men's & boys' trousers & slacks; jeans: men's, youths' & boys'; women's & misses' outerwear; jeans: women's, misses' & juniors'; jeans: girls', children's & infants'
PA: Trlg Intermediate Holdings, Llc
1888 Rosecrans Ave
Manhattan Beach CA 90266
323 266-3072

(P-3021)
VF CONTEMPORARY BRANDS INC
777 S Alameda St Bldg 1, Los Angeles
(90021-1633)
PHONE.....................213 747-7002
EMP: 11
SALES (est): 1.3MM
SALES (corp-wide): 12.3B **Publicly Held**
SIC: 2325 2321
PA: V.F. Corporation
105 Corporate Center Blvd
Greensboro NC 27408
336 424-6000

2326 Men's & Boys' Work Clothing

(P-3022)
ADWEAR INC
Also Called: Tutti
850 S Broadway Ste 400, Los Angeles
(90014-3235)
PHONE.....................213 629-2535
Dairi Hariri, *President*
Louesette Cohen, *Treasurer*
Kristina Ritz-Alspach, *Accounts Exec*
EMP: 15 EST: 1993
SQ FT: 20,000
SALES: 5MM **Privately Held**
WEB: www.baseballjacket.com
SIC: 2326 Work pants

(P-3023)
ALPINESTARS USA
2780 W 237th St, Torrance (90505-5270)
PHONE.....................310 891-0222
Giovanni Mazzarolo, *CEO*
◆ EMP: 10
SQ FT: 28,380
SALES (est): 2.5MM
SALES (corp-wide): 1.5MM **Privately Held**
WEB: www.alpinestars.com
SIC: 2326 2331 Men's & boys' work clothing; women's & misses' blouses & shirts
HQ: Alpinestars Spa
Viale Enrico Fermi 5
Asolo TV 31011
042 352-86

(P-3024)
ALVARADO DYE & KNITTING MILL
30542 Union City Blvd, Union City
(94587-1598)
P.O. Box 38, Brisbane (94005-0038)
PHONE.....................510 324-8892
Raymond Chan, *President*
▲ EMP: 50
SALES (est): 3.3MM **Privately Held**
WEB: www.alvaradomills.com
SIC: 2326 Men's & boys' work clothing

(P-3025)
AMERICAN GIANT INC
161 Natoma St Fl 2, San Francisco
(94105-3746)
PHONE.....................415 529-2429
Bayard Winthrop, *President*
Pete Dinh, *CFO*
Tate Huffard, *Opers Mgr*
Chris Lentz, *Production*
Robinson Mallory, *Production*
EMP: 10
SALES (est): 1.3MM **Privately Held**
SIC: 2326 Work uniforms

(P-3026)
BEN F DAVIS COMPANY (PA)
Also Called: Ben Davis
3140 Kerner Blvd Ste G, San Rafael
(94901-5435)
PHONE..............................415 382-1000
Frank L Davis, *President*
Mike Davis, *Manager*
▲ EMP: 10
SALES (est): 18.9MM Privately Held
WEB: www.bendavis.com
SIC: 2326 Work pants

(P-3027)
BUNKERHILL INDUS GROUP INC
Also Called: Big Front Uniforms
4535 Huntington Dr S, Los Angeles
(90032-1940)
PHONE..............................323 227-4222
EMP: 15
SALES: 950K Privately Held
SIC: 2326

(P-3028)
BUY INSTA SLIM INC
Also Called: Instantfigure
17831 Sky Park Cir Ste C, Irvine
(92614-6105)
PHONE..............................949 263-2301
Eeman Jalili, *CEO*
Monir Jalili, *President*
Ehsan Jalili, *Vice Pres*
Houshang Jalili, *Vice Pres*
▲ EMP: 14 EST: 2010
SALES: 5MM Privately Held
SIC: 2326 5961 7389 Men's & boys' work
clothing; women's apparel, mail order;

(P-3029)
CINTAS CORPORATION
1679 Entp Blvd Ste 10, West Sacramento
(95691)
PHONE..............................916 375-8633
Ken Eslick, *Branch Mgr*
EMP: 15
SALES (corp-wide): 6.8B Publicly Held
WEB: www.cintas-corp.com
SIC: 2326 Work uniforms
PA: Cintas Corporation
6800 Cintas Blvd
Cincinnati OH 45262
513 459-1200

(P-3030)
COH-FB LLC
Also Called: Fabric Brand
5715 Bickett St, Huntington Park
(90255-2624)
PHONE..............................323 923-1240
Christine Soh, *Director*
Amy William, *President*
Simon Miller,
EMP: 50 EST: 2015
SQ FT: 500
SALES (est): 1.7MM Privately Held
SIC: 2326 Work garments, except rain-
coats: waterproof

(P-3031)
COOL JAMS INC
11206 Spencerport Way, San Diego
(92131-2912)
PHONE..............................858 566-6165
Anita Mahaffey, *President*
▲ EMP: 15
SALES (est): 935.8K Privately Held
SIC: 2326 5651 5136 Men's & boys' work
clothing; family clothing stores; men's &
boys' clothing

(P-3032)
**DAVID GARMENT CUTNG
FUSING SVC**
5008 S Boyle Ave, Vernon (90058-3904)
PHONE..............................323 583-9885
David Alvarado, *President*
Mario Alvarado, *Vice Pres*
▲ EMP: 15
SQ FT: 15,000
SALES (est): 1.4MM Privately Held
WEB: www.davidsclothier.com
SIC: 2326 2339 Men's & boys' work cloth-
ing; women's & misses' athletic clothing &
sportswear

(P-3033)
DEIST ENGINEERING INC
Also Called: Deist Safety Equipment
2623 N San Fernando Rd, Los Angeles
(90065-1316)
PHONE..............................818 240-7866
Jim F Deist, *President*
Kirk Miller, *CFO*
Marian Deist, *Vice Pres*
Sean Sousa, *Admin Sec*
Joe Hasen, *Purch Mgr*
▲ EMP: 32
SQ FT: 15,000
SALES (est): 2.5MM Privately Held
WEB: www.deist.com
SIC: 2326 3545 Overalls & coveralls; ma-
chine tool accessories

(P-3034)
GOLD BELT LINE INC
1547 Jayken Way Ste C, Chula Vista
(91911-4677)
PHONE..............................619 424-5544
Jonnie Simon, *CEO*
Alan Simon, *President*
Simon Al, *Manager*
EMP: 10
SQ FT: 6,000
SALES (est): 670K Privately Held
WEB: www.goldbeltline.com
SIC: 2326 Industrial garments, men's &
boys'

(P-3035)
HAUS OF GREY LLC
Also Called: Matte Grey
10930 Portal Dr, Los Alamitos
(90720-2519)
PHONE..............................562 270-4739
Travis Johnson, *President*
Ashley Johnson, *Project Leader*
Kelli Marie Riley,
Kami Riley, *Director*
EMP: 10
SALES (est): 1.6MM Privately Held
SIC: 2326 2335 5136 Men's & boys' work
clothing; women's, juniors' & misses'
dresses; men's & boys' clothing

(P-3036)
HOT TOPIC INC (DH)
Also Called: Shockhound
18305 San Jose Ave, City of Industry
(91748-1237)
PHONE..............................626 839-4681
Steve Vranes, *CEO*
Cindy Boden, *Vice Pres*
Elizabeth Haynes, *Vice Pres*
Kelly McGuire-Diehl, *Vice Pres*
Sue McPherson-Spissu, *Vice Pres*
◆ EMP: 800
SQ FT: 250,000
SALES (est): 2.3B Privately Held
WEB: www.hottopic.com
SIC: 2326 5699 5632 Men's & boys' work
clothing; designers, apparel; apparel ac-
cessories

(P-3037)
**IMAGE APPAREL FOR
BUSINESS INC**
1618 E Edinger Ave, Santa Ana
(92705-5019)
PHONE..............................714 541-5247
Keith Knerr, *CEO*
Robert Duffield, *Controller*
EMP: 25
SALES (est): 1.3MM Privately Held
SIC: 2326 2339 2353 7213 Men's &
boys' work clothing; uniforms, athletic:
women's, misses' & juniors'; uniform hats
& caps; linen supply

(P-3038)
**IMAGE SOLUTIONS APPAREL
INC**
19571 Magellan Dr, Torrance (90502-1136)
PHONE..............................310 464-8991
Christopher Kelley, *President*
Hong Tran, *Vice Pres*
Danielle Sorge, *Executive Asst*
Raj Sharma, *Info Tech Dir*
Gendron Katie, *Technology*
▲ EMP: 35
SQ FT: 4,500

SALES (est): 10MM Privately Held
WEB: www.eimagesolutions.com
SIC: 2326 Work uniforms

(P-3039)
INDIE SOURCE INC
1933 S Broadway Ste 1168, Los Angeles
(90007-4501)
PHONE..............................424 200-2027
Jesse Dombrowiak, *Officer*
Sam Simon, *Director*
EMP: 20
SALES: 750K Privately Held
SIC: 2326 7336 Men's & boys' work cloth-
ing; graphic arts & related design

(P-3040)
KIM & ROY CO INC
Also Called: Cnc Clothing
2924 E Ana St, Compton (90221-5603)
PHONE..............................310 762-1896
Hahn J Kim, *President*
▲ EMP: 10
SALES: 9.5MM Privately Held
SIC: 2326 Industrial garments, men's &
boys

(P-3041)
KNK APPAREL INC
223 W Rosecrans Ave, Gardena
(90248-1831)
PHONE..............................310 768-3333
John Kang, *President*
EMP: 250
SQ FT: 90,000
SALES (est): 14.4MM Privately Held
WEB: www.knktreasures.com
SIC: 2326 2339 Men's & boys' work cloth-
ing; women's & misses' outerwear

(P-3042)
LA TRIUMPH INC
Also Called: Medgear
13336 Alondra Blvd, Cerritos (90703-2205)
PHONE..............................562 404-7657
Hasina Lakhani, *CEO*
Amin Lakhani, *President*
▲ EMP: 24
SQ FT: 40,000
SALES (est): 2.8MM Privately Held
WEB: www.medgear.com
SIC: 2326 Medical & hospital uniforms,
men's; work uniforms

(P-3043)
MATSUN AMERICA CORP
4070 Greystone Dr Ste B, Ontario
(91761-3103)
PHONE..............................909 930-0779
Yo R Song, *President*
Bob Wang, *General Mgr*
EMP: 14 EST: 2011
SQ FT: 40,000
SALES (est): 728.9K Privately Held
SIC: 2326 5136 Men's & boys' work cloth-
ing; men's & boys' clothing

(P-3044)
MENS WEARHOUSE
6100 Stevenson Blvd, Fremont
(94538-2490)
PHONE..............................510 657-9821
EMP: 48
SALES (est): 9MM Privately Held
SIC: 2326

(P-3045)
MEXAPPAREL INC (PA)
2344 E 38th St, Vernon (90058-1627)
PHONE..............................323 364-8600
Maria Maniatis, *President*
Fred Kalmar, *CFO*
Hubert Guez, *Vice Pres*
Nomaan Yousef, *Controller*
EMP: 14
SQ FT: 277,000
SALES (est): 2.3MM Privately Held
SIC: 2326 Service apparel (baker, barber,
lab, etc.), washable: men's

(P-3046)
MINACHEE INC
1248 S Flower St, Los Angeles
(90015-2117)
PHONE..............................213 745-8100
EMP: 15

SALES (corp-wide): 2.5MM Privately
Held
SIC: 2326 Men's & boys' work clothing
PA: Minachee, Inc.
832 S Los Angeles St A
Los Angeles CA 90014
310 989-3535

(P-3047)
PAIGE LLC (HQ)
Also Called: Paige Premium Denim
10119 Jefferson Blvd, Culver City
(90232-3519)
PHONE..............................310 733-2100
Michael Geller, *President*
Paige Adams-Geller, *Officer*
Lindsay Weitz, *Merchandising*
Laura B Bodycott, *Accounts Exec*
◆ EMP: 150
SQ FT: 40,000
SALES (est): 34.1MM Privately Held
SIC: 2326 2331 Men's & boys' work cloth-
ing; women's & misses' blouses & shirts
PA: Ppd Holding, Llc
10119 Jefferson Blvd
Culver City CA 90232
310 733-2100

(P-3048)
PROVIDENCE INDUSTRIES LLC
Also Called: Mydyer.com
3833 Mcgowen St, Long Beach
(90808-1702)
PHONE..............................562 420-9091
Daniel S Kang, *President*
Dan Kang, *President*
James Lee, *CFO*
Jennifer Gim, *Vice Pres*
Krystal Park, *Admin Sec*
◆ EMP: 60
SQ FT: 10,000
SALES (est): 25.9MM Privately Held
WEB: www.mydyer.com
SIC: 2326 2331 Men's & boys' work cloth-
ing; blouses, women's & juniors': made
from purchased material

(P-3049)
PURE COTTON INCORPORATED
2221 S Main St Fl 2, Los Angeles
(90007-1427)
PHONE..............................213 507-3270
Kyung H Choi, *CEO*
EMP: 100 EST: 2006
SALES (est): 3.9MM Privately Held
SIC: 2326 Industrial garments, men's &
boys'

(P-3050)
ROF LLC
Also Called: Ring of Fire
7800 Arprt Bus Pkwy Ste B, Van Nuys
(91406)
PHONE..............................818 933-4000
Isaac Bitton,
Eran Bitton,
▲ EMP: 45
SQ FT: 60,000
SALES (est): 21.8MM Privately Held
SIC: 2326 Men's & boys' work clothing

(P-3051)
SECURA INC
Also Called: Suttini
6965 El Camino Re Ste 105, Oceanside
(92054)
PHONE..............................760 804-7313
EMP: 70
SQ FT: 4,000
SALES (est): 4.9MM Privately Held
SIC: 2326

(P-3052)
SEOLLEM CORPORATION
2856 E Pico Blvd, Los Angeles
(90023-3610)
PHONE..............................323 265-3266
Bong Ja Yoo, *CEO*
EMP: 12
SALES (est): 1.3MM Privately Held
SIC: 2326 Men's & boys' work clothing

(P-3053)
SEW FORTH INC
2350 Central Ave, Duarte (91010-2919)
PHONE..............................323 725-3500

Samuel Androus, *CEO*
◆ **EMP:** 25
SQ FT: 26,000
SALES (est): 4.8MM **Privately Held**
WEB: www.sewforth.com
SIC: 2326 Men's & boys' work clothing

(P-3054)
SKIRT INC
Also Called: Sofi Clothing
2600 E 8th St, Los Angeles (90023-2104)
PHONE..................................213 553-1134
Susan Miller, *President*
Kari Spitz, *Vice Pres*
EMP: 12 **EST:** 2001
SQ FT: 3,000
SALES: 1.5MM **Privately Held**
SIC: 2326 Men's & boys' work clothing

(P-3055)
STRATEGIC DISTRIBUTION L P
9800 De Soto Ave, Chatsworth
(91311-4411)
PHONE..................................818 671-2100
Michael Singer, *CEO*
Dan Hosch, *Accounts Exec*
▲ **EMP:** 240 **EST:** 2003
SALES (est): 42.7MM **Privately Held**
SIC: 2326 2337 3143 3144 Work uniforms; medical & hospital uniforms,
men's; uniforms, except athletic:
women's, misses & juniors'; men's
footwear, except athletic; women's
footwear, except athletic; uniforms & work
clothing; shoes
PA: Strategic Partners, Inc.
9800 De Soto Ave
Chatsworth CA 91311

(P-3056)
TECHNICHE SOLUTIONS
Also Called: Techniche International
2575 Pioneer Ave Ste 101, Vista
(92081-8450)
PHONE..................................619 818-0071
Doug Frost, *CEO*
◆ **EMP:** 25
SALES (est): 2.5MM **Privately Held**
SIC: 2326 Men's & boys' work clothing

(P-3057)
US GARMENT LLC
4440 E 26th St, Vernon (90058-4318)
P.O. Box 23368, Los Angeles (90023-0368)
PHONE..................................323 415-6464
Jae K Chung, *Mng Member*
Wesley J Chung,
▲ **EMP:** 35
SALES (est): 3.8MM **Privately Held**
SIC: 2326 Men's & boys' work clothing

(P-3058)
WAY OUT WEST INC
15760 Ventura Blvd # 1730, Encino
(91436-3048)
PHONE..................................310 769-6937
Michael C Goldberg, *President*
Mark J Goldberg, *President*
Michael Goldberg, *CEO*
▲ **EMP:** 40 **EST:** 1979
SALES (est): 5.8MM **Privately Held**
WEB: www.wayoutwestinc.com
SIC: 2326 2385 Industrial garments,
men's & boys'; waterproof outerwear

(P-3059)
WEST COAST GARMENT MFG
70 Elmira St, San Francisco (94124-1911)
PHONE..................................415 896-1772
Katherine Ng, *President*
Erica Ku, *Admin Sec*
▲ **EMP:** 38
SQ FT: 10,000
SALES: 9.2MM **Privately Held**
SIC: 2326 2369 2339 Industrial garments,
men's & boys'; girls' & children's outer-
wear; women's & misses' outerwear

┌─────────────────────────┐
│   **2329 Men's & Boys'**   │
│   **Clothing, NEC**   │
└─────────────────────────┘

(P-3060)
3 POINT DISTRIBUTION LLC
Also Called: Ezekiel
170 Technology Dr, Irvine (92618-2401)
PHONE..................................949 266-2700
Steven A Kurtzman,
Mike Martin, *Natl Sales Mgr*
Erica Dominguez,
Daniel Kurtzman,
▲ **EMP:** 20
SQ FT: 42,000
SALES (est): 3.4MM **Privately Held**
WEB: www.3-point.org
SIC: 2329 Men's & boys' sportswear & ath-
letic clothing

(P-3061)
A AND G INC (HQ)
Also Called: Alstyle Apparel
11296 Harrel St, Jurupa Valley
(91752-3715)
PHONE..................................714 765-0400
Keith S Walters, *President*
Gloria Del Mundo, *Administration*
Aziz Kazi, *Purch Agent*
Kevin Potter, *VP Mfg*
Chris Caldwell, *Marketing Staff*
◆ **EMP:** 627
SALES (est): 179.4MM
SALES (corp-wide): 2.9B **Privately Held**
WEB: www.murina.com
SIC: 2329 2253 Athletic (warmup, sweat &
jogging) suits: men's & boys'; T-shirts &
tops, knit
PA: Gildan Activewear Inc
600 Boul De Maisonneuve O 33eme
etage
Montreal QC H3A 3
514 735-2023

(P-3062)
ACTIVEAPPAREL INC (PA)
11076 Venture Dr, Jurupa Valley
(91752-3234)
PHONE..................................951 361-0060
Wasif M Siddique, *President*
Khan Baloch, *Admin Sec*
▲ **EMP:** 19
SQ FT: 30,000
SALES (est): 11.4MM **Privately Held**
WEB: www.activeapparel.net
SIC: 2329 2339 7389 Men's & boys'
sportswear & athletic clothing; women's &
misses' athletic clothing & sportswear;
sewing contractor

(P-3063)
ADIDAS NORTH AMERICA INC
Also Called: Adidas Outlet Store Vacaville
378 Nut Tree Rd, Vacaville (95687-3233)
PHONE..................................707 446-1070
Wibur Grapes, *Manager*
EMP: 20
SALES (corp-wide): 25B **Privately Held**
WEB: www.role.noris.net
SIC: 2329 Athletic (warmup, sweat & jog-
ging) suits: men's & boys'; men's & boys'
athletic uniforms; knickers, dress (sepa-
rate): men's & boys'
HQ: Adidas North America, Inc.
3449 N Anchor St Ste 500
Portland OR 97217
971 234-2300

(P-3064)
ALONA APPAREL INC
Also Called: Positano
1651 Mateo St, Los Angeles (90021-2854)
PHONE..................................323 232-1548
EMP: 10
SALES (est): 976.4K **Privately Held**
SIC: 2329 2321

(P-3065)
AMERICAN FASHION GROUP
INC (PA)
1430 E Washington Blvd, Los Angeles
(90021-3040)
P.O. Box 15755 (90015-0755)
PHONE..................................213 748-2100
Ali Saleh, *President*

Mohamad Saleh, *CFO*
▲ **EMP:** 10
SQ FT: 24,000
SALES (est): 1MM **Privately Held**
SIC: 2329 Men's & boys' sportswear & ath-
letic clothing

(P-3066)
ANDARI FASHION INC
9626 Telstar Ave, El Monte (91731-3004)
PHONE..................................626 575-2759
WEI Chen Wang, *President*
Lillian Wang, *President*
Charles Chang, *Vice Pres*
◆ **EMP:** 120
SQ FT: 50,000
SALES (est): 13.4MM **Privately Held**
WEB: www.andari.com
SIC: 2329 2339 2253 5199 Sweaters &
sweater jackets: men's & boys'; women's
& misses' accessories; sweaters &
sweater coats, knit; art goods & supplies;
knit goods

(P-3067)
ANGELS GARMENTS
Also Called: Angel Manufacturing
525 E 12th St Ste 107, Los Angeles
(90015-2645)
PHONE..................................213 748-0581
Jae R Kim, *Owner*
EMP: 15
SALES (est): 1.2MM **Privately Held**
WEB: www.angelsgarment.com
SIC: 2329 2339 2361 Men's & boys'
sportswear & athletic clothing; women's &
misses' outerwear; girls' & children's
dresses, blouses & shirts

(P-3068)
ANTAEUS FASHIONS GROUP
INC
2400 Chico Ave, South El Monte
(91733-1613)
PHONE..................................626 452-0797
Yungchieh Lin, *CEO*
Peter Lin, *CFO*
Michael Lin, *Executive*
Shangwen Lin, *Admin Sec*
Sammi Mach, *Accounts Mgr*
▲ **EMP:** 35
SQ FT: 10,000
SALES (est): 4.3MM **Privately Held**
SIC: 2329 2339 Men's & boys' sportswear
& athletic clothing; women's & misses'
athletic clothing & sportswear

(P-3069)
ARIES 33 LLC
3400 S Main St, Los Angeles (90007-4412)
PHONE..................................310 355-8330
Daniel Guez, *CEO*
Robin Saeks, *CFO*
EMP: 20 **EST:** 2017
SQ FT: 28,000
SALES: 15MM **Privately Held**
SIC: 2329 7389 2339 Men's & boys'
sportswear & athletic clothing; apparel de-
signers, commercial; women's & misses'
outerwear

(P-3070)
B O A INC
580 W Lambert Rd Ste L, Brea
(92821-3913)
PHONE..................................714 256-8960
David Fleming, *President*
Pamela Fleming, *Vice Pres*
▲ **EMP:** 34
SQ FT: 6,000
SALES (est): 3.1MM **Privately Held**
SIC: 2329 2337 2339 Men's & boys'
sportswear & athletic clothing; women's &
misses' suits & coats; women's & misses'
outerwear

(P-3071)
BOARDRIDERS INC (DH)
5600 Argosy Ave Ste 100, Huntington
Beach (92649-1063)
PHONE..................................714 889-2200
Dave Tanner, *CEO*
Thomas Chambolle, *President*
Greg Healy, *President*
Shannan North, *President*
Nate Smith, *President*

▼ **EMP:** 200
SALES (est): 285.1MM
SALES (corp-wide): 43B **Publicly Held**
WEB: www.quiksilverusa.com
SIC: 2329 2339 3949 5136 Men's &
boys' sportswear & athletic clothing;
women's & misses' athletic clothing &
sportswear; sporting & athletic goods;
winter sports equipment; skateboards;
windsurfing boards (sailboards) & equipment; sportswear, men's & boys'; sportswear, women's & children's

(P-3072)
BODY GLOVE INTERNATIONAL
LLC
6255 W Sunset Blvd # 650, Hollywood
(90028-7403)
PHONE..................................310 374-3441
Michael Devirgilio, *President*
Cory M Baker, *COO*
Warren Clamen, *CFO*
Nick Meistrell, *Mktg Dir*
◆ **EMP:** 17
SALES (est): 837.5K **Privately Held**
SIC: 2329 2339 2369 3069 Bathing suits
& swimwear: men's & boys'; bathing suits:
women's, misses' & juniors'; bathing suits
& swimwear: girls', children's & infants';
wet suits, rubber; shorts (outerwear):
men's, youths' & boys'; men's & boys'
clothing; apparel belts, men's & boys';
men's & boys' outerwear; shirts, men's &
boys'

(P-3073)
CORAL HEAD INC (PA)
Also Called: Hawaiian Island Creations
1988 W 169th St, Gardena (90247-5254)
PHONE..................................310 366-7712
Ronald Yoshida, *Partner*
Clarence Hara, *Vice Pres*
Craig Hara, *Vice Pres*
▲ **EMP:** 10
SQ FT: 6,600
SALES (est): 1.6MM **Privately Held**
SIC: 2329 Men's & boys' sportswear & ath-
letic clothing

(P-3074)
DC SHOES INC (DH)
5600 Argosy Ave Ste 100, Huntington
Beach (92649-1063)
PHONE..................................714 889-4206
Charles Exon, *CEO*
Brad Holman, *CFO*
Scott Fullerton, *Vice Pres*
Jeff Shine, *Vice Pres*
Jonathan Fischbein, *Technical Staff*
◆ **EMP:** 81
SQ FT: 100,000
SALES (est): 31.2MM
SALES (corp-wide): 43B **Publicly Held**
WEB: www.dcshoes.com
SIC: 2329 5136 5137 5139 Men's &
boys' sportswear & athletic clothing; ski &
snow clothing: men's & boys'; men's &
boys' clothing; women's & children's
clothing; footwear
HQ: Boardriders, Inc.
5600 Argosy Ave Ste 100
Huntington Beach CA 92649
714 889-2200

(P-3075)
DHY INC
Also Called: Darrow
922 Duncan Ave, Manhattan Beach
(90266-6626)
PHONE..................................310 376-7512
David Yates, *President*
Betty Yates, *Treasurer*
Tracy Vanpelt, *Admin Sec*
EMP: 40
SQ FT: 24,000
SALES: 1.5MM **Privately Held**
SIC: 2329 2339 2369 2331 Men's &
boys' sportswear & athletic clothing;
sportswear, women's; girls' & children's
outerwear; women's & misses' blouses &
shirts; men's & boys' furnishings

▲ = Import ▼ = Export
◆ = Import/Export

(P-3076)
DRIVEN CONCEPTS INC
4040 W Carriage Dr, Santa Ana
(92704-6303)
PHONE..............................714 549-2170
Brian Hirth, *CEO*
Gary Hunt, *President*
Harish Naran, *CFO*
Leila Drager, *Exec VP*
EMP: 10
SQ FT: 50,000
SALES: 1.8MM **Privately Held**
WEB: www.drivenconcepts.com
SIC: 2329 2253 Men's & boys' sportswear
& athletic clothing; T-shirts & tops, knit

(P-3077)
E8 DENIM HOUSE LLC
309 E 8th St Fl 5, Los Angeles
(90014-2200)
PHONE..............................310 386-4413
Carlo Ghailian, *CEO*
Mark Davis, *President*
Steve Ajamian, *CFO*
▲ **EMP:** 10
SQ FT: 10,000
SALES (est): 141.7K
SALES (corp-wide): 35MM **Privately
Held**
SIC: 2329 2339 Men's & boys' sportswear
& athletic clothing; women's & misses'
athletic clothing & sportswear
PA: Castma, Inc.
309 E 8th St Fl 5
Los Angeles CA 90014
213 769-4545

(P-3078)
**EDMUND KIM INTERNATIONAL
INC (PA)**
2880 E Ana St, Compton (90221-5602)
PHONE..............................310 604-1100
Edmund K Kim, *President*
Reza Farmehr, *CFO*
◆ **EMP:** 20
SALES (est): 34.3MM **Privately Held**
WEB: www.ekii.com
SIC: 2329 2261 7218 2253 Athletic
(warmup, sweat & jogging) suits: men's &
boys'; dyeing cotton broadwoven fabrics;
industrial launderers; dresses & skirts;
blouses, shirts, pants & suits; commercial
printing, lithographic

(P-3079)
FEAR OF GOD LLC
1200 S Santa Fe Ave Ste A, Los Angeles
(90021-1789)
PHONE..............................310 466-9751
EMP: 36 **Privately Held**
SIC: 2329 Sweaters & sweater jackets:
men's & boys'
PA: Fear Of God, Llc
3940 Lrl Cyn Blvd Ste 42
Studio City CA 91604

(P-3080)
FEAR OF GOD LLC (PA)
3940 Lrl Cyn Blvd Ste 42, Studio City
(91604-3709)
PHONE..............................213 235-7985
Jerry Manuel, *Mng Member*
Glenn Milus, *CFO*
Lao Lee, *Manager*
EMP: 13
SALES (est): 4.6MM **Privately Held**
SIC: 2329 Sweaters & sweater jackets:
men's & boys'

(P-3081)
FETISH GROUP INC (PA)
Also Called: Tag Rag
1013 S Los Angeles St # 700, Los Angeles
(90015-1782)
PHONE..............................323 587-7873
Raphael Sabbah, *CEO*
Orly Dahan, *Vice Pres*
▲ **EMP:** 47
SQ FT: 28,000
SALES (est): 5MM **Privately Held**
WEB: www.tagrag.com
SIC: 2329 2339 2369 Men's & boys'
sportswear & athletic clothing; women's &
misses' athletic clothing & sportswear;
girls' & children's outerwear

(P-3082)
FIERRA DESIGN INC
Also Called: Fierra Design CL Manufactures
1359 Channing St, Los Angeles
(90021-2410)
PHONE..............................213 622-2426
Haim Iber, *President*
EMP: 30
SQ FT: 35,000
SALES (est): 1.3MM **Privately Held**
SIC: 2329 Men's & boys' sportswear & ath-
letic clothing

(P-3083)
FIVE KEYS INC
Also Called: Mount Seven
150 E Broadway Ave, Atwater
(95301-4562)
PHONE..............................209 358-7971
Mohan Johal, *Officer*
Bob Johal, *Controller*
EMP: 40
SQ FT: 21,000
SALES (est): 3.8MM **Privately Held**
WEB: www.fivekeys.com
SIC: 2329 5632 7389 Men's & boys'
sportswear & athletic clothing; women's
accessory & specialty stores; sewing con-
tractor

(P-3084)
FOURBRO INC
13772 A Better Way, Garden Grove
(92843-3906)
PHONE..............................714 277-3858
Rasheed Hussain, *President*
Mohamed Abuthahir, *Corp Secy*
▲ **EMP:** 14
SQ FT: 34,000
SALES (est): 1.3MM **Privately Held**
WEB: www.fourbro.com
SIC: 2329 2331 2321 Men's & boys'
sportswear & athletic clothing; women's &
misses' blouses & shirts; men's & boys'
furnishings

(P-3085)
FUNNY-BUNNY INC (PA)
Also Called: Cachcach
1513b E Saint Gertrude Pl, Santa Ana
(92705-5309)
PHONE..............................714 957-1114
Paul Kohne, *President*
▲ **EMP:** 95
SQ FT: 25,000
SALES (est): 8.7MM **Privately Held**
WEB: www.cachcach.com
SIC: 2329 2369 Men's & boys' sportswear
& athletic clothing; slacks: girls' & chil-
dren's

(P-3086)
GLOBAL CASUALS INC
18505 S Broadway, Gardena (90248-4632)
PHONE..............................310 817-2828
Jack Tsao, *General Mgr*
▲ **EMP:** 15
SQ FT: 2,000
SALES (est): 1.2MM
SALES (corp-wide): 101.6MM **Privately
Held**
WEB: www.unionbay.com
SIC: 2329 Men's & boys' sportswear & ath-
letic clothing
PA: Seattle Pacific Industries, Inc.
1633 Westlake Ave N Ste 3
Seattle WA 98109
253 872-8822

(P-3087)
GUESS INC
Guess Factory Store 3122
8300 Arroyo Cir Ste 270, Gilroy
(95020-7335)
PHONE..............................408 847-3400
May Satsain, *Manager*
EMP: 20
SALES (corp-wide): 2.6B **Publicly Held**
WEB: www.guess.com
SIC: 2329 2331 Men's & boys' sportswear
& athletic clothing; women's & misses'
blouses & shirts
PA: Guess , Inc.
1444 S Alameda St
Los Angeles CA 90021
213 765-3100

(P-3088)
HOT SHOPPE DESIGNS INC
1323 Calle Avanzado, San Clemente
(92673-6351)
PHONE..............................949 487-2828
David Marietti, *CEO*
Max Frost, *Opers Staff*
▲ **EMP:** 15
SQ FT: 6,500
SALES (est): 149.5K **Privately Held**
WEB: www.hotshoppedesigns.com
SIC: 2329 5136 7336 7389 Riding
clothes:, men's, youths' & boys'; shirts,
men's & boys'; package design; lettering
& sign painting services

(P-3089)
HURLEY INTERNATIONAL LLC
100 Citadel Dr Ste 433, Commerce
(90040-1595)
PHONE..............................323 728-1821
Oscar Gomez, *Branch Mgr*
Chance King, *Vice Pres*
Garcia Leeann, *Store Mgr*
Velarde Teresa, *IT Specialist*
Juanita Altamirano, *Prdtn Mgr*
EMP: 11
SALES (corp-wide): 39.1B **Publicly Held**
SIC: 2329 5621 5611 Men's & boys'
sportswear & athletic clothing; women's
clothing stores; men's & boys' clothing
stores
HQ: Hurley International Llc
1945g Placentia Ave
Costa Mesa CA 92627
949 548-9375

(P-3090)
HURLEY INTERNATIONAL LLC
321 Nut Tree Rd, Vacaville (95687-3242)
PHONE..............................707 446-6300
EMP: 105
SALES (corp-wide): 39.1B **Publicly Held**
SIC: 2329 Men's & boys' sportswear & ath-
letic clothing
HQ: Hurley International Llc
1945g Placentia Ave
Costa Mesa CA 92627
949 548-9375

(P-3091)
**HURLEY INTERNATIONAL LLC
(HQ)**
1945g Placentia Ave, Costa Mesa
(92627-3420)
PHONE..............................949 548-9375
John Schweitzer, *CEO*
Leone Duquesnay, *Store Mgr*
Michael Prenovost, *Accounting Mgr*
Tim Carney, *Credit Staff*
Michael Lee, *Prdtn Mgr*
◆ **EMP:** 200
SALES (est): 96.1MM
SALES (corp-wide): 39.1B **Publicly Held**
WEB: www.hurley.com
SIC: 2329 5137 Knickers, dress (sepa-
rate): men's & boys'; women's & chil-
dren's clothing
PA: Nike, Inc.
1 Sw Bowerman Dr
Beaverton OR 97005
503 671-6453

(P-3092)
HYLETE INC
564 Stevens Ave, Solana Beach
(92075-2054)
PHONE..............................858 225-8998
Ron L Wilson II, *Ch of Bd*
Pete Dirksing, *Vice Pres*
Scott Kennerly, *Vice Pres*
Matthew Paulson, *Vice Pres*
Jamie Wardlow, *VP Mktg*
EMP: 27
SQ FT: 4,300
SALES (est): 3.9MM **Privately Held**
SIC: 2329 2339 5091 Athletic (warmup,
sweat & jogging) suits: men's & boys';
women's & misses' athletic clothing &
sportswear; athletic clothing: women's,
misses' & juniors'; athletic goods

(P-3093)
IMAGE STAR LLC
Also Called: Reflective Images
42 Digital Dr Ste 10, Novato (94949-5762)
PHONE..............................415 883-5815
Angelika Sultan,
Kristen Gregoriev,
EMP: 11
SQ FT: 2,640
SALES (est): 411.2K **Privately Held**
SIC: 2329 2759 Men's & boys' sportswear
& athletic clothing; screen printing

(P-3094)
**INTERNATIONAL TREND - 3
CORP**
Also Called: Trinity - 4
7103 Marcelle St, Paramount
(90723-4840)
PHONE..............................562 360-5185
Steve Shin, *President*
EMP: 20
SQ FT: 15,000
SALES (est): 1.6MM **Privately Held**
SIC: 2329 2339 Men's & boys' sportswear
& athletic clothing; athletic clothing:
women's, misses' & juniors'

(P-3095)
J K STAR CORP
1123 N Stanford Ave, Los Angeles
(90059-3516)
PHONE..............................310 538-0185
▲ **EMP:** 80
SQ FT: 50,000
SALES (est): 3.7MM **Privately Held**
SIC: 2329 2339

(P-3096)
JEFFREY RUDES LLC
9550 Heather Rd, Beverly Hills
(90210-1739)
PHONE..............................310 281-0800
Jeffrey Rudes, *Mng Member*
EMP: 10 **EST:** 2014
SQ FT: 2,900
SALES (est): 1.9MM **Privately Held**
SIC: 2329 Knickers, dress (separate):
men's & boys'

(P-3097)
JS APPAREL INC
1751 E Del Amo Blvd, Carson
(90746-2938)
PHONE..............................310 631-6333
Ki S Kim, *CEO*
▲ **EMP:** 99
SALES (est): 17.4MM **Privately Held**
WEB: www.jsapparel.net
SIC: 2329 2339 Men's & boys' sportswear
& athletic clothing; women's & misses'
outerwear

(P-3098)
KOKATAT INC
5350 Ericson Way, Arcata (95521-9277)
PHONE..............................707 822-7621
Stephen O Meara, *President*
Kit Mann, *Vice Pres*
Aaron McVanner, *IT/INT Sup*
Jordan Jones, *Technology*
Michele Bisgrove, *Human Res Mgr*
◆ **EMP:** 100
SQ FT: 30,000
SALES (est): 11.7MM **Privately Held**
WEB: www.kokatat.com
SIC: 2329 2339 Men's & boys' sportswear
& athletic clothing; women's & misses'
athletic clothing & sportswear

(P-3099)
KORAL LLC
Also Called: Koral Active Wear
5124 Pacific Blvd, Vernon (90058-2218)
PHONE..............................323 391-1060
Marcelo Kugel, *Mng Member*
Liz Hampshire,
Peter Koral,
Ilana Kugel,
EMP: 36
SALES: 7MM **Privately Held**
SIC: 2329 2339 Men's & boys' sportswear
& athletic clothing; women's & misses'
athletic clothing & sportswear

PRODUCTS & SVCS

(P-3100)
KRISSY OP SHINS USA INC
Also Called: International Baggyz
2408 S Broadway, Los Angeles
(90007-2716)
PHONE..............................213 747-2591
Hae Shin, *President*
Donna Shin, *Vice Pres*
EMP: 80
SALES: 2.7MM **Privately Held**
WEB: www.kos-usa.com
SIC: 2329 Men's & boys' sportswear & athletic clothing

(P-3101)
LEEMARC INDUSTRIES LLC
Also Called: Canari
2471 Coral St, Vista (92081-8431)
PHONE..............................760 598-0505
Christopher Robinson, *Mng Member*
▲ EMP: 55
SQ FT: 40,000
SALES (est): 8MM **Privately Held**
WEB: www.canari.com
SIC: 2329 2339 Athletic (warmup, sweat & jogging) suits: men's & boys'; women's & misses' outerwear

(P-3102)
LEEMAX INTERNATIONAL INC
Also Called: Ranboy Sportswear
1182 Via Escalante, Chula Vista
(91910-8141)
PHONE..............................619 208-2355
David L Shen, *President*
Juan Jose, *Manager*
EMP: 30
SQ FT: 3,000
SALES: 2MM **Privately Held**
SIC: 2329 Men's & boys' sportswear & athletic clothing

(P-3103)
LEVI STRAUSS INTERNATIONAL (HQ)
1155 Battery St, San Francisco
(94111-1264)
PHONE..............................415 501-6000
Michael Howard, *President*
John Anderson, *President*
S Lindsay Webbe, *President*
Robert Friedman, *Principal*
▲ EMP: 10 EST: 1965
SQ FT: 25,000
SALES (est): 1.8MM
SALES (corp-wide): 5.5B **Publicly Held**
SIC: 2329 2339 Men's & boys' sportswear & athletic clothing; women's & misses' outerwear
PA: Levi Strauss & Co.
1155 Battery St
San Francisco CA 94111
415 501-6000

(P-3104)
LIQUID GRAPHICS INC
2701 S Harbor Blvd Unit A, Santa Ana
(92704-5839)
PHONE..............................949 486-3588
Josh Merrell, *President*
Mark Hyman, *CFO*
Tiffany Jenkins, *Controller*
▲ EMP: 130 EST: 1997
SQ FT: 100,000
SALES: 25MM **Privately Held**
SIC: 2329 Men's & boys' sportswear & athletic clothing

(P-3105)
LOST INTERNATIONAL LLC
170 Technology Dr, Irvine (92618-2401)
PHONE..............................949 600-6950
Mike Reola, *Mng Member*
Matt Biolos,
Joel Cooper,
▲ EMP: 15
SALES (est): 1.7MM **Privately Held**
SIC: 2329 Athletic (warmup, sweat & jogging) suits: men's & boys'

(P-3106)
MAD APPAREL INC
Also Called: Athos Works
201 Arch St, Redwood City (94062-1305)
PHONE..............................800 714-9697
Dhananja Jayalath, *CEO*

Lindsey Cruz, *Officer*
Hamid Butte, *Vice Pres*
Christine Toha, *Office Mgr*
Ryan Matsumura, *Software Dev*
EMP: 33
SQ FT: 5,800
SALES (est): 4.4MM **Privately Held**
SIC: 2329 2339 Men's & boys' sportswear & athletic clothing; women's & misses' athletic clothing & sportswear

(P-3107)
MELAMED INTERNATIONAL INC (PA)
Also Called: Phantom
113 N Palm Dr, Beverly Hills (90210-5506)
PHONE..............................310 271-8585
Shahram Melamed, *President*
Dr Ruben Melamed, *Ch of Bd*
Farshad Melamed, *Director*
Michelle Melamed, *Director*
EMP: 12
SALES (est): 910.4K **Privately Held**
WEB: www.melamedinternational.com
SIC: 2329 2339 2369 5136 Men's & boys' sportswear & athletic clothing; women's & misses' athletic clothing & sportswear; girls' & children's outerwear; men's & boys' clothing; women's & children's clothing

(P-3108)
MIHOLIN INC
Also Called: Spikey Wear
1500 S Bradshaw Ave, Monterey Park
(91754-5426)
PHONE..............................213 820-8225
Peter Yoo, *President*
MI Young Song, *Vice Pres*
EMP: 10 EST: 2001
SQ FT: 7,600
SALES: 800K **Privately Held**
SIC: 2329 Men's & boys' sportswear & athletic clothing

(P-3109)
NORQUIST SALVAGE CORP INC
Also Called: Thrift Town
5005 Stockton Blvd Ste B, Sacramento
(95820-5424)
PHONE..............................916 454-0435
Rita Cheshire, *Manager*
EMP: 25
SALES (corp-wide): 120.7MM **Privately Held**
WEB: www.thrifttown.com
SIC: 2329 5932 3944 2731 Men's & boys' sportswear & athletic clothing; used merchandise stores; games, toys & children's vehicles; book publishing; women's & misses' outerwear
PA: Norquist Salvage Corporation, Inc.
2151 Prof Dr Ste 200
Roseville CA 95661
916 787-1070

(P-3110)
NORQUIST SALVAGE CORP INC
Also Called: Thrift Town
410 El Camino Ave, Sacramento
(95815-2937)
PHONE..............................916 922-9942
Donna Lunquist, *Manager*
EMP: 30
SALES (corp-wide): 120.7MM **Privately Held**
WEB: www.thrifttown.com
SIC: 2329 5932 Men's & boys' sportswear & athletic clothing; clothing, secondhand
PA: Norquist Salvage Corporation, Inc.
2151 Prof Dr Ste 200
Roseville CA 95661
916 787-1070

(P-3111)
OLAES ENTERPRISES INC
Also Called: Olaes Design & Marketing
13860 Stowe Dr, Poway (92064-8800)
PHONE..............................858 679-4450
Anthony Olaes, *President*
▲ EMP: 20
SQ FT: 28,000
SALES: 23.5MM **Privately Held**
WEB: www.olaesdesign.com
SIC: 2329 Men's & boys' athletic uniforms

(P-3112)
PEOPLE TREND INC
4801 Staunton Ave, Vernon (90058-1944)
PHONE..............................213 995-5555
Shahram Sharafian, *President*
EMP: 12 EST: 2011
SALES: 3.9MM **Privately Held**
SIC: 2329 Down-filled clothing: men's & boys'; men's & boys' sportswear & athletic clothing; athletic (warmup, sweat & jogging) suits: men's & boys'; riding clothes:, men's, youths' & boys'

(P-3113)
QOR LLC
775 Baywood Dr Ste 312, Petaluma
(94954-5500)
P.O. Box 1020 (94953-1020)
PHONE..............................707 658-2539
Joe Teno, *Mng Member*
Kelly Cooper, *Officer*
Lori Overton, *Info Tech Dir*
▲ EMP: 11
SALES (est): 1.9MM **Privately Held**
SIC: 2329 Athletic (warmup, sweat & jogging) suits: men's & boys'

(P-3114)
QUANTUM CONCEPT INC
5701 S Eastrn Ave Ste 220, Commerce
(90040)
PHONE..............................323 888-8601
Sung Tack Cho, *CEO*
◆ EMP: 13
SQ FT: 12,000
SALES (est): 1.5MM **Privately Held**
WEB: www.sqwear.com
SIC: 2329 5136 Athletic (warmup, sweat & jogging) suits: men's & boys'; men's & boys' clothing

(P-3115)
SAUVAGE INC (PA)
7717 Formula Pl, San Diego (92121-2419)
PHONE..............................858 408-0100
Elizabeth Southwood, *President*
Simon Southwood, *Corp Secy*
EMP: 18
SQ FT: 10,000
SALES (est): 1.6MM **Privately Held**
WEB: www.sauvagewear.com
SIC: 2329 2339 Men's & boys' sportswear & athletic clothing; bathing suits & swimwear: men's & boys'; bathing suits: women's, misses & juniors'; sportswear, women's

(P-3116)
SPORTSROBE INC
8654 Hayden Pl, Culver City (90232-2902)
PHONE..............................310 559-3999
Allen Ruegsegger, *President*
Mary Ann Ruegsegger, *Vice Pres*
EMP: 49
SQ FT: 14,000
SALES (est): 3.9MM **Privately Held**
SIC: 2329 Baseball uniforms: men's, youths' & boys'; football uniforms: men's, youths' & boys'

(P-3117)
ST CYCLEWEAR/GALLOP LLC
Also Called: S T Cycle Wear
1200 Billy Mitchell Dr D, El Cajon
(92020-1184)
PHONE..............................619 449-9191
Bruce Powell, *Mng Member*
Phin Kheng, *Accountant*
▲ EMP: 13 EST: 1981
SQ FT: 3,700
SALES (est): 1.4MM **Privately Held**
WEB: www.stcyclewear.com
SIC: 2329 Athletic (warmup, sweat & jogging) suits: men's & boys'; men's & boys' leather, wool & down-filled outerwear

(P-3118)
STEADY CLOTHING INC
1711 Newport Cir, Santa Ana (92705-5111)
PHONE..............................714 444-2058
Eric Anthony, *President*
Joshua Brownfield, *Vice Pres*
Johnny Baldaray, *Webmaster*
▲ EMP: 17
SQ FT: 10,000

SALES (est): 2.3MM **Privately Held**
WEB: www.steadyclothing.com
SIC: 2329 2339 Men's & boys' sportswear & athletic clothing; sportswear, women's

(P-3119)
STRAIGHT DOWN SPORTSWEAR (PA)
Also Called: Straight Down Clothing Co
625 Clarion Ct, San Luis Obispo
(93401-8177)
PHONE..............................805 543-3086
Mike Rowley, *President*
Steve Petterson, *Vice Pres*
▲ EMP: 20
SQ FT: 21,000
SALES (est): 2.6MM **Privately Held**
WEB: www.straightdown.com
SIC: 2329 2339 Men's & boys' sportswear & athletic clothing; women's & misses' outerwear

(P-3120)
STREAMLINE DSIGN SLKSCREEN INC (PA)
Also Called: Old Guys Rule
1299 S Wells Rd, Ventura (93004-1901)
PHONE..............................805 884-1025
Thom Hill, *CEO*
▲ EMP: 54
SQ FT: 33,000
SALES (est): 13.9MM **Privately Held**
SIC: 2329 5136 5611 Men's & boys' sportswear & athletic clothing; men's & boys' clothing; men's & boys' clothing stores

(P-3121)
SUNFLOWER IMPORTS INC
412 W Pico Blvd, Los Angeles
(90015-2404)
PHONE..............................213 748-3444
Premkumar Sakhrani, *Principal*
▲ EMP: 11
SQ FT: 15,000
SALES (est): 902.4K **Privately Held**
WEB: www.sunflowerimports.com
SIC: 2329 2339 Shirt & slack suits: men's, youths' & boys'; women's & misses' athletic clothing & sportswear

(P-3122)
SURF RIDE
1609 Ord Way, Oceanside (92056-3599)
PHONE..............................760 433-4020
John Ennis, *Principal*
Susan Goddard, *Buyer*
EMP: 16 EST: 2007
SALES (est): 2MM **Privately Held**
SIC: 2329 5941 Men's & boys' sportswear & athletic clothing; skateboarding equipment

(P-3123)
TARTAN FASHION INC
4357 Rowland Ave, El Monte (91731-1119)
PHONE..............................626 575-2828
Joann Sun, *President*
◆ EMP: 20
SQ FT: 20,363
SALES (est): 1.8MM **Privately Held**
WEB: www.tartan168.com
SIC: 2329 Men's & boys' sportswear & athletic clothing

(P-3124)
TRAVISMATHEW LLC
15202 Graham St, Huntington Beach
(92649-1109)
PHONE..............................562 799-6900
Travis Brasher, *CEO*
Nick Beranek,
John Kruger,
Chris Rossassen,
▲ EMP: 17
SALES (est): 2.9MM
SALES (corp-wide): 1.2B **Publicly Held**
SIC: 2329 5699 Athletic (warmup, sweat & jogging) suits: men's & boys'; sports apparel
PA: Callaway Golf Company
2180 Rutherford Rd
Carlsbad CA 92008
760 931-1771

▲ = Import ▼=Export
◆ =Import/Export

(P-3125)
TRUWEST INC
5592 Engineer Dr, Huntington Beach (92649-1122)
P.O. Box 1855 (92647-1855)
PHONE..................................714 895-2444
Lee Westwell, *President*
Gil Westwell, *Treasurer*
Gary Westwell, *Vice Pres*
Norm Westwell, *Vice Pres*
EMP: 28
SQ FT: 13,000
SALES (est): 3MM **Privately Held**
WEB: www.truwest.com
SIC: 2329 2339 Men's & boys' sportswear & athletic clothing; women's & misses' athletic clothing & sportswear

(P-3126)
UNILETE INC
18774 Ashford Ln, Huntington Beach (92648-7032)
P.O. Box 1520 (92647-1520)
PHONE..................................714 557-1271
Jonathan Oe, *President*
EMP: 10 **EST:** 2000
SALES: 300K **Privately Held**
SIC: 2329 2339 Athletic (warmup, sweat & jogging) suits: men's & boys'; athletic clothing: women's, misses' & juniors'

(P-3127)
UV SKINZ INC (PA)
13775 Mono Way Ste A, Sonora (95370-8857)
PHONE..................................209 536-9200
Rhonda R Sparks, *President*
Gerri Rusch, *Manager*
▲ **EMP:** 10
SQ FT: 3,500
SALES (est): 848.3K **Privately Held**
SIC: 2329 Men's & boys' sportswear & athletic clothing

(P-3128)
VF OUTDOOR LLC (HQ)
Also Called: North Face, The
2701 Harbor Bay Pkwy, Alameda (94502-3041)
P.O. Box 372670, Denver CO (80237-6670)
PHONE..................................510 618-3500
Scott Baxter, *President*
Alexandria Roberts, *Bd of Directors*
Jim Gerson, *Vice Pres*
Douglas L Hassman, *Vice Pres*
Becky Avila, *Store Mgr*
▲ **EMP:** 250 **EST:** 1994
SQ FT: 151,085
SALES (est): 348.4MM
SALES (corp-wide): 13.8MM **Publicly Held**
WEB: www.thenorthface.com
SIC: 2329 2339 3949 2394 Men's & boys' leather, wool & down-filled outerwear; ski & snow clothing: men's & boys'; women's & misses' outerwear; camping equipment & supplies; tents: made from purchased materials; sleeping bags; camping & backpacking equipment; skiing equipment
PA: V.F. Corporation
105 Corporate Center Blvd
Greensboro NC 27408
336 424-6000

(P-3129)
WARNACO SWIMWEAR INC (DH)
Also Called: Warnaco Swimwear Products
1201 W 5th St Ste 1200, Los Angeles (90017-2019)
PHONE..................................323 837-6000
Linda J Wachner, *Ch of Bd*
Kathy Van Ness, *President*
Roger Williams, *President*
Antonio Alvarez, *CEO*
Stanley S Lerstein, *CEO*
◆ **EMP:** 50
SQ FT: 10,000

SALES (est): 45.4MM
SALES (corp-wide): 9.6B **Publicly Held**
SIC: 2329 2339 2321 3949 Athletic (warmup, sweat & jogging) suits: men's & boys'; baseball uniforms: men's, youths' & boys'; ski & snow clothing: men's & boys'; bathing suits & swimwear: men's & boys'; bathing suits: women's, misses' & juniors'; ski jackets & pants: women's, misses' & juniors'; athletic clothing: women's, misses' & juniors'; men's & boys' sports & polo shirts; water sports equipment; sports apparel; military goods & regalia; bathing suits
HQ: Warnaco Inc.
501 Fashion Ave Fl 14
New York NY 10018
212 287-8000

(P-3130)
WATT ENTERPRISE INC
Also Called: Pacific Coast Sportswear
10575 Bechler River Ave, Fountain Valley (92708-6908)
PHONE..................................714 963-0781
Al Watt Jr, *President*
Lisa Hahn, *Manager*
EMP: 12
SALES (est): 1.3MM **Privately Held**
WEB: www.pcsportswear.com
SIC: 2329 2339 5091 Men's & boys' sportswear & athletic clothing; women's & misses' athletic clothing & sportswear; athletic goods

(P-3131)
ZEENI INC
Also Called: Prieto Sports
9536 Gidley St, Temple City (91780-4213)
PHONE..................................626 350-1024
Hassan Zeenni, *President*
Mercedes Zeenni, *Treasurer*
▲ **EMP:** 15
SQ FT: 11,000
SALES (est): 1.9MM **Privately Held**
WEB: www.prietosports.com
SIC: 2329 Baseball uniforms: men's, youths' & boys'

(P-3132)
ZK ENTERPRISES INC
Also Called: Unique Sales
4368 District Blvd, Vernon (90058-3124)
PHONE..................................213 622-7012
Ron Kelfer, *President*
Kathy Kelfer, *Vice Pres*
Ralph Barragan, *Prdtn Mgr*
EMP: 40
SQ FT: 13,000
SALES (est): 5MM **Privately Held**
WEB: www.uniquesalesco.com
SIC: 2329 2339 Athletic (warmup, sweat & jogging) suits: men's & boys'; jogging & warmup suits: women's, misses' & juniors'

2331 Women's & Misses' Blouses

(P-3133)
4 WHAT ITS WORTH INC (PA)
Also Called: Tyte Jeans
5815 Smithway St, Commerce (90040-1605)
PHONE..................................323 728-4503
Alden Halpern, *President*
◆ **EMP:** 10
SQ FT: 38,000
SALES (est): 8.9MM **Privately Held**
WEB: www.tyte.com
SIC: 2331 2329 Women's & misses' blouses & shirts; knickers, dress (separate): men's & boys'

(P-3134)
ACTIVE KNITWEAR RESOURCES INC
Also Called: Gypsy Heart
322 S Date Ave, Alhambra (91803-1404)
PHONE..................................626 308-1328
▲ **EMP:** 19
SQ FT: 22,000
SALES (est): 2.4MM **Privately Held**
WEB: www.activeknitwear.com
SIC: 2331 7389

(P-3135)
ALL STAR CLOTHING INC
Also Called: Big Bang Clothing
4507 Staunton Ave, Vernon (90058-1936)
PHONE..................................323 233-7773
Sam Lee, *Principal*
EMP: 12
SQ FT: 6,000
SALES (est): 788.2K **Privately Held**
SIC: 2331 5137 Women's & misses' blouses & shirts; women's & children's clothing

(P-3136)
ALLIANCE APPAREL INC
Also Called: Blu Heaven
3422 Garfield Ave, Commerce (90040-3104)
PHONE..................................323 888-8900
Tae Hoo Shin, *President*
Michael Park, *Vice Pres*
▲ **EMP:** 40
SQ FT: 17,500
SALES (est): 4.4MM **Privately Held**
WEB: www.bluheaven.net
SIC: 2331 Blouses, women's & juniors': made from purchased material

(P-3137)
AMERTEX INTERNATIONAL INC
2108 Orange St, Alhambra (91803-1427)
PHONE..................................626 570-9409
Amy Wong, *President*
Victor Wong, *Admin Sec*
▲ **EMP:** 50
SQ FT: 25,000
SALES (est): 12.5MM **Privately Held**
WEB: www.amertex.net
SIC: 2331 2335 2337 2339 Women's & misses' blouses & shirts; women's, juniors' & misses' dresses; women's & misses' suits & coats; sportswear, women's

(P-3138)
ATREVETE INC
Also Called: Staccato
2055 E 51st St, Vernon (90058-2818)
PHONE..................................323 277-5551
Sarah Moon, *Owner*
Bernard Chung, *Sales Mgr*
▲ **EMP:** 17
SALES (est): 1.4MM **Privately Held**
SIC: 2331 Women's & misses' blouses & shirts

(P-3139)
BAILEY 44 LLC
4700 S Boyle Ave, Vernon (90058-3000)
PHONE..................................213 228-1930
Shelli Segal, *Mng Member*
Linda Heiman, *Buyer*
Carlos Leiva, *Prdtn Mgr*
Alex Zalewski, *Director*
Paola Nieto, *Associate*
EMP: 25
SALES (est): 3.5MM **Privately Held**
SIC: 2331 5621 Blouses, women's & juniors': made from purchased material; shirts, women's & juniors': made from purchased materials; T-shirts & tops, women's: made from purchased materials; boutiques

(P-3140)
BERESHITH INC (PA)
Also Called: Love In
1015 Crocker St, Los Angeles (90021-2051)
PHONE..................................213 749-7304
Kyung Hae Lee Chang, *CEO*
Helen Chang, *Director*
EMP: 10 **EST:** 2010
SALES (est): 1.6MM **Privately Held**
SIC: 2331 2335 2361 Women's & misses' blouses & shirts; women's, juniors' & misses' dresses; girls' & children's blouses & shirts

(P-3141)
BLTEE LLC
7101 Telegraph Rd, Montebello (90640-6511)
P.O. Box 2762, Santa Fe Springs (90670-0762)
PHONE..................................213 802-1736

Elano Miguel Elias, *Mng Member*
EMP: 45
SQ FT: 4,900
SALES (est): 10.5MM **Privately Held**
SIC: 2331 5136 Women's & misses' blouses & shirts; shirts, men's & boys'

(P-3142)
BLUPRINT CLOTHING CORP
5600 Bandini Blvd, Bell (90201-6407)
PHONE..................................323 780-4347
Ju Hyun Kim, *CEO*
Liz Lee, *Vice Pres*
Jake Lee, *Technology*
Gina Balag, *Controller*
Ginalyn Balag, *Controller*
▲ **EMP:** 72
SALES: 30MM **Privately Held**
SIC: 2331 Women's & misses' blouses & shirts; blouses, women's & juniors': made from purchased material; shirts, women's & juniors': made from purchased materials

(P-3143)
BOULEVARD STYLE INC
Also Called: Blvd
1680 E 40th Pl, Los Angeles (90011-2223)
PHONE..................................213 749-1551
Joseph Huh, *Principal*
EMP: 13 **Privately Held**
SIC: 2331 Women's & misses' blouses & shirts
PA: Boulevard Style, Inc.
1015 Crocker St Ste 27
Los Angeles CA 90021

(P-3144)
BOULEVARD STYLE INC (PA)
Also Called: In Style
1015 Crocker St Ste 27, Los Angeles (90021-2051)
PHONE..................................213 749-1551
Joseph Huh, *CEO*
EMP: 15
SALES (est): 2.7MM **Privately Held**
SIC: 2331 Women's & misses' blouses & shirts

(P-3145)
BYER CALIFORNIA (PA)
66 Potrero Ave, San Francisco (94103-4800)
PHONE..................................415 626-7844
Allan G Byer, *CEO*
Ed Manburg, *CFO*
Marian Byer, *Corp Secy*
Barbara Berling, *Vice Pres*
Janis Byer, *Vice Pres*
▲ **EMP:** 575
SQ FT: 230,000
SALES (est): 347.6MM **Privately Held**
WEB: www.byer.com
SIC: 2331 Women's & misses' blouses & shirts

(P-3146)
BYER CALIFORNIA
3740 Livermore Outlets Dr, Livermore (94551-4215)
PHONE..................................925 245-0184
EMP: 67
SALES (corp-wide): 372.3MM **Privately Held**
SIC: 2331
PA: Byer California
66 Potrero Ave
San Francisco CA 94103
415 626-7844

(P-3147)
C-QUEST INC
Also Called: Ava James
1439 S Herbert Ave, Commerce (90023-4047)
PHONE..................................323 980-1400
Nam Paik, *CEO*
Sung C Choi, *Admin Sec*
◆ **EMP:** 55
SQ FT: 100,000
SALES (est): 8.1MM **Privately Held**
WEB: www.chereamie.com
SIC: 2331 Women's & misses' blouses & shirts

(P-3148)
CAVERN CLUB LLC
Also Called: Liverpool Jeans
1708 Aeros Way, Montebello (90640-6504)
PHONE.....................323 837-9800
Doron Kadosh,
Benjamin Goldstein,
Ronald Perilman,
EMP: 10 EST: 2012
SQ FT: 65,000
SALES (est): 1MM Privately Held
SIC: 2331 Women's & misses' blouses &
shirts

(P-3149)
CLOTHING BY FRENZII INC
905 Mateo St, Los Angeles (90021-1713)
PHONE.....................213 670-0265
Sung-Kyu William Kang, CEO
William Kang, COO
EMP: 16 EST: 2001
SQ FT: 8,950
SALES (est): 1.7MM Privately Held
SIC: 2331 5137 Women's & misses'
blouses & shirts; women's & children's
clothing; women's & children's dresses,
suits, skirts & blouses

(P-3150)
COLON MANUFACTURING INC
(PA)
Also Called: Coc Inc
1100 S San Pedro St, Los Angeles
(90015-2328)
PHONE.....................213 749-6149
Thomas T Byun, President
Julia Anna Byun, Admin Sec
EMP: 19
SALES (est): 1.7MM Privately Held
WEB: www.healthwear.org
SIC: 2331 2335 2337 Women's & misses'
blouses & shirts; women's, juniors' &
misses' dresses; women's & misses' suits
& coats

(P-3151)
CURE APPAREL LLC
Also Called: Liberty Love
3338 S Malt Ave, Commerce (90040-3126)
PHONE.....................562 927-7460
Mohammad R Seilabi, Mng Member
Amir Seilabi, Vice Pres
▲ EMP: 15
SQ FT: 5,000
SALES (est): 2.1MM Privately Held
SIC: 2331 Blouses, women's & juniors':
made from purchased material

(P-3152)
CUT & TRIM INC
20847 Betron St, Woodland Hills
(91364-3351)
PHONE.....................818 264-0101
Jon Bernstein, President
Janet Bernstein, Vice Pres
EMP: 11
SQ FT: 10,000
SALES (est): 1.2MM Privately Held
SIC: 2331 Women's & misses' blouses &
shirts

(P-3153)
D & R BROTHERS INC
Also Called: Visage Ladies Fashions
952 S Broadway 2, Los Angeles
(90015-1610)
PHONE.....................213 747-4309
Rafi Khosrow Shaoulian, President
Danny Shaoulian, Vice Pres
EMP: 45
SQ FT: 40,000
SALES (est): 3.7MM Privately Held
WEB: www.drbrothers.com
SIC: 2331 8741 5136 T-shirts & tops,
women's: made from purchased materi-
als; management services; shirts, men's
& boys'

(P-3154)
DELTA SPORTSWEAR INC
331 S Hale Ave, Fullerton (92831-4805)
PHONE.....................714 568-1102
Imran Parekh, President
Muhamed Y Wadalawala, CFO
EMP: 10
SQ FT: 30,000

SALES (est): 1.2MM Privately Held
WEB: www.delpacific.com
SIC: 2331 T-shirts & tops, women's: made
from purchased materials

(P-3155)
DIDI OF CALIFORNIA INC
5816 Piedmont Ave, Los Angeles
(90042-4244)
PHONE.....................323 256-4514
Aldo Garrolini, President
EMP: 25
SQ FT: 10,000
SALES (est): 1.9MM Privately Held
SIC: 2331 2339 Blouses, women's & jun-
iors': made from purchased material;
women's & misses' outerwear

(P-3156)
DRESS TO KILL INC
Also Called: Jane Mohr Design
15500 Erwin St Ste 1089, Van Nuys
(91411-1027)
PHONE.....................818 994-3890
Jane Mohr, CEO
▲ EMP: 12
SQ FT: 1,400
SALES (est): 955.2K Privately Held
SIC: 2331 Women's & misses' blouses &
shirts

(P-3157)
EASTWEST CLOTHING INC (PA)
Also Called: Language Los Angeles
40 E Verdugo Ave, Burbank (91502-1931)
PHONE.....................323 980-1177
Michael Schreier, CEO
Arvril Ozen, COO
▲ EMP: 22
SQ FT: 10,000
SALES (est): 5.2MM Privately Held
SIC: 2331 Women's & misses' blouses &
shirts

(P-3158)
ERGE DESIGNS LLC
4770 E 48th St, Vernon (90058-2702)
PHONE.....................310 614-9197
David Berg, Mng Member
Frank Quijada, Partner
EMP: 10
SQ FT: 30,000
SALES (est): 1.5MM Privately Held
SIC: 2331 Blouses, women's & juniors':
made from purchased material

(P-3159)
FORTUNE CASUALS LLC (PA)
Also Called: Judy Ann
10119 Jefferson Blvd, Culver City
(90232-3519)
PHONE.....................310 733-2100
Fred Kayne, Mng Member
Michael Geller,
Walt Lacher,
◆ EMP: 110
SQ FT: 40,000
SALES (est): 9.5MM Privately Held
WEB: www.fortunecasuals.com
SIC: 2331 2339 2321 T-shirts & tops,
women's: made from purchased materi-
als; slacks: women's, misses' & juniors';
men's & boys' furnishings

(P-3160)
GIANNO CO LTD
13546 Vintage Pl, Chino (91710-5243)
PHONE.....................909 628-6928
Peter Chang, President
▲ EMP: 10
SALES (est): 949.3K Privately Held
WEB: www.giannousa.com
SIC: 2331 Women's & misses' blouses &
shirts

(P-3161)
GLORIA LANCE INC (PA)
Also Called: Electric Designs
15616 S Broadway, Gardena (90248-2211)
PHONE.....................310 767-4400
Robert Hempling, President
Gloria Lopez, Treasurer
Zvia Hempling, Vice Pres
Miguel Lopez, Admin Sec
David Leman, Purchasing
◆ EMP: 90

SQ FT: 25,000
SALES (est): 18.3MM Privately Held
SIC: 2331 2339 2335 Blouses, women's
& juniors': made from purchased material;
sportswear, women's; bridal & formal
gowns

(P-3162)
GRAU DESIGN INC
1133 N Highland Ave, Los Angeles (90038)
P.O. Box 93156 (90093-0156)
PHONE.....................323 461-4462
Claudia Marie Grau, President
Mel Grau, Treasurer
Ann Grau, Vice Pres
EMP: 10
SQ FT: 2,000
SALES (est): 590.8K Privately Held
SIC: 2331 2335 2337 Women's & misses'
blouses & shirts; women's, juniors' &
misses' dresses; women's & misses' suits
& coats

(P-3163)
GROUP MARTIN LLC
JOHNATHON
3400 S Main St, Los Angeles (90007-4412)
PHONE.....................323 235-1555
Yaniv Dirman,
Eli Cohen,
EMP: 30
SALES (est): 1.2MM Privately Held
SIC: 2331 Women's & misses' blouses &
shirts

(P-3164)
GURU KNITS INC
Also Called: Antex Knitting Mills
225 W 38th St, Los Angeles (90037-1405)
PHONE.....................323 235-9424
Kevin Port, CEO
◆ EMP: 60
SALES (est): 8.8MM Privately Held
SIC: 2331 2361 Women's & misses'
blouses & shirts; blouses: girls', children's
& infants'

(P-3165)
GUSB INC
219 E 32nd St, Los Angeles (90011-1917)
PHONE.....................323 233-0044
Scott Changsup Lee, CEO
▲ EMP: 15
SQ FT: 10,000
SALES (est): 1.1MM Privately Held
SIC: 2331 2335 2337 2339 Women's &
misses' blouses & shirts; women's, jun-
iors' & misses' dresses; women's &
misses' suits & coats; women's & misses'
outerwear

(P-3166)
H & L APPAREL ENTERPRISE
INC
2202 E Anderson St, Vernon (90058-3451)
PHONE.....................323 589-1563
EMP: 11 EST: 2013
SQ FT: 20,000
SALES (est): 1MM Privately Held
SIC: 2331

(P-3167)
HARKHAM INDUSTRIES INC
(PA)
Also Called: Jonathan Martin
857 S San Pedro St # 300, Los Angeles
(90014-2432)
PHONE.....................323 586-4600
Uri Harkham, President
◆ EMP: 50
SQ FT: 140,000
SALES (est): 5.5MM Privately Held
SIC: 2331 2335 2337 2339 Blouses,
women's & juniors': made from purchased
material; women's, juniors' & misses'
dresses; skirts, separate: women's,
misses' & juniors'; women's & misses'
outerwear

(P-3168)
J HEYRI INC
Also Called: Everleigh
6900 S Alameda St, Huntington Park
(90255-3619)
PHONE.....................323 588-1234

Tiffany Lin, President
Sunny Choi, CEO
Sunny S Choi, Vice Pres
Alexis Kwak, Vice Pres
▲ EMP: 20
SQ FT: 3,000
SALES (est): 2.4MM Privately Held
SIC: 2331 Women's & misses' blouses &
shirts

(P-3169)
K TOO
Also Called: K-Too
800 E 12th St Ste 117, Los Angeles
(90021-2199)
PHONE.....................213 747-7766
Jae Hee Kim, CEO
Erik Kim, Vice Pres
Kelley Kim, Princpl
Audrey Kim, Exec Dir
◆ EMP: 41
SALES (est): 16.2MM Privately Held
SIC: 2331 Women's & misses' blouses &
shirts

(P-3170)
KAMIRAN INC
Also Called: Mesmerize
1415 Maple Ave Ste 220, Los Angeles
(90015-3103)
PHONE.....................213 746-9161
Kamram Hakimi, President
Kambi Hakimi, Vice Pres
▲ EMP: 13
SQ FT: 6,000
SALES (est): 1.6MM Privately Held
WEB: www.kamikam.com
SIC: 2331 Women's & misses' blouses &
shirts

(P-3171)
KATHY IRELAND WORLDWIDE
39 Princeton Dr, Rancho Mirage
(92270-3115)
P.O. Box 1410 (92270-1052)
PHONE.....................310 557-2700
Kathy Ireland, CEO
Stephen Roseberry, President
Erik Sterling, CFO
Steve Glick, Exec VP
Bialik Benjamin, Vice Pres
EMP: 11
SALES (est): 1.3MM Privately Held
SIC: 2331 2335 2337 5023 Women's &
misses' blouses & shirts; women's, jun-
iors' & misses' dresses; women's &
misses' suits & coats; rugs

(P-3172)
KOMEX INTERNATIONAL INC
Also Called: Bubblegum USA
736 E 29th St, Los Angeles (90011-2014)
PHONE.....................323 233-9005
John J Inn, President
Laura Hong, Vice Pres
Paul Sanghyon Inn, Vice Pres
◆ EMP: 40
SQ FT: 60,000
SALES (est): 4.4MM Privately Held
WEB: www.bubblegumusa.com
SIC: 2331 2329 2339 2325 Women's &
misses' blouses & shirts; men's & boys'
sportswear & athletic clothing; women's &
misses' outerwear; men's & boys'
trousers & slacks

(P-3173)
LA MAMBA LLC
242 S Anderson St, Los Angeles
(90033-3205)
PHONE.....................323 526-3526
Vera Campbell,
Stephen Brown,
Denni Kopelan,
▲ EMP: 25
SALES (est): 2.3MM Privately Held
SIC: 2331 Blouses, women's & juniors':
made from purchased material

(P-3174)
LF SPORTSWEAR INC (PA)
Also Called: Furst
5333 Mcconnell Ave, Los Angeles
(90066-7025)
PHONE.....................310 437-4100
Phillip L Furst, CEO

Marsha Furst, *Vice Pres*
Steve Katz, *Vice Pres*
Stephanie Ocon, *Human Res Dir*
▲ **EMP:** 30
SQ FT: 35,000
SALES (est): 16.2MM **Privately Held**
WEB: www.lfstores.com
SIC: 2331 2335 5137 2211 Women's & misses' blouses & shirts; women's & children's dresses, suits, skirts & blouses; denims

(P-3175)
LILI BUTLER STUDIO INC
Also Called: The Rupp Butler Studio
7950 Redwood Dr Ste 16, Cotati
(94931-3054)
PHONE...................707 793-0222
Lili Butler, *President*
EMP: 17
SALES (est): 1.8MM **Privately Held**
WEB: www.lilibutler.com
SIC: 2331 2335 2337 5621 Women's & misses' blouses & shirts; women's, juniors' & misses' dresses; women's & misses' suits & coats; women's clothing stores

(P-3176)
LOVE MARKS INC (PA)
Also Called: Kiddo By Katie
2050 E 51st St, Vernon (90058-2819)
PHONE...................323 859-8770
Samuel Paik, *President*
▲ **EMP:** 17 EST: 2012
SALES (est): 6.2MM **Privately Held**
SIC: 2331 Women's & misses' blouses & shirts

(P-3177)
LSPACE AMERICA LLC
Also Called: L Space
9821 Irvine Center Dr, Irvine (92618-4307)
PHONE...................949 596-8726
Paul Carr, *Mng Member*
Lauren Kula, *CFO*
◆ **EMP:** 20
SALES (est): 1.6MM **Privately Held**
SIC: 2331 2253 Women's & misses' blouses & shirts; bathing suits & swimwear, knit

(P-3178)
LYRIC CULTURE LLC
2520 W 6th St Ste 250, Los Angeles
(90057-3199)
PHONE...................323 581-3511
Jason Schutzer, *Mng Member*
Elliot Schutzer,
EMP: 10 EST: 2014
SQ FT: 53,000
SALES (est): 857.5K **Privately Held**
SIC: 2331 T-shirts & tops, women's: made from purchased materials

(P-3179)
MAKING IT BIG INC
1375 Corp Ctr Pkwy Ste A, Santa Rosa
(95407-5076)
PHONE...................707 795-1995
Tracy Amiral, *President*
Kristina Chan, *Marketing Staff*
EMP: 24
SALES (est): 3.2MM **Privately Held**
WEB: www.amiral.org
SIC: 2331 2335 2337 2339 Women's & misses' blouses & shirts; women's, juniors' & misses' dresses; women's & misses' suits & coats; women's & misses' outerwear; women's apparel, mail order; women's clothing stores

(P-3180)
MF INC
Also Called: Welovefine
2010 E 15th St, Los Angeles (90021-2823)
PHONE...................213 627-2498
Danish Gajiani, *CEO*
Faizan Bakali, *President*
Bill Bussiere, *CFO*
Dean Allen, *Chief Mktg Ofcr*
Amanda Winter, *Production*
▲ **EMP:** 120
SQ FT: 700,000

SALES (est): 25MM
SALES (corp-wide): 173MM **Privately Held**
WEB: www.rubygloom.com
SIC: 2331 2253 T-shirts & tops, women's: made from purchased materials; shirts, women's & juniors': made from purchased materials; T-shirts & tops, knit
PA: Mad Engine, Llc
6740 Cobra Way Ste 100
San Diego CA 92121
858 558-5270

(P-3181)
MONROW INC
1404 S Main St Ste C, Los Angeles
(90015-2566)
PHONE...................213 741-6007
Megan George, *President*
Ashley Sarbinoff, *Sales Staff*
EMP: 29
SALES: 12.1MM **Privately Held**
SIC: 2331 T-shirts & tops, women's: made from purchased materials

(P-3182)
MXF DESIGNS INC
Also Called: Nally & Millie
1601 Perrino Pl Ste A, Los Angeles
(90023-2662)
PHONE...................323 266-1451
James Park, *President*
Nally Park, *Shareholder*
▼ **EMP:** 95
SQ FT: 64,000
SALES: 11MM **Privately Held**
SIC: 2331 Blouses, women's & juniors': made from purchased material

(P-3183)
MYMICHELLE COMPANY LLC (HQ)
Also Called: My Michelle
13077 Temple Ave, La Puente
(91746-1418)
PHONE...................626 934-4166
Arthur Gordon, *President*
Caren Belair, *President*
Perri Cohen, *President*
Susan Stokes, *President*
Roger D Joseph, *Treasurer*
▲ **EMP:** 300
SQ FT: 600,000
SALES (est): 21.4MM
SALES (corp-wide): 594MM **Privately Held**
WEB: www.kellwoodco.com
SIC: 2331 2337 2335 2361 Blouses, women's & juniors': made from purchased material; shirts, women's & juniors': made from purchased materials; skirts, separate: women's, misses' & juniors'; dresses, paper: cut & sewn; blouses: girls', children's & infants'; shirts: girls', children's & infants'; girls' & children's outerwear; women's & misses' athletic clothing & sportswear
PA: Kellwood Company, Llc
600 Kellwood Pkwy Ste 110
Chesterfield MO 63017
314 576-3100

(P-3184)
NOAHS ARK INTERNATIONAL INC
Also Called: Cheol Lee
2319 E 8th St, Los Angeles (90021-1732)
PHONE...................714 521-1235
Cheol Woo Lee, *President*
EMP: 12
SQ FT: 3,000
SALES: 2.9MM **Privately Held**
SIC: 2331 Blouses, women's & juniors': made from purchased material

(P-3185)
NORTH BAY RHBLITATION SVCS INC
Also Called: North Bay Industries
875 Airport Rd, Monterey (93940)
PHONE...................831 372-4094
Robert Hutt, *Branch Mgr*
EMP: 30

SALES (corp-wide): 16.2MM **Privately Held**
WEB: www.nbrs.org
SIC: 2331 8331 2399 7389 Shirts, women's & misses': made from purchased materials; community service employment training program; flags, fabric; sewing contractor
PA: North Bay Rehabilitation Services, Inc.
649 Martin Ave
Rohnert Park CA 94928
707 585-1991

(P-3186)
NOTHING TO WEAR INC (PA)
Also Called: Figure 8
630 Maple Ave, Torrance (90503-5001)
PHONE...................310 328-0408
Cindy Nunes Freeman, *President*
Darrin Freeman, *CFO*
Julie L Santiago, *Production*
◆ **EMP:** 35
SQ FT: 18,000
SALES (est): 7.7MM **Privately Held**
WEB: www.subtletones.com
SIC: 2331 2335 2339 Women's & misses' blouses & shirts; women's, juniors' & misses' dresses; women's & misses' accessories

(P-3187)
OAKLEY INC (DH)
1 Icon, Foothill Ranch (92610-3000)
PHONE...................949 951-0991
Colin Baden, *President*
Jim Jannard, *Ch of Bd*
D Scott Olivet, *Ch of Bd*
Don Krause, *President*
Gianluca Tagliabue, *CFO*
◆ **EMP:** 900
SQ FT: 550,000
SALES (est): 1B
SALES (corp-wide): 1.4MM **Privately Held**
WEB: www.oakley.com
SIC: 2331 2339 3021 3873 Women's & misses' blouses & shirts; women's & misses' outerwear; rubber & plastics footwear; watches, clocks, watchcases & parts; men's footwear, except athletic; glasses, sun or glare

(P-3188)
OUTDOOR LFSTYLE COLLECTIVE LLC
Also Called: Mad Hueys, The
829 Windcrest Dr, Carlsbad (92011-3715)
PHONE...................858 336-5580
Patrick J Connell, *Mng Member*
Pj Connell, *General Mgr*
▲ **EMP:** 12 EST: 2014
SQ FT: 5,000
SALES: 500K **Privately Held**
SIC: 2331 2329 5136 5137 Women's & misses' blouses & shirts; shirt & slack suits: men's, youths' & boys'; men's & boys' clothing; women's & children's clothing

(P-3189)
PROJECT SOCIAL T LLC
615 S Clarence St, Los Angeles
(90023-1107)
PHONE...................323 266-4500
Mike Chodler, *Mng Member*
EMP: 30
SALES: 15MM **Privately Held**
SIC: 2331 5137 5621 Women's & misses' blouses & shirts; women's & children's clothing; women's clothing stores

(P-3190)
SADIE & SAGE INC (PA)
Also Called: Sage The Label
1900 E 25th St, Los Angeles (90058-1130)
PHONE...................213 234-2188
Sinae Kim, *CEO*
Steven Kim, *Admin Sec*
Ryan Shelton, *Media Spec*
Shannon Barnes, *Education*
▲ **EMP:** 10 EST: 2015
SALES (est): 2.3MM **Privately Held**
SIC: 2331 5137 Women's & misses' blouses & shirts; women's & children's clothing

(P-3191)
SANCTUARY CLOTHING INC
3611 N San Fernando Blvd, Burbank
(91505-1043)
PHONE...................818 505-0018
Ken Polanco, *President*
Debra Polanco, *Vice Pres*
EMP: 40
SALES (est): 3.3MM **Privately Held**
WEB: www.sanctuaryclothing.com
SIC: 2331 Women's & misses' blouses & shirts

(P-3192)
SENSE FASHION CORPORATION
Also Called: Sense Fashions
2415 Merced Ave, South El Monte
(91733-1921)
PHONE...................626 454-3381
June Ho, *President*
Charles Loh, *Vice Pres*
◆ **EMP:** 30
SQ FT: 14,000
SALES: 2.1MM **Privately Held**
SIC: 2331 2339 2329 Blouses, women's & juniors': made from purchased material; shirts, women's & juniors': made from purchased materials; sportswear, women's; men's & boys' sportswear & athletic clothing

(P-3193)
SEWING EXPERTS INC
227 Lincoln St, Calexico (92231-2257)
PHONE...................760 357-8525
Mike Fletes, *President*
EMP: 35
SALES (est): 2.8MM **Privately Held**
SIC: 2331 2329 Women's & misses' blouses & shirts; shirt & slack suits: men's, youths' & boys'

(P-3194)
SHIMMER FASHION
555 Broadway Ste 134, Chula Vista
(91910-5382)
PHONE...................619 426-7781
EMP: 15
SALES (est): 784.7K **Privately Held**
SIC: 2331

(P-3195)
STYLE PLUS INC (PA)
Also Called: Wanna B
2807 S Olive St, Los Angeles
(90007-3339)
PHONE...................213 205-8408
Eun Kyoung Shin, *CEO*
Kenny Kim, *CFO*
EMP: 12
SALES (est): 3.3MM **Privately Held**
SIC: 2331 Women's & misses' blouses & shirts

(P-3196)
TEAM FASHION
2303 E 55th St, Vernon (90058-3435)
PHONE...................323 589-3388
EMP: 15
SQ FT: 80,000
SALES (est): 1.6MM **Privately Held**
SIC: 2331

(P-3197)
THREE BROTHERS CUTTING
8416 Otis St, South Gate (90280-2515)
PHONE...................323 564-4774
Jose Hernandez, *Owner*
EMP: 15
SALES (est): 677.2K **Privately Held**
SIC: 2331 Blouses, women's & juniors': made from purchased material

(P-3198)
THREE DOTS LLC
7340 Lampson Ave, Garden Grove
(92841-2902)
PHONE...................714 799-6333
Sharon Lebon,
Bruno Lenon,
▲ **EMP:** 72

SALES (est): 9.1MM
SALES (corp-wide): 17.6MM Privately Held
WEB: www.threedots.net
SIC: 2331 T-shirts & tops, women's: made from purchased materials
PA: Three Dots, Inc.
   11791 Monarch St
   Garden Grove CA 92841
   714 799-6333

(P-3199)
THREE PLUS ONE INC
Also Called: Audrey 3plus1
3007 Fruitland Ave, Vernon (90058-3626)
PHONE.....................213 623-3070
Kim Yon MI, President
Durey Kim,
EMP: 14 EST: 2007
SALES (est): 1.1MM Privately Held
SIC: 2331 Women's & misses' blouses & shirts

(P-3200)
TIANELLO INC
Also Called: Tianello By Steve Barraza
138 W 38th St, Los Angeles (90037-1404)
PHONE.....................323 231-0599
Steven Barraza, President
Kent Bailey, CFO
Barraza Steve, Vice Pres
Angel Orellana, Cust Mgr
Paul Farnacio, Manager
▲ EMP: 185
SQ FT: 25,000
SALES (est): 23.5MM Privately Held
WEB: www.tianello.com
SIC: 2331 5621 2339 Women's & misses' blouses & shirts; women's clothing stores; women's & misses' outerwear

(P-3201)
TRIXXI CLOTHING COMPANY INC (PA)
6817 E Acco St, Commerce (90040-1901)
PHONE.....................323 585-4200
Annette Soufrine, CEO
Leslie Flores, President
Janet Edwards, Controller
▲ EMP: 41
SQ FT: 35,000
SALES (est): 36.4MM Privately Held
WEB: www.trixxigirl.com
SIC: 2331 5621 Blouses, women's & juniors': made from purchased material; women's specialty clothing stores

(P-3202)
TWO STAR DOG INC (PA)
Also Called: Body Dope
1329 9th St, Berkeley (94710-1502)
PHONE.....................510 525-1100
Steven Boutrous, President
Allan Boutrous, Vice Pres
Attas Boutrous, Vice Pres
Stella Boutrous Carakasi, Vice Pres
Allegra Alvarado, Admin Asst
▲ EMP: 34
SQ FT: 25,000
SALES (est): 4.9MM Privately Held
SIC: 2331 Women's & misses' blouses & shirts

(P-3203)
UBST INC
373 Van Ness Ave, Torrance (90501-1484)
PHONE.....................424 222-9908
Ju Chun, CEO
EMP: 11
SALES: 7.9MM Privately Held
SIC: 2331 Shirts, women's & juniors': made from purchased materials

(P-3204)
UMGEE USA INC
1565 E 23rd St, Los Angeles (90011-1801)
PHONE.....................323 526-9138
Boyng Ki GI, President
◆ EMP: 18
SALES (est): 839.9K Privately Held
SIC: 2331 2335 Women's & misses' blouses & shirts; women's, juniors' & misses' dresses

(P-3205)
UNGER FABRIK LLC (PA)
18525 Railroad St, City of Industry (91748-1316)
PHONE.....................626 469-8080
Yongbin Luo, CEO
Celso Ong, Controller
◆ EMP: 110
SQ FT: 300,000
SALES (est): 49.5MM Privately Held
WEB: www.ungerfab.com
SIC: 2331 Women's & misses' blouses & shirts

(P-3206)
US PREMIER INC
624 S Clarence St, Los Angeles (90023-1108)
PHONE.....................323 267-4463
Tae Lee, President
EMP: 12
SQ FT: 8,000
SALES (est): 2.5MM Privately Held
SIC: 2331 2329 Women's & misses' blouses & shirts; knickers, dress (separate): men's & boys'

(P-3207)
VEEZEE INC
Also Called: Honulua Surf Co
121 Waterworks Way, Irvine (92618-7719)
PHONE.....................949 265-0800
Paul Naude, President
▲ EMP: 20
SALES (est): 1.8MM
SALES (corp-wide): 43B Publicly Held
SIC: 2331 5099 Women's & misses' blouses & shirts; sunglasses
HQ: Billabong International Limited
   1 Billabong Pl
   Burleigh Heads QLD 4220

(P-3208)
W5 CONCEPTS INC
2049 E 38th St, Vernon (90058-1614)
PHONE.....................323 231-2415
Kyung Eun Kim, CEO
Nancy Ramirez, Manager
EMP: 20
SQ FT: 3,800
SALES (est): 2.4MM Privately Held
SIC: 2331 Women's & misses' blouses & shirts

2335 Women's & Misses' Dresses

(P-3209)
4 YOU APPAREL INC
Also Called: Egen
2944 E 44th St, Vernon (90058-2430)
PHONE.....................323 583-4242
Joo Sung Son, President
▲ EMP: 15 EST: 2000
SQ FT: 53,420
SALES (est): 1.3MM Privately Held
WEB: www.4youapparel.com
SIC: 2335 Women's, juniors' & misses' dresses

(P-3210)
ADRIENNE DRESSES INC
719 S Los Angeles St # 827, Los Angeles (90014-2129)
PHONE.....................213 622-8557
Miriam G Rosa, President
EMP: 16
SQ FT: 1,796
SALES (est): 1.2MM Privately Held
SIC: 2335 Women's, juniors' & misses' dresses

(P-3211)
ALMACK LINERS INC
9541 Cozycroft Ave, Chatsworth (91311-5102)
PHONE.....................818 718-5878
Susana Almack, President
EMP: 25
SQ FT: 3,000

SALES (est): 3.2MM Privately Held
WEB: www.almackliners.com
SIC: 2335 2329 Women's, juniors' & misses' dresses; men's & boys' sportswear & athletic clothing

(P-3212)
AM RETAIL GROUP INC
Also Called: Dkny
100 Citadel Dr, Commerce (90040-1580)
PHONE.....................323 728-8996
EMP: 157
SALES (corp-wide): 3B Publicly Held
SIC: 2335 Women's, juniors' & misses' dresses
HQ: Am Retail Group, Inc.
   7401 Boone Ave N
   Brooklyn Park MN 55428

(P-3213)
AMMIEL ENTERPRISE INC
Also Called: Wasabi Mint
1100 S San Pedro St C01, Los Angeles (90015-2385)
PHONE.....................213 973-5032
Jong S Byun, CEO
▼ EMP: 12
SALES (est): 2.5MM Privately Held
SIC: 2335 Women's, juniors' & misses' dresses

(P-3214)
AQUARIUS RAGS LLC (PA)
Also Called: ABS By Allen Schwartz
1218 S Santa Fe Ave, Los Angeles (90021-1745)
PHONE.....................213 895-4400
Allen Schwartz, Mng Member
Kirk Foster,
Armand Marciano,
▲ EMP: 14
SQ FT: 50,000
SALES (est): 14.5MM Privately Held
SIC: 2335 Women's, juniors' & misses' dresses

(P-3215)
AWAKE INC
Also Called: Jem Sportswear
10711 Walker St, Cypress (90630-4720)
PHONE.....................818 365-9361
Jeffrey A Marine, CEO
Orna Stark, President
▲ EMP: 100
SQ FT: 65,000
SALES (est): 11.5MM Privately Held
SIC: 2335 Women's, juniors' & misses' dresses

(P-3216)
AZAZIE INC
148 E Brokaw Rd, San Jose (95112-4203)
PHONE.....................650 963-9420
Qi Zhong, CEO
Karen Luo, Marketing Staff
Rachel Hogue, Manager
EMP: 12
SALES (est): 1.3MM Privately Held
SIC: 2335 Gowns, formal

(P-3217)
B & Y GLOBAL SOURCING LLC
801 S Grand Ave Ste 475, Los Angeles (90017-4622)
PHONE.....................213 891-1112
Norbert Baroukh,
Jack Remoke,
Eddie Yuen,
▲ EMP: 13
SQ FT: 2,000
SALES (est): 1.2MM Privately Held
SIC: 2335 Women's, juniors' & misses' dresses

(P-3218)
BD IMPOTEX LLC
Also Called: Sweet Girl
2623 S San Pedro St, Los Angeles (90011-1521)
PHONE.....................323 521-1500
Shaiful Alam, Mng Member
Shoyebul Islam,
▲ EMP: 10
SQ FT: 18,000

SALES: 25MM Privately Held
SIC: 2335 5137 Women's, juniors' & misses' dresses; women's & children's clothing

(P-3219)
BEE DARLIN INC (PA)
Also Called: Bee Darlin and Be Smart
1875 E 22nd St, Los Angeles (90058-1033)
PHONE.....................213 749-2116
Steve Namm, President
Jill Namm, Treasurer
Edwina Von Bjorn, Principal
▲ EMP: 100
SQ FT: 30,000
SALES (est): 19MM Privately Held
SIC: 2335 Dresses, paper: cut & sewn

(P-3220)
BELLASPOSA WEDDING CENTER
11450 4th St Ste 103, Rancho Cucamonga (91730-9024)
PHONE.....................909 758-0176
Hsin-Hung Lu, CEO
EMP: 12
SALES (est): 1.1MM Privately Held
SIC: 2335 Wedding gowns & dresses

(P-3221)
CAROL ANDERSON INC (PA)
Also Called: Carol Anderson By Invitation
18700 S Laurel Park Rd, Rancho Dominguez (90220-6003)
PHONE.....................310 638-3333
Jan Janura, President
Carol M Anderson, President
Jan A Janura, President
◆ EMP: 25 EST: 1977
SQ FT: 50,000
SALES (est): 8.7MM Privately Held
SIC: 2335 2339 Women's, juniors' & misses' dresses; shorts (outerwear): women's, misses' & juniors'

(P-3222)
CENTURY SEWING CO
421 S Raymond Ave, Alhambra (91803-1532)
PHONE.....................626 289-0533
Margaret Fong, Partner
EMP: 30
SQ FT: 5,000
SALES (est): 1.8MM Privately Held
SIC: 2335 Dresses, paper: cut & sewn

(P-3223)
CHOON INC (PA)
Also Called: Pezeme
520 Mateo St, Los Angeles (90013-2243)
PHONE.....................213 225-2500
Choon S Nakamura, President
Daniel Nakamura, Vice Pres
▲ EMP: 32 EST: 1972
SQ FT: 35,000
SALES (est): 4.8MM Privately Held
WEB: www.choon.com
SIC: 2335 Women's, juniors' & misses' dresses

(P-3224)
COMPLETE CLOTHING COMPANY (PA)
Also Called: Willow & Clay
4950 E 49th St, Vernon (90058-2736)
PHONE.....................323 277-1470
Eleanor M Sanchez, President
Fil Torres, Controller
▲ EMP: 60
SQ FT: 30,000
SALES (est): 16.5MM Privately Held
WEB: www.originalzinc.com
SIC: 2335 2339 2337 2331 Women's, juniors' & misses' dresses; sportswear, women's; women's & misses' suits & coats; women's & misses' blouses & shirts

(P-3225)
DANBEE INC
3360 E Pico Blvd, Los Angeles (90023-3729)
PHONE.....................323 780-0077
Hae MI Choi, President
Ann Choi, Admin Sec
EMP: 12

SALES (est): 1.1MM **Privately Held**
SIC: **2335** Women's, juniors' & misses'
dresses

(P-3226)
ELLE BOUTIQUE
200 E Garvey Ave Ste 105, Monterey Park
(91755-1859)
PHONE.....................626 307-9882
Danny Kiang, *Owner*
EMP: 12
SQ FT: 2,000
SALES (est): 550K **Privately Held**
SIC: **2335** 5621 Ensemble dresses:
women's, misses' & juniors'; dress shops

(P-3227)
GAZE USA INC
1665 Mateo St, Los Angeles (90021-2854)
PHONE.....................213 622-0022
EMP: 18
SALES: 12MM **Privately Held**
SIC: **2335**

(P-3228)
GINZA COLLECTION DESIGN INC
6015 Obispo Ave, Long Beach
(90805-3756)
PHONE.....................562 531-1116
Ty Yeh, *President*
Julee Klopp, *Executive*
WEI Chen Yeh, *Admin Sec*
EMP: 40
SALES (est): 2.5MM
SALES (corp-wide): 6.2MM **Privately Held**
WEB: www.avantidesign.net
SIC: **2335** Wedding gowns & dresses
PA: Private Label By G Inc
6015 Obispo Ave
Long Beach CA 90805
562 531-1116

(P-3229)
GREEN MOCHI LLC
Also Called: 12th Street By Cynthia Vincent
834 S Broadway Ste Mezz, Los Angeles
(90014-3501)
PHONE.....................213 225-2250
Cynthia Vincent,
Armen Gregorian,
▲ **EMP:** 12
SALES (est): 1.2MM **Privately Held**
SIC: **2335** 3144 Women's, juniors' &
misses' dresses; dress shoes, women's

(P-3230)
HUANG QI
4700 Miller Dr Ste H, Temple City
(91780-3757)
PHONE.....................626 442-6808
EMP: 15
SALES (est): 640.5K **Privately Held**
SIC: **2335**

(P-3231)
IRENE KASMER INC
315 S Bedford Dr, Beverly Hills
(90212-3724)
PHONE.....................310 553-8986
Irene Kasmer, *President*
Gerald Kasmer, *Vice Pres*
EMP: 15 **EST:** 1967
SALES (est): 1.2MM **Privately Held**
SIC: **2335** 2331 Dresses, paper: cut &
sewn; blouses, women's & juniors': made
from purchased material

(P-3232)
J C TRIMMING COMPANY INC
Also Called: JC Industries
3800 S Hill St, Los Angeles (90037-1416)
PHONE.....................323 235-4458
Eric Shin, *CEO*
Hyunjin Wang, *Accountant*
Dawn Woods, *Manager*
◆ **EMP:** 50
SALES (est): 12.1MM **Privately Held**
SIC: **2335** 2326 Women's, juniors' &
misses' dresses; men's & boys' work
clothing

(P-3233)
JADE APPAREL INC
1625 S Greenwood Ave, Montebello
(90640-6534)
PHONE.....................323 867-9800
Joe H Cho, *President*
Jason Kim, *Vice Pres*
▲ **EMP:** 32 **EST:** 2000
SQ FT: 25,000
SALES (est): 5.5MM **Privately Held**
WEB: www.jadeapparel.net
SIC: **2335** Women's, juniors' & misses'
dresses

(P-3234)
JAY-CEE BLOUSE CO INC
Also Called: La Rose of California
823 Maple Ave Ste 200, Los Angeles
(90014-2232)
PHONE.....................213 622-0116
Stephen Roseman, *President*
Edith Roseman, *Vice Pres*
Richard Roseman, *Vice Pres*
EMP: 108
SALES (est): 7.1MM **Privately Held**
SIC: **2335** 2331 Women's, juniors' &
misses' dresses; blouses, women's & jun-
iors': made from purchased material

(P-3235)
JODI KRISTOPHER LLC (PA)
Also Called: City Triangles
1950 Naomi Ave, Los Angeles
(90011-1342)
PHONE.....................323 890-8000
Ira Rosenberg, *President*
Ellen Delosh-Bacher, *Shareholder*
Jan Smith, *Shareholder*
Ira Fogelman, *CFO*
Alice Rosenberg, *Admin Sec*
▲ **EMP:** 200
SQ FT: 100,000
SALES (est): 28.8MM **Privately Held**
SIC: **2335** Women's, juniors' & misses'
dresses

(P-3236)
JOHNNY WAS COLLECTION INC (PA)
Also Called: Johnny Was Showroom
2423 E 23rd St, Los Angeles (90058-1201)
PHONE.....................323 231-8222
Eli Levite, *President*
▼ **EMP:** 26
SQ FT: 30,000
SALES (est): 3.6MM **Privately Held**
SIC: **2335** Women's, juniors' & misses'
dresses

(P-3237)
KATHRINE BAUMANN BEVERLY HILLS
Also Called: Katherine Baumann Collectibles
9040 W Sunset Blvd # 208, West Holly-
wood (90069-1851)
PHONE.....................310 274-7441
Kathrine Baumann, *President*
EMP: 37
SQ FT: 6,000
SALES (est): 3.4MM **Privately Held**
SIC: **2335** Women's, juniors' & misses'
dresses

(P-3238)
L Y Z LTD (PA)
Also Called: Lily Samii Collection
210 Post St, San Francisco (94108-5102)
PHONE.....................415 445-9505
Lily Samii, *President*
Laleh Eskandari, *Treasurer*
EMP: 17 **EST:** 1969
SQ FT: 7,200
SALES (est): 1.8MM **Privately Held**
WEB: www.lilysamii.com
SIC: **2335** 5621 Women's, juniors' &
misses' dresses; dress shops

(P-3239)
LA SICILIANA INC
Also Called: La Siciliana Dressmaking
8674 Washington Blvd, Culver City
(90232-7460)
PHONE.....................323 870-4155
Tindara Mollica, *President*
Anthony Mollica, *Admin Sec*

EMP: 40 **EST:** 1967
SQ FT: 10,000
SALES (est): 2.6MM **Privately Held**
WEB: www.lasiciliana.com
SIC: **2335** 2339 Women's, juniors' &
misses' dresses; women's & misses' out-
erwear

(P-3240)
LAVISH CLOTHING INC
245 W 28th St, Los Angeles (90007-3312)
PHONE.....................213 745-5400
Song Kyung Choi, *President*
EMP: 15
SQ FT: 25,000
SALES: 4.5MM **Privately Held**
SIC: **2335** Women's, juniors' & misses'
dresses

(P-3241)
LCI LAUNDRY INC
Also Called: Laundry By Shelli Segal
5835 S Eastrn Ave Ste 100, Commerce
(90040)
PHONE.....................323 767-1900
Paul Sharron, *Ch of Bd*
Paula Schneider, *President*
▲ **EMP:** 125 **EST:** 1976
SQ FT: 58,000
SALES (est): 8.3MM
SALES (corp-wide): 6B **Publicly Held**
SIC: **2335** 2339 2331 Dresses, paper: cut
& sewn; women's & misses' athletic cloth-
ing & sportswear; women's & misses'
blouses & shirts
HQ: Kate Spade Holdings Llc
2 Park Ave Fl 8
New York NY 10016
212 354-4900

(P-3242)
LEES FASHIONS INC
1157 Monterey Pl, Encinitas (92024-1340)
PHONE.....................760 753-2408
Lee Torti, *President*
Loretta Torti, *Vice Pres*
EMP: 25
SQ FT: 5,000
SALES (est): 1.8MM **Privately Held**
SIC: **2335** 2331 2339 Women's, juniors' &
misses' dresses; blouses, women's & jun-
iors': made from purchased material;
slacks: women's, misses' & juniors'

(P-3243)
LOTUS ORIENT CORP (PA)
Also Called: Venus Bridal Gowns
411 S California St, San Gabriel
(91776-2527)
P.O. Box 280 (91778-0280)
PHONE.....................626 285-5796
Eugene Wu, *President*
▲ **EMP:** 17
SQ FT: 6,400
SALES (est): 1.7MM **Privately Held**
SIC: **2335** 5621 Wedding gowns &
dresses; bridal shops

(P-3244)
MISS KIM INC
Also Called: Miss Cristina
1015 San Julian St, Los Angeles
(90015-2311)
PHONE.....................213 747-4011
Leticia Alvarez, *CEO*
Sung H Kim, *CFO*
EMP: 16
SALES: 2.5MM **Privately Held**
SIC: **2335** 5137 Ensemble dresses:
women's, misses' & juniors'; dresses

(P-3245)
NIGHT FASHION INC
Also Called: Fashion 1001 Nights
628 W 30th St Ofc C, Los Angeles
(90007-4629)
PHONE.....................213 747-8740
David Kahenassa, *President*
▲ **EMP:** 34
SQ FT: 30,000
SALES (est): 2.2MM **Privately Held**
WEB: www.fashion1001nights.com
SIC: **2335** Bridal & formal gowns

(P-3246)
NOVA PRINT INC
2100 S Fairview St, Santa Ana
(92704-4516)
PHONE.....................951 525-4040
Douglas Gay, *CEO*
Michelle Gay, *COO*
Sharon Reyne, *Sales Staff*
EMP: 12
SQ FT: 4,000
SALES: 600K **Privately Held**
SIC: **2335** 2262 Dresses, paper: cut &
sewn; roller printing: manmade fiber & silk
broadwoven fabrics

(P-3247)
PACIFIC BOULEVARD INC
Also Called: Verde
5075 Pacific Blvd, Vernon (90058-2215)
PHONE.....................323 581-1656
Joe Ramos, *President*
EMP: 15
SALES (est): 853.7K **Privately Held**
SIC: **2335** Women's, juniors' & misses'
dresses

(P-3248)
PALIHUSE HLLWAY RSIDENCES ASSN
8465 Holloway Dr, West Hollywood
(90069-4258)
PHONE.....................323 656-4100
Kirsten Leigh Pratt, *CEO*
Kazu Namise, *Comms Dir*
Matt Fisher, *Principal*
Nicole Castaneda, *Director*
EMP: 10
SALES (est): 1MM **Privately Held**
SIC: **2335** Housedresses

(P-3249)
PRIVATE BRAND MDSG CORP
Also Called: Jody of California
214 W Olympic Blvd, Los Angeles
(90015-1605)
PHONE.....................213 749-0191
William Berman, *President*
Rochelle Berman, *Corp Secy*
Marc Schwartz, *VP Prdtn*
John Berman, *VP Sales*
EMP: 23
SQ FT: 6,000
SALES (est): 2.7MM **Privately Held**
WEB: www.jodyca.com
SIC: **2335** 2339 Women's, juniors' &
misses' dresses; sportswear, women's

(P-3250)
PRIVATE LABEL BY G INC (PA)
6015 Obispo Ave, Long Beach
(90805-3756)
PHONE.....................562 531-1116
Ty Yeh, *President*
WEI Chen Yeh, *Treasurer*
Marian Tran, *Vice Pres*
▲ **EMP:** 25
SQ FT: 5,000
SALES (est): 6.2MM **Privately Held**
WEB: www.privatelabelbyg.com
SIC: **2335** Wedding gowns & dresses

(P-3251)
PROMISES PROMISES INC
Also Called: Broadway Pl
3121 S Grand Ave, Los Angeles
(90007-3816)
PHONE.....................213 749-7725
Eugene M Hardy, *President*
▲ **EMP:** 29 **EST:** 1978
SALES (est): 3.9MM **Privately Held**
WEB: www.promisespromises.com
SIC: **2335** Women's, juniors' & misses'
dresses

(P-3252)
PROTREND LTD (HQ)
Also Called: Nicola
6001 E Washington Blvd, Commerce
(90040-2451)
PHONE.....................323 832-9323
Peter Kim, *President*
Eunice Kim, *CEO*
▲ **EMP:** 13
SQ FT: 22,000

SALES (est): 1.9MM
SALES (corp-wide): 2MM **Privately Held**
WEB: www.saymeekinc.com
SIC: 2335 Women's, juniors' & misses' dresses
PA: K Saymee Inc
6409 Gayhart St
Commerce CA 90040
323 832-9323

(P-3253)
STOP STARING DESIGNS
1151 Goodrick Dr, Tehachapi (93561-1517)
PHONE....................213 627-1480
Alicia Estrada, *CEO*
James Atyeo, *CFO*
EMP: 27
SQ FT: 2,500
SALES (est): 942.4K **Privately Held**
WEB: www.stopstaringclothing.com
SIC: 2335 Women's, juniors' & misses' dresses

(P-3254)
STUDIO KRP LLC
6133 Bonsall Dr, Malibu (90265-3824)
PHONE....................310 589-5777
Carol Rosenstein, *CEO*
EMP: 13
SQ FT: 1,500
SALES: 3MM **Privately Held**
SIC: 2335 Women's, juniors' & misses' dresses

(P-3255)
SWEET INSPIRATIONS INC
17770 Ridgeway Rd, Granada Hills (91344-2131)
PHONE....................310 886-9010
Chieko Kamisato, *President*
Bebe Ganaja, *Corp Secy*
EMP: 30 **EST:** 1974
SQ FT: 30,000
SALES (est): 1.4MM **Privately Held**
WEB: www.sweetinspiration.com
SIC: 2335 Women's, juniors' & misses' dresses

(P-3256)
TONY MARTERIE & ASSOCIATES
Also Called: North Coast Industries
28 Liberty Ship Way Fl 2, Sausalito (94965-3320)
P.O. Box 2018 (94966-2018)
PHONE....................415 331-7150
Tony Marterie, *President*
Roxanne Marterie, *Vice Pres*
Robert Ghiorci, *Manager*
▲ **EMP:** 25
SQ FT: 27,000
SALES (est): 2.9MM **Privately Held**
SIC: 2335 2339 Women's, juniors' & misses' dresses; women's & misses' outerwear

(P-3257)
TWO STAR DOG INC
Also Called: Stella Carakasi
1329 9th St, Berkeley (94710-1502)
PHONE....................510 525-1100
Allan Boutrous, *Creative Dir*
EMP: 16 **Privately Held**
SIC: 2335 Women's, juniors' & misses' dresses
PA: Two Star Dog Inc.
1329 9th St
Berkeley CA 94710

(P-3258)
URBAN OUTFITTERS INC
Also Called: Urban Outfitters Store 18
139 W Colorado Blvd, Pasadena (91105-1924)
PHONE....................626 449-1818
Allie Enoch, *Manager*
EMP: 30
SALES (corp-wide): 3.9B **Publicly Held**
WEB: www.urbanoutfittersinc.com
SIC: 2335 5611 5719 Women's, juniors' & misses' dresses; men's & boys' clothing stores; kitchenware

PA: Urban Outfitters, Inc.
5000 S Broad St
Philadelphia PA 19112
215 454-5500

(P-3259)
URU BY KRISTINE ST RRIK INC
Also Called: U R U
622 Aero Way, Escondido (92029-1201)
PHONE....................760 745-1800
Ken Brown, *President*
Kristine Garrett, *Admin Sec*
▲ **EMP:** 16
SQ FT: 7,700
SALES: 2.1MM **Privately Held**
SIC: 2335 2384 2339 2331 Women's, juniors' & misses' dresses; robes & dressing gowns; women's & misses' outerwear; women's & misses' blouses & shirts

(P-3260)
VALMAS INC
Also Called: Sam & Lavi
1233 S Boyle Ave, Los Angeles (90023-2601)
PHONE....................323 677-2211
Sam Arasteh, *President*
Emily Chen, *Manager*
▲ **EMP:** 20
SALES (est): 1.5MM **Privately Held**
SIC: 2335 Women's, juniors' & misses' dresses

(P-3261)
YMI JEANSWEAR INC (PA)
1155 S Boyle Ave, Los Angeles (90023-2109)
PHONE....................323 581-7700
Moshe Moshezaga, *CEO*
David Vered, *President*
Michael Godigian, *Vice Pres*
Michael Silvestri, *Vice Pres*
Ann Puig, *Production*
▲ **EMP:** 15
SALES (est): 13.1MM **Privately Held**
WEB: www.ymijeans.com
SIC: 2335 Women's, juniors' & misses' dresses

2337 Women's & Misses' Suits, Coats & Skirts

(P-3262)
ANN LILLI CORP (PA)
1010 B St Ste 209, San Rafael (94901-2919)
PHONE....................415 482-9444
Don Kamler, *Principal*
Jo Schuman, *Principal*
EMP: 63
SALES (est): 5.7MM **Privately Held**
SIC: 2337 Women's & misses' suits & coats

(P-3263)
CALIFORNIA FASHION CLUB INC (PA)
Also Called: Lisa & ME
207 S 9th Ave, La Puente (91746-3310)
P.O. Box 880, San Gabriel (91778-0880)
PHONE....................626 575-1838
Sandy Wai Nga Chen, *President*
William Chen, *Vice Pres*
▲ **EMP:** 11
SQ FT: 1,100
SALES: 2MM **Privately Held**
SIC: 2337 2331 Women's & misses' suits & coats; women's & misses' blouses & shirts

(P-3264)
DANOC MANUFACTURING CORP INC
Also Called: Danoc Embroidery
6015 Power Inn Rd Ste A, Sacramento (95824-2336)
PHONE....................916 455-2876
Tom Land, *President*
EMP: 16
SQ FT: 1,500

SALES (est): 1.3MM **Privately Held**
WEB: www.danoc.com
SIC: 2337 2326 Uniforms, except athletic: women's, misses' & juniors'; industrial garments, men's & boys'; work garments, except raincoats: waterproof

(P-3265)
DBG SUBSIDIARY INC
Also Called: Joe's Jeans
1500 N El Centro Ave # 150, Los Angeles (90028-9223)
PHONE....................323 837-3700
Marc B Crossman, *President*
Steve Harris, *Credit Staff*
Lea Lloyd, *Site Mgr*
▲ **EMP:** 150
SALES (est): 14.1MM
SALES (corp-wide): 596.6MM **Publicly Held**
SIC: 2337 Women's & misses' suits & coats
PA: Centric Brands Inc.
350 5th Ave Fl 6
New York NY 10118
646 582-6000

(P-3266)
FASHION QUEEN MANIA INC
800 E 12th St Ste 428, Los Angeles (90021-2245)
PHONE....................213 788-7310
Hee Young Moon, *CEO*
EMP: 20 **EST:** 2017
SALES (est): 615.4K **Privately Held**
SIC: 2337 Skirts, separate: women's, misses' & juniors'

(P-3267)
KAYO OF CALIFORNIA (PA)
161 W 39th St, Los Angeles (90037-1080)
PHONE....................323 233-6107
Jack Ostrovsky, *Ch of Bd*
Jeffrey Michaels, *CEO*
Annabelle Wall, *CFO*
Jonathan Kaye, *Vice Pres*
Jonathon Kaye, *Vice Pres*
◆ **EMP:** 45 **EST:** 1968
SQ FT: 24,000
SALES (est): 8.4MM **Privately Held**
WEB: www.kayo.com
SIC: 2337 2339 Skirts, separate: women's, misses' & juniors'; sportswear, women's; shorts (outerwear): women's, misses' & juniors'; slacks: women's, misses' & juniors'

(P-3268)
KELLER CLASSICS INC (PA)
Also Called: Nannette Keller
19628 Country Oaks St, Tehachapi (93561-8490)
PHONE....................805 524-1322
Nannette Keller, *President*
Roger Keller, *CFO*
Richard Scott, *Admin Sec*
EMP: 35
SQ FT: 12,000
SALES (est): 3.6MM **Privately Held**
WEB: www.kellerclassics.com
SIC: 2337 5621 Women's & misses' suits & skirts; women's clothing stores

(P-3269)
KOMAROV ENTERPRISES INC
Also Called: Kisca
1936 Mateo St, Los Angeles (90021-2833)
PHONE....................213 244-7000
Dimitri Komarov, *President*
Dimitri Leiberman, *Vice Pres*
Dimitry Liberman, *Vice Pres*
Ashley Segal, *Vice Pres*
Jose Rojas, *Accounting Mgr*
▲ **EMP:** 75
SQ FT: 25,000
SALES (est): 8.7MM **Privately Held**
WEB: www.komarovinc.com
SIC: 2337 2331 Women's & misses' suits & coats; women's & misses' blouses & shirts

(P-3270)
NORTH HOLLYWOOD UNIFORM INC
Also Called: North Hollywood Uniform Group
7328 Laurel Canyon Blvd, North Hollywood (91605-3710)
PHONE....................818 503-5931
Virginia Gray, *President*
EMP: 15
SALES (est): 1MM **Privately Held**
SIC: 2337 2329 5137 Uniforms, except athletic: women's, misses' & juniors'; men's & boys' athletic uniforms; uniforms, women's & children's

(P-3271)
OFF PRICE NETWORK LLC
10544 Dunleer Dr, Los Angeles (90064-4318)
PHONE....................213 477-8205
Diana Murray,
EMP: 30
SQ FT: 56,500
SALES (est): 2.6MM **Privately Held**
WEB: www.offprice.net
SIC: 2337 Women's & misses' suits & coats

(P-3272)
POETRY CORPORATION (PA)
2111 Long Beach Ave, Los Angeles (90058-1023)
PHONE....................213 765-8957
Seong H Lee, *CEO*
▲ **EMP:** 24 **EST:** 1998
SQ FT: 50,000
SALES (est): 4.1MM **Privately Held**
SIC: 2337 Women's & misses' suits & coats

(P-3273)
R B III ASSOCIATES INC
Also Called: Teamwork Athletic Apparel
166 Newport Dr, San Marcos (92069-1467)
PHONE....................760 471-5370
Matthew Lehrer, *CEO*
Dave Caserta, *President*
Andy Lehrer, *Vice Pres*
Brianna Wagner, *Administration*
Maria Vega, *Accountant*
▲ **EMP:** 150
SQ FT: 110,000
SALES (est): 22.9MM **Privately Held**
WEB: www.fcsite1.com
SIC: 2337 2329 Uniforms, except athletic: women's, misses' & juniors'; men's & boys' athletic uniforms

(P-3274)
RENEE C
127 E 9th St Ste 506, Los Angeles (90015-1735)
PHONE....................213 741-0095
Jin Young Song, *Principal*
EMP: 17
SALES (est): 661K **Privately Held**
SIC: 2337 Women's & misses' suits & coats

(P-3275)
RUBEL MARGUERITE MFG CO
27 Pier, San Francisco (94111-1038)
PHONE....................415 362-2626
EMP: 12 **EST:** 1952
SQ FT: 20,000
SALES (est): 1MM **Privately Held**
SIC: 2337

(P-3276)
S STUDIO INC
Also Called: Sue Wong
3030 W 6th St, Los Angeles (90020-1506)
PHONE....................213 388-7400
Dieter Raabe, *President*
Sue Wong, *Ch of Bd*
Josh Homann, *Manager*
▲ **EMP:** 60
SQ FT: 28,000
SALES (est): 22.5MM **Privately Held**
WEB: www.suewong.com
SIC: 2337 Women's & misses' suits & skirts

▲ = Import ▼=Export
◆ =Import/Export

(P-3277)
SCHOOL APPAREL INC (PA)
Also Called: A Career Apparel
838 Mitten Rd, Burlingame (94010-1304)
PHONE..................650 777-4500
Kenneth Knoss, *CEO*
Ryan Knoss, *Ch of Bd*
Bernice B Knoss, *Treasurer*
Vincent Knoss, *Chief Mktg Ofcr*
Marty Crowley, *Vice Pres*
◆ **EMP:** 137
SALES (est): 60.8MM **Privately Held**
WEB: www.schoolapparel.com
SIC: 2337 2311 2326 Uniforms, except athletic: women's, misses' & juniors'; men's & boys' uniforms; work uniforms

(P-3278)
TOPSON DOWNS CALIFORNIA INC
3545 Motor Ave, Los Angeles (90034-4806)
PHONE..................310 558-0300
Kris Scott, *Branch Mgr*
Alex Perez, *Info Tech Mgr*
EMP: 35
SALES (corp-wide): 280.2MM **Privately Held**
SIC: 2337 5621 Women's & misses' suits & coats; ready-to-wear apparel, women's
PA: Topson Downs Of California, Inc.,
3840 Watseka Ave
Culver City CA 90232
310 558-0300

2339 Women's & Misses' Outerwear, NEC

(P-3279)
AARON CORPORATION
Also Called: J P Sportswear
1820 E 41st St, Vernon (90058-1534)
PHONE..................323 235-5959
Paul Shechet, *President*
Francisco Balleste, *Vice Pres*
Ana Almeida, *Plant Mgr*
Eli Shechet, *Marketing Staff*
▲ **EMP:** 170 **EST:** 1955
SQ FT: 41,000
SALES (est): 22.9MM **Privately Held**
WEB: www.jpsportswear.net
SIC: 2339 Women's & misses' athletic clothing & sportswear

(P-3280)
AB&R INC
Also Called: Billy Blues
5849 Smithway St, Commerce (90040-1605)
PHONE..................323 727-0007
Rene Allison Thomas, *President*
William Scott Curtis, *Vice Pres*
▲ **EMP:** 22
SQ FT: 10,500
SALES (est): 2.1MM **Privately Held**
SIC: 2339 Women's & misses' outerwear

(P-3281)
ABS BY ALLEN SCHWARTZ LLC (HQ)
1218 S Santa Fe Ave, Los Angeles (90021-1745)
PHONE..................213 895-4400
Allen Schwartz,
Kirk Foster, *CFO*
Camelia Torre, *IT/INT Sup*
▲ **EMP:** 37
SQ FT: 50,000
SALES (est): 13.4MM
SALES (corp-wide): 14.5MM **Privately Held**
WEB: www.harmonycollection.com
SIC: 2339 5621 Women's & misses' outerwear; women's clothing stores
PA: Aquarius Rags, Llc
1218 S Santa Fe Ave
Los Angeles CA 90021
213 895-4400

(P-3282)
ABS CLOTHING COLLECTION INC
Also Called: A.B.S. By Allen Schwartz
1218 S Santa Fe Ave, Los Angeles (90021-1745)
PHONE..................213 895-4400
Allen Schwartz, *President*
Johnny Schwartz, *Manager*
EMP: 15
SALES (est): 1.9MM **Privately Held**
SIC: 2339 5621 Women's & misses' outerwear; women's clothing stores

(P-3283)
ALBION KNITTING MILLS INC
2152 Sacramento St, Los Angeles (90021-1722)
PHONE..................213 624-7740
George Ainslie, *President*
EMP: 28 **EST:** 1923
SQ FT: 15,000
SALES (est): 2.2MM **Privately Held**
SIC: 2339 2329 2253 Uniforms, athletic: women's, misses' & juniors'; jackets (suede, leatherette, etc.), sport: men's & boys; knit outerwear mills

(P-3284)
AMBIANCE USA INC (PA)
Also Called: Ambiance Apparel
2415 E 15th St, Los Angeles (90021-2936)
PHONE..................323 587-0007
Sang B Noh, *CEO*
◆ **EMP:** 100
SALES (est): 4.3MM **Privately Held**
SIC: 2339 Women's & misses' outerwear

(P-3285)
APPAREL ENTERPRISES CO INC
1900 Wilson Ave Ste B, National City (91950-5532)
PHONE..................619 474-6916
Duy Nguyentran, *President*
Uyen Dao, *Vice Pres*
◆ **EMP:** 20 **EST:** 2001
SALES (est): 1.9MM **Privately Held**
SIC: 2339 Women's & misses' outerwear

(P-3286)
APPAREL LIMITED INC
Also Called: Kangol
3011 E Pico Blvd, Los Angeles (90023-3611)
PHONE..................323 859-2430
Masud Sarshar, *CEO*
Maryam Toofer, *President*
▼ **EMP:** 90
SQ FT: 71,000
SALES (est): 8.1MM **Privately Held**
SIC: 2339 Women's & misses' athletic clothing & sportswear

(P-3287)
APPAREL PROD SVCS GLOBL LLC
Also Called: APS Global
8954 Lurline Ave, Chatsworth (91311-6103)
PHONE..................818 700-3700
Clayton Medley,
Richard Cohen,
Paul Stanley,
◆ **EMP:** 42
SQ FT: 15,000
SALES (est): 7.5MM **Privately Held**
WEB: www.apscorp.org
SIC: 2339 2329 Women's & misses' athletic clothing & sportswear; men's & boys' sportswear & athletic clothing

(P-3288)
ASSOLUTO INC
Also Called: Molly Max
215 S Santa Fe Ave Apt 5, Los Angeles (90012-4350)
PHONE..................213 748-1116
Ugo Capasso, *CEO*
▲ **EMP:** 16
SQ FT: 2,600
SALES (est): 1.8MM **Privately Held**
WEB: www.gigigirl.com
SIC: 2339 Women's & misses' athletic clothing & sportswear

(P-3289)
AVID LYFE INC
3133 Tiger Run Ct Ste 109, Carlsbad (92010-6704)
PHONE..................888 510-2517
Lindsey Hunziker, *CEO*
EMP: 12
SALES (est): 1.3MM **Privately Held**
SIC: 2339 3498 2326 Athletic clothing: women's, misses' & juniors'; fabricated pipe & fittings; men's & boys' work clothing

(P-3290)
AZTECA JEANS INC
6600 Avalon Blvd, Los Angeles (90003-1959)
PHONE..................323 758-7721
EMP: 50
SALES (est): 3.4MM **Privately Held**
SIC: 2339

(P-3291)
BABETTE (PA)
867 Newton Carey Jr Way, Oakland (94607-1596)
PHONE..................510 625-8500
Babette Pinsky, *President*
Steven Pinsky, *CFO*
Elfriede Griffey, *Admin Sec*
▲ **EMP:** 37
SQ FT: 28,000
SALES (est): 6.8MM **Privately Held**
WEB: www.babettesf.com
SIC: 2339 2369 Sportswear, women's; women's & misses' jackets & coats, except sportswear; girls' & children's outerwear

(P-3292)
BARE NOTHINGS INC (PA)
17705 Sampson Ln, Huntington Beach (92647-6790)
PHONE..................714 848-8532
Ann Mase, *President*
Ronald Mase, *Treasurer*
EMP: 22
SALES (est): 2.4MM **Privately Held**
WEB: www.barenothings.com
SIC: 2339 Bathing suits: women's, misses' & juniors'

(P-3293)
BB CO INC
Also Called: Wild Lizard
1753 E 21st St, Los Angeles (90058-1006)
PHONE..................213 747-4701
Kyoung K Frazier, *President*
▲ **EMP:** 30
SQ FT: 22,000
SALES (est): 4.2MM **Privately Held**
SIC: 2339 Women's & misses' athletic clothing & sportswear

(P-3294)
BCBG MAXAZRIA ENTRMT LLC
2761 Fruitland Ave, Vernon (90058-3607)
PHONE..................323 277-4713
Max Azria,
Charles Cohenm,
EMP: 10
SALES (est): 791.4K **Privately Held**
SIC: 2339 5137 5621 Women's & misses' outerwear; women's & children's clothing; women's clothing stores

(P-3295)
BIDU INC
756 E Wash Blvd Ste B, Los Angeles (90021-3017)
PHONE..................213 748-4433
Walter Shim, *President*
EMP: 11
SALES (est): 1.3MM **Privately Held**
WEB: www.bidu.com
SIC: 2339 7389 Women's & misses' outerwear; sewing contractor

(P-3296)
BIG BANG CLOTHING INC (PA)
Also Called: Big Bang Clothing Co
4507 Staunton Ave, Vernon (90058-1936)
PHONE..................323 233-7773
Sam Seungwoo Lee, *President*
EMP: 10
SQ FT: 9,000
SALES (est): 1.5MM **Privately Held**
WEB: www.bigbangclothing.com
SIC: 2339 Women's & misses' athletic clothing & sportswear

(P-3297)
BLACK SILVER ENTERPRISES INC (PA)
Also Called: Gracie Collection
6024 Paseo Delicias, Rancho Santa Fe (92067)
PHONE..................858 623-9220
Un MI Lee, *President*
Seya Mahvi, *CEO*
EMP: 11
SQ FT: 1,500
SALES (est): 802.8K **Privately Held**
SIC: 2339 Women's & misses' outerwear

(P-3298)
BURNING TORCH INC
1738 Cordova St, Los Angeles (90007-1129)
PHONE..................323 733-7700
Karyn Craven, *President*
Gracie Minijarez, *Bookkeeper*
Rose Marron, *Prdtn Mgr*
▲ **EMP:** 20
SQ FT: 5,000
SALES (est): 2.3MM **Privately Held**
WEB: www.burningtorchinc.com
SIC: 2339 Sportswear, women's

(P-3299)
C & Y INVESTMENT INC
Also Called: Girl Talk Clothing
946 E 29th St, Los Angeles (90011-2034)
PHONE..................323 267-9000
Carrie Jooyon Yi, *CEO*
Michael Yi, *CFO*
EMP: 11
SQ FT: 8,000
SALES: 2.5MM **Privately Held**
SIC: 2339 Aprons, except rubber or plastic: women's, misses', juniors'

(P-3300)
C P SHADES INC (PA)
403 Coloma St, Sausalito (94965-2827)
PHONE..................415 331-4581
David Weinstein, *President*
Denise Weinstein, *Treasurer*
Alison Pownall, *Vice Pres*
Bianca Chui, *Executive*
Cyndi Pettibone, *Office Mgr*
▲ **EMP:** 17
SQ FT: 40,405
SALES (est): 81.1MM **Privately Held**
SIC: 2339 5621 Women's & misses' athletic clothing & sportswear; sportswear, women's; women's sportswear

(P-3301)
CAMP SMIDGEMORE INC (DH)
Also Called: Renee Claire Inc
3641 10th Ave, Los Angeles (90018-4114)
PHONE..................323 634-0333
Wendy Luttrel, *CEO*
Renee Bertrand, *President*
▲ **EMP:** 22
SQ FT: 13,000
SALES (est): 5.3MM
SALES (corp-wide): 260MM **Privately Held**
SIC: 2339 2341 Women's & misses' outerwear; pajamas & bedjackets: women's & children's
HQ: Komar Intimates, Llc
90 Hudson St
Jersey City NJ 07302
212 725-1500

(P-3302)
CAROL WIOR INC
Also Called: Slimsuit
7533 Garfield Ave, Bell (90201-4817)
PHONE..................562 927-0052
Carol Wior, *President*
Troy Berg, *CEO*
Lucy Weddell, *Treasurer*
Niki Wior, *Vice Pres*
Julie Wilson, *Admin Sec*
▲ **EMP:** 70
SQ FT: 77,000

PRODUCTS & SVCS

SALES (est): 6.7MM **Privately Held**
SIC: 2339 5699 Bathing suits: women's, misses' & juniors'; sportswear, women's; beachwear: women's, misses' & juniors'; bathing suits

(P-3303)
CEE SPORTSWEAR
6409 Gayhart St, Commerce (90040-2505)
PHONE..............................323 726-8158
Paul Bogner, *President*
▲ **EMP:** 20 **EST:** 1958
SQ FT: 57,000
SALES (est): 2.4MM **Privately Held**
SIC: 2339 Maternity clothing

(P-3304)
CITIZENS OF HUMANITY LLC (PA)
Also Called: Goldsign
5715 Bickett St, Huntington Park (90255-2624)
PHONE..............................323 923-1240
Jerome Dahan, *CEO*
Amy Williams, *President*
Shelley Barham, *Vice Pres*
Sarah Stratford, *Executive*
Daniel Pulido, *Administration*
▲ **EMP:** 70
SQ FT: 70,000
SALES (est): 81MM **Privately Held**
WEB: www.citizensofhumanity.com
SIC: 2339 Jeans: women's, misses' & juniors'

(P-3305)
CLASSIC TEES INC
4915 Walnut Grove Ave, San Gabriel (91776-2021)
PHONE..............................626 607-0255
Paul Chauderson, *President*
Connie Lam, *Vice Pres*
EMP: 35
SQ FT: 15,000
SALES (est): 3.2MM **Privately Held**
WEB: www.classic-tees.com
SIC: 2339 Women's & misses' athletic clothing & sportswear

(P-3306)
CLOTHING ILLUSTRATED INC (PA)
Also Called: Love Stitch
2014 E 15th St, Los Angeles (90021-2823)
PHONE..............................213 403-9950
Danny Forouzesh, *President*
Cyrous Forouzesh, *CFO*
▲ **EMP:** 40
SALES (est): 6.2MM **Privately Held**
SIC: 2339 Women's & misses' outerwear

(P-3307)
CLOVER GARMENTS INC
2565 3rd St Ste 232, San Francisco (94107-3160)
PHONE..............................415 826-6909
Florence Lo, *President*
▲ **EMP:** 70
SQ FT: 10,000
SALES (est): 5.9MM **Privately Held**
SIC: 2339 2329 Sportswear, women's; men's & boys' sportswear & athletic clothing

(P-3308)
CONNECTED APPAREL COMPANY LLC (PA)
Also Called: Next Up
6015 Bandini Blvd, Commerce (90040-2904)
PHONE..............................323 890-8000
Jay Balaban, *Mng Member*
Ira Fogelman, *CFO*
Ellen Delloshbacher,
Alice Rosenberg,
Jan Smith,
▲ **EMP:** 25
SQ FT: 50,000
SALES (est): 4.7MM **Privately Held**
WEB: www.connectedapparel.com
SIC: 2339 Athletic clothing: women's, misses' & juniors'

(P-3309)
CREW KNITWEAR LLC (PA)
Also Called: Hiatus
660 S Myers St, Los Angeles (90023-1015)
PHONE..............................323 526-3888
Peter Jung, *CEO*
Christine Pisano, *Accounts Mgr*
▲ **EMP:** 52
SQ FT: 39,000
SALES (est): 16.6MM **Privately Held**
WEB: www.crewknitwear.com
SIC: 2339 Women's & misses' outerwear

(P-3310)
CUT LOOSE (PA)
101 Williams Ave, San Francisco (94124-2619)
PHONE..............................415 822-2031
Will Wenham, *President*
Rosemarie Ovian, *Vice Pres*
◆ **EMP:** 63
SQ FT: 17,000
SALES (est): 9.4MM **Privately Held**
WEB: www.cutloose.com
SIC: 2339 5621 2331 Sportswear, women's; women's clothing stores; women's & misses' blouses & shirts

(P-3311)
D&A UNLIMITED INC
2700 Rose Ave Ste J, Signal Hill (90755-1929)
PHONE..............................562 336-1528
David Anthony, *CEO*
Anna Anthony, *President*
EMP: 25
SALES (est): 300K **Privately Held**
SIC: 2339 Women's & misses' athletic clothing & sportswear

(P-3312)
DARBO MANUFACTURING COMPANY
363 Glenoaks St, Brea (92821-2117)
PHONE..............................714 529-7693
EMP: 25
SQ FT: 7,500
SALES (est): 1.2MM **Privately Held**
WEB: www.dancewearforyou.com
SIC: 2339 2369 2389

(P-3313)
DASH SPORTSWEAR
Also Called: Dash Sportwear
2624 Geraldine St, Los Angeles (90011-1829)
PHONE..............................323 846-2640
Ho Suk Kim, *Owner*
EMP: 20
SQ FT: 13,000
SALES (est): 1.3MM **Privately Held**
SIC: 2339 5131 Women's & misses' outerwear; piece goods & other fabrics

(P-3314)
DDA HOLDINGS INC
Also Called: A Commom Thread
834 S Broadway Ste 1100, Los Angeles (90014-3510)
PHONE..............................213 624-5200
Anthony Graham, *CEO*
Sandra Balestier, *President*
▲ **EMP:** 18
SQ FT: 15,000
SALES (est): 2.7MM **Privately Held**
SIC: 2339 Women's & misses' athletic clothing & sportswear

(P-3315)
DE SOTO CLOTHING INC
Also Called: De Soto Sport
7584 Trade St, San Diego (92121-2412)
PHONE..............................858 578-6672
Emilio De Soto II, *President*
Dan Neyenhuis, *Shareholder*
Marta Lundgren, *Admin Sec*
▲ **EMP:** 15
SQ FT: 5,600
SALES (est): 1.4MM **Privately Held**
WEB: www.desotosport.com
SIC: 2339 2329 Women's & misses' athletic clothing & sportswear; men's & boys' sportswear & athletic clothing

(P-3316)
DESIGN CONCEPTS INC
4625 E 50th St, Vernon (90058-3223)
PHONE..............................323 277-4771
Michael Park, *President*
▲ **EMP:** 15
SALES (est): 133.4K **Privately Held**
SIC: 2339 Women's & misses' athletic clothing & sportswear

(P-3317)
DESIGN TODAYS INC (PA)
725 E Wash Blvd Fl 2nd, Los Angeles (90021-3069)
PHONE..............................213 745-3091
Sung OK Hong, *President*
EMP: 53
SQ FT: 12,000
SALES (est): 4MM **Privately Held**
WEB: www.designtodays.com
SIC: 2339 Women's & misses' outerwear

(P-3318)
DHM INTERNATIONAL CORP
Also Called: Sunshine Enterprises
901 Monterey Pass Rd, Monterey Park (91754-3610)
PHONE..............................323 263-3888
Scott Yuen, *President*
Joe Yuen, *Vice Pres*
Ross Yuen, *Vice Pres*
▲ **EMP:** 90
SQ FT: 28,000
SALES (est): 9.2MM **Privately Held**
SIC: 2339 2326 Women's & misses' outerwear; men's & boys' work clothing

(P-3319)
DMBM LLC
2445 E 12th St Ste C, Los Angeles (90021-2954)
PHONE..............................714 321-6032
David Chong, *Owner*
EMP: 25 **Privately Held**
WEB: www.dmbmla.com
SIC: 2339 2369 Women's & misses' outerwear; girls' & children's outerwear
PA: Dmbm, Llc
2701 S Santa Fe Ave
Vernon CA

(P-3320)
DOSA INC
850 S Broadway Ste 700, Los Angeles (90014-3238)
PHONE..............................213 627-3672
Christina Kim, *President*
Meghan Murphy, *Prdtn Mgr*
▲ **EMP:** 30
SQ FT: 15,000
SALES (est): 2.8MM **Privately Held**
SIC: 2339 Sportswear, women's

(P-3321)
EQUESTRIAN DESIGNS LLC
91 2nd St Ste A, Buellton (93427-9471)
PHONE..............................805 686-4455
Iona Marshall, *Mng Member*
EMP: 25
SQ FT: 6,000
SALES (est): 2.4MM **Privately Held**
WEB: www.equestriandesigns.net
SIC: 2339 Women's & misses' outerwear

(P-3322)
ESKA INC
Also Called: Event Spice Wear
3631 Union Pacific Ave, Los Angeles (90023-3255)
PHONE..............................323 268-2134
Suk Eun Cho, *President*
▲ **EMP:** 25
SQ FT: 1,660
SALES (est): 3.4MM **Privately Held**
WEB: www.eska.com
SIC: 2339 Athletic clothing: women's, misses' & juniors'

(P-3323)
EVER-GLORY INTL GROUP INC
1009 Becklee Rd, Glendora (91741-2201)
P.O. Box 855 (91740-0855)
PHONE..............................626 859-6638
Jessie Hsu, *Manager*
EMP: 10

SALES (corp-wide): 3.9MM **Privately Held**
SIC: 2339 Women's & misses' outerwear
HQ: Ever-Glory International Group Apparel Inc.
No. 509, Chengxin Ave., Jiangning Technical Economic Development
Nanjing 21110
255 209-6879

(P-3324)
FASHION TODAY INC
Also Called: Mon Amie
1100 S San Pedro St Ste A, Los Angeles (90015-2328)
PHONE..............................213 744-1636
John Sung, *CFO*
EMP: 22 **Privately Held**
SIC: 2339 Women's & misses' jackets & coats, except sportswear
PA: Fashion Today, Inc.
3100 S Grand Ave Fl 3
Los Angeles CA 90007

(P-3325)
FASHION TODAY INC (PA)
Also Called: Mon Amie
3100 S Grand Ave Fl 3, Los Angeles (90007-3815)
PHONE..............................213 744-1636
Kwang Pyo Hong, *CEO*
Sung Hwan Hong, *President*
EMP: 11
SQ FT: 10,000
SALES: 10MM **Privately Held**
SIC: 2339 Athletic clothing: women's, misses' & juniors'

(P-3326)
FAST SPORTSWEAR INC
6400 E Washington Blvd, Commerce (90040-1820)
PHONE..............................323 720-1078
Young Kuen Kim, *President*
Sook In Kim, *Vice Pres*
EMP: 70
SQ FT: 200,000
SALES (est): 4.9MM **Privately Held**
SIC: 2339 Sportswear, women's

(P-3327)
FELLYR INTERNATIONAL INC
Also Called: Fenini
13453 Brooks Dr Ste B, Baldwin Park (91706-2255)
PHONE..............................626 960-5111
Sandra Yang, *President*
EMP: 14
SQ FT: 10,000
SALES (est): 1.9MM **Privately Held**
SIC: 2339 5085 Women's & misses' athletic clothing & sportswear; commercial containers

(P-3328)
GAZE USA INC
1665 Mateo St, Los Angeles (90021-2854)
PHONE..............................213 622-0022
Ji S Hong, *CEO*
Stephen S Whang, *President*
EMP: 25 **EST:** 2010
SALES (est): 2.9MM **Privately Held**
SIC: 2339 5651 3999 Women's & misses' athletic clothing & sportswear; unisex clothing stores; bristles, dressing of

(P-3329)
GLIMA INC
11133 Vanowen St Ste A, North Hollywood (91605-6379)
PHONE..............................818 980-9686
AVI Levy, *CEO*
EMP: 12
SALES (est): 1.1MM **Privately Held**
WEB: www.glima.com
SIC: 2339 Athletic clothing: women's, misses' & juniors'

(P-3330)
GOLDEN COAST SPORTSWEAR INC
1140 E Howell Ave, Anaheim (92805-6452)
P.O. Box 3370 (92803-3370)
PHONE..............................714 704-4655
Mark Casale, *President*

▲ = Import ▼=Export
◆ =Import/Export

Katy Kunzweiler, *President*
EMP: 50 **EST:** 1982
SALES (est): 5.4MM **Privately Held**
SIC: 2339 2329 Sportswear, women's;
men's & boys' sportswear & athletic cloth-
ing

(P-3331)
GOLF APPAREL BRANDS INC
Also Called: La Mode
3824 W 113th St, Inglewood (90303-2606)
PHONE....................................310 327-5188
Edward J Kahn, *President*
Miriam Mencia, *CFO*
W Barry Kahn, *Vice Pres*
◆ **EMP:** 140
SALES (est): 11.6MM **Privately Held**
WEB: www.golf-apparel-brands.com
SIC: 2339 Women's & misses' outerwear

(P-3332)
GYPSY 05 INC
3200 Union Pacific Ave, Los Angeles
(90023-4203)
PHONE....................................323 265-2700
Dotan Shoham, *President*
Catalina Dado, *Accounting Mgr*
▲ **EMP:** 20
SALES (est): 2.2MM **Privately Held**
SIC: 2339 Women's & misses' athletic
clothing & sportswear

(P-3333)
H STARLET LLC
3447 S Main St, Los Angeles (90007-4413)
PHONE....................................323 235-8777
Brad Zions,
Heidi Cornell,
▲ **EMP:** 10
SALES (est): 1.5MM **Privately Held**
SIC: 2339 Women's & misses' athletic
clothing & sportswear

(P-3334)
HANK PLAYER INC
4303 Lemp Ave, Studio City (91604-2814)
PHONE....................................818 856-6079
EMP: 10
SQ FT: 6,000
SALES (est): 76.4K **Privately Held**
WEB: www.hank.com
SIC: 2339 5136

(P-3335)
HEARTS DELIGHT
4035 N Ventura Ave, Ventura (93001-1163)
PHONE....................................805 648-7123
Deborah Mesker, *Owner*
EMP: 27
SQ FT: 2,000
SALES (est): 2.1MM **Privately Held**
SIC: 2339 5621 Women's & misses' outer-
wear; boutiques

(P-3336)
HEY BABY OF CALIFORNIA
11238 Peoria St Ste C, Sun Valley
(91352-1663)
PHONE....................................818 504-2060
Pam Lengua, *Partner*
Anita Lengua, *Partner*
Rick Lengua, *Partner*
EMP: 42
SQ FT: 3,500
SALES (est): 1.5MM **Privately Held**
SIC: 2339 Bathing suits: women's, misses'
& juniors'

(P-3337)
HIP & HIP INC (PA)
Also Called: Angels
1100 S San Pedro St D07, Los Angeles
(90015-2328)
PHONE....................................310 494-6742
Jung Ae Park, *President*
EMP: 20 **EST:** 1997
SQ FT: 30,000
SALES (est): 1.4MM **Privately Held**
SIC: 2339 Women's & misses' outerwear

(P-3338)
HONEY PUNCH INC (PA)
1535 Rio Vista Ave, Los Angeles
(90023-2619)
PHONE....................................323 800-3812
Tae Sung Kang, *President*

Huyon Kang, *Vice Pres*
▲ **EMP:** 15
SALES (est): 2.2MM **Privately Held**
SIC: 2339 5621 Women's & misses' ath-
letic clothing & sportswear; women's
clothing stores

(P-3339)
I JOAH (PA)
1721 Wall St, Los Angeles (90015-3718)
PHONE....................................213 742-0500
Peter Song, *President*
▲ **EMP:** 10
SALES (est): 3.2MM **Privately Held**
WEB: www.ms1-misopeusa.com
SIC: 2339 Women's & misses' athletic
clothing & sportswear

(P-3340)
J & F DESIGN INC
Also Called: Next Generation
2042 Garfield Ave, Commerce
(90040-1804)
PHONE....................................323 526-4444
Jack Farshi, *President*
◆ **EMP:** 67
SQ FT: 100,000
SALES (est): 8.8MM **Privately Held**
SIC: 2339 Sportswear, women's

(P-3341)
JAMES KIM YOUNG
1215 W Walnut St, Compton (90220-5009)
PHONE....................................310 605-5328
James Young, *Principal*
EMP: 40
SALES (est): 1.7MM **Privately Held**
SIC: 2339 Women's & misses' outerwear

(P-3342)
JAMM INDUSTRIES CORP
Also Called: Bordeaux
2425 E 12th St, Los Angeles (90021-2906)
PHONE....................................213 622-0555
Afshin Raminfar, *CEO*
▲ **EMP:** 39
SQ FT: 15,000
SALES (est): 4.8MM **Privately Held**
SIC: 2339 Service apparel, washable:
women's

(P-3343)
JAPANESE WEEKEND INC (PA)
496 S Airport Blvd, South San Francisco
(94080-6911)
PHONE....................................415 621-0555
Barbara White, *President*
▲ **EMP:** 25
SQ FT: 6,000
SALES (est): 4.6MM **Privately Held**
WEB: www.japaneseweekend.com
SIC: 2339 5621 Maternity clothing; mater-
nity wear

(P-3344)
JAYA APPAREL GROUP LLC (PA)
5175 S Soto St, Vernon (90058-3620)
PHONE....................................323 584-3500
Jane Siskin, *CEO*
Don Lewis, *Officer*
Salvador Lopez, *Graphic Designe*
Maila Santos, *Finance Mgr*
Muhammad Gwaduri, *Controller*
◆ **EMP:** 80
SQ FT: 170,000
SALES (est): 70MM **Privately Held**
SIC: 2339 2337 Women's & misses' jack-
ets & coats, except sportswear; shorts
(outerwear): women's, misses' & juniors';
women's & misses' suits & skirts

(P-3345)
JD/CMC INC
Also Called: Color ME Cotton
2834 E 11th St, Los Angeles (90023-3406)
PHONE....................................818 767-2260
Mari Tatevosian, *President*
Anait Grigorian, *Admin Sec*
◆ **EMP:** 35
SQ FT: 12,000
SALES (est): 688.1K **Privately Held**
WEB: www.vreseis.com
SIC: 2339 Women's & misses' outerwear

(P-3346)
JINX INC
N Stanley Ave, Los Angeles (90008)
PHONE....................................818 399-4544
Sean Gailey, *CEO*
EMP: 50
SALES (est): 1MM **Privately Held**
SIC: 2339 3944 Maternity clothing;
games, toys & children's vehicles

(P-3347)
JNJ APPAREL INC
3838 S Santa Fe Ave, Vernon
(90058-1713)
PHONE....................................323 584-9700
Chan Hyoung Park, *President*
▲ **EMP:** 30
SQ FT: 10,000
SALES (est): 3.4MM **Privately Held**
SIC: 2339 Women's & misses' athletic
clothing & sportswear

(P-3348)
**JOLYN CLOTHING COMPANY
LLC**
150 5th St Ste 100, Huntington Beach
(92648-5139)
PHONE....................................714 794-2149
Warren Lief Pedersen, *President*
Brandon Molina, *COO*
Ann Dawson, *Vice Pres*
Kelsea Smith, *Sales Dir*
Tanya Gandy, *Sales Staff*
EMP: 30
SALES (est): 2.1MM **Privately Held**
SIC: 2339 5621 Women's & misses' ath-
letic clothing & sportswear; women's
sportswear

(P-3349)
JOY ACTIVE
13324 Estrella Ave, Gardena (90248-1519)
PHONE....................................310 660-0022
Jong Lim, *President*
EMP: 85
SALES (est): 3.1MM **Privately Held**
SIC: 2339 Women's & misses' outerwear

(P-3350)
JT DESIGN STUDIO INC (PA)
Also Called: 860, Shameless, Hot Wire
860 S Los Angeles St # 912, Los Angeles
(90014-3319)
PHONE....................................213 891-1500
Ted Cooper, *President*
Robert Grossman, *Vice Pres*
▲ **EMP:** 24 **EST:** 1998
SALES (est): 4MM **Privately Held**
WEB: www.shamelessclothing.com
SIC: 2339 Women's & misses' athletic
clothing & sportswear

(P-3351)
JUST FOR WRAPS INC (PA)
Also Called: A-List
5745 Rickenbacker Rd, Commerce
(90040-3052)
PHONE....................................213 239-0503
Vrajesh Lal, *CEO*
Rakesh Lal, *Vice Pres*
Edna Asuncion, *Accounting Mgr*
Alyssa Knowlton, *Sales Staff*
Bukul Chawla, *Manager*
▲ **EMP:** 130
SQ FT: 105,000
SALES (est): 25.2MM **Privately Held**
WEB: www.wrapper.com
SIC: 2339 2335 2337 Sportswear,
women's; women's, juniors' & misses'
dresses; women's & misses' suits & coats

(P-3352)
KAYO OF CALIFORNIA
11854 Alameda St, Lynwood (90262-4019)
PHONE....................................310 605-2693
Sandra Salgado, *Branch Mgr*
Wendy Swafford, *Planning*
EMP: 10
SALES (corp-wide): 8.4MM **Privately
Held**
SIC: 2339 Women's & misses' accessories
PA: Kayo Of California
161 W 39th St
Los Angeles CA 90037
323 233-6107

(P-3353)
KC EXCLUSIVE INC (PA)
Also Called: Zenana
1100 S San Pedro St, Los Angeles
(90015-2328)
PHONE....................................213 749-0088
Seok Jun Choi, *CEO*
Cindy Lee, *Accountant*
◆ **EMP:** 59
SALES (est): 10.2MM **Privately Held**
SIC: 2339 Women's & misses' athletic
clothing & sportswear

(P-3354)
**KENNETH MILLER CLOTHING
INC**
210 E Olympic Blvd # 208, Los Angeles
(90015-1775)
P.O. Box 79293 (90079-0293)
PHONE....................................213 746-8866
Rabin Babazadeh, *CEO*
◆ **EMP:** 22
SQ FT: 6,000
SALES (est): 2.2MM **Privately Held**
SIC: 2339 Women's & misses' jackets &
coats, except sportswear

(P-3355)
KIM & CAMI PRODUCTIONS INC
Also Called: Kim and Cami
2950 Leonis Blvd, Vernon (90058-2916)
PHONE....................................323 584-1300
Kimberly A Hiatt, *President*
Cami Gasmer, *Vice Pres*
▲ **EMP:** 22
SQ FT: 1,000
SALES (est): 4MM **Privately Held**
SIC: 2339 Sportswear, women's

(P-3356)
KLK FORTE INDUSTRY INC (PA)
Also Called: Honey Punch
1535 Rio Vista Ave, Los Angeles
(90023-2619)
PHONE....................................323 415-9181
Katherine Kim, *CEO*
◆ **EMP:** 45 **EST:** 2012
SQ FT: 30,000
SALES (est): 100K **Privately Held**
SIC: 2339 Women's & misses' outerwear

(P-3357)
KORAL INDUSTRIES LLC (PA)
Also Called: Koral Los Angeles
5124 Pacific Blvd, Vernon (90058-2218)
PHONE....................................323 585-5343
David Koral,
Peter Koral,
▲ **EMP:** 52
SQ FT: 60,000
SALES (est): 6.5MM **Privately Held**
SIC: 2339 Service apparel, washable:
women's

(P-3358)
KYMSTA CORP
1506 W 12th St, Los Angeles (90015-2013)
PHONE....................................213 380-8118
Roxanne Heptner, *President*
Arthur Pereira, *CFO*
EMP: 30
SQ FT: 25,000
SALES (est): 2.3MM **Privately Held**
WEB: www.kymsta.com
SIC: 2339 Women's & misses' athletic
clothing & sportswear

(P-3359)
L Y A GROUP INC
1317 S Grand Ave, Los Angeles
(90015-3008)
PHONE....................................213 683-1123
Claudia L Blanco, *CEO*
Augustin Ramirez, *President*
▲ **EMP:** 18
SALES (est): 4.2MM **Privately Held**
SIC: 2339 Jeans: women's, misses' & jun-
iors'

(P-3360)
LAC BLEU INC
3817 S Santa Fe Ave, Vernon
(90058-1712)
PHONE....................................213 973-5335
Kevin Chong, *Branch Mgr*

EMP: 10
SALES (corp-wide): 5.5MM **Privately Held**
SIC: 2339 Women's & misses' outerwear
PA: Lac Bleu, Inc.
　1145 Towne Ave Ste 9
　Los Angeles CA 90021
　213 973-5335

(P-3361)
LAT LLC
Also Called: G Girl
2052 E Vernon Ave, Vernon (90058-1613)
PHONE...............................323 233-3017
Simon Cho, *Mng Member*
▲ EMP: 40
SQ FT: 20,000
SALES: 12MM **Privately Held**
SIC: 2339 Women's & misses' outerwear

(P-3362)
LEE THOMAS INC (PA)
13800 S Figueroa St, Los Angeles
(90061-1026)
PHONE...............................310 532-7560
Lee Opolinsky, *President*
Thomas Mahoney, *Vice Pres*
EMP: 30
SQ FT: 45,000
SALES (est): 1.9MM **Privately Held**
SIC: 2339 Women's & misses' athletic
　clothing & sportswear

(P-3363)
LEFTY PRODUCTION CO LLC
318 W 9th St Ste 1010, Los Angeles
(90015-1546)
PHONE...............................323 515-9266
Marta Abrams, *Mng Member*
EMP: 18 EST: 2012
SALES (est): 1.9MM **Privately Held**
SIC: 2339 Athletic clothing: women's,
　misses' & juniors'

(P-3364)
LISA AND LESLEY CO
Also Called: Lisa & Lesley Fashion ACC
14140 Ventura Blvd # 101, Sherman Oaks
(91423-2750)
P.O. Box 1958, Studio City (91614-0958)
PHONE...............................323 877-9878
Lisa Rosson, *Partner*
Lesley Rosson, *Partner*
EMP: 10
SALES (est): 966.8K **Privately Held**
SIC: 2339 Women's & misses' athletic
　clothing & sportswear

(P-3365)
M STEVENS INC
Also Called: Stevens, M Dancewear & Design
1925 Blake Ave, Los Angeles (90039-3807)
PHONE...............................323 661-2147
Norma Winner, *President*
Gayle Davis, *Vice Pres*
Sonya Cohen, *Manager*
EMP: 10
SQ FT: 3,500
SALES (est): 1.2MM **Privately Held**
WEB: www.solipsist.org
SIC: 2339 Women's & misses' athletic
　clothing & sportswear

(P-3366)
**MANHATTAN BEACHWEAR INC
(DH)**
Also Called: La Blanca Swimwear
10700 Valley View St, Cypress
(90630-4835)
PHONE...............................714 892-7354
Lindsay Shumlas, *CEO*
Sergio Onaga, *Graphic Designe*
Julie Wilson, *Human Res Dir*
Veronica Thompson, *Payroll Mgr*
Felicia Pearson, *Purch Mgr*
◆ EMP: 200
SQ FT: 81,000
SALES (est): 153MM **Privately Held**
SIC: 2339 Bathing suits: women's, misses'
　& juniors'; beachwear: women's, misses'
　& juniors'; athletic clothing: women's,
　misses' & juniors'; sportswear, women's

(P-3367)
MANHATTAN BEACHWEAR INC
10700 Valley View St, Cypress
(90630-4835)
PHONE...............................714 892-7354
EMP: 100
SALES (corp-wide): 229.8MM **Privately
Held**
SIC: 2339
PA: Manhattan Beachwear, Inc.
　10700 Valley View St
　Cypress CA 90630
　714 892-7354

(P-3368)
MARCEA INC
1742 Crenshaw Blvd, Torrance
(90501-3311)
P.O. Box 48317, Los Angeles (90048-0317)
PHONE...............................213 746-5191
Marcia D Lane, *President*
EMP: 12
SQ FT: 2,500
SALES (est): 154.6K **Privately Held**
WEB: www.marcea.com
SIC: 2339 Sportswear, women's

(P-3369)
MARGARET OLEARY INC (PA)
50 Dorman Ave, San Francisco
(94124-1807)
PHONE...............................415 354-6663
Margaret O'Leary, *CEO*
▲ EMP: 70
SQ FT: 16,000
SALES (est): 16MM **Privately Held**
WEB: www.moleary.com
SIC: 2339 2253 Sportswear, women's; knit
　outerwear mills

(P-3370)
MARIKA LLC
5553-B Bandini Blvd, Bell (90201)
PHONE...............................323 888-7755
Frank M Zarabi, *Mng Member*
Patrick Shaowl,
▲ EMP: 100
SQ FT: 160,000
SALES (est): 109.3MM **Privately Held**
SIC: 2339 Athletic clothing: women's,
　misses' & juniors'; women's & misses
　athletic clothing & sportswear

(P-3371)
MARINA SPORTSWEAR INC
Also Called: Marina Industries
3766 S Main St, Los Angeles (90007-4419)
PHONE...............................323 232-2012
Marina Galdamez, *President*
Mondie Saenz, *Opers Staff*
EMP: 70
SQ FT: 12,000
SALES (est): 2MM **Privately Held**
SIC: 2339 2329 Sportswear, women's;
　men's & boys' sportswear & athletic cloth-
　ing

(P-3372)
MAX LEON INC (PA)
Also Called: Max Studio.com
3100 New York Dr, Pasadena
(91107-1524)
P.O. Box 70879 (91117-7879)
PHONE...............................626 797-6886
Leon Max, *President*
Jolene Abercromby, *Manager*
▲ EMP: 100
SQ FT: 65,000
SALES (est): 106.7MM **Privately Held**
WEB: www.maxstudio.com
SIC: 2339 5632 Sportswear, women's; ap-
　parel accessories

(P-3373)
MGT INDUSTRIES INC (PA)
Also Called: California Dynasty
13889 S Figueroa St, Los Angeles
(90061-1025)
PHONE...............................310 516-5900
Jeffrey P Mirvis, *CEO*
Alessandra Strahl, *President*
Phil Nathanson, *CFO*
Mike Brooks, *Vice Pres*
Tom Stevenson, *Vice Pres*
▲ EMP: 115
SQ FT: 82,000

SALES (est): 51.4MM **Privately Held**
SIC: 2339 Women's & misses' outerwear

(P-3374)
MIMI CHICA (PA)
Also Called: Mimi Chica Design
161 W 33rd St, Los Angeles (90007-4106)
PHONE...............................323 264-9278
Paul Spoleti, *President*
EMP: 18
SALES (est): 3.5MM **Privately Held**
WEB: www.mimichica.com
SIC: 2339 Women's & misses' culottes,
　knickers & shorts; jeans: women's,
　misses' & juniors'; slacks: women's,
　misses' & juniors'

(P-3375)
MONTEREY CANYON LLC (PA)
1515 E 15th St, Los Angeles (90021-2711)
PHONE...............................213 741-0209
Fabian Oberfeld,
Richard Sneider,
▲ EMP: 70 EST: 1977
SALES (est): 4.7MM **Privately Held**
WEB: www.canyon-sports.com
SIC: 2339 Sportswear, women's

(P-3376)
NEXXEN APPAREL INC (PA)
Also Called: Check It Out
1555 Los Palos St, Los Angeles
(90023-3218)
PHONE...............................323 267-9900
Jai Sim, *President*
Carol Chang, *Vice Pres*
Billy Sim, *Vice Pres*
EMP: 18
SQ FT: 10,000
SALES (est): 2.9MM **Privately Held**
SIC: 2339 Women's & misses' outerwear

(P-3377)
NILS INC (PA)
Also Called: Nils Skiwear
3151 Airway Ave Ste V, Costa Mesa
(92626-4627)
PHONE...............................714 755-1600
Nils Andersson, *CEO*
Richard Leffler, *President*
▲ EMP: 15 EST: 1953
SALES (est): 3.1MM **Privately Held**
WEB: www.nilsskiwear.com
SIC: 2339 Women's & misses' athletic
　clothing & sportswear; ski jackets &
　pants: women's, misses' & juniors'; snow
　suits: women's, misses' & juniors'

(P-3378)
NOOSHIN INC
Also Called: Nooshin Blanque
555 Chalette Dr, Beverly Hills
(90210-1915)
PHONE...............................310 559-5766
Nooshin Malakzad, *President*
Chas Chesler, *Executive*
Newsha Malakzad, *Admin Sec*
EMP: 10
SQ FT: 8,000
SALES (est): 1.4MM **Privately Held**
SIC: 2339 Sportswear, women's

(P-3379)
OAK APPAREL INC
Also Called: Jemstone
1363 Elwood St, Los Angeles
(90021-2412)
PHONE...............................213 489-9766
Eun S Kim, *CEO*
▲ EMP: 10
SQ FT: 5,000
SALES (est): 5MM **Privately Held**
SIC: 2339 Women's & misses' outerwear

(P-3380)
ODETTE CHRISTIANE LLC
Also Called: Dresses.com
21521 Blythe St, Canoga Park
(91304-4910)
PHONE...............................818 883-0410
Joseph Sweeney,
Odette Sweeney,
Tor Sweeney,
EMP: 12
SQ FT: 5,000

SALES (est): 3MM **Privately Held**
WEB: www.oscardresses.com
SIC: 2339 Sportswear, women's

(P-3381)
PACE SPORTSWEAR INC
12781 Monarch St, Garden Grove
(92841-3920)
PHONE...............................714 891-8716
Leonor Saavedra, *CEO*
Maria Marsh, *President*
▲ EMP: 13
SQ FT: 6,500
SALES: 785.8K **Privately Held**
WEB: www.pacesportswear.com
SIC: 2339 2329 Athletic clothing:
　women's, misses' & juniors'; athletic
　(warmup, sweat & jogging) suits: men's &
　boys'

(P-3382)
PACIFIC ATHLETIC WEAR INC
7340 Lampson Ave, Garden Grove
(92841-2902)
PHONE...............................714 751-8006
John Hillenbrand, *President*
Gabriela Hillenbrand, *Executive*
▲ EMP: 70
SALES (est): 7.7MM **Privately Held**
WEB: www.pawman.com
SIC: 2339 Uniforms, athletic: women's,
　misses' & juniors'

(P-3383)
PATTERSON KINCAID LLC
5175 S Soto St, Vernon (90058-3620)
PHONE...............................323 584-3559
Jane Siskin, *Mng Member*
Jilali Elbasri,
◆ EMP: 12
SQ FT: 35,000
SALES (est): 783K
SALES (corp-wide): 23.8MM **Privately
Held**
SIC: 2339 Women's & misses' outerwear
PA: Jaya Apparel Group Llc
　5175 S Soto St
　Vernon CA 90058
　323 584-3500

(P-3384)
PEEP INC
Also Called: Peep Studio
720 Towne Ave, Los Angeles (90021-1418)
PHONE...............................213 748-5500
Kamran Samooha, *President*
▲ EMP: 20
SQ FT: 2,000
SALES (est): 2MM **Privately Held**
WEB: www.marshmallowpeeps.com
SIC: 2339 Sportswear, women's

(P-3385)
**PERFORMANCE APPAREL
CORP**
Also Called: Hot Chillys
174 Suburban Rd Ste 100, San Luis Obispo
(93401-7522)
PHONE...............................805 541-0989
Jon Df Stanfield, *Chairman*
Shirley Skinner, *Human Res Dir*
▲ EMP: 10
SALES (est): 2.9MM
SALES (corp-wide): 99.5MM **Privately
Held**
WEB: www.hotchillys.com
SIC: 2339 Athletic clothing: women's,
　misses' & juniors'; bathing suits: women's,
　misses' & juniors'
HQ: Stanfield's Limited
　1 Logan St
　Truro NS B2N 5
　902 895-5406

(P-3386)
PETER K INC (PA)
Also Called: Next ERA
5175 S Soto St, Vernon (90058-3620)
PHONE...............................323 585-5343
Peter Koral, *President*
▲ EMP: 41 EST: 1982
SALES (est): 8.4MM **Privately Held**
SIC: 2339 2369 Sportswear, women's;
　girls' & children's outerwear

▲ = Import ▼=Export
◆ =Import/Export

(P-3387)
PICCONE APPAREL CORP
6444 Fleet St, Commerce (90040-1710)
PHONE..................................310 559-6702
Robin Piccone, *President*
Rita Piccone, *Vice Pres*
Tony Andreu, *Controller*
▲ EMP: 30
SALES (est): 3.3MM **Privately Held**
WEB: www.dominioncorde.com
SIC: 2339 Women's & misses' outerwear

(P-3388)
PIERRE MITRI (PA)
Also Called: Watch L.A.
1138 Wall St, Los Angeles (90015-2320)
PHONE..................................213 747-1838
Pierre D Mitri, *Owner*
▲ EMP: 17
SQ FT: 6,000
SALES (est): 2.6MM **Privately Held**
WEB: www.watchla.com
SIC: 2339 Jeans: women's, misses' & jun-
iors'; women's & misses' athletic clothing
& sportswear

(P-3389)
PIET RETIEF INC
Also Called: Peter Cohen Companies
1914 6th Ave, Los Angeles (90018-1124)
PHONE..................................323 732-8312
Peter Cohen, *President*
Anna Cohen, *Treasurer*
Lee Stuart Cox, *Vice Pres*
EMP: 34
SQ FT: 4,800
SALES (est): 3.5MM **Privately Held**
WEB: www.petercohen.net
SIC: 2339 Sportswear, women's

(P-3390)
POINT CONCEPTION INC
Also Called: Kechika
23121 Arroyo Vis Ste A, Rcho STA Marg
(92688-2609)
PHONE..................................949 589-6890
Jeff Jung, *CEO*
Jamie Jung, *President*
◆ EMP: 35
SQ FT: 20,000
SALES (est): 3.8MM **Privately Held**
WEB: www.pointconception.com
SIC: 2339 Bathing suits: women's, misses'
& juniors'; sportswear, women's

(P-3391)
POLYMOND DK INC
777 E 10th St Ste 110, Los Angeles
(90021-2083)
PHONE..................................213 327-0771
EMP: 30
SALES (corp-wide): 2.3MM **Privately
Held**
SIC: 2339 5136 Women's & misses' ath-
letic clothing & sportswear; men's & boys'
clothing
PA: Polymond Dk, Inc.
655 S Santa Fe Ave
Los Angeles CA 90021
213 327-0771

(P-3392)
PRODUCE APPAREL INC
23383 Saint Andrews, Mission Viejo
(92692-1538)
PHONE..................................949 472-9434
Scott Machock, *President*
Helen Machock, *Vice Pres*
▲ EMP: 15
SQ FT: 5,000
SALES (est): 2.1MM **Privately Held**
WEB: www.produceapparel.com
SIC: 2339 5621 Sportswear, women's;
women's clothing stores

(P-3393)
PURE ALLURE INC
Also Called: Pure Allure Accessories
4005 Avenida De La Plata, Oceanside
(92056-5843)
PHONE..................................760 966-3650
Dale A Grose, *President*
Daylene Grose, *Vice Pres*
▲ EMP: 100
SQ FT: 6,000
SALES (est): 6.7MM **Privately Held**
WEB: www.pureallure.com
SIC: 2339 5137 3961 Women's & misses'
accessories; women's & children's acces-
sories; costume jewelry

(P-3394)
**PUTNAM ACCESSORY GROUP
INC**
4455 Fruitland Ave, Vernon (90058-3222)
PHONE..................................323 306-1330
John Putnam, *President*
▲ EMP: 20 EST: 2012
SALES (est): 2.1MM **Privately Held**
SIC: 2339 2389 Women's & misses' ac-
cessories; men's miscellaneous acces-
sories

(P-3395)
Q&A7 LLC
Also Called: Q&A Clothing
2155 E 7th St Ste 150, Los Angeles
(90023-1032)
PHONE..................................323 364-4250
Aaron Voref,
Nicholas Rozansky,
◆ EMP: 19
SQ FT: 10,000
SALES (est): 8.2MM **Privately Held**
SIC: 2339 5137 Women's & misses' ath-
letic clothing & sportswear; athletic cloth-
ing: women's, misses' & juniors'; women's
& children's clothing

(P-3396)
R & W INC
6351 Rege St 100 A & 300, Huntington
Park (90255)
PHONE..................................323 589-1374
Wendy Kim, *CEO*
EMP: 13
SALES (est): 1.2MM **Privately Held**
SIC: 2339 Women's & misses' outerwear

(P-3397)
RAJ MANUFACTURING LLC
2692 Dow Ave, Tustin (92780-7208)
PHONE..................................714 838-3110
Joseph Binotto,
EMP: 19
SALES (est): 2.2MM **Privately Held**
SIC: 2339 Bathing suits: women's, misses'
& juniors'

(P-3398)
RHAPSODY CLOTHING INC
Also Called: Epilogue and Arrested
810 E Pico Blvd Ste 24, Los Angeles
(90021-2375)
PHONE..................................213 614-8887
Bryan Kang, *CEO*
Yoon MI Kang, *Vice Pres*
Joi Dela Rama, *Manager*
▲ EMP: 65
SALES (est): 8.2MM **Privately Held**
WEB: www.rhapsodyclothing.com
SIC: 2339 Shorts (outerwear): women's,
misses' & juniors'; jeans: women's,
misses' & juniors'

(P-3399)
RIAH FASHION INC
1820 E 46th St, Vernon (90058-1948)
PHONE..................................323 325-7308
Jose Alejandro Kim, *CEO*
Eunice Jung, *CFO*
EMP: 10 EST: 2008
SQ FT: 4,550
SALES (est): 1MM **Privately Held**
SIC: 2339 5122 5944 5621 Women's &
misses' accessories; cosmetics; jewelry
stores; women's clothing stores

(P-3400)
ROTAX INCORPORATED
Also Called: Gamma
2940 Leonis Blvd, Vernon (90058-2916)
PHONE..................................323 589-5999
Arthur Torssien, *President*
Ripsick Kepenekian, *Vice Pres*
▲ EMP: 40
SALES (est): 210.1K **Privately Held**
WEB: www.rotax.com
SIC: 2339 2329 Women's & misses' outer-
wear; men's & boys' sportswear & athletic
clothing

(P-3401)
ROYAL APPAREL INC
4331 Baldwin Ave, El Monte (91731-1103)
PHONE..................................626 579-5168
Kung-Shih Yang, *President*
Sheena Yang, *Corp Secy*
Michael Hsu, *Vice Pres*
▲ EMP: 70
SQ FT: 24,000
SALES (est): 5.6MM **Privately Held**
WEB: www.royalapparel.com
SIC: 2339 Leotards: women's, misses' &
juniors'; women's & misses' athletic cloth-
ing & sportswear

(P-3402)
SECOND GENERATION INC
Also Called: Fish Bowl
1950 Naomi Ave, Los Angeles
(90011-1342)
PHONE..................................213 743-8700
Michael Weisberg, *CEO*
Dale Kaufman, *CFO*
▲ EMP: 68
SQ FT: 11,000
SALES (est): 13.9MM **Privately Held**
SIC: 2339 5621 Women's & misses' ath-
letic clothing & sportswear; women's
clothing stores

(P-3403)
SESSIONS
60 Old El Pueblo Rd, Scotts Valley
(95066-3540)
PHONE..................................831 461-5080
Joel Gomez, *CEO*
Cindy Busenhart, *President*
▲ EMP: 40
SQ FT: 20,000
SALES (est): 4.6MM **Privately Held**
WEB: www.sessions.com
SIC: 2339 5941 2329 Ski jackets & pants:
women's, misses' & juniors'; snow suits:
women's, misses' & juniors'; sporting
goods & bicycle shops; ski & snow cloth-
ing: men's & boys'

(P-3404)
SEW SPORTY
2215 La Mirada Dr, Vista (92081-8828)
PHONE..................................760 599-0585
Loralynn Williams, *Partner*
David Sheeron, *Partner*
▲ EMP: 20
SQ FT: 8,000
SALES: 1MM **Privately Held**
WEB: www.sewsporty.com
SIC: 2339 2329 Uniforms, athletic:
women's, misses' & juniors'; men's &
boys' athletic uniforms

(P-3405)
SFO APPAREL
41 Park Pl 43, Brisbane (94005-1306)
PHONE..................................415 468-8816
Peter Mou, *President*
▲ EMP: 140
SQ FT: 20,000
SALES (est): 16.3MM **Privately Held**
SIC: 2339 Women's & misses' athletic
clothing & sportswear; beachwear:
women's, misses' & juniors'

(P-3406)
SIHO CORPORATION
Also Called: Annianna
5750 Grace Pl, Commerce (90022-4121)
PHONE..................................323 721-4000
Hanni Hilman, *President*
Jason Teng, *CFO*
EMP: 15
SQ FT: 3,000
SALES (est): 5MM **Privately Held**
SIC: 2339 Women's & misses' outerwear

(P-3407)
SKY LUXURY CORP
3001 Humboldt St, Los Angeles
(90031-1830)
PHONE..................................323 940-0111
Peter Kane, *President*
EMP: 21
SQ FT: 8,000
SALES (est): 2.1MM **Privately Held**
SIC: 2339 5661 Women's & misses' outer-
wear; shoes, orthopedic

(P-3408)
SMB CLOTHING INC
Also Called: Top Ten
1016 Towne Ave Unit 104, Los Angeles
(90021-2078)
PHONE..................................213 489-4949
Sally Michull Baek, *CEO*
Yong Koo Hyung, *CFO*
EMP: 10
SALES (est): 1.2MM **Privately Held**
SIC: 2339 5137 Sportswear, women's;
sportswear, women's & children's

(P-3409)
**SOLE SURVIVOR
CORPORATION**
Also Called: Gramicci Comfort Engineered
28632 Roadside Dr Ste 200, Agoura Hills
(91301-6088)
PHONE..................................818 338-3760
Donald N Love, *CEO*
▲ EMP: 145
SQ FT: 46,000
SALES (est): 9.6MM **Privately Held**
SIC: 2339 2329 5137 5136 Sportswear,
women's; men's & boys' sportswear &
athletic clothing; women's & children's
clothing; men's & boys' clothing

(P-3410)
SPIRIT CLOTHING COMPANY
Also Called: Spirit Activewear
2211 E 37th St, Vernon (90058-1427)
PHONE..................................213 784-0251
Jake Pitaszink, *President*
◆ EMP: 25
SQ FT: 19,000
SALES (est): 3.8MM **Privately Held**
WEB: www.spiritactivewear.com
SIC: 2339 2329 Athletic clothing:
women's, misses' & juniors'; men's &
boys' sportswear & athletic clothing

(P-3411)
SSC APPAREL INC
Also Called: Soprano
2025 Long Beach Ave, Los Angeles
(90058-1021)
P.O. Box 1358, Lomita (90717-5358)
PHONE..................................213 746-0200
Julie Kim, *CEO*
Alexis Kim, *President*
Gary Kim, *Sales Executive*
▲ EMP: 23
SQ FT: 20,000
SALES (est): 3.4MM **Privately Held**
WEB: www.soprano.com
SIC: 2339 Women's & misses' athletic
clothing & sportswear

(P-3412)
ST JOHN KNITS INC (DH)
17522 Armstrong Ave, Irvine (92614-5876)
PHONE..................................949 863-1171
Bruce Fetter, *CEO*
EMP: 111
SALES (est): 170.1MM
SALES (corp-wide): 507.1MM **Privately
Held**
SIC: 2339 2253 2389 Women's & misses'
accessories; knit outerwear mills; men's
miscellaneous accessories
HQ: St. John Knits International, Incorpo-
rated
17522 Armstrong Ave
Irvine CA 92614
949 863-1171

(P-3413)
ST JOHN KNITS INTL INC (HQ)
Also Called: St John Knits
17522 Armstrong Ave, Irvine (92614-5876)
PHONE..................................949 863-1171
Geoffroy Van Raemdonck, *CEO*
James Kelley, *Partner*
Bernd Beetz, *Ch of Bd*
Glenn McMahon, *CEO*
Bruce Fetter, *COO*
◆ EMP: 150
SQ FT: 71,100
SALES (est): 507.1MM **Privately Held**
WEB: www.stjohnknits.com
SIC: 2339 Sportswear, women's; scarves,
hoods, headbands, etc.: women's; jack-
ets, untailored: women's, misses' & jun-
iors'; slacks: women's, misses' & juniors'

PA: Gray Vestar Investors Llc
　17622 Armstrong Ave
　Irvine CA 92614
　949 863-1171

(P-3414)
STAPLES INC
731 S Spring St Ste 300, Los Angeles
(90014-2922)
PHONE....................213 623-4395
Gary Brownstein, *President*
EMP: 15 **EST:** 2002
SALES (est): 852.3K **Privately Held**
SIC: 2339 2335 Sportswear, women's;
women's, juniors' & misses' dresses

(P-3415)
STAR AVE
514 E 8th St Ste 500, Los Angeles
(90014-2335)
PHONE....................213 623-5799
Hyon Seun Kim, *Owner*
EMP: 25 **EST:** 1998
SALES (est): 1.1MM **Privately Held**
SIC: 2339 Athletic clothing: women's,
misses' & juniors'

(P-3416)
STELLA FASHIONS INC
1015 Crocker St Ste Q04, Los Angeles
(90021-2063)
PHONE....................213 746-6889
Yun Lee, *President*
Jung Lee, *Treasurer*
EMP: 20 **EST:** 1998
SQ FT: 5,000
SALES: 6MM **Privately Held**
SIC: 2339 Athletic clothing: women's,
misses' & juniors'; women's & misses'
athletic clothing & sportswear

(P-3417)
STONY APPAREL CORP (PA)
Also Called: Eyeshadow
1500 S Evergreen Ave, Los Angeles
(90023-3618)
PHONE....................323 981-9080
Tony Litman, *CEO*
William Tolcher, *COO*
Ben Quan, *Vice Pres*
Dean Wiener, *Vice Pres*
Stephen B Maiman, *Admin Sec*
▲ **EMP:** 200
SQ FT: 200,000
SALES (est): 58.2MM **Privately Held**
SIC: 2339 Women's & misses' athletic
clothing & sportswear

(P-3418)
SUSY CLOTHING CO
2256 Hollister Ter, Glendale (91206-3031)
PHONE....................818 500-7879
Gevork Koshkakaryan, *Owner*
EMP: 27
SALES: 650K **Privately Held**
SIC: 2339 Athletic clothing: women's,
misses' & juniors'

(P-3419)
SWIMWEAR
Also Called: T. H. E. Swimwear
1961 Hawkins Cir, Los Angeles
(90001-2255)
PHONE....................323 584-7536
Thomas J Hartigan, *President*
Mary E Hartigan, *Vice Pres*
Michael V Hartigan, *Vice Pres*
EMP: 35
SQ FT: 30,000
SALES: 1.5MM **Privately Held**
WEB: www.theswimwear.com
SIC: 2339 Bathing suits: women's, misses'
& juniors'

(P-3420)
T-BAGS LLC
Also Called: Misa Los Angeles
1530 E 25th St, Los Angeles (90011-1814)
PHONE....................323 225-9525
Mehrdad Fahrat,
Shadi Askari, *Principal*
EMP: 10
SALES (est): 1.3MM **Privately Held**
SIC: 2339 Athletic clothing: women's,
misses' & juniors'

(P-3421)
TCJ MANUFACTURING LLC
Also Called: Velvet Heart
2744 E 11th St, Los Angeles (90023-3404)
PHONE....................213 488-8400
Gabrielle Tsabag, *Mng Member*
Moshe Tsabag,
▲ **EMP:** 22
SALES (est): 3.4MM **Privately Held**
SIC: 2339 Athletic clothing: women's,
misses' & juniors'

(P-3422)
TCW TRENDS INC
2886 Columbia St, Torrance (90503-3808)
PHONE....................310 533-5177
Charanjiv S Mansingh, *President*
Prerana Sachdev Khanna, *Vice Pres*
Gurvinder Singh Sandhu, *Vice Pres*
DK Sachdev, *IT/INT Sup*
Rohaidah Chehassan, *Finance Dir*
▲ **EMP:** 18
SQ FT: 10,000
SALES (est): 25.2MM **Privately Held**
SIC: 2339 2326 5137 Aprons, except rub-
ber or plastic: women's, misses', juniors';
men's & boys' work clothing; coordinate
sets: women's, children's infants'

(P-3423)
TEMPTED APPAREL CORP
4516 Loma Vista Ave, Vernon
(90058-2602)
PHONE....................323 859-2480
Steven Schoenholz, *President*
Donna Ericastillo, *Executive*
Steve Schoholds, *Administration*
Moy Valentin, *Controller*
Regina Pugliese, *Opers Staff*
▲ **EMP:** 50
SALES (est): 5.4MM **Privately Held**
SIC: 2339 Women's & misses' outerwear

(P-3424)
**TOAD & CO INTERNATIONAL
INC (PA)**
2020 Alameda Padre Serra, Santa Barbara
(93103-1756)
P.O. Box 21508 (93121-1508)
PHONE....................805 957-1474
Gordon Seabury, *President*
Lindsay Faulding, *Buyer*
Lindsey Hawkins, *Production*
Steven McCann, *Marketing Mgr*
Nina Brito, *Sales Staff*
▲ **EMP:** 50
SQ FT: 7,000
SALES (est): 10.3MM **Privately Held**
SIC: 2339 2329 Women's & misses' ath-
letic clothing & sportswear; men's & boys'
sportswear & athletic clothing

(P-3425)
TOSKA INC
Also Called: Tz
1100 S San Pedro St I06, Los Angeles
(90015-2387)
PHONE....................213 746-0088
Nancy Choi, *President*
Rachel Johnson, *Bookkeeper*
▲ **EMP:** 15
SALES (est): 1.4MM **Privately Held**
SIC: 2339 5137 Women's & misses' outer-
wear; women's & children's clothing

(P-3426)
TOUCH ME FASHION INC
Also Called: Teen Bell
906 E 60th St, Los Angeles (90001-1017)
PHONE....................323 234-9200
Hyun Soon Chung, *President*
▲ **EMP:** 29
SALES (est): 3.3MM **Privately Held**
SIC: 2339 Women's & misses' outerwear

(P-3427)
**TRANSGLOBAL APPAREL
GROUP INC**
12362 Knott St, Garden Grove
(92841-2802)
PHONE....................714 890-9200
Andrew Su, *President*
Timmic Su, *CFO*
EMP: 10

SALES: 10.5MM **Privately Held**
SIC: 2339 Women's & misses' outerwear

(P-3428)
TRES BIEN INC (PA)
1016 Towne Ave Unit 113, Los Angeles
(90021-2078)
PHONE....................213 747-3366
Daejae Kim, *CEO*
Joseph Kim, *Mktg Dir*
▲ **EMP:** 12
SALES (est): 1.5MM **Privately Held**
SIC: 2339 Athletic clothing: women's,
misses' & juniors'

(P-3429)
UNIQUE APPAREL INC
3777 S Main St, Los Angeles (90007-4420)
PHONE....................213 321-8192
Suzie Kang, *President*
▲ **EMP:** 80
SALES (est): 4.7MM **Privately Held**
SIC: 2339 Jeans: women's, misses' & jun-
iors'

(P-3430)
VICTORY CUSTOM ATHLETICS
2001 Anchor Ct Ste A, Newbury Park
(91320-1615)
PHONE....................818 349-8476
Mike Le Cocq, *Partner*
Carlos Yniguez, *Partner*
Tommy Kimmerle, *Graphic Designe*
EMP: 54
SQ FT: 5,500
SALES (est): 5.6MM **Privately Held**
WEB: www.victory-la.com
SIC: 2339 2329 Athletic clothing:
women's, misses' & juniors'; athletic
(warmup, sweat & jogging) suits: men's &
boys'

(P-3431)
**VICTORY PROFESSIONAL
PRODUCTS**
Also Called: Victory Koredrry
5601 Engineer Dr, Huntington Beach
(92649-1123)
PHONE....................714 887-0621
Marc Spitaleri, *President*
▲ **EMP:** 28
SQ FT: 8,500
SALES: 3MM **Privately Held**
WEB: www.victorywetsuits.com
SIC: 2339 2329 2393 Women's & misses'
athletic clothing & sportswear; men's &
boys' sportswear & athletic clothing; tex-
tile bags

(P-3432)
VISIONMAX INC
Also Called: Ficcare
17232 Railroad St, City of Industry
(91748-1021)
PHONE....................626 839-1602
Janet Lau, *President*
Ing Chen, *Executive*
▲ **EMP:** 10
SALES (est): 1.1MM **Privately Held**
SIC: 2339 Women's & misses' accessories

(P-3433)
W & W CONCEPT INC
Also Called: Perseption
4890 S Alameda St, Vernon (90058-2806)
PHONE....................323 233-9202
Wonsook Chong, *President*
Jay Joo, *CEO*
▲ **EMP:** 55
SQ FT: 45,000
SALES (est): 17.3MM **Privately Held**
WEB: www.perseption.com
SIC: 2339 Sportswear, women's

(P-3434)
WEARABLE INTEGRITY INC
Also Called: Barbara Lesser
1360 E 17th St, Los Angeles (90021-3024)
PHONE....................213 748-6044
Mark Lesser, *President*
Barbara Lesser, *Vice Pres*
▲ **EMP:** 22
SQ FT: 20,000

SALES (est): 2.5MM **Privately Held**
WEB: www.barbaralesser.com
SIC: 2339 5137 2335 Women's & misses'
outerwear; women's & children's sportswear & swimsuits; women's, juniors' &
misses' dresses

(P-3435)
YH TEXPERT CORPORATION
Also Called: Urbanista
5052 Cecelia St, South Gate (90280-3511)
PHONE....................323 562-8800
Alexander Han, *CEO*
John Park, *Vice Pres*
Yoon Lee, *Accounts Mgr*
▲ **EMP:** 11
SQ FT: 6,000
SALES: 7MM **Privately Held**
WEB: www.texpert.net
SIC: 2339 5137 Women's & misses' ath-
letic clothing & sportswear; athletic cloth-
ing: women's, misses' & juniors';
maternity clothing; women's & children's
clothing

(P-3436)
YMI JEANSWEAR INC
1015 Wall St Ste 115, Los Angeles
(90015-2392)
PHONE....................213 746-6681
Ronan Vered, *Branch Mgr*
EMP: 55
SALES (corp-wide): 13.1MM **Privately
Held**
WEB: www.ymijeans.com
SIC: 2339 2325 Jeans: women's, misses'
& juniors'; men's & boys' jeans & dunga-
rees
PA: Y.M.I. Jeanswear, Inc,
　1155 S Boyle Ave
　Los Angeles CA 90023
　323 581-7700

┌────────────────────────────┐
│ **2341 Women's, Misses' &** │
│ **Children's Underwear &** │
│ **Nightwear**   │
└────────────────────────────┘

(P-3437)
402 SHOES INC
Also Called: Trashy Lingerie
402 N La Cienega Blvd, West Hollywood
(90048-1907)
PHONE....................323 655-5437
Mitchell Shrier, *President*
Deirdre Miller, *CFO*
Tracy Shrier, *Admin Sec*
Randy Shrier,
EMP: 23
SQ FT: 6,000
SALES (est): 1.9MM **Privately Held**
SIC: 2341 5632 2322 Women's & chil-
dren's nightwear; lingerie & corsets (un-
derwear); men's & boys' underwear &
nightwear

(P-3438)
**ADVANCE LATEX PRODUCTS
INC**
Also Called: International Molders
6915 Woodley Ave B, Van Nuys
(91406-4844)
PHONE....................310 559-8300
Blanch Howard, *CEO*
Michael Wellman, *President*
▲ **EMP:** 30
SQ FT: 40,000
SALES (est): 2.6MM **Privately Held**
SIC: 2341 Women's & children's under-
wear

(P-3439)
**AFR APPAREL INTERNATIONAL
INC**
Also Called: Parisa Lingerie & Swim Wear
19401 Business Center Dr, Northridge
(91324-3506)
PHONE....................818 773-5000
Amir Moghadam, *President*
Brenda J Moghadam, *Exec VP*
Brenda Moghadam, *Vice Pres*
Michael Arens, *Office Mgr*
▲ **EMP:** 60

▲ = Import ▼=Export
◆ =Import/Export

SQ FT: 46,000
SALES: 25MM **Privately Held**
WEB: www.parisausa.com
SIC: **2341** 2342 2369 5137 Women's & children's nightwear; bras, girdles & allied garments; bathing suits & swimwear; girls', children's & infants'; lingerie

(P-3440)
CALOR APPAREL GROUP INTL CORP
Also Called: True Grit
884 W 16th St, Newport Beach (92663-2802)
PHONE..................................949 548-9095
Bruce W Bennett III, *CEO*
John R Provine, *Treasurer*
Liz Bennett, *Vice Pres*
▲ EMP: 28
SQ FT: 7,000
SALES (est): 2.8MM **Privately Held**
SIC: **2341** 2329 2342 5961 Women's & children's underwear; men's & boys' sportswear & athletic clothing; bras, girdles & allied garments; mail order house; women's apparel, mail order

(P-3441)
FARR WEST FASHIONS
580 Cathedral Dr, Aptos (95003-3407)
PHONE..................................831 661-5039
Charles Farr, *President*
John E Farr Jr, *Chairman*
Iris Farr, *Admin Sec*
EMP: 13
SQ FT: 9,600
SALES (est): 792.1K **Privately Held**
WEB: www.farrwest.com
SIC: **2341** Chemises, camisoles & teddies: women's & children's; nightgowns & negligees: women's & children's; women's & children's nightwear

(P-3442)
HONEST COMPANY INC (PA)
12130 Millennium Ste 500, Playa Vista (90094-2946)
PHONE..................................310 917-9199
Nick Vlahos, *CEO*
David Parker, *COO*
Jessica Alba, *Officer*
Christopher Gavigan, *Officer*
Janis Hoyt, *Officer*
◆ EMP: 187
SALES (est): 108.4MM **Privately Held**
SIC: **2341** 2833 Panties: women's, misses', children's & infants'; vitamins, natural or synthetic: bulk, uncompounded

(P-3443)
LITO
3730 Union Pacific Ave, Los Angeles (90023-3229)
PHONE..................................323 260-4692
Lee Garvin, *Manager*
▲ EMP: 40 EST: 2013
SALES (est): 1.4MM **Privately Held**
SIC: **2341** Women's & children's undergarments

(P-3444)
MAIDENFORM LLC
100 Citadel Dr Ste 323, Commerce (90040-1592)
PHONE..................................323 724-9558
EMP: 178
SALES (corp-wide): 5.7B **Publicly Held**
SIC: **2341**
HQ: Maidenform Llc
1000 E Hanes Mill Rd
Winston Salem NC 27105
336 519-8080

(P-3445)
NATIONAL CORSET SUPPLY HOUSE (PA)
Also Called: Louden Madelon
3240 E 26th St, Vernon (90058-8008)
PHONE..................................323 261-0265
Roy Schlobohm, *CEO*
Kirk Schlobohm, *Controller*
Dora Schlobohm, *Persnl Mgr*
Al Saenz, *Plant Mgr*
Steve Boxer, *Sales Executive*
▲ EMP: 65 EST: 1948
SQ FT: 25,000

SALES (est): 10.7MM **Privately Held**
WEB: www.shirleyofhollywood.com
SIC: **2341** 5137 Women's & children's undergarments; corsets

(P-3446)
NEFFUL USA INC
18563 Gale Ave, City of Industry (91748-1339)
PHONE..................................626 839-6657
Toshiya Kanijo, *President*
Akira Mori, *Vice Pres*
▲ EMP: 10
SALES (est): 1.2MM **Privately Held**
WEB: www.neffulusa.com
SIC: **2341** Women's & children's undergarments

(P-3447)
SAN FRANCISCO NETWORK
Also Called: Sunday Brunch
2171 Francisco Blvd E G, San Rafael (94901-5542)
PHONE..................................415 468-1110
Leonard Eber, *Ch of Bd*
Karen Neuberger, *President*
Richard N Compton, *CFO*
▲ EMP: 33
SQ FT: 3,000
SALES (est): 1.9MM **Privately Held**
SIC: **2341** Women's & children's nightwear

(P-3448)
SELECTRA INDUSTRIES CORP
5166 Alcoa Ave, Vernon (90058-3716)
PHONE..................................323 581-8500
John Neman, *President*
Malek Neman, *CFO*
Mark Neman, *Admin Sec*
▲ EMP: 85 EST: 2000
SQ FT: 30,000
SALES (est): 10.9MM **Privately Held**
WEB: www.selectraindustries.com
SIC: **2341** 2339 Women's & children's underwear; sportswear, women's

(P-3449)
SUNNYSIDE LLC
Also Called: Sundry Clothing
3763 S Hill St, Los Angeles (90007-4339)
PHONE..................................213 745-3070
Matthieu Leblan, *Mng Member*
Amy Willens, *Controller*
EMP: 10 EST: 2014
SALES (est): 1.7MM **Privately Held**
SIC: **2341** 5621 5961 Women's & children's undergarments; ready-to-wear apparel, women's;

(P-3450)
T L CARE INC
1459 San Mateo Ave, South San Francisco (94080-6504)
P.O. Box 77087, San Francisco (94107-0087)
PHONE..................................650 589-3659
Estelle Lee, *CEO*
R Timothy Leister, *CFO*
Diane Leister, *Admin Sec*
▲ EMP: 10
SQ FT: 5,000
SALES: 5MM **Privately Held**
WEB: www.tlcare.com
SIC: **2341** 2342 2385 5137 Women's & children's undergarments; maternity bras & corsets; waterproof outerwear; bibs, waterproof: made from purchased materials; diaper covers, waterproof: made from purchased materials; baby goods; diapers; infants' wear; infant furnishings & equipment

2342 Brassieres, Girdles & Garments

(P-3451)
BRAGEL INTERNATIONAL INC
Also Called: Brava
3383 Pomona Blvd, Pomona (91768-3297)
PHONE..................................909 598-8808
Clotilde Chen, *CEO*
Kenny Chen, *Shareholder*
Alice Chen, *Treasurer*
▲ EMP: 45

SQ FT: 30,000
SALES (est): 6.9MM **Privately Held**
WEB: www.bragel.com
SIC: **2342** Brassieres

(P-3452)
FOH GROUP INC (PA)
Also Called: Movie Star
6255 W Sunset Blvd # 2212, Los Angeles (90028-7403)
PHONE..................................323 466-5151
Thomas J Lynch, *Ch of Bd*
Thomas Rende, *CFO*
◆ EMP: 41
SQ FT: 23,000
SALES: 86.5MM **Privately Held**
SIC: **2342** 2339 5621 5632 Bras, girdles & allied garments; women's & misses' outerwear; women's & misses' athletic clothing & sportswear; jeans: women's, misses' & juniors'; women's clothing stores; ready-to-wear apparel, women's; teenage apparel; women's accessory & specialty stores; apparel accessories; women's dancewear, hosiery & lingerie; handbags; women's & children's nightwear

(P-3453)
INSTYLE PRINTING INC
2115 Central Ave, South El Monte (91733-2117)
PHONE..................................626 575-2725
Vicky Yang, *President*
EMP: 30
SALES (est): 1.5MM **Privately Held**
SIC: **2342** 2326 Foundation garments, women's; industrial garments, men's & boys'

(P-3454)
METRIC PRODUCTS INC (PA)
4630 Leahy St, Culver City (90232-3515)
PHONE..................................310 815-9000
Shirley Magidson, *President*
Rita Haft, *Vice Pres*
Debra Magidson, *Admin Sec*
Ted Quantz, *VP Sales*
▲ EMP: 20
SQ FT: 25,000
SALES (est): 9.8MM **Privately Held**
WEB: www.metric-products.com
SIC: **2342** 3496 Brassieres; fabrics, woven wire

(P-3455)
MSA WEST LLC
16161 Ventura Blvd C326, Encino (91436-2522)
PHONE..................................213 536-9880
ARI Aalfon, *Mng Member*
◆ EMP: 20 EST: 2016
SALES (est): 2MM **Privately Held**
SIC: **2342** Bras, girdles & allied garments

(P-3456)
OFFLINE INC (PA)
2250 Maple Ave, Los Angeles (90011-1190)
PHONE..................................213 742-9001
Charles Park, *President*
Nina Kim, *Creative Dir*
Karen Park, *Admin Sec*
▲ EMP: 45
SQ FT: 50,000
SALES (est): 6.2MM **Privately Held**
WEB: www.offlineinc.com
SIC: **2342** 2326 Foundation garments, women's; industrial garments, men's & boys'

(P-3457)
ORANGE CORPORATION
1430 S Grande Vista Ave, Los Angeles (90023-3717)
PHONE..................................323 266-0700
OK Kyong Lee, *President*
EMP: 10 EST: 1997
SQ FT: 20,000
SALES (est): 1MM **Privately Held**
SIC: **2342** Foundation garments, women's

(P-3458)
SOFTMAX INC
Also Called: Greige Gods Boking PO AP Group
2341 E 49th St Fl 2, Vernon (90058-2820)
PHONE..................................213 718-2100
David Jung, *CEO*
EMP: 12
SQ FT: 6,000
SALES: 500K **Privately Held**
SIC: **2342** 5137 Foundation garments, women's; women's & children's clothing

(P-3459)
SUGARED + BRONZED LLC
13033 Ventura Blvd, Studio City (91604-2219)
PHONE..................................747 264-0477
EMP: 74
SALES (corp-wide): 5.5MM **Privately Held**
SIC: **2342** Bras, girdles & allied garments
PA: Sugared + Bronzed, Llc
34241 Pacific Coast Hwy
Dana Point CA 92629
410 493-3467

2353 Hats, Caps & Millinery

(P-3460)
AGRON INC
2440 S Sepulveda Blvd # 201, Los Angeles (90064-1748)
PHONE..................................310 473-7223
Wade Siegel, *President*
Ron Adams, *Sales Mgr*
Charlie Digiulian, *Cust Mgr*
Greg Thomsen, *Director*
Nicholas Setter, *Manager*
▲ EMP: 60
SQ FT: 10,000
SALES (est): 9.5MM **Privately Held**
WEB: www.agron.com
SIC: **2353** 2393 3949 3171 Hats, caps & millinery; canvas bags; sporting & athletic goods; women's handbags & purses

(P-3461)
AUGUST HAT COMPANY INC (PA)
Also Called: August Accessories
850 Calle Plano Ste M, Camarillo (93012-8570)
PHONE..................................805 983-4651
Roque Valladares, *President*
Ann Valladares, *Corp Secy*
▲ EMP: 23
SQ FT: 11,000
SALES (est): 3.7MM **Privately Held**
WEB: www.augustacc.com
SIC: **2353** 2381 2339 Hats, caps & millinery; fabric dress & work gloves; scarves, hoods, headbands, etc.: women's

(P-3462)
CALI-FAME LOS ANGELES INC
Also Called: Kennedy Athletics
20934 S Santa Fe Ave, Carson (90810-1131)
PHONE..................................310 747-5263
Michael G Kennedy, *CEO*
Brian Kennedy, *President*
Linelle Kennedy, *Corp Secy*
Tim Kennedy, *Vice Pres*
Timothy Kennedy, *Vice Pres*
▲ EMP: 92
SQ FT: 30,000
SALES (est): 11.2MM **Privately Held**
WEB: www.califame.com
SIC: **2353** Uniform hats & caps

(P-3463)
CALIFORNIA CUSTOM CAPS
2319 Sastre Ave, South El Monte (91733-2655)
PHONE..................................626 454-1766
Robn Trung Tran, *Principal*
EMP: 25
SALES (est): 2.1MM **Privately Held**
WEB: www.californiacustomcaps.com
SIC: **2353** Hats & caps

P R O D U C T S & S V C S

(P-3464)
CAREER CAP CORPORATION
1680 Industrial Blvd, Chula Vista
(91911-3922)
PHONE..................................619 575-2277
Jim Ghashghaee, *President*
Jack Frise, *Vice Pres*
EMP: 48
SQ FT: 5,100
SALES: 1.6MM **Privately Held**
WEB: www.careercap.com
SIC: 2353 Baseball caps

(P-3465)
GOORIN BROS INC (PA)
1890 Bryant St Ste 208, San Francisco
(94110-7410)
PHONE..................................415 431-9196
Benjamin T Goorin, *CEO*
Jim Curly, *CFO*
Vincent Laurel, *Accounting Mgr*
Mercy Ung, *Production*
Nathaniel Pearce, *Marketing Staff*
▲ EMP: 30 EST: 1895
SALES (est): 12.9MM **Privately Held**
WEB: www.goorin.com
SIC: 2353 Hats & caps

(P-3466)
GOORIN BROSINC
23787 Eichler St Ste E, Hayward
(94545-2760)
EMP: 15
SALES (corp-wide): 6MM **Privately Held**
SIC: 2353
PA: Goorin Bros.Inc.
    1269 Howard St
    San Francisco CA 94110
    415 431-9196

(P-3467)
HEADMASTER INC (PA)
3000 S Croddy Way, Santa Ana
(92704-6305)
PHONE..................................714 556-5244
Dong J Park, *President*
Jimmy J Park, *Vice Pres*
▲ EMP: 21
SQ FT: 35,000
SALES (est): 1.9MM **Privately Held**
WEB: www.headmaster.com
SIC: 2353 Hats: cloth, straw & felt

(P-3468)
LEGENDARY HOLDINGS INC
Also Called: Legendary Headwear
2295 Paseo De Las America, San Diego
(92154-7909)
PHONE..................................619 872-6100
▲ EMP: 38
SQ FT: 13,300
SALES (est): 5MM **Privately Held**
WEB: www.legendaryholdings.com
SIC: 2353 Hats, caps & millinery

(P-3469)
LOUISE GREEN MILLINERY CO INC
1616 Cotner Ave, Los Angeles
(90025-3304)
PHONE..................................310 479-1881
Lawrence Green, *President*
Louise Green, *Partner*
▲ EMP: 12
SQ FT: 9,000
SALES (est): 1.3MM **Privately Held**
WEB: www.louisegreen.com
SIC: 2353 5137 Millinery; women's & children's clothing

(P-3470)
NIKE INC
20001 Ellipse, Foothill Ranch
(92610-3001)
PHONE..................................949 768-4000
Matt Ross, *Manager*
EMP: 15
SALES (corp-wide): 39.1B **Publicly Held**
WEB: www.nike.com
SIC: 2353 5137 5136 Baseball caps; women's & children's clothing; men's & boys' clothing
PA: Nike, Inc.
    1 Sw Bowerman Dr
    Beaverton OR 97005
    503 671-6453

(P-3471)
ONE HAT ONE HAND LLC
1335 Yosemite Ave, San Francisco
(94124-3319)
PHONE..................................415 822-2020
Chrisray Collins,
Erin Johnson, *Vice Pres*
Marcus Guillard,
EMP: 42 EST: 2008
SQ FT: 19,000
SALES (est): 3.7MM **Privately Held**
SIC: 2353 Hats, caps & millinery

2361 Children's & Infants' Dresses & Blouses

(P-3472)
A THANKS MILLION INC
8195 Mercury Ct Ste 140, San Diego
(92111-1231)
PHONE..................................858 432-7744
Lowell J Cohen, *CEO*
Peter Mouostaos, *President*
Ian Barrow, *COO*
Greg Dona, *General Mgr*
◆ EMP: 19
SALES (est): 2.6MM **Privately Held**
SIC: 2361 2329 T-shirts & tops: girls', children's & infants'; shirt & slack suits: men's, youths' & boys'

(P-3473)
ALL ACCESS APPAREL INC (PA)
Also Called: Self Esteem
1515 Gage Rd, Montebello (90640-6613)
PHONE..................................323 889-4300
Richard Clareman, *CEO*
Michael Conway, *CFO*
Andrea Rankin, *Exec VP*
◆ EMP: 134
SQ FT: 122,000
SALES (est): 119.3MM **Privately Held**
WEB: www.selfesteemclothing.com
SIC: 2361 2335 2331 Girls' & children's dresses, blouses & shirts; women's, juniors' & misses' dresses; women's & misses' blouses & shirts

(P-3474)
AST SPORTSWEAR INC (PA)
2701 E Imperial Hwy, Brea (92821-6713)
P.O. Box 17219, Anaheim (92817-7219)
PHONE..................................714 223-2030
Shoaib Dadabhoy, *CEO*
Taher Dadabhoy, *Admin Sec*
▲ EMP: 56
SQ FT: 42,000
SALES (est): 64.1MM **Privately Held**
WEB: www.astsportswear.com
SIC: 2361 2331 5699 T-shirts & tops: girls', children's & infants'; T-shirts & tops, women's: made from purchased materials; sports apparel

(P-3475)
AVALON APPAREL LLC (PA)
Also Called: Disorderly Kids
2520 W 6th St, Los Angeles (90057-3174)
PHONE..................................323 581-3511
Elliot Schutzer, *Mng Member*
Dede Venegas, *COO*
Terri Cohen,
Jill Grossman,
Jason Schutzer,
EMP: 165
SQ FT: 5,000
SALES (est): 17.5MM **Privately Held**
SIC: 2361 Girls' & children's dresses, blouses & shirts

(P-3476)
COTTON GENERATION INC
Also Called: Trouble At The Mill
6051 Maywood Ave, Huntington Park
(90255-3211)
PHONE..................................323 581-8555
Mohamad Toluee, *President*
Masoud Parvinjah, *Vice Pres*
EMP: 50
SQ FT: 45,000
SALES (est): 4.6MM **Privately Held**
SIC: 2361 2339 7389 T-shirts & tops: girls', children's & infants'; sportswear, women's; textile & apparel services

(P-3477)
CRESTONE LLC
Also Called: Hazel Clothes
1852 E 46th St, Vernon (90058-1948)
PHONE..................................323 588-8857
Robert Cho, *Mng Member*
Maria Madriz, *Production*
Ruben Romero, *Sales Mgr*
Janet Cho, *Mng Member*
▲ EMP: 30
SQ FT: 10,000
SALES (est): 4MM **Privately Held**
SIC: 2361 2331 Girls' & children's dresses, blouses & shirts; women's & misses' blouses & shirts

(P-3478)
EVY OF CALIFORNIA INC (HQ)
Also Called: La Touch
2042 Garfield Ave, Commerce
(90040-1804)
P.O. Box 812030, Los Angeles (90081-0018)
PHONE..................................213 746-4647
Kurt Krieser, *President*
Kevin Krieser, *COO*
Checrag Peer, *CFO*
Cheryl Kimble, *Software Engr*
Esther Aguire, *Human Res Dir*
▲ EMP: 136
SQ FT: 50,000
SALES (est): 16.5MM
SALES (corp-wide): 670.2MM **Privately Held**
WEB: www.evy.com
SIC: 2361 2369 Dresses: girls', children's & infants'; warm-up, jogging & sweat suits: girls' & children's
PA: Hybrid Promotions, Llc
    10711 Walker St
    Cypress CA 90630
    714 952-3866

(P-3479)
JESSICA MCCLINTOCK INC (PA)
2307 Broadway St, San Francisco
(94115-1291)
PHONE..................................415 553-8200
Jessica Mc Clintock, *President*
▲ EMP: 150 EST: 1970
SQ FT: 120,000
SALES (est): 53MM **Privately Held**
WEB: www.jessicamcclintock.com
SIC: 2361 2335 2844 Dresses: girls', children's & infants'; women's, juniors' & misses' dresses; perfumes, natural or synthetic

(P-3480)
KENNETH CRONON INC
10413 Haines Canyon Ave, Tujunga
(91042-2031)
PHONE..................................818 632-4972
Kenneth Cronon, *President*
EMP: 12
SALES (est): 401.9K **Privately Held**
SIC: 2361 Girls' & children's dresses, blouses & shirts

(P-3481)
KWDZ MANUFACTURING LLC (PA)
337 S Anderson St, Los Angeles
(90033-3742)
PHONE..................................323 526-3526
Vera Campbell,
Gene Bonilla,
▲ EMP: 75
SQ FT: 45,000
SALES (est): 19.5MM **Privately Held**
SIC: 2361 T-shirts & tops: girls', children's & infants'

(P-3482)
L A S A M INC
Also Called: Natural Elements
3844 S Santa Fe Ave, Vernon
(90058-1713)
PHONE..................................323 586-8717
Sandy Maroney, *President*
Dennis Maroney, *Admin Sec*
EMP: 14 EST: 1981
SQ FT: 5,000

SALES (est): 1MM **Privately Held**
WEB: www.lasam.net
SIC: 2361 Girls' & children's dresses, blouses & shirts

(P-3483)
LIDA CHILDRENS WEAR INC
3113 E California Blvd, Pasadena
(91107-5352)
PHONE..................................626 967-8868
◆ EMP: 50
SALES (est): 3.7MM **Privately Held**
WEB: www.lidachildren.com
SIC: 2361 2311 2369 2335

(P-3484)
MARNA RO LLC
818 S Broadway Ste 800, Los Angeles
(90014-3228)
PHONE..................................310 801-5788
Dee Drexler, *CEO*
EMP: 10
SALES (est): 1.2MM **Privately Held**
SIC: 2361 2335 3171 3151 Girls' & children's dresses, blouses & shirts; women's, juniors' & misses' dresses; women's handbags & purses; leather gloves & mittens; shirt & slack suits: men's, youths' & boys'

(P-3485)
MISYD CORP (PA)
Also Called: Ruby Rox
30 Fremont Pl, Los Angeles (90005-3858)
PHONE..................................213 742-1800
Robert Borman, *President*
Joseph Hanasab, *CFO*
▲ EMP: 79
SQ FT: 35,000
SALES (est): 11.5MM **Privately Held**
SIC: 2361 Shirts: girls', children's & infants'

(P-3486)
PEEK ARENT YOU CURIOUS INC (PA)
425 2nd St Ste 405, San Francisco
(94107-1420)
PHONE..................................415 512-7335
Maria Cristina Canales, *CEO*
Jason Klein, *CFO*
Gregory Onken, *Admin Sec*
▲ EMP: 86
SQ FT: 2,000
SALES (est): 7.8MM **Privately Held**
SIC: 2361 2369 5641 5661 Girls' & children's dresses, blouses & shirts; girls' & children's outerwear; children's & infants' wear stores; children's shoes

(P-3487)
ROSE GENUINE INC
Also Called: Jinelle
834 S Broadway Ste 1100, Los Angeles
(90014-3510)
P.O. Box 555970 (90055-0970)
PHONE..................................213 747-4120
John Golshan, *President*
Mike Golshan, *Admin Sec*
▲ EMP: 15
SQ FT: 15,000
SALES (est): 2.1MM **Privately Held**
SIC: 2361 Dresses: girls', children's & infants'

(P-3488)
RSDG INTERNATIONAL INC
2127 Aralia St, Newport Beach
(92660-4131)
P.O. Box 4032, Diamond Bar (91765-0032)
PHONE..................................626 256-4190
Ralph Silva, *President*
▲ EMP: 24
SQ FT: 9,000
SALES: 6MM **Privately Held**
SIC: 2361 Girls' & children's dresses, blouses & shirts

(P-3489)
S SEDGHI INC (PA)
Also Called: Lavender Alley
2416 W 7th St, Los Angeles (90057-3904)
P.O. Box 361338 (90036-9330)
PHONE..................................213 745-2019
Shohreh Sedghi, *Principal*
▲ EMP: 22

▲ = Import ▼=Export
◆ =Import/Export

SALES (est): 2.2MM **Privately Held**
SIC: 2361 Girls' & children's dresses, blouses & shirts

(P-3490)
WILDTHINGS SNAP-ONS INC
4 De Luca Pl, San Rafael (94901-3909)
P.O. Box 3635 (94912-3635)
PHONE..................................415 457-0112
Patricia Phillips, *President*
▲ EMP: 10
SQ FT: 1,500
SALES: 500K **Privately Held**
SIC: 2361 T-shirts & tops: girls', children's & infants'

(P-3491)
WINSTAR TEXTILE INC
16815 E Johnson Dr, City of Industry (91745-2417)
PHONE..................................626 357-1133
Der Yeu Lu, *CEO*
Davis Lu, *President*
Huimin Dou, *Principal*
▲ EMP: 20 EST: 1999
SQ FT: 3,400
SALES (est): 3.2MM **Privately Held**
WEB: www.winstartextile.com
SIC: 2361 Blouses: girls', children's & infants'; men's & boys' trousers & slacks

---

2369 Girls' & Infants' Outerwear, NEC

(P-3492)
BABY GUESS INC
1444 S Alameda St, Los Angeles (90021-2433)
PHONE..................................213 765-3100
Maurice Marciano, *Ch of Bd*
EMP: 50
SALES (est): 356.1K
SALES (corp-wide): 2.6B **Publicly Held**
WEB: www.guess.com
SIC: 2369 Jackets: girls', children's & infants'; skirts: girls', children's & infants'; slacks: girls' & children's
PA: Guess , Inc.
1444 S Alameda St
Los Angeles CA 90021
213 765-3100

(P-3493)
FLAP HAPPY INC
2857 E 11th St, Los Angeles (90023-3405)
PHONE..................................310 453-3527
Laurie Snyder, *President*
Walter Snyder, *Vice Pres*
EMP: 20
SQ FT: 12,000
SALES (est): 3MM **Privately Held**
WEB: www.flaphappy.com
SIC: 2369 2353 Girls' & children's outerwear; hats & caps

(P-3494)
MACK & REISS INC
Also Called: Biscotti and Kate Mack
5601 San Leandro St Ste 3, Oakland (94621-4433)
PHONE..................................510 434-9122
Bernadette Reiss, *President*
Robert Mack, *Corp Secy*
▲ EMP: 85
SQ FT: 75,000
SALES (est): 9.5MM **Privately Held**
WEB: www.biscottiinc.com
SIC: 2369 Girls' & children's outerwear

(P-3495)
RMLA INC
Also Called: La Chic
1972 E 20th St, Vernon (90058-1005)
PHONE..................................213 749-4333
Ralph Maya, *CEO*
Jan Adamcyk, *Bd of Directors*
▲ EMP: 55
SALES (est): 7.2MM **Privately Held**
WEB: www.rmla.com
SIC: 2369 Girls' & children's outerwear

(P-3496)
TRLG INTERMEDIATE HOLDINGS LLC (PA)
1888 Rosecrans Ave, Manhattan Beach (90266-3712)
PHONE..................................323 266-3072
Dalli Snyder, *CFO*
Alan Weiss, *Vice Pres*
Eugene Davis, *Director*
Tony Di Paolo, *Director*
Lisa Gavales, *Director*
◆ EMP: 12
SQ FT: 119,000
SALES: 350MM **Privately Held**
SIC: 2369 2325 2339 Girls' & children's outerwear; men's & boys' trousers & slacks; women's & misses' outerwear

(P-3497)
VESTURE GROUP INCORPORATED
Also Called: Pinky Los Angeles
3405 W Pacific Ave, Burbank (91505-1555)
PHONE..................................818 842-0200
Robert Galishoff, *CEO*
Gail Lupacchini, *Vice Pres*
▲ EMP: 48
SQ FT: 3,500
SALES (est): 7.1MM **Privately Held**
SIC: 2369 2335 Skirts: girls', children's & infants'; women's, juniors' & misses' dresses

---

2371 Fur Goods

(P-3498)
BOND FURS INC
114 W Lime Ave, Monrovia (91016-2841)
PHONE..................................626 471-9912
Steven Zaslaw, *President*
EMP: 12
SQ FT: 3,000
SALES (est): 963.2K **Privately Held**
WEB: www.bondfurs.com
SIC: 2371 5632 3999 Coats, fur; fur apparel, made to custom order; furs

(P-3499)
FUR ACCENTS LLC
349 W Grove Ave, Orange (92865-3205)
PHONE..................................714 403-5286
Steven Goodyear, *Mng Member*
EMP: 15
SALES: 2MM **Privately Held**
SIC: 2371 5632 Fur goods; fur apparel

(P-3500)
LARRY B LLC
Also Called: Dicker & Dicker Beverly Hills
215 S Robertson Blvd, Beverly Hills (90211-2810)
PHONE..................................310 652-3877
Lawrence Charles Becker,
EMP: 11
SQ FT: 1,200
SALES (est): 942K **Privately Held**
SIC: 2371 5199 5632 Apparel, fur; leather, leather goods & furs; fur apparel

(P-3501)
SEIRUS INNOVATIVE ACC INC
Also Called: Seirus Innovation
13975 Danielson St, Poway (92064-6889)
PHONE..................................858 513-1212
Michael Carey, *President*
Wendy Carey, *CFO*
Joe Edwards, *Treasurer*
Joseph H Edwards, *Treasurer*
Robert Murphy, *Vice Pres*
▲ EMP: 65
SQ FT: 11,000
SALES (est): 4.9MM **Privately Held**
WEB: www.seirus.com
SIC: 2371 Apparel, fur

2381 Dress & Work Gloves

(P-3502)
MECHANIX WEAR LLC (PA)
28525 Witherspoon Pkwy, Valencia (91355-5417)
PHONE..................................800 222-4296

Michael Hale, *CEO*
Bari Waalk, *COO*
Jamie Mearns, *CFO*
Kevin Reynolds, *CFO*
Sherrie Hale, *Admin Sec*
▲ EMP: 98
SQ FT: 24,000
SALES (est): 23.6MM **Privately Held**
WEB: www.mechanixwear.com
SIC: 2381 7218 Fabric dress & work gloves; safety glove supply

(P-3503)
ORBITA CORP (PA)
Also Called: Estam
1136 Crocker St, Los Angeles (90021-2014)
PHONE..................................213 746-4783
Dae Seung Park, *President*
▲ EMP: 15
SALES (est): 4.5MM **Privately Held**
SIC: 2381 Fabric dress & work gloves

2384 Robes & Dressing Gowns

(P-3504)
TERRY TOWN CORPORATION
8851 Kerns St Ste 100, San Diego (92154-6298)
PHONE..................................619 421-5354
Saip Ereren, *CEO*
Norma Lozano,
Aaron Bradley, *Manager*
Jasmine Sengur, *Manager*
◆ EMP: 19
SALES: 16.7MM **Privately Held**
SIC: 2384 5023 5719 Bathrobes, men's & women's: made from purchased materials; linens & towels; bedding (sheets, blankets, spreads & pillows)

(P-3505)
VICTOIRE LLC
Also Called: Robeworks
955 S Meridian Ave, Alhambra (91803-1249)
PHONE..................................323 225-0101
Vincent Rojas,
Kathleen Rojas, *Exec Dir*
Kenneth Nim,
EMP: 12
SQ FT: 5,000
SALES (est): 1MM **Privately Held**
SIC: 2384 Robes & dressing gowns

2386 Leather & Sheep Lined Clothing

(P-3506)
AJG INC
Also Called: Astrologie California
7220 E Slauson Ave, Commerce (90040-3625)
PHONE..................................323 346-0171
Angelo Ghailian, *CEO*
▲ EMP: 20
SALES (est): 8.9MM **Privately Held**
SIC: 2386 5131 5199 Leather & sheep-lined clothing; knit fabrics; fabrics, yarns & knit goods

(P-3507)
AWCC CORPORATION
434 N Coast Hwy, Laguna Beach (92651-1630)
PHONE..................................949 497-6313
Bob Turner, *President*
▲ EMP: 10
SALES (est): 1MM **Privately Held**
WEB: www.pacificrimdirect.com
SIC: 2386 Garments, leather

(P-3508)
BARRY COSTELLO
319 Broad St, Nevada City (95959-2405)
PHONE..................................530 265-3300
Margaret Costello, *Manager*
EMP: 14

SALES (corp-wide): 1.7MM **Privately Held**
WEB: www.furtraders.com
SIC: 2386 Leather & sheep-lined clothing
PA: Barry Costello
233 Broad St
Nevada City CA
530 265-3300

(P-3509)
BATES INDUSTRIES INC
Also Called: Bates Leathers
3671 Industry Ave Ste C5, Lakewood (90712-4159)
PHONE..................................562 426-8668
Dana L Grindle, *President*
Dawn Grindle, *President*
Lori Montez, *Treasurer*
▲ EMP: 10 EST: 1939
SQ FT: 4,300
SALES (est): 660K **Privately Held**
WEB: www.batesleathers.com
SIC: 2386 Garments, leather

(P-3510)
CHROME HEARTS LLC (PA)
921 N Mansfield Ave, Los Angeles (90038-2311)
PHONE..................................323 957-7544
Richard Stark, *Mng Member*
Adrian Taylor, *CFO*
Peter Struthers, *Office Mgr*
John Lippian, *IT/INT Sup*
Alexa-Jade Lawson, *Technology*
▲ EMP: 50
SQ FT: 50,000
SALES (est): 16.4MM **Privately Held**
WEB: www.chromehearts.com
SIC: 2386 3911 2511 2371 Leather & sheep-lined clothing; jewelry, precious metal; wood household furniture; fur goods

(P-3511)
CORONADO LEATHER CO INC
1961 Main St, San Diego (92113-2129)
PHONE..................................619 238-0265
Brent Laulom, *President*
EMP: 15
SQ FT: 2,100
SALES (est): 2MM **Privately Held**
WEB: www.coronadoleather.com
SIC: 2386 3111 Garments, leather; handbag leather

(P-3512)
DISTINCTIVE INDS TEXAS INC
9419 Ann St, Santa Fe Springs (90670-2613)
PHONE..................................323 889-5766
Dwight Forrester, *Branch Mgr*
EMP: 34
SALES (corp-wide): 13.6MM **Privately Held**
SIC: 2386 Coats & jackets, leather & sheep-lined
PA: Distinctive Industries Of Texas, Inc.
4516 Seton Pkwy 135
Austin TX 78752
512 491-3500

(P-3513)
DISTINCTIVE INDS TEXAS INC
Also Called: Roadwire Distinctive Inds
10618 Shoemaker Ave, Santa Fe Springs (90670-4038)
PHONE..................................512 491-3500
Dwight Forrester, *Principal*
EMP: 28
SALES (corp-wide): 13.6MM **Privately Held**
SIC: 2386 Leather & sheep-lined clothing
PA: Distinctive Industries Of Texas, Inc.
4516 Seton Pkwy 135
Austin TX 78752
512 491-3500

(P-3514)
EURO BELLO USA
10660 Wilshire Blvd, Los Angeles (90024-4522)
PHONE..................................213 446-2818
Bijan Israel, *President*
Natalio Oscar, *Manager*
EMP: 46 EST: 2014
SQ FT: 20,000

P R O D U C T S & S V C S

SALES: 18MM **Privately Held**
SIC: **2386** 2211 Garments, leather; apparel & outerwear fabrics, cotton

(P-3515)
GB SPORT SF LLC
Also Called: Golden Bear Sportswear
200 Potrero Ave, San Francisco
(94103-4815)
PHONE.....................415 863-6171
Ronald Gilmere, *Mng Member*
EMP: 20
SALES (est): 508.6K **Privately Held**
SIC: **2386** Leather & sheep-lined clothing

(P-3516)
HD GARMENT SOLUTIONS INC
13351 Riverside Dr, Sherman Oaks
(91423-2542)
PHONE.....................323 581-6000
Ron Mansuri, *President*
EMP: 20 EST: 2011
SQ FT: 2,000
SALES (est): 1.7MM **Privately Held**
SIC: **2386** Garments, leather

(P-3517)
JEJOMI DESIGNS INC
Also Called: Long Pine Leathers
2626 Fruitland Ave, Vernon (90058-2220)
PHONE.....................323 584-4211
Jorge Castellon, *President*
Cecilia Polanco, *Treasurer*
Susan Castellon, *Vice Pres*
▲ EMP: 35
SQ FT: 9,200
SALES: 3.6MM **Privately Held**
SIC: **2386** Coats & jackets, leather & sheep-lined

(P-3518)
JOHNSON LEATHER CORPORATION (PA)
1833 Polk St, San Francisco (94109-3003)
PHONE.....................415 775-7393
Johnson Tam, *President*
▲ EMP: 12
SQ FT: 3,000
SALES (est): 1MM **Privately Held**
WEB: www.johnsonleather.com
SIC: **2386** 5699 5136 5137 Garments, leather; leather garments; leather & sheep lined clothing, men's & boys'; leather & sheep lined clothing, women's & children's

(P-3519)
KRASNES INC
Also Called: Cop Shopper
2222 Commercial St, San Diego
(92113-1111)
PHONE.....................619 232-2066
Jerry Krasne, *President*
Gail Wilson, *CFO*
Kurt Krasne, *Vice Pres*
Susie Godinez, *Sales Staff*
▲ EMP: 90
SQ FT: 28,000
SALES (est): 10.6MM **Privately Held**
WEB: www.triplek.com
SIC: **2386** 3484 Leather & sheep-lined clothing; small arms

(P-3520)
MR S LEATHER
Also Called: Fetters U.S.A.
385 8th St, San Francisco (94103-4423)
PHONE.....................415 863-7764
Richard Hunter, *President*
Tchukon Hunter, *Vice Pres*
Jonathan Schroder, *General Mgr*
▲ EMP: 45
SQ FT: 15,000
SALES: 4.8MM **Privately Held**
WEB: www.mr-s-leather-fetters.com
SIC: **2386** 5699 5136 Garments, leather; leather garments; men's & boys' clothing; men's & boys' furnishings

(P-3521)
OHECK LLC
5830 Bickett St, Huntington Park
(90255-2627)
PHONE.....................323 923-2700
Eric Jweon, *Mng Member*
EMP: 250 EST: 2012

SQ FT: 52,000
SALES (est): 25MM **Privately Held**
SIC: **2386** Garments, leather

(P-3522)
SCULLY SPORTSWEAR INC
Also Called: Oakridge
1701 Pacific Ave, Oxnard (93033-2745)
PHONE.....................805 483-6339
Daniel J Scully III, *CEO*
Robert Swink, *Vice Pres*
Laina Tucker, *Graphic Designe*
Linda Hanson, *Human Res Mgr*
Charlane Gage, *Sales Staff*
▲ EMP: 60
SQ FT: 80,000
SALES (est): 8.6MM **Privately Held**
SIC: **2386** 5099 Coats & jackets, leather & sheep-lined; garments, leather; luggage; cases, carrying

(P-3523)
SUPERLAMB INC
Also Called: Sheepskin Specialties
8026 Miramar Rd, San Diego
(92126-4320)
PHONE.....................858 566-2031
Lindsay Gulliver, *CEO*
Elizabeth Gulliver, *Vice Pres*
▼ EMP: 15
SQ FT: 7,000
SALES (est): 1.6MM **Privately Held**
WEB: www.superlambfootwear.com
SIC: **2386** Leather & sheep-lined clothing

(P-3524)
TEX SHOEMAKER & SON INC
19034 E Donington St, Glendora
(91741-1900)
PHONE.....................909 592-2071
EMP: 10
SQ FT: 32,000
SALES: 300K **Privately Held**
WEB: www.texshoemaker.com
SIC: **2386** 5941 3172

(P-3525)
WALZ CAPS INC
2215 La Mirada Dr, Vista (92081-8828)
PHONE.....................760 683-9259
Michael Gilstrap, *President*
Michael R Gilstrap, *President*
EMP: 30
SALES (est): 289.8K **Privately Held**
SIC: **2386** Hats & caps, leather

2387 Apparel Belts

(P-3526)
ARCADE BELTS INC (PA)
150 Alpine Meadows Rd, Alpine Meadows
(96146-9880)
P.O. Box 2728, Olympic Valley (96146-2728)
PHONE.....................530 580-8089
Tristan Queen, *President*
David Bronkie, *Corp Secy*
EMP: 22
SALES (est): 7.9MM **Privately Held**
SIC: **2387** Apparel belts

(P-3527)
BELTS BY SIMON INC
14382 Chambers Rd, Tustin (92780-6912)
PHONE.....................714 573-0303
Saeed Tavassoli, *President*
▲ EMP: 65
SQ FT: 4,000
SALES (est): 6.3MM **Privately Held**
SIC: **2387** Apparel belts

(P-3528)
BRIGHTON COLLECTIBLES LLC
10250 Santa Monica Blvd, Los Angeles
(90067-6482)
PHONE.....................626 961-9381
EMP: 22
SALES (corp-wide): 310.5MM **Privately Held**
SIC: **2387** Apparel belts
PA: Brighton Collectibles, Llc
14022 Nelson Ave
City Of Industry CA 91746
626 961-9381

(P-3529)
CABORCA LEATHER LLC
4275 Peaceful Glen Rd, Vacaville
(95688-9507)
PHONE.....................707 463-7607
Paul L Clapham,
Paul Clapham, *President*
Ron Davis, *Vice Pres*
Jim Hess, *VP Finance*
▲ EMP: 35
SALES (est): 2.7MM **Privately Held**
SIC: **2387** 5136 Apparel belts; apparel belts, men's & boys'

(P-3530)
ELITE FASHION ACCESSORIES INC
7141 N Warren Ave, Fresno (93711-7150)
PHONE.....................559 435-0225
Diane Daddian, *President*
Laurie Sivas, *Treasurer*
Paul Sivas, *Vice Pres*
Jeanet Sivas, *Director*
EMP: 10
SQ FT: 20,000
SALES: 3.5MM **Privately Held**
WEB: www.warehouseexpress.com
SIC: **2387** Apparel belts

(P-3531)
LEJON OF CALIFORNIA INC
Also Called: Lejon Tulliani
1229 Railroad St, Corona (92882-1838)
PHONE.....................951 736-1229
John W Shirinian, *President*
Jack Shirinian, *Admin Sec*
▲ EMP: 40
SQ FT: 33,000
SALES: 6MM **Privately Held**
WEB: www.lejon.com
SIC: **2387** 3172 Apparel belts; personal leather goods

(P-3532)
MARKAP INC
20382 Hermana Cir, Lake Forest
(92630-8701)
PHONE.....................949 240-1418
Gavin Kaplan, *CEO*
Mark Naude, *CFO*
▲ EMP: 48
SQ FT: 27,000
SALES (est): 3.5MM **Privately Held**
WEB: www.anotherline.com
SIC: **2387** Apparel belts

(P-3533)
STREETS AHEAD INC
Also Called: Hyde
5510 S Soto St Unit B, Vernon
(90058-3623)
PHONE.....................323 277-0860
David Sack, *CEO*
Michael Fructuoso, *Controller*
Michelle Sack, *Sales Dir*
▲ EMP: 20
SQ FT: 28,000
SALES (est): 3.8MM **Privately Held**
SIC: **2387** Apparel belts

(P-3534)
WESTSIDE ACCESSORIES INC (PA)
8920 Vernon Ave Ste 128, Montclair
(91763-1663)
PHONE.....................626 858-5452
Carol Cantagallo, *President*
▲ EMP: 21
SALES (est): 2MM **Privately Held**
WEB: www.westsideaccessories.com
SIC: **2387** Apparel belts

2389 Apparel & Accessories, NEC

(P-3535)
32 BAR BLUES LLC
1015 Cindy Ln B, Carpinteria (93013-2905)
PHONE.....................805 962-6665
Steve Meronk, *Mng Member*
Stephen Meronk, *Vice Pres*
Bruce Willard, *Managing Dir*
Sondra Williamson, *Merchandising*

David Brown, *Agent*
▲ EMP: 13 EST: 2011
SALES (est): 1.8MM **Privately Held**
SIC: **2389** Men's miscellaneous accessories

(P-3536)
ACADEMIC CH CHOIR GWNS MFG INC
Also Called: Academic Cap & Gown
20644 Superior St, Chatsworth
(91311-4414)
PHONE.....................818 886-8697
Mike Cronan, *President*
Evelyn Cronan, *Vice Pres*
Mark Cronan, *Vice Pres*
Lois Montoya, *Regl Sales Mgr*
▲ EMP: 30 EST: 1947
SQ FT: 13,000
SALES: 24.3MM **Privately Held**
WEB: www.academicapparel.com
SIC: **2389** 2353 Clergymen's vestments; hats, caps & millinery

(P-3537)
ALEXANDERS TEXTILE PDTS INC
Also Called: Alexander's Costumes
200 N D St, San Bernardino (92401-1702)
PHONE.....................951 276-2500
▲ EMP: 15
SQ FT: 16,000
SALES (est): 2.2MM **Privately Held**
WEB: www.merseyworld.com
SIC: **2389** 2299 5099 2339

(P-3538)
AMERICAN APPAREL (USA) LLC
747 Warehouse St, Los Angeles
(90021-1106)
P.O. Box 5129, Brandon MS (39047-5129)
PHONE.....................213 488-0226
Dov Charney,
▲ EMP: 18
SALES (est): 2.6MM **Privately Held**
WEB: www.americanapparel.net
SIC: **2389** 5961 Men's miscellaneous accessories; women's apparel, mail order

(P-3539)
AMERICAN COSTUME CORP
12980 Raymer St, North Hollywood
(91605-4276)
PHONE.....................818 432-4350
Luster Bayless, *Chairman*
Diana Foster, *President*
EMP: 10
SQ FT: 30,000
SALES (est): 1.3MM **Privately Held**
SIC: **2389** Costumes

(P-3540)
AMERICAN GARMENT COMPANY
Also Called: Laila Jayde Dda
16230 Manning Way, Cerritos
(90703-2223)
PHONE.....................562 483-8300
Justin Lee, *CEO*
David Laduke, *President*
EMP: 10
SALES: 5MM **Privately Held**
SIC: **2389** Men's miscellaneous accessories

(P-3541)
APP WINDDOWN LLC (HQ)
Also Called: American Apparel
747 Warehouse St, Los Angeles
(90021-1106)
P.O. Box 5129, Brandon MS (39047-5129)
PHONE.....................213 488-0226
Chelsea Grayson, *CEO*
Alma Amaya, *President*
◆ EMP: 28
SALES: 608.8MM
SALES (corp-wide): 2.9B **Privately Held**
WEB: www.americanapparel.net
SIC: **2389** 2311 2331 Men's miscellaneous accessories; men's & boys' suits & coats; women's & misses' blouses & shirts

▲ = Import ▼=Export
◆ =Import/Export

PA: Gildan Activewear Inc
600 Boul De Maisonneuve O 33eme etage
Montreal QC H3A 3
514 735-2023

(P-3542)
B2 APPAREL INC
Also Called: Bb Apparel
219 E 32nd St, Los Angeles (90011-1917)
PHONE..............................323 233-0044
Scott Lee, *President*
EMP: 15
SQ FT: 20,000
SALES (est): 10MM **Privately Held**
SIC: 2389 Footlets

(P-3543)
BRIGHTON COLLECTIBLES LLC
1195 Broadway Plz, Walnut Creek (94596-5130)
PHONE..............................925 932-1500
Jerry Kohl, *Branch Mgr*
EMP: 17
SALES (corp-wide): 310.5MM **Privately Held**
SIC: 2389 Men's miscellaneous accessories
PA: Brighton Collectibles, Llc
14022 Nelson Ave
City Of Industry CA 91746
626 961-9381

(P-3544)
CALIFRNIA CSTUME CLLCTIONS INC (PA)
Also Called: California Costume Int'l
210 S Anderson St, Los Angeles (90033-3205)
PHONE..............................323 262-8383
Tak Kwan Woo, *CEO*
Peter Woo, *President*
Charles Woo, *Treasurer*
Quinton Young, *Info Tech Mgr*
Wendy Chung, *Accountant*
◆ **EMP:** 46
SQ FT: 300,000
SALES (est): 38.6MM **Privately Held**
WEB: www.californiacostumes.com
SIC: 2389 5092 Costumes; toys

(P-3545)
CENTER THTRE GROUP LOS ANGELES
Also Called: Center Thatre Group Costume Sp
2856 E 11th St, Los Angeles (90023-3406)
PHONE..............................213 972-3751
Michael Thompson, *Branch Mgr*
EMP: 30
SALES (corp-wide): 48.8MM **Privately Held**
WEB: www.ctgla.org
SIC: 2389 Theatrical costumes
PA: Center Theatre Group Of Los Angeles
601 W Temple St
Los Angeles CA 90012
213 972-7344

(P-3546)
CHAGALL DESIGN LIMITED
20625 Belshaw Ave, Carson (90746-3507)
PHONE..............................310 537-9530
Jacques De Groot, *President*
Mannix Delfino-De Groot, *Vice Pres*
EMP: 12
SQ FT: 8,000
SALES (est): 1.1MM **Privately Held**
WEB: www.chagalldesign.com
SIC: 2389 Clergymen's vestments

(P-3547)
CHARADES LLC (PA)
14438 Don Julian Rd, City of Industry (91746-3101)
PHONE..............................626 435-0077
Jerry B Beck,
Howard Beige,
Mark Beige,
▲ **EMP:** 240
SQ FT: 100,000
SALES (est): 34.8MM **Privately Held**
WEB: www.charadescostumes.com
SIC: 2389 Costumes

(P-3548)
COMPUTERIZED FASHION SVCS INC
Also Called: Pride Sash
3341 Jack Northrop Ave, Hawthorne (90250-4426)
PHONE..............................310 973-0106
Louis Boksenbaum, *President*
Joelle Boksenbaum, *Vice Pres*
▲ **EMP:** 13
SALES (est): 1MM **Privately Held**
SIC: 2389 Uniforms & vestments

(P-3549)
CUSTOM CHARACTERS INC
621 Thompson Ave, Glendale (91201-2032)
PHONE..............................818 507-5940
Ryan Rhodes, *President*
Drew Herron, *Treasurer*
Victoria Arcenale, *Accounting Mgr*
EMP: 18
SQ FT: 5,200
SALES (est): 1.7MM **Privately Held**
WEB: www.customcharacters.com
SIC: 2389 3999 Costumes; stage hardware & equipment, except lighting

(P-3550)
DECKERS OUTDOOR CORPORATION (PA)
250 Coromar Dr, Goleta (93117-3697)
PHONE..............................805 967-7611
David Powers, *President*
Michael F Devine III, *Ch of Bd*
David E Lafitte, *COO*
Steven J Fasching, *CFO*
Chris Wisner, *Executive*
▲ **EMP:** 277
SQ FT: 185,000
SALES (est): 2B **Publicly Held**
WEB: www.deckers.com
SIC: 2389 2339 3021 Men's miscellaneous accessories; women's & misses' accessories; sandals, rubber

(P-3551)
DIAMOND COLLECTION LLC
Also Called: Charades
14438 Don Julian Rd, City of Industry (91746-3101)
PHONE..............................626 435-0077
Marc Lavich, *Principal*
EMP: 30
SALES (est): 2.7MM **Privately Held**
SIC: 2389 5137 Costumes; dresses

(P-3552)
DISGUISE INC (HQ)
12120 Kear Pl, Poway (92064-7132)
PHONE..............................858 391-3600
Stephen Berman, *CEO*
Benoit Pousset, *President*
Magento Theme, *Mfg Staff*
◆ **EMP:** 31
SQ FT: 206,000
SALES (est): 12.9MM **Publicly Held**
WEB: www.disguise.com
SIC: 2389 7299 Costumes; costume rental

(P-3553)
DISNEY ENTERPRISES INC
1313 S Harbor Blvd, Anaheim (92802-2309)
PHONE..............................407 397-6000
Marlene Madrid, *Manager*
EMP: 100
SALES (corp-wide): 90.2B **Publicly Held**
SIC: 2389 Theatrical costumes
HQ: Disney Enterprises, Inc.
500 S Buena Vista St
Burbank CA 91521
818 560-1000

(P-3554)
GILLI INC
1100 S San Pedro St C07, Los Angeles (90015-2385)
PHONE..............................213 744-9808
Hae Yun Suh, *Branch Mgr*
EMP: 15
SALES (corp-wide): 7MM **Privately Held**
SIC: 2389 5137 Uniforms & vestments; women's & children's clothing

PA: Gilli, Inc.
2939 Bandini Blvd
Vernon CA 90058
323 235-3722

(P-3555)
GOOD TIME USA INC
1100 S San Pedro St K04, Los Angeles (90015-2328)
PHONE..............................213 741-0100
Simon Lee, *CEO*
EMP: 11
SALES (est): 284K **Privately Held**
SIC: 2389 5137 Men's miscellaneous accessories; women's & children's clothing

(P-3556)
HQ BRANDS LLC
Also Called: House of Quirky
860 S Los Angeles St # 326, Los Angeles (90014-3322)
PHONE..............................213 627-7922
Melissa Tong, *Mng Member*
EMP: 10
SQ FT: 5,000
SALES (est): 906.7K **Privately Held**
SIC: 2389 Disposable garments & accessories

(P-3557)
INCHARACTER COSTUMES LLC
4560 Alvarado Canyon Rd 1d, San Diego (92120-4309)
PHONE..............................858 552-3600
Robert S Pickens, *COO*
Robert Emmerman, *Vice Pres*
Norma Floriano, *Vice Pres*
Tippy Larkin, *Accountant*
Robert Torre, *Controller*
▲ **EMP:** 50
SQ FT: 46,800
SALES (est): 17MM **Privately Held**
WEB: www.incharacter.com
SIC: 2389 Costumes

(P-3558)
IRONHEAD STUDIOS INC
7616 Ventura Canyon Ave, Van Nuys (91402-6372)
PHONE..............................818 901-7561
Jose Fernandez, *CEO*
Patricia Stoddard, *Admin Sec*
EMP: 19
SALES (est): 670K **Privately Held**
SIC: 2389 7922 Costumes; costume & scenery design services

(P-3559)
J&C TAPOCIK INC
Also Called: Express ID
2941 Mcallister St, Riverside (92503-6111)
PHONE..............................951 351-4333
Claudette Tapocik, *President*
John C Tapocik, *Corp Secy*
Mike Tapocik, *Vice Pres*
▲ **EMP:** 10
SQ FT: 30,000
SALES (est): 1MM **Privately Held**
SIC: 2389 2321 Men's miscellaneous accessories; men's & boys' furnishings

(P-3560)
JUST SAYING INC
800 S Date Ave, Alhambra (91803-1414)
PHONE..............................888 512-5007
Tony Lau, *President*
EMP: 10
SALES (est): 702K **Privately Held**
SIC: 2389 Apparel & accessories

(P-3561)
KATIE K INC
5601 Bickett St, Vernon (90058-3605)
PHONE..............................323 589-3030
Mimi Kim, *President*
▲ **EMP:** 10
SQ FT: 4,000
SALES (est): 1.6MM **Privately Held**
SIC: 2389 Uniforms & vestments

(P-3562)
KINARY INC
2542 Troy Ave, South El Monte (91733-1428)
PHONE..............................626 575-7873
Kim Chung, *President*

EMP: 30
SALES (est): 1.5MM **Privately Held**
SIC: 2389 Uniforms & vestments

(P-3563)
LAKEVIEW INNOVATIONS INC
11391 Sunrise Gold Cir # 100, Rancho Cordova (95742-7212)
PHONE..............................212 502-6702
Scott Colquitt, *President*
Harry Mull, *CFO*
▲ **EMP:** 10
SALES (est): 2.2MM **Privately Held**
SIC: 2389 Cummerbunds

(P-3564)
LE CHEF COSTUMIER INC
825 Western Ave Ste 21, Glendale (91201-2385)
PHONE..............................818 242-0868
Jason Vaughan, *CEO*
EMP: 20
SALES (est): 1.3MM **Privately Held**
SIC: 2389 Costumes

(P-3565)
LETS GO APPAREL INC (PA)
Also Called: Uptown
1729 E Washington Blvd, Los Angeles (90021-3124)
PHONE..............................213 863-1767
Chang Wha Yoon, *President*
▼ **EMP:** 17
SQ FT: 30,000
SALES: 8.5MM **Privately Held**
SIC: 2389 5661 5632 Academic vestments (caps & gowns); shoes, custom; apparel accessories

(P-3566)
LLC MARSH PERKINS
80080 Via Pessaro, La Quinta (92253-7581)
PHONE..............................760 880-4558
Diane Lohman,
EMP: 15
SALES (est): 400.1K **Privately Held**
SIC: 2389 Apparel & accessories

(P-3567)
LOVESTRENGTH LLC
865 Arbor Glen Ln, Vista (92081-7913)
PHONE..............................760 481-9951
Deborah Cappellazo, *Mng Member*
Wendy Wiltsey, *Master*
EMP: 11 **EST:** 2010
SALES (est): 898.5K **Privately Held**
SIC: 2389 Apparel & accessories

(P-3568)
MASK U S INC
3121 Main St Ste F, Chula Vista (91911-5765)
PHONE..............................619 476-9041
David P Bragg, *CEO*
Martha Bragg, *Treasurer*
▲ **EMP:** 14
SQ FT: 8,000
SALES (est): 1.3MM **Privately Held**
WEB: www.maskus.com
SIC: 2389 Costumes

(P-3569)
MAURY RAZON
Also Called: L R Associates
74 W Cochran St Ste A, Simi Valley (93065-6268)
PHONE..............................818 989-6246
Maury Razon, *Owner*
EMP: 15
SQ FT: 5,000
SALES (est): 1.2MM **Privately Held**
SIC: 2389 2353 Uniforms & vestments; hats & caps

(P-3570)
MDC INTERIOR SOLUTIONS LLC
Also Called: Komar Apparel Supply
6900 E Washington Blvd, Los Angeles (90040-1908)
PHONE..............................800 621-4006
Gary Rothschild, *Manager*
EMP: 75

P
R
O
D
U
C
T
S

&

S
V
C
S

SALES (corp-wide): 93.8MM **Privately Held**
SIC: **2389** Men's miscellaneous accessories
PA: Mdc Interior Solutions, Llc
400 High Grove Blvd
Glendale Heights IL 60139
847 437-4000

(P-3571)
ML KISHIGO MFG CO LLC
2901 Daimler St, Santa Ana (92705-5810)
PHONE..................................949 852-1963
Loren H Wall, *CEO*
Karen Wall, *Vice Pres*
▲ EMP: 86
SQ FT: 24,000
SALES (est): 15.7MM
SALES (corp-wide): 11.6B **Privately Held**
WEB: www.mlkishigo.com
SIC: **2389** Men's miscellaneous accessories
PA: Bunzl Public Limited Company
York House, 45 Seymour Street
London W1H 7
207 725-5000

(P-3572)
NICOLE FULLERTON
Also Called: Pendragon Costumes
27821 Pine Crest Pl, Castaic (91384-4129)
PHONE..................................661 257-0406
Nicole Fullerton, *Owner*
EMP: 12
SALES: 500K **Privately Held**
SIC: **2389** 5621 Costumes; women's clothing stores

(P-3573)
PARADISE RANCH
Also Called: Molly's Custom Silver
2900 Adams St Ste C8, Riverside (92504-7915)
PHONE..................................951 776-7736
Randy Rush, *CEO*
Molly Rush, *President*
EMP: 12
SQ FT: 2,000
SALES: 4MM **Privately Held**
SIC: **2389** Men's miscellaneous accessories

(P-3574)
POLERAX USA
909 S Greenwood Ave Ste K, Montebello (90640-5836)
PHONE..................................323 477-1866
Kyung J Lee, *President*
EMP: 18
SALES (est): 1MM **Privately Held**
SIC: **2389** Apparel & accessories

(P-3575)
R & R INDUSTRIES INC
204 Avenida Fabricante, San Clemente (92672-7538)
PHONE..................................949 361-9238
Robert Pare, *President*
Roger Poulin, *Treasurer*
Neil Samuels, *Vice Pres*
◆ EMP: 30
SQ FT: 8,150
SALES (est): 3.3MM **Privately Held**
SIC: **2389** Uniforms & vestments

(P-3576)
RG COSTUMES & ACCESSORIES INC
726 Arrow Grand Cir, Covina (91722-2147)
PHONE..................................626 858-9559
Roger Lee, *President*
Michael Lee, *Vice Pres*
▲ EMP: 30
SQ FT: 21,000
SALES: 1.9MM **Privately Held**
SIC: **2389** 7299 Costumes; costume rental

(P-3577)
RM 518 MANAGEMENT LLC
Also Called: S M U
719 S Los Angeles St, Los Angeles (90014-2109)
PHONE..................................213 624-6788
Randall Beatty,
Victor Kaplan,
Mike Price,

MEI Price,
▲ EMP: 23
SQ FT: 3,000
SALES (est): 1.3MM **Privately Held**
SIC: **2389** Men's miscellaneous accessories

(P-3578)
SHAFTON INC
6932 Tujunga Ave, North Hollywood (91605-6212)
PHONE..................................818 985-5025
David Janzow, *President*
Becky Allen, *Corp Secy*
Linda Putnam, *Supervisor*
EMP: 17 EST: 1975
SQ FT: 7,000
SALES (est): 1.6MM **Privately Held**
WEB: www.shaftoninc.com
SIC: **2389** Theatrical costumes

(P-3579)
SILVIAS COSTUMES
4964 Hollywood Blvd, Los Angeles (90027-6108)
PHONE..................................323 661-2142
Silvia Tchakmakjian, *CEO*
Micheal Majian, *President*
EMP: 20
SQ FT: 6,000
SALES (est): 1.8MM **Privately Held**
SIC: **2389** Masquerade costumes

(P-3580)
SKATE GROUP INC
830 E 14th Pl, Los Angeles (90021-2120)
PHONE..................................213 749-6651
Kevin Neman, *President*
EMP: 10
SALES (est): 1.1MM **Privately Held**
SIC: **2389** Disposable garments & accessories

(P-3581)
SUSPENDER FACTORY INC
Also Called: Suspender Factory of S F
1425 63rd St, Emeryville (94608-2188)
PHONE..................................510 547-5400
John Nemec, *President*
▲ EMP: 35
SQ FT: 6,000
SALES (est): 5MM **Privately Held**
SIC: **2389** 2387 Suspenders; apparel belts

(P-3582)
TRUE WARRIOR LLC
21226 Lone Star Way, Santa Clarita (91390-4226)
PHONE..................................661 237-6588
Edward Luster,
EMP: 20 EST: 2017
SALES (est): 508.6K **Privately Held**
SIC: **2389** 3069 Apparel & accessories; boot or shoe products, rubber

(P-3583)
UNDERWRAPS COSTUME CORPORATION
Also Called: Underwraps Costumes Inc.
9600 Irondale Ave, Chatsworth (91311-5008)
P.O. Box 9603, Canoga Park (91309-0603)
PHONE..................................818 349-5300
Payman Shaffa, *CEO*
Irene Shaffa, *Vice Pres*
▲ EMP: 16
SQ FT: 45,000
SALES (est): 6.8MM **Privately Held**
SIC: **2389** Costumes

(P-3584)
WALT DISNEY IMAGINEERING
1200 N Miller St Unit D, Anaheim (92806-1954)
PHONE..................................714 781-3152
EMP: 150
SALES (corp-wide): 90.2B **Publicly Held**
SIC: **2389** Masquerade costumes; theatrical costumes
HQ: Walt Disney Imagineering Research & Development, Inc.
1401 Flower St
Glendale CA 91201
818 544-6500

(P-3585)
X SUBLIMATION INC
2837 S Olive St, Los Angeles (90007-3339)
PHONE..................................213 700-1024
Terry Park, *President*
EMP: 10
SALES (est): 660.3K **Privately Held**
SIC: **2389** Disposable garments & accessories

2391 Curtains & Draperies

(P-3586)
AMERICAN BLINDS AND DRAP INC
30776 Huntwood Ave, Hayward (94544-7002)
PHONE..................................510 487-3500
Paul Russo, *President*
EMP: 50 EST: 1961
SQ FT: 30,000
SALES (est): 4.8MM **Privately Held**
WEB: www.americandrape.com
SIC: **2391** 2591 Draperies, plastic & textile: from purchased materials; mini blinds

(P-3587)
AMTEX CALIFORNIA INC
Also Called: Ameritex International
113 S Utah St, Los Angeles (90033-3213)
PHONE..................................323 859-2200
Saq Hafeez, *President*
Alia Hafeez, *Vice Pres*
◆ EMP: 45 EST: 1991
SQ FT: 40,000
SALES (est): 5.7MM **Privately Held**
WEB: www.ameritexinternational.com
SIC: **2391** 2392 5023 Draperies, plastic & textile: from purchased materials; bedspreads & bed sets: made from purchased materials; curtains; bedspreads

(P-3588)
D & M DRAPERIES INC
Also Called: Dan-Mar Custom Draperies
323 W Maple Ave, Monrovia (91016-3331)
PHONE..................................626 256-1993
Marcos Barron, *President*
Danny Luna, *Vice Pres*
EMP: 15
SALES (est): 880K **Privately Held**
SIC: **2391** Curtains & draperies

(P-3589)
ILONA DRAPERIES INC
19617 Bruces Pl, Canyon Country (91351-4841)
PHONE..................................818 840-8811
Fred Winter, *President*
Keith Winter, *Treasurer*
Carol Winter, *Vice Pres*
EMP: 30
SALES (est): 2.7MM **Privately Held**
WEB: www.ilonadraperies.com
SIC: **2391** 2392 Draperies, plastic & textile: from purchased materials; comforters & quilts: made from purchased materials

(P-3590)
M L INTERIORS INC
Also Called: Mark Levine Window Coverings
151 Shipyard Way Ste 4, Newport Beach (92663-4460)
PHONE..................................949 723-5001
Mark Levine, *President*
Debby Levine, *Corp Secy*
EMP: 23
SQ FT: 6,000
SALES (est): 1.7MM **Privately Held**
SIC: **2391** 7389 2392 Curtains & draperies; interior decorating; bedspreads & bed sets: made from purchased materials

(P-3591)
MANZER CORPORATION
Also Called: Pacific Drapery
3801 30th St, San Diego (92104-3609)
PHONE..................................619 295-6031
Kathleen McAveney, *Owner*
EMP: 20
SQ FT: 2,000

SALES (est): 1.4MM **Privately Held**
SIC: **2391** 2221 Draperies, plastic & textile: from purchased materials; broadwoven fabric mills, manmade

(P-3592)
MBF INTERIORS INC
Also Called: Modern Blind Factory
7831 Ostrow St, San Diego (92111-3602)
PHONE..................................858 565-2944
Behrooz Farhood, *President*
EMP: 25 EST: 1973
SQ FT: 24,000
SALES: 3MM **Privately Held**
SIC: **2391** 2591 5714 5719 Draperies, plastic & textile: from purchased materials; blinds vertical; draperies; vertical blinds

(P-3593)
MCCARTHYS DRAPERIES INC
Also Called: Rubio Fabrics
6955 Luther Dr, Sacramento (95823-1805)
PHONE..................................916 422-0155
Vern McCarthy, *President*
Eugenia McCarthy, *Vice Pres*
EMP: 35 EST: 1958
SQ FT: 10,000
SALES (est): 2.7MM **Privately Held**
SIC: **2391** 5131 2591 Draperies, plastic & textile: from purchased materials; piece goods & notions; drapery hardware & blinds & shades

(P-3594)
PATS DECORATING SERVICE INC
2532 Strozier Ave, South El Monte (91733-2020)
PHONE..................................323 585-5073
Maria Lopez, *President*
EMP: 15
SQ FT: 36,000
SALES (est): 1.7MM **Privately Held**
WEB: www.patsdecorator.com
SIC: **2391** 2392 5714 5719 Draperies, plastic & textile: from purchased materials; bedspreads & bed sets: made from purchased materials; draperies; bedding (sheets, blankets, spreads & pillows)

(P-3595)
ROYAL DRAPERY MANUFACTURING
Also Called: Royal Drapery and Interiors
3149 California Blvd K, NAPA (94558-3334)
PHONE..................................707 226-2022
Peter Lomonaco, *Partner*
Sharon Lomonaco, *Partner*
EMP: 13
SALES: 450K **Privately Held**
SIC: **2391** 5714 Draperies, plastic & textile: from purchased materials; draperies

(P-3596)
S & K THEATRICAL DRAP INC
Also Called: Sk Drapes
7313 Varna Ave, North Hollywood (91605-4009)
PHONE..................................818 503-0596
Carmela Skogman, *President*
Michael Skoaman, *Vice Pres*
Damian Schmidt, *Prdtn Mgr*
Kevin Skogman, *Sales Staff*
EMP: 16
SALES (est): 2.2MM **Privately Held**
WEB: www.sktheatricaldraperies.com
SIC: **2391** Draperies, plastic & textile: from purchased materials

(P-3597)
SEW WHAT INC
Also Called: Rent What
1978 E Gladwick St, Compton (90220-6201)
PHONE..................................310 639-6000
Megan Duckett, *President*
Adam Duckett, *Vice Pres*
◆ EMP: 35
SQ FT: 15,000
SALES (est): 4.5MM **Privately Held**
WEB: www.sewwhat.com
SIC: **2391** 5049 Curtains & draperies; theatrical equipment & supplies

(P-3598)
SUPERIOR WINDOW COVERINGS INC
7683 N San Fernando Rd, Burbank (91505-1073)
PHONE....................818 762-6685
Marco Bonilla, *President*
Mario Murillo, *Info Tech Dir*
Diana Castillo, *Sales Staff*
▲ EMP: 35
SQ FT: 4,000
SALES (est): 3.5MM **Privately Held**
WEB: www.superiorshades.com
SIC: 2391 2591 Draperies, plastic & textile: from purchased materials; blinds vertical

---

2392 House furnishings: Textile

(P-3599)
AMERICA ASIA TRADE PROMOTION
Also Called: A A Trader
4633 Old Ironsides Dr # 400, Santa Clara (95054-1807)
P.O. Box 3331 (95055-3331)
PHONE....................408 970-8868
EMP: 10
SALES (est): 580K **Privately Held**
SIC: 2392 2511 2512 2834

(P-3600)
ANATOMIC GLOBAL INC
1241 Old Temescal Rd # 103, Corona (92881-7266)
PHONE....................800 874-7237
David Farley, *CEO*
▲ EMP: 115
SQ FT: 55,000
SALES (est): 29.9MM **Privately Held**
WEB: www.anatomicconcepts.com
SIC: 2392 Bedspreads & bed sets: made from purchased materials

(P-3601)
ART MASTERPIECE GALLERY
4950 S Santa Fe Ave, Vernon (90058-2106)
PHONE....................323 277-9448
Peter Leogrande, *President*
Randy Greenberg, *CEO*
Glenn Knecht, *Vice Pres*
▲ EMP: 14
SQ FT: 120,000
SALES (est): 1.1MM **Privately Held**
SIC: 2392 Household furnishings

(P-3602)
BEME INTERNATIONAL LLC
7333 Ronson Rd, San Diego (92111-1404)
PHONE....................858 751-0580
Peisheng Qian,
Ed File, *Engineer*
Brian Graves,
Zhiwei David Xu,
Danne Sadler, *Director*
▲ EMP: 21 EST: 1998
SALES (est): 3MM **Privately Held**
WEB: www.beme.net
SIC: 2392 Household furnishings

(P-3603)
BOJER INC
177 S Peckham Rd, Azusa (91702-3237)
PHONE....................626 334-1711
Doris Gabai, *President*
Joey Gabai, *Vice Pres*
Shelly Gabai, *Sales Mgr*
EMP: 20
SQ FT: 12,974
SALES (est): 1.6MM **Privately Held**
WEB: www.bojerinc.com
SIC: 2392 Cushions & pillows

(P-3604)
BRENTWOOD ORIGINALS INC (PA)
20639 S Fordyce Ave, Carson (90810-1019)
PHONE....................310 637-6804
Loren H Sweet, *President*
Bill Bronstein, *Senior VP*

Tom Rose, *Senior VP*
Craig Torrey, *Senior VP*
Joel Fierberg, *Vice Pres*
◆ EMP: 650
SQ FT: 1,200,000
SALES (est): 145.3MM **Privately Held**
WEB: www.brentwoodoriginals.com
SIC: 2392 Cushions & pillows

(P-3605)
BURTON CHING LTD
432 N Canal St Ste 5, South San Francisco (94080-4666)
PHONE....................415 522-5520
Sen Ching, *Owner*
Tony Ching, *Partner*
John Cerney, *Manager*
EMP: 14
SALES (est): 650K **Privately Held**
WEB: www.burtonching.com
SIC: 2392 5932 Household furnishings; used merchandise stores

(P-3606)
CALIFORNIA FEATHER INDS INC
2241 E 49th St, Vernon (90058-2822)
PHONE....................323 585-5800
Jeff Goldman, *President*
Paras Jain, *Vice Pres*
Anhil Mehta, *Vice Pres*
EMP: 11
SQ FT: 45,000
SALES (est): 810K **Privately Held**
SIC: 2392 Cushions & pillows

(P-3607)
CJ PRODUCTS INC
Also Called: Pillow Pets
4087 Calle Platino, Oceanside (92056-5805)
PHONE....................760 444-4217
Clint Telfer, *President*
Julie Caravaggio, *Sales Staff*
Molly King, *Sales Staff*
Caleb Barber, *Art Dir*
Heidi H Niehart, *Director*
◆ EMP: 15 EST: 2008
SQ FT: 20,000
SALES (est): 1.6MM **Privately Held**
SIC: 2392 Cushions & pillows

(P-3608)
CLASSIC SLIPCOVER INC
4300 District Blvd, Vernon (90058-3110)
PHONE....................323 583-0804
David Illulian, *CEO*
Chris Wroolie, *President*
▲ EMP: 20
SQ FT: 15,000
SALES (est): 2.1MM **Privately Held**
WEB: www.classicslipcovers.com
SIC: 2392 5714 Slipcovers: made of fabric, plastic etc.; slip covers

(P-3609)
COTTON TALE DESIGNS INC
16291 Sierra Ridge Way, Hacienda Heights (91745-5545)
PHONE....................714 435-9558
Larry D Aspegren, *President*
Nina Selby, *President*
Larry Aspegren, *Vice Pres*
▲ EMP: 20
SQ FT: 16,500
SALES (est): 2.2MM **Privately Held**
WEB: www.cottontaledesigns.com
SIC: 2392 2361 2211 Household furnishings; girls' & children's dresses, blouses & shirts; bed sheeting, cotton

(P-3610)
CUSHION WORKS
68929 Perez Rd Ste B, Cathedral City (92234-7283)
PHONE....................760 321-7808
Dia Davis, *President*
EMP: 10
SALES (est): 430.3K **Privately Held**
SIC: 2392 Cushions & pillows

(P-3611)
CUSTOM QUILTING INC
2832 Walnut Ave Ste D, Tustin (92780-7002)
PHONE....................714 731-7271
Alfredo Zermeno, *Owner*

Elda Zermeno, *Vice Pres*
EMP: 28
SALES (est): 3.2MM **Privately Held**
SIC: 2392 5719 Bedspreads & bed sets: made from purchased materials; bedding (sheets, blankets, spreads & pillows)

(P-3612)
DRAPES 4 SHOW INC
12811 Foothill Blvd, Sylmar (91342-5316)
PHONE....................818 838-0852
Karen Honigberg, *President*
Jason Honigberg, *Sales Mgr*
Tyler Recesso, *Accounts Exec*
◆ EMP: 25
SQ FT: 3,500
SALES (est): 3.7MM **Privately Held**
WEB: www.drapes.com
SIC: 2392 Tablecloths & table settings

(P-3613)
DREAMS DUVETS & BED LINENS
Also Called: Dreams Duvets & Linens
921 Howard St, San Francisco (94103-4108)
PHONE....................415 543-1800
Kusum Jain, *President*
EMP: 11
SQ FT: 17,000
SALES: 900K **Privately Held**
SIC: 2392 5719 7699 Comforters & quilts: made from purchased materials; beddings & linens; general household repair services

(P-3614)
DV KAP INC
Also Called: Canaan Company
426 W Bedford Ave, Fresno (93711-6858)
PHONE....................559 435-5575
Dan Sivas, *CEO*
Khach Sivas, *Manager*
◆ EMP: 50
SQ FT: 25,000
SALES (est): 7.5MM **Privately Held**
WEB: www.canaancompany.com
SIC: 2392 Cushions & pillows

(P-3615)
FABRIC WALLS INC
322 Harriet St, San Francisco (94103-4716)
PHONE....................415 863-2711
Donald Piermarini, *President*
Ray Bollinger, *Vice Pres*
EMP: 11 EST: 1974
SQ FT: 2,000
SALES (est): 1.3MM **Privately Held**
SIC: 2392 2391 Household furnishings; curtains, window: made from purchased materials

(P-3616)
FARALLON BRANDS INC (PA)
Also Called: Peanut Shell
33300 Central Ave, Union City (94587-2044)
PHONE....................510 550-4299
Michael Roach, *CEO*
William T Tauscher, *Ch of Bd*
Laura Tauscher, *COO*
Yvonne Ortiz, *Vice Pres*
Jill Hudson, *VP Sales*
◆ EMP: 17
SQ FT: 27,000
SALES (est): 2.4MM **Privately Held**
SIC: 2392 3944 Blankets, comforters & beddings; baby carriages & restraint seats

(P-3617)
HOMETEX CORPORATION
1743 Continental Ln, Escondido (92029-4328)
PHONE....................619 661-0400
Shoaib Kothawala, *President*
James Houlihan, *Vice Pres*
EMP: 30
SALES (est): 1.9MM **Privately Held**
SIC: 2392 Towels, fabric & nonwoven: made from purchased materials

(P-3618)
HUDSON & COMPANY LLC
Also Called: Spirit Throws
100 Irene Ave, Roseville (95678-3226)
P.O. Box 968 (95678-0968)
PHONE....................916 774-6465
Shannon Hudson, *Mng Member*
▼ EMP: 23
SQ FT: 984
SALES (est): 1.2MM **Privately Held**
SIC: 2392 Blankets, comforters & beddings

(P-3619)
INSTANT TUCK INC
9663 Santa Monica Blvd, Beverly Hills (90210-4303)
PHONE....................310 955-8824
Adrian Gluck, *CEO*
EMP: 30
SALES (est): 727.3K **Privately Held**
SIC: 2392 Mattress pads

(P-3620)
JR WATKINS LLC
101 Mission St, San Francisco (94105-1705)
PHONE....................415 477-8500
Michael Fox, *CEO*
Dan Swander, *Partner*
Chris Folena, *CFO*
EMP: 22
SALES (est): 617.7K **Privately Held**
SIC: 2392 5963 Household furnishings; home related products, direct sales

(P-3621)
KLEEN MAID INC
11450 Sheldon St, Sun Valley (91352-1121)
PHONE....................323 581-3000
Sean Solouki, *CEO*
Kamyar Solouki, *President*
Hamid Moghaven, *Vice Pres*
◆ EMP: 27
SALES (est): 11.2MM **Privately Held**
WEB: www.kleenmaidinc.com
SIC: 2392 3991 Mops, floor & dust; brushes, household or industrial

(P-3622)
KUMI KOOKOON
18018 S Western Ave, Gardena (90248-3624)
PHONE....................310 515-8811
Jennifer S Chang, *Owner*
▲ EMP: 13
SALES (est): 1.2MM **Privately Held**
WEB: www.kumikookoon.com
SIC: 2392 Blankets, comforters & beddings

(P-3623)
LAMBS & IVY INC
Also Called: Bed Time Originals
2042 E Maple Ave, El Segundo (90245-5008)
PHONE....................310 322-3800
Barbara Laiken, *President*
Dan Simone, *CFO*
Cathy Ravdin, *Vice Pres*
Cristina Muresean, *Production*
Stephanie Elias, *Director*
◆ EMP: 60
SQ FT: 30,000
SALES (est): 6.9MM **Privately Held**
WEB: www.lambsandivy.com
SIC: 2392 Blankets, comforters & beddings

(P-3624)
MAGNOLIA LANE SOFT HM FURN INC
Also Called: Designs With Fabric
187 Utah Ave, South San Francisco (94080-6712)
PHONE....................650 624-0700
Kathleen Redmond, *President*
Mary McWilliams, *Admin Sec*
Laura Skinner, *Project Mgr*
Judy Powers, *Marketing Staff*
EMP: 20
SQ FT: 5,000
SALES (est): 1.8MM **Privately Held**
WEB: www.designswithfabric.com
SIC: 2392 2391 Cushions & pillows; blankets, comforters & beddings; draperies, plastic & textile: from purchased materials

PRODUCTS & SVCS

(P-3625)
MATTEO LLC
1000 E Cesar E Chavez Ave, Los Angeles
(90033-1204)
PHONE.....................................213 617-2813
Matthew Lenoci, *Mng Member*
▲ EMP: 50
SQ FT: 25,000
SALES (est): 8.1MM **Privately Held**
WEB: www.matteohome.com
SIC: 2392 Blankets, comforters & beddings

(P-3626)
MAX FISCHER & SONS INC
Also Called: Acme Wiping Materials
1327 Palmetto St, Los Angeles
(90013-2228)
PHONE.....................................213 624-8756
Marilyn Fischer, *President*
Marla Fischer, *Vice Pres*
EMP: 20
SQ FT: 50,000
SALES (est): 2MM **Privately Held**
SIC: 2392 Towels, fabric & nonwoven:
  made from purchased materials

(P-3627)
**MICRONOVA MANUFACTURING
INC**
3431 Lomita Blvd, Torrance (90505-5010)
PHONE.....................................310 784-6990
Audrey J Reynolds Lowman, *CEO*
Bridgett Butler, *Executive Asst*
Debra Southard, *Finance*
Jenny Farney, *Human Res Mgr*
Heidi Garlick, *Purch Mgr*
▲ EMP: 30
SQ FT: 28,310
SALES (est): 5.6MM **Privately Held**
WEB: www.micronova-mfg.com
SIC: 2392 Mops, floor & dust

(P-3628)
**NORTHWESTERN CONVERTING
CO**
Also Called: Premier Mop & Broom
2395 Railroad St, Corona (92880-5411)
PHONE.....................................800 959-3402
Tom Buckles, *President*
Thomas M Buckles, *President*
▲ EMP: 100
SALES (est): 15.2MM **Privately Held**
WEB: www.premiermop.com
SIC: 2392 Household furnishings

(P-3629)
OMNIA LEATHER MOTION INC
Also Called: Cathy Ireland Home
4950 Edison Ave, Chino (91710-5713)
PHONE.....................................909 393-4400
Peter Zolferino, *President*
Luie Nastri, *Vice Pres*
Michael Rutheford, *Sales Staff*
▲ EMP: 200
SALES (est): 23.6MM **Privately Held**
WEB: www.omnialeather.com
SIC: 2392 Household furnishings

(P-3630)
ONE BELLA CASA INC
Also Called: Artehouse
101 Lucas Valley Rd # 130, San Rafael
(94903-1791)
PHONE.....................................707 746-8300
Gary Sattin, *CEO*
▲ EMP: 24 EST: 2013
SQ FT: 10,000
SALES: 22MM **Privately Held**
SIC: 2392 3952 Pillows, bed: made from
  purchased materials; canvas, prepared
  on frames: artists'

(P-3631)
**PACIFIC CAST FTHER CUSHION
LLC (DH)**
7600 Industry Ave, Pico Rivera
(90660-4302)
PHONE.....................................562 801-9995
◆ EMP: 110
SQ FT: 100,000
SALES (est): 25.1MM
SALES (corp-wide): 1B **Privately Held**
WEB: www.pcfcushion.com
SIC: 2392 Cushions & pillows

HQ: Pacific Coast Feather, Llc
  1736 4th Ave S Ste B
  Seattle WA 98134
  206 624-1057

(P-3632)
PACIFIC COAST FEATHER LLC
8500 Rex Rd, Pico Rivera (90660-3779)
PHONE.....................................562 222-5560
Rudy Garza, *Branch Mgr*
EMP: 150
SALES (corp-wide): 1B **Privately Held**
WEB: www.pacificcoast.com
SIC: 2392 Cushions & pillows
HQ: Pacific Coast Feather, Llc
  1736 4th Ave S Ste B
  Seattle WA 98134
  206 624-1057

(P-3633)
**PACIFIC COAST HOME FURN
INC (PA)**
Also Called: Sherry Kline
2424 Saybrook Ave, Commerce
(90040-2510)
PHONE.....................................323 838-7808
Parviz Banafshe, *President*
Shahrokh Samani, *CFO*
▲ EMP: 19
SQ FT: 35,000
SALES (est): 3.4MM **Privately Held**
SIC: 2392 3261 Cushions & pillows; bath-
  room accessories/fittings, vitreous china
  or earthenware

(P-3634)
PACIFIC URETHANES LLC
1671 Champagne Ave Ste A, Ontario
(91761-3660)
PHONE.....................................909 390-8400
Darrell Nance, *Mng Member*
Neil Silverman,
▲ EMP: 200
SQ FT: 250,000
SALES (est): 97.2MM
SALES (corp-wide): 4.2B **Publicly Held**
SIC: 2392 5021 Blankets, comforters &
  beddings; beds & bedding
PA: Leggett & Platt, Incorporated
  1 Leggett Rd
  Carthage MO 64836
  417 358-8131

(P-3635)
PALERMO PRODUCTS LLC
16935 Saticoy St, Van Nuys (91406-2128)
PHONE.....................................949 201-9066
James Hoseini, *CEO*
Ali Hahseni, *Vice Pres*
Alex Araeloui, *Manager*
EMP: 15
SALES: 1.5MM **Privately Held**
SIC: 2392 Household furnishings

(P-3636)
**PRO-MART INDUSTRIES INC
(PA)**
Also Called: Promart Dazz
17421 Von Karman Ave, Irvine
(92614-6205)
PHONE.....................................949 428-7700
Azad Sabounjian, *CEO*
▲ EMP: 40
SQ FT: 120,000
SALES (est): 8.2MM **Privately Held**
WEB: www.deltanovaltd.com
SIC: 2392 Bags, laundry: made from pur-
  chased materials

(P-3637)
QUILTING HOUSE
16872 Millikan Ave, Irvine (92606-5012)
PHONE.....................................949 476-7090
Richard Shields, *Owner*
Sheri Shields, *Co-Owner*
EMP: 40
SQ FT: 16,000
SALES (est): 3.6MM **Privately Held**
WEB: www.quiltinghouse.com
SIC: 2392 2391 Cushions & pillows; bed-
  spreads & bed sets: made from pur-
  chased materials; pillows, bed: made
  from purchased materials; curtains &
  draperies

(P-3638)
**RELIANCE UPHOLSTERY SUP
CO INC**
Also Called: Reliance Carpet Cushion
5942 Santa Fe Ave, Huntington Park
(90255-2733)
P.O. Box 58584, Vernon (90058-0584)
PHONE.....................................323 321-2300
Ronald J Greitzer, *CEO*
Stanley Grietzer, *President*
Sheldon P Wallach, *CFO*
EMP: 95
SQ FT: 360,000
SALES (est): 9MM **Privately Held**
SIC: 2392 Linings, carpet: textile, except
  felt; cushions & pillows

(P-3639)
ROYAL BLUE INC
9025 Wilshire Blvd # 301, Beverly Hills
(90211-1831)
PHONE.....................................310 888-0156
Diana Moinian, *President*
▲ EMP: 21
SALES: 2MM **Privately Held**
WEB: www.royalblueintl.com
SIC: 2392 2299 Household furnishings;
  towels & towelings, linen & linen-and-cot-
  ton mixtures

(P-3640)
SIBYL SHEPARD INC
Also Called: Sarris Interiors
8225 Alondra Blvd, Paramount
(90723-4401)
PHONE.....................................562 531-8612
C Nicholas Sarris, *President*
Chris Andrew Sarris, *Vice Pres*
Byron Sarris, *Director*
EMP: 20 EST: 1957
SQ FT: 15,000
SALES (est): 2MM **Privately Held**
WEB: www.sarrisinteriors.com
SIC: 2392 Bedspreads & bed sets: made
  from purchased materials; towels, fabric &
  nonwoven: made from purchased materi-
  als; washcloths & bath mitts: made from
  purchased materials; shower curtains:
  made from purchased materials

(P-3641)
SILVER EAGLE CORPORATION
Also Called: Woodmark Manufacturing
2655 Land Ave, Sacramento (95815-2383)
PHONE.....................................916 925-6843
Mark E Bristow, *President*
Bill Bristow, *Vice Pres*
Pat Bristow, *Admin Sec*
EMP: 30
SQ FT: 40,000
SALES (est): 3.8MM **Privately Held**
SIC: 2392 Household furnishings

(P-3642)
**SPENCER N ENTERPRISES LLC
(DH)**
Also Called: Spencer Home Decor
425 S Lemon Ave, City of Industry
(91789-2911)
PHONE.....................................909 895-8495
Jeffrey Werner, *President*
Charles F Kuehne, *CFO*
▲ EMP: 41
SQ FT: 100,000
SALES (est): 18.1MM **Privately Held**
SIC: 2392 Cushions & pillows

(P-3643)
STANDARD FIBER LLC (PA)
577 Airport Blvd Ste 200, Burlingame
(94010-2052)
PHONE.....................................650 872-6528
Welles Alexander Gray III, *President*
Kim Garcia, *Office Admin*
▲ EMP: 40
SQ FT: 13,000
SALES (est): 52.4MM **Privately Held**
WEB: www.stdfiber.com
SIC: 2392 5021 Blankets, comforters &
  beddings; cushions & pillows; beds &
  bedding

(P-3644)
SUNRISE PILLOW CO INC
2215 Merced Ave, El Monte (91733-2622)
PHONE.....................................626 401-9283
Adnan K Hermas, *President*
EMP: 16
SQ FT: 11,500
SALES (est): 1.3MM **Privately Held**
SIC: 2392 5719 Pillows, bed: made from
  purchased materials; bedding (sheets,
  blankets, spreads & pillows)

(P-3645)
THOMAS WEST INC (PA)
Also Called: T W I
470 Mercury Dr, Sunnyvale (94085-4706)
PHONE.....................................408 481-3850
Tom West, *CEO*
Dr Steve Kirtley, *COO*
Martin Wohlert, *Info Tech Dir*
Suli Holani, *Prdtn Mgr*
▲ EMP: 27
SQ FT: 43,000
SALES (est): 4.5MM **Privately Held**
WEB: www.thomaswest.com
SIC: 2392 Towels, dishcloths & dust cloths

(P-3646)
THOREEN DESIGNS INC
930 W 16th St Ste C1, Costa Mesa
(92627-4337)
PHONE.....................................949 645-0981
Cheryl Thoreen, *President*
Nicole Coffey, *Prgrmr*
EMP: 32
SQ FT: 2,500
SALES: 1MM **Privately Held**
SIC: 2392 5023 5719 Pillows, bed: made
  from purchased materials; bedspreads;
  bedding (sheets, blankets, spreads & pil-
  lows)

(P-3647)
**UNIVERSAL CUSHION
COMPANY INC (PA)**
Also Called: Cloud Nine Comforts
3121 Fujita St, Torrance (90505-4006)
PHONE.....................................323 887-8000
Sharyl G Bloom, *President*
Sharyl Bloom, *President*
Isabel Incoing, *Executive*
▲ EMP: 34
SQ FT: 17,000
SALES (est): 4.4MM **Privately Held**
WEB: www.universalcushion.com
SIC: 2392 2221 2211 Cushions & pillows;
  comforters & quilts: made from purchased
  materials; pillowcases: made from pur-
  chased materials; comforters & quilts,
  manmade fiber & silk; sheets & sheetings,
  cotton; pillowcases; piques, cotton

(P-3648)
VFT INC
Also Called: Vertical Fiber Technologies
1040 S Vail Ave, Montebello (90640-6020)
PHONE.....................................323 728-2280
John Chang, *President*
▲ EMP: 40 EST: 1998
SQ FT: 70,000
SALES (est): 6.4MM **Privately Held**
WEB: www.bedtimelinens.com
SIC: 2392 Household furnishings

(P-3649)
WASATCH CO
Also Called: Wasatch Import
11000 Wright Rd, Lynwood (90262-3153)
PHONE.....................................310 637-6160
Abdul Wahab, *President*
Yosuf Haroon, *Vice Pres*
▲ EMP: 12
SQ FT: 50,000
SALES (est): 6.7MM **Privately Held**
SIC: 2392 Towels, dishcloths & dust cloths;
  tablecloths & table settings; bedspreads &
  bed sets: made from purchased materi-
  als; mattress pads

(P-3650)
WOOF & POOF INC
388 Orange St, Chico (95928-5091)
PHONE.....................................530 895-0693
Debra Headley, *President*
▲ EMP: 30
SQ FT: 14,000

▲ = Import ▼=Export
◆ =Import/Export

SALES (est): 2.3MM **Privately Held**
WEB: www.woofpoof.com
SIC: 2392 Pillows, bed: made from purchased materials

(P-3651)
XIMENEZ ICONS
Also Called: Goddess of Gadgets
1107 Fair Oaks Ave Ste 11, South
Pasadena (91030-3311)
PHONE...............................310 344-6670
Lisa Rodgers, *CEO*
EMP: 10 EST: 2017
SALES (est): 493K **Privately Held**
SIC: 2392 Household furnishings

2393 Textile Bags

(P-3652)
ACTION BAG & COVER INC
18401 Mount Langley St, Fountain Valley
(92708-6904)
PHONE...............................714 965-7777
Byung Ki Lee, *President*
▲ EMP: 80 EST: 1978
SQ FT: 15,000
SALES (est): 8.1MM **Privately Held**
WEB: www.actionbaginc.com
SIC: 2393 Canvas bags

(P-3653)
AMERICAN SPORT BAGS INC
1485 E Warner Ave, Santa Ana
(92705-5434)
PHONE...............................714 547-8013
Camacho Alvarez, *President*
Mary Ann Alvarez, *Treasurer*
EMP: 35
SQ FT: 5,000
SALES (est): 3.2MM **Privately Held**
SIC: 2393 3949 3161 Textile bags; sporting & athletic goods; luggage

(P-3654)
CHICOECO INC
Also Called: Chicobag
747 Fortress St, Chico (95973-9012)
PHONE...............................530 342-4426
Andrew Keller, *President*
Crystal Viars, *Sales Mgr*
Victor Cantu, *Sales Associate*
Maddie Roberts, *Sales Associate*
Nau Mazari, *Marketing Staff*
▲ EMP: 30
SALES (est): 4.3MM **Privately Held**
WEB: www.chicobag.com
SIC: 2393 Textile bags

(P-3655)
CONTINENTAL MARKETING SVC INC
15381 Proctor Ave, City of Industry
(91745-1022)
PHONE...............................626 626-8888
Dawn Du, *President*
EMP: 17
SALES (est): 2MM **Privately Held**
SIC: 2393 Bags & containers, except sleeping bags: textile

(P-3656)
CTA MANUFACTURING INC
Also Called: Bagmasters
1160 California Ave, Corona (92881-3324)
PHONE...............................951 280-2400
Richard Gayne Whittier, *President*
Gayne Whittier, *Vice Pres*
Michael Webb, *Social Dir*
Darren Taylor, *Mktg Coord*
▲ EMP: 40 EST: 1922
SQ FT: 23,000
SALES (est): 6.1MM **Privately Held**
WEB: www.ctamfg.com
SIC: 2393 Textile bags

(P-3657)
CUSHION WORKS INC
3320 18th St, San Francisco (94110-1905)
PHONE...............................415 552-6220
Susan Schroeder, *President*
EMP: 10
SQ FT: 15,000

SALES: 1.2MM **Privately Held**
WEB: www.cushionworks.com
SIC: 2393 Cushions, except spring & carpet: purchased materials

(P-3658)
GLEASON CORPORATION (PA)
10474 Santa Monica Blvd # 400, Los Angeles (90025-6932)
PHONE...............................310 470-6001
Harry Kotler, *President*
Howard Seinman, *COO*
Jeff Leggat, *Treasurer*
Shirley Kotler, *Vice Pres*
Jim Kerr, *Information Mgr*
◆ EMP: 11 EST: 1946
SQ FT: 8,000
SALES: 17MM **Privately Held**
WEB: www.gleasoncorporation.com
SIC: 2393 2399 5083 Textile bags; hammocks & other net products; lawn machinery & equipment

(P-3659)
GOLD CREST INDUSTRIES INC
1018 E Acacia St, Ontario (91761-4553)
P.O. Box 3280 (91761-0928)
PHONE...............................909 930-9069
Jose Garcia, *President*
Frank Castillo, *Manager*
EMP: 40
SQ FT: 14,000
SALES (est): 3.6MM **Privately Held**
WEB: www.goldcrestind.com
SIC: 2393 3999 2392 Cushions, except spring & carpet: purchased materials; garden umbrellas; household furnishings

(P-3660)
JANSPORT INC (HQ)
2601 Harbor Bay Pkwy, Alameda
(94502-3042)
P.O. Box 372670, Denver CO (80237-6670)
PHONE...............................510 814-7400
Mackey McDonald, *President*
Julia Holenstein, *Graphic Designe*
◆ EMP: 10
SALES (est): 1.2MM
SALES (corp-wide): 13.8MM **Publicly Held**
WEB: www.vfc.com
SIC: 2393 Bags & containers, except sleeping bags: textile
PA: V.F. Corporation
105 Corporate Center Blvd
Greensboro NC 27408
336 424-6000

(P-3661)
JU-JU-BE INTL LLC (PA)
15300 Barranca Pkwy # 100, Irvine
(92618-2256)
PHONE...............................877 258-5823
Joseph J Croft, *President*
Rachelle Croft, *Vice Pres*
Tracie Schor, *Vice Pres*
Nicole Eckert, *Marketing Mgr*
Erin Fischer, *Sales Staff*
▲ EMP: 28
SALES (est): 2MM **Privately Held**
SIC: 2393 Bags & containers, except sleeping bags: textile

(P-3662)
OUTDOOR RECREATION GROUP (PA)
Also Called: Outdoor Products
3450 Mount Vernon Dr, View Park
(90008-4936)
PHONE...............................323 226-0830
Joel Altshule, *Ch of Bd*
Andrew Altshule, *CEO*
Robert Guzman, *Sr Associate*
Chelsea Stockton, *Manager*
◆ EMP: 37
SQ FT: 90,000
SALES (est): 15.5MM **Privately Held**
WEB: www.fieldline.com
SIC: 2393 3949 Textile bags; camping equipment & supplies

(P-3663)
RICKSHAW BAGWORKS INC
904 22nd St, San Francisco (94107-3427)
PHONE...............................415 904-8368

Mark Dwight, *CEO*
Joseph Montana, *Marketing Staff*
Caroline Ikeji, *Manager*
▲ EMP: 26
SALES (est): 3.5MM **Privately Held**
SIC: 2393 Textile bags

(P-3664)
RIVERSIDE TENT & AWNING CO
231 E Alcandro Blvd Ste A, Riverside
(92508)
PHONE...............................951 683-1925
Chilton E Burt, *President*
Betty Burt, *Vice Pres*
▲ EMP: 12 EST: 1919
SQ FT: 20,000
SALES: 1.5MM **Privately Held**
SIC: 2393 2394 Canvas bags; canvas & related products

(P-3665)
SPECIAL FORCES CUSTOM GEAR INC
2949 Hoover Ave, National City (91950)
PHONE...............................619 241-5453
Juan Vazquez, *President*
EMP: 38
SQ FT: 18,500
SALES (est): 1.2MM **Privately Held**
SIC: 2393 Bags & containers, except sleeping bags: textile

(P-3666)
TIMBUK2 DESIGNS INC
2031 Cessna Dr, Vacaville (95688-8874)
PHONE...............................800 865-2513
Chris Garcia, *Manager*
EMP: 25 **Privately Held**
SIC: 2393 Canvas bags
PA: Timbuk2 Designs, Inc.
583 Shotwell St
San Francisco CA 94110

(P-3667)
TIMBUK2 DESIGNS INC (PA)
583 Shotwell St, San Francisco
(94110-1915)
PHONE...............................415 252-4300
Patricia Cazzato, *CEO*
Tony Meneghetti, *CFO*
Geoff Mather, *Store Mgr*
Jesse Gillingham, *Business Mgr*
Kyle Tan, *Analyst*
▲ EMP: 60
SQ FT: 30,000
SALES (est): 14.2MM **Privately Held**
WEB: www.timbuk2.com
SIC: 2393 Canvas bags

(P-3668)
WESSCO INTERNATIONAL LTD A C (PA)
11400 W Olympic Blvd # 450, Los Angeles
(90064-1550)
PHONE...............................310 477-4272
Robert Bregman, *President*
Nick Bregman, *COO*
Tyler Shepodd, *CFO*
Alex Silva, *Creative Dir*
Miranda Kuhl, *Admin Asst*
◆ EMP: 30
SQ FT: 7,000
SALES (est): 54.2MM **Privately Held**
WEB: www.wessco.net
SIC: 2393 Textile bags

(P-3669)
WORLD TEXTILE AND BAG INC
4680 Pell Dr Ste B, Sacramento
(95838-2082)
PHONE...............................916 922-9222
Richard Quinley, *CEO*
EMP: 33
SALES (est): 4.3MM **Privately Held**
SIC: 2393 Textile bags

(P-3670)
YAMAMOTO OF ORIENT INC
Also Called: Yamamotoyama of America
12475 Mills Ave, Chino (91710-2078)
PHONE...............................909 591-7654
Willy Gomez, *Branch Mgr*
EMP: 10 **Privately Held**
SIC: 2393 Tea bags, fabric: made from purchased materials

HQ: Yamamoto Of Orient, Inc.
122 Voyager St
Pomona CA 91768
909 594-7356

2394 Canvas Prdts

(P-3671)
A-AZTEC RENTS & SELLS INC (PA)
Also Called: Aztec Tents
2665 Columbia St, Torrance (90503-3801)
PHONE...............................310 347-3010
Chuck Miller, *CEO*
Alex Kouzmanoff, *Vice Pres*
David Bradley, *General Mgr*
Claudia Garza, *Executive Asst*
Eric Vanderploeg, *Financial Exec*
◆ EMP: 125
SQ FT: 70,000
SALES (est): 16.9MM **Privately Held**
WEB: www.aztectent.com
SIC: 2394 Canvas & related products

(P-3672)
ABC SUN CONTROL LLC
7241 Ethel Ave, North Hollywood
(91605-4215)
PHONE...............................818 982-6989
Donald B Smallwood,
Martina Smallwood, *Vice Pres*
Martina H Smallwood,
▲ EMP: 16
SQ FT: 30,000
SALES (est): 2.5MM **Privately Held**
WEB: www.abcsuncontrol.com
SIC: 2394 Awnings, fabric: made from purchased materials

(P-3673)
BAY AREA CANVAS INC
2362 De La Cruz Blvd, Santa Clara
(95050-2921)
PHONE...............................408 727-4314
Chris Ferretti, *CEO*
Kevin Zierman, *Partner*
EMP: 12
SQ FT: 4,000
SALES (est): 1.3MM **Privately Held**
WEB: www.bayareaawning.com
SIC: 2394 Awnings, fabric: made from purchased materials

(P-3674)
BRAMPTON MTHESEN FABR PDTS INC
Also Called: Sullivan & Brampton
1688 Abram Ct, San Leandro
(94577-3227)
PHONE...............................510 483-7771
Fax: 510 483-7723
EMP: 20
SQ FT: 40,000
SALES (est): 1.9MM **Privately Held**
WEB: www.sullivanandbrampton.com
SIC: 2394 2519 2393

(P-3675)
CANVAS AWNING CO INC
325 W Main St, Ontario (91762-3843)
PHONE...............................909 447-5100
Mark Burg, *President*
Roseanna Burg, *Vice Pres*
EMP: 18
SALES (est): 1.5MM **Privately Held**
WEB: www.apexstructures.com
SIC: 2394 Awnings, fabric: made from purchased materials

(P-3676)
CANVAS CONCEPTS INC
649 Anita St Ste A2, Chula Vista
(91911-4658)
PHONE...............................619 424-3428
Robert A Mackenzie, *President*
Olivia Appel, *Corp Secy*
Anton Silvernagel, *Vice Pres*
Dale Kalar, *VP Sales*
EMP: 18
SQ FT: 9,600
SALES: 1.3MM **Privately Held**
WEB: www.canvasstore.com
SIC: 2394 Awnings, fabric: made from purchased materials

(P-3677)
CANVAS SPECIALTY INC
1309 S Eastern Ave, Commerce
(90040-5610)
PHONE.....................323 722-1156
Gregory Naiman, *President*
Richard P Naiman, *Exec VP*
▲ EMP: 25
SQ FT: 84,000
SALES (est): 2.9MM **Privately Held**
WEB: www.can-spec.com
SIC: 2394 5199 Tarpaulins, fabric: made from purchased materials; canvas products

(P-3678)
CARAVAN CANOPY INTL INC
14600 Alondra Blvd, La Mirada
(90638-5603)
PHONE.....................714 367-3000
Lindy Jung Park, *CEO*
David Hudrlik, *President*
▲ EMP: 50
SQ FT: 50,000
SALES (est): 8.1MM **Privately Held**
WEB: www.caravanintl.com
SIC: 2394 Canvas & related products

(P-3679)
CASTILLO MARITESS
Also Called: American Supply
1490 S Vineyard Ave Ste G, Ontario
(91761-8043)
P.O. Box 2322, Chino (91708-2322)
PHONE.....................949 216-0468
Maritess Castillo, *Owner*
Von Castillo, *Co-Owner*
EMP: 16
SQ FT: 1,600
SALES: 400K **Privately Held**
SIC: 2394 Liners & covers, fabric: made from purchased materials

(P-3680)
CITY CANVAS
1381 N 10th St, San Jose (95112-2804)
PHONE.....................408 287-2688
John M Cerrito, *President*
EMP: 13
SQ FT: 10,000
SALES: 1.5MM **Privately Held**
WEB: www.citycanvas.com
SIC: 2394 7699 Awnings, fabric: made from purchased materials; awning repair shop

(P-3681)
E-Z UP DIRECTCOM
Also Called: EZ Up Factory Store
1900 2nd St, Colton (92324)
PHONE.....................909 426-0060
Rose Kilstrom,
EMP: 25
SALES (est): 2.5MM **Privately Held**
WEB: www.ezupdirect.com
SIC: 2394 Shades, canvas: made from purchased materials

(P-3682)
EIDE INDUSTRIES INC
16215 Piuma Ave, Cerritos (90703-1528)
PHONE.....................562 402-8335
Don Araiza, *President*
Jesus Borrego, *Vice Pres*
Dan Neill, *Vice Pres*
Joe Belli, *Admin Sec*
Matt Aulbach, *Project Mgr*
◆ EMP: 80
SQ FT: 41,000
SALES (est): 14.9MM **Privately Held**
WEB: www.eideindustries.com
SIC: 2394 Tents: made from purchased materials; awnings, fabric: made from purchased materials

(P-3683)
FRAMETENT INC
Also Called: Central Tent
26480 Summit Cir, Santa Clarita
(91350-2991)
PHONE.....................661 290-3375
Nattha Chunapongse, *President*
◆ EMP: 30

SALES (est): 5.4MM **Privately Held**
WEB: www.centraltent.com
SIC: 2394 5999 Tents: made from purchased materials; tents

(P-3684)
GOLDEN FLEECE DESIGNS INC
441 S Victory Blvd, Burbank (91502-2353)
PHONE.....................323 849-1901
Antoinette Argyropoulos, *President*
Symeon Argyropoulos, *Chairman*
Maria Argyropoulos, *Vice Pres*
EMP: 15
SQ FT: 16,000
SALES (est): 1.5MM **Privately Held**
SIC: 2394 5199 Canvas & related products; advertising specialties

(P-3685)
GUARDIAN CORPORATE SERVICES
Also Called: Acme Awning & Canvas Co
2814 University Ave Frnt, San Diego
(92104-2993)
PHONE.....................619 295-2646
EMP: 25
SQ FT: 1,000
SALES: 3.2MM
SALES (corp-wide): 156.9MM **Privately Held**
SIC: 2394
HQ: Reassure Companies Services Limited
Windsor House Ironmasters Way
Telford TF3 4
843 372-9142

(P-3686)
HARBOR CUSTOM CANVAS
733 W Anaheim St, Long Beach
(90813-2819)
PHONE.....................562 436-7708
Daniel Loggans, *CEO*
EMP: 10
SQ FT: 7,500
SALES (est): 1.1MM **Privately Held**
WEB: www.harborcustomcanvas.com
SIC: 2394 Liners & covers, fabric: made from purchased materials

(P-3687)
INTERNATIONAL E-Z UP INC (PA)
1900 2nd St, Norco (92860-2803)
PHONE.....................800 457-4233
William Bradford Smith, *CEO*
Mark Carter, *Ch of Bd*
Brad Smith, *President*
Jason Miller, *Software Dev*
Raymond Garcia, *Technology*
◆ EMP: 100
SQ FT: 115,000
SALES (est): 18.6MM **Privately Held**
WEB: www.ezup.com
SIC: 2394 Shades, canvas: made from purchased materials

(P-3688)
INTERNATIONAL TENTS & SUPPLIES
1720 1st St, San Fernando (91340-2711)
PHONE.....................818 599-6258
▲ EMP: 10 EST: 2008
SALES (est): 530K **Privately Held**
SIC: 2394

(P-3689)
KENSINGTON PROTECTIVE PRODUCTS
151 N Reservoir St, Pomona (91767-5709)
PHONE.....................909 469-1240
Anthony Gatto, *President*
Becky Hasbath, *Admin Sec*
▲ EMP: 12
SALES (est): 907.2K **Privately Held**
WEB: www.kensingtonproducts.com
SIC: 2394 3199 Awnings, fabric: made from purchased materials; saddles or parts

(P-3690)
LARSENS INC
1041 17th Ave Ste A, Santa Cruz
(95062-3070)
PHONE.....................831 476-3009
Kurt W Larsen, *President*

Susan Larsen, *Vice Pres*
EMP: 15 EST: 1972
SQ FT: 6,000
SALES (est): 2MM **Privately Held**
WEB: www.larsensails.com
SIC: 2394 Sails: made from purchased materials

(P-3691)
MODESTO TENT AND AWNING INC
Also Called: Mid-Valley Tarp Service
4448 Sisk Rd, Modesto (95356-8729)
PHONE.....................209 545-1607
Robert Valk, *President*
Leonard Rigg, *Corp Secy*
▲ EMP: 12
SQ FT: 26,000
SALES (est): 1.4MM **Privately Held**
WEB: www.modestotentandawning.com
SIC: 2394 2399 7359 5999 Awnings, fabric: made from purchased materials; tarpaulins, fabric: made from purchased materials; banners, made from fabric; tent & tarpaulin rental; tents; signs, not made in custom sign painting shops; truck equipment & parts

(P-3692)
N J P SPORTS INC
548 Arden Ave, Glendale (91203-1012)
P.O. Box 1469 (91209-1469)
PHONE.....................818 247-3914
Norman J Perry, *President*
Regina Perry, *Vice Pres*
EMP: 15 EST: 1969
SALES (est): 1.7MM **Privately Held**
WEB: www.njpsports.com
SIC: 2394 5999 3949 2298 Canvas & related products; canvas products; sporting & athletic goods; cordage & twine

(P-3693)
NATHAN KIMMEL COMPANY LLC
4880 Valley Blvd, Los Angeles
(90032-3315)
PHONE.....................213 627-8556
Carol Jean Schary, *Mng Member*
Dat Trust,
EMP: 13
SALES (est): 2.1MM **Privately Held**
WEB: www.nathankimmel.com
SIC: 2394 5085 Tarpaulins, fabric: made from purchased materials; industrial supplies

(P-3694)
NORTH SAILS GROUP LLC
Also Called: North Sails One Design
4630 Santa Fe St, San Diego
(92109-1601)
PHONE.....................619 226-1415
Vince Brun, *Owner*
Celeste Palumbo, *Office Mgr*
Sean Neely, *Engineer*
Chris Buncke, *Sales Associate*
Michael Richelsen, *Director*
EMP: 60
SQ FT: 11,592 **Privately Held**
WEB: www.northsails.com
SIC: 2394 Sails: made from purchased materials
HQ: North Sails Group, Llc
125 Old Gate Ln Ste 7
Milford CT 06460
203 874-7548

(P-3695)
PACIFIC PLAY TENTS INC
2801 E 12th St, Los Angeles (90023-3621)
PHONE.....................323 269-0431
Victor Preisler, *CEO*
Brian Jablan, *Vice Pres*
Andrea Alexanian, *Graphic Designe*
▲ EMP: 13
SQ FT: 75,000
SALES (est): 1.6MM **Privately Held**
WEB: www.pacificplaytents.com
SIC: 2394 5941 5092 3944 Tents: made from purchased materials; sporting goods & bicycle shops; toys; games, toys & children's vehicles

(P-3696)
PACIFIC TENT AND AWNING
Also Called: Awnings
7295 N Palm Bluffs Ave, Fresno
(93711-5737)
PHONE.....................559 436-8147
Ken Bricker, *Principal*
Michael Mygind, *Partner*
EMP: 10
SQ FT: 3,000
SALES (est): 1MM **Privately Held**
SIC: 2394 Awnings, fabric: made from purchased materials

(P-3697)
PALO ALTO AWNING INC
1381 N 10th St, San Jose (95112-2804)
PHONE.....................650 968-4270
John M Cerrito, *President*
Robert Terry, *General Mgr*
EMP: 16 EST: 1993
SQ FT: 4,800
SALES: 1MM **Privately Held**
SIC: 2394 5999 Awnings, fabric: made from purchased materials; awnings

(P-3698)
PARADISE MANUFACTURING CO INC
Also Called: Arden/Paradise Manufacturing
13364 Aerospace Dr 100, Victorville
(92394-7902)
PHONE.....................909 477-3460
Robert Sachs, *President*
Michael Sachs, *Vice Pres*
EMP: 150
SALES (est): 12.2MM **Privately Held**
SIC: 2394 Air cushions & mattresses, canvas; canvas awnings & canopies

(P-3699)
PHILIP A STITT AGENCY
Also Called: Capitol Tarpaulin Co
3900 Stockton Blvd, Sacramento
(95820-2913)
PHONE.....................916 451-2801
Martin Stitt, *President*
Philip L Stitt, *Corp Secy*
Richard Pechal, *Vice Pres*
EMP: 15
SQ FT: 13,000
SALES (est): 1.1MM **Privately Held**
WEB: www.captarp.com
SIC: 2394 Tarpaulins, fabric: made from purchased materials; tents: made from purchased materials; awnings, fabric: made from purchased materials

(P-3700)
POLYAIR INTER PACK INC
1692 Jenks Dr Ste 102, Corona
(92880-2513)
PHONE.....................951 737-7125
Jim Higgins, *Branch Mgr*
EMP: 80
SALES (est): 9.9MM **Privately Held**
SIC: 2394 5199 Tarpaulins, fabric: made from purchased materials; liners & covers, fabric: made from purchased materials; packaging materials

(P-3701)
REDWOOD EMPIRE AWNG & FURN CO
3547 Santa Rosa Ave, Santa Rosa
(95407-8270)
PHONE.....................707 633-8156
Marilyn Lenney, *President*
Gregory Lenney, *Treasurer*
Leon Lenney, *Treasurer*
Greg Lenney, *Vice Pres*
Micheal Lenney, *Admin Sec*
EMP: 11
SQ FT: 8,000
SALES: 1.5MM **Privately Held**
WEB: www.reaco.com
SIC: 2394 5999 8742 Awnings, fabric: made from purchased materials; awnings; industrial consultant

(P-3702)
S A FIELDS INC
Also Called: Tent City Canvas House
3328 N Duke Ave, Fresno (93727-7803)
PHONE.....................559 292-1221

▲ = Import ▼=Export
◆ =Import/Export

Stephen A Fields, *President*
Susan Fields, *Admin Sec*
EMP: 16
SQ FT: 10,000
SALES (est): 1.6MM **Privately Held**
WEB: www.tentcitycanvashouse.com
SIC: 2394 Canvas & related products

(P-3703)
SAN JOSE AWNING COMPANY INC
755 Chestnut St Ste E, San Jose
(95110-1832)
PHONE..................................408 350-7000
Michael Yaholkovsky, *President*
Tracie Ho, *Admin Asst*
Evelyn Trang, *Production*
EMP: 14
SQ FT: 8,800
SALES (est): 2MM **Privately Held**
WEB: www.sanjoseawning.com
SIC: 2394 Awnings, fabric: made from purchased materials

(P-3704)
SCHULZ LEATHER CO INC
Also Called: Schulz Industries
16247 Minnesota Ave, Paramount
(90723-4915)
PHONE..................................562 633-1081
Robert Schulz, *President*
Lillian Schulz, *Corp Secy*
Bob Schulz, *General Mgr*
EMP: 25
SQ FT: 12,000
SALES (est): 2.9MM **Privately Held**
WEB: www.fodbuster.com
SIC: 2394 2393 3161 2273 Liners & covers, fabric: made from purchased materials; bags & containers, except sleeping bags: textile; luggage; carpets & rugs; narrow fabric mills; broadwoven fabric mills, manmade

(P-3705)
SEMCO AEROSPACE
9637 Owensmouth Ave, Chatsworth
(91311-4804)
PHONE..................................818 678-9381
Joseph Sember, *President*
EMP: 10
SALES (est): 650.6K **Privately Held**
SIC: 2394 3357 Air cushions & mattresses, canvas; aluminum wire & cable

(P-3706)
SHELTER SYSTEMS
224 Walnut St, Menlo Park (94025-2613)
PHONE..................................650 323-6202
Robert Gillis, *Owner*
EMP: 10
SALES (est): 946.2K **Privately Held**
WEB: www.shelter-systems.com
SIC: 2394 Tents: made from purchased materials

(P-3707)
STARK MFG CO
Also Called: Stark Awning & Canvas
76 Broadway, Chula Vista (91910-1422)
PHONE..................................619 425-5880
Turner Stark, *Chairman*
Robert Donegan, *Info Tech Mgr*
Gene Lentfer, *Mktg Dir*
Steve Hegyi, *Manager*
EMP: 29 **EST:** 1953
SQ FT: 3,500
SALES (est): 3.9MM **Privately Held**
WEB: www.starkmfgco.com
SIC: 2394 3444 Awnings, fabric: made from purchased materials; sheet metalwork

(P-3708)
SUPERIOR AWNING INC
14555 Titus St, Panorama City
(91402-4920)
PHONE..................................818 780-7200
Brian Hotchkiss, *President*
Julie Hotchkiss, *Vice Pres*
EMP: 40
SQ FT: 11,776

SALES (est): 3.9MM **Privately Held**
WEB: www.superiorawning.com
SIC: 2394 5999 3444 Awnings, fabric: made from purchased materials; awnings; sheet metalwork

(P-3709)
TARPS & TIE-DOWNS INC (PA)
24967 Huntwood Ave, Hayward
(94544-1814)
PHONE..................................510 782-8772
David Lee, *President*
Todd Stiles, *VP Bus Dvlpt*
Cindy C Cortes, *Branch Mgr*
Michael Chun, *General Mgr*
▲ **EMP:** 10
SQ FT: 12,000
SALES (est): 8.7MM **Privately Held**
SIC: 2394 Tarpaulins, fabric: made from purchased materials

(P-3710)
TEMPTROL INDUSTRIES INC
3909 Onawa Ct, Antelope (95843-2412)
PHONE..................................916 344-4457
Richard D Koscinski, *President*
EMP: 12
SQ FT: 11,000
SALES (est): 3.5MM **Privately Held**
SIC: 2394 Canvas & related products

(P-3711)
TRANSPORTATION EQUIPMENT INC (PA)
Also Called: Pulltarps Manufacturing
1404 N Marshall Ave, El Cajon
(92020-1521)
PHONE..................................619 449-8860
Nathan Lynn Chenowth, *President*
Bryan Elzey, *General Mgr*
Edgar Maigue, *Production*
Rodger Hubbard, *Manager*
▲ **EMP:** 40
SQ FT: 20,000
SALES (est): 7.6MM **Privately Held**
WEB: www.pulltarps.com
SIC: 2394 3479 Tarpaulins, fabric: made from purchased materials; bonderizing of metal or metal products

(P-3712)
ULLMAN SAILS INC (PA)
2710 S Croddy Way, Santa Ana
(92704-5206)
PHONE..................................714 432-1860
Bruce Cooper, *President*
EMP: 15
SQ FT: 10,900
SALES (est): 2.7MM **Privately Held**
WEB: www.ullmansails.com
SIC: 2394 Sails: made from purchased materials

(P-3713)
VINYL FABRICATIONS INC
2690 5th Ave, Oroville (95965-5824)
PHONE..................................530 532-1236
Michael G Smith, *President*
Bonita Charron, *Treasurer*
EMP: 10
SQ FT: 12,000
SALES (est): 443.5K **Privately Held**
WEB: www.vinylfabricators.com
SIC: 2394 Liners & covers, fabric: made from purchased materials

(P-3714)
WEST COAST CANVAS (PA)
1242 W Fremont St, Stockton
(95203-2624)
PHONE..................................209 333-0243
Curtis G Page, *Owner*
Sandy Galli, *Benefits Mgr*
EMP: 15
SALES (est): 1.4MM **Privately Held**
WEB: www.westcoastcanvas.com
SIC: 2394 Liners & covers, fabric: made from purchased materials; convertible tops, canvas or boat: from purchased materials; awnings, fabric: made from purchased materials

(P-3715)
WESTCOAST COMPANIES INC
Also Called: Westcoast Elevator Pads
725-729 E Washington Blvd, Pasadena
(91104)
PHONE..................................626 794-9330
Leslie Malloy, *President*
EMP: 10
SQ FT: 8,000
SALES: 1.5MM **Privately Held**
SIC: 2394 Air cushions & mattresses, canvas

(P-3716)
WINDTAMER TARPS
13704 Hanford Armona Rd B2, Hanford
(93230-9263)
P.O. Box 645, Lemoore (93245-0645)
PHONE..................................559 584-2080
Bobby Lee, *Owner*
EMP: 15
SQ FT: 10,000
SALES: 720K **Privately Held**
SIC: 2394 Tarpaulins, fabric: made from purchased materials

2395 Pleating & Stitching For The Trade

(P-3717)
AAA GARMENTS & LETTERING INC
Also Called: Competitor Golf & Tennis AP
9309 La Riviera Dr Ste C, Sacramento
(95826-2437)
PHONE..................................916 363-4590
James L Lortz, *President*
Barbara Beringer, *Office Mgr*
EMP: 14
SQ FT: 5,600
SALES (est): 1.1MM **Privately Held**
SIC: 2395 Emblems, embroidered; embroidery & art needlework

(P-3718)
AAA PRINTING BY WIZARD
8961 W Sunset Blvd Ste 1d, West Hollywood (90069-1886)
PHONE..................................310 285-0505
Michael Norman, *Owner*
EMP: 30
SALES (est): 1.9MM **Privately Held**
SIC: 2395 Embroidery products, except schiffli machine

(P-3719)
ACADEMY AWNING INC
1501 Beach St, Montebello (90640-5431)
PHONE..................................800 422-9646
James D Richman, *President*
Maury Rice, *Corp Secy*
Tom Shapiro, *Vice Pres*
EMP: 25
SALES (est): 3.7MM **Privately Held**
WEB: www.academyawning.com
SIC: 2395 5999 Quilted fabrics or cloth; awnings

(P-3720)
ACE PLEATING & STITCHING INC
2351 E 49th St, Vernon (90058-2820)
PHONE..................................323 582-8213
Jorge Nevarez Sr, *President*
Jorge Nevarez Jr, *Vice Pres*
EMP: 25
SALES (est): 1.9MM **Privately Held**
WEB: www.acepleatinginc.com
SIC: 2395 Pleating & tucking, for the trade

(P-3721)
ALL-STAR MKTG & PROMOTIONS INC
Also Called: All-Star Logo
8715 Aviation Blvd, Inglewood
(90301-2003)
PHONE..................................323 582-4880
Edmond Moossighi, *Vice Pres*
▲ **EMP:** 10
SQ FT: 10,000
SALES: 2MM **Privately Held**
WEB: www.allstarlogo.com
SIC: 2395 Embroidery & art needlework

(P-3722)
AMERICAN QUILTING COMPANY INC
Also Called: Antaky Quilting Company
1540 Calzona St, Los Angeles
(90023-3254)
PHONE..................................323 233-2500
Derek Antaky, *CEO*
Elias Antaky Jr, *Vice Pres*
▲ **EMP:** 30
SALES (est): 2.5MM **Privately Held**
WEB: www.antakyquilting.com
SIC: 2395 Quilting, for the trade

(P-3723)
ANAHEIM EMBROIDERY INC
Also Called: KB Design Enterprises
1230 N Jefferson St Ste C, Anaheim
(92807-1631)
PHONE..................................714 563-5220
Kent D Brush, *President*
Kent Brush, *President*
Catherine Brush, *Vice Pres*
EMP: 30
SQ FT: 10,000
SALES (est): 3.9MM **Privately Held**
WEB: www.anaheimembroidery.com
SIC: 2395 2396 Embroidery products, except schiffli machine; automotive & apparel trimmings

(P-3724)
B J EMBROIDERY & SCREENPRINT
272 E Smith St, Ukiah (95482-4411)
PHONE..................................707 463-2767
Walt Richey, *Owner*
EMP: 12 **EST:** 2000
SALES (est): 601.2K **Privately Held**
SIC: 2395 Emblems, embroidered

(P-3725)
BEST- IN- WEST
Also Called: Best-In-West Emblem Co
2279 Eagle Glen Pkwy, Corona
(92883-0790)
PHONE..................................909 947-6507
Eric Roberts, *President*
Heriberto Perez, *Treasurer*
Beatriz Roberts, *Admin Sec*
EMP: 50
SQ FT: 15,000
SALES (est): 4.1MM **Privately Held**
WEB: www.bestinwest.net
SIC: 2395 2759 Embroidery products, except schiffli machine; commercial printing

(P-3726)
CADEN CONCEPTS LLC
13412 Ventura Blvd # 300, Sherman Oaks
(91423-6201)
PHONE..................................323 651-1190
Lori Caden, *Mng Member*
Kari Caden,
Warren Friedman,
▲ **EMP:** 12
SQ FT: 3,900
SALES (est): 1.6MM **Privately Held**
WEB: www.cadenconcepts.com
SIC: 2395 Embroidery products, except schiffli machine

(P-3727)
CAL NOR EMBROIDERY & SPC
4208 Douglas Blvd Ste 100, Granite Bay
(95746-5909)
PHONE..................................916 786-3131
Jim Thyken, *Partner*
Dana Thyken, *Partner*
Amy Schneider, *Mktg Dir*
Ann Colvin, *Manager*
EMP: 10
SALES (est): 700K **Privately Held**
WEB: www.norcallogos.com
SIC: 2395 Embroidery products, except schiffli machine

(P-3728)
CAL STITCH EMBROIDERY INC
2057 Hunter Rd, Chino Hills (91709-5219)
PHONE..................................909 465-5448
Johnny Ko, *President*
Judy Ko, *Vice Pres*
EMP: 18
SQ FT: 8,000

(PA)=Parent Co (HQ)=Headquarters (DH)=Div Headquarters
✿ = New Business established in last 2 years

SALES (est): 1.1MM **Privately Held**
WEB: www.calsportswear.com
SIC: 2395 Embroidery products, except
　schiffli machine

(P-3729)
CECILIAS DESIGNS INC
6862 Vanscoy Ave, North Hollywood
(91605-5330)
PHONE....................................323 584-6151
Edgar Miron, *President*
Julio Miron, *Vice Pres*
Marlyn Mendenhall, *Admin Sec*
EMP: 30
SQ FT: 10,000
SALES (est): 2.2MM **Privately Held**
SIC: 2395 Embroidery products, except
　schiffli machine

(P-3730)
CHRISTINE ALEXANDER INC
110 E 9th St Ste B336, Los Angeles
(90079-3336)
PHONE....................................213 488-1114
EMP: 24 **Privately Held**
SIC: 2395

(P-3731)
CLASSIC GRAPHIX
12152 Woodruff Ave, Downey
(90241-5606)
PHONE....................................562 940-0806
Judy Bathurst, *President*
Jeff Bathurst, *Corp Secy*
Scott Bathurst, *Vice Pres*
EMP: 12
SQ FT: 15,000
SALES (est): 1MM **Privately Held**
WEB: www.classicgraphix.com
SIC: 2395 2759 Emblems, embroidered;
　screen printing

(P-3732)
CLASSIC QUILTING
1471 E Warner Ave, Santa Ana
(92705-5434)
PHONE....................................714 558-8312
Rosa Aceves, *Owner*
EMP: 10
SALES (est): 390K **Privately Held**
SIC: 2395 2211 Quilted fabrics or cloth;
　sheets, bedding & table cloths: cotton

(P-3733)
COASTAL EMBROIDERY INC
2263 Pickwick Dr, Camarillo (93010-6409)
PHONE....................................805 383-5593
Brian Tillquist, *CEO*
Don Tillquist, *Treasurer*
EMP: 12
SALES (est): 693.4K **Privately Held**
WEB: www.coastalemb.net
SIC: 2395 Embroidery products, except
　schiffli machine; embroidery & art needle-
　work

(P-3734)
COLORSTITCH INC
3100 S Croddy Way, Santa Ana
(92704-6346)
PHONE....................................714 754-4220
Federico P Garcia, *President*
EMP: 10
SALES (est): 807.8K **Privately Held**
WEB: www.colorstitch.biz
SIC: 2395 Embroidery products, except
　schiffli machine

(P-3735)
COMPUTERIZED EMBROIDERY CO
Also Called: C.E.C.
673 E Cooley Dr Ste 101, Colton
(92324-4016)
PHONE....................................909 825-3841
Ruben Duran Jr, *Owner*
Karen Duran, *Co-Owner*
▲ **EMP:** 10
SQ FT: 200
SALES (est): 737K **Privately Held**
WEB: www.cecembroidery.com
SIC: 2395 2759 5699 Embroidery prod-
　ucts, except schiffli machine; commercial
　printing; customized clothing & apparel

(P-3736)
DCL PRODUCTIONS
1284 Missouri St, San Francisco
(94107-3310)
PHONE....................................415 826-2200
David Christopher Long, *Owner*
EMP: 12 **EST:** 1995
SQ FT: 7,500
SALES (est): 1.4MM **Privately Held**
WEB: www.dclproductions.com
SIC: 2395 2759 Embroidery & art needle-
　work; promotional printing; screen printing

(P-3737)
DOUBLE V INDUSTRIES
Also Called: Bluefrog Embroidery
717 Whitney St, San Leandro (94577-1117)
PHONE....................................510 347-3764
Michael P Givvin, *President*
Lesa Schultz, *Office Mgr*
Nancy Rumrill, *Accountant*
Winnie Cheung, *Production*
EMP: 40
SQ FT: 10,000
SALES (est): 4.3MM **Privately Held**
WEB: www.bluefrogemb.com
SIC: 2395 Embroidery & art needlework

(P-3738)
DUDEN ENTERPRISES INC
Also Called: Bryngelson Prints
2025 W Park Ave Ste 4, Redlands
(92373-6274)
P.O. Box 1690, Yucaipa (92399-1438)
PHONE....................................909 795-0160
Harlan Duden, *President*
Frank Wisener, *Treasurer*
Lisa Duden, *Admin Sec*
▲ **EMP:** 10
SQ FT: 5,000
SALES (est): 955K **Privately Held**
SIC: 2395 2396 Embroidery & art needle-
　work; screen printing on fabric articles

(P-3739)
E J Y CORPORATION
Also Called: Dlt Co
151 W 33rd St, Los Angeles (90007-4106)
PHONE....................................213 748-1700
Eun Kim, *President*
▲ **EMP:** 35 **EST:** 1999
SQ FT: 8,250
SALES (est): 2.3MM **Privately Held**
WEB: www.dltco.com
SIC: 2395 Embroidery products, except
　schiffli machine

(P-3740)
EMBROIDERTEX WEST LTD (PA)
435 E 16th St, Los Angeles (90015-3726)
PHONE....................................213 749-4319
Leonard Kleiderman, *President*
EMP: 15 **EST:** 1977
SQ FT: 13,000
SALES (est): 5.3MM **Privately Held**
SIC: 2395 2397 Embroidery products, ex-
　cept schiffli machine; schiffli machine em-
　broideries

(P-3741)
EMBROIDERY BY P & J INC
301 E Arrow Hwy Ste 104, San Dimas
(91773-3364)
PHONE....................................909 592-2622
Pat Smith, *President*
EMP: 10
SALES (est): 841K **Privately Held**
WEB: www.embbypj.com
SIC: 2395 Embroidery products, except
　schiffli machine; embroidery & art needle-
　work

(P-3742)
EMBROIDERY ONE CORP
1359 Channing St, Los Angeles
(90021-2410)
PHONE....................................213 572-0280
Danny Yektafar, *President*
Sassan Yektafar, *Bd of Directors*
John Mora, *Manager*
Danny Yekta, *Manager*
EMP: 20
SQ FT: 4,600

SALES (est): 1.1MM **Privately Held**
WEB: www.embroidery-one.com
SIC: 2395 Embroidery products, except
　schiffli machine; embroidery & art needle-
　work

(P-3743)
EMBROIDERY OUTLET
Also Called: Discount Outlet
10460 Magnolia Ave, Riverside
(92505-1812)
PHONE....................................951 687-1750
Yong Jeon, *Owner*
EMP: 10
SALES (est): 323.2K **Privately Held**
SIC: 2395 5699 Embroidery products, ex-
　cept schiffli machine; uniforms & work
　clothing

(P-3744)
EQUIPMENT DE SPORT USA INC
Also Called: Elan Blanc
39301 Badger St Ste 500, Palm Desert
(92211-1162)
PHONE....................................760 772-5544
Sharon Elaine Burr, *President*
Brian Burr, *Vice Pres*
▼ **EMP:** 17
SQ FT: 2,500
SALES (est): 960.6K **Privately Held**
SIC: 2395 Embroidery & art needlework

(P-3745)
HOLCOMB PRODUCTS INC
Also Called: California Embroidery
6751 N Blackstone Ave # 103, Fresno
(93710-3500)
PHONE....................................559 822-2067
Gary Holcomb, *President*
Wilma Holcomb, *Vice Pres*
EMP: 10
SALES (est): 882.4K **Privately Held**
WEB: www.californiaembroidery.com
SIC: 2395 Embroidery products, except
　schiffli machine; embroidery & art needle-
　work

(P-3746)
LA PALM FURNITURES & ACC INC (PA)
Also Called: Royal Plasticware
1650 W Artesia Blvd, Gardena
(90248-3217)
PHONE....................................310 217-2700
Dorra Ngan, *CEO*
Donna Sada, *Vice Pres*
Shawn Morse, *Sales Staff*
Gino Lam, *Director*
John Lee, *Director*
▲ **EMP:** 70
SQ FT: 30,000
SALES (est): 5.3MM **Privately Held**
WEB: www.apolloemb.com
SIC: 2395 Embroidery products, except
　schiffli machine

(P-3747)
LOGO JOES INC
41695 Elm St Ste 101, Murrieta
(92562-1406)
PHONE....................................951 461-0388
Joseph Gisis, *CEO*
EMP: 10
SALES (est): 290.5K **Privately Held**
SIC: 2395 Embroidery products, except
　schiffli machine

(P-3748)
M AND M SPORTS
Also Called: M and M Apparel
14288 Central Ave Ste A, Chino
(91710-5779)
PHONE....................................909 548-3371
Edward J Martin, *Owner*
Sarah Solomon,
EMP: 11
SALES (est): 800K **Privately Held**
WEB: www.mandmapparel.com
SIC: 2395 2261 2262 2396 Embroidery
　products, except schiffli machine; screen
　printing of cotton broadwoven fabrics;
　screen printing: manmade fiber & silk
　broadwoven fabrics; screen printing on
　fabric articles; athletic (warmup, sweat &
　jogging) suits: men's & boys'

(P-3749)
MELMARC PRODUCTS INC
752 S Campus Ave, Ontario (91761-1728)
PHONE....................................714 549-2170
Brian Hirth, *President*
Leila Drager, *COO*
Harish Naran, *CFO*
Eddie Mejia, *Vice Pres*
Christine Tomogen, *Executive*
▲ **EMP:** 330
SQ FT: 85,000
SALES (est): 80.1MM **Privately Held**
WEB: www.melmarc.com
SIC: 2395 2396 Pleating & stitching;
　screen printing on fabric articles

(P-3750)
NATIONAL EMBLEM INC (PA)
3925 E Vernon St, Long Beach
(90815-1727)
P.O. Box 15680 (90815-0680)
PHONE....................................310 515-5055
Milton H Lubin Sr, *President*
Milton H Lubin Jr, *Vice Pres*
▲ **EMP:** 250
SQ FT: 60,000
SALES (est): 46.9MM **Privately Held**
WEB: www.nationalemblem.com
SIC: 2395 2396 Emblems, embroidered;
　automotive & apparel trimmings

(P-3751)
OUTLOOK RESOURCES INC
Also Called: Leftbank Art
14930 Alondra Blvd, La Mirada
(90638-5752)
PHONE....................................714 522-2452
Chris Hyun, *President*
Quinn Blackman, *Office Mgr*
Janell Jernigan, *Administration*
▲ **EMP:** 100
SALES (est): 11.6MM **Privately Held**
WEB: www.leftbankart.com
SIC: 2395 5999 Pleating & stitching; art
　dealers

(P-3752)
PRODUCTION EMBROIDERY INC
1235 Activity Dr Ste D, Vista (92081-8562)
PHONE....................................760 727-7407
Andy Cao, *President*
EMP: 13
SALES (est): 500K **Privately Held**
WEB: www.proembroidery.net
SIC: 2395 Emblems, embroidered

(P-3753)
R & R INDUSTRIES INC
1923 S Santa Fe Ave, Los Angeles
(90021-2917)
PHONE....................................323 581-6000
Ron Mansuri, *President*
EMP: 29
SALES: 1.8MM **Privately Held**
SIC: 2395 Embroidery & art needlework

(P-3754)
REBECCA INTERNATIONAL INC
4587 E 48th St, Vernon (90058-3201)
PHONE....................................323 973-2602
Eli Kahen, *Owner*
EMP: 25
SQ FT: 1,500
SALES: 2MM **Privately Held**
SIC: 2395 2759 7299 Embroidery prod-
　ucts, except schiffli machine; screen print-
　ing; stitching services

(P-3755)
RPM EMBROIDERY INC
1614 Babcock St, Costa Mesa
(92627-4330)
P.O. Box 11847 (92627-0847)
PHONE....................................949 650-0085
Bekki Prather, *Vice Pres*
Doug Prather, *Owner*
EMP: 12
SALES (est): 84.7K **Privately Held**
SIC: 2395 Embroidery products, except
　schiffli machine

(P-3756)
SAN FRANSTITCHCO INC
624 Portal St Ste A, Cotati (94931-3069)
PHONE....................................707 795-6891
Darrel Kolse, *President*

▲ = Import ▼=Export
◆ =Import/Export

EMP: 15
SALES (est): 1.3MM **Privately Held**
SIC: 2395 Embroidery products, except schiffli machine

(P-3757)
SKY SIGNS & GRAPHICS
15340 San Fernnd Missn Bl, Mission Hills (91345-1122)
PHONE..................................818 898-3802
Alvarez Rene, *Owner*
EMP: 18
SALES (est): 1.2MM **Privately Held**
SIC: 2395 3479 5699 1799 Embroidery products, except schiffli machine; engraving jewelry silverware, or metal; miscellaneous apparel & accessories; sign installation & maintenance; signs & advertising specialties

(P-3758)
STITCH FACTORY
Also Called: Stitch Service
120 W 131st St, Los Angeles (90061-1616)
PHONE..................................310 523-3337
Luis Salguero, *Owner*
EMP: 15
SALES: 222K **Privately Held**
SIC: 2395 2396 Embroidery products, except schiffli machine; automotive & apparel trimmings

(P-3759)
SUNDANCE UNIFORM & EMBROIDERY
Also Called: Sundance Uniforms & Embroidery
4050 Durock Rd Ste 13, Shingle Springs (95682-8450)
PHONE..................................530 676-6900
Laurie Oliver, *CEO*
Danny Oliver, *President*
Lori Oliver, *Vice Pres*
EMP: 13 **EST:** 1995
SALES (est): 1MM **Privately Held**
SIC: 2395 5699 2759 Embroidery products, except schiffli machine; uniforms & work clothing; screen printing

(P-3760)
SUPERIOR EMBLEM & EMBROIDERY
2601 S Hill St, Los Angeles (90007-2705)
PHONE..................................213 747-4103
David Park, *President*
Young Park, *Treasurer*
Cathy Hong, *Vice Pres*
H E Park, *Admin Sec*
John Park, *Manager*
EMP: 45
SQ FT: 9,500
SALES (est): 2.4MM **Privately Held**
SIC: 2395 Emblems, embroidered

(P-3761)
TAIGA EMBROIDERY INC
12368 Valley Blvd Ste 114, El Monte (91732-3668)
PHONE..................................626 448-4812
Tomoko Ishida, *President*
EMP: 15
SALES: 508K **Privately Held**
SIC: 2395 Embroidery products, except schiffli machine

(P-3762)
TSS EMBROIDERY INC
3432 Royal Ridge Rd, Chino Hills (91709-1422)
PHONE..................................909 590-1383
EMP: 10
SALES: 300K **Privately Held**
SIC: 2395

(P-3763)
VFLY CORPORATION
Also Called: V Fly
4137 Peck Rd, El Monte (91732-2249)
PHONE..................................626 575-3115
LI Shiu Yu, *President*
▲ **EMP:** 10
SALES (est): 735.1K **Privately Held**
SIC: 2395 2396 Embroidery & art needlework; automotive & apparel trimmings

(P-3764)
WINNING TEAM INC
24922 Anza Dr Ste E, Valencia (91355-1228)
P.O. Box 802197 (91380-2197)
PHONE..................................661 295-1428
Harris G Birken, *President*
EMP: 12
SQ FT: 6,000
SALES (est): 1MM **Privately Held**
WEB: www.thewinningteam.com
SIC: 2395 2253 Embroidery products, except schiffli machine; jackets, knit

---

2396 Automotive Trimmings, Apparel Findings, Related Prdts

(P-3765)
ABSOLUTE SCREEN GRAPHICS INC
2131 S Hellman Ave Ste A, Ontario (91761-8004)
PHONE..................................909 923-1227
Ernest Ferraras, *President*
EMP: 11
SALES (est): 660K **Privately Held**
SIC: 2396 Screen printing on fabric articles

(P-3766)
ABSOLUTE SCREENPRINT INC
333 Cliffwood Park St, Brea (92821-4104)
P.O. Box 9069 (92822-9069)
PHONE..................................714 529-2120
Steven Restivo, *CEO*
Andrea Restivo, *CFO*
Robert Bargelski, *General Mgr*
▲ **EMP:** 250
SQ FT: 65,000
SALES (est): 41.4MM **Privately Held**
WEB: www.absolutescreenprint.com
SIC: 2396 3993 2759 Screen printing on fabric articles; signs & advertising specialties; screen printing

(P-3767)
ACCURATE SCREEN PROCESSING
3538 Foothill Blvd, La Crescenta (91214-1828)
PHONE..................................818 957-3965
Fax: 818 957-6445
EMP: 15
SQ FT: 2,320
SALES (est): 1.1MM
SALES (corp-wide): 2.8MM **Privately Held**
SIC: 2396
PA: Accurate Dial & Nameplate Inc
329 Mira Loma Ave
Glendale CA 91204
323 245-9181

(P-3768)
AD SPECIAL TS EMB SCREEN PRTG
202 Bella Vista Rd Ste B, Vacaville (95687-5412)
PHONE..................................707 452-7272
Mike Anderson, *President*
Donald McKimmy, *Vice Pres*
Lela Anderson, *Admin Sec*
EMP: 12
SQ FT: 6,300
SALES: 900K **Privately Held**
WEB: www.adspecialts.com
SIC: 2396 2395 5941 5699 Screen printing on fabric articles; embroidery & art needlework; sporting goods & bicycle shops; sports apparel

(P-3769)
ALPHA IMPRESSIONS INC
4161 S Main St, Los Angeles (90037-2297)
P.O. Box 3156 (90051-1156)
PHONE..................................323 234-8221
Joseph H Dudas, *President*
Linda I Dudas, *Admin Sec*
EMP: 13
SQ FT: 3,000

SALES (est): 1MM **Privately Held**
WEB: www.alphaimpressions.com
SIC: 2396 2752 Fabric printing & stamping; commercial printing, lithographic

(P-3770)
APPLECORE
1200 Harkness St, Manhattan Beach (90266-4218)
P.O. Box 3734, Wofford Heights (93285-3734)
PHONE..................................310 567-6768
Roberta Schannep, *Owner*
EMP: 18
SALES (est): 948.4K **Privately Held**
WEB: www.applecore.net
SIC: 2396 Screen printing on fabric articles

(P-3771)
ATELIER LUXURY GROUP LLC
Also Called: Amiri
1330 Channing St, Los Angeles (90021-2411)
PHONE..................................310 751-2444
Michael Amiri, *CEO*
EMP: 35
SQ FT: 30,000
SALES (est): 685.4K **Privately Held**
SIC: 2396 2311 2321 2331 Apparel & other linings, except millinery; men's & boys' suits & coats; men's & boys' furnishings; women's & misses' blouses & shirts; men's miscellaneous accessories

(P-3772)
ATOMIC MONKEY INDUSTRIES INC
946 Calle Amanecer, San Clemente (92673-6221)
PHONE..................................949 415-8846
Michael P Lynn, *Principal*
James R Lynn, *Principal*
EMP: 10
SQ FT: 2,000
SALES (est): 580K **Privately Held**
SIC: 2396 Automotive trimmings, fabric

(P-3773)
BANDMERCH LLC
3120 W Empire Ave, Burbank (91504-3107)
PHONE..................................818 736-4800
Joseph Bongiovi, *President*
▲ **EMP:** 33
SALES (est): 16.2MM **Privately Held**
SIC: 2396 Fabric printing & stamping
HQ: Aeg Presents Llc
425 W 11th St
Los Angeles CA 90015
323 930-5700

(P-3774)
BEL AIRE BRIDAL INC
Also Called: Bel Aire Bridal Accessories
23002 Mariposa Ave, Torrance (90502-2605)
PHONE..................................310 325-8160
Joyce Smith, *President*
Stephanie Smith, *Shareholder*
Eric D Smith, *Vice Pres*
▲ **EMP:** 22 **EST:** 1960
SQ FT: 12,000
SALES (est): 2.3MM **Privately Held**
WEB: www.belairebridal.com
SIC: 2396 2353 Veils & veiling: bridal, funeral, etc.; hats, caps & millinery

(P-3775)
BRUCK BRAID COMPANY
1200 S Santa Fe Ave, Los Angeles (90021-1789)
PHONE..................................213 627-7611
Gino Nasear, *Owner*
Ronald Jacobs, *President*
Ellen Jacobs, *Vice Pres*
EMP: 40
SQ FT: 90,000
SALES (est): 3.1MM **Privately Held**
SIC: 2396 Trimming, fabric

(P-3776)
C S DASH COVER INC
14020 Paramount Blvd, Paramount (90723-2606)
PHONE..................................562 790-8300
Cameron Zada, *President*

Diana Berg, *General Mgr*
Karsten Berg, *General Mgr*
▲ **EMP:** 16
SQ FT: 3,200
SALES (est): 1.7MM **Privately Held**
WEB: www.csdashcovers.com
SIC: 2396 5521 Automotive trimmings, fabric; used car dealers

(P-3777)
CALIBER SCREENPRINTING INC
1101 S Hope St, El Centro (92243-3452)
PHONE..................................760 353-3499
Oscar Quintero, *CEO*
EMP: 10
SQ FT: 2,400
SALES (est): 981.6K **Privately Held**
SIC: 2396 Screen printing on fabric articles

(P-3778)
CALIFORNIA CSTM FURN & UPHL CO
Also Called: Andrew Morgan Furniture
3325 San Pasqual Trl, Escondido (92025-7543)
PHONE..................................760 727-1444
Marie Cunning, *Owner*
EMP: 20
SALES (est): 1.5MM **Privately Held**
WEB: www.andrewmorganfurniture.com
SIC: 2396 2514 2512 2511 Furniture trimmings, fabric; metal household furniture; upholstered household furniture; wood household furniture; household furnishings; curtains & draperies

(P-3779)
CALIFORNIA SILKSCREEN
Also Called: Calif Silk Screen
1507 Plaza Del Amo, Torrance (90501-4935)
PHONE..................................310 320-5111
Beverly Collins, *Vice Pres*
EMP: 14 **EST:** 1976
SQ FT: 7,400
SALES: 900K **Privately Held**
SIC: 2396 Screen printing on fabric articles

(P-3780)
CKCC INC
Also Called: Nissi Trim
2125 Bay St, Los Angeles (90021-1707)
PHONE..................................213 629-0939
Thuong T Nguyen, *CEO*
EMP: 20 **EST:** 2014
SALES (est): 22.9MM **Privately Held**
WEB: www.nissi-inc.com
SIC: 2396 Trimming, fabric

(P-3781)
CONTAINER DECORATING INC
12 Homestead Ct, Danville (94506-1410)
PHONE..................................510 489-9212
Joe Gallegos, *President*
Vickie Gallegos, *Treasurer*
EMP: 10
SALES: 350K **Privately Held**
SIC: 2396 Printing & embossing on plastics fabric articles

(P-3782)
D AND J MARKETING INC
Also Called: DJM Suspension
580 W 184th St, Gardena (90248-4202)
PHONE..................................310 538-1583
Jeffery J Ullmann, *President*
Mark Dunham, *Vice Pres*
▲ **EMP:** 32
SQ FT: 18,000
SALES (est): 3.3MM **Privately Held**
WEB: www.djmsuspension.com
SIC: 2396 2531 3714 Automotive trimmings, fabric; public building & related furniture; motor vehicle parts & accessories

(P-3783)
DECOR AUTO INC
1709 W Washington Blvd, Los Angeles (90007-1121)
PHONE..................................323 733-9025
Susan K Wheaton, *President*
Susan Wheaton, *President*
Moon Wheaton, *Vice Pres*
EMP: 11
SQ FT: 4,930

SALES (est): 700K Privately Held
WEB: www.decorauto.com
SIC: 2396 Automotive & apparel trimmings

(P-3784)
DISTINCTIVE INDUSTRIES
Also Called: Specialty Division
10618 Shoemaker Ave, Santa Fe Springs
(90670-4038)
PHONE...............................800 421-9777
Dwight Forrister, CEO
Aaron Forrister, Vice Pres
▲ **EMP:** 410
SQ FT: 110,000
SALES (est): 34MM Privately Held
WEB: www.distinctiveindustries.com
SIC: 2396 3086 Automotive trimmings,
fabric; plastics foam products

(P-3785)
DJ SAFETY INC
2623 N San Fernando Rd, Los Angeles
(90065-1316)
PHONE...............................323 221-0000
Joe Hansen, President
Sandra Andres, Shareholder
Darlene Hansen, Shareholder
▲ **EMP:** 20 **EST:** 1996
SQ FT: 11,000
SALES: 2.5MM Privately Held
WEB: www.dj-ltd.com
SIC: 2396 Automotive & apparel trimmings

(P-3786)
FOUR SEASONS DESIGN INC (PA)
2451 Britannia Blvd, San Diego
(92154-7405)
PHONE...............................619 761-5151
John Borsini, President
▲ **EMP:** 200
SALES (est): 28.6MM Privately Held
WEB: www.rudeboyz.net
SIC: 2396 Screen printing on fabric articles

(P-3787)
FULTON ACRES INC
Also Called: Headgear Plus Promo
1330 Commerce St Ste A, Petaluma
(94954-7493)
PHONE...............................707 762-2280
David Trisko, Manager
Kristine Trisko, Managing Prtnr
Jose Rodriguez, Technology
EMP: 10
SQ FT: 9,000
SALES: 2MM Privately Held
WEB: www.headgearplus.com
SIC: 2396 2395 5136 Screen printing on
fabric articles; embroidery & art needle-
work; sportswear, men's & boys'

(P-3788)
FUTURIS AUTOMOTIVE (CA) LLC
6601 Overlake Pl, Newark (94560-1009)
PHONE...............................510 771-2300
Merv Dunn, CEO
Mervin Dunn, Bd of Directors
Walter Cooke, Program Mgr
Lieu Lien, Administration
Gerald Rust, Technical Mgr
▲ **EMP:** 280
SQ FT: 22,000
SALES (est): 10.1MM Privately Held
SIC: 2396 Automotive trimmings, fabric
HQ: Futuris Automotive (Us) Inc.
14925 W 11 Mile Rd
Oak Park MI 48237
248 439-7800

(P-3789)
G&A APPAREL GROUP
Also Called: G&A Bias Les
3610 S Broadway, Los Angeles
(90007-4430)
PHONE...............................323 234-1746
EMP: 30
SQ FT: 4,000
SALES (est): 2.4MM Privately Held
SIC: 2396

(P-3790)
GP DESIGN INC
1185 W Mahalo Pl, Compton (90220-5444)
PHONE...............................310 638-8737
Glenn Aoyama, President

Margaret Aoyama, Treasurer
EMP: 15
SQ FT: 8,000
SALES: 1MM **Privately Held**
SIC: 2396 Screen printing on fabric articles

(P-3791)
GRAPHIC PRINTS INC
Also Called: Pipeline
1200 Kona Dr, Compton (90220-5405)
P.O. Box 459, Gardena (90248-0459)
PHONE...............................310 768-0474
Alan Greenberg, CEO
Tamotsu Inouye, COO
Richard Greenberg, Corp Secy
EMP: 45
SQ FT: 22,000
SALES (est): 5.6MM Privately Held
WEB: www.graphicprints.net
SIC: 2396 2339 2329 Screen printing on
fabric articles; women's & misses' athletic
clothing & sportswear; men's & boys'
sportswear & athletic clothing

(P-3792)
HAMBLY STUDIOS INC
23980 Spalding Ave, Los Altos
(94024-6349)
PHONE...............................408 496-1100
Harry Hambly, President
EMP: 40 **EST:** 1959
SQ FT: 16,000
SALES (est): 3.5MM Privately Held
SIC: 2396 2672 Screen printing on fabric
articles; coated & laminated paper

(P-3793)
JAMES GANG COMPANY
4851 Newport Ave, San Diego
(92107-3110)
PHONE...............................619 225-1283
Leigh Ann Bearce, Partner
James Berdeguez, Partner
Elizabeth Berdeguez, CFO
Paul Bearce, Vice Pres
EMP: 13 **EST:** 2011
SALES (est): 1.3MM Privately Held
SIC: 2396 2752 2261 Screen printing on
fabric articles; commercial printing, offset;
business form & card printing, litho-
graphic; screen printing of cotton broad-
woven fabrics

(P-3794)
KAPAN - KENT COMPANY INC
2675 Vista Pacific Dr, Oceanside
(92056-3500)
PHONE...............................760 631-1716
Arnold Kapen Sr, President
Stefanie Baird, Vice Pres
Kipp Anders, Sales Staff
Brittany Torres, Sales Staff
Kaitlyn McClelland, Manager
▲ **EMP:** 35
SQ FT: 30,023
SALES (est): 4.6MM Privately Held
WEB: www.kapankent.com
SIC: 2396 3231 Screen printing on fabric
articles; decorated glassware: chipped,
engraved, etched, etc.

(P-3795)
KNIT FIT INC
112 W 9th St Ste 230, Los Angeles
(90015-1636)
PHONE...............................213 673-4731
Barry Wolin, President
▲ **EMP:** 18
SQ FT: 8,500
SALES (est): 1.2MM Privately Held
SIC: 2396 7389 Apparel & other linings,
except millinery; textile & apparel services

(P-3796)
LEMOR TRIMS INC
830 Venice Blvd, Los Angeles
(90015-3228)
PHONE...............................213 741-1646
Romel Acosta, President
▲ **EMP:** 15
SALES (est): 1.3MM Privately Held
SIC: 2396 Apparel findings & trimmings

(P-3797)
LOGOS PLUS INC
Also Called: Original Letterman Jacket Co
8130 Rosecrans Ave, Paramount
(90723-2754)
PHONE...............................562 634-3009
Attorney Frenzel, Owner
Michael Jessick, President
Murray Gardner, Treasurer
Maria Jessick, Director
EMP: 12
SQ FT: 11,000
SALES (est): 440K Privately Held
SIC: 2396 Screen printing on fabric
articles; embroidery & art needlework

(P-3798)
LUNA MORA LLC
Also Called: Blur Leather
1240 S Corning St Apt 306, Los Angeles
(90035-2481)
PHONE...............................310 550-6979
Farshid Javaheri, Principal
▲ **EMP:** 11
SQ FT: 2,000
SALES (est): 772.6K Privately Held
SIC: 2396 Apparel & other linings, except
millinery

(P-3799)
MAGNA CHARGER INC
1990 Knoll Dr Ste A, Ventura (93003-7309)
PHONE...............................805 642-8833
Jerry Magnuson, President
Edward Tresback, Vice Pres
Maureen Magnuson, Admin Sec
EMP: 65
SALES (est): 3.7MM Privately Held
WEB: www.magnacharger.net
SIC: 2396 Automotive & apparel trimmings

(P-3800)
METRO NOVELTY & PLEATING CO
906 Thayer Ave, Los Angeles
(90024-3314)
PHONE...............................213 748-1201
Manny Fingson, President
Martin Telleria, Vice Pres
Nader Pakravan, Principal
▲ **EMP:** 80
SQ FT: 52,000
SALES (est): 5.1MM Privately Held
SIC: 2396 2387 5099 Trimming, fabric;
apparel belts; novelties, durable

(P-3801)
MIKE FELLOWS
28913 Arnold Dr, Sonoma (95476-9738)
PHONE...............................707 938-0278
Mike Fellows, Owner
EMP: 20
SALES (est): 1.1MM Privately Held
WEB: www.inmotion.net
SIC: 2396 2759 Screen printing on fabric
articles; screen printing

(P-3802)
MONICA BRUCE DESIGNS INC
Also Called: Inmotion
28913 Arnold Dr, Sonoma (95476-9738)
PHONE...............................707 938-0277
T Michael Fellows, President
Nick Castro, Vice Pres
Doug Scott, Art Dir
EMP: 17 **EST:** 1974
SQ FT: 9,000
SALES (est): 1.9MM Privately Held
SIC: 2396 Screen printing on fabric
articles; embroidery & art needlework

(P-3803)
NEXT DAY PRINTED TEES
Also Called: Swim Cap Company , The
3523 Main St Ste 601, Chula Vista
(91911-0803)
PHONE...............................619 420-8618
Timothy B Lewis, President
Carmen Nichols, CFO
Mary Jane Lewis, Senior VP
Christopher Lewis, Vice Pres
Jane Lewis, Vice Pres
EMP: 16
SQ FT: 9,000

SALES (est): 2.2MM Privately Held
WEB: www.ndpt.com
SIC: 2396 5699 Screen printing on fabric
articles; customized clothing & apparel

(P-3804)
NORTH AMERICAN TEXTILE CO LLC (PA)
Also Called: N A T C O
346 W Cerritos Ave, Glendale
(91204-2704)
PHONE...............................818 409-0019
Esteban E Arslanian Sr,
Armine Madanyan, Graphic Designe
Armando Arslanian,
Carlos Arslanian,
▲ **EMP:** 35
SQ FT: 18,000
SALES (est): 7.3MM Privately Held
WEB: www.natcolabel.com
SIC: 2396 7389 Apparel findings & trim-
mings; textile & apparel services

(P-3805)
OSUMO INC
Also Called: Fabrix
1933 Republic Ave, San Leandro
(94577-4220)
PHONE...............................510 346-6888
M Sung, President
Michael Sung, President
EMP: 10 **EST:** 1978
SALES: 500K Privately Held
WEB: www.osumo.com
SIC: 2396 Screen printing on fabric articles

(P-3806)
PANGEA SILKSCREEN
110 Howard St Ste A, Petaluma
(94952-2922)
PHONE...............................707 778-0110
Richard Nakagawa, President
Michelle Caldwell, Vice Pres
EMP: 25
SQ FT: 10,500
SALES (est): 2.5MM Privately Held
WEB: www.pangeapromo.com
SIC: 2396 2395 Screen printing on fabric
articles; embroidery & art needlework

(P-3807)
PARTSFLEX INC
6700 Brem Ln Ste 4, Gilroy (95020-7021)
PHONE...............................408 677-7121
Max Alsedda, President
EMP: 25
SQ FT: 10,000
SALES (est): 624.7K Privately Held
SIC: 2396 5013 Automotive & apparel
trimmings; automotive supplies & parts

(P-3808)
PLASTECH SPECIALTIES COMPANY (PA)
4645 Portofino Cir, Cypress (90630-6806)
PHONE...............................626 357-6839
Mike Delaney, CEO
Patrick L Delaney, President
EMP: 12
SQ FT: 14,000
SALES (est): 782.3K Privately Held
WEB: www.plastechspec.com
SIC: 2396 Printing & embossing on plas-
tics fabric articles

(P-3809)
R B T INC
Also Called: Ink Throwers
2240 Encinitas Blvd, Encinitas
(92024-4345)
PHONE...............................619 781-8802
Tom Butler, CEO
EMP: 14
SALES (est): 1.7MM Privately Held
SIC: 2396 Screen printing on fabric articles

(P-3810)
RC APPAREL INC
3104 Markridge Rd, La Crescenta
(91214-1332)
PHONE...............................818 541-1994
▲ **EMP:** 12
SALES (est): 2MM Privately Held
SIC: 2396

▲ = Import ▼=Export
◆ =Import/Export

(P-3811)
ROYAL TRIM
2529 Chambers St, Vernon (90058-2107)
PHONE......................................323 583-2121
Farzad Pakravan, *President*
▲ EMP: 25
SQ FT: 30,000
SALES (est): 2.2MM **Privately Held**
SIC: 2396 2395 Apparel findings & trimmings; pleating & stitching

(P-3812)
SECURITY TEXTILE CORPORATION
1457 E Washington Blvd, Los Angeles (90021-3039)
PHONE......................................213 747-2673
Doug Weitman, *CEO*
Brian Weitman, *President*
Mary Larimore, *Human Res Mgr*
Jeff Waldman, *Sales Dir*
▲ EMP: 80
SQ FT: 85,000
SALES (est): 7MM **Privately Held**
SIC: 2396 5131 Automotive & apparel trimmings; sewing supplies & notions

(P-3813)
SIMSO TEX SUBLIMATION (PA)
3028 E Las Hermanas St, Compton (90221-5511)
PHONE......................................310 885-9717
Joe Simsoly, *CEO*
Eli Simsollo, *President*
Kaden Simsolo, *Admin Sec*
▲ EMP: 80 EST: 2001
SQ FT: 38,000
SALES (est): 8.2MM **Privately Held**
WEB: www.simsotex.com
SIC: 2396 Fabric printing & stamping

(P-3814)
SJ&L BIAS BINDING & TEX CO INC
Also Called: Superior Bias Trims
1950 E 20th St, Vernon (90058-1005)
PHONE......................................213 747-5271
Lynn Menichiwi, *CEO*
Joseph Menichini, *Vice Pres*
▲ EMP: 50
SQ FT: 11,000
SALES (est): 5.5MM **Privately Held**
SIC: 2396 Pads, shoulder: for coats, suits, etc.

(P-3815)
SMOOTHREADS INC
Also Called: 2.95 Guys
13750 Stowe Dr Ste A, Poway (92064-8828)
PHONE......................................800 536-5959
Lance Beesley, *President*
▲ EMP: 28
SQ FT: 12,000
SALES (est): 3.6MM **Privately Held**
WEB: www.295guys.com
SIC: 2396 2395 Screen printing on fabric articles; embroidery products, except schiffli machine

(P-3816)
STANDARD BIAS BINDING CO INC
4621 Pacific Blvd, Vernon (90058-2221)
P.O. Box 58025, Los Angeles (90058-0025)
PHONE......................................323 277-9763
Rex Bollar, *President*
Loree Bollar, *Treasurer*
EMP: 36
SQ FT: 20,800
SALES (est): 2.6MM **Privately Held**
SIC: 2396 Automotive & apparel trimmings

(P-3817)
STAR FISH INC
410 Talbert St, Daly City (94014-1623)
PHONE......................................415 468-6688
Sieu Khac, *Administration*
Sieu MA, *President*
EMP: 10
SALES: 1MM **Privately Held**
SIC: 2396 Screen printing on fabric articles

(P-3818)
SUPER VIAS & TRIM
3651 S Main St E, Los Angeles (90007-4417)
PHONE......................................323 233-2556
EMP: 12
SALES (est): 1.1MM **Privately Held**
SIC: 2396 7389

(P-3819)
SURFSIDE PRINTS INC
2686 Johnson Dr Ste D, Ventura (93003-7245)
PHONE......................................805 620-0052
Matthew Whitney, *President*
Nicole Whitney, *CFO*
EMP: 10
SQ FT: 2,475
SALES: 850K **Privately Held**
SIC: 2396 2395 2621 2759 Fabric printing & stamping; emblems, embroidered; book, bond & printing papers; promotional printing

(P-3820)
TEAM COLOR INC
Also Called: Team Color Screen Printing
837 W 18th St, Costa Mesa (92627-4410)
PHONE......................................949 646-6486
William Andrew Wolfe, *President*
Julie Wolfe, *Vice Pres*
Julio Delgado, *Prdtn Mgr*
EMP: 40
SALES (est): 4.9MM **Privately Held**
SIC: 2396 2759 Screen printing on fabric articles; screen printing

(P-3821)
UNIQUE SCREEN PRINTING INC
Also Called: Yang's Screen Printing
2115 Central Ave, South El Monte (91733-2117)
PHONE......................................626 575-2725
Lu Hui-Chin Yang, *President*
EMP: 30
SQ FT: 2,000
SALES: 400K **Privately Held**
SIC: 2396 Screen printing on fabric articles

(P-3822)
VALLEY IMAGES
1925 Kyle Park Ct, San Jose (95125-1029)
PHONE......................................408 279-6777
Carlo Strangis, *Partner*
Robert Malik, *Partner*
Eric King, *Graphic Designe*
EMP: 17
SQ FT: 10,201
SALES (est): 1.3MM **Privately Held**
WEB: www.valleyimages.com
SIC: 2396 Screen printing on fabric articles

(P-3823)
VOELKER SENSORS INC
3790 El Camino Real, Palo Alto (94306-3314)
PHONE......................................650 361-0570
Joe Hedges, *President*
Paul Voelker, *CEO*
EMP: 15
SQ FT: 1,000
SALES (est): 1.3MM **Privately Held**
WEB: www.vsi-oil.com
SIC: 2396 Automotive & apparel trimmings

(P-3824)
WESTSIDE RESEARCH INC
4293 County Road 99w, Orland (95963-9153)
PHONE......................................530 330-0085
Tim Dexter, *President*
Karen Dexter, *Vice Pres*
▲ EMP: 15
SALES (est): 1.5MM **Privately Held**
WEB: www.westsideresearch.com
SIC: 2396 Automotive & apparel trimmings

(P-3825)
WORLD UPHOLSTERY & TRIM INC
1320 E Main St, Santa Paula (93060-2926)
PHONE......................................805 921-0100
Michael May, *President*
Fran Adler, *Vice Pres*
EMP: 11
SALES: 800K **Privately Held**
WEB: www.worlduph.com
SIC: 2396 Automotive trimmings, fabric

2399 Fabricated Textile Prdts, NEC

(P-3826)
A LOT TO SAY INC
1541 S Vineyard Ave, Ontario (91761-7717)
PHONE......................................925 964-5079
Armando Herrera, *Branch Mgr*
EMP: 15 **Privately Held**
SIC: 2399 2361 Banners, made from fabric; girls' & children's blouses & shirts
PA: A Lot To Say, Inc.
4155 Blackhawk
Danville CA 94506
-

(P-3827)
A LOT TO SAY INC (PA)
4155 Blackhawk, Danville (94506)
PHONE......................................877 366-8448
Jennifer Spannich Danmiller, *CEO*
Alisson Spannich Powers, *COO*
EMP: 15
SALES (est): 2.6MM **Privately Held**
SIC: 2399 Banners, made from fabric

(P-3828)
AAA FLAG & BANNER MFG CO INC
Also Called: A A A Sign & Banner Mfg Co
8966 National Blvd, Los Angeles (90034-3308)
PHONE......................................310 836-3341
Howard Furst, *President*
EMP: 200
SALES (corp-wide): 31.9MM **Privately Held**
WEB: www.aaaflag.com
SIC: 2399 3993 Banners, pennants & flags; signs & advertising specialties
PA: Aaa Flag & Banner Mfg Co Inc
8937 National Blvd
Los Angeles CA 90034
310 836-3200

(P-3829)
ACTION EMBROIDERY CORP (PA)
1315 Brooks St, Ontario (91762-3612)
PHONE......................................909 983-1359
Ira Newman, *President*
Steven Mendelow, *Treasurer*
▲ EMP: 120
SQ FT: 12,000
SALES (est): 28.1MM **Privately Held**
WEB: www.actionemb.com
SIC: 2399 2395 Emblems, badges & insignia; from purchased materials; pleating & stitching

(P-3830)
AIRBORNE SYSTEMS N AMER CA INC
3100 W Segerstrom Ave, Santa Ana (92704-5812)
PHONE......................................714 662-1400
Bryce Wiedeman, *President*
Sean P Maroney, *Treasurer*
Terrance M Paradie, *Principal*
Halle F Terrion, *Admin Sec*
▼ EMP: 161
SQ FT: 160,000
SALES (est): 49.1MM
SALES (corp-wide): 3.8B **Publicly Held**
WEB: www.irvinaerospace.com
SIC: 2399 Parachutes
HQ: Airborne Systems North America Inc.
5800 Magnolia Ave
Pennsauken NJ 08109
856 663-1275

(P-3831)
AMERICAN HORSE PRODUCTS
Also Called: Inerfab
31896 Plaza Dr Ste C4, San Juan Capistrano (92675-3736)
PHONE......................................949 248-5300
James Carter, *CEO*
Diane Carter, *Vice Pres*
EMP: 12
SQ FT: 12,000
SALES: 3.5MM **Privately Held**
SIC: 2399 5699 Horse & pet accessories, textile; riding apparel

(P-3832)
AMZR INC
Also Called: Adco Products
29115 Avenue Valleyview, Valencia (91355-5443)
PHONE......................................800 541-2326
Alan Ein, *President*
Morgan Ein, *Vice Pres*
Robert Martin, *Vice Pres*
▲ EMP: 150 EST: 1955
SQ FT: 250,000
SALES (est): 70.9MM
SALES (corp-wide): 116.6MM **Privately Held**
WEB: www.adcoprod.com
SIC: 2399 Automotive covers, except seat & tire covers
PA: Covercraft Industries, Llc
100 Enterprise
Pauls Valley OK 73075
405 238-9651

(P-3833)
AUTOLIV SAFETY TECHNOLOGY INC
2475 Paseo D Las Amrcs, San Diego (92154)
PHONE......................................619 662-8000
Bradley J Murray, *President*
Raymond B Pekar, *Treasurer*
Anthony J Nellis, *Admin Sec*
EMP: 1003
SALES (est): 19.6K
SALES (corp-wide): 8.6B **Publicly Held**
SIC: 2399 Seat belts, automobile & aircraft
PA: Autoliv, Inc.
3350 Airport Rd
Ogden UT 84405
801 629-9800

(P-3834)
CABEAU INC
21700 Oxnard St Ste 900, Woodland Hills (91367-7569)
PHONE......................................877 962-2232
David Sternlight, *CEO*
Ryan Hilterbran, *Vice Pres*
Nicholle Natividad, *Accountant*
Duy Nguyen, *Controller*
Shane Ferris, *Opers Staff*
▲ EMP: 25
SALES (est): 1.5MM **Privately Held**
WEB: www.completesupportpillow.com
SIC: 2399 Emblems, badges & insignia

(P-3835)
CAL TRENDS ACCESSORIES LLC
Also Called: Cal Trend Automotive Products
2121 S Anne St, Santa Ana (92704-4408)
PHONE......................................714 708-5115
Roger Loomis,
Mike Wadhera, *CIO*
Cesar Hernandez, *Plant Mgr*
EMP: 22
SALES (est): 2.5MM **Privately Held**
WEB: www.caltrend.com
SIC: 2399 3751 3714 Automotive covers, except seat & tire covers; motorcycle accessories; motor vehicle parts & accessories

(P-3836)
DISPLAY FABRICATION GROUP INC
1231 N Miller St Ste 100, Anaheim (92806-1950)
PHONE......................................714 373-2100
Luis Ocampo, *President*
Craig Moloney, *VP Opers*
Leslie McCarter, *Director*
Johnson Lindsey, *Manager*
◆ EMP: 50
SQ FT: 100,000
SALES: 274.4K **Privately Held**
SIC: 2399 Belting, fabric: made from purchased materials

(P-3837)
DRAKE ENTERPRISES INCORPORATED
Also Called: Big D Products
490 Watt Dr, Fairfield (94534-1663)
PHONE..........................707 864-3077
Glenn Drake, *President*
▲ EMP: 67
SQ FT: 55,000
SALES (est): 6.4MM **Privately Held**
WEB: www.bigdblankets.com
SIC: 2399 Horse blankets; horse & pet accessories, textile

(P-3838)
DSY EDUCATIONAL CORPORATION
Also Called: Main Street Banner
525 Maple St, Carpinteria (93013-2070)
P.O. Box 41829, Santa Barbara (93140-1829)
PHONE..........................805 684-8111
David Yothers, *President*
Sharon Yothers, *Corp Secy*
Jeannie Dominguez, *Assistant*
EMP: 11
SQ FT: 15,000
SALES (est): 1MM **Privately Held**
WEB: www.mainstreetbanner.com
SIC: 2399 7336 Banners, made from fabric; flags, fabric; commercial art & graphic design

(P-3839)
EEVELLE LLC
2270 Cosmos Ct Ste 100, Carlsbad (92011-1558)
PHONE..........................760 434-2231
Charles McKee, *Mng Member*
Carlos Carrasco, *Purch Agent*
▲ EMP: 24
SALES (est): 1.5MM **Privately Held**
WEB: www.eevelle.com
SIC: 2399 Automotive covers, except seat & tire covers

(P-3840)
EXXEL OUTDOORS INC
343 Baldwin Park Blvd, City of Industry (91746-1406)
PHONE..........................626 369-7278
EMP: 254
SALES (corp-wide): 124.9MM **Privately Held**
SIC: 2399 Sleeping bags
PA: Exxel Outdoors, Inc.
   300 American Blvd
   Haleyville AL 35565
   205 486-5258

(P-3841)
FALCON AUTOMOTIVE INC
1305 E Wakeham Ave, Santa Ana (92705-4145)
PHONE..........................714 569-1085
Peter Eberhardt, *President*
▲ EMP: 30
SQ FT: 16,000
SALES (est): 2.5MM **Privately Held**
SIC: 2399 2273 3714 Automotive covers, except seat & tire covers; seat covers, automobile; automobile floor coverings, except rubber or plastic; motor vehicle parts & accessories

(P-3842)
FLAGCRAFTERS INC
1120 Bay Blvd Ste E, Chula Vista (91911-7169)
PHONE..........................619 585-1044
Janet Crowe, *CEO*
Robert Crowe, *President*
Barbara Ayers, *Vice Pres*
EMP: 20
SALES (est): 1.6MM **Privately Held**
WEB: www.flagcrafters.com
SIC: 2399 Banners, made from fabric; flags, fabric

(P-3843)
FLEXSYSTEMS USA INC
1308 N Magnolia Ave Ste J, El Cajon (92020-1646)
PHONE..........................619 401-1858
Diane Chapman, *President*
▲ EMP: 25
SALES (est): 3.4MM **Privately Held**
WEB: www.flexsystems.com
SIC: 2399 2396 Emblems, badges & insignia; pet collars, leashes, etc.: non-leather; apparel findings & trimmings

(P-3844)
FXC CORPORATION
Guardian Parachute Division
3050 Red Hill Ave, Costa Mesa (92626-4524)
PHONE..........................714 557-8032
Frank X Chevrier, *Manager*
EMP: 75
SALES (corp-wide): 14.7MM **Privately Held**
WEB: www.fxcguardian.com
SIC: 2399 3429 Parachutes; parachute hardware
PA: Fxc Corporation
   3050 Red Hill Ave
   Costa Mesa CA 92626
   714 556-7400

(P-3845)
HIGH ENERGY SPORTS INC
1081 N Shepard St Ste A, Anaheim (92806-2819)
PHONE..........................714 632-3323
Elizabeth Rothman, *President*
EMP: 15
SQ FT: 3,600
SALES (est): 1.4MM **Privately Held**
WEB: www.highenergysports.com
SIC: 2399 Parachutes

(P-3846)
HITEX DYEING & FINISHING INC
355 Vineland Ave, City of Industry (91746-2321)
PHONE..........................626 363-0160
Young C Kim, *President*
▲ EMP: 40 EST: 2010
SALES (est): 458.8K **Privately Held**
SIC: 2399 2257 Nets, launderers & dyers; dyeing & finishing circular knit fabrics

(P-3847)
JESSIE STEELE INC
1020 The Alameda, San Jose (95126-3139)
PHONE..........................510 204-0991
Helena J Steele, *President*
Larry Philipps, *COO*
◆ EMP: 11
SALES (est): 1.4MM **Privately Held**
WEB: www.jessiesteele.com
SIC: 2399 Aprons, breast (harness)

(P-3848)
MADDOX DEFENSE INC
Also Called: Stinger Solar Kits
6549 Mission Gorge Rd # 112, San Diego (92120-2306)
PHONE..........................818 378-8246
Jason Maddox, *CEO*
EMP: 15
SALES (est): 1.4MM **Privately Held**
SIC: 2399 2394 5099 Military insignia, textile; convertible tops, canvas or boat: from purchased materials; lifesaving & survival equipment (non-medical)

(P-3849)
MARIE JOANN DESIGNS INC
630 S Jefferson St Ste H, Placentia (92870-6639)
PHONE..........................714 996-0550
Fred Hughes, *Partner*
Joann Marie Dextradeur, *Partner*
▲ EMP: 13
SQ FT: 2,000
SALES (est): 1.2MM **Privately Held**
WEB: www.jmdinc.net
SIC: 2399 5199 Emblems, badges & insignia; gifts & novelties

(P-3850)
MOTORLAMB INTERNATIONAL ACC
Also Called: Blue Ribbon Sheepskin
8055 Clairemont Mesa Blvd # 108, San Diego (92111-1620)
PHONE..........................858 569-8111
Selwyn Klein, *President*
EMP: 10 EST: 1979
SQ FT: 4,400
SALES (est): 644.8K **Privately Held**
SIC: 2399 5531 Seat covers, automobile; automotive accessories

(P-3851)
NORTH BAY RHBLITATION SVCS INC (PA)
Also Called: North Bay Industries
649 Martin Ave, Rohnert Park (94928-2050)
PHONE..........................707 585-1991
Robert Hutt, *CEO*
William Stewart, *Ch of Bd*
Bella Hutt, *CFO*
Liz Sutton, *Exec VP*
Roxanne Muse, *Human Res Mgr*
EMP: 230
SQ FT: 18,000
SALES: 16.2MM **Privately Held**
WEB: www.nbrs.org
SIC: 2399 0782 8331 Banners, pennants & flags; lawn services; community service employment training program; vocational rehabilitation agency

(P-3852)
PATCH PLACE
1724 S Grove Ave Ste A, Ontario (91761-4564)
PHONE..........................909 947-3023
Eric Roberts, *Owner*
EMP: 50
SALES (est): 3.7MM **Privately Held**
WEB: www.thepatchplace.com
SIC: 2399 Emblems, badges & insignia

(P-3853)
PRESTIGE FLAG & BANNER CO
591 Camino Dela Reina 917, San Diego (92108)
PHONE..........................619 497-2220
Mike Roberts, *President*
Dave Fenimore, *COO*
Stuart Fried, *Vice Pres*
Tiffany Rogers, *Accounting Mgr*
Paul Ballard, *Commissioner*
▼ EMP: 100
SQ FT: 8,000
SALES (est): 9.9MM **Privately Held**
WEB: www.prestigeflag.com
SIC: 2399 Flags, fabric

(P-3854)
RANKS BIG DATA
2453 Naglee Rd, Tracy (95304-7324)
PHONE..........................510 830-6926
Nathan Sharma, *CEO*
EMP: 149 EST: 2010
SQ FT: 2,000
SALES (est): 6.9MM **Privately Held**
SIC: 2399 8748 Hand woven apparel; business consulting; energy conservation consultant

(P-3855)
REFLEX CORPORATION
1825 Aston Ave Ste A, Carlsbad (92008-7341)
PHONE..........................760 931-9009
John C Levy Jr, *President*
Annika Risher, *COO*
Kathleen Coawn, *CFO*
▲ EMP: 20
SQ FT: 20,000
SALES (est): 2.1MM **Privately Held**
WEB: www.premiumtufflock.com
SIC: 2399 Horse & pet accessories, textile; pet collars, leashes, etc.: non-leather

(P-3856)
ROYAL RIDERS
120 Mast St Ste B, Morgan Hill (95037-5154)
PHONE..........................408 779-1997
Janet Graham, *Owner*
▲ EMP: 11
SQ FT: 5,500
SALES (est): 836.5K **Privately Held**
SIC: 2399 Horse blankets

(P-3857)
RUTH TRAINING CENTER SEW MCHS
328 E 24th St, Los Angeles (90011-1029)
PHONE..........................213 748-8033
Lilian Herrera, *President*
EMP: 10 EST: 1998
SALES (est): 560K **Privately Held**
SIC: 2399 7999 Fabricated textile products; sewing instruction

(P-3858)
SAMPLING INTERNATIONAL LLC (PA)
Also Called: Levolor
2942 Century Pl, Costa Mesa (92626-4324)
PHONE..........................949 305-5333
Dean Treister, *Managing Dir*
Anthony Lynch, *Director*
▲ EMP: 11 EST: 2007
SALES (est): 2.5MM **Privately Held**
SIC: 2399 Book covers, fabric

(P-3859)
SCOTTEX INC
12828 S Broadway, Los Angeles (90061-1116)
PHONE..........................310 516-1411
Stanley Jung, *President*
▲ EMP: 11
SQ FT: 19,000
SALES (est): 1.8MM **Privately Held**
WEB: www.scottex.net
SIC: 2399 Hand woven & crocheted products

(P-3860)
SEABORN CANVAS
435 N Harbor Blvd Ste B1, San Pedro (90731-2271)
PHONE..........................310 519-1208
Juanita Wade, *Owner*
▼ EMP: 25
SQ FT: 5,000
SALES (est): 1.1MM **Privately Held**
SIC: 2399 2394 Banners, pennants & flags; flags, fabric; canvas & related products

(P-3861)
SEVENTH HEAVEN INC
Also Called: Western Mountaineering
1025 S 5th St, San Jose (95112-3927)
PHONE..........................408 287-8945
Gary Schaezlein, *Sales Mgr*
Gary Peterson, *Prdtn Mgr*
▲ EMP: 30
SQ FT: 12,000
SALES (est): 3.7MM **Privately Held**
WEB: www.westernmountaineering.com
SIC: 2399 2392 2329 Sleeping bags; comforters & quilts: made from purchased materials; down-filled clothing: men's & boys'

(P-3862)
TB KAWASHIMA USA INC
19200 Von Karman Ave # 870, Irvine (92612-8523)
PHONE..........................714 389-5310
Masanori Sawa, *Branch Mgr*
EMP: 10 **Privately Held**
SIC: 2399 Aprons, breast (harness)
HQ: Tb Kawashima Usa, Inc.
   412 Groves St
   Lugoff SC 29078
   803 421-0033

(P-3863)
UNIVERSITY BLANKET & FLAG CORP (PA)
1111 Orange Ave Ste C, Coronado (92118-3432)
PHONE..........................619 435-4100
Carroll Gerbel, *President*
Linda Gerbel, *Vice Pres*
▲ EMP: 10
SQ FT: 1,000
SALES (est): 2.2MM **Privately Held**
WEB: www.ubflag.com
SIC: 2399 2392 Flags, fabric; blankets: made from purchased materials

(P-3864)
USA PRODUCTS GROUP INC (PA)
Also Called: Progrip Cargo Control
1300 E Vine St, Lodi (95240-3148)
P.O. Box 1750 (95241-1750)
PHONE..............................209 334-1460
Stephen D Jackson, *President*
Yolanda Bernasconi, *Executive*
Sandy O Omstead, *Administration*
Shirley Callaham, *Buyer*
Seth Talbot, *Marketing Staff*
▲ EMP: 30
SALES (est): 8.4MM **Privately Held**
SIC: 2399 3949 Seat covers, automobile; bags, golf

(P-3865)
VANGUARD INDUSTRIES EAST INC
2440 Impala Dr, Carlsbad (92010-7226)
PHONE..............................800 433-1334
William M Gershen, *Branch Mgr*
Melinda Kindred, *Purchasing*
Glenn Deans, *Natl Sales Mgr*
Rochelle Debicki, *Sales Staff*
EMP: 73
SALES (corp-wide): 13.4MM **Privately Held**
SIC: 2399 Military insignia, textile
PA: Vanguard Industries East, Inc.
1172 Azalea Garden Rd
Norfolk VA 23502
800 221-1264

(P-3866)
VANGUARD INDUSTRIES WEST INC (PA)
2440 Impala Dr, Carlsbad (92010-7226)
PHONE..............................760 438-4437
William M Gershen, *President*
Michael Harrison, *Vice Pres*
Bill Gershen, *Principal*
Cindy Mortrud, *General Mgr*
David Thomas, *Info Tech Dir*
▲ EMP: 107
SQ FT: 36,000
SALES (est): 14.2MM **Privately Held**
SIC: 2399 2395 Military insignia, textile; pleating & stitching

(P-3867)
WEST COAST SHEEPSKIN IMPORT
14056 Whittier Blvd, Whittier (90605-2041)
PHONE..............................562 945-5151
Fax: 562 698-3946
EMP: 10
SQ FT: 6,000
SALES (est): 245K **Privately Held**
SIC: 2399 5013 5531

(P-3868)
YOUNG SUNG USA INC
1122 S Alvarado St, Los Angeles (90006-4110)
PHONE..............................213 427-2580
Pyung Kwon, *President*
▲ EMP: 15
SQ FT: 15,600
SALES (est): 1.6MM **Privately Held**
SIC: 2399 Seat covers, automobile

2411 Logging

(P-3869)
A&M TIMBER INC
4002 Alta Mesa Dr, Redding (96002-3732)
PHONE..............................530 515-1740
Joseph D Atchley III, *President*
Clay Montgomery, *Corp Secy*
EMP: 11
SALES (est): 730K **Privately Held**
SIC: 2411 Logging

(P-3870)
ALDERMAN TIMBER COMPANY INC
Also Called: Alderman Logging
17180 Alderman Rd, Sonora (95370-8909)
P.O. Box 127, Soulsbyville (95372-0127)
PHONE..............................209 532-9636
Keith Alderman, *President*

Linda Alderman, *Corp Secy*
Roger Alderman, *Vice Pres*
EMP: 14
SQ FT: 12,020
SALES (est): 1.8MM **Privately Held**
SIC: 2411 Logging camps & contractors

(P-3871)
AMUNDSON TOM TMBER FLLING CNTR
14615 River Oaks Dr, Red Bluff (96080-9338)
PHONE..............................530 529-0504
Thomas Amundson, *Owner*
EMP: 10
SALES (est): 720K **Privately Held**
SIC: 2411 Timber, cut at logging camp

(P-3872)
ANDERSON LOGGING INC
1296 N Main St, Fort Bragg (95437-8407)
P.O. Box 1266 (95437-1266)
PHONE..............................707 964-2770
Michael Anderson, *President*
Joseph Anderson, *Vice Pres*
Maribelle Anderson, *Admin Sec*
EMP: 100 EST: 1977
SQ FT: 3,000
SALES (est): 10.1MM **Privately Held**
SIC: 2411 4212 Logging camps & contractors; lumber (log) trucking, local

(P-3873)
APEX ENTERPRISES INC
687 Oro Dam Blvd E 4, Oroville (95965-5725)
PHONE..............................530 871-0732
Logan Bamford, *President*
Debbie McCann, *Manager*
EMP: 12 EST: 2017
SALES (est): 1.1MM **Privately Held**
SIC: 2411 Logging

(P-3874)
AUBERRY FOREST PRODUCTS INC
32177 Auberry Rd, Auberry (93602-9603)
P.O. Box 233 (93602-0233)
PHONE..............................559 855-6255
Darlene Allen, *President*
Matthew Allen, *President*
EMP: 17
SQ FT: 600
SALES (est): 1.5MM **Privately Held**
WEB: www.auberryforestproducts.com
SIC: 2411 Logging

(P-3875)
BIG HILL LOGGING & RD BUILDING (PA)
680 Sutter St, Yuba City (95991-4218)
PHONE..............................530 673-4155
Macarthur Siller, *President*
McArthur Siller, *President*
Janet Siller, *Vice Pres*
Dane Siller, *Admin Sec*
EMP: 27
SQ FT: 1,726
SALES: 5MM **Privately Held**
SIC: 2411 1611 Logging camps & contractors; highway & street construction

(P-3876)
BUNDY AND SONS INC
15196 Mountain Shadows Dr, Redding (96001-9544)
PHONE..............................530 246-3868
William J Bundy, *President*
Terrice Bundy, *Vice Pres*
EMP: 22
SQ FT: 2,000
SALES (est): 3.7MM **Privately Held**
SIC: 2411 Logging camps & contractors

(P-3877)
CHUCK L LOGGING INC
6527 Big Springs Rd, Montague (96064-9105)
PHONE..............................530 459-3842
Charles Hedin, *President*
Sandy Hedin, *Corp Secy*
EMP: 45
SALES (est): 4MM **Privately Held**
SIC: 2411 Logging camps & contractors

(P-3878)
D L STOY LOGGING CO
17302 Mountain View Rd, Greenville (95947-9750)
PHONE..............................530 283-3292
Douglas L Stoy, *Owner*
EMP: 11
SALES: 1.4MM **Privately Held**
SIC: 2411 Logging camps & contractors

(P-3879)
DAN ARENS AND SON INC
Also Called: Arens Brothers Logging
5780 Ridgeway Dr, Pollock Pines (95726-9533)
P.O. Box 1142 (95726-1142)
PHONE..............................530 644-6307
Dan Arens, *CEO*
Jerry Arens, *CFO*
Levi Arens, *Admin Sec*
Craig Irish, *Director*
EMP: 12
SQ FT: 2,000
SALES (est): 1.8MM **Privately Held**
WEB: www.danarensi.com
SIC: 2411 Logging camps & contractors

(P-3880)
DAVE RICHARDSON TRUCKING
Also Called: R & B Logging
8817 Lwer Lttle Shasta Rd, Montague (96064-9699)
PHONE..............................530 459-5088
Dave Richardson, *Owner*
Deborah Richardson, *Co-Owner*
EMP: 18 EST: 1974
SALES: 2MM **Privately Held**
SIC: 2411 4212 Logging camps & contractors; lumber (log) trucking, local

(P-3881)
DEL LOGGING INC
101 Punkin Center Rd, Bieber (96009)
P.O. Box 246 (96009-0246)
PHONE..............................530 294-5492
Russ Hawkins, *President*
Helen Hawkins, *Corp Secy*
EMP: 42
SQ FT: 450
SALES (est): 2.4MM **Privately Held**
SIC: 2411 Logging camps & contractors

(P-3882)
FORD LOGGING INC
Also Called: Pacific Earthscape
1225 Central Ave Ste 11, McKinleyville (95519-5301)
PHONE..............................707 840-9442
Delman Ford, *President*
Heath Ford, *Treasurer*
Glenn Ford, *Vice Pres*
Derek Ford, *Admin Sec*
EMP: 20
SALES: 600K **Privately Held**
SIC: 2411 1611 Logging camps & contractors; gravel or dirt road construction

(P-3883)
FRANKLIN LOGGING INC
11906 Wilson Way, Redding (96003)
P.O. Box 1303, Bella Vista (96008-1303)
PHONE..............................530 549-4924
Dianne Franklin, *President*
Bruce Olsen, *Vice Pres*
EMP: 25 EST: 1950
SQ FT: 1,700
SALES (est): 3.6MM **Privately Held**
SIC: 2411 Logging camps & contractors

(P-3884)
FRAY LOGGING INC
10619 Jim Brady Rd, Jamestown (95327-9518)
PHONE..............................209 984-5968
Richard N Fray, *President*
Susan Fray, *Treasurer*
EMP: 20
SALES (est): 2.1MM **Privately Held**
SIC: 2411 Logging camps & contractors

(P-3885)
H&M LOGGING
442 S Franklin St, Fort Bragg (95437-4803)
PHONE..............................707 964-2340
Richard Hautala, *President*

EMP: 10
SALES (est): 820K **Privately Held**
SIC: 2411 Logging camps & contractors

(P-3886)
HOOPA FOREST INDUSTRIES
778 Marshall Ln, Hoopa (95546-9762)
P.O. Box 759 (95546-0759)
PHONE..............................530 625-4281
Merwin Clark, *CEO*
EMP: 29
SALES (est): 2.7MM **Privately Held**
SIC: 2411 Logging
PA: Hoopa Valley Tribal Council
11860 State Highway 96
Hoopa CA 95546
530 625-4211

(P-3887)
HUFFMAN LOGGING CO INC
1155 Huffman Dr, Fortuna (95540-3337)
PHONE..............................707 725-4335
EMP: 45
SALES (est): 2.9MM **Privately Held**
SIC: 2411

(P-3888)
IVERSON & LOGGING INC
41575 Little Lake Rd, Mendocino (95460-9784)
PHONE..............................707 937-0028
Walter R Iverson, *President*
Marlene E Iverson, *Corp Secy*
Donald Iverson, *Bd of Directors*
EMP: 13
SALES: 900K **Privately Held**
SIC: 2411 1629 Logging camps & contractors; land preparation construction

(P-3889)
J W BAMFORD INC
Also Called: Bamford Equipment
4288 State Highway 70, Oroville (95965-8340)
PHONE..............................530 533-0732
Joel Bamford, *President*
James W Bamford, *Trustee*
James Bamford, *Vice Pres*
Lori Curtis, *Vice Pres*
EMP: 16
SQ FT: 8,000
SALES (est): 4MM **Privately Held**
WEB: www.bamfordequipment.com
SIC: 2411 Logging

(P-3890)
JAMES A HEADRICK II/ELIZABETH
Also Called: Headrick Logging
7194 Bridge St, Anderson (96007-9496)
PHONE..............................530 247-8000
James Headrick, *Owner*
Elizabeth Headrick, *Co-Owner*
EMP: 55
SQ FT: 4,500
SALES (est): 6.3MM **Privately Held**
SIC: 2411 Logging camps & contractors

(P-3891)
JOHN WHEELER LOGGING INC
13570 State Highway 36 E, Red Bluff (96080-8878)
P.O. Box 339 (96080-0339)
PHONE..............................530 527-2993
Dave Holder, *President*
Vern Mc Coshum, *Vice Pres*
EMP: 105 EST: 1966
SQ FT: 3,500
SALES (est): 13.6MM **Privately Held**
SIC: 2411 4212 Logging camps & contractors; local trucking, without storage

(P-3892)
LESLIE ENVIRONMENTAL INDS LLC
17617 Buttercup Cir, Sonora (95370-9700)
PHONE..............................209 840-1664
Colleen Leslie,
EMP: 12
SALES (est): 381.6K **Privately Held**
SIC: 2411 Logging camps & contractors

(P-3893)
LIVING WATERS LOGGING INC
1159 Stromberg Ave, Arcata (95521-5121)
PHONE..................................707 822-3955
Kim Vanden Plas, *President*
Saundra Vanden Plas, *Admin Sec*
EMP: 12
SALES (est): 1.1MM **Privately Held**
SIC: 2411 Logging camps & contractors

(P-3894)
M & M LOGGING INC
Also Called: Contract Logging
7800 N Old Stage Rd, Weed (96094-9510)
P.O. Box 429 (96094-0429)
PHONE..................................530 938-0745
Timothy E Miller, *Principal*
EMP: 10
SALES (est): 1MM **Privately Held**
SIC: 2411 Logging

(P-3895)
MARK CRAWFORD LOGGING INC
26 Walker Creek Rd, Seiad Valley (96086)
P.O. Box 720 (96086-0720)
PHONE..................................530 496-3272
Mark Crawford, *President*
Sherry Crawford, *Admin Sec*
EMP: 10
SALES (est): 3MM **Privately Held**
SIC: 2411 Logging

(P-3896)
MARTIN FISCHER LOGGING INC
1165 Skull Flat Rd, West Point (95255)
P.O. Box 146 (95255-0146)
PHONE..................................209 293-4847
Martin M Fischer, *President*
Lillian Fischer, *Admin Sec*
EMP: 11
SALES (est): 1.1MM **Privately Held**
SIC: 2411 Logging camps & contractors

(P-3897)
MATTHEWS SKYLINE LOGGING INC
10100 East Rd, Potter Valley (95469-9773)
P.O. Box 419, Calpella (95418-0419)
PHONE..................................707 743-2890
Cecil Matthews, *President*
Betty Matthews, *Admin Sec*
EMP: 32 EST: 1977
SQ FT: 20,000
SALES (est): 3MM **Privately Held**
SIC: 2411 Logging camps & contractors

(P-3898)
MESSER LOGGING INC
32111 Rock Hill Ln, Auberry (93602-9771)
PHONE..................................559 855-3160
Timothy Messer, *President*
Tery Messer, *CFO*
Hayley Ferguson, *Corp Secy*
EMP: 20
SALES (est): 3.3MM **Privately Held**
SIC: 2411 Logging camps & contractors

(P-3899)
NORTHWEST SKYLINE LOGGING INC
725 Lower Airport Rd, Happy Camp (96039)
P.O. Box 144, Round Mountain (96084-0144)
PHONE..................................530 493-5150
Tom Forcher, *President*
Anton Forcher, *Corp Secy*
Elena Norman, *Admin Sec*
EMP: 10
SALES (est): 943.5K **Privately Held**
SIC: 2411 Logging camps & contractors

(P-3900)
PACIFIC TIMBER CONTRACTING
690 Jacobsen Way, Ferndale (95536)
P.O. Box 44 (95536-0044)
PHONE..................................707 498-1374
David Walters, *Owner*
EMP: 10
SALES: 950K **Privately Held**
SIC: 2411 Logging camps & contractors

(P-3901)
PHILBRICK INC
Also Called: Philbrick Logging & Trucking
32180 Airport Rd, Fort Bragg (95437-9509)
P.O. Box 1288 (95437-1288)
PHONE..................................707 964-2277
Jerry D Philbrick, *President*
EMP: 48
SQ FT: 500
SALES: 4MM **Privately Held**
WEB: www.philbrick.com
SIC: 2411 Logging camps & contractors

(P-3902)
ROACH BROS INC
23550 Shady Ln, Fort Bragg (95437-8421)
PHONE..................................707 964-9240
Leroy Roach, *President*
Sybil Roach, *Treasurer*
Gary Roach, *Vice Pres*
Sally Roach, *Admin Sec*
EMP: 70
SALES (est): 5.8MM **Privately Held**
WEB: www.roachbros.com
SIC: 2411 Logging camps & contractors

(P-3903)
ROUNDS LOGGING COMPANY
4350 Lynbrook Loop Apt 1, Redding (96003-6853)
PHONE..................................530 247-0517
Roger Rounds, *President*
Stacie Rounds, *Admin Sec*
EMP: 45
SQ FT: 1,200
SALES (est): 5.3MM **Privately Held**
SIC: 2411 Logging camps & contractors

(P-3904)
SHASTA GREEN INC
Also Called: Franklin Logging
35586a State Hwy 299 E, Burney (96013-4048)
PHONE..................................530 335-4924
Diane Franklin, *President*
Keith Tiner, *Vice Pres*
EMP: 50
SQ FT: 1,500
SALES (est): 7.9MM **Privately Held**
WEB: www.shastagreen.com
SIC: 2411 Logging camps & contractors

(P-3905)
SHUSTERS LOGGING INC
750 E Valley St, Willits (95490-9749)
PHONE..................................707 459-4131
Steve Shuster, *President*
Marv Lawrence, *Corp Secy*
Phillip L Shuster, *Vice Pres*
EMP: 75
SQ FT: 2,300
SALES (est): 6.1MM **Privately Held**
SIC: 2411 Logging

(P-3906)
SIERRA RESOURCE MANAGEMENT INC
12015 La Grange Rd, Jamestown (95327-9724)
PHONE..................................209 984-1146
Mike Albrecht, *President*
Stacy Dodge, *Vice Pres*
EMP: 25
SQ FT: 4,500
SALES (est): 3MM **Privately Held**
WEB: www.sierraresource.org
SIC: 2411 Logging camps & contractors

(P-3907)
SILLER BROTHERS INC (PA)
Also Called: Siller Aviation
1250 Smith Rd, Yuba City (95991-6948)
P.O. Box 1585 (95992-1585)
PHONE..................................530 673-0734
Tom Siller, *President*
Hunt Norris, *CFO*
Jack Parnell, *Chairman*
Andrew Jansen, *Vice Pres*
Jim Staas, *Supervisor*
EMP: 55
SALES (est): 9.5MM **Privately Held**
SIC: 2411 2421 Logging camps & contractors; sawmills & planing mills, general

(P-3908)
SKYLINE ALTERATIONS INC
6727 Deschutes Rd, Anderson (96007-8492)
PHONE..................................530 549-4010
Dawn M Sherman, *President*
EMP: 24
SALES (corp-wide): 1.2MM **Privately Held**
SIC: 2411 Logging
PA: Skyline Alterations, Inc.
10771 Cheshire Way
Palo Cedro CA 96073
530 549-4010

(P-3909)
SOPER-WHEELER COMPANY LLC (PA)
19855 Barton Hill Rd, Strawberry Valley (95981-9700)
PHONE..................................530 675-2343
David Westcott, *CEO*
Daniel Krueger, *President*
Paul Violet, *Vice Pres*
Paul Violett, *Vice Pres*
Anne Bigalow, *Asst Treas*
EMP: 30
SQ FT: 30,000
SALES: 10MM **Privately Held**
SIC: 2411 Logging camps & contractors

(P-3910)
STEVE MORRIS
Also Called: Steve Morris Logging & Contg
1500 Glendale Dr, McKinleyville (95519-9208)
PHONE..................................707 822-8537
Steve Morris, *Owner*
EMP: 10
SALES: 3MM **Privately Held**
SIC: 2411 Logging camps & contractors

(P-3911)
TS LOGGING
18121 Rays Rd, Philo (95466)
P.O. Box 31 (95466-0031)
PHONE..................................707 895-3751
Timothy Slotte, *Owner*
EMP: 11
SALES (est): 1.4MM **Privately Held**
SIC: 2411 Logging camps & contractors

(P-3912)
TUBIT ENTERPRISES INC
21640 S Vallejo St, Burney (96013-9778)
P.O. Box 1019 (96013-1019)
PHONE..................................530 335-5085
Douglas Lindgren, *CEO*
Richard Lindgren, *President*
EMP: 40
SQ FT: 3,000
SALES: 1MM **Privately Held**
SIC: 2411 Logging camps & contractors

(P-3913)
US DOOR AND FENCE LLC
3880 Garner Rd, Riverside (92501-1066)
PHONE..................................951 300-0010
Gang Wu, *Owner*
Nick Anis, *Vice Pres*
Aizhen Chen, *Mng Member*
Chunjie Sun, *Mng Member*
Yicheng Sun, *Mng Member*
▲ EMP: 15 EST: 2012
SQ FT: 30,000
SALES: 1.7MM
SALES (corp-wide): 14.1MM **Privately Held**
SIC: 2411 3089 3315 3442 Rails, fence; round or split; fences, gates & accessories: plastic; fence gates posts & fittings: steel; screen & storm doors & windows; screen doors, metal; storm doors or windows, metal; metal doors; fences, gates, posts & flagpoles; metal doors, sash & trim
PA: Ningbo Win Success Machinery Co.,Ltd
No. 228 Jinchuan Road , Zhenhai Economic Development Zone.
Ningbo 31520
574 863-0767

(P-3914)
WARNER ENTERPRISES INC
1577 Beltline Rd, Redding (96003-1407)
PHONE..................................530 241-4000
Paul Warner, *President*
Gary Warner, *Vice Pres*
EMP: 30
SQ FT: 9,000
SALES (est): 3.8MM **Privately Held**
WEB: www.wagner-webworks.com
SIC: 2411 Wood chips, produced in the field; logging camps & contractors

(P-3915)
WASHBURN GROVE MANAGEMENT INC
27781 Fairview Ave, Hemet (92544-8521)
PHONE..................................909 322-4690
Dennis Washburn, *President*
David Washburn, *Vice Pres*
EMP: 25
SALES (est): 2.7MM **Privately Held**
SIC: 2411 0783 Logging; ornamental shrub & tree services

(P-3916)
WELL ANALYSIS CORPORATION INC (PA)
Also Called: Welaco
5500 Woodmere Dr, Bakersfield (93313-2776)
P.O. Box 20008 (93390-0008)
PHONE..................................661 283-9510
Judy L Bebout, *CEO*
Dan Bebout, *Treasurer*
Brenda Muniozguren, *Vice Pres*
Robert Muniozguren, *Admin Sec*
Chuck Obrien, *Safety Mgr*
▲ EMP: 28
SQ FT: 1,400
SALES (est): 4.4MM **Privately Held**
WEB: www.welaco.com
SIC: 2411 1389 Logging; oil field services

(P-3917)
WEST COAST TIMBER CORP
6221 Apache Rd, Westminster (92683-1919)
PHONE..................................714 893-4374
EMP: 15
SALES: 700K **Privately Held**
SIC: 2411

(P-3918)
WHEELER LUMBER CO INC
Also Called: Jim Wheeler Logging
2407 Cathy Rd, Miranda (95553)
P.O. Box 294 (95553-0294)
PHONE..................................707 943-3424
Jimmie Wheeler, *President*
H D Wheeler, *Vice Pres*
EMP: 10 EST: 1969
SALES (est): 815.9K **Privately Held**
SIC: 2411 5211 Logging camps & contractors; planing mill products & lumber

(P-3919)
WILLIAM R SCHMITT
Also Called: Schmitt Superior Classics
18135 Clear Creek Rd, Redding (96001-5233)
PHONE..................................530 243-3069
William R Schmitt, *Owner*
Sylvia Schmitt, *Co-Owner*
Ken Rice, *Manager*
EMP: 20
SALES (est): 1.6MM **Privately Held**
SIC: 2411 4212 5521 Logging; lumber (log) trucking, local; automobiles, used cars only; antique automobiles

(P-3920)
WIRTA LOGGING INC
970 Kandy Ln, Portola (96122-9631)
PHONE..................................928 440-3446
Mike Wirta, *President*
EMP: 20
SALES (est): 1.1MM **Privately Held**
SIC: 2411 Logging camps & contractors

(P-3921)
WITTEN LOGGING
4600 Kelso Creek Rd, Weldon (93283-9687)
PHONE..................................760 378-3640

▲ = Import ▼=Export
◆ =Import/Export

Jess Witten, *Owner*
EMP: 10
SALES (est): 718.7K **Privately Held**
SIC: 2411 Logging camps & contractors

(P-3922)
WYLATTI RESOURCE MGT INC
23601 Cemetery Ln, Covelo (95428-9773)
P.O. Box 575 (95428-0575)
PHONE..................................707 983-8135
Brian K Hurt, *President*
EMP: 20
SALES (est): 3MM **Privately Held**
SIC: 2411 1611 1622 1442 Logging; general contractor, highway & street construction; bridge construction; construction sand & gravel; dump truck haulage; heavy machinery transport, local

---
2421 Saw & Planing Mills

(P-3923)
AMERICAN WOOD FIBERS INC
4560 Skyway Dr, Marysville (95901)
P.O. Box 788 (95901-0021)
PHONE..................................530 741-3700
Mark Medearis, *Manager*
EMP: 12 **Privately Held**
WEB: www.awf.com
SIC: 2421 Sawdust & shavings
PA: American Wood Fibers, Inc.
9740 Patuxent
Columbia MD 21046

(P-3924)
ARTESIA SAWDUST PRODUCTS INC
13434 S Ontario Ave, Ontario (91761-7956)
PHONE..................................909 947-5983
Brigitte De Laura-Espinoza, *President*
Anthony Espinoza, *Vice Pres*
EMP: 35
SQ FT: 2,700
SALES (est): 5.8MM **Privately Held**
WEB: www.artesiasawdust.com
SIC: 2421 Sawdust & shavings; wood chips, produced at mill

(P-3925)
AUTUMN MILLING CO INC
621 26th St, Manhattan Beach (90266-2228)
PHONE..................................310 635-0703
Charles E Jordan, *President*
Janet Jordan, *Treasurer*
Craig Jordan, *Vice Pres*
EMP: 20
SALES (est): 2.3MM
SALES (corp-wide): 2.4MM **Privately Held**
SIC: 2421 Sawmills & planing mills, general
PA: C E Jordan Hardwood Co Inc
20930 S Alameda St
Long Beach CA 90810
310 635-0703

(P-3926)
B P JOHN RECYCLE INC
Also Called: B P John Hauling
38875 Avenida La Cresta, Murrieta (92562-9155)
PHONE..................................951 696-1144
Edward F Metzler, *President*
Lynda Metzler, *Admin Sec*
EMP: 20
SALES: 5MM **Privately Held**
SIC: 2421 4212 Fuelwood, from mill waste; light haulage & cartage, local

(P-3927)
BLASTED WOOD PRODUCTS INC
Also Called: Insignia
7108 Santa Rita Cir, Buena Park (90620-3189)
PHONE..................................714 237-1600
Joseph L Westbrook, *CEO*
Joseph Westbrook, *President*
EMP: 10
SALES (est): 1.9MM **Privately Held**
SIC: 2421 Lumber: rough, sawed or planed

(P-3928)
CABINETS GALORE ORANGE COUNTY
Also Called: Cabinets Galore Oc
9279 Cabot Dr Ste D, San Diego (92126-4364)
PHONE..................................858 586-0555
Barry Jacobs, *President*
ADI Jacobs, *Vice Pres*
Luke Breandt, *Principal*
EMP: 20
SQ FT: 10,000
SALES: 3MM **Privately Held**
SIC: 2421 1751 Furniture dimension stock, softwood; cabinet & finish carpentry

(P-3929)
CHAPMAN DESIGNS INC
8333 Secura Way, Santa Fe Springs (90670-2213)
P.O. Box 2155, Whittier (90610-2155)
PHONE..................................562 698-4600
Michael Chapman, *President*
John Chapman, *Vice Pres*
EMP: 25
SQ FT: 16,000
SALES (est): 3.5MM **Privately Held**
WEB: www.chapmandesignsinc.com
SIC: 2421 Specialty sawmill products

(P-3930)
COLLINS PINE COMPANY
500 Main St, Chester (96020)
P.O. Box 796 (96020-0796)
PHONE..................................530 258-2111
Chris Verderber, *Branch Mgr*
EMP: 262
SALES (corp-wide): 105.8MM **Privately Held**
WEB: www.collinswood.com
SIC: 2421 Sawmills & planing mills, general
PA: Collins Pine Company
29100 Sw Town Center Lo
Wilsonville OR 97070
503 227-1219

(P-3931)
CROSSROADS RECYCLED LUMBER LLC
58500 Hancock Way, North Fork (93643)
P.O. Box 928 (93643-0928)
PHONE..................................559 877-3645
Toll Free:..................................888
Marc Mandell, *Mng Member*
EMP: 10
SQ FT: 30,000
SALES (est): 627K **Privately Held**
WEB: www.crossroadslumber.com
SIC: 2421 5932 Lumber: rough, sawed or planed; building materials, secondhand

(P-3932)
D LAURENCE GATES LTD
2671 Crow Canyon Rd, San Ramon (94583-1519)
PHONE..................................925 736-8176
David Gates, *CEO*
EMP: 25
SQ FT: 3,500
SALES (est): 812.9K **Privately Held**
SIC: 2421 3272 5031 Building & structural materials, wood; building materials, except block or brick: concrete; concrete stuctural support & building material; building materials, interior; building materials, exterior

(P-3933)
HAGLE LUMBER COMPANY INC
3100 Somis Rd, Somis (93066-9549)
P.O. Box 120 (93066-0120)
PHONE..................................805 987-3887
Ralph Hagle, *CEO*
Rick Hagle, *President*
Joe Ferreira, *Vice Pres*
Denise Beck, *Executive*
Javier Hurtado, *Foreman/Supr*
EMP: 30
SQ FT: 3,000
SALES (est): 11.4MM **Privately Held**
WEB: www.haglelumber.com
SIC: 2421 Sawmills & planing mills, general

(P-3934)
HAMAR WOOD PARQUET COMPANY
Also Called: Royal Custom Parquet
9303 Greenleaf Ave, Santa Fe Springs (90670-3029)
PHONE..................................562 944-8885
Jeffrey Hamar, *President*
EMP: 20
SALES (est): 1.4MM **Privately Held**
SIC: 2421 Flooring (dressed lumber), softwood

(P-3935)
HMR BUILDING SYSTEMS LLC
620 Newport Center Dr # 12, Newport Beach (92660-6420)
PHONE..................................951 749-4700
Ronald Simon,
RSI Holding LLC,
▲ EMP: 15
SQ FT: 90,000
SALES (est): 2.7MM **Privately Held**
SIC: 2421 Building & structural materials, wood
PA: Rsi Holding Llc
620 Nwport Ctr Dr Fl 12 Flr 12
Newport Beach CA 92660
-

(P-3936)
I & E LATH MILL INC
8701 School Rd, Philo (95466)
P.O. Box 9 (95466-0009)
PHONE..................................707 895-3380
Rodney Island, *President*
Virginia Island, *Corp Secy*
EMP: 35
SQ FT: 40,000
SALES (est): 5.3MM **Privately Held**
SIC: 2421 2411 Lumber: rough, sawed or planed; snow fence lath; logging

(P-3937)
JACK MCMAHON LANDSCAPE
Also Called: Jack McMahon Landscaping Svcs
21 Miriam Dr, Calistoga (94515-1335)
PHONE..................................707 942-1122
Jack McMahon, *Owner*
EMP: 10
SALES (est): 550K **Privately Held**
SIC: 2421 0781 Flooring (dressed lumber), softwood; landscape services

(P-3938)
LINDGREN LUMBER CO
3851 W End Ct, Arcata (95521)
PHONE..................................707 822-6519
Joe Lindgren, *Owner*
EMP: 10
SQ FT: 8,400
SALES (est): 824.2K **Privately Held**
WEB: www.lindgrenlumber.com
SIC: 2421 Lath, made in sawmills & lathmills

(P-3939)
NORTH CAL WOOD PRODUCTS INC
700 Kunzler Ranch Rd, Ukiah (95482-3264)
P.O. Box 1534 (95482-1534)
PHONE..................................707 462-0686
Frank Van Vranken, *President*
Tony Fernandez, *Vice Pres*
Charles Currey, *Admin Sec*
EMP: 50
SQ FT: 8,000
SALES: 4MM **Privately Held**
SIC: 2421 2431 2435 Lumber: rough, sawed or planed; lath, made in sawmills & lathmills; panel work, wood; hardwood veneer & plywood

(P-3940)
PLUM CREEK TIMBERLANDS LP
615 N Benson Ave, Upland (91786-5076)
PHONE..................................909 949-2255
EMP: 117
SALES (corp-wide): 7.2B **Publicly Held**
SIC: 2421

HQ: Plum Creek Timberlands, L.P.
601 Union St Ste 3100
Seattle WA 98101
206 467-3600

(P-3941)
PLUM VALLEY INC
Also Called: Pacific Wood Milling Reload
3308 Cyclone Ct, Cottonwood (96022)
P.O. Box 1485 (96022-1485)
PHONE..................................530 262-6262
Donald E Frank, *CEO*
Jackie Tonner, *Manager*
Mary Victor, *Manager*
EMP: 20
SQ FT: 5,000
SALES (est): 339.2K **Privately Held**
WEB: www.plumvalley.com
SIC: 2421 Lumber: rough, sawed or planed

(P-3942)
RAFAEL SANDOVAL
Also Called: Lathrop Woodworks
16175 Mckinley Ave, Lathrop (95330-9703)
PHONE..................................209 858-4173
Rafael Sandoval, *Owner*
▲ EMP: 45
SQ FT: 1,000
SALES (est): 5.5MM **Privately Held**
WEB: www.dmv.ca.gov
SIC: 2421 Outdoor wood structural products; specialty sawmill products

(P-3943)
REGAL CUSTOM MILLWORK INC
301 E Santa Ana St, Anaheim (92805-3954)
P.O. Box 879 (92815-0879)
PHONE..................................714 632-2488
Shirley Reel, *President*
Don Reel, *Shareholder*
Gilbert Reel, *CFO*
EMP: 17
SALES: 2.6MM **Privately Held**
SIC: 2421 5211 Custom sawmill; millwork & lumber

(P-3944)
REUSER INC
370 Santana Dr, Cloverdale (95425-4224)
PHONE..................................707 894-4224
Bruce Reuser, *President*
John Reuser, *Vice Pres*
EMP: 15
SQ FT: 5,000
SALES (est): 3.1MM **Privately Held**
WEB: www.reuserinc.com
SIC: 2421 2875 Sawdust & shavings; wood chips, produced at mill; fertilizers, mixing only

(P-3945)
SAMSGAZEBOSCOM INC
Also Called: Sams Crftsman Style Pfab Gzbos
132 E 163rd St, Gardena (90248-2804)
PHONE..................................310 523-3778
Sam Goeku, *President*
EMP: 10
SQ FT: 12,320
SALES (est): 1.6MM **Privately Held**
WEB: www.samsgazebos.com
SIC: 2421 5211 Outdoor wood structural products; lumber products

(P-3946)
SCHMIDBAUER LUMBER INC (PA)
Also Called: Pacific Clears
1099 W Waterfront Dr, Eureka (95501-0170)
P.O. Box 152 (95502-0152)
PHONE..................................707 443-7024
Frank Schmidbauer, *Principal*
Duane Martin, *Treasurer*
Mary Schmidbauer, *Vice Pres*
▲ EMP: 210
SQ FT: 200,000
SALES (est): 47.6MM **Privately Held**
SIC: 2421 5211 Sawmills & planing mills, general; lumber & other building materials

(P-3947)
SCHMIDBAUER LUMBER INC
Pacific Clears
1017 Samoa Blvd, Arcata (95521-6605)
P.O. Box 1141 (95518-1141)
PHONE..................................707 822-7607
Lee Iorg, *Sales/Mktg Mgr*
Lee Liorg, *Plant Mgr*
EMP: 30
SQ FT: 3,000
SALES (corp-wide): 47.6MM **Privately Held**
SIC: 2421 5211 Resawing lumber into smaller dimensions; planing mill products & lumber
PA: Schmidbauer Lumber, Inc.
1099 W Waterfront Dr
Eureka CA 95501
707 443-7024

(P-3948)
SELL LUMBER CORPORATION
7887 Eastside Rd, Redding (96001-8307)
P.O. Box 990788 (96099-0788)
PHONE..................................530 241-2085
Robert H Sell Sr, *CEO*
Verleen Rath, *Vice Pres*
EMP: 12
SQ FT: 2,000
SALES (est): 2.2MM **Privately Held**
WEB: www.selllumber.com
SIC: 2421 Sawmills & planing mills, general

(P-3949)
SETZER FOREST PRODUCTS INC
Also Called: Millwork Div
1980 Kusel Rd, Oroville (95966-9528)
PHONE..................................530 534-8100
Terry Dunn, *Manager*
Carol Parlin, *Controller*
Don May, *Manager*
EMP: 115
SALES (corp-wide): 50.5MM **Privately Held**
WEB: www.setzerforest.com
SIC: 2421 2431 Cut stock, softwood; millwork
PA: Forest Setzer Products Inc
2555 3rd St Ste 200
Sacramento CA 95818
916 442-2555

(P-3950)
SIERRA PACIFIC INDUSTRIES
2771 Bechelli Ln, Redding (96002-1924)
PHONE..................................530 226-5181
Sheri Dunmoyer, *Admin Asst*
David Kiff, *Accountant*
Greg Thom, *Plant Mgr*
Mark Bosetti, *Manager*
John Phillips, *Manager*
EMP: 13
SALES (corp-wide): 1.2B **Privately Held**
SIC: 2421 Lumber: rough, sawed or planed
PA: Sierra Pacific Industries
19794 Riverside Ave
Anderson CA 96007
530 378-8000

(P-3951)
SIERRA PACIFIC INDUSTRIES (PA)
19794 Riverside Ave, Anderson (96007-4908)
P.O. Box 496028, Redding (96049-6028)
PHONE..................................530 378-8000
George Emmerson, *President*
Mark Emmerson, *Chairman*
Dominic Truniger, *Vice Pres*
Dave Freeburn, *Regional Mgr*
Scott Henson, *Regional Mgr*
◆ **EMP:** 100
SQ FT: 37,000
SALES (est): 1.2B **Privately Held**
WEB: www.sierrapacificind.com
SIC: 2421 2431 Lumber: rough, sawed or planed; millwork; windows, wood

(P-3952)
SIERRA PACIFIC INDUSTRIES
14980 Camage Ave, Sonora (95370-9287)
P.O. Box 247, Standard (95373-0247)
PHONE..................................530 378-8301

Rod Johnson, *Opers-Prdtn-Mfg*
Rod Meier, *Engineer*
Pang Leung, *Sales Mgr*
James Marston, *Sales Staff*
David Porter, *Sales Staff*
EMP: 150
SALES (corp-wide): 1.2B **Privately Held**
WEB: www.sierrapacificind.com
SIC: 2421 Lumber: rough, sawed or planed
PA: Sierra Pacific Industries
19794 Riverside Ave
Anderson CA 96007
530 378-8000

(P-3953)
SIERRA PACIFIC INDUSTRIES
36336 Highway 299 E, Burney (96013)
PHONE..................................530 378-8301
Ed Fischer, *Branch Mgr*
EMP: 13
SALES (corp-wide): 1.2B **Privately Held**
SIC: 2421 Sawmills & planing mills, general
PA: Sierra Pacific Industries
19794 Riverside Ave
Anderson CA 96007
530 378-8000

(P-3954)
SIERRA PACIFIC INDUSTRIES
3025 S 5th Ave, Oroville (95965-5855)
P.O. Box 2198 (95965-2198)
PHONE..................................530 532-6630
Scott Meek, *Branch Mgr*
Mike Vinum, *Plant Mgr*
EMP: 161
SALES (corp-wide): 1.2B **Privately Held**
WEB: www.sierrapacificind.com
SIC: 2421 2431 Lumber: rough, sawed or planed; millwork; windows, wood
PA: Sierra Pacific Industries
19794 Riverside Ave
Anderson CA 96007
530 378-8000

(P-3955)
SIERRA PACIFIC INDUSTRIES
Hwy 299 E, Burney (96013)
P.O. Box 2677 (96013-2677)
PHONE..................................530 335-3681
Ed Fisher, *Branch Mgr*
Nadine Raymond, *Safety Mgr*
EMP: 150
SQ FT: 1,000
SALES (corp-wide): 1.2B **Privately Held**
WEB: www.sierrapacificind.com
SIC: 2421 Lumber: rough, sawed or planed
PA: Sierra Pacific Industries
19794 Riverside Ave
Anderson CA 96007
530 378-8000

(P-3956)
SIERRA PACIFIC INDUSTRIES
3735 El Cajon Ave, Shasta Lake (96019-9211)
PHONE..................................530 275-8851
Darrell Dearman, *Branch Mgr*
EMP: 120
SALES (corp-wide): 1.2B **Privately Held**
WEB: www.sierrapacificind.com
SIC: 2421 2426 Lumber: rough, sawed or planed; hardwood dimension & flooring mills
PA: Sierra Pacific Industries
19794 Riverside Ave
Anderson CA 96007
530 378-8000

(P-3957)
SIERRA PACIFIC INDUSTRIES
19758 Riverside Ave, Anderson (96007-4908)
P.O. Box 10939 (96007-1939)
PHONE..................................530 365-3721
Shane Young, *Division Mgr*
EMP: 420
SALES (corp-wide): 1.2B **Privately Held**
WEB: www.sierrapacificind.com
SIC: 2421 Lumber: rough, sawed or planed
PA: Sierra Pacific Industries
19794 Riverside Ave
Anderson CA 96007
530 378-8000

(P-3958)
SIERRA PACIFIC INDUSTRIES
3950 Carson Rd, Camino (95709-9347)
P.O. Box 680 (95709-0680)
PHONE..................................530 644-2311
Brian Coyle, *Branch Mgr*
EMP: 300
SALES (corp-wide): 1.2B **Privately Held**
WEB: www.sierrapacificind.com
SIC: 2421 Lumber: rough, sawed or planed
PA: Sierra Pacific Industries
19794 Riverside Ave
Anderson CA 96007
530 378-8000

(P-3959)
SIERRA PACIFIC INDUSTRIES
1440 Lincoln Blvd, Lincoln (95648-9105)
P.O. Box 670 (95648-0670)
PHONE..................................916 645-1631
Dan Quarton, *Branch Mgr*
Alan Gulko, *Executive*
EMP: 300
SALES (corp-wide): 1.2B **Privately Held**
WEB: www.sierrapacificind.com
SIC: 2421 Lumber: rough, sawed or planed
PA: Sierra Pacific Industries
19794 Riverside Ave
Anderson CA 96007
530 378-8000

(P-3960)
SIERRA PACIFIC INDUSTRIES
Window Division
11605 Reading Rd, Red Bluff (96080-6702)
P.O. Box 8489 (96080-8489)
PHONE..................................530 527-9620
Bob Taylor, *Manager*
Jan Stephens, *Research*
EMP: 500
SALES (corp-wide): 1.2B **Privately Held**
WEB: www.sierrapacificind.com
SIC: 2421 Sawmills & planing mills, general
PA: Sierra Pacific Industries
19794 Riverside Ave
Anderson CA 96007
530 378-8000

(P-3961)
SIMPSON TIMBER COMPANY
1165 Maple Creek Rd, Korbel (95550-9613)
P.O. Box 68 (95550-0068)
PHONE..................................707 668-4566
EMP: 12
SALES (est): 1.5MM **Privately Held**
WEB: www.simpsoncalifornia.com
SIC: 2421

(P-3962)
STRATA FOREST PRODUCTS INC (PA)
Also Called: Profile Planing Mill
2600 S Susan St, Santa Ana (92704-5816)
PHONE..................................714 751-0800
Richard W Hormuth, *President*
John Hormuth, *President*
▲ **EMP:** 53
SQ FT: 38,000
SALES (est): 9.9MM **Privately Held**
WEB: www.strataforest.com
SIC: 2421 Planing mills

(P-3963)
SUNSET MOULDING CO (PA)
2231 Paseo Rd, Live Oak (95953-9721)
P.O. Box 326, Yuba City (95992-0326)
PHONE..................................530 790-2700
John A Morrison, *CEO*
Wendy Forren, *CFO*
Michel Morrison, *Vice Pres*
Mark Westlake, *Vice Pres*
▲ **EMP:** 50
SALES (est): 24.3MM **Privately Held**
WEB: www.sunsetmoulding.com
SIC: 2421 2431 Cut stock, softwood; moldings, wood: unfinished & prefinished

(P-3964)
TRINITY RIVER LUMBER COMPANY (PA)
1375 Main St, Weaverville (96093)
P.O. Box 249 (96093-0249)
PHONE..................................530 623-5561

Frank A Schmidbauer, *CEO*
Dee Sanders, *Vice Pres*
▲ **EMP:** 150
SQ FT: 10,000
SALES (est): 26.3MM **Privately Held**
SIC: 2421 Lumber: rough, sawed or planed

(P-3965)
WEYERHAEUSER COMPANY
Marketing Sales & Dist Div
27027 Weyerhauser Way, Santa Clarita (91351-4953)
PHONE..................................661 250-3500
Cameron Ylant, *Manager*
EMP: 40
SQ FT: 51,063
SALES (corp-wide): 7.4B **Publicly Held**
SIC: 2421 Sawmills & planing mills, general
PA: Weyerhaeuser Company
220 Occidental Ave S
Seattle WA 98104
206 539-3000

(P-3966)
WEYERHAEUSER COMPANY
2700 S California St, Stockton (95206-3223)
PHONE..................................209 942-1825
John Copenhever, *Manager*
EMP: 12
SALES (corp-wide): 7.4B **Publicly Held**
SIC: 2421 Lumber: rough, sawed or planed
PA: Weyerhaeuser Company
220 Occidental Ave S
Seattle WA 98104
206 539-3000

(P-3967)
WILLITS REDWOOD COMPANY INC
220 Franklin Ave, Willits (95490-4132)
PHONE..................................707 459-4549
Bruce Burton, *President*
Chris Baldo, *Vice Pres*
EMP: 24 EST: 1975
SQ FT: 500
SALES (est): 3.7MM **Privately Held**
WEB: www.willitsredwood.com
SIC: 2421 Custom sawmill

2426 Hardwood Dimension & Flooring Mills

(P-3968)
BAXSTRA INC
Also Called: Martin Erattrud Co
1224 W 132nd St, Gardena (90247-1506)
PHONE..................................323 770-4171
Patrick Baxter, *President*
Allan Stratford, *Owner*
EMP: 100
SALES (est): 6MM **Privately Held**
WEB: www.martinbrattrud.com
SIC: 2426 Frames for upholstered furniture, wood

(P-3969)
BECKER WOODWORKING
847 E 108th St, Los Angeles (90059-1005)
PHONE..................................323 564-2441
Boyd Becker, *Owner*
EMP: 12 EST: 1975
SQ FT: 11,500
SALES: 550K **Privately Held**
SIC: 2426 2499 Hardwood dimension & flooring mills; decorative wood & woodwork

(P-3970)
BIG OAK HARDWOOD FLOOR CO INC
1731 Leslie St, San Mateo (94402-2409)
PHONE..................................650 591-8651
Richard Mack, *President*
Robert Connor, *Treasurer*
EMP: 58
SQ FT: 7,500
SALES (est): 6.2MM **Privately Held**
SIC: 2426 Flooring, hardwood

▲ = Import ▼ = Export
◆ = Import/Export

(P-3971)
CALIFORNIA PRO-SPECS INC
Also Called: Production Specialties
2240 15th Ave, Sacramento (95822-1504)
PHONE..................................916 455-9890
Stephen J Luther, *President*
Nancy Luther, *Vice Pres*
EMP: 25
SQ FT: 31,000
SALES (est): 2.5MM **Privately Held**
SIC: 2426 2511 2435 2434 Furniture dimension stock, hardwood; novelty furniture: wood; hardwood veneer & plywood; wood kitchen cabinets

(P-3972)
DESERT SHUTTERS INC
33907 Robles Dr, Dana Point (92629-2268)
PHONE..................................949 388-8344
Tom Schuster, *President*
EMP: 20
SQ FT: 3,500
SALES (est): 2.4MM **Privately Held**
WEB: www.desertshutters.com
SIC: 2426 2431 Shuttle blocks, hardwood; millwork

(P-3973)
EXCAVO LLC
13428 Maxella Ave Ste 409, Marina Del Rey (90292-5620)
PHONE..................................310 823-7670
EMP: 15
SQ FT: 2,250
SALES (est): 1.4MM **Privately Held**
WEB: www.excavofurniture.com
SIC: 2426

(P-3974)
FURNITURE TECHNOLOGIES INC
17227 Columbus St, Adelanto (92301)
P.O. Box 1076 (92301-1076)
PHONE..................................760 246-9180
Kenneth Drum, *CEO*
Martin Garcia, *Manager*
EMP: 24
SQ FT: 31,000
SALES (est): 4.6MM **Privately Held**
SIC: 2426 Furniture stock & parts, hardwood

(P-3975)
HALLMARK FLOORS INC (PA)
2360 S Archibald Ave, Ontario (91761-8520)
PHONE..................................909 947-7736
Zheng Qing Pan, *President*
Sylvia Bulanek, *Marketing Mgr*
▲ EMP: 28
SALES: 3.5MM **Privately Held**
SIC: 2426 Flooring, hardwood

(P-3976)
HV INDUSTRIES INC
13688 Newhope St, Garden Grove (92843-3712)
PHONE..................................651 233-5676
Vu Ho, *Manager*
John Ho, *Manager*
EMP: 10
SALES (est): 518.4K **Privately Held**
SIC: 2426 3569 3069 3542 Textile machinery accessories, hardwood; lubrication machinery, automatic; reclaimed rubber (reworked by manufacturing processes); presses: hydraulic & pneumatic, mechanical & manual

(P-3977)
LA HARDWOOD FLOORING INC (PA)
Also Called: Eternity Flooring
9880 San Fernando Rd, Pacoima (91331-2603)
PHONE..................................818 361-0099
Doron Gal, *President*
Eliyahu Shuat, *Principal*
▲ EMP: 17
SQ FT: 12,000
SALES (est): 5.1MM **Privately Held**
SIC: 2426 5211 Flooring, hardwood; flooring, wood

(P-3978)
MCMURTRIE & MCMURTRIE INC
Also Called: Tru-Wood Products
915 W 5th St, Azusa (91702-3311)
P.O. Box 1940, Monrovia (91017-5940)
PHONE..................................626 815-0177
Richard McMurtrie, *CEO*
Bill Cherry, *Corp Secy*
▲ EMP: 70
SQ FT: 97,000
SALES (est): 8.4MM **Privately Held**
SIC: 2426 2431 5031 Frames for upholstered furniture, wood; trim, wood; lumber, plywood & millwork

(P-3979)
MONTCLAIR WOOD CORPORATION
545 N Mountain Ave # 104, Upland (91786-5054)
PHONE..................................909 985-0302
John Slavek Grey, *President*
Louis Jimenez, *Vice Pres*
Melissa Lee, *Director*
EMP: 106
SQ FT: 70,000
SALES (est): 16.7MM **Privately Held**
SIC: 2426 5031 Furniture stock & parts, hardwood; lumber: rough, dressed & finished

(P-3980)
O INDUSTRIES CORPORATION
1930 W 139th St, Gardena (90249-2408)
P.O. Box 779, Dana Point (92629-0779)
PHONE..................................310 719-2289
Rhonda Oerding, *CEO*
William Oerding, *COO*
▼ EMP: 15
SALES: 3MM **Privately Held**
SIC: 2426 Flooring, hardwood

(P-3981)
PARQUET BY DIAN INC
16601 S Main St, Gardena (90248-2722)
PHONE..................................310 527-3779
Anatoli Efros, *CEO*
Dima Efros, *President*
EMP: 92
SALES: 12MM **Privately Held**
WEB: www.parquet.com
SIC: 2426 Parquet flooring, hardwood

(P-3982)
QEP CO INC
Also Called: Qep
4200 Santa Ana St, Ontario (91761-1539)
PHONE..................................909 622-3537
Marco Garcia, *Branch Mgr*
EMP: 15
SALES (corp-wide): 334.6MM **Publicly Held**
SIC: 2426 5023 Hardwood dimension & flooring mills; floor coverings
PA: Q.E.P. Co., Inc.
    1001 Brkn Snd Pkwy Nw A
    Boca Raton FL 33487
    561 994-5550

(P-3983)
RONALD D TESON INC
Also Called: California Frames
13945 Mckinley Ave, Los Angeles (90059-3501)
P.O. Box 869, Sunset Beach (90742-0869)
PHONE..................................310 532-5987
Ronald D Teson, *President*
EMP: 34
SQ FT: 18,000
SALES (est): 2.6MM **Privately Held**
WEB: www.californiaframes.com
SIC: 2426 Frames for upholstered furniture, wood

(P-3984)
RTMEX INC
Also Called: Best Redwood
1202 Piper Ranch Rd, San Diego (92154-7714)
P.O. Box 8662, Chula Vista (91912-8662)
PHONE..................................619 391-9913
Jorje Sampietro, *President*
Charlie Burgas, *Sales Mgr*
EMP: 108
SQ FT: 15,000

SALES: 50K **Privately Held**
SIC: 2426 Carvings, furniture: wood

(P-3985)
SYNFONIA FLOORS INC
1550 S Anaheim Blvd Ste A, Anaheim (92805-6218)
PHONE..................................714 300-0770
Aj Ghafari, *Director*
EMP: 15
SQ FT: 6,000
SALES: 1MM **Privately Held**
SIC: 2426 Flooring, hardwood

2429 Special Prdt Sawmills, NEC

(P-3986)
CHARLOIS COOPERAGE USA
1285 S Foothill Blvd, Cloverdale (95425-3254)
PHONE..................................707 224-2377
Sylvain Charlois, *CEO*
Caroline Hale, *Opers Mgr*
▲ EMP: 14 EST: 2010
SALES (est): 2.3MM **Privately Held**
SIC: 2429 Heading, barrel (cooperage stock): sawed or split

(P-3987)
TONELERIA NACIONAL USA INC
Also Called: Tncoopers
21481 8th St E Ste 20c, Sonoma (95476-9292)
P.O. Box 1815 (95476-1815)
PHONE..................................707 501-8728
Alejandro Fantoni, *CEO*
Alexander Schnaidt, *General Mgr*
EMP: 17
SALES (est): 1.9MM **Privately Held**
SIC: 2429 Barrels & barrel parts

2431 Millwork

(P-3988)
A & R DOORS INC
Also Called: A & R Pre-Hung Door
41 5th St Frnt, Hollister (95023-3975)
PHONE..................................831 637-8139
Ruben L Rodriguez, *President*
Albert Rodriguez, *Vice Pres*
EMP: 14
SQ FT: 8,000
SALES: 2.2MM **Privately Held**
WEB: www.aandrdoors.com
SIC: 2431 Doors, wood

(P-3989)
A WORLD OF MOULDING
3041 S Main St, Santa Ana (92707-4250)
PHONE..................................714 361-9308
Michael Leymon, *President*
EMP: 20
SQ FT: 12,000
SALES (est): 1.8MM **Privately Held**
WEB: www.worldofmoulding.com
SIC: 2431 Moldings, wood: unfinished & prefinished

(P-3990)
AAB GARAGE DOOR INC
25333 Pennsylvania Ave, Lomita (90717-2025)
PHONE..................................310 530-3637
Fatih Qeblwy, *President*
EMP: 11
SALES (est): 1.2MM **Privately Held**
SIC: 2431 Garage doors, overhead: wood

(P-3991)
ABC CUSTOM WOOD SHUTTERS INC
Also Called: Golden West Shutters
20561 Pascal Way, Lake Forest (92630-8119)
PHONE..................................949 595-0300
David Harris, *Vice Pres*
John Stahman, *Vice Pres*
EMP: 35

SALES (est): 2.2MM **Privately Held**
SIC: 2431 Door shutters, wood; window shutters, wood

(P-3992)
ANDERCO INC
540 Airpark Dr, Fullerton (92833-2503)
PHONE..................................714 446-9508
Peter Johnson, *President*
Ralph Johnson, *Vice Pres*
Aaron Olson, *CPA*
▲ EMP: 50
SQ FT: 70,000
SALES (est): 8.3MM **Privately Held**
SIC: 2431 5031 Door frames, wood; doors & windows

(P-3993)
ANLIN INDUSTRIES
Also Called: Anlin Window Systems
1665 Tollhouse Rd, Clovis (93611-0523)
PHONE..................................800 287-7996
Thomas Anton Vidmar, *Principal*
Harry Parisi, *CFO*
Eric Vidmar, *Corp Secy*
Stan Fikes, *Vice Pres*
Greg Vidmar, *Vice Pres*
EMP: 250
SQ FT: 188,000
SALES (est): 51MM **Privately Held**
SIC: 2431 Windows & window parts & trim, wood

(P-3994)
APEX INTERIOR SOURCE INC
30555 Roseview Ln, Thousand Palms (92276-2916)
PHONE..................................760 343-1919
Dennis Silva, *President*
EMP: 20
SQ FT: 3,000
SALES (est): 1.7MM **Privately Held**
SIC: 2431 Windows & window parts & trim, wood

(P-3995)
APEX SPECIALTY CNSTR ENTPS
Also Called: Apex Door & Frame
17461 Poplar St, Hesperia (92345-6563)
PHONE..................................714 334-1118
Oscar Gonzalez, *President*
Virgina Gonzalez, *Vice Pres*
EMP: 16
SQ FT: 2,500
SALES (est): 1.3MM **Privately Held**
WEB: www.apexdoorandframe.com
SIC: 2431 Door frames, wood

(P-3996)
ARCH-RITE INC
1062 N Armando St, Anaheim (92806-2605)
P.O. Box 6207, Fullerton (92834-6207)
PHONE..................................714 630-9305
Michael Barry, *President*
George Goodwin, *Vice Pres*
EMP: 14
SQ FT: 15,000
SALES: 1.2MM **Privately Held**
WEB: www.arch-rite.com
SIC: 2431 Windows & window parts & trim, wood; doors & door parts & trim, wood

(P-3997)
ARCHITCTRAL MLLWK SLUTIONS INC
2565 Progress St, Vista (92081-8423)
PHONE..................................760 510-6440
Ricardo E Alcantara, *President*
Terry Alcantara, *CFO*
EMP: 15
SQ FT: 8,850
SALES: 1MM **Privately Held**
SIC: 2431 Millwork

(P-3998)
ARCHITCTRAL MLLWK SNTA BARBARA
Also Called: Manufacturers of Wood Products
8 N Nopal St, Santa Barbara (93103-3317)
P.O. Box 4699 (93140-4699)
PHONE..................................805 965-7011
Thomas G Mathews, *President*
Ronald Mathews, *Shareholder*
Glenice Mathews, *CEO*
Joseph J Mathews, *Vice Pres*

PRODUCTS & SVCS

Lisa Mathews, *Accounting Mgr*
EMP: 40
SQ FT: 10,000
SALES (est): 7.5MM **Privately Held**
WEB: www.archmill.com
SIC: 2431 Millwork

(P-3999)
ART GLASS ETC INC
Also Called: AG Millworks
3111 Golf Course Dr, Ventura
(93003-7604)
PHONE.................805 644-4494
Rachid El Etel, *President*
Aida El Etel, *CFO*
Laura Graybill, *Manager*
▲ **EMP:** 50
SALES (est): 7.4MM **Privately Held**
WEB: www.artglassandmetal.com
SIC: 2431 Doors & door parts & trim,
wood; windows & window parts & trim,
wood

(P-4000)
AVALON SHUTTERS INC
3407 N Perris Blvd, Perris (92571-3100)
PHONE.................909 937-4900
Douglas Noel Serbin, *CEO*
Tammy Vincent, *Accountant*
Jody Strickland, *Safety Mgr*
Trish Long, *Sales Staff*
Doreen Graybill, *Cust Mgr*
▲ **EMP:** 215
SQ FT: 85,000
SALES: 20MM **Privately Held**
WEB: www.avalonshutters.net
SIC: 2431 Window shutters, wood; door
shutters, wood; blinds (shutters), wood

(P-4001)
B & G MILLWORKS
12522 Lakeland Rd, Santa Fe Springs
(90670-3940)
PHONE.................562 944-4599
Gene Harden, *Partner*
Brad Simons, *Partner*
EMP: 14
SALES (est): 1.9MM **Privately Held**
WEB: www.bgmillworks.com
SIC: 2431 1751 5084 Millwork; carpentry
work; woodworking machinery

(P-4002)
**BAKERSFIELD WOODWORKS
INC**
3416 Big Trail Ave, Bakersfield
(93313-5071)
PHONE.................661 282-8492
EMP: 10
SALES (est): 1.1MM **Privately Held**
WEB: www.bakersfieldwoodworksinc.com
SIC: 2431

(P-4003)
**BLOSSOM APPLE MOULDING &
MLLWK**
Also Called: Apple Blossom Mould Mill Work
2411 Old Crow Canyon Rd L, San Ramon
(94583-1240)
PHONE.................925 820-2345
Donald Utley, *Owner*
EMP: 22
SALES (est): 3.2MM **Privately Held**
SIC: 2431 5031 Millwork; lumber, plywood
& millwork

(P-4004)
BMC EAST LLC
Also Called: Precision Milling
161 W Cypress Ave, Burbank
(91502-1739)
PHONE.................818 842-8139
Todd Righplery, *Manager*
EMP: 18
SQ FT: 2,092 **Publicly Held**
WEB: www.stockbuildingsupply.com
SIC: 2431 Millwork
HQ: Bmc East, Llc
8020 Arco Corp Dr Ste 400
Raleigh NC 27617
919 431-1000

(P-4005)
BROOKS MILLWORK COMPANY
13551 Yorba Ave, Chino (91710-5057)
PHONE.................562 920-3000

Michael B Brooks, *Owner*
EMP: 11
SALES (est): 1.6MM **Privately Held**
SIC: 2431 5211 Moldings, wood: unfin-
ished & prefinished; millwork & lumber

(P-4006)
CA SKYHOOK INC
4149 Cartagena Dr Ste B, San Diego
(92115-6724)
PHONE.................619 229-2169
John Reinhold, *President*
Gaye Reinhold, *CFO*
EMP: 23
SQ FT: 12,500
SALES (est): 2.2MM **Privately Held**
SIC: 2431 Staircases, stairs & railings

(P-4007)
CALIFORNIA CAB & STORE FIX
8472 Carbide Ct, Sacramento
(95828-5609)
PHONE.................916 386-1340
Bruce D Nicolson, *President*
EMP: 45
SQ FT: 20,640
SALES (est): 5MM **Privately Held**
SIC: 2431 2541 Millwork; table or counter
tops, plastic laminated

(P-4008)
CALIFORNIA DECOR
Also Called: Salon Brandy
541 E Pine St, Compton (90222-2817)
PHONE.................310 603-9944
James Lee Jenkins, *President*
Richard Mars, *Corp Secy*
EMP: 23
SQ FT: 36,000
SALES: 1.4MM **Privately Held**
WEB: www.californiadecor.com
SIC: 2431 7359 2522 2512 Woodwork,
interior & ornamental; equipment rental &
leasing; office furniture, except wood; up-
holstered household furniture; wood
household furniture

(P-4009)
**CALIFORNIA DELUXE WINDOW
INDUS (PA)**
Also Called: California Blind Company
20735 Superior St, Chatsworth
(91311-4416)
PHONE.................818 349-5566
Aaron Adirim, *President*
EMP: 50
SQ FT: 60,000
SALES (est): 12.6MM **Privately Held**
SIC: 2431 2824 Windows & window parts
& trim, wood; vinyl fibers

(P-4010)
**CALIFORNIA KIT CAB DOOR
CORP**
Also Called: Cal Door
1800 Abbott St, Salinas (93901-4534)
PHONE.................831 784-5142
Jorg Bruckner, *Principal*
EMP: 200
SALES (corp-wide): 65.3MM **Privately
Held**
SIC: 2431 Doors & door parts & trim, wood
PA: California Kitchen Cabinet Door Corpo-
ration
400 Cochrane Cir
Morgan Hill CA 95037
408 782-5700

(P-4011)
CALIFORNIA MILLWORKS CORP
Also Called: California Classics
27772 Avenue Scott, Santa Clarita
(91355-3417)
PHONE.................661 294-2345
Steven Gadol, *President*
Lay Cho, *President*
Steven Godol, *President*
Edmond Cho, *Vice Pres*
EMP: 22
SQ FT: 149,000
SALES (est): 417.4K
SALES (corp-wide): 4.5MM **Privately
Held**
WEB: www.california-classics.com
SIC: 2431 Doors, wood; windows & win-
dow parts & trim, wood

PA: Old English Milling And Woodworks,
Inc
27772 Avenue Scott
Santa Clarita CA 91355
661 294-9171

(P-4012)
**CALIFRNIA MANTEL FIREPLACE
INC (PA)**
4141 N Freeway Blvd, Sacramento
(95834-1209)
P.O. Box 340037 (95834-0037)
PHONE.................916 925-5775
Stephen Casey, *President*
EMP: 45
SQ FT: 7,000
SALES (est): 7.5MM **Privately Held**
SIC: 2431 3272 Mantels, wood; mantels,
concrete

(P-4013)
CAMELIA CITY MILLWORK INC
7831 Clifton Rd, Sacramento (95826-4324)
PHONE.................916 451-2454
Angelo Bertagnini, *President*
Karen Bertagnini, *Vice Pres*
EMP: 11
SQ FT: 7,000
SALES (est): 1.5MM **Privately Held**
SIC: 2431 2434 Millwork; wood kitchen
cabinets

(P-4014)
CANYON GRAPHICS INC
6680 Cobra Way, San Diego (92121-4107)
PHONE.................858 646-0444
Scott Moncrieff, *CEO*
Paul Billimoria, *Vice Pres*
Tracy Francis, *Info Tech Dir*
Warren Johnson, *Info Tech Dir*
Carmelo Rioflorido, *Engineer*
EMP: 60
SQ FT: 34,500
SALES (est): 11MM **Privately Held**
WEB: www.canyongraphics.com
SIC: 2431 2754 Moldings & baseboards,
ornamental & trim; labels: gravure printing

(P-4015)
CARL NERSESIAN
Also Called: California Blind Company
13415 Saticoy St, North Hollywood
(91605-3413)
PHONE.................818 888-0111
Carl Nersesian, *Owner*
Lisa Kianoun, *Executive Asst*
EMP: 15
SQ FT: 6,000
SALES: 2MM **Privately Held**
WEB: www.californiablinds.com
SIC: 2431 2591 5023 5714 Blinds (shut-
ters), wood; window blinds; vertical blinds;
drapery & upholstery stores; window fur-
nishings

(P-4016)
CASA GRANDE WOODWORKS
4230 Cloud Way, Paso Robles
(93446-8378)
PHONE.................805 226-2040
Jeff Casagrande, *Principal*
EMP: 20 **EST:** 2011
SALES (est): 2MM **Privately Held**
SIC: 2431 Millwork

(P-4017)
CHARLES GEMEINER CABINETS
3225 Exposition Pl, Los Angeles
(90018-4032)
PHONE.................323 299-8696
Charles Gemeiner, *Owner*
EMP: 27
SQ FT: 20,000
SALES: 800K **Privately Held**
SIC: 2431 1751 Millwork; cabinet building
& installation

(P-4018)
**COMMERCIAL CASEWORK INC
(PA)**
Also Called: Madera Fina
41780 Christy St, Fremont (94538-5106)
PHONE.................510 657-7933
William M Palmer, *CEO*
Lee Bassard, *Project Mgr*
Ben Castellon, *Project Mgr*

Richard Topete, *Engineer*
EMP: 58
SQ FT: 35,000
SALES (est): 10.1MM **Privately Held**
WEB: www.commercialcasework.com
SIC: 2431 2541 Millwork; office fixtures,
wood

(P-4019)
**COMMERCIAL MTL & DOOR SUP
INC**
Also Called: Commercial Mill & Builders Sup
1210 Ames Ave, Milpitas (95035-6306)
P.O. Box 612708, San Jose (95161-2708)
PHONE.................408 432-3383
Gerald Zisch, *President*
Dennis Henslye, *Treasurer*
Ronald Bowron, *Vice Pres*
EMP: 12
SQ FT: 30,000
SALES (est): 1.7MM **Privately Held**
SIC: 2431 5031 Doors, wood; lumber, ply-
wood & millwork

(P-4020)
**COMPOSITE TECHNOLOGY INTL
INC**
Also Called: Composite Technology Intl
1730 I St Ste 100, Sacramento
(95811-3015)
PHONE.................916 551-1850
J Griffin Reid, *CEO*
Cynthia Reid, *Corp Secy*
Griffin Reid, *Vice Pres*
Joseph Falmer, *VP Finance*
◆ **EMP:** 46
SQ FT: 3,000
SALES (est): 9.3MM **Privately Held**
SIC: 2431 5023 8711 3999 Moldings,
wood: unfinished & prefinished; frames &
framing, picture & mirror; sanitary engi-
neers; barber & beauty shop equipment

(P-4021)
COPPA WOODWORKING INC
1231 Paraiso St, San Pedro (90731-1334)
PHONE.................310 548-4142
Ciro C Coppa, *President*
Carol Coppa, *Vice Pres*
▼ **EMP:** 10
SQ FT: 9,000
SALES (est): 1.4MM **Privately Held**
WEB: www.coppawoodworking.com
SIC: 2431 2511 5712 5211 Door screens,
wood frame; wood lawn & garden furni-
ture; outdoor & garden furniture; screens,
door & window

(P-4022)
CPS WOOD WORKS INC
1257 E 9th St, Pomona (91766-3830)
PHONE.................909 326-1102
Oscar Gomez, *CEO*
EMP: 13
SALES (est): 175.2K **Privately Held**
SIC: 2431 Woodwork, interior & ornamen-
tal

(P-4023)
**CREATIVE CONCEPTS AND
DESIGN**
8460 Freedom Ln, Winters (95694-9681)
PHONE.................707 812-9320
William Nylander, *Owner*
EMP: 10 **EST:** 2013
SALES (est): 427.8K **Privately Held**
SIC: 2431 7389 Millwork;

(P-4024)
**CRESTMARK
ARCHITRACTURAL MILL**
5640 West End Rd, Arcata (95521-9202)
PHONE.................707 822-4034
Scott David Olsen, *Principal*
Tio Escarda, *Project Mgr*
EMP: 45
SALES: 1.7MM **Privately Held**
WEB: www.crestmarkam.com
SIC: 2431 Millwork

▲ = Import ▼=Export
◆ =Import/Export

(P-4025)

CUSTOM MULDINGS SASH DOORS INC
7732 Densmore Ave Ste A, Van Nuys (91406-1919)
PHONE..................................818 787-7367
Peter Montano Jr, *President*
Antonio Jose Garcia, *Vice Pres*
Jose I Garcia, *Vice Pres*
EMP: 11
SQ FT: 4,800
SALES: 950K **Privately Held**
SIC: 2431 Door sashes, wood

(P-4026)

CUSTOM QUALITY DOOR & TRIM INC
1116 Bradford Cir, Corona (92882-1874)
PHONE..................................951 278-0066
Michael Leroy Hughes, *CEO*
Shawn Hughes, *President*
Leah Ortiz, *Controller*
EMP: 13
SALES (est): 3.2MM **Privately Held**
SIC: 2431 Doors & door parts & trim, wood

(P-4027)

CUSTOM WINDOW DESIGN INC
3242 Production Ave, Oceanside (92058-1308)
PHONE..................................760 439-6213
Mark Alvey, *President*
Andrew Alvey, *Admin Sec*
EMP: 30
SQ FT: 30,000
SALES (est): 3.9MM **Privately Held**
WEB: www.customwindowdesign.com
SIC: 2431 Doors, wood; door frames, wood; windows, wood; window frames, wood

(P-4028)

D & L MOULDING AND LUMBER CO
1044 N Soldano Ave, Azusa (91702-2135)
PHONE..................................626 444-0134
EMP: 11
SQ FT: 6,000
SALES (est): 820.5K **Privately Held**
SIC: 2431

(P-4029)

D S MCGEE ENTERPRISES INC
3240 Trade Center Dr, Riverside (92507-3432)
PHONE..................................951 378-8473
Dennis McGee, *President*
Sherrie McGee, *Corp Secy*
Diane Peake, *Manager*
EMP: 45
SQ FT: 4,500
SALES (est): 8MM **Privately Held**
SIC: 2431 Woodwork, interior & ornamental; moldings, wood: unfinished & prefinished

(P-4030)

DAY STAR INDUSTRIES
13727 Excelsior Dr, Santa Fe Springs (90670-5104)
PHONE..................................562 926-8800
Dan R Prigmore, *President*
Anne Prigmore, *Treasurer*
Christine Robertson, *Project Mgr*
EMP: 19
SALES (est): 2.9MM **Privately Held**
SIC: 2431 Millwork

(P-4031)

DE LARSHE CABINETRY LLC
Also Called: L-G Wood Products
2000 S Reservoir St, Pomona (91766-5545)
PHONE..................................909 627-2757
Scott League, *Mng Member*
Jeff Cregger,
EMP: 40
SQ FT: 19,500
SALES (est): 6.2MM **Privately Held**
SIC: 2431 2448 Staircases & stairs, wood; wood pallets & skids

(P-4032)

DECORE-ATIVE SPECIALTIES (PA)
2772 Peck Rd, Monrovia (91016-5005)
PHONE..................................626 254-9191
Jack Lansford Sr, *CEO*
Jack Lansford Jr, *President*
Billie Lansford, *Treasurer*
Eric Lansford, *Senior VP*
Bridget Morris, *Vice Pres*
▲ **EMP:** 650
SALES (est): 178.5MM **Privately Held**
WEB: www.decore.com
SIC: 2431 Millwork

(P-4033)

DECORE-ATIVE SPECIALTIES
4414 Azusa Canyon Rd, Irwindale (91706-2740)
PHONE..................................626 960-7731
David Thompson, *Branch Mgr*
EMP: 230
SALES (corp-wide): 178.5MM **Privately Held**
SIC: 2431 Millwork
PA: Decore-Ative Specialties
2772 Peck Rd
Monrovia CA 91016
626 254-9191

(P-4034)

DECORE-ATIVE SPECIALTIES
104 Gate Eats Stock Blvd, Elk Grove (95624)
PHONE..................................916 686-4700
Jack Albright, *Manager*
EMP: 240
SALES (corp-wide): 178.5MM **Privately Held**
WEB: www.decore.com
SIC: 2431 Doors, wood
PA: Decore-Ative Specialties
2772 Peck Rd
Monrovia CA 91016
626 254-9191

(P-4035)

DIAMOND WOODCRAFT
Also Called: Diamond Doors
2197 Ruth Ave Ste 1, South Lake Tahoe (96150-4340)
PHONE..................................530 541-0866
Robert Beaty, *Owner*
EMP: 12 **EST:** 1958
SQ FT: 9,000
SALES (est): 1.2MM **Privately Held**
WEB: www.diamondwoodcraft.com
SIC: 2431 Millwork

(P-4036)

DOOR & HARDWARE INSTALLERS INC
Also Called: Cabinet & Millwork Installers
14300 Davenport Rd Ste 1a, Santa Clarita (91390-5004)
PHONE..................................661 298-9383
Arthur Benson, *President*
Ardith Swanger, *Info Tech Mgr*
EMP: 30 **EST:** 1995
SQ FT: 15,000
SALES (est): 4.6MM **Privately Held**
SIC: 2431 Doors & door parts & trim, wood

(P-4037)

DOORS PLUS INC
314 N Main St, Lodi (95240-0604)
P.O. Box 934 (95241-0934)
PHONE..................................209 463-3667
Douglas Larsson, *President*
Susie Larsson, *Treasurer*
▲ **EMP:** 14
SQ FT: 16,000
SALES (est): 2.6MM **Privately Held**
WEB: www.doorsplusonline.com
SIC: 2431 Doors, wood; window frames, wood

(P-4038)

DORRIS LUMBER AND MOULDING CO (PA)
3453 Ramona Ave Ste 5, Sacramento (95826-3828)
PHONE..................................916 452-7531
Joshua Tyler, *President*
Nels Israelson, *Shareholder*

E Chase Israelson, *Ch of Bd*
Dennis Murcko, *CFO*
Larry White, *Vice Pres*
▲ **EMP:** 145
SALES (est): 22.5MM **Privately Held**
WEB: www.dorrismoulding.com
SIC: 2431 Moldings, wood: unfinished & prefinished

(P-4039)

DREES WOOD PRODUCTS INC
14020 Orange Ave, Paramount (90723-2018)
PHONE..................................562 633-7337
Ed Drees, *Manager*
EMP: 50
SALES (corp-wide): 16.4MM **Privately Held**
WEB: www.dreeswood.com
SIC: 2431 Doors, wood
PA: Drees Wood Products, Inc.
14003 Orange Ave
Paramount CA 90723
562 633-7337

(P-4040)

DREES WOOD PRODUCTS INC (PA)
14003 Orange Ave, Paramount (90723-2017)
PHONE..................................562 633-7337
Ed Drees, *CEO*
Paula Smith, *Credit Mgr*
EMP: 50
SALES (est): 16.4MM **Privately Held**
WEB: www.dreeswood.com
SIC: 2431 Doors, wood

(P-4041)

EAGLE MOULDING COMPANY 1 (PA)
1625 Tierra Buena Rd, Yuba City (95993-8854)
PHONE..................................530 673-6517
Constance Mc Cool, *President*
Kevin P Mc Cool, *Vice Pres*
▲ **EMP:** 28
SQ FT: 44,000
SALES (est): 3.2MM **Privately Held**
WEB: www.eagleco.en.alibaba.com
SIC: 2431 Moldings, wood: unfinished & prefinished

(P-4042)

EL & EL WOOD PRODUCTS CORP (PA)
6011 Schaefer Ave, Chino (91710-7043)
P.O. Box 5105 (91708-5105)
PHONE..................................909 591-0339
Cathy Vidas, *President*
Paul Conley, *Vice Pres*
Bryan Leonard, *Creative Dir*
Jeremy Brainard, *Info Tech Mgr*
Flavia Silva, *Accounting Mgr*
▲ **EMP:** 140 **EST:** 1963
SQ FT: 72,000
SALES (est): 25.2MM **Privately Held**
WEB: www.elandelwoodproducts.com
SIC: 2431 Millwork

(P-4043)

EUROPEAN ELEGANCE WOODWORK
12243 Foothill Blvd, Sylmar (91342-6002)
PHONE..................................818 570-9401
Laszlo Balazs, *Principal*
EMP: 10
SALES (est): 1.3MM **Privately Held**
SIC: 2431 Millwork

(P-4044)

FINELINE WOODWORKING INC
Also Called: Fineline Architectural Mllwk
1139 Baker St, Costa Mesa (92626-4114)
PHONE..................................714 540-5468
Marc Butman, *CEO*
Jon Muller, *COO*
Tom Crone, *CFO*
Stephen Chiang, *IT/INT Sup*
Grant Vanderboom, *Project Mgr*
EMP: 60
SQ FT: 20,000
SALES (est): 6.4MM **Privately Held**
SIC: 2431 Millwork

(P-4045)

FRENCH CUSTOM SHUTTERS INC
Also Called: Wholesales Shutter Specialist
9248 Olive Dr, Spring Valley (91977-2305)
PHONE..................................619 667-2636
Jim French, *President*
Marty French, *Vice Pres*
EMP: 14
SQ FT: 6,000
SALES (est): 2MM **Privately Held**
WEB: www.frenchshutters.com
SIC: 2431 Door frames, wood

(P-4046)

G A DOORS INC
Also Called: Grand American Millwork
15140 Desman Rd, La Mirada (90638-5737)
P.O. Box 805 (90637-0805)
PHONE..................................714 739-1144
Norman Nilsen, *President*
John Nilsen, *Vice Pres*
EMP: 56
SQ FT: 16,000
SALES (est): 5.6MM **Privately Held**
SIC: 2431 Doors, wood; window shutters, wood

(P-4047)

G AND S MILLING CO
Also Called: Island Mountain Lumber
23205 Live Oak Rd, Willits (95490-9707)
PHONE..................................707 459-0294
Fred Galten, *Owner*
Christine Galten, *Principal*
EMP: 30
SALES: 1.7MM **Privately Held**
SIC: 2431 2421 2426 Millwork; sawmills & planing mills, general; hardwood dimension & flooring mills

(P-4048)

GARAGE DOORS INCORPORATED
147 Martha St, San Jose (95112-5814)
PHONE..................................408 293-7443
Scott Jensen, *President*
Nancy Jensen, *Treasurer*
EMP: 60
SQ FT: 45,000
SALES (est): 9.5MM **Privately Held**
WEB: www.garagedoorsinc.com
SIC: 2431 5031 Garage doors, overhead: wood; doors, garage

(P-4049)

GLOBAL DOORS CORP
1340 E 6th St, Los Angeles (90021-1272)
PHONE..................................213 622-2003
Tal Hassid, *President*
David Niedermaier, *Partner*
EMP: 48
SALES (est): 3.5MM **Privately Held**
SIC: 2431 Doors, wood

(P-4050)

GMJ WOODWORKING
2365 Mountain View Dr, Escondido (92027-4951)
PHONE..................................760 294-7428
Christopher Laughton, *Owner*
EMP: 20 **EST:** 2007
SALES (est): 812K **Privately Held**
SIC: 2431 1522 Millwork; residential construction

(P-4051)

GONZALEZ FELICIANO
Also Called: Paradise Kitchen Doors
1583 E Grand Ave, Pomona (91766-3808)
PHONE..................................909 236-1372
Feliciano Gonzalez, *Owner*
EMP: 15 **EST:** 2015
SALES (est): 1.5MM **Privately Held**
SIC: 2431 Doors, wood

(P-4052)

HALEY BROS INC (HQ)
6291 Orangethorpe Ave, Buena Park (90620-1339)
PHONE..................................714 670-2112
Thomas J Cobb, *CEO*
Barry Reynolds, *General Mgr*
Thomas Cobb, *Admin Sec*

Ingrid Bradford, *Human Resources*
Ismael Chavez, *Purch Agent*
▲ **EMP:** 200
SQ FT: 24,000
SALES (est): 31MM
SALES (corp-wide): 92.5MM **Privately Held**
WEB: www.haleybros.com
SIC: 2431 Doors, wood
PA: T. M. Cobb Company
　　500 Palmyrita Ave
　　Riverside CA 92507
　　951 248-2400

(P-4053)
HALLE-HOPPER LLC
Also Called: Trim Quick Co
630 Parkridge Ave, Norco (92860-3124)
PHONE..................................951 284-7373
EMP: 20
SQ FT: 70,000
SALES (est): 3.8MM **Privately Held**
SIC: 2431 Window trim, wood

(P-4054)
HAND CRFTED DUTCHMAN DOORS INC
770 Stonebridge Dr, Tracy (95376-2812)
PHONE..................................209 833-7378
Larry B Vis, *President*
Donna Vis, *CFO*
EMP: 40
SQ FT: 16,000
SALES (est): 6.6MM **Privately Held**
WEB: www.dutchmandoors.com
SIC: 2431 2434 Doors, wood; wood
　　kitchen cabinets

(P-4055)
HIS LIFE WOODWORKS
15107 S Main St, Gardena (90248-1923)
PHONE..................................310 756-0170
John Johnson Jr, *President*
Garrett Brim, *Vice Pres*
Anne Schmidt, *Controller*
EMP: 40
SQ FT: 15,000
SALES: 2.8MM **Privately Held**
WEB: www.hislifewoodworks.com
SIC: 2431 Millwork

(P-4056)
HOSPITALITY WOOD PRODUCTS INC
7206 E Gage Ave, Commerce (90040-3813)
PHONE..................................562 806-5564
Michael Romero, *President*
Carlos Escalante, *Treasurer*
Victor Garcia, *Vice Pres*
EMP: 17 **EST:** 2001
SALES (est): 2.4MM **Privately Held**
SIC: 2431 Interior & ornamental woodwork
　　& trim

(P-4057)
HOWIES MOULDING INC
8032 Allport Ave, Santa Fe Springs (90670-2102)
PHONE..................................562 698-0261
Howard F Holmes, *President*
Michael Holmes, *Shareholder*
Phyllis Holmes, *Treasurer*
▲ **EMP:** 10 **EST:** 1963
SQ FT: 8,000
SALES (est): 1.4MM **Privately Held**
SIC: 2431 Moldings, wood: unfinished &
　　prefinished

(P-4058)
ICI ARCHITECTURAL MILLWORK INC
6820 Brynhurst Ave, Los Angeles (90043-4664)
PHONE..................................323 759-4993
Izhak Korin, *CEO*
Robert A Babayan, *President*
Byron Bailey, *Project Mgr*
EMP: 15 **EST:** 2007
SALES (est): 2.1MM **Privately Held**
SIC: 2431 Millwork

(P-4059)
IDX LOS ANGELES LLC
Also Called: Universal Forest Products
5005 E Philadelphia St, Ontario (91761-2816)
PHONE..................................909 212-8333
Graham Fownes, *General Mgr*
◆ **EMP:** 109
SALES (est): 16.1MM
SALES (corp-wide): 4.4B **Publicly Held**
SIC: 2431 Millwork
PA: Universal Forest Products, Inc.
　　2801 E Beltline Ave Ne
　　Grand Rapids MI 49525
　　616 364-6161

(P-4060)
J & J QUALITY DOOR INC
Also Called: Quality Door & Trim
741 S Airport Way, Stockton (95205-6126)
PHONE..................................209 948-5013
Jeffery Dean Cannon, *CEO*
Steve Cantrell, *President*
Debbie Sue Cantrell, *CFO*
EMP: 35
SALES (est): 6.9MM **Privately Held**
WEB: www.qualitydoor.net
SIC: 2431 Doors, wood

(P-4061)
J RS WOODWORKS INC
300 W Robles Ave Ste B, Santa Rosa (95407-8168)
P.O. Box 9491 (95405-1491)
PHONE..................................707 588-8255
Richard Hoffman, *President*
EMP: 10
SQ FT: 5,750
SALES (est): 1.5MM **Privately Held**
SIC: 2431 Millwork

(P-4062)
J SUMMITT INC
Also Called: Summit Forest Products
13834 Bettencourt St, Cerritos (90703-1010)
PHONE..................................562 236-5744
Jim Summit, *Branch Mgr*
EMP: 27 **Privately Held**
WEB: www.jmsummitt.net
SIC: 2431 Millwork
PA: J. Summitt, Inc.
　　13834 Bettencourt St
　　Cerritos CA 90703

(P-4063)
JELD-WEN INC
Also Called: International Wood Products
3760 Convoy St Ste 111, San Diego (92111-3743)
PHONE..................................800 468-3667
Hugo Hernadez, *Manager*
EMP: 23 **Publicly Held**
SIC: 2431 Doors, wood
HQ: Jeld-Wen, Inc.
　　2645 Silver Crescent Dr
　　Charlotte NC 28273
　　800 535-3936

(P-4064)
JELD-WEN INC
Jeld-Wen Doors
3901 Cincinnati Ave, Rocklin (95765-1303)
PHONE..................................916 782-4900
Roald Pederson, *Manager*
EMP: 115 **Publicly Held**
WEB: www.jeld-wen.com
SIC: 2431 5211 Doors, wood; door & win-
　　dow products
HQ: Jeld-Wen, Inc.
　　2645 Silver Crescent Dr
　　Charlotte NC 28273
　　800 535-3936

(P-4065)
JENSEN DOOR SYSTEMS INC
160 Vallecitos De Oro, San Marcos (92069-1435)
PHONE..................................760 736-4036
Tim Jensen, *President*
Lisa Jensen, *Vice Pres*
EMP: 11
SALES (est): 1.3MM **Privately Held**
WEB: www.jensendoorsystems.com
SIC: 2431 Doors, wood

(P-4066)
JOHN L STATON INC
1214 5th St, Berkeley (94710-1306)
PHONE..................................510 527-3114
Loretta Penning, *President*
John L Staton, *Shareholder*
EMP: 70
SALES (est): 6.4MM **Privately Held**
SIC: 2431 Doors, wood; window frames,
　　wood; window shutters, wood

(P-4067)
KARLS CUSTOM SASH AND DOORS
Also Called: Karl's Sash & Doors
18292 Gothard St, Huntington Beach (92648-1225)
PHONE..................................714 842-7877
Anton Seitz, *Managing Prtnr*
EMP: 23 **EST:** 1980
SQ FT: 9,900
SALES (est): 2.2MM **Privately Held**
SIC: 2431 Door sashes, wood; doors,
　　wood

(P-4068)
KASTLE STAIR INC (PA)
7422 Mountjoy Dr, Huntington Beach (92648-1231)
PHONE..................................714 596-2600
Rose Phillips, *President*
EMP: 20
SALES (est): 6MM **Privately Held**
WEB: www.kastlestair.com
SIC: 2431 Staircases & stairs, wood

(P-4069)
KATZIRS FLOOR & HM DESIGN INC
Also Called: National Hardwood Flooring & M
14742 Calvert St, Van Nuys (91411-2705)
PHONE..................................818 988-9663
Omer Katzir, *President*
EMP: 15
SQ FT: 13,310
SALES (corp-wide): 10.8MM **Privately Held**
WEB: www.nationalhardwood.com
SIC: 2431 Millwork
PA: Katzir's Floor And Home Design, Inc.
　　14959 Delano St
　　Van Nuys CA 91411
　　818 988-9663

(P-4070)
KLS DOORS LLC
Chaparral A Division Kls Door
501 Kettering Dr, Ontario (91761-8150)
PHONE..................................909 605-6468
Varry Methvin, *Branch Mgr*
EMP: 29
SALES (corp-wide): 3.8MM **Privately Held**
SIC: 2431 Doors & door parts & trim, wood
PA: Kls Doors Llc
　　501 Kettering Dr
　　Ontario CA 91761
　　909 605-6468

(P-4071)
L & L CUSTOM SHUTTERS INC
3133 Yukon Ave, Costa Mesa (92626-2921)
PHONE..................................714 996-9539
Larry Allen, *President*
Lillian Allen, *Treasurer*
Ralph Gerardo, *Vice Pres*
EMP: 135
SQ FT: 9,000
SALES (est): 12.6MM **Privately Held**
SIC: 2431 Window shutters, wood

(P-4072)
L J SMITH INC
25956 Commercentre Dr, Lake Forest (92630-8815)
PHONE..................................949 609-0544
Danny Umemoto, *Manager*
EMP: 15
SALES (corp-wide): 227.6MM **Privately Held**
WEB: www.ljsmith.com
SIC: 2431 Millwork

HQ: L. J. Smith, Inc.
　　35280 Scio Bowerston Rd
　　Bowerston OH 44695
　　740 269-2221

(P-4073)
L&F WOOD LLC
Also Called: Boardhouse
416 E Alondra Blvd, Gardena (90248-2902)
PHONE..................................310 400-5569
Russell Walker, *Mng Member*
Michael Dutko,
Mike Dutko,
Christine A Meyer,
▲ **EMP:** 15 **EST:** 2012
SQ FT: 20,000
SALES: 3.7MM **Privately Held**
SIC: 2431 5211 5031 Millwork; millwork &
　　lumber; millwork

(P-4074)
LEEPERS WOOD TURNING CO INC (PA)
Also Called: Leeper's Stair Products
341 Bonnie Cir Ste 104, Corona (92880-2895)
P.O. Box 17098, Long Beach (90807-7098)
PHONE..................................562 422-6525
Michael Skinner, *President*
Barbara Skinner, *Ch of Bd*
Molly Rubio, *Treasurer*
◆ **EMP:** 95 **EST:** 1946
SQ FT: 29,000
SALES (est): 11MM **Privately Held**
WEB: www.stairproducts.com
SIC: 2431 Staircases & stairs, wood; stair-
　　cases, stairs & railings

(P-4075)
LIBERTY VALLEY DOORS INC
6005 Gravenstein Hwy, Cotati (94931-9756)
P.O. Box 176 (94931-0176)
PHONE..................................707 795-8040
Michael Pastryk, *President*
John Kenny, *Admin Sec*
EMP: 18
SQ FT: 15,000
SALES (est): 1.8MM **Privately Held**
WEB: www.libertyvalleydoors.com
SIC: 2431 Doors, wood

(P-4076)
LOWPENSKY MOULDING
900 Palou Ave, San Francisco (94124-3429)
PHONE..................................415 822-7422
Theodore M Lowpensky, *Owner*
Todd Lowpensky, *Office Mgr*
EMP: 15
SQ FT: 13,000
SALES (est): 1.8MM **Privately Held**
WEB: www.lowpensky.com
SIC: 2431 Moldings, wood: unfinished &
　　prefinished

(P-4077)
LRB MILLWORK & CASEWORK INC
2760 S Iowa Ave, Colton (92324-5801)
PHONE..................................951 328-0105
Rene Alberto Bernhardt, *President*
EMP: 16
SQ FT: 34,979
SALES (est): 2.6MM **Privately Held**
SIC: 2431 Millwork

(P-4078)
LUXOR INDUSTRIES INTERNATIONAL
1250 E Franklin Ave, Pomona (91766-5449)
PHONE..................................909 469-4757
Randy Rodriguez, *President*
EMP: 30
SQ FT: 36,000
SALES (est): 2.9MM **Privately Held**
SIC: 2431 Millwork

(P-4079)
MABREY PRODUCTS INC
200 Ryan Ave, Chico (95973-9032)
P.O. Box 1345 (95927-1345)
PHONE..................................530 895-3799

Douglas Tobey, *President*
EMP: 12
SQ FT: 5,000
SALES: 600K **Privately Held**
WEB: www.mabreyproducts.com
SIC: 2431 Woodwork, interior & ornamental

(P-4080)
MAR VISTA WOOD PRODUCTS INC
7343 Pierce Ave, Whittier (90602-1112)
PHONE................................562 698-2024
Judy Wu, *President*
EMP: 10
SALES (est): 1.1MM **Privately Held**
SIC: 2431 Moldings & baseboards, ornamental & trim

(P-4081)
MASONITE ENTRY DOOR CORP
25100 Globe St, Moreno Valley
(92551-9528)
PHONE................................951 243-2261
Lawrence Repar, *President*
▲ **EMP:** 11
SALES (est): 1.8MM **Privately Held**
SIC: 2431 Doors, wood

(P-4082)
MASONITE INTERNATIONAL CORP
Also Called: Delta Door Company
433 W Scotts Ave, Stockton (95203-3320)
PHONE................................209 948-0637
Steve Beckham, *Manager*
EMP: 50
SALES (corp-wide): 2.1B **Publicly Held**
WEB: www.masoniteinternational.com
SIC: 2431 5211 Doors, wood; doors, wood or metal, except storm
PA: Masonite International Corporation
201 N Franklin St Ste 300
Tampa FL 33602
800 895-2723

(P-4083)
MATRIX CAB PARTS INC
Also Called: Matrix Millwork
7950 Woodley Ave Ste B, Van Nuys
(91406-1261)
PHONE................................818 782-7022
Anthony Abiad, *President*
Julie Antunez, *Office Mgr*
EMP: 11
SQ FT: 9,000
SALES: 2MM **Privately Held**
WEB: www.matrixcabparts.com
SIC: 2431 5251 Millwork; hardware

(P-4084)
METAL TEK ENGINEERING INC
7426 Cherry Ave Ste 210, Fontana
(92336-4263)
PHONE................................909 821-4158
Moises Lopez, *President*
EMP: 20 **EST:** 2004
SQ FT: 2,000
SALES: 1.2MM **Privately Held**
SIC: 2431 Staircases, stairs & railings

(P-4085)
MILLCRAFT INC
2850 E White Star Ave, Anaheim
(92806-2517)
PHONE................................714 632-9621
Lars Eppick, *President*
Philip De Marco, *Treasurer*
Reginald Skipcott, *Vice Pres*
Ray Pfeifer, *Admin Sec*
EMP: 70
SQ FT: 34,000
SALES (est): 10MM **Privately Held**
WEB: www.millcraft.info
SIC: 2431 2434 Doors, wood; wood kitchen cabinets

(P-4086)
MILLER WOODWORKING INC
1429 259th St, Harbor City (90710-3326)
PHONE................................310 257-6806
Steve Miller, *President*
EMP: 20
SQ FT: 17,000
SALES (est): 4.2MM **Privately Held**
SIC: 2431 Millwork

(P-4087)
MILLWORK CO
607 Brazos St Ste C, Ramona
(92065-1884)
PHONE................................760 788-1533
Gregory J Lucas, *CEO*
EMP: 16
SALES (est): 2.2MM **Privately Held**
SIC: 2431 Millwork

(P-4088)
MILLWORKS BY DESIGN INC
2248 Townsgate Rd Ste 1, Westlake Village
(91361-2441)
PHONE................................818 597-1326
Daniel S Parish, *CEO*
Zachary D Eglit, *President*
Adam Henninger, *Project Mgr*
▲ **EMP:** 30
SALES (est): 5.9MM **Privately Held**
SIC: 2431 Millwork

(P-4089)
MOLDINGS PLUS INC
1856 S Grove Ave, Ontario (91761-5613)
PHONE................................909 947-3310
Robert Bryant, *President*
Steve Totri, *Vice Pres*
Roy Harrod, *Sales Mgr*
▲ **EMP:** 20 **EST:** 1972
SQ FT: 13,500
SALES (est): 4.2MM **Privately Held**
WEB: www.moldingsplusinc.com
SIC: 2431 Moldings, wood: unfinished & prefinished; doors & door parts & trim, wood; moldings & baseboards, ornamental & trim

(P-4090)
MONTY VENTSAM INC
Also Called: Ventsam Sash & Door Mfg Co
9495 San Fernando Rd, Sun Valley
(91352-1421)
PHONE................................818 768-6424
Monty Ventsam, *President*
EMP: 12
SQ FT: 8,000
SALES: 1.5MM **Privately Held**
SIC: 2431 5211 Door sashes, wood; door trim, wood; door & window products

(P-4091)
MRR MOULDING INDUSTRIES INC
Also Called: Accurate Moulding Mirror Work
125 N Mary Ave Spc 42, Sunnyvale
(94086-4819)
PHONE................................510 794-8116
EMP: 12
SQ FT: 22,000
SALES (est): 1.5MM **Privately Held**
WEB: www.accuratemoulding.com
SIC: 2431

(P-4092)
NEST ENVIRONMENTS INC
530 E Dyer Rd, Santa Ana (92707-3737)
PHONE................................714 979-5500
Staci Bina, *Principal*
EMP: 10
SALES (est): 1MM **Privately Held**
SIC: 2431 Millwork

(P-4093)
NEVADA WINDOW SUPPLY INC
Also Called: ATI Windows
1455 Columbia Ave, Riverside
(92507-2013)
PHONE................................951 300-0100
Stephan Schwartz, *CEO*
Daniel Schwartz, *President*
Stephen Schwartz, *CEO*
EMP: 13 **EST:** 2005
SALES (est): 3.6MM **Privately Held**
SIC: 2431 Window frames, wood

(P-4094)
NEWMAN BROS CALIFORNIA INC (PA)
Also Called: A-1 Grit Co
1901 Massachusetts Ave, Riverside
(92507-2618)
P.O. Box 5675 (92517-5675)
PHONE................................951 782-0102
Harold Newman, *CEO*

EMP: 20
SALES (est): 3.6MM **Privately Held**
SIC: 2431 3291 5199 8711 Millwork; grit, steel; architects' supplies (non-durable); consulting engineer

(P-4095)
NICKS DOORS INC
Also Called: Nick's Cabinet Doors
1052 W Kirkwall Rd, Azusa (91702-5126)
PHONE................................626 812-6491
Nicolas Huizar, *President*
Anna Huizar, *Treasurer*
Sal Huizar, *Vice Pres*
Socorro Huizar, *Admin Sec*
EMP: 15
SQ FT: 32,000
SALES (est): 2MM **Privately Held**
SIC: 2431 5211 Doors, wood; door & window products

(P-4096)
NORTH BAY PLYWOOD INC
510 Northbay Dr, NAPA (94559-1426)
P.O. Box 2338 (94558-0518)
PHONE................................707 224-7849
Thomas H Lowenstein, *President*
Janice Leann Lowenstein, *Treasurer*
John Claudino, *Superintendent*
EMP: 39
SQ FT: 24,000
SALES (est): 10MM **Privately Held**
WEB: www.northbayplywood.com
SIC: 2431 2599 5211 2434 Doors, wood; cabinets, factory; cabinets, kitchen; doors, wood or metal, except storm; wood kitchen cabinets

(P-4097)
NORTHERN CALIFORNIA STAIR
Also Called: California Stairs
7150 Alexander St, Gilroy (95020-6609)
P.O. Box 536 (95021-0536)
PHONE................................408 847-0106
Warner Gartner, *President*
EMP: 10
SALES (est): 1.1MM **Privately Held**
SIC: 2431 Staircases & stairs, wood

(P-4098)
OAK-IT INC
143 Business Center Dr, Corona
(92880-1757)
PHONE................................951 735-5973
Lori Barrett, *President*
EMP: 31
SALES (est): 5.6MM **Privately Held**
SIC: 2431 Millwork

(P-4099)
OLD ENGLISH MIL & WOODWORKS (PA)
Also Called: Old English Mil & Woodworks
27772 Avenue Scott, Santa Clarita
(91355-3417)
PHONE................................661 294-9171
Lay Cho, *President*
Edmond Cho, *Vice Pres*
EMP: 30 **EST:** 1977
SQ FT: 30,000
SALES: 4.5MM **Privately Held**
WEB: www.valencialumber.com
SIC: 2431 2439 1751 Staircases & stairs, wood; window frames, wood; door frames, wood; structural wood members; carpentry work

(P-4100)
ORANGE WOODWORKS INC
1215 N Parker St, Orange (92867-4613)
PHONE................................714 997-2600
Jeff McMillian, *President*
Amanda Marchant, *Manager*
EMP: 45
SQ FT: 120,000
SALES (est): 7.6MM **Privately Held**
WEB: www.orangewoodworks.com
SIC: 2431 Millwork

(P-4101)
PACIFIC ARCHTECTURAL MLLWK INC
1031 S Leslie St, La Habra (90631-6843)
PHONE................................714 525-2059
John Higman, *Branch Mgr*
EMP: 10

SALES (corp-wide): 19MM **Privately Held**
SIC: 2431 Window shutters, wood
PA: Pacific Architectural Millwork, Inc.
1435 Pioneer St
Brea CA 92821
562 905-3200

(P-4102)
PACIFIC ARCHITECTURAL MLLWK INC (PA)
Also Called: Reveal Windows & Doors
1435 Pioneer St, Brea (92821-3721)
PHONE................................562 905-3200
John Higman, *CEO*
Roy Gustin, *Vice Pres*
Alice Vanberpool, *Vice Pres*
Randy Bradley, *Network Mgr*
Mike Jubran, *Project Mgr*
▲ **EMP:** 100
SQ FT: 31,000
SALES (est): 19MM **Privately Held**
WEB: www.pacmillwork.com
SIC: 2431 Planing mill, millwork

(P-4103)
PACIFIC DOOR & CABINET COMPANY
7050 N Harrison Ave, Pinedale
(93650-1008)
PHONE................................559 439-3822
Duane Failla, *President*
Gail Baker, *Executive*
Janet Failla, *Human Resources*
Terry Freeman, *Sales Executive*
EMP: 30
SQ FT: 16,000
SALES (est): 5.6MM **Privately Held**
WEB: www.pacificdoorinc.com
SIC: 2431 3442 Doors, wood; windows, wood; metal doors, sash & trim

(P-4104)
PACIFIC MDF PRODUCTS INC (PA)
Also Called: Pac Trim
4312 Anthony Ct Ste A, Rocklin
(95677-2174)
PHONE................................916 660-1882
Clifford Stokes, *President*
Geri Grommett, *General Mgr*
Scott Clapp, *Controller*
Joel Dahlgren, *Plant Mgr*
Rick Miller, *Foreman/Supr*
▲ **EMP:** 50
SQ FT: 55,000
SALES (est): 21.9MM **Privately Held**
WEB: www.pactrim.com
SIC: 2431 Moldings, wood: unfinished & prefinished

(P-4105)
PARAMOUNT WINDOWS & DOORS
Also Called: Paramount Window & Doors
723 W Mill St, San Bernardino
(92410-3347)
PHONE................................909 888-4688
Don Mc Farland, *CEO*
EMP: 17
SQ FT: 10,000
SALES (est): 163.9K **Privately Held**
SIC: 2431 5211 Windows & window parts & trim, wood; doors & door parts & trim, wood; door & window products

(P-4106)
PAULA KELLER
Also Called: San Pedro Garage Door and Repr
1044 S Gaffey St, San Pedro (90731-4072)
PHONE................................310 833-1894
Paula Keller, *Owner*
EMP: 16
SALES (est): 1.5MM **Privately Held**
SIC: 2431 Garage doors, overhead: wood

(P-4107)
PERFECT PLANK CO
2850 S 5th Ave, Oroville (95965-5851)
PHONE................................530 533-7606
EMP: 14
SQ FT: 10,000

SALES (corp-wide): 2MM **Privately Held**
WEB: www.perfectplank.com
SIC: 2431 Millwork
PA: Perfect Plank Co.
2850 S 5th Ave
Oroville CA
530 533-7606

(P-4108)
PHILLIPS LOBUE & WILSON MLLWK
300 E Santa Ana St, Anaheim
(92805-3953)
PHONE..................................951 331-5714
Richard Phillips, *President*
Ken Lobue, *President*
Randy Wilson, *Admin Sec*
EMP: 15
SQ FT: 2,000
SALES (est): 1.3MM **Privately Held**
SIC: 2431 Millwork

(P-4109)
PINECRAFT CUSTOM SHUTTERS INC
Also Called: Sterling Shutters
946 W 17th St, Costa Mesa (92627-4403)
P.O. Box 2417, Newport Beach (92659-1417)
PHONE..................................949 642-9317
Frank L Gerardo Sr, *President*
Anthony Gerardo, *Vice Pres*
EMP: 50 EST: 1964
SQ FT: 12,000
SALES (est): 5MM **Privately Held**
SIC: 2431 Door shutters, wood

(P-4110)
PRECISION COMPANIES INC
Also Called: Precision Doors & Millwork
15088 La Palma Dr, Chino (91710-9669)
PHONE..................................909 548-2700
Joseph J Felix, *President*
Marcia Felix, *Corp Secy*
EMP: 15
SQ FT: 5,000
SALES: 4.5MM **Privately Held**
WEB: www.predoor.com
SIC: 2431 3441 3442 Millwork; fabricated structural metal; metal doors, sash & trim

(P-4111)
PRECISION MILLWORK LLC
14300 Davenport Rd Ste 4a, Agua Dulce
(91390-5000)
PHONE..................................661 402-5021
Ardith Swanger, *Mng Member*
Miguel Pena,
Michelle St John,
EMP: 15
SQ FT: 5,000
SALES: 8MM **Privately Held**
SIC: 2431 Millwork

(P-4112)
RAU RESTORATION
Also Called: Rau William Automotive Wdwrk
2027 Pontius Ave, Los Angeles
(90025-5613)
PHONE..................................310 445-1128
William Rau, *President*
EMP: 15
SQ FT: 4,000
SALES: 1.2MM **Privately Held**
WEB: www.rau-autowood.com
SIC: 2431 Interior & ornamental woodwork & trim

(P-4113)
REDWOOD MILLING COMPANY LLC
12055 Old Redwood Hwy, Healdsburg
(95448-9238)
PHONE..................................707 433-1343
Steven I Pankowski, *Partner*
Ronald Pankowski, *Partner*
EMP: 20
SALES (est): 1.7MM **Privately Held**
SIC: 2431 Moldings, wood: unfinished & prefinished

(P-4114)
RENAISSANCE WDWRK & DESIGN INC
7605 Hazeltine Ave Unit B, Van Nuys
(91405-1423)
PHONE..................................818 787-7238
Will Windrow, *Branch Mgr*
EMP: 15
SALES (corp-wide): 8MM **Privately Held**
SIC: 2431 Millwork
PA: Renaissance Woodwork & Design, Inc.
22531 Ventura Blvd
Woodland Hills CA 91364
818 222-2771

(P-4115)
RENAISSNCE FRNCH DORS SASH INC (PA)
Also Called: Renaissance Doors & Windows
38 Segada, Rcho STA Marg (92688-2744)
PHONE..................................714 578-0090
Michael Jenkins, *President*
James Jenkins, *Corp Secy*
Thomas Jenkins, *Vice Pres*
EMP: 129
SQ FT: 75,000
SALES (est): 7.1MM **Privately Held**
WEB: www.renaissancedoors.com
SIC: 2431 Doors, wood

(P-4116)
RITESCREEN INC
33444 Western Ave, Union City
(94587-3202)
P.O. Box 965 (94587-0965)
PHONE..................................800 949-4174
Art Lucero, *General Mgr*
EMP: 13
SALES (est): 810K **Privately Held**
SIC: 2431 Door screens, wood frame

(P-4117)
RIVER CITY MILLWORK INC
3045 Fite Cir, Sacramento (95827-1814)
PHONE..................................916 364-8981
Paul Parks, *President*
Valerie Parks, *Corp Secy*
Doug Parker, *General Mgr*
Linda Tatum, *Office Mgr*
EMP: 33
SQ FT: 24,000
SALES (est): 7.5MM **Privately Held**
SIC: 2431 2434 Moldings, wood: unfinished & prefinished; wood kitchen cabinets

(P-4118)
RTA SALES INC
Also Called: Shutters By Angel Co
210 E Avenue L Ste A, Lancaster
(93535-4613)
PHONE..................................661 942-3553
Ralph Arellano, *President*
EMP: 17 EST: 1996
SQ FT: 22,000
SALES (est): 2.2MM **Privately Held**
SIC: 2431 Window shutters, wood

(P-4119)
SADDLEBACK STAIR & MILLWORK
23291 Peralta Dr Ste B4, Laguna Hills
(92653-1426)
PHONE..................................949 460-0384
Miles Densmore, *President*
Irene Densmore, *Vice Pres*
EMP: 13
SALES (est): 1.4MM **Privately Held**
SIC: 2431 Staircases & stairs, wood

(P-4120)
SAN FRANCISCO VICTORIANA INC
2070 Newcomb Ave, San Francisco
(94124-1615)
PHONE..................................415 648-0313
Gary Root, *President*
▲ EMP: 10 EST: 1971
SQ FT: 25,000
SALES (est): 1.1MM **Privately Held**
WEB: www.sfvictoriana.com
SIC: 2431 Exterior & ornamental woodwork & trim

(P-4121)
SBS AMERICA LLC (PA)
Also Called: San Benito Shutter
1600 Lana Way, Hollister (95023-2532)
PHONE..................................831 637-8700
Jordan Bastable, *Mng Member*
Jillian Shaw, *Accountant*
Michelle Lee,
William S Lee,
Lisa Flaherty, *Manager*
▲ EMP: 70
SQ FT: 112,000
SALES (est): 18MM **Privately Held**
WEB: www.sanbenitoshutter.com
SIC: 2431 Blinds (shutters), wood

(P-4122)
SETZER FOREST PRODUCTS INC (PA)
2555 3rd St Ste 200, Sacramento
(95818-1196)
PHONE..................................916 442-2555
D Mark Kable, *CEO*
Hardie Setzer, *Shareholder*
Garner Setzer, *President*
Mark Setzer, *Chief Mktg Ofcr*
Jeff Setzer, *Vice Pres*
▲ EMP: 160 EST: 1927
SALES (est): 50.5MM **Privately Held**
WEB: www.setzerforest.com
SIC: 2431 2441 Moldings, wood: unfinished & prefinished; box shook, wood

(P-4123)
SIERRA LUMBER MANUFACTURERS
375 W Hazelton Ave, Stockton
(95203-3306)
P.O. Box 6216 (95206-0216)
PHONE..................................209 943-7777
Bob Long, *President*
▼ EMP: 190
SQ FT: 65,000
SALES (est): 20.8MM
SALES (corp-wide): 2.1B **Publicly Held**
WEB: www.sierralumber.com
SIC: 2431 2421 2435 Doors, wood; cut stock, softwood; hardwood veneer & plywood
HQ: Masonite Corporation
201 N Franklin St Ste 300
Tampa FL 33602
813 877-2726

(P-4124)
SIERRA PACIFIC INDUSTRIES
Alameda Rd, Corning (96021)
PHONE..................................530 824-2474
Kendall Pierson, *Vice Pres*
Troi Shilts, *Sales Staff*
EMP: 400
SALES (corp-wide): 1.2B **Privately Held**
WEB: www.sierrapacificind.com
SIC: 2431 2426 2421 Millwork; hardwood dimension & flooring mills; sawmills & planing mills, general
PA: Sierra Pacific Industries
19794 Riverside Ave
Anderson CA 96007
530 378-8000

(P-4125)
SIERRA WOODWORKING INC
960 6th St Ste 101a, Norco (92860-1440)
PHONE..................................949 493-4528
Maurice Kendall, *President*
EMP: 22
SQ FT: 10,000
SALES (est): 3.6MM **Privately Held**
WEB: www.sierrawoodworking.com
SIC: 2431 2541 2521 2439 Millwork; cabinets, except refrigerated: show, display, etc.: wood; wood office furniture; structural wood members; wood kitchen cabinets; decorative wood & woodwork

(P-4126)
SISKIYOU FOREST PRODUCTS (PA)
6275 State Highway 273, Anderson
(96007)
PHONE..................................530 378-6980
Fred Duchi, *President*
Bill Duchi, *Vice Pres*
Monte Acquistapace, *Sales Associate*

▲ EMP: 48 EST: 1974
SQ FT: 2,280
SALES (est): 10.4MM **Privately Held**
WEB: www.siskiyouforestproducts.com
SIC: 2431 5031 Millwork; lumber, plywood & millwork

(P-4127)
SKYCO SHADING SYSTEMS INC
3411 W Fordham Ave, Santa Ana
(92704-4422)
PHONE..................................714 708-3038
Sandra Young, *President*
▲ EMP: 28
SQ FT: 16,000
SALES (est): 5.2MM **Privately Held**
WEB: www.skycoshade.com
SIC: 2431 Awnings, blinds & shutters, wood

(P-4128)
SOUTH COAST STAIRS INC
30251 Tomas, Rcho STA Marg
(92688-2123)
PHONE..................................949 858-1685
Chris Galloway, *President*
Mary Galloway, *Vice Pres*
Tamera Selchau, *Admin Sec*
EMP: 40
SQ FT: 2,000
SALES (est): 4.8MM **Privately Held**
SIC: 2431 2439 5211 Staircases & stairs, wood; structural wood members; millwork & lumber

(P-4129)
STEINER & MATEER INC
Also Called: Shuttercraft of California
8333 Secura Way, Santa Fe Springs
(90670-2299)
PHONE..................................562 464-9082
Richard K Oliver, *President*
EMP: 30
SQ FT: 20,000
SALES (est): 3.8MM **Privately Held**
SIC: 2431 Louver doors, wood; window shutters, wood

(P-4130)
STEVE BRUNER
Also Called: Tali Pak Lumber Milling
81 Hwy 175, Hopland (95449)
PHONE..................................707 744-1103
Steve Bruner, *Owner*
EMP: 20
SQ FT: 1,000
SALES (est): 1.7MM **Privately Held**
SIC: 2431 Millwork

(P-4131)
SUMMIT WINDOW PRODUCTS INC
6336 Patterson Pass Rd F, Livermore
(94550-9577)
PHONE..................................408 526-1600
Ron Clementi, *President*
Nick Sabic, *Vice Pres*
EMP: 54
SQ FT: 15,000
SALES (est): 5.7MM **Privately Held**
WEB: www.summitwindowproducts.com
SIC: 2431 Window shutters, wood

(P-4132)
SUN MOUNTAIN INC
2 Henry Adams St Ste 150, San Francisco
(94103-5045)
PHONE..................................415 852-2320
EMP: 25
SALES (corp-wide): 12.1MM **Privately Held**
SIC: 2431 Millwork
PA: Sun Mountain, Inc.
140 Commerce Rd
Berthoud CO 80513
970 532-2105

(P-4133)
SUNRISE WOOD PRODUCTS INC
Also Called: Sunrise Shutters
6701 11th Ave, Los Angeles (90043-4729)
P.O. Box 43998 (90043-0998)
PHONE..................................323 971-6540
Detlef Guttke, *President*

▲ = Import ▼ = Export
◆ = Import/Export

Erika Guttke, *Corp Secy*
EMP: 25
SQ FT: 11,000
SALES (est): 3.2MM **Privately Held**
SIC: 2431 Window shutters, wood

(P-4134)
SUNWOOD DOORS INC
21176 S Alameda St, Long Beach (90810-1207)
PHONE..................................562 951-9401
Oscar Alvarez, *President*
▲ **EMP:** 31
SALES (est): 3.9MM **Privately Held**
SIC: 2431 5211 Millwork; garage doors, sale & installation

(P-4135)
SURE GUARD SOCAL
Also Called: Sure Guard Windows
11702 Anabel Ave, Garden Grove (92843-3711)
PHONE..................................714 556-5497
Charles Nguyen, *Partner*
EMP: 10
SALES (est): 546.8K **Privately Held**
SIC: 2431 Windows & window parts & trim, wood

(P-4136)
T M COBB COMPANY (PA)
Also Called: Haley Bros
500 Palmyrita Ave, Riverside (92507-1196)
PHONE..................................951 248-2400
Jeffrey Cobb, *President*
Vince French, *CFO*
Thomas J Cobb, *Vice Pres*
Peter Bonilla, *Administration*
Yoshiko Miyazaki, *Administration*
▲ **EMP:** 23
SALES (est): 92.5MM **Privately Held**
WEB: www.tmcobbco.com
SIC: 2431 3442 Door frames, wood; window & door frames

(P-4137)
T M COBB COMPANY
Also Called: Haley Brothers
2651 E Roosevelt St, Stockton (95205-3825)
PHONE..................................209 948-5358
John Jenkins, *Branch Mgr*
Katrina O'Boyle, *Office Mgr*
Carlos Vizcarra, *Purchasing*
EMP: 55
SQ FT: 1,200
SALES (corp-wide): 92.5MM **Privately Held**
WEB: www.tmcobbco.com
SIC: 2431 Doors, wood
PA: T. M. Cobb Company
500 Palmyrita Ave
Riverside CA 92507
951 248-2400

(P-4138)
T M COBB COMPANY
Haley Bros Inc A Div T M Cobb
6291 Orangethorpe Ave, Buena Park (90620-1339)
PHONE..................................714 670-2112
Thomas J Cobb, *President*
EMP: 40
SQ FT: 7,966
SALES (corp-wide): 92.5MM **Privately Held**
WEB: www.tmcobbco.com
SIC: 2431 Doors, wood; moldings, wood: unfinished & prefinished
PA: T. M. Cobb Company
500 Palmyrita Ave
Riverside CA 92507
951 248-2400

(P-4139)
TAIT CABINETRY WOODWORKS
6572 Whitman Ct, Riverside (92506-4905)
PHONE..................................951 776-1192
Bruce Tait, *Principal*
EMP: 10
SALES (est): 710K **Privately Held**
SIC: 2431 Millwork

(P-4140)
THOMAS TELLEZ
Also Called: Wallace
100 Taylor Way, Blue Lake (95525)
P.O. Box 708 (95525-0708)
PHONE..................................707 668-1825
Thomas Tellez, *Owner*
EMP: 20
SALES (est): 2.1MM **Privately Held**
SIC: 2431 3547 8712 Millwork; bar mills; architectural services

(P-4141)
TMR EXECUTIVE INTERIORS INC
1287 W Nielsen Ave, Fresno (93706)
PHONE..................................559 346-0631
Jamie Russell, *President*
Timothy Russell, *Vice Pres*
EMP: 19
SQ FT: 21,000
SALES (est): 2.4MM **Privately Held**
SIC: 2431 1751 Millwork; cabinet & finish carpentry

(P-4142)
TRANSDESIGN INC
Also Called: Foam Design Center
440 19th St, Bakersfield (93301-4908)
PHONE..................................661 631-1062
Joe Tran, *President*
Julie Pham, *Vice Pres*
EMP: 10
SALES (est): 1.3MM **Privately Held**
SIC: 2431 Millwork

(P-4143)
TRAVIS AMERICAN GROUP LLC
Also Called: Travis Industries
11450 Sheldon St, Sun Valley (91352-1121)
PHONE..................................714 258-1200
Thomas D Bell, *President*
Stephen Saponaro, *VP Finance*
Lyle Zastrow, *VP Opers*
Robert Kincaid,
Robert Levine,
EMP: 150
SQ FT: 5,300
SALES (est): 10.7MM **Privately Held**
SIC: 2431 2499 2426 2591 Moldings, wood: unfinished & prefinished; veneer work, inlaid; furniture stock & parts, hardwood; venetian blinds; paints, varnishes & supplies

(P-4144)
UNITY FOREST PRODUCTS INC
1162 Putman Ave, Yuba City (95991-7216)
P.O. Box 1849 (95992-1849)
PHONE..................................530 671-7152
Enita Elphick, *President*
Ryan Smith, *Treasurer*
Michael Smith, *Vice Pres*
Mike Smith, *Vice Pres*
Shawn Nelson, *Admin Sec*
EMP: 48
SQ FT: 4,200
SALES: 11MM **Privately Held**
WEB: www.unityforest.com
SIC: 2431 Millwork

(P-4145)
VICTORIAN SHUTTERS INC (PA)
Also Called: Golden State Shutters
305 Industrial Way Frnt, Dixon (95620-9769)
PHONE..................................707 678-1776
Richard Scholten, *President*
Cornelius J Scholten, *Vice Pres*
Melinda Scholten, *Admin Sec*
EMP: 13 **EST:** 1931
SQ FT: 20,000
SALES: 750K **Privately Held**
WEB: www.goldenstateshutters.com
SIC: 2431 5211 Window shutters, wood; door & window products

(P-4146)
W B POWELL INC
630 Parkridge Ave, Norco (92860-3124)
PHONE..................................951 270-0095
Charles G Mayhew, *CEO*
Chuck Mayhew, *President*
Doug Westra, *CFO*
Steve Wimberly, *Senior VP*

Jack Bacon, *Vice Pres*
EMP: 30
SALES (est): 5.7MM
SALES (corp-wide): 7.2MM **Privately Held**
WEB: www.foldcraft.com
SIC: 2431 2439 Millwork; structural wood members
PA: Foldcraft Co.
14400 Southcross Dr W # 200
Burnsville MN 55306
507 789-5111

(P-4147)
WESTERN INTEGRATED MTLS INC (PA)
3310 E 59th St, Long Beach (90805-4504)
PHONE..................................562 634-2823
Larry Farrah, *President*
Edward G Farrah, *Vice Pres*
Jim Halbrook, *Principal*
Debra Price, *Principal*
Alex Rojas, *Principal*
▲ **EMP:** 30
SQ FT: 20,000
SALES (est): 4.4MM **Privately Held**
WEB: www.western-integrated.com
SIC: 2431 3442 Millwork; window & door frames

(P-4148)
WESTGATE HARDWOODS INC (PA)
9296 Midway, Durham (95938-9779)
PHONE..................................530 892-0300
Ivan Hoath, *President*
Becky Hoath, *Corp Secy*
Ivan Hoath III, *Vice Pres*
Craig Jones, *Draft/Design*
Tom Greminger, *Sales Executive*
EMP: 22
SQ FT: 10,000
SALES (est): 6MM **Privately Held**
WEB: www.westgatehardwoods.com
SIC: 2431 5031 Millwork; lumber: rough, dressed & finished

(P-4149)
WHOLESALE SHUTTER COMPANY INC
411 Olive Ave, Beaumont (92223-2640)
PHONE..................................951 845-8786
Sabiha Patel, *CEO*
▲ **EMP:** 11
SQ FT: 10,000
SALES (est): 920K **Privately Held**
WEB: www.wholesaleshutter.com
SIC: 2431 Door shutters, wood; blinds (shutters), wood

(P-4150)
WILCO BUILDING CORPORATION
2005 Palma Dr Ste A, Ventura (93003-5750)
PHONE..................................805 765-4188
Benjamin Wilson, *CEO*
EMP: 15
SQ FT: 9,000
SALES (est): 2.2MM **Privately Held**
SIC: 2431 8741 1542 Millwork; construction management; restaurant construction

(P-4151)
WINDOW & DOOR SHOP INC (PA)
185 Industrial St, San Francisco (94124-1927)
PHONE..................................415 282-6192
Javier Garcia, *President*
Fred Ochoa, *Treasurer*
Jose Ochoa, *Admin Sec*
Diane Larson, *Project Mgr*
EMP: 14
SQ FT: 9,000
SALES (est): 1.6MM **Privately Held**
WEB: www.windowanddoorshop.com
SIC: 2431 5211 Doors, wood; windows, wood; door & window products

(P-4152)
WINDOW PRODUCTS MANAGEMENT INC
Also Called: Wpm
5917 Olivas Park Dr Ste F, Ventura (93003-7613)
PHONE..................................805 677-6800
John Norman Edwards, *President*
EMP: 10
SALES (est): 1.3MM **Privately Held**
SIC: 2431 2591 Windows & window parts & trim, wood; window shutters, wood; window shades

(P-4153)
WINDSOR WILLITS COMPANY (PA)
Also Called: Windsor Mill
7950 Redwood Dr Ste 4, Cotati (94931-3054)
PHONE..................................707 665-9663
Craig Flynn, *President*
Douglas Sherer, *CFO*
Alrene Flynn, *Admin Sec*
Mary Shaw, *Human Res Mgr*
Jim Walls, *Plant Mgr*
▲ **EMP:** 29
SQ FT: 50,000
SALES (est): 13.8MM **Privately Held**
WEB: www.windsorone.com
SIC: 2431 Moldings, wood: unfinished & prefinished

(P-4154)
WINDSOR WILLITS COMPANY
Also Called: Windsor Mill
661 Railroad Ave, Willits (95490-3942)
PHONE..................................707 459-8568
John Hankins, *Opers-Prdtn-Mfg*
Charlie Holum, *Buyer*
EMP: 40
SALES (corp-wide): 13.8MM **Privately Held**
WEB: www.windsorone.com
SIC: 2431 2439 Moldings, wood: unfinished & prefinished; moldings & baseboards, ornamental & trim; structural wood members
PA: Windsor Willits Company
7950 Redwood Dr Ste 4
Cotati CA 94931
707 665-9663

(P-4155)
WOOD CONNECTION INC
4701 N Star Way, Modesto (95356-9567)
PHONE..................................209 577-1044
William W Fenstermacher, *President*
Judy L Fenstermacher, *Admin Sec*
EMP: 25
SQ FT: 11,400
SALES (est): 4.3MM **Privately Held**
SIC: 2431 2434 Millwork; wood kitchen cabinets

(P-4156)
WOODWORK PIONEERS CORP
1757 S Claudina Way, Anaheim (92805-6544)
PHONE..................................714 991-1017
Karina Avalos, *President*
EMP: 50
SALES (est): 2MM **Privately Held**
SIC: 2431 Millwork

(P-4157)
WTI JKB INC (PA)
Also Called: Woodtech Industries
405 Aldo Ave, Santa Clara (95054-2302)
PHONE..................................408 297-8579
Joe Becher, *President*
◆ **EMP:** 10
SQ FT: 10,000
SALES (est): 1.4MM **Privately Held**
SIC: 2431 2541 Millwork; cabinets, except refrigerated: show, display, etc.: wood

(P-4158)
YOUNG & FAMILY INC
Also Called: Quality Doors & Trim
64 Soda Bay Rd, Lakeport (95453-5609)
P.O. Box 897 (95453-0897)
PHONE..................................707 263-8877
Hilary Young, *President*
Andrew Young, *Vice Pres*

P
R
O
D
U
C
T
S

&

S
V
C
S

EMP: 25
SQ FT: 11,400
SALES (est): 3.2MM **Privately Held**
SIC: 2431 2434 Doors, wood; wood kitchen cabinets

(P-4159)
YUBA RIVER MOULDING MLLWK INC (PA)
Also Called: Cal Yuba Investments
3757 Feather River Blvd, Olivehurst (95961-9615)
P.O. Box 1078, Yuba City (95992-1078)
PHONE..................................530 742-2168
Thomas C Williams Sr, *Ch of Bd*
Thomas C Williams Jr, *President*
Jolyne Williams, *Treasurer*
Damon Munsee, *Vice Pres*
Andrea Watson, *Department Mgr*
▲ **EMP:** 41 **EST:** 1977
SQ FT: 200,000
SALES: 10.7MM **Privately Held**
SIC: 2431 6512 Moldings, wood: unfinished & prefinished; commercial & industrial building operation

---
2434 Wood Kitchen

(P-4160)
A PLUS CABINETS INC
83930 Dr Carreon Blvd, Indio (92201-7177)
PHONE..................................760 322-5262
Rhett Ferrell, *President*
EMP: 12
SQ FT: 2,500
SALES (est): 1.6MM **Privately Held**
SIC: 2434 Wood kitchen cabinets

(P-4161)
ACCRACUTT CABINETS
2238 S Phoenix Ave, Ontario (91761-5833)
PHONE..................................951 685-7322
William Ball, *Owner*
EMP: 10
SALES (est): 984.2K **Privately Held**
WEB: www.accracutt.com
SIC: 2434 Wood kitchen cabinets

(P-4162)
ALDER CREEK MILLWORK
8409 Rovana Cir Ste 7, Sacramento (95828-2539)
PHONE..................................916 379-9831
John R Loomis, *Owner*
EMP: 30
SALES (est): 1.5MM **Privately Held**
SIC: 2434 Wood kitchen cabinets

(P-4163)
ALEX DESIGN INC
8541 Younger Creek Dr # 400, Sacramento (95828-1037)
PHONE..................................916 386-8020
Lazaro Martinez, *Branch Mgr*
EMP: 12
SALES (corp-wide): 827.6K **Privately Held**
SIC: 2434 Wood kitchen cabinets
PA: Alex Design, Inc.
8517 Florin Rd
Sacramento CA 95828
916 706-0059

(P-4164)
ARANDAS WOODCRAFT INC
137 W 157th St, Gardena (90248-2225)
P.O. Box 3954 (90247-7507)
PHONE..................................310 538-9945
EMP: 40
SQ FT: 19,000
SALES (est): 4.7MM **Privately Held**
WEB: www.arandaswoodcraft.com
SIC: 2434 2541

(P-4165)
ARCHITECTURAL WOOD DESIGN INC
Also Called: Carpentry Millwork
5672 E Dayton Ave, Fresno (93727-7801)
PHONE..................................559 292-9104
Phillip D Farnsworth, *President*
Corey Farnsworth, *Vice Pres*
Riley Farnsworth, *Project Mgr*

EMP: 40
SQ FT: 16,000
SALES: 8MM **Privately Held**
SIC: 2434 Wood kitchen cabinets

(P-4166)
ARTCRAFTERS CABINETS INC
5446 Cleon Ave, North Hollywood (91601-2897)
PHONE..................................818 752-8960
Jack R Walter, *President*
Steve Counter, *Vice Pres*
Sharon E Walter, *Vice Pres*
Dawn Kunihiro, *Office Mgr*
Bob Schindler, *VP Opers*
EMP: 50
SQ FT: 20,000
SALES (est): 5.5MM **Privately Held**
WEB: www.artcrafter.com
SIC: 2434 2521 2431 Wood kitchen cabinets; wood office furniture; millwork

(P-4167)
BARBOSA CABINETS INC
2020 E Grant Line Rd, Tracy (95304-8525)
PHONE..................................209 836-2501
Edward Barbosa, *President*
Ron Barbosa, *Vice Pres*
Johnny Horton, *Project Mgr*
Peter Lontz, *Project Mgr*
Carene Brandrup, *Accounting Mgr*
▲ **EMP:** 346
SQ FT: 300,000
SALES (est): 57.1MM **Privately Held**
WEB: www.barcab.com
SIC: 2434 Wood kitchen cabinets

(P-4168)
BELLATERRA HOME LLC
8372 Tiogawoods Dr # 180, Sacramento (95828-5066)
PHONE..................................916 896-3188
Betty Cheung, *President*
▲ **EMP:** 10
SALES (est): 1.5MM **Privately Held**
SIC: 2434 5719 5211 Vanities, bathroom: wood; mirrors; counter tops

(P-4169)
BIRCHWOOD CABINETS SONORA INC
Also Called: Bcsi
14375 Cuesta Ct, Sonora (95370-8223)
PHONE..................................209 532-1417
Lee F Erickson, *President*
Carrie Erickson, *Vice Pres*
EMP: 19
SQ FT: 10,000
SALES (est): 2.1MM **Privately Held**
SIC: 2434 Vanities, bathroom: wood

(P-4170)
BLUEGATE SURFACE WORKS INC
15936 Downey Ave, Paramount (90723-5116)
PHONE..................................562 630-9005
Charles Anthony Gallagher, *Owner*
EMP: 11
SALES (est): 995K **Privately Held**
SIC: 2434 5031 5211 Wood kitchen cabinets; kitchen cabinets; cabinets, kitchen; counter tops

(P-4171)
C & C BUILT-IN INC
Also Called: Build-In C & C
2000 Lana Way, Hollister (95023-2500)
PHONE..................................831 635-5880
Hyung Ki Han, *President*
EMP: 20
SALES (est): 2MM **Privately Held**
SIC: 2434 Wood kitchen cabinets

(P-4172)
CABINET CONCEPTS
131 S Eucla Ave, San Dimas (91773-2901)
PHONE..................................909 599-9191
Joe Arnold, *President*
EMP: 10
SALES: 800K **Privately Held**
SIC: 2434 Wood kitchen cabinets

(P-4173)
CABINET MASTER & SON INC
667 E Edna Pl, Covina (91723-1314)
PHONE..................................626 332-0300
EMP: 14
SALES (corp-wide): 1MM **Privately Held**
SIC: 2434 Wood kitchen cabinets
PA: Cabinet Master & Son Inc
5429 Via Corona St
Los Angeles CA 90022
323 727-9717

(P-4174)
CABINETS & DOORS DIRECT INC
858 E 1st St, Pomona (91766-2004)
PHONE..................................909 629-3388
Sam Ho, *President*
EMP: 12
SALES (est): 1MM **Privately Held**
SIC: 2434 Wood kitchen cabinets

(P-4175)
CABINETS 2000 LLC
Also Called: Cabinets 2000, Inc.
11100 Firestone Blvd, Norwalk (90650-2269)
PHONE..................................562 868-0909
Frank Hamadani, *Chairman*
Nematollah Abdollahi, *President*
Sherwood Prusso, *President*
Azam Abdollahi, *CFO*
Sue Abdollahi, *CFO*
EMP: 180
SQ FT: 103,000
SALES (est): 40.8MM
SALES (corp-wide): 190.5MM **Privately Held**
WEB: www.cabinets2000.com
SIC: 2434 1751 Wood kitchen cabinets; cabinet & finish carpentry
PA: Acproducts, Inc.
3551 Plano Pkwy Ste 200
The Colony TX 75056
214 469-3000

(P-4176)
CABINETS BY ANDY INC
2411 Central Ave, McKinleyville (95519-3615)
PHONE..................................707 839-0220
Andy Dickey, *President*
EMP: 15
SQ FT: 10,000
SALES (est): 1.2MM **Privately Held**
WEB: www.cabinetsbyandy.com
SIC: 2434 Wood kitchen cabinets

(P-4177)
CALIFORNIA DESIGNERS CHOICE
547 Constitution Ave F, Camarillo (93012-8572)
PHONE..................................805 987-5820
Mark Mulchay, *President*
Russell Leavitt, *Admin Sec*
Michelle Cekov, *Bookkeeper*
EMP: 38
SALES (est): 5.5MM **Privately Held**
WEB: www.cdcc-inc.com
SIC: 2434 Wood kitchen cabinets

(P-4178)
CALIFORNIA KIT CAB DOOR CORP (PA)
Also Called: California Door
400 Cochrane Cir, Morgan Hill (95037-2859)
PHONE..................................408 782-5700
Edward Joseph Rossi, *Principal*
Ron Ianni, *CFO*
Rebecca Bolanos, *Executive*
Amber Linse, *Executive*
Melissa Naranjo, *Executive*
◆ **EMP:** 100
SQ FT: 260,000
SALES (est): 65.3MM **Privately Held**
WEB: www.caldoor.com
SIC: 2434 2431 Wood kitchen cabinets; millwork

(P-4179)
CALIFORNIA WOODWORKING INC
1726 Ives Ave, Oxnard (93033-4072)
PHONE..................................805 982-9090
Edward Vickery, *President*
Lucas Vickery, *Vice Pres*
Rj Pranski, *General Mgr*
Susan Vickery, *Admin Sec*
Maria G Reyes, *Project Mgr*
EMP: 30
SQ FT: 8,000
SALES (est): 3.1MM **Privately Held**
WEB: www.calwoodinc.com
SIC: 2434 Wood kitchen cabinets

(P-4180)
CENTRAL VALLEY CABINET MFG
Also Called: Vern Lackey
10739 14th Ave, Armona (93202)
P.O. Box 1211 (93202-1211)
PHONE..................................559 584-8441
Vern Lackey, *President*
EMP: 10
SALES (est): 954.2K **Privately Held**
SIC: 2434 Wood kitchen cabinets

(P-4181)
CHAMPION INSTALLS INC
9631 Elk Grove Florin Rd, Elk Grove (95624-2225)
PHONE..................................916 627-0929
Brock Rhodes, *Principal*
EMP: 18
SALES (est): 1.9MM **Privately Held**
SIC: 2434 Wood kitchen cabinets

(P-4182)
CLASSIC MILL & CABINET
Also Called: Classic Innovations
590 Santana Dr, Cloverdale (95425-4296)
PHONE..................................707 894-9800
Tony Mertes, *President*
Ms Billie Siemsen, *Manager*
Chad Stephens, *Accounts Mgr*
▲ **EMP:** 37
SQ FT: 35,000
SALES (est): 3.8MM **Privately Held**
SIC: 2434 Wood kitchen cabinets

(P-4183)
CORONA MILLWORKS COMPANY (PA)
5572 Edison Ave, Chino (91710-6936)
PHONE..................................909 606-3288
Jose Corona, *CEO*
Kathy Medina, *Controller*
Darren Dean, *Sales Mgr*
Jesus Aguilar, *Manager*
▲ **EMP:** 81
SQ FT: 8,700
SALES: 12MM **Privately Held**
WEB: www.coronamillworks.com
SIC: 2434 Wood kitchen cabinets

(P-4184)
CUSTOM FURNITURE DESIGN INC
Also Called: Entertainment Centers Plus
3340 Sunrise Blvd Ste F, Rancho Cordova (95742-7316)
PHONE..................................916 631-6300
Dan Gwiazdon, *President*
EMP: 20
SQ FT: 13,000
SALES (est): 1.8MM **Privately Held**
WEB: www.cfdsacto.com
SIC: 2434 Wood kitchen cabinets

(P-4185)
CUSTOM INSTALLATIONS
1452 Hawks Vista Ln, Alpine (91901-3338)
P.O. Box 550 (91903-0550)
PHONE..................................619 445-0692
Dale Hinriths, *Owner*
EMP: 13
SALES (est): 870.2K **Privately Held**
WEB: www.custominstallations.com
SIC: 2434 Wood kitchen cabinets

▲ = Import ▼=Export
◆ =Import/Export

(P-4186)
D & D CBNETS - SVAGE DSGNS INC
1478 Sky Harbor Dr, Olivehurst (95961-7418)
PHONE..................................530 634-9713
Peter D Giordano, *President*
EMP: 30
SALES (est): 6.3MM **Privately Held**
SIC: 2434 Wood kitchen cabinets

(P-4187)
DAVID BEARD
Also Called: Beards Custom Cabinets
821 Twin View Blvd, Redding (96003-2002)
PHONE..................................530 244-1248
David Beard, *Owner*
EMP: 16
SQ FT: 8,550
SALES (est): 1.6MM **Privately Held**
WEB: www.davidbeard.com
SIC: 2434 2521 2541 Wood kitchen cabinets; cabinets, office: wood; cabinets, lockers & shelving

(P-4188)
DECORATIVE CONSTRUCTION
614 E Badillo St, Covina (91723-2804)
PHONE..................................626 862-6814
Gary Mathieu, *Principal*
EMP: 14
SALES (est): 1.3MM **Privately Held**
SIC: 2434 Wood kitchen cabinets

(P-4189)
DOORS UNLIMITED
Also Called: Timberline Molding
1316 Armorlite Dr, San Marcos (92069-1342)
PHONE..................................760 744-5590
Marvin Wait, *Partner*
Susan Wait, *Partner*
EMP: 12
SQ FT: 7,500
SALES (est): 1.5MM **Privately Held**
SIC: 2434 Wood kitchen cabinets

(P-4190)
DREAMS CLOSETS
13030 Ramona Blvd Unit 9, Baldwin Park (91706-3759)
PHONE..................................626 641-5070
Armando Padilla, *Owner*
EMP: 11
SALES: 200K **Privately Held**
SIC: 2434 Vanities, bathroom: wood

(P-4191)
ENCORE FINE CABINETRY INC
14748 Highway 41 Ste B, Madera (93636-8904)
PHONE..................................559 822-4333
Edward Fenton, *President*
Chelsea Takemoto, *Office Admin*
EMP: 14 EST: 2000
SQ FT: 32,000
SALES (est): 1.7MM **Privately Held**
WEB: www.encorefinecabinetry.com
SIC: 2434 Wood kitchen cabinets

(P-4192)
EUROPEAN WOODWORK
7531 Suzi Ln, Westminster (92683-4359)
PHONE..................................714 892-8831
Anthony Dunatov, *Owner*
EMP: 10
SQ FT: 4,800
SALES (est): 1MM **Privately Held**
WEB: www.europeanwoodworksinc.com
SIC: 2434 Wood kitchen cabinets

(P-4193)
EXCEL CABINETS INC
225 Jason Ct, Corona (92879-6199)
PHONE..................................951 279-4545
Charles W Ketzel, *CEO*
Sandra Ketzel, *Corp Secy*
Kevin Ketzel, *Vice Pres*
Keith A Ketzel, *Sales Executive*
▲ EMP: 35
SALES (est): 6MM **Privately Held**
WEB: www.excelcabinetsinc.com
SIC: 2434 Wood kitchen cabinets

(P-4194)
EXPRESSION IN WOOD
1738 Brackett St, La Verne (91750-5855)
PHONE..................................909 596-8496
Darrell Covey, *CEO*
Nathan Covey, *President*
Nancy Feng, *Human Res Mgr*
EMP: 11
SQ FT: 4,500
SALES: 1MM **Privately Held**
WEB: www.expressioninwood.com
SIC: 2434 1751 5045 Wood kitchen cabinets; cabinet building & installation; computers, peripherals & software

(P-4195)
FALTON CUSTOM CABINETS INC
667 High Tech Pkwy, Oakdale (95361)
PHONE..................................209 845-9823
Jose Ismerio, *Vice Pres*
Antonio Munz, *President*
EMP: 11
SALES (est): 88.3K **Privately Held**
SIC: 2434 Wood kitchen cabinets

(P-4196)
FINELINE CARPENTRY INC
1297 Old County Rd, Belmont (94002-3920)
PHONE..................................650 592-2442
Mac Bean, *President*
Cheryl Bean, *Vice Pres*
EMP: 25
SQ FT: 15,000
SALES (est): 4MM **Privately Held**
WEB: www.finelinecarpentry.com
SIC: 2434 Wood kitchen cabinets

(P-4197)
FINISHING TOUCH MOULDING INC
6190 Corte Del Cedro, Carlsbad (92011-1515)
PHONE..................................760 444-1019
Roland Chaney, *President*
EMP: 55 EST: 2013
SALES (est): 4.1MM **Privately Held**
SIC: 2434 1751 Wood kitchen cabinets; carpentry work

(P-4198)
FITUCCI LLC
14753 Oxnard St, Van Nuys (91411-3122)
PHONE..................................818 785-3841
Eric Fituci, *Mng Member*
EMP: 11
SALES (est): 1.1MM **Privately Held**
SIC: 2434 Wood kitchen cabinets

(P-4199)
FRANKS CABINET SHOP INC
11204 San Diego St, Lamont (93241-2453)
PHONE..................................661 845-0781
Ronnie Jung, *President*
Doris Jung, *Treasurer*
Anetta Jung, *Admin Sec*
EMP: 15 EST: 1956
SQ FT: 32,000
SALES (est): 1.5MM **Privately Held**
SIC: 2434 2541 5211 Wood kitchen cabinets; wood partitions & fixtures; lumber products

(P-4200)
GALLERY CABINET CONNECTION
5783 E Shields Ave, Fresno (93727-7821)
PHONE..................................559 294-7007
Herb Falk, *President*
EMP: 11
SALES (est): 1.2MM **Privately Held**
SIC: 2434 Wood kitchen cabinets

(P-4201)
GALLEYS PLUS CUSTOM CABINETS
1432 E 6th St, Corona (92879-1713)
PHONE..................................951 278-4596
Bob Ballenger, *President*
EMP: 10
SQ FT: 5,000

SALES (est): 1.2MM **Privately Held**
SIC: 2434 2599 2521 2541 Wood kitchen cabinets; cabinets, factory; cabinets, office: wood; cabinets, except refrigerated: show, display, etc.: wood; cabinets: show, display or storage: except wood

(P-4202)
GRAND CABINETS AND STONE INC
1583 Entp Blvd Ste 20, West Sacramento (95691)
PHONE..................................510 759-3268
Yong Heng Luo, *Branch Mgr*
EMP: 11
SALES (corp-wide): 871.9K **Privately Held**
SIC: 2434 Wood kitchen cabinets
PA: Grand Cabinets And Stone Inc
10368 Hite Cir
Elk Grove CA 95757
916 270-7207

(P-4203)
HEART WOOD MANUFACTURING INC
Also Called: Heartwood Cabinets
5860 Obata Way, Gilroy (95020-7038)
P.O. Box 2552 (95021-2552)
PHONE..................................408 848-9750
David Boll, *President*
Eileen Boll, *Vice Pres*
EMP: 55
SQ FT: 25,000
SALES (est): 7.4MM **Privately Held**
SIC: 2434 2511 2431 Wood kitchen cabinets; wood household furniture; millwork

(P-4204)
HERITAGE WOODWORKING CO INC
4633 Mountain Lakes Blvd, Redding (96003-1450)
PHONE..................................530 243-7215
James Boisselle, *Owner*
Nora Boisselle, *Corp Secy*
EMP: 20
SQ FT: 14,720
SALES: 2.5MM **Privately Held**
SIC: 2434 Vanities, bathroom: wood

(P-4205)
HILKERS CUSTOM CABINETS INC
504 N Greco Ct, San Jacinto (92582-3877)
PHONE..................................951 487-7640
Daniel D Hilker, *President*
EMP: 10
SALES (est): 895.6K **Privately Held**
SIC: 2434 Wood kitchen cabinets

(P-4206)
HOLLANDS CUSTOM CABINETS INC
14511 Olde Highway 80, El Cajon (92021-2877)
PHONE..................................619 443-6081
Robert Holland, *President*
Jed Richard, *Vice Pres*
EMP: 25
SQ FT: 10,000
SALES (est): 3.7MM **Privately Held**
SIC: 2434 Wood kitchen cabinets

(P-4207)
I AND E CABINETS INC
14660 Raymer St, Van Nuys (91405-1217)
PHONE..................................818 933-6480
Israel Chlomovitz, *CEO*
Ettie Chlomovitz, *Corp Secy*
EMP: 34
SQ FT: 9,000
SALES: 5MM **Privately Held**
SIC: 2434 Wood kitchen cabinets

(P-4208)
IDO CABINET INC
1551 Minnesota St, San Francisco (94107-3521)
PHONE..................................415 282-1683
James Yu, *President*
Jenny Kong, *Vice Pres*
EMP: 13
SQ FT: 10,000

SALES (est): 1.2MM **Privately Held**
SIC: 2434 Wood kitchen cabinets

(P-4209)
INDIGO DESIGNS
16607 Reed St, Fontana (92336-2528)
PHONE..................................909 997-0854
George Ramirez, *Partner*
EMP: 10
SALES (est): 531.3K **Privately Held**
SIC: 2434 Wood kitchen cabinets

(P-4210)
JKF CONSTRUCTION INC
460 E Easy St Ste 102, Simi Valley (93065-1868)
PHONE..................................805 583-4228
Jon Flugum, *President*
EMP: 14
SALES (est): 1.4MM **Privately Held**
SIC: 2434 Wood kitchen cabinets

(P-4211)
JM KITCHEN CABINETS
702 E Gage Ave, Los Angeles (90001-1514)
PHONE..................................323 752-6520
Jose Maltonado, *Owner*
▲ EMP: 13
SALES (est): 1.2MM **Privately Held**
SIC: 2434 Wood kitchen cabinets

(P-4212)
JOHN HEWITT
Also Called: Cabinet Crafters
12759 E Brandt Rd Ste G, Lockeford (95237-9561)
P.O. Box 454 (95237-0454)
PHONE..................................209 727-9534
John Hewitt, *Owner*
EMP: 11
SQ FT: 6,000
SALES: 750K **Privately Held**
SIC: 2434 Wood kitchen cabinets

(P-4213)
JR STEPHENS COMPANY
5208 Boyd Rd, Arcata (95521-4410)
PHONE..................................707 825-0100
Jim Stephens, *President*
Bryan Stephens, *CFO*
Josh Stephens, *Vice Pres*
Rosalie Stephens, *Admin Sec*
EMP: 40
SALES: 6MM **Privately Held**
WEB: www.jrsco.net
SIC: 2434 Wood kitchen cabinets

(P-4214)
K & Z CABINET CO INC
1450 S Grove Ave, Ontario (91761-4523)
PHONE..................................909 947-3567
Dennis Chan, *President*
Jennifer Zeigler, *Administration*
Mike Twyford, *Plant Mgr*
Troy Zerillo, *Sr Project Mgr*
EMP: 60 EST: 1975
SQ FT: 59,000
SALES: 12.2MM **Privately Held**
SIC: 2434 2431 Wood kitchen cabinets; millwork

(P-4215)
KENEY MANUFACTURING CO (PA)
Also Called: Keney's Cabinets
586 Broadway Ave, Atwater (95301-4408)
P.O. Box 518 (95301-0518)
PHONE..................................209 358-6474
Robert Hernandez, *Partner*
Rodney Haygood, *Partner*
EMP: 16
SALES (est): 1.4MM **Privately Held**
SIC: 2434 Wood kitchen cabinets

(P-4216)
KEYSTONE CABINETRY INC
3110 N Clybourn Ave, Burbank (91505-1050)
PHONE..................................818 565-3330
Julian Sahagun, *CEO*
Amber Sahagun, *COO*
EMP: 10
SQ FT: 8,000

PRODUCTS & SVCS

SALES (est): 1.3MM **Privately Held**
WEB: www.keystonecabinetry.com
SIC: 2434 Wood kitchen cabinets

(P-4217)
KITCHEN POST INC
8617 Baseline Rd, Rancho Cucamonga
(91730-1111)
PHONE.............................909 948-6768
Randy Ludwig, *President*
EMP: 13
SALES (est): 1.9MM **Privately Held**
SIC: 2434 Wood kitchen cabinets

(P-4218)
KITCHENS NOW INC
20 Blue Sky Ct, Sacramento (95828-1015)
PHONE.............................916 229-8222
Douglas Carl Schubert, *CEO*
Kevin Sexton, *COO*
Xavier Salazar, *Project Mgr*
EMP: 17
SALES (est): 2.5MM **Privately Held**
SIC: 2434 Wood kitchen cabinets

(P-4219)
**KOBIS WINDOWS & DOORS
MFG INC**
7326 Laurel Canyon Blvd, North Hollywood
(91605-3710)
PHONE.............................818 764-6400
Kobi Louria, *CEO*
▲ EMP: 25 EST: 1999
SALES (est): 6.1MM **Privately Held**
SIC: 2434 2431 1522 Vanities, bathroom:
wood; millwork; residential construction

(P-4220)
LA BATH VANITY INC
2222 Davie Ave, Commerce (90040-1708)
PHONE.............................909 303-3323
EMP: 16 **Privately Held**
SIC: 2434 Vanities, bathroom: wood
PA: La Bath Vanity Inc.
1071 W 9th St
Upland CA 91786
-

(P-4221)
LACKEY WOODWORKING INC
2730 Chanticleer Ave, Santa Cruz
(95065-1812)
PHONE.............................831 462-0528
John E Lackey, *President*
Kathy Lackey, *Principal*
EMP: 13 EST: 1974
SQ FT: 6,000
SALES: 750K **Privately Held**
WEB: www.lackeywoodworking.com
SIC: 2434 2541 2431 2511 Wood kitchen
cabinets; cabinets, except refrigerated:
show, display, etc.: wood; doors, wood;
wood household furniture; signboards,
wood

(P-4222)
M AND M CABINETS INC
33238 Central Ave, Union City
(94587-2010)
PHONE.............................510 324-4034
Mark Mc Gee, *President*
Tim Mc Gee, *Treasurer*
Shirley Milburn, *Vice Pres*
EMP: 10
SQ FT: 2,500
SALES (est): 1.4MM **Privately Held**
SIC: 2434 Wood kitchen cabinets

(P-4223)
MASTERBRAND CABINETS INC
3700 S Riverside Ave, Colton
(92324-3329)
PHONE.............................951 686-3614
Michael Mejia, *Manager*
EMP: 50
SALES (corp-wide): 5.4B **Publicly Held**
WEB: www.mbcabinets.com
SIC: 2434 Wood kitchen cabinets
HQ: Masterbrand Cabinets, Inc.
1 Masterbrand Cabinets Dr
Jasper IN 47546
812 482-2527

(P-4224)
MILLBROOK KITCHENS INC
15960 Downey Ave, Paramount
(90723-5116)
PHONE.............................310 684-3366
▲ EMP: 15
SQ FT: 450,000
SALES: 450K **Privately Held**
SIC: 2434 1799

(P-4225)
MILLWOOD CABINET CO INC
2321 Virginia Ave, Bakersfield
(93307-2545)
PHONE.............................661 327-0371
David T Millwood Jr, *President*
Sandra Millwood, *Treasurer*
Diana Shackelford, *Admin Sec*
EMP: 23
SQ FT: 18,000
SALES (est): 4.3MM **Privately Held**
SIC: 2434 2541 Wood kitchen cabinets;
wood partitions & fixtures

(P-4226)
MISSION BELL MFG CO INC
25656 Schulte Ct, Tracy (95377-8643)
PHONE.............................209 229-7280
Terry Silva, *Manager*
EMP: 25
SALES (corp-wide): 21MM **Privately
Held**
SIC: 2434 2431 Wood kitchen cabinets;
millwork
PA: Mission Bell Mfg. Co., Inc.
16100 Jacqueline Ct
Morgan Hill CA 95037
408 778-2036

(P-4227)
MITCHELL DEAN COLLINS
12771 Monarch St, Garden Grove
(92841-3920)
P.O. Box 48, Sunset Beach (90742-0048)
PHONE.............................714 894-6767
Mitchell Collins, *Owner*
Sophia Staveley, *Office Mgr*
EMP: 10
SALES (est): 1.1MM **Privately Held**
SIC: 2434 Wood kitchen cabinets

(P-4228)
NORM TESSIER CABINETS INC
11989 6th St, Rancho Cucamonga
(91730-6133)
PHONE.............................909 987-8955
David L Beavers, *President*
Denise Beavers, *Vice Pres*
Jennifer Beavers, *Office Mgr*
EMP: 35 EST: 1978
SQ FT: 20,000
SALES: 2MM **Privately Held**
WEB: www.normtessiercabinets.com
SIC: 2434 Wood kitchen cabinets

(P-4229)
**PACIFIC HARDWOOD
CABINETRY**
2811 Dowd Dr, Santa Rosa (95407-7897)
PHONE.............................707 528-8627
Daniel G Bauman, *Owner*
EMP: 30
SQ FT: 41,000
SALES (est): 2.4MM **Privately Held**
SIC: 2434 Wood kitchen cabinets

(P-4230)
PATRICKS CABINETS
10160 Redwood Ave, Fontana
(92335-6237)
P.O. Box 787, Yucaipa (92399-0787)
PHONE.............................909 823-2524
Chris Dyer, *Owner*
EMP: 12
SQ FT: 10,000
SALES (est): 1.4MM **Privately Held**
SIC: 2434 Vanities, bathroom: wood

(P-4231)
PELICAN WOODWORKS
560 Birch St Ste 2, Lake Elsinore
(92530-2726)
PHONE.............................951 674-7821
Richard Mancuso, *Partner*
Frank Mc Whirt, *Partner*

EMP: 25
SQ FT: 11,000
SALES (est): 2.5MM **Privately Held**
SIC: 2434 2541 Wood kitchen cabinets;
counters or counter display cases, wood

(P-4232)
PROGRESSIVE WOODWORK
2255 Ceanothus Ave, Chico (95926-1661)
P.O. Box 1371 (95927-1371)
PHONE.............................530 343-2211
Gary Mc Connell, *Owner*
EMP: 15 EST: 1992
SQ FT: 10,000
SALES: 500K **Privately Held**
SIC: 2434 Vanities, bathroom: wood

(P-4233)
**QUALITY CABINET AND
FIXTURE CO (HQ)**
7955 Saint Andrews Ave, San Diego
(92154-8224)
PHONE.............................619 266-1011
Michael J Floyd, *CEO*
Donald Paradise, *Ch of Bd*
Tim Paradise, *President*
Andrew Meek, *CFO*
Nicholas P Willems, *CFO*
▲ EMP: 24
SQ FT: 55,000
SALES: 3.9MM
SALES (corp-wide): 25.4MM **Privately
Held**
WEB: www.qcfc.com
SIC: 2434 Wood kitchen cabinets
PA: Glenn Rieder, Inc.
6520 W Becher Pl
Milwaukee WI 53219
414 449-2888

(P-4234)
QUALITY CRAFT CABINETS INC
504 E Duarte Rd, Monrovia (91016-4604)
PHONE.............................626 358-2021
Andrew Riccardo, *President*
Steve Riccardo, *Vice Pres*
EMP: 14 EST: 1966
SQ FT: 8,000
SALES (est): 1.4MM **Privately Held**
SIC: 2434 Wood kitchen cabinets

(P-4235)
QUALITY WOODWORKS INC
261a Redel Rd, San Marcos (92078-4347)
PHONE.............................760 744-4748
Greg Durmer, *President*
Charles Somers, *Vice Pres*
EMP: 28
SQ FT: 10,000
SALES (est): 3.2MM **Privately Held**
SIC: 2434 Wood kitchen cabinets

(P-4236)
**R A JENSON MANUFACTURING
CO**
1337 Van Dyke Ave, San Francisco
(94124-3312)
PHONE.............................415 822-2732
Richard A Jenson, *President*
Rita Jenson, *Vice Pres*
Ron Smith, *Vice Pres*
Laura Jenson, *Admin Sec*
Richard Bailen,
EMP: 15 EST: 1960
SQ FT: 7,500
SALES (est): 1.7MM **Privately Held**
SIC: 2434 Vanities, bathroom: wood

(P-4237)
**RAWSON CUSTOM CABINETS
INC (PA)**
16890 Church St Bldg 1a, Morgan Hill
(95037-5114)
PHONE.............................408 779-9838
Dennis Rawson, *President*
Patricia Rawson, *Admin Sec*
Luke Nervig, *Design Engr*
Fred Agustinez, *Prdtn Mgr*
EMP: 24 EST: 1975
SQ FT: 19,300
SALES (est): 1.6MM **Privately Held**
WEB: www.rawson-cabinets.com
SIC: 2434 Wood kitchen cabinets

(P-4238)
REGAL KITCHENS LLC
3480 Sunset Ln, Oxnard (93035-4129)
PHONE.............................786 953-6578
Tony Pace, *President*
George Flack, *CFO*
Robert Sweeney,
◆ EMP: 200 EST: 1957
SQ FT: 168,000
SALES (est): 20.3MM **Privately Held**
WEB: www.regalkitchensinc.com
SIC: 2434 Wood kitchen cabinets

(P-4239)
ROCHAS CABINETS
108 Industrial Park Dr # 17, Manteca
(95337-6128)
PHONE.............................209 239-2367
Anthony Rocha, *Partner*
Jared Rocha, *Partner*
Joe Rocha, *Partner*
EMP: 10
SQ FT: 10,500
SALES: 1MM **Privately Held**
SIC: 2434 Vanities, bathroom: wood

(P-4240)
ROYAL CABINETS INC
1299 E Phillips Blvd, Pomona
(91766-5429)
PHONE.............................909 629-8565
Clay Smith, *President*
Bill Roan, *COO*
Kris Wengel, *Buyer*
▲ EMP: 600
SQ FT: 70,000
SALES (est): 72.6MM **Privately Held**
WEB: www.royalcabinets.com
SIC: 2434 2511 Wood kitchen cabinets;
wood household furniture

(P-4241)
ROYAL INDUSTRIES INC
Also Called: Royal Cabinets
1299 E Phillips Blvd, Pomona
(91766-5429)
PHONE.............................909 629-8565
Clay R Smith, *CEO*
Dan McGinn, *President*
Gus Danjoi, *CFO*
Kathy Goodrow, *Admin Sec*
EMP: 130
SALES (est): 17.5MM **Privately Held**
SIC: 2434 Vanities, bathroom: wood

(P-4242)
**RUCKER MILL & CABINET
WORKS**
5828 Mother Lode Dr, Placerville
(95667-8233)
PHONE.............................530 621-0236
John Rucker, *President*
Janice Rucker, *Admin Sec*
EMP: 12
SQ FT: 8,800
SALES (est): 1.1MM **Privately Held**
SIC: 2434 2431 1751 Wood kitchen cabi-
nets; millwork; cabinet & finish carpentry

(P-4243)
S M G CUSTOM CABINETS INC
5750 Alder Ave, Sacramento (95828-1112)
PHONE.............................916 381-5999
Stephen M Gelasakis, *President*
Mike Gelasakis, *Vice Pres*
Maria Gelasakis, *Admin Sec*
EMP: 20
SQ FT: 22,000
SALES (est): 2MM **Privately Held**
SIC: 2434 Wood kitchen cabinets

(P-4244)
SAGE INTERIOR INC
9 Aspen Tree Ln, Irvine (92612-2202)
PHONE.............................949 654-0184
Majid Kiani, *President*
EMP: 12
SALES (est): 2MM **Privately Held**
SIC: 2434 Wood kitchen cabinets

(P-4245)
SAN DIEGO CABINETS INC
2001 Lendee Dr, Escondido (92025-6351)
PHONE.............................760 747-3100
Sky Polselli, *President*

EMP: 30
SALES (est): 2.8MM **Privately Held**
SIC: 2434 Wood kitchen cabinets

(P-4246)
SANTA MONICA MILLWORKS
2568 Channel Dr Ste C, Ventura
(93003-4563)
PHONE..................................805 643-0010
William Lunche, *President*
EMP: 20
SALES (est): 1.7MM **Privately Held**
SIC: 2434 Wood kitchen cabinets

(P-4247)
SE INDUSTRIES INC
300 W Collins Ave, Orange (92867-5506)
PHONE..................................714 744-3200
Jan Schaffer, *President*
EMP: 12
SQ FT: 27,000
SALES (est): 1.3MM **Privately Held**
WEB: www.seindustries.net
SIC: 2434 Wood kitchen cabinets

(P-4248)
SLIGH CABINETS INC
105 Calle Propano, Paso Robles
(93446-3929)
PHONE..................................805 239-2550
Steve Sligh, *President*
EMP: 14
SQ FT: 30,000
SALES (est): 2.1MM **Privately Held**
WEB: www.slighcabinets.com
SIC: 2434 Vanities, bathroom: wood

(P-4249)
SOUTHCOAST CABINET INC (PA)
755 Pinefalls Ave, Walnut (91789-3027)
PHONE..................................909 594-3089
Dante M Senese, *CEO*
John Lopez, *President*
Danny Mendoza, *Info Tech Dir*
Ron St Jean, *Safety Mgr*
Scott Fibrow, *Opers Mgr*
EMP: 50
SQ FT: 108,000
SALES (est): 12.6MM **Privately Held**
WEB: www.southcoastcabinet.com
SIC: 2434 Wood kitchen cabinets

(P-4250)
STEVE AND CYNTHIA KIZANIS
Also Called: Kizanis Custom Cabinets
2483 Washington Ave, San Leandro
(94577-5920)
PHONE..................................510 352-2832
Steve Kizanis, *Owner*
Cynthia Kizanis, *Co-Owner*
John Fillipucci, *Sales Associate*
EMP: 13
SQ FT: 10,000
SALES (est): 740K **Privately Held**
SIC: 2434 Wood kitchen cabinets

(P-4251)
SUPERIOR MILLWORK OF SB INC
7330 Hollister Ave Ste B, Goleta
(93117-2868)
PHONE..................................805 685-1744
Joseph Morin, *President*
Diana Morin, *CFO*
EMP: 24 EST: 1972
SQ FT: 10,000
SALES (est): 2MM **Privately Held**
SIC: 2434 2431 Wood kitchen cabinets;
millwork

(P-4252)
T L CLARK CO INC
Also Called: Orion Woodcraft
3430 Kurtz St, San Diego (92110-4429)
PHONE..................................619 230-1400
Thomas Clark, *President*
EMP: 18
SQ FT: 8,000
SALES: 1MM **Privately Held**
WEB: www.orionwoodcraft.com
SIC: 2434 2499 Wood kitchen cabinets;
laundry products, wood

(P-4253)
TARA ENTERPRISES INC
27023 Mack Bean Pkwy, Valencia (91355)
PHONE..................................661 510-2206
EMP: 15
SALES (est): 1.2MM **Privately Held**
SIC: 2434

(P-4254)
TONUSA LLC
Also Called: Contemporary Bath.com
16770 E Johnson Dr, City of Industry
(91745-2414)
PHONE..................................626 961-8700
Yin M Ng,
Christine Hsu, *Opers Staff*
James Ng,
Dan Yu Chan Tseng,
▲ EMP: 15
SQ FT: 4,000
SALES (est): 2.3MM **Privately Held**
SIC: 2434 Vanities, bathroom: wood

(P-4255)
TRUE DESIGN INC
9427 Norwalk Blvd, Santa Fe Springs
(90670-2943)
PHONE..................................562 699-2001
Hani ABI Naked, *CEO*
Thomas Cavelti, *CFO*
EMP: 15 EST: 2014
SQ FT: 17,000
SALES: 3MM **Privately Held**
SIC: 2434 Wood kitchen cabinets

(P-4256)
TURLOCK CABINET SHOP INC
1475 West Ave S, Turlock (95380-5740)
PHONE..................................209 632-1311
Richard Lopes, *President*
Carolyn Lopes, *Admin Sec*
EMP: 11
SQ FT: 8,600
SALES (est): 1.1MM **Privately Held**
SIC: 2434 Wood kitchen cabinets

(P-4257)
ULTRA BUILT KITCHENS INC
1814 E 43rd St, Los Angeles (90058-1517)
PHONE..................................323 232-3362
Iris Yanes, *President*
Eduardo Yanes, *Treasurer*
Daisy Blanco, *Vice Pres*
EMP: 28
SQ FT: 18,000
SALES (est): 3.7MM **Privately Held**
WEB: www.ultrabuiltkitchens.net
SIC: 2434 Vanities, bathroom: wood

(P-4258)
UNITED CABINET COMPANY INC
1510 S Mountain View Ave, San Bernardino
(92408-3134)
PHONE..................................909 796-3015
Dennis Rice, *President*
Gayle L Rice, *Shareholder*
Doris Rice, *Corp Secy*
Jeffery Westrom, *Vice Pres*
EMP: 20
SQ FT: 10,000
SALES (est): 1.8MM **Privately Held**
SIC: 2434 Wood kitchen cabinets

(P-4259)
UNITED GRANITE & CABINETS LLC
5225 Central Ave, Richmond (94804-5805)
PHONE..................................510 558-8999
Paul Yu, *Owner*
Simon Yu CHI Ao, *Principal*
Simon Y Ao, *Principal*
▲ EMP: 13
SALES (est): 630K **Privately Held**
SIC: 2434 Wood kitchen cabinets

(P-4260)
VALET CSTM CABINETS & CLOSETS
1190 Dell Ave Ste J, Campbell
(95008-6614)
PHONE..................................408 374-4407
Larry Fox, *President*
EMP: 11

SALES (est): 982.8K **Privately Held**
SIC: 2434 Wood kitchen cabinets

(P-4261)
VALLEY CASEWORK INC
1112 Cleghorn Way, Alpine (91901-2907)
PHONE..................................619 579-6886
Fax: 619 579-0701
EMP: 60
SQ FT: 15,000
SALES (est): 5.9MM **Privately Held**
WEB: www.valleycasework.com
SIC: 2434

(P-4262)
VCSD INC
Also Called: Valley Cabinet
585 Vernon Way, El Cajon (92020-1934)
PHONE..................................619 579-6886
Larry Doyle, *President*
Susan Raymond, *CFO*
Christy Campbell, *Prgrmr*
EMP: 49 EST: 2011
SALES (est): 6.9MM **Privately Held**
SIC: 2434 Wood kitchen cabinets

(P-4263)
VILLAGE COLLECTION INC
1303 Elmer St A, Belmont (94002-4010)
PHONE..................................650 594-1635
Martin Phelps, *President*
Debbie Janssen, *Vice Pres*
EMP: 11
SQ FT: 18,000
SALES: 2MM **Privately Held**
WEB: www.thevillagecollection.net
SIC: 2434 5211 1521 Wood kitchen cabi-
nets; cabinets, kitchen; counter tops; sin-
gle-family housing construction

(P-4264)
W L RUBOTTOM CO
320 W Lewis St, Ventura (93001-1335)
PHONE..................................805 648-6943
Gary McCoy, *President*
Lawrence Rubottom, *Vice Pres*
Dene Hawthorne, *Accounting Dir*
Mark Rubottom, *VP Opers*
EMP: 55 EST: 1946
SQ FT: 40,000
SALES (est): 7.9MM **Privately Held**
WEB: www.rubottomco.com
SIC: 2434 Wood kitchen cabinets

(P-4265)
WEST PACIFIC CABINET MFG
3121 Swetzer Rd Ste A, Loomis
(95650-9586)
PHONE..................................916 652-6840
Steven Dietz, *President*
Cindy Dietz, *Vice Pres*
EMP: 19
SQ FT: 7,200
SALES (est): 1.8MM **Privately Held**
WEB: www.westpacificcabinets.com
SIC: 2434 2521 Wood kitchen cabinets;
cabinets, office: wood

(P-4266)
WILLIAMS CABINETS INC
2011 Frontier Trl, Anderson (96007-3008)
P.O. Box 915 (96007-0915)
PHONE..................................530 365-8421
Ronald E Raab, *President*
EMP: 10 EST: 1967
SQ FT: 7,000
SALES (est): 600K **Privately Held**
SIC: 2434 Vanities, bathroom: wood

(P-4267)
WOODEN BRIDGE INC
483 Reynolds Cir, San Jose (95112-1122)
PHONE..................................408 436-9663
David Baeza, *President*
Dave Toubrn, *Co-Owner*
EMP: 15
SALES (est): 2MM **Privately Held**
WEB: www.woodenbridge.com
SIC: 2434 Wood kitchen cabinets

(P-4268)
WOODIE WOODPECKERS WOODWORKS
21268 Deering Ct, Canoga Park
(91304-5015)
PHONE..................................818 999-2090

Darlene Somers, *CFO*
EMP: 20
SQ FT: 15,000
SALES (est): 2.8MM **Privately Held**
SIC: 2434 Wood kitchen cabinets

(P-4269)
WOODLINE PARTNERS INC
Also Called: Woodline Cabinets
5165 Fulton Dr, Fairfield (94534-1638)
PHONE..................................707 864-5445
Grant Paxton, *President*
Paul McKay, *CFO*
Lloyd Alexander, *Opers Mgr*
EMP: 49
SQ FT: 37,500
SALES (est): 6.4MM **Privately Held**
SIC: 2434 Wood kitchen cabinets

(P-4270)
WOODPECKER CABINET INC
21512 Nordhoff St, Chatsworth
(91311-5822)
PHONE..................................310 404-4805
Izaac Sananes, *CEO*
River Cook, *Manager*
EMP: 20
SALES: 1.2MM **Privately Held**
SIC: 2434 1799 Wood kitchen cabinets;
kitchen cabinet installation

(P-4271)
WYNDHAM COLLECTION LLC
1175 Aviation Pl, San Fernando
(91340-1460)
PHONE..................................888 522-8476
Martin Symes, *Mng Member*
Harry Parsamyan,
Sammy Parsamyan,
EMP: 26
SQ FT: 100,000
SALES (est): 306K **Privately Held**
SIC: 2434 Vanities, bathroom: wood

(P-4272)
YOUNGS CUSTOM CABINET INC
1760 Yosemite Ave, San Francisco
(94124-2622)
PHONE..................................415 822-8313
Yong X Xiao, *President*
EMP: 10
SALES (est): 905.3K **Privately Held**
SIC: 2434 Vanities, bathroom: wood

2435 Hardwood Veneer & Plywood

(P-4273)
ARCHITECTURAL PLYWOOD INC
Also Called: API
7104 Case Ave, North Hollywood
(91605-6301)
PHONE..................................818 255-1900
Ernie Huber, *President*
EMP: 20
SQ FT: 35,000
SALES (est): 2.2MM **Privately Held**
WEB: www.apiply.com
SIC: 2435 Plywood, hardwood or hard-
wood faced

(P-4274)
GENERAL VENEER MFG CO
8652 Otis St, South Gate (90280-3292)
P.O. Box 1607 (90280-1607)
PHONE..................................323 564-2661
William Dewitt, *President*
Ed Bewitt, *Treasurer*
Ed Dewitt, *Treasurer*
Ed Witt, *Treasurer*
Douglas Bradley, *Vice Pres*
EMP: 50 EST: 1942
SQ FT: 200,000
SALES: 8.8MM **Privately Held**
WEB: www.generalveneer.com
SIC: 2435 3365 Hardwood veneer & ply-
wood; aerospace castings, aluminum

PRODUCTS & SVCS

(P-4275)
JC HANSCOM INC
Also Called: Panel Works
11830 Wakeman St, Santa Fe Springs
(90670-2129)
PHONE.....................562 789-9955
John C Hanscom, *President*
Marsha Hanscom, *Vice Pres*
EMP: 16
SQ FT: 23,000
SALES (est): 2.5MM **Privately Held**
WEB: www.panelworks.com
SIC: 2435 Panels, hardwood plywood

(P-4276)
MADRID INC
7800 Industry Ave, Pico Rivera
(90660-4306)
PHONE.....................562 404-9941
Bob Ellis, *President*
EMP: 10
SQ FT: 25,000
SALES (est): 1.7MM **Privately Held**
WEB: www.madridinc.com
SIC: 2435 2511 Hardwood veneer & ply-
wood; wood household furniture

(P-4277)
MALAKAN INC (PA)
412 1/2 S Central Ave, Glendale
(91204-1602)
PHONE.....................310 910-9270
Radik Khachatryan, *President*
▲ **EMP:** 17
SQ FT: 8,000
SALES (est): 2.8MM **Privately Held**
SIC: 2435 Hardwood veneer & plywood

(P-4278)
**PACIFIC PANEL PRODUCTS
CORP**
15601 Arrow Hwy, Irwindale (91706-2004)
P.O. Box 2204 (91706-1126)
PHONE.....................626 851-0444
Jon R Dickey, *CEO*
Cory Dickey, *Plant Mgr*
Jeff Elliot, *Sales Staff*
▲ **EMP:** 39
SQ FT: 79,800
SALES (est): 8.2MM **Privately Held**
WEB: www.pacificpanel.com
SIC: 2435 Panels, hardwood plywood

(P-4279)
PLYCRAFT INDUSTRIES INC
Also Called: Concepts & Wood
2100 E Slauson Ave, Huntington Park
(90255-2727)
PHONE.....................323 587-8101
Ashley Joffe, *President*
Nathan Joffe, *CFO*
Donald R Greenberg, *Exec VP*
George Samoya, *CIO*
▲ **EMP:** 180
SQ FT: 71,187
SALES: 56MM **Privately Held**
SIC: 2435 Plywood, hardwood or hard-
wood faced; veneer stock, hardwood

(P-4280)
SONORA FACE CO
5233 Randolph St, Maywood (90270-3448)
PHONE.....................323 560-8188
Ossiel Calvillo, *President*
▲ **EMP:** 24
SQ FT: 20,000
SALES (est): 3.8MM **Privately Held**
SIC: 2435 Veneer stock, hardwood

(P-4281)
SPACEWALL INC
Also Called: Spacewall West Slotwall Mfg
350 E Crowther Ave, Placentia
(92870-6419)
PHONE.....................714 961-1300
Terry Sexton, *Manager*
EMP: 12
SQ FT: 15,605
SALES (corp-wide): 6.5MM **Privately
Held**
WEB: www.spacewall.com
SIC: 2435 5046 Hardwood veneer & ply-
wood; store fixtures & display equipment

PA: Spacewall, Inc.
4509 Stonegate Indus Blvd
Stone Mountain GA 30083
404 294-9564

(P-4282)
**SWANER HARDWOOD CO INC
(PA)**
5 W Magnolia Blvd, Burbank (91502-1776)
PHONE.....................818 953-5350
Keith M Swaner, *CEO*
Gary Swaner, *President*
Stephen Haag, *Treasurer*
Beverly Swaner, *Admin Sec*
David Layland, *Administration*
▲ **EMP:** 70
SQ FT: 4,500
SALES: 83MM **Privately Held**
WEB: www.swanerhardwood.com
SIC: 2435 5031 Hardwood veneer & ply-
wood; lumber: rough, dressed & finished;
plywood

(P-4283)
**TIMBER PRODUCTS CO LTD
PARTNR**
Also Called: Yreka Division
130 N Phillipe Ln, Yreka (96097-9014)
P.O. Box 766 (96097-0766)
PHONE.....................530 842-2310
Pete Himmel, *Branch Mgr*
Tracy Arasmith, *Maintence Staff*
EMP: 116
SALES (corp-wide): 340.8MM **Privately
Held**
WEB: www.sor.teamtp.com
SIC: 2435 2436 Veneer stock, hardwood;
softwood veneer & plywood
PA: Timber Products Co. Limited Partner-
ship
305 S 4th St
Springfield OR 97477
541 747-4577

(P-4284)
**WOODSOURCE
INTERNATIONAL**
2201 Dominguez St, Torrance
(90501-1418)
P.O. Box 153, Saint James MO (65559-
0153)
PHONE.....................310 328-9663
Chris Margetis, *Partner*
Dennis Prock, *General Ptnr*
EMP: 10
SALES (est): 111K **Privately Held**
SIC: 2435 Hardwood veneer & plywood

**2439 Structural Wood
Members, NEC**

(P-4285)
**ADVANTAGE TRUSS COMPANY
LLC**
2025 San Juan Rd, Hollister (95023-9601)
PHONE.....................831 635-0377
Jennifer Pfeiffer, *CEO*
EMP: 25 **EST:** 2000
SALES: 3.4MM **Privately Held**
SIC: 2439 1522 Trusses, wooden roof;
residential construction

(P-4286)
ALL-TRUSS INC
22700 Broadway, Sonoma (95476-8233)
PHONE.....................707 938-5595
Robert L Biggs, *President*
EMP: 20
SALES (est): 3.4MM **Privately Held**
WEB: www.alltruss.netfirms.com
SIC: 2439 Trusses, wooden roof

(P-4287)
AMERICAN PACIFIC TRUSS INC
Also Called: American Truss
24265 Rue De Cezanne, Laguna Niguel
(92677-6107)
PHONE.....................949 363-1691
Nouraddin Kharazmi, *CEO*
EMP: 25
SALES (est): 2.3MM **Privately Held**
SIC: 2439 Trusses, wooden roof

(P-4288)
**AUTOMATED BLDG
COMPONENTS INC**
2853 S Orange Ave, Fresno (93725-1921)
PHONE.....................559 485-8232
David Cervantes, *President*
Violet Cervantes, *Treasurer*
Gabriel Cervantes, *Vice Pres*
EMP: 13
SQ FT: 15,669
SALES (est): 1.8MM **Privately Held**
WEB: www.automatedbuildingcompo-
nents.com
SIC: 2439 Trusses, wooden roof

(P-4289)
BETTER BUILT TRUSS INC
251 E 4th St, Ripon (95366-2774)
P.O. Box 1319 (95366-1319)
PHONE.....................209 869-4545
Jeff Qualle, *President*
David Sanders, *President*
Rick Soto, *Engineer*
Mariana Cardoso, *Controller*
Melissa Dugan, *Controller*
EMP: 50 **EST:** 2010
SALES (est): 9.4MM **Privately Held**
SIC: 2439 Trusses, wooden roof

(P-4290)
**BROWN & HONEYCUTT TRUSS
SYSTMS**
16775 Smoke Tree St, Hesperia
(92345-6165)
P.O. Box 401804 (92340-1804)
PHONE.....................760 244-8887
Michael Hough, *President*
EMP: 45
SQ FT: 1,800
SALES (est): 4.7MM **Privately Held**
WEB: www.bhtruss.com
SIC: 2439 Trusses, wooden roof

(P-4291)
CAL-ASIA TRUSS INC
10547 E Stockton Blvd, Elk Grove
(95624-9743)
PHONE.....................916 685-5648
Richard Avery, *Manager*
EMP: 46
SALES (corp-wide): 5MM **Privately Held**
WEB: www.cal-asia.com
SIC: 2439 Trusses, wooden roof
PA: Cal-Asia Truss, Inc.
2300 Clayton Rd Ste 1400
Concord CA 94520
925 680-7701

(P-4292)
CALIFORNIA TRUSFRAME LLC
144 Commerce Way, Sanger (93657)
PHONE.....................951 657-7491
EMP: 434 **Privately Held**
SIC: 2439 Trusses, wooden roof
PA: California Trusframe, Llc
25220 Hancock Ave Ste 350
Murrieta CA 92562

(P-4293)
CALIFORNIA TRUSFRAME LLC
23665 Cajalco Rd, Perris (92570-8181)
PHONE.....................951 657-7491
EMP: 145 **Privately Held**
SIC: 2439 Trusses, wooden roof
PA: California Trusframe, Llc
25220 Hancock Ave Ste 350
Murrieta CA 92562

(P-4294)
**CALIFORNIA TRUSFRAME LLC
(PA)**
Also Called: Ctf
25220 Hancock Ave Ste 350, Murrieta
(92562-0903)
PHONE.....................951 350-4880
Steve Stroder, *Chairman*
Susan Engquist, *CFO*
Kenneth Cloyd, *Chairman*
EMP: 107
SQ FT: 5,000
SALES: 110MM **Privately Held**
SIC: 2439 Trusses, wooden roof

(P-4295)
CALIFORNIA TRUSS COMPANY
2800 Tully Rd, Hughson (95326-9640)
PHONE.....................209 883-8000
Kenneth Cloyd, *President*
EMP: 30
SALES (corp-wide): 35.5MM **Privately
Held**
SIC: 2439 Trusses, wooden roof
PA: California Truss Company
23665 Cajalco Rd
Perris CA 92570
951 657-7491

(P-4296)
COMMERCIAL TRUSS CO
Also Called: Alliance Trutrus
10731 Treena St Ste 207, San Diego
(92131-1041)
PHONE.....................858 693-1771
Dan Hershey, *President*
EMP: 50
SALES (est): 20MM **Privately Held**
SIC: 2439 Structural wood members

(P-4297)
**COMPU TECH LUMBER
PRODUCTS**
1980 Huntington Ct, Fairfield (94533-9753)
PHONE.....................707 437-6683
Walter L Young, *President*
Michael Blazer, *CFO*
Greg Young, *Vice Pres*
EMP: 80
SQ FT: 94,657
SALES (est): 11.9MM **Privately Held**
SIC: 2439 2431 1742 Trusses, wooden
roof; doors & door parts & trim, wood;
plastering, plain or ornamental

(P-4298)
CY TRUSS
10715 E American Ave, Del Rey
(93616-9703)
P.O. Box 188 (93616-0188)
PHONE.....................559 888-2160
Dave Campos, *Owner*
EMP: 30
SALES: 1MM **Privately Held**
SIC: 2439 Trusses, wooden roof

(P-4299)
DIAMOND TRUSS
12462 Charles Dr, Grass Valley
(95945-9371)
PHONE.....................530 477-1477
Joseph C Droivold, *Principal*
EMP: 12
SALES (est): 1.5MM **Privately Held**
SIC: 2439 Trusses, wooden roof

(P-4300)
EL DORADO TRUSS COINC
300 Industrial Dr, Placerville (95667-6828)
PHONE.....................530 622-1264
Steve Stewart, *President*
Edith Stewart, *Corp Secy*
EMP: 45
SQ FT: 15,000
SALES (est): 5.9MM **Privately Held**
SIC: 2439 Trusses, wooden roof

(P-4301)
ENTRUSSED LLC
5065 Commercial Pl, Sheridan
(95681-9601)
PHONE.....................916 753-5406
Dale Ebberts, *Mng Member*
EMP: 10
SQ FT: 720
SALES (est): 546.4K **Privately Held**
SIC: 2439 Trusses, except roof: laminated
lumber

(P-4302)
**GOLDENWOOD TRUSS
CORPORATION**
11032 Nardo St, Ventura (93004-3210)
PHONE.....................805 659-2520
Kevin Tollefson, *President*
Darin Ranson, *Vice Pres*
Myron Hodgson, *Admin Sec*
EMP: 80

SALES (est): 12.9MM **Privately Held**
WEB: www.goldenwoodtruss.com
SIC: 2439 Trusses, wooden roof

(P-4303)
HAISCH CONSTRUCTION CO INC
Also Called: Systems Plus Lumber
1800 S Barney Rd, Anderson (96007-9703)
PHONE...................................530 378-6800
Matthew C Haisch, *CEO*
Bill Ivey, *Corp Secy*
Douglas C Haisch, *Principal*
Tony Lobue, *Program Mgr*
EMP: 18 EST: 1968
SQ FT: 10,000
SALES (est): 3.9MM **Privately Held**
WEB: www.systplus.com
SIC: 2439 3441 Trusses, wooden roof; fabricated structural metal

(P-4304)
HANSON TRUSS INC
13950 Yorba Ave, Chino (91710-5520)
PHONE...................................909 591-9256
Donald R Hanson, *President*
Tom Hanson, *Corp Secy*
Mark McMullen, *Sales Staff*
EMP: 300
SQ FT: 4,000
SALES (est): 33.2MM **Privately Held**
SIC: 2439 Trusses, wooden roof

(P-4305)
HANSON TRUSS COMPONENTS INC
4476 Skyway Dr, Olivehurst (95961-7477)
P.O. Box 31, Marysville (95901-0001)
PHONE...................................530 740-7750
Steven L Hanson, *President*
EMP: 60
SALES: 6MM **Privately Held**
SIC: 2439 Trusses, except roof: laminated lumber

(P-4306)
HIGH SIERRA TRUSS COMPANY INC
1201 S K St, Tulare (93274-6424)
PHONE...................................559 688-6611
Oral E Micham, *President*
EMP: 14
SQ FT: 800
SALES (est): 1.9MM **Privately Held**
SIC: 2439 Arches, laminated lumber

(P-4307)
HOMEWOOD COMPONENTS INC
Also Called: Homewood Truss
5033 Feather River Blvd, Marysville (95901)
P.O. Box 5010 (95901-8501)
PHONE...................................530 743-8855
Hamid Noorani, *President*
Lain Moss, *Treasurer*
Adam Noorani, *Director*
EMP: 65
SQ FT: 120,000
SALES (est): 7.4MM **Privately Held**
SIC: 2439 Trusses, wooden roof; trusses, except roof: laminated lumber

(P-4308)
INLAND TRUSS INC (PA)
275 W Rider St, Perris (92571-3225)
PHONE...................................951 300-1758
Dan Irwin, *President*
Ernie Castro, *Treasurer*
Daniel Irwin, *Executive*
Jason Irwin, *Sales Mgr*
Debbie Meier, *Manager*
EMP: 66
SQ FT: 1,200
SALES (est): 5.1MM **Privately Held**
SIC: 2439 Trusses, wooden roof

(P-4309)
INLAND VALLEY TRUSS INC
150 N Sinclair Ave, Stockton (95215-5132)
PHONE...................................209 943-4710
Daniel Irwin, *President*
Dan Irwin, *President*
EMP: 11

SALES (est): 1.4MM **Privately Held**
WEB: www.inlandvalleytruss.com
SIC: 2439 Trusses, wooden roof
PA: Inland Empire Truss, Inc.
275 W Rider St
Perris CA 92571

(P-4310)
INTER MOUNTAIN TRUSS & GIRDER
596 Armstrong Way, Oakdale (95361-9367)
PHONE...................................209 847-9184
Paul Girard, *President*
Lance B Lester, *Treasurer*
EMP: 18
SQ FT: 1,632
SALES (est): 2.4MM **Privately Held**
SIC: 2439 Trusses, wooden roof

(P-4311)
JIM ELLIS
Also Called: Ellis Truss Company
16797 Live Oak St, Hesperia (92345-6209)
PHONE...................................760 244-8566
Jim Ellis, *Owner*
Sherry Vanillo, *CFO*
EMP: 15
SQ FT: 4,328
SALES (est): 1.3MM **Privately Held**
SIC: 2439 Trusses, wooden roof

(P-4312)
KATERRA INC
2302 Paradise Rd, Tracy (95304-8530)
PHONE...................................623 236-5322
Matt Ryan, *Branch Mgr*
EMP: 400
SALES (corp-wide): 151.2MM **Privately Held**
SIC: 2439 2421 2434 Trusses, wooden roof; lumber: rough, sawed or planed; wood kitchen cabinets
PA: Katerra Inc.
2494 Sand Hill Rd Ste 100
Menlo Park CA 94025
650 422-3572

(P-4313)
LASSEN FOREST PRODUCTS INC
22829 Casale Rd, Red Bluff (96080)
P.O. Box 8520 (96080-8520)
PHONE...................................530 527-7677
Peter Brunello Jr, *President*
EMP: 42
SQ FT: 30,000
SALES (est): 5.8MM **Privately Held**
SIC: 2439 5031 Structural wood members; lumber, plywood & millwork

(P-4314)
PACIFIC COAST SUPPLY LLC
Also Called: Pacific Supply
5550 Roseville Rd, North Highlands (95660-5038)
PHONE...................................916 339-8100
Wayne Tibke, *Branch Mgr*
Heather Miller, *Administration*
Leslie Blomquist, *Tax Mgr*
EMP: 19
SALES (corp-wide): 1.5B **Privately Held**
SIC: 2439 Trusses, wooden roof
HQ: Pacific Coast Supply, Llc
4290 Roseville Rd
North Highlands CA 95660
916 971-2301

(P-4315)
PRODUCTION TRUSS INC
9925 Prospect Ave Ste E, Santee (92071-4376)
P.O. Box 711662 (92072-1662)
PHONE...................................619 258-8792
David Bruno, *President*
EMP: 10 EST: 1998
SQ FT: 20,000
SALES (est): 103.7K **Privately Held**
SIC: 2439 Trusses, wooden roof

(P-4316)
REDBUILT LLC
Also Called: Trus Joist Macmillan
5088 Edison Ave, Chino (91710-5715)
PHONE...................................909 465-1215

Helder Pamplona, *Branch Mgr*
EMP: 35
SQ FT: 38,940
SALES (corp-wide): 2.9B **Privately Held**
SIC: 2439 Timbers, structural: laminated lumber
HQ: Redbuilt Llc
200 E Mallard Dr
Boise ID 83706

(P-4317)
SIMPSON STRONG-TIE COMPANY INC
12246 Holly St, Riverside (92509-2314)
PHONE...................................714 871-8373
Dave Bastian, *Branch Mgr*
Andre El-Khoury, *Plant Mgr*
EMP: 250
SQ FT: 40,845
SALES (corp-wide): 1B **Publicly Held**
SIC: 2439 3429 Structural wood members; manufactured hardware (general)
HQ: Simpson Strong-Tie Company Inc.
5956 W Las Positas Blvd
Pleasanton CA 94588
925 560-9000

(P-4318)
SOUTHERN CALIFORNIA COMPONENTS
9927 C Ave, Hesperia (92345-6048)
P.O. Box 401550 (92340-1550)
PHONE...................................760 949-5144
James Mc Cabe, *President*
EMP: 62
SQ FT: 2,000
SALES (est): 5MM **Privately Held**
WEB: www.socalcomp.com
SIC: 2439 Trusses, wooden roof

(P-4319)
SPATES FABRICATORS INC
85435 Middleton, Thermal (92274-9619)
PHONE...................................760 397-4122
Tom Spates, *President*
David Spates, *Vice Pres*
Frankie Spates, *Admin Sec*
Philip Spates, *Project Mgr*
Troy Guard, *Accounts Mgr*
EMP: 51 EST: 1976
SQ FT: 40,000
SALES (est): 20.2MM **Privately Held**
WEB: www.spates.com
SIC: 2439 Trusses, except roof: laminated lumber; trusses, wooden roof

(P-4320)
STONE TRUSS INC (PA)
507 Jones Rd, Oceanside (92058-1217)
PHONE...................................760 967-6171
Valerie Thomas, *Mng Member*
Steven Hall, *Principal*
Charles Signorino, *Principal*
EMP: 12
SQ FT: 80
SALES: 621.5K **Privately Held**
SIC: 2439 Trusses, wooden roof

(P-4321)
STRUCTURAL WOOD SYSTEMS
505 San Bernardino Blvd, Ridgecrest (93555-8236)
PHONE...................................760 375-2772
Gary Allred, *Owner*
EMP: 10
SQ FT: 1,000
SALES (est): 897.2K **Privately Held**
SIC: 2439 Trusses, except roof: laminated lumber

(P-4322)
T L TIMMERMAN CONSTRUCTION
Also Called: Timco
9845 Santa Fe Ave E, Hesperia (92345-6216)
P.O. Box 402563 (92340-2563)
PHONE...................................760 244-2532
Timothy L Timmerman, *President*
Anita Timmerman, *Vice Pres*
EMP: 30 EST: 1976
SQ FT: 7,700
SALES (est): 3.7MM **Privately Held**
SIC: 2439 Trusses, wooden roof

(P-4323)
TRI STATE TRUSS CORPORATION
600 River Rd, Needles (92363)
P.O. Box 628 (92363-0628)
PHONE...................................760 326-3868
Richard C Huebner, *CEO*
Mike Terry, *President*
EMP: 18 EST: 1978
SQ FT: 1,500
SALES (est): 2.7MM **Privately Held**
SIC: 2439 Trusses, wooden roof; trusses, except roof: laminated lumber

(P-4324)
TRI-CO BUILDING SUPPLY INC
Also Called: Truspro
695 Obispo St, Guadalupe (93434-1631)
P.O. Box 850 (93434-0850)
PHONE...................................805 343-2555
Patrick A Herring Sr, *President*
Memory Herring, *Corp Secy*
Steve Herring, *Vice Pres*
EMP: 51 EST: 1975
SQ FT: 2,500
SALES (est): 7.3MM **Privately Held**
SIC: 2439 Trusses, wooden roof

(P-4325)
TRI-K TRUSS COMPANY
453 S Main St, Porterville (93257-5323)
PHONE...................................559 784-8511
Larry Hansen, *President*
Ginger Hansen, *Vice Pres*
EMP: 16
SQ FT: 2,200
SALES (est): 2.5MM **Privately Held**
WEB: www.tri-k-truss.com
SIC: 2439 Trusses, wooden roof

(P-4326)
TRUSS ENGINEERING INC
477 Zeff Rd, Modesto (95351-3943)
P.O. Box 580210 (95358-0005)
PHONE...................................209 527-6387
Lawrence O Brien, *President*
EMP: 20
SQ FT: 14,000
SALES (est): 3MM **Privately Held**
WEB: www.trussengineering.com
SIC: 2439 Trusses, wooden roof

2441 Wood Boxes

(P-4327)
A & J INDUSTRIES INC
Also Called: A & J Manufacturing
1430 240th St, Harbor City (90710-1307)
P.O. Box 90596, Los Angeles (90009-0596)
PHONE...................................310 216-2170
Patrick Doucette, *CEO*
Keith Bell, *Admin Sec*
◆ EMP: 18 EST: 1945
SQ FT: 40,000
SALES: 3MM **Privately Held**
WEB: www.ajcases.com
SIC: 2441 Chests & trunks, wood; tool chests, wood; shipping cases, wood: nailed or lock corner; packing cases, wood: nailed or lock corner

(P-4328)
ARBO BOX INC
2900 Supply Ave, Commerce (90040-2708)
PHONE...................................562 404-2726
Robert Wharton, *CEO*
EMP: 45
SQ FT: 14,200
SALES: 2.4MM **Privately Held**
WEB: www.arbobox.com
SIC: 2441 Nailed wood boxes & shook

(P-4329)
ARMORED GROUP INC
Also Called: Innerspace Cases
11555 Cantara St, North Hollywood (91605-1652)
PHONE...................................818 767-3030
Louis Kaye, *President*
Loretta Kaye, *Corp Secy*
Joshua Kaye, *Info Tech Mgr*
EMP: 25 EST: 1986
SQ FT: 15,000

PRODUCTS & SVCS

SALES (est): 4.5MM **Privately Held**
WEB: www.innerspacecases.com
SIC: 2441 Cases, wood

(P-4330)
BASAW MANUFACTURING INC (PA)
7300 Varna Ave, North Hollywood (91605-4008)
PHONE..............................818 765-6650
Robert Allen, *President*
Hugh Mullen, *Treasurer*
Eleazar Padilla, *Vice Pres*
Jorge Cea,
Martha Rivera,
▲ **EMP:** 32
SQ FT: 63,165
SALES (est): 8.6MM **Privately Held**
WEB: www.basaw.com
SIC: 2441 7389 Shipping cases, wood: nailed or lock corner; packaging & labeling services

(P-4331)
BASAW SERVICES INC
7300 Varna Ave, North Hollywood (91605-4008)
PHONE..............................818 765-6650
Robert Allen, *Vice Pres*
EMP: 50
SALES (corp-wide): 8.6MM **Privately Held**
WEB: www.basaw.com
SIC: 2441 Shipping cases, wood: nailed or lock corner
PA: Basaw Manufacturing Inc
   7300 Varna Ave
   North Hollywood CA 91605
   818 765-6650

(P-4332)
BASAW SERVICES INC
13340 Raymer St, North Hollywood (91605-4101)
PHONE..............................818 765-6650
Robert Allen, *Manager*
EMP: 40
SALES (corp-wide): 8.6MM **Privately Held**
WEB: www.basaw.com
SIC: 2441 Shipping cases, wood: nailed or lock corner
PA: Basaw Manufacturing Inc
   7300 Varna Ave
   North Hollywood CA 91605
   818 765-6650

(P-4333)
CAL-COAST PKG & CRATING INC
2040 E 220th St, Carson (90810-1603)
PHONE..............................310 518-7215
Dale Loughry, *President*
▲ **EMP:** 35 **EST:** 1957
SQ FT: 58,000
SALES (est): 3.9MM **Privately Held**
WEB: www.calcoastpacking.com
SIC: 2441 2449 Shipping cases, wood: nailed or lock corner; wood containers

(P-4334)
CASE HARDIGG CENTER
651 Barrington Ave Ste A, Ontario (91764-5115)
PHONE..............................413 665-2163
Natalie Cohen, *Manager*
EMP: 10
SALES (est): 943K **Privately Held**
SIC: 2441 Shipping cases, wood: nailed or lock corner

(P-4335)
EL CAMINO WOOD PRODUCTS
16816 S Broadway, Gardena (90248-3110)
PHONE..............................310 768-3447
Donald Bailey Jr, *Owner*
EMP: 10
SQ FT: 4,000
SALES (est): 716.9K **Privately Held**
SIC: 2441 Boxes, wood

(P-4336)
FCA LLC
3810 Transport St, Ventura (93003-5126)
PHONE..............................805 477-9901
Carol S Kilburg, *President*

EMP: 18 **Privately Held**
SIC: 2441 Cases, wood
PA: Fca, Llc
   7601 John Deere Pkwy
   Moline IL 61265
   -

(P-4337)
JAN-AL INNERPRIZES INC
Also Called: Jan-Al Cases
3339 Union Pacific Ave, Los Angeles (90023-3812)
P.O. Box 23337 (90023-0337)
PHONE..............................323 260-7212
Miriam Alejandro, *President*
Mark Oneill, *Treasurer*
Jan Michael Alejandro, *Vice Pres*
Dianne Parker, *Financial Exec*
Mercedes Johnson,
EMP: 30
SQ FT: 16,000
SALES (est): 2.4MM **Privately Held**
WEB: www.janalcase.com
SIC: 2441 Cases, wood

(P-4338)
LARSON PACKAGING COMPANY LLC
1000 Yosemite Dr, Milpitas (95035-5410)
PHONE..............................408 946-4971
Mark A Hoffman, *Mng Member*
Ray Horner, *COO*
Tom Moore, *Design Engr*
Arnold Hoffman,
Gold Hoffman,
EMP: 48 **EST:** 1967
SQ FT: 30,000
SALES (est): 10.7MM **Privately Held**
SIC: 2441 2448 2421 Nailed wood boxes & shook; pallets, wood; sawmills & planing mills, general

(P-4339)
MEZA PALLET INC
14619 Merrill Ave, Fontana (92335-4219)
PHONE..............................909 829-0223
Leodegario G Meza, *President*
Michael Meza, *President*
EMP: 15
SALES (est): 3MM **Privately Held**
SIC: 2441 Ammunition boxes, wood

(P-4340)
NEFAB PACKAGING INC
8477 Central Ave, Newark (94560-3431)
PHONE..............................408 678-2500
Ana Gonzales, *Branch Mgr*
EMP: 98
SALES (corp-wide): 496.7MM **Privately Held**
SIC: 2441 5113 5199 Shipping cases, wood: nailed or lock corner; cardboard & products; packaging materials
HQ: Nefab Packaging, Inc.
   204 Airline Dr Ste 100
   Coppell TX 75019
   469 444-5264

(P-4341)
NELSON CASE CORPORATION
650 S Jefferson St Ste A, Placentia (92870-6640)
PHONE..............................714 528-2215
Edward Bobadilla, *CEO*
John Bovadilla Jr, *CEO*
Virginia Sandburg, *CFO*
Ernie Contreras, *Purch Mgr*
Scott Mana, *Sales Associate*
EMP: 19
SALES (est): 3.9MM **Privately Held**
WEB: www.nelsoncasecorp.com
SIC: 2441 5199 5099 2449 Packing cases, wood: nailed or lock corner; shipping cases, wood: nailed or lock corner; bags, baskets & cases; cases, carrying; shipping cases, wood: wirebound

(P-4342)
PROCASES INC
Also Called: Az-Iz Case Co
4626 E 48th St, Vernon (90058-3228)
PHONE..............................323 585-4447
Afshin Zakhor, *President*
▲ **EMP:** 10
SQ FT: 10,080

SALES: 1.5MM **Privately Held**
WEB: www.procases.com
SIC: 2441 Shipping cases, wood: nailed or lock corner

(P-4343)
UNIQUE DRAWER BOXES INC
9435 Bond Ave, El Cajon (92021-2874)
PHONE..............................619 873-4240
Mark Plas, *President*
Margaret Plas, *Vice Pres*
EMP: 14
SALES (est): 2.4MM **Privately Held**
WEB: www.quickdrawer.com
SIC: 2441 Boxes, wood

2448 Wood Pallets & Skids

(P-4344)
AAA PALLET RECYCLING & MFG INC
23120 Oleander Ave, Perris (92570-5662)
PHONE..............................951 681-7748
Tyson Paulis, *CEO*
EMP: 22
SQ FT: 152,460
SALES: 5MM **Privately Held**
SIC: 2448 Wood pallets & skids

(P-4345)
ALL BAY PALLET COMPANY INC (PA)
24993 Tarman Ave, Hayward (94544-2119)
PHONE..............................510 636-4131
Eladio Garcia Padilla, *President*
EMP: 36
SQ FT: 50,000
SALES: 2.1MM **Privately Held**
SIC: 2448 2449 Pallets, wood; wood containers

(P-4346)
ALL GOOD PALLETS INC
1055 Diamond St, Stockton (95205-7020)
PHONE..............................209 467-7000
Jack Nagra, *Manager*
EMP: 20
SALES (corp-wide): 3.2MM **Privately Held**
SIC: 2448 Wood pallets & skids
PA: All Good Pallets, Inc.
   6756 Central Ave Ste E
   Newark CA 94560
   510 794-4700

(P-4347)
ARNIES SUPPLY SERVICE LTD (PA)
1541 N Ditman Ave, Los Angeles (90063-2501)
P.O. Box 26, Monterey Park (91754-0026)
PHONE..............................323 263-1696
Arnold Espino, *President*
Madeline Espino, *Treasurer*
Maria Espino, *Admin Sec*
EMP: 25 **EST:** 1975
SALES (est): 6.6MM **Privately Held**
SIC: 2448 Pallets, wood & wood with metal

(P-4348)
ATLAS PALLET CORP
600 Industry Rd, Pittsburg (94565-2767)
P.O. Box 1363 (94565-0136)
PHONE..............................925 432-6261
La Sang Lim, *Principal*
EMP: 12 **EST:** 1969
SQ FT: 6,000
SALES (est): 1.9MM **Privately Held**
SIC: 2448 Pallets, wood; pallets, wood & wood with metal

(P-4349)
AZTEC TECHNOLOGY CORPORATION
14022 Slover Ave, Fontana (92337-7039)
PHONE..............................909 350-8830
Dale Aldey, *Manager*
EMP: 12
SALES (corp-wide): 9.5MM **Privately Held**
WEB: www.azteccontainer.com
SIC: 2448 Cargo containers, wood & wood with metal

PA: Aztec Technology Corporation
   2550 S Santa Fe Ave
   Vista CA 92084
   760 727-2300

(P-4350)
BIG GZ PALLETS
1181 S Wilson Way, Stockton (95205-7053)
P.O. Box 55140 (95205-8640)
PHONE..............................209 465-0351
Ronal Grijalva, *Owner*
EMP: 10
SALES (est): 1.7MM **Privately Held**
SIC: 2448 Pallets, wood; pallets, wood & wood with metal

(P-4351)
BIG VALLEY PALLET
2512 Paulson Rd, Turlock (95380-9757)
P.O. Box 1998 (95381-1998)
PHONE..............................209 632-7687
Mike Atwood, *President*
Jim Atwood, *Vice Pres*
Janice Atwood, *Office Mgr*
EMP: 30
SQ FT: 3,000
SALES (est): 4.7MM **Privately Held**
SIC: 2448 Pallets, wood

(P-4352)
BRUCE IVERSEN
Also Called: B&B Pallet Company
439 E Carlin Ave, Compton (90222-2309)
PHONE..............................310 537-4168
Bruce Iversen, *Owner*
EMP: 42 **EST:** 1965
SQ FT: 20,000
SALES: 5MM **Privately Held**
SIC: 2448 2421 Pallets, wood; sawdust & shavings

(P-4353)
C PALLETS FROM BKERSFIELD CALL
2508 E Brundage Ln, Bakersfield (93307-2812)
P.O. Box 367, Delano (93216-0367)
PHONE..............................661 833-2801
Isaias Correa, *Owner*
C Pallets, *Owner*
EMP: 12
SALES (est): 960K **Privately Held**
SIC: 2448 5085 4789 Pallets, wood & wood with metal; plastic pallets; cargo loading & unloading services

(P-4354)
CELERINOS PALLETS
1320 Mateo St, Los Angeles (90021-1747)
PHONE..............................626 923-4182
Edgar Reyes, *Owner*
EMP: 15 **EST:** 2011
SALES (est): 1.2MM **Privately Held**
SIC: 2448 Pallets, wood & wood with metal

(P-4355)
CENTRAL PALLETS
1881 E Market St, Stockton (95205-5673)
PHONE..............................209 462-3019
Rene Torres, *Owner*
EMP: 15
SALES (est): 1.5MM **Privately Held**
SIC: 2448 Pallets, wood & wood with metal

(P-4356)
CHEP (USA) INC
Also Called: Bay Area Pallette Company
2276 Wilbur Ln, Antioch (94509-8510)
PHONE..............................925 234-4970
Vince Sheldon, *Manager*
EMP: 55 **Privately Held**
WEB: www.ifcosystems.com
SIC: 2448 5085 Pallets, wood; industrial supplies
HQ: Chep (U.S.A.) Inc.
   5897 Windward Pkwy
   Alpharetta GA 30005
   770 668-8100

(P-4357)
COMMERCIAL LBR & PALLET CO INC (PA)
135 Long Ln, City of Industry (91746-2633)
PHONE..............................626 968-0631

Raymond Gutierrez, *President*
Jason Gutierrez, *Sales Executive*
EMP: 150
SQ FT: 10,000
SALES (est): 56.4MM **Privately Held**
SIC: 2448 5031 Pallets, wood; lumber:
  rough, dressed & finished

(P-4358)
CORREA PALLET INC (PA)
Also Called: National Wholesale Lumber
13036 Avenue 76, Pixley (93256-9458)
PHONE..............................559 757-1790
Martin Correa, *President*
EMP: 50
SALES (est): 9.4MM **Privately Held**
SIC: 2448 Pallets, wood

(P-4359)
CROWN PALLET COMPANY INC
15151 Salt Lake Ave, La Puente
(91746-3316)
PHONE..............................626 937-6565
Robert Miller, *President*
▲ **EMP:** 20
SQ FT: 400
SALES (est): 2.7MM **Privately Held**
SIC: 2448 2441 Pallets, wood; nailed
  wood boxes & shook

(P-4360)
CUTTER LUMBER PRODUCTS
4004 S El Dorado St, Stockton
(95206-3759)
PHONE..............................209 982-4477
Tony Palma, *Manager*
EMP: 50
SALES (est): 4.8MM
SALES (corp-wide): 11.3MM **Privately
Held**
WEB: www.cutterlumber.com
SIC: 2448 Pallets, wood
PA: Cutter Lumber Products
  10 Rickenbacker Cir
  Livermore CA 94551
  925 443-5959

(P-4361)
D L B PALLETS (PA)
4510 Rutile St, Riverside (92509-2649)
P.O. Box 10513, San Bernardino (92423-
0513)
PHONE..............................951 360-9896
Daniel Bodbyl, *President*
Anna Bodbyl, *Treasurer*
EMP: 15
SALES (est): 3.3MM **Privately Held**
SIC: 2448 5031 Pallets, wood; pallets,
  wood

(P-4362)
DEL RIO WEST PALLETS
3845 S El Dorado St, Stockton
(95206-3760)
PHONE..............................209 983-8215
Candy Villalobos, *Owner*
EMP: 24
SALES (est): 3.9MM **Privately Held**
SIC: 2448 Pallets, wood & wood with metal

(P-4363)
E & R PALLETS INC
4247 Campbell St, Riverside (92509-2618)
PHONE..............................951 790-1212
Ronnie Cortez, *Administration*
EMP: 10
SALES (est): 1.2MM **Privately Held**
SIC: 2448 Pallets, wood

(P-4364)
E VASQUEZ DISTRIBUTORS INC
Also Called: Oxnard Pallet Company
4524 E Pleasant Valley Rd, Oxnard
(93033-2309)
P.O. Box 1748 (93032-1748)
PHONE..............................805 487-8458
Elias Vasquez Jr, *President*
Beatrice Vasquez, *CFO*
Vannessa Vasquez, *Vice Pres*
EMP: 30
SQ FT: 480
SALES: 5.8MM **Privately Held**
SIC: 2448 4214 Pallets, wood; local truck-
  ing with storage

(P-4365)
EL PELADO LLC
Also Called: Sonoma Pacific Company
1180 Fremont Dr, Sonoma (95476-9257)
PHONE..............................707 938-2877
Tommy Thompson, *Owner*
EMP: 44
SQ FT: 326,699
SALES: 5MM **Privately Held**
SIC: 2448 Wood pallets & skids

(P-4366)
FIVE STAR LUMBER COMPANY LLC
655 Brunken Ave, Salinas (93901-4362)
PHONE..............................831 422-4493
Gary Beasley, *Manager*
EMP: 20
SALES (corp-wide): 18.5MM **Privately
Held**
SIC: 2448 Pallets, wood
PA: Five Star Lumber Company Llc
  6899 Smith Ave
  Newark CA 94560
  510 795-7204

(P-4367)
FIVE STAR LUMBER COMPANY LLC (PA)
Also Called: Five Star Pallet Co
6899 Smith Ave, Newark (94560-4223)
PHONE..............................510 795-7204
Marco Beretta, *President*
Bruce Beretta,
David Beretta,
Sandra Beretta,
▲ **EMP:** 25 **EST:** 1981
SQ FT: 20,000
SALES: 18.5MM **Privately Held**
SIC: 2448 5031 Pallets, wood; lumber:
  rough, dressed & finished

(P-4368)
G O PALLETS INC
15642 Slover Ave, Fontana (92337-7362)
PHONE..............................909 823-4663
Guatalupe Ojeda, *President*
Lina Montes, *Office Mgr*
EMP: 22
SALES (est): 3.4MM **Privately Held**
SIC: 2448 Pallets, wood

(P-4369)
HANNIBAL LAFAYETTE
Also Called: D & L Pallet Company
10758 Fremont Ave, Ontario (91762-3909)
PHONE..............................909 322-0600
Lafayette Hannibal, *Branch Mgr*
EMP: 11
SALES (corp-wide): 200K **Privately Held**
SIC: 2448 Wood pallets & skids
PA: Lafayette Hannibal
  1554 W Holt Ave
  Pomona CA 91768
  909 322-0600

(P-4370)
HARDING CONTAINERS INTL INC
4000 Santa Fe Ave, Long Beach
(90810-1832)
PHONE..............................310 549-7272
Victor Hsing, *President*
Keith R Mayer, *Vice Pres*
▲ **EMP:** 20
SQ FT: 1,000
SALES (est): 3.4MM **Privately Held**
SIC: 2448 Cargo containers, wood & wood
  with metal

(P-4371)
IDEAL PALLET SYSTEM INC
7422 Cedar Dr, Huntington Beach
(92647-5498)
P.O. Box 2300 (92647-0300)
PHONE..............................714 847-9657
Toll Free:.............................877 -
Melvin Mermelstein, *President*
Edie Mermelstein, *CFO*
EMP: 15
SQ FT: 3,500
SALES (est): 1.8MM **Privately Held**
WEB: www.idealpallet.com
SIC: 2448 Pallets, wood

(P-4372)
IFCO SYSTEMS NORTH AMERICA INC
14750 Miller Ave, Fontana (92336-1685)
PHONE..............................909 356-0697
EMP: 46 **Privately Held**
SIC: 2448
HQ: Ifco Systems North America, Inc.
  13100 Nw Fwy Ste 625
  Houston TX 77040
  -

(P-4373)
IFCO SYSTEMS US LLC
8950 Rochester Ave # 150, Rancho Cuca-
monga (91730-5541)
PHONE..............................909 484-4332
Mike Ellis, *Principal*
Marcus Blood, *General Mgr*
Tony Flores, *General Mgr*
Ben Hiott, *General Mgr*
Eric Smith, *General Mgr*
EMP: 47 **Privately Held**
SIC: 2448 Pallets, wood
HQ: Ifco Systems Us, Llc
  3030 N Rocky Point Dr W # 300
  Tampa FL 33607

(P-4374)
INCA PALLETS SUPPLY INC
1349 S East End Ave, Pomona
(91766-5412)
PHONE..............................909 622-1414
Zuleica Quimones, *President*
EMP: 29
SALES (est): 4.3MM **Privately Held**
SIC: 2448 7699 Pallets, wood; pallet re-
  pair

(P-4375)
J & A PALLET ACCESSORY INC
6607 Doolittle Ave Ste A, Riverside
(92503-1471)
PHONE..............................951 785-1594
Omar Sosa, *President*
Sonia Sanchez-Sosa, *Vice Pres*
EMP: 12
SALES (est): 2.4MM **Privately Held**
SIC: 2448 Pallets, wood

(P-4376)
JC PALLET CO
5800 State Rd Spc 13, Bakersfield
(93308-3039)
P.O. Box 81196 (93380-1196)
PHONE..............................661 393-2229
Jack Chalmers, *Owner*
EMP: 10
SQ FT: 6,000
SALES (est): 887.2K **Privately Held**
SIC: 2448 2449 Pallets, wood; wood con-
  tainers

(P-4377)
LONG BEACH WOODWORKS LLC
Also Called: Pacific Pallet Co
1261 Highland Ave, Glendale (91202-2055)
PHONE..............................562 437-2293
Steven P Amato,
Pamela Amato, *Office Mgr*
Sam Amato,
EMP: 14
SQ FT: 2,000
SALES (est): 2.4MM **Privately Held**
WEB: www.pacificpallet.com
SIC: 2448 Pallets, wood

(P-4378)
LOPEZ PALLETS INC
11080 Redwood Ave, Fontana
(92337-7130)
P.O. Box 847, Rancho Cucamonga (91729-
0847)
PHONE..............................909 823-0865
Jesus M Lopez, *President*
EMP: 16
SQ FT: 700
SALES (est): 1.5MM **Privately Held**
SIC: 2448 7699 Pallets, wood; skids,
  wood; pallet repair

(P-4379)
M C WOODWORK
747 E 60th St, Los Angeles (90001-1030)
PHONE..............................323 233-0954
Mario Contreares, *Owner*
EMP: 18
SALES (est): 1.1MM **Privately Held**
SIC: 2448 Wood pallets & skids

(P-4380)
MARTINEZ PALLET SERVICES LLC
671 Mariposa Rd, Modesto (95354-4145)
P.O. Box 2854, Turlock (95381-2854)
PHONE..............................209 968-1393
Jose Martinez,
Oscar Barcelo,
EMP: 14 **EST:** 2014
SALES (est): 818.4K **Privately Held**
SIC: 2448 Pallets, wood

(P-4381)
MEDINA WOOD PRODUCTS INC
26342 S Banta Rd, Tracy (95304-8157)
P.O. Box 1037 (95378-1037)
PHONE..............................209 832-4523
Salvador David Medina, *President*
Irene Medina, *CFO*
EMP: 14
SQ FT: 700
SALES (est): 2.1MM **Privately Held**
SIC: 2448 Pallets, wood

(P-4382)
P & R PALLETS INC
2301 Porter St, Los Angeles (90021-2509)
PHONE..............................213 327-1104
Juan Reyes, *President*
Mary luelas, *Manager*
EMP: 25
SQ FT: 5,520
SALES (est): 1.7MM **Privately Held**
WEB: www.prpallets.com
SIC: 2448 Pallets, wood

(P-4383)
P T M INC
10842 Road 28 1/2, Madera (93637-8504)
P.O. Box 602 (93639-0602)
PHONE..............................559 673-1552
John Gonzales, *President*
Herbert Carlos, *Associate Dir*
EMP: 15
SALES (est): 1.4MM **Privately Held**
SIC: 2448 7699 Pallets, wood; pallet re-
  pair

(P-4384)
PACIFIC COAST PALLETS INC
15151 Salt Lake Ave, La Puente
(91746-3316)
PHONE..............................626 937-6565
Richard Reeves, *President*
EMP: 20 **EST:** 1979
SQ FT: 600
SALES: 1MM **Privately Held**
WEB: www.pacificcoastpallets.com
SIC: 2448 7699 Pallets, wood; pallet re-
  pair

(P-4385)
PACIFIC PALLET EXCHANGE INC
3350 51st Ave, Sacramento (95823)
PHONE..............................916 448-5589
Ricardo Zepeda, *President*
Douglas Schnabel, *President*
Glenna Schnabel, *CFO*
EMP: 30
SQ FT: 77,537
SALES: 3MM **Privately Held**
SIC: 2448 Pallets, wood

(P-4386)
PACKAGING SPECIALISTS INC
Also Called: PSI
3663 Feather River Blvd, Plumas Lake
(95961-9616)
P.O. Box 10, Olivehurst (95961-0010)
PHONE..............................530 742-8441
Gary Allen, *CEO*
David Allen, *President*
Mary Allen, *Admin Sec*
EMP: 14

P
R
O
D
U
C
T
S

&

S
V
C
S

SALES (est): 2.7MM **Privately Held**
SIC: 2448 Pallets, wood

(P-4387)
PALLET DEPOT INC (PA)
19049 Avenue 242, Lindsay (93247-9698)
PHONE..................916 645-0490
Jamie Anderson, *President*
Mike Anderson, *Vice Pres*
Sharon Anderson, *Director*
EMP: 70
SALES (est): 6.6MM **Privately Held**
SIC: 2448 Pallets, wood & wood with metal

(P-4388)
PALLET MASTERS INC
655 E Florence Ave, Los Angeles
(90001-2319)
PHONE..................323 758-1713
Stephen H Anderson, *President*
Tim Hwang, *Controller*
EMP: 55
SQ FT: 105,000
SALES (est): 8.8MM **Privately Held**
SIC: 2448 2441 2439 Pallets, wood;
skids, wood; boxes, wood; structural
wood members

(P-4389)
PALLET RECOVERY SERVICE INC
3401 Gaffery Rd, Tracy (95304-9345)
P.O. Box 35, Westley (95387-0035)
PHONE..................209 496-5074
Lisa E Kilcoyne, *President*
Matt Haugrud, *Vice Pres*
John Kilcoyne, *Vice Pres*
EMP: 14 EST: 2008
SALES (est): 2.6MM **Privately Held**
SIC: 2448 Pallets, wood

(P-4390)
PALLETS 4 LESS INC
750 Ceres Ave, Los Angeles (90021-1516)
P.O. Box 21096 (90021-0096)
PHONE..................213 377-7813
Gabriel Diaz, *President*
Oralia Tarra, *Admin Sec*
EMP: 10
SALES (est): 1MM **Privately Held**
SIC: 2448 Pallets, wood

(P-4391)
PALLETS UNLIMITED INC
2390 Athens Ave, Lincoln (95648-9508)
P.O. Box 1656 (95648-1443)
PHONE..................916 408-1914
Nick Mehalakis, *President*
EMP: 18 EST: 2010
SALES (est): 3MM **Privately Held**
SIC: 2448 Pallets, wood

(P-4392)
PREFERRED PALLETS INC
288 E Santa Ana Ave, Bloomington
(92316-2918)
P.O. Box 1652, Rancho Cucamonga
(91729-1652)
PHONE..................909 875-7540
Laura Gonzalez, *President*
EMP: 12
SQ FT: 2,000
SALES (est): 1.9MM **Privately Held**
SIC: 2448 7699 Pallets, wood; pallet re-
pair

(P-4393)
PREMIUM PALLET INC
2000 Pomona Blvd, Pomona (91768-3323)
PHONE..................909 868-9621
Agusting Perez, *President*
EMP: 10
SALES (est): 1.6MM **Privately Held**
SIC: 2448 Pallets, wood & wood with metal

(P-4394)
PRIORITY PALLET INC
1060 E Third St, Beaumont (92223-3020)
PHONE..................951 769-9399
Raymond Guiterrez, *President*
EMP: 150
SALES (est): 16.2MM **Privately Held**
SIC: 2448 Pallets, wood

(P-4395)
RH PRODUCTS INC
Also Called: Rh Wood Products
6756 Central Ave Ste E, Newark
(94560-5923)
P.O. Box 1188 (94560-6188)
PHONE..................510 794-6676
Richard Huetteman, *President*
EMP: 30
SQ FT: 23,000
SALES: 1.5MM **Privately Held**
SIC: 2448 Pallets, wood & metal combina-
tion

(P-4396)
RM PALLETS INC
2512 Paulson Rd, Turlock (95380)
PHONE..................209 632-9887
Georgina Ceja, *CEO*
EMP: 15 EST: 2015
SALES (est): 173.2K **Privately Held**
SIC: 2448 Pallets, wood & wood with metal

(P-4397)
ROGER R CARUSO ENTERPRISES INC
Also Called: Century Pallets
2911 Norton Ave, Lynwood (90262-1810)
PHONE..................714 778-6006
Roger R Caruso, *President*
Rose Caruso, *Admin Sec*
▲ EMP: 20
SQ FT: 92,000
SALES (est): 3.2MM **Privately Held**
WEB: www.centurypallet.com
SIC: 2448 Pallets, wood

(P-4398)
SATCO INC (PA)
1601 E El Segundo Blvd, El Segundo
(90245-4334)
PHONE..................310 322-4719
Micheal Proctor, *President*
Vincent Voong, *COO*
Richard Weis, *CFO*
Mary Looker, *Admin Sec*
Chris Remensperger, *Info Tech Mgr*
▲ EMP: 125 EST: 1968
SQ FT: 27,000
SALES (est): 66.7MM **Privately Held**
WEB: www.satco-inc.com
SIC: 2448 Cargo containers, wood & metal
combination

(P-4399)
SELMA PALLET INC
1651 Pacific St, Selma (93662-9336)
P.O. Box 615 (93662-0615)
PHONE..................559 896-7171
Lupe Romero, *President*
Vera Romero, *Vice Pres*
Lynette Romero Wilson, *Admin Sec*
EMP: 50
SQ FT: 1,000
SALES (est): 9.6MM **Privately Held**
SIC: 2448 Pallets, wood; skids, wood

(P-4400)
SONOMA PACIFIC COMPANY LLC
1180 Fremont Dr, Sonoma (95476-9257)
P.O. Box 1251 (95476-1251)
PHONE..................707 938-2877
Scott Gillum, *Branch Mgr*
EMP: 60
SQ FT: 10,000
SALES (est): 8.3MM
SALES (corp-wide): 8.2MM **Privately Held**
WEB: www.sonpac.com
SIC: 2448 Pallets, wood
PA: Sonoma Pacific Company, Llc
100 W Canyon Crest Rd # 204
Alpine UT 84004
972 899-5980

(P-4401)
STANDARD LUMBER COMPANY INC (HQ)
Also Called: United Wholesale Lumber Co
8009 W Doe Ave, Visalia (93291-9284)
PHONE..................559 651-2037
Thomas J Thayer, *CEO*
John Garcia, *Manager*
Adele M Greene, *Manager*

EMP: 35
SQ FT: 10,000
SALES: 15.1MM
SALES (corp-wide): 222.6MM **Privately Held**
WEB: www.uwlco.com
SIC: 2448 2441 Pallets, wood; nailed
wood boxes & shook
PA: Fruit Growers Supply Company Inc
27770 N Entrmt Dr Fl 3 Flr 3
Valencia CA 91355
661 290-8704

(P-4402)
TRIPLE A PALLETS INC
Also Called: Ayala and Son Pallets
3555 S Academy Ave, Sanger
(93657-9566)
P.O. Box 1380 (93657-1380)
PHONE..................559 313-7636
Arturo Ayala, *Principal*
EMP: 15
SALES (est): 710.2K **Privately Held**
SIC: 2448 Pallets, wood

(P-4403)
UNITED PALLET SERVICES INC
4043 Crows Landing Rd, Modesto
(95358-9404)
PHONE..................209 538-5844
Wayne Randall, *President*
Darrel Roberson, *Vice Pres*
Amber McMahon, *Admin Sec*
Callen Cochran, *Business Mgr*
Ryan Roberson, *Sales Staff*
EMP: 150
SQ FT: 46,884
SALES (est): 26.3MM **Privately Held**
WEB: www.palts4u.com
SIC: 2448 7699 Pallets, wood; pallet re-
pair

(P-4404)
VILLA PALLET LLC
6756 Central Ave, Hayward (94544)
PHONE..................510 794-6676
Pati Patrick, *Office Mgr*
EMP: 14 EST: 2010
SALES (est): 903.2K **Privately Held**
SIC: 2448 Wood pallets & skids

(P-4405)
WALKER STREET PALLETS LLC
801 Ohlone Pkwy, Watsonville
(95076-7016)
P.O. Box 2568 (95077-2568)
PHONE..................831 724-6088
Rick Thayer,
EMP: 15
SQ FT: 1,200
SALES: 4MM **Privately Held**
SIC: 2448 Pallets, wood

(P-4406)
WEST COAST PALLETS INC
680 Janopaul Ave, Modesto (95351-3983)
PHONE..................209 524-3587
Gabriela Perez, *CEO*
EMP: 12
SQ FT: 87,120
SALES (est): 446.8K **Privately Held**
SIC: 2448 Wood pallets & skids

(P-4407)
WESTERN PLLET SUP LGISTICS LLC
7675 W 11th St, Tracy (95304-8831)
P.O. Box 1208 (95378-1208)
PHONE..................209 836-1968
Justine Quinton, *Mng Member*
EMP: 10
SALES (est): 1.5MM **Privately Held**
SIC: 2448 Wood pallets & skids

(P-4408)
WESTSIDE PALLET INC
2138 L St, Newman (95360)
P.O. Box 786 (95360-0786)
PHONE..................209 862-3941
Bernadine Rocha, *President*
Carolyn Beach, *Vice Pres*
EMP: 55 EST: 1994
SQ FT: 10,000
SALES: 7MM **Privately Held**
SIC: 2448 Pallets, wood; skids, wood

(P-4409)
WILMINGTON WOODWORKS INC
318 E C St, Wilmington (90744-6614)
P.O. Box 581 (90748-0581)
PHONE..................310 834-1015
Ronald Young, *President*
Pat Mace, *Shareholder*
EMP: 25
SALES (est): 2.9MM **Privately Held**
WEB: www.wilmwoodworks.com
SIC: 2448 Pallets, wood

2449 Wood Containers, NEC

(P-4410)
ADVANCED PACKAGING & CRATING
15432 Electronic Ln, Huntington Beach
(92649-1334)
PHONE..................714 892-1702
Tippi Longo, *President*
EMP: 10
SQ FT: 6,000
SALES (est): 1.3MM **Privately Held**
SIC: 2449 4783 Containers, plywood &
veneer wood; packing goods for shipping

(P-4411)
APEX DRUM COMPANY INC
Also Called: Apex Container Services
6226 Ferguson Dr, Commerce
(90022-5399)
PHONE..................323 721-8994
Abe Michlin, *CEO*
Sybil Flom, *Admin Sec*
Noah Flom, *Director*
EMP: 19
SQ FT: 40,000
SALES (est): 3.5MM **Privately Held**
WEB: www.apexdrum.com
SIC: 2449 5085 Containers, plywood &
veneer wood; shipping cases & drums,
wood: wirebound & plywood; cooperage
stock; drums, new or reconditioned

(P-4412)
BACKYARD UNLIMITED (PA)
4765 Pacific St, Rocklin (95677-2407)
PHONE..................916 630-7433
Nathan Martin, *Principal*
EMP: 13
SALES (est): 1.9MM **Privately Held**
SIC: 2449 Chicken coops (crates), wood:
wirebound

(P-4413)
BROWN WOOD PRODUCTS INC
310 Devonshire Blvd, San Carlos
(94070-1633)
PHONE..................650 593-9875
Richard Russell, *President*
Bonnie Russell, *Vice Pres*
EMP: 32
SQ FT: 35,000
SALES (est): 1.4MM **Privately Held**
SIC: 2449 5084 2441 Shipping cases &
drums, wood: wirebound & plywood; in-
dustrial machinery & equipment; nailed
wood boxes & shook

(P-4414)
CORRWOOD CONTAINERS
7182 Rasmussen Ave, Visalia
(93291-9405)
P.O. Box 670, Goshen (93227-0670)
PHONE..................559 651-0335
Don Nepinsky, *President*
Candace Nepinsky, *Corp Secy*
▲ EMP: 31
SQ FT: 70,000
SALES: 16MM **Privately Held**
SIC: 2449 Shipping cases, wood: wire-
bound

(P-4415)
DEMPTOS NAPA COOPERAGE (HQ)
1050 Soscol Ferry Rd, NAPA (94558-6228)
PHONE..................707 257-2628
Jerome Francois, *President*
William Jamieson, *Vice Pres*
◆ EMP: 32 EST: 1982

SQ FT: 27,500
SALES (est): 7.3MM
SALES (corp-wide): 46MM **Privately
Held**
WEB: www.demptosusa.com
SIC: **2449** 5085 Barrels, wood: coopered;
barrels, new or reconditioned
PA: Tonnellerie Francois Freres
Tonnellerie Daniel Chapelle
Saint-Romain 21190
966 876-052

(P-4416)
INNERSTAVE LLC
Also Called: Custom Cooperage Innerstave
21660 8th St E Ste B, Sonoma
(95476-2828)
PHONE..................................707 996-8781
Brian Daw,
Carl Dillon, *General Mgr*
Jacques Dowd, *General Mgr*
Alicia McBride, *General Mgr*
Candy Vanhemert, *Controller*
◆ EMP: 28
SALES (est): 5.4MM **Privately Held**
WEB: www.innerstave.com
SIC: **2449** 5085 5182 Wood containers;
commercial containers; wine & distilled
beverages

(P-4417)
**JDC DEVELOPMENT GROUP
INC**
Also Called: Dggr Packaging Crating & Foam
1321 N Blue Gum St, Anaheim
(92806-1750)
PHONE..................................714 575-1108
Joseph Dibenedetto Jr, *President*
Joseph Di Benedetto Jr, *President*
EMP: 35
SALES (est): 3.7MM **Privately Held**
WEB: www.jdpack.com
SIC: **2449** 2631 Rectangular boxes &
crates, wood; container, packaging &
boxboard

(P-4418)
JOHN DANIEL GONZALEZ
Also Called: Custom Wood Products
13458 E Industrial Dr, Parlier (93648-9678)
P.O. Box 783 (93648-0783)
PHONE..................................559 646-6621
John Daniel Gonzalez, *Owner*
Jennifer Gonzalez, *Co-Owner*
EMP: 43
SQ FT: 14,000
SALES (est): 2.9MM **Privately Held**
SIC: **2449** Wood containers

(P-4419)
**JOHNSTONS TRADING POST
INC**
11 N Pioneer Ave, Woodland (95776-5907)
PHONE..................................530 661-6152
James B Johnston, *CEO*
Cary Johnston, *Vice Pres*
Gloria Johnston, *Admin Sec*
EMP: 50
SQ FT: 112,000
SALES (est): 8.4MM **Privately Held**
SIC: **2449** 4225 Wood containers; general
warehousing & storage

(P-4420)
LESTER BOX INC
Also Called: Lester Box & Manufacturing
1470 Seabright Ave, Long Beach
(90813-1152)
PHONE..................................562 437-5123
Steven S Amato, *President*
EMP: 12
SQ FT: 10,360
SALES (est): 2.1MM **Privately Held**
WEB: www.lesterbox.com
SIC: **2449** Boxes, wood: wirebound

(P-4421)
MARIBA CORPORATION
158 N Glendora Ave Ste W, Glendora
(91741-3352)
PHONE..................................626 963-6775
Ray Malki, *CEO*
Richard Malki, *President*
EMP: 10
SQ FT: 10,000

SALES (est): 820K **Privately Held**
WEB: www.mariba.com
SIC: **2449** Wood containers

(P-4422)
OBENTEC INC
Also Called: Laptop Lunches
500 Chestnut St Ste 225, Santa Cruz
(95060-3675)
PHONE..................................831 457-0301
Tammy Pelstring, *President*
Amy Hemmert, *President*
Summer Cornish, *Marketing Staff*
▲ EMP: 10
SQ FT: 1,000
SALES (est): 1.3MM **Privately Held**
SIC: **2449** 2731 Food containers, wood:
wirebound; book publishing

(P-4423)
OMEGA CASE COMPANY INC
2231 N Hollywood Way, Burbank
(91505-1113)
PHONE..................................818 238-9263
Omar Gonzales, *Owner*
Cris Vargas, *Opers Mgr*
Randy Velasquez, *Sales Staff*
EMP: 30
SALES (est): 4MM **Privately Held**
WEB: www.omegacase.com
SIC: **2449** Shipping cases & drums, wood:
wirebound & plywood

(P-4424)
PICNIC AT ASCOT INC
3237 W 131st St, Hawthorne (90250-5514)
PHONE..................................310 674-3098
Paul Whitlock, *President*
Jill Brown, *Vice Pres*
Elsa Laguna, *Marketing Staff*
◆ EMP: 30
SQ FT: 20,000
SALES (est): 6.1MM **Privately Held**
WEB: www.picnicatascot.com
SIC: **2449** 5947 Baskets: fruit & vegetable,
round stave, till, etc.; gift, novelty & sou-
venir shop

(P-4425)
RED RIVER LUMBER CO
Also Called: Barrel Merchants
2959 Saint Helena Hwy N, Saint Helena
(94574-9703)
PHONE..................................707 963-1251
EMP: 20
SQ FT: 1,200
SALES (est): 1.6MM **Privately Held**
SIC: **2449**

(P-4426)
SAN JUAN SPECIALTY PDTS INC
4149 Avenida De La Plata, Oceanside
(92056-6002)
PHONE..................................888 342-8262
Barney Rigney, *President*
Kathryn Rigney, *Admin Sec*
EMP: 11
SQ FT: 1,900
SALES (est): 51.8K **Privately Held**
SIC: **2449** Wood containers

(P-4427)
**SEGUIN MOREAU HOLDINGS
INC (PA)**
151 Camino Dorado, NAPA (94558-6213)
PHONE..................................707 252-3408
Thomas Martin, *President*
Justin Moye, *Sales Staff*
▲ EMP: 57
SALES (est): 6.5MM **Privately Held**
SIC: **2449** 5085 Barrels, wood: coopered;
barrels, new or reconditioned

(P-4428)
**SPECILIZED PACKG SOLUTIONS
INC**
Also Called: Specilzed Packg Solutions-Wood
38505 Cherry St Ste H, Newark
(94560-4700)
P.O. Box 3042, Fremont (94539-0304)
PHONE..................................510 494-5670
Karen Besso, *CEO*
Terrence Besso, *Vice Pres*
Lisa Matthews, *Executive*
▲ EMP: 50
SQ FT: 63,000

SALES (est): 11.8MM **Privately Held**
SIC: **2449** 2653 5113 3086 Rectangular
boxes & crates, wood; sheets, corrugated: made from purchased materials;
corrugated & solid fiber boxes; plastics
foam products

(P-4429)
T & R LUMBER COMPANY (PA)
8685 Etiwanda Ave, Rancho Cucamonga
(91739-9611)
P.O. Box 2484 (91729-2484)
PHONE..................................909 899-2383
Cheryl L Guardia, *President*
Philip Guardia, *Vice Pres*
Dennis Anderson, *Opers Staff*
Nicole Jackson, *Sales Associate*
Steve Reynolds, *Associate*
▲ EMP: 73
SQ FT: 4,600
SALES (est): 11.9MM **Privately Held**
SIC: **2449** 2499 2441 Boxes, wood: wire-
bound; handles, poles, dowels & stakes:
wood; nailed wood boxes & shook

(P-4430)
**TONNELLERIE FRANCAISE
FRENCH C**
Also Called: Nadalie USA
1401 Tubbs Ln, Calistoga (94515-9726)
P.O. Box 798 (94515-0798)
PHONE..................................707 942-9301
Jean Jacques Nadalie, *CEO*
Alain Poisson, *Vice Pres*
Frederic Pavon, *Prdtn Mgr*
Kevin Andre, *Sales Staff*
April Moulton, *Sales Staff*
▲ EMP: 18
SQ FT: 12,000
SALES (est): 3.4MM
SALES (corp-wide): 32.4MM **Privately
Held**
WEB: www.nadalieusa.com
SIC: **2449** Barrels, wood: coopered
PA: Tonnelerie Nadalie
99 Rue Lafont
Ludon-Medoc 33290
557 100-200

(P-4431)
**TONNELLERIE RADOUX USA
INC**
480 Aviation Blvd, Santa Rosa
(95403-1069)
PHONE..................................707 284-2888
Christen Liarg, *President*
Phillip Doray, *Corp Secy*
Janette Bass, *Administration*
Maud Fitzpatrick, *Technology*
Andrea Chappell, *Sales Associate*
▲ EMP: 17
SQ FT: 25,000
SALES (est): 3.2MM
SALES (corp-wide): 46MM **Privately
Held**
WEB: www.tonnellieradoux.com
SIC: **2449** Vats, wood: coopered
HQ: Tonnelerie Radoux
10 Avenue Faidherbe
Jonzac 17500
546 480-065

(P-4432)
WINE COUNTRY CASES INC
621 Airpark Rd, NAPA (94558-6272)
PHONE..................................707 967-4805
Dan C Pina, *President*
EMP: 87
SQ FT: 5,500
SALES (est): 6.7MM **Privately Held**
WEB: www.winecountrycases.com
SIC: **2449** 2657 Butter crates, wood: wire-
bound; folding paperboard boxes

(P-4433)
WOOD BOX SPECIALTIES INC
23308 Kidder St, Hayward (94545-1633)
PHONE..................................510 786-1600
Terry Tressell, *President*
EMP: 10
SALES: 500K **Privately Held**
WEB: www.woodboxspecialties.com
SIC: **2449** 5199 2541 Wood containers;
gift baskets; store & office display cases
& fixtures

(P-4434)
**WOOD-N-WOOD PRODUCTS
CAL INC (PA)**
2247 W Birch Ave, Fresno (93711-0442)
PHONE..................................559 896-3636
Rodney Allen Scary, *CEO*
Susan Scarry, *Treasurer*
EMP: 38
SQ FT: 15,000
SALES (est): 3.9MM **Privately Held**
SIC: **2449** Wood containers

(P-4435)
**WOOD-N-WOOD PRODUCTS
CAL INC**
13598 S Golden State Blvd, Selma (93662)
PHONE..................................559 896-3636
Rick Murillo, *Manager*
EMP: 20
SALES (corp-wide): 3.9MM **Privately
Held**
SIC: **2449** Containers, plywood & veneer
wood
PA: Wood-N-Wood Products Of California,
Inc.
2247 W Birch Ave
Fresno CA 93711
559 896-3636

(P-4436)
WOOD-N-WOOD PRODUCTS INC
Also Called: Wood-N-Wood Products Cal
2247 W Birch Ave, Fresno (93711-0442)
PHONE..................................559 896-3636
Allen Scarry, *Branch Mgr*
EMP: 15
SALES (corp-wide): 5.3MM **Privately
Held**
SIC: **2449** Rectangular boxes & crates,
wood
PA: Wood-N-Wood Products Inc
3750 S Hwy 287
Corsicana TX
-

2451 Mobile Homes

(P-4437)
10100 HOLDINGS INC (PA)
10100 Santa Monica Blvd # 1050, Los An-
geles (90067-4003)
PHONE..................................310 552-0705
Ernest L Thesman, *President*
EMP: 12
SALES (est): 20.7MM **Privately Held**
SIC: **2451** 6515 Mobile homes; mobile
home site operators

(P-4438)
BERGER MODULAR
350 Crescent Dr, Galt (95632-1605)
PHONE..................................209 329-9368
Kimberly E Berger, *Owner*
EMP: 11
SALES: 500K **Privately Held**
SIC: **2451** Mobile homes, personal or pri-
vate use

(P-4439)
CASTAIC LAKE R V PARK INC
Also Called: Castaic R V Park
31540 Ridge Route Rd, Castaic
(91384-3358)
PHONE..................................661 257-3340
Arthur Staudigel, *President*
C Dan Foote, *Treasurer*
Clyde Widrig, *Vice Pres*
Robert C Tallent, *Admin Sec*
EMP: 15
SALES (est): 1.7MM **Privately Held**
WEB: www.castaiclakervpark.com
SIC: **2451** 5411 7011 5921 Mobile
homes; grocery stores, independent; ho-
tels & motels; liquor stores

(P-4440)
CAVCO INDUSTRIES INC
Also Called: Fleetwood Homes
7007 Jurupa Ave, Riverside (92504-1015)
P.O. Box 49991 (92514-1991)
PHONE..................................951 688-5353
Mike Hayes, *Branch Mgr*
EMP: 215

SALES (corp-wide): 962.7MM **Publicly Held**
SIC: 2451 2452 Mobile homes; prefabricated buildings, wood
PA: Cavco Industries, Inc.
3636 N Central Ave # 1200
Phoenix AZ 85012
602 256-6263

(P-4441)
CLAYTON HOMES INC
Also Called: CMH Manufacturing West
9998 Old Placerville Rd, Sacramento (95827-3557)
PHONE................................916 363-2681
Alen Limley, *Branch Mgr*
EMP: 13
SALES (corp-wide): 225.3B **Publicly Held**
SIC: 2451 Mobile homes, personal or private use
HQ: Clayton Homes, Inc.
5000 Clayton Rd
Maryville TN 37804
865 380-3000

(P-4442)
CLAYTON HOMES INC
Also Called: Golden West Homes
3100 N Perris Blvd, Perris (92571-3242)
PHONE................................951 657-1611
John Drean, *Branch Mgr*
EMP: 150
SALES (corp-wide): 225.3B **Publicly Held**
WEB: www.clayton.net
SIC: 2451 Mobile homes, personal or private use
HQ: Clayton Homes, Inc.
5000 Clayton Rd
Maryville TN 37804
865 380-3000

(P-4443)
D-MAC INC
1105 E Discovery Ln, Anaheim (92801-1121)
PHONE................................714 808-3918
David A Wade, *Owner*
Leo Hernandez, *Controller*
Mike Marks, *Sales Staff*
EMP: 26 EST: 1998
SALES (est): 4.4MM **Privately Held**
WEB: www.d-mac.com
SIC: 2451 5039 5032 Mobile home frames; structural assemblies, prefabricated: non-wood; paving materials; plastering materials

(P-4444)
DVELE INC
25525 Redlands Blvd, Loma Linda (92354-2009)
P.O. Box 1710 (92354-0150)
PHONE................................909 796-2561
EMP: 45
SALES (corp-wide): 2.9MM **Privately Held**
SIC: 2451 2452 Mobile homes, except recreational; prefabricated buildings, wood
PA: Dvele, Inc.
2201 Market St
San Francisco CA
-

(P-4445)
DVELE OMEGA CORPORATION
Also Called: Hallmark Southwest
25525 Redlands Blvd, Loma Linda (92354-2009)
P.O. Box 1710 (92354-0150)
PHONE................................909 796-2561
Luca Brammer, *President*
EMP: 100
SQ FT: 5,000
SALES (est): 6.6MM **Privately Held**
SIC: 2451 2452 Mobile homes, personal or private use; mobile homes, industrial or commercial use; prefabricated wood buildings; modular homes, prefabricated, wood; panels & sections, prefabricated, wood

(P-4446)
FLEETWOOD ENTERPRISES INC
351 Corporate Terrace Cir, Corona (92879-6028)
PHONE................................951 750-1971
Kent Wemsel, *Branch Mgr*
EMP: 402
SALES (corp-wide): 2.6B **Privately Held**
SIC: 2451 Mobile homes, personal or private use
HQ: Fleetwood Enterprises, Inc.
1351 Pomona Rd Ste 230
Corona CA 92882
951 354-3000

(P-4447)
FLEETWOOD HOMES CALIFORNIA INC (DH)
7007 Jurupa Ave, Riverside (92504-1015)
P.O. Box 7638 (92513-7638)
PHONE................................951 351-2494
Elvin Smith, *President*
Lyle N Larkin, *Treasurer*
Boyd R Plowman, *Exec VP*
Roger L Howsmon, *Senior VP*
Forrest D Theobald, *Senior VP*
▲ EMP: 28
SQ FT: 262,900
SALES (est): 30.5MM
SALES (corp-wide): 2.6B **Privately Held**
SIC: 2451 Mobile homes
HQ: Fleetwood Enterprises, Inc.
1351 Pomona Rd Ste 230
Corona CA 92882
951 354-3000

(P-4448)
FLEETWOOD HOMES OF FLORIDA (DH)
3125 Myers St, Riverside (92503-5527)
P.O. Box 7638 (92513-7638)
PHONE................................909 261-4274
Edward B Caudill, *President*
Boyd R Plowman, *CFO*
Lyle N Larkin, *Treasurer*
Forrest D Theobald, *Senior VP*
▲ EMP: 16
SQ FT: 262,900
SALES (est): 6.2MM
SALES (corp-wide): 2.6B **Privately Held**
SIC: 2451 Mobile homes, except recreational
HQ: Fleetwood Enterprises, Inc.
1351 Pomona Rd Ste 230
Corona CA 92882
951 354-3000

(P-4449)
FLEETWOOD HOMES OF IDAHO INC
3125 Myers St, Riverside (92503-5527)
P.O. Box 7698 (92513-7698)
PHONE................................951 354-3000
Edward B Caudill, *President*
Boyd R Plowman, *CFO*
Lyle Larkin, *Treasurer*
Roger L Howsmon, *Senior VP*
Forrest D Theobald, *Senior VP*
EMP: 200
SQ FT: 262,900
SALES (est): 15.4MM
SALES (corp-wide): 2.6B **Privately Held**
SIC: 2451 Mobile homes
HQ: Fleetwood Enterprises, Inc.
1351 Pomona Rd Ste 230
Corona CA 92882
951 354-3000

(P-4450)
FLEETWOOD HOMES OF KENTUCKY (DH)
1351 Pomona Rd Ste 230, Corona (92882-7165)
PHONE................................800 688-1745
Elden L Smith, *Principal*
Boyd R Plowman, *CFO*
Roger L Howsmon, *Treasurer*
Forrest D Theobald, *Senior VP*
Lyle N Larkin, *Vice Pres*
EMP: 13 EST: 1998
SALES (est): 10.9MM
SALES (corp-wide): 2.6B **Privately Held**
SIC: 2451 Mobile homes

HQ: Fleetwood Enterprises, Inc.
1351 Pomona Rd Ste 230
Corona CA 92882
951 354-3000

(P-4451)
FLEETWOOD HOMES OF VIRGINIA
3125 Myers St, Riverside (92503-5527)
P.O. Box 7638 (92513-7638)
PHONE................................951 351-3500
Elden L Smith, *Principal*
Edward B Caudill, *President*
Boyd R Plowman, *CFO*
Lyle N Larkin, *Treasurer*
Roger L Howsmon, *Senior VP*
EMP: 180 EST: 1968
SQ FT: 262,900
SALES (est): 12MM
SALES (corp-wide): 2.6B **Privately Held**
SIC: 2451 Mobile homes
HQ: Fleetwood Enterprises, Inc.
1351 Pomona Rd Ste 230
Corona CA 92882
951 354-3000

(P-4452)
INCEPTION HOMES INC
Also Called: Advantage Homes
12640 Beach Blvd, Stanton (90680-4008)
PHONE................................714 890-1883
Tom Randall, *Branch Mgr*
EMP: 10
SALES (corp-wide): 6.9MM **Privately Held**
SIC: 2451 Mobile homes
PA: Inception Homes, Inc.
2890 Monterey Hwy
San Jose CA 95111
408 239-4859

2452 Prefabricated Wood Buildings & Cmpnts

(P-4453)
ADAPTIVE SHELTERS LLC
427 E 17th St Ste F268, Costa Mesa (92627-3201)
PHONE................................949 923-5444
Matthew Bays, *Mng Member*
Dave Arfin, *Mng Member*
EMP: 50
SALES: 15MM **Privately Held**
SIC: 2452 Modular homes, prefabricated, wood

(P-4454)
ALAN PRE-FAB BUILDING CORP
17817 Evelyn Ave, Gardena (90248-3735)
PHONE................................310 538-0333
Toll Free:................................888 -
John W Andrus, *President*
Bill Andrus, *Vice Pres*
Bret Andrus, *Vice Pres*
Ann Andrus, *Admin Sec*
EMP: 13
SQ FT: 49,000
SALES (est): 1.8MM **Privately Held**
WEB: www.alanprefab.com
SIC: 2452 7359 Prefabricated wood buildings; equipment rental & leasing

(P-4455)
ALL AMERICAN MODULAR LLC
750 Spaans Dr Ste F, Galt (95632-8609)
PHONE................................209 744-0400
Ranse Gale, *Branch Mgr*
EMP: 12
SALES (corp-wide): 2.2MM **Privately Held**
SIC: 2452 Prefabricated wood buildings
PA: All American Modular Llc
13631 Montfort Ave
Herald CA 95638
209 747-1788

(P-4456)
AMERICAN MODULAR SYSTEMS INC
Also Called: AMS
787 Spreckels Ave, Manteca (95336-6002)
PHONE................................209 825-1921
Daniel Sarich, *President*
Tony Sarich, *Vice Pres*

EMP: 100
SQ FT: 85,000
SALES (est): 37.1MM **Privately Held**
SIC: 2452 1542 Modular homes, prefabricated, wood; nonresidential construction

(P-4457)
APPLIED POLYTECH SYSTEMS INC
Also Called: A P S
26000 Springbrook Ave # 102, Santa Clarita (91350-2592)
PHONE................................818 504-9261
Christine Wagner, *President*
Chris Wagner, *Data Proc Dir*
EMP: 30
SQ FT: 6,000
SALES (est): 4.1MM **Privately Held**
SIC: 2452 Prefabricated wood buildings

(P-4458)
CALIFORNIA LEISURE PRODUCTS
265 Thomas St, Ukiah (95482-5823)
PHONE................................707 462-2106
Greg Farmer, *Owner*
EMP: 13
SALES (est): 1.2MM **Privately Held**
WEB: www.califleisureproducts.com
SIC: 2452 5999 Prefabricated buildings, wood; spas & hot tubs

(P-4459)
GARY DOUPNIK MANUFACTURING INC
3237 Rippey Rd, Loomis (95650-7654)
P.O. Box 527 (95650-0527)
PHONE................................916 652-9291
Sherie Edgar, *President*
Gary Doupnik Sr, *Treasurer*
Gary Doupnik Jr, *Vice Pres*
Jt Doupnik, *Vice Pres*
Kirtus Doupnik, *Vice Pres*
EMP: 60
SQ FT: 4,000
SALES (est): 6.9MM **Privately Held**
WEB: www.gdmfg.com
SIC: 2452 3448 Prefabricated buildings, wood; prefabricated metal buildings

(P-4460)
GLOBAL DIVERSIFIED INDS INC (PA)
1200 Airport Dr, Chowchilla (93610-9344)
P.O. Box 32, Atwater (95301-0032)
PHONE................................559 665-5800
Phillip Hamilton, *President*
Adam N Debard, *Corp Secy*
EMP: 50
SQ FT: 100,000
SALES (est): 5.3MM **Privately Held**
WEB: www.gdvi.net
SIC: 2452 Modular homes, prefabricated, wood

(P-4461)
GLOBAL MODULAR INC (HQ)
1200 Airport Dr, Chowchilla (93610-9344)
P.O. Box 369 (93610-0369)
PHONE................................559 665-5800
Adam De Bard, *President*
Milo King, *Admin Sec*
EMP: 30
SALES: 4.8MM
SALES (corp-wide): 5.3MM **Privately Held**
WEB: www.gdvi.net
SIC: 2452 Prefabricated wood buildings
PA: Global Diversified Industries, Inc.
1200 Airport Dr
Chowchilla CA 93610
559 665-5800

(P-4462)
INTERMODAL STRUCTURES INC
Also Called: Imod Structures
251 Bagley St, Vallejo (94592-1057)
PHONE................................415 887-2211
Craig Severance, *CEO*
John Diserens,
Reed B Walker,
EMP: 13
SQ FT: 600

SALES (est): 1.7MM **Privately Held**
SIC: 2452 Modular homes, prefabricated, wood

(P-4463)
JET CUTTING SOLUTIONS INC
10853 Bell Ct, Rancho Cucamonga (91730-4835)
PHONE..................................909 948-2424
Louis Mammooito, *CEO*
Thomas Ribas, *President*
EMP: 10
SALES (est): 2.1MM **Privately Held**
SIC: 2452 Prefabricated wood buildings

(P-4464)
MCCARTHY RANCH
15425 Los Gatos Blvd # 102, Los Gatos (95032-2541)
PHONE..................................408 356-2300
Joe McCarthy, *Owner*
EMP: 12
SALES (est): 2.1MM **Privately Held**
SIC: 2452 Farm & agricultural buildings, prefabricated wood

(P-4465)
PLH PRODUCTS INC
6655 Knott Ave, Buena Park (90620-1129)
PHONE..................................714 739-6622
Seung Woo Lee, *Ch of Bd*
Kyung Min Park, *President*
Won Yong Lee, *CFO*
◆ EMP: 29
SALES: 38.5MM **Privately Held**
WEB: www.healthmatesauna.com
SIC: 2452 2449 5999 Sauna rooms, prefabricated, wood; hot tubs, wood; sauna equipment & supplies

(P-4466)
TUFF SHED INC
931 Cadillac Ct, Milpitas (95035-3053)
PHONE..................................408 935-8833
Rod Miller, *Manager*
EMP: 11
SALES (corp-wide): 292.4MM **Privately Held**
SIC: 2452 Prefabricated wood buildings
PA: Tuff Shed, Inc.
1777 S Harrison St # 600
Denver CO 80210
303 753-8833

(P-4467)
TUFF SHED INC
1401 Franquette Ave, Concord (94520-7956)
PHONE..................................925 681-3492
Penny Gerald, *Branch Mgr*
EMP: 13
SALES (corp-wide): 292.4MM **Privately Held**
SIC: 2452 Prefabricated wood buildings
PA: Tuff Shed, Inc.
1777 S Harrison St # 600
Denver CO 80210
303 753-8833

(P-4468)
UNITED PARTITION SYSTEMS INC
2180 S Hellman Ave, Ontario (91761-7700)
PHONE..................................909 947-1077
Mike Kaminski, *CEO*
Robert Kaminski, *CFO*
Bryan Leisure, *Regional Mgr*
Sue Kaminski, *Admin Sec*
EMP: 10
SQ FT: 13,000
SALES (est): 2MM **Privately Held**
WEB: www.unitedpartition.com
SIC: 2452 3448 2541 1542 Prefabricated metal buildings; partitions for floor attachment, prefabricated, wood; commercial & office buildings, prefabricated erection; panels & sections, prefabricated, wood

(P-4469)
US CONTAINER AND HOUSING CO
22320 Fthill Blvd Ste 450, Hayward (94541)
PHONE..................................844 762-8242
Terry Keeney, *CEO*
Jerrold Johnson, *CFO*

EMP: 20 EST: 2014
SALES: 10MM **Privately Held**
SIC: 2452 1522 3444 1542 Panels & sections, prefabricated, wood; residential construction; metal housings, enclosures, casings & other containers; commercial & office building, new construction

(P-4470)
WALDEN STRUCTURES INC
1000 Bristol St N 126, Newport Beach (92660-8916)
PHONE..................................909 389-9100
Charlie Walden, *Owner*
Curtis H Claire, *COO*
Michael J Dominici, *CFO*
EMP: 89
SQ FT: 150,000
SALES (est): 68.9MM **Privately Held**
WEB: www.waldenstructures.com
SIC: 2452 Modular homes, prefabricated, wood

2491 Wood Preserving

(P-4471)
BLUE LAKE ROUNDSTOCK CO LLC
19195 Latona Rd, Anderson (96007-9421)
PHONE..................................530 515-7007
Robert Hambrecht,
Glenn Zane,
EMP: 12 EST: 2009
SQ FT: 500
SALES (est): 1.4MM **Privately Held**
SIC: 2491 Poles, posts & pilings: treated wood

(P-4472)
CALIFORNIA CASCADE INDUSTRIES
7512 14th Ave, Sacramento (95820-3539)
P.O. Box 130026 (95853-0026)
PHONE..................................916 736-3353
Stuart D Heath, *President*
Stu Heath, *President*
Richard Rose, *CFO*
Kyle Keaton, *Corp Secy*
Harvey Molatore, *General Mgr*
EMP: 200
SQ FT: 6,500
SALES (est): 67.7MM **Privately Held**
WEB: www.californiacascade.com
SIC: 2491 2421 Wood preserving; sawmills & planing mills, general
PA: Canwel Building Materials Group Ltd
1055 Georgia St W Suite 1100
Vancouver BC V6E 0
604 432-1400

(P-4473)
CALIFORNIA CASCADE-WOODLAND
Also Called: Western Wood Treating
1492 Churchill Downs Ave, Woodland (95776-6113)
P.O. Box 1443 (95776-1443)
PHONE..................................530 666-1261
Henry Feenstra, *President*
EMP: 15
SQ FT: 1,000
SALES (est): 3MM **Privately Held**
SIC: 2491 Structural lumber & timber, treated wood

(P-4474)
CHARLES JJ INC
Also Called: Used Pellet Co
4115 S Orange Ave, Fresno (93725-9367)
PHONE..................................559 264-6664
Jeffrey Seib, *President*
EMP: 40
SALES (est): 3.9MM **Privately Held**
SIC: 2491 Wood preserving

(P-4475)
COAST WOOD PRESERVING INC (PA)
600 W Glenwood Ave, Turlock (95380-6232)
P.O. Box 1805 (95381-1805)
PHONE..................................209 632-9931
Micheal Logsdon, *President*
Gene Piepila, *Corp Secy*
EMP: 11
SQ FT: 13,200
SALES (est): 1MM **Privately Held**
SIC: 2491 Wood preserving

(P-4476)
CONRAD WOOD PRESERVING CO
7085 Eddy Rd Unit C, Arbuckle (95912-9789)
PHONE..................................530 476-2894
Fred Noah, *Branch Mgr*
EMP: 14
SALES (corp-wide): 36.3MM **Privately Held**
SIC: 2491 Wood preserving
PA: Conrad Wood Preserving Co.
68765 Wildwood Rd
North Bend OR 97459
800 356-7146

(P-4477)
EAST BAY FIXTURE COMPANY
941 Aileen St, Oakland (94608-2805)
PHONE..................................510 652-4421
Richard Laible, *President*
Frances Laible, *Corp Secy*
Jenny Laible, *Supervisor*
EMP: 50
SQ FT: 32,000
SALES (est): 7.6MM **Privately Held**
WEB: www.ebfc.com
SIC: 2491 2541 Millwork, treated wood; office fixtures, wood

(P-4478)
JH BAXTER A CAL LTD PARTNR (PA)
1700 S El Camino Real, San Mateo (94402-3047)
P.O. Box 5902 (94402-5902)
PHONE..................................650 349-0201
Georgia B Krause, *Managing Prtnr*
Richard Keeley, *Partner*
Sandra Lavino, *Partner*
Robert Stockton, *Partner*
Paul Krotts, *Controller*
EMP: 50
SQ FT: 2,000
SALES (est): 7.2MM **Privately Held**
WEB: www.acza.com
SIC: 2491 Poles & pole crossarms, treated wood

(P-4479)
PACIFIC STATES TREATING INC
422 Mill St, Weed (96094-2261)
PHONE..................................530 938-4408
Roger A Burch, *President*
EMP: 12
SALES (est): 1.8MM **Privately Held**
SIC: 2491 Wood preserving

(P-4480)
PACIFIC WD PRSERVING-NEW STINE
5601 District Blvd, Bakersfield (93313-2129)
PHONE..................................661 617-6385
Richard Jackson, *President*
EMP: 19
SALES (est): 2.8MM **Privately Held**
SIC: 2491 Preserving (creosoting) of wood

(P-4481)
SC BLUWOOD INC
2604 El Camino Real Ste B, Carlsbad (92008-1205)
PHONE..................................909 519-5470
Stephen Conboy, *President*
EMP: 30
SALES (est): 1.6MM **Privately Held**
SIC: 2491 Structural lumber & timber, treated wood

(P-4482)
THUNDERBOLT SALES INC
3400 Patterson Rd, Riverbank (95367-2998)
P.O. Box 890 (95367-0890)
PHONE..................................209 869-4561
T W Ted Seybold, *President*
T W Seybold, *President*
Don De Vries, *Vice Pres*
Leonard Lovalvo, *Vice Pres*
EMP: 20
SALES (est): 2.1MM
SALES (corp-wide): 7.3MM **Privately Held**
SIC: 2491 Wood preserving
PA: Thunderbolt Wood Treating Co., Inc.
3400 Patterson Rd
Riverbank CA
209 869-4561

2493 Reconstituted Wood Prdts

(P-4483)
CALPLANT I LLC
6101 State Highway 162, Willows (95988)
P.O. Box 1338 (95988-1338)
PHONE..................................530 570-0542
Gerald Uhland, *CEO*
Chris Motley, *CFO*
James Boyd,
Suzy Boyd, *Manager*
EMP: 23 EST: 2008
SALES (est): 64.3K
SALES (corp-wide): 1.2MM **Privately Held**
SIC: 2493 Reconstituted wood products
PA: Calplant I Holdco, Llc
6101 State Highway 162
Willows CA 95988
530 570-0542

(P-4484)
CALPLANT I HOLDCO LLC (PA)
6101 State Highway 162, Willows (95988)
P.O. Box 1338 (95988-1338)
PHONE..................................530 570-0542
Gerald Uhland, *CEO*
Chris Motley, *CFO*
EMP: 23
SALES (est): 1.2MM **Privately Held**
SIC: 2493 Reconstituted wood products

(P-4485)
PANOLAM INDUSTRIES INTL INC
Also Called: Pionite
8535 Oakwood Pl Ste A, Rancho Cucamonga (91730-4864)
PHONE..................................909 581-1970
John Fulkerson, *Manager*
Zena Colwill, *Manager*
EMP: 20 **Privately Held**
SIC: 2493 Particleboard products
PA: Panolam Industries International, Inc.
1 Corporate Dr Ste 725
Shelton CT 06484

(P-4486)
REGARDS ENTERPRISES INC
Also Called: Quality Marble & Granite
731 S Taylor Ave, Ontario (91761-1847)
PHONE..................................909 983-0655
Evan Cohen, *CEO*
▲ EMP: 19
SQ FT: 95,000
SALES (est): 2.5MM **Privately Held**
SIC: 2493 3281 Marbleboard (stone face hard board); granite, cut & shaped

(P-4487)
STANDARD INDUSTRIES INC
Also Called: GAF Materials
11800 Industry Ave, Fontana (92337-6936)
PHONE..................................951 360-4274
H S Bray, *Manager*
Elizabeth Pardo, *Accounting Mgr*
Elizabeth M Logan, *Purchasing*
EMP: 119
SQ FT: 14,000
SALES (corp-wide): 2.5B **Privately Held**
SIC: 2493 2952 Insulation & roofing material, reconstituted wood; asphalt felts & coatings

PRODUCTS & SVCS

HQ: Standard Industries Inc.
1 Campus Dr
Parsippany NJ 07054

2499 Wood Prdts, NEC

(P-4488)
A E T C O INC
2825 Metropolitan Pl, Pomona
(91767-1853)
P.O. Box 458, San Dimas (91773-0458)
PHONE..........................909 593-2521
Anthony Taylor, *President*
Jeanne Shinogle, *Vice Pres*
Barbara Taylor, *Admin Sec*
EMP: 35
SQ FT: 12,500
SALES (est): 4.5MM **Privately Held**
WEB: www.aetcoinc.com
SIC: 2499 3429 3842 2326 Policemen's
clubs, wood; handcuffs & leg irons; surgical
appliances & supplies; men's & boys'
work clothing

(P-4489)
ALACO LADDER COMPANY
5167 G St, Chino (91710-5143)
PHONE..........................909 591-7561
Gil Jacobs, *President*
Mario Garcia, *Vice Pres*
▼ **EMP:** 25
SQ FT: 26,000
SALES (est): 2.1MM
SALES (corp-wide): 3.2MM **Privately Held**
SIC: 2499 3354 3499 Ladders, wood; aluminum
extruded products; metal ladders;
ladders, portable: metal
PA: B, E & P Enterprises, Llc
5167 G St
Chino CA 91710
909 591-7561

(P-4490)
AMARAL INDUSTRIES COMMON LAW
20993 Foothill Blvd 144, Hayward
(94541-1511)
PHONE..........................510 569-8669
C Tony Amaral, *Owner*
Delia Dagumo, *Co-Owner*
EMP: 52
SALES (est): 2.1MM **Privately Held**
SIC: 2499 8699 8412 Fencing, docks &
other outdoor wood structural products;
reading rooms & other cultural organizations;
museums & art galleries; museum

(P-4491)
APPLIED SILVER INC
26254 Eden Landing Rd, Hayward
(94545-3717)
PHONE..........................888 939-4747
Sean Morham, *CEO*
Elizabeth Hutt Pollard, *Ch of Bd*
Paul McCabe, *CFO*
Joyce Wang, *Office Mgr*
Keith Copenhagen, *Engineer*
EMP: 11
SALES (est): 1.1MM **Privately Held**
SIC: 2499 5719 Laundry products, wood;
linens

(P-4492)
B E & P ENTERPRISES LLC (PA)
Also Called: Alaco Ladder Company
5167 G St, Chino (91710-5143)
PHONE..........................909 591-7561
Mario Garcia, *Vice Pres*
Sue Ritchey, *Sales Executive*
Stephen Bernstein,
Fred Evans,
Gil Jacobs,
EMP: 25
SALES (est): 3.2MM **Privately Held**
SIC: 2499 3499 3354 Ladders, wood; ladders,
portable: metal; aluminum extruded
products

(P-4493)
BK SEMS USA INC
4 Executive Park Ste 270, Irvine (92614)
PHONE..........................949 390-7120

EMP: 19 **EST:** 2002
SALES (est): 3MM **Privately Held**
SIC: 2499

(P-4494)
BRENT-WOOD PRODUCTS INC
777 E Rosecrans Ave, Los Angeles
(90059-3563)
P.O. Box 59178 (90059-0178)
PHONE..........................800 400-7335
Lawrence D Hobbs, *CEO*
Birgitta Olin, *President*
Anna Pinili, *Corp Secy*
Jordan Hobbs, *Consultant*
▼ **EMP:** 30 **EST:** 1963
SQ FT: 26,000
SALES (est): 6.5MM **Privately Held**
SIC: 2499 Reels, plywood

(P-4495)
CALIFORNIA CEDAR PRODUCTS CO (PA)
2385 Arch Airport Rd # 500, Stockton
(95206-4403)
PHONE..........................209 932-5002
Charles Berolzheimer, *President*
Vincent Bricka, *COO*
Susan Macintyre, *CFO*
Troy White, *VP Finance*
Andrea Montgomery, *Accountant*
▲ **EMP:** 50 **EST:** 1920
SQ FT: 10,000
SALES (est): 81.2MM **Privately Held**
WEB: www.calcedar.com
SIC: 2499 Pencil slats, wood; logs of sawdust
& wood particles, pressed

(P-4496)
CARRIS REELS CALIFORNIA INC (HQ)
2100 W Almond Ave, Madera (93637-5203)
P.O. Box 88 (93639-0088)
PHONE..........................559 674-0804
William Carris, *Ch of Bd*
Dave Ferraro, *President*
David Fitzgerald, *CFO*
David Ferraro, *Vice Pres*
Linda Gallipo, *Asst Treas*
▲ **EMP:** 30 **EST:** 1966
SALES (est): 3.5MM **Privately Held**
SIC: 2499 2448 Spools, reels & pulleys:
wood; reels, plywood; pallets, wood

(P-4497)
CONTINENTAL COMPONENTS LLC
243 S Escondido Blvd, Escondido
(92025-4116)
PHONE..........................760 480-4420
Judd Lafountain, *Branch Mgr*
EMP: 15
SALES (corp-wide): 1.5MM **Privately Held**
SIC: 2499 Applicators, wood
PA: Continental Components, L.L.C.
5617 Ne Portland Hwy
Portland OR 97218
503 281-8701

(P-4498)
COOLING TOWER RESOURCES INC (PA)
Also Called: C T R
1470 Grove St, Healdsburg (95448-4700)
P.O. Box 159 (95448-0159)
PHONE..........................707 433-3900
Gordon Martin, *CEO*
Terri Martin, *Corp Secy*
Brad Pirrung, *Sales Executive*
Justin Davis, *Marketing Staff*
◆ **EMP:** 20
SQ FT: 1,200
SALES (est): 6.1MM **Privately Held**
WEB: www.cooltower.com
SIC: 2499 Cooling towers, wood or wood &
sheet metal combination

(P-4499)
CRI 2000 LP (PA)
Also Called: Lso
2245 San Diego Ave # 125, San Diego
(92110-2942)
PHONE..........................619 542-1975
Mitchell G Lynn, *Partner*
Mitchel Lynn, *Managing Prtnr*

Luis Torres, *General Mgr*
Rose Darrow, *Research*
Kristina Au, *Human Res Dir*
◆ **EMP:** 60
SQ FT: 10,000
SALES (est): 12.6MM **Privately Held**
SIC: 2499 5112 5049 5092 Picture frame
molding, finished; office supplies; school
supplies; arts & crafts equipment & supplies;
photographic equipment & supplies

(P-4500)
DELGADO BROTHERS LLC
647 E 59th St, Los Angeles (90001-1001)
PHONE..........................323 233-9793
Felipe Delgado, *Partner*
Antonio Delgado, *Partner*
Rafael Delgado Jr, *Partner*
Ramiro Delgado, *Partner*
▲ **EMP:** 25 **EST:** 2006
SQ FT: 105,000
SALES (est): 3.4MM **Privately Held**
WEB: www.delgadobrothers.com
SIC: 2499 Picture frame molding, finished;
picture & mirror frames, wood

(P-4501)
FAITH INDUSTRIES INC
Also Called: Western Wood
4117 Pearl St, Lake Elsinore (92530-2023)
PHONE..........................951 351-1486
Jeff Loupe, *President*
Dan Morgan, *CFO*
EMP: 25 **EST:** 1962
SQ FT: 86,000
SALES (est): 1.6MM **Privately Held**
SIC: 2499 Decorative wood & woodwork

(P-4502)
FORMSOLVER INC
Also Called: Framatic Company
3041 N North Coolidge Ave, Los Angeles
(90039-3413)
PHONE..........................323 664-7888
David Dedlow, *President*
Edwina Dedlow, *Vice Pres*
Vicente Diaz, *Technology*
Donna Ruckman, *Controller*
▲ **EMP:** 33
SQ FT: 12,500
SALES (est): 4.5MM **Privately Held**
WEB: www.framatic.com
SIC: 2499 Picture frame molding, finished

(P-4503)
FOSTER PLANING MILL CO
1258 W 58th St, Los Angeles (90037-3917)
PHONE..........................323 759-9156
Robert Stanley, *President*
EMP: 14 **EST:** 1937
SQ FT: 15,000
SALES (est): 1.5MM **Privately Held**
SIC: 2499 2431 Picture & mirror frames,
wood; venetian blind slats, wood

(P-4504)
GL WOODWORKING INC
Also Called: Millers Woodworking
14341 Franklin Ave, Tustin (92780-7010)
PHONE..........................949 515-2192
Grant Miller, *Owner*
EMP: 63
SALES (est): 6.7MM **Privately Held**
SIC: 2499 Decorative wood & woodwork

(P-4505)
GLC GENERAL INC
Also Called: Linen Liners
100 W Walnut Ave, Fullerton (92832-2345)
PHONE..........................714 870-9825
Gary L Cox, *President*
▲ **EMP:** 12 **EST:** 1962
SQ FT: 1,000
SALES (est): 2.1MM **Privately Held**
WEB: www.linenliners.com
SIC: 2499 Picture frame molding, finished;
picture & mirror frames, wood

(P-4506)
GOLDEN VANTAGE LLC
8807 Rochester Ave, Rancho Cucamonga
(91730-4913)
PHONE..........................626 255-3362
Canlin Chen, *Mng Member*
Anfeng Huang, *Mng Member*
▲ **EMP:** 10

SQ FT: 55,000
SALES (est): 7.2MM **Privately Held**
SIC: 2499 5074 Kitchen, bathroom &
household ware: wood; plumbing & hydronic
heating supplies

(P-4507)
J & S STAKES INC
3157 Greenwood Heights Dr, Kneeland
(95549-8912)
PHONE..........................707 668-5647
EMP: 18
SQ FT: 21,000
SALES (est): 2MM **Privately Held**
SIC: 2499

(P-4508)
JERRY SOLOMON ENTERPRISES INC
Also Called: Jerry Slmon Cstm Picture Frmng
5221 W Jefferson Blvd, Los Angeles
(90016-3815)
PHONE..........................323 556-2265
Jerry Solomon, *President*
Arlyn Solomon, *Corp Secy*
Fred Solomon, *Vice Pres*
▲ **EMP:** 50
SQ FT: 60,000
SALES (est): 4.7MM **Privately Held**
WEB: www.solomonframe.com
SIC: 2499 5999 3231 Picture & mirror
frames, wood; picture frames, ready
made; products of purchased glass

(P-4509)
JIMO ENTERPRISES
6001 Santa Monica Blvd, Los Angeles
(90038-1807)
PHONE..........................323 469-0805
Larry Neuberg, *Owner*
▲ **EMP:** 20
SALES (est): 1MM **Privately Held**
SIC: 2499 Picture & mirror frames, wood

(P-4510)
KENS STAKES & SUPPLIES
193 S Mariposa Ave, Visalia (93292-9242)
PHONE..........................559 747-1313
Joseph Hallmeyer, *President*
Barbara Hallmeyer, *Vice Pres*
EMP: 10
SQ FT: 12,000
SALES (est): 1.5MM **Privately Held**
SIC: 2499 5049 Handles, poles, dowels &
stakes: wood; surveyors' instruments

(P-4511)
KUTZIN & KUTZIN INC
Also Called: Custom Framing Service
14726 Oxnard St, Van Nuys (91411-3121)
P.O. Box 57438, Sherman Oaks (91413-2438)
PHONE..........................818 994-0242
EMP: 11
SALES: 900K **Privately Held**
SIC: 2499 3952 Picture & mirror frames,
wood; frames for artists' canvases

(P-4512)
LARSON-JUHL US LLC
Also Called: Larson Picture Frames
12206 Bell Ranch Dr, Santa Fe Springs
(90670-3361)
PHONE..........................562 946-6873
Anthony Eikenberry, *Manager*
EMP: 24
SALES (corp-wide): 225.3B **Publicly Held**
SIC: 2499 Picture & mirror frames, wood
HQ: Larson-Juhl Us Llc
3900 Steve Reynolds Blvd
Norcross GA 30093
770 279-5200

(P-4513)
LARSON-JUHL US LLC
5365 Industrial Way, Benicia (94510-1026)
PHONE..........................707 747-0555
EMP: 20
SALES (corp-wide): 225.3B **Publicly Held**
SIC: 2499 3231 Picture & mirror frames,
wood; products of purchased glass

▲ = Import ▼ =Export
◆ =Import/Export

HQ: Larson-Juhl Us Llc
3900 Steve Reynolds Blvd
Norcross GA 30093
770 279-5200

(P-4514)
MADERA CONCEPTS
Also Called: Absolute Woods Products
55b Depot Rd, Goleta (93117-3430)
PHONE..................................805 692-0053
Jeffrey A Wayco, *Partner*
Antonio G Gonzales, *Partner*
▲ EMP: 15
SALES (est): 800K **Privately Held**
WEB: www.maderaconcepts.com
SIC: 2499 Decorative wood & woodwork

(P-4515)
MAGIC-FLIGHT GENERAL MFG INC
3417 Hancock St, San Diego (92110-4307)
P.O. Box 3758, Rancho Santa Fe (92067-3758)
PHONE..................................619 288-4638
Forrest Landry, *CEO*
Tamara Ward, *CFO*
EMP: 130
SQ FT: 35,000
SALES (est): 10MM **Privately Held**
SIC: 2499 Woodenware, kitchen & household

(P-4516)
MOLDING COMPANY
1987 Russell Ave, Santa Clara (95054-2035)
PHONE..................................408 748-6968
Doug Randall, *President*
EMP: 25
SALES (est): 2.4MM **Privately Held**
SIC: 2499 Decorative wood & woodwork

(P-4517)
MONARCH ART & FRAME INC
7700 Gloria Ave, Van Nuys (91406-1819)
PHONE..................................818 373-6180
Jaime V Mizrahi, *CEO*
EMP: 50
SQ FT: 16,000
SALES (est): 6.2MM **Privately Held**
WEB: www.themonarchcollection.com
SIC: 2499 Picture & mirror frames, wood;
picture frame molding, finished

(P-4518)
MWW INC
Also Called: Modern Woodworks
7945 Deering Ave, Canoga Park (91304-5009)
PHONE..................................800 575-3475
George Mekhtarian, *CEO*
Allen Mekhtarian, *Vice Pres*
▲ EMP: 35
SQ FT: 10,000
SALES (est): 6.1MM **Privately Held**
SIC: 2499 Carved & turned wood

(P-4519)
OUTDOOR DIMENSIONS LLC
5325 E Hunter Ave, Anaheim (92807-2054)
PHONE..................................714 578-9555
Donald Pickler, *President*
Brian Pickler, *Vice Pres*
Pam Rogers, *Executive*
Jennifer Ryan, *Executive*
Angel Luna, *Project Mgr*
EMP: 160 EST: 1974
SQ FT: 80,000
SALES (est): 34.4MM **Privately Held**
WEB: www.outdoordimensions.com
SIC: 2499 3993 3281 Signboards, wood;
signs & advertising specialties; cut stone
& stone products

(P-4520)
PICTURE THIS FRAMING INC
631 S State College Blvd, Fullerton (92831-5115)
PHONE..................................714 447-8749
Neil Oleary, *President*
Neil O'Leary, *President*
Ginger Greenleaf, *Vice Pres*
EMP: 15
SQ FT: 8,000

SALES (est): 2MM **Privately Held**
WEB: www.picturethisframing.com
SIC: 2499 Picture & mirror frames, wood

(P-4521)
PORTOCORK AMERICA INC
164 Gateway Rd E, NAPA (94558-7576)
PHONE..................................707 258-3930
Dustin Mowe, *President*
Jose Santos, *Vice Pres*
Isabelle Sodini, *Director*
▼ EMP: 12
SALES (est): 2.5MM **Privately Held**
WEB: www.portocork.com
SIC: 2499 Corks, bottle
HQ: Amorim - ServiCos E GestAo, S.A.
Rua De Meladas, 380
Mozelos Vfr 4535-
227 475-400

(P-4522)
PRO TOUR MEMORABILIA LLC
Also Called: Ptm Images
700 N San Vicente Blvd G696, West Hollywood (90069-5073)
P.O. Box 15084, Beverly Hills (90209-1084)
PHONE..................................424 303-7200
Jonathan Bass,
▲ EMP: 25
SQ FT: 8,000
SALES (est): 6.7MM **Privately Held**
WEB: www.ptmimages.com
SIC: 2499 Picture & mirror frames, wood

(P-4523)
QUALITY FIRST WOODWORKS INC
1264 N Lakeview Ave, Anaheim (92807-1831)
PHONE..................................714 632-0480
Mark Nappy, *President*
Chad Nappy, *Corp Secy*
Randy Dell, *Vice Pres*
EMP: 115
SQ FT: 30,000
SALES: 14MM **Privately Held**
WEB: www.qualityfirstwoodworks.com
SIC: 2499 1751 Decorative wood & woodwork; cabinet building & installation

(P-4524)
RAPHAELS INC
2780 Sweetwater Spgs Blvd, Spring Valley (91977-7136)
PHONE..................................619 670-7999
Scott Brummitt, *CEO*
Richard J Hennen, *President*
▲ EMP: 17 EST: 1976
SQ FT: 300,000
SALES (est): 2.8MM **Privately Held**
WEB: www.raphaelstoday.com
SIC: 2499 Picture & mirror frames, wood

(P-4525)
REDWORKS INDUSTRIES LLC
23986 Aliso Creek Rd, Laguna Niguel (92677-3908)
PHONE..................................949 334-7081
Melissa Soto,
Juan C Soto,
Melissa P Soto,
EMP: 35
SQ FT: 15,000
SALES: 950K **Privately Held**
SIC: 2499 Applicators, wood

(P-4526)
RICH XIBERTA USA INC
450 Aaron St, Cotati (94931-3068)
PHONE..................................707 795-1800
Ferran Botifoll, *General Mgr*
Andrea Fishbein, *Accounts Mgr*
Steve Romeo, *Accounts Mgr*
▲ EMP: 10
SQ FT: 11,000
SALES (est): 1.9MM **Privately Held**
WEB: www.xiberta.com
SIC: 2499 5085 Cork & cork products; bottler supplies
HQ: Rich Xiberta Sa
Travesia Taronja, S/N
Caldes De Malavella 17455
972 472-727

(P-4527)
ROMA MOULDING INC
6230 N Irwindale Ave, Irwindale (91702-3208)
PHONE..................................626 334-2539
Jon Mathews, *Manager*
EMP: 20
SALES (corp-wide): 28.8MM **Privately Held**
SIC: 2499 5023 Picture frame molding, finished; frames & framing, picture & mirror
PA: Roma Moulding Inc
360 Hanlan Rd
Woodbridge ON L4L 3
905 850-1500

(P-4528)
ROSS FABRICATION & WELDING INC
1154 Basta Ave, Bakersfield (93308-4477)
PHONE..................................661 393-1242
Jeffrey Ross, *President*
Julie Ross, *CFO*
EMP: 14
SALES (est): 1.6MM **Privately Held**
SIC: 2499 Food handling & processing products, wood

(P-4529)
S & S WOODCARVER INC
Also Called: American Carousel
13 San Rafael Pl, Laguna Niguel (92677-7623)
PHONE..................................714 258-2222
Sid Askari, *CEO*
Sy Vakhsourpour, *President*
EMP: 28
SALES: 2.5MM **Privately Held**
WEB: www.americancarousel.com
SIC: 2499 Carved & turned wood

(P-4530)
S&S SIGNATURE MILL WORKS INC
5951 Jetton Ln Ste C6, Loomis (95650-9593)
PHONE..................................916 652-1046
Gary Stephens, *Owner*
EMP: 15
SQ FT: 4,000
SALES: 1MM **Privately Held**
SIC: 2499 1751 Decorative wood & woodwork; cabinet & finish carpentry

(P-4531)
SEVEN WELLS LLC
Also Called: I.E. Distribution
14801 Able Ln Ste 102, Huntington Beach (92647-2059)
PHONE..................................213 305-4775
John Dickenson, *Manager*
Barry Lublin, *CFO*
▲ EMP: 14
SALES (est): 1.5MM **Privately Held**
SIC: 2499 Shoe & boot products, wood

(P-4532)
SHASTA FOREST PRODUCTS INC (PA)
1412 Montague Rd, Yreka (96097-9659)
P.O. Box 777 (96097-0777)
PHONE..................................530 842-0527
Richard W Conroy, *President*
William Hall, *Vice Pres*
Karen Cunningham, *Admin Sec*
EMP: 42
SQ FT: 3,500
SALES: 10.7MM **Privately Held**
WEB: www.shastabark.com
SIC: 2499 Mulch, wood & bark

(P-4533)
SHASTA FOREST PRODUCTS INC
1423 Montague Rd, Yreka (96097-9659)
P.O. Box 777 (96097-0777)
PHONE..................................530 842-2787
Bill Hall, *Manager*
EMP: 30
SALES (corp-wide): 10.7MM **Privately Held**
WEB: www.shastabark.com
SIC: 2499 2421 Mulch, wood & bark; sawmills & planing mills, general

PA: Shasta Forest Products, Inc.
1412 Montague Rd
Yreka CA 96097
530 842-0527

(P-4534)
SHELTER INTERNATIONAL INC
6310 Corsair St, Commerce (90040-2504)
PHONE..................................323 888-8856
Shawn Arshad, *President*
EMP: 50
SALES (est): 115.6K **Privately Held**
SIC: 2499 Decorative wood & woodwork

(P-4535)
SHINE COMPANY INC
3535 Philadelphia St, Chino (91710-2089)
PHONE..................................909 590-5005
Wallace Chen, *President*
Margarita Chen, *Vice Pres*
Gideon Yambot, *Accounts Mgr*
▲ EMP: 10
SQ FT: 50,000
SALES (est): 870K **Privately Held**
WEB: www.shineco.com
SIC: 2499 Decorative wood & woodwork

(P-4536)
SOUTHERN CALIFORNIA MULCH INC
30141 Antelope Rd 116, Menifee (92584-7001)
PHONE..................................951 352-5355
Elisabeth Michelle Brownton, *CEO*
EMP: 12
SALES (est): 266K **Privately Held**
SIC: 2499 5999 Mulch or sawdust products, wood; rock & stone specimens

(P-4537)
SURVEY STAKE AND MARKER INC
Also Called: Nichols Lumber
13470 Dalewood St, Baldwin Park (91706-5834)
PHONE..................................626 960-4802
Judith A Nichols, *President*
Evelyn M Rumsey, *Vice Pres*
Charles F Nichols, *Admin Sec*
Charles Nichols, *Admin Sec*
EMP: 18
SQ FT: 3,000
SALES (est): 1.5MM **Privately Held**
SIC: 2499 Surveyors' stakes, wood

(P-4538)
SYBMAN INC
Also Called: PICTURE SOURCE OF CALIFORNIA
9911 Gidley St, El Monte (91731-1111)
PHONE..................................626 579-9911
Angky Dharmosetio, *President*
Kusno Wongsodirdjo, *Vice Pres*
Ferry Soendjojo, *Admin Sec*
◆ EMP: 10
SQ FT: 6,000
SALES: 605.9K **Privately Held**
WEB: www.hotelart.com
SIC: 2499 Picture frame molding, finished

(P-4539)
TIMMONS WOOD PRODUCTS INC
4675 Wade Ave, Perris (92571-7494)
PHONE..................................951 940-4700
Eddie Timmons, *President*
EMP: 13
SQ FT: 45,000
SALES (est): 1.3MM **Privately Held**
SIC: 2499 Handles, poles, dowels & stakes: wood

(P-4540)
TREND MARKETING CORPORATION
Also Called: Trend Frames
3025 Beyer Blvd Ste 102, San Diego (92154-3432)
PHONE..................................800 468-7363
Sam Ceci, *President*
EMP: 100 EST: 1976
SQ FT: 7,512

SALES (est): 10.8MM **Privately Held**
WEB: www.go-trend.com
SIC: 2499 3999 Picture & mirror frames, wood; novelties, bric-a-brac & hobby kits

(P-4541)
UNIVERSITY FRAMES INC
3060 E Miraloma Ave, Anaheim (92806-1810)
PHONE.....................714 575-5100
John G Winn, *CEO*
Diane Winn, *Vice Pres*
Tami Demint, *Accounting Mgr*
Danny Winn, *Opers Mgr*
Andrea Arczynski, *Director*
▲ **EMP:** 50
SQ FT: 20,000
SALES (est): 9.6MM **Privately Held**
WEB: www.universityframes.com
SIC: 2499 5999 Picture frame molding, finished; picture frames, ready made

(P-4542)
WALTON COMPANY INC
17900 Sampson Ln, Huntington Beach (92647-7149)
PHONE.....................714 847-8800
Don Walton, *President*
▼ **EMP:** 15
SQ FT: 12,000
SALES (est): 1.3MM **Privately Held**
SIC: 2499 Cork & cork products

(P-4543)
WILDLIFE IN WOOD INC
165 E Liberty Ave, Anaheim (92801-1014)
PHONE.....................714 773-5816
Devra Robledo, *President*
EMP: 18 EST: 1976
SQ FT: 12,000
SALES (est): 2.2MM **Privately Held**
SIC: 2499 8011 Decorative wood & woodwork; novelties, wood fiber; furniture inlays (veneers); engraved wood products; offices & clinics of medical doctors

(P-4544)
YTI ENTERPRISES INC
Also Called: Laminating Technologies
1260 S State College Pkwy, Anaheim (92806-5240)
PHONE.....................714 632-8696
Judith Rochverger, *President*
Jair N Rochverger, *CFO*
EMP: 15
SQ FT: 16,500
SALES (est): 2MM **Privately Held**
SIC: 2499 Seats, toilet

```
2511 Wood Household
Furniture
```

(P-4545)
ALDER & CO LLC
412 Wallace St, Bakersfield (93307-1447)
PHONE.....................661 326-0320
Bryan Shimp,
Adriana Caceres, *Partner*
Jose Luis Garcia,
Adan Perez,
Humberto Cobian, *Mng Member*
EMP: 16
SQ FT: 10,000
SALES: 800K **Privately Held**
WEB: www.alderandco.com
SIC: 2511 Wood household furniture

(P-4546)
AMERICAN CRAFTSMEN CORPORATION
273 N Hill Ave, Pasadena (91106-1531)
PHONE.....................626 793-3329
James L Key, *President*
EMP: 10 EST: 1948
SQ FT: 3,301
SALES (est): 1.1MM **Privately Held**
SIC: 2511 2434 Wood household furniture; wood kitchen cabinets

(P-4547)
AMISH COUNTRY GAZEBOS INC
739 E Francis St, Ontario (91761-5514)
PHONE.....................800 700-1777
Chet Beiler, *President*

EMP: 12
SALES (est): 1.6MM **Privately Held**
SIC: 2511 5031 1521 Garden furniture: wood; structural assemblies, prefabricated: wood; patio & deck construction & repair

(P-4548)
ART OF MUSE LLC
Also Called: Oly
2222 5th St, Berkeley (94710-2217)
PHONE.....................510 644-1870
Brad Huntzinger, *President*
Kate McIntyre, *Vice Pres*
▲ **EMP:** 24
SALES (est): 3.6MM **Privately Held**
SIC: 2511 2521 Wood household furniture; wood office furniture

(P-4549)
ARTS CUSTOM CABINETS INC
897 E Tulare Rd, Lindsay (93247-2244)
P.O. Box 218 (93247-0218)
PHONE.....................559 562-2766
Art Serna, *President*
Leonor Dela Fuente Serna, *Admin Sec*
EMP: 19
SQ FT: 45,000
SALES (est): 2.2MM **Privately Held**
WEB: www.artscc.com
SIC: 2511 2434 Kitchen & dining room furniture; vanities, bathroom: wood

(P-4550)
ASPEN BRANDS CORPORATION
1305 E Wakeham Ave, Santa Ana (92705-4145)
PHONE.....................702 946-9430
Michael Rocha, *CEO*
▲ **EMP:** 14
SALES (est): 427.5K **Privately Held**
SIC: 2511 3231 3641 5021 Chairs, household, except upholstered: wood; tables, household: wood; products of purchased glass; electric light bulbs, complete; tables, occasional; chairs; glassware; lighting fixtures

(P-4551)
AW INDUSTRIES INC
Also Called: Skog Furniture
1810 S Reservoir St, Pomona (91766-5541)
PHONE.....................909 629-1500
Ted Wong, *President*
Beatrice Wong, *Admin Sec*
EMP: 55
SQ FT: 46,000
SALES (est): 6.4MM **Privately Held**
WEB: www.awindustries.com
SIC: 2511 Wood household furniture

(P-4552)
BAU FURNITURE MANUFACTURING (PA)
23811 Aliso Creek Rd # 134, Laguna Niguel (92677-3902)
PHONE.....................949 643-2729
Thomas Bau, *President*
Linda Bau, *President*
EMP: 40
SQ FT: 43,000
SALES (est): 3.4MM **Privately Held**
WEB: www.baufurniture.com
SIC: 2511 2512 2521 Tables, household: wood; chairs, household, except upholstered: wood; upholstered household furniture; tables, office; chairs, office; padded, upholstered or plain: wood

(P-4553)
BEAUTY CRAFT FURNITURE CORP
Also Called: California House
3316 51st Ave, Sacramento (95823-1089)
PHONE.....................916 428-2238
Steven Start, *President*
Dee Start, *Ch of Bd*
▲ **EMP:** 44
SQ FT: 65,000
SALES (est): 7MM **Privately Held**
SIC: 2511 Wood game room furniture

(P-4554)
BENT FIR COMPANY
3598 Manzanita Ave, Nice (95464)
P.O. Box 506 (95464-0506)
PHONE.....................707 274-6628
Robert Alvord, *Owner*
EMP: 11
SQ FT: 6,000
SALES: 600K **Privately Held**
SIC: 2511 2431 Screens, privacy: wood; doors, wood

(P-4555)
BERKELEY MLLWK & FURN CO INC
Also Called: Berkeley Mills
2830 7th St, Berkeley (94710-2703)
PHONE.....................510 549-2854
Eugene Agress, *President*
Luong Lee Dinh, *Vice Pres*
Scott Pew, *Vice Pres*
EMP: 43
SQ FT: 18,000
SALES (est): 4.6MM **Privately Held**
WEB: www.berkeleymills.com
SIC: 2511 2541 2434 Wood household furniture; wood partitions & fixtures; wood kitchen cabinets

(P-4556)
BIG TREE FURNITURE & INDS INC (PA)
760 S Vail Ave, Montebello (90640-4954)
PHONE.....................310 894-7500
Joe Ho, *CEO*
▲ **EMP:** 44
SALES (est): 8.8MM **Privately Held**
SIC: 2511 Wood household furniture

(P-4557)
BLANK AND CABLES INC
3100 E 10th St, Oakland (94601-2914)
P.O. Box 7229 (94601-0229)
PHONE.....................415 648-3842
Jeremy Bradley, *CEO*
EMP: 10
SQ FT: 11,000
SALES (est): 1.6MM **Privately Held**
WEB: www.blankandcables.com
SIC: 2511 2514 Wood household furniture; metal household furniture

(P-4558)
BRADSHAW KIRCHOFER HOME FURN
22926 Mariposa Ave, Torrance (90502-2603)
PHONE.....................310 325-0010
John Kirchofer, *Co-Owner*
Ann Kirchofer, *Co-Owner*
EMP: 12 EST: 1995
SQ FT: 10,000
SALES (est): 1.3MM **Privately Held**
WEB: www.bradshawkirchofer.com
SIC: 2511 Wood household furniture

(P-4559)
CALIFORNIA BEDROOMS INC
95 Santa Fe Ave, Fresno (93721-3034)
PHONE.....................559 233-7050
Elias Serrano, *President*
▲ **EMP:** 40
SALES (est): 4.8MM **Privately Held**
SIC: 2511 Wood bedroom furniture

(P-4560)
CB MILL INC
1232 Connecticut St, San Francisco (94107-3352)
PHONE.....................415 386-5309
EMP: 19 EST: 2001
SQ FT: 16,000
SALES (est): 2.2MM **Privately Held**
WEB: www.cbmill.net
SIC: 2511

(P-4561)
CONCEPTS BY J INC
834 E 108th St, Los Angeles (90059-1006)
P.O. Box 88249 (90009-8249)
PHONE.....................323 564-9988
Jay Meepos, *President*
EMP: 20
SQ FT: 12,100

SALES (est): 2MM **Privately Held**
WEB: www.conceptsbyq.com
SIC: 2511 Wood household furniture

(P-4562)
CRESCENT WOODWORKING CO LTD
Also Called: Ayca Furniture
400 Ramona Ave Ste 212, Corona (92879-1443)
PHONE.....................909 673-9955
▲ **EMP:** 12
SQ FT: 32,000
SALES (est): 1.5MM
SALES (corp-wide): 10.3MM **Privately Held**
WEB: www.crescentwoodworking.com
SIC: 2511
PA: Tianjin Sayca Wood Co., Ltd.
In Hailong Warehousing And Transportation Center, No.5035, Jinta
Tianjin 30045
222 532-3876

(P-4563)
CYPRESS FURNITURE INC
26602 Corporate Ave, Hayward (94545-3919)
PHONE.....................510 723-4890
James Berrens, *President*
Charles Oliver, *Admin Sec*
EMP: 10
SQ FT: 15,000
SALES (est): 700K **Privately Held**
WEB: www.cypressfurniture.com
SIC: 2511 Bed frames, except water bed frames: wood

(P-4564)
DATELINE PRODUCTS LLC
1375 E Base Line St Ste B, San Bernardino (92410-4063)
PHONE.....................909 888-9785
Robert Prescaro, *CFO*
Joe Garofalo, *President*
Rodger Reynoso, *Vice Pres*
◆ **EMP:** 12
SQ FT: 20,000
SALES (est): 1.3MM **Privately Held**
WEB: www.datelineproducts.com
SIC: 2511 Wood household furniture

(P-4565)
DOUG MOCKETT & COMPANY INC
1915 Abalone Ave, Torrance (90501-3706)
P.O. Box 3333, Manhattan Beach (90266-1333)
PHONE.....................310 318-2491
Susan Darby Gordon, *President*
Edwin Deacruz, *Executive*
Sonia Marie H Mockett, *Admin Sec*
May Beck, *Administration*
Martha Gonzales, *Human Res Dir*
▲ **EMP:** 40
SALES (est): 9.3MM **Privately Held**
WEB: www.mockett.com
SIC: 2511 Unassembled or unfinished furniture, household: wood

(P-4566)
EDMONS UNQUE FURN STONE GLLERY (PA)
5174 Melrose Ave, Los Angeles (90038-4117)
PHONE.....................323 462-5787
Edmon Simonian, *President*
EMP: 10
SQ FT: 10,000
SALES (est): 1MM **Privately Held**
SIC: 2511 Wood household furniture

(P-4567)
ELEMENTS BY GRAPEVINE INC
18251 N Highway 88, Lockeford (95237-9716)
P.O. Box 1458 (95237-1458)
PHONE.....................209 727-3711
Isaac Kubryk, *President*
Renee Kubryk, *Vice Pres*
▲ **EMP:** 45 EST: 1979
SQ FT: 60,000

▲ = Import ▼=Export
◆ =Import/Export

SALES: 15MM **Privately Held**
WEB: www.wizkids.com
SIC: 2511 2519 Tables, household: wood;
lawn & garden furniture, except wood &
metal

(P-4568)
EMANUEL MOREZ INC
Also Called: Amos Art Studio
8754 Yolanda Ave, Northridge
(91324-3831)
PHONE....................818 780-2787
Amos Stockfish, *President*
▲ EMP: 30
SQ FT: 26,000
SALES: 3MM **Privately Held**
WEB: www.emanuelmorez.com
SIC: 2511 2499 1751 Wood household
furniture; decorative wood & woodwork;
carved & turned wood; cabinet & finish
carpentry

(P-4569)
EURODESIGN LTD (PA)
62 Chester Cir, Los Altos (94022-1246)
PHONE....................650 948-5160
Edward G Wildanger, *President*
Paula P Wildanger, *Corp Secy*
EMP: 15
SALES: 3MM **Privately Held**
SIC: 2511 5712 Wood household furniture;
furniture stores

(P-4570)
FEDERAL PRISON INDUSTRIES
Also Called: Unicor
3600 Guard Rd, Lompoc (93436-2705)
PHONE....................805 736-4154
Steve Southall, *Superintendent*
EMP: 245 **Publicly Held**
WEB: www.unicor.gov
SIC: 2511 2759 3993 9223 Wood house-
hold furniture; commercial printing; signs
& advertising specialties; correctional in-
stitutions;
HQ: Federal Prison Industries, Inc
320 1st St Nw
Washington DC 20534
202 305-3500

(P-4571)
FREMARC INDUSTRIES INC
(PA)
Also Called: Fremarc Designs
18810 San Jose Ave, City of Industry
(91748-1325)
PHONE....................626 965-0802
Maurice M Donenfeld, *President*
Harriette Donenfeld, *Corp Secy*
▲ EMP: 82
SQ FT: 45,000
SALES (est): 10.5MM **Privately Held**
WEB: www.fremarc.com
SIC: 2511 Wood household furniture

(P-4572)
FRENCH TRADITION (PA)
13700 Crenshaw Blvd, Gardena
(90249-2348)
PHONE....................310 719-9977
Franck Valles, *President*
Julie Valles, *Vice Pres*
EMP: 15
SQ FT: 7,000
SALES (est): 2.1MM **Privately Held**
WEB: www.thefrenchtradition.com
SIC: 2511 Wood household furniture

(P-4573)
FURNITURE TECHNICS INC
Also Called: Furniture Techniques
2900 Supply Ave, Commerce (90040-2708)
PHONE....................562 802-0261
Cesar Rousseau, *President*
Ricardo Flores, *Admin Sec*
EMP: 25
SALES: 266.4K **Privately Held**
SIC: 2511 2426 Wood household furniture;
furniture stock & parts, hardwood

(P-4574)
HANSENS OAK INC (PA)
166 E Broadway Ave, Atwater
(95301-4562)
PHONE....................209 357-3424
Michael Hansen, *President*

Robert Glenney, *Vice Pres*
▲ EMP: 14
SALES (est): 1.3MM **Privately Held**
SIC: 2511 Dining room furniture: wood;
chairs, household, except upholstered:
wood; desks, household: wood

(P-4575)
HOLLYWOOD CHAIRS
Also Called: Totally Bamboo
1880 Diamond St, San Marcos
(92078-5100)
PHONE....................760 471-6600
Joanne Chen, *President*
Tom Sullivan, *CEO*
Melanie Tomaschke, *Executive*
Jim Baltad, *Project Mgr*
Blaine Maas, *Controller*
◆ EMP: 12
SQ FT: 10,000
SALES (est): 2.4MM **Privately Held**
WEB: www.totallybamboo.com
SIC: 2511 Wood household furniture

(P-4576)
IMPERIAL CUSTOM CABINET
INC
8093 Lemon Grove Way, Lemon Grove
(91945-1913)
PHONE....................619 461-4093
Art Schiele, *President*
EMP: 15 EST: 1971
SQ FT: 10,000
SALES (est): 1.8MM **Privately Held**
SIC: 2511 2434 Wood household furniture;
wood kitchen cabinets

(P-4577)
INTERIOR WOOD DESIGN INC
334 Sacramento St Ste 1, Auburn
(95603-5510)
PHONE....................530 888-7707
Tim Hanson, *President*
Tim Fariss, *Vice Pres*
Mark Hanson, *VP Mktg*
EMP: 10
SQ FT: 5,000
SALES (est): 1.1MM **Privately Held**
WEB: www.interiorwooddesign.com
SIC: 2511 2521 Wood household furniture;
cabinets, office: wood

(P-4578)
JOES CUSTOM FURN & FRAMES
6402 Whittier Blvd, Los Angeles
(90022-4604)
PHONE....................323 721-1881
Joe Cypert Jr, *Partner*
Manuel Cypert, *Partner*
EMP: 10
SQ FT: 2,000
SALES (est): 1.3MM **Privately Held**
SIC: 2511 5932 7641 Wood household
furniture; furniture, secondhand; furniture
repair & maintenance

(P-4579)
JP PRODUCTS LLC
2054 Davie Ave, Commerce (90040-1705)
PHONE....................310 237-6237
Patrick Mooney, *Mng Member*
Jacqueline Mooney, *Mng Member*
EMP: 46
SQ FT: 35,000
SALES (est): 3.5MM **Privately Held**
SIC: 2511 Wood household furniture

(P-4580)
JUAN BRAMBILA SR
Also Called: Brambila's Draperies
5018 Venice Blvd, Los Angeles
(90019-5308)
PHONE....................323 939-8312
Juan Brambila Sr, *Owner*
Ana Brambila, *Co-Owner*
EMP: 16
SQ FT: 8,000
SALES (est): 1.8MM **Privately Held**
SIC: 2511 2392 2391 5023 Bed frames,
except water bed frames: wood; bed-
spreads & bed sets: made from pur-
chased materials; draperies, plastic &
textile: from purchased materials;
draperies

(P-4581)
KEHOE CUSTOM WOOD
DESIGNS
1320 N Miller St Ste D, Anaheim
(92806-1414)
PHONE....................714 993-0444
Joseph T Kehoe, *President*
EMP: 10
SQ FT: 5,000
SALES (est): 819K **Privately Held**
SIC: 2511 2517 2521 Wood household
furniture; wood television & radio cabi-
nets; cabinets, office: wood

(P-4582)
KERROCK COUNTERTOPS INC
(PA)
Also Called: Lisac Construction
1450 Dell Ave Ste C, Campbell
(95008-6600)
PHONE....................510 441-2300
William G Lisac, *President*
▲ EMP: 20
SALES: 1.6MM **Privately Held**
WEB: www.kerrock.com
SIC: 2511 5211 1799 Wood household
furniture; cabinets, kitchen; counter top in-
stallation

(P-4583)
KINWAI USA INC
2265 Davis Ct, Hayward (94545-1113)
PHONE....................510 780-9388
Chongwei Zhao, *President*
Daniel Murphy, *Project Mgr*
Alexis Chang, *Sales Staff*
▲ EMP: 20
SALES (est): 2.3MM **Privately Held**
SIC: 2511 5021 Wood household furniture;
household furniture

(P-4584)
KUSHWOOD CHAIR INC
1290 E Elm St, Ontario (91761-4025)
PHONE....................909 930-2100
Daniel Kusvhinikov, *President*
Roger Douglas, *Vice Pres*
EMP: 250 EST: 1979
SQ FT: 450,000
SALES (est): 18.9MM **Privately Held**
SIC: 2511 2521 Wood office furniture;
unassembled or unfinished furniture,
household: wood

(P-4585)
LA CANDELARIA
MANUFACTURING
Also Called: La Candelaria Furniture Mfr
2790 M L King Jr Blvd, Lynwood (90262)
PHONE....................310 763-0112
Felipe Contreras, *Owner*
Antonio Garcia, *Co-Owner*
EMP: 10
SQ FT: 1,200
SALES (est): 675.8K **Privately Held**
SIC: 2511 Wood stands & chests, except
bedside stands; wood bedroom furniture

(P-4586)
LANPAR INC
Also Called: Oakwood Interiors
1333 S Bon View Ave, Ontario
(91761-4404)
PHONE....................541 484-1962
Nick Lanphier, *Ch of Bd*
EMP: 255
SQ FT: 180,000
SALES (est): 19.8MM **Privately Held**
WEB: www.fineoak.com
SIC: 2511 Wood bedroom furniture

(P-4587)
LUNDIA
449 Borrego Ct, San Dimas (91773-2971)
PHONE....................888 989-1370
Robert Norden, *CEO*
EMP: 280
SALES (est): 6.4MM **Privately Held**
SIC: 2511 Wood household furniture

(P-4588)
M F G EUROTEC INC
Also Called: BV WILMS
84464 Cabazon Center Dr, Indio
(92201-6200)
PHONE....................760 863-0033
Jody R Williams, *President*
A R Williams, *Treasurer*
William Vinton Williams, *Principal*
Jason Williams, *Admin Sec*
EMP: 20
SQ FT: 18,500
SALES: 755.2K **Privately Held**
WEB: www.bvwilms.com
SIC: 2511 5211 1751 Wood household
furniture; cabinets, kitchen; cabinet & fin-
ish carpentry

(P-4589)
MAGNUSSEN HOME
FURNISHINGS INC
2155 Excise Ave Ste B, Ontario
(91761-8536)
PHONE....................336 841-4424
Jeff Cook, *Branch Mgr*
Martin Torres, *Manager*
EMP: 11
SALES (corp-wide): 57.5MM **Privately
Held**
SIC: 2511 Wood household furniture
HQ: Magnussen Holdings Usa, Inc.
4523 Green Point Dr # 109
Greensboro NC 27410
336 841-4424

(P-4590)
MCGUNAGLE WILLIAM H &
SONS MFG (PA)
Also Called: Mack Wall Bed Systems
971 Transport Way Ste B, Petaluma
(94954-1402)
PHONE....................707 762-7900
William H Mc Gunagle, *President*
Nancy Mc Gunagle, *Vice Pres*
EMP: 10
SALES: 225K **Privately Held**
WEB: www.mackwallbedsystems.com
SIC: 2511 5712 Bedspring frames: wood;
furniture stores

(P-4591)
MICHAELS FURNITURE
COMPANY INC
15 Koch Rd Ste J, Corte Madera
(94925-1231)
PHONE....................916 381-9086
Gary Friedman, *CEO*
Mike Bollum, *General Mgr*
▲ EMP: 300
SQ FT: 150,000
SALES (est): 25.6MM
SALES (corp-wide): 2.5B **Publicly Held**
WEB: www.restorationhardware.com
SIC: 2511 Wood household furniture
HQ: Restoration Hardware, Inc.
15 Koch Rd Ste K
Corte Madera CA 94925
415 924-1005

(P-4592)
MID CENTURY IMPORTS INC
5333 Cahuenga Blvd, North Hollywood
(91601-3431)
PHONE....................818 509-3050
David Pierce, *President*
▲ EMP: 10
SALES (est): 901.6K **Privately Held**
SIC: 2511 Wood household furniture

(P-4593)
MIKHAIL DARAFEEV INC (PA)
5075 Edison Ave, Chino (91710-5716)
PHONE....................909 613-1818
Antonina Darafeev, *President*
Paul Darafeev, *Treasurer*
George Darafeev, *Admin Sec*
▲ EMP: 50 EST: 1957
SALES (est): 18.2MM **Privately Held**
WEB: www.darafeev.com
SIC: 2511 Stools, household: wood

PRODUCTS & SVCS

(P-4594)
MILLER & PIDSKALNY CSTM WDWRK
1940 Blair Ave, Santa Ana (92705-5707)
PHONE..........................949 250-8508
Lawrence P Miller, *President*
EMP: 15
SQ FT: 3,500
SALES (est): 1.3MM **Privately Held**
WEB: www.millerpid.com
SIC: 2511 2512 2431 Wood household furniture; upholstered household furniture; staircases, stairs & railings

(P-4595)
MINTON-SPIDELL INC (PA)
8467 Steller Dr, Culver City (90232-2424)
PHONE..........................310 836-0403
Maurice N Spidell, *President*
Rick Nelson, *Sales Executive*
Rick A Nelson, *Agent*
EMP: 19 **EST:** 1959
SQ FT: 9,000
SALES (est): 1.5MM **Privately Held**
WEB: www.minton-spidell.com
SIC: 2511 Wood household furniture

(P-4596)
MOD SHOP
15610 S Main St, Gardena (90248-2219)
PHONE..........................310 523-1008
John Bernard, *Owner*
▲ **EMP:** 50
SALES (est): 4MM **Privately Held**
SIC: 2511 Wood household furniture

(P-4597)
MODERN BAMBOO INCORPORATED
5853 Virmar Ave, Oakland (94618-1536)
PHONE..........................925 820-2804
Anthony Marschak, *President*
Rod Suzuki, *CFO*
EMP: 12
SALES (est): 842.7K **Privately Held**
SIC: 2511 Wood household furniture

(P-4598)
NEWCO INTERNATIONAL INC
Also Called: Harmony Kids
13600 Vaughn St, San Fernando (91340-3017)
PHONE..........................818 834-7100
Howard Napolske, *President*
Ernest Johnston, *Vice Pres*
▲ **EMP:** 350
SQ FT: 20,000
SALES (est): 36.2MM **Privately Held**
WEB: www.harmonykids.com
SIC: 2511 Children's wood furniture

(P-4599)
NOVA LIFESTYLE INC (PA)
6565 E Washington Blvd, Commerce (90040-1821)
PHONE..........................323 888-9999
Thanh H Lam, *Ch of Bd*
Jeffery Chuang, *CFO*
Huy La, *Bd of Directors*
Steven Qiang Liu, *Vice Pres*
Min Su, *Admin Sec*
EMP: 22
SALES: 88.6MM **Publicly Held**
SIC: 2511 2512 Wood household furniture; upholstered household furniture; chairs: upholstered on wood frames

(P-4600)
OAK TREE FURNITURE INC
13681 Newport Ave Ste 8, Tustin (92780-7815)
PHONE..........................562 944-0754
Tim Sopp, *President*
Elaine Sopp, *Vice Pres*
▲ **EMP:** 70 **EST:** 1977
SALES (est): 7.9MM **Privately Held**
WEB: www.otfinc.net
SIC: 2511 Wood household furniture

(P-4601)
P J MILLIGAN COMPANY LLC (PA)
Also Called: P J Milligan & Associates
436 E Gutierrez St, Santa Barbara (93101-1709)
PHONE..........................805 963-4038
Patrick Milligan, *CEO*
▲ **EMP:** 13
SQ FT: 18,000
SALES: 2.5MM **Privately Held**
WEB: www.pjmilligan.com
SIC: 2511 5712 Wood household furniture; furniture stores

(P-4602)
PLUSH HOME INC
6507 Lindenhurst Ave, Los Angeles (90048-4733)
PHONE..........................323 852-1912
Steven Ho, *President*
EMP: 20
SALES (est): 2.4MM **Privately Held**
WEB: www.plushhome.com
SIC: 2511 7389 Wood household furniture; interior designer

(P-4603)
QUALITY SHEDS INC
33210 Bailey Park Blvd, Menifee (92584-9584)
PHONE..........................951 672-6750
Matt Poturich, *Owner*
Jack Roy, *Administration*
EMP: 11
SQ FT: 3,700
SALES (est): 1.5MM **Privately Held**
SIC: 2511 Storage chests, household: wood

(P-4604)
RADFORD CABINETS INC
216 E Avenue K8, Lancaster (93535-4527)
PHONE..........................661 729-8931
Steven Radford, *President*
Robert Mendoza, *Vice Pres*
Sue Allen, *Executive*
Sharon Radford, *Admin Sec*
EMP: 70
SQ FT: 20,000
SALES (est): 9.1MM **Privately Held**
WEB: www.radfordcabinets.com
SIC: 2511 2434 2521 Kitchen & dining room furniture; wood kitchen cabinets; cabinets, office: wood

(P-4605)
RANDOLPH & HEIN
720 E 59th St, Los Angeles (90001-1004)
PHONE..........................323 233-6010
Mohammad Ali Karbalai, *Administration*
Payam Karbalai, *Marketing Staff*
▲ **EMP:** 10
SALES (est): 1MM **Privately Held**
SIC: 2511 5712 Wood household furniture; furniture stores

(P-4606)
RODS UNFINISHED FURNITURE
1121 S Meridian Ave, Alhambra (91803-1218)
PHONE..........................626 281-9855
Juan C Rodriguez Sr, *President*
Ann Rodriguez, *Treasurer*
John Rodriguez Jr, *Vice Pres*
EMP: 20 **EST:** 1982
SQ FT: 25,000
SALES (est): 1.8MM **Privately Held**
SIC: 2511 Unassembled or unfinished furniture, household:

(P-4607)
ROSETTI GENNARO FURNITURE
6833 Brynhurst Ave, Los Angeles (90043-4665)
PHONE..........................323 750-7794
Gennaro Rosetti, *Owner*
EMP: 33
SQ FT: 15,000
SALES (est): 2.4MM **Privately Held**
SIC: 2511 2426 2521 Wood household furniture; hardwood dimension & flooring mills; wood office furniture

(P-4608)
RUSS BASSETT CORP
Also Called: Group Five
8189 Byron Rd, Whittier (90606-2615)
PHONE..........................562 945-2445
Mike Dressendorfer, *CEO*
Peter Fink, *President*
Sasha Johnson, *President*
Clinton Losey, *Sales Engr*
Kellen Smith, *Sales Engr*
▲ **EMP:** 115
SQ FT: 112,000
SALES (est): 25.6MM **Privately Held**
WEB: www.russbassett.com
SIC: 2511 Wood household furniture

(P-4609)
S D M FURNITURE CO INC
Also Called: Sdm
4620 W Jefferson Blvd, Los Angeles (90016-4007)
PHONE..........................323 936-0295
Victor Cohen, *President*
Martha Cohen, *Treasurer*
Michael Cohen, *Vice Pres*
EMP: 14
SQ FT: 6,000
SALES (est): 1.5MM **Privately Held**
SIC: 2511 Wood household furniture

(P-4610)
SAN DIEGO ARCFT INTERIORS INC
2940 Hoover Ave, National City (91950-7218)
PHONE..........................619 474-1997
Juan Carlos Vasquez, *President*
Carlos Vazquez, *General Mgr*
▲ **EMP:** 23
SALES: 1MM **Privately Held**
SIC: 2511 Chairs, household, except upholstered: wood

(P-4611)
SANDBERG FURNITURE MFG CO INC (PA)
5705 Alcoa Ave, Vernon (90058-3794)
P.O. Box 58291, Los Angeles (90058-0291)
PHONE..........................323 582-0711
John Sandberg, *CEO*
Mark Nixon, *Senior VP*
Michael Bagwell, *Vice Pres*
Bill Hall, *Vice Pres*
Linda Hart, *Credit Mgr*
▲ **EMP:** 225
SALES (est): 75MM **Privately Held**
SIC: 2511 Wood bedroom furniture

(P-4612)
STUART DAVID INC (PA)
Also Called: Stuart's Fine Furniture
3419 Railroad Ave, Ceres (95307-3623)
P.O. Box 1009 (95307-1009)
PHONE..........................209 537-7449
David Neilson, *President*
Della Nielson, *CFO*
Greg Willden, *Sales Mgr*
Della Maria Nielson, *Accounts Mgr*
EMP: 35
SQ FT: 79,000
SALES (est): 4.7MM **Privately Held**
WEB: www.stuarts.net
SIC: 2511 Wood household furniture

(P-4613)
SUMMERTREE INTERIORS INC
4111 Buchanan St, Riverside (92503-4812)
PHONE..........................951 549-0590
Pockets Alvarez, *President*
EMP: 10
SALES (est): 1.2MM **Privately Held**
SIC: 2511 Wood household furniture

(P-4614)
SUMMIT FURNITURE INC (PA)
5 Harris Ct Bldg W, Monterey (93940-5755)
PHONE..........................831 375-7811
Jane Sieberts, *President*
Patty Parker, *CFO*
Patricia Parker, *Corp Secy*
Hilary Gustafsson, *Sales Dir*
◆ **EMP:** 13
SQ FT: 30,000

SALES (est): 1.8MM **Privately Held**
SIC: 2511 Wood household furniture

(P-4615)
TEXTURED DESIGN FURNITURE
Also Called: Texture Design
1303 S Claudina St, Anaheim (92805-6235)
PHONE..........................714 502-9121
J Luis Gonzales, *President*
▲ **EMP:** 40
SQ FT: 34,000
SALES: 4MM **Privately Held**
WEB: www.texturedesign.com
SIC: 2511 Wood household furniture

(P-4616)
TREND MANOR FURN MFG CO INC
17047 Gale Ave, City of Industry (91745-1808)
PHONE..........................626 964-6493
Theodore Vecchione, *President*
▲ **EMP:** 42 **EST:** 1946
SQ FT: 63,000
SALES (est): 5.2MM **Privately Held**
SIC: 2511 Wood household furniture

(P-4617)
UNIVERSAL INTERIOR INDUSTRIES
4111 Buchanan St, Riverside (92503-4812)
PHONE..........................951 743-5446
Pockets Alvarez, *President*
Marvella Garcia, *Vice Pres*
Pockets Alarez, *Principal*
EMP: 12
SALES (est): 1MM **Privately Held**
SIC: 2511 Wood household furniture

(P-4618)
WALMSLEY DESIGN
3825 Willat Ave Bldg A, Culver City (90232-2306)
PHONE..........................310 836-0772
Ian Walmsley, *Owner*
EMP: 10
SQ FT: 3,000
SALES: 500K **Privately Held**
SIC: 2511 Wood household furniture

(P-4619)
WEST COAST CATRG TRCKS MFG INC
1217 Goodrich Blvd, Commerce (90022-5124)
PHONE..........................323 278-1279
Juan Gomez, *President*
Jesus Gomez, *Director*
EMP: 12
SQ FT: 18,000
SALES (est): 1.2MM **Privately Held**
WEB: www.westcoastcateringtrucks.com
SIC: 2511 Stands, household, wood

(P-4620)
WEST WORLD MANUFACTURING INC
Also Called: West-World Co
6420 Federal Blvd Ste F, Lemon Grove (91945-1339)
P.O. Box 152780, San Diego (92195-2780)
PHONE..........................619 287-4403
Richard Mossay, *President*
EMP: 12 **EST:** 1977
SQ FT: 6,000
SALES: 1MM **Privately Held**
SIC: 2511 3083 2541 3089 Wood household furniture; plastic finished products, laminated; cabinets, except refrigerated: show, display, etc.: wood; plastic kitchenware, tableware & houseware; wood kitchen cabinets

(P-4621)
WESTERN DOVETAIL INCORPORATED
1101 Nimitz Ave Ste 209, Vallejo (94592-1034)
P.O. Box 1592 (94590-0159)
PHONE..........................707 556-3683
Maxfield Hunter, *Principal*
Joshua Hunter, *Director*
EMP: 22
SQ FT: 1,000

SALES: 3.3MM **Privately Held**
WEB: www.drawer.com
SIC: 2511 Wood household furniture

(P-4622)
WHALEN LLC (DH)
Also Called: Whalen Furniture Manufacturing
1578 Air Wing Rd, San Diego
(92154-7706)
PHONE..................619 423-9948
Dow Famulak, *President*
Paul Coscarelli, *Vice Pres*
David Levinson, *Vice Pres*
Myrna Gonzalez, *Executive*
Alba Wylie, *Executive*
◆ EMP: 113
SQ FT: 100,000
SALES (est): 30.7MM **Privately Held**
WEB: www.whalenfurniture.com
SIC: 2511 Wood household furniture

(P-4623)
WILD WOOD DESIGNS INC
Also Called: Wildwood Designs
1607 E Edinger Ave Ste P, Santa Ana
(92705-5017)
PHONE..................714 543-6549
Matthew Taylor, *President*
EMP: 10
SQ FT: 1,600
SALES: 500K **Privately Held**
WEB: www.wildwooddesigns.com
SIC: 2511 2434 Wood household furniture;
wood kitchen cabinets

(P-4624)
WOOD TECH INC
4611 Malat St, Oakland (94601-4903)
PHONE..................510 534-4930
Juan D Figueroa, *CEO*
Herbert Vega, *Controller*
EMP: 70
SQ FT: 92,000
SALES (est): 9.2MM **Privately Held**
WEB: www.woodtechonline.com
SIC: 2511 2521 Wood household furniture;
wood office furniture

(P-4625)
WOODLAND BEDROOMS INC
3423 Merced St, Los Angeles
(90065-1660)
PHONE..................562 408-1558
Gustavo Loza, *President*
Delia Loza, *Vice Pres*
▲ EMP: 75
SQ FT: 60,000
SALES (est): 6.6MM **Privately Held**
SIC: 2511 Wood household furniture

(P-4626)
WOODWORKS
107 Nunes Rd, Watsonville (95076-9627)
P.O. Box 227, Freedom (95019-0227)
PHONE..................831 688-8420
Christopher Holmstrom, *Owner*
EMP: 10
SALES (est): 602.9K **Privately Held**
SIC: 2511 2431 Wood household furniture;
door frames, wood

2512 Wood Household Furniture, Upholstered

(P-4627)
A RUDIN INC (PA)
Also Called: A Rudin Designs
6062 Alcoa Ave, Vernon (90058-3902)
PHONE..................323 589-5547
Arnold Rudin, *President*
Ralph Rudin, *Vice Pres*
Louis Dechristopher, *Sales Staff*
Chloe Lubrano, *Sales Staff*
▲ EMP: 92
SQ FT: 117,000
SALES (est): 12.5MM **Privately Held**
SIC: 2512 5021 Upholstered household
furniture; household furniture

(P-4628)
AMERASIA FURNITURE COMPONENTS
2772 Norton Ave, Lynwood (90262-1835)
PHONE..................310 638-0570

Khue Van Cao, *CEO*
Alfred Varela Jr, *President*
▲ EMP: 29
SQ FT: 55,000
SALES (est): 3.3MM **Privately Held**
SIC: 2512 Upholstered household furniture

(P-4629)
BEST QUALITY FURNITURE MFG INC
5400 E Francis St, Ontario (91761-3603)
P.O. Box 310795, Fontana (92331-0795)
PHONE..................909 230-6440
Khoa Van Ta, *CEO*
Craig Alford, *Vice Pres*
▲ EMP: 100 EST: 1996
SALES (est): 9.5MM **Privately Held**
WEB: www.bestqualityfurniture.com
SIC: 2512 5021 2511 Upholstered house-
hold furniture; household furniture; wood
household furniture

(P-4630)
BURTON JAMES INC
428 Turnbull Canyon Rd, City of Industry
(91745-1011)
PHONE..................626 961-7221
Raymond Zoref, *CEO*
Harry Robbins, *CFO*
Brandy Wong, *Director*
EMP: 80
SQ FT: 28,000
SALES (est): 12.4MM **Privately Held**
WEB: www.burtonjames.com
SIC: 2512 Upholstered household furniture

(P-4631)
CISCO BROS CORP
938 E 60th St, Los Angeles (90001-1017)
PHONE..................323 778-8612
Ysenia Mota, *Manager*
EMP: 15 **Privately Held**
SIC: 2512 Upholstered household furniture
PA: Cisco Bros. Corp.
5955 S Western Ave
Los Angeles CA 90047

(P-4632)
CISCO BROS CORP (PA)
Also Called: Cisco & Brothers Designs
5955 S Western Ave, Los Angeles
(90047-1124)
PHONE..................323 778-8612
Francisco Pinedo, *CEO*
Alba E Pinedo, *Exec VP*
Lorena Ashby, *Vice Pres*
Kahou Lei, *Software Engr*
◆ EMP: 145
SQ FT: 100,000
SALES (est): 48.2MM **Privately Held**
WEB: www.ciscobrothers.com
SIC: 2512 Upholstered household furniture

(P-4633)
COMMERCIAL INTR RESOURCES INC
Also Called: Contract Resources
6077 Rickenbacker Rd, Commerce
(90040-3031)
PHONE..................562 926-5885
Roberta Tuchman, *CEO*
Stanley Rice, *President*
Barbara Rice, *Corp Secy*
Stephanie Lesko, *Vice Pres*
Juan Morales, *Vice Pres*
EMP: 65
SQ FT: 28,000
SALES (est): 8.9MM **Privately Held**
WEB: www.bprco.com
SIC: 2512 Upholstered household furniture

(P-4634)
CORTEZ FURNITURE MFG INC
2423 E 58th St, Los Angeles (90058-3511)
PHONE..................323 581-5935
Antonio Flores, *President*
EMP: 15
SALES (corp-wide): 800K **Privately Held**
SIC: 2512 Upholstered household furniture
PA: Cortez Furniture Manufacturing, Inc.
2444 E 57th St
Vernon CA 90058
323 581-5935

(P-4635)
CUSTOM UPHOLSTERED FURN INC
Also Called: Upholstery Workroom
5000 W Jefferson Blvd, Los Angeles
(90016-3925)
PHONE..................323 731-3033
EMP: 14
SALES (est): 982.6K **Privately Held**
SIC: 2512

(P-4636)
DAVES INTERIORS INC
Also Called: Life Style West
1579 N Main St, Orange (92867-3439)
PHONE..................714 998-5554
David Navarro, *President*
Denise Navarro, *Treasurer*
Rachel Navarro, *Vice Pres*
Kay Ames, *Admin Sec*
▲ EMP: 25
SQ FT: 12,500
SALES (est): 3.1MM **Privately Held**
WEB: www.davesinteriors.com
SIC: 2512 7641 2511 Upholstered house-
hold furniture; reupholstery; wood house-
hold furniture

(P-4637)
DECOR FABRICS INC
Also Called: Decor International
6515 Mckinley Ave, Los Angeles
(90001-1519)
PHONE..................323 752-2200
Freshath Kashani, *President*
EMP: 25
SQ FT: 25,000
SALES: 2MM **Privately Held**
SIC: 2512 2521 Upholstered household
furniture; wood office furniture

(P-4638)
DELLAROBBIA INC (PA)
119 Waterworks Way, Irvine (92618-3110)
PHONE..................949 251-9532
David Soonlan, *President*
Sunee Soonlan, *Admin Sec*
▲ EMP: 48
SQ FT: 27,000
SALES (est): 3.7MM **Privately Held**
WEB: www.dellarobbiausa.com
SIC: 2512 Upholstered household furniture

(P-4639)
EBANISTA INC (PA)
2015 Newport Blvd, Costa Mesa
(92627-2161)
PHONE..................949 650-6397
Abby Menhenett, *Principal*
EMP: 20
SALES (est): 9MM **Privately Held**
SIC: 2512 Living room furniture: uphol-
stered on wood frames

(P-4640)
EJ LAUREN LLC
Also Called: Ejl
9400 Hall Rd, Downey (90241-5365)
PHONE..................562 803-1113
Antonio Ocampo, *Mng Member*
▲ EMP: 50
SQ FT: 20,000
SALES (est): 7.2MM **Privately Held**
SIC: 2512 Upholstered household furniture

(P-4641)
FUTON EXPRESS
10309 Vacco St, South El Monte
(91733-3315)
PHONE..................626 443-8684
GI Cheng LI, *Owner*
▲ EMP: 10
SALES (est): 576.3K **Privately Held**
WEB: www.futonexpress.net
SIC: 2512 Upholstered household furniture

(P-4642)
GENESIS TC INC
Also Called: Genesis 2000
524 Hofgaarden St, La Puente
(91744-5529)
PHONE..................626 968-4455
Anthony Moreno, *President*
Marvin Alperin, *Principal*
EMP: 12

SALES (est): 1.6MM **Privately Held**
SIC: 2512 Wood upholstered chairs &
couches

(P-4643)
GOMEN FURNITURE MFG INC
11612 Wright Rd, Lynwood (90262-3945)
PHONE..................310 635-4894
Leonardo Gonzalez, *President*
▲ EMP: 30
SALES (est): 4MM **Privately Held**
WEB: www.gomenfurniture.com
SIC: 2512 7641 Upholstered household
furniture; upholstery work

(P-4644)
GUY CHADDOCK & COMPANY (PA)
1100 La Avenida St, Mountain View
(94043-1452)
PHONE..................408 907-9200
EMP: 230
SQ FT: 75,000
SALES (est): 21.9MM **Privately Held**
SIC: 2512 2521 2511

(P-4645)
HAMMER COLLECTION INC
14427 S Main St, Gardena (90248-1913)
P.O. Box 2458, Manhattan Beach (90267-
2458)
PHONE..................310 515-0276
Frank Hammer, *President*
Eva Hammer, *Vice Pres*
▲ EMP: 41
SQ FT: 30,000
SALES (est): 4.2MM **Privately Held**
SIC: 2512 2511 Upholstered household
furniture; wood household furniture

(P-4646)
HARBOR FURNITURE MANUFACTURING (PA)
Also Called: Harbor House
12508 Center St, South Gate (90280-8079)
PHONE..................323 636-1201
Malcolm Tuttleton Jr, *President*
Brent Tuttleton, *Vice Pres*
▲ EMP: 40 EST: 1929
SQ FT: 40,000
SALES (est): 2MM **Privately Held**
SIC: 2512 2511 6514 2521 Upholstered
household furniture; wood household fur-
niture; dwelling operators, except apart-
ments; wood office furniture

(P-4647)
J F FITZGERALD COMPANY INC
Also Called: Fitzgerald Designers & Mfrs
2750 19th St, San Francisco (94110-2124)
PHONE..................415 648-6161
Charles James Willin Jr, *President*
Michael Willin, *Vice Pres*
EMP: 19
SQ FT: 15,000
SALES: 1.5MM **Privately Held**
SIC: 2512 Upholstered household furniture

(P-4648)
JENSON CUSTOM FURNITURE INC
Also Called: Infiniti
2161 S Dupont Dr, Anaheim (92806-6102)
PHONE..................714 634-8145
Florence Simpson, *President*
Mary Anne Simpson, *Treasurer*
Anthony Simpson, *Vice Pres*
EMP: 75
SQ FT: 27,000
SALES (est): 7.6MM **Privately Held**
SIC: 2512 Upholstered household furniture

(P-4649)
JONATHAN LOUIS INTL LTD
12919 S Figueroa St, Los Angeles
(90061-1134)
PHONE..................213 622-6114
EMP: 469
SALES (corp-wide): 170.5MM **Privately Held**
SIC: 2512 Upholstered household furniture
PA: Jonathan Louis International Ltd.
544 W 130th St
Gardena CA 90248
323 770-3330

(P-4650)
JONATHAN LOUIS INTL LTD (PA)
544 W 130th St, Gardena (90248-1502)
PHONE..................................323 770-3330
Juan Valle, *CEO*
Javier Sanchez, *Partner*
Maribel Corona, *Office Admin*
Cas Koza, *Admin Sec*
Ushan Dalwis, *CIO*
▲ EMP: 141
SQ FT: 55,000
SALES (est): 170.5MM **Privately Held**
WEB: www.jonathanlouis.net
SIC: 2512 Upholstered household furniture

(P-4651)
KAY CHESTERFIELD INC
6365 Coliseum Way, Oakland
(94621-3719)
PHONE..................................510 533-5565
Kriss Kokoefer, *President*
Joanne H Jones, *Vice Pres*
Kevelynne Ely, *Engineer*
EMP: 14
SQ FT: 10,000
SALES (est): 2.1MM **Privately Held**
WEB: www.reupholster.com
SIC: 2512 7641 Upholstered household
furniture; upholstery work

(P-4652)
LA FAMOSA MANUFACTURE INC
6600 Mckinley Ave, Los Angeles
(90001-1522)
PHONE..................................323 241-3100
Gabriela Dalvamez, *President*
EMP: 14
SALES (est): 698.6K **Privately Held**
SIC: 2512 Couches, sofas & davenports:
upholstered on wood frames

(P-4653)
LITTLE CASTLE FURNITURE CO INC
301 Todd Ct, Oxnard (93030-5192)
P.O. Box 4254, Westlake Village (91359-
1254)
PHONE..................................805 278-4646
Kayvan Torabian, *President*
▲ EMP: 45
SQ FT: 9,000
SALES (est): 10.7MM **Privately Held**
WEB: www.littlecastleinc.com
SIC: 2512 Upholstered household furniture

(P-4654)
LOCKHART FURNITURE MFG INC
Also Called: Lockhart Collection
13659 Rosecrans Ave Ste B, Santa Fe
Springs (90670-5036)
PHONE..................................562 404-0561
Joseph Lockhart, *President*
Daniel Lockhart, *Vice Pres*
EMP: 75
SALES (est): 8.6MM **Privately Held**
WEB: www.lockhartcollection.com
SIC: 2512 Upholstered household furniture

(P-4655)
MARCO FINE FURNITURE INC
650 Potrero Ave, San Francisco
(94110-2117)
P.O. Box 590659 (94159-0659)
PHONE..................................415 285-3235
◆ EMP: 20
SQ FT: 23,000
SALES (est): 1.9MM **Privately Held**
WEB: www.marcofinefurniture.com
SIC: 2512

(P-4656)
MARGE CARSON INC (PA)
1260 E Grand Ave, Pomona (91766-3801)
P.O. Box 1283 (91769-1283)
PHONE..................................626 571-1111
James Labarge, *CEO*
Dominic Ching, *CFO*
Laura Lady, *Executive*
Maria Campos, *Buyer*
Irma Jaramillo, *Buyer*
▲ EMP: 82 EST: 1951
SQ FT: 88,000

SALES (est): 21.3MM **Privately Held**
WEB: www.margecarson.com
SIC: 2512 2511 Living room furniture: upholstered on wood frames; wood household furniture

(P-4657)
MARLIN DESIGNS LLC
1900 E Warner Ave Ste J, Santa Ana
(92705-5549)
PHONE..................................949 637-7257
Ronald Whitlock, *Mng Member*
EMP: 150
SALES: 13MM **Privately Held**
WEB: www.marlin-designs.com
SIC: 2512 Upholstered household furniture

(P-4658)
MARTIN/BRATTRUD INC
1224 W 132nd St, Gardena (90247-1566)
PHONE..................................323 770-4171
Allan G Stratford, *President*
Patrick Baxter, *Vice Pres*
Martin Brattrud, *Vice Pres*
EMP: 95
SQ FT: 38,000
SALES (est): 15.9MM **Privately Held**
SIC: 2512 2511 Upholstered household
furniture; tables, household: wood

(P-4659)
MONTE ALLEN INTERIORS INC
1505 W 139th St, Gardena (90249-2603)
PHONE..................................310 380-4640
ESA Maki, *Owner*
ESA Yla-Soininmaki, *Partner*
Timo Yla-Soininmaki, *Partner*
EMP: 40
SALES (est): 4.7MM **Privately Held**
WEB: www.monteallen.com
SIC: 2512 7641 2211 2511 Upholstered
household furniture; reupholstery & furni-
ture repair; slip cover fabrics, cotton;
wood household furniture

(P-4660)
MPB FURNITURE CORPORATION
414 W Ridgecrest Blvd, Ridgecrest
(93555-4015)
PHONE..................................760 375-4800
Mike McGee, *President*
Bill Farris, *General Mgr*
EMP: 12
SQ FT: 18,000
SALES (est): 1.3MM **Privately Held**
SIC: 2512 Upholstered household furniture

(P-4661)
MULHOLLAND BROTHERS (PA)
1710 4th St, Berkeley (94710-1711)
PHONE..................................415 824-5995
Jay Holland, *President*
Guy Holland, *Vice Pres*
▲ EMP: 26
SALES (est): 8.1MM **Privately Held**
WEB: www.mulhollandbrothers.com
SIC: 2512 5199 3161 Upholstered house-
hold furniture; leather, leather goods &
furs; cases, carrying

(P-4662)
OLD BONES CO
Also Called: Old Bones Company
641 Paularino Ave, Costa Mesa
(92626-3033)
PHONE..................................714 641-2800
Sheia Jalalvand, *Owner*
EMP: 12
SQ FT: 3,800
SALES (est): 732.6K **Privately Held**
SIC: 2512 Living room furniture: uphol-
stered on wood frames

(P-4663)
R J VINCENT INC
Also Called: Devon Furniture
1030 Abbot Ave, San Gabriel (91776-2902)
PHONE..................................626 448-1509
Sanh Phung, *President*
Luu Nguyen, *Treasurer*
▲ EMP: 25
SQ FT: 17,000

SALES (est): 1.3MM **Privately Held**
WEB: www.rjvincent.com
SIC: 2512 2511 Living room furniture: upholstered on wood frames; wood household furniture

(P-4664)
RAMON LOPEZ
Also Called: G R Furniture Manufacturing
9729 Alpaca St, South El Monte
(91733-3028)
PHONE..................................626 575-3891
Ramon Lopez, *Owner*
EMP: 14
SQ FT: 9,000
SALES (est): 690K **Privately Held**
WEB: www.ramonlopez.com
SIC: 2512 Living room furniture: uphol-
stered on wood frames

(P-4665)
RC FURNITURE INC
1111 Jellick Ave, City of Industry
(91748-1212)
PHONE..................................626 964-4100
Rene Cazares, *President*
Nora Pineda, *Human Res Mgr*
▲ EMP: 81
SQ FT: 25,000
SALES (est): 16.3MM **Privately Held**
WEB: www.rcfurniture.com
SIC: 2512 5021 Upholstered household
furniture; furniture

(P-4666)
REGAL FURNITURE MANUFACTURING
6007 S St Andrews Pl # 2, Los Angeles
(90047-1334)
PHONE..................................323 971-9185
Harvey Jacobson, *President*
Ron Jacobson, *Vice Pres*
EMP: 17 EST: 1945
SQ FT: 20,000
SALES (est): 1.9MM **Privately Held**
SIC: 2512 2426 Living room furniture: up-
holstered on wood frames; frames for up-
holstered furniture, wood

(P-4667)
REPUBLIC FURNITURE MFG INC
2241 E 49th St, Vernon (90058-2822)
PHONE..................................323 235-2144
Karen Rosen-Hirsch, *President*
Judy Rosen, *Vice Pres*
EMP: 42
SQ FT: 38,000
SALES (est): 5MM **Privately Held**
SIC: 2512 2515 Living room furniture: up-
holstered on wood frames; mattresses &
bedsprings

(P-4668)
ROMAN UPHOLSTERY MANUFACTURING
2008 Cotner Ave, Los Angeles
(90025-5604)
PHONE..................................310 479-3252
Steven Hipsman, *President*
Arthur J Hipsman, *Treasurer*
EMP: 11 EST: 1963
SQ FT: 5,000
SALES: 900K **Privately Held**
SIC: 2512 7641 Upholstered household
furniture; reupholstery

(P-4669)
ROYAL CUSTOM DESIGNS INC
13951 Monte Vista Ave, Chino
(91710-5536)
PHONE..................................909 591-8990
Raya Trietsch, *President*
Darius Panah, *CEO*
George Trietsch, *Treasurer*
Jack Sissoyev, *CIO*
Iris Tan, *Accounting Mgr*
▲ EMP: 120 EST: 1970
SQ FT: 35,000
SALES (est): 19.5MM **Privately Held**
WEB: www.royalcustomdesigns.com
SIC: 2512 Upholstered household furniture

(P-4670)
SOFA U LOVE (PA)
Also Called: Factory Showroom Exchange
1207 N Western Ave, Los Angeles
(90029-1018)
PHONE..................................323 464-3397
Varougan Karapetian, *President*
EMP: 22
SQ FT: 22,000
SALES (est): 5.6MM **Privately Held**
WEB: www.sofaulove.com
SIC: 2512 5712 Upholstered household
furniture; furniture stores

(P-4671)
SOLE DESIGNS INC
11685 Mcbean Dr, El Monte (91732-1104)
PHONE..................................626 452-8642
Linda Le, *CEO*
Lam Tran, *President*
▲ EMP: 17
SQ FT: 8,000
SALES (est): 2.2MM **Privately Held**
WEB: www.soledesigns.com
SIC: 2512 Upholstered household furniture

(P-4672)
STITCH INDUSTRIES INC
Also Called: Joybird
6055 E Wash Blvd Ste 900, Commerce
(90040-2453)
PHONE..................................888 282-0842
Kurt L Darrow, *CEO*
EMP: 50
SALES (est): 14.3MM
SALES (corp-wide): 1.7B **Publicly Held**
SIC: 2512 5961 5712 Upholstered house-
hold furniture; catalog & mail-order
houses; furniture stores
PA: La-Z-Boy Incorporated
1 Lazboy Dr
Monroe MI 48162
734 242-1444

(P-4673)
SUPERB CHAIR CORPORATION
Also Called: Patricia Edwards
6861 Watcher St, Commerce (90040-3715)
PHONE..................................562 776-1771
Audrey Smith, *President*
James E Smith, *Vice Pres*
Julie Smith, *Vice Pres*
EMP: 35
SQ FT: 36,000
SALES (est): 4.5MM **Privately Held**
WEB: www.patriciaedwards.com
SIC: 2512 Living room furniture: uphol-
stered on wood frames; chairs: uphol-
stered on wood frames; couches, sofas &
davenports: upholstered on wood frames

(P-4674)
TERRA FURNITURE INC
549 E Edna Pl, Covina (91723-1311)
PHONE..................................626 912-8523
Gary Stafford, *President*
▲ EMP: 41
SQ FT: 57,600
SALES (est): 5.4MM **Privately Held**
WEB: www.terrafurniture.com
SIC: 2512 2514 2522 2511 Upholstered
household furniture; metal household fur-
niture; office furniture, except wood; wood
lawn & garden furniture

(P-4675)
UPHOLSTERY FACTORY INC (PA)
Also Called: Home Collection Fine Furniture
74757 Joni Dr Ste 1, Palm Desert
(92260-2057)
PHONE..................................760 341-6865
Salvador Hernandez, *President*
Fernando Hernandez, *Vice Pres*
Sandra Hernandez, *Admin Sec*
EMP: 14
SQ FT: 13,200
SALES: 700K **Privately Held**
WEB: www.homecollectionfurniture.com
SIC: 2512 7641 2511 Couches, sofas &
davenports: upholstered on wood frames;
chairs: upholstered on wood frames; up-
holstery work; dining room furniture: wood

▲ = Import ▼=Export
◆ =Import/Export

(P-4676)
VAN SARK INC (PA)
Also Called: Dependable Furniture Mfg Co
888 Doolittle Dr, San Leandro
(94577-1020)
PHONE....................510 635-1111
Kevin Sarkisian, *President*
Baltazar Garcia, *Prdtn Mgr*
▲ EMP: 50
SQ FT: 75,000
SALES (est): 13.4MM **Privately Held**
WEB: www.dfmonline.com
SIC: 2512 Wood upholstered chairs &
couches

(P-4677)
VIOSKI INC
1625 S Magnolia Ave, Monrovia
(91016-4509)
PHONE....................626 359-4571
Douglas Desantis, *CEO*
EMP: 13
SALES: 1.3MM **Privately Held**
SIC: 2512 Couches, sofas & davenports:
upholstered on wood frames

(P-4678)
YEN-NHAI INC
Also Called: Nathan Anthony Furniture
4940 District Blvd, Vernon (90058-2718)
PHONE....................323 584-1315
Khai MAI, *President*
Randy Gleckman, *Natl Sales Mgr*
EMP: 40
SALES (est): 5.8MM **Privately Held**
SIC: 2512 Upholstered household furniture

2514 Metal Household Furniture

(P-4679)
A A CATER TRUCK MFG CO INC
Also Called: Hizco Truck Body
750 E Slauson Ave, Los Angeles
(90011-5236)
PHONE....................323 233-2343
Vahe Karapetian, *President*
Alex Mitchell, *MIS Mgr*
Richard Gomez, *Engineer*
ARA Agabjanian, *Purch Agent*
EMP: 75
SQ FT: 60,000
SALES (est): 8MM **Privately Held**
SIC: 2514 7538 Metal household furniture;
general truck repair

(P-4680)
AIRFLEX5D LLC
Also Called: Advaning
12282 Knott St, Garden Grove
(92841-2825)
PHONE....................855 574-0158
Wendy Lin, *Exec VP*
EMP: 10
SQ FT: 20,000
SALES (est): 753.8K **Privately Held**
SIC: 2514 Garden furniture, metal

(P-4681)
ALL AMERICAN FRAME & BEDG CORP
4641 Ardine St, Cudahy (90201-5801)
PHONE....................323 773-7415
Don Diep, *President*
Suzuyo Diep, *Admin Sec*
▲ EMP: 24
SQ FT: 10,600
SALES (est): 3MM **Privately Held**
SIC: 2514 Beds, including folding & cabi-
net, household: metal; frames for box
springs or bedsprings: metal

(P-4682)
ANVIL ARTS INC
1137 N Fountain Way, Anaheim
(92806-2009)
P.O. Box 4445, Orange (92863-4445)
PHONE....................714 630-2870
Gary Benson, *President*
EMP: 10
SQ FT: 7,000
SALES (est): 1MM **Privately Held**
SIC: 2514 3646 Metal household furniture;
ornamental lighting fixtures, commercial

(P-4683)
ATLANTIC REPRESENTATIONS INC
Also Called: Snowsound USA
10018 Santa Fe Springs Rd, Santa Fe
Springs (90670-2922)
P.O. Box 2399 (90670-0399)
PHONE....................562 903-9550
Leo Dardashti, *CEO*
Shahriar Dardashti, *President*
Farnaz Dardashti, *Vice Pres*
Mari Garibaldi, *Controller*
▲ EMP: 30
SQ FT: 150,000
SALES (est): 23.4MM **Privately Held**
WEB: www.atlantic-inc.com
SIC: 2514 2511 Metal household furniture;
wood household furniture

(P-4684)
ATLAS SURVIVAL SHELTERS LLC
7407 Telegraph Rd, Montebello
(90640-6515)
PHONE....................323 727-7084
Ronal D Hubbard, *Mng Member*
EMP: 25
SQ FT: 30,000
SALES: 3MM **Privately Held**
SIC: 2514 Beds, including folding & cabi-
net, household: metal

(P-4685)
BEST LIVING INTERNATIONAL INC
12234 Florence Ave, Santa Fe Springs
(90670-3806)
PHONE....................626 625-2911
Wenjie Kuang, *Principal*
EMP: 10
SQ FT: 40,000
SALES (est): 355.2K **Privately Held**
SIC: 2514 Metal lawn & garden furniture

(P-4686)
BULTHAUP CORP
153 S Robertson Blvd, Los Angeles
(90048-3207)
PHONE....................310 288-3875
Fax: 310 288-3885
EMP: 11
SALES (est): 1.1MM
SALES (corp-wide): 157.6MM **Privately Held**
SIC: 2514
PA: Bulthaup Gmbh & Co Kg
Werkstr. 4-6
Bodenkirchen 84155
874 180-0

(P-4687)
CASUALWAY USA LLC
Also Called: Casualway Home & Garden
1623 Lola Way, Oxnard (93030-5080)
PHONE....................805 660-7408
Guoxiang Wu,
Jian He, *Co-Owner*
Ralph Ybarra, *Vice Pres*
EMP: 99
SALES (est): 2.1MM **Privately Held**
SIC: 2514 Garden furniture, metal

(P-4688)
COSMO IMPORT & EXPORT LLC (PA)
3919 Channel Dr, West Sacramento
(95691-3431)
PHONE....................916 209-5500
Jennifer Hayes, *CEO*
EMP: 20
SQ FT: 100,000
SALES: 60MM **Privately Held**
SIC: 2514 Garden furniture, metal

(P-4689)
CURVE LINE METAL CORPORATION
Also Called: J H Castro
9705 Klingerman St, South El Monte
(91733-1728)
PHONE....................626 448-5956
Angelica Rodriguez, *President*
EMP: 12
SQ FT: 12,000

SALES (est): 1.5MM **Privately Held**
SIC: 2514 Backs & seats for metal household furniture

(P-4690)
EARTHLITE LLC (DH)
990 Joshua Way, Vista (92081-7855)
P.O. Box 51245, Los Angeles (90051-5245)
PHONE....................760 599-1112
James Chenevey, *CEO*
Richard Clark, *Technical Staff*
Erica Coble, *Business Mgr*
Ken Howard, *Purch Agent*
Oscar Mendez, *Mfg Staff*
◆ EMP: 106
SQ FT: 68,000
SALES (est): 42MM
SALES (corp-wide): 14.6MM **Privately Held**
WEB: www.earthlite.com
SIC: 2514 5091 2531 Tables, household:
metal; spa equipment & supplies; chairs,
portable folding
HQ: Earthlite Holdings, Llc
150 E 58th St Fl 37
New York NY 10155
212 317-2004

(P-4691)
INNOVATIVE DESIGNS & MFG INC
1067 W 5th St, Azusa (91702-3313)
PHONE....................626 812-4422
Ted Koroghlian, *CEO*
Peter Koroghlian, *General Mgr*
EMP: 10
SQ FT: 15,000
SALES (est): 686.4K **Privately Held**
WEB: www.idmfurnishings.com
SIC: 2514 1542 Metal household furniture;
commercial & office building contractors

(P-4692)
JBI LLC
Also Called: Buchbinder, Jay Industries
18521 S Santa Fe Ave, Compton
(90221-5624)
PHONE....................310 537-2910
Claudio Luna, *Manager*
EMP: 36
SALES (corp-wide): 52.9MM **Privately Held**
WEB: www.jbiindustries.com
SIC: 2514 2221 2511 Tables, household:
metal; fiberglass fabrics; wood household
furniture
PA: Jbi, Llc
2650 E El Presidio St
Long Beach CA 90810
310 886-8034

(P-4693)
KOLKKA JOHN
Also Called: Kolkka Furniture Design & Mfg
1300 Green Island Rd, Vallejo
(94503-9658)
PHONE....................707 554-3660
Fernando Flores, *Manager*
EMP: 29
SALES (corp-wide): 4.8MM **Privately Held**
SIC: 2514 Metal household furniture
PA: Kolkka, John
871 Charter St
Redwood City CA 94063
650 327-5001

(P-4694)
LEE SANDUSKY CORPORATION
Also Called: SANDUSKY LEE CORPORA-
TION
16125 Widmere Rd, Arvin (93203-9307)
P.O. Box 517 (93203-0517)
PHONE....................661 854-5551
Jim Coontz, *Branch Mgr*
Koleen Kelly, *Sales Executive*
EMP: 50
SALES (corp-wide): 32.8MM **Privately Held**
WEB: www.sanduskycabinets.com
SIC: 2514 2522 Metal household furniture;
office furniture, except wood
PA: Sandusky Lee Llc
80 Keystone St
Littlestown PA 17340
717 359-4111

(P-4695)
LUIS WTKINS CSTM WRUGHT IR LLC
Also Called: Watkins, Luis
3737 S Durango Ave, Los Angeles
(90034-3314)
PHONE....................310 836-5655
Ines Madison,
Freddy Fuentes,
EMP: 24
SQ FT: 5,000
SALES (est): 3.1MM **Privately Held**
SIC: 2514 3645 Metal household furniture;
residential lighting fixtures

(P-4696)
OAK LAND FURNITURE
Also Called: Oak Land Company
2462 Main St Ste D, Chula Vista
(91911-4694)
PHONE....................619 424-8758
Sasan Moazzam, *President*
EMP: 17
SQ FT: 8,000
SALES (est): 2MM **Privately Held**
SIC: 2514 2515 Metal bedroom furniture;
mattresses & bedsprings

(P-4697)
PACIFIC CASUAL LLC
1060 Avenida Acaso, Camarillo
(93012-8712)
PHONE....................805 445-8310
Rick Stephens, *Mng Member*
Dale C Boles, *CEO*
Shaun Sweeney, *Vice Pres*
Toni Wilson, *Finance*
Latrenda Bernard, *Opers Staff*
▲ EMP: 35
SQ FT: 29,000
SALES (est): 5.1MM **Privately Held**
SIC: 2514 Metal lawn & garden furniture

(P-4698)
PEREZ BROTHERS
Also Called: Perez Bros Ornamental Iron
19607 Prairie St, Northridge (91324-2426)
PHONE....................818 780-8482
Juan A Perez, *Owner*
Raul Perez, *Manager*
EMP: 10
SALES (est): 1.1MM **Privately Held**
SIC: 2514 Metal kitchen & dining room fur-
niture

(P-4699)
RSI HOME PRODUCTS INC (HQ)
400 E Orangethorpe Ave, Anaheim
(92801-1046)
PHONE....................714 449-2200
Alex Calabrese, *CEO*
David Lowrie, *CFO*
Jeff Hoeft, *Exec VP*
Jonathan Keefe, *Vice Pres*
Kreig Rugh, *Vice Pres*
▲ EMP: 700
SQ FT: 675,000
SALES (est): 1B
SALES (corp-wide): 1.6B **Publicly Held**
SIC: 2514 2541 3281 2434 Kitchen cabi-
nets: metal; medicine cabinets & vanities:
metal; counter & sink tops; cut stone &
stone products; wood kitchen cabinets
PA: American Woodmark Corporation
561 Shady Elm Rd
Winchester VA 22602
540 665-9100

(P-4700)
RSI HOME PRODUCTS INC
620 Newport Center Dr # 1200, Newport
Beach (92660-8012)
PHONE....................949 720-1116
Ken Snellings, *General Mgr*
EMP: 1000
SALES (corp-wide): 1.6B **Publicly Held**
SIC: 2514 2541 1751 Metal household
furniture; wood partitions & fixtures; cabi-
net & finish carpentry
HQ: Rsi Home Products, Inc.
400 E Orangethorpe Ave
Anaheim CA 92801
714 449-2200

P R O D U C T S & S V C S

(P-4701)
RSI HOME PRODUCTS MFG INC
400 E Orangethorpe Ave, Anaheim
(92801-1046)
P.O. Box 4120 (92803-4120)
PHONE.............................714 449-2200
Thomas Chieffe, *CEO*
Jeff Hoeft, *President*
▲ EMP: 100
SALES (est): 25.8MM
SALES (corp-wide): 1.6B **Publicly Held**
SIC: 2514 2541 3281 2434 Kitchen cabinets: metal; medicine cabinets & vanities: metal; counter & sink tops; cut stone & stone products; wood kitchen cabinets
HQ: Rsi Home Products, Inc.
400 E Orangethorpe Ave
Anaheim CA 92801
714 449-2200

(P-4702)
SURROUNDING ELEMENTS LLC
33051 Calle Aviador Ste A, San Juan
Capistrano (92675-4780)
PHONE.............................949 582-9000
Moss Shacter, *Mng Member*
Anthony C Geach,
EMP: 20
SQ FT: 15,000
SALES (est): 2.4MM **Privately Held**
WEB: www.surroundingelements.com
SIC: 2514 Lawn furniture: metal

(P-4703)
THOMAS LUNDBERG
Also Called: Lundberg Designs
2620 3rd St, San Francisco (94107-3115)
PHONE.............................415 695-0110
Thomas Lundberg, *Owner*
EMP: 12
SQ FT: 5,000
SALES (est): 1.2MM **Privately Held**
WEB: www.lundbergdesign.com
SIC: 2514 Metal household furniture

(P-4704)
TK CLASSICS LLC
3771 Channel Dr 100, West Sacramento
(95691-3421)
PHONE.............................916 209-5500
Jennifer Hayes, *CEO*
EMP: 20
SQ FT: 100,000
SALES: 60MM **Privately Held**
SIC: 2514 Garden furniture, metal
PA: Cosmo Import & Export, Llc
3919 Channel Dr
West Sacramento CA 95691
916 209-5500

(P-4705)
**TROPITONE FURNITURE CO
INC (HQ)**
5 Marconi, Irvine (92618-2594)
PHONE.............................949 595-2000
Randy Danielson, *Exec VP*
Walter Cornelison, *Vice Pres*
Rebecca Cotogno, *General Mgr*
Clinton Cornelison, *Technology*
Anne C Mattson, *Credit Mgr*
◆ EMP: 300 EST: 1954
SQ FT: 100,000
SALES: 100MM **Privately Held**
WEB: www.tropitone.com
SIC: 2514 2522 Garden furniture, metal; camp furniture: metal; office furniture, except wood

(P-4706)
URBAN STEEL DESIGNS INC
4679 18th St Unit A, San Francisco
(94114-1833)
PHONE.............................415 305-2570
Jens Schlueter, *CEO*
EMP: 12
SALES (est): 1.3MM **Privately Held**
SIC: 2514 5712 2542 Metal household furniture; custom made furniture, except cabinets; partitions & fixtures, except wood

(P-4707)
VICTOR MARTIN INC
Also Called: Corsican Furniture
1640 W 132nd St, Gardena (90249-2039)
PHONE.............................323 587-3101

Martin Perfit, *President*
Marvin Alperin, *Principal*
EMP: 140
SQ FT: 100,000
SALES (est): 7.5MM **Privately Held**
WEB: www.victormartin.com
SIC: 2514 Beds, including folding & cabinet, household: metal

(P-4708)
WESLEY ALLEN INC (PA)
Also Called: Iron Beds of America
1001 E 60th St, Los Angeles (90001-1098)
PHONE.............................323 231-4275
Victor Sawan, *CEO*
Fran Chesaux, *Administration*
Daniel Molina, *Purchasing*
▲ EMP: 140
SQ FT: 100,000
SALES (est): 20.2MM **Privately Held**
WEB: www.wesleyallen.com
SIC: 2514 Metal household furniture

**2515 Mattresses &
Bedsprings**

(P-4709)
AIR DREAMS MATTRESSES
3266 Rosemead Blvd, El Monte
(91731-2807)
PHONE.............................626 573-5733
Felipe Carlos, *Owner*
EMP: 12
SQ FT: 12,000
SALES (est): 1MM **Privately Held**
SIC: 2515 2512 5712 5021 Mattresses, innerspring or box spring; upholstered household furniture; mattresses; mattresses

(P-4710)
AMERICAN NATIONAL MFG INC
252 Mariah Cir, Corona (92879-1751)
PHONE.............................951 273-7888
Eve Miller, *President*
Craig Miller, *Vice Pres*
▲ EMP: 110
SQ FT: 75,000
SALES (est): 20.5MM **Privately Held**
WEB: www.americannationalmfg.com
SIC: 2515 5712 Mattresses & bedsprings; furniture stores

(P-4711)
**AMF SUPPORT SURFACES INC
(DH)**
1691 N Delilah St, Corona (92879-1885)
PHONE.............................951 549-6800
Fredrick Kohnke, *CEO*
Carole A Wyatt, *President*
Charles C Wyatt, *President*
Curt Wyatt, *CEO*
Kara Johan, *COO*
▲ EMP: 162 EST: 1932
SQ FT: 40,000
SALES (est): 26.4MM
SALES (corp-wide): 2.8B **Publicly Held**
WEB: www.amfsupport.com
SIC: 2515 Mattresses, containing felt, foam rubber, urethane, etc.
HQ: Anodyne Medical Device, Inc.
1069 State Road 46 E
Batesville IN 47006
954 340-0500

(P-4712)
BIG SLEEP FUTON INC
Also Called: Big Tree Big Sleep
760 S Vail Ave, Montebello (90640-4954)
PHONE.............................800 647-2671
Ying He, *CEO*
Robert Pecorara, *President*
▲ EMP: 22
SALES (est): 3.1MM **Privately Held**
SIC: 2515 Sleep furniture

(P-4713)
BRENTWOOD HOME LLC (PA)
Also Called: Silverrest
701 Burning Tree Rd Ste A, Fullerton
(92833-1451)
PHONE.............................562 949-3759
Vy Nguyen, *President*
EMP: 128 EST: 2015

SQ FT: 80,000
SALES (est): 32.7MM **Privately Held**
SIC: 2515 5021 5712 Mattresses, containing felt, foam rubber, urethane, etc.; mattresses; mattresses

(P-4714)
BRENTWOOD HOME LLC
2301 E 7th St Ste 417, Los Angeles
(90023-1035)
PHONE.............................213 457-7626
Vy Nguyen, *President*
Oscar Ruiz, *Opers Staff*
EMP: 12
SALES (corp-wide): 32.7MM **Privately
Held**
SIC: 2515 5021 5712 Mattresses, containing felt, foam rubber, urethane, etc.; mattresses; mattresses
PA: Brentwood Home, Llc
701 Burning Tree Rd Ste A
Fullerton CA 92833
562 949-3759

(P-4715)
**COMFORT-PEDIC MATTRESS
USA**
Also Called: Resta Mattress
9080 Charles Smith Ave, Rancho Cucamonga (91730-5566)
PHONE.............................909 810-2600
Raouf Ghobrial, *President*
EMP: 10
SALES: 2MM **Privately Held**
WEB: www.comfortpedicmattress.com
SIC: 2515 5021 5712 Mattresses & bedsprings; mattresses; mattresses

(P-4716)
CRISTAL MATERIALS INC
6825 Mckinley Ave, Los Angeles
(90001-1525)
PHONE.............................323 855-1688
Luis Ponce, *CEO*
EMP: 10 EST: 2013
SALES (est): 1.7MM **Privately Held**
SIC: 2515 5999 3086 Mattresses, containing felt, foam rubber, urethane, etc.; foam & foam products; plastics foam products

(P-4717)
CUEVAS MATTRESS INC
Also Called: Springpudic
3504 E Olympic Blvd, Los Angeles
(90023-3924)
PHONE.............................310 631-8382
Isabel Cuevas, *President*
EMP: 14
SALES (corp-wide): 1.1MM **Privately
Held**
SIC: 2515 Mattresses & bedsprings
PA: Cuevas Mattress Inc.
5843 S Broadway
Los Angeles CA 90003
310 631-8382

(P-4718)
DELLA ROBBIA INC
796 E Harrison St, Corona (92879-1348)
PHONE.............................951 372-9199
David Soonlan, *President*
▲ EMP: 20
SQ FT: 72,000
SALES: 5MM **Privately Held**
SIC: 2515 Sofa beds (convertible sofas)

(P-4719)
ES KLUFT & COMPANY INC (PA)
11096 Jersey Blvd Ste 101, Rancho Cucamonga (91730-5158)
PHONE.............................909 373-4211
David Binke, *CEO*
Ron Bruneau, *COO*
Alan Docherty, *CFO*
Alwyna Luceno, *Office Mgr*
Celia Correa, *Accounting Mgr*
◆ EMP: 176
SALES (est): 63.1MM **Privately Held**
WEB: www.kluftmattress.com
SIC: 2515 Mattresses, innerspring or box spring

(P-4720)
GOLDEN MATTRESS CO INC
4231 Firestone Blvd, South Gate
(90280-3223)
PHONE.............................323 887-1888
San Dang, *CEO*
Phuc Nguyen, *Vice Pres*
▲ EMP: 52
SQ FT: 33,000
SALES (est): 7.1MM **Privately Held**
SIC: 2515 5021 Mattresses & foundations; mattresses

(P-4721)
**HANDCRAFT MATTRESS
COMPANY**
1131 Baker St, Costa Mesa (92626-4114)
PHONE.............................714 241-8316
Dave Ogle, *CEO*
EMP: 12
SQ FT: 16,000
SALES (est): 1.6MM **Privately Held**
WEB: www.hmcwest.com
SIC: 2515 Mattresses & foundations

(P-4722)
**HOSPITALITY SLEEP SYSTEMS
INC**
107 E Rialto Ave, San Bernardino
(92408-1128)
PHONE.............................909 387-9779
Cristiana Solorio, *CEO*
EMP: 11
SALES (est): 1.3MM **Privately Held**
SIC: 2515 Mattresses & foundations; mattresses, innerspring or box spring

(P-4723)
INNOVATIVE R ADVANCED (PA)
Also Called: Smart Foam Pads
23101 Lake Center Dr # 100, Lake Forest
(92630-2801)
PHONE.............................949 273-8100
Robert Doherty, *CEO*
Timothy G Woodward, *COO*
Michael Seffer, *CFO*
EMP: 15
SQ FT: 4,000
SALES: 1.2MM **Publicly Held**
SIC: 2515 Mattresses, containing felt, foam rubber, urethane, etc.

(P-4724)
INNOVATIVE R ADVANCED
3401 Etiwanda Ave, Jurupa Valley
(91752-1128)
PHONE.............................949 273-8100
Brad Bannister, *Manager*
EMP: 30
SALES (corp-wide): 1.2MM **Publicly Held**
SIC: 2515 Mattresses, containing felt, foam rubber, urethane, etc.
PA: Advanced Innovative Recovery Technologies, Inc.
23101 Lake Center Dr # 100
Lake Forest CA 92630
949 273-8100

(P-4725)
JONA GLOBAL TRADING INC
Also Called: Foam Depot
245 S 8th Ave, La Puente (91746-3210)
PHONE.............................626 855-2588
Jack Hung, *President*
▲ EMP: 10
SALES (est): 942.2K **Privately Held**
SIC: 2515 Mattresses, containing felt, foam rubber, urethane, etc.

(P-4726)
KINGDOM MATTRESS INC
Also Called: Kingdom Matress Company
17920 S Figueroa St, Gardena
(90248-4211)
PHONE.............................562 630-5531
Jose Flores, *President*
EMP: 35
SALES (est): 4.3MM **Privately Held**
SIC: 2515 Mattresses & bedsprings

▲ = Import ▼=Export
◆ =Import/Export

(P-4727)
LEGGETT & PLATT INCORPORATED
Also Called: Lpcc 6008
1050 S Dupont Ave, Ontario (91761-1578)
PHONE..................909 937-1010
Barry Kubasak, *Manager*
EMP: 96
SALES (corp-wide): 4.2B **Publicly Held**
SIC: 2515 Mattresses, innerspring or box spring
PA: Leggett & Platt, Incorporated
1 Leggett Rd
Carthage MO 64836
417 358-8131

(P-4728)
LEGGETT & PLATT INCORPORATED
Whittier 0e00
12352 Whittier Blvd, Whittier (90602-1015)
PHONE..................562 945-2641
Ray Wolven, *Branch Mgr*
Jorge Cruz, *Maint Spvr*
EMP: 73
SQ FT: 226,000
SALES (corp-wide): 4.2B **Publicly Held**
WEB: www.leggett.com
SIC: 2515 2511 Mattresses & bedsprings; wood household furniture
PA: Leggett & Platt, Incorporated
1 Leggett Rd
Carthage MO 64836
417 358-8131

(P-4729)
MARSPRING CORPORATION
4920 S Boyle Ave, Vernon (90058-3017)
PHONE..................800 522-5252
Ronald Greitzer, *Manager*
EMP: 34
SALES (corp-wide): 10.3MM **Privately Held**
WEB: www.marflex.com
SIC: 2515 Spring cushions
PA: Marspring Corporation
4920 S Boyle Ave
Vernon CA 90058
323 589-5637

(P-4730)
MARSPRING CORPORATION
Also Called: Los Angeles Fiber Co
5190 S Santa Fe Ave, Vernon (90058-3532)
P.O. Box 58643, Los Angeles (90058-0643)
PHONE..................310 484-6849
Ronald Greitzer, *President*
EMP: 34
SALES (corp-wide): 10.3MM **Privately Held**
WEB: www.marflex.com
SIC: 2515 Spring cushions
PA: Marspring Corporation
4920 S Boyle Ave
Vernon CA 90058
323 589-5637

(P-4731)
MBC MATTRESS CO INC
19270 Envoy Ave, Corona (92881-3839)
PHONE..................951 371-8044
Charles H Mumford, *President*
Micheal Gargaliss, *Vice Pres*
EMP: 25
SALES (est): 3.2MM **Privately Held**
SIC: 2515 Mattresses, innerspring or box spring

(P-4732)
MIRACLE BEDDING CORPORATION
3700 Capitol Ave, City of Industry (90601-1731)
PHONE..................562 908-2370
CAM Hua, *President*
CAM Tu Hua, *President*
Quyen Lieu, *Treasurer*
▲ EMP: 50
SQ FT: 100,000
SALES (est): 5.3MM **Privately Held**
SIC: 2515 5719 5712 Mattresses, containing felt, foam rubber, urethane, etc.; mattresses, innerspring or box spring; bedding (sheets, blankets, spreads & pillows); mattresses

(P-4733)
NATIONAL BEDDING COMPANY LLC
Also Called: Serta International
6818 Patterson Pass Rd, Livermore (94550-4230)
PHONE..................925 373-1350
Michael Traub, *President*
EMP: 200
SALES (est): 5.9MM **Privately Held**
SIC: 2515 Mattresses & bedsprings
PA: Serta Simmons Bedding, Llc
2451 Industry Ave
Atlanta GA 30360

(P-4734)
ORGANIC MATTRESSES INC
Also Called: OMI
1335 Harter Pkwy, Yuba City (95993-2604)
PHONE..................530 790-6723
Walt Bader, *President*
Jeri Kemmer, *Opers Spvr*
Whitney Roe, *Sales Staff*
▲ EMP: 35
SQ FT: 60,000
SALES (est): 6.4MM **Privately Held**
WEB: www.omimattress.com
SIC: 2515 Mattresses & foundations

(P-4735)
PARAMOUNT MATTRESS INC
2900 E Olympic Blvd, Los Angeles (90023-3431)
PHONE..................323 264-3451
Hector Hernandez, *President*
▼ EMP: 10
SQ FT: 10,000
SALES: 650K **Privately Held**
WEB: www.paramountmatt.com
SIC: 2515 Mattresses, innerspring or box spring

(P-4736)
PLEASANT MATTRESS INC
Also Called: McRoskey Mattress
1687 Market St, San Francisco (94103-1237)
PHONE..................415 874-7540
Paul Deming, *Branch Mgr*
Marina Polyak, *Sales Staff*
EMP: 14
SALES (corp-wide): 22.8MM **Privately Held**
WEB: www.mcroskey.com
SIC: 2515 Mattresses & foundations
PA: Pleasant Mattress, Inc.
375 S West Ave
Fresno CA 93706
559 268-6446

(P-4737)
PLEASANT MATTRESS INC (PA)
Also Called: Cannon Sleep Products
375 S West Ave, Fresno (93706-1341)
PHONE..................559 268-6446
Herbert Morgenstern, *President*
Stephanie Aguilar, *Treasurer*
Judy Davis, *Vice Pres*
Pao Vang, *MIS Mgr*
Russell Raymond, *Opers Staff*
◆ EMP: 86 EST: 1948
SQ FT: 100,000
SALES (est): 22.8MM **Privately Held**
WEB: www.cannonsleep.com
SIC: 2515 Mattresses & foundations

(P-4738)
PURA NATURALS INC
3401 Etiwanda Ave, Jurupa Valley (91752-1128)
PHONE..................949 273-8100
Brad Bannister, *Manager*
EMP: 30
SALES (corp-wide): 1.2MM **Publicly Held**
SIC: 2515 Mattresses, containing felt, foam rubber, urethane, etc.

HQ: Pura Naturals, Inc.
23101 Lake Center Dr # 100
Lake Forest CA 92630
949 273-8100

(P-4739)
RGR DIVERSIFIED SERVICES INC
5635 Panorama Dr, Whittier (90601-2428)
PHONE..................562 522-0028
Arthur G Rios, *President*
EMP: 15
SALES (est): 1.2MM **Privately Held**
SIC: 2515 Mattresses & bedsprings

(P-4740)
ROYAL-PEDIC MATTRESS MFG LLC
Also Called: Royalpedic Mattress Mfg
331 N Fries Ave, Wilmington (90744-5624)
PHONE..................310 518-5420
Tony E Keleman, *Manager*
EMP: 25
SALES (est): 2.2MM
SALES (corp-wide): 3.1MM **Privately Held**
WEB: www.royalpedic.com
SIC: 2515 5021 5712 Mattresses & bedsprings; mattresses, innerspring or box spring; mattresses; mattresses
PA: Royal-Pedic Mattress Manufacturing, Llc
341 N Robertson Blvd
Beverly Hills CA 90211
310 278-9594

(P-4741)
SEALY MATTRESS MFG CO INC
1130 7th St, Richmond (94801-2103)
PHONE..................510 235-7171
Curt Maszun, *Branch Mgr*
EMP: 200
SQ FT: 238,000
SALES (corp-wide): 2.7B **Publicly Held**
SIC: 2515 Mattresses, innerspring or box spring
HQ: Sealy Mattress Manufacturing Company, Llc
1 Office Parkway Rd
Trinity NC 27370
336 861-3500

(P-4742)
SKY RIDER EQUIPMENT CO INC
1180 N Blue Gum St, Anaheim (92806-2409)
PHONE..................714 632-6890
Martin Villegas, *CEO*
Carl Gray, *President*
Dev Donnelley, *Vice Pres*
Karl Keranen, *Vice Pres*
Desiree Avila, *Executive Asst*
▲ EMP: 30
SQ FT: 12,000
SALES (est): 6MM **Privately Held**
WEB: www.sky-rider.com
SIC: 2515 7349 5719 Foundations & platforms; window cleaning; window shades

(P-4743)
SLEEPRITE INDUSTRIES INC
Also Called: Restonic/San Francisco
1492 Rollins Rd, Burlingame (94010-2307)
P.O. Box 814 (94011-0710)
PHONE..................650 344-1980
Jeffrey S Karp, *President*
Elaine Karp, *Corp Secy*
Randall H Karp, *Vice Pres*
▼ EMP: 25 EST: 1968
SQ FT: 30,000
SALES (est): 4.2MM **Privately Held**
SIC: 2515 Mattresses, containing felt, foam rubber, urethane, etc.; mattresses, innerspring or box spring

(P-4744)
SOUTH BAY INTERNATIONAL INC
8570 Hickory Ave, Rancho Cucamonga (91739-9632)
PHONE..................909 718-5000
Guohai Tang, *President*
Daniella Serven, *CEO*
Wendiao Hou, *CFO*
Weijun She, *Admin Sec*

▲ EMP: 25
SALES (est): 32.2MM **Privately Held**
SIC: 2515 Mattresses & bedsprings

(P-4745)
SPECFOAM LLC
13215 Marlay Ave, Fontana (92337-6942)
PHONE..................951 685-3626
Hector Jimenez,
EMP: 18
SQ FT: 26,000
SALES (est): 2.3MM **Privately Held**
SIC: 2515 Mattresses, containing felt, foam rubber, urethane, etc.

(P-4746)
SQUARE DEAL MATTRESS FACTORY
Also Called: Square Deal Mat Fctry & Uphl
1354 Humboldt Ave, Chico (95928-5952)
PHONE..................530 342-2510
Lois Lash, *President*
Richard Lash, *President*
EMP: 24
SQ FT: 6,000
SALES (est): 2.6MM **Privately Held**
WEB: www.squaredealmattress.com
SIC: 2515 Mattresses & bedsprings; furniture stores

(P-4747)
SSB MANUFACTURING COMPANY
20100 S Alameda St, Compton (90221-6208)
PHONE..................770 512-7700
Tito Lampon, *General Mgr*
Michael King, *Controller*
EMP: 108 **Privately Held**
WEB: www.simmonscompany.com
SIC: 2515 5021 Bedsprings, assembled; box springs, assembled; mattresses
HQ: Ssb Manufacturing Company
1 Concourse Pkwy Ste 800
Atlanta GA 30328
770 512-7700

(P-4748)
VISIONARY SLEEP LLC
2060 S Wineville Ave A, Ontario (91761-3633)
PHONE..................909 605-2010
Carter Gronbach, *Manager*
EMP: 58
SALES (corp-wide): 4MM **Privately Held**
SIC: 2515 Mattresses, innerspring or box spring
PA: Visionary Sleep, Llc
Moon Lake Blvd Ste 205
Hoffman Estates IL 60169
812 945-4155

(P-4749)
WICKLINE BEDDING ENTP CORP
Also Called: Sleep Therapy
1199 Elfin Forest Rd E, San Marcos (92078-1077)
PHONE..................760 747-7761
Kuan-Yu Chen, *Principal*
Jack Chen, *CEO*
▲ EMP: 30
SALES (est): 4.5MM **Privately Held**
SIC: 2515 Mattresses, innerspring or box spring

(P-4750)
WILLIAMS FOAM INC
12961 San Fernando Rd, Sylmar (91342-3656)
PHONE..................818 833-4343
William Ramirez, *President*
▲ EMP: 12
SQ FT: 30,000
SALES: 2MM **Privately Held**
WEB: www.williamsfoam.com
SIC: 2515 3069 3086 Mattresses, containing felt, foam rubber, urethane, etc.; foam rubber; plastics foam products

(P-4751)
ZINUS INC (HQ)
1951 Fairway Dr Ste A, San Leandro (94577-5643)
PHONE..................925 417-2100

P R O D U C T S & S V C S

Youn Jae Lee, *President*
Brad Song, *Office Admin*
Jiyun Jeong, *Accounting Mgr*
Soojin Lee, *Accounting Mgr*
Stephanie TSO, *Accountant*
▲ EMP: 70
SQ FT: 155,000
SALES: 123.8MM **Privately Held**
WEB: www.zinus.com
SIC: 2515 Chair & couch springs, assembled

2517 Wood T V, Radio, Phono & Sewing Cabinets

(P-4752)
ANA GLOBAL LLC
2360 Marconi Ct, San Diego (92154-7241)
PHONE................................619 482-9990
MD Anwarul Hoque, *Purchasing*
Yesenia Rivera, *Purchasing*
Mamoru Kojima, *Marketing Staff*
Yoshiaki Nishiba,
Anisuz Zaman,
▲ EMP: 800
SALES (est): 149.3MM **Privately Held**
SIC: 2517 5999 Television cabinets, wood; medical apparatus & supplies

(P-4753)
GILBERT MARTIN WDWKG CO INC (PA)
Also Called: Martin Furniture
2345 Britannia Blvd, San Diego (92154-8313)
PHONE................................800 268-5669
Gilbert Martin, *President*
Mark Mitchell, *Vice Pres*
Rich Hartig, *QC Mgr*
Vincent Noel, *Sales Staff*
Alberto Enriquez, *Manager*
◆ EMP: 30
SQ FT: 210,000
SALES (est): 47.8MM **Privately Held**
WEB: www.martinfurniture.com
SIC: 2517 2511 2521 5021 Home entertainment unit cabinets, wood; stereo cabinets, wood; television cabinets, wood; wood household furniture; wood office furniture; furniture stores

(P-4754)
PARKER HOUSE MFG CO INC
Also Called: Parker House International
6300 Providence Way, Eastvale (92880-9636)
PHONE................................800 628-1319
Chris Lupo, *President*
Arlene M Zonni, *COO*
Maria R Lupo, *Corp Secy*
Victor Zonni, *Chief Mktg Ofcr*
Robert Glick, *Vice Pres*
▲ EMP: 30
SQ FT: 135,000
SALES (est): 15.9MM **Privately Held**
SIC: 2517 2511 Wood television & radio cabinets; bookcases, household: wood

(P-4755)
SPARTAK ENTERPRISES INC
11186 Venture Dr, Mira Loma (91752-1194)
PHONE................................951 360-0610
Armen Babayan, *President*
EMP: 30
SQ FT: 40,000
SALES (est): 4.4MM **Privately Held**
WEB: www.spartakent.com
SIC: 2517 2522 Wood television & radio cabinets; office furniture, except wood

(P-4756)
TOCABI AMERICA CORPORATION
333 H St Ste 5007, Chula Vista (91910-5561)
P.O. Box 5397 (91912-5397)
PHONE................................619 661-6136
▲ EMP: 23
SALES (est): 2MM **Privately Held**
WEB: www.tocabi.com
SIC: 2517 2542 2521 2511

(P-4757)
WEBB MASSEY CO INC
201 W Carleton Ave, Orange (92867-3678)
P.O. Box 4969 (92863-4969)
PHONE................................714 639-6012
EMP: 32
SALES (est): 1.7MM **Privately Held**
SIC: 2517

(P-4758)
ZELCO CABINET MFG INC
298 W Robles Ave, Santa Rosa (95407-8118)
PHONE................................707 584-1121
Zelco Cecich-Karuzic, *President*
Paula Cecich-Karuzic, *Vice Pres*
Margo Abraham, *Admin Sec*
EMP: 10
SQ FT: 12,000
SALES (est): 1MM **Privately Held**
SIC: 2517 2434 Home entertainment unit cabinets, wood; wood kitchen cabinets

2519 Household Furniture, NEC

(P-4759)
ACRYLIC DISTRIBUTION CORP
8501 Lankershim Blvd, Sun Valley (91352-3127)
PHONE................................818 767-8448
Shlomi Haziza, *Principal*
Soli Amor, *Treasurer*
Nick Enriques, *General Mgr*
▲ EMP: 75
SALES (est): 9.7MM **Privately Held**
WEB: www.hstudio.com
SIC: 2519 Furniture, household: glass, fiberglass & plastic

(P-4760)
ALVARADO ALTA CALIDAD LLC
Also Called: Alvarado Alta Clidad Cstm Furn
2907 Humboldt St, Los Angeles (90031-1828)
PHONE................................323 222-0038
Robert Alvarado,
EMP: 12
SQ FT: 10,000
SALES: 1.5MM **Privately Held**
SIC: 2519 Household furniture, except wood or metal: upholstered

(P-4761)
AMERICAN FURNITURE ALIANCE INC
9141 Arrow Rte, Rancho Cucamonga (91730-4414)
PHONE................................323 804-5242
John Chang, *CEO*
Paul Chien, *Director*
EMP: 10
SQ FT: 1,000
SALES (est): 2MM **Privately Held**
SIC: 2519 3291 ; tripoli

(P-4762)
ARKTURA LLC (PA)
18225 S Figueroa St, Gardena (90248-4216)
PHONE................................310 532-1050
Chris Kabatsi, *CEO*
▲ EMP: 30
SALES: 9MM **Privately Held**
SIC: 2519 Furniture, household: glass, fiberglass & plastic

(P-4763)
BAKER INTERIORS FURNITURE CO
Also Called: McGuire Furniture
101 Henry Adams St # 350, San Francisco (94103-5222)
PHONE................................415 626-1414
EMP: 45 **Privately Held**
SIC: 2519 2511 2512 Rattan furniture: padded or plain; wood household furniture; upholstered household furniture
HQ: Baker Interiors Furniture Company
1 Baker Way
Connelly Springs NC 28612
828 397-1440

(P-4764)
CALIFRNIA FURN COLLECTIONS INC
Also Called: Artifacts International
150 Reed Ct Ste A, Chula Vista (91911-5890)
PHONE................................619 621-2455
Eric Vogt, *President*
Omaha Manzanilla, *Vice Pres*
Monica Reyes, *Accounting Mgr*
EMP: 114
SQ FT: 40,000
SALES (est): 9.9MM **Privately Held**
WEB: www.artifactsinternational.com
SIC: 2519 2514 2511 2512 Household furniture, except wood or metal: upholstered; metal household furniture; household furniture: upholstered on metal frames; wood household furniture; upholstered household furniture

(P-4765)
DWELL HOME INC
39962 Cedar Blvd Ste 277, Newark (94560-5326)
PHONE................................877 864-5752
EMP: 10
SALES (est): 840K **Privately Held**
SIC: 2519

(P-4766)
MEADOW DECOR INC
1477 E Cedar St Ste A, Ontario (91761-8330)
PHONE................................909 923-2558
Jun Chen, *CEO*
David Mok, *Ch of Bd*
John Chen, *President*
Lily Chen, *Vice Pres*
Jiali Zhang, *Principal*
▲ EMP: 13
SQ FT: 24,000
SALES (est): 4MM **Privately Held**
SIC: 2519 2392 Lawn & garden furniture, except wood & metal; cushions & pillows

(P-4767)
NEXT DAY FRAME INC
11560 Wright Rd, Lynwood (90262-3944)
PHONE................................310 886-0851
Nancy Abelar, *CEO*
EMP: 65
SALES (est): 5MM **Privately Held**
SIC: 2519 Household furniture, except wood or metal: upholstered

(P-4768)
NICHOLAS MICHAEL DESIGNS INC
2330 Raymer Ave, Fullerton (92833-2515)
PHONE................................714 562-8101
Michael A Cimarueti, *CEO*
Bruce Triolo, *VP Sales*
▲ EMP: 120
SALES (est): 18.7MM **Privately Held**
SIC: 2519 Household furniture, except wood or metal: upholstered

(P-4769)
PATIO & DOOR OUTLET INC (PA)
Also Called: Patio Outlet
410 W Fletcher Ave, Orange (92865-2612)
PHONE................................714 974-9900
Christopher Lyons, *President*
▲ EMP: 23
SQ FT: 200,000
SALES (est): 2.6MM **Privately Held**
SIC: 2519 5712 2514 5031 Garden furniture, except wood, metal, stone or concrete; outdoor & garden furniture; garden furniture, metal; lumber, plywood & millwork; furniture

(P-4770)
PF PLASTICS INC
Also Called: Crystal Craft
2044 Wright Ave, La Verne (91750-5821)
PHONE................................909 392-4488
Parviz Youssefy, *President*
EMP: 13
SQ FT: 10,300

SALES (est): 1.5MM **Privately Held**
WEB: www.crystalcraft.com
SIC: 2519 2541 Household furniture, except wood or metal: upholstered; display fixtures, wood; store fixtures, wood

(P-4771)
PRC COMPOSITES LLC
1400 S Campus Ave, Ontario (91761-4330)
PHONE................................909 391-2006
John Upsher, *Mng Member*
Gene Gregory,
EMP: 99 EST: 2014
SALES (est): 17.7MM **Privately Held**
SIC: 2519 Furniture, household: glass, fiberglass & plastic

(P-4772)
RECYCLED SPACES INC
Also Called: High Camp Home
10191 Donner Pass Rd # 1, Truckee (96161-0408)
P.O. Box 10358 (96162-0358)
PHONE................................530 587-3394
Diana Vincent, *CEO*
Teresa Mersky, *President*
▲ EMP: 15
SALES (est): 2.1MM **Privately Held**
WEB: www.highcamphome.com
SIC: 2519 5712 Lawn & garden furniture, except wood & metal; furniture stores

(P-4773)
SEATING COMPONENT MFG INC
3951 E Miraloma Ave, Anaheim (92806-6201)
PHONE................................714 693-3376
Daryl Fossier, *President*
EMP: 12
SQ FT: 12,000
SALES (est): 1.5MM **Privately Held**
SIC: 2519 Fiberglass furniture, household: padded or plain

(P-4774)
STONE YARD INC
Also Called: Carlsbad Manufacturing
6056 Corte Del Cedro, Carlsbad (92011-1514)
PHONE................................858 586-1580
Mitchell Brean, *President*
◆ EMP: 45
SALES (est): 4.4MM **Privately Held**
WEB: www.stoneyardinc.com
SIC: 2519 Household furniture, except wood or metal: upholstered

(P-4775)
TAZI DESIGNS
2660 Bridgeway, Sausalito (94965-1482)
PHONE................................415 503-0013
Hicham Tazi, *Owner*
▲ EMP: 10
SALES (est): 1.1MM **Privately Held**
SIC: 2519 Household furniture

(P-4776)
VINOTEMP INTERNATIONAL CORP (PA)
16782 Von Karman Ave # 15, Irvine (92606-2417)
PHONE................................310 886-3332
India Hynes, *CEO*
India Ravel, *CFO*
Kevin Henry, *Business Dir*
Alvin Patrick, *General Mgr*
Karen Philvin, *General Mgr*
▲ EMP: 70
SQ FT: 70,000
SALES (est): 13.1MM **Privately Held**
WEB: www.vinotemp.com
SIC: 2519 Household furniture, except wood or metal: upholstered

(P-4777)
WISE LIVING INC
2001 W 60th St, Los Angeles (90047-1037)
PHONE................................323 541-0410
Jose A Pinedo, *CEO*
Jeff Fitch, *Representative*
EMP: 35
SALES (est): 5.1MM **Privately Held**
SIC: 2519 Household furniture, except wood or metal: upholstered

▲ = Import ▼=Export
◆ =Import/Export

2521 Wood Office Furniture

(P-4778)
A M CABINETS INC (PA)
239 E Gardena Blvd, Gardena (90248-2813)
PHONE.............................310 532-1919
Alex H Mc Kay Jr, *President*
Travis McKay, *General Mgr*
Nancy Wolfinger, *Admin Sec*
Nicole Wilson, *Admin Asst*
Anthony Duggan, *Project Mgr*
EMP: 90
SQ FT: 35,000
SALES (est): 20.4MM **Privately Held**
WEB: www.amcabinets.com
SIC: 2521 2434 2541 Wood office furniture; wood kitchen cabinets; counters or counter display cases, wood

(P-4779)
ACTION LAMINATES LLC
3400 Investment Blvd, Hayward (94545-3811)
PHONE.............................510 259-6217
Daniel Johnston,
EMP: 13
SQ FT: 12,000
SALES (est): 2.1MM **Privately Held**
WEB: www.actionlaminates.com
SIC: 2521 Wood office furniture

(P-4780)
AMERICON
900 Flynn Rd, Camarillo (93012-8703)
PHONE.............................805 987-0412
Bill Farrah, *President*
EMP: 17
SQ FT: 30,000
SALES (est): 4MM **Privately Held**
WEB: www.americon-usa.com
SIC: 2521 3663 Wood office furniture; radio & TV communications equipment

(P-4781)
AMPINE LLC
11610 Ampine Fibreform Rd, Sutter Creek (95685-9686)
PHONE.............................209 223-1690
Terry Velasco, *General Mgr*
EMP: 112
SALES (corp-wide): 340.8MM **Privately Held**
SIC: 2521 Wood office furniture
HQ: Ampine, Llc
11300 Ridge Rd
Martell CA 95654
209 223-6091

(P-4782)
AMQ SOLUTIONS LLC (HQ)
764 Walsh Ave, Santa Clara (95050-2613)
PHONE.............................877 801-0370
James P Keane, *President*
▲ EMP: 14
SALES (est): 2.7MM
SALES (corp-wide): 3.4B **Publicly Held**
SIC: 2521 2522 5021 Wood office desks & tables; office chairs, benches & stools, except wood; office furniture
PA: Steelcase Inc.
901 44th St Se
Grand Rapids MI 49508
616 247-2710

(P-4783)
ANDERSON DESK INC
7510 Airway Rd Ste 7, San Diego (92154-8303)
PHONE.............................619 671-1040
Mark Baker, *President*
Jose Campos, *Info Tech Mgr*
▲ EMP: 300
SALES (est): 27.9MM
SALES (corp-wide): 3.4B **Publicly Held**
SIC: 2521 Wood office furniture
PA: Steelcase Inc.
901 44th St Se
Grand Rapids MI 49508
616 247-2710

(P-4784)
ANTIQUE DESIGNS LTD INC
916 W Hyde Park Blvd, Inglewood (90302-3308)
PHONE.............................310 671-5400
▲ EMP: 31
SQ FT: 6,000
SALES: 120K **Privately Held**
WEB: www.antiquedesigns.net
SIC: 2521 2426 2511

(P-4785)
ARTISTIC CONCEPTS
3293 N San Fernando Rd, Los Angeles (90065-1414)
PHONE.............................323 257-8101
Oscar Mejia, *President*
EMP: 10
SQ FT: 3,000
SALES (est): 808.1K **Privately Held**
WEB: www.laform.com
SIC: 2521 Cabinets, office: wood

(P-4786)
BAUSMAN AND COMPANY INC (PA)
1500 Crafton Ave Bldg 124, Mentone (92359-1304)
PHONE.............................909 947-0139
Craig L Johnson, *CEO*
Craig Johnson, *CEO*
Robert Williams, *Vice Pres*
EMP: 249 EST: 1971
SALES (est): 34.7MM **Privately Held**
WEB: www.bausman.net
SIC: 2521 2511 Wood office furniture; wood household furniture

(P-4787)
BKON INTERIOR SOUTION
15330 Allen St, Paramount (90723-4012)
PHONE.............................562 408-1655
Jong Lee, *Owner*
Terry Kim, *Co-Owner*
EMP: 10
SQ FT: 10,000
SALES (est): 1.1MM **Privately Held**
SIC: 2521 2431 Cabinets, office: wood; interior & ornamental woodwork & trim

(P-4788)
CAPITOL STORE FIXTURES
Also Called: Capitol Components
4220 Pell Dr Ste C, Sacramento (95838-2575)
PHONE.............................916 646-9096
Toll Free:.............................888
Jim Pelc, *President*
Vicki Pelc, *Vice Pres*
EMP: 25
SQ FT: 24,000
SALES (est): 3.6MM **Privately Held**
WEB: www.csfixtures.com
SIC: 2521 5046 Cabinets, office: wood; shelving, commercial & industrial

(P-4789)
CASEWORX INC
1130 Research Dr, Redlands (92374-4562)
PHONE.............................909 799-8550
Bruce Humphrey, *President*
Melissa Fletcher, *Office Mgr*
▲ EMP: 37
SQ FT: 28,000
SALES (est): 5.9MM **Privately Held**
SIC: 2521 Cabinets, office: wood

(P-4790)
CENTRAL COAST CABINETS
111a Lee Rd, Watsonville (95076-9422)
PHONE.............................831 724-2992
Kelly Souza, *Co-Owner*
Todd Souza, *Co-Owner*
EMP: 10
SQ FT: 34,000
SALES (est): 1.2MM **Privately Held**
SIC: 2521 2434 Cabinets, office: wood; wood kitchen cabinets

(P-4791)
COLOMBARAS CABINET & MLLWK INC
421 4th St, Woodland (95695-4011)
PHONE.............................530 662-2665
Craig Colombara, *President*
Eileen Colombara, *CFO*
Raymond Colombara, *Vice Pres*
Elaine Scarlett, *Admin Sec*
EMP: 10
SQ FT: 11,000
SALES (est): 1.5MM **Privately Held**
WEB: www.colombaras.com
SIC: 2521 5251 2541 2434 Cabinets, office: wood; builders' hardware; sink tops, plastic laminated; table or counter tops, plastic laminated; vanities, bathroom: wood

(P-4792)
COMMERCIAL FURNITURE
1261 N Lakeview Ave, Anaheim (92807-1834)
PHONE.............................714 350-7045
Bob Gomez, *President*
EMP: 20
SQ FT: 8,500
SALES (est): 2MM **Privately Held**
WEB: www.commfurn.com
SIC: 2521 7641 Wood office furniture; upholstery work

(P-4793)
CREATIVE WOOD PRODUCTS INC
900 77th Ave, Oakland (94621-2573)
PHONE.............................510 635-5399
Jose Mendes, *President*
Polly Peggs Mendes, *CFO*
Polly Mendes, *Safety Mgr*
Michelle Caluag, *Marketing Mgr*
▲ EMP: 120 EST: 1964
SQ FT: 85,000
SALES (est): 20.1MM **Privately Held**
WEB: www.creativewood.net
SIC: 2521 Desks, office: wood

(P-4794)
CRI SUB 1 (DH)
Also Called: E O C
1715 S Anderson Ave, Compton (90220-5005)
PHONE.............................310 537-1657
Ken Bodger, *CEO*
Richard L Sinclair Jr, *President*
Charles Hess, *Vice Pres*
▲ EMP: 15
SQ FT: 120,000
SALES (est): 1.6MM
SALES (corp-wide): 70.7MM **Privately Held**
WEB: www.eoccorp.com
SIC: 2521 Cabinets, office: wood; chairs, office: padded, upholstered or plain: wood; panel systems & partitions (free-standing), office: wood

(P-4795)
DESKMAKERS INC
6525 Flotilla St, Commerce (90040-1713)
PHONE.............................323 264-2260
Philip K Polishook, *CEO*
Daniel Boiles, *Vice Pres*
John Bornstein, *Vice Pres*
April Simental, *Finance*
Jose Bugarin, *Opers Staff*
◆ EMP: 50
SQ FT: 105,000
SALES (est): 10.2MM **Privately Held**
SIC: 2521 Desks, office: wood

(P-4796)
FAUSTINOS CHAIR FACTORY INC
2425 S Malt Ave, Commerce (90040-3201)
P.O. Box 911515, Los Angeles (90091-1239)
PHONE.............................323 724-8055
Faustino Limon, *President*
Bertha Mancilla,
▲ EMP: 50
SQ FT: 90,000
SALES (est): 7.3MM **Privately Held**
WEB: www.faustinoschairfactory.com
SIC: 2521 Wood office furniture

(P-4797)
FORTRESS INC
Also Called: Off Broadway
1721 Wright Ave, La Verne (91750-5841)
PHONE.............................909 593-8600
Donald I Wolper, *President*
Nancy Ancheta, *Controller*
▲ EMP: 35 EST: 1959
SQ FT: 100
SALES (est): 5.5MM **Privately Held**
WEB: www.fortresseating.com
SIC: 2521 2522 Chairs, office: padded, upholstered or plain: wood; chairs, office: padded or plain, except wood

(P-4798)
GALTECH COMPUTER CORPORATION
Also Called: Galtech International
501 Flynn Rd, Camarillo (93012-8756)
P.O. Box 305, Newbury Park (91319-0305)
PHONE.............................805 376-1060
Fei Lin Ko, *CEO*
Jim Lai, *Shareholder*
Robert Ko, *President*
▲ EMP: 20
SQ FT: 32,000
SALES (est): 11.9MM **Privately Held**
WEB: www.galtechcorp.com
SIC: 2521 Benches, office: wood

(P-4799)
GARFIELD COMMERCIAL ENTPS
15977 Heron Ave, La Mirada (90638-5512)
PHONE.............................714 690-5959
Simon Yao, *President*
EMP: 49 EST: 2015
SALES (est): 3.7MM **Privately Held**
SIC: 2521 2531 2519 2512 Wood office furniture; school furniture; household furniture; chairs: upholstered on wood frames

(P-4800)
GRAHAM LEE ASSOCIATES INC
8674 Atlantic Ave, South Gate (90280-3502)
PHONE.............................323 581-8203
Charles Graham, *President*
Michael Chu, *Shareholder*
Brian Krueger, *Shareholder*
Ywart Lee, *Vice Pres*
EMP: 17
SQ FT: 11,000
SALES (est): 1.4MM **Privately Held**
WEB: www.grahamlee.com
SIC: 2521 Cabinets, office: wood

(P-4801)
HERMAN MILLER INC
2740 Zanker Rd Ste 150, San Jose (95134-2132)
PHONE.............................408 432-5730
Marcus Lohela, *Principal*
EMP: 24
SALES (corp-wide): 2.5B **Publicly Held**
SIC: 2521 Wood office furniture
PA: Herman Miller, Inc.
855 E Main Ave
Zeeland MI 49464
616 654-3000

(P-4802)
HPL CONTRACT INC
525 Baldwin Rd, Patterson (95363-8859)
PHONE.............................209 892-1717
Frank Stratiotis, *President*
Jim Robertson, *Vice Pres*
EMP: 17
SQ FT: 7,200
SALES (est): 3.9MM **Privately Held**
WEB: www.hplcontract.com
SIC: 2521 Wood office furniture

(P-4803)
INTERIOR WOOD OF SAN DIEGO
1215 W Nutmeg St, San Diego (92101-1230)
PHONE.............................619 295-6469
Alan Marshall, *President*
EMP: 32
SQ FT: 10,000
SALES (est): 3.9MM **Privately Held**
WEB: www.interiorwood.com
SIC: 2521 Cabinets, office: wood

(P-4804)
IRONIES LLC
2222 5th St, Berkeley (94710-2217)
PHONE.............................510 644-2100
Kathleen McIntyre, *President*

EMP: 35
SALES (est): 6.2MM **Privately Held**
WEB: www.ironies.com
SIC: 2521 Wood office furniture

(P-4805)
J & C CUSTOM CABINETS INC
11451 Elks Cir, Rancho Cordova
(95742-7355)
PHONE..................916 638-3400
Chris Christie, *Ch of Bd*
James E Farrell, *President*
EMP: 20
SQ FT: 20,000
SALES: 2.8MM **Privately Held**
SIC: 2521 2434 Cabinets, office: wood;
wood kitchen cabinets

(P-4806)
KINGS CABINET SYSTEMS
426 Park Ave, Hanford (93230-4440)
PHONE..................559 584-9662
Fax: 559 584-9670
EMP: 13 **EST:** 1977
SQ FT: 12,500
SALES (est): 1.2MM **Privately Held**
SIC: 2521

(P-4807)
KNOLL INC
555 W 5th St Ste 3100, Los Angeles
(90013-1018)
PHONE..................310 289-5800
Rosa Sinnott, *Manager*
EMP: 25 **Publicly Held**
WEB: www.knoll.com
SIC: 2521 Wood office furniture
PA: Knoll, Inc.
1235 Water St
East Greenville PA 18041

(P-4808)
LIGNUM VITAE CABINET
1625 16th St, Oakland (94607-1541)
PHONE..................510 444-2030
James Martin, *Owner*
EMP: 10 **EST:** 1976
SALES (est): 1MM **Privately Held**
WEB: www.lignumvitae.com
SIC: 2521 2511 5712 7389 Wood office
furniture; wood household furniture; cabi-
net work, custom;

(P-4809)
MONTBLEAU & ASSOCIATES INC (PA)
555 Raven St, San Diego (92102-4523)
PHONE..................619 263-5550
Ron P Montbleau, *President*
Laura Everds, *CFO*
Barton Ward, *Exec VP*
David Zammit, *Vice Pres*
Marti Montbleau, *Admin Sec*
EMP: 90 **EST:** 1980
SQ FT: 32,000
SALES (est): 17.7MM **Privately Held**
WEB: www.montbleau.com
SIC: 2521 1751 2434 Wood office furni-
ture; cabinet building & installation; wood
kitchen cabinets

(P-4810)
NAKAMURA-BEEMAN INC
8520 Wellsford Pl, Santa Fe Springs
(90670-2226)
PHONE..................562 696-1400
Mike Beeman, *President*
Jack Loudermill, *Opers Mgr*
EMP: 40 **EST:** 1978
SQ FT: 20,000
SALES (est): 6.3MM **Privately Held**
WEB: www.nbifixtures.com
SIC: 2521 3429 2541 Wood office furni-
ture; cabinet hardware; display fixtures,
wood

(P-4811)
NEW MAVERICK DESK INC
15100 S Figueroa St, Gardena
(90248-1724)
PHONE..................310 217-1554
John Long, *CEO*
Rich Mealey, *President*
Ted Jaroszewicz, *CEO*
Donald Clark, *Purchasing*

Jamie Sameshima, *Manager*
▲ **EMP:** 150
SQ FT: 1,000
SALES (est): 19.8MM **Privately Held**
SIC: 2521 Wood office furniture
HQ: Workstream Inc.
3158 Production Dr
Fairfield OH 45014

(P-4812)
NORSTAR OFFICE PRODUCTS INC (PA)
Also Called: Boss
5353 Jillson St, Commerce (90040-2115)
PHONE..................323 262-1919
William W Huang, *President*
◆ **EMP:** 40
SQ FT: 150,000
SALES (est): 247.7MM **Privately Held**
WEB: www.bosschair.com
SIC: 2521 2522 Chairs, office: padded,
upholstered or plain: wood; chairs, office:
padded or plain, except wood

(P-4813)
NORTHWOOD DESIGN PARTNERS INC
1550 Atlantic St, Union City (94587-2006)
PHONE..................510 731-6505
Michael Hayes, *CEO*
Josh Michael Hayes, *President*
Gcc Coyle, *Exec VP*
Sowmya Sankar, *Design Engr*
Fernando Bernasconi, *VP Opers*
EMP: 38
SQ FT: 2,000
SALES (est): 7.4MM **Privately Held**
SIC: 2521 2431 Wood office furniture; mill-
work

(P-4814)
OAK DESIGN CORPORATION
13272 6th St, Chino (91710-4108)
PHONE..................909 628-9597
Ismaell Castellanos, *President*
Julio Salas, *President*
EMP: 25
SALES (est): 3.1MM **Privately Held**
WEB: www.oakdesigns.net
SIC: 2521 2434 2511 Wood office furni-
ture; wood kitchen cabinets; wood bed-
room furniture

(P-4815)
OFFICE CHAIRS INC
Also Called: Oci
14815 Radburn Ave, Santa Fe Springs
(90670-5319)
PHONE..................562 802-0464
Sharon Klapper, *President*
Joseph J Klapper Jr, *Corp Secy*
Donald J Simek, *Exec VP*
Jay Klapper, *Technology*
▲ **EMP:** 60 **EST:** 1974
SQ FT: 60,000
SALES (est): 10.3MM **Privately Held**
WEB: www.officechairs.net
SIC: 2521 2512 Wood office furniture;
chairs: upholstered on wood frames

(P-4816)
OFS BRANDS HOLDINGS INC
5559 Mcfadden Ave, Huntington Beach
(92649-1317)
PHONE..................714 903-2257
Craig Baker, *President*
EMP: 11
SALES (est): 1.9MM **Privately Held**
SIC: 2521 Wood office furniture

(P-4817)
OHIO INC
630 Treat Ave, San Francisco
(94110-2016)
PHONE..................415 647-6446
David Pierce, *President*
Nicholas Ruiz, *Opers Staff*
EMP: 13 **EST:** 1996
SQ FT: 7,000
SALES (est): 500K **Privately Held**
SIC: 2521 Wood office furniture

(P-4818)
RAINBOW MANUFACTURING CO INC
1504 W 58th St, Los Angeles (90062-2824)
PHONE..................323 778-2093
David Azari, *President*
Rachel Azari, *Vice Pres*
Moshe Azari, *Admin Sec*
▲ **EMP:** 10
SQ FT: 9,000
SALES (est): 1.3MM **Privately Held**
SIC: 2521 Wood office furniture

(P-4819)
RBF GROUP INTERNATIONAL
Also Called: Rbf Lifestyle Holdings
1441 W 2nd St, Pomona (91766-1202)
PHONE..................626 333-5700
Robert Brown, *CEO*
Chris Hernandez, *Controller*
▲ **EMP:** 19
SALES (est): 2.1MM **Privately Held**
SIC: 2521 Chairs, office: padded, uphol-
stered or plain: wood

(P-4820)
S & H CABINETS AND MFG INC
10860 Mulberry Ave, Fontana
(92337-7027)
PHONE..................909 357-0551
Michael Hansen, *CEO*
Rich Hansen, *Manager*
EMP: 40 **EST:** 1954
SQ FT: 22,000
SALES (est): 6.2MM **Privately Held**
WEB: www.shcabinets.com
SIC: 2521 2541 2431 Cabinets, office:
wood; table or counter tops, plastic lami-
nated; millwork

(P-4821)
SARDO BUS & COACH UPHOLSTERY
512 W Rosecrans Ave, Gardena
(90248-1515)
PHONE..................800 654-3824
Jim Kemme, *Manager*
EMP: 60
SALES: 950K **Privately Held**
SIC: 2521 2512 Chairs, office: padded,
upholstered or plain: wood; couches,
sofas & davenports: upholstered on wood
frames

(P-4822)
STOLO CABINETS INC (PA)
Also Called: Stolo Custom Cabinets
860 Challenger St, Brea (92821-2946)
PHONE..................714 529-7303
Gary Stolo, *Vice Pres*
Robert F Stolo, *Treasurer*
Justin Stolo, *Vice Pres*
Jo Nagel, *Admin Asst*
Mark Amador, *Prgrmr*
EMP: 45
SQ FT: 15,000
SALES (est): 7.9MM **Privately Held**
WEB: www.stolocabinets.com
SIC: 2521 Cabinets, office: wood

(P-4823)
TRINITY OFFICE FURNITURE INC
1050 W Rialto Ave, San Bernardino
(92410-2376)
P.O. Box 1526, Wildomar (92595-1526)
PHONE..................909 888-5551
James B Kesterson, *President*
Marci Kesterson, *Admin Sec*
▲ **EMP:** 70
SQ FT: 135,000
SALES (est): 5.4MM **Privately Held**
SIC: 2521 2511 5021 Wood office furni-
ture; wood household furniture; office fur-
niture

(P-4824)
VALLEY OAKS INDUSTRIES
Also Called: Valley Oak Cabinets
3550 E Highway 246 Ste Ae, Santa Ynez
(93460-9480)
P.O. Box 1097 (93460-1097)
PHONE..................805 688-2754
Tom Carlson, *President*
Kim Carlson, *Vice Pres*

EMP: 17
SALES (est): 2.5MM **Privately Held**
WEB: www.valleyoakindustries.com
SIC: 2521 2511 Wood office furniture;
wood household furniture

(P-4825)
ZENBOOTH INC
650 University Ave # 10, Berkeley
(94710-1946)
PHONE..................510 646-8368
Sam Johnson, *CEO*
EMP: 24 **EST:** 2016
SALES (est): 3.6MM **Privately Held**
SIC: 2521 Wood office furniture

(P-4826)
ZUO MODERN CONTEMPORARY INC (PA)
80 Swan Way Ste 300, Oakland
(94621-1440)
PHONE..................510 777-1030
Luis Ruesga, *CEO*
Steven Poon, *COO*
Terry Tam, *CFO*
Roberto Chavez, *Branch Mgr*
Eljuris Ceballos, *Opers Staff*
◆ **EMP:** 26
SQ FT: 64,000
SALES: 25.4MM **Privately Held**
WEB: www.zuomod.com
SIC: 2521 3645 Wood office furniture; res-
idential lighting fixtures

2522 Office Furniture, Except Wood

(P-4827)
AMERICAN FURNITURE SYSTEMS INC
Also Called: Advantage Custom Fixtures
14105 Avalon Blvd, Los Angeles
(90061-2637)
P.O. Box 1235, San Gabriel (91778-1235)
PHONE..................626 457-9900
Allen Sterris, *President*
EMP: 34
SQ FT: 50,000
SALES: 2.5MM **Privately Held**
WEB: www.americanfurnituresys.com
SIC: 2522 5411 Office furniture, except
wood; convenience stores

(P-4828)
ANGELL & GIROUX INC
2727 Alcazar St, Los Angeles (90033-1196)
PHONE..................323 269-8596
Richard M Hart, *CEO*
Carol A Hart, *Vice Pres*
Kenneth Hart, *Vice Pres*
Rosemary Vazquez, *Executive*
EMP: 52
SQ FT: 13,000
SALES (est): 9.9MM **Privately Held**
WEB: www.angellandgiroux.com
SIC: 2522 3479 Cabinets, office: except
wood; painting, coating & hot dipping;
enameling, including porcelain, of metal
products

(P-4829)
ARTE DE MEXICO INC (PA)
1000 Chestnut St, Burbank (91506-1623)
PHONE..................818 753-4559
Gerald J Stoffers, *CEO*
▲ **EMP:** 90
SQ FT: 103,000
SALES (est): 22.5MM **Privately Held**
WEB: www.artedemexico.com
SIC: 2522 3645 Office furniture, except
wood; residential lighting fixtures

(P-4830)
BENCH-TEK SOLUTIONS LLC
525 Aldo Ave, Santa Clara (95054-2205)
P.O. Box 640818, San Jose (95164-0818)
PHONE..................408 653-1100
Maria Castellon,
Jorge Castellon,
▼ **EMP:** 13
SQ FT: 8,000

SALES: 4MM **Privately Held**
WEB: www.bench-tek.com
SIC: **2522** 2599 Benches, office: except wood; work benches, factory

(P-4831)
D3 INC (PA)
Also Called: 9 To 5 Seating
3211 Jack Northrop Ave, Hawthorne (90250-4424)
PHONE....................................310 223-2200
Darius Mir, *CEO*
Susan Mir, *Vice Pres*
David Effio, *Software Dev*
Tom Jackson, *Technician*
Refugio Leanos, *Prdtn Mgr*
◆ EMP: 103
SQ FT: 50,000
SALES (est): 20.1MM **Privately Held**
WEB: www.9to5seating.com
SIC: **2522** Chairs, office: padded or plain, except wood

(P-4832)
ELITE MFG CORP
Also Called: Elite Modern
12143 Altamar Pl, Santa Fe Springs (90670-2501)
PHONE....................................888 354-8356
Peter Luong, *CEO*
Michael Luong, *CFO*
Robinson Ho, *Vice Pres*
▲ EMP: 102
SQ FT: 62,000
SALES (est): 17.7MM **Privately Held**
SIC: **2522** 2514 Office furniture, except wood; metal household furniture

(P-4833)
ENCORE SEATING INC
5692 Fresca Dr, La Palma (90623-1048)
PHONE....................................562 926-1969
Casey Journigan, *President*
Chris Burgess, *Vice Pres*
▲ EMP: 100
SQ FT: 53,000
SALES (est): 7.5MM **Privately Held**
WEB: www.encoreseating.com
SIC: **2522** Chairs, office: padded or plain, except wood

(P-4834)
ERGODIRECT INC
1601 Old County Rd, San Carlos (94070-5204)
PHONE....................................650 654-4300
Nasser M Moshiri, *President*
Nazan Meysami, *General Mgr*
EMP: 10
SALES (est): 1.3MM **Privately Held**
SIC: **2522** Office furniture, except wood

(P-4835)
ERGONONMIC COMFORT DESIGN INC
9140 Stellar Ct Ste B, Corona (92883-4902)
P.O. Box 79018 (92877-0167)
PHONE....................................951 277-1558
Aldolfo Agramonte, *President*
Patricia Agramonte, *Vice Pres*
Veronica Luna, *Manager*
▲ EMP: 18
SQ FT: 22,000
SALES (est): 3.6MM **Privately Held**
WEB: www.ecdonline.net
SIC: **2522** Office chairs, benches & stools, except wood

(P-4836)
EXEMPLIS LLC
Also Called: Sit On It
6280 Artesia Blvd, Buena Park (90620-1004)
PHONE....................................714 995-4800
Paul Devries, *Manager*
EMP: 35 **Privately Held**
SIC: **2522** 2521 2512 Chairs, office: padded or plain, except wood; wood office furniture; upholstered household furniture
PA: Exemplis Llc
6415 Katella Ave
Cypress CA 90630

(P-4837)
EXEMPLIS LLC
Also Called: Ideon
6280 Artesia Blvd, Buena Park (90620-1004)
PHONE....................................714 898-5500
Craig Dumity, *Director*
EMP: 260 **Privately Held**
SIC: **2522** 5021 Chairs, office: padded or plain, except wood; furniture
PA: Exemplis Llc
6415 Katella Ave
Cypress CA 90630

(P-4838)
EXEMPLIS LLC (PA)
Also Called: Sitonit
6415 Katella Ave, Cypress (90630-5245)
PHONE....................................714 995-4800
Paul Devries, *CEO*
Patrick Sommerfield, *Exec VP*
Jared Abramowitz, *Vice Pres*
Ryan Dibble, *Vice Pres*
Kevin Mulcahy, *Vice Pres*
◆ EMP: 40
SQ FT: 20,000
SALES (est): 137.4MM **Privately Held**
SIC: **2522** Chairs, office: padded or plain, except wood

(P-4839)
HAWORTH INC
144 N Robertson Blvd # 202, West Hollywood (90048-3109)
PHONE....................................310 854-7633
EMP: 17
SALES (corp-wide): 1.2B **Privately Held**
SIC: **2522** 5021
HQ: Haworth, Inc.
1 Haworth Ctr
Holland MI 49423
616 393-3000

(P-4840)
HNI CORPORATION
3780 Pell Cir, Sacramento (95838-2528)
PHONE....................................916 927-0400
EMP: 318
SALES (corp-wide): 2.2B **Publicly Held**
SIC: **2522** Office furniture, except wood
PA: Hni Corporation
600 E 2nd St
Muscatine IA 52761
563 272-7400

(P-4841)
KORDEN INC
611 S Palmetto Ave, Ontario (91762-4124)
PHONE....................................909 988-8979
Barjona S Meek, *Principal*
Thomas Mc Cormick, *President*
Jim Ethridge, *Exec VP*
EMP: 13 **EST:** 1949
SQ FT: 75,000
SALES (est): 3MM **Privately Held**
WEB: www.korden.com
SIC: **2522** Stools, office: except wood

(P-4842)
MARK RESOURCES LLC (PA)
1962 22nd Ave, San Francisco (94116-1209)
PHONE....................................415 515-5540
Lloyd Mark,
David Mark,
EMP: 10
SQ FT: 2,500
SALES (est): 840.4K **Privately Held**
SIC: **2522** 7221 8742 8711 Office furniture, except wood; photographer, still or video; business planning & organizing services; designing: ship, boat, machine & product

(P-4843)
MC-DOWELL-CRAIG MFGCO (PA)
Also Called: McDowell Craig
13146 Firestone Blvd, Santa Fe Springs (90670-5517)
PHONE....................................714 521-7170
Brent McDowell, *Admin Sec*
EMP: 12
SQ FT: 125,000

SALES (est): 2.3MM **Privately Held**
WEB: www.mcdowell-craig.com
SIC: **2522** Cabinets, office: except wood

(P-4844)
MCDOWELL & CRAIG OFF SYSTEMS
Also Called: McDowell-Craig Office Furn
13146 Firestone Blvd, Norwalk (90650)
P.O. Box 349 (90651-0349)
PHONE....................................562 921-4441
Brent G McDowell, *President*
Jeffrey C McDowell, *Admin Sec*
EMP: 70
SQ FT: 117,000
SALES (est): 8.3MM **Privately Held**
WEB: www.mcdowellcraig.com
SIC: **2522** Office furniture, except wood

(P-4845)
MODULAR OFFICE SOLUTIONS INC
11701 6th St, Rancho Cucamonga (91730-6030)
PHONE....................................909 476-4200
Daniel G Coelho, *CEO*
Jorge E Robles, *President*
▲ EMP: 100 **EST:** 1999
SQ FT: 173,000
SALES (est): 9.8MM **Privately Held**
SIC: **2522** 2521 Office furniture, except wood; wood office furniture

(P-4846)
OFFICE MASTER INC
1110 Mildred St, Ontario (91761-3512)
PHONE....................................909 392-5678
William Chow, *CEO*
Wallace Hwang, *Vice Pres*
Linda Hsu, *Manager*
◆ EMP: 60
SQ FT: 70,000
SALES (est): 12.4MM **Privately Held**
WEB: www.office-master.com
SIC: **2522** Office chairs, benches & stools, except wood

(P-4847)
RDM INDUSTRIAL PRODUCTS INC
1652 Watson Ct, Milpitas (95035-6822)
PHONE....................................408 945-8400
Ricky Vigil, *President*
Kristi Cubillo, *Info Tech Mgr*
Kristi Ehrhorn, *Manager*
Michele Gomez, *Manager*
Lynn Tweedie, *Assistant*
EMP: 18 **EST:** 1976
SQ FT: 17,000
SALES: 3MM **Privately Held**
WEB: www.rdm-ind.com
SIC: **2522** 5712 2521 Cabinets, office: except wood; cabinet work, custom; custom made furniture, except cabinets; office furniture; cabinets, office: wood

(P-4848)
SISNEROS INC
Also Called: Sisneros Office Furntiure
12717 Los Nietos Rd, Santa Fe Springs (90670-3007)
PHONE....................................562 777-9797
Luis Sisneros, *President*
Margarita Sisneros, *Vice Pres*
EMP: 20
SQ FT: 20,000
SALES (est): 2.7MM **Privately Held**
SIC: **2522** Office furniture, except wood

(P-4849)
STEELCASE INC
111 Rhode Island St, San Francisco (94103-5200)
PHONE....................................415 865-0261
EMP: 263
SALES (corp-wide): 3.4B **Publicly Held**
SIC: **2522** Office furniture, except wood
PA: Steelcase Inc.
901 44th St Se
Grand Rapids MI 49508
616 247-2710

(P-4850)
Z-LINE DESIGNS INC (PA)
2410 San Ramon Valley Blv, San Ramon (94583-1791)
PHONE....................................925 743-4000
James Sexton, *President*
John Negovetich, *Treasurer*
Rick Lamb, *Vice Pres*
Pauleen Sexton, *Admin Sec*
Jason Peralta, *Administration*
◆ EMP: 90
SQ FT: 13,000
SALES (est): 10.9MM **Privately Held**
WEB: www.z-linedesigns.com
SIC: **2522** Office furniture, except wood

2531 Public Building & Related Furniture

(P-4851)
AEROFOAM INDUSTRIES INC
Also Called: QUALITY FOAM PACKAGING
31855 Corydon St, Lake Elsinore (92530-8501)
PHONE....................................951 245-4429
Noel Castellon Jr, *President*
Ruth Castellon, *Treasurer*
James Barrett, *Vice Pres*
Jim Barrett, *Vice Pres*
Castellon Noel, *Vice Pres*
▲ EMP: 80
SQ FT: 150,000
SALES: 21.2MM **Privately Held**
SIC: **2531** Seats, aircraft

(P-4852)
AIRO INDUSTRIES COMPANY
429 Jessie St, San Fernando (91340-2541)
PHONE....................................818 838-1008
Bahram Salem, *President*
Mike Salem, *Vice Pres*
Adam Lari, *Materials Mgr*
Shakila Ardakani, *Marketing Staff*
Ryan Ranjbar, *Sales Staff*
▲ EMP: 25
SQ FT: 20,000
SALES (est): 4.1MM **Privately Held**
WEB: www.airoindustries.com
SIC: **2531** 4581 Seats, aircraft; aircraft upholstery repair

(P-4853)
ALUMINUM SEATING INC
555 Tennis Court Ln, San Bernardino (92408-1615)
PHONE....................................909 884-9449
Sakorn Sirirat, *President*
Quy Van Dang, *Vice Pres*
EMP: 10
SQ FT: 15,000
SALES (est): 828.6K **Privately Held**
SIC: **2531** Stadium seating

(P-4854)
COD USA INC
Also Called: Creative Outdoor Distrs USA
25954 Commercentre Dr, Lake Forest (92630-8815)
PHONE....................................949 381-7367
Heather Smulson, *President*
Brian Horowitz, *CEO*
Barbara Tolbert, *COO*
◆ EMP: 23
SQ FT: 34,000
SALES (est): 4.1MM **Privately Held**
SIC: **2531** Chairs, portable folding; chairs, table & arm

(P-4855)
COUNTY OF MARIN
Also Called: Parks and Open Space
3501 Civic Center Dr, San Rafael (94903-4112)
PHONE....................................415 446-4414
Linda Dahl, *Director*
EMP: 70 **Privately Held**
SIC: **2531** 9111 Picnic tables or benches, park; county supervisors' & executives' offices
PA: County Of Marin
3501 Civic Center Dr # 258
San Rafael CA 94903
415 473-6358

(P-4856)
DANG THA
Also Called: Skyline Seating
13050 Hoover St, Westminster
(92683-2388)
PHONE.....................714 898-0989
Tha Dang, *Owner*
EMP: 15
SQ FT: 3,000
SALES (est): 1.1MM **Privately Held**
SIC: 2531 Seats, automobile

(P-4857)
DEFOE FURNITURE FOR KIDS INC
910 S Grove Ave, Ontario (91761-3435)
PHONE.....................909 947-4459
John G Defoe, *President*
Narcisa Defoe, *Treasurer*
EMP: 16
SQ FT: 17,000
SALES (est): 2.4MM **Privately Held**
SIC: 2531 School furniture

(P-4858)
ECR4KIDS LP
Also Called: Early Childhood Resources
4370 Jutland Dr, San Diego (92117-3642)
PHONE.....................619 323-2005
Mitchell Lynn,
Steve McMahon, *Purch Mgr*
Jamie Lasky, *Purchasing*
Ashley McElravy, *Marketing Mgr*
Ashley West, *Marketing Mgr*
◆ EMP: 23
SALES (est): 11.5MM **Privately Held**
WEB: www.ecr4kids.com
SIC: 2531 3944 2511 5021 Chairs, table
& arm; craft & hobby kits & sets; chil-
dren's wood furniture; chairs; public build-
ing furniture; arts & crafts equipment &
supplies
PA: Cri 2000, L.P.
2245 San Diego Ave # 125
San Diego CA 92110
-

(P-4859)
ERA PRODUCTS INC
1130 Benedict Canyon Dr, Beverly Hills
(90210-2726)
PHONE.....................310 324-4908
Marlene Alter, *President*
Roy H Alter, *Vice Pres*
EMP: 16
SQ FT: 56,792
SALES (est): 4MM **Privately Held**
WEB: www.eraproducts.com
SIC: 2531 Vehicle furniture

(P-4860)
FUTUREFLITE INC
806 Calle Plano, Camarillo (93012-8557)
PHONE.....................818 653-2145
Andrew S Kanigowski, *CEO*
EMP: 15
SALES (est): 2.2MM **Privately Held**
WEB: www.futureflite.com
SIC: 2531 Seats, aircraft

(P-4861)
IJOT DEVELOPMENT INC
11360b Pleasant Valley Rd, Penn Valley
(95946-9000)
PHONE.....................925 258-9909
Michael Gompertz, *President*
▲ EMP: 1600
SQ FT: 12,000
SALES (est): 78.1MM **Privately Held**
SIC: 2531 2599 Public building & related
furniture; work benches, factory

(P-4862)
JOHNSON CONTROLS INC
5770 Warland Dr Ste A, Cypress
(90630-5047)
PHONE.....................562 799-8882
Dough Beebe, *Manager*
EMP: 150 **Privately Held**
SIC: 2531 1711 5075 5065 Seats, automobile; heating systems repair & maintenance; warm air heating & air
conditioning; electronic parts & equipment

HQ: Johnson Controls, Inc.
5757 N Green Bay Ave
Milwaukee WI 53209
414 524-1200

(P-4863)
KINGS RIVER CASTING INC
1350 North Ave, Sanger (93657-3742)
PHONE.....................559 875-8250
Patrick Henry, *President*
Merry Henry, *Corp Secy*
▼ EMP: 15
SQ FT: 30,000
SALES (est): 1.8MM **Privately Held**
SIC: 2531 3648 2599 Benches for public
buildings; street lighting fixtures; bar furni-
ture

(P-4864)
LOUIS SARDO UPHOLSTERY INC (PA)
Also Called: Sardo Bus & Coach Upholstery
512 W Rosecrans Ave, Gardena
(90248-1515)
PHONE.....................310 327-0532
Louis Sardo, *President*
Jeanie Sardo, *Vice Pres*
Kathy Cruse, *Natl Sales Mgr*
Betty Sahranavard, *Director*
EMP: 65
SQ FT: 10,000
SALES (est): 13.9MM **Privately Held**
SIC: 2531 3713 7641 Seats, automobile;
truck & bus bodies; reupholstery & furni-
ture repair

(P-4865)
MORTECH MANUFACTURING CO INC
411 N Aerojet Dr, Azusa (91702-3253)
PHONE.....................626 334-1471
Gino Joseph, *CEO*
Christy Haines, *CFO*
Paul Joseph, *Vice Pres*
Michael Kubacik, *Vice Pres*
Yvonne Rios, *Admin Asst*
◆ EMP: 42
SQ FT: 43,000
SALES (est): 9.9MM **Privately Held**
WEB: www.mortechmfg.com
SIC: 2531 5087 Altars & pulpits; funeral di-
rectors' equipment & supplies

(P-4866)
NEWHOUSE UPHOLSTERY
Also Called: Newhouse Upholstery Mfg
2309 Edwards Ave, El Monte (91733-2041)
P.O. Box 3201 (91733-0201)
PHONE.....................626 444-1370
Ed Stevenson, *President*
Maria Stevenson, *Corp Secy*
EMP: 20 EST: 1953
SQ FT: 18,000
SALES (est): 3.1MM **Privately Held**
WEB: www.newhouserv.com
SIC: 2531 Vehicle furniture

(P-4867)
ORBO CORPORATION
Also Called: Eurotec Seating
1000 S Euclid St, La Habra (90631-6806)
PHONE.....................562 806-6171
Oscar Galvez, *President*
Ricardo Galvez, *Vice Pres*
Alex Osorio, *Accounts Exec*
EMP: 50
SALES (est): 2.7MM **Privately Held**
SIC: 2531 Seats, automobile

(P-4868)
PACIFIC HOSPITALITY DESIGN INC
Also Called: PH Design
2620 S Malt Ave, Commerce (90040-3206)
PHONE.....................323 587-4289
Gilberto Martinez, *CEO*
Ana Martinez, *Vice Pres*
EMP: 25
SQ FT: 14,000
SALES (est): 4.5MM **Privately Held**
WEB: www.phdesign.com
SIC: 2531 Public building & related furni-
ture

(P-4869)
PRIMED PRODUCTIONS INC
1443 E Washington Blvd, Pasadena
(91104-2650)
PHONE.....................626 216-5822
Jax Pascua, *President*
EMP: 18
SALES (est): 1.6MM **Privately Held**
SIC: 2531 Bleacher seating, portable

(P-4870)
REDART CORPORATION
Also Called: Beard Seats
2549 Eastbluff Dr, Newport Beach
(92660-3500)
PHONE.....................714 774-9444
Tim Sousamian, *President*
▲ EMP: 14
SQ FT: 10,000
SALES (est): 1.5MM **Privately Held**
WEB: www.redart.com
SIC: 2531 2298 Seats, automobile; cargo
nets

(P-4871)
SEATING CONCEPTS LLC
4229 Ponderosa Ave Ste B, San Diego
(92123-1519)
PHONE.....................619 491-3159
Juan Carlos Letayf, *Mng Member*
Laz Briceno, *CFO*
Taylor Heilbronner, *Business Mgr*
Jose Letayf,
◆ EMP: 30
SALES (est): 6.8MM **Privately Held**
WEB: www.seatingconcepts.com
SIC: 2531 5021 Theater furniture; chairs

(P-4872)
SERIOUS ENERGY INC (PA)
Also Called: Serious Windows
1250 Elko Dr, Sunnyvale (94089-2213)
PHONE.....................408 541-8000
Kevin Surace, *CEO*
Mark Mitchell, *COO*
Russ Lampert, *CFO*
Sandra Vaughan, *Chief Mktg Ofcr*
Scott Morgan, *Senior VP*
▲ EMP: 55
SALES (est): 12.6MM **Privately Held**
WEB: www.quietsolution.com
SIC: 2531 Public building & related furni-
ture

(P-4873)
STEARNS PARK
Also Called: Long Beach City of
4520 E 23rd St, Long Beach (90815-1806)
PHONE.....................562 570-1685
Garcia Elyse, *Principal*
EMP: 30
SALES: 400K **Privately Held**
SIC: 2531 Picnic tables or benches, park

(P-4874)
TALIMAR SYSTEMS INC
3105 W Alpine St, Santa Ana (92704-6911)
PHONE.....................714 557-4884
David Wesdell, *President*
David G Wesdell, *President*
Alejandro Bonell, *Project Mgr*
Patty Boris, *Project Mgr*
Brandon Wesdell, *Project Mgr*
▲ EMP: 37
SQ FT: 11,000
SALES (est): 6.2MM **Privately Held**
WEB: www.talimarsystems.com
SIC: 2531 5712 7389 5932 Public build-
ing & related furniture; furniture stores;
merchandise liquidators; office furniture,
secondhand

(P-4875)
VILLA FURNITURE MFG CO
Also Called: Villa International
13760 Midway St, Cerritos (90703-2331)
PHONE.....................714 535-7272
Andrew M Greenthal, *President*
John Hermosillo, *Plant Mgr*
Mike Ramirez, *Natl Sales Mgr*
Michael Battaglia, *Manager*
▲ EMP: 125
SQ FT: 75,000
SALES (est): 24.2MM **Privately Held**
SIC: 2531 2522 Vehicle furniture; office
furniture, except wood

(P-4876)
VIRCO MFG CORPORATION (PA)
2027 Harpers Way, Torrance (90501-1524)
PHONE.....................310 533-0474
Robert A Virtue, *Ch of Bd*
Douglas A Virtue, *President*
J Scott Bell, *COO*
Robert E Dose, *CFO*
Alexander Cappello, *Bd of Directors*
◆ EMP: 277
SQ FT: 560,000
SALES (est): 200.7MM **Publicly Held**
WEB: www.virco.com
SIC: 2531 2522 2511 School furniture;
chairs, portable folding; chairs, table &
arm; office furniture, except wood; chairs,
office: padded or plain, except wood; ta-
bles, office: except wood; wood house-
hold furniture

(P-4877)
YANFENG US AUTOMOTIVE
30559 San Antonio St, Hayward
(94544-7101)
PHONE.....................616 886-3622
Phillip George, *Branch Mgr*
EMP: 20
SALES (corp-wide): 55MM **Privately
Held**
SIC: 2531 Seats, automobile
HQ: Yanfeng Us Automotive Interior Sys-
tems I Llc
41935 W 12 Mile Rd
Novi MI 48377
248 319-7333

2541 Wood, Office & Store Fixtures

(P-4878)
ALEMAD INC
2061 Freeway Dr Ste C, Woodland
(95776-9506)
PHONE.....................530 661-1697
Mike Ware, *President*
EMP: 40
SQ FT: 20,000
SALES (est): 3.5MM **Privately Held**
WEB: www.weretops.com
SIC: 2541 5999 1799 Counter & sink
tops; monuments & tombstones; counter
top installation

(P-4879)
ALL AMERICAN CABINETRY INC
Also Called: All American Sterile Coat
13901 Saticoy St, Van Nuys (91402-6521)
PHONE.....................818 376-0500
Chris Zepatos, *President*
EMP: 60
SALES (est): 6.3MM **Privately Held**
SIC: 2541 Cabinets, lockers & shelving

(P-4880)
AMTREND CORPORATION
1458 Manhattan Ave, Fullerton
(92831-5222)
PHONE.....................714 630-2070
Hamid A Malik, *President*
Javeeda Malik, *CEO*
Rosa Rubio, *Human Res Mgr*
Luis Orozco, *Plant Mgr*
EMP: 85 EST: 1980
SQ FT: 45,000
SALES (est): 16.8MM **Privately Held**
WEB: www.amtrend.com
SIC: 2541 2521 7641 2512 Wood parti-
tions & fixtures; wood office furniture; up-
holstery work; upholstered household
furniture

(P-4881)
ARCHITECTURAL WOODWORKING CO
582 Monterey Pass Rd, Monterey Park
(91754-2417)
PHONE.....................626 570-4125
John K Heydorff, *President*
John F Heydorff, *Shareholder*
Thomas C Heydorff, *CFO*
Richard A Schaub, *Admin Sec*
Blanca Bonilla, *Accounting Mgr*

▲ = Import ▼=Export
◆ =Import/Export

EMP: 100 EST: 1963
SQ FT: 60,000
SALES (est): 14.4MM Privately Held
WEB: www.architecturalwoodwork.com
SIC: **2541** 1751 Office fixtures, wood; cabinets, except refrigerated: show, display, etc.: wood; display fixtures, wood; partitions for floor attachment, prefabricated: wood; carpentry work

(P-4882)
ARNOLD & EGAN MANUFACTURING CO
1515 Griffith St, San Francisco (94124-3412)
PHONE.....................................415 822-2700
Kenneth Egan, *CEO*
Rose Egan, *CFO*
Donna Egan, *Admin Sec*
EMP: 20
SQ FT: 10,000
SALES (est): 3.8MM Privately Held
SIC: **2541** 2521 2434 2431 Wood partitions & fixtures; wood office furniture; wood kitchen cabinets; millwork

(P-4883)
ATLAS GRANITE & STONE
2560 Grennan Ct, Rancho Cordova (95742-6318)
PHONE.....................................916 638-7100
Steve Zabetian, *Owner*
▲ EMP: 10 EST: 2000
SQ FT: 7,000
SALES (est): 1.7MM Privately Held
WEB: www.atlasgranite.com
SIC: **2541** 5722 Counter & sink tops; kitchens, complete (sinks, cabinets, etc.)

(P-4884)
BLOCK TOPS INC (PA)
1321 S Sunkist St, Anaheim (92806-5614)
PHONE.....................................714 978-5080
Vanessa Bates, *CEO*
Nate Kolenski, *President*
Don Lewis, *Branch Mgr*
Alfonso Aramburo, *Plant Mgr*
▲ EMP: 34 EST: 1977
SQ FT: 10,000
SALES (est): 8.2MM Privately Held
WEB: www.blocktops.com
SIC: **2541** 2519 3281 2821 Table or counter tops, plastic laminated; furniture, household: glass, fiberglass & plastic; cut stone & stone products; plastics materials & resins

(P-4885)
BRIGGS & SONS
1225 E Macarthur St, Sonoma (95476-3811)
P.O. Box 1469 (95476-1469)
PHONE.....................................707 938-4325
Mike Briggs, *Owner*
Patricia Briggs, *Principal*
EMP: 11
SQ FT: 8,000
SALES: 1.3MM Privately Held
SIC: **2541** 1751 Store fixtures, wood; cabinets, except refrigerated: show, display, etc.: wood; cabinet & finish carpentry

(P-4886)
BRISTOL OMEGA INC
9441 Opal Ave Ste 2, Mentone (92359-9900)
PHONE.....................................909 794-6862
Ralf G Zacky, *CEO*
EMP: 27 EST: 1993
SALES: 1.2MM Privately Held
SIC: **2541** 1611 Wood partitions & fixtures; general contractor, highway & street construction

(P-4887)
CABINET COMPANY INC
Also Called: Complete Kitchen & Bath
416 Crown Point Cir Ste 7, Grass Valley (95945-9558)
PHONE.....................................530 273-7533
Joshua L Emrich, *President*
EMP: 10

SALES (est): 750K **Privately Held**
WEB: www.thecabinetcompany.com
SIC: **2541** 2521 5211 1799 Cabinets, lockers & shelving; wood office furniture; bookcases, office: wood; closets, interiors & accessories; counter top installation; cabinet & finish carpentry

(P-4888)
CALIFORNIA MFG CABINETRY INC
Also Called: C M C
1474 E Francis St, Ontario (91761-5791)
PHONE.....................................909 930-3632
Miguel Jimenez, *President*
Mike Jimmez, *Vice Pres*
EMP: 15
SALES (est): 2MM Privately Held
SIC: **2541** 2434 2431 Cabinets, except refrigerated: show, display, etc.: wood; wood kitchen cabinets; millwork

(P-4889)
CCM ENTERPRISES
9366 Abraham Way, Santee (92071-2861)
PHONE.....................................619 562-2605
Cody Nosko, *Manager*
EMP: 10 **Privately Held**
WEB: www.ccmmfg.com
SIC: **2541** 3083 Counter & sink tops; laminated plastics plate & sheet
PA: Ccm Enterprises
10848 Wheatlands Ave
Santee CA 92071

(P-4890)
CCM ENTERPRISES (PA)
10848 Wheatlands Ave, Santee (92071-2855)
PHONE.....................................619 562-2605
Cody L Nosko, *CEO*
Duane Nosco, *Vice Pres*
Virginia Jaggi, *Admin Sec*
EMP: 60
SQ FT: 67,543
SALES (est): 8.1MM Privately Held
WEB: www.ccmmfg.com
SIC: **2541** 1799 Counter & sink tops; kitchen & bathroom remodeling; kitchen cabinet installation

(P-4891)
CHICO CUSTOM COUNTER
3080 Thorntree Dr Ste 45, Chico (95973-9503)
PHONE.....................................530 894-8123
Shane Barker, *Owner*
EMP: 12
SQ FT: 6,000
SALES (est): 1MM Privately Held
SIC: **2541** Counters or counter display cases, wood

(P-4892)
CLOSETS BY DESIGN INC
3860 Capitol Ave, City of Industry (90601-1733)
PHONE.....................................562 699-9945
Frank Melkonian, *President*
Gerard Thompson, *CFO*
EMP: 185
SALES (est): 20.7MM Privately Held
SIC: **2541** 2521 Lockers, except refrigerated: wood; wood office filing cabinets & bookcases

(P-4893)
COLUMBIA SHOWCASE & CAB CO INC
11034 Sherman Way Ste A, Sun Valley (91352-4915)
PHONE.....................................818 765-9710
Samuel M Patterson Jr, *CEO*
James E Barnett, *Co-COB*
Samuel M Patterson Sr, *Co-COB*
Joe Patterson, *Senior VP*
James Haley, *Project Mgr*
▲ EMP: 125
SQ FT: 170,000
SALES (est): 26MM Privately Held
WEB: www.columbiashowcase.com
SIC: **2541** 1542 Cabinets, except refrigerated: show, display, etc.: wood; commercial & office building contractors

---

(P-4894)
CTA FIXTURES INC
5721 Santa Ana St Ste B, Ontario (91761-8617)
PHONE.....................................909 390-6744
Carlos Gutierrez, *CEO*
▲ EMP: 62
SQ FT: 90,000
SALES (est): 9.6MM Privately Held
WEB: www.ctafixtures.com
SIC: **2541** Wood partitions & fixtures

(P-4895)
CUSTOM DISPLAYS INC
411 W 157th St, Gardena (90248-2118)
PHONE.....................................323 770-8074
Thomas Otani, *President*
Ben Hasuike, *Vice Pres*
EMP: 30
SQ FT: 16,000
SALES (est): 3.7MM Privately Held
WEB: www.customdisplays.com
SIC: **2541** 3827 3993 Display fixtures, wood; triplet magnifying instruments, optical; signs & advertising specialties

(P-4896)
DENNIS REEVES INC
Also Called: Reeves Enterprises
1350 Palomares St Ste A, La Verne (91750-5230)
PHONE.....................................909 392-9999
Dennis L Reeves, *President*
Denise Reeves, *CFO*
Brad Reeves, *Vice Pres*
Dennis Reeves, *General Mgr*
EMP: 10
SQ FT: 20,000
SALES (est): 1.8MM Privately Held
SIC: **2541** 1751 Store fixtures, wood; cabinet building & installation

(P-4897)
DESIGN WORKSHOPS
486 Lesser St, Oakland (94601-4902)
PHONE.....................................510 434-0727
Richard G Bourdon, *President*
David Keystone, *CFO*
Tad Beach, *Vice Pres*
EMP: 10
SQ FT: 45,000
SALES (est): 1.8MM Privately Held
WEB: www.design-workshops.com
SIC: **2541** 2521 2517 2434 Cabinets, except refrigerated: show, display, etc.: wood; wood office furniture; wood television & radio cabinets; wood kitchen cabinets

(P-4898)
DIMENSIONS UNLIMITED
1080 Nimitz Ave Ste 400, Vallejo (94592-1009)
PHONE.....................................707 552-6800
John Ewer, *President*
Jane B Ewer, *Principal*
Jane Ewer, *Admin Sec*
EMP: 15
SQ FT: 9,300
SALES: 1.4MM Privately Held
WEB: www.dimensions-unlimited.com
SIC: **2541** 1751 Cabinets, except refrigerated: show, display, etc.: wood; lockers, except refrigerated: wood; cabinet & finish carpentry; customized furniture & cabinets

(P-4899)
ELEMENTS MANUFACTURING INC
115 Harvey West Blvd C, Santa Cruz (95060-2168)
PHONE.....................................831 421-9440
Ken Ketch, *President*
Kristy Stormes, *Partner*
Alan Stormes, *Admin Sec*
David Wright, *Opers Staff*
EMP: 20
SQ FT: 15,000
SALES (est): 1.3MM Privately Held
WEB: www.elementsmfg.com
SIC: **2541** Cabinets, lockers & shelving; counter & sink tops

---

(P-4900)
EMERZIAN WOODWORKING INC
2555 N Argyle Ave, Fresno (93727-1378)
PHONE.....................................559 292-2448
Tom Emerzian, *Owner*
EMP: 40
SQ FT: 46,000
SALES (est): 5.6MM Privately Held
WEB: www.emerzianwoodworking.com
SIC: **2541** 2434 Showcases, except refrigerated: wood; wood kitchen cabinets

(P-4901)
EUROPEAN WHOLESALE COUNTER
10051 Prospect Ave, Santee (92071-4321)
PHONE.....................................619 562-0565
Pete Sciarrino, *CEO*
EMP: 150
SQ FT: 40,000
SALES (est): 14.6MM Privately Held
SIC: **2541** 1799 Counter & sink tops; cabinets, lockers & shelving; counter top installation

(P-4902)
F-J-E INC
Also Called: Jf Fixtures & Design
546 W Esther St, Long Beach (90813-1529)
PHONE.....................................562 437-7466
Frank Ernandes, *President*
Barbara Ernandes, *Admin Sec*
EMP: 25
SQ FT: 26,000
SALES: 3.1MM Privately Held
WEB: www.jffixtures.com
SIC: **2541** 2542 Store fixtures, wood; fixtures, store: except wood

(P-4903)
FAIRMONT GLOBAL LLC (PA)
Also Called: Fairmont Designs
2010 Jimmy Durante Blvd, Del Mar (92014-2237)
PHONE.....................................415 320-2929
Robert Shapiro,
Michael Shapiro,
Tery Young,
EMP: 10
SALES (est): 5.6MM
SALES (corp-wide): 5.1MM Privately Held
SIC: **2541** 7389 Store & office display cases & fixtures; design services

(P-4904)
FIXTURES BY DESIGN LLC
2951 Saturn St Ste Unitb, Brea (92821-6206)
PHONE.....................................714 572-5406
Lorrain Sandoval Obrien, *CEO*
Mark Cooper, *Vice Pres*
EMP: 15
SQ FT: 5,900
SALES: 1.4MM
SALES (corp-wide): 2.5MM Privately Held
SIC: **2541** Store fixtures, wood
PA: Obrien Systems Llc
21123 Via Santiago
Yorba Linda CA 92887
714 485-2179

(P-4905)
GREG IAN ISLANDS INC
Also Called: Igi
123b E Montecito Ave B, Sierra Madre (91024-1923)
PHONE.....................................626 355-0019
EMP: 20
SALES (est): 1.8MM Privately Held
SIC: **2541**

(P-4906)
GRENEKER FURNITURE
3110 E 12th St, Los Angeles (90023-3616)
PHONE.....................................323 263-9000
Erik Johnson, *Owner*
EMP: 30
SQ FT: 100,000
SALES (est): 3.4MM Privately Held
SIC: **2541** 2542 Display fixtures, wood; fixtures: display, office or store: except wood

PRODUCTS & SVCS

(P-4907)
H & M CABINET COMPANY
1565 La Mirada Dr, San Marcos
(92078-2425)
PHONE..................760 744-0559
EMP: 10
SALES (est): 640K **Privately Held**
SIC: 2541

(P-4908)
H AND M INDUSTRIES LLC
Also Called: Specialty Science Counter Tops
855 Rancho Conejo Blvd, Newbury Park
(91320-1714)
PHONE..................805 499-5100
Steve Coats,
Mike Downey,
Mary Fields,
Gloria Kaiser,
EMP: 12
SQ FT: 15,000
SALES (est): 990K **Privately Held**
SIC: 2541 Table or counter tops, plastic laminated

(P-4909)
HEMISPHERE DESIGN & MFG LLC
28895 Industry Dr, Valencia (91355-5419)
PHONE..................661 294-9500
Timothy Arnold, *Mng Member*
EMP: 15 EST: 2013
SALES (est): 3MM **Privately Held**
SIC: 2541 7389 Store & office display cases & fixtures; design services

(P-4910)
HERITAGE CABINET CO INC
21740 Marilla St, Chatsworth (91311-4125)
PHONE..................818 786-4900
Robert Geyer, *Owner*
Kathy Geyer, *Corp Secy*
EMP: 12
SQ FT: 12,000
SALES (est): 1.4MM **Privately Held**
WEB: www.heritagecabinet.com
SIC: 2541 5211 2521 2517 Cabinets, except refrigerated: show, display, etc.: wood; lumber & other building materials; wood office furniture; wood television & radio cabinets; wood kitchen cabinets; millwork

(P-4911)
IDEAL PRODUCTS INC
4501 Etiwanda Ave, Jurupa Valley
(91752-1445)
P.O. Box 4090, Ontario (91761-1006)
PHONE..................951 727-8600
Robert L Martin Jr, *CEO*
Virginia Martin, *Vice Pres*
EMP: 35 EST: 1976
SQ FT: 20,000
SALES (est): 7MM **Privately Held**
WEB: www.idealockers.com
SIC: 2541 Lockers, except refrigerated: wood

(P-4912)
IVARS CABINET SHOP INC (PA)
Also Called: Ivar's Displays
2314 E Locust Ct, Ontario (91761-7637)
PHONE..................909 923-2761
Ivan Gundersen, *President*
Karl Gundersen, *CEO*
Jason Gundersen, *CFO*
Linda Pulice, *Vice Pres*
Rose Marie Aunario, *Accounts Mgr*
▲ **EMP:** 109
SQ FT: 95,000
SALES: 16.3MM **Privately Held**
WEB: www.ivarsdisplay.com
SIC: 2541 2542 Store fixtures, wood; shelving, office & store: except wood

(P-4913)
J P B JEWELRY BOX CO (PA)
2428 Dallas St, Los Angeles (90031-1013)
PHONE..................323 225-0500
Jerry Borodian, *Partner*
Josephine Borodian, *Partner*
Robert Todd, *Vice Pres*
▲ **EMP:** 15
SQ FT: 14,000

SALES: 1MM **Privately Held**
SIC: 2541 2441 3172 Wood partitions & fixtures; nailed wood boxes & shook; cases, jewelry

(P-4914)
JUDITH VON HOPF INC
1525 W 13th St Ste H, Upland
(91786-7528)
PHONE..................909 481-1884
Judith P Hopf, *CEO*
▲ **EMP:** 25
SALES (est): 4MM **Privately Held**
WEB: www.judithvonhopf.com
SIC: 2541 Display fixtures, wood

(P-4915)
KALANICO INC
Also Called: Salsam Manufacturing Co
1036 Chantilly Cir, Santa Ana
(92705-6108)
PHONE..................714 532-5770
Carl Eisler, *President*
Donna Eisler, *Admin Sec*
EMP: 15 EST: 1971
SQ FT: 20,000
SALES: 750K **Privately Held**
WEB: www.salsam.com
SIC: 2541 Cabinets, except refrigerated: show, display, etc.: wood; showcases, except refrigerated: wood

(P-4916)
KEYS CABINETRY INC
20 Pimentel Ct Ste B14, Novato
(94949-5688)
PHONE..................415 382-1466
Steven Cheavacci, *President*
EMP: 10
SQ FT: 4,000
SALES (est): 730K **Privately Held**
SIC: 2541 Cabinets, except refrigerated: show, display, etc.: wood

(P-4917)
KILLION INDUSTRIES INC (PA)
1380 Poinsettia Ave, Vista (92081-8504)
PHONE..................760 727-5102
Richard W Killion, *President*
Larry Edward, *Vice Pres*
Paul Bramhall, *Opers Staff*
▲ **EMP:** 80 EST: 1981
SQ FT: 185,000
SALES (est): 36.8MM **Privately Held**
SIC: 2541 Store & office display cases & fixtures; display fixtures, wood; counters or counter display cases, wood

(P-4918)
L & N FIXTURES INC
2214 Tyler Ave, El Monte (91733-2710)
PHONE..................323 686-0041
Louis Pierotti, *President*
EMP: 31 EST: 1970
SQ FT: 16,000
SALES: 2MM **Privately Held**
SIC: 2541 1799 2521 2434 Store fixtures, wood; office furniture installation; wood office furniture; wood kitchen cabinets

(P-4919)
LA CABINET & MILLWORK INC
Also Called: Bromack
3005 Humboldt St, Los Angeles
(90031-1830)
PHONE..................323 227-5000
Leonard Lumpkin, *President*
Kurt Webster, *Treasurer*
Oscar Gonzalez, *Vice Pres*
Brown S McPherson III, *Vice Pres*
Robert Rieger, *Vice Pres*
EMP: 25
SQ FT: 17,000
SALES: 1MM **Privately Held**
SIC: 2541 1799 2434 1751 Counters or counter display cases, wood; counter top installation; wood kitchen cabinets; carpentry work

(P-4920)
LEGGETT & PLATT INCORPORATED
Also Called: Leggett & Platt 0302
29120 Commerce Center Dr # 1, Valencia
(91355-5404)
PHONE..................661 775-8500
EMP: 30
SALES (corp-wide): 3.7B **Publicly Held**
SIC: 2541
PA: Leggett & Platt, Incorporated
1 Leggett Rd
Carthage MO 64836
417 358-8131

(P-4921)
LEONARDS CARPET SERVICE INC (PA)
Also Called: Xgrass Turf Direct
1121 N Red Gum St, Anaheim
(92806-2582)
PHONE..................714 630-1930
Leonard Nagel, *President*
Joel Nagel, *CEO*
▲ **EMP:** 75
SQ FT: 52,000
SALES (est): 33.3MM **Privately Held**
WEB: www.lcsdesign.com
SIC: 2541 1771 1799 Table or counter tops, plastic laminated; flooring contractor; artificial turf installation

(P-4922)
NICO NAT MFG CORP
Also Called: Niconat Manufacturing
2624 Yates Ave, Commerce (90040-2622)
PHONE..................323 721-1900
Jose Valdez, *CEO*
Francisco Valdez, *Shareholder*
Valerie Castillo, *Assistant*
EMP: 45 EST: 2008
SALES (est): 8.7MM **Privately Held**
SIC: 2541 Store & office display cases & fixtures

(P-4923)
NORTHBAY STONE WRKS CNTERTOPS
849 Sweetser Ave, Novato (94945-2428)
PHONE..................415 898-0200
Greg Palmer, *Partner*
Mark Miltenberger, *Partner*
EMP: 13
SQ FT: 5,000
SALES (est): 1.2MM **Privately Held**
WEB: www.nbstoneworks.com
SIC: 2541 5211 Counter & sink tops; counter tops

(P-4924)
NYCETEK INC
Also Called: Rack Master
555 W Lambert Rd Ste F, Brea
(92821-3917)
PHONE..................714 671-3860
Nelson Chang, *President*
Yvonne Chang, *CFO*
▲ **EMP:** 10
SALES (est): 780K **Privately Held**
WEB: www.nycetek.com
SIC: 2541 Display fixtures, wood

(P-4925)
OAK-IT INC
845 Sandhill Ave, Carson (90746-1210)
P.O. Box 4733, Downey (90241-1733)
PHONE..................310 719-3999
Lori Barrett, *President*
Sean Kittiko, *Treasurer*
◆ **EMP:** 40
SQ FT: 8,000
SALES (est): 5.3MM **Privately Held**
SIC: 2541 2431 5046 Store fixtures, wood; cabinets, except refrigerated: show, display, etc.: wood; millwork; store fixtures

(P-4926)
OLDE WORLD CORPORATION
Also Called: Great Spaces USA
360 Grogan Ave, Merced (95341-6446)
PHONE..................209 384-1337
Richard T Conas, *President*
Jan Conas, *Vice Pres*
EMP: 20

SQ FT: 35,000
SALES (est): 3.9MM **Privately Held**
SIC: 2541 Store & office display cases & fixtures

(P-4927)
OMNI ENCLOSURES INC
Also Called: Omni Pacific
505 Raleigh Ave, El Cajon (92020-3139)
PHONE..................619 579-6664
Thomas P Burke, *President*
Tara Burke, *General Mgr*
Mendoza Tracey, *Info Tech Mgr*
Mike Burke, *Manager*
Kathleen Uno-Kolb, *Accounts Exec*
▲ **EMP:** 27
SQ FT: 20,000
SALES (est): 4.3MM **Privately Held**
WEB: www.omnipacific.com
SIC: 2541 Office fixtures, wood

(P-4928)
OTANEZ NEW CREATIONS
7179 E Columbus Dr, Anaheim
(92807-4530)
PHONE..................951 808-9663
Joe Otanez, *President*
Olga Otanez, *Treasurer*
EMP: 13
SQ FT: 10,000
SALES (est): 1.1MM **Privately Held**
SIC: 2541 1751 Wood partitions & fixtures; cabinet & finish carpentry

(P-4929)
PACIFIC WESTLINE INC
1536 W Embassy St, Anaheim
(92802-1016)
PHONE..................714 956-2442
Daniel G McLeith, *CEO*
John Lara, *Office Mgr*
EMP: 90
SQ FT: 62,000
SALES (est): 13.2MM **Privately Held**
WEB: www.pacificwestline.com
SIC: 2541 2431 Cabinets, except refrigerated: show, display, etc.: wood; millwork

(P-4930)
PAZZULLA PLASTICS INC
165 Emilia Ln, Fallbrook (92028-2686)
PHONE..................714 847-2541
Sam Pazzulla, *Owner*
EMP: 20
SQ FT: 7,800
SALES (est): 1.4MM **Privately Held**
WEB: www.pazzullaplastics.com
SIC: 2541 Table or counter tops, plastic laminated

(P-4931)
PG EMMINGER INC
4036 Pacheco Blvd A, Martinez
(94553-2224)
PHONE..................925 313-5830
Philip G Emminger, *President*
Mike Graham, *Project Mgr*
EMP: 22
SQ FT: 10,000
SALES (est): 3.8MM **Privately Held**
SIC: 2541 Wood partitions & fixtures

(P-4932)
PLANET ONE PRODUCTS INC (PA)
Also Called: Le Cache Premium Wine Cabinets
1445 N Mcdowell Blvd, Petaluma
(94954-6516)
PHONE..................707 794-8000
Ben Z Argov, *President*
Bruce Kirsten, *Treasurer*
Keith Sedwick, *Vice Pres*
Doug McAlpine, *Engineer*
▲ **EMP:** 27
SQ FT: 18,000
SALES (est): 4.8MM **Privately Held**
WEB: www.lecache.com
SIC: 2541 Cabinets, except refrigerated: show, display, etc.: wood

(P-4933)
PYRAMID SYSTEMS INC
10105 8 3/4 Ave, Hanford (93230-4769)
PHONE..................559 582-9345
David Gunter, *President*

2020 California
Manufacturers Register

▲ = Import ▼=Export
◆ =Import/Export

Lori Pollard, *Exec VP*
Amber Ratt, *Admin Sec*
EMP: 25
SQ FT: 12,000
SALES (est): 3.5MM **Privately Held**
SIC: 2541 Wood partitions & fixtures

(P-4934)
QUALITY COUNTERTOPS INC
17853 Santiago Blvd # 107, Villa Park
(92861-4113)
PHONE...................................909 597-6888
Rick Rambo, *President*
Tammy Rambo, *Vice Pres*
EMP: 15
SQ FT: 14,000
SALES (est): 1.8MM **Privately Held**
SIC: 2541 1799 Wood partitions & fixtures;
counter top installation

(P-4935)
RON & DIANA VANATTA
Also Called: R C I
332 Sacramento St, Auburn (95603-5510)
PHONE...................................530 888-0200
Ron Vannatta, *Owner*
Diana Vannatta, *Co-Owner*
EMP: 14
SQ FT: 5,000
SALES (est): 1.6MM **Privately Held**
WEB: www.rcitops.com
SIC: 2541 5211 1799 1751 Table or
counter tops, plastic laminated; cabinets,
kitchen; counter top installation; cabinet &
finish carpentry

(P-4936)
SCIENTIFIC SURFACE INDS INC
Also Called: Ssi Surfaces
855 Rancho Conejo Blvd, Newbury Park
(91320-1714)
PHONE...................................805 499-5100
David Marquez, *Vice Pres*
EMP: 16
SQ FT: 10,000
SALES (est): 1MM **Privately Held**
SIC: 2541 Counter & sink tops

(P-4937)
SHASTA WOOD PRODUCTS
19751 Hirsch Ct, Anderson (96007-4945)
P.O. Box 1101, Cottonwood (96022-1101)
PHONE...................................530 378-6880
Jeff Aboud, *President*
Tamara Aboud, *CEO*
Cheryl Aboud, *Treasurer*
Thomas Aboud, *Vice Pres*
EMP: 20 **EST:** 1986
SQ FT: 12,000
SALES (est): 3.9MM **Privately Held**
WEB: www.shastawoodproducts.com
SIC: 2541 2499 2434 Cabinets, lockers &
shelving; counter & sink tops; kitchen,
bathroom & household ware: wood; wood
kitchen cabinets

(P-4938)
SHOW OFFS
1696 W Mill St Unit 10, Colton
(92324-1074)
PHONE...................................909 885-5223
Dave Snavely, *Owner*
EMP: 23
SQ FT: 18,000
SALES (est): 2.4MM **Privately Held**
WEB: www.showoffsdisplay.com
SIC: 2541 2542 5046 Display fixtures,
wood; racks, merchandise display or stor-
age: except wood; store fixtures

(P-4939)
SISTONE INC
15530 Lanark St, Van Nuys (91406-1411)
PHONE...................................818 988-9918
Yair Sisso, *President*
Arthur Sistone, *Technology*
EMP: 30
SALES (est): 4.3MM **Privately Held**
WEB: www.sistoneinc.com-.gif
SIC: 2541 Counter & sink tops

(P-4940)
SPALINGER ENTERPRISES INC
Also Called: Skyline Cabinet & Millworks
800 S Mount Vernon Ave, Bakersfield
(93307-2889)
PHONE...................................661 834-4550
David Spalinger, *President*
Melody Spalinger, *Corp Secy*
J W Spalinger, *Vice Pres*
▲ **EMP:** 12
SQ FT: 8,500
SALES (est): 1.5MM **Privately Held**
SIC: 2541 Cabinets, except refrigerated:
show, display, etc.: wood

(P-4941)
SPOONERS WOODWORKS INC
12460 Kirkham Ct, Poway (92064-6819)
PHONE...................................858 679-9086
Tom Spooner, *President*
Thomas Spooner, *CEO*
Valerie Spooner, *Treasurer*
Jim Spooner, *Vice Pres*
Stephen Spooner, *Vice Pres*
EMP: 85
SQ FT: 22,000
SALES (est): 17.3MM **Privately Held**
WEB: www.spoonerwoodworks.com
SIC: 2541 Store fixtures, wood

(P-4942)
SUBA MFG INC
921 Bayshore Rd, Benicia (94510-2990)
PHONE...................................707 745-0358
Jack Bell, *President*
Sue Bell, *Admin Sec*
Scott Cody, *Marketing Staff*
EMP: 23
SQ FT: 40,000
SALES (est): 3.8MM **Privately Held**
SIC: 2541 3083 Table or counter tops,
plastic laminated; laminated plastics plate
& sheet

(P-4943)
SULLIVAN COUNTER TOPS INC
1189 65th St, Oakland (94608-1108)
PHONE...................................510 652-2337
Thomas C Sullivan, *President*
EMP: 26
SQ FT: 10,000
SALES (est): 4.4MM **Privately Held**
WEB: www.sullivancountertops.com
SIC: 2541 2821 Counter & sink tops; table
or counter tops, plastic laminated; plastics
materials & resins

(P-4944)
SURFACE TECHNIQUES CORPORATION (PA)
Also Called: Surface Technology
25673 Nickel Pl, Hayward (94545-3221)
PHONE...................................510 887-6000
Howard Berger, *President*
EMP: 30
SQ FT: 13,000
SALES (est): 21.7MM **Privately Held**
SIC: 2541 Counters or counter display
cases, wood

(P-4945)
SW FIXTURES INC
3940 Valley Blvd Ste C, Walnut
(91789-1541)
PHONE...................................909 595-2506
Daniel Zachary, *President*
Daniel Farinella, *Design Engr*
Brian Welsh, *Opers Mgr*
EMP: 18
SQ FT: 22,500
SALES (est): 3.4MM **Privately Held**
SIC: 2541 2431 Display fixtures, wood;
planing mill, millwork

(P-4946)
T M COBB COMPANY
Also Called: Haley Brothers
1592 E San Bernardino Ave, San
Bernardino (92408-2929)
PHONE...................................909 796-6969
Thomas J Cobb, *Branch Mgr*
EMP: 150
SQ FT: 1,000

SALES (corp-wide): 92.5MM **Privately Held**
WEB: www.tmcobbco.com
SIC: 2541 2431 5211 Wood partitions &
fixtures; millwork; door & window products
PA: T. M. Cobb Company
500 Palmyrita Ave
Riverside CA 92507
951 248-2400

(P-4947)
TAMALPAIS COML CABINETRY INC
200 9th St, Richmond (94801-3146)
P.O. Box 2169 (94802-1169)
PHONE...................................510 231-6800
John Kenner, *President*
EMP: 30
SQ FT: 23,000
SALES (est): 5.2MM **Privately Held**
WEB: www.tamcab.com
SIC: 2541 Cabinets, lockers & shelving

(P-4948)
TECHNIQUE DESIGNS INC
63665 19th Ave, North Palm Springs
(92258)
P.O. Box 550, Morongo Valley (92256-
0550)
PHONE...................................760 904-6223
Bruce Watts, *President*
Danelle Watts, *Admin Sec*
EMP: 14
SQ FT: 6,000
SALES (est): 3.2MM **Privately Held**
SIC: 2541 Wood partitions & fixtures

(P-4949)
TEMEKA ADVERTISING INC
Also Called: Temeka Group
9073 Pulsar Ct, Corona (92883-7357)
PHONE...................................951 277-2525
Michael D Wilson, *CEO*
Paul Mieboer, *Shareholder*
Marlene Kelly, *CFO*
Trina Richards, *Accounts Exec*
▲ **EMP:** 55
SQ FT: 24,000
SALES: 10MM **Privately Held**
SIC: 2541 Store & office display cases &
fixtures

(P-4950)
TONY GLAZING SPECIALTIES CO
Also Called: Fixtures Unlimited
13011 S Normandie Ave, Gardena
(90249-2125)
PHONE...................................323 770-8400
Tony Bressickello Sr, *President*
Anthony Bressickello Jr, *Treasurer*
EMP: 10 **EST:** 1946
SQ FT: 15,000
SALES (est): 1.1MM **Privately Held**
SIC: 2541 1542 7922 Store fixtures,
wood; commercial & office building, new
construction; commercial & office build-
ings, renovation & repair; theatrical rental
services

(P-4951)
TROSAK CABINETS INC
1478 Alpine Pl, San Marcos (92078-3801)
PHONE...................................760 744-9042
Matthew Trosak, *President*
Richard Trosak, *Vice Pres*
EMP: 16
SQ FT: 9,500
SALES (est): 2.3MM **Privately Held**
WEB: www.trosak.com
SIC: 2541 1751 Cabinets, except refriger-
ated: show, display, etc.: wood; cabinet &
finish carpentry

(P-4952)
V TWEST INC
16222 Phoebe Ave, La Mirada
(90638-5610)
PHONE...................................714 521-2167
Douglas Edward Clausen, *Branch Mgr*
EMP: 12
SALES (corp-wide): 197.9MM **Privately Held**
SIC: 2541 Counter & sink tops

HQ: V T.West Inc.
1000 Industrial Park
Holstein IA 51025
-

(P-4953)
VIEW RITE MANUFACTURING
455 Allan St, Daly City (94014-1627)
PHONE...................................415 468-3856
Brad Somberg, *President*
Nha Nguyen, *Vice Pres*
EMP: 50
SQ FT: 78,000
SALES (est): 8MM **Privately Held**
SIC: 2541 2542 Store fixtures, wood; fix-
tures, store: except wood

(P-4954)
WALLACE WOOD PRODUCTS
Also Called: Corte Custom Case
1247 S Buena Vista St C, San Jacinto
(92583-4664)
PHONE...................................951 654-9311
Roy Wallace, *Owner*
EMP: 12 **Privately Held**
SIC: 2541 Wood partitions & fixtures
PA: Wallace Wood Products
1247 S Buena Vista St C
San Jacinto CA 92583

(P-4955)
WEST COAST FIXTURES INC (PA)
511 Stone Rd, Benicia (94510-1113)
PHONE...................................707 752-6373
Rick D Dade, *President*
Barry Nash, *Vice Pres*
EMP: 45
SQ FT: 12,500
SALES (est): 12MM **Privately Held**
SIC: 2541 Display fixtures, wood

(P-4956)
WOODCRAFTERS INTERNATIONAL
946 Calle Amanecer Ste C, San Clemente
(92673-6221)
PHONE...................................949 498-0739
Marvin G Dennis, *President*
EMP: 10
SQ FT: 4,700
SALES (est): 600K **Privately Held**
WEB: www.woodcraftersintl.com
SIC: 2541 Cabinets, except refrigerated:
show, display, etc.: wood; counters or
counter display cases, wood; table or
counter tops, plastic laminated

(P-4957)
WOODLAND PRODUCTS CO INC
10825 7th St Ste C, Rancho Cucamonga
(91730-5402)
PHONE...................................909 622-3456
Frank Robertson, *President*
Judith Louise Robertson, *Treasurer*
EMP: 10 **EST:** 1959
SQ FT: 50,000
SALES (est): 1.2MM **Privately Held**
SIC: 2541 Wood partitions & fixtures

(P-4958)
WOODSMITHS ARCHITECTURAL CASEW
2709 Del Monte St, West Sacramento
(95691-3811)
PHONE...................................916 456-8871
Eric Smith, *CEO*
Anthony Anderson, *Principal*
EMP: 13
SALES (est): 2.2MM **Privately Held**
WEB: www.woodsmiths.biz
SIC: 2541 Cabinets, except refrigerated:
show, display, etc.: wood

(P-4959)
YOSHIMASA DISPLAY CASE INC
108 Pico St, Pomona (91766-2137)
PHONE...................................213 637-9999
Toro Hayashi, *President*
Michael Y Yoo, *Principal*
Alma Kim, *Manager*
▲ **EMP:** 35 **EST:** 2011
SQ FT: 15,000

SALES: 2.5MM **Privately Held**
SIC: 2541 3564 Store & office display cases & fixtures; aircurtains (blower)

2542 Partitions & Fixtures, Except Wood

(P-4960)
ACCURATE LAMINATED PDTS INC
1826 Dawns Way, Fullerton (92831-5523)
PHONE..............................714 632-2773
Daniel Dunn, *President*
Patricia Dunn, *Vice Pres*
Karen Evans, *Project Mgr*
Aaron Grim, *Project Mgr*
Ken Muller, *Project Mgr*
EMP: 30
SQ FT: 5,000
SALES (est): 5.1MM **Privately Held**
WEB: www.accuratelaminated.com
SIC: 2542 Bar fixtures, except wood; cabinets: show, display or storage: except wood

(P-4961)
ADVANCED EQUIPMENT CORPORATION (PA)
2401 W Commonwealth Ave, Fullerton (92833-2999)
PHONE..............................714 635-5350
Wesley B Dickson, *Owner*
W Dickson, *President*
W Scott Dickson, *CEO*
Lynn Stanco, *Corp Secy*
Frank Manning, *Senior VP*
◆ **EMP:** 50
SQ FT: 51,000
SALES (est): 10.9MM **Privately Held**
SIC: 2542 2541 Partitions for floor attachment, prefabricated: except wood; wood partitions & fixtures

(P-4962)
ALFRED PICON
Also Called: Superior Manufacturing
7644 Emil Ave, Bell (90201-4940)
PHONE..............................562 928-2561
Alfred Picon, *Owner*
EMP: 14
SQ FT: 7,000
SALES (est): 810K **Privately Held**
SIC: 2542 Showcases (not refrigerated): except wood; stands, merchandise display: except wood

(P-4963)
BRIAN KLAAS INC
11101 Tuxford St, Sun Valley (91352-2632)
PHONE..............................818 394-9881
Brian Klaas, *President*
EMP: 10
SALES (est): 951.2K **Privately Held**
SIC: 2542 Cabinets: show, display or storage: except wood

(P-4964)
BRITCAN INC
Also Called: Rich Limited
3809 Ocean Ranch Blvd # 110, Oceanside (92056-8606)
PHONE..............................760 722-2300
James B Hollen, *CEO*
◆ **EMP:** 20
SQ FT: 23,000
SALES (est): 5.1MM **Privately Held**
WEB: www.richltd.com
SIC: 2542 3089 Racks, merchandise display or storage: except wood; air mattresses, plastic

(P-4965)
BURKE DISPLAY SYSTEMS INC
55 S Peak, Laguna Niguel (92677-2903)
PHONE..............................949 248-0091
Robert Burke, *President*
EMP: 35
SQ FT: 1,000
SALES (est): 400.2K **Privately Held**
WEB: www.burkedisplays.us
SIC: 2542 Fixtures, store: except wood

(P-4966)
CAL PARTITIONS INC
23814 President Ave, Harbor City (90710-1390)
PHONE..............................310 539-1911
Alan Anderson, *President*
Sarah Anderson, *Treasurer*
Keith Peckham, *VP Sls/Mktg*
Sami Anderson, *Sales Staff*
EMP: 19
SQ FT: 13,000
SALES (est): 2.3MM **Privately Held**
WEB: www.calpartitions.com
SIC: 2542 5046 3231 2631 Partitions for floor attachment, prefabricated: except wood; partitions; products of purchased glass; paperboard mills; wood partitions & fixtures; office furniture, except wood

(P-4967)
CALIFORNIA COUNTERTOP INC (PA)
7811 Alvarado Rd, La Mesa (91942-0665)
PHONE..............................619 460-0205
Wayne J Krumenacker, *President*
EMP: 20
SQ FT: 8,300
SALES (est): 1.4MM **Privately Held**
WEB: www.californiacountertop.com
SIC: 2542 1799 3241 5211 Counters or counter display cases: except wood; counter top installation; wood partitions & fixtures; cabinets, kitchen

(P-4968)
CARDENAS ENTERPRISES INC
Also Called: J C Rack Systems
339 W Norman Ave, Arcadia (91007-8042)
PHONE..............................323 588-0137
John Cardenas, *President*
Maria Cardenas, *Vice Pres*
EMP: 17 **EST:** 1977
SALES: 1MM **Privately Held**
WEB: www.versatilegunrack.com
SIC: 2542 Garment racks: except wood

(P-4969)
CCI MAIL & SHIPPING SYSTEMS
Also Called: C C I Mling-Shipping Eqp Suppl
369 Estrella St, Ventura (93003)
PHONE..............................805 658-9123
Annette Klein, *Partner*
Paul Klein, *Partner*
EMP: 10
SALES (est): 1.1MM **Privately Held**
SIC: 2542 5044 Postal lock boxes, mail racks & related products; mailing machines

(P-4970)
COIN GLLERY OF SAN FRNCSCO INC
Also Called: Presentation Systems
951 Hensley St, Richmond (94801-2114)
PHONE..............................510 236-8882
Cory Marcus, *President*
Jim Blake, *Vice Pres*
Fancisco Mejia, *Vice Pres*
EMP: 19
SQ FT: 25,000
SALES: 10MM **Privately Held**
SIC: 2542 3999 3131 Stands, merchandise display: except wood; coins & tokens, non-currency; inner parts for shoes

(P-4971)
CRYSTOLON INC
7223 Sycamore St, Commerce (90040-2713)
P.O. Box 58323, Los Angeles (90058-0323)
PHONE..............................323 725-3482
Marki Leonard, *President*
Russell R Moore, *Corp Secy*
EMP: 50
SQ FT: 13,000
SALES (est): 4.3MM **Privately Held**
SIC: 2542 5046 Fixtures, store: except wood; store fixtures

(P-4972)
CUTTING EDGE CREATIVE LLC
8155 Byron Rd, Whittier (90606-2615)
PHONE..............................562 907-7007
Jennifer Franklin, *Mng Member*
Daniel Esquer, *Prdtn Mgr*

Ward Lookabaugh,
▲ **EMP:** 75
SQ FT: 40,000
SALES (est): 12.3MM **Privately Held**
WEB: www.weldedfixtures.com
SIC: 2542 3496 7319 Racks, merchandise display or storage: except wood; miscellaneous fabricated wire products; display advertising service

(P-4973)
DESIGN IMAGERY
3621 Ortega St, San Francisco (94122-4033)
PHONE..............................650 589-6464
EMP: 10
SQ FT: 7,000
SALES: 1MM **Privately Held**
WEB: www.designimagery.com
SIC: 2542

(P-4974)
DURACITE
Also Called: Mark One Counter Top Designs
2636 N Argyle Ave, Fresno (93727-1303)
PHONE..............................559 346-1181
Fadi Halabi, *CEO*
EMP: 10
SQ FT: 2,700
SALES (est): 609K **Privately Held**
SIC: 2542 Counters or counter display cases: except wood

(P-4975)
EVOLV SURFACES INC
Also Called: Fox Marble & Granite
1315 Armstrong Ave, San Francisco (94124-3608)
PHONE..............................415 671-0635
Charles McLaughlin, *President*
▲ **EMP:** 122
SQ FT: 16,613
SALES (est): 21.2MM **Privately Held**
WEB: www.fox-marble.com
SIC: 2542 5032 Counters or counter display cases: except wood; marble building stone

(P-4976)
FELBRO INC
3666 E Olympic Blvd, Los Angeles (90023-3147)
PHONE..............................323 263-8686
Howard Feldner, *Ch of Bd*
Norman Feldner, *CEO*
Ricardo Navarro, *Technical Staff*
Conrad Natac, *Controller*
Jeffrey Feldner, *VP Mfg*
◆ **EMP:** 180
SQ FT: 75,000
SALES (est): 39.6MM **Privately Held**
WEB: www.felbro-inc.com
SIC: 2542 Racks, merchandise display or storage: except wood

(P-4977)
FIELD MANUFACTURING CORP (PA)
1751 Torrance Blvd Ste H, Torrance (90501-1726)
PHONE..............................310 781-9292
Patrick Field, *President*
▲ **EMP:** 36
SQ FT: 20,000
SALES (est): 12.6MM **Privately Held**
WEB: www.fieldmfg.com
SIC: 2542 3089 Partitions & fixtures, except wood; injection molding of plastics

(P-4978)
GIANNELLI CABINET MFG CO
8835 Shirley Ave, Northridge (91324-3412)
PHONE..............................818 882-9787
John Giannelli, *President*
EMP: 10
SQ FT: 17,000
SALES (est): 1.5MM **Privately Held**
SIC: 2542 1751 2541 2434 Cabinets: show, display or storage: except wood; cabinet & finish carpentry; wood partitions & fixtures; wood kitchen cabinets

(P-4979)
GLOBAL STEEL PRODUCTS CORP
Also Called: Global Specialties Direct
936 61st St, Oakland (94608-1307)
PHONE..............................510 652-2060
Steve Allen, *Manager*
EMP: 25
SQ FT: 13,600
SALES (corp-wide): 201.7MM **Privately Held**
WEB: www.globalpartitions.com
SIC: 2542 5023 5021 5046 Partitions for floor attachment, prefabricated: except wood; home furnishings; furniture; partitions
HQ: Global Steel Products Corp
95 Marcus Blvd
Deer Park NY 11729
631 586-3455

(P-4980)
HANNIBAL MATERIAL HANDLING
2230 E 38th St, Vernon (90058-1629)
PHONE..............................323 587-4060
Blanton Bartlett, *President*
Heidy Moon, *Vice Pres*
Steve Roger, *Vice Pres*
▼ **EMP:** 214
SQ FT: 163,000
SALES (est): 40.4MM
SALES (corp-wide): 60.2MM **Privately Held**
WEB: www.hannibalindustries.com
SIC: 2542 Partitions & fixtures, except wood
PA: Hannibal Industries, Inc.
3851 S Santa Fe Ave
Vernon CA 90058
323 513-1200

(P-4981)
HUFCOR CALIFORNIA INC (HQ)
Also Called: Hufcor Airwall Since 1900
2380 E Artesia Blvd, Long Beach (90805-1708)
P.O. Box 1149, Bellflower (90707-1149)
PHONE..............................562 634-3116
Andy Espineira, *President*
J Michael Borden, *CEO*
Mike Borden, *Chairman*
Frank Scott, *Treasurer*
EMP: 56
SQ FT: 87,000
SALES (est): 44.2MM
SALES (corp-wide): 233.7MM **Privately Held**
SIC: 2542 5046 Partitions & fixtures, except wood; partitions
PA: Hufcor, Inc.
2101 Kennedy Rd
Janesville WI 53545
608 756-1241

(P-4982)
IDX CORPORATION
5655 Silver Creek Vly Rd, San Jose (95138-2473)
PHONE..............................408 270-8094
Carl Vitale, *Principal*
EMP: 122
SALES (corp-wide): 4.4B **Publicly Held**
SIC: 2542 Office & store showcases & display fixtures
HQ: Idx Corporation
1 Rider Trail Plaza Dr
Earth City MO 63045
314 739-4120

(P-4983)
IMPERIAL SHADE VENETIAN BLIND
Also Called: Imperial Shade Venetian Blind
909 E 59th St, Los Angeles (90001-1007)
PHONE..............................323 233-4391
Sue Joe, *Branch Mgr*
EMP: 10
SALES (corp-wide): 9.2MM **Privately Held**
SIC: 2542 1541 Counters or counter display cases: except wood; industrial buildings & warehouses

▲ = Import ▼=Export
◆ =Import/Export

PA: Imperial Shade And Venetian Blind Co.
4362 S Broadway
Los Angeles CA 90037
323 232-4901

(P-4984)
INTERIOR CORNER USA INC
2714 Stingle Ave, Rosemead (91770-3329)
PHONE..................................626 452-8833
Jacob Tsang-CHI Poon, *President*
▲ **EMP:** 10 **EST:** 2003
SQ FT: 10,052
SALES (est): 1.1MM **Privately Held**
SIC: 2542 Fixtures, office: except wood

(P-4985)
JCM INDUSTRIES INC (PA)
Also Called: Advance Storage Products
15302 Pipeline Ln, Huntington Beach
(92649-1138)
PHONE..................................714 902-9000
John Vr Krummell, *President*
Ken Blankenhorn, *President*
John Warren, *CFO*
JP Hoeft, *Vice Pres*
Jeff Howard, *Vice Pres*
▼ **EMP:** 21
SQ FT: 10,000
SALES (est): 33.7MM **Privately Held**
WEB: www.rackbargains.com
SIC: 2542 Racks, merchandise display or
storage: except wood

(P-4986)
JOHNS FORMICA SHOP INC
2439 Piner Rd, Santa Rosa (95403-2356)
PHONE..................................707 544-8585
John Deas, *President*
Ellen Deas, *Vice Pres*
EMP: 15
SQ FT: 4,500
SALES (est): 2.5MM **Privately Held**
WEB: www.johnsformicashop.com
SIC: 2542 2434 Counters or counter dis-
play cases: except wood; wood kitchen
cabinets

(P-4987)
M S F INC
1100 Industrial Rd Ste 18, San Carlos
(94070-4131)
PHONE..................................650 592-0239
Sabino F Madariaga, *President*
Mike Jaca, *Vice Pres*
Brian Madariaga, *Vice Pres*
EMP: 12
SALES (est): 3MM **Privately Held**
WEB: www.msf.net
SIC: 2542 Partitions & fixtures, except
wood

(P-4988)
M3 PRODUCTS INC
Also Called: J Roberts Design
335 N Puente St Ste E, Brea (92821-5274)
PHONE..................................626 371-1900
Heejung Yu, *President*
EMP: 15
SALES (est): 1.9MM **Privately Held**
SIC: 2542 Fixtures, store: except wood

(P-4989)
MAGNA-POLE PRODUCTS INC
(PA)
Also Called: Hang-UPS Unlimited
1904 14th St Ste 107, Santa Monica
(90404-4600)
PHONE..................................310 453-3806
Scott Freeman, *President*
◆ **EMP:** 16 **EST:** 1962
SQ FT: 15,000
SALES (est): 2.6MM **Privately Held**
WEB: www.hangups.com
SIC: 2542 Partitions & fixtures, except
wood

(P-4990)
MERCHANDISING SYSTEMS
INC
381 Claire Pl, Menlo Park (94025-5354)
P.O. Box 2423, Union City (94587-7423)
PHONE..................................510 477-9100
Kyle Robinson, *President*
Mary Lynn Robinson, *Treasurer*
▲ **EMP:** 50

SALES (est): 6.4MM **Privately Held**
WEB: www.msmdisplays.com
SIC: 2542 Partitions & fixtures, except
wood

(P-4991)
MICHAEL T MINGIONE
Also Called: 2 Spec Mfg
2885 Aiello Dr Ste D, San Jose
(95111-2188)
PHONE..................................408 365-1544
Michael Mingione, *Owner*
EMP: 10
SQ FT: 34,000
SALES: 1MM **Privately Held**
SIC: 2542 Postal lock boxes, mail racks &
related products

(P-4992)
NEW GREENSCREEN
INCORPORATED
Also Called: Impac International
5500 Jurupa St, Ontario (91761-3668)
PHONE..................................800 767-9378
Kory Levoy, *Branch Mgr*
EMP: 20 **Privately Held**
WEB: www.pmpwest.com
SIC: 2542 3444 Cabinets: show, display or
storage: except wood; sheet metalwork
PA: New Greenscreen, Incorporated
5500 Jurupa St
Ontario CA 91761

(P-4993)
ONQ SOLUTIONS INC (PA)
24540 Clawiter Rd, Hayward (94545-2222)
PHONE..................................650 262-4150
Paul Chapuis, *President*
Laura Metz, *Vice Pres*
EMP: 31
SQ FT: 1,700
SALES (est): 5.5MM **Privately Held**
SIC: 2542 Stands, merchandise display:
except wood

(P-4994)
PACIFIC FIXTURE COMPANY INC
12860 San Fernando Rd B1, Sylmar
(91342-3725)
P.O. Box 920844 (91392-0844)
PHONE..................................818 362-2130
Keith Stark, *President*
EMP: 14
SQ FT: 15,000
SALES (est): 2.6MM **Privately Held**
WEB: www.pacificfixture.com
SIC: 2542 Partitions & fixtures, except
wood

(P-4995)
PACIFIC MANUFACTURING MGT
INC
Also Called: Greneker Solutions
3110 E 12th St, Los Angeles (90023-3616)
PHONE..................................323 263-9000
Erik Johnson, *President*
Steven Beckman, *COO*
Gerry Clark, *Project Mgr*
▲ **EMP:** 60
SQ FT: 60,000
SALES (est): 13.7MM **Privately Held**
WEB: www.grenekersolutions.com
SIC: 2542 2541 Fixtures: display, office or
store: except wood; display fixtures, wood

(P-4996)
PALOMAR CASEWORK INC
4275 Clearview Dr, Carlsbad (92008-3632)
PHONE..................................760 941-9860
EMP: 18
SQ FT: 15,000
SALES (est): 2.1MM **Privately Held**
SIC: 2542 2541

(P-4997)
PLASTIC TOPS INC
521 E Jamie Ave, La Habra (90631-6842)
PHONE..................................714 738-8128
Paul Ackerman, *President*
Gene Versluys, *Vice Pres*
Don Gauthier, *Sales Mgr*
EMP: 14
SQ FT: 9,500

SALES (est): 3.3MM **Privately Held**
SIC: 2542 8011 Counters or counter display cases: except wood; offices & clinics
of medical doctors

(P-4998)
RAP SECURITY INC
4630 Cecilia St, Cudahy (90201-5814)
PHONE..................................323 560-3493
Angelo Palmer, *President*
Tina Martinez, *COO*
Bob Palmer, *Vice Pres*
Marki Leonard, *General Mgr*
▲ **EMP:** 55
SQ FT: 40,000
SALES (est): 8.8MM **Privately Held**
WEB: www.rapstfx.com
SIC: 2542 Fixtures, store: except wood

(P-4999)
REEVE STORE EQUIPMENT
COMPANY (PA)
9131 Bermudez St, Pico Rivera
(90660-4507)
PHONE..................................562 949-2535
John Frackelton, *President*
Mary Ann Crysler, *CFO*
Mary Crysler, *CFO*
Robert Frackelton, *Vice Pres*
Maynor Rueno, *Controller*
▲ **EMP:** 100 **EST:** 1932
SQ FT: 170,000
SALES (est): 17MM **Privately Held**
SIC: 2542 3471 Counters or counter dis-
play cases: except wood; electroplating of
metals or formed products

(P-5000)
SALSBURY INDUSTRIES INC
(PA)
18300 Central Ave, Carson (90746-4008)
PHONE..................................323 846-6700
Dennis Fraher, *President*
Michael N Lobasso, *CFO*
John Fraher, *Chairman*
Brian Fraher, *Vice Pres*
Stefanie Cruz, *Accountant*
◆ **EMP:** 229
SQ FT: 600,000
SALES (est): 73.9MM **Privately Held**
WEB: www.mailboxes.com
SIC: 2542 Locker boxes, postal service:
except wood; postal lock boxes, mail
racks & related products

(P-5001)
SAMSON PRODUCTS INC
Also Called: J L Industries
6285 Randolph St, Commerce
(90040-3514)
PHONE..................................323 726-9070
John Reissner, *President*
Robert Dunn, *President*
Richard McNamara, *Manager*
EMP: 480 **EST:** 1955
SQ FT: 20,000
SALES (est): 54.3MM
SALES (corp-wide): 154.2MM **Privately
Held**
WEB: www.samsonproducts.com
SIC: 2542 Cabinets: show, display or stor-
age: except wood
PA: Activar, Inc.
9700 Newton Ave S
Bloomington MN 55431
952 944-3533

(P-5002)
SANTA CRUZ INDUSTRIES INC
129 Bulkhead, Santa Cruz (95060-2701)
P.O. Box 37 (95063-0037)
PHONE..................................831 423-9211
Walter Poterbin, *President*
Marvin Christie, *Vice Pres*
Cathy Poterbin, *Vice Pres*
▲ **EMP:** 10 **EST:** 1954
SALES (est): 960K **Privately Held**
WEB: www.santacruzind.com
SIC: 2542 Office & store showcases & dis-
play fixtures

(P-5003)
STEVES PLATING
CORPORATION
3111 N San Fernando Blvd, Burbank
(91504-2527)
PHONE..................................818 842-2184
Terry Knezevich, *CEO*
Roger C Knezevich, *Corp Secy*
EMP: 140 **EST:** 1956
SQ FT: 80,000
SALES (est): 18.7MM **Privately Held**
WEB: www.stevesplating.com
SIC: 2542 3446 3471 7692 Fixtures,
store: except wood; ladders, for perma-
nent installation: metal; railings, prefabri-
cated metal; plating of metals or formed
products; welding repair; fabricated pipe
& fittings

(P-5004)
STRAFFORD INTL GROUP INC
Also Called: Sig
877 Island Ave Unit 704, San Diego
(92101-7152)
PHONE..................................619 446-6960
Keith S Robinson, *President*
▲ **EMP:** 17
SQ FT: 2,000
SALES (est): 3.2MM **Privately Held**
SIC: 2542 8742 Fixtures, office: except
wood; business consultant

(P-5005)
TEAMMATE BUILDERS INC
Also Called: Formatop
281 E Mcglincy Ln Frnt, Campbell
(95008-4946)
PHONE..................................408 377-9000
Toll Free:..................................888 -
Fax: 408 377-6972
EMP: 19
SQ FT: 12,000
SALES (est): 1.9MM **Privately Held**
WEB: www.formatopusa.com
SIC: 2542

(P-5006)
TEICHMAN ENTERPRISES INC
Also Called: T & H Store Fixtures
6100 Bandini Blvd, Commerce
(90040-3112)
PHONE..................................323 278-9000
Ruth Teichman, *President*
Alan Teichman, *Treasurer*
Sol Teichman, *Corp Secy*
Bernard Teichman, *Vice Pres*
Sidney Teichman, *Vice Pres*
▲ **EMP:** 50
SALES (est): 9.5MM **Privately Held**
WEB: www.teichman.net
SIC: 2542 Fixtures: display, office or store:
except wood

(P-5007)
TRINITY ENGINEERING
583 Martin Ave, Rohnert Park
(94928-2060)
PHONE..................................707 585-2959
Bruce D Omholt, *CEO*
Michael Johnston, *President*
Ronald R Milard, *President*
Denise R Palmer, *CFO*
Ellen Tackett, *Executive Asst*
EMP: 23
SQ FT: 18,000
SALES (est): 3.5MM **Privately Held**
WEB: www.trinityengineering.com
SIC: 2542 8711 Fixtures: display, office or
store: except wood; designing: ship, boat,
machine & product

(P-5008)
TURTLE STORAGE LTD
Also Called: American Bicycle Security Co
401 S Beckwith Rd, Santa Paula
(93060-3047)
P.O. Box 7359, Ventura (93006-7359)
PHONE..................................805 933-3688
Thomas Volk, *President*
Thomas M Volk, *CEO*
EMP: 20
SQ FT: 16,000
SALES (est): 2.7MM **Privately Held**
WEB: www.ameribike.com
SIC: 2542 1799 Lockers (not refrigerated):
except wood; fiberglass work

PRODUCTS & SVCS

(P-5009)
UNIWEB INC (PA)
222 S Promenade Ave, Corona
(92879-1743)
PHONE.....................951 279-7999
Karl F Weber, *CEO*
John McDonnell, *Vice Pres*
Denise Savaria, *Accounting Mgr*
Sam Gibson, *Purchasing*
Brent Abbott, *Purch Agent*
▲ **EMP:** 90 **EST:** 1979
SQ FT: 170,000
SALES (est): 14.2MM **Privately Held**
WEB: www.uniwebinc.com
SIC: 2542 Fixtures: display, office or store:
except wood

(P-5010)
VERLO INDUSTRIES INC
10762 Chestnut Ave, Stanton
(90680-2434)
PHONE.....................714 236-2191
Kreig Lopour, *President*
EMP: 40
SQ FT: 16,000
SALES (est): 6.5MM **Privately Held**
SIC: 2542 2522 Racks, merchandise dis-
play or storage: except wood; office furni-
ture, except wood

(P-5011)
WBP ASSOCIATES INC
2017 Seaman Ave, South El Monte
(91733-2626)
PHONE.....................626 575-0747
William Pope, *President*
Robert Pope, *Vice Pres*
EMP: 19
SQ FT: 6,500
SALES: 1MM **Privately Held**
SIC: 2542 1799 Counters or counter dis-
play cases: except wood; counter top in-
stallation

(P-5012)
**WESTERN PCF STOR
SOLUTIONS INC (PA)**
300 E Arrow Hwy, San Dimas
(91773-3339)
PHONE.....................909 451-0303
Tom Rogers, *President*
Peter G Dunn, *Ch of Bd*
Bill Whitehouse, *Vice Pres*
Mike Guerrero, *VP Engrg*
Joe Cascio, *Sales Staff*
EMP: 100
SQ FT: 165,000
SALES (est): 23MM **Privately Held**
WEB: www.wpss.com
SIC: 2542 Shelving, office & store: except
wood

2591 Drapery Hardware,
Window Blinds & Shades

(P-5013)
**ALL STRONG INDUSTRY (USA)
INC (PA)**
326 Paseo Tesoro, Walnut (91789-2725)
PHONE.....................909 598-6494
Pei-Hsiang Hsu, *Ch of Bd*
Frank Hsu, *Vice Pres*
▲ **EMP:** 30
SQ FT: 52,000
SALES (est): 5.8MM **Privately Held**
WEB: www.allstrongusa.com
SIC: 2591 Mini blinds; window shades

(P-5014)
**ALRO CSTM DRAPERY
INSTALLATION**
809 San Antonio Rd Ste 1, Palo Alto
(94303-4626)
PHONE.....................650 847-4343
Alfred Robledo, *Admin Sec*
Mar Y Sol Alvarado, *President*
EMP: 10 **EST:** 2016
SALES (est): 416.1K **Privately Held**
SIC: 2591 5714 Drapery hardware &
blinds & shades; curtains

(P-5015)
AMBASSADOR INDUSTRIES
2754 W Temple St, Los Angeles
(90026-4795)
PHONE.....................213 383-1171
Mike Lahav, *Owner*
EMP: 10
SQ FT: 20,000
SALES (est): 959.8K **Privately Held**
WEB: www.ambassadorindustries.com
SIC: 2591 5719 5023 Window blinds;
blinds vertical; window shades; window
furnishings; vertical blinds

(P-5016)
**BONDED WINDOW COVERINGS
INC**
7831 Ostrow St, San Diego (92111-3602)
P.O. Box 710130 (92171-0130)
PHONE.....................858 974-7700
Lee Howard Tandet, *President*
Mitch Adler, *Info Tech Dir*
EMP: 40
SALES (est): 4.4MM **Privately Held**
WEB: www.bondedwindowcoverings.com
SIC: 2591 Drapery hardware & blinds &
shades

(P-5017)
C & M WOOD INDUSTRIES
17229 Lemon St Ste D, Hesperia
(92345-5125)
PHONE.....................760 949-3292
Calvin Lam, *President*
Roger McCarvel, *Vice Pres*
▲ **EMP:** 155
SQ FT: 55,000
SALES (est): 13.1MM **Privately Held**
WEB: www.cmwood.com
SIC: 2591 Venetian blinds

(P-5018)
CAROLS ROMAN SHADES INC
130 Mason Cir Ste K, Concord
(94520-1246)
PHONE.....................925 674-9622
Carol Krystoff Lawton, *President*
EMP: 50
SQ FT: 4,033
SALES (est): 7.6MM **Privately Held**
WEB: www.carolsromanshades.com
SIC: 2591 Window shades

(P-5019)
CENTURY BLINDS INC
300 S Promenade Ave, Corona
(92879-1754)
PHONE.....................951 734-3762
Mitch Shapiro, *CEO*
Gene Sierra, *Controller*
Richard Cervantes, *Purch Mgr*
Alan Kramer, *Sales Mgr*
Lysa Bertsche, *Sales Staff*
▲ **EMP:** 100
SALES (est): 17MM **Privately Held**
WEB: www.centuryblindsinc.com
SIC: 2591 3429 5719 5023 Blinds verti-
cal; manufactured hardware (general);
vertical blinds; vertical blinds
HQ: Hunter Douglas Scandinavia Ab
Kristineholmsvagen 14a
Alingsas 441 3
322 775-00

(P-5020)
DISCOUNT BLIND CENTER
16074 Grand Ave, Lake Elsinore
(92530-1418)
PHONE.....................951 678-3980
Richard M Caty, *Owner*
John Caty, *Partner*
EMP: 10
SALES: 250K **Privately Held**
SIC: 2591 1799 Window blinds; window
treatment installation

(P-5021)
ELWIN INC
6910 8th St, Buena Park (90620-1036)
PHONE.....................714 752-6962
Josh W Kim, *CEO*
EMP: 20
SALES (est): 2.2MM **Privately Held**
SIC: 2591 5719 Window blinds; window
shades

(P-5022)
HADCO PRODUCTS INC
Also Called: Sierra Sunscreens
3345 Sunrise Blvd Ste 5, Rancho Cordova
(95742-7309)
PHONE.....................916 966-2409
Daniel A Wilmoth, *President*
EMP: 11
SQ FT: 3,800
SALES (est): 1.2MM **Privately Held**
SIC: 2591 1799 5211 1521 Window
shade rollers & fittings; window treatment
installation; screens, door & window; patio
& deck construction & repair

(P-5023)
HAUSER & SONS INC
Also Called: Hauser Shade
150 S 2nd St, Richmond (94804-2110)
PHONE.....................510 234-8850
Ken Hauser, *President*
Susan Hauser, *Treasurer*
Robert Hauser, *Vice Pres*
Marilyn Hauser, *Admin Sec*
Jones Victoria, *Marketing Staff*
▲ **EMP:** 13 **EST:** 1910
SQ FT: 18,000
SALES (est): 1.9MM **Privately Held**
WEB: www.hausershade.com
SIC: 2591 Window shades

(P-5024)
**HD WINDOW FASHIONS INC
(DH)**
Also Called: M & B Window Fashions
1818 Oak St, Los Angeles (90015-3302)
PHONE.....................213 749-6333
Wayne Gourlay, *President*
Dominique Au Yeung, *General Mgr*
Isha Garcia, *Human Res Mgr*
▲ **EMP:** 500
SQ FT: 200,000
SALES (est): 42.1MM **Privately Held**
SIC: 2591 Mini blinds; venetian blinds; win-
dow shades; blinds vertical
HQ: Hunter Douglas Inc.
1 Blue Hill Plz Ste 1569
Pearl River NY 10965
845 664-7000

(P-5025)
**HT WINDOW FASHIONS
CORPORATION (PA)**
Also Called: Richview By Tehdex
770 Epperson Dr, City of Industry
(91748-1336)
PHONE.....................626 839-8866
Lynne Lee, *President*
Greg Miles, *VP Sales*
William Liu, *Mktg Dir*
▲ **EMP:** 60
SQ FT: 34,000
SALES (est): 9.6MM **Privately Held**
WEB: www.richview.com
SIC: 2591 Blinds vertical; window blinds

(P-5026)
**HUNTER DOUGLAS
FABRICATIONS**
Also Called: Win-Glo Window Coverings
842 Charcot Ave, San Jose (95131-2210)
PHONE.....................408 435-8844
Jerry Fuchs, *President*
Ajit Mehra, *Treasurer*
Steve Pirylis, *Vice Pres*
Tom Hill, *Admin Sec*
Quintana Adriana, *HR Admin*
EMP: 275 **EST:** 1930
SQ FT: 76,000
SALES (est): 32.3MM **Privately Held**
SIC: 2591 Window blinds; blinds vertical;
venetian blinds; window shades
PA: Hunter Douglas N.V.
Dokweg 19
Willemstad

(P-5027)
JC WINDOW FASHIONS INC
6400 Fleet St, Commerce (90040-1710)
PHONE.....................909 364-8888
Jennifer Chiao, *CEO*
▲ **EMP:** 28

SALES (est): 4.2MM **Privately Held**
SIC: 2591 Drapery hardware & blinds &
shades

(P-5028)
KITTRICH CORPORATION (PA)
1585 W Mission Blvd, Pomona
(91766-1233)
PHONE.....................714 736-1000
Robert Friedland, *CEO*
Sylvia Fong-Trein, *Director*
◆ **EMP:** 130
SQ FT: 237,000
SALES (est): 161.1MM **Privately Held**
WEB: www.kittrich.com
SIC: 2591 2392 2381 Blinds vertical;
household furnishings; fabric dress &
work gloves

(P-5029)
L C PRINGLE SALES INC (PA)
Also Called: Pringle's Draperies
12020 Western Ave, Garden Grove
(92841-2913)
PHONE.....................714 892-1524
Larry C Pringle, *President*
Pamela Pringle Skinner, *Corp Secy*
Susan Pringle Kusinsky, *Vice Pres*
Carolyn Pringle, *Vice Pres*
Curtis L Pringle, *Vice Pres*
EMP: 30
SQ FT: 11,000
SALES (est): 3MM **Privately Held**
SIC: 2591 7216 2391 7211 Blinds verti-
cal; mini blinds; curtain cleaning & repair;
draperies, plastic & textile: from pur-
chased materials; power laundries, family
& commercial

(P-5030)
LA VOIES OF SAN JOSE
Also Called: Donald La Voie
2096 Lincoln Ave, San Jose (95125-3539)
PHONE.....................408 297-1285
Donald La Voie, *Owner*
EMP: 10
SQ FT: 4,867
SALES: 1.5MM **Privately Held**
WEB: www.lavoiesofsj.com
SIC: 2591 5231 5719 5714 Window
shades; wallpaper; window furnishings;
upholstery materials

(P-5031)
MILLER MANUFACTURING INC
Also Called: Silent Servant
165 Cascade Ct, Rohnert Park
(94928-1601)
PHONE.....................707 584-9528
Tom Miller, *President*
Joanne Miller, *Vice Pres*
Steve Miller, *Admin Sec*
Jim Miller, *Foreman/Supr*
▲ **EMP:** 10
SQ FT: 10,400
SALES (est): 1.3MM **Privately Held**
WEB: www.silentservant.com
SIC: 2591 3534 3442 3479 Curtain &
drapery rods, poles & fixtures; dumbwait-
ers; metal doors, sash & trim; etching &
engraving

(P-5032)
MILLERTON BUILDERS INC
Also Called: Vinyl Specialties
4714 E Home Ave, Fresno (93703-4509)
PHONE.....................559 252-0490
Frank Spencer, *President*
Matthew Carlton, *Treasurer*
Matt Carlton, *Corp Secy*
EMP: 25
SQ FT: 20,000
SALES: 3MM **Privately Held**
SIC: 2591 Drapery hardware & blinds &
shades

(P-5033)
PHASE II PRODUCTS INC (PA)
501 W Broadway Ste 2090, San Diego
(92101-8563)
PHONE.....................619 236-9699
Charles Hunt, *CEO*
John Bowie, *CFO*
Gordon Peiper, *Vice Pres*
Elizabeth Soper, *Project Leader*
▲ **EMP:** 30

▲ = Import ▼=Export
◆ =Import/Export

SQ FT: 4,800
SALES (est): 4.8MM
SALES (corp-wide): 4.5MM Privately
Held
SIC: 2591 Drapery hardware & blinds &
shades

(P-5034)
PLASTIC VIEW ATC INC
4585 Runway St Ste B, Simi Valley
(93063-3479)
PHONE..................................805 520-9390
Ryan Voges, *President*
EMP: 10
SQ FT: 5,400
SALES: 1.4MM Privately Held
WEB: www.pvatc.com
SIC: 2591 Window shades

(P-5035)
REMEDY BLINDS INC
220 W Central Ave, Santa Ana
(92707-3416)
PHONE..................................714 245-0186
Craig Briggs, *President*
Grace Briggs, *Corp Secy*
◆ EMP: 55
SQ FT: 21,000
SALES (est): 7.1MM Privately Held
SIC: 2591 2431 Window blinds; window
shades; window shutters, wood

(P-5036)
ROLL-A-SHADE INC (PA)
12101 Madera Way, Riverside
(92503-4849)
PHONE..................................951 245-5077
Tyrone Pereira, *President*
Ric Berg, *Vice Pres*
▲ EMP: 22
SQ FT: 10,000
SALES (est): 6.9MM Privately Held
SIC: 2591 1799 Window shades; window
treatment installation

(P-5037)
SHADES UNLIMITED INC
Also Called: Redi Shades
361 Blodgett St, Cotati (94931-8700)
PHONE..................................707 285-2233
Kevin D Wohlert, *CEO*
Joe Militello, *CEO*
Joe Metger, *CFO*
Christine Zabaneh, *CFO*
Yelena Pavlik, *Marketing Staff*
▲ EMP: 18
SALES (est): 3.7MM Privately Held
WEB: www.redishade.com
SIC: 2591 Window shades

(P-5038)
SHOWDOGS INC
Also Called: Wholesale Shade
168 S Pacific St, San Marcos
(92078-2527)
PHONE..................................760 603-3269
Patrick Howe, *President*
EMP: 30
SQ FT: 10,000
SALES: 1MM Privately Held
SIC: 2591 Blinds vertical

(P-5039)
SKAGFIELD CORPORATION
Also Called: Skandia Industries
2225 Avenida Costa Este, San Diego
(92154-6238)
PHONE..................................858 635-7777
Larry Sack, *Branch Mgr*
Pete Stewart, *Administration*
Dana Kissie, *Human Res Dir*
EMP: 300
SALES (corp-wide): 16.8MM Privately
Held
SIC: 2591 Window blinds
PA: Skagfield Corporation
270 Crossway Rd
Tallahassee FL 32305
850 878-1144

(P-5040)
SPEED-O-PIN INTERNATIONAL
1401 Freeman Ave, Long Beach
(90804-2518)
PHONE..................................562 433-4911
Jeffrey Jacobson, *President*

EMP: 12
SQ FT: 20,000
SALES (est): 1.2MM Privately Held
SIC: 2591 2672 Drapery hardware &
blinds & shades; coated & laminated
paper

(P-5041)
**SPRINGS WINDOW FASHIONS
LLC**
Also Called: Graber Blinds
6754 Calle De Linea, San Diego
(92154-8021)
PHONE..................................877 792-0002
EMP: 10
SALES (corp-wide): 3B Privately Held
SIC: 2591 Blinds vertical
HQ: Springs Window Fashions, Llc
7549 Graber Rd
Middleton WI 53562
608 836-1011

(P-5042)
VERTICAL DOORS INC
Also Called: Vdi Motor Sports
542 3rd St, Lake Elsinore (92530-2729)
PHONE..................................951 273-1069
Rob Baum, *President*
EMP: 18
SALES (est): 3.5MM Privately Held
WEB: www.verticaldoors.com
SIC: 2591 Blinds vertical

(P-5043)
WEBB DESIGNS INC
Also Called: Webbshade
40300 Greenwood Way, Oakhurst
(93644-9566)
P.O. Box 215 (93644-0215)
PHONE..................................559 641-5400
Mike Benbrook, *President*
Allison Benbrook, *Vice Pres*
▼ EMP: 18
SQ FT: 9,000
SALES: 1.8MM Privately Held
SIC: 2591 Window shades

(P-5044)
**XENTRIC DRAPERY HARDWARE
INC**
11001 Sutter Ave, Pacoima (91331-2457)
PHONE..................................818 897-0444
Carlos Contreras, *President*
Erika Luna Contreras, *Vice Pres*
▲ EMP: 10
SALES (est): 1.4MM Privately Held
SIC: 2591 Blinds vertical

**2599 Furniture & Fixtures,
NEC**

(P-5045)
1PERFECTCHOICE
21908 Valley Blvd, Walnut (91789-0938)
PHONE..................................909 594-8855
CHI Ching Lin, *CEO*
Brian Lin, *CFO*
EMP: 18
SQ FT: 5,000
SALES: 2.1MM Privately Held
SIC: 2599 5021 5712 Hospital furniture,
except beds; furniture; furniture stores

(P-5046)
ACCENT MANUFACTURING INC
105 Leavesley Rd Bldg 3d, Gilroy
(95020-3688)
PHONE..................................408 846-9993
Joe Catanzaro, *President*
Esther Catanzaro, *Corp Secy*
Frank Catanzaro, *Vice Pres*
EMP: 20
SQ FT: 30,000
SALES (est): 2.9MM Privately Held
WEB: www.accentmfg.com
SIC: 2599 2431 5031 2434 Cabinets,
factory; doors & door parts & trim, wood;
lumber, plywood & millwork; wood kitchen
cabinets

(P-5047)
AFN SERVICES LLC
Also Called: Socialight, The
368 E Campbell Ave, Campbell
(95008-2029)
PHONE..................................408 364-1564
EMP: 40
SQ FT: 2,200
SALES: 250K Privately Held
SIC: 2599 5813 7929

(P-5048)
**ALEGACY FOODSERVICE
PRODUCTS**
12683 Corral Pl, Santa Fe Springs
(90670-4748)
PHONE..................................562 320-3100
Jesse Gross, *Principal*
Brett Gross, *President*
Eric Gross, *Vice Pres*
Christine Trujillo, *Accountant*
Les Palmer, *Sales Dir*
◆ EMP: 60
SQ FT: 130,000
SALES (est): 8.7MM Privately Held
WEB: www.alegacy.com
SIC: 2599 3263 Carts, restaurant equip-
ment; cookware, fine earthenware

(P-5049)
**AMKO RESTAURANT
FURNITURE INC**
5833 Avalon Blvd, Los Angeles
(90003-1307)
PHONE..................................323 234-0388
Seong Gyun Shin, *President*
Soon Jo Shin, *CFO*
Shin Tae, *Info Tech Dir*
▲ EMP: 23
SQ FT: 18,000
SALES (est): 3.5MM Privately Held
WEB: www.chairimports.com
SIC: 2599 Restaurant furniture, wood or
metal

(P-5050)
**BAY VALVE SERVICE & ENGRG
LLC**
3948 Teal Ct, Benicia (94510-1202)
PHONE..................................707 748-7166
Rob Sterry, *Branch Mgr*
Scott Allen, *Manager*
EMP: 25
SALES (corp-wide): 54.3MM Privately
Held
SIC: 2599 Bar, restaurant & cafeteria furni-
ture
PA: Bay Valve Service & Engineering, Llc
4385 S 133rd St
Tukwila WA 98168
206 782-7800

(P-5051)
BENCH-CRAFT INC
4005 Artesia Ave, Fullerton (92833-2519)
PHONE..................................714 523-3322
Theodor Steinhilber, *President*
John Boyd, *CFO*
David Spivy, *CFO*
EMP: 10 EST: 1985
SQ FT: 35,000
SALES (est): 1.8MM
SALES (corp-wide): 4.6MM Privately
Held
WEB: www.bench-craft.com
SIC: 2599 Work benches, factory
PA: Stein Industries, Inc.
4005 Artesia Ave
Fullerton CA 92833
714 522-4560

(P-5052)
BENCHPRO INC
Also Called: Bench Depot
23949 Tecate Mission Rd, Tecate (91980)
P.O. Box G (91980-0958)
PHONE..................................619 478-9400
Jay David Lissner, *President*
Daniel Drake, *General Mgr*
Coy Marchino, *Info Tech Mgr*
Susengno Sutijo, *Info Tech Mgr*
▲ EMP: 188
SQ FT: 155,000

SALES (est): 34.2MM Privately Held
WEB: www.benchpro.com
SIC: 2599 Work benches, factory

(P-5053)
**COMMERCIAL CSTM STING
UPHL INC**
12601 Western Ave, Garden Grove
(92841-4014)
PHONE..................................714 850-0520
Robert Francis, *CEO*
▲ EMP: 90
SQ FT: 50,000
SALES (est): 20.5MM Privately Held
WEB: www.commercialcustomseating.com
SIC: 2599 Restaurant furniture, wood or
metal

(P-5054)
DAVID HAID
8619 Crocker St, Los Angeles
(90003-3516)
PHONE..................................323 752-8096
EMP: 20 Privately Held
WEB: www.oasisfurniture.net
SIC: 2599 5199 Factory furniture & fix-
tures; advertising specialties
PA: David Haid
3931 Topanga Canyon Blvd
Malibu CA 90265

(P-5055)
DIVISADERO 500 LLC
Also Called: Mad Zone
502 Divisadero St, San Francisco
(94117-2213)
PHONE..................................415 572-6062
Michael J Krouse, *President*
EMP: 18 EST: 2010
SALES (est): 1MM Privately Held
SIC: 2599 Bar, restaurant & cafeteria furni-
ture

(P-5056)
ELEGANCE UPHOLSTERY INC
11803 Slauson Ave Unit A, Ontario (91762)
PHONE..................................562 698-2584
Ricardo Vargas, *CEO*
EMP: 16
SALES (est): 2.2MM Privately Held
SIC: 2599 7641 Bar, restaurant & cafeteria
furniture; restaurant furniture, wood or
metal; bowling establishment furniture; re-
upholstery & furniture repair; reupholstery

(P-5057)
ELITE CABINETRY INC
25755 Jefferson Ave, Murrieta
(92562-6903)
PHONE..................................951 698-5050
Paul Silva, *President*
EMP: 14
SQ FT: 8,200
SALES (est): 1.8MM Privately Held
WEB: www.elitecabinetry.com
SIC: 2599 Cabinets, factory

(P-5058)
ELKAY INTERIOR SYSTEMS INC
225 Santa Monica Blvd, Santa Monica
(90401-2207)
PHONE..................................800 837-8373
Laurie Schmidt, *Branch Mgr*
EMP: 10
SALES (corp-wide): 1.1B Privately Held
WEB: www.isiamerica.com
SIC: 2599 2511 Restaurant furniture,
wood or metal; wood household furniture
HQ: Elkay Interior Systems Inc.
241 N Broadway Ste 600
Milwaukee WI 53202
414 224-0957

(P-5059)
ERGONOM CORPORATION
Also Called: E R G International
361 Bernoulli Cir, Oxnard (93030-5164)
PHONE..................................805 981-9978
George Zaki, *CEO*
Roy Zaki, *President*
Donna Shelton, *Assistant*
◆ EMP: 90

SALES: 25.4MM **Privately Held**
WEB: www.erginternational.com
SIC: 2599 2531 Hospital furniture, except beds; hotel furniture; school furniture

(P-5060)
FIXTURE DESIGN & MFG CO
Also Called: F D M
4848 Lakeview Ave Ste E, Yorba Linda (92886-3452)
P.O. Box 819, Anaheim (92815-0819)
PHONE.....................714 776-3104
David T Carlson, *President*
Judy McArthur, *Corp Secy*
Doreen Carlson, *Vice Pres*
EMP: 30
SQ FT: 40,000
SALES: 6MM **Privately Held**
WEB: www.fixturedesign.com
SIC: 2599 Bar, restaurant & cafeteria furniture

(P-5061)
FORBES INDUSTRIES DIV
1933 E Locust St, Ontario (91761-7608)
PHONE.....................909 923-4559
Tim Sweetland, *President*
Peter Sweetland, *Vice Pres*
▼ EMP: 210
SQ FT: 110,000
SALES (est): 26.3MM
SALES (corp-wide): 41.8MM **Privately Held**
WEB: www.forbesindustries.com
SIC: 2599 Carts, restaurant equipment
PA: The Winsford Corporation
1933 E Locust St
Ontario CA 91761
909 923-4559

(P-5062)
GLP DESIGNS INC
Also Called: Antique Designs
916 W Hyde Park Blvd, Inglewood (90302-3308)
PHONE.....................310 652-6800
Keith G Hudson, *Vice Pres*
Keith Hudson, *Vice Pres*
EMP: 15
SALES: 950K **Privately Held**
SIC: 2599 Furniture & fixtures

(P-5063)
HARMONY INFINITE INC
Also Called: Best Slip Cover Company
12918 Bloomfield St, Studio City (91604-1401)
PHONE.....................818 780-4569
Stuart Dones, *CEO*
Joan Dones, *Corp Secy*
Joshua Siegel, *Vice Pres*
EMP: 16
SALES (est): 3.6MM **Privately Held**
SIC: 2599 Factory furniture & fixtures

(P-5064)
HIRE ELEGANCE
8333 Arjons Dr Ste E, San Diego (92126-6320)
PHONE.....................858 740-7862
Stuart Simble, *Principal*
EMP: 10
SALES (est): 1.4MM **Privately Held**
SIC: 2599 Furniture & fixtures

(P-5065)
HURLEYS LP
Also Called: Hurleys Restaurant & Bar
1516 King Ave, NAPA (94559-1524)
PHONE.....................707 944-2345
Robert Hurley, *Owner*
EMP: 60
SALES (est): 6.9MM **Privately Held**
WEB: www.hurleysrestaurant.com
SIC: 2599 Bar, restaurant & cafeteria furniture

(P-5066)
IAC INDUSTRIES
3010 Saturn St Ste 205, Brea (92821-6220)
PHONE.....................714 990-8997
Nancy Bonee, *Purch Mgr*
John Notti, *Opers Staff*
Jessica Urioste, *Marketing Staff*
Rosa Gomez, *Sales Staff*

Jessica Haderer, *Sales Staff*
EMP: 40
SALES (corp-wide): 12.6MM **Privately Held**
SIC: 2599 Bar furniture
PA: Iac Industries
3831 S Bullard Ave
Goodyear AZ 85338
714 990-8997

(P-5067)
J&T DESIGNS LLC
1463 W El Segundo Blvd, Compton (90222-1144)
PHONE.....................310 868-5190
Joe Galindo,
EMP: 35
SQ FT: 15,000
SALES (est): 3.6MM **Privately Held**
WEB: www.jtdesigns.net
SIC: 2599 Factory furniture & fixtures

(P-5068)
JBI LLC (PA)
Also Called: Jbl Interiors
2650 E El Presidio St, Long Beach (90810-1142)
PHONE.....................310 886-8034
Pete Jensen, *Manager*
Buck Miko, *Officer*
Joseph Parisi, *Senior VP*
Jack Potter, *Vice Pres*
Robert Rivas, *Business Dir*
◆ EMP: 200
SQ FT: 270,000
SALES (est): 52.9MM **Privately Held**
WEB: www.jbiindustries.com
SIC: 2599 5046 Restaurant furniture, wood or metal; restaurant equipment & supplies

(P-5069)
K&K WORLD INC
721 W Wedgewood Ln, La Habra (90631-7664)
PHONE.....................714 234-6237
Sun Suk Kang, *President*
▲ EMP: 35
SALES: 950K **Privately Held**
SIC: 2599 Furniture & fixtures

(P-5070)
KOUZOUIANS FINE CUSTOM FURN
Also Called: Kouzouian Custom Furniture
18586 Caspian Ct, Granada Hills (91344-2010)
PHONE.....................818 772-1212
Hartyoun Kouzouian, *President*
Diana Kouzouian, *CFO*
EMP: 25
SQ FT: 20,000
SALES (est): 2.8MM **Privately Held**
SIC: 2599 Hotel furniture

(P-5071)
M DAMICO INC
Also Called: Mjd Cabinets
12650 Highway 67 Ste E, Lakeside (92040-1132)
PHONE.....................619 390-5858
Mark D'Amico, *President*
Maryanne D'Amico, *Treasurer*
Nick D'Amico, *Vice Pres*
EMP: 20
SQ FT: 6,000
SALES (est): 1.6MM **Privately Held**
SIC: 2599 Cabinets, factory

(P-5072)
MAKE BEVERAGE HOLDINGS LLC
2569 Tea Leaf Ln, Tustin (92782-2001)
PHONE.....................949 923-8238
Jeffrey Duggan, *Principal*
EMP: 20
SALES (est): 685.6K **Privately Held**
SIC: 2599 Bar, restaurant & cafeteria furniture

(P-5073)
MASHINDUSTRIES INC
7150 Village Dr, Buena Park (90621-2261)
PHONE.....................714 736-9600
Bernard Brucha, *CEO*
Michelle Blemel, *Admin Sec*

EMP: 47
SALES: 3MM **Privately Held**
SIC: 2599 Factory furniture & fixtures

(P-5074)
NLP FURNITURE INDUSTRIES INC
1425 Corporate Center Dr # 200, San Diego (92154-6629)
P.O. Box 530659 (92153-0659)
PHONE.....................619 661-5170
Joseph B Cabrera, *President*
Louis J Rodriguez, *Vice Pres*
▲ EMP: 134
SQ FT: 9,000
SALES (est): 11.3MM **Privately Held**
WEB: www.nlpfurniture.com
SIC: 2599 Hospital furniture, except beds

(P-5075)
PANDA BOWL
11940 Edinger Ave, Fountain Valley (92708-1211)
PHONE.....................714 418-0299
Victor Cheng, *Owner*
EMP: 12
SALES (est): 1.4MM **Privately Held**
SIC: 2599 Food wagons, restaurant

(P-5076)
PRODUCTION SYSTEMS GROUP INC
Also Called: Production Industries
895 Beacon St, Brea (92821-2905)
PHONE.....................714 990-8997
EMP: 40
SQ FT: 50,000
SALES: 5MM
SALES (corp-wide): 12.6MM **Privately Held**
SIC: 2599
PA: Iac Industries
895 Beacon St
Brea CA 85338
714 990-8997

(P-5077)
R & J FABRICATORS INC
1121 Railroad St Ste 102, Corona (92882-8219)
PHONE.....................951 817-0300
James Ciarletta, *CEO*
Jay Warren Ciarletta, *Vice Pres*
Danny Carlson, *Sales Staff*
EMP: 20
SQ FT: 20,000
SALES (est): 3.8MM **Privately Held**
SIC: 2599 Restaurant furniture, wood or metal

(P-5078)
RICHTER FURNITURE MFG 2002
Also Called: Richter Furniture Mfr Rfm
28720 Canwood St Ste 108, Agoura Hills (91301-9745)
PHONE.....................323 588-7900
EMP: 150
SALES (est): 10.1MM **Privately Held**
SIC: 2599 Factory furniture & fixtures

(P-5079)
RIVER CITY
Also Called: River City Restaurant
505 Lincoln Ave, NAPA (94558-3610)
P.O. Box 2553 (94558-0255)
PHONE.....................707 253-1111
Assaad Barazi, *President*
EMP: 45
SQ FT: 6,000
SALES (est): 5.1MM **Privately Held**
SIC: 2599 5812 Bar, restaurant & cafeteria furniture; eating places

(P-5080)
ROTH WOOD PRODUCTS LTD
2260 Canoas Garden Ave, San Jose (95125-2007)
PHONE.....................408 723-8888
Robert E Roth, *CEO*
Marilyn Roth, *Treasurer*
EMP: 40 EST: 1974
SQ FT: 12,800
SALES (est): 5.6MM **Privately Held**
WEB: www.rothwoodproducts.com
SIC: 2599 2434 Cabinets, factory; wood kitchen cabinets

(P-5081)
SAMMONS EQUIPMENT MFG CORP
Also Called: Shammi Industries
390 Meyer Cir Ste A, Corona (92879-6617)
PHONE.....................951 340-3419
Bhupinder Saggu, *President*
David Duke, *Manager*
▲ EMP: 14 EST: 1932
SQ FT: 39,000
SALES (est): 2.6MM **Privately Held**
WEB: www.sammonsequipment.com
SIC: 2599 Carts, restaurant equipment

(P-5082)
STAINLESS FIXTURES INC
1250 E Franklin Ave, Pomona (91766-5449)
PHONE.....................909 622-1615
Randy Rodriguez, *President*
Armando Gonzalez, *Project Mgr*
EMP: 35
SQ FT: 36,000
SALES (est): 11.7MM **Privately Held**
SIC: 2599 Restaurant furniture, wood or metal; hotel furniture

(P-5083)
STANFORD FURNITURE MFG INC
5851 Alder Ave Ste A, Sacramento (95828-1126)
PHONE.....................916 387-5300
Alireza Angha, *President*
EMP: 28
SALES (est): 4.1MM **Privately Held**
SIC: 2599 Factory furniture & fixtures

(P-5084)
TAHITI CABINETS INC
5419 E La Palma Ave, Anaheim (92807-2022)
PHONE.....................714 693-0618
Mark Ramsey, *President*
Doreen Ramsey, *Admin Sec*
Carrie Olson, *Project Mgr*
Jessica Parra, *Purch Mgr*
Jaime Acosta, *Opers Mgr*
EMP: 58
SQ FT: 32,000
SALES (est): 12.3MM **Privately Held**
WEB: www.tahiticabinets.com
SIC: 2599 2431 2434 Cabinets, factory; millwork; wood kitchen cabinets

(P-5085)
THOMAS CRAVEN WOOD FINISHERS
15746 W Arminta St, Simi Valley (93065)
PHONE.....................805 341-7713
Thomas Craven, *President*
EMP: 11
SALES: 600K **Privately Held**
SIC: 2599 2491 7641 Furniture & fixtures; wood preserving; furniture repair & maintenance

(P-5086)
TRATTORIA AMICI/AMERICANA LLC
783 Americana Way, Glendale (91210-1507)
PHONE.....................818 502-1220
Tancredi Deluca, *CEO*
EMP: 10
SALES (est): 1.4MM **Privately Held**
SIC: 2599 Food wagons, restaurant

(P-5087)
ULTIMATE JUMPERS INC
14924 Arrow Hwy Ste A, Baldwin Park (91706-1849)
PHONE.....................626 337-3086
Tigran Thenteretshyan, *President*
Vazgen Melikyan, *Vice Pres*
EMP: 15
SQ FT: 11,500
SALES: 1.1MM **Privately Held**
SIC: 2599 Inflatable beds

(P-5088)
VISIBILITY SOLUTIONS INC
320 E Dyer Rd, Santa Ana (92707-3740)
PHONE.....................714 434-7040
Jeffrey Jacobson, *President*

▲ = Import ▼=Export
◆ =Import/Export

Marty Jacobson, *Vice Pres*
EMP: 13
SALES (est): 860K **Privately Held**
WEB: www.visibilitysolutions.com
SIC: 2599 Inflatable beds

(P-5089)
WESTERN MILL FABRICATORS INC
615 Fee Ana St, Placentia (92870-6704)
PHONE..................................714 993-3667
Kimball Boyack, *CEO*
EMP: 30
SQ FT: 25,000
SALES (est): 4.9MM **Privately Held**
WEB: www.wmfinc.com
SIC: 2599 Bar, restaurant & cafeteria furniture

2611 Pulp Mills

(P-5090)
ARNA TRADING INC (PA)
Also Called: Simba Recycling
2892 S Santa Fe Ave # 109, San Marcos (92069-6022)
PHONE..................................760 940-2775
Ash Shah, *President*
▼ **EMP:** 15
SQ FT: 20,000
SALES (est): 3.7MM **Privately Held**
WEB: www.simbaint.com
SIC: 2611 Pulp mills, mechanical & recycling processing; kraft (sulfate) pulp

(P-5091)
BEYOND ULTIMATE LLC
360 S 9th Ave, City of Industry (91746-3311)
PHONE..................................626 330-9777
Janak Patel,
Dipak Patel,
EMP: 10
SALES (est): 1.3MM **Privately Held**
SIC: 2611 Pulp manufactured from waste or recycled paper

(P-5092)
CENCAL RECYCLING LLC
501 Port Road 22, Stockton (95203-2909)
PHONE..................................209 546-8000
Steve Sutta, *Mng Member*
EMP: 16
SQ FT: 104,400
SALES (est): 2.2MM **Privately Held**
WEB: www.cencalrecycling.com
SIC: 2611 Pulp mills, mechanical & recycling processing

(P-5093)
INLAND PCF RESOURCE RECOVERY
12650 Slughter Hse Cyn Rd, Lakeside (92040)
P.O. Box 123 (92040-0123)
PHONE..................................619 390-1418
Lloyd Maynard, *President*
Ralph Esquivel, *Vice Pres*
EMP: 32
SALES (est): 2.5MM **Privately Held**
SIC: 2611 Pulp manufactured from waste or recycled paper

(P-5094)
NEW GREEN DAY LLC
1710 E 111th St, Los Angeles (90059-1910)
P.O. Box 72147 (90002-0147)
PHONE..................................323 566-7603
Brian Kelly, *CEO*
Virgialeo San Victors, *Accountant*
Randi Yamamoto, *Accountant*
David Holt,
Kirk Sanford, *Mng Member*
EMP: 25
SQ FT: 25,000
SALES (est): 6MM **Privately Held**
SIC: 2611 Pulp manufactured from waste or recycled paper

(P-5095)
WESTERN PACIFIC PULP AND PAPER (HQ)
9400 Hall Rd, Downey (90241-5365)
PHONE..................................562 803-4401
Ralph Ho, *Ch of Bd*
Kevin Duncombe, *CEO*
Jim Forkey, *Vice Pres*
Kyle Duncombe, *General Mgr*
Alisha Martinson, *Accounting Mgr*
▼ **EMP:** 51
SALES (est): 16.4MM
SALES (corp-wide): 15.6MM **Privately Held**
SIC: 2611 5093 Pulp manufactured from waste or recycled paper; waste paper
PA: Y. F. International
180 Park Rd
Burlingame CA 94010
650 342-6560

2621 Paper Mills

(P-5096)
ACME UNITED CORPORATION
630 Young St, Santa Ana (92705-5633)
PHONE..................................714 557-2001
EMP: 22
SALES (corp-wide): 137.3MM **Publicly Held**
SIC: 2621 Absorbent paper
PA: Acme United Corporation
55 Walls Dr Ste 201
Fairfield CT 06824
203 254-6060

(P-5097)
ALLEN REED COMPANY INC
Also Called: Chicwrap
25000 Avenue Stanford # 208, Valencia (91355-4596)
PHONE..................................310 575-8704
Ian Kaiser, *President*
Michael Kaiser, *Ch of Bd*
Garry Pearson, *CEO*
Sean Allen Neiberger, *Vice Pres*
Antonette Bellows, *Opers Mgr*
EMP: 10
SALES (est): 1.2MM **Privately Held**
SIC: 2621 3353 Parchment paper; foil, aluminum

(P-5098)
ATTENDS HEALTHCARE PDTS INC
1941 N White Ave, La Verne (91750-5663)
P.O. Box 1060 (91750-0960)
PHONE..................................909 392-1200
Dave Franklin, *Branch Mgr*
EMP: 190
SALES (corp-wide): 5.1B **Privately Held**
SIC: 2621 Sanitary tissue paper; absorbent paper; tissue paper
HQ: Attends Healthcare Products Inc.
8020 Arco Corp Dr Ste 200
Raleigh NC 27617
252 752-1100

(P-5099)
BOISE CASCADE COMPANY
12030 S Harlan Rd, Lathrop (95330-8768)
PHONE..................................209 983-4114
Brad Terrell, *Branch Mgr*
Kim Jackson, *Consultant*
EMP: 40
SALES (corp-wide): 5B **Publicly Held**
SIC: 2621 2679 Paper mills; building paper, laminated: made from purchased material
PA: Boise Cascade Company
1111 W Jefferson St # 300
Boise ID 83702
208 384-6161

(P-5100)
CLEARWATER PAPER CORPORATION
1320 Willow Pass Rd # 550, Concord (94520-5232)
PHONE..................................925 947-4700
Mark Ohleyer, *Principal*
Mike Cameron, *Engineer*
EMP: 600 **Publicly Held**
SIC: 2621 2631 Paper mills; paperboard mills
PA: Clearwater Paper Corporation
601 W Riverside Ave # 1100
Spokane WA 99201

(P-5101)
D D OFFICE PRODUCTS INC
Also Called: Liberty Paper
5025 Hampton St, Vernon (90058-2133)
P.O. Box 58026 (90058-0026)
PHONE..................................323 582-3400
Alex Ismail, *CEO*
Anwar Lalani, *President*
Benazir Ismael, *CFO*
Abdul Ismail, *Vice Pres*
Celia Goldman, *Human Resources*
▲ **EMP:** 25
SQ FT: 22,000
SALES: 36.6MM **Privately Held**
WEB: www.libertypp.com
SIC: 2621 5112 5044 5045 Printing paper; stationery & office supplies; office equipment; computers & accessories, personal & home entertainment; hardware; furniture

(P-5102)
DOCUMENT PROC SOLUTIONS INC
535 Main St Ste 317, Martinez (94553-1102)
PHONE..................................925 839-1182
EMP: 35
SALES (corp-wide): 8.5MM **Privately Held**
SIC: 2621 Paper mills
PA: Document Processing Solutions, Inc.
590 W Lambert Rd
Brea CA 92821
714 482-2060

(P-5103)
EAGLE RIDGE PAPER LTD (HQ)
Also Called: Eagleridge Paper CA
100 S Anaheim Blvd # 250, Anaheim (92805-3848)
PHONE..................................714 780-1799
Yeoh Khai Sun, *President*
▲ **EMP:** 20
SALES (est): 2.8MM
SALES (corp-wide): 22.6MM **Privately Held**
SIC: 2621 Printing paper
PA: Eagle Ridge Paper Ltd
20 Hereford St Unit 15
Brampton ON L6Y 0
888 324-5399

(P-5104)
ENVELOPE PRODUCTS CO
Also Called: Epco
2882 W Cromwell Ave, Fresno (93711-0353)
PHONE..................................925 939-5173
Alex Macdonald, *Chairman*
Darlene Macdonald, *President*
Janine Eldred, *Vice Pres*
EMP: 26
SQ FT: 23,000
SALES (est): 3.5MM **Privately Held**
WEB: www.epco-envelopes.com
SIC: 2621 2761 Envelope paper; manifold business forms

(P-5105)
FLEENOR COMPANY INC
4201 E Fremont St, Stockton (95215-4814)
P.O. Box 14438, Oakland (94614-2438)
PHONE..................................209 932-0329
Ramon Cavares, *Branch Mgr*
Anthony Guido, *CFO*
EMP: 50
SALES (corp-wide): 21MM **Privately Held**
WEB: www.fleenorpaper.com
SIC: 2621 Paper mills
PA: Fleenor Company, Inc
2225 Harbor Bay Pkwy
Alameda CA 94502
800 433-2531

(P-5106)
GLOBAL PAPER SOLUTIONS INC
100 S Anaheim Blvd # 250, Anaheim (92805-3872)
PHONE..................................714 687-6102
CHI MI Chung, *President*
◆ **EMP:** 30
SALES (est): 8.9MM **Privately Held**
SIC: 2621 Paper mills

(P-5107)
GRAPHIC PACKAGING INTL LLC
Also Called: International Paper
1600 Kelsey Rd, Visalia (93291)
P.O. Box 4349 (93278-4349)
PHONE..................................559 651-3535
Robert E Eades, *Opers-Prdtn-Mfg*
EMP: 150 **Publicly Held**
WEB: www.internationalpaper.com
SIC: 2621 Paper mills
HQ: Graphic Packaging International, Llc
1500 Riveredge Pkwy # 100
Atlanta GA 30328

(P-5108)
HARVARD LABEL LLC
Also Called: Harvard Card Systems
111 Baldwin Park Blvd, City of Industry (91746-1402)
PHONE..................................626 333-8881
Michael Tang, *CEO*
David Banducci, *President*
Almon Lin, *Information Mgr*
▲ **EMP:** 115
SQ FT: 125,000
SALES (est): 40MM **Privately Held**
WEB: www.harvardlabel.com
SIC: 2621 2675 2752 Greeting card paper; stencil cards, die-cut: made from purchased materials; cards, lithographed
PA: Plasticard - Locktech International, Llc
1220 Trade Dr
North Las Vegas NV 89030

(P-5109)
IMAGE SQUARE INC
Also Called: Image Square Copy & Print
1627 Stanford St, Santa Monica (90404-4113)
PHONE..................................310 586-2333
Kavian Soudbakhsh, *President*
Ashkan Soudbakhsh, *President*
Sepideh Soudbakhsh, *Admin Sec*
Thomas Allison, *Mktg Dir*
EMP: 11
SQ FT: 2,400
SALES (est): 2.6MM **Privately Held**
WEB: www.imagesquare.com
SIC: 2621 Printing paper

(P-5110)
INTERNATIONAL PAPER COMPANY
42305 Albrae St, Fremont (94538-3392)
PHONE..................................510 490-5887
Jay Casos, *Manager*
EMP: 50
SQ FT: 60,805
SALES (corp-wide): 23.3B **Publicly Held**
WEB: www.internationalpaper.com
SIC: 2621 Paper mills
PA: International Paper Company
6400 Poplar Ave
Memphis TN 38197
901 419-9000

(P-5111)
INTERNATIONAL PAPER COMPANY
900 N Plaza Dr, Visalia (93291-8826)
PHONE..................................559 651-1416
Derek Miller, *Branch Mgr*
EMP: 133
SALES (corp-wide): 23.3B **Publicly Held**
WEB: www.internationalpaper.com
SIC: 2621 Paper mills
PA: International Paper Company
6400 Poplar Ave
Memphis TN 38197
901 419-9000

P R O D U C T S   &   S V C S

(P-5112)
INTERNATIONAL PAPER COMPANY
1111 N Anderson Rd, Exeter (93221-9370)
PHONE..........................559 592-7279
Rick Goddard, *Branch Mgr*
EMP: 60
SALES (corp-wide): 23.3B **Publicly Held**
WEB: www.internationalpaper.com
SIC: 2621 Paper mills
PA: International Paper Company
    6400 Poplar Ave
    Memphis TN 38197
    901 419-9000

(P-5113)
INTERNATIONAL PAPER COMPANY
10268 Waterman Rd, Elk Grove
(95624-9403)
PHONE..........................916 685-9000
Dave Carpenter, *Branch Mgr*
Neil Gates, *Engineer*
Ted Maloney, *Sales Executive*
Karla Moore, *Sales Staff*
EMP: 100
SALES (corp-wide): 23.3B **Publicly Held**
WEB: www.internationalpaper.com
SIC: 2621 Paper mills
PA: International Paper Company
    6400 Poplar Ave
    Memphis TN 38197
    901 419-9000

(P-5114)
INTERNATIONAL PAPER COMPANY
6211 Descanso Ave, Buena Park
(90620-1012)
PHONE..........................714 736-0296
Brian Evans, *Branch Mgr*
EMP: 168
SALES (corp-wide): 23.3B **Publicly Held**
SIC: 2621 Paper mills
PA: International Paper Company
    6400 Poplar Ave
    Memphis TN 38197
    901 419-9000

(P-5115)
INTERNATIONAL PAPER COMPANY
6791 Alexander St, Gilroy (95020-6679)
PHONE..........................408 846-2060
David Washer, *General Mgr*
EMP: 65
SALES (corp-wide): 23.3B **Publicly Held**
SIC: 2621 Printing paper
PA: International Paper Company
    6400 Poplar Ave
    Memphis TN 38197
    901 419-9000

(P-5116)
INTERNATIONAL PAPER COMPANY
2000 Pleasant Valley Rd, Camarillo
(93010-8543)
PHONE..........................805 933-4347
EMP: 11
SALES (corp-wide): 23.3B **Publicly Held**
SIC: 2621 Paper mills
PA: International Paper Company
    6400 Poplar Ave
    Memphis TN 38197
    901 419-9000

(P-5117)
INTERNATIONAL PAPER COMPANY
19615 S Susana Rd, Compton
(90221-5717)
PHONE..........................310 639-2310
Joseph Winters, *General Mgr*
Patricia Ruiz, *Purchasing*
EMP: 13
SALES (corp-wide): 23.3B **Publicly Held**
SIC: 2621 Paper mills
PA: International Paper Company
    6400 Poplar Ave
    Memphis TN 38197
    901 419-9000

(P-5118)
INTERNATIONAL PAPER COMPANY
1000 Muscat Ave, Sanger (93657-4001)
PHONE..........................559 875-3311
EMP: 16
SALES (corp-wide): 23.3B **Publicly Held**
SIC: 2621 Paper mills
PA: International Paper Company
    6400 Poplar Ave
    Memphis TN 38197
    901 419-9000

(P-5119)
INTERNATIONAL PAPER COMPANY
14150 Artesia Blvd, Cerritos (90703-7032)
PHONE..........................562 404-1856
Manuel Gutierrez, *Branch Mgr*
EMP: 10
SALES (corp-wide): 23.3B **Publicly Held**
SIC: 2621 Paper mills
PA: International Paper Company
    6400 Poplar Ave
    Memphis TN 38197
    901 419-9000

(P-5120)
INTERNATIONAL PAPER COMPANY
11205 Knott Ave Ste A, Cypress
(90630-5489)
PHONE..........................714 889-4900
EMP: 10
SALES (corp-wide): 23.3B **Publicly Held**
SIC: 2621 Paper mills
PA: International Paper Company
    6400 Poplar Ave
    Memphis TN 38197
    901 419-9000

(P-5121)
INTERNATIONAL PAPER COMPANY
12851 Alondra Blvd, Norwalk (90650-6838)
PHONE..........................562 483-6680
John Faraci, *President*
EMP: 13
SALES (corp-wide): 23.3B **Publicly Held**
SIC: 2621 Paper mills
PA: International Paper Company
    6400 Poplar Ave
    Memphis TN 38197
    901 419-9000

(P-5122)
INTERNATIONAL PAPER COMPANY
1345 Harkins Rd, Salinas (93901-4408)
PHONE..........................831 755-2100
EMP: 11
SALES (corp-wide): 23.3B **Publicly Held**
SIC: 2621 Paper mills
PA: International Paper Company
    6400 Poplar Ave
    Memphis TN 38197
    901 419-9000

(P-5123)
INTERNATIONAL PAPER COMPANY
6400 Jamieson Way, Gilroy (95020-6620)
PHONE..........................408 847-6400
Michael Hayford, *Branch Mgr*
EMP: 92
SALES (corp-wide): 23.3B **Publicly Held**
WEB: www.tin.com
SIC: 2621 Paper mills
PA: International Paper Company
    6400 Poplar Ave
    Memphis TN 38197
    901 419-9000

(P-5124)
INTERNATIONAL PAPER COMPANY
1714 Cebrian St, West Sacramento
(95691-3819)
PHONE..........................916 371-4634
Clark Weiss, *Opers Staff*
EMP: 40
SALES (corp-wide): 23.3B **Publicly Held**
WEB: www.internationalpaper.com
SIC: 2621 Paper mills

PA: International Paper Company
    6400 Poplar Ave
    Memphis TN 38197
    901 419-9000

(P-5125)
INTERNATIONAL PAPER COMPANY
9211 Norwalk Blvd, Santa Fe Springs
(90670-2923)
PHONE..........................562 692-9465
Lee Bekiarian, *Branch Mgr*
EMP: 150
SALES (corp-wide): 23.3B **Publicly Held**
WEB: www.tin.com
SIC: 2621 Paper mills
PA: International Paper Company
    6400 Poplar Ave
    Memphis TN 38197
    901 419-9000

(P-5126)
INTERNATIONAL PAPER COMPANY
1350 E 223rd St, Carson (90745-4381)
PHONE..........................310 549-5525
Melanie Kastner, *Branch Mgr*
EMP: 150
SALES (corp-wide): 23.3B **Publicly Held**
WEB: www.internationalpaper.com
SIC: 2621 Paper mills
PA: International Paper Company
    6400 Poplar Ave
    Memphis TN 38197
    901 419-9000

(P-5127)
INTERNATIONAL PAPER COMPANY
6485 Descanso Ave, Buena Park
(90620-1016)
PHONE..........................562 868-2246
Bob Dickens, *General Mgr*
EMP: 84
SQ FT: 74,826
SALES (corp-wide): 23.3B **Publicly Held**
WEB: www.internationalpaper.com
SIC: 2621 Paper mills
PA: International Paper Company
    6400 Poplar Ave
    Memphis TN 38197
    901 419-9000

(P-5128)
KIMBERLY-CLARK CORPORATION
2001 E Orangethorpe Ave, Fullerton
(92831-5396)
PHONE..........................714 578-0705
Rick Tucker, *Branch Mgr*
Gary Hardesty, *Safety Mgr*
Joanne Han, *Manager*
EMP: 410
SQ FT: 3,000
SALES (corp-wide): 18.4B **Publicly Held**
WEB: www.kimberly-clark.com
SIC: 2621 2676 Sanitary tissue paper;
sanitary paper products
PA: Kimberly-Clark Corporation
    351 Phelps Dr
    Irving TX 75038
    972 281-1200

(P-5129)
KIMBERLY-CLARK CORPORATION
15260 Ventura Blvd # 1410, Van Nuys
(91403-5307)
PHONE..........................818 986-2430
Troy Moore, *Branch Mgr*
EMP: 10
SQ FT: 3,000
SALES (corp-wide): 18.4B **Publicly Held**
WEB: www.kimberly-clark.com
SIC: 2621 2676 Sanitary tissue paper; in-
fant & baby paper products
PA: Kimberly-Clark Corporation
    351 Phelps Dr
    Irving TX 75038
    972 281-1200

(P-5130)
KUI CO INC
266 Calle Pintoresco, San Clemente
(92672-7504)
PHONE..........................949 369-7949
Terry Daum, *President*
Sandy Daum, *CFO*
EMP: 40
SQ FT: 14,800
SALES: 3.5MM **Privately Held**
WEB: www.kuico.com
SIC: 2621 3089 Molded pulp products;
plastic processing

(P-5131)
MAILWORKS INC
2513 Folex Way, Spring Valley
(91978-2038)
PHONE..........................619 670-2365
Robert Hodges, *President*
EMP: 30
SALES (est): 5.6MM **Privately Held**
SIC: 2621 Printing paper

(P-5132)
METHOD HOME PRODUCTS
637 Commercial St Fl 3, San Francisco
(94111-6515)
PHONE..........................415 568-4600
Steve Jurvetson, *Owner*
EMP: 13
SALES (est): 2.5MM **Privately Held**
SIC: 2621 Cleansing paper

(P-5133)
NAKAGAWA MANUFACTURING USA INC
8652 Thornton Ave, Newark (94560-3330)
PHONE..........................510 782-0197
Yuzuru Isshiki, *CEO*
Shinji Aoki, *President*
Tetsuya Isshiki, *President*
◆ EMP: 40
SQ FT: 40,000
SALES (est): 9.7MM **Privately Held**
WEB: www.nakagawa-usa.com
SIC: 2621 Specialty papers
HQ: Nakagawa Mfg.Co., Ltd.
    2-5-21, Nishikicho
    Warabi STM 335-0

(P-5134)
NASHUA CORPORATION
Rittenhouse
13341 Cambridge St, Santa Fe Springs
(90670-4903)
PHONE..........................323 583-8828
EMP: 80
SQ FT: 57,600
SALES (corp-wide): 1.9B **Publicly Held**
SIC: 2621
HQ: Nashua Corporation
    59 Daniel Webster Hwy A
    Merrimack NH 03054
    603 880-1100

(P-5135)
NATIONAL SALES INC
825 F St Ste 600, West Sacramento
(95605-2389)
PHONE..........................916 912-2894
Majid Pasha, *President*
EMP: 12
SALES (est): 1.1MM **Privately Held**
SIC: 2621 Toilet tissue stock

(P-5136)
NEW-INDY CONTAINERBOARD LLC (DH)
Also Called: International Paper
3500 Porsche Way Ste 150, Ontario
(91764-4969)
P.O. Box 519, Port Hueneme (93044-0519)
PHONE..........................909 296-3400
Richard Hartman, *CEO*
Mike Conkey, *Vice Pres*
Zhen Han, *Engineer*
Jeff Branch, *Purch Mgr*
Blake Perkins, *Manager*
▲ EMP: 95
SALES: 332.3K
SALES (corp-wide): 257.8MM **Privately Held**
SIC: 2621 Paper mills

HQ: New-Indy Containerboard Hold Co Llc
5100 Jurupa St
Foxboro MA 02035
508 384-4230

(P-5137)
NEW-INDY ONTARIO LLC
Also Called: New-Indy Containerboard
5100 Jurupa St, Ontario (91761-3618)
PHONE.................................909 390-1055
Richard Hartman, *CEO*
Mike Conkey, *Vice Pres*
Scott Conant, *General Mgr*
Antonio Magdaleno, *Project Engr*
George Johnston, *Maint Spvr*
EMP: 110
SALES: 345MM
SALES (corp-wide): 257.8MM **Privately Held**
SIC: 2621 Paper mills
HQ: New-Indy Containerboard Llc
3500 Porsche Way Ste 150
Ontario CA 91764
909 296-3400

(P-5138)
NEW-INDY OXNARD LLC
Also Called: New-Indy Containerboard
5936 Perkins Rd, Oxnard (93033-9044)
P.O. Box 519, Port Hueneme (93044-0519)
PHONE.................................805 986-3881
Richard Hartman, *CEO*
Mike Conkey, *Vice Pres*
▲ EMP: 224 EST: 2012
SALES (est): 310.5MM
SALES (corp-wide): 257.8MM **Privately Held**
SIC: 2621 Paper mills
HQ: New-Indy Containerboard Llc
3500 Porsche Way Ste 150
Ontario CA 91764
909 296-3400

(P-5139)
NOVACART
Also Called: Novacart USA
512 W Ohio Ave, Richmond (94804-2040)
P.O. Box 70579 (94807-0579)
PHONE.................................510 215-8999
Toll Free:.................................877 -
Giorgio Angahileri, *President*
Guadalupe Gonzalez, *Accounting Mgr*
Terry Schepper, *Prdtn Mgr*
Joe Miglia, *Manager*
Harla Rairigh, *Manager*
◆ EMP: 42
SQ FT: 35,000
SALES: 7MM
SALES (corp-wide): 107.6K **Privately Held**
WEB: www.novacartusa.com
SIC: 2621 Molded pulp products
HQ: Novacart Spa
Via Europa 1
Garbagnate Monastero LC 23846
031 858-611

(P-5140)
OEM MATERIALS & SUPPLIES INC
1500 Ritchey St, Santa Ana (92705-4731)
PHONE.................................714 564-9600
Randall K Johnson, *CEO*
Wendy R King, *President*
EMP: 20
SALES (est): 7.9MM **Privately Held**
SIC: 2621 2631 5084 2671 Wrapping & packaging papers; container, packaging & boxboard; processing & packaging equipment; packaging paper & plastics film, coated & laminated

(P-5141)
PACIFIC MILLENNIUM US CORP
12526 High Bluff Dr # 300, San Diego (92130-2064)
PHONE.................................858 450-1505
Richard Tan, *President*
EMP: 17
SALES (est): 2MM **Privately Held**
SIC: 2621 Writing paper

(P-5142)
PAPER GROUP COMPANY LLC
15201 Woodlawn Ave # 200, Tustin (92780-6449)
PHONE.................................714 566-0025
Marie Van Vugt, *Mng Member*
▲ EMP: 40
SQ FT: 42,000
SALES (est): 7.8MM **Privately Held**
SIC: 2621 Facial tissue stock

(P-5143)
PAPER SURCE CONVERTING MFG INC
Also Called: Soft-Touch Tissue
4800 S Santa Fe Ave, Vernon (90058-2104)
PHONE.................................323 583-3800
Jacob Khobian, *CEO*
Jonathan Khodabakhsh, *VP Opers*
▲ EMP: 50
SQ FT: 55,000
SALES (est): 21.1MM **Privately Held**
WEB: www.papersourcemfg.com
SIC: 2621 Tissue paper

(P-5144)
PPS PACKAGING COMPANY
Also Called: Continental Enterprises
3189 E Manning Ave, Fowler (93625-9749)
P.O. Box 427 (93625-0427)
PHONE.................................559 834-1641
Thomas Wilson, *Ch of Bd*
Ray Casuga, *President*
Joni Hill, *CEO*
Jeff Thorp, *Purch Mgr*
Galen Van Aalsburg, *Sales Staff*
▲ EMP: 75
SQ FT: 108,000
SALES (est): 19.2MM **Privately Held**
WEB: www.ppspackaging.com
SIC: 2621 Packaging paper

(P-5145)
PRATT INDUSTRIES INC
2643 Industrial Pkwy Ofc, Santa Maria (93455-1536)
PHONE.................................805 348-1097
Robert Mann, *President*
EMP: 20
SALES (corp-wide): 2.5B **Privately Held**
WEB: www.rmp.com
SIC: 2621 Paper mills
PA: Pratt Industries, Inc.
1800 Sarasot Bus Pkwy Ne C
Conyers GA 30013
770 918-5678

(P-5146)
PRATT INDUSTRIES INC
Also Called: Robert Mann Packaging
3931 Oceanic Dr, Oceanside (92056-5846)
PHONE.................................760 966-9170
Steve Clarke, *Branch Mgr*
EMP: 26
SQ FT: 13,000
SALES (corp-wide): 2.5B **Privately Held**
SIC: 2621 Packaging paper
PA: Pratt Industries, Inc.
1800 Sarasot Bus Pkwy Ne C
Conyers GA 30013
770 918-5678

(P-5147)
PRATT INDUSTRIES INC
2131 E Louise Ave, Lathrop (95330-9607)
PHONE.................................770 922-0117
Ron McComas, *General Mgr*
EMP: 110
SALES (corp-wide): 2.5B **Privately Held**
SIC: 2621 Packaging paper
PA: Pratt Industries, Inc.
1800 Sarasot Bus Pkwy Ne C
Conyers GA 30013
770 918-5678

(P-5148)
RONPAK INC
10900 San Sevaine Way, Jurupa Valley (91752-1138)
PHONE.................................951 685-3800
Paul Warg, *Opers-Prdtn-Mfg*
Valerie Casas, *QA Dir*
Charlotte Reese, *Manager*
EMP: 49

SALES (corp-wide): 57.1MM **Privately Held**
WEB: www.ronpak.com
SIC: 2621 2673 2671 Bag paper; bags: plastic, laminated & coated; packaging paper & plastics film, coated & laminated
PA: Ronpak, Inc
1 Nathan Sedley Rd
Shreveport LA 71115
318 219-4300

(P-5149)
SAN DIEGO DAILY TRANSCRIPT
34 Emerald Gln, Laguna Niguel (92677-9379)
P.O. Box 85469, San Diego (92186-5469)
PHONE.................................619 232-4381
Ed Frederickson, *President*
EMP: 63 EST: 1886
SQ FT: 30,000
SALES (est): 10.4MM
SALES (corp-wide): 12.5MM **Privately Held**
WEB: www.sddt.com
SIC: 2621 4813 Printing paper;
PA: Calcomco, Inc.
5544 S Red Pine Cir
Kalamazoo MI 49009
313 885-9228

(P-5150)
SIERRA HYGIENE PRODUCTS LLC
4749 Bennett Dr Ste B, Livermore (94551-4806)
PHONE.................................925 371-7173
Doug Johnson,
John Perterson,
▼ EMP: 10
SQ FT: 1,600
SALES (est): 1.9MM **Privately Held**
WEB: www.sierrahygiene.com
SIC: 2621 Tissue paper

(P-5151)
SMALL PAPER CO INC
2559 E 56th St, Huntington Park (90255-2516)
PHONE.................................323 277-0525
Federico Rodriguez, *President*
Gracia Rodriguez, *Principal*
EMP: 10
SALES (est): 1.6MM **Privately Held**
SIC: 2621 Paper mills

(P-5152)
SMITHCORP INC
Also Called: Green Field Paper Company
7196 Clairemont Mesa Blvd, San Diego (92111-1005)
PHONE.................................888 402-9979
Frederick Smith, *President*
Shari Smith, *CEO*
EMP: 10
SALES (est): 1.9MM **Privately Held**
SIC: 2621 Wrapping & packaging papers

(P-5153)
SPILL MAGIC INC
630 Young St, Santa Ana (92705-5633)
PHONE.................................714 557-2001
Susan Wampler, *President*
David Wampler, *Vice Pres*
▲ EMP: 22
SQ FT: 30,000
SALES (est): 950.4K **Privately Held**
WEB: www.spillmagic.com
SIC: 2621 Absorbent paper

(P-5154)
ZIP NOTES LLC
2822 Van Ness Ave, San Francisco (94109-1426)
PHONE.................................415 931-8020
Maurice Kanbar, *President*
Darryl Cooper, *Director*
EMP: 10
SQ FT: 6,800
SALES (est): 900K **Privately Held**
SIC: 2621 Stationery, envelope & tablet papers

2631 Paperboard Mills

(P-5155)
ALL STARS PACKAGING INC
Also Called: All Stars Packaging & Display
13851 Roswell Ave Ste H, Chino (91710-5471)
PHONE.................................626 664-3797
Elizabeth Pereyra, *Principal*
EMP: 12
SALES (est): 800K **Privately Held**
SIC: 2631 Container, packaging & boxboard

(P-5156)
AMIMON INC
2350 Mission College Blvd # 190, Santa Clara (95054-1542)
PHONE.................................650 641-3191
EMP: 13
SALES (est): 1.8MM **Privately Held**
SIC: 2631
PA: Amimon Ltd
26 Zarchin Alexander
Raanana 43662
996 292-00

(P-5157)
BUZZ CONVERTING INC
4343 E Fremont St, Stockton (95215-4032)
PHONE.................................209 948-1341
Merlin Davis Jr, *President*
Jeff Vandan Baum, *General Mgr*
EMP: 17
SQ FT: 35,000
SALES (est): 2.5MM **Privately Held**
SIC: 2631 Chip board

(P-5158)
C B SHEETS INC
13901 Carmenita Rd, Santa Fe Springs (90670-4916)
PHONE.................................562 921-1223
John Widera, *CEO*
Mackey Davis, *President*
EMP: 21
SALES (est): 3.5MM
SALES (corp-wide): 21.7MM **Privately Held**
SIC: 2631 Cardboard
PA: California Box Company
13901 Carmenita Rd
Santa Fe Springs CA 90670
562 921-1223

(P-5159)
CALIFORNIA TRADE CONVERTERS
13299 Louvre St, Pacoima (91331-2319)
PHONE.................................818 899-1455
Carlos Martinez, *President*
EMP: 25
SALES (est): 1.7MM **Privately Held**
SIC: 2631 2675 Paperboard mills; paper die-cutting

(P-5160)
DERIK PLASTICS INDUSTRIES INC
2540 Corp Pl Ste B100, Monterey Park (91754)
PHONE.................................626 371-7799
Derik Zhang, *President*
EMP: 700
SALES (est): 35.3MM **Privately Held**
SIC: 2631 Container, packaging & boxboard

(P-5161)
FIRST CLASS PACKAGING INC
280 Cypress Ln Ste D, El Cajon (92020-1662)
PHONE.................................619 579-7166
Sandra L Brock, *President*
Hector Gonzalez, *Prdtn Mgr*
EMP: 22
SQ FT: 18,500
SALES (est): 6.4MM **Privately Held**
WEB: www.firstclasspack.com
SIC: 2631 2449 3086 5085 Packaging board; rectangular boxes & crates, wood; plastics foam products; bins & containers, storage; corrugated & solid fiber boxes; nailed wood boxes & shook

(P-5162)
GRAPHIC PACKAGING INTL LLC
1600 Barranca Pkwy, Irvine (92606-4823)
PHONE..................................949 250-0900
Wendy Shute, *Sales Staff*
Ottie Gamboz, *Telecom Exec*
Cheryl Kennard, *Controller*
Rob Moynan, *Director*
Wayne Reichenthaler, *Manager*
EMP: 240 **Publicly Held**
SIC: 2631 Folding boxboard
HQ: Graphic Packaging International, Llc
1500 Riveredge Pkwy # 100
Atlanta GA 30328

(P-5163)
INTERNATIONAL PAPER COMPANY
660 Mariposa Rd, Modesto (95354-4130)
P.O. Box 3171 (95353-3171)
PHONE..................................209 526-4700
Rick Fritz, *Branch Mgr*
Sue Lewis,
Matt Yelland, *Manager*
EMP: 130
SQ FT: 165,196
SALES (corp-wide): 23.3B **Publicly Held**
WEB: www.internationalpaper.com
SIC: 2631 2653 Corrugating medium; corrugated & solid fiber boxes
PA: International Paper Company
6400 Poplar Ave
Memphis TN 38197
901 419-9000

(P-5164)
INTERNATIONAL PAPER COMPANY
3551 E Francis St, Ontario (91761-2926)
PHONE..................................909 605-2540
Jim Elder, *Opers-Prdtn-Mfg*
EMP: 61
SALES (corp-wide): 23.3B **Publicly Held**
WEB: www.internationalpaper.com
SIC: 2631 2672 2621 Setup boxboard; coated & laminated paper; paper mills
PA: International Paper Company
6400 Poplar Ave
Memphis TN 38197
901 419-9000

(P-5165)
INTERPRESS TECHNOLOGIES INC (HQ)
1120 Del Paso Rd, Sacramento (95834-7737)
PHONE..................................916 929-9771
Roderick W Miner, *President*
Peter Fox, *President*
Angie Young, *Office Mgr*
Randall Laveau, *Business Mgr*
◆ **EMP:** 50
SQ FT: 20,000
SALES: 30MM **Privately Held**
WEB: www.interpresstechnologies.com
SIC: 2631 Folding boxboard
PA: R. W. Miner Corporation
260 California St Ste 300
San Francisco CA 94111
415 781-2626

(P-5166)
LOS ANGELES BOARD MILLS INC
Also Called: Los Angeles Ppr Box & Bd Mills
6027 S Eastern Ave, Commerce (90040-3413)
PHONE..................................323 685-8900
William H Kewell III, *President*
Carol A Kewell, *Corp Secy*
EMP: 150
SQ FT: 300,000
SALES (est): 28.9MM **Privately Held**
WEB: www.lapb.com
SIC: 2631 2652 2653 5113 Folding boxboard; setup paperboard boxes; boxes, corrugated: made from purchased materials; industrial & personal service paper; folding paperboard boxes

(P-5167)
MAXCO SUPPLY INC
2059 E Olsen Ave, Reedley (93654)
P.O. Box 814, Parlier (93648-0814)
PHONE..................................559 638-8449
Roy Ortega, *Manager*
EMP: 60
SQ FT: 50,550
SALES (corp-wide): 149.5MM **Privately Held**
SIC: 2631 Cardboard
PA: Maxco Supply, Inc.
605 S Zediker Ave
Parlier CA 93648
559 646-8449

(P-5168)
MAXON AUTO CORPORATION
8599 Enterprise Way, Chino (91710-9306)
PHONE..................................626 400-6464
Xinxiang Wang, *CEO*
▲ **EMP:** 10
SALES (est): 1.1MM **Privately Held**
SIC: 2631 Automobile board

(P-5169)
ONE UP MANUFACTURING LLC
2555 E Del Amo Blvd, Compton (90221-6001)
PHONE..................................310 749-8347
Nielson Ballon, *Mng Member*
Kavish Mehta,
Nathan Miller,
EMP: 25
SQ FT: 15,000
SALES: 500K **Privately Held**
SIC: 2631 Container, packaging & boxboard

(P-5170)
ORGANIC BOTTLE DCTG CO LLC
Also Called: Zion Packaging
575 Alcoa Cir Ste B, Corona (92880-9203)
PHONE..................................951 335-4600
Gary Martin,
EMP: 20 **EST:** 2013
SALES: 2MM **Privately Held**
SIC: 2631 2759 Container, packaging & boxboard; screen printing

(P-5171)
PACKAGING DIST ASSEMBLY GROUP
Also Called: Pda Group
24730 Avenue Rockefeller, Valencia (91355-3465)
PHONE..................................661 607-0600
▲ **EMP:** 14
SALES (est): 2.2MM **Privately Held**
SIC: 2631 Container, packaging & boxboard

(P-5172)
SANTA ANA PACKAGING INC
14655 Firestone Blvd, La Mirada (90638-5916)
PHONE..................................714 670-6397
Ning Yen, *CEO*
Michael Nguyen, *General Mgr*
▲ **EMP:** 10
SALES (est): 2.5MM **Privately Held**
SIC: 2631 Container, packaging & boxboard

(P-5173)
SIMPLE CONTAINER SOLUTIONS INC
Also Called: Insulated Products
250 W Artesia Blvd, Rancho Dominguez (90220-5500)
PHONE..................................310 638-0900
Charles Veiseh, *President*
▲ **EMP:** 27
SQ FT: 100,000
SALES: 21MM **Privately Held**
SIC: 2631 Container, packaging & boxboard

(P-5174)
SONOCO PRODUCTS COMPANY
Also Called: Sonoco Industrial Products Div
166 Baldwin Park Blvd, City of Industry (91746-1498)
PHONE..................................626 369-6611

Dhamo Srinivasan, *Opers-Prdtn-Mfg*
Garrett Sizemore, *Engineer*
Khaleda Hamid, *Director*
Ralph Henderson, *Director*
Mitchell Gainey, *Manager*
EMP: 100
SALES (corp-wide): 5.3B **Publicly Held**
WEB: www.sonoco.com
SIC: 2631 2611 Paperboard mills; pulp mills
PA: Sonoco Products Company
1 N 2nd St
Hartsville SC 29550
843 383-7000

(P-5175)
SONOCO PRODUCTS COMPANY
12851 Leyva St, Norwalk (90650-6853)
PHONE..................................562 921-0881
Jeff Blaine, *Opers-Prdtn-Mfg*
Pat Majors, *Technician*
Cedric Mudlong, *Controller*
Angel Ortiz, *Prdtn Mgr*
Paul Kamholz, *Manager*
EMP: 55
SQ FT: 164,934
SALES (corp-wide): 5.3B **Publicly Held**
WEB: www.sonoco.com
SIC: 2631 2655 Paperboard mills; fiber cans, drums & similar products
PA: Sonoco Products Company
1 N 2nd St
Hartsville SC 29550
843 383-7000

(P-5176)
UNION CARBIDE CORPORATION
19206 Hawthorne Blvd, Torrance (90503-1590)
PHONE..................................310 214-5300
Patrick E Gottschalk, *Principal*
EMP: 60
SQ FT: 15,269
SALES (corp-wide): 61B **Publicly Held**
SIC: 2631 Latex board
HQ: Union Carbide Corporation
1254 Enclave Pkwy
Houston TX 77077
281 966-2727

(P-5177)
WALLY INTERNATIONAL INC (PA)
20520 E Walnut Dr N, Walnut (91789-2925)
PHONE..................................805 444-7764
Yibin Gu, *CEO*
Fend Zhou, *Vice Pres*
EMP: 200 **EST:** 2015
SALES: 2.6MM **Privately Held**
SIC: 2631 3423 Container, packaging & boxboard; hand & edge tools

(P-5178)
WESTROCK CP LLC
2710 O St, Bakersfield (93301-2446)
PHONE..................................661 327-3841
Judy Walker, *Office Mgr*
EMP: 10
SALES (corp-wide): 16.2B **Publicly Held**
WEB: www.sto.com
SIC: 2631 Paperboard mills
HQ: Westrock Cp, Llc
1000 Abernathy Rd
Atlanta GA 30328

(P-5179)
WESTROCK CP LLC
205 E Alma Ave, San Jose (95112-5902)
PHONE..................................770 448-2193
David Blavin, *Controller*
EMP: 35
SALES (corp-wide): 16.2B **Publicly Held**
WEB: www.sto.com
SIC: 2631 Paperboard mills
HQ: Westrock Cp, Llc
1000 Abernathy Rd
Atlanta GA 30328

(P-5180)
WESTROCK CP LLC
3003 N San Fernando Blvd, Burbank (91504-2525)
PHONE..................................818 557-1500

Sue Woldanski, *Manager*
EMP: 25
SALES (corp-wide): 16.2B **Publicly Held**
WEB: www.smurfit-stone.com
SIC: 2631 Container board
HQ: Westrock Cp, Llc
1000 Abernathy Rd
Atlanta GA 30328

(P-5181)
WESTROCK CP LLC
24 S Thorne Ave, Fresno (93706-1460)
P.O. Box 12303 (93777-2303)
PHONE..................................559 441-1166
Bob Kuhn, *Manager*
EMP: 19
SALES (corp-wide): 16.2B **Publicly Held**
WEB: www.sto.com
SIC: 2631 Paperboard mills
HQ: Westrock Cp, Llc
1000 Abernathy Rd
Atlanta GA 30328

(P-5182)
WESTROCK CP LLC
4800 Florin Perkins Rd, Sacramento (95826-4813)
PHONE..................................916 379-2200
Richard Garmsen, *Manager*
EMP: 50
SALES (corp-wide): 16.2B **Publicly Held**
WEB: www.sto.com
SIC: 2631 2611 Paperboard mills; pulp mills
HQ: Westrock Cp, Llc
1000 Abernathy Rd
Atlanta GA 30328

(P-5183)
WESTROCK CP LLC
2540 S Main St, Santa Ana (92707-3430)
PHONE..................................714 641-8891
Rob Allen, *General Mgr*
EMP: 20
SALES (corp-wide): 16.2B **Publicly Held**
WEB: www.sto.com
SIC: 2631 Paperboard mills
HQ: Westrock Cp, Llc
1000 Abernathy Rd
Atlanta GA 30328

(P-5184)
WESTROCK CP LLC
Smurfit Stone Container
15300 Marquardt Ave, Santa Fe Springs (90670)
PHONE..................................714 523-3550
Robert Simonds, *Manager*
EMP: 55
SALES (corp-wide): 16.2B **Publicly Held**
WEB: www.sto.com
SIC: 2631 Paperboard mills
HQ: Westrock Cp, Llc
1000 Abernathy Rd
Atlanta GA 30328

(P-5185)
WESTROCK MWV LLC
15750 Mountain Ave, Chino (91708-9120)
PHONE..................................909 597-2197
Pete Miller, *COO*
EMP: 300
SALES (corp-wide): 16.2B **Publicly Held**
WEB: www.meadwestvaco.com
SIC: 2631 Paperboard mills
HQ: Westrock Mwv, Llc
501 S 5th St
Richmond VA 23219
804 444-1000

(P-5186)
ZAPP PACKAGING INC
1921 S Business Pkwy, Ontario (91761-8539)
PHONE..................................909 930-1500
Vincent Randazzo, *CEO*
William L Finn, *CEO*
Bruce Altshuler, *Corp Secy*
Amy Finn, *Project Mgr*
▲ **EMP:** 60 **EST:** 1931
SQ FT: 80,000

▲ = Import ▼=Export
◆ =Import/Export

SALES (est): 10.3MM **Privately Held**
WEB: www.finnindustriesinc.com
SIC: **2631** Folding boxboard; setup
boxboard

2652 Set-Up Paperboard Boxes

(P-5187)
CUSTOM PAPER PRODUCTS
2360 Teagarden St, San Leandro
(94577-4341)
PHONE..................510 352-6880
Robert W Field Jr, *President*
Frank Leyva, *COO*
Blake Field, *Vice Pres*
Greg Wall, *Regl Sales Mgr*
Cameron Field, *Sales Staff*
EMP: 70
SQ FT: 100,000
SALES (est): 16.1MM **Privately Held**
WEB: www.custompaperproducts.com
SIC: **2652 3089** Filing boxes, paperboard:
made from purchased materials; boxes,
plastic

(P-5188)
DAVID DULEY
700 La Cresta Blvd, San Marcos (92079)
PHONE..................619 449-8556
David Daley, *Owner*
EMP: 55
SALES (est): 4.1MM **Privately Held**
SIC: **2652** Setup paperboard boxes

(P-5189)
JAMACO ENTERPRISES INC
Also Called: Westcoast Business Solutions
5331 Derry Ave Ste L, Agoura Hills
(91301-3386)
PHONE..................818 991-2050
Bradley C Schwartz, *President*
Amber Benavidez, *Accounts Mgr*
Jennelle Miyagawa, *Accounts Mgr*
EMP: 10 EST: 1998
SQ FT: 2,500
SALES (est): 2.2MM **Privately Held**
WEB: www.solutionspartner.com
SIC: **2652 2754 2759 2761** Filing boxes,
paperboard: made from purchased mate-
rials; business forms: gravure printing;
seals, gravure printing; stationery:
gravure printing; financial note & certificate printing & engraving; continuous
forms, office & business; embossing
seals, corporate & official; value-added
resellers, computer systems

(P-5190)
MOZAIK LLC
2330 Artesia Ave Ste B, Fullerton
(92833-2566)
PHONE..................562 207-1900
Paul Bellamy, *Mng Member*
Laurie Hilton,
Kevin Stein,
▲ EMP: 12
SQ FT: 27,000
SALES (est): 12MM **Privately Held**
SIC: **2652** Filing boxes, paperboard: made
from purchased materials

(P-5191)
PACIFIC PAPER BOX COMPANY (PA)
3928 Encino Hills Pl, Encino (91436-3804)
PHONE..................323 771-7733
Craig T Harrison, *CEO*
Bud Erhardt, *President*
EMP: 31
SQ FT: 70,000
SALES (est): 5.6MM **Privately Held**
WEB: www.pacificpaperbox.com
SIC: **2652** Boxes, newsboard, metal
edged: made from purchased materials

(P-5192)
WESTROCK RKT LLC
1854 E Home Ave, Fresno (93703-3636)
PHONE..................559 441-1181
Wes Gentles, *General Mgr*
EMP: 12
SQ FT: 50,000

SALES (corp-wide): 16.2B **Publicly Held**
WEB: www.rocktenn.com
SIC: **2652 2631** Setup paperboard boxes;
paperboard mills
HQ: Westrock Rkt, Llc
1000 Abernathy Rd Ste 125
Atlanta GA 30328
770 448-2193

2653 Corrugated & Solid Fiber Boxes

(P-5193)
ABEX DISPLAY SYSTEMS INC (PA)
Also Called: Abex Exhibit Systems
355 Parkside Dr, San Fernando
(91340-3036)
PHONE..................800 537-0231
Robbie Blumenfeld, *President*
Max Candiotty, *Vice Pres*
Alan Go, *Information Mgr*
Art Perez, *Prdtn Mgr*
George Contorinis, *Marketing Staff*
◆ EMP: 110
SQ FT: 85,000
SALES (est): 22.3MM **Privately Held**
WEB: www.abex.com
SIC: **2653 2541** Display items, solid fiber:
made from purchased materials; store &
office display cases & fixtures

(P-5194)
ADVANCE PAPER BOX COMPANY
Also Called: Packaging Spectrum
6100 S Gramercy Pl, Los Angeles
(90047-1397)
PHONE..................323 750-2550
Martin Gardner, *CEO*
Carlo Mendoza, *CFO*
Nick Silk, *Treasurer*
Devan Gardner, *Vice Pres*
Katherine Munoz, *Human Res Dir*
▲ EMP: 250
SQ FT: 500,000
SALES (est): 80.9MM **Privately Held**
WEB: www.packagingspectrum.com
SIC: **2653 3082** Boxes, corrugated: made
from purchased materials; boxes, solid
fiber: made from purchased materials; un-
supported plastics profile shapes

(P-5195)
AMERICAN CONTAINERS INC
813 W Luce St Ste B, Stockton
(95203-4937)
PHONE..................209 460-1127
Robert Calverly, *Branch Mgr*
EMP: 25
SALES (corp-wide): 33.8MM **Privately Held**
SIC: **2653** Corrugated boxes, partitions,
display items, sheets & pad
PA: American Containers, Inc
2526 Western Ave
Plymouth IN 46563
574 936-4068

(P-5196)
ANDROP PACKAGING INC
Also Called: Ontario Foam Products
4400 E Francis St, Ontario (91761-2327)
PHONE..................909 605-8842
Cesar Flores, *President*
▲ EMP: 23 EST: 1974
SQ FT: 52,000
SALES (est): 6.3MM **Privately Held**
WEB: www.androppackaging.com
SIC: **2653 3086** Boxes, corrugated: made
from purchased materials; plastics foam
products

(P-5197)
AWARD PACKAGING SPC CORP
12855 Midway Pl, Cerritos (90703-2141)
PHONE..................323 727-1200
Alfred Espinoza, *CEO*
Virginia S Espinoza, *Treasurer*
EMP: 40
SQ FT: 800
SALES (est): 10.3MM **Privately Held**
SIC: **2653** Boxes, corrugated: made from
purchased materials

(P-5198)
BAY CITIES CONTAINER CORP (PA)
5138 Industry Ave, Pico Rivera
(90660-2550)
PHONE..................562 948-3751
Greg A Tucker, *CEO*
Brett Kirkpatrick, *COO*
Patrick Donohoe, *CFO*
Gil Biberstein, *Sales Executive*
Gabriel Perez, *Manager*
▲ EMP: 143 EST: 1956
SALES (est): 65.6MM **Privately Held**
WEB: www.bay-cities.com
SIC: **2653 3993 5113** Boxes, corrugated:
made from purchased materials; display
items, corrugated: made from purchased
materials; signs & advertising specialties;
corrugated & solid fiber boxes; folding pa-
perboard boxes

(P-5199)
BAYCORR PACKAGING LLC (PA)
Also Called: Heritage Paper Co
6850 Brisa St, Livermore (94550-2521)
P.O. Box 44441, San Francisco (94144-
0001)
PHONE..................925 449-1148
John Tatum, *CEO*
▲ EMP: 130
SQ FT: 129,000
SALES (est): 31.6MM **Privately Held**
WEB: www.heritagepaper.com
SIC: **2653 5113** Boxes, corrugated: made
from purchased materials; corrugated &
solid fiber boxes

(P-5200)
BEST BOX COMPANY INC
Also Called: A1 Carton Co
8011 Beach St, Los Angeles (90001-3424)
PHONE..................323 589-6088
Jay Kim, *President*
EMP: 15
SQ FT: 38,000
SALES (est): 1.1MM **Privately Held**
WEB: www.best-box.com
SIC: **2653** Boxes, corrugated: made from
purchased materials

(P-5201)
BLOWER-DEMPSAY CORPORATION
Also Called: Pacific Western Container
4044 W Garry Ave, Santa Ana
(92704-6300)
PHONE..................714 547-9266
Ken Ito, *Manager*
EMP: 100
SQ FT: 30,000
SALES (corp-wide): 142.6MM **Privately Held**
SIC: **2653 5199 5113** Boxes, corrugated:
made from purchased materials; packag-
ing materials; corrugated & solid fiber
boxes
PA: Blower-Dempsay Corporation
4042 W Garry Ave
Santa Ana CA 92704
714 481-3800

(P-5202)
BLUE RIBBON CONT & DISPLAY INC
11106 Shoemaker Ave, Santa Fe Springs
(90670-4647)
PHONE..................562 944-1217
Kenneth G Overfield, *President*
EMP: 15
SQ FT: 32,000
SALES (est): 3.3MM **Privately Held**
WEB: www.brcbox.com
SIC: **2653 5199 5113** Boxes, corrugated:
made from purchased materials; packag-
ing materials; boxes & containers

(P-5203)
CAL SHEETS LLC
1212 Performance Dr, Stockton
(95206-4925)
P.O. Box 30370 (95213-0370)
PHONE..................209 234-3300
Rick Goddard, *CEO*
Scott Sherman, *President*
Pete Brodie, *CFO*

Joe Escobar, *Mng Member*
◆ EMP: 68
SQ FT: 203,000
SALES (est): 26.4MM
SALES (corp-wide): 222.8MM **Privately Held**
WEB: www.calsheets.com
SIC: **2653** Sheets, corrugated: made from
purchased materials
PA: Golden West Packaging Group Llc
8333 24th Ave
Sacramento CA 95826
404 345-8365

(P-5204)
CALIFORNIA BOX II
8949 Toronto Ave, Rancho Cucamonga
(91730-5412)
PHONE..................909 944-9202
John Widera, *CEO*
Mackey Davis, *Vice Pres*
EMP: 45
SQ FT: 100,000
SALES (est): 9.4MM **Privately Held**
WEB: www.calbox.com
SIC: **2653 5113** Boxes, corrugated: made
from purchased materials; corrugated &
solid fiber boxes

(P-5205)
CAPITAL CORRUGATED LLC
Also Called: Capital Corrugated and Carton
8333 24th Ave, Sacramento (95826-4809)
P.O. Box 278060 (95827-8060)
PHONE..................916 388-7848
Dennis D Watson, *President*
Nhi Willis, *Project Mgr*
Mike Riley, *Sales Mgr*
▲ EMP: 80
SQ FT: 124,000
SALES (est): 26.4MM
SALES (corp-wide): 222.8MM **Privately Held**
WEB: www.capitalcorrugated.com
SIC: **2653** Boxes, corrugated: made from
purchased materials; display items, corru-
gated: made from purchased materials;
sheets, corrugated: made from purchased
materials; partitions, corrugated: made
from purchased materials
PA: Golden West Packaging Group Llc
8333 24th Ave
Sacramento CA 95826
404 345-8365

(P-5206)
CD CONTAINER INC
Also Called: Carton Design
7343 Paramount Blvd, Pico Rivera
(90660-3713)
PHONE..................562 948-1910
Juan De La Cruz, *President*
Jose De La Cruz, *CFO*
▲ EMP: 70
SQ FT: 46,000
SALES (est): 16.3MM **Privately Held**
SIC: **2653** Boxes, corrugated: made from
purchased materials

(P-5207)
CITY PAPER BOX CO
652 E 61st St, Los Angeles (90001-1021)
PHONE..................323 231-5990
Stanley Goodrich, *President*
Maurey Friedman, *Vice Pres*
Frieda Goodrich, *Vice Pres*
Michael Goodrich, *Vice Pres*
Abe Friedman, *Executive*
EMP: 16
SQ FT: 9,000
SALES (est): 2.9MM **Privately Held**
SIC: **2653** Boxes, corrugated: made from
purchased materials

(P-5208)
COASTAL CONTAINER INC
8455 Loch Lomond Dr, Pico Rivera
(90660-2508)
PHONE..................562 801-4595
Richard Rudell, *President*
Roberta Noble, *Treasurer*
EMP: 30
SQ FT: 3,000

SALES (est): 5.8MM **Privately Held**
WEB: www.coastalcontainer.com
SIC: 2653 5113 Boxes, corrugated: made from purchased materials; corrugated & solid fiber boxes

(P-5209)
COLOR-BOX LLC
Also Called: Georgia-Pacific
1275 S Granada Dr, Madera (93637-4803)
PHONE..............................559 674-1049
Tim McCoy, *Manager*
Brad Alling, *Maint Spvr*
EMP: 50
SQ FT: 107,424
SALES (corp-wide): 40.6B **Privately Held**
WEB: www.gp.com
SIC: 2653 2657 Corrugated & solid fiber boxes; folding paperboard boxes
HQ: Color-Box Llc
623 S G St
Richmond IN 47374
765 966-7588

(P-5210)
COMMANDER PACKAGING WEST INC
602 S Rockefeller Ave D, Ontario (91761-8191)
PHONE..............................714 921-9350
Joseph F Kindlon, *Ch of Bd*
Brian R Webber, *President*
EMP: 37
SQ FT: 48,000
SALES (est): 8MM
SALES (corp-wide): 10.8MM **Privately Held**
WEB: www.commanderpackagingwest.com
SIC: 2653 7389 5113 Boxes, corrugated: made from purchased materials; packaging & labeling services; corrugated & solid fiber boxes
PA: Cano Container Corporation
3920 Enterprise Ct Ste A
Aurora IL 60504
630 585-7500

(P-5211)
COMPRO PACKAGING LLC
Also Called: Bayline
1600 Atlantic St, Union City (94587-2017)
PHONE..............................510 475-0118
Michael Ramelot, *President*
John Roberts, *Ch of Bd*
Donald Cook, *Vice Pres*
EMP: 50
SQ FT: 75,000
SALES (est): 4.2MM **Privately Held**
SIC: 2653 2679 5113 Boxes, corrugated: made from purchased materials; corrugated paper: made from purchased material; industrial & personal service paper

(P-5212)
CORRU-KRAFT IV
1911 E Rosslynn Ave, Fullerton (92831-5141)
PHONE..............................714 773-0124
Bob Dunford, *Principal*
Paul Sartin, *General Mgr*
EMP: 14
SALES (est): 4.8MM **Privately Held**
SIC: 2653 Boxes, corrugated: made from purchased materials

(P-5213)
CORRUGADOS DE BAJA CALIFORNIA
2475 Paseo De Las A, San Diego (92154)
PHONE..............................619 662-8672
Smurfit Kappa, *Owner*
Eduardo Lopez, *Manager*
EMP: 900
SALES (est): 228.8MM **Privately Held**
SIC: 2653 Corrugated & solid fiber boxes

(P-5214)
CORRUGATED PACKAGING PDTS INC
27403 Industrial Blvd, Hayward (94545-3348)
PHONE..............................650 615-9180
Christopher Grandov, *President*
Linda Grandov, *Admin Sec*
EMP: 25 **EST:** 1960

SQ FT: 2,000
SALES (est): 7MM **Privately Held**
SIC: 2653 2631 Corrugated & solid fiber boxes; paperboard mills

(P-5215)
CROCKETT GRAPHICS INC (PA)
Also Called: Folding Cartons
980 Avenida Acaso, Camarillo (93012-8759)
PHONE..............................805 987-8577
Edward Randall Crockett, *President*
Rod K Rieth, *Treasurer*
Mike Mullens, *Vice Pres*
Russ Collins, *Human Res Dir*
Glen Brown, *Sales Staff*
▲ **EMP:** 60
SALES (est): 19MM **Privately Held**
WEB: www.garedgraphics.com
SIC: 2653 Corrugated boxes, partitions, display items, sheets & pad

(P-5216)
CROWN CARTON COMPANY INC
1820 E 48th Pl, Vernon (90058-1946)
PHONE..............................323 582-3053
Jeffrey P Marks, *President*
Kyle Johnson, *Vice Pres*
EMP: 20
SQ FT: 28,000
SALES (est): 4MM **Privately Held**
WEB: www.crowncarton.com
SIC: 2653 Boxes, corrugated: made from purchased materials

(P-5217)
CUSTOM PAD AND PARTITION INC
1100 Richard Ave, Santa Clara (95050-2800)
PHONE..............................408 970-9711
James L Jones, *CEO*
Janice Jones, *Treasurer*
Cathy Crowder, *Purchasing*
Chip Peto, *Purchasing*
Norman Chow, *Manager*
EMP: 65
SQ FT: 60,000
SALES (est): 21.7MM **Privately Held**
WEB: www.custompad.com
SIC: 2653 Pads, corrugated: made from purchased materials; partitions, corrugated: made from purchased materials; boxes, corrugated: made from purchased materials

(P-5218)
ECKO PRODUCTS GROUP LLC
Also Called: Ecko Print & Packaging
740 S Milliken Ave Ste C, Ontario (91761-7842)
PHONE..............................909 628-5678
Eric Rogers, *CFO*
Christopher Hively, *President*
Jennifer Pearce, *Accountant*
Brandon Proctor,
Amanda Alexander, *Cust Mgr*
▲ **EMP:** 23
SQ FT: 17,000
SALES (est): 9.6MM **Privately Held**
SIC: 2653 5085 2759 Boxes, corrugated: made from purchased materials; abrasives & adhesives; commercial printing

(P-5219)
EMPIRE CONTAINER CORPORATION
1161 E Walnut St, Carson (90746-1382)
PHONE..............................310 537-8190
Donald Simmons, *President*
Patrick Fox, *Shareholder*
Gregory V Hall, *Principal*
▲ **EMP:** 66 **EST:** 1970
SQ FT: 61,000
SALES (est): 20.7MM **Privately Held**
WEB: www.empirecontainercorp.com
SIC: 2653 3578 Boxes, corrugated: made from purchased materials; point-of-sale devices

(P-5220)
EXPRESS CONTAINER INC
560 Iowa St, Redlands (92373-8060)
P.O. Box 230 (92373-0064)
PHONE..............................909 798-3857
Gilles Roy, *President*
EMP: 22
SQ FT: 25,000
SALES (est): 4.8MM **Privately Held**
WEB: www.expresscontainer.com
SIC: 2653 Boxes, corrugated: made from purchased materials

(P-5221)
FRUIT GROWERS SUPPLY COMPANY (PA)
27770 N Entrmt Dr Fl 3 Flr 3, Valencia (91355)
PHONE..............................661 290-8704
Jim Phillips, *CEO*
Charles Boyce, *CFO*
William O Knox, *Vice Pres*
Mark Lindgren, *Executive*
John W Eacker, *Regional Mgr*
◆ **EMP:** 50
SQ FT: 10,000
SALES (est): 222.6MM **Privately Held**
WEB: www.fruitgrowers.com
SIC: 2653 0811 5191 2448 Boxes, corrugated: made from purchased materials; timber tracts; farm supplies; fertilizer & fertilizer materials; pallets, wood; cardboard & products

(P-5222)
FRUIT GROWERS SUPPLY COMPANY
Also Called: F G S Packing Services
674 E Myer Ave, Exeter (93221-9644)
PHONE..............................559 592-6550
Bruce Adams, *Manager*
Michael Fontes, *Officer*
EMP: 12
SQ FT: 5,240
SALES (corp-wide): 222.6MM **Privately Held**
SIC: 2653 Boxes, corrugated: made from purchased materials
PA: Fruit Growers Supply Company Inc
27770 N Entrmt Dr Fl 3 Flr 3
Valencia CA 91355
661 290-8704

(P-5223)
GABRIEL CONTAINER CO (PA)
Also Called: Recycled Paper Products
8844 Millergrove Dr, Santa Fe Springs (90670-2013)
P.O. Box 3188 (90670-0188)
PHONE..............................562 699-1051
Ronald H Gabriel, *President*
Agnes Gabriel, *Admin Sec*
Anush Gabriel,
▲ **EMP:** 199 **EST:** 1935
SQ FT: 72,000
SALES (est): 38.2MM **Privately Held**
WEB: www.gabrielcontainer.com
SIC: 2653 2621 Boxes, corrugated: made from purchased materials; paper mills

(P-5224)
GEM BOX OF WEST
2430 S Hill St, Los Angeles (90007-2720)
PHONE..............................213 748-4875
Sang Up Park, *President*
Suizie Park, *Admin Sec*
▲ **EMP:** 26
SQ FT: 135,000
SALES (est): 3.8MM **Privately Held**
SIC: 2653 5094 Solid fiber boxes, partitions, display items & sheets; jewelers' findings

(P-5225)
GENERAL CONTAINER
5450 Dodds Ave, Buena Park (90621-1209)
PHONE..............................714 562-8700
Tim Black, *President*
Tim G Black, *President*
Patty Black, *Admin Sec*
Debbie McMillen, *Accounting Mgr*
Scott Black, *Sales Staff*
EMP: 75 **EST:** 1976
SQ FT: 62,000

SALES (est): 21.8MM **Privately Held**
SIC: 2653 Boxes, corrugated: made from purchased materials

(P-5226)
GEORGIA-PACIFIC LLC
2400 Lapham Dr, Modesto (95354-4003)
PHONE..............................209 522-5201
David Rieser, *General Mgr*
Dan Brasher, *Manager*
EMP: 150
SALES (corp-wide): 40.6B **Privately Held**
WEB: www.gp.com
SIC: 2653 Boxes, corrugated: made from purchased materials
HQ: Georgia-Pacific Llc
133 Peachtree St Nw
Atlanta GA 30303
404 652-4000

(P-5227)
GEORGIA-PACIFIC LLC
249 E Grand Ave, South San Francisco (94080-4804)
P.O. Box 2407 (94083)
PHONE..............................650 873-7800
Ron Huff, *Branch Mgr*
EMP: 225
SALES (corp-wide): 40.6B **Privately Held**
WEB: www.gp.com
SIC: 2653 5113 Boxes, corrugated: made from purchased materials; corrugated & solid fiber boxes
HQ: Georgia-Pacific Llc
133 Peachtree St Nw
Atlanta GA 30303
404 652-4000

(P-5228)
GEORGIA-PACIFIC LLC
24600 Avenue 13, Madera (93637-9019)
P.O. Box 1327 (93639-1327)
PHONE..............................559 674-4685
Steve Mindt, *General Mgr*
Joe Antonino, *Sales Staff*
EMP: 150
SALES (corp-wide): 40.6B **Privately Held**
WEB: www.gp.com
SIC: 2653 5113 Boxes, corrugated: made from purchased materials; corrugated & solid fiber boxes
HQ: Georgia-Pacific Llc
133 Peachtree St Nw
Atlanta GA 30303
404 652-4000

(P-5229)
GLOBAL PACKAGING SOLUTIONS INC
6259 Progressive Dr # 200, San Diego (92154-6644)
PHONE..............................619 710-2661
Jawed Ghias, *CEO*
Henry Romo, *Shareholder*
Rajnikanth Parikh, *Treasurer*
Anila Parikh, *Principal*
Tariq Butt, *Admin Sec*
▲ **EMP:** 280
SALES (est): 8.4MM **Privately Held**
SIC: 2653 3089 Corrugated & solid fiber boxes; injection molding of plastics
PA: Global Packaging Solutions, S.A. De C.V.
Calle 7 Norte No.108
Tijuana B.C. 22444

(P-5230)
GOLDEN WEST PACKG GROUP LLC (PA)
8333 24th Ave, Sacramento (95826-4809)
PHONE..............................404 345-8365
Brad Jordan, *President*
EMP: 381
SALES (est): 222.8MM **Privately Held**
SIC: 2653 Boxes, corrugated: made from purchased materials

(P-5231)
GOLDENCORR SHEETS LLC
13890 Nelson Ave, City of Industry (91746-2050)
P.O. Box 90968 (91715-0968)
PHONE..............................626 369-6446
Tom Anderson, *Mng Member*
John Perullo, *President*

▲ = Import ▼=Export
◆ =Import/Export

Jeffrey Erseluis, *Mng Member*
Glen Tucker, *Mng Member*
John Webb, *Mng Member*
▲ **EMP:** 150
SALES (est): 49.1MM **Privately Held**
SIC: 2653 Corrugated boxes, partitions, display items, sheets & pad

(P-5232)
GRAPHICPAK CORPORATION
760 S Vail Ave, Montebello (90640-4954)
PHONE..............................323 306-3054
Robert Berger, *CEO*
Peter Butzloff, *Vice Pres*
EMP: 10
SQ FT: 33,000
SALES (est): 2.8MM **Privately Held**
WEB: www.graphicpak.com
SIC: 2653 Corrugated & solid fiber boxes

(P-5233)
HARVEST CONTAINER COMPANY
24476 Road 216, Lindsay (93247-8222)
P.O. Box 697 (93247-0697)
PHONE..............................559 562-1394
Dennis A Del Rio, *Exec VP*
Fred Lo Bue, *President*
Robert Reniers, *Corp Secy*
Phil Enghusen, *Executive*
Dennis Del Rio, *General Mgr*
▲ **EMP:** 45
SQ FT: 104,000
SALES (est): 12.9MM **Privately Held**
WEB: www.harvestcontainer.com
SIC: 2653 Boxes, corrugated: made from purchased materials

(P-5234)
HERITAGE CONTAINER INC
4777 Felspar St, Riverside (92509-3040)
P.O. Box 605, Mira Loma (91752-0605)
PHONE..............................951 360-1900
Richard Gabriel, *CEO*
Thomas Gabriel, *President*
Nancy Zuniga, *Vice Pres*
Tom Gabriel, *Executive*
Charlie Cashen, *Purchasing*
EMP: 55
SQ FT: 95,000
SALES: 15MM **Privately Held**
WEB: www.heritagecontainer.com
SIC: 2653 5199 Boxes, corrugated: made from purchased materials; packaging materials

(P-5235)
HERITAGE PAPER CO (HQ)
2400 S Grand Ave, Santa Ana (92705-5211)
PHONE..............................714 540-9737
Ron Scagliotti, *CEO*
Lenet Derksen, *CFO*
Bill Bumstead, *Vice Pres*
Terri Sloane, *Department Mgr*
Hugh Lovelace, *Sales Mgr*
▲ **EMP:** 75
SQ FT: 150,000
SALES (est): 24.6MM
SALES (corp-wide): 158.2MM **Privately Held**
WEB: www.heritage-paper.net
SIC: 2653 5199 Boxes, corrugated: made from purchased materials; packaging materials
PA: Pioneer Packing, Inc.
2430 S Grand Ave
Santa Ana CA 92705
714 540-9751

(P-5236)
HOLLINGER METAL EDGE INC
356 S Coyote Ln, Anaheim (92808-1354)
PHONE..............................323 721-7800
Robert J Henderson, *CEO*
Annie Riddle, *Vice Pres*
▼ **EMP:** 20
SALES (est): 3.8MM **Privately Held**
WEB: www.metaledgeinc.com
SIC: 2653 Boxes, corrugated: made from purchased materials; boxes, solid fiber: made from purchased materials

(P-5237)
INTERNATIONAL PAPER COMPANY
601 E Ball Rd, Anaheim (92805-5910)
PHONE..............................714 776-6060
Terry Tockey, *Branch Mgr*
EMP: 140
SALES (corp-wide): 23.3B **Publicly Held**
WEB: www.internationalpaper.com
SIC: 2653 Boxes, corrugated: made from purchased materials
PA: International Paper Company
6400 Poplar Ave
Memphis TN 38197
901 419-9000

(P-5238)
INTERNATIONAL PAPER COMPANY
11211 Greenstone Ave, Santa Fe Springs (90670-4616)
PHONE..............................323 946-6100
Marc Bailey, *General Mgr*
EMP: 145
SALES (corp-wide): 23.3B **Publicly Held**
SIC: 2653 Boxes, corrugated: made from purchased materials
PA: International Paper Company
6400 Poplar Ave
Memphis TN 38197
901 419-9000

(P-5239)
INTERNATIONAL PAPER COMPANY
3550 Bozzano Rd, Stockton (95215-9100)
PHONE..............................209 931-9005
Doc Parris, *Manager*
Rebecca Wynn, *Finance*
EMP: 40
SALES (corp-wide): 23.3B **Publicly Held**
WEB: www.internationalpaper.com
SIC: 2653 Boxes, corrugated: made from purchased materials
PA: International Paper Company
6400 Poplar Ave
Memphis TN 38197
901 419-9000

(P-5240)
JELLCO CONTAINER INC
1151 N Tustin Ave, Anaheim (92807-1736)
PHONE..............................714 666-2728
Jeff Erselius, *President*
Rick Leininger, *CFO*
Ralph Ramirez, *Opers-Prdtn-Mfg*
Rod Eggleston, *Sales Staff*
EMP: 72
SQ FT: 42,000
SALES (est): 24.6MM **Privately Held**
WEB: www.jellco.com
SIC: 2653 Boxes, corrugated: made from purchased materials

(P-5241)
JSJ INC CORRUGATED
10700 Jersey Blvd, Rancho Cucamonga (91730-5116)
PHONE..............................909 987-4746
Joseph G Alba, *President*
EMP: 12
SALES (est): 1MM **Privately Held**
SIC: 2653 Boxes, corrugated: made from purchased materials

(P-5242)
KAWEAH CONTAINER INC (HQ)
7101 Avenue 304, Visalia (93291-9479)
P.O. Box 6940 (93290-6940)
PHONE..............................559 651-7846
Robert J Reeves, *CEO*
William Ring, *Human Res Dir*
Kevin Finerty, *Sales Staff*
▲ **EMP:** 75
SQ FT: 30,000
SALES (est): 21.7MM
SALES (corp-wide): 100.4MM **Privately Held**
SIC: 2653 Boxes, corrugated: made from purchased materials
PA: Wileman Bros. & Elliott, Inc.
40232 Road 128
Cutler CA 93615
559 651-8378

(P-5243)
LIBERTY CONTAINER COMPANY
Also Called: Key Container
4224 Santa Ana St, South Gate (90280-2557)
PHONE..............................323 564-4211
Robert J Watts, *President*
William J Watts, *Vice Pres*
▲ **EMP:** 110
SQ FT: 300,000
SALES (est): 25.7MM **Privately Held**
WEB: www.keycontainer.com
SIC: 2653 Boxes, corrugated: made from purchased materials

(P-5244)
LIBERTY DIVERSIFIED INTL INC
Also Called: Harbor Packaging
13100 Danielson St, Poway (92064-6840)
PHONE..............................858 391-7302
Lauren De-Cerbo, *Accountant*
EMP: 245
SALES (corp-wide): 387.6MM **Privately Held**
SIC: 2653 5199 Boxes, corrugated: made from purchased materials; packaging materials
PA: Liberty Diversified International, Inc.
5600 Highway 169 N
New Hope MN 55428
763 536-6600

(P-5245)
MENASHA PACKAGING COMPANY LLC
305 Resource Dr Ste 100, Bloomington (92316-3528)
PHONE..............................951 374-5281
EMP: 30
SALES (corp-wide): 1.8B **Privately Held**
SIC: 2653 Boxes, corrugated: made from purchased materials
HQ: Menasha Packaging Company, Llc
1645 Bergstrom Rd
Neenah WI 54956
920 751-1000

(P-5246)
MENASHA PACKAGING COMPANY LLC
8110 Sorensen Ave, Santa Fe Springs (90670-2122)
PHONE..............................562 698-3705
Hector Gonzalez, *Prdtn Mgr*
EMP: 84
SALES (corp-wide): 1.8B **Privately Held**
WEB: www.menasha.com
SIC: 2653 Boxes, corrugated: made from purchased materials
HQ: Menasha Packaging Company, Llc
1645 Bergstrom Rd
Neenah WI 54956
920 751-1000

(P-5247)
MONTEBELLO CONTAINER CO LLC
14333 Macaw St, La Mirada (90638-5208)
P.O. Box 788 (90637-0788)
PHONE..............................714 994-2351
Al Perez, *CFO*
EMP: 100 **Privately Held**
WEB: www.montcc.com
SIC: 2653 5113 Boxes, corrugated: made from purchased materials; corrugated & solid fiber boxes
HQ: Montebello Container Company Llc
13220 Molette St
Santa Fe Springs CA 90670
562 404-6221

(P-5248)
NUMATECH WEST (KMP) LLC
Also Called: Kmp Numatech Pacific
1201 E Lexington Ave, Pomona (91766-5520)
P.O. Box 357, Placentia (92871-0357)
PHONE..............................909 706-3627
John Neate, *Mng Member*
Robert Sliter, *General Mgr*
Rodelieta Clavin, *Director*
▲ **EMP:** 100
SQ FT: 65,000

SALES (est): 14.2MM
SALES (corp-wide): 49.8MM **Privately Held**
SIC: 2653 Boxes, corrugated: made from purchased materials
PA: Nw Packaging Llc
1201 E Lexington Ave
Pomona CA 91766
909 706-3627

(P-5249)
ORANGE CONTAINER INC
1984 E Mcfadden Ave, Santa Ana (92705-4706)
PHONE..............................714 547-9617
Harold Bankhead, *President*
Terry Schnabel, *Vice Pres*
EMP: 60
SQ FT: 25,000
SALES (est): 7MM **Privately Held**
WEB: www.orangecontainer.com
SIC: 2653 Boxes, corrugated: made from purchased materials

(P-5250)
PACIFIC QUALITY PACKAGING CORP
660 Neptune Ave, Brea (92821-2909)
PHONE..............................714 257-1234
Frederick H Chau, *President*
Chris Chau, *Project Mgr*
▲ **EMP:** 65
SQ FT: 44,000
SALES (est): 14.2MM **Privately Held**
SIC: 2653 3993 Boxes, corrugated: made from purchased materials; signs & advertising specialties

(P-5251)
PACIFIC SOUTHWEST CONT LLC
Also Called: PSC
9525 W Nicholas Ct, Visalia (93291-9468)
PHONE..............................559 651-5500
Don Mayol, *Opers Staff*
Palmira Crane, *Opers Staff*
Mike Kipp, *Manager*
EMP: 89
SALES (corp-wide): 159.4MM **Privately Held**
SIC: 2653 Boxes, corrugated: made from purchased materials
PA: Pacific Southwest Container, Llc
4530 Leckron Rd
Modesto CA 95357
209 526-0444

(P-5252)
PACKAGEONE INC (PA)
Also Called: All West Container
1100 Union St, San Francisco (94109-2019)
P.O. Box 27095 (94127-0095)
PHONE..............................650 761-3339
Richard Pfaff, *President*
Christopher Grandov, *Vice Pres*
▼ **EMP:** 44 **EST:** 1958
SQ FT: 129,000
SALES (est): 7.5MM **Privately Held**
WEB: www.allwestcontainer.com
SIC: 2653 Boxes, corrugated: made from purchased materials

(P-5253)
PACKAGING CORPORATION AMERICA
Also Called: PCA/Los Angeles 349
4240 Bandini Blvd, Vernon (90058-4207)
PHONE..............................323 263-7581
Mark Beyma, *Branch Mgr*
Marie Madariaga, *Executive*
Juliet Valle, *Executive*
Richard Thomas, *Plant Mgr*
EMP: 100
SALES (corp-wide): 7B **Publicly Held**
WEB: www.packagingcorp.com
SIC: 2653 Boxes, corrugated: made from purchased materials
PA: Packaging Corporation Of America
1 N Field Ct
Lake Forest IL 60045
847 482-3000

(P-5254)
PACKAGING CORPORATION AMERICA
Also Called: PCA/South Gate 378
9700 E Frontage Rd Ste 20, South Gate (90280-5421)
PHONE.................................562 927-7741
Eric Thorntoon, *Branch Mgr*
Margie Torre, *Human Res Mgr*
Michael Hinton, *Safety Mgr*
Lora Thalley, *Cust Mgr*
EMP: 230
SALES (corp-wide): 7B **Publicly Held**
WEB: www.packagingcorp.com
SIC: 2653 Boxes, corrugated: made from purchased materials
PA: Packaging Corporation Of America
1 N Field Ct
Lake Forest IL 60045
847 482-3000

(P-5255)
PACKAGING PLUS
3816 S Willow Ave Ste 102, Fresno (93725-9241)
PHONE.................................209 858-9200
Robert Crossman, *President*
Alecia Crossman, *Vice Pres*
Michelle Reid, *Manager*
▲ EMP: 32
SQ FT: 60,000
SALES (est): 6.1MM **Privately Held**
SIC: 2653 Sheets, corrugated: made from purchased materials

(P-5256)
PACTIV LLC
4545 Qantas Ln, Stockton (95206-3982)
PHONE.................................209 983-1930
Muhammad Subhan, *Engineer*
Trena Huerta, *HR Admin*
John Chamberlain, *Plant Engr*
Thomas Maxey, *Maintence Staff*
Jeff Frese, *Manager*
EMP: 1300
SALES (corp-wide): 14.1MM **Privately Held**
SIC: 2653 2656 2652 Boxes, corrugated: made from purchased materials; sanitary food containers; setup paperboard boxes
HQ: Pactiv Llc
1900 W Field Ct
Lake Forest IL 60045
847 482-2000

(P-5257)
PCA CENTRAL CAL CORRUGATED LLC
Also Called: Packaging America - Sacramento
4841 Urbani Ave, McClellan (95652-2025)
PHONE.................................916 614-0580
Bob Bruna, *General Mgr*
EMP: 146
SALES (corp-wide): 7B **Publicly Held**
SIC: 2653 Corrugated & solid fiber boxes
HQ: Pca Central California Corrugated, Llc
1955 W Field Ct
Lake Forest IL 60045
847 482-3000

(P-5258)
PK1 INC (HQ)
Also Called: American River Packaging
4225 Pell Dr, Sacramento (95838-2533)
PHONE.................................916 858-1300
Thomas Kandris, *CEO*
Ronald Frederick, *CFO*
Ron Frederick, *VP Finance*
Jessica Clark, *Human Res Dir*
Steve Farinelli, *Opers Mgr*
▲ EMP: 100
SQ FT: 240,000
SALES (est): 21.1MM
SALES (corp-wide): 222.8MM **Privately Held**
WEB: www.arpkg.com
SIC: 2653 5113 4783 Boxes, corrugated: made from purchased materials; industrial & personal service paper; packing goods for shipping
PA: Golden West Packaging Group Llc
8333 24th Ave
Sacramento CA 95826
404 345-8365

(P-5259)
PNC PROACTIVE NTHRN CONT LLC
602 S Rockefeller Ave A, Ontario (91761-8190)
PHONE.................................909 390-5624
Gary Hartog, *Mng Member*
▲ EMP: 50
SQ FT: 362,000
SALES (est): 8.7MM **Privately Held**
SIC: 2653 Boxes, corrugated: made from purchased materials
PA: Fourth Third Llc
375 Park Ave Ste 3304
New York NY

(P-5260)
PROACTIVE PACKG & DISPLAY LLC (DH)
602 S Rockefeller Ave, Ontario (91761-8190)
PHONE.................................909 390-5624
Richard Hartman, *CEO*
▲ EMP: 55
SQ FT: 164,000
SALES (est): 14.9MM
SALES (corp-wide): 257.8MM **Privately Held**
WEB: www.proactivepkg.com
SIC: 2653 Boxes, corrugated: made from purchased materials
HQ: New-Indy Containerboard Llc
3500 Porsche Way Ste 150
Ontario CA 91764
909 296-3400

(P-5261)
PROGRESSIVE PACKG GROUP INC (PA)
18931 Portola Dr Ste C, Salinas (93908-1295)
P.O. Box 2268 (93902-2268)
PHONE.................................831 424-2942
Eli Riddle, *President*
Barry Jhonston, *CFO*
EMP: 22
SQ FT: 1,700
SALES (est): 5.7MM **Privately Held**
SIC: 2653 Boxes, corrugated: made from purchased materials

(P-5262)
RICARDO OCHOA
Also Called: Northwest Pallets
281 N Pioneer Ave, Woodland (95776)
PHONE.................................530 668-1152
Ricardo Ochoa, *Owner*
EMP: 17
SQ FT: 17,500
SALES (est): 2.1MM **Privately Held**
SIC: 2653 2448 Pallets, corrugated: made from purchased materials; wood pallets & skids

(P-5263)
RTS PACKAGING LLC
14103 Borate St, Santa Fe Springs (90670-5342)
PHONE.................................562 356-6550
Doud Hensley, *General Mgr*
EMP: 50
SALES (corp-wide): 16.2B **Publicly Held**
WEB: www.rtspackaging.com
SIC: 2653 2631 Pads, solid fiber: made from purchased materials; paperboard mills
HQ: Rts Packaging, Llc
504 Thrasher St
Norcross GA 30071
800 558-6984

(P-5264)
SAN DIEGO CRATING & PKG INC
12678 Brookprinter Pl, Poway (92064-6809)
PHONE.................................858 748-0100
Jacqueline H Peterson, *Principal*
Lee Peterson, *President*
EMP: 17
SQ FT: 12,000

SALES (est): 1.1MM **Privately Held**
WEB: www.sdcrate.com
SIC: 2653 4783 Boxes, corrugated: made from purchased materials; crating goods for shipping; packing goods for shipping

(P-5265)
SCOPE PACKAGING INC
Also Called: Sp
13400 Nelson Ave, City of Industry (91746-2331)
PHONE.................................714 998-4411
Mike E Flinn, *CEO*
Cindy Baker, *Vice Pres*
▲ EMP: 45
SQ FT: 70,000
SALES (est): 12.2MM **Privately Held**
WEB: www.kraftdesigns.com
SIC: 2653 7389 Boxes, corrugated: made from purchased materials; packaging & labeling services

(P-5266)
SMURFIT KAPPA NORTH AMER LLC
440 Baldwin Park Blvd, City of Industry (91746-1407)
PHONE.................................626 322-2123
EMP: 413 **Privately Held**
SIC: 2653 2671 2657
HQ: Smurfit Kappa North America Llc
13400 Nelson Ave
City Of Industry CA 75062
626 333-6363

(P-5267)
SONOCO CORRFLEX LLC
1225 Grand Central Ave, Glendale (91201-2425)
PHONE.................................818 507-7477
John Kack, *Regl Sales Mgr*
EMP: 17
SALES (corp-wide): 5.3B **Publicly Held**
SIC: 2653 Display items, corrugated: made from purchased materials
HQ: Sonoco Display & Packaging, Llc
555 Aureole St
Winston Salem NC 27107

(P-5268)
SONOCO PRTECTIVE SOLUTIONS INC
3466 Enterprise Ave, Hayward (94545-3219)
PHONE.................................510 785-0220
Rob Hazelton, *Manager*
Dolores Odgers, *Executive*
Raj Vanapalli, *Info Tech Dir*
Sanjay Maharaj, *Manager*
EMP: 60
SQ FT: 125,975
SALES (corp-wide): 5.3B **Publicly Held**
WEB: www.tuscarora.com
SIC: 2653 3086 Boxes, corrugated: made from purchased materials; plastics foam products
HQ: Sonoco Protective Solutions, Inc.
1 N 2nd St
Hartsville SC 29550
843 383-7000

(P-5269)
SOUTHLAND CONTAINER CORP
Also Called: Concept Packaging Group
1600 Champagne Ave, Ontario (91761-3612)
PHONE.................................909 937-9781
Tom Heinz, *Branch Mgr*
EMP: 15
SALES (corp-wide): 897.8MM **Privately Held**
WEB: www.concept-pkg.com
SIC: 2653 Boxes, corrugated: made from purchased materials
PA: Southland Container Corporation
60 Fairview Church Rd
Spartanburg SC 29303
864 578-0085

(P-5270)
SOVEREIGN PACKAGING INC
8420 Kass Dr, Buena Park (90621-3808)
PHONE.................................714 670-6811
David Pittman, *President*
Sheryl Dreiling, *Vice Pres*

Bibiana N Boerio, *Managing Dir*
EMP: 24
SQ FT: 25,000
SALES (est): 2.8MM **Privately Held**
WEB: www.sovereignpackaging.com
SIC: 2653 7336 5113 Boxes, corrugated: made from purchased materials; package design; corrugated & solid fiber boxes

(P-5271)
WESTROCK CONVERTING COMPANY
16110 Cosmos St, Moreno Valley (92551-7308)
PHONE.................................951 601-4164
Tony Rangel, *General Mgr*
EMP: 18
SALES (corp-wide): 16.2B **Publicly Held**
SIC: 2653 Partitions, solid fiber: made from purchased materials
HQ: Westrock Converting, Llc
1000 Abernathy Rd Ste 125
Atlanta GA 30328
770 448-2193

(P-5272)
WESTROCK CP LLC
Also Called: Smurfit-Stone Container
201 S Hillview Dr, Milpitas (95035-5417)
PHONE.................................408 946-3600
Derek Bonner, *Branch Mgr*
EMP: 146
SALES (corp-wide): 16.2B **Publicly Held**
WEB: www.smurfit-stone.com
SIC: 2653 5113 Boxes, corrugated: made from purchased materials; corrugated & solid fiber boxes
HQ: Westrock Cp, Llc
1000 Abernathy Rd
Atlanta GA 30328

(P-5273)
WESTROCK CP LLC
Also Called: Smurfit-Stone Container
13833 Freeway Dr, Santa Fe Springs (90670-5701)
PHONE.................................714 523-3550
Manny Loera, *Branch Mgr*
EMP: 125
SQ FT: 265,000
SALES (corp-wide): 16.2B **Publicly Held**
WEB: www.smurfit-stone.com
SIC: 2653 Boxes, corrugated: made from purchased materials
HQ: Westrock Cp, Llc
1000 Abernathy Rd
Atlanta GA 30328

(P-5274)
WESTROCK CP LLC
1078 Merrill St, Salinas (93901-4409)
PHONE.................................831 424-1831
Jimmy Murkison, *General Mgr*
EMP: 120
SALES (corp-wide): 16.2B **Publicly Held**
WEB: www.smurfit-stone.com
SIC: 2653 Boxes, corrugated: made from purchased materials
HQ: Westrock Cp, Llc
1000 Abernathy Rd
Atlanta GA 30328

(P-5275)
WESTROCK CP LLC
185 N Smith Ave, Corona (92880-1739)
PHONE.................................951 734-1870
David Tichchch, *Branch Mgr*
EMP: 117
SALES (corp-wide): 16.2B **Publicly Held**
WEB: www.smurfit-stone.com
SIC: 2653 5113 Boxes, corrugated: made from purchased materials; corrugated & solid fiber boxes
HQ: Westrock Cp, Llc
1000 Abernathy Rd
Atlanta GA 30328

(P-5276)
WESTROCK CP LLC
Also Called: West Rock
201 S Hillview Dr, Milpitas (95035-5417)
PHONE.................................408 946-3600

▲ = Import ▼=Export
◆ =Import/Export

Russell Asp, *Branch Mgr*
EMP: 150
SALES (corp-wide): 16.2B **Publicly Held**
WEB: www.sto.com
SIC: 2653 Boxes, corrugated: made from
purchased materials
HQ: Westrock Cp, Llc
1000 Abernathy Rd
Atlanta GA 30328
-

(P-5277)
WESTROCK CP LLC
Also Called: Corpak of Tulare
701 E Continental Ave, Tulare
(93274-6813)
PHONE...................................559 685-1102
Eric Miller, *Branch Mgr*
EMP: 70
SALES (corp-wide): 16.2B **Publicly Held**
SIC: 2653 Boxes, corrugated: made from
purchased materials
HQ: Westrock Cp, Llc
1000 Abernathy Rd
Atlanta GA 30328

(P-5278)
WESTROCK CP LLC
3366 E Muscat Ave, Fresno (93725-2624)
PHONE...................................559 519-7240
Bernardo Thomas,
EMP: 101
SALES (corp-wide): 16.2B **Publicly Held**
SIC: 2653 2631 2655 Boxes, corrugated:
made from purchased materials; partitions, corrugated: made from purchased
materials; partitions, solid fiber: made
from purchased materials; container
board; boxboard; folding boxboard; liner-
board; tubes, fiber or paper: made from
purchased material; fiber cores, reels &
bobbins; drums, fiber: made from purchased material
HQ: Westrock Cp, Llc
1000 Abernathy Rd
Atlanta GA 30328

(P-5279)
WESTROCK RKT COMPANY
749 N Poplar St, Orange (92868-1013)
PHONE...................................714 978-2895
Bob Appoloney, *Branch Mgr*
EMP: 161
SALES (corp-wide): 16.2B **Publicly Held**
SIC: 2653 Boxes, corrugated: made from
purchased materials
HQ: Westrock Rkt, Llc
1000 Abernathy Rd Ste 125
Atlanta GA 30328
770 448-2193

(P-5280)
WESTROCK RKT COMPANY
3366 E Muscat Ave, Fresno (93725-2624)
PHONE...................................559 497-1662
Thomas Bernardo, *Branch Mgr*
EMP: 161
SALES (corp-wide): 16.2B **Publicly Held**
SIC: 2653 Hampers, solid fiber: made from
purchased materials; boxes, corrugated:
made from purchased materials
HQ: Westrock Rkt, Llc
1000 Abernathy Rd Ste 125
Atlanta GA 30328
770 448-2193

(P-5281)
WESTROCK RKT COMPANY
Also Called: Alliance Display & Packaging
100 E Tujunga Ave Ste 102, Burbank
(91502-1963)
PHONE...................................818 729-0610
Allen Kinder, *Branch Mgr*
EMP: 20
SALES (corp-wide): 16.2B **Publicly Held**
WEB: www.rocktenn.com
SIC: 2653 Boxes, corrugated: made from
purchased materials
HQ: Westrock Rkt, Llc
1000 Abernathy Rd Ste 125
Atlanta GA 30328
770 448-2193

(P-5282)
WESTROCK RKT COMPANY
536 S 2nd Ave, Covina (91723-3043)
PHONE...................................626 859-7633
EMP: 161
SALES (corp-wide): 16B **Publicly Held**
SIC: 2653 2679
HQ: Westrock Rkt Company
504 Thrasher St
Norcross GA 30328
770 448-2193

(P-5283)
WESTROCK USC INC
13820 Mica St, Santa Fe Springs
(90670-5728)
PHONE...................................562 282-0000
EMP: 11
SALES (corp-wide): 16.2B **Publicly Held**
SIC: 2653 Corrugated & solid fiber boxes
HQ: Westrock Usc, Inc.
1000 Abernathy Rd
Atlanta GA 30328
770 448-2193

(P-5284)
WESTROCK USC INC
13833 Freeway Dr, Santa Fe Springs
(90670-5701)
PHONE...................................562 282-4200
David Weissberg, *CEO*
EMP: 12
SALES (corp-wide): 16.2B **Publicly Held**
SIC: 2653 Boxes, corrugated: made from
purchased materials
HQ: Westrock Usc, Inc.
1000 Abernathy Rd
Atlanta GA 30328
770 448-2193

(P-5285)
WEYERHAEUSER COMPANY
Also Called: Los Angeles Sales Office-North
543 Country Club Dr, Simi Valley
(93065-0637)
PHONE...................................800 238-3676
Ralph Hathaway, *Branch Mgr*
EMP: 147
SALES (corp-wide): 7.4B **Publicly Held**
SIC: 2653 Corrugated boxes, partitions,
display items, sheets & pad
PA: Weyerhaeuser Company
220 Occidental Ave S
Seattle WA 98104
206 539-3000

2655 Fiber Cans, Tubes & Drums

(P-5286)
ADMAIL WEST INC
800 N 10th St Ste F, Sacramento
(95811-0342)
PHONE...................................916 554-5755
Mike Mc Bride, *Manager*
EMP: 95
SALES (corp-wide): 12.8MM **Privately Held**
SIC: 2655 Fiber shipping & mailing con-
tainers
PA: Admail West, Inc.
521 N 10th St
Sacramento CA 95811
916 442-3613

(P-5287)
CALIFORNIA COMPOSITE CONT CORP
22770 Perry St, Perris (92570-9725)
PHONE...................................951 940-9343
Jerry Martin, *President*
Richard Hull, *Vice Pres*
▲ **EMP:** 25
SQ FT: 18,000
SALES (est): 6.2MM **Privately Held**
SIC: 2655 Cans, fiber: made from pur-
chased material

(P-5288)
CARAUSTAR INDUSTRIES INC
Newark Recovery & Recycling
800b W Church St, Stockton (95203-3206)
P.O. Box 58044, Santa Clara (95052-8044)
PHONE...................................209 464-6590

Mark Vincent, *Opers-Prdtn-Mfg*
Kabrina Cabalar, *Admin Asst*
EMP: 250
SQ FT: 480,000
SALES (corp-wide): 3.8B **Publicly Held**
WEB: www.newarkgroup.com
SIC: 2655 Fiber cans, drums & similar
products
HQ: Caraustar Industries, Inc.
5000 Austell Powder Sprin
Austell GA 30106
770 948-3101

(P-5289)
CARAUSTAR INDUSTRIES INC
4502 E Airport Dr, Ontario (91761-7820)
PHONE...................................951 685-5544
D Wever Paul Potter, *Manager*
EMP: 43
SALES (corp-wide): 3.8B **Publicly Held**
WEB:
www.newarkpaperboardproducts.com
SIC: 2655 Tubes, fiber or paper: made
from purchased material
HQ: Caraustar Industries, Inc.
5000 Austell Powder Sprin
Austell GA 30106
770 948-3101

(P-5290)
CARAUSTAR INDUSTRIES INC
Also Called: California Paperboard
525 Mathew St, Santa Clara (95050-3001)
P.O. Box 58044 (95052-8044)
PHONE...................................408 845-7600
Stephen G Blankenship, *Manager*
Larry Lacotti, *Marketing Staff*
EMP: 120
SQ FT: 61,005
SALES (corp-wide): 3.8B **Publicly Held**
WEB: www.newarkgroup.com
SIC: 2655 Fiber cans, drums & similar
products
HQ: Caraustar Industries, Inc.
5000 Austell Powder Sprin
Austell GA 30106
770 948-3101

(P-5291)
COMPOSITE SUPPORT AND SLTNS IN
767 W Channel St, San Pedro
(90731-1411)
PHONE...................................310 514-3162
Clem Hill, *President*
Hilde Hiel, *Admin Sec*
EMP: 16
SALES (est): 1.4MM **Privately Held**
SIC: 2655 Cans, composite: foil-fiber &
other: from purchased fiber

(P-5292)
DORCO ELECTRONICS INC
Also Called: Dorco Fiberglass Products
13540 Larwin Cir, Santa Fe Springs
(90670-5031)
PHONE...................................562 623-1133
Ted Casmer, *President*
Gary Dexter, *Vice Pres*
EMP: 16 **EST:** 1958
SQ FT: 7,000
SALES (est): 3MM **Privately Held**
WEB: www.dorco.com
SIC: 2655 Bobbins, fiber: made from pur-
chased material

(P-5293)
GREEN PRODUCTS PACKAGING CORP
Also Called: California Composite Container
22770 Perry St, Perris (92570-9725)
PHONE...................................951 940-9343
Paul Z Rachina, *CEO*
Corina Rachina, *Corp Secy*
EMP: 14
SQ FT: 28,000
SALES (est): 2.1MM **Privately Held**
SIC: 2655 Ammunition cans or tubes,
board laminated with metal foil

(P-5294)
GREIF INC
2400 Cooper Ave, Merced (95348-4310)
P.O. Box 2146 (95344-0146)
PHONE...................................209 383-4396
Farrell Smith, *Manager*

Larry Allen, *Sales Executive*
EMP: 75
SALES (corp-wide): 3.8B **Publicly Held**
WEB: www.greif.com
SIC: 2655 Fiber cans, drums & similar
products
PA: Greif, Inc.
425 Winter Rd
Delaware OH 43015
740 549-6000

(P-5295)
GREIF INC
Also Called: Western Division
235 San Pedro Ave, Morgan Hill
(95037-5236)
PHONE...................................408 779-2161
John Saldate, *Plant Mgr*
Amanda Woodward, *Purch Mgr*
Fran Sorci, *Manager*
Evan Thomas, *Manager*
EMP: 72
SQ FT: 105,731
SALES (corp-wide): 3.8B **Publicly Held**
WEB: www.greif.com
SIC: 2655 Drums, fiber: made from pur-
chased material
PA: Greif, Inc.
425 Winter Rd
Delaware OH 43015
740 549-6000

(P-5296)
GREIF INC
Western Division
5701 Fresca Dr, La Palma (90623-1009)
PHONE...................................714 523-9580
George Grace, *Manager*
Rey Cardenas, *QC Mgr*
Bob Gentry, *Production*
EMP: 60
SQ FT: 72,000
SALES (corp-wide): 3.8B **Publicly Held**
WEB: www.greif.com
SIC: 2655 5085 3412 2674 Drums, fiber:
made from purchased material; commer-
cial containers; metal barrels, drums &
pails; bags: uncoated paper & multiwall
PA: Greif, Inc.
425 Winter Rd
Delaware OH 43015
740 549-6000

(P-5297)
HUHTAMAKI INC
8450 Gerber Rd, Sacramento
(95828-3712)
PHONE...................................916 688-4938
Carl Graf, *Opers Spvr*
EMP: 12
SALES (corp-wide): 3.5B **Privately Held**
SIC: 2655 Fiber cans, drums & similar
products
HQ: Huhtamaki, Inc.
9201 Packaging Dr
De Soto KS 66018
913 583-3025

(P-5298)
ICSH PARENT INC
1540 S Greenwood Ave, Montebello
(90640-6536)
P.O. Box 2067 (90640-1467)
PHONE...................................323 724-8507
Charles Veniez, *President*
EMP: 98
SALES (est): 8.9MM **Privately Held**
SIC: 2655 5085 Fiber cans, drums & con-
tainers; drums, fiber: made from pur-
chased material; drums, new or
reconditioned

(P-5299)
PACIFIC PAPER TUBE INC (PA)
4343 E Fremont St, Stockton (95215-4032)
PHONE...................................510 562-8823
Toll Free:...................................888 -
Patrick Wallace, *President*
Colleen Wallace, *Vice Pres*
Nancy Wallace, *Admin Sec*
▲ **EMP:** 50
SQ FT: 85,000
SALES (est): 23.4MM **Privately Held**
WEB: www.pacificpapertube.com
SIC: 2655 Tubes, fiber or paper: made
from purchased material

(P-5300)
PLASTOPAN INDUSTRIES INC (PA)
812 E 59th St, Los Angeles (90001-1006)
PHONE..................................323 231-2225
Ronald D Miller, *President*
Martin L Miller, *Vice Pres*
Sofia G Miller, *Vice Pres*
Catherine M Bump, *Admin Sec*
Eric J Scala, *Accountant*
EMP: 40
SQ FT: 48,000
SALES: 3.1MM **Privately Held**
WEB: www.plastopan.com
SIC: 2655 Fiber cans, drums & similar products

(P-5301)
RECTANGULAR TUBING INC
Also Called: Rti
333 Newquist Pl, City of Industry (91745-1027)
PHONE..................................626 333-7884
Dennis Sherlin, *President*
Emily Sherlin, *CFO*
Perry Regf,
EMP: 10 **EST:** 1959
SQ FT: 6,000
SALES (est): 1.5MM **Privately Held**
WEB: www.rectube.com
SIC: 2655 3496 Tubes, fiber or paper: made from purchased material; miscellaneous fabricated wire products

(P-5302)
SGL COMPOSITES INC (DH)
1551 W 139th St, Gardena (90249-2603)
PHONE..................................424 329-5250
David Otterson, *CEO*
Jeff Schade, *Vice Pres*
Joe Greco, *Prdtn Mgr*
Simon Ricks, *Manager*
▼ **EMP:** 90
SALES (est): 29.1MM
SALES (corp-wide): 1.2B **Privately Held**
SIC: 2655 Fiber cans, drums & similar products
HQ: Sgl Carbon, Llc
　10715 David Taylor Dr # 460
　Charlotte NC 28262
　704 593-5100

(P-5303)
SPIRAL PPR TUBE & CORE CO INC
5200 Industry Ave, Pico Rivera (90660-2506)
PHONE..................................562 801-9705
George Hibard, *CEO*
Summer Hibard, *Vice Pres*
▲ **EMP:** 45
SQ FT: 40,000
SALES (est): 11MM **Privately Held**
SIC: 2655 Fiber cans, drums & similar products

(P-5304)
STABLCOR TECHNOLOGY INC
17011 Beach Blvd Ste 900, Huntington Beach (92647-5998)
PHONE..................................714 375-6644
Doug S Schneider, *President*
EMP: 10
SQ FT: 3,000
SALES (est): 985.7K **Privately Held**
SIC: 2655 Cans, composite: foil-fiber & other: from purchased fiber

(P-5305)
TUBE-TAINER INC
8174 Byron Rd, Whittier (90606-2616)
PHONE..................................562 945-3711
Mike Mundia, *President*
▲ **EMP:** 45 **EST:** 1967
SQ FT: 44,000
SALES (est): 2.1MM **Privately Held**
WEB: www.tubetainer.com
SIC: 2655 Tubes, fiber or paper: made from purchased material

---

2656 Sanitary Food Containers

(P-5306)
AMSCAN INC
Ampro
804 W Town And Country Rd, Orange (92868-4712)
PHONE..................................714 972-2626
James Bell, *Branch Mgr*
EMP: 52
SALES (corp-wide): 2.4B **Publicly Held**
SIC: 2656 Cups, paper: made from purchased material
HQ: Amscan Inc.
　80 Grasslands Rd Ste 3
　Elmsford NY 10523
　914 345-2020

(P-5307)
GEORGIA-PACIFIC LLC
3630 E Wawona Ave Ste 104, Fresno (93725-9028)
PHONE..................................559 485-4900
Daniel August, *General Mgr*
EMP: 225
SALES (corp-wide): 40.6B **Privately Held**
WEB: www.gp.com
SIC: 2656 Sanitary food containers
HQ: Georgia-Pacific Llc
　133 Peachtree St Nw
　Atlanta GA 30303
　404 652-4000

(P-5308)
LOLLICUP USA INC (HQ)
Also Called: Lollicup Tea Zone
6185 Kimball Ave, Chino (91708-9126)
PHONE..................................626 965-8882
Alan Yu, *President*
Marvin Cheng, *Vice Pres*
Amy Tsen, *Vice Pres*
Billy Pham, *Site Mgr*
Vanessa Yu, *Sales Staff*
◆ **EMP:** 33 **EST:** 2000
SQ FT: 9,800
SALES (est): 13.7MM
SALES (corp-wide): 175.4MM **Privately Held**
WEB: www.lollicupstore.com
SIC: 2656 Paper cups, plates, dishes & utensils
PA: Karat Packaging Inc.
　6185 Kimball Ave
　Chino CA 91708
　626 965-8882

(P-5309)
S W C GROUP INC
Also Called: Carryoutsupplies.com
2399 Bateman Ave, Duarte (91010-3313)
PHONE..................................888 982-1628
Jimmy Chan, *CEO*
◆ **EMP:** 30
SQ FT: 18,000
SALES: 8MM **Privately Held**
SIC: 2656 Sanitary food containers

(P-5310)
YOCUP COMPANY
13711 S Main St, Los Angeles (90061-2165)
PHONE..................................310 884-9888
Jian Yin Liang, *President*
▲ **EMP:** 14 **EST:** 2009
SALES (est): 619.6K **Privately Held**
SIC: 2656 Cups, paper: made from purchased material

2657 Folding Paperboard Boxes

(P-5311)
BOXES R US INC
Also Called: Ultimate Paper Box Company
15051 Don Julian Rd, City of Industry (91746-3302)
PHONE..................................626 820-5410
Janak P Patel, *President*
Dipak Patel, *Vice Pres*
Eric Haikara, *Sales Mgr*
Damon Francis, *Accounts Mgr*
▲ **EMP:** 70
SQ FT: 38,000
SALES (est): 24.2MM **Privately Held**
SIC: 2657 Folding paperboard boxes

(P-5312)
CRAFTON CARTON
31790 Hayman St, Hayward (94544-7934)
PHONE..................................510 441-5985
Glenn Boatley, *President*
Diane Boatley, *Vice Pres*
EMP: 20
SQ FT: 20,000
SALES (est): 3.3MM **Privately Held**
WEB: www.sierrapack.com
SIC: 2657 Folding paperboard boxes

(P-5313)
EVERETT GRAPHICS INC
7300 Edgewater Dr, Oakland (94621-3006)
PHONE..................................510 577-6777
Munson Wittman Everett, *President*
Mark Carlson, *CFO*
John F Everett, *Vice Pres*
John Everett, *Admin Sec*
Adrienne Dikitanan, *Administration*
▲ **EMP:** 75
SQ FT: 100,000
SALES (est): 34.9MM **Privately Held**
WEB: www.everettgraphics.com
SIC: 2657 Folding paperboard boxes

(P-5314)
ROYAL PAPER BOX CO CALIFORNIA (PA)
1105 S Maple Ave, Montebello (90640-6007)
P.O. Box 458 (90640-0458)
PHONE..................................323 728-7041
Jim Hodges, *CEO*
Darryl Carlson, *Vice Pres*
Scott Larson, *Vice Pres*
Steve Perez, *Vice Pres*
Andy Polanco, *Vice Pres*
▲ **EMP:** 117
SQ FT: 172,500
SALES: 50MM **Privately Held**
WEB: www.royalpaperbox.com
SIC: 2657 Folding paperboard boxes

(P-5315)
SAN DIEGO PAPER BOX CO INC
10605 Jamacha Blvd, Spring Valley (91978-2098)
PHONE..................................619 660-9566
Richard D Chapman, *President*
Reyna Paniagua, *Admin Asst*
EMP: 30 **EST:** 1906
SQ FT: 100,000
SALES (est): 8.1MM **Privately Held**
WEB: www.sdpbc.com
SIC: 2657 Folding paperboard boxes

(P-5316)
T & T BOX COMPANY INC
Also Called: Thomas Container & Packaging
1353 Philadelphia St, Pomona (91766-5554)
PHONE..................................909 465-0848
Thomas Murphy, *CEO*
Andy Murphy, *Vice Pres*
EMP: 22
SQ FT: 60,000
SALES (est): 4.7MM **Privately Held**
WEB: www.thomascontainer.com
SIC: 2657 2653 Folding paperboard boxes; corrugated & solid fiber boxes

(P-5317)
THERMAL BAGS BY INGRID INC
5801 Skylab Rd, Huntington Beach (92647-2051)
PHONE..................................847 836-4400
Ingrid Kosar, *Owner*
Mary Denicolo, *Sales Mgr*
▲ **EMP:** 18
SALES (est): 3.9MM **Privately Held**
WEB: www.thermalbags.com
SIC: 2657 Food containers, folding: made from purchased material

(P-5318)
TWPM INC
Also Called: 3 Ball Co
15320 Valley View Ave, La Mirada (90638-5236)
PHONE..................................714 522-8881
Seon H Sohn, *Principal*
Nancy Hwang, *CFO*
EMP: 11
SQ FT: 10,000
SALES: 1MM **Privately Held**
SIC: 2657 Food containers, folding: made from purchased material

(P-5319)
UNITED PAPER BOX INC
Also Called: California Button
1530 Lakeview Loop, Anaheim (92807-1819)
PHONE..................................714 777-8383
Ron Silverstein, *President*
John Hynes, *Exec VP*
H Rosie Silverstein, *Admin Sec*
EMP: 20
SALES (est): 1.7MM **Privately Held**
WEB: www.californiabutton.com
SIC: 2657 3544 7389 5113 Folding paperboard boxes; special dies, tools, jigs & fixtures; laminating service; bags, paper & disposable plastic

(P-5320)
YAVAR MANUFACTURING CO INC
Also Called: National Packaging Products
1900 S Tubeway Ave, Commerce (90040-1612)
PHONE..................................323 722-2040
Massoud Afari, *CEO*
▲ **EMP:** 23
SQ FT: 50,000
SALES (est): 5.9MM **Privately Held**
SIC: 2657 Folding paperboard boxes

2671 Paper Coating & Laminating for Packaging

(P-5321)
AMCOR FLEXIBLES LLC
5425 Broadway St, American Canyon (94503-9678)
PHONE..................................707 257-6481
Richard Evans, *Branch Mgr*
Rodrigo Lecot, *Vice Pres*
Brad Philip, *Engineer*
George Bodreau, *Finance Mgr*
Michele Evans, *Analyst*
EMP: 135 **Privately Held**
SIC: 2671 2621 2821 3081 Plastic film, coated or laminated for packaging; packaging paper; plastics materials & resins; packing materials, plastic sheet; closures, stamped metal
HQ: Amcor Flexibles Llc
　2150 E Lake Cook Rd
　Buffalo Grove IL 60089
　224 313-7000

(P-5322)
AMCOR FLEXIBLES LLC
5416 Union Pacific Ave, Commerce (90022-5117)
PHONE..................................323 721-6777
Graeme Liebelt, *Branch Mgr*
EMP: 135 **Privately Held**
SIC: 2671 2621 2821 3081 Plastic film, coated or laminated for packaging; packaging paper; plastics materials & resins; packing materials, plastic sheet; closures, stamped metal
HQ: Amcor Flexibles Llc
　2150 E Lake Cook Rd
　Buffalo Grove IL 60089
　224 313-7000

(P-5323)
ATRA INTERNATIONAL TRADERS INC
3301 Leonis Blvd, Vernon (90058-3013)
PHONE..................................562 864-3885
Alex Patel, *President*
▼ **EMP:** 30

SALES (est): 4.7MM **Privately Held**
SIC: 2671 Packaging paper & plastics film, coated & laminated

(P-5324)
AUDIO VIDEO COLOR CORPORATION (PA)
Also Called: Avc
17707 S Santa Fe Ave, Compton (90221-5419)
PHONE..................424 213-7500
Kali J Limath, *CEO*
Jim Hardiman, *President*
Guy Marrom, *Exec VP*
▲ EMP: 86
SQ FT: 78,000
SALES (est): 68.1MM **Privately Held**
WEB: www.avccorp.com
SIC: 2671 Packaging paper & plastics film, coated & laminated

(P-5325)
BEU INDUSTRIES INC
2937 E Maria St, E Rncho Dmngz (90221-5801)
PHONE.................310 885-9626
Jeffrey Beu, *President*
Ken Beu Jr, *Vice Pres*
EMP: 30
SALES (est): 3.8MM **Privately Held**
SIC: 2671 Packaging paper & plastics film, coated & laminated

(P-5326)
CARRYOUT BAGS INC (PA)
3592 Rosemead Blvd # 513, Rosemead (91770-2053)
PHONE.................626 279-7000
Daniel Emrani, *CEO*
EMP: 10
SALES (est): 5.4MM **Privately Held**
SIC: 2671 Plastic film, coated or laminated for packaging

(P-5327)
ESHIELDS LLC
2307 Country Clb Vista St, Glendora (91741-4060)
PHONE.................909 305-8848
Andrew Mason, *Mng Member*
David Clifford,
Eleanora Clifford,
Theani Davis, *Director*
▲ EMP: 32 EST: 2006
SQ FT: 1,500
SALES (est): 5.6MM **Privately Held**
SIC: 2671 Plastic film, coated or laminated for packaging

(P-5328)
GLOBAL LINK SOURCING INC
41690 Corporate Center Ct, Murrieta (92562-7084)
PHONE.................951 698-1977
Jullie Annet, *President*
Mike Deigan, *VP Bus Dvlpt*
Lanette Johnson, *Office Mgr*
Tony Montalbano, *Graphic Designe*
▲ EMP: 70
SQ FT: 80,000
SALES (est): 15MM **Privately Held**
SIC: 2671 Packaging paper & plastics film, coated & laminated

(P-5329)
GREAT NORTHERN CORPORATION
Laminations West
12075 Cabernet Dr, Fontana (92337-7703)
PHONE.................951 361-4770
Josh Coldiron, *Plant Mgr*
Sally Brewer, *Executive*
EMP: 35
SALES (corp-wide): 521.9MM **Privately Held**
SIC: 2671 Paper coated or laminated for packaging
PA: Great Northern Corporation
395 Stroebe Rd
Appleton WI 54914
920 739-3671

(P-5330)
LIFE LINE PACKAGING INC
Also Called: Life Line Products
1250 Pierre Way, El Cajon (92021-4608)
PHONE.................619 444-2737
Miguel Lackenbacher, *President*
EMP: 15
SQ FT: 16,000
SALES (est): 907.5K **Privately Held**
WEB: www.lifelinepackaging.com
SIC: 2671 3089 5113 7336 Thermoplastic coated paper for packaging; thermoformed finished plastic products; shipping supplies; package design

(P-5331)
MICHELSEN PACKAGING CO CAL
Also Called: Michelsen Packaging California
4165 S Cherry Ave, Fresno (93706-5709)
P.O. Box 10109 (93745-0109)
PHONE.................559 237-3819
Dan Keck, *President*
Debbie Falcon, *Office Mgr*
Jason Cline, *Plant Mgr*
Chad Gregerson, *Regl Sales Mgr*
EMP: 25
SALES (corp-wide): 74.6MM **Privately Held**
SIC: 2671 2674 Packaging paper & plastics film, coated & laminated; paper bags: made from purchased materials
PA: Michelsen Packaging Company Of California
202 N 2nd Ave
Yakima WA 98902
509 248-6270

(P-5332)
NORMAN PAPER AND FOAM CO INC
Also Called: Norman International
4501 S Santa Fe Ave, Vernon (90058-2129)
PHONE.................323 582-7132
Norman Levine, *President*
Christopher Werner, *CFO*
Ellen Levine, *Corp Secy*
Chris Werner, *Vice Pres*
Dawnn Winter, *Vice Pres*
▲ EMP: 23 EST: 1980
SQ FT: 40,000
SALES (est): 5.8MM **Privately Held**
SIC: 2671 3086 2673 Packaging paper & plastics film, coated & laminated; packaging & shipping materials, foamed plastic; bags: plastic, laminated & coated

(P-5333)
OSIO INTERNATIONAL INC
2550 E Cerritos Ave, Anaheim (92806-5627)
PHONE.................714 935-9700
Don H Kwon, *CEO*
Rick Whipple, *Vice Pres*
Matthew Hendricks, *General Mgr*
Carol Blackwell, *Accounting Mgr*
▲ EMP: 11
SQ FT: 7,500
SALES (est): 12MM **Privately Held**
WEB: www.osiopack.com
SIC: 2671 8711 Paper coated or laminated for packaging; industrial engineers

(P-5334)
PACIFIC SOUTHWEST CONT LLC (PA)
4530 Leckron Rd, Modesto (95357-0517)
PHONE.................209 526-0444
John W Mayol, *Mng Member*
Lester H Mangold, *CFO*
Kevin Allen, *Vice Pres*
Art Holdridge, *Technician*
Richard Rapp, *Technician*
▲ EMP: 347
SQ FT: 129,600
SALES (est): 159.4MM **Privately Held**
SIC: 2671 2657 3086 2653 Packaging paper & plastics film, coated & laminated; folding paperboard boxes; packaging & shipping materials, foamed plastic; boxes, corrugated: made from purchased materials; commercial printing, lithographic

(P-5335)
PACIFIC SOUTHWEST CONT LLC
671 Mariposa Rd, Modesto (95354-4145)
PHONE.................209 526-0444
EMP: 11
SALES (corp-wide): 159.4MM **Privately Held**
SIC: 2671 2657 3086 2653 Packaging paper & plastics film, coated & laminated; folding paperboard boxes; packaging & shipping materials, foamed plastic; boxes, corrugated: made from purchased materials; commercial printing, lithographic
PA: Pacific Southwest Container, Llc
4530 Leckron Rd
Modesto CA 95357
209 526-0444

(P-5336)
PAPERCUTTERS INC
6023 Bandini Blvd, Los Angeles (90040-2904)
PHONE.................323 888-1330
Susan Feinstein, *President*
Joyce Feinstein, *Corp Secy*
Beth Feinstein, *Vice Pres*
▲ EMP: 21
SQ FT: 20,000
SALES (est): 4.9MM **Privately Held**
WEB: www.papercutters.net
SIC: 2671 5113 Packaging paper & plastics film, coated & laminated; paper & products, wrapping or coarse

(P-5337)
PGAC CORP (PA)
9630 Ridgehaven Ct Ste B, San Diego (92123-5605)
PHONE.................858 560-8213
Mark Grantham, *President*
Florentina Shields, *Vice Pres*
EMP: 75
SALES (est): 86.8MM **Privately Held**
SIC: 2671 Paper coated or laminated for packaging

(P-5338)
PRECISION LABEL INC
659 Benet Rd, Oceanside (92058-1208)
P.O. Box 766, Solana Beach (92075-0766)
PHONE.................760 757-7533
Robert A Wilcox, *President*
EMP: 30 EST: 1991
SQ FT: 7,000
SALES (est): 7.8MM **Privately Held**
SIC: 2671 2759 Packaging paper & plastics film, coated & laminated; labels & seals: printing

(P-5339)
QUALITY CONTAINER CORP
866 Towne Center Dr, Pomona (91767-5902)
P.O. Box 1297, Claremont (91711-1297)
PHONE.................909 482-1850
Edward J Kaleff, *CEO*
EMP: 18
SALES (est): 5.7MM **Privately Held**
SIC: 2671 Packaging paper & plastics film, coated & laminated

(P-5340)
SAMCO PLASTICS INC
Also Called: Sambrailo Packaging
1260 W Beach St, Watsonville (95076)
P.O. Box 50090 (95077-5090)
PHONE.................831 761-1392
William Sambrailo, *President*
Mark Sambrailo, *President*
Michael Sambrailo, *Vice Pres*
EMP: 12
SQ FT: 30,000
SALES (est): 1.4MM **Privately Held**
SIC: 2671 Plastic film, coated or laminated for packaging

(P-5341)
STERIPAX INC
5412 Research Dr, Huntington Beach (92649-1542)
PHONE.................714 892-8811
Steve Pearce, *President*
Linda Pearce, *Vice Pres*
▲ EMP: 47
SQ FT: 10,000
SALES (est): 27.9MM **Privately Held**
WEB: www.steripaxinc.com
SIC: 2671 Packaging paper & plastics film, coated & laminated

(P-5342)
SUMMIT INTERNATIONAL PACKG INC
Also Called: Western Summit Manufacturing
30200 Cartier Dr, Rancho Palos Verdes (90275-5722)
PHONE.................626 333-3333
Donald Clark, *President*
EMP: 85
SQ FT: 58,000
SALES (est): 11.3MM **Privately Held**
SIC: 2671 Plastic film, coated or laminated for packaging

(P-5343)
SUSTAINABLE FIBR SOLUTIONS LLC (PA)
30950 Rancho Viejo Rd, San Juan Capistrano (92675-1764)
PHONE.................949 265-8287
Raymond Taccolini, *President*
Diana Higby, *Accountant*
EMP: 11
SALES (est): 1.5MM **Privately Held**
SIC: 2671 Packaging paper & plastics film, coated & laminated

(P-5344)
TECHFLEX PACKAGING LLC
Also Called: Xsential
13771 Gramercy Pl, Gardena (90249-2470)
PHONE.................424 266-9400
Burt Siegelman,
Neil Kinney,
▲ EMP: 52
SALES (est): 15MM **Privately Held**
SIC: 2671 Plastic film, coated or laminated for packaging

(P-5345)
THERMECH CORPORATION
Also Called: Thermech Engineering
1773 W Lincoln Ave Ste I, Anaheim (92801-6713)
PHONE.................714 533-3183
Jim Shah, *CEO*
Richard Gorman, *President*
Sonia Bounds, *Purchasing*
EMP: 23
SQ FT: 24,000
SALES (est): 4.7MM **Privately Held**
WEB: www.thermech.com
SIC: 2671 3083 Packaging paper & plastics film, coated & laminated; plastic finished products, laminated

(P-5346)
TRIUNE ENTERPRISES INC
Also Called: Triune Enterprises Mfg
13711 S Normandie Ave, Gardena (90249-2609)
PHONE.................310 719-1600
John Christman, *CEO*
Sidney Arouh, *Vice Pres*
Donald Alhanati, *Admin Sec*
◆ EMP: 23
SQ FT: 29,000
SALES (est): 6.7MM **Privately Held**
SIC: 2671 5162 Plastic film, coated or laminated for packaging; resinous impregnated paper for packaging; plastics materials & basic shapes

(P-5347)
UOP LLC
2100 E Orangethorpe Ave, Anaheim (92806-1227)
PHONE.................714 870-7590
Lorraine Manandik, *Manager*
EMP: 30
SALES (corp-wide): 41.8B **Publicly Held**
SIC: 2671 Packaging paper & plastics film, coated & laminated
HQ: Uop Llc
25 E Algonquin Rd
Des Plaines IL 60016
847 391-2000

(P-5348)
VINYL TECHNOLOGY INC
200 Railroad Ave, Monrovia (91016-4643)
PHONE..................................626 443-5257
Carlos A Mollura, *Ch of Bd*
Daniel Mullora, *CEO*
Haydee Mollura, *Corp Secy*
Rodney Mollura, *Exec VP*
Carlos Mollura Jr, *Vice Pres*
▲ **EMP:** 200
SQ FT: 68,000
SALES (est): 72.3MM **Privately Held**
WEB: www.vinyltechnology.com
SIC: 2671 7389 Plastic film, coated or laminated for packaging; sewing contractor

---

2672 Paper Coating & Laminating, Exc for Packaging

(P-5349)
AVERY DENNISON CORPORATION (PA)
207 N Goode Ave, Glendale (91203-1301)
PHONE..................................626 304-2000
Mitchell R Butier, *Ch of Bd*
Georges Gravanis, *President*
Gregory S Lovins, *CFO*
Julia Stewart, *Bd of Directors*
Anne Hill, *Officer*
EMP: 277
SALES: 7.1B **Publicly Held**
WEB: www.avery.com
SIC: 2672 3081 3497 2678 Adhesive papers, labels or tapes: from purchased material; gummed paper: made from purchased materials; coated paper, except photographic, carbon or abrasive; unsupported plastics film & sheet; metal foil & leaf; notebooks: made from purchased paper

(P-5350)
AVERY DENNISON CORPORATION
50 Pointe Dr, Brea (92821-3652)
PHONE..................................714 674-8500
Rick Alonzo, *Manager*
Paul Prince, *Regional Mgr*
Coleen Alberico, *Human Res Mgr*
Carrie Knipfer, *Marketing Staff*
Tony Hill, *Facilities Mgr*
EMP: 400
SALES (corp-wide): 7.1B **Publicly Held**
WEB: www.avery.com
SIC: 2672 3081 3497 2678 Adhesive papers, labels or tapes: from purchased material; unsupported plastics film & sheet; metal foil & leaf; stationery products; pens & mechanical pencils; adhesives & sealants
PA: Avery Dennison Corporation
207 N Goode Ave
Glendale CA 91203
626 304-2000

(P-5351)
AVERY DENNISON CORPORATION
751 N Todd Ave, Azusa (91702-2244)
PHONE..................................626 938-7239
EMP: 115
SALES (corp-wide): 7.1B **Publicly Held**
SIC: 2672 3081 3497 2678 Adhesive papers, labels or tapes: from purchased material; gummed paper: made from purchased materials; coated paper, except photographic, carbon or abrasive; unsupported plastics film & sheet; metal foil & leaf; notebooks: made from purchased paper
PA: Avery Dennison Corporation
207 N Goode Ave
Glendale CA 91203
626 304-2000

(P-5352)
AVERY DENNISON CORPORATION
11195 Eucalyptus St, Rancho Cucamonga (91730-3836)
PHONE..................................909 987-4631
Marta E Corfaelb, *Manager*
EMP: 125
SALES (corp-wide): 7.1B **Publicly Held**
WEB: www.avery.com
SIC: 2672 Tape, pressure sensitive: made from purchased materials
PA: Avery Dennison Corporation
207 N Goode Ave
Glendale CA 91203
626 304-2000

(P-5353)
AVERY DENNISON CORPORATION
10721 Jasmine St, Fontana (92337-8200)
PHONE..................................909 428-4238
Bruce Elliott, *Manager*
EMP: 115
SALES (corp-wide): 7.1B **Publicly Held**
WEB: www.avery.com
SIC: 2672 Coated paper, except photographic, carbon or abrasive
PA: Avery Dennison Corporation
207 N Goode Ave
Glendale CA 91203
626 304-2000

(P-5354)
AVERY DENNISON CORPORATION
2900 Bradley St, Pasadena (91107-1560)
PHONE..................................626 304-2000
Dave Edwards, *Vice Pres*
Herman Hartono, *Engineer*
EMP: 120
SQ FT: 67,580
SALES (corp-wide): 7.1B **Publicly Held**
WEB: www.avery.com
SIC: 2672 2679 Adhesive papers, labels or tapes: from purchased material; coated paper, except photographic, carbon or abrasive; labels, paper: made from purchased material
PA: Avery Dennison Corporation
207 N Goode Ave
Glendale CA 91203
626 304-2000

(P-5355)
AVERY DENNISON CORPORATION
5819 Telegraph Rd, Commerce (90040-1515)
PHONE..................................323 728-8888
Justman Morley, *Branch Mgr*
EMP: 115
SALES (corp-wide): 7.1B **Publicly Held**
SIC: 2672 Adhesive backed films, foams & foils
PA: Avery Dennison Corporation
207 N Goode Ave
Glendale CA 91203
626 304-2000

(P-5356)
AVERY DENNISON CORPORATION
2743 Thompson Creek Rd, Pomona (91767-1861)
PHONE..................................626 304-2000
Jeffrey Stites, *Branch Mgr*
EMP: 115
SALES (corp-wide): 7.1B **Publicly Held**
SIC: 2672 Adhesive backed films, foams & foils
PA: Avery Dennison Corporation
207 N Goode Ave
Glendale CA 91203
626 304-2000

(P-5357)
BECKERS FABRICATION INC
Also Called: B F I Labels
22465 La Palma Ave, Yorba Linda (92887-3803)
PHONE..................................714 692-1600
Mark Becker, *CEO*
Dan Becker, *President*
David Beilfuss, *General Mgr*

James Steven, *Sales Staff*
Alma Fierro, *Accounts Mgr*
EMP: 24
SQ FT: 6,500
SALES (est): 6.5MM **Privately Held**
WEB: www.beckersfab.com
SIC: 2672 2759 Coated & laminated paper; screen printing

(P-5358)
BLC WC INC
Imperial Marking
2935 Whipple Rd, Union City (94587-1207)
PHONE..................................510 471-4100
John Kramer, *Manager*
EMP: 36
SALES (corp-wide): 16.2MM **Privately Held**
WEB: www.bestlabel.com
SIC: 2672 2671 Coated & laminated paper; packaging paper & plastics film, coated & laminated
PA: Blc Wc, Inc.
13260 Moore St
Cerritos CA 90703
562 926-1452

(P-5359)
CINTON
Also Called: West Coast Labels
620 Richfield Rd, Placentia (92870-6727)
PHONE..................................714 961-8808
Salvatore Scaffide, *President*
Romona Scaffide, *Vice Pres*
Cindi Montgomery, *Admin Sec*
Mark Trahanovski, *Mktg Dir*
Alie Delgado, *Sales Staff*
EMP: 46
SQ FT: 23,000
SALES (est): 10.4MM **Privately Held**
WEB: www.westcoastlabels.com
SIC: 2672 2679 Coated & laminated paper; labels, paper: made from purchased material

(P-5360)
CLARIANT CORPORATION
926 S 8th St, Colton (92324-3500)
P.O. Box 610 (92324-0610)
PHONE..................................909 825-1793
Kenneth Golder, *President*
Paul Gusman, *Site Mgr*
Jerri Traylor, *Manager*
EMP: 32
SALES (corp-wide): 6.6B **Privately Held**
SIC: 2672 7389 5199 Coated & laminated paper; packaging & labeling services; packaging materials
HQ: Clariant Corporation
4000 Monroe Rd
Charlotte NC 28205
704 331-7000

(P-5361)
EDWARDS ASSOC CMMNICATIONS INC (PA)
Also Called: Edwards Label
2277 Knoll Dr Ste A, Ventura (93003-5878)
PHONE..................................805 658-2626
Joel Horacio Gomez-Avila, *President*
John Edwards, *President*
Lisa Hernandez, *Engineer*
Garrett Boys, *Human Resources*
Melyssa Ho, *Mfg Staff*
EMP: 300
SQ FT: 44,000
SALES (est): 67.9MM **Privately Held**
SIC: 2672 Labels (unprinted), gummed: made from purchased materials; adhesive papers, labels or tapes: from purchased material

(P-5362)
HARRIS INDUSTRIES INC (PA)
5181 Argosy Ave, Huntington Beach (92649-1058)
P.O. Box 3269 (92605-3269)
PHONE..................................714 898-8048
William Helzer, *President*
Gail Helzer, *Corp Secy*
Joel Castillo, *Vice Pres*
◆ **EMP:** 60
SQ FT: 25,000
SALES (est): 21.3MM **Privately Held**
SIC: 2672 Tape, pressure sensitive: made from purchased materials

(P-5363)
HIS COMPANY INC
Precision Converting
400 E Parkridge Ave # 101, Corona (92879-6618)
PHONE..................................951 493-0200
George Cailloueepe, *Director*
EMP: 18
SALES (corp-wide): 263.1MM **Privately Held**
SIC: 2672 Adhesive backed films, foams & foils
PA: His Company, Inc.
6650 Concord Park Dr
Houston TX 77040
713 934-1600

(P-5364)
KING ABRASIVES INC
1942 National Ave, Hayward (94545-1710)
PHONE..................................510 785-8100
David D, *Co-CEO*
◆ **EMP:** 12
SALES: 200K **Privately Held**
SIC: 2672 3291 Adhesive papers, labels or tapes: from purchased material; abrasive wheels & grindstones, not artificial

(P-5365)
LABEL SERVICE INC
20008 Normandie Ave, Torrance (90502-1210)
PHONE..................................310 329-5605
Russell Nakada, *President*
Minoru Nakada, *Shareholder*
Peter Nakada, *Shareholder*
Kanji Yasutomi, *Shareholder*
EMP: 13
SQ FT: 7,700
SALES: 1.2MM **Privately Held**
SIC: 2672 2752 2679 Labels (unprinted), gummed: made from purchased materials; commercial printing, offset; labels, paper: made from purchased material

(P-5366)
LOGIC TECHNOLOGY INC (PA)
1138 W Evelyn Ave, Sunnyvale (94086-5742)
PHONE..................................408 530-1007
Henry Tan, *President*
EMP: 12 **EST:** 1971
SQ FT: 7,500
SALES (est): 2.1MM **Privately Held**
SIC: 2672 Coated & laminated paper

(P-5367)
MARCAFLEX INC
2 Seville Dr, San Rafael (94903-1561)
PHONE..................................415 472-4423
Mario Cataldi, *President*
EMP: 15
SALES (est): 2.2MM **Privately Held**
WEB: www.marcaflex.com
SIC: 2672 3961 Labels (unprinted), gummed: made from purchased materials; keychains, except precious metal

(P-5368)
MILLER PRODUCTS INC
Also Called: Mpi Label Systems
2315 Station Dr, Stockton (95215-7928)
P.O. Box 5543 (95205-0543)
PHONE..................................209 467-2470
Spencer Cser, *Principal*
EMP: 60
SALES (corp-wide): 36.3MM **Privately Held**
SIC: 2672 2679 2759 Adhesive papers, labels or tapes: from purchased material; labels, paper: made from purchased material; commercial printing
PA: Miller Products, Inc.
450 Courtney Rd
Sebring OH 44672
330 938-2134

(P-5369)
MPS LANSING INC
Also Called: John Henry Packaging West
101 H St Ste M, Petaluma (94952-5100)
PHONE..................................707 778-1250
Dan Welty, *President*
EMP: 30

▲ = Import ▼=Export
◆ =Import/Export

SALES (corp-wide): 16.2B **Publicly Held**
WEB: www.thejohnhenrycompany.com
SIC: 2672 2754 Coated & laminated paper; commercial printing, gravure
HQ: Lansing Mps Inc
   5800 W Grand River Ave
   Lansing MI 48906
   517 323-9000

(P-5370)
NITTO AMERICAS INC (HQ)
Also Called: Permacel-Automotive
48500 Fremont Blvd, Fremont (94538-6579)
PHONE......................510 445-5400
Toru Takeuchi, *Ch of Bd*
Yoichiro Sakuma, *President*
Steve Evans, *CFO*
Aryo Nikopour, *Vice Pres*
Jeff Wolbert, *General Mgr*
◆ **EMP:** 125 **EST:** 1968
SQ FT: 168,000
SALES (est): 334MM **Privately Held**
SIC: 2672 3589 5162 5065 Tape, pressure sensitive: made from purchased materials; water treatment equipment, industrial; plastics products; electronic parts

(P-5371)
PRECISION DYNAMICS CORPORATION (HQ)
Also Called: Pdc-Identicard
25124 Sprngfeld Ct Ste 20, Valencia (91355)
PHONE......................818 897-1111
J Michael Nauman, *CEO*
Robin Barber, *Vice Pres*
Robert Case, *Vice Pres*
John Park, *Vice Pres*
Kris Oberdick, *Admin Asst*
◆ **EMP:** 184 **EST:** 1956
SQ FT: 75,000
SALES (corp-wide): 85.4MM
SALES (corp-wide): 1.1B **Publicly Held**
WEB: www.pdcorp.com
SIC: 2672 2754 5047 3069 Adhesive papers, labels or tapes: from purchased material; labels (unprinted), gummed: made from purchased materials; labels: gravure printing; instruments, surgical & medical; tape, pressure sensitive: rubber
PA: Brady Corporation
   6555 W Good Hope Rd
   Milwaukee WI 53223
   414 358-6600

(P-5372)
RICHARDS LABEL CO INC
17291 Mount Herrmann St, Fountain Valley (92708-4117)
PHONE......................714 529-1791
Kyle Richards, *President*
Leigh Richards, *Treasurer*
Gary Richards, *Vice Pres*
Julie Sagat - Ofc, *Manager*
EMP: 12
SQ FT: 6,300
SALES (est): 1.4MM **Privately Held**
WEB: www.richardslabel.com
SIC: 2672 Labels (unprinted), gummed: made from purchased materials

(P-5373)
SCAPA TAPES NORTH AMERICA LLC
540 N Oak St, Inglewood (90302-2942)
PHONE......................310 419-0567
Kevin Ryan, *Branch Mgr*
EMP: 42
SALES (corp-wide): 401.1MM **Privately Held**
SIC: 2672 Adhesive papers, labels or tapes: from purchased material
HQ: Scapa Tapes North America Llc
   111 Great Pond Dr
   Windsor CT 06095
   860 688-8000

(P-5374)
SEAL METHODS INC (PA)
11915 Shoemaker Ave, Santa Fe Springs (90670-4717)
P.O. Box 2604 (90670-0604)
PHONE......................562 944-0291
Eugene Welter, *Principal*

Joseph Evans, *General Mgr*
Geri Welter, *Admin Sec*
Michael O'Donnell, *Business Mgr*
Kari Welter, *Purch Mgr*
▲ **EMP:** 90 **EST:** 1974
SQ FT: 75,000
SALES (est): 31.2MM **Privately Held**
WEB: www.sealmethodsinc.com
SIC: 2672 3053 5085 Masking tape: made from purchased materials; tape, pressure sensitive: made from purchased materials; gaskets, all materials; packing, rubber; gaskets; seals, industrial

(P-5375)
TAPE & LABEL CONVERTERS INC
8231 Allport Ave, Santa Fe Springs (90670-2105)
P.O. Box 398, Pico Rivera (90660-0398)
PHONE......................562 945-3486
Toll Free:......................888 -
Robert Varela Jr, *President*
Jeanette Verela, *Admin Sec*
Roger Varela, *Sales Staff*
EMP: 20
SQ FT: 3,625
SALES (est): 3.7MM **Privately Held**
SIC: 2672 2782 2752 2671 Labels (unprinted), gummed: made from purchased materials; blankbooks & looseleaf binders; commercial printing, lithographic; packaging paper & plastics film, coated & laminated

(P-5376)
TAPE FACTORY INC
Also Called: American Decal Company
11899 Lotus Ave, Fountain Valley (92708-2637)
PHONE......................714 979-7742
Paul Riccobon, *President*
EMP: 20
SQ FT: 17,000
SALES (est): 5.2MM **Privately Held**
SIC: 2672 Tape, pressure sensitive: made from purchased materials

(P-5377)
UPM RAFLATAC INC
1105 Auto Center Dr, Ontario (91761-2213)
PHONE......................909 390-4657
Alan Punch, *Manager*
EMP: 20
SALES (corp-wide): 12B **Privately Held**
WEB: www.raflatac.com
SIC: 2672 2679 Coated & laminated paper; labels, paper: made from purchased material
HQ: Upm Raflatac, Inc.
   400 Broadpointe Dr
   Mills River NC 28759
   828 651-4800

(P-5378)
VERSATRACTION INC
1424 Ritchey St Ste C, Santa Ana (92705-4757)
PHONE......................714 973-4589
Jason Neu, *President*
EMP: 17
SQ FT: 5,000
SALES (est): 2.6MM **Privately Held**
SIC: 2672 Adhesive backed films, foams & foils

(P-5379)
VINTAGE 99 LABEL MFG INC
611 Enterprise Ct, Livermore (94550-5200)
PHONE......................925 294-5270
Mark Gonzales, *CEO*
Kathy Gonzales, *President*
Samantha Gomez, *Creative Dir*
Brian Lloyd, *Sales Dir*
Daniel Hughes, *Manager*
EMP: 21 **EST:** 1999
SALES (est): 5.7MM **Privately Held**
WEB: www.vintage99.com
SIC: 2672 2752 Adhesive papers, labels or tapes: from purchased material; commercial printing, lithographic

(P-5380)
WESTROCK CP LLC
2363 Boulevard Cir Ste 4, Walnut Creek (94595-1173)
PHONE......................925 946-0842
Robert Scheer, *Manager*
EMP: 88
SALES (corp-wide): 16.2B **Publicly Held**
WEB: www.smurfit-stone.com
SIC: 2672 Coated & laminated paper
HQ: Westrock Cp, Llc
   1000 Abernathy Rd
   Atlanta GA 30328

2673 Bags: Plastics, Laminated & Coated

(P-5381)
ADAMANT ENTERPRISE INC
2326 Jurado Ave, Hacienda Heights (91745-4423)
PHONE......................626 934-3399
Angie WEI, *CEO*
Yung C WEI, *Vice Pres*
Teresa WEI, *Admin Sec*
▲ **EMP:** 35
SQ FT: 40,000
SALES (est): 7.3MM **Privately Held**
SIC: 2673 Plastic & pliofilm bags

(P-5382)
ADVANCED ADBAG PACKAGING INC
597 Quarry Rd, San Carlos (94070-6222)
P.O. Box 1048 (94070-1048)
PHONE......................650 591-1625
Carmen Nevaro, *President*
Dan Bridgeman, *Vice Pres*
Kevin Neadeau, *Vice Pres*
▲ **EMP:** 10 **EST:** 1981
SALES (est): 2.3MM **Privately Held**
WEB: www.adbag-inc.com
SIC: 2673 Cellophane bags, unprinted: made from purchased materials

(P-5383)
ALLSTATE PLASTICS LLC
1763 Sabre St, Hayward (94545-1015)
PHONE......................510 783-9600
Angela Leung, *Mng Member*
Yau CHI Leung,
◆ **EMP:** 17
SQ FT: 26,538
SALES (est): 4.2MM **Privately Held**
SIC: 2673 Plastic & pliofilm bags

(P-5384)
ASIA PLASTICS INC
9347 Rush St, South El Monte (91733-2544)
PHONE......................626 448-8100
Kent Ung, *CEO*
Hung Tran, *CFO*
Tracy Ung, *Corp Secy*
▲ **EMP:** 20 **EST:** 1982
SQ FT: 11,000
SALES (est): 3.9MM **Privately Held**
WEB: www.asiaplastics.com
SIC: 2673 Plastic bags: made from purchased materials

(P-5385)
C H K MANUFACTURING INC
960 98th Ave, Oakland (94603-2347)
PHONE......................510 632-5637
Chio-Hsiung Kuo, *President*
EMP: 50
SQ FT: 30,000
SALES: 10.8MM **Privately Held**
SIC: 2673 Plastic bags: made from purchased materials

(P-5386)
CALIFORNIA PLASTIX INC
1319 E 3rd St, Pomona (91766-2212)
PHONE......................909 629-8288
Danny Farshadfar, *President*
Touraj Tour, *Vice Pres*
▼ **EMP:** 25
SQ FT: 44,000

SALES: 4MM **Privately Held**
SIC: 2673 3089 Garment & wardrobe bags, (plastic film); extruded finished plastic products

(P-5387)
CALTEX PLASTICS INC (PA)
2380 E 51st St, Vernon (90058-2813)
PHONE......................800 584-7303
Ruth Rosenfeld, *CEO*
Rafael Rosenfeld, *CFO*
Jin Kim, *Executive*
Stephen Graves, *General Mgr*
Fred Movey, *Controller*
▲ **EMP:** 50
SQ FT: 35,000
SALES (est): 8.5MM **Privately Held**
WEB: www.caltexplastics.com
SIC: 2673 Trash bags (plastic film): made from purchased materials

(P-5388)
CENTRAL VALLEY PROFESSIONAL SE
Also Called: Central Valley Prof Svcs
8207 Mondo Ln, Oakdale (95361-8135)
PHONE......................209 847-7832
David A Racher, *President*
John Hassapakis, *Vice Pres*
▲ **EMP:** 13
SQ FT: 12,400
SALES (est): 1.8MM **Privately Held**
SIC: 2673 2385 3423 3089 Pliofilm bags: made from purchased materials; aprons, waterproof: made from purchased materials; knives, agricultural or industrial; injection molding of plastics

(P-5389)
CF&B MANUFACTURING INC
Also Called: Cleanroom Film & Bags
1405 N Manzanita St, Orange (92867-3603)
P.O. Box 807, Atwood (92811-0807)
PHONE......................714 744-8361
James Fruth, *President*
Brad Mello, *General Mgr*
Peggy Pearce, *Sales Staff*
EMP: 20
SQ FT: 10,000
SALES (est): 3MM **Privately Held**
SIC: 2673 Plastic bags: made from purchased materials

(P-5390)
CLEAR IMAGE INC (PA)
Also Called: Clearbags
4949 Windplay Dr Ste 100, El Dorado Hills (95762-9318)
PHONE......................916 933-4700
Benny Dyal Wilkins, *President*
Dave Pavao, *Vice Pres*
Laura Wilkins, *Admin Sec*
Aaron Johnson, *Administration*
Dave Deppner, *Info Tech Mgr*
◆ **EMP:** 41
SQ FT: 35,000
SALES (est): 7.6MM **Privately Held**
WEB: www.clearbags.com
SIC: 2673 5112 Bags: plastic, laminated & coated; envelopes

(P-5391)
CLW PLASTIC BAG MFG CO INC
13060 Park St, Santa Fe Springs (90670-4032)
PHONE......................562 903-8878
Yo Fu Lee, *President*
Wen-CHI Wu, *Vice Pres*
▲ **EMP:** 10
SALES (est): 2MM **Privately Held**
SIC: 2673 Plastic bags: made from purchased materials

(P-5392)
COMMAND PACKAGING LLC
3840 E 26th St, Vernon (90058-4107)
PHONE......................323 980-0918
Dhu Thompson,
Vickie Niesley, *Executive*
Avelino Garcia, *Engineer*
Bridgette Martinez, *Credit Staff*
Michael Manville, *Controller*
▲ **EMP:** 200
SQ FT: 170,000

SALES (est): 83.5MM **Privately Held**
WEB: www.restaurantbags.com
SIC: 2673 Bags: plastic, laminated &
coated
PA: Delta Plastics Of The South, Llc
8801 Frazier Pike
Little Rock AR 72206

(P-5393)
CROWN POLY INC
Also Called: Pull-N-Pac
5700 Bickett St, Huntington Park
(90255-2625)
PHONE...................323 268-1298
Ebrahim Simhaee, *CEO*
Zichen Xiao, *Engineer*
Bertha Padilla, *Human Res Dir*
Timothy Kim, *Plant Mgr*
Marc Isveck, *Sales Mgr*
◆ **EMP:** 150
SQ FT: 40,000
SALES (est): 93.5MM **Privately Held**
WEB: www.crownpoly.com
SIC: 2673 Plastic bags: made from pur-
chased materials

(P-5394)
DURABAG COMPANY INC
1432 Santa Fe Dr, Tustin (92780-6417)
PHONE...................714 259-8811
Frank C S Huang, *Vice Pres*
Daniel Huang, *Vice Pres*
Feng Jung Huang, *Director*
▲ **EMP:** 70
SQ FT: 150,000
SALES (est): 28.9MM **Privately Held**
WEB: www.durabag.net
SIC: 2673 Food storage & frozen food
bags, plastic; trash bags (plastic film):
made from purchased materials; plastic
bags: made from purchased materials

(P-5395)
E-Z PLASTIC PACKAGING CORP
2051 Garfield Ave, Commerce
(90040-1803)
PHONE...................323 887-0123
Sui TAC LI, *President*
Nam LI, *Vice Pres*
EMP: 25 **EST:** 1996
SQ FT: 75,000
SALES: 5MM **Privately Held**
SIC: 2673 Bags: plastic, laminated &
coated

(P-5396)
EPSILON PLASTICS INC
3100 E Harcourt St, Compton
(90221-5506)
PHONE...................310 609-1320
Jim Gifford, *Administration*
Luz Franco, *Office Mgr*
Fred Stabile, *Plant Mgr*
Tamayo Covarrubias, *Mfg Staff*
Tracie Castillo, *Sales Executive*
EMP: 75
SQ FT: 39,963 **Privately Held**
SIC: 2673 Bags: plastic, laminated &
coated
HQ: Epsilon Plastics Inc.
Page & Schuyler Ave 8
Lyndhurst NJ 07071
201 933-6000

(P-5397)
GHAZAL & SONS INC (PA)
Also Called: All American Plastic & Packg
3020 Hoover Ave, National City
(91950-7220)
PHONE...................619 474-6677
Munther Ghazal, *President*
Duraid Ghazal, *Treasurer*
Betool Y Elia, *Vice Pres*
Mike Ghazal, *Vice Pres*
Norman M Ghazal, *Admin Sec*
▼ **EMP:** 75
SQ FT: 50,000
SALES: 5MM **Privately Held**
WEB: www.aaplastic.com
SIC: 2673 Plastic bags: made from pur-
chased materials

(P-5398)
GREAT AMERICAN PACKAGING
4361 S Soto St, Vernon (90058-2311)
PHONE...................323 582-2247
Greg Gurewitz, *President*
Bruce Carter, *President*
Marlene Gurewitz, *CFO*
Cheryl Gartin, *Purch Agent*
Bob Clarke, *Sales Mgr*
EMP: 50
SQ FT: 40,000
SALES (est): 13.4MM **Privately Held**
WEB: www.greatampack.com
SIC: 2673 3081 3082 Plastic bags: made
from purchased materials; plastic film &
sheet; unsupported plastics profile
shapes

(P-5399)
HEAT FACTORY INC
2793 Loker Ave W, Carlsbad (92010-6601)
PHONE...................760 734-5300
Chris Treptow, *CEO*
Chris Parks, *COO*
Deron Degraw, *Design Engr*
Marian Strohmeyer, *Finance*
▲ **EMP:** 35
SQ FT: 40,000
SALES (est): 8.4MM **Privately Held**
SIC: 2673 2381 Bags: plastic, laminated &
coated; fabric dress & work gloves

(P-5400)
HERITAGE BAG COMPANY
12320 4th St, Rancho Cucamonga
(91730-6123)
PHONE...................909 899-5554
John Eberhard, *Manager*
Victor Garibay, *Plant Mgr*
EMP: 10
SALES (corp-wide): 2.9B **Privately Held**
WEB: www.heritage-bag.com
SIC: 2673 Plastic bags: made from pur-
chased materials
HQ: Heritage Bag Company
501 Gateway Pkwy
Roanoke TX 76262
972 241-5525

(P-5401)
LIBERTY PACKG & EXTRUDING INC
3015 Supply Ave, Commerce (90040-2709)
PHONE...................323 722-5124
Derek De Heras, *CEO*
Bonnie Hudson, *CEO*
Mary Anne Bove, *Treasurer*
Mary Hudson, *Vice Pres*
Lola Jones, *Principal*
EMP: 40
SQ FT: 25,000
SALES (est): 9.1MM **Privately Held**
WEB: www.libertypkg.com
SIC: 2673 7389 Plastic & pliofilm bags;
packaging & labeling services

(P-5402)
M & M PRINTED BAG INC
5651 Kimball Ct, Chino (91710-9121)
PHONE...................909 393-5537
Ernest N Taylor, *CEO*
Jeff Taylor, *President*
Gay Taylor, *Corp Secy*
▲ **EMP:** 32
SQ FT: 24,000
SALES (est): 8.5MM **Privately Held**
SIC: 2673 Plastic bags: made from pur-
chased materials

(P-5403)
MERCURY PLASTICS INC (PA)
14825 Salt Lake Ave, City of Industry
(91746-3131)
PHONE...................626 961-0165
Benjamin Deutsch, *CEO*
Stanley Tzenkov, *Exec VP*
Kamyar Mirdamadi, *Vice Pres*
Yathira Munoz, *VP Mfg*
▲ **EMP:** 415
SQ FT: 140,000
SALES (est): 164.2MM **Privately Held**
SIC: 2673 2759 3089 Plastic bags: made
from purchased materials; bags, plastic:
printing; plastic containers, except foam

(P-5404)
METRO POLY CORPORATION
1651 Aurora Dr, San Leandro
(94577-3101)
PHONE...................510 357-9898
Peter Kung, *Principal*
▲ **EMP:** 48
SQ FT: 40,000
SALES: 17.6MM **Privately Held**
SIC: 2673 Plastic bags: made from pur-
chased materials

(P-5405)
MIXED BAG DESIGNS INC
1744 Rollins Rd, Burlingame (94010-2208)
PHONE...................650 239-5358
Jan E Mercer, *CEO*
▲ **EMP:** 100
SALES (est): 7.6MM **Privately Held**
SIC: 2673 Cellophane bags, unprinted:
made from purchased materials

(P-5406)
MOHAWK WESTERN PLASTICS INC
1496 Arrow Hwy, La Verne (91750-5219)
P.O. Box 463 (91750-0463)
PHONE...................909 593-7547
John R Mordoff, *CEO*
J Christopher Mordoff, *President*
EMP: 40 **EST:** 1965
SQ FT: 28,000
SALES (est): 10.1MM **Privately Held**
WEB: www.mohawkwestern.com
SIC: 2673 3081 Plastic bags: made from
purchased materials; unsupported plas-
tics film & sheet

(P-5407)
NELSON BANNER INC
5720 Labath Ave, Rohnert Park
(94928-2039)
PHONE...................707 585-9942
A J Nelson, *President*
C R Nelson, *Vice Pres*
EMP: 28
SQ FT: 3,500
SALES: 1.3MM **Privately Held**
SIC: 2673 Bags: plastic, laminated &
coated

(P-5408)
OMEGA PLASTICS CORP
Also Called: Omega Extruding
9614 Lucas Ranch Rd Ste D, Rancho Cu-
camonga (91730-5787)
PHONE...................909 987-8716
EMP: 125 **Privately Held**
SIC: 2673 Plastic bags: made from pur-
chased materials
HQ: Omega Plastics Corp.
Page & Schuyler Ave Ste 5
Lyndhurst NJ 07071
201 507-9100

(P-5409)
PACKIT LLC
875 S Westlake Blvd, Westlake Village
(91361-2902)
PHONE...................805 496-2999
Melissa Kieling, *Mng Member*
Melissa Zuk, *Graphic Designe*
Paula Service, *Controller*
Amanda Bianchi, *Sales Mgr*
Charles Brofman,
◆ **EMP:** 10
SALES (est): 2.9MM **Privately Held**
SIC: 2673 Food storage & trash bags
(plastic)

(P-5410)
PANIC PLASTICS
1652 W 11th St, Upland (91786-3511)
PHONE...................909 946-5529
Miles Bruce, *Principal*
John Inglese, *Sales Dir*
EMP: 19
SALES (est): 3.1MM **Privately Held**
SIC: 2673 Bags: plastic, laminated &
coated

(P-5411)
PREMIER PLASTICS INC
6070 Peachtree St, Commerce
(90040-4012)
PHONE...................213 725-0502
George Mann, *President*
Harvey Deutsch, *Treasurer*
Sallo Schreiber, *Admin Sec*
EMP: 20
SALES: 1.3MM **Privately Held**
SIC: 2673 Bags: plastic, laminated &
coated; plastic & pliofilm bags

(P-5412)
PRINTPACK INC
5870 Stoneridge Mall Rd # 200, Pleasanton
(94588-3704)
PHONE...................925 469-0601
Doug Brow, *Manager*
Jack Gigantino, *Technology*
Tony Santos, *Technology*
Christel Sundin, *Technology*
David Willard, *Technology*
EMP: 188
SALES (corp-wide): 1.3B **Privately Held**
WEB: www.printpack.com
SIC: 2673 3081 Bags: plastic, laminated &
coated; plastic film & sheet
HQ: Printpack, Inc.
2800 Overlook Pkwy Ne
Atlanta GA 30339
404 460-7000

(P-5413)
PURFECT PACKAGING
5420 Brooks St, Montclair (91763-4520)
PHONE...................909 460-7363
Marlene Froechlich, *President*
Roland Blazys, *Vice Pres*
▲ **EMP:** 15
SQ FT: 7,000
SALES (est): 2MM **Privately Held**
SIC: 2673 Bags: plastic, laminated &
coated

(P-5414)
RCRV INC
Also Called: Rock Revival
4619 S Alameda St, Vernon (90058-2012)
PHONE...................323 235-7332
EMP: 17
SALES (corp-wide): 59.2MM **Privately
Held**
SIC: 2673 5137 Garment & wardrobe
bags, (plastic film); women's & children's
clothing
PA: Rcrv, Inc.
4715 S Alameda St
Vernon CA 90058
323 235-7354

(P-5415)
REPUBLIC BAG INC (PA)
580 E Harrison St, Corona (92879-1344)
PHONE...................951 734-9740
Richard Schroeder, *CEO*
Chris Mayer, *Senior VP*
Steven Fritz, *Vice Pres*
Mark Teo, *Principal*
Artemio Gonzalez, *Plant Mgr*
▲ **EMP:** 130
SQ FT: 59,000
SALES (est): 33.9MM **Privately Held**
SIC: 2673 Plastic bags: made from pur-
chased materials

(P-5416)
ROPLAST INDUSTRIES INC
3155 S 5th Ave, Oroville (95965-5858)
PHONE...................530 532-9500
Robert C Berman, *Chairman*
Robert Bateman, *President*
◆ **EMP:** 110
SQ FT: 160,000
SALES (est): 47.6MM **Privately Held**
WEB: www.roplast.com
SIC: 2673 Plastic bags: made from pur-
chased materials

(P-5417)
SAVENSEALCOM LTD
Also Called: Shieldnseal
15478 Applewood Ln, Nevada City
(95959-9712)
PHONE...................530 478-0238
Larry Heiniemi, *President*

▲ = Import ▼=Export
◆ =Import/Export

▲ EMP: 10 EST: 2011
SALES: 1.6MM Privately Held
SIC: 2673 Food storage & frozen food bags, plastic

(P-5418)
SEALED AIR CORPORATION
16201 Commerce Way, Cerritos (90703-2324)
PHONE..................201 791-7600
Brian Duncan, Branch Mgr
Greg Beauregard, Regl Sales Mgr
EMP: 20
SALES (corp-wide): 4.7B Publicly Held
WEB: www.sealedair.com
SIC: 2673 Food storage & frozen food bags, plastic
PA: Sealed Air Corporation
2415 Cascade Pointe Blvd
Charlotte NC 28208
980 221-3235

(P-5419)
SEALED AIR CORPORATION
Also Called: Special Products Group
2311 Boswell Rd Ste 8, Chula Vista (91914-3512)
PHONE..................619 421-9003
David Rader, Manager
Dave Rader, Mfg Staff
Michael Wilson, Production
EMP: 25
SALES (corp-wide): 4.7B Publicly Held
WEB: www.sealedair.com
SIC: 2673 Bags: plastic, laminated & coated
PA: Sealed Air Corporation
2415 Cascade Pointe Blvd
Charlotte NC 28208
980 221-3235

(P-5420)
SIUS PRODUCTS-DISTRIBUTOR INC (PA)
700 Kevin Ct, Oakland (94621-4040)
PHONE..................510 382-1700
Kuai Cheong Siu, CEO
Peter Siu, Vice Pres
John Huynh, General Mgr
▲ EMP: 18
SQ FT: 45,000
SALES (est): 3.7MM Privately Held
WEB: www.siusproducts.com
SIC: 2673 Plastic bags: made from purchased materials

(P-5421)
SORMA USA LLC
9810 W Ferguson Ave, Visalia (93291-2450)
PHONE..................559 651-1269
Rick Goddard, Vice Pres
Steve McCartha, Plant Mgr
Laura Pena, Production
▲ EMP: 350
SALES (est): 61.9MM
SALES (corp-wide): 33MM Privately Held
SIC: 2673 3565 Bags: plastic, laminated & coated; packaging machinery
PA: Sorma Spa
Via Don Federico Tosatto 8
Venezia VE 30174

(P-5422)
SUN PLASTICS INC
7140 E Slauson Ave, Commerce (90040-3663)
PHONE..................323 888-6999
Vahan Bagamian, President
Movses Shrikian, Admin Sec
EMP: 50
SQ FT: 60,000
SALES (est): 11.5MM Privately Held
WEB: www.sunplastics.com
SIC: 2673 Plastic bags: made from purchased materials

(P-5423)
TDI2 CUSTOM PACKAGING INC
3400 W Fordham Ave, Santa Ana (92704-4422)
PHONE..................714 751-6782
Stephen Deniger, CEO
Catharina Deniger, Admin Sec

EMP: 17
SQ FT: 19,000
SALES (est): 3.9MM Privately Held
SIC: 2673 Trash bags (plastic film): made from purchased materials

(P-5424)
TRANS WESTERN POLYMERS INC
7539 Las Positas Rd, Livermore (94551-8202)
P.O. Box 2399, Appleton WI (54912-2399)
PHONE..................925 449-7800
Joon B Bai, Ch of Bd
Stephen Bai, President
Matthew Kim, Vice Pres
Joe Lagana, Sales Executive
▲ EMP: 400
SQ FT: 100,000
SALES (est): 148.9MM Privately Held
SIC: 2673 5023 3089 Plastic bags: made from purchased materials; kitchen tools & utensils; tableware, plastic

(P-5425)
TRANSCONTINENTAL US LLC
Also Called: Coveris
10801 Iona Ave, Hanford (93230-9415)
PHONE..................559 585-2040
Walter Gerst, Branch Mgr
David Serpa, General Mgr
EMP: 140
SALES (corp-wide): 1.6B Privately Held
WEB: www.exopack.com
SIC: 2673 Bags: plastic, laminated & coated
HQ: Transcontinental Us Llc
8600 W Br Mw Ave 800n
Chicago IL 60631
773 877-3300

(P-5426)
TRANSCONTINENTAL US LLC
Also Called: Coveris
5601 Santa Ana St, Ontario (91761-8622)
PHONE..................909 390-8866
EMP: 20
SALES (corp-wide): 1.6B Privately Held
WEB: www.exopack.com
SIC: 2673 Bags: plastic, laminated & coated
HQ: Transcontinental Us Llc
8600 W Br Mw Ave 800n
Chicago IL 60631
773 877-3300

(P-5427)
TUNG FEI PLASTIC INC
Also Called: Wheaton International
1859 Sabre St, Hayward (94545-1023)
PHONE..................510 783-9688
Rick Liu, President
Ming Liu, Admin Sec
▲ EMP: 10
SQ FT: 20,000
SALES (est): 1.7MM Privately Held
WEB: www.tfplastic.com
SIC: 2673 Plastic bags: made from purchased materials

(P-5428)
UC PLASTIC MANUFACTURE INC
3202 Diablo Ave, Hayward (94545-2780)
PHONE..................510 785-6777
Jesse K Tseng, President
▲ EMP: 30
SQ FT: 10,000
SALES (est): 4.4MM Privately Held
SIC: 2673 Bags: plastic, laminated & coated

(P-5429)
UNI-POLY INC
2040 Williams St, San Leandro (94577)
PHONE..................510 357-9898
Alex Eduardo, Manager
EMP: 18
SALES (corp-wide): 8.7MM Privately Held
SIC: 2673 Plastic & plioflim bags
PA: Uni-Poly, Inc.
1651 Aurora Dr
San Leandro CA 94577
510 357-9898

(P-5430)
UNIVERSAL PLASTIC BAGS MFG INC
1309 S Wanamaker Ave, Ontario (91761-2237)
PHONE..................909 218-2247
Narendra L Babaria, President
Rajendra Babaria, Vice Pres
▲ EMP: 19
SQ FT: 25,000
SALES (est): 6.4MM Privately Held
SIC: 2673 Bags: plastic, laminated & coated

(P-5431)
WESTERN STATES PACKAGING INC
13276 Paxton St, Pacoima (91331-2356)
PHONE..................818 686-6045
Richard Joyce, President
Mark Pickrell, Vice Pres
Rocco Loosbrock, Marketing Staff
Lee Joice, Sales Staff
▲ EMP: 50
SQ FT: 35,000
SALES (est): 12.4MM Privately Held
WEB: www.westernstatespackaging.com
SIC: 2673 5113 5162 Plastic bags: made from purchased materials; bags, paper & disposable plastic; plastics materials

2674 Bags: Uncoated Paper & Multiwall

(P-5432)
ACME BAG CO INC (PA)
Also Called: California Bag
440 N Pioneer Ave Ste 300, Woodland (95776-6139)
PHONE..................530 662-6130
David Rosenberg, CEO
Paresh Shah, General Mgr
Tony Panelli, Accounts Exec
◆ EMP: 19
SQ FT: 40,000
SALES (est): 3.8MM Privately Held
WEB: www.sacbag.com
SIC: 2674 5199 5191 2673 Bags: uncoated paper & multiwall; bags, textile; greenhouse equipment & supplies; bags: plastic, laminated & coated; textile bags; broadwoven fabric mills, cotton

(P-5433)
BAGCRAFTPAPERCON I LLC
Also Called: Papercon Packaging Division
515 Turnball Canyon Rd, City of Industry (91745-1118)
PHONE..................626 961-6766
Hector Lourido, Manager
EMP: 100
SALES (corp-wide): 2.9B Privately Held
WEB: www.packaging-dynamics.com
SIC: 2674 2671 Bags: uncoated paper & multiwall; packaging paper & plastics film, coated & laminated
HQ: Bagcraftpapercon I, Llc
3900 W 43rd St
Chicago IL 60632
620 856-2800

(P-5434)
CALIFORNIA PAPER BAG INC
1829 Dana St Ste A, Glendale (91201-2026)
PHONE..................818 240-6717
Felix Perez, President
Olga Perez, Treasurer
Tony Perez, Vice Pres
▲ EMP: 10
SQ FT: 22,000
SALES (est): 1.4MM Privately Held
SIC: 2674 Bags: uncoated paper & multiwall

(P-5435)
CTS CEMENT MANUFACTURING CORP
13846 Firestone Blvd, Santa Fe Springs (90670-5807)
PHONE..................562 802-2660
Jim Scanlan, Manager
EMP: 34

SALES (corp-wide): 43MM Privately Held
WEB: www.ctscement.com
SIC: 2674 Cement bags: made from purchased materials
PA: Cts Cement Manufacturing Corporation
12442 Knott St
Garden Grove CA 92841
714 379-8260

(P-5436)
E-Z MIX INC
3355 Industrial Dr, Bloomington (92316-3543)
PHONE..................909 874-7686
Bobbie Telcamp, Principal
EMP: 28
SALES (est): 3.7MM Privately Held
WEB: www.e-zmix.com
SIC: 2674 3241 Bags: uncoated paper & multiwall; cement, hydraulic
PA: E-Z Mix Inc.
11450 Tuxford St
Sun Valley CA 91352

(P-5437)
E-Z MIX INC (PA)
11450 Tuxford St, Sun Valley (91352-2638)
PHONE..................818 768-0568
William Frenzel, CEO
Sunjiv Parekh, CEO
Moises Inestroza, Accounting Mgr
Bobby Tellkamp, Sales Mgr
EMP: 33
SQ FT: 50,000
SALES (est): 14.1MM Privately Held
WEB: www.e-zmix.com
SIC: 2674 Cement bags: made from purchased materials

(P-5438)
E-Z MIX INC
4125 Breakwater Ave Ste E, Hayward (94545-3600)
PHONE..................510 782-8010
Richard Vega, Branch Mgr
EMP: 31 Privately Held
WEB: www.e-zmix.com
SIC: 2674 Bags: uncoated paper & multiwall
PA: E-Z Mix Inc.
11450 Tuxford St
Sun Valley CA 91352

(P-5439)
ENDPAK PACKAGING INC
9101 Perkins St, Pico Rivera (90660-4512)
PHONE..................562 801-0281
Edgar A Garcia, CEO
Carlos Garcia, President
EMP: 90
SQ FT: 45,600
SALES (est): 30.1MM Privately Held
WEB: www.endpak.com
SIC: 2674 5199 Paper bags: made from purchased materials; packaging materials

(P-5440)
LANGSTON COMPANIES INC
2500 S K St, Tulare (93274-6874)
PHONE..................559 688-3839
Joe Hart, Branch Mgr
EMP: 25
SQ FT: 26,000
SALES (corp-wide): 68.2MM Privately Held
SIC: 2674 Shipping bags or sacks, including multiwall & heavy duty
PA: Langston Companies, Inc.
1760 S 3rd St
Memphis TN 38109
901 774-4440

(P-5441)
MAHIVR
5405 Alton Pkwy, Irvine (92604-3717)
PHONE..................949 559-5470
Carlynn Cassidy, Manager
Babul Sheth, Officer
EMP: 10
SALES (est): 980.2K Privately Held
SIC: 2674 Shipping & shopping bags or sacks

(PA)=Parent Co (HQ)=Headquarters (DH)=Div Headquarters
✪ = New Business established in last 2 years

PRODUCTS & SVCS

(P-5442)
PACOBOND INC
9800 Glenoaks Blvd, Sun Valley
(91352-1041)
PHONE..................................818 768-5002
Arsine Seraydarian, *CEO*
Gerard Seradarian, *President*
▲ EMP: 50
SQ FT: 45,000
SALES (est): 9.1MM **Privately Held**
SIC: 2674 5162 Shopping bags: made
from purchased materials; plastics materials

(P-5443)
ROMEO PACKING COMPANY
106 Princeton Ave, Half Moon Bay
(94019-4035)
PHONE..................................650 728-3393
Charles Romeo, *President*
Frank Romeo, *Treasurer*
Joey Romeo, *Vice Pres*
Constance Romeo, *Admin Sec*
EMP: 22
SQ FT: 40,000
SALES (est): 5MM **Privately Held**
WEB: www.romeopacking.com
SIC: 2674 2873 Paper bags: made from
purchased materials; fertilizers: natural
(organic), except compost

(P-5444)
SILICON 360 LLC
801 Buckeye Ct, Milpitas (95035-7408)
PHONE..................................408 432-1790
Zafar Malik,
EMP: 10
SALES (est): 979.5K **Privately Held**
SIC: 2674 Bags: uncoated paper & multiwall

(P-5445)
WOLFPACK GEAR INC
3765 S Higuera St Ste 150, San Luis
Obispo (93401-1569)
P.O. Box 2538, Paso Robles (93447-2538)
PHONE..................................805 439-1911
Michael Oberndorfer, *President*
Ronald Darin Sanders, *Vice Pres*
EMP: 11
SQ FT: 1,700
SALES (est): 2.8MM **Privately Held**
SIC: 2674 Bags: uncoated paper & multiwall

2675 Die-Cut Paper & Board

(P-5446)
APEX DIE CORPORATION
840 Cherry Ln, San Carlos (94070-3394)
PHONE..................................650 592-6350
Thomas J Cullen, *Chairman*
Kevin Cullen, *President*
Eva Cummings, *CFO*
Chris J Cullen, *Vice Pres*
Judy Grilli, *Accountant*
EMP: 55
SQ FT: 33,800
SALES (est): 11.4MM **Privately Held**
WEB: www.apexdie.com
SIC: 2675 2759 2672 Die-cut paper &
board; embossing on paper; coated &
laminated paper

(P-5447)
ARCHITECTURAL FOAMSTONE INC
9757 Glenoaks Blvd, Sun Valley
(91352-1013)
PHONE..................................818 767-4500
Ruben Jimenez, *President*
EMP: 17
SQ FT: 9,000
SALES (est): 3.2MM **Privately Held**
SIC: 2675 3086 Die-cut paper & board;
plastics foam products

(P-5448)
IMPERIAL DIE CUTTING INC
800 Richards Blvd, Sacramento
(95811-0315)
PHONE..................................916 443-6142
Brent Rabe, *President*
Jennifer Rabe, *Vice Pres*

EMP: 35
SQ FT: 13,000
SALES (est): 6.4MM **Privately Held**
WEB: www.imperialdie.com
SIC: 2675 3469 2759 Die-cut paper &
board; metal stampings; commercial printing

(P-5449)
J J FOIL COMPANY INC
650 W Freedom Ave, Orange
(92865-2537)
PHONE..................................714 998-9920
Tiffany Dang, *President*
EMP: 45
SQ FT: 18,000
SALES (est): 10.2MM **Privately Held**
WEB: www.jjfoil.com
SIC: 2675 2759 Paper die-cutting; embossing on paper

(P-5450)
K & D GRAPHICS
Also Called: K & D Graphics Prtg & Packg
1432 N Main St Ste C, Orange
(92867-3450)
PHONE..................................714 639-8900
Don Chew, *CEO*
Montri Chew, *CFO*
Bebe Chew, *Vice Pres*
Gus Chew, *Vice Pres*
Kim Chew, *Admin Sec*
▲ EMP: 48
SQ FT: 75,500
SALES (est): 7.9MM **Privately Held**
WEB: www.kdgpp.com
SIC: 2675 2752 Die-cut paper & board;
commercial printing, offset

(P-5451)
PRESENTATION FOLDER INC
1130 N Main St, Orange (92867-3421)
PHONE..................................714 289-7000
Joseph Tardie Jr, *President*
Joseph Tardie Sr, *Vice Pres*
▲ EMP: 45
SQ FT: 70,000
SALES (est): 11MM **Privately Held**
WEB: www.presentationfolder.com
SIC: 2675 2759 2672 Folders, filing, die-
cut: made from purchased materials;
paper die-cutting; embossing on paper;
coated & laminated paper

(P-5452)
R & J RULE & DIE INC
Also Called: R & J Paper Box
701 Sturbridge Dr, La Habra (90631-6324)
PHONE..................................562 945-7535
Jim Fuller, *President*
Ray Fuller, *Shareholder*
Vera Fuller, *Shareholder*
EMP: 10
SQ FT: 10,000
SALES (est): 800K **Privately Held**
SIC: 2675 Paper die-cutting

(P-5453)
RAINBOW SYMPHONY INC
6860 Canby Ave Ste 120, Reseda
(91335-8710)
PHONE..................................818 708-8400
Mark Margolis, *President*
Sophia Margolis, *Marketing Mgr*
▲ EMP: 12
SQ FT: 2,100
SALES (est): 1.7MM **Privately Held**
WEB: www.rainbowsymphony.com
SIC: 2675 Paper die-cutting

(P-5454)
SHAMROCK DIE CUTTING COMPANY
3020 Meyerloa Ln, Pasadena (91107-1133)
PHONE..................................323 266-4556
Carole Lorenzini, *President*
Sean M Lorenzini, *Treasurer*
Sadie Chism, *Vice Pres*
EMP: 40
SQ FT: 12,000
SALES (est): 3.3MM **Privately Held**
SIC: 2675 3544 2789 Die-cut paper &
board; special dies, tools, jigs & fixtures;
bookbinding & related work

(P-5455)
TOPS SLT INC
8550 Chetle Ave Ste B, Whittier
(90606-2662)
PHONE..................................562 968-2000
EMP: 148
SALES (corp-wide): 10.4B **Publicly Held**
SIC: 2675
HQ: Tops Slt, Inc.
225 Broadhollow Rd 184w
Melville NY 11747
631 675-5700

(P-5456)
WINDSOR HOUSE INVESTMENTS INC
Also Called: Colortone
12250 Coast Dr, Whittier (90601-1607)
PHONE..................................323 261-0231
Carl Price, *President*
EMP: 25 EST: 1938
SALES (est): 6MM **Privately Held**
WEB: www.colortonegrafx.com
SIC: 2675 2752 2843 2796 Paper die-
cutting; decals, lithographed; surface ac-
tive agents; platemaking services;
bookbinding & related work; automotive &
apparel trimmings

2676 Sanitary Paper Prdts

(P-5457)
ALLIED WEST PAPER CORP
11101 Etiwanda Ave # 100, Fontana
(92337-6984)
PHONE..................................909 349-0710
Ray Ovanessian, *CEO*
Eric Ovanessian, *Vice Pres*
Mike Ovanessian, *Vice Pres*
Rick Williams, *Sales Mgr*
▲ EMP: 95
SQ FT: 300,000
SALES (est): 51MM **Privately Held**
WEB: www.alliedwestpaper.com
SIC: 2676 Napkins, paper: made from pur-
chased paper

(P-5458)
AXENT CORPORATION LIMITED
Also Called: Axent USA
3 Musick, Irvine (92618-1638)
PHONE..................................949 900-4349
LI Feiyu, *Principal*
▲ EMP: 25 EST: 2008
SALES (est): 5.5MM **Privately Held**
SIC: 2676 2499 Sanitary paper products;
seats, toilet

(P-5459)
BABY BOX COMPANY INC (PA)
1601 Vine St, Los Angeles (90028-8806)
PHONE..................................844 422-2926
Jennifer Clary-Haberer, *CEO*
Michelle Vick, *Principal*
Kevin Haberer, *CTO*
▲ EMP: 13
SALES (est): 2MM **Privately Held**
SIC: 2676 5137 5113 Infant & baby paper
products; baby goods; boxes & containers

(P-5460)
DEPENDBLE INCONTINENCE SUP INC
Also Called: Dis
590 S Vincent Ave, Azusa (91702-5130)
PHONE..................................626 812-0044
Mike Cholakian, *CEO*
Harry Kemangian, *CFO*
▼ EMP: 15
SQ FT: 25,000
SALES (est): 16MM **Privately Held**
WEB: www.disbriefs.com
SIC: 2676 Diapers, paper (disposable):
made from purchased paper

(P-5461)
GEORGIA PACIFIC HOLDINGS INC
13208 Hadley St Apt 1, Whittier
(90601-4531)
PHONE..................................626 926-1474
Jorge Arroyo, *CEO*
EMP: 860

SQ FT: 1,000
SALES (est): 135.1MM **Privately Held**
SALES (corp-wide): 40.6B **Privately Held**
SIC: 2676 2656 2435 2821 Sanitary
paper products; sanitary food containers;
hardwood veneer & plywood; plastics materials & resins
PA: Koch Industries, Inc.
4111 E 37th St N
Wichita KS 67220
316 828-5500

(P-5462)
HAIN CELESTIAL GROUP INC
8468 Warner Dr, Culver City (90232-2429)
PHONE..................................310 945-4300
EMP: 10 **Publicly Held**
SIC: 2676 Towels, napkins & tissue paper
products
PA: The Hain Celestial Group Inc
1111 Marcus Ave Ste 100
New Hyde Park NY 11042

(P-5463)
JOHNSON & JOHNSON
3509 Langdon Cmn, Fremont
(94538-5403)
PHONE..................................650 237-4878
Phil Palin, *Principal*
EMP: 80
SALES (corp-wide): 81.5B **Publicly Held**
SIC: 2676 Feminine hygiene paper prod-
ucts
PA: Johnson & Johnson
1 Johnson And Johnson Plz
New Brunswick NJ 08933
732 524-0400

(P-5464)
PRINCESS PAPER INC
4455 Fruitland Ave, Vernon (90058-3222)
PHONE..................................323 588-4777
Abraham Hakimi, *President*
▲ EMP: 45
SQ FT: 150,000
SALES (est): 12MM **Privately Held**
WEB: www.princesspaper.com
SIC: 2676 Towels, napkins & tissue paper
products; toilet paper: made from pur-
chased paper

(P-5465)
PROCTER & GAMBLE PAPER PDTS CO
800 N Rice Ave, Oxnard (93030-8910)
PHONE..................................805 485-8871
Shirley Boone, *Manager*
Kyle Field, *Information Mgr*
John Zaragoza, *Project Leader*
Martin Boyd, *Technology*
Joe Santos, *Engineer*
EMP: 500
SALES (corp-wide): 67.6B **Publicly Held**
SIC: 2676 Towels, paper: made from pur-
chased paper
HQ: The Procter & Gamble Paper Products
Company
1 Procter And Gamble Plz
Cincinnati OH 45202
513 983-1100

(P-5466)
RAEL INC
13915 Cerritos Corprt Dr D, Cerritos
(90703-2469)
PHONE..................................800 573-1516
Aness Han, *CEO*
Yanghee Park, *President*
EMP: 20 EST: 2017
SALES (est): 3.7MM **Privately Held**
SIC: 2676 Feminine hygiene paper prod-
ucts

(P-5467)
ROCHESTER MIDLAND CORPORATION
7275 Sycamore Canyon Blvd # 101, River-
side (92508-2326)
PHONE..................................800 388-4762
Brenda Barr, *Branch Mgr*
Aaron Stapf, *Sales Mgr*
EMP: 22

▲ = Import ▼=Export
◆ =Import/Export

SALES (corp-wide): 129.4MM **Privately Held**
WEB: www.rochestermidland.com
SIC: 2676 5087 8732 2899 Feminine hygiene paper products; cleaning & maintenance equipment & supplies; commercial nonphysical research; chemical preparations; floor waxes
PA: Rochester Midland Corporation
155 Paragon Dr
Rochester NY 14624
585 336-2200

2677 Envelopes

(P-5468)
CENVEO WORLDWIDE LIMITED
150 N Myers St, Los Angeles (90033-2109)
PHONE..................................323 261-7171
Ed Binder, *Branch Mgr*
Kirk Bennett, *Sales Staff*
EMP: 65
SQ FT: 156,100
SALES (corp-wide): 2.6B **Privately Held**
WEB: www.mail-well.com
SIC: 2677 2752 2759 Envelopes; commercial printing, lithographic; labels & seals: printing
HQ: Cenveo Worldwide Limited
200 First Stamford Pl # 2
Stamford CT 06902
203 595-3000

(P-5469)
CLEANSMART SOLUTIONS INC
Also Called: San Francisco Envelope
47422 Kato Rd, Fremont (94538-7319)
PHONE..................................650 871-9123
Don Clark, *Branch Mgr*
EMP: 30
SALES (corp-wide): 49MM **Privately Held**
WEB: www.jcpaper.com
SIC: 2677 Envelopes
PA: Cleansmart Solutions Inc.
47422 Kato Rd
Fremont CA 94538
510 413-4700

(P-5470)
GOLDEN WEST ENVELOPE CORP
1009 Morton St, Alameda (94501-3904)
PHONE..................................510 452-5419
Raymond Mazur, *President*
Gert Mazur, *Vice Pres*
EMP: 25
SQ FT: 17,000
SALES: 1MM **Privately Held**
WEB: www.goldenwestenvelope.com
SIC: 2677 2752 Envelopes; commercial printing, offset

(P-5471)
INLAND ENVELOPE COMPANY
150 N Park Ave, Pomona (91768-3835)
PHONE..................................909 622-2016
Bernard Kloenne, *CEO*
Otilia Kloenne, *Admin Sec*
EMP: 55
SQ FT: 45,000
SALES (est): 20.4MM **Privately Held**
WEB: www.inlandenvelope.com
SIC: 2677 Envelopes

(P-5472)
J R C INDUSTRIES INC
11804 Wakeman St, Santa Fe Springs (90670-2129)
PHONE..................................562 698-0171
Leonard Fishelberg, *CEO*
EMP: 67 EST: 1976
SQ FT: 32,000
SALES (est): 13.8MM **Privately Held**
SIC: 2677 Envelopes

(P-5473)
LA ENVELOPE INCORPORATED
1053 S Vail Ave, Montebello (90640-6019)
PHONE..................................323 838-9300
Gary T Earls, *President*
Louise Earls, *Admin Sec*
EMP: 35
SQ FT: 25,000

SALES (est): 9MM **Privately Held**
WEB: www.laenvelope.com
SIC: 2677 2752 Envelopes; commercial printing, offset

(P-5474)
SEABOARD ENVELOPE CO INC
15601 Cypress Ave, Irwindale (91706-2120)
P.O. Box 2225, Baldwin Park (91706-1134)
PHONE..................................626 960-4559
Ronald Neidringhaus, *President*
Richard Riggle, *Vice Pres*
Valerie Niedringhaus, *QC Mgr*
EMP: 25
SQ FT: 72,000
SALES (est): 7.5MM **Privately Held**
WEB: www.seaboardenvelope.com
SIC: 2677 Envelopes

(P-5475)
SOUTHLAND ENVELOPE COMPANY INC
10111 Riverford Rd, Lakeside (92040-2741)
PHONE..................................619 449-3553
Dianne Gonzalez, *CEO*
Frank Soloman Jr, *President*
Rita Soloman, *Vice Pres*
Mike Brockett, *Plant Mgr*
Del Rivera, *Marketing Staff*
EMP: 115 EST: 1970
SQ FT: 80,000
SALES (est): 45.2MM **Privately Held**
WEB: www.southlandenvelope.com
SIC: 2677 Envelopes

(P-5476)
VISION ENVELOPE & PRTG CO INC (PA)
13707 S Figueroa St, Los Angeles (90061-1045)
PHONE..................................310 324-7062
Mark Fisher, *Principal*
Michael J Leeny, *Vice Pres*
Chase Smith, *Sales Staff*
EMP: 50
SQ FT: 45,000
SALES (est): 7.9MM **Privately Held**
SIC: 2677 2752 Envelopes; commercial printing, offset

(P-5477)
WESTERN STATES ENVELOPE CORP
2301 Raymer Ave, Fullerton (92833-2514)
P.O. Box 2607 (92837-0607)
PHONE..................................714 449-0909
Lisa Hoehle, *President*
Giovanni Portanova, *Maintence Staff*
Jing Zaide, *Maintence Staff*
EMP: 60
SQ FT: 24,000
SALES (est): 15.8MM **Privately Held**
SIC: 2677 Envelopes

2678 Stationery Prdts

(P-5478)
AVERY PRODUCTS CORPORATION
6987 Calle De Linea # 101, San Diego (92154-8016)
PHONE..................................619 671-1022
Geoff Martin, *President*
EMP: 44
SALES (corp-wide): 3.9B **Privately Held**
SIC: 2678 Stationery products
HQ: Avery Products Corporation
50 Pointe Dr
Brea CA 92821
714 675-8500

(P-5479)
AVERY PRODUCTS CORPORATION (DH)
50 Pointe Dr, Brea (92821-3652)
PHONE..................................714 675-8500
Geoff Martin, *President*
Mark Cooper, *Vice Pres*
Jeff Lattanzio, *Vice Pres*
Jeffery Jett, *Regional Mgr*
Bohdan Sirota, *Admin Sec*

◆ EMP: 274
SALES (est): 264.3MM
SALES (corp-wide): 3.9B **Privately Held**
SIC: 2678 3951 2672 2891 Notebooks: made from purchased paper; markers, soft tip (felt, fabric, plastic, etc.); labels (unprinted), gummed: made from purchased materials; adhesives
HQ: Ccl Industries Corporation
15 Controls Dr
Shelton CT 06484
203 926-1253

(P-5480)
ETERNAL STAR CORPORATION
17813 S Main St Ste 101, Gardena (90248-3542)
PHONE..................................310 768-1945
▲ EMP: 30
SQ FT: 250,000
SALES (est): 4.1MM **Privately Held**
SIC: 2678 2782

(P-5481)
LADY JAYNE LP
10833 Valley View St # 420, Cypress (90630-5045)
▲ EMP: 10
SQ FT: 28,000
SALES (est): 1.5MM
SALES (corp-wide): 380.1MM **Privately Held**
WEB: www.ladyjayneltd.com
SIC: 2678
PA: R.A.F. Industries, Inc.
165 Township Line Rd # 2100
Jenkintown PA 19046
215 572-0738

(P-5482)
MILLS ASAP REPROGRAPHICS (PA)
495 Morro Bay Blvd, Morro Bay (93442-2143)
P.O. Box 1678 (93443-1678)
PHONE..................................805 772-2019
Roger R Marlin, *Owner*
EMP: 18
SQ FT: 4,000
SALES (est): 2MM **Privately Held**
WEB: www.asapreprographics.com
SIC: 2678 5943 5999 Memorandum books, notebooks & looseleaf filler paper; office forms & supplies; writing supplies; artists' supplies & materials

(P-5483)
MRS GROSSMANS PAPER COMPANY
Also Called: Paragon Label
3810 Cypress Dr, Petaluma (94954-5613)
PHONE..................................707 763-1700
Fax: 707 763-7121
▲ EMP: 100 EST: 1975
SQ FT: 11,000
SALES (est): 22.9MM **Privately Held**
WEB: www.paragonlabel.com
SIC: 2678 2679 2759 2752

(P-5484)
PENCIL GRIP INC (PA)
21200 Superior St Ste A, Chatsworth (91311-4324)
P.O. Box 3787 (91313-3787)
PHONE..................................310 315-3545
Alexander Provda, *CEO*
Asher Provda, *CEO*
Julia Boyle, *Vice Pres*
Theresa Baker, *Finance*
Steve George, *Director*
◆ EMP: 17
SQ FT: 12,000
SALES (est): 2.9MM **Privately Held**
WEB: www.pencilgrip.com
SIC: 2678 Stationery products

(P-5485)
TREE HOUSE PAD & PAPER INC
2341 Pomona Rd Ste 108, Corona (92880-6973)
PHONE..................................800 213-4184
David Moncrief, *President*
Darrin Monroe, *Vice Pres*
Rebekah Radford, *Finance Mgr*
John Huitsing, *Controller*
EMP: 55

SQ FT: 50,000
SALES (est): 16MM **Privately Held**
WEB: www.treehousepaper.com
SIC: 2678 Stationery products

(P-5486)
VIVA HOLDINGS LLC (PA)
Also Called: Viva Concepts
700 N Central Ave Ste 220, Glendale (91203-1240)
PHONE..................................818 243-1363
Farid Tabibzadeh,
Majid Tabibzadeh, *Principal*
EMP: 18
SALES (est): 12.1MM **Privately Held**
SIC: 2678 Memorandum books, except printed: purchased materials

(P-5487)
VIVA PRINT LLC (HQ)
1025 N Brand Blvd Ste 300, Glendale (91202-3633)
PHONE..................................818 243-1363
Greg Hughes Sr, *CEO*
Greg Hughes Jr, *COO*
Randy Nobis, *Prdtn Mgr*
EMP: 10
SQ FT: 28,000
SALES (est): 2.1MM
SALES (corp-wide): 12.1MM **Privately Held**
SIC: 2678 Memorandum books, except printed: purchased materials
PA: Viva Holdings, Llc
700 N Central Ave Ste 220
Glendale CA 91203
818 243-1363

2679 Converted Paper Prdts, NEC

(P-5488)
A A LABEL INC (PA)
Also Called: All American Label
6958 Sierra Ct, Dublin (94568-2641)
PHONE..................................925 803-5709
Bradley Brown, *CEO*
Cynthia Brown, *Vice Pres*
Irene George, *Sales Staff*
Marci Hector, *Sales Staff*
Mike Anderson, *Manager*
▲ EMP: 25
SQ FT: 25,000
SALES (est): 5.2MM **Privately Held**
WEB: www.allamericanlabel.net
SIC: 2679 Labels, paper: made from purchased material

(P-5489)
A PLUS LABEL INCORPORATED
3215 W Warner Ave, Santa Ana (92704-5314)
PHONE..................................714 229-9811
Nick Phan, *President*
Thi Phan, *Controller*
EMP: 40
SQ FT: 6,400
SALES: 2.5MM **Privately Held**
WEB: www.apluslabel.com
SIC: 2679 Tags & labels, paper

(P-5490)
ALL LABEL INC
Also Called: K1 Packaging
17989 Arenth Ave, City of Industry (91748-1126)
PHONE..................................626 964-6744
Jui Yun Tsai, *President*
▲ EMP: 10
SQ FT: 36,876
SALES (est): 2MM **Privately Held**
SIC: 2679 Labels, paper: made from purchased material

(P-5491)
AMERICAN GRAPHIC BOARD INC
5880 E Slauson Ave, Commerce (90040-3018)
PHONE..................................323 721-0585
Don Zeccola, *President*
Michael Carmody, *CFO*
Peter Kang, *Admin Sec*
▲ EMP: 35

PRODUCTS & SVCS

SQ FT: 135,000
SALES (est): 6.9MM **Privately Held**
SIC: 2679 Paperboard products, converted

(P-5492)
AMERICAN INDEX AND FILES LLC
2900 E Miraloma Ave Ste B, Anaheim (92806-1871)
PHONE..................................714 630-3360
Peggy Alvardo, *CEO*
Randy Swanson, *Office Mgr*
Eddie Alvarado,
EMP: 10
SALES (est): 1.6MM **Privately Held**
SIC: 2679 Cardboard products, except die-cut

(P-5493)
APPLE PAPER CONVERTING INC
3800 E Miraloma Ave, Anaheim (92806-2108)
P.O. Box 768, Atwood (92811-0768)
PHONE..................................714 632-3195
Jorge Daniel Podboj, *President*
Louis Salavar, *President*
George Podboj, *Vice Pres*
EMP: 20
SALES (est): 2.5MM **Privately Held**
SIC: 2679 Paper products, converted

(P-5494)
ARTISSIMO DESIGNS LLC (HQ)
2100 E Grand Ave Ste 400, El Segundo (90245-5055)
PHONE..................................310 906-3700
Ravi Bhagavatula, *CEO*
Jennifer Hao, *Accountant*
Diane Dempsey, *VP Sales*
▲ EMP: 50
SQ FT: 13,000
SALES (est): 73MM **Privately Held**
SIC: 2679 Wallboard, decorated: made from purchased material
PA: Excelsior Capital Partners, Llc
4695 Macarthur Ct Ste 370
Newport Beach CA 92660
949 566-8110

(P-5495)
ARTISTRY IN MOTION INC
19411 Londelius St, Northridge (91324-3512)
PHONE..................................818 994-7388
Roger Wachtell, *CEO*
Richard Graves, *President*
EMP: 22
SALES (est): 2.9MM **Privately Held**
WEB: www.artistryinmotion.com
SIC: 2679 5947 Confetti: made from purchased material; gifts & novelties

(P-5496)
BOWEN PRINTING INC
Also Called: Bowen Enterprises
380 Coogan Way, El Cajon (92020-1976)
PHONE..................................619 440-8605
Newell B Bowen, *President*
EMP: 12
SQ FT: 8,000
SALES (est): 1.3MM **Privately Held**
WEB: www.bowenprinting.com
SIC: 2679 2752 Labels, paper: made from purchased material; commercial printing, offset

(P-5497)
BRUSH DANCE INC
165 N Redwood Dr Ste 200, San Rafael (94903-1971)
PHONE..................................415 491-4950
Marc A Lesser, *CEO*
Johanna Malen, *President*
◆ EMP: 14
SQ FT: 7,000
SALES (est): 1.9MM **Privately Held**
SIC: 2679 Paper products, converted

(P-5498)
CALPACO PAPERS INC (PA)
3155 Universe Dr, Jurupa Valley (91752-3252)
PHONE..................................323 767-2800
Paul Maier, *President*
Francis A Maier, *Chairman*

▲ EMP: 136
SQ FT: 606,000
SALES (est): 8.1MM **Privately Held**
WEB: www.calpaco.com
SIC: 2679 5111 Paper products, converted; printing & writing paper

(P-5499)
CENVEO WORLDWIDE LIMITED
6250 S Boyle Ave, Vernon (90058-3937)
PHONE..................................323 262-6000
Kevin Johnson, *Branch Mgr*
Susan Torres, *Hum Res Coord*
Larry Lindwall, *Purch Agent*
Stephen Spear, *Manager*
EMP: 125
SQ FT: 135,212
SALES (corp-wide): 2.6B **Privately Held**
WEB: www.mail-well.com
SIC: 2679 5112 Tags & labels, paper; envelopes
HQ: Cenveo Worldwide Limited
200 First Stamford Pl # 2
Stamford CT 06902
203 595-3000

(P-5500)
COAST TO COAST LABEL INC (PA)
18401 Bandilier Cir, Fountain Valley (92708-7012)
PHONE..................................657 203-2583
Renee Anastasia, *CEO*
Dana Anastasia, *President*
▼ EMP: 12
SQ FT: 3,000
SALES (est): 1.5MM **Privately Held**
WEB: www.coasttocoastlabel.com
SIC: 2679 Labels, paper: made from purchased material

(P-5501)
COLORTECH LABEL INC
1230 S Sherman St, Anaheim (92805-6455)
PHONE..................................714 999-5545
Randy Montram, *President*
EMP: 13
SALES (est): 1.1MM **Privately Held**
SIC: 2679 Labels, paper: made from purchased material

(P-5502)
CONTINENTAL DATALABEL INC
Also Called: American Single Sheets
211 Business Center Ct, Redlands (92373-4404)
PHONE..................................909 307-3600
Patrick Flynn, *Branch Mgr*
Ron Kruger, *CTO*
EMP: 30
SALES (corp-wide): 31.5MM **Privately Held**
WEB: www.compulabel.com
SIC: 2679 2672 Labels, paper: made from purchased material; coated & laminated paper
PA: Continental Datalabel, Inc.
1855 Fox Ln
Elgin IL 60123
847 742-1600

(P-5503)
CROWN PAPER CONVERTING INC
1380 S Bon View Ave, Ontario (91761-4403)
P.O. Box 3277 (91761-0928)
PHONE..................................909 923-5226
Bruce Hale, *Principal*
Lisa Hale, *Vice Pres*
EMP: 40
SQ FT: 34,000
SALES (est): 11.4MM **Privately Held**
SIC: 2679 Paper products, converted

(P-5504)
DATA LABEL PRODUCTS INC
840 N Cummings Rd, Covina (91724-2505)
PHONE..................................626 915-6478
David Jensen, *President*
EMP: 10 EST: 1964

SALES (est): 1.2MM **Privately Held**
WEB: www.datalabelproducts.com
SIC: 2679 2752 Labels, paper: made from purchased material; commercial printing, lithographic

(P-5505)
DIETZGEN CORPORATION
1522 E Bentley Dr, Corona (92879-1741)
PHONE..................................951 278-3259
Darren A Letang, *President*
Alfonso Herrera, *Manager*
EMP: 22
SALES (corp-wide): 44.6MM **Privately Held**
SIC: 2679 Paper products, converted
PA: Dietzgen Corporation
121 Kelsey Ln Ste G
Tampa FL 33619
813 286-4767

(P-5506)
DIGITAL LABEL SOLUTIONS INC
22745 Old Canal Rd, Yorba Linda (92887-4603)
PHONE..................................714 982-5000
Joel H Mark, *CEO*
Sandy Petersen, *Vice Pres*
Suzie Dobyns, *Admin Sec*
EMP: 29
SQ FT: 14,000
SALES (est): 6.3MM **Privately Held**
SIC: 2679 Tags & labels, paper

(P-5507)
FDS MANUFACTURING COMPANY (PA)
2200 S Reservoir St, Pomona (91766-6408)
P.O. Box 3120 (91769-3120)
PHONE..................................909 591-1733
Robert B Stevenson, *CEO*
Samuel B Stevenson, *Chairman*
Chuck O'Connor, *Vice Pres*
Kevin Stevenson, *Vice Pres*
Todd Lawrence, *Controller*
▲ EMP: 150
SQ FT: 240,000
SALES (est): 36.5MM **Privately Held**
WEB: www.fdsmfg.com
SIC: 2679 3089 Corrugated paper: made from purchased material; plastic containers, except foam

(P-5508)
FLEENOR COMPANY INC (PA)
Also Called: Fleenor Paper Company
2225 Harbor Bay Pkwy, Alameda (94502-3026)
P.O. Box 14438, Oakland (94614-2438)
PHONE..................................800 433-2531
Rebecca Fleenor, *President*
Janine Rochex, *CFO*
Yesenia Zelaya, *Office Mgr*
Barb Chasey, *Purch Mgr*
Mauricio Saucedo, *Plant Mgr*
◆ EMP: 40
SALES (est): 21MM **Privately Held**
WEB: www.fleenorpaper.com
SIC: 2679 Paper products, converted; paperboard products, converted

(P-5509)
GM NAMEPLATE INC
2095 Otoole Ave, San Jose (95131-1374)
PHONE..................................408 435-1666
Bruce Cleckley, *Sales Mgr*
Mike Bogle, *Program Mgr*
Jacob Leon, *Engineer*
John Perez, *Purch Mgr*
Ron Saxon, *QC Mgr*
EMP: 127
SQ FT: 24,600
SALES (corp-wide): 315.4MM **Privately Held**
SIC: 2679 3479 3993 2752 Labels, paper: made from purchased material; name plates: engraved, etched, etc.; signs & advertising specialties; commercial printing, lithographic; packaging paper & plastics film, coated & laminated
PA: Gm Nameplate, Inc.
2040 15th Ave W
Seattle WA 98119
206 284-2200

(P-5510)
GOLDEN KRAFT INC
15500 Valley View Ave, La Mirada (90638-5230)
PHONE..................................562 926-8888
Dan August, *General Mgr*
EMP: 92 EST: 1982
SQ FT: 63,200
SALES (est): 15MM
SALES (corp-wide): 40.6B **Privately Held**
SIC: 2679 2631 Corrugated paper: made from purchased material; paperboard mills
HQ: Georgia-Pacific Corrugated Iii Llc
5645 W 82nd St
Indianapolis IN 46278

(P-5511)
HCL LABELS INC
1800 Green Hills Rd # 104, Scotts Valley (95066-4984)
PHONE..................................800 421-6710
Fernando Nell, *President*
Benjamin Nell, *Vice Pres*
Alicia Dayton, *Controller*
Rajiv Prakash, *Senior Mgr*
EMP: 11
SQ FT: 3,974
SALES (est): 1.4MM **Privately Held**
WEB: www.hclco.com
SIC: 2679 5099 5131 2759 Labels, paper: made from purchased material; signs, except electric; labels; commercial printing; labels & seals: printing

(P-5512)
LABL HOLDING CORPORATION
W/S Packaging Fullerton
531 Airpark Dr, Fullerton (92833-2501)
PHONE..................................714 992-2574
William Harper, *Manager*
EMP: 81 **Privately Held**
WEB: www.wspackaging.com
SIC: 2679 2671 2759 Labels, paper: made from purchased material; packaging paper & plastics film, coated & laminated; labels & seals: printing
HQ: Labl Holding Corporation
4053 Clough Woods Dr
Batavia OH 45103
920 866-6300

(P-5513)
MAIN STREET KITCHENS
37 Quail Ct Ste 200, Walnut Creek (94596-8722)
PHONE..................................925 944-0153
Scott J Westby, *Owner*
EMP: 15 EST: 2001
SALES: 1.3MM **Privately Held**
WEB: www.mainstreetkitchens.com
SIC: 2679 5031 1799 Building paper, laminated: made from purchased material; building materials, interior; kitchen & bathroom remodeling

(P-5514)
NATIONAL RECYCLING CORPORATION
1312 Kirkham St, Oakland (94607-2257)
PHONE..................................510 268-1022
Richard Wang, *President*
▼ EMP: 18
SQ FT: 80,000
SALES (est): 3.2MM **Privately Held**
SIC: 2679 4953 Paper products, converted; recycling, waste materials

(P-5515)
NCLA INC
1388 W Foothill Blvd, Azusa (91702-2846)
PHONE..................................562 926-6252
John McGee, *President*
EMP: 19
SALES (est): 4.4MM **Privately Held**
WEB: www.ncla.net
SIC: 2679 3083 Paper products, converted; plastic finished products, laminated

(P-5516)
NOVIPAX INC (DH)
Also Called: Paper-Pak Industries
1941 N White Ave, La Verne (91750-5663)
PHONE..................................909 392-1750

▲ = Import ▼=Export
◆ =Import/Export

Ron Leach, *CEO*
Rich Beu, *President*
Jeffrey Williams, *CFO*
Sophia Smeragliuolo, *Research*
Lindsay Riehle, *Technical Staff*
◆ **EMP:** 100
SQ FT: 100,000
SALES (est): 48.1MM
SALES (corp-wide): 2.9B **Privately Held**
WEB: www.paperpakindustries.com
SIC: 2679 Building, insulating & packaging
   paper
HQ: Novipax Llc
   2215 York Rd Ste 504
   Oak Brook IL 60523
   630 686-2735

(P-5517)
P & R PAPER SUPPLY CO INC
1350 Piper Ranch Rd, San Diego
(92154-7708)
PHONE..................619 671-2400
Bruce Overmeyer, *Manager*
EMP: 19
SALES (corp-wide): 102.2MM **Privately
Held**
SIC: 2679 2621 Paper products, con-
   verted; paper mills
PA: P. & R. Paper Supply Company, Inc.
   1898 E Colton Ave
   Redlands CA 92374
   909 389-1811

(P-5518)
PACIFIC PPRBD CONVERTING LLC (PA)
8865 Utica Ave Ste A, Rancho Cucamonga
(91730-5144)
PHONE..................909 476-6466
Bill Donahue, *CEO*
John Todora, *General Mgr*
EMP: 25
SALES (est): 4.7MM **Privately Held**
WEB: www.bmxpaper.com
SIC: 2679 Paper products, converted

(P-5519)
PACTIV CORPORATION
9700 Bell Ranch Dr, Santa Fe Springs
(90670-2950)
PHONE..................562 944-0052
Carlos Ruiz, *Branch Mgr*
John Fernandez, *VP Finance*
EMP: 35
SALES (corp-wide): 14.1MM **Privately
Held**
WEB: www.pactiv.com
SIC: 2679 2671 2631 Honeycomb core &
   board: made from purchased material;
   packaging paper & plastics film, coated &
   laminated; paperboard mills
HQ: Pactiv Llc
   1900 W Field Ct
   Lake Forest IL 60045
   847 482-2000

(P-5520)
PAPER PULP & FILM
Also Called: Fresno Paper Express
2822 S Maple Ave, Fresno (93725-2207)
PHONE..................559 233-1151
G Carol Jones, *CEO*
Tal Cloud, *President*
Meredith Orman, *Admin Sec*
▲ **EMP:** 40
SQ FT: 120,000
SALES (est): 19.4MM **Privately Held**
WEB: www.paperconverter.com
SIC: 2679 4213 Wrappers, paper (un-
   printed): made from purchased material;
   heavy hauling

(P-5521)
PARADIGM LABEL INC
10258 Birtcher Dr, Jurupa Valley
(91752-1827)
PHONE..................951 372-9212
Curtis Harton, *CEO*
Elda Withrow, *Opers Staff*
EMP: 15
SQ FT: 15,000
SALES (est): 3.9MM **Privately Held**
SIC: 2679 Labels, paper: made from pur-
   chased material

(P-5522)
POSITIVE CONCEPTS INC (PA)
Also Called: Ameri-Fax
2021 N Glassell St, Orange (92865-3305)
PHONE..................714 685-5800
Lambert C Thom, *CEO*
George Manzur, *President*
▼ **EMP:** 22
SQ FT: 20,000
SALES (est): 4.7MM **Privately Held**
WEB: www.posconcepts.com
SIC: 2679 5084 Paper products, con-
   verted; machine tools & accessories

(P-5523)
PRIME CONVERTING CORPORATION
9121 Pittsbrgh Ave Ste 100, Rancho Cuca-
monga (91730)
P.O. Box 3207 (91729-3207)
PHONE..................909 476-9500
Robert J Nielsen, *President*
▲ **EMP:** 24
SALES (est): 12MM **Privately Held**
WEB: www.primeconvertingcorp.com
SIC: 2679 Paper products, converted

(P-5524)
PROGRESSIVE LABEL INC
2545 Yates Ave, Commerce (90040-2619)
P.O. Box 911430, Los Angeles (90091-
1238)
PHONE..................323 415-9770
Gus Garcia, *President*
David Lawrence, *Shareholder*
Adam Flores, *Vice Pres*
Julie Lawrence, *Admin Sec*
Regina Sitt, *Purchasing*
▲ **EMP:** 39
SQ FT: 18,000
SALES (est): 8.9MM **Privately Held**
WEB: www.progressivelabel.com
SIC: 2679 2672 2671 2241 Tags & la-
   bels, paper; coated & laminated paper;
   packaging paper & plastics film, coated &
   laminated; narrow fabric mills

(P-5525)
QUADRIGA USA ENTERPRISES INC
Also Called: Commercial and Security Labels
28410 Witherspoon Pkwy, Valencia
(91355-4167)
PHONE..................888 669-9994
Aram Mehrabyan, *CEO*
Ashot Mehrabyan, *CFO*
Vahan Arakelyan, *General Mgr*
Mher Mehrabyan, *Admin Sec*
EMP: 14
SQ FT: 18,200
SALES (est): 403.4K **Privately Held**
SIC: 2679 5131 7389 2672 Tags & la-
   bels, paper; labels; packaging & labeling
   services; adhesive papers, labels or
   tapes: from purchased material; labels &
   seals: printing

(P-5526)
RTS PACKAGING LLC
1900 Wardrobe Ave, Merced (95341-6447)
PHONE..................209 722-2787
Mike Myer, *Manager*
EMP: 71
SQ FT: 32,400
SALES (corp-wide): 14.8B **Publicly Held**
WEB: www.rtspackaging.com
SIC: 2679 2631 Paperboard products,
   converted; paperboard mills
HQ: Rts Packaging, Llc
   504 Thrasher St
   Norcross GA 30071
   800 558-6984

(P-5527)
SACHS INDUSTRIES INC
Also Called: Custom Label
801 Kate Ln, Woodland (95776-5733)
PHONE..................631 242-9000
EMP: 18
SQ FT: 12,000
SALES (est): 2.3MM **Privately Held**
SIC: 2679 5113

(P-5528)
SALINAS VALLEY WAX PAPER CO
1111 Abbott St, Salinas (93901-4501)
P.O. Box 68 (93902-0068)
PHONE..................831 424-2747
Charles Nelson, *CEO*
Bill Zimmerman, *Vice Pres*
Chris Zimmerman, *Admin Sec*
Ivonne Prado, *Human Resources*
▲ **EMP:** 49
SQ FT: 50,000
SALES (est): 10.2MM **Privately Held**
WEB: www.salinasvalleywaxpapercom-
pany.com
SIC: 2679 2672 Paper products, con-
   verted; coated & laminated paper

(P-5529)
SAPPI NORTH AMERICA INC
333 S Anita Dr Ste 840, Orange
(92868-3320)
PHONE..................714 456-0600
Brent Demichael, *Branch Mgr*
EMP: 60
SALES (corp-wide): 5.3B **Privately Held**
SIC: 2679 Paper products, converted
HQ: Sappi North America, Inc.
   255 State St Fl 4
   Boston MA 02109
   617 423-7300

(P-5530)
SIGN OF TIMES INC
4950 S Santa Fe Ave, Vernon
(90058-2106)
PHONE..................323 826-9766
Mark Roginson, *President*
▲ **EMP:** 20
SALES (est): 1.8MM **Privately Held**
WEB: www.signofthetimes.com
SIC: 2679 Wallboard, decorated: made
   from purchased material

(P-5531)
SIGNODE INDUSTRIAL GROUP LLC
Also Called: Down River
3901 Navone Rd, Stockton (95215-9311)
PHONE..................209 931-0917
Humberto Laguna, *Branch Mgr*
EMP: 92
SALES (corp-wide): 11.1B **Publicly Held**
SIC: 2679 2655 Paper products, con-
   verted; ammunition cans or tubes, board
   laminated with metal foil
HQ: Signode Industrial Group Llc
   3650 W Lake Ave
   Glenview IL 60026
   847 724-7500

(P-5532)
SUNRISE MFG INC (PA)
2665 Mercantile Dr, Rancho Cordova
(95742-6521)
PHONE..................916 635-6262
James Sewell, *CEO*
Matt Sewell, *Vice Pres*
Justin Sewell, *General Mgr*
Jessica Morris, *Office Mgr*
Teri Bradley, *CTO*
▲ **EMP:** 25
SQ FT: 72,000
SALES (est): 8.7MM **Privately Held**
WEB: www.sunrisemfg.com
SIC: 2679 Building, insulating & packaging
   paper

(P-5533)
SUPERIOR RADIANT INSUL INC
175 Principia Ct, Claremont (91711-4657)
PHONE..................909 305-1450
David Dittemore, *President*
Linda Dittemore, *Admin Sec*
EMP: 10
SALES (est): 2MM **Privately Held**
SIC: 2679 Insulating paper: batts, fills &
   blankets

(P-5534)
TAB LABEL INC
21 Hegenberger Ct, Oakland (94621-1321)
P.O. Box 6266 (94603-0266)
PHONE..................510 638-4411
EMP: 17

(P-5535)
SQ FT: 11,000
SALES (est): 223.8K **Privately Held**
WEB: www.tablabel.com
SIC: 2679

(P-5535)
TAGTIME U S A INC
4601 District Blvd, Vernon (90058-2731)
PHONE..................323 587-1555
Cort Johnson, *President*
Mindy Knox, *Vice Pres*
Mark Lonneker, *Vice Pres*
Jim Maier, *Vice Pres*
Darryl Rudnick, *Vice Pres*
▲ **EMP:** 480
SQ FT: 23,000
SALES (est): 64.9MM **Privately Held**
WEB: www.tagtimeusa.com
SIC: 2679 Labels, paper: made from pur-
   chased material

(P-5536)
TAPP LABEL INC (HQ)
161 S Vasco Rd L, Livermore
(94551-5130)
PHONE..................707 252-8300
John Attayek, *CEO*
Jeff Licht, *Vice Pres*
Brooks Denny, *Business Dir*
Doug Smith, *Business Dir*
Dawn Graves, *Credit Staff*
EMP: 11
SALES (est): 2.5MM
SALES (corp-wide): 18MM **Privately
Held**
SIC: 2679 Labels, paper: made from pur-
   chased material
PA: Tltc Holdings Inc
   6270 205 St
   Langley BC
   604 533-3294

(P-5537)
TEKNI-PLEX INC
Also Called: Natvar
19555 Arenth Ave, City of Industry
(91748-1403)
PHONE..................909 589-4366
Joleen Kennelley, *Branch Mgr*
Jesus Barrios, *Engineer*
Alberto Hernandez, *Engineer*
Jerry Wombold, *Marketing Staff*
EMP: 163
SALES (corp-wide): 1.1B **Privately Held**
WEB: www.dolco.net
SIC: 2679 3061 Egg cartons, molded pulp:
   made from purchased material; medical &
   surgical rubber tubing (extruded & lathe-
   cut)
PA: Tekni-Plex, Inc.
   460 E Swedesford Rd # 3000
   Wayne PA 19087
   484 690-1520

(P-5538)
TLC LOGISTICS INC
Also Called: Western Die Cutting and Prtg
3109 Casitas Ave, Los Angeles
(90039-2410)
PHONE..................323 665-0474
Jerry Lavinsky, *President*
EMP: 10
SQ FT: 7,000
SALES (est): 1.4MM **Privately Held**
SIC: 2679 Paper products, converted

(P-5539)
TOTAL PAPER AND PACKAGING INC
2175 Agate Ct Unit A, Simi Valley
(93065-1839)
PHONE..................818 885-1072
Rajiv Kaushal, *President*
▲ **EMP:** 13
SALES: 5MM **Privately Held**
SIC: 2679 Paper products, converted

(P-5540)
WORLD CENTRIC
1400 Valley House Dr # 220, Rohnert Park
(94928-4940)
PHONE..................707 241-9190
Aseem Das, *CEO*
Mark Marinozzi, *Vice Pres*
Mark Stephany, *Vice Pres*
Brandon Lourenzo, *Planning*

Matt Wynkoop, *Business Anlyst*
◆ **EMP:** 17
SALES (est): 9.2MM **Privately Held**
SIC: 2679 2675 5113 Plates, pressed &
molded pulp: from purchased material;
die-cut paper & board; industrial & personal service paper

(P-5541)
Z B P INC
Also Called: Z-Barten Productions
2871 E Pico Blvd, Los Angeles
(90023-3609)
PHONE...................................323 266-3363
Dale Zabel, *President*
Nancy Andersen, *Principal*
Jane Berse, *Principal*
Paula Greenberg, *Principal*
Howard Kuykendall, *Principal*
▲ **EMP:** 12
SQ FT: 20,000
SALES (est): 1.3MM **Privately Held**
WEB: www.confetti.com
SIC: 2679 2678 Novelties, paper: made
from purchased material; stationery prod-
ucts

2711 Newspapers:
Publishing & Printing

(P-5542)
2100 FREEDOM INC (HQ)
625 N Grand Ave, Santa Ana (92701-4347)
PHONE...................................714 796-7000
Richard E Mirman, *CEO*
Aaron Kushner, *CEO*
EMP: 100
SALES (est): 371.7MM
SALES (corp-wide): 2.5B **Privately Held**
SIC: 2711 2721 7313 2741 Newspapers,
publishing & printing; periodicals; news-
paper advertising representative; miscel-
laneous publishing; newspapers, home
delivery, not by printers or publishers;
PA: 2100 Trust, Llc
625 N Grand Ave
Santa Ana CA 92701
877 469-7344

(P-5543)
5800 SUNSET PRODUCTIONS
INC
Also Called: Tribune Studios
5800 W Sunset Blvd, Los Angeles
(90028-6607)
PHONE...................................323 460-3987
EMP: 13
SALES (est): 3.4MM
SALES (corp-wide): 2B **Publicly Held**
SIC: 2711
PA: Tribune Media Company
435 N Michigan Ave Fl 2
Chicago IL 60654
212 210-2786

(P-5544)
ACORN NEWSPAPER INC
30423 Canwood St Ste 108, Agoura Hills
(91301-4313)
PHONE...................................818 706-0266
Jim Rule, *President*
EMP: 30
SQ FT: 3,000
SALES (est): 1.7MM **Privately Held**
WEB: www.theacorn.com
SIC: 2711 Newspapers: publishing only,
not printed on site

(P-5545)
ADVERTISER PERCEPTIONS
3009 Deer Meadow Dr, Danville
(94506-2134)
PHONE...................................925 648-3902
Kenneth M Pearl, *CEO*
Kevin Mannion, *Exec VP*
Frank Papsadore, *Programmer Anys*
EMP: 20 **EST:** 2008
SALES (est): 1.2MM **Privately Held**
SIC: 2711 Newspapers: publishing only,
not printed on site

(P-5546)
ALAMEDA NEWSPAPERS INC
(DH)
Also Called: Times Herald
22533 Foothill Blvd, Hayward
(94541-4109)
PHONE...................................510 783-6111
Joh Schueler, *President*
P Scott McKibben, *President*
EMP: 250
SQ FT: 50,000
SALES (est): 65.1MM
SALES (corp-wide): 4.2B **Privately Held**
WEB: www.newsschool.com
SIC: 2711 Newspapers, publishing & print-
ing

(P-5547)
ALAMEDA NEWSPAPERS INC
Also Called: San Mateo Times
1080 S Amphlett Blvd, San Mateo
(94402-1802)
PHONE...................................650 348-4321
Dan Cruey, *Manager*
EMP: 80
SALES (corp-wide): 4.2B **Privately Held**
WEB: www.newsschool.com
SIC: 2711 Newspapers: publishing only,
not printed on site; newspapers, publish-
ing & printing
HQ: Alameda Newspapers, Inc
22533 Foothill Blvd
Hayward CA 94541
510 783-6111

(P-5548)
AMERICAN CITY BUS
JOURNALS INC
Also Called: Sacramento Business Journal
555 Capitol Mall Ste 200, Sacramento
(95814-4557)
P.O. Box 189249 (95818-9249)
PHONE...................................916 447-7661
Mike Trainor, *General Mgr*
EMP: 29
SALES (corp-wide): 1.3B **Privately Held**
SIC: 2711 Newspapers: publishing only,
not printed on site
HQ: American City Business Journals, Inc.
120 W Morehead St Ste 400
Charlotte NC 28202
704 973-1000

(P-5549)
AMMI PUBLISHING INC
Also Called: Ark Newspaper, The
1550 Tiburon Blvd Ste D, Belvedere
Tiburon (94920-2537)
P.O. Box 1054 (94920-4054)
PHONE...................................415 435-2652
Allison Kern, *President*
Jeff Dempsey, *Editor*
EMP: 10
SQ FT: 1,000
SALES (est): 618.8K **Privately Held**
WEB: www.thearknewspaper.com
SIC: 2711 Newspapers: publishing only,
not printed on site

(P-5550)
AMPERSAND PUBLISHING LLC
(PA)
Also Called: Santa Barbara News-Press Info
715 Anacapa St, Santa Barbara
(93101-2203)
P.O. Box 1359 (93102-1359)
PHONE...................................805 564-5200
Wendy McCaw,
Sharon Moore, *President*
John A Royston, *Info Tech Dir*
Yoland Apodaca, *Human Res Dir*
Gabriele Huth, *Advt Staff*
EMP: 30
SQ FT: 65,000
SALES (est): 27.6MM **Privately Held**
WEB: www.newspress.com
SIC: 2711 Newspapers: publishing only,
not printed on site

(P-5551)
ANG NEWSPAPER GROUP INC
(DH)
Also Called: Pacifica Tribune
1301 Grant Ave B, Novato (94945-3143)
P.O. Box 1159, Pacifica (94044-6159)
PHONE...................................650 359-6666
Cynthia Caldwell, *Manager*
Dean Singelton, *President*
Chris Hunter, *Principal*
Barbara Pagan, *Manager*
EMP: 14
SQ FT: 4,500
SALES: 1.4MM
SALES (corp-wide): 4.2B **Privately Held**
WEB: www.pacificatribune.com
SIC: 2711 Commercial printing & newspa-
per publishing combined

(P-5552)
ANTELOPE VALLEY
NEWSPAPERS INC
Also Called: Antelope Valley Press
44939 10th St W, Lancaster (93534-2313)
PHONE...................................661 940-1000
Tammy Valdes, *Manager*
EMP: 42
SALES (corp-wide): 13.6MM **Privately
Held**
SIC: 2711 7313 2741 Newspapers: pub-
lishing only, not printed on site; newspa-
per advertising representative;
miscellaneous publishing
PA: Antelope Valley Newspapers Inc.
37404 Sierra Hwy
Palmdale CA
661 273-2700

(P-5553)
ARGONAUT
5355 Mcconnell Ave, Los Angeles
(90066-7025)
PHONE...................................310 822-1629
David Asper Johnson, *President*
George Drury Smith, *CFO*
EMP: 27 **EST:** 1971
SQ FT: 10,000
SALES: 2MM **Privately Held**
WEB: www.argonautnewspaper.com
SIC: 2711 Newspapers: publishing only,
not printed on site

(P-5554)
ASIA PACIFIC CALIFORNIA INC
(PA)
Also Called: China Press, The
1648 Gilbreth Rd, Burlingame
(94010-1408)
PHONE...................................650 513-6189
Yining Xie, *President*
▲ **EMP:** 16
SQ FT: 13,000
SALES (est): 3.2MM **Privately Held**
SIC: 2711 Newspapers, publishing & print-
ing

(P-5555)
ASIA PACIFIC CALIFORNIA INC
Also Called: The China Press
923 E Valley Blvd Ste 203, San Gabriel
(91776-3684)
PHONE...................................626 281-8500
Non Hiand, *General Mgr*
EMP: 35 **Privately Held**
SIC: 2711 Newspapers
PA: Asia Pacific California Inc
1648 Gilbreth Rd
Burlingame CA 94010

(P-5556)
ASIAN WEEK (PA)
809 Sacramento St, San Francisco
(94108-2116)
PHONE...................................415 397-0220
James Fang, *President*
EMP: 10
SQ FT: 10,000
SALES (est): 3.2MM **Privately Held**
WEB: www.asianweek.com
SIC: 2711 2721 Newspapers: publishing
only, not printed on site; television sched-
ules: publishing & printing

(P-5557)
ASSOCIATED DESERT
NEWSPAPER (DH)
Also Called: Imperial Valley Press
205 N 8th St, El Centro (92243-2301)
P.O. Box 2641 (92244-2641)
PHONE...................................760 337-3400
Mayer Malone, *President*
David Leone, *President*
Teresa Zimmer, *CFO*
John Yanni, *Treasurer*
Clifford James, *Admin Sec*
EMP: 40
SQ FT: 30,000
SALES (est): 5.3MM
SALES (corp-wide): 1B **Publicly Held**
WEB: www.ivpressonline.com
SIC: 2711 Newspapers, publishing & print-
ing; commercial printing & newspaper
publishing combined
HQ: Schurz Communications, Inc.
1301 E Douglas Rd Ste 200
Mishawaka IN 46545
574 247-7237

(P-5558)
ASSOCIATED STUDENTS UCLA
Also Called: Asucla Publications
308 Westwood Plz Ste 118, Los Angeles
(90095-8355)
PHONE...................................310 825-2787
Arvli Ward, *Manager*
EMP: 200
SALES (corp-wide): 42.7MM **Privately
Held**
SIC: 2711 2741 2721 Newspapers: pub-
lishing only, not printed on site; miscella-
neous publishing; periodicals
PA: Associated Students U.C.L.A.
308 Westwood Plz
Los Angeles CA 90095
310 825-4321

(P-5559)
AUBURN JOURNAL INC (HQ)
1030 High St, Auburn (95603-4707)
P.O. Box 5910 (95604-5910)
PHONE...................................530 885-5656
Craig Dennis, *President*
Tony Hazarian, *Owner*
Martin Cody, *President*
William J Brehm Sr, *Vice Pres*
Moana Brehm, *Admin Sec*
EMP: 23
SQ FT: 18,000
SALES (est): 38.3MM
SALES (corp-wide): 224.8MM **Privately
Held**
SIC: 2711 Commercial printing & newspa-
per publishing combined; newspapers,
publishing & printing
PA: Brehm Communications, Inc.
16644 W Bernardo Dr # 300
San Diego CA 92127
858 451-6200

(P-5560)
AUBURN JOURNAL INC
Also Called: Colfax Record
1030 High St, Auburn (95603-4707)
PHONE...................................530 346-2232
Todd Frantz, *Principal*
EMP: 100
SALES (corp-wide): 224.8MM **Privately
Held**
SIC: 2711 7313 Newspapers: publishing
only, not printed on site; newspaper ad-
vertising representative
HQ: Auburn Journal Inc
1030 High St
Auburn CA 95603
530 885-5656

(P-5561)
AZTECA NEWS
1532 E Wellington Ave, Santa Ana
(92701-3235)
PHONE...................................714 972-9912
Rosana Romano, *Owner*
EMP: 10
SALES (est): 462.1K **Privately Held**
WEB: www.aztecanews.com
SIC: 2711 Newspapers

(P-5562)
BALITA MEDIA INC
Also Called: Weekend Balita
2629 Foothill Blvd, La Crescenta
(91214-3511)
PHONE..................................818 552-4503
Luchie Allen, *CEO*
Ruby Allen, *Principal*
Ramonsito Mendoza, *Admin Sec*
Myra Portes, *Advt Staff*
EMP: 22
SALES: 2MM **Privately Held**
WEB: www.balita.com
SIC: 2711 Newspapers, publishing & printing

(P-5563)
BAR MEDIA INC
Also Called: Bay Area Reporter
44 Gough St Ste 204, San Francisco
(94103-5424)
PHONE..................................415 861-5019
Michael Yamashita, *President*
Thomas E Horn, *Ch of Bd*
Patrick Brown, *CFO*
Todd Vogt, *Admin Sec*
Cynthia Laird, *Editor*
EMP: 15
SQ FT: 1,258
SALES (est): 103.8K **Privately Held**
SIC: 2711 Newspapers: publishing only, not printed on site

(P-5564)
BAY GUARDIAN COMPANY
Also Called: San Francisco Bay Guardian
135 Micaicaippi St, San Francisco (94107)
PHONE..................................415 255-3100
Bruce Brugman, *President*
Jean Brugman, *President*
EMP: 70 **EST:** 1966
SQ FT: 28,000
SALES (est): 3.6MM **Privately Held**
SIC: 2711 Newspapers, publishing & printing

(P-5565)
BEACON MEDIA INC
125 E Chestnut Ave, Monrovia
(91016-3411)
PHONE..................................626 301-1010
Jesse Dillon, *CEO*
Fred Bankston, *Manager*
Jose Correa, *Accounts Mgr*
EMP: 10
SALES (est): 848.7K **Privately Held**
SIC: 2711 2759 Newspapers: publishing only, not printed on site; commercial printing

(P-5566)
BEVERLY HILLS COURIER INC
499 N Canon Dr Ste 100, Beverly Hills
(90210-6192)
PHONE..................................310 278-1322
Clifton Smith, *President*
March Schwartz, *President*
EMP: 20
SQ FT: 10,000
SALES (est): 1.3MM **Privately Held**
WEB: www.bhcourier.com
SIC: 2711 Newspapers, publishing & printing

(P-5567)
BIOCENTURY PUBLICATIONS INC (PA)
1235 Radio Rd Ste 100, Redwood City
(94065-1315)
P.O. Box 1246, San Carlos (94070-1246)
PHONE..................................650 595-5333
David Flores, *President*
Selina Koch, *Assoc Editor*
Michael Schuppenhauer PH, *Senior Editor*
EMP: 35
SALES (est): 2.9MM **Privately Held**
SIC: 2711 2721 Newspapers; periodicals

(P-5568)
BREHM COMMUNICATIONS INC
Also Called: Folsom Telegraph
921 Sutter St, Folsom (95630-2441)
PHONE..................................916 985-2581
Jeff Royce, *Manager*
EMP: 12

SALES (corp-wide): 224.8MM **Privately Held**
WEB: www.brehmcommunications.com
SIC: 2711 Newspapers, publishing & printing
PA: Brehm Communications, Inc.
16644 W Bernardo Dr # 300
San Diego CA 92127
858 451-6200

(P-5569)
BRENTWOOD PRESS & PUBG LLC
Also Called: Brentwood Yellow Pages
248 Oak St, Brentwood (94513-1337)
PHONE..................................925 516-4757
Jimmy Chamores Mg Mem, *Principal*
Sherrie Hamilton, *Graphic Designe*
Eric Kinnaird, *Production*
Jimmy Chamores, *Mng Member*
Lonnie Tapia, *Publisher*
EMP: 45
SQ FT: 3,500
SALES (est): 1MM **Privately Held**
SIC: 2711 Newspapers: publishing only, not printed on site

(P-5570)
BUENA PARK ANAHEIM INDEPENDENT
9551 Valley View St, Cypress (90630)
PHONE..................................714 952-8505
Eddie Verdugo, *President*
EMP: 20
SALES (est): 553.6K **Privately Held**
SIC: 2711 Newspapers, publishing & printing

(P-5571)
BULLDOG REPORTER
124 Linden St, Oakland (94607-2538)
PHONE..................................510 596-9300
EMP: 16
SALES (est): 3MM **Privately Held**
SIC: 2711

(P-5572)
BUSINESS JRNL PUBLICATIONS INC
125 S Market St 11, San Jose
(95113-2292)
PHONE..................................408 295-3800
Italo Jimenez, *Manager*
EMP: 43
SALES (corp-wide): 1.3B **Privately Held**
WEB: www.tampabaybusinessjournal.com
SIC: 2711 Newspapers: publishing only, not printed on site
HQ: Business Journal Publications, Inc.
4350 W Cypress St Ste 800
Tampa FL 33607

(P-5573)
BUSINESS JRNL PUBLICATIONS INC
Also Called: San Francisco Business Time
275 Battery St Ste 600, San Francisco
(94111-3376)
PHONE..................................415 989-2522
Mary Huss, *Principal*
Jim Gardner, *Manager*
Kierstyn Moore, *Accounts Exec*
EMP: 45
SALES (corp-wide): 1.3B **Privately Held**
WEB: www.tampabaybusinessjournal.com
SIC: 2711 Newspapers: publishing only, not printed on site
HQ: Business Journal Publications, Inc.
4350 W Cypress St Ste 800
Tampa FL 33607

(P-5574)
CALAVERAS FIRST CO INC
Also Called: Calaveras Enterprise
15 Main St, San Andreas (95249)
P.O. Box 1197 (95249-1197)
PHONE..................................209 754-3861
Ralph Alldredge, *President*
EMP: 30
SQ FT: 8,000
SALES (est): 1.8MM **Privately Held**
SIC: 2711 Newspapers: publishing only, not printed on site

(P-5575)
CALI TODAY DAILY NEWSPAPER
1310 Tully Rd Ste 105, San Jose
(95122-3054)
PHONE..................................408 297-8271
Nan Nguyen, *President*
EMP: 14
SALES (est): 590.9K **Privately Held**
SIC: 2711 Newspapers, publishing & printing

(P-5576)
CALIFORNIA COMMUNITY NEWS LLC (HQ)
5091 4th St, Irwindale (91706-2173)
PHONE..................................626 472-5297
Eddy Hartenstein, *President*
Judy Kendall, *Vice Pres*
Julie Xanders, *Admin Sec*
EMP: 349
SQ FT: 324,000
SALES (est): 53.9MM
SALES (corp-wide): 1B **Publicly Held**
SIC: 2711 Newspapers, publishing & printing; commercial printing & newspaper publishing combined
PA: Tribune Publishing Company
160 N Stetson Ave
Chicago IL 60601
312 222-9100

(P-5577)
CALIFORNIA NEWSPAPERS INC
Also Called: Marin Independent Journal
150 Alameda Del Prado, Novato
(94949-6665)
PHONE..................................415 883-8600
Roger Grossman, *President*
Mario Bendingan, *President*
EMP: 526
SQ FT: 60,000
SALES (est): 25.2MM
SALES (corp-wide): 4.2B **Privately Held**
WEB: www.marinij.com
SIC: 2711 Commercial printing & newspaper publishing combined; newspapers, publishing & printing
HQ: California Newspapers Limited Partnership
605 E Huntington Dr # 100
Monrovia CA 91016
626 962-8811

(P-5578)
CALIFORNIA NEWSPAPERS PARTNR (PA)
Also Called: Mng Newspapers
4 N 2nd St Ste 800, San Jose
(95113-1317)
PHONE..................................408 920-5333
Steven B Rossi, *President*
Meredith Macdaniel, *Executive*
Marie Chavarria, *Sales Staff*
EMP: 149
SALES (est): 9.3MM
SALES (corp-wide): 22.1MM **Privately Held**
SIC: 2711 Newspapers: publishing only, not printed on site

(P-5579)
CALIFRNIA NWSPAPERS LTD PARTNR (DH)
Also Called: Inland Valley Daily Bulletin
605 E Huntington Dr # 100, Monrovia
(91016-6352)
P.O. Box 1259, Covina (91722-0259)
PHONE..................................626 962-8811
Ron Hasse, *President*
Jim Maurer, *Vice Pres*
Mark Welches, *Vice Pres*
Michelle Vielma, *Sales Staff*
Rich Archbold, *Director*
EMP: 450 **EST:** 1997
SALES (est): 237.9MM
SALES (corp-wide): 4.2B **Privately Held**
WEB: www.sgvtribune.com
SIC: 2711 Newspapers: publishing only, not printed on site

(P-5580)
CALIFRNIA NWSPAPERS LTD PARTNR
Also Called: Inland Valley Daily Bulletin
9616 Archibald Ave # 100, Rancho Cucamonga (91730-7939)
PHONE..................................909 987-6397
Bob Balzer, *Manager*
Christine Burt, *Executive Asst*
Curt Annett, *Sales Mgr*
EMP: 275
SQ FT: 88,304
SALES (corp-wide): 4.2B **Privately Held**
WEB: www.sgvtribune.com
SIC: 2711 Newspapers, publishing & printing
HQ: California Newspapers Limited Partnership
605 E Huntington Dr # 100
Monrovia CA 91016
626 962-8811

(P-5581)
CALIFRNIA NWSPAPERS LTD PARTNR
Also Called: Redlands Daily Facts
19 E Citrus Ave Ste 102, Redlands
(92373-4763)
PHONE..................................909 793-3221
Peggy Del Torro, *Manager*
EMP: 35
SQ FT: 8,301
SALES (corp-wide): 4.2B **Privately Held**
WEB: www.sgvtribune.com
SIC: 2711 7313 Newspapers, publishing & printing; newspaper advertising representative
HQ: California Newspapers Limited Partnership
605 E Huntington Dr # 100
Monrovia CA 91016
626 962-8811

(P-5582)
CALIFRNIA NWSPAPERS LTD PARTNR
Also Called: Media News
5399 Clark Rd, Paradise (95969-6325)
P.O. Box 70 (95967-0070)
PHONE..................................530 877-4413
Steve McCormick, *Controller*
Rick Silva, *Manager*
EMP: 185
SALES (corp-wide): 4.2B **Privately Held**
WEB: www.sgvtribune.com
SIC: 2711 2796 2791 2789 Newspapers: publishing only, not printed on site; platemaking services; typesetting; bookbinding & related work; commercial printing, lithographic
HQ: California Newspapers Limited Partnership
605 E Huntington Dr # 100
Monrovia CA 91016
626 962-8811

(P-5583)
CALIMESA NEWS MIRROR
1007 Calimesa Blvd Ste D, Calimesa
(92320-1143)
PHONE..................................909 795-8145
Jerry Bean, *CEO*
EMP: 20
SALES (est): 568.7K **Privately Held**
SIC: 2711 Newspapers

(P-5584)
CARMEL COMMUNICATIONS INC
Also Called: Carmel Pine Cone, The
734 Lighthouse Ave, Pacific Grove
(93950-2522)
PHONE..................................831 274-8593
Paul Miller, *Treasurer*
Nicholas Shaw, *Vice Pres*
Kevin Wandra, *Director*
EMP: 14
SALES (est): 312.5K **Privately Held**
SIC: 2711 Commercial printing & newspaper publishing combined

(P-5585)
CHAMPION PBLICATIONS CHINO INC
Also Called: Champion Newspapers
13179 9th St, Chino (91710-4216)
P.O. Box 607 (91708-0607)
PHONE..................................909 628-5501
Allen P McCombs, *President*
Bill McCombs, *Treasurer*
Gretchen McCombs, *Vice Pres*
Linda Fenner, *Sales Staff*
EMP: 21
SQ FT: 6,500
SALES (est): 1.5MM **Privately Held**
WEB: www.chinochampion.com
SIC: 2711 Newspapers, publishing & printing
PA: Golden State Newspapers Llc
95 W 11th St Ste 101
Tracy CA 95376
209 835-3030

(P-5586)
CHICO COMMUNITY PUBLISHING (PA)
Also Called: Reno News & Review
353 E 2nd St, Chico (95928-5469)
PHONE..................................530 894-2300
Jeff Von Kaenel, *CEO*
Jeff Vonkaenel, *President*
Charles Marcks, *CFO*
Valentina Flynn, *Vice Pres*
Deborah Redmond, *Admin Sec*
EMP: 40
SQ FT: 7,200
SALES (est): 9.6MM **Privately Held**
WEB: www.newsreview.com
SIC: 2711 Newspapers, publishing & printing

(P-5587)
CHICO COMMUNITY PUBLISHING
Also Called: Sacramento News & Review
1124 Del Paso Blvd, Sacramento (95815-3607)
PHONE..................................916 498-1234
Angela Hanson, *Manager*
Michelle Carl, *Publications*
Jason Cassidy, *Editor*
EMP: 60
SALES (corp-wide): 9.6MM **Privately Held**
WEB: www.newsreview.com
SIC: 2711 Newspapers, publishing & printing
PA: Chico Community Publishing Inc
353 E 2nd St
Chico CA 95928
530 894-2300

(P-5588)
CHINA PRESS
2121 W Mission Rd Ste 103, Alhambra (91803-1433)
PHONE..................................626 281-8500
Fax: 626 281-8400
▲ EMP: 10
SALES (est): 799.2K **Privately Held**
SIC: 2711

(P-5589)
CHRISTIAN MUSIC TODAY INC
Also Called: Spirit West Coast
80 Gilman Ave Ste 2, Campbell (95008-3013)
PHONE..................................408 377-9232
John Robertson, *President*
Allan Stark, *Treasurer*
David Martinez, *Admin Sec*
Jon Robberson, *Relg Ldr*
EMP: 12
SQ FT: 1,200
SALES: 751.7K **Privately Held**
WEB: www.spiritwestcoast.org
SIC: 2711 Newspapers: publishing only, not printed on site

(P-5590)
CHRISTIAN SCIENCE CHURCH
Also Called: First Church Christ, Scientist
120 E Valerio St, Santa Barbara (93101-1914)
PHONE..................................805 966-6661
Fredrick Hunter, *Pastor*

Ann Flury, *Representative*
EMP: 20
SALES (est): 861.3K **Privately Held**
WEB: www.christiansciencechurch.com
SIC: 2711 Newspapers

(P-5591)
CHRISTIAN TODAY INC
354 S Normandie Ave # 101, Los Angeles (90020-3183)
PHONE..................................323 931-0505
Jong Chun Suh, *CEO*
Young Bin Lee, *President*
▲ EMP: 10
SQ FT: 2,000
SALES: 160K **Privately Held**
SIC: 2711 Newspapers

(P-5592)
CIVIC CENTER NEWS INC
Also Called: Los Angeles Downtown News
1264 W 1st St, Los Angeles (90026-5831)
PHONE..................................213 481-1448
Susan R Laris, *President*
EMP: 20
SQ FT: 2,366
SALES (est): 1.3MM **Privately Held**
SIC: 2711 Newspapers: publishing only, not printed on site

(P-5593)
CLAREMONT COURIER
114 Olive St, Claremont (91711-4924)
PHONE..................................909 621-4761
Peter Weinberger, *Owner*
EMP: 20
SQ FT: 4,000
SALES (est): 1.3MM **Privately Held**
WEB: www.claremontcourier.com
SIC: 2711 Newspapers: publishing only, not printed on site

(P-5594)
COAST NEWS
315 S Coast Highway 101 W, Encinitas (92024-3555)
P.O. Box 232550 (92023-2550)
PHONE..................................760 436-9737
James Kydd, *CEO*
Phyllis Mitchell, *Graphic Designe*
Sue Otto, *Sales Staff*
Savannah Lang, *Manager*
EMP: 30
SALES (est): 1.8MM **Privately Held**
WEB: www.thecoastnews.com
SIC: 2711 2741 Newspapers, publishing & printing; miscellaneous publishing

(P-5595)
COMMUNITY CLOSE-UP WESTMINSTER
1771 S Lewis St, Anaheim (92805-6439)
PHONE..................................714 704-5811
EMP: 61
SALES (est): 6.6MM
SALES (corp-wide): 2.3B **Privately Held**
SIC: 2711
HQ: Freedom Communications, Inc.
625 N Grand Ave
Santa Ana CA 92701
714 796-7000

(P-5596)
COMMUNITY MEDIA CORPORATION
19100 Crest Ave Apt 26, Castro Valley (94546-2864)
PHONE..................................657 337-0200
Alene Renne Whiten, *Branch Mgr*
EMP: 68 **Privately Held**
SIC: 2711 Newspapers, publishing & printing
PA: Community Media Corporation
5119 Ball Rd
Cypress CA 90630

(P-5597)
COMMUNITY MEDIA CORPORATION (PA)
Also Called: San Dego Nghborhood Newspapers
5119 Ball Rd, Cypress (90630-3645)
PHONE..................................714 220-0292
Kathy Verdugo, *President*

Daniel Verdugo, *COO*
Linda Townson, *Vice Pres*
Franco Te, *Director*
Eddie Verdugo, *Publisher*
EMP: 12
SQ FT: 4,000
SALES (est): 6.7MM **Privately Held**
WEB: www.community-media.com
SIC: 2711 Newspapers, publishing & printing

(P-5598)
CONTRA COSTA NEWSPAPERS INC (DH)
Also Called: Contra Costa Times
175 Lennon Ln Ste 100, Walnut Creek (94598-2466)
PHONE..................................925 935-2525
George Riggs, *CEO*
John Armstrong, *President*
Chris Boisvert, *Info Tech Dir*
Mike Lefkow, *Editor*
EMP: 1000
SQ FT: 180,000
SALES (est): 158.1MM
SALES (corp-wide): 4.2B **Privately Held**
WEB: www.contracostatimes.com
SIC: 2711 Newspapers, publishing & printing

(P-5599)
CONTRA COSTA NEWSPAPERS INC
1516 Oak St, Alameda (94501-2947)
PHONE..................................510 748-1683
John Kawomoto, *Branch Mgr*
Connie Rux, *Editor*
EMP: 273
SALES (corp-wide): 4.2B **Privately Held**
SIC: 2711 Newspapers, publishing & printing
HQ: Contra Costa Newspapers, Inc.
175 Lennon Ln Ste 100
Walnut Creek CA 94598
925 935-2525

(P-5600)
CONTRA COSTA NEWSPAPERS INC
127 Spring St, Pleasanton (94566-6623)
PHONE..................................925 847-2123
Kelly Gust, *Principal*
EMP: 91
SALES (corp-wide): 4.2B **Privately Held**
SIC: 2711 Newspapers, publishing & printing
HQ: Contra Costa Newspapers, Inc.
175 Lennon Ln Ste 100
Walnut Creek CA 94598
925 935-2525

(P-5601)
CONTRA COSTA NEWSPAPERS INC
2205 Dean Lesher Dr, Concord (94520)
PHONE..................................925 977-8520
Gary Gomes, *Manager*
EMP: 140
SALES (corp-wide): 4.2B **Privately Held**
WEB: www.contracostatimes.com
SIC: 2711 Newspapers, publishing & printing
HQ: Contra Costa Newspapers, Inc.
175 Lennon Ln Ste 100
Walnut Creek CA 94598
925 935-2525

(P-5602)
CONTRA COSTA NEWSPAPERS INC
Also Called: Brentwood News
1700 Cavallo Rd, Antioch (94509-1930)
PHONE..................................925 634-2125
EMP: 10
SALES (corp-wide): 4.3B **Privately Held**
SIC: 2711
HQ: Contra Costa Newspapers, Inc.
175 Lennon Ln Ste 100
Walnut Creek CA 94598
925 935-2525

(P-5603)
COPLEY PRESS INC
Also Called: Union Tribune
1152 Armorlite Dr, San Marcos (92069-1441)
P.O. Box 120191, San Diego (92112-0191)
PHONE..................................760 752-6700
EMP: 16
SQ FT: 44,044
SALES (corp-wide): 92.6MM **Privately Held**
SIC: 2711 7383 7313
PA: The Copley Press Inc
7776 Ivanhoe Ave
La Jolla CA 92037
858 454-0411

(P-5604)
CYCLE NEWS INC (PA)
Also Called: CN Publishing Group
17771 Mitchell N, Irvine (92614-6028)
PHONE..................................949 863-7082
Sharon Clayton, *President*
Michelle Baird, *Editor*
EMP: 37
SQ FT: 10,000
SALES (est): 2.6MM **Privately Held**
WEB: www.watercraft.com
SIC: 2711 Newspapers, publishing & printing

(P-5605)
DAILY COMPUTING SOLUTIONS INC
3521 Foxglove Rd, Glendale (91206-4817)
PHONE..................................818 240-5400
Artin Kasparian, *President*
EMP: 10
SALES (est): 161.7K **Privately Held**
SIC: 2711 Newspapers, publishing & printing

(P-5606)
DAILY DOSES LLC
13150 Saticoy St, North Hollywood (91605-3402)
PHONE..................................858 220-0076
Daniel Andrade, *Branch Mgr*
EMP: 21
SALES (corp-wide): 1.3MM **Privately Held**
SIC: 2711 Newspapers, publishing & printing
PA: Daily Doses, Llc
1130 S Shenandoah St
Los Angeles CA 90035
858 220-0076

(P-5607)
DAILY JOURNAL
1720 S Amphlett Blvd # 123, San Mateo (94402-2710)
PHONE..................................650 344-5200
Jerry Lee, *Owner*
EMP: 20
SALES (est): 645.7K **Privately Held**
SIC: 2711 Newspapers, publishing & printing

(P-5608)
DAILY JOURNAL CORPORATION (PA)
915 E 1st St, Los Angeles (90012-4042)
PHONE..................................213 229-5300
Gerald L Salzman, *President*
Charles T Munger, *Ch of Bd*
Ani Ghahreman, *President*
John Patrick Guerin, *Vice Ch Bd*
Peter Kaufman, *Bd of Directors*
EMP: 116
SQ FT: 34,000
SALES: 40.7MM **Publicly Held**
WEB: www.dailyjournal.com
SIC: 2711 2721 7313 7372 Newspapers, publishing & printing; magazines: publishing & printing; newspaper advertising representative; prepackaged software

(P-5609)
DAILY JOURNAL CORPORATION
Also Called: San Francisco Daily Journal
44 Montgomery St Ste 500, San Francisco (94104-4607)
PHONE..................................415 296-2400
Ray Reynolds, *Branch Mgr*

Chuleenan Svetvilas, *Manager*
EMP: 80
SALES (corp-wide): 40.7MM **Publicly Held**
WEB: www.dailyjournal.com
SIC: 2711 2721 Newspapers, publishing & printing; periodicals
PA: Daily Journal Corporation
  915 E 1st St
  Los Angeles CA 90012
  213 229-5300

(P-5610)
DAILY RECORDER
901 H St Ste 312, Sacramento (95814-1808)
PHONE..............................916 444-2355
Chris Nofuente, *Manager*
EMP: 12
SALES (est): 431.8K **Privately Held**
SIC: 2711 Newspapers, publishing & printing

(P-5611)
DAILY REVIEW
Also Called: A and G News Papers
3317 Arden Rd, Hayward (94545-3903)
PHONE..................................510 783-6111
Steve Cressoub, *CFO*
EMP: 30
SALES (est): 1.3MM **Privately Held**
WEB: www.thedailyreview.com
SIC: 2711 Newspapers, publishing & printing

(P-5612)
DAILY SPORTS SEOUL USA INC
626 S Kingsley Dr, Los Angeles (90005-2318)
PHONE..................................213 487-9331
Jang Hee Lee, *President*
EMP: 30
SALES (est): 1.9MM **Privately Held**
SIC: 2711 Commercial printing & newspaper publishing combined; newspapers, publishing & printing

(P-5613)
DAILYMEDIA INC (PA)
8 E Figueroa St Ste 220, Santa Barbara (93101-2716)
PHONE..................................541 821-5207
Scott Blum, *President*
Jessica Roady, *Bookkeeper*
EMP: 19
SQ FT: 5,000
SALES (est): 1MM **Privately Held**
SIC: 2711 Newspapers, publishing & printing

(P-5614)
DESERT SUN PUBLISHING CO (HQ)
Also Called: Desert Sun The
750 N Gene Autry Trl, Palm Springs (92262-5463)
PHONE..................................760 322-8889
Denise Fleig, *Executive*
Sonia Parra, *Executive*
Joe Myers, *Credit Mgr*
Sara Weaver, *Sales Mgr*
Adrienne Montoya, *Manager*
EMP: 200 **EST:** 1974
SQ FT: 30,621
SALES (est): 44.7MM
SALES (corp-wide): 2.9B **Publicly Held**
WEB: www.thedesertsun.com
SIC: 2711 Newspapers, publishing & printing
PA: Gannett Co., Inc.
  7950 Jones Branch Dr
  Mc Lean VA 22102
  703 854-6000

(P-5615)
DIGITAL FIRST MEDIA LLC
Also Called: Orange County Register, The
625 N Grand Ave, Santa Ana (92701-4347)
P.O. Box 61056, Anaheim (92803-6156)
PHONE..................................714 796-7000
Toll Free:..................................877 -
Chris Anderson, *Manager*
N Christian Anderson, *President*
Jon Merendino, *Vice Pres*
Cathy Taylor, *Vice Pres*
Ching Lee, *Executive*

EMP: 900
SQ FT: 144,000
SALES (corp-wide): 4.2B **Privately Held**
WEB: www.freedom.com
SIC: 2711 Commercial printing & newspaper publishing combined
PA: Digital First Media, Llc
  101 W Colfax Ave Fl 11
  Denver CO
  -

(P-5616)
DISPATCHER NEWSPAPER
1188 Franklin St Fl 4, San Francisco (94109-6800)
PHONE..................................415 775-0533
Robert McElireth, *President*
Sam Alvarado, *Director*
Joe Cabrales, *Director*
EMP: 25
SALES (est): 863.3K **Privately Held**
SIC: 2711 Newspapers

(P-5617)
DIXON TRIBUNE
145 E A St, Dixon (95620-3599)
PHONE..................................707 678-5594
David Payne, *Owner*
EMP: 17
SALES (est): 773.5K **Privately Held**
SIC: 2711 Newspapers, publishing & printing

(P-5618)
DOW JONES & COMPANY INC
201 California St Fl 13, San Francisco (94111-5002)
PHONE..................................415 765-6131
Steve Yoder, *Chief*
Nancy Werthan, *Office Mgr*
Katie Purchase, *Sales Staff*
Paul Solari, *Sales Staff*
Lee Khan, *Accounts Mgr*
EMP: 20
SALES (corp-wide): 10B **Publicly Held**
SIC: 2711 Newspapers, publishing & printing
HQ: Dow Jones & Company, Inc.
  1211 Avenue Of The Americ
  New York NY 10036
  609 627-2999

(P-5619)
DOW JONES LMG STOCKTON INC
Also Called: Record The
530 E Market St, Stockton (95202-3009)
P.O. Box 900 (95201-0900)
PHONE..................................209 943-6397
Deitra Kenoly, *President*
Roger Coover, *President*
Stewart Willis, *Info Tech Mgr*
Kenneth Damilano, *Technical Staff*
Dave Kelso, *Finance Dir*
EMP: 208
SALES (est): 12.2MM
SALES (corp-wide): 1.5B **Privately Held**
SIC: 2711 Newspapers, publishing & printing
HQ: Local Media Group, Inc.
  40 Mulberry St
  Middletown NY 10940
  845 341-1100

(P-5620)
DOWNEY PATRIOT
8301 Florence Ave Ste 100, Downey (90240-3946)
PHONE..................................562 904-3668
Jennifer Dekay-Gibins, *Owner*
EMP: 10
SALES (est): 637.5K **Privately Held**
SIC: 2711 Newspapers

(P-5621)
E Z BUY E Z SELL RECYCLER CORP (DH)
Also Called: Recycler Classified
4954 Van Nuys Blvd # 201, Sherman Oaks (91403-1719)
PHONE..................................310 886-7808
Niki Ruokosuo, *President*
Jim Fullmer, *VP Finance*
EMP: 200
SQ FT: 13,000

SALES (est): 33.1MM
SALES (corp-wide): 2.7B **Publicly Held**
WEB: www.recycler.com
SIC: 2711 2741 Newspapers: publishing only, not printed on site; miscellaneous publishing
HQ: Tribune Media Company
  515 N State St Ste 2400
  Chicago IL 60654
  312 222-3394

(P-5622)
EAGLE NEWSPAPERS LLC
Also Called: Coronado Eagle
1224 10th St Ste 103, Coronado (92118-3419)
PHONE..................................619 437-8800
Dean Eckenroth,
EMP: 20
SQ FT: 1,350
SALES (est): 1.2MM **Privately Held**
WEB: www.eaglenewsca.com
SIC: 2711 Newspapers: publishing only, not printed on site

(P-5623)
EAST COUNTY GAZETTE
Also Called: Alcine Gazette
270 E Douglas Ave, El Cajon (92020-4514)
P.O. Box 697 (92022-0697)
PHONE..................................619 444-5774
Debbie Norman, *Owner*
EMP: 10
SALES (est): 581K **Privately Held**
SIC: 2711 Newspapers: publishing only, not printed on site; newspapers, publishing & printing

(P-5624)
EASY AD INCORPORATED
155 S Harvard St, Hemet (92543-4233)
PHONE..................................951 658-2244
Winston Greene Jr, *President*
EMP: 35
SALES (est): 1.7MM **Privately Held**
SIC: 2711 2741 Newspapers: publishing only, not printed on site; miscellaneous publishing

(P-5625)
EASY READER INC
832 Hermosa Ave, Hermosa Beach (90254-4116)
P.O. Box 427 (90254-0427)
PHONE..................................310 372-4611
Kevin Cody, *President*
Richard Budman, *COO*
Adrienne Slaughter, *Technology*
Tamar Gillotti, *Accounts Mgr*
Bondo Wyszpolski, *Editor*
EMP: 30 **EST:** 1970
SQ FT: 3,400
SALES (est): 1.7MM **Privately Held**
WEB: www.hermosawave.net
SIC: 2711 Newspapers: publishing only, not printed on site

(P-5626)
EL DORADO GOLD PANNER INC
Also Called: Gold Panner, The
247 Placerville Dr, Placerville (95667-3911)
PHONE..................................530 626-5057
Jerry Moore, *President*
EMP: 10
SALES (est): 490K **Privately Held**
SIC: 2711 Newspapers: publishing only, not printed on site

(P-5627)
EL DORADO NEWSPAPERS INC (DH)
Also Called: Clovis Independent
2100 Q St, Sacramento (95816-6816)
P.O. Box 15779 (95852-0779)
PHONE..................................916 321-1826
Karole Morgan-Prager, *Admin Sec*
Anna Ramseier, *Prdtn Mgr*
Bill Gutierrez, *Adv Mgr*
EMP: 200
SALES (est): 18.5MM
SALES (corp-wide): 807.2MM **Publicly Held**
WEB: www.clovisindependent.com
SIC: 2711 Commercial printing & newspaper publishing combined; newspapers, publishing & printing

HQ: Mcclatchy Newspapers, Inc.
  2100 Q St
  Sacramento CA 95816
  916 321-1855

(P-5628)
EL OBSERVADOR PUBLICATIONS INC
1042 W Hedding St Ste 250, San Jose (95126-1206)
PHONE..................................408 938-1700
Hilbert Morales, *President*
Monica Amador, *Vice Pres*
Elizabeth J Rose-Morales, *Vice Pres*
EMP: 10
SQ FT: 1,400
SALES (est): 765.1K **Privately Held**
WEB: www.el-observador.com
SIC: 2711 Newspapers: publishing only, not printed on site

(P-5629)
EL POPULAR SPANISH NEWSPAPER
404 Truxtun Ave, Bakersfield (93301-5316)
PHONE..................................661 325-7725
George Camacho, *Partner*
EMP: 10 **EST:** 1983
SALES (est): 586.4K **Privately Held**
WEB: www.elpopularnews.com
SIC: 2711 Newspapers: publishing only, not printed on site

(P-5630)
EMBARCADERO PUBLISHING COMPANY (PA)
Also Called: Country Almanac
450 Cambridge Ave, Palo Alto (94306-1507)
P.O. Box 1610 (94302-1610)
PHONE..................................650 964-6300
William Johnson, *President*
Frank Bravo, *Info Tech Dir*
Kristin Brown, *Prdtn Mgr*
Janice Hoogner, *Advt Staff*
Rosemary Lewkowitz, *Advt Staff*
EMP: 132
SQ FT: 4,500
SALES (est): 12.3MM **Privately Held**
WEB: www.paweekly.com
SIC: 2711 Commercial printing & newspaper publishing combined; newspapers, publishing & printing

(P-5631)
EXIN LLC
1213 Evans Ave, San Francisco (94124-1717)
PHONE..................................415 359-2600
Ted Fang, *President*
Florence Fang, *Ch of Bd*
James Fang, *Treasurer*
EMP: 120 **EST:** 2000
SQ FT: 27,526
SALES (est): 4.2MM **Privately Held**
SIC: 2711 Newspapers: publishing only, not printed on site

(P-5632)
FEATHER PUBLISHING COMPANY INC (PA)
Also Called: Feather River Bulletin
287 Lawrence St, Quincy (95971-9477)
P.O. Box B (95971-3586)
PHONE..................................530 283-0800
Michael C Taborski, *President*
Keri B Taborski, *Vice Pres*
Holly Buus, *Manager*
EMP: 30
SALES (est): 7.5MM **Privately Held**
WEB: www.plumasnews.com
SIC: 2711 2752 Newspapers, publishing & printing; lithographing on metal

(P-5633)
FEATHER PUBLISHING COMPANY INC
Also Called: Lassen County Times
100 Grand Ave, Susanville (96130-4451)
PHONE..................................530 257-5321
Sam Williams, *Manager*
EMP: 15

PRODUCTS & SVCS

SALES (corp-wide): 7.5MM **Privately Held**
WEB: www.plumasnews.com
SIC: **2711** 2759 Newspapers, publishing & printing; newspapers: printing
PA: Feather Publishing Company, Incorporated
    287 Lawrence St
    Quincy CA 95971
    530 283-0800

(P-5634)
FOOTHILLS SUN-GAZETTE
Also Called: Foothills Advertiser
120 N E St, Exeter (93221-1729)
P.O. Box 7 (93221-0007)
PHONE.................................559 592-3171
Katie Byrne, *President*
Wsley Byrne, *Treasurer*
Reggie Ellis, *Vice Pres*
William Brown, *Principal*
EMP: 20
SQ FT: 5,000
SALES (est): 1.3MM **Privately Held**
WEB: www.theexetersun.com
SIC: **2711** Newspapers: publishing only, not printed on site

(P-5635)
FREEDOM COMMUNICATIONS INC
Also Called: Orange County Register
22481 Aspan St, El Toro (92630-1630)
PHONE.................................949 454-7300
EMP: 50
SALES (corp-wide): 2.5B **Privately Held**
SIC: **2711**
HQ: Freedom Communications Inc
    625 N Grand Ave
    Santa Ana CA 92701
    714 796-7000

(P-5636)
GANNETT CO INC
U S A Today
10960 Wilshire Blvd, Los Angeles (90024-3702)
PHONE.................................310 444-2120
Gary Pietsch, *Director*
EMP: 20
SALES (corp-wide): 2.9B **Publicly Held**
WEB: www.gannett.com
SIC: **2711** Newspapers, publishing & printing
PA: Gannett Co., Inc.
    7950 Jones Branch Dr
    Mc Lean VA 22102
    703 854-6000

(P-5637)
GANNETT CO INC
Also Called: Tulare Advance Register
330 N West St, Tulare (93274)
PHONE.................................559 688-0521
Amy Pack, *Manager*
EMP: 120
SALES (corp-wide): 2.9B **Publicly Held**
WEB: www.gannett.com
SIC: **2711** Newspapers, publishing & printing
PA: Gannett Co., Inc.
    7950 Jones Branch Dr
    Mc Lean VA 22102
    703 854-6000

(P-5638)
GANNETT CO INC
Also Called: Desert Sun, The
750 N Gene Autry Trl, Palm Springs (92262-5463)
PHONE.................................760 322-8889
EMP: 77
SALES (corp-wide): 2.9B **Publicly Held**
WEB: www.gannett.com
SIC: **2711** Newspapers
PA: Gannett Co., Inc.
    7950 Jones Branch Dr
    Mc Lean VA 22102
    703 854-6000

(P-5639)
GARDENA VALLEY NEWS INC
Also Called: Valley News Gardens
15005 S Vermont Ave, Gardena (90247-3004)
P.O. Box 219 (90248-0219)
PHONE.................................310 329-6351
George D Algie, *President*
Ruriko Yatabe, *Corp Secy*
Robert Von Gorres, *Sales Mgr*
EMP: 40
SQ FT: 8,200
SALES (est): 2.6MM **Privately Held**
WEB: www.gardenavalleynews.com
SIC: **2711** Commercial printing & newspaper publishing combined

(P-5640)
GATEHOUSE MEDIA LLC
Also Called: Fort Bragg Advocate-News
690 S Main St, Fort Bragg (95437-5108)
P.O. Box 1188 (95437-1188)
PHONE.................................707 964-5642
Stan Andreson, *Enginr/R&D Mgr*
EMP: 19
SQ FT: 3,500
SALES (corp-wide): 1.5B **Privately Held**
WEB: www.fortsmith.com
SIC: **2711** Newspapers: publishing only, not printed on site
HQ: Gatehouse Media, Llc
    175 Sullys Trl Fl 3
    Pittsford NY 14534
    585 598-0030

(P-5641)
GATEHOUSE MEDIA LLC
Also Called: Siskiyou Daily News
309 S Broadway St, Yreka (96097-2905)
P.O. Box 127, Mount Shasta (96067-0127)
PHONE.................................530 842-5777
Rod Ows, *Branch Mgr*
EMP: 24
SALES (corp-wide): 1.5B **Privately Held**
WEB: www.gatehousemedia.com
SIC: **2711** Newspapers, publishing & printing
HQ: Gatehouse Media, Llc
    175 Sullys Trl Fl 3
    Pittsford NY 14534
    585 598-0030

(P-5642)
GATEHOUSE MEDIA LLC
Also Called: Chico Enterprise Record
400 E Park Ave, Chico (95928-7127)
P.O. Box 9 (95927-0009)
PHONE.................................530 891-1234
Wolf Rosenburg, *Branch Mgr*
EMP: 70
SALES (corp-wide): 1.5B **Privately Held**
WEB: www.fortsmith.com
SIC: **2711** Newspapers, publishing & printing
HQ: Gatehouse Media, Llc
    175 Sullys Trl Fl 3
    Pittsford NY 14534
    585 598-0030

(P-5643)
GAZETTE MEDIA CO LLC
Also Called: Sacramento Gazette, The
770 L St Ste 950, Sacramento (95814-3361)
P.O. Box 293956 (95829-3956)
PHONE.................................916 567-9654
David Fong, *Mng Member*
EMP: 10
SALES (est): 600.1K **Privately Held**
SIC: **2711** Newspapers: publishing only, not printed on site

(P-5644)
GAZETTE NEWSPAPERS
Also Called: Grunion Gazette
5225 E 2nd St, Long Beach (90803-5326)
PHONE.................................562 433-2000
Simmon Grief, *Principal*
Julie McKibbin, *Assistant*
Jennifer Epstein, *Editor*
EMP: 20
SQ FT: 2,600
SALES (est): 1.3MM **Privately Held**
WEB: www.gazettes.com
SIC: **2711** Newspapers, publishing & printing

(P-5645)
GIBSON PRINTING & PUBLISHING
Also Called: Benicia Herald
820 1st St, Benicia (94510-3216)
P.O. Box 65 (94510-0065)
PHONE.................................707 745-0733
Pam Poppee, *Manager*
EMP: 18
SALES (corp-wide): 4.4MM **Privately Held**
SIC: **2711** 7313 Newspapers: publishing only, not printed on site; newspaper advertising representative
PA: Gibson Printing & Publishing
    544 Curtola Pkwy
    Vallejo CA

(P-5646)
GIBSON PRINTING & PUBLISHING
Also Called: Martinez News Gazette
802 Alhambra Ave, Martinez (94553-1604)
P.O. Box 151 (94553-0015)
PHONE.................................925 228-6400
Dale Lorren, *Manager*
Stephen Shores, *Adv Dir*
EMP: 10
SALES (corp-wide): 4.4MM **Privately Held**
SIC: **2711** Newspapers: publishing only, not printed on site
PA: Gibson Printing & Publishing
    544 Curtola Pkwy
    Vallejo CA

(P-5647)
GIBSON PRINTING & PUBLISHING
Also Called: Dixon Tribune
145 E A St, Dixon (95620-3531)
PHONE.................................707 678-5594
David Payne, *Owner*
EMP: 10
SALES (corp-wide): 4.4MM **Privately Held**
SIC: **2711** Commercial printing & newspaper publishing combined
PA: Gibson Printing & Publishing
    544 Curtola Pkwy
    Vallejo CA

(P-5648)
GRACE COMMUNICATIONS INC (PA)
Also Called: Metropolitan News Company
210 S Spring St, Los Angeles (90012-3710)
P.O. Box 86308 (90086-0308)
PHONE.................................213 628-4384
Joann W Grace, *President*
Roger M Grace, *Vice Pres*
Terry Yoshikawa, *Admin Asst*
Veronica Lopez, *Advt Staff*
EMP: 43 EST: 1901
SQ FT: 21,000
SALES (est): 6.8MM **Privately Held**
SIC: **2711** Newspapers, publishing & printing; newspapers: publishing only, not printed on site

(P-5649)
GREAT NORTHERN WHEELS DEALS
Also Called: Wheels and Deals
810 Lake Blvd Ste C, Redding (96003-2200)
PHONE.................................530 533-2134
Fax: 530 533-1531
EMP: 33
SQ FT: 2,400
SALES: 2MM **Privately Held**
WEB: www.wheelsanddeals.com
SIC: **2711** 7313

(P-5650)
GUM SUN TIMES INC (PA)
Also Called: Chinese Times
625 Kearny St, San Francisco (94108-1849)
PHONE.................................415 379-6788
Michael Lamm, *President*

See B Hom, *President*
Harrison Lim, *President*
EMP: 30
SQ FT: 9,000
SALES (est): 1.3MM **Privately Held**
SIC: **2711** Newspapers: publishing only, not printed on site

(P-5651)
HANFORD SENTINEL INC
Also Called: Pulitzer Community Newspapers
300 W 6th St, Hanford (93230-4518)
P.O. Box 9 (93232-0009)
PHONE.................................559 582-0471
Randy Rickman, *President*
Mark Daniel, *Vice Pres*
Rusty Williamson, *Advt Staff*
Joyce Chambers, *Manager*
EMP: 90
SQ FT: 16,000
SALES (est): 5.2MM
SALES (corp-wide): 593.9MM **Publicly Held**
WEB: www.newzcentral.com
SIC: **2711** Commercial printing & newspaper publishing combined; newspapers, publishing & printing
HQ: Pulitzer Inc
    900 N Tucker Blvd
    Saint Louis MO 63101
    314 340-8000

(P-5652)
HARRELL HOLDINGS (PA)
1707 Eye St Ste 102, Bakersfield (93301-5208)
P.O. Box 440 (93302-0440)
PHONE.................................661 322-5627
Richard Beene, *President*
Logan Molen, *COO*
Michelle Hirst, *CFO*
Virginia Fritts Moorhouse, *Chairman*
John Arthur, *Vice Pres*
EMP: 190
SALES (est): 21.4MM **Privately Held**
WEB: www.bakersfield.net
SIC: **2711** Commercial printing & newspaper publishing combined; newspapers, publishing & printing

(P-5653)
HARTE HANKS INC
2830 Orbiter St, Brea (92821-6224)
PHONE.................................714 577-4462
Pete Gorman, *Branch Mgr*
EMP: 32
SALES (corp-wide): 284.6MM **Publicly Held**
SIC: **2711** Newspapers, publishing & printing
PA: Harte Hanks, Inc.
    9601 Mcallister Fwy # 610
    San Antonio TX 78216
    210 829-9000

(P-5654)
HARTE HANKS INC
Also Called: Pennysaver
150 N Santa Anita Ave # 300, Arcadia (91006-3113)
PHONE.................................626 251-4500
Jannie Goodman, *Sales/Mktg Mgr*
EMP: 13
SALES (corp-wide): 284.6MM **Publicly Held**
SIC: **2711** 7313 Newspapers, publishing & printing; newspaper advertising representative
PA: Harte Hanks, Inc.
    9601 Mcallister Fwy # 610
    San Antonio TX 78216
    210 829-9000

(P-5655)
HEARST COMMUNICATIONS INC
7916 Arcade Lake Ln, Citrus Heights (95610-5165)
PHONE.................................916 725-8694
EMP: 251
SALES (corp-wide): 8.3B **Privately Held**
SIC: **2711** Newspapers, publishing & printing

HQ: Hearst Communications, Inc.
300 W 57th St
New York NY 10019
212 649-2000

(P-5656)
HEARST COMMUNICATIONS INC
Chronicle Books
680 2nd St, San Francisco (94107-2015)
PHONE..................................415 537-4200
Nion McEvoy, *Manager*
EMP: 160
SALES (corp-wide): 8.3B **Privately Held**
WEB: www.telegram.com
SIC: 2711 Newspapers, publishing & printing
HQ: Hearst Communications, Inc.
300 W 57th St
New York NY 10019
212 649-2000

(P-5657)
HEARST CORPORATION
Also Called: HEARST CORPORATION THE
224 Reindollar Ave, Marina (93933-3857)
PHONE..................................831 582-9605
Joel Doss, *Manager*
EMP: 247
SALES (corp-wide): 8.3B **Privately Held**
WEB: www.hearstcorp.com
SIC: 2711 Newspapers
PA: The Hearst Corporation
300 W 57th St Fl 42
New York NY 10019
212 649-2000

(P-5658)
HEARST CORPORATION
Sunical Land and Livestock Div
5 3rd St Ste 200, San Francisco
(94103-3299)
PHONE..................................415 777-0600
Stephen Hurst, *Manager*
EMP: 13
SALES (corp-wide): 8.3B **Privately Held**
WEB: www.hearstcorp.com
SIC: 2711 Newspapers
PA: The Hearst Corporation
300 W 57th St Fl 42
New York NY 10019
212 649-2000

(P-5659)
HEARTS FOR LONG BEACH INC
5225 E 2nd St, Long Beach (90803-5326)
PHONE..................................562 433-2000
Simmon Grief, *Principal*
EMP: 20 EST: 1977
SALES: 4.3K **Privately Held**
WEB: www.heartsforhounds.com
SIC: 2711 Newspapers, publishing & printing

(P-5660)
HERBURGER PUBLICATIONS INC (PA)
Also Called: Galt Herald
604 N Lincoln Way, Galt (95632-8601)
P.O. Box 307 (95632-0307)
PHONE..................................916 685-5533
Roy Herburger, *President*
David Herburger, *Vice Pres*
EMP: 60 EST: 1903
SQ FT: 10,000
SALES (est): 6.1MM **Privately Held**
WEB: www.herburger.net
SIC: 2711 Commercial printing & newspaper publishing combined

(P-5661)
HERBURGER PUBLICATIONS INC
Also Called: Elk Grove Citizen
8970 Elk Grove Blvd, Elk Grove
(95624-1971)
P.O. Box 1777 (95759-1777)
PHONE..................................916 685-3945
Cameron Macdonald, *Principal*
EMP: 10

SALES (corp-wide): 6.1MM **Privately Held**
WEB: www.herburger.net
SIC: 2711 7313 Newspapers, publishing & printing; newspaper advertising representative
PA: Herburger Publications, Inc
604 N Lincoln Way
Galt CA 95632
916 685-5533

(P-5662)
HESPERIA RESORTER
Also Called: Apple Valley News
16925 Main St Ste A, Hesperia
(92345-6038)
P.O. Box 400937 (92340-0937)
PHONE..................................760 244-0021
Ray Pryke, *Owner*
EMP: 25
SALES (est): 1.3MM **Privately Held**
SIC: 2711 Newspapers

(P-5663)
HI-DESERT PUBLISHING COMPANY
Also Called: Yuciapa & Calimesa News Mirror
35154 Yucaipa Blvd, Yucaipa (92399-4339)
P.O. Box 760 (92399-0760)
PHONE..................................909 797-9101
Fax: 909 797-0502
EMP: 27
SALES (corp-wide): 213.8MM **Privately Held**
SIC: 2711
HQ: Hi-Desert Publishing Company
56445 29 Palms Hwy
Yucca Valley CA 92284
760 365-3315

(P-5664)
HI-DESERT PUBLISHING COMPANY
Also Called: Mountain News & Shopper
28200 Highway 189 O-1, Lake Arrowhead
(92352-9700)
P.O. Box 2410 (92352-2410)
PHONE..................................909 336-3555
Harry Bradley, *Sales/Mktg Mgr*
EMP: 23
SALES (corp-wide): 224.8MM **Privately Held**
WEB: www.hidesertstar.com
SIC: 2711 Commercial printing & newspaper publishing combined
HQ: Hi-Desert Publishing Company
56445 29 Palms Hwy
Yucca Valley CA 92284

(P-5665)
HI-DESERT PUBLISHING COMPANY (HQ)
56445 29 Palms Hwy, Yucca Valley
(92284-2861)
PHONE..................................760 365-3315
Cindy Melland, *Publisher*
Stacy Moore, *Editor*
EMP: 70
SALES (est): 24.6MM
SALES (corp-wide): 224.8MM **Privately Held**
WEB: www.hidesertstar.com
SIC: 2711 Newspapers, publishing & printing
PA: Brehm Communications, Inc.
16644 W Bernardo Dr # 300
San Diego CA 92127
858 451-6200

(P-5666)
HORIZON CAL PUBLICATIONS
Also Called: Mammoth Times
452 Old Mammoth Rd, Mammoth Lakes
(93546-2013)
P.O. Box 3929 (93546-3929)
PHONE..................................760 934-3929
David J Radler, *President*
EMP: 15
SQ FT: 2,100
SALES: 2MM **Privately Held**
WEB: www.mammothtimes.com
SIC: 2711 Newspapers

(P-5667)
HORIZON PUBLICATIONS INC
Also Called: Inyo Register, The
407 W Line St Ste 8, Bishop (93514-3321)
PHONE..................................760 873-3535
Bob Reitz, *Branch Mgr*
Terrance Vestal, *Editor*
EMP: 16
SALES (corp-wide): 71.5MM **Privately Held**
WEB: www.malvern-online.com
SIC: 2711 Newspapers
PA: Horizon Publications, Inc.
1120 N Carbon St Ste 100
Marion IL 62959
618 993-1711

(P-5668)
HUGHES PRICE & SHARP INC
Also Called: Bargain Mart Classifieds
5200 Lankershim Blvd # 850, North Hollywood (91601-3155)
PHONE..................................865 675-6278
Jose Ortiz, *President*
A Eugene Hughes, *Treasurer*
EMP: 20
SALES (est): 1.1MM **Privately Held**
WEB: www.bargainmartclassifieds.com
SIC: 2711 Newspapers: publishing only, not printed on site

(P-5669)
HUMBOLDT NEWSPAPER INC
Also Called: Times-Standard
930 6th St, Eureka (95501-1112)
P.O. Box 3580 (95502-3580)
PHONE..................................707 442-1711
Stephan J Sosinski, *Publisher*
Ron Maloney, *Manager*
EMP: 526
SQ FT: 49,872
SALES (est): 21.9MM **Privately Held**
WEB: www.times-standard.com
SIC: 2711 Newspapers: publishing only, not printed on site

(P-5670)
INDEPENDENT COAST OBSERVER
Also Called: I. C. O.
38500 S Highway 1, Gualala (95445-8592)
P.O. Box 1200 (95445-1200)
PHONE..................................707 884-3501
Stephen McLaughlin, *President*
EMP: 15
SQ FT: 2,000
SALES (est): 862.2K **Privately Held**
WEB: www.independentcoastobserver.com
SIC: 2711 Commercial printing & newspaper publishing combined

(P-5671)
INDEPNDENT BRKLEY STDNT PUBG I
Also Called: Daily Californian
2483 Hearst Ave, Berkeley (94709-1320)
P.O. Box 1949 (94701-1949)
PHONE..................................510 548-8300
Karim Doumar, *President*
Bryan Wang, *Chief Mktg Ofcr*
Carmelia Muljadi, *Marketing Mgr*
EMP: 100
SQ FT: 4,100
SALES: 694K **Privately Held**
SIC: 2711 7372 Newspapers: publishing only, not printed on site; application computer software

(P-5672)
INDIA-WEST PUBLICATIONS INC (PA)
933 Macarthur Blvd, San Leandro
(94577-3062)
PHONE..................................510 383-1140
Ramesh Murarka, *President*
Bina Murarka, *Corp Secy*
Divya Kumar, *Associate*
EMP: 21
SQ FT: 7,000
SALES (est): 1.8MM **Privately Held**
SIC: 2711 Newspapers: publishing only, not printed on site

(P-5673)
INLAND EMPIRE CMNTY NEWSPAPERS
Also Called: Rialto Record
1809 Commercenter W, San Bernardino
(92408-3303)
P.O. Box 110, Colton (92324-0110)
PHONE..................................909 381-9898
William B Harrison, *President*
EMP: 25 EST: 1948
SQ FT: 4,000
SALES (est): 1.2MM **Privately Held**
SIC: 2711 Newspapers: publishing only, not printed on site

(P-5674)
INLAND VALLEY NEWS INC
2009 Porter Field Way C, Upland
(91786-2196)
PHONE..................................909 949-3099
Gloria Morrow, *President*
Tommy Morrow, *Admin Sec*
▲ EMP: 15
SALES: 105.4K **Privately Held**
WEB: www.inlandvalleynews.com
SIC: 2711 Newspapers: publishing only, not printed on site

(P-5675)
INLAND VALLEY PUBISING CO
Also Called: Independent, The
2250 1st St, Livermore (94550-3143)
P.O. Box 1198 (94551-1198)
PHONE..................................925 243-8000
Joan Seppala, *President*
EMP: 12
SQ FT: 5,000
SALES: 850K **Privately Held**
WEB: www.independentnews.com
SIC: 2711 Newspapers: publishing only, not printed on site

(P-5676)
INTERNATIONAL DAILY NEWS INC (PA)
870 Monterey Pass Rd, Monterey Park
(91754-3688)
PHONE..................................323 265-1317
Jessica G Elnitiarta, *President*
▲ EMP: 20
SQ FT: 10,000
SALES (est): 3.7MM **Privately Held**
WEB: www.chinesetoday.com
SIC: 2711 Newspapers, publishing & printing

(P-5677)
INVESTORS BUSINESS DAILY INC (HQ)
12655 Beatrice St, Los Angeles
(90066-7303)
PHONE..................................310 448-6000
William O'Neil, *President*
Kathy Sherman, *Vice Pres*
Brian Gonzales, *Education*
Alexandra Torzilli, *Director*
▲ EMP: 200
SQ FT: 180,000
SALES (est): 30.3MM
SALES (corp-wide): 231.5MM **Privately Held**
WEB: www.investors.com
SIC: 2711 Newspapers, publishing & printing
PA: Data Analysis Inc.
12655 Beatrice St
Los Angeles CA 90066
310 448-6800

(P-5678)
JOONG-ANG DAILY NEWS CAL INC (HQ)
Also Called: Korea Daily
690 Wilshire Pl, Los Angeles (90005-3930)
PHONE..................................213 368-2500
Kae Hong Ko, *CEO*
In Taek Park, *President*
Yoonsoo Kim, *General Mgr*
Jung Lee, *General Mgr*
Sang Park, *Administration*
▲ EMP: 200 EST: 1974
SQ FT: 70,000

SALES (est): 98MM Privately Held
WEB: www.joongangusa.com
SIC: 2711 Commercial printing & newspaper publishing combined

(P-5679)
JOONG-ANG DAILY NEWS CAL INC
Also Called: Korea Central
8269 Garden Grove Blvd, Garden Grove (92844-1010)
PHONE.....................714 638-2341
Chung Park, *Manager*
EMP: 10 **Privately Held**
WEB: www.joongangusa.com
SIC: 2711 Newspapers, publishing & printing
HQ: The Joong-Ang Daily News California Inc
690 Wilshire Pl
Los Angeles CA 90005
213 368-2500

(P-5680)
JOURNAL OF BOCOMMUNICATION INC
2772 Woodwardia Dr, Los Angeles (90077-2121)
PHONE.....................310 475-4708
Robert C Turner, *Principal*
Carol Gray, *Business Mgr*
EMP: 15
SALES: 0 **Privately Held**
SIC: 2711 Newspapers, publishing & printing

(P-5681)
KAAR DRECT MAIL FLFILLMENT LLC
1225 Expo Way Ste 160, San Diego (92154)
PHONE.....................619 382-3670
Sohela Aragon, *CEO*
Jennifer Solis, *Executive Asst*
Juan Rodriguez, *Opers Mgr*
EMP: 25
SALES (est): 2.4MM Privately Held
SIC: 2711 5963 2752 8742 Commercial printing & newspaper publishing combined; direct sales, telemarketing; publication printing, lithographic; marketing consulting services; pamphlets: printing only, not published on site

(P-5682)
KING RUSTLER
522 Broadway St Ste A, King City (93930-3243)
P.O. Box 710 (93930-0710)
PHONE.....................831 385-4880
Tom Cross, *Partner*
EMP: 15
SALES (est): 544.9K Privately Held
SIC: 2711 5812 Newspapers, publishing & printing; eating places

(P-5683)
KOREA CENTRAL DAILY NEWS
Also Called: Joongang Dily Nwssan Francisco
33288 Central Ave, Union City (94587-2010)
PHONE.....................213 368-2500
Kim Pansoo, *President*
Yeon T Lee, *President*
Sunny Ui Lee, *Treasurer*
▲ **EMP:** 17
SQ FT: 23,000
SALES: 2MM **Privately Held**
SIC: 2711 Newspapers, publishing & printing

(P-5684)
KOREA DAILY NEWS & KOREA TIMES
8134 Capwell Dr, Oakland (94621-2110)
PHONE.....................510 777-1111
Jae Chang, *President*
EMP: 30
SALES (est): 1.3MM Privately Held
SIC: 2711 Newspapers, publishing & printing

(P-5685)
KOREA TIMES LOS ANGELES INC
Also Called: Korea Times San Francisco, The
8134 Capwell Dr, Oakland (94621-2110)
PHONE.....................510 777-1111
Sung CHI, *Manager*
EMP: 30
SALES (corp-wide): 85.3MM Privately Held
WEB: www.koreatimeshawaii.com
SIC: 2711 Newspapers, publishing & printing
PA: The Korea Times Los Angeles Inc
3731 Wilshire Blvd
Los Angeles CA 90010
323 692-2000

(P-5686)
KOREA TIMES LOS ANGELES INC
9572 Garden Grove Blvd, Garden Grove (92844-1514)
PHONE.....................714 530-6001
Cangy Lee, *Manager*
EMP: 10
SALES (corp-wide): 85.3MM Privately Held
WEB: www.koreatimeshawaii.com
SIC: 2711 Newspapers, publishing & printing
PA: The Korea Times Los Angeles Inc
3731 Wilshire Blvd
Los Angeles CA 90010
323 692-2000

(P-5687)
KYOCHARO USA LLC
3807 Wilshire Blvd # 518, Los Angeles (90010-3113)
PHONE.....................213 383-1236
Im Kyu Sim, *Owner*
▲ **EMP:** 15
SALES: 1MM **Privately Held**
SIC: 2711 Newspapers, publishing & printing

(P-5688)
LA OPINION LP (HQ)
Also Called: Lozano Enterprises
915 Wilshire Blvd Ste 915 # 915, Los Angeles (90017-3474)
PHONE.....................213 896-2196
Monica C Lozano, *CEO*
Lozano Communications, *General Ptnr*
La Opini N, *Vice Pres*
Maria Amezcua, *Executive*
Paula Gamez, *Technology*
EMP: 54
SALES (est): 31.8MM
SALES (corp-wide): 65.3MM Privately Held
WEB: www.laopinion.com
SIC: 2711 Newspapers, publishing & printing
PA: Impremedia, Llc
1 Metrotech Ctr Fl 18
Brooklyn NY 11201
212 807-4600

(P-5689)
LA OPINION LP
210 E Washington Blvd, Los Angeles (90015-3603)
PHONE.....................213 896-2222
Carlos Marina, *Manager*
EMP: 100
SALES (corp-wide): 65.3MM Privately Held
WEB: www.laopinion.com
SIC: 2711 Newspapers, publishing & printing
HQ: La Opinion, L.P.
915 Wilshire Blvd Ste 915 # 915
Los Angeles CA 90017
213 896-2196

(P-5690)
LA TIMES
202 W 1st St Ste 500, Los Angeles (90012-4401)
PHONE.....................213 237-2279
Raymond Jansen, *CEO*
EMP: 13

SALES (est): 1.1MM Privately Held
SIC: 2711 Newspapers, publishing & printing

(P-5691)
LA WEEKLY
Also Called: L A Weekly
724 S Spring St Ste 700, Los Angeles (90014-2943)
P.O. Box 5052, Culver City (90231-5052)
PHONE.....................310 574-7100
Mike Sigman, *President*
Whitney Crossley, *Advt Staff*
Joel Lara, *Sales Staff*
Shana N Dambrot, *Editor*
Michele Stueven, *Editor*
EMP: 150
SALES (est): 10.3MM
SALES (corp-wide): 25MM Privately Held
WEB: www.laweekly.com
SIC: 2711 Newspapers, publishing & printing
PA: Village Voice Media Llc
36 Cooper Sq Fl 433333
New York NY
212 475-3300

(P-5692)
LAGUNA BEACH ALES & LAGERS LLC
31611 Florence Ave, Laguna Beach (92651-8281)
PHONE.....................949 228-4496
Michael Lombardo, *Principal*
EMP: 11
SALES (est): 835.8K Privately Held
SIC: 2711 Newspapers

(P-5693)
LAKE COUNTY PUBLISHING CO (DH)
Also Called: Lake County Record-Bee
2150 S Main St, Lakeport (95453-5620)
P.O. Box 849 (95453-0849)
PHONE.....................707 263-5636
Edward Mead, *President*
EMP: 69
SALES (est): 4.7MM
SALES (corp-wide): 4.2B Privately Held
SIC: 2711 Newspapers, publishing & printing

(P-5694)
LAPRENSA SAN DIEGO
220 Glover Ave Apt E, Chula Vista (91910-2657)
PHONE.....................619 425-7400
Daniel Munoz, *Principal*
EMP: 10
SALES (est): 379.5K Privately Held
SIC: 2711 Newspapers, publishing & printing

(P-5695)
LATINA & ASSOCIATES INC (PA)
Also Called: El Latino Newspaper
1105 Broadway, Chula Vista (91911-2767)
P.O. Box 120550, San Diego (92112-0550)
PHONE.....................619 426-1491
Fanny Miller, *CEO*
EMP: 38 **EST:** 1985
SQ FT: 2,500
SALES (est): 2.3MM Privately Held
WEB: www.ellatino.net
SIC: 2711 Newspapers: publishing only, not printed on site

(P-5696)
LEE CENTRAL CAL NEWSPAPERS
Also Called: Selma Enterprise
2045 Grant St, Selma (93662-3508)
P.O. Box 100 (93662-0100)
PHONE.....................559 896-1976
Manuel Collazo, *Director*
EMP: 50
SALES (est): 2.2MM
SALES (corp-wide): 593.9MM Publicly Held
WEB: www.selmaenterprise.com
SIC: 2711 2752 Commercial printing & newspaper publishing combined; lithographing on metal

PA: Lee Enterprises, Incorporated
201 N Harrison St Ste 600
Davenport IA 52801
563 383-2100

(P-5697)
LEE ENTERPRISES INCORPORATED
Also Called: Santa Maria Times
3200 Skyway Dr, Santa Maria (93455-1824)
PHONE.....................805 925-2691
Cynthia Schur, *Manager*
EMP: 140
SALES (corp-wide): 593.9MM Publicly Held
WEB: www.lee.net
SIC: 2711 Commercial printing & newspaper publishing combined
PA: Lee Enterprises, Incorporated
201 N Harrison St Ste 600
Davenport IA 52801
563 383-2100

(P-5698)
LELAND STANFORD JUNIOR UNIV
Also Called: Stanford University Press
500 Broadway St, Redwood City (94063-3199)
PHONE.....................650 723-9434
Geoffrey Burn, *Director*
Jean Kim, *Finance*
Anne Jain, *Production*
Gigi Mark, *Production*
Linda Stewart, *Marketing Staff*
EMP: 30
SALES (corp-wide): 11.3B Privately Held
SIC: 2711 2731 Newspapers; book publishing
PA: Leland Stanford Junior University
450 Jane Stanford Way
Stanford CA 94305
650 723-2300

(P-5699)
LITTLE SAIGON NEWS INC
Also Called: Saigon Nho
13861 Seaboard Cir, Garden Grove (92843-3908)
PHONE.....................714 265-0800
Brigitte L Huynh, *CEO*
Brigitte Huynh, *President*
EMP: 17
SQ FT: 16,370
SALES (est): 1.4MM Privately Held
SIC: 2711 Newspapers, publishing & printing

(P-5700)
LIVE JOURNAL INC
6363 Skyline Blvd, Oakland (94611-1042)
PHONE.....................415 230-3600
Andrew Paulson, *President*
Steffanie Gravelle, *CFO*
Brenden Delzer, *Editor*
EMP: 33
SALES (est): 2.5MM Privately Held
SIC: 2711 Newspapers, publishing & printing

(P-5701)
LMG NATIONAL PUBLISHING INC
Also Called: Daily Press
13891 Park Ave, Victorville (92392-2435)
P.O. Box 1389 (92393-1389)
PHONE.....................760 241-7744
Albert Frattura, *Manager*
David Schrimpf, *Webmaster*
EMP: 100
SALES (corp-wide): 1.5B Privately Held
SIC: 2711 2752 Newspapers, publishing & printing; commercial printing, lithographic
HQ: Lmg National Publishing, Inc.
350 Willowbrook Office Pa
Fairport NY 14450
585 598-6874

(P-5702)
LODI NEWS SENTINEL
Also Called: Lodi Mail Express
125 N Church St, Lodi (95240-2197)
P.O. Box 1360 (95241-1360)
PHONE.....................209 369-2761

Frederick E Weybret, *Ch of Bd*
Alcyon Weybret, *Shareholder*
James Weybret, *Shareholder*
Martin Weybret, *President*
▲ EMP: 90
SQ FT: 19,000
SALES (est): 5.5MM **Privately Held**
WEB: www.lodinews.com
SIC: 2711 Commercial printing & newspaper publishing combined; newspapers, publishing & printing

(P-5703)
LOS ANGELES SENTINEL INC
Also Called: La Sentinel Newspaper
3800 Crenshaw Blvd, Los Angeles
(90008-1813)
PHONE.....................323 299-3800
Jennifer Thomas, *President*
Brik Booker, *CEO*
Tracy Mitchell, *Controller*
EMP: 51
SALES (est): 3.8MM **Privately Held**
WEB: www.losangelessentinel.com
SIC: 2711 Newspapers, publishing & printing

(P-5704)
**LOS ANGLES TMES
CMMNCTIONS LLC (PA)**
2300 E Imperial Hwy, El Segundo
(90245-2813)
PHONE.....................213 237-5000
Ross Levinsohn, *CEO*
Chris Argentieri, *COO*
Don Reis, *Officer*
Crane Kenney, *Vice Pres*
Hillary Manning, *Vice Pres*
▲ EMP: 192
SQ FT: 162,000
SALES (est): 846.2MM **Privately Held**
WEB: www.latimes.com
SIC: 2711 Newspapers, publishing & printing

(P-5705)
**LOS ANGLES TMES
CMMNCTIONS LLC**
1717 4th St Ste 100, Santa Monica
(90401-3319)
PHONE.....................310 450-6666
Greg Bertness, *Manager*
Karen Melick, *Project Mgr*
EMP: 100
SQ FT: 4,000
SALES (corp-wide): 846.2MM **Privately Held**
SIC: 2711 Newspapers
PA: Los Angeles Times Communications, Llc
2300 E Imperial Hwy
El Segundo CA 90245
213 237-5000

(P-5706)
**LOS ANGLES TMES
CMMNCTIONS LLC**
1245 S Longwood Ave, Los Angeles
(90019-1759)
PHONE.....................213 237-7203
John Madigan, *Branch Mgr*
EMP: 115
SALES (corp-wide): 846.2MM **Privately Held**
SIC: 2711 Newspapers, publishing & printing
PA: Los Angeles Times Communications, Llc
2300 E Imperial Hwy
El Segundo CA 90245
213 237-5000

(P-5707)
**LOS ANGLES TMES
CMMNCTIONS LLC**
10540 Talbert Ave 300w, Fountain Valley
(92708-6027)
P.O. Box 2008, Costa Mesa (92628-2008)
PHONE.....................714 966-5600
Judith L Sweeney, *President*
Cindy Allen, *Marketing Mgr*
EMP: 411
SQ FT: 60,000

SALES (corp-wide): 846.2MM **Privately Held**
SIC: 2711 Newspapers: publishing only, not printed on site
PA: Los Angeles Times Communications, Llc
2300 E Imperial Hwy
El Segundo CA 90245
213 237-5000

(P-5708)
**LOS ANGLES TMES
CMMNCTIONS LLC**
Also Called: Glendale Times
1011 E Wilson Ave Fl 2, Glendale
(91206-4535)
PHONE.....................818 637-3203
Judee Kendall, *General Mgr*
EMP: 65
SALES (corp-wide): 846.2MM **Privately Held**
SIC: 2711 Newspapers, publishing & printing
PA: Los Angeles Times Communications, Llc
2300 E Imperial Hwy
El Segundo CA 90245
213 237-5000

(P-5709)
**LOS ANGLES TMES
CMMNCTIONS LLC**
705 Pine St, Paso Robles (93446-2860)
PHONE.....................805 238-2720
EMP: 37
SALES (corp-wide): 846.2MM **Privately Held**
SIC: 2711 Newspapers
PA: Los Angeles Times Communications, Llc
2300 E Imperial Hwy
El Segundo CA 90245
213 237-5000

(P-5710)
**LOS ANGLES TMES
CMMNCTIONS LLC**
388 Market St Ste 1550, San Francisco
(94111-5355)
PHONE.....................415 274-9000
EMP: 13
SALES (corp-wide): 769.2MM **Privately Held**
SIC: 2711
PA: Los Angeles Times Communications, Llc
2300 E Imperial Hwy
El Segundo CA 90245
213 237-5000

(P-5711)
**LOS ANGLES TMES
CMMNCTIONS LLC**
Also Called: La Canada Valley Sun
1061 Valley Sun Ln, La Canada Flintridge
(91011-3283)
P.O. Box 38, La Canada (91012-0038)
PHONE.....................818 790-8774
Carol Cormacie, *Manager*
Olga Albarado, *Controller*
Elaine Zinngrabe, *Publisher*
EMP: 35
SALES (corp-wide): 846.2MM **Privately Held**
SIC: 2711 Newspapers: publishing only, not printed on site
PA: Los Angeles Times Communications, Llc
2300 E Imperial Hwy
El Segundo CA 90245
213 237-5000

(P-5712)
**LOS ANGLES TMES
CMMNCTIONS LLC**
10427 San Sevaine Way E, Jurupa Valley
(91752-1199)
PHONE.....................951 683-6066
Darlene Masi, *Branch Mgr*
EMP: 38
SALES (corp-wide): 846.2MM **Privately Held**
SIC: 2711 Newspapers, publishing & printing

PA: Los Angeles Times Communications, Llc
2300 E Imperial Hwy
El Segundo CA 90245
213 237-5000

(P-5713)
**LOS ANGLES TMES
CMMNCTIONS LLC**
Also Called: Lats International
145 S Spring St, Los Angeles
(90012-4053)
PHONE.....................213 237-7987
EMP: 30
SALES (corp-wide): 769.2MM **Privately Held**
SIC: 2711 2741
PA: Los Angeles Times Communications, Llc
2300 E Imperial Hwy
El Segundo CA 90245
213 237-5000

(P-5714)
**LOS ANGLES TMES
CMMNCTIONS LLC**
Also Called: L A Times Olympic Plant
2000 E 8th St, Los Angeles (90021-2474)
PHONE.....................213 237-5691
EMP: 240
SALES (corp-wide): 846.2MM **Privately Held**
SIC: 2711 Newspapers, publishing & printing
PA: Los Angeles Times Communications, Llc
2300 E Imperial Hwy
El Segundo CA 90245
213 237-5000

(P-5715)
**LOS ANGLES TMES
CMMNCTIONS LLC**
2001 E Cashdan St, Compton
(90220-6438)
PHONE.....................310 638-9414
Sandy Sao, *Manager*
EMP: 14
SALES (corp-wide): 846.2MM **Privately Held**
SIC: 2711 Newspapers, publishing & printing
PA: Los Angeles Times Communications, Llc
2300 E Imperial Hwy
El Segundo CA 90245
213 237-5000

(P-5716)
**MADERA PRINTING & PUBG CO
INC**
2890 Falcon Dr, Madera (93637-9287)
PHONE.....................559 674-2424
Charles P Doud, *President*
EMP: 35
SQ FT: 15,000
SALES (est): 1.7MM **Privately Held**
WEB: www.maderatribune.net
SIC: 2711 Newspapers

(P-5717)
**MAINSTREET MEDIA GROUP
LLC**
6400 Monterey Rd, Gilroy (95020-6628)
P.O. Box 516 (95021-0516)
PHONE.....................408 842-6400
Anthony A Allegretti, *CEO*
Stephen P Staloch, *COO*
Christopher L Lake, *CFO*
Dana Arvig, *Vice Pres*
EMP: 180
SQ FT: 25,000
SALES (est): 10.5MM **Privately Held**
WEB: www.mainstreetmediagroup.com
SIC: 2711 Newspapers, publishing & printing

(P-5718)
MALIBU ENTERPRISES INC
Also Called: Surfside News
28990 Pacific Coast Hwy # 108, Malibu
(90265-3952)
P.O. Box 6854 (90264-6854)
PHONE.....................310 457-2112
Anne C Soble, *President*

EMP: 24
SQ FT: 2,100
SALES (est): 108.9K **Privately Held**
SIC: 2711 5994 Newspapers: publishing only, not printed on site; news dealers & newsstands

(P-5719)
MALIBU TIMES INC
3864 Las Flores Canyon Rd, Malibu
(90265-5295)
P.O. Box 1127 (90265-1127)
PHONE.....................310 456-5507
Arnold York, *President*
Karen York, *Vice Pres*
EMP: 15
SQ FT: 2,000
SALES (est): 1.1MM **Privately Held**
WEB: www.malibutimes.com
SIC: 2711 Newspapers: publishing only, not printed on site

(P-5720)
MAMMOTH MEDIA INC
1447 2nd St, Santa Monica (90401-3404)
PHONE.....................310 393-3024
Benoit Vatere, *CEO*
Mike Jones, *Chairman*
EMP: 64 EST: 2016
SALES (est): 1.9MM **Privately Held**
SIC: 2711 Newspapers

(P-5721)
MANNIS COMMUNICATIONS INC
Also Called: The Beacon
1621 Grand Ave Ste C, San Diego
(92109-4458)
PHONE.....................858 270-3103
Julie M Hoisington, *CEO*
David Mannis, *President*
EMP: 25
SALES (est): 1.4MM **Privately Held**
SIC: 2711 Newspapers

(P-5722)
MANNIS COMMUNICATIONS INC
Also Called: San Diego Cmnty Newsppr Group
4645 Caca St Fl 2 Flr 2, San Diego
(92109)
P.O. Box 9550 (92169-0550)
PHONE.....................858 270-3103
David Mannis, *President*
Julie Mannis, *Vice Pres*
EMP: 35
SQ FT: 3,000
SALES (est): 1.9MM **Privately Held**
WEB: www.sdnews.com
SIC: 2711 Newspapers: publishing only, not printed on site

(P-5723)
MARIN SCOPE INCORPORATED
Also Called: Marin Scope Newspapers
1301b Grant Ave, Novato (94945-3143)
P.O. Box 8 (94948-0008)
PHONE.....................415 892-1516
Dijay Mallya, *Principal*
Vijay Mallya, *President*
EMP: 20
SQ FT: 3,400
SALES (est): 1.2MM **Privately Held**
WEB: www.marinscope.com
SIC: 2711 Newspapers, publishing & printing

(P-5724)
MARIN SCOPE INCORPORATED
Also Called: San Rfl-Trra Linda Newspointer
700 Larkspur Landing Cir, Larkspur
(94939-1715)
PHONE.....................415 892-1516
Paul A Anderson, *President*
John Igan, *Principal*
EMP: 29 EST: 1971
SQ FT: 6,000
SALES (est): 1.4MM **Privately Held**
SIC: 2711 Newspapers, publishing & printing

(P-5725)
MARIPOSA GAZETTE & MINER
Also Called: Mountain Life
5180 Hwy 140 Ste B, Mariposa (95338)
PHONE.....................209 966-2500
Robert Daniel Tucker, *Owner*

(PA)=Parent Co (HQ)=Headquarters (DH)=Div Headquarters
✿ = New Business established in last 2 years

Shantel Sojka, *Sales Staff*
Dan Tucker, *Publisher*
EMP: 12
SQ FT: 3,000
SALES (est): 612.4K **Privately Held**
SIC: 2711 Newspapers, publishing & printing

(P-5726)
MARKETING BULLETIN BOARD
639 Olive Rd, Santa Barbara (93108-1442)
PHONE...............................805 455-2255
Walter E Owen III, *Principal*
Walter Owen, *Principal*
EMP: 10 **EST:** 2008
SALES (est): 634.3K **Privately Held**
SIC: 2711 Newspapers, publishing & printing

(P-5727)
MCCLATCHY COMPANY (PA)
2100 Q St, Sacramento (95816-6816)
P.O. Box 15779 (95852-0779)
PHONE...............................916 321-1844
Craig I Forman, *President*
Kevin S McClatchy, *Ch of Bd*
Elaine Lintecum, *CFO*
Alan Saxe, *Exec VP*
Terrance Geiger, *Vice Pres*
EMP: 224
SALES: 807.2MM **Publicly Held**
WEB: www.mcclatchy.com
SIC: 2711 Newspapers: publishing only, not printed on site

(P-5728)
MCCLATCHY NEWSPAPERS INC (HQ)
Also Called: Sacramento Bee
2100 Q St, Sacramento (95816-6899)
P.O. Box 15779 (95852-0779)
PHONE...............................916 321-1855
Erwin Potts, *Ch of Bd*
James P Smith, *Treasurer*
Carrie Vawter-Yousfi, *Executive*
Jamileh Smith, *Controller*
Roger Tafoya, *Manager*
▲ **EMP:** 2500
SALES (est): 988.4MM
SALES (corp-wide): 807.2MM **Publicly Held**
WEB: www.sacbee.com
SIC: 2711 2759 7375 Newspapers, publishing & printing; commercial printing; online data base information retrieval
PA: The Mcclatchy Company
　2100 Q St
　Sacramento CA 95816
　916 321-1844

(P-5729)
MCCLATCHY NEWSPAPERS INC
Fresno Bee, The
1626 E St, Fresno (93706-2006)
P.O. Box 51485, Livonia MI (48151-5485)
PHONE...............................559 441-6111
William Fleet, *Publisher*
Keith Buchanan, *Info Tech Mgr*
Gary Funk, *Info Tech Mgr*
Carlos Davidson, *Technology*
Cathy Santana, *Manager*
EMP: 300
SQ FT: 80,000
SALES (corp-wide): 807.2MM **Publicly Held**
WEB: www.sacbee.com
SIC: 2711 Newspapers, publishing & printing
HQ: Mcclatchy Newspapers, Inc.
　2100 Q St
　Sacramento CA 95816
　916 321-1855

(P-5730)
MCCLATCHY NEWSPAPERS INC
Also Called: Modesto Bee, The
948 11th St 300, Modesto (95354-2308)
P.O. Box 510626, Livonia MI (48151-6626)
PHONE...............................305 740-8440
Karen Ruho, *Branch Mgr*
Juanita Toth, *Accounts Mgr*
Kyndal Dunbar, *Consultant*
EMP: 18

SALES (corp-wide): 807.2MM **Publicly Held**
SIC: 2711 Newspapers, publishing & printing
HQ: Mcclatchy Newspapers, Inc.
　2100 Q St
　Sacramento CA 95816
　916 321-1855

(P-5731)
MCCLATCHY NEWSPAPERS INC
Also Called: El Sol
1325 H St, Modesto (95354-2427)
P.O. Box 3928 (95352-3928)
PHONE...............................209 238-4636
Olivia Ruiz, *Manager*
EMP: 500
SALES (corp-wide): 807.2MM **Publicly Held**
WEB: www.sacbee.com
SIC: 2711 Newspapers, publishing & printing
HQ: Mcclatchy Newspapers, Inc.
　2100 Q St
　Sacramento CA 95816
　916 321-1855

(P-5732)
MCCLATCHY NEWSPAPERS INC
Also Called: Los Banos Enterprise
907 6th St, Los Banos (93635-4215)
PHONE...............................209 826-3831
Gene Lieb, *Manager*
EMP: 95
SALES (corp-wide): 807.2MM **Publicly Held**
WEB: www.sacbee.com
SIC: 2711 Newspapers, publishing & printing
HQ: Mcclatchy Newspapers, Inc.
　2100 Q St
　Sacramento CA 95816
　916 321-1855

(P-5733)
MCCLATCHY NEWSPAPERS INC
Also Called: Merced Sun Star
1190 W Olive Ave Ste F, Merced (95348-1960)
P.O. Box 739 (95341-0739)
PHONE...............................209 722-1511
Allen Portman, *Manager*
EMP: 140
SALES (corp-wide): 807.2MM **Publicly Held**
WEB: www.sacbee.com
SIC: 2711 2759 7375 Newspapers, publishing & printing; commercial printing; online data base information retrieval
HQ: Mcclatchy Newspapers, Inc.
　2100 Q St
　Sacramento CA 95816
　916 321-1855

(P-5734)
MCCLATCHY NEWSPAPERS INC
Also Called: Modesto Bee Circulation
948 11th St Ste 30, Modesto (95354-2340)
P.O. Box 5256 (95352-5256)
PHONE...............................209 587-2250
Wes Horan, *Manager*
EMP: 300
SALES (corp-wide): 807.2MM **Publicly Held**
WEB: www.sacbee.com
SIC: 2711 2721 Newspapers, publishing & printing; periodicals
HQ: Mcclatchy Newspapers, Inc.
　2100 Q St
　Sacramento CA 95816
　916 321-1855

(P-5735)
MCCLATCHY NEWSPAPERS INC
Also Called: Silicon Vly Cmnty Newspapers
4 N 2nd St Ste 800, San Jose (95113-1317)
PHONE...............................408 200-1000
David Cohen, *Principal*
EMP: 68
SALES (corp-wide): 807.2MM **Publicly Held**
WEB: www.sacbee.com
SIC: 2711 Newspapers, publishing & printing

HQ: Mcclatchy Newspapers, Inc.
　2100 Q St
　Sacramento CA 95816
　916 321-1855

(P-5736)
MCCLATCHY NEWSPAPERS INC
Also Called: San Luis Tribune
3825 S Higuera St, San Luis Obispo (93401-7438)
P.O. Box 112 (93406-0112)
PHONE...............................805 781-7800
Paso Robles, *Branch Mgr*
EMP: 180
SALES (corp-wide): 807.2MM **Publicly Held**
WEB: www.sacbee.com
SIC: 2711 Newspapers, publishing & printing
HQ: Mcclatchy Newspapers, Inc.
　2100 Q St
　Sacramento CA 95816
　916 321-1855

(P-5737)
MCNAUGHTON NEWSPAPERS
Also Called: D Davis Enterprise
315 G St, Davis (95616-4119)
P.O. Box 1470 (95617-1470)
PHONE...............................530 756-0800
Foy McNaughton, *Owner*
Richard B Mc Naughton, *Admin Sec*
Shelley Butler, *Human Resources*
Linda Dubois, *Assoc Editor*
Bob Dunning, *Director*
EMP: 60
SALES (est): 3.8MM **Privately Held**
WEB: www.davisenterprise.com
SIC: 2711 Commercial printing & newspaper publishing combined; newspapers, publishing & printing

(P-5738)
MCNAUGHTON NEWSPAPERS INC (PA)
Also Called: Daily Republic
1250 Texas St, Fairfield (94533-5748)
P.O. Box 47 (94533-0747)
PHONE...............................707 425-4646
Foy Mc Naughton, *President*
R Burt Mc Naughton, *Corp Secy*
▲ **EMP:** 99 **EST:** 1855
SQ FT: 35,000
SALES (est): 13MM **Privately Held**
WEB: www.dailyrepublic.com
SIC: 2711 Commercial printing & newspaper publishing combined; newspapers, publishing & printing

(P-5739)
MEDIA NEWS GROUP
Also Called: Willits News
77 W Commercial St, Willits (95490-3021)
P.O. Box 628 (95490-0628)
PHONE...............................707 459-4643
Kevin McConnell, *President*
EMP: 10
SQ FT: 4,000
SALES (est): 659K
SALES (corp-wide): 4.2B **Privately Held**
WEB: www.willitsnews.com
SIC: 2711 Commercial printing & newspaper publishing combined; newspapers, publishing & printing
HQ: Medianews Group, Inc.
　101 W Colfax Ave Ste 1100
　Denver CO 80202

(P-5740)
MEDIANEWS GROUP INC
Long Beach Press-Telegram
300 Oceangate Ste 150, Long Beach (90802-6801)
PHONE...............................562 435-1161
Barbie Brodeur, *Branch Mgr*
Tom Kelly, *Officer*
EMP: 99
SALES (corp-wide): 4.2B **Privately Held**
SIC: 2711 Newspapers, publishing & printing
HQ: Medianews Group, Inc.
　101 W Colfax Ave Ste 1100
　Denver CO 80202

(P-5741)
MEDIANEWS GROUP INC
Also Called: Daily News
21860 Burbank Blvd # 200, Woodland Hills (91367-6477)
P.O. Box 4200 (91365-4200)
PHONE...............................818 713-3000
Douglas Hanes, *Publisher*
Gloria Arango, *Vice Pres*
Elizabeth Chou, *Author*
Julie Buggy-Corlette, *Manager*
Daniel Aitken, *Editor*
EMP: 700
SALES (corp-wide): 4.2B **Privately Held**
SIC: 2711 Newspapers, publishing & printing
HQ: Medianews Group, Inc.
　101 W Colfax Ave Ste 1100
　Denver CO 80202

(P-5742)
MEDIANEWS GROUP INC
Also Called: Daily Breeze
5215 Torrance Blvd, Torrance (90503-4009)
PHONE...............................310 540-5511
Michael J Koren, *Vice Pres*
Sandy Mazza, *Relations*
Deena Knight, *Accounts Exec*
EMP: 157
SALES (corp-wide): 4.2B **Privately Held**
SIC: 2711 Newspapers, publishing & printing
HQ: Medianews Group, Inc.
　101 W Colfax Ave Ste 1100
　Denver CO 80202
-

(P-5743)
MEDIANEWS GROUP INC
Also Called: Convertly
4 N 2nd St Ste 800, San Jose (95113-1317)
PHONE...............................408 920-5713
Michael Koren, *CFO*
EMP: 500
SALES (corp-wide): 4.2B **Privately Held**
SIC: 2711 Newspapers, publishing & printing
HQ: Medianews Group, Inc.
　101 W Colfax Ave Ste 1100
　Denver CO 80202

(P-5744)
MEDIANEWS GROUP INC
Also Called: Daily News
255 Constitution Dr, Menlo Park (94025-1108)
PHONE...............................650 391-1000
Nisook Lee, *Branch Mgr*
EMP: 157
SALES (corp-wide): 4.2B **Privately Held**
WEB: www.sacbee.com
SIC: 2711 Newspapers, publishing & printing
HQ: Medianews Group, Inc.
　101 W Colfax Ave Ste 1100
　Denver CO 80202
-

(P-5745)
MEDIANEWS GROUP INC
Also Called: Daily Democrat, The
711 Main St, Woodland (95695-3406)
P.O. Box 730 (95776-0730)
PHONE...............................530 662-5421
John Fenric, *General Mgr*
EMP: 30
SALES (corp-wide): 4.2B **Privately Held**
WEB: www.fortsmith.com
SIC: 2711 Newspapers, publishing & printing
HQ: Medianews Group, Inc.
　101 W Colfax Ave Ste 1100
　Denver CO 80202

▲ = Import ▼=Export
◆ =Import/Export

(P-5746)
MEDIANEWS GROUP INC
Also Called: Daily News
24800 Ave Rockefeller, Valencia
(91355-3467)
P.O. Box 4200, Woodland Hills (91365-4200)
PHONE..............................661 257-5200
EMP: 200
SALES (corp-wide): 4.3B Privately Held
SIC: 2711 2752
HQ: Medianews Group, Inc.
    101 W Colfax Ave Ste 1100
    Denver CO 80202

(P-5747)
MEDIANEWS GROUP INC
14913 Lakeshore Dr, Clearlake
(95422-8503)
PHONE..............................707 994-6656
EMP: 157
SALES (corp-wide): 4.2B Privately Held
SIC: 2711 Newspapers
HQ: Medianews Group, Inc.
    101 W Colfax Ave Ste 1100
    Denver CO 80202

(P-5748)
MEDIANEWS GROUP INC
Also Called: Red Bluff Daily News
728 Main St, Red Bluff (96080-3342)
PHONE..............................530 527-2151
Jay Harn, Principal
EMP: 35
SALES (corp-wide): 4.2B Privately Held
WEB: www.fortsmith.com
SIC: 2711 2752 Newspapers, publishing &
printing; commercial printing, lithographic
HQ: Medianews Group, Inc.
    101 W Colfax Ave Ste 1100
    Denver CO 80202

(P-5749)
MEDLEYCOM INCORPORATED
Also Called: Adultfriendfinder
910 E Hamilton Ave Fl 6, Campbell
(95008-0655)
PHONE..............................408 745-5418
Anthony Previte, CEO
Gavin Towey, Administration
Kevin Schmidt, Technical Staff
EMP: 19
SALES (est): 1.5MM Privately Held
SIC: 2711 Newspapers, publishing & print-
ing

(P-5750)
METRO PUBLISHING INC
Also Called: Metro Santa Cruz Newspaper
1205 Pacific Ave Ste 301, Santa Cruz
(95060-3936)
PHONE..............................831 457-9000
Debra Whizin, Manager
EMP: 15
SALES (corp-wide): 10MM Privately
Held
WEB: www.metcruz.com
SIC: 2711 Newspapers, publishing & print-
ing
PA: Metro Publishing, Inc.
    380 S 1st St
    San Jose CA
    408 298-8000

(P-5751)
METRO PUBLISHING INC
Also Called: Metrosa
847 5th St, Santa Rosa (95404-4526)
PHONE..............................707 527-1200
Rosemary Olson, Manager
EMP: 13
SALES (corp-wide): 10MM Privately
Held
WEB: www.metcruz.com
SIC: 2711 8611 Newspapers, publishing &
printing; business associations
PA: Metro Publishing, Inc.
    380 S 1st St
    San Jose CA
    408 298-8000

(P-5752)
METROPOLITAN NEWS COMPANY
Also Called: Riverside Bulletin & Jurupa Th
3540 12th St, Riverside (92501-3802)
P.O. Box 60859, Los Angeles (90060-0859)
PHONE..............................951 369-5890
Roger Gray, President
EMP: 29 EST: 1998
SALES (est): 590.3K Privately Held
SIC: 2711 Newspapers: publishing only,
not printed on site

(P-5753)
MID VALLEY PUBLICATION
Also Called: Merced County Times
2221 K St, Merced (95340-3868)
PHONE..............................209 383-0433
John Derby, President
EMP: 25
SQ FT: 1,238
SALES (est): 732.3K Privately Held
SIC: 2711 Newspapers, publishing & print-
ing

(P-5754)
MIDVALLEY PUBLISHING INC
Also Called: Orange Cove Mountain Times
1130 G St, Reedley (93654-3004)
P.O. Box 432 (93654-0432)
PHONE..............................559 638-2244
Fred Hall, President
Janie Lucio, Advt Staff
Beth Warmerdam, Editor
EMP: 35
SALES (est): 2.1MM Privately Held
SIC: 2711 Newspapers, publishing & print-
ing

(P-5755)
MIDVALLEY PUBLISHING INC
Also Called: Fowler Ensinger
740 N St, Sanger (93657-3114)
PHONE..............................559 875-2511
Fred Hall, Publisher
Pete Penner, Ch of Bd
Floyd Barsoon, Treasurer
Norma Hage, Vice Pres
Rosemary Kallio, Admin Sec
EMP: 25
SQ FT: 5,650
SALES (est): 1.4MM Privately Held
SIC: 2711 2752 Newspapers, publishing &
printing; commercial printing, lithographic

(P-5756)
MILPITAS POST NEWSPAPERS INC
59 Marylinn Dr, Milpitas (95035-4311)
PHONE..............................408 262-2454
Rob Devincenzi, Principal
Matthew Jew, Executive
EMP: 13
SALES (est): 672.7K Privately Held
SIC: 2711 Newspapers

(P-5757)
MLIM LLC
350 Camino De La Reina, San Diego
(92108-3007)
PHONE..............................619 299-3131
Douglas Manchester, Chairman
John Lynch, CEO
Ryan Kiesel, CFO
EMP: 766
SALES (est): 118.1MM
SALES (corp-wide): 1B Publicly Held
SIC: 2711 Newspapers, publishing & print-
ing
PA: Tribune Publishing Company
    160 N Stetson Ave
    Chicago IL 60601
    312 222-9100

(P-5758)
MONTEREY COUNTY HERALD COMPANY (DH)
Also Called: Monterey Herald
2200 Garden Rd 101, Monterey
(93940-5329)
PHONE..............................831 372-3311
Gary Omerick, President
Mardi Browning, Director
Davide V Leal, Manager
EMP: 30

SALES (est): 7.3MM
SALES (corp-wide): 4.2B Privately Held
SIC: 2711 Commercial printing & newspaper publishing combined; newspapers,
publishing & printing

(P-5759)
MONTEREY COUNTY WEEKLY
Also Called: Exchange, The
668 Williams Ave, Seaside (93955-5736)
PHONE..............................831 393-3348
Bradley Zeve, President
George Kassal, Executive
Keely Richter, Business Dir
Kevin Smith, Director
Mark Anderson, Manager
EMP: 22
SQ FT: 3,300
SALES (est): 1.5MM Privately Held
WEB: www.montereycountyweekly.com
SIC: 2711 2791 Newspapers: publishing
only, not printed on site; typesetting

(P-5760)
MOONSHINE INK
10137 Riverside Dr, Truckee (96161-0303)
P.O. Box 4003 (96160-4403)
PHONE..............................530 587-3607
Mayumi Elegado, Owner
EMP: 20
SALES (est): 615.9K Privately Held
SIC: 2711 Newspapers

(P-5761)
MORRIS MULTIMEDIA INC
Also Called: Signal Newspaper, The
24000 Creekside Rd, Santa Clarita
(91355-1726)
P.O. Box 801870 (91380-1870)
PHONE..............................661 259-1234
Jay Harn, Branch Mgr
EMP: 100
SALES (corp-wide): 285.7MM Privately
Held
WEB: www.morrismultimedia.com
SIC: 2711 Newspapers: publishing only,
not printed on site
PA: Morris Multimedia, Inc.
    27 Abercorn St
    Savannah GA 31401
    912 233-1281

(P-5762)
MORRIS NEWSPAPER CORP CAL (HQ)
Also Called: Manteca Bulletin
531 E Yosemite Ave, Manteca
(95336-5806)
P.O. Box 1958 (95336-1156)
PHONE..............................209 249-3500
Jennifer Merrick, Director
Dennis Wyatt, Director
EMP: 65
SQ FT: 8,000
SALES (est): 5.8MM
SALES (corp-wide): 285.7MM Privately
Held
WEB: www.mantecabulletin.com
SIC: 2711 6531 Newspapers, publishing &
printing; real estate agents & managers
PA: Morris Multimedia, Inc.
    27 Abercorn St
    Savannah GA 31401
    912 233-1281

(P-5763)
MORRIS PUBLICATIONS (PA)
Also Called: Advertiser, The
122 S 3rd Ave, Oakdale (95361-3935)
P.O. Box 278 (95361-0278)
PHONE..............................209 847-3021
Drew Savage, General Mgr
EMP: 40 EST: 1888
SQ FT: 5,000
SALES (est): 3.1MM Privately Held
WEB: www.oakdaleleader.com
SIC: 2711 2752 8999 Commercial printing
& newspaper publishing combined; photo-
offset printing; newspaper column writing

(P-5764)
MOTHER LODE PRINTING & PUBG CO
Also Called: Mountain Democrat
2889 Ray Lawyer Dr, Placerville
(95667-3914)
P.O. Box 1088 (95667-1088)
PHONE..............................530 344-5030
James Webb, Publisher
Susie Graunstadt, Advt Staff
Liz Hansen, Advt Staff
Jon Meyer, Advt Staff
Ruth Pietrowski, Manager
EMP: 74 EST: 1851
SQ FT: 19,400
SALES (est): 3.7MM Privately Held
WEB: www.mtdemocrat.com
SIC: 2711 Commercial printing & newspa-
per publishing combined

(P-5765)
MOUNT ROSE PUBLISHING CO INC
Also Called: Sierra Sun Newspaper
10775 Pioneer Trl, Truckee (96161-0232)
P.O. Box 2973 (96160-2973)
PHONE..............................530 587-6061
Jody Poe, Manager
EMP: 10
SALES (est): 468.7K
SALES (corp-wide): 650K Privately Held
WEB: www.tahoeworld.com
SIC: 2711 Newspapers: publishing only,
not printed on site
PA: Mount Rose Publishing Co Inc
    395 N Lake Blvd Ste A
    Tahoe City CA 96145
    530 583-3487

(P-5766)
MOUNT ROSE PUBLISHING CO INC (PA)
Also Called: Tahoe World
395 N Lake Blvd Ste A, Tahoe City (96145)
PHONE..............................530 583-3487
Scott McElhaney, President
EMP: 12
SQ FT: 1,350
SALES (est): 650K Privately Held
WEB: www.tahoeworld.com
SIC: 2711 Newspapers: publishing only,
not printed on site

(P-5767)
MOUNTAIN VIEW VOICE
450 Cambridge Ave, Palo Alto
(94306-1507)
P.O. Box 405, Mountain View (94042-0405)
PHONE..............................650 326-8210
William Johnson, President
EMP: 40
SALES (est): 1.1MM Privately Held
WEB: www.mv-voice.com
SIC: 2711 Newspapers, publishing & print-
ing

(P-5768)
MY BURBANKCOM INC
10061 Rverside Dr Ste 520, Toluca Lake
(91602)
PHONE..............................818 842-2140
Craig Sherwood, President
Ross A Benson, Manager
Lisa Paredes, Editor
EMP: 10
SALES (est): 130.6K Privately Held
SIC: 2711 Newspapers, publishing & print-
ing

(P-5769)
NAPA VALLEY PUBLISHING CO
Also Called: NAPA Valley Register
1615 Soscol Ave, NAPA (94559-1901)
P.O. Box 150 (94559-0050)
PHONE..............................707 226-3711
Carson Pierce, Director
Tracy Hardee, Data Proc Staff
Marty James, Editor
Philip Marshall, Accounts Exec
Phyllis Mauceri, Accounts Exec
EMP: 74
SALES (corp-wide): 10.1MM Privately
Held
SIC: 2711 Newspapers: publishing only,
not printed on site

PA: Napa Valley Publishing Co
1615 Soscol Ave
Napa CA 94559
707 226-3711

(P-5770)
NAPA VALLEY PUBLISHING CO (PA)
Also Called: NAPA Register
1615 Soscol Ave, NAPA (94559-1901)
PHONE..................................707 226-3711
E W Scripps, *Ch of Bd*
Betty Knight Scripps, *Vice Chairman*
EMP: 26 **EST:** 1958
SALES (est): 10.1MM **Privately Held**
SIC: 2711 Newspapers: publishing only, not printed on site

(P-5771)
NATIONAL HOT ROD ASSOCIATION
Also Called: National Dragster Magazine
2220 E Route 66, Glendora (91740-4694)
PHONE..................................626 250-2300
Adrian Pierson, *Manager*
EMP: 50
SALES (corp-wide): 99.2MM **Privately Held**
WEB: www.nhra.com
SIC: 2711 2721 Newspapers: publishing only, not printed on site; periodicals
PA: National Hot Rod Association
2035 E Financial Way
Glendora CA 91741
626 914-4761

(P-5772)
NATIONAL MEDIA INC (HQ)
Also Called: Beach Reporter
609 Deep Valley Dr # 200, Rllng HLS Est (90274-3629)
P.O. Box 2609, Pls Vrds Pnsl (90274-8609)
PHONE..................................310 377-6877
Stephen C Laxineta, *President*
Simon M Tam, *President*
William Dean Singleton, *CEO*
EMP: 30
SQ FT: 12,000
SALES (est): 5.4MM
SALES (corp-wide): 4.2B **Privately Held**
WEB: www.pvnews.com
SIC: 2711 Newspapers: publishing only, not printed on site

(P-5773)
NATIONAL MEDIA INC
Also Called: Beach Reporter, The
2615 Pcf Cast Hwy Ste 329, Hermosa Beach (90254)
PHONE..................................310 372-0388
Richard Frank, *Publisher*
Alejandro Gonzalez, *Graphic Designe*
Michael Hixon, *Editor*
Jim Curnutt, *Accounts Exec*
Jenifer Lemon, *Accounts Exec*
EMP: 24
SALES (corp-wide): 4.2B **Privately Held**
WEB: www.pvnews.com
SIC: 2711 Newspapers: publishing only, not printed on site
HQ: National Media, Inc.
609 Deep Valley Dr # 200
Rllng Hls Est CA 90274
310 377-6877

(P-5774)
NEVADA COUNTY PUBLISHING CO
Also Called: Union, The
464 Sutton Way, Grass Valley (95945-4102)
PHONE..................................530 273-9561
Jeff Akerman, *Publisher*
Mary Davis, *Social Dir*
Carole Bukovich, *Adv Dir*
Patrick Connolly, *Adv Dir*
Julia Stidham, *Adv Dir*
▼ **EMP:** 650
SQ FT: 13,000
SALES (est): 24.8MM
SALES (corp-wide): 137.7MM **Privately Held**
WEB: www.sierrasun.com
SIC: 2711 Newspapers, publishing & printing

PA: Swift Communications, Inc.
580 Mallory Way
Carson City NV 89701
775 850-7676

(P-5775)
NEW INCORPORATION NOW
12323 Imperial Hwy, Norwalk (90650-8304)
PHONE..................................562 484-3020
Lee Cantafio, *CEO*
EMP: 18
SALES (est): 663.6K **Privately Held**
SIC: 2711 8231 Newspapers, publishing & printing; documentation center

(P-5776)
NEWLON ROUGE LLC
Also Called: Santa Monica Daily Press
1640 5th St Ste 218, Santa Monica (90401-3325)
PHONE..................................310 458-7737
Ross Furukawa, *President*
Jenny Medina, *Executive*
David Ganforth,
Carolyn Sackariason,
Matthew Hall, *Editor*
EMP: 12
SALES (est): 724.5K **Privately Held**
WEB: www.smdp.com
SIC: 2711 Commercial printing & newspaper publishing combined; newspapers, publishing & printing

(P-5777)
NEWS MEDIA CORPORATION
Also Called: Watsonvlle Register-Pajaronian
21 Brennan St Ste 18, Watsonville (95076-4337)
PHONE..................................831 761-7300
Tom Cross, *Principal*
EMP: 55 **Privately Held**
WEB: www.newsmediacorporation.com
SIC: 2711 Newspapers, publishing & printing
PA: News Media Corporation
211 E Il Route 38
Rochelle IL

(P-5778)
NEWS MEDIA INC
Also Called: Paso Robles Press
502 First St, Paso Robles (93446-3763)
P.O. Box 427 (93447-0427)
PHONE..................................805 237-6060
Richard D Reddick, *President*
EMP: 20 **EST:** 2000
SALES (est): 846.9K **Privately Held**
WEB: www.darlastephenson.com
SIC: 2711 Newspapers, publishing & printing

(P-5779)
NGUOI VIETNAMESE PEOPLE INC (PA)
Also Called: Nguoi Viet Newspaper
14771 Moran St, Westminster (92683-5553)
PHONE..................................714 892-9414
Dat Pham, *Chairman*
Hoang Tong, *CEO*
Dieu Le, *Vice Pres*
▲ **EMP:** 30
SQ FT: 10,000
SALES (est): 4.8MM **Privately Held**
WEB: www.nguoi-viet.com
SIC: 2711 5994 2741 Newspapers: publishing only, not printed on site; news dealers & newsstands; miscellaneous publishing

(P-5780)
NORTH AREA NEWS (PA)
2612 El Camino Ave, Sacramento (95821-5937)
P.O. Box 214245 (95821-0245)
PHONE..................................916 486-1248
Tom Hoey, *President*
Joanne Hoey, *Corp Secy*
John Hoey, *Vice Pres*
EMP: 14
SQ FT: 2,400
SALES (est): 2.6MM **Privately Held**
SIC: 2711 Newspapers

(P-5781)
NORTH COAST JOURNAL INC
310 F St, Eureka (95501-1006)
PHONE..................................707 442-1400
Judy Hodgson, *President*
Chuck Leifhman, *General Mgr*
EMP: 18
SALES (est): 1.2MM **Privately Held**
WEB: www.northcoastjournal.com
SIC: 2711 Newspapers, publishing & printing

(P-5782)
NORTH COUNTY TIMES (DH)
Also Called: Californian, The
350 Camino De La Reina, San Diego (92108-3007)
PHONE..................................800 533-8830
▲ **EMP:** 250 **EST:** 1962
SQ FT: 45,000
SALES (est): 24.5MM
SALES (corp-wide): 593.9MM **Publicly Held**
WEB: www.nctimes.com
SIC: 2711 Newspapers, publishing & printing
HQ: Lee Publications, Inc.
4600 E 53rd St
Davenport IA 52807
563 383-2100

(P-5783)
NORTH COUNTY TIMES
28441 Rancho California R, Temecula (92590-3618)
PHONE..................................951 676-4315
Claude Reinke, *Manager*
EMP: 50
SALES (corp-wide): 593.9MM **Publicly Held**
WEB: www.nctimes.com
SIC: 2711 Newspapers, publishing & printing
HQ: North County Times
350 Camino De La Reina
San Diego CA 92108
800 533-8830

(P-5784)
NORTH VALLEY NEWSPAPERS INC
Also Called: Valley Post
2676 Gateway Dr, Anderson (96007-3530)
P.O. Box 492397, Redding (96049-2397)
PHONE..................................530 365-2797
Douglas Hirsch, *President*
EMP: 15
SALES (est): 817.8K **Privately Held**
SIC: 2711 Newspapers, publishing & printing

(P-5785)
NOTICIERO SEMANAL ADVERTISING
Also Called: Porterville Recorder
115 E Oak Ave, Porterville (93257-3807)
P.O. Box 151 (93258-0151)
PHONE..................................559 784-5000
Paul Mauney, *Principal*
Terry Feagin, *Accounting Mgr*
EMP: 65
SALES (est): 1.8MM **Privately Held**
SIC: 2711 7313 Newspapers, publishing & printing; newspaper advertising representative

(P-5786)
OAKLAND TRIBUNE INC
Also Called: Tribune, The
600 Grand Ave 308, Oakland (94610-3548)
PHONE..................................510 208-6300
John Armstrong, *President*
Doug Van Sant, *Producer*
◆ **EMP:** 800
SALES (est): 20.6MM
SALES (corp-wide): 4.2B **Privately Held**
SIC: 2711 Newspapers, publishing & printing
HQ: Medianews Group, Inc.
101 W Colfax Ave Ste 1100
Denver CO 80202

(P-5787)
OBSERVER NEWSPAPER
1844 Lincoln Blvd, Santa Monica (90404-4506)
P.O. Box 5652 (90409-5652)
PHONE..................................310 452-9900
David Ganezer, *President*
EMP: 20
SALES: 500K **Privately Held**
SIC: 2711 Newspapers, publishing & printing

(P-5788)
OLYMPIC CASCADE PUBLISHING (DH)
Also Called: Puyallup Herald
2100 Q St, Sacramento (95816-6816)
P.O. Box 15779 (95852-0779)
PHONE..................................916 321-1000
Steven Robinson, *Vice Pres*
Marion Dodd, *Corp Secy*
EMP: 45
SQ FT: 5,100
SALES (est): 4.6MM
SALES (corp-wide): 807.2MM **Publicly Held**
WEB: www.puyallupherald.com
SIC: 2711 Commercial printing & newspaper publishing combined; newspapers, publishing & printing
HQ: Mcclatchy Newspapers, Inc.
2100 Q St
Sacramento CA 95816
916 321-1855

(P-5789)
OUTWORD NEWS MAGAZINE
Also Called: Outword Newsmagazine
1 Ebbtide Ct, Sacramento (95831-2406)
PHONE..................................916 329-9280
Fred Palmer, *President*
EMP: 45
SALES (est): 1.7MM **Privately Held**
WEB: www.outwordmagazine.com
SIC: 2711 Newspapers

(P-5790)
PACIFIC COAST BUS TIMES INC
14 E Carrillo St Ste A, Santa Barbara (93101-2769)
PHONE..................................805 560-6950
Henry Dubroff, *President*
Linda Brock, *Executive*
Jennifer Carusa, *Marketing Staff*
Glenn Rabinowitz, *Manager*
Marlize Van Romburgh, *Editor*
EMP: 13
SQ FT: 2,200
SALES (est): 898.6K **Privately Held**
WEB: www.pacbiztimes.com
SIC: 2711 Newspapers, publishing & printing

(P-5791)
PACIFIC NORTHWEST PUBG CO INC
2100 Q St, Sacramento (95816-6816)
PHONE..................................916 321-1828
Patrick Talmantes, *Director*
EMP: 300 **EST:** 1905
SQ FT: 100,000
SALES (est): 26.7MM
SALES (corp-wide): 2.9B **Publicly Held**
WEB: www.tallahassee.com
SIC: 2711 Newspapers, publishing & printing
HQ: Gannett River States Publishing Corporation
7950 Jones Branch Dr
Mc Lean VA 22102
703 284-6000

(P-5792)
PACIFIC PRESS CORPORATION
Also Called: Viet Nam Daily Newspaper
2350 S 10th St, San Jose (95112-4109)
PHONE..................................408 292-3422
Can Nguyen, *President*
Giang Nguyen, *Corp Secy*
EMP: 30
SQ FT: 10,000
SALES (est): 1.6MM **Privately Held**
SIC: 2711 2752 Newspapers: publishing only, not printed on site; commercial printing, lithographic

(P-5793)
PASADENA NEWSPAPERS INC (PA)
Also Called: Pasadena Star-News
2 N Lake Ave Ste 150, Pasadena
(91101-1896)
PHONE.................................626 578-6300
Dean Singleton, *President*
Melene Alfonso, *Vice Pres*
▲ **EMP:** 190
SQ FT: 80,000
SALES (est): 32.5MM **Privately Held**
WEB: www.pasadenastarnews.com
SIC: 2711 7313 Commercial printing & newspaper publishing combined; newspaper advertising representative

(P-5794)
PASADENA NEWSPAPERS INC
Also Called: Eureka Times-Standard
930 6th St, Eureka (95501-1112)
P.O. Box 3580 (95502-3580)
PHONE.................................707 442-1711
Gerry Adolph, *Manager*
EMP: 135
SQ FT: 49,872
SALES (corp-wide): 32.5MM **Privately Held**
WEB: www.pasadenastarnews.com
SIC: 2711 2752 Newspapers: publishing only, not printed on site; commercial printing, lithographic
PA: Pasadena Newspapers Inc
2 N Lake Ave Ste 150
Pasadena CA 91101
626 578-6300

(P-5795)
PENNYSAVER
Also Called: Harthanks
1520 N Mountain Ave # 121, Ontario
(91762-1132)
PHONE.................................909 467-8500
Mike Paulsin, *President*
EMP: 50
SALES (est): 2MM **Privately Held**
WEB: www.hhshoppers.com
SIC: 2711 Newspapers, publishing & printing

(P-5796)
PERIODICO EL VIDA
Also Called: Vida Newspaper
130 Palm Dr, Oxnard (93030-4979)
PHONE.................................805 483-1008
Manuel Munoz, *Owner*
EMP: 37
SALES (est): 1.2MM **Privately Held**
SIC: 2711 Newspapers, publishing & printing

(P-5797)
PHIL BLAZER ENTERPRISES INC
Also Called: Jewish News
15315 Magnolia Blvd # 101, Sherman Oaks
(91403-1100)
PHONE.................................818 786-4000
Phil Blazer, *President*
EMP: 10 **EST:** 1972
SQ FT: 3,000
SALES: 823.3K **Privately Held**
SIC: 2711 7812 Newspapers: publishing only, not printed on site; television film production

(P-5798)
PLANETART LLC (DH)
23801 Calabasas Rd # 2005, Calabasas
(91302-1547)
PHONE.................................818 436-3600
Roger Bloxberg,
EMP: 50
SALES: 18MM
SALES (corp-wide): 1.4MM **Privately Held**
SIC: 2711 Newspapers
HQ: Avanquest North America Llc
23801 Calabasas Rd # 2005
Calabasas CA 91302
818 591-9600

(P-5799)
POLITEZER NEWSPAERS INC
Also Called: Grover City Press
260 Station Way Ste F, Arroyo Grande
(93420-3359)
PHONE.................................805 929-3864
Emily Slater, *Manager*
Cynthia Schur, *President*
Vern Ahrendes, *Manager*
EMP: 13 **EST:** 1963
SQ FT: 12,000
SALES (est): 670K **Privately Held**
WEB: www.timespressrecorder.com
SIC: 2711 Newspapers, publishing & printing

(P-5800)
POPULAR TV NETWORKS LLC
8307 Rugby Pl, Los Angeles (90046-1527)
PHONE.................................323 822-3324
Marvin Jarrett, *Principal*
Jaclynn Jarrett, *Principal*
EMP: 10 **EST:** 2014
SALES (est): 409.5K **Privately Held**
SIC: 2711 7389 Newspapers, publishing & printing;

(P-5801)
POST NEWSPAPER GROUP
360 14th St Ste B05, Oakland
(94612-3200)
PHONE.................................510 287-8200
Paul Cobb, *Principal*
EMP: 12
SALES (est): 15.3K **Privately Held**
SIC: 2711 Newspapers, publishing & printing

(P-5802)
PRECINCT REPORTER
Also Called: Precinct Reporter Newsprs
357 W 2nd St Ste 1a, San Bernardino
(92401-1824)
PHONE.................................909 889-0597
Brian Townsend, *Partner*
EMP: 10
SALES (est): 631.1K **Privately Held**
SIC: 2711 7313 Job printing & newspaper publishing combined; newspaper advertising representative

(P-5803)
PREMIER MEDIA INC
Also Called: India Journal
13353 Alondra Blvd # 115, Santa Fe
Springs (90670-5545)
PHONE.................................562 802-9720
Navneet Chugh, *President*
Parminder Singh, *General Mgr*
EMP: 11
SQ FT: 2,100
SALES (est): 646.1K **Privately Held**
WEB: www.indiajournal.com
SIC: 2711 8732 Newspapers: publishing only, not printed on site; commercial nonphysical research

(P-5804)
PRESS-ENTERPRISE COMPANY (PA)
3450 14th St, Riverside (92501-3878)
P.O. Box 792 (92502-0792)
PHONE.................................951 684-1200
Ronald Redfern, *President*
Ed Lasak, *CFO*
Sue Barry, *Vice Pres*
Kathy Weiermiller, *Vice Pres*
Ezra Greenhouse, *Editor*
▲ **EMP:** 700
SQ FT: 190,000
SALES (est): 158.4MM **Privately Held**
SIC: 2711 Commercial printing & newspaper publishing combined; newspapers, publishing & printing

(P-5805)
PRESS-ENTERPRISE COMPANY
3450 14th St, Riverside (92501-3878)
PHONE.................................951 684-1200
EMP: 15
SALES (corp-wide): 158.4MM **Privately Held**
SIC: 2711 Newspapers, publishing & printing

(P-5812)
SAIGON TIMES INC
9234 Valley Blvd, Rosemead (91770-1922)
P.O. Box 428 (91770-0428)
PHONE.................................626 288-2696

PA: Press-Enterprise Company
3450 14th St
Riverside CA 92501
951 684-1200

(P-5806)
RAFU SHIMPO
Also Called: L A Japanese Daily News
701 E 3rd St Ste 130, Los Angeles
(90013-1789)
PHONE.................................213 629-2231
Michael M Komai, *President*
Gail Miyasaki, *Office Mgr*
Michael Culross, *Editor*
Gwen Muranaka, *Editor*
EMP: 20 **EST:** 1903
SQ FT: 20,000
SALES: 52K **Privately Held**
WEB: www.rafu.com
SIC: 2711 Newspapers, publishing & printing

(P-5807)
RAMONA HOME JOURNAL
726 D St, Ramona (92065-2330)
PHONE.................................760 788-8148
Carol Kinney, *Owner*
EMP: 10 **EST:** 1998
SALES (est): 451.3K **Privately Held**
SIC: 2711 Newspapers, publishing & printing

(P-5808)
RANCHO CUCAMONGA MAVERICK
Also Called: Rancho Cucamonga Today
7349 Milliken Ave Ste 110, Rancho Cucamonga (91730-7435)
PHONE.................................909 466-6445
Rex Gutierrez, *Owner*
EMP: 10
SALES (est): 350K **Privately Held**
SIC: 2711 Newspapers

(P-5809)
REPORTER
Also Called: Media News Groups
916 Cotting Ln, Vacaville (95688-9338)
PHONE.................................707 448-6401
Jody Lodevick, *President*
Rowena Nguyen, *Sales Staff*
Kimberly Fu, *Manager*
Joel Rosenbaum, *Manager*
Richard Bammer, *Relations*
EMP: 91
SQ FT: 40,000
SALES (est): 5.6MM **Privately Held**
WEB: www.thereporter.com
SIC: 2711 Commercial printing & newspaper publishing combined; newspapers, publishing & printing

(P-5810)
RIDER CIRCULATION SERVICES
Also Called: Rcs
1324 Cypress Ave, Los Angeles
(90065-1220)
PHONE.................................323 344-1200
John Dorman, *President*
Michael Werner, *Vice Pres*
▲ **EMP:** 10
SQ FT: 8,500
SALES: 4.4MM **Privately Held**
WEB: www.gorcs.com
SIC: 2711 Newspapers, publishing & printing

(P-5811)
RJ MEDIA
Also Called: India Post
1860 Mowry Ave Ste 200, Fremont
(94538-1730)
PHONE.................................510 938-8667
Romesh K Japra, *President*
Naresh Sodhi, *Executive*
Vidya Sethuraman, *Editor*
EMP: 10 **EST:** 2005
SALES (est): 265.7K **Privately Held**
SIC: 2711 Newspapers, publishing & printing

Hap Tu Thai, *President*
Katherine Le, *Manager*
EMP: 10
SQ FT: 3,285
SALES (est): 437.4K **Privately Held**
WEB: www.saigontimes.net
SIC: 2711 Commercial printing & newspaper publishing combined

(P-5813)
SALINAS NEWSPAPERS LLC
Also Called: Salinas Newspapers Inc
1093 S Main St Ste 101, Salinas
(93901-2362)
P.O. Box 81091 (93912-1000)
PHONE.................................831 424-2221
Paula Goudraw, *President*
EMP: 150
SQ FT: 8,000
SALES (est): 22.3MM
SALES (corp-wide): 2.9B **Publicly Held**
WEB: www.californianprepress.com
SIC: 2711 Newspapers, publishing & printing
PA: Gannett Co., Inc.
7950 Jones Branch Dr
Mc Lean VA 22102
703 854-6000

(P-5814)
SAN CLEMENTE TIMES LLC
34932 Calle Del Sol Ste B, Capistrano
Beach (92624-1664)
PHONE.................................949 388-7700
Norb Garrett,
Fiat Luxe MGT,
EMP: 10
SALES (est): 736.6K **Privately Held**
SIC: 2711 Commercial printing & newspaper publishing combined; newspapers, publishing & printing

(P-5815)
SAN DIEGO UNION-TRIBUNE LLC
San Diego Union Tribune
600 B St Ste 1201, San Diego
(92101-4505)
P.O. Box 120191 (92112-0191)
PHONE.................................619 299-3131
Roy E Gene Bell, *CEO*
EMP: 99
SQ FT: 400,000 **Privately Held**
WEB: www.copleynewspapers.com
SIC: 2711 7313 Newspapers: publishing only, not printed on site; newspaper advertising representative
PA: The San Diego Union-Tribune Llc
600 B St Ste 1201
San Diego CA 92101

(P-5816)
SAN DIEGO UNION-TRIBUNE LLC (PA)
Also Called: San Diego Union Tribune, The
600 B St Ste 1201, San Diego
(92101-4505)
P.O. Box 120191 (92112-0191)
PHONE.................................619 299-3131
Jeff Light, *President*
Katie Musolf, *Executive*
Patty Rangel, *Executive*
EMP: 600
SALES (est): 155MM **Privately Held**
SIC: 2711 7313 7383 Newspapers: publishing only, not printed on site; newspaper advertising representative; news reporting services for newspapers & periodicals

(P-5817)
SAN JOSE BUSINESS JOURNAL
125 S Market St Ste 1100, San Jose
(95113-2286)
PHONE.................................408 295-3800
Dick Kruez, *Publisher*
Italo Jimenez, *Business Mgr*
EMP: 45
SALES (est): 2.2MM
SALES (corp-wide): 1.3B **Privately Held**
SIC: 2711 2741 Newspapers, publishing & printing; miscellaneous publishing

HQ: American City Business Journals, Inc.
120 W Morehead St Ste 400
Charlotte NC 28202
704 973-1000

(P-5818)
SAN JOSE MERCURY-NEWS LLC (DH)
4 N 2nd St Fl 8, San Jose (95113-1308)
PHONE.....................408 920-5000
Michael Hopkins,
Bud Geracie, *Executive*
Astrid Garcia, *Principal*
Mindy Kiernan, *Principal*
Joseph T Natoli, *Principal*
EMP: 1000
SQ FT: 400,000
SALES (est): 115.8MM
SALES (corp-wide): 4.2B **Privately Held**
WEB: www.mercurynews.com
SIC: 2711 Commercial printing & newspaper publishing combined; newspapers, publishing & printing

(P-5819)
SAN MATEO DAILY NEWS
255 Constitution Dr, Menlo Park
(94025-1108)
PHONE.....................650 327-9090
Dave Price, *President*
EMP: 50
SALES (est): 2.3MM **Privately Held**
SIC: 2711 Newspapers, publishing & printing

(P-5820)
SANTA BARBARA INDEPENDENT INC
12 E Figueroa St, Santa Barbara
(93101-2709)
PHONE.....................805 965-5205
M Partridge Poette, *President*
Tanya Guiliacci, *Opers Mgr*
Emily Cosentino, *Marketing Staff*
Brandon Fastman, *Relations*
EMP: 40
SQ FT: 5,000
SALES (est): 2.6MM **Privately Held**
WEB: www.independant.com
SIC: 2711 Newspapers: publishing only, not printed on site

(P-5821)
SANTA MARIA TIMES INC
3200 Skyway Dr, Santa Maria
(93455-1896)
P.O. Box 400 (93456-0400)
PHONE.....................805 925-2691
Dan Cotter, *Manager*
George Fischer, *Prdtn Dir*
Ed Galanski, *Sales Staff*
Mike Chaldu, *Editor*
Marga Cooley, *Editor*
EMP: 120
SALES (corp-wide): 5.4MM **Privately Held**
SIC: 2711 Newspapers, publishing & printing
PA: Santa Maria Times, Inc
7701 Forsyth Blvd # 1000
Saint Louis MO 63105
314 340-8890

(P-5822)
SANTA ROSA PRESS DEMOCRAT INC (HQ)
Also Called: Press Democrat, The
427 Mendocino Ave, Santa Rosa
(95401-6313)
P.O. Box 569 (95402-0569)
PHONE.....................707 546-2020
Michael J Parman, *President*
Alexa Williams, *Accounts Exec*
EMP: 270
SALES (est): 75MM **Privately Held**
WEB: www.sonomatraveler.com
SIC: 2711 Newspapers, publishing & printing
PA: Sonoma Media Investments, Llc
427 Mendocino Ave
Santa Rosa CA 95401
707 546-2020

(P-5823)
SCRIPPS MEDIA INC
Also Called: Ventura County Star
771 E Daily Dr Ste 300, Camarillo
(93010-0781)
PHONE.....................805 437-0000
Shanna Cannon,
Maria Camargo, *Marketing Staff*
Gerardo Gallegos, *Council Mbr*
Darrin Peschka, *Director*
Vallie Brown, *Supervisor*
EMP: 175
SALES (est): 7.7MM
SALES (corp-wide): 2.9B **Publicly Held**
WEB: www.scripps.com
SIC: 2711 Newspapers
HQ: Journal Media Group, Inc.
333 W State St
Milwaukee WI 53203
414 224-2000

(P-5824)
SENTINEL PRINTING & PUBLISHING
Also Called: Dinuba Sentinel
145 S L St, Dinuba (93618-2324)
PHONE.....................559 591-4632
Bob Raison, *Manager*
EMP: 17 EST: 1909
SQ FT: 7,500
SALES (est): 735.3K **Privately Held**
WEB: www.dinubasentinel.com
SIC: 2711 Commercial printing & newspaper publishing combined

(P-5825)
SIERRA VIEW INC
Also Called: News Review, The
109 N Sanders St, Ridgecrest
(93555-3848)
PHONE.....................760 371-4301
Patricia Farris, *President*
Pat Farris, *Publisher*
EMP: 25
SQ FT: 2,800
SALES: 450K **Privately Held**
SIC: 2711 Newspapers: publishing only, not printed on site

(P-5826)
SIGNAL
Also Called: Newhall Signal
26330 Diamond Pl Ste 100, Santa Clarita
(91350-5819)
P.O. Box 801870 (91380-1870)
PHONE.....................661 259-1234
Charles Morris, *President*
Chris Budman, *Vice Pres*
Dawn Begley, *Executive*
Karen Bennett, *Graphic Designe*
Abner Gutierrez, *Graphic Designe*
EMP: 98
SQ FT: 32,000
SALES (est): 6.3MM
SALES (corp-wide): 285.7MM **Privately Held**
WEB: www.sclarita.com
SIC: 2711 Newspapers, publishing & printing
PA: Morris Multimedia, Inc.
27 Abercorn St
Savannah GA 31401
912 233-1281

(P-5827)
SING TAO NEWSPAPERS (HQ)
Also Called: Sing Tao Daily
1818 Gilbreth Rd Ste 108, Burlingame
(94010-1217)
PHONE.....................650 808-8800
Robin Mui, *CEO*
Florence TSO, *General Mgr*
Kelvin Yeung, *Info Tech Mgr*
Angel Law, *Accountant*
Germaine Louie, *Human Res Mgr*
▲ EMP: 75
SQ FT: 22,000
SALES (est): 14.8MM **Privately Held**
WEB: www.singtaousa.com
SIC: 2711 Commercial printing & newspaper publishing combined

(P-5828)
SING TAO NEWSPAPERS LTD
Also Called: Sing Tao Nwspapers Los Angeles
17059 Green Dr, City of Industry
(91745-1812)
PHONE.....................626 839-8200
Sau K Cheung, *Manager*
EMP: 52 **Privately Held**
WEB: www.singtao.com
SIC: 2711 Newspapers, publishing & printing
PA: Sing Tao Limited
Sing Tao News Corporation Bldg
Tseung Kwan O NT

(P-5829)
SLO NEW TIMES INC
Also Called: New Times Media Group
1010 Marsh St, San Luis Obispo
(93401-3630)
PHONE.....................805 546-8208
Bob Rucker, *CEO*
Jason Gann, *Adv Dir*
Jim Parsons, *Manager*
Ryah Cooley, *Editor*
Caleb Wiseblood, *Editor*
EMP: 30
SALES (est): 1.5MM **Privately Held**
WEB: www.newtimesslo.com
SIC: 2711 Newspapers: publishing only, not printed on site

(P-5830)
SONOMA INDEX-TRIBUNE
Also Called: Sonoma Valley Publishing
117 W Napa St Ste A, Sonoma
(95476-6691)
P.O. Box C (95476-0209)
PHONE.....................707 938-2111
William Lynch, *President*
James Lynch, *Corp Secy*
Jean Lynch, *Vice Pres*
EMP: 55
SQ FT: 17,000
SALES (est): 2.9MM **Privately Held**
WEB: www.sonomanews.com
SIC: 2711 Commercial printing & newspaper publishing combined

(P-5831)
SONOMA WEST PUBLISHERS INC (PA)
Also Called: Sonoma West Times & News
135 S Main St, Sebastopol (95472-4258)
P.O. Box 518, Healdsburg (95448-0518)
PHONE.....................707 823-7845
Jeff Mays, *President*
Sandra M Mays, *Treasurer*
Sarah Bradbury, *Vice Pres*
EMP: 12
SALES (est): 1.9MM **Privately Held**
WEB: www.sonomawest.com
SIC: 2711 Newspapers: publishing only, not printed on site

(P-5832)
SOUTH COAST PUBLISHING INC
Also Called: Long Beach Business Journal
2599 E 28th St Ste 212, Long Beach
(90755-2139)
PHONE.....................562 988-1222
George Economides, *President*
Samantha Mehlinger, *Assoc Editor*
▲ EMP: 10
SALES (est): 742.8K **Privately Held**
WEB: www.lbbj.com
SIC: 2711 Newspapers, publishing & printing

(P-5833)
SOUTH COUNTY NEWSPAPERS LLC
Also Called: Soledad Bee
522 Broadway St Ste B, King City
(93930-3243)
P.O. Box 710 (93930-0710)
PHONE.....................831 385-4880
Tricia Bergeron, *General Mgr*
Jeremy Burke, *Mng Member*
EMP: 10

SALES (est): 667.9K **Privately Held**
WEB: www.newsmediacorporation.com
SIC: 2711 Newspapers, publishing & printing
PA: News Media Corporation
211 E Il Route 38
Rochelle IL

(P-5834)
SOUTHLAND PUBLISHING INC (PA)
Also Called: Ventura County Reporter
50 S Delacey Ave Ste 200, Pasadena
(91105)
PHONE.....................626 584-1500
Michael Flannery, *President*
David Comden, *Vice Pres*
Chris Jay, *Author*
EMP: 13
SALES (est): 1.4MM **Privately Held**
WEB: www.vcreporter.com
SIC: 2711 Newspapers: publishing only, not printed on site

(P-5835)
SPORTS MEDICINE INFO NETWORK
8737 Beverly Blvd Ste 303, West Hollywood
(90048-1839)
PHONE.....................310 659-6889
Robert Carp, *Owner*
EMP: 10 EST: 2001
SALES (est): 320.6K **Privately Held**
WEB: www.sportsmedinfo.net
SIC: 2711 Newspapers

(P-5836)
SR3 SOLUTIONS LLC
Also Called: S R 3
13136 Saticoy St, North Hollywood
(91605-3438)
PHONE.....................818 255-3131
Richard Kaltman, *Mng Member*
Jon Kaltman, *Mng Member*
EMP: 10
SQ FT: 24,000
SALES (est): 713.2K **Privately Held**
SIC: 2711 Commercial printing & newspaper publishing combined

(P-5837)
ST LOUIS POST-DISPATCH LLC
Also Called: Novato Advance Newspaper
1068 Machin Ave, Novato (94945-2458)
P.O. Box 8 (94948-0008)
PHONE.....................415 892-1516
William C Haigwood, *Manager*
EMP: 43
SALES (corp-wide): 593.9MM **Publicly Held**
SIC: 2711 Newspapers, publishing & printing
HQ: St. Louis Post-Dispatch Llc
900 N Tucker Blvd
Saint Louis MO 63101
314 340-8000

(P-5838)
ST LOUIS POST-DISPATCH LLC
Also Called: Argus Courier
830 Petaluma Blvd N, Petaluma
(94952-2109)
P.O. Box 1091 (94953-1091)
PHONE.....................707 762-4541
John Burnes, *Branch Mgr*
EMP: 25
SQ FT: 10,000
SALES (corp-wide): 593.9MM **Publicly Held**
SIC: 2711 Newspapers, publishing & printing
HQ: St. Louis Post-Dispatch Llc
900 N Tucker Blvd
Saint Louis MO 63101
314 340-8000

(P-5839)
ST LOUIS POST-DISPATCH LLC
Also Called: Daily Midway Driller
800 Center St, Taft (93268-3129)
PHONE.....................661 763-3171
John Watkins, *Branch Mgr*
EMP: 10

SALES (corp-wide): 593.9MM **Publicly Held**
SIC: 2711 Newspapers, publishing & printing
HQ: St. Louis Post-Dispatch Llc
900 N Tucker Blvd
Saint Louis MO 63101
314 340-8000

(P-5840)
STANFORD DAILY PUBLISHING CORP
Also Called: STANFORD DAILY, THE
456 Panama Mall, Stanford (94305-5294)
PHONE..............................650 723-2555
Alice Brown, *President*
Wes Radez, *Vice Pres*
EMP: 40
SQ FT: 2,300
SALES: 563.1K **Privately Held**
SIC: 2711 Newspapers: publishing only, not printed on site

(P-5841)
STATE HORNET
6000 J St, Sacramento (95819-2605)
PHONE..............................916 278-6583
Claire Morgan, *Editor*
Margherita Beale, *Manager*
EMP: 70
SALES (est): 3.2MM **Privately Held**
WEB: www.statehornet.com
SIC: 2711 Newspapers
HQ: California State University, Sacramento
6000 J St Ste 2200
Sacramento CA 95819

(P-5842)
SUN COMPANY SAN BERNARDINO CAL (PA)
Also Called: San Bernardino County Sun, The
4030 Georgia Blvd, San Bernardino (92407-1847)
PHONE..............................909 889-9666
Bob Balzer, *President*
Douglass H McCorkindale, *Principal*
Gustavo Ortiz, *MIS Dir*
Theresa Almanza, *Technology*
Louise Kopitch, *VP Human Res*
EMP: 400
SQ FT: 110,000
SALES (est): 42MM **Privately Held**
SIC: 2711 Newspapers, publishing & printing

(P-5843)
SUN REPORTER PUBLISHING INC
Also Called: Sun Reporter Newspaper
1286 Fillmore St, San Francisco (94115-4111)
PHONE..............................415 671-1000
Amelia Ward, *President*
EMP: 15
SALES (est): 1.1MM **Privately Held**
WEB: www.sunreporter.com
SIC: 2711 8661 Newspapers: publishing only, not printed on site; religious organizations

(P-5844)
TACOMA NEWS INC (DH)
2100 Q St, Sacramento (95816-6816)
PHONE..............................916 321-1846
Elizabeth F Brenner, *President*
Elaine Lintecum, *Treasurer*
Robert J Weil, *Vice Pres*
Karole Morgan-Prager, *Admin Sec*
EMP: 500
SALES (est): 43.9MM
SALES (corp-wide): 807.2MM **Publicly Held**
WEB: www.tacomanews.com
SIC: 2711 Newspapers, publishing & printing
HQ: Mcclatchy Newspapers, Inc.
2100 Q St
Sacramento CA 95816
916 321-1855

(P-5845)
TAKE A BREAK PAPER
263 W Olive Ave 307, Burbank (91502-1825)
PHONE..............................323 333-7773
Albert Moran, *Partner*
EMP: 30 **EST:** 2013
SALES (est): 474.8K **Privately Held**
SIC: 2711 Newspapers, publishing & printing

(P-5846)
TARGET MEDIA PARTNERS OPER LLC
5900 Wilshire Blvd # 550, Los Angeles (90036-5013)
PHONE..............................323 930-3123
Mark Schiffmacher, *CEO*
EMP: 40
SALES (est): 1MM **Privately Held**
SIC: 2711 Newspapers

(P-5847)
TEHACHAPI NEWS INC (PA)
Also Called: Southeast Kern Weekender
411 N Mill St, Tehachapi (93561-1351)
P.O. Box 1840 (93581-1840)
PHONE..............................661 822-6828
Al Criseli, *President*
William J Mead, *President*
Elizabeth S Mead, *Corp Secy*
Betty J Autery, *Advt Staff*
Sandra Honea, *Advt Staff*
EMP: 17 **EST:** 1943
SQ FT: 2,400
SALES (est): 1.1MM **Privately Held**
WEB: www.tehachapinews.com
SIC: 2711 Newspapers, publishing & printing

(P-5848)
THE VALLEY BUSINESS JURNL INC
40335 Winchester Rd # 128, Temecula (92591-5500)
PHONE..............................951 461-0400
Linda Wunderlich, *President*
EMP: 15
SALES (est): 699.8K **Privately Held**
WEB: www.valleybusinessjournal.com
SIC: 2711 Newspapers, publishing & printing

(P-5849)
TIDINGS
Also Called: VIDA NUEVA
3424 Wilshire Blvd, Los Angeles (90010-2263)
PHONE..............................213 637-7360
Roger Mahoney, *President*
EMP: 30
SALES (est): 1.9MM **Privately Held**
WEB: www.the-tidings.com
SIC: 2711 Newspapers: publishing only, not printed on site

(P-5850)
TIMES MEDIA INC
Also Called: Bellou Publishing
1900 Camden Ave, San Jose (95124-2942)
PHONE..............................408 494-7000
William D Bellou, *CEO*
Sandy Bellou, *Human Res Mgr*
Brigitte Jones, *Manager*
Jeanne Carbone, *Editor*
EMP: 14
SALES (est): 861.5K **Privately Held**
WEB: www.almadentimes.com
SIC: 2711 Newspapers, publishing & printing

(P-5851)
TRACY PRESS INC
145 W 10th St, Tracy (95376-3952)
P.O. Box 419 (95378-0419)
PHONE..............................209 835-3030
Robert S Matthews, *President*
Tom Matthews, *Vice Pres*
Maggie Jauregui, *Graphic Designe*
William Fleet, *VP Mktg*
EMP: 30
SQ FT: 20,000

SALES (est): 2.2MM **Privately Held**
WEB: www.tracypress.com
SIC: 2711 Commercial printing & newspaper publishing combined; newspapers, publishing & printing

(P-5852)
TRIBE MEDIA CORP
Also Called: JEWISH JOURNAL, THE
3250 Wilshire Blvd, Los Angeles (90010-1577)
PHONE..............................213 368-1661
Rob Eshman, *Publisher*
Marty Finkelstein, *Exec Dir*
Sara Budisantoso, *Traffic Mgr*
EMP: 27
SQ FT: 4,500
SALES: 4.4MM **Privately Held**
WEB: www.jewishjournal.com
SIC: 2711 Newspapers, publishing & printing

(P-5853)
TRIBUNE LOS ANGELES INC
202 W 1st St Ste 500, Los Angeles (90012-4401)
PHONE..............................213 237-5000
EMP: 13
SALES (est): 773.5K
SALES (corp-wide): 2.7B **Publicly Held**
WEB: www.tribune.com
SIC: 2711 Newspapers, publishing & printing
HQ: Tribune Media Company
515 N State St Ste 2400
Chicago IL 60654
312 222-3394

(P-5854)
TURLOCK JOURNAL
138 S Center St, Turlock (95380-4508)
P.O. Box 800 (95381-0800)
PHONE..............................209 634-9141
Olaf Frandsen, *Principal*
Charles Webber, *Advt Staff*
Kristina Hacker, *Editor*
EMP: 11
SALES (est): 722.3K **Privately Held**
SIC: 2711 Commercial printing & newspaper publishing combined; newspapers, publishing & printing

(P-5855)
TXD INTERNATIONAL USA INC
2336 S Vineyard Ave A, Ontario (91761-7767)
PHONE..............................909 947-6568
Rodolfo J Galvez Cordova, *CEO*
Francisco Galvez Vernis, *Vice Pres*
Armando Herrera, *Admin Sec*
▲ **EMP:** 15
SQ FT: 8,500
SALES (est): 1.7MM **Privately Held**
SIC: 2711 2752 2211 2262 Commercial printing & newspaper publishing combined; promotional printing, lithographic; print cloths, cotton; printing: manmade fiber & silk broadwoven fabrics; printing of narrow fabrics

(P-5856)
VALLEY COMMUNITY NEWSPAPER
1109 Markham Way, Sacramento (95818-2913)
PHONE..............................916 429-9901
George Macko, *President*
Sally King, *Editor*
EMP: 10
SALES (est): 716.6K **Privately Held**
WEB: www.valcomnews.com
SIC: 2711 Newspapers: publishing only, not printed on site

(P-5857)
VANGIE L CORTES
Also Called: Asian America Business Journal
9466 Black Mountain Rd, San Diego (92126-4550)
PHONE..............................858 578-6807
Vangie L Cortes, *Owner*
EMP: 21
SALES (est): 70K **Privately Held**
SIC: 2711 Newspapers: publishing only, not printed on site

(P-5858)
VENTURA COUNTY STAR
771 E Daily Dr Ste 300, Camarillo (93010-0781)
PHONE..............................805 437-0138
George H Cogswell III, *President*
EMP: 14
SALES (est): 1.1MM **Privately Held**
WEB: www.vcstar.com
SIC: 2711 Newspapers: publishing only, not printed on site

(P-5859)
VIETNMESE AMRCN MDIA CORP VAMC
Also Called: Vien Dong Daily News
14891 Moran St, Westminster (92683-5535)
PHONE..............................714 379-2851
Hoang Tong, *Exec Dir*
Nga Le, *Manager*
EMP: 19
SALES: 950K **Privately Held**
SIC: 2711 Newspapers: publishing only, not printed on site

(P-5860)
VILLAGE VOICE MEDIA
Also Called: Eastbay Express
318 Harrison St Ste 302, Oakland (94607-4134)
PHONE..............................510 879-3700
Josh Fromson, *Principal*
Nicole Heirich, *Executive*
Sara Herrera, *Accounts Exec*
EMP: 54
SQ FT: 7,400
SALES (est): 3MM **Privately Held**
WEB: www.eastbayexpress.com
SIC: 2711 5812 Newspapers, publishing & printing; eating places

(P-5861)
VILLLAGE NEWS INC
Also Called: Fallbrook Bonsall Village News
41740 Enterprise Cir S, Temecula (92590-4881)
PHONE..............................760 451-3488
Julie Reeder, *President*
Michelle Howard, *Advt Staff*
EMP: 23
SQ FT: 1,500
SALES (est): 1.6MM **Privately Held**
WEB: www.thevillagenews.com
SIC: 2711 Newspapers: publishing only, not printed on site

(P-5862)
WAVE COMMUNITY NEWSPAPERS INC (PA)
Also Called: The Wave
3731 Wilshire Blvd # 840, Los Angeles (90010-2830)
PHONE..............................323 290-3000
Pluria Marshall, *President*
Andy Wiedlin, *Officer*
▲ **EMP:** 30
SQ FT: 15,000
SALES (est): 1.8MM **Privately Held**
SIC: 2711 Commercial printing & newspaper publishing combined; newspapers, publishing & printing

(P-5863)
WESTERN HELLENIC JOURNAL INC
1839 Ygnacio Valley Rd, Walnut Creek (94598-3214)
PHONE..............................925 939-3900
Fanis Economidis, *President*
EMP: 34
SALES (est): 162.2K **Privately Held**
SIC: 2711 Newspapers, publishing & printing

(P-5864)
WESTERN OUTDOORS PUBLICATIONS (PA)
Also Called: Western Outdoor News
1211 Puerta Del Sol # 270, San Clemente (92673-6306)
P.O. Box 73370 (92673-0113)
PHONE..............................949 366-0030
Robert Twilegar, *President*
Lori Twilegar, *Admin Sec*

Gloria Sievers, *Graphic Designe*
Chuck Buhagiar, *Sls & Mktg Exec*
Bill Egan, *Director*
EMP: 42
SALES (est): 3.3MM **Privately Held**
WEB: www.wonews.com
SIC: 2711 2721 Newspapers: publishing only, not printed on site; periodicals

(P-5865)
WESTERN STATES WEEKLIES INC
Also Called: Long Beach Navy Dispatch
6312 Riverdale St, San Diego
(92120-3310)
P.O. Box 600600 (92160-0600)
PHONE.................................619 280-2988
Sara Hagerty, *President*
EMP: 10
SALES (est): 520K **Privately Held**
WEB: www.navynews.com
SIC: 2711 2721 Newspapers: publishing only, not printed on site; periodicals

(P-5866)
WICK COMMUNICATIONS CO
Also Called: Kern Valley Sun
6404 Lake Isabella Blvd, Lake Isabella
(93240-9475)
P.O. Box 3074 (93240-3074)
PHONE.................................760 379-3667
Cliff Urfeth, *Manager*
EMP: 31
SALES (corp-wide): 79.4MM **Privately Held**
WEB: www.hmbreview.com
SIC: 2711 Newspapers, publishing & printing
HQ: Wick Communications Co.
333 W Wilcox Dr Ste 302
Sierra Vista AZ 85635
520 458-0200

(P-5867)
WICK COMMUNICATIONS CO
Also Called: Half Moon Bay Review
714 Kelly St, Half Moon Bay (94019-1919)
P.O. Box 68 (94019-0068)
PHONE.................................650 726-4424
Debra Godshall, *Principal*
EMP: 25
SALES (corp-wide): 79.4MM **Privately Held**
WEB: www.hmbreview.com
SIC: 2711 6531 Newspapers, publishing & printing; real estate agents & managers
HQ: Wick Communications Co.
333 W Wilcox Dr Ste 302
Sierra Vista AZ 85635
520 458-0200

(P-5868)
WINTON TIMES
Also Called: Mid Valley Publications
6950 Gerard Ave, Winton (95388)
P.O. Box 65 (95388-0065)
PHONE.................................209 358-5311
John M Derby, *Owner*
EMP: 25
SQ FT: 5,000
SALES (est): 1.1MM **Privately Held**
SIC: 2711 2752 Newspapers, publishing & printing; commercial printing, lithographic

(P-5869)
WORLD JOURNAL INC (PA)
231 Adrian Rd, Millbrae (94030-3102)
PHONE.................................650 692-9936
Pl Ly Wang, *President*
Shiun Yi Hsia, *CEO*
Cary Cheng, *Executive*
Joe Hung, *Executive*
Susan Chung, *Sales Staff*
▲ **EMP:** 98
SQ FT: 15,000
SALES (est): 14.6MM **Privately Held**
WEB: www.chinesenews.com
SIC: 2711 Newspapers, publishing & printing

(P-5870)
WORLD JOURNAL LA LLC (HQ)
1588 Corporate Center Dr, Monterey Park
(91754-7624)
PHONE.................................323 268-4982
James Guon, *CEO*

Susan Chung, *Sales Staff*
James Guo, *Manager*
Michelle Han, *Accounts Exec*
▲ **EMP:** 170 **EST:** 1981
SQ FT: 45,000
SALES (est): 24.4MM **Privately Held**
WEB: www.chinesedailynews.com
SIC: 2711 Newspapers: publishing only, not printed on site

(P-5871)
YNEZ CORPORATION
432 2nd St, Solvang (93463)
P.O. Box 647 (93464-0647)
PHONE.................................805 688-5522
Peggy Johnson, *President*
EMP: 16 **EST:** 1974
SQ FT: 8,000
SALES (est): 1.1MM
SALES (corp-wide): 593.9MM **Publicly Held**
SIC: 2711 Newspapers, publishing & printing
PA: Lee Enterprises, Incorporated
201 N Harrison St Ste 600
Davenport IA 52801
563 383-2100

2721 Periodicals: Publishing & Printing

(P-5872)
18 MEDIA INC (PA)
Also Called: Gentry Magazine
873 Santa Cruz Ave # 206, Menlo Park
(94025-4635)
PHONE.................................650 324-1818
Elsie Sloriani, *Ch of Bd*
Sloan Citron, *President*
DOT Juby, *CFO*
Sara Shaw, *Vice Pres*
Collier Granberry, *Executive*
EMP: 13
SQ FT: 2,500
SALES (est): 1.8MM **Privately Held**
WEB: www.18media.com
SIC: 2721 Magazines: publishing only, not printed on site

(P-5873)
909 MEDIA GROUP INC
Also Called: 909 Magazine
100 N Euclid Ave Ste 202, Upland
(91786-8315)
PHONE.................................909 608-7426
Marc Grossman, *Branch Mgr*
EMP: 15
SALES (corp-wide): 700K **Privately Held**
SIC: 2721 7389 Magazines: publishing only, not printed on site; advertising, promotional & trade show services
PA: 909 Media Group Inc.
100 N Euclid Ave Ste 202
Upland CA 91786
909 252-7224

(P-5874)
ACTIVE INTEREST MEDIA INC (PA)
Also Called: A I M
300 Continental Blvd # 650, El Segundo
(90245-5067)
PHONE.................................310 356-4100
Efrem Zimbalist, *President*
Lauren Depalma, *Assoc VP*
John Ruscin, *Exec VP*
Mitchell H Faigen, *Senior VP*
Pete Sheinbaum, *Senior VP*
EMP: 70
SALES (est): 113.1MM **Privately Held**
WEB: www.activeinterestmedia.com
SIC: 2721 Magazines: publishing only, not printed on site

(P-5875)
ADAMS TRADE PRESS LP (PA)
Also Called: Adams Business Media
420 S Palm Canyon Dr, Palm Springs
(92262-7304)
PHONE.................................760 318-7000
Mark Adams, *Partner*
EMP: 30
SQ FT: 2,000

SALES (est): 2.2MM **Privately Held**
WEB: www.adamsbevgroup.com
SIC: 2721 Periodicals: publishing only

(P-5876)
AEROTECH NEWS AND REVIEW INC (PA)
Also Called: Bullseye
220 E Avenue K4 Ste 7, Lancaster
(93535-4687)
P.O. Box 1332 (93584-1332)
PHONE.................................520 623-9321
Paul Kinison, *President*
Bill Whitham, *Executive*
EMP: 45
SQ FT: 2,000
SALES (est): 3.7MM **Privately Held**
SIC: 2721 2741 2752 Trade journals: publishing only, not printed on site; miscellaneous publishing; commercial printing, lithographic

(P-5877)
AFFLUENT TARGET MARKETING INC
Also Called: Affluent Living Publication
3855 E La Palma Ave # 250, Anaheim
(92807-1765)
P.O. Box 18507 (92817-8507)
PHONE.................................714 446-6280
Wally Hicks, *President*
Debbie Mesna, *Executive*
Deborah Mesna, *Executive*
Elizabeth Orozco, *Manager*
EMP: 26
SQ FT: 3,500
SALES (est): 3.8MM **Privately Held**
SIC: 2721 Magazines: publishing only, not printed on site

(P-5878)
AKN HOLDINGS LLC (PA)
10250 Constellation Blvd, Los Angeles
(90067-6200)
PHONE.................................310 432-7100
Andrew Nikou,
Daniel Abrams, *Senior VP*
Matthias Gundlach, *Principal*
EMP: 11
SALES (est): 676.7MM **Privately Held**
WEB: www.opengatecapital.com
SIC: 2721 6799 8621 Magazines: publishing & printing; investors; professional membership organizations

(P-5879)
ALM MEDIA HOLDINGS INC
Also Called: American Lawyer Media
1035 Market St Ste 500, San Francisco
(94103-1650)
PHONE.................................415 490-1054
Christopher Braun, *Manager*
Jason Doiy, *Editor*
Nicole Nakama, *Representative*
EMP: 30
SALES (corp-wide): 181.8MM **Privately Held**
SIC: 2721 Periodicals: publishing & printing
PA: Alm Media Holdings, Inc.
120 Broadway Fl 5
New York NY 10271
212 457-9400

(P-5880)
APPAREL NEWS GROUP
Also Called: California Apparel News
110 E 9th St Ste A777, Los Angeles
(90079-1777)
PHONE.................................213 327-1002
EMP: 40
SALES (est): 3.7MM
SALES (corp-wide): 4.5MM **Privately Held**
WEB: www.apparelnews.net
SIC: 2721
PA: Mnm Corporation
110 E 9th St Ste A777
Los Angeles CA 90079
213 627-3737

(P-5881)
APPLIED MATERIALS INC
3330 Scott Blvd Bldg 6, Santa Clara
(95054-3101)
PHONE.................................408 727-5555

Debbie Noris, *Branch Mgr*
Thorsten Kril, *Technical Staff*
Martin Seamons, *Engineer*
Kirk Liebscher, *Senior Engr*
EMP: 14
SALES (corp-wide): 17.2B **Publicly Held**
WEB: www.appliedmaterials.com
SIC: 2721 3559 Periodicals; semiconductor manufacturing machinery
PA: Applied Materials, Inc.
3050 Bowers Ave
Santa Clara CA 95054
408 727-5555

(P-5882)
APRESS L P
Also Called: Appress
2588 Telegraph Ave, Berkeley
(94704-2920)
PHONE.................................510 549-5930
Gary Cornell, *CEO*
EMP: 12
SALES (est): 131.2K **Privately Held**
WEB: www.apress.com
SIC: 2721 Magazines: publishing & printing

(P-5883)
ARSENIC INC
530 S Hewitt St Unit 119, Los Angeles
(90013-2290)
PHONE.................................310 701-7559
Amanda Micallef, *President*
EMP: 15
SALES (est): 1MM **Privately Held**
SIC: 2721 Magazines: publishing only, not printed on site

(P-5884)
AUTO CLUB ENTERPRISES
Also Called: Westway Magazine
3333 Fairview Rd, Costa Mesa
(92626-1610)
PHONE.................................714 885-2376
Tamara Hill, *Principal*
EMP: 278
SALES (corp-wide): 3.4B **Privately Held**
WEB: www.aaa-newmexico.com
SIC: 2721 Periodicals
PA: Auto Club Enterprises
3333 Fairview Rd Msa451
Costa Mesa CA 92626
714 850-5111

(P-5885)
BACKSTAGE WEST
5055 Wilshire Blvd 5, Los Angeles
(90036-6100)
PHONE.................................323 525-2356
Jamie Young, *Principal*
EMP: 20
SALES (est): 695.4K **Privately Held**
WEB: www.backstagewest.com
SIC: 2721 Magazines: publishing only, not printed on site

(P-5886)
BASS ANGLER
Also Called: Bass Angler Magazine
2500 Shadow Mountain Ct, San Ramon
(94583-1823)
PHONE.................................925 362-3190
Mark Lassagne, *President*
EMP: 11
SALES (est): 500K **Privately Held**
SIC: 2721 7311 Magazines: publishing only, not printed on site; advertising agencies

(P-5887)
BEAR BROTHERS ENTERPRISES LTD
777 E Tahqtz Cyn Way # 200, Palm Springs
(92262-6784)
PHONE.................................914 588-6885
Steve Harris, *President*
Michael Goldberg, *Vice Pres*
EMP: 30
SQ FT: 800
SALES (est): 1.8MM **Privately Held**
SIC: 2721 Magazines: publishing & printing

(P-5888)

BELMONT PUBLICATIONS INC
Also Called: Dimensions of Dental Hygiene
3621 S Harbor Blvd # 265, Santa Ana
(92704-8905)
PHONE..................714 825-1234
Lorene G Kent, *President*
EMP: 10
SALES (est): 1.3MM **Privately Held**
WEB:
www.dimensionsofdentalhygiene.com
SIC: 2721 Magazines: publishing only, not printed on site

(P-5889)

BENTLEY MANAGEMENT CORPORATION
Also Called: Players International Publ
8060 Melrose Ave Ste 210, Los Angeles
(90046-7037)
PHONE..................323 653-8060
Bentley Morris, *Vice Pres*
Bentley Morriss, *Vice Pres*
Tom Morney, *Director*
EMP: 10
SQ FT: 3,000
SALES (est): 581.2K **Privately Held**
SIC: 2721 Magazines: publishing & printing

(P-5890)

BONNIER CORPORATION
15255 Alton Pkwy, Irvine (92618-2367)
PHONE..................760 707-0100
Jeremy Thompson, *Owner*
EMP: 88
SALES (corp-wide): 2.9B **Privately Held**
SIC: 2721 Magazines: publishing only, not printed on site
HQ: Bonnier Corporation
460 N Orlando Ave Ste 200
Winter Park FL 32789

(P-5891)

BOWTIE INC
Also Called: Pet Product News
3 Burroughs, Irvine (92618-2804)
P.O. Box 6050, Mission Viejo (92690-6050)
PHONE..................949 855-8822
Peter Bullhagen, *President*
EMP: 80
SALES (corp-wide): 56.1MM **Privately Held**
WEB: www.bowtieinc.com
SIC: 2721 0752 2731 Magazines: publishing & printing; animal specialty services; book publishing
HQ: Bowtie, Inc.
500 N Brand Blvd Ste 600
Glendale CA 91203
213 385-2222

(P-5892)

BRIDGE USA INC
20817 S Western Ave, Torrance
(90501-1804)
PHONE..................310 532-5921
Yoshihiro Ishii, *President*
EMP: 20
SQ FT: 6,000
SALES (est): 2.3MM **Privately Held**
SIC: 2721 7311 Magazines: publishing only, not printed on site; advertising agencies

(P-5893)

BRIGHT BUSINESS MEDIA LLC
Also Called: Smart Meetings
475 Gate 5 Rd Ste 235, Sausalito
(94965-2877)
PHONE..................415 339-9355
Marin Bright,
John Decesare, *Vice Pres*
Luc Troussieux, *Principal*
EMP: 10
SALES (est): 1.8MM **Privately Held**
WEB: www.smartmtgs.com
SIC: 2721 Magazines: publishing only, not printed on site

(P-5894)

BUILDER & DEVELOPER MAGAZINES
Also Called: Peninsula Publishing
1602 Monrovia Ave, Newport Beach
(92663-2808)
PHONE..................949 631-0308
Nick Slevin, *Partner*
Stuart Cochrane, *Partner*
EMP: 10
SALES (est): 937.5K **Privately Held**
WEB: www.bdmag.com
SIC: 2721 Magazines: publishing only, not printed on site

(P-5895)

BUSINESS EXTENSION BUREAU
Also Called: Western Real Estate News
500 S Airport Blvd, South San Francisco
(94080-6912)
PHONE..................650 737-5700
Gil Chin, *President*
Steven Hufford, *Technical Staff*
Robert Stallard, *QC Mgr*
Jeff Childers, *Account Dir*
EMP: 20
SQ FT: 7,000
SALES: 1MM **Privately Held**
SIC: 2721 7331 2752 Trade journals: publishing & printing; direct mail advertising services; commercial printing, lithographic

(P-5896)

BUSINESS JOURNAL
Also Called: Fresno Business Journal
1315 Van Ness Ave Ste 200, Fresno
(93721-1729)
P.O. Box 126 (93707-0126)
PHONE..................559 490-3400
Gordon M Webster Jr, *President*
Kaysi Curtin, *Sales Staff*
EMP: 24 EST: 1886
SALES (est): 2.5MM **Privately Held**
WEB: www.thebusinessjournal.com
SIC: 2721 2711 Trade journals: publishing only, not printed on site; newspapers

(P-5897)

BUTANE PROPANE NEWS INC
338 E Foothill Blvd, Arcadia (91006-2542)
P.O. Box 660698 (91066-0698)
PHONE..................626 357-2168
Natalia Peal, *President*
Nanette Dougall, *Vice Pres*
EMP: 10
SQ FT: 1,750
SALES (est): 790K **Privately Held**
WEB: www.bpnews.com
SIC: 2721 2741 Magazines: publishing & printing; business service newsletters: publishing & printing

(P-5898)

CBJ LP
Also Called: San Fernando Valley Bus Jurnl
21550 Oxnard St, Woodland Hills
(91367-7100)
PHONE..................818 676-1750
Pegi Matsuda, *Manager*
Charles Crumpley, *Editor*
EMP: 12
SALES (corp-wide): 31.5MM **Privately Held**
WEB: www.ocbj.com
SIC: 2721 Magazines: publishing only, not printed on site
PA: Cbj, L.P.
7101 College Blvd # 1100
Shawnee Mission KS
913 451-9000

(P-5899)

CBJ LP
Also Called: Los Angeles Business Journal
5700 Wilshire Blvd # 170, Los Angeles
(90036-7205)
PHONE..................323 549-5225
Matt Toledo, *Branch Mgr*
Nina Bays, *Prdtn Dir*
Elizabeth Gravier, *Natl Sales Mgr*
Sarah Ewald, *Manager*
Nicole Hamre, *Manager*
EMP: 40

SALES (corp-wide): 31.5MM **Privately Held**
WEB: www.ocbj.com
SIC: 2721 2711 8742 Periodicals: publishing only; trade journals: publishing only, not printed on site; newspapers; general management consultant
PA: Cbj, L.P.
7101 College Blvd # 1100
Shawnee Mission KS
913 451-9000

(P-5900)

CBJ LP
Also Called: San Diego Business Journal
4909 Murphy Canyon Rd # 200, San Diego
(92123-4349)
PHONE..................858 277-6359
Armon Mills, *Principal*
Jeffrey Blease, *Partner*
EMP: 25
SQ FT: 10,000
SALES (corp-wide): 31.5MM **Privately Held**
WEB: www.ocbj.com
SIC: 2721 2741 2711 Trade journals: publishing & printing; miscellaneous publishing; newspapers
PA: Cbj, L.P.
7101 College Blvd # 1100
Shawnee Mission KS
913 451-9000

(P-5901)

CBJ LP
Also Called: Orange County Business Journal
18500 Von Karman Ave # 150, Irvine
(92612-0504)
PHONE..................949 833-8373
Janet Cox, *Manager*
Diana Leonard, *Vice Pres*
Cynthia Newcomb, *Executive Asst*
Courtney Zani, *Administration*
Martin Nilchian, *Technology*
EMP: 40
SALES (corp-wide): 31.5MM **Privately Held**
WEB: www.ocbj.com
SIC: 2721 2711 7313 Trade journals: publishing only, not printed on site; newspapers; newspaper advertising representative
PA: Cbj, L.P.
7101 College Blvd # 1100
Shawnee Mission KS
913 451-9000

(P-5902)

CHALLENGE PUBLICATIONS INC
21835 Nordhoff St, Chatsworth
(91311-5712)
PHONE..................818 700-6868
Edwin A Schnepf, *President*
Susan Duprey, *Mng Officer*
EMP: 20
SQ FT: 30,000
SALES (est): 2MM **Privately Held**
WEB: www.challengeweb.com
SIC: 2721 Magazines: publishing & printing

(P-5903)

CHET COOPER
Also Called: C2 Publishing
1001 W 17th St, Costa Mesa (92627-4512)
P.O. Box 10878 (92627-0271)
PHONE..................949 854-8700
Chet Cooper, *Owner*
Pamela K Johnson, *Director*
EMP: 12
SALES (est): 968.8K **Privately Held**
WEB: www.abilitymagazine.com
SIC: 2721 Magazines: publishing only, not printed on site

(P-5904)

CHURM PUBLISHING INC (PA)
Also Called: O.C. Metro Magazine
1451 Quail St Ste 201, Newport Beach
(92660-2741)
PHONE..................714 796-7000
Steve Churm, *President*
Brian O'Neill, *CFO*
Peter Churm, *Vice Pres*
EMP: 47
SQ FT: 7,000

SALES (est): 3MM **Privately Held**
WEB: www.ocfamily.com
SIC: 2721 Trade journals: publishing & printing

(P-5905)

CLIQUE BRANDS INC (PA)
Also Called: Who What Wear
750 N San Vicnte Blvd Re800, West Hollywood (90069-5788)
PHONE..................323 648-5619
Katherine Power, *CEO*
Hilary Kerr, *President*
Mika Onishi, *COO*
Alexandra Taylor, *Exec Dir*
Katie Macias, *Web Dvlpr*
EMP: 32
SQ FT: 2,200
SALES (est): 5MM **Privately Held**
SIC: 2721 Magazines: publishing only, not printed on site

(P-5906)

COIN DEALER NEWSLETTER INC
2034 262nd St, Lomita (90717-3416)
PHONE..................310 515-7369
Pauline Miladin, *President*
EMP: 12
SALES (est): 1.4MM **Privately Held**
WEB: www.greysheet.com
SIC: 2721 Periodicals: publishing only

(P-5907)

COMPETITOR GROUP INC (HQ)
Also Called: Competitor Magazine
6420 Sequence Dr, San Diego
(92121-4313)
PHONE..................858 450-6510
David Abeles, *CEO*
Scott Dickey, *President*
Steve Gintowt, *COO*
Barrett Garrison, *CFO*
Keith Kendrick, *Chief Mktg Ofcr*
▲ EMP: 191
SQ FT: 56,796
SALES (est): 126.4MM
SALES (corp-wide): 127MM **Privately Held**
SIC: 2721 7941 Magazines: publishing & printing; sports promotion
PA: Calera Capital Management, Inc.
580 California St # 2200
San Francisco CA 94104
415 632-5200

(P-5908)

COMPETITOR MAGAZINE
10179 Hudiken St Ste 100, San Diego
(92121)
PHONE..................858 768-6800
Bob Babbitt, *President*
Lois Schwartz, *Vice Pres*
EMP: 20
SQ FT: 2,500
SALES (est): 2.3MM **Privately Held**
SIC: 2721 Magazines: publishing only, not printed on site

(P-5909)

COMSTOCK PUBLISHING INC
Also Called: Comstock's Magazine
2335 American River Dr # 301, Sacramento
(95825-7088)
PHONE..................916 364-1000
Comstockca Exc, *Vice Pres*
Winnie Comstockcarlson, *Exec VP*
Clayton Blakley, *Vice Pres*
Randy Brink, *Vice Pres*
Ryan Montoya, *Vice Pres*
EMP: 15
SQ FT: 1,600
SALES (est): 1.6MM **Privately Held**
SIC: 2721 Magazines: publishing only, not printed on site

(P-5910)

CONTINENTAL FEATURE/ NEWS SVC
501 W Broadway Ste C, San Diego
(92101-3520)
PHONE..................858 492-8696
Gary P Salamone, *Owner*
EMP: 50

(PA)=Parent Co (HQ)=Headquarters (DH)=Div Headquarters
✪ = New Business established in last 2 years

2721 - Periodicals: Publishing & Printing County (P-5911)

SALES (est): 2.5MM **Privately Held**
SIC: 2721 4899 7383 7389 Periodicals: publishing & printing; data communication services; news syndicates; personal service agents, brokers & bureaus

(P-5911)
COYNE & BLANCHARD INC
Also Called: Communication Arts
110 Constitution Dr, Menlo Park (94025-1107)
PHONE...................650 326-6040
Patrick Coyne, *President*
Martha Coyne, *Corp Secy*
Eric Coyne, *Vice Pres*
Lois Vega, *Executive*
Jiping Hu, *Sr Software Eng*
EMP: 20
SQ FT: 7,500
SALES (est): 2.4MM **Privately Held**
WEB: www.creativehotlist.com
SIC: 2721 Magazines: publishing only, not printed on site

(P-5912)
CREATIVE AGE PUBLICATIONS INC
Also Called: Nailpro
7628 Densmore Ave, Van Nuys (91406-2042)
PHONE...................818 782-7328
Deborah Carver, *President*
Mindy Rosiejka, *CFO*
Diane Jones, *Adv Dir*
Andrew Smith, *Mktg Dir*
Jamie Andrew, *Marketing Staff*
EMP: 50
SQ FT: 14,000
SALES (est): 7.1MM **Privately Held**
WEB: www.creativeage.com
SIC: 2721 2731 Magazines: publishing only, not printed on site; book publishing

(P-5913)
CURTCO MEDIA GROUP LLC
29160 Heathercliff Rd # 1, Malibu (90265-6310)
P.O. Box 6934 (90264-6934)
PHONE...................310 589-7700
Samantha Brooks, *Principal*
EMP: 12 EST: 2010
SALES (est): 1.3MM **Privately Held**
SIC: 2721 Magazines: publishing & printing

(P-5914)
DAILY GRAPHS INC
Also Called: Daily Graphics
12655 Beatrice St, Los Angeles (90066-7306)
PHONE...................310 448-6843
William Oneil, *President*
William O'Neil, *President*
Don Drake, *Treasurer*
EMP: 20
SALES (est): 971.1K
SALES (corp-wide): 231.5MM **Privately Held**
WEB: www.dailygraphs.com
SIC: 2721 7371 Magazines: publishing only, not printed on site; custom computer programming services
HQ: O'neil Securities, Incorporated
12655 Beatrice St
Los Angeles CA 90066
310 448-6800

(P-5915)
DAISY PUBLISHING COMPANY INC
Also Called: Hi-Torque Publications
25233 Anza Dr, Santa Clarita (91355-1289)
PHONE...................661 295-1910
Roland Hinz, *President*
Lila Hinz, *Vice Pres*
Carl Husfeld, *Safety Mgr*
Robb Mesecher, *Adv Dir*
Chris Stangl, *Adv Mgr*
EMP: 55 EST: 1969
SQ FT: 16,000
SALES (est): 11.5MM **Privately Held**
WEB: www.dirtbikemagazine.com
SIC: 2721 Magazines: publishing & printing

(P-5916)
DAN M SWOFFORD
728 Cherry St, Chico (95928-5143)
PHONE...................530 343-9994
EMP: 10
SALES (est): 480K **Privately Held**
SIC: 2721

(P-5917)
DESERT PUBLICATIONS INC (PA)
Also Called: Desert Grafics
303 N Indian Canyon Dr, Palm Springs (92262-6015)
P.O. Box 2724 (92263-2724)
PHONE...................760 325-2333
Franklin Jones, *Principal*
Stuart Funk, *Creative Dir*
Todd May, *Info Tech Dir*
Rima Dorsey, *Adv Dir*
Maryanne Coury, *Director*
EMP: 49
SQ FT: 25,000
SALES (est): 7.5MM **Privately Held**
WEB: www.jonesagency.com
SIC: 2721 7311 Magazines: publishing only, not printed on site; advertising agencies

(P-5918)
DESIGN JOURNAL INC
Also Called: Design La
1720 20th St Ste 201, Santa Monica (90404-3944)
P.O. Box 993, Pacific Palisades (90272-0993)
PHONE...................310 394-4394
John Platter, *President*
John Moses, *Admin Sec*
EMP: 15
SALES (est): 1.8MM **Privately Held**
WEB: www.adexawards.com
SIC: 2721 7311 8742 Magazines: publishing only, not printed on site; advertising agencies; marketing consulting services

(P-5919)
DIABLO COUNTRY MAGAZINE INC
Also Called: Diablo Custom Publishing
2520 Camino Diablo, Walnut Creek (94597-3939)
PHONE...................925 943-1111
Steven J Rivera, *President*
Eileen Cunningham, *COO*
Brendan C Casey, *CFO*
Dave Bergeron, *Creative Dir*
Alex Ackerman, *Info Tech Mgr*
▲ EMP: 40 EST: 1979
SQ FT: 7,640
SALES (est): 6.5MM **Privately Held**
WEB: www.dcpubs.com
SIC: 2721 2741 Magazines: publishing only, not printed on site; miscellaneous publishing

(P-5920)
DISNEY PUBLISHING WORLDWIDE (DH)
500 S Buena Vista St, Burbank (91521-0001)
PHONE...................212 633-4400
R Russell Hampton Jr, *Chairman*
Robert W Hernandez, *Senior VP*
▲ EMP: 100
SALES (est): 35MM
SALES (corp-wide): 90.2B **Publicly Held**
SIC: 2721 Magazines: publishing only, not printed on site
HQ: Disney Enterprises, Inc.
500 S Buena Vista St
Burbank CA 91521
818 560-1000

(P-5921)
DISTINCTIVE PRPTS NAPA VLY
1615 2nd St, NAPA (94559-2818)
PHONE...................707 256-2251
Randy Principe, *Director*
Priscilla Lara, *Manager*
EMP: 100 EST: 1984
SALES: 2MM **Privately Held**
WEB: www.napanews.com
SIC: 2721 Periodicals

(P-5922)
DIVERSITYCOMM INC
Also Called: Diversity In Steam
18 Technology Dr Ste 170, Irvine (92618-2313)
PHONE...................949 825-5777
Mona Lisa Faris, *President*
Richard Abboud, *General Mgr*
Erika Ulloa, *Executive Asst*
Rosario Diaz, *Research*
Pamela Burke, *Human Resources*
EMP: 12
SQ FT: 1,700
SALES: 1.5MM **Privately Held**
WEB: www.hnmagazine.com
SIC: 2721 Magazines: publishing only, not printed on site

(P-5923)
DOW THEORY LETTERS INC
7590 Fay Ave Ste 404, La Jolla (92037-4872)
PHONE...................858 454-0481
Richard Russell, *President*
Fay Russell, *Vice Pres*
EMP: 10 EST: 1958
SQ FT: 1,500
SALES (est): 1.2MM **Privately Held**
WEB: www.dowtheoryletters.com
SIC: 2721 Statistical reports (periodicals): publishing only

(P-5924)
DREAM COMMUNICATIONS INC
Also Called: Dream Homes Magazine
2431 Morena Blvd, San Diego (92110-4139)
PHONE...................619 275-9100
Michael Vlassis, *President*
EMP: 15
SQ FT: 4,732
SALES (est): 1.6MM **Privately Held**
WEB: www.dreamhomesmagazine.com
SIC: 2721 Magazines: publishing & printing

(P-5925)
DUB PUBLISHING INC
Also Called: Dub Custom Auto Show
11803 Smith Ave, Santa Fe Springs (90670-3226)
P.O. Box 91471, City of Industry (91715-1471)
PHONE...................626 336-3821
Myles Kovacs, *President*
Haythem Haddad, *Art Dir*
Herman Flores, *Director*
▲ EMP: 10
SQ FT: 5,000
SALES (est): 2.9MM **Privately Held**
WEB: www.dubmagazine.com
SIC: 2721 Magazines: publishing only, not printed on site

(P-5926)
DUNCAN MCINTOSH COMPANY INC (PA)
Also Called: Sea Magazine
18475 Bandilier Cir, Fountain Valley (92708-7012)
PHONE...................949 660-6150
Duncan R McIntosh, *CEO*
Teresa McIntosh, *Corp Secy*
Dave Kelsen, *Info Tech Dir*
Rick Avila, *Opers Staff*
Janette Hood, *Adv Dir*
EMP: 35
SQ FT: 15,728
SALES (est): 5.1MM **Privately Held**
WEB: www.seamag.com
SIC: 2721 7389 Magazines: publishing & printing; trade show arrangement

(P-5927)
DWELL LIFE INC (PA)
595 Pacific Ave 4, San Francisco (94133-4669)
PHONE...................415 373-5100
Michela Abrams, *CEO*
Amy Lloyd, *Partner*
Trey Walker, *Engineer*
Jenna Page, *Marketing Mgr*
Lara H Deam, *Manager*
▲ EMP: 40

SALES: 20MM **Privately Held**
WEB: www.dwellmag.com
SIC: 2721 7389 Magazines: publishing & printing; advertising, promotional & trade show services

(P-5928)
E H PUBLISHING INC
Also Called: Security Sales & Integration
3520 Challenger St, Torrance (90503-1640)
PHONE...................310 533-2400
Scott Goldfine, *Editor*
Tom Green, *Chief*
Amy Lanphear, *Manager*
Rodney Bosch, *Senior Editor*
EMP: 24 **Privately Held**
SIC: 2721 Magazines: publishing & printing
PA: E H Publishing, Inc.
111 Speen St Ste 200
Framingham MA 01701

(P-5929)
ELISID MAGAZINE
1450 University Ave F168, Riverside (92507-4467)
PHONE...................619 990-9999
EMP: 20
SALES (est): 1.2MM **Privately Held**
SIC: 2721

(P-5930)
EMERALD EXPOSITIONS LLC
Also Called: Vnu Business
31910 Del Obispo St # 200, San Juan Capistrano (92675-3182)
PHONE...................949 226-5754
Denise Bashem, *Branch Mgr*
EMP: 70
SALES (corp-wide): 380.7MM **Publicly Held**
SIC: 2721 7389 Trade journals: publishing only, not printed on site; promoters of shows & exhibitions
HQ: Emerald Expositions, Llc
31910 Del Obispo St # 200
San Juan Capistrano CA 92675

(P-5931)
EMERALD EXPOSITIONS LLC
5055 Wilshire Blvd # 600, Los Angeles (90036-6100)
PHONE...................323 525-2000
Eric Mika, *Branch Mgr*
EMP: 60
SALES (corp-wide): 380.7MM **Publicly Held**
SIC: 2721 Trade journals: publishing only, not printed on site
HQ: Emerald Expositions, Llc
31910 Del Obispo St # 200
San Juan Capistrano CA 92675

(P-5932)
ENTER MUSIC PUBLISHING INC
Also Called: Drum Magazine
1346 The Alameda Ste 7, San Jose (95126-5006)
PHONE...................408 971-9794
Phillip Hood, *President*
Connie Hood, *Treasurer*
Andrew Doerschuk, *Vice Pres*
EMP: 14
SQ FT: 3,000
SALES (est): 1.7MM **Privately Held**
WEB: www.drummagazine.com
SIC: 2721 Magazines: publishing only, not printed on site

(P-5933)
ENTREPRENEUR MEDIA INC (PA)
Also Called: Entrepeneur Magazine
18061 Fitch, Irvine (92614-6018)
P.O. Box 19787 (92623-9787)
PHONE...................949 261-2325
Ryan Shea, *CEO*
Neil Perlman, *President*
Joe Goodman, *CFO*
Bill Shaw, *Officer*
Ronald Young, *Admin Sec*
▲ EMP: 80
SQ FT: 30,000

▲ = Import ▼ = Export
◆ = Import/Export

SALES (est): 16.4MM **Privately Held**
SIC: **2721** Magazines: publishing & printing

(P-5934)
EXCELLENCE MAGAZINE INC
Also Called: Ross Periodicals
42 Digital Dr Ste 5, Novato (94949-5762)
PHONE...............................415 382-0582
Tom Toldrian, *President*
EMP: 14
SQ FT: 2,850
SALES (est): 1.4MM **Privately Held**
WEB: www.rossperiodicals.com
SIC: **2721** Magazines: publishing only, not
printed on site

(P-5935)
FLAUNT MAGAZINE
1422 N Highland Ave, Los Angeles
(90028-7611)
PHONE...............................323 836-1044
Luis A Barajas Jr, *President*
Jose Abella, *Office Mgr*
Amy Slocum, *Manager*
Britton Litow, *Assistant*
Angus Donohoo, *Senior Editor*
▲ EMP: 18
SQ FT: 8,500
SALES (est): 903.5K **Privately Held**
WEB: www.flauntmagazine.com
SIC: **2721** Magazines: publishing & printing

(P-5936)
FORESTER COMMUNICATIONS INC
Also Called: Grading and Excavating Mag
2946 De La Vina St, Santa Barbara
(93105-3310)
P.O. Box 3100 (93130-3100)
PHONE...............................805 682-1300
Daniel Waldman, *President*
John Richardson, *Info Tech Dir*
Doug Mlyn, *Prdtn Mgr*
John Trotti, *VP Mktg*
Janice Kaspersen, *Marketing Mgr*
EMP: 30
SQ FT: 4,500
SALES (est): 3.8MM **Privately Held**
WEB: www.forester.net
SIC: **2721** Magazines: publishing only, not
printed on site

(P-5937)
FORTY-NINERS PUBLICATION
1250 Bellflower Blvd Csul, Long Beach
(90840-0001)
PHONE...............................562 985-5568
Dr William A Mulligan, *Owner*
Beverly Munson, *Manager*
EMP: 10
SALES (est): 549.7K **Privately Held**
SIC: **2721** Magazines: publishing & printing

(P-5938)
FOUNDATION FOR NAT PROGRESS
Also Called: Mother Jones Magazine
222 Sutter St Ste 600, San Francisco
(94108-4457)
PHONE...............................415 321-1700
Madeleine Buckingham, *CFO*
Marisa Endicott, *Fellow*
EMP: 39 EST: 1975
SQ FT: 13,500
SALES: 16.5MM **Privately Held**
SIC: **2721** Magazines: publishing & printing

(P-5939)
FRANCHISE UPDATE INC
Also Called: Franchise Update Media Group
6489 Camden Ave Ste 204, San Jose
(95120-2851)
P.O. Box 20547 (95160-0547)
PHONE...............................408 402-5681
Therese Thilgen, *CEO*
Jamie N Hage, *Partner*
Andrew P Loewinger, *Partner*
Carolyn G Nussbaum, *Partner*
Arthur L Pressman, *Partner*
EMP: 15
SALES (est): 1.8MM **Privately Held**
WEB: www.franchise-update.com
SIC: **2721** Magazines: publishing only, not
printed on site

(P-5940)
FREEDOM OF PRESS FOUNDATION
601 Van Ness Ave Ste E731, San Francisco
(94102-3200)
PHONE...............................510 995-0780
Trevor Timm, *Exec Dir*
EMP: 16
SALES: 5.9MM **Privately Held**
SIC: **2721** Periodicals

(P-5941)
FUTURE US INC (HQ)
1390 Market St Ste 200, San Francisco
(94102-5404)
P.O. Box 22418, Pasadena (91185-0001)
PHONE...............................650 238-2400
Rachelle Considine, *CEO*
Charlie Speight, *Senior VP*
Rhoda Bueno, *Vice Pres*
Stacy Gaines, *Vice Pres*
Isaac Ugay, *Vice Pres*
EMP: 91
SALES (est): 55MM
SALES (corp-wide): 158.8MM **Privately Held**
WEB: www.futurenetworkusa.com
SIC: **2721** Magazines: publishing only, not
printed on site
PA: Future Plc
Quay House
Bath BA1 1
122 544-2244

(P-5942)
GAMMON LLC
Also Called: Sonoma Business Magazine
1410 Neotomas Ave Ste 200, Santa Rosa
(95405-7533)
PHONE...............................707 575-8282
Norman Rosinski, *Principal*
John Dennis,
Joni Rosinski,
EMP: 12 EST: 2000
SALES: 1MM **Privately Held**
SIC: **2721** Periodicals

(P-5943)
GANNETT CO INC
Also Called: Nurseweek Publishing
1156 Aster Ave Ste C, Sunnyvale
(94086-6810)
PHONE...............................800 859-2091
Andy Baldwin, *Manager*
EMP: 30
SALES (corp-wide): 2.9B **Publicly Held**
WEB: www.gannett.com
SIC: **2721** Magazines: publishing only, not
printed on site
PA: Gannett Co., Inc.
7950 Jones Branch Dr
Mc Lean VA 22102
703 854-6000

(P-5944)
GOLD PROSPECTORS ASSN OF AMER
Also Called: Gold Prospectors Assn Amer
25819 Jefferson Ave # 110, Murrieta
(92562-6964)
P.O. Box 891509, Temecula (92589-1509)
PHONE...............................951 699-4749
Thomas H Massie, *President*
Kevin Hoagland, *Exec Dir*
Richard Dixon, *Admin Sec*
Michael Lukes, *Finance Mgr*
Dominic Ricci, *Opers Staff*
EMP: 20
SALES (est): 2.5MM **Privately Held**
WEB: www.goldprospectors.com
SIC: **2721** 4833 Magazines: publishing
only, not printed on site; television broad-
casting stations

(P-5945)
GRAPHIC FILM GROUP LLC (PA)
1901 Avenue Of The Stars, Los Angeles
(90067-6001)
PHONE...............................310 887-6330
Scott Walterschied, *Chairman*
Ranford Schlei, *Chairman*
Randy Mendhlsohn, *Principal*
EMP: 15

SALES (est): 1MM **Privately Held**
SIC: **2721** 7812 Television schedules:
publishing & printing; video production

(P-5946)
GREATDAD LLC
Also Called: Pregnancy Magazine
2337 Vallejo St, San Francisco
(94123-4711)
PHONE...............................415 572-8181
Paul Banas, *Owner*
EMP: 10
SALES (est): 686.5K **Privately Held**
SIC: **2721** Magazines: publishing & printing

(P-5947)
H S N CONSULTANTS INC
Also Called: Nilson Report, The
1110 Eugenia Pl Ste 100, Carpinteria
(93013-2080)
PHONE...............................805 684-8800
David Robertson, *President*
Alistair Mills, *Director*
Lori Fulmer, *Manager*
Alarice Parsons, *Manager*
Lisa Cervantes, *Editor*
EMP: 10 EST: 1970
SALES: 2MM **Privately Held**
WEB: www.nilsonreport.com
SIC: **2721** Periodicals

(P-5948)
HARTLE MEDIA VENTURES LLC
Also Called: 7x7
680 2nd St, San Francisco (94107-2015)
PHONE...............................415 362-7797
EMP: 20
SQ FT: 2,000
SALES (est): 2.1MM **Privately Held**
WEB: www.allegiscapital.com
SIC: **2721**

(P-5949)
HAYMARKET WORLDWIDE INC
17030 Red Hill Ave, Irvine (92614-5626)
PHONE...............................949 417-6700
Peter Foubister, *CEO*
▲ EMP: 30
SQ FT: 4,000
SALES (est): 2.8MM
SALES (corp-wide): 219.2MM **Privately Held**
WEB: www.haymarketworldwide.com
SIC: **2721** Magazines: publishing only, not
printed on site
HQ: Haymarket Media, Inc.
275 7th Ave Fl 10
New York NY 10001
646 638-6000

(P-5950)
HEARST CORPORATION
Also Called: Examiner Special Projects Div
3000 Ocean Park Blvd, Santa Monica
(90405-3020)
PHONE...............................310 752-1040
Amory Jack Cooke, *Manager*
Liz Manley, *Sales Staff*
Sandy Adamski, *Director*
EMP: 14
SALES (corp-wide): 8.3B **Privately Held**
WEB: www.hearstcorp.com
SIC: **2721** Magazines: publishing only, not
printed on site
PA: The Hearst Corporation
300 W 57th St Fl 42
New York NY 10019
212 649-2000

(P-5951)
HEARST CORPORATION
Also Called: Cycle World Magazine
15255 Alton Pkwy Ste 300, Irvine
(92618-2603)
PHONE...............................760 707-0100
Nancy Laporte, *Manager*
EMP: 60
SALES (corp-wide): 8.3B **Privately Held**
WEB: www.popphoto.com
SIC: **2721** Magazines: publishing & printing
PA: The Hearst Corporation
300 W 57th St Fl 42
New York NY 10019
212 649-2000

(P-5952)
HEARST CORPORATION
1 Wyntoon Rd, Mccloud (96057)
P.O. Box 1600, McCloud (96057-1600)
PHONE...............................530 964-3131
Pat Patterson, *Manager*
EMP: 25
SALES (corp-wide): 8.3B **Privately Held**
WEB: www.hearstcorp.com
SIC: **2721** Magazines: publishing only, not
printed on site
PA: The Hearst Corporation
300 W 57th St Fl 42
New York NY 10019
212 649-2000

(P-5953)
HELEN NOBLE
Also Called: Military Magazine
2120 28th St, Sacramento (95818-1910)
PHONE...............................916 457-8990
Armond Nobel, *Owner*
Helen Nobel, *Owner*
EMP: 11
SALES (est): 595.8K **Privately Held**
WEB: www.milmag.com
SIC: **2721** Magazines: publishing only, not
printed on site

(P-5954)
HIC CORPORATION (PA)
Also Called: Heavy Duty Trucking
38 Executive Park Ste 300, Irvine
(92614-6755)
PHONE...............................949 261-1636
Doug Condra, *Principal*
Sean Thornton, *Sales Staff*
Stephane Babcock, *Manager*
EMP: 15
SALES (est): 2.3MM **Privately Held**
WEB: www.heavydutytrucking.com
SIC: **2721** Magazines: publishing only, not
printed on site

(P-5955)
HISPANIC BUSINESS INC
Also Called: Hispanic Business Magazine
5385 Hollister Ave # 204, Santa Barbara
(93111-2389)
PHONE...............................805 964-4554
Jesus Chavarria, *President*
Bonnie Chavarria, *Corp Secy*
EMP: 13
SQ FT: 40,000
SALES (est): 1.8MM **Privately Held**
WEB: www.hirediversity.com
SIC: **2721** 7375 7389 Magazines: pub-
lishing only, not printed on site; data base
information retrieval; trade show arrange-
ment

(P-5956)
HITS MAGAZINE INC (PA)
Also Called: Music Market Update
6906 Hollywood Blvd Fl 2, Los Angeles
(90028-6104)
PHONE...............................323 946-7600
Dennis Lavinthal, *President*
Lenny Beer, *Principal*
Robert Moore, *Technology*
EMP: 19
SALES (est): 5.4MM **Privately Held**
WEB: www.hitsmagazine.com
SIC: **2721** Magazines: publishing only, not
printed on site

(P-5957)
HW HOLDCO LLC
555 Anton Blvd Ste 950, Costa Mesa
(92626-7811)
PHONE...............................714 540-8500
Jeff Meyers, *Manager*
Julie Supinski, *Vice Pres*
Nathan Lancaster, *Sr Ntwrk Engine*
Jenna Mahoney, *Opers Staff*
Dave Macintosh, *VP Sales*
EMP: 50
SALES (corp-wide): 164.8MM **Privately Held**
WEB: www.toolsofthetrade.org
SIC: **2721** Trade journals: publishing only,
not printed on site
PA: Hw Holdco, Llc
1 Thomas Cir Nw Ste 600
Washington DC 20005
202 452-0800

P
R
O
D
U
C
T
S
&
S
V
C
S

(P-5958)
HWF CONSTRUCTION INC
3685 Fruitvale Ave, Bakersfield
(93308-5107)
PHONE...................................661 587-3590
Robert Hinelsy, *President*
EMP: 15
SALES: 32.2MM **Privately Held**
SIC: 2721 Magazines: publishing only, not printed on site

(P-5959)
IDG CONSUMER & SMB INC (DH)
Also Called: PC World Online
501 2nd St, San Francisco (94107-1469)
PHONE...................................415 243-0500
Colin Crawford, *President*
Michael Kisseberth, *President*
Edward B Bloom, *Vice Pres*
Kevin C Krull, *Vice Pres*
Miriam Karlin, *Admin Sec*
EMP: 116
SQ FT: 21,000
SALES (est): 12.7MM
SALES (corp-wide): 1.7B **Privately Held**
WEB: www.pcworld.com
SIC: 2721 Magazines: publishing only, not printed on site; periodicals: publishing only
HQ: Idg Communications, Inc.
   5 Speen St
   Framingham MA 01701
   508 872-8200

(P-5960)
IDG GAMES MEDIA GROUP INC
Also Called: Gamepro Magazine
555 12th St, Oakland (94607-4046)
PHONE...................................510 768-2700
John Rousseau, *President*
EMP: 50
SALES (est): 3MM
SALES (corp-wide): 1.7B **Privately Held**
WEB: www.gamepro.com
SIC: 2721 Trade journals: publishing only, not printed on site
HQ: Idg Communications, Inc.
   5 Speen St
   Framingham MA 01701
   508 872-8200

(P-5961)
IMAGE MAGAZINE INC
5001 Birch St, Newport Beach
(92660-2116)
PHONE...................................949 608-5188
Dean Dingman, *President*
EMP: 26
SALES (est): 1.8MM **Privately Held**
SIC: 2721 5994 Periodicals; magazine stand

(P-5962)
INFOFAX INC
305 Nord Ave, Chico (95926-4710)
P.O. Box 4191 (95927-4191)
PHONE...................................530 895-0431
John Scott, *President*
EMP: 12
SQ FT: 2,041
SALES: 500K **Privately Held**
SIC: 2721 Statistical reports (periodicals): publishing only

(P-5963)
INFOKOREA INC
Also Called: Radio Korea USA
626 S Kingsley Dr, Los Angeles
(90005-2318)
PHONE...................................213 487-1580
Fax: 213 487-7744
▲ EMP: 30
SALES (est): 2.3MM **Privately Held**
SIC: 2721 4832

(P-5964)
INFORMA MEDIA INC
Also Called: Enviormental Business Intl
4452 Park Blvd Ste 306, San Diego
(92116-4049)
PHONE...................................619 295-7685
Grant Ferrier, *Principal*
Susan Johnson, *Administration*
Richard White, *Business Mgr*
Lucy Green, *Sales Mgr*

Tim Johnson, *Facilities Mgr*
EMP: 20
SALES (corp-wide): 3B **Privately Held**
WEB: www.penton.com
SIC: 2721 Magazines: publishing & printing
HQ: Informa Media, Inc.
   605 3rd Ave Fl 22
   New York NY 10158
   212 204-4200

(P-5965)
INFORMA MEDIA INC
11500 W Olympic Blvd, Los Angeles
(90064-1524)
PHONE...................................301 755-0162
EMP: 62
SALES (corp-wide): 3B **Privately Held**
SIC: 2721 Magazines: publishing only, not printed on site
HQ: Informa Media, Inc.
   605 3rd Ave Fl 22
   New York NY 10158
   212 204-4200

(P-5966)
INFOWORLD MEDIA GROUP INC (DH)
501 2nd St Ste 500, San Francisco
(94107-4133)
PHONE...................................415 243-4344
Robert Ostrow, *CEO*
Patrick J Mc Govern, *Ch of Bd*
William P Murphy, *Treasurer*
Betty Chen, *Chief Mktg Ofcr*
Virginia Hines, *Vice Pres*
▲ EMP: 75
SQ FT: 50,000
SALES (est): 8.4MM
SALES (corp-wide): 1.7B **Privately Held**
WEB: www.infoworld.com
SIC: 2721 2741 7389 Magazines: publishing only, not printed on site; newsletter publishing; trade show arrangement
HQ: Idg Communications, Inc.
   5 Speen St
   Framingham MA 01701
   508 872-8200

(P-5967)
INLAND EMPIRE MEDIA GROUP INC
Also Called: Inland Empire Magazine
3400 Central Ave Ste 160, Riverside
(92506-2183)
PHONE...................................951 682-3026
Don Lorenzi, *President*
Richard Lorenzi, *Admin Sec*
EMP: 15 EST: 1972
SQ FT: 1,700
SALES (est): 1.9MM **Privately Held**
WEB: www.inlandempiremagazine.com
SIC: 2721 Magazines: publishing & printing; magazines: publishing only, not printed on site

(P-5968)
INTERNET INDUSTRY PUBLISHING
315 Pacific Ave, San Francisco
(94111-1701)
PHONE...................................415 733-5400
Jonathan Wright, *Executive*
EMP: 50
SALES (est): 1.7MM
SALES (corp-wide): 1.7B **Privately Held**
WEB: www.workscape.net
SIC: 2721 Magazines: publishing only, not printed on site
PA: International Data Group, Inc.
   1 Exeter Plz Fl 15
   Boston MA 02116
   508 875-5000

(P-5969)
KELLEY BLUE BOOK CO INC (DH)
195 Technology Dr, Irvine (92618-2402)
P.O. Box 19691 (92623-9691)
PHONE...................................949 770-7704
Jared Rowe, *CEO*
John Morrison, *CFO*
Susan Brown, *Vice Pres*
Leo Drew, *Vice Pres*
Andrea Suh, *Comms Mgr*
EMP: 92

SALES (est): 87.5MM
SALES (corp-wide): 32.3B **Privately Held**
WEB: www.kbb.com
SIC: 2721 Trade journals: publishing only, not printed on site
HQ: Autotrader.Com, Inc.
   3003 Summit Blvd Fl 200
   Brookhaven GA 30319
   404 568-8000

(P-5970)
KNIGHT PUBLISHING CORP
8060 Melrose Ave Ste 210, Los Angeles
(90046-7037)
PHONE...................................323 653-8060
Bentley Morriss, *President*
EMP: 20
SQ FT: 3,000
SALES (est): 1.5MM **Privately Held**
SIC: 2721 2759 Magazines: publishing only, not printed on site; periodicals: printing

(P-5971)
L F P INC (PA)
Also Called: Flynt, Larry Publishing
8484 Wilshire Blvd # 900, Beverly Hills
(90211-3218)
PHONE...................................323 651-3525
Larry Flynt, *Ch of Bd*
Michael H Klein, *President*
Tony Cochi, *Exec VP*
Philip Del Rio, *Vice Pres*
Jade Ramirez, *Executive Asst*
▲ EMP: 100 EST: 1976
SQ FT: 10,000
SALES (est): 29.6MM **Privately Held**
SIC: 2721 Magazines: publishing & printing

(P-5972)
LA PARENT MAGAZINE (PA)
5855 Topanga Canyon Blvd # 150, Woodland Hills (91367-4685)
PHONE...................................818 264-2222
Madelyn Calabrese, *Manager*
Lisa Giuntoli, *Sales Staff*
Elena Epstein, *Director*
EMP: 20
SQ FT: 2,500
SALES (est): 1.1MM **Privately Held**
SIC: 2721 Magazines: publishing only, not printed on site

(P-5973)
LANDSCAPE COMMUNICATIONS INC
Also Called: Landscape Contract National
14771 Plaza Dr Ste A, Tustin (92780-2779)
P.O. Box 1126 (92781-1126)
PHONE...................................714 979-5276
George Schmok, *President*
Alexander Theologidy, *Education*
Matt Henderson, *Contractor*
Foley Lana, *Contractor*
Mike Dahl, *Editor*
EMP: 25
SQ FT: 1,618
SALES (est): 2.8MM **Privately Held**
WEB: www.landscapeonline.com
SIC: 2721 Trade journals: publishing only, not printed on site

(P-5974)
LATINO AMERICANOS REVISTA
82723 Miles Ave, Indio (92201-4229)
PHONE...................................760 342-2312
Patricia Parrilla, *Owner*
EMP: 10
SALES (est): 702.3K **Privately Held**
WEB: www.latinoamericanos.com
SIC: 2721 8721 Magazines: publishing & printing; certified public accountant

(P-5975)
LATITUDE 38 PUBLISHING COMPANY
15 Locust Ave, Mill Valley (94941-2899)
PHONE...................................415 383-8200
Richard L Spindler, *President*
Penny Clayton, *Bookkeeper*
Mitch Perkins, *Advt Staff*
John Arndt, *Publisher*
EMP: 10
SQ FT: 2,000

SALES (est): 1.1MM **Privately Held**
WEB: www.latitude38.com
SIC: 2721 Magazines: publishing only, not printed on site

(P-5976)
LAUFER MEDIA INC
Also Called: Tiger Beat Magazine
330 N Brand Blvd Ste 1150, Glendale
(91203-2339)
PHONE...................................818 291-8408
Scott D Laufer, *President*
EMP: 11
SALES (est): 2.3MM **Privately Held**
SIC: 2721 Magazines: publishing only, not printed on site

(P-5977)
LIFE MEDIA INC
Also Called: Black Media News
7657 Winnetka Ave Ste 504, Winnetka
(91306-2677)
PHONE...................................800 201-9440
Phil Tucker, *President*
Art Allen, *CFO*
EMP: 50
SALES: 10MM **Privately Held**
WEB: www.lifemedia.ca
SIC: 2721 Magazines: publishing only, not printed on site

(P-5978)
LINE PUBLICATIONS INC
Also Called: Movieline Magazine
9800 S La Cienega Blvd # 10, Inglewood
(90301-4440)
PHONE...................................310 234-9501
EMP: 15
SALES (est): 1.4MM **Privately Held**
WEB: www.movieline.com
SIC: 2721

(P-5979)
LOS ANGELES BUS JURNL ASSOC
5700 Wilshire Blvd # 170, Los Angeles
(90036-7205)
PHONE...................................323 549-5225
Matt Toledo, *President*
Darrin Sennott, *Vice Pres*
EMP: 45
SALES (est): 3.8MM **Privately Held**
SIC: 2721 Magazines: publishing only, not printed on site

(P-5980)
LUNDBERG SURVEY INC
911 Via Alondra, Camarillo (93012-8048)
PHONE...................................805 383-2400
Trilby Lundberg, *President*
EMP: 35
SALES (est): 3.2MM **Privately Held**
WEB: www.lundbergsurvey.com
SIC: 2721 8748 2741 Statistical reports (periodicals): publishing only; business consulting; miscellaneous publishing

(P-5981)
LUTHER E GIBSON INC
Also Called: Gibson Radio and Publishing Co
544 Curtola Pkwy, Vallejo (94590-6925)
P.O. Box 3067 (94590-0674)
PHONE...................................707 643-6104
David Payne, *President*
Maggie Keane, *General Mgr*
Toni Kirsch, *Director*
EMP: 25
SALES (est): 1.6MM **Privately Held**
SIC: 2721 Periodicals

(P-5982)
MAC PUBLISHING LLC (HQ)
Also Called: Macworld Magazine
501 2nd St Ste 500, San Francisco
(94107-4133)
PHONE...................................415 243-0505
Colin Crawford, *President*
Stephen Daniels, *President*
Bill Cappel, *Opers Staff*
Kevin Greene, *Sales Executive*
EMP: 20
SALES (est): 2.9MM
SALES (corp-wide): 1.7B **Privately Held**
WEB: www.macworld.com
SIC: 2721 Magazines: publishing only, not printed on site

▲ = Import ▼=Export
◆ =Import/Export

PA: International Data Group, Inc.
1 Exeter Plz Fl 15
Boston MA 02116
508 875-5000

(P-5983)
MAGAZINE PUBLISHERS SVC INC
350 E St, Santa Rosa (95404-4437)
PHONE....................707 571-7610
Ronald E Allen Jr, *President*
EMP: 99
SALES (est): 5.8MM **Privately Held**
SIC: 2721 Magazines: publishing & printing

(P-5984)
MAKE COMMUNITY LLC
708 Gravenstein Hwy N, Sebastopol (95472-2808)
P.O. Box 239 (95473-0239)
PHONE....................707 548-0833
Dale Dougherty, *Mng Member*
EMP: 16
SALES: 250K **Privately Held**
SIC: 2721 Magazines: publishing only, not printed on site

(P-5985)
MARIN MAGAZINE INC
1 Harbor Dr Ste 208, Sausalito (94965-1434)
PHONE....................415 332-4800
Nikki Wood, *President*
Peter Thomas, *Production*
Michele Johnson, *Adv Dir*
Leah Bronson, *Manager*
Jessica Gliddon, *Editor*
EMP: 12
SQ FT: 2,500
SALES (est): 1.6MM **Privately Held**
WEB: www.marinmagazine.com
SIC: 2721 7313 Magazines: publishing only, not printed on site; printed media advertising representatives

(P-5986)
MCKINNON ENTERPRISES
Also Called: San Dego HM Grdn Lfestyles Mag
4577 Viewridge Ave, San Diego (92123-1623)
P.O. Box 719001 (92171-9001)
PHONE....................858 571-1818
Michael Dean McKinnon, *Partner*
Katharine Phillips, *Mktg Coord*
Liz Crocker, *Director*
Wendy Generes, *Editor*
EMP: 20
SALES (est): 2MM **Privately Held**
WEB: www.mediaza.com
SIC: 2721 Magazines: publishing only, not printed on site

(P-5987)
MEYERS PUBLISHING INC
799 Camarillo Springs Rd, Camarillo (93012-9468)
PHONE....................805 445-8881
Len Meyers, *CEO*
Andrew Meyers, *President*
Lana Meyers, *CFO*
Lee Denton, *Controller*
Mark Horowitz, *Adv Dir*
EMP: 12
SALES (est): 1.6MM **Privately Held**
WEB: www.meyerspublishing.com
SIC: 2721 Magazines: publishing only, not printed on site

(P-5988)
MHB GROUP INC
Also Called: Mobile Home Park Magazines
1240 Mountain Vw Alviso C, Sunnyvale (94089)
PHONE....................408 744-1011
Elizabeth Tripp, *President*
Clifford Shores, *Shareholder*
Dana Sketchley, *Shareholder*
Rosemary Walsh, *Shareholder*
EMP: 25
SQ FT: 3,500
SALES (est): 2.5MM **Privately Held**
WEB: www.mobilehomeparkmagazines.com
SIC: 2721 6531 Trade journals: publishing & printing; real estate listing services

(P-5989)
MINGO ENTERPRISES INC
Also Called: Ad Review
1209 Solano Ave Ste B, Albany (94706-1768)
P.O. Box 6071 (94706-0071)
PHONE....................510 528-3044
Liz Tellefsen, *President*
Scott Malmberg, *Marketing Staff*
EMP: 16
SQ FT: 500
SALES (est): 1.4MM **Privately Held**
SIC: 2721 Trade journals: publishing only, not printed on site

(P-5990)
MNM CORPORATION (PA)
Also Called: Apparel Newsgroup, The
110 E 9th St Ste A777, Los Angeles (90079-1777)
PHONE....................213 627-3737
Martin Wernicke, *CEO*
Howard Greller, *Officer*
Molly Rhodes, *General Mgr*
Jim Patel, *CPA*
Terry Martinez, *Sales Executive*
▲ **EMP:** 25
SQ FT: 11,000
SALES (est): 3.4MM **Privately Held**
WEB: www.singnet.com.sg
SIC: 2721 8721 Magazines: publishing only, not printed on site; accounting, auditing & bookkeeping

(P-5991)
MODERN LUXURY MEDIA LLC (HQ)
Also Called: Angeleno Magazine
243 Vallejo St, San Francisco (94111-1511)
PHONE....................404 443-0004
Michael B Kong, *Mng Member*
John Carroll, *President*
Michael Dickey, *President*
Leslie Wolfson, *President*
Katie Suhr, *Executive*
▲ **EMP:** 40
SALES (est): 13MM
SALES (corp-wide): 41MM **Privately Held**
SIC: 2721 Magazines: publishing only, not printed on site
PA: Dickey Publishing, Inc.
3280 Peachtree Rd Ne S
Atlanta GA 30305
404 949-0700

(P-5992)
MUSIC CONNECTION INC
Also Called: Music Connection Magazine
16130 Ventura Blvd # 540, Encino (91436-2503)
PHONE....................818 995-0101
J Michael Dolan, *President*
Eric Bettelli, *CEO*
EMP: 11 **EST:** 1977
SALES (est): 1.1MM **Privately Held**
WEB: www.musicconnection.com
SIC: 2721 Magazines: publishing only, not printed on site

(P-5993)
NATIVE AMERICAN MEDIA
Also Called: Native Canadian Media
10806 1/2 Wilshire Blvd, Los Angeles (90024)
PHONE....................310 475-6845
Mike Roberts, *President*
EMP: 12
SALES (est): 1.3MM **Privately Held**
SIC: 2721 Magazines: publishing only, not printed on site

(P-5994)
OMICS GROUP INC
731 Gull Ave, Foster City (94404-1329)
PHONE....................650 268-9744
Srinu B Gedela, *Branch Mgr*
EMP: 460
SALES (corp-wide): 46.3MM **Privately Held**
SIC: 2721 Trade journals: publishing & printing
PA: Omics Group Inc
2360 Corp Cir Ste 400
Henderson NV 89074
888 843-8169

(P-5995)
ORANGE CNTY MLT-HSING SVC CORP
525 Cabrillo Park Dr # 125, Santa Ana (92701-5017)
PHONE....................714 245-9500
Alan Daugher, *President*
EMP: 12
SALES (est): 1.1MM **Privately Held**
WEB: www.aaoc.com
SIC: 2721 Magazines: publishing only, not printed on site
PA: Apartment Association Of Orange County
525 Cabrillo Park Dr # 125
Santa Ana CA 92701
714 245-9500

(P-5996)
ORANGE COAST KOMMUNICATIONS
Also Called: Orange Coast Magazine
1124 Main St Ste A, Irvine (92614-6757)
PHONE....................949 862-1133
Gary Thoe, *President*
Kevin Jimenez, *Sales Staff*
Jeana Arakal, *Mktg Coord*
Sofia Gutierrez, *Mktg Coord*
Mindy Benham, *Director*
EMP: 26
SQ FT: 14,000
SALES (est): 3.2MM
SALES (corp-wide): 114.1MM **Publicly Held**
WEB: www.orangecoastmagazine.com
SIC: 2721 5812 Magazines: publishing only, not printed on site; eating places
HQ: Emmis Publishing, L.P.
40 Monument Cir Ste 100
Indianapolis IN 46204

(P-5997)
PACIFIC SUN
847 5th St, Santa Rosa (95404-4526)
PHONE....................415 488-8100
Gina Channell-Allen, *Principal*
EMP: 12
SALES (est): 908.4K **Privately Held**
SIC: 2721 Periodicals

(P-5998)
PAISANO PUBLICATIONS LLC (PA)
Also Called: V Twin Magazine
28210 Dorothy Dr, Agoura Hills (91301-2693)
PHONE....................818 889-8740
John Lagana, *CEO*
Joseph Teresi, *Chairman*
Beverly Barragan, *Exec VP*
Dave Nichols, *Vice Pres*
Karen Johnson, *Controller*
EMP: 113
SQ FT: 40,000
SALES (est): 13.2MM **Privately Held**
WEB: www.paisanopub.com
SIC: 2721 Magazines: publishing only, not printed on site

(P-5999)
PAISANO PUBLICATIONS INC
Also Called: V/ Twins
28210 Dorothy Dr, Agoura Hills (91301-2693)
P.O. Box 3000 (91376-3000)
PHONE....................818 889-8740
Bill Prather, *President*
Robert Davis, *Treasurer*
Allen Ribakoff, *Vice Pres*
Joseph Teresi, *Admin Sec*
Beverly Jermyn, *Human Res Dir*
EMP: 65
SALES: 30MM
SALES (corp-wide): 13.2MM **Privately Held**
WEB: www.paisanopub.com
SIC: 2721 7812 Magazines: publishing & printing; commercials, television: tape or film
PA: Paisano Publications, Llc
28210 Dorothy Dr
Agoura Hills CA 91301
818 889-8740

(P-6000)
PENHOUSE MEDIA GROUP INC
11601 Wilshire Blvd Fl 5, Los Angeles (90025-1995)
PHONE....................310 575-4835
Harlan Baum, *Principal*
EMP: 32
SALES (corp-wide): 11.5MM **Privately Held**
SIC: 2721 Magazines: publishing only, not printed on site
PA: Penhouse Media Group Incorporated
11 Penn Plz Fl 12
New York NY 10001
212 702-6000

(P-6001)
PENINSULA PUBLISHING INC
1602 Monrovia Ave, Newport Beach (92663-2808)
PHONE....................949 631-1307
Nick Slevin, *President*
Chris Comer, *Exec Dir*
Nick Kosan, *Natl Sales Mgr*
Rona Fiedler, *Sales Mgr*
Georgina Slim, *Sales Mgr*
EMP: 50 **EST:** 1998
SALES (est): 1.8MM **Privately Held**
WEB: www.optionsmag.com
SIC: 2721 Magazines: publishing & printing

(P-6002)
PFANNER COMMUNICATIONS INC
Also Called: Sportscar
3334 E Coast Hwy Ste 162, Corona Del Mar (92625-2328)
PHONE....................714 227-3579
Paul Pfanner, *President*
EMP: 17
SQ FT: 4,000
SALES (est): 1.3MM **Privately Held**
SIC: 2721 8742 Magazines: publishing & printing; marketing consulting services

(P-6003)
PINPOINT MEDIA GROUP INC
Also Called: The Orgnal Los Angeles APT Mag
3188 Airway Ave Ste L, Costa Mesa (92626-4652)
PHONE....................714 545-5640
EMP: 15 **EST:** 1991
SQ FT: 900
SALES (est): 1.1MM **Privately Held**
SIC: 2721

(P-6004)
PLAYBOY ENTERPRISES INC
10960 Wilshire Blvd # 2200, Los Angeles (90024-3702)
PHONE....................310 424-1800
John Luther, *Manager*
David Israel, *CFO*
Daisha McDaniel, *Admin Asst*
Jessica Lewis, *Marketing Staff*
Marya Gullo, *Director*
EMP: 79
SALES (corp-wide): 45.6MM **Privately Held**
WEB: www.playboy.com
SIC: 2721 Magazines: publishing & printing
PA: Playboy Enterprises, Inc.
9346 Civic Center Dr # 200
Beverly Hills CA 90210
310 424-1800

(P-6005)
PLAYBOY JAPAN INC
9346 Civic Center Dr # 200, Beverly Hills (90210-3604)
PHONE....................310 424-1800
John Lumpkin, *Executive*
Jonathan Homan, *Advt Staff*
Tamar Aprahamian, *Director*
Bryce Anderson, *Manager*
Gabriela Cifuentes, *Manager*
EMP: 16
SALES (est): 725.8K
SALES (corp-wide): 45.6MM **Privately Held**
SIC: 2721 Magazines: publishing & printing
PA: Playboy Enterprises, Inc.
9346 Civic Center Dr # 200
Beverly Hills CA 90210
310 424-1800

(P-6006)
POLLSTAR LLC (PA)
Also Called: Pollstar.com
1100 Glendon Ave Ste 2100, Los Angeles
(90024-3592)
PHONE..................559 271-7900
Gary Bongiovanni, *President*
Gary Smith, *CEO*
Bridgette Walker, *Director*
Chad Ivie, *Associate*
EMP: 58
SALES (est): 8MM **Privately Held**
WEB: www.pollstar.com
SIC: 2721 Trade journals: publishing only,
not printed on site

(P-6007)
PROMEDIA COMPANIES
Also Called: National Mustang Racers Assn
3518 W Lake Center Dr D, Santa Ana
(92704-6979)
PHONE..................714 444-2426
Steve Wolcott, *Partner*
James Lawrence, *Partner*
Judy Keaton, *Executive*
Justin Hudson, *Recruiter*
Jim Campisano, *Sales Dir*
EMP: 13
SQ FT: 3,000
SALES (est): 2MM **Privately Held**
WEB: www.fasteststreetcar.com
SIC: 2721 Magazines: publishing only,
printed on site

(P-6008)
**PUBLISHERS DEVELOPMENT
CORP**
Also Called: American Handgunner and Guns
13741 Danielson St Ste A, Poway
(92064-6895)
PHONE..................858 605-0200
Thomas Von Rosen, *CEO*
Thomas M Hollander, *Vice Pres*
Maryellen Bridge, *Chief*
EMP: 40
SALES (est): 6.6MM **Privately Held**
WEB: www.fmgnews.com
SIC: 2721 Magazines: publishing only, not
printed on site

(P-6009)
QG PRINTING CORP
6688 Box Springs Blvd, Riverside
(92507-0726)
PHONE..................951 571-2500
Ken Eazell, *Manager*
EMP: 230
SALES (corp-wide): 4.1B **Publicly Held**
WEB: www.qwdys.com
SIC: 2721 2752 Periodicals; commercial
printing, lithographic
HQ: Qg Printing Corp.
N61w23044 Harrys Way
Sussex WI 53089

(P-6010)
QUALITY CIRCLE INSTITUTE INC
Also Called: Quality Digest
555 East Ave, Chico (95926-1204)
PHONE..................530 893-4095
Mike Richman, *Manager*
Taran March, *Director*
April Johnson, *Manager*
EMP: 14
SALES (corp-wide): 1.6MM **Privately
Held**
WEB: www.qualitydigest.com
SIC: 2721 8742 Periodicals; management
consulting services
PA: Quality Circle Institute, Inc
633 Orange St Ste 3
Chico CA
530 893-4095

(P-6011)
R T C GROUP
Also Called: Cots Journal Magazine
905 Calle Amanecer # 150, San Clemente
(92673-6226)
PHONE..................949 226-2000
John Reardon, *Owner*
EMP: 20

SALES (est): 2.3MM **Privately Held**
WEB: www.rtcgroup.com
SIC: 2721 Magazines: publishing only, not
printed on site

(P-6012)
**RACER MEDIA & MARKETING
INC**
17030 Red Hill Ave, Irvine (92614-5626)
PHONE..................949 417-6700
William Sparks, *COO*
Paul Pfanner, *President*
EMP: 14
SQ FT: 4,500
SALES (est): 1.4MM **Privately Held**
SIC: 2721 Magazines: publishing only, not
printed on site

(P-6013)
**RANGEFINDER PUBLISHING CO
INC**
Also Called: After Capture
11835 W Olympic Blvd 550e, Los Angeles
(90064-5001)
PHONE..................310 846-4770
Stephen Sheanin, *President*
EMP: 18
SQ FT: 12,000
SALES (est): 1.7MM
SALES (corp-wide): 380.7MM **Publicly
Held**
WEB: www.rfpublishing.com
SIC: 2721 Magazines: publishing only, not
printed on site
HQ: Emerald Expositions, Llc
31910 Del Obispo St # 200
San Juan Capistrano CA 92675

(P-6014)
READER MAGAZINE
108 Orange St Ste 11, Redlands
(92373-4719)
PHONE..................909 335-8100
Chris Theater, *President*
EMP: 11
SALES (est): 823.5K **Privately Held**
SIC: 2721 Magazines: publishing only, not
printed on site

(P-6015)
RECRUITMENT SERVICES INC
Also Called: Working Nurse
3600 Wilshire Blvd Ste 15, Los Angeles
(90010-2603)
PHONE..................213 364-1960
Randy Goldring, *President*
Catherine Rhodes, *Publisher*
EMP: 12
SALES (est): 950K **Privately Held**
SIC: 2721 Periodicals

(P-6016)
REFINITIV US LLC
50 California St, San Francisco
(94111-4624)
PHONE..................415 344-6000
Andrea Lavoie, *Principal*
EMP: 345 **Publicly Held**
WEB: www.tfn.com
SIC: 2721 Periodicals
HQ: Refinitiv Us Llc
3 Times Sq
New York NY 10036
646 223-4000

(P-6017)
RELX INC
Also Called: Lexisnexis Matthew Bender
201 Mission St Fl 26, San Francisco
(94105-1831)
PHONE..................415 908-3200
Isabela Sonnenberg, *Principal*
EMP: 49
SALES (corp-wide): 9.6B **Privately Held**
SIC: 2721 2731 7389 Trade journals:
publishing only, not printed on site; books:
publishing only; trade show arrangement
HQ: Relx Inc.
230 Park Ave Ste 700
New York NY 10169
212 309-8100

(P-6018)
RHODES PUBLICATIONS INC
Also Called: Working World
3600 Wilshire Blvd # 1526, Los Angeles
(90010-2619)
PHONE..................213 385-4781
Catherine Rhodes, *President*
Richard Rhodes, *President*
EMP: 12
SALES (est): 1.1MM **Privately Held**
SIC: 2721 Magazines: publishing & printing

(P-6019)
**ROADRACING WORLD
PUBLISHING**
Also Called: .com
581 Birch St Ste C, Lake Elsinore
(92530-2746)
P.O. Box 1428 (92531-1428)
PHONE..................951 245-6411
Trudy Ulrich, *President*
John Ulrich, *Vice Pres*
Stephen Zarra, *Graphic Designe*
Hayley Ulrich, *Marketing Staff*
Chris Ulrich,
▲ EMP: 10
SQ FT: 1,500
SALES (est): 1.8MM **Privately Held**
WEB: www.roadracingworld.com
SIC: 2721 Magazines: publishing only, not
printed on site

(P-6020)
ROBB CURTCO MEDIA LLC
29160 Heathercliff Rd # 200, Malibu
(90265-6306)
PHONE..................310 589-7700
EMP: 33
SALES (corp-wide): 17.6MM **Privately
Held**
SIC: 2721 Magazines: publishing & printing
PA: Curtco Robb Media Llc
29160 Heathercliff Rd # 1
Malibu CA 90265
310 589-7700

(P-6021)
RUNNERS WORLD MAGAZINE
2101 Rosecrans Ave # 6200, El Segundo
(90245-4749)
PHONE..................310 615-4567
Steve Murphy, *President*
EMP: 17 EST: 1966
SALES (est): 552.6K **Privately Held**
SIC: 2721 Magazines: publishing only, not
printed on site

(P-6022)
**SAN DIEGO FAMILY MAGAZINE
LLC**
1475 6th Ave Ste 500, San Diego
(92101-3200)
P.O. Box 23960 (92193-3960)
PHONE..................619 685-6970
Sharon Bay,
Larry Bay,
EMP: 11
SQ FT: 4,000
SALES (est): 1.3MM **Privately Held**
WEB: www.sandiegofamily.com
SIC: 2721 Magazines: publishing & printing

(P-6023)
**SAN DIEGO MAGAZINE PUBG
CO**
707 Broadway Ste 1100, San Diego
(92101-5315)
PHONE..................619 230-9292
James Fitzpatrick, *CEO*
EMP: 30
SQ FT: 10,000
SALES (est): 8.1MM
SALES (corp-wide): 3.4MM **Privately
Held**
WEB: www.sandiegomag.com
SIC: 2721 Magazines: publishing only, not
printed on site
PA: Curtco Publishing Llc
29160 Heathercliff Rd # 1
Malibu CA 90265
310 589-7700

(P-6024)
SCI PUBLISHING INC
Also Called: Sportscar International
42 Digital Dr Ste 5, Novato (94949-5762)
P.O. Box 1529, Ross (94957-1529)
PHONE..................415 382-0580
Thomas Toldrian, *President*
EMP: 11
SALES (est): 717.1K
SALES (corp-wide): 1.5MM **Privately
Held**
SIC: 2721 Magazines: publishing only, not
printed on site
PA: Ross Periodicals, Inc
42 Digital Dr Ste 5
Novato CA
415 382-0580

(P-6025)
SELECT COMMUNICATIONS INC
Also Called: Los Altos Town Crier
138 Main St, Los Altos (94022-2905)
PHONE..................650 948-9000
Paul D Nyberg, *President*
Elizabeth Nyberg, *Vice Pres*
Chris Redden, *Director*
Bruce Barton, *Editor*
Howard Bischoff, *Publisher*
EMP: 20
SQ FT: 3,600
SALES: 1.5MM **Privately Held**
WEB: www.losaltosonline.com
SIC: 2721 2711 Magazines: publishing
only, not printed on site; newspapers,
publishing & printing

(P-6026)
SERBIN COMMUNICATIONS INC
Also Called: Photographer's Forum
813 Reddick St, Santa Barbara
(93103-3124)
PHONE..................805 963-0439
Glen Serbin, *President*
Susan Baraz, *Director*
◆ EMP: 15
SQ FT: 3,000
SALES (est): 1.8MM **Privately Held**
WEB: www.serbin.com
SIC: 2721 7335 Magazines: publishing
only, not printed on site; commercial pho-
tography

(P-6027)
**SIDNEY MILLERS BLACK RADIO
EX**
Also Called: Black Radio Exclusive Magazine
15030 Ventura Blvd # 864, Sherman Oaks
(91403-5470)
PHONE..................818 907-9959
Susan Miller, *President*
EMP: 27 EST: 1978
SQ FT: 4,600
SALES (est): 1.9MM **Privately Held**
WEB: www.bremagazine.com
SIC: 2721 Magazines: publishing only, not
printed on site

(P-6028)
SMITH PUBLISHING INC
Also Called: Santa Barbara Magazine
2064 Alameda Padre Serra # 120, Santa
Barbara (93103-1704)
PHONE..................805 965-5999
Jennifer Smithhale, *President*
Jennifer Smith-Hale, *President*
EMP: 10
SALES (est): 1.1MM **Privately Held**
WEB: www.sbmag.com
SIC: 2721 Magazines: publishing only, not
printed on site

(P-6029)
**SOCCER LEARNING SYSTEMS
INC**
17610 Murphy Pkwy, Lathrop (95330-8629)
P.O. Box 765, Salida (95368-0765)
PHONE..................209 858-4300
Patrick Mc Quaid, *President*
Patrick McQuaid, *Managing Prtnr*
EMP: 10
SALES (est): 1MM **Privately Held**
WEB: www.soccerbooks.com
SIC: 2721 Periodicals

▲ = Import ▼=Export
◆ =Import/Export

(P-6030)
SOCIETY FOR THE ADVANCEMENT OF
Also Called: Sampe
21680 Gateway Center Dr # 300, Diamond Bar (91765-2453)
PHONE..................626 521-9460
Gregg Balko, *CEO*
Patty Hunt, *Sales Mgr*
Priscilla Heredia, *Manager*
EMP: 12 **EST:** 1944
SQ FT: 5,789
SALES: 258K **Privately Held**
SIC: 2721 Periodicals: publishing only

(P-6031)
SPIRITUAL COUNTERFEITS PRJ INC
Also Called: S C P
2606 Dwight Way, Berkeley (94704-3029)
P.O. Box 40015, Pasadena (91114-7015)
PHONE..................510 540-0300
Tal Brooke, *President*
EMP: 10
SQ FT: 3,284
SALES: 101.7K **Privately Held**
WEB: www.scp-inc.org
SIC: 2721 2741 Trade journals: publishing only, not printed on site; newsletter publishing

(P-6032)
SPORTS PUBLICATIONS INC (PA)
Also Called: Swimming World Magazine
228 Nevada St, El Segundo (90245-4210)
PHONE..................310 607-9956
Richard Deal, *President*
▲ **EMP:** 13 **EST:** 1960
SALES (est): 1MM **Privately Held**
SIC: 2721 Magazines: publishing & printing

(P-6033)
STYLE MEDIA GROUP INC
120 Blue Ravine Rd Ste 5, Folsom (95630-4752)
P.O. Box 925 (95763-0925)
PHONE..................916 988-9888
Terence Carroll, *CEO*
Wendy Sipple, *COO*
Ray Burgess, *Graphic Designe*
Emily Peter, *Assoc Editor*
Tom Gherini, *Accounts Mgr*
EMP: 22 **EST:** 2003
SALES (est): 2.1MM **Privately Held**
SIC: 2721 Magazines: publishing only, not printed on site

(P-6034)
SUBDIRECT LLC (PA)
Also Called: Subco
653 W Fallbrook Ave # 101, Fresno (93711-5503)
PHONE..................559 321-0449
Kelly Vucovich,
Lindsay Vanacker, *CFO*
Jonathan Eropkin, *CTO*
Susan T Dietrich, *Marketing Staff*
Lindsay Van Acker,
EMP: 16
SQ FT: 10,000
SALES (est): 2.4MM **Privately Held**
SIC: 2721 Magazines: publishing & printing

(P-6035)
SUNSET PUBLISHING CORPORATION (HQ)
Also Called: Sunset Magazine
55 Harrison St Ste 150, Oakland (94607-3772)
P.O. Box 62375, Tampa FL (33662-2375)
PHONE..................800 777-0117
Kevin Lynch, *Vice Pres*
Christopher Kevorkian, *Vice Pres*
Mark Okean, *Vice Pres*
Christina Olsen, *Vice Pres*
Lorinda Reichert, *Vice Pres*
EMP: 150 **EST:** 1928
SQ FT: 56,000

SALES (est): 15.5MM
SALES (corp-wide): 38.3MM **Privately Held**
WEB: www.sunset.com
SIC: 2721 2731 Magazines: publishing only, not printed on site; books: publishing only
PA: Regent, Lp
9720 Wilshire Blvd
Beverly Hills CA 90212
310 299-4100

(P-6036)
SYNTHESIS
210 W 6th St, Chico (95928-5510)
PHONE..................530 899-7708
William Fishkin, *Owner*
EMP: 25
SQ FT: 1,600
SALES (est): 1.8MM **Privately Held**
WEB: www.synthesis.net
SIC: 2721 Periodicals

(P-6037)
T C MEDIA INC
Also Called: Pacific Rim Publishing
40748 Encyclopedia Cir, Fremont (94538-2473)
PHONE..................510 656-5100
Thomas OH, *President*
Joan Chien, *Admin Sec*
Gigi C OH, *Publisher*
EMP: 10
SQ FT: 40,000
SALES (est): 992K **Privately Held**
WEB: www.martialartsmart.com
SIC: 2721 7812 5941 8743 Magazines: publishing only, not printed on site; video tape production; martial arts equipment & supplies; promotion service

(P-6038)
TEN ENTHUSIAST NETWORK LLC
Transworld Snowboarding
2052 Corte Del Nogal # 100, Carlsbad (92011-1498)
PHONE..................760 722-7777
Scott Dickey, *CEO*
Ashley Otte, *General Mgr*
Mozelle Martinez, *Office Mgr*
Paul Kobriger, *Mktg Dir*
Mike Fitzgerald, *Sales Staff*
EMP: 125 **Privately Held**
SIC: 2721 Periodicals
PA: Ten Publishing Media, Llc
831 S Douglas St Ste 100
El Segundo CA 90245

(P-6039)
TENNIS MEDIA CO LLC
814 S Westgate Ave # 100, Los Angeles (90049-5662)
PHONE..................310 966-8182
Jeffrey Williams, *Mng Member*
Steve Furgals, *President*
Michael Sultan, *CFO*
EMP: 10
SALES (est): 7MM **Privately Held**
SIC: 2721 Magazines: publishing & printing

(P-6040)
THEATER PUBLICATIONS INC
Also Called: Pisani Printing II
3485 Victor St, Santa Clara (95054-2319)
P.O. Box 4743 (95056-4743)
PHONE..................408 748-1600
Michael Pisani, *President*
Gail Pisani, *Vice Pres*
EMP: 10
SQ FT: 3,000
SALES (est): 1.2MM **Privately Held**
WEB: www.theaterpublications.com
SIC: 2721 2752 Magazines: publishing & printing; commercial printing, lithographic

(P-6041)
TI GOTHAM INC
2 Embarcadero Ctr, San Francisco (94111-3823)
PHONE..................415 434-5244
Tim Richards, *Manager*
EMP: 33

SALES (corp-wide): 3.1B **Publicly Held**
SIC: 2721 Magazines: publishing only, not printed on site
HQ: Ti Gotham Inc.
225 Liberty St
New York NY 10281
212 522-1212

(P-6042)
TL ENTERPRISES LLC (DH)
Also Called: Highways Magazine
2750 Park View Ct Ste 240, Oxnard (93036-5458)
PHONE..................805 981-8393
Marcus Lemonis, *President*
Thomas Wolfe, *CFO*
Tom Wolfe, *CFO*
Stephen Adams, *Chairman*
Dale Hendrix, *Controller*
EMP: 24
SALES (est): 22.6MM
SALES (corp-wide): 488.7MM **Privately Held**
WEB: www.motorhomemagazine.com
SIC: 2721 Magazines: publishing only, not printed on site

(P-6043)
TOURISM DEVELOPMENT CORP (PA)
Also Called: Where Orange County Magazine
3679 Motor Ave Ste 300, Los Angeles (90034-5762)
PHONE..................310 280-2880
Jeff Levy, *President*
Leanne Killian, *Executive*
Benjamin Epstein, *Chief*
▲ **EMP:** 10
SQ FT: 3,000
SALES (est): 2.1MM **Privately Held**
SIC: 2721 Magazines: publishing only, not printed on site

(P-6044)
TRANSFORMATIONNET MEDIA LLC
Also Called: Realtalkla
1640 N Spring St, Los Angeles (90012-1927)
PHONE..................310 476-5259
Jay M Levin, *CEO*
Karen Fund,
Sridhar RAO,
EMP: 35 **EST:** 1999
SQ FT: 7,200
SALES (est): 2.1MM **Privately Held**
WEB: www.realtalkla.com
SIC: 2721 Magazines: publishing & printing

(P-6045)
TWELVE SIGNS INC
Also Called: Starscroll
3369 S Robertson Blvd, Los Angeles (90034)
PHONE..................310 553-8000
Richard W Housman, *President*
H Kim, *Vice Pres*
EMP: 100
SQ FT: 25,000
SALES (est): 9.1MM **Privately Held**
WEB: www.starmatch.com
SIC: 2721 Magazines: publishing only, not printed on site

(P-6046)
UBM CANON LLC (DH)
2901 28th St Ste 100, Santa Monica (90405-2975)
PHONE..................310 445-4200
Sally Shankland, *President*
Scott Schulman, *CEO*
Brian Field, *COO*
Rudolf Hotter, *COO*
David Cox, *CFO*
EMP: 122
SQ FT: 50,000
SALES (est): 60.3MM
SALES (corp-wide): 1.3B **Privately Held**
WEB: www.cancom.com
SIC: 2721 7389 Magazines: publishing only, not printed on site; trade show arrangement
HQ: Ubm, Llc
1983 Marcus Ave Ste 250
New Hyde Park NY 11042
516 562-7800

(P-6047)
UBM LLC
18301 Von Karman Ave # 920, Irvine (92612-1009)
PHONE..................415 947-6770
Sharon Fibelkorn, *Manager*
Steve Weitzner, *President*
Jennifer Reidy, *Training Spec*
R C Johnson, *Editor*
EMP: 55
SALES (corp-wide): 1.3B **Privately Held**
WEB: www.cmp.com
SIC: 2721 2741 Periodicals: publishing only; miscellaneous publishing
HQ: Ubm, Llc
1983 Marcus Ave Ste 250
New Hyde Park NY 11042
516 562-7800

(P-6048)
UBM LLC
Also Called: Cmp Healthcare Media
303 2nd St Ste 900s, San Francisco (94107-1375)
PHONE..................415 947-6488
Armand Derhacobian, *Director*
EMP: 128
SALES (corp-wide): 1.3B **Privately Held**
WEB: www.cmp.com
SIC: 2721 Magazines: publishing & printing
HQ: Ubm, Llc
1983 Marcus Ave Ste 250
New Hyde Park NY 11042
516 562-7800

(P-6049)
UBM TECHWEB (DH)
303 Secon St Tower Fl 9 9 Stower, San Francisco (94107)
PHONE..................415 947-6000
Paul Miller, *CEO*
Marco Pardi, *President*
John Dennehy, *CFO*
Deirdre Blake, *Bd of Directors*
Lenny Heymann, *Exec VP*
EMP: 14
SALES (est): 9.1MM
SALES (corp-wide): 1.3B **Privately Held**
SIC: 2721 Magazines: publishing only, not printed on site
HQ: Ubm, Llc
1983 Marcus Ave Ste 250
New Hyde Park NY 11042
516 562-7800

(P-6050)
UNION PUBLICATIONS INC
653 Wellesley Ave, Kensington (94708-1009)
PHONE..................510 525-6300
EMP: 11
SALES (est): 1MM **Privately Held**
SIC: 2721 2759

(P-6051)
UNITED ADVG PUBLICATIONS INC
Also Called: For Rent
3017 Douglas Blvd, Roseville (95661-3848)
PHONE..................916 746-2300
Dee Dahl, *Exec Dir*
EMP: 21 **Privately Held**
WEB: www.tradeonline.com
SIC: 2721 Magazines: publishing & printing
HQ: United Advertising Publications, Inc.
1331 L St Nw Ste 2
Washington DC 20005
210 377-3116

(P-6052)
UNIVERSAL MEDICAL PRESS INC
2443 Fillmore St, San Francisco (94115-1814)
PHONE..................415 436-9790
Thomas F Laszlo, *President*
EMP: 12
SALES (est): 944.3K **Privately Held**
SIC: 2721 8011 Trade journals: publishing only, not printed on site; offices & clinics of medical doctors

(P-6053)
VIDEOMAKER INC
Also Called: Smart TV & Sound
645 Mangrove Ave, Chico (95926-3946)
P.O. Box 4591 (95927-4591)
PHONE...................................530 891-8410
Matthew York, *President*
Patrice York, *Treasurer*
Gabrielle Green, *Executive*
Terra Yurkovic, *Business Dir*
Michael Delzell, *Sales Staff*
EMP: 36
SQ FT: 8,000
SALES (est): 4MM **Privately Held**
WEB: www.litewheels.com
SIC: 2721 7812 Magazines: publishing only, not printed on site; motion picture & video production

(P-6054)
VISTANOMICS INC
3450 Ocean View Blvd Frnt, Glendale (91208-3301)
PHONE...................................818 249-1236
Gary W Short, *President*
EMP: 10
SQ FT: 800
SALES (est): 1.2MM **Privately Held**
SIC: 2721 3829 Periodicals: publishing only; measuring & controlling devices

(P-6055)
VIZ MEDIA LLC
Also Called: Viz Media Music
1355 Market St Ste 200, San Francisco (94103-1460)
P.O. Box 77010 (94107-0010)
PHONE...................................415 546-7073
Hidemi Fukuhara, *CEO*
Brad Woods, *Chief Mktg Ofcr*
Akane Matsuo, *Vice Pres*
James Stutz, *Vice Pres*
Keith Beasley, *Web Dvlpr*
▲ EMP: 153
SALES (est): 37.5MM **Privately Held**
WEB: www.viz.com
SIC: 2721 2731 7819 6794 Comic books: publishing only, not printed on site; books: publishing only; video tape or disk reproduction; copyright buying & licensing; prerecorded records & tapes
PA: Shogakukan Inc.
2-3-1, Hitotsubashi
Chiyoda-Ku TKY 101-0

(P-6056)
WEIDER LEASING INC
21100 Erwin St, Woodland Hills (91367-3712)
PHONE...................................818 884-6800
EMP: 100
SQ FT: 32,000
SALES (est): 4.7MM **Privately Held**
SIC: 2721

(P-6057)
WELLS MEDIA GROUP INC (PA)
Also Called: Insurance Journal
3570 Camino Delrio N 20, San Diego (92108)
PHONE...................................619 584-1100
Mark Wells, *President*
Steven Johnston, *CFO*
Mindy Trammell, *Sales Staff*
Don Jergler, *Editor*
EMP: 22 EST: 1923
SQ FT: 3,600
SALES (est): 2.1MM **Privately Held**
WEB: www.insurancejrnl.com
SIC: 2721 8111 Magazines: publishing & printing; legal services

(P-6058)
WINE COMMUNICATIONS GROUP
Also Called: Wine Business Monthly
35 Maple St, Sonoma (95476-7014)
PHONE...................................707 939-0822
Eric Jorgensen, *President*
Liz Netherton, *Social Dir*
Jacki Kardum, *Office Mgr*
EMP: 15

SALES: 2MM **Privately Held**
WEB: www.winebusinessmonthly.com
SIC: 2721 Magazines: publishing only, not printed on site

(P-6059)
WIRED VENTURES INC
520 3rd St Ste 305, San Francisco (94107-6805)
PHONE...................................415 276-8400
Louis Rossetto, *Ch of Bd*
Jane Metcalfe, *Principal*
Megan Molteni, *Research*
Ron Licata, *Prdtn Dir*
Mj Milchanoski, *Merchandising*
EMP: 175
SALES (est): 37.8MM **Privately Held**
SIC: 2721 6719 Magazines: publishing only, not printed on site; investment holding companies, except banks

(P-6060)
WORLD TARIFF LIMITED
Also Called: Worldtariff
220 Montgomery St Ste 448, San Francisco (94104-3536)
PHONE...................................415 391-7501
G Edmund Clark, *President*
EMP: 25
SQ FT: 5,335
SALES (est): 1.6MM
SALES (corp-wide): 69.6B **Publicly Held**
WEB: www.worldtariff.com
SIC: 2721 Statistical reports (periodicals): publishing & printing
HQ: Fedex Trade Networks, Inc.
6075 Poplar Ave Ste 300
Memphis TN 38119
901 684-4800

(P-6061)
WSR PUBLISHING INC (PA)
Also Called: Widescreen Review
27645 Commerce Center Dr, Temecula (92590-2521)
P.O. Box 2587 (92593-2587)
PHONE...................................951 676-4914
Gary Reber, *President*
Mary M Reber, *Exec VP*
Tricia Spears, *Assoc Editor*
EMP: 14
SQ FT: 7,000
SALES: 1.9MM **Privately Held**
WEB: www.surroundmusic.net
SIC: 2721 5731 Magazines: publishing only, not printed on site; radio, television & electronic stores

(P-6062)
XPLAIN CORPORATION
Also Called: Mactech Magazine
705 Lakefield Rd Ste I, Westlake Village (91361-5903)
P.O. Box 5200 (91359-5200)
PHONE...................................805 494-9797
Neil Ticktin, *President*
Andrea Sniderman, *Ch of Bd*
EMP: 15
SALES (est): 1.1MM **Privately Held**
WEB: www.xplain.com
SIC: 2721 5994 Magazines: publishing only, not printed on site; magazine stand

(P-6063)
ZOASIS CORPORATION
1960 E Grand Ave Ste 555, El Segundo (90245-5099)
PHONE...................................800 745-4725
Douglas Drew, *CEO*
David Aucoin, *President*
Lisa Moise, *Vice Pres*
EMP: 39
SQ FT: 7,000
SALES (est): 3.1MM **Privately Held**
WEB: www.zoasis.com
SIC: 2721 8742 7375 Periodicals: publishing only; marketing consulting services; information retrieval services

---

2731 Books: Publishing & Printing

(P-6064)
5 BALL INC
Also Called: Bikernet.com
200 Broad Ave, Wilmington (90744-5812)
PHONE...................................310 830-0630
Keith Ball, *President*
Jason Douglass, *Vice Pres*
Ladd Terry, *Vice Pres*
Ben Lamboeuf, *Adv Dir*
EMP: 12 EST: 1995
SQ FT: 2,000
SALES: 34.4K **Privately Held**
WEB: www.bikernet.com
SIC: 2731 Book publishing

(P-6065)
A B C-CLIO INC (PA)
Also Called: ABC-Clio
147 Castilian Dr, Goleta (93117-5505)
P.O. Box 1911, Santa Barbara (93116-1911)
PHONE...................................805 968-1911
Ronald Boehm, *CEO*
Marlys Boehm, *Admin Sec*
Mark Lacommare, *Info Tech Mgr*
Chris Martinich, *Software Dev*
Jimi Derouen, *Business Anlyst*
EMP: 115 EST: 1955
SALES (est): 14.7MM **Privately Held**
WEB: www.abc-clio.com
SIC: 2731 Books: publishing only

(P-6066)
ABC - CLIO LLC
147 Castilian Dr, Goleta (93117-5505)
P.O. Box 1911, Santa Barbara (93116-1911)
PHONE...................................800 368-6868
Becky A Snyder,
Vince Burns, *Vice Pres*
Julie Dunbar, *Manager*
Patrick Hall, *Editor*
Jennifer Hutchinson, *Editor*
EMP: 14
SALES (est): 1.1MM **Privately Held**
SIC: 2731 Book publishing

(P-6067)
ALAN WOFSY FINE ARTS LLC
Also Called: Dow Frosini
1109 Geary Blvd, San Francisco (94109-6815)
P.O. Box 2210 (94126-2210)
PHONE...................................415 292-6500
Alan Wofsy, *Mng Member*
Andrew Redkin, *Marketing Staff*
EMP: 10 EST: 1969
SQ FT: 500
SALES (est): 19.1K **Privately Held**
WEB: www.art-books.com
SIC: 2731 5192 8412 Books: publishing only; books; art gallery

(P-6068)
ALFRED MUSIC GROUP INC (PA)
16320 Roscoe Blvd Ste 100, Van Nuys (91406-1216)
PHONE...................................818 891-5999
Steven Manus, *CEO*
Ron Manus, *President*
Elise Keil, *General Mgr*
Paul Melancon, *Sales Staff*
EMP: 20
SALES (est): 1.6MM **Privately Held**
SIC: 2731 Book music: publishing & printing

(P-6069)
ALPHA PUBLISHING CORPORATION
Also Called: McDowell Publishers
337 N Vineyard Ave # 240, Ontario (91764-4453)
PHONE...................................909 464-0500
Taki Khan, *President*
EMP: 35
SQ FT: 4,500
SALES: 9MM **Privately Held**
SIC: 2731 5961 Book publishing; books, mail order (except book clubs)

(P-6070)
AMAZING FACTS INTERNATIONAL
Also Called: Amazing Facts Ministries
6615 Sierra College Blvd, Roseville (95746-7366)
P.O. Box 1058 (95678-8058)
PHONE...................................916 434-3880
Allen Hrenyk, *Principal*
Doug Batchelor, *President*
EMP: 85
SALES (est): 1.7MM **Privately Held**
SIC: 2731 Books: publishing only

(P-6071)
AMERICAN PUBLISHING CORP
2143 E Convention Center, Ontario (91764-5635)
PHONE...................................909 390-7548
Taki Khan, *President*
EMP: 26
SQ FT: 11,000
SALES: 8MM **Privately Held**
SIC: 2731 Book publishing

(P-6072)
ANTHEM MUSIC & MEDIA FUND LLC
Also Called: Bicycle Music Co, The
5750 Wilshire Blvd Fl 4th, Los Angeles (90036-7201)
PHONE...................................310 286-6600
Jake Wisely, *CEO*
Michael Pizzuto, *Senior VP*
Steve Toland, *Vice Pres*
Marty Willard, *Vice Pres*
Maeline Younger, *Manager*
EMP: 14
SALES (est): 1.3MM **Privately Held**
SIC: 2731 Book music: publishing & printing

(P-6073)
AVN MEDIA NETWORK INC
Also Called: Adult Video News
9400 Penfield Ave, Chatsworth (91311-6549)
PHONE...................................818 718-5788
Tony Rios, *CEO*
Roy Karch, *Bd of Directors*
Timothy Ferencz, *Executive*
Jesse Dena, *Creative Dir*
Marlene Amata, *Controller*
EMP: 30
SQ FT: 15,000
SALES (est): 3.9MM **Privately Held**
SIC: 2731 2721 Book publishing; periodicals

(P-6074)
BERRETT-KOEHLER PUBLISHERS INC (PA)
1333 Broadway Ste 1000, Oakland (94612-1926)
PHONE...................................510 817-2277
Steven Piersanti, *President*
▲ EMP: 20
SQ FT: 5,400
SALES (est): 3MM **Privately Held**
WEB: www.bkpub.com
SIC: 2731 Books: publishing only

(P-6075)
BERTELSMANN INC
Also Called: Arvato Services
29011 Commerce Center Dr, Valencia (91355-4195)
PHONE...................................661 702-2700
Janet Adams, *Manager*
EMP: 400
SALES (corp-wide): 75.3MM **Privately Held**
WEB: www.bertelsmann.com
SIC: 2731 Book publishing
HQ: Bertelsmann, Inc.
1745 Broadway Fl 20
New York NY 10019
212 782-1000

▲ = Import ▼=Export
◆ =Import/Export

(P-6076)
BEST VALUE TEXTBOOKS LLC
Also Called: BVT Publishing
  410 Hemsted Dr Ste 100, Redding
  (96002-0164)
  P.O. Box 492831 (96049-2831)
  PHONE................................530 222-5980
  Jason James, *Mng Member*
  Richard Schofield, *Business Dir*
  Erik Lineback, *Software Dev*
  EMP: 22
  SQ FT: 2,000
  SALES (est): 4.6MM **Privately Held**
  WEB: www.bestvaluetextbooks.com
  SIC: 2731 Textbooks: publishing & printing

(P-6077)
BETTER CHINESE LLC
  150 W Iowa Ave Ste 104, Sunnyvale
  (94086-6179)
  P.O. Box 695, Palo Alto (94302-0695)
  PHONE................................650 384-0902
  James Lin, *Mng Member*
  Helen Yung, *Vice Pres*
  Yuan LI, *Office Mgr*
  ▲ **EMP:** 10
  SALES (est): 1.2MM **Privately Held**
  SIC: 2731 Book publishing

(P-6078)
BHAKTIVEDANTA BOOK TR INTL INC
Also Called: Bbt
  9701 Venus Blvd Ste A, Los Angeles
  (90034)
  PHONE................................310 837-5284
  Emil Beca, *President*
  Stuart Kadetz, *Treasurer*
  Gil Sanchez, *Admin Sec*
  ▲ **EMP:** 12
  SQ FT: 5,000
  SALES (est): 652.3K **Privately Held**
  WEB: www.mcremo.com
  SIC: 2731 Books: publishing only

(P-6079)
BLUE MTN CTR OF MEDITATION INC
Also Called: NILGIRI PRESS
  3600 Tomales Rd, Tomales (94971)
  P.O. Box 256 (94971-0256)
  PHONE................................707 878-2369
  Christine Easwaran, *President*
  Debbie McMurray, *President*
  Lisa Bishop, *Director*
  Joan Barnicle, *Manager*
  John Suerstedt, *Manager*
  EMP: 20
  SQ FT: 1,800
  SALES: 1.4MM **Privately Held**
  WEB: www.bluemountaincenter.org
  SIC: 2731 8661 Books: publishing & printing; religious organizations

(P-6080)
BLURB INC
  580 California St Fl 3, San Francisco
  (94104-1024)
  PHONE................................415 364-6300
  Eileen Gittins, *CEO*
  Kelly Leach, *General Mgr*
  Adam Hobbi, *Software Engr*
  Krista Jackson, *Software Engr*
  Brady Kroupa, *Project Mgr*
  EMP: 54
  SALES (est): 11.8MM **Privately Held**
  SIC: 2731 Books: publishing only

(P-6081)
BRIDGE PUBLICATIONS INC (PA)
Also Called: Bpi Records
  5600 E Olympic Blvd, Commerce
  (90022-5128)
  PHONE................................323 888-6200
  Blake Silber, *CEO*
  Lis Astrupgaard, *President*
  Helen Lumbroso, *Vice Pres*
  Suzanne Riley, *Vice Pres*
  Laura Lan, *Executive*
  ▲ **EMP:** 40
  SQ FT: 15,000
  SALES (est): 18.4MM **Privately Held**
  SIC: 2731 3652 Books: publishing only; pre-recorded records & tapes

(P-6082)
BRYAN EDWARDS PUBLISHING CO
Also Called: Flash Anatomy
  2185 N Orange Olive Rd # 3, Orange
  (92865-3300)
  PHONE................................714 634-0264
  Bryan Edward Nash, *President*
  EMP: 10
  SALES (est): 994K **Privately Held**
  SIC: 2731 Books: publishing only

(P-6083)
CENGAGE LEARNING INC
Education To Go
  40880 County Center Dr G, Temecula
  (92591-6024)
  P.O. Box 760 (92593-0760)
  PHONE................................951 719-1878
  Jerry Weissberg, *Branch Mgr*
  EMP: 35 **Privately Held**
  WEB: www.thomsonlearning.com
  SIC: 2731 Textbooks: publishing & printing
  PA: Cengage Learning, Inc.
    200 Pier 4 Blvd Ste 400
    Boston MA 02210

(P-6084)
CENTER FOR CLLBRTIVE CLASSROOM
  1001 Marina Village Pkwy # 110, Alameda
  (94501-1092)
  PHONE................................510 533-0213
  Roger King, *CEO*
  Victor Young, *President*
  Brent Welling, *Vice Pres*
  Peter Brunn, *Vice Pres*
  Joshua Callman, *Associate Dir*
  ▲ **EMP:** 99
  SQ FT: 15,000
  SALES (est): 14MM **Privately Held**
  WEB: www.devstu.org
  SIC: 2731 8299 Book publishing; personal development school

(P-6085)
CENTERSOURCE SYSTEMS LLC
  60 Commerce Ln Ste D, Cloverdale
  (95425-4230)
  PHONE................................707 838-1061
  David Gibbs, *General Mgr*
  Jeanne Gibbs,
  Carolyn Rankin,
  Susan Rankin,
  ▲ **EMP:** 10
  SQ FT: 4,000
  SALES (est): 1MM **Privately Held**
  WEB: www.centersourcesystems.com
  SIC: 2731 8748 Book publishing; business consulting

(P-6086)
CEQUAL PRODUCTS INC
  1328 16th St, Santa Monica (90404-1804)
  PHONE................................310 458-0441
  ▲ **EMP:** 10
  SALES (est): 840K **Privately Held**
  WEB: www.cequal.com
  SIC: 2731 7812 8741

(P-6087)
CHICK PUBLICATIONS INC
  8780 Archibald Ave, Rancho Cucamonga
  (91730-4697)
  P.O. Box 3500, Ontario (91761-1019)
  PHONE................................909 987-0771
  Jack T Chick, *President*
  Ronald Rockney, *Treasurer*
  George A Collins, *Vice Pres*
  Ron Rockney, *Sales Mgr*
  David Daniels, *Author*
  ◆ **EMP:** 35 **EST:** 1961
  SQ FT: 10,000
  SALES (est): 3.9MM **Privately Held**
  WEB: www.chick.com
  SIC: 2731 5961 Books: publishing only; mail order house

(P-6088)
CHRONICLE BOOKS LLC
  680 2nd St, San Francisco (94107-2015)
  PHONE................................415 537-4200
  Nion McEvoy,
  Beth Weber, *Associate Dir*
  Wendy Thorpe, *Admin Sec*
  Paul Gore, *CIO*
  Madeline Moe, *Software Dev*
  ▲ **EMP:** 160
  SALES: 22.1MM
  SALES (corp-wide): 29.9MM **Privately Held**
  WEB: www.chroniclebooks.com
  SIC: 2731 Books: publishing only
  PA: The Mcevoy Group Llc
    680 2nd St
    San Francisco CA 94107
    415 537-4200

(P-6089)
CLP APG LLC
Also Called: Clp Apg, Inc.
  1700 4th St, Berkeley (94710-1711)
  PHONE................................510 528-1444
  Charles B Winton, *Ch of Bd*
  Susan Reich, *President*
  EMP: 90
  SQ FT: 14,000
  SALES (est): 3.9MM
  SALES (corp-wide): 140.4MM **Privately Held**
  SIC: 2731 Books: publishing only
  PA: Clp Pb, Llc
    1290 Ave Of The Amrcas
    New York NY 10104
    212 340-8100

(P-6090)
COGNELLA INC
Also Called: University Readers
  3970 Sorrento Valley Blvd # 500, San Diego
  (92121-1416)
  PHONE................................858 552-1120
  Bassin Hamadeh, *CEO*
  Ryan Bailey, *Vice Pres*
  Mike Simpson, *Vice Pres*
  Dave Wilson, *Vice Pres*
  Miguel Macias, *Graphic Designe*
  EMP: 65
  SQ FT: 8,000
  SALES (est): 7.8MM **Privately Held**
  WEB: www.universityreaders.com
  SIC: 2731 Textbooks: publishing only, not printed on site

(P-6091)
CONCORD MUSIC GROUP INC (PA)
  5750 Wilshire Blvd # 450, Los Angeles
  (90036-3697)
  PHONE................................310 385-4455
  Glen Barros, *CEO*
  Edward Ginis, *President*
  Gene Rumsey, *President*
  Bob Valentine, *CFO*
  John Burk, *Officer*
  ▲ **EMP:** 89
  SQ FT: 8,000
  SALES (est): 33.5MM **Privately Held**
  SIC: 2731 Book music: publishing & printing

(P-6092)
COUNCIL OAK BOOKS LLC
  2822 Van Ness Ave, San Francisco
  (94109-1426)
  PHONE................................415 931-7700
  Mitchell Wortzman, *CFO*
  David Kanbar,
  Maurice Kanbar,
  ▲ **EMP:** 12
  SALES (est): 1MM **Privately Held**
  WEB: www.counciloakbooks.com
  SIC: 2731 5192 Books: publishing only; books

(P-6093)
CPP/BELWIN INC
  16320 Roscoe Blvd Ste 100, Van Nuys
  (91406-1216)
  PHONE................................818 891-5999
  Steven Manus, *President*
  ▲ **EMP:** 31
  SQ FT: 142,000
  SALES (est): 1.9MM **Privately Held**
  SIC: 2731 Book music: publishing only, not printed on site
  PA: Alfred Music Group Inc.
    16320 Roscoe Blvd Ste 100
    Van Nuys CA 91406

(P-6094)
CREATIVE TEACHING PRESS INC (PA)
  6262 Katella Ave, Cypress (90630-5204)
  PHONE................................714 799-2100
  James M Connelly, *CEO*
  Luella Connelly, *Chairman*
  Patrick Connelly, *Treasurer*
  Susan Connelly, *Admin Sec*
  Mike Kennedy, *Administration*
  ◆ **EMP:** 61
  SQ FT: 85,000
  SALES (est): 12.6MM **Privately Held**
  WEB: www.creativeteaching.com
  SIC: 2731 Books: publishing only

(P-6095)
DAVID KORDANSKY GALLERY INC (PA)
  5130 Edgewood Pl, Los Angeles
  (90019-1619)
  PHONE................................323 935-3030
  David Kordansky, *President*
  Michele Barbati, *Administration*
  Athena Denos, *Administration*
  Chloe Ginnegar, *Administration*
  Corynne Pless, *Administration*
  ▲ **EMP:** 30
  SQ FT: 16,150
  SALES (est): 520K **Privately Held**
  SIC: 2731 Book publishing

(P-6096)
DAWN SIGN PRESS INC
  6130 Nancy Ridge Dr, San Diego
  (92121-3223)
  PHONE................................858 625-0600
  Joe Dannis, *CEO*
  Tina Jo Breindel, *Treasurer*
  Rebecca Ryan, *Vice Pres*
  Thomas Schlegel, *Admin Sec*
  Leigh Ainsworth, *Inv Control Mgr*
  ◆ **EMP:** 28
  SQ FT: 16,500
  SALES: 7.7MM **Privately Held**
  WEB: www.dawnsign.com
  SIC: 2731 Books: publishing only

(P-6097)
DHARMA MUDRANALAYA (PA)
Also Called: Dharma Publishing
  35788 Hauser Bridge Rd, Cazadero
  (95421-9611)
  PHONE................................707 847-3380
  Arnaud Maitland, *CEO*
  Tarthang Tulku, *President*
  Debbie Black, *Vice Pres*
  Matthew Breit, *Technology*
  Rima Tamar, *Sales Dir*
  ▲ **EMP:** 21
  SQ FT: 16,000
  SALES: 376.1K **Privately Held**
  WEB: www.dharmapublishing.com
  SIC: 2731 7336 Books: publishing & printing; commercial art & graphic design

(P-6098)
DISNEY BOOK GROUP LLC (DH)
Also Called: Hyperion Books For Children
  500 S Buena Vista St, Burbank
  (91521-0001)
  PHONE................................818 560-1000
  Russell R Hampton Jr, *President*
  Marsha L Reed, *Admin Sec*
  EMP: 13
  SALES (est): 1.4MM
  SALES (corp-wide): 90.2B **Publicly Held**
  SIC: 2731 Book publishing

(P-6099)
EDUCATIONAL IDEAS INCORPORATED
Also Called: Ballard & Tighe Publishers
  471 Atlas St, Brea (92821-3118)
  P.O. Box 219 (92822-0219)
  PHONE................................714 990-4332
  Dorothy Roberts, *Ch of Bd*
  Mark Espinola, *CEO*
  Sari Luoma, *Vice Pres*
  Fred Tan, *Vice Pres*
  Kent Roberts, *Admin Sec*
  ▲ **EMP:** 30
  SQ FT: 12,000

PRODUCTS & SVCS

SALES (est): 3.2MM **Privately Held**
WEB: www.ballard-tighe.com
SIC: 2731 Textbooks: publishing only, not
printed on site

(P-6100)
ELAINE GILL INC
Also Called: Crossing Press, The
6001 Shellmound St Fl 4th, Emeryville
(94608-1968)
PHONE..................................510 559-1600
Philip Wood, *President*
Joann Deck, *Vice Pres*
EMP: 15 EST: 1966
SQ FT: 14,800
SALES (est): 960K **Privately Held**
SIC: 2731 Books: publishing only

(P-6101)
EVAN-MOOR CORPORATION (HQ)
Also Called: Evan-Moor Educational Publr
18 Lower Ragsdale Dr, Monterey
(93940-5746)
PHONE..................................831 649-5901
William E Evans, *President*
Joellen Moore, *Vice Pres*
Dave Miller, *Finance*
James F O'Donnell III, *VP Sales*
Kirsten Schmieg-Watters, *Sales Dir*
▲ EMP: 30
SQ FT: 20,000
SALES (est): 10MM
SALES (corp-wide): 16.7MM **Privately Held**
WEB: www.evan-moor.com
SIC: 2731 Books: publishing & printing
PA: Lincoln Learning Solutions, Inc.
294 Massachusetts Ave
Rochester PA 15074
724 764-7200

(P-6102)
FONDO DE CULTURA ECONOMICA
2293 Verus St, San Diego (92154-4704)
PHONE..................................619 429-0455
Rovolso Pataky, *Manager*
EMP: 10
SQ FT: 7,822 **Privately Held**
WEB: www.fondodeculturaeconomica.com
SIC: 2731 Textbooks: publishing only, not
printed on site; books: publishing only
HQ: Fondo De Cultura Economica
Carr. Picacho - Ajusco No. 227
Ciudad De Mexico CDMX 14738

(P-6103)
FOUR M STUDIOS
Also Called: Meredith Publishing
201 Mission St Fl 12, San Francisco
(94105-1888)
PHONE..................................415 249-2362
Tamara Marcsisak, *Manager*
Albert Murillo, *Accounts Exec*
EMP: 80
SALES (corp-wide): 3.1B **Publicly Held**
WEB: www.meredith.com
SIC: 2731 Book publishing; periodi-
cals
PA: Meredith Corporation
1716 Locust St
Des Moines IA 50309
515 284-3000

(P-6104)
GALAXY PRESS INC
6115-6121 Malburg Way, Vernon (90058)
PHONE..................................323 399-3433
Mich Breuer, *General Mgr*
EMP: 25
SALES (est): 904.5K **Privately Held**
SIC: 2731 Book publishing

(P-6105)
GANDER PUBLISHING INC
450 Front St, Avila Beach (93424-3551)
P.O. Box 780 (93424-0780)
PHONE..................................805 541-5523
Nanci L Bell, *CEO*
▲ EMP: 18
SQ FT: 5,000
SALES (est): 1.8MM **Privately Held**
WEB: www.ganderpublishing.net
SIC: 2731 Books: publishing only

(P-6106)
GOFF CORPORATION
Also Called: Palace Press International
10 Paul Dr, San Rafael (94903-2102)
PHONE..................................415 526-1370
Raoul Goff, *President*
▲ EMP: 30
SALES (est): 2.5MM **Privately Held**
WEB: www.palacepress.com
SIC: 2731 2796 Books: publishing & print-
ing; color separations for printing

(P-6107)
HARPERCOLLINS PUBLISHERS LLC
353 Sacramento St Ste 500, San Francisco
(94111-3637)
PHONE..................................415 477-4400
Diane Gedymin, *Manager*
Annette Bourland, *Vice Pres*
Brittani Dimare, *Production*
Linda Tozer, *Marketing Mgr*
Tara Feehan, *Director*
EMP: 35
SALES (corp-wide): 10B **Publicly Held**
WEB: www.harpercollins.com
SIC: 2731 Book publishing
HQ: Harpercollins Publishers L.L.C.
195 Broadway
New York NY 10007
212 207-7000

(P-6108)
HESPERIAN HEALTH GUIDES (PA)
1919 Addison St Ste 304, Berkeley
(94704-1143)
PHONE..................................510 845-1447
Sarah Shannon, *Director*
Salma Suleyman, *Officer*
Mary A Buckley, *Business Mgr*
Robin Young, *Marketing Staff*
Todd Jailer, *Publications*
EMP: 20
SQ FT: 1,600
SALES: 1.8MM **Privately Held**
WEB: www.hesperian.org
SIC: 2731 2741 8399 8641 Books: pub-
lishing only; miscellaneous publishing;
community development groups; civic so-
cial & fraternal associations

(P-6109)
HEYDAY
Also Called: Heyday Books
1808 San Pablo Ave Apt A, Berkeley
(94702-1795)
P.O. Box 9145 (94709-0145)
PHONE..................................510 549-3564
Malcolm Margolin, *Exec Dir*
Steve Wasserman, *Exec Dir*
Ashley Ingram, *Graphic Designe*
Diane Lee, *Prdtn Dir*
Linda Yamane, *Editor*
▲ EMP: 12
SALES: 2MM **Privately Held**
WEB: www.heydaybooks.com
SIC: 2731 2721 Books: publishing only;
magazines: publishing only, not printed on
site

(P-6110)
HOLLOWAY HOUSE PUBLISHING CO
8060 Melrose Ave Fl 3, Los Angeles
(90046-7039)
PHONE..................................323 653-8060
Bentley Morris, *President*
Mark Marsh, *Manager*
EMP: 15 EST: 1961
SQ FT: 5,000
SALES (est): 1.3MM **Privately Held**
SIC: 2731 Books: publishing only

(P-6111)
HOUGHTON MIFFLIN HARCOURT PUBG
Also Called: Harcourt Trade Publishers
525 B St Ste 1900, San Diego
(92101-4495)
PHONE..................................617 351-5000
Barbara Fisch, *Branch Mgr*
EMP: 17

SALES (corp-wide): 1.3B **Publicly Held**
SIC: 2731 Textbooks: publishing only, not
printed on site
HQ: Houghton Mifflin Harcourt Publishing
Company
125 High St Ste 900
Boston MA 02110
617 351-5000

(P-6112)
INSIGHT EDITIONS LP
800 A St Ste B, San Rafael (94901-3011)
P.O. Box 3088 (94912-3088)
PHONE..................................415 526-1370
Raoul Goff, *CEO*
Michael Madden, *COO*
Lina Palma, *Vice Pres*
Sadie Crofts, *Production*
Lauren Lepera, *Production*
▲ EMP: 100
SALES (est): 16.7MM **Privately Held**
SIC: 2731 2721 Books: publishing only;
comic books: publishing only, not printed
on site

(P-6113)
INSPIRED PROPERTIES LLC
14320 Ventura Blvd 181, Sherman Oaks
(91423-2717)
PHONE..................................818 430-9634
Ron Belk, *Mng Member*
EMP: 27
SALES (est): 2.3MM **Privately Held**
SIC: 2731 Book publishing

(P-6114)
J S PALUCH CO INC
9400 Norwalk Blvd, Santa Fe Springs
(90670-6105)
P.O. Box 4368 (90670-1380)
PHONE..................................562 692-0484
Lee Corbasque, *Manager*
John Gossage, *Foreman/Supr*
EMP: 50
SQ FT: 47,232
SALES (corp-wide): 87.6MM **Privately Held**
WEB: www.jspaluch.com
SIC: 2731 8743 2721 Book publishing;
sales promotion; periodicals
PA: J. S. Paluch Co., Inc.
3708 River Rd Ste 400
Franklin Park IL 60131
847 678-9300

(P-6115)
JO SONJAS FOLK ART STUDIO
2136 3rd St, Eureka (95501-0814)
P.O. Box 9080 (95502-9080)
PHONE..................................707 445-9306
Jerry Jansen, *President*
Jo Sonja Jansen, *Vice Pres*
Mark Jansen, *Manager*
▲ EMP: 10 EST: 1975
SQ FT: 10,000
SALES (est): 690K **Privately Held**
SIC: 2731 8299 2721 Books: publishing
only; art school, except commercial; peri-
odicals

(P-6116)
JOHN WILEY & SONS INC
Also Called: Jossey-Bass Publishers
1 Montgomery St Ste 1200, San Francisco
(94104-4594)
PHONE..................................415 433-1740
Steve Robinson, *Manager*
Barry Davis, *Exec VP*
Aref Matin, *Exec VP*
Christopher Caridi, *Vice Pres*
Kevin Monaco, *Vice Pres*
EMP: 154
SALES (corp-wide): 1.8B **Publicly Held**
WEB: www.wiley.com
SIC: 2731 2741 Textbooks: publishing
only, not printed on site; miscellaneous
publishing
PA: John Wiley & Sons, Inc.
111 River St Ste 2000
Hoboken NJ 07030
201 748-6000

(P-6117)
JUDY O PRODUCTIONS INC
4858 W Pico Blvd Ste 331, Los Angeles
(90019-4225)
PHONE..................................323 938-8513
Judy Ostarch, *President*
▲ EMP: 28 EST: 1999
SALES (est): 182.7K **Privately Held**
WEB: www.judyoproductions.com
SIC: 2731 Book publishing

(P-6118)
LITTLE EINSTEINS LLC
500 S Buena Vista St, Burbank
(91521-0001)
P.O. Box 25020, Glendale (91221-5020)
PHONE..................................818 560-1000
Julie Aigner-Clark,
Susan McLain, *Vice Pres*
EMP: 13
SQ FT: 6,000
SALES (est): 773.2K
SALES (corp-wide): 90.2B **Publicly Held**
SIC: 2731 3695 Books: publishing & print-
ing; video recording tape, blank
HQ: Twdc Enterprises 18 Corp.
500 S Buena Vista St
Burbank CA 91521

(P-6119)
MARSHALL & SWIFT/BOECKH LLC
777 S Figueroa St Fl 12, Los Angeles
(90017-5878)
PHONE..................................213 683-9000
Tony Reisz, *CEO*
Norrine Brydon, *Vice Pres*
Mike Fisher, *Info Tech Dir*
Randy Stastny, *IT/INT Sup*
Rick Carlberg, *VP Opers*
EMP: 16
SALES (corp-wide): 1.7B **Publicly Held**
SIC: 2731 2741 Pamphlets: publishing &
printing; miscellaneous publishing
HQ: Marshall & Swift/Boeckh, Llc
10001 W Innovation Dr # 100
Milwaukee WI 53226
262 780-2800

(P-6120)
MCEVOY PROPERTIES LLC
680 2nd St, San Francisco (94107-2015)
PHONE..................................415 537-4200
Nion McEvoy,
EMP: 163
SALES (est): 985.2K **Privately Held**
SIC: 2731 Book publishing

(P-6121)
MCKEAGUE PATPATRICK
Also Called: XYZ Text Book
1339 Marsh St, San Luis Obispo
(93401-3315)
PHONE..................................805 541-4593
Patpatrick McKeague, *Owner*
Staci Truelson, *Project Mgr*
EMP: 10
SALES (est): 530K **Privately Held**
SIC: 2731 Textbooks: publishing only, not
printed on site

(P-6122)
MERIDIAN TECHNICAL SALES INC
520 Alder Dr, Milpitas (95035-7443)
PHONE..................................408 526-2000
David Dilling, *President*
Ray Bautista, *Vice Pres*
Nick Creighton, *Technical Staff*
Brandy Thomas, *Marketing Staff*
Brian Hedayati, *Sales Staff*
EMP: 20
SALES (est): 2MM **Privately Held**
SIC: 2731 7313 Books: publishing only;
electronic media advertising representa-
tives

(P-6123)
MIKE MURACH & ASSOCIATES
4340 N Knoll Ave, Fresno (93722-7825)
PHONE..................................559 440-9071
Michael Murach, *President*
Georgia Murach, *Admin Sec*
Joel Murach, *Technical Staff*

▲ = Import ▼=Export
◆ =Import/Export

EMP: 12 EST: 1972
SALES (est): 1.5MM **Privately Held**
WEB: www.murach.com
SIC: 2731 Textbooks: publishing only, not
printed on site

(P-6124)
NARCOTICS ANONYMOUS
WORLD SERV
Also Called: World Service Office
19737 Nordhoff Pl, Chatsworth
(91311-6606)
P.O. Box 9999, Van Nuys (91409-9099)
PHONE...................................818 773-9999
Anthony Edmondson, *CEO*
Stephan Lantos, *Info Tech Mgr*
▲ EMP: 45
SQ FT: 35,000
SALES: 7.9MM **Privately Held**
SIC: 2731 Books: publishing only; pam-
phlets: publishing only, not printed on site

(P-6125)
NATIONAL DIRECTORY
SERVICES
19698 View Forever Ln, Grass Valley
(95945-8883)
PHONE...................................530 268-8636
EMP: 20 EST: 1989
SALES (est): 1.4MM **Privately Held**
WEB: www.lucchesivineyards.com
SIC: 2731 2741

(P-6126)
NATIONAL LAW DIGEST INC
Also Called: Times Publishing
23844 Hawthorne Blvd # 200, Torrance
(90505-5945)
PHONE...................................310 791-9975
Vijay Fadia, *President*
EMP: 20
SALES (est): 1.2MM **Privately Held**
WEB: www.timespublishing.com
SIC: 2731 2721 Books: publishing only;
periodicals: publishing only

(P-6127)
NATURAL STD RES
COLLABORATION
3120 W March Ln Fl 1, Stockton
(95219-2368)
PHONE...................................617 591-3300
EMP: 20
SQ FT: 2,000
SALES: 2.5MM **Privately Held**
SIC: 2731

(P-6128)
NEW HARBINGER
PUBLICATIONS INC (PA)
5674 Shattuck Ave, Oakland (94609-1662)
PHONE...................................510 652-0215
Matt McKay, *President*
Heather Garnos, *Vice Pres*
Minoo Irvani, *Executive*
Jesse Burson, *Project Mgr*
Neocles Serafimidis, *Technology*
▲ EMP: 33
SQ FT: 6,500
SALES: 14.6MM **Privately Held**
WEB: www.newharbinger.com
SIC: 2731 3652 Books: publishing only;
master records or tapes, preparation of

(P-6129)
NOLO
950 Parker St, Berkeley (94710-2524)
PHONE...................................510 549-1976
Bob Dubow, *CEO*
Laurence Nathanson, *Vice Pres*
John Plessas, *Vice Pres*
Mark Stuhr, *Vice Pres*
Jackie Thompson, *Vice Pres*
EMP: 120
SQ FT: 25,000
SALES (est): 11MM
SALES (corp-wide): 284.6MM **Privately**
Held
WEB: www.nolo.com
SIC: 2731 8111 8742 Books: publishing
only; legal services; marketing consulting
services

PA: Internet Brands, Inc.
909 N Pacific Coast Hwy # 11
El Segundo CA 90245
310 280-4000

(P-6130)
NORMAN & GLOBUS INC
Also Called: Science Wiz Summer Camp
4128 Lakeside Dr, Richmond (94806-1941)
P.O. Box 20533, El Sobrante (94820-0533)
PHONE...................................510 222-2638
Penelope A Norman, *CEO*
▲ EMP: 12
SQ FT: 4,000
SALES (est): 1.7MM **Privately Held**
WEB: www.electrowiz.com
SIC: 2731 Books: publishing only

(P-6131)
OREILLY MEDIA INC (PA)
Also Called: Safari Books Online
1005 Gravenstein Hwy N, Sebastopol
(95472-2811)
PHONE...................................707 827-7000
Timothy F O'Reilly, *President*
Maria Manrique, *CFO*
Karen Hebert-Maccaro, *Officer*
Mark Jacobs, *Officer*
Jim Stogdill, *Officer*
▲ EMP: 150
SQ FT: 90,000
SALES (est): 114.7MM **Privately Held**
WEB: www.oreilly.com
SIC: 2731 2741 8231 Books: publishing
only; ; libraries

(P-6132)
PALACE PRINTING & DESIGN
LP
800 A St, San Rafael (94901-3011)
PHONE...................................415 526-1370
Raoul Goff, *President*
Sreed Haran, *Sales Staff*
▲ EMP: 20
SALES (est): 1.2MM **Privately Held**
SIC: 2731 Books: publishing & printing

(P-6133)
PAM DEE PUBLISHING
303 Talbot Ave, Santa Rosa (95405-4534)
PHONE...................................707 542-1528
Pamela Atchison, *Owner*
EMP: 10
SALES (est): 500.6K **Privately Held**
SIC: 2731 Book publishing

(P-6134)
PEARSON EDUCATION INC
Also Called: Scott Foresman Pearson Edu-
catn
3700 Inland Empire Blvd, Ontario
(91764-4906)
PHONE...................................800 653-1918
Mark Moyer, *Branch Mgr*
EMP: 10
SALES (corp-wide): 5.3B **Privately Held**
WEB: www.phgenit.com
SIC: 2731 Book publishing
HQ: Pearson Education, Inc.
221 River St
Hoboken NJ 07030
201 236-7000

(P-6135)
PEARSON EDUCATION INC
1301 Sansome St, San Francisco
(94111-1122)
PHONE...................................415 402-2500
Benjamin Cummings, *Manager*
Donae Viertel, *Technology*
EMP: 20
SALES (corp-wide): 5.3B **Privately Held**
WEB: www.phgenit.com
SIC: 2731 Book publishing
HQ: Pearson Education, Inc.
221 River St
Hoboken NJ 07030
201 236-7000

(P-6136)
PLAYERS PRESS INC
Fulton Ave, Studio City (91604)
PHONE...................................818 789-4980
William Landes, *President*
June Heal, *President*
Sharon Gorrell, *Senior VP*

Marjorie Clapper, *Admin Sec*
EMP: 33
SALES (est): 2.6MM **Privately Held**
SIC: 2731 Books: publishing & printing

(P-6137)
PLURAL PUBLISHING INC
5521 Ruffin Rd, San Diego (92123-1314)
PHONE...................................858 492-1555
Sadanand Singh, *President*
Valerie Johns, *General Mgr*
Janis Pilla, *Office Mgr*
Brian Summerville, *Controller*
Sandy Doyle, *Production*
▲ EMP: 15
SALES (est): 2MM **Privately Held**
WEB: www.pluralpublishing.com
SIC: 2731 Textbooks: publishing only, not
printed on site

(P-6138)
PRACTICE MANAGEMENT INFO
CORP (PA)
Also Called: Pmic
4727 Wilshire Blvd # 302, Los Angeles
(90010-3806)
PHONE...................................323 954-0224
James B Davis, *President*
Michelle Cuevas, *Opers Mgr*
Charles Ekin, *Representative*
◆ EMP: 35
SQ FT: 6,000
SALES (est): 4.3MM **Privately Held**
WEB: www.medicalbookstore.com
SIC: 2731 7372 Book publishing; business
oriented computer software

(P-6139)
PRIMA GAMES INC
Also Called: Prima Publishing
2990 Lava Ridge Ct # 120, Roseville
(95661-3076)
PHONE...................................916 787-7000
Richard Sarnoff, *President*
Julie Asbury, *Director*
EMP: 180
SALES (est): 12.6MM **Privately Held**
WEB: www.primagames.com
SIC: 2731 Books: publishing only

(P-6140)
QUEENSHIP PUBLISHING
COMPANY
5951 Encina Rd Ste 100, Goleta
(93117-6251)
P.O. Box 220 (93116-0220)
PHONE...................................805 692-0043
David Schaeffer, *President*
EMP: 12
SALES: 129.7K **Privately Held**
WEB: www.queenship.org
SIC: 2731 Books: publishing only

(P-6141)
RICKY READER LLC
6715 Mckinley Ave Unit B, Los Angeles
(90001-1591)
PHONE...................................323 231-4322
Dennis Brown, *President*
EMP: 10
SALES (est): 292.2K **Privately Held**
SIC: 2731 Books: publishing only

(P-6142)
ROBERT W CAMERON & CO
INC
Also Called: Cameroncompany
149 Kentucky St Ste 7, Petaluma
(94952-2940)
PHONE...................................707 769-1617
Robert Cameron, *Ch of Bd*
Christopher Roger Gruener, *CEO*
Tracy Davis, *Treasurer*
Linda Henry, *Admin Sec*
▲ EMP: 20
SQ FT: 8,000
SALES (est): 798.6K **Privately Held**
WEB: www.rwcameronlaw.ca
SIC: 2731 Books: publishing only

(P-6143)
SADDLEBACK EDUCATIONAL
INC
151 Kalmus Dr Ste J1, Costa Mesa
(92626-5973)
PHONE...................................714 640-5224
Arianne M McHugh, *President*
Amber Dormanesh, *Prdtn Mgr*
▲ EMP: 20
SQ FT: 5,000
SALES (est): 3.1MM **Privately Held**
WEB: www.sdlback.com
SIC: 2731 5192 Book publishing; books

(P-6144)
SCHOLASTIC INC
4821 Charter St, Baldwin Park
(91706-2195)
PHONE...................................626 337-9996
Karen Stearn, *Branch Mgr*
EMP: 28
SALES (corp-wide): 1.6B **Publicly Held**
WEB: www.scholasticdealer.com
SIC: 2731 Textbooks: publishing only, not
printed on site
HQ: Scholastic Inc.
557 Broadway Lbby 1
New York NY 10012
212 343-6100

(P-6145)
SECRET ROAD MUSIC PUBG
INC
5850 Foothill Dr, Los Angeles
(90068-3622)
PHONE...................................323 464-1234
Lynn Grossman, *CEO*
EMP: 15 EST: 2010
SALES (est): 657.9K **Privately Held**
SIC: 2731 Books: publishing & printing

(P-6146)
SMILEY GROUP INC (PA)
4434 Crenshaw Blvd, Los Angeles
(90043-1208)
PHONE...................................323 290-4690
Tavis Smiley, *President*
Kimberly McFarland, *Executive Asst*
EMP: 10
SALES (est): 1.1MM **Privately Held**
WEB: www.tavistalks.com
SIC: 2731 Book publishing

(P-6147)
SOCIETY FOR THE STUDY NTIV
ART
Also Called: North Atlantic Books
2526 Mrtin Lther King Jr, Berkeley
(94704-2607)
PHONE...................................510 549-4270
Douglas Reil, *CEO*
Lindy Hough, *Treasurer*
Richard Grossinger, *Exec Dir*
Alla Spector, *Finance Dir*
Bryan Lovitz, *Purch Dir*
▲ EMP: 25
SQ FT: 6,000
SALES: 3.9MM **Privately Held**
WEB: www.northatlanticbooks.com
SIC: 2731 Books: publishing only

(P-6148)
STAMATS COMMUNICATIONS
INC
Also Called: Stamats Travel Group
550 Montgomery St Ste 750, San Francisco
(94111-2557)
PHONE...................................800 358-0388
Peters Stamats, *Branch Mgr*
EMP: 20
SALES (corp-wide): 21.8MM **Privately**
Held
WEB: www.stamatsinfo.com
SIC: 2731 2721 Pamphlets: publishing
only, not printed on site; magazines: pub-
lishing only, not printed on site
PA: Stamats Communications, Inc.
615 5th St Se
Cedar Rapids IA 52401
319 364-6167

(P-6149)
STONEYBROOK PUBLISHING INC
10815 Rncho Brnrdo Rd Ste, San Diego (92127)
PHONE..............................858 674-4600
Aaron Combs, *President*
Dave Stone, *CEO*
EMP: 21
SALES (est): 2.1MM **Privately Held**
WEB: www.dcmspec.com
SIC: 2731 2741 7331 Pamphlets: publishing only, not printed on site; newsletter publishing; direct mail advertising services

(P-6150)
TASCHEN AMERICA LLC (PA)
6671 W Sunset Blvd, Los Angeles (90028-7175)
PHONE..............................323 463-4441
Elissa Gomez, *Director*
Iris Ploetzer, *Admin Asst*
Creed Poulson, *Pub Rel Mgr*
Bernard Cummings, *Sales Staff*
Debra Schram, *Sales Staff*
▲ EMP: 13
SQ FT: 5,000
SALES (est): 2.2MM **Privately Held**
SIC: 2731 Books: publishing only

(P-6151)
TEACHER CREATED MATERIALS INC
5301 Oceanus Dr, Huntington Beach (92649-1030)
P.O. Box 1040 (92647-1040)
PHONE..............................714 891-2273
Rachelle Cracchiolo, *CEO*
Corinne Burton, *President*
Rich Levitt, *COO*
Kimberly Carlton, *Officer*
Eric Lemoine, *Officer*
▲ EMP: 110
SQ FT: 10,000
SALES (est): 21.2MM **Privately Held**
WEB: www.tcmpub.com
SIC: 2731 Textbooks: publishing only, not printed on site

(P-6152)
TEACHER CREATED RESOURCES INC
12621 Western Ave, Garden Grove (92841-4014)
PHONE..............................714 230-7060
Mary Diane Smith, *CEO*
Dan Bauer, *Graphic Designe*
Lisa Lemos, *Purchasing*
Dianne Kelly, *Marketing Staff*
Al Jobes, *Sales Staff*
◆ EMP: 100
SALES (est): 14.3MM **Privately Held**
SIC: 2731 Textbooks: publishing only, not printed on site

(P-6153)
TEACHERS CURRICULUM INST LLC (PA)
2440 W El Cam, Mountain View (94040)
P.O. Box 1327, Rancho Cordova (95741-1327)
PHONE..............................800 497-6138
Bert Bower, *Mng Member*
Nathan Wellborne, *Software Dev*
Jodi Forrest, *Prdtn Mgr*
Sarah Osentowski, *Production*
Christy Sanders, *Manager*
EMP: 24
SQ FT: 7,994
SALES: 28MM **Privately Held**
WEB: www.teachtci.com
SIC: 2731 8748 Books: publishing only; educational consultant

(P-6154)
THE MICROFILM COMPANY OF CAL
Also Called: Library Reproduction Service
14214 S Figueroa St, Los Angeles (90061-1034)
PHONE..............................310 354-2610
Joan Miller, *President*
Peter Jones, *Vice Pres*
EMP: 15 EST: 1946

SQ FT: 7,000
SALES (est): 1.5MM **Privately Held**
WEB: www.lrs-largeprint.com
SIC: 2731 7389 Books: publishing & printing; microfilm recording & developing service

(P-6155)
TOKYOPOP INC
5200 W Century Blvd Fl 7, Los Angeles (90045-5926)
PHONE..............................323 920-5967
Stuart J Levy, *President*
John Parker, *Vice Pres*
◆ EMP: 90
SQ FT: 8,699
SALES (est): 5.9MM **Privately Held**
WEB: www.tokyopop.com
SIC: 2731 3652 7812 7371 Books: publishing only; compact laser discs, prerecorded; video tape production; custom computer programming services; periodicals; entertainment promotion

(P-6156)
TORAH-AURA PRODUCTIONS INC
2710 Supply Ave, Commerce (90040-2704)
PHONE..............................323 585-1847
▲ EMP: 13 EST: 1982
SQ FT: 15,000
SALES (est): 1.3MM **Privately Held**
WEB: www.torahaura.com
SIC: 2731

(P-6157)
TRUCK CLUB PUBLISHING INC
7807 Telegraph Rd Ste H, Montebello (90640-6528)
PHONE..............................323 726-8620
Miguel A Machuca, *President*
EMP: 20
SALES (est): 1.9MM **Privately Held**
WEB: www.truckclubmagazine.com
SIC: 2731 Book publishing

(P-6158)
UNIVERSITY CAL PRESS FUNDATION (PA)
155 Grand Ave Ste 400, Oakland (94612-3764)
PHONE..............................510 642-4247
Lynne Withey, *President*
Richard C Atkinson, *President*
Mike Buczkowski, *Chief Mktg Ofcr*
Karen Maider, *Principal*
Deanna Evans, *Exec Dir*
▲ EMP: 100
SALES (est): 7.8MM **Privately Held**
SIC: 2731 Books: publishing only

(P-6159)
UNIVERSITY CAL PRESS FUNDATION
2000 Center St Ste 303, Berkeley (94704-1200)
PHONE..............................510 642-4247
Rebecca Symon, *Principal*
EMP: 25
SALES (corp-wide): 7.8MM **Privately Held**
SIC: 2731 Books: publishing only
PA: University Of California Press Foundation
155 Grand Ave Ste 400
Oakland CA 94612
510 642-4247

(P-6160)
UNIVERSITY CALIFORNIA BERKELEY
Also Called: University of California Press
155 Grand Ave Ste 400, Oakland (94612-3764)
PHONE..............................510 642-4247
Allison Mudditt, *Branch Mgr*
Anna Weidman, *CFO*
Brendan Tinney, *Officer*
Lynn Withey, *Administration*
Carolyn Wu, *Administration*
EMP: 20 **Privately Held**
WEB: www.law.berkeley.edu
SIC: 2731 8221 9411 Book publishing; university; administration of educational programs;

HQ: The University California Berkeley
200 Clfrnia Hall Spc 1500
Berkeley CA 94720
510 642-6000

(P-6161)
WEST PUBLISHING CORPORATION
Also Called: The Rutter Group
633 W 5th St Ste 2300, Los Angeles (90071-2049)
PHONE..............................800 747-3161
William Rutter, *Branch Mgr*
Bruce E Cooperman, *Partner*
Robert H Fairbank, *Partner*
Dennis L Greenwald, *Partner*
Mark Hagarty, *Partner*
EMP: 50
SALES (corp-wide): 10.6B **Publicly Held**
WEB: www.ruttergroup.com
SIC: 2731 8111 Book publishing; general practice attorney, lawyer
HQ: West Publishing Corporation
610 Opperman Dr
Eagan MN 55123
651 687-7000

(P-6162)
WHATEVER PUBLISHING INC
Also Called: New World Library
14 Pamaron Way Ste 1, Novato (94949-6215)
PHONE..............................415 884-2100
Marc Allen, *President*
Victoria Clarke, *CEO*
▲ EMP: 18
SQ FT: 6,000
SALES (est): 2.2MM **Privately Held**
WEB: www.newworldlibrary.com
SIC: 2731 Books: publishing only

(P-6163)
WILSHIRE BOOK COMPANY INC
22647 Ventura Blvd, Woodland Hills (91364-1416)
PHONE..............................818 700-1522
Melvin Powers, *President*
EMP: 22
SQ FT: 15,000
SALES: 5MM **Privately Held**
WEB: www.mpowers.com
SIC: 2731 5961 Textbooks: publishing only, not printed on site; mail order house

(P-6164)
WIXEN MUSIC PUBLISHING INC
24025 Park Sorrento # 130, Calabasas (91302-4018)
PHONE..............................818 591-7355
Randall Wixen, *President*
Matthew Fowler, *Client Mgr*
EMP: 15
SALES (est): 1.8MM **Privately Held**
WEB: www.wixenmusic.com
SIC: 2731 8111 Book music: publishing & printing; legal services

(P-6165)
WORKBOOK INC
110 N Doheny Dr, Beverly Hills (90211-1811)
PHONE..............................323 856-0008
Alexis Scott, *Principal*
Andy Carey, *Director*
Jacqueline Lopez, *Assistant*
Zach Thomas, *Editor*
▲ EMP: 20
SALES (est): 2.2MM **Privately Held**
SIC: 2731 Book publishing

(P-6166)
WORLD HARMONY ORGANIZATION
World Harmony Institute
514 Arballo Dr, San Francisco (94132-2163)
PHONE..............................415 246-6886
Francis Cw Fung, *President*
EMP: 10 **Privately Held**
SIC: 2731 Book publishing
PA: World Harmony Organization
24301 Suthland Dr Ste 405
Hayward CA 94545

(P-6167)
WORLDVIEW PROJECT
2445 Morena Blvd Ste 210, San Diego (92110-4157)
PHONE..............................858 964-0709
Thomas Johnston O Neill, *President*
Chris Bengs, *Principal*
William James, *Principal*
Shari Johnston-O'neill, *Principal*
EMP: 15
SALES (est): 13.6K **Privately Held**
WEB: www.worldviewpress.org
SIC: 2731 Book publishing

(P-6168)
YOSEMITE NATURAL HISTORY ASSN
Also Called: Yosemite Association
5020 El Portal Rd, El Portal (95318)
P.O. Box 230 (95318-0230)
PHONE..............................209 379-2646
Steven P Medley, *President*
Beth Pratt, *CFO*
Patricia Wight, *Admin Sec*
▲ EMP: 63
SQ FT: 1,500
SALES (est): 2.5MM **Privately Held**
WEB: www.yosemite.org
SIC: 2731 5942 Books: publishing only; book stores

(P-6169)
ZOOM BOOKZ LLC
10000 Fairway Dr Ste 140, Roseville (95678-3553)
PHONE..............................800 662-9982
Viktor Oleynik, *Mng Member*
EMP: 10
SALES (est): 368.2K **Privately Held**
SIC: 2731 4212 Book publishing; delivery service, vehicular

2732 Book Printing, Not Publishing

(P-6170)
CONSOLIDATED PRINTERS INC
2630 8th St, Berkeley (94710-2588)
PHONE..............................510 843-8524
Lawrence A Hawkins, *CEO*
Jim Fassett, *Vice Pres*
Paula Dudley, *Human Resources*
Ken Thorsen, *VP Mfg*
Mike Fave, *Mktg Dir*
EMP: 50
SQ FT: 60,000
SALES (est): 11.5MM **Privately Held**
WEB: www.consoprinters.com
SIC: 2732 2752 Books: printing & binding; commercial printing, lithographic

(P-6171)
COREFACT CORPORATION
20936 Cabot Blvd, Hayward (94545-1129)
PHONE..............................866 777-3986
Christopher Burnley, *President*
Jim Hammarstrom, *Vice Pres*
Cynthia Kwok, *Vice Pres*
Lisa Harris, *Graphic Designe*
Alex Kalajakis, *Graphic Designe*
EMP: 10
SQ FT: 16,000
SALES (est): 2.1MM **Privately Held**
SIC: 2732 7371 Book printing; computer software development

(P-6172)
HAMPTON-BROWN COMPANY LLC
1 Lower Ragsdale Dr # 1200, Monterey (93940-5749)
PHONE..............................831 620-6001
EMP: 10 EST: 2011
SALES (est): 510K **Privately Held**
SIC: 2732

2741 Misc Publishing

(P-6173)
ACCEPTED CO
2229 S Canfield Ave, Los Angeles
(90034-1114)
PHONE.................................310 815-9553
Linda Abraham, *President*
Mark Abraham, *CFO*
Jen Weld, *Regl Sales Mgr*
Sara Wolff, *Marketing Staff*
Cydney Foote, *Sr Consultant*
EMP: 14
SALES (est): 881.9K **Privately Held**
WEB: www.accepted.com
SIC: 2741 Miscellaneous publishing

(P-6174)
ADVANCED PUBLISHING TECH INC
1105 N Hollywood Way, Burbank
(91505-2528)
PHONE.................................818 557-3035
D Kraai, *Owner*
EMP: 18 **Privately Held**
SIC: 2741 Miscellaneous publishing
PA: Advanced Publishing Technology, Inc.
123 S Victory Blvd
Burbank CA 91502

(P-6175)
AGI PUBLISHING INC (PA)
Also Called: Valley Yellow Pages
1850 N Gateway Blvd # 152, Fresno
(93727-1600)
PHONE.................................559 251-8888
Sieg A Fischer, *CEO*
Steve Spring, *CFO*
Michael Schilling, *Treasurer*
Dominic D'Innocenti, *Senior VP*
Dominick Innocenti, *Vice Pres*
EMP: 50
SQ FT: 19,000
SALES (est): 128.2MM **Privately Held**
WEB: www.valleyyellowpages.com
SIC: 2741 Directories, telephone: publish-
ing only, not printed on site

(P-6176)
AGI PUBLISHING INC
Also Called: Valley Yellow Pages
1850 N Gateway Blvd # 152, Fresno
(93727-1600)
PHONE.................................559 251-8888
Karen Donner, *Human Res Mgr*
EMP: 136
SALES (corp-wide): 128.2MM **Privately
Held**
WEB: www.valleyyellowpages.com
SIC: 2741 Directories, telephone: publish-
ing only, not printed on site
PA: Agi Publishing, Inc.
1850 N Gateway Blvd # 152
Fresno CA 93727
559 251-8888

(P-6177)
AIR MARKETING
516 E 7th St, Long Beach (90813-4504)
PHONE.................................562 208-3990
Francisco Dominguez, *President*
EMP: 10
SALES (est): 269.4K **Privately Held**
SIC: 2741

(P-6178)
AIRCRAFT TECHNICAL PUBLISHERS (PA)
Also Called: Atp
2000 Sierra Point Pkwy # 501, Brisbane
(94005-1874)
PHONE.................................415 330-9500
Rick Noble, *CEO*
Stephen Gray, *CFO*
Mark Culpepper,
Ken Aubrey, *Officer*
Victor Sanchez, *Vice Pres*
EMP: 69
SQ FT: 28,000
SALES (est): 11.9MM **Privately Held**
WEB: www.atp.com
SIC: 2741 Miscellaneous publishing

(P-6179)
ALAMEDA DIRECTORY INC
Also Called: Oakland Magazine
1416 Park Ave, Alameda (94501-4520)
PHONE.................................510 747-1060
Tracy McKean, *President*
EMP: 16
SALES (est): 834.2K **Privately Held**
WEB: www.oaklandmagazine.com
SIC: 2741 Directories, telephone: publish-
ing only, not printed on site

(P-6180)
ALPHA I PUBLISHING INC
28400 Coachman Ln, Highland
(92346-2721)
P.O. Box 635 (92346-0635)
PHONE.................................909 862-9572
John Tillman, *President*
Shirley Hirst, *Vice Pres*
Roberta Tillman, *Vice Pres*
EMP: 11
SQ FT: 3,400
SALES (est): 760.9K **Privately Held**
WEB: www.alpha1pub.com
SIC: 2741 7311 Directories, telephone:
publishing only, not printed on site; adver-
tising agencies

(P-6181)
AMERICAN CLUBS LLC
Also Called: American Cellar Wine Club
4550 E Thousand Oaks Blvd, Westlake Vil-
lage (91362-3820)
PHONE.................................805 496-1218
Larry Dutra,
James Perdue,
EMP: 16 EST: 1997
SQ FT: 2,500
SALES (est): 1.4MM **Privately Held**
WEB: www.acwc.com
SIC: 2741 7331 Atlas, map & guide pub-
lishing; direct mail advertising services

(P-6182)
AMERICAN HISTORIC INNS INC
249 Forest Ave, Laguna Beach
(92651-2104)
P.O. Box 669, Dana Point (92629-0669)
PHONE.................................949 499-8070
Deborah Sakach, *CEO*
Jamee Danihels, *Office Mgr*
Diane Ringler, *Marketing Staff*
EMP: 16
SQ FT: 1,800
SALES (est): 1.3MM **Privately Held**
SIC: 2741 7011 Directories: publishing
only, not printed on site; hotels & motels

(P-6183)
AMERICAN SECURITY EDUCATORS
8734 Cleta St Ste E, Downey
(90241-5279)
P.O. Box 1337 (90240-0337)
PHONE.................................562 928-1847
Georgia Gonos Ananias, *President*
Dean Ananias, *Exec VP*
EMP: 10
SALES (est): 630K **Privately Held**
WEB: www.americansecurityeducators.com
SIC: 2741 8322 Miscellaneous publishing;
individual & family services

(P-6184)
AMERICAN SOCIETY OF COMPOSERS
Also Called: Ascap
7920 W Sunset Blvd # 300, Los Angeles
(90046-3300)
PHONE.................................323 883-1000
Daniel Gonzales, *General Mgr*
Moya Ashman, *Manager*
EMP: 30
SALES (corp-wide): 155.7MM **Privately
Held**
WEB: www.ascap.com
SIC: 2741 Miscellaneous publishing
PA: American Society Of Composers, Au-
thors And Publishers
250 W 57th St Ste 1300
New York NY 10107
212 621-6000

(P-6185)
AMERICAN SYSTEM PUBLICATIONS
3018 Carmel St, Los Angeles
(90065-1401)
P.O. Box 476, Pasadena (91102-0476)
PHONE.................................323 259-1867
Maureen Calney, *President*
EMP: 49
SALES (est): 3.4MM **Privately Held**
SIC: 2741 Miscellaneous publishing

(P-6186)
APARTMENT DIRECTORY OF L A
Also Called: Apartment Drctry L A-South Bay
2515 S Western Ave Ste 13, San Pedro
(90732-4643)
PHONE.................................310 832-0354
Glenn Kurtz, *Partner*
Armida Kurtz, *Partner*
EMP: 14
SALES (est): 953.8K **Privately Held**
SIC: 2741 7331 Directories: publishing &
printing; mailing list compilers

(P-6187)
ARENA PRESS
Also Called: Academic Therapy Publications
20 Leveroni Ct, Novato (94949-5746)
PHONE.................................415 883-3314
Anna Arena, *Administration*
EMP: 12 EST: 1980
SALES (est): 1MM **Privately Held**
WEB: www.academictherapy.com
SIC: 2741 Miscellaneous publishing

(P-6188)
ART BRAND STUDIOS LLC (PA)
18715 Madrone Pkwy, Morgan Hill
(95037-2876)
PHONE.................................408 201-5000
Steve Loveless,
EMP: 50
SQ FT: 40,000
SALES (est): 12MM **Privately Held**
SIC: 2741 6794 Art copy & poster publish-
ing; copyright buying & licensing

(P-6189)
ART IMPRESSIONS INC
23586 Calabasas Rd # 210, Calabasas
(91302-1319)
PHONE.................................818 591-0105
▲ **EMP:** 12
SALES (est): 1.2MM **Privately Held**
SIC: 2741

(P-6190)
ASSOC STUDENTS UNIVERSITY CA
Also Called: Bsr
112 Hearst Gym Rm 4520, Berkeley
(94720-3611)
PHONE.................................510 590-7874
Asako Miyakawa, *Branch Mgr*
EMP: 40
SALES (corp-wide): 1.9MM **Privately
Held**
SIC: 2741 8299 Miscellaneous publishing;
educational services
PA: Associated Students Of The University
Of California
Bancroft Way 400 Eshleman St Ban-
croft W
Berkeley CA 94704
510 642-5420

(P-6191)
ASSOCIATED DESERT SHOPPERS (DH)
Also Called: The White Sheet
73400 Highway 111, Palm Desert
(92260-3908)
PHONE.................................760 346-1729
Harold Paradis, *President*
Esperanza Barrett, *Treasurer*
Rey Verdugo Sr, *Vice Pres*
Joe Ayala, *MIS Staff*
EMP: 75
SQ FT: 4,000

SALES (est): 14.1MM
SALES (corp-wide): 1B **Publicly Held**
WEB: www.desertshoppers.net
SIC: 2741 7313 Shopping news: publish-
ing & printing; newspaper advertising rep-
resentative
HQ: Schurz Communications, Inc.
1301 E Douglas Rd Ste 200
Mishawaka IN 46545
574 247-7237

(P-6192)
AT&T CORP
Also Called: Advertising Solutions
8954 Rio San Diego Dr # 604, San Diego
(92108-1659)
PHONE.................................619 521-6100
Vanita Thurston, *Manager*
EMP: 222
SALES (corp-wide): 170.7B **Publicly
Held**
SIC: 2741 Miscellaneous publishing
HQ: At&T Corp.
1 At&T Way
Bedminster NJ 07921
800 403-3302

(P-6193)
AT&T CORP
Also Called: SBC
370 3rd St Rm 714, San Francisco
(94107-1250)
PHONE.................................415 542-9000
Tom Miller, *Manager*
EMP: 500
SALES (corp-wide): 170.7B **Publicly
Held**
WEB: www.swbell.com
SIC: 2741 4812 4813 Directories, telephone: publishing only, not printed on
site; cellular telephone services; paging
services; radio pager (beeper) communication services; data telephone communications; local telephone communications;
long distance telephone communications
HQ: At&T Corp.
1 At&T Way
Bedminster NJ 07921
800 403-3302

(P-6194)
AUDIENCE INC
5670 Wilshire Blvd # 100, Los Angeles
(90036-5686)
PHONE.................................323 413-2370
Oliver Luckett, *CEO*
Kate McLean, *President*
Jeffery Pressman, *COO*
EMP: 45
SALES (est): 4.5MM **Privately Held**
SIC: 2741 Miscellaneous publishing
PA: Al Ahli Holding Group
Dubai Al-Ain Road Route 66, Dubai
Outlet City, Blue Glasses
Dubai
442 346-66

(P-6195)
AUTOMOTIVE LEASE GUIDE ALG INC
120 Broadway Ste 200, Santa Monica
(90401-2385)
P.O. Box 61207, Santa Barbara (93160-
1207)
PHONE.................................424 258-8026
James Nguyen, *President*
Michael Guthrie, *CFO*
Eric Lyman, *Vice Pres*
Oliver Strauss, *Vice Pres*
Valeri Tompkins, *Vice Pres*
EMP: 44
SALES (est): 3.7MM
SALES (corp-wide): 353.5MM **Publicly
Held**
WEB: www.dealertrack.com
SIC: 2741 Guides: publishing only, not
printed on site
PA: Truecar, Inc.
120 Broadway Ste 200
Santa Monica CA 90401
800 200-2000

(P-6196)
B C YELLOW PAGES
1001 Bille Rd, Paradise (95969-3319)
PHONE.................................530 876-8616

(PA)=Parent Co (HQ)=Headquarters (DH)=Div Headquarters
✿ = New Business established in last 2 years

2020 California
Manufacturers Register

259

PRODUCTS & SVCS

Marco Orlando, *President*
EMP: 10
SALES (est): 420.8K **Privately Held**
SIC: 2741 Telephone & other directory
publishing

(P-6197)
B-FLAT PUBLISHING LLC
Also Called: Royce Records
9616 Macarthur Blvd, Oakland
(94605-4748)
PHONE..................510 639-7170
EMP: 13
SALES (est): 1MM **Privately Held**
SIC: 2741

(P-6198)
BAY AR YELLOW PAGES
46292 Warm Springs Blvd, Fremont
(94539-7997)
PHONE..................650 558-8888
Hua Su, *Manager*
EMP: 10
SALES (est): 366.1K **Privately Held**
SIC: 2741 Telephone & other directory
publishing

(P-6199)
**BINGO PUBLISHERS
INCORPORATED**
24881 Alicia Pkwy Ste E, Laguna Hills
(92653-4617)
PHONE..................949 581-5410
Charles Sloan, *President*
EMP: 20
SQ FT: 3,000
SALES: 1.5MM **Privately Held**
SIC: 2741 Miscellaneous publishing

(P-6200)
BIRDCAGE PRESS LLC
2320 Bowdoin St, Palo Alto (94306-1216)
PHONE..................650 462-6300
Wanda O Reilly, *Manager*
Maureen Kravitz, *Vice Pres*
Kelly Davis, *Graphic Designe*
EMP: 12
SALES (est): 1MM **Privately Held**
WEB: www.birdcagepress.com
SIC: 2741 Miscellaneous publishing

(P-6201)
BIRDEYE INC (PA)
250 Cambridge Ave Ste 103, Palo Alto
(94306-1554)
PHONE..................800 561-3357
Navee Gupta, *CEO*
Evan Manning, *Partner*
Rachel Randall, *Partner*
Chris Aker, *Officer*
Janelle Johnson, *Vice Pres*
EMP: 47
SALES (est): 13MM **Privately Held**
SIC: 2741

(P-6202)
**BLUE BOOK PUBLISHERS INC
(PA)**
Also Called: Coastal Graphics
9820 Willow Creek Rd # 410, San Diego
(92131-1115)
P.O. Box 561, La Jolla (92038-0561)
PHONE..................858 454-7939
Richard L Levin, *President*
Stephen Milne, *Exec VP*
Susan Davidson, *Vice Pres*
Brian Husebye, *Vice Pres*
Scott Levin, *Vice Pres*
EMP: 55
SQ FT: 13,000
SALES (est): 3.9MM **Privately Held**
WEB: www.lajollabluebook.com
SIC: 2741 Directories, telephone: publish-
ing only, not printed on site; guides: pub-
lishing only, not printed on site

(P-6203)
BLUEWATER PUBLISHING LLC
9040 Brentwood Blvd Ste B, Brentwood
(94513-4052)
P.O. Box 1598 (94513-3598)
PHONE..................925 634-0880
Karen J Spann,
James Spann,
Karen Spann,
EMP: 10

SQ FT: 2,000
SALES (est): 869.6K **Privately Held**
SIC: 2741 Miscellaneous publishing

(P-6204)
BOOKPACK INC
Also Called: Ulysses Press
3286 Adeline St Ste 1, Berkeley
(94703-2484)
P.O. Box 3440 (94703-0440)
PHONE..................510 601-8301
Ray Riegert, *President*
Leslie Henriques, *Corp Secy*
Claire Chun, *Prdtn Mgr*
▲ **EMP:** 10
SQ FT: 1,250
SALES (est): 1.1MM **Privately Held**
WEB: www.ulyssespress.com
SIC: 2741 2731 Guides: publishing only,
not printed on site; book clubs: publishing
only, not printed on site

(P-6205)
**BROADVISION RCAO
BROADVISI**
585 Broadway St, Redwood City
(94063-3122)
PHONE..................650 261-5100
Asher Kotz, *Partner*
Neil Pisane, *President*
Raina Arnold, *Program Mgr*
Ricky Nguyen, *CTO*
Chris Winquist, *Sales Staff*
EMP: 13 **EST:** 2008
SALES (est): 1.2MM **Privately Held**
SIC: 2741 Miscellaneous publishing

(P-6206)
**BROWNTROUT PUBLISHERS
INC (PA)**
201 Continental Blvd # 200, El Segundo
(90245-4514)
PHONE..................424 290-6122
William Michael Brown, *CEO*
Gray Peterson, *Vice Pres*
Femie Mueller, *Planning*
Neal Potter, *Finance*
Joleen Obrien, *Prdtn Mgr*
▲ **EMP:** 40
SQ FT: 11,000
SALES (est): 21.3MM **Privately Held**
SIC: 2741 Miscellaneous publishing

(P-6207)
BRUD INC
837 N Spring St Ste 101, Los Angeles
(90012-2594)
PHONE..................310 806-2283
Trevor McFedries, *President*
EMP: 17
SALES (est): 997.4K **Privately Held**
SIC: 2741

(P-6208)
BUY AND SELL PRESS INC
605 Broadway, Jackson (95642-2420)
PHONE..................209 223-3333
Emilio Prunetti, *President*
Craig Murphy, *Treasurer*
Dan Barnett, *Vice Pres*
Hazel Prunetti, *Admin Sec*
Donna Murphy, *Director*
EMP: 18
SQ FT: 2,000
SALES (est): 1.3MM **Privately Held**
WEB: www.buynsel.com
SIC: 2741 6512 Shopping news: publish-
ing & printing; nonresidential building op-
erators

(P-6209)
C PUBLISHING LLC
Also Called: C Magazine
1543 7th St Ste 202, Santa Monica
(90401-2645)
PHONE..................310 393-3800
Jennifer Smith Hale,
Nick Hale, *CFO*
Sandy Hubbard, *Info Tech Dir*
Debbie Flynn, *Director*
Avery Travis, *Director*
EMP: 25
SALES (est): 3.4MM **Privately Held**
SIC: 2741 Miscellaneous publishing

(P-6210)
C&T PUBLISHING INC
1651 Challenge Dr, Concord (94520-5206)
PHONE..................925 677-0377
J Todd Hensley, *CEO*
▲ **EMP:** 43
SQ FT: 12,250
SALES (est): 5.4MM **Privately Held**
WEB: www.ctpub.com
SIC: 2741 Miscellaneous publishing

(P-6211)
CASUAL FRIDAYS INC
Also Called: Social Media Day San Diego
3990 Old Town Ave A203, San Diego
(92110-2930)
PHONE..................858 433-1442
Tyler Anderson, *CEO*
William Vieux, *Vice Pres*
Michael Crump, *Principal*
EMP: 25
SALES (est): 1.3MM **Privately Held**
SIC: 2741

(P-6212)
CHI-AM COMICS DAILY INC
Also Called: Katherine Shih
673 Monterey Pass Rd, Monterey Park
(91754-2418)
PHONE..................626 281-2989
Katherine Shih, *President*
EMP: 10
SALES (est): 523.3K **Privately Held**
SIC: 2741 6531 Miscellaneous publishing;
real estate agents & managers

(P-6213)
**CHINESE OVERSEAS MKTG SVC
CORP**
33420 Alvarado Niles Rd, Union City
(94587-3110)
PHONE..................510 476-0880
Alan KAO, *President*
EMP: 50
SALES (corp-wide): 1.5MM **Privately
Held**
WEB: www.ccyp.com
SIC: 2741 7389 Directories, telephone:
publishing only, not printed on site; trade
show arrangement
PA: Chinese Overseas Marketing Service
Corporation
3940 Rosemead Blvd
Rosemead CA 91770
626 280-8588

(P-6214)
**CHINESE OVERSEAS MKTG SVC
CORP**
Also Called: Chinese Consumer Yellow
Pages
46292 Warm Springs Blvd, Fremont
(94539-7997)
PHONE..................626 280-8588
Gorden KAO, *Branch Mgr*
EMP: 40
SALES (corp-wide): 1.5MM **Privately
Held**
WEB: www.ccyp.com
SIC: 2741 7389 8742 Directories, tele-
phone: publishing only, not printed on
site; trade show arrangement; marketing
consulting services
PA: Chinese Overseas Marketing Service
Corporation
3940 Rosemead Blvd
Rosemead CA 91770
626 280-8588

(P-6215)
**CHINESE OVERSEAS MKTG SVC
CORP (PA)**
Also Called: Chinese Consumer Yellow
Pages
3940 Rosemead Blvd, Rosemead
(91770-1952)
PHONE..................626 280-8588
Alan KAO, *President*
Gorden KAO, *Director*
Alice Chen, *Accounts Exec*
▲ **EMP:** 60
SQ FT: 9,298

SALES: 1.5MM **Privately Held**
WEB: www.ccyp.com
SIC: 2741 7389 8742 Directories, telephone: publishing only, not printed on
site; trade show arrangement; marketing
consulting services

(P-6216)
COBRA SYSTEMS
Remindersstickers Div
3521 E Enterprise Dr, Anaheim
(92807-1604)
PHONE..................714 688-7992
Wendy Mazurier, *Branch Mgr*
EMP: 10
SALES (corp-wide): 4MM **Privately Held**
SIC: 2741 Miscellaneous publishing
PA: Cobra Systems
3521 E Enterprise Dr
Anaheim CA 92807
714 688-7999

(P-6217)
**CRITTENDEN PUBLISHING INC
(HQ)**
45 Leveroni Ct Ste 204, Novato
(94949-5721)
P.O. Box 1150 (94948-1150)
PHONE..................415 475-1522
Alan Crittenden, *CEO*
Allen Crittenden, *President*
David Berger, *Principal*
Teresa Moody, *Principal*
Eva Nickel-Raudio, *Human Res Mgr*
EMP: 19 **EST:** 1980
SQ FT: 9,500
SALES (est): 1.8MM
SALES (corp-wide): 6.6MM **Privately
Held**
WEB: www.crittendenonline.com
SIC: 2741 2721 Newsletter publishing; pe-
riodicals
PA: Crittenden Research Inc
45 Leveroni Ct
Novato CA
415 475-1576

(P-6218)
CTG I LLC
Also Called: Cleantech Group
600 California St Fl 11, San Francisco
(94108-2727)
PHONE..................415 233-9700
Richard Youngman, *CEO*
Nicholas Parker, *Co-Founder*
Keith Raab, *Co-Founder*
Jules Besnainou, *Director*
Stephen Marcus, *Director*
EMP: 12
SALES (est): 573.3K **Privately Held**
SIC: 2741 Miscellaneous publishing

(P-6219)
DAISY SCOUT PUBLISHING
1200 N Barsten Way, Anaheim
(92806-1822)
PHONE..................714 630-6611
Athena Cox, *Owner*
EMP: 10
SALES (est): 656.4K **Privately Held**
SIC: 2741 Miscellaneous publishing

(P-6220)
DANIELS INC (PA)
Also Called: Big Nickel
74745 Leslie Ave, Palm Desert
(92260-2030)
PHONE..................801 621-3355
Daniel Murphy, *President*
Dennis Porter, *Corp Secy*
EMP: 23
SQ FT: 10,000
SALES: 1.5MM **Privately Held**
SIC: 2741 Shopping news: publishing &
printing

(P-6221)
DINNER ON A DOLLAR INC
10249 Caminito Pitaya, San Diego
(92131-2010)
PHONE..................858 693-3939
EMP: 11
SALES (est): 730K **Privately Held**
SIC: 2741

▲ = Import ▼=Export
◆ =Import/Export

(P-6222)
DIVERSIFIED PRINTERS INC
12834 Maxwell Dr, Tustin (92782-0914)
PHONE..............................714 994-3400
Kenneth Bittner, *President*
Paul R Nassar, *CFO*
Jerry Tominaga, *Exec VP*
EMP: 51
SQ FT: 105,000
SALES (est): 9.8MM **Privately Held**
WEB: www.diversifiedprinters.com
SIC: 2741 2759 2789 Directories: publish-
ing & printing; commercial printing; book-
binding & related work

(P-6223)
DLIVE INC
19450 Stevens Creek Blvd, Cupertino
(95014-2503)
PHONE..............................650 491-9555
Charles Wayn, *CEO*
EMP: 20
SALES (est): 619.3K **Privately Held**
SIC: 2741

(P-6224)
ECONODAY INC
3730 Mt Diablo Blvd # 340, Lafayette
(94549-3641)
P.O. Box 954 (94549-0954)
PHONE..............................925 299-5350
Cynthia Parker, *President*
June Moberg, *Admin Sec*
Anne Picker, *Deputy Dir*
EMP: 17
SQ FT: 1,200
SALES: 1MM **Privately Held**
WEB: www.econoday.com
SIC: 2741 · Miscellaneous publishing

(P-6225)
ECT NEWS NETWORK INC
16133 Ventura Blvd # 700, Encino
(91436-2403)
P.O. Box 18500 (91416-8500)
PHONE..............................818 461-9700
Richard Kern, *Principal*
EMP: 15
SALES (est): 982.2K **Privately Held**
WEB: www.ectnews.com
SIC: 2741

(P-6226)
EDIRECT PUBLISHING INC
Also Called: Resumemailman
3451 Via Montebello # 192, Carlsbad
(92009-8492)
PHONE..............................760 602-8300
Lee Marc, *CEO*
Melisa Cochran, *Opers Staff*
EMP: 12
SALES (est): 917.7K **Privately Held**
WEB: www.execs-direct.com
SIC: 2741 5961   ;

(P-6227)
EL CLASIFICADO
1125 Goodrich Blvd, Commerce
(90022-5104)
P.O. Box 227310, Los Angeles (90022-
0750)
PHONE..............................323 278-5310
EMP: 100
SALES (corp-wide): 11.2MM **Privately
Held**
SIC: 2741
PA: El Clasificado
   11205 Imperial Hwy
   Norwalk CA 90650
   323 837-4095

(P-6228)
ELSEVIER INC
525 B St Ste 1650, San Diego
(92101-4497)
PHONE..............................619 231-6616
Kristen Chrisman, *Branch Mgr*
Sal Gelardi, *Senior VP*
Allan Wright, *Marketing Mgr*
Brenna Coffey, *Senior Mgr*
Steven Emmert, *Director*
EMP: 67
SALES (corp-wide): 9.6B **Privately Held**
SIC: 2741 Miscellaneous publishing

HQ: Elsevier Inc.
   230 Park Ave Fl 8
   New York NY 10169
   212 989-5800

(P-6229)
EMPLOYERWARE LLC
Also Called: Poster Compliance Center
3687 Mt Diablo Blvd 100a, Lafayette
(94549-3777)
PHONE..............................925 283-9735
Maurice Levich,
Terry Hughes, *Controller*
Eileen Kearnes, *Cust Mgr*
Margaret Lennon, *Manager*
EMP: 33
SQ FT: 2,500
SALES (est): 3.1MM **Privately Held**
WEB: www.employerware.com
SIC: 2741 8748 Miscellaneous publishing;
publishing consultant

(P-6230)
EQUITY FORD RESEARCH
11722 Sorrento Valley Rd I, San Diego
(92121-1021)
PHONE..............................858 755-1327
Timothy R Alward, *President*
Jonathan Worrall, *Chairman*
Richard Segarra, *CTO*
Stephen Cicero, *Software Dev*
Albert Chan, *Financial Analy*
EMP: 18
SQ FT: 5,500
SALES (est): 1.3MM **Privately Held**
WEB: www.fordupdate.com
SIC: 2741 6282 Miscellaneous publishing;
investment advice

(P-6231)
EXPRESS CHIPPING
418 Goetz Ave, Santa Ana (92707-3710)
PHONE..............................562 789-8058
Mike Pla, *Owner*
John Pla, *President*
EMP: 12
SALES (est): 1.1MM **Privately Held**
SIC: 2741 Miscellaneous publishing

(P-6232)
EXPRESS FOLDING
21250 Hawthorne Blvd, Torrance
(90503-5506)
PHONE..............................310 316-6762
Mark Nelson, *Owner*
EMP: 45
SALES (est): 1.4MM **Privately Held**
SIC: 2741 Miscellaneous publishing

(P-6233)
EXPRESS IT DELIVERS
168 Mason Way Ste B5, City of Industry
(91746-2339)
PHONE..............................626 855-1294
Paul Grassia, *Owner*
EMP: 50
SALES (est): 1.3MM **Privately Held**
SIC: 2741 Miscellaneous publishing

(P-6234)
**FEDERAL BUYERS GUIDE INC
(PA)**
Also Called: Government Travel Directory
324 Palm Ave, Santa Barbara
(93101-1727)
P.O. Box 41108 (93140-1108)
PHONE..............................805 963-7470
Stuart Miller, *President*
Cory Oltmer, *CFO*
Afzal Hussain, *Exec VP*
EMP: 12
SQ FT: 3,500
SALES (est): 1.2MM **Privately Held**
WEB: www.federalbuyersguideinc.com
SIC: 2741 Guides: publishing & printing

(P-6235)
FINAL DATA INC
5950 Canoga Ave Ste 220, Woodland Hills
(91367-5066)
PHONE..............................818 835-9560
Chae Lee, *President*
Akira Katanosaka, *Vice Pres*
EMP: 30
SALES: 2.7MM **Privately Held**
SIC: 2741 Miscellaneous publishing

(P-6236)
FINDDOCTR INC
9550 Bolsa Ave Ste 213, Westminster
(92683-5947)
PHONE..............................657 888-2629
Thu Thai, *President*
EMP: 10
SALES (est): 261K **Privately Held**
SIC: 2741

(P-6237)
FIRST DATABANK INC (DH)
Also Called: First Data Bank
701 Gateway Blvd Ste 600, South San
Francisco (94080-7084)
PHONE..............................800 633-3453
Gregory H Dorn, *President*
Don Nielsen, *President*
James Schultz, *Treasurer*
Bob Katter, *Exec VP*
Clifton Louie, *Exec VP*
EMP: 74
SALES (est): 27.5MM
SALES (corp-wide): 8.3B **Privately Held**
WEB: www.firstdatabank.com
SIC: 2741 7375 Technical manuals: pub-
lishing only, not printed on site; micropub-
lishing; information retrieval services; data
base information retrieval
HQ: Hearst Business Media Corp
   2620 Barrett Rd
   Gainesville GA 30507
   770 532-4111

(P-6238)
FOODBEAST INC
305 W 4th St, Santa Ana (92701-4502)
PHONE..............................949 344-2634
Geoff Kutnick, *CEO*
Geoffrey Kutnick, *Partner*
Elie Ayrouth, *President*
Rudolph Chaney, *CTO*
Evan Lancaster, *Internal Med*
EMP: 16
SQ FT: 2,500
SALES: 2MM **Privately Held**
SIC: 2741

(P-6239)
FRANKLIN COVEY CO
3333 Michelson Dr Ste 400, Irvine
(92612-1684)
PHONE..............................949 788-8102
Maryann Bothers, *Manager*
EMP: 23
SALES (corp-wide): 209.7MM **Publicly
Held**
SIC: 2741 Miscellaneous publishing
PA: Franklin Covey Co.
   2200 W Parkway Blvd
   Salt Lake City UT 84119
   801 817-1776

(P-6240)
FRONTIERS MEDIA LLC
Also Called: Frontiers Magazine
5657 Wilshire Blvd # 470, Los Angeles
(90036-3736)
PHONE..............................323 930-3220
EMP: 50
SALES: 3.7MM **Privately Held**
SIC: 2741

(P-6241)
FUNDX INVESTMENT GROUP
Also Called: Fundex Investment Group
235 Montgomery St # 1049, San Francisco
(94104-3008)
PHONE..............................415 986-7979
Janet Brown, *President*
Jeffrey Smith, *Principal*
Dannielle Kimpel, *Executive Asst*
Jason Browne, *Portfolio Mgr*
EMP: 18
SQ FT: 2,000
SALES (est): 2MM **Privately Held**
WEB: www.dal-investment.com
SIC: 2741 6282 Newsletter publishing; in-
vestment advisory service

(P-6242)
GAYOT PUBLICATIONS
1744 Sunset Ave, Santa Monica
(90405-5920)
PHONE..............................323 965-3529
Andry Gayot, *Owner*

Jeremy Jeffers, *Business Mgr*
Jana Montgomery, *Personnel*
Becky Sauer, *Assoc Editor*
Harriet Callier, *Manager*
EMP: 20
SALES (est): 996.9K **Privately Held**
SIC: 2741 Miscellaneous publishing

(P-6243)
GLOBAL COMPLIANCE INC
Also Called: Compliance Poster
438 W Chestnut Ave Ste A, Monrovia
(91016-1129)
P.O. Box 607 (91017-0607)
PHONE..............................626 303-6855
Patricia A Blum, *President*
John Nielsen, *Corp Comm Staff*
EMP: 25
SALES (est): 3.5MM **Privately Held**
WEB: www.complianceposter.com
SIC: 2741 Posters: publishing & printing

(P-6244)
GMM INC
Also Called: Creative Industry Handbooks
10152 Riverside Dr, Toluca Lake
(91602-2532)
PHONE..............................323 874-1600
Carl Rovsek, *President*
Blythe Rovsek, *Vice Pres*
EMP: 20
SALES (est): 1.7MM **Privately Held**
WEB: www.creativehandbook.com
SIC: 2741 Newsletter publishing

(P-6245)
GOFF INVESTMENT GROUP LLC
Also Called: Global Printing Sourcing & Dev
135 3rd St Ste 150, San Rafael
(94901-3531)
PHONE..............................415 456-2934
Steven Goff, *Managing Dir*
▲ **EMP:** 11
SQ FT: 3,000
SALES (est): 1.7MM **Privately Held**
WEB: www.globalpsd.com
SIC: 2741 Miscellaneous publishing

(P-6246)
GOOD WORLDWIDE LLC
6380 Wilshire Blvd # 1500, Los Angeles
(90048-5003)
PHONE..............................323 206-6495
Ben Goldhirsh,
Michelle Medlock, *Manager*
EMP: 44
SALES: 950K **Privately Held**
SIC: 2741 Miscellaneous publishing

(P-6247)
GRAPHIQ LLC
101a Innovation Pl, Santa Barbara
(93108-2268)
P.O. Box 1259, Summerland (93067-1259)
PHONE..............................805 335-2433
Kevin Oconnor, *President*
Ivan Bercovich, *President*
Victoria Roebuck, *Executive*
Scott Leonard, *CTO*
Dan Tobin, *Director*
EMP: 120 EST: 2009
SALES: 9.9MM **Publicly Held**
SIC: 2741 4813   ;
PA: Amazon.Com, Inc.
   410 Terry Ave N
   Seattle WA 98109

(P-6248)
**GUADALUPE ASSOCIATES INC
(PA)**
Also Called: Ignatius Press
1348 10th Ave, San Francisco
(94122-2304)
PHONE..............................415 387-2324
Mark Brumley, *CEO*
Jack Gergurich, *Accountant*
Meryl Amland, *Production*
Carolyn Lemon, *Production*
Vivian Dudro, *Assoc Editor*
◆ **EMP:** 15
SQ FT: 1,500
SALES: 2.9MM **Privately Held**
WEB: www.catecheticalresources.com
SIC: 2741 2731 Miscellaneous publishing;
books: publishing only

PRODUCTS & SVCS

(P-6249)
HADLEY MEDIA INC
1665 S Ranch Santa Fe Rd, San Marcos
(92078)
PHONE......................................800 270-2084
Patrick Hadley, *President*
Daniel Hadley, *Principal*
Katherine Hadley, *Project Mgr*
EMP: 15
SALES (est): 1.1MM **Privately Held**
WEB: www.hadleymedia.com
SIC: 2741 Catalogs: publishing only, not
printed on site

(P-6250)
HEALTHLINE MEDIA INC
660 3rd St, San Francisco (94107-1927)
PHONE......................................415 281-3100
David Kopp, *CEO*
Cheryl Kim, *CFO*
Andy Atherton, *Senior VP*
Laurie Dewan, *Vice Pres*
Tracy Rosecrans, *Vice Pres*
EMP: 300
SALES (est): 46MM **Privately Held**
SIC: 2741

(P-6251)
HIGHWIRE PRESS INC (PA)
15575 Los Gatos Blvd A, Los Gatos
(95032-2569)
PHONE......................................650 721-6388
Dan Filby, *CEO*
EMP: 26
SALES (est): 2.9MM **Privately Held**
SIC: 2741 Miscellaneous publishing

(P-6252)
**HOMEFACTS MANAGEMENT
LLC**
Also Called: Homefacts.com
1 Venture Ste 300, Irvine (92618-7416)
PHONE......................................949 502-8300
Cabell Cobbs, *Principal*
EMP: 15
SQ FT: 3,750
SALES (est): 545.6K **Privately Held**
SIC: 2741

(P-6253)
HOMESTEAD PUBLISHING INC
4388 17th St, San Francisco (94114-1888)
PHONE......................................307 733-6248
Carl A Schreier, *President*
EMP: 20
SALES (est): 1.2MM **Privately Held**
SIC: 2741 Miscellaneous publishing

(P-6254)
IBISWORLD INC
11755 Wilshire Blvd # 1100, Los Angeles
(90025-1506)
PHONE......................................212 626-6794
Justin Ruthven, *President*
EMP: 50
SALES (est): 1.4MM **Privately Held**
WEB: www.ibisworld.com
SIC: 2741 Miscellaneous publishing

(P-6255)
INFORMA BUSINESS MEDIA INC
Sourceesb
16815 Von Karman Ave # 150, Irvine
(92606-2406)
PHONE......................................949 252-1146
Tam Nguyen, *Branch Mgr*
EMP: 30
SALES (corp-wide): 3B **Privately Held**
SIC: 2741 Directories: publishing only, not
printed on site
HQ: Informa Business Media, Inc.
605 3rd Ave
New York NY 10158
212 204-4200

(P-6256)
**INGRAM PUBLISHER SERVICES
LLC**
1700 4th St, Berkeley (94710-1711)
PHONE......................................510 528-1444
Richard C Freese, *President*
Geoffrey V Sutton, *Author*
EMP: 67
SALES (corp-wide): 3.9B **Privately Held**
SIC: 2741 Miscellaneous publishing

HQ: Ingram Publisher Services Llc
1 Ingram Blvd
La Vergne TN 37086
615 213-5000

(P-6257)
**INSTITUTIONAL REAL ESTATE
(PA)**
1475 N Broadway Ste 300, Walnut Creek
(94596-4643)
PHONE......................................925 933-4040
Geoffrey Dohrmann, *CEO*
Nyia Dohrman, *President*
Erika Cohen, *COO*
Jonathan A Schein, *Senior VP*
Jenny Guerrero, *Accounting Mgr*
EMP: 20
SQ FT: 3,000
SALES (est): 1.3MM **Privately Held**
WEB: www.irei.com
SIC: 2741 8742 8748 2721 Newsletter
publishing; real estate consultant; busi-
ness consulting; periodicals

(P-6258)
**JACK BRAIN AND ASSOCIATES
INC**
20819 Nunes Ave, Castro Valley
(94546-5741)
PHONE......................................510 889-1360
Jack Brain, *President*
Karrie Brain Marsh, *Treasurer*
Shirley Brain, *Admin Sec*
EMP: 10
SQ FT: 4,000
SALES (est): 820K **Privately Held**
WEB: www.jackbrain.com
SIC: 2741 6513 Newsletter publishing;
apartment building operators

(P-6259)
JENNIS GROUP LLC
Also Called: Pinecone Press
1631 Placentia Ave, Costa Mesa
(92627-4311)
PHONE......................................714 227-7972
Debra Jennis, *President*
Alex Jennis, *Principal*
Walter Jennis, *Principal*
EMP: 11
SALES (est): 700K **Privately Held**
SIC: 2741 2621 Miscellaneous publishing;
magazine paper

(P-6260)
JIGSAW DATA CORPORATION
900 Concar Dr, San Mateo (94402-2600)
PHONE......................................650 235-8400
James Fowler, *President*
Barry Friefield, *Partner*
Steven Klei, *CFO*
Garth Moulton, *Vice Pres*
EMP: 16
SALES (est): 1.5MM
SALES (corp-wide): 13.2B **Publicly Held**
SIC: 2741 Telephone & other directory
publishing
PA: Salesforce.Com, Inc.
415 Mission St Fl 3
San Francisco CA 94105
415 901-7000

(P-6261)
**JONES GLYN PRODUCTIONS
INC**
1945 Camino Vida Roble M, Carlsbad
(92008-6529)
PHONE......................................760 431-8955
EMP: 10
SQ FT: 4,500
SALES (est): 879.8K **Privately Held**
WEB: www.glynjones.com
SIC: 2741

(P-6262)
JOSEPH CHARLES WHITSON
Also Called: Adventures In Personal Cmpt
154 Auburn Way, Vacaville (95688-3561)
PHONE......................................707 694-8806
Joseph C Whitson, *Principal*
EMP: 10
SALES (est): 65.1K **Privately Held**
SIC: 2741 Miscellaneous publishing

(P-6263)
JOURNEYWORKS PUBLISHING
763 Chestnut St, Santa Cruz (95060-3751)
P.O. Box 8466 (95061-8466)
PHONE......................................831 423-1400
Steven Bignell, *President*
EMP: 16
SQ FT: 5,200
SALES (est): 2MM **Privately Held**
WEB: www.journeyworks.com
SIC: 2741 Miscellaneous publishing

(P-6264)
JUMPER MEDIA LLC
4747 Morena Blvd Ste 201, San Diego
(92117-3467)
PHONE......................................831 333-6202
Colton Bollinger, *CEO*
Gian Pepe,
Peter Sercia,
EMP: 99
SALES (est): 4.3MM **Privately Held**
SIC: 2741

(P-6265)
KAN GROUP CORP
3807 Wilshire Blvd # 518, Los Angeles
(90010-3101)
PHONE......................................213 383-1236
Michelle Parks, *President*
EMP: 15
SALES (est): 691.4K **Privately Held**
SIC: 2741 Miscellaneous publishing

(P-6266)
KUDOS&CO INC
470 Ramona St, Palo Alto (94301-1707)
PHONE......................................650 799-9104
Ole Vidar Hestaas, *CEO*
EMP: 25
SALES (est): 616.5K **Privately Held**
SIC: 2741

(P-6267)
**LA XPRESS AIR & HEATING
SVCS**
6400 E Wash Blvd Ste 121, Commerce
(90040-1820)
PHONE......................................310 856-9678
Jesus A Chavez, *CEO*
EMP: 67 EST: 2013
SALES (est): 108.4K **Privately Held**
SIC: 2741 Miscellaneous publishing

(P-6268)
LARSON BROTHERS
5665 E Westover Ave # 101, Fresno
(93727-8650)
PHONE......................................559 292-8161
Jeff Larson, *Partner*
Tom Larson, *Partner*
Luz Ehrastom, *Office Mgr*
EMP: 12
SQ FT: 2,500
SALES (est): 1.2MM **Privately Held**
WEB: www.larsonbrothers.com
SIC: 2741 7221 Yearbooks: publishing &
printing; school photographer

(P-6269)
LEADMMATIC LLC
5154 Don Pio Dr, Woodland Hills
(91364-1730)
PHONE......................................310 857-4511
Aaron Beck, *Branch Mgr*
EMP: 21
SALES (corp-wide): 2.5MM **Privately
Held**
SIC: 2741
PA: Leadmmatic, Llc
15021 Ventura Blvd # 104
Sherman Oaks CA 91403
310 857-4511

(P-6270)
LEE & FIELDS PUBLISHING INC
3731 Wilshire Blvd # 940, Los Angeles
(90010-2827)
PHONE......................................213 380-5858
Edward Y Lee, *President*
EMP: 12
SALES (est): 820K **Privately Held**
SIC: 2741 Miscellaneous publishing

(P-6271)
**LELAND STANFORD JUNIOR
UNIV**
Also Called: Stanford University Libraries
557 Escondido Mall, Stanford
(94305-6001)
PHONE......................................650 723-5553
Robert Phillips, *Branch Mgr*
Odile Disch-Bhadkamka, *Managing Dir*
Debbie Barros, *Administration*
Alicia Middleton, *Research*
Angela Vidergar, *Research*
EMP: 106
SQ FT: 10,000
SALES (corp-wide): 11.3B **Privately Held**
SIC: 2741 8221 Miscellaneous publishing;
university
PA: Leland Stanford Junior University
450 Jane Stanford Way
Stanford CA 94305
650 723-2300

(P-6272)
**LELAND STANFORD JUNIOR
UNIV**
Also Called: Stanford Humanities Review
424 Matison Ave, Stanford (94305)
PHONE......................................650 723-3052
Stefano Franch, *Editor*
EMP: 103
SALES (corp-wide): 11.3B **Privately Held**
SIC: 2741 8221 Miscellaneous publishing;
university
PA: Leland Stanford Junior University
450 Jane Stanford Way
Stanford CA 94305
650 723-2300

(P-6273)
**LELAND STANFORD JUNIOR
UNIV**
Also Called: Institute For Intl Studies
559 Nathan Abbott Way, Stanford
(94305-8602)
PHONE......................................650 723-4455
Larry Kramer, *Principal*
EMP: 100
SALES (corp-wide): 11.3B **Privately Held**
SIC: 2741 8221 2721 Technical manuals:
publishing & printing; colleges universities
& professional schools; periodicals
PA: Leland Stanford Junior University
450 Jane Stanford Way
Stanford CA 94305
650 723-2300

(P-6274)
LOG(N) LLC
5651 Dreyer Pl, Oakland (94619-3109)
PHONE......................................323 839-4538
Jinal Jhaveri, *Mng Member*
Forum Desai, *COO*
Diane Tiu, *General Mgr*
EMP: 12
SALES (est): 795.7K **Privately Held**
SIC: 2741 7379 ; computer related con-
sulting services

(P-6275)
LYRA CORPORATION
Also Called: M & H Type Composition &
Fndry
1802 Hays St, San Francisco (94129-1197)
PHONE......................................415 668-2546
Andrew Hoyem, *President*
Barry Traub, *Admin Sec*
EMP: 11 EST: 1961
SQ FT: 10,000
SALES (est): 1.4MM **Privately Held**
WEB: www.arionpress.com
SIC: 2741 Miscellaneous publishing

(P-6276)
M G A INVESTMENT CO INC
Also Called: Easy Ad Magazine
3211 Broad St Ste 201, San Luis Obispo
(93401-6770)
PHONE......................................805 543-9050
Jackie Koda, *Administration*
EMP: 15
SQ FT: 2,000

SALES (est): 1.6MM **Privately Held**
WEB: www.photo-ad.com
SIC: 2741 2721 Shopping news: publishing only, not printed on site; magazines: publishing only, not printed on site

(P-6277)
MARCOA MEDIA LLC (PA)
9955 Black Mountain Rd, San Diego (92126-4514)
P.O. Box 509100 (92150-9100)
PHONE..........................858 635-9627
Michael Martella, *Mng Member*
Scott Ogan, *Exec Dir*
Anthony Kuh, *Project Mgr*
Smith Robin, *Project Mgr*
Alfonso Santana, *Graphic Designe*
EMP: 40
SQ FT: 40,000
SALES (est): 13MM **Privately Held**
WEB: www.marcoa.com
SIC: 2741 Atlas, map & guide publishing

(P-6278)
MARCOA QUALITY PUBLISHING LLC
9955 Black Mountain Rd, San Diego (92126-4514)
P.O. Box 509100 (92150-9100)
PHONE..........................858 695-9600
Quinn Smith,
EMP: 99
SALES (est): 950K **Privately Held**
SIC: 2741 Miscellaneous publishing

(P-6279)
MCCORMACKS GUIDES INC
3211 Elmquist Ct, Martinez (94553-3150)
P.O. Box 190 (94553-0190)
PHONE..........................925 229-1869
Don McCormack, *President*
EMP: 10
SALES (est): 91.7K **Privately Held**
SIC: 2741 Guides: publishing only, not printed on site

(P-6280)
MESGONA CORPORATION
12534 Moorpark St Apt H, Studio City (91604-1357)
PHONE..........................310 926-3238
Seyedrasool Sadrieh, *President*
EMP: 10
SALES (est): 261K **Privately Held**
SIC: 2741

(P-6281)
MID MICHIGAN TRADING POST LTD
Also Called: Wheeler Deeler
5200 Lankershim Blvd # 350, North Hollywood (91601-3155)
P.O. Box 389, Dimondale MI (48821-0389)
PHONE..........................517 323-9020
Patrick D Karslake, *President*
Gretchen Karslake, *Admin Sec*
EMP: 90
SQ FT: 3,200
SALES (est): 6.3MM **Privately Held**
WEB: www.wheelerdeeler.com
SIC: 2741 2752 2721 Shopping news: publishing only, not printed on site; commercial printing, offset; periodicals

(P-6282)
MIGHTY NETWORKS INC
2690 N Beachwood Dr Fl 2, Los Angeles (90068-2308)
PHONE..........................323 464-1050
David Gale, *CEO*
Carol Levey, *Consultant*
EMP: 12
SALES (est): 1.3MM **Privately Held**
SIC: 2741

(P-6283)
MITCHELL REPAIR INFO CO LLC (HQ)
Also Called: Mitchell1
14145 Danielson St Ste A, Poway (92064-8827)
PHONE..........................858 391-5000
David Ellingen,
Ken Young, *Exec VP*
David Niemiec, *Vice Pres*

Lon Mok, *Administration*
Michael Nolan, *Administration*
EMP: 20 **EST:** 1996
SALES (est): 37.5MM
SALES (corp-wide): 3.7B **Publicly Held**
WEB: www.mitchellrepair.com
SIC: 2741 2731 5251 Technical manuals: publishing only, not printed on site; book publishing; hardware
PA: Snap-On Incorporated
2801 80th St
Kenosha WI 53143
262 656-5200

(P-6284)
MODERNPRO LLC
15 Woodcrest Ln, Aliso Viejo (92656-2125)
PHONE..........................949 232-2148
Scott Esposto, *President*
EMP: 10
SALES (est): 615.9K **Privately Held**
SIC: 2741 7812 7221 8748 ; motion picture & video production; music video production; photographer, still or video; business consulting

(P-6285)
MONGABAYORG CORPORATION
37 W Summit Dr, Emerald Hills (94062-3340)
PHONE..........................209 315-5573
Rhett Butler, *President*
EMP: 24 **EST:** 2011
SALES (est): 1.1MM **Privately Held**
SIC: 2741

(P-6286)
MOTHERLY INC
1725 Oakdell Dr, Menlo Park (94025-5735)
PHONE..........................917 860-9926
Christina Cubeta, *COO*
EMP: 24
SALES (est): 600K **Privately Held**
SIC: 2741

(P-6287)
MPC NETWORKCOM INC
440 Fair Dr Ste 233, Costa Mesa (92626-6294)
PHONE..........................949 873-1002
Rich D'Alessio, *CEO*
Dennis D'Alessio, *Ch of Bd*
EMP: 10
SALES (est): 863.9K **Privately Held**
SIC: 2741 Directories: publishing only, not printed on site

(P-6288)
MYANIMELIST LLC
Also Called: Mal
505 Howard St Ste 201, San Francisco (94105-3262)
PHONE..........................714 423-8289
Kyohei Tomida, *Mng Member*
Hiro Tokuda,
EMP: 15
SALES (est): 500K **Privately Held**
SIC: 2741
PA: Media Do Holdings Co., Ltd.
1-1-1, Hitotsubashi
Chiyoda-Ku TKY 100-0

(P-6289)
MYERS-BRIGGS COMPANY (PA)
Also Called: Cpp
185 N Wolfe Rd, Sunnyvale (94086-5212)
PHONE..........................650 969-8901
Jeffrey Hayes, *President*
Marion McGovern, *Ch of Bd*
Carl Thoresen, *Ch of Bd*
Calvin W Finch, *Senior VP*
Andrew Bell, *Vice Pres*
EMP: 100
SQ FT: 16,000
SALES (est): 35.8MM **Privately Held**
SIC: 2741 Miscellaneous publishing

(P-6290)
MYVOICEGIG LLC
12517 Wedgwood Cir, Tustin (92780-2879)
PHONE..........................714 702-6006
D Elery Werner, *CEO*
EMP: 11 **EST:** 2014
SALES (est): 650K **Privately Held**
SIC: 2741

(P-6291)
NATIONAL APPRAISAL GUIDES INC
Also Called: Nada Appraisal Guide
3186 Airway Ave Ste K, Costa Mesa (92626-4650)
PHONE..........................714 556-8511
Donald D Christy Jr, *President*
Jody Christy, *Corp Secy*
Robin Lewis, *Vice Pres*
Troy Snyder, *Marketing Mgr*
Matt Kollar, *Manager*
EMP: 33
SQ FT: 20,000
SALES (est): 5MM **Privately Held**
WEB: www.aircraftprice.com
SIC: 2741 Guides: publishing & printing

(P-6292)
NEIL A KJOS MUSIC COMPANY (PA)
4382 Jutland Dr, San Diego (92117-3642)
P.O. Box 178270 (92177-8270)
PHONE..........................858 270-9800
Ryan Nowlin, *President*
Neil A Kjos Jr, *Ch of Bd*
Barbara G Kjos, *Chairman*
◆ **EMP:** 40
SQ FT: 72,000
SALES (est): 6.8MM **Privately Held**
WEB: www.kjos.com
SIC: 2741 Music books: publishing & printing; music, sheet: publishing & printing

(P-6293)
NEIL PATEL DIGITAL LLC
750 B St Ste 2600, San Diego (92101-8175)
PHONE..........................619 356-8119
Mike Kamo,
EMP: 25
SALES (est): 560.4K **Privately Held**
SIC: 2741

(P-6294)
NETFLIX INC (PA)
100 Winchester Cir, Los Gatos (95032-1815)
PHONE..........................408 540-3700
Reed Hastings, *Ch of Bd*
Alexis Martin Woodall, *President*
Spencer Neumann, *CFO*
Jonathan Friedland, *Ch Credit Ofcr*
Jackie Lee-Joe, *Chief Mktg Ofcr*
EMP: 166
SQ FT: 600,000
SALES: 15.7B **Publicly Held**
SIC: 2741 7841 ; video disk/tape rental to the general public

(P-6295)
NETMARBLE US INC
600 Wilshire Blvd # 1100, Los Angeles (90017-3249)
PHONE..........................714 276-1196
Chul Min Sim, *CEO*
Joon Yoon, *Marketing Mgr*
Nicole Kim, *Marketing Staff*
EMP: 15
SQ FT: 2,500
SALES: 10MM
SALES (corp-wide): 1B **Privately Held**
SIC: 2741 5734 Miscellaneous publishing; software, computer games
PA: Netmarble Corporation
20/F G-Valley Biz Plaza
Seoul 08379
821 588-5180

(P-6296)
NEXTAG INC (PA)
555 Twin Dolphin Dr # 370, Redwood City (94065-2133)
PHONE..........................650 645-4700
Chris Hart, *CEO*
EMP: 97
SALES (est): 66.3MM
SALES (corp-wide): 68.7MM **Privately Held**
WEB: www.nextag.com
SIC: 2741 Shopping news: publishing & printing

(P-6297)
NEXTCLIENTCOM INC
25012 Avenue Kearny, Valencia (91355-1253)
PHONE..........................661 222-7755
Lawrence J Tjan, *President*
Karen E Sugihara, *Admin Sec*
Enrique Aguilar, *Web Dvlpr*
Jonathan Tjan, *Web Dvlpr*
Cindy Rodriguez, *Personnel Assit*
EMP: 14
SALES (est): 1.7MM **Privately Held**
SIC: 2741 8742 7336 Newsletter publishing; marketing consulting services; commercial art & graphic design

(P-6298)
NO STARCH PRESS INC
245 8th St, San Francisco (94103-3910)
PHONE..........................415 863-9900
William Pollock, *President*
Laurel Chun, *Production*
Riley Hoffman, *Production*
Julia Borden, *Sales Staff*
Ming Choi,
▲ **EMP:** 18
SQ FT: 8,000
SALES (est): 1.9MM **Privately Held**
WEB: www.nostarch.com
SIC: 2741 Miscellaneous publishing

(P-6299)
NYABENGA LLC
Also Called: Thehomemag Bay Area
9020 Brentwood Blvd Ste A, Brentwood (94513-4048)
PHONE..........................925 418-4221
David Pritchett, *President*
Mark Pistor, *Shareholder*
Rachel Pritchett, *Principal*
EMP: 10
SQ FT: 1,200
SALES: 1MM **Privately Held**
SIC: 2741 7311 Miscellaneous publishing; advertising agencies

(P-6300)
ONE INTERNET AMERICA LLC
350 S Milliken Ave Ste E, Ontario (91761-7845)
PHONE..........................951 377-8844
Leisser Barrera,
EMP: 17
SALES (est): 3.2MM **Privately Held**
SIC: 2741

(P-6301)
ONNET USA INC
2870 Zanker Rd Ste 205, San Jose (95134-2133)
PHONE..........................408 457-3992
Kyongwan Son, *CEO*
Yeon Pak, *Office Mgr*
EMP: 26
SALES (est): 2MM **Privately Held**
SIC: 2741 Miscellaneous publishing
HQ: Onnet Co., Ltd.
9/F Sampyung-Dong
Seongnam 13487

(P-6302)
OPEN-XCHANGE INC (PA)
530 Lytton Ave Fl 2, Palo Alto (94301-1541)
P.O. Box 143, Ardsley On Hudson NY (10503-0143)
PHONE..........................914 332-5720
Rafael Laguna, *President*
Richard Seibt, *Ch of Bd*
Carsten Dirks, *COO*
Monika Schroeder, *CFO*
Jurgen Geck, *CTO*
EMP: 10
SALES: 16.7MM **Privately Held**
SIC: 2741 Guides: publishing & printing

(P-6303)
ORB MEDIA BROADCASTING INC
3125 W Beverly Blvd, Montebello (90640-2216)
PHONE..........................323 246-4524
Yoel Berrios, *CEO*
Wendell Frohwein, *Shareholder*
Adrian Mendoza, *Shareholder*

EMP: 10
SALES: 200K **Privately Held**
SIC: 2741 Miscellaneous publishing

(P-6304)
OUTREACH SLUTIONS AS A SVC LLC
980 9th St Fl 16, Sacramento
(95814-2736)
PHONE..................................800 824-8573
William Molina,
EMP: 10
SALES (est): 304.1K **Privately Held**
SIC: 2741

(P-6305)
PARROT COMMUNICATIONS INTL INC
Also Called: Parrot Media Network
26321 Ferry Ct, Santa Clarita
(91350-2998)
PHONE..................................818 567-4700
Robert W Mertz, *CEO*
▲ **EMP:** 50
SQ FT: 60,000
SALES (est): 5.8MM **Privately Held**
WEB: www.parrotmedia.com
SIC: 2741 7331 4822 7375 Directories: publishing only, not printed on site; direct mail advertising services; facsimile transmission services; information retrieval services; prepackaged software

(P-6306)
PEACHPIT PRESS
1301 Sansome St, San Francisco
(94111-1122)
PHONE..................................415 336-6831
M Carreiro, *Director*
Diane Heuel, *Director*
Tracey Croom, *Editor*
EMP: 40 EST: 2013
SALES (est): 141.3K **Privately Held**
SIC: 2741 Miscellaneous publishing

(P-6307)
PENROSE STUDIOS INC
223 Mississippi St Ste 3, San Francisco
(94107-2501)
PHONE..................................703 354-1801
Eugene Chung, *CEO*
EMP: 15
SALES (est): 402.6K **Privately Held**
SIC: 2741

(P-6308)
PERFORMMEDIACOM INC WHICH
4500 Great America Pkwy, Santa Clara
(95054-1283)
PHONE..................................858 336-8121
Leo Polanowski, *CEO*
EMP: 14
SALES (est): 345.6K **Privately Held**
SIC: 2741

(P-6309)
PERSONAL AWARENESS SYSTEMS
Also Called: Persona International
767 Bridgeway Ste 3b, Sausalito
(94965-2193)
P.O. Box 100 (94966-0100)
PHONE..................................415 331-3900
Jon Gornstein, *Ch of Bd*
Leah Rosenthal, *President*
Quan Lieu Keongam, *Vice Pres*
EMP: 15
SALES (est): 1.3MM **Privately Held**
WEB: www.personaglobal.com
SIC: 2741 8742 Technical manual & paper publishing; management consulting services

(P-6310)
PLANNED PARENTHOOD LOS ANGELES
1578 Colorado Blvd Ste 13, Los Angeles
(90041-1452)
PHONE..................................323 256-1717
Sheri Bonner, *CEO*
EMP: 48
SALES (corp-wide): 63.9MM **Privately Held**
SIC: 2741 Miscellaneous publishing

PA: Planned Parenthood Los Angeles, Inc
400 W 30th St
Los Angeles CA 90007
213 284-3200

(P-6311)
PLAYBOY ENTERPRISES INTL INC
Also Called: Peei
10960 Wilshire Blvd # 2200, Los Angeles
(90024-3808)
PHONE..................................310 424-1800
Christopher Pachler, *Exec VP*
Hugh Heffner, *Officer*
EMP: 100
SALES: 3MM
SALES (corp-wide): 45.6MM **Privately Held**
SIC: 2741 Miscellaneous publishing
PA: Playboy Enterprises, Inc.
9346 Civic Center Dr # 200
Beverly Hills CA 90210
310 424-1800

(P-6312)
POPSUGAR INC
3523 Eastham Dr, Culver City
(90232-2440)
PHONE..................................310 562-8049
Sarah Siegel, *Branch Mgr*
EMP: 10 **Privately Held**
SIC: 2741 Miscellaneous publishing
PA: Popsugar Inc.
111 Sutter St Fl 16
San Francisco CA 94104

(P-6313)
POPSUGAR INC (PA)
111 Sutter St Fl 16, San Francisco
(94104-4541)
PHONE..................................415 391-7576
Brian Sugar, *CEO*
Sean Macnew, *CFO*
Anna Fieler, *Chief Mktg Ofcr*
Geoff Schiller, *Officer*
Alex McNealy, *Exec VP*
▲ **EMP:** 150
SALES (est): 32.5MM **Privately Held**
SIC: 2741 Miscellaneous publishing

(P-6314)
POSITIVE PUBLISHING INC
449 Nautilus St, La Jolla (92037-5968)
P.O. Box 8648 (92038-8648)
PHONE..................................858 551-0889
Anthony Kampmann, *CEO*
Rose Kampmann, *Vice Pres*
Patricia Kampmann, *Admin Sec*
▲ **EMP:** 18
SALES (est): 1.4MM **Privately Held**
WEB: www.pospub.com
SIC: 2741 Miscellaneous publishing

(P-6315)
PPL ENTERTAINMENT GROUP INC (PA)
Also Called: Pollybyrd Publications Limited
468 N Camden Dr, Beverly Hills
(90210-4507)
P.O. Box 261488, Encino (91426-1488)
PHONE..................................310 860-7499
Jaeson James Jarrett, *CEO*
Suzette L Cuseo, *President*
Maximus Z Diamond, *Exec VP*
Michael J Hochberg, *Vice Pres*
Jake Q Montana, *Vice Pres*
EMP: 25
SQ FT: 3,000
SALES (est): 1.3MM **Privately Held**
SIC: 2741 7389 3652 Music book & sheet music publishing; recording studio, noncommercial records; compact laser discs, prerecorded

(P-6316)
PRIORITY POSTING AND PUBG INC
17501 Irvine Blvd Ste 1, Tustin
(92780-3147)
PHONE..................................714 338-2568
Thomas Haacker, *President*
Maureen Haacker, *Vice Pres*
EMP: 25
SQ FT: 3,000

SALES (est): 2.5MM **Privately Held**
WEB: www.priorityposting.com
SIC: 2741 Miscellaneous publishing

(P-6317)
PRISON RIDE SHARE NETWORK
Also Called: Prison Rideshare Network
1541 S California Ave, Compton
(90221-4924)
PHONE..................................314 703-5245
Keisha Joseph-Beard, *Owner*
EMP: 20
SALES (est): 492.2K **Privately Held**
SIC: 2741 8742 4729 Telephone & other directory publishing; transportation consultant; carpool/vanpool arrangement

(P-6318)
PROFORMATIVE INC
99 Almaden Blvd Ste 975, San Jose
(95113-1616)
PHONE..................................408 400-3993
John Kogan, *Principal*
Greg Stout, *CTO*
Lina Beltran, *Sales Staff*
Misty Worley, *Sales Staff*
EMP: 17
SALES (est): 1.7MM **Privately Held**
SIC: 2741 Miscellaneous publishing

(P-6319)
PROOF READING LLC
3905 State St Ste 7-516, Santa Barbara
(93105-3138)
PHONE..................................650 438-9438
Darren Shafae, *Principal*
EMP: 12
SALES (corp-wide): 873.8K **Privately Held**
SIC: 2741 Miscellaneous publishing
PA: Proof Reading, Llc
664 Natoma St
San Francisco CA 94103
866 433-4867

(P-6320)
PROTOTYPE INDUSTRIES INC (PA)
26035 Acero Ste 100, Mission Viejo
(92691-7951)
PHONE..................................949 680-4890
Irene Grigoriadis, *President*
Victor Ramirez, *CTO*
Tom Rochin, *Manager*
Donna Warner, *Manager*
EMP: 23
SQ FT: 4,000
SALES (est): 1.9MM **Privately Held**
WEB: www.prototypeindustries.com
SIC: 2741 2752 Miscellaneous publishing; commercial printing, offset

(P-6321)
PROVIDENCE PUBLICATIONS LLC
1620 Santa, Roseville (95661)
P.O. Box 2610, Granite Bay (95746-2610)
PHONE..................................916 774-4000
J Dale Debber, *Managing Dir*
Janet M Debber,
EMP: 30
SQ FT: 7,904
SALES (est): 207.5K **Privately Held**
SIC: 2741 Miscellaneous publishing

(P-6322)
QUADRIGA AMERICAS LLC
17800 S Main St Ste 113, Gardena
(90248-3511)
PHONE..................................424 634-4900
EMP: 21
SALES (corp-wide): 242.1K **Privately Held**
SIC: 2741
HQ: Quadriga Americas, Llc
480 Olde Worthington Rd # 350
Westerville OH 43082
614 890-6090

(P-6323)
RANGEME INC
665 3rd St Ste 415, San Francisco
(94107-1968)
PHONE..................................415 351-9268
Nicky Jackson, *CEO*
EMP: 12

SALES (est): 334.3K **Privately Held**
SIC: 2741
PA: Efficient Collaborative Retail Marketing Company, Llc
27070 Miles Rd Ste A
Solon OH 44139

(P-6324)
RASPADOXPRESS
8610 Van Nuys Blvd, Panorama City
(91402-7205)
PHONE..................................818 892-6969
Oscar Limon, *Branch Mgr*
EMP: 13
SALES (corp-wide): 1.1MM **Privately Held**
SIC: 2741 Miscellaneous publishing
PA: Raspadoxpress
9765 Laurel Canyon Blvd
Pacoima CA 91331
818 890-4111

(P-6325)
RATEBEER LLC
Also Called: Ratebeer.com
1381 Velma Ave, Santa Rosa
(95403-7218)
PHONE..................................302 476-2337
Joseph Tucker, *Principal*
EMP: 95
SALES (est): 2.7MM **Privately Held**
SIC: 2741

(P-6326)
REAL MARKETING
9955 Black Mountain Rd, San Diego
(92126-4514)
PHONE..................................858 847-0335
David Collins, *President*
▼ **EMP:** 28
SQ FT: 4,000
SALES (est): 3.7MM **Privately Held**
SIC: 2741 2759 2721 Newsletter publishing; promotional printing; magazines: publishing & printing

(P-6327)
REDDIT INC (PA)
548 Market St, San Francisco
(94104-5401)
PHONE..................................415 666-2330
Steve Huffman, *Founder*
Alexis Ohanian, *Founder*
Zubair Jandali, *Senior VP*
Katelin Holloway, *Vice Pres*
Ricky Ramirez, *Administration*
EMP: 20 EST: 2011
SALES (est): 3.6MM **Privately Held**
SIC: 2741

(P-6328)
REGENT PUBLISHING SERVICES
5355 Mira Sorrento Pl # 100, San Diego
(92121-3803)
PHONE..................................760 510-1936
Valerie Harwell, *Principal*
EMP: 40 **Privately Held**
SIC: 2741 Miscellaneous publishing
PA: Regent Publishing Services Limited
Rm B&C 7/F Genesis
Wong Chuk Hang HK

(P-6329)
REMBA PARTNERS LLC
1419 E Adams Blvd, Los Angeles
(90011-1819)
PHONE..................................310 858-8495
Luis Remba,
EMP: 10
SALES: 900K **Privately Held**
WEB: www.mixografia.com
SIC: 2741 8748 Art copy: publishing & printing; business consulting

(P-6330)
RETAIL CONTENT SERVICE INC
440 N Wolfe Rd, Sunnyvale (94085-3869)
PHONE..................................415 890-2097
Zakhar Dikhtyar, *CEO*
EMP: 45
SALES (est): 1MM **Privately Held**
SIC: 2741

▲ = Import ▼=Export
◆ =Import/Export

(P-6331)
RJW & ASSOC
31700 Dunraven Ct Ste 100, Thousand
Oaks (91361-4513)
PHONE...................................818 706-0289
Ron Weilbacher, *Owner*
EMP: 12
SALES (est): 587.2K **Privately Held**
SIC: 2741 Miscellaneous publishing

(P-6332)
ROCK RAG INC
913 N Highland Ave, Los Angeles
(90038-2412)
P.O. Box 827, Burbank (91503-0827)
PHONE...................................818 919-9364
Kimberly Fields, *President*
EMP: 12
SALES (est): 496K **Privately Held**
SIC: 2741 Miscellaneous publishing

(P-6333)
**RONDOR MUSIC
INTERNATIONAL (PA)**
2440 S Sepulveda Blvd # 119, Los Angeles
(90064-1784)
PHONE...................................310 235-4800
Lance Freed, *President*
Dan Bess, *Vice Pres*
Wendy Goldstein, *Vice Pres*
Anna Hall, *Vice Pres*
James Harrington, *Vice Pres*
EMP: 12
SQ FT: 25,000
SALES (est): 5.9MM **Privately Held**
SIC: 2741 Music, sheet: publishing only,
not printed on site

(P-6334)
**SAN DEGO GOGRAPHIC INFO
SOURCE**
Also Called: Sangis
5510 Overland Ave Ste 230, San Diego
(92123-1239)
PHONE...................................858 874-7000
Brad Lind, *Exec Dir*
EMP: 14 EST: 1997
SQ FT: 4,000
SALES (est): 1.3MM **Privately Held**
WEB: www.sangis.com
SIC: 2741 Maps: publishing & printing

(P-6335)
SAN DIEGO GUIDE INC
Also Called: San Diegan
6370 Lusk Blvd Ste F202, San Diego
(92121-2755)
PHONE...................................858 877-3217
Barry M Berndes, *President*
EMP: 20
SQ FT: 2,500
SALES (est): 1.7MM **Privately Held**
WEB: www.sandiegan.com
SIC: 2741 Guides: publishing only, not
printed on site

(P-6336)
**SANTA BARBARA MUSIC
PUBLISHING**
260 Loma Media Rd, Santa Barbara
(93103-2154)
PHONE...................................805 962-5800
Barbara Harlow, *President*
EMP: 20
SALES (est): 1.5MM **Privately Held**
WEB: www.sbmp.com
SIC: 2741 Music book & sheet music pub-
lishing

(P-6337)
SCRIBBLE PRESS INC
1109 Montana Ave, Santa Monica
(90403-1609)
P.O. Box 20743, New York NY (10021-
0075)
PHONE...................................212 288-2928
EMP: 30
SALES (est): 2.2MM
SALES (corp-wide): 5.2MM **Privately
Held**
SIC: 2741
PA: Make Meaning, Inc.
1100 La Avenida St Ste A
Mountain View CA 94043
646 307-5906

(P-6338)
SELFOPTIMA INC
1601 S De Anza Blvd # 255, Cupertino
(95014-5347)
P.O. Box 3502, Saratoga (95070-1502)
PHONE...................................408 217-8667
Nader Vasseghi, *CEO*
Bill Gray, *Chief Mktg Ofcr*
EMP: 11
SQ FT: 3,500
SALES (est): 684.1K **Privately Held**
SIC: 2741

(P-6339)
SIXTEEN RIVERS PRESS INC
1195 Green St, San Francisco
(94109-2060)
P.O. Box 640663 (94164-0663)
PHONE...................................415 273-1303
Margaret Kaufman, *President*
Sharon Olson, *Treasurer*
EMP: 14
SALES: 23.5K **Privately Held**
SIC: 2741 Miscellaneous publishing

(P-6340)
SOCIALWISE INC
Also Called: Rallio
400 Spectrum Center Dr # 1250, Irvine
(92618-5030)
PHONE...................................949 861-3900
Chuck Goetschel, *CEO*
EMP: 10
SALES: 1MM **Privately Held**
SIC: 2741

(P-6341)
SODAMAIL LLC
1300 Valley House Dr # 100, Rohnert Park
(94928-4927)
PHONE...................................707 794-1289
Lauren R Elliott, *President*
Cliff Allen, *Vice Pres*
EMP: 11 EST: 1997
SALES (est): 657.9K **Privately Held**
WEB: www.sodamail.com
SIC: 2741 Newsletter publishing

(P-6342)
**SONGS MUSIC PUBLISHING
LLC**
7656 W Sunset Blvd, Los Angeles
(90046-2724)
PHONE...................................323 939-3511
Carianne Marshall, *Branch Mgr*
EMP: 15 **Privately Held**
SIC: 2741 Miscellaneous publishing
PA: Songs Music Publishing, Llc
307 7th Ave Rm 904
New York NY 10001

(P-6343)
**SONY/ATV MUSIC PUBLISHING
LLC**
10635 Santa Monica Blvd # 300, Los Ange-
les (90025-8314)
PHONE...................................310 441-1300
Irwin Robinson, *Manager*
EMP: 30 **Privately Held**
SIC: 2741 5736 Music book & sheet music
publishing; sheet music
HQ: Sony/Atv Music Publishing Llc
25 Madison Ave Fl 24
New York NY 10010
212 833-7730

(P-6344)
SPARKCENTRAL INC (PA)
535 Mission St Fl 14, San Francisco
(94105-3253)
PHONE...................................866 559-6229
Joe Gagnon, *CEO*
Matthew Finneran, *Principal*
Cameron Halstead, *Marketing Staff*
EMP: 18
SQ FT: 1,400
SALES (est): 790.2K **Privately Held**
SIC: 2741 4899 Miscellaneous publishing;
data communication services

(P-6345)
SPIDELL PUBLISHING INC
1134 N Gilbert St, Anaheim (92801-1401)
P.O. Box 61044 (92803-6144)
PHONE...................................714 776-7850
Lynn Freer, *President*
Richard Derby, *Technician*
Tim Hilger, *CPA*
Anthony Abeyta, *Production*
Ashley Counts, *Director*
EMP: 20 EST: 1975
SQ FT: 2,500
SALES (est): 2.4MM **Privately Held**
WEB: www.spidell.com
SIC: 2741 Guides: publishing only, not
printed on site

(P-6346)
SPROUT INC
475 Brannan St Ste 410, San Francisco
(94107-5421)
PHONE...................................415 894-9629
Carnet Williams, *CEO*
Matthew McNeely, *Vice Pres*
Adam Taisch, *Vice Pres*
EMP: 10
SALES (est): 598.7K **Privately Held**
SIC: 2741 7311 ; advertising agencies
PA: Inmobi Technologies Private Limited
6th, 7th And 8th Floor
Bengaluru KA 56010

(P-6347)
**STAFFING INDUSTRY ANALYSTS
INC**
Also Called: Staffing Industry Report
1975 W El Cmno Rl 304, Mountain View
(94040)
PHONE...................................650 390-6200
Ron Mester, *CEO*
Barry Asin, *President*
EMP: 35
SQ FT: 4,307
SALES (est): 3MM
SALES (corp-wide): 225MM **Privately
Held**
WEB: www.staffingindustry.com
SIC: 2741 Newsletter publishing
PA: Crain Communications, Inc.
1155 Gratiot Ave
Detroit MI 48207
313 446-6000

(P-6348)
STREETWISE REPORTS LLC
755 Baywood Dr Fl 2, Petaluma
(94954-5510)
P.O. Box 1099, Kenwood (95452-1099)
PHONE...................................707 981-8999
Karen Roche, *President*
Ron Tomassini, *Web Dvlpr*
Kevin Jaillet, *Marketing Staff*
Paul Guedes, *Contractor*
Kieran Magee, *Publisher*
EMP: 25 EST: 2011
SALES (est): 1.5MM **Privately Held**
SIC: 2741

(P-6349)
**STRING LETTER PUBLISHING
INC**
Also Called: Acoustic Guitar Magazine
941 Marina Way S Ste E, Richmond
(94804-3768)
PHONE...................................510 215-0010
David Lusterman, *President*
Greg Sutton, *Sales Mgr*
Lyzy Lusterman, *Director*
Lynn Fischer, *Manager*
Phil Hood, *Publisher*
EMP: 25
SALES: 3.8MM **Privately Held**
SIC: 2741 Miscellaneous publishing

(P-6350)
STUDIO SYSTEMS INC (PA)
5700 Wilshire Blvd # 600, Los Angeles
(90036-3659)
PHONE...................................323 634-3400
Gary Hiller, *President*
Anthony Pinga, *Director*
EMP: 20
SQ FT: 13,000

SALES (est): 2.5MM **Privately Held**
SIC: 2741 Miscellaneous publishing

(P-6351)
SUPERMEDIA LLC
1215 W Center St Ste 102, Manteca
(95337-4280)
PHONE...................................209 472-6011
Renee Fink, *Branch Mgr*
EMP: 254
SALES (corp-wide): 1.6B **Privately Held**
SIC: 2741 Directories, telephone: publish-
ing only, not printed on site
HQ: Supermedia Llc
2200 W Airfield Dr
Dfw Airport TX 75261
972 453-7000

(P-6352)
SUPERMEDIA LLC
3401 Centre Lake Dr # 500, Ontario
(91761-1217)
PHONE...................................909 390-5000
Shelly Long, *General Mgr*
EMP: 254
SALES (corp-wide): 1.6B **Privately Held**
SIC: 2741 Directories, telephone: publish-
ing only, not printed on site
HQ: Supermedia Llc
2200 W Airfield Dr
Dfw Airport TX 75261
972 453-7000

(P-6353)
SUPERMEDIA LLC
1270 E Garvey St, Covina (91724-3658)
PHONE...................................626 331-9440
EMP: 254
SALES (corp-wide): 1.8B **Privately Held**
SIC: 2741
HQ: Supermedia Llc
2200 W Airfield Dr
Dfw Airport TX 75261
972 453-7000

(P-6354)
SUPERMEDIA LLC
Also Called: Verizon
3131 Katella Ave, Los Alamitos
(90720-2335)
P.O. Box 3770 (90720-0377)
PHONE...................................562 594-5101
Del Humenik, *Manager*
EMP: 400
SQ FT: 150,078
SALES (corp-wide): 1.6B **Privately Held**
WEB: www.verizon.superpages.com
SIC: 2741 7372 2791 Directories, tele-
phone: publishing only, not printed on
site; prepackaged software; typesetting
HQ: Supermedia Llc
2200 W Airfield Dr
Dfw Airport TX 75261
972 453-7000

(P-6355)
SUPERMEDIA LLC
Also Called: Verizon
1200 Melody Ln Ste 100, Roseville
(95678-5189)
PHONE...................................916 782-6866
Robert Collins, *Branch Mgr*
EMP: 254
SALES (corp-wide): 1.6B **Privately Held**
WEB: www.verizon.superpages.com
SIC: 2741 Telephone & other directory
publishing
HQ: Supermedia Llc
2200 W Airfield Dr
Dfw Airport TX 75261
972 453-7000

(P-6356)
TABOR COMMUNICATIONS INC
Also Called: Hpcwire
8445 Camino Santa Fe # 101, San Diego
(92121-2649)
PHONE...................................858 625-0070
Debra Goldfarb, *President*
Thomas Taber, *Ch of Bd*
EMP: 20
SQ FT: 15,000
SALES: 1.7MM **Privately Held**
WEB: www.hpcwire.com
SIC: 2741 Miscellaneous publishing

PRODUCTS & SVCS

(P-6357)
TELLME NETWORKS INC
1065 La Avenida St, Mountain View
(94043-1421)
PHONE.................................650 693-1009
John Lamacchia, *Chairman*
Robert Komin, *CFO*
▲ EMP: 330 EST: 1999
SALES (est): 24.2MM
SALES (corp-wide): 125.8B **Publicly Held**
WEB: www.tellme.com
SIC: 2741 4812 Telephone & other directory publishing; radio telephone communication
PA: Microsoft Corporation
1 Microsoft Way
Redmond WA 98052
425 882-8080

(P-6358)
THOMSON REUTERS CORPORATION
163 Albert Pl, Costa Mesa (92627-1744)
PHONE.................................949 400-7782
EMP: 325
SALES (corp-wide): 10.6B **Publicly Held**
SIC: 2741 Miscellaneous publishing
HQ: Thomson Reuters Corporation
3 Times Sq
New York NY 10036
646 223-4000

(P-6359)
TOP ART LLC
8830 Rehco Rd Ste G, San Diego
(92121-3263)
PHONE.................................858 554-0102
Keith Circosta, *Mng Member*
Kim Cox, *Opers Mgr*
▲ EMP: 13
SQ FT: 2,600
SALES (est): 1.3MM **Privately Held**
WEB: www.ericwaugh.com
SIC: 2741 Art copy & poster publishing

(P-6360)
TOTAL MEDIA ENTERPRISES INC
Also Called: The Hispanic News
16235 Montbrook St, La Puente
(91744-3231)
PHONE.................................626 961-7887
Patricia Rago, *Owner*
EMP: 15 EST: 1995
SQ FT: 2,475
SALES (est): 876.1K **Privately Held**
SIC: 2741 Newsletter publishing

(P-6361)
TOUCANED INC
1716 Brommer St, Santa Cruz
(95062-3002)
PHONE.................................831 464-0508
Kathleen Middleton, *President*
EMP: 15
SALES (est): 1.5MM **Privately Held**
WEB: www.toucaned.com
SIC: 2741 8742 Miscellaneous publishing; hospital & health services consultant

(P-6362)
TRAYLOR MANAGEMENT INC (PA)
Also Called: Map Masters
12120 Tech Center Dr B, Poway
(92064-7149)
P.O. Box 720699, San Diego (92172-0699)
PHONE.................................858 486-7700
Natalie Carlson, *CEO*
Dana Ertley, *President*
EMP: 12
SQ FT: 3,200
SALES (est): 1MM **Privately Held**
WEB: www.century-publishing.com
SIC: 2741 Maps: publishing only, not printed on site; directories: publishing only, not printed on site; guides: publishing only, not printed on site

(P-6363)
TSE WORLDWIDE PRESS INC
Also Called: United Yearbook Printing Svcs
9830 6th St Ste 101, Rancho Cucamonga
(91730-7969)
PHONE.................................909 989-8282
Sarah TSE, *CEO*
Jayde Porte, *Marketing Staff*
▲ EMP: 20
SQ FT: 4,000
SALES (est): 1.6MM **Privately Held**
SIC: 2741 Miscellaneous publishing

(P-6364)
TWITCH INTERACTIVE INC
350 Bush St Ste 2, San Francisco
(94104-2879)
PHONE.................................415 919-5000
Emmett Shear, *CEO*
Kevin Lin, *COO*
John Sutton, *CFO*
Doug Scott, *Chief Mktg Ofcr*
Lenke Taylor,
EMP: 1146 EST: 2006
SALES: 228MM **Publicly Held**
SIC: 2741
PA: Amazon.Com, Inc.
410 Terry Ave N
Seattle WA 98109

(P-6365)
TYLOON MEDIA CORPORATION
6168 Fielding St, Chino (91710-1350)
PHONE.................................626 330-5838
Bary Su, *CEO*
EMP: 10
SALES (est): 315.9K **Privately Held**
SIC: 2741

(P-6366)
UNITED REPORTING PUBG CORP
1835 Iron Point Rd # 100, Folsom
(95630-8771)
P.O. Box 41037, Sacramento (95841-0037)
PHONE.................................916 542-7501
Paul Curry, *CEO*
EMP: 35
SQ FT: 3,399
SALES (est): 1MM **Privately Held**
SIC: 2741 Miscellaneous publishing

(P-6367)
UNIVERSAL DIRECTORY PUBLISHING
Also Called: Elson Alexander
2995 E White Star Ave, Anaheim
(92806-2630)
PHONE.................................714 994-6025
Stanley Pesner, *President*
Lila Pesner, *Vice Pres*
EMP: 40 EST: 1967
SQ FT: 4,000
SALES (est): 2.4MM **Privately Held**
SIC: 2741 Directories: publishing only, not printed on site

(P-6368)
UNIVERSAL MUSIC PUBLISHING INC
2100 Colorado Ave, Santa Monica
(90404-3504)
PHONE.................................310 235-4700
Jody Gerson, *CEO*
Ryan Hill, *Managing Dir*
Hector Rivera, *Sales Dir*
Robert-Jan Voorbraak, *Manager*
Wendy Wilson, *Manager*
EMP: 15
SALES (est): 1MM **Privately Held**
SIC: 2741 Miscellaneous publishing

(P-6369)
UNIVOCITY MEDIA INC
2901 E Alejo Rd Bldg 4, Palm Springs
(92262-6251)
P.O. Box 2086 (92263-2086)
PHONE.................................760 904-5200
John McMullen, *President*
Haddon Libby, *CFO*
Haddon Lebby, *Officer*
EMP: 11

SALES: 170K **Privately Held**
SIC: 2741 7372 ; application computer software

(P-6370)
UPPER DECK COMPANY
5830 El Camino Real, Carlsbad
(92008-8816)
PHONE.................................800 873-7332
Jason Masherah, *President*
Don Utic, *Treasurer*
EMP: 120
SQ FT: 33,424
SALES (est): 11.9MM **Privately Held**
SIC: 2741 Music books: publishing & printing

(P-6371)
VALLEY PUBLICATIONS
27259 One Half Camp Plnty, Canyon Country (91351)
PHONE.................................661 298-5330
Douglas D Sutton, *Partner*
Doug Sutton,
Darren Watson,
EMP: 15
SQ FT: 1,500
SALES (est): 1.3MM **Privately Held**
SIC: 2741 Newsletter publishing

(P-6372)
VANISHING VISTAS
Also Called: Richard E Cox Interprizes
5043 Midas Ave, Rocklin (95677-2200)
P.O. Box 1491 (95677-7491)
PHONE.................................916 624-1237
Richard Cox, *President*
EMP: 37
SALES (est): 862.3K **Privately Held**
SIC: 2741 Miscellaneous publishing

(P-6373)
VEREDATECH LLC
4645 Vereda Mar Del Sol, San Diego
(92130-8628)
PHONE.................................858 342-6468
Raja Habib,
EMP: 10
SALES (est): 261K **Privately Held**
SIC: 2741

(P-6374)
VIPOLOGY INC
1278 Center Court Dr, Covina
(91724-3601)
PHONE.................................626 502-8661
Chris Peaslee, *CEO*
Brian Pinkus, *CFO*
Thomas Pinkus, *Admin Sec*
EMP: 10
SQ FT: 10,000
SALES (est): 315.9K **Privately Held**
SIC: 2741 4813 7371 ; ; software programming applications

(P-6375)
VISION PUBLICATIONS INC
Also Called: Vision Design Studio
3745 Long Beach Blvd, Long Beach
(90807-3340)
PHONE.................................562 597-4000
Carl Patrick Dene, *President*
Jeff Ye, *Info Tech Mgr*
EMP: 28 EST: 2000
SALES (est): 388.8K **Privately Held**
SIC: 2741 7311 Miscellaneous publishing; advertising agencies

(P-6376)
VOTEBLAST INC
8478 Hollywood Blvd, Los Angeles
(90069-1511)
PHONE.................................650 387-9147
Ardeshir Falaki, *Principal*
EMP: 21
SALES (est): 811K **Privately Held**
SIC: 2741

(P-6377)
VOXARA LLC
5737 Kanan Rd Ste 700, Agoura Hills
(91301-1601)
PHONE.................................844 869-2721
Alec R Nakashima,
EMP: 12

SALES: 850K **Privately Held**
SIC: 2741

(P-6378)
VOYAGER LEARNING COMPANY
2060 Lynx Pl Unit G, Ontario (91761)
PHONE.................................909 923-3120
EMP: 16 **Publicly Held**
SIC: 2741
HQ: Voyager Learning Company
17855 Dallas Pkwy Ste 400
Dallas TX 75287
214 932-9500

(P-6379)
VRTCAL MARKETS INC
10 E Yanonali St, Santa Barbara
(93101-1875)
PHONE.................................228 313-3327
Todd Wooten, *President*
EMP: 12
SALES (est): 334.3K **Privately Held**
SIC: 2741

(P-6380)
WARNER/CHAPPELL MUSIC INC (DH)
10585 Santa Monica Blvd # 200, Los Angeles (90025-4926)
PHONE.................................310 441-8600
Cameron Strang, *CEO*
Scott Francis, *President*
Ira Pianko, *COO*
Brian Roberts, *CFO*
Edgar Miles Bronfman, *Chairman*
EMP: 110 EST: 1984
SQ FT: 35,000
SALES (est): 90.1MM **Privately Held**
SIC: 2741 Music book & sheet music publishing

(P-6381)
WCITIESCOM INC
1212 Broadway Ste 500, Oakland
(94612-1807)
PHONE.................................415 495-8090
Fraser Campbell, *CEO*
Landon Moblad, *Business Dir*
Fraser Find, *Sales Staff*
Nathan Cranford, *Manager*
EMP: 12 EST: 2003
SALES (est): 351K **Privately Held**
WEB: www.wcities.com
SIC: 2741 Telephone & other directory publishing

(P-6382)
WEDDINGCHANNELCOM INC
5757 Wilshire Blvd # 504, Los Angeles
(90036-5810)
PHONE.................................213 599-4100
Adam Berger, *President*
Donald Drapkin, *Chairman*
Lee Essmer, *Vice Pres*
Greg Franchina, *CIO*
EMP: 125 EST: 1996
SQ FT: 18,000
SALES (est): 6.7MM
SALES (corp-wide): 160.5MM **Privately Held**
SIC: 2741 5621 Miscellaneous publishing; women's clothing stores
HQ: Xo Group Inc.
195 Broadway Fl 25
New York NY 10007

(P-6383)
WILSON IMAGING AND PUBLISHING
305 N 2nd Ave Pmb 324, Upland
(91786-6064)
PHONE.................................909 931-1818
Kent Wilson, *President*
EMP: 11
SALES (est): 1MM **Privately Held**
SIC: 2741 Miscellaneous publishing

(P-6384)
XOMV MEDIA CORPORATION
9465 Wilshire Blvd, Beverly Hills
(90212-2612)
PHONE.................................424 284-4024
Marissa Webber, *President*
EMP: 20 EST: 2015

SALES (est): 868.3K **Privately Held**
SIC: 2741

(P-6385)
YAMAGATA AMERICA INC
3760 Convoy St Ste 219, San Diego
(92111-3744)
PHONE..............................858 751-1010
Yasuhide Fujimoto, *President*
Annelies De Vliegher, *Senior Mgr*
EMP: 19
SQ FT: 4,630
SALES: 8.4MM **Privately Held**
WEB: www.yamagataamerica.com
SIC: 2741 Technical manuals: publishing &
printing
HQ: Yamagata Holdings America, Inc.
3760 Convoy St Ste 219
San Diego CA 92111
619 889-4566

(P-6386)
YB MEDIA LLC
1534 Plaza Ln 146, Burlingame
(94010-3204)
PHONE..............................310 467-5804
Benjamin Maggin, *CEO*
EMP: 20
SALES (est): 611.7K **Privately Held**
SIC: 2741

(P-6387)
YELLOW PAGES INC
24931 Nellie Gail Rd, Laguna Hills
(92653-5821)
PHONE..............................714 776-0534
Maria Salivar, *Branch Mgr*
EMP: 20
SALES (corp-wide): 7.3MM **Privately
Held**
WEB: www.ypinc.net
SIC: 2741 Telephone & other directory
publishing
PA: Yellow Pages, Inc.
222 N Main St
New City NY 10956
845 639-6060

**2752 Commercial Printing:
Lithographic**

(P-6388)
365 PRINTING INC
14747 Artesia Blvd Ste 3a, La Mirada
(90638-6003)
PHONE..............................714 752-6990
Chang Lee, *President*
EMP: 15
SQ FT: 3,300
SALES (est): 1.2MM **Privately Held**
SIC: 2752 Commercial printing, litho-
graphic

(P-6389)
A & J ENTERPRISES INC
Also Called: USA Printing
7925 Santa Monica Blvd, West Hollywood
(90046-5181)
PHONE..............................323 654-5902
Amir Shirian, *President*
Steve Ordyke, *Prdtn Mgr*
EMP: 12 EST: 1968
SQ FT: 12,000
SALES (est): 2.4MM **Privately Held**
SIC: 2752 Commercial printing, offset

(P-6390)
**ABACUS PRINTING &
GRAPHICS INC**
Also Called: Abacus Prtg & Digital Graphics
23806 Strathern St, West Hills
(91304-6133)
PHONE..............................818 929-6740
Robert D Posard, *President*
Ricki Posard, *Vice Pres*
EMP: 10
SALES (est): 1.6MM **Privately Held**
SIC: 2752 Color lithography

(P-6391)
ABC PRINTING INC
1090 S Milpitas Blvd, Milpitas
(95035-6307)
PHONE..............................408 263-1118

Danny Luong, *President*
Diana Wong, *Treasurer*
EMP: 15
SQ FT: 8,000
SALES: 1.6MM **Privately Held**
SIC: 2752 Commercial printing, offset

(P-6392)
ACE COMMERCIAL INC
Also Called: Press Colorcom
10310 Pioneer Blvd Ste 1, Santa Fe
Springs (90670-3737)
PHONE..............................562 946-6664
Andrew H Choi, *CEO*
Ozzie Villalobos, *Manager*
Eugene Yoo, *Accounts Mgr*
Mike Cabrera, *Accounts Exec*
Michael Kim, *Accounts Exec*
EMP: 40
SQ FT: 22,000
SALES (est): 10.6MM **Privately Held**
WEB: www.acecommercial.com
SIC: 2752 7331 2791 2789 Commercial
printing, offset; direct mail advertising
services; typesetting; bookbinding & re-
lated work; die-cut paper & board

(P-6393)
ACE GRAPHICS INC
5351 Bonsai Ave, Moorpark (93021-1785)
PHONE..............................213 746-5100
Ricardo Huambachano, *President*
EMP: 13
SQ FT: 11,000
SALES (est): 223.5K **Privately Held**
WEB: www.acegraphicsinc.com
SIC: 2752 Commercial printing, offset

(P-6394)
ACME PRESS INC
Also Called: California Lithographers
2312 Stanwell Dr, Concord (94520-4809)
P.O. Box 5698 (94524-0698)
PHONE..............................925 682-1111
Mardjan Taheripour, *CEO*
Bahman Taheripour, *Vice Pres*
Kenneth Vonberg, *Info Tech Dir*
Sean Healy, *Project Mgr*
Eli Lucero, *Technology*
EMP: 87
SQ FT: 36,000
SALES (est): 20.7MM **Privately Held**
WEB: www.calitho.com
SIC: 2752 Commercial printing, offset

(P-6395)
ACP VENTURES
Also Called: Allegro Copy & Print
3340 Mt Diablo Blvd Ste B, Lafayette
(94549-4076)
PHONE..............................925 297-0100
Peter Smyth, *President*
Karen Smyth, *Vice Pres*
EMP: 19
SQ FT: 6,300
SALES (est): 2.6MM **Privately Held**
WEB: www.allegrocp.com
SIC: 2752 2791 2789 7331 Commercial
printing, offset; typesetting; bookbinding &
related work; mailing service

(P-6396)
ADMAIL-EXPRESS INC
31640 Hayman St, Hayward (94544-7122)
PHONE..............................510 471-6200
Brian M Schott, *CEO*
Paul Sekins, *General Mgr*
EMP: 45
SQ FT: 55,000
SALES (est): 8.2MM **Privately Held**
WEB: www.admail.com
SIC: 2752 Commercial printing, offset

(P-6397)
ADVANCED COLOR GRAPHICS
Also Called: Acg Ecopack
1921 S Business Pkwy, Ontario
(91761-8539)
PHONE..............................909 930-1500
Steve Thompson, *President*
Mike Mullens, *Vice Pres*
EMP: 60
SQ FT: 70,000
SALES: 8MM **Privately Held**
WEB: www.acg-online.com
SIC: 2752 Commercial printing, offset

(P-6398)
ADVERTISING SERVICES
Also Called: Menu Services
7697 9th St, Buena Park (90621-2898)
PHONE..............................714 522-2781
Orris Abbott, *Owner*
EMP: 25
SQ FT: 30,000 **Privately Held**
WEB: www.advertisingservices.com
SIC: 2752 Menus, lithographed

(P-6399)
AKIDO PRINTING INC
Also Called: Promotion Xpress Prtg Graphics
2096 Merced St, San Leandro
(94577-3230)
PHONE..............................510 357-0238
Thanh Do, *President*
Stella Phan, *CFO*
EMP: 11
SQ FT: 12,000
SALES (est): 2MM **Privately Held**
SIC: 2752 Commercial printing, offset

(P-6400)
ALAN HAMILTON INDUSTRIES
Also Called: Hamilton & Associates
21020 Lassen St, Chatsworth
(91311-4241)
PHONE..............................818 885-5121
Richard A Hamilton, *Ch of Bd*
EMP: 85
SQ FT: 14,700
SALES (est): 749.1K **Privately Held**
WEB: www.hamilton-inc.com
SIC: 2752 2759 Commercial printing, litho-
graphic; commercial printing

(P-6401)
**ALEXANDER BUSINESS
SUPPLIES**
Also Called: Alexander Color Printing
21500 Wyandotte St # 110, Canoga Park
(91303-1566)
PHONE..............................818 346-1820
Alexander Frankel, *President*
Diane Frankel, *Vice Pres*
EMP: 10
SQ FT: 3,000
SALES (est): 1.5MM **Privately Held**
SIC: 2752 5734 5943 Commercial print-
ing, offset; modems, monitors, terminals
& disk drives: computers; office forms &
supplies

(P-6402)
ALL CITY PRINTING INC
1061 Howard St, San Francisco
(94103-2822)
PHONE..............................415 861-8088
Tony Ngi, *President*
EMP: 10
SQ FT: 7,000
SALES (est): 1.7MM **Privately Held**
WEB: www.allcityprinting.com
SIC: 2752 Commercial printing, offset

(P-6403)
ALLEGRA
434 9th St, San Francisco (94103-4411)
PHONE..............................415 824-9610
Takashi Yomshmu, *President*
Nora Chan, *CFO*
To Chuk Kong, *Vice Pres*
▲ EMP: 15
SQ FT: 6,000
SALES (est): 1.9MM **Privately Held**
WEB: www.goldendragonprint.com
SIC: 2752 Commercial printing, offset

(P-6404)
ALLIED PRINTING COMPANY
1912 O St, Sacramento (95811-5210)
PHONE..............................916 442-1373
Matthew G Zellmer, *Owner*
EMP: 10
SQ FT: 4,200
SALES (est): 720K **Privately Held**
SIC: 2752 2759 Commercial printing, off-
set: letters, circular or form: lithographed;
letterpress printing

(P-6405)
ALLURA PRINTING INC
185 Paularino Ave Ste B, Costa Mesa
(92626-3324)
PHONE..............................714 433-0200
David Gagnon, *CEO*
Rene Gagnon, *Vice Pres*
EMP: 12
SALES: 500K **Privately Held**
SIC: 2752 Commercial printing, offset

(P-6406)
ALLYN JAMES INC
6575 Trinity Ct Ste B, Dublin (94568-2643)
PHONE..............................925 828-5530
Mark Cady, *President*
Mark W Cady, *President*
Curtis J Mc Carthy, *Vice Pres*
EMP: 16
SALES: 1.8MM **Privately Held**
WEB: www.jamesallyn.com
SIC: 2752 Commercial printing, offset

(P-6407)
**ALPHA PRINTING & GRAPHICS
INC**
12758 Schabarum Ave, Irwindale
(91706-6801)
PHONE..............................626 851-9800
Stacey Chen, *President*
Kelly Ngo, *CEO*
▲ EMP: 20
SQ FT: 5,000
SALES (est): 4.8MM **Privately Held**
WEB: www.alphaprinting.com
SIC: 2752 Commercial printing, offset

(P-6408)
**AMERICAN LITHOGRAPHERS
INC**
Also Called: Pacific Standard Print
2629 5th St, Sacramento (95818-2802)
PHONE..............................916 441-5392
Joe R Davis, *CEO*
Tom Mueller, *President*
Peter Bachelor, *Accounts Exec*
EMP: 70
SQ FT: 60,000
SALES (est): 13.8MM
SALES (corp-wide): 6.8B **Publicly Held**
WEB: www.printpsp.com/
SIC: 2752 2759 Commercial printing, off-
set; commercial printing
HQ: Consolidated Graphics, Inc.
5858 Westheimer Rd # 200
Houston TX 77057
713 787-0977

(P-6409)
**AMERICAN PCF PRTRS
COLLEGE INC**
Also Called: Kenny The Printer
17931 Sky Park Cir, Irvine (92614-6312)
PHONE..............................949 250-3212
David Smith, *CEO*
Cal Laird, *CFO*
EMP: 36 EST: 1981
SQ FT: 22,000
SALES (est): 7.8MM **Privately Held**
WEB: www.kennytheprinter.com
SIC: 2752 Commercial printing, offset

(P-6410)
**AMERICAN PRINTING & COPY
INC**
1100 Obrien Dr, Menlo Park (94025-1411)
PHONE..............................650 325-2322
Kamran Motamedi, *President*
Cynthia Motamedi, *Vice Pres*
Brady Hopkins, *Principal*
Kanak Sesha, *Principal*
Dan Tamada, *Principal*
EMP: 14
SQ FT: 1,400
SALES (est): 2.6MM **Privately Held**
SIC: 2752 7334 Commercial printing, off-
set; photocopying & duplicating services

(P-6411)
AMERICAN PRINTING & DESIGN
14622 Ventura Blvd # 102, Sherman Oaks
(91403-3600)
PHONE..............................310 287-0460
Michael Kenner, *President*
EMP: 20 EST: 1981

PRODUCTS & SVCS

SQ FT: 40,000
SALES: 2MM **Privately Held**
SIC: 2752 Commercial printing, offset; catalogs, lithographed

(P-6412)
AMERICHIP INC (PA)
19032 S Vermont Ave, Gardena
(90248-4412)
PHONE..................................310 323-3697
Timothy Clegg, *CEO*
Keven Clegg, *President*
Primoz Samardzija, *Exec VP*
John Clegg, *Vice Pres*
Michael Ronk, *Vice Pres*
▲ EMP: 56
SQ FT: 30,000
SALES (est): 10.9MM **Privately Held**
WEB: www.americhip.com
SIC: 2752 Promotional printing, lithographic

(P-6413)
AMPLIGRAPHIX
Also Called: Central Printing & Graphics
1768 Glenwood Dr, Bakersfield
(93306-4230)
PHONE..................................661 321-3150
Sherry Darke, *President*
Craig C Combs, *Admin Sec*
EMP: 10 EST: 1957
SQ FT: 4,500
SALES (est): 760K **Privately Held**
WEB: www.central-printing.com
SIC: 2752 Commercial printing, offset

(P-6414)
ANCHORED PRINTS INC
635 N Eckhoff St Ste Q, Orange
(92868-1048)
PHONE..................................714 929-9317
Samuel Schinhofen, *CEO*
EMP: 23
SALES (est): 756.6K **Privately Held**
SIC: 2752 Commercial printing, lithographic

(P-6415)
ANTO OFFSET PRINTING
1101 5th St, Berkeley (94710-1201)
PHONE..................................510 843-8454
Alexder Cingoz, *Partner*
Antrenge Cingoz, *Partner*
EMP: 11 EST: 1977
SQ FT: 10,000
SALES (est): 1.1MM **Privately Held**
SIC: 2752 Commercial printing, offset

(P-6416)
ANY BUDGET PRINTING & MAILING
8170 Ronson Rd Ste L, San Diego
(92111-2008)
PHONE..................................858 278-3151
Charlie Silveria, *Owner*
Terry Silveria, *Co-Owner*
EMP: 14
SQ FT: 1,500
SALES (est): 1.3MM **Privately Held**
WEB: www.anybudget.com
SIC: 2752 Commercial printing, offset

(P-6417)
API MARKETING
Also Called: Auburn Printers and Mfg
13020 Earhart Ave, Auburn (95602-9536)
PHONE..................................916 632-1946
Merrill Kagan-Weston, *President*
Brad Weston, *Vice Pres*
Kelley Buxton, *Opers Mgr*
EMP: 17
SQ FT: 10,000
SALES: 1.7MM **Privately Held**
WEB: www.auburnprint.com
SIC: 2752 Commercial printing, offset; catalogs, lithographed; circulars, lithographed

(P-6418)
ARDEN & HOWE PRINTING INC
Also Called: Signature Press
430 17th St, Sacramento (95811-1004)
PHONE..................................916 444-7154
Chris Martinez, *President*
EMP: 10 EST: 1978
SQ FT: 8,000

SALES (est): 1.2MM **Privately Held**
SIC: 2752 2759 Commercial printing, offset; letterpress printing

(P-6419)
ARROWHEAD PRESS INC
220 W Maple Ave Ste B, Monrovia
(91016-3393)
PHONE..................................626 358-1168
Diana Marie Sims, *CEO*
Ken Shannon, *Marketing Staff*
Charlie Hodge, *Sales Staff*
Frances Harsono, *Manager*
Annie Stickle, *Receptionist*
EMP: 28 EST: 1973
SQ FT: 9,000
SALES (est): 6.2MM **Privately Held**
WEB: www.arrowheadpress.com
SIC: 2752 2789 Commercial printing, offset; bookbinding & related work

(P-6420)
ARSH INCORPORATED
Also Called: Copyland /Zip2print
2300 Stevens Creek Blvd, San Jose
(95128-1650)
PHONE..................................408 971-2722
Frank Ettefgh, *President*
Robert Caballero, *Manager*
EMP: 10 EST: 1995
SALES: 1.5MM **Privately Held**
SIC: 2752 5099 5999 Commercial printing, offset; signs, except electric; banners

(P-6421)
ASIA AMERICA ENTERPRISE INC
Also Called: America Printing
1321 N Carolan Ave, Burlingame
(94010-2401)
PHONE..................................650 348-2333
Macy Mak, *CEO*
Ryan Mak, *Corp Secy*
EMP: 20
SQ FT: 27,000
SALES (est): 3.4MM **Privately Held**
WEB: www.americaprinting.com
SIC: 2752 Commercial printing, offset

(P-6422)
AUTUMN PRESS INC (PA)
Also Called: Autumn Express
945 Camelia St, Berkeley (94710-1437)
PHONE..................................510 654-4545
Miguel Alson, *President*
Gordon Empey, *Exec VP*
Theresa Thornton, *Vice Pres*
EMP: 20
SQ FT: 15,000
SALES (est): 2.6MM **Privately Held**
WEB: www.autumnpress.com
SIC: 2752 Commercial printing, offset

(P-6423)
AVION GRAPHICS INC
27192 Burbank, Foothill Ranch
(92610-2503)
PHONE..................................949 472-0438
Craig Greiner, *President*
Mary Kay Swanson, *Shareholder*
Michele Morris, *Vice Pres*
Mark Macdonald, *Prdtn Mgr*
Tiffany Davis, *Sales Staff*
EMP: 33
SQ FT: 6,800
SALES (est): 8.8MM **Privately Held**
WEB: www.aviongraphics.com
SIC: 2752 7336 3993 5999 Decals, lithographed; commercial art & graphic design; signs & advertising specialties; decals; aircraft & parts

(P-6424)
AVOY CORP
114 Greenbank Ave, Piedmont
(94611-4336)
PHONE..................................510 295-8055
Sedrick A Tydus, *Branch Mgr*
EMP: 16 **Privately Held**
SIC: 2752 Commercial printing, offset
PA: Avoy Corp.
    2406 Webster St
    Oakland CA 94612
    -

(P-6425)
AVOY CORP (PA)
Also Called: Minuteman Press Oakland
2406 Webster St, Oakland (94612-3118)
PHONE..................................510 832-7746
Sedrick A Tydus, *CEO*
EMP: 15
SALES (est): 1.9MM **Privately Held**
SIC: 2752 Commercial printing, lithographic

(P-6426)
AZPIRE PRINT & MEDIAWORKS LLC
10555 Clarkson Rd, Los Angeles
(90064-4315)
PHONE..................................310 736-5952
Hardat N Pariag, *President*
EMP: 19
SALES: 500K **Privately Held**
SIC: 2752 7389 Commercial printing, offset;

(P-6427)
B & D LITHO GROUP INC
325 N Ponderosa Ave, Ontario
(91761-1530)
PHONE..................................909 390-0903
Steve Gaynor, *Principal*
Roussel Pierre, *Info Tech Dir*
Christine Van Empel, *Engineer*
EMP: 22
SALES (corp-wide): 400.7MM **Publicly Held**
SIC: 2752 Commercial printing, offset
HQ: B & D Litho Group, Inc.
    3820 N 38th Ave
    Phoenix AZ 85019
    602 269-2526

(P-6428)
B AND Z PRINTING INC
1300 E Wakeham Ave B, Santa Ana
(92705-4145)
PHONE..................................714 892-2000
Frank Buono, *President*
James Zimmer, *Admin Sec*
EMP: 45
SQ FT: 40,000
SALES (est): 7.3MM **Privately Held**
WEB: www.bandzprinting.com
SIC: 2752 2789 Commercial printing, offset; bookbinding & related work

(P-6429)
B BRAYS CARD INC
12053 Mariposa Rd, Victorville (92394)
PHONE..................................760 265-4720
Melvin Bray, *Principal*
EMP: 12 EST: 2013
SALES (est): 1MM **Privately Held**
SIC: 2752 Business form & card printing, lithographic

(P-6430)
B K HARRIS INC
Also Called: Presstime
3574 E Enterprise Dr, Anaheim
(92807-1627)
PHONE..................................714 630-8780
Bryan Kerl, *President*
Marcelle Kerl, *Admin Sec*
EMP: 10
SALES (est): 1.2MM **Privately Held**
WEB: www.presstimeprinters.com
SIC: 2752 Commercial printing, lithographic

(P-6431)
BABYLON PRINTING INC
Also Called: Medius
1800 Dobbin Dr, San Jose (95133-1701)
PHONE..................................408 519-5000
Daisy Zaia, *CEO*
George Zaia, *Vice Pres*
Gene Joudy, *Exec Dir*
Michael Zaia, *Info Tech Dir*
Miruna Williams, *Marketing Staff*
◆ EMP: 43
SQ FT: 110,000
SALES: 14.7MM **Privately Held**
WEB: www.mediuscorp.com
SIC: 2752 Commercial printing, offset

(P-6432)
BACCHUS PRESS INC (PA)
1287 66th St, Emeryville (94608-1198)
PHONE..................................510 420-5800
Monsoor Assadi, *President*
Karen Schreiber, *Sales Staff*
Sue Kent, *Manager*
Jerry Blueford, *Supervisor*
EMP: 20
SQ FT: 10,000
SALES (est): 3.7MM **Privately Held**
WEB: www.bacchuspress.com
SIC: 2752 Commercial printing, offset

(P-6433)
BACHUR & ASSOCIATES
1950 Homestead Rd, Santa Clara
(95050-6936)
PHONE..................................408 988-5861
Jerry Bachur, *Owner*
EMP: 12
SALES: 600K **Privately Held**
WEB: www.bachur-n-associates.com
SIC: 2752 8748 Photolithographic printing; systems analysis & engineering consulting services

(P-6434)
BAISE ENTERPRISES INC
Also Called: Sutter Printing
3258 Stockton Blvd, Sacramento
(95820-1418)
PHONE..................................916 446-0167
Craig Baise, *President*
EMP: 13
SALES (est): 1.2MM **Privately Held**
WEB: www.sutterprinting.com
SIC: 2752 7334 2791 2759 Commercial printing, offset; photocopying & duplicating services; typesetting, computer controlled; commercial printing; commercial art & graphic design

(P-6435)
BARLOW AND SONS PRINTING INC
Also Called: Barlow Printing
481 Aaron St, Cotati (94931-3081)
PHONE..................................707 664-9773
Patrick Barlow, *President*
Ken Reed, *Vice Pres*
EMP: 15
SQ FT: 20,000
SALES (est): 3.2MM **Privately Held**
WEB: www.barlowprinting.com
SIC: 2752 Letters, circular or form: lithographed; commercial printing, offset

(P-6436)
BARRYS PRINTING INC
Also Called: All About Printing
9005 Eton Ave Ste D, Canoga Park
(91304-6534)
PHONE..................................818 998-8600
Barry Shapiro, *CEO*
EMP: 30
SALES (est): 4.9MM **Privately Held**
WEB: www.dotgraphics.net
SIC: 2752 7334 Commercial printing, offset; photocopying & duplicating services

(P-6437)
BATCHLDER BUS CMMNICATIONS INC
Also Called: AlphaGraphics
2900 Standiford Ave Ste 5, Modesto
(95350-6575)
PHONE..................................209 577-2222
Ardem Batchelder, *President*
EMP: 12
SALES (est): 1.4MM **Privately Held**
SIC: 2752 7331 Commercial printing, lithographic; mailing list compilers

(P-6438)
BATIDA INC
Also Called: Western Lithographics
3187 Airway Ave Ste B, Costa Mesa
(92626-4603)
PHONE..................................714 557-4597
George Petty, *Vice Pres*
Parie Petty, *President*
Phyllis Petty, *Treasurer*
EMP: 11 EST: 1970
SQ FT: 4,200

SALES (est): 2MM **Privately Held**
WEB: www.westernlithographics.com
SIC: 2752 Commercial printing, offset

(P-6439)
BAY CENTRAL PRINTING INC
33401 Western Ave, Union City
(94587-3201)
PHONE..................................510 429-9111
Michael H Mahmoudi, *President*
Bana Mahmoudi, *Sales Staff*
EMP: 14
SQ FT: 2,500
SALES (est): 2.5MM **Privately Held**
WEB: www.baycentralprinting.com
SIC: 2752 Commercial printing, offset

(P-6440)
BBC CORP
Also Called: Enterprise Printing
4286 N Star Dr, Shingle Springs
(95682-5003)
PHONE..................................530 677-4009
Chris K Mulligan, *President*
Bertha J Mulligan, *Treasurer*
EMP: 29
SALES (est): 2.4MM **Privately Held**
SIC: 2752 Commercial printing, lithographic

(P-6441)
BENJAMIN LEWIS INC
Also Called: Studio Two Black Diamond Prtg
23042 Alcalde Dr Ste C, Laguna Hills
(92653-1326)
PHONE..................................949 859-5119
Jeff Benjamin, *President*
Eddie Chung, *Cust Mgr*
EMP: 13
SALES (est): 1.4MM **Privately Held**
SIC: 2752 Commercial printing, offset

(P-6442)
BENJAMIN LITHO INC
1810 Oakland Rd Ste F, San Jose
(95131-2316)
PHONE..................................408 232-3800
Ronald Habit, *President*
Matt Bonnett, *Production*
▲ EMP: 10
SQ FT: 1,040
SALES (est): 1.2MM **Privately Held**
WEB: www.benjaminlitho.com
SIC: 2752 5199 2759 Commercial printing, lithographic; gifts & novelties; screen printing

(P-6443)
BENNETT INDUSTRIES INC
Also Called: Graphic Source, The
4304 Redwood Hwy 200, San Rafael
(94903-2103)
PHONE..................................415 482-9000
Christie Lo, *President*
Lori Lopin, *CFO*
Jeff Lo, *Officer*
Jeffrey Lo, *Vice Pres*
Joe Brooks, *Project Mgr*
▲ EMP: 13
SQ FT: 2,500
SALES (est): 2.4MM **Privately Held**
WEB: www.graphic-source.com
SIC: 2752 Commercial printing, offset

(P-6444)
BENTLEY PRTG & GRAPHICS INC
1608 Sierra Madre Cir, Placentia
(92870-6626)
PHONE..................................714 636-1622
Thomas Bentley, *President*
Donna Aigner, *Manager*
EMP: 11
SQ FT: 3,500
SALES (est): 1.3MM **Privately Held**
WEB: www.bentleyprint.com
SIC: 2752 2791 Commercial printing, offset; typesetting

(P-6445)
BERT-CO INDUSTRIES INC (PA)
2150 S Parco Ave, Ontario (91761-5768)
P.O. Box 4150 (91761-1068)
PHONE..................................323 669-5700
Charles F Stay, *CEO*
Rose Vanderzanden, *CFO*

Stefan De Paz, *Finance*
Constantin S Tz, *Director*
▲ EMP: 106 EST: 1984
SQ FT: 120,000
SALES: 50MM **Privately Held**
WEB: www.bert-co.com
SIC: 2752 Commercial printing, lithographic

(P-6446)
BETTER INSTANT COPY
512 S San Vicente Blvd # 1, Los Angeles
(90048-4645)
P.O. Box 17734, Beverly Hills (90209-3734)
PHONE..................................323 782-6934
Boaz Rasael, *Owner*
EMP: 10
SALES (est): 1.1MM **Privately Held**
SIC: 2752 Commercial printing, offset

(P-6447)
BIBBERO SYSTEMS INC (HQ)
1300 N Mcdowell Blvd, Petaluma
(94954-1180)
PHONE..................................800 242-2376
Michael Buckley, *President*
Joan Buckley, *Corp Secy*
EMP: 29 EST: 1953
SQ FT: 60,000
SALES (est): 4.1MM
SALES (corp-wide): 7.9MM **Privately Held**
WEB: www.bibbero.com
SIC: 2752 2759 Offset & photolithographic printing; business forms; printing
PA: Professional Filing Systems, Inc.
5076 Winters Chapel Rd # 200
Atlanta GA 30360
770 396-4994

(P-6448)
BIG INK PRINTING
1711 Branham Ln Ste A5, San Jose
(95118-5223)
PHONE..................................408 624-1204
Dion Berry, *Principal*
EMP: 10 EST: 2013
SALES (est): 905.8K **Privately Held**
SIC: 2752 Commercial printing, offset

(P-6449)
BIG TIME DIGITAL
1250 E 223rd St Ste 111, Carson
(90745-4277)
PHONE..................................714 752-5959
Jeanette F Reale, *Mng Member*
EMP: 13
SALES (est): 1.7MM **Privately Held**
SIC: 2752 Commercial printing, lithographic

(P-6450)
BIG3D
Also Called: Big3d.com
2794 N Larkin Ave, Fresno (93727-1315)
PHONE..................................559 233-3380
Thomas K Saville Jr, *President*
Tom Saville, *President*
Laura McKee, *Sales Staff*
▲ EMP: 25
SQ FT: 25,000
SALES (est): 4.1MM **Privately Held**
WEB: www.big3d.com
SIC: 2752 Commercial printing, lithographic

(P-6451)
BIZ LAUNCHERS INC
1075 Linda Vista Dr, San Marcos
(92078-2621)
PHONE..................................760 744-6604
Jon Dixon, *Principal*
Brian Peeples, *Graphic Designe*
EMP: 14
SALES (est): 2.1MM **Privately Held**
SIC: 2752 Commercial printing, lithographic

(P-6452)
BLUEBARRY ENTERPRISES INC
Also Called: PIP Printing
16525 Sherman Way Ste C11, Van Nuys
(91406-3786)
PHONE..................................818 956-0912
Michael Bluestein, *President*

EMP: 10
SQ FT: 1,200
SALES (est): 1.1MM **Privately Held**
SIC: 2752 Commercial printing, offset

(P-6453)
BOHNS PRINTING
656 W Lancaster Blvd, Lancaster
(93534-3127)
PHONE..................................661 948-8081
Roger Hemme, *Owner*
Shirley Hemme, *Co-Owner*
EMP: 10
SQ FT: 6,500
SALES (est): 901.1K **Privately Held**
SIC: 2752 Commercial printing, offset

(P-6454)
BOSS LITHO INC
2380 Peck Rd, City of Industry
(90601-1601)
PHONE..................................626 912-7088
Jean Paul Nataf, *President*
Tim Chen, *Marketing Staff*
EMP: 42
SALES (est): 10MM **Privately Held**
WEB: www.bosslitho.com
SIC: 2752 Commercial printing, offset

(P-6455)
BOSS PRINTING INC
3403 W Macarthur Blvd, Santa Ana
(92704-6805)
PHONE..................................714 545-2677
Todd Gibb, *President*
Whitaker Christa, *Office Mgr*
EMP: 10
SQ FT: 11,500
SALES (est): 968K **Privately Held**
SIC: 2752 Commercial printing, lithographic

(P-6456)
BOX CO INC
7575 Britannia Park Pl, San Diego
(92154-7418)
PHONE..................................619 661-8090
Richard Barragan, *President*
Maggie Barragan, *Corp Secy*
▲ EMP: 16
SQ FT: 16,000
SALES (est): 3.8MM **Privately Held**
WEB: www.theboxcoinc.com
SIC: 2752 2657 Commercial printing, lithographic; folding paperboard boxes

(P-6457)
BRAND IDENTITY INC
9520 Flintridge Way, Orangevale
(95662-5713)
PHONE..................................916 553-0000
Peter Stelmaszczyk, *CEO*
Kasia Stelmaszczyk, *Vice Pres*
EMP: 11 EST: 1994
SQ FT: 6,000
SALES (est): 1.1MM **Privately Held**
WEB: www.thebrandidentity.com
SIC: 2752 Commercial printing, offset

(P-6458)
BREHM COMMUNICATIONS INC (PA)
Also Called: B C I
16644 W Bernardo Dr # 300, San Diego
(92127-1901)
P.O. Box 28429 (92198-0429)
PHONE..................................858 451-6200
Bill Brehm Jr, *President*
W J Brehm, *Chairman*
Tom Taylor, *Vice Pres*
Mona Brehm, *Admin Sec*
EMP: 47 EST: 1919
SQ FT: 6,000
SALES (est): 224.8MM **Privately Held**
WEB: www.brehmcommunications.com
SIC: 2752 2711 Commercial printing, offset; commercial printing & newspaper publishing combined

(P-6459)
BRUNETTES PRINTING SERVICE
Also Called: Brunette Printing
742 E Washington Blvd, Los Angeles
(90021-3077)
PHONE..................................213 749-7441
Ed Volen, *President*

Mark Volen, *Vice Pres*
Renee Volen, *Admin Sec*
EMP: 10
SQ FT: 5,200
SALES (est): 1.4MM **Privately Held**
SIC: 2752 2759 Commercial printing, offset; letterpress printing

(P-6460)
BRYAN PRESS INC
1011 S Stimson Ave, City of Industry
(91745-1630)
PHONE..................................626 961-9257
K Bryan, *President*
Brad Bryan, *Sales Mgr*
EMP: 18
SALES (est): 2.6MM **Privately Held**
SIC: 2752 Commercial printing, lithographic

(P-6461)
BULLFROG PRINTING AND GRAPHICS
1261 S Wright St, Santa Ana (92705-4511)
P.O. Box 11402 (92711-1402)
PHONE..................................714 641-0220
Steven Sealy, *Owner*
EMP: 10
SALES (est): 1.1MM **Privately Held**
SIC: 2752 Commercial printing, offset

(P-6462)
BUSINESS FULFILLMENT SVCS INC
Also Called: B F S Printing Bulk Mail Etc
791 Plumas St, Yuba City (95991-4437)
PHONE..................................530 671-7006
Adel Mitchell, *President*
EMP: 10
SQ FT: 2,500
SALES: 340K **Privately Held**
SIC: 2752 Commercial printing, offset

(P-6463)
BUSINESS WITH PLEASURE
1 Victor Sq, Scotts Valley (95066-3575)
PHONE..................................831 430-9711
Marcelo Siero, *Owner*
EMP: 10
SQ FT: 5,500
SALES (est): 1MM **Privately Held**
SIC: 2752 5943 5947 Commercial printing, offset; office forms & supplies; gift, novelty & souvenir shop

(P-6464)
C T V INC
Also Called: Imperial Printing
481 Vandell Way, Campbell (95008-6907)
PHONE..................................408 378-1606
Melvin Cardoza, *President*
Ron Cardoza, *Vice Pres*
Sharon Cardoza, *Vice Pres*
Kris Salazar, *Vice Pres*
Christina Rodriguez, *Bookkeeper*
EMP: 13
SALES (est): 2MM **Privately Held**
SIC: 2752 Commercial printing, offset

(P-6465)
C4 LITHO
27020 Daisy Cir, Yorba Linda (92887-4233)
PHONE..................................714 259-1073
Su T Dang,
Stacey Dang,
EMP: 17
SALES (est): 3.5MM **Privately Held**
SIC: 2752 Commercial printing, offset

(P-6466)
CAL SOUTHERN GRAPHICS CORP
8432 Steller Dr, Culver City (90232-2425)
PHONE..................................310 559-3600
Timothy Toomey, *CEO*
Saeed Amir, *Controller*
Amir Saeed, *Controller*
Donya Toomey, *Purchasing*
Jonas Hanelin, *Sales Staff*
▲ EMP: 82
SQ FT: 32,000

PRODUCTS & SVCS

SALES: 20MM **Privately Held**
WEB: www.socalgraph.com
SIC: 2752 2759 2754 Lithographing on metal; commercial printing; commercial printing, gravure

(P-6467)
CALIFORNIA MASTER PRINTERS
Also Called: Gold Leaf Cigar Co
796 N Todd Ave, Azusa (91702-2227)
PHONE.................................626 812-8930
Tony Lazzeri, *President*
Arthur Lazzeri, *Vice Pres*
Beverly Lazzeri, *Vice Pres*
EMP: 10
SQ FT: 8,000
SALES (est): 847K **Privately Held**
SIC: 2752 Commercial printing, offset

(P-6468)
CALIFORNIA SCENE PUBLISHING
8360 Juniper Creek Ln, San Diego
(92126-1072)
PHONE.................................858 635-9400
Leo Sismanis, *President*
▲ **EMP:** 10
SQ FT: 6,200
SALES (est): 1.1MM **Privately Held**
WEB: www.calscene.com
SIC: 2752 Post cards, picture: lithographed

(P-6469)
CALIFRNIA INTEGRATED MEDIA INC (PA)
Also Called: AlphaGraphics
3000 Kerner Blvd, San Rafael
(94901-5413)
PHONE.................................415 627-8310
Manuel Torres, *CEO*
EMP: 13 **EST:** 2015
SALES (est): 2.5MM **Privately Held**
SIC: 2752 Commercial printing, lithographic

(P-6470)
CAMPBELL GRAPHICS INC
156 N 2nd St, Campbell (95008-2024)
PHONE.................................408 371-6411
Laverne G Lamar, *President*
Jean Lamar, *Corp Secy*
EMP: 24
SQ FT: 10,000
SALES (est): 2.9MM **Privately Held**
WEB: www.cgprint.com
SIC: 2752 Commercial printing, offset

(P-6471)
CANDLELIGHT PRESS INC
26752 Oak Ave Ste F, Canyon Country
(91351-6675)
PHONE.................................323 299-3798
Richard E Rice, *President*
EMP: 20
SQ FT: 15,000
SALES: 1.8MM **Privately Held**
WEB: www.candlelightpress.com
SIC: 2752 Commercial printing, lithographic

(P-6472)
CANDU GRAPHICS
5737 Kanan Rd Ste 132, Agoura Hills
(91301-1601)
PHONE.................................310 822-1620
Michael Dutra, *President*
EMP: 10
SALES: 1.3MM **Privately Held**
SIC: 2752 Commercial printing, offset

(P-6473)
CARL & IRVING PRINTERS INC
161 N N St, Tulare (93274-4226)
P.O. Box 627 (93275-0627)
PHONE.................................559 686-8354
James Gonsalves, *President*
Arlene Gonsalves, *Corp Secy*
EMP: 10
SQ FT: 11,000
SALES (est): 991.6K **Privately Held**
SIC: 2752 2759 Commercial printing, offset; letterpress printing

(P-6474)
CASEY PRINTING INC
398 E San Antonio Dr, King City
(93930-2509)
P.O. Box 913 (93930-0913)
PHONE.................................831 385-3221
Richard Casey, *President*
EMP: 48
SQ FT: 31,000
SALES (est): 7.7MM **Privately Held**
WEB: www.caseyprinting.com
SIC: 2752 Commercial printing, offset

(P-6475)
CDR GRAPHICS INC (PA)
2299 Westwood Blvd, Los Angeles
(90064-2017)
PHONE.................................310 474-7600
Homan Hadawi, *President*
EMP: 24
SQ FT: 4,610
SALES (est): 3.1MM **Privately Held**
SIC: 2752 Commercial printing, lithographic

(P-6476)
CEC PRINT SOLUTIONS INC
30971 San Benito St, Hayward
(94544-7936)
PHONE.................................510 670-0160
Amit Chokshi, *President*
Mary Beth Cahill, *Office Mgr*
Pratik Dakwala, *Mktg Dir*
Richard Fish, *Accounts Exec*
▲ **EMP:** 12 **EST:** 1976
SQ FT: 26,000
SALES (est): 2.8MM **Privately Held**
WEB: www.cecprinting.com
SIC: 2752 Commercial printing, offset; business forms, lithographed

(P-6477)
CENTRAL BUSINESS FORMS INC
Also Called: Central Printing Group
289 Foster City Blvd B, Foster City
(94404-1100)
PHONE.................................650 548-0918
Jeanine M Morgan, *President*
Michelle L Cabral, *Corp Secy*
EMP: 18
SQ FT: 22,800
SALES (est): 3.5MM **Privately Held**
WEB: www.cpgusa.com
SIC: 2752 Commercial printing, offset

(P-6478)
CENVEO WORLDWIDE LIMITED
665 3rd St Ste 505, San Francisco
(94107-1956)
PHONE.................................415 821-7171
Coleen Schoenatide, *Branch Mgr*
EMP: 80
SALES (corp-wide): 2.6B **Privately Held**
SIC: 2752 Commercial printing, offset
HQ: Cenveo Worldwide Limited
200 First Stamford Pl # 2
Stamford CT 06902
203 595-3000

(P-6479)
CH IMAGE INC
Also Called: Cater Line , The
15350 Valley Blvd, City of Industry
(91746-3335)
PHONE.................................626 336-6063
▲ **EMP:** 15 **EST:** 1999
SALES (est): 1.2MM **Privately Held**
SIC: 2752

(P-6480)
CHALLENGE GRAPHICS INC
16611 Roscoe Pl, North Hills (91343-6104)
PHONE.................................818 892-0123
Robert F Ritter, *President*
Kathy Burtoft, *Treasurer*
Sally A Ritter, *Vice Pres*
Tara Curtis, *Admin Sec*
EMP: 25
SQ FT: 17,000
SALES (est): 2.5MM **Privately Held**
WEB: www.challenge-graphics.com
SIC: 2752 Commercial printing, offset

(P-6481)
CHECCHI ENTERPRISES INC
Also Called: Harvest Printing Company
19849 Riverside Ave, Anderson
(96007-4909)
PHONE.................................530 378-1207
Tom Watega, *President*
Diana Watega, *Bookkeeper*
Joni Sargent, *Manager*
EMP: 15
SQ FT: 10,200
SALES (est): 2.4MM **Privately Held**
WEB: www.harvestprinting.com
SIC: 2752 Commercial printing, offset

(P-6482)
CHILD EVNGELISM FELLOWSHIP INC
2201 Mount Vernon Ave, Bakersfield
(93306-3341)
P.O. Box 60735 (93386-0735)
PHONE.................................661 873-9032
EMP: 41
SALES (corp-wide): 24.4MM **Privately Held**
SIC: 2752 Commercial printing, lithographic
PA: Child Evangelism Fellowship Incorporated
17482 Highway M
Warrenton MO 63383
636 456-4321

(P-6483)
CHIMES PRINTING INCORPORATED
1065 Hensley St, Richmond (94801-2116)
PHONE.................................510 235-2388
Thomas C Pimm, *President*
EMP: 12 **EST:** 1989
SALES (est): 1.7MM **Privately Held**
SIC: 2752 Commercial printing, offset

(P-6484)
CHROMATIC INC LITHOGRAPHERS
127 Concord St, Glendale (91203-2456)
PHONE.................................818 242-5785
Keith Sevigny, *President*
Mary Gene Sevigny, *CEO*
Michael Sevigny, *Vice Pres*
Sandy Orozco, *Admin Asst*
Marlene Lunn, *Administration*
▲ **EMP:** 32
SQ FT: 30,000
SALES (est): 7.2MM **Privately Held**
SIC: 2752 Commercial printing, offset

(P-6485)
CHUP CORPORATION
Also Called: Color Digit
2990 Airway Ave Ste A, Costa Mesa
(92626-6037)
PHONE.................................949 455-0676
Mohsen Kaeni, *President*
Hadi Kaeni, *Vice Pres*
Hamid Kaeni, *Admin Sec*
EMP: 15
SQ FT: 11,000
SALES (est): 4.1MM **Privately Held**
SIC: 2752 2796 Commercial printing, offset; color separations for printing

(P-6486)
CLASSIC LITHO & DESIGN INC
340 Maple Ave, Torrance (90503-2600)
PHONE.................................310 224-5200
Masoud Nikravan, *CEO*
Firouzeh Nikravan, *President*
Henry Guzman, *Project Mgr*
Bill Obr, *Project Mgr*
Craig Elferdink, *Manager*
EMP: 30 **EST:** 1976
SQ FT: 12,500
SALES: 5.2MM **Privately Held**
WEB: www.classiclitho.com
SIC: 2752 Commercial printing, offset

(P-6487)
CLEAR IMAGE PRINTING INC
12744 San Fernando Rd # 200, Sylmar
(91342-3856)
PHONE.................................818 547-4684
Anthony Toven, *President*
Jessica Slepicka, *Executive*

Dejirlene Concha, *Bookkeeper*
Sammantha Toven, *Sales Staff*
EMP: 28
SQ FT: 18,000
SALES (est): 8MM **Privately Held**
SIC: 2752 Commercial printing, offset

(P-6488)
CLIC LLC
Also Called: Andresen
855 Stanton Rd 300, Burlingame
(94010-1403)
PHONE.................................415 421-2900
Michael Hicks, *Mng Member*
Andresen Family Trust, *Mng Member*
EMP: 18
SALES (est): 3.9MM **Privately Held**
WEB: www.andresen.com
SIC: 2752 7374 Commercial printing, lithographic; computer graphics service

(P-6489)
CMY IMAGE CORPORATION
Also Called: Compandsave
33268 Central Ave, Union City
(94587-2010)
PHONE.................................510 516-6668
Andrew Yeung, *CEO*
EMP: 15 **EST:** 2013
SALES: 6MM **Privately Held**
SIC: 2752 Photo-offset printing

(P-6490)
CMYK ENTERPRISE INC
Also Called: Cmyk Prints and Promotions.com
1950 W Fremont St, Stockton
(95203-2041)
PHONE.................................209 229-7230
Nick Michael Pappas, *President*
Amy Gephart,
▲ **EMP:** 12
SQ FT: 30,000
SALES (est): 2.5MM **Privately Held**
SIC: 2752 7389 8743 Commercial printing, lithographic; packaging & labeling services; promotion service

(P-6491)
CO-COLOR
Also Called: Co/Color Division
650 W Terrace Dr, San Dimas
(91773-2908)
PHONE.................................909 394-7888
Fax: 909 394-7897
EMP: 12 **EST:** 1969
SQ FT: 12,000
SALES (est): 3.6MM **Privately Held**
SIC: 2752

(P-6492)
COAST COLOR PRINTING INC
Also Called: Sunset Printing
16301 S Broadway, Gardena (90248-2709)
PHONE.................................310 352-3560
Dennis Lanfre, *CEO*
Michael Lanfre, *Vice Pres*
Kimberly Lanfre-Brubaker, *Vice Pres*
EMP: 10
SQ FT: 6,000
SALES: 1.7MM **Privately Held**
SIC: 2752 Commercial printing, lithographic

(P-6493)
COLE PRINT & MARKETING
2001 Salvio St Ste 25, Concord
(94520-2059)
PHONE.................................925 276-2344
Chris Cole, *Owner*
EMP: 11 **EST:** 2010
SALES (est): 1.3MM **Privately Held**
SIC: 2752 Commercial printing, lithographic

(P-6494)
COLOR INC
1600 Flower St, Glendale (91201-2319)
PHONE.................................818 240-1350
Barry D Hamm, *President*
James E Hamm, *Vice Pres*
Chris Nava, *Accounts Exec*
EMP: 35
SQ FT: 16,000

▲ = Import ▼=Export
◆ =Import/Export

SALES (est): 6MM **Privately Held**
SIC: 2752 2796 Color lithography; publication printing, lithographic; platemaking services

(P-6495)
COLOR SERVICE INC
40 E Verdugo Ave, Burbank (91502-1931)
PHONE.................................323 283-4793
Patrick F Seeholzer, *President*
Patrick Seeholzer, *Bd of Directors*
Michael Mahoney, *Vice Pres*
EMP: 42
SQ FT: 30,000
SALES (est): 4.6MM **Privately Held**
WEB: www.colorservice.com
SIC: 2752 Commercial printing, lithographic

(P-6496)
COLOR TONE INC
Also Called: Colortone Digital
2475 Estand Way, Pleasant Hill (94523-3911)
PHONE.................................925 680-2695
Bobby Santos, *President*
EMP: 10
SQ FT: 8,500
SALES: 1.6MM **Privately Held**
SIC: 2752 Commercial printing, offset

(P-6497)
COLORCOM INC
2437 S Eastern Ave, Commerce (90040-1414)
PHONE.................................323 246-4640
John Youn, *President*
Young Kim, *Shareholder*
Paul Yoo, *General Mgr*
EMP: 16
SALES (est): 3.4MM **Privately Held**
WEB: www.colorcom.net
SIC: 2752 Commercial printing, offset

(P-6498)
COLORFAST DYE & PRINT HSE INC
5075 Pacific Blvd, Vernon (90058-2215)
PHONE.................................323 581-1656
Enrique Ruiz, *President*
Jose Ramos, *Vice Pres*
EMP: 107
SQ FT: 30,000
SALES (est): 9.3MM **Privately Held**
SIC: 2752 2396 2269 Commercial printing, lithographic; screen printing on fabric articles; dyeing: raw stock yarn & narrow fabrics

(P-6499)
COLORFX INC
11050 Randall St, Sun Valley (91352-2621)
P.O. Box 12357, La Crescenta (91224-5357)
PHONE.................................818 767-7671
Razmik Avedissian, *CEO*
Arby Avedissian, *Vice Pres*
Yolanda Avedissian, *Admin Sec*
EMP: 50
SQ FT: 28,000
SALES (est): 8.4MM **Privately Held**
WEB: www.colorfxweb.com
SIC: 2752 Commercial printing, offset

(P-6500)
COLORMARX CORPORATION
Also Called: PIP Printing
4825 Auburn Blvd, Sacramento (95841-3603)
PHONE.................................916 334-0334
Kabrina K McNaught, *President*
Ray McNaught, *Vice Pres*
EMP: 11
SQ FT: 5,600
SALES (est): 2MM **Privately Held**
SIC: 2752 Commercial printing, offset

(P-6501)
COLORPRINT
1570 Gilbreth Rd, Burlingame (94010-1605)
PHONE.................................650 697-7611
Mark Jaffe, *Owner*
Irene Jhin, *Partner*
Genevieve Soriano, *Technology*
Paige Sawyer, *Opers Mgr*

Madsen Lorraine, *VP Sales*
EMP: 10
SQ FT: 3,200
SALES (est): 900K **Privately Held**
WEB: www.colorprint.com
SIC: 2752 7334 Commercial printing, offset; photocopying & duplicating services

(P-6502)
COMMERCE PRINTERS INC
3201 Halladay St, Santa Ana (92705-5628)
PHONE.................................714 549-5002
Cheryl Toscas, *CEO*
Thomas Toscas, *Owner*
Jay Toscas, *Manager*
▲ EMP: 20
SQ FT: 8,000
SALES (est): 3.5MM **Privately Held**
SIC: 2752 Commercial printing, offset

(P-6503)
COMMERCIAL CLEAR PRINT INC
9025 Fullbright Ave, Chatsworth (91311-6126)
PHONE.................................818 709-1220
Geoffrey Pick, *President*
Colleen Pick, *Vice Pres*
Blaine Waldman, *Project Mgr*
EMP: 10
SQ FT: 4,900
SALES (est): 2.1MM **Privately Held**
WEB: www.clearprint.com
SIC: 2752 7336 2759 Commercial printing, offset; commercial art & graphic design; commercial printing

(P-6504)
COMMUNICART
1589 Laurelwood Rd, Santa Clara (95054-2744)
PHONE.................................408 970-0922
Ken Azebu, *President*
Diane Ogami, *CEO*
Chiyo Ogami, *Treasurer*
Richard Ogami, *Vice Pres*
EMP: 10
SQ FT: 6,300
SALES (est): 870K **Privately Held**
WEB: www.communicart.com
SIC: 2752 2791 Commercial printing, offset; typesetting

(P-6505)
COMMUNITY PRINTERS INC
1827 Soquel Ave, Santa Cruz (95062-1385)
PHONE.................................831 426-4682
Joe Chavez, *President*
Shelly D'Amour, *CFO*
Mischa Kandinksy, *Treasurer*
Andy Bacon, *Project Mgr*
EMP: 32
SQ FT: 10,000
SALES: 4.9MM
SALES (corp-wide): 316.3K **Privately Held**
WEB: www.comprinters.com
SIC: 2752 Commercial printing, offset
PA: Eschaton Foundation
612 Ocean St
Santa Cruz CA 95060
831 423-1626

(P-6506)
COMSTOCK PRESS
2117 San Jose Ave, Alameda (94501-4915)
PHONE.................................510 522-4115
Fritz Zehender, *Owner*
EMP: 22
SALES: 1.5MM **Privately Held**
SIC: 2752 Commercial printing, offset

(P-6507)
CONTINENTAL GRAPHICS CORP
Also Called: Continental Engineering Svcs
6910 Carroll Rd, San Diego (92121-2211)
PHONE.................................858 552-6520
Manuel Defaria, *Branch Mgr*
Bruce Robinson, *Administration*
Matthew Labruyere, *Technology*
EMP: 500

SALES (corp-wide): 101.1B **Publicly Held**
WEB: www.cdgnow.com
SIC: 2752 7336 Promotional printing, lithographic; graphic arts & related design
HQ: Continental Graphics Corporation
4060 N Lakewood Blvd
Long Beach CA 90808
714 503-4200

(P-6508)
CONTINENTAL GRAPHICS CORP
Also Called: Continental Data Graphics
4060 N Lakewood Blvd 8015fl, Long Beach (90808-1700)
PHONE.................................714 827-1752
Warren Smith, *Manager*
EMP: 1080
SALES (corp-wide): 101.1B **Publicly Held**
WEB: www.cdgnow.com
SIC: 2752 7336 Promotional printing, lithographic; graphic arts & related design
HQ: Continental Graphics Corporation
4060 N Lakewood Blvd
Long Beach CA 90808
714 503-4200

(P-6509)
CONTINENTAL GRAPHICS CORP
9302 Pttsbrgh Ave Ste 100, Rancho Cucamonga (91730)
PHONE.................................909 758-9800
Steve Meade, *Branch Mgr*
EMP: 30
SALES (corp-wide): 101.1B **Publicly Held**
WEB: www.cdgnow.com
SIC: 2752 7336 Promotional printing, lithographic; graphic arts & related design
HQ: Continental Graphics Corporation
4060 N Lakewood Blvd
Long Beach CA 90808
714 503-4200

(P-6510)
CONTINENTAL GRAPHICS CORP
Also Called: Continental Data Graphics
222 N Pacific Coast Hwy # 300, El Segundo (90245-5648)
PHONE.................................310 662-2307
Mike Parvin, *Manager*
Warren Smith, *Vice Pres*
Thomas Spangler, *Vice Pres*
EMP: 20
SALES (corp-wide): 101.1B **Publicly Held**
WEB: www.cdgnow.com
SIC: 2752 7336 Promotional printing, lithographic; graphic arts & related design
HQ: Continental Graphics Corporation
4060 N Lakewood Blvd
Long Beach CA 90808
714 503-4200

(P-6511)
CONTINENTAL GRAPHIX
166 Riviera Dr, San Rafael (94901-1554)
PHONE.................................415 864-2345
Barry Schwartz, *President*
EMP: 25
SALES (est): 2.2MM **Privately Held**
WEB: www.continentalgraphix.com
SIC: 2752 7334 Commercial printing, offset; photocopying & duplicating services

(P-6512)
COPY 1 INC
Also Called: Digital One Legal Solutions
77 Battery St Fl 2, San Francisco (94111-5544)
PHONE.................................415 986-0111
Young Park, *President*
EMP: 25
SALES (est): 3.6MM **Privately Held**
SIC: 2752 Commercial printing, offset

(P-6513)
COPY SOLUTIONS INC
919 S Fremont Ave Ste 398, Alhambra (91803-4701)
PHONE.................................323 307-0900
Roger Zhao, *President*
EMP: 20
SQ FT: 5,000

SALES (est): 3.7MM **Privately Held**
WEB: www.copysolution.com
SIC: 2752 Commercial printing, lithographic

(P-6514)
COPYMAT SALINAS LLC
44 W Gabilan St, Salinas (93901-2731)
PHONE.................................831 753-0471
Barbara Mazzei,
EMP: 12
SQ FT: 4,000
SALES (est): 1.6MM **Privately Held**
SIC: 2752 Commercial printing, offset

(P-6515)
CORPORATE GRAPHICS & PRINTING
335 Science Dr, Moorpark (93021-2092)
PHONE.................................805 529-5333
Harry A Stidham, *President*
Harry Stidham, *President*
John Bird, *Vice Pres*
Warren Bachtel, *Accounts Exec*
EMP: 17
SQ FT: 20,000
SALES: 3MM **Privately Held**
WEB: www.corp-graphics.com
SIC: 2752 Commercial printing, offset

(P-6516)
CORPORATE GRAPHICS INTL INC
Also Called: Corporate Graphics West
4909 Alcoa Ave, Vernon (90058-3022)
PHONE.................................323 826-3440
Robert Gonynor, *General Mgr*
EMP: 85
SALES (corp-wide): 2.8B **Privately Held**
SIC: 2752 2759 Commercial printing, offset; lithographing on metal; embossing on paper
HQ: Corporate Graphics International, Inc.
1885 Northway Dr
North Mankato MN 56003
507 625-4400

(P-6517)
COYLE REPRODUCTIONS INC (PA)
2850 Orbiter St, Brea (92821-6224)
PHONE.................................866 269-5373
Frank T Cutrone Jr, *CEO*
Frank T Cutrone, *Ch of Bd*
Jason De Soto, *Exec VP*
Rosa Hernandez, *Office Mgr*
Kiri Chhoy, *Administration*
EMP: 140 EST: 1963
SQ FT: 85,000
SALES (est): 37.3MM **Privately Held**
WEB: www.coylerepro.com
SIC: 2752 2759 Commercial printing, offset; screen printing; posters, including billboards: printing

(P-6518)
CPRINT HOLDINGS LLC
1901 E 7th Pl, Los Angeles (90021-1601)
PHONE.................................213 488-0456
Sean Saberi, *President*
EMP: 15 EST: 2015
SALES: 2MM **Privately Held**
SIC: 2752 Commercial printing, offset

(P-6519)
CPS PRINTING
2304 Faraday Ave, Carlsbad (92008-7216)
PHONE.................................760 494-9000
Philip M Lurie, *President*
Kimberly Manning, *CFO*
EMP: 72
SQ FT: 23,000
SALES (est): 15.4MM **Privately Held**
WEB: www.cpsprinting.com
SIC: 2752 Commercial printing, offset

(P-6520)
CREAMER PRINTING CO
1413 N La Brea Ave, Inglewood (90302-1218)
PHONE.................................310 671-9491
Fred John Creamer III, *President*
Lawrence Creamer, *CFO*
Edmund J Creamer, *Corp Secy*
EMP: 15 EST: 1924

SQ FT: 10,000
SALES (est): 2.2MM **Privately Held**
SIC: 2752 2759 Commercial printing, off-set; flexographic printing

(P-6521)
CREATIVE COLOR PRINTING INC
1605 Railroad St, Corona (92880-2503)
PHONE..................................951 737-4551
Rudy Resner, *President*
Steve Rebel, *Sales Staff*
EMP: 11 **EST:** 1982
SQ FT: 8,000
SALES (est): 1.8MM **Privately Held**
WEB: www.creativecolorprinting.com
SIC: 2752 Commercial printing, offset

(P-6522)
CREATIVE PRESS LLC
1600 E Ball Rd, Anaheim (92805-5990)
PHONE..................................714 774-5060
Michael L Patton, *President*
Tony Ramirez, *Executive*
Tina Seybert, *Technology*
Kevin McHugh, *Foreman/Supr*
Mike Patton, *Marketing Mgr*
EMP: 65
SQ FT: 31,000
SALES (est): 21.6MM **Privately Held**
WEB: www.creativepressinc.net
SIC: 2752 2791 2789 Commercial printing, offset; typesetting; bookbinding & related work

(P-6523)
CRESCENT INC
1196 N Osprey Cir, Anaheim (92807-1709)
PHONE..................................714 992-6030
Reza Mohkami, *President*
Tahereh Mohkami, *Treasurer*
Ira Heshmati, *Vice Pres*
EMP: 25
SQ FT: 10,000
SALES (est): 3.9MM **Privately Held**
WEB: www.printprinting.com
SIC: 2752 7549 Commercial printing, offset; do-it-yourself garages

(P-6524)
CRESTEC USA INC
Also Called: Crestec Los Angeles
2410 Mira Mar Ave, Long Beach (90815-1756)
PHONE..................................310 327-9000
Tsuyoshi Kaneko, *CEO*
Mike Burk, *Vice Pres*
Steven Strother, *General Mgr*
Isabel Bocanegra, *Admin Sec*
Michael Fleder, *Engineer*
▲ **EMP:** 50 **EST:** 1967
SALES (est): 10.2MM **Privately Held**
WEB: www.crestecla.com
SIC: 2752 Commercial printing, offset
PA: Crestec Inc.
    676, Kasaishindencho, Higashi-Ku
    Hamamatsu SZO 431-3
    -

(P-6525)
CTS PRINTING
9920 Jordan Cir, Santa Fe Springs (90670-3346)
PHONE..................................562 941-8420
EMP: 10
SALES (est): 580K **Privately Held**
WEB: www.ctsll.com
SIC: 2752

(P-6526)
CUSTOM ART SERVICES CORP
Also Called: Colorplak.com
37110 Mesa Rd, Temecula (92592-8650)
PHONE..................................951 302-9889
Marvin Ellerby Farr, *CEO*
Melodie Faith Farr, *President*
Anita Park, *Master*
EMP: 10 **EST:** 2008
SALES: 750K **Privately Held**
SIC: 2752 7699 Photo-offset printing; picture framing, custom

(P-6527)
CUSTOM LITHOGRAPH
7006 Stanford Ave, Los Angeles (90001-1583)
PHONE..................................323 778-7751
Robert D Hanel, *President*
John Sebourn, *CFO*
Pamela Sebourn, *Admin Sec*
EMP: 20 **EST:** 1958
SQ FT: 92,000
SALES (est): 3.1MM **Privately Held**
WEB: www.customlithograph.com
SIC: 2752 Commercial printing, offset

(P-6528)
CYU LITHOGRAPHICS INC
Also Called: Choice Lithographics
6951 Oran Cir, Buena Park (90621-3305)
PHONE..................................888 878-9898
Michael Wang, *President*
▲ **EMP:** 25
SQ FT: 13,000
SALES: 3MM **Privately Held**
WEB: www.choicelitho.com
SIC: 2752 2721 Color lithography; magazines: publishing only, not printed on site

(P-6529)
D & J PRINTING INC
Also Called: Sinclair Printing Company
600 W Technology Dr, Palmdale (93551-3748)
PHONE..................................661 775-4586
Donna Beltran, *Branch Mgr*
Justin Smith, *Representative*
EMP: 100
SALES (corp-wide): 536.1MM **Privately Held**
SIC: 2752 Commercial printing, offset
HQ: D. & J. Printing, Inc.
    3323 Oak St
    Brainerd MN 56401
    218 829-2877

(P-6530)
D BENHAM CORPORATION
Also Called: KEBERT REPROGRAPHICS
10969 Wheatlands Ave A, Santee (92071-5619)
PHONE..................................619 448-8079
Dewey Kebert, *President*
Sandra Kebert, *Admin Sec*
Ryan Morse, *Web Dvlpr*
EMP: 10
SQ FT: 8,000
SALES: 850K **Privately Held**
WEB: www.kebertreprographics.com
SIC: 2752 Offset & photolithographic printing

(P-6531)
DAKOTA PRESS INC
14400 Doolittle Dr, San Leandro (94577-5546)
PHONE..................................510 895-1300
Mary Reid, *President*
Gary Reid, *Vice Pres*
EMP: 15
SALES (est): 3.6MM **Privately Held**
SIC: 2752 Commercial printing, lithographic

(P-6532)
DARE LITHOWORKS INC
Also Called: Rabbit Lithographics
13512 Vintage Pl Ste A, Chino (91710-5207)
PHONE..................................213 250-9062
Armand Dabuet, *President*
Ernand Dabuet, *Treasurer*
Reine Dabuet, *Vice Pres*
Renwick Dabuet, *Admin Sec*
EMP: 10
SQ FT: 6,000
SALES (est): 1.7MM **Privately Held**
WEB: www.rabbitlitho.com
SIC: 2752 Commercial printing, offset

(P-6533)
DAVID B ANDERSON
Also Called: Central Coast Printing
921 Huston St, Grover Beach (93433-3108)
PHONE..................................805 489-0661
David B Anderson, *Owner*
Gail Speer, *Admin Sec*

Doug Speer, *Plant Mgr*
EMP: 26 **EST:** 1978
SQ FT: 17,000
SALES (est): 3.5MM **Privately Held**
SIC: 2752 Commercial printing, offset

(P-6534)
DBC PRINTING INCORPORATED
Also Called: Vanguard Printing
220 Bernoulli Cir, Oxnard (93030-8012)
PHONE..................................805 988-8855
Jeff D Cox, *CEO*
Justin Cox, *Sales Staff*
Dina Masters, *Accounts Mgr*
EMP: 14
SQ FT: 14,000
SALES (est): 2.5MM **Privately Held**
SIC: 2752 Offset & photolithographic printing

(P-6535)
DENNIS BOLTON ENTERPRISES INC
7285 Coldwater Canyon Ave, North Hollywood (91605-4204)
PHONE..................................818 982-1800
Dennis Bolton, *President*
Osvaldo Acosta, *Treasurer*
Max Guerrero, *Vice Pres*
Carlo Bernal, *Admin Sec*
EMP: 23
SQ FT: 14,780
SALES (est): 3.1MM **Privately Held**
WEB: www.printingbydbe.com
SIC: 2752 7334 7311 Commercial printing, offset; photocopying & duplicating services; advertising consultant

(P-6536)
DESIGNER PRINTING INC
Also Called: Igraphix
638 Washington St, San Francisco (94111-2106)
PHONE..................................415 989-0008
Wade Lai, *President*
▲ **EMP:** 17
SQ FT: 8,500
SALES (est): 1.7MM **Privately Held**
WEB: www.designerprinting.com
SIC: 2752 Commercial printing, offset

(P-6537)
DF GRAFIX INC
13871 Danielson St, Poway (92064-6891)
PHONE..................................858 866-0858
David P Fox, *President*
◆ **EMP:** 10
SALES (est): 2MM **Privately Held**
SIC: 2752 Commercial printing, offset

(P-6538)
DIEGO & SON PRINTING INC
2277 National Ave, San Diego (92113-3614)
P.O. Box 13100 (92170-3100)
PHONE..................................619 233-5373
Nicholas Aguilera, *President*
Isabelle Aguilera, *Corp Secy*
Rebecca Aguilera, *Vice Pres*
Rebecca Aguilera-Gardin, *Vice Pres*
Elizabeth Fitzsimons, *Vice Pres*
EMP: 22
SALES (est): 4.3MM **Privately Held**
WEB: www.diegoandson.com
SIC: 2752 2759 Commercial printing, offset; commercial printing

(P-6539)
DIGI PRINT PLUS
9670 Research Dr, Irvine (92618-4666)
PHONE..................................949 770-5000
Farhad Omidvar, *CEO*
EMP: 11
SALES (est): 1.4MM **Privately Held**
SIC: 2752 Commercial printing, offset

(P-6540)
DIGITAL MANIA INC
Also Called: Copymat
455 Market St Ste 180, San Francisco (94105-2476)
PHONE..................................415 896-0500
Darius Meykadah, *President*
EMP: 20
SALES: 4.5MM **Privately Held**
SIC: 2752 Commercial printing, offset

(P-6541)
DIGITAL ONE PRINTING INC
13367 Kirkham Way 110, Poway (92064-7118)
PHONE..................................858 278-2228
Micheal Clark, *President*
Dave Picinich, *Vice Pres*
EMP: 10
SALES (est): 1.3MM **Privately Held**
SIC: 2752 Commercial printing, lithographic

(P-6542)
DIGITAL PRINTING SYSTEMS INC (PA)
777 N Georgia Ave, Azusa (91702-2207)
PHONE..................................626 815-1888
Donald J Nores, *CEO*
Peter Young, *CEO*
Doug Gabriel, *CFO*
Joyce Nores, *Treasurer*
Jim Nores, *Vice Pres*
◆ **EMP:** 75
SQ FT: 30,640
SALES (est): 20.1MM **Privately Held**
WEB: www.dpstickets.com
SIC: 2752 Tickets, lithographed

(P-6543)
DIRECT LABEL & TAG LLC
11909 Telegraph Rd, Santa Fe Springs (90670-3785)
PHONE..................................562 948-4499
Edward Rosen, *Mng Member*
Jeffrey Gampel,
▲ **EMP:** 21
SQ FT: 2,700
SALES (est): 1.2MM **Privately Held**
SIC: 2752 2754 3577 5131 Tags, lithographed; labels: gravure printing; bar code (magnetic ink) printers; labels

(P-6544)
DISCOUNT INSTANT PRINTING
175 S Thurston Ave, Los Angeles (90049-3128)
PHONE..................................213 622-4347
Kamran Nazarian, *Partner*
Kiu Nazarian, *Partner*
EMP: 12
SQ FT: 3,400
SALES (est): 1.1MM **Privately Held**
SIC: 2752 Commercial printing, lithographic

(P-6545)
DIVERSIFIED LITHO SERVICES
Also Called: DLS
4462 E Airport Dr, Ontario (91761-7804)
PHONE..................................714 558-2995
Geoffrey Gruber, *Owner*
EMP: 10
SALES (est): 1.2MM **Privately Held**
WEB: www.dlsgroup.net
SIC: 2752 Commercial printing, lithographic

(P-6546)
DLA DOCUMENT SERVICES
4231 San Pedro Rd, Port Hueneme (93043-4308)
PHONE..................................805 982-4310
Mark Shadinger, *Manager*
EMP: 28 **Publicly Held**
SIC: 2752 9711 Commercial printing, lithographic; national security;
HQ: Dla Document Services
    5450 Carlisle Pike Bldg 9
    Mechanicsburg PA 17050
    717 605-2362

(P-6547)
DOCUMOTION RESEARCH INC
2020 S Eastwood Ave, Santa Ana (92705-5208)
PHONE..................................714 662-3800
Joel Van Boom, *President*
EMP: 17
SQ FT: 10,000
SALES (est): 3.2MM **Privately Held**
SIC: 2752 Commercial printing, lithographic

▲ = Import ▼=Export
◆ =Import/Export

(P-6548)
DOLPHIN PRESS INC
264 S Maple Ave, South San Francisco (94080-6304)
PHONE..................................650 873-9092
Gary Swanson, *President*
Marsha Fontes, *Vice Pres*
EMP: 14
SQ FT: 4,200
SALES (est): 1.8MM **Privately Held**
SIC: 2752 Commercial printing, lithographic

(P-6549)
DOT COPY INC
Also Called: DOT Graphics
9655 De Soto Ave, Chatsworth (91311-5013)
PHONE..................................818 341-6666
Brian Whiteman, *CEO*
Jamie Gordon, *Executive*
Crystal Sessions, *Purchasing*
Ernest Edwards, *Mfg Staff*
Brian Berent, *Sales Staff*
EMP: 49
SALES (est): 10.7MM **Privately Held**
SIC: 2752 Commercial printing, offset

(P-6550)
DOT CORP
1801 S Standard Ave, Santa Ana (92707-2465)
PHONE..................................714 708-5960
Sherry Gardner, *Credit Mgr*
Kathy Payne, *VP Sales*
Ruben Gonzalez, *Director*
Scott Pohle, *Director*
Richard Alvarez, *Manager*
EMP: 23
SALES (corp-wide): 2.5MM **Privately Held**
SIC: 2752 Commercial printing, lithographic
PA: The Dot Corp
2525 Pullman St
Santa Ana CA 92705
714 708-5800

(P-6551)
DOT PRINTER INC (PA)
2424 Mcgaw Ave, Irvine (92614-5834)
PHONE..................................949 474-1100
Bruce M Carson, *President*
Stan Lowe, *COO*
James Voss, *CFO*
Jim Voss, *CFO*
Laura Parker, *Senior VP*
▲ EMP: 170
SQ FT: 40,000
SALES (est): 56.5MM **Privately Held**
WEB: www.dotprinter.com
SIC: 2752 2732 3555 Commercial printing, lithographic; book printing; printing trades machinery

(P-6552)
DSJ PRINTING INC
1703 Stewart St, Santa Monica (90404-4021)
PHONE..................................310 828-8051
Jeffrey L Vaughan, *President*
Jeffrey Vaughan Jr, *Vice Pres*
Stacie Vaughan, *Graphic Designe*
Brandon Vaughan, *Prdtn Mgr*
Rodrigo Lima, *Production*
EMP: 13
SQ FT: 3,000
SALES (est): 2MM **Privately Held**
WEB: www.dsjprinting.com
SIC: 2752 2759 Commercial printing, offset; letterpress printing

(P-6553)
DUMONT PRINTING INC
Also Called: Dumont Printing & Mailing
1333 G St, Fresno (93706-1634)
P.O. Box 12726 (93779-2726)
PHONE..................................559 485-6311
Susan Denise Moore, *CEO*
Susan Moore, *President*
▼ EMP: 42
SQ FT: 21,000

SALES (est): 10.4MM **Privately Held**
WEB: www.dumontprinting.com
SIC: 2752 2759 7331 7334 Commercial printing, offset; commercial printing; direct mail advertising services; photocopying & duplicating services; signs & advertising specialties; subscription fulfillment services: magazine, newspaper, etc.

(P-6554)
DUNCAN PRESS INC
25 W Lockeford St, Lodi (95240-2125)
P.O. Box 1627 (95241-1627)
PHONE..................................209 462-5245
Michael Bedford, *President*
Steven Bedford, *Corp Secy*
EMP: 13
SALES (est): 1MM **Privately Held**
SIC: 2752 Commercial printing, offset

(P-6555)
EARTH PRINT INC
Also Called: Cr Print
31115 Via Colinas Ste 301, Westlake Village (91362-4507)
PHONE..................................818 879-6050
Jim Friedl, *President*
Edward Corridori, *Admin Sec*
Mike Corridori, *VP Sales*
Michael Keane, *Manager*
EMP: 19
SQ FT: 7,500
SALES (est): 3.4MM **Privately Held**
WEB: www.crprint.com
SIC: 2752 7334 Commercial printing, offset; photocopying & duplicating services

(P-6556)
EAST WEST PRINTING
7433 Lampson Ave, Garden Grove (92841-2903)
PHONE..................................714 899-7885
Fax: 714 899-7886
EMP: 11
SQ FT: 1,200
SALES (est): 1.4MM **Privately Held**
SIC: 2752

(P-6557)
ECLIPSE PRTG & GRAPHICS LLC
Also Called: James Litho
4462 E Airport Dr, Ontario (91761-7804)
PHONE..................................909 390-2452
Jeff James, *Mng Member*
Sue James,
EMP: 20 EST: 1999
SQ FT: 25,000
SALES (est): 5.5MM **Privately Held**
SIC: 2752 Commercial printing, offset

(P-6558)
ECON-O-PLATE INC
Also Called: Pacific Rim Printers & Mailers
5760 Hannum Ave, Culver City (90230-6501)
PHONE..................................310 342-5900
Robert Brothers, *President*
Richard Gonzales, *President*
Brad Carl, *Treasurer*
Leslie Rice, *Office Mgr*
Frank Tellez, *Programmer Anys*
EMP: 15
SQ FT: 15,000
SALES (est): 3.9MM **Privately Held**
WEB: www.pacificrimprinters.com
SIC: 2752 7331 Commercial printing, offset; mailing service

(P-6559)
ECONOMY PRINT & IMAGE INC
Also Called: Economy Printing
7515 Metropolitan Dr, San Diego (92108-4403)
PHONE..................................619 295-4455
John Ferrari, *President*
Greg Hunt, *Accounts Mgr*
EMP: 16
SQ FT: 7,200
SALES (est): 2.3MM **Privately Held**
WEB: www.economyprint.com
SIC: 2752 Commercial printing, offset

(P-6560)
ECONOMY PRINTING
Also Called: Economy Printing Image
12642 Stoutwood St, Poway (92064-6430)
PHONE..................................858 679-8630
Robert Baird, *Owner*
EMP: 15
SALES (est): 974.8K **Privately Held**
SIC: 2752 Offset & photolithographic printing

(P-6561)
EDGEWOOD PRESS INC
1130 N Main St, Orange (92867-3421)
PHONE..................................714 516-2455
Carol Altvater, *President*
Ernest Altvater Jr, *Corp Secy*
John M Atwell, *Vice Pres*
EMP: 14
SQ FT: 12,000
SALES (est): 1.2MM **Privately Held**
WEB: www.folderfacts.com
SIC: 2752 Commercial printing, offset

(P-6562)
EDITION ONE GROUP
2080 2nd St, Berkeley (94710-1907)
PHONE..................................510 705-1930
Ben Zlotkin, *Owner*
EMP: 10 EST: 2010
SALES (est): 905.7K **Privately Held**
SIC: 2752 Commercial printing, lithographic

(P-6563)
ELITE 4 PRINT INC
851 E Walnut St, Carson (90746-1214)
PHONE..................................310 366-1344
Keith Kyong, *Principal*
▲ EMP: 20
SALES (est): 3.9MM **Privately Held**
SIC: 2752 Commercial printing, offset

(P-6564)
ELLEGRA PRINT & IMAGING
1419 Santa Fe Ave, Long Beach (90813-1236)
PHONE..................................562 432-2931
Connie Bucks, *President*
Richard W Mc Hale Jr, *Shareholder*
Mike Bucks, *Vice Pres*
EMP: 10
SQ FT: 7,000
SALES (est): 926.5K **Privately Held**
SIC: 2752 Commercial printing, offset

(P-6565)
EPAC TECHNOLOGIES INC (PA)
2561 Grant Ave, San Leandro (94579-2501)
PHONE..................................510 317-7979
Sasha Dobrovolsky, *CEO*
James Gentilcore, *President*
Jose Perez, *President*
Kathy Torru, *Executive*
Steve Mintz, *CTO*
▲ EMP: 105 EST: 1998
SALES (est): 26.8MM **Privately Held**
WEB: www.epac.com
SIC: 2752 Commercial printing, lithographic

(P-6566)
ESCHATON FOUNDATION (PA)
Also Called: Resource Ctr For Nonviolence
612 Ocean St, Santa Cruz (95060-4006)
PHONE..................................831 423-1626
Barbara Hayes,
Peter Klotz-Chamberlin, *Corp Secy*
Jane Weed, *Vice Pres*
Tom Helman, *Exec Dir*
Robert Muller, *Admin Sec*
EMP: 60
SQ FT: 2,000
SALES: 316.3K **Privately Held**
WEB: www.rcnv.org
SIC: 2752 8399 Commercial printing, lithographic; council for social agency

(P-6567)
ESSENCE PRINTING INC (PA)
270 Oyster Point Blvd, South San Francisco (94080-1911)
PHONE..................................650 952-5072
Sue WEI, *President*
Herbert WEI, *CEO*

Edwin WEI Jr, *Vice Pres*
Hanson Shiu, *Project Mgr*
EMP: 82 EST: 1988
SQ FT: 40,000
SALES (est): 13.5MM **Privately Held**
WEB: www.essenceprinting.com
SIC: 2752 Commercial printing, offset

(P-6568)
FALLBROOK PRINTING CORP
Also Called: Fallbrook Communications
504 E Alvarado St Ste 110, Fallbrook (92028-2363)
PHONE..................................760 731-2020
Randall C Folin, *President*
Sean Redmond, *Director*
EMP: 10
SQ FT: 8,000
SALES (est): 1.7MM **Privately Held**
WEB: www.fallbrookprinting.com
SIC: 2752 Commercial printing, offset

(P-6569)
FAUST PRINTING INC
8656 Utica Ave Ste 100, Rancho Cucamonga (91730-4860)
P.O. Box 721713, Pinon Hills (92372-1713)
PHONE..................................909 980-1577
Donald F Faust Jr, *President*
Greg Faust, *Shareholder*
Tom Faust, *Shareholder*
Rosemary Faust, *Ch of Bd*
Jim Buccholz, *CFO*
EMP: 30
SQ FT: 20,000
SALES: 5.5MM **Privately Held**
WEB: www.faustprinting.com
SIC: 2752 2796 Commercial printing, offset; letterpress plates, preparation of; embossing plates for printing

(P-6570)
FBPRODUCTIONS INC
12722 Rverside Dr Ste 204, Valley Village (91607)
PHONE..................................818 773-9337
Frank Barbarino, *President*
David Wohl, *CEO*
Jerry Cheney, *Vice Pres*
EMP: 100
SQ FT: 60,000
SALES (est): 13.2MM **Privately Held**
WEB: www.fbonline.com
SIC: 2752 2675 Commercial printing, offset; die-cut paper & board

(P-6571)
FED EX KINKOS OFC & PRINT CTR
255 W Stanley Ave, Ventura (93001-1313)
PHONE..................................805 604-6000
Robin Jo Ann, *Vice Pres*
EMP: 15
SALES (est): 2MM **Privately Held**
SIC: 2752 Commercial printing, lithographic

(P-6572)
FIREBRAND MEDIA LLC
Also Called: Laguna Beach Magazine
580 Broadway St Ste 301, Laguna Beach (92651-4328)
PHONE..................................949 715-4100
Vincent Zepezauer, *Mng Member*
Steve Zepezauer, *CEO*
Chris Mattingley, *Executive*
Sonia Chung, *Creative Dir*
Cindy Mendaros, *Office Mgr*
EMP: 25
SQ FT: 5,000
SALES: 2MM **Privately Held**
SIC: 2752 Commercial printing, lithographic

(P-6573)
FIRST IMPRESSIONS PRINTING
25030 Viking St, Hayward (94545-2704)
PHONE..................................510 784-0811
Gary E Stang, *President*
Jennifer Stang, *Admin Sec*
EMP: 20
SQ FT: 10,000
SALES (est): 3MM **Privately Held**
SIC: 2752 Commercial printing, offset

(P-6574)
FISHER PRINTING INC (PA)
2257 N Pacific St, Orange (92865-2615)
PHONE..................................714 998-9200
Thomas Fischer, *Chairman*
Will Fischer, *CEO*
Tom Scarpati, *COO*
Matt Shobe, *Relg Ldr*
EMP: 150 **EST:** 1933
SQ FT: 60,000
SALES (est): 60.1MM **Privately Held**
WEB: www.fisherprinting.com
SIC: 2752 Commercial printing, offset

(P-6575)
FIVE-STAR GRAPHICS INC
2628 Woodbury Dr, Torrance (90503-7374)
PHONE..................................310 325-6881
Shirley Fuerst, *President*
Barry Fuerst, *President*
Robert Fuerst, *President*
EMP: 18
SQ FT: 11,000
SALES (est): 2.2MM **Privately Held**
SIC: 2752 Commercial printing, offset

(P-6576)
FIZZY COLOR LLC
3561 Homestead Rd Ste 231, Santa Clara (95051-5161)
PHONE..................................408 623-6705
Joseph Zojaji, *Owner*
EMP: 10
SALES: 1.5MM **Privately Held**
SIC: 2752 Commercial printing, lithographic

(P-6577)
FONG BROTHERS PRINTING INC (PA)
320 Valley Dr, Brisbane (94005-1208)
PHONE..................................415 467-1050
Tony D Fong, *President*
Susie Woo, *CFO*
Eugene Fong, *Vice Pres*
Paul Fong, *Vice Pres*
Peter Fong, *Vice Pres*
▲ **EMP:** 150
SQ FT: 105,000
SALES (est): 47.4MM **Privately Held**
WEB: www.fbp.com
SIC: 2752 Commercial printing, offset

(P-6578)
FONG FONG PRTRS LTHGRPHERS INC
3009 65th St, Sacramento (95820-2021)
PHONE..................................916 739-1313
Karen Cotton, *CEO*
Marsha Fong, *Corp Secy*
May L Fong, *Vice Pres*
Curtis Fong, *Sales Mgr*
EMP: 43
SQ FT: 50,000
SALES: 8MM **Privately Held**
SIC: 2752 Commercial printing, offset

(P-6579)
FOOTHILL PRITNG & GRAPHICS/ C (PA)
2245 Highway 49, Angels Camp (95222-9579)
P.O. Box 338 (95222-0338)
PHONE..................................209 736-4332
James D Klann, *President*
▲ **EMP:** 12
SQ FT: 5,000
SALES (est): 1.9MM **Privately Held**
WEB: www.foothillprinting.com
SIC: 2752 Commercial printing, offset

(P-6580)
FOREST INVESTMENT GROUP INC
Also Called: Unicorn Group
83 Hamilton Dr Ste 100, Novato (94949-5674)
PHONE..................................415 459-2330
David A Brooks, *CEO*
Mark Schmidt, *Vice Pres*
EMP: 15
SQ FT: 8,000

SALES: 1.7MM **Privately Held**
SIC: 2752 2791 2789 7334 Commercial printing, offset; typesetting; bookbinding & related work; photocopying & duplicating services

(P-6581)
FOSTER PRINTING COMPANY INC
700 E Alton Ave, Santa Ana (92705-5610)
PHONE..................................714 731-2000
Dennis M Blackburn, *CEO*
Steve Gutmann, *Plant Mgr*
Kris Blackburn, *VP Sales*
EMP: 65
SQ FT: 35,000
SALES (est): 12.5MM **Privately Held**
WEB: www.fosterprint.com
SIC: 2752 Commercial printing, offset

(P-6582)
FOUR COLORCOM
Also Called: Cal Printing
2300 Stevens Creek Blvd, San Jose (95128-1650)
PHONE..................................408 436-7574
Shawn Malakiman, *President*
Manuela Malakiman, *Treasurer*
EMP: 16
SQ FT: 10,000
SALES (est): 2.7MM **Privately Held**
SIC: 2752 7374 Commercial printing, offset; computer graphics service; optical scanning data service

(P-6583)
FPC GRAPHICS INC
2682 Market St, Riverside (92501-2126)
P.O. Box 192 (92502-0192)
PHONE..................................951 686-0232
Michael S Vaughan, *President*
EMP: 35 **EST:** 1955
SQ FT: 35,000
SALES (est): 4.3MM **Privately Held**
WEB: www.fpcgraphics.com
SIC: 2752 7336 7311 2791 Commercial printing, offset; commercial art & graphic design; advertising agencies; typesetting

(P-6584)
FRANCHISE SERVICES INC (PA)
26722 Plaza, Mission Viejo (92691-8051)
PHONE..................................949 348-5400
Don F Lowe, *Ch of Bd*
Daniel J Conger, *CFO*
Daniel Conger, *CFO*
Dan Beck, *Exec VP*
John Clampitt, *Vice Pres*
EMP: 20 **EST:** 1968
SQ FT: 44,000
SALES: 19.9MM **Privately Held**
WEB: www.franserv.com
SIC: 2752 6159 Commercial printing, lithographic; machinery & equipment finance leasing

(P-6585)
FRICKE-PARKS PRESS INC
Also Called: F-P Press
33250 Transit Ave, Union City (94587-2035)
PHONE..................................510 489-6543
Robert C Parks, *Ch of Bd*
David Brown, *President*
Patti Parks, *Vice Pres*
Lupe Girgis, *Human Resources*
EMP: 60
SQ FT: 50,000
SALES (est): 11.9MM **Privately Held**
WEB: www.fricke-parks.com
SIC: 2752 Commercial printing, offset

(P-6586)
FRUITRIDGE PRTG LITHOGRAPH INC (PA)
3258 Stockton Blvd, Sacramento (95820-1418)
PHONE..................................916 452-9213
Susan Hausmann, *President*
Karen Young, *Vice Pres*
EMP: 39 **EST:** 1965
SQ FT: 28,500
SALES (est): 7.6MM **Privately Held**
WEB: www.fruitridge.com
SIC: 2752 2796 Color lithography; platemaking services

(P-6587)
FULL COLOR BUSINESS
Also Called: Full Color Bus Cds & Flyers
2620 El Camino Ave, Sacramento (95821-5902)
PHONE..................................916 218-7845
William Lewis, *Owner*
EMP: 10
SALES (est): 1.6MM **Privately Held**
SIC: 2752 Business form & card printing, lithographic

(P-6588)
FULLERTON PRINTING INC
Also Called: Bixby Knolls Prtg & Graphics
315 N Lemon St, Fullerton (92832-2030)
PHONE..................................714 870-7500
Donald Moreland, *President*
Bryan D Moreland, *Officer*
EMP: 12
SQ FT: 3,737
SALES (est): 1.3MM **Privately Held**
WEB: www.fullertonprinting.com
SIC: 2752 Commercial printing, offset

(P-6589)
GENESIS PRINTING
5872 W Pico Blvd, Los Angeles (90019-3715)
PHONE..................................323 965-7935
Liborio Lozano, *Owner*
EMP: 15
SQ FT: 6,864
SALES (est): 1.4MM **Privately Held**
SIC: 2752 Commercial printing, offset

(P-6590)
GEORGE CORIATY
Also Called: Sir Speedy
7240 Greenleaf Ave, Whittier (90602-1312)
PHONE..................................562 698-7513
George Coriaty, *Owner*
Richard Coriaty, *Manager*
EMP: 32
SQ FT: 12,000
SALES: 12.4MM **Privately Held**
WEB: www.sswhittier.com
SIC: 2752 7334 Commercial printing, lithographic; photocopying & duplicating services

(P-6591)
GIANT HORSE PRINTING INC
1336 San Mateo Ave, South San Francisco (94080-6501)
PHONE..................................650 875-7137
Steve MA, *President*
EMP: 15
SQ FT: 15,000
SALES (est): 1.9MM **Privately Held**
WEB: www.gianthorse.com
SIC: 2752 2732 2791 Commercial printing, offset; books: printing only; typographic composition, for the printing trade

(P-6592)
GOLDEN COLOR PRINTING INC
9353 Rush St, South El Monte (91733-2544)
PHONE..................................626 455-0850
Deng-Muh Yen, *President*
EMP: 21
SQ FT: 11,000
SALES (est): 3.5MM **Privately Held**
SIC: 2752 Color lithography

(P-6593)
GOLDEN GATE LITHO
11144 Golf Links Rd, Oakland (94605-5799)
PHONE..................................510 568-5335
Don Asher, *President*
Saundra Davis, *Professor*
EMP: 10
SQ FT: 13,000
SALES: 1.3MM **Privately Held**
WEB: www.goldengatelitho.com
SIC: 2752 Cards, lithographed; commercial printing, offset

(P-6594)
GRAPHIC COLOR SYSTEMS INC
Also Called: Continental Colorcraft
1166 W Garvey Ave, Monterey Park (91754-2511)
PHONE..................................323 283-3000

Andy Scheidegger, *President*
Maria Donhauser, *Treasurer*
Linda Clarke, *Vice Pres*
Kathleen Ryan, *Executive*
Ellen Crabb, *Project Mgr*
EMP: 52
SQ FT: 28,000
SALES (est): 13MM **Privately Held**
WEB: www.continentalcolorcraft.com
SIC: 2752 2796 2791 2759 Commercial printing, offset; color separations for printing; typesetting; commercial printing

(P-6595)
GRAPHIC FOX INC
3124 Thorntree Dr, Chico (95973-9068)
PHONE..................................530 895-1359
Larry Laney, *President*
Michael Ritsch, *Sales Mgr*
EMP: 14
SQ FT: 5,000
SALES (est): 1.9MM **Privately Held**
SIC: 2752 Commercial printing, offset

(P-6596)
GRAPHIC VISIONS INC
7119 Fair Ave, North Hollywood (91605-6304)
PHONE..................................818 845-8393
Randall Avazian, *CEO*
Patrick Bird, *Partner*
Kenneth Langer, *President*
Jodi Shapiro, *Bookkeeper*
Michael Beauregard, *VP Mfg*
▲ **EMP:** 23
SALES (est): 5.7MM **Privately Held**
SIC: 2752 Commercial printing, offset

(P-6597)
GRAPHIX PRESS INC
13814 Del Sur St, San Fernando (91340-3440)
PHONE..................................818 834-8520
Steve Reder, *President*
James Cohen, *Exec VP*
EMP: 50
SQ FT: 35,000
SALES (est): 5.2MM **Privately Held**
SIC: 2752 Commercial printing, lithographic

(P-6598)
GRIFFITHS SERVICES INC
Also Called: Griffiths Printing
121 S Old Springs Rd, Anaheim (92808-1247)
PHONE..................................714 685-7700
Ron Griffith, *President*
Allison Griffiths, *General Mgr*
Evan Brown, *Plant Mgr*
EMP: 30
SQ FT: 6,600
SALES: 4MM **Privately Held**
SIC: 2752 Commercial printing, offset

(P-6599)
GSL FINE LITHOGRAPHERS
8386 Rovana Cir, Sacramento (95828-2527)
PHONE..................................916 231-1410
Joe R Davis, *Ch of Bd*
Darian Koberl, *President*
Bob Keller, *Executive*
Worthen Ken, *Executive*
Chanel Decker, *Principal*
EMP: 38
SQ FT: 24,000
SALES: 6.1MM
SALES (corp-wide): 6.8B **Publicly Held**
WEB: www.gslitho.com
SIC: 2752 Commercial printing, offset
HQ: Consolidated Graphics, Inc.
5858 Westheimer Rd # 200
Houston TX 77057
713 787-0977

(P-6600)
GUEST CHEX INC
Also Called: Guestchex
7697 9th St, Buena Park (90621-2898)
PHONE..................................714 522-1860
EMP: 10
SALES (est): 840K **Privately Held**
SIC: 2752

(P-6601)
H J S GRAPHICS
Also Called: Printing Connection , The
3533 Old Conejo Rd # 104, Newbury Park
(91320-2156)
PHONE...................................818 782-5490
Henry Steenackers, *President*
EMP: 15
SALES (est): 2.6MM **Privately Held**
WEB: www.printcnx.net
SIC: 2752 Commercial printing, offset

(P-6602)
H&H IMAGING INC
Also Called: H&H Platemakers
375 Alabama St Ste 150, San Francisco
(94110-7333)
PHONE...................................415 431-4731
Kenneth Mitchell, *President*
Mark Davis, *General Mgr*
EMP: 10 EST: 1964
SQ FT: 10,000
SALES (est): 2MM **Privately Held**
SIC: 2752 Commercial printing, offset

(P-6603)
HALL LETTER SHOP INC
5200 Rosedale Hwy, Bakersfield
(93308-6000)
PHONE...................................661 327-3228
Catherine A Dounies, *President*
Greg Dounies, *General Mgr*
EMP: 13
SALES (est): 1.3MM **Privately Held**
WEB: www.hallprintmail.com
SIC: 2752 7331 2791 2789 Commercial
printing, offset; mailing service; typeset-
ting, computer controlled; binding only:
books, pamphlets, magazines, etc.

(P-6604)
HANDBILL PRINTERS LP
820 E Parkridge Ave, Corona (92879-6611)
PHONE...................................951 547-5910
Don J Messick, *President*
Dane Messick, *Partner*
Kenneth Messick, *Partner*
Mark Messick, *Partner*
Michael Messick, *Partner*
EMP: 45
SQ FT: 62,500
SALES (est): 28.2MM **Privately Held**
WEB: www.hbprinters.com
SIC: 2752 7336 Commercial printing, off-
set; graphic arts & related design

(P-6605)
HARMAN PRESS
Also Called: Harman Envelopes
6840 Vineland Ave, North Hollywood
(91605-6409)
PHONE...................................818 432-0570
Jay Goldner, *President*
Phillip Goldner, *Vice Pres*
Deborah Goldner-Watson, *Admin Sec*
Sundee Shehyn, *Analyst*
Pilar Banas, *Purchasing*
EMP: 38 EST: 1963
SQ FT: 10,000
SALES (est): 9.6MM **Privately Held**
WEB: www.harmanpress.com
SIC: 2752 Commercial printing, offset

(P-6606)
HAVANA GRAPHIC CENTER INC
Also Called: Zada International Printing
9250 Independence Ave # 109, Chatsworth
(91311-5904)
PHONE...................................818 841-3774
George Zada, *CEO*
Kenarique Zada, *Treasurer*
EMP: 20
SALES (est): 2.9MM **Privately Held**
SIC: 2752 2759 Lithographing on metal;
flexographic printing

(P-6607)
HELENS PLACE INC
Also Called: Printing Rsources Southern Cal
893 W 9th St, Upland (91786-4541)
PHONE...................................909 981-5715
Nancy De Diemar Jones, *President*
Patrick C Jones, *Corp Secy*
EMP: 15
SQ FT: 5,400

SALES (est): 2MM **Privately Held**
WEB: www.printingresources.com
SIC: 2752 7331 Commercial printing, off-
set; mailing service

(P-6608)
HENRY L HUDSON (PA)
Also Called: Graphic Systems
403 N G St, Lompoc (93436-5317)
PHONE...................................805 736-2737
Henry L Hudson, *Owner*
Ryan Bruemmer, *Department Mgr*
Michael Hudson, *Systems Staff*
Pat Saul, *Manager*
EMP: 12
SQ FT: 3,200
SALES (est): 1.4MM **Privately Held**
WEB: www.gsprinters.com
SIC: 2752 2791 7334 Commercial print-
ing, offset; typesetting; blueprinting serv-
ice

(P-6609)
HERALD PRINTING LTD (PA)
1242 Los Angeles Ave, Ventura
(93004-1920)
PHONE...................................805 647-1870
Eric Linquist, *President*
Cathy Linquist, *Corp Secy*
EMP: 10
SQ FT: 1,500
SALES (est): 1.3MM **Privately Held**
WEB: www.heraldprinting.net
SIC: 2752 Commercial printing, offset;
color lithography

(P-6610)
**HERDELL PRINTING &
LITHOGRAPHY**
340 Mccormick St, Saint Helena
(94574-1457)
P.O. Box 72 (94574-0072)
PHONE...................................707 963-3634
Michael Herdell, *President*
Patricia A Herdell, *Admin Sec*
Patty Ditomaso, *Controller*
EMP: 26
SQ FT: 22,200
SALES (est): 6.1MM **Privately Held**
SIC: 2752 Commercial printing, offset; lith-
ographing on metal

(P-6611)
HERITAGE PAPER CO
17740 Shideler Pkwy, Lathrop
(95330-9356)
PHONE...................................925 449-1148
EMP: 13
SALES (est): 1.7MM **Privately Held**
SIC: 2752 Commercial printing, litho-
graphic

(P-6612)
**HERRICK RETAIL
CORPORATION TH**
Also Called: AlphaGraphics
2923 Saturn St Ste D, Brea (92821-6260)
PHONE...................................714 256-9543
Bill Herrik, *Owner*
Janet Herrik, *Co-Owner*
EMP: 10
SALES (est): 877.7K **Privately Held**
SIC: 2752 Commercial printing, litho-
graphic

(P-6613)
HI REZ DIGITAL SOLUTIONS
1235 Activity Dr Ste E, Vista (92081-8562)
PHONE...................................760 597-2650
Drew Hendricks, *Owner*
EMP: 10
SQ FT: 2,900
SALES (est): 718.3K **Privately Held**
WEB: www.hirezdigital.com
SIC: 2752 Commercial printing, offset

(P-6614)
HIGH FIVE INC
Also Called: Printech
1452 Manhattan Ave, Fullerton
(92831-5222)
PHONE...................................714 847-2200
Steve Kramer, *President*
Alan Kramer, *CFO*
Katherine Kramer, *Corp Secy*
▼ EMP: 27

SQ FT: 12,800
SALES (est): 4.9MM **Privately Held**
WEB: www.printechusa.com
SIC: 2752 Commercial printing, offset

(P-6615)
HNC PRINTING SERVICES LLC
Also Called: Business Point Impressions
5125 Port Chicago Hwy, Concord
(94520-1216)
PHONE...................................925 771-2080
Cynthia Yee,
EMP: 17
SALES (est): 1.7MM **Privately Held**
SIC: 2752 Commercial printing, litho-
graphic

(P-6616)
HO TAI PRINTING CO INC
Also Called: Ho Tai Printing & Book Store
723 Clay St Ste 725, San Francisco
(94108-1802)
PHONE...................................415 421-4218
Tak Pui TSE, *President*
Christy Ng, *Admin Sec*
▲ EMP: 10 EST: 1974
SQ FT: 1,000
SALES (est): 1MM **Privately Held**
SIC: 2752 5942 5943 Commercial print-
ing, offset; book stores; stationery stores

(P-6617)
HOUSE OF PRINT & COPY
1501 E Main St, Grass Valley
(95945-5229)
PHONE...................................530 273-1000
Patti Ferree, *Owner*
EMP: 11
SQ FT: 2,000
SALES (est): 1.5MM **Privately Held**
SIC: 2752 7334 Commercial printing, off-
set; photocopying & duplicating services

(P-6618)
HOUSE OF PRINTING INC
3336 E Colorado Blvd, Pasadena
(91107-3885)
PHONE...................................626 793-7034
Eugene F Pittroff Sr, *President*
Marguerite Pittroff, *Treasurer*
Walter E Pittroff, *Vice Pres*
Edna Pittroff, *Admin Sec*
EMP: 22
SQ FT: 6,500
SALES (est): 3MM **Privately Held**
SIC: 2752 2791 2789 Commercial print-
ing, offset; typesetting; bookbinding & re-
lated work

(P-6619)
HUNTFORD PRINTING
Also Called: Huntford Printing & Graphics
275 Dempsey Rd, Milpitas (95035-5556)
PHONE...................................408 957-5000
George Loughborough, *President*
Charles H Loughborough, *Vice Pres*
Larry Nadeau, *Admin Sec*
EMP: 24
SQ FT: 10,000
SALES: 3.5MM **Privately Held**
WEB: www.huntford.com
SIC: 2752 Commercial printing, offset

(P-6620)
HYDE PRINTING AND GRAPHICS
2748 Willow Pass Rd, Concord
(94519-2546)
PHONE...................................925 686-4933
Patrick Hyde, *President*
AVI Ben-ARI, *Vice Pres*
Heidi Cheary, *Office Mgr*
Craig Levine, *Sales Mgr*
EMP: 12
SQ FT: 6,000
SALES (est): 1.4MM **Privately Held**
WEB: www.hydeprinting.com
SIC: 2752 Commercial printing, offset

(P-6621)
**I COLOR PRINTING & MAILING
INC**
1450 W 228th St Ste 12, Torrance
(90501-5081)
PHONE...................................310 947-1452
Sameer Khan, *Branch Mgr*
EMP: 10 **Privately Held**

SIC: 2752 Commercial printing, offset
PA: I Color Printing & Mailing Inc.
13000 S Broadway
Los Angeles CA 90061

(P-6622)
**I COLOR PRINTING & MAILING
INC (PA)**
Also Called: Icolorprinting.net
13000 S Broadway, Los Angeles
(90061-1120)
PHONE...................................310 997-1452
Mohammed Adil Khan, *CEO*
EMP: 10
SALES (est): 4.3MM **Privately Held**
SIC: 2752 Commercial printing, offset

(P-6623)
ICLAVIS LLC
8222 Allport Ave, Santa Fe Springs
(90670-2106)
PHONE...................................310 503-6847
David Chavez, *Principal*
EMP: 10 EST: 2014
SQ FT: 20,000
SALES (est): 580.1K **Privately Held**
SIC: 2752 Tag, ticket & schedule printing:
lithographic

(P-6624)
**IDEA PRINTING & GRAPHICS
INC**
1921 E Main St, Visalia (93292-6714)
PHONE...................................559 733-4149
James Laber, *President*
Ben Flores, *Graphic Designe*
Ruby Laber, *Cust Mgr*
Jeff Gooding, *Representative*
EMP: 11
SQ FT: 8,000
SALES (est): 1.7MM **Privately Held**
WEB: www.ideaprinting.net
SIC: 2752 7334 Commercial printing, off-
set; photocopying & duplicating services

(P-6625)
IDEAL GRAPHICS INC
1458 N Hundley St, Anaheim (92806-1322)
PHONE...................................714 632-3398
Patric Fung, *President*
Frank Liang, *Vice Pres*
EMP: 17
SQ FT: 7,500
SALES (est): 2.2MM **Privately Held**
SIC: 2752 Offset & photolithographic print-
ing

(P-6626)
IDEAL PRINTING CO INC
17855 Maclaren St, City of Industry
(91744-5799)
PHONE...................................626 964-2019
Richard Mancino, *President*
Yolanda Mancino, *Vice Pres*
EMP: 20 EST: 1961
SQ FT: 30,000
SALES (est): 2.5MM **Privately Held**
WEB: www.idealprintingcompany.com
SIC: 2752 Commercial printing, offset

(P-6627)
**IMAGE DISTRIBUTION
SERVICES**
3191 W Temple Ave Ste 180, Pomona
(91768-3254)
PHONE...................................909 599-7680
EMP: 16
SALES (corp-wide): 8.1MM **Privately
Held**
SIC: 2752 Commercial printing, offset
PA: Image Distribution Services Inc
60 Bunsen
Irvine CA 92618
949 754-9000

(P-6628)
**IMAGE DISTRIBUTION
SERVICES (PA)**
Also Called: Image Printing Solutions
60 Bunsen, Irvine (92618-4210)
PHONE...................................949 754-9000
Joe Fries, *CEO*
William Kaszton, *President*
Chris Paul, *CFO*

Jim Spellman, *Vice Pres*
EMP: 48
SQ FT: 15,000
SALES (est): 8.1MM **Privately Held**
SIC: 2752 5943 Commercial printing, offset; office forms & supplies

(P-6629)
IMAGEMOVER INC
10051 Bradley Ave, Pacoima (91331-2202)
PHONE.................................818 485-8840
Ben Taylor, *President*
EMP: 17
SALES (est): 3.1MM **Privately Held**
SIC: 2752 Commercial printing, lithographic

(P-6630)
IMAGEX INC
5990 Stoneridge Dr # 112, Pleasanton (94588-4517)
PHONE.................................925 474-8100
Stan Poitras, *President*
Cathy Brandt, *Executive*
EMP: 17
SALES (est): 3.3MM **Privately Held**
SIC: 2752 Commercial printing, offset; advertising posters, lithographed; business form & card printing, lithographic

(P-6631)
IMPACT PRINTING & GRAPHICS
15150 Sierra Bonita Ln, Chino (91710-8903)
PHONE.................................909 614-1678
Bill McGinley, *President*
Sarah Jensen, *Human Resources*
EMP: 25
SQ FT: 14,000
SALES (est): 4MM **Privately Held**
WEB: www.impact-printing.com
SIC: 2752 Commercial printing, lithographic

(P-6632)
IMPERIAL PRINTERS INC (PA)
Also Called: Imperial Printers Rocket Copy
430 W Main St, El Centro (92243-3019)
PHONE.................................760 352-4374
Rudy Rodgruegos, *President*
Rodolfo Rodriguez, *Vice Pres*
Marvin Wieben Jr, *Vice Pres*
EMP: 18
SQ FT: 8,725
SALES (est): 2MM **Privately Held**
WEB: www.imperialprinters.com
SIC: 2752 2796 Commercial printing, offset; letterpress plates, preparation of

(P-6633)
IMPRESS COMMUNICATIONS INC
9320 Lurline Ave, Chatsworth (91311-6041)
PHONE.................................818 701-8800
Paul Marino, *President*
Stefanie Cogger, *Executive Asst*
Samir Danshka, *Info Tech Dir*
Jeff Park, *Info Tech Mgr*
Toba Oluyide, *Technology*
▲ **EMP:** 92
SQ FT: 50,000
SALES: 15MM **Privately Held**
WEB: www.impress1.com
SIC: 2752 7336 7319 Commercial printing, offset; commercial art & graphic design; display advertising service

(P-6634)
IN TO INK
6959 Colorado Ave, La Mesa (91942-1107)
PHONE.................................858 271-6363
Larry Pyle, *Partner*
Theresa Pyle, *Partner*
EMP: 12
SQ FT: 3,250
SALES (est): 1.7MM **Privately Held**
WEB: www.intoink.com
SIC: 2752 Commercial printing, offset

(P-6635)
INDEPENDENT PRINTING CO INC (PA)
Also Called: Ipco Printing
1530 Franklin Canyon Rd, Martinez (94553-9607)
PHONE.................................925 229-5050
Kurt Brombacher, *President*
Lisa Brombacher, *Admin Sec*
Lisa Olson, *Admin Sec*
EMP: 40 **EST:** 1910
SQ FT: 7,000
SALES (est): 5.5MM **Privately Held**
SIC: 2752 Commercial printing, offset

(P-6636)
INDUSTRY COLOR PRINTING INC
11642 Washington Blvd, Whittier (90606-2425)
P.O. Box 1903, Rancho Cucamonga (91729-1903)
PHONE.................................626 961-2403
Rafael Osorio, *President*
Miriam Osorio, *Treasurer*
EMP: 20 **EST:** 1976
SALES (est): 2.2MM **Privately Held**
WEB: www.icpprint.com
SIC: 2752 Commercial printing, offset

(P-6637)
INK & COLOR INC
Also Called: Acuprint
5920 Bowcroft St, Los Angeles (90016-4302)
PHONE.................................310 280-6060
Saman Sowlaty, *CEO*
Jane Corish, *Vice Pres*
Mojgan Sowalty, *Vice Pres*
Jose Garcia, *Technician*
Dena Limpert, *Bookkeeper*
▲ **EMP:** 30
SQ FT: 17,000
SALES (est): 6.2MM **Privately Held**
WEB: www.acuprint.net
SIC: 2752 Commercial printing, offset

(P-6638)
INK SPOT INC
9737 Bell Ranch Dr, Santa Fe Springs (90670-2951)
PHONE.................................626 338-4500
Somsak Reuanglith, *CEO*
Betty Ching, *Sales Staff*
EMP: 26
SALES (est): 4.8MM **Privately Held**
SIC: 2752 Commercial printing, offset

(P-6639)
INKOVATION INC (PA)
13659 Excelsior Dr, Santa Fe Springs (90670-5103)
PHONE.................................800 465-4174
Janak Savaliya, *President*
EMP: 22
SALES (est): 5.6MM **Privately Held**
SIC: 2752 Commercial printing, offset

(P-6640)
INKWRIGHT LLC
5822 Research Dr, Huntington Beach (92649-1348)
PHONE.................................714 892-3300
Danny Nichols,
EMP: 30
SALES (est): 6.4MM **Privately Held**
SIC: 2752 Offset & photolithographic printing

(P-6641)
INLAND LITHO LLC
Also Called: Inland Group
4305 E La Palma Ave, Anaheim (92807-1843)
PHONE.................................714 993-6000
Steve Urbanovitch, *Marketing Mgr*
Kathy Urbanovitch,
EMP: 60
SQ FT: 40,000
SALES (est): 17.4MM **Privately Held**
SIC: 2752 Commercial printing, offset

(P-6642)
INSTANT IMPRINTS FRANCHISING
6615 Flanders Dr Ste B, San Diego (92121-2963)
PHONE.................................858 642-4848
Leo Kats, *President*
Lev Kats, *CEO*
Jim Blackburn, *Exec VP*
EMP: 22
SQ FT: 20,000
SALES (est): 2.4MM **Privately Held**
SIC: 2752 Commercial printing, lithographic

(P-6643)
INSTANT WEB LLC
Also Called: Iwco Direct - Downey
7300 Flores St, Downey (90242-4010)
PHONE.................................562 658-2020
Jake Hertel, *Branch Mgr*
EMP: 240
SALES (corp-wide): 819.8MM **Publicly Held**
SIC: 2752 Commercial printing, lithographic
HQ: Instant Web, Llc
7951 Powers Blvd
Chanhassen MN 55317
952 474-0961

(P-6644)
INSUA GRAPHICS INCORPORATED
9121 Glenoaks Blvd, Sun Valley (91352-2612)
PHONE.................................818 767-7007
Jose Miguel Insua, *CEO*
Albert Insua, *Treasurer*
Eric Insua, *Vice Pres*
▲ **EMP:** 35 **EST:** 1996
SQ FT: 28,000
SALES (est): 7MM **Privately Held**
SIC: 2752 Commercial printing, offset

(P-6645)
INTEGRATED COMMUNICATIONS INC
1411 W 190th St Ste 110, Gardena (90248-4370)
PHONE.................................310 851-8066
Peter Levshin, *CEO*
David Humphrey, *President*
▲ **EMP:** 24
SQ FT: 5,000
SALES (est): 4.1MM **Privately Held**
WEB: www.icla.com
SIC: 2752 Commercial printing, lithographic

(P-6646)
INTEGRATED DIGITAL MEDIA (PA)
Also Called: AlphaGraphics
840 Sansome St, San Francisco (94111-1508)
PHONE.................................415 986-4091
Manuel Torres, *Principal*
EMP: 25 **EST:** 2010
SALES (est): 9.4MM **Privately Held**
SIC: 2752 Commercial printing, lithographic

(P-6647)
INTEGRATED DIGITAL MEDIA
Also Called: AlphaGraphics
156 2nd St, San Francisco (94105-3724)
PHONE.................................415 882-9390
EMP: 33
SALES (corp-wide): 9.4MM **Privately Held**
SIC: 2752 Commercial printing, lithographic
PA: Integrated Digital Media
840 Sansome St
San Francisco CA 94111
415 986-4091

(P-6648)
INTELICARE DIRECT INC
Also Called: Instant Checkmate
9596 Chesapeake Dr Ste A, San Diego (92123-1346)
PHONE.................................702 765-0867
Kristian Kibak, *CEO*

Brandon Wright, *Mng Member*
EMP: 17 **EST:** 2014
SALES (est): 3.6MM **Privately Held**
SIC: 2752 Commercial printing, lithographic

(P-6649)
INTER-CITY PRINTING CO INC
Also Called: Madison Street Press
614 Madison St, Oakland (94607-4726)
PHONE.................................510 451-4775
Paul Murai, *President*
Miok Murai, *Admin Sec*
Marlene Cornelius, *VP Sales*
Christopher Dougherty, *Marketing Mgr*
Keith Rice, *Accounts Exec*
EMP: 17
SQ FT: 6,500
SALES (est): 3.9MM **Privately Held**
WEB: www.madison-st-press.com
SIC: 2752 Commercial printing, offset

(P-6650)
INTERLINK INC
Also Called: Precision Plastics Printing
3845 E Coronado St, Anaheim (92807-1649)
PHONE.................................714 905-7700
Bob Bhagat, *President*
Hathin Bhagat, *Principal*
Rudy Sabhaya, *Info Tech Mgr*
Juan Brown, *Sales Staff*
▲ **EMP:** 85
SQ FT: 50,000
SALES (est): 20MM **Privately Held**
SIC: 2752 Commercial printing, lithographic

(P-6651)
INTERNATIONAL PRINTING & TYPSG
14535 Hamlin St, Van Nuys (91411-1608)
PHONE.................................818 787-6804
Todd M Wallace, *President*
Joyce Wallace, *CFO*
EMP: 15
SQ FT: 3,000
SALES (est): 1.2MM **Privately Held**
SIC: 2752 2791 Commercial printing, offset; typesetting, computer controlled

(P-6652)
IPS PRINTING INC
2020 K St, Sacramento (95811-4217)
PHONE.................................916 442-8961
Richard Peterson, *President*
Ken Peterson, *Vice Pres*
Steve Bralley, *Executive*
Chris Semkiw, *Manager*
Tim Stults, *Manager*
EMP: 31
SQ FT: 9,000
SALES (est): 3.9MM **Privately Held**
SIC: 2752 2791 Photolithographic printing; typesetting

(P-6653)
ISLAND COLOR INC
3972 Barranca Pkwy J521, Irvine (92606-1204)
PHONE.................................714 352-5888
David E Pauley, *President*
EMP: 10
SALES (est): 1.2MM **Privately Held**
SIC: 2752 Commercial printing, lithographic

(P-6654)
J & D BUSINESS FORMS INC
Also Called: JD Printing and Mailing
650 W Terrace Dr, San Dimas (91773-2908)
PHONE.................................626 914-1777
EMP: 11
SQ FT: 20,000
SALES (est): 1.5MM **Privately Held**
SIC: 2752 3577

(P-6655)
J E J PRINT INC
673 Monterey Pass Rd, Monterey Park (91754-2418)
PHONE.................................626 281-8989
Catherine Shih, *Manager*
EMP: 18

▲ = Import ▼=Export
◆ =Import/Export

SALES (est): 1.8MM **Privately Held**
SIC: 2752 Commercial printing, lithographic

(P-6656)
J R RAPID PRINT INC
909 S Cucamonga Ave # 104, Ontario (91761-1973)
PHONE.................................909 947-4868
Rita Wong, *President*
EMP: 10
SQ FT: 1,200
SALES (est): 1.5MM **Privately Held**
SIC: 2752 Commercial printing, offset

(P-6657)
J S M PRODUCTIONS INC
Also Called: PIP Printing
537 E Florida Ave, Hemet (92543-4333)
PHONE.................................951 929-5771
John E Mullany, *President*
EMP: 13
SQ FT: 3,500
SALES (est): 2MM **Privately Held**
SIC: 2752 Commercial printing, offset

(P-6658)
J&L PRESS INC (PA)
1218 W 163rd St, Gardena (90247-4432)
PHONE.................................818 549-8344
Mark Iwakiri, *CEO*
John Iwakiri, *Vice Pres*
EMP: 15
SQ FT: 6,700
SALES (est): 2.2MM **Privately Held**
SIC: 2752 Commercial printing, offset

(P-6659)
JA FERRARI PRINT IMAGING LLC
Also Called: Allegra Print & Imaging
7515 Metro Dr Ste 405, San Diego (92108)
PHONE.................................619 295-8307
John Ferrari, *Mng Member*
EMP: 15
SALES (est): 2.3MM **Privately Held**
SIC: 2752 Commercial printing, offset

(P-6660)
JAMES GANG CUSTOM PRINTING
Also Called: James Gang Graphics & Printing
4851 Newport Ave, San Diego (92107-3110)
PHONE.................................619 225-1283
Pat James, *President*
EMP: 12 EST: 1964
SQ FT: 5,000
SALES (est): 1.1MM **Privately Held**
SIC: 2752 7331 Commercial printing, offset; direct mail advertising services

(P-6661)
JAPAN GRAPHICS CORP
1820 W 220th St Ste 210, Torrance (90501-0697)
PHONE.................................310 222-8639
Tai Makino, *President*
Hatsue Makino, *Vice Pres*
EMP: 21
SQ FT: 3,800
SALES (est): 2.9MM **Privately Held**
WEB: www.japangraphics.com
SIC: 2752 Commercial printing, offset

(P-6662)
JAY BREWER
Also Called: Jawen Enterprises
926 Turquoise St Ste A, San Diego (92109-1186)
PHONE.................................858 488-4871
Jay Brewer, *Owner*
EMP: 10
SQ FT: 7,780
SALES (est): 1.5MM **Privately Held**
WEB: www.jaybrewer.com
SIC: 2752 Commercial printing, offset

(P-6663)
JD BUSINESS SOLUTIONS INC
Also Called: Printing Impressions
1351 Holiday Hill Rd, Goleta (93117-1815)
P.O. Box 1729 (93116-1729)
PHONE.................................805 962-8193
James Denion, *President*

Michael Gregory, *Principal*
Jeannine Denion, *Admin Sec*
EMP: 20
SQ FT: 9,000
SALES (est): 3.7MM **Privately Held**
SIC: 2752 Commercial printing, offset

(P-6664)
JEB-PHI INC
Also Called: PIP Printing
10417 Lakewood Blvd, Downey (90241-2744)
PHONE.................................562 861-0863
Bruce Pansky, *President*
Belinda Pansky, *Corp Secy*
Phillip Pansky, *Vice Pres*
Heather Kelly, *Sales Mgr*
Landy Pansky, *Sales Mgr*
EMP: 22
SQ FT: 2,900
SALES (est): 3.4MM **Privately Held**
SIC: 2752 Commercial printing, offset

(P-6665)
JENSEN GRAPHICS & PRINTING
Also Called: D I Printing
18270 Spyglass Rd, Hidden Valley Lake (95467-8655)
P.O. Box 7295, Clearlake (95422-7295)
PHONE.................................707 987-8966
William Jensen, *President*
Linda Jensen, *Corp Secy*
Jack Jensen, *Vice Pres*
EMP: 10
SQ FT: 3,400
SALES (est): 932.3K **Privately Held**
SIC: 2752 Commercial printing, offset

(P-6666)
JJ LITHOGRAPHICS INC
Also Called: Jj Printing
8607 Dice Rd, Santa Fe Springs (90670-2511)
PHONE.................................562 698-0280
Shulin Chiu, *CEO*
Hung-Nan Chen, *President*
Derek Lee, *General Mgr*
Chen Edward, *Prdtn Mgr*
Leo Tsai, *Marketing Mgr*
▲ EMP: 10
SQ FT: 4,000
SALES (est): 2.1MM **Privately Held**
SIC: 2752 Commercial printing, lithographic

(P-6667)
JORLIND ENTERPRISES INC
Also Called: Kwik Kopy Printing
28570 Marguerite Pkwy # 108, Mission Viejo (92692-3713)
PHONE.................................949 364-2309
David Leckness, *President*
▲ EMP: 10
SQ FT: 1,100
SALES (est): 1.4MM **Privately Held**
SIC: 2752 Commercial printing, offset

(P-6668)
JOSEF MENDELOVITZ
Also Called: Power Printing
11240 Explorer Rd, La Mesa (91941-7276)
PHONE.................................619 231-3555
Josef Mendelovitz, *Owner*
EMP: 12
SALES (est): 940K **Privately Held**
SIC: 2752 Commercial printing, lithographic

(P-6669)
JP GRAPHICS INC
3310 Woodward Ave, Santa Clara (95054-2627)
PHONE.................................408 235-8821
Joan Escover, *CEO*
David McLintock, *President*
Michael Iburg, *General Mgr*
Suean Shank, *Admin Asst*
Mike Day, *Project Mgr*
▲ EMP: 40
SQ FT: 14,000
SALES (est): 7MM **Privately Held**
SIC: 2752 Commercial printing, offset

(P-6670)
JSL PARTNERS INC
Also Called: AlphaGraphics
1294 Anvilwood Ct, Sunnyvale (94089-2200)
PHONE.................................408 747-9000
Jeff Lerner, *President*
Jill Learner, *Vice Pres*
Melissa Bright, *Office Mgr*
Chris Riggs, *Project Mgr*
David Buzza, *Director*
EMP: 12 EST: 1997
SQ FT: 7,500
SALES (est): 2.2MM **Privately Held**
SIC: 2752 Commercial printing, lithographic

(P-6671)
JUNO GRAPHICS
16334 S Avalon Blvd, Gardena (90248-2910)
PHONE.................................310 329-0126
Chang Kim, *Owner*
▲ EMP: 14
SQ FT: 11,000
SALES (est): 1.5MM **Privately Held**
SIC: 2752 7389 Commercial printing, offset; printing broker

(P-6672)
K-1 PACKAGING GROUP
2001 W Mission Blvd, Pomona (91766-1020)
PHONE.................................626 964-9384
EMP: 29 **Privately Held**
SIC: 2752 Offset & photolithographic printing
PA: K-1 Packaging Group
17989 Arenth Ave
City Of Industry CA 91748
-

(P-6673)
K-1 PACKAGING GROUP (PA)
17989 Arenth Ave, City of Industry (91748-1126)
PHONE.................................626 964-9384
Mike Tsai, *President*
Lynn An, *Asst Admin*
Fred Liu, *Data Proc Exec*
Cindy Parker, *Purch Mgr*
Jennie Chang, *Marketing Staff*
▲ EMP: 91
SALES (est): 19.9MM **Privately Held**
WEB: www.k1packaging.com
SIC: 2752 Offset & photolithographic printing

(P-6674)
KELMSCOTT COMMUNICATIONS LLC
Also Called: Orange County Printing
2485 Da Vinci, Irvine (92614-5844)
PHONE.................................949 475-1900
Paz Calaci, *Branch Mgr*
EMP: 11
SALES (corp-wide): 6.8B **Publicly Held**
WEB: www.ocpc.com
SIC: 2752 Commercial printing, offset
HQ: Kelmscott Communications Llc
5858 Westheimer Rd # 410
Houston TX 77057
713 787-0977

(P-6675)
KEYLINE LITHOGRAPHY INC
Also Called: Key Line Litho
1726 W 180th St, Gardena (90248-3600)
PHONE.................................310 538-8618
Danny Wong, *President*
EMP: 10
SQ FT: 4,000
SALES (est): 1.4MM **Privately Held**
WEB: www.keylinelitho.com
SIC: 2752 Commercial printing, offset

(P-6676)
KINDRED LITHO INCORPORATED
10833 Bell Ct, Rancho Cucamonga (91730-4835)
PHONE.................................909 944-4015
Kurt Kindred, *President*
Cherie Kindred, *Admin Sec*
EMP: 13 EST: 1971

SQ FT: 8,000
SALES (est): 2MM **Privately Held**
SIC: 2752 Commercial printing, offset

(P-6677)
KINGS PRINTING CORP
Also Called: King's Printing
5401 Linda Vista Rd # 401, San Diego (92110-2402)
PHONE.................................619 297-6000
Sabbel Aguilar, *President*
Tony Capulong, *Treasurer*
Michael Wong, *Vice Pres*
Stephanie Adamson, *Store Mgr*
Camie Nguyen, *Manager*
EMP: 20
SQ FT: 5,200
SALES (est): 2.3MM **Privately Held**
SIC: 2752 Commercial printing, offset

(P-6678)
KK GRAPHICS INC
1336 San Mateo Ave, South San Francisco (94080-6501)
PHONE.................................415 468-1057
Moon MA, *CEO*
Julie MA, *Finance*
EMP: 10 EST: 1979
SQ FT: 5,000
SALES: 2.6MM **Privately Held**
SIC: 2752 Commercial printing, lithographic

(P-6679)
KM PRINTING PRODUCTION INC
218 Longden Ave, Irwindale (91706-1328)
PHONE.................................626 821-0008
Chim Moon Ming, *President*
Kerwin Ngo, *Vice Pres*
Wendy Lui, *Accounting Mgr*
EMP: 18
SQ FT: 600
SALES (est): 2.8MM **Privately Held**
WEB: www.kmppi.com
SIC: 2752 Commercial printing, offset

(P-6680)
KORE PRINT SOLUTIONS INC
20974 Corsair Blvd, Hayward (94545-1002)
PHONE.................................510 445-1638
Ken Chapman, *President*
EMP: 10
SALES (est): 1.4MM **Privately Held**
SIC: 2752 Commercial printing, offset

(P-6681)
KOVIN CORPORATION INC
Also Called: Neb Cal Printing
9240 Mira Este Ct, San Diego (92126-6336)
PHONE.................................858 558-0100
Mervin Kodesh, *President*
Sandra Kodesh, *Vice Pres*
EMP: 30
SQ FT: 10,000
SALES (est): 5.5MM **Privately Held**
WEB: www.nebcal.com
SIC: 2752 2789 Commercial printing, offset; bookbinding & related work

(P-6682)
KP LLC (PA)
13951 Washington Ave, San Leandro (94578-3220)
PHONE.................................510 346-0729
Joe Atturio, *CEO*
Jill Gardner, *Vice Pres*
Heather Burroughs, *Program Mgr*
Rachel Lee, *Program Mgr*
Ben Tsai, *Data Proc Staff*
▲ EMP: 80 EST: 1929
SQ FT: 12,000
SALES (est): 107.8MM **Privately Held**
WEB: www.kpcorporation.com
SIC: 2752 7334 7331 7374 Commercial printing, offset; photocopying & duplicating services; direct mail advertising services; computer graphics service; subscription fulfillment services: magazine, newspaper, etc.; marketing consulting services

(P-6683)
KP LLC
K/P Graphics-Salem Division
13951 Washington Ave, San Leandro
(94578-3220)
PHONE....................510 346-0729
Keith Whittier, *Manager*
David Gibson, *Systems Admin*
Amee Adair, *Accounting Mgr*
EMP: 25
SALES (corp-wide): 107.8MM **Privately Held**
WEB: www.kpcorporation.com
SIC: 2752 8742 7331 2796 Commercial printing, offset; management consulting services; direct mail advertising services; platemaking services; partitions & fixtures, except wood
PA: Kp Llc
13951 Washington Ave
San Leandro CA 94578
510 346-0729

(P-6684)
KP LLC
Also Called: K P Graphics
1134 Enterprise St, Stockton (95204-2316)
P.O. Box 8900 (95208-0900)
PHONE....................209 466-6761
Roberta Morris, *Manager*
EMP: 20
SQ FT: 10,000
SALES (corp-wide): 107.8MM **Privately Held**
WEB: www.kpcorporation.com
SIC: 2752 Commercial printing, offset
PA: Kp Llc
13951 Washington Ave
San Leandro CA 94578
510 346-0729

(P-6685)
KYUNG IN PRINTING INC
Also Called: Printing Manufacturer
7920 Airway Rd Ste A8, San Diego
(92154-8311)
PHONE....................619 662-3920
Sung Hwan Lee, *President*
Kay Park, *CFO*
▲ EMP: 198
SQ FT: 36,000
SALES: 33.4MM **Privately Held**
WEB: www.pl-america.com
SIC: 2752 Commercial printing, offset

(P-6686)
L & L PRINTERS CARLSBAD LLC
Also Called: Specialist Media Group
6200 Yarrow Dr, Carlsbad (92011-1537)
PHONE....................760 477-0321
William Anderson, *President*
Frank Scorzelli, *CFO*
EMP: 50
SALES (est): 12.2MM **Privately Held**
SIC: 2752 Commercial printing, offset

(P-6687)
L & L PRINTERS INC
6200 Yarrow Dr, Carlsbad (92011-1537)
PHONE....................858 278-4300
William Anderson, *President*
Nancy Byron, *CFO*
Sally Anderson, *Vice Pres*
Michael Kenney, *Vice Pres*
Jay Pardo, *Vice Pres*
EMP: 13
SQ FT: 7,500
SALES (est): 4.2MM **Privately Held**
WEB: www.llprinters.com
SIC: 2752 Commercial printing, offset

(P-6688)
L T LITHO & PRINTING CO
16811 Noyes Ave, Irvine (92606-5122)
PHONE....................949 466-8584
Craig Thomas, *President*
Mark Thomas, *CEO*
EMP: 26
SQ FT: 16,000
SALES (est): 3.9MM **Privately Held**
WEB: www.ltlitho.net
SIC: 2752 2759 Commercial printing, lithographic; commercial printing

(P-6689)
LA BROTHERS ENTERPRISE INC
Also Called: Oscar Printing
57 Columbia Sq, San Francisco
(94103-4015)
PHONE....................415 626-8818
Jeffrey La, *President*
Steve La, *Corp Secy*
▲ EMP: 24
SQ FT: 8,000
SALES (est): 3.8MM **Privately Held**
WEB: www.oscarprinting.com
SIC: 2752 2759 Commercial printing, offset; letterpress printing

(P-6690)
LA PRINTING & GRAPHICS INC
Also Called: L A PRESS
13951 S Main St, Los Angeles
(90061-2140)
PHONE....................310 527-4526
Kevin Sheu Chhim Kaing, *CEO*
Sheu C Kevin Kaing, *President*
Lor Yik, *Admin Sec*
EMP: 26
SQ FT: 32,000
SALES (est): 4.8MM **Privately Held**
SIC: 2752 Commercial printing, offset

(P-6691)
LAHLOUH INC
1649 Adrian Rd, Burlingame (94010-2103)
P.O. Box 4345 (94011-4345)
PHONE....................650 692-6600
John Lahlouh, *President*
Fadi Lahlouh, *Vice Pres*
Michael Lahlouh, *Admin Sec*
▲ EMP: 185
SALES (est): 64MM **Privately Held**
WEB: www.colorcopyprinting.com
SIC: 2752 Commercial printing, offset

(P-6692)
LAVA PRODUCTS INC
3168 Airway Ave, Costa Mesa
(92626-4608)
PHONE....................949 951-7191
Michael Freitas, *CEO*
David Howard, *Vice Pres*
Dean Passaglia, *Creative Dir*
Rhonda Stutz, *General Mgr*
Chris Joyce, *Sales Staff*
▲ EMP: 22
SQ FT: 13,500
SALES (est): 5.5MM **Privately Held**
WEB: www.lavaproducts.com
SIC: 2752 Commercial printing, offset

(P-6693)
LAYTON PRINTING & MAILING
1538 Arrow Hwy, La Verne (91750-5318)
PHONE....................909 592-4419
Michael Layton, *President*
Mary Ellen Layton, *Admin Sec*
EMP: 18
SQ FT: 20,000
SALES (est): 3.7MM **Privately Held**
WEB: www.laytonprinting.com
SIC: 2752 Commercial printing, offset

(P-6694)
LEE AUGUSTYN INC
9390 7th St Ste A, Rancho Cucamonga
(91730-5669)
PHONE....................909 483-0688
Kevin Brown, *President*
EMP: 10 EST: 1991
SQ FT: 1,600
SALES (est): 1MM **Privately Held**
SIC: 2752 Commercial printing, lithographic

(P-6695)
LEE MAXTON INC
Also Called: Minuteman Press
10844 Edison Ct, Rancho Cucamonga
(91730-3868)
PHONE....................909 483-0688
Kevin Browm, *President*
EMP: 12
SALES (est): 1.6MM **Privately Held**
SIC: 2752 Commercial printing, lithographic

(P-6696)
LEEWOOD PRESS INC
1407 Indiana St, San Francisco
(94107-3515)
PHONE....................415 896-0513
Tom W Lee, *President*
EMP: 20
SQ FT: 19,000
SALES (est): 3.9MM **Privately Held**
WEB: www.leewoodpress.com
SIC: 2752 Commercial printing, offset

(P-6697)
LEGAL VISION GROUP LLC
1880 Century Park E # 209, Los Angeles
(90067-1600)
PHONE....................310 945-5550
Michelle Cano, *President*
EMP: 30
SALES (est): 1MM **Privately Held**
SIC: 2752 7389 7374 7335 Commercial printing, lithographic; mailing & messenger services; data processing & preparation; commercial photography; title abstract offices

(P-6698)
LEO LAM INC
Also Called: A & M Printing
3589 Nevada St Ste A, Pleasanton
(94566-6323)
PHONE....................925 484-3690
Leo Lam, *President*
Amy Chan, *CEO*
Maria Johnston, *Graphic Designe*
EMP: 30
SQ FT: 13,000
SALES (est): 5.3MM **Privately Held**
WEB: www.anmprinting.com
SIC: 2752 7331 2789 Commercial printing, offset; direct mail advertising services; bookbinding & related work

(P-6699)
LESTER LITHOGRAPH INC
1128 N Gilbert St, Anaheim (92801-1412)
PHONE....................714 491-3981
Robert Miller, *CEO*
Larry Lester, *COO*
Larita Miller, *CFO*
Jim Witt, *Exec VP*
James Witt, *Vice Pres*
EMP: 50
SQ FT: 25,000
SALES (est): 9.4MM **Privately Held**
WEB: www.lesterlitho.com
SIC: 2752 Commercial printing, offset

(P-6700)
LETTERHEAD FACTORY INC
1007 E Dominguez St Ste H, Carson
(90746-7252)
PHONE....................310 538-3321
Richard W Rice, *CEO*
EMP: 15
SQ FT: 5,000
SALES (est): 2.8MM **Privately Held**
WEB: www.letterheadfactory.com
SIC: 2752 Commercial printing, offset

(P-6701)
LIBERTY PRINTING INC
2601 Teepee Dr, Stockton (95205-2421)
P.O. Box 275, Clements (95227-0275)
PHONE....................209 467-8800
Dorothy Baker, *President*
Dan Mossbarger, *Vice Pres*
Jim Mossbarger, *Vice Pres*
EMP: 20
SQ FT: 40,000
SALES (est): 2.1MM **Privately Held**
WEB: www.libertyprinting.net
SIC: 2752 2789 Commercial printing, lithographic; bookbinding & related work

(P-6702)
LICHER DIRECT MAIL INC
980 Seco St, Pasadena (91103-2816)
PHONE....................626 795-3333
Wayne Licher Sr, *President*
Besse Licher, *Corp Secy*
Wayne Licher Jr, *Vice Pres*
Tony Huynh, *Prdtn Mgr*
EMP: 20
SQ FT: 17,000

SALES (est): 3.4MM **Privately Held**
SIC: 2752 7331 Commercial printing, offset; direct mail advertising services

(P-6703)
LIGHTS FANTASTIC
Also Called: Screen Machine
2408 Lincoln Village Dr, San Jose
(95125-2741)
PHONE....................408 266-2787
Clay Wescott, *President*
EMP: 24 EST: 2003
SQ FT: 1,200
SALES: 175K **Privately Held**
SIC: 2752 1799 7389 Offset & photolithographic printing; screening contractor: window, door, etc.;

(P-6704)
LITHOGRAPHIX INC (PA)
12250 Crenshaw Blvd, Hawthorne
(90250-3332)
PHONE....................323 770-1000
Herbert Zebrack, *President*
Gary Bates, *President*
Linh Bober, *CFO*
Victor Wolfe, *CFO*
Jeffrey Zebrack, *Corp Secy*
▲ EMP: 305
SQ FT: 250,000
SALES (est): 117.2MM **Privately Held**
WEB: www.lithoxprep.com
SIC: 2752 2759 Commercial printing, offset; commercial printing

(P-6705)
LITHOTYPE COMPANY INC (PA)
333 Point San Bruno Blvd, South San Francisco (94080-4917)
PHONE....................650 871-1750
Aphos Ikonomou, *President*
Penelope Rich, *CEO*
Linda Sartori, *CFO*
Bob Shoreen, *Senior VP*
Carl Haynes, *Vice Pres*
▲ EMP: 65
SQ FT: 41,000
SALES: 39MM **Privately Held**
WEB: www.lithotype.com
SIC: 2752 Wrappers, lithographed

(P-6706)
LL BAKER INC
Also Called: Printing Solutions
431 N Hale Ave, Escondido (92029-1421)
PHONE....................760 741-9899
Monika Baker, *President*
Mike Baker, *Vice Pres*
EMP: 10
SQ FT: 3,000
SALES (est): 1.7MM **Privately Held**
WEB: www.printing-solutions.biz
SIC: 2752 Commercial printing, offset

(P-6707)
LOMA LINDA UNIVERSITY
Also Called: University Printing
24951 Stewart St, Loma Linda
(92350-1712)
PHONE....................909 558-4552
Jennifer Rowland, *Manager*
Billy Hughes, *Education*
EMP: 25
SALES (corp-wide): 269.1MM **Privately Held**
WEB: www.llu.edu
SIC: 2752 Commercial printing, lithographic
PA: Loma Linda University
11060 Anderson St
Loma Linda CA 92350
909 558-4540

(P-6708)
LOMBARD ENTERPRISES INC
Also Called: Lombard Graphics
3619 San Gbriel Rver Pkwy, Pico Rivera
(90660-1403)
PHONE....................562 692-7070
Stephen R Lombard, *President*
Ross Lombard, *Vice Pres*
EMP: 20
SQ FT: 10,000
SALES (est): 3.6MM **Privately Held**
WEB: www.lombardgraphics.com
SIC: 2752 Commercial printing, offset

▲ = Import ▼=Export
◆ =Import/Export

(P-6709)
LOUIS ROESCH COMPANY
289 Foster City Blvd B, Foster City
(94404-1100)
PHONE.............................650 212-2052
EMP: 10
SALES (est): 860K Privately Held
SIC: 2752

(P-6710)
LSHUVER INC
3880 Redondo Beach Blvd, Torrance
(90504-1114)
PHONE.............................310 323-2326
Lewis Schuver, President
EMP: 12
SQ FT: 25,000
SALES (est): 1.8MM Privately Held
WEB: www.majorfulfillment.com
SIC: 2752 Commercial printing, offset

(P-6711)
LUCE COMMUNICATIONS LLC
Also Called: ABG Communications
3810 Wabash Dr, Jurupa Valley
(91752-1143)
PHONE.............................951 361-7404
Joel Luce, CEO
Dan Ablett, President
Vicki Ruff, Vice Pres
Humberto Quintanar, Principal
Dave Warren, Network Mgr
EMP: 40
SQ FT: 50,000
SALES (est): 11.4MM Privately Held
WEB: www.abgonline.com
SIC: 2752 2899 4822 7331 Business
forms, lithographed; ; electronic mail;
mailing service

(P-6712)
MAILRITE PRINT & MAIL INC
834 Striker Ave Ste C, Sacramento
(95834-1169)
PHONE.............................916 927-6245
Reimah Reinert, CEO
Robyn Christensen, Administration
Richard Reed, Accounts Exec
EMP: 22
SQ FT: 20,000
SALES (est): 3.8MM Privately Held
SIC: 2752 Commercial printing, offset

(P-6713)
MAN-GROVE INDUSTRIES INC
Also Called: Lithocraft Co
1201 N Miller St, Anaheim (92806-1933)
PHONE.............................714 630-3020
Bradley L Thurman, President
Colleen Cosgrove, Vice Pres
Robert Navarro, Vice Pres
John Cosgrove, Admin Sec
David Stouder, Administration
EMP: 64
SQ FT: 45,000
SALES (est): 18.5MM Privately Held
SIC: 2752 Commercial printing, offset

(P-6714)
MARIN COUNTY COPY SHOPS INC
Also Called: Copy Shop & Printing Co, The
901 C St, San Rafael (94901-2805)
PHONE.............................415 457-5600
Richard Goldstein, President
Howard Goldstein, Treasurer
Edythe Goldstein, Admin Sec
EMP: 10
SQ FT: 5,000
SALES (est): 1.1MM Privately Held
SIC: 2752 7334 Commercial printing, off-
set; photocopying & duplicating services

(P-6715)
MARRS PRINTING INC
Also Called: Mars Printing and Packaging
860 Tucker Ln, City of Industry
(91789-2914)
PHONE.............................909 594-9459
Walter H Marrs, CEO
Jackie Marrs, Treasurer
Teresa Grigsby, Vice Pres
Teresa Grisby, Vice Pres
Scott Marrs, Vice Pres
EMP: 82
SQ FT: 27,000

SALES (est): 16.9MM Privately Held
WEB: www.marrsprint.net
SIC: 2752 Commercial printing, offset

(P-6716)
MASKLESS LITHOGRAPHY INC
2550 Zanker Rd, San Jose (95131-1127)
P.O. Box 641537 (95164-1537)
PHONE.............................408 433-1864
William D Meisburger, President
William Wr Elder, CEO
William Pappani, CFO
▲ EMP: 14
SALES (est): 2.1MM Privately Held
WEB: www.maskless.com
SIC: 2752 Commercial printing, offset

(P-6717)
MASS GROUP
Also Called: Mass Press
1959 Kingsdale Ave, Redondo Beach
(90278-3417)
PHONE.............................310 214-2000
Michael Davoudian, President
EMP: 25
SQ FT: 4,500
SALES (est): 3.1MM Privately Held
WEB: www.masspress.com
SIC: 2752 Commercial printing, offset

(P-6718)
MASTER PRODUCTIONS INC
8310 Miramar Mall Ste A, San Diego
(92121-2576)
PHONE.............................858 677-0037
David Ekeroth, President
Joy Ekeroth, Treasurer
George Ekeroth, Vice Pres
Joshua Miskovsky, Information Mgr
EMP: 10
SQ FT: 7,600
SALES (est): 1.4MM Privately Held
WEB: www.master4printing.com
SIC: 2752 Commercial printing, offset

(P-6719)
MATSUDA HOUSE PRINTING INC
Also Called: B & G House of Printing
1825 W 169th St Ste A, Gardena
(90247-5270)
PHONE.............................310 532-1533
Benjamin Matsuda, CEO
Patsy Matsuda, Treasurer
Darren Matsuda, Vice Pres
Rick Morimura, Sales Staff
▲ EMP: 31
SALES (est): 5.3MM Privately Held
SIC: 2752 Lithographing on metal; com-
mercial printing, offset

(P-6720)
MCPRINT CORP
Also Called: McPrint Direct
327 E Commercial St, Pomona
(91767-5505)
PHONE.............................714 632-9966
Yusheng Shew, President
EMP: 13
SALES (est): 207.1K Privately Held
SIC: 2752 2759 Commercial printing, litho-
graphic; post cards, picture: printing

(P-6721)
MEGAPRINT DIGITAL PRTG CORP
1404 Old County Rd, Belmont
(94002-3928)
PHONE.............................650 517-0200
Lee R Browner, CEO
EMP: 13
SALES (est): 1.9MM Privately Held
SIC: 2752 Commercial printing, offset

(P-6722)
MEKONG PRINTING INC
Also Called: Mk Printing
2421 W 1st St, Santa Ana (92703-3509)
PHONE.............................714 558-9595
Hoan Truong, President
Nancy Luu, Vice Pres
EMP: 22
SQ FT: 20,000
SALES (est): 3.5MM Privately Held
WEB: www.mekongprinting.com
SIC: 2752 Commercial printing, offset

(P-6723)
MENDOCINO LITHOGRAPHERS
Also Called: Mendo Litho
100 N Franklin St, Fort Bragg
(95437-3603)
PHONE.............................707 964-0062
Phil Sharples, Owner
EMP: 10
SQ FT: 3,525
SALES (est): 1MM Privately Held
WEB: www.mendolitho.com
SIC: 2752 Commercial printing, offset

(P-6724)
MERIDIAN GRAPHICS INC
2652 Dow Ave, Tustin (92780-7208)
PHONE.............................949 833-3500
Paul Valencia, Senior VP
David Melin, President
Craig Miller, Corp Secy
Irene Saengsouvanna, Controller
Lisa Hartman, Human Resources
▲ EMP: 65
SQ FT: 40,000
SALES (est): 24.3MM Privately Held
WEB: www.mglitho.com
SIC: 2752 2759 Commercial printing, off-
set; letterpress printing

(P-6725)
MERILIZ INCORPORATED (PA)
Also Called: Dome Printing and Lithograph
2031 Dome Ln, McClellan (95652-2033)
PHONE.............................916 923-3663
Tim Poole, President
Timothy M Poole, President
Bob Poole, Chief Mktg Ofcr
Dave Baker, Vice Pres
Eric Carle, Vice Pres
EMP: 120 EST: 1947
SQ FT: 340,000
SALES (est): 33.6MM Privately Held
WEB: www.domeprinting.com
SIC: 2752 Commercial printing, offset

(P-6726)
METRO DIGITAL PRINTING INC
3311 W Macarthur Blvd, Santa Ana
(92704-6803)
PHONE.............................714 545-8400
Mike Jafari, President
Sherri Taheri, Treasurer
EMP: 30
SQ FT: 15,000
SALES (est): 3.6MM Privately Held
SIC: 2752 Commercial printing, litho-
graphic

(P-6727)
MICROPRINT INC
133 Puente Ave, City of Industry
(91746-2302)
PHONE.............................626 369-1950
Stone Liu, President
Chung Chien Peng, Shareholder
Teresa Peng, Shareholder
TSE Hung Liu, CEO
MEI Wong Chen, Admin Sec
▲ EMP: 20
SQ FT: 10,000
SALES (est): 3.2MM Privately Held
SIC: 2752 Commercial printing, offset

(P-6728)
MICROSCALE INDUSTRIES INC
18435 Bandilier Cir, Fountain Valley
(92708-7012)
PHONE.............................714 593-1422
David Williams, President
David Khai-Vu, Info Tech Dir
EMP: 18
SQ FT: 10,626
SALES: 1.4MM Privately Held
WEB: www.microscale.com
SIC: 2752 5945 Decals, lithographed;
hobby, toy & game shops

(P-6729)
MIKE PRINTER INC
6933 Woodley Ave, Van Nuys
(91406-4844)
PHONE.............................818 902-9922
Mike Domash, President
Roy Shirakata, Manager
EMP: 10
SQ FT: 12,000

SALES (est): 1.5MM Privately Held
WEB: www.miketheprinter.com
SIC: 2752 Commercial printing, offset

(P-6730)
MINUTE MAN ENVMTL SYSTEMS INC
830 W 16th St, Costa Mesa (92627-4331)
PHONE.............................949 637-5446
John Agamalian, President
EMP: 21 EST: 2010
SALES (est): 1.6MM Privately Held
SIC: 2752 Commercial printing, litho-
graphic

(P-6731)
MIR PRINTING & GRAPHICS
21333 Deering Ct, Canoga Park
(91304-5018)
PHONE.............................818 313-9333
Robert Mirzakhaian, CEO
EMP: 10
SALES (est): 1.2MM Privately Held
SIC: 2752 Commercial printing, offset

(P-6732)
MODEM GRAPHIC INC
18600 San Jose Ave, City of Industry
(91748-1366)
PHONE.............................626 912-7088
Willis Wang, President
Kevin Chen, Vice Pres
▲ EMP: 80
SQ FT: 15,000
SALES (est): 842.2K Privately Held
WEB: www.modemgraphics.com
SIC: 2752 Commercial printing, litho-
graphic

(P-6733)
MOJAVE COPY & PRINTING INC
12402 Industrial Blvd E10, Victorville
(92395-5875)
PHONE.............................760 241-7898
Howard Kack, President
EMP: 14
SQ FT: 5,500
SALES (est): 3.1MM Privately Held
SIC: 2752 Commercial printing, offset

(P-6734)
MOLINO COMPANY
Also Called: Melcast
13712 Alondra Blvd, Cerritos (90703-2316)
PHONE.............................323 726-1000
Melchor Castano, President
Cesar Dua, Pediatrics
EMP: 85
SQ FT: 200,000
SALES (est): 11.9MM Privately Held
SIC: 2752 Commercial printing, offset

(P-6735)
MONARCH LITHO INC (PA)
1501 Date St, Montebello (90640-6324)
PHONE.............................323 727-0300
Robert Lopez, President
Victor Neri, Corp Secy
George Lopez, Vice Pres
Jose Badia, General Mgr
Mariano Balbuena, Info Tech Dir
EMP: 50
SQ FT: 153,000
SALES (est): 55.5MM Privately Held
WEB: www.monarchlitho.com
SIC: 2752 Commercial printing, offset; ad-
vertising posters, lithographed

(P-6736)
MONTEREY GRAPHICS INC
23505 Crenshaw Blvd # 137, Torrance
(90505-5221)
P.O. Box 3398 (90510-3398)
PHONE.............................310 787-3370
Larry Bird, President
Tami Bird, Vice Pres
EMP: 10
SQ FT: 2,400
SALES (est): 3.2MM Privately Held
WEB: www.montereygraphics.com
SIC: 2752 7336 Commercial printing, off-
set; graphic arts & related design

PRODUCTS & SVCS

(P-6737)
MONTEREY SIGNS INC
555 Broadway Ave, Seaside (93955-4250)
PHONE.................................831 632-0490
Shawn Adams, *President*
Anjanette Adams, *CFO*
EMP: 12
SQ FT: 28,000
SALES: 450K Privately Held
SIC: 2752 7389 Commercial printing, lithographic; lettering & sign painting services

(P-6738)
MONTERO PRINTING INC
Also Called: Economy Printing Service
2 Harris Ct Ste A6, Monterey (93940-7817)
PHONE.................................831 655-5511
Francisco Montero, *President*
Diane Montero, *CFO*
EMP: 20
SQ FT: 2,600
SALES: 800K Privately Held
WEB: www.economyprintingservice.com
SIC: 2752 Commercial printing, offset

(P-6739)
MOQUIN PRESS INC
555 Harbor Blvd, Belmont (94002-4020)
PHONE.................................650 592-0575
Gregory A Mocquin, *Founder*
EMP: 60
SQ FT: 22,000
SALES (est): 14.6MM Privately Held
WEB: www.moquinpress.com
SIC: 2752 Commercial printing, offset

(P-6740)
MULTI PACKAGING SOLUTIONS INC
2350 W Empire Ave 150, Burbank (91504-3350)
PHONE.................................818 638-0216
Rick Dickson, *Vice Pres*
Rick N Dickson, *Vice Pres*
Moises Bermudez, *Technology*
EMP: 35
SALES (corp-wide): 16.2B Publicly Held
WEB: www.ivyhill-cinram.com
SIC: 2752 Color lithography
HQ: Multi Packaging Solutions, Inc.
   885 3rd Ave Fl 28
   New York NY 10022
   -

(P-6741)
MY SIGN DESIGN LLC
4821 Lankershim Blvd F145, North Hollywood (91601-4538)
PHONE.................................818 384-0800
Alan Nudel, *CEO*
EMP: 10
SQ FT: 25,000
SALES (est): 399.7K Privately Held
SIC: 2752 5999 3993 Commercial printing, offset; banners, flags, decals & posters; advertising artwork

(P-6742)
N M H INC
Also Called: MGF Graphics
19426 Londelius St, Northridge (91324-3511)
PHONE.................................818 843-8522
Michael Fitleberg, *President*
EMP: 12
SQ FT: 5,100
SALES (est): 1.4MM Privately Held
WEB: www.mgfgraphics.com
SIC: 2752 2791 2789 Commercial printing, offset; typesetting; bookbinding & related work

(P-6743)
NAPA PRINTING & GRAPHICS CTR (PA)
Also Called: NAPA Desktop Publishing
630 Airpark Rd Ste D, NAPA (94558-7528)
PHONE.................................707 257-6555
John Dunbar, *President*
Jeff Gerlomes, *Vice Pres*
Dennis Burdick, *Executive Asst*
Don Thiess, *Administration*
Kristi Hanan, *Sales Staff*
▲ EMP: 13 EST: 1981
SQ FT: 4,000

SALES (est): 1.8MM Privately Held
WEB: www.napaprinting.com
SIC: 2752 7334 2791 7331 Commercial printing, offset; photocopying & duplicating services; typesetting; direct mail advertising services

(P-6744)
NATIONAL GRAPHICS LLC
Also Called: Jano Graphics
4893 Mcgrath St, Ventura (93003-7719)
PHONE.................................805 644-9212
Mike Scher, *President*
John Armstrong, *Administration*
Steve Dreyer, *Sales Staff*
Junior Gaona, *Accounts Mgr*
EMP: 40 EST: 1960
SQ FT: 15,000
SALES (est): 9.2MM Privately Held
WEB: www.janographics.com
SIC: 2752 Commercial printing, offset

(P-6745)
NETWORK PRINTING & COPY CENTER
12155 Flint Pl, Poway (92064-7107)
PHONE.................................858 695-8221
Henry Cook, *Partner*
Bob Cook, *Partner*
EMP: 10
SQ FT: 5,000
SALES: 900K Privately Held
WEB: www.nwp1.com
SIC: 2752 7336 7334 Photo-offset printing; graphic arts & related design; photocopying & duplicating services

(P-6746)
NEWPORT MESA USD CAMPUS C
2985 Bear St, Costa Mesa (92626-4300)
PHONE.................................714 424-8939
Mellissia Christensen, *Principal*
EMP: 13
SALES (est): 3.1MM Privately Held
SIC: 2752 Commercial printing, lithographic

(P-6747)
NEYENESCH PRINTERS INC
2750 Kettner Blvd, San Diego (92101-1295)
P.O. Box 81184 (92138-1184)
PHONE.................................619 297-2281
Carl A Bentley, *CEO*
Clifford Neyenesch, *Ch of Bd*
Dave Pauley, *President*
Kandy Neyenesch, *CFO*
Mark Harlos, *Vice Pres*
EMP: 70 EST: 1899
SQ FT: 30,000
SALES (est): 16.9MM Privately Held
WEB: www.neyenesch.com
SIC: 2752 Commercial printing, offset

(P-6748)
NG JOHN
Also Called: Copy Mill
780 Van Ness Ave, San Francisco (94102-3218)
PHONE.................................415 929-7188
John Ng, *Owner*
▲ EMP: 10
SALES (est): 1MM Privately Held
SIC: 2752 Commercial printing, offset

(P-6749)
NIKNEJAD INC
Also Called: Colornet
6855 Hayvenhurst Ave, Van Nuys (91406-4718)
PHONE.................................310 478-8363
Kamran Niknejad, *President*
Sima Fouladi, *Vice Pres*
Rashid Yassamy, *Vice Pres*
Temo Moreno, *Project Mgr*
EMP: 40 EST: 1981
SQ FT: 5,000
SALES (est): 7.7MM Privately Held
SIC: 2752 7336 2791 Commercial printing, offset; graphic arts & related design; typesetting

(P-6750)
NO BOUNDARIES INC
Also Called: Greenbox Art and Culture
789 Gateway Center Way, San Diego (92102-4539)
PHONE.................................619 266-2349
Thomas Capp, *CEO*
▲ EMP: 50
SQ FT: 3,500
SALES (est): 9.1MM Privately Held
WEB: www.oopsydaisy.com
SIC: 2752 Commercial printing, offset

(P-6751)
NONSTOP PRINTING INC
6226 Santa Monica Blvd, Los Angeles (90038-1704)
PHONE.................................323 464-1640
Kenneth Chan, *Partner*
EMP: 11
SQ FT: 8,000
SALES (est): 1.4MM Privately Held
SIC: 2752 7334 Commercial printing, offset; photocopying & duplicating services

(P-6752)
NORCAL PRINTING INC (PA)
1555 Yosemite Ave Ste 28, San Francisco (94124-3272)
PHONE.................................415 282-8856
MEI Lee, *President*
Tim Anderer, *Vice Pres*
Kim Lee, *Vice Pres*
▲ EMP: 13
SQ FT: 12,400
SALES (est): 1.6MM Privately Held
WEB: www.norcalprinting.com
SIC: 2752 Commercial printing, offset

(P-6753)
NORSAL PRINTING INC
20255 Prairie St, Chatsworth (91311-6025)
PHONE.................................818 886-4164
Salvatore Dapello, *President*
Eric Floyd, *Vice Pres*
Patricia V Dapello, *Admin Sec*
EMP: 13
SQ FT: 4,500
SALES (est): 1.4MM Privately Held
SIC: 2752 2759 Commercial printing, offset; commercial printing

(P-6754)
NSS ENTERPRISES
Also Called: Cyber Press
3380 Viso Ct, Santa Clara (95054-2625)
PHONE.................................408 970-9200
Chuck Nijmeh, *President*
Adam Zeno, *Vice Pres*
EMP: 22
SALES: 3.6MM Privately Held
WEB: www.cyber-press.net
SIC: 2752 Commercial printing, offset

(P-6755)
OAKMEAD PRTG & REPRODUCTION
233 E Weddell Dr Ste G, Sunnyvale (94089-1659)
PHONE.................................408 734-5505
Toll Free:.................................888 -
Tony Ngo, *President*
EMP: 50
SQ FT: 2,000
SALES (est): 3MM Privately Held
WEB: www.oakmead.com
SIC: 2752 2791 Commercial printing, offset; typesetting, computer controlled

(P-6756)
OCPC INC
Also Called: The Orange County Printing Co
2485 Da Vinci, Irvine (92614-5844)
PHONE.................................949 475-1900
Miguel Jacobowitz, *COO*
Moises Ramirez, *Info Tech Mgr*
Matt Schwartz, *Technology*
Luis Delgadillo, *Production*
Lac Pham, *Production*
EMP: 60
SQ FT: 18,000
SALES (est): 11.3MM Privately Held
SIC: 2752 Commercial printing, offset

(P-6757)
ODCOMBE PRESS (NASHVILLE)
Also Called: Haynes Publications
859 Lawrence Dr, Newbury Park (91320-2232)
PHONE.................................615 793-5414
John H Haynes, *Ch of Bd*
▲ EMP: 30
SALES (est): 4.3MM
SALES (corp-wide): 47.1MM Privately Held
WEB: www.hays.plc.uk
SIC: 2752 Commercial printing, lithographic
PA: Haynes Publishing Group Public Limited Company
   Sparkford
   Yeovil BA22
   196 344-0635

(P-6758)
OMEGA GRAPHICS PRINTING HOLLYW
6000 Fountain Ave, Los Angeles (90028-8311)
PHONE.................................213 784-5200
MAI Vong, *CEO*
EMP: 10
SQ FT: 1,100
SALES: 150K Privately Held
SIC: 2752 Commercial printing, offset

(P-6759)
ON PRESS PRINTING SERVICE INC
1440 Richardson St, San Bernardino (92408-2962)
PHONE.................................909 799-9599
Grant Rumary, *President*
Annie Boyd, *Treasurer*
EMP: 14
SQ FT: 15,000
SALES (est): 1.1MM Privately Held
SIC: 2752 2759 Commercial printing, offset; commercial printing

(P-6760)
ONEIL DIGITAL SOLUTIONS LLC
12655 Beatrice St, Los Angeles (90066-7300)
PHONE.................................310 448-6407
David Woodley, *Controller*
EMP: 201
SALES (corp-wide): 231.5MM Privately Held
SIC: 2752 5045 7389 Commercial printing, lithographic; computer software; mailbox rental & related service
HQ: O'neil Digital Solutions, Llc
   3100 E Plano Pkwy
   Plano TX

(P-6761)
ORANGE COAST REPROGRAPHICS INC
Also Called: Mouse Graphics
659 W 19th St, Costa Mesa (92627-2715)
PHONE.................................949 548-5571
Constance Mary Lane, *CEO*
EMP: 22
SQ FT: 9,000
SALES (est): 4.5MM Privately Held
WEB: www.sendmouse.com
SIC: 2752 7336 2789 2759 Commercial printing, lithographic; commercial art & graphic design; bookbinding & related work; commercial printing

(P-6762)
ORCHARD PRINTING
325 Aleut Ct, Fremont (94539-6871)
PHONE.................................510 490-1736
Steven T Karris, *Owner*
EMP: 11
SQ FT: 6,700
SALES (est): 530K Privately Held
SIC: 2752 Publication printing, lithographic

(P-6763)
PACFUL INC (PA)
11311 White Rock Rd # 100, Rancho Cordova (95742-6876)
PHONE.................................916 233-1488
Jennfier Jo Hudek, *CEO*

Rhonda Lepera, *Controller*
Felipe Roque, *Accounts Mgr*
◆ **EMP:** 57
SALES (est): 19.9MM **Privately Held**
SIC: 2752 7389 Commercial printing, off-set; rug binding

(P-6764)
PACFUL INC
131 Glenn Way Ste 4, San Carlos
(94070-6259)
PHONE..................................650 200-4252
EMP: 72 **Privately Held**
SIC: 2752 7389 Commercial printing, litho-graphic; rug binding
PA: Pacful, Inc.
11311 White Rock Rd # 100
Rancho Cordova CA 95742

(P-6765)
PACIFIC IMAGING
Also Called: Pacific Printing
9687 Distribution Ave, San Diego
(92121-2307)
PHONE..................................858 536-2600
Steve Cook, *President*
EMP: 17
SQ FT: 8,250
SALES (est): 1.4MM **Privately Held**
WEB: www.pac-print.com
SIC: 2752 7336 Commercial printing, off-set; graphic arts & related design

(P-6766)
PACIFIC WEST LITHO INC
3291 E Miraloma Ave, Anaheim
(92806-1910)
PHONE..................................714 579-0868
Chang Che Chou, *CEO*
Robin Dean, *Office Mgr*
EMP: 70
SQ FT: 24,000
SALES (est): 11.7MM **Privately Held**
WEB: www.pacificwestlitho.com
SIC: 2752 Lithographing on metal; com-mercial printing, offset

(P-6767)
PAR GLOBAL RESOURCES INC
2005 De La Cruz Blvd # 111, Santa Clara
(95050-3030)
PHONE..................................408 982-5515
Paul Craft Hathaway, *President*
Jane Hathaway, *Admin Sec*
EMP: 12
SALES (est): 2.2MM **Privately Held**
WEB: www.par-global.com
SIC: 2752 Commercial printing, offset

(P-6768)
PARADISE PRINTING INC
13474 Pumice St, Norwalk (90650-5247)
PHONE..................................714 228-9628
Paul B Pistone, *CEO*
EMP: 25
SQ FT: 48,000
SALES (est): 5.4MM **Privately Held**
SIC: 2752 Commercial printing, offset

(P-6769)
PARKER PRINTING INC
11240 Young River Ave, Fountain Valley
(92708-4109)
PHONE..................................714 444-4550
Marie Colacchio, *President*
Bernie P Colacchio, *Vice Pres*
EMP: 12
SQ FT: 12,000
SALES (est): 2.4MM **Privately Held**
WEB: www.parkerprinting.com
SIC: 2752 Commercial printing, offset

(P-6770)
PARS PUBLISHING CORP
Also Called: Grapheex
4485 Runway St, Simi Valley (93063-3436)
PHONE..................................818 280-0540
Mehran Kiankarimi, *President*
Mike Kian, *President*
Allan Yegani, *Treasurer*
Mahnaz Shidfar, *Vice Pres*
Vincent Fisher, *Admin Sec*
EMP: 54
SQ FT: 40,000

SALES (est): 7.2MM **Privately Held**
WEB: www.grapheex.com
SIC: 2752 Commercial printing, offset

(P-6771)
PATSONS PRESS
Also Called: Patsons Media Group
3000 Scott Blvd Ste 101, Santa Clara
(95054-3321)
PHONE..................................408 567-0911
Patricia Dellamano, *President*
Joseph Dellamano, *Corp Secy*
Mark Dellamano, *Vice Pres*
Greg Hall, *Info Tech Mgr*
Veronica Smoot, *Sales Staff*
EMP: 50
SALES (est): 8.1MM **Privately Held**
WEB: www.patsons.com
SIC: 2752 Commercial printing, offset

(P-6772)
PAUL BAKER PRINTING INC
220 Riverside Ave, Roseville (95678-3146)
PHONE..................................916 969-8317
Kasey Cotulla, *President*
James Davis, *Vice Pres*
Bonnie Townsend, *Admin Asst*
Maggie Soderman, *Sales Staff*
EMP: 32
SQ FT: 8,500
SALES (est): 5.9MM **Privately Held**
WEB: www.pbaker.com
SIC: 2752 Commercial printing, offset

(P-6773)
PAUL SILVER ENTERPRISES INC
Also Called: Quick Silver Prtg & Graphics
9155 Alabama Ave Ste F, Chatsworth
(91311-5873)
PHONE..................................818 998-9900
Paul Silver, *President*
Ava Silver, *Vice Pres*
▲ **EMP:** 10
SALES (est): 1.6MM **Privately Held**
WEB: www.quicksilverprint.com
SIC: 2752 8743 2759 Commercial print-ing, offset; promotion service; advertising literature: printing

(P-6774)
PDF PRINT COMMUNICATIONS INC (PA)
2630 E 28th St, Long Beach (90755-2202)
PHONE..................................562 426-6978
Robert Albert Mullaney, *CEO*
Shirley Mullaney, *Corp Secy*
Kevin J Mullaney, *Vice Pres*
EMP: 52
SQ FT: 23,000
SALES (est): 16.3MM **Privately Held**
WEB: www.pacificdataforms.com
SIC: 2752 2761 Commercial printing, off-set; manifold business forms

(P-6775)
PERAZZA PRINTS LLC (PA)
25 Crescent Dr Ste A349, Pleasant Hill
(94523-5508)
PHONE..................................925 681-2458
Michael Perillo, *Principal*
EMP: 14
SALES (est): 6MM **Privately Held**
SIC: 2752 Commercial printing, litho-graphic

(P-6776)
PERAZZA PRINTS LLC
2495 Estand Way, Pleasant Hill
(94523-3911)
PHONE..................................925 567-3395
EMP: 28
SALES (corp-wide): 6MM **Privately Held**
SIC: 2752 Commercial printing, litho-graphic
PA: Perazza Prints Llc
25 Crescent Dr Ste A349
Pleasant Hill CA 94523
925 681-2458

(P-6777)
PERFECT IMAGE PRINTING INC
3223 Monier Cir, Rancho Cordova
(95742-6807)
PHONE..................................916 631-8350
James Van Hill, *CEO*
Anita Van Hill, *CFO*

EMP: 10
SQ FT: 7,500
SALES (est): 1.6MM **Privately Held**
SIC: 2752 Commercial printing, litho-graphic

(P-6778)
PERFORMANCE PRINTING CENTER
4380 Redwood Hwy Ste B8, San Rafael
(94903-2110)
P.O. Box 3675 (94912-3675)
PHONE..................................415 485-5878
Barbara Echo, *President*
Mike Murnin, *Sales Staff*
EMP: 25
SALES (est): 2.5MM **Privately Held**
WEB: www.printingcenter.com
SIC: 2752 Commercial printing, offset

(P-6779)
PFANSTIEL PUBLISHERS & PRTRS
Also Called: Pfanstiel Printing
3010 E Anaheim St, Long Beach
(90804-3802)
PHONE..................................562 438-5641
Craig Pfanstiel, *President*
Charlotte J Pfanstiel, *Treasurer*
Denise Pfanstiel, *Corp Secy*
EMP: 10
SQ FT: 6,000
SALES (est): 1.2MM **Privately Held**
WEB: www.pfanstielprinters.com
SIC: 2752 2711 Commercial printing, off-set; newspapers, publishing & printing

(P-6780)
PGI PACIFIC GRAPHICS INTL
14938 Nelson Ave, City of Industry
(91744-4330)
PHONE..................................626 336-7707
Yvonne Castillo Wasson, *CEO*
Ricardo Wasson, *Vice Pres*
Trey Brooks, *Director*
EMP: 25
SQ FT: 17,000
SALES (est): 4.5MM **Privately Held**
SIC: 2752 2759 8742 7331 Commercial printing, offset; commercial printing; mar-keting consulting services; mailing service

(P-6781)
PHOTONIC CORP
5800 Uplander Way Ste 100, Culver City
(90230-6608)
PHONE..................................310 642-7975
Birendra Dutt, *President*
Marco Ramirez, *Technology*
EMP: 12
SALES (est): 1.5MM **Privately Held**
SIC: 2752 Commercial printing, litho-graphic

(P-6782)
PINE GROVE INDUSTRIES INC
Also Called: Custom Printing
2001 Cabot Pl, Oxnard (93030-2666)
PHONE..................................805 485-3700
Charles Utts, *President*
Becky Utts, *Vice Pres*
Kristen Utts, *Accounting Mgr*
EMP: 39
SQ FT: 10,000
SALES (est): 8.9MM **Privately Held**
SIC: 2752 Commercial printing, offset

(P-6783)
PINNACLE DIVERSIFIED INC
Also Called: Pinnacle Press
1248 San Luis Obispo St, Hayward
(94544-7916)
PHONE..................................510 400-7929
Jason Kim, *President*
Rui Wang, *Vice Pres*
EMP: 17
SQ FT: 13,000
SALES (est): 2.6MM **Privately Held**
SIC: 2752 Commercial printing, litho-graphic

(P-6784)
PIP PRINTING PALO ALTO INC
2233 El Camino Real, Palo Alto
(94306-1541)
PHONE..................................650 323-8388

Michael Maystead, *CEO*
EMP: 10
SQ FT: 2,500
SALES (est): 2MM **Privately Held**
SIC: 2752 Commercial printing, offset

(P-6785)
PM CORPORATE GROUP INC
Also Called: PM Packaging
2285 Michael Faraday Dr, San Diego
(92154-7926)
PHONE..................................619 498-9199
Ramona Schmidt, *President*
Gayle Cronin, *Vice Pres*
Steve Reder, *Vice Pres*
EMP: 240
SALES (est): 25.8MM **Privately Held**
SIC: 2752 Commercial printing, offset

(P-6786)
PM LITHOGRAPHERS INC
Also Called: Promedia Printers
7600 Linley Ln, Canoga Park (91304-5224)
PHONE..................................818 704-2626
Victor J Gelfo, *President*
Holly Gelfo, *Treasurer*
EMP: 14
SQ FT: 4,000
SALES: 1.3MM **Privately Held**
SIC: 2752 Commercial printing, offset

(P-6787)
PMRCA INC (PA)
Also Called: Witts Everything For Office
20437 Brian Way Ste B, Tehachapi
(93561-6764)
P.O. Box 1334 (93581-1334)
PHONE..................................661 822-6760
Mika Amato, *President*
Paul M Amato, *Vice Pres*
Cara Dominguez, *Graphic Designe*
EMP: 11
SQ FT: 8,000
SALES (est): 2.7MM **Privately Held**
WEB: www.governmentauction.com
SIC: 2752 5943 Offset & photolithographic printing; office forms & supplies

(P-6788)
POSTAL INSTANT PRESS INC (HQ)
Also Called: PIP Printing
26722 Plaza, Mission Viejo (92691-8051)
P.O. Box 9077 (92690-9077)
PHONE..................................949 348-5000
Dan Lowe, *Ch of Bd*
Richard Low, *President*
Dan Conger, *CFO*
David C Rice, *Vice Pres*
Ines Farris, *Office Mgr*
EMP: 40
SQ FT: 25,000
SALES: 2.2MM
SALES (corp-wide): 19.9MM **Privately Held**
WEB: www.pip.com
SIC: 2752 6159 Commercial printing, off-set; machinery & equipment finance leas-ing
PA: Franchise Services, Inc.
26722 Plaza
Mission Viejo CA 92691
949 348-5400

(P-6789)
PRE-PRESS INTERNATIONAL
Also Called: Digital Pre-Press Intl
20 S Linden Ave Ste 4a, South San Fran-cisco (94080-6425)
PHONE..................................415 216-0031
Sanjay Sakhuja, *President*
EMP: 37
SQ FT: 20,710
SALES: 6MM **Privately Held**
SIC: 2752 Commercial printing, litho-graphic

(P-6790)
PRECISION LITHO INC
1185 Joshua Way, Vista (92081-7892)
PHONE..................................760 727-9400
Bill Anderson, *President*
Mike Gacnik, *President*
John Krebs, *Vice Pres*
Kent Wright, *Vice Pres*
EMP: 35 **EST:** 1981

SQ FT: 40,000
SALES (est): 5.8MM
SALES (corp-wide): 6.8B **Publicly Held**
WEB: www.plitho.com
SIC: 2752 Commercial printing, lithographic
HQ: Consolidated Graphics, Inc.
　5858 Westheimer Rd # 200
　Houston TX 77057
　713 787-0977

(P-6791)
PRECISION OFFSET INC
Also Called: Precision Services Group
15201 Woodlawn Ave, Tustin (92780-6449)
PHONE.....................949 752-1714
Lawrence Smith, *President*
Greg Cocroft, *Vice Pres*
Kevin Smith, *Sales Mgr*
Lydia Avina, *Manager*
Faith Pantel, *Manager*
EMP: 75
SQ FT: 15,000
SALES (est): 20.5MM **Privately Held**
WEB: www.precisionoffset.net
SIC: 2752 Commercial printing, offset

(P-6792)
PRESSNET EXPRESS INC
7283 Engineer Rd Ste Ab, San Diego (92111-1414)
PHONE.....................858 694-0070
Sam Levine, *CEO*
Yoav Levine, *President*
Jose Garcia, *Prdtn Mgr*
EMP: 15
SQ FT: 5,000
SALES (est): 2.4MM **Privately Held**
WEB: www.pressnetexpress.com
SIC: 2752 Commercial printing, offset

(P-6793)
PRIMARY COLOR SYSTEMS CORP (PA)
11130 Holder St, Cypress (90630-5162)
PHONE.....................949 660-7080
Daniel Hirt, *President*
Ronald Hirt, *Shareholder*
Michael Hirt, *Vice Pres*
Paul Wartman, *Vice Pres*
Anna Strenger, *Project Leader*
▲ **EMP:** 292 **EST:** 1984
SQ FT: 40,000
SALES: 61MM **Privately Held**
WEB: www.primarycolor.com
SIC: 2752 2759 Commercial printing, offset; commercial printing

(P-6794)
PRINT & MAIL SOLUTIONS INC
Also Called: AlphaGraphics
1322 Blue Oaks Blvd # 100, Roseville (95678-7051)
PHONE.....................916 782-5489
Guy Vasconcellos, *CEO*
Linda Vasconcellos, *Vice Pres*
EMP: 12
SQ FT: 4,500
SALES (est): 2MM **Privately Held**
SIC: 2752 Commercial printing, lithographic

(P-6795)
PRINT N SAVE INC
2120 E Howell Ave Ste 414, Anaheim (92806-6029)
PHONE.....................714 634-1133
Roy Anderson, *Vice Pres*
Maud Anderson, *President*
EMP: 10
SQ FT: 3,845
SALES (est): 1.1MM **Privately Held**
SIC: 2752 Commercial printing, offset

(P-6796)
PRINT SMITH INC
8047 Soquel Dr, Aptos (95003-3928)
PHONE.....................831 688-1538
Peter Truman, *President*
Kimberly Ann Truman, *Admin Sec*
EMP: 10
SQ FT: 3,200

SALES (est): 1MM **Privately Held**
WEB: www.printsmith.com
SIC: 2752 7334 7338 7374 Commercial printing, offset; photocopying & duplicating services; word processing service; data processing & preparation

(P-6797)
PRINT-N-STUFF INC
Also Called: Galaxy Press
1300 Galaxy Way Ste 3, Concord (94520-4922)
PHONE.....................925 798-3212
Tom J Meyer, *President*
Robert Meyer, *Vice Pres*
Tom Meyer, *Principal*
EMP: 10
SQ FT: 6,900
SALES (est): 1.7MM **Privately Held**
WEB: www.galaxypress.net
SIC: 2752 Commercial printing, offset

(P-6798)
PRINTCOM INC
Also Called: Minuteman Press
14675 Titus St, Van Nuys (91402-4922)
PHONE.....................818 891-8282
Pamela K Berg, *President*
Kevin Berg, *Vice Pres*
EMP: 13
SQ FT: 5,100
SALES (est): 1.4MM **Privately Held**
WEB: www.minutemanpressla.com
SIC: 2752 Commercial printing, lithographic

(P-6799)
PRINTEFEX INC
401 W Los Feliz Rd Ste C, Glendale (91204-2772)
PHONE.....................818 240-2400
Rouben Ovanespour, *Co-Owner*
Seth Ovanespour, *Co-Owner*
Arbi Sarian, *Sales Staff*
EMP: 10
SQ FT: 1,150
SALES (est): 1.5MM **Privately Held**
WEB: www.printefex.com
SIC: 2752 7384 2759 Commercial printing, offset; photofinishing laboratory; commercial printing

(P-6800)
PRINTERPREZZ INC
4026 Clipper Ct, Fremont (94538-6540)
PHONE.....................510 225-8412
Shrinivas Shetty, *CEO*
Shri Shetty, *CEO*
EMP: 18
SALES (est): 122.8K **Privately Held**
SIC: 2752 Commercial printing, lithographic

(P-6801)
PRINTERY INC
1762 Kaiser Ave, Irvine (92614-5706)
PHONE.....................949 757-1930
Massis Chahbazian, *CEO*
Denise Acosta, *Finance Mgr*
Emma Macmillan, *Manager*
Mike Wilson, *Manager*
▲ **EMP:** 15
SQ FT: 10,000
SALES (est): 3.9MM **Privately Held**
SIC: 2752 Commercial printing, offset

(P-6802)
PRINTFIRM INC
21352 Nordhoff St Ste 104, Chatsworth (91311-6908)
PHONE.....................818 992-1005
Masis Artounian, *President*
EMP: 13
SALES (est): 1.8MM **Privately Held**
SIC: 2752 Commercial printing, lithographic

(P-6803)
PRINTING DIVISION INC
1933 N Main St, Orange (92865-4101)
PHONE.....................714 685-0111
Richard Baca, *CEO*
Sam Nooriala, *CFO*
Samuel Nooriala, *CFO*
EMP: 13
SQ FT: 6,800

SALES (est): 2MM **Privately Held**
WEB: www.printdivinc.com
SIC: 2752 Commercial printing, offset

(P-6804)
PRINTING ISLAND CORPORATION
11535 Martens River Cir, Fountain Valley (92708-4201)
PHONE.....................714 668-1000
Philip Wang, *President*
Denise Pham, *Admin Sec*
EMP: 11
SALES (est): 1.2MM **Privately Held**
WEB: www.printingisland.com
SIC: 2752 Commercial printing, offset

(P-6805)
PRINTING MANAGEMENT ASSOCIATES
17128 Edwards Rd, Cerritos (90703-2424)
PHONE.....................562 407-9977
Jeffrey Brady, *CEO*
Michael Lane, *President*
Clif McDougall, *Exec VP*
Rich Russell, *Vice Pres*
Steve Doerr, *Executive*
▲ **EMP:** 19
SQ FT: 12,600
SALES (est): 3MM **Privately Held**
WEB: www.printmgt.com
SIC: 2752 5111 Commercial printing, offset; printing paper

(P-6806)
PRINTING PALACE INC (PA)
2300 Lincoln Blvd, Santa Monica (90405-2530)
PHONE.....................310 451-5151
Eli Albek, *President*
EMP: 20
SQ FT: 8,000
SALES (est): 1.4MM **Privately Held**
WEB: www.printingpalace.com
SIC: 2752 Commercial printing, offset

(P-6807)
PRINTING SAFARI CO
Also Called: Safari Signs
9855 Topanga Canyon Blvd, Chatsworth (91311-4044)
PHONE.....................818 709-3752
Doris Potvin, *Partner*
Ingrid Lindquist, *Partner*
Rick Carranza, *General Mgr*
EMP: 12
SQ FT: 3,800
SALES (est): 1.4MM **Privately Held**
WEB: www.printingsafari.com
SIC: 2752 Commercial printing, offset

(P-6808)
PRINTIVITY (PA)
8840 Kenamar Dr Ste 405, San Diego (92121-2450)
PHONE.....................877 649-5463
Lawrence Chou, *Owner*
Craig Watkins, *Production*
Rishi Patel, *Manager*
EMP: 15
SALES (est): 3.1MM **Privately Held**
SIC: 2752 Commercial printing, lithographic

(P-6809)
PRINTOGRAPH INC
7625 N San Fernando Rd, Burbank (91505-1073)
PHONE.....................818 252-3000
Kristina Keshishyan, *Principal*
EMP: 13
SALES (est): 2.4MM **Privately Held**
SIC: 2752 Commercial printing, lithographic

(P-6810)
PRINTRUNNER LLC
Also Called: U-Nited Printing and Copy Ctr
8000 Haskell Ave, Van Nuys (91406-1321)
PHONE.....................888 296-5760
Dean Rabbani, *Principal*
Mike Zaya, *President*
Adam Berger, *CEO*
Kamie Davison, *Controller*
EMP: 30
SQ FT: 50,000

SALES (est): 490.5K **Privately Held**
WEB: www.printrunner.com
SIC: 2752 Commercial printing, lithographic

(P-6811)
PRINTS CHARMN INC (PA)
11560 Tennessee Ave, Los Angeles (90064-1513)
PHONE.....................310 312-0904
Maxine Elster-Pearlman, *President*
Maxine A Elster, *Owner*
EMP: 11
SQ FT: 1,000
SALES (est): 1MM **Privately Held**
WEB: www.printscharmn.com
SIC: 2752 Commercial printing, lithographic

(P-6812)
PRO DOCUMENT SOLUTIONS INC (PA)
1760 Commerce Way, Paso Robles (93446-3620)
PHONE.....................805 238-6680
George Phillips, *President*
Ryan Mazon, *Plant Supt*
Zac Alvarez, *Supervisor*
▲ **EMP:** 92
SQ FT: 35,000
SALES (est): 31.2MM **Privately Held**
WEB: www.prodocumentsolutions.com
SIC: 2752 Business forms, lithographed

(P-6813)
PROCESSORS MAILING INC
Also Called: Processors The
761 N Dodsworth Ave, Covina (91724-2408)
PHONE.....................626 358-5075
Fax: 626 358-5607
EMP: 30 **EST:** 1974
SQ FT: 8,000
SALES (est): 4MM **Privately Held**
WEB: www.theprocessors.com
SIC: 2752 7331 2791

(P-6814)
PROFESSIONAL PRINT & MAIL INC
2818 E Hamilton Ave, Fresno (93721-3209)
PHONE.....................559 237-7468
Doug Carlile, *President*
Rorberta Carlile, *Executive*
Laurie Wax, *General Mgr*
Roberta L Carlile, *Admin Sec*
Russ Fowler, *Opers Mgr*
EMP: 30 **EST:** 1985
SQ FT: 20,000
SALES: 3.4MM **Privately Held**
WEB: www.printfresno.com
SIC: 2752 7331 5999 Commercial printing, offset; mailing service; banners, flags, decals & posters

(P-6815)
PROGRAPHICS INC
9200 Lower Azusa Rd, Rosemead (91770-1593)
PHONE.....................626 287-0417
Christina Stevens, *CEO*
Timothy Stevens, *President*
Elizabeth Cawley, *Vice Pres*
Jaime Colacio, *Vice Pres*
EMP: 39 **EST:** 1967
SQ FT: 23,000
SALES (est): 13.7MM **Privately Held**
WEB: www.prographicsllc.com
SIC: 2752 Commercial printing, offset

(P-6816)
PRPCO
Also Called: Poor Richard's Press
2226 Beebee St, San Luis Obispo (93401-5505)
PHONE.....................805 543-6844
Todd P Ventura, *President*
Mary Monroe, *CFO*
Richard C Blake, *Vice Pres*
EMP: 35
SALES (est): 3.6MM **Privately Held**
SIC: 2752 Commercial printing, lithographic

▲ = Import ▼=Export
◆ =Import/Export

(P-6817)
PYRAMID GRAPHICS
Also Called: Pyramid Printing and Graphics
325 Harbor Way, South San Francisco
(94080-6919)
PHONE..............................650 871-0290
Kingman Leung, *President*
Nancy Tam, *Treasurer*
Larry Phan, *General Mgr*
EMP: 16
SQ FT: 4,000
SALES (est): 2.2MM **Privately Held**
WEB: www.pyramidgraphics.net
SIC: 2752 7374 7336 Commercial print-
ing, offset; data processing & preparation;
commercial art & graphic design

(P-6818)
Q TEAM
Also Called: Ryan Press
6400 Dale St, Buena Park (90621-3115)
PHONE..............................714 228-4465
Donna Quibodeaux, *President*
James Quibodeaux, *Treasurer*
Mike Quibodeaux, *Vice Pres*
EMP: 16
SQ FT: 13,000
SALES (est): 4.1MM **Privately Held**
WEB: www.ryanpress.com
SIC: 2752 Commercial printing, offset

(P-6819)
QG LLC
Worldcolor Merced
2201 Cooper Ave, Merced (95348-4307)
PHONE..............................209 384-0444
EMP: 611
SALES (corp-wide): 4.1B **Publicly Held**
WEB: www.qwdys.com
SIC: 2752 Commercial printing, offset
HQ: Qg, Llc
N61w23044 Harrys Way
Sussex WI 53089
-

(P-6820)
QG PRINTING II CORP
Also Called: Quad Graphics
6688 Box Springs Blvd, Riverside
(92507-0726)
PHONE..............................951 571-2500
Georg Decker, *Branch Mgr*
Tony Moyer, *Technology*
Steve Lund, *Maintence Staff*
EMP: 519
SALES (corp-wide): 4.1B **Publicly Held**
SIC: 2752 Commercial printing, offset
HQ: Qg Printing Ii Corp.
N61w23044 Harrys Way
Sussex WI 53089

(P-6821)
QUAD/GRAPHICS INC
17871 Park Plaza Dr # 150, Cerritos
(90703-9317)
PHONE..............................310 751-3900
Jeff Wunrow, *Managing Dir*
Richard Larson, *Controller*
EMP: 12
SALES (corp-wide): 4.1B **Publicly Held**
WEB: www.qg.com
SIC: 2752 Commercial printing, litho-
graphic
PA: Quad/Graphics Inc.
N61w23044 Harrys Way
Sussex WI 53089
414 566-6000

(P-6822)
QUAD/GRAPHICS INC
7190 Jurupa Ave, Riverside (92504-1016)
PHONE..............................951 689-1122
Uli Oels, *General Mgr*
EMP: 250
SQ FT: 30,000
SALES (corp-wide): 4.1B **Publicly Held**
WEB: www.vertisinc.com
SIC: 2752 7336 Commercial printing, off-
set; commercial art & graphic design
PA: Quad/Graphics Inc.
N61w23044 Harrys Way
Sussex WI 53089
414 566-6000

(P-6823)
QUAD/GRAPHICS INC
350 Rhode Island St # 110, San Francisco
(94103-5188)
PHONE..............................415 267-3700
Bruce Vogen, *Manager*
EMP: 509
SALES (corp-wide): 4.1B **Publicly Held**
SIC: 2752 Commercial printing, offset
PA: Quad/Graphics Inc.
N61w23044 Harrys Way
Sussex WI 53089
414 566-6000

(P-6824)
QUAD/GRAPHICS INC
2201 Cooper Ave, Merced (95348-4307)
PHONE..............................209 384-0444
Freider Debiasi, *Branch Mgr*
Susan Grofe, *Buyer*
Frank Nofuentes, *Mfg Mgr*
Dave Hall, *Maintence Staff*
EMP: 463
SALES (corp-wide): 4.1B **Publicly Held**
SIC: 2752 Commercial printing, offset
PA: Quad/Graphics Inc.
N61w23044 Harrys Way
Sussex WI 53089
414 566-6000

(P-6825)
QUADCO PRINTING INC
2535 Zanella Way, Chico (95928-7146)
PHONE..............................530 894-4061
Richard Braak, *President*
Sherryl Garcia Braak, *CFO*
EMP: 18 EST: 1978
SQ FT: 15,000
SALES: 1.5MM **Privately Held**
WEB: www.quadcoprinting.com
SIC: 2752 Commercial printing, offset

(P-6826)
QUEEN BEACH PRINTERS INC
937 Pine Ave, Long Beach (90813-4375)
P.O. Box 540 (90801-0540)
PHONE..............................562 436-8201
Nicholas W Edwards, *CEO*
William L Edwards Sr, *President*
Bill Edwards Jr, *COO*
William L Edwards Jr, *COO*
Virginia Noyes, *Vice Pres*
EMP: 30 EST: 1944
SQ FT: 25,000
SALES (est): 4.8MM **Privately Held**
WEB: www.qbprinters.com
SIC: 2752 7336 Commercial printing, off-
set; commercial art & graphic design

(P-6827)
R GOODLOE & ASSOCIATES INC
Also Called: Rga
25602 Alicia Pkwy, Laguna Hills
(92653-5309)
PHONE..............................714 380-3900
Robert A Goodloe, *President*
Robert Goodloe, *President*
Lavinia Goodloe, *Vice Pres*
EMP: 11
SALES (est): 1.5MM **Privately Held**
SIC: 2752 Commercial printing, offset

(P-6828)
R R DONNELLEY & SONS COMPANY
Also Called: Moore Business Forms
1050 Aviator Dr, Vacaville (95688-8900)
PHONE..............................707 446-6195
Mark George, *Branch Mgr*
EMP: 15
SALES (corp-wide): 6.8B **Publicly Held**
WEB: www.moore.com
SIC: 2752 Commercial printing, litho-
graphic
PA: R. R. Donnelley & Sons Company
35 W Wacker Dr
Chicago IL 60601
312 326-8000

(P-6829)
R R DONNELLEY & SONS COMPANY
Also Called: R R Donnelley
955 Gateway Center Way, San Diego
(92102-4542)
PHONE..............................619 527-4600
Boyd Richardson, *Branch Mgr*
EMP: 204
SALES (corp-wide): 6.8B **Publicly Held**
SIC: 2752 Commercial printing, litho-
graphic
PA: R. R. Donnelley & Sons Company
35 W Wacker Dr
Chicago IL 60601
312 326-8000

(P-6830)
R R DONNELLEY & SONS COMPANY
Also Called: R R Donnelley Coml Press Plant
960 Gateway Center Way, San Diego
(92102-4542)
PHONE..............................619 527-4600
Jim Rosenberg, *Manager*
EMP: 150
SALES (corp-wide): 6.8B **Publicly Held**
WEB: www.rrdonnelley.com
SIC: 2752 Commercial printing, litho-
graphic
PA: R. R. Donnelley & Sons Company
35 W Wacker Dr
Chicago IL 60601
312 326-8000

(P-6831)
RAINBOW MAGNETICS INCORPORATED
1 Whatney, Irvine (92618-2806)
PHONE..............................714 540-4777
Robert Knapp, *President*
Jennifer Knapp, *CFO*
▲ EMP: 25 EST: 1974
SQ FT: 13,174
SALES (est): 3.5MM **Privately Held**
WEB: www.rainbowmagnetics.com
SIC: 2752 3993 Commercial printing, off-
set; advertising novelties

(P-6832)
RAINTREE BUSINESS PRODUCTS
Also Called: B C T
23101 Terra Dr, Laguna Hills (92653-1320)
PHONE..............................949 859-0801
Joseph H Rachal Jr, *President*
Donna C Rachal, *Vice Pres*
EMP: 20
SQ FT: 7,000
SALES (est): 2.5MM **Privately Held**
WEB: www.bctlaguna.com
SIC: 2752 Commercial printing, litho-
graphic

(P-6833)
RANCHO BERNARDO PRINTING INC
1519 Industrial Ave Ste D, Escondido
(92029-1363)
P.O. Box 461101 (92046-1101)
PHONE..............................858 486-4540
Steve Swadell, *President*
Loyd Beth Swadell, *Shareholder*
EMP: 11
SALES (est): 1.6MM **Privately Held**
WEB: www.rbprinting.com
SIC: 2752 Commercial printing, offset

(P-6834)
RANROY COMPANY
8320 Camino Santa Fe # 200, San Diego
(92121-2659)
PHONE..............................858 571-8800
Randall S Roy, *President*
Mindy Staton, *Technology*
Jennifer San Nicolas, *Accounts Mgr*
EMP: 25
SQ FT: 20,000
SALES (est): 1.4MM **Privately Held**
WEB: www.ranroy.com
SIC: 2752 5112 Commercial printing, off-
set; envelopes

(P-6835)
RAPID PRINTERS INC
Also Called: Minuteman Press
201 Foam St, Monterey (93940-1400)
PHONE..............................831 373-1822
Cory Sloan, *President*
Jean Angley, *President*
Mike Djubasak, *President*
Allison Brye Baker, *Vice Pres*
Jean Djubasak, *Vice Pres*
EMP: 12 EST: 1981
SQ FT: 6,900
SALES (est): 3.2MM **Privately Held**
WEB: www.rapidprinters.com
SIC: 2752 2791 2789 Commercial print-
ing, offset; typesetting; bookbinding & re-
lated work

(P-6836)
RAYMONDS LITTLE PRINT SHOP INC
Also Called: Jim Little Raymonds Print Shop
41454 Christy St, Fremont (94538-5105)
PHONE..............................510 353-3608
Raymond Lei, *President*
EMP: 450
SQ FT: 100,000
SALES: 10MM
SALES (corp-wide): 192.5MM **Privately Held**
SIC: 2752 Commercial printing, litho-
graphic
PA: Ooshirts Inc.
41454 Christy St
Fremont CA 94538
866 660-8667

(P-6837)
RDS GROUP INC
Also Called: RDS Printing and Graphics Ctr
1714 E Grevillea Ct, Ontario (91761-8035)
PHONE..............................909 923-8831
Robert Saiz, *President*
Theresa Saiz, *Vice Pres*
EMP: 10
SQ FT: 10,000
SALES (est): 1.6MM **Privately Held**
WEB: www.rdsprinting.com
SIC: 2752 Commercial printing, offset

(P-6838)
READY INDUSTRIES INC
Also Called: Ready Reproductions
1520 E 15th St, Los Angeles (90021-2712)
PHONE..............................213 749-2041
E H Reitz, *CEO*
Chuck Nix, *Treasurer*
EMP: 16
SQ FT: 15,000
SALES (est): 2.2MM **Privately Held**
WEB: www.readyrepro.com
SIC: 2752 Photolithographic printing

(P-6839)
RED BRICK CORPORATION
Also Called: Design Printing
5364 Venice Blvd, Los Angeles
(90019-5240)
PHONE..............................323 549-9444
Parviz Bina, *CEO*
Bijan Bina, *Vice Pres*
Wendy Galope, *Accountant*
Jay Goodman, *Purch Agent*
Bob Hart, *Prdtn Mgr*
EMP: 18
SQ FT: 8,000
SALES (est): 3.8MM **Privately Held**
SIC: 2752 Commercial printing, offset

(P-6840)
REDDING PRINTING CO INC (PA)
1130 Continental St, Redding
(96001-0799)
PHONE..............................530 243-0525
Ken Peterson, *President*
Richard Peterson, *Corp Secy*
Mel Phelps, *Graphic Designe*
EMP: 30
SQ FT: 14,000
SALES (est): 2.6MM **Privately Held**
WEB: www.reddingprinting.com
SIC: 2752 Commercial printing, offset

PRODUCTS & SVCS

(P-6841)
REDSHARK GROUP INC
166 Saint Helena Ct, Danville
(94526-5523)
PHONE...................................925 837-3490
Gregory Sharkey, *President*
Kevin Kurbenknabe, *Vice Pres*
EMP: 11
SALES (est): 1.9MM **Privately Held**
WEB: www.redsharkgroup.com
SIC: 2752 Commercial printing, litho-
graphic

(P-6842)
**REGULUS INTGRTED
SOLUTIONS LLC**
860 Latour Ct, NAPA (94558-6258)
PHONE...................................707 254-4000
Vartan Berejikyan, *Manager*
EMP: 28
SALES (corp-wide): 1.5B **Publicly Held**
WEB: www.regulusgroup.com
SIC: 2752 7389 3861 2759 Commercial
printing, lithographic; microfilm recording
& developing service; photographic equip-
ment & supplies; commercial printing
HQ: Regulus Integrated Solutions Llc
9645-L Part Blvd
Charlotte NC 28216
704 904-8759

(P-6843)
REPRO MAGIC
8585 Miramar Pl, San Diego (92121-2529)
PHONE...................................858 277-2488
Ali Rashidi, *President*
Ricardo Mendoza, *Plant Mgr*
Kia Talai, *Marketing Staff*
Rick Webster, *Representative*
Joe Sigurdson, *Accounts Exec*
EMP: 12 **EST:** 1997
SQ FT: 6,000
SALES (est): 3.1MM **Privately Held**
WEB: www.repromagic.com
SIC: 2752 Commercial printing, offset

(P-6844)
RIVAS INDUSTRIES INC
Also Called: Omega Graphics
6687 Havenhurst St, Eastvale
(92880-3797)
PHONE...................................951 880-8638
Ricardo Rivas, *President*
Luz Rivas, *Vice Pres*
EMP: 16
SQ FT: 18,000
SALES (est): 1.5MM **Privately Held**
SIC: 2752 Color lithography

(P-6845)
**RIVER CITY PRINT AND MAIL
INC**
2431 Mercantile Dr Ste G, Rancho Cordova
(95742-6252)
PHONE...................................916 638-8400
Michael S Hagen, *President*
EMP: 10
SALES (est): 1.6MM **Privately Held**
SIC: 2752 Commercial printing, offset

(P-6846)
RIVER CITY PRINTERS LLC
4251 Gateway Park Blvd, Sacramento
(95834-1975)
PHONE...................................916 638-8400
Kasey Cotulla, *Mng Member*
Eric Fields, *Vice Pres*
Jim Davis,
EMP: 35
SALES (est): 8.6MM **Privately Held**
SIC: 2752 Commercial printing, offset

(P-6847)
RMS PRINTING LLC
5331 Derry Ave Ste N, Agoura Hills
(91301-3384)
PHONE...................................818 707-2625
EMP: 14
SALES (est): 2MM **Privately Held**
SIC: 2752 Commercial printing, offset

(P-6848)
RNJ PRINTING CORPORATION
16005 S Broadway, Gardena (90248-2417)
PHONE...................................310 638-7768
John Samuel Osten, *President*
Rose Cecola Osten, *CFO*
EMP: 16
SQ FT: 8,000
SALES (est): 2.6MM **Privately Held**
WEB: www.rnjprinting.com
SIC: 2752 2796 Commercial printing, off-
set; letterpress plates, preparation of

(P-6849)
**RR DONNELLEY & SONS
COMPANY**
3837 Producers Dr, Stockton (95206-4217)
PHONE...................................209 983-6700
EMP: 389
SALES (corp-wide): 6.8B **Publicly Held**
SIC: 2752 Commercial printing, lithographic
PA: R. R. Donnelley & Sons Company
35 W Wacker Dr
Chicago IL 60601
312 326-8000

(P-6850)
RUSH PRESS INC
Also Called: Arts & Crafts Press
955 Gateway Center Way, San Diego
(92102-4542)
PHONE...................................619 296-7874
Joe R Davis, *CEO*
Gene Valles, *President*
Jim Art, *Vice Pres*
Doug Stemet, *Technology*
Jim C Art, *Manager*
EMP: 48
SALES (est): 7MM
SALES (corp-wide): 6.8B **Publicly Held**
WEB: www.rushpress.com
SIC: 2752 Commercial printing, offset
HQ: Consolidated Graphics, Inc.
5858 Westheimer Rd # 200
Houston TX 77057
713 787-0977

(P-6851)
S & S PRINTERS
2100 W Lincoln Ave Ste A, Anaheim
(92801-5641)
PHONE...................................714 535-5592
Bann Ratankee, *President*
EMP: 32
SQ FT: 10,000
SALES (est): 1.2MM **Privately Held**
SIC: 2752 2759 Commercial printing, off-
set; letterpress printing

(P-6852)
**SACRAMENTO ENVELOPE CO
INC**
773 Northport Dr Ste C-A, West Sacra-
mento (95691-2176)
PHONE...................................916 371-4747
Dominic Tringali, *President*
Lisa Tringali, *Corp Secy*
Lisa Cofield, *Admin Sec*
EMP: 10
SQ FT: 8,000
SALES: 2.7MM **Privately Held**
WEB: www.sacenvelope.com
SIC: 2752 Commercial printing, offset

(P-6853)
**SAN FRANCISCO PRINT MEDIA
CO (PA)**
835 Market St Ste 550, San Francisco
(94103-1906)
PHONE...................................415 487-2594
David Black, *CEO*
Curran Jay, *Officer*
Katherine Mackinnon, *Executive*
Patrick Brown, *General Mgr*
Cristiane Storfner, *Human Res Mgr*
EMP: 23
SALES (est): 8.4MM **Privately Held**
SIC: 2752 Commercial printing, litho-
graphic

(P-6854)
SARI ART & PRINTING INC
3733 San Gabriel River Pk, Pico Rivera
(90660-1460)
PHONE...................................626 305-0888
Theresa MEI Ching Tan, *CEO*
▲ EMP: 10

SALES (est): 2.3MM **Privately Held**
SIC: 2752 Commercial printing, lithographic

(P-6855)
SCHOLASTIC SPORTS INC
4878 Ronson Ct Ste Kl, San Diego
(92111-1806)
PHONE...................................858 496-9221
Jill Spindle, *President*
Sam Spindlee, *Vice Pres*
Reggie Segal, *Manager*
EMP: 90
SQ FT: 5,500
SALES (est): 867.6K **Privately Held**
SIC: 2752 Commercial printing, litho-
graphic

(P-6856)
SEDAS PRINTING INC
5335 Santa Monica Blvd, Los Angeles
(90029-1105)
PHONE...................................323 469-1034
John Rashidi, *President*
Seda Rashidi, *Vice Pres*
EMP: 15
SQ FT: 8,000
SALES (est): 1.4MM **Privately Held**
WEB: www.sedasprinting.com
SIC: 2752 Commercial printing, offset

(P-6857)
SEEGERS INDUSTRIES INC
Also Called: Seeger's Printing
210 N Center St, Turlock (95380-4003)
PHONE...................................209 667-2750
Arthur W Seeger, *President*
Richard Berger, *Treasurer*
Toni Jevert,
Nancy Wallen, *Consultant*
EMP: 15
SQ FT: 7,100
SALES (est): 2.1MM **Privately Held**
WEB: www.seegersprinting.com
SIC: 2752 Photo-offset printing; commer-
cial printing, offset

(P-6858)
SELECT GRAPHICS
11931 Euclid St, Garden Grove
(92840-2200)
PHONE...................................714 537-5250
Yung Phan, *Principal*
Laura Reeves, *Graphic Designe*
Christina Pham, *Accountant*
Jennifer Pham, *Marketing Staff*
EMP: 12
SQ FT: 2,703
SALES: 1.5MM **Privately Held**
SIC: 2752 2759 Commercial printing, off-
set; commercial printing

(P-6859)
SERVICE PRESS INC
935 Tanklage Rd, San Carlos
(94070-3222)
PHONE...................................650 592-3484
Keith Thompson, *President*
▲ EMP: 10
SQ FT: 2,000
SALES (est): 1.7MM **Privately Held**
WEB: www.servicepressinc.com
SIC: 2752 Commercial printing, offset

(P-6860)
SHIFT CALENDARS INC
Also Called: Graphics United
809 N Glendora Ave, Covina (91724-2529)
PHONE...................................626 967-5862
Robert Breaux Jr, *President*
Brenda Moreno, *Office Mgr*
EMP: 15
SQ FT: 6,500
SALES (est): 2.9MM **Privately Held**
WEB: www.graphicsunited.com
SIC: 2752 Commercial printing, offset

(P-6861)
SHORETT PRINTING INC
Also Called: Crown Printers Anaheim
250 W Rialto Ave, San Bernardino
(92408-1017)
PHONE...................................714 956-9001
Charles D Shorett Jr, *Branch Mgr*
EMP: 10

SALES (est): 558.3K
SALES (corp-wide): 6.4MM **Privately
Held**
WEB: www.crownconnect.com
SIC: 2752 Commercial printing, offset
PA: Shorett Printing, Inc.
250 W Rialto Ave
San Bernardino CA 92408
714 545-4689

(P-6862)
**SIERRA OFFICE SYSTEMS PDTS
INC (PA)**
Also Called: Sierra Office Supply & Prtg
9950 Horn Rd Ste 5, Sacramento
(95827-1905)
PHONE...................................916 369-0491
Michael Kipp, *CEO*
Jason Gallivan, *COO*
Rick Holmes, *Executive*
Mary Theis, *Admin Sec*
Dan Paul, *Technology*
EMP: 100
SQ FT: 28,000
SALES (est): 31MM **Privately Held**
WEB: www.sierrabg.com
SIC: 2752 5712 5943 Commercial print-
ing, offset; office furniture; office forms &
supplies

(P-6863)
SORENSON PUBLISHING INC
Also Called: Prestige Printing
12925 Alcosta Blvd Ste 6, San Ramon
(94583-1341)
PHONE...................................925 866-1514
Fax: 925 866-0533
EMP: 10
SQ FT: 3,200
SALES (est): 990K **Privately Held**
WEB: www.prestigeprinting.com
SIC: 2752

(P-6864)
**SOURCE PRINT MEDIA
SOLUTIONS**
29108 Summer Oak Ct, Santa Clarita
(91390-4192)
PHONE...................................661 263-1880
Matthew L Pearson, *CEO*
Mary K Pearson, *Vice Pres*
EMP: 12
SALES (est): 1.9MM **Privately Held**
WEB: www.sourceprintmedia.com
SIC: 2752 Commercial printing, offset

(P-6865)
SOURCING GROUP LLC
1672 Delta Ct, Hayward (94544-7043)
PHONE...................................510 471-4749
EMP: 30
SALES (corp-wide): 60MM **Privately
Held**
SIC: 2752 2761
PA: Sourcing Group The Llc
77 Water St Ste 902
New York NY 10005
646 572-7520

(P-6866)
**SOUTHWEST OFFSET PRTG CO
INC (PA)**
13650 Gramercy Pl, Gardena
(90249-2453)
PHONE...................................310 965-9154
Greg McDonald, *CEO*
Matt Choate, *President*
Mark Franco, *President*
Art Spear, *CFO*
Bill Elliott, *Vice Pres*
▲ EMP: 300
SQ FT: 45,000
SALES (est): 115.9MM **Privately Held**
WEB: www.southwestoffset.com
SIC: 2752 Commercial printing, offset

(P-6867)
**SPECTRATEK TECHNOLOGIES
INC (PA)**
9834 Jordan Cir, Santa Fe Springs
(90670-3303)
PHONE...................................310 822-2400
Michael Foster, *CEO*
Terry Conway, *CFO*
Tamika Gordon, *Vice Pres*

Michael Wanlass, *Principal*
Pankaj Jangira, *Director*
▲ **EMP:** 58
SQ FT: 74,000
SALES (est): 23.1MM **Privately Held**
WEB: www.spectratek.net
SIC: 2752 Commercial printing, offset

(P-6868)
SPECTRUM GRAFIX INC
141 10th St, San Francisco (94103-2604)
P.O. Box 884961 (94188-4961)
PHONE..................................415 648-2400
Bill Forman, *President*
John Shea, *General Mgr*
Bart Forman, *Sales Staff*
EMP: 10
SQ FT: 2,500
SALES (est): 1.6MM **Privately Held**
WEB: www.spectrumgrafix.com
SIC: 2752 2789 5112 Offset & photolithographic printing; binding only: books, pamphlets, magazines, etc.; envelopes

(P-6869)
SPECTRUM LITHOGRAPH INC
4300 Business Center Dr, Fremont
(94538-6358)
PHONE..................................510 438-9192
Fernandino Pereira, *President*
Fernanda Pereira, *CFO*
EMP: 27
SQ FT: 46,000
SALES (est): 7MM **Privately Held**
WEB: www.spectrumlithograph.com
SIC: 2752 Commercial printing, offset

(P-6870)
SPRINT COPY CENTER INC
175 N Main St, Sebastopol (95472-3448)
PHONE..................................707 823-3900
Ron Hudelson, *President*
Stephen Liebling, *Manager*
EMP: 11
SALES (est): 500K **Privately Held**
SIC: 2752 7334 Commercial printing, offset; photocopying & duplicating services

(P-6871)
STOCKON MAILING & PRINTING
4133 Postal Ave, Stockton (95204-2318)
P.O. Box 8374 (95208-0374)
PHONE..................................209 466-6741
James S Huiras Jr, *President*
James Huiras Sr, *Shareholder*
Nancy Huiras, *Shareholder*
Kelly Hartemann, *Treasurer*
EMP: 18
SQ FT: 12,000
SALES (est): 1.5MM **Privately Held**
SIC: 2752 7331 Lithographing on metal; addressing service; mailing service

(P-6872)
STOUGHTON PRINTING CO
130 N Sunset Ave, City of Industry
(91744-3595)
PHONE..................................626 961-3678
Jack Stoughton Jr, *President*
Clay Stoughton, *Vice Pres*
EMP: 27
SQ FT: 21,000
SALES (est): 5.6MM **Privately Held**
WEB: www.stoughtonprinting.com
SIC: 2752 Commercial printing, offset

(P-6873)
STRAHMCOLOR
3000 Kerner Blvd, San Rafael
(94901-5413)
P.O. Box 9445 (94912-9445)
PHONE..................................415 459-5409
Jason Strahm, *President*
EMP: 12 **EST:** 1980
SQ FT: 10,000
SALES (est): 1.7MM **Privately Held**
WEB: www.strahmcom.com
SIC: 2752 Commercial printing, offset

(P-6874)
STREETER PRINTING
Also Called: Goodway Printing
13865 Sagewood Dr Ste C, Poway
(92064-1403)
PHONE..................................858 278-6611
Adrienne Streeter, *Partner*

EMP: 20
SQ FT: 5,000
SALES (est): 1.8MM **Privately Held**
SIC: 2752 7336 Lithographing on metal; commercial art & graphic design

(P-6875)
STREETER PRINTING INC
9880 Via Pasar Ste C, San Diego
(92126-4575)
PHONE..................................858 566-0866
Adrienne Streeter, *President*
Jack Streeter, *Vice Pres*
Ingrid Nehmitz, *Accounting Mgr*
EMP: 16 **EST:** 1980
SQ FT: 11,000
SALES (est): 3.5MM **Privately Held**
WEB: www.streeterprinting.com
SIC: 2752 Commercial printing, offset

(P-6876)
STUDIO TWO PRINTING INC
Also Called: Studio Two Graphics and Prtg
23042 Alcalde Dr Ste C, Laguna Hills
(92653-1326)
PHONE..................................949 859-5119
Thomas Lewis, *President*
Dori Lewis, *Corp Secy*
Jeff Benjamin, *Vice Pres*
EMP: 28
SALES (est): 3.9MM **Privately Held**
SIC: 2752 7336 Commercial printing, offset; commercial art & graphic design; graphic arts & related design

(P-6877)
SUMI PRINTING & BINDING INC
Also Called: Sumi Office Services
1139 E Janis St, Carson (90746-1306)
PHONE..................................310 769-1600
Roland Sumi, *President*
EMP: 14
SALES (est): 2.8MM **Privately Held**
WEB: www.sumiprinting.com
SIC: 2752 Commercial printing, lithographic

(P-6878)
SUPERIOR GRAPHIC PACKAGING INC
Also Called: Superior Lithographics
3055 Bandini Blvd, Vernon (90058-4109)
PHONE..................................323 263-8400
Douglas Rawson, *CEO*
Alex Rabino, *Admin Mgr*
Carla Drago, *Purchasing*
Brian Bones, *Production*
Lee Pennock, *Production*
▲ **EMP:** 90
SQ FT: 60,000
SALES (est): 22.7MM **Privately Held**
SIC: 2752 Commercial printing, offset

(P-6879)
SUPERPRINT LITHOGRAPHICS INC
8332 Secura Way, Santa Fe Springs
(90670-2204)
PHONE..................................562 698-8001
Chao-Tung Chen, *CEO*
Roy Chen, *President*
Michael Chen, *General Mgr*
Erika Delun, *Accountant*
Sal Dipasquale, *Sales Staff*
EMP: 15
SQ FT: 30,000
SALES (est): 3.8MM **Privately Held**
WEB: www.roychen.com
SIC: 2752 Commercial printing, offset

(P-6880)
SUPREME GRAPHICS INC
3403 Jack Northrop Ave, Hawthorne
(90250-4428)
PHONE..................................310 531-8300
Ramin Kohanteb, *President*
EMP: 18
SALES (est): 3.2MM **Privately Held**
WEB: www.supremegraphic.com
SIC: 2752 Commercial printing, offset

(P-6881)
SWANKY PRINTS LLC
42309 Winchester Rd Ste D, Temecula
(92590-4859)
PHONE..................................760 407-9265

Eugene Swank, *Branch Mgr*
EMP: 16
SALES (corp-wide): 1.2MM **Privately Held**
SIC: 2752 Commercial printing, lithographic
PA: Swanky Prints Llc
46382 Lone Pine Dr
Temecula CA 92592
760 452-5110

(P-6882)
T & V PRINTING INC
7101 Jurupa Ave Ste 3, Riverside
(92504-1029)
PHONE..................................951 353-8470
Vince A Castelluccio, *CEO*
EMP: 11
SQ FT: 5,000
SALES (est): 1.4MM **Privately Held**
SIC: 2752 Commercial printing, offset

(P-6883)
TAGS & LABELS
Also Called: Label Art of California
290 27th St, Oakland (94612-3821)
PHONE..................................510 465-1125
David Masri, *President*
Daniel Masri, *General Mgr*
EMP: 30 **EST:** 1965
SALES (est): 4.2MM **Privately Held**
SIC: 2752 Commercial printing, lithographic

(P-6884)
TAJEN GRAPHICS INC
Also Called: Apollo Printing & Graphics
2100 W Lincoln Ave Ste B, Anaheim
(92801-5642)
PHONE..................................714 527-3122
Dhansukhlal Ratanjee, *President*
Ken Ratanjee, *Vice Pres*
EMP: 30
SQ FT: 1,800
SALES (est): 5.7MM **Privately Held**
WEB: Www.apganaheim.com
SIC: 2752 2791 Commercial printing, offset; typesetting, computer controlled

(P-6885)
TAM PRINTING INC
2961 E White Star Ave, Anaheim
(92806-2630)
PHONE..................................714 224-4488
Tam Bui, *President*
CHI Trinh, *Manager*
EMP: 19
SQ FT: 10,000
SALES (est): 2.7MM **Privately Held**
WEB: www.tamprinting.com
SIC: 2752 Offset & photolithographic printing

(P-6886)
TECHNOLOGY TRAINING CORP
Also Called: Avalon Communications
3238 W 131st St, Hawthorne (90250-5517)
PHONE..................................310 644-7777
Richard D Lytle, *President*
EMP: 80
SALES (corp-wide): 8.8MM **Privately Held**
WEB: www.ttcus.com
SIC: 2752 7331 3577 Commercial printing, offset; direct mail advertising services; computer peripheral equipment
PA: Technology Training Corp
369 Van Ness Way Ste 735
Torrance CA 90501
310 320-8110

(P-6887)
TEEFOR 2 INC
5460 Vine St, Ontario (91710-5247)
PHONE..................................909 613-0055
Larry Lazalde, *CEO*
EMP: 16 **EST:** 2012
SALES (est): 2.7MM **Privately Held**
SIC: 2752 Commercial printing, lithographic

(P-6888)
TEK LABELS AND PRINTING INC
472 Vista Way, Milpitas (95035-5406)
PHONE..................................408 586-8107

Jim Dibona, *President*
David Hinds, *Vice Pres*
EMP: 25
SALES (est): 2.7MM **Privately Held**
WEB: www.teklabel.com
SIC: 2752 Commercial printing, lithographic

(P-6889)
THE LIGATURE INC (HQ)
Also Called: Echelon Fine Printing
4909 Alcoa Ave, Vernon (90058-3022)
PHONE..................................323 585-6000
Tom Clifford, *Vice Pres*
Dave Meyer, *Vice Pres*
Linda H Pennell, *Admin Sec*
Denyse Owens, *VP Finance*
Joseph Fontana, *Director*
EMP: 50 **EST:** 1920
SQ FT: 47,415
SALES (est): 12.6MM
SALES (corp-wide): 2.8B **Privately Held**
WEB: www.theligature.com
SIC: 2752 2759 Commercial printing, offset; invitation & stationery printing & engraving
PA: Taylor Corporation
1725 Roe Crest Dr
North Mankato MN 56003
507 625-2828

(P-6890)
TIME PRTG SOLUTIONS PROVIDER
1614 D St, Sacramento (95814-1014)
PHONE..................................916 446-6152
Andy Poole, *President*
Dena Poole, *CFO*
EMP: 10
SALES (est): 120K **Privately Held**
SIC: 2752 Commercial printing, offset

(P-6891)
TIMES LITHO INC
300 S Grand Ave Ste 1200, Los Angeles
(90071-3122)
PHONE..................................503 359-0300
William T Beckwith, *President*
Richard Bunker, *Vice Pres*
EMP: 49
SQ FT: 70,000
SALES (est): 2.7MM **Privately Held**
SIC: 2752 0752 Animal specialty services; color lithography

(P-6892)
TOMS PRINTING INC
1819 E St, Sacramento (95811-1018)
PHONE..................................916 444-7788
Daniel Tom, *President*
Mel Tom, *Treasurer*
Robert Tom, *Vice Pres*
Rebecca Tom, *Admin Sec*
EMP: 16
SQ FT: 9,600
SALES (est): 2.1MM **Privately Held**
WEB: www.toms-printing.com
SIC: 2752 Lithographing on metal; commercial printing, offset

(P-6893)
TOUCH LITHO COMPANY
7215 E Gage Ave, Commerce
(90040-3812)
PHONE..................................562 927-8899
Michael Wu, *President*
Jimmy Magpayo, *Manager*
▲ **EMP:** 15
SQ FT: 6,000
SALES (est): 2.9MM **Privately Held**
SIC: 2752 Commercial printing, offset

(P-6894)
TRACKSTAR PRINTING INC
1140 W Mahalo Pl, Compton (90220-5443)
PHONE..................................310 216-1275
Larry Migliazzo, *President*
Patricia A Migliazzo, *Admin Sec*
▲ **EMP:** 12
SQ FT: 2,600
SALES (est): 2MM **Privately Held**
WEB: www.trackstarla.com
SIC: 2752 Commercial printing, offset

P R O D U C T S & S V C S

(P-6895)
TRADE PRINTING SERVICES LLC
2080 Las Palmas Dr, Carlsbad (92011-1570)
PHONE...............................760 496-0230
Jim Simpson,
Jason Karches,
EMP: 24
SALES (est): 3MM **Privately Held**
WEB: www.tradeprintingsvc.com
SIC: 2752 Commercial printing, offset

(P-6896)
TRANSWORLD PRINTING SVCS INC
Also Called: T P S
152 Whitcomb Ave, Colfax (95713-9036)
PHONE...............................209 982-1511
Edwin McClenton, CEO
Daphyne Brown, President
Dennis Vera, Manager
EMP: 15
SALES (est): 2.1MM **Privately Held**
SIC: 2752 Commercial printing, offset

(P-6897)
TREND OFFSET PRINTING SVCS INC
3701 Catalina St, Los Alamitos (90720-2402)
PHONE...............................859 449-2900
EMP: 110
SALES (corp-wide): 337.5MM **Privately Held**
SIC: 2752 Commercial printing, offset
PA: Trend Offset Printing Services, Inc.
     3701 Catalina St
     Los Alamitos CA 90720
     562 598-2446

(P-6898)
TREND OFFSET PRINTING SVCS INC (PA)
3701 Catalina St, Los Alamitos (90720-2402)
P.O. Box 3008 (90720-1308)
PHONE...............................562 598-2446
Anthony Jacob Lienau, Ch of Bd
Todd Nelson, CEO
Munir Ahmed, COO
Thomas Balutis, CFO
Adam Lienau, CFO
▲ EMP: 650
SQ FT: 300,000
SALES (est): 337.5MM **Privately Held**
WEB: www.trendoffset.com
SIC: 2752 Commercial printing, offset

(P-6899)
TREND OFFSET PRINTING SVCS INC
3791 Catalina St, Los Alamitos (90720-2402)
PHONE...............................562 598-2446
Paul Rhilindger, Manager
Clark King, Sales Executive
Norman Webster, Cust Mgr
Mike Day, Director
EMP: 425
SALES (corp-wide): 337.5MM **Privately Held**
WEB: www.trendoffset.com
SIC: 2752 2732 Commercial printing, offset; books: printing & binding
PA: Trend Offset Printing Services, Inc.
     3701 Catalina St
     Los Alamitos CA 90720
     562 598-2446

(P-6900)
TRI PRINT LLC
Also Called: Hangtags.com
7573 Slater Ave Ste C, Huntington Beach (92647-7754)
PHONE...............................714 847-1400
Ronald P Herrema,
Pamela Herrema, Vice Pres
▲ EMP: 16
SALES (est): 2.9MM **Privately Held**
WEB: www.triprint.com
SIC: 2752 Commercial printing, offset

(P-6901)
TRIBAL PRINT SOURCE
36146 Pala Temecula Rd, Pala (92059)
PHONE...............................760 597-2650
Drew Hendricks, Director
Jonathan Connelly, Prdtn Mgr
EMP: 12 EST: 2011
SALES (est): 1.1MM **Privately Held**
SIC: 2752 Commercial printing, lithographic

(P-6902)
TRINITY MARKETING LLC
Also Called: Prestige Printing & Graphics
12925 Alcosta Blvd Ste 6, San Ramon (94583-1341)
PHONE...............................925 866-1514
Rose Maloney, Mng Member
Chris Maloney,
EMP: 10
SALES (est): 1.5MM **Privately Held**
SIC: 2752 Commercial printing, offset

(P-6903)
TULIP PUBG & GRAPHICS INC
Also Called: Greener Printer
1003 Canal Blvd, Richmond (94804-3549)
PHONE...............................510 898-0000
Mario Assadi, Principal
Andrea Larson, Accounting Mgr
EMP: 28
SQ FT: 40,000
SALES (est): 6.1MM **Privately Held**
WEB: www.tulipnet.com
SIC: 2752 Commercial printing, offset

(P-6904)
TYPECRAFT INC
Also Called: Typecraft Wood & Jones
2040 E Walnut St, Pasadena (91107-5804)
PHONE...............................626 795-8093
D Harry Montgomery, President
Jeffrey J Gish, Vice Pres
Jeffrey Gish, Vice Pres
Mark Burks, Plant Mgr
Tim Silverlake, Manager
EMP: 38
SQ FT: 19,000
SALES (est): 6.6MM **Privately Held**
WEB: www.typecraft.com
SIC: 2752 Commercial printing, offset; circulars, lithographed; posters, lithographed

(P-6905)
TYT LLC (HQ)
Also Called: PS Print, LLC
2861 Mandela Pkwy, Oakland (94608-4011)
PHONE...............................510 444-3933
Andy Comly, Mng Member
Gilbert Estrada, Plant Mgr
Sonia Mansfield, Marketing Staff
Chris Strabley, Maintence Staff
Frank Young, Mng Member
▼ EMP: 110
SQ FT: 55,000
SALES (est): 8MM
SALES (corp-wide): 2B **Publicly Held**
WEB: www.psprint.com
SIC: 2752 Commercial printing, offset
PA: Deluxe Corporation
     3680 Victoria St N
     Shoreview MN 55126
     651 483-7111

(P-6906)
ULTIMATE PRINT SOURCE INC
Also Called: Printing 4him
2070 S Hellman Ave, Ontario (91761-8018)
PHONE...............................909 947-5292
Jeffrey J Ferrazzano, CEO
Edith Le Leux, Treasurer
Desiree Ferrazzano, Vice Pres
Jon Le Leux, Admin Sec
EMP: 30
SQ FT: 20,000
SALES (est): 5.5MM **Privately Held**
WEB: www.ultimateprintsource.com
SIC: 2752 Commercial printing, offset

(P-6907)
UNI SPORT INC
16933 Gramercy Pl, Gardena (90247-5207)
PHONE...............................310 217-4587
Thomas Hebert, President

Kris Beasley, General Mgr
Carlos Ortiz, General Mgr
EMP: 25
SQ FT: 10,000
SALES (est): 3.2MM **Privately Held**
SIC: 2752 Commercial printing, lithographic

(P-6908)
UNIQUE IMAGE INC
19365 Bus Center Dr Ste 4, Northridge (91324-3581)
PHONE...............................818 727-7785
Wafa Kanan, President
Mika Kyprianides, Creative Dir
Michael Lloyd, Mktg Dir
EMP: 17 EST: 1993
SQ FT: 15,400
SALES (est): 3.1MM **Privately Held**
SIC: 2752 2741 7311 7331 Commercial printing, lithographic; miscellaneous publishing; advertising agencies; direct mail advertising services; commercial art & graphic design; public relations services

(P-6909)
UNITED CRAFTSMEN PRINITING
Also Called: Craftsman Printing
6660 Via Del Oro, San Jose (95119-1392)
PHONE...............................408 224-6464
Joan Falkenstein, President
EMP: 27
SQ FT: 17,900
SALES (est): 6MM **Privately Held**
SIC: 2752 Commercial printing, offset

(P-6910)
UNIVERSAL PRINTING SERVICES
Also Called: Color Tech Commercial Printing
26012 Atlantic Ocean Dr, Lake Forest (92630-8843)
PHONE...............................951 788-1500
Gregg Baxter, President
Sharon Baxter, Vice Pres
EMP: 14
SQ FT: 2,800
SALES (est): 3.8MM **Privately Held**
WEB: www.colortechprinting.com
SIC: 2752 Commercial printing, lithographic

(P-6911)
UPPER DECK COMPANY LLC
5830 El Camino Real, Carlsbad (92008-8816)
PHONE...............................800 873-7332
Richard Mc William, CEO
Jason Masherah, President
Roz Nowicki, Exec VP
Tom Farrell, Vice Pres
Richard Bonora, Business Dir
▲ EMP: 400
SQ FT: 247,000
SALES (est): 113.7MM **Privately Held**
SIC: 2752 5947 Souvenir cards, lithographed; gift, novelty & souvenir shop

(P-6912)
USA PRINTER COMPANY LLC
Also Called: USA Printer Guy
41571 Corning Pl Ste 115, Murrieta (92562-7066)
PHONE...............................800 279-7768
Gordon Wood, President
▲ EMP: 10 EST: 2010
SALES (est): 1.3MM **Privately Held**
SIC: 2752 Commercial printing, offset

(P-6913)
UTAP PRINTING CO INC
1423 San Mateo Ave, South San Francisco (94080-6504)
PHONE...............................650 588-2818
Patrick Y Chin, President
EMP: 13
SQ FT: 5,200
SALES (est): 2MM **Privately Held**
WEB: www.utap.com
SIC: 2752 Commercial printing, offset

(P-6914)
V3 PRINTING CORPORATION
Also Called: V 3
200 N Elevar St, Oxnard (93030-7969)
PHONE...............................805 981-2600

David Wilson, President
Michael Szanger, Vice Pres
Harkie Ford, Executive
Tom Hinkle, Executive
Richard Mantor, Executive
EMP: 80
SQ FT: 4,000
SALES (est): 21.1MM **Privately Held**
WEB: www.venturaprint.com
SIC: 2752 Lithographing on metal; commercial printing, offset

(P-6915)
VALLEY BUSINESS PRINTERS INC
Also Called: Valley Printers
16230 Filbert St, Sylmar (91342-1039)
PHONE...............................818 362-7771
Michael Flannery, CEO
Bruce Bolkin, President
Karen S Flannery, Corp Secy
▲ EMP: 92
SQ FT: 110,000
SALES (est): 16.4MM **Privately Held**
SIC: 2752 2759 Commercial printing, offset; commercial printing

(P-6916)
VANARD LITHOGRAPHERS INC
3220 Kurtz St, San Diego (92110-4426)
PHONE...............................619 291-5571
Annette Fritzenkotter, President
EMP: 28
SQ FT: 25,000
SALES (est): 3.5MM **Privately Held**
WEB: www.vanard.com
SIC: 2752 Commercial printing, offset

(P-6917)
VANS INSTANT PRINTERS INC
221 E San Bernardino Rd, Covina (91723-1624)
PHONE...............................626 966-1708
William J Hammnett, Owner
EMP: 11
SALES (est): 605.7K **Privately Held**
SIC: 2752 Commercial printing, offset

(P-6918)
VARIABLE IMAGE PRINTING
16540 Aston Ste A, Irvine (92606-4805)
PHONE...............................949 296-1444
Paul O Brien, President
Bob Stewart, Vice Pres
EMP: 18 EST: 2000
SQ FT: 12,400
SALES (est): 2.4MM **Privately Held**
WEB: www.variableimageprinting.com
SIC: 2752 Commercial printing, offset

(P-6919)
VARIABLE IMAGE PRINTING
9020 Kenamar Dr Ste 204, San Diego (92121-2431)
PHONE...............................858 530-2443
Paul O'Brien, President
Paul Obrien, President
Bob Stewart, Vice Pres
EMP: 30
SALES (est): 2.2MM **Privately Held**
SIC: 2752 Commercial printing, offset

(P-6920)
VDP DIRECT LLC (PA)
5520 Ruffin Rd Ste 111, San Diego (92123-1320)
P.O. Box 910027 (92191-0027)
PHONE...............................858 300-4510
Jimmy Lakdawala,
Steven England, Info Tech Dir
Janice Lakdawala,
EMP: 25
SQ FT: 12,500
SALES (est): 6MM **Privately Held**
SIC: 2752 Commercial printing, offset

(P-6921)
VELO3D INC
511 Division St, Campbell (95008-6905)
PHONE...............................408 666-5309
Benny Buller, CEO
EMP: 120
SQ FT: 17,000
SALES (est): 351.7K **Privately Held**
SIC: 2752 Commercial printing, lithographic

▲ = Import ▼=Export
◆ =Import/Export

(P-6922)
VERTICAL PRINTING & GRAPHICS
2240 Encinitas Blvd Ste F, Encinitas (92024-4345)
PHONE..................................760 334-2004
Laura Beulke, *President*
EMP: 12
SQ FT: 1,000
SALES (est): 1.9MM **Privately Held**
WEB: www.verticalprinting.com
SIC: 2752 Commercial printing, offset

(P-6923)
VILLAGE INSTANT PRINTING INC
Also Called: Park's Prtg & Lithographic Co
1515 10th St, Modesto (95354-0726)
PHONE..................................209 576-2568
Austin E Parks, *President*
Michelle Neilsen, *Corp Secy*
Frank Parks, *Vice Pres*
Patricia Parks Minnix, *Director*
EMP: 40 EST: 1974
SQ FT: 10,000
SALES (est): 8.3MM **Privately Held**
SIC: 2752 Commercial printing, offset

(P-6924)
VOMELA SPECIALTY COMPANY
9810 Bell Ranch Dr, Santa Fe Springs (90670-2952)
PHONE..................................562 944-3853
Loren Maxwell, *Branch Mgr*
EMP: 23
SALES (corp-wide): 128.5MM **Privately Held**
SIC: 2752 7336 Poster & decal printing, lithographic; commercial art & graphic design
PA: Vomela Specialty Company
845 Minnehaha Ave E
Saint Paul MN 55106
651 228-2200

(P-6925)
WALKER LITHOGRAPH
Also Called: Walker Printing
20869 Walnut St, Red Bluff (96080-9704)
PHONE..................................530 527-2142
Neal Gagliano, *Partner*
Chris Gagliano, *Partner*
Cris Gagliano, *Chairman*
EMP: 14 EST: 1996
SQ FT: 5,000
SALES (est): 2.1MM **Privately Held**
WEB: www.walkerlitho.com
SIC: 2752 Commercial printing, offset

(P-6926)
WANDA MATRANGA
Also Called: Printing Place, The
41651 Corporate Way Ste 5, Palm Desert (92260-1987)
P.O. Box 12827 (92255-2827)
PHONE..................................760 773-4701
Wanda Matranga, *Owner*
Larry Espinola, *Project Mgr*
Karen Schroeder, *Accounts Exec*
EMP: 12
SQ FT: 7,000
SALES (est): 1.4MM **Privately Held**
WEB: www.theprintingplace.net
SIC: 2752 Commercial printing, offset

(P-6927)
WARREN PRINTING & MAILING INC
5000 Eagle Rock Blvd, Los Angeles (90041-1908)
PHONE..................................323 258-2621
Robert H Warren, *President*
Victoria Warren, *Vice Pres*
EMP: 10
SQ FT: 5,661
SALES (est): 1.4MM **Privately Held**
WEB: www.print-mail.com
SIC: 2752 7331 2759 Commercial printing, offset; direct mail advertising services; commercial printing

(P-6928)
WE DO GRAPHICS INC
1150 N Main St, Orange (92867-3421)
PHONE..................................714 997-7390
Douglas K Le Mieux, *President*
Heidi G Le Mieux, *Vice Pres*
Steven I Lehrer, *Vice Pres*
Laura Lehrer, *Manager*
▲ EMP: 25
SQ FT: 23,000
SALES (est): 4.3MM **Privately Held**
WEB: www.wedographics.com
SIC: 2752 Commercial printing, offset

(P-6929)
WEBER PRINTING COMPANY INC
1124 E Del Amo Blvd, Carson (90746-3180)
PHONE..................................310 639-5064
Richard M Weber, *President*
Lynda Slack, *CFO*
Steven Weber, *Vice Pres*
Ron Lamantia, *Technology*
EMP: 35
SQ FT: 30,000
SALES (est): 6.4MM **Privately Held**
SIC: 2752 Photo-offset printing

(P-6930)
WELLPRINT INC
380 E 1st St Ste B, Tustin (92780-3211)
PHONE..................................714 838-3962
Rick Mandell, *President*
EMP: 10 EST: 1971
SQ FT: 3,300
SALES (est): 780K **Privately Held**
WEB: www.wellprint.com
SIC: 2752 7334 Commercial printing, offset; photocopying & duplicating services

(P-6931)
WEST COAST BUSINESS PRTRS INC
Also Called: West Coast Digital
9822 Independence Ave, Chatsworth (91311-4319)
PHONE..................................818 709-4980
Arthur Worthington, *President*
Patricia Worthington, *Admin Sec*
EMP: 13
SQ FT: 10,000
SALES (est): 1.9MM **Privately Held**
WEB: www.wcdigital.com
SIC: 2752 5112 2759 Commercial printing, offset; envelopes; commercial printing

(P-6932)
WESTCOTT PRESS INC
1121 W Isabel St, Burbank (91506-1405)
PHONE..................................626 794-7716
Jeffrey W Carpenter, *President*
Mila Carpenter, *Corp Secy*
Neil W Carpenter, *Vice Pres*
Darnell Diaz, *Office Mgr*
Dave Matthews, *Prdtn Mgr*
EMP: 12
SQ FT: 10,000
SALES (est): 1.8MM **Privately Held**
WEB: www.westcottpress.com
SIC: 2752 Commercial printing, offset

(P-6933)
WESTERN METAL DCTG CO COIL DIV
Also Called: Cucamonga Division
8875 Industrial Ln, Rancho Cucamonga (91730-4529)
PHONE..................................909 987-2506
EMP: 11
SQ FT: 95,000
SALES: 1MM **Privately Held**
WEB: www.western-metal.com
SIC: 2752 Lithographing on metal

(P-6934)
WESTERN PRTG & GRAPHICS LLC (PA)
Also Called: Western Printing and Label
17931 Sky Park Cir, Irvine (92614-6312)
PHONE..................................714 532-3946
Aaron David Smith,
Cynthia Joan Smith,
EMP: 23 EST: 1981
SQ FT: 11,000

(P-6935)
WESTERN TRADE PRINTING INC
5695 E Shields Ave, Fresno (93727-7819)
PHONE..................................559 251-8595
Claude Teisinger, *President*
Christine Langney, *Corp Secy*
Erlinda Teisinger, *Vice Pres*
▲ EMP: 14
SQ FT: 19,000
SALES (est): 2.6MM **Privately Held**
WEB: www.westerntradeprinting.com
SIC: 2752 Commercial printing, lithographic

(P-6936)
WESTERN WEB INC
1900 Bendixsen St Ste 2, Samoa (95564-9525)
P.O. Box 278 (95564-0278)
PHONE..................................707 444-6236
Stephen Jackson, *President*
Michael Morris, *Vice Pres*
Ryan Barsanti, *Accounts Mgr*
EMP: 21 EST: 2010
SQ FT: 25,400
SALES: 3MM **Privately Held**
SIC: 2752 Commercial printing, offset

(P-6937)
WESTMINSTER PRESS INC
4906 W 1st St, Santa Ana (92703-3110)
PHONE..................................714 210-2881
Gary Tang, *CEO*
Thoai Tang, *Vice Pres*
Tri Tang, *Vice Pres*
EMP: 50
SQ FT: 10,000
SALES (est): 8MM **Privately Held**
SIC: 2752 Color lithography

(P-6938)
WESTROCK CP LLC
MPS Corona
2577 Research Dr, Corona (92882-7607)
PHONE..................................951 273-7900
Steven Voorhees, *CEO*
EMP: 64
SALES (corp-wide): 16.2B **Publicly Held**
SIC: 2752 Commercial printing, offset
HQ: Westrock Cp, Llc
1000 Abernathy Rd
Atlanta GA 30328
-

(P-6939)
WILLEY PRINTING COMPANY INC (PA)
1405 10th St, Modesto (95354-0724)
P.O. Box 886 (95353-0886)
PHONE..................................209 524-4811
Jerry Sauls, *President*
Mary Alice Willey, *Vice Pres*
Barbara Haynes, *Bookkeeper*
EMP: 30 EST: 1946
SQ FT: 20,000
SALES (est): 2.5MM **Privately Held**
SIC: 2752 Commercial printing, offset

(P-6940)
WILLIAM J HAMMETT INC
Also Called: Grand Printing
221 E San Bernardino Rd, Covina (91723-1624)
PHONE..................................626 966-1708
William Hammett, *President*
EMP: 10
SQ FT: 4,500
SALES: 600K **Privately Held**
WEB: www.grandprinting.com
SIC: 2752 Commercial printing, offset; lithographing on metal

(P-6941)
WIRZ & CO
444 Colton Ave, Colton (92324-3019)
PHONE..................................909 825-6970
Charles Fred Wirz, *Owner*
Kelly Gettings, *Marketing Staff*
EMP: 18

SQ FT: 8,000
SALES (est): 1.8MM **Privately Held**
SIC: 2752 Commercial printing, offset

(P-6942)
WISSINGS INC
Also Called: Printing Shoppe, The
9906 Mesa Rim Rd, San Diego (92121-2910)
PHONE..................................858 625-4111
Jerry Wissing, *President*
Nancy Wissing, *Corp Secy*
EMP: 14 EST: 1981
SQ FT: 8,600
SALES (est): 2.4MM **Privately Held**
WEB: www.printingshoppe.com
SIC: 2752 Commercial printing, offset

(P-6943)
WS PACKAGING-BLAKE PRINTERY (DH)
2222 Beebee St, San Luis Obispo (93401-5505)
PHONE..................................805 543-6843
Michael P Glavin, *CEO*
Jay K Tomcheck, *VP Finance*
EMP: 19
SQ FT: 40,000
SALES (est): 6.9MM **Privately Held**
SIC: 2752 Commercial printing, offset
HQ: Labl Holding Corporation
4053 Clough Woods Dr
Batavia OH 45103
920 866-6300

(P-6944)
WS PACKAGING-BLAKE PRINTERY
Also Called: Poor Richards Press
2224 Beebee St, San Luis Obispo (93401-5505)
PHONE..................................805 543-6844
Bruce Dickinson, *Branch Mgr*
EMP: 30
SQ FT: 3,500 **Privately Held**
SIC: 2752 2621 2791 Commercial printing, offset; wrapping paper; typesetting, computer controlled
HQ: Ws Packaging-Blake Printery
2222 Beebee St
San Luis Obispo CA 93401
805 543-6843

(P-6945)
WTPC INC
Also Called: World Trade Printing Company
12082 Western Ave, Garden Grove (92841-2913)
PHONE..................................714 903-2500
Joe Ratanjee, *CEO*
▲ EMP: 30
SQ FT: 25,000
SALES (est): 8MM **Privately Held**
WEB: www.wtpcenter.com
SIC: 2752 Commercial printing, lithographic

(P-6946)
X-IGENT PRINTING INC
1001 Goodrich Blvd, Commerce (90022-5102)
PHONE..................................323 837-9779
Omar Rodriguez, *President*
Norma Cerzanges, *Office Mgr*
EMP: 15
SQ FT: 6,000
SALES (est): 2.3MM **Privately Held**
WEB: www.xigentsolutions.com
SIC: 2752 Commercial printing, offset

(P-6947)
ZADA GRAPHICS INC
Also Called: Micro-DOT
11180 Lewis Hill Dr, Santa Clarita (91390-2890)
PHONE..................................323 321-8940
Helen Zada, *President*
Sam H Zada, *Corp Secy*
Allan Zada, *Vice Pres*
John Cameron, *General Mgr*
EMP: 12
SALES: 1.2MM **Privately Held**
WEB: www.zadagraphics.com
SIC: 2752 2759 Commercial printing, offset; letterpress printing

(P-6948)
ZAP PRINTING INCORPORATED
Also Called: Zap Printing and Graphics
127 Radio Rd, Corona (92879-1724)
P.O. Box 1208 (92878-1208)
PHONE..................................951 734-8181
Paula A Montanez, *CEO*
Eugene Montanez, *President*
John Janik, *Graphic Designe*
EMP: 11
SQ FT: 7,000
SALES (est): 2MM **Privately Held**
SIC: 2752 3993 2759 Commercial printing, offset; signs & advertising specialties; commercial printing

(P-6949)
ZIP PRINT INC (PA)
Also Called: Valprint
1257 G St, Fresno (93706-1610)
P.O. Box 12332 (93777-2332)
PHONE..................................559 486-3112
Jack Emerian, *President*
Darryl Hanoian, *Vice Pres*
Angie Orosco, *Manager*
EMP: 50
SQ FT: 7,500
SALES (est): 8.5MM **Privately Held**
SIC: 2752 7334 7331 2791 Commercial printing, offset; photocopying & duplicating services; direct mail advertising services; typesetting; bookbinding & related work; commercial printing

(P-6950)
ZOO PRINTING INC (PA)
Also Called: Zoo Printing Trade Printer
25152 Springfield Ct # 280, Valencia (91355-1078)
PHONE..................................310 253-7751
Dan Doron, *President*
Maria Camins, *Vice Pres*
Sako Sahaghian, *Info Tech Mgr*
Shawn Mahoney, *Prgrmr*
Jeff Bentz, *Plant Mgr*
▲ EMP: 88
SALES (est): 18.9MM **Privately Held**
SIC: 2752 Commercial printing, offset

2754 Commercial Printing: Gravure

(P-6951)
ALNA ENVELOPE COMPANY INC
1567 E 25th St, Los Angeles (90011-1887)
PHONE..................................323 235-3161
Al Azus, *President*
Hedi Azus, *Treasurer*
Max Candiotty, *Vice Pres*
Jose Caldera, *Prdtn Mgr*
EMP: 35 EST: 1955
SQ FT: 14,000
SALES (est): 3.7MM **Privately Held**
WEB: www.alnaenvelope.com
SIC: 2754 2759 Envelopes: gravure printing; commercial printing

(P-6952)
COSMOJET INC
9601 Cozycroft Ave Ste 2, Chatsworth (91311-5183)
PHONE..................................818 773-6544
Serge Kapustin, *President*
Olga Kapustin, *CFO*
▲ EMP: 10 EST: 1999
SQ FT: 10,000
SALES (est): 442.8K **Privately Held**
SIC: 2754 8742 Labels: gravure printing; marketing consulting services

(P-6953)
FERNQVIST RETAIL SYSTEMS INC (HQ)
Also Called: Fernqvist Labeling Solutions
2544 Leghorn St, Mountain View (94043-1614)
PHONE..................................650 428-0330
Tom Vargas, *CEO*
Jim Clark, *President*
Teresa Caputo, *Officer*
EMP: 16
SQ FT: 6,100
SALES: 3.8MM **Privately Held**
WEB: www.fernqvist.com
SIC: 2754 5734 Labels: gravure printing; printers & plotters: computers
PA: Epic Labeling Solutions, Inc.
2544 Leghorn St
Mountain View CA 94043
650 428-0330

(P-6954)
FILET MENU INC
1830 S La Cienega Blvd, Los Angeles (90035-4652)
PHONE..................................310 202-8000
Michael R Levine, *President*
EMP: 22
SQ FT: 28,000
SALES (est): 179.4K **Privately Held**
SIC: 2754 2759 Commercial printing, gravure; commercial printing

(P-6955)
FONGS GRAPHICS & PRINTING INC
7743 Garvey Ave, Rosemead (91770-3068)
PHONE..................................626 307-1898
Chak M Fong, *President*
Annie Ng, *Art Dir*
Daphne Fong, *Manager*
▲ EMP: 20
SQ FT: 1,300
SALES (est): 1.9MM **Privately Held**
WEB: www.fongsmenu.com
SIC: 2754 7336 Menus: gravure printing; commercial art & graphic design

(P-6956)
INSTITUTE OF ELECTRICAL AND EL
Also Called: Ieee Computer Society
10662 Los Vaqueros Cir, Los Alamitos (90720-2513)
P.O. Box 3014 (90720)
PHONE..................................714 821-8380
Linda Ashworth, *Administration*
Ronald Hoelzeman, *Vice Pres*
Anabell St Vincent, *Database Admin*
David Grier, *Chief*
Carlos Jimenez,
EMP: 85
SALES (corp-wide): 494.3MM **Privately Held**
SIC: 2754 Publication printing, gravure
PA: The Institute Of Electrical And Electronics Engineers Incorporated
445 Hoes Ln
Piscataway NJ 08854
212 419-7900

(P-6957)
KMR LABEL LLC
Also Called: Axiom Label Group
1360 W Walnut Pkwy, Compton (90220-5029)
PHONE..................................310 603-8910
Kieron Delahunt, *General Mgr*
Jennifer Curby, *Executive*
Tony Dennis, *Controller*
Connie Hui, *Controller*
McHugh Keith, *Controller*
EMP: 50 EST: 1972
SQ FT: 24,000
SALES (est): 8.6MM **Privately Held**
WEB: www.axiomlabel.com
SIC: 2754 2752 Labels: gravure printing; commercial printing, lithographic

(P-6958)
MC ALLISTER INDUSTRIES INC (PA)
731 S Highway 101 Ste 2, Solana Beach (92075-2629)
PHONE..................................858 755-0683
Robert Mc Allister, *President*
▲ EMP: 20
SQ FT: 2,500
SALES (est): 1.9MM **Privately Held**
WEB: www.mcallisterindustries.com
SIC: 2754 Cards, except greeting: gravure printing

(P-6959)
MILLENNIUM GRAPHICS INC
3443 Park Pl, Pleasanton (94588-2936)
PHONE..................................925 602-0635
Frank Baltazar, *President*
Christine Baltazar, *Vice Pres*
EMP: 11
SALES: 400K **Privately Held**
SIC: 2754 Commercial printing, gravure

(P-6960)
MONTEREY BAY OFFICE PDTS INC
1700 Wyatt Dr, Santa Clara (95054-1526)
PHONE..................................408 727-4627
Kellie S Murphy, *Branch Mgr*
Armando Gonzalez, *Exec VP*
EMP: 12
SALES (corp-wide): 10.8MM **Privately Held**
SIC: 2754 Business form & card printing, gravure
PA: Monterey Bay Office Products Inc.
325 Victor St Ste A
Salinas CA 93907
831 646-8080

(P-6961)
ONEIL CAPITAL MANAGEMENT
Also Called: O'Neil Data Systems, Inc.
12655 Beatrice St, Los Angeles (90066-7300)
PHONE..................................310 448-6400
William O Neil, *CEO*
Linda Clapper, *Vice Pres*
Bill Hickey, *VP Bus Dvlpt*
Joanna Cannon, *Office Mgr*
Gregg White, *Info Tech Dir*
▲ EMP: 92
SQ FT: 70,000
SALES (est): 28.3MM
SALES (corp-wide): 231.5MM **Privately Held**
WEB: www.oneildata.com
SIC: 2754 2732 2741 2711 Catalogs: gravure printing, not published on site; book printing; miscellaneous publishing; newspapers
PA: Data Analysis Inc.
12655 Beatrice St
Los Angeles CA 90066
310 448-6800

(P-6962)
QPE INC
Also Called: Quality Packaging and Engrg
1372 Mcgaw Ave, Irvine (92614-5539)
PHONE..................................949 263-0381
Kirk WEI, *President*
Joseph S Chiang, *Corp Secy*
Ted Wan, *Manager*
◆ EMP: 18
SQ FT: 10,000
SALES: 6MM **Privately Held**
SIC: 2754 7389 Labels: gravure printing; packaging & labeling services

(P-6963)
R R DONNELLEY & SONS COMPANY
Also Called: Donnelley Financial
1 Embarcadero Ctr Ste 200, San Francisco (94111-3644)
PHONE..................................415 362-2300
Joyce Battisite, *Manager*
Dawnet Beverley, *Manager*
EMP: 40
SALES (corp-wide): 6.8B **Publicly Held**
WEB: www.rrdonnelley.com
SIC: 2754 2752 Directories: gravure printing, not published on site; commercial printing, lithographic
PA: R. R. Donnelley & Sons Company
35 W Wacker Dr
Chicago IL 60601
312 326-8000

(P-6964)
SOLUTION BOX INC
Also Called: Ideal Print Solutions
1923 Avenida Plaza Real, Oceanside (92056-6024)
PHONE..................................949 387-3223
Larry Corrado, *President*
Amber Ramsey, *Office Mgr*
EMP: 11
SQ FT: 6,000
SALES (est): 3.5MM **Privately Held**
SIC: 2754 Labels: gravure printing

(P-6965)
TAYLOR COMMUNICATIONS INC
330 E Lambert Rd Ste 100, Brea (92821-4100)
PHONE..................................866 541-0937
EMP: 14
SALES (corp-wide): 2.8B **Privately Held**
SIC: 2754 Commercial printing, gravure
HQ: Taylor Communications, Inc.
1725 Roe Crest Dr
North Mankato MN 56003
507 625-2828

(P-6966)
WESTERN SHELD ACQUISITIONS LLC
Also Called: Western Shield Label
2146 E Gladwick St, Rancho Dominguez (90220-6203)
PHONE..................................310 527-6212
Graham C Weaver, *Mng Member*
Thomas Moyer, *President*
Frank Connelly, *CEO*
Rod Couser, *Vice Pres*
Lee Baba, *Manager*
EMP: 28
SQ FT: 17,000
SALES (est): 5MM **Privately Held**
WEB: www.westernshield.com
SIC: 2754 3172 2752 Labels: gravure printing; tobacco pouches; coupons, lithographed

2759 Commercial Printing

(P-6967)
4 OVER LLC (HQ)
5900 San Fernando Rd D, Glendale (91202-2773)
PHONE..................................818 246-1170
Zarik Megerdichian, *CEO*
Tina Hartounian, *President*
Ian Barrett, *Vice Pres*
Amber Solorzano, *Admin Asst*
Ryan West, *Web Dvlpr*
▲ EMP: 277 EST: 2001
SALES (est): 190.6MM **Privately Held**
WEB: www.4over.com
SIC: 2759 7336 Commercial printing; commercial art & graphic design

(P-6968)
4 OVER LLC
1225 Los Angeles St, Glendale (91204-2403)
PHONE..................................818 246-1170
Erika Takenaka, *Principal*
Dean Rossi, *Controller*
EMP: 15
SALES (corp-wide): 190.6MM **Privately Held**
SIC: 2759 Screen printing
HQ: 4 Over, Llc
5900 San Fernando Rd D
Glendale CA 91202
818 246-1170

(P-6969)
6480 CORPORATION
Also Called: First Press
7230 Coldwater Canyon Ave, North Hollywood (91605-4203)
PHONE..................................818 765-9670
Daniel Mamane, *President*
Richard Eliazar, *General Mgr*
EMP: 23
SQ FT: 25,000
SALES (est): 17.4K **Privately Held**
SIC: 2759 3695 Bag, wrapper & seal printing & engraving; magnetic & optical recording media

(P-6970)
A F E INDUSTRIES INC (PA)
13233 Barton Cir, Whittier (90605-3255)
P.O. Box 3303, Santa Fe Springs (90670-1303)
PHONE..................................562 944-6889
Fred Elhami, *President*

Ruth Elhami, *Corp Secy*
Tiffany Elhami, *Chief Mktg Ofcr*
EMP: 94
SQ FT: 27,000
SALES (est): 13MM **Privately Held**
SIC: 2759 Screen printing; imprinting; letterpress printing

(P-6971)
ABC IMAGING OF WASHINGTON
17240 Red Hill Ave, Irvine (92614-5628)
PHONE....................949 419-3728
EMP: 50
SALES (corp-wide): 213.2MM **Privately Held**
SIC: 2759 Commercial printing
PA: Abc Imaging Of Washington, Inc
5290 Shawnee Rd Ste 300
Alexandria VA 22312
202 429-8870

(P-6972)
ABLE CARD LLC
1388 W Foothill Blvd, Azusa (91702-2846)
PHONE....................626 969-1888
Herman Ho, *President*
Donny Yu, *Vice Pres*
EMP: 20
SALES (est): 3.2MM **Privately Held**
SIC: 2759 Commercial printing

(P-6973)
ADAMS LABEL COMPANY LLC (PA)
6052 Industrial Way Ste G, Livermore (94551-9711)
PHONE....................925 371-5393
David Bowyer, *CEO*
EMP: 14 **EST:** 2014
SALES (est): 2.9MM **Privately Held**
SIC: 2759 3565 Labels & seals: printing; labeling machines, industrial

(P-6974)
ADCRAFT PRODUCTS CO INC
1230 S Sherman St, Anaheim (92805-6455)
PHONE....................714 776-1230
Randy C Mottram, *President*
Keith A Mottram, *Vice Pres*
Laural Gadison, *Manager*
EMP: 27
SALES (est): 5.6MM **Privately Held**
SIC: 2759 Screen printing

(P-6975)
ADVANCE SCREEN GRAPHIC
5720 Union Pacific Ave, Commerce (90022-5135)
PHONE....................323 724-9910
Raymundo Alcaraz, *President*
Umberto Contreras, *Treasurer*
Jose Luis Contreras, *Vice Pres*
Juan Felix, *Admin Sec*
EMP: 15
SQ FT: 22,000
SALES (est): 1.7MM **Privately Held**
SIC: 2759 Screen printing

(P-6976)
ADVANCED VSUAL IMAGE DSIGN LLC
Also Called: Avid Ink
229 N Sherman Ave, Irvine (92614)
PHONE....................951 279-2138
Robert D Davis, *CEO*
Jennie Enholm,
▲ **EMP:** 200
SQ FT: 20,000
SALES (est): 31.4MM **Privately Held**
SIC: 2759 Screen printing

(P-6977)
ADVANCED WEB OFFSET INC
Also Called: Awo
2260 Oak Ridge Way, Vista (92081-8341)
PHONE....................760 727-1700
Stephen F Shoemaker, *President*
Dan Armstrong, *General Mgr*
David Altomare, *Admin Sec*
Darcy Alvarado, *Bookkeeper*
Laura McGowan, *Human Res Mgr*
EMP: 75
SQ FT: 65,000

SALES (est): 14.4MM **Privately Held**
WEB: www.awoink.com
SIC: 2759 2752 Newspapers: printing; offset & photolithographic printing

(P-6978)
ADVANTAGE BUSINESS FORMS INC
102 N Riverside Ave, Rialto (92376-5922)
PHONE....................909 875-7163
Kevin M Danko, *CEO*
Keith Sabo, *Sales Staff*
Debi Southern, *Supervisor*
EMP: 12
SQ FT: 10,000
SALES (est): 1.2MM **Privately Held**
WEB: www.abfprints.com
SIC: 2759 7323 Commercial printing; credit reporting services

(P-6979)
ALL FORMS EXPRESS
17572 Griffin Ln, Huntington Beach (92647-6791)
PHONE....................714 596-8641
Brent Millville, *President*
EMP: 11
SALES (est): 642.2K **Privately Held**
SIC: 2759 Commercial printing

(P-6980)
ALL SPORTS SERVICES INC
Also Called: Sportsco
1814 Commercenter W Ste G, San Bernardino (92408-3332)
PHONE....................909 885-4626
Ray C Imbriana, *President*
Bob Forrest, *Corp Secy*
David Epperson, *Vice Pres*
EMP: 11
SALES (est): 1.2MM **Privately Held**
WEB: www.teamsportsco.com
SIC: 2759 Screen printing

(P-6981)
ALL-STAR LETTERING INC
9419 Ann St, Santa Fe Springs (90670-2613)
PHONE....................562 404-5995
Paul Possemato, *President*
Palma Possemato, *Treasurer*
Susan Possemato, *Vice Pres*
Arcadio Aguayo, *General Mgr*
Matt Crum, *Graphic Designe*
EMP: 45 **EST:** 1969
SALES (est): 6.3MM **Privately Held**
WEB: www.allstarlettering.com
SIC: 2759 3555 2396 Screen printing; printing trades machinery; automotive & apparel trimmings

(P-6982)
ALLIANCE MULTIMEDIA LLC
2033 San Elijo Ave Ste 20, Cardiff (92007-1726)
PHONE....................760 522-3455
Bill McCaffrey, *Mng Member*
Steve Reiley, *Creative Dir*
EMP: 12
SALES: 1.5MM **Privately Held**
SIC: 2759 7374 7812 7941 Publication printing; computer graphics service; video production; sports promotion

(P-6983)
ALLIANCE TAGS
9235 Trade Pl, San Diego (92126-6313)
P.O. Box 537, La Jolla (92038-0537)
PHONE....................858 549-7297
Bricks Keifer, *General Mgr*
Tessie Mills, *Administration*
EMP: 22
SALES (est): 1.9MM **Privately Held**
WEB: www.alliancetag.com
SIC: 2759 3993 2671 Labels & seals: printing; signs & advertising specialties; packaging paper & plastics film, coated & laminated

(P-6984)
ALROS LABEL CO INC
Also Called: Alros Lebel Co
14200 Aetna St, Van Nuys (91401-3433)
PHONE....................818 781-2403
Alfredo Rosales, *President*
Dalia Masjuam, *Corp Secy*

Maria L Rosales, *Vice Pres*
Maria Rosales, *Vice Pres*
EMP: 12 **EST:** 1976
SQ FT: 5,000
SALES: 900K **Privately Held**
SIC: 2759 Labels & seals: printing

(P-6985)
AMERICAN FOIL & EMBOSING INC
35 Musick, Irvine (92618-1638)
PHONE....................949 580-0080
Abdul A Hussain, *President*
EMP: 10
SQ FT: 3,600
SALES (est): 1.4MM **Privately Held**
WEB: www.americanfoil.com
SIC: 2759 Commercial printing

(P-6986)
AMERICAN NON STOP LABEL CORP
Also Called: American Label Co
16221 Arthur St, Cerritos (90703-2130)
PHONE....................562 921-9437
George Loayza, *CEO*
John Lincoln, *Shareholder*
▲ **EMP:** 19
SQ FT: 20,000
SALES (est): 3.7MM **Privately Held**
WEB: www.americanlabelco.com
SIC: 2759 Flexographic printing

(P-6987)
AMERICAN ZABIN INTL INC
3933 S Hill St, Los Angeles (90037-1313)
PHONE....................213 746-3770
Alan Faiola, *CEO*
Steven Garfinkle, *President*
Eric Sedso, *Vice Pres*
▲ **EMP:** 32
SQ FT: 18,000
SALES: 10MM **Privately Held**
SIC: 2759 Tags: printing

(P-6988)
AMIGO CUSTOM SCREEN PRINTS LLC
6351 Yarrow Dr Ste A&B, Carlsbad (92011-1545)
PHONE....................760 525-5593
Robert Lusitana,
EMP: 30
SALES (est): 3.3MM **Privately Held**
SIC: 2759 Screen printing

(P-6989)
APPAREL UNIFIED LLC
12136 Del Vista Dr, La Mirada (90638-1402)
PHONE....................562 639-7233
Richard Bermejo,
EMP: 10
SQ FT: 10,000
SALES (est): 334.8K **Privately Held**
SIC: 2759 Letterpress & screen printing

(P-6990)
AQUA PRIETA TEES LLC
33398 Paseo El Lazo, San Juan Capistrano (92675-1001)
PHONE....................714 719-2000
Jamey Darter, *Mng Member*
EMP: 12
SALES (est): 1.2MM **Privately Held**
SIC: 2759 Screen printing

(P-6991)
ARACA MERCHANDISE LP
Araca Ink
459 Park Ave, San Fernando (91340-2525)
PHONE....................818 743-5400
Judy Courney, *Manager*
EMP: 20 **Privately Held**
SIC: 2759 Screen printing
HQ: Araca Merchandise L.P.
545 W 45th St Fl 10
New York NY 10036

(P-6992)
ARTEEZ
Also Called: J & J Screen Printing
3600 Sunrise Blvd Ste 4, Rancho Cordova (95742-7340)
PHONE....................916 631-0473
John Kim, *Owner*
EMP: 10
SQ FT: 5,000
SALES (est): 1.2MM **Privately Held**
WEB: www.arteez.com
SIC: 2759 2396 Screen printing; automotive & apparel trimmings

(P-6993)
ARTISAN NAMEPLATE AWARDS CORP
Also Called: Weber Precision Graphics
2730 S Shannon St, Santa Ana (92704-5232)
PHONE....................714 556-6222
Henry G Weber, *President*
Margaret Weber, *Corp Secy*
Jeff Johnson, *Exec VP*
Manny Estrada, *General Mgr*
Nacho Cuevas, *Purch Mgr*
EMP: 33
SQ FT: 12,160
SALES (est): 6.3MM **Privately Held**
WEB: www.weberpg.com
SIC: 2759 3479 Labels & seals: printing; coating of metals with plastic or resins

(P-6994)
ARTISAN SCREEN PRINTING INC
1055 W 5th St, Azusa (91702-3313)
PHONE....................626 815-2700
Vasant N Doabria, *President*
C P Kheni, *Corp Secy*
Praful Bajaria, *Vice Pres*
▲ **EMP:** 120
SQ FT: 90,000
SALES (est): 16.2MM **Privately Held**
SIC: 2759 Screen printing

(P-6995)
ASHKA PRINT LLC
600 E Wash Blvd Ste W4, Los Angeles (90015-3731)
PHONE....................323 980-6008
Sung Lee,
EMP: 30
SALES (est): 836.9K **Privately Held**
SIC: 2759 Screen printing

(P-6996)
B & B LABEL INC
2357 Thompson Way, Santa Maria (93455-1050)
PHONE....................805 922-0332
Stephen Brookshire, *President*
Brian McCormick, *Vice Pres*
Cathy Brookshire, *Admin Sec*
EMP: 12
SQ FT: 6,000
SALES (est): 1.3MM **Privately Held**
WEB: www.bblabel.com
SIC: 2759 Flexographic printing

(P-6997)
BASIC BUSINESS FORMS INC
561 Kinetic Dr Ste A, Oxnard (93030-7947)
PHONE....................805 278-4551
EMP: 30
SALES (est): 2.7MM **Privately Held**
SIC: 2759 2761

(P-6998)
BERT-CO INDUSTRIES INC
2150 S Parco Ave, Ontario (91761-5768)
PHONE....................323 669-5700
Vince Savasta, *Branch Mgr*
EMP: 11
SQ FT: 89,149
SALES (corp-wide): 50MM **Privately Held**
WEB: www.bert-co.com
SIC: 2759 2752 Commercial printing; commercial printing, lithographic
PA: Bert-Co Industries, Inc.
2150 S Parco Ave
Ontario CA 91761
323 669-5700

PRODUCTS & SVCS

(P-6999)
BIZINKCOM LLC
9822 Independence Ave, Chatsworth
(91311-4319)
PHONE..................................818 676-0766
Tom Pelino,
EMP: 12 EST: 1995
SALES (est): 1.5MM **Privately Held**
SIC: 2759 Commercial printing

(P-7000)
BJS UKIAH EMBROIDERY
272 E Smith St, Ukiah (95482-4411)
PHONE..................................707 463-2767
Walt Richey, *Owner*
EMP: 10
SALES (est): 550K **Privately Held**
SIC: 2759 Screen printing

(P-7001)
BLACKBURN ALTON INVSTMENTS LLC
Also Called: Foster Print
700 E Alton Ave, Santa Ana (92705-5610)
PHONE..................................714 731-2000
Dennis M Blackburn,
EMP: 34 EST: 2011
SALES (est): 1.7MM **Privately Held**
SIC: 2759 Commercial printing

(P-7002)
BLC WC INC (PA)
Also Called: Imperial Marking Systems
13260 Moore St, Cerritos (90703-2228)
PHONE..................................562 926-1452
Ernest Wong, *President*
Timothy Koontz, *CFO*
Donald Ingle, *Admin Sec*
Pat Ortiz, *Persnl Dir*
Gary Ingle, *Opers Mgr*
EMP: 120 EST: 1989
SQ FT: 60,000
SALES (est): 16.2MM **Privately Held**
WEB: www.bestlabel.com
SIC: 2759 Commercial printing

(P-7003)
BOONE PRINTING & GRAPHICS INC
70 S Kellogg Ave Ste 8, Goleta
(93117-6408)
PHONE..................................805 683-2349
Andrew Ochsner, *President*
Rob Grayson, *Creative Dir*
Dave Tanner, *General Mgr*
Scott Tate, *Info Tech Dir*
Robert Galle, *Project Mgr*
EMP: 52
SQ FT: 15,000
SALES (est): 11.2MM **Privately Held**
WEB: www.boonegraphics.net
SIC: 2759 Commercial printing

(P-7004)
BORDEN DECAL COMPANY INC
870 Harrison St Unit 101, San Francisco
(94107-2254)
PHONE..................................415 431-1587
Richard Parmelee, *President*
Sharon Parmelee, *Treasurer*
Mark Flagg, *Vice Pres*
Christina Lau, *QC Mgr*
EMP: 20 EST: 1923
SQ FT: 15,000
SALES (est): 2.3MM **Privately Held**
WEB: www.bordendecal.com
SIC: 2759 2396 Decals: printing; automotive & apparel trimmings

(P-7005)
BRAND INK INC
3801 Oceanic Dr Ste 103, Oceanside
(92056-5850)
P.O. Box 4007, Carlsbad (92018-4007)
PHONE..................................760 721-4465
Todd Liotine, *President*
EMP: 30
SQ FT: 12,000
SALES (est): 4.3MM **Privately Held**
SIC: 2759 Screen printing

(P-7006)
BRAVO DESIGN INC
150 E Olive Ave Ste 304, Burbank
(91502-1850)
PHONE..................................818 563-1385
Dan Arriola, *CEO*
Ramon Buensuceso, *COO*
John Jurado, *Graphic Designe*
EMP: 12 EST: 2001
SALES (est): 1MM **Privately Held**
WEB: www.bravodesigninc.com
SIC: 2759 Advertising literature: printing

(P-7007)
BREAKAWAY PRESS INC
9620 Topanga Canyon Pl A, Chatsworth
(91311-0868)
PHONE..................................818 727-7388
Cynthia Friedman, *President*
Telly Shammas, *General Mgr*
Carole Kimmel, *Office Mgr*
EMP: 21
SQ FT: 3,000
SALES (est): 3.5MM **Privately Held**
WEB: www.breakawaypress.com
SIC: 2759 Commercial printing

(P-7008)
BRETT CORP
Also Called: So Cal Graphics
8316 Clairemont Mesa Blvd # 105, San
Diego (92111-1316)
PHONE..................................858 292-4919
Bret Catcott, *President*
Jessi Catcott, *Office Mgr*
Keri Catcott, *Admin Sec*
Lee Evans, *MIS Mgr*
EMP: 20
SQ FT: 4,500
SALES (est): 2.8MM **Privately Held**
WEB: www.socalgraphics.com
SIC: 2759 7336 Commercial printing;
graphic arts & related design

(P-7009)
BRIXEN & SONS INC
2100 S Fairview St, Santa Ana
(92704-4516)
PHONE..................................714 566-1444
Martin Corey Brixen, *President*
Son Nguyen, *Treasurer*
Gabriel Oseguera, *Manager*
▲ EMP: 27
SQ FT: 32,000
SALES (est): 5.3MM **Privately Held**
WEB: www.brixen.com
SIC: 2759 3993 Screen printing; signs &
advertising specialties

(P-7010)
C & H LETTERPRESS INC
3400 W Castor St, Santa Ana
(92704-3910)
PHONE..................................714 438-1350
Hernan A Pineda, *President*
Suzanne Harrison, *Treasurer*
EMP: 14
SQ FT: 8,600
SALES (est): 7.2MM **Privately Held**
WEB: www.chletterpress.com
SIC: 2759 Letterpress printing

(P-7011)
C T L PRINTING INDS INC
Also Called: Cal Tape & Label
1741 W Lincoln Ave Ste A, Anaheim
(92801-6716)
PHONE..................................714 635-2980
James Edward Hudson, *CEO*
J J Hudson, *Ch of Bd*
Dave Adams, *Principal*
Joanna Guzman, *Manager*
EMP: 25
SQ FT: 8,950
SALES (est): 4.9MM **Privately Held**
WEB: www.caltapeandlabel.com
SIC: 2759 Labels & seals: printing; decals:
printing

(P-7012)
CAL SPRINGS LLC
6250 N Irwindale Ave, Irwindale
(91702-3208)
PHONE..................................562 943-5599
▲ EMP: 54

SALES (est): 4.6MM **Privately Held**
SIC: 2759 3069 3751 5149

(P-7013)
CALICO TAG & LABEL INC
13233 Barton Cir, Whittier (90605-3255)
P.O. Box 3303, Santa Fe Springs (90670-
1303)
PHONE..................................562 944-6889
Fred Elhami, *President*
Ruth Elhami, *Vice Pres*
EMP: 13
SQ FT: 15,012
SALES (est): 966.5K **Privately Held**
WEB: www.calicotag.com
SIC: 2759 Tags: printing; labels & seals:
printing
PA: A F E Industries Inc.
13233 Barton Cir
Whittier CA 90605

(P-7014)
CALIFORNIA PRTG SOLUTIONS INC
1950 W Park Ave, Redlands (92373-3133)
P.O. Box 11451, San Bernardino (92423-
1451)
PHONE..................................909 307-2032
Mark Smith, *President*
▲ EMP: 22
SQ FT: 20,000
SALES (est): 2.9MM **Privately Held**
WEB: www.printingsolutions.net
SIC: 2759 Promotional printing

(P-7015)
CAMEO CRAFTS
Also Called: York Label
4995 Hillsdale Cir, El Dorado Hills
(95762-5707)
PHONE..................................513 381-1480
John McKernan, *CEO*
Scott Grigsby, *VP Opers*
Kevin Grigsby, *VP Sales*
EMP: 21
SQ FT: 30,000
SALES (est): 1.9MM **Privately Held**
WEB: www.yorklabel.com
SIC: 2759 Flexographic printing

(P-7016)
CASA MEXICO ENTERPRISES INC
3156 Foothill Blvd Ste G, La Crescenta
(91214-4258)
PHONE..................................888 411-9530
Eric Leyva Buccio, *President*
EMP: 10
SALES (est): 368.3K **Privately Held**
SIC: 2759 Promotional printing

(P-7017)
CCL LABEL INC
Pharmaceutical Label Systems
576 College Commerce Way, Upland
(91786-4377)
PHONE..................................909 608-2655
Kieorn Delahunt, *Branch Mgr*
Jan Burnett, *Manager*
EMP: 130
SQ FT: 43,000
SALES: 14.9MM
SALES (corp-wide): 3.9B **Privately Held**
SIC: 2759 Labels & seals: printing
HQ: Ccl Label, Inc.
161 Worcester Rd Ste 603
Framingham MA 01701
508 872-4511

(P-7018)
CCL LABEL (DELAWARE) INC
576 College Commerce Way, Upland
(91786-4377)
PHONE..................................909 608-2260
Kieron Delahunt, *Manager*
EMP: 150
SALES (corp-wide): 3.9B **Privately Held**
SIC: 2759 Labels & seals: printing
HQ: Ccl Label (Delaware), Inc.
15 Controls Dr
Shelton CT 06484
203 926-1253

(P-7019)
CEE -JAY RESEARCH & SALES LLC
920 W 10th St, Azusa (91702-1936)
PHONE..................................626 815-1530
Bert Banta, *Mng Member*
EMP: 30
SALES (est): 4.3MM **Privately Held**
WEB: www.cee-jay.com
SIC: 2759 2679 3429 Tags: printing; tags,
paper (unprinted): made from purchased
paper; manufactured hardware (general)

(P-7020)
CENTURY PUBLISHING
Also Called: Community Adviser Newspaper
218 N Murray St, Banning (92220-5512)
P.O. Box 727 (92220-0018)
PHONE..................................951 849-4586
Gerald Bean, *Owner*
Art Reyes, *General Mgr*
Virginia Bradford, *Office Mgr*
EMP: 15
SALES (est): 1.7MM **Privately Held**
WEB: www.recordgazette.net
SIC: 2759 7313 2711 Commercial print-
ing; newspaper advertising representa-
tive; newspapers

(P-7021)
CHEMTEX PRINT USA INC
3061 E Maria St, Compton (90221-5803)
PHONE..................................310 900-1818
Carolyn Tan, *President*
Dominic Tan, *Vice Pres*
▲ EMP: 25
SQ FT: 50,000
SALES (est): 2.2MM **Privately Held**
WEB: www.ctxprint.com
SIC: 2759 7389 Textile printing rolls: en-
graving; textile & apparel services

(P-7022)
CHURCH SCIENTOLOGY INTL
Freedon Publishing
6331 Hollywood Blvd # 801, Los Angeles
(90028-4698)
PHONE..................................323 960-3500
Aron Mason, *Principal*
EMP: 100
SALES (corp-wide): 114.6MM **Privately
Held**
SIC: 2759 7313 Publication printing; mag-
azine advertising representative
PA: Church Of Scientology International
6331 Hollywood Blvd # 801
Los Angeles CA 90028
323 960-3500

(P-7023)
CITY & COUNTY OF SAN FRANCISCO
Also Called: Administrative Services
875 Stevenson St Ste 125, San Francisco
(94103-0952)
PHONE..................................415 557-5251
David German, *Manager*
EMP: 20 **Privately Held**
SIC: 2759 9199 Commercial printing; gen-
eral government administration; ;
PA: City & County Of San Francisco
1 Dr Carlton B Goodlett P
San Francisco CA 94102
415 554-7500

(P-7024)
CLAREMONT INSTITUTE STATESMANS (PA)
Also Called: CLAREMONT INSTITUTE, THE
1317 W Foothill Blvd # 120, Upland
(91786-3676)
PHONE..................................909 981-2200
Michael Pack, *President*
John Marini, *Bd of Directors*
Ryan Williams, *Officer*
Larry Greenfield, *Vice Pres*
Matthew Peterson, *Vice Pres*
EMP: 21
SQ FT: 3,600
SALES: 4.7MM **Privately Held**
SIC: 2759 8733 Publication printing; re-
search institute

▲ = Import ▼=Export
◆ =Import/Export

(P-7025)
CLIFF DIGITAL
14700 S Main St, Gardena (90248-1959)
PHONE..................................310 323-5600
David Thomas, *President*
EMP: 11
SQ FT: 4,500
SALES (est): 896.5K **Privately Held**
SIC: 2759 7374 Screen printing; computer graphics service

(P-7026)
COASTAL TAG & LABEL INC
13233 Barton Cir, Whittier (90605-3255)
P.O. Box 3303, Santa Fe Springs (90670-1303)
PHONE..................................562 946-4318
Fred Elhami, *President*
Ruth Elhami, *Admin Sec*
EMP: 94
SALES (est): 10.6MM **Privately Held**
WEB: www.afeindustries.com
SIC: 2759 2672 2671 Labels & seals: printing; tags: printing; coated & laminated paper; packaging paper & plastics film, coated & laminated
PA: A F E Industries Inc.
13233 Barton Cir
Whittier CA 90605

(P-7027)
COASTWIDE TAG & LABEL CO
7647 Industry Ave, Pico Rivera (90660-4301)
PHONE..................................323 721-1501
Jay Sullivan, *President*
Jerry Sullivan, *Vice Pres*
EMP: 25 EST: 1946
SQ FT: 6,000
SALES (est): 3.5MM **Privately Held**
SIC: 2759 Labels & seals: printing; tags: printing

(P-7028)
COLLOTYPE LABELS USA INC (HQ)
Also Called: Multi-Color NAPA
21 Executive Way, NAPA (94558-6271)
PHONE..................................707 603-2500
Nigel Vinecombe, *CEO*
David Buse, *President*
Mike Huntsinger, *Vice Pres*
Angel Galvez, *Human Res Mgr*
Ken Wood, *Purchasing*
▲ EMP: 72
SQ FT: 14,500
SALES (est): 19.9MM
SALES (corp-wide): 1.7B **Privately Held**
WEB: www.collotype.com
SIC: 2759 Labels & seals: printing
PA: Multi-Color Corporation
4053 Clough Woods Dr
Batavia OH 45103
513 381-1480

(P-7029)
COLLOTYPE LABELS USA INC
Also Called: Multicolor
21684 8th St E, Sonoma (95476-2815)
PHONE..................................707 931-7400
EMP: 14
SALES (corp-wide): 1.7B **Privately Held**
SIC: 2759 Labels & seals: printing
HQ: Collotype Labels Usa Inc.
21 Executive Way
Napa CA 94558
707 603-2500

(P-7030)
COLMOL INC
Also Called: King Graphics
8517 Production Ave, San Diego (92121-2204)
PHONE..................................858 693-7575
Sean P Mundy, *CEO*
▲ EMP: 45
SQ FT: 14,000
SALES (est): 10.7MM **Privately Held**
WEB: www.kinggraph.com
SIC: 2759 Screen printing

(P-7031)
COLOR DEPOT INC
512 State St, Glendale (91203-1524)
PHONE..................................818 500-9033

Thomas Hovsepian, *President*
Anna Hovsepian, *CFO*
Lilit Shamiryan, *Graphic Designe*
EMP: 14
SQ FT: 2,800
SALES: 1MM **Privately Held**
SIC: 2759 7336 2732 2752 Commercial printing; commercial art & graphic design; book printing; commercial printing, lithographic

(P-7032)
COLOUR DROP
1388 Sutter St Ste 508, San Francisco (94109-5452)
PHONE..................................415 353-5720
Tipu Barber, *Owner*
EMP: 10
SALES: 1MM **Privately Held**
WEB: www.colourdrop.com
SIC: 2759 Commercial printing

(P-7033)
CONSOLIDATED GRAPHICS INC
Anderson La
3550 Tyburn St, Los Angeles (90065-1427)
PHONE..................................323 460-4115
Luke Westlake, *Vice Pres*
Tuan Pham, *Vice Pres*
Kevin Polley, *VP Bus Dvlpt*
Ann Lydecker, *Executive*
Aakruti Patel, *Technology*
EMP: 95
SALES (corp-wide): 6.8B **Publicly Held**
SIC: 2759 2752 Commercial printing; letterpress printing; screen printing; commercial printing, offset
HQ: Consolidated Graphics, Inc.
5858 Westheimer Rd # 200
Houston TX 77057
713 787-0977

(P-7034)
CONTENT MANAGEMENT CORPORATION
Also Called: C M C
4287 Technology Dr, Fremont (94538-6339)
PHONE..................................510 505-1100
Tom Pipkin, *CEO*
Zack Tsuji, *President*
Charles Price, *Project Mgr*
Jennifer Jones-Boyd, *Accounting Mgr*
EMP: 17
SQ FT: 8,000
SALES (est): 3MM **Privately Held**
WEB: www.cmcondemand.com
SIC: 2759 Commercial printing

(P-7035)
CORPORATE IMPRESSIONS LA INC
Also Called: Dorado Pkg
10742 Burbank Blvd, North Hollywood (91601-2516)
PHONE..................................818 761-9295
Jennifer L Freund, *President*
Gary Gonzales, *Project Mgr*
Sandy Benson, *Business Mgr*
Mike Recchia, *Plant Mgr*
EMP: 27 EST: 1982
SQ FT: 10,000
SALES (est): 4.7MM **Privately Held**
WEB: www.corporateimpressions.com
SIC: 2759 7389 Screen printing; packaging & labeling services

(P-7036)
CORPRINT INCORPORATED
Also Called: Total Brand Delivery
4235 Mission Oaks Blvd, Camarillo (93010)
PHONE..................................818 839-5316
Marc Lewis, *President*
EMP: 15
SALES (est): 3.5MM **Privately Held**
WEB: www.corprintinc.com
SIC: 2759 Business forms: printing

(P-7037)
COSMO FIBER CORPORATION (PA)
1802 Santo Domingo Ave, Duarte (91010-2933)
PHONE..................................626 256-6098

Sidney Ru, *President*
Sissy Ru, *Admin Sec*
Iris Kwok, *Manager*
Salina Brill, *Accounts Mgr*
▲ EMP: 33
SQ FT: 4,000
SALES (est): 6.3MM **Privately Held**
WEB: www.cosmofiber.com
SIC: 2759 7389 Promotional printing; advertising, promotional & trade show services

(P-7038)
COUNTY OF MONTEREY
Also Called: Monterey Coun Graphic Comm
855 E Laurel Dr Ste C, Salinas (93905-1300)
PHONE..................................831 755-4790
Virgil Schwab, *Branch Mgr*
EMP: 10 **Privately Held**
WEB: www.montereycountyfarmbureau.org
SIC: 2759 9111 2752 Commercial printing; county supervisors' & executives' offices; commercial printing, lithographic
PA: County Of Monterey
168 W Alisal St Fl 2
Salinas CA 93901
831 755-5040

(P-7039)
CR & A CUSTOM APPAREL INC
Also Called: Cr & A Custom
312 W Pico Blvd, Los Angeles (90015-2437)
PHONE..................................213 749-4440
Masoud RAD, *COO*
Carmen RAD, *President*
Matthew Otis, *Project Mgr*
Dino Maquiddang, *Controller*
Dennis Bise, *VP Opers*
▲ EMP: 30
SQ FT: 26,500
SALES: 6.5MM **Privately Held**
WEB: www.cracustom.com
SIC: 2759 Posters, including billboards: printing

(P-7040)
CREO INC
Also Called: Screaming Squeegee
50 Fullerton Ct Ste 107, Sacramento (95825-6205)
PHONE..................................530 756-1477
Greg Garcia, *President*
EMP: 11
SQ FT: 2,400
SALES (est): 1.2MM **Privately Held**
WEB: www.squeegee.com
SIC: 2759 Screen printing

(P-7041)
CUSTOM LABEL AND DECAL LLC
3392 Investment Blvd, Hayward (94545-3809)
PHONE..................................510 876-0000
Colin Ho-Tseung Jr, *Mng Member*
Wade Ignacio, *Sales Mgr*
Scott Dickes,
Dick Parmelee,
Connie Gouveia, *Cust Mgr*
EMP: 20
SQ FT: 25,000
SALES (est): 3.5MM **Privately Held**
WEB: www.customlabel.com
SIC: 2759 2752 2672 Labels & seals: printing; commercial printing, lithographic; coated & laminated paper

(P-7042)
CUSTOMPLANETCOM INC
12180 Ridgecrest Rd # 314, Victorville (92395-7798)
PHONE..................................760 508-2648
Chris Taylor, *Principal*
Hannah Taylor, *Manager*
EMP: 15
SALES (est): 1.9MM **Privately Held**
SIC: 2759 Screen printing

(P-7043)
DATAPAGE INC
5577 Sheila St, Commerce (90040-1424)
P.O. Box 911188, Los Angeles (90091-1188)
PHONE..................................323 725-7500

Barbara Martine, *President*
Grady Martine, *Vice Pres*
Thirkield Thomas, *Opers Spvr*
EMP: 10
SALES (est): 990K **Privately Held**
WEB: www.datapageinc.com
SIC: 2759 Laser printing

(P-7044)
DELTA WEB PRINTING INC
Also Called: Delta Web Printing & Bindery
1871 Enterprise Blvd, West Sacramento (95691-3423)
PHONE..................................916 375-0044
James Davis, *President*
Kasey Cotulla, *Vice Pres*
Linda Gould, *Bookkeeper*
Eric Cormier, *Plant Mgr*
EMP: 22
SQ FT: 30,000
SALES (est): 4.3MM **Privately Held**
SIC: 2759 2789 Screen printing; binding & repair of books, magazines & pamphlets

(P-7045)
DIGITAL ROOM HOLDINGS INC (PA)
Also Called: New Printing
8000 Haskell Ave, Van Nuys (91406-1321)
PHONE..................................310 575-4440
Michael Turner, *Officer*
Brett Zane, *CFO*
Joyce Price, *VP Bus Dvlpt*
Kareem Edwards, *Office Mgr*
Daeron Lockett, *Info Tech Dir*
▲ EMP: 101
SALES (est): 82.4MM **Privately Held**
WEB: www.digitalroom.com
SIC: 2759 7336 Commercial printing; graphic arts & related design

(P-7046)
DIGITALPRO INC
Also Called: Dpi Direct
13257 Kirkham Way, Poway (92064-7116)
PHONE..................................858 874-7750
Sam Mousavi, *President*
Mohammed Khaki, *Vice Pres*
Paul Moebius, *Vice Pres*
EMP: 65
SQ FT: 38,000
SALES (est): 9.4MM **Privately Held**
WEB: www.digitalpro.com
SIC: 2759 Screen printing

(P-7047)
DIRECT EDGE SCREENWORKS INC
430 W Collins Ave, Orange (92867-5508)
PHONE..................................714 579-3686
Ryan Clark, *President*
Ryan Bruecknru, *Vice Pres*
Nicksharo Oshiro, *Vice Pres*
Tim Standon, *Vice Pres*
EMP: 19
SQ FT: 20,000
SALES: 3MM **Privately Held**
SIC: 2759 Screen printing

(P-7048)
DISPLAY ADVERTISING INC
1837 Van Ness Ave, Fresno (93721-1190)
PHONE..................................559 266-0231
Dave O' Brien, *President*
EMP: 10
SQ FT: 16,000
SALES: 900K **Privately Held**
SIC: 2759 Screen printing

(P-7049)
DIVERSIFIED IMAGES INC
27955 Beale Ct, Valencia (91355-1211)
PHONE..................................661 702-0003
Robert W Waycott, *President*
Barbara Waycott, *Vice Pres*
Bill Waycott, *General Mgr*
EMP: 12
SQ FT: 16,000
SALES (est): 880K **Privately Held**
WEB: www.diversifiedimages.com
SIC: 2759 2752 3479 Screen printing; decals, lithographed; etching & engraving

(P-7050)
DM LUXURY LLC
875 Prospect St Ste 300, La Jolla
(92037-4264)
PHONE...............................858 366-9721
EMP: 144
SALES (corp-wide): 79.5MM **Privately
Held**
SIC: 2759 Advertising literature: printing
PA: Dm Luxury, Llc
　3414 Peachtree Rd Ne # 480
　Atlanta GA 30326
　404 443-1180

(P-7051)
**DREAMTEAM BUSINESS GROUP
LLC**
Also Called: Rlf Print Shop
5261 E Kings Canyon Rd # 101, Fresno
(93727-4083)
PHONE...............................559 430-7676
Nehemiah Fane,
Dwayne Taylor,
EMP: 10
SQ FT: 5,000
SALES (est): 971.1K **Privately Held**
SIC: 2759 Commercial printing

(P-7052)
DYNAMIC SERVICES INC
27091 Burbank, El Toro (92610-2505)
PHONE...............................949 458-2553
Zoltan F Csik, President
EMP: 10
SQ FT: 8,500
SALES: 1.4MM **Privately Held**
WEB: www.dynamicservice.com
SIC: 2759 5734 3565 2679 Labels &
seals: printing; printers & plotters: com-
puters; labeling machines, industrial; la-
bels, paper: made from purchased
material

(P-7053)
E Z MARTIN STICK LABELS INC
12921 Sunnyside Pl, Santa Fe Springs
(90670-4645)
PHONE...............................562 906-1577
Francisco Martinez, President
Sylvia Martinez, Treasurer
Moncia Martinez, Admin Sec
EMP: 18
SQ FT: 14,800
SALES (est): 2MM **Privately Held**
WEB: www.ezstick.com
SIC: 2759 Labels & seals: printing

(P-7054)
EARL HAYS PRESS
10707 Sherman Way, Sun Valley
(91352-5155)
PHONE...............................818 765-0700
Rafael Hernandez Jr, Partner
Paul Crumrine, Partner
EMP: 16
SQ FT: 8,000
SALES: 1.5MM **Privately Held**
SIC: 2759 7829 Card printing & engraving,
except greeting; motion picture distribu-
tion services

(P-7055)
**ELECTRONIC PRTG SOLUTIONS
LLC**
4879 Ronson Ct Ste C, San Diego
(92111-1811)
PHONE...............................858 576-3000
Grant Freeman, Mng Member
Brian Bell,
Janice Freeman,
EMP: 20
SQ FT: 7,600
SALES: 3.2MM **Privately Held**
WEB: www.epsolution.com
SIC: 2759 2732 Magazines: printing; book
printing

(P-7056)
**ELECTRONICS FOR IMAGING
INC (HQ)**
Also Called: Efi
6750 Dumbarton Cir, Fremont
(94555-3616)
PHONE...............................650 357-3500
Marc Olin, COO

Grant Fitz, CFO
▲ EMP: 50
SQ FT: 119,000
SALES: 1B **Privately Held**
WEB: www.vutek.com
SIC: 2759 3955 Commercial printing; print
cartridges for laser & other computer
printers
PA: East Private Holdings Ii, Llc
　6750 Dumbarton Cir
　Fremont CA 94555
　650 357-3500

(P-7057)
**ELITE COLOR TECHNOLOGIES
INC**
851 E Walnut St, Carson (90746-1214)
PHONE...............................310 324-3040
Ki Kyong, President
▲ EMP: 12
SQ FT: 15,000
SALES (est): 2.1MM **Privately Held**
SIC: 2759 Commercial printing

(P-7058)
EPICSON INC
Also Called: Candroy Embroidery
8250 Cmino Santa Fe Ste A, San Diego
(92121)
P.O. Box 131, La Jolla (92038-0131)
PHONE...............................858 558-5757
Miranda R Amid, Principal
EMP: 15
SALES (est): 1.6MM **Privately Held**
SIC: 2759 Screen printing

(P-7059)
**EUROSTAMPA NORTH AMERICA
INC**
2545 Napa Vly, NAPA (94558)
PHONE...............................707 927-4848
Pat Hoe, Plant Mgr
EMP: 18
SALES (corp-wide): 152K **Privately Held**
SIC: 2759 Labels & seals: printing
HQ: Eurostampa North America Inc.
　1440 Seymour Ave
　Cincinnati OH 45237

(P-7060)
EXCALIBER SYSTEMS INC
185 Los Vientos Dr, Newbury Park
(91320-2810)
PHONE...............................805 376-1366
Mark Bliskel, President
Mark Sponsler, President
George Sponsler, Vice Pres
EMP: 40
SALES (est): 8MM **Privately Held**
SIC: 2759 Souvenir cards: printing

(P-7061)
EXECUPRINT INC
9650 Topanga Canyon Pl E, Chatsworth
(91311-4104)
PHONE...............................818 993-8184
Amin Farag, Partner
Bassem Farag, Partner
Esther Farag, Partner
Michael Farag, Partner
Kevin Mehle, Representative
EMP: 10 EST: 1975
SQ FT: 6,000
SALES (est): 2.1MM **Privately Held**
WEB: www.execuprint.com
SIC: 2759 7374 2752 Ready prints; com-
puter graphics service; commercial print-
ing, offset

(P-7062)
**EXPRESS BUSINESS SYSTEMS
INC**
9155 Trade Pl, San Diego (92126-4377)
P.O. Box 537, La Jolla (92038-0537)
PHONE...............................858 549-9828
Briggs Keiffer, President
Maureen O'Malley, Corp Secy
EMP: 37
SQ FT: 7,000

SALES (est): 3.8MM **Privately Held**
WEB: www.expresscorp.com
SIC: 2759 3993 2672 2671 Labels &
seals: printing; signs & advertising specialties; coated & laminated paper; packaging paper & plastics film, coated &
laminated; labels, paper: made from purchased material

(P-7063)
FACE FIRST SCREEN PRINT INC
33049 Calle Aviador Ste C, San Juan
Capistrano (92675-4785)
PHONE...............................949 443-9895
John Theaders, President
▲ EMP: 23
SQ FT: 4,800
SALES (est): 2.4MM **Privately Held**
SIC: 2759 5699 Screen printing; cus-
tomized clothing & apparel

(P-7064)
**FISHER PRINTING & STAMPING
CO**
5038 Venice Blvd, Los Angeles
(90019-5310)
PHONE...............................323 933-9193
John E Becca, Owner
EMP: 10
SQ FT: 2,000
SALES: 900K **Privately Held**
SIC: 2759 2752 Embossing on paper; let-
terpress printing; commercial printing, lith-
ographic

(P-7065)
**FLANNIGANS MERCHANDISING
INC**
15803 Stagg St, Van Nuys (91406-1922)
PHONE...............................818 785-7428
Nathan Boles, President
EMP: 20
SQ FT: 10,000
SALES: 750K **Privately Held**
SIC: 2759 Screen printing

(P-7066)
FLOYD DENNEE
Also Called: A B C Press
2780 Walnut Ave, Signal Hill (90755-1832)
PHONE...............................562 595-6024
Floyd Dennee, Owner
Ruth Denee, Co-Owner
EMP: 10 EST: 1945
SQ FT: 5,000
SALES: 1.2MM **Privately Held**
WEB: www.abcpres.com
SIC: 2759 Announcements: engraved

(P-7067)
FOILFLEX PRODUCTS INC
24963 Avenue Tibbitts, Valencia
(91355-3427)
PHONE...............................661 702-0775
Michael Dekel, President
Ned Washburn, Vice Pres
▲ EMP: 14
SQ FT: 17,000
SALES (est): 3.5MM **Privately Held**
WEB: www.foilflex.com
SIC: 2759 Flexographic printing

(P-7068)
FORWARD PRINTING & DESIGN
9331 Burr St, Oakland (94605-4313)
PHONE...............................510 535-2222
Daniel Corcoran, Principal
Joyce Corcoran, CFO
Daniel Phelan, Project Mgr
Lemanuel Shelley, Opers Mgr
EMP: 16
SALES (est): 2.1MM **Privately Held**
SIC: 2759 Screen printing

(P-7069)
**FRANKLIN LEE ENTERPRISES
LLC**
Also Called: Conveyor Group
2419 Imprl Bus Park Dr, Imperial
(92251-4004)
PHONE...............................760 355-1500
Aaron Popejoy,
Hartnoll Nicholson,
EMP: 10

SALES (est): 1.1MM **Privately Held**
WEB: www.conveyorgroup.com
SIC: 2759 5734 7335 7375 Commercial
printing; computer software & accessories; commercial photography; on-line
data base information retrieval

(P-7070)
G PRINTING INC
456 W Broadway, Glendale (91204-1209)
PHONE...............................818 246-1156
George Ouzounian, President
John Melkonian, Vice Pres
Gary Worth, Manager
EMP: 11 EST: 1974
SQ FT: 8,000
SALES: 952.7K **Privately Held**
SIC: 2759 Catalogs: printing; business
forms: printing; menus: printing; letter-
press printing

(P-7071)
G2 GRAPHIC SERVICE INC
5510 Cleon Ave, North Hollywood
(91601-2835)
PHONE...............................818 623-3100
John C Beard, CEO
Joe Cotrupe, President
Pamela Beard-Cotrupe, CEO
Rob Cashman, Vice Pres
Scott Dewinkeleer, Vice Pres
◆ EMP: 52
SQ FT: 35,000
SALES (est): 12.5MM **Privately Held**
WEB: www.g2online.com
SIC: 2759 7331 Commercial printing; di-
rect mail advertising services

(P-7072)
GACHUPIN ENTERPRISES LLC
Also Called: Speedwear
5671 Engineer Dr, Huntington Beach
(92649-1123)
PHONE...............................714 375-4111
Kai Gachupin, Owner
Tony Bustamante, Graphic Designe
Mike Thomas, Accounting Mgr
Will Marquez, Prdtn Mgr
Darren Ellis, Sales Staff
▲ EMP: 40
SQ FT: 11,000
SALES: 1.9MM **Privately Held**
SIC: 2759 7389 3949 Screen printing;
embroidering of advertising on shirts, etc.;
sporting & athletic goods

(P-7073)
GEO LABELS INC
1180 E Francis St Ste G, Ontario
(91761-4802)
P.O. Box 3009 (91761-0901)
PHONE...............................909 923-6832
George Contreras, President
Elena Conteras, Admin Sec
EMP: 12
SQ FT: 16,000
SALES (est): 1.5MM **Privately Held**
SIC: 2759 Labels & seals: printing

(P-7074)
GOLDEN APPLEXX CO INC
19805 Harrison Ave, Walnut (91789-2849)
PHONE...............................909 594-9788
Peter Lee, President
Shio R Lee, Vice Pres
Shio-Ru Lee, Vice Pres
◆ EMP: 40
SALES (est): 4.8MM **Privately Held**
WEB: www.goldenapplexx.com
SIC: 2759 2396 Promotional printing; au-
tomotive & apparel trimmings

(P-7075)
GRAPHIC PACKAGING INTL LLC
Also Called: Sierra Pacific Packaging
525 Airport Pkwy, Oroville (95965-9248)
PHONE...............................530 533-1058
Allen Ennis, Branch Mgr
Vincent Geiger, Engineer
Stefanie Garcia, Human Resources
Alyson Lazarus, Safety Mgr
Josh Rasmussen, Manager
EMP: 160 **Publicly Held**

▲ = Import ▼=Export
◆ =Import/Export

SIC: 2759 2752 2671 2631 Commercial printing; commercial printing, lithographic; packaging paper & plastics film, coated & laminated; paperboard mills
HQ: Graphic Packaging International, Llc
1500 Riveredge Pkwy # 100
Atlanta GA 30328

(P-7076)
GRAPHIC SYSTEMS
1693 Mission Dr Ste C101, Solvang (93463-3608)
PHONE..............................805 686-0705
Heather Bedford, *Owner*
EMP: 16 EST: 1981
SALES (est): 856.5K **Privately Held**
SIC: 2759 Commercial printing

(P-7077)
GRAPHIC TRENDS INCORPORATED
7301 Adams St, Paramount (90723-4007)
PHONE..............................562 531-2339
Kieu V Tran, *Principal*
Allen Gasper, *Info Tech Mgr*
Albert Beserra, *Purch Dir*
Cesar Arambula, *Supervisor*
EMP: 40
SQ FT: 20,984
SALES (est): 7.6MM **Privately Held**
WEB: www.graphictrends.net
SIC: 2759 7336 Screen printing; graphic arts & related design

(P-7078)
GRAPHICS FACTORY INC
21344 Superior St, Chatsworth (91311-4312)
PHONE..............................818 727-9040
Jeffrey Hampsten, *President*
Lisa Hampsten, *CFO*
EMP: 10
SQ FT: 5,000
SALES (est): 1.2MM **Privately Held**
SIC: 2759 Commercial printing

(P-7079)
GRAPHICS INK LITHOGRAPHY LLC
5531 Foxtail Loop, Carlsbad (92010-7153)
PHONE..............................760 438-9052
EMP: 10 EST: 1998
SQ FT: 4,000
SALES: 1.2MM **Privately Held**
SIC: 2759

(P-7080)
GREAT WESTERN PACKAGING LLC
8230-8240 Haskell Ave, Van Nuys (91406)
PHONE..............................818 464-3800
Michael C Warner, *Mng Member*
Denise Scanlon, *Executive*
Howard Metz, *MIS Mgr*
Misty Bright, *Project Mgr*
Charles Wesley, *Purch Mgr*
EMP: 68 EST: 1970
SALES (est): 11.2MM **Privately Held**
SIC: 2759 Commercial printing

(P-7081)
GREATHOUSE SCREEN PRINTING
Also Called: Gsp
5644 Kearny Mesa Rd Ste E, San Diego (92111-1311)
PHONE..............................858 279-4939
Shawn Greathouse, *Owner*
EMP: 12
SQ FT: 5,000
SALES (est): 1.2MM **Privately Held**
SIC: 2759 Screen printing

(P-7082)
GREEN SHEET INC
5830 Commerce Blvd Ste B, Rohnert Park (94928-1666)
P.O. Box 750878, Petaluma (94975-0878)
PHONE..............................707 284-1684
Paul Green, *President*
Brandee Wolfe, *President*
Kat Doherty, *Office Mgr*
Richard Aston, *Sales Staff*
Danielle Thorpe, *Director*

EMP: 10
SQ FT: 2,300
SALES (est): 1.4MM **Privately Held**
WEB: www.thegreensheet.com
SIC: 2759 Magazines: printing

(P-7083)
GUANO RECORDS LLC
26298 Jaylene St, Murrieta (92563-4940)
PHONE..............................714 263-5398
Breian Russell, *CEO*
EMP: 10
SALES (est): 368.3K **Privately Held**
SIC: 2759 7389 Music sheet: printing;

(P-7084)
GUTIERREZ GRADING
1505 E Phillips Blvd, Pomona (91766-5435)
PHONE..............................909 397-8717
Geronimo Gutierrez, *Owner*
EMP: 10
SALES (est): 946.4K **Privately Held**
SIC: 2759 Commercial printing

(P-7085)
H2 CARDS INC
Also Called: Igraphix
638 Washington St, San Francisco (94111-2106)
PHONE..............................415 788-7888
Wade Lai, *President*
Opal Tsui, *Executive*
▲ EMP: 10
SALES (est): 1.8MM **Privately Held**
SIC: 2759 7336 7313 7312 Commercial printing; commercial art & graphic design; radio advertising representative; printed media advertising representatives; outdoor advertising services; billboard advertising

(P-7086)
HB PRODUCTS LLC
5671 Engineer Dr, Huntington Beach (92649-1123)
PHONE..............................714 799-6967
Robert Mannarelli,
John Abramson, *Vice Pres*
EMP: 20
SALES (est): 3MM **Privately Held**
SIC: 2759 Screen printing

(P-7087)
HUDSON PRINTING INC
2780 Loker Ave W, Carlsbad (92010-6611)
PHONE..............................760 602-1260
James Fairweather, *President*
Anne Fairweather, *Treasurer*
Tom Fairweather, *Vice Pres*
Ashley Fairweather, *Production*
Jennifer Redmond, *Production*
EMP: 23
SQ FT: 6,000
SALES (est): 5.5MM **Privately Held**
SIC: 2759 2752 Screen printing; commercial printing, offset

(P-7088)
HYX TECH CORP
13620 Benson Ave Ste B, Chino (91710-5201)
PHONE..............................951 907-3386
Yaxian Huang, *President*
EMP: 12
SALES (est): 549.4K **Privately Held**
SIC: 2759 Commercial printing

(P-7089)
I E P FULL SERVICE PRINTING
1501 Cortland Ave, San Francisco (94110-5769)
PHONE..............................415 648-6002
Michael Kim, *Principal*
EMP: 14 EST: 2000
SALES (est): 861.3K **Privately Held**
SIC: 2759 Commercial printing

(P-7090)
IC INK IMAGE CO INC
Also Called: Legends Apparel & I C Ink
4627 E Fremont St, Stockton (95215-4010)
P.O. Box 4487 (95204-0487)
PHONE..............................209 931-3040
Tom Sousa, *President*
EMP: 20

SQ FT: 25,000
SALES (est): 3.6MM **Privately Held**
SIC: 2759 2396 2395 Screen printing; automotive & apparel trimmings; pleating & stitching

(P-7091)
ICON SCREENING INC
Also Called: Icon Screen Printing
1108 W Grove Ave, Orange (92865-4131)
PHONE..............................714 630-4266
Bryan Huber, *CEO*
Mike Zaremba, *Production*
EMP: 13 EST: 2011
SALES (est): 674.4K **Privately Held**
SIC: 2759 Screen printing

(P-7092)
ID SUPPLY
15182 Triton Ln Ste 101, Huntington Beach (92649-1076)
PHONE..............................714 728-6478
Brandon Rddach, *President*
EMP: 17
SALES (est): 153.9K **Privately Held**
SIC: 2759 Letterpress & screen printing; screen printing

(P-7093)
IGRAPHICS (PA)
Also Called: Precision Printers
165 Spring Hill Dr, Grass Valley (95945-5936)
PHONE..............................530 273-2200
James G Clay, *Owner*
Patrick Keown, *COO*
David Clay, *Mng Member*
EMP: 25
SQ FT: 15,000
SALES (est): 1.7MM **Privately Held**
WEB: www.igraphicspp.com
SIC: 2759 7389 3993 2671 Screen printing; printing broker; signs & advertising specialties; packaging paper & plastics film, coated & laminated; automotive & apparel trimmings

(P-7094)
IN HOUSE CUSTOM DECALS
Also Called: In House Stickers
2300 S Reservoir St # 308, Pomona (91766-6458)
PHONE..............................909 613-1403
Frank Caldron, *Owner*
▲ EMP: 13 EST: 1996
SALES (est): 240.3K **Privately Held**
SIC: 2759 Decals: printing

(P-7095)
INDEX PRINTING INC
Also Called: Tuesday Review, The
1021 Fresno St, Newman (95360-1303)
P.O. Box 878 (95360-0878)
PHONE..............................209 862-2222
Susan Mattos, *President*
EMP: 13
SALES (est): 685.2K **Privately Held**
SIC: 2759 Commercial printing

(P-7096)
INDIAN INK SCREEN PRINT
1351 Logan Ave Ste A, Costa Mesa (92626-4096)
PHONE..............................714 437-0882
Doug Winbury, *President*
Paul Schmitt, *Vice Pres*
Mark Oblow, *Admin Sec*
EMP: 40
SQ FT: 25,000
SALES: 2MM **Privately Held**
WEB: www.giantsk8dist.com
SIC: 2759 2396 Screen printing; automotive & apparel trimmings

(P-7097)
INFOIMAGE OF CALIFORNIA INC (PA)
141 Jefferson Dr, Menlo Park (94025-1114)
PHONE..............................650 473-6388
Howard Lee, *President*
Rose Lee, *COO*
Lilly Fong, *CFO*
Lenora Lee, *CFO*
Tomas Lee, *Officer*
EMP: 85

SALES (est): 16.2MM **Privately Held**
WEB: www.infoimageinc.com
SIC: 2759 7331 7374 Laser printing; mailing service; data processing service

(P-7098)
INK FX CORPORATION
2031 S Lynx Ave, Ontario (91761-8011)
PHONE..............................909 673-1950
Joe Metz, *President*
Mike Machrone, *CEO*
Lydia Matz, *Financial Exec*
EMP: 25
SQ FT: 12,000
SALES (est): 3.5MM **Privately Held**
WEB: www.inkfx.net
SIC: 2759 Screen printing

(P-7099)
INTEGRATED BUSINESS NETWORK
28310 Roadside Dr Ste 136, Agoura Hills (91301-4950)
PHONE..............................818 879-0670
EMP: 10
SALES (est): 612.8K **Privately Held**
SIC: 2759

(P-7100)
INTER COLOR PLUS INTER
13234 Sherman Way Ste 6, North Hollywood (91605-7711)
PHONE..............................818 764-5034
Oscar Moleno, *Owner*
Patricia Abrim, *Admin Sec*
EMP: 28
SALES: 38K **Privately Held**
SIC: 2759 Commercial printing

(P-7101)
INTERNTIONAL COLOR POSTERS INC
Also Called: ICP West
8081 Orangethorpe Ave, Buena Park (90621-3801)
PHONE..............................949 768-1005
Eric Guerineau, *President*
▲ EMP: 50
SQ FT: 26,000
SALES (est): 5.9MM **Privately Held**
WEB: www.icpwest.com
SIC: 2759 Screen printing

(P-7102)
INVESTMENT ENTERPRISES INC (PA)
Also Called: Great Western Litho
8230 Haskell Ave Ste 8240, Van Nuys (91406-1322)
PHONE..............................818 464-3800
Michael Warner, *President*
Jack Wickson, *Vice Pres*
Denise Scanlon, *Executive*
EMP: 43 EST: 1970
SALES (est): 13.6MM **Privately Held**
SIC: 2759 Magazines: printing

(P-7103)
IRIS GROUP INC
Also Called: Modern Postcard
1675 Faraday Ave, Carlsbad (92008-7314)
PHONE..............................760 431-1103
Steve Hoffman, *CEO*
Pam Sepesi, *Technology*
Jessica Biondo, *Marketing Staff*
Brian Cortez, *Marketing Staff*
Ken Cox, *Marketing Staff*
EMP: 250
SQ FT: 75,000
SALES (est): 60.1MM **Privately Held**
WEB: www.modernpostcard.com
SIC: 2759 5961 Commercial printing; mail order house

(P-7104)
JOHN LOMPA
Also Called: Trade Lithography
720 Harbour Way S Ste A, Richmond (94804-3631)
PHONE..............................510 965-6501
John Lompa, *Owner*
Mike Porter, *Manager*
EMP: 15
SQ FT: 14,000

SALES (est): 2.5MM **Privately Held**
SIC: 2759 Commercial printing

(P-7105)
K S PRINTING INC
710 E Parkridge Ave # 105, Corona
(92879-1097)
PHONE.....................................951 268-5180
Ralph Azar, *President*
▲ EMP: 12
SQ FT: 20,000
SALES: 100K **Privately Held**
WEB: www.ksprintingonline.com
SIC: 2759 Commercial printing

(P-7106)
KIERAN LABEL CORP
2321 Siempre Viva Ct # 101, San Diego
(92154-6301)
PHONE.....................................619 449-4457
Denis Vanier, *CEO*
Bill Walker, *Sr Corp Ofcr*
Teiko Watanabe, *Accountant*
Karl Morgan, *Controller*
Jeannette Franks,
▲ EMP: 44 EST: 1979
SALES (est): 12.4MM **Privately Held**
SIC: 2759 Commercial printing

(P-7107)
KJM ENTERPRISES INC
8148 Auberge Cir, San Diego
(92127-4204)
PHONE.....................................858 537-2490
Kevin Murray, *President*
▲ EMP: 40
SQ FT: 16,000
SALES (est): 7.8MM **Privately Held**
WEB: www.kjmscreenprints.com
SIC: 2759 Screen printing

(P-7108)
L A SUPPLY CO
Also Called: Label House
18005 Sky Park Cir Ste A, Irvine
(92614-6514)
P.O. Box 14876 (92623-4876)
PHONE.....................................949 470-9900
Randolph William Austin, *CEO*
Ron Middlekauff, *Manager*
▲ EMP: 31 EST: 1947
SQ FT: 35,000
SALES (est): 5.3MM **Privately Held**
SIC: 2759 2752 2672 2396 Labels &
seals: printing; commercial printing, litho-
graphic; coated & laminated paper; auto-
motive & apparel trimmings; service
establishment equipment

(P-7109)
LABEL ART-EASY STIK LABELS
Also Called: Label Art of California
290 27th St, Oakland (94612-3821)
PHONE.....................................510 465-1125
David S Masri, *President*
Daniel Masri, *Vice Pres*
Elizabeth Masri, *Admin Sec*
EMP: 25
SALES (est): 4.2MM **Privately Held**
WEB: www.instantlabel.com
SIC: 2759 Labels & seals: printing

(P-7110)
LABEL IMPRESSIONS INC
1831 W Sequoia Ave, Orange
(92868-1017)
PHONE.....................................714 634-3466
Jeffrey Salisbury, *CEO*
Kevin Deallen, *Vice Pres*
Carolyn Deyoe, *Vice Pres*
Ramy Zada, *Opers Staff*
Travis Graham, *Production*
EMP: 42
SQ FT: 15,000
SALES (est): 8.1MM **Privately Held**
WEB: www.labelimpressions.com
SIC: 2759 Labels & seals: printing

(P-7111)
LABEL MASTERS INC
3188 N Marks Ave Ste 112, Fresno
(93722-4940)
PHONE.....................................559 445-1208
Roger A Cooper, *President*
Kathleen Cooper, *Vice Pres*
EMP: 12 EST: 1979

SQ FT: 10,000
SALES (est): 1.5MM **Privately Held**
WEB: www.labelmastersinc.com
SIC: 2759 2752 Flexographic printing;
commercial printing, offset

(P-7112)
LABEL PRODUCTIONS OF CAL
42068 Winchester Rd, Temecula
(92590-4804)
PHONE.....................................951 296-1881
Steven Hamelback, *President*
Susanna F Hamelback, *Vice Pres*
EMP: 12
SQ FT: 17,425
SALES (est): 2.9MM **Privately Held**
SIC: 2759 Commercial printing

(P-7113)
LABEL SPECIALTIES INC
704 Dunn Way, Placentia (92870-6805)
PHONE.....................................714 961-8074
Michael A Gyure, *President*
Tom Wetterhus, *Vice Pres*
EMP: 18
SQ FT: 11,000
SALES (est): 3.8MM **Privately Held**
WEB: www.labelspec.com
SIC: 2759 Labels & seals: printing

(P-7114)
LABELING HURST SYSTEMS LLC
Also Called: Hurst International
20747 Dearborn St, Chatsworth
(91311-5914)
P.O. Box 5169 (91313-5169)
PHONE.....................................818 701-0710
Aron Lichtenberg, *President*
▲ EMP: 18
SQ FT: 12,875
SALES (est): 4.8MM **Privately Held**
SIC: 2759 Labels & seals: printing

(P-7115)
LABELTRONIX LLC
Also Called: Rethink Label Systems
2419 E Winston Rd, Anaheim
(92806-5544)
PHONE.....................................800 429-4321
Daniel Blair,
Louie Mendoza, *Engineer*
Meghan Lievanos, *Opers Staff*
Monique Holguin, *Production*
Eric Shepard,
▲ EMP: 73
SQ FT: 48,000
SALES: 19MM **Privately Held**
WEB: www.labeltronix.com
SIC: 2759 Labels & seals: printing

(P-7116)
LANDMARK LABEL MANUFACTURING
39611 Eureka Dr, Newark (94560-4806)
PHONE.....................................510 651-5551
Peter Offerman, *President*
Peter Offermann, *President*
EMP: 48
SQ FT: 24,000
SALES (est): 4.5MM
SALES (corp-wide): 236.4MM **Privately Held**
WEB: www.landmarklabel.com
SIC: 2759 2672 Labels & seals: printing;
coated & laminated paper
HQ: Cellotape, Inc.
39611 Eureka Dr
Newark CA 94560
510 651-5551

(P-7117)
LAWEB OFFSET PRINTING INC
Also Called: Chinese-La Daily News
9639 Telstar Ave, El Monte (91731-3003)
PHONE.....................................626 454-2469
Walter Chang, *President*
Ya-Tang Fu, *Shareholder*
CHI-Kwang Chiang, *Treasurer*
Jason Lee, *Accounting Mgr*
▲ EMP: 165
SQ FT: 29,730
SALES (est): 16.2MM **Privately Held**
WEB: www.laweboffset.com
SIC: 2759 2752 Newspapers: printing;
commercial printing, offset

(P-7118)
LCA PROMOTIONS INC
9545 Cozycroft Ave, Chatsworth
(91311-5102)
PHONE.....................................818 773-9170
Terrence R Aleck, *President*
EMP: 20
SQ FT: 6,200
SALES (est): 2.8MM **Privately Held**
WEB: www.lcapromotions.com
SIC: 2759 Screen printing

(P-7119)
LEGACY GRAPHICS LLC
1120 Bay Blvd Ste E, Chula Vista
(91911-7169)
PHONE.....................................619 585-1044
Janet Crowe, *Mng Member*
EMP: 10
SALES: 950K **Privately Held**
SIC: 2759 2399 3993 5999 Commercial
printing; banners, pennants & flags; banners, made from fabric; signs & advertising specialties; banners, flags, decals &
posters; commercial art & graphic design

(P-7120)
LEGION CREATIVE GROUP
1680 Vine St Ste 700, Los Angeles
(90028-8833)
PHONE.....................................323 498-1100
Kathleen Fliller, *Owner*
EMP: 25
SALES: 40MM **Privately Held**
SIC: 2759 Advertising literature: printing

(P-7121)
LIMPUS PRINTS INC
Also Called: Insight System Exchange
1820 S Santa Fe St, Santa Ana
(92705-4815)
PHONE.....................................714 545-5078
Pat Pester, *President*
EMP: 14 EST: 1997
SALES (est): 2.1MM **Privately Held**
SIC: 2759 Screen printing

(P-7122)
LITHOGRAPHIX INC
6200 Yarrow Dr, Carlsbad (92011-1537)
PHONE.....................................760 438-3456
Carl Davenport, *Manager*
EMP: 75
SALES (corp-wide): 117.2MM **Privately Held**
WEB: www.lithoxprep.com
SIC: 2759 2796 2789 2752 Screen print-
ing; platemaking services; bookbinding &
related work; commercial printing, litho-
graphic
PA: Lithographix, Inc.
12250 Crenshaw Blvd
Hawthorne CA 90250
323 770-1000

(P-7123)
LITHOTECH INTERNATIONAL LLC
9950 Baldwin Pl, El Monte (91731-2204)
PHONE.....................................626 443-4210
Shen Yen,
Shih-Yi Yang,
▲ EMP: 42
SALES (est): 4.1MM **Privately Held**
WEB: www.pop-international.com
SIC: 2759 Commercial printing

(P-7124)
LITHOTECHS INC
9950 Baldwin Pl, El Monte (91731-2204)
PHONE.....................................626 433-1333
Shen Yen, *CEO*
EMP: 12
SQ FT: 16,000
SALES (est): 2.3MM **Privately Held**
SIC: 2759 Commercial printing

(P-7125)
LPS AGENCY SALES AND POSTING
3210 El Camino Real # 200, Irvine
(92602-1368)
PHONE.....................................714 247-7500
Richard Teal, *Branch Mgr*
Danny Laughlin, *Info Tech Mgr*

EMP: 21
SALES (corp-wide): 500K **Privately Held**
SIC: 2759 Publication printing
PA: Lps Agency Sales And Posting Inc
3210 El Camino Real # 200
Irvine CA 92602
714 247-7503

(P-7126)
LUCKY DEVIL LLC
431 Atlas St, Brea (92821-3118)
PHONE.....................................714 990-2237
Timothy J Worcester,
EMP: 10
SALES (est): 1.2MM **Privately Held**
SIC: 2759 Screen printing

(P-7127)
LUCKY STAR SILKSCREEN LLC
Also Called: Golden Star Silk Screen
5767 E Washington Blvd, Commerce
(90040-2228)
PHONE.....................................323 728-4071
Timmy Trieu, *Mng Member*
Dino Ha,
EMP: 41
SALES (est): 1.2MM **Privately Held**
SIC: 2759 Screen printing

(P-7128)
M B C REPROGRAPHICS INC
Also Called: Mesa Reprographics
5560 Ruffin Rd Ste 5, San Diego
(92123-1332)
PHONE.....................................858 541-1500
Michael Atkins, *President*
Phyllis Atkins, *Admin Sec*
Karen Atkins, *Prdtn Mgr*
Olsen Greg, *Sales Mgr*
EMP: 22
SQ FT: 4,500
SALES (est): 3.8MM **Privately Held**
WEB: www.mesablueprint.com
SIC: 2759 7334 Commercial printing;
blueprinting service

(P-7129)
MAINETTI USA INC
17511 S Susana Rd, Compton
(90221-5405)
PHONE.....................................562 741-2920
Gabino Banuelos, *Branch Mgr*
Denise Gaudet, *Manager*
Santiago Rangel, *Manager*
EMP: 15
SALES (corp-wide): 12.5MM **Privately Held**
SIC: 2759 3089 Bag, wrapper & seal print-
ing & engraving; clothes hangers, plastic
HQ: Mainetti Usa Inc.
300 Mac Ln
Keasbey NJ 08832
201 215-2900

(P-7130)
MARCO FINE ARTS
4860 W 147th St, Hawthorne (90250-6706)
PHONE.....................................310 615-1818
Al Marco, *Principal*
Gabriella Carlstroem, *Manager*
▲ EMP: 80
SQ FT: 10,000
SALES (est): 12.5MM **Privately Held**
WEB: www.marcofinearts.com
SIC: 2759 5199 5023 Commercial print-
ing; art goods; frames & framing, picture
& mirror

(P-7131)
MARIA CORPORATION
Also Called: Reprodox
2760 S Harbor Blvd Ste C, Santa Ana
(92704-5827)
PHONE.....................................714 751-2460
Maria Cutler, *CEO*
Kevin David Cutler, *CFO*
Ulises Lopez, *Admin Sec*
EMP: 10
SQ FT: 3,200
SALES (est): 955.2K **Privately Held**
SIC: 2759 Commercial printing

▲ = Import ▼=Export
◆ =Import/Export

(P-7132)
MATRIX DOCUMENT IMAGING INC
527 E Rowland St Ste 214, Covina (91723-3267)
PHONE...............................626 966-9959
Thomas Smith, *President*
Mercedes Uribe, *Vice Pres*
EMP: 51
SALES (est): 5.9MM **Privately Held**
SIC: 2759 8111 Laser printing; legal services

(P-7133)
MEPCO LABEL SYSTEMS
1313 S Stockton St, Lodi (95240-5942)
PHONE...............................209 946-0201
Jennifer Tracy, *CEO*
Tom Gassner, *President*
Alfred M Gassner, *CEO*
Carol Gassner, *CEO*
Karl Gassner, *Exec VP*
EMP: 96
SQ FT: 83,000
SALES (est): 18.7MM **Privately Held**
WEB: www.mepcolabel.com
SIC: 2759 Publication printing; labels & seals: printing

(P-7134)
MERRILL CORPORATION
350 S Grand Ave Ste 3000, Los Angeles (90071-3424)
PHONE...............................213 253-5900
William Brahos, *Director*
Robert Stobie, *Vice Pres*
Matthew Weiss, *Software Dev*
Paulo Kneip, *Sr Project Mgr*
Manuel Tabb, *Manager*
EMP: 88
SALES (corp-wide): 566.6MM **Privately Held**
SIC: 2759 Commercial printing
PA: Merrill Corporation
1 Merrill Cir
Saint Paul MN 55108
651 646-4501

(P-7135)
MERRILL CORPORATION
10716 Reagan St, Los Alamitos (90720-2431)
PHONE...............................714 690-2200
Brian Merrill, *President*
Scott Beebe, *Accounts Mgr*
EMP: 88
SALES (corp-wide): 566.6MM **Privately Held**
SIC: 2759 Commercial printing
PA: Merrill Corporation
1 Merrill Cir
Saint Paul MN 55108
651 646-4501

(P-7136)
MERRILL CORPORATION
1731 Embarcadero Rd # 100, Palo Alto (94303-3339)
PHONE...............................650 493-1400
Don Conception, *Manager*
EMP: 30
SALES (corp-wide): 566.6MM **Privately Held**
WEB: www.merrillcorp.com
SIC: 2759 Commercial printing
PA: Merrill Corporation
1 Merrill Cir
Saint Paul MN 55108
651 646-4501

(P-7137)
MERRILL CORPORATION
8899 University Center Ln # 200, San Diego (92122-1065)
PHONE...............................858 623-0300
Jon Silgester, *Manager*
Ramiro Avalos, *Sr Project Mgr*
EMP: 87
SALES (corp-wide): 566.6MM **Privately Held**
WEB: www.merrillcorp.com
SIC: 2759 Commercial printing
PA: Merrill Corporation
1 Merrill Cir
Saint Paul MN 55108
651 646-4501

(P-7138)
MERRILL CORPORATION
14500 Reservation Rd, Salinas (93908-9251)
PHONE...............................831 759-9300
Brian Merrill, *Branch Mgr*
EMP: 15
SALES (corp-wide): 566.6MM **Privately Held**
WEB: www.merrillcorp.com
SIC: 2759 Commercial printing
PA: Merrill Corporation
1 Merrill Cir
Saint Paul MN 55108
651 646-4501

(P-7139)
MERRILL CORPORATION
Also Called: Merrill/Orange County
1900 Avenue Of The Stars # 1200, Los Angeles (90067-4403)
PHONE...............................949 252-9449
Nancy Dagostino, *Manager*
EMP: 12
SALES (corp-wide): 566.6MM **Privately Held**
WEB: www.merrillcorp.com
SIC: 2759 Financial note & certificate printing & engraving
PA: Merrill Corporation
1 Merrill Cir
Saint Paul MN 55108
651 646-4501

(P-7140)
MERRILL CORPORATION INC
10635 Santa Monica Blvd # 350, Los Angeles (90025-8300)
PHONE...............................310 552-5288
Fax: 310 552-5299
EMP: 25
SALES (corp-wide): 691.4MM **Privately Held**
SIC: 2759
PA: Merrill Corporation
1 Merrill Cir
Saint Paul MN 55108
651 646-4501

(P-7141)
MESA LABEL EXPRESS INC
13257 Kirkham Way, Poway (92064-7116)
PHONE...............................858 668-2820
James Teeter, *President*
Mary Ellen Teeter, *Treasurer*
EMP: 14
SQ FT: 10,000
SALES (est): 2.7MM **Privately Held**
WEB: www.mesalabel.com
SIC: 2759 2672 Labels & seals: printing; adhesive papers, labels or tapes: from purchased material

(P-7142)
MIDONNA INC
Also Called: Blue Engravers
1375 Caspian Ave, Long Beach (90813-2649)
PHONE...............................562 983-5140
Michael Leonar, *President*
EMP: 14
SALES (est): 700K **Privately Held**
SIC: 2759 Engraving

(P-7143)
MILLION CORPORATION
Also Called: Able Card Corporation
1300 W Optical Dr Ste 600, Irwindale (91702-3285)
PHONE...............................626 969-1888
Herman Ho, *CEO*
Donny Yu, *CFO*
Hector Dominguez, *Vice Pres*
EMP: 70
SQ FT: 45,000
SALES (est): 7.1MM **Privately Held**
WEB: www.ablecard.com
SIC: 2759 Commercial printing
PA: First Nations Capital Partners, Llc
7676 Hazard Center Dr # 5
San Diego CA 92108

(P-7144)
MIXONIC
1145 Polk St Ste A, San Francisco (94109-5541)
PHONE...............................866 838-5067
Robert Jacobson, *CEO*
EMP: 12
SALES (est): 27.1K **Privately Held**
WEB: www.mixonic.com
SIC: 2759 Commercial printing

(P-7145)
MORRISSEY BROS PRINTERS INC
929 E Slauson Ave, Los Angeles (90011-5239)
PHONE...............................323 233-7197
Donisle R Morrissey Jr, *President*
John B Jones, *Treasurer*
D R Morrisey III, *Vice Pres*
Jeanne Morrissey, *Admin Sec*
EMP: 25
SQ FT: 15,000
SALES (est): 2.9MM **Privately Held**
SIC: 2759 2752 7389 5111 Flexographic printing; commercial printing, lithographic; brokers' services; printing & writing paper; stationery stores; packaging paper & plastics film, coated & laminated

(P-7146)
NATIONWIDE PRINTING SVCS INC
400 Camino Vista Verde, San Clemente (92673-6815)
PHONE...............................714 258-7899
Lewis Gray, *President*
EMP: 10
SALES (est): 630K **Privately Held**
SIC: 2759 Commercial printing

(P-7147)
NELSON NAME PLATE COMPANY (PA)
Also Called: Nelson-Miller
2800 Casitas Ave, Los Angeles (90039-2942)
PHONE...............................323 663-3971
Hosmel Galan, *CEO*
Jim Kaldem, *President*
David Balce, *CFO*
Thomas Cassutt, *Co-President*
David Lazier, *Co-President*
▲ EMP: 182
SQ FT: 87,000
SALES (est): 62MM **Privately Held**
WEB: www.nelsonusa.com
SIC: 2759 3479 3993 2796 Screen printing; name plates: engraved, etched, etc.; signs & advertising specialties; platemaking services

(P-7148)
NEW DIRECTION SILK SCREEN
Also Called: Screenprintit.com
2328 Auburn Blvd Ste 2, Sacramento (95821-1706)
PHONE...............................916 971-3939
Ray Wise, *Owner*
EMP: 18
SQ FT: 18,000
SALES (est): 1.9MM **Privately Held**
WEB: www.screenprintit.com
SIC: 2759 5199 7389 Screen printing; advertising specialties; embroidering of advertising on shirts, etc.

(P-7149)
NORMEL INC
Also Called: Edward's Industries
12841 Blmfeld St Unit 104, Studio City (91604)
PHONE...............................818 504-4041
Milton Friedman, *President*
Norma Friedman, *Admin Sec*
▲ EMP: 18
SALES (est): 2.1MM **Privately Held**
WEB: www.edwardsindustries.com
SIC: 2759 Commercial printing

(P-7150)
NORTHERN CALIFORNIA LABELS INC
12809 Marquardt Ave, Santa Fe Springs (90670-4827)
P.O. Box 1693, La Mirada (90637-1693)
PHONE...............................562 802-8528
Ron Broussard, *President*
Alice Broussard, *Corp Secy*
EMP: 10
SQ FT: 6,000
SALES (est): 1.2MM **Privately Held**
WEB: www.nclabels.com
SIC: 2759 2752 Labels & seals: printing; commercial printing, lithographic

(P-7151)
ODDBOX HOLDINGS INC
Also Called: Purple Porcupine
16842 Hale Ave, Irvine (92606-5021)
PHONE...............................949 474-9222
Mark Swart, *Principal*
Carla Turna, *Principal*
Matthew Degroat, *Manager*
EMP: 11
SALES (est): 1.4MM **Privately Held**
SIC: 2759 Flexographic printing

(P-7152)
OFFICELOCALE INC
275 E Hillcrest Dr # 160, Thousand Oaks (91360-5827)
PHONE...............................805 777-8866
Zeeshan Husain, *Administration*
EMP: 11 EST: 2014
SALES (est): 1.1MM **Privately Held**
SIC: 2759 Commercial printing

(P-7153)
OKI GRAPHICS INC
2148 Zanker Rd, San Jose (95131-2113)
PHONE...............................408 451-9294
Yoon OH Kim, *President*
EMP: 16
SALES (est): 2MM **Privately Held**
WEB: www.okigraphics.com
SIC: 2759 Commercial printing

(P-7154)
OLYMPIC PRESS INC
461 Nelo St, Santa Clara (95054-2145)
PHONE...............................408 496-6222
Becky Bayot, *President*
Oliver Bayot, *Vice Pres*
EMP: 16
SALES (est): 1.6MM **Privately Held**
WEB: www.olympicpress.com
SIC: 2759 Letterpress printing

(P-7155)
OMEGA GRAPHICS PRINTING INC
7710 Kester Ave, Van Nuys (91405-1104)
PHONE...............................818 374-9189
Peter Smith, *President*
EMP: 12 EST: 2012
SALES (est): 1MM **Privately Held**
SIC: 2759 7336 Commercial printing; commercial art & graphic design

(P-7156)
ONE STOP LABEL CORPORATION
1641 S Baker Ave, Ontario (91761-8025)
PHONE...............................909 230-9380
Maria Navarro, *President*
Jorge Navarro, *Vice Pres*
EMP: 19
SQ FT: 12,000
SALES (est): 3.8MM **Privately Held**
WEB: www.onestoplabel.com
SIC: 2759 Labels & seals: printing

(P-7157)
OOSHIRTS INC (PA)
41454 Christy St, Fremont (94538-5105)
PHONE...............................866 660-8667
Raymond Lei, *President*
Rick Barger, *Facilities Mgr*
◆ EMP: 60
SALES (est): 192.5MM **Privately Held**
SIC: 2759 Screen printing

(P-7158)
OPTEC LASER SYSTEMS LLC
11622 El Camino Real, San Diego
(92130-2049)
PHONE.................................858 220-1070
John Roy,
EMP: 25
SALES (est): 1.1MM **Privately Held**
SIC: 2759 Laser printing

(P-7159)
ORANGE CIRCLE STUDIO CORP
Also Called: Studio OH
8687 Research Dr Ste 150, Irvine
(92618-4290)
PHONE.................................949 727-0800
Daniel Whang, *CEO*
Scott Whang, *Chairman*
Felicity Day, *Office Mgr*
Walter Robertson, *Director*
◆ EMP: 56
SQ FT: 10,000
SALES (est): 26MM **Privately Held**
SIC: 2759 Calendars: printing

(P-7160)
ORANGE CNTY PRTG GRAPHICS INC
303 Broadway St Ste 108, Laguna Beach
(92651-1816)
PHONE.................................949 464-9898
Joe Attie, *CEO*
EMP: 11
SALES (est): 179K **Privately Held**
SIC: 2759 7336 Commercial printing;
graphic arts & related design

(P-7161)
ORANGE COUNTY LABEL CO INC
301 W Dyer Rd Ste D, Santa Ana
(92707-3450)
PHONE.................................714 437-1010
Jerome Mattert, *President*
Jef Mattert, *Opers Mgr*
EMP: 13 EST: 1995
SQ FT: 3,500
SALES (est): 805.2K **Privately Held**
WEB: www.oclabel.com
SIC: 2759 Labels & seals: printing

(P-7162)
ORORA VISUAL LLC
1600 E Valencia Dr, Fullerton (92831-4735)
PHONE.................................714 879-2400
James R Hamel, *President*
▲ EMP: 100
SALES (est): 10.9MM **Privately Held**
WEB: www.graphictech.net
SIC: 2759 Screen printing

(P-7163)
ORORA VISUAL TX LLC
3116 W Avenue 32, Los Angeles
(90065-2317)
PHONE.................................323 258-4111
EMP: 70 **Privately Held**
SIC: 2759 Commercial printing
HQ: Orora Visual Tx Llc
3210 Innovative Way
Mesquite TX 75149
972 289-0705

(P-7164)
P E N INC
Also Called: News Publishers' Press
215 Allen Ave, Glendale (91201-2803)
PHONE.................................818 954-0775
Richard E Jutras, *CEO*
Jeffrey Jutras, *President*
Joven Calingo, *Info Tech Dir*
Cindy Morrison, *Controller*
Robert Garcia, *Plant Mgr*
EMP: 30 EST: 1978
SQ FT: 11,000
SALES (est): 3.3MM **Privately Held**
WEB: www.newspublisherspress.com
SIC: 2759 Newspapers: printing

(P-7165)
PACIFIC COLOR GRAPHICS INC
6336 Patterson Pass Rd A, Livermore
(94550-9577)
PHONE.................................925 600-3006
David A Rekart, *President*

Lynette Rekart, *CFO*
Rob Edwards, *Sales Mgr*
Chris Grimes, *Manager*
David Lamarche, *Accounts Exec*
EMP: 14
SQ FT: 1,200
SALES (est): 2.8MM **Privately Held**
WEB: www.pacificcolor.net
SIC: 2759 Screen printing

(P-7166)
PACIFIC CONTAINERPRINT INC
5951 Riverside Dr Apt 4, Chino
(91710-4477)
PHONE.................................909 465-0365
Michael E Wever, *President*
Debra Wever, *Treasurer*
Daniel P Wever, *Vice Pres*
EMP: 28
SQ FT: 9,300
SALES (est): 700K **Privately Held**
SIC: 2759 3993 Screen printing; signs &
advertising specialties

(P-7167)
PACIFIC LABEL INC
1511 E Edinger Ave, Santa Ana
(92705-4907)
PHONE.................................714 237-1276
Nick Valestrino, *President*
EMP: 98
SQ FT: 22,000
SALES (est): 10.1MM **Privately Held**
WEB: www.lable.com
SIC: 2759 Commercial printing

(P-7168)
PACIFIC THERMOGRAPHY
9550 Jellico Ave, Northridge (91325-2029)
PHONE.................................323 938-3349
Chang C Pak, *Owner*
Steven Pak, *Owner*
EMP: 20
SQ FT: 4,500
SALES (est): 1.7MM **Privately Held**
WEB: www.ptcprint.com
SIC: 2759 2752 Thermography; commer-
cial printing, offset

(P-7169)
PADYWELL CORP
835 Meridian St, Duarte (91010-3587)
PHONE.................................626 359-9149
▲ EMP: 20
SQ FT: 7,825
SALES (est): 1.4MM **Privately Held**
SIC: 2759

(P-7170)
PAW PRINTS INC
3166 Bay Rd, Redwood City (94063-3907)
PHONE.................................650 365-4077
John Garibaldi, *President*
Antionette Garibaldi, *Vice Pres*
EMP: 11
SALES: 800K **Privately Held**
WEB: www.pawprints.org
SIC: 2759 5199 3993 Screen printing; ad-
vertising specialties; signs & advertising
specialties

(P-7171)
PAX TAG & LABEL INC
9528 Rush St Ste C, El Monte
(91733-1551)
PHONE.................................626 579-2000
Michael Brown, *President*
EMP: 20
SQ FT: 10,000
SALES (est): 2.2MM **Privately Held**
WEB: www.paxtag.com
SIC: 2759 2679 Tags: printing; tags, paper
(unprinted): made from purchased paper

(P-7172)
PERFORMANCE LABEL INTL INC
6825 Gateway Park Dr # 1, San Diego
(92154-7530)
PHONE.................................619 429-6870
Harold Dreis, *President*
EMP: 12
SQ FT: 8,400
SALES (est): 1.9MM **Privately Held**
WEB: www.performancelabel.com
SIC: 2759 Screen printing

(P-7173)
PHEONICIA INC
710 E Parkridge Ave # 105, Corona
(92879-1097)
PHONE.................................951 268-5180
Ralph Azar, *CEO*
EMP: 10
SALES: 1.6MM **Privately Held**
SIC: 2759 Commercial printing

(P-7174)
PIXSCAN
Also Called: Scanart
1259 Park Ave, Emeryville (94608-3630)
PHONE.................................510 595-2222
Frederic Lompa, *President*
Kathy Lompa, *CFO*
EMP: 10
SQ FT: 5,000
SALES (est): 2.1MM **Privately Held**
WEB: www.scanart.com
SIC: 2759 Commercial printing

(P-7175)
PLASTI-PRINT INC
1620 Gilbreth Rd, Burlingame
(94010-1405)
PHONE.................................650 652-4950
Peter Vigil, *President*
Helen Vigil, *Corp Secy*
Adolf Vigil, *Vice Pres*
Rodney Vigil, *Vice Pres*
EMP: 10
SALES (est): 700K **Privately Held**
WEB: www.plasti-print.com
SIC: 2759 7389 2672 2396 Screen print-
ing; letterpress printing; laminating serv-
ice; coated & laminated paper;
automotive & apparel trimmings

(P-7176)
POLYCRAFT INC
42075 Avenida Alvarado, Temecula
(92590-3486)
PHONE.................................951 296-0860
William D Verstegen, *President*
Bryan Nealy, *Principal*
Patricia Verstegen, *Principal*
EMP: 20
SQ FT: 21,000
SALES (est): 1.6MM **Privately Held**
WEB: www.polycraftinc.com
SIC: 2759 2671 Screen printing; packag-
ing paper & plastics film, coated & lami-
nated

(P-7177)
POPULAR PRINTERS INC
3210 San Gabriel Blvd, Rosemead
(91770-2540)
PHONE.................................626 307-4281
Lihung Wang, *President*
Timothy Chu, *Vice Pres*
EMP: 10
SQ FT: 5,000
SALES (est): 1MM **Privately Held**
SIC: 2759 Commercial printing

(P-7178)
POSTCARD PRESS INC (PA)
Also Called: Next Day Flyers
8000 Haskell Ave, Van Nuys (91406-1321)
PHONE.................................310 747-3800
David Handmaker, *President*
◆ EMP: 31 EST: 1996
SALES (est): 8.5MM **Privately Held**
WEB: www.nextdayflyers.com
SIC: 2759 Visiting cards (including busi-
ness): printing

(P-7179)
PRESIDENT ENTERPRISE INC
Also Called: Lotus Labels
700 Columbia St, Brea (92821-2914)
PHONE.................................714 671-9577
George Wu, *President*
Lindsey Hand, *Sales Staff*
▲ EMP: 20
SQ FT: 22,000
SALES (est): 3.6MM **Privately Held**
WEB: www.lotuslabels.net
SIC: 2759 Labels & seals: printing

(P-7180)
PRESTIGE FOIL INC
13531 Fairmont Way, Tustin (92780-1808)
PHONE.................................714 556-1431
Charles Wingard, *President*
Anne Considine Wingard, *Corp Secy*
Mike Wingard, *Vice Pres*
Phil Wingard, *Vice Pres*
Phillip Wingard, *Principal*
EMP: 10
SQ FT: 5,000
SALES (est): 1.1MM **Privately Held**
SIC: 2759 Embossing on paper

(P-7181)
PRIMARY COLOR SYSTEMS CORP
401 Coral Cir, El Segundo (90245-4622)
PHONE.................................310 841-0250
Ed Philipps, *Branch Mgr*
Drew Haygeman, *Vice Pres*
Ed Phillips, *Division Mgr*
Zachary Peelor, *Project Mgr*
Brittany Webster, *Asst Controller*
EMP: 100
SALES (corp-wide): 61MM **Privately Held**
WEB: www.primarycolor.com
SIC: 2759 2752 Commercial printing;
commercial printing, lithographic
PA: Primary Color Systems Corporation
11130 Holder St
Cypress CA 90630
949 660-7080

(P-7182)
PRINT INK INC
Also Called: Build Your Own Garment
6918 Sierra Ct, Dublin (94568-2641)
PHONE.................................925 829-3950
Cathileen Marchese, *President*
EMP: 24
SALES (est): 2.8MM **Privately Held**
WEB: www.byoglogo.com
SIC: 2759 Screen printing

(P-7183)
PRINTING AND MARKETING INC
33200 Transit Ave, Union City
(94587-2035)
PHONE.................................510 931-7000
Stacy Mudd, *President*
Francisco Quiteno, *Manager*
EMP: 10
SALES (est): 856K **Privately Held**
SIC: 2759 5699 2754 Commercial print-
ing; T-shirts, custom printed; promotional
printing, gravure

(P-7184)
PRODIGY PRESS INC
1136 W Evelyn Ave, Sunnyvale
(94086-5742)
PHONE.................................408 962-0396
Alireza Azadan, *President*
EMP: 10
SALES (est): 1.9MM **Privately Held**
WEB: www.prodigypress.com
SIC: 2759 Advertising literature: printing

(P-7185)
PROFESSNAL RPRGRAPHIC SVCS INC
Also Called: Pro Group
17731 Cowan, Irvine (92614-6009)
PHONE.................................949 748-5400
Cindy Kennedy, *President*
Thomas Brian Kennedy, *CFO*
EMP: 25
SALES (est): 8MM **Privately Held**
SIC: 2759 Commercial printing

(P-7186)
PROGRAPHICS SCREENPRINTING INC
1975 Diamond St, San Marcos
(92078-5122)
PHONE.................................760 744-4555
Bruce Heid, *President*
Barbara Heid, *Vice Pres*
EMP: 41
SQ FT: 18,000

▲ = Import ▼=Export
◆ =Import/Export

SALES (est): 6.4MM **Privately Held**
SIC: 2759 3993 2396 5112 Screen printing; signs & advertising specialties; automotive & apparel trimmings; pens &/or pencils; embroidery products, except schiffli machine

(P-7187)
PROGRSSIVE INTGRATED SOLUTIONS
Also Called: Progressive Manufacturing
3700 E Miraloma Ave, Anaheim (92806-2107)
PHONE.....................714 237-0980
Rodney Dean Boehme, *President*
Doug Woodward, *Vice Pres*
EMP: 76
SQ FT: 30,000
SALES (est): 10.1MM **Privately Held**
SIC: 2759 2752 Envelopes: printing; commercial printing, offset

(P-7188)
QINGMU INTERNATIONAL INC
1055 Park View Dr Ste 119, Covina (91724-3735)
PHONE.....................626 965-7277
EMP: 50
SALES (est): 2.1MM **Privately Held**
SIC: 2759

(P-7189)
QUANTUM CHROMODYNAMICS INC
3703 W 190th St, Torrance (90504-5706)
PHONE.....................310 329-5000
David Hills, *President*
EMP: 15
SALES (est): 960K **Privately Held**
WEB: www.hillslasermarking.com
SIC: 2759 7389 Laser printing; engraving service

(P-7190)
QUEST INDUSTRIES LLC
Also Called: Quest Inds - Stockton Plant
2518 Boeing Way, Stockton (95206-3937)
PHONE.....................209 234-0202
Ryan Reid, *Branch Mgr*
EMP: 18
SALES (corp-wide): 19.4MM **Privately Held**
WEB: www.questllc.com
SIC: 2759 Labels & seals: printing
PA: Quest Industries Llc
15 Bleeker St Ste 202
Millburn NJ 07041
908 851-9070

(P-7191)
QUIKTURN PROF SCRNPRINTING INC
567 S Melrose St, Placentia (92870-6305)
PHONE.....................800 784-5419
Bill Allen, *CEO*
EMP: 15
SALES (est): 2.5MM **Privately Held**
SIC: 2759 Commercial printing

(P-7192)
R R DONNELLEY & SONS COMPANY
Also Called: R R Donnelley Financial
1888 Century Park E # 1650, Los Angeles (90067-1734)
PHONE.....................310 789-4100
Summer Carmichael, *Manager*
EMP: 11
SALES (corp-wide): 6.8B **Publicly Held**
WEB: www.rrdonnelley.com
SIC: 2759 Financial note & certificate printing & engraving
PA: R. R. Donnelley & Sons Company
35 W Wacker Dr
Chicago IL 60601
312 326-8000

(P-7193)
RAINBOW SUBLYMATION INC
2438 E 11th St, Los Angeles (90021-2938)
PHONE.....................213 489-5001
▲ EMP: 37
SALES (est): 2.7MM **Privately Held**
SIC: 2759

(P-7194)
RAOUL TEXTILES INC
Also Called: Raoul's Hand-Screened Yardage
110 Los Aguajes Ave, Santa Barbara (93101-3818)
PHONE.....................805 965-1694
Salley McQuillan, *President*
EMP: 16 EST: 2004
SALES (est): 1.9MM **Privately Held**
WEB: www.raoultextiles.com
SIC: 2759 Screen printing

(P-7195)
RESOURCE LABEL GROUP LLC
Also Called: Spectrum Label
30803 San Clemente St, Hayward (94544-7136)
PHONE.....................510 477-0707
EMP: 49
SALES (corp-wide): 238MM **Privately Held**
SIC: 2759 Flexographic printing
PA: Resource Label Group, Llc
147 Seaboard Ln
Franklin TN 37067
615 661-5900

(P-7196)
RESPONSE ENVELOPE INC (PA)
1340 S Baker Ave, Ontario (91761-7742)
PHONE.....................909 923-5855
Jonas Ulrich, *CEO*
Philip Ulrich, *Vice Pres*
▲ EMP: 104
SQ FT: 85,000
SALES (est): 19MM **Privately Held**
WEB: www.response-envelope.com
SIC: 2759 2677 Envelopes: printing; envelopes

(P-7197)
RESPONSE GRAPHICS IN PRINT
1065 La Mirada St, Laguna Beach (92651-3569)
PHONE.....................949 376-8701
▲ EMP: 12
SALES (est): 450K **Privately Held**
SIC: 2759

(P-7198)
RETAIL PRINT MEDIA INC
2355 Crenshaw Blvd # 135, Torrance (90501-3341)
PHONE.....................424 488-6950
Raymond Young, *CEO*
Karli Sikich, *COO*
Erika Whitmore, *Director*
Angelina Jungo, *Account Dir*
EMP: 35 EST: 2015
SALES (est): 3.6MM **Privately Held**
SIC: 2759 7371 Advertising literature: printing; computer software writing services

(P-7199)
REVOLUTION SCREENING INC (PA)
2523 Evergreen Ave, West Sacramento (95691-3013)
PHONE.....................916 604-6865
EMP: 15
SALES (est): 2.5MM **Privately Held**
SIC: 2759 Screen printing

(P-7200)
RHEETECH SALES & SERVICES INC
2401 S Main St, Los Angeles (90007-2727)
PHONE.....................213 749-9111
Brian Rhee, *President*
▲ EMP: 10
SQ FT: 10,000
SALES (est): 1.2MM **Privately Held**
WEB: www.prinsupply.com
SIC: 2759 Screen printing

(P-7201)
RJ ACQUISITION CORP (PA)
Also Called: Ad Art Company
3260 E 26th St, Vernon (90058-8008)
PHONE.....................323 318-1107
Joe M Demarco, *President*
Roger Keech, *CEO*
Todd Conrad, *Vice Pres*
Andrew Gorman, *Vice Pres*

Joseph Demarco, *Executive*
▲ EMP: 215
SQ FT: 200,000
SALES (est): 75.7MM **Privately Held**
WEB: www.adartco.com
SIC: 2759 Screen printing

(P-7202)
ROBERT R WIX INC (PA)
Also Called: Valley Printing
2140 Pine St, Ceres (95307-3620)
PHONE.....................209 537-4561
Robert R Wix, *President*
Linny Goodrich, *Vice Pres*
Tom Mink, *Vice Pres*
Mia Wix, *Manager*
EMP: 32 EST: 1959
SQ FT: 31,000
SALES (est): 5.5MM **Privately Held**
WEB: www.valleyptg.com
SIC: 2759 2752 2672 2671 Letterpress printing; commercial printing, offset; coated & laminated paper; packaging paper & plastics film, coated & laminated

(P-7203)
ROBINSON PRINTING INC
42685 Rio Nedo, Temecula (92590-3711)
PHONE.....................951 296-0300
David Robinson, *CEO*
Jeff Blount, *President*
Dennis Dibiasi, *President*
Mike Robinson, *President*
Steve Robinson, *Vice Pres*
▲ EMP: 25
SQ FT: 24,000
SALES (est): 4.4MM **Privately Held**
WEB: www.robinsonprinting.com
SIC: 2759 2621 Screen printing; packaging paper

(P-7204)
RR DONNELLEY & SONS COMPANY
Also Called: Donnelley Financial
19200 Von Karman Ave # 700, Irvine (92612-8518)
PHONE.....................949 852-1933
Ben Puente, *General Mgr*
Jeff Balcof, *Manager*
EMP: 40
SALES (corp-wide): 6.8B **Publicly Held**
WEB: www.rrdonnelllc.com
SIC: 2759 Commercial printing
PA: R. R. Donnelley & Sons Company
35 W Wacker Dr
Chicago IL 60601
312 326-8000

(P-7205)
RR DONNELLEY & SONS COMPANY
Los Angeles Manufacturing Div
19681 Pacific Gateway Dr, Torrance (90502-1116)
PHONE.....................310 516-3100
Barbara Dowell, *Data Proc Dir*
Edee Del Negro, *Purch Mgr*
EMP: 600
SQ FT: 80,000
SALES (corp-wide): 6.8B **Publicly Held**
WEB: www.rrdonnelley.com
SIC: 2759 2752 Publication printing; commercial printing, lithographic
PA: R. R. Donnelley & Sons Company
35 W Wacker Dr
Chicago IL 60601
312 326-8000

(P-7206)
SAFE PUBLISHING COMPANY
5775 Lindero Canyon Rd, Westlake Village (91362-4013)
PHONE.....................805 973-1300
John Gooden, *President*
EMP: 70 EST: 1976
SQ FT: 96,000
SALES (est): 5.4MM **Privately Held**
WEB: www.inside12x12.com
SIC: 2759 8748 8742 8741 Promotional printing; business consulting; management consulting services; management services; information retrieval services; special warehousing & storage

(P-7207)
SAN BRNRDINO CMNTY COLLEGE DST
Also Called: Print Shop
701 S Mount Vernon Ave, San Bernardino (92410-2705)
PHONE.....................909 888-6511
Louie Chavira, *Supervisor*
EMP: 163
SALES (corp-wide): 46.5MM **Privately Held**
WEB: www.sbvc.sbccd.cc.ca.us
SIC: 2759 Commercial printing
PA: San Bernardino Community College District
114 S Del Rosa Dr
San Bernardino CA 92408
909 382-4000

(P-7208)
SCREEN ART INC
15162 Triton Ln, Huntington Beach (92649-1041)
PHONE.....................714 891-4185
James K Proctor, *President*
EMP: 17
SQ FT: 8,400
SALES (est): 2.2MM **Privately Held**
WEB: www.screenartinc.com
SIC: 2759 Screen printing

(P-7209)
SCREEN PRINTERS RESOURCE INC
1251 Burton St, Fullerton (92831-5211)
PHONE.....................714 441-1155
Frank Sator, *President*
▲ EMP: 16
SQ FT: 20,000
SALES (est): 2.7MM **Privately Held**
WEB: www.spresource.com
SIC: 2759 Screen printing

(P-7210)
SCREENWORKS CO TIM
Also Called: Tcth Screenworks
1705 W 134th St, Gardena (90249-2032)
PHONE.....................310 532-7239
Cheryl Hughes, *President*
EMP: 20
SALES (est): 1.8MM **Privately Held**
SIC: 2759 Screen printing

(P-7211)
SHIHS PRINTING
673 Monterey Pass Rd, Monterey Park (91754-2418)
PHONE.....................626 281-2989
Catherine Shih, *Owner*
EMP: 15 EST: 1989
SALES (est): 934.2K **Privately Held**
SIC: 2759 Magazines: printing

(P-7212)
SHORETT PRINTING INC (PA)
Also Called: Crown Printers
250 W Rialto Ave, San Bernardino (92408-1017)
PHONE.....................714 545-4689
Charles D Shorett Jr, *CEO*
John Shorett, *Vice Pres*
Mike Brusig, *Executive*
Erin Franco, *Business Mgr*
Eric Shorett, *Sales Staff*
EMP: 40 EST: 1970
SALES (est): 6.4MM **Privately Held**
WEB: www.crownconnect.com
SIC: 2759 2752 Commercial printing; commercial printing, offset

(P-7213)
SINCLAIR SYSTEMS INTL LLC
3115 S Willow Ave, Fresno (93725-9349)
PHONE.....................559 233-4500
Erik A Gregerson, *President*
Edward Clapp, *CFO*
Paula Cooke, *Bd of Directors*
Colin Woodward, *Officer*
Slaten Vansaun, *Technology*
▲ EMP: 11
SQ FT: 4,100

(PA)=Parent Co (HQ)=Headquarters (DH)=Div Headquarters
✿ = New Business established in last 2 years

2020 California
Manufacturers Register

297

PRODUCTS & SVCS

SALES (est): 3.2MM
SALES (corp-wide): 93.8MM **Privately Held**
WEB: www.sinclair-intl.com
SIC: 2759 7389 2672 Decals: printing; packaging & labeling services; coated & laminated paper
HQ: Sinclair International Limited
Jarrold Way Bowthorpe Employment Area
Norwich NR5 9

(P-7214)
SINE-TIFIC SOLUTIONS INC
1701 Fortune Dr Ste C, San Jose
(95131-1702)
PHONE..........................408 432-3434
Bruce McGuire, *President*
Franklin Pennell, *Vice Pres*
EMP: 12
SQ FT: 6,000
SALES (est): 2MM **Privately Held**
WEB: www.engravers.com
SIC: 2759 7389 Screen printing; engraving service

(P-7215)
SIRENA INCORPORATED
Also Called: Los Angeles Wraps
22717 S Western Ave, Torrance
(90501-4952)
PHONE..........................866 548-5353
Brandon Park, *CEO*
EMP: 16
SQ FT: 10,000
SALES: 1.5MM **Privately Held**
SIC: 2759 Commercial printing

(P-7216)
SKIVA GRAPHICS SCREEN PRTG INC
2258 Rutherford Rd Ste A, Carlsbad
(92008-8824)
PHONE..........................760 602-9124
Leon Monfort, *President*
EMP: 40
SQ FT: 42,078
SALES (est): 14.5MM **Privately Held**
WEB: www.skivagraphics.com
SIC: 2759 7336 3993 Screen printing; commercial art & graphic design; signs & advertising specialties

(P-7217)
SMITH PRINTING CORPORATION
17344 Eastman, Irvine (92614-5522)
P.O. Box 18211 (92623-8211)
PHONE..........................949 250-9709
Michael Brian Smith, *President*
EMP: 12
SALES (est): 677.4K **Privately Held**
SIC: 2759 2631 Commercial printing; packaging board

(P-7218)
SOFT TOUCH INC
Also Called: Mojado Bros
1830 E Miraloma Ave Ste C, Placentia
(92870-6744)
PHONE..........................714 524-3382
Mike Rodriguez, *President*
EMP: 10
SQ FT: 7,300
SALES (est): 885.6K **Privately Held**
SIC: 2759 Screen printing

(P-7219)
SONOMA PINS ETC CORPORATION
Also Called: Sonoma Promotional Solutions
841 W Napa St, Sonoma (95476-6414)
PHONE..........................707 996-9956
Bernard Friedman, *President*
Judy Friedman, *Exec VP*
Barb Wendel, *Graphic Designe*
Jacob Powell, *Business Mgr*
Nickolai Mathison, *VP Sales*
▲ **EMP:** 99
SQ FT: 600
SALES (est): 11.6MM **Privately Held**
WEB: www.sonoma88188.com
SIC: 2759 Promotional printing

(P-7220)
SOUTH SWELL SCREEN ARTS
8440 Production Ave, San Diego
(92121-2203)
PHONE..........................858 566-3095
Allen Repashy, *Owner*
EMP: 10
SQ FT: 6,000
SALES (est): 910.2K **Privately Held**
WEB: www.southswellcorp.com
SIC: 2759 3993 2396 Screen printing; signs & advertising specialties; automotive & apparel trimmings

(P-7221)
SOUTHWEST OFFSET PRTG CO INC
Also Called: San Francisco Offset Printing
587 Charcot Ave, San Jose (95131-2202)
PHONE..........................408 232-5160
Ed Tervol, *Branch Mgr*
EMP: 85
SALES (corp-wide): 115.9MM **Privately Held**
WEB: www.southwestoffset.com
SIC: 2759 2789 2752 Commercial printing; bookbinding & related work; commercial printing, lithographic
PA: Southwest Offset Printing Co., Inc.
13650 Gramercy Pl
Gardena CA 90249
310 965-9154

(P-7222)
SPARTAN
444 E Taylor St, San Jose (95112-3137)
PHONE..........................800 743-6950
EMP: 22 **EST:** 2014
SALES (est): 800.5K **Privately Held**
SIC: 2759 Screen printing

(P-7223)
SPECIALIZED SCREEN PRINTING
18435 Bandilier Cir, Fountain Valley
(92708-7012)
PHONE..........................714 964-1230
David Williams, *CEO*
Jim Keisker, *President*
Mark Brown, *Info Tech Dir*
EMP: 32
SQ FT: 20,000
SALES (est): 4.2MM **Privately Held**
WEB: www.specializedscreenprinting.com
SIC: 2759 2752 2396 Screen printing; commercial printing, lithographic; automotive & apparel trimmings

(P-7224)
SPECTRAPRINT INC
24 Moody Ct, San Rafael (94901-1029)
PHONE..........................415 460-1228
EMP: 16
SQ FT: 12,800
SALES (est): 1.8MM **Privately Held**
WEB: www.spectraprintinc.com
SIC: 2759

(P-7225)
SPINELLI GRAPHIC INC
10621 Bloomfield St Ste 2, Los Alamitos
(90720-6729)
PHONE..........................562 431-3232
Joseph Spinelli, *President*
Renee Spinelli, *Admin Sec*
EMP: 11
SALES: 1.2MM **Privately Held**
WEB: www.spinelligraphics.com
SIC: 2759 2752 Screen printing; commercial printing, lithographic

(P-7226)
SPREAD EFFECT LLC
7580 Fay Ave Ste 304, La Jolla
(92037-4849)
PHONE..........................888 705-1127
Ryan Sandberg, *CEO*
Alyssa Vincent, *Director*
EMP: 29
SALES (est): 440.8K
SALES (corp-wide): 4.7MM **Privately Held**
SIC: 2759 Advertising literature: printing

PA: Adduco Media, Llc
3130 W Maple Loop Dr
Lehi UT 84043
385 204-3242

(P-7227)
STEVEN LABEL CORPORATION
9046 Sorensen Ave, Santa Fe Springs
(90670-2641)
PHONE..........................562 906-2612
John McCullough, *Controller*
Karyn Will, *Controller*
EMP: 10
SALES (corp-wide): 54.2MM **Privately Held**
WEB: www.stevenlabel.com
SIC: 2759 Letterpress printing; screen printing; flexographic printing
PA: Steven Label Corporation
11926 Burke St
Santa Fe Springs CA 90670
562 698-9971

(P-7228)
STEVEN LABEL CORPORATION
11926 Burke St, Santa Fe Springs
(90670-2546)
PHONE..........................562 698-9971
EMP: 10
SALES (corp-wide): 54.2MM **Privately Held**
WEB: www.stevenlabel.com
SIC: 2759 Letterpress printing; screen printing; flexographic printing
PA: Steven Label Corporation
11926 Burke St
Santa Fe Springs CA 90670
562 698-9971

(P-7229)
STICKER HUB INC
Also Called: Plush Printing
1452 Manhattan Ave, Fullerton
(92831-5222)
PHONE..........................714 912-8457
Sean W Wigand, *CEO*
EMP: 11 **EST:** 2010
SALES (est): 1.1MM **Privately Held**
SIC: 2759 Commercial printing

(P-7230)
STONE PUBLISHING INC (PA)
Also Called: Almaden
2549 Scott Blvd, Santa Clara (95050-2508)
PHONE..........................408 450-7910
Eric Stern, *Ch of Bd*
Chris Siebert, *CEO*
Almos Adorjan, *Vice Pres*
Audrey Paulson, *Administration*
Dave Marks, *Info Tech Mgr*
EMP: 110
SQ FT: 100,000
SALES: 30MM **Privately Held**
WEB: www.almadenpress.com
SIC: 2759 Promotional printing

(P-7231)
STRATEGIC PRTG SOLUTION INC
3731 San Gabriel River Pk, Pico Rivera
(90660-1498)
PHONE..........................562 242-5880
Sarabjit Singh Bedi, *CEO*
EMP: 11
SALES (est): 172.7K **Privately Held**
SIC: 2759 Commercial printing
PA: Strategic Designs Private Limited
46/6,
New Delhi DL

(P-7232)
STREAMLINE DSIGN SLKSCREEN INC
Also Called: Iron and Resin
1328 N Ventura Ave, Ventura (93001-1546)
PHONE..........................805 884-1025
Tom Hill, *President*
EMP: 10 **Privately Held**
SIC: 2759 Screen printing
PA: Streamline Design & Silkscreen, Inc.
1299 S Wells Rd
Ventura CA 93004

(P-7233)
SUNWEST PRINTING INC
118 E Airport Dr Ste 209, San Bernardino
(92408-3419)
PHONE..........................909 890-3898
Nick Lopez, *President*
John Lopez, *Vice Pres*
EMP: 12
SQ FT: 8,500
SALES (est): 1.8MM **Privately Held**
WEB: www.sunwestprint.com
SIC: 2759 2789 Screen printing; bookbinding & related work

(P-7234)
SUPER COLOR DIGITAL LLC (PA)
16761 Hale Ave, Irvine (92606-5006)
PHONE..........................949 622-0010
Peyman Rashtchi, *Mng Member*
▲ **EMP:** 25
SQ FT: 48,043
SALES (est): 66.2MM **Privately Held**
SIC: 2759 Commercial printing

(P-7235)
SUPERIOR PRINTING INC
Also Called: Superior Press
9440 Norwalk Blvd, Santa Fe Springs
(90670-2928)
PHONE..........................888 590-7998
Robert Traut, *President*
Jason Traut, *Treasurer*
Frank Marquez, *Vice Pres*
Steve Traut, *Vice Pres*
Kevin Traut, *Admin Sec*
EMP: 95
SQ FT: 32,000
SALES (est): 25.2MM **Privately Held**
WEB: www.superior-press.com
SIC: 2759 5112 Commercial printing; business forms

(P-7236)
SYNECTIC PACKAGING INC
1201 San Luis Obispo St, Hayward
(94544-7915)
PHONE..........................650 474-0132
Joe Iskander, *President*
Gil Dulong, *Vice Pres*
Dave Hoydal, *Vice Pres*
Andy Pena, *Vice Pres*
▲ **EMP:** 10
SQ FT: 10,000
SALES (est): 1.3MM **Privately Held**
SIC: 2759 5999 Flexographic printing; packaging materials: boxes, padding, etc.

(P-7237)
TACKETT VOLUME PRESS INC
1348 Terminal St, West Sacramento
(95691-3515)
PHONE..........................916 374-8991
Ron Tackett, *President*
EMP: 28
SQ FT: 45,000
SALES (est): 6.2MM **Privately Held**
WEB: www.volumepress.com
SIC: 2759 Commercial printing

(P-7238)
TAILGATE PRINTING INC
2930 S Fairview St, Santa Ana
(92704-6503)
PHONE..........................714 966-3035
Maria C Vega, *President*
Colleen Madrid, *Executive*
EMP: 147
SQ FT: 80,000
SALES (est): 8.8MM **Privately Held**
SIC: 2759 Letterpress printing

(P-7239)
TARGET MEDIA PARTNERS (HQ)
Also Called: Target Mdia Prtners Intractive
5200 Lankershim Blvd, North Hollywood
(91601-3155)
PHONE..........................323 930-3123
Dave Duckwitz, *CEO*
Mark Salcido, *Senior VP*
Boris Bronshteyn, *Vice Pres*
Jason Hays, *Vice Pres*
Eve Minogue, *Vice Pres*
EMP: 15

▲ = Import ▼=Export
◆ =Import/Export

SALES (est): 2.5MM
SALES (corp-wide): 24.4MM **Privately Held**
WEB: www.targetmediapartners.com
SIC: **2759** 7331 Commercial printing; direct mail advertising services
PA: Responselogix, Inc.
    6991 E Camelback Rd B300
    Scottsdale AZ 85251
    408 220-6545

(P-7240)
TAYLOR GRAPHICS INC
1582 Browning, Irvine (92606-4807)
PHONE..................................949 752-5200
Dean S Taylor, *CEO*
Carla Spicer, *Admin Sec*
EMP: 23
SQ FT: 7,500
SALES (est): 4.1MM **Privately Held**
SIC: **2759** Screen printing

(P-7241)
TEC COLOR CRAFT (PA)
Also Called: TEC Color Craft Products
1860 Wright Ave, La Verne (91750-5824)
PHONE..................................909 392-9000
Edgar A Frenkiel, *CEO*
Dave Marsh, *Purchasing*
Martin Serrano, *Prdtn Mgr*
Jim Evans, *VP Sales*
Blake Frenkiel, *Marketing Mgr*
▲ EMP: 40
SQ FT: 8,000
SALES (est): 6.2MM **Privately Held**
WEB: www.teccolorcraft.com
SIC: **2759** Screen printing

(P-7242)
TECHNICAL SCREEN PRINTING INC
677 N Hariton St, Orange (92868-1311)
PHONE..................................714 541-8590
Robert Golino, *President*
Barbara Golino, *Vice Pres*
EMP: 35
SQ FT: 18,000
SALES (est): 3.5MM **Privately Held**
SIC: **2759** 2752 2396 Screen printing; commercial printing, lithographic; automotive & apparel trimmings

(P-7243)
TELECARD LLC
220 Bingham Dr Ste 101, San Marcos (92069-1482)
PHONE..................................760 752-1700
Alan Saloner, *Mng Member*
EMP: 15
SALES (est): 570K **Privately Held**
SIC: **2759** Visiting cards (including business): printing .

(P-7244)
TEMECULA T-SHIRT PRINTERS INC
41607 Enterprise Cir N A, Temecula (92590-5684)
PHONE..................................951 296-0184
Kenneth Dawkins, *President*
EMP: 15
SALES (est): 469.5K **Privately Held**
SIC: **2759** Screen printing

(P-7245)
TERRAMAR GRAPHICS INC
5345 Townsgate Rd Ste 330, Westlake Village (91361)
PHONE..................................805 529-8845
Elaine Mc Coy, *Owner*
Stan Lazuka, *Sales Staff*
EMP: 14
SQ FT: 4,000
SALES (est): 1.5MM **Privately Held**
SIC: **2759** 5112 Business forms: printing; business forms

(P-7246)
TEXTILE 2000 SCREEN PRINTING
Also Called: Frontline Military Apparel
8675 Miralani Dr, San Diego (92126-4355)
PHONE..................................858 735-8521
Keith Gentry, *Owner*
Colin Wickersheim, *Accounts Exec*

EMP: 23 EST: 1999
SALES (est): 1.5MM **Privately Held**
SIC: **2759** Screen printing

(P-7247)
THE LIGATURE INC
Echelon Fine Printing
750 Gilmore St, Berkeley (94710)
PHONE..................................510 526-5181
Baird Conner, *General Mgr*
EMP: 30
SALES (corp-wide): 2.8B **Privately Held**
WEB: www.theligature.com
SIC: **2759** 2752 Commercial printing; commercial printing, lithographic
HQ: The Ligature Inc
    4909 Alcoa Ave
    Vernon CA 90058
    323 585-6000

(P-7248)
THERAPEUTIC RES FACULTY LLC
3120 W March Ln, Stockton (95219-2368)
PHONE..................................209 472-2240
Wes Crews, *CEO*
EMP: 200
SALES (est): 4MM **Privately Held**
SIC: **2759** Publication printing

(P-7249)
THERMCRAFT INC
3762 Bradview Dr, Sacramento (95827-9702)
PHONE..................................916 363-9411
Ray Summers, *President*
Maurine Summers, *Vice Pres*
EMP: 16
SQ FT: 4,600
SALES (est): 2.4MM **Privately Held**
WEB: www.thermcraft.com
SIC: **2759** Commercial printing

(P-7250)
THREE MAN CORPORATION
Also Called: San Diego Printers
10025 Huennekens St, San Diego (92121-2957)
PHONE..................................858 684-5200
John Barros, *President*
Wayne Ihms, *Vice Pres*
EMP: 20
SQ FT: 14,000
SALES (est): 3.7MM **Privately Held**
WEB: www.sdprinters.com
SIC: **2759** 2752 Commercial printing; commercial printing, lithographic

(P-7251)
TJ GIANT LLC
12623 Cisneros Ln, Santa Fe Springs (90670-3373)
PHONE..................................562 906-1060
Peter D Ahn,
EMP: 900 EST: 2008
SQ FT: 1,500
SALES (est): 5.1MM **Privately Held**
SIC: **2759** Screen printing

(P-7252)
TOP PRINTING & GRAPHIC INC
1210 N Knollwood Cir, Anaheim (92801-1309)
PHONE..................................714 484-9200
Kyu H Yoon, *President*
EMP: 10
SQ FT: 14,000
SALES (est): 605K **Privately Held**
SIC: **2759** Commercial printing

(P-7253)
TOTTY PRINTING
18946 Spectacular Bid Ln, Yorba Linda (92886-7000)
PHONE..................................714 633-7081
Thomas Totty, *Owner*
EMP: 10
SALES (est): 991.2K **Privately Held**
WEB: www.tottyprinting.com
SIC: **2759** Screen printing

(P-7254)
TRADE ONLY SCREEN PRINTING INC
Also Called: Curry Graphics
23482 Foley St, Hayward (94545-5308)
P.O. Box 5698, Concord (94524-0698)
PHONE..................................510 887-2020
Patrick T Bryson, *President*
Richard Ayres, *President*
EMP: 20
SQ FT: 15,000
SALES (est): 2.5MM **Privately Held**
SIC: **2759** 2396 Screen printing; promotional printing; automotive & apparel trimmings

(P-7255)
TRANSCONTINENTAL NRTHERN CA 20
47540 Kato Rd, Fremont (94538-7303)
PHONE..................................510 580-7700
Brian Reid, *CEO*
Francois Olivier, *Principal*
Vivian Marzin McKay, *Finance*
▲ EMP: 200
SALES (est): 42MM
SALES (corp-wide): 1.6B **Privately Held**
SIC: **2759** Magazines: printing
PA: Transcontinental Inc
    1 Place Ville-Marie Bureau 3240
    Montreal QC H3B 0
    514 954-4000

(P-7256)
TRI-CITY TECHNOLOGIES INC
Also Called: Tri-City Print & Mail
2615 Del Monte St, West Sacramento (95691-3809)
PHONE..................................916 503-5300
Charles F Sievers Jr, *President*
EMP: 16
SQ FT: 10,000
SALES (est): 1.5MM **Privately Held**
WEB: www.tricitytech.net
SIC: **2759** 7331 Advertising literature: printing; direct mail advertising services

(P-7257)
TRISAR INC
2200 W Orangewood Ave # 235, Orange (92868-1975)
PHONE..................................714 972-2626
James Bell, *President*
▲ EMP: 40
SALES (est): 4.4MM
SALES (corp-wide): 2.4B **Publicly Held**
SIC: **2759** 2261 Screen printing; screen printing of cotton broadwoven fabrics
HQ: Amscan Inc.
    80 Grasslands Rd Ste 3
    Elmsford NY 10523
    914 345-2020

(P-7258)
TURNER GROUP PUBLICATIONS INC
27788 Klaus Ct, Hayward (94542-2366)
PHONE...............................:408 297-3299
EMP: 11
SALES (est): 2MM **Privately Held**
SIC: **2759**

(P-7259)
UNITECH DECO INC
Also Called: Unitech Industries
19731 Bahama St, Northridge (91324-3304)
PHONE..................................818 700-1373
Merle Wurm, *President*
Tina Wurm-Donikian, *Treasurer*
EMP: 34
SQ FT: 9,000
SALES (est): 3.8MM **Privately Held**
SIC: **2759** 2789 2396 Bag, wrapper & seal printing & engraving; bookbinding & related work; automotive & apparel trimmings

(P-7260)
UNIVERSAL LABEL PRINTERS INC
Also Called: Unilabel
13003 Los Nietos Rd, Santa Fe Springs (90670-3348)
P.O. Box 3648 (90670-1648)
PHONE..................................562 944-0234
John Walsh, *President*
Patricia Walsh, *Treasurer*
Jack Walsh, *Vice Pres*
Kathleen Mulcahey, *Admin Sec*
Paul Mulcahey, *Human Res Mgr*
EMP: 22
SQ FT: 30,000
SALES (est): 3.2MM **Privately Held**
WEB: www.universallabel.com
SIC: **2759** Labels & seals: printing; tags: printing

(P-7261)
US1COM INC
715 Southpoint Blvd Ste D, Petaluma (94954-6836)
P.O. Box 3303, Santa Fe Springs (90670-1303)
PHONE..................................707 781-2560
EMP: 17
SQ FT: 5,417
SALES: 614.2K **Privately Held**
WEB: www.us1com.com
SIC: **2759**
PA: A F E Industries Inc.
    13233 Barton Cir
    Whittier CA 90605

(P-7262)
VENTURA PRINTING INC (PA)
Also Called: V3
200 N Elevar St, Oxnard (93030-7969)
PHONE..................................805 981-2600
David Wilson, *President*
▲ EMP: 100
SALES (est): 14.6MM **Privately Held**
SIC: **2759** Commercial printing

(P-7263)
VITACHROME GRAPHICS INC
3710 Park Pl, Montrose (91020-1623)
P.O. Box 2924, Santa Fe Springs (90670-0924)
PHONE..................................818 957-0900
Gary Durbin, *President*
Tony Won, *Vice Pres*
Jeanne De Guzman, *Opers Mgr*
EMP: 45
SQ FT: 43,000
SALES (est): 5.4MM **Privately Held**
WEB: www.vitachrome.com
SIC: **2759** Decals: printing; screen printing; labels & seals: printing

(P-7264)
VOMAR PRODUCTS INC
7800 Deering Ave, Canoga Park (91304-5005)
PHONE..................................818 610-5115
Paul Van Ostrand, *CEO*
Herbert Paul Van Ostrand, *President*
Jason Van Ostrand, *Vice Pres*
John Barmaan, *General Mgr*
Anh Nguyen, *Info Tech Mgr*
EMP: 38
SQ FT: 29,000
SALES (est): 6.1MM **Privately Held**
WEB: www.vomarproducts.com
SIC: **2759** 3993 Commercial printing; name plates: except engraved, etched, etc.: metal

(P-7265)
WARREN PACKAGING INC
1722 E Grevillea Ct, Ontario (91761-8035)
PHONE..................................909 923-0613
Philip Chaffey Warren, *CEO*
Mike Dittenber, *Exec Dir*
Kristen Ackerman, *Sales Staff*
Philip Warren, *Sales Staff*
EMP: 12
SQ FT: 7,000
SALES (est): 7MM **Privately Held**
SIC: **2759** Commercial printing

(P-7266)
WAY OF THE WORLD INC
170 Commercial St, Sunnyvale
(94086-5201)
PHONE..............................408 616-7700
Mark Johnson, *President*
Karen Thomas, *Vice Pres*
EMP: 10
SQ FT: 5,000
SALES (est): 1.2MM **Privately Held**
SIC: 2759 Commercial printing

(P-7267)
WES GO INC
Also Called: GP Color Imaging Group
8211 Lankershim Blvd, North Hollywood
(91605-1614)
PHONE..............................818 504-1200
Wesley Adams, *CEO*
Thomas Wilhelm, *President*
Wes Adams, *Info Tech Mgr*
Jorge Galvez, *Prdtn Mgr*
▲ EMP: 24
SALES (est): 3.6MM **Privately Held**
WEB: www.gpcolor.com
SIC: 2759 Posters, including billboards:
printing

(P-7268)
WESTERN DIE & PRINTING CORP
3109 Casitas Ave, Los Angeles
(90039-2410)
PHONE..............................323 665-0474
Saied Toobian, *President*
▲ EMP: 12
SALES (est): 1.5MM **Privately Held**
SIC: 2759 Commercial printing

(P-7269)
WESTERN ROTO ENGRAVERS INC
Also Called: W R E Colortech
1225 6th St, Berkeley (94710-1488)
PHONE..............................510 525-2950
Bill Mackay, *Manager*
Kathleen Harrelson, *CFO*
Daniel Comerford, *Vice Pres*
John Comerford, *VP Bus Dvlpt*
EMP: 12
SALES (corp-wide): 11.7MM **Privately Held**
WEB: www.wrecolor.com
SIC: 2759 2796 Engraving; plates & cylinders for rotogravure printing
PA: Western Roto Engravers, Incorporated
533 Banner Ave
Greensboro NC 27401
336 275-9821

(P-7270)
WESTERN YANKEE INC
13233 Barton Cir, Whittier (90605-3255)
PHONE..............................562 944-6889
Fred Elhami, *President*
EMP: 30
SQ FT: 18,000
SALES: 2.2MM **Privately Held**
WEB: www.westernyankee.com
SIC: 2759 Letterpress & screen printing;
imprinting; letterpress printing
PA: A F E Industries Inc.
13233 Barton Cir
Whittier CA 90605

(P-7271)
WHATS HAPPENING TRI CITY
Also Called: Tri City Voice
39120 Argonaut Way # 335, Fremont
(94538-1304)
PHONE..............................510 494-1999
William Marshak, *Owner*
Sharon Marshak, *Co-Owner*
EMP: 30
SALES (est): 2.2MM **Privately Held**
SIC: 2759 5192 Magazines: printing;
newspapers: printing; newspapers

(P-7272)
WILSONS ART STUDIO INC
Also Called: Solutions Unlimited
501 S Acacia Ave, Fullerton (92831-5101)
PHONE..............................714 870-7030
William L Goetsch, *President*

Roberta C Goetsch, *Corp Secy*
N Jim Goetsch, *Vice Pres*
EMP: 63 EST: 1958
SQ FT: 50,000
SALES (est): 8.1MM **Privately Held**
SIC: 2759 2396 Screen printing; automotive & apparel trimmings

(P-7273)
WINTFLASH INC
Also Called: Print Shop, The
13720 De Alcala Dr, La Mirada
(90638-3622)
PHONE..............................562 944-6548
Scott Flasher, *President*
Joy Flasher, *Corp Secy*
EMP: 11 EST: 1997
SQ FT: 3,000
SALES (est): 600K **Privately Held**
SIC: 2759 Commercial printing

(P-7274)
WIZARD GRAPHICS INC
411 Otterson Dr Ste 20, Chico
(95928-8241)
P.O. Box 7650 (95927-7650)
PHONE..............................530 893-3636
Merlin Newkirk, *President*
EMP: 15
SQ FT: 10,000
SALES (est): 1.1MM **Privately Held**
SIC: 2759 Commercial printing

(P-7275)
XYZ GRAPHICS INC (PA)
190 Lombard St, San Francisco
(94111-1111)
PHONE..............................415 227-9972
Steven Waterloo, *President*
Charlie Boyle, *Exec VP*
Sean McGlynn, *Exec VP*
Sean Mc Glynn, *Vice Pres*
John Gatewood, *Project Mgr*
EMP: 29
SQ FT: 8,500
SALES (est): 4MM **Privately Held**
WEB: www.xygraphics.com
SIC: 2759 Commercial printing

(P-7276)
YELLOW LETTERS INC
5908 Dartmoor Wood Ave, Bakersfield
(93314-8012)
PHONE..............................661 864-7860
Michael Quarles, *Owner*
EMP: 12
SALES (est): 1.7MM **Privately Held**
SIC: 2759 Commercial printing

(P-7277)
YENOR INC
Also Called: Library Mosacis
5640 W 63rd St, Los Angeles
(90056-2013)
PHONE..............................310 410-1573
Raymond Rony, *President*
EMP: 10
SALES: 175K **Privately Held**
SIC: 2759 Magazines: printing

(P-7278)
ZUZA
2304 Faraday Ave, Carlsbad (92008-7216)
PHONE..............................760 438-9411
EMP: 50 EST: 2011
SALES (est): 4.3MM **Privately Held**
SIC: 2759

2761 Manifold Business Forms

(P-7279)
APPERSON INC (PA)
17315 Studebaker Rd # 209, Cerritos
(90703-2508)
PHONE..............................562 356-3333
Kelly Doherty, *CEO*
William Apperson, *Ch of Bd*
Brian Apperson, *Vice Pres*
Lori Guaderrama, *Marketing Staff*
▲ EMP: 70
SQ FT: 80,080

SALES (est): 22MM **Privately Held**
WEB: www.appersonprint.com
SIC: 2761 Continuous forms, office & business

(P-7280)
BESTFORMS INC
1135 Avenida Acaso, Camarillo
(93012-8740)
PHONE..............................805 388-0503
Joe Valdez, *President*
Joy Macfarlane, *CFO*
Patrick Valdez, *Vice Pres*
Pat Valdez, *VP Sales*
Jill Smith, *Sales Staff*
EMP: 48
SQ FT: 31,000
SALES (est): 8.4MM **Privately Held**
WEB: www.bestforms.com
SIC: 2761 Manifold business forms

(P-7281)
COMPLYRIGHT DISTRIBUTION SVCS
3451 Jupiter Ct, Oxnard (93030-8957)
PHONE..............................805 981-0992
Richard Roddis, *CEO*
EMP: 44
SALES (est): 822.5K
SALES (corp-wide): 2.8B **Privately Held**
SIC: 2761 Manifold business forms
PA: Taylor Corporation
1725 Roe Crest Dr
North Mankato MN 56003
507 625-2828

(P-7282)
ENNIS INC
298 Sherwood Rd, Paso Robles
(93446-3546)
PHONE..............................805 238-1144
Terry Reynolds, *Manager*
EMP: 113
SALES (corp-wide): 400.7MM **Publicly Held**
WEB: www.ennis.com
SIC: 2761 3955 2621 Manifold business forms; carbon paper for typewriters, sales books, etc.; writing paper
PA: Ennis, Inc.
2441 Presidential Pkwy
Midlothian TX 76065
972 775-9801

(P-7283)
PRINTEGRA CORP
379 Earhart Way, Livermore (94551-9509)
PHONE..............................925 373-6368
Vinny Dinicola, *Manager*
EMP: 22
SALES (corp-wide): 400.7MM **Publicly Held**
WEB: www.printegra.com
SIC: 2761 2782 Continuous forms, office & business; blankbooks & looseleaf binders
HQ: Printegra Corp
5040 Highlands Pkwy Se
Smyrna GA 30082
770 487-5151

(P-7284)
RR DONNELLEY & SONS COMPANY
1765 Challenge Way # 220, Sacramento
(95815-5000)
PHONE..............................916 929-8632
Steve Sherbondy, *Branch Mgr*
EMP: 10
SALES (corp-wide): 6.8B **Publicly Held**
WEB: www.moore.com
SIC: 2761 Computer forms, manifold or continuous
PA: R. R. Donnelley & Sons Company
35 W Wacker Dr
Chicago IL 60601
312 326-8000

(P-7285)
RR DONNELLEY & SONS COMPANY
Also Called: Forms Division
19200 Von Karman Ave # 700, Irvine
(92612-8518)
PHONE..............................949 476-0505

Gordon Gaudett, *Branch Mgr*
EMP: 40
SALES (corp-wide): 6.8B **Publicly Held**
WEB: www.moore.com
SIC: 2761 Computer forms, manifold or continuous
PA: R. R. Donnelley & Sons Company
35 W Wacker Dr
Chicago IL 60601
312 326-8000

(P-7286)
TAYLOR COMMUNICATIONS INC
8972 Cuyamaca St, Corona (92883-2102)
PHONE..............................951 203-9011
Edward Arminta, *Branch Mgr*
EMP: 24
SALES (corp-wide): 2.8B **Privately Held**
SIC: 2761 Manifold business forms
HQ: Taylor Communications, Inc.
1725 Roe Crest Dr
North Mankato MN 56003
507 625-2828

(P-7287)
TAYLOR COMMUNICATIONS INC
1300 Ethan Way Ste 675, Sacramento
(95825-2295)
P.O. Box 255366 (95865-5366)
PHONE..............................916 927-1891
Pegge Kiszely, *Branch Mgr*
EMP: 14
SALES (corp-wide): 2.8B **Privately Held**
WEB: www.stdreg.com
SIC: 2761 Manifold business forms
HQ: Taylor Communications, Inc.
1725 Roe Crest Dr
North Mankato MN 56003
507 625-2828

(P-7288)
TAYLOR COMMUNICATIONS INC
5151 Murphy Canyon Rd # 100, San Diego
(92123-4440)
PHONE..............................866 541-0937
Steven Wickman, *Branch Mgr*
EMP: 10
SALES (corp-wide): 2.8B **Privately Held**
WEB: www.stdreg.com
SIC: 2761 Manifold business forms
HQ: Taylor Communications, Inc.
1725 Roe Crest Dr
North Mankato MN 56003
507 625-2828

(P-7289)
TAYLOR COMMUNICATIONS INC
3885 Seaport Blvd Ste 40, West Sacramento (95691-3527)
PHONE..............................916 340-0200
John Joyce, *Branch Mgr*
Toshio Hayashi, *Sr Software Eng*
Inna Uskova, *Buyer*
EMP: 75
SALES (corp-wide): 2.8B **Privately Held**
WEB: www.stdreg.com
SIC: 2761 Manifold business forms
HQ: Taylor Communications, Inc.
1725 Roe Crest Dr
North Mankato MN 56003
507 625-2828

(P-7290)
TAYLOR COMMUNICATIONS INC
535 Anton Blvd Ste 530, Costa Mesa
(92626-1947)
PHONE..............................714 708-2005
EMP: 20
SALES (corp-wide): 2.8B **Privately Held**
WEB: www.stdreg.com
SIC: 2761 Manifold business forms
HQ: Taylor Communications, Inc.
1725 Roe Crest Dr
North Mankato MN 56003
507 625-2828

(P-7291)
TAYLOR COMMUNICATIONS INC
400 N Tustin Ave Ste 275, Santa Ana
(92705-3885)
PHONE..............................714 664-8865
Don Chelius, *Manager*
EMP: 22
SALES (corp-wide): 2.8B **Privately Held**
WEB: www.stdreg.com
SIC: 2761 Manifold business forms

▲ = Import ▼=Export
◆ =Import/Export

HQ: Taylor Communications, Inc.
1725 Roe Crest Dr
North Mankato MN 56003
507 625-2828

(P-7292)
TAYLOR COMMUNICATIONS INC
10390 Coloma Rd Ste 7, Rancho Cordova
(95670-2152)
PHONE..............................916 368-1200
John Miller, *Manager*
EMP: 13
SALES (corp-wide): 2.8B **Privately Held**
WEB: www.stdreg.com
SIC: 2761 Manifold business forms
HQ: Taylor Communications, Inc.
1725 Roe Crest Dr
North Mankato MN 56003
507 625-2828

(P-7293)
TST/IMPRESO CALIFORNIA INC
10589 Business Dr, Fontana (92337-8223)
PHONE..............................909 357-7190
Marshall Sorokwasz, *President*
▲ EMP: 15
SQ FT: 30,000
SALES (est): 1.9MM
SALES (corp-wide): 83.3MM **Publicly Held**
SIC: 2761 Continuous forms, office & business
HQ: Tst/Impreso, Inc.
652 Southwestern Blvd
Coppell TX 75019
972 462-0100

(P-7294)
WRIGHT BUSINESS FORMS INC
Also Called: Wright Business Graphics Calif
13602 12th St Ste A, Chino (91710-5200)
P.O. Box 20489, Portland OR (97294-0489)
PHONE..............................909 614-6700
Gene Snitker, *Principal*
Steve Dupas, *Cust Mgr*
EMP: 50
SALES (corp-wide): 400.7MM **Publicly Held**
WEB: www.wrightbg.com
SIC: 2761 Manifold business forms
HQ: Wright Business Graphics Llc
18440 Ne San Rafael St
Portland OR 97230
800 547-8397

2771 Greeting Card Publishing

(P-7295)
FOUND IMAGE PRESS INC
5225 Riley St, San Diego (92110-2620)
PHONE..............................619 282-3452
Barry Bell, *Co-Owner*
Catherine Bell, *Co-Owner*
EMP: 13
SQ FT: 6,250
SALES: 1MM **Privately Held**
WEB: www.foundimage.com
SIC: 2771 5199 Greeting cards; calendars

(P-7296)
JUMPING CRACKER BEANS LLC
1588 Camden Village Cir, San Jose
(95124-6582)
PHONE..............................408 265-0658
Judith Dugan,
Julia Dugan,
EMP: 10
SALES (est): 1.2MM **Privately Held**
SIC: 2771 Greeting cards

(P-7297)
PUNKPOST INC
41 Federal St Unit 4, San Francisco
(94107-4199)
PHONE..............................415 818-7677
Alexis Monson, *CEO*
Santiago Prieto, *President*
EMP: 27
SALES: 100K **Privately Held**
SIC: 2771 7389 Greeting cards;

(P-7298)
SCHURMAN FINE PAPERS
22500 Town Cir, Moreno Valley
(92553-7509)
PHONE..............................951 653-1934
EMP: 158
SALES (corp-wide): 265.8MM **Privately Held**
SIC: 2771
PA: Schurman Retail Group
500 Chadbourne Rd
Fairfield CA 37072
707 428-0200

(P-7299)
SPS STUDIOS INC
7917 Ivanhoe Ave, La Jolla (92037-4512)
P.O. Box 1046 (92038-1046)
PHONE..............................858 456-2336
EMP: 33 **Privately Held**
SIC: 2771
PA: Sps Studios, Inc.
2905 Wilderness Pl # 100
Boulder CO 80301
303 449-0536

(P-7300)
STAR ROUTE LLC
4522 Henley Ct, Westlake Village
(91361-4307)
P.O. Box 6101, Thousand Oaks (91359-6101)
PHONE..............................805 405-8510
Tom Jankowski, *President*
Don Ko, *Director*
EMP: 12
SQ FT: 2,000
SALES: 600K **Privately Held**
SIC: 2771 Greeting cards

2782 Blankbooks & Looseleaf Binders

(P-7301)
ABISCO PRODUCTS CO
5925 E Washington Blvd, Commerce
(90040-2412)
PHONE..............................562 906-9330
EMP: 25
SQ FT: 10,000
SALES (est): 2.7MM **Privately Held**
WEB: www.abiscoproducts.com
SIC: 2782 2675

(P-7302)
AD INDUSTRIES LLC (PA)
Also Called: California Calendar
14071 Peyton Dr Unit 2170, Chino Hills
(91709-7195)
P.O. Box 8315, La Verne (91750-8315)
PHONE..............................818 765-4200
Steven Anderson, *Mng Member*
Karen Anderson, *Partner*
Rob Rose, *Partner*
Ralph Moscoloni, *Sales Staff*
▲ EMP: 10
SQ FT: 50,000
SALES (est): 1.6MM **Privately Held**
WEB: www.adind.com
SIC: 2782 Looseleaf binders & devices

(P-7303)
BINDERS EXPRESS INC
13800 Gramercy Pl, Gardena
(90249-2457)
PHONE..............................310 329-4811
Moti Taragano, *President*
Frank Naranjo, *Vice Pres*
EMP: 10
SALES (est): 1.4MM **Privately Held**
WEB: www.bindersexpress.com
SIC: 2782 Checkbooks

(P-7304)
BLAZAR COMMUNICATIONS CORP
Also Called: Blazar Mailing Solutions
17951 Sky Park Cir Ste K, Irvine
(92614-4353)
PHONE..............................949 336-7115
Jay Rajcevich, *President*
David Haimes, *COO*
Marilyn Norman, *Treasurer*
EMP: 11

SALES (est): 1.5MM **Privately Held**
SIC: 2782 3589 7374 8748 Account books; shredders, industrial & commercial; data entry service; communications consulting

(P-7305)
CACHE PHLOW ENTERPRISE
1894 Lynwood Dr Apt D, Concord
(94519-1158)
P.O. Box 415 (94522-0415)
PHONE..............................925 609-8649
Aaron Morris, *Partner*
EMP: 10
SALES (est): 478.4K **Privately Held**
SIC: 2782 Record albums

(P-7306)
CHAMELEON LIKE INC
Also Called: Chameleon Books & Journals
345 Kishimura Dr, Gilroy (95020-3653)
PHONE..............................408 847-3661
Pierre Martichoux, *President*
Daniel Busatto, *Vice Pres*
Amanda Gil, *Admin Asst*
Zepeda Jose, *Graphic Designe*
Sophia Corona, *Sales Associate*
▲ EMP: 34
SQ FT: 12,000
SALES (est): 6.4MM **Privately Held**
WEB: www.chameleonlike.com
SIC: 2782 Blankbooks & looseleaf binders

(P-7307)
CHECKWORKS INC
315 Cloverleaf Dr Ste J, Baldwin Park
(91706-6510)
P.O. Box 60065, City of Industry (91716-0065)
PHONE..............................626 333-1444
Aloysious J Uniack, *President*
Aloysius J Uniack, *President*
Christen Mc Kiernan, *Admin Sec*
Rodica Bohm, *Controller*
EMP: 55
SQ FT: 15,000
SALES (est): 7.6MM **Privately Held**
WEB: www.checkworks.com
SIC: 2782 Checkbooks

(P-7308)
CONTINENTAL BDR SPECIALTY CORP (PA)
407 W Compton Blvd, Gardena
(90248-1703)
PHONE..............................310 324-8227
Andrew Lisardi, *CEO*
Jack Gray, *Vice Pres*
▼ EMP: 120 EST: 1978
SQ FT: 31,000
SALES (est): 11.9MM **Privately Held**
SIC: 2782 2759 2675 2396 Looseleaf binders & devices; commercial printing; die-cut paper & board; automotive & apparel trimmings

(P-7309)
DELUXE CORPORATION
Also Called: Deluxe Financial Services
1551 Dell Ave, Campbell (95008-6903)
P.O. Box 328800, Los Gatos (95032)
PHONE..............................408 370-8801
Randy Bueford, *Manager*
EMP: 100
SALES (corp-wide): 2B **Publicly Held**
SIC: 2782 Checkbooks
PA: Deluxe Corporation
3680 Victoria St N
Shoreview MN 55126
651 483-7111

(P-7310)
DELUXE CORPORATION
2861 Mandela Pkwy, Oakland
(94608-4011)
PHONE..............................651 483-7100
EMP: 278
SALES (corp-wide): 2B **Publicly Held**
SIC: 2782 Checkbooks
PA: Deluxe Corporation
3680 Victoria St N
Shoreview MN 55126
651 483-7111

(P-7311)
DELUXE CORPORATION
Also Called: Deluxe Check Printers
42933 Business Ctr Pkwy, Lancaster
(93535-4515)
PHONE..............................661 942-1144
Shannon Holcomb, *General Mgr*
EMP: 460
SQ FT: 67,253
SALES (corp-wide): 2B **Publicly Held**
WEB: www.dlx.com
SIC: 2782 2761 2759 Checkbooks; manifold business forms; commercial printing
PA: Deluxe Corporation
3680 Victoria St N
Shoreview MN 55126
651 483-7111

(P-7312)
DOCUPAK INC
17515 Valley View Ave, Cerritos
(90703-7002)
PHONE..............................714 670-7944
William Lyons, *President*
John Flores, *CFO*
Pat Lyons, *Vice Pres*
EMP: 50
SQ FT: 27,000
SALES (est): 5.8MM **Privately Held**
SIC: 2782 Looseleaf binders & devices

(P-7313)
LIFETOUCH NAT SCHL STUDIOS INC
2860 Fair St, Chico (95928-8804)
PHONE..............................530 345-3993
Robert Evans, *Manager*
Phil Lawry, *Technology*
Ryan Cranney, *Engineer*
Sherron Stoltenberg, *Regional*
EMP: 100
SQ FT: 53,000
SALES (corp-wide): 1.9B **Privately Held**
SIC: 2782 7221 Account books; photographer, still or video
HQ: Lifetouch National School Studios Inc.
11000 Viking Dr Ste 300
Eden Prairie MN 55344
952 826-4000

(P-7314)
PIONEER PHOTO ALBUMS INC (PA)
9801 Deering Ave, Chatsworth
(91311-4398)
P.O. Box 2497 (91313-2497)
PHONE..............................818 882-2161
Shell Plutsky, *CEO*
Jason Reubens, *President*
Eric Bisquera, *COO*
Tiffany Boxer, *Vice Pres*
Rick Collies, *Vice Pres*
▲ EMP: 150
SQ FT: 100,000
SALES (est): 14.3MM **Privately Held**
WEB: www.pioneerphotoalbums.com
SIC: 2782 Albums

(P-7315)
RR DONNELLEY & SONS COMPANY
Also Called: RR Donnelley Financial
855 N California Ave A, Palo Alto (94303)
PHONE..............................650 845-6600
James Alley, *General Mgr*
EMP: 50
SALES (corp-wide): 6.8B **Publicly Held**
WEB: www.rrdonnelley.com
SIC: 2782 2759 Blankbooks & looseleaf binders; commercial printing
PA: R. R. Donnelley & Sons Company
35 W Wacker Dr
Chicago IL 60601
312 326-8000

(P-7316)
SHARON HAVRILUK
Also Called: American Mailing & Prtg Svc
1164 N Kraemer Pl, Anaheim (92806-1922)
PHONE..............................714 630-1313
Sharon Havriluk, *Owner*
Jennifer Hill, *COO*
EMP: 20
SQ FT: 10,000

PRODUCTS & SVCS

SALES (est): 2.8MM **Privately Held**
WEB: www.ampls.com
SIC: 2782 7331 Account books; mailing
list compilers; mailing service

(P-7317)
SONG BEOUNG
Also Called: Viva Photo Albums Company
501 Murphy Ranch Rd # 148, Milpitas
(95035-7930)
PHONE......................................510 670-8788
Beoung Song, *Owner*
▲ EMP: 13
SALES (est): 987.9K **Privately Held**
SIC: 2782 Scrapbooks, albums & diaries

(P-7318)
SUNNY PRODUCTS INC
Also Called: Pacific Trendz
1989 S Campus Ave, Ontario (91761-5410)
PHONE......................................909 923-4128
Seungsik Jang, *CEO*
SOO Chang, *President*
Rock Chon, *Vice Pres*
◆ EMP: 12
SQ FT: 12,000
SALES (est): 1.7MM **Privately Held**
WEB: www.sunnyproducts.com
SIC: 2782 Albums

(P-7319)
ULTRA PRO ACQUISITION LLC
6049 E Slauson Ave, Commerce
(90040-3007)
PHONE......................................323 725-1975
▲ EMP: 120
SALES (est): 6.1MM **Privately Held**
SIC: 2782 Library binders, looseleaf
PA: Marlin Equity Partners, Llc
338 Pier Ave
Hermosa Beach CA 90254

(P-7320)
**ULTRA PRO INTERNATIONAL
LLC (PA)**
Also Called: Jolly Roger Games
6049 E Slauson Ave, Commerce
(90040-3007)
PHONE......................................323 890-2100
Sheldon Rosenberg, *Mng Member*
Jay Kuo, *Vice Pres*
Justin Cole, *Project Mgr*
Ray Lei, *Accountant*
Mario Herrera, *Production*
▲ EMP: 62
SALES (est): 17.8MM **Privately Held**
SIC: 2782 Scrapbooks, albums & diaries

(P-7321)
US PACKAGERS INC
Also Called: West Coast Binders
13620 Crenshaw Blvd, Gardena
(90249-2347)
PHONE......................................310 327-7721
Policarpio Adriano, *President*
Juvenal Chiwawa, *Vice Pres*
EMP: 25 EST: 2011
SQ FT: 10,000
SALES (est): 1.2MM **Privately Held**
SIC: 2782 Blankbooks & looseleaf binders

(P-7322)
VAGRANT RECORDS INC
6351 Wilshire Blvd # 101, Los Angeles
(90048-5021)
PHONE......................................323 302-0100
Richard A Egan, *President*
Jon Cohen, *Vice Pres*
EMP: 20
SALES (est): 2.5MM **Privately Held**
WEB: www.vagrantrecords.com
SIC: 2782 5735 Record albums; records

(P-7323)
VAPOR DELUX INC (PA)
5221 Lankershim Blvd, North Hollywood
(91601-3110)
PHONE......................................818 856-3750
Ry R Chalme, *Administration*
EMP: 15
SALES (est): 3.8MM **Privately Held**
SIC: 2782 Checkbooks

(P-7324)
VIATECH PUBG SOLUTIONS INC
5668 E 61st St, Commerce (90040-3408)
PHONE......................................323 721-3629
Erik Treutlein, *Manager*
Larry Kambas, *Business Mgr*
Kevin Miller, *Business Mgr*
Walter Rosalind, *Accountant*
Cindy Sherman, *Purch Agent*
EMP: 56
SALES (corp-wide): 55MM **Privately
Held**
SIC: 2782 2741 Blankbooks & looseleaf
binders; miscellaneous publishing
PA: Viatech Publishing Solutions, Inc.
11935 N Stemmons Fwy
Dallas TX 75234
214 827-8151

2789 Bookbinding

(P-7325)
ACE BINDERY INC
10549 Dale Ave, Stanton (90680-2641)
PHONE......................................714 220-0232
Soon Chang, *President*
EMP: 13
SQ FT: 10,000
SALES (est): 1.1MM **Privately Held**
SIC: 2789 Bookbinding & related work

(P-7326)
B J BINDERY
833 S Grand Ave, Santa Ana (92705-4117)
PHONE......................................714 835-7342
Naresh Arya, *CEO*
Renu Arya, *Vice Pres*
▲ EMP: 80 EST: 1970
SQ FT: 29,000
SALES (est): 9.3MM **Privately Held**
WEB: www.bjbindery.com
SIC: 2789 Binding only: books, pamphlets,
magazines, etc.

(P-7327)
BARGAS BINDERY
1658 Scenicview Dr, San Leandro
(94577-5333)
PHONE......................................510 357-7901
Bernard Richard Wade, *Owner*
EMP: 10
SQ FT: 9,500
SALES (est): 602.5K **Privately Held**
SIC: 2789 Binding only: books, pamphlets,
magazines, etc.

(P-7328)
CAL BIND
Also Called: Mechanical Bookbinding
4700 Littlejohn St, Baldwin Park
(91706-2274)
PHONE......................................626 338-3699
Chris Stern, *President*
Mary Ellen Nardoza, *Vice Pres*
EMP: 50 EST: 1949
SQ FT: 21,000
SALES (est): 4.4MM **Privately Held**
WEB: www.calbind.com
SIC: 2789 Bookbinding & repairing: trade,
edition, library, etc.

(P-7329)
D A M BINDERY INC
Also Called: Bindery , The
7949 Stromesa Ct Ste B, San Diego
(92126-6338)
PHONE......................................858 621-7000
Sarah Sabor, *President*
Richard Sabor, *Treasurer*
Laurel Smith, *Vice Pres*
EMP: 10
SQ FT: 13,700
SALES (est): 1MM **Privately Held**
WEB: www.thebinderyinc.com
SIC: 2789 Bookbinding & related work

(P-7330)
DYNAMIC BINDERY INC
170 S Arrowhead Ave, San Bernardino
(92408-1303)
PHONE......................................909 884-1296
James Jameson, *President*
Lewane Stephenson, *Vice Pres*
EMP: 18

SQ FT: 12,000
SALES (est): 2MM **Privately Held**
SIC: 2789 Binding only: books, pamphlets,
magazines, etc.

(P-7331)
GOLDEN RULE BINDERY INC
Also Called: Golden Rule Packaging
1315 Hot Springs Way # 102, Vista
(92081-7878)
PHONE......................................760 471-2013
Jerry Kiley, *President*
Fred Antor, *Treasurer*
EMP: 22
SQ FT: 6,400
SALES (est): 3.1MM **Privately Held**
WEB: www.goldenrulebindery.com
SIC: 2789 Bookbinding & related work

(P-7332)
GRAPHICS BINDERY
16611 Roscoe Pl, North Hills (91343-6104)
PHONE......................................818 886-2463
Steve Silverman, *Owner*
EMP: 16
SQ FT: 5,000
SALES (est): 1.1MM **Privately Held**
SIC: 2789 Trade binding services

(P-7333)
HONG FAT DYE CUTTING CO
2103 Sastre Ave, South El Monte
(91733-2651)
PHONE......................................626 452-0382
Shing Koo, *Owner*
▲ EMP: 10 EST: 1993
SALES: 650K **Privately Held**
SIC: 2789 Paper cutting

(P-7334)
**INVESTMENT LAND
APPRAISERS**
Also Called: Supreme Bindery
333 E 157th St, Gardena (90248-2512)
PHONE......................................310 819-8831
EMP: 11
SALES (corp-wide): 699.3K **Privately
Held**
SIC: 2789
PA: Investment Land Appraisers, Inc
4208 W 175th Pl
Torrance CA
310 532-3850

(P-7335)
JAMES CLARK
Also Called: Fresno Trade Bindery & Mailing
1766 N Helm Ave Ste 105, Fresno
(93727-1627)
PHONE......................................559 456-3893
James Clark, *Owner*
Michael Clark, *General Mgr*
EMP: 10
SQ FT: 7,500
SALES: 500K **Privately Held**
WEB: www.jamesclark.com
SIC: 2789 Bookbinding & related work

(P-7336)
JIM PERRY
Also Called: Action Color Card
13611 Northlands Rd, Eastvale
(92880-0769)
PHONE......................................909 947-0747
Jim Perry, *Owner*
EMP: 30
SALES (est): 1.9MM **Privately Held**
SIC: 2789 2782 Swatches & samples;
blankbooks & looseleaf binders

(P-7337)
**JS TRADE BINDERY SERVICES
INC**
435 Harbor Blvd, Belmont (94002-4019)
PHONE......................................650 486-1475
Jai Kumar, *President*
Rita Kumar, *Officer*
Raj Lal, *Human Res Mgr*
Puente Armando, *Production*
EMP: 61
SQ FT: 40,000
SALES (est): 7.8MM **Privately Held**
WEB: www.jsbindery.com
SIC: 2789 Trade binding services

(P-7338)
**KATER-CRAFTS
INCORPORATED**
Also Called: Book Binders
4860 Gregg Rd, Pico Rivera (90660-2107)
PHONE......................................562 692-0665
Bruce Kavin, *President*
Richard Kavin, *Vice Pres*
EMP: 40
SQ FT: 20,000
SALES (est): 4MM **Privately Held**
WEB: www.katercrafts.com
SIC: 2789 Bookbinding & repairing: trade,
edition, library, etc.

(P-7339)
M M BOOK BINDERY
1826 W 169th St, Gardena (90247-5252)
P.O. Box 3307, Torrance (90510-3307)
PHONE......................................310 532-0780
Stephen M Goodman, *Administration*
EMP: 16
SALES (est): 2.7MM **Privately Held**
SIC: 2789 Bookbinding & related work

(P-7340)
**ONTARIO BINDING COMPANY
INC**
15951 Promontory Rd, Chino Hills
(91709-2371)
PHONE......................................909 947-7866
Maria Doerzapf, *President*
Luis Sanchez, *Treasurer*
EMP: 67
SQ FT: 25,000
SALES (est): 6.5MM **Privately Held**
WEB: www.ontariobinding.com
SIC: 2789 2675 Binding only: books, pam-
phlets, magazines, etc.; die-cut paper &
board

(P-7341)
**PACIFIC COAST GRAPHICS
BINDERY**
12250 Coast Dr, Whittier (90601-1607)
PHONE......................................562 908-5900
OK K Chang, *President*
EMP: 35
SQ FT: 20,000
SALES (est): 1.4MM **Privately Held**
SIC: 2789 Binding & repair of books, mag-
azines & pamphlets

(P-7342)
PACIFICO BINDERY INC
544 W Angus Ave, Orange (92868-1302)
PHONE......................................714 744-1510
Richard G Zinke, *President*
EMP: 20
SALES (est): 2.2MM **Privately Held**
WEB: www.pacificobindery.com
SIC: 2789 Binding only: books, pamphlets,
magazines, etc.

(P-7343)
ROBERT A KERL
Also Called: Southwest Trade Bindery
8930 Quartz Ave, Northridge (91324-3339)
PHONE......................................818 341-9281
Robert A Kerl Jr, *Owner*
EMP: 22
SALES (est): 1.5MM **Privately Held**
SIC: 2789 Trade binding services

(P-7344)
ROSS BINDERY INC
15310 Spring Ave, Santa Fe Springs
(90670-5644)
PHONE......................................562 623-4565
George Jackson, *CEO*
Desiree Reyna, *Accounting Dir*
Jaime Cerda, *Production*
John Gaynor, *Manager*
Alisa Sanchez, *Receptionist*
▲ EMP: 120
SQ FT: 65,000
SALES (est): 17.3MM **Privately Held**
WEB: www.rossbindery.com
SIC: 2789 Pamphlets, binding

(P-7345)
S & S BINDERY INC
2366 1st St, La Verne (91750-5545)
PHONE......................................909 596-2213
Steve Thompson, *President*

Scott Fehrensen, *Vice Pres*
▼ **EMP:** 20
SQ FT: 13,750
SALES (est): 2.6MM **Privately Held**
SIC: 2789 Bookbinding & related work

(P-7346)
S K DIGITAL IMAGING INC
7686 Miramar Rd Ste A, San Diego
(92126-4236)
PHONE..............................858 408-0732
Sean E Kaye, *President*
Gerald Kaye, *CFO*
EMP: 13
SALES (est): 1.8MM **Privately Held**
SIC: 2789 2752 Trade binding services;
commercial printing, lithographic

(P-7347)
SACRAMENTAL COLOR COIL
Also Called: D Bindery
8541 Thys Ct, Sacramento (95828-1006)
PHONE..............................916 383-9588
Darrell Johnston, *President*
May Johnston, *Vice Pres*
EMP: 20
SQ FT: 2,880
SALES: 750K **Privately Held**
SIC: 2789 Binding & repair of books, mag-
azines & pamphlets

(P-7348)
SILVER PRESS INC
940 Rincon Cir, San Jose (95131-1313)
PHONE..............................408 435-0449
Chin U Kim, *President*
Yoon Kim, *Vice Pres*
EMP: 10
SQ FT: 9,996
SALES (est): 1MM **Privately Held**
SIC: 2789 Bookbinding & related work

(P-7349)
SOMERSET TRAVELLER INC
Also Called: Somerset Printing
2765 Comstock Cir, Belmont (94002-2904)
PHONE..............................650 593-7350
Allan W Jaffe, *President*
Isac Gutfreund, *Treasurer*
EMP: 16
SQ FT: 8,000
SALES: 2.8MM **Privately Held**
SIC: 2789 2752 Bookbinding & related
work; commercial printing, offset

(P-7350)
**SOUTHERN CAL BNDERY
MILING INC**
10661 Business Dr, Fontana (92337-8212)
PHONE..............................909 829-1949
Rex Miller, *President*
EMP: 75
SQ FT: 51,000
SALES (est): 6.8MM **Privately Held**
SIC: 2789 7331 Binding & repair of books,
magazines & pamphlets; mailing service

(P-7351)
SPECIALTY GRAPHICS INC
1998 Republic Ave, San Leandro
(94577-4224)
PHONE..............................510 351-7705
Angela Plowman, *President*
Kyle Forrest, *Partner*
Deborah Waltmire, *Admin Sec*
EMP: 15
SQ FT: 37,000
SALES (est): 2.2MM **Privately Held**
WEB: www.sgica.com
SIC: 2789 2732 Trade binding services;
books: printing only

(P-7352)
SPEEDY BINDERY INC
4386 Jutland Dr, San Diego (92117-3642)
PHONE..............................619 275-0261
Fozi Awad Khouri, *President*
Victor Khouri, *Vice Pres*
EMP: 26
SQ FT: 20,000
SALES (est): 2.8MM **Privately Held**
SIC: 2789 7389 2675 Binding only:
books, pamphlets, magazines, etc.; lami-
nating service; die-cut paper & board

(P-7353)
**WESCO MOUNTING & FINISHING
INC**
5450 Dodds Ave, Buena Park
(90621-1209)
PHONE..............................714 562-0122
Tim Black, *President*
EMP: 25
SQ FT: 32,000
SALES (est): 2.6MM **Privately Held**
SIC: 2789 Paper cutting

2791 Typesetting

(P-7354)
AUTOMATION PRINTING CO (PA)
1230 Long Beach Ave, Los Angeles
(90021-2320)
PHONE..............................213 488-1230
David Tobman, *President*
Ann Tobman, *Corp Secy*
Art Tolentino, *Opers Mgr*
John Rangel, *Plant Mgr*
Terry Harrison, *Sales Mgr*
EMP: 39 **EST:** 1949
SQ FT: 30,000
SALES (est): 5.7MM **Privately Held**
WEB: www.automationtaft.com
SIC: 2791 2796 2759 2732 Typesetting;
platemaking services; commercial print-
ing; book printing; commercial printing,
offset

(P-7355)
BARKERBLUE INC
363 N Amphlett Blvd, San Mateo
(94401-1806)
PHONE..............................650 696-2100
Eugene A Klein, *CEO*
Michael Callaghan, *CFO*
Konstantin Koshelev, *Senior VP*
Mallory Satarzadh, *Sales Staff*
Carmen Edelman, *Cust Mgr*
EMP: 35
SQ FT: 15,000
SALES (est): 5.1MM **Privately Held**
WEB: www.barkerblue.com
SIC: 2791 7334 Typesetting; blueprinting
service

(P-7356)
DAKOTA PRESS
14400 Doolittle Dr, San Leandro
(94577-5546)
PHONE..............................510 895-1300
Mary Reid, *President*
Perry Mundorff, *Vice Pres*
EMP: 15
SQ FT: 11,000
SALES (est): 2MM **Privately Held**
WEB: www.dakotapress.com
SIC: 2791 2789 2761 2752 Typesetting;
bookbinding & related work; manifold
business forms; commercial printing, off-
set

(P-7357)
FOLGERGRAPHICS INC
21093 Forbes Ave, Hayward (94545-1115)
PHONE..............................510 293-2294
Richard L Folger, *CEO*
Patricia A Folger, *Vice Pres*
EMP: 40
SQ FT: 16,000
SALES (est): 6.7MM **Privately Held**
WEB: www.folgergraphics.com
SIC: 2791 2752 Typesetting; commercial
printing, offset

(P-7358)
GOLDING PUBLICATIONS
Also Called: Friday Flier
31558 Railroad Canyon Rd, Canyon Lake
(92587-9427)
PHONE..............................951 244-1966
Charles G Golding, *Owner*
Dona Jessup, *Executive*
Marti Norris, *Executive*
EMP: 11
SALES (est): 1.1MM **Privately Held**
WEB: www.goldingpublications.com
SIC: 2791 Typesetting

(P-7359)
NORCO PRINTING INC
440 Hester St, San Leandro (94577-1024)
PHONE..............................510 569-2200
Ricky C Damiani, *President*
Rick C Damiani, *President*
Rose Damiani, *Vice Pres*
Catherine Simi, *Sales Executive*
EMP: 15
SALES (est): 2.1MM **Privately Held**
WEB: www.norcoprint.com
SIC: 2791 2759 2752 2789 Typesetting;
letterpress & screen printing; commercial
printing, offset; bookbinding & related
work; manifold business forms

(P-7360)
RAPID LASERGRAPHICS (HQ)
836 Harrison St, San Francisco
(94107-1125)
PHONE..............................415 957-5840
Bent Kjolby, *President*
John Perkins, *Vice Pres*
EMP: 13
SALES (est): 1.3MM
SALES (corp-wide): 3.3MM **Privately
Held**
SIC: 2791 2752 7336 Typesetting; color li-
thography; graphic arts & related design
PA: Rapid Typographers Company Inc
836 Harrison St
San Francisco CA 94107
415 957-5840

(P-7361)
**RAPID TYPOGRAPHERS
COMPANY (PA)**
Also Called: Rapid Lasergraphics
836 Harrison St, San Francisco
(94107-1125)
PHONE..............................415 957-5840
Bent Kjolby, *President*
John Perkins, *Vice Pres*
EMP: 45
SQ FT: 12,000
SALES (est): 3.3MM **Privately Held**
WEB: www.rapidgraphics.com
SIC: 2791 2752 7336 2759 Typesetting;
color lithography; graphic arts & related
design; commercial printing

(P-7362)
SYSTEMS PRINTING INC
14311 Chambers Rd, Tustin (92780-6911)
PHONE..............................714 832-4677
Kevin Williams, *President*
EMP: 11
SQ FT: 3,600
SALES: 1MM **Privately Held**
WEB: www.allegraprint.com
SIC: 2791 7334 2752 Typesetting; photo-
copying & duplicating services; commer-
cial printing, lithographic

(P-7363)
TAS GROUP INC
Also Called: Vision Press
2333 San Ramon Vly Blvd, San Ramon
(94583-1763)
PHONE..............................925 551-3700
Andy Lion, *President*
Robert Carda, *CFO*
Steve Commerford, *Vice Pres*
EMP: 10
SALES (est): 910K **Privately Held**
SIC: 2791 Typesetting

(P-7364)
THOMPSON TYPE INC
3687 Voltaire St, San Diego (92106-1297)
PHONE..............................619 224-3137
John Pierce, *President*
Alma Bell, *Production*
EMP: 24
SQ FT: 12,000
SALES (est): 2.4MM **Privately Held**
WEB: www.thompsontype.com
SIC: 2791 Hand composition typesetting

(P-7365)
ULTRATYPE & GRAPHICS
1929 Hancock St Ste D, San Diego
(92110-2062)
PHONE..............................858 541-1894
EMP: 10
SQ FT: 2,800

SALES (est): 746.2K **Privately Held**
SIC: 2791 7336

(P-7366)
**WILSTED & TAYLOR PUBG
SVCS**
430 40th St, Oakland (94609-2691)
PHONE..............................510 428-9087
Christine Taylor, *Partner*
Leroy Wilsted, *Partner*
EMP: 10 **EST:** 1979
SQ FT: 1,000
SALES (est): 1.1MM **Privately Held**
WEB: www.wilstedandtaylor.com
SIC: 2791 7389 2731 Typesetting; design,
commercial & industrial; book publishing

2796 Platemaking & Related Svcs

(P-7367)
ACTION GRAPHIC ARTS INC
13065 Raintree Pl, Chino (91710-4637)
PHONE..............................626 443-3113
Dennis Ward, *President*
Clyde Bergman, *Vice Pres*
Francy Ward, *Admin Sec*
EMP: 10 **EST:** 1960
SQ FT: 5,000
SALES (est): 790K **Privately Held**
SIC: 2796 Color separations for printing

(P-7368)
AFT CORPORATION
Also Called: Andresen Digital Pre-Press
1815c Centinela Ave, Santa Monica
(90404-4203)
PHONE..............................310 576-1007
William Andresen, *President*
Ann Verkuilen, *CFO*
Chuck Henk, *Treasurer*
Glen Rosuck, *Vice Pres*
EMP: 21
SQ FT: 4,200
SALES (est): 2.3MM **Privately Held**
SIC: 2796 Color separations for printing

(P-7369)
**COAST ENGRAVING
COMPANIES**
Also Called: Coast Creative Nameplates
1097 N 5th St, San Jose (95112-4449)
PHONE..............................408 297-2555
Ida Wool, *President*
Fred A Wool Jr, *CFO*
Matt Wool, *Director*
EMP: 40 **EST:** 1970
SQ FT: 10,000
SALES (est): 4.3MM **Privately Held**
WEB: www.coaste.com
SIC: 2796 2752 2759 Engraving on cop-
per, steel, wood or rubber: printing plates;
lithographic plates, positives or negatives;
commercial printing, lithographic; com-
mercial printing

(P-7370)
EFFECTIVE GRAPHICS INC
40 E Verdugo Ave, Burbank (91502-1931)
PHONE..............................310 323-2223
Roger Sanders, *CEO*
David Curtis, *President*
Michael Vascellaro, *CFO*
EMP: 55
SQ FT: 47,970
SALES (est): 6.6MM **Privately Held**
WEB: www.effectivegraphics.com
SIC: 2796 2752 Color separations for
printing; commercial printing, lithographic

(P-7371)
FLEXLINE INC
15405 Cornet St, Santa Fe Springs
(90670-5533)
PHONE..............................562 921-4141
John Bateman, *President*
William Hall, *Vice Pres*
Dave Saguin, *Art Dir*
EMP: 28
SALES (est): 3.1MM **Privately Held**
WEB: www.flexlineinc.com
SIC: 2796 2759 3555 Platemaking serv-
ices; commercial printing; printing plates

(P-7372)
GEMINI - G E L
8365 Melrose Ave, Los Angeles
(90069-5419)
PHONE...........................323 651-0513
Sidney B Felsen, *President*
Stanley Grinstein, *Treasurer*
EMP: 20
SQ FT: 6,000
SALES (est): 2.2MM **Privately Held**
WEB: www.geminigel.com
SIC: 2796 2752 Etching on copper, steel,
wood or rubber: printing plates; commer-
cial printing, lithographic

(P-7373)
GRAFICO INC
15320 Cornet St, Santa Fe Springs
(90670-5532)
PHONE...........................562 404-4976
Dan Koon, *CEO*
Daniel Koon, *President*
Meredith Dugan, *CFO*
▲ EMP: 15
SQ FT: 23,500
SALES (est): 1.7MM **Privately Held**
WEB: www.grafico.com
SIC: 2796 7336 2791 Color separations
for printing; commercial art & graphic de-
sign; typesetting

(P-7374)
GRAPHIC DIES INC
12335 Florence Ave, Santa Fe Springs
(90670-3807)
P.O. Box 4343 (90670-1355)
PHONE...........................562 946-1802
Paul Bushaw, *President*
Estelle Bushaw, *Treasurer*
Janice Bushaw, *Admin Sec*
EMP: 10 EST: 1967
SQ FT: 5,129
SALES: 400K **Privately Held**
WEB: www.graphicdiesinc.com
SIC: 2796 Photoengraving plates, linecuts
or halftones

(P-7375)
HEADLINE GRAPHICS INC
2259 Flatiron Way, San Marcos
(92078-2143)
PHONE...........................760 436-0133
Gerald Anderson, *President*
Debra Anderson, *Vice Pres*
EMP: 30
SALES (est): 2.9MM **Privately Held**
WEB: www.headlinegraphics.com
SIC: 2796 7336 2791 Color separations
for printing; graphic arts & related design;
commercial art & illustration; typesetting;
computer controlled

(P-7376)
HEINZ WEBER INCORPORATED
13025 Park Pl Unit 402, Hawthorne
(90250-0995)
PHONE...........................310 477-3561
Heinz Weber, *President*
EMP: 45
SQ FT: 5,000
SALES (est): 5MM **Privately Held**
WEB: www.heinzweber.com
SIC: 2796 Color separations for printing

(P-7377)
INLAND COLOR GRAPHICS
2054 Tandem, Norco (92860-3609)
PHONE...........................951 493-2999
Carl J Vitolo, *President*
EMP: 10
SQ FT: 10,000
SALES (est): 1.5MM **Privately Held**
WEB: www.icgcolor.com
SIC: 2796 Color separations for printing

(P-7378)
JAGUAR LITHO
INCORPORATED
Also Called: J & L Imaging Center
1500 S Sunkist St Ste I, Anaheim
(92806-5815)
PHONE...........................714 978-1821
Joe Vitolo, *President*
Sue Vitolo, *Treasurer*
EMP: 10
SQ FT: 6,500

SALES (est): 1.1MM **Privately Held**
WEB: www.jaguarlitho.com
SIC: 2796 Color separations for printing

(P-7379)
MASTER ARTS INC
Also Called: Master Arts Engraving
3737 E Miraloma Ave, Anaheim
(92806-2100)
PHONE...........................714 240-4550
Elgin Chalayan, *President*
Rick Workman, *General Mgr*
Mike Liberto, *Cust Mgr*
EMP: 15
SQ FT: 10,000
SALES (est): 2.3MM **Privately Held**
SIC: 2796 3555 Platemaking services;
printing plates

(P-7380)
ONE COLOR COMMUNICATIONS
LLC
Also Called: One Color Communications
1851 Harbor Bay Pkwy, Alameda
(94502-3010)
PHONE...........................510 263-1840
Stephen Kozel, *Mng Member*
Tim Wilson, *Branch Mgr*
Kim Fogarty,
Tom Kozel,
EMP: 75
SQ FT: 40,000
SALES (est): 5.6MM **Privately Held**
SIC: 2796 Color separations for printing

(P-7381)
SGK LLC
Also Called: Schawk
650 Townsend St Ste 160, San Francisco
(94103-6258)
PHONE...........................415 438-6700
Leslie Ungar, *Manager*
EMP: 100
SALES (corp-wide): 1.6B **Publicly Held**
WEB: www.schawk.com
SIC: 2796 7374 Color separations for
printing; computer graphics service
HQ: Sgk, Llc
1695 S River Rd
Des Plaines IL 60018
847 827-9494

(P-7382)
SGK LLC
Also Called: Schawk
3116 W Avenue 32, Los Angeles
(90065-2317)
PHONE...........................323 258-4111
Joe Kellenberger, *Principal*
EMP: 150
SQ FT: 75,850
SALES (corp-wide): 1.6B **Publicly Held**
WEB: www.schawk.com
SIC: 2796 Lithographic plates, positives or
negatives
HQ: Sgk, Llc
1695 S River Rd
Des Plaines IL 60018
847 827-9494

2812 Alkalies & Chlorine

(P-7383)
ARKEMA INC
Also Called: Arkema Coating Resins
19206 Hawthorne Blvd, Torrance
(90503-1505)
PHONE...........................310 214-5327
EMP: 124
SALES (corp-wide): 98.4MM **Privately
Held**
SIC: 2812 2819 2869 2899 Chlorine,
compressed or liquefied; industrial inor-
ganic chemicals; industrial organic chemi-
cals; metal treating compounds; plastics
pipe
HQ: Arkema Inc.
900 First Ave
King Of Prussia PA 19406
610 205-7000

(P-7384)
CHURCH & DWIGHT CO INC
31266 Avenue 12, Madera (93638-8328)
PHONE...........................559 661-2790
David Johnston, *Manager*
Christine Reichmuth, *Controller*
EMP: 20
SALES (corp-wide): 4.1B **Publicly Held**
WEB: www.churchdwight.com
SIC: 2812 Sodium bicarbonate
PA: Church & Dwight Co., Inc.
500 Charles Ewing Blvd
Ewing NJ 08628
609 806-1200

(P-7385)
CLOROX COMPANY
VOLUNTARY
1221 Broadway Ste 1300, Oakland
(94612-1871)
P.O. Box 24305 (94623-1305)
PHONE...........................510 271-7000
EMP: 15
SALES: 3.5MM **Privately Held**
SIC: 2812 Chlorine, compressed or lique-
fied

(P-7386)
CLOROX SALES COMPANY
530 Idaho Ave, Escondido (92025-5226)
PHONE...........................760 432-8362
EMP: 25
SALES (corp-wide): 5.5B **Publicly Held**
SIC: 2812
HQ: The Clorox Sales Company
1221 Broadway Ste 13
Oakland CA 94612
510 271-7000

(P-7387)
FMC CORPORATION
201 Cousteau Pl, Davis (95618-5412)
PHONE...........................530 753-6718
Bijou Abraham, *Engineer*
EMP: 95
SALES (corp-wide): 4.7B **Publicly Held**
SIC: 2812 Soda ash, sodium carbonate
(anhydrous)
PA: Fmc Corporation
2929 Walnut St
Philadelphia PA 19104
215 299-6000

(P-7388)
HASA INC
1251 Loveridge Rd, Pittsburg
(94565-2803)
PHONE...........................661 259-5848
Lisa Wilson, *Manager*
EMP: 30
SALES (corp-wide): 72.3MM **Privately
Held**
WEB: www.hasapool.com
SIC: 2812 Chlorine, compressed or lique-
fied
PA: Hasa, Inc.
23119 Drayton St
Santa Clarita CA 91350
661 259-5848

(P-7389)
HILL BROTHERS CHEMICAL
COMPANY
Also Called: Desert Brand
15017 Clark Ave, City of Industry
(91745-1409)
PHONE...........................626 333-2251
Ron Hill, *President*
Toni Dakovich, *Purch Mgr*
Paco Lozan, *Traffic Mgr*
Bobby Conrad, *Sales Staff*
EMP: 18
SQ FT: 17,203
SALES (est): 5MM
SALES (corp-wide): 110.9MM **Privately
Held**
WEB: www.durafiber.com
SIC: 2812 2851 2819 Chlorine, com-
pressed or liquefied; paints & allied prod-
ucts; industrial inorganic chemicals
PA: Hill Brothers Chemical Company
1675 N Main St
Orange CA 92867
714 998-8800

(P-7390)
JCI JONES CHEMICALS INC
1401 Del Amo Blvd, Torrance (90501-1630)
PHONE...........................310 523-1629
Mike Reddinton, *Manager*
EMP: 35
SALES (corp-wide): 179MM **Privately
Held**
WEB: www.jcichem.com
SIC: 2812 2899 Alkalies; chlorine, com-
pressed or liquefied; chemical prepara-
tions
PA: Jci Jones Chemicals, Inc.
1765 Ringling Blvd # 200
Sarasota FL 34236
941 330-1537

(P-7391)
OLIN CHLOR ALKALI LOGISTICS
Also Called: Chlor Alkali Products & Vinyls
11600 Pike St, Santa Fe Springs
(90670-2938)
PHONE...........................562 692-0510
John Bilac, *Branch Mgr*
EMP: 136
SALES (corp-wide): 6.9B **Publicly Held**
SIC: 2812 Alkalies & chlorine
HQ: Olin Chlor Alkali Logistics Inc
490 Stuart Rd Ne
Cleveland TN 37312
423 336-4850

(P-7392)
SCC CHEMICAL CORPORATION
Also Called: All Pure Pool Service
32215 Dunlap Blvd, Yucaipa (92399-1756)
P.O. Box 2021, Redlands (92373-0621)
PHONE...........................909 796-8369
Chris Padgett, *CEO*
Mark Reichmann, *Director*
EMP: 12
SALES: 1.2MM **Privately Held**
SIC: 2812 Chlorine, compressed or lique-
fied

2813 Industrial Gases

(P-7393)
AIR LIQUID HEALTHCARE
12460 Arrow Rte, Rancho Cucamonga
(91739-9682)
PHONE...........................909 899-4633
Gerald Berger, *Principal*
EMP: 26
SALES (est): 4.8MM **Privately Held**
SIC: 2813 8099 Oxygen, compressed or
liquefied; health & allied services

(P-7394)
AIR PRODUCTS AND
CHEMICALS INC
8934 Dice Rd, Santa Fe Springs
(90670-2518)
PHONE...........................562 944-3873
EMP: 50
SALES (corp-wide): 8.9B **Publicly Held**
WEB: www.airproducts.com
SIC: 2813 2869 Oxygen, compressed or
liquefied; amines, acids, salts, esters
PA: Air Products And Chemicals, Inc.
7201 Hamilton Blvd
Allentown PA 18195
610 481-4911

(P-7395)
AIR PRODUCTS AND
CHEMICALS INC
23300 S Alameda St, Carson (90810-1921)
PHONE...........................310 847-7300
Matt Pitcher, *Manager*
EMP: 10
SALES (corp-wide): 8.9B **Publicly Held**
WEB: www.airproducts.com
SIC: 2813 Industrial gases
PA: Air Products And Chemicals, Inc.
7201 Hamilton Blvd
Allentown PA 18195
610 481-4911

▲ = Import ▼=Export
◆ =Import/Export

(P-7396)
AIR PRODUCTS AND CHEMICALS INC
901 W 12th St, Long Beach (90813-2813)
PHONE....................................562 437-0462
Shelly Stuart, *Branch Mgr*
EMP: 25
SALES (corp-wide): 8.9B **Publicly Held**
WEB: www.airproducts.com
SIC: 2813 Industrial gases
PA: Air Products And Chemicals, Inc.
7201 Hamilton Blvd
Allentown PA 18195
610 481-4911

(P-7397)
AIR PRODUCTS AND CHEMICALS INC
400 Macarthur Blvd, Newport Beach (92660)
PHONE....................................949 474-1860
Max Monestime, *Branch Mgr*
EMP: 11
SALES (corp-wide): 8.9B **Publicly Held**
WEB: www.airproducts.com
SIC: 2813 5169 Industrial gases; industrial gases
PA: Air Products And Chemicals, Inc.
7201 Hamilton Blvd
Allentown PA 18195
610 481-4911

(P-7398)
AIR PRODUCTS AND CHEMICALS INC
1969 Palomar Oaks Way, Carlsbad (92011-1307)
PHONE....................................760 931-9555
Ileen Turner, *Site Mgr*
Mary McAdams, *Manager*
EMP: 175
SALES (corp-wide): 8.9B **Publicly Held**
WEB: www.airproducts.com
SIC: 2813 3625 2899 2865 Industrial gases; relays & industrial controls; chemical preparations; cyclic crudes & intermediates
PA: Air Products And Chemicals, Inc.
7201 Hamilton Blvd
Allentown PA 18195
610 481-4911

(P-7399)
AIR PRODUCTS AND CHEMICALS INC
700 N Henry Ford Ave, Wilmington (90744-6717)
PHONE....................................310 952-9172
Jim Click, *Branch Mgr*
EMP: 20
SALES (corp-wide): 8.9B **Publicly Held**
WEB: www.airproducts.com
SIC: 2813 Industrial gases
PA: Air Products And Chemicals, Inc.
7201 Hamilton Blvd
Allentown PA 18195
610 481-4911

(P-7400)
AIR SOURCE INDUSTRIES
3976 Cherry Ave, Long Beach (90807-3727)
PHONE....................................562 426-4017
Robert L Bowers, *CEO*
Richard Smith, *Vice Pres*
EMP: 14
SALES (est): 3.6MM **Privately Held**
WEB: www.air-source.com
SIC: 2813 5999 Industrial gases; convalescent equipment & supplies

(P-7401)
AIRGAS USA LLC
315 Harbor Way, South San Francisco (94080-6919)
PHONE....................................650 873-4212
EMP: 12
SALES (corp-wide): 164.2MM **Privately Held**
SIC: 2813 5999 5169
HQ: Airgas Usa, Llc
259 N Radnor Chester Rd # 100
Radnor PA 19087
610 687-5253

(P-7402)
AIRGAS USA LLC
1415 Grand Ave, San Marcos (92078-2405)
PHONE....................................760 744-1472
Fernando Anzaldua, *Branch Mgr*
EMP: 25
SQ FT: 22,032
SALES (corp-wide): 125.9MM **Privately Held**
WEB: www.airgas.com
SIC: 2813 5084 3443 Industrial gases; welding machinery & equipment; weldments
HQ: Airgas Usa, Llc
259 N Radnor Chester Rd
Radnor PA 19087
610 687-5253

(P-7403)
AIRGAS USA LLC
9810 Jordan Cir, Santa Fe Springs (90670-3303)
PHONE....................................562 946-8394
Ruthie Cox, *Manager*
Loyd E Wright, *Agent*
EMP: 50
SALES (corp-wide): 125.9MM **Privately Held**
SIC: 2813 5999 5169 Industrial gases; ice; dry ice
HQ: Airgas Usa, Llc
259 N Radnor Chester Rd
Radnor PA 19087
610 687-5253

(P-7404)
AIRGAS USA LLC
700 Decoto Rd, Union City (94587-3513)
PHONE....................................510 429-4200
Bob Oconnor, *Manager*
EMP: 56
SQ FT: 35,886
SALES (corp-wide): 125.9MM **Privately Held**
WEB: www.airliquide.com
SIC: 2813 5084 Industrial gases; industrial machinery & equipment
HQ: Airgas Usa, Llc
259 N Radnor Chester Rd
Radnor PA 19087
610 687-5253

(P-7405)
AIRGAS USA LLC
1750 Clinton Dr, Concord (94521-2015)
PHONE....................................925 969-0419
EMP: 17
SALES (corp-wide): 125.9MM **Privately Held**
SIC: 2813 Industrial gases
HQ: Airgas Usa, Llc
259 N Radnor Chester Rd
Radnor PA 19087
610 687-5253

(P-7406)
AIRGAS USA LLC
8832 Dice Rd, Santa Fe Springs (90670-2516)
PHONE....................................562 945-1383
Rafael Motta, *Branch Mgr*
Cynthia Aragundi, *Plant Mgr*
EMP: 44
SQ FT: 29,887
SALES (corp-wide): 125.9MM **Privately Held**
WEB: www.airliquide.com
SIC: 2813 5084 Industrial gases; industrial machinery & equipment
HQ: Airgas Usa, Llc
259 N Radnor Chester Rd
Radnor PA 19087
610 687-5253

(P-7407)
AIRGAS USA LLC
Also Called: California Dental Group
7254 Coldwater Canyon Ave, North Hollywood (91605-4203)
PHONE....................................818 787-6010
Jack Storm, *Branch Mgr*
EMP: 10
SALES (corp-wide): 125.9MM **Privately Held**
SIC: 2813 Industrial gases

HQ: Airgas Usa, Llc
259 N Radnor Chester Rd
Radnor PA 19087
610 687-5253

(P-7408)
AIRGAS USA LLC
46409 Landing Pkwy, Fremont (94538-6496)
PHONE....................................510 624-4000
Scott Anderson, *Branch Mgr*
EMP: 40
SQ FT: 10,000
SALES (corp-wide): 125.9MM **Privately Held**
WEB: www.airliquide.com
SIC: 2813 Industrial gases
HQ: Airgas Usa, Llc
259 N Radnor Chester Rd
Radnor PA 19087
610 687-5253

(P-7409)
AIRGAS USA LLC
9756 Santa Fe Springs Rd, Santa Fe Springs (90670-2920)
PHONE....................................562 906-8700
Cynthia Aragundi, *Manager*
EMP: 30
SALES (corp-wide): 125.9MM **Privately Held**
WEB: www.airliquide.com
SIC: 2813 5169 Industrial gases; oxygen
HQ: Airgas Usa, Llc
259 N Radnor Chester Rd
Radnor PA 19087
610 687-5253

(P-7410)
AIRGAS USA LLC
311 Kentucky St, Bakersfield (93305-4229)
PHONE....................................661 201-8107
Roy Neal, *Branch Mgr*
EMP: 20
SALES (corp-wide): 125.9MM **Privately Held**
WEB: www.airliquide.com
SIC: 2813 2911 5084 Industrial gases; petroleum refining; materials handling machinery
HQ: Airgas Usa, Llc
259 N Radnor Chester Rd
Radnor PA 19087
610 687-5253

(P-7411)
AIRGAS USA LLC
12550 Arrow Rte, Rancho Cucamonga (91739-9683)
PHONE....................................909 899-4670
Dave Erickson, *Branch Mgr*
EMP: 17
SALES (corp-wide): 125.9MM **Privately Held**
SIC: 2813 Industrial gases
HQ: Airgas Usa, Llc
259 N Radnor Chester Rd
Radnor PA 19087
610 687-5253

(P-7412)
AMERICAN AIR LIQUIDE INC (DH)
46409 Landing Pkwy, Fremont (94538-6496)
PHONE....................................510 624-4000
Benoit Potier, *Chairman*
Pierre Dufour, *President*
Scott Krapf, *CFO*
Gregory Alexander, *Treasurer*
Jean-Pierre Duprieu, *Exec VP*
◆ EMP: 90
SQ FT: 40,000
SALES (est): 314.8MM
SALES (corp-wide): 125.9MM **Privately Held**
SIC: 2813 5084 3533 4931 Industrial gases; welding machinery & equipment; oil & gas drilling rigs & equipment; electric & other services combined
HQ: Air Liquide International
75 Quai D Orsay
Paris
140 625-555

(P-7413)
FOLLMER DEVELOPMENT INC
Also Called: Fd
840 Tourmaline Dr, Newbury Park (91320-1205)
PHONE....................................805 498-4531
Christopher H Follmer, *CEO*
Garrett Follmer, *President*
Helen Follmer, *Treasurer*
David McKenzie, *Vice Pres*
Dan Follmer, *Principal*
▼ EMP: 41
SQ FT: 35,000
SALES (est): 20.7MM **Privately Held**
WEB: www.follmerdevelopment.com
SIC: 2813 Aerosols

(P-7414)
LINDE GAS NORTH AMERICA LLC
Also Called: Lifegas
614 S Glenwood Pl, Burbank (91506-2820)
PHONE....................................626 855-8344
EMP: 19
SALES (corp-wide): 20.1B **Privately Held**
SIC: 2813
HQ: Linde Gas North America Llc
200 Somerset Corp Blvd # 7000
Bridgewater NJ 08807
-

(P-7415)
LINDE GAS NORTH AMERICA LLC
Also Called: Lifegas
680 Baldwin Park Blvd, City of Industry (91746-1501)
PHONE....................................626 780-3104
Alan Underwood, *Principal*
Eric Mozell, *Research*
EMP: 19 **Privately Held**
SIC: 2813 Nitrogen; oxygen, compressed or liquefied
HQ: Linde Gas North America Llc
200 Somerset Corp Blvd # 7000
Bridgewater NJ 08807

(P-7416)
MATHESON TRI-GAS INC
16125 Ornelas St, Irwindale (91706-2037)
PHONE....................................626 334-2905
Fermin Reyes, *Manager*
Joe Cassidy, *Engineer*
David Barlow, *Opers Staff*
Chris Russell, *Opers Staff*
Gary Carbonari, *Sales Engr*
EMP: 25
SQ FT: 19,472 **Privately Held**
WEB: www.matheson-trigas.com
SIC: 2813 5169 Industrial gases; industrial gases
HQ: Matheson Tri-Gas, Inc.
150 Allen Rd Ste 302
Basking Ridge NJ 07920
908 991-9200

(P-7417)
MATHESON TRI-GAS INC
6925 Central Ave, Newark (94560-3940)
PHONE....................................510 714-3026
Tae-Byung Park, *Finance*
EMP: 16 **Privately Held**
SIC: 2813 Industrial gases
HQ: Matheson Tri-Gas, Inc.
150 Allen Rd Ste 302
Basking Ridge NJ 07920
908 991-9200

(P-7418)
MATHESON TRI-GAS INC
8800 Utica Ave, Rancho Cucamonga (91730-5104)
PHONE....................................909 758-5464
Gary Harper, *Branch Mgr*
EMP: 20
SQ FT: 5,560 **Privately Held**
WEB: www.matheson-trigas.com
SIC: 2813 5084 3494 Industrial gases; welding machinery & equipment; valves & pipe fittings
HQ: Matheson Tri-Gas, Inc.
150 Allen Rd Ste 302
Basking Ridge NJ 07920
908 991-9200

PRODUCTS & SVCS

(P-7419)
MATHESON TRI-GAS INC
6775 Central Ave, Newark (94560-3936)
PHONE.................................510 793-2559
Rob Peetz, *Division Mgr*
Scott Kallman, *COO*
EMP: 90
SQ FT: 19,281 **Privately Held**
WEB: www.matheson-trigas.com
SIC: **2813** 5084 3494 Industrial gases;
　welding machinery & equipment; valves &
　pipe fittings
HQ: Matheson Tri-Gas, Inc.
　　150 Allen Rd Ste 302
　　Basking Ridge NJ 07920
　　908 991-9200

(P-7420)
MATHESON TRI-GAS INC
5555 District Blvd, Vernon (90058-4017)
PHONE.................................323 773-2777
Robin Reynolds, *Manager*
EMP: 15 **Privately Held**
SIC: **2813** 5084 5169 Industrial gases;
　welding machinery & equipment; indus-
　trial gases
HQ: Matheson Tri-Gas, Inc.
　　150 Allen Rd Ste 302
　　Basking Ridge NJ 07920
　　908 991-9200

(P-7421)
MESSER LLC
Also Called: Cryostar USA
13117 Meyer Rd, Whittier (90605-3555)
PHONE.................................562 903-1290
Mark Sutton, *Branch Mgr*
EMP: 17
SALES (corp-wide): 1.4B **Privately Held**
SIC: **2813** 3561 Oxygen, compressed or
　liquefied; pumps & pumping equipment
HQ: Messer Llc
　　200 Somerset Corp Blvd # 7000
　　Bridgewater NJ 08807
　　908 464-8100

(P-7422)
MESSER LLC
2535 Del Amo Blvd, Torrance (90503-1706)
PHONE.................................310 533-8394
Jason Lacasella, *Branch Mgr*
EMP: 20
SALES (corp-wide): 1.4B **Privately Held**
SIC: **2813** Carbon dioxide
HQ: Messer Llc
　　200 Somerset Corp Blvd # 7000
　　Bridgewater NJ 08807
　　908 464-8100

(P-7423)
MESSER LLC
Also Called: Boc Gases
731 W Cutting Blvd, Richmond
(94804-2023)
PHONE.................................510 233-8911
Ken Marquardt, *Opers-Prdtn-Mfg*
Gregory Vreeburg, *Mktg Dir*
EMP: 18
SALES (corp-wide): 1.4B **Privately Held**
SIC: **2813** Oxygen, compressed or lique-
　fied
HQ: Messer Llc
　　200 Somerset Corp Blvd # 7000
　　Bridgewater NJ 08807
　　908 464-8100

(P-7424)
MESSER LLC
5858 88th St, Sacramento (95828-1104)
PHONE.................................916 381-1606
Steve Morgan, *Branch Mgr*
EMP: 20
SALES (corp-wide): 1.4B **Privately Held**
SIC: **2813** Nitrogen; oxygen, compressed
　or liquefied
HQ: Messer Llc
　　200 Somerset Corp Blvd # 7000
　　Bridgewater NJ 08807
　　908 464-8100

(P-7425)
MESSER LLC
B O C Edwards/Temescal
4569 Las Positas Rd Ste C, Livermore
(94551-8865)
PHONE.................................925 371-4170

Gregg S Wallace, *Manager*
EMP: 33
SALES (corp-wide): 1.4B **Privately Held**
SIC: **2813** Oxygen, compressed or lique-
　fied
HQ: Messer Llc
　　200 Somerset Corp Blvd # 7000
　　Bridgewater NJ 08807
　　908 464-8100

(P-7426)
MESSER LLC
660 Baldwin Park Blvd, City of Industry
(91746-1501)
PHONE.................................626 855-8366
Mike Colvin, *Branch Mgr*
EMP: 60
SALES (corp-wide): 1.4B **Privately Held**
SIC: **2813** Nitrogen; oxygen, compressed
　or liquefied
HQ: Messer Llc
　　200 Somerset Corp Blvd # 7000
　　Bridgewater NJ 08807
　　908 464-8100

(P-7427)
PRAXAIR INC
2430 Camino Ramon Ste 310, San Ramon
(94583-4321)
PHONE.................................925 866-6800
Mark Plant, *Director*
D L Pierce, *Marketing Mgr*
EMP: 12 **Privately Held**
SIC: **2813** Industrial gases
HQ: Praxair, Inc.
　　10 Riverview Dr
　　Danbury CT 06810
　　203 837-2000

(P-7428)
PRAXAIR INC
2000 Loveridge Rd, Pittsburg (94565-4114)
PHONE.................................925 427-1051
Sturt Becker, *Manager*
Alberto Castro, *Engineer*
EMP: 60 **Privately Held**
SIC: **2813** Industrial gases
HQ: Praxair, Inc.
　　10 Riverview Dr
　　Danbury CT 06810
　　203 837-2000

(P-7429)
PRAXAIR INC
2006 E 223rd St, Long Beach
(90810-1609)
PHONE.................................310 816-1066
Stu Lehmann, *Manager*
Juan Pelaez, *Director*
EMP: 20 **Privately Held**
SIC: **2813** Industrial gases
HQ: Praxair, Inc.
　　10 Riverview Dr
　　Danbury CT 06810
　　203 837-2000

(P-7430)
PRAXAIR INC
10728 Prospect Ave Ste A, Santee
(92071-4558)
PHONE.................................619 596-4558
Wayne Yakich, *Owner*
EMP: 20 **Privately Held**
SIC: **2813** Industrial gases
HQ: Praxair, Inc.
　　10 Riverview Dr
　　Danbury CT 06810
　　203 837-2000

(P-7431)
PRAXAIR INC
112 W Olive Ave, Madera (93637-5433)
PHONE.................................559 674-7306
Jimmy Schulte, *Branch Mgr*
EMP: 20 **Privately Held**
SIC: **2813** Industrial gases
HQ: Praxair, Inc.
　　10 Riverview Dr
　　Danbury CT 06810
　　203 837-2000

(P-7432)
PRAXAIR INC
2995 Atlas Rd, San Pablo (94806-1167)
PHONE.................................510 223-9593
EMP: 20

SALES (corp-wide): 11.9B **Publicly Held**
SIC: **2813**
PA: Praxair, Inc.
　　39 Old Ridgebury Rd
　　Danbury CT 06810
　　203 837-2000

(P-7433)
PRAXAIR INC
305 E Haley St Ste A, Santa Barbara
(93101-1723)
PHONE.................................805 966-0829
Karl Grimm, *Manager*
EMP: 16 **Privately Held**
SIC: **2813** Industrial gases
HQ: Praxair, Inc.
　　10 Riverview Dr
　　Danbury CT 06810
　　203 837-2000

(P-7434)
PRAXAIR INC
8300 Atlantic Ave, Cudahy (90201-5808)
PHONE.................................323 562-5200
Don Hamric, *Manager*
EMP: 14 **Privately Held**
SIC: **2813** Industrial gases
HQ: Praxair, Inc.
　　10 Riverview Dr
　　Danbury CT 06810
　　203 837-2000

(P-7435)
PRAXAIR INC
3331 Buck Owens Blvd, Bakersfield
(93308-6323)
PHONE.................................661 861-6421
Mark Cooper, *Manager*
EMP: 20 **Privately Held**
SIC: **2813** Industrial gases
HQ: Praxair, Inc.
　　10 Riverview Dr
　　Danbury CT 06810
　　203 837-2000

(P-7436)
PRAXAIR INC
3505 Buck Owens Blvd, Bakersfield
(93308-4919)
PHONE.................................661 327-5336
Mark Cooper, *General Mgr*
EMP: 25 **Privately Held**
SIC: **2813** Industrial gases
HQ: Praxair, Inc.
　　10 Riverview Dr
　　Danbury CT 06810
　　203 837-2000

(P-7437)
PRAXAIR INC
3994 Bayshore Blvd, Brisbane
(94005-1404)
PHONE.................................415 657-9880
EMP: 21 **Privately Held**
SIC: **2813** Oxygen, compressed or lique-
　fied
HQ: Praxair, Inc.
　　10 Riverview Dr
　　Danbury CT 06810
　　203 837-2000

(P-7438)
PRAXAIR INC
5705 E Airport Dr, Ontario (91761-8611)
PHONE.................................909 390-0283
M M Stenberg, *Branch Mgr*
EMP: 65 **Privately Held**
SIC: **2813** Industrial gases
HQ: Praxair, Inc.
　　10 Riverview Dr
　　Danbury CT 06810
　　203 837-2000

(P-7439)
PRAXAIR INC
7501 Foothills Blvd, Roseville
(95747-6504)
PHONE.................................916 786-3900
EMP: 15 **Privately Held**
SIC: **2813** Industrial gases
HQ: Praxair, Inc.
　　10 Riverview Dr
　　Danbury CT 06810
　　203 837-2000

(P-7440)
PRAXAIR INC
331 E Channel Rd, Benicia (94510-1127)
PHONE.................................707 745-5328
John Alford, *Manager*
EMP: 20 **Privately Held**
SIC: **2813** Industrial gases
HQ: Praxair, Inc.
　　10 Riverview Dr
　　Danbury CT 06810
　　203 837-2000

(P-7441)
PRAXAIR DISTRIBUTION INC
2771 S Maple Ave, Fresno (93725-2117)
PHONE.................................559 237-5521
Keith Martinez, *Branch Mgr*
EMP: 33
SQ FT: 11,800 **Privately Held**
SIC: **2813** Acetylene
HQ: Praxair Distribution, Inc.
　　10 Riverview Dr
　　Danbury CT 06810
　　203 837-2000

(P-7442)
PRAXAIR DISTRIBUTION INC
500 Harrington St Ste G, Corona
(92880-6735)
PHONE.................................951 736-8113
Laura Johnston, *Principal*
EMP: 47 **Privately Held**
SIC: **2813** Industrial gases
HQ: Praxair Distribution, Inc.
　　10 Riverview Dr
　　Danbury CT 06810
　　203 837-2000

(P-7443)
PRAXAIR DISTRIBUTION INC
305 E Haley St, Santa Barbara
(93101-1723)
PHONE.................................805 966-0829
Bret Glasspoole, *Manager*
EMP: 47 **Privately Held**
SIC: **2813** Industrial gases
HQ: Praxair Distribution, Inc.
　　10 Riverview Dr
　　Danbury CT 06810
　　203 837-2000

(P-7444)
PRAXAIR DISTRIBUTION INC
5508 Vineland Ave, North Hollywood
(91601-2729)
PHONE.................................818 760-2011
Stephen Schultz, *Manager*
EMP: 13 **Privately Held**
SIC: **2813** Industrial gases
HQ: Praxair Distribution, Inc.
　　10 Riverview Dr
　　Danbury CT 06810
　　203 837-2000

(P-7445)
PRAXAIR DISTRIBUTION INC
455 E Wooley Rd, Oxnard (93030-7224)
PHONE.................................805 487-2742
Craig Haggmark, *Manager*
John Whitt, *Manager*
EMP: 12 **Privately Held**
SIC: **2813** Industrial gases
HQ: Praxair Distribution, Inc.
　　10 Riverview Dr
　　Danbury CT 06810
　　203 837-2000

(P-7446)
PRAXAIR DISTRIBUTION INC
215 San Jose Ave, San Jose (95125-1009)
PHONE.................................408 995-6089
Brian Anderson, *Manager*
EMP: 12 **Privately Held**
SIC: **2813** Industrial gases
HQ: Praxair Distribution, Inc.
　　10 Riverview Dr
　　Danbury CT 06810
　　203 837-2000

(P-7447)
PRAXAIR DISTRIBUTION INC
1545 E Edinger Ave, Santa Ana
(92705-4907)
PHONE.................................714 547-6684
Janice Webber, *Manager*
EMP: 50 **Privately Held**

▲ = Import ▼=Export
◆ =Import/Export

SIC: 2813 Oxygen, compressed or liquefied
HQ: Praxair Distribution, Inc.
10 Riverview Dr
Danbury CT 06810
203 837-2000

(P-7448)
PRAXAIR DISTRIBUTION INC
2020 De La Cruz Blvd, Santa Clara
(95050)
PHONE.................................408 748-1722
Pete Krieger, *Branch Mgr*
EMP: 47 **Privately Held**
SIC: 2813 Industrial gases
HQ: Praxair Distribution, Inc.
10 Riverview Dr
Danbury CT 06810
203 837-2000

(P-7449)
PRAXAIR DISTRIBUTION INC
19200 Hawthorne Blvd, Torrance
(90503-1505)
PHONE.................................310 371-1254
Fred Casey, *Branch Mgr*
O'Neal Summers, *Plant Mgr*
Karina Rusnak, *Assistant*
EMP: 70 **Privately Held**
SIC: 2813 Industrial gases
HQ: Praxair Distribution, Inc.
10 Riverview Dr
Danbury CT 06810
203 837-2000

(P-7450)
**SHIELD REALTY CALIFORNIA
INC (PA)**
Also Called: Shield CA
5165 G St, Chino (91710-5143)
P.O. Box 190, Canton MA (02021-0190)
PHONE.................................909 628-4707
George P Bates, *President*
Todd A Johnston, *Vice Pres*
A Bruce Simpson, *Vice Pres*
Troy D Wilson, *Vice Pres*
Louis A Sgarzi, *Admin Sec*
▲ EMP: 43
SQ FT: 30,000
SALES (est): 21.9MM **Privately Held**
SIC: 2813 Aerosols

(P-7451)
TECH AIR NORTHERN CAL LLC
Also Called: Alliance Welding Supplies
140 S Montgomery St, San Jose
(95110-2520)
PHONE.................................408 293-9353
Chris Gremich, *Manager*
EMP: 11
SALES (corp-wide): 4.8MM **Privately
Held**
SIC: 2813 Industrial gases
PA: Tech Air Of Northern California, Llc
50 Mill Plain Rd
Danbury CT 06811
203 792-1834

(P-7452)
TECH AIR NORTHERN CAL LLC
Also Called: Alliance Welding Supplies
800 Greenville Rd, Livermore
(94550-9241)
PHONE.................................925 449-9353
Mark Harrill, *Manager*
EMP: 11
SALES (corp-wide): 4.8MM **Privately
Held**
SIC: 2813 Industrial gases
PA: Tech Air Of Northern California, Llc
50 Mill Plain Rd
Danbury CT 06811
203 792-1834

(P-7453)
TECH AIR NORTHERN CAL LLC
1224 6th St, Berkeley (94710-1402)
PHONE.................................510 524-9353
Larry McDonnell, *Manager*
EMP: 11
SALES (corp-wide): 4.8MM **Privately
Held**
SIC: 2813 Industrial gases

PA: Tech Air Of Northern California, Llc
50 Mill Plain Rd
Danbury CT 06811
203 792-1834

(P-7454)
TECH AIR NORTHERN CAL LLC
1135 Erickson Rd, Concord (94520-3799)
PHONE.................................925 568-9353
Mike Jones, *Manager*
EMP: 11
SALES (corp-wide): 4.8MM **Privately
Held**
SIC: 2813 Industrial gases
PA: Tech Air Of Northern California, Llc
50 Mill Plain Rd
Danbury CT 06811
203 792-1834

(P-7455)
TECH AIR NORTHERN CAL LLC
820 Industrial Rd, San Carlos
(94070-3319)
PHONE.................................650 593-9353
Juan Aguirre, *Manager*
EMP: 11
SALES (corp-wide): 4.8MM **Privately
Held**
SIC: 2813 Industrial gases
PA: Tech Air Of Northern California, Llc
50 Mill Plain Rd
Danbury CT 06811
203 792-1834

(P-7456)
TECH AIR NORTHERN CAL LLC
Also Called: Alliance Welding Supplies
4445 Jensen St, Oakland (94601-3939)
PHONE.................................510 533-9353
Chris Calegari, *Manager*
EMP: 11
SALES (corp-wide): 4.8MM **Privately
Held**
SIC: 2813 Industrial gases
PA: Tech Air Of Northern California, Llc
50 Mill Plain Rd
Danbury CT 06811
203 792-1834

2816 Inorganic Pigments

(P-7457)
**COLORWEN INTERNATIONAL
CORP**
951 Lawson St, City of Industry
(91748-1121)
PHONE.................................626 363-8855
Chin Huang, *Principal*
▲ EMP: 10
SALES (est): 1MM **Privately Held**
SIC: 2816 Color pigments

(P-7458)
DAY-GLO COLOR CORP
4615 Ardine St, Cudahy (90201-5821)
PHONE.................................323 560-2000
Joe Cummings, *Opers-Prdtn-Mfg*
EMP: 19
SQ FT: 100,000
SALES (corp-wide): 5.5B **Publicly Held**
WEB: www.dayglo.com
SIC: 2816 5169 2865 2851 Inorganic pig-
ments; synthetic resins, rubber & plastic
materials; color pigments, organic; paints
& allied products
HQ: Day-Glo Color Corp.
4515 Saint Clair Ave
Cleveland OH 44103
216 391-7070

(P-7459)
GENERAL CARBON COMPANY
7542 Maie Ave, Los Angeles (90001-2637)
PHONE.................................323 588-9291
Renee Aukers, *President*
Julio Negrete, *Vice Pres*
Mark Attwater, *Business Mgr*
▲ EMP: 12
SQ FT: 10,000
SALES (est): 3.1MM **Privately Held**
WEB: www.generalcarboncompany.com
SIC: 2816 Lamp black

(P-7460)
PLASTIC COLOR TECHNOLOGY
3010 Spyglass Ct, Chino Hills
(91709-2488)
PHONE.................................909 597-9230
Xavier Benegas, *Owner*
EMP: 15
SQ FT: 9,500
SALES (est): 1.8MM **Privately Held**
SIC: 2816 Metallic & mineral pigments

(P-7461)
RYVEC INC
251 E Palais Rd, Anaheim (92805-6239)
PHONE.................................714 520-5592
Michael Ryan, *CEO*
Steve Ryan, *Sales Mgr*
◆ EMP: 26
SQ FT: 43,000
SALES (est): 7MM **Privately Held**
WEB: www.ryvec.com
SIC: 2816 2865 2821 Color pigments;
dyes & pigments; polyurethane resins

(P-7462)
SOLOMON COLORS INC
1371 Laurel Ave, Rialto (92376-3011)
PHONE.................................909 484-9156
Jeff Bowers, *Branch Mgr*
Larry Parish, *Vice Pres*
Steve Laforce, *Info Tech Mgr*
Cecilia Lenihan, *Purchasing*
Tanya Bryant, *Marketing Staff*
EMP: 37
SQ FT: 80,000
SALES (corp-wide): 35.7MM **Privately
Held**
WEB: www.solomoncolors.com
SIC: 2816 Inorganic pigments
PA: Solomon Colors, Inc.
4050 Color Plant Rd
Springfield IL 62702
217 522-3112

(P-7463)
SPECTRA COLOR INC
9116 Stellar Ct, Corona (92883-4923)
PHONE.................................951 277-0200
Robert Shedd, *President*
John Shedd, *Admin Sec*
▲ EMP: 42
SQ FT: 40,000
SALES (est): 13MM **Privately Held**
SIC: 2816 3089 2821 Color pigments;
coloring & finishing of plastic products;
plastics materials & resins

(P-7464)
**STANFORD MATERIALS
CORPORATION**
23661 Birtcher Dr, Lake Forest
(92630-1770)
PHONE.................................949 380-7362
▲ EMP: 13
SALES (est): 2.1MM **Privately Held**
SIC: 2816

(P-7465)
VENATOR AMERICAS LLC
Davis Colors
3700 E Olympic Blvd, Los Angeles
(90023-3123)
P.O. Box 23100 (90023-0100)
PHONE.................................323 269-7311
Nick Paris, *Vice Pres*
George Armstrong, *Engineer*
Joe Hernandez, *Buyer*
EMP: 70
SQ FT: 540,000
SALES (corp-wide): 9.3B **Publicly Held**
WEB: www.rockwoodpigments.com
SIC: 2816 2865 Inorganic pigments; cyclic
crudes & intermediates
HQ: Venator Americas Llc
7011 Muirkirk Rd
Beltsville MD 20705
301 210-3400

2819 Indl Inorganic
Chemicals, NEC

(P-7466)
**ADVANCED CHEMICAL TECH
INC**
8728 Utica Ave, Rancho Cucamonga
(91730-5115)
PHONE.................................800 527-9607
Daniel Anthony Earley, *CEO*
EMP: 40 EST: 1996
SQ FT: 18,698
SALES (est): 11.4MM **Privately Held**
SIC: 2819 2899 5169 Industrial inorganic
chemicals; antiscaling compounds, boiler;
water treating compounds; anti-corrosion
products; industrial chemicals

(P-7467)
**AIR LIQUIDE ELECTRONICS US
LP**
Also Called: Aloha
46401 Landing Pkwy, Fremont
(94538-6496)
PHONE.................................510 624-4338
Don Swetnam, *Branch Mgr*
EMP: 45
SALES (corp-wide): 125.9MM **Privately
Held**
SIC: 2819 Industrial inorganic chemicals
HQ: Air Liquide Electronics U.S. Lp
9101 Lyndon B Johnson Fwy # 800
Dallas TX 75243
972 301-5200

(P-7468)
AMCOR MANUFACTURING INC
500 Winmoore Way, Modesto
(95358-5750)
PHONE.................................209 581-9687
Michael Harvey, *President*
Michael Archibald, *Vice Pres*
EMP: 22
SQ FT: 36,000
SALES: 2.9MM **Privately Held**
SIC: 2819 Industrial inorganic chemicals

(P-7469)
**AMERICAN LITHIUM ENERGY
CORP**
2261 Rutherford Rd, Carlsbad
(92008-8815)
PHONE.................................760 599-7388
Jiang Fan, *Presidenter*
Robert Spotnitz, *CTO*
▲ EMP: 15
SALES (est): 1.5MM **Privately Held**
SIC: 2819 3692 5063 Lithium com-
pounds, inorganic; dry cell batteries, sin-
gle or multiple cell; storage batteries,
industrial

(P-7470)
AMERICAS STYRENICS LLC
305 Crenshaw Blvd, Torrance
(90503-1701)
PHONE.................................424 488-3757
Brad Crocker, *Branch Mgr*
Tyler Staggs, *Engineer*
Lisa Jones, *Human Res Dir*
Peter Ott, *VP Opers*
Matt Stoker, *Manager*
EMP: 11 **Privately Held**
SIC: 2819 Industrial inorganic chemicals
PA: Americas Styrenics Llc
24 Waterway Ave Ste 1200
The Woodlands TX 77380

(P-7471)
**BD BISCNCES SYSTEMS
RGENTS INC**
2350 Qume Dr, San Jose (95131-1812)
PHONE.................................408 518-5024
EMP: 103
SALES (corp-wide): 1.2MM **Privately
Held**
SIC: 2819
PA: Bd Biosciences, Systems And
Reagents, Inc.
1 Becton Dr
Franklin Lakes NJ 07417
201 847-6800

P
R
O
D
U
C
T
S

&

S
V
C
S

(P-7472)
BIOLARGO INC (PA)
Also Called: BIO2
14921 Chestnut St, Westminster
(92683-5215)
PHONE...................................949 643-9540
Dennis P Calvert, *Ch of Bd*
Charles K Dargan II, *CFO*
Charles Dargan, *CFO*
Joseph L Provenzano, *Vice Pres*
Kenneth R Code, *Security Dir*
EMP: 23
SQ FT: 9,000
SALES: 1.3MM **Publicly Held**
SIC: 2819 Iodine, elemental

(P-7473)
CAL-PAC CHEMICAL CO INC
6231 Maywood Ave, Huntington Park
(90255-4530)
PHONE...................................323 585-2178
Charles F Duane, *President*
EMP: 17
SQ FT: 37,000
SALES (est): 3.9MM **Privately Held**
SIC: 2819 Industrial inorganic chemicals

(P-7474)
CALGON CARBON CORPORATION
501 Hatchery Rd, Blue Lake (95525)
P.O. Box 857 (95525-0857)
PHONE...................................707 668-5637
Lee Brown, *Manager*
EMP: 13 **Privately Held**
WEB: www.calgoncarbon.com
SIC: 2819 Charcoal (carbon), activated
HQ: Calgon Carbon Corporation
3000 Gsk Dr
Moon Township PA 15108
412 787-6700

(P-7475)
CALIFORNIA CARBON COMPANY INC
2825 E Grant St, Wilmington (90744-4033)
PHONE...................................562 436-1962
Franklin Liu, *President*
Rita L Wu, *Treasurer*
Richard Liu, *Vice Pres*
▲ EMP: 17
SQ FT: 10,000
SALES (est): 3.5MM **Privately Held**
WEB: www.californiacarbon.com
SIC: 2819 Carbides

(P-7476)
CALIFORNIA SILICA PRODUCTS LLC
12808 Rancho Rd, Adelanto (92301-2719)
PHONE...................................909 947-0028
Randall Humphreys, *Branch Mgr*
EMP: 19
SALES (corp-wide): 866K **Privately Held**
SIC: 2819 Silica compounds
PA: California Silica Products, Llc
1420 S Bon View Ave
Ontario CA 91761
760 885-5358

(P-7477)
CALIFORNIA SULPHUR COMPANY
2250 E Pacific Coast Hwy, Wilmington
(90744-2917)
P.O. Box 176 (90748-0176)
PHONE...................................562 437-0768
John Babbitt, *Principal*
Cheryl Rocha, *Manager*
▼ EMP: 28
SQ FT: 900
SALES (est): 6.4MM **Privately Held**
WEB: www.calsulco.com
SIC: 2819 Industrial inorganic chemicals

(P-7478)
CAR SOUND EXHAUST SYSTEM INC
Environmental Catalyst Tech
1901 Corporate Ctr, Oceanside
(92056-5831)
PHONE...................................949 888-1625
Steve Kasprisin,

EMP: 20
SALES (corp-wide): 101.4MM **Privately Held**
SIC: 2819 Catalysts, chemical
PA: Car Sound Exhaust System, Inc.
1901 Corporate Ctr
Oceanside CA 92056
949 858-5900

(P-7479)
CARBOMER INC
6324 Ferris Sq Ste B, San Diego
(92121-3238)
P.O. Box 261026 (92196-1026)
PHONE...................................858 552-0992
Manssur Yalpani, *President*
EMP: 85
SALES (est): 17.3K **Privately Held**
SIC: 2819 Industrial inorganic chemicals

(P-7480)
CDTI ADVANCED MATERIALS INC (PA)
1700 Fiske Pl, Oxnard (93033-1863)
PHONE...................................805 639-9458
Matthew Beale, *President*
Lon E Bell, *Ch of Bd*
Peter J Chase, *COO*
Tracy A Kern, *CFO*
Stephen J Golden, *Vice Pres*
EMP: 47
SQ FT: 52,000
SALES: 28.3MM **Privately Held**
WEB: www.cdti.com
SIC: 2819 3823 Catalysts, chemical; industrial instrmnts msrmnt display/control process variable

(P-7481)
CHEMTRADE CHEMICALS US LLC
501 Nichols Rd, Bay Point (94565-1002)
PHONE...................................925 458-7300
Brad Klock, *General Mgr*
EMP: 30
SALES (corp-wide): 1.2B **Privately Held**
SIC: 2819 Industrial inorganic chemicals
HQ: Chemtrade Chemicals Us Llc
90 E Halsey Rd
Parsippany NJ 07054

(P-7482)
CHEMTRADE CHEMICALS US LLC
525 Castro St, Richmond (94801-2104)
PHONE...................................510 232-7193
Thomas Brafford, *Manager*
Ernestina Diaz, *Opers Mgr*
EMP: 37
SALES (corp-wide): 1.2B **Privately Held**
SIC: 2819 Sulfuric acid, oleum
HQ: Chemtrade Chemicals Us Llc
90 E Halsey Rd
Parsippany NJ 07054

(P-7483)
CLEARCHEM DIAGNOSTICS INC
1710 E Grevillea Ct, Ontario (91761-8035)
PHONE...................................714 734-8041
Robert Stone, *President*
Kent Fleck, *Vice Pres*
EMP: 12 EST: 2001
SQ FT: 12,000
SALES (est): 2.7MM **Privately Held**
SIC: 2819 3559 8711 Chemicals, reagent grade: refined from technical grade; chemical machinery & equipment; electrical or electronic engineering

(P-7484)
CODEXIS INC (PA)
200 Penobscot Dr, Redwood City
(94063-4718)
PHONE...................................650 421-8100
John J Nicols, *President*
Bernard J Kelley, *Ch of Bd*
Gordon Sangster, *CFO*
Patrick Yang, *Bd of Directors*
Laurie Heilmann, *Senior VP*
EMP: 116
SQ FT: 107,200

SALES: 60.5MM **Publicly Held**
WEB: www.codexis.com
SIC: 2819 2869 8731 Catalysts, chemical; industrial organic chemicals; commercial research laboratory

(P-7485)
DOW CHEMICAL COMPANY
7380 Morton Ave, Newark (94560-4200)
PHONE...................................510 797-2281
James Oswald, *Branch Mgr*
EMP: 120
SALES (corp-wide): 61B **Publicly Held**
SIC: 2819 Industrial inorganic chemicals
HQ: The Dow Chemical Company
2211 H H Dow Way
Midland MI 48642
989 636-1000

(P-7486)
DOW CHEMICAL COMPANY
14445 Alondra Blvd, La Mirada
(90638-5504)
PHONE...................................714 228-4700
Jim Ryan, *Branch Mgr*
EMP: 200
SQ FT: 29,287
SALES (corp-wide): 61B **Publicly Held**
SIC: 2819 2821 Industrial inorganic chemicals; plastics materials & resins
HQ: The Dow Chemical Company
2211 H H Dow Way
Midland MI 48642
989 636-1000

(P-7487)
ECO SERVICES OPERATIONS CORP
100 Mococo Rd, Martinez (94553-1314)
PHONE...................................925 313-8224
Darrel Hodge, *Plant Mgr*
Jim Cesen, *Opers Mgr*
Roger Yackel, *Director*
Brett Jacks, *Manager*
EMP: 42
SALES (corp-wide): 1.6B **Publicly Held**
WEB: www.food.us.rhodia.com
SIC: 2819 Sulfuric acid, oleum
HQ: Eco Services Operations Corp.
300 Lindenwood Dr
Malvern PA 19355
610 251-9118

(P-7488)
ECO SERVICES OPERATIONS CORP
20720 S Wilmington Ave, Long Beach
(90810-1034)
PHONE...................................310 885-6719
Stephen Caro, *Branch Mgr*
EMP: 51
SALES (corp-wide): 1.6B **Publicly Held**
SIC: 2819 Sulfuric acid, oleum
HQ: Eco Services Operations Corp.
300 Lindenwood Dr
Malvern PA 19355
610 251-9118

(P-7489)
ELEMENT MATERIALS LLC
4936 E Pontiac Way, Fresno (93727-7449)
PHONE...................................559 304-1008
Michael Braham, *Principal*
EMP: 10
SALES (est): 1.9MM **Privately Held**
SIC: 2819 Elements

(P-7490)
ELEMENT SIX TECH US CORP
3901 Burton Dr, Santa Clara (95054-1583)
PHONE...................................408 986-8184
Adrian Wilson, *President*
EMP: 17
SALES (est): 3.2MM **Privately Held**
SIC: 2819 Industrial inorganic chemicals
PA: Element Six Sa
Rue Charles Martel 58
Luxembourg
268 647-08

(P-7491)
ENKI TECHNOLOGY INC
1035 Walsh Ave, Santa Clara
(95050-2645)
PHONE...................................408 383-9034
Kevin Kopczynski, *CEO*

Tom Colson, *COO*
Paul Kidman, *Vice Pres*
Brenor Brophy, *CTO*
Sina Maghsoodi, *Engineer*
▲ EMP: 13
SQ FT: 8,000
SALES (est): 2.4MM **Privately Held**
SIC: 2819 Silica compounds

(P-7492)
ENVIRNMENTAL CATALYST TECH LLC
3937 Ocean Ranch Blvd, Oceanside
(92056)
PHONE...................................949 459-3870
Steve Kasprisin,
Gennaro Paolone, *President*
Paul Applebee, *Mfg Spvr*
Kathy Paolone,
Laurie Paolone,
▲ EMP: 20
SALES (est): 5.8MM
SALES (corp-wide): 101.4MM **Privately Held**
SIC: 2819 Catalysts, chemical
PA: Car Sound Exhaust System, Inc.
1901 Corporate Ctr
Oceanside CA 92056
949 858-5900

(P-7493)
ERG AEROSPACE CORPORATION
Also Called: Erg Materials and Aerospace
964 Stanford Ave, Oakland (94608-2323)
PHONE...................................510 658-9785
Mitchell Hall, *CEO*
Berry Seamon, *Maintence Staff*
EMP: 70
SQ FT: 60,000
SALES (est): 6.8MM **Privately Held**
WEB: www.ergaerospace.com
SIC: 2819 Aluminum compounds

(P-7494)
ERNEST PACKAGING SOLUTIONS (PA)
2825 S Elm Ave Ste 103, Fresno
(93706-5460)
PHONE...................................800 757-4968
Tim Wilson, *President*
A Charles Wilson, *Chairman*
Brian Porter, *Vice Pres*
Kenny Briggs, *General Mgr*
Edward Cho, *Manager*
EMP: 45
SQ FT: 50,000
SALES (est): 8.3MM **Privately Held**
SIC: 2819 5191 5087 Industrial inorganic chemicals; chemicals, agricultural; cleaning & maintenance equipment & supplies; janitors' supplies

(P-7495)
ERNEST PACKAGING SOLUTIONS
8670 Fruitridge Rd # 300, Sacramento
(95826-9735)
PHONE...................................800 486-7222
Charles Wilson, *Owner*
EMP: 30
SALES (corp-wide): 8.3MM **Privately Held**
SIC: 2819 Industrial inorganic chemicals
PA: Ernest Packaging Solutions
2825 S Elm Ave Ste 103
Fresno CA 93706
800 757-4968

(P-7496)
FERRO CORPORATION
1395 Aspen Way, Vista (92081-8350)
PHONE...................................442 224-6100
Mike Steele, *Manager*
EMP: 10
SALES (corp-wide): 1.6B **Publicly Held**
WEB: www.ferro.com
SIC: 2819 Industrial inorganic chemicals
PA: Ferro Corporation
6060 Parkland Blvd # 250
Mayfield Heights OH 44124
216 875-5600

▲ = Import ▼=Export
◆ =Import/Export

(P-7497)
FLORIDE PRODUCTS LLC (PA)
2867 Vail Ave, Commerce (90040-2613)
PHONE................................323 201-4363
EMP: 23
SALES (est): 19.1MM **Privately Held**
SIC: 2819

(P-7498)
GE-HITACHI NUCLEAR ENERGY
Also Called: GE Vallecitos Nuclear Center
6705 Vallecitos Rd, Sunol (94586-9524)
PHONE................................925 862-4382
David Turner, Manager
EMP: 72
SALES (corp-wide): 121.6B **Publicly Held**
SIC: 2819 Nuclear fuel & cores, inorganic
HQ: Ge-Hitachi Nuclear Energy America Llc
3901 Castle Hayne Rd
Wilmington NC 28401

(P-7499)
HALDOR TOPSOE INC
Also Called: Refining Technology Division
770 The Cy Dr S Ste 8400, Orange
(92868)
PHONE................................714 621-3800
F Emmett Bingham, President
EMP: 10
SALES (corp-wide): 862MM **Publicly Held**
SIC: 2819 8711 Catalysts, chemical; chemical engineering
HQ: Haldor Topsoe, Inc.
17629 El Cam
Houston TX 77058
281 228-5000

(P-7500)
HONEYWELL INTERNATIONAL INC
3500 Garrett Dr, Santa Clara (95054-2827)
PHONE................................408 962-2000
Paul Raymond, Vice Pres
EMP: 100
SALES (corp-wide): 41.8B **Publicly Held**
WEB: www.honeywell.com
SIC: 2819 3674 Chemicals, reagent grade: refined from technical grade; semiconductors & related devices
PA: Honeywell International Inc.
300 S Tryon St
Charlotte NC 28202
973 455-2000

(P-7501)
JVIC CATALYST SERVICES LLC
18025 S Broadway, Carson (90745)
PHONE................................310 327-0991
Rodney Woody, Manager
EMP: 40 **Privately Held**
WEB: www.cat-tech.com
SIC: 2819 Catalysts, chemical
HQ: Jvic Catalyst Services, Llc
4040 Red Bluff Rd
Pasadena TX 77503
713 568-2600

(P-7502)
KEMIRA WATER SOLUTIONS INC
14000 San Bernardino Ave, Fontana
(92335-5258)
PHONE................................909 350-5678
Keith Heasley, Manager
Randy Prater, Technical Staff
John Vanderkolk, Technical Staff
Matthew Stegura, Site Mgr
Pete Broderick, Sales Mgr
EMP: 21
SALES (corp-wide): 2.9B **Privately Held**
WEB: www.kemiron.com
SIC: 2819 Industrial inorganic chemicals
HQ: Kemira Water Solutions, Inc.
1000 Parkwood Cir Se # 500
Atlanta GA 30339
770 436-1542

(P-7503)
MATERIA INC (PA)
60 N San Gabriel Blvd, Pasadena
(91107-3748)
PHONE................................626 584-8400

Christopher Murphy, President
Scott Krog, CFO
Cliff Post, Vice Pres
Mark S Trimmer, Vice Pres
Trina Harding, Planning
▲ EMP: 120
SQ FT: 30,000
SALES (est): 27.1MM **Privately Held**
WEB: www.materia-inc.com
SIC: 2819 Catalysts, chemical

(P-7504)
MATTERHORN FILTER CORPORATION
125 W Victoria St, Gardena (90248-3522)
PHONE................................310 329-8073
Joseph Silva, President
▲ EMP: 11
SALES (est): 1.6MM **Privately Held**
SIC: 2819 Charcoal (carbon), activated

(P-7505)
MERELEX CORPORATION
Also Called: American Elements
10884 Weyburn Ave, Los Angeles
(90024-2917)
PHONE................................310 208-0551
Michael Silver, President
Gabriel Leis, Buyer
Brian Lim, Opers Staff
Keri Keinath, Sales Engr
Scott Michel, Manager
▲ EMP: 22 EST: 1996
SALES (est): 6.5MM **Privately Held**
SIC: 2819 Chemicals, high purity: refined from technical grade

(P-7506)
MISSION PARK HOTEL LP
Also Called: Element Santa Clara
1950 Wyatt Dr, Santa Clara (95054-1544)
PHONE................................408 809-3838
Mona Rigdon, Principal
Brent Lower, Principal
EMP: 38
SALES (est): 3.8MM **Privately Held**
SIC: 2819 Elements

(P-7507)
MONOLITH MATERIALS INC
1700 Seaport Blvd Ste 110, Redwood City
(94063-5572)
PHONE................................650 933-4957
Pete Johnson, CEO
Bill Brady, Chairman
Jose Bahury, Vice Pres
Ned Hardman, Vice Pres
Roscoe Taylor, Vice Pres
EMP: 26
SQ FT: 3,500
SALES (est): 10.8MM **Privately Held**
SIC: 2819 Chemicals, high purity: refined from technical grade

(P-7508)
MORAVEK BIOCHEMICALS INC (PA)
577 Mercury Ln, Brea (92821-4831)
PHONE................................714 990-2018
Paul Moravek, President
Joseph Moravek, President
Helen Moravek, Corp Secy
Ivana Moravek, Info Tech Mgr
Lia Barnes, Production
▲ EMP: 25 EST: 1976
SQ FT: 6,000
SALES (est): 4.1MM **Privately Held**
SIC: 2819 Industrial inorganic chemicals

(P-7509)
MORGAN ADVANCED CERAMICS INC
13079 Earhart Ave, Auburn (95602-9536)
PHONE................................530 823-3401
John Stang, CEO
James A West, President
Chester Chiu, Info Tech Mgr
Frank Ravera, Maintence Staff
▲ EMP: 167
SQ FT: 80,000
SALES (est): 29.9MM
SALES (corp-wide): 1.3B **Privately Held**
SIC: 2819 3356 3264 Aluminum oxide; zirconium & zirconium alloy bars, sheets, strip, etc.; porcelain electrical supplies

HQ: Morganite Industries Inc.
4000 Westchase Blvd # 170
Raleigh NC 27607
919 821-1253

(P-7510)
NALCO COMPANY LLC
Also Called: Nalco Champion
6321 District Blvd, Bakersfield
(93313-2143)
PHONE................................661 834-0454
Tom Pappas, Manager
Matt Knickrehm, Manager
Doc Monical, Manager
EMP: 15
SQ FT: 5,000
SALES (corp-wide): 14.6B **Publicly Held**
WEB: www.champ-tech.com
SIC: 2819 7349 Industrial inorganic chemicals; chemical cleaning services
HQ: Nalco Company Llc
1601 W Diehl Rd
Naperville IL 60563
630 305-1000

(P-7511)
NCH CORPORATION
Also Called: Mohawk Laboratories Division
932 Kifer Rd, Sunnyvale (94086-5206)
P.O. Box 152126, Irving TX (75015-2126)
PHONE................................972 438-0211
Gerald Ikeda, Branch Mgr
Edward Trambley, Office Admin
EMP: 12
SQ FT: 53,000
SALES (corp-wide): 1B **Privately Held**
WEB: www.nch.com
SIC: 2819 4226 5169 2842 Industrial inorganic chemicals; special warehousing & storage; chemicals & allied products; specialty cleaning, polishes & sanitation goods
PA: Nch Corporation
2727 Chemsearch Blvd
Irving TX 75062
972 438-0211

(P-7512)
NIPPON CARBIDE INDS USA INC
13856 Bettencourt St, Cerritos
(90703-1010)
PHONE................................562 777-1810
EMP: 15 **Privately Held**
SIC: 2819 Carbides
HQ: Nippon Carbide Industries (Usa), Inc.
12981 Florence Ave
Santa Fe Springs CA 90670
562 777-1810

(P-7513)
OMYA CALIFORNIA INC
Also Called: O M Y A
7299 Crystal Creek Rd, Lucerne Valley
(92356-8646)
PHONE................................760 248-7306
Anthony Colak, CEO
James Reddy, President
Leonard Eisenberg, Admin Sec
Richard Bushart, Technical Staff
David Moore, Manager
▲ EMP: 100
SQ FT: 6,000
SALES (est): 25MM
SALES (corp-wide): 3.9B **Privately Held**
SIC: 2819 8741 3281 Calcium compounds & salts, inorganic; management services; cut stone & stone products
HQ: Omya Industries, Inc
9987 Carver Rd Ste 300
Blue Ash OH 45242
513 387-4600

(P-7514)
OXBOW ACTIVATED CARBON LLC
2535 Jason Ct, Oceanside (92056-3592)
PHONE................................760 630-5724
Mark McCormick, Vice Pres
EMP: 25
SALES (corp-wide): 444.9MM **Privately Held**
SIC: 2819 Charcoal (carbon), activated
HQ: Oxbow Activated Carbon Llc
1601 Forum Pl Ste 1400
West Palm Beach FL 33401
561 907-5400

(P-7515)
PCT-GW CARBIDE TOOLS USA INC
13701 Excelsior Dr, Santa Fe Springs
(90670-5104)
PHONE................................562 921-7898
Shamir Seth, President
▲ EMP: 50
SALES (est): 758.8K **Privately Held**
SIC: 2819 Carbides

(P-7516)
PERIMETER SOLUTIONS LP
Wildfire Control Division
10667 Jersey Blvd, Rancho Cucamonga
(91730-5110)
PHONE................................909 983-0772
Vinayak Sharma, Manager
EMP: 20 **Privately Held**
SIC: 2819 Industrial inorganic chemicals
HQ: Perimeter Solutions Lp
8000 Maryland Ave Ste 350
Saint Louis MO 63105
314 983-7500

(P-7517)
PHIBRO-TECH INC
8851 Dice Rd, Santa Fe Springs
(90670-2515)
PHONE................................562 698-8036
Mark Alling, Manager
Alonso Alatorre, Lab Dir
Jeff Dorfman, MIS Dir
Jim Ferguson, Maintence Staff
Jerry Mesinger, Manager
EMP: 50
SALES (corp-wide): 828MM **Publicly Held**
WEB: www.phibrochem.com
SIC: 2819 2899 Inorganic metal compounds or salts; chemical preparations
HQ: Phibro-Tech, Inc.
300 Frank W Burr Blvd # 21
Teaneck NJ 07666

(P-7518)
PICKERING LABORATORIES INC
1280 Space Park Way, Mountain View
(94043-1434)
PHONE................................650 694-6700
Michael Pickering, President
James Murphy, Vice Pres
Jim Murphy, Vice Pres
Mike Gottschalk, Principal
David Mazawa, Principal
EMP: 22
SQ FT: 17,000
SALES (est): 6.5MM **Privately Held**
WEB: www.pickeringlabs.com
SIC: 2819 3826 2899 Chemicals, reagent grade: refined from technical grade; liquid chromatographic instruments; chemical preparations

(P-7519)
PQ CORPORATION
8401 Quartz Ave, South Gate
(90280-2536)
PHONE................................323 326-1100
Jim Olivier, Manager
William Berkey, Analyst
EMP: 11
SALES (corp-wide): 1.6B **Publicly Held**
WEB: www.pqcorp.com
SIC: 2819 Industrial inorganic chemicals
HQ: Pq Corporation
300 Lindenwood Dr
Malvern PA 19355
610 651-4200

(P-7520)
QUALITY CAR CARE PRODUCTS INC
2734 Huntington Dr, Duarte (91010-2301)
PHONE................................626 359-9174
Edward R Justice Jr, President
EMP: 30
SQ FT: 25,000
SALES (est): 6.2MM **Privately Held**
SIC: 2819 Industrial inorganic chemicals

(P-7521)
REAGENT CHEMICAL & RES INC
Also Called: White Fire Tagets
1454 S Sunnyside Ave, San Bernardino
(92408-2810)
PHONE..............................909 796-4059
Dan Sumnter, *Branch Mgr*
Phil Murray, *Sales Staff*
EMP: 20
SQ FT: 99,400
SALES (corp-wide): 517MM **Privately
Held**
WEB: www.biotarget.com
SIC: 2819 3949 Sulfur, recovered or re-
fined, incl. from sour natural gas; targets,
archery & rifle shooting
PA: Reagent Chemical & Research, Inc.
115 Rte 202
Ringoes NJ 08551
908 284-2800

(P-7522)
SHELL CATALYSTS & TECH LP
1001 N Todd Ave, Azusa (91702-1602)
PHONE..............................626 334-1241
Bill Holmes, *Branch Mgr*
Lisa Segal, *Executive*
EMP: 70
SQ FT: 50,000
SALES (corp-wide): 388.3B **Privately
Held**
WEB: www.criterioncatalysts.com
SIC: 2819 Catalysts, chemical
HQ: Shell Catalysts & Technologies Lp
910 Louisiana St Ste 2900
Houston TX 77002
713 241-3000

(P-7523)
SHELL CATALYSTS & TECH LP
2840 Willow Pass Rd, Bay Point
(94565-3237)
P.O. Box 5159, Pittsburg (94565-0659)
PHONE..............................925 458-9045
William Howell, *Manager*
EMP: 100
SALES (corp-wide): 388.3B **Privately
Held**
WEB: www.criterioncatalysts.com
SIC: 2819 Catalysts, chemical
HQ: Shell Catalysts & Technologies Lp
910 Louisiana St Ste 2900
Houston TX 77002
713 241-3000

(P-7524)
SHELL CHEMICAL LP
10 Mococo Rd, Martinez (94553-1340)
PHONE..............................925 313-8601
Marj Leeds, *Manager*
EMP: 65
SALES (corp-wide): 388.3B **Privately
Held**
SIC: 2819 Catalysts, chemical
HQ: Shell Chemical Lp
910 Louisiana St
Houston TX 77002
855 697-4355

(P-7525)
SIGNA CHEMISTRY INC
720 Olive Dr Ste Cd, Davis (95616-4740)
PHONE..............................212 933-4101
EMP: 25
SALES (corp-wide): 8.9MM **Privately
Held**
SIC: 2819 3511
PA: Signa Chemistry, Inc.
445 Park Ave Ste 937
New York NY 10017
212 933-4101

(P-7526)
**SMARTWASH SOLUTIONS LLC
(HQ)**
1129 Harkins Rd, Salinas (93901-4407)
PHONE..............................831 676-9750
Bruce Taylor,
Abraham Richardson, *Technician*
▲ EMP: 15
SALES (est): 4MM **Privately Held**
SIC: 2819 Chemicals, high purity: refined
from technical grade

(P-7527)
SOLDO CAPITAL INC (DH)
4695 Macarthur Ct # 1200, Newport Beach
(92660-8859)
P.O. Box 746, Bluffton SC (29910-0746)
PHONE..............................800 659-6745
Dan Stahl, *Vice Pres*
EMP: 27
SQ FT: 2,000
SALES (est): 4.4MM
SALES (corp-wide): 454.2MM **Publicly
Held**
WEB: www.ohp.com
SIC: 2819 Industrial inorganic chemicals
HQ: Amvac Chemical Corporation
4695 Macarthur Ct # 1200
Newport Beach CA 92660
323 264-3910

(P-7528)
SOLVAY USA INC
Also Called: Marchem Solvay Group
20851 S Santa Fe Ave, Long Beach
(90810-1130)
PHONE..............................310 669-5300
Maria Johnson, *Manager*
EMP: 17
SALES (corp-wide): 12.8MM **Privately
Held**
SIC: 2819 Industrial inorganic chemicals
HQ: Solvay Usa Inc.
504 Carnegie Ctr
Princeton NJ 08540
609 860-4000

(P-7529)
TESSENDERLO KERLEY INC
5247 E Central Ave, Fresno (93725)
PHONE..............................559 485-0114
Vince Roggentine, *General Mgr*
EMP: 40 **Privately Held**
WEB: www.mprserve.com
SIC: 2819 Industrial inorganic chemicals
HQ: Tessenderlo Kerley, Inc.
2255 N 44th St Ste 300
Phoenix AZ 85008
602 889-8300

(P-7530)
TIGER-SUL PRODUCTS LLC
61 Stork Rd, Stockton (95203-8200)
PHONE..............................209 451-2725
EMP: 12 EST: 2008
SALES (est): 2.7MM **Privately Held**
SIC: 2819 Industrial inorganic chemicals

(P-7531)
**TOKYO OHKA KOGYO AMERICA
INC**
Also Called: Tok America
190 Topaz St, Milpitas (95035-5429)
PHONE..............................408 956-9901
Yoshi Arai, *Manager*
EMP: 13
SQ FT: 12,560 **Privately Held**
WEB: www.ohka.com
SIC: 2819 3674 Industrial inorganic chem-
icals; semiconductors & related devices
HQ: Tokyo Ohka Kogyo America, Inc.
4600 Ne Brookwood Pkwy
Hillsboro OR 97124

(P-7532)
US BORAX INC
14486 Borax Rd, Boron (93516-2017)
PHONE..............................760 762-7000
Joe A Carrabba, *Branch Mgr*
Doug Batchelor, *MIS Dir*
Saman Naerges, *Analyst*
EMP: 900
SALES (corp-wide): 40.5B **Privately Held**
WEB: www.borax.com
SIC: 2819 Industrial inorganic chemicals
HQ: U.S. Borax Inc.
8051 E Maplewood Ave # 100
Greenwood Village CO 80111
303 713-5000

(P-7533)
US BORAX INC
300 Falcon St, Wilmington (90744-6407)
PHONE..............................310 522-5300
Robert F Shaw, *President*
EMP: 182

SALES (corp-wide): 40.5B **Privately Held**
WEB: www.borax.com
SIC: 2819 2899 Industrial inorganic chem-
icals; chemical preparations
HQ: U.S. Borax Inc.
8051 E Maplewood Ave # 100
Greenwood Village CO 80111
303 713-5000

(P-7534)
**VACUUM ENGRG & MTLS CO
INC**
390 Reed St, Santa Clara (95050-3108)
PHONE..............................408 871-9900
John S Kavanaugh Jr, *Ch of Bd*
Stephanie McConnell, *CFO*
EMP: 30
SQ FT: 16,500
SALES (est): 9MM **Privately Held**
WEB: www.vem-co.com
SIC: 2819 3399 3499 Chemicals, high pu-
rity: refined from technical grade; powder,
metal; friction material, made from pow-
dered metal

(P-7535)
VENUS LABORATORIES INC
Earth Friendly Products
11150 Hope St, Cypress (90630-5236)
PHONE..............................714 891-3100
Firas Jamal, *Manager*
Mike Palmatier, *CFO*
Belinda Diaz, *Purch Agent*
Monika Hanks, *Marketing Staff*
Amber Enriquez, *General Counsel*
EMP: 70
SALES (corp-wide): 76.7MM **Privately
Held**
SIC: 2819 2844 2842 2841 Industrial in-
organic chemicals; toilet preparations;
specialty cleaning, polishes & sanitation
goods; soap & other detergents
PA: Venus Laboratories, Inc.
111 S Rohlwing Rd
Addison IL 60101
630 595-1900

(P-7536)
W R GRACE & CO
Also Called: W R Grace Construction Pdts
7237 E Gage Ave, Commerce
(90040-3812)
PHONE..............................562 927-8513
Suzanne Parsons, *Manager*
EMP: 15
SQ FT: 18,595
SALES (corp-wide): 1.9B **Publicly Held**
WEB: www.grace.com
SIC: 2819 Industrial inorganic chemicals
PA: W. R. Grace & Co.
7500 Grace Dr
Columbia MD 21044
410 531-4000

(P-7537)
W R GRACE & CO
252 W Larch Rd Ste H, Tracy
(95304-1638)
PHONE..............................209 839-2800
EMP: 164
SALES (corp-wide): 3.1B **Publicly Held**
SIC: 2819
PA: W. R. Grace & Co.
7500 Grace Dr
Columbia MD 21044
410 531-4000

(P-7538)
ZI CHEMICALS
8605 Santa Monica Blvd, Los Angeles
(90069-4109)
PHONE..............................818 827-1301
Barnaby L Zelman, *Owner*
▼ EMP: 11
SALES (est): 1.3MM **Privately Held**
WEB: www.zichemicals.com
SIC: 2819 Industrial inorganic chemicals

**2821 Plastics, Mtrls &
Nonvulcanizable Elastomers**

(P-7539)
ACP NOXTAT INC
1112 E Washington Ave, Santa Ana
(92701-4221)
PHONE..............................714 547-5477
Anthony Floyd Richard, *President*
Tracee Huwe, *COO*
Anthony Richard, *Info Tech Dir*
EMP: 20
SALES (est): 4.5MM **Privately Held**
WEB: www.noxtat.com
SIC: 2821 Plastics materials & resins

(P-7540)
**ALPHA CORPORATION OF
TENNESSEE**
Also Called: Alpha-Owens Corning
19991 Seaton Ave, Perris (92570-8724)
PHONE..............................951 657-5161
John Mulrine, *Enginr/R&D Mgr*
EMP: 60
SALES (corp-wide): 242.1K **Privately
Held**
WEB: www.glasteel.com
SIC: 2821 Polyethylene resins
HQ: The Alpha Corporation Of Tennessee
955 Highway 57
Collierville TN 38017
901 854-2800

(P-7541)
**AMERICAN LIQUID PACKAGING
SYST (PA)**
Also Called: Chemtex International
440 N Wolfe Rd, Sunnyvale (94085-3869)
PHONE..............................408 524-7474
Saeed Amidhozour, *President*
Rahim Amidhozour, *CFO*
▼ EMP: 40
SQ FT: 25,000
SALES (est): 117.8MM **Privately Held**
SIC: 2821 Plastics materials & resins

(P-7542)
APTCO LLC (PA)
31381 Pond Rd Bldg 2, Mc Farland
(93250-9795)
PHONE..............................661 792-2107
Jim Banuelos, *Mng Member*
Scott Hakl,
◆ EMP: 43
SALES (est): 15.9MM **Privately Held**
WEB: www.aptcollc.com
SIC: 2821 Thermoplastic materials

(P-7543)
BAMBERGER POLYMERS INC
145 S State College Blvd # 100, Brea
(92821-5824)
PHONE..............................714 672-4740
Chris Landis, *Branch Mgr*
EMP: 10 **Privately Held**
WEB: www.bambergerpolymers.com
SIC: 2821 Plastics materials & resins
HQ: Bamberger Polymers, Inc.
2 Jericho Plz Ste 109
Jericho NY 11753

(P-7544)
BD CLASSIC ENTERPRIZES INC
12903 Sunshine Ave, Santa Fe Springs
(90670-4732)
P.O. Box 2445 (90670-0445)
PHONE..............................562 944-6177
Fred S Benson, *CEO*
Matt Benson, *Vice Pres*
Frederick Benson, *Info Tech Dir*
Patricia Ashford, *Purch Mgr*
Gene Vega, *Sales Mgr*
▲ EMP: 16
SQ FT: 15,000
SALES (est): 6.5MM **Privately Held**
WEB: www.bdcepoxysystems.com
SIC: 2821 Epoxy resins

▲ = Import ▼=Export
◆ =Import/Export

(P-7545)
BJB ENTERPRISES INC
14791 Franklin Ave, Tustin (92780-7215)
PHONE..............................714 734-8450
Brian Stransky, *President*
Terry McGinnis, *Technical Staff*
Troy Peterson, *Technical Staff*
Joel Severin, *Technical Staff*
Joseph Castillo, *Mfg Staff*
EMP: 27
SQ FT: 38,000
SALES (est): 7.1MM **Privately Held**
WEB: www.bjbenterprises.com
SIC: 2821 3087 5162 Polyurethane
resins; custom compound purchased
resins; plastics materials & basic shapes

(P-7546)
BOLCOF PLSTIC MTLS
STHEAST INC
Also Called: Bolcof Port Polymers
960 W 10th St, Azusa (91702-1936)
PHONE..............................800 621-2681
Ralph Bolcof, *CEO*
Keith Eitzen, *President*
Carol Bolcof, *Corp Secy*
Jeffrey Tunstall, *Vice Pres*
Gail Lieberman, *Administration*
▲ EMP: 10
SQ FT: 50,000
SALES (est): 2.2MM
SALES (corp-wide): 243MM **Privately Held**
SIC: 2821 Plastics materials & resins
PA: Port Plastics, Inc.
5800 Campus Circle Dr E 150a
Irving TX 75063
469 299-7000

(P-7547)
CERTAINTEED CORPORATION
Also Called: saint gobain certainteed pipe
300 S Beckman Rd, Lodi (95240-3103)
PHONE..............................209 365-7500
Dave Eugins, *Plant Mgr*
EMP: 200
SALES (corp-wide): 215.9MM **Privately Held**
SIC: 2821 Plastics materials & resins
HQ: Certainteed Llc
20 Moores Rd
Malvern PA 19355
610 893-5000

(P-7548)
CLARIANT CORPORATION
3350 W Bayshore Rd, Palo Alto
(94303-4238)
PHONE..............................650 494-1749
Kenneth Golder, *President*
EMP: 225
SALES (corp-wide): 6.6B **Privately Held**
SIC: 2821 Plastics materials & resins
HQ: Clariant Corporation
4000 Monroe Rd
Charlotte NC 28205
704 331-7000

(P-7549)
COASTAL ENTERPRISES
1925 W Collins Ave, Orange (92867-5426)
P.O. Box 4875 (92863-4875)
PHONE..............................714 771-4969
Chuck Miller, *Owner*
Krystle Rhodes, *Office Admin*
▲ EMP: 20
SQ FT: 25,000
SALES (est): 3.5MM **Privately Held**
WEB: www.precisionboard.com
SIC: 2821 Plastics materials & resins

(P-7550)
COSMIC PLASTICS INC (PA)
28410 Industry Dr, Valencia (91355-4108)
PHONE..............................661 257-3274
George Luh, *CEO*
Edwin Luh, *Vice Pres*
Eddie Cantrell, *Manager*
◆ EMP: 30
SQ FT: 846,000
SALES: 5MM **Privately Held**
WEB: www.cosmicplastics.com
SIC: 2821 Plastics materials & resins

(P-7551)
CROSSFIELD PRODUCTS CORP
(PA)
Also Called: Dex-O-Tex Division
3000 E Harcourt St, Compton
(90221-5589)
PHONE..............................310 886-9100
Richard Watt, *Ch of Bd*
W Brad Watt, *President*
Ronald Borum, *Exec VP*
▲ EMP: 47
SQ FT: 23,000
SALES (est): 17.2MM **Privately Held**
WEB: www.crossfieldproducts.com
SIC: 2821 Plastics materials & resins

(P-7552)
CYTEC ENGINEERED
MATERIALS INC
1191 N Hawk Cir, Anaheim (92807-1723)
PHONE..............................714 632-8444
George Slayton, *Branch Mgr*
EMP: 20
SALES (corp-wide): 12.8MM **Privately Held**
WEB: www.cytecengineeredmaterials.com
SIC: 2821 2822 Plastics materials &
resins; synthetic rubber
HQ: Cytec Engineered Materials Inc.
2085 E Tech Cir Ste 200
Tempe AZ 85284

(P-7553)
CYTEC ENGINEERED
MATERIALS INC
645 N Cypress St, Orange (92867-6603)
PHONE..............................714 630-9400
Ron Martin, *Branch Mgr*
EMP: 130
SQ FT: 300,000
SALES (corp-wide): 12.8MM **Privately Held**
WEB: www.cytecengineeredmaterials.com
SIC: 2821 Molding compounds, plastics
HQ: Cytec Engineered Materials Inc.
2085 E Tech Cir Ste 200
Tempe AZ 85284

(P-7554)
DOW CHEMICAL CO
FOUNDATION
11266 Jersey Blvd, Rancho Cucamonga
(91730-5114)
P.O. Box 748 (91729-0748)
PHONE..............................909 476-4127
Steve Rynders, *Principal*
EMP: 36
SALES (corp-wide): 61B **Publicly Held**
SIC: 2821 Thermoplastic materials
HQ: The Dow Chemical Company Foundation
2030 Dow Ctr
Midland MI 48674
989 636-1000

(P-7555)
DOW CHEMICAL COMPANY
901 Loveridge Rd, Pittsburg (94565-2811)
P.O. Box 1398 (94565-0398)
PHONE..............................925 432-3165
Larry Reeves, *Branch Mgr*
EMP: 75
SQ FT: 17,280
SALES (corp-wide): 61B **Publicly Held**
WEB: www.dow.com
SIC: 2821 2879 2851 Thermoplastic materials; agricultural chemicals; paints & allied products
HQ: The Dow Chemical Company
2211 H H Dow Way
Midland MI 48642
989 636-1000

(P-7556)
DOW CHEMICAL COMPANY
25500 Whitesell St, Hayward (94545-3615)
PHONE..............................510 786-0100
◆ EMP: 249
SALES (corp-wide): 61B **Publicly Held**
SIC: 2821 Thermoplastic materials

HQ: The Dow Chemical Company
2211 H H Dow Way
Midland MI 48642
989 636-1000

(P-7557)
EASTMAN PERFORMANCE
FILMS LLC
Also Called: Cpfilms Distribution Center
4110 E La Palma Ave, Anaheim
(92807-1814)
PHONE..............................714 634-0900
Greg McKay, *Branch Mgr*
EMP: 20 **Publicly Held**
SIC: 2821 Plastics materials & resins
HQ: Eastman Performance Films, Llc
4210 The Great Rd
Fieldale VA 24089
276 627-3000

(P-7558)
EASTMAN PERFORMANCE
FILMS LLC
21019 Osborne St, Canoga Park
(91304-1744)
PHONE..............................818 882-5744
Joseph Gordon, *Branch Mgr*
EMP: 43 **Publicly Held**
SIC: 2821 Plastics materials & resins
HQ: Eastman Performance Films, Llc
4210 The Great Rd
Fieldale VA 24089
276 627-3000

(P-7559)
EEZER PRODUCTS INC
4734 E Home Ave, Fresno (93703-4509)
PHONE..............................559 255-4140
Leighton Sjostrand, *President*
▲ EMP: 21
SQ FT: 20,000
SALES: 2MM **Privately Held**
WEB: www.eezer.com
SIC: 2821 Plastics materials & resins

(P-7560)
ELASCO INC
Also Called: E Sales
11377 Markon Dr, Garden Grove
(92841-1402)
PHONE..............................714 373-4767
Henry Larrucea, *President*
David Schindler, *President*
Gary Stull, *CFO*
Janet Lurrucea, *Vice Pres*
▲ EMP: 100
SQ FT: 28,000
SALES (est): 20.6MM **Privately Held**
WEB: www.elascourethane.com
SIC: 2821 2891 2822 Polyurethane
resins; adhesives & sealants; synthetic
rubber

(P-7561)
ELITE GLOBAL SOLUTIONS INC
19732 Descartes, Foothill Ranch
(92610-2621)
PHONE..............................949 709-4872
Garry Mazzone, *President*
Tracie Mazzone, *Project Mgr*
Rhett Boyer, *Purchasing*
Jim Neace, *Marketing Mgr*
Linda Alvarez, *Sales Staff*
◆ EMP: 14
SALES (est): 3.7MM **Privately Held**
SIC: 2821 5023 Melamine resins,
melamine-formaldehyde; kitchenware

(P-7562)
ENVIRONMENTAL
TECHNOLOGY INC
Also Called: Eti
300 S Bay Depot Rd, Fields Landing
(95537)
P.O. Box 365 (95537-0365)
PHONE..............................707 443-9323
David C Fonsen, *President*
Deborah Fonsen, *Treasurer*
Carol Miller, *Office Mgr*
Andrew Cranfill, *Production*
Don Adele, *Manager*
◆ EMP: 25
SQ FT: 3,000

SALES (est): 6.2MM
SALES (corp-wide): 13.1MM **Privately Held**
WEB: www.eti-usa.com
SIC: 2821 Thermoplastic materials
PA: Polytek Development Corp.
55 Hilton St
Easton PA 18042
610 559-8620

(P-7563)
FERCO COLOR &
COMPOUNDING INC
Also Called: Ferco Plastic Products
5498 Vine St, Chino (91710-5247)
PHONE..............................909 930-0773
Jennifer Thaw, *Principal*
EMP: 48
SQ FT: 20,000
SALES: 16.9MM **Privately Held**
WEB: www.fercocolor.com
SIC: 2821 2865 Polyethylene resins;
polypropylene resins; color pigments, organic

(P-7564)
HENNIS ENTERPRISES INC
2646 Palma Dr Ste 430, Ventura
(93003-7798)
PHONE..............................805 477-0257
Rodney Hennis, *President*
Christopher Hennis, *Treasurer*
EMP: 20 EST: 1975
SQ FT: 10,000
SALES (est): 3.6MM **Privately Held**
WEB: www.hennisenterprises.com
SIC: 2821 Polyurethane resins

(P-7565)
HEXCEL CORPORATION
11711 Dublin Blvd, Dublin (94568-2898)
PHONE..............................925 551-4900
Robert Petrisko, *Branch Mgr*
Patrick Winterlich, *Exec VP*
John Bonema, *General Mgr*
Gene Cunliffe, *Technician*
Lilia Cruz, *Research*
EMP: 59
SALES (corp-wide): 2.1B **Publicly Held**
WEB: www.hexcel.com
SIC: 2821 Plastics materials & resins
PA: Hexcel Corporation
281 Tresser Blvd Ste 1503
Stamford CT 06901
203 969-0666

(P-7566)
HOFFMAN PLASTIC
COMPOUNDS INC
16616 Garfield Ave, Paramount
(90723-5305)
PHONE..............................323 636-3346
Ronald P Hoffman, *President*
Susan Hoffman, *Treasurer*
▲ EMP: 66
SQ FT: 46,000
SALES (est): 18.9MM **Privately Held**
SIC: 2821 3087 Polyvinyl chloride resins
(PVC); custom compound purchased
resins

(P-7567)
HUNTSMAN ADVANCED
MATERIALS AM
5121 W San Fernando Rd, Los Angeles
(90039-1011)
PHONE..............................818 265-7221
Glenn Bauernschmidt, *Manager*
Marlene Stirbys, *Vice Pres*
Maggie Escriva, *Office Mgr*
Paul Hu, *Manager*
Floyd Sylvester, *Manager*
EMP: 120
SALES (corp-wide): 9.3B **Publicly Held**
SIC: 2821 Plastics materials & resins
HQ: Huntsman Advanced Materials Americas Llc
10003 Woodloch Forest Dr # 260
The Woodlands TX 77380
281 719-6000

(P-7568)
INDUSPAC CALIFORNIA INC
Also Called: Pacific Foam
1550 Champagne Ave, Ontario
(91761-3600)
PHONE.....................909 390-4422
Keith Tatum, General Mgr
EMP: 11
SALES (corp-wide): 119.4MM Privately
Held
SIC: 2821 Polyethylene resins
HQ: Induspac California, Inc.
　21062 Forbes Ave
　Hayward CA 94545

(P-7569)
INDUSPAC CALIFORNIA INC (HQ)
Also Called: Western Foam
21062 Forbes Ave, Hayward (94545-1116)
PHONE.....................510 324-3626
John McAuslan, CEO
EMP: 46
SQ FT: 200,000
SALES (est): 10.3MM
SALES (corp-wide): 119.4MM Privately
Held
WEB: www.macfarlanegroup.net
SIC: 2821 Polyethylene resins
PA: Groupe Emballage Specialise S.E.C.
　3300 Rte Transcanadienne
　Pointe-Claire QC H9R 1
　514 636-7951

(P-7570)
INTERPLASTIC CORPORATION
Also Called: Silmar Division
12335 S Van Ness Ave, Hawthorne
(90250-3320)
PHONE.....................323 757-1801
Doug Johnson, Branch Mgr
EMP: 50
SQ FT: 56,425
SALES (corp-wide): 271.4MM Privately
Held
WEB: www.interplastic.com
SIC: 2821 5169 Plastics materials &
　resins; synthetic resins, rubber & plastic
　materials
PA: Interplastic Corporation
　1225 Willow Lake Blvd
　Saint Paul MN 55110
　651 481-6860

(P-7571)
INTERPLASTIC CORPORATION
Also Called: North American Composites
611 Gilmore Ave Ste C, Stockton
(95203-4910)
PHONE.....................209 932-0396
Jeremy Locke, Manager
EMP: 10
SALES (corp-wide): 271.4MM Privately
Held
WEB: www.interplastic.com
SIC: 2821 Plastics materials & resins
PA: Interplastic Corporation
　1225 Willow Lake Blvd
　Saint Paul MN 55110
　651 481-6860

(P-7572)
IPP PLASTICS PRODUCTS INC
4610 Littlejohn St, Baldwin Park
(91706-2267)
PHONE.....................626 357-1178
Russell Wayne King, President
EMP: 10
SALES (est): 931.5K Privately Held
SIC: 2821 Molding compounds, plastics

(P-7573)
ITW PLYMERS SALANTS N AMER INC
Pacific Polymers
12271 Monarch St, Garden Grove
(92841-2906)
PHONE.....................714 898-0025
Robert Seiple, Branch Mgr
EMP: 25

SALES (corp-wide): 1.5B Publicly Held
SIC: 2821 2822 2851 2891 Plastics ma-
　terials & resins; synthetic rubber; paints &
　allied products; adhesives & sealants; as-
　phalt felts & coatings
HQ: Itw Polymers Sealants North America
　Inc.
　111 S Nursery Rd
　Irving TX 75060
　972 438-9111

(P-7574)
IVEX PROTECTIVE PACKAGING INC
Also Called: IVEX Ontario
1550 Champagne Ave, Ontario
(91761-3600)
PHONE.....................909 390-4422
Steve Darby, General Mgr
EMP: 29
SALES (corp-wide): 119.4MM Privately
Held
SIC: 2821 Polyethylene resins
HQ: Ivex Protective Packaging Inc.
　2600 Campbell Rd
　Sidney OH 45365
　937 498-9298

(P-7575)
J-M MANUFACTURING COMPANY INC
Also Called: JM Eagle
23711 Rider St, Perris (92570-7114)
PHONE.....................951 657-7400
Robert Johnson, Manager
EMP: 70
SALES (corp-wide): 1B Privately Held
SIC: 2821 Polyvinyl chloride resins (PVC)
PA: J-M Manufacturing Company, Inc.
　5200 W Century Blvd
　Los Angeles CA 90045
　800 621-4404

(P-7576)
J-M MANUFACTURING COMPANY INC
10990 Hemlock Ave, Fontana
(92337-7250)
PHONE.....................909 822-3009
Stephen Yang, Manager
EMP: 84
SQ FT: 72,000
SALES (corp-wide): 1B Privately Held
SIC: 2821 3084 5051 3085 Polyvinyl
　chloride resins (PVC); plastics pipe; pipe
　& tubing, steel; plastics bottles
PA: J-M Manufacturing Company, Inc.
　5200 W Century Blvd
　Los Angeles CA 90045
　800 621-4404

(P-7577)
J-M MANUFACTURING COMPANY INC
1051 Sperry Rd, Stockton (95206-3931)
PHONE.....................209 982-1500
David Chen, Manager
Jaime Ramirez, Executive
EMP: 110
SALES (corp-wide): 1B Privately Held
SIC: 2821 3084 Polyvinyl chloride resins
　(PVC); plastics pipe
PA: J-M Manufacturing Company, Inc.
　5200 W Century Blvd
　Los Angeles CA 90045
　800 621-4404

(P-7578)
K C A ENGINEERED PLASTICS INC (PA)
580 California St Ste 22, San Francisco
(94104-1000)
PHONE.....................415 433-4494
C Sedgwick Dienst, CEO
Sedgwick Dienst, CEO
EMP: 100
SQ FT: 32,000
SALES (est): 6.2MM Privately Held
SIC: 2821 3089 Plastics materials &
　resins; injection molding of plastics

(P-7579)
KURARAY AMERICA INC
2 Park Plz Ste 480, Irvine (92614-3512)
PHONE.....................949 476-9600

EMP: 18 Privately Held
SIC: 2821 Vinyl resins
HQ: Kuraray America, Inc.
　2625 Bay Area Blvd # 600
　Houston TX 77058

(P-7580)
MANGO MATERIALS INC
800 Buchanan St, Berkeley (94710-1105)
P.O. Box 11, Palo Alto (94302-0011)
PHONE.....................650 440-0430
Molly Morse, CEO
Anne Schauer-Gimenez, Vice Pres
Nancy Schauer, Admin Asst
Allison Pieja, CTO
EMP: 19
SALES (est): 626.9K Privately Held
SIC: 2821 Plastics materials & resins

(P-7581)
MAPEI CORPORATION
5415 Industrial Pkwy, San Bernardino
(92407-1803)
PHONE.....................909 475-4100
Jose Granillo, Manager
Ron Pickinpaugh, Purch Mgr
EMP: 40 Privately Held
SIC: 2821 Acrylic resins
HQ: Mapei Corporation
　1144 E Newport Center Dr
　Deerfield Beach FL 33442
　954 246-8888

(P-7582)
MOLDING ACQUISITION CORP
Also Called: Rotoplas
2651 Cooper Ave, Merced (95348-4315)
PHONE.....................209 723-5000
Juan Negrete, Branch Mgr
EMP: 15 Privately Held
SIC: 2821 Molding compounds, plastics
HQ: Molding Acquisition Corp.
　685 John B Sias Mem
　Fort Worth TX 76134
　209 723-5000

(P-7583)
NATURAL ENVMTL PROTECTION CO
Also Called: Nepco
750 S Reservoir St, Pomona (91766-3815)
PHONE.....................909 620-8028
Young Su Shin, President
▲ EMP: 31
SQ FT: 3,600
SALES (est): 6.8MM Privately Held
SIC: 2821 Polystyrene resins
PA: Gum Sung Industry Co., Ltd.
　57-6 Gubong-Gil, Donghwa-Myeon
　Jangseong 57242

(P-7584)
NEW TECHNOLOGY PLASTICS INC
7110 Fenwick Ln, Westminster
(92683-5248)
PHONE.....................562 941-6034
Gregory A Nelson, President
EMP: 35
SALES (est): 8.9MM Privately Held
SIC: 2821 5162 Molding compounds,
　plastics; plastics materials & basic shapes

(P-7585)
NO LIFT NAILS INC
3211 S Shannon St, Santa Ana
(92704-6352)
PHONE.....................714 897-0070
Laurence H Gaertner, President
Thomas A Gaertner, Vice Pres
EMP: 12
SALES (est): 1.8MM Privately Held
WEB: www.noliftnails.com
SIC: 2821 2844 Acrylic resins; manicure
　preparations

(P-7586)
NORTH AMERICAN COMPOSITES CO
Also Called: Interplastic
4990 Vanderbilt St, Ontario (91761-2202)
PHONE.....................909 605-8977
Mark Prost, Vice Pres

David Englesgard, Vice Pres
ARA Berberian, Sales Staff
▲ EMP: 20
SALES (est): 2.3MM Privately Held
SIC: 2821 Plastics materials & resins

(P-7587)
NORTH AMRCN SPECIALTY PDTS LLC
300 S Beckman Rd, Lodi (95240-3103)
PHONE.....................209 365-7500
Joseph Bondi,
EMP: 11 Publicly Held
SIC: 2821 Plastics materials & resins
HQ: North American Specialty Products Llc
　993 Old Eagle School Rd
　Wayne PA 19087
　484 253-4545

(P-7588)
NUSIL TECHNOLOGY LLC
Also Called: Nusil Silicone Technology
1000 Cindy Ln, Carpinteria (93013-2906)
PHONE.....................805 684-8780
Giavonnie Jones, Manager
EMP: 100
SALES (corp-wide): 1.4B Publicly Held
SIC: 2821 Silicone resins
HQ: Nusil Technology Llc
　1050 Cindy Ln
　Carpinteria CA 93013
　805 684-8780

(P-7589)
ORION PLASTICS CORPORATION
700 W Carob St, Compton (90220-5225)
PHONE.....................310 223-0370
Patricia Conkling, Principal
Fred Conkling, President
Wayne Moore, Business Dir
Daniel Gitzke, Accounts Mgr
▲ EMP: 75 EST: 2000
SQ FT: 60,000
SALES: 26MM Privately Held
WEB: www.orionplastics.net
SIC: 2821 Plastics materials & resins

(P-7590)
PERFORMANCE MATERIALS CORP (PA)
Also Called: Tencate Performance Composite
1150 Calle Suerte, Camarillo (93012-8051)
PHONE.....................805 482-1722
Thomas W Smith, President
Michelle Larios, Admin Asst
▲ EMP: 100
SQ FT: 50,000
SALES (est): 22.8MM Privately Held
WEB: www.performancematerials.com
SIC: 2821 Plastics materials & resins

(P-7591)
PHARMAPACK NORTH AMERICA CORP
5095 E Airport Dr, Ontario (91761-4701)
PHONE.....................909 390-1888
Xianjun Qi, President
Douglas Powanda, Vice Pres
▲ EMP: 10 EST: 2014
SQ FT: 10,000
SALES (est): 2.1MM
SALES (corp-wide): 29.5MM Privately
Held
SIC: 2821 5162 Plastics materials &
　resins; plastics materials & basic shapes
PA: Pharmapack Technologies Corporation
　No.16 Huangqishan Road, Yonghe
　Economic Zone, Etdz
　Guangzhou 51135
　208 221-5907

(P-7592)
PLASKOLITE WEST LLC
Also Called: Plaskolite West, Inc.
2225 E Del Amo Blvd, Compton
(90220-6303)
PHONE.....................310 637-2103
Mitch Grindley, President
Rick Larkin, CFO
▲ EMP: 30
SALES (est): 10.7MM
SALES (corp-wide): 294.5MM Privately
Held
SIC: 2821 Acrylic resins

▲ = Import ▼=Export
◆ =Import/Export

PA: Plaskolite, Llc
400 W Nationwide Blvd # 400
Columbus OH 43215
614 294-3281

(P-7593)
PLASTIC MART INC
43535 Gadsden Ave Ste F, Lancaster
(93534-6147)
PHONE..............................310 268-1404
James Nahigian, *President*
Ralph Kafesjian, *Vice Pres*
Gary Phillips, *Admin Sec*
EMP: 30
SALES (est): 4.7MM **Privately Held**
WEB: www.plasticmart.net
SIC: 2821 5211 5162 Plastics materials &
resins; lumber & other building materials;
plastics materials & basic shapes

(P-7594)
POLY PROCESSING COMPANY
LLC
8055 Ash St, French Camp (95231-9667)
P.O. Box 80 (95231-0080)
PHONE..............................209 982-4904
Dixon Abell, *Mng Member*
Shawn Newbury, *Design Engr*
EMP: 279
SQ FT: 75,000
SALES (est): 34.9MM
SALES (corp-wide): 276.8MM **Privately**
Held
SIC: 2821 3443 Molding compounds,
plastics; fabricated plate work (boiler
shop)
PA: Abell Corporation
2500 Sterlington Rd
Monroe LA 71203
318 343-7565

(P-7595)
POLYNT COMPOSITES USA INC
2801 Lynwood Rd, Lynwood (90262-4009)
PHONE..............................310 886-1070
Jason Webb, *Branch Mgr*
Michael Gardea, *Manager*
EMP: 11
SALES (corp-wide): 2.4B **Privately Held**
SIC: 2821 Plastics materials & resins
HQ: Polynt Composites Usa Inc.
99 E Cottage Ave
Carpentersville IL 60110

(P-7596)
POLYONE CORPORATION
2104 E 223rd St, Carson (90810-1611)
P.O. Box 9077, Long Beach (90810-0077)
PHONE..............................310 513-7100
Rod Myers, *Branch Mgr*
Maria Furtak, *Regl Sales Mgr*
Tom Moore, *Regl Sales Mgr*
Geoff Kendle, *Manager*
EMP: 60 **Publicly Held**
WEB: www.polyone.com
SIC: 2821 Polyvinyl chloride resins (PVC);
vinyl resins
PA: Polyone Corporation
33587 Walker Rd
Avon Lake OH 44012

(P-7597)
POLYONE CORPORATION
11400 Newport Dr Ste A, Rancho Cuca-
monga (91730-5511)
PHONE..............................909 987-0253
Tim Lee, *Manager*
EMP: 40 **Publicly Held**
WEB: www.polyone.com
SIC: 2821 Plastics materials & resins
PA: Polyone Corporation
33587 Walker Rd
Avon Lake OH 44012
-

(P-7598)
PPP LLC
5991 Alcoa Ave, Vernon (90058-3920)
PHONE..............................323 581-6058
Tim Guth,
Evelyn Garcia, *Mng Member*
EMP: 10
SQ FT: 81,000

SALES (est): 1.4MM **Privately Held**
SIC: 2821 Polyethylene resins

(P-7599)
PRIME CONDUIT INC
1776 E Beamer St, Woodland
(95776-6218)
PHONE..............................530 669-0160
Tom Godosky, *Branch Mgr*
EMP: 27 **Privately Held**
SIC: 2821 Polyvinyl chloride resins (PVC)
PA: Prime Conduit, Inc.
23240 Chagrin Blvd # 405
Beachwood OH 44122

(P-7600)
PROFESSIONAL PLASTICS INC
Also Called: Dva Professsional Plastic
2940 Ramco St Ste 100, West Sacramento
(95691-6408)
PHONE..............................916 374-4580
David Fowler, *Manager*
EMP: 11
SALES (corp-wide): 121.3MM **Privately**
Held
WEB: www.professionalplastics.com
SIC: 2821 Plastics materials & resins
PA: Professional Plastics, Inc.
1810 E Valencia Dr
Fullerton CA 92831
714 446-6500

(P-7601)
QUALITY IMAGE INC
15130 Illinois Ave, Paramount
(90723-4107)
PHONE..............................562 259-9872
Susie Alofaituli, *President*
Robert Cabrera, *Vice Pres*
Roberto Cabrera, *Vice Pres*
EMP: 20
SQ FT: 9,000
SALES (est): 1.8MM **Privately Held**
WEB: www.qualityimageinc.com
SIC: 2821 Plastics materials & resins

(P-7602)
R K FABRICATION INC
1283 N Grove St, Anaheim (92806-2114)
PHONE..............................714 630-9654
Roger King, *CEO*
Sarah King, *Treasurer*
Brandon Scrimes, *Manager*
EMP: 18
SQ FT: 10,000
SALES (est): 4.8MM **Privately Held**
WEB: www.rkfabrication.com
SIC: 2821 3714 1799 Plastics materials &
resins; exhaust systems & parts, motor
vehicle; fiberglass work

(P-7603)
REICHHOLD LLC 2
Also Called: Reichhold Chemicals
237 S Motor Ave, Azusa (91702-3228)
PHONE..............................626 334-4974
Steward Fletcher, *Branch Mgr*
EMP: 14
SALES (corp-wide): 128MM **Privately**
Held
WEB: www.reichhold.com
SIC: 2821 2851 Plastics materials &
resins; paints & allied products
PA: Reichhold Llc 2
1035 Swabia Ct
Durham NC 27703
919 990-7500

(P-7604)
ROA PACIFIC INC
1225 Exposition Way, San Diego
(92154-6663)
PHONE..............................619 565-2800
Cristina Thalia Mulligan, *CEO*
Randy Roa, *Principal*
EMP: 11
SALES (est): 1.8MM **Privately Held**
SIC: 2821 Molding compounds, plastics

(P-7605)
RONCELLI PLASTICS INC
330 W Duarte Rd, Monrovia (91016-4584)
PHONE..............................800 250-6516
Gino Roncelli, *CEO*
Riley Cole, *President*

Bingo Roncelli, *Corp Secy*
Don Mehling, *Manager*
EMP: 61 **EST:** 1970
SQ FT: 11,000
SALES (est): 16.7MM **Privately Held**
WEB: www.roncelliplastics.com
SIC: 2821 Plastics materials & resins

(P-7606)
S R S M INC
Also Called: Vm International
945 E Church St, Riverside (92507-1103)
PHONE..............................310 952-9000
Roya Vazin, *CEO*
Moe Ii Afsari, *Manager*
▲ **EMP:** 120 **EST:** 1996
SQ FT: 250,000
SALES (est): 37.7MM **Privately Held**
WEB: www.srsm.com
SIC: 2821 5023 Plastics materials &
resins; kitchenware

(P-7607)
SAINT-GOBAIN PRFMCE PLAS
CORP
7301 Orangewood Ave, Garden Grove
(92841-1411)
PHONE..............................714 893-0470
Greg Maki, *Branch Mgr*
John Leary, *Manager*
EMP: 190
SALES (corp-wide): 215.9MM **Privately**
Held
SIC: 2821 Plastics materials & resins
HQ: Saint-Gobain Performance Plastics
Corporation
31500 Solon Rd
Solon OH 44139
440 836-6900

(P-7608)
SENTRY INDUSTRIES INC
1245 Brooks St, Ontario (91762-3609)
PHONE..............................909 986-3642
William Dubble, *President*
Aileen Dubble, *Treasurer*
▲ **EMP:** 10
SQ FT: 10,000
SALES: 1MM **Privately Held**
SIC: 2821 Acrylic resins

(P-7609)
SHOCKING TECHNOLOGIES INC
5870 Hellyer Ave, San Jose (95138-1004)
PHONE..............................831 331-4558
Lex A Kosowsky, *President*
▼ **EMP:** 42
SQ FT: 52,000
SALES (est): 6MM **Privately Held**
SIC: 2821 Polymethyl methacrylate resins
(plexiglass)

(P-7610)
SILFINE AMERICA INC
1750 Cleveland Ave, San Jose
(95126-1903)
PHONE..............................408 823-8663
Seung Yong Lim, *President*
Jeffrey Harte, *Exec VP*
▲ **EMP:** 65
SQ FT: 1,600
SALES: 7MM **Privately Held**
SIC: 2821 Silicone resins

(P-7611)
SILPAK INC (PA)
470 E Bonita Ave, Pomona (91767-1928)
PHONE..............................909 625-0056
Philip Galarneau, *President*
Janice A Galarneau, *Vice Pres*
EMP: 15
SQ FT: 13,850
SALES (est): 2.6MM **Privately Held**
WEB: www.silpak.com
SIC: 2821 Plastics materials & resins

(P-7612)
SOUTHERN CALIFORNIA PLAS
INC
3122 Maple St, Santa Ana (92707-4408)
PHONE..............................714 751-7084
Anthony Codet, *President*
▲ **EMP:** 54
SQ FT: 240,000
SALES (est): 12.1MM **Privately Held**
SIC: 2821 Plastics materials & resins

(P-7613)
SOUTHWALL TECHNOLOGIES
INC (DH)
3788 Fabian Way, Palo Alto (94303-4601)
PHONE..............................650 798-1285
B Travis Smith, *CEO*
Mallorie Burak,
Michael Vargas, *VP Admin*
◆ **EMP:** 43
SQ FT: 30,174
SALES (est): 15.6MM **Publicly Held**
WEB: www.southwall.com
SIC: 2821 Plastics materials & resins
HQ: Solutia Inc.
575 Maryville Centre Dr
Saint Louis MO 63141
423 229-2000

(P-7614)
SPHERE ALLIANCE INC
Also Called: Advanced Aircraft Seal
3051 Myers St, Riverside (92503-5525)
PHONE..............................951 352-2400
Daryl Silva, *CEO*
Robert Balderas, *Engineer*
EMP: 37
SALES (est): 9.9MM **Privately Held**
SIC: 2821 Plastics materials & resins

(P-7615)
STEPAN COMPANY
Also Called: Anaheim Plant
1208 N Patt St, Anaheim (92801-2549)
PHONE..............................714 776-9870
Tom Szczeblowski, *Manager*
EMP: 32
SQ FT: 10,412
SALES (corp-wide): 1.9B **Publicly Held**
WEB: www.stepan.com
SIC: 2821 2843 Plastics materials &
resins; surface active agents
PA: Stepan Company
22 W Frontage Rd
Northfield IL 60093
847 446-7500

(P-7616)
TA AEROSPACE CO
Also Called: Ta Division
28065 Franklin Pkwy, Valencia
(91355-4117)
PHONE..............................661 702-0448
Jim Sweeney, *President*
EMP: 180
SQ FT: 78,124
SALES (corp-wide): 3.8B **Publicly Held**
WEB: www.kirkhill.com
SIC: 2821 3429 Elastomers, nonvulcaniz-
able (plastics); clamps, metal
HQ: Ta Aerospace Co.
28065 Franklin Pkwy
Valencia CA 91355
661 775-1100

(P-7617)
TAMMY TAYLOR NAILS INC
2001 E Deere Ave, Santa Ana
(92705-5724)
PHONE..............................949 250-9287
Tammy Taylor, *President*
▼ **EMP:** 45
SQ FT: 11,500
SALES (est): 8.2MM **Privately Held**
SIC: 2821 7231 5087 Acrylic resins;
beauty shops; beauty parlor equipment &
supplies

(P-7618)
TAP PLASTICS INC A CAL CORP
(PA)
3011 Alvarado St Ste A, San Leandro
(94577-5707)
PHONE..............................510 357-3755
David Freeberg, *President*
Carole L Bremer, *CFO*
Robert J Wilson, *Vice Pres*
Debra Kawano, *Human Resources*
EMP: 15 **EST:** 1952
SQ FT: 4,000
SALES (est): 62.3MM **Privately Held**
WEB: www.tapplastics.com
SIC: 2821 5162 Acrylic resins; resins, syn-
thetic

(PA)=Parent Co (HQ)=Headquarters (DH)=Div Headquarters
✪ = New Business established in last 2 years

(P-7619)
TECHMER PM INC
18420 S Laurel Park Rd, Compton
(90220-6015)
PHONE....................................310 632-9211
John R Manuck, *President*
Craig Burnett, *VP Opers*
◆ **EMP:** 500
SQ FT: 40,000
SALES (est): 128.2MM **Privately Held**
WEB: www.techmerpm.com
SIC: 2821 Plastics materials & resins

(P-7620)
TEKNOR APEX COMPANY
Maclin Company
420 S 6th Ave, City of Industry
(91746-3128)
P.O. Box 2307, La Puente (91746-0307)
PHONE....................................626 968-4656
Tony Patrizio, *Manager*
Jon Riley, *Vice Pres*
Gary Gruslin, *Info Tech Dir*
James Wynne, *Info Tech Mgr*
Robin Keeley, *Prgrmr*
EMP: 199
SALES (corp-wide): 845.9MM **Privately Held**
SIC: 2821 3081 3089 Vinyl resins; unsupported plastics film & sheet; plastic processing
PA: Teknor Apex Company
505 Central Ave
Pawtucket RI 02861
401 725-8000

(P-7621)
TUFF STUFF PRODUCTS
9600 Road 256, Terra Bella (93270-9732)
PHONE....................................559 535-5778
Maximilian B Lee, *President*
▲ **EMP:** 500 **EST:** 1999
SALES (est): 68.2MM **Privately Held**
WEB: www.tufftubs.com
SIC: 2821 Plastics materials & resins

(P-7622)
UREMET CORPORATION
3026 Orange Ave, Santa Ana (92707-4248)
PHONE....................................714 641-8813
Steve Zamollo, *CEO*
Mark Moore, *President*
John Cockriel, *Vice Pres*
▲ **EMP:** 26
SQ FT: 9,500
SALES (est): 6MM **Privately Held**
WEB: www.uremet.com
SIC: 2821 Polyurethane resins

(P-7623)
US BLANKS LLC (PA)
14700 S San Pedro St, Gardena
(90248-2001)
P.O. Box 486 (90248-0486)
PHONE....................................310 225-6774
Jeff Holtby,
Kimberly Thress,
▲ **EMP:** 48
SALES (est): 8.8MM **Privately Held**
SIC: 2821 Plastics materials & resins

(P-7624)
VIRTUAL COMPOSITES CO INC
584 Explorer St, Brea (92821-3108)
PHONE....................................714 256-8850
Wayne R Howard, *President*
EMP: 10
SALES (est): 1.6MM **Privately Held**
SIC: 2821 Plastics materials & resins

(P-7625)
XERXES CORPORATION
1210 N Tustin Ave, Anaheim (92807-1617)
PHONE....................................714 630-0012
Rudy Tapia, *Manager*
Kathy Demuth, *CFO*
Jan R Arciszewski, *Vice Pres*
Gerardo Zendejas, *Vice Pres*
Shawn Roach, *VP Mfg*
EMP: 100
SALES (corp-wide): 100.8MM **Privately Held**
WEB: www.xerxescorp.com
SIC: 2821 5999 3444 Polystyrene resins; fiberglass materials, except insulation; sheet metalwork

PA: Xerxes Corporation
7901 Xerxes Ave S Ste 201
Minneapolis MN 55431
952 887-1890

2822 Synthetic Rubber (Vulcanizable Elastomers)

(P-7626)
CALIFORNIA INDUSTRIAL RBR CO
1690 Sierra Ave, Yuba City (95993-8981)
PHONE....................................530 674-2444
Andy Campos, *Branch Mgr*
EMP: 20
SQ FT: 4,800
SALES (corp-wide): 56.5MM **Privately Held**
SIC: 2822 2891 3496 3241 Synthetic rubber; adhesives; conveyor belts; cement, hydraulic; agricultural chemicals
PA: California Industrial Rubber Co, Inc
2539 S Cherry Ave
Fresno CA 93706
559 268-7321

(P-7627)
COI RUBBER PRODUCTS INC
19255 San Jose Ave, City of Industry
(91748-1418)
PHONE....................................626 965-9966
David Chao, *CEO*
EMP: 450
SQ FT: 2,500
SALES (est): 627.1K **Privately Held**
SIC: 2822 Butadiene-acrylonitrile, nitrile rubbers, NBR

(P-7628)
CRITICALPOINT CAPITAL LLC
Arlon Materials For Elec Div
9433 Hyssop Dr, Rancho Cucamonga
(91730-6107)
PHONE....................................909 987-9533
Roy Baulmer, *Branch Mgr*
EMP: 100
SALES (corp-wide): 18MM **Privately Held**
WEB: www.arlon.com
SIC: 2822 3672 2821 Silicone rubbers; printed circuit boards; plastics materials & resins
PA: Criticalpoint Capital, Llc
2121 Rosecrans Ave # 2330
El Segundo CA 90245
310 321-4400

(P-7629)
FLEX TECHNOLOGIES INC
Also Called: Silicone Hose
15151 S Main St, Gardena (90248-1923)
PHONE....................................310 323-1801
Timothy Coory, *President*
Joe Coory, *CFO*
Carla Mc Millen, *Personnel Exec*
▲ **EMP:** 10
SQ FT: 10,000
SALES (est): 2.1MM **Privately Held**
WEB: www.siliconehose.com
SIC: 2822 3599 Silicone rubbers; flexible metal hose, tubing & bellows

(P-7630)
HANDY SERVICE CORPORATION
1043 S Melrose St Ste A, Placentia
(92870-7133)
PHONE....................................714 632-7832
Sandra Sherman, *President*
Anne Didion, *Corp Secy*
Sandy Sherman, *Administration*
EMP: 10
SQ FT: 6,700
SALES (est): 1.5MM **Privately Held**
SIC: 2822 Silicone rubbers

(P-7631)
KIRKHILL INC (HQ)
Also Called: Sfs
300 E Cypress St, Brea (92821-4007)
PHONE....................................714 529-4901
Annette Oneal, *President*
Annette O'Neal, *President*
Ronnel Jamir, *Mfg Staff*

EMP: 23
SALES: 95MM
SALES (corp-wide): 3.8B **Publicly Held**
SIC: 2822 Synthetic rubber
PA: Transdigm Group Incorporated
1301 E 9th St Ste 3000
Cleveland OH 44114
216 706-2960

(P-7632)
LTI HOLDINGS INC (HQ)
Also Called: Boyd
600 S Mcclure Rd, Modesto (95357-0520)
PHONE....................................209 236-1111
Mitch Aiello, *President*
Kurt Wetzel, *CFO*
▲ **EMP:** 15
SALES (est): 886.5MM
SALES (corp-wide): 915.2MM **Privately Held**
SIC: 2822 3069 Synthetic rubber; hard rubber & molded rubber products; rubber automotive products
PA: Snow Phipps Group, Llc
667 Madison Ave Fl 18
New York NY 10065
212 508-3300

(P-7633)
WCE PRODUCTS INC
Also Called: West Coast Enterprizes
7542 Santa Rita Cir, Stanton (90680-3433)
PHONE....................................714 895-4381
Van G Zeitz, *President*
▲ **EMP:** 13
SQ FT: 12,000
SALES (est): 2.4MM **Privately Held**
SIC: 2822 Synthetic rubber

2824 Synthetic Organic Fibers, Exc Cellulosic

(P-7634)
ARCLINE INVESTMENT MGT LP (PA)
4 Embarcadero Ctr # 3460, San Francisco
(94111-4106)
PHONE....................................415 801-4570
Rajeev Amara, *CEO*
EMP: 15
SALES (est): 53.9MM **Privately Held**
SIC: 2824 Elastomeric fibers

(P-7635)
DAL-TILE CORPORATION
7865 Ostrow St, San Diego (92111-3602)
PHONE....................................858 565-7767
Scott Hambor, *Manager*
EMP: 10
SALES (corp-wide): 9.9B **Publicly Held**
WEB: www.mohawk.com
SIC: 2824 5032 Organic fibers, noncellulosic; ceramic wall & floor tile
HQ: Dal-Tile Corporation
7834 C F Hawn Fwy
Dallas TX 75217
214 398-1411

(P-7636)
DAL-TILE CORPORATION
16201 Stagg St, Van Nuys (91406-1716)
PHONE....................................818 787-3224
Scott Phiser, *Branch Mgr*
EMP: 20
SALES (corp-wide): 9.9B **Publicly Held**
WEB: www.mohawk.com
SIC: 2824 5032 Organic fibers, noncellulosic; ceramic wall & floor tile
HQ: Dal-Tile Corporation
7834 C F Hawn Fwy
Dallas TX 75217
214 398-1411

(P-7637)
DAL-TILE CORPORATION
3550 Tyburn St, Los Angeles (90065-1427)
P.O. Box 170730, Dallas TX (75217-0730)
PHONE....................................323 257-7553
Dan Bargreen, *Branch Mgr*
EMP: 12

SALES (corp-wide): 9.9B **Publicly Held**
WEB: www.mohawk.com
SIC: 2824 5032 1743 Organic fibers, noncellulosic; ceramic wall & floor tile; tile installation, ceramic
HQ: Dal-Tile Corporation
7834 C F Hawn Fwy
Dallas TX 75217
214 398-1411

(P-7638)
ENERGY LANE INC
Also Called: Pitbull Energy Bar
6767 W Sunset Blvd 8152, Los Angeles
(90028-7177)
PHONE....................................323 962-5020
Bobby Robertson, *President*
Biviana Carillo, *COO*
EMP: 10
SALES (est): 1.1MM **Privately Held**
SIC: 2824 Protein fibers

(P-7639)
INTEGRTED POLYMR SOLUTIONS INC (HQ)
3701 E Conant St, Long Beach
(90808-1783)
PHONE....................................562 354-2920
Rajeev Amara, *CEO*
▲ **EMP:** 15
SQ FT: 55,000
SALES (est): 53.9MM **Privately Held**
WEB: www.sandersind.com
SIC: 2824 Elastomeric fibers
PA: Arcline Investment Management Lp
4 Embarcadero Ctr # 3460
San Francisco CA 94111
415 801-4570

(P-7640)
LAGIER RANCHES INC
16161 Murphy Rd, Escalon (95320-9755)
P.O. Box 89, Ripon (95366-0089)
PHONE....................................209 982-5618
John E Lagier, *President*
Casey Havre, *Corp Secy*
EMP: 12
SQ FT: 6,000
SALES (est): 2.2MM **Privately Held**
WEB: www.lagierranches.com
SIC: 2824 Organic fibers, noncellulosic

(P-7641)
ST PAUL BRANDS INC
11555 Monarch St Ste B, Garden Grove
(92841-1814)
PHONE....................................714 903-1000
Jimmy Ngo, *President*
Henry Smith, *Vice Pres*
▲ **EMP:** 25
SALES (est): 2MM **Privately Held**
SIC: 2824 Protein fibers

(P-7642)
TURNER FIBERFILL INC
1600 Date St, Montebello (90640-6371)
P.O. Box 460 (90640-0460)
PHONE....................................323 724-7957
Paul Turner, *President*
▲ **EMP:** 35
SALES (est): 13.1MM **Privately Held**
SIC: 2824 Polyester fibers

(P-7643)
VYBION INC
584 Oak St, Monterey (93940-1321)
PHONE....................................607 227-2502
Lee A Henderson, *Ch of Bd*
EMP: 16
SQ FT: 2,500
SALES (est): 856.4K **Privately Held**
SIC: 2824 Protein fibers

2833 Medicinal Chemicals & Botanical Prdts

(P-7644)
AMERICAN INGREDIENTS INC
2929 E White Star Ave, Anaheim
(92806-2628)
PHONE....................................714 630-6000
Howard Simon, *President*
Andrea Bauer, *Treasurer*
▲ **EMP:** 14

▲ = Import ▼=Export
◆ =Import/Export

SALES (est): 3.1MM
SALES (corp-wide): 3.7B **Publicly Held**
WEB: www.amer-ing.com
SIC: **2833** Medicinals & botanicals
HQ: Pharmachem Laboratories, Llc
   265 Harrison Tpke
   Kearny NJ 07032
   201 246-1000

(P-7645)
ANIMAL NUTRITION INDS INC
Also Called: Interntnal Veterinary Sciences
5602 E La Palma Ave, Anaheim
(92807-2110)
PHONE...................................949 583-2920
ARA Bohchalian, *CEO*
Norma Wilson, *Office Mgr*
Kevin Park, *Controller*
EMP: 10
SQ FT: 4,000
SALES: 300K **Privately Held**
SIC: **2833** Medicinal chemicals

(P-7646)
BIO-RAD LABORATORIES INC
Bio-RAD E C S
9500 Jeronimo Rd, Irvine (92618-2017)
PHONE...................................949 598-1200
Kelly Knapps, *Branch Mgr*
Danny Nguyen, *Project Engr*
Patrick Ogrady, *Engineer*
EMP: 140
SALES (corp-wide): 2.2B **Publicly Held**
WEB: www.bio-rad.com
SIC: **2833** 2835 Medicinals & botanicals;
in vitro & in vivo diagnostic substances
PA: Bio-Rad Laboratories, Inc.
   1000 Alfred Nobel Dr
   Hercules CA 94547
   510 724-7000

(P-7647)
CARGILL INCORPORATED
600 N Gilbert St, Fullerton (92833-2555)
PHONE...................................714 449-6708
Steve Hoemoller, *Manager*
EMP: 56
SALES (corp-wide): 114.7B **Privately Held**
WEB: www.cargill.com
SIC: **2833** 2079 5199 Vegetable oils, me-
dicinal grade: refined or concentrated; ed-
ible fats & oils; oils, animal or vegetable
PA: Cargill, Incorporated
   15407 Mcginty Rd W
   Wayzata MN 55391
   952 742-7575

(P-7648)
CHROMADEX CORPORATION (PA)
10005 Muirlands Blvd G, Irvine
(92618-2538)
PHONE...................................949 419-0288
Robert Fried, *CEO*
Frank Jaksch Jr, *Ch of Bd*
Kevin Farr, *CFO*
Mark Friedman, *Admin Sec*
EMP: 73
SQ FT: 15,000
SALES: 31.5MM **Publicly Held**
SIC: **2833** Botanical products, medicinal:
ground, graded or milled

(P-7649)
CHULADA INC
Also Called: Chulada Spices Herbs & Snacks
640 S Flower St, Burbank (91502-2011)
PHONE...................................818 841-6536
Hector D Alvarez, *President*
EMP: 30
SQ FT: 12,000
SALES (est): 4.4MM **Privately Held**
SIC: **2833** 2099 Drugs & herbs: grading,
grinding & milling; seasonings & spices

(P-7650)
COSMO - PHARM INC
Also Called: Nature's Glory
11751 Vose St Ste 53, North Hollywood
(91605-5736)
PHONE...................................818 764-0246
Ashwin Patel, *President*
Urmila Patel, *Corp Secy*
Rajen Patel, *Exec VP*
▼ EMP: 40

SQ FT: 45,000
SALES (est): 7.1MM **Privately Held**
WEB: www.naturesglory.com
SIC: **2833** 2048 Vitamins, natural or syn-
thetic: bulk, uncompounded; prepared
feeds

(P-7651)
CREATIONS GRDN NATURAL FD MKTS
Also Called: Cgnfm
24849 Anza Dr, Valencia (91355-1259)
PHONE...................................661 877-4280
Dino Guglielmelli, *President*
EMP: 250 EST: 1999
SALES: 3.3MM **Privately Held**
SIC: **2833** Medicinals & botanicals

(P-7652)
CV SCIENCES INC (PA)
10070 Barnes Canyon Rd # 10, San Diego
(92121-2722)
PHONE...................................866 290-2157
Joseph Dowling, *CEO*
Michael Mona III, *President*
Joerg Grasser, *CFO*
Karina Sainz, *Executive*
Alex Becker, *Accounts Mgr*
EMP: 38
SQ FT: 30,000
SALES: 48.2MM **Privately Held**
SIC: **2833** Medicinals & botanicals

(P-7653)
DOCTORS SIGNATURE SALES
Also Called: Life Force International
495 Raleigh Ave, El Cajon (92020-3137)
PHONE...................................800 531-4877
Ron Hillman, *President*
Geraldine L Hillman, *Ch of Bd*
Kathleen Meadows, *Vice Pres*
Marjorie Lynn, *Admin Sec*
Barbara Frontella, *Sales Staff*
▲ EMP: 23
SQ FT: 24,000
SALES (est): 15.6MM **Privately Held**
WEB: www.lifeforce.net
SIC: **2833** 2048 Drugs & herbs: grading,
grinding & milling; prepared feeds

(P-7654)
ELYPTOL INC
2500 Broadway Ste F125, Santa Monica
(90404-3080)
PHONE...................................424 500-8099
Timothy O'Connor, *CEO*
EMP: 10
SALES (est): 846.7K **Privately Held**
SIC: **2833** 2834 Medicinals & botanicals;
ointments

(P-7655)
ENVITA LABS LLC
Also Called: Hero Nutritional
1900 Carnegie Ave Ste A, Santa Ana
(92705-5557)
PHONE...................................800 500-4376
Jennifer Hodges, *CEO*
Ben Bratcher,
Stephanie Magill,
Estela Schnelle,
Kelly Springer,
EMP: 30
SQ FT: 15,953
SALES (est): 9.5MM **Privately Held**
WEB: www.heronutritionals.com
SIC: **2833** Vitamins, natural or synthetic:
bulk, uncompounded

(P-7656)
ERBAVIVA INC
Also Called: Erba Organics
19831 Nordhoff Pl Ste 116, Chatsworth
(91311-6614)
PHONE...................................818 998-7112
Robin Brown, *CEO*
Anna C Brown, *Vice Pres*
Jason Lee, *Opers Mgr*
◆ EMP: 20
SQ FT: 10,000
SALES (est): 5.9MM **Privately Held**
WEB: www.erbaviva.com
SIC: **2833** Organic medicinal chemicals:
bulk, uncompounded

(P-7657)
ETHOS NATURAL MEDICINE LLC
Also Called: Etha Natural Medicine
1950 Cordell Ct Ste 105, El Cajon
(92020-0923)
PHONE...................................858 267-7599
Victor Chung, *Mng Member*
Kendra Price, *General Mgr*
Alexander Karp,
EMP: 10
SQ FT: 2,727
SALES: 1.1MM **Privately Held**
SIC: **2833** Alkaloids & other botanical
based products

(P-7658)
EVOLIFE SCIENTIFIC LLC
1452 E 33rd St, Signal Hill (90755-5200)
PHONE...................................888 750-0310
Alan Castro,
EMP: 23
SALES (est): 951.5K **Privately Held**
SIC: **2833** Medicinals & botanicals

(P-7659)
EXCELSIOR NUTRITION INC
Also Called: 4excelsior
1206 N Miller St Unit D, Anaheim
(92806-1960)
PHONE...................................657 999-5188
Yisheng Lin, *President*
Angela Duan, *COO*
Jennifer Wu, *CFO*
Jian Wu, *CFO*
EMP: 48
SQ FT: 78,000
SALES (est): 2.3MM **Privately Held**
SIC: **2833** Medicinals & botanicals

(P-7660)
FITPRO USA LLC
1911 2nd St, Livermore (94550-4426)
PHONE...................................877 645-5776
Kostandinos Malliarodakis, *CEO*
Ericca Hoffman, *COO*
Michael Zumpano, *CFO*
Kevin Cruz, *CIO*
Barbara Harrington, *Controller*
EMP: 10
SALES: 865K **Privately Held**
SIC: **2833** 2026 Botanical products, me-
dicinal: ground, graded or milled; milk
drinks, flavored

(P-7661)
FUJISAWA BRISTOL CORPORATION
69848 Highway 111, Rancho Mirage
(92270-2837)
P.O. Box 2040 (92270-1054)
PHONE...................................760 324-1488
Gregory Ackerman, *President*
Maureen Kelly, *Corp Secy*
Nancy Lane, *Exec VP*
Nancy J Ackerman, *Principal*
EMP: 60
SQ FT: 35,000
SALES: 20MM **Privately Held**
SIC: **2833** 2844 Vitamins, natural or syn-
thetic: bulk, uncompounded; face creams
or lotions

(P-7662)
GE HEALTHCARE INC
Also Called: GE Health Care
4877 Mercury St, San Diego (92111-2104)
PHONE...................................858 279-9382
George Starks, *Manager*
EMP: 20
SALES (corp-wide): 121.6B **Publicly Held**
SIC: **2833** Medicinals & botanicals
HQ: Ge Healthcare Inc.
   100 Results Way
   Marlborough MA 01752
   800 526-3593

(P-7663)
GE NUTRIENTS INC
Also Called: Gencor
19700 Fairchild Ste 330, Irvine
(92612-2529)
PHONE...................................949 502-5760
Jith Veeravalli, *CEO*
Gita Kasiri, *Manager*
▲ EMP: 10 EST: 2014

SALES (est): 196.9K **Privately Held**
SIC: **2833** Drugs & herbs: grading, grinding
& milling

(P-7664)
GREEN ACRES CANNABIS LLC
6256 3rd St, San Francisco (94124-3110)
PHONE...................................415 657-3484
Ramona Davis, *Mng Member*
Janiece Addison,
Tiya Addison,
Claudia Smith,
EMP: 26
SALES (est): 2.3MM **Privately Held**
SIC: **2833** Medicinals & botanicals

(P-7665)
GREEN CURES INC
20201 Sherman Way Ste 101, Winnetka
(91306-3269)
PHONE...................................818 773-3929
EMP: 34
SALES (est): 3MM **Privately Held**
SIC: **2833**

(P-7666)
HALL HEALTH AND LONGEVITY CNTR
916 Main St, Venice (90291-3376)
PHONE...................................310 566-6690
Longevity Center, *Principal*
EMP: 16
SALES (corp-wide): 1.7MM **Privately Held**
SIC: **2833** Hormones or derivatives
PA: Hall Health And Longevity Center, A
   Professional Corporation
   1321 7th St
   Santa Monica CA 90401
   310 566-6688

(P-7667)
HERB KAN COMPANY INC
380 Encinal St Ste 100, Santa Cruz
(95060-2178)
PHONE...................................831 438-9450
Lise Groleau, *President*
▲ EMP: 17
SALES (est): 3MM **Privately Held**
WEB: www.kanherb.com
SIC: **2833** Adrenal derivatives

(P-7668)
HERBAL SCIENCE INTERNATIONAL
205 Russell St, City of Industry
(91744-3940)
PHONE...................................626 333-9998
William Chang, *President*
▲ EMP: 15
SALES (est): 1.2MM **Privately Held**
WEB: www.hsusa.net
SIC: **2833** 5499 Medicinals & botanicals;
spices & herbs

(P-7669)
IMP INTERNATIONAL INC (PA)
Also Called: Unichem Enterprises
1905 S Lynx Ave, Ontario (91761-8055)
PHONE...................................909 321-1000
Chentao Hang, *President*
▲ EMP: 38
SQ FT: 40,000
SALES (est): 5.9MM **Privately Held**
SIC: **2833** 2869 Vitamins, natural or syn-
thetic: bulk, uncompounded; sweeteners,
synthetic

(P-7670)
INTERHEALTH NUTRACEUTICALS INC
5451 Industrial Way, Benicia (94510-1010)
PHONE...................................800 783-4636
Paul Dijkstra, *CEO*
Navpreet Singh, *COO*
Mary Helen Lucero, *CFO*
Kim Lee, *Accountant*
▲ EMP: 30
SQ FT: 33,000
SALES (est): 8.2MM
SALES (corp-wide): 5.5B **Privately Held**
WEB: www.interhealthusa.com
SIC: **2833** Vitamins, natural or synthetic:
bulk, uncompounded

PA: Lonza Group Ag
Munchensteinerstr. 38
Basel BS 4052
613 168-111

(P-7671)
INTERNTNAL MDCTION SYSTEMS LTD
Also Called: IMS
10642 El Poche St, South El Monte
(91733-3408)
PHONE..................626 459-5586
EMP: 13
SALES (corp-wide): 210.4MM Publicly Held
SIC: 2833
HQ: International Medication Systems, Ltd.
1886 Santa Anita Ave
South El Monte CA 91733
626 442-6757

(P-7672)
J & D LABORATORIES INC
2710 Progress St, Vista (92081-8449)
PHONE..................844 453-5227
David Wood, CEO
▲ EMP: 300
SQ FT: 32,000
SALES (est): 92.5MM
SALES (corp-wide): 167.9MM Privately Held
WEB: www.jdlaboratories.com
SIC: 2833 2834 Vitamins, natural or synthetic: bulk, uncompounded; pharmaceutical preparations
HQ: Captek Softgel International, Inc.
16218 Arthur St
Cerritos CA 90703

(P-7673)
JOHN A THOMSON PHD
Also Called: Huntington Company
12610 Saticoy St S, North Hollywood
(91605-4313)
PHONE..................323 877-5186
John A Thomson, Owner
▼ EMP: 20 EST: 1936
SALES (est): 3.4MM Privately Held
WEB: www.superthrive.com
SIC: 2833 Medicinals & botanicals

(P-7674)
MULTIVITAMIN DIRECT INC
2178 Paragon Dr, San Jose (95131-1305)
PHONE..................408 573-7276
▲ EMP: 21
SQ FT: 5,000
SALES: 3.5MM Privately Held
SIC: 2833

(P-7675)
NATURAL WONDERS CA INC
Also Called: Nature Creation
7240 Eton Ave, Canoga Park (91303-1505)
PHONE..................818 593-2001
Hagay Mizrahi, President
▲ EMP: 15
SQ FT: 20,000
SALES (est): 2.6MM Privately Held
SIC: 2833 5122 Medicinals & botanicals; botanical products, medicinal: ground, graded or milled

(P-7676)
NATURES BOUNTY CO
901 E 233rd St, Carson (90745-6204)
PHONE..................310 952-7107
Colleen Davis, Branch Mgr
Cesar Cortez, Info Tech Mgr
Roxanne Bladenn, Purch Mgr
EMP: 19 Publicly Held
WEB: www.nbty.com
SIC: 2833 Medicinals & botanicals
HQ: The Nature's Bounty Co
2100 Smithtown Ave
Ronkonkoma NY 11779
631 200-2000

(P-7677)
NATURES BOUNTY CO
7366 Orangewood Ave, Garden Grove
(92841-1412)
PHONE..................714 898-9936
Lily Mu, Branch Mgr
Marco Ortega, Plant Mgr

Tim Unger, Relations
EMP: 19 Publicly Held
WEB: www.nbty.com
SIC: 2833 Vitamins, natural or synthetic: bulk, uncompounded
HQ: The Nature's Bounty Co
2100 Smithtown Ave
Ronkonkoma NY 11779
631 200-2000

(P-7678)
NITRO 2 GO INC
1420 Richardson St, San Bernardino
(92408-2962)
PHONE..................909 864-4886
Jeff Diehl, President
▲ EMP: 35
SQ FT: 6,000
SALES (est): 7.3MM Privately Held
WEB: www.nitro2go.com
SIC: 2833 Drugs & herbs: grading, grinding & milling

(P-7679)
NU-HEALTH PRODUCTS CO
Also Called: Nu Health Products
20875 Currier Rd, Walnut (91789-3081)
PHONE..................909 869-0666
Lynn Leung, President
Amanda Fu, Purch Mgr
▲ EMP: 25
SQ FT: 12,000
SALES (est): 4MM Privately Held
WEB: www.nu-health.com
SIC: 2833 2048 5149 Vitamins, natural or synthetic: bulk, uncompounded; drugs & herbs: grading, grinding & milling; prepared feeds; organic & diet foods

(P-7680)
OPTIMUM BIOENERGY INTL CORP
2463 Pomona Rd, Corona (92880-6931)
PHONE..................714 903-8872
Louis LI, President
Judy LI, Vice Pres
▲ EMP: 15
SQ FT: 5,000
SALES: 1.2MM Privately Held
SIC: 2833 Vitamins, natural or synthetic: bulk, uncompounded

(P-7681)
PHARMAVITE LLC (DH)
8531 Fallbrook Ave, West Hills
(91304-3232)
P.O. Box 9606, Mission Hills (91346-9606)
PHONE..................818 221-6200
Jeff Boutelle, CEO
Bob McQuillan, President
Rhonda Hoffman, Chief Mktg Ofcr
Dave Larson, Division VP
Bryan Donaldson, Exec VP
▲ EMP: 172 EST: 2002
SQ FT: 45,000
SALES (est): 284.3MM Privately Held
WEB: www.pharmavite.com
SIC: 2833 2834 Vitamins, natural or synthetic: bulk, uncompounded; pharmaceutical preparations
HQ: Otsuka America, Inc.
1 Embarcadero Ctr # 2020
San Francisco CA 94111
415 986-5300

(P-7682)
PHARMAVITE LLC
1150 Aviation Pl, San Fernando
(91340-1460)
PHONE..................818 221-6200
Jim Jordan, Exec VP
Octavio Padilla, Technician
Alejandro Cervantes, Research
Manmeet Salh, Research
Haik Parkahni, Engineer
EMP: 300 Privately Held
WEB: www.pharmavite.com
SIC: 2833 Vitamins, natural or synthetic: bulk, uncompounded
HQ: Pharmavite Llc
8531 Fallbrook Ave
West Hills CA 91304
818 221-6200

(P-7683)
POTNETWORK HOLDINGS INC
3278 Wilshire Blvd, Los Angeles
(90010-1402)
PHONE..................800 915-3060
EMP: 10
SALES (corp-wide): 14.3MM Privately Held
SIC: 2833 5122 5521 Medicinals & botanicals; medicinals & botanicals; automobiles, used cars only
PA: Potnetwork Holdings, Inc.
3531 Griffin Rd
Fort Lauderdale FL 33312
800 433-0127

(P-7684)
PRO TEAM AXIS LLC
Also Called: Cbd Axis
1725 Harding Ave Unit A, National City
(91950-5509)
PHONE..................833 333-2947
Armando Baylon, Mng Member
Isac Rodriguez,
EMP: 10
SQ FT: 2,000
SALES: 1.2MM Privately Held
SIC: 2833 Adrenal derivatives

(P-7685)
PROMEGA BIOSCIENCES LLC
277 Granada Dr, San Luis Obispo
(93401-7396)
PHONE..................805 544-8524
Kristen Yetter, Finance
Jeff Richardson, MIS Mgr
Sergiy Levin, Research
Poncho Meisenheimer, Research
Ce Shi, Research
EMP: 55
SQ FT: 40,000
SALES (est): 13MM
SALES (corp-wide): 420.8MM Privately Held
WEB: www.promega.com
SIC: 2833 2835 Medicinal chemicals; in vitro & in vivo diagnostic substances
PA: Promega Corporation
2800 Woods Hollow Rd
Fitchburg WI 53711
608 274-4330

(P-7686)
PROTHENA CORP PUB LTD CO
331 Oyster Point Blvd, South San Francisco (94080-1913)
PHONE..................650 837-8550
Gene Kinney, CEO
Bill Homan, Officer
David McNinch, Officer
Pam Farmer, Vice Pres
Bill Yates, Vice Pres
EMP: 11
SALES (est): 1.8MM Privately Held
SIC: 2833 Medicinals & botanicals

(P-7687)
RON TEEGUARDEN ENTERPRISES INC (PA)
Also Called: Dragon Herbs
5670 Wilshire Blvd # 1500, Los Angeles
(90036-5660)
PHONE..................323 556-8188
Ron Teagarden, President
Yanlin Teeguarden, Principal
Ricah Rejano, Executive Asst
◆ EMP: 33
SQ FT: 13,000
SALES (est): 4.7MM Privately Held
WEB: www.dragonherbs.com
SIC: 2833 5122 Drugs & herbs: grading, grinding & milling; medicinals & botanicals

(P-7688)
RYZER-RX LLC
5575 La Jolla Blvd, La Jolla (92037-7612)
PHONE..................858 454-7477
David Nava, Info Tech Dir
EMP: 10
SQ FT: 5,000
SALES (est): 18.4K Privately Held
SIC: 2833 5122 Drugs & herbs: grading, grinding & milling; vitamins & minerals

(P-7689)
S K LABORATORIES INC
Also Called: S K Labs
5420 E La Palma Ave, Anaheim
(92807-2023)
PHONE..................714 695-9800
Bansi Patel, President
Ramila B Patel, Admin Sec
▲ EMP: 100
SQ FT: 60,000
SALES: 25MM Privately Held
WEB: www.sklabs.com
SIC: 2833 Vitamins, natural or synthetic: bulk, uncompounded

(P-7690)
S&B PHARMA INC
Also Called: Norac Pharma
405 S Motor Ave, Azusa (91702-3232)
PHONE..................626 334-2908
Dr Daniel Levin, President
Emerich Eisenreich, Research
Frank Parrish, Technology
John Ernest, Plant Engr
Richard Wong, Products
▲ EMP: 61
SALES (est): 14.2MM Privately Held
SIC: 2833 8731 2834 Medicinals & botanicals; commercial physical research; pharmaceutical preparations

(P-7691)
SABRE SCIENCES INC
2233 Faraday Ave Ste K, Carlsbad
(92008-7214)
PHONE..................760 448-2750
Victor Salerno, President
Anna Salerno, Treasurer
Michael Borkin, Principal
Jennifer Lewis, Mng Member
EMP: 18
SQ FT: 8,000
SALES (est): 3.6MM Privately Held
WEB: www.sabresciences.com
SIC: 2833 8731 Hormones or derivatives; commercial physical research

(P-7692)
SAPPHIRE ENERGY INC
10996 Torreyana Rd # 280, San Diego
(92121-1161)
PHONE..................858 768-4700
James Levine, CEO
Thomas Willardson, CFO
Steven Goldby, Bd of Directors
Jim Astwood, Senior VP
Craig Behnke, Vice Pres
EMP: 55
SALES (est): 23.1MM Privately Held
SIC: 2833 Medicinals & botanicals

(P-7693)
SELECT SUPPLEMENTS INC
2390 Oak Ridge Way, Vista (92081-8345)
PHONE..................760 431-7509
Joar A Opheim, CEO
Hector Gudino, COO
▲ EMP: 32
SQ FT: 36,000
SALES (est): 12.3MM Privately Held
SIC: 2833 Medicinals & botanicals

(P-7694)
SPRUCE BIOSCIENCES INC
1700 Montgomery St # 212, San Francisco
(94111-1023)
PHONE..................415 655-3803
Alexis Howerton, CEO
David Moriarty, Vice Pres
EMP: 18
SALES (est): 3.3MM Privately Held
SIC: 2833 Endocrine products

(P-7695)
STAUBER PRFMCE INGREDIENTS (HQ)
4120 N Palm St, Fullerton (92835-1026)
PHONE..................714 441-3900
Patrick Hawkins, President
Shirley Rozeboom, Senior VP
Pat Wratschko, Vice Pres
Sheri Esswein, VP Bus Dvlpt
Katie Laughlin, Executive
EMP: 139

▲ = Import ▼=Export
◆ =Import/Export

SALES (est): 8.5MM
SALES (corp-wide): 556.3MM **Publicly Held**
SIC: 2833 Medicinals & botanicals
PA: Hawkins, Inc.
2381 Rosegate
Roseville MN 55113
612 331-6910

(P-7696)
THRESHOLD ENTERPRISES LTD
165 Technology Dr, Watsonville (95076-2448)
PHONE..................................831 425-3955
EMP: 18
SALES (corp-wide): 172MM **Privately Held**
SIC: 2833 2099 Vitamins, natural or synthetic: bulk, uncompounded; food preparations
PA: Threshold Enterprises Ltd.
23 Janis Way
Scotts Valley CA 95066
831 438-6851

(P-7697)
THRESHOLD ENTERPRISES LTD (PA)
Also Called: Vanguard Marketing
23 Janis Way, Scotts Valley (95066-3546)
PHONE..................................831 438-6851
Tom Grillea, *CEO*
Ira L Goldberg, *CEO*
Daniel Goldberg, *Managing Dir*
Matt McNair, *Admin Asst*
Ken Grunstra, *Administration*
◆ **EMP:** 277
SQ FT: 100,000
SALES (est): 172MM **Privately Held**
WEB: www.planetaryformulas.com
SIC: 2833 Vitamins, natural or synthetic: bulk, uncompounded

(P-7698)
THRESHOLD ENTERPRISES LTD
11 Janis Way, Scotts Valley (95066-3537)
PHONE..................................831 461-6413
Scott Laforce, *Controller*
EMP: 54
SALES (corp-wide): 172MM **Privately Held**
WEB: www.planetaryformulas.com
SIC: 2833 5122 Vitamins, natural or synthetic: bulk, uncompounded; vitamins & minerals
PA: Threshold Enterprises Ltd.
23 Janis Way
Scotts Valley CA 95066
831 438-6851

(P-7699)
THRESHOLD ENTERPRISES LTD
19 Janis Way Scotts Vly Scotts Valle, Scotts Valley (95066)
PHONE..................................831 461-6343
EMP: 30
SALES (corp-wide): 172MM **Privately Held**
WEB: www.planetaryformulas.com
SIC: 2833 Vitamins, natural or synthetic: bulk, uncompounded
PA: Threshold Enterprises Ltd.
23 Janis Way
Scotts Valley CA 95066
831 438-6851

(P-7700)
THRESHOLD ENTERPRISES LTD
2280 Delaware Ave, Santa Cruz (95060-5707)
PHONE..................................831 466-4014
Charles Powell, *General Mgr*
EMP: 36
SALES (corp-wide): 172MM **Privately Held**
SIC: 2833 Vitamins, natural or synthetic: bulk, uncompounded
PA: Threshold Enterprises Ltd.
23 Janis Way
Scotts Valley CA 95066
831 438-6851

(P-7701)
UNI-CAPS LLC
540 Lambert Rd, Brea (92821)
PHONE..................................714 529-8400

Sang H Kim, *Mng Member*
▲ **EMP:** 30
SALES (est): 14.4MM **Privately Held**
SIC: 2833 Vitamins, natural or synthetic: bulk, uncompounded

(P-7702)
VISION SMART CENTER INC
123 Astronaut E S Onizuka, Los Angeles (90012-3864)
PHONE..................................213 625-1740
Eddie Shiojima, *CEO*
Yuya Aoyama, *Opers Mgr*
EMP: 10
SQ FT: 2,000
SALES (est): 730K **Privately Held**
SIC: 2833 Vitamins, natural or synthetic: bulk, uncompounded

(P-7703)
VITAJOY USA INC
14165 Ramona Ave, Chino (91710-5753)
PHONE..................................626 965-8830
Dan Gu, *CEO*
Charles Kuo, *Vice Pres*
▲ **EMP:** 10 **EST:** 2012
SALES (est): 2.7MM **Privately Held**
SIC: 2833 Vitamins, natural or synthetic: bulk, uncompounded

(P-7704)
WESTAR NUTRITION CORP
350 Paularino Ave, Costa Mesa (92626-4616)
PHONE..................................949 645-6100
David Fan, *President*
Lucy Fan, *Vice Pres*
▼ **EMP:** 240
SQ FT: 55,000
SALES (est): 34.3MM **Privately Held**
SIC: 2833 2834 2844 7389 Vitamins, natural or synthetic: bulk, uncompounded; pharmaceutical preparations; cosmetic preparations; packaging & labeling services

(P-7705)
WINNING LABORATORIES INC
Also Called: Natutac
16218 Arthur St, Cerritos (90703-2131)
PHONE..................................562 921-6880
James Hao, *President*
Lydia Hao, *Vice Pres*
▲ **EMP:** 16
SQ FT: 90,000
SALES (est): 9.2MM **Privately Held**
WEB: www.silverspurcorp.com
SIC: 2833 Medicinals & botanicals
PA: Silver Spur Corporation
16010 Shoemaker Ave
Cerritos CA 90703
562 921-6880

2834 Pharmaceuticals

(P-7706)
3M COMPANY
19901 Nordhoff St, Northridge (91324-3213)
P.O. Box 1001 (91328-1001)
PHONE..................................818 341-1300
Carol Beesley, *Branch Mgr*
Peter Luedtke, *Engineer*
Jacob Rosander, *Manager*
EMP: 400
SALES (corp-wide): 32.7B **Publicly Held**
WEB: www.mmm.com
SIC: 2834 Pharmaceutical preparations
PA: 3m Company
3m Center
Saint Paul MN 55144
651 733-1110

(P-7707)
89BIO INC
535 Mission St Fl 14, San Francisco (94105-3253)
PHONE..................................415 500-4614
Rohan Palekar, *CEO*
Ram Waisbourd, *COO*
Ryan Martins, *CFO*
Hank Mansbach, *Chief Mktg Ofcr*
Quoc Le-Nguyen, *Officer*
EMP: 14

SALES (est): 1.4MM **Privately Held**
SIC: 2834 Pharmaceutical preparations

(P-7708)
A Q PHARMACEUTICALS INC
11555 Monarch St Ste C, Garden Grove (92841-1814)
PHONE..................................714 903-1000
Tracy Nguyen, *President*
Henry Smith, *Vice Pres*
▲ **EMP:** 30
SQ FT: 3,000
SALES (est): 5.5MM **Privately Held**
WEB: www.aqpharmaceuticals.com
SIC: 2834 Pharmaceutical preparations

(P-7709)
ABBOTT LABORATORIES
15900 Valley View Ct, Sylmar (91342-3577)
PHONE..................................818 493-2388
Dee Vetter, *Principal*
Tinsley Maness, *Executive*
Aubrey Mullenix, *Administration*
Jacob Hanggi, *Network Enginr*
Bryan Brust, *Sales Staff*
EMP: 27
SALES (corp-wide): 30.5B **Publicly Held**
SIC: 2834 Pharmaceutical preparations
PA: Abbott Laboratories
100 Abbott Park Rd
Abbott Park IL 60064
224 667-6100

(P-7710)
ABBOTT LABORATORIES
41888 Motor Car Pkwy, Temecula (92591-4651)
P.O. Box 9018 (92589-9018)
PHONE..................................951 914-3000
Matthew Holmes, *Branch Mgr*
EMP: 45
SALES (corp-wide): 30.5B **Publicly Held**
SIC: 2834 Pharmaceutical preparations
PA: Abbott Laboratories
100 Abbott Park Rd
Abbott Park IL 60064
224 667-6100

(P-7711)
ABBOTT NUTRITION
2302 Courage Dr, Fairfield (94533)
PHONE..................................707 399-1100
EMP: 17
SALES (est): 3.7MM **Privately Held**
SIC: 2834 Pharmaceutical preparations

(P-7712)
ABBOTT NUTRITION MFG INC (HQ)
2351 N Watney Way Ste C, Fairfield (94533-6726)
PHONE..................................707 399-1100
Mark Shaffar, *Vice Pres*
Mel Williamson, *Principal*
▼ **EMP:** 183
SALES (est): 54.8MM
SALES (corp-wide): 30.5B **Publicly Held**
WEB: www.abbott.com
SIC: 2834 Vitamin, nutrient & hematinic preparations for human use
PA: Abbott Laboratories
100 Abbott Park Rd
Abbott Park IL 60064
224 667-6100

(P-7713)
ABBOTT VASCULAR INC
26531 Ynez Rd, Temecula (92591-4630)
PHONE..................................951 941-2400
Ronald Dollens, *Branch Mgr*
Erik Bomstad, *Program Mgr*
Cornel Ciurea, *Administration*
Judy Fairchild, *Network Mgr*
Schmitz Brian, *Business Anlyst*
EMP: 500
SALES (corp-wide): 30.5B **Publicly Held**
SIC: 2834 Pharmaceutical preparations
HQ: Abbott Vascular Inc.
3200 Lakeside Dr
Santa Clara CA 95054
408 845-3000

(P-7714)
ABCO LABORATORIES INC (PA)
Also Called: Baron Brand Spices
2450 S Watney Way, Fairfield (94533-6730)
P.O. Box 2519 (94533-0251)
PHONE..................................707 427-1818
Allen Baron, *President*
Greg Northam, *President*
Eric Whitaker, *Exec VP*
Adrian Cesana, *CIO*
Hamed Malekan, *Research*
▲ **EMP:** 100
SQ FT: 29,000
SALES (est): 22.6MM **Privately Held**
WEB: www.abcolabs.com
SIC: 2834 2099 Vitamin preparations; spices, including grinding

(P-7715)
ABRAXIS BIOSCIENCE INC
Also Called: American Bioscience
2730 Wilshire Blvd # 110, Santa Monica (90403-4743)
PHONE..................................310 883-1300
EMP: 75
SALES (corp-wide): 15.2B **Privately Held**
SIC: 2834 Pharmaceutical preparations
HQ: Abraxis Bioscience, Inc.
86 Morris Ave
Summit NJ 07901

(P-7716)
ABRAXIS BIOSCIENCE LLC (DH)
11755 Wilshire Blvd Fl 20, Los Angeles (90025-1543)
PHONE..................................800 564-0216
Leon O Moulder Jr,
Rick Rodgers Sr,
Patrick Soon-Shiong MD,
EMP: 232
SALES (est): 95.4MM
SALES (corp-wide): 15.2B **Privately Held**
SIC: 2834 Pharmaceutical preparations

(P-7717)
ACADIA PHARMACEUTICALS INC (PA)
3611 Valley Centre Dr # 300, San Diego (92130-3331)
PHONE..................................858 558-2871
Stephen R Davis, *President*
Stephen R Biggar, *Ch of Bd*
Srdjan Stankovic, *President*
Elena Ridloff, *CFO*
Michael J Yang, *Ch Credit Ofcr*
▲ **EMP:** 425
SQ FT: 78,000
SALES: 223.8MM **Publicly Held**
WEB: www.acadia-pharm.com
SIC: 2834 8731 Pharmaceutical preparations; medical research, commercial

(P-7718)
ACELRX PHARMACEUTICALS INC
351 Galveston Dr, Redwood City (94063-4736)
PHONE..................................650 216-3500
Vincent J Angotti, *CEO*
Adrian Adams, *Ch of Bd*
Raffi Asadorian, *CFO*
Pamela P Palmer, *Chief Mktg Ofcr*
Badri Dasu, *Officer*
EMP: 61
SQ FT: 25,893
SALES: 2.1MM **Privately Held**
WEB: www.acelrx.com
SIC: 2834 Pharmaceutical preparations

(P-7719)
ACHAOGEN INC (PA)
1 Tower Pl Ste 400, South San Francisco (94080-1832)
PHONE..................................650 800-3636
Kenneth J Hillan, *President*
Bryan E Roberts, *Ch of Bd*
Liz Bhatt, *COO*
Blake Wise, *COO*
Zeryn Sarpangal, *CFO*
EMP: 155
SQ FT: 16,000

PRODUCTS & SVCS

SALES: 8.7MM **Privately Held**
WEB: www.achaogen.com
SIC: **2834** Pharmaceutical preparations

(P-7720)
ACOLOGIX INC
3960 Point Eden Way, Hayward
(94545-3719)
PHONE.................................510 512-7200
Yoshinari Kumagai, *President*
R Scott Greer, *Ch of Bd*
John J Buckley, *CFO*
Dawn McGuire, *Chief Mktg Ofcr*
David M Rosen, *Senior VP*
EMP: 37
SQ FT: 5,244
SALES (est): 5.3MM **Privately Held**
WEB: www.acologix.com
SIC: **2834** Drugs acting on the gastrointestinal or genitourinary system

(P-7721)
ACTAVALON INC
3210 Merryfield Row, San Diego
(92121-1126)
PHONE.................................949 244-5684
Gail Wesley Hatfield, *CEO*
G Wesley Hatfield, *CEO*
EMP: 12
SALES (est): 1.7MM **Privately Held**
SIC: **2834** Proprietary drug products

(P-7722)
ACTAVIS LLC
132 Business Center Dr, Corona
(92880-1724)
PHONE.................................951 493-5582
EMP: 13 **Privately Held**
SIC: **2834** Pharmaceutical preparations
HQ: Actavis Llc
　　5 Giralda Farms
　　Madison NJ 07940
　　862 261-7000

(P-7723)
ACTAVIS LLC
311 Bonnie Cir, Corona (92880-2882)
P.O. Box 1149 (92878-1149)
PHONE.................................909 270-1400
Allen Chao, *Branch Mgr*
Abigail Jenkins, *President*
Sigurdur Olafsson, *Exec VP*
Patrick Brunner, *Senior VP*
David A Buchen, *Senior VP*
EMP: 79 **Privately Held**
SIC: **2834** Pharmaceutical preparations
HQ: Actavis Llc
　　5 Giralda Farms
　　Madison NJ 07940
　　862 261-7000

(P-7724)
ACTELION PHRMACEUTICALS US INC (DH)
5000 Shoreline Ct Ste 200, South San
Francisco (94080-1956)
PHONE.................................650 624-6900
Bill Fairey, *President*
Simon Buckingham, *President*
Rajiv Patni, *Senior VP*
Douglas B Snyder, *Senior VP*
Jean Marc Bellemin, *Vice Pres*
EMP: 26 EST: 1998
SALES (est): 21.2MM
SALES (corp-wide): 81.5B **Publicly Held**
SIC: **2834** Pharmaceutical preparations
HQ: Actelion Pharmaceuticals Ltd
　　Gewerbestrasse 16
　　Allschwil BL 4123
　　615 656-565

(P-7725)
ADAMAS PHARMACEUTICALS INC (PA)
1900 Powell St Ste 1000, Emeryville
(94608-1839)
PHONE.................................510 450-3500
Neil McFarlane, *CEO*
Alfred G Merriweather, *CFO*
Jennifer J Rhodes, *Ch Credit Ofcr*
Vijay Shreedhar, *Ch Credit Ofcr*
Martha Demski, *Bd of Directors*
EMP: 97
SQ FT: 37,626

SALES: 571K **Publicly Held**
WEB: www.adamaspharma.com
SIC: **2834** Drugs acting on the central
nervous system & sense organs

(P-7726)
ADAMIS PHARMACEUTICALS CORP (PA)
11682 El Cmino Real Ste 3, San Diego
(92130)
PHONE.................................858 997-2400
Dennis Carlo, *President*
Richard C Williams, *Ch of Bd*
Dennis J Carlo, *President*
Robert O Hopkins, *CFO*
Ronald B Moss, *Chief Mktg Ofcr*
EMP: 41
SQ FT: 7,525
SALES: 15MM **Publicly Held**
WEB: www.cellegy.com
SIC: **2834** Pharmaceutical preparations

(P-7727)
ADIANA INC
1240 Elko Dr, Sunnyvale (94089-2212)
PHONE.................................650 421-2900
Paul Goeld, *CEO*
EMP: 30
SQ FT: 12,000
SALES (est): 2.4MM
SALES (corp-wide): 3.2B **Publicly Held**
WEB: www.adiana.com
SIC: **2834** 8731 Pharmaceutical preparations; commercial physical research
HQ: Cytyc Corporation
　　250 Campus Dr
　　Marlborough MA 01752
　　508 263-2900

(P-7728)
ADURO BIOTECH INC (PA)
740 Heinz Ave, Berkeley (94710-2748)
PHONE.................................510 848-4400
Stephen T Isaacs, *Ch of Bd*
Dimitry SA Nuyten, *Chief Mktg Ofcr*
Thomas W Dubensky Jr, *Officer*
Andrea Elsas, *Officer*
Blaine Templeman, *Officer*
EMP: 90
SQ FT: 25,000
SALES: 15MM **Publicly Held**
SIC: **2834** 8731 Pharmaceutical preparations; commercial physical research

(P-7729)
ADVANCED CHEMBLOCKS INC
Also Called: A Chemblock
849 Mitten Rd Ste 101, Burlingame
(94010-1308)
PHONE.................................650 692-2368
Robert Du, *President*
EMP: 10 EST: 2009
SQ FT: 500
SALES (est): 3.5MM **Privately Held**
SIC: **2834** 8711 Pharmaceutical preparations; chemical engineering

(P-7730)
ADVANTAGE PHARMACEUTICALS
4363 Pacific St, Rocklin (95677-2117)
PHONE.................................916 630-4960
Arthur Whitney, *President*
EMP: 10
SALES (est): 1.4MM **Privately Held**
SIC: **2834** Pharmaceutical preparations

(P-7731)
AGOURON PHARMACEUTICALS INC (HQ)
10777 Science Center Dr, San Diego
(92121-1111)
PHONE.................................858 622-3000
Catherine Mackey PHD, *Senior VP*
EMP: 50
SALES (est): 54.6MM
SALES (corp-wide): 53.6B **Publicly Held**
WEB: www.agouron.com
SIC: **2834** 5122 8731 Pharmaceutical preparations; pharmaceuticals; commercial physical research
PA: Pfizer Inc.
　　235 E 42nd St
　　New York NY 10017
　　212 733-2323

(P-7732)
AGRAQUEST INC (DH)
Also Called: Bayer Cropscience
890 Embarcadero Dr, West Sacramento
(95605-1503)
PHONE.................................866 992-2937
James Blome, *CEO*
Michael Mille, *COO*
Joel R Jung, *CFO*
▲ EMP: 54
SQ FT: 28,000
SALES (est): 32.5MM
SALES (corp-wide): 45.3B **Privately Held**
WEB: www.agraquest.com
SIC: **2834** Pharmaceutical preparations
HQ: Bayer Cropscience Ag
　　Alfred-Nobel-Str. 50
　　Monheim Am Rhein 40789
　　217 338-0

(P-7733)
AIMMUNE THERAPEUTICS INC
8000 Marina Blvd Ste 300, Brisbane
(94005-1884)
PHONE.................................650 614-5220
Jayson Dallas, *CEO*
Mark D McDade, *Ch of Bd*
Eric H Bjerkholt, *CFO*
Andrew Oxtoby, *Ch Credit Ofcr*
Gregory Behar, *Bd of Directors*
EMP: 131
SQ FT: 53,000
SALES (est): 30.3MM **Privately Held**
SIC: **2834** Pharmaceutical preparations

(P-7734)
AKARANTA INC
Also Called: Sierra Pharmacy
8661 Baseline Rd, Rancho Cucamonga
(91730-1111)
PHONE.................................909 989-9800
Pradeep K Amin, *CEO*
EMP: 10
SALES (est): 1.8MM **Privately Held**
SIC: **2834** 5999 Pharmaceutical preparations; medical apparatus & supplies

(P-7735)
ALCON MANUFACTURING LTD (PA)
15800 Alton Pkwy, Irvine (92618-3818)
PHONE.................................949 753-1393
Ken Lickel, *Principal*
▲ EMP: 15 EST: 1945
SALES (est): 2.1MM **Privately Held**
SIC: **2834** 8011 Veterinary pharmaceutical preparations; eyes, ears, nose & throat specialist: physician/surgeon

(P-7736)
ALLAKOS INC
975 Island Dr Ste 201, Redwood City
(94065-5173)
PHONE.................................650 597-5002
Robert Alexander, *President*
Daniel Janney, *Ch of Bd*
Adam Tomasi, *COO*
Henrik Rasmussen, *Chief Mktg Ofcr*
EMP: 44 EST: 2012
SQ FT: 10,142
SALES (est): 17.2MM **Privately Held**
SIC: **2834** Pharmaceutical preparations

(P-7737)
ALLERGAN INC
735 Workman Mill Rd, Whittier (90601)
PHONE.................................512 527-6688
EMP: 194 **Privately Held**
SIC: **2834** Drugs acting on the central nervous system & sense organs
HQ: Allergan, Inc.
　　5 Giralda Farms
　　Madison NJ 07940
　　862 261-7000

(P-7738)
ALLERGAN SALES LLC
Also Called: Bioscience Laboratories
503 Vandell Way Ste A, Campbell
(95008-6924)
PHONE.................................408 376-3001
Tom Kawata, *Surgery Dir*
EMP: 38 **Privately Held**
SIC: **2834** Pharmaceutical preparations

HQ: Allergan Sales, Llc
　　2525 Dupont Dr
　　Irvine CA 92612
　　862 261-7000

(P-7739)
ALLERGAN SALES LLC
Also Called: Analytical Sciences
18655a Teller Ave, Irvine (92612-1610)
PHONE.................................714 246-2288
Dilip R Choudhury PHD, *Manager*
EMP: 28 **Privately Held**
SIC: **2834** Pharmaceutical preparations
HQ: Allergan Sales, Llc
　　2525 Dupont Dr
　　Irvine CA 92612
　　862 261-7000

(P-7740)
ALLERGAN SALES LLC (DH)
2525 Dupont Dr, Irvine (92612-1599)
P.O. Box 19534 (92623-9534)
PHONE.................................862 261-7000
Brenton L Saunders, *President*
Matthew M Walsh, *CFO*
Alex Kelly, *Ch Credit Ofcr*
William Meury, *Ch Credit Ofcr*
A Robert D Bailey,
▲ EMP: 600
SQ FT: 10,000
SALES (est): 334.3MM **Privately Held**
WEB: www.myallerganbenefits.com
SIC: **2834** Pharmaceutical preparations
HQ: Allergan, Inc.
　　5 Giralda Farms
　　Madison NJ 07940
　　862 261-7000

(P-7741)
ALLERGAN SPCLTY THRPEUTICS INC
2525 Dupont Dr, Irvine (92612-1599)
PHONE.................................714 246-4500
David Pyott, *President*
Michelle Davis, *Executive*
William Glass, *Surgery Dir*
Scott Johnson, *Regional Mgr*
Lisa Purmort, *Executive Asst*
EMP: 1500 EST: 1997
SALES (est): 208.5MM **Privately Held**
WEB: www.allergan.com
SIC: **2834** Pharmaceutical preparations
HQ: Allergan, Inc.
　　5 Giralda Farms
　　Madison NJ 07940
　　862 261-7000

(P-7742)
ALLERGAN USA INC
Also Called: Pacific Communications
18581 Teller Ave, Irvine (92612-1627)
P.O. Box 19534 (92623-9534)
PHONE.................................714 427-1900
David E I Pyott, *CEO*
Craig Sullivan, *President*
Jeffrey L Edwards, *CFO*
James M Hindman, *Treasurer*
Kun Kim, *Vice Pres*
EMP: 2000
SALES (est): 228.8MM **Privately Held**
WEB: www.espritpharma.com
SIC: **2834** Druggists' preparations (pharmaceuticals)
HQ: Allergan, Inc.
　　5 Giralda Farms
　　Madison NJ 07940
　　862 261-7000

(P-7743)
ALLERGY RESEARCH GROUP LLC
Also Called: Nutricology
2300 N Loop Rd, Alameda (94502-8009)
PHONE.................................510 263-2000
Stephen Levine, *Ch of Bd*
Manfred Salomon, *CEO*
Susan Levine, *Vice Pres*
Laura Johnson, *Controller*
Dan Mallar, *Sales Staff*
▲ EMP: 50
SQ FT: 29,821
SALES (est): 14.2MM **Privately Held**
WEB: www.allergyresearchgroup.com
SIC: **2834** Vitamin, nutrient & hematinic preparations for human use

▲ = Import ▼=Export
◆ =Import/Export

(P-7744)
ALTAVIZ LLC (PA)
13766 Alton Pkwy Ste 143, Irvine
(92618-1619)
PHONE...................................949 656-4003
John Huculak, *Mng Member*
Steven Ziemba, *Exec VP*
Jack Auld, *Principal*
Matthew Latourette, *Office Admin*
Heckler Paul, *Project Engr*
EMP: 10
SALES (est): 1.6MM **Privately Held**
SIC: 2834 8731 Pharmaceutical prepara-
tions; biotechnical research, commercial

(P-7745)
ALZA CORPORATION (HQ)
Also Called: Alza Pharmaceuticals
700 Eubanks Dr, Vacaville (95688-9470)
PHONE...................................707 453-6400
Katie Fitz Chaddock, *President*
David Danks, *Vice Pres*
Patrick Hannon, *General Mgr*
Jose Avena, *Engineer*
Brian Putney, *Mfg Staff*
▲ EMP: 800
SQ FT: 74,500
SALES (est): 286.6MM
SALES (corp-wide): 81.5B **Publicly Held**
WEB: www.alza.com
SIC: 2834 Pharmaceutical preparations
PA: Johnson & Johnson
1 Johnson And Johnson Plz
New Brunswick NJ 08933
732 524-0400

(P-7746)
**AMBIT BIOSCIENCES
CORPORATION**
10201 Wtridge Cir Ste 200, San Diego
(92121)
PHONE...................................858 334-2100
Michael A Martino, *President*
Faheem Hasnain, *Ch of Bd*
Alan Fuhrman, *CFO*
Annette North, *Senior VP*
Mario Orlando, *Senior VP*
EMP: 53
SQ FT: 20,000
SALES: 27MM **Privately Held**
WEB: www.ambitbio.com
SIC: 2834 Pharmaceutical preparations
PA: Daiichi Sankyo Company, Limited
3-5-1, Nihombashihoncho
Chuo-Ku TKY 103-0

(P-7747)
AMBRX INC
10975 N Torrey Pines Rd # 100, La Jolla
(92037-1051)
PHONE...................................858 875-2400
Tiecheng Qiao, *CEO*
John D Diekman, *Ch of Bd*
Simon Allen, *Officer*
Yong-Jiang HEI, *Officer*
Peter Kiener, *Officer*
EMP: 56
SALES: 20.4MM **Privately Held**
SIC: 2834 Druggists' preparations (phar-
maceuticals)

(P-7748)
AMF PHARMA LLC
1931 S Lynx Ave, Ontario (91761-8055)
PHONE...................................909 930-9599
Zi Meng, *COO*
Jeanne Liu, *Research*
EMP: 23
SALES (est): 4.9MM **Privately Held**
SIC: 2834 Pharmaceutical preparations

(P-7749)
AMGEN INC
1909 Oak Terrace Ln, Newbury Park
(91320-1732)
PHONE...................................805 499-0512
Sarah Westwood, *Administration*
Jeff Weisiger, *Exec Dir*
Pam McCaslin, *Manager*
EMP: 16
SALES (corp-wide): 23.7B **Publicly Held**
SIC: 2834 Pharmaceutical preparations

PA: Amgen Inc.
1 Amgen Center Dr
Thousand Oaks CA 91320
805 447-1000

(P-7750)
AMGEN INC
1120 Veterans Blvd, South San Francisco
(94080-1985)
PHONE...................................650 244-2000
David V Goeddel, *Site Mgr*
Shanling Shen, *Executive*
Ramon Rivera, *Exec Dir*
Alisa Bredo, *Technical Mgr*
Pete Ricci, *Technician*
EMP: 25
SALES (corp-wide): 23.7B **Publicly Held**
WEB: www.amgen.com
SIC: 2834 Pharmaceutical preparations
PA: Amgen Inc.
1 Amgen Center Dr
Thousand Oaks CA 91320
805 447-1000

(P-7751)
AMGEN INC
1840 De Havilland Dr, Newbury Park
(91320-1789)
PHONE...................................805 447-1000
Gordon M Binder, *Manager*
Barry Cherney, *Exec Dir*
Narimon Honarpour, *Exec Dir*
Lionel Aguayo, *Admin Sec*
Sahba Tafazoli, *Planning*
EMP: 60
SALES (corp-wide): 23.7B **Publicly Held**
WEB: www.amgen.com
SIC: 2834 Pharmaceutical preparations
PA: Amgen Inc.
1 Amgen Center Dr
Thousand Oaks CA 91320
805 447-1000

(P-7752)
**AMPAC FINE CHEMICALS LLC
(HQ)**
Highway 50 And Hazel Ave, Rancho Cor-
dova (95741)
P.O. Box 1718 (95741-1718)
PHONE...................................916 357-6880
Aslam Malik, *President*
Jeff Butler, *Vice Pres*
William Dubay, *Vice Pres*
Linda Ferguson, *Vice Pres*
Lisa Stuart, *Executive Asst*
▲ EMP: 277
SQ FT: 235,000
SALES (est): 130.7MM **Privately Held**
WEB: www.apfc.com
SIC: 2834 Pharmaceutical preparations

(P-7753)
AMPAC FINE CHEMICALS LLC
Also Called: Ampac Analytical
1100 Windfield Way, El Dorado Hills
(95762-9622)
PHONE...................................916 245-6500
Renato Murrer, *Branch Mgr*
EMP: 18 **Privately Held**
SIC: 2834 Digitalis pharmaceutical prepa-
rations
HQ: Ampac Fine Chemicals Llc
Highway 50 And Hazel Ave
Rancho Cordova CA 95741
916 357-6880

(P-7754)
**AMPHASTAR
PHARMACEUTICALS INC (PA)**
11570 6th St, Rancho Cucamonga
(91730-6025)
PHONE...................................909 980-9484
Jack Yongfeng Zhang, *CEO*
Mary Ziping Luo, *Ch of Bd*
Jason B Shandell, *President*
Bill Peters, *CFO*
William J Peters, *CFO*
▲ EMP: 140 EST: 1996
SQ FT: 267,674
SALES: 294.6MM **Publicly Held**
WEB: www.amphastar.com
SIC: 2834 Pharmaceutical preparations

(P-7755)
**AMYLIN PHARMACEUTICALS
LLC**
9373 Twn Cntr Dr 150, San Diego (92101)
PHONE...................................858 552-2200
Fax: 858 552-2212
EMP: 70
SALES (corp-wide): 16.5B **Publicly Held**
SIC: 2834 8731
HQ: Amylin Pharmaceuticals, Llc
1800 Concord Pike
Wilmington DE 19897
858 552-2200

(P-7756)
ANABOLIC INCORPORATED
Also Called: Vitamer Laboratories
17802 Gillette Ave, Irvine (92614-6502)
P.O. Box 19516 (92623-9516)
PHONE...................................949 863-0340
Steven R Brown, *President*
Jane Drinkwalter, *Vice Pres*
▲ EMP: 95
SALES (est): 11.8MM **Privately Held**
WEB: www.anaboliclabs.com
SIC: 2834 Vitamin preparations

(P-7757)
ANABOLIC LABORATORIES INC
26021 Commercentre Dr, Lake Forest
(92630-8853)
P.O. Box 19516, Irvine (92623-9516)
PHONE...................................949 863-0340
Steven Brown, *President*
EMP: 12
SALES (est): 1.6MM **Privately Held**
SIC: 2834 Pharmaceutical preparations

(P-7758)
**ANACOR PHARMACEUTICALS
INC**
1020 E Meadow Cir, Palo Alto
(94303-4230)
PHONE...................................650 543-7500
EMP: 20
SALES (corp-wide): 20.6MM **Publicly
Held**
SIC: 2834
PA: Anacor Pharmaceuticals, Inc.
1020 E Meadow Cir
Palo Alto CA 10017
650 543-7500

(P-7759)
**ANCHEN PHARMACEUTICALS
INC**
5 Goodyear, Irvine (92618-2000)
PHONE...................................949 639-8100
Phillip Brancazio, *Owner*
Bennie Navarro, *Prdtn Mgr*
EMP: 10 **Privately Held**
SIC: 2834 Druggists' preparations (phar-
maceuticals)
HQ: Anchen Pharmaceuticals, Inc.
9601 Jeronimo Rd
Irvine CA 92618
949 639-8100

(P-7760)
ANIVIVE LIFESCIENCES INC
3250 Airflite Way 400, Long Beach
(90807-5312)
PHONE...................................714 931-7810
Kwansun Ahn, *CEO*
Warren Rickard, *Principal*
Dylan Balsz, *Exec Dir*
EMP: 10
SALES (est): 402.6K **Privately Held**
SIC: 2834 Pharmaceutical preparations

(P-7761)
APEXIGEN INC
75 Shoreway Rd Ste C, San Carlos
(94070-2727)
PHONE...................................650 931-6236
Xiaodong Yang, *President*
Mark Nevins, *President*
Frances Rena Bahjat, *Vice Pres*
Ovid Trifan, *Vice Pres*
Ovid C Trifan, *Vice Pres*
EMP: 28
SALES (est): 5.9MM **Privately Held**
SIC: 2834 Pharmaceutical preparations

(P-7762)
ARADIGM CORPORATION (PA)
39655 Eureka Dr, Newark (94560-4806)
PHONE...................................510 265-9000
Igor Gonda, *President*
Virgil D Thompson, *Ch of Bd*
Nancy E Pecota, *CFO*
Juergen Froehlich, *Chief Mktg Ofcr*
Huiying Wu, *Research*
EMP: 23
SQ FT: 72,000
SALES: 14.4MM **Publicly Held**
WEB: www.aradigm.com
SIC: 2834 Drugs acting on the respiratory
system

(P-7763)
ARDELYX INC
34175 Ardenwood Blvd, Fremont
(94555-3653)
PHONE...................................510 745-1700
Michael Raab, *President*
Mark Kaufmann, *CFO*
Elizabeth Grammer, *Exec VP*
Bryan Shaw, *Vice Pres*
Amy Chao, *Executive Asst*
EMP: 86
SQ FT: 61,784
SALES: 2.6MM **Privately Held**
SIC: 2834 8731 Pharmaceutical prepara-
tions; biotechnical research, commercial

(P-7764)
**ARENA PHARMACEUTICALS
INC (PA)**
6154 Nancy Ridge Dr, San Diego
(92121-3223)
PHONE...................................858 453-7200
Amit D Munshi, *President*
Kevin R Lind, *CFO*
Robert Lisicki, *Ch Credit Ofcr*
Randall E Woods, *Bd of Directors*
Preston Klassen, *Chief Mktg Ofcr*
EMP: 56
SQ FT: 131,000
SALES: 17.9MM **Publicly Held**
WEB: www.arenapharm.com
SIC: 2834 Pharmaceutical preparations

(P-7765)
ARETE THERAPEUTICS INC
52 Buena Vista Ter, San Francisco
(94117-4111)
PHONE...................................650 737-4600
Garrett Roper, *Principal*
EMP: 12
SALES (est): 2.1MM **Privately Held**
SIC: 2834 Druggists' preparations (phar-
maceuticals)

(P-7766)
**ARIDIS PHARMACEUTICALS
INC**
5941 Optical Ct, San Jose (95138-1410)
PHONE...................................408 385-1742
Vu Truong, *CEO*
Eric Patzer, *Ch of Bd*
Fred Kurland, *CFO*
Paul Mendelman, *Chief Mktg Ofcr*
Andy Kelson, *Research*
EMP: 31
SQ FT: 4,500
SALES: 2.7MM **Privately Held**
WEB: www.aridispharma.com
SIC: 2834 Pharmaceutical preparations

(P-7767)
ARMO BIOSCIENCES INC
575 Chesapeake Dr, Redwood City
(94063-4724)
PHONE...................................650 779-5075
Peter Van Vlasselaer, *President*
Herb Cross, *CFO*
Joseph Leveque, *Chief Mktg Ofcr*
Russell Kawahata, *Vice Pres*
Clinton Musil, *Vice Pres*
EMP: 21 EST: 2010
SQ FT: 11,388
SALES: 2.7MM
SALES (corp-wide): 24.5B **Publicly Held**
SIC: 2834 Pharmaceutical preparations
PA: Eli Lilly And Company
Lilly Corporate Ctr
Indianapolis IN 46285
317 276-2000

(P-7768)
ARROWHEAD
PHARMACEUTICALS INC (PA)
225 S Lake Ave Ste 1050, Pasadena
(91101-4820)
PHONE..........................626 304-3400
Christopher Anzalone, *President*
Douglass Given, *Ch of Bd*
Bruce Given, *COO*
Ken Myszkowski, *CFO*
Kenneth A Myszkowski, *CFO*
EMP: 11
SQ FT: 8,500
SALES: 16.1MM **Publicly Held**
WEB: www.arrowres.com
SIC: 2834 8731 Pharmaceutical preparations; biological research

(P-7769)
ASCENDIS PHARMA INC
500 Emerson St, Palo Alto (94301-1607)
PHONE..........................650 352-8389
Jan Mller Mikkelsen, *President*
Flemming Steen Jensen, *President*
Scott T Smith, *CFO*
Michael Wolff Jensen, *Chairman*
Jonathan Leff MD, *Officer*
EMP: 16 EST: 2013
SALES (est): 95.4K
SALES (corp-wide): 12.1MM **Privately Held**
SIC: 2834 Pharmaceutical preparations
PA: Ascendis Pharma A/S
    Tuborg Boulevard 12
    Hellerup 2900
    702 222-44

(P-7770)
ASCLEMED USA INC
379 Van Ness Ave Ste 1403, Torrance
(90501-7211)
PHONE..........................310 218-4146
Robert Nickell, *President*
Joseph J Dekellis, *Admin Sec*
▲ EMP: 11
SQ FT: 8,500
SALES (est): 1.7MM **Privately Held**
SIC: 2834 Pharmaceutical preparations

(P-7771)
ASKGENE PHARMA INC
5217 Verdugo Way Ste A, Camarillo
(93012-8642)
PHONE..........................805 807-9868
Jeff Lu, *CEO*
Robert Wynner, *Principal*
Donggou He, *Director*
EMP: 12 EST: 2012
SALES (est): 2.6MM **Privately Held**
SIC: 2834 Pharmaceutical preparations

(P-7772)
ASSEMBLY BIOSCIENCES INC
331 Oyster Point Blvd, South San Francisco (94080-1913)
PHONE..........................415 978-2163
Anthony Altig, *Bd of Directors*
Myron Z Holubiak, *Bd of Directors*
Helen S Kim, *Bd of Directors*
Jennifer Troia, *Vice Pres*
EMP: 13
SALES (corp-wide): 14.8MM **Publicly Held**
SIC: 2834 Pharmaceutical preparations
PA: Assembly Biosciences, Inc.
    11711 N Meridian St # 310
    Carmel IN 46032
    317 210-9311

(P-7773)
ASTEX PHARMACEUTICALS INC (DH)
4420 Rosewood Dr Ste 200, Pleasanton
(94588-3008)
PHONE..........................925 560-0100
James Manuso, *President*
Michael Molkentin, *CFO*
Mohammad Azab, *Chief Mktg Ofcr*
EMP: 80
SQ FT: 37,000
SALES (est): 19.8MM **Privately Held**
WEB: www.supergen.com
SIC: 2834 Pharmaceutical preparations

HQ: Otsuka America, Inc.
    1 Embarcadero Ctr # 2020
    San Francisco CA 94111
    415 986-5300

(P-7774)
ASTRAZENECA
PHARMACEUTICALS LP
200 Cardinal Way, Redwood City
(94063-4702)
PHONE..........................650 305-2600
Ed Louie, *Branch Mgr*
EMP: 26
SALES (corp-wide): 22B **Privately Held**
SIC: 2834 Druggists' preparations (pharmaceuticals)
HQ: Astrazeneca Pharmaceuticals Lp
    1 Medimmune Way
    Gaithersburg MD 20878

(P-7775)
ATARA BIOTHERAPEUTICS INC
2380 Conejo Spectrum St # 200, Newbury
Park (91320-1444)
PHONE..........................805 623-4211
Christpher Haqq, *Manager*
Eric Dobmeier, *Bd of Directors*
Matthew Fust, *Bd of Directors*
John Craighead, *Vice Pres*
Zung Thai, *Vice Pres*
EMP: 10
SALES (corp-wide): 83.5MM **Publicly Held**
SIC: 2834 Pharmaceutical preparations
PA: Atara Biotherapeutics, Inc.
    611 Gateway Blvd Ste 900
    South San Francisco CA 94080
    650 278-8930

(P-7776)
ATXCO INC
3030 Bunker Hill St # 325, San Diego
(92109-5754)
PHONE..........................650 334-2079
Robert Williamson, *CEO*
EMP: 21
SALES (est): 882K **Privately Held**
SIC: 2834 Pharmaceutical preparations

(P-7777)
AURITEC PHARMACEUTICALS INC
2285 E Foothill Blvd, Pasadena
(91107-3658)
PHONE..........................424 272-9501
Thomas Smith, *President*
Frederic Ransom, *President*
Amanda Malone, *Vice Pres*
Sarjan Shah, *Associate Dir*
Meredith Blake, *General Mgr*
EMP: 13
SQ FT: 250
SALES (est): 2MM **Privately Held**
WEB: www.auritecpharma.com
SIC: 2834 Proprietary drug products

(P-7778)
AURO PHARMACEUTICALS INC
511 S Harbor Blvd Ste F, La Habra
(90631-9375)
PHONE..........................562 352-9630
Nayan Patel, *Manager*
Ashwin Patel, *Treasurer*
Yogesh Patel, *Admin Sec*
EMP: 15 EST: 2013
SALES (est): 886.8K **Privately Held**
SIC: 2834 Druggists' preparations (pharmaceuticals)

(P-7779)
AURO PHARMACIES INC
Also Called: Central Drugs
511 S Harbor Blvd Ste F, La Habra
(90631-9375)
PHONE..........................562 352-9630
Nayan Patel, *Branch Mgr*
EMP: 30
SALES (corp-wide): 15MM **Privately Held**
SIC: 2834 Pharmaceutical preparations
PA: Auro Pharmacies, Inc.
    520 W La Habra Blvd
    La Habra CA 90631
    562 691-6754

(P-7780)
AUSPEX PHARMACEUTICALS INC
3333 N Torrey Pines Ct, La Jolla
(92037-1023)
P.O. Box 49272, Los Angeles (90049-0272)
PHONE..........................858 558-2400
Larry Downey, *President*
Deborah A Griffin, *CFO*
Austin D Kim, *Admin Sec*
Kjersti Horais, *QC Mgr*
EMP: 30
SALES (est): 6.5MM
SALES (corp-wide): 5B **Privately Held**
WEB: www.auspexpharma.com
SIC: 2834 Pharmaceutical preparations
PA: Teva Pharmaceutical Industries Limited
    5 Bazel
    Petah Tikva 49510
    392 672-67

(P-7781)
AVANIR PHARMACEUTICALS INC (HQ)
30 Enterprise Ste 400, Aliso Viejo
(92656-7106)
PHONE..........................949 389-6700
Rohan Palekar, *President*
Gregory J Flesher, *Senior VP*
Richard Malamut, *Senior VP*
Joao Siffert, *Senior VP*
Dan Dalton, *Vice Pres*
EMP: 151
SQ FT: 69,000
SALES (est): 132.3MM **Privately Held**
SIC: 2834 Pharmaceutical preparations

(P-7782)
AVID BIOSERVICES INC (PA)
2642 Michelle Dr Ste 200, Tustin
(92780-7019)
PHONE..........................714 508-6000
Richard B Hancock, *CEO*
Joseph Carleone, *Ch of Bd*
Richard Richieri, *COO*
Daniel Hart, *CFO*
Mark R Ziebell, *Vice Pres*
EMP: 186
SQ FT: 183,000
SALES: 53.6MM **Publicly Held**
WEB: www.peregrineinc.com
SIC: 2834 Pharmaceutical preparations

(P-7783)
BACHEM AMERICAS INC
Also Called: Bachem Vista BSD
1271 Avenida Chelsea, Vista (92081-8315)
PHONE..........................888 422-2436
Brian Gregg, *President*
EMP: 17
SALES (corp-wide): 115.6MM **Privately Held**
SIC: 2834 Pharmaceutical preparations
HQ: Bachem Americas, Inc.
    3132 Kashiwa St
    Torrance CA 90505
    310 784-4440

(P-7784)
BAUSCH & LOMB INCORPORATED
50 Technology Dr, Irvine (92618-2301)
PHONE..........................949 788-6000
EMP: 75
SALES (corp-wide): 5.7B **Privately Held**
SIC: 2834
HQ: Bausch & Lomb Incorporated
    1 Bausch And Lomb Pl
    Rochester NY 08807
    585 338-5442

(P-7785)
BAUSCH HEALTH AMERICAS INC
50 Technology Dr, Irvine (92618-2301)
PHONE..........................800 548-5100
Robert Ingram, *Bd of Directors*
Scott Horton, *Vice Pres*
Marisol Davis, *Finance*
EMP: 15
SALES (corp-wide): 8.3B **Privately Held**
SIC: 2834 Pharmaceutical preparations

HQ: Bausch Health Americas, Inc.
    400 Somerset Corp Blvd
    Bridgewater NJ 08807
    908 927-1400

(P-7786)
BAXALTA INCORPORATED
4501 Colorado Blvd, Los Angeles
(90039-1103)
PHONE..........................818 240-5600
Raul Navarro, *Branch Mgr*
Linda Wong, *Lab Dir*
Eladio Alvarez, *General Mgr*
John Swenson, *Research*
Jason Guu, *Technical Staff*
EMP: 1000
SALES (corp-wide): 15.1B **Privately Held**
SIC: 2834 Pharmaceutical preparations
HQ: Baxalta Incorporated
    1200 Lakeside Dr
    Bannockburn IL 60015
    224 940-2000

(P-7787)
BAXALTA US INC
15903 Strathern St, Van Nuys
(91406-1313)
PHONE..........................818 947-5600
Jeff Miller, *Branch Mgr*
EMP: 80
SALES (corp-wide): 15.1B **Privately Held**
SIC: 2834 Pharmaceutical preparations
HQ: Baxalta Us Inc.
    1200 Lakeside Dr
    Bannockburn IL 60015
    224 948-2000

(P-7788)
BAXALTA US INC
1455 Lawrence Dr, Thousand Oaks
(91320-1311)
PHONE..........................805 375-6807
Greg Bower, *Manager*
EMP: 10
SALES (corp-wide): 15.1B **Privately Held**
SIC: 2834 Pharmaceutical preparations
HQ: Baxalta Us Inc.
    1200 Lakeside Dr
    Bannockburn IL 60015
    224 948-2000

(P-7789)
BAXTER HEALTHCARE CORPORATION
Baxter Hospital Supply
4551 E Philadelphia St, Ontario
(91761-2316)
PHONE..........................303 222-6837
Richard S Justin, *Opers-Prdtn-Mfg*
EMP: 150
SALES (corp-wide): 11.1B **Publicly Held**
SIC: 2834 Pharmaceutical preparations
HQ: Baxter Healthcare Corporation
    1 Baxter Pkwy
    Deerfield IL 60015
    224 948-2000

(P-7790)
BAXTER INTERNATIONAL INC
2024 W Winton Ave, Hayward
(94545-1208)
PHONE..........................510 723-2000
Elden Naea, *Branch Mgr*
Lucy West, *MIS Mgr*
MEI Tan, *Research*
Nancy Chui, *Engineer*
Alan Montemayor, *Engineer*
EMP: 11
SALES (corp-wide): 11.1B **Publicly Held**
SIC: 2834 Pharmaceutical preparations
PA: Baxter International Inc.
    1 Baxter Pkwy
    Deerfield IL 60015
    224 948-2000

(P-7791)
BAYER HEALTHCARE LLC
455 Mission Bay Blvd S # 493, San Francisco (94158-2158)
PHONE..........................415 437-5800
Douglas Schneider, *Manager*
Nicole Schmidt, *Research*
Arnel Agapito, *Manager*
Kristin Beyer, *Manager*
Patrick Jones, *Associate*
EMP: 252

▲ = Import ▼=Export
◆ =Import/Export

SALES (corp-wide): 45.3B **Privately Held**
SIC: 2834 Pharmaceutical preparations
HQ: Bayer Healthcare Llc
100 Bayer Blvd
Whippany NJ 07981
862 404-3000

(P-7792)
BAYER HEALTHCARE LLC
5885 Hollis St, Emeryville (94608-2404)
PHONE..............................510 597-6150
Anita Bawa, *Branch Mgr*
EMP: 104
SALES (corp-wide): 45.3B **Privately Held**
SIC: 2834 Pharmaceutical preparations
HQ: Bayer Healthcare Llc
100 Bayer Blvd
Whippany NJ 07981
862 404-3000

(P-7793)
BAYER HEALTHCARE LLC
800 Dwight Way, Berkeley (94710-2428)
PHONE..............................510 705-7545
Paul Heiden, *Branch Mgr*
Shachi Sharma, *Associate Dir*
Shawn Gagnon, *Planning*
Laura Yee, *Project Mgr*
Jason Divine, *Recruiter*
EMP: 134
SALES (corp-wide): 45.3B **Privately Held**
SIC: 2834 Pharmaceutical preparations
HQ: Bayer Healthcare Llc
100 Bayer Blvd
Whippany NJ 07981
862 404-3000

(P-7794)
BAYER HEALTHCARE LLC
Biological Products Division
717 Potter St Street-2, Berkeley
(94710-2722)
PHONE..............................510 705-7539
Jay Keasling, *Branch Mgr*
EMP: 252
SALES (corp-wide): 45.3B **Privately Held**
SIC: 2834 Pharmaceutical preparations
HQ: Bayer Healthcare Llc
100 Bayer Blvd
Whippany NJ 07981
862 404-3000

(P-7795)
BAYER HEALTHCARE LLC
747 Grayson St, Berkeley (94710)
P.O. Box 6314, Wheeling WV (26003-
0734)
PHONE..............................510 705-4421
EMP: 134
SQ FT: 1,964
SALES (corp-wide): 45.3B **Privately Held**
SIC: 2834 Pharmaceutical preparations
HQ: Bayer Healthcare Llc
100 Bayer Blvd
Whippany NJ 07981
862 404-3000

(P-7796)
BAYER HEALTHCARE LLC
2448 6th St, Berkeley (94710-2414)
PHONE..............................510 705-4914
Stan Pinder, *President*
EMP: 134
SALES (corp-wide): 45.3B **Privately Held**
SIC: 2834 Pharmaceutical preparations
HQ: Bayer Healthcare Llc
100 Bayer Blvd
Whippany NJ 07981
862 404-3000

(P-7797)
BAYER HEALTHCARE LLC
Also Called: Bayer Diabetes Care
510 Oakmead Pkwy, Sunnyvale
(94085-4022)
PHONE..............................408 499-0606
Joseph Ruggiero, *Manager*
Steve Smart, *Analyst*
Ying LI, *Manager*
EMP: 60
SALES (corp-wide): 45.3B **Privately Held**
SIC: 2834 Pharmaceutical preparations
HQ: Bayer Healthcare Llc
100 Bayer Blvd
Whippany NJ 07981
862 404-3000

(P-7798)
BAYER HLTHCARE PHRMCTICALS INC
Also Called: Berlex Bioscience
455 Mission Bay Blvd S, San Francisco
(94158-2158)
P.O. Box 4099, Richmond (94804-0099)
PHONE..............................510 262-5000
David A Scrimger, *Manager*
Cr Willis Jr, *Vice Pres*
Dove Thiess, *Consultant*
EMP: 400
SALES (corp-wide): 45.3B **Privately Held**
SIC: 2834 8731 Pharmaceutical prepara-
tions; commercial physical research
HQ: Bayer Healthcare Pharmaceuticals Inc.
100 Bayer Blvd
Whippany NJ 07981
862 404-3000

(P-7799)
BAYLISS BOTANICALS LLC
17 W Rio Bonito Rd, Biggs (95917)
PHONE..............................530 868-5466
Pedro Convalez, *Mng Member*
EMP: 10 EST: 2010
SALES (est): 46K **Privately Held**
SIC: 2834 Extracts of botanicals: pow-
dered, pilular, solid or fluid

(P-7800)
BEAUTY & HEALTH INTERNATIONAL (PA)
7541 Anthony Ave, Garden Grove
(92841-4005)
P.O. Box 890, Westminster (92684-0890)
PHONE..............................714 903-9730
Charles G Myung, *President*
John Myuong, *Manager*
▲ EMP: 20
SQ FT: 12,000
SALES (est): 5.5MM **Privately Held**
WEB: www.nutriwell.net
SIC: 2834 2844 5122 5149 Vitamin
preparations; cosmetic preparations; vita-
mins & minerals; cosmetics; health foods;
health & dietetic food stores

(P-7801)
BERKELEY NUTRITIONAL MFG CORP
Also Called: Protein Research
1852 Rutan Dr, Livermore (94551-7635)
PHONE..............................925 243-6300
Robert Matheson, *President*
Melissa Dethardt, *Vice Pres*
Ashley Matheson, *Vice Pres*
Gary Troxel, *Vice Pres*
▲ EMP: 60
SQ FT: 53,900
SALES (est): 17.7MM **Privately Held**
WEB: www.proteinresearch.com
SIC: 2834 Vitamin preparations

(P-7802)
BIMEDA INC
5539 Ayon Ave, Irwindale (91706-2057)
PHONE..............................626 815-1680
Tim Tynan, *Branch Mgr*
EMP: 14
SALES (corp-wide): 70.9MM **Privately
Held**
WEB: www.bimeda.com
SIC: 2834 3841 Veterinary pharmaceutical
preparations; surgical & medical instru-
ments
HQ: Bimeda Inc.
1 Tower Ln Ste 2250
Oakbrook Terrace IL 60181
630 928-0361

(P-7803)
BIO-NUTRACEUTICALS INC
Also Called: Bni
21820 Marilla St, Chatsworth (91311-4127)
PHONE..............................818 727-0246
Gerald Farris, *President*
Yesenia Ortega, *Admin Asst*
Denise Ruiz, *Human Res Mgr*
Dawn Hernandez, *Purchasing*
Patty Farris, *Sales Staff*
EMP: 69
SALES (est): 16.4MM **Privately Held**
SIC: 2834 Tablets, pharmaceutical

(P-7804)
BIOCALTH INTERNATIONAL INC
1920 Wright Ave, La Verne (91750-5819)
PHONE..............................909 267-3988
Jackson Wen, *CEO*
▲ EMP: 12
SQ FT: 22,000
SALES (est): 1.6MM **Privately Held**
SIC: 2834 Vitamin, nutrient & hematinic
preparations for human use

(P-7805)
BIOELECTRON TECHNOLOGY CORP (PA)
350 Bernardo Ave, Mountain View
(94043-5207)
PHONE..............................650 641-9200
Guy Miller, *CEO*
James Gibson, *CFO*
Jim Gibson, *CFO*
Steve Bobzin, *Vice Pres*
Phil Leonard, *Vice Pres*
EMP: 20
SALES (est): 3.5MM **Privately Held**
SIC: 2834 Pharmaceutical preparations

(P-7806)
BIOKEY INC
44370 Old Warm Springs Bl, Fremont
(94538-6148)
PHONE..............................510 668-0881
San-Laung Chow, *President*
George Lee, *President*
Paul Dickinson, *QC Mgr*
▼ EMP: 20 EST: 2000
SQ FT: 28,000
SALES: 2MM **Privately Held**
SIC: 2834 Pharmaceutical preparations

(P-7807)
BIOMARIN PHARMACEUTICAL INC (PA)
770 Lindaro St, San Rafael (94901-3991)
PHONE..............................415 506-6700
Jean-Jacques Bienaime, *Ch of Bd*
Daniel Spiegelman, *CFO*
Jeff Ajer, *Ch Credit Ofcr*
Robert A Baffi, *Exec VP*
G Eric Davis, *Exec VP*
EMP: 350
SQ FT: 391,700
SALES: 1.4B **Publicly Held**
WEB: www.biomarinpharm.com
SIC: 2834 2835 Pharmaceutical prepara-
tions; enzyme & isoenzyme diagnostic
agents

(P-7808)
BIOMARIN PHARMACEUTICAL INC
21 Pimentel Ct, Novato (94949-5661)
PHONE..............................415 506-3258
Santhi Sengpraseuth, *Branch Mgr*
Luisa Bigornia, *Vice Pres*
Joshua Lilienstein, *Associate Dir*
Nicole Miller, *Associate Dir*
Lucy Crockett, *Research*
EMP: 10
SALES (corp-wide): 1.4B **Publicly Held**
SIC: 2834 Pharmaceutical preparations
PA: Biomarin Pharmaceutical Inc.
770 Lindaro St
San Rafael CA 94901
415 506-6700

(P-7809)
BIOMARIN PHARMACEUTICAL INC
79 Digital Dr, Novato (94949-5788)
PHONE..............................415 218-7386
Rachel Foreman, *Research*
EMP: 16
SALES (corp-wide): 1.4B **Publicly Held**
SIC: 2834 Pharmaceutical preparations
PA: Biomarin Pharmaceutical Inc.
770 Lindaro St
San Rafael CA 94901
415 506-6700

(P-7810)
BIONORICA LLC
903 Calle Amanecer # 110, San Clemente
(92673-6251)
PHONE..............................949 361-4900
Scott C Bukow, *Mng Member*

Amy Bukow,
EMP: 12
SALES (est): 1.9MM **Privately Held**
SIC: 2834 Cough medicines

(P-7811)
BIOPHARMX CORPORATION (PA)
115 Nicholson Ln, San Jose (95134-1359)
PHONE..............................650 889-5020
David S Tierney, *CEO*
Michael Hubbard, *Ch of Bd*
Anja Krammer, *President*
Steven M Bosacki, *COO*
Greg Kitchener, *Officer*
EMP: 27
SQ FT: 12,203
SALES: 57K **Publicly Held**
SIC: 2834 Pharmaceutical preparations

(P-7812)
BIORX PHARMACEUTICALS INC
Also Called: Biorx Laboratories
6465 Corvette St, Commerce
(90040-1702)
PHONE..............................323 725-3100
Amin Jack, *President*
EMP: 32
SALES: 11MM **Privately Held**
SIC: 2834 2844 Pharmaceutical prepara-
tions; toilet preparations

(P-7813)
BIOVAIL TECHNOLOGIES LTD
1 Enterprise, Aliso Viejo (92656-2606)
PHONE..............................703 995-2400
David Tierney, *President*
EMP: 125
SQ FT: 55,000
SALES (est): 20.5MM
SALES (corp-wide): 8.3B **Privately Held**
SIC: 2834 8731 3841 2087 Pharmaceuti-
cal preparations; commercial physical re-
search; surgical & medical instruments;
flavoring extracts & syrups
PA: Bausch Health Companies Inc
2150 Boul Saint-Elzear O
Sainte-Rose QC H7L 4
514 744-6792

(P-7814)
BIOZONE LABORATORIES INC (DH)
Also Called: Bio-Zone Laboratories
580 Garcia Ave, Pittsburg (94565-4901)
PHONE..............................925 473-1000
Richard Fischler, *Mng Member*
Kristin Morris, *Business Mgr*
Darlene Bowers, *Purch Agent*
Tung Ngo, *Asst Director*
Brent Godfrey, *Director*
▲ EMP: 13
SQ FT: 52,000
SALES (est): 3MM
SALES (corp-wide): 6.4MM **Publicly Held**
WEB: www.biozonelabs.com
SIC: 2834 Pharmaceutical preparations

(P-7815)
BIOZONE LABORATORIES INC
701 Willow Pass Rd Ste 8, Pittsburg
(94565-1803)
PHONE..............................925 431-1010
Amhed Shaikh, *Manager*
EMP: 40
SALES (corp-wide): 6.4MM **Publicly Held**
SIC: 2834 5122 8071 Pharmaceutical
preparations; drugs, proprietaries & sun-
dries; biological laboratory
HQ: Biozone Laboratories, Inc.
580 Garcia Ave
Pittsburg CA 94565
925 473-1000

(P-7816)
BOSCOGEN INC
8 Chrysler, Irvine (92618-2008)
PHONE..............................949 380-4317
Lymae Chang, *Vice Pres*
EMP: 21 **Privately Held**
SIC: 2834 Druggists' preparations (phar-
maceuticals)
HQ: Boscogen, Inc
11 Morgan
Irvine CA 92618

PRODUCTS & SVCS

(P-7817)
BRIDGEBIO PHARMA INC
421 Kipling St, Palo Alto (94301-1530)
PHONE..................................650 391-9740
Neil Kumar, *CEO*
Brian C Stephenson, *CFO*
Michael Henderson, *Senior VP*
Cameron Turtle, *Senior VP*
Uma Sinha, *Security Dir*
EMP: 152
SQ FT: 3,900
SALES (est): 5.5MM **Privately Held**
SIC: 2834 8731 Pharmaceutical prepara-
tions; biotechnical research, commercial

(P-7818)
C S BIO CO (PA)
20 Kelly Ct, Menlo Park (94025-1418)
PHONE..................................650 322-1111
Heng WEI Chang, *CEO*
Dario Slavazza, *President*
Bill Dong, *Info Tech Mgr*
Jason Chang, *VP Opers*
Antinea Chair, *Opers Mgr*
▲ EMP: 10
SQ FT: 5,000
SALES (est): 2.6MM **Privately Held**
WEB: www.csbio.com
SIC: 2834 Pharmaceutical preparations

(P-7819)
C8 MEDISENSORS INC
6375 San Ignacio Ave, San Jose
(95119-1200)
PHONE..................................408 623-7281
John B Kaiser, *CEO*
Fred Toney, *CFO*
Rudy Hofmeister, *Exec VP*
Viet Ngo, *Vice Pres*
EMP: 30
SQ FT: 50,000
SALES (est): 10.8MM **Privately Held**
SIC: 2834 Pharmaceutical preparations

(P-7820)
**CALIFORNIA NATURAL
VITAMINS**
Also Called: The Vitamin Barn
9044 Independence Ave, Canoga Park
(91304-1742)
PHONE..................................818 772-8441
Gene Arnold, *President*
EMP: 22
SALES (est): 3MM **Privately Held**
WEB: www.thevitaminbarn.com
SIC: 2834 Vitamin preparations

(P-7821)
**CALIFORNIA
PHARMACEUTICALS LLC**
768 Calle Plano, Camarillo (93012-8555)
PHONE..................................805 482-3737
Edgar Lozano, *Manager*
EMP: 19 EST: 2008
SALES (est): 3.1MM **Privately Held**
SIC: 2834 Pharmaceutical preparations

(P-7822)
CALIMMUNE INC
129 N Hill Ave Ste 105, Pasadena
(91106-1961)
PHONE..................................310 806-6240
Mary Santos, *Manager*
EMP: 14 **Privately Held**
SIC: 2834 Pharmaceutical preparations
HQ: Calimmune, Inc.
35 N Lake Ave Ste 600
Pasadena CA 91101
-

(P-7823)
CALIMMUNE INC (DH)
35 N Lake Ave Ste 600, Pasadena
(91101-4194)
PHONE..................................310 806-6240
Alan Willis, *President*
John Levy, *Treasurer*
Margo Lunsford, *Admin Sec*
EMP: 12
SALES (est): 2.1MM **Privately Held**
SIC: 2834 Pharmaceutical preparations
HQ: Cslb Holdings Inc.
1020 1st Ave
King Of Prussia PA 19406
610 878-4000

(P-7824)
CALITHERA BIOSCIENCES INC
343 Oyster Point Blvd, South San Fran-
cisco (94080-1913)
PHONE..................................650 870-1000
Susan M Molineaux, *President*
Deepika Pakianathan, *Bd of Directors*
Curtis Hecht, *Officer*
Mark K Bennett, *Senior VP*
Christopher J Molineaux, *Senior VP*
EMP: 44
SALES (est): 22.2MM **Privately Held**
SIC: 2834 8731 Pharmaceutical prepara-
tions; biotechnical research, commercial

(P-7825)
CALMOSEPTINE INC
16602 Burke Ln, Huntington Beach
(92647-4536)
PHONE..................................714 848-2949
Gregory Dixon, *CEO*
▲ EMP: 10
SQ FT: 5,368
SALES (est): 2.9MM **Privately Held**
WEB: www.calmoseptine.com
SIC: 2834 Ointments

(P-7826)
CAMTEK LLC
2645 Nina St, Pasadena (91107-3710)
PHONE..................................626 508-1700
Delbert White, *President*
EMP: 10
SQ FT: 15,000
SALES: 900K **Privately Held**
SIC: 2834 1541 Pharmaceutical prepara-
tions; pharmaceutical manufacturing plant
construction

(P-7827)
**CANTABIO PHARMACEUTICALS
INC**
1250 Oakmead Pkwy Ste 210, Sunnyvale
(94085-4035)
PHONE..................................408 501-8893
Gergely Toth, *CEO*
EMP: 12 EST: 2016
SQ FT: 3,800
SALES (est): 579.9K **Privately Held**
SIC: 2834 Pharmaceutical preparations

(P-7828)
**CAPRICOR THERAPEUTICS INC
(PA)**
8840 Wilshire Blvd Fl 2, Beverly Hills
(90211-2606)
PHONE..................................310 358-3200
Linda Marban, *President*
Frank Litvack, *Ch of Bd*
Deborah Ascheim, *Chief Mktg Ofcr*
Anthony Bergmann, *Officer*
Karen G Krasney, *Exec VP*
EMP: 19
SALES: 1.6MM **Publicly Held**
SIC: 2834 Pharmaceutical preparations

(P-7829)
**CAPTEK SOFTGEL INTL INC
(DH)**
16218 Arthur St, Cerritos (90703-2131)
PHONE..................................562 921-9511
David Wood, *CEO*
Danielle Conner, *COO*
Fon Wong, *CFO*
▲ EMP: 300
SQ FT: 90,000
SALES (est): 167.9MM **Privately Held**
WEB: www.capteksoftgel.com
SIC: 2834 Vitamin, nutrient & hematinic
preparations for human use
HQ: Captek Midco, Inc.
16218 Arthur St
Cerritos CA 90703
562 921-9511

(P-7830)
CARDINAL HEALTH 414 LLC
640 S Jefferson St, Placentia (92870-6600)
PHONE..................................714 572-9900
Shanam Biglari, *Manager*
Van Tran, *Pharmacy Dir*
Rachi Pichon, *Pharmacist*
EMP: 35

SALES (corp-wide): 145.5B **Publicly
Held**
WEB: www.syncor.com
SIC: 2834 5912 Pharmaceutical prepara-
tions; drug stores & proprietary stores
HQ: Cardinal Health 414, Llc
7000 Cardinal Pl
Dublin OH 43017
614 757-5000

(P-7831)
CAREFUSION CORPORATION
1100 Bird Center Dr, Palm Springs
(92262-8000)
PHONE..................................760 778-7200
Carol Zilm, *President*
Charles Kinnear, *Supervisor*
Francisco Flores, *Associate*
EMP: 17
SALES (corp-wide): 15.9B **Publicly Held**
SIC: 2834 Pharmaceutical preparations
HQ: Carefusion Corporation
3750 Torrey View Ct
San Diego CA 92130

(P-7832)
**CARLSBAD TECHNOLOGY INC
(DH)**
5922 Farnsworth Ct # 102, Carlsbad
(92008-7398)
PHONE..................................760 431-8284
Robert Wan, *CEO*
Andy Cheng, *COO*
Howard Marcus, *Vice Pres*
Shawn Stewart, *VP Bus Dvlpt*
Sally Vynck, *Executive*
▲ EMP: 96
SQ FT: 27,000
SALES: 20MM **Privately Held**
WEB: www.carlsbadtech.com
SIC: 2834 Druggists' preparations (phar-
maceuticals)

(P-7833)
CARLSBAD TECHNOLOGY INC
5923 Balfour Ct, Carlsbad (92008-7304)
PHONE..................................760 431-8284
Robert Wan, *CEO*
WEI Yung Lee, *CEO*
Cheong Yik, *Technology*
Wen Young, *Opers Dir*
Song Gao, *Maint Spvr*
EMP: 70 **Privately Held**
SIC: 2834 Druggists' preparations (phar-
maceuticals)
HQ: Carlsbad Technology Inc.
5922 Farnsworth Ct # 102
Carlsbad CA 92008

(P-7834)
CATALINA LIFESCIENCES INC
Also Called: A Division of Metagenics
25 Enterprise Ste 200, Aliso Viejo
(92656-2713)
PHONE..................................800 898-6888
Thomas Kinder, *President*
▼ EMP: 26
SQ FT: 7,800
SALES (est): 4.6MM
SALES (corp-wide): 8.7B **Privately Held**
SIC: 2834 Vitamin, nutrient & hematinic
preparations for human use
HQ: Metagenics, Inc.
25 Enterprise Ste 200
Aliso Viejo CA 92656
949 366-0818

(P-7835)
**CATALYST BIOSCIENCES INC
(PA)**
611 Gateway Blvd Ste 710, South San
Francisco (94080-7029)
PHONE..................................650 266-8674
Nassim Usman, *President*
Howard Levy, *Chief Mktg Ofcr*
Grant Blouse, *Vice Pres*
Linda Neuman, *Vice Pres*
Faisal Shawwa, *Finance*
EMP: 13
SQ FT: 12,965
SALES: 6K **Publicly Held**
WEB: www.targacept.com
SIC: 2834 Pharmaceutical preparations

(P-7836)
**CENTRAL ADMXTURE PHRM
SVCS INC (DH)**
Also Called: Caps
2525 Mcgaw Ave, Irvine (92614-5841)
P.O. Box 19791 (92623-9791)
PHONE..................................949 660-2000
Tom Wilverding, *President*
Alex Lee, *Administration*
Lisa Segal, *Controller*
EMP: 10
SALES (est): 101.7MM
SALES (corp-wide): 2.6MM **Privately
Held**
WEB: www.capspharmacy.com
SIC: 2834 5122 Pharmaceutical prepara-
tions; pharmaceuticals
HQ: B. Braun Medical Inc.
824 12th Ave
Bethlehem PA 18018
610 691-5400

(P-7837)
**CENTRAL ADMXTURE PHRM
SVCS INC**
Also Called: C A P S
10370 Slusher Dr Ste 6, Santa Fe Springs
(90670-6067)
PHONE..................................562 941-9595
Gary Grandfield, *Branch Mgr*
Peter Huang, *Prdtn Mgr*
EMP: 30
SALES (corp-wide): 2.6MM **Privately
Held**
WEB: www.capspharmacy.com
SIC: 2834 5122 Pharmaceutical prepara-
tions; pharmaceuticals
HQ: Central Admixture Pharmacy Services,
Inc.
2525 Mcgaw Ave
Irvine CA 92614
-

(P-7838)
**CENTRAL ADMXTURE PHRM
SVCS INC**
7935 Dunbrook Rd Ste C, San Diego
(92126-6322)
PHONE..................................858 578-1380
Mike Rainey, *Owner*
EMP: 24
SALES (corp-wide): 2.6MM **Privately
Held**
WEB: www.capspharmacy.com
SIC: 2834 Pharmaceutical preparations
HQ: Central Admixture Pharmacy Services,
Inc.
2525 Mcgaw Ave
Irvine CA 92614
-

(P-7839)
CH LABORATORIES INC (PA)
1243 W 130th St, Gardena (90247-1501)
PHONE..................................310 516-8273
Brid Nolan, *President*
EMP: 25
SQ FT: 30,000
SALES (est): 2.7MM **Privately Held**
WEB: www.chlaboratories.com
SIC: 2834 Vitamin preparations

(P-7840)
CHA BIO & DIOSTECH CO LTD
3731 Wilshire Blvd # 850, Los Angeles
(90010-2830)
PHONE..................................213 487-3211
Kyung Rae Kim, *Director*
EMP: 95 EST: 2011
SALES (est): 5.3MM **Privately Held**
SIC: 2834 Pharmaceutical preparations

(P-7841)
CHEMOCENTRYX INC (PA)
850 Maude Ave, Mountain View
(94043-4022)
PHONE..................................650 210-2900
Thomas J Schall, *Ch of Bd*
William C Fairey Jr, *COO*
Markus J Cappel, *Treasurer*
Thomas Schall, *Bd of Directors*
Petrus Bekker, *Officer*
EMP: 66
SQ FT: 35,755

▲ = Import ▼=Export
◆ =Import/Export

SALES: 42.8MM **Publicly Held**
WEB: www.chemocentryx.com
SIC: 2834 Drugs affecting parasitic & infective diseases

(P-7842)
CITRAGEN PHARMACEUTICALS INC
3789 Spinnaker Ct, Fremont (94538-6537)
PHONE.................510 249-9066
Ravichandran Mahalingam, *CEO*
Ravi Jayapal, *Vice Pres*
EMP: 10
SALES (est) 1.6MM **Privately Held**
SIC: 2834 Pharmaceutical preparations

(P-7843)
CLINICAL FORMULA LLC
888 W 16th St, Newport Beach (92663-2802)
PHONE.................949 631-0149
Ken Kutanakit, *CEO*
▲ EMP: 10
SALES (est) 990K **Privately Held**
SIC: 2834 Dermatologicals

(P-7844)
COHBAR INC
1455 Adams Dr Ste 2050, Menlo Park (94025-1438)
PHONE.................650 446-7888
Steven Engle, *CEO*
Albion J Fitzgerald, *Ch of Bd*
Jon L Stern, *COO*
Jon Stern, *COO*
Jeffrey F Biunno, *CFO*
EMP: 12
SALES (est) 2.3MM **Privately Held**
SIC: 2834 8731 Pharmaceutical preparations; medical research, commercial

(P-7845)
COLBY PHARMACEUTICAL COMPANY (PA)
1095 Colby Ave Ste C, Menlo Park (94025-2334)
PHONE.................650 333-3150
David A Zarling, *CEO*
EMP: 13
SQ FT: 1,623
SALES (est) 1.6MM **Privately Held**
SIC: 2834 Pharmaceutical preparations

(P-7846)
COLLIDION INC (PA)
1770 Corporate Cir, Petaluma (94954-6924)
PHONE.................707 668-7600
Hoji Alimi, *Ch of Bd*
William Watson, *President*
Sameer Harish, *Finance Dir*
EMP: 10
SALES (est) 1.2MM **Privately Held**
SIC: 2834 Pharmaceutical preparations

(P-7847)
COMPRHNSIVE CRDVSCLAR SPCALIST (PA)
220 S 1st St Ste 101, Alhambra (91801-3705)
PHONE.................626 281-8663
Peter Fung, *President*
Annie Saovalaksakul, *Assistant*
EMP: 34
SALES (est) 6.1MM **Privately Held**
SIC: 2834 8111 Drugs acting on the cardiovascular system, except diagnostic; legal services

(P-7848)
CONCENTRIC ANALGESICS INC
1824 Jackson St Apt A, San Francisco (94109-2871)
PHONE.................415 771-5129
John F Donovan, *Owner*
Mike A Royal, *Officer*
EMP: 10
SALES (est) 411.9K **Privately Held**
SIC: 2834 Analgesics

(P-7849)
CONTINENTAL VITAMIN CO INC
Also Called: Cvc Specialties
4510 S Boyle Ave, Vernon (90058-2418)
PHONE.................323 581-0176

Ron Beckenfeld, *President*
Lillian Beckenfeld, *Vice Pres*
Dee Dee Garcia, *Admin Sec*
Luis Castro, *VP Human Res*
Ron Deckenfield, *Sales Executive*
EMP: 60
SQ FT: 80,000
SALES: 8MM **Privately Held**
WEB: www.cvc4health.com
SIC: 2834 5122 Vitamin preparations; vitamins & minerals

(P-7850)
CORCEPT THERAPEUTICS INC
149 Commonwealth Dr, Menlo Park (94025-1133)
PHONE.................650 327-3270
Joseph K Belanoff, *President*
James N Wilson, *Ch of Bd*
G Charles Robb, *CFO*
George Baker, *Bd of Directors*
Daniel Bradbury, *Bd of Directors*
EMP: 136
SQ FT: 23,473
SALES: 251.2MM **Privately Held**
WEB: www.corcept.com
SIC: 2834 Pharmaceutical preparations

(P-7851)
CORE SUPPLEMENT TECHNOLOGY
4665 North Ave, Oceanside (92056-3511)
P.O. Box 3010, La Mesa (91944-3010)
PHONE.................760 452-7364
EMP: 11
SALES (est) 1.8MM **Privately Held**
SIC: 2834 Pharmaceutical preparations

(P-7852)
CORIUM INC (HQ)
Also Called: Corium International, Inc.
235 Constitution Dr, Menlo Park (94025-1108)
PHONE.................650 298-8255
Peter D Staple, *President*
Joseph J Sarret, *Officer*
Christina Dickerson, *Vice Pres*
Parminder Singh, *Vice Pres*
Niall Murphy, *Controller*
EMP: 150
SQ FT: 25,000
SALES: 31.8MM **Privately Held**
WEB: www.coriumintl.com
SIC: 2834 8731 2836 Pharmaceutical preparations; biological research; biological products, except diagnostic
PA: Gurnet Point Capital Llc
55 Cambridge Pkwy Ste 401
Cambridge MA 02142
617 588-4902

(P-7853)
CORTEXYME INC (PA)
269 E Grand Ave, South San Francisco (94080-4804)
PHONE.................415 910-5717
Casey C Lynch, *Ch of Bd*
Christopher Lowe, *CFO*
Michael Detke, *Chief Mktg Ofcr*
Leslie Holsinger, *Exec VP*
Kristen Gafric, *Senior VP*
EMP: 19 EST: 2014
SQ FT: 3,185
SALES (est) 2.5MM **Publicly Held**
SIC: 2834 8731 Pharmaceutical preparations; commercial physical research; biological research

(P-7854)
CORVUS PHARMACEUTICALS INC
863 Mitten Rd Ste 102, Burlingame (94010-1311)
PHONE.................650 900-4520
Richard A Miller, *Ch of Bd*
Leiv Lea, *CFO*
Mehrdad Mobasher, *Chief Mktg Ofcr*
Joseph J Buggy, *Exec VP*
Daniel W Hunt, *Senior VP*
EMP: 55
SQ FT: 28,633
SALES (est) 12.6MM **Privately Held**
SIC: 2834 Pharmaceutical preparations

(P-7855)
COUGAR BIOTECHNOLOGY INC
10990 Wilshire Blvd # 1200, Los Angeles (90024-3913)
PHONE.................310 943-8040
Alan H Auerbach, *President*
Arie S Belldegrun MD, *Ch of Bd*
Charles Eyler, *Treasurer*
Gloria Lee MD, *Vice Pres*
Cheryl Collett, *Controller*
EMP: 58
SQ FT: 7,300
SALES (est) 7.9MM
SALES (corp-wide): 81.5B **Publicly Held**
WEB: www.cougarbiotechnology.com
SIC: 2834 Drugs affecting neoplasms & endrocrine systems
PA: Johnson & Johnson
1 Johnson And Johnson Plz
New Brunswick NJ 08933
732 524-0400

(P-7856)
CREEKSIDE MANAGED CARE
879 2nd St, Santa Rosa (95404-4621)
PHONE.................707 578-0399
David Medina, *Owner*
EMP: 17
SALES (est) 1.3MM **Privately Held**
SIC: 2834 Pharmaceutical preparations

(P-7857)
CRINETICS PHARMACEUTICALS INC
10222 Barnes Canyon Rd # 200, San Diego (92121-2711)
PHONE.................858 450-6464
R Scott Struthers, *President*
Wendell Wierenga, *Ch of Bd*
Marc Wilson, *CFO*
Alan Krasner, *Chief Mktg Ofcr*
Stephen F Betz, *Vice Pres*
EMP: 36
SQ FT: 29,499
SALES: 2.4MM **Privately Held**
SIC: 2834 Pharmaceutical preparations

(P-7858)
CRISI MEDICAL SYSTEMS INC
9191 Towne Centre Dr # 330, San Diego (92122-6243)
PHONE.................858 754-8640
Michael Perry, *CEO*
EMP: 12
SALES (est) 1.6MM
SALES (corp-wide): 15.9B **Publicly Held**
SIC: 2834 3061 Intravenous solutions; medical & surgical rubber tubing (extruded & lathe-cut)
PA: Becton, Dickinson And Company
1 Becton Dr
Franklin Lakes NJ 07417
201 847-6800

(P-7859)
CSPC HEALTHCARE INC
Also Called: Cspc Nutritionals
1221 W State St, Ontario (91762-4015)
PHONE.................909 395-5272
Jiapan Gao, *CEO*
Jessica Franco, *Manager*
EMP: 21
SALES (est) 6.8MM **Privately Held**
SIC: 2834 Druggists' preparations (pharmaceuticals)

(P-7860)
CYMABAY THERAPEUTICS INC (PA)
7575 Gateway Blvd Ste 110, Newark (94560-1194)
PHONE.................510 293-8800
Sujal A Shah, *President*
Robert J Wills, *Ch of Bd*
Pol Boudes, *Chief Mktg Ofcr*
Charles A McWherter, *Senior VP*
Klara Dickinson, *Vice Pres*
EMP: 26
SQ FT: 17,698
SALES: 10MM **Publicly Held**
WEB: www.metabolex.com
SIC: 2834 Druggists' preparations (pharmaceuticals)

(P-7861)
CYTOKINETICS INCORPORATED (PA)
280 E Grand Ave, South San Francisco (94080-4808)
PHONE.................650 624-3000
Robert I Blum, *President*
L Patrick Gage, *Ch of Bd*
Ching Jaw, *CFO*
Fady I Malik, *Exec VP*
David W Cragg, *Senior VP*
EMP: 137
SQ FT: 81,587
SALES: 31.5MM **Publicly Held**
WEB: www.cytokinetics.com
SIC: 2834 8731 Pharmaceutical preparations; biotechnical research, commercial

(P-7862)
CYTOMX THERAPEUTICS INC
151 Oyster Point Blvd # 40, South San Francisco (94080-1840)
PHONE.................650 515-3185
Sean A McCarthy, *Ch of Bd*
Debanjan Ray, *CFO*
Frederick Gluck, *Bd of Directors*
Rachel W Humphrey, *Chief Mktg Ofcr*
Michael Kavanaugh, *Officer*
EMP: 139
SQ FT: 76,000
SALES: 59.5MM **Privately Held**
SIC: 2834 Pharmaceutical preparations

(P-7863)
DANIEL LORIA NOVARTIS
4560 Horton St, Emeryville (94608-2916)
PHONE.................510 655-8729
Daniel Loria Novartis, *Principal*
Shenny Antony, *Officer*
Sanjay Shukla, *Vice Pres*
Elizabeth Adefioye, *Executive*
Nancy N Dougherty, *Associate Dir*
EMP: 37 EST: 2010
SALES (est) 7MM **Privately Held**
SIC: 2834 Pharmaceutical preparations

(P-7864)
DARE BIOSCIENCE INC
3655 Nobel Dr Ste 260, San Diego (92122-1050)
PHONE.................858 926-7655
Sabrina Johnson, *President*
William H Rastetter, *Ch of Bd*
Sabrina Martucci Johnson, *President*
EMP: 14
SALES (est) 1.8MM **Privately Held**
WEB: www.tempopharmaceuticals.com
SIC: 2834 Pharmaceutical preparations; druggists' preparations (pharmaceuticals)

(P-7865)
DBV INC
17120 Valley View Ave, La Mirada (90638-5828)
PHONE.................562 404-9714
Jeffrey Best, *Branch Mgr*
EMP: 21
SALES (corp-wide): 1.3MM **Privately Held**
SIC: 2834 Pharmaceutical preparations
PA: Dbv Inc
314 N Vista St
Los Angeles CA 90036
323 857-5577

(P-7866)
DELMAR PHARMACEUTICAL INC
3475 Edison Way Ste R, Menlo Park (94025-1821)
PHONE.................650 269-1984
Saiid Zarrabian, *President*
Jeffrey Bacha, *President*
Scott Praill, *CFO*
Erich Mohr, *Chairman*
Dennis M Brown, *Principal*
EMP: 10
SALES (est) 1MM **Privately Held**
SIC: 2834 Druggists' preparations (pharmaceuticals)

PRODUCTS & SVCS

(P-7867)
DENDREON PHARMACEUTICALS INC
1700 Saturn Way, Seal Beach
(90740-5618)
PHONE.....................562 253-3931
EMP: 13
SALES (corp-wide): 215.7MM Privately Held
SIC: 2834
HQ: Dendreon Pharmaceuticals Llc
1700 Saturn Way
Seal Beach CA 90740
562 252-7500

(P-7868)
DENDREON PHARMACEUTICALS LLC (HQ)
1700 Saturn Way, Seal Beach
(90740-5618)
PHONE.....................562 252-7500
James Caggiano, CEO
Christina Yi, COO
Chris Carr, CFO
Matthew Kemp, Ch Credit Ofcr
Bruce A Brown, Senior VP
EMP: 50
SALES (est): 146.9MM
SALES (corp-wide): 2B Privately Held
SIC: 2834 Pharmaceutical preparations
PA: Nanjing Xinjiekou Department Store
Co., Ltd.
No.1,Zhongshan South Rd.,Qinhuai
District
Nanjing 21000
258 471-5188

(P-7869)
DERMIRA INC
275 Middlefield Rd # 150, Menlo Park
(94025-4008)
PHONE.....................650 421-7200
Thomas G Wiggans, Ch of Bd
Andrew L Guggenhime, CFO
Lori Lyons-Williams, Ch Credit Ofcr
Eugene A Bauer, Chief Mktg Ofcr
Christopher M Griffith, Officer
EMP: 333
SQ FT: 68,990
SALES: 42.3MM Privately Held
SIC: 2834 Pharmaceutical preparations

(P-7870)
DESIGNERX PHARMACEUTICALS INC
4941 Allison Pkwy Ste B, Vacaville
(95688-8794)
PHONE.....................707 451-0441
Bor-Wen Wu, CEO
WEI-Jen Kung, President
▲ EMP: 14
SQ FT: 18,000
SALES (est): 4MM Privately Held
WEB: www.drxpharma.com
SIC: 2834 Pharmaceutical preparations

(P-7871)
DIABLO CLINICAL RESEARCH INC
2255 Ygnacio Valley Rd M, Walnut Creek
(94598-3347)
PHONE.....................925 930-7267
Richard Weinstein, President
EMP: 22
SQ FT: 2,200
SALES: 600K Privately Held
WEB: www.diablocin.com
SIC: 2834 8011 Pharmaceutical preparations; offices & clinics of medical doctors

(P-7872)
DLC LABORATORIES INC
Also Called: De La Cruz Products
7008 Marcelle St, Paramount
(90723-4839)
PHONE.....................562 602-2184
Spero Kessaris, President
Sonia Perez, Admin Asst
Judy De Rocha, Purchasing
▲ EMP: 14 EST: 1963
SQ FT: 16,000
SALES (est): 5.9MM Privately Held
WEB: www.dlclaboratories.com
SIC: 2834 2844 Vitamin preparations; shampoos, rinses, conditioners: hair

(P-7873)
DR J SKINCLINIC INC
Also Called: Drj Organics
13834 Bettencourt St, Cerritos
(90703-1010)
PHONE.....................562 474-8861
Young Min Choi, CEO
▲ EMP: 11
SQ FT: 15,000
SALES (est): 3MM Privately Held
SIC: 2834 5122 Pharmaceutical preparations; cosmetics
PA: Pharma Research Products Co.,Ltd.
Daejun-Dong
Gangneung 25452

(P-7874)
DURECT CORPORATION (PA)
10260 Bubb Rd, Cupertino (95014-4166)
PHONE.....................408 777-1417
James E Brown, President
Felix Theeuwes, Ch of Bd
Matthew J Hogan, CFO
Terrence Blaschke, Bd of Directors
Jon Saxe, Bd of Directors
EMP: 93
SALES: 18.5MM Publicly Held
WEB: www.durect.com
SIC: 2834 Drugs acting on the central nervous system & sense organs

(P-7875)
DURECT CORPORATION
10240 Bubb Rd, Cupertino (95014-4166)
PHONE.....................408 777-1417
James Brown, CEO
Jian LI, Vice Pres
EMP: 10
SALES (est): 1MM Privately Held
SIC: 2834 Pharmaceutical preparations

(P-7876)
EIDON INC
Also Called: Mortgage Company, The
12330 Stowe Dr, Poway (92064-6802)
PHONE.....................800 700-1169
Richard M Wagner, President
Rishon Wagner, Treasurer
Bruno Zvirzin, Opers Mgr
EMP: 10
SQ FT: 11,500
SALES: 2.5MM Privately Held
WEB: www.eidon.com
SIC: 2834 Vitamin, nutrient & hematinic preparations for human use

(P-7877)
ELI LILLY AND COMPANY
Also Called: Elanco Animal Health
63 Via Ricardo, Newbury Park
(91320-7000)
PHONE.....................805 499-5475
Robert Reingold, Branch Mgr
Dan Cella, Manager
EMP: 144
SALES (corp-wide): 24.5B Publicly Held
WEB: www.lilly.com
SIC: 2834 Pharmaceutical preparations
PA: Eli Lilly And Company
Lilly Corporate Ctr
Indianapolis IN 46285
317 276-2000

(P-7878)
EMI HOLDING INC (HQ)
21250 Hawthorne Blvd B, Torrance
(90503-5506)
PHONE.....................310 214-0065
George C Carpenter IV, President
EMP: 13 EST: 2007
SALES: 15MM
SALES (corp-wide): 1.3MM Publicly Held
SIC: 2834 Pharmaceutical preparations
PA: Emmaus Life Sciences, Inc.
21250 Hawthorne Blvd
Torrance CA 90503
310 214-0065

(P-7879)
EMMAUS MEDICAL INC (DH)
21250 Hawthorne Blvd # 800, Torrance
(90503-5506)
PHONE.....................310 214-0065
Yutaka Niihara, President
Willis Lee, COO

EMP: 13
SQ FT: 4,500
SALES (est): 1.4MM
SALES (corp-wide): 1.3MM Publicly Held
WEB: www.emmausmedical.com
SIC: 2834 Pharmaceutical preparations
HQ: Emi Holding, Inc.
21250 Hawthorne Blvd B
Torrance CA 90503
310 214-0065

(P-7880)
ENVY MEDICAL INC (HQ)
9414 Eton Ave, Chatsworth (91311-5862)
PHONE.....................818 874-2700
Arash A Khazei, CEO
Ken Karasiuk, COO
Michael McNamara, Bd of Directors
Bob Ingersoll, Vice Pres
Khoa Bui, IT/INT Sup
▲ EMP: 15
SALES (est): 2.3MM Privately Held
SIC: 2834 Dermatologicals

(P-7881)
ESCIENT PHARMACEUTICALS INC
10578 Science Center Dr # 250, San Diego
(92121-1147)
PHONE.....................858 617-8236
Alain Baron, CEO
William Hodder, Officer
Kristin Taylo, Vice Pres
EMP: 14
SALES (est): 1MM Privately Held
SIC: 2834 Pharmaceutical preparations

(P-7882)
ESSENTIAL PHARMACEUTICAL CORP
1906 W Holt Ave, Pomona (91768-3351)
PHONE.....................909 623-4565
Bruce Lin, CEO
PO Chia Lin, Treasurer
▲ EMP: 20 EST: 1986
SQ FT: 7,642
SALES (est): 4.9MM Privately Held
SIC: 2834 Vitamin preparations

(P-7883)
EVOFEM BIOSCIENCES INC (PA)
12400 High Bluff Dr, San Diego
(92130-3077)
PHONE.....................858 550-1900
Saundra Pelletier, CEO
Thomas Lynch, Ch of Bd
Justin J File, CFO
Russ Barrans, Ch Credit Ofcr
Kelly Culwell, Chief Mktg Ofcr
EMP: 18
SALES (est): 2.1MM Publicly Held
SIC: 2834 Pharmaceutical preparations

(P-7884)
EVOLUS INC (DH)
520 Nwport Ctr Dr Ste 120, Newport Beach
(92660)
PHONE.....................949 284-4555
David Moatazedi, President
Vikram Malik, Ch of Bd
David Gill, Bd of Directors
Michael Jafar, Chief Mktg Ofcr
Michael M Jafar, Chief Mktg Ofcr
EMP: 63
SQ FT: 17,758
SALES (est): 7.2MM
SALES (corp-wide): 36.8MM Publicly Held
SIC: 2834 Pharmaceutical preparations
HQ: Alphaeon Corporation
17901 Von Karman Ave # 150
Irvine CA 92614
949 284-4555

(P-7885)
EXELIXIS INC
169 Harbor Way, South San Francisco
(94080-6109)
PHONE.....................650 837-8254
EMP: 200 Publicly Held
SIC: 2834

PA: Exelixis, Inc.
210 E Grand Ave
South San Francisco CA 94502
-

(P-7886)
EXELIXIS INC
1851 Harbor Bay Pkwy, Alameda
(94502-3016)
PHONE.....................650 837-7000
EMP: 129 Publicly Held
SIC: 2834
PA: Exelixis, Inc.
210 E Grand Ave
South San Francisco CA 94502
-

(P-7887)
EXELIXIS INC (PA)
1851 Harbor Bay Pkwy, Alameda
(94502-3010)
PHONE.....................650 837-7000
Michael M Morrissey, President
Stelios Papadopoulos, Ch of Bd
Gisela M Schwab, President
Christopher J Senner, CFO
Charles Cohen, Bd of Directors
EMP: 57
SALES: 853.8MM Publicly Held
WEB: www.exelixis.com
SIC: 2834 8731 Pharmaceutical preparations; commercial physical research; biological research

(P-7888)
FAMILY MEDICINE CENTER TORR
2841 Lomita Blvd Ste 220, Torrance
(90505-5111)
PHONE.....................310 326-8600
Terence M Hammer, Principal
EMP: 15
SALES (est): 3.1MM Privately Held
SIC: 2834 Medicines, capsuled or ampuled

(P-7889)
FARMHOUSE CULTURE INC (PA)
182 Lewis Rd, Royal Oaks (95076-5352)
P.O. Box 2049, Watsonville (95077-2049)
PHONE.....................831 466-0499
John Tucker, CEO
John Wells, CFO
Sue Rains, Accounting Mgr
EMP: 45
SALES (est): 18MM Privately Held
SIC: 2834 Vitamin, nutrient & hematinic preparations for human use

(P-7890)
FIBROGEN INC (PA)
409 Illinois St, San Francisco (94158-2509)
PHONE.....................415 978-1200
James A Schoeneck, CEO
Pat Cotroneo, CFO
K Peony Yu, Chief Mktg Ofcr
Christine Chung, Vice Pres
Elias Kouchakji, Vice Pres
EMP: 169
SQ FT: 234,000
SALES: 212.9MM Publicly Held
WEB: www.fibrogen.com
SIC: 2834 Pharmaceutical preparations

(P-7891)
FIVE PRIME THERAPEUTICS INC
111 Oyster Point Blvd, South San Francisco
(94080-1910)
PHONE.....................415 365-5600
William Ringo, CEO
David V Smith, CFO
Sheila Gujrathi, Bd of Directors
Garry Nicholson, Bd of Directors
Helen Collins, Chief Mktg Ofcr
EMP: 216
SQ FT: 115,466
SALES: 49.8MM Privately Held
WEB: www.fiveprime.com
SIC: 2834 8733 Pharmaceutical preparations; biotechnical research, noncommercial

(P-7892)
FOREST LABORATORIES LLC
12021 Dolly Way, Moreno Valley
(92555-2007)
PHONE......................................951 941-0024
Garrettt R Campbell, *Branch Mgr*
EMP: 75 **Privately Held**
SIC: 2834 Pharmaceutical preparations
HQ: Forest Laboratories, Llc
909 3rd Ave Fl 23
New York NY 10022

(P-7893)
FORMEX LLC
11011 Torreyana Rd # 100, San Diego
(92121-1104)
PHONE......................................858 529-6600
Cyrus K Mirsaidi, *President*
Ian Wisenberg, *CFO*
Blair West, *Officer*
J Blair West, *Security Dir*
Leigh Peeleman, *Human Resources*
EMP: 32
SQ FT: 44,000
SALES (est): 7.7MM
SALES (corp-wide): 19.7MM **Privately Held**
SIC: 2834 8731 8071 Tablets, pharmaceutical; biological research; testing laboratories
PA: Bioduro Llc
11011 Torreyana Rd
San Diego CA 92121
858 529-6600

(P-7894)
FORMULATION TECHNOLOGY INC
571 Armstrong Way, Oakdale
(95361-9367)
P.O. Box 1895 (95361-1895)
PHONE......................................209 847-0331
Keith W Hensley, *President*
Mary G Hangley, *Shareholder*
April Houck, *Shareholder*
Celia Meese, *Corp Secy*
Jed Meese, *Vice Pres*
▲ EMP: 49 EST: 1981
SQ FT: 15,000
SALES (est): 11.9MM **Privately Held**
WEB: www.formulationtech.com
SIC: 2834 Vitamin preparations

(P-7895)
FORMUREX INC
2470 Wilcox Rd, Stockton (95215-2319)
PHONE......................................209 931-2040
Dongxiao Tony Zhang, *President*
Xiaoling LI, *Officer*
Sreenath Konanki, *Info Tech Mgr*
Bhaskara Jasti, *Director*
EMP: 10
SQ FT: 8,000
SALES (est): 1.5MM **Privately Held**
WEB: www.formurex.com
SIC: 2834 Pharmaceutical preparations

(P-7896)
FORTY SEVEN INC
1490 Obrien Dr Ste A, Menlo Park
(94025-1499)
PHONE......................................650 352-4150
Mark A McCamish, *President*
Ann D Rhoads, *CFO*
Chris H Takimoto, *Chief Mktg Ofcr*
Norman Kruse, *Counsel*
EMP: 57
SALES (est): 19.9MM **Privately Held**
SIC: 2834 8731 Pharmaceutical preparations; biotechnical research, commercial

(P-7897)
FREMONT AMGEN INC (HQ)
6397 Kaiser Dr, Fremont (94555-3602)
PHONE......................................510 284-6500
Kevin Sharer, *President*
H Ward Wolff, *CFO*
Gisela M Schwab, *Officer*
Kristen M Anderson, *Senior VP*
Donald R Joseph, *Senior VP*
▲ EMP: 375
SQ FT: 516,000

SALES (est): 47.5MM
SALES (corp-wide): 23.7B **Publicly Held**
SIC: 2834 Extracts of botanicals: powdered, pilular, solid or fluid; antibiotics, packaged
PA: Amgen Inc.
1 Amgen Center Dr
Thousand Oaks CA 91320
805 447-1000

(P-7898)
FRESENIUS USA INC (DH)
Also Called: Fresenius Medical Care
4040 Nelson Ave, Concord (94520-1200)
PHONE......................................925 288-4218
Ronald J Kuerbitz, *CEO*
Mark Costanzo, *President*
Ben Lipps, *President*
Angelo Moesslang, *CFO*
Mark Fawcett, *Treasurer*
▲ EMP: 220 EST: 1974
SQ FT: 85,000
SALES (est): 768.2MM
SALES (corp-wide): 18.9B **Privately Held**
SIC: 2834 3841 2835 3842 Intravenous solutions; solutions, pharmaceutical; hemodialysis apparatus; IV transfusion apparatus; blood transfusion equipment; blood derivative diagnostic agents; surgical appliances & supplies; biological products, except diagnostic

(P-7899)
FRONTIER MEDICINES
151 Oyster Point Blvd # 200, South San Francisco (94080-1841)
PHONE......................................650 457-1005
Chris Varma, *CEO*
EMP: 50
SALES (est): 1.8MM **Privately Held**
SIC: 2834 Medicines, capsuled or ampuled

(P-7900)
GENELABS TECHNOLOGIES INC (HQ)
505 Penobscot Dr, Redwood City
(94063-4737)
P.O. Box 13398, Durham NC (27709-3398)
PHONE......................................415 297-2901
Frederick W Driscoll, *President*
Gerald Suh, *Owner*
Irene A Chow, *Ch of Bd*
Ronald C Griffith PHD, *Officer*
Heather Criss Keller, *Vice Pres*
EMP: 18
SQ FT: 50,000
SALES (est): 4.7MM
SALES (corp-wide): 39.5B **Privately Held**
WEB: www.genelabs.com
SIC: 2834 Proprietary drug products
PA: Glaxosmithkline Plc
G S K House
Brentford MIDDX TW8 9
208 047-5000

(P-7901)
GENENTECH INC
1000 New Horizons Way, Vacaville
(95688-9431)
PHONE......................................707 454-1000
Frank Jackson, *General Mgr*
Ekaterine Kortkhonjia, *Officer*
Thomas Glenn, *Administration*
Cassi Godfrey, *Administration*
Jim Thein, *Administration*
EMP: 25
SALES (corp-wide): 57.2B **Privately Held**
WEB: www.gene.com
SIC: 2834 Pharmaceutical preparations
HQ: Genentech, Inc.
1 Dna Way
South San Francisco CA 94080
650 225-1000

(P-7902)
GENENTECH INC (DH)
1 Dna Way, South San Francisco
(94080-4990)
P.O. Box 4354, Portland OR (97208-4354)
PHONE......................................650 225-1000
Ian Clark, *CEO*
Pascal Soriot, *COO*
Steve Krognes, *CFO*
Hal Barron, *Chief Mktg Ofcr*
Rick Kentz, *Officer*
◆ EMP: 2000 EST: 1987

SQ FT: 140,000
SALES (est): 3.4B
SALES (corp-wide): 57.2B **Privately Held**
WEB: www.gene.com
SIC: 2834 Hormone preparations
HQ: Roche Holdings, Inc.
1 Dna Way
South San Francisco CA 94080
650 225-1000

(P-7903)
GENENTECH INC
465 E Grand Ave Ms432, South San Francisco (94080-6225)
PHONE......................................408 963-8759
EMP: 19
SALES (corp-wide): 57.2B **Privately Held**
SIC: 2834 Pharmaceutical preparations
HQ: Genentech, Inc.
1 Dna Way
South San Francisco CA 94080
650 225-1000

(P-7904)
GENENTECH INC
1 Antibody Way, Oceanside (92056-5701)
PHONE......................................760 231-2440
AMR Elkhayat, *Director*
Cheryl Mata, *Admin Asst*
Scott Hodulik, *Administration*
Anthony Reynoso, *Info Tech Mgr*
Bahar Dahi, *Engineer*
EMP: 300
SALES (corp-wide): 57.2B **Privately Held**
WEB: www.gene.com
SIC: 2834 Pharmaceutical preparations
HQ: Genentech, Inc.
1 Dna Way
South San Francisco CA 94080
650 225-1000

(P-7905)
GENENTECH INC
550 Broadway St, Redwood City
(94063-3115)
PHONE......................................650 216-2900
Jay Edwards, *Corp Comm Staff*
Michael Ash, *Director*
Martin Majchrowicz, *Director*
Christy Rolfson, *Director*
EMP: 300
SALES (corp-wide): 57.2B **Privately Held**
WEB: www.gene.com
SIC: 2834 Pharmaceutical preparations
HQ: Genentech, Inc.
1 Dna Way
South San Francisco CA 94080
650 225-1000

(P-7906)
GENENTECH INC
431 Grandview Dr Bldg 27, South San Francisco (94080)
PHONE......................................650 225-3214
Rick Rouleau, *Manager*
EMP: 15
SALES (corp-wide): 57.2B **Privately Held**
WEB: www.gene.com
SIC: 2834 Pharmaceutical preparations
HQ: Genentech, Inc.
1 Dna Way
South San Francisco CA 94080
650 225-1000

(P-7907)
GENENTECH INC
1 Dna Way, South San Francisco
(94080-4990)
PHONE......................................650 225-1000
Severin Schwan, *Branch Mgr*
EMP: 193
SALES (corp-wide): 57.2B **Privately Held**
WEB: www.gene.com
SIC: 2834 Pharmaceutical preparations
HQ: Genentech, Inc.
1 Dna Way
South San Francisco CA 94080
650 225-1000

(P-7908)
GENENTECH USA INC
1 Dna Way, South San Francisco
(94080-4990)
PHONE......................................650 225-1000
Ian T Clark, *Principal*
Leonard Kanavy, *Principal*

Frederick C Kentz III, *Principal*
Steve Krognes, *Principal*
Kyle Rounseville, *Engineer*
▲ EMP: 1992
SALES (est): 222MM
SALES (corp-wide): 57.2B **Privately Held**
WEB: www.gene.com
SIC: 2834 Hormone preparations
HQ: Genentech, Inc.
1 Dna Way
South San Francisco CA 94080
650 225-1000

(P-7909)
GENOPIS INC
10390 Pacific Center Ct, San Diego
(92121-4340)
PHONE......................................858 875-4700
Sun Young Kim, *CEO*
Keith Hall, *COO*
EMP: 24
SQ FT: 68,400
SALES: 500K **Privately Held**
SIC: 2834 Pharmaceutical preparations

(P-7910)
GENSIA SICOR INC (HQ)
19 Hughes, Irvine (92618-1902)
PHONE......................................949 455-4700
Carlo Salvi, *Vice Chairman*
▲ EMP: 800
SQ FT: 170,000
SALES (est): 99.6MM
SALES (corp-wide): 5B **Privately Held**
WEB: www.sicorinc.com
SIC: 2834 8731 Drugs acting on the cardiovascular system, except diagnostic; medical research, commercial
PA: Teva Pharmaceutical Industries Limited
5 Bazel
Petah Tikva 49510
392 672-67

(P-7911)
GENZYME CORPORATION
Also Called: Genzyme Genetics
655 E Huntington Dr, Monrovia
(91016-3636)
PHONE......................................800 255-1616
Jane Willis, *Branch Mgr*
James Bartley, *Director*
Shoshanna Clark, *Director*
Laura George, *Manager*
Lisa Valenti, *Manager*
EMP: 80 **Privately Held**
WEB: www.genzyme.com
SIC: 2834 Pharmaceutical preparations
HQ: Genzyme Corporation
50 Binney St
Cambridge MA 02142
617 252-7500

(P-7912)
GERON CORPORATION (PA)
149 Commonwealth Dr # 2070, Menlo Park
(94025-1133)
PHONE......................................650 473-7700
John A Scarlett, *Ch of Bd*
Olivia K Bloom, *CFO*
Daniel Bradbury, *Bd of Directors*
Karin Eastham, *Bd of Directors*
Robert Spiegel, *Bd of Directors*
EMP: 20
SQ FT: 14,500
SALES: 1MM **Publicly Held**
WEB: www.geron.com
SIC: 2834 Pharmaceutical preparations

(P-7913)
GILEAD COLORADO INC
333 Lakeside Dr, Foster City (94404-1394)
PHONE......................................650 574-3000
J William Freytag, *President*
John Milligan, *President*
Joseph L Turner, *CFO*
Michael R Bristow, *Officer*
Richard J Gorczynski, *Senior VP*
EMP: 110
SQ FT: 40,000
SALES (est): 15.3MM
SALES (corp-wide): 22.1B **Publicly Held**
WEB: www.myogen.com
SIC: 2834 Pharmaceutical preparations

P R O D U C T S & S V C S

PA: Gilead Sciences, Inc.
333 Lakeside Dr.
Foster City CA 94404
650 574-3000

(P-7914)
GILEAD PALO ALTO INC
Also Called: Gilead Scientist
650 Cliffside Dr, San Dimas (91773-2957)
PHONE..............................909 394-4000
Chris Beley, *CEO*
EMP: 300
SALES (corp-wide): 22.1B **Publicly Held**
SIC: 2834 Drugs acting on the cardiovascular system, except diagnostic
HQ: Alto Gilead Palo Inc
333 Lakeside Dr
Foster City CA 94404
-

(P-7915)
GILEAD PALO ALTO INC (HQ)
333 Lakeside Dr, Foster City (94404-1394)
PHONE..............................650 384-8500
John C Martin, *Chairman*
Louis Lange PHD, *Ch of Bd*
John F Milligan, *President*
Daniel K Spiegelman, *CFO*
Brent K Blackburn PHD, *Senior VP*
EMP: 63
SALES (est): 65.2MM
SALES (corp-wide): 22.1B **Publicly Held**
WEB: www.cvt.com
SIC: 2834 8731 Drugs acting on the cardiovascular system, except diagnostic; commercial physical research
PA: Gilead Sciences, Inc.
333 Lakeside Dr
Foster City CA 94404
650 574-3000

(P-7916)
GILEAD SCIENCES INC (PA)
333 Lakeside Dr, Foster City (94404-1394)
PHONE..............................650 574-3000
Daniel Oday, *CEO*
Robin L Washington, *CFO*
Nicholas Moore, *Bd of Directors*
Per Wold-Olsen, *Bd of Directors*
Gregg H Alton,
▲ **EMP:** 289
SALES: 22.1B **Publicly Held**
WEB: www.gilead.com
SIC: 2834 Pharmaceutical preparations

(P-7917)
GILEAD SCIENCES INC
542 W Covina Blvd, San Dimas (91773-2955)
PHONE..............................909 394-4090
Arthur Chiles, *Manager*
EMP: 19
SALES (corp-wide): 22.1B **Publicly Held**
WEB: www.gilead.com
SIC: 2834 Pharmaceutical preparations
PA: Gilead Sciences, Inc.
333 Lakeside Dr
Foster City CA 94404
650 574-3000

(P-7918)
GILEAD SCIENCES INC
Also Called: Nexstar Pharmaceutical
650 Cliffside Dr, San Dimas (91773-2957)
PHONE..............................909 394-4000
Christin Eley, *Principal*
Catherine Kuo, *Engineer*
Linda Lintao, *Manager*
Andrea Ocampo, *Manager*
EMP: 183
SALES (corp-wide): 22.1B **Publicly Held**
WEB: www.gilead.com
SIC: 2834 Drugs affecting parasitic & infective diseases
PA: Gilead Sciences, Inc.
333 Lakeside Dr
Foster City CA 94404
650 574-3000

(P-7919)
GLAXOSMITHKLINE CONSUMER
2020 E Vine Ave, Fresno (93706-5458)
PHONE..............................559 650-1550
Mark Bullard, *Branch Mgr*
EMP: 99

SALES (corp-wide): 39.5B **Privately Held**
SIC: 2834 Pharmaceutical preparations
HQ: Glaxosmithkline Consumer Healthcare, L.P.
184 Libery Corner Rd
Warren NJ 07059
-

(P-7920)
GLAXOSMITHKLINE LLC
11205 Creekside Ct, Dublin (94568-3511)
PHONE..............................925 833-1551
Mary Lewis, *Branch Mgr*
EMP: 26
SALES (corp-wide): 39.5B **Privately Held**
SIC: 2834 Pharmaceutical preparations
HQ: Glaxosmithkline Llc
5 Crescent Dr
Philadelphia PA 19112
215 751-4000

(P-7921)
GLAXOSMITHKLINE LLC
2399 Hummingbird St, Chula Vista (91915-2420)
PHONE..............................619 863-0399
EMP: 26
SALES (corp-wide): 39.5B **Privately Held**
SIC: 2834 Pharmaceutical preparations
HQ: Glaxosmithkline Llc
5 Crescent Dr
Philadelphia PA 19112
215 751-4000

(P-7922)
GLOBAL BLOOD THERAPEUTICS INC (PA)
Also Called: Gbt
171 Oyster Point Blvd # 30, South San Francisco (94080-1910)
PHONE..............................650 741-7700
Ted W Love, *President*
Jeffrey Farrow, *CFO*
David L Johnson, *Ch Credit Ofcr*
Tricia Suvari,
Jung E Choi, *Officer*
EMP: 87
SQ FT: 67,185
SALES (est): 27.9MM **Publicly Held**
SIC: 2834 8731 Pharmaceutical preparations; biological research

(P-7923)
GLOBAL FUTURE CITY HOLDING INC
2 Park Plz Ste 400, Irvine (92614-8514)
PHONE..............................949 769-3550
Michael R Dunn, *Ch of Bd*
EMP: 10
SQ FT: 5,824
SALES: 3.5MM **Privately Held**
SIC: 2834 2087 Pharmaceutical preparations; concentrates, drink

(P-7924)
GMP GLOBAL NUTRITION INC
13653 Central Ave, Chino (91710-5108)
PHONE..............................909 628-8889
Maggie P Liu, *CEO*
▲ **EMP:** 12
SALES (est): 2.3MM **Privately Held**
SIC: 2834 Pharmaceutical preparations

(P-7925)
GMP LABORATORIES AMERICA INC
2931 E La Jolla St, Anaheim (92806-1306)
PHONE..............................714 630-2467
Mohammad Ishaq, *CEO*
Suhail Ishaq, *President*
Yusuf Ishaq, *COO*
Farheena Shakil, *Research*
Naresh Davda, *Accountant*
▲ **EMP:** 92
SQ FT: 90,000
SALES (est): 22.1MM **Privately Held**
WEB: www.gmplabs.com
SIC: 2834 Pharmaceutical preparations

(P-7926)
GRAND MEADOWS INC
1607 W Orange Grove Ave E, Orange (92868-1128)
PHONE..............................714 628-1690
Nicholas Hartog, *President*

Angela Slater, *CFO*
▲ **EMP:** 10
SQ FT: 8,260
SALES: 2.8MM **Privately Held**
WEB: www.grandmeadows.com
SIC: 2834 Veterinary pharmaceutical preparations

(P-7927)
GREENWICH BIOSCIENCES INC (HQ)
5750 Fleet St Ste 200, Carlsbad (92008-4709)
PHONE..............................760 795-2200
Julian Gangolli, *President*
Justin Gover, *CEO*
Scott Giacobello, *CFO*
Kenneth Sommerville, *Vice Pres*
Shelly Applegate, *VP Human Res*
EMP: 32 **EST:** 2013
SQ FT: 4,911
SALES (est): 9.7MM
SALES (corp-wide): 24.9MM **Privately Held**
SIC: 2834 Pharmaceutical preparations
PA: Gw Pharmaceuticals Plc
Sovereign House
Cambridge CAMBS
122 326-6800

(P-7928)
GU
1204 10th St, Berkeley (94710-1509)
PHONE..............................510 527-4664
Bill Vaughn, *Owner*
EMP: 27
SALES (est): 6.6MM **Privately Held**
SIC: 2834 Vitamin, nutrient & hematinic preparations for human use

(P-7929)
GUARDION HEALTH SCIENCES INC (PA)
15150 Avenue Of Science # 20, San Diego (92128-3405)
PHONE..............................858 605-9055
Michael Favish, *Ch of Bd*
John Townsend,
David W Evans, *Security Dir*
Vincent J Roth, *Admin Sec*
EMP: 10
SALES (est): 942.1K **Publicly Held**
SIC: 2834 Pharmaceutical preparations

(P-7930)
H J HARKINS COMPANY INC
Also Called: Pharma Pac
1400 W Grand Ave Ste F, Grover Beach (93433-4221)
PHONE..............................805 929-1333
Norma Jean Erenius, *CEO*
Charles Smith, *President*
Norma Erenius, *Officer*
Mary Graham, *Administration*
Leonard Lutz, *Technology*
EMP: 50
SQ FT: 10,000
SALES (est): 8.5MM **Privately Held**
SIC: 2834 Pharmaceutical preparations

(P-7931)
HAHNEMANN LABORTORIES INC
Also Called: Hahnemann Homeopathic Pharmacy
1940 4th St, San Rafael (94901-2671)
PHONE..............................415 451-6978
April Eya, *President*
Roslyn Ball, *Manager*
EMP: 15
SALES (est): 1.4MM **Privately Held**
WEB: www.hahnemannlabs.com
SIC: 2834 Medicines, capsuled or ampuled

(P-7932)
HANDA PHARMACEUTICALS LLC
1732 N 1st St Ste 200, San Jose (95112-4518)
PHONE..............................510 354-2888
Stephen D Cary, *Principal*
Beth Hill, *Research*
Todd Morrison, *Engineer*
EMP: 13

SALES (est): 2.2MM **Privately Held**
SIC: 2834 Pharmaceutical preparations
PA: Handa Pharmaceuticals, Inc.
3f-1, 3f-2, No. 23, Nanke 3rd Rd.
Tainan City 74147

(P-7933)
HARBOR BIOSCIENCES INC (PA)
Also Called: (A DEVELOPMENT STAGE COMPANY)
9191 Towne Centre Dr # 409, San Diego (92122-1225)
PHONE..............................858 587-9333
James M Fincke PHD, *CEO*
Robert W Weber, *CFO*
Christopher L Reading PHD, *Officer*
Dwight R Stickney MD, *Officer*
Steven Gordziel, *Vice Pres*
EMP: 19
SALES: 146K **Publicly Held**
WEB: www.holliseden.com
SIC: 2834 Pharmaceutical preparations

(P-7934)
HARPERS PHARMACY INC
Also Called: Ameripharma
132 S Anita Dr Ste 210, Orange (92868-3317)
PHONE..............................877 778-3773
Andrew A Harper, *CEO*
Gor Mnatsakanyan, *Principal*
EMP: 187
SALES (est): 90K **Privately Held**
SIC: 2834 Pharmaceutical preparations

(P-7935)
HARROW HEALTH INC (PA)
12264 El Camino Real # 350, San Diego (92130-0001)
PHONE..............................858 704-4040
Andrew R Boll, *CFO*
Mark L Baum, *CEO*
Steven Austin, *Bd of Directors*
Larry Dillaha, *Chief Mktg Ofcr*
Pramod Sharma, *Vice Pres*
EMP: 37
SQ FT: 10,200
SALES: 41.3MM **Publicly Held**
SIC: 2834 Pharmaceutical preparations

(P-7936)
HEALTH NATURALS INC
13 Navarre, Irvine (92612-7700)
PHONE..............................714 259-1821
Ruby Ableman, *President*
Steven Jacobson, *Principal*
◆ **EMP:** 15
SALES (est): 1.4MM **Privately Held**
SIC: 2834 Vitamin preparations

(P-7937)
HERON THERAPEUTICS INC (PA)
4242 Campus Point Ct # 200, San Diego (92121-1513)
PHONE..............................858 251-4400
Barry D Quart, *CEO*
Kevin C Tang, *Ch of Bd*
Robert H Rosen, *President*
Robert E Hoffman, *CFO*
John Poyhonen, *Ch Credit Ofcr*
EMP: 145
SQ FT: 28,275
SALES: 77.4MM **Publicly Held**
WEB: www.appharma.com
SIC: 2834 Pharmaceutical preparations

(P-7938)
IDEAYA BIOSCIENCES INC
7000 Shoreline Ct Ste 350, South San Francisco (94080-7604)
PHONE..............................650 443-6209
Yujiro Hata, *President*
John Diekman, *Ch of Bd*
Julie Hambleton, *Chief Mktg Ofcr*
Michael Dillon, *Senior VP*
Jeffrey Hager, *Senior VP*
EMP: 58
SALES (est): 17.5MM **Privately Held**
SIC: 2834 Pharmaceutical preparations

(P-7939)
IGENICA INC
863 Mitten Rd Ste 102, Burlingame
(94010-1311)
PHONE..................................650 231-4320
Mary Haak-Frendscho, *CEO*
David Goeddel, *Ch of Bd*
Mike Rothe, *President*
Hans Van Houte, *CFO*
Thi-Sau Migone, *Officer*
EMP: 40
SALES (est): 12.7MM **Privately Held**
SIC: 2834 Druggists' preparations (phar-
maceuticals)

(P-7940)
IGM BIOSCIENCES INC
325 E Middlefield Rd, Mountain View
(94043-4003)
PHONE..................................650 965-7873
Fred Schwarzer, *President*
Michael Loberg, *Ch of Bd*
Misbah Tahir, *CFO*
Daniel Chen, *Chief Mktg Ofcr*
Ramesh Baliga, *Vice Pres*
EMP: 51 EST: 1993
SQ FT: 34,000
SALES (est): 15.5MM
SALES (corp-wide): 862MM **Publicly
Held**
SIC: 2834 Pharmaceutical preparations
PA: Haldor Topsoe Holding A/S
Haldor Topsoes Alle 1
Kongens Lyngby 2800
458 784-94

(P-7941)
IGNYTA INC (PA)
1 Dna Way, South San Francisco
(94080-4918)
PHONE..................................858 255-5959
Jonathan E Lim, *Ch of Bd*
Zachary Hornby, *COO*
Jacob Chacko, *CFO*
Pratik Multani, *Chief Mktg Ofcr*
Jason Christiansen, *Vice Pres*
EMP: 68
SALES (est): 16MM **Privately Held**
SIC: 2834 Pharmaceutical preparations

(P-7942)
IMMUNE DESIGN CORP
601 Gateway Blvd Ste 250, South San
Francisco (94080-7403)
PHONE..................................650 225-0214
EMP: 20
SALES (corp-wide): 2.2MM **Privately
Held**
SIC: 2834 8731 Pharmaceutical prepara-
tions; commercial physical research;
biotechnical research, commercial
PA: Immune Design Corp.
1616 Eastlake Ave E
Seattle WA 98102
206 682-0645

(P-7943)
IMMUNIC INC
15222 Ave Of Science B, San Diego
(92128-3422)
PHONE..................................858 673-6840
Duane D Nash, *President*
Faheem Hasnain, *Ch of Bd*
Sanjay S Patel, *CFO*
Michael V Swanson, *CFO*
Robert A Ashley, *Exec VP*
EMP: 10
SQ FT: 19,000
SALES (est): 3.3MM **Privately Held**
WEB: www.vitaltherapies.com
SIC: 2834 Pharmaceutical preparations

(P-7944)
IMPAX LABORATORIES INC
31047 Genstar Rd, Hayward (94544-7831)
PHONE..................................510 240-6000
Larry Hsu, *CEO*
EMP: 58
SALES (corp-wide): 1.6B **Publicly Held**
SIC: 2834 Pharmaceutical preparations
HQ: Impax Laboratories, Llc
30831 Huntwood Ave
Hayward CA 94544
510 240-6000

(P-7945)
IMPAX LABORATORIES LLC
(DH)
30831 Huntwood Ave, Hayward
(94544-7003)
PHONE..................................510 240-6000
Paul M Bisaro, *President*
Robert L Burr, *Ch of Bd*
Douglas S Boothe, *President*
Michael J Nestor, *President*
Bryan M Reasons, *CFO*
▲ EMP: 600
SQ FT: 45,000
SALES: 775.7MM
SALES (corp-wide): 1.6B **Publicly Held**
WEB: www.impaxlabs.com
SIC: 2834 Pharmaceutical preparations

(P-7946)
IMPAX LABORATORIES LLC
Impax Generics
30831 Huntwood Ave, Hayward
(94544-7003)
PHONE..................................510 240-6000
EMP: 27
SALES (corp-wide): 1.6B **Publicly Held**
SIC: 2834 Pharmaceutical preparations
HQ: Impax Laboratories, Llc
30831 Huntwood Ave
Hayward CA 94544
510 240-6000

(P-7947)
IMPAX LABORATORIES LLC
30941 San Clemente St, Hayward
(94544-7128)
PHONE..................................510 476-2000
Mark C Shaw, *Branch Mgr*
EMP: 13
SALES (corp-wide): 1.6B **Publicly Held**
SIC: 2834 Pharmaceutical preparations
HQ: Impax Laboratories, Llc
30831 Huntwood Ave
Hayward CA 94544
510 240-6000

(P-7948)
IMPAX LABORATORIES USA
LLC
30831 Huntwood Ave, Hayward
(94544-7003)
PHONE..................................510 240-6000
Larry Hsu PHD, *CEO*
EMP: 11
SALES (est): 238.1K
SALES (corp-wide): 1.6B **Publicly Held**
SIC: 2834 Pharmaceutical preparations
HQ: Impax Laboratories, Llc
30831 Huntwood Ave
Hayward CA 94544
510 240-6000

(P-7949)
INCARDA THERAPEUTICS INC
39899 Balentine Dr # 185, Newark
(94560-5361)
PHONE..................................510 422-5522
Grace Colon, *President*
Carlos Schuler, *COO*
Luiz Belardinelli, *Chief Mktg Ofcr*
Robert L Roden, *Vice Pres*
Tavita Tung, *Executive Asst*
EMP: 20
SALES (est): 321K **Privately Held**
SIC: 2834 Pharmaceutical preparations

(P-7950)
INNOVIVA INC (PA)
2000 Sierra Point Pkwy # 500, Brisbane
(94005-1830)
PHONE..................................650 238-9600
Geoffrey Hulme, *CEO*
Marianne Zhen,
EMP: 12 EST: 1997
SQ FT: 8,427
SALES: 261MM **Publicly Held**
WEB: www.theravance.com
SIC: 2834 Drugs acting on the respiratory
system

(P-7951)
INOVIO PHARMACEUTICALS
INC
10480 Wateridge Cir, San Diego
(92121-5773)
PHONE..................................267 440-4200
Peter Kies, *CFO*
Paul Stead, *President*
Scott White, *Vice Pres*
Jennifer Lata, *Associate Dir*
Trevor Smith, *Associate Dir*
EMP: 25 **Publicly Held**
SIC: 2834 Pharmaceutical preparations
PA: Inovio Pharmaceuticals, Inc.
660 W Germantown Pike
Plymouth Meeting PA 19462

(P-7952)
INSPYR THERAPEUTICS INC
(PA)
31200 Via Colinas Ste 200, Westlake Vil-
lage (91362-3959)
PHONE..................................818 661-6302
Christopher Lowe, *President*
Peter E Grebow, *Ch of Bd*
Russell Richerson, *COO*
Ronald Shazer, *Chief Mktg Ofcr*
David Maloney, *Vice Pres*
EMP: 10
SALES (est): 870.2K **Publicly Held**
SIC: 2834 Pharmaceutical preparations

(P-7953)
INSTACURE HEALING
PRODUCTS
235 N Moorpark Rd # 2022, Thousand
Oaks (91358-7001)
PHONE..................................818 222-9600
David Traub, *Owner*
EMP: 33 EST: 2015
SQ FT: 6,000
SALES: 3MM **Privately Held**
SIC: 2834 Lip balms

(P-7954)
INTERCEPT
PHARMACEUTICALS INC
4760 Eastgate Mall, San Diego
(92121-1970)
PHONE..................................646 747-1005
Mark Pruzanski, *CEO*
Greg Wong, *President*
Lily Kinninger, *Associate Dir*
EMP: 14 **Publicly Held**
SIC: 2834 Pharmaceutical preparations
PA: Intercept Pharmaceuticals, Inc.
10 Hudson Yards Fl 37
New York NY 10001

(P-7955)
INTERMUNE INC (DH)
1 Dna Way, South San Francisco
(94080-4918)
PHONE..................................415 466-4383
Daniel G Welch, *President*
John C Hodgman, *CFO*
Jonathan A Leff, *Exec VP*
Sean P Nolan, *Exec VP*
Andrew Powell, *Exec VP*
EMP: 215
SQ FT: 56,000
SALES: 70.3MM
SALES (corp-wide): 57.2B **Privately Held**
WEB: www.intermune.com
SIC: 2834 8731 Pharmaceutical prepara-
tions; medical research, commercial
HQ: Roche Holdings, Inc.
1 Dna Way
South San Francisco CA 94080
650 225-1000

(P-7956)
INTERNATIONAL STEM CELL
CORP (PA)
5950 Priestly Dr, Carlsbad (92008-8849)
PHONE..................................760 940-6383
Andrey Semechkin, *Ch of Bd*
Donald A Wright, *Ch of Bd*
Russell Kern, *Exec VP*
Sophia Garnette, *Vice Pres*
EMP: 47
SQ FT: 9,848

SALES: 11MM **Publicly Held**
WEB: www.intlstemcell.com
SIC: 2834 Pharmaceutical preparations

(P-7957)
INTERNATIONAL VITAMIN CORP
Also Called: Adam Nutrition, A Division Ivc
11010 Hopkins St Ste B, Mira Loma
(91752-3279)
PHONE..................................951 361-1120
Iliu Elisara, *Branch Mgr*
John Torphy, *Senior VP*
Maynor Zamora, *Opers Mgr*
EMP: 125 **Privately Held**
SIC: 2834 Vitamin, nutrient & hematinic
preparations for human use
PA: International Vitamin Corp
1 Park Plz Ste 800
Irvine CA 92614

(P-7958)
INTERNATIONAL VITAMIN CORP
(PA)
Also Called: I V C
1 Park Plz Ste 800, Irvine (92614-5998)
PHONE..................................949 664-5500
Steven Dai, *President*
Glenn Davis, *COO*
Eva Pinto, *Treasurer*
Jeff Moran, *Vice Pres*
Stephen Rosenman, *Vice Pres*
▲ EMP: 400
SQ FT: 166,000
SALES (est): 469MM **Privately Held**
SIC: 2834 5149 8099 Vitamin prepara-
tions; organic & diet foods; nutrition serv-
ices

(P-7959)
INTERNTNAL HMEOPATHIC MFG
DIST
7108 De Soto Ave Ste 105, Canoga Park
(91303-3230)
PHONE..................................818 884-8040
James Rojas, *President*
Christopher Powell, *Sales Staff*
EMP: 18
SQ FT: 4,000
SALES: 1.4MM **Privately Held**
SIC: 2834 Vitamin preparations

(P-7960)
INTERNTNAL MDCTION
SYSTEMS LTD
Also Called: IMS
1886 Santa Anita Ave, South El Monte
(91733-3414)
PHONE..................................626 442-6757
Jack Zhang, *President*
Mary Luo Zhang, *COO*
Mary Luo, *Chairman*
Bernard Chu, *CIO*
Carmen Rueda, *CTO*
▲ EMP: 720
SALES (est): 228.8MM
SALES (corp-wide): 294.6MM **Publicly
Held**
WEB: www.ims-limited.com
SIC: 2834 2833 3841 Drugs acting on the
central nervous system & sense organs;
anesthetics, in bulk form; surgical & med-
ical instruments
PA: Amphastar Pharmaceuticals Inc
11570 6th St
Rancho Cucamonga CA 91730
909 980-9484

(P-7961)
IONIS PHARMACEUTICALS INC
2282 Faraday Ave, Carlsbad (92008-7208)
PHONE..................................760 603-3567
Stanley Crooke, *Branch Mgr*
Breaux Castleman, *Bd of Directors*
Joseph Loscalzo, *Bd of Directors*
Jessie Daly, *Vice Pres*
Richard S Geary, *Vice Pres*
EMP: 22
SALES (corp-wide): 599.6MM **Publicly
Held**
SIC: 2834 Pharmaceutical preparations
PA: Ionis Pharmaceuticals, Inc.
2855 Gazelle Ct
Carlsbad CA 92010
760 931-9200

PRODUCTS & SVCS

(P-7962)
IONIS PHARMACEUTICALS INC (PA)
2855 Gazelle Ct, Carlsbad (92010-6670)
PHONE..............................760 931-9200
Stanley T Crooke, *Ch of Bd*
Patrick R O'Neil, *Senior VP*
▲ EMP: 262
SALES: 599.6MM **Publicly Held**
WEB: www.isispharm.com
SIC: 2834 8731 3845 Pharmaceutical preparations; medical research, commercial; electromedical equipment

(P-7963)
IOVANCE BIOTHERAPEUTICS INC (PA)
999 Skyway Rd Ste 150, San Carlos (94070-2724)
PHONE..............................650 260-7120
Maria Fardis, *President*
Wayne P Rothbaum, *Ch of Bd*
Gregory T Schiffman, *CFO*
Friedrich Graf Finckenstein, *Chief Mktg Ofcr*
Steven A Fischkoff, *Chief Mktg Ofcr*
EMP: 23
SALES (est): 6.8MM **Publicly Held**
SIC: 2834 Pharmaceutical preparations

(P-7964)
IRISYS LLC
6828 Nncy Rdge Dr Ste 100, San Diego (92121)
PHONE..............................858 623-1520
Gerald Yakatan, *Mng Member*
Robert Gianini,
Jean Wang,
EMP: 49
SQ FT: 24,100
SALES (est): 9.7MM **Privately Held**
SIC: 2834 Druggists' preparations (pharmaceuticals)
PA: Irisys, Inc.
6828 Nncy Rdge Dr Ste 100
San Diego CA 92121

(P-7965)
ISIS PHARMACEUTICALS
1767 Avenida Segovia, Oceanside (92056-6230)
PHONE..............................760 603-2631
Gregory Hardee, *Vice Pres*
Jason Ferrone, *Vice Pres*
Frank Rigo, *Associate Dir*
Lijian Chen, *Director*
Yvonne Tami, *Manager*
EMP: 16
SALES (est): 2.1MM **Privately Held**
SIC: 2834 Pharmaceutical preparations

(P-7966)
JAGUAR HEALTH INC (PA)
Also Called: JAGUAR ANIMAL HEALTH
201 Mission St Ste 2375, San Francisco (94105-1839)
PHONE..............................415 371-8300
James J Bochnowski, *Ch of Bd*
Lisa A Conte, *President*
Karen S Wright, *CFO*
Jonathan Wolin, *Ch Credit Ofcr*
Steven R King, *Exec VP*
EMP: 23
SQ FT: 6,008
SALES: 4.4MM **Publicly Held**
SIC: 2834 0752 Veterinary pharmaceutical preparations; animal specialty services

(P-7967)
JAMES STEWART
Also Called: Diagnostic Reagents
8931 S Vermont Ave, Los Angeles (90044-4833)
PHONE..............................323 778-1687
EMP: 22
SQ FT: 4,200
SALES (est): 2.1MM **Privately Held**
SIC: 2834

(P-7968)
JANSSEN BIOPHARMA INC
Also Called: Alios Biopharma, Inc.
260 E Grand Ave, South San Francisco (94080-4811)
PHONE..............................650 635-5500
Lawrence Blatt MD, *President*
Leonid Beigelman MD, *Security Dir*
Derrick De Leon, *Info Tech Dir*
EMP: 26
SALES (est): 9.3MM
SALES (corp-wide): 81.5B **Publicly Held**
SIC: 2834 Pharmaceutical preparations
PA: Johnson & Johnson
1 Johnson And Johnson Plz
New Brunswick NJ 08933
732 524-0400

(P-7969)
JANSSEN RESEARCH & DEV LLC
3210 Merryfield Row, San Diego (92121-1126)
PHONE..............................858 450-2000
Steve Schuetzle, *Manager*
EMP: 228
SALES (corp-wide): 81.5B **Publicly Held**
WEB: www.jnjpharmarnd.com
SIC: 2834 Pharmaceutical preparations
HQ: Janssen Research & Development, Llc
920 Us Highway 202
Raritan NJ 08869
908 704-4000

(P-7970)
JARROW INDUSTRIES INC
12246 Hawkins St, Santa Fe Springs (90670-3365)
PHONE..............................562 906-1919
Jarrow Rogovin, *Ch of Bd*
Mohammed Khalid, *President*
David Chen, *CFO*
Ben Khowong, *Treasurer*
Arianna Gonzales, *Manager*
▲ EMP: 140
SQ FT: 125,000
SALES (est): 51.4MM **Privately Held**
WEB: www.jiimfg.com
SIC: 2834 Vitamin preparations

(P-7971)
JAZZ PHARMACEUTICALS INC (HQ)
3170 Porter Dr, Palo Alto (94304-1212)
PHONE..............................650 496-3777
Bruce C Cozadd, *Ch of Bd*
Kathryn E Falberg, *CFO*
Russell J Cox, *Exec VP*
Jeffrey Tobias, *Exec VP*
Laurie Hurley, *Vice Pres*
▲ EMP: 163
SALES: 1.6B **Privately Held**
SIC: 2834 Drugs acting on the central nervous system & sense organs

(P-7972)
K & K LABORATORIES INC
2160 Warmlands Ave, Vista (92084-3338)
PHONE..............................760 758-2352
Alex Kononchuk Jr, *President*
Linda Kononchuk, *Admin Sec*
EMP: 35
SQ FT: 20,000
SALES (est): 4.2MM **Privately Held**
SIC: 2834 Vitamin, nutrient & hematinic preparations for human use

(P-7973)
KALYPSYS INC
333 S Grand Ave Ste 4070, Los Angeles (90071-1544)
P.O. Box 1390, Solana Beach (92075-7390)
PHONE..............................858 552-0674
August Watanabe, *Ch of Bd*
John McKearn, *CEO*
David C Tiemeier, *COO*
EMP: 110
SQ FT: 42,000
SALES (est): 16.6MM **Privately Held**
WEB: www.kalypsys.com
SIC: 2834 Pharmaceutical preparations

(P-7974)
KANAMAX INTERNATIONAL INC (PA)
10618 Rush St, South El Monte (91733-3432)
PHONE..............................213 399-3398
Kelvin Ng, *President*
▲ EMP: 15
SQ FT: 3,000
SALES (est): 1.9MM **Privately Held**
SIC: 2834 Liniments

(P-7975)
KATE SOMERVILLE SKINCARE LLC (HQ)
144 S Beverly Dr Ste 500, Beverly Hills (90212-3023)
PHONE..............................323 655-7546
Kate Somerville, *Mng Member*
Susan Beal, *CTO*
Jeff Hansen,
Laura Shaff,
Michelle Taylor,
▲ EMP: 51
SALES (est): 13.7MM
SALES (corp-wide): 58.3B **Privately Held**
SIC: 2834 5122 Pharmaceutical preparations; toiletries; cosmetics; perfumes
PA: Unilever N.V.
Weena 455
Rotterdam
102 174-000

(P-7976)
KAVI SKIN SOLUTIONS INC (PA)
700 Larkspur Landing Cir, Larkspur (94939-1715)
PHONE..............................415 839-5156
Kaveh Alizadeh, *President*
▲ EMP: 38
SQ FT: 2,400
SALES (est): 2.5MM **Privately Held**
SIC: 2834 Pharmaceutical preparations

(P-7977)
KC PHARMACEUTICALS INC (PA)
3201 Producer Way, Pomona (91768-3916)
PHONE..............................909 598-9499
L T Khouw, *Ch of Bd*
Joseph Sutedjo, *President*
Dr Pramuditya Oen, *CEO*
Cecilio Joaquin, *Engineer*
Edwin Koo, *QC Mgr*
▲ EMP: 93
SQ FT: 20,000
SALES (est): 36MM **Privately Held**
SIC: 2834 Solutions, pharmaceutical; cough medicines; cold remedies; antacids

(P-7978)
KC PHARMACEUTICALS INC
3220 Producer Way, Pomona (91768-3915)
PHONE..............................909 598-9499
Paul Kartiko, *Manager*
EMP: 50
SALES (est): 7.5MM
SALES (corp-wide): 36MM **Privately Held**
SIC: 2834 Solutions, pharmaceutical
PA: Kc Pharmaceuticals Inc.
3201 Producer Way
Pomona CA 91768
909 598-9499

(P-7979)
KEZAR LIFE SCIENCES INC
4000 Shoreline Ct Ste 300, South San Francisco (94080-2005)
PHONE..............................650 822-5600
John Fowler, *CEO*
Jean-Pierre Sommadossi, *Ch of Bd*
Christopher Kirk, *President*
Marc L Belsky, *CFO*
Niti Goel, *Chief Mktg Ofcr*
EMP: 20
SQ FT: 24,357
SALES (est): 5MM **Privately Held**
SIC: 2834 Pharmaceutical preparations

(P-7980)
KINDRED BIOSCIENCES INC (PA)
1555 Bayshore Hwy Ste 200, Burlingame (94010-1617)
PHONE..............................650 701-7901
Richard Chin, *President*
Denise M Bevers, *President*
Wendy Wee, *CFO*
Raymond Townsend, *Bd of Directors*
Stephen Sundlof, *Exec VP*
EMP: 41 EST: 2012
SALES: 1.9MM **Publicly Held**
SIC: 2834 Veterinary pharmaceutical preparations

(P-7981)
KODIAK SCIENCES INC (PA)
2631 Hanover St, Palo Alto (94304-1118)
PHONE..............................650 281-0850
Victor Perlroth, *Ch of Bd*
John A Borgeson, *CFO*
Jason Ehrlich, *Chief Mktg Ofcr*
Hong Liang, *Senior VP*
EMP: 28
SQ FT: 11,000
SALES (est): 3.1MM **Publicly Held**
SIC: 2834 Pharmaceutical preparations

(P-7982)
KOSAN BIOSCIENCES INCORPORATED
3832 Bay Center Pl, Hayward (94545-3619)
P.O. Box 4000, Princeton NJ (08543-4000)
PHONE..............................650 995-7356
Helen S Kim, *President*
Peter Davis PHD, *Ch of Bd*
Gary S Titus, *CFO*
Peter J Licari PHD, *Senior VP*
Jonathan K Wright, *Senior VP*
EMP: 91
SALES (est): 10MM
SALES (corp-wide): 22.5B **Publicly Held**
WEB: www.kosan.com
SIC: 2834 8731 Pharmaceutical preparations; commercial research laboratory
PA: Bristol-Myers Squibb Company
430 E 29th St Fl 14
New York NY 10016
212 546-4000

(P-7983)
KYOWA KIRIN PHRM RES INC (HQ)
9420 Athena Cir, La Jolla (92037-1387)
PHONE..............................858 952-7000
Kinya Ohgami, *President*
Hiroshi Makino, *Director*
▲ EMP: 45
SQ FT: 3,000
SALES (est): 14.1MM **Privately Held**
SIC: 2834 Pharmaceutical preparations

(P-7984)
KYTHERA BIOPHARMACEUTICALS INC
30930 Russell Ranch Rd # 3, Westlake Village (91362-7378)
PHONE..............................818 587-4500
A R D Bailey, *President*
A Robert D Bailey, *President*
John W Smither, *CFO*
Elisabeth A Sandoval, *Ch Credit Ofcr*
Frederick Beddingfield III, *Chief Mktg Ofcr*
EMP: 106
SQ FT: 33,198
SALES (est): 16.6MM **Privately Held**
SIC: 2834 Dermatologicals
PA: Allergan Public Limited Company
Clonshaugh Business And Technology Park
Dublin

(P-7985)
L-NUTRA INC
8240 Zitola Ter, Playa Del Rey (90293-7834)
PHONE..............................310 245-1724
Fabrizio Schirano, *CEO*
EMP: 16 **Privately Held**
SIC: 2834 Pharmaceutical preparations

▲ = Import ▼=Export
◆ =Import/Export

PA: L-Nutra Inc.
8000 Beverly Blvd
Los Angeles CA 90048

(P-7986)
LABORATORIOS CAMACHO INC
9349 Melvin Ave Ste 1, Northridge
(91324-2480)
P.O. Box 2363, Los Angeles (90078-2363)
PHONE..............................818 764-2748
Jorge Camacho, *President*
Gioconda Camacho, *Vice Pres*
EMP: 10
SQ FT: 3,500
SALES (est): 1.8MM **Privately Held**
WEB: www.laboratorioscamacho.com
SIC: 2834 Adrenal pharmaceutical preparations

(P-7987)
LEADING BIOSCIENCES INC
5800 Armada Dr Ste 210, Carlsbad
(92008-4611)
PHONE..............................858 395-6099
Greg Doyle, *CEO*
JD Finley, *CFO*
Clark Straw, *Chairman*
EMP: 10
SALES (est): 1.3MM **Privately Held**
SIC: 2834 Pharmaceutical preparations

(P-7988)
LEINER HEALTH PRODUCTS INC
7366 Orangewood Ave, Garden Grove
(92841-1412)
PHONE..............................714 898-9936
James Smith, *Manager*
EMP: 315 **Publicly Held**
WEB: www.leiner.com
SIC: 2834 2844 2833 5122 Vitamin, nutrient & hematinic preparations for human use; toilet preparations; medicinals & botanicals; vitamins & minerals
HQ: Leiner Health Products, Inc.
901 E 233rd St
Carson CA 90745
631 200-2000

(P-7989)
LEINER HEALTH PRODUCTS INC
27655b Avenue Hopkins, Valencia
(91355-3493)
PHONE..............................661 775-1422
EMP: 100 **Publicly Held**
SIC: 2834
HQ: Leiner Health Products, Inc.
901 E 233rd St
Carson CA 90745
631 200-2000

(P-7990)
LEITERS ENTERPRISES INC
Also Called: Leiter's Compounding
17 Great Oaks Blvd, San Jose
(95119-1359)
PHONE..............................800 292-6772
Bob Zollars, *Ch of Bd*
Jim Cunniff, *CEO*
Charles Leiter, *Vice Pres*
EMP: 84 EST: 2013
SALES (est): 22.3MM **Privately Held**
SIC: 2834 Druggists' preparations (pharmaceuticals)

(P-7991)
LIEF ORGANICS LLC
Also Called: Lief Labs
28901 28903 Ave Paine, Valencia (91355)
PHONE..............................661 775-2500
Adel Villalobos, *CEO*
Nathan Cox, *Vice Pres*
Victor Leyson, *VP Finance*
EMP: 30 EST: 2008
SALES (est): 13.4MM **Privately Held**
SIC: 2834 Adrenal pharmaceutical preparations

(P-7992)
LIFEBLOOM CORPORATION
Also Called: B&A Health Products Co
925 W Lambert Rd Ste B, Brea
(92821-2943)
PHONE..............................562 944-6800
Sam Ahn, *CEO*

Chong Ahn, *Vice Pres*
David Kim, *Purch Mgr*
Cathy Ahn, *Opers Mgr*
◆ EMP: 20
SALES (est): 6MM **Privately Held**
SIC: 2834 Vitamin preparations

(P-7993)
LIGAND PHARMACEUTICALS INC
10275 Science Center Dr, San Diego
(92121-1117)
PHONE..............................858 550-7500
Matt Witte, *President*
EMP: 21
SALES (est): 3.6MM **Privately Held**
SIC: 2834 Pharmaceutical preparations

(P-7994)
LIGAND PHARMACEUTICALS INC (PA)
3911 Sorrento Valley Blvd # 110, San Diego
(92121-1457)
PHONE..............................858 550-7500
John L Higgins, *CEO*
Matthew W Foehr, *President*
Matthew Korenberg, *CFO*
Charles S Berkman, *Senior VP*
EMP: 62
SQ FT: 5,000
SALES (est): 251.4MM **Publicly Held**
WEB: www.ligand.com
SIC: 2834 Pharmaceutical preparations

(P-7995)
LILLY BIOTECHNOLOGY CENTER
10290 Campus Point Dr, San Diego
(92121-1522)
PHONE..............................858 597-4990
Maegan Arnett, *Research*
Vincent Truax, *Director*
EMP: 14
SALES (est): 5.8MM **Privately Held**
SIC: 2834 Pharmaceutical preparations

(P-7996)
LILLY MING INTERNATIONAL INC
16 Trinity, Irvine (92612-3271)
PHONE..............................949 266-4836
Liming Wang Lilly, *President*
EMP: 10
SALES (est): 1MM **Privately Held**
SIC: 2834 Pharmaceutical preparations

(P-7997)
LIQUID BIOSCIENCE INC
26895 Aliso Creek Rd B800, Aliso Viejo
(92656-5301)
PHONE..............................949 432-9559
Matthew Nunez, *CEO*
EMP: 10
SALES (est): 409.5K **Privately Held**
SIC: 2834 Medicines, capsuled or ampuled

(P-7998)
LOBOB LABORATORIES INC
1440 Atteberry Ln, San Jose (95131-1410)
PHONE..............................408 324-0381
Robert M Lohr, *President*
EMP: 35 EST: 1964
SQ FT: 20,000
SALES (est): 5.1MM **Privately Held**
WEB: www.loboblabs.com
SIC: 2834 3851 2841 Solutions, pharmaceutical; ophthalmic goods; soap & other detergents

(P-7999)
M & L PHARMACEUTICALS INC
629 S Allen St, San Bernardino
(92408-2250)
PHONE..............................909 890-0078
Jorge Molina Jr, *President*
Guadalupe Molina, *Corp Secy*
EMP: 15
SQ FT: 6,000
SALES (est): 3.2MM **Privately Held**
WEB: www.mlpharmaceutical.com
SIC: 2834 Vitamin preparations

(P-8000)
MABVAX THRPEUTICS HOLDINGS INC (PA)
11535 Sorrento Valley Rd, San Diego
(92121-1309)
PHONE..............................858 259-9405
J David Hansen, *Ch of Bd*
Paul W Maffuid, *Exec VP*
Paul Resnick, *Vice Pres*
Ritsuko Sawada, *Associate Dir*
Jonah Rainey, *Exec Dir*
EMP: 11
SQ FT: 14,971
SALES (est): 1.6MM **Publicly Held**
WEB: www.telik.com
SIC: 2834 Pharmaceutical preparations

(P-8001)
MACROGENICS WEST INC
3280 Byshore Blvd Ste 200, Brisbane
(94005)
PHONE..............................650 624-2600
Scott Koenig, *President*
Ezio Bonvini, *President*
EMP: 16
SALES (est): 3.6MM **Privately Held**
SIC: 2834 Druggists' preparations (pharmaceuticals)

(P-8002)
MANNKIND CORPORATION (PA)
30930 Russell Ranch Rd # 300, Westlake
Village (91362-7379)
PHONE..............................818 661-5000
Michael E Castagna, *CEO*
Kent Kresa, *Ch of Bd*
Steven B Binder, *CFO*
Steven Binder, *CFO*
Matthew Pfeffer, *CFO*
▲ EMP: 250
SQ FT: 24,475
SALES (est): 27.8MM **Publicly Held**
WEB: www.mannkindcorp.com
SIC: 2834 8731 Pharmaceutical preparations; biotechnical research, commercial

(P-8003)
MCKENNA LABS INC (PA)
1601 E Orangethorpe Ave, Fullerton
(92831-5230)
PHONE..............................714 687-6888
Dennis Alexander Owen, *President*
Irina Samofalova, *Vice Pres*
Francine Sakamoto, *Controller*
Raquel Carey, *Purch Dir*
Amanda Hernandez, *Purch Agent*
◆ EMP: 40
SQ FT: 62,000
SALES (est): 18.9MM **Privately Held**
WEB: www.mckennalabs.com
SIC: 2834 2844 Pharmaceutical preparations; toilet preparations

(P-8004)
MED-PHARMEX INC
2727 Thompson Creek Rd, Pomona
(91767-1861)
PHONE..............................909 593-7875
Avinash Ghanekar, *President*
Gerald Macedo, *CEO*
▲ EMP: 12
SQ FT: 18,000
SALES (est): 4.9MM **Privately Held**
SIC: 2834 Pharmaceutical preparations

(P-8005)
MEDICINES360 (PA)
Also Called: M360
353 Sacramento St Ste 300, San Francisco
(94111-3688)
PHONE..............................415 951-8700
Jessica Grossman, *CEO*
Pamela Weir, *COO*
Bradley Luke, *CFO*
Mark Busch, *Vice Pres*
Autumn Ehnow, *Vice Pres*
EMP: 14
SQ FT: 15,000
SALES: 23.3MM **Privately Held**
SIC: 2834 Pharmaceutical preparations

(P-8006)
MEDIMMUNE LLC
Also Called: Medimmune Vaccines
297 Bernardo Ave, Mountain View
(94043-5205)
PHONE..............................650 603-2000
David Mott, *CEO*
Nicole Bleckwenn, *Associate Dir*
Kudla Joseph, *Associate Dir*
Bob Laughner, *Associate Dir*
Elias Bernal, *Technician*
EMP: 275
SALES (corp-wide): 22B **Privately Held**
WEB: www.medimmune.com
SIC: 2834 Pharmaceutical preparations
HQ: Medimmune, Llc
1 Medimmune Way
Gaithersburg MD 20878
301 398-0000

(P-8007)
MEDIVATION INC (HQ)
Also Called: Xtandi
525 Market St Ste 3600, San Francisco
(94105-2747)
PHONE..............................415 543-3470
David T Hung, *President*
Marion McCourt, *COO*
Jennifer Jarrett, *CFO*
Mohammad Hirmand, *Chief Mktg Ofcr*
Joseph Lobacki, *Officer*
EMP: 201
SQ FT: 143,000
SALES: 943.2MM
SALES (corp-wide): 53.6B **Publicly Held**
WEB: www.medivation.net
SIC: 2834 Adrenal pharmaceutical preparations
PA: Pfizer Inc.
235 E 42nd St
New York NY 10017
212 733-2323

(P-8008)
MEI PHARMA INC
3611 Vly Cntre Dr Ste 500, San Diego
(92130)
PHONE..............................858 369-7100
Daniel P Gold, *President*
Christine A White, *Ch of Bd*
David M Urso, *COO*
Brian G Drazba, *CFO*
Robert D Mass, *Chief Mktg Ofcr*
EMP: 25
SQ FT: 13,700
SALES: 4.9MM **Privately Held**
SIC: 2834 Pharmaceutical preparations

(P-8009)
MENLO THERAPEUTICS INC
200 Cardinal Way Ste 200 # 200, Redwood
City (94063-4703)
PHONE..............................650 486-1416
Steven Basta, *President*
Kristine Ball, *CFO*
Ronald A Krasnow, *Ch Credit Ofcr*
Scott Whitcup, *Bd of Directors*
Paul Kwon, *Security Dir*
EMP: 48 EST: 2011
SQ FT: 14,000
SALES: 10.6MM **Privately Held**
SIC: 2834 Pharmaceutical preparations

(P-8010)
MERCK & CO INC
901 California Ave, Palo Alto (94304-1104)
PHONE..............................650 496-6400
John T Curnutte, *President*
Jeanne Baker, *Research*
Wendy Blumenschein, *Research*
Patricia Bourne, *Research*
Grigori Ermakov, *Research*
EMP: 100
SALES (corp-wide): 42.2B **Publicly Held**
SIC: 2834 Pharmaceutical preparations
PA: Merck & Co., Inc.
2000 Galloping Hill Rd
Kenilworth NJ 07033
908 740-4000

(P-8011)
MERCK SHARP & DOHME CORP
8355 Aero Dr, San Diego (92123-1718)
P.O. Box 23576 (92193-3576)
PHONE..............................619 292-4900
Peter Kovacs, *President*

PRODUCTS & SVCS

Pamela Sears, *Vice Pres*
EMP: 100
SALES (corp-wide): 42.2B **Publicly Held**
SIC: 2834 Pharmaceutical preparations
HQ: Merck Sharp & Dohme Corp.
2000 Galloping Hill Rd
Kenilworth NJ 07033
908 740-4000

(P-8012)
METABASIS THERAPEUTICS INC
11085 N Torrey Pines Rd # 300, La Jolla
(92037-1015)
PHONE................................858 550-7500
John L Higgins, *President*
Constance C Bienfait, *Vice Pres*
R Wayne Frost, *Vice Pres*
Molly A Holman, *Vice Pres*
Julie C Cunningham, *Commissioner*
EMP: 18 **EST:** 1997
SQ FT: 82,000
SALES (est): 2.9MM
SALES (corp-wide): 251.4MM **Publicly Held**
WEB: www.mbasis.com
SIC: 2834 Pharmaceutical preparations
PA: Ligand Pharmaceuticals Incorporated
3911 Sorrento Valley Blvd # 110
San Diego CA 92121
858 550-7500

(P-8013)
MGFSO LLC
Also Called: Medigreens
7372 Siena Dr, Huntington Beach
(92648-6825)
PHONE................................949 500-7645
Mark Nashed,
John Paboojian,
Kelly Rossow-Soto,
EMP: 10
SQ FT: 5,227,200
SALES: 500K **Privately Held**
SIC: 2834 Pharmaceutical preparations

(P-8014)
MIRATI THERAPEUTICS INC
9393 Twne Cntre Dr Ste 20, San Diego
(92121)
PHONE................................858 332-3410
Charles M Baum, *President*
Faheem Hasnain, *Ch of Bd*
Rodney W Lappe, *Ch of Bd*
Jamie A Donadio, *CFO*
Jamie Donadio, *CFO*
EMP: 19
SQ FT: 18,000
SALES: 12.9MM **Privately Held**
SIC: 2834 8731 Pharmaceutical preparations; biotechnical research, commercial

(P-8015)
MIRUM PHARMACEUTICALS INC
950 Tower Ln Ste 1050, Foster City
(94404-4251)
PHONE................................650 667-4085
Christopher Peetz, *President*
Michael Grey, *Chairman*
Ed Tucker, *Chief Mktg Ofcr*
Ian Clements, *Senior VP*
Pamela Vig, *Security Dir*
EMP: 24
SQ FT: 6,000
SALES (est): 449.1K **Privately Held**
SIC: 2834 Pharmaceutical preparations

(P-8016)
MOM ENTERPRISES INC
1003 W Cutting Blvd # 110, Richmond
(94804-2092)
P.O. Box 6524, San Rafael (94903-0524)
PHONE................................415 526-2710
Roshan Kaderali, *CEO*
Shiraz Kaderali, *President*
Yasmin Kaderali, *CEO*
April Howell, *Vice Pres*
EMP: 10
SQ FT: 3,000
SALES: 11.6MM **Privately Held**
SIC: 2834 Antacids; extracts of botanicals: powdered, pilular, solid or fluid

(P-8017)
MURAD LLC (HQ)
2121 Park Pl Fl 1, El Segundo
(90245-4843)
PHONE................................310 726-0600
Howard Murad MD, *President*
Elizabeth Ashmun, *Chief Mktg Ofcr*
Olia Botchev, *Vice Pres*
Missy Gilmore, *Vice Pres*
Van Vuong, *Vice Pres*
▲ **EMP:** 160
SQ FT: 8,000
SALES (est): 52.2MM
SALES (corp-wide): 58.3B **Privately Held**
SIC: 2834 5122 Vitamin, nutrient & hematinic preparations for human use; vitamin preparations; pharmaceuticals; proprietary (patent) medicines
PA: Unilever N.V.
Weena 455
Rotterdam
102 174-000

(P-8018)
MYA INTERNATIONAL INC
3517 Main St Ste 304, Chula Vista
(91911-0800)
PHONE................................619 429-6012
Ana Martins, *CEO*
Michael Martins, *President*
◆ **EMP:** 13
SALES (est): 2.9MM **Privately Held**
SIC: 2834 Vitamin, nutrient & hematinic preparations for human use

(P-8019)
MYLAN PHARMACEUTICALS INC
150 Industrial Rd, San Carlos
(94070-6256)
PHONE................................650 631-3100
G Fukumitsu, *Principal*
Dan Miller, *Associate Dir*
Michael Schillaci, *Research*
Nelson Todd, *Engineer*
Chuck Kreider, *Director*
EMP: 56
SALES (corp-wide): 204.1K **Privately Held**
WEB: www.novartis.com
SIC: 2834 Veterinary pharmaceutical preparations
HQ: Mylan Pharmaceuticals Inc.
781 Chestnut Ridge Rd
Morgantown WV 26505
304 599-2595

(P-8020)
MYOGENIX INCORPORATED
2309 A St, Santa Maria (93455-1072)
PHONE................................800 950-0348
Adam G Nielson, *President*
▲ **EMP:** 12
SALES (est): 2.2MM **Privately Held**
WEB: www.myogenix.com
SIC: 2834 Pharmaceutical preparations

(P-8021)
MYOKARDIA INC (PA)
333 Allerton Ave, South San Francisco
(94080-4816)
PHONE................................650 741-0900
Tassos Gianakakos, *President*
Taylor C Harris, *CFO*
William Fairey, *Ch Credit Ofcr*
Kevin Starr, *Bd of Directors*
June Lee, *Exec VP*
EMP: 93
SQ FT: 34,400
SALES: 33.5MM **Publicly Held**
SIC: 2834 Drugs acting on the cardiovascular system, except diagnostic

(P-8022)
NADIN COMPANY
1815 Flower St, Glendale (91201-2024)
PHONE................................818 500-8908
EMP: 25
SQ FT: 35,000
SALES (est): 2.2MM **Privately Held**
SIC: 2834

(P-8023)
NATROL LLC (DH)
21411 Prairie St, Chatsworth (91311-5829)
PHONE................................818 739-6000

Tom Zimmerman, *CEO*
Ivan Milenkovic, *Administration*
Edgar Rodriguez, *Comp Lab Dir*
Michael Berinde, *Info Tech Mgr*
Rosa Guzman, *Technology*
◆ **EMP:** 179 **EST:** 2015
SALES (est): 105.3MM
SALES (corp-wide): 1.6B **Privately Held**
SIC: 2834 Pharmaceutical preparations
HQ: Aurobindo Pharma U.S.A., Inc.
279 Prnctn Hightstown Rd
East Windsor NJ 08520
732 839-9400

(P-8024)
NATURA-GENICS INC
6952 Buckeye St, Chino (91710-8248)
PHONE................................909 597-6676
Renzo Bustamante, *President*
Grace Juliono, *QC Mgr*
▲ **EMP:** 10
SALES (est): 2.2MM **Privately Held**
SIC: 2834 Vitamin preparations

(P-8025)
NATURAL ALTERNATIVES INTL INC (PA)
Also Called: Nai
1535 Faraday Ave, Carlsbad (92008-7319)
PHONE................................760 736-7700
Mark A Ledoux, *Ch of Bd*
▲ **EMP:** 50 **EST:** 1980
SQ FT: 20,981
SALES: 132.4MM **Publicly Held**
WEB: www.nai-online.com
SIC: 2834 Pharmaceutical preparations

(P-8026)
NATURESTAR BIO TECH INC
1175 S Grove Ave Ste 101, Ontario
(91761-3470)
PHONE................................909 930-1878
Liqiong Fei, *President*
EMP: 15
SALES (est): 2MM **Privately Held**
WEB: www.naturestarusa.com
SIC: 2834 Vitamin, nutrient & hematinic preparations for human use

(P-8027)
NBTY MANUFACTURING LLC
Also Called: Nature's Bounty
5115 E La Palma Ave, Anaheim
(92807-2018)
PHONE................................714 765-8323
Steve Cahillane, *CEO*
Majid Khodaparast, *Research*
Lily Mu, *Training Dir*
Scott Ludwig, *Recruiter*
Hans Lindgren,
▼ **EMP:** 224
SALES (est): 36.4MM **Publicly Held**
WEB: www.nbtymfg.com
SIC: 2834 Vitamin preparations
HQ: The Nature's Bounty Co
2100 Smithtown Ave
Ronkonkoma NY 11779
631 200-2000

(P-8028)
NEILMED PHARMACEUTICALS INC
601 Aviation Blvd, Santa Rosa
(95403-1025)
PHONE................................707 525-3784
Kaetan Mehta MD, *CEO*
Nina Mehta, *President*
Ken Di, *CFO*
Ajit Mehta, *VP Bus Dvlpt*
Daniel Barba, *Graphic Designe*
▲ **EMP:** 300
SALES (est): 107.3MM **Privately Held**
WEB: www.nasalrinse.com
SIC: 2834 Pharmaceutical preparations

(P-8029)
NEKTAR THERAPEUTICS
150 Industrial Rd, San Carlos
(94070-6256)
PHONE................................650 622-1790
Carlo Di Fonzo, *Vice Pres*
Dorian Rinella, *Vice Pres*
Mary Tagliaferri, *Vice Pres*
Sunny Xie, *Vice Pres*
Kerry Ellis, *Executive Asst*
EMP: 20 **Publicly Held**

SIC: 2834 Pharmaceutical preparations
PA: Nektar Therapeutics
455 Mission Bay Blvd S
San Francisco CA 94158

(P-8030)
NEKTAR THERAPEUTICS (PA)
455 Mission Bay Blvd S, San Francisco
(94158-2158)
PHONE................................415 482-5300
Howard W Robin, *President*
Jonathan Zalevsky, *Development*
Stephen K Doberstein, *Fellow*
EMP: 280
SQ FT: 126,285
SALES: 1.1B **Publicly Held**
SIC: 2834 Pharmaceutical preparations

(P-8031)
NERVEDA INC
3888 Quarter Mile Dr, San Diego
(92130-1291)
PHONE................................858 705-2365
CAM Gallagher, *Principal*
EMP: 72
SALES (est): 5.7MM **Privately Held**
SIC: 2834 Pharmaceutical preparations

(P-8032)
NEUROCRINE BIOSCIENCES INC (PA)
Also Called: Ingrezza
12780 El Camino Real # 100, San Diego
(92130-2042)
PHONE................................858 617-7600
Kevin C Gorman, *CEO*
EMP: 232
SQ FT: 140,000
SALES: 451.2MM **Publicly Held**
WEB: www.neurocrine.com
SIC: 2834 2833 Pituitary gland pharmaceutical preparations; drugs acting on the central nervous system & sense organs; endocrine products

(P-8033)
NEXGEN PHARMA INC (PA)
46 Corporate Park Ste 100, Irvine
(92606-3121)
P.O. Box 19516 (92623-9516)
PHONE................................949 863-0340
Steven Brown, *CEO*
Gary P Korngold, *President*
Mark Nishi, *CFO*
Gene Nakagawa, *Exec VP*
Dr Deepak Thassu, *Vice Pres*
EMP: 190
SQ FT: 50,000
SALES (est): 57MM **Privately Held**
WEB: www.vitamer.com
SIC: 2834 Pharmaceutical preparations

(P-8034)
NEXGEN PHARMA INC
17802 Gillette Ave, Irvine (92614-6502)
PHONE................................949 260-3702
Ian Gibson, *Vice Pres*
EMP: 45
SALES (corp-wide): 57MM **Privately Held**
WEB: www.vitamer.com
SIC: 2834 Vitamin, nutrient & hematinic preparations for human use
PA: Nexgen Pharma, Inc.
46 Corporate Park Ste 100
Irvine CA 92606
949 863-0340

(P-8035)
NEXGEN PHARMA INC
17802 Gillette Ave, Irvine (92614-6502)
PHONE................................949 863-0340
Steve Brown, *President*
EMP: 15
SQ FT: 26,152
SALES (corp-wide): 57MM **Privately Held**
WEB: www.vitamer.com
SIC: 2834 Vitamin, nutrient & hematinic preparations for human use
PA: Nexgen Pharma, Inc.
46 Corporate Park Ste 100
Irvine CA 92606
949 863-0340

▲ = Import ▼=Export
◆ =Import/Export

(P-8036)
NEXT PHARMACEUTICALS INC
360 Espinosa Rd, Salinas (93907-8895)
PHONE..................................831 621-8712
Charles Kosmont, *President*
Robert Garrison, *Chairman*
EMP: 50
SALES (est): 5.5MM **Privately Held**
WEB: www.nextpharmaceuticals.com
SIC: 2834 Vitamin, nutrient & hematinic preparations for human use; vitamin preparations

(P-8037)
NEXTPHARMA TECH USA INC
Also Called: Bioserv
5340 Eastgate Mall, San Diego (92121-2804)
PHONE..................................858 450-3123
Franck Latrille, *CEO*
Danny John, *Purchasing*
EMP: 27
SQ FT: 38,000
SALES (est): 5.9MM
SALES (corp-wide): 10.2K **Privately Held**
WEB: www.bioservcorp.com
SIC: 2834 2835 Pharmaceutical preparations; microbiology & virology diagnostic products
HQ: Nextpharma Technologies Holding Limited
1 Tannery House
Woking
-

(P-8038)
NGM BIOPHARMACEUTICALS INC
Also Called: NGMBIO
333 Oyster Point Blvd, South San Francisco (94080-1978)
PHONE..................................650 243-5555
David J Woodhouse, *CEO*
Tamas Blandl, *Vice Pres*
Alex Depaoli, *Vice Pres*
Wenyan Shen, *Vice Pres*
Hui Tian, *Vice Pres*
EMP: 164
SQ FT: 122,000
SALES: 108.6MM **Privately Held**
SIC: 2834 Pharmaceutical preparations

(P-8039)
NHK LABORATORIES (PA)
12230 Florence Ave, Santa Fe Springs (90670-3806)
PHONE..................................562 903-5835
M Amirul Karim, *CEO*
Shafiel Ahmed, *CFO*
Nasima A Karim, *Vice Pres*
Shabbir Akand, *Executive*
Rolando Sabilia, *Controller*
▲ EMP: 95
SQ FT: 90,000
SALES (est): 19.2MM **Privately Held**
WEB: www.nhklabs.com
SIC: 2834 5122 Vitamin preparations; vitamins & minerals

(P-8040)
NIVAGEN PHARMACEUTICALS INC
3050 Fite Cir Ste 100, Sacramento (95827-1818)
PHONE..................................916 364-1662
Jwalant S Shukla, *President*
Ray Walker, *Exec VP*
Thomas Henry, *Vice Pres*
Anand Shukla, *Vice Pres*
Chris Welton, *Controller*
EMP: 25 EST: 2009
SALES (est): 2.2MM **Privately Held**
SIC: 2834 Pharmaceutical preparations

(P-8041)
NOVABAY PHARMACEUTICALS INC
2000 Powell St Ste 1150, Emeryville (94608-1866)
PHONE..................................510 899-8800
Justin Hall, *President*
Paul E Freiman, *Ch of Bd*
Jason Raleigh, *CFO*
▲ EMP: 33
SQ FT: 7,799

SALES: 12.5MM **Privately Held**
SIC: 2834 Drugs acting on the central nervous system & sense organs

(P-8042)
NOVARTIS CORPORATION
3115 Merryfield Row, San Diego (92121-1125)
PHONE..................................858 812-1741
Joerg Reinhardt, *Chairman*
Shelley Chang, *Associate*
EMP: 56
SALES (corp-wide): 51.9B **Privately Held**
SIC: 2834 Pharmaceutical preparations
HQ: Novartis Corporation
1 S Ridgedale Ave Ste 1 # 1
East Hanover NJ 07936
212 307-1122

(P-8043)
NOVARTIS INST FOR BIOMEDICAL R
5300 Chiron Way, Emeryville (94608-2966)
PHONE..................................510 923-4248
EMP: 11
SALES (corp-wide): 51.9B **Privately Held**
SIC: 2834 Pharmaceutical preparations
HQ: Novartis Institutes For Biomedical Research, Inc.
250 Massachusetts Ave
Cambridge MA 02139
617 871-8000

(P-8044)
NOVUS THERAPEUTICS INC
19900 Macarthur Blvd # 550, Irvine (92612-8426)
PHONE..................................949 238-8090
Gregory J Flesher, *CEO*
Keith A Katkin, *Ch of Bd*
Catherine C Turkel, *President*
Jon S Kuwahara, *Senior VP*
EMP: 10
SQ FT: 5,197
SALES (est): 1.6MM **Privately Held**
SIC: 2834 Pharmaceutical preparations

(P-8045)
NUTRAWISE HEALTH & BEAUTY CORP (PA)
Also Called: Nutrawise Corporation
9600 Toledo Way, Irvine (92618-1808)
PHONE..................................949 900-2400
Darren Rude, *CEO*
Patty Terzo-Rude, *President*
Theresa Rude, *Treasurer*
Heidi Kaufman, *Planning*
Maurice Munoz, *Technology*
EMP: 62 EST: 2009
SQ FT: 130,000
SALES: 48MM **Privately Held**
SIC: 2834 Vitamin, nutrient & hematinic preparations for human use

(P-8046)
NUTRITION RESOURCE INC (PA)
Also Called: Nutribiotic
865 Parallel Dr, Lakeport (95453-5707)
P.O. Box 238 (95453-0238)
PHONE..................................707 263-0411
Richard Perry, *President*
Kenny Ridgeway, *Marketing Staff*
◆ EMP: 16
SQ FT: 20,000
SALES (est): 4.3MM **Privately Held**
WEB: www.nutribiotic.com
SIC: 2834 2844 2841 2023 Vitamin preparations; ointments; toothpastes or powders, dentifrices; soap: granulated, liquid, cake, flaked or chip; dietary supplements, dairy & non-dairy based

(P-8047)
NUTRITIONAL ENGINEERING INC
1208 Avenida Chelsea, Vista (92081-8315)
PHONE..................................760 599-5200
Ted Laoudis, *CEO*
EMP: 12
SQ FT: 12,000
SALES (est): 3.4MM **Privately Held**
WEB: www.herbalman.com
SIC: 2834 Vitamin preparations

(P-8048)
OBAGI COSMECEUTICALS LLC (PA)
Also Called: Obagi Medical
3760 Kilroy Airport Way, Long Beach (90806-2443)
PHONE..................................800 636-7546
Jamie Castle, *President*
Mark T Taylor, *Senior VP*
Lisa Errecart, *Vice Pres*
Trish Mentas, *Controller*
Mike Leclair, *Regl Sales Mgr*
EMP: 60
SQ FT: 30,884
SALES (est): 38.6MM **Privately Held**
SIC: 2834 Pharmaceutical preparations

(P-8049)
OCULEVE INC
4410 Rosewood Dr, Pleasanton (94588-3050)
PHONE..................................415 745-3784
Michael D Ackermann, *President*
EMP: 15
SALES (est): 3.5MM **Privately Held**
SIC: 2834 Pharmaceutical preparations
PA: Allergan Public Limited Company
Clonshaugh Business And Technology Park
Dublin

(P-8050)
OCUNEXUS THERAPEUTICS INC
12481 High Bluff Dr D, San Diego (92130-3585)
PHONE..................................858 480-2403
Bradford J Duft, *President*
Tracey Sunderland, *COO*
David Paul, *CFO*
David Pool, *CFO*
David E Eisenbud, *Officer*
EMP: 14
SALES (est): 2.2MM **Privately Held**
SIC: 2834 Pharmaceutical preparations

(P-8051)
ODONATE THERAPEUTICS INC
4747 Executive Dr Ste 510, San Diego (92121-3100)
PHONE..................................858 731-8180
Kevin C Tang, *Ch of Bd*
John G Lemkey, *COO*
Michael Hearne, *CFO*
Jeff L Vacirca, *Vice Ch Bd*
Joseph P O'Connell, *Chief Mktg Ofcr*
EMP: 130
SQ FT: 8,365
SALES (est): 1.1MM **Privately Held**
SIC: 2834 Pharmaceutical preparations

(P-8052)
ONCOMED PHARMACEUTICALS INC
800 Chesapeake Dr, Redwood City (94063-4748)
PHONE..................................650 995-8200
Denise Scots-Knight, *CEO*
EMP: 56
SQ FT: 45,690
SALES: 44.4MM **Privately Held**
WEB: www.oncomed.com
SIC: 2834 Pharmaceutical preparations
HQ: Mereo Us Holdings Inc.
800 Chesapeake Dr
Redwood City CA 94063
650 995-8200

(P-8053)
ONCTERNAL THERAPEUTICS INC (PA)
12230 El Camino Real, San Diego (92130-2090)
PHONE..................................858 434-1113
James B Breitmeyer, *President*
David F Hale, *Ch of Bd*
Richard G Vincent, *CFO*
Frank Hsu, *Officer*
Rajesh Krishnan, *Senior VP*
EMP: 21 EST: 1997
SALES (est): 2.5MM **Publicly Held**
WEB: www.gtxinc.com
SIC: 2834 8733 Pharmaceutical preparations; medical research

(P-8054)
ONYX PHARMACEUTICALS INC
1 Amgen Center Dr, Newbury Park (91320-1730)
PHONE..................................650 266-0000
Pablo Cagnoni, *President*
Helen Torley, *COO*
Matthew K Fust, *CFO*
Juergen Lasowski PHD, *Exec VP*
Suzanne M Shema Jdl, *Exec VP*
EMP: 741
SQ FT: 297,111
SALES (est): 228.8MM
SALES (corp-wide): 23.7B **Publicly Held**
WEB: www.onyx-pharm.com
SIC: 2834 8049 Drugs affecting parasitic & infective diseases; occupational therapist
PA: Amgen Inc.
1 Amgen Center Dr
Thousand Oaks CA 91320
805 447-1000

(P-8055)
OPIANT PHARMACEUTICALS INC
201 Santa Monica Blvd # 500, Santa Monica (90401-2213)
PHONE..................................310 598-5410
Roger Crystal, *CEO*
David O'Toole, *CFO*
Aziz Mottiwala, *Ch Credit Ofcr*
Phil Skolnick, *Officer*
Rahsaan Thompson, *General Counsel*
EMP: 16
SQ FT: 1,500
SALES: 13.9MM **Privately Held**
SIC: 2834 Pharmaceutical preparations

(P-8056)
OREXIGEN THERAPEUTICS INC
3344 N Torrey Pines Ct # 200, La Jolla (92037-1024)
PHONE..................................858 875-8600
Thomas P Lynch, *President*
Lota S Zoth, *Ch of Bd*
Tom Lynch, *Exec VP*
Daniel Cooper, *Vice Pres*
Armando Cortes, *Vice Pres*
EMP: 100
SQ FT: 29,935
SALES: 33.7MM
SALES (corp-wide): 1.3MM **Publicly Held**
WEB: www.robinson-pilaw.com
SIC: 2834 Pharmaceutical preparations
HQ: Nalpropion Pharmaceuticals, Inc.
10 N Park Pl Ste 201
Morristown NJ 07960
858 875-8600

(P-8057)
ORIC PHARMACEUTICALS INC
240 E Grand Ave, South San Francisco (94080-4811)
PHONE..................................650 918-8818
Jacob Chacko, *CEO*
Rich Heyman, *Ch of Bd*
Dominic Piscitelli, *CFO*
Pratik Multani, *Chief Mktg Ofcr*
Leonard Reyno, *Chief Mktg Ofcr*
EMP: 34
SALES (est): 8.4MM **Privately Held**
SIC: 2834 Pharmaceutical preparations

(P-8058)
OTONOMY INC
4796 Executive Dr, San Diego (92121-3090)
PHONE..................................619 323-2200
David A Weber, *President*
Jay Lichter, *Ch of Bd*
Paul E Cayer, *CFO*
Kathie Bishop, *Security Dir*
Robert Michael Savel II, *CTO*
EMP: 53
SQ FT: 62,000
SALES: 745K **Privately Held**
SIC: 2834 8731 Pharmaceutical preparations; biological research

(P-8059)
P & L DEVELOPMENT LLC
Also Called: Pl Development
11840 Alameda St, Lynwood (90262-4019)
PHONE..................................310 763-1377
James L Medford, *President*
EMP: 30 **Privately Held**

SIC: 2834 Pharmaceutical preparations
PA: P & L Development, Llc
609 Cantiague Rock Rd 2a
Westbury NY 11590

(P-8060)
PACIFIC PHARMASCIENCE INC
23052 Alcalde Dr Ste A, Laguna Hills
(92653-1327)
PHONE.....................................949 916-6955
Robert L Orr, *President*
EMP: 10
SALES (est): 1.3MM Privately Held
SIC: 2834 8748 Pharmaceutical preparations; testing services

(P-8061)
PACIFIC SHORE HOLDINGS INC
Also Called: Nature-Cide
8236 Remmet Ave, Canoga Park
(91304-4156)
PHONE.....................................818 998-0996
Matthew Mills, *President*
Ronald J Tchorzewski, *CFO*
David E Toomey, *Exec VP*
Jennifer Mills, *Admin Sec*
▲ EMP: 12
SQ FT: 13,000
SALES (est): 2.6MM Privately Held
SIC: 2834 2879 Pharmaceutical preparations; pesticides, agricultural or household
PA: Med-X, Inc.
8236 Remmet Ave
Canoga Park CA 91304
818 349-2870

(P-8062)
PACIRA PHARMACEUTICALS INC
10450 Science Center Dr, San Diego
(92121-1119)
PHONE.....................................858 678-3950
Dave Stack, *President*
James S Scibetta, *CFO*
Taunia Markvicka, *Senior VP*
Gordon Schooley, *Senior VP*
Richard Scranton, *Vice Pres*
▲ EMP: 80
SQ FT: 82,000
SALES (est): 26.9MM Publicly Held
SIC: 2834 Pharmaceutical preparations
PA: Pacira Pharmaceuticals, Inc.
5 Sylvan Way Ste 300
Parsippany NJ 07054

(P-8063)
PEARL MANAGEMENT GROUP INC
14950 Delano St, Van Nuys (91411-2122)
PHONE.....................................818 217-0218
Michael Ben Perlman, *Branch Mgr*
EMP: 23
SALES (corp-wide): 2.9MM Privately Held
SIC: 2834 Pharmaceutical preparations
PA: Pearl Management Group Inc.
3217 Oakley Dr
Los Angeles CA 90068
818 383-0095

(P-8064)
PEGASUS MED SERVICES/RENALAB
3570 Sibley Ln, Templeton (93465-9472)
PHONE.....................................805 226-8350
Gil McGuff, *President*
EMP: 15
SALES (est): 1.2MM Privately Held
SIC: 2834 Pharmaceutical preparations

(P-8065)
PEREZ DISTRIBUTING FRESNO INC (PA)
103 S Academy Ave, Sanger (93657-2428)
P.O. Box 579 (93657-0579)
PHONE.....................................800 638-3512
Emeterio P Perez, *President*
Alma Perez, *Vice Pres*
▲ EMP: 27
SQ FT: 16,000

SALES (est): 4.9MM Privately Held
WEB: www.perezdistfresno.com
SIC: 2834 Druggists' preparations (pharmaceuticals)

(P-8066)
PFENEX INC
10790 Roselle St, San Diego (92121-1508)
PHONE.....................................858 352-4400
Jason Grenfell-Gardner, *Ch of Bd*
Evert B Schimmelpennink, *President*
Shawn A Scranton, *COO*
Susan A Knudson, *CFO*
Paul Wagner, *CFO*
EMP: 67
SQ FT: 46,959
SALES: 14.8MM Privately Held
SIC: 2834 Pharmaceutical preparations

(P-8067)
PFIZER HEALTH SOLUTIONS INC
2400 Broadway Ste 500, Santa Monica
(90404-3072)
PHONE.....................................310 586-2550
Alan Lang, *Branch Mgr*
EMP: 10
SALES (corp-wide): 53.6B Publicly Held
SIC: 2834 Pharmaceutical preparations
HQ: Pfizer Health Solutions Inc
150 E 42nd St Bsmt 2
New York NY 10017
314 274-1360

(P-8068)
PFIZER INC
11095 Torreyana Rd, San Diego
(92121-1104)
PHONE.....................................858 622-7325
Cheryl Garner, *Manager*
Rick Bailey, *VP Human Res*
EMP: 148
SALES (corp-wide): 53.6B Publicly Held
SIC: 2834 Pharmaceutical preparations
PA: Pfizer Inc.
235 E 42nd St
New York NY 10017
212 733-2323

(P-8069)
PFIZER INC
10646 Science Center Dr, San Diego
(92121-1150)
PHONE.....................................858 622-3001
Mary Mateja, *Manager*
Ying Jiang, *Research*
Cory Painter, *Research*
Max Parker, *Research*
Stephanie Salts, *Research*
EMP: 2000
SALES (corp-wide): 53.6B Publicly Held
WEB: www.pfizer.com
SIC: 2834 Pharmaceutical preparations
PA: Pfizer Inc.
235 E 42nd St
New York NY 10017
212 733-2323

(P-8070)
PH LABS ADVANCED NUTRITION
9760 Via De La Amistad, San Diego
(92154-7210)
PHONE.....................................619 240-3263
EMP: 11 EST: 2014
SALES (est): 1.8MM Privately Held
SIC: 2834 Druggists' preparations (pharmaceuticals)

(P-8071)
PHARMA ALLIANCE GROUP INC
Also Called: Lab Ecx.com
28518 Constellation Rd, Valencia
(91355-5082)
PHONE.....................................661 294-7955
Marvin Delgado, *President*
Amit Marfatia, *Vice Pres*
Bharat Zaveri, *Vice Pres*
Vilma Delgado, *Admin Sec*
◆ EMP: 13
SQ FT: 4,000
SALES (est): 3MM Privately Held
SIC: 2834 Pharmaceutical preparations

(P-8072)
PHARMACEUTIC LITHO LABEL INC
3990 Royal Ave, Simi Valley (93063-3380)
PHONE.....................................805 285-5162
Timothy Laurence, *President*
Tom Moore, *President*
Rick Machale, *Vice Pres*
Diana Fonseca, *Asst Controller*
Lyuba Ross, *Controller*
▲ EMP: 85
SQ FT: 32,000
SALES (est): 35MM Privately Held
WEB: www.pharmaceuticlitho.com
SIC: 2834 Pharmaceutical preparations

(P-8073)
PHARMACYCLICS LLC (HQ)
995 E Arques Ave, Sunnyvale
(94085-4521)
PHONE.....................................408 215-3000
Wulff-Erik Von Borcke, *President*
Sumita Ray, *Officer*
Ramses Erdtmann, *Exec VP*
Gregory Hemmi, *Vice Pres*
Christine Huh, *Vice Pres*
EMP: 208
SALES (est): 385.8MM
SALES (corp-wide): 32.7B Publicly Held
SIC: 2834 Pharmaceutical preparations
PA: Abbvie Inc.
1 N Waukegan Rd
North Chicago IL 60064
847 932-7900

(P-8074)
PHATHOM PHARMACEUTICALS INC
70 Willow Rd Ste 200, Menlo Park
(94025-3652)
PHONE.....................................650 325-5156
David Socks, *CEO*
EMP: 12
SALES (est): 793.1K Privately Held
SIC: 2834 Pharmaceutical preparations

(P-8075)
PHOENIX PHARMACEUTICALS INC
330 Beach Rd, Burlingame (94010-2004)
PHONE.....................................650 558-8898
Jaw-Kang Chang, *President*
Eng Tau, *COO*
Chang Jaw, *Info Tech Dir*
Laurent Ginestet-Araki, *Technical Staff*
Chentao Wang, *Marketing Mgr*
EMP: 20
SQ FT: 5,000
SALES (est): 7MM Privately Held
WEB: www.phoenixpeptide.com
SIC: 2834 8731 Pharmaceutical preparations; commercial physical research

(P-8076)
PHYTO TECH CORP
Also Called: Blue California Company
30111 Tomas, Rcho STA Marg
(92688-2125)
PHONE.....................................949 635-1990
Steven Chen, *President*
▲ EMP: 25
SQ FT: 50,000
SALES (est): 6.1MM Privately Held
SIC: 2834 Vitamin, nutrient & hematinic preparations for human use

(P-8077)
PIONYR IMMUNOTHERAPEUTICS INC
953 Indiana St, San Francisco
(94107-3007)
PHONE.....................................415 226-7503
Steven P James, *President*
Alicia Levey, *Officer*
Kevin Baker, *Senior VP*
Monte Montgomery, *Senior VP*
Leonard Reyno, *Senior VP*
EMP: 17
SALES (est): 5MM Privately Held
SIC: 2834 Pharmaceutical preparations

(P-8078)
PLEXXIKON INC
91 Bolivar Dr, Berkeley (94710-2210)
PHONE.....................................510 647-4000

Gideon Bollag, *CEO*
Paul Lin, *COO*
Joseph Young, *Treasurer*
Edward Mathers, *Bd of Directors*
Keith B Nolop MD, *Chief Mktg Ofcr*
EMP: 44
SQ FT: 10,000
SALES (est): 13.4MM Privately Held
WEB: www.plexxicon.com
SIC: 2834 Tablets, pharmaceutical
PA: Daiichi Sankyo Company, Limited
3-5-1, Nihombashihoncho
Chuo-Ku TKY 103-0

(P-8079)
POLARIS PHARMACEUTICALS INC
9373 Towne Centre Dr # 150, San Diego
(92121-3027)
PHONE.....................................858 452-6688
Bor Wen Wu, *CEO*
Shaw T Chen, *Exec VP*
John Bomalaski, *Vice Pres*
Chang Philip, *Exec Dir*
Richard Showalter, *Exec Dir*
EMP: 28
SALES: 6MM Privately Held
SIC: 2834 Pharmaceutical preparations

(P-8080)
PORTOLA PHARMACEUTICALS INC (PA)
270 E Grand Ave, South San Francisco
(94080-4811)
PHONE.....................................650 246-7300
Scott Garland, *CEO*
Mardi C Dier, *CFO*
Sheldon Koenig, *Ch Credit Ofcr*
David Stump, *Bd of Directors*
Ernie Meyer, *Officer*
EMP: 148
SQ FT: 74,000
SALES: 40.1MM Publicly Held
SIC: 2834 Pharmaceutical preparations

(P-8081)
PREFERRED PHARMACEUTICALS INC
1250 N Lakeview Ave Ste O, Anaheim
(92807-1801)
PHONE.....................................714 777-3729
Robert Kent, *President*
Mike Kent, *Vice Pres*
EMP: 10
SALES (est): 2.6MM Privately Held
SIC: 2834 Pharmaceutical preparations

(P-8082)
PRESIDIO PHARMACEUTICALS INC
1700 Owens St Ste 585, San Francisco
(94158-0008)
PHONE.....................................415 655-7560
Leo Redmond, *President*
H Daniel Perez, *President*
EMP: 19
SQ FT: 8,000
SALES (est): 3.4MM Privately Held
WEB: www.presidiopharma.com
SIC: 2834 Pharmaceutical preparations

(P-8083)
PRIMAPHARMA INC
3443 Tripp Ct, San Diego (92121-1032)
PHONE.....................................858 259-0969
Mark Livingston, *President*
Larry Braga, *Vice Pres*
Tony Dziabo, *Vice Pres*
Sarah Dziabo, *Associate Dir*
Nayaz Ahmed, *Director*
EMP: 35
SQ FT: 24,000
SALES: 5.2MM Privately Held
SIC: 2834 Pharmaceutical preparations

(P-8084)
PRINCIPIA BIOPHARMA INC
220 E Grand Ave, South San Francisco
(94080-4811)
PHONE.....................................650 416-7700
Martin Babler, *President*
Alan B Colowick, *Ch of Bd*
Christopher Y Chai, *CFO*
Dolca Thomas, *Chief Mktg Ofcr*

▲ = Import ▼=Export
◆ =Import/Export

Roy Hardiman, *Officer*
EMP: 69 **EST:** 2011
SQ FT: 47,500
SALES: 69.1MM **Privately Held**
SIC: 2834 Pharmaceutical preparations

(P-8085)
PRO-FORM MANUFACTURING LLC
Also Called: Pro-Form Laboratories
5001 Industrial Way, Benicia (94510-1017)
PHONE..................................707 752-9010
EMP: 124
SALES (est): 3.8MM **Privately Held**
SIC: 2834 5499 5149 Vitamin preparations; health & dietetic food stores; organic & diet foods

(P-8086)
PROMETHEUS BIOSCIENCES INC
9410 Carroll Park Dr, San Diego (92121-5201)
PHONE..................................858 200-7888
Mark C McKenna, *CEO*
Mike Walther, *Ch Credit Ofcr*
EMP: 20
SALES (est): 131.8K **Privately Held**
SIC: 2834 Pharmaceutical preparations

(P-8087)
PROMETHEUS LABORATORIES INC
9410 Carroll Park Dr, San Diego (92121-5201)
PHONE..................................858 824-0895
Warren Cresswell, *CEO*
Jenny Alonso, *Vice Pres*
Robert Carlson, *Vice Pres*
Larry Mimms PHD, *Vice Pres*
Frederick Fletcher, *Vice Pres*
EMP: 405
SQ FT: 99,000
SALES (est): 125.2MM
SALES (corp-wide): 92B **Privately Held**
WEB: www.prometheuslabs.com
SIC: 2834 8011 Pharmaceutical preparations; offices & clinics of medical doctors
HQ: Nestle Health Science Sa
Batiment 4
Epalinges VD 1066
216 326-100

(P-8088)
PROTAB LABORATORIES
25902 Towne Centre Dr, Foothill Ranch (92610-3436)
PHONE..................................949 635-1930
Min W Chen, *CEO*
Xiao Zhou, *Co-Owner*
Shafiqul Islam, *Vice Pres*
Randy L Pollan, *Vice Pres*
Joanne Hsu, *Administration*
▲ **EMP:** 60
SQ FT: 100,000
SALES (est): 15.7MM **Privately Held**
SIC: 2834 Vitamin preparations

(P-8089)
PROTAGONIST THERAPEUTICS INC
7707 Gateway Blvd Ste 140, Newark (94560-1160)
PHONE..................................510 474-0170
Dinesh V Patel, *President*
Harold E Selick, *Ch of Bd*
Donald Kalkofen, *CFO*
Suneel Gupta, *Officer*
David Y Liu, *Security Dir*
EMP: 62
SQ FT: 42,877
SALES: 30.9MM **Privately Held**
SIC: 2834 8731 Pharmaceutical preparations; commercial physical research

(P-8090)
PUMA BIOTECHNOLOGY INC (PA)
10880 Wilshire Blvd # 2150, Los Angeles (90024-4106)
P.O. Box 64945, Saint Paul MN (55164-0945)
PHONE..................................424 248-6500
Alan H Auerbach, *Ch of Bd*
Charles R Eyler, *Treasurer*

Steven Lo, *Ch Credit Ofcr*
Jay Moyes, *Bd of Directors*
Troy Wilson, *Bd of Directors*
EMP: 69
SQ FT: 25,700
SALES: 250.9MM **Publicly Held**
SIC: 2834 Pharmaceutical preparations

(P-8091)
PURETEK CORPORATION
7900 Nelson Rd Unit A, Panorama City (91402-6828)
PHONE..................................818 361-3949
Jeff Pressman, *Branch Mgr*
EMP: 130
SALES (est): 17MM **Privately Held**
SIC: 2834 2844 Pharmaceutical preparations; cosmetic preparations
PA: Puretek Corporation
1145 Arroyo St Ste D
San Fernando CA 91340

(P-8092)
PURETEK CORPORATION (PA)
1145 Arroyo St Ste D, San Fernando (91340-1839)
PHONE..................................818 361-3316
Barry Pressman, *CEO*
Jeff Pressman, *Info Tech Mgr*
Nicki Chew, *Research*
Ann Huang, *Research*
Maria Gutierrez, *Business Mgr*
◆ **EMP:** 50
SQ FT: 114,000
SALES: 38MM **Privately Held**
WEB: www.pharmapure.net
SIC: 2834 Pharmaceutical preparations

(P-8093)
QUANTICEL PHARMACUETICALS INC
9393 Towne Centre Dr # 110, San Diego (92121-3070)
PHONE..................................858 956-3747
Steve Kaldor, *Branch Mgr*
EMP: 20 **Privately Held**
SIC: 2834 Pharmaceutical preparations
PA: Quanticel Pharmacueticals, Inc.
1500 Owens St Ste 500
San Francisco CA 94158

(P-8094)
QUARK PHARMACEUTICALS INC (DH)
7999 Gateway Blvd Ste 310, Newark (94560-1188)
PHONE..................................510 402-4020
Daniel Zurr, *President*
Philip B Simon, *Ch of Bd*
Rami Skaliter, *COO*
Joseph Rubinfeld, *Vice Ch Bd*
Elena Feinstein, *Officer*
EMP: 25
SALES (est): 7.4MM **Privately Held**
WEB: www.qbi.co.il
SIC: 2834 Pharmaceutical preparations

(P-8095)
QUOREX PHARM INC (PA)
2232 Rutherford Rd, Carlsbad (92008-8814)
PHONE..................................760 602-1910
Robert Robb, *President*
Gary JG Atkinson, *CFO*
Krzysztof Appelt, *Exec VP*
Jeffrey Stein, *Exec VP*
Donald Mc Carthy, *Controller*
EMP: 42
SQ FT: 23,500
SALES (est): 2.8MM **Privately Held**
SIC: 2834 Pharmaceutical preparations

(P-8096)
RAFFAELLO RESEARCH LABS
120 The Village Unit 109, Redondo Beach (90277-2561)
PHONE..................................310 618-8754
Rafael Akyuz, *President*
Linda Akyuz, *Treasurer*
EMP: 15
SQ FT: 12,500
SALES (est): 1.8MM **Privately Held**
SIC: 2834 Pharmaceutical preparations

(P-8097)
RANDAL OPTIMAL NUTRIENTS LLC
Also Called: Vimco
1595 Hampton Way, Santa Rosa (95407-6844)
P.O. Box 7328 (95407-0328)
PHONE..................................707 528-1800
William A Robotham, *President*
Lynn J Brinker, *Corp Secy*
Donna Coats, *Vice Pres*
Linda Aceves, *Purchasing*
EMP: 32
SQ FT: 22,500
SALES (est): 8.3MM **Privately Held**
WEB: www.randalnutritional.com
SIC: 2834 5122 Vitamin preparations; drugs, proprietaries & sundries

(P-8098)
RAPT THERAPEUTICS INC
561 Eccles Ave, South San Francisco (94080-1906)
PHONE..................................650 489-9000
Brian Wong, *President*
Eric Hall, *CFO*
William Ho, *Chief Mktg Ofcr*
David Wustrow, *Senior VP*
Paul Kassner, *Vice Pres*
EMP: 62
SQ FT: 36,754
SALES (est): 17.5MM **Privately Held**
SIC: 2834 8731 Pharmaceutical preparations; biotechnical research, commercial

(P-8099)
RAPTOR PHARMACEUTICALS INC
7 Hamilton Landing # 100, Novato (94949-8209)
PHONE..................................415 408-6200
Julie Anne Smith, *CEO*
Rick Timmers, *Business Mgr*
EMP: 28 **EST:** 2005
SALES (est): 57.1K **Privately Held**
SIC: 2834 Pharmaceutical preparations
HQ: Horizon Pharmaceutical Llc
7 Hamilton Landing # 100
Novato CA 94949

(P-8100)
RECEPTOS INC
3033 Science Park Rd # 300, San Diego (92121-1166)
PHONE..................................858 652-5700
Faheem Hasnain, *President*
Graham Cooper, *CFO*
Marcus F Boehm, *Founder*
Shiela Gujrathi, *Chief Mktg Ofcr*
Christian Wego, *Senior VP*
EMP: 32
SALES: 5.9MM
SALES (corp-wide): 15.2B **Privately Held**
SIC: 2834 Pharmaceutical preparations
PA: Celgene Corporation
86 Morris Ave
Summit NJ 07901
908 673-9000

(P-8101)
REDWOOD SCIENTIFIC TECH INC
11450 Sheldon St, Sun Valley (91352-1121)
PHONE..................................310 693-5401
Jason E Cardiff, *President*
Jacques Poujade, *Treasurer*
M Salah Zaki, *Chief Mktg Ofcr*
Eunjung Cardiff, *Admin Sec*
Rhonda Pearlman, *General Counsel*
EMP: 24
SALES (est): 667.1K **Privately Held**
SIC: 2834 Druggists' preparations (pharmaceuticals)

(P-8102)
RELYPSA INC
100 Cardinal Way, Redwood City (94063-4755)
PHONE..................................650 421-9500
John A Orwin, *CEO*
Patrick Treanor, *President*
Kristine M Ball, *CFO*
Lance Berman, *Officer*

Stephen D Harrison, *Officer*
EMP: 406
SQ FT: 93,904
SALES: 18.5MM
SALES (corp-wide): 1.5B **Privately Held**
WEB: www.relypsa.com
SIC: 2834 Pharmaceutical preparations
PA: Vifor Pharma Ag
Rechenstrasse 37
St. Gallen SG 9014
588 518-484

(P-8103)
RESEARCH WAY LL LLC
Also Called: Research Way Partners
1900 Main St Ste 375, Irvine (92614-7332)
PHONE..................................608 830-6300
Justin Komppa, *Senior Partner*
EMP: 14
SALES (est): 682K **Privately Held**
SIC: 2834 Tablets, pharmaceutical

(P-8104)
RETROPHIN INC (PA)
3721 Vly Cntre Dr Ste 200, San Diego (92130)
PHONE..................................760 260-8600
Eric Dube, *President*
Neil F McFarlane, *COO*
Laura M Clague, *CFO*
Peter Heerma, *Ch Credit Ofcr*
Noah L Rosenberg, *Officer*
EMP: 92
SQ FT: 23,107
SALES: 164.2MM **Publicly Held**
SIC: 2834 8731 Pharmaceutical preparations; biotechnical research, commercial

(P-8105)
REVANCE THERAPEUTICS INC
7555 Gateway Blvd, Newark (94560-1152)
PHONE..................................510 742-3400
Mark Foley, *President*
Abhay Joshi, *COO*
Tobin C Schilke, *CFO*
Todd E Zavodnick, *Ch Credit Ofcr*
Robert Byrnes, *Bd of Directors*
EMP: 134
SQ FT: 90,000
SALES: 3.7MM **Privately Held**
WEB: www.revance.com
SIC: 2834 Pharmaceutical preparations

(P-8106)
REZOLUTE INC (PA)
570 El Camino Rd, Redwood City (94063)
PHONE..................................303 222-2128
Nevan C Elam, *Ch of Bd*
Keith Vendola, *CFO*
Hoyoung Huh, *Vice Ch Bd*
Sankaram Mantripragada, *Security Dir*
EMP: 20 **EST:** 2010
SQ FT: 27,000
SALES (est): 4.3MM **Publicly Held**
SIC: 2834 Pharmaceutical preparations

(P-8107)
RIGEL PHARMACEUTICALS INC (PA)
1180 Veterans Blvd, South San Francisco (94080-1985)
PHONE..................................650 624-1100
Raul R Rodriguez, *President*
Dean Schorno, *CFO*
Eldon C Mayer III, *Ch Credit Ofcr*
Bradford S Goodwin, *Bd of Directors*
Elliott B Grossbard, *Chief Mktg Ofcr*
EMP: 126
SQ FT: 147,000
SALES: 44.5MM **Publicly Held**
WEB: www.rigel.com
SIC: 2834 8733 Pharmaceutical preparations; medical research

(P-8108)
RINAT NEUROSCIENCE CORP
230 E Grand Ave, South San Francisco (94080-4811)
PHONE..................................650 615-7300
Patrick Lynn, *President*
Arnon Rosenthal, *CTO*
C Fletcher Payne, *Finance*
EMP: 16

PRODUCTS & SVCS

SALES (est): 3.3MM
SALES (corp-wide): 53.6B **Publicly Held**
WEB: www.rinatneuro.com
SIC: 2834 Druggists' preparations (pharmaceuticals)
PA: Pfizer Inc.
　235 E 42nd St
　New York NY 10017
　212 733-2323

(P-8109)
ROBINSON PHARMA INC
3701 W Warner Ave, Santa Ana (92704-5218)
PHONE..........................714 241-0235
Tam H Nguyen, *CEO*
EMP: 65 **Privately Held**
SIC: 2834 7389 Pharmaceutical preparations; packaging & labeling services
PA: Robinson Pharma, Inc.
　3330 S Harbor Blvd
　Santa Ana CA 92704

(P-8110)
ROBINSON PHARMA INC (PA)
3330 S Harbor Blvd, Santa Ana (92704-6831)
PHONE..........................714 241-0235
Tam H Nguyen, *CEO*
Tuong Nguyen, *President*
Rebecca Castillo, *Vice Pres*
Zue Delaney, *Vice Pres*
Shah Neil, *Vice Pres*
◆ **EMP:** 310
SQ FT: 124,000
SALES (est): 149.8MM **Privately Held**
WEB: www.robinsonpharma.com
SIC: 2834 Vitamin preparations

(P-8111)
ROBINSON PHARMA INC
2811 S Harbor Blvd, Santa Ana (92704-5805)
PHONE..........................714 241-0235
Tam Nguyen, *President*
EMP: 102 **Privately Held**
SIC: 2834 Pharmaceutical preparations
PA: Robinson Pharma, Inc.
　3330 S Harbor Blvd
　Santa Ana CA 92704

(P-8112)
ROCHE MOLECULAR SYSTEMS INC
1145 Atlantic Ave Ste 100, Alameda (94501-1145)
PHONE..........................510 814-2800
Terrance Taford, *Branch Mgr*
EMP: 135
SALES (corp-wide): 57.2B **Privately Held**
SIC: 2834 Pharmaceutical preparations
HQ: Roche Molecular Systems, Inc.
　4300 Hacienda Dr
　Pleasanton CA 94588

(P-8113)
ROCHE MOLECULAR SYSTEMS INC (DH)
4300 Hacienda Dr, Pleasanton (94588-2722)
P.O. Box 9002 (94566-9002)
PHONE..........................925 730-8000
Paul Brown, *President*
Donald Cole, *Information Mgr*
Peggy Gore, *Information Mgr*
Michael Fellenzer, *Technology*
Isabelle Dauphin, *Technical Staff*
◆ **EMP:** 400
SALES (est): 336.1MM
SALES (corp-wide): 57.2B **Privately Held**
SIC: 2834 Pharmaceutical preparations
HQ: Roche Holdings, Inc.
　1 Dna Way
　South San Francisco CA 94080
　650 225-1000

(P-8114)
ROCHE PHARMACEUTICALS
4300 Hacienda Dr, Pleasanton (94588-2722)
PHONE..........................908 635-5692
Fidel Fampo, *Principal*
Yimin Wang, *Officer*

Eslie Dennis, *Vice Pres*
Maria Horga, *Vice Pres*
Walter Koch, *Vice Pres*
EMP: 37
SALES (est): 4.5MM **Privately Held**
SIC: 2834 Pharmaceutical preparations

(P-8115)
ROSE CHEM INTL - USA CORP
25 Rainbow Fls, Irvine (92603-3439)
PHONE..........................678 510-8864
Minh Nguyen Thi Thanh, *CEO*
Son Ngoc Ha, *CFO*
Lich Thi Thanh Nguyen, *Admin Sec*
EMP: 30 **EST:** 2015
SALES (est): 1.3MM **Privately Held**
SIC: 2834 Pharmaceutical preparations

(P-8116)
RXD NOVA PHARMACEUTICALS INC
2010 Cessna Dr, Vacaville (95688-8712)
PHONE..........................610 952-7242
Jianning Liu, *CEO*
EMP: 15 **EST:** 2017
SALES (est): 2.7MM **Privately Held**
SIC: 2834 Pharmaceutical preparations

(P-8117)
SAMSON PHARMACEUTICALS INC
2027 Leo Ave, Commerce (90040-1626)
PHONE..........................323 722-3066
Jay Kassir, *President*
Kevin Yan, *QA Dir*
Kakeena Pina, *Research*
Jennifer Chan, *Marketing Staff*
Elsa Sanchez, *Sales Staff*
▲ **EMP:** 40
SALES (est): 9.3MM **Privately Held**
SIC: 2834 Pharmaceutical preparations

(P-8118)
SANOFI US SERVICES INC
185 Berry St, San Francisco (94107-5705)
PHONE..........................415 856-5000
EMP: 136
SALES (corp-wide): 609.6MM **Privately Held**
SIC: 2834
HQ: Sanofi Us Services Inc.
　55 Corporate Dr
　Bridgewater NJ 08807
　336 407-4994

(P-8119)
SANTA CRUZ NUTRITIONALS
2200 Delaware Ave, Santa Cruz (95060-5707)
PHONE..........................831 457-3200
Michael Westhusing, *CEO*
Randy Bridges, *COO*
Matt Kemme, *Senior VP*
Anthony Romaine, *Info Tech Mgr*
▲ **EMP:** 400
SQ FT: 200,000
SALES (est): 212MM **Privately Held**
WEB: www.harmonyfoods.com
SIC: 2834 2064 Vitamin, nutrient & hematinic preparations for human use; candy & other confectionery products

(P-8120)
SANTARUS INC
3611 Vly Cntre Dr Ste 400, San Diego (92130)
PHONE..........................858 314-5700
Blake Boland, *Principal*
EMP: 20
SALES (est): 2.7MM **Privately Held**
SIC: 2834 5122 Pharmaceutical preparations; pharmaceuticals

(P-8121)
SATSUMA PHARMACEUTICALS INC
400 Oyster Point Blvd # 221, South San Francisco (94080-1952)
PHONE..........................650 410-3200
John Kollins, *President*
Tom O'Neil, *CFO*
Detlef Albrecht, *Chief Mktg Ofcr*
Mic Iwashima, *Vice Pres*
Robert Schultz, *Vice Pres*
EMP: 11

SQ FT: 4,148
SALES (est): 265.2K **Privately Held**
SIC: 2834 Pharmaceutical preparations

(P-8122)
SCICLONE PHARMACEUTICALS INC (HQ)
950 Tower Ln Ste 900, Foster City (94404-2125)
PHONE..........................650 358-3456
Friedhelm Blobel, *President*
Wilson W Cheung, *CFO*
Carey Chern, *Ch Credit Ofcr*
Raymond A Low, *Controller*
EMP: 40
SQ FT: 11,900
SALES: 160.1MM **Privately Held**
WEB: www.scln.com
SIC: 2834 Druggists' preparations (pharmaceuticals)

(P-8123)
SENJU USA INC
21700 Oxnard St Ste 1070, Woodland Hills (91367-8103)
PHONE..........................818 719-7190
AG Katayama, *President*
EMP: 15
SALES (est): 2.6MM **Privately Held**
SIC: 2834 Druggists' preparations (pharmaceuticals)
PA: Senju Pharmaceutical Co.,Ltd.
　3-1-9, Kawaramachi, Chuo-Ku
　Osaka OSK 541-0

(P-8124)
SENSORY NEUROSTIMULATION INC
Also Called: Relaxis
　1235 Puerta Del Sol # 600, San Clemente (92673-6309)
PHONE..........................949 492-0550
Fred Burbank, *CEO*
Michael Jones, *COO*
Tiffany Jones, *Consultant*
EMP: 11
SQ FT: 4,000
SALES: 60K **Privately Held**
SIC: 2834 5122 Druggists' preparations (pharmaceuticals); drugs & drug proprietaries

(P-8125)
SENTYNL THERAPEUTICS INC
420 Stevens Ave Ste 200, Solana Beach (92075-2078)
PHONE..........................888 227-8725
Matt Heck, *CEO*
Daniel Stokely, *CFO*
Paul Maccini, *Officer*
Shawn Scranton, *Officer*
Michael Hercz, *Vice Pres*
EMP: 30 **EST:** 2011
SALES: 50MM
SALES (corp-wide): 875.9MM **Privately Held**
SIC: 2834 Pharmaceutical preparations
PA: Cadila Healthcare Limited
　Zydus Corporate Park,Scheme No. 63,
　Survey No. 536,
　Ahmedabad GJ 38248
　792 686-8100

(P-8126)
SEYCHELLE ENVMTL TECH INC
32963 Calle Perfecto, San Juan Capistrano (92675-4705)
PHONE..........................949 234-1999
Carl Palmer, *Branch Mgr*
EMP: 14 **Publicly Held**
SIC: 2834 Chlorination tablets & kits (water purification)
PA: Seychelle Environmental Technologies, Inc.
　22 Journey
　Aliso Viejo CA 92656

(P-8127)
SHIRE
1445 Lawrence Dr, Newbury Park (91320-1311)
PHONE..........................805 372-3000
John Sandstrom, *Principal*
Jimmy Vu, *Technical Staff*

Chris Lewallyn, *Director*
Bill Krosky, *Manager*
EMP: 12
SALES (est): 2MM **Privately Held**
SIC: 2834 Pharmaceutical preparations

(P-8128)
SHIRE RGENERATIVE MEDICINE INC
10933 N Torrey Pines Rd # 200, La Jolla (92037-1054)
PHONE..........................858 202-0673
Jennifer Cassidy, *Branch Mgr*
EMP: 20
SALES (corp-wide): 15.1B **Privately Held**
SIC: 2834 Pharmaceutical preparations
HQ: Shire Regenerative Medicine, Inc.
　36 Church Ln
　Westport CT 06880
　877 422-4463

(P-8129)
SHIRE RGENERATIVE MEDICINE INC
10933 N Torrey Pines Rd # 200, La Jolla (92037-1054)
PHONE..........................858 754-3700
EMP: 100
SALES (corp-wide): 15.1B **Privately Held**
SIC: 2834 Pharmaceutical preparations
HQ: Shire Regenerative Medicine, Inc.
　36 Church Ln
　Westport CT 06880
　877 422-4463

(P-8130)
SHIRE RGENERATIVE MEDICINE INC
Also Called: Advanced Biohealing.com
　11095 Torreyana Rd, San Diego (92121-1104)
PHONE..........................858 754-5396
Kathy McGee, *Branch Mgr*
Dean Tozer, *Senior VP*
Donald Ayers, *Manager*
EMP: 90
SALES (corp-wide): 15.1B **Privately Held**
WEB: www.advancedtissue.com
SIC: 2834 Pharmaceutical preparations
HQ: Shire Regenerative Medicine, Inc.
　36 Church Ln
　Westport CT 06880
　877 422-4463

(P-8131)
SIGNAL PHARMACEUTICALS LLC
10300 Campus Point Dr # 100, San Diego (92121-1504)
PHONE..........................858 795-4700
Alan J Lewis PHD, *President*
R Michael Gendreau, *Chief Mktg Ofcr*
Shripad Bhagwat, *Vice Pres*
David R Webb, *Vice Pres*
EMP: 134
SQ FT: 78,202
SALES (est): 21MM
SALES (corp-wide): 15.2B **Privately Held**
SIC: 2834 Pharmaceutical preparations
PA: Celgene Corporation
　86 Morris Ave
　Summit NJ 07901
　908 673-9000

(P-8132)
SILLAJEN BIOTHERAPEUTICS INC
450 Sansome St Ste 650, San Francisco (94111-3380)
PHONE..........................415 281-8886
Laurent Fischer, *President*
David H Kirn, *Chief Mktg Ofcr*
James M Burke, *Vice Pres*
Deborah Campagna, *Senior Mgr*
Robbi Sera, *Director*
EMP: 15
SALES (est): 3MM **Privately Held**
SIC: 2834 Pharmaceutical preparations
PA: Sillajen Usa, Inc.
　450 Sansome St Ste 650
　San Francisco CA 94111
　415 281-8886

▲ = Import ▼=Export
◆ =Import/Export

(P-8133)
SIMPSON INDUSTRIES INC
Also Called: Simpsonsimpson Industries
1093 E Bedmar St, Carson (90746-3601)
PHONE...................................310 605-1224
Rick Simpson, *CEO*
Robert Simpson, *COO*
EMP: 50
SALES (est): 5.7MM Privately Held
SIC: 2834 Proprietary drug products

(P-8134)
SIRNA THERAPEUTICS INC
1700 Owens St, San Francisco
(94158-0004)
PHONE...................................415 512-7200
Howard W Robin, *President*
Gregory L Weaver, *CFO*
Roberto Guerciolini, *Chief Mktg Ofcr*
Barry Polisky, *Senior VP*
J Michael French, *Development*
EMP: 68
SALES (est): 5.9MM
SALES (corp-wide): 74.9MM Publicly
Held
WEB: www.sirna.com
SIC: 2834 Pharmaceutical preparations
PA: Alnylam Pharmaceuticals, Inc.
300 3rd St Ste 3
Cambridge MA 02142
617 551-8200

(P-8135)
SKYEPHARMA INC
10450 Science Center Dr, San Diego
(92121-1119)
PHONE...................................858 678-3950
Steve Thornton, *President*
Geraldine Venthoye, *Vice Pres*
EMP: 14
SALES (est): 2.2MM Privately Held
SIC: 2834 Pharmaceutical preparations

(P-8136)
SOFT GEL TECHNOLOGIES INC
(HQ)
6982 Bandini Blvd, Commerce
(90040-3326)
PHONE...................................323 726-0700
Steve Holtby, *CEO*
Ronald Udell, *President*
Hiroshi Kishimoto, *Treasurer*
Joann Falgado, *Office Mgr*
Santiago J Hernandez, *Info Tech Mgr*
▲ EMP: 100
SQ FT: 21,000
SALES (est): 25.9MM Privately Held
WEB: www.soft-gel.com
SIC: 2834 Medicines, capsuled or ampuled

(P-8137)
SOLENO THERAPEUTICS INC
(PA)
1235 Radio Rd Ste 110, Redwood City
(94065-1315)
PHONE...................................650 213-8444
Anish Bhatnagar, *President*
Ernest Mario, *Ch of Bd*
Jonathan R Wolter, *CFO*
Marco Gutierrez, *Sales Staff*
Jeremy Chan, *Accounts Mgr*
EMP: 12 EST: 1999
SQ FT: 8,171
SALES (est): 2MM Publicly Held
WEB: www.capnia.com
SIC: 2834 Pharmaceutical preparations

(P-8138)
SOVA PHARMACEUTICALS INC
11099 N Torrey Pines Rd, La Jolla
(92037-1029)
PHONE...................................858 750-4700
Jay Lichter, *CEO*
EMP: 10
SALES (est): 1.3MM Privately Held
SIC: 2834 Pharmaceutical preparations

(P-8139)
SQUAREBAR INC
1035 22nd Ave Unit 8, Oakland
(94606-5271)
PHONE...................................530 412-0209
Alamedans Sarah, *Principal*
Andrew Gordon, *Principal*
EMP: 10

SALES (est): 1.7MM Privately Held
SIC: 2834 Vitamin, nutrient & hematinic
preparations for human use

(P-8140)
ST JUDE MEDICAL LLC
Also Called: Sjm Facility
2375 Morse Ave, Irvine (92614-6233)
PHONE...................................949 769-5000
Ron Calvarese, *Vice Pres*
Kim Nguyn, *Info Tech Mgr*
Minh Ngyuen, *Info Tech Mgr*
Jennifer Alvarado, *Technician*
Mark Vu, *Supervisor*
EMP: 25
SALES (corp-wide): 30.5B Publicly Held
SIC: 2834 Pharmaceutical preparations
HQ: St. Jude Medical, Llc
1 Saint Jude Medical Dr
Saint Paul MN 55117
651 756-2000

(P-8141)
STA PHARMACEUTICAL US LLC
6114 Nancy Ridge Dr, San Diego
(92121-3223)
PHONE...................................609 606-6499
Chen Hui, *CFO*
EMP: 40
SALES (est): 1.1MM Privately Held
SIC: 2834 Pharmaceutical preparations

(P-8142)
STANDARD HOMEOPATHIC CO
(PA)
Also Called: Hyland's Homeopathic
204 W 131st St, Los Angeles (90061-1676)
P.O. Box 61067 (90061-0067)
PHONE...................................310 768-0700
John Pborneman, *CEO*
John P Borneman III, *Ch of Bd*
Dan Krombach, *CFO*
Jeannine Taillac, *Admin Asst*
Margot Moore,
▲ EMP: 100
SQ FT: 21,000
SALES (est): 27.6MM Privately Held
WEB: www.hylands.com
SIC: 2834 5912 Pharmaceutical prepara-
tions; drug stores

(P-8143)
STANDARD HOMEOPATHIC CO
Also Called: Hyland Homeopathic
108 W Walnut St Fl 1, Gardena
(90248-3107)
PHONE...................................424 224-4127
Janet Okubo, *Principal*
EMP: 22
SALES (corp-wide): 27.6MM Privately
Held
SIC: 2834 Pharmaceutical preparations
PA: Standard Homeopathic Co.
204 W 131st St
Los Angeles CA 90061
310 768-0700

(P-8144)
STASON PHARMACEUTICALS
INC (PA)
Also Called: IMT-Stason Laboratories
11 Morgan, Irvine (92618-2005)
PHONE...................................949 380-0752
Harry Fan, *CEO*
Karl Weinrich, *Officer*
Cedrick Le, *Technical Staff*
Steven Cheng, *Prdtn Mgr*
▲ EMP: 48
SQ FT: 37,149
SALES (est): 13.4MM Privately Held
SIC: 2834 Pharmaceutical preparations

(P-8145)
STEADYMED THERAPEUTICS
INC
2603 Camino Ramon Ste 350, San Ramon
(94583-9127)
P.O. Box 2147 (94583-7147)
PHONE...................................925 361-7111
Jonathan Rigby, *President*
Peter Noymer, *Exec VP*
EMP: 15
SALES (est): 2.6MM Privately Held
SIC: 2834 Tranquilizers or mental drug
preparations

(P-8146)
STELLAR BIOTECHNOLOGIES
INC
332 E Scott St, Port Hueneme
(93041-2939)
PHONE...................................805 488-2147
Frank Oakes, *Ch of Bd*
Catherine Brisson, *COO*
Kathi Niffenegger, *CFO*
Gregory Baxter, *Exec VP*
Darrell Brookstein, *Exec VP*
EMP: 12
SALES: 211.8K
SALES (corp-wide): 2.2MM Privately
Held
WEB: www.stellarbiotech.com
SIC: 2834 Adrenal pharmaceutical prepa-
rations
PA: Edesa Biotech Inc
100 Spy Crt
Markham ON L3R 5
905 475-1234

(P-8147)
STERISYN INC
11969 Challenger Ct, Moorpark
(93021-7119)
PHONE...................................805 991-9694
Julie Anne, *Administration*
Timothy Henry, *CEO*
EMP: 30
SALES (est): 2MM Privately Held
SIC: 2834 Pharmaceutical preparations

(P-8148)
SUHEUNG-AMERICA
CORPORATION (HQ)
428 Saturn St, Brea (92821-1710)
PHONE...................................714 854-9882
Joo Hwan Yang, *President*
Ki Hoon Kim, *Principal*
Kevin Lee, *Technical Staff*
▲ EMP: 17
SALES (est): 2.2MM Privately Held
SIC: 2834 2899 3769 Medicines, cap-
suled or ampuled; gelatin capsules; space
capsules

(P-8149)
SUNBIO INC
57 Claremont Ave, Orinda (94563-2135)
PHONE...................................925 876-0439
EMP: 35
SQ FT: 8,000
SALES (est): 2.4MM Privately Held
SIC: 2834 Pharmaceutical preparations

(P-8150)
SUNESIS PHARMACEUTICALS
INC (PA)
395 Oyster Point Blvd # 400, South San
Francisco (94080-1995)
PHONE...................................650 266-3500
Dayton Misfeldt, *CEO*
James W Young, *Ch of Bd*
Parvinder S Hyare, *Senior VP*
William Quinn, *Senior VP*
Stephen Nava, *Vice Pres*
EMP: 34
SQ FT: 15,378
SALES: 237K Publicly Held
WEB: www.sunesis.com
SIC: 2834 Pharmaceutical preparations

(P-8151)
SUPERNUTRITION
Also Called: Forever Young
3034 Jordan Rd, Oakland (94602-3531)
PHONE...................................510 446-7980
Cathy Mooney, *Owner*
EMP: 30
SALES (est): 3.4MM Privately Held
WEB: www.supernutritionusa.com
SIC: 2834 Vitamin preparations

(P-8152)
SYNTHORX INC
11099 N Torrey Pines Rd, La Jolla
(92037-1029)
PHONE...................................858 750-4700
Laura Shawver, *President*
Jay Lichter, *Ch of Bd*
Pratik Shah, *Ch of Bd*
Tighe Reardon, *CFO*
Joseph Leveque, *Chief Mktg Ofcr*

EMP: 25
SQ FT: 8,636
SALES (est): 7.3MM Privately Held
SIC: 2834 8731 Pharmaceutical prepara-
tions; biotechnical research, commercial

(P-8153)
TALON THERAPEUTICS INC
157 Technology Dr, Irvine (92618-2402)
PHONE...................................949 788-6700
Joseph W Turgeon, *CEO*
EMP: 241
SQ FT: 50,000
SALES: 186MM Publicly Held
WEB: www.hanabiosciences.com
SIC: 2834 8731 Pharmaceutical prepara-
tions; commercial physical research
PA: Spectrum Pharmaceuticals, Inc.
11500 S Estrn Ave Ste 240
Henderson NV 89052

(P-8154)
TANOX INC (DH)
1 Dna Way, South San Francisco
(94080-4918)
PHONE...................................650 851-1607
Stephen G Juelsgaard, *President*
Zhengbin Yao, *Vice Pres*
Robert C Bast,
▲ EMP: 124
SQ FT: 111,000
SALES (est): 18.3MM
SALES (corp-wide): 57.2B Privately Held
SIC: 2834 Pharmaceutical preparations
HQ: Genentech, Inc.
1 Dna Way
South San Francisco CA 94080
650 225-1000

(P-8155)
TARSAL PHARMACEUTICALS
INC
3909 Oceanic Dr Ste 401, Oceanside
(92056-5853)
PHONE...................................818 919-9723
Ashak Fakous Botros, *CEO*
EMP: 20
SQ FT: 6,005
SALES (est): 846.9K Privately Held
SIC: 2834 Pharmaceutical preparations

(P-8156)
TEIKOKU PHARMA USA INC
(HQ)
1718 Ringwood Ave, San Jose
(95131-1711)
PHONE...................................408 501-1800
Masahisa Kitagawa, *President*
Ichiro Mori, *COO*
Atsumu Matsushita, *CFO*
Tetsuto Nagata, *Exec VP*
Larry Caldwell, *Vice Pres*
▲ EMP: 60
SALES (est): 16.2MM Privately Held
WEB: www.teikokuusa.com
SIC: 2834 Pharmaceutical preparations

(P-8157)
TESORX PHARMA LLC
3670 W Temple Ave, Pomona
(91768-2588)
PHONE...................................909 595-0500
Ramachandran Thirucote, *CEO*
Willem A Robberts, *President*
Guru Betageri PHD, *Founder*
Karl Bean, *Director*
EMP: 19
SALES (est): 3.1MM Privately Held
SIC: 2834 Pharmaceutical preparations

(P-8158)
TEVA PARENTERAL MEDICINES
INC
19 Hughes, Irvine (92618-1902)
P.O. Box 57049 (92619-7049)
PHONE...................................949 455-4700
Phillip Frost, *Ch of Bd*
Karin Shanahan, *CEO*
Amir Elstein, *Vice Ch Bd*
Nir Baron, *Senior VP*
Iris Beck-Codner, *Vice Pres*
▲ EMP: 830
SQ FT: 148,000

PRODUCTS & SVCS

SALES (est): 209.9MM
SALES (corp-wide): 5B **Privately Held**
WEB: www.lemmon.com
SIC: **2834** Pills, pharmaceutical
HQ: Teva Pharmaceuticals Usa, Inc.
1090 Horsham Rd
North Wales PA 19454
215 591-3000

(P-8159)
TEVA PHARMACEUTICALS USA INC
19 Hughes, Irvine (92618-1902)
PHONE...............................949 457-2828
John Case, *Executive*
Binky Evidente, *General Mgr*
Mary Bazensky, *Executive Asst*
Edward Smith, *Engineer*
Cheng-Hsien Wang, *Engineer*
EMP: 35
SALES (corp-wide): 5B **Privately Held**
SIC: **2834** 2833 Pharmaceutical preparations; medicinals & botanicals; penicillin: bulk, uncompounded; antibiotics
HQ: Teva Pharmaceuticals Usa, Inc.
1090 Horsham Rd
North Wales PA 19454
215 591-3000

(P-8160)
TFX INTERNATIONAL
Also Called: Platt Medical Center
72785 Frank Sinatra Dr, Rancho Mirage (92270-3205)
PHONE...............................760 836-3232
Michael Platt, *Owner*
EMP: 12
SALES (est): 2MM **Privately Held**
WEB: www.drplatt.com
SIC: **2834** 8011 7299 Hormone preparations; specialized medical practitioners, except internal; personal appearance services

(P-8161)
THERAVANCE BIOPHARMA US INC
901 Gateway Blvd, South San Francisco (94080-7024)
PHONE...............................650 808-6000
Rick Winningham, *CEO*
Frank Pasqualone, *Senior VP*
Kit Chiu, *Associate Dir*
Paul Fatheree, *Associate Dir*
James Wertman, *Associate Dir*
EMP: 244
SALES (est): 88.6MM **Privately Held**
SIC: **2834** Pharmaceutical preparations
PA: Theravance Biopharma Inc
C/O Maples Corporate Services Ltd
George Town GR CAYMAN

(P-8162)
THERAVNCE BPHRMA ANTBOTICS INC
901 Gateway Blvd, South San Francisco (94080-7024)
PHONE...............................877 275-6930
Rick Winningham, *CEO*
EMP: 200
SALES (est): 11.3MM **Privately Held**
SIC: **2834** Pharmaceutical preparations
PA: Theravance Biopharma Inc
C/O Maples Corporate Services Ltd
George Town GR CAYMAN

(P-8163)
THORX LABORATORIES INC
30831 Huntwood Ave, Hayward (94544-7003)
PHONE...............................510 240-6000
Frederick Wilkinson, *Principal*
EMP: 15
SALES (est): 214.3K
SALES (corp-wide): 1.6B **Publicly Held**
SIC: **2834** Pharmaceutical preparations
HQ: Impax Laboratories, Llc
30831 Huntwood Ave
Hayward CA 94544
510 240-6000

(P-8164)
TITAN MEDICAL ENTERPRISES INC
Also Called: US Apothecary Crown Labs
11100 Greenstone Ave, Santa Fe Springs (90670-4640)
PHONE...............................562 903-7236
James L McDaniel, *President*
James McDaniel, *President*
EMP: 15
SQ FT: 12,000
SALES (est): 3.9MM **Privately Held**
SIC: **2834** Vitamin preparations

(P-8165)
TITAN PHARMACEUTICALS INC (PA)
400 Oyster Point Blvd # 505, South San Francisco (94080-1958)
PHONE...............................650 244-4990
Sunil Bhonsle, *President*
Marc Rubin, *Ch of Bd*
Dane D Hallberg, *Officer*
EMP: 13
SQ FT: 9,255
SALES (est): 6.6MM **Publicly Held**
WEB: www.titanpharm.com
SIC: **2834** Drugs acting on the central nervous system & sense organs

(P-8166)
TOCAGEN INC
4242 Campus Point Ct # 500, San Diego (92121-1513)
PHONE...............................858 412-8400
Martin J Duvall, *CEO*
Faheem Hasnain, *Ch of Bd*
Mark Foletta, *CFO*
Asha Das, *Chief Mktg Ofcr*
Jamey Skillings, *Chief Mktg Ofcr*
EMP: 67
SQ FT: 19,000
SALES (est): 18MM **Privately Held**
SIC: **2834** Pharmaceutical preparations

(P-8167)
TRACON PHARMACEUTICALS INC (PA)
4350 La Jolla Village Dr # 800, San Diego (92122-1247)
PHONE...............................858 550-0780
Charles P Theuer, *President*
Bonne Adams, *Exec VP*
Sharon Real, *Exec VP*
Scott Brown,
EMP: 26
SQ FT: 10,458
SALES (est): 3MM **Publicly Held**
WEB: www.traconpharma.com
SIC: **2834** 2836 8731 Pharmaceutical preparations; biological products, except diagnostic; biotechnical research, commercial

(P-8168)
TRAGARA PHARMACEUTICALS INC
12481 High Bluff Dr # 150, San Diego (92130-3585)
PHONE...............................760 208-6900
Scott Megaffin, *CEO*
Thomas Estok, *President*
Dennis Bilski, *Vice Pres*
Chris Lemasters, *Principal*
EMP: 17
SALES (est): 2.7MM **Privately Held**
SIC: **2834** Pharmaceutical preparations

(P-8169)
TRICIDA INC
7000 Shoreline Ct Ste 201, South San Francisco (94080-7603)
PHONE...............................415 429-7800
Gerrit Klaerner, *President*
Klaus R Veitinger, *Ch of Bd*
Geoffrey M Parker, *CFO*
Susannah Cantrell, *Ch Credit Ofcr*
Janet Dorling, *Officer*
EMP: 76
SQ FT: 26,987
SALES (est): 8.2MM **Privately Held**
SIC: **2834** Pharmaceutical preparations

(P-8170)
TRIUS THERAPEUTICS LLC
4747 Executive Dr # 1100, San Diego (92121-3095)
PHONE...............................858 452-0370
Jeffrey Stein, *President*
David S Kabakoff, *Ch of Bd*
John P Schmid, *CFO*
Kenneth Bartizal, *Officer*
John Finn, *Officer*
EMP: 90
SQ FT: 39,000
SALES (est): 14.2MM
SALES (corp-wide): 42.2B **Publicly Held**
WEB: www.triusrx.com
SIC: **2834** Antibiotics, packaged
HQ: Cubist Pharmaceuticals Llc
2000 Galloping Hill Rd
Kenilworth NJ 07033

(P-8171)
TURNING POINT THERAPEUTICS INC
10628 Science Center Dr # 200, San Diego (92121-1128)
PHONE...............................858 926-5251
Athena Countouriotis, *President*
Jingrong Jean Cui, *Ch of Bd*
Annette North, *Exec VP*
Brian Baker, *Vice Pres*
Jane Ung, *Research*
EMP: 50
SQ FT: 18,029
SALES (est): 12.2MM **Privately Held**
SIC: **2834** Pharmaceutical preparations

(P-8172)
UCSF SCHOOL OF PHARMACY
Also Called: Drug Product Services Lab
3333 California St, San Francisco (94118-1981)
PHONE...............................415 476-1444
Marcus Ferrone, *Director*
EMP: 10
SALES (est): 1MM **Privately Held**
SIC: **2834** Pharmaceutical preparations

(P-8173)
ULTRAGENYX PHARMACEUTICAL INC (PA)
60 Leveroni Ct, Novato (94949-5746)
PHONE...............................415 483-8800
Emil D Kakkis, *President*
Wladimir Hogenhuis, *COO*
Shalini Sharp, *CFO*
Bill Aliski, *Bd of Directors*
Camille L Bedrosian, *Chief Mktg Ofcr*
EMP: 238
SQ FT: 129,500
SALES (est): 51.5MM **Publicly Held**
SIC: **2834** Pharmaceutical preparations

(P-8174)
UROVANT SCIENCES INC (HQ)
5281 California Ave # 100, Irvine (92617-3218)
PHONE...............................949 226-6029
Keith Katkin, *President*
Christine Ocampo, *Senior VP*
EMP: 40
SQ FT: 8,000
SALES (est): 7.3MM **Privately Held**
SIC: **2834** Pharmaceutical preparations

(P-8175)
US WHOLESALE DRUG CORP
2611 N San Fernando Rd, Los Angeles (90065-1316)
PHONE...............................323 227-4258
Virginia Farha, *President*
EMP: 12
SALES (est): 1.4MM **Privately Held**
SIC: **2834** Pharmaceutical preparations

(P-8176)
VAXART INC (PA)
290 Utah Ave Ste 200, South San Francisco (94080-6801)
PHONE...............................650 550-3500
Wouter W Latour, *President*
Richard J Markham, *Ch of Bd*
Margaret Echerd, *Officer*
Wouter Latour, *Officer*
Brant Biehn, *Senior VP*

EMP: 34
SALES: 4.1MM **Publicly Held**
WEB: www.nabi.com
SIC: **2834** 2836 Pharmaceutical preparations; drugs affecting parasitic & infective diseases; vaccines & other immunizing products

(P-8177)
VERSEON CORPORATION
47071 Bayside Pkwy, Fremont (94538-6517)
PHONE...............................510 255-9000
EMP: 12
SALES (corp-wide): 7.2MM **Privately Held**
SIC: **2834** Druggists' preparations (pharmaceuticals)
PA: Verseon Corporation
48820 Kato Rd Ste 100b
Fremont CA 94538
510 668-1622

(P-8178)
VERSEON CORPORATION (PA)
48820 Kato Rd Ste 100b, Fremont (94538-7323)
PHONE...............................510 668-1622
Adityo Prakash, *President*
Eniko Fodor, *COO*
David Kita, *Vice Pres*
Kevin Short, *Director*
David Williams, *Director*
EMP: 35
SQ FT: 8,000
SALES (est): 7.2MM **Privately Held**
WEB: www.verseon.com
SIC: **2834** Druggists' preparations (pharmaceuticals)

(P-8179)
VERUS PHARMACEUTICALS INC
11455 El Camino Real # 460, San Diego (92130-2088)
PHONE...............................858 436-1600
Robert W Keith, *President*
CAM Garner, *Ch of Bd*
Richard Vincent, *CFO*
Ahmet S Tutuncu, *Vice Pres*
Adam Simpson, *General Counsel*
EMP: 16
SQ FT: 13,000
SALES (est): 3.1MM **Privately Held**
WEB: www.veruspharm.com
SIC: **2834** Pharmaceutical preparations

(P-8180)
VIBRANT CARE PHARMACY INC
7400 Macarthur Blvd Ste B, Oakland (94605-2939)
PHONE...............................510 638-9851
Kalpesh Patel, *CEO*
EMP: 15 EST: 2015
SALES (est): 975.5K **Privately Held**
SIC: **2834** 5912 Chlorination tablets & kits (water purification); drug stores

(P-8181)
VIKING THERAPEUTICS INC
12340 El Cmino Real Ste 2, San Diego (92130)
PHONE...............................858 704-4660
Brian Lian, *President*
Lawson Macartney, *Ch of Bd*
Morneau Michael, *CFO*
Michael Morneau, *CFO*
Amy Broidrick, *Vice Pres*
EMP: 12
SQ FT: 7,049
SALES (est): 2.5MM **Privately Held**
SIC: **2834** Pharmaceutical preparations

(P-8182)
VITABEST NUTRITION INC
Also Called: Vit Best
2802 Dow Ave, Tustin (92780-7212)
PHONE...............................714 832-9700
Gale Bensussen, *President*
Toni Clubb, *CFO*
Bing Jiang, *Admin Sec*
EMP: 275
SQ FT: 200,000

SALES (est): 76.4MM
SALES (corp-wide): 413.8MM **Privately Held**
SIC: 2834 Vitamin preparations
PA: Xiamen Kingdomway Group Company No. 299, Sunshine West Road, Xinyang Industrial Zone, Haicang Xiamen 36102
592 651-1111

(P-8183)
VITAGEN ACQUISITION CORP
15222 Avenue Of Science B, San Diego (92128-3422)
PHONE...............................858 673-6840
Robert A Ashley, *COO*
EMP: 12
SALES (est): 2MM **Privately Held**
SIC: 2834 Pharmaceutical preparations

(P-8184)
VIVUS INC (PA)
900 E Hamilton Ave # 550, Campbell (95008-0643)
PHONE...............................650 934-5200
John Amos, *CEO*
David Y Norton, *Ch of Bd*
Ken Suh, *President*
Thomas B King, *CEO*
Scott Oehrlein, *COO*
EMP: 49
SQ FT: 45,240
SALES: 65MM **Publicly Held**
WEB: www.vivus.com
SIC: 2834 Druggists' preparations (pharmaceuticals); proprietary drug products

(P-8185)
VM DISCOVERY INC
45535 Northport Loop E, Fremont (94538-6461)
PHONE...............................510 818-1018
Jay Wu, *CEO*
Maggie Wang, *Project Mgr*
Sandy Wong, *Manager*
EMP: 10
SALES (est): 1.5MM **Privately Held**
WEB: www.vmdiscovery.com
SIC: 2834 Druggists' preparations (pharmaceuticals)

(P-8186)
WEST COAST LABORATORIES INC
156 E 162nd St, Gardena (90248-2802)
PHONE...............................310 527-6163
Maurice Ovadia, *Manager*
EMP: 35
SQ FT: 4,000
SALES (corp-wide): 7.3MM **Privately Held**
WEB: www.westcoastlabsinc.com
SIC: 2834 Vitamin preparations
PA: West Coast Laboratories, Inc.
116 E Alondra Blvd
Gardena CA 90248
323 321-4774

(P-8187)
WEST COAST LABORATORIES INC (PA)
116 E Alondra Blvd, Gardena (90248-2806)
PHONE...............................323 321-4774
Maurice Ovadia, *President*
Jamil Shad, *Treasurer*
Naim Abdullah, *Vice Pres*
Anwar Abdullah, *Admin Sec*
EMP: 15
SQ FT: 4,000
SALES (est): 7.3MM **Privately Held**
WEB: www.westcoastlabsinc.com
SIC: 2834 Vitamin preparations

(P-8188)
WILLPOWER LABS INC
Also Called: Mealenders
3318 California St Apt 4, San Francisco (94118-1996)
PHONE...............................415 805-1518
Mark Bernstein, *CEO*
EMP: 10
SALES: 1.2MM **Privately Held**
SIC: 2834 Lozenges, pharmaceutical

(P-8189)
WRIGHT PHARMA INC
700 Kiernan Ave Ste A, Modesto (95356-9329)
PHONE...............................209 549-9771
Eric Fogleman, *Branch Mgr*
EMP: 20
SALES (corp-wide): 4.9MM **Privately Held**
SIC: 2834 2023 Pharmaceutical preparations; dietary supplements, dairy & non-dairy based
PA: Wright Pharma, Inc.
201 Energy Pkwy Ste 400
Lafayette LA 70508
337 783-3096

(P-8190)
XENCOR INC
111 W Lemon Ave, Monrovia (91016-2809)
PHONE...............................626 305-5900
Bassil I Dahiyat, *President*
Paul Foster, *Chief Mktg Ofcr*
John R Desjarlais, *Senior VP*
Celia Eckert, *Vice Pres*
Jeremy Grunstein, *Vice Pres*
EMP: 114
SQ FT: 48,000
SALES: 40.6MM **Privately Held**
SIC: 2834 Pharmaceutical preparations

(P-8191)
XOMA CORPORATION (PA)
2200 Powell St Ste 310, Emeryville (94608-2792)
PHONE...............................510 204-7200
James R Neal, *CEO*
W Denman Van Ness, *Ch of Bd*
Thomas Burns, *CFO*
Patrick Scannon, *Exec VP*
Daniel P Cafaro, *Vice Pres*
EMP: 12
SALES: 5.3MM **Publicly Held**
WEB: www.xoma.com
SIC: 2834 Pharmaceutical preparations

(P-8192)
YOUCARE PHARMA (USA) INC
132 Business Center Dr, Corona (92880-1724)
P.O. Box 668 (92878-0668)
PHONE...............................951 258-3114
Weishi Yu, *CEO*
EMP: 60 EST: 2015
SQ FT: 160,000
SALES (est): 8.1MM **Privately Held**
SIC: 2834 Pharmaceutical preparations
HQ: Youcare Pharmaceutical Group Co., Ltd.
No.6, Hongda Middle Road, Economic & Technology Development Zone
Beijing 10017
106 786-5666

(P-8193)
ZACHARON PHARMACEUTICALS INC
105 Digital Dr, Novato (94949-8703)
PHONE...............................415 506-6700
George Eric Davis, *CEO*
Douglas Downs, *CFO*
Charles Glass, *Senior VP*
Brett E Crawford, *Vice Pres*
Shripad Bhagwat, *Security Dir*
EMP: 10
SQ FT: 5,000
SALES: 1.1MM
SALES (corp-wide): 1.4B **Publicly Held**
SIC: 2834 Pharmaceutical preparations
PA: Biomarin Pharmaceutical Inc.
770 Lindaro St
San Rafael CA 94901
415 506-6700

(P-8194)
ZELZAH PHARMACY INC (PA)
Also Called: Good Neighbor Pharmacy
17911 Ventura Blvd, Encino (91316-3618)
PHONE...............................818 609-0692
Pejman Javaheri, *Principal*
EMP: 11
SALES (est): 6.8MM **Privately Held**
SIC: 2834 5912 Druggists' preparations (pharmaceuticals); drug stores

(P-8195)
ZOGENIX INC (PA)
5959 Horton St Ste 500, Emeryville (94608-2120)
PHONE...............................510 550-8300
Stephen J Farr, *President*
Ann D Rhoads, *CFO*
Louis Bock, *Bd of Directors*
James Breitmeyer, *Bd of Directors*
Erle Mast, *Bd of Directors*
EMP: 23
SQ FT: 22,000
SALES (est): 9.8MM **Publicly Held**
SIC: 2834 Pharmaceutical preparations; drugs acting on the central nervous system & sense organs

(P-8196)
ZOSANO PHARMA CORPORATION (PA)
34790 Ardentech Ct, Fremont (94555-3657)
PHONE...............................510 745-1200
John P Walker, *Ch of Bd*
Greg Kitchener, *CFO*
Hayley Lewis, *Senior VP*
Dushyant Pathak, *Senior VP*
Donald Kellerman, *Vice Pres*
EMP: 36
SALES (est): 10.4MM **Publicly Held**
SIC: 2834 Pharmaceutical preparations

(P-8197)
ZS PHARMA INC
1100 Park Pl Fl 3, San Mateo (94403-1599)
PHONE...............................650 753-1823
EMP: 14 EST: 2017
SALES (est): 4.1MM **Privately Held**
SIC: 2834 Pharmaceutical preparations

2835 Diagnostic Substances

(P-8198)
ABBOTT DIABETES CARE INC (HQ)
Also Called: Medisense
1420 Harbor Bay Pkwy, Alameda (94502-7080)
PHONE...............................510 749-5400
Lawrence W Huffman, *Vice Pres*
Robert D Brownell, *Principal*
Adam Heller, *Principal*
Charles T Liamos, *Principal*
▲ EMP: 250
SQ FT: 54,500
SALES (est): 134.3MM
SALES (corp-wide): 30.5B **Publicly Held**
WEB: www.abbottdiabetescare.com
SIC: 2835 3845 3823 In vitro diagnostics; electromedical equipment; industrial instrmnts msrmnt display/control process variable
PA: Abbott Laboratories
100 Abbott Park Rd
Abbott Park IL 60064
224 667-6100

(P-8199)
ACROMETRIX CORPORATION
46500 Kato Rd, Fremont (94538-7310)
PHONE...............................707 746-8888
David Hoffmeister, *CEO*
Michael Eck, *President*
Tambi McCarthy, *VP Human Res*
EMP: 45
SQ FT: 26,000
SALES (est): 11.4MM **Privately Held**
WEB: www.acrometrix.com
SIC: 2835 In vitro & in vivo diagnostic substances

(P-8200)
ADEZA BIOMEDICAL CORPORATION
1240 Elko Dr, Sunnyvale (94089-2212)
PHONE...............................408 745-6491
Emory V Anderson, *President*
Andrew E Senyei, *Ch of Bd*
Mark D Fischer Colbrie, *CFO*
Durlin E Hickok, *Vice Pres*
Robert O Hussa, *Vice Pres*
EMP: 103

SQ FT: 22,600
SALES (est): 12.3MM
SALES (corp-wide): 3.2B **Publicly Held**
WEB: www.cytyc.com
SIC: 2835 Pregnancy test kits
HQ: Cytyc Corporation
250 Campus Dr
Marlborough MA 01752
508 263-2900

(P-8201)
ALERE INC
Also Called: Cholestech
6465 National Dr, Livermore (94550-8808)
PHONE...............................510 732-7200
Gregory Bennett, *Branch Mgr*
Ya-Ling King, *Director*
EMP: 375
SALES (corp-wide): 30.5B **Publicly Held**
SIC: 2835 Pregnancy test kits
HQ: Alere Inc.
51 Sawyer Rd Ste 200
Waltham MA 02453
781 647-3900

(P-8202)
ALERE SAN DIEGO INC
9975 Summers Ridge Rd, San Diego (92121-2997)
PHONE...............................858 455-4808
John Yonkin, *President*
Gary A King, *Vice Pres*
Mark Gladwell, *Principal*
S Elaine Walton, *QA Dir*
Heidi Langbein Allen, *Opers Mgr*
▲ EMP: 1003
SQ FT: 350,000
SALES (est): 228.8MM
SALES (corp-wide): 30.5B **Publicly Held**
WEB: www.biosite.com
SIC: 2835 In vitro & in vivo diagnostic substances
HQ: Alere Inc.
51 Sawyer Rd Ste 200
Waltham MA 02453
781 647-3900

(P-8203)
ALFA SCIENTIFIC DESIGNS INC
13200 Gregg St, Poway (92064-7121)
PHONE...............................858 513-3888
Chai Bunyagidj, *President*
Naishu Wang, *Ch of Bd*
Claudia Shen, *Treasurer*
Angela Shen, *Vice Pres*
Cathy Parsons, *Mktg Dir*
▲ EMP: 88
SQ FT: 39,000
SALES: 13MM **Privately Held**
WEB: www.alfascientific.com
SIC: 2835 In vitro & in vivo diagnostic substances

(P-8204)
ANTIBODIES INCORPORATED
25242 County Road 95, Davis (95616)
P.O. Box 1560 (95617-1560)
PHONE...............................800 824-8540
Richard Krogsrud, *President*
Will Fry, *Manager*
Ricardo Rodarte, *Manager*
EMP: 18
SQ FT: 23,000
SALES (est): 4.2MM **Privately Held**
WEB: www.antibodiesinc.com
SIC: 2835 2836 In vitro & in vivo diagnostic substances; serums

(P-8205)
B D PHARMINGEN INC (HQ)
10975 Torreyana Rd, San Diego (92121-1106)
PHONE...............................858 812-8800
William Kozy, *President*
Andrew Lasp, *General Mgr*
EMP: 12
SQ FT: 80,000
SALES (est): 45.2MM
SALES (corp-wide): 15.9B **Publicly Held**
WEB: www.pharmingen.com
SIC: 2835 In vitro & in vivo diagnostic substances
PA: Becton, Dickinson And Company
1 Becton Dr
Franklin Lakes NJ 07417
201 847-6800

(P-8206)
BECKMAN INSTRUMENTS INC
2500 N Harbor Blvd, Fullerton
(92835-2600)
PHONE...............714 871-4848
John Collette, *President*
Steve Blanc, *District Mgr*
Angela Garrick, *Info Tech Dir*
Tamara Martinez, *Analyst*
Claudine Vo, *Human Res Dir*
EMP: 23
SALES (est): 359.7K **Privately Held**
SIC: 2835 In vitro & in vivo diagnostic substances

(P-8207)
BIOSERV CORPORATION
Also Called: Bioserve
5340 Eastgate Mall, San Diego
(92121-2804)
PHONE...............917 817-1326
Henry Ji, *President*
Kevin Herde, *Vice Pres*
Jay Schrier, *Vice Pres*
Rhonda Nichols, *QA Dir*
Joanne Busalacchi, *Project Mgr*
EMP: 27
SALES (est): 7.2MM
SALES (corp-wide): 21.1MM **Publicly Held**
SIC: 2835 2834 In vitro & in vivo diagnostic substances; pharmaceutical preparations
PA: Sorrento Therapeutics, Inc.
4955 Directors Pl
San Diego CA 92121
858 203-4100

(P-8208)
BIOSOURCE INTERNATIONAL INC
5791 Van Allen Way, Carlsbad
(92008-7321)
PHONE...............805 659-5759
Terrance J Bieker, *President*
Jean-Pierre L Conte, *Ch of Bd*
Alan Edrick, *CFO*
Kevin J Reagan PHD, *Exec VP*
Jozef Vangenechten, *Exec VP*
EMP: 167
SQ FT: 51,821
SALES (est): 44.3MM **Privately Held**
WEB: www.biofluids.com
SIC: 2835 In vitro & in vivo diagnostic substances

(P-8209)
BIOSPACIFIC INC (DH)
5980 Horton St Ste 360, Emeryville
(94608-2058)
PHONE...............510 652-6155
Sandy Koshkin, *President*
EMP: 10
SQ FT: 2,800
SALES (est): 904.4K
SALES (corp-wide): 714MM **Publicly Held**
WEB: www.biospacific.com
SIC: 2835 In vitro diagnostics
HQ: Research And Diagnostic Systems, Inc.
614 Mckinley Pl Ne
Minneapolis MN 55413
612 379-2956

(P-8210)
BLACKTHORN THERAPEUTICS INC
780 Brannan St, San Francisco
(94103-4919)
PHONE...............415 548-5401
William J Martin, *CEO*
Annette Madrid, *Officer*
Bill Martin, *Officer*
Laura Hansen, *Vice Pres*
Monique Levy, *Security Dir*
EMP: 35
SALES (est): 5.3MM **Privately Held**
SIC: 2835 Microbiology & virology diagnostic products

(P-8211)
CANCER GENETICS INC
1640 Marengo St Ste 7, Los Angeles
(90033-1057)
PHONE...............323 224-3900
Ernesto Pena, *Technician*
Lara Sislian, *Technician*
Annette Gascon, *Human Res Mgr*
EMP: 113
SALES (corp-wide): 27.4MM **Publicly Held**
SIC: 2835 In vivo diagnostics
PA: Cancer Genetics, Inc.
201 Route 17 Fl 2
Rutherford NJ 07070
201 528-9200

(P-8212)
CELL MARQUE CORPORATION
6600 Sierra College Blvd, Rocklin
(95677-4306)
PHONE...............916 746-8900
Nora Lacey, *President*
David Zembo, *CFO*
Paul Ardi, *Vice Pres*
EMP: 42
SALES (est): 10.7MM
SALES (corp-wide): 16.9B **Privately Held**
WEB: www.cellmarque.com
SIC: 2835 In vitro & in vivo diagnostic substances
HQ: Sigma-Aldrich Corporation
3050 Spruce St
Saint Louis MO 63103
314 771-5765

(P-8213)
CELLESTA INC
10554 Caminito Alvarez, San Diego
(92126-5785)
PHONE...............858 552-0888
Jia Xu, *President*
EMP: 15
SALES (est): 931.8K **Privately Held**
SIC: 2835 In vitro & in vivo diagnostic substances

(P-8214)
CEPHEID
632 E Caribbean Dr, Sunnyvale
(94089-1108)
PHONE...............408 548-9104
EMP: 12
SALES (est): 1.7MM **Privately Held**
SIC: 2835 In vitro & in vivo diagnostic substances

(P-8215)
CHRONIX BIOMEDICAL INC (PA)
5941 Optical Ct Ste 203e, San Jose
(95138-1410)
PHONE...............408 960-2306
Howard Urnovitz, *President*
William Boeger, *Vice Pres*
Paul Freiman, *Admin Sec*
EMP: 10
SALES (est): 1.3MM **Privately Held**
WEB: www.chronixbiomedical.com
SIC: 2835 In vitro & in vivo diagnostic substances

(P-8216)
CLEARLIGHT DIAGNOSTICS LLC
428 Oakmead Pkwy, Sunnyvale
(94085-4708)
PHONE...............928 525-4290
Laurie Goodman, *CEO*
EMP: 10 EST: 2015
SALES (est): 725.4K **Privately Held**
SIC: 2835 Cytology & histology diagnostic agents

(P-8217)
CUE HEALTH INC
11175 Flintkote Ave, San Diego
(92121-1209)
PHONE...............256 651-1656
Ayub Khattak, *CEO*
Brad Younggren, *Chief Mktg Ofcr*
Clint Sever,
Robin Farias-Eisner, *Surgeon*
Dino Di Carlo, *Advisor*
EMP: 50
SQ FT: 7,557

SALES (est): 3MM **Privately Held**
SIC: 2835 In vitro diagnostics

(P-8218)
DANISCO US INC (DH)
Also Called: Genencor International
925 Page Mill Rd, Palo Alto (94304-1013)
PHONE...............650 846-7500
James C Collins, *CEO*
Scott Power, *Vice Pres*
Xing Xia, *Administration*
Gopal Stewart, *Info Tech Mgr*
Chao Zhu, *Research*
◆ EMP: 200
SQ FT: 128,000
SALES (est): 272.6MM
SALES (corp-wide): 30.6B **Publicly Held**
SIC: 2835 8731 2899 2869 In vitro & in vivo diagnostic substances; commercial physical research; chemical preparations; industrial organic chemicals
HQ: E. I. Du Pont De Nemours And Company
974 Centre Rd Bldg 735
Wilmington DE 19805
302 485-3000

(P-8219)
DIAGNOSTICS FOR REAL WORLD LTD (PA)
845 Embedded Way, San Jose
(95138-1085)
PHONE...............408 773-1511
Helen H Lee, *President*
Vivian Laitila, *Director*
Craig Wisniewski, *Director*
EMP: 13
SALES (est): 1.7MM **Privately Held**
WEB: www.drw-ltd.com
SIC: 2835 In vitro & in vivo diagnostic substances

(P-8220)
DIASORIN MOLECULAR LLC
11331 Valley View St, Cypress
(90630-5300)
PHONE...............562 240-6500
Carlo Rosa, *CEO*
Mauro Priolo, *CFO*
Michelle Tabb, *Officer*
Shelly Barber, *Sales Staff*
David Du, *Senior Mgr*
EMP: 200
SALES: 90MM
SALES (corp-wide): 416.8MM **Privately Held**
SIC: 2835 5047 In vitro diagnostics; diagnostic equipment, medical
HQ: Diasorin Inc.
1951 Northwestern Ave S
Stillwater MN 55082
651 439-9710

(P-8221)
EPICUREN DISCOVERY
26081 Merit Cir Ste 116, Laguna Hills
(92653-7017)
PHONE...............949 588-5807
Colleen Lohrman, *President*
Tamara Miyao, *Vice Pres*
Janae Muzzy, *Vice Pres*
Kendall Clark, *Executive*
Brian Douglas, *Project Mgr*
▲ EMP: 65
SQ FT: 20,000
SALES (est): 17.1MM **Privately Held**
SIC: 2835 Enzyme & isoenzyme diagnostic agents

(P-8222)
FUJIFILM WAKO DIAGNOSTICS US
Also Called: Wako Life Sciences, Inc.
1025 Terra Bella Ave A, Mountain View
(94043-1829)
PHONE...............650 210-9153
Shinji Satomura, *CEO*
EMP: 40
SALES (est): 8.7MM **Privately Held**
SIC: 2835 5047 In vitro & in vivo diagnostic substances; diagnostic equipment, medical

HQ: Fujifilm Wako Holdings U.S.A. Corporation
1600 Bellwood Rd
North Chesterfield VA 23237

(P-8223)
FULLER LABORATORIES
1312 E Valencia Dr, Fullerton (92831-4758)
PHONE...............714 525-7660
Lee Fuller, *President*
Lynn Fuller, *Corp Secy*
▼ EMP: 19
SQ FT: 12,500
SALES (est): 7.3MM **Privately Held**
WEB: www.fullerlabs.com
SIC: 2835 Microbiology & virology diagnostic products

(P-8224)
GEN-PROBE INCORPORATED
10210 Genetic Center Dr, San Diego
(92121-4394)
PHONE...............858 410-8000
Gene Walther, *Principal*
Jeff Burns, *Program Mgr*
Daniel Corrales, *General Mgr*
George Neblina, *Administration*
Jeanne Woodard, *Information Mgr*
EMP: 74
SALES (corp-wide): 741MM **Privately Held**
SIC: 2835 In vitro diagnostics; microbiology & virology diagnostic products
HQ: Gen-Probe Incorporated
250 Campus Dr
Marlborough MA 01752
508 263-8937

(P-8225)
GIT AMERICA INC
230 Commerce Ste 190, Irvine
(92602-1336)
PHONE...............714 433-2180
Simon Park, *President*
▲ EMP: 11
SALES (est): 16.1MM **Privately Held**
WEB: www.gitauto.com
SIC: 2835 7371 In vitro & in vivo diagnostic substances; computer software development

(P-8226)
GNOSIS INTERNATIONAL LLC
8008 Westbury Ave, San Diego
(92126-2134)
PHONE...............858 254-6369
Chinh Vu, *CFO*
EMP: 20
SALES (est): 2.5MM **Privately Held**
SIC: 2835 In vitro & in vivo diagnostic substances

(P-8227)
HELICA BIOSYSTEMS INC
3310 W Macarthur Blvd, Santa Ana
(92704-6804)
PHONE...............714 578-7830
Wondu Wolde Mariam, *President*
Wondu Wolde-Mariam, *Executive*
Jess Hinton, *Technician*
Thu Huynh, *Research*
Sheila Ray, *Opers Staff*
EMP: 17
SQ FT: 7,500
SALES (est): 2MM **Privately Held**
WEB: www.helica.com
SIC: 2835 2836 In vitro diagnostics; biological products, except diagnostic

(P-8228)
HYGIENA LLC (PA)
941 Avenida Acaso, Camarillo
(93012-8755)
PHONE...............805 388-2383
Steven Nason, *CEO*
Susan Nason, *Vice Pres*
Paul Meighan, *Research*
Tyler Stephens, *Technical Staff*
Stacy Stoltenberg, *Technical Staff*
EMP: 127
SQ FT: 30,000

▲ = Import ▼=Export
◆ =Import/Export

SALES (est): 101.3MM **Privately Held**
WEB: www.hygiena.com
SIC: 2835 3812 8731 Microbiology & virology diagnostic products; search & detection systems & instruments; biological research

(P-8229)
IMMUNOSCIENCE LLC
6780 Sierra Ct Ste M, Dublin (94568-2630)
PHONE..................................925 400-6055
Robert J Nagy, *Branch Mgr*
EMP: 19
SALES (corp-wide): 4.4MM **Privately Held**
SIC: 2835 Microbiology & virology diagnostic products
PA: Immunoscience Llc
6780 Sierra Ct Ste M
Dublin CA 94568
925 460-8111

(P-8230)
INDI MOLECULAR INC
6160 Bristol Pkwy, Culver City (90230-6694)
PHONE..................................310 417-4999
Al Luderer, *CEO*
Heather Agnew, *Vice Pres*
EMP: 11 EST: 2013
SALES (est): 348.8K **Privately Held**
SIC: 2835 In vitro diagnostics
PA: Biodesix, Inc.
2970 Wilderness Pl # 120
Boulder CO 80301

(P-8231)
INNOMINATA
Also Called: Genbio
15222 Avenue Of Science A, San Diego (92158-3422)
PHONE..................................858 592-9300
Fred Adler, *Partner*
David Lynette, *Partner*
▲ EMP: 18
SALES (est): 3.7MM **Privately Held**
WEB: www.genbio.com
SIC: 2835 In vitro diagnostics

(P-8232)
INNOVACON INC
9975 Summers Ridge Rd, San Diego (92121-2997)
PHONE..................................858 805-8900
John Bridgen, *CEO*
Jixun Lin, *President*
▲ EMP: 70
SALES (est): 10.8MM
SALES (corp-wide): 30.5B **Publicly Held**
SIC: 2835 In vitro & in vivo diagnostic substances
HQ: Alere Inc.
51 Sawyer Rd-Ste 200
Waltham MA 02453
781 647-3900

(P-8233)
INTERNATIONAL IMMUNOLOGY CORP
25549 Adams Ave, Murrieta (92562-9747)
P.O. Box 972 (92564-0972)
PHONE..................................951 677-5629
Shunsaku Shibota, *President*
▲ EMP: 42 EST: 1982
SQ FT: 20,000
SALES (est): 8.5MM **Privately Held**
WEB: www.iicsera.com
SIC: 2835 2836 In vitro & in vivo diagnostic substances; biological products, except diagnostic

(P-8234)
LIFE TECHNOLOGIES CORPORATION (HQ)
5781 Van Allen Way, Carlsbad (92008-7321)
P.O. Box 1039 (92018-1039)
PHONE..................................760 603-7200
Seth Hoogasian, *CEO*
Seth H Hoogasian, *CEO*
John A Cottingham, *Officer*
Peggy Lio, *Admin Sec*
Tom Dulan, *IT/INT Sup*
◆ EMP: 140

SALES (est): 3.2B
SALES (corp-wide): 24.3B **Publicly Held**
WEB: www.lifetechnologies.com
SIC: 2835 2836 In vitro & in vivo diagnostic substances; biological products, except diagnostic
PA: Thermo Fisher Scientific Inc.
168 3rd Ave
Waltham MA 02451
781 622-1000

(P-8235)
LIFEOME BIOLABS INC
10054 Mesa Ridge Ct, San Diego (92121-2945)
PHONE..................................619 302-0129
Zheng Chaojun, *President*
EMP: 19
SALES (corp-wide): 1.6MM **Privately Held**
SIC: 2835 8731 Microbiology & virology diagnostic products; biological research; biotechnical research, commercial
PA: Lifeome Biolabs Inc.
1895 Avenida Del Oro # 6554
Oceanside CA 92056
619 302-0129

(P-8236)
MEDICAL ANALYSIS SYSTEMS INC (DH)
46360 Fremont Blvd, Fremont (94538-6406)
PHONE..................................510 979-5000
Steve Kondor, *President*
Eric Scheinerman, *CFO*
Darwin Richardson, *Vice Pres*
EMP: 150
SQ FT: 180,000
SALES (est): 7.5MM
SALES (corp-wide): 24.3B **Publicly Held**
WEB: www.mas-inc.com
SIC: 2835 Blood derivative diagnostic agents
HQ: Fisher Scientific International Llc
81 Wyman St
Waltham MA 02451
781 622-1000

(P-8237)
METRA BIOSYSTEMS INC (HQ)
2981 Copper Rd, Santa Clara (95051)
PHONE..................................408 616-4300
John Tamerius, *Manager*
Bill Sommer, *Asst Controller*
EMP: 50
SQ FT: 24,000
SALES (est): 11.9MM
SALES (corp-wide): 522.2MM **Publicly Held**
SIC: 2835 In vitro & in vivo diagnostic substances
PA: Quidel Corporation
12544 High Bluff Dr # 200
San Diego CA 92130
858 552-1100

(P-8238)
MICROPOINT BIOSCIENCE INC
3521 Leonard Ct, Santa Clara (95054-2043)
PHONE..................................408 588-1682
Nan Zhang, *CEO*
▲ EMP: 30
SALES (est): 6.7MM
SALES (corp-wide): 17.3MM **Privately Held**
SIC: 2835 In vitro & in vivo diagnostic substances
PA: Micropoint Biotechnologies Co., Ltd.
2/3/6f,Taiping Health Building, No. 3
Shekou Industrial 5th Roa
Shenzhen 51806
755 866-7390

(P-8239)
MILLPLEDGE NORTH AMERICA INC
5310 Derry Ave Ste S&T, Agoura Hills (91301-4509)
PHONE..................................310 215-0400
▲ EMP: 11
SALES (est): 1.9MM **Privately Held**
SIC: 2835 8734 5122 Veterinary diagnostic substances; veterinary testing; pharmaceuticals

HQ: Millpledge Limited
Whinleys Estate
Retford NOTTS

(P-8240)
MINDRAY DS USA INC
Also Called: Mindray Innvtion Ctr Slcon Vly
2100 Gold St, San Jose (95002-3700)
PHONE..................................650 230-2800
EMP: 18 **Privately Held**
SIC: 2835 3841 3845 In vitro diagnostics; surgical & medical instruments; patient monitoring apparatus
HQ: Mindray Ds Usa, Inc.
800 Macarthur Blvd
Mahwah NJ 07430

(P-8241)
MONOGRAM BIOSCIENCES INC
345 Oyster Point Blvd, South San Francisco (94080-1913)
PHONE..................................650 635-1100
Floyd S Eberts III, *CEO*
Kathy L Hibbs, *Senior VP*
William J Welch, *Senior VP*
Kenneth N Hitchner, *Vice Pres*
Kay Limoli, *Associate Dir*
EMP: 382
SQ FT: 41,000
SALES (est): 60.9MM **Publicly Held**
WEB: www.monogrambio.com
SIC: 2835 In vitro & in vivo diagnostic substances
PA: Laboratory Corporation Of America Holdings
358 S Main St
Burlington NC 27215

(P-8242)
NOVA-ONE DIAGNOSTICS LLC
Also Called: Nod
22287 Mulholland Hwy, Calabasas (91302-5157)
PHONE..................................818 348-1543
Jonathan Gilchrist,
Roseanne Gilchrist,
EMP: 70
SALES (est): 6.6MM **Privately Held**
SIC: 2835 In vitro & in vivo diagnostic substances

(P-8243)
NOVARTIS PHARMACEUTICALS CORP
Also Called: Novartis Biophrmctcl Ops-Vcvll
2010 Cessna Dr, Vacaville (95688-8712)
PHONE..................................707 452-8081
Chris Busstioneau, *Manager*
EMP: 50
SALES (corp-wide): 51.9B **Privately Held**
WEB: www.chiron.com
SIC: 2835 2834 In vitro & in vivo diagnostic substances; pharmaceutical preparations
HQ: Novartis Pharmaceuticals Corporation
1 Health Plz
East Hanover NJ 07936
862 778-8300

(P-8244)
ONE LAMBDA INC (HQ)
21001 Kittridge St, Canoga Park (91303-2801)
PHONE..................................818 702-0042
Seth H Hoogasian, *CEO*
George M Ayoub, *President*
James Keegan, *CFO*
Don Arii, *Vice Pres*
Emiko Terasaki, *Admin Sec*
EMP: 83
SQ FT: 53,000
SALES (est): 75.4MM
SALES (corp-wide): 24.3B **Publicly Held**
WEB: www.onelambda.com
SIC: 2835 In vitro & in vivo diagnostic substances
PA: Thermo Fisher Scientific Inc.
168 3rd Ave
Waltham MA 02451
781 622-1000

(P-8245)
ORTHO-CLINICAL DIAGNOSTICS INC
1401 Red Hawk Cir E307, Fremont (94538-4747)
PHONE..................................908 704-5910
EMP: 33
SALES (corp-wide): 594.4MM **Privately Held**
SIC: 2835 Blood derivative diagnostic agents
PA: Ortho-Clinical Diagnostics, Inc.
1001 Route 202
Raritan NJ 08869
908 218-8000

(P-8246)
ORTHO-CLINICAL DIAGNOSTICS INC
612 W Katella Ave Ste B, Orange (92867-4608)
PHONE..................................714 639-2323
Robert Black, *Branch Mgr*
EMP: 20
SQ FT: 2,200
SALES (corp-wide): 594.4MM **Privately Held**
WEB: www.orthoclinical.com
SIC: 2835 Blood derivative diagnostic agents
PA: Ortho-Clinical Diagnostics, Inc.
1001 Route 202
Raritan NJ 08869
908 218-8000

(P-8247)
PACIFIC BIOTECH INC
10165 Mckellar Ct, San Diego (92121-4201)
PHONE..................................858 552-1100
Wayne Kay, *President*
EMP: 220
SQ FT: 70,000
SALES (est): 10.9MM
SALES (corp-wide): 522.2MM **Publicly Held**
WEB: www.quidel.com
SIC: 2835 Pregnancy test kits
PA: Quidel Corporation
12544 High Bluff Dr # 200
San Diego CA 92130
858 552-1100

(P-8248)
PROZYME INC
3832 Bay Center Pl, Hayward (94545-3619)
PHONE..................................510 638-6900
Sergey Vlasenko, *President*
C Richard Hutchinson, *VP Info Sys*
EMP: 47
SQ FT: 20,000
SALES (est): 11.3MM
SALES (corp-wide): 4.9B **Publicly Held**
WEB: www.prozyme.com
SIC: 2835 Blood derivative diagnostic agents
PA: Agilent Technologies, Inc.
5301 Stevens Creek Blvd
Santa Clara CA 95051
408 345-8886

(P-8249)
QUANDX INC
2176 Ringwood Ave, San Jose (95131-1720)
PHONE..................................650 262-4140
Xiaojun Lei, *CEO*
▲ EMP: 10 EST: 2010
SALES (est): 907.7K **Privately Held**
SIC: 2835 In vitro diagnostics

(P-8250)
QUANTIMETRIX CORPORATION
2005 Manhattan Beach Blvd, Redondo Beach (90278-1205)
PHONE..................................310 536-0006
Monty Ban, *President*
Edward Cleek, *CEO*
Abdee Akhavan, *CFO*
EMP: 70
SQ FT: 86,400

SALES (est): 18.3MM **Privately Held**
WEB: www.4qc.com
SIC: 2835 In vitro & in vivo diagnostic substances

(P-8251)
QUIDEL CORPORATION (PA)
12544 High Bluff Dr # 200, San Diego
(92130-3050)
PHONE..................................858 552-1100
Douglas C Bryant, *President*
Kenneth F Buechler, *Ch of Bd*
Randall J Steward, *CFO*
Michael D Abney Jr, *Senior VP*
Robert J Bujarski, *Senior VP*
EMP: 277 EST: 1979
SQ FT: 30,000
SALES: 522.2MM **Publicly Held**
WEB: www.quidel.com
SIC: 2835 Pregnancy test kits

(P-8252)
**SCANTIBODIES LABORATORY
INC (PA)**
9336 Abraham Way, Santee (92071-2861)
PHONE..................................619 258-9300
Thomas L Cantor, *CEO*
John Van Duzer, *COO*
Cheryl Cantor, *Vice Pres*
Gerardo Magana, *Business Dir*
Joe Pascual, *Research*
▲ EMP: 240
SQ FT: 60,500
SALES (est): 101.9MM **Privately Held**
WEB: www.scantibodies.com
SIC: 2835 Pregnancy test kits

(P-8253)
**SEKISUI AMERICA
CORPORATION**
Genzyme Diagnostics
6659 Top Gun St, San Diego (92121-4113)
PHONE..................................858 452-3198
Brian Danieli, *Branch Mgr*
Theresa Narciso, *Manager*
EMP: 21 **Privately Held**
WEB: www.genzyme.com
SIC: 2835 In vitro & in vivo diagnostic substances
HQ: Sekisui America Corporation
333 Meadowlands Pkwy
Secaucus NJ 07094
201 423-7960

(P-8254)
SEQUENTA LLC
329 Oyster Point Blvd, South San Francisco (94080-1913)
PHONE..................................650 243-3900
Tom Willis, *CEO*
Malek Faham, *Security Dir*
EMP: 60
SALES (est): 9.2MM **Publicly Held**
SIC: 2835 2836 In vitro & in vivo diagnostic substances; biological products, except diagnostic
PA: Adaptive Biotechnologies Corporation
1551 Eastlake Ave E # 200
Seattle WA 98102

(P-8255)
SERADYN INC
46360 Fremont Blvd, Fremont
(94538-6406)
PHONE..................................317 610-3800
Mark Roberts, *President*
EMP: 90
SQ FT: 40,000
SALES (est): 7.9MM
SALES (corp-wide): 24.3B **Publicly Held**
WEB: www.seradyn.com
SIC: 2835 Microbiology & virology diagnostic products
HQ: Fisher Scientific International Llc
81 Wyman St
Waltham MA 02451
781 622-1000

(P-8256)
**SIEMENS HLTHCARE
DGNOSTICS INC**
Also Called: Siemens Medical Solutions
5210 Pacific Concourse Dr, Los Angeles
(90045-6900)
PHONE..................................310 645-8200
Anthony Bihl, *Branch Mgr*
EMP: 55
SALES (corp-wide): 95B **Privately Held**
WEB: www.dpcweb.com
SIC: 2835 Veterinary diagnostic substances
HQ: Siemens Healthcare Diagnostics Inc.
511 Benedict Ave
Tarrytown NY 10591
914 631-8000

(P-8257)
**SIEMENS HLTHCARE
DGNOSTICS INC**
2040 Enterprise Blvd, West Sacramento
(95691-5045)
PHONE..................................916 372-1900
Rick Lee, *Manager*
EMP: 25
SALES (corp-wide): 95B **Privately Held**
WEB: www.dpcweb.com
SIC: 2835 In vitro & in vivo diagnostic substances
HQ: Siemens Healthcare Diagnostics Inc.
511 Benedict Ave
Tarrytown NY 10591
914 631-8000

(P-8258)
SINGULAR BIO INC
455 Mission Bay Blvd S # 145, San Francisco (94158-2159)
PHONE..................................415 553-8773
Hywel Jones, *CEO*
EMP: 12
SALES (est): 339K **Privately Held**
SIC: 2835 In vitro diagnostics

(P-8259)
SOFIE BIOSCIENCES INC (PA)
160 Briston Pkwy Ste 200, Culver City
(90230)
PHONE..................................310 215-3159
Patrick W Phelps, *CEO*
Michael Phelps, *Ch of Bd*
Johannes Czernin, *Managing Dir*
Ruben Guzman, *Engineer*
Philipp Czernin, *Finance Dir*
EMP: 35
SQ FT: 3,500
SALES (est): 171.6MM **Privately Held**
SIC: 2835 In vitro diagnostics

(P-8260)
SOURCE BIO INC
43379 Bus Pk Dr Ste 100, Temecula
(92590-3687)
PHONE..................................951 676-1000
Duane Pinkerton, *President*
Theresa Pinkerton, *Exec VP*
◆ EMP: 10
SALES (est): 1.2MM **Privately Held**
WEB: www.sourcebioinc.com
SIC: 2835 Blood derivative diagnostic agents

(P-8261)
SPRING BIOSCIENCE CORP
4300 Hacienda Dr, Pleasanton
(94588-2722)
PHONE..................................925 474-8463
Meghan Lehrkamp, *Manager*
EMP: 809
SALES (est): 97.5MM
SALES (corp-wide): 57.2B **Privately Held**
WEB: www.springbio.com
SIC: 2835 In vitro & in vivo diagnostic substances
HQ: Ventana Medical Systems, Inc.
1910 E Innovation Park Dr
Oro Valley AZ 85755
520 887-2155

(P-8262)
SYNBIOTICS LLC
16420 Via Esprillo, San Diego
(92127-1702)
PHONE..................................858 451-3771

Keith A Butler, *Branch Mgr*
Frank Clifford, *Vice Pres*
Michael Woodard, *Exec Dir*
Sarah Chalangaran, *Director*
EMP: 20
SALES (corp-wide): 5.8B **Publicly Held**
SIC: 2835 Veterinary diagnostic substances
HQ: Synbiotics Llc
12200 Nw Ambassador
Kansas City MO 64163
816 464-3500

(P-8263)
SYNTRON BIORESEARCH INC
2774 Loker Ave W, Carlsbad (92010-6610)
PHONE..................................760 930-2200
Charles Yu, *President*
Ted Chen, *Vice Pres*
▲ EMP: 278
SALES (est): 44.5MM **Privately Held**
WEB: www.syntron.net
SIC: 2835 In vitro & in vivo diagnostic substances; biologicals & allied products

(P-8264)
TECO DIAGNOSTICS
1268 N Lakeview Ave, Anaheim
(92807-1831)
PHONE..................................714 693-7788
K C Chen, *President*
Kelly Chen, *Research*
Hui-Ling Koh, *Research*
Aquil Merchant, *Research*
Dhaval Waghela, *Research*
◆ EMP: 70
SQ FT: 40,000
SALES (est): 16.8MM **Privately Held**
WEB: www.tecodiag.com
SIC: 2835 5049 In vitro & in vivo diagnostic substances; laboratory equipment, except medical or dental

(P-8265)
TROVAGENE INC
11055 Flintkote Ave Ste A, San Diego
(92121-1220)
PHONE..................................858 952-7570
Thomas H Adams, *Ch of Bd*
Mark Erlander, *Officer*
Leilani Smith, *Executive Asst*
Sandra Silberman,
EMP: 13
SQ FT: 26,100
SALES: 378.3K **Privately Held**
SIC: 2835 2836 In vitro & in vivo diagnostic substances; biological products, except diagnostic

---

**2836 Biological Prdts, Exc
Diagnostic Substances**

(P-8266)
ABZENA (SAN DIEGO) INC
8810 Rehco Rd Ste E, San Diego
(92121-3262)
PHONE..................................858 550-4094
John Burton, *CEO*
Gary Pierce, *President*
Leigh N Pierce, *CTO*
EMP: 12
SQ FT: 7,245
SALES (est): 4.1MM
SALES (corp-wide): 222K **Privately Held**
WEB: www.pacificgmp.com
SIC: 2836 Biological products, except diagnostic
HQ: Abzena Limited
Babraham Hall
Cambridge CAMBS CB22
122 390-3498

(P-8267)
**ADVERUM BIOTECHNOLOGIES
INC**
1035 Obrien Dr Ste A, Menlo Park
(94025-1408)
PHONE..................................650 272-6269
Leone Patterson, *President*
Paul B Cleveland, *Ch of Bd*
Patrick Machado, *Ch of Bd*

Thomas Leung, *CFO*
Linda Neuman, *Chief Mktg Ofcr*
EMP: 78
SQ FT: 36,000
SALES: 1.6MM **Privately Held**
SIC: 2836 8731 Biological products, except diagnostic; biotechnical research, commercial

(P-8268)
ALLIANCE ANALYTICAL INC
355 Fairview Way, Milpitas (95035-3024)
PHONE..................................800 916-5600
John H Muliken III, *President*
EMP: 25
SALES (est): 5.6MM **Privately Held**
SIC: 2836 5049 Biological products, except diagnostic; laboratory equipment, except medical or dental

(P-8269)
**ALTA ADVANCED
TECHNOLOGIES INC**
760 E Sunkist St, Ontario (91761-1861)
PHONE..................................909 983-2973
Steven G Boland Jr, *President*
▲ EMP: 45
SQ FT: 12,723
SALES: 6MM **Privately Held**
SIC: 2836 2851 3827 Biological products, except diagnostic; coating, air curing; lens coating equipment

(P-8270)
AMGEN INC (PA)
1 Amgen Center Dr, Thousand Oaks
(91320-1799)
PHONE..................................805 447-1000
Robert A Bradway, *Ch of Bd*
David W Meline, *CFO*
Cynthia M Patton, *Ch Credit Ofcr*
Murdo Gordon, *Exec VP*
David M Reese, *Exec VP*
◆ EMP: 2577
SALES: 23.7B **Publicly Held**
WEB: www.amgen.com
SIC: 2836 Biological products, except diagnostic

(P-8271)
AMGEN USA INC (HQ)
1 Amgen Center Dr, Thousand Oaks
(91320-1799)
PHONE..................................805 447-1000
Kevin W Sharer, *CEO*
EMP: 99
SALES (est): 1.5MM
SALES (corp-wide): 23.7B **Publicly Held**
SIC: 2836 Biological products, except diagnostic
PA: Amgen Inc.
1 Amgen Center Dr
Thousand Oaks CA 91320
805 447-1000

(P-8272)
**ARMATA PHARMACEUTICALS
INC (PA)**
4503 Glencoe Ave, Marina Del Rey
(90292-6372)
PHONE..................................310 655-2928
Todd R Patrick, *CEO*
Brian Varnum, *President*
Steve R Martin, *CFO*
EMP: 56
SALES (est): 8.2MM **Publicly Held**
WEB: www.targen.com
SIC: 2836 Biological products, except diagnostic

(P-8273)
**ATARA BIOTHERAPEUTICS INC
(PA)**
611 Gateway Blvd Ste 900, South San
Francisco (94080-7029)
PHONE..................................650 278-8930
Pascal Touchon, *President*
Utpal Koppikar, *CFO*
Mitchall G Clark, *Officer*
Christopher Haqq, *Exec VP*
Joe Newell, *Exec VP*
EMP: 117
SQ FT: 13,670

SALES (est): 83.5MM **Publicly Held**
SIC: **2836** 8731 Biological products, except diagnostic; biotechnical research, commercial; medical research, commercial

(P-8274)
ATARA BIOTHERAPEUTICS INC
2430 Conejo Spectrum St, Thousand Oaks (91320-1445)
PHONE..................................805 309-9534
EMP: 19
SALES (corp-wide): 83.5MM **Publicly Held**
SIC: **2836** Biological products, except diagnostic
PA: Atara Biotherapeutics, Inc.
611 Gateway Blvd Ste 900
South San Francisco CA 94080
650 278-8930

(P-8275)
ATRECA INC
500 Saginaw Dr, Redwood City (94063-4750)
PHONE..................................650 595-2595
John A Orwin, *President*
Norman Michael Greenberg, *Officer*
Tito A Serafini, *Officer*
Andrew Swinnerton, *Associate Dir*
Guy Cavet, *CTO*
EMP: 85
SQ FT: 41,124
SALES (est): 23.6MM **Privately Held**
SIC: **2836** Biological products, except diagnostic

(P-8276)
ATYR PHARMA INC
3545 John Hopkins Ct # 2, San Diego (92121-1108)
PHONE..................................858 731-8389
Sanjay S Shukla, *President*
John K Clarke, *Ch of Bd*
EMP: 42
SQ FT: 24,494
SALES (est): 16.2MM **Privately Held**
SIC: **2836** 2834 Biological products, except diagnostic; pharmaceutical preparations

(P-8277)
AUDENTES THERAPEUTICS INC (PA)
600 California St Fl 17, San Francisco (94108-2725)
PHONE..................................415 818-1001
Matthew Patterson, *Ch of Bd*
Natalie Holles, *President*
Thomas Soloway, *CFO*
Eric B Mosbrooker, *Ch Credit Ofcr*
Edward R Conner, *Chief Mktg Ofcr*
EMP: 115 EST: 2012
SQ FT: 29,496
SALES (est): 35.7MM **Publicly Held**
SIC: **2836** Biological products, except diagnostic

(P-8278)
AZURE BIOSYSTEMS INC
6747 Sierra Ct Ste A, Dublin (94568-2651)
PHONE..................................925 307-7127
Alnoor Mohamedali Shivji, *CEO*
Lisa Isailovic, *Marketing Staff*
▲ EMP: 40
SALES (est): 8.2MM **Privately Held**
SIC: **2836** Biological products, except diagnostic

(P-8279)
B-BRIDGE INTERNATIONAL INC
3350 Scott Blvd Bldg 29, Santa Clara (95054-3105)
PHONE..................................408 252-6200
Hiroyuki Masumoto, *CEO*
▲ EMP: 30
SALES (est): 6.5MM **Privately Held**
WEB: www.b-bridge.com
SIC: **2836** Biological products, except diagnostic

(P-8280)
BACHEM AMERICAS INC (DH)
Also Called: Bachem California
3132 Kashiwa St, Torrance (90505-4087)
PHONE..................................310 784-4440

Brian Gregg, *CEO*
Jessica Novak, *Partner*
Michael Brenk, *CFO*
Peter Hutchings, *Vice Pres*
Fariba Jashnian, *Vice Pres*
▲ EMP: 206
SQ FT: 70,000
SALES (est): 73.8MM
SALES (corp-wide): 115.6MM **Privately Held**
SIC: **2836** 2834 Biological products, except diagnostic; pharmaceutical preparations
HQ: Bachem Holding Ag
Hauptstrasse 144
Bubendorf BL 4416
619 352-333

(P-8281)
BACHEM BIOSCIENCE INC
3132 Kashiwa St, Torrance (90505-4087)
PHONE..................................310 784-7322
Peter Grogg, *Ch of Bd*
Cara Zeno, *Admin Asst*
David Floyd, *Controller*
▲ EMP: 37
SALES (est): 5.9MM
SALES (corp-wide): 115.6MM **Privately Held**
SIC: **2836** 2899 Biological products, except diagnostic; chemical preparations
HQ: Bachem Holding Ag
Hauptstrasse 144
Bubendorf BL 4416
619 352-333

(P-8282)
BIOLEGEND INC (PA)
8999 Biolegend Way, San Diego (92121-2284)
PHONE..................................858 455-9588
Gene Lay, *President*
Bill Kullback, *CFO*
Kim Clark, *Vice Pres*
William Godfrey, *Program Mgr*
Richard Alouche, *General Mgr*
◆ EMP: 206
SQ FT: 75,000
SALES (est): 114.2MM
SALES (corp-wide): 107.7MM **Privately Held**
WEB: www.biolegend.com
SIC: **2836** Biological products, except diagnostic

(P-8283)
BIOMER TECHNOLOGY LLC
1233 Quarry Ln 135, Pleasanton (94566-8452)
PHONE..................................925 426-0787
Cheng Chou,
Steve Lee,
EMP: 10
SQ FT: 3,000
SALES (est): 1.5MM **Privately Held**
WEB: www.biomertech.com
SIC: **2836** 8731 Biological products, except diagnostic; biotechnical research, commercial

(P-8284)
BIOSEARCH TECHNOLOGIES INC (DH)
Also Called: Lgc Biosearch Technologies
2199 S Mcdowell Blvd, Petaluma (94954-6904)
PHONE..................................415 883-8400
Ronald M Cook, *CEO*
Bernard Slack, *Technology*
Mikey Songster, *Technology*
Kathleen Ritter, *Project Engr*
Nik Von Atzigen, *QC Mgr*
EMP: 120
SQ FT: 121,000
SALES (est): 28MM **Privately Held**
WEB: www.btidna.com
SIC: **2836** 2899 2835 2869 Biological products, except diagnostic; chemical preparations; in vitro diagnostics; industrial organic chemicals
HQ: Lgc Science Group Limited
Queens Road
Teddington MIDDX
208 943-7000

(P-8285)
CELPROGEN INC
3914 Del Amo Blvd Ste 901, Torrance (90503-2175)
PHONE..................................310 542-8822
Jay Sharma, *President*
▼ EMP: 10
SQ FT: 5,000
SALES (est): 2MM **Privately Held**
WEB: www.celprogen.com
SIC: **2836** Biological products, except diagnostic

(P-8286)
CENTERLINE PRECISION INC
2265 Calle Del Mundo, Santa Clara (95054-1006)
PHONE..................................408 988-4380
Ricardo Rengifo, *CEO*
EMP: 13
SQ FT: 5,000
SALES (est): 1.3MM **Privately Held**
WEB: www.centerlinep.com
SIC: **2836** Biological products, except diagnostic

(P-8287)
CERUS CORPORATION (PA)
2550 Stanwell Dr Ste 300, Concord (94520-4813)
PHONE..................................925 288-6000
William M Greenman, *President*
Kevin D Green, *CFO*
Timothy Anderson, *Bd of Directors*
Laurence M Corash, *Chief Mktg Ofcr*
Chrystal N Menard,
▲ EMP: 173
SQ FT: 36,029
SALES: 60.9MM **Publicly Held**
WEB: www.cerus.com
SIC: **2836** Biological products, except diagnostic

(P-8288)
CHECKERSPOT INC
740 Heinz Ave, Berkeley (94710-2748)
PHONE..................................510 239-7921
Charles Dimmler, *CEO*
EMP: 10
SQ FT: 1,000
SALES (est): 131.8K **Privately Held**
SIC: **2836** Biological products, except diagnostic

(P-8289)
CIDARA THERAPEUTICS INC (PA)
6310 Nncy Rdge Dr Ste 101, San Diego (92121)
PHONE..................................858 752-6170
Jeffrey L Stein, *President*
Scott M Rocklage, *Ch of Bd*
Paul Daruwala, *COO*
James Levine, *CFO*
Taylor Sandison, *Chief Mktg Ofcr*
EMP: 56 EST: 2012
SQ FT: 29,638
SALES (est): 14.2MM **Publicly Held**
SIC: **2836** 8731 Biological products, except diagnostic; biotechnical research, commercial

(P-8290)
CLINIQA CORPORATION (HQ)
495 Enterprise St, San Marcos (92078-4364)
PHONE..................................760 744-1900
Kevin Gould, *President*
C Granger Haugh, *CEO*
Dean Harriman, *CFO*
Larry Beaty, *Vice Pres*
Shing Kwan, *Vice Pres*
▼ EMP: 76
SQ FT: 25,000
SALES (est): 18.5MM
SALES (corp-wide): 714MM **Publicly Held**
WEB: www.cliniqa.com
SIC: **2836** Biological products, except diagnostic
PA: Bio-Techne Corporation
614 Mckinley Pl Ne
Minneapolis MN 55413
612 379-8854

(P-8291)
COHERUS BIOSCIENCES INC
Also Called: Coherus Analytical Laboratory
4014 Cmino Ranchero Ste A, Camarillo (93012)
PHONE..................................805 445-7051
EMP: 92
SALES (corp-wide): 1.5MM **Publicly Held**
SIC: **2836** Biological products, except diagnostic
PA: Coherus Biosciences, Inc.
333 Twin Dolphin Dr # 600
Redwood City CA 94065
650 649-3530

(P-8292)
CYTRX CORPORATION (PA)
11726 San Vicente Blvd # 650, Los Angeles (90049-5079)
PHONE..................................310 826-5648
Steven A Kriegsman, *Ch of Bd*
Eric L Curtis, *President*
John Y Caloz, *CFO*
Shanta Chawla, *Senior VP*
Felix Kratz, *Vice Pres*
EMP: 20
SQ FT: 5,739
SALES: 250K **Publicly Held**
SIC: **2836** Biological products, except diagnostic

(P-8293)
DENALI THERAPEUTICS INC (PA)
161 Oyster Point Blvd, South San Francisco (94080-1910)
PHONE..................................650 866-8548
Ryan J Watts, *President*
Vicki Sato, *Ch of Bd*
Alexander O Schuth, *COO*
Steve E Krognes, *CFO*
Carole Ho, *Chief Mktg Ofcr*
EMP: 107
SALES: 129.1MM **Publicly Held**
SIC: **2836** 2834 Biological products, except diagnostic; pharmaceutical preparations

(P-8294)
DYNAVAX TECHNOLOGIES CORP (PA)
2100 Powell St Ste 900, Emeryville (94608-1844)
PHONE..................................510 848-5100
Eddie Gray, *CEO*
EMP: 154
SQ FT: 55,200
SALES: 8.2MM **Publicly Held**
WEB: www.dynavax.com
SIC: **2836** 8731 Biological products, except diagnostic; biological research; commercial physical research

(P-8295)
EIGER BIOPHARMACEUTICALS INC (PA)
2155 Park Blvd, Palo Alto (94306-1543)
PHONE..................................650 272-6138
David Cory, *President*
David Apelian, *COO*
SRI Ryali, *CFO*
Jeffrey Glenn, *Bd of Directors*
EMP: 10
SQ FT: 1,570
SALES: 2.5MM **Publicly Held**
WEB: www.celladon.net
SIC: **2836** 3845 Biological products, except diagnostic; cardiographs

(P-8296)
EMD MILLIPORE CORPORATION
Also Called: Bioscience Research Reagents
28820 Single Oak Dr, Temecula (92590-3607)
PHONE..................................951 676-8080
John Ambroziak, *Manager*
Patrick Schneider, *Vice Pres*
Helmut Pacher, *Director*
EMP: 180
SALES (corp-wide): 16.9B **Privately Held**
WEB: www.millipore.com
SIC: **2836** 2835 3826 Biological products, except diagnostic; vaccines; in vitro & in vivo diagnostic substances; liquid testing apparatus

PRODUCTS & SVCS

HQ: Emd Millipore Corporation
400 Summit Dr
Burlington MA 01803
781 533-6000

(P-8297)
EQUILLIUM INC
2223 Avenida De La Playa, La Jolla
(92037-3200)
PHONE....................858 412-5302
Daniel M Bradbury, *Ch of Bd*
Bruce D Steel, *President*
Jason A Keyes, *CFO*
Krishna R Polu, *Chief Mktg Ofcr*
Stephen Connelly, *Security Dir*
EMP: 11
SQ FT: 1,750
SALES (est): 1.3MM **Privately Held**
SIC: 2836 Biological products, except diagnostic

(P-8298)
EVOLVA INC
80 E Sir Francis Drake Bl, Larkspur
(94939-1709)
PHONE....................415 448-5451
Murali P Muthuwamy, *President*
Jorgen Hansen, *Officer*
Hannah Gertjegerdes, *Executive Asst*
Grace Park, *Research*
Kari Thomas, *Research*
EMP: 15
SQ FT: 11,000
SALES: 5.8MM
SALES (corp-wide): 8.9MM **Privately Held**
SIC: 2836 Biological products, except diagnostic
HQ: Evolva Ag
Duggingerstrasse 23
Reinach BL 4153
614 852-000

(P-8299)
EXPRESSION SYSTEMS LLC (PA)
2537 2nd St, Davis (95618-5475)
PHONE....................877 877-7421
David Hedin,
EMP: 27
SQ FT: 27,000
SALES: 2MM **Privately Held**
WEB: www.expressionsystems.com
SIC: 2836 Culture media

(P-8300)
FATE THERAPEUTICS INC
3535 General Atomics Ct # 20, San Diego
(92121-1140)
PHONE....................858 875-1800
William H Rastetter, *Ch of Bd*
J Scott Wolchko, *President*
John D Mendlein, *Vice Ch Bd*
Sarah Cooley, *Senior VP*
Wen Bo Wang, *Senior VP*
EMP: 11 EST: 2007
SQ FT: 48,000
SALES: 4.7MM **Privately Held**
SIC: 2836 8731 Biological products, except diagnostic; biotechnical research, commercial

(P-8301)
FLASH BACK USA
1535 Templeton Rd, Templeton
(93465-9694)
PHONE....................805 434-0321
Andrew McArthur, *President*
EMP: 16
SALES (est): 1.5MM **Privately Held**
SIC: 2836 Veterinary biological products

(P-8302)
FUJIFILM IRVINE SCIENTIFIC INC
Also Called: Irvine Scientific
1830 E Warner Ave, Santa Ana
(92705-5505)
PHONE....................949 261-7800
Yutaka Yamaguchi, *CEO*
Akiko Ohno, *President*
Ryo Iguchi, *CFO*
Toru Naganuma, *Officer*
Fiona Barry, *Executive*
▲ EMP: 150
SQ FT: 20,000

SALES: 31.9MM **Privately Held**
WEB: www.irvinesci.com
SIC: 2836 5047 Blood derivatives; culture media; medical laboratory equipment
HQ: Fujifilm Holdings America Corporation
200 Summit Lake Dr Fl 2
Valhalla NY 10595
914 789-8100

(P-8303)
FUSION 360 INC
677 E Olive Ave, Turlock (95380-4013)
P.O. Box 1004 (95381-1004)
PHONE....................209 632-0139
Thomas Yamashita PHD, *President*
Alfredo Lara, *Technical Staff*
Robert Buenrostro, *Consultant*
EMP: 12
SALES (est): 1.1MM **Privately Held**
SIC: 2836 Biological products, except diagnostic

(P-8304)
GILEAD SCIENCES INC
4049 Avenida De La Plata, Oceanside
(92056-5802)
PHONE....................760 945-7701
EMP: 14
SALES (corp-wide): 22.1B **Publicly Held**
SIC: 2836 Biological products, except diagnostic
PA: Gilead Sciences, Inc.
333 Lakeside Dr
Foster City CA 94404
650 574-3000

(P-8305)
GRIFOLS BIOLOGICALS LLC (DH)
2410 Lillyvale Ave, Los Angeles
(90032-3514)
PHONE....................323 225-2221
Greg Rich, *CEO*
Max Debrouwer, *CFO*
David Bell, *Vice Pres*
Kevin Sullivan, *Research*
Lynette Thomas, *Training Spec*
▲ EMP: 277
SALES (est): 187.8MM
SALES (corp-wide): 741MM **Privately Held**
WEB: www.alphather.com
SIC: 2836 2834 Plasmas; pharmaceutical preparations
HQ: Grifols Shared Services North America, Inc.
2410 Lillyvale Ave
Los Angeles CA 90032
323 225-2221

(P-8306)
GRITSTONE ONCOLOGY INC (PA)
5858 Horton St Ste 210, Emeryville
(94608-2006)
PHONE....................510 871-6100
Andrew Allen, *President*
Jean-Marc Bellemin, *CFO*
Raphael Rousseau, *Chief Mktg Ofcr*
Matthew Hawryluk, *Exec VP*
Erin Jones, *Exec VP*
EMP: 109
SQ FT: 13,100
SALES: 1.1MM **Publicly Held**
SIC: 2836 Biological products, except diagnostic

(P-8307)
HALOZYME THERAPEUTICS INC (PA)
11388 Sorrento Valley Rd # 200, San Diego
(92121-1345)
PHONE....................858 794-8889
Connie L Matsui, *Ch of Bd*
Helen I Torley, *President*
Laurie D Stelzer, *CFO*
Harry J Leonhardt, *Ch Credit Ofcr*
Alison A Armour, *Senior VP*
EMP: 84 EST: 1998
SQ FT: 76,000
SALES: 151.8MM **Publicly Held**
WEB: www.halozyme.com
SIC: 2836 2834 Biological products, except diagnostic; pharmaceutical preparations

(P-8308)
HEMOSTAT LABORATORIES INC (PA)
515 Industrial Way, Dixon (95620-9779)
P.O. Box 790 (95620-0790)
PHONE....................707 678-9594
Jim Mc Elligott, *President*
Gordon Murphy, *Vice Pres*
Kate Murphy, *General Mgr*
EMP: 20
SQ FT: 9,500
SALES (est): 3.1MM **Privately Held**
WEB: www.hemostat.com
SIC: 2836 2673 Blood derivatives; plastic & pliofilm bags

(P-8309)
HONGENE BIOTECH CORPORATION
29520 Kohoutek Way, Union City
(94587-1221)
PHONE....................650 520-9678
WEI Jiang, *Owner*
EMP: 12
SALES: 800K **Privately Held**
SIC: 2836 Biological products, except diagnostic

(P-8310)
HYGIEIA BIOLOGICAL LABS (PA)
1785 E Main St Ste 4, Woodland
(95776-6206)
P.O. Box 8300 (95776-8300)
PHONE....................530 661-1442
James L Wallis, *President*
Barry Kersting, *Prdtn Mgr*
EMP: 20
SQ FT: 4,000
SALES (est): 3.2MM **Privately Held**
WEB: www.hygieialabs.com
SIC: 2836 5047 Veterinary biological products; veterinarians' equipment & supplies

(P-8311)
INFRATAB
4347 Raytheon Rd Unit 6, Oxnard
(93033-8225)
PHONE....................805 986-8880
Therese E Myers, *Principal*
Stanton Kaye, *Principal*
EMP: 25
SQ FT: 15,000
SALES (est): 3.5MM **Privately Held**
WEB: www.infratab.com
SIC: 2836 Biological products, except diagnostic

(P-8312)
INTEGRATED DNA TECH INC
6828 Nncy Rdge Dr Ste 400, San Diego
(92121)
PHONE....................858 410-6677
Jack Jacobs, *Vice Pres*
Dean E Daggett, *Agent*
Jeff Wolking, *Agent*
EMP: 17
SALES (corp-wide): 19.8B **Publicly Held**
SIC: 2836 Biological products, except diagnostic
HQ: Integrated Dna Technologies, Inc.
1710 Commercial Park
Coralville IA 52241
847 745-1700

(P-8313)
LIFE TECHNOLOGIES CORPORATION
Also Called: Supplier Diversity Program
5791 Van Allen Way, Carlsbad
(92008-7321)
PHONE....................760 918-4259
Melissa Roberts, *Engineer*
David Daly, *Oncology*
Brian Patch, *Senior Mgr*
Armin Spura, *Director*
Jennifer Gericke, *Manager*
EMP: 100
SALES (corp-wide): 24.3B **Publicly Held**
SIC: 2836 Biological products, except diagnostic
HQ: Life Technologies Corporation
5781 Van Allen Way
Carlsbad CA 92008
760 603-7200

(P-8314)
LINEAGE CELL THERAPEUTICS INC (PA)
2173 Salk Ave Ste 200, Carlsbad
(92008-7354)
PHONE....................510 521-3390
Brian M Culley, *CEO*
Neal Bradsher, *Bd of Directors*
Edward D Wirth III, *Chief Mktg Ofcr*
Tony Kalajian, *Officer*
Gary S Hogge, *Senior VP*
EMP: 79
SALES: 4.9MM **Publicly Held**
WEB: www.biotimeinc.com
SIC: 2836 8731 Biological products, except diagnostic; biotechnical research, commercial

(P-8315)
LIST BIOLOGICAL LABS INC
Also Called: List Labs
540 Division St, Campbell (95008-6906)
PHONE....................408 866-6363
Karen Crawford, *President*
Debra Booth, *Vice Pres*
Debra Dye, *Vice Pres*
Linda Eaton, *Vice Pres*
Megan Dawson, *Administration*
▼ EMP: 25
SQ FT: 11,000
SALES (est): 8.3MM **Privately Held**
WEB: www.listlabs.com
SIC: 2836 Biological products, except diagnostic

(P-8316)
NANTKWEST INC
9920 Jefferson Blvd, Culver City
(90232-3506)
PHONE....................858 633-0300
EMP: 10
SALES (corp-wide): 1.3MM **Publicly Held**
SIC: 2836 Biological products, except diagnostic
HQ: Nantkwest, Inc.
3530 John Hopkins Ct
San Diego CA 92121

(P-8317)
NANTKWEST INC (HQ)
3530 John Hopkins Ct, San Diego
(92121-1121)
PHONE....................805 633-0300
Patrick Soon-Shiong, *Ch of Bd*
Barry J Simon, *President*
Sonja Nelson, *CFO*
Steve Gorlin, *Vice Ch Bd*
John Lee, *Senior VP*
EMP: 31
SQ FT: 44,681
SALES: 47K
SALES (corp-wide): 1.3MM **Publicly Held**
SIC: 2836 Biological products, except diagnostic
PA: Cambridge Equities, Lp
9922 Jefferson Blvd
Culver City CA 90232
858 350-2300

(P-8318)
NITTOBO AMERICA INC
25549 Adams Ave, Murrieta (92562-9747)
PHONE....................951 677-5629
Tatsuo Sakae, *President*
◆ EMP: 97
SQ FT: 3,049,200
SALES: 18.8MM **Privately Held**
SIC: 2836 Biological products, except diagnostic
PA: Nitto Boseki Co., Ltd.
2-4-1, Kojimachi
Chiyoda-Ku TKY 102-0

(P-8319)
ORGANOVO INC
6275 Nncy Rdge Dr Ste 110, San Diego
(92121)
PHONE....................858 224-1000
Taylor Crouch, *CEO*
Craig Kussman, *CFO*
Sharon Presnell, *Officer*
Eric Davis, *Exec VP*
Susan Daugherty, *Senior VP*
EMP: 111

▲ = Import ▼=Export
◆ =Import/Export

SALES (est): 1.6MM
SALES (corp-wide): 3MM **Publicly Held**
SIC: 2836 Biological products, except diagnostic
PA: Organovo Holdings, Inc.
   6275 Nncy Rdge Dr Ste 110
   San Diego CA 92121
   858 224-1000

(P-8320)
PDL BIOPHARMA INC
1500 Seaport Blvd, Redwood City
(94063-5540)
PHONE..............................650 454-1000
Daniel Levitt, *Branch Mgr*
EMP: 40
SALES (corp-wide): 198.1MM **Publicly Held**
WEB: www.pdl.com
SIC: 2836 Biological products, except diagnostic
PA: Pdl Biopharma, Inc.
   932 Southwood Blvd
   Incline Village NV 89451
   775 832-8500

(P-8321)
PHL ASSOCIATES INC
24711 County Road 100a, Davis
(95616-9410)
PHONE..............................530 753-5881
Jeff Wichmann, *President*
Mary Holmes, *Admin Sec*
Patricia Hanzo, *Admin Asst*
Gene Huh, *Technician*
Dr Howard Gray, *Director*
EMP: 10 **EST:** 1960
SQ FT: 7,000
SALES (est): 1.6MM **Privately Held**
WEB: www.phlassociates.com
SIC: 2836 Vaccines; veterinary biological products

(P-8322)
PLASVACC USA INC
1535 Templeton Rd, Templeton
(93465-9694)
PHONE..............................805 434-0321
Andrew McArthur, *President*
EMP: 15
SALES (est): 1MM **Privately Held**
WEB: www.plasvaccusa.com
SIC: 2836 Biological products, except diagnostic

(P-8323)
PROLACTA BIOSCIENCE INC
(PA)
757 Baldwin Park Blvd, City of Industry
(91746-1504)
PHONE..............................626 599-9260
Scott A Elster, *CEO*
Joseph Fournell, *Vice Pres*
Alan Kofsky, *Vice Pres*
Susan Neumann, *Vice Pres*
Emily Tung, *Vice Pres*
▼ **EMP:** 132
SQ FT: 65,000
SALES (est): 45.4MM **Privately Held**
WEB: www.prolacta.com
SIC: 2836 Biological products, except diagnostic

(P-8324)
PROTEUS DIGITAL HEALTH INC
3956 Point Eden Way, Hayward
(94545-3719)
PHONE..............................650 632-4031
Andrew Thompson, *Principal*
Neela Paykel, *Vice Pres*
Peter Bjeletich, *Senior Mgr*
Jenny Amistoso, *Supervisor*
EMP: 168
SALES (corp-wide): 185.2MM **Privately Held**
SIC: 2836 Biological products, except diagnostic
PA: Proteus Digital Health, Inc.
   2600 Bridge Pkwy
   Redwood City CA 94065
   650 632-4031

(P-8325)
PROTEUS DIGITAL HEALTH INC
(PA)
2600 Bridge Pkwy, Redwood City
(94065-6136)
PHONE..............................650 632-4031
Andrew Thompson, *CEO*
Ben Costello, *Senior VP*
Sean Handel, *Senior VP*
Kenneth Chee, *Vice Pres*
Christopher Reggiardo, *Vice Pres*
▲ **EMP:** 250
SALES (est): 185.2MM **Privately Held**
WEB: www.proteusbiomedical.com
SIC: 2836 Biological products, except diagnostic

(P-8326)
RAINIER THERAPEUTICS INC
1040 Davis St Ste 202, San Leandro
(94577-1519)
PHONE..............................925 413-6140
Scott D Myers, *Ch of Bd*
Graeme Currie, *COO*
Julie Eastland, *CFO*
Esteban Abella, *Chief Mktg Ofcr*
Max Barker, *Vice Pres*
EMP: 13
SALES (est): 1.8MM **Privately Held**
SIC: 2836 Biological products, except diagnostic

(P-8327)
SAGE (PA)
1410 Monument Blvd, Concord
(94520-4368)
PHONE..............................925 288-4827
Marc Weinstein, *COO*
Brian McIntosh, *Vice Pres*
Sam Castle-Scott, *Director*
Emily Hanwell, *Director*
Jeremy Renshaw, *Director*
EMP: 27
SALES (est): 9.6MM **Privately Held**
SIC: 2836 Veterinary biological products

(P-8328)
SANTA CRUZ BIOTECHNOLOGY INC
2145 Delaware Ave, Santa Cruz
(95060-5706)
PHONE..............................831 457-3800
Matt Mullin, *Branch Mgr*
Kathryn Beswetherick, *Research*
Taylor Deibel, *Research*
Melanie Laur, *Research*
Sarah Riddick, *Research*
EMP: 42 **Privately Held**
SIC: 2836 Biological products, except diagnostic
PA: Santa Cruz Biotechnology, Inc.
   10410 Finnell St
   Dallas TX 75220
   -

(P-8329)
SCRIPPS LABORATORIES INC
6838 Flanders Dr, San Diego (92121-2904)
PHONE..............................858 546-5800
Simon C Khoury, *President*
William Adams, *Sales Dir*
EMP: 20 **EST:** 1984
SQ FT: 32,000
SALES: 3.6MM
SALES (corp-wide): 2.1B **Privately Held**
WEB: www.scrippslabs.com
SIC: 2836 2835 Biological products, except diagnostic; in vitro & in vivo diagnostic substances
PA: Scripps Health
   10140 Campus Point Dr Ax415
   San Diego CA 92121
   800 727-4777

(P-8330)
SINUSYS CORPORATION
4030 Fabian Way, Palo Alto (94303-4607)
PHONE..............................650 213-9988
R Hoxie, *Officer*
Robert Hoxie, *Officer*
Lloyd Griese, *Vice Pres*
Christopher Schneider, *Technology*
EMP: 13

SALES (est): 2.5MM **Privately Held**
SIC: 2836 Biological products, except diagnostic

(P-8331)
SUTRO BIOPHARMA INC (PA)
310 Utah Ave Ste 150, South San Francisco (94080-6803)
PHONE..............................650 392-8412
William J Newell, *CEO*
Connie Matsui, *Ch of Bd*
Edward Albini, *CFO*
Arturo Molina, *Chief Mktg Ofcr*
Shabbir T Anik, *Officer*
EMP: 120
SQ FT: 52,200
SALES: 38.4MM **Publicly Held**
WEB: www.f-a-b-inc.com
SIC: 2836 Biological products, except diagnostic

(P-8332)
VECTOR LABORATORIES INC
(PA)
30 Ingold Rd, Burlingame (94010-2206)
PHONE..............................650 697-3600
James S Whitehead, *President*
William Cahalan, *Vice Pres*
Ravi Vinayak, *General Mgr*
Carine Edder, *Research*
Brian Kanagy, *Research*
◆ **EMP:** 52
SQ FT: 65,000
SALES (est): 12.7MM **Privately Held**
SIC: 2836 2899 Biological products, except diagnostic; chemical preparations

(P-8333)
VITALITY EXTRACTS LLC
1350 Columbia St Unit 701, San Diego
(92101-3456)
PHONE..............................844 429-6580
Ryder Sloat, *CEO*
EMP: 10
SALES (est): 81.8K **Privately Held**
SIC: 2836 Extracts

2841 Soap & Detergents

(P-8334)
ADVANCED BIOCATALYTICS CORP
18010 Sky Park Cir # 130, Irvine
(92614-6456)
PHONE..............................949 442-0880
Chris Harano, *President*
Guillermo Torres, *COO*
Karen Frawley, *Accountant*
EMP: 12 **EST:** 1996
SALES (est): 1.9MM **Privately Held**
WEB: www.abiocat.com
SIC: 2841 Detergents, synthetic organic or inorganic alkaline

(P-8335)
ALL ONE GOD FAITH INC (PA)
Also Called: Dr. Bronners Magic Soaps
1335 Park Center Dr, Vista (92081-8357)
P.O. Box 1958 (92085-1958)
PHONE..............................844 937-2551
David Bronner, *CEO*
Trudy Bronner, *CFO*
◆ **EMP:** 240
SQ FT: 126,000
SALES (est): 90.2MM **Privately Held**
SIC: 2841 2834 2844 Soap: granulated, liquid, cake, flaked or chip; lip balms; lotions, shaving; face creams or lotions; suntan lotions & oils

(P-8336)
AMERICAS FINEST PRODUCTS
1639 9th St, Santa Monica (90404-3703)
PHONE..............................310 450-6555
Frank Kagarakis, *President*
Gilberto Barragan, *Vice Pres*
EMP: 20
SQ FT: 5,600
SALES (est): 3.8MM **Privately Held**
SIC: 2841 2899 Soap & other detergents; chemical preparations

(P-8337)
CUSTOM BLENDERS CORPORATION
39 California Ave Ste 108, Pleasanton
(94566-6279)
PHONE..............................510 635-4352
Debra Westlund, *President*
Stanley Westlund, *Chairman*
Gary Westlund, *Vice Pres*
David Westlund, *General Mgr*
EMP: 11
SQ FT: 26,000
SALES: 210K **Privately Held**
WEB: www.lehmanmfg.com
SIC: 2841 2842 2899 Soap: granulated, liquid, cake, flaked or chip; cleaning or polishing preparations; water treating compounds

(P-8338)
ECOLAB INC
18383 Railroad St, City of Industry
(91748-1218)
PHONE..............................626 935-1212
Mike Travis, *Branch Mgr*
David Reed, *District Mgr*
EMP: 10
SQ FT: 50,000
SALES (corp-wide): 14.6B **Publicly Held**
WEB: www.ecolab.com
SIC: 2841 Detergents, synthetic organic or inorganic alkaline
PA: Ecolab Inc.
   1 Ecolab Pl
   Saint Paul MN 55102
   800 232-6522

(P-8339)
ECOLAB INC
3160 Crow Canyon Pl # 200, San Ramon
(94583-1100)
PHONE..............................925 215-8008
Sharon Haley, *Branch Mgr*
EMP: 61
SALES (corp-wide): 14.6B **Publicly Held**
SIC: 2841 Soap & other detergents
PA: Ecolab Inc.
   1 Ecolab Pl
   Saint Paul MN 55102
   800 232-6522

(P-8340)
FOLEX CO
2505 Folex Way, Spring Valley
(91978-2038)
P.O. Box 789, Tualatin OR (97062-0789)
PHONE..............................619 670-5588
Barrett Lash, *President*
Patty Lash, *Treasurer*
EMP: 11
SQ FT: 21,000
SALES (est): 2.2MM **Privately Held**
WEB: www.folexeast.com
SIC: 2841 Textile soap

(P-8341)
GREEN SOAP INC
450 E Grant Line Rd 1, Tracy (95376-2811)
PHONE..............................925 240-5546
Theresa Anne Ennis, *CEO*
Michael Long, *Prdtn Mgr*
EMP: 11 **EST:** 2010
SQ FT: 20,000
SALES (est): 2.6MM **Privately Held**
SIC: 2841 5999 Soap & other detergents; toiletries, cosmetics & perfumes

(P-8342)
KINGMAN INDUSTRIES INC
26370 Beckman Ct Ste A, Murrieta
(92562-1005)
PHONE..............................951 698-1812
Barbara Mandel, *CEO*
Paul Mandel Jr, *President*
Mitch Mayer, *President*
▲ **EMP:** 20
SQ FT: 23,000
SALES: 4MM **Privately Held**
WEB: www.kingmanindustries.com
SIC: 2841 2869 5169 5122 Soap & other detergents; industrial organic chemicals; detergents & soaps, except specialty cleaning; cosmetics

(P-8343)
LIFEKIND PRODUCTS INC
333 Crown Point Cir # 225, Grass Valley
(95945-9538)
P.O. Box 1774 (95945-1774)
PHONE..........................530 477-5395
Walter Bader, *President*
EMP: 21
SALES (est): 3.6MM **Privately Held**
WEB: www.lifekind.com
SIC: 2841 2515 Detergents, synthetic organic or inorganic alkaline; mattresses & bedsprings

(P-8344)
MISSION KLEENSWEEP PROD INC
Also Called: Mission Laboratories
13644 Live Oak Ln, Baldwin Park
(91706-1317)
PHONE..........................323 223-1405
Toll Free:..........................888
Helen Rosenbaum, *President*
EMP: 53
SQ FT: 75,000
SALES (est): 16.4MM **Privately Held**
WEB: www.missionlabs.net
SIC: 2841 2842 Soap & other detergents; specialty cleaning, polishes & sanitation goods

(P-8345)
NUGENTEC OILFIELD CHEM LLC
1155 Park Ave, Emeryville (94608-3631)
PHONE..........................707 891-3012
Donato Polignone, *President*
▼ **EMP:** 34 **EST:** 2011
SALES (est): 2.9MM
SALES (corp-wide): 7.6MM **Privately Held**
SIC: 2841 2899 1389 Soap & other detergents; chemical preparations; oil field services
PA: Nugeneration Technologies, Llc
1155 Park Ave
Emeryville CA 94608
707 820-4080

(P-8346)
P & L DEVELOPMENT LLC
Also Called: Pl Development
11865 Alameda St, Lynwood (90262-4022)
PHONE..........................323 567-2482
Jim Smith, *General Mgr*
EMP: 125 **Privately Held**
WEB: www.aaroninindustriesinc.com
SIC: 2841 2844 2834 Soap & other detergents; toilet preparations; pharmaceutical preparations
PA: P & L Development, Llc
609 Cantiague Rock Rd 2a
Westbury NY 11590

(P-8347)
PANROSA ENTERPRISES INC
550 Monica Cir Ste 101, Corona
(92880-5496)
PHONE..........................951 339-5888
Peter Chengjian Pan, *President*
Jingwen Zhao, *CFO*
Chenyang Sun, *Admin Sec*
Shirley Zhang, *Accountant*
▲ **EMP:** 60
SALES (est): 1.9MM **Privately Held**
WEB: www.panrosa.com
SIC: 2841 Soap & other detergents

(P-8348)
PROCTER & GAMBLE MFG CO
8201 Fruitridge Rd, Sacramento
(95826-4716)
PHONE..........................916 383-3800
Bob Randall, *Branch Mgr*
Sylvia Quick, *Purchasing*
Kevin McKittrick, *Manager*
EMP: 130
SALES (corp-wide): 67.6B **Publicly Held**
SIC: 2841 Detergents, synthetic organic or inorganic alkaline

HQ: The Procter & Gamble Manufacturing Company
1 Procter And Gamble Plz
Cincinnati OH 45202
513 983-1100

(P-8349)
PROCTER & GAMBLE MFG CO
18125 Rowland St, City of Industry
(91748-1235)
PHONE..........................513 627-4678
Ashley Tucker, *Branch Mgr*
EMP: 371
SALES (corp-wide): 67.6B **Publicly Held**
SIC: 2841 2079 2099 2844 Detergents, synthetic organic or inorganic alkaline; shortening & other solid edible fats; peanut butter; toilet preparations; cake mixes, prepared: from purchased flour
HQ: The Procter & Gamble Manufacturing Company
1 Procter And Gamble Plz
Cincinnati OH 45202
513 983-1100

(P-8350)
SHUGAR SOAPWORKS INC
5955 Rickenbacker Rd, Commerce
(90040-3029)
PHONE..........................323 234-2874
▲ **EMP:** 10
SQ FT: 10,000
SALES (est): 1.3MM **Privately Held**
WEB: www.shugarsoapworks.com
SIC: 2841

(P-8351)
SOUTHERN CALIFORNIA SOAP CO
2700 Tanager Ave, Commerce
(90040-2721)
PHONE..........................323 888-1332
Robert Bergin, *President*
Linda Lafrenais, *Controller*
EMP: 10
SQ FT: 35,000
SALES (est): 1.3MM **Privately Held**
SIC: 2841 Soap & other detergents

(P-8352)
STAR PACIFIC INC
27462 Sunrise Farm Rd, Los Altos Hills
(94022-3221)
PHONE..........................510 471-6555
John Miller, *President*
Lee Price, *Treasurer*
Ed Kubiak, *Vice Pres*
EMP: 20
SQ FT: 57,000
SALES (est): 3.6MM **Privately Held**
SIC: 2841 Soap & other detergents

(P-8353)
TUULA INC
Also Called: Destiny Boutique
26019 Jefferson Ave Ste D, Murrieta
(92562-6986)
PHONE..........................858 761-6045
Tuula Hakkanen, *President*
Martin Hotte, *Vice Pres*
EMP: 12
SQ FT: 2,800
SALES: 5MM **Privately Held**
SIC: 2841 Detergents, synthetic organic or inorganic alkaline

(P-8354)
UNIVERSAL SURFACE TECHLGY INC
Also Called: UST
13023 S Main St, Los Angeles
(90061-1605)
PHONE..........................310 352-6969
Fax: 310 352-6970
▲ **EMP:** 35
SQ FT: 30,000
SALES (est): 4.8MM **Privately Held**
SIC: 2841

(P-8355)
VALUE PRODUCTS INC
Also Called: Pride Line Products
2128 Industrial Dr, Stockton (95206-4936)
PHONE..........................209 345-3817
Douglas Hall, *President*
Erica Hall, *Corp Secy*

June Guanzon, *Technician*
Silverio Fernandez, *Prdtn Mgr*
Mark Hall, *Products*
EMP: 25
SQ FT: 34,000
SALES (est): 4.8MM **Privately Held**
WEB: www.valueproductsinc.com
SIC: 2841 Detergents, synthetic organic or inorganic alkaline

---

2842 Spec Cleaning, Polishing & Sanitation Preparations

(P-8356)
2ND GEN PRODUCTIONS INC
Also Called: Mark V Products
400 El Sobrante Rd, Corona (92879-5755)
PHONE..........................800 877-6282
Mark Marchese, *CEO*
Dora Marchese, *President*
Frank Marchese, *Vice Pres*
Robert Marchese, *Admin Sec*
Winnie Sanchez, *Accounting Mgr*
EMP: 19
SALES (est): 1MM **Privately Held**
SIC: 2842 5013 Waxes for wood, leather & other materials; polishing preparations & related products; automotive supplies

(P-8357)
3D INTERNATIONAL LLC
Also Called: 3d Detailing Products For The
20724 Cntre Pnte Pkwy Uni, Santa Clarita
(91350)
PHONE..........................661 250-2020
▲ **EMP:** 45
SQ FT: 30,000
SALES (est): 12.7MM **Privately Held**
WEB: www.3dproducts.com
SIC: 2842 Polishing preparations & related products

(P-8358)
3D/INTERNATIONAL INC
20724 Centre Pointe Pkwy # 1, Santa Clarita (91350-2980)
PHONE..........................661 250-2020
Tony Goren, *Manager*
EMP: 80
SALES (corp-wide): 3.5B **Publicly Held**
SIC: 2842 Automobile polish
HQ: 3d/International, Inc.
2200 West Loop S Ste 200
Houston TX 77027
713 871-7000

(P-8359)
ALDRAN CHEMICAL INC
1313 N Carolan Ave, Burlingame
(94010-2401)
PHONE..........................650 347-8242
Robert Mitch Drangle, *President*
EMP: 26
SQ FT: 19,000
SALES (est): 3.7MM **Privately Held**
WEB: www.aldranchemical.com
SIC: 2842 Cleaning or polishing preparations

(P-8360)
ALLBRITE CAR CARE PRODUCTS
1201 N Las Brisas St, Anaheim
(92806-1823)
PHONE..........................714 666-8683
Jitu Jhaveri, *CEO*
Sarla Jhaveri, *Vice Pres*
EMP: 10
SQ FT: 8,110
SALES (est): 2.3MM **Privately Held**
SIC: 2842 5087 Specialty cleaning preparations; carwash equipment & supplies

(P-8361)
AMREP INC (DH)
1555 S Cucamonga Ave, Ontario
(91761-4512)
PHONE..........................909 923-0430
Lou Purvis, *CEO*
Kevin J Gallagher, *CEO*
Mark R Bachmann, *CFO*
Philip A Theodore, *Admin Sec*

◆ **EMP:** 180
SQ FT: 125,000
SALES (est): 104.5MM
SALES (corp-wide): 1B **Privately Held**
WEB: www.amrep.com
SIC: 2842 2079 2911 2869 Specialty cleaning preparations; sanitation preparations, disinfectants & deodorants; edible oil products, except corn oil; greases, lubricating; industrial organic chemicals; soap & other detergents; industrial inorganic chemicals
HQ: Zep Inc.
3330 Cumberland Blvd Se # 700
Atlanta GA 30339
877 428-9937

(P-8362)
ANGELUS SHOE POLISH CO INC
Also Called: Angelus Formulations
12060 Florence Ave, Santa Fe Springs
(90670-4406)
P.O. Box 3066, Cerritos (90703-3066)
PHONE..........................562 941-4242
Paul T Angelos, *President*
Linda Angelus, *Vice Pres*
Myrtle Angelus, *Vice Pres*
▲ **EMP:** 12 **EST:** 1907
SQ FT: 10,000
SALES (est): 3.5MM **Privately Held**
WEB: www.pacit4u.com
SIC: 2842 4783 Shoe polish or cleaner; packing & crating

(P-8363)
AQUA MIX INC
250 Benjamin Dr, Corona (92879-6508)
PHONE..........................951 256-3040
Rick Baldini, *President*
Manuel G Magallanes, *Ch of Bd*
Jill Magallanes, *Vice Pres*
William Tran, *Vice Pres*
EMP: 64
SQ FT: 74,000
SALES (est): 8.7MM **Privately Held**
WEB: www.aquamix.com
SIC: 2842 2891 Specialty cleaning preparations; sealants
HQ: Custom Building Products, Inc.
7711 Center Ave Ste 500
Huntington Beach CA 92647
800 272-8786

(P-8364)
AUTO-CHLOR SYSTEM WASH INC
16141 Hart St, Van Nuys (91406-3904)
PHONE..........................818 376-0940
Brian Gate, *Manager*
Mark Benz, *Manager*
EMP: 15
SALES (corp-wide): 61.9MM **Privately Held**
SIC: 2842 Laundry cleaning preparations
PA: Auto-Chlor System Of Washington, Inc.
450 Ferguson Dr
Mountain View CA 94043
650 967-3085

(P-8365)
AWESOME PRODUCTS INC (PA)
Also Called: La's Totally Awesome
6370 Altura Blvd, Buena Park
(90620-1001)
PHONE..........................714 562-8873
Loksarang D Hardas, *CEO*
Norma Martinez, *VP Opers*
◆ **EMP:** 125
SQ FT: 250,000
SALES (est): 61.3MM **Privately Held**
WEB: www.awesomeproducts.com
SIC: 2842 Cleaning or polishing preparations

(P-8366)
BAF INDUSTRIES (PA)
Also Called: Pro Wax
1451 Edinger Ave Ste F, Tustin
(92780-6250)
PHONE..........................714 258-8055
Michael P Bell, *CEO*
Otis F Bell, *President*
▲ **EMP:** 42 **EST:** 1935
SQ FT: 44,000

▲ = Import ▼=Export
◆ =Import/Export

SALES (est): 9.1MM **Privately Held**
WEB: www.prowax.com
SIC: **2842** Cleaning or polishing preparations

(P-8367)
BEST SANITIZERS INC
310 Prvdnce Mine Rd # 120, Nevada City (95959-2981)
P.O. Box 1360, Penn Valley (95946-1360)
PHONE..................................530 265-1800
Hillard T Witt, *President*
Ed Hay, *Vice Pres*
Ryan Witt, *Vice Pres*
◆ EMP: 52
SQ FT: 10,000
SALES: 20MM **Privately Held**
WEB: www.bestsanitizers.com
SIC: **2842** Sanitation preparations

(P-8368)
BLUE CROSS LABORATORIES INC (PA)
20950 Centre Pointe Pkwy, Santa Clarita (91350-2975)
PHONE..................................661 255-0955
Darrell Mahler, *President*
Glenn Mahler, *Corp Secy*
◆ EMP: 160
SQ FT: 100,000
SALES (est): 39.9MM **Privately Held**
WEB: www.bc-labs.com
SIC: **2842 2844** Cleaning or polishing preparations; toilet preparations

(P-8369)
BRACTON SOSAFE INC
Also Called: Bracton Beer Line Cleaners
1061 N Shepard St Ste E, Anaheim (92806-2818)
PHONE..................................714 632-8499
Michael Hunter, *President*
EMP: 10
SALES (est): 907.3K **Privately Held**
SIC: **2842** Specialty cleaning, polishes & sanitation goods

(P-8370)
BUSHNELL INDUSTRIES INC
7449 Avenue 304, Visalia (93291)
P.O. Box 429, Goshen (93227-0429)
PHONE..................................559 651-9039
Robert Bushnell, *President*
EMP: 12
SQ FT: 11,000
SALES (est): 2.5MM **Privately Held**
WEB: www.bushii.com
SIC: **2842 7699** Specialty cleaning, polishes & sanitation goods; agricultural equipment repair services

(P-8371)
C & S PRODUCTS CA INC (PA)
Also Called: Coco Dry
1345 S Parkside Pl, Ontario (91761-4556)
PHONE..................................909 218-8971
James Stevens, *President*
Kevin Calvo, *Principal*
Lou Ferrero, *Principal*
Bill Habeger, *Principal*
Skip Hodgetts, *Principal*
EMP: 12
SQ FT: 14,000
SALES (est): 484K **Privately Held**
SIC: **2842** Sweeping compounds, oil or water absorbent, clay or sawdust

(P-8372)
CHEMCOR CHEMICAL CORPORATION
13770 Benson Ave, Chino (91710-7000)
PHONE..................................909 590-7234
Dave Tarquin, *CEO*
Frank Tarquin, *Vice Pres*
Brent Tarquin, *Purch Mgr*
▲ EMP: 10
SQ FT: 25,000
SALES (est): 4.1MM **Privately Held**
SIC: **2842 5169** Specialty cleaning, polishes & sanitation goods; chemicals & allied products

(P-8373)
CILAJET LLC
16425 Ishida Ave, Gardena (90248-2924)
PHONE..................................310 320-8000

Jaci Warren, *President*
EMP: 25
SALES (est): 4.4MM **Privately Held**
SIC: **2842** 7542 Automobile polish; washing & polishing, automotive

(P-8374)
CLEANLOGIC LLC
4051 S Broadway, Los Angeles (90037-1030)
PHONE..................................310 261-3001
Robert Smerling, *Mng Member*
EMP: 50
SALES (est): 1.8MM **Privately Held**
SIC: **2842 3582 3589 7699** Laundry cleaning preparations; drycleaning equipment & machinery, commercial; servicing machines, except dry cleaning, laundry: coin-oper.; machinery cleaning; biotechnical research, commercial

(P-8375)
CLOROX COMPANY (PA)
1221 Broadway Ste 1300, Oakland (94612-1871)
PHONE..................................510 271-7000
Benno Dorer, *Ch of Bd*
Kevin B Jacobsen, *CFO*
Eric Reynolds, *Chief Mktg Ofcr*
Denise Garner, *Officer*
Matthew Laszlo, *Officer*
▼ EMP: 277 EST: 1913
SALES: 6.2B **Publicly Held**
WEB: www.clorox.com
SIC: **2842 2673 2035 2844** Laundry cleaning preparations; polishing preparations & related products; food storage & frozen food bags, plastic; seasonings & sauces, except tomato & dry; dressings, salad: raw & cooked (except dry mixes); seasonings, meat sauces (except tomato & dry); cosmetic preparations; insecticides & pesticides

(P-8376)
CLOROX COMPANY
11940 S Harlan Rd, Lathrop (95330-8767)
PHONE..................................209 234-1094
EMP: 19
SALES (corp-wide): 6.2B **Publicly Held**
SIC: **2842** Specialty cleaning, polishes & sanitation goods
PA: The Clorox Company
1221 Broadway Ste 1300
Oakland CA 94612
510 271-7000

(P-8377)
CLOROX COMPANY
4900 Johnson Dr, Pleasanton (94588-3308)
PHONE..................................925 368-6000
Wayne L Delker, *President*
EMP: 19
SALES (corp-wide): 6.2B **Publicly Held**
SIC: **2842** Specialty cleaning, polishes & sanitation goods
PA: The Clorox Company
1221 Broadway Ste 1300
Oakland CA 94612
510 271-7000

(P-8378)
CLOROX MANUFACTURING COMPANY (HQ)
Also Called: Clorox Products Mfg Co
1221 Broadway, Oakland (94612-1837)
PHONE..................................510 271-7000
T E Bailey, *CEO*
Karen M Rose, *Treasurer*
Suzanne Thompson, *Vice Pres*
Roland Castro, *Senior Mgr*
◆ EMP: 180
SALES (est): 338.3MM
SALES (corp-wide): 6.2B **Publicly Held**
SIC: **2842** Specialty cleaning, polishes & sanitation goods
PA: The Clorox Company
1221 Broadway Ste 1300
Oakland CA 94612
510 271-7000

(P-8379)
CLOROX PRODUCTS MFG CO
2600 Huntington Dr, Fairfield (94533-9736)
PHONE..................................707 437-1051

Scott Johnston, *Manager*
Atul Patel, *Opers Staff*
EMP: 55
SALES (corp-wide): 6.2B **Publicly Held**
SIC: **2842** Bleaches, household: dry or liquid
HQ: Clorox Manufacturing Company
1221 Broadway
Oakland CA 94612
-

(P-8380)
CLOROX PRODUCTS MFG CO
2300 W San Bernardino Ave, Redlands (92374-5000)
PHONE..................................909 307-2756
EMP: 85
SALES (corp-wide): 6.2B **Publicly Held**
SIC: **2842** Specialty cleaning, polishes & sanitation goods
HQ: Clorox Manufacturing Company
1221 Broadway
Oakland CA 94612

(P-8381)
COCO PRODUCTS LLC
1345 S Parkside Pl, Ontario (91761-4556)
PHONE..................................909 218-8971
Steven Parker, *Mng Member*
EMP: 12
SQ FT: 14,000
SALES (est): 1.1MM **Privately Held**
SIC: **2842** Sweeping compounds, oil or water absorbent, clay or sawdust

(P-8382)
EARTH LAB INC
5016 Maplewood Ave Apt B, Los Angeles (90004-3081)
PHONE..................................888 835-2276
Jawon Suh, *CEO*
EMP: 10
SALES (est): 616.9K **Privately Held**
SIC: **2842 5169** Sanitation preparations, disinfectants & deodorants; specialty cleaning & sanitation preparations

(P-8383)
FACTORY DIRECT DIST CORP
1001 B Ave Ste 100, San Diego (92118-3422)
PHONE..................................619 435-3437
Edwin Michael Furey, *CEO*
Ed Furey, *Principal*
Michael Oconnor, *Principal*
John C Otten, *Principal*
EMP: 10
SALES (est): 2MM **Privately Held**
WEB: www.factorydirectcorp.com
SIC: **2842 2851** Specialty cleaning, polishes & sanitation goods; paints & allied products

(P-8384)
GEA FARM TECHNOLOGIES INC
Also Called: W S West
2717 S 4th St, Fresno (93725-1938)
PHONE..................................559 497-5074
Warren Dorathy, *Manager*
EMP: 40
SALES (corp-wide): 5.5B **Privately Held**
WEB: www.westfaliasurge.com
SIC: **2842** Specialty cleaning, polishes & sanitation goods
HQ: Gea Farm Technologies, Inc.
1880 Country Farm Dr
Naperville IL 60563
630 548-8200

(P-8385)
GOODWIN AMMONIA COMPANY (PA)
12102 Industry St, Garden Grove (92841-2814)
PHONE..................................714 894-0531
Tom Goodwin, *President*
Janice Fleet, *Corp Secy*
Gary Goodwin, *Vice Pres*
Jason Woods, *Human Res Dir*
◆ EMP: 15 EST: 1922
SQ FT: 58,000
SALES (est): 31.9MM **Privately Held**
SIC: **2842** Automobile polish

(P-8386)
GRANITE GOLD INC
12780 Danielson Ct Ste A, Poway (92064-8857)
PHONE..................................858 499-8933
Leonard Sciarrino, *President*
Scott Martin, *COO*
Leonard Pellegrino, *Exec VP*
Mike Rose, *Vice Pres*
Dan Tucker, *Manager*
▲ EMP: 10
SALES (est): 2.5MM **Privately Held**
SIC: **2842** Cleaning or polishing preparations

(P-8387)
GRANITIZE PRODUCTS INC
11022 Vulcan St, South Gate (90280-7621)
P.O. Box 2306 (90280-9306)
PHONE..................................562 923-5438
Tony Raymondo, *CEO*
Marty Raymondo, *COO*
Betty Raymondo, *Corp Secy*
Randy Bair, *General Mgr*
Joy Eastwood, *Office Mgr*
◆ EMP: 75
SQ FT: 30,000
SALES (est): 21.1MM **Privately Held**
WEB: www.granitize.com
SIC: **2842** Automobile polish; cleaning or polishing preparations

(P-8388)
HOCKING INTERNATIONAL LABS INC (PA)
980 Rancheros Dr, San Marcos (92069-3029)
P.O. Box 462785, Escondido (92046-2785)
PHONE..................................760 432-5277
Bert E Hocking Jr, *CEO*
Mike Walther, *President*
Sherry Hocking, *Corp Secy*
Krista Castberg, *Vice Pres*
Shelly Allman, *Buyer*
▲ EMP: 21
SQ FT: 15,000
SALES (est): 9.9MM **Privately Held**
WEB: www.hockingintl.com
SIC: **2842 5087** Specialty cleaning preparations; service establishment equipment

(P-8389)
HOME & BODY COMPANY (PA)
Also Called: Direct Chemicals
18352 Enterprise Ln, Huntington Beach (92648-1206)
PHONE..................................714 842-8000
Hazem H Haddad, *President*
Nadene Haddad, *Admin Sec*
▲ EMP: 34
SALES (est): 3.5MM **Privately Held**
WEB: www.directchemicals.com
SIC: **2842 2841 2899 2844** Bleaches, household: dry or liquid; textile soap; essential oils; face creams or lotions

(P-8390)
JASON MARKK INC
329 E 2nd St, Los Angeles (90012-4202)
PHONE..................................213 687-7060
Jason M Angsuvarn, *CEO*
Gheren Vitte, *Marketing Staff*
Luis Osuna, *Sales Staff*
Jino Jinowat, *Manager*
Franda Lay, *Manager*
▲ EMP: 34 EST: 2007
SALES (est): 805.8K **Privately Held**
SIC: **2842** Shoe polish or cleaner

(P-8391)
KIK-SOCAL INC
Also Called: K I K
9028 Dice Rd, Santa Fe Springs (90670-2520)
PHONE..................................562 946-6427
Jeffrey M Nodland, *CEO*
Stratis Katsiris, *President*
William Smith, *President*
Ben W Kaak, *CFO*
Greg Wiese, *General Mgr*
EMP: 3000
SQ FT: 3,000,000

P
R
O
D
U
C
T
S

&

S
V
C
S

SALES (corp-wide): 3.2MM **Privately Held**
SIC: 2842 Bleaches, household: dry or liquid; fabric softeners; ammonia, household; cleaning or polishing preparations
HQ: Kik International Houston Inc
2921 Corder St
Houston TX 77054
713 747-8710

(P-8392)
LAB-CLEAN LLC
3627 Briggeman Dr, Los Alamitos
(90720-2475)
PHONE..................714 689-0063
Mark Cunningham, *Prgrmr*
Cathy Poe, *Administration*
Matthew Bays,
EMP: 25
SQ FT: 40,000
SALES (est): 4.9MM **Privately Held**
SIC: 2842 Cleaning or polishing preparations

(P-8393)
LMC ENTERPRISES (PA)
Also Called: Chemco Products Company
6401 Alondra Blvd, Paramount
(90723-3758)
PHONE..................562 602-2116
Elaine S Cooper, *CEO*
Janis Utz, *President*
John D Grimes, *COO*
Shawn Carroll, *CFO*
Michael Bourgeois, *Vice Pres*
EMP: 70 EST: 1962
SQ FT: 15,000
SALES (est): 25.3MM **Privately Held**
WEB: www.chemcoprod.com
SIC: 2842 Cleaning or polishing preparations; floor waxes

(P-8394)
LMC ENTERPRISES
Also Called: Flo-Kem
19402 S Susana Rd, Compton
(90221-5712)
PHONE..................310 632-7124
Elaine Cooper, *CEO*
Steven Hamstrom, *Executive*
June Massa, *General Mgr*
Roxanne Hibbard, *Credit Mgr*
Beth Edwards, *Purch Agent*
EMP: 50
SQ FT: 20,000
SALES (corp-wide): 25.3MM **Privately Held**
SIC: 2842 Cleaning or polishing preparations; floor waxes
PA: Lmc Enterprises
6401 Alondra Blvd
Paramount CA 90723
562 602-2116

(P-8395)
M P M BUILDING SERVICES INC
Also Called: Mpm & Associates
7011 Hayvenhurst Ave F, Van Nuys
(91406-3822)
PHONE..................818 708-9676
Paul Davis, *President*
Mike Danesh, *Vice Pres*
EMP: 60
SQ FT: 35,000
SALES (est): 4.3MM **Privately Held**
WEB: www.mpmco.com
SIC: 2842 Specialty cleaning, polishes & sanitation goods

(P-8396)
MEGUIARS INC (HQ)
Also Called: Brilliant Solutions
17991 Mitchell S, Irvine (92614-6015)
PHONE..................949 752-8000
Barry J Meguiar, *President*
Michael W Meguiar, *Ch of Bd*
Mary Swanson, *Principal*
Catherine E Bayless, *Admin Sec*
Jamie Cruz, *Admin Asst*
◆ EMP: 50
SALES (est): 80.3MM
SALES (corp-wide): 32.7B **Publicly Held**
WEB: www.meguiars.com
SIC: 2842 Cleaning or polishing preparations; automobile polish; furniture polish or wax

PA: 3m Company
3m Center
Saint Paul MN 55144
651 733-1110

(P-8397)
MORGAN GALLACHER INC
Also Called: Custom Chemical Formulators
8707 Millergrove Dr, Santa Fe Springs
(90670-2001)
PHONE..................562 695-1232
Harriet Von Luft, *Ch of Bd*
David M Smith, *President*
Sufian Phoa, *VP Finance*
▼ EMP: 46
SQ FT: 100,000
SALES (est): 10.7MM **Privately Held**
WEB: www.customchem.com
SIC: 2842 5169 Cleaning or polishing preparations; industrial chemicals

(P-8398)
MOTSENBOCKER ADVANCED DEVELOPM (PA)
Also Called: Lift Off
4901 Morena Blvd Ste 806, San Diego
(92117-7327)
P.O. Box 90947 (92169-2947)
PHONE..................858 581-0222
Gregg Motsenbocker, *President*
Skip Motsenbocker, *COO*
Lori Motsenbocker, *Treasurer*
Patty Brooks, *Marketing Mgr*
EMP: 15
SQ FT: 8,600
SALES (est): 3.3MM **Privately Held**
WEB: www.liftoffinc.com
SIC: 2842 6794 Wax removers; patent owners & lessors

(P-8399)
NEOGEN CORPORATION
Also Called: Preserved
1355 Paulson Rd, Turlock (95380-5541)
PHONE..................209 664-1683
EMP: 28
SALES (corp-wide): 414.1MM **Publicly Held**
SIC: 2842 Sanitation preparations; cleaning or polishing preparations
PA: Neogen Corporation
620 Lesher Pl
Lansing MI 48912
517 372-9200

(P-8400)
OIL-DRI CORPORATION AMERICA
950 Petroleum Club Rd, Taft (93268-9748)
P.O. Box 1277 (93268-1277)
PHONE..................661 765-7194
Patrick Gollihar, *Project Mgr*
EMP: 10
SALES (corp-wide): 277MM **Publicly Held**
SIC: 2842 Sweeping compounds, oil or water absorbent, clay or sawdust
PA: Oil-Dri Corporation Of America
410 N Michigan Ave Fl 4
Chicago IL 60611
312 321-1515

(P-8401)
OMEGA INDUSTRIAL SUPPLY INC
101 Grobric Ct, Fairfield (94534-1673)
PHONE..................707 864-8164
Adam Brady, *CEO*
Lori Rehn, *President*
Pam Wilcox, *Purchasing*
Kerry Mahoney, *Manager*
Niki Ryan, *Accounts Mgr*
EMP: 35
SQ FT: 10,000
SALES (est): 8.4MM **Privately Held**
WEB: www.onlyomega.com
SIC: 2842 5169 Sanitation preparations; chemicals & allied products

(P-8402)
PACE INTERNATIONAL LLC
1104 N Nevada St, Visalia (93291)
PHONE..................559 651-4877
Gorge Lobisser,
Michelle Smith, *Technical Mgr*

Scott Christie, *Engineer*
Eric Gordon, *Engineer*
Timothy Clarke, *Finance Dir*
EMP: 29 **Privately Held**
WEB: www.paceint.com
SIC: 2842 2879 2873 2899 Specialty cleaning preparations; agricultural chemicals; plant foods, mixed: from plants making nitrog. fertilizers; water treating compounds; emulsifiers, except food & pharmaceutical; cutting oils, blending: made from purchased materials
HQ: Pace International, Llc
5661 Branch Rd
Wapato WA 98951
800 936-6750

(P-8403)
PARADISE ROAD LLC
5872 Engineer Dr, Huntington Beach
(92649-1166)
PHONE..................714 894-1779
Lou Basenese, *President*
Tim Miller, *CEO*
▲ EMP: 25
SALES (est): 2.8MM **Privately Held**
SIC: 2842 Specialty cleaning, polishes & sanitation goods

(P-8404)
PARK-RAND ENTERPRISES INC
Also Called: Meri Gol Products Limited
39630 Fairway Dr Apt 218, Palmdale
(93551-7570)
PHONE..................818 362-2565
Joseph N Gray, *President*
Robert C Swick, *Vice Pres*
EMP: 10
SALES (est): 820K **Privately Held**
SIC: 2842 Ammonia, household

(P-8405)
PATRIOT POLISHING COMPANY
47260 Wrangler Rd, Aguanga
(92536-9518)
PHONE..................310 903-7409
Raymond Esfandi, *CFO*
EMP: 15
SALES (est): 785.8K **Privately Held**
SIC: 2842 Metal polish

(P-8406)
PEERLESS MATERIALS COMPANY (PA)
4442 E 26th St, Vernon (90058-4318)
P.O. Box 33228, Los Angeles (90033-0228)
PHONE..................323 266-0313
Louis J Buty, *President*
Peter H Pritchard, *Vice Pres*
Peter Pritchard, *Human Res Mgr*
Mandy Wright, *Opers Staff*
Hank Hahn, *Sales Associate*
▲ EMP: 36
SQ FT: 35,000
SALES (est): 4.7MM **Privately Held**
SIC: 2842 Sweeping compounds, oil or water absorbent, clay or sawdust

(P-8407)
PLANET INC
Also Called: Planet Products
15791 Coleman Valley Rd, Occidental
(95465-9304)
P.O. Box 156 (95465-0156)
PHONE..................250 478-8171
Allen Stedman, *President*
Larry Brucia, *President*
Shandra Robson, *Prdtn Mgr*
EMP: 10
SQ FT: 1,500
SALES (est): 134.2K **Privately Held**
WEB: www.planetinc.com
SIC: 2842 Specialty cleaning, polishes & sanitation goods

(P-8408)
PRODUCTION CHEMICAL MFG INC (PA)
Also Called: Production Car Care Products
1000 E Channel St, Stockton (95205-4942)
PHONE..................209 943-7337
Lewyn Boler, *President*
Blanche Boler, *Admin Sec*
EMP: 12 EST: 1979
SQ FT: 7,500

SALES (est): 5.9MM **Privately Held**
SIC: 2842 Cleaning or polishing preparations

(P-8409)
PURE BIOSCIENCE INC (PA)
1725 Gillespie Way, El Cajon (92020-1015)
PHONE..................619 596-8600
Tom Y Lee, *Ch of Bd*
Tom Myers, *COO*
Mark Elliott, *CFO*
Gary Cohee, *Bd of Directors*
Bridget Tinsley, *Senior VP*
EMP: 13
SQ FT: 7,400
SALES: 1.9MM **Publicly Held**
WEB: www.purebio.com
SIC: 2842 2879 Disinfectants, household or industrial plant; agricultural chemicals

(P-8410)
PURICLE INC
11799 Jersey Blvd, Rancho Cucamonga
(91730-4936)
PHONE..................909 466-7125
Elisa Sim, *President*
EMP: 50
SQ FT: 37,000
SALES (est): 9.8MM **Privately Held**
WEB: www.puricle.com
SIC: 2842 Disinfectants, household or industrial plant

(P-8411)
QUANTUM GLOBAL TECH LLC
Also Called: Quantum Clean
1710 Ringwood Ave, San Jose
(95131-1711)
PHONE..................408 487-1770
Scott Nicholas, *CEO*
Michael Johnson, *Manager*
EMP: 23
SALES (corp-wide): 1.1B **Publicly Held**
SIC: 2842 Specialty cleaning, polishes & sanitation goods
HQ: Quantum Global Technologies, Llc
1900 Am Dr Ste 200
Quakertown PA 18951
215 892-9300

(P-8412)
QUANTUM GLOBAL TECH LLC
Also Called: Quantumclean
44010 Fremont Blvd, Fremont
(94538-6042)
PHONE..................510 687-8000
Michael Bonner, *Engineer*
EMP: 49
SALES (corp-wide): 1.1B **Publicly Held**
SIC: 2842 Specialty cleaning, polishes & sanitation goods
HQ: Quantum Global Technologies, Llc
1900 Am Dr Ste 200
Quakertown PA 18951
215 892-9300

(P-8413)
REFLECTECH INC
Also Called: Reflection Technology
5861 88th St Ste 100, Sacramento
(95828-1132)
PHONE..................916 388-7821
Dave Nugent, *President*
Ed Russell, *CFO*
Pete Hoffman, *Vice Pres*
EMP: 12
SQ FT: 12,000
SALES (est): 2.2MM **Privately Held**
SIC: 2842 Specialty cleaning preparations

(P-8414)
RENU CHEM INC
Also Called: Finish Renu Car Care
572 Malloy Ct, Corona (92880-2045)
PHONE..................951 736-8072
Jim Moreno, *CEO*
Nanette Moreno, *President*
EMP: 10 EST: 2008
SQ FT: 15,000
SALES: 1.4MM **Privately Held**
SIC: 2842 Automobile polish

▲ = Import ▼=Export
◆ =Import/Export

(P-8415)
SANACT INC (PA)
Also Called: Roto-Rooter
1274 Dupont Ct, Manteca (95336-6003)
PHONE..................................925 464-2761
Rodney Allen Wray, *CEO*
▼ **EMP:** 11
SQ FT: 7,000
SALES: 11.4MM **Privately Held**
SIC: 2842 5169 5074 Specialty cleaning preparations; specialty cleaning & sanitation preparations; plumbing fittings & supplies

(P-8416)
SANITEK PRODUCTS INC
3959 Goodwin Ave, Los Angeles (90039-1187)
PHONE..................................323 245-6781
Robert L Moseley, *President*
David Moseley, *Treasurer*
▲ **EMP:** 13 **EST:** 1941
SQ FT: 25,000
SALES (est): 3.2MM **Privately Held**
WEB: www.sanitek.com
SIC: 2842 2899 2992 2891 Sanitation preparations, disinfectants & deodorants; fire retardant chemicals; lubricating oils & greases; adhesives & sealants; agricultural chemicals; soap & other detergents

(P-8417)
SECONDWIND PRODUCTS INC
4301 Second Wind Way, Paso Robles (93446-6304)
P.O. Box 2300 (93447-2300)
PHONE..................................805 239-2555
Gus Blythe, *President*
Ken Fontes, *CFO*
EMP: 27
SQ FT: 24,250
SALES (est): 2.6MM **Privately Held**
WEB: www.2ndwind.com
SIC: 2842 3089 3131 3021 Stain removers; shoe polish or cleaner; soling strips, boot or shoe: plastic; footwear cut stock; rubber & plastics footwear; women's & misses' outerwear

(P-8418)
SOAPTRONIC LLC
20562 Crescent Bay Dr, Lake Forest (92630-8845)
PHONE..................................949 465-8955
Horst Binderbauer, *Mng Member*
◆ **EMP:** 25
SALES (est): 6.8MM **Privately Held**
WEB: www.soaptronic.com
SIC: 2842 2841 Sanitation preparations, disinfectants & deodorants; soap & other detergents

(P-8419)
SUNSHINE MAKERS INC (PA)
Also Called: Simple Green
15922 Pacific Coast Hwy, Huntington Beach (92649-1894)
PHONE..................................562 795-6000
Bruce P Fabrizio, *President*
Pat Sheehan, *Exec VP*
Carol Chapin, *Vice Pres*
Rose Concilia, *Vice Pres*
Jeffrey Hyder, *Vice Pres*
▼ **EMP:** 51
SQ FT: 25,000
SALES (est): 10.1MM **Privately Held**
WEB: www.simplegreen.com
SIC: 2842 Cleaning or polishing preparations; degreasing solvent; specialty cleaning preparations

(P-8420)
SURF CITY GARAGE
5872 Engineer Dr, Huntington Beach (92649-1166)
PHONE..................................714 894-1707
Timothy D Miller, *President*
Matt Rigdon, *President*
▲ **EMP:** 33
SQ FT: 22,000
SALES (est): 6.9MM **Privately Held**
SIC: 2842 Cleaning or polishing preparations

(P-8421)
SURTEC INC
Also Called: Surtec System , The
1880 N Macarthur Dr, Tracy (95376-2841)
PHONE..................................209 820-3700
William A Fields, *President*
Don C Fromm, *Treasurer*
Don Fromm, *Vice Pres*
◆ **EMP:** 50
SQ FT: 87,000
SALES (est): 15.5MM **Privately Held**
WEB: www.surtecsystem.com
SIC: 2842 5087 Specialty cleaning preparations; floor machinery, maintenance

(P-8422)
ULTRA CHEM LABS CORP
4581 Brickell Privado St, Ontario (91761-7828)
PHONE..................................909 605-1640
Christopher Shieh, *President*
Cesar Castro, *Admin Sec*
▲ **EMP:** 15
SQ FT: 19,000
SALES (est): 2.5MM **Privately Held**
SIC: 2842 Floor waxes

(P-8423)
US CONTINENTAL MARKETING INC (PA)
310 Reed Cir, Corona (92879-1349)
PHONE..................................951 808-8888
David Lee Williams, *President*
◆ **EMP:** 90
SQ FT: 40,000
SALES (est): 35.5MM **Privately Held**
WEB: www.uscontinental.com
SIC: 2842 Leather dressings & finishes; shoe polish or cleaner

(P-8424)
WITT HILLARD
Also Called: Saraya Healthcare
310 Providence Mine Rd, Nevada City (95959-2982)
PHONE..................................530 510-0756
Hillard Witt, *Owner*
Cindi Linville, *Manager*
EMP: 35 **EST:** 2015
SQ FT: 55,000
SALES (est): 1.3MM **Privately Held**
SIC: 2842 Sanitation preparations, disinfectants & deodorants

2843 Surface Active & Finishing Agents, Sulfonated Oils

(P-8425)
ANTERRA GROUP INC
25255 Cabot Rd Ste 215, Laguna Hills (92653-5508)
PHONE..................................949 215-0658
Anthony J Terranova, *President*
Tracee H Terranova, *Vice Pres*
Natalie Rosin, *Marketing Staff*
Carlos Zatarain, *Consultant*
EMP: 10
SALES (est): 1.9MM **Privately Held**
SIC: 2843 Processing assistants

(P-8426)
CENTRAL GREASE COMPANY INC
17771 W Gettysburg Ave, Kerman (93630-9537)
PHONE..................................559 846-9607
Morrie Kiseloff, *Administration*
EMP: 2
SALES (est): 2.6MM **Privately Held**
SIC: 2843 Oils & greases

(P-8427)
CHEMEOR INC
727 Arrow Grand Cir, Covina (91722-2148)
PHONE..................................626 966-3808
Yongchun Tang, *Ch of Bd*
Pat Mills, *CEO*
Patrick Shuler, *CFO*
Carl Aften, *Vice Pres*
Herb Juppe, *Vice Pres*
▲ **EMP:** 40

SQ FT: 16,000
SALES (est): 19.5MM **Privately Held**
SIC: 2843 1389 2911 Surface active agents; chemically treating wells; aromatic chemical products

(P-8428)
HENKEL US OPERATIONS CORP
20021 S Susana Rd, Compton (90221-5721)
PHONE..................................310 764-4600
Sarah Liao, *Info Tech Mgr*
Selene Hernandez, *Technician*
Khanh Trinh, *Maintence Staff*
Mitch Stutz, *Manager*
Qizhuo Zhuo, *Manager*
EMP: 175
SALES (corp-wide): 22.7B **Privately Held**
SIC: 2843 Surface active agents
HQ: Henkel Us Operations Corporation
1 Henkel Way
Rocky Hill CT 06067
860 571-5100

(P-8429)
JUSTICE BROS DIST CO INC
Also Called: Justice Bros-J B Car Care Pdts
2734 Huntington Dr, Duarte (91010-2301)
PHONE..................................626 359-9174
Edward R Justice Sr, *Ch of Bd*
Edward R Justice Jr, *President*
▲ **EMP:** 25
SQ FT: 33,000
SALES (est): 5.3MM **Privately Held**
WEB: www.justicebrothers.com
SIC: 2843 2899 Surface active agents; chemical preparations

2844 Perfumes, Cosmetics & Toilet Preparations

(P-8430)
220 LABORATORIES INC
2321 3rd St, Riverside (92507-3306)
PHONE..................................951 683-2912
Ian Sishman, *Manager*
EMP: 150 **Privately Held**
WEB: www.220labs.com
SIC: 2844 5122 5087 Cosmetic preparations; cosmetics, perfumes & hair products; beauty parlor equipment & supplies
PA: 220 Laboratories Inc.
2375 3rd St
Riverside CA 92507

(P-8431)
220 LABORATORIES INC (PA)
2375 3rd St, Riverside (92507-3306)
PHONE..................................951 683-2912
Yoram Fishman, *CEO*
Ian Fishman, *President*
Mike Herzog, *Vice Pres*
Gary Wilson, *General Mgr*
George Allison, *Info Tech Mgr*
▲ **EMP:** 104
SQ FT: 130,000
SALES (est): 50.7MM **Privately Held**
WEB: www.220labs.com
SIC: 2844 Cosmetic preparations

(P-8432)
ADVANCED INST OF SKIN CARE
Also Called: Mineral Essence
7225 Fulton Ave, North Hollywood (91605-4111)
PHONE..................................818 765-2606
David Kohanbash, *President*
EMP: 10
SQ FT: 8,000
SALES (est): 1.1MM **Privately Held**
SIC: 2844 Cosmetic preparations

(P-8433)
ADVANCED SKIN & HAIR INC
Also Called: Revivogen
12121 Wilshire Blvd # 1012, Los Angeles (90025-1176)
PHONE..................................310 442-9700
Alex Khadavi, *CEO*
Alan Shargani, *President*
Sheri Carrie, *Office Mgr*
Jennifer Kay, *Accounts Mgr*
▲ **EMP:** 10

SALES (est): 1.7MM **Privately Held**
WEB: www.clearogen.com
SIC: 2844 Cosmetic preparations; hair preparations, including shampoos

(P-8434)
ALLURE LABS INC
30901 Wiegman Ct, Hayward (94544-7809)
PHONE..................................510 489-8896
Sam Dhatt, *CEO*
Renu Dhatt, *Vice Pres*
Sumeet Dhatt, *Info Tech Dir*
Amruta Shetye, *Buyer*
Carlos Torres, *Manager*
▲ **EMP:** 30
SQ FT: 50,000
SALES (est): 9MM **Privately Held**
WEB: www.allurecosmetic.com
SIC: 2844 Cosmetic preparations

(P-8435)
AMERICAN INTL INDS INC
Also Called: Aii Beauty
2220 Gaspar Ave, Commerce (90040-1516)
PHONE..................................323 728-2999
David Eisenstein, *CEO*
Pedro Curiel, *Branch Mgr*
Theresa Cooper, *Manager*
◆ **EMP:** 1100
SQ FT: 224,000
SALES (est): 185.3MM **Privately Held**
SIC: 2844 Toilet preparations

(P-8436)
AMPAC USA INC
3343 Industrial Dr Ste 2, Santa Rosa (95403-2060)
PHONE..................................707 571-1754
Roy Kuppenbender, *President*
David A Bade, *COO*
Nancy M Lanz, *Admin Sec*
▲ **EMP:** 11
SQ FT: 3,000
SALES: 1.2MM **Privately Held**
WEB: www.ampac-usa.com
SIC: 2844 Cosmetic preparations

(P-8437)
ANDALOU NATURALS
1470 Cader Ln, Petaluma (94954-5644)
PHONE..................................415 446-9470
Stacey Kelly Egide, *CEO*
Mark A Egide, *President*
Erin Sellers, *Regl Sales Mgr*
Jonathan Cranford, *Sales Staff*
Rachel Henry, *Sales Staff*
▲ **EMP:** 14
SALES (est): 3.7MM **Privately Held**
SIC: 2844 Shampoos, rinses, conditioners: hair; face creams or lotions

(P-8438)
ARCHIPELAGO INC
Also Called: Archipelago Botanicals
2440 E 38th St, Vernon (90058-1708)
PHONE..................................213 743-9200
David Klass, *CEO*
Gregory Corzine, *Admin Sec*
Alexi Mintz, *CTO*
Gloria Rivera, *Prdtn Mgr*
Anisha Gupta, *Marketing Staff*
◆ **EMP:** 110
SALES (est): 27.8MM **Privately Held**
WEB: www.archipelago-usa.com
SIC: 2844 3999 Toilet preparations; candles

(P-8439)
ARMINAK SOLUTIONS LLC
Also Called: Chrislie
1361 Mountain View Cir, Azusa (91702-1649)
PHONE..................................626 385-5858
Helga Arminak, *President*
EMP: 22
SQ FT: 55,000
SALES: 10MM **Privately Held**
SIC: 2844 Toilet preparations

(P-8440)
AWARE PRODUCTS INC
9250 Mason Ave, Chatsworth (91311-6005)
PHONE..................................818 206-6700

Joe Pender, *President*
Jeff Baum, *Info Tech Dir*
Fernando Velasco, *Director*
EMP: 23
SALES (est): 7.9MM **Privately Held**
SIC: 2844 Toilet preparations

(P-8441)
AWARE PRODUCTS LLC
9250 Mason Ave, Chatsworth
(91311-6005)
PHONE.............................818 206-6700
Chuck Greenberg, *CEO*
Lawrence Balingit, *CFO*
Penny L Hutchinson, *Vice Pres*
Michelle Jimenez, *Vice Pres*
Ni'kita Wilson, *Vice Pres*
▲ **EMP:** 150
SQ FT: 60,000
SALES (est): 79.3MM
SALES (corp-wide): 24.9MM **Privately Held**
WEB: www.awareproducts.com
SIC: 2844 Hair preparations, including shampoos
PA: Vpi Holding Company, Llc
676 N Michigan Ave
Chicago IL 60611
312 255-4800

(P-8442)
BATH PETALS INC
Also Called: Bath Promotions
15620 S Figueroa St, Gardena
(90248-2127)
PHONE.............................310 532-4532
EMP: 10
SQ FT: 5,000
SALES: 395K **Privately Held**
WEB: www.bathpetals.com
SIC: 2844

(P-8443)
BELLAVUOS
417 N Azusa Ave, West Covina
(91791-1348)
PHONE.............................626 653-0121
Etunaah Nguyen, *Owner*
EMP: 19
SALES (est): 1.2MM **Privately Held**
SIC: 2844 Manicure preparations

(P-8444)
BIO CREATIVE ENTERPRISES
Also Called: Bio Creative Labs
350 Kalmus Dr, Costa Mesa (92626-6013)
PHONE.............................714 352-3600
Jason Freeman, *CEO*
▲ **EMP:** 15
SALES (est): 3.6MM **Privately Held**
WEB: www.source1enterprises.com
SIC: 2844 Toilet preparations

(P-8445)
BLACK PHOENIX INC
Also Called: Black Phoenix Alchemy Lab
12120 Sherman Way, North Hollywood
(91605-5501)
PHONE.............................818 506-9404
Elizabeth Barrial, *CEO*
Brian Constantine, *President*
EMP: 10
SQ FT: 3,000
SALES (est): 1.7MM **Privately Held**
SIC: 2844 Toilet preparations

(P-8446)
BLUE CROSS BEAUTY PRODUCTS INC
557 Jessie St, San Fernando (91340-2542)
PHONE.............................818 896-8681
Ray J Friedman, *Ch of Bd*
Mark Friedman, *President*
Lorraine Friedman, *Corp Secy*
▲ **EMP:** 35 **EST:** 1942
SQ FT: 12,000
SALES (est): 7.1MM **Privately Held**
SIC: 2844 Manicure preparations

(P-8447)
BLUEFIELD ASSOCIATES INC
14900 Hilton Dr, Fontana (92336-4026)
PHONE.............................909 476-6027
Iheatu N Obioha, *CEO*
Chimere K Obioha, *Vice Pres*
Tembi Sukuta, *Vice Pres*

Sunil Ram, *QC Mgr*
Chimere Obioha, *Marketing Staff*
◆ **EMP:** 30
SQ FT: 30,000
SALES (est): 7.5MM **Privately Held**
WEB: www.bluefieldinc.com
SIC: 2844 5122 Cosmetic preparations; cosmetics, perfumes & hair products

(P-8448)
BOINCA INC (PA)
15000 S Avalon Blvd Ste F, Gardena
(90248-2035)
PHONE.............................714 809-6313
Edward Bae, *CEO*
Andrew Kim, *Principal*
EMP: 14
SALES: 5.1MM **Privately Held**
SIC: 2844 Toilet preparations

(P-8449)
BOINCA INC
Also Called: Arctic Fox
1611 S Rancho Santa Fe Rd, San Marcos
(92078-5157)
PHONE.............................619 398-7252
Edward Bae, *Branch Mgr*
EMP: 10
SALES (corp-wide): 5.1MM **Privately Held**
SIC: 2844 Hair coloring preparations
PA: Boinca Inc.
15000 S Avalon Blvd Ste F
Gardena CA 90248
714 809-6313

(P-8450)
BOTANICALABS INC
21900 Plummer St, Chatsworth
(91311-4001)
PHONE.............................818 466-5639
Kevin Wachs, *CEO*
Joseph Wachs, *Vice Pres*
Salvador Rodriguez, *Prdtn Mgr*
▲ **EMP:** 12
SALES (est): 3.3MM **Privately Held**
SIC: 2844 Shampoos, rinses, conditioners: hair

(P-8451)
BOTANX LLC
3357 E Miraloma Ave # 156, Anaheim
(92806-1937)
PHONE.............................714 854-1601
James McGee, *Mng Member*
▲ **EMP:** 50
SALES (est): 10.3MM **Privately Held**
SIC: 2844 Cosmetic preparations

(P-8452)
BUDS COTTON INC
1240 N Fee Ana St, Anaheim (92807-1817)
P.O. Box 18073 (92817-8073)
PHONE.............................714 223-7800
Dewitt Paul, *Ch of Bd*
Barry Williams, *President*
Carol Aarsleff, *Accountant*
Matt Paul, *VP Sales*
▲ **EMP:** 30
SQ FT: 30,000
SALES (est): 6.9MM **Privately Held**
WEB: www.cottonbuds.com
SIC: 2844 Toilet preparations

(P-8453)
C A BOTANA INTERNATIONAL INC (PA)
9365 Waples St Ste A, San Diego
(92121-3904)
PHONE.............................858 450-1717
Ursula Wagstaff Kuster, *CEO*
Dieter Kuster, *President*
Jim Lee, *CFO*
Laraine Poveromo, *Marketing Staff*
▲ **EMP:** 20
SALES (est): 4.8MM **Privately Held**
WEB: www.ca-botana.com
SIC: 2844 Face creams or lotions; cosmetic preparations

(P-8454)
CALI CHEM INC
Also Called: Be Beauty
14271 Corp Dr Ste B, Garden Grove
(92843)
PHONE.............................714 265-3740

Tung Doan, *CEO*
Duc Doan, *President*
Amy Doan, *Admin Sec*
▲ **EMP:** 25
SQ FT: 50,000
SALES (est): 6.2MM **Privately Held**
SIC: 2844 Face creams or lotions

(P-8455)
CALIFORNIA INTERFILL INC
8178 Mar Vista Ct, Riverside (92504-4324)
PHONE.............................951 351-2619
Thomas E Boyes, *President*
▲ **EMP:** 15
SQ FT: 20,000
SALES: 3.2MM **Privately Held**
SIC: 2844 Cosmetic preparations

(P-8456)
CARDINAL LABORATORIES INC
Also Called: Westwood Laboratories
710 S Ayon Ave, Azusa (91702-5123)
PHONE.............................626 610-1200
Tony Devos, *President*
Cheryl Kohorst, *CFO*
Deborah Pierce, *CFO*
Paul Schirmer, *Executive*
◆ **EMP:** 70 **EST:** 1971
SALES (est): 11.9MM **Privately Held**
WEB: www.cardinalpet.com
SIC: 2844 Face creams or lotions

(P-8457)
CLASSIC COSMETICS INC
9601 Irondale Ave, Chatsworth
(91311-5009)
PHONE.............................818 773-9042
EMP: 18
SALES (corp-wide): 27.6MM **Privately Held**
SIC: 2844 Toilet preparations
PA: Classic Cosmetics, Inc.
9530 De Soto Ave
Chatsworth CA 91311
818 773-9042

(P-8458)
CLASSIC COSMETICS INC (PA)
9530 De Soto Ave, Chatsworth
(91311-5010)
PHONE.............................818 773-9042
Ida Csiszar, *CEO*
Frank Csiszar, *Corp Secy*
Steve Csiszar, *Vice Pres*
Larry Tapia, *Opers Staff*
▲ **EMP:** 125
SQ FT: 70,000
SALES (est): 27.6MM **Privately Held**
WEB: www.classiccosmetics.com
SIC: 2844 Cosmetic preparations

(P-8459)
COLONIAL ENTERPRISES INC
10620 Mulberry Ave, Fontana
(92337-7025)
PHONE.............................909 822-8700
Louis Navarro, *COO*
EMP: 40
SALES: 2.5MM **Privately Held**
SIC: 2844 2087 Shampoos, rinses, conditioners: hair; powders, drink

(P-8460)
COLOR DESIGN LABORATORY
19151 Parthenia St Ste H, Northridge
(91324-5126)
PHONE.............................818 341-5100
Gilberto Amparo, *CEO*
Maria Amparo, *President*
Maria Gonzalez, *COO*
▲ **EMP:** 50
SQ FT: 9,000
SALES: 5MM **Privately Held**
SIC: 2844 Cosmetic preparations

(P-8461)
COLORFUL PRODUCTS CORPORATION
996 Lawrence Dr Ste 301, Newbury Park
(91320-6020)
PHONE.............................805 498-2195
Cyril Faries, *President*
▲ **EMP:** 10
SQ FT: 18,000
SALES (est): 1.6MM **Privately Held**
SIC: 2844 Toilet preparations

PA: Inter Pacific Industries Inc
996 Lawrence Dr Ste 301
Newbury Park CA 91320
805 498-2195

(P-8462)
COLUMBIA COSMETICS MFRS INC (PA)
1661 Timothy Dr, San Leandro
(94577-2311)
PHONE.............................510 562-5900
Rachel Rendel, *CEO*
Paul Northam, *Info Tech Mgr*
Melissa Ramos, *Purch Agent*
Gregory Northam, *VP Opers*
Chrissy Phelps, *Sales Staff*
▲ **EMP:** 80
SQ FT: 31,000
SALES (est): 21MM **Privately Held**
SIC: 2844 Cosmetic preparations

(P-8463)
CONOPCO INC
1400 Waterloo Rd, Stockton (95205-3743)
PHONE.............................209 466-9580
Max Nicholson, *Branch Mgr*
EMP: 150
SALES (corp-wide): 58.3B **Privately Held**
SIC: 2844 Toilet preparations
HQ: Conopco, Inc.
700 Sylvan Ave
Englewood Cliffs NJ 07632
201 894-7760

(P-8464)
COOLA LLC
Also Called: Coola Suncare
3200 Lionshead Ave, Carlsbad
(92010-4712)
PHONE.............................760 940-2125
Christopher J Birchby, *Manager*
Belinda Colesanti, *CFO*
Melissa Mao, *Vice Pres*
Bill Neubauer, *Vice Pres*
Eric Gangnath, *Creative Dir*
EMP: 40
SALES (est): 602.6K **Privately Held**
SIC: 2844 5722 Suntan lotions & oils; suntanning equipment & supplies

(P-8465)
CORE TECH PRODUCTS INC
1850 Sunnyside Ct, Bakersfield
(93308-6823)
PHONE.............................661 833-1572
James Boone, *CEO*
Brad Bierman, *President*
Cindy Hayef, *Treasurer*
EMP: 10
SQ FT: 5,000
SALES: 3MM **Privately Held**
SIC: 2844 Face creams or lotions

(P-8466)
CORETEX PRODUCTS INC (PA)
1850 Sunnyside Ct, Bakersfield
(93308-6823)
PHONE.............................661 834-6805
James Boone, *Chairman*
Brad Bierman, *President*
Richard B Bierman, *CEO*
Matt Brummett, *Prdtn Mgr*
▲ **EMP:** 14
SQ FT: 14,000
SALES (est): 3.1MM **Privately Held**
WEB: www.coretexproducts.com
SIC: 2844 Suntan lotions & oils

(P-8467)
COSMEDICA SKINCARE
2208 Srra Madows Dr Ste A, Rocklin
(95677)
PHONE.............................800 922-5280
Lucia Conway, *President*
Lucia Shin, *Principal*
EMP: 10
SQ FT: 2,000
SALES (est): 1.2MM **Privately Held**
SIC: 2844 5961 Face creams or lotions; catalog & mail-order houses

(P-8468)
COSMETIC ENTERPRISES LTD
12848 Pierce St, Pacoima (91331-2524)
PHONE.............................818 896-5355
Richard Saute, *President*

▲ = Import ▼=Export
◆ =Import/Export

Arda Saute, *Treasurer*
Debbie Cadis, *Office Admin*
Paul Hwang, *Info Tech Mgr*
Laura Flores, *Human Res Dir*
▲ **EMP:** 19
SQ FT: 65,000
SALES (est): 6.5MM **Privately Held**
WEB: www.cosmeticent.com
SIC: 2844 Hair preparations, including shampoos; cosmetic preparations

(P-8469)
COSMETIC GROUP USA INC
8430 Tujunga Ave, Sun Valley (91352-3934)
PHONE..................................818 767-2889
Andrea Chuchvara, *CEO*
Julio Lara, *Vice Pres*
Giselle Poinier, *Project Mgr*
Jeff Engels, *Engineer*
Omar Combet, *Accountant*
▼ **EMP:** 180 **EST:** 1984
SQ FT: 80,000
SALES: 25MM **Privately Held**
WEB: www.colorfactoryla.com
SIC: 2844 Cosmetic preparations

(P-8470)
COSMO INTERNATIONAL CORP
Also Called: Cosmo International Fragrances
9200 W Sunset Blvd # 401, West Hollywood (90069-3502)
PHONE..................................310 271-1100
Axel Van Liempt, *Branch Mgr*
EMP: 32
SALES (corp-wide): 58MM **Privately Held**
SIC: 2844 Perfumes, natural or synthetic
PA: Cosmo International Corp.
2455 E Sunrise Blvd # 720
Fort Lauderdale FL 33304
954 566-1516

(P-8471)
COSMOBEAUTI LABS & MFG INC
Also Called: Cosmo Beauty Lab & Mfg
480 E Arrow Hwy, San Dimas (91773-3340)
PHONE..................................909 971-9832
Barbara Choi, *President*
Kenneth Lim, *Sales Staff*
▲ **EMP:** 15
SQ FT: 10,000
SALES (est): 3.3MM **Privately Held**
SIC: 2844 Face creams or lotions

(P-8472)
COSMOLARA INC
Also Called: Healthspecialty
8339 Allport Ave, Santa Fe Springs (90670-2107)
PHONE..................................562 273-0348
Anil Badlani, *CEO*
▲ **EMP:** 10
SALES (est): 2.3MM **Privately Held**
SIC: 2844 2676 3999 Hair preparations, including shampoos; infant & baby paper products; hair & hair-based products

(P-8473)
COSWAY COMPANY INC
14805 S Maple Ave, Gardena (90248-1994)
PHONE..................................310 527-9135
Jose Lozano, *Manager*
EMP: 50
SALES (corp-wide): 31.3MM **Privately Held**
WEB: www.coswayco.com
SIC: 2844 5699 Face creams or lotions; bathing suits
PA: Cosway Company, Inc.
20633 S Fordyce Ave
Carson CA 90810
310 900-4100

(P-8474)
COSWAY COMPANY INC (PA)
20633 S Fordyce Ave, Carson (90810-1019)
PHONE..................................310 900-4100
Richard L Hough, *CEO*
Maggie Martinez, *Planning*
Radesh Narine, *Engrg Dir*
Luis Rendon, *Research*

Jose Garcia, *Technology*
▲ **EMP:** 20
SALES (est): 31.3MM **Privately Held**
WEB: www.coswayco.com
SIC: 2844 Face creams or lotions; cosmetic preparations; shampoos, rinses, conditioners: hair

(P-8475)
CREATIVE IMAGE SYSTEMS INC
1921 E Acacia St, Ontario (91761-7921)
PHONE..................................909 947-8588
Steve Hong, *President*
Vivian Shiffman, *Manager*
◆ **EMP:** 12
SQ FT: 20,000
SALES (est): 2.3MM **Privately Held**
WEB: www.creativeimagesystems.com
SIC: 2844 Hair coloring preparations

(P-8476)
DAVID PIRROTTA DIST INC
7424 1/2 W Sunset Blvd # 5, Los Angeles (90046-3446)
PHONE..................................323 645-7456
David Pirrotta, *CEO*
EMP: 12
SQ FT: 1,000
SALES (est): 980K **Privately Held**
SIC: 2844 Toilet preparations

(P-8477)
DAVIDS NATURAL TOOTHPASTE
40292 Rosewell Ct, Temecula (92591-7599)
PHONE..................................949 933-1185
Eric Buss, *President*
EMP: 10 **EST:** 2015
SALES (est): 599.5K **Privately Held**
SIC: 2844 Toothpastes or powders, dentifrices

(P-8478)
DEN-MAT CORPORATION (DH)
236 S Broadway St, Orcutt (93455)
PHONE..................................805 922-8491
Robert L Ibsen, *CEO*
Noreen Freitas, *Exec VP*
▲ **EMP:** 500
SQ FT: 2,500
SALES (est): 86.3MM
SALES (corp-wide): 144.6MM **Privately Held**
WEB: www.denmat.com
SIC: 2844 3843 Toothpastes or powders, dentifrices; dental materials

(P-8479)
DEN-MAT CORPORATION
21515 Vanowen St Ste 200, Canoga Park (91303-2715)
PHONE..................................800 445-0345
Robert Brennis, *Manager*
EMP: 35
SALES (corp-wide): 144.6MM **Privately Held**
WEB: www.denmat.com
SIC: 2844 Toothpastes or powders, dentifrices
HQ: Den-Mat Corporation
236 S Broadway St
Orcutt CA 93455
805 922-8491

(P-8480)
DERMACARE NEUROSCIENCE INST
2580 Corporate Pl F109, Monterey Park (91754-7633)
PHONE..................................323 780-2981
EMP: 10
SALES (corp-wide): 782.3K **Privately Held**
SIC: 2844
PA: Dermacare Neuroscience Institute
9595 Wilshire Blvd # 900
Beverly Hills CA 90212
310 271-7888

(P-8481)
DERMALOGICA LLC (HQ)
Also Called: Dermal Group, The
1535 Beachey Pl, Carson (90746-4005)
PHONE..................................310 900-4000
Aurelian Lis, *President*

Mathew Divaris, *Vice Pres*
Ivor Gordon, *Vice Pres*
Ram Reddy, *Vice Pres*
Jennifer Gaw, *Associate Dir*
◆ **EMP:** 150
SQ FT: 52,000
SALES (est): 125.4MM
SALES (corp-wide): 58.3B **Privately Held**
SIC: 2844 Cosmetic preparations
PA: Unilever N.V.
Weena 455
Rotterdam
102 174-000

(P-8482)
DERMANEW LLC (PA)
436 Smithwood Dr, Beverly Hills (90212-4214)
PHONE..................................626 442-2813
Dean Rhoades, *CEO*
Amby Longhoffer, *President*
▲ **EMP:** 11
SQ FT: 4,000
SALES (est): 907.2K **Privately Held**
WEB: www.dermanew.com
SIC: 2844 2834 Cosmetic preparations; dermatologicals

(P-8483)
DIAMOND WIPES INTL INC (PA)
Also Called: D W I
4651 Schaefer Ave, Chino (91710-5542)
PHONE..................................909 230-9888
Eve Yen, *CEO*
Angie Injian, *Senior VP*
Vivian Kul, *Vice Pres*
William LI, *Vice Pres*
Anthony Reyes, *Vice Pres*
▲ **EMP:** 100
SALES (est): 29.5MM **Privately Held**
WEB: www.diamondwipes.com
SIC: 2844 Towelettes, premoistened

(P-8484)
EBA DESIGN INC
Also Called: Eba Performance Makeup
760 W 16th St Ste D, Costa Mesa (92627-4319)
PHONE..................................714 417-9222
Jarosian Turek, *President*
Katie N Zaslow, *Recruiter*
Lenka Urbanova, *Opers Staff*
Alden Silvestre, *Sales Staff*
▲ **EMP:** 12
SALES (est): 2.5MM **Privately Held**
SIC: 2844 Cosmetic preparations

(P-8485)
ECOLY INTERNATIONAL INC
Also Called: Sea Critters
5800 Bristol Pkwy Ste 700, Culver City (90230-6993)
PHONE..................................818 718-6982
Jim Morrison, *CEO*
EMP: 40
SQ FT: 2,200
SALES (est): 5.4MM **Privately Held**
SIC: 2844 5122 Hair preparations, including shampoos; drugs, proprietaries & sundries

(P-8486)
EDDIES PERFUME & COSMTC CO INC
20929 Ventura Blvd, Woodland Hills (91364-2334)
PHONE..................................818 341-1717
Edmund Zafrani, *President*
Haim Zafrani, *Principal*
◆ **EMP:** 20
SQ FT: 15,000
SALES (est): 22.5MM **Privately Held**
WEB: www.eddiesperfume.com
SIC: 2844 5122 Perfumes, natural or synthetic; drugs, proprietaries & sundries

(P-8487)
EDEN BEAUTY CONCEPTS INC
Also Called: Eufora
3215 Executive Rdg, Vista (92081-8527)
PHONE..................................760 330-9941
Don Bewley, *Vice Pres*
Fred Phillips, *Vice Pres*
Elaine Jeffries, *Accounting Mgr*
Selena Schanning, *Purch Mgr*
Kathleen Summers, *Mktg Dir*

▲ **EMP:** 20
SQ FT: 10,000
SALES (est): 6MM **Privately Held**
WEB: www.eufora.com
SIC: 2844 Shampoos, rinses, conditioners: hair; face creams or lotions; beauty salon & barber shop equipment & supplies

(P-8488)
ELF BEAUTY INC (PA)
570 10th St, Oakland (94607-4038)
PHONE..................................510 210-8602
Tarang P Amin, *Ch of Bd*
John P Bailey, *President*
Richard F Baruch Jr, *Ch Credit Ofcr*
Kory Marchisotto, *Chief Mktg Ofcr*
Allison Malkin, *Officer*
EMP: 25
SALES: 267.4MM **Publicly Held**
SIC: 2844 5122 5999 Cosmetic preparations; cosmetics; cosmetics

(P-8489)
ENORMAREL INC
9200 Mason Ave, Chatsworth (91311-6005)
PHONE..................................818 882-4666
EMP: 10
SALES (est): 841.4K **Privately Held**
WEB: www.enormarel.com
SIC: 2844

(P-8490)
EVERBRANDS INC
10547 W Pico Blvd, Los Angeles (90064-2319)
PHONE..................................855 595-2999
Michael Florman, *CEO*
Joshua Wallace, *President*
EMP: 15
SQ FT: 6,000
SALES: 1.8MM **Privately Held**
SIC: 2844 Oral preparations; cosmetic preparations

(P-8491)
EXQUISITE CORPORATION
Also Called: Exquisite Mfg & Filling Serv
5000 Rivergrade Rd, Baldwin Park (91706-1405)
PHONE..................................626 856-0200
Lily Gozaly, *President*
▲ **EMP:** 30
SQ FT: 20,000
SALES (est): 5.6MM **Privately Held**
SIC: 2844 Toilet preparations

(P-8492)
FENCHEM INC (PA)
15308 El Prado Rd, Chino (91710-7659)
PHONE..................................909 597-8880
Shufeng Fan, *CEO*
Liang Chunyi, *Sales Mgr*
Brian English, *Sales Mgr*
Jason Betts, *Accounts Mgr*
Ryan Fortner, *Accounts Mgr*
▲ **EMP:** 10
SALES (est): 1.8MM **Privately Held**
SIC: 2844 Cosmetic preparations

(P-8493)
FMK LABS INC
1690 N Delilah St, Corona (92879-1866)
PHONE..................................951 736-1212
Alex Minsung Kim, *CEO*
Dylan Kim, *Vice Pres*
Brittany Garay, *Admin Asst*
Steven Thieken, *Purch Dir*
Steven Chavez, *Sales Staff*
▲ **EMP:** 35
SALES (est): 8.6MM **Privately Held**
SIC: 2844 Cosmetic preparations

(P-8494)
FNC MEDICAL CORPORATION
Also Called: Show Off Time
6000 Leland St, Ventura (93003-7605)
PHONE..................................805 644-7576
Samuel S Pattillo, *President*
Samuel Pattillo, *President*
Synora Pattillo, *Vice Pres*
EMP: 20
SQ FT: 36,000
SALES (est): 4.7MM **Privately Held**
SIC: 2844 Cosmetic preparations

PRODUCTS & SVCS

(P-8495)
FULL SPECTRUM OMEGA INC
12832 Nutwood St, Garden Grove
(92840-6312)
PHONE..............................714 866-0039
Richard Brumfield, *CEO*
Guillermo Avina, *CFO*
EMP: 10
SALES (est): 211.6K **Privately Held**
SIC: 2844 7389 2834 Suntan lotions &
oils; ; tinctures, pharmaceutical

(P-8496)
GABELS COSMETICS INC
126 S Avenue 18, Los Angeles
(90031-1777)
PHONE..............................323 221-2430
Sufian Phoa, *CEO*
EMP: 11
SQ FT: 20,000
SALES (est): 1MM **Privately Held**
SIC: 2844 Hair preparations, including
shampoos; cosmetic preparations

(P-8497)
GENERITECH CORPORATION
4967 E Lansing Way, Fresno (93727-7408)
PHONE..............................559 346-0233
Gregory Banks, *President*
Norma Banks, *Vice Pres*
▲ **EMP:** 10
SQ FT: 5,000
SALES: 250K **Privately Held**
SIC: 2844 2834 Cosmetic preparations;
pharmaceutical preparations

(P-8498)
GIOVANNI COSMETICS INC
Also Called: Giovanni Hair Care & Cosmetics
2064 E University Dr, Rancho Dominguez
(90220-6419)
P.O. Box 6990, Beverly Hills (90212-6990)
PHONE..............................310 952-9960
Giovanni J Guidotti, *CEO*
Arthur Guidotti, *Owner*
Peter Stathis, *President*
James Guidotti, *CFO*
Misty Andrade, *Accountant*
◆ **EMP:** 56
SALES (est): 13.5MM **Privately Held**
SIC: 2844 5122 5999 Cosmetic prepara-
tions; cosmetics, perfumes & hair prod-
ucts; cosmetics

(P-8499)
**GLAM AND GLITS NAIL DESIGN
INC**
Also Called: Kiara Sky Professional Nails
8700 Swigert Ct Unit 209, Bakersfield
(93311-9696)
PHONE..............................661 393-4800
Khoa Duong, *CEO*
▲ **EMP:** 65
SALES (est): 458.7K **Privately Held**
SIC: 2844 Manicure preparations

(P-8500)
GLOBAL SALES INC
Also Called: Aniise Skin Care
1732 Westwood Blvd, Los Angeles
(90024-5608)
PHONE..............................310 474-7700
Sheida Kimiabakhsh, *CEO*
Sharareh Kimiabakhsh, *Vice Pres*
Vafa Khoshbin, *Principal*
▲ **EMP:** 23 **EST:** 2011
SALES (est): 4.2MM **Privately Held**
SIC: 2844 5999 Hair preparations, includ-
ing shampoos; face creams or lotions; toi-
letries, cosmetics & perfumes

(P-8501)
GORDON LABORATORIES INC
751 E Artesia Blvd, Carson (90746-1202)
PHONE..............................310 327-5240
Michael Pereira, *CFO*
Lewis Bealer, *Officer*
Marco Pereira, *Vice Pres*
Laura Gutierrez, *Research*
Nina Varma, *Asst Controller*
▲ **EMP:** 120 **EST:** 1967
SQ FT: 100,000
SALES: 32MM **Privately Held**
SIC: 2844 Cosmetic preparations

(P-8502)
**GRAHAM WEBB
INTERNATIONAL INC (DH)**
6109 De Soto Ave, Woodland Hills
(91367-3709)
PHONE..............................760 918-3600
Rick Kornbluth, *President*
Thomas P Baumann, *Vice Pres*
EMP: 70
SQ FT: 30,000
SALES (est): 6.3MM **Publicly Held**
WEB: www.grahamwebb.com
SIC: 2844 Hair preparations, including
shampoos
HQ: Wella Corporation
4500 Park Granada
Calabasas CA 91302
818 999-5112

(P-8503)
GRATEFUL NATURALS CORP
213 Walter Ave, Newbury Park
(91320-4343)
PHONE..............................323 379-4553
Monica Mayer, *Principal*
EMP: 17
SALES (est): 2.2MM **Privately Held**
SIC: 2844 Toilet preparations

(P-8504)
GS COSMECEUTICAL USA INC
131 Pullman St, Livermore (94551-5128)
PHONE..............................925 371-5000
Gurpreet S Sangha, *CEO*
Gurkirpal Sandhu, *COO*
Varinder Sangha, *CFO*
▲ **EMP:** 40
SQ FT: 60,000
SALES (est): 15.2MM **Privately Held**
SIC: 2844 Face creams or lotions; cos-
metic preparations

(P-8505)
GSCM VENTURES INC
Also Called: Pacific Naturals
12924 Pierce St, Pacoima (91331-2526)
PHONE..............................818 303-2600
Gary McNelley, *President*
Gary Neeley, *President*
David Rivero, *Vice Pres*
▼ **EMP:** 30
SQ FT: 5,000
SALES (est): 9.3MM **Privately Held**
WEB: www.websupportcenter.com
SIC: 2844 Toilet preparations

(P-8506)
H2O PLUS LLC (PA)
111 Sutter St Fl 22, San Francisco
(94104-4540)
PHONE..............................312 377-2132
Joy Chen, *President*
Robert Seidl, *CEO*
◆ **EMP:** 90
SQ FT: 82,000
SALES (est): 25.1MM **Privately Held**
SIC: 2844 5999 5122 Toilet preparations;
cosmetics; cosmetics

(P-8507)
HAIN CELESTIAL GROUP INC
Also Called: Jason's Natural
5630 Rickenbacker Rd, Bell (90201-6412)
PHONE..............................323 859-0553
David Vazquez, *Branch Mgr*
EMP: 150 **Publicly Held**
SIC: 2844 Toilet preparations
PA: The Hain Celestial Group Inc
1111 Marcus Ave Ste 100
New Hyde Park NY 11042

(P-8508)
HAIN CELESTIAL GROUP INC
2201 S Mcdowell Boulevard, Petaluma
(94954-7626)
PHONE..............................707 347-1200
Esther Larson, *Branch Mgr*
EMP: 56 **Publicly Held**
WEB: www.hain-celestial.com
SIC: 2844 Deodorants, personal
PA: The Hain Celestial Group Inc
1111 Marcus Ave Ste 100
New Hyde Park NY 11042

(P-8509)
HAND & NAIL HARMONY INC
Also Called: Hand and Nail Harmony
1545 Moonstone, Brea (92821-2876)
PHONE..............................714 773-9758
Danny Haile, *CEO*
David Daniel, *President*
Gari-Dawn Tingler, *Vice Pres*
Napoleon Espinoza, *General Mgr*
Kristin La Roque, *Marketing Mgr*
◆ **EMP:** 68
SALES (est): 23.6MM **Privately Held**
SIC: 2844 Cosmetic preparations

(P-8510)
**HARBER ALL NATURAL
PRODUCTS**
1440 3rd St, Riverside (92507-3481)
PHONE..............................347 921-1004
Bruce Harrison, *President*
Eric Traughber, *Vice Pres*
EMP: 11
SQ FT: 25,000
SALES (est): 1MM
SALES (corp-wide): 2MM **Privately Held**
SIC: 2844 2079 Hair preparations, includ-
ing shampoos; suntan lotions & oils; face
creams or lotions; cooking oils, except
corn: vegetable refined
PA: Harber Foods Llc
1440 3rd St Ste 25
Riverside CA 92507
347 921-1004

(P-8511)
HARBER FOODS LLC (PA)
1440 3rd St Ste 25, Riverside
(92507-3462)
PHONE..............................347 921-1004
Bruce Harrison, *President*
Eric Traughber, *Vice Pres*
EMP: 10
SQ FT: 25,000
SALES: 2MM **Privately Held**
SIC: 2844 4213 2035 2038 Hair prepara-
tions, including shampoos; face creams
or lotions; suntan lotions & oils; refriger-
ated products transport; mayonnaise;
breakfasts, frozen & packaged; dinners,
frozen & packaged

(P-8512)
HONE & STROP INC
1617 Franklin St Apt 6, Santa Monica
(90404-4239)
PHONE..............................424 262-4474
Rodney Bell, *CEO*
EMP: 12
SALES (est): 1MM **Privately Held**
SIC: 2844 5122 Depilatories (cosmetic);
cosmetics

(P-8513)
HYDRABRUSH INC
701 S Andreasen Dr Ste C, Escondido
(92029-1950)
PHONE..............................760 743-5160
Kenneth Hegemann, *President*
▲ **EMP:** 12
SQ FT: 10,000
SALES: 130.5K **Privately Held**
SIC: 2844 Oral preparations

(P-8514)
IBG HOLDINGS INC
24841 Avenue Tibbitts, Valencia
(91355-3405)
PHONE..............................661 702-8680
Richard Mayne, *President*
Marissa Pomerantz, *Vice Pres*
▲ **EMP:** 20
SQ FT: 5,000
SALES (est): 3.3MM **Privately Held**
SIC: 2844 Cosmetic preparations

(P-8515)
**INNOVATIVE BIOSCIENCES
CORP**
Also Called: Innovative Body Science
1849 Diamond St, San Marcos
(92078-5127)
PHONE..............................760 603-0772
Michelle Barton, *President*
▲ **EMP:** 20
SQ FT: 16,000

SALES (est): 4.9MM **Privately Held**
WEB: www.innovativebodyscience.com
SIC: 2844 8742 Toilet preparations; man-
agement consulting services

(P-8516)
**INNOVATIVE COSMETIC LABS
INC**
9740 Cozycroft Ave, Chatsworth
(91311-4401)
PHONE..............................818 349-1121
David Stearn, *CEO*
Lynda Miles, *Vice Pres*
EMP: 15
SALES (est): 3.9MM **Privately Held**
SIC: 2844 Cosmetic preparations

(P-8517)
**INTERNATIONAL ABRASIVE
MFG CO**
1517 N Harmony Cir, Anaheim
(92807-6003)
PHONE..............................714 779-9970
James George, *President*
◆ **EMP:** 35
SALES: 670K **Privately Held**
WEB: www.inmnails.com
SIC: 2844 3423 3291 Manicure prepara-
tions; hand & edge tools; abrasive prod-
ucts

(P-8518)
**INTERNATIONAL BEAUTY PDTS
LLC (PA)**
Also Called: Jerome Russell
8200 Remmet Ave, Canoga Park
(91304-4156)
PHONE..............................818 999-1222
Jim Perry, *Vice Pres*
Jerome Russell, *Principal*
Sherry Hughes, *Manager*
EMP: 11
SQ FT: 1,000
SALES (est): 6MM **Privately Held**
WEB: www.jeromerussell.com
SIC: 2844 Toilet preparations

(P-8519)
IWEN NATURALS
4150 Mystic View Ct, Hayward
(94542-2166)
PHONE..............................510 589-8019
I-Wen WEI, *Owner*
EMP: 10
SALES (est): 467.5K **Privately Held**
SIC: 2844 5999 Cosmetic preparations;
cosmetics

(P-8520)
JAPONESQUE LLC
2420 Camino Ramon Ste 250, San Ramon
(94583-4319)
PHONE..............................925 866-6670
Rich Conti, *CEO*
Catherine West-Jancoski, *Executive Asst*
Anh Tran, *Director*
▲ **EMP:** 16
SQ FT: 4,500
SALES (est): 4.3MM **Privately Held**
WEB: www.japonesque.com
SIC: 2844 5122 Cosmetic preparations;
cosmetics

(P-8521)
JIVAGO INC (PA)
9454 Wilshire Blvd # 600, Beverly Hills
(90212-2931)
PHONE..............................310 205-5535
Ilana V Jivago, *President*
◆ **EMP:** 15
SQ FT: 4,000
SALES (est): 3.8MM **Privately Held**
WEB: www.jivagoinc.com
SIC: 2844 Perfumes & colognes; face
creams or lotions

(P-8522)
JOAR LABS INC
4115 San Fernando Rd, Glendale
(91204-2517)
PHONE..............................818 243-0700
Arturo Martinez, *President*
▲ **EMP:** 40
SQ FT: 15,000

SALES (est): 5.6MM **Privately Held**
SIC: 2844 2833 Cosmetic preparations; vitamins, natural or synthetic: bulk, uncompounded

(P-8523)
JOHNSON & JOHNSON CONSUMER INC
Also Called: Neutrogena
5760 W 96th St, Los Angeles (90045-5544)
PHONE..................................310 642-1150
EMP: 47
SALES (corp-wide): 81.5B **Publicly Held**
WEB: www.neutrogena.com
SIC: 2844 Toilet preparations
HQ: Johnson & Johnson Consumer Inc.
  199 Grandview Rd
  Skillman NJ 08558
  908 874-1000

(P-8524)
JOICO LABORATORIES INC
488 E Santa Clara St # 301, Arcadia
(91006-7229)
PHONE..................................626 321-4100
Sara Jones, *President*
Akira Mochizuki, *Exec VP*
Takahiro Iwabuchi, *Director*
▲ **EMP:** 200 **EST:** 1976
SALES (est): 25.7MM
SALES (corp-wide): 22.7B **Privately Held**
WEB: www.joico.com
SIC: 2844 Hair preparations, including shampoos; cosmetic preparations
HQ: Zotos International, Inc.
  100 Tokeneke Rd
  Darien CT 06820
  203 655-8911

(P-8525)
KAMSUT INCORPORATED
Also Called: Kama Sutra
2151 Anchor Ct, Thousand Oaks
(91320-1604)
PHONE..................................805 495-7479
Joseph Bolstad, *President*
Jacqueline Kane, *Vice Pres*
Nick Nugwynne, *Opers Mgr*
Patrick Trematerra, *Marketing Mgr*
Christine Marsden, *Accounts Mgr*
▲ **EMP:** 20
SQ FT: 8,000
SALES (est): 4.4MM **Privately Held**
WEB: www.kamasutra.com
SIC: 2844 Cosmetic preparations

(P-8526)
KELLY TEEGARDEN ORGANICS LLC
Also Called: Kto
6524 Platt Ave Ste 224, West Hills
(91307-3218)
PHONE..................................818 518-0707
Kelly Teegarden,
Amber Hunter, *General Mgr*
EMP: 12
SALES (est): 2.6MM **Privately Held**
SIC: 2844 Lipsticks

(P-8527)
KIM LAUBE & COMPANY INC
Also Called: Kelco
2221 Statham Blvd, Oxnard (93033-3913)
PHONE..................................805 240-1300
Kim E Laube, *President*
Jacqueline Laube, *Sales Staff*
◆ **EMP:** 40
SALES (est): 7.4MM **Privately Held**
WEB: www.kimlaubeco.com
SIC: 2844 3999 Hair preparations, including shampoos; shampoos, rinses, conditioners: hair; hair clippers for human use, hand & electric; pet supplies

(P-8528)
KUM KANG TRADING USAINC
Also Called: Black N Gold
6433 Alondra Blvd, Paramount
(90723-3758)
PHONE..................................562 531-6111
Yoon OH, *President*
◆ **EMP:** 12
SQ FT: 20,000
SALES (est): 2.3MM **Privately Held**
SIC: 2844 Hair preparations, including shampoos

(P-8529)
KUSTOMER KINETICS INC
136 E Saint Joseph St A, Arcadia
(91006-7151)
PHONE..................................626 445-6161
Jay Berger, *President*
William H Berger, *President*
EMP: 10
SALES (est): 1.4MM **Privately Held**
WEB: www.kustomerkinetics.com
SIC: 2844 Perfumes, natural or synthetic

(P-8530)
LANZA RESEARCH INTERNATIONAL
429 Santa Monica Blvd # 510, Santa Monica (90401-3401)
PHONE..................................310 393-5227
Robert De Lanza, *President*
Jo-Ann Stamp, *Corp Secy*
Dana Story, *Exec VP*
EMP: 75
SQ FT: 40,000
SALES (est): 6.4MM **Privately Held**
WEB: www.davexlabs.com
SIC: 2844 5122 Shampoos, rinses, conditioners: hair; cosmetics

(P-8531)
LEE PHARMACEUTICALS
1434 Santa Anita Ave, South El Monte
(91733-3312)
PHONE..................................626 442-3141
Ronald G Lee, *CEO*
Mike Agresti, *CFO*
▲ **EMP:** 82
SALES (est): 17.2MM **Privately Held**
WEB: www.leepharmaceuticals.com
SIC: 2844 2834 3843 Manicure preparations; depilatories (cosmetic); pharmaceutical preparations; enamels, dentists'; cement, dental

(P-8532)
LENUS HANDCRAFTED
3323 Thorn St, San Diego (92104-4747)
PHONE..................................619 200-4266
Laura Lisauskas, *Principal*
EMP: 10
SALES: 80K **Privately Held**
SIC: 2844 7389 Face creams or lotions;

(P-8533)
LIBBY LABORATORIES INC
1700 6th St, Berkeley (94710-1806)
PHONE..................................510 527-5400
Susan Libby, *President*
Gordon Libby, *Treasurer*
Charles Mendoza, *Info Tech Mgr*
George Pieri, *Plant Engr*
James Pirie, *Plant Engr*
EMP: 23
SQ FT: 25,000
SALES (est): 2.3MM **Privately Held**
WEB: www.libbylabs.com
SIC: 2844 2834 2899 Cosmetic preparations; pharmaceutical preparations; solutions, pharmaceutical; chemical preparations

(P-8534)
LIQUID TECHNOLOGIES INC
14425 Yorba Ave, Chino (91710-5733)
PHONE..................................909 393-9475
John Maruszewski, *CEO*
Marc Tomberlin, *CFO*
▲ **EMP:** 30
SALES (est): 8MM **Privately Held**
WEB: www.liquidtek.com
SIC: 2844 Hair preparations, including shampoos

(P-8535)
LLC BAKER CUMMINS
580 Garcia Ave, Pittsburg (94565-4901)
PHONE..................................925 732-9338
Evan Warshawsky, *President*
EMP: 75
SALES (est): 2.5MM **Privately Held**
SIC: 2844 2834 Cosmetic preparations; pharmaceutical preparations

(P-8536)
LYNEX COMPANY INC
375 Digital Dr, Morgan Hill (95037-2880)
PHONE..................................408 778-7884
Lien Nguyen, *President*
Nicholas Dinh, *Vice Pres*
▲ **EMP:** 10
SQ FT: 1,500
SALES (est): 1.5MM **Privately Held**
WEB: www.lynex.com
SIC: 2844 Toilet preparations

(P-8537)
MASTEY DE PARIS INC
25413 Rye Canyon Rd, Valencia
(91355-1269)
PHONE..................................661 257-4814
Stephen Mastey, *President*
Lesley Mastey, *Admin Sec*
EMP: 50
SQ FT: 63,000
SALES (est): 5.3MM **Privately Held**
SIC: 2844 Hair preparations, including shampoos

(P-8538)
MERLE NORMAN COSMETICS INC (PA)
9130 Bellanca Ave, Los Angeles
(90045-4772)
PHONE..................................310 641-3000
Jack B Nethercutt, *Ch of Bd*
Amy Hackbart, *COO*
Michael Cassidy, *CFO*
Helen Nethercutt, *Vice Ch Bd*
Travis Richards, *Bd of Directors*
▲ **EMP:** 345 **EST:** 1974
SQ FT: 354,000
SALES: 64MM **Privately Held**
WEB: www.merlenorman.com
SIC: 2844 5999 Cosmetic preparations; cosmetics

(P-8539)
MILESTONES PRODUCTS INC
Also Called: Q Perfumes
1965 S Tubeway Ave, Commerce
(90040-1611)
PHONE..................................323 728-3434
Edmond Sabet, *President*
▲ **EMP:** 10
SQ FT: 30,000
SALES (est): 3.1MM **Privately Held**
WEB: www.qperfumes.net
SIC: 2844 Perfumes & colognes

(P-8540)
MIXED CHICKS LLC
21218 Vanowen St, Canoga Park
(91303-2823)
PHONE..................................818 888-4008
Wendi Levy, *Mng Member*
Djata Grant, *Officer*
Kim Etheredge,
Brad Kaaya,
◆ **EMP:** 10
SALES (est): 1.5MM **Privately Held**
SIC: 2844 5122 Hair preparations, including shampoos; cosmetics

(P-8541)
MOSAIC DISTRIBUTORS LLC
Also Called: Chella
507 Calle San Pablo, Camarillo
(93012-8550)
PHONE..................................805 383-7711
Chris Kolodziejski, *CEO*
EMP: 10 **EST:** 2012
SALES (est): 1.3MM **Privately Held**
SIC: 2844 5122 Cosmetic preparations; face creams or lotions; cosmetics

(P-8542)
MOSAIC MARKETING PARTNERS LLC
Also Called: Chella Professional Skin Care
507 Calle San Pablo, Camarillo
(93012-8550)
PHONE..................................805 383-7711
Chris Kolodziejski,
▲ **EMP:** 10
SQ FT: 4,900
SALES (est): 644.2K **Privately Held**
SIC: 2844 Cosmetic preparations; face creams or lotions

(P-8543)
MY WORLD STYLES LLC
Also Called: Players Circle Barbershop
16 Dutton Ave, San Leandro (94577-2839)
PHONE..................................800 355-4008
Allen Richard, *CEO*
EMP: 10
SQ FT: 2,000
SALES (est): 857.9K **Privately Held**
SIC: 2844 7241 Face creams or lotions; barber college

(P-8544)
NAKED PRINCESS WORLDWIDE LLC (PA)
11766 Wilshire Blvd Fl 9, Los Angeles
(90025-6548)
PHONE..................................310 271-1199
Jordana Woodland, *CEO*
Cari Deutsch, *Production*
▲ **EMP:** 15
SALES (est): 1.4MM **Privately Held**
SIC: 2844 Cosmetic preparations

(P-8545)
NATURES BABY PRODUCTS INC
Also Called: Nature's Baby Organics
58 Dartmouth Dr, Rancho Mirage
(92270-3162)
PHONE..................................818 521-5054
Phil Wolvek, *CEO*
Adena Surabian, *President*
Beverly Wolvek, *Corp Secy*
▼ **EMP:** 10
SQ FT: 30,000
SALES (est): 1.4MM **Privately Held**
SIC: 2844 5137 Powder: baby, face, talcum or toilet; baby goods

(P-8546)
NEUTRADERM INC
20660 Nordhoff St, Chatsworth
(91311-6114)
PHONE..................................818 534-3190
Samuel D Raoof, *CEO*
Toora J Raoof, *Principal*
Jake Salzaruoo, *Purch Mgr*
Tino Osuna, *VP Opers*
▲ **EMP:** 25
SALES (est): 10.2MM **Privately Held**
SIC: 2844 Cosmetic preparations

(P-8547)
NEW FRAGRANCE CONTINENTAL
Also Called: La Natura
5033 Exposition Blvd, Los Angeles
(90016-3913)
PHONE..................................323 766-0060
Sabina Chazanas, *President*
Alejandro Chazanas, *Vice Pres*
Carina Chazanas, *Director*
EMP: 12
SQ FT: 5,000
SALES: 668.3K **Privately Held**
WEB: www.lanatura.com
SIC: 2844 Cosmetic preparations

(P-8548)
NIX MOUTHWASH
19925 Stevens Creek Blvd, Cupertino
(95014-2300)
PHONE..................................888 909-9088
Bea Janonis, *CEO*
EMP: 50
SALES (est): 1.8MM **Privately Held**
SIC: 2844 Mouthwashes

(P-8549)
NUVORA INC
3350 Scott Blvd Ste 502, Santa Clara
(95054-3108)
PHONE..................................408 856-2200
Jerry Gin, *President*
EMP: 20
SQ FT: 8,000
SALES (est): 3.5MM **Privately Held**
SIC: 2844 Oral preparations

(P-8550)
OLAPLEX LLC (PA)
1482 E Valley Rd Ste 701, Santa Barbara
(93108-1200)
PHONE..................................805 258-7680

Dean Christal,
Tyler Krebs, *Vice Pres*
EMP: 14
SALES: 2MM **Privately Held**
SIC: 2844 Hair preparations, including
shampoos

(P-8551)
ORAL ESSENTIALS INC
436 N Roxbury Dr, Beverly Hills
(90210-5026)
PHONE..........................888 773-5273
Kourosh Maddahi, *CEO*
Caroline Heerwagon, *COO*
Linda Kloeffer, *CFO*
Justin Maddahi, *Chief Mktg Ofcr*
Brent Burden, *VP Sales*
EMP: 13 **EST:** 2014
SALES (est): 162.9K **Privately Held**
SIC: 2844 Toothpastes or powders, denti-
frices

(P-8552)
ORLY INTERNATIONAL INC
Also Called: Sparitual
7710 Haskell Ave, Van Nuys (91406-1905)
PHONE..........................818 994-1001
Jeff Pink, *President*
◆ **EMP:** 100 **EST:** 1977
SQ FT: 65,000
SALES (est): 36.8MM **Privately Held**
WEB: www.orlybeauty.com
SIC: 2844 Cosmetic preparations

(P-8553)
PACIFIC WORLD CORPORATION (PA)
100 Technology Dr Ste 200, Irvine
(92618-2466)
PHONE..........................949 598-2400
James Colleran, *CEO*
Joseph Fracassi, *President*
Joseph Jaeger, *COO*
Joel Carden, *Exec VP*
Craig Finney, *Exec VP*
◆ **EMP:** 99
SQ FT: 30,000
SALES (est): 29.5MM **Privately Held**
WEB: www.nailene.com
SIC: 2844 3421 3999 Cosmetic prepara-
tions; clippers, fingernail & toenail; finger-
nails, artificial

(P-8554)
PANCO MENS PRODUCTS INC
45605 Citrus Ave, Indio (92201-3451)
PHONE..........................760 342-4368
Gene Pantuso, *President*
EMP: 15 **EST:** 1964
SQ FT: 40,000
SALES (est): 2.6MM **Privately Held**
SIC: 2844 Toilet preparations; face creams
or lotions; lotions, shaving; shampoos,
rinses, conditioners: hair

(P-8555)
PBH MARKETING INC
Also Called: Paul Brown Hawaii
9960 Glenoaks Blvd Ste C, Sun Valley
(91352-1066)
PHONE..........................818 374-9000
Paul Brown, *President*
▲ **EMP:** 10
SALES (est): 1.2MM **Privately Held**
SIC: 2844 Hair preparations, including
shampoos

(P-8556)
PERSON & COVEY INC
616 Allen Ave, Glendale (91201-2014)
P.O. Box 25018 (91221-5018)
PHONE..........................818 937-5000
Lorne Person Jr, *CEO*
Lorne Person Sr, *Ch of Bd*
Sue Person, *Vice Pres*
Bill Morelli, *CIO*
William Marquardt, *MIS Dir*
EMP: 45 **EST:** 1941
SQ FT: 36,000
SALES (est): 9.4MM **Privately Held**
WEB: www.personandcovey.com
SIC: 2844 2834 Cosmetic preparations;
dermatologicals

(P-8557)
PETRA-1 LP
12386 Osborne Pl, Pacoima (91331-2013)
PHONE..........................866 334-3702
Benjamin Whitham, *Partner*
EMP: 15
SALES (est): 886.8K **Privately Held**
SIC: 2844 Toilet preparations

(P-8558)
PHYSICANS FORMULA HOLDINGS INC (HQ)
22067 Ferrero, Walnut (91789-5214)
PHONE..........................626 334-3395
Ingrid Jackel, *CEO*
Jeffrey P Rogers, *President*
Leslie H Keegan, *Senior VP*
Chad Boise, *Exec Sec*
▲ **EMP:** 33
SQ FT: 82,000
SALES (est): 28.3MM
SALES (corp-wide): 283.8MM **Privately
Held**
SIC: 2844 5122 Cosmetic preparations;
drugs, proprietaries & sundries
PA: Markwins International Corp
22067 Ferrero
Walnut CA 91789
909 595-8898

(P-8559)
PHYSICIANS FORMULA INC (DH)
22067 Ferrero, City of Industry
(91789-5214)
PHONE..........................626 334-3395
Ingrid Jackel, *Ch of Bd*
Jeff Rogers, *President*
Joseph J Jaeger, *CFO*
Rick Kirchhoff, *Vice Pres*
Manuel Scates, *Purchasing*
▲ **EMP:** 57
SQ FT: 82,800
SALES (est): 28.3MM
SALES (corp-wide): 283.8MM **Privately
Held**
WEB: www.physiciansformula.com
SIC: 2844 Cosmetic preparations

(P-8560)
PHYSICIANS FORMULA INC
250 S 9th Ave, City of Industry
(91746-3309)
PHONE..........................626 334-3395
Jennifer Sharp, *Branch Mgr*
EMP: 100
SALES (corp-wide): 283.8MM **Privately
Held**
WEB: www.physiciansformula.com
SIC: 2844 Cosmetic preparations
HQ: Physicians Formula, Inc.
22067 Ferrero
City Of Industry CA 91789
626 334-3395

(P-8561)
PHYSICIANS FORMULA INC
753 Arrow Grand Cir, Covina (91722-2148)
PHONE..........................626 334-3395
Vivian Durra, *Branch Mgr*
EMP: 100
SALES (corp-wide): 283.8MM **Privately
Held**
WEB: www.physiciansformula.com
SIC: 2844 Cosmetic preparations
HQ: Physicians Formula, Inc.
22067 Ferrero
City Of Industry CA 91789
626 334-3395

(P-8562)
PHYSICIANS FORMULA COSMT INC
22067 Ferrero, City of Industry
(91789-5214)
PHONE..........................626 334-3395
Jeffrey P Rogers, *President*
Joseph J Jaeger, *CFO*
EMP: 147
SALES (est): 24.3K
SALES (corp-wide): 283.8MM **Privately
Held**
SIC: 2844 Cosmetic preparations

HQ: Physicians Formula, Inc.
22067 Ferrero
City Of Industry CA 91789
626 334-3395

(P-8563)
PLEROS LLC
Also Called: Neomen
2825 E Tahquitz Cyn W, Palm Springs
(92262-6906)
PHONE..........................442 275-6764
Peter Zhu, *COO*
EMP: 10
SQ FT: 2,000
SALES (est): 2MM **Privately Held**
SIC: 2844 5999 Cosmetic preparations;
cosmetics

(P-8564)
PRESTIGE COSMETICS INC
17780 Gothard St, Huntington Beach
(92647-6216)
PHONE..........................714 375-0395
Sarjula Sanghvi, *President*
EMP: 11
SQ FT: 10,000
SALES (est): 1.9MM **Privately Held**
SIC: 2844 5122 Cosmetic preparations;
cosmetics

(P-8565)
PRETIKA CORPORATION
16 Salermo, Laguna Niguel (92677-9032)
PHONE..........................949 481-8818
Thomas E Nichols, *President*
◆ **EMP:** 26
SQ FT: 22,500
SALES (est): 4.6MM **Privately Held**
WEB: www.pretika.com
SIC: 2844 Cosmetic preparations

(P-8566)
PRIMA FLEUR BOTANICALS INC
84 Galli Dr, Novato (94949-5706)
PHONE..........................415 455-0957
Marianne Griffeth, *President*
Ron Griffeth, *Corp Secy*
Donna Lenoue, *Office Admin*
Christina Mitaine, *Purch Mgr*
Stacy Huang, *Sales Staff*
▲ **EMP:** 16
SQ FT: 5,000
SALES (est): 4MM **Privately Held**
WEB: www.primafleur.com
SIC: 2844 5169 Suntan lotions & oils; es-
sential oils

(P-8567)
PRINCE DEVELOPMENT LLC
Also Called: Prince Reigns
23302 Oxnard St, Woodland Hills
(91367-3123)
PHONE..........................866 774-6234
Edouard Joseph, *Mng Member*
Christine Joseph,
▼ **EMP:** 12
SQ FT: 3,800
SALES (est): 2MM **Privately Held**
SIC: 2844 Cosmetic preparations

(P-8568)
PRISHA COSMETICS INC
9260 Owensmouth Ave, Chatsworth
(91311-5853)
PHONE..........................818 773-8784
Riken Shah, *President*
Luci Murillo, *Exec Dir*
▲ **EMP:** 11
SQ FT: 6,800
SALES (est): 2.4MM **Privately Held**
SIC: 2844 Cosmetic preparations

(P-8569)
PROFESSIONAL SKIN CARE INC (PA)
Also Called: Only You Rx Skin Care
25028 Avenue Kearny, Valencia
(91355-1253)
P.O. Box 753, Lafayette (94549-0753)
PHONE..........................661 257-7771
Dr James Paige, *President*
▲ **EMP:** 30
SQ FT: 25,000

SALES (est): 3.7MM **Privately Held**
SIC: 2844 5122 5087 Cosmetic preparations; drugs, proprietaries & sundries;
cosmetics; beauty parlor equipment &
supplies

(P-8570)
PURA NATURALS INC (HQ)
23101 Lake Center Dr # 100, Lake Forest
(92630-2801)
PHONE..........................949 273-8100
Robert Doherty, *CEO*
Derek Duhame, *President*
Robert Switzer, *Admin Sec*
Jim Breech, *VP Sales*
EMP: 15
SQ FT: 4,000
SALES: 377K
SALES (corp-wide): 1.2MM **Publicly Held**
SIC: 2844 Cosmetic preparations
PA: Advanced Innovative Recovery Tech-
nologies, Inc.
23101 Lake Center Dr # 100
Lake Forest CA 92630
949 273-8100

(P-8571)
REVLON INC
Creative Nail Design
1125 Joshua Way Ste 12, Vista
(92081-7840)
PHONE..........................760 599-2900
Jim Northstrum, *Director*
Jan Arnold, *VP Human Res*
EMP: 50 **Publicly Held**
WEB: www.revlon.com
SIC: 2844 Manicure preparations
PA: Revlon, Inc.
1 New York Plz Fl 49
New York NY 10004

(P-8572)
RMF SALT HOLDINGS LLC
Also Called: San Francisco Bath Salt Co
2217 S Shore Ctr 200, Alameda
(94501-8073)
PHONE..........................510 477-9600
Lee J Williamson, *President*
◆ **EMP:** 16
SALES (est): 4.6MM
SALES (corp-wide): 35.4MM **Privately
Held**
WEB: www.sfbsc.com
SIC: 2844 5149 Bath salts; salt, edible
PA: Red Monkey Foods, Inc.
6751 W Kings St
Springfield MO 65802
417 319-7300

(P-8573)
ROBANDA INTERNATIONAL INC
Also Called: World Amenities
8260 Cmino Santa Fe Ste A, San Diego
(92121)
PHONE..........................619 276-7660
David Lieb, *President*
Gerald Leib, *Ch of Bd*
Helen Lieb, *CFO*
Anthony Lieb, *Vice Pres*
▲ **EMP:** 28
SQ FT: 20,000
SALES (est): 10.8MM **Privately Held**
WEB: www.robanda.com
SIC: 2844 Cosmetic preparations

(P-8574)
SAMUEL RAOOF
Also Called: Brandmd Skin Care
20660 Nordhoff St, Chatsworth
(91311-6114)
PHONE..........................818 534-3180
Samuel Raoof, *Owner*
EMP: 20 **EST:** 2014
SALES (est): 1.4MM **Privately Held**
SIC: 2844 Deodorants, personal

(P-8575)
SANDRA SPARKS & ASSOCIATES
2510 Peninsula Rd, Oxnard (93035-2962)
PHONE..........................805 985-2057
Sandra Sparks, *Owner*
EMP: 13
SALES (est): 825K **Privately Held**
SIC: 2844 Cosmetic preparations

▲ = Import ▼=Export
◆ =Import/Export

(P-8576)
SANTEE COSMETICS USA
13202 Estrella Ave, Gardena (90248-1520)
PHONE..................................310 329-2305
Jacklyn Kim, *Owner*
▲ EMP: 10 EST: 2008
SALES: 1MM **Privately Held**
SIC: 2844 Cosmetic preparations

(P-8577)
SAYDEL INC (PA)
Also Called: Nina Religion
2475 E Slauson Ave, Huntington Park
(90255-2887)
PHONE..................................323 585-2800
Santo Gil Orta, *President*
Michael Orta, *Vice Pres*
EMP: 15 EST: 1968
SQ FT: 11,000
SALES: 552.8K **Privately Held**
WEB: www.saydel.com
SIC: 2844 5049 5999 Perfumes, natural
or synthetic; religious supplies; religious
goods

(P-8578)
SHADOW HOLDINGS LLC (PA)
Also Called: Bocchi Laboratories
26455 Ruether Ave, Santa Clarita
(91350-2621)
PHONE..................................661 252-3807
Robert Bocchi,
Patrick Kelley,
Joe Pender,
EMP: 34
SQ FT: 88,500
SALES (est): 79.4MM **Privately Held**
SIC: 2844 Toilet preparations

(P-8579)
SHADOW HOLDINGS LLC
Also Called: Bocchi Laboratories
26421 Ruether Ave, Santa Clarita
(91350-2621)
PHONE..................................661 252-3807
Robert J Bocchi, *Mng Member*
EMP: 166
SQ FT: 86,200
SALES (corp-wide): 79.4MM **Privately
Held**
WEB: www.bocchilabs.com
SIC: 2844 Toilet preparations
PA: Shadow Holdings, Llc
26455 Ruether Ave
Santa Clarita CA 91350
661 252-3807

(P-8580)
SHEER DESIGN INC
6309 Esplanade, Playa Del Rey
(90293-7581)
PHONE..................................310 306-2121
Mark Friedland, *President*
EMP: 60
SALES (est): 6.7MM **Privately Held**
SIC: 2844 Cosmetic preparations

(P-8581)
SHINE & PRETTY (USA) CORP
456 Constitution Ave, Camarillo
(93012-8529)
PHONE..................................805 388-8581
Edward Sheu, *President*
▲ EMP: 10
SQ FT: 13,400
SALES (est): 1.3MM **Privately Held**
SIC: 2844 Cosmetic preparations

(P-8582)
SMALL WORLD TRADING CO
Also Called: Eo Products
90 Windward Way, San Rafael
(94901-7200)
PHONE..................................415 945-1900
Susan Griffin-Black, *CEO*
Brad Black, *Principal*
EMP: 103
SQ FT: 40,000
SALES (est): 19.9MM **Privately Held**
WEB: www.eoproducts.com
SIC: 2844 Hair preparations, including
shampoos; concentrates, perfume

(P-8583)
**SMASHBOX BEAUTY
COSMETICS INC**
Also Called: Smashbox Cosmetics
8538 Warner Dr, Culver City (90232-2431)
PHONE..................................310 558-1490
Sara Moss, *CEO*
Karen Quimby, *Vice Pres*
Jill Tomandl, *Vice Pres*
Tricia Veteri, *Vice Pres*
Bronson Page, *Exec Dir*
◆ EMP: 120
SQ FT: 20,000
SALES (est): 25.3MM **Publicly Held**
WEB: www.smashbox.com
SIC: 2844 Toilet preparations
PA: The Estee Lauder Companies Inc
767 5th Ave Fl 1
New York NY 10153

(P-8584)
**SMITH & VANDIVER
CORPORATION**
Also Called: Sinclair & Valentine
480 Airport Blvd, Watsonville (95076-2002)
PHONE..................................831 722-9526
Jeffrey K Slaboden, *CEO*
Irvaz Husic, *Vice Pres*
Corliss Deome, *Info Tech Mgr*
Vikki Vance, *Accounting Mgr*
▲ EMP: 75
SQ FT: 55,000
SALES (est): 31.9MM **Privately Held**
WEB: www.smith-vandiver.com
SIC: 2844 Cosmetic preparations

(P-8585)
SOAP & WATER LLC
11450 Sheldon St, Sun Valley
(91352-1121)
PHONE..................................310 639-3990
Jill Belasco,
EMP: 20
SQ FT: 80,000
SALES (est): 1.6MM **Privately Held**
SIC: 2844 Face creams or lotions

(P-8586)
SPA GIRL CORPORATION
3100 W Warner Ave Ste 11, Santa Ana
(92704-5331)
PHONE..................................714 444-1040
Kerrie La Bianco, *CEO*
EMP: 20
SQ FT: 2,500
SALES: 5MM **Privately Held**
SIC: 2844 Cosmetic preparations

(P-8587)
SPATZ CORPORATION
Also Called: Spatz Laboratories
1600 Westar Dr, Oxnard (93033-2423)
PHONE..................................805 487-2122
Joel Lynn Nelson, *CEO*
John Nelson, *COO*
George Jefferson, *CFO*
Laura Nelson, *Vice Pres*
Maria Zendejas, *Executive*
▲ EMP: 145 EST: 1954
SQ FT: 62,000
SALES (est): 79.7MM **Privately Held**
WEB: www.spatzlabs.com
SIC: 2844 3089 Cosmetic preparations;
plastic containers, except foam

(P-8588)
STEARNS CORPORATION
Also Called: Derma E
2130 Ward Ave, Simi Valley (93065-1851)
PHONE..................................805 582-2710
Brenda Wu, *President*
Linda Miles, *President*
Barbara Roll, *Officer*
Gina Ferrato, *Sales Staff*
▲ EMP: 25
SALES (est): 6.1MM
SALES (corp-wide): 45MM **Privately
Held**
SIC: 2844 Face creams or lotions
PA: Topix Pharmaceuticals Inc.
5200 New Horizons Blvd
Amityville NY 11701
631 226-7979

(P-8589)
SUMBODY UNION STREET LLC
118 N Main St, Sebastopol (95472-3447)
PHONE..................................707 823-4043
Kila Peterson,
Deborah Burnes,
EMP: 20
SALES (est): 2.1MM **Privately Held**
WEB: www.sumbody.com
SIC: 2844 5999 Toilet preparations; toi-
letries, cosmetics & perfumes

(P-8590)
SUN DEEP INC
Also Called: Sun Deep Cosmetics
31285 San Clemente St B, Hayward
(94544-7814)
P.O. Box 2814, Danville (94526-7814)
PHONE..................................510 441-2525
Jay Gill, *CEO*
Prabhleen S Gill, *President*
Ravi Gill, *Corp Secy*
Sundeep Gill, *Vice Pres*
▲ EMP: 40
SQ FT: 40,000
SALES (est): 8MM **Privately Held**
WEB: www.sundeepinc.com
SIC: 2844 5122 Cosmetic preparations;
toilet preparations; cosmetics, perfumes &
hair products

(P-8591)
SUNEVA MEDICAL INC (PA)
5870 Pacific Center Blvd, San Diego
(92121-4204)
PHONE..................................858 550-9999
Patricia Altavilla, *CEO*
Joseph A Newcomb, *CFO*
Stewart M Brown, *Vice Pres*
Nicola Selley, *Vice Pres*
Steven C Trider, *Vice Pres*
EMP: 45 EST: 2009
SALES (est): 7.9MM **Privately Held**
SIC: 2844 3842 Cosmetic preparations;
cosmetic restorations

(P-8592)
TENDER LOVING THINGS INC
Also Called: Happy Company, The
26203 Prod Ave Ste 4, Hayward (94545)
PHONE..................................510 300-1260
Mark Juarez, *CEO*
Alan Widdoss, *CFO*
EMP: 20
SQ FT: 20,000
SALES (est): 3.8MM **Privately Held**
WEB: www.thehappycompany.com
SIC: 2844 2499 5122 Toilet preparations;
novelties, wood fiber; drugs, proprietaries
& sundries

(P-8593)
THIBIANT INTERNATIONAL INC
Also Called: Kdc-One
20320 Prairie St, Chatsworth (91311-6026)
PHONE..................................818 709-1345
Nicholas Whitley, *CEO*
Omri Nahman, *CFO*
Fernando Fernandez, *Research*
Surendra Dhanaraj, *Analyst*
Martin Tremblay, *CPA*
◆ EMP: 450
SQ FT: 350,000
SALES (est): 228.8MM
SALES (corp-wide): 300K **Privately Held**
WEB: www.thibiantspa.com
SIC: 2844 Cosmetic preparations
HQ: Knowlton Development Corporation
Inc
255 Boul Roland-Therrien Bureau 100
Longueuil QC J4H 4
450 243-2000

(P-8594)
TRADEMARK COSMETIC INC
545 Columbia Ave, Riverside (92507-2183)
PHONE..................................951 683-2631
David Ryngler, *CEO*
Joy Boiani, *CFO*
Eko Handoko, *Vice Pres*
Jessica Burrola, *Purch Mgr*
▲ EMP: 38
SQ FT: 38,000

SALES (est): 11.5MM **Privately Held**
WEB: www.trademarkcosmetics.com
SIC: 2844 7231 5999 5122 Hair preparations, including shampoos; beauty shops;
cosmetics; cosmetics

(P-8595)
TRANS-INDIA PRODUCTS INC
Also Called: Shikai Products
3330 Coffey Ln Ste A&B, Santa Rosa
(95403-1917)
P.O. Box 2866 (95405-0866)
PHONE..................................707 544-0298
Dennis Sepp, *President*
Jason Sepp, *CEO*
Carol Sepp, *Corp Secy*
Vasant Telang, *Vice Pres*
▲ EMP: 25
SQ FT: 30,000
SALES (est): 6.4MM **Privately Held**
WEB: www.shikai.com
SIC: 2844 Face creams or lotions; cos-
metic preparations

(P-8596)
TU-K INDUSTRIES INC
5702 Firestone Pl, South Gate
(90280-3714)
PHONE..................................562 927-3365
Alpin K Kaler, *President*
Eleanor Kaler, *Corp Secy*
Arman Cornell, *Manager*
▲ EMP: 30 EST: 1970
SQ FT: 40,000
SALES: 3.5MM **Privately Held**
WEB: www.2kindustries.com
SIC: 2844 Cosmetic preparations

(P-8597)
URBAN DECAL LLC (HQ)
Also Called: Urban Decay Cosmetics
833 W 16th St, Newport Beach
(92663-2801)
PHONE..................................949 574-9712
Adel Hamdan, *Mng Member*
John Ferrari, *Treasurer*
Jennifer Broadway, *Assoc VP*
Paula Floyd, *Senior VP*
Carolea Fields, *Vice Pres*
▲ EMP: 35
SQ FT: 6,500
SALES (est): 6.6MM
SALES (corp-wide): 4.4B **Privately Held**
WEB: www.urbandecay.com
SIC: 2844 5122 Cosmetic preparations;
cosmetics, perfumes & hair products
PA: L'oreal
Kerastase Mizani Oreal Prof Paris Essi
Paris 8e Arrondissement 75008
140 206-000

(P-8598)
US COTTON LLC
7100 W Sunnyview Ave, Visalia
(93291-9639)
PHONE..................................559 651-3015
Gary S Jordan, *Principal*
EMP: 293
SALES (corp-wide): 1.4B **Privately Held**
SIC: 2844 Toilet preparations
HQ: U.S. Cotton, Llc
531 Cotton Blossom Cir
Gastonia NC 28054
216 676-6400

(P-8599)
USP INC
Also Called: Enjoy Haircare
1818 Ord Way, Oceanside (92056-1502)
PHONE..................................760 842-7700
Patrick Dockry, *Principal*
Gordon Fletcher, *Vice Pres*
▲ EMP: 60
SQ FT: 60,000
SALES (est): 18MM **Privately Held**
SIC: 2844 Hair preparations, including
shampoos

(P-8600)
**V MANUFACTURING LOGISTICS
INC**
20501 Earlgate St, Walnut (91789-2909)
PHONE..................................909 869-6200
Florence Nacino, *President*
Beatriz Betancourt, *Executive Asst*
▲ EMP: 20

SALES: 2MM **Privately Held**
SIC: 2844 Cosmetic preparations

(P-8601)
VEGE - KURL INC
Also Called: Vege-Tech Company
412 W Cypress St, Glendale (91204-2402)
PHONE..............................818 956-5582
Eric W Huffman, *President*
Helen Huffman, *Corp Secy*
EMP: 60
SALES (est): 17.7MM **Privately Held**
WEB: www.vegekurl.com
SIC: 2844 2833 5122 Shampoos, rinses,
conditioners: hair; medicinals & botani-
cals; cosmetics, perfumes & hair products

(P-8602)
VERDE COSMETIC LABS LLC
19845 Nordhokk St, Northridge (91324)
PHONE..............................818 284-4080
John Mizialko, *President*
Linda Mile,
David Stearn,
EMP: 14
SQ FT: 13,000
SALES: 3.5MM **Privately Held**
SIC: 2844 Cosmetic preparations

(P-8603)
VIC COSMETICS LLC
3420 Bristol St Ste 517, Costa Mesa
(92626-7170)
PHONE..............................949 330-7668
Edward Le,
Jessica Le,
EMP: 10
SALES (est): 409.5K **Privately Held**
SIC: 2844 Cosmetic preparations; depilato-
ries (cosmetic); lipsticks

(P-8604)
VIE PRODUCTS INC
9663 Santa Monica Blvd, Beverly Hills
(90210-4303)
PHONE..............................310 684-3566
Kevin Seib, *President*
EMP: 20
WEB: www.vieproducts.com
SIC: 2844 Cosmetic preparations

(P-8605)
VITALITY INST MED PDTS INC
Also Called: VI Aesthetics
6121 Santa Monica Blvd, Los Angeles
(90038-1700)
PHONE..............................310 587-1910
Laleh Taheri, *CEO*
Amanda Lucas, *Sales Staff*
EMP: 12 EST: 2005
SALES (est): 2.9MM **Privately Held**
SIC: 2844 Cosmetic preparations

(P-8606)
VS VINCENZO LTD INC
34700 Pacific Coast Hwy, Capistrano
Beach (92624-1351)
PHONE..............................949 388-8791
Vincent Michael Spinnato, *President*
Christian Hernandez, *Treasurer*
EMP: 10
SQ FT: 1,400
SALES (est): 1.1MM **Privately Held**
SIC: 2844 Toilet preparations

(P-8607)
**WESTRIDGE LABORATORIES
INC**
1671 E Saint Andrew Pl, Santa Ana
(92705-4932)
PHONE..............................714 259-9400
Gregg Richard Haskell, *CEO*
Catherine Mazzacco, *Vice Pres*
John Speelman, *Vice Pres*
John Spielman, *Vice Pres*
Rhonda Jongsma, *Admin Asst*
▲ EMP: 28
SALES (est): 8.1MM **Privately Held**
WEB: www.idlube.com
SIC: 2844 Cosmetic preparations

(P-8608)
**WESTWOOD LABORATORIES
INC (PA)**
710 S Ayon Ave, Azusa (91702-5123)
PHONE..............................626 969-3305
Tony De Vos, *CEO*
Paul Schirmer, *President*
Cheryl Kohorst, *CFO*
▲ EMP: 50
SALES (est): 13.2MM **Privately Held**
SIC: 2844 Toilet preparations

(P-8609)
YES TO INC
Also Called: Yes To Carrots
177 E Colo Blvd Ste 110, Pasadena
(91105)
PHONE..............................626 365-1976
Ingrid Jackel, *CEO*
Lance Kalish, *Shareholder*
Ido Leffler, *Shareholder*
Manuel Scates, *Vice Pres*
Valerie Castro, *Associate Dir*
▲ EMP: 40
SQ FT: 3,000
SALES: 0 **Privately Held**
SIC: 2844 5122 Face creams or lotions;
cosmetic preparations; hair preparations,
including shampoos; cosmetics

(P-8610)
YOUNG NAILS INC
1149 N Patt St, Anaheim (92801-2568)
PHONE..............................714 992-1400
Habib Bishara Salo, *CEO*
Greg Salo, *President*
Young Salo, *Vice Pres*
▲ EMP: 18
SQ FT: 19,000
SALES (est): 6.1MM **Privately Held**
WEB: www.youngnails.com
SIC: 2844 Manicure preparations

(P-8611)
ZERRAN INTERNATIONAL CORP
Also Called: Www.zerran.com
12880 Pierce St, Pacoima (91331-2524)
PHONE..............................818 897-5494
Steven Saute, *President*
Richard Saute, *Shareholder*
Robert Saute, *Shareholder*
▲ EMP: 13
SALES (est): 2.4MM **Privately Held**
WEB: www.zerran.com
SIC: 2844 5122 Hair preparations, includ-
ing shampoos; hair preparations

(P-8612)
ZION HEALTH INC
Also Called: Adama Minerals
430 E Grand Ave, South San Francisco
(94080-6207)
P.O. Box 282249, San Francisco (94128-
2249)
PHONE..............................650 520-4313
Haim Zion, *Principal*
Marie Holmes, *Mktg Dir*
Angela Kray, *Sales Staff*
Josh Jordan, *Manager*
EMP: 11
SALES (est): 622.7K **Privately Held**
SIC: 2844 Shampoos, rinses, conditioners:
hair; lotions, shaving; deodorants, per-
sonal

(P-8613)
ZO SKIN HEALTH INC (PA)
9685 Research Dr, Irvine (92618-4657)
PHONE..............................949 988-7524
Mark Williams, *CEO*
Kevin Cornett, *CFO*
Frank Fazio, *Vice Pres*
Rick Woodin, *Vice Pres*
Dara Burton, *Executive*
▲ EMP: 80
SQ FT: 12,000
SALES (est): 21.1MM **Privately Held**
SIC: 2844 Face creams or lotions

(P-8614)
ZOTOS INTERNATIONAL INC
Joico Laboratories Division
488 E Santa Clara St # 301, Arcadia
(91006-7229)
PHONE..............................626 321-4100
Annie Hu, *Branch Mgr*

EMP: 30
SALES (corp-wide): 22.7B **Privately Held**
WEB: www.zotos.com
SIC: 2844 Hair preparations, including
shampoos; cosmetic preparations
HQ: Zotos International, Inc.
100 Tokeneke Rd
Darien CT 06820
203 655-8911

**2851 Paints, Varnishes,
Lacquers, Enamels**

(P-8615)
AEGIS INDUSTRIES INC
Also Called: Atlas Computer Centers
2360 Thompson Way Ste A, Santa Maria
(93455-1095)
P.O. Box 6558 (93456-6558)
PHONE..............................805 922-2700
Robert Dickerson, *President*
EMP: 10
SALES (est): 1.1MM **Privately Held**
SIC: 2851 2891 5198 Paints, waterproof;
sealants; paints

(P-8616)
ALLIED COATINGS INC
1125 Linda Vista Dr # 104, San Marcos
(92078-3819)
PHONE..............................800 630-2375
Donald J Palazzo, *Principal*
EMP: 15
SALES (est): 2.4MM **Privately Held**
SIC: 2851 Vinyl coatings, strippable

(P-8617)
**AMAZON ENVIRONMENTAL INC
(PA)**
Also Called: Amazon Paint
779 Palmyrita Ave, Riverside (92507-1811)
P.O. Box 9306, Whittier (90608-9306)
PHONE..............................951 588-0206
Craig Elzinga, *President*
John P Segala, *Vice Pres*
Vince Martinez, *Supervisor*
EMP: 21
SQ FT: 12,000
SALES (est): 5MM **Privately Held**
WEB: www.amazonpaint.com
SIC: 2851 Paints & allied products

(P-8618)
AMERICA WOOD FINISHES INC
728 E 59th St, Los Angeles (90001-1004)
PHONE..............................323 232-8256
Manuel Padilla, *President*
Elvira Padilla, *Admin Sec*
▲ EMP: 15
SALES (est): 2.4MM **Privately Held**
SIC: 2851 Paints, waterproof

(P-8619)
**BEHR HOLDINGS
CORPORATION (HQ)**
3400 W Segerstrom Ave, Santa Ana
(92704-6405)
PHONE..............................714 545-7101
Jeff Filley, *President*
EMP: 2000
SALES (est): 1.5B
SALES (corp-wide): 8.3B **Publicly Held**
SIC: 2851 Paints & paint additives; stains:
varnish, oil or wax; varnishes
PA: Masco Corporation
17450 College Pkwy
Livonia MI 48152
313 274-7400

(P-8620)
BEHR PROCESS CORPORATION
1603 W Alton Ave, Santa Ana
(92704-7258)
PHONE..............................714 545-7101
Jeffrey D Filley, *Branch Mgr*
EMP: 23
SQ FT: 54,819
SALES (corp-wide): 8.3B **Publicly Held**
WEB: www.behr.com
SIC: 2851 Paints & allied products
HQ: Behr Process Corporation
1801 E Saint Andrew Pl
Santa Ana CA 92705

(P-8621)
**BEHR PROCESS CORPORATION
(DH)**
Also Called: Behr Paint Company
1801 E Saint Andrew Pl, Santa Ana
(92705-5044)
PHONE..............................714 545-7101
Jeffrey D Filley, *President*
Jonathan Sullivan, *Senior VP*
Greg Brod, *Vice Pres*
Sarah Furnari, *Vice Pres*
John Hoskins, *Vice Pres*
▼ EMP: 700
SQ FT: 220,000
SALES: 1.5B
SALES (corp-wide): 8.3B **Publicly Held**
SIC: 2851 Paints & paint additives; stains:
varnish, oil or wax; varnishes

(P-8622)
BEHR PROCESS CORPORATION
3400 W Garry Ave, Santa Ana
(92704-6421)
PHONE..............................714 545-7101
Jeffrey D Filley, *Principal*
EMP: 91
SALES (corp-wide): 8.3B **Publicly Held**
SIC: 2851 Paints & paint additives
HQ: Behr Process Corporation
1801 E Saint Andrew Pl
Santa Ana CA 92705
-

(P-8623)
BEHR PROCESS CORPORATION
3130 S Harbor Blvd # 400, Santa Ana
(92704-6820)
PHONE..............................714 545-7101
Jeffrey D Filley, *Branch Mgr*
EMP: 87
SALES (corp-wide): 8.3B **Publicly Held**
SIC: 2851 Paints & paint additives
HQ: Behr Process Corporation
1801 E Saint Andrew Pl
Santa Ana CA 92705

(P-8624)
BEHR PROCESS CORPORATION
3500 W Segerstrom Ave, Santa Ana
(92704-6406)
PHONE..............................714 545-7101
Jeffrey D Filley, *Branch Mgr*
EMP: 18
SALES (corp-wide): 8.3B **Publicly Held**
SIC: 2851 Paints & paint additives
HQ: Behr Process Corporation
1801 E Saint Andrew Pl
Santa Ana CA 92705

(P-8625)
BEHR PROCESS CORPORATION
1995 S Standard Ave, Santa Ana
(92707-3004)
PHONE..............................714 545-7101
Jeffrey D Filley, *Branch Mgr*
Dave Hobson, *Director*
EMP: 65
SALES (corp-wide): 8.3B **Publicly Held**
SIC: 2851 Paints & paint additives
HQ: Behr Process Corporation
1801 E Saint Andrew Pl
Santa Ana CA 92705
-

(P-8626)
BEHR SALES INC (HQ)
Also Called: Behr Paint Corp.
3400 W Segerstrom Ave, Santa Ana
(92704-6405)
PHONE..............................714 545-7101
Jeffrey D Filley, *CEO*
Jonathan M Sullivan, *CFO*
Anthony Demiro, *Senior VP*
Michelle Comagon, *Executive*
Jessica Barr, *Training Spec*
EMP: 124 EST: 1948
SQ FT: 54,000
SALES (est): 553.5MM
SALES (corp-wide): 8.3B **Publicly Held**
SIC: 2851 Paints & paint additives; stains:
varnish, oil or wax

▲ = Import ▼=Export
◆ =Import/Export

PA: Masco Corporation
17450 College Pkwy
Livonia MI 48152
313 274-7400

(P-8627)
CAL WEST SPCIALTY COATINGS INC
1058 W Evelyn Ave Ste 10, Sunnyvale (94086-5794)
PHONE..............................408 720-7440
Edward Woodhall, *President*
Brian Wong, *CFO*
▲ EMP: 10
SQ FT: 10,000
SALES (est): 1.6MM **Privately Held**
WEB: www.cal-west.net
SIC: 2851 2899 Lacquers, varnishes, enamels & other coatings; chemical preparations

(P-8628)
CARBOLINE COMPANY
5533 Brooks St, Montclair (91763-4547)
PHONE..............................909 459-1090
Jose Fernandez, *Manager*
Vernon Lowdon, *Engineer*
Russell Spotten, *Sales Staff*
EMP: 20
SALES (corp-wide): 5.5B **Publicly Held**
SIC: 2851 Lacquers, varnishes, enamels & other coatings
HQ: Carboline Company
2150 Schuetz Rd Fl.1
Saint Louis MO 63146
314 644-1000

(P-8629)
CARBONYTE SYSTEMS INCORPORATED
3 Wayne Ct Ste A, Sacramento (95829-1306)
PHONE..............................916 387-0316
Gordon Rayner, *President*
William Coe, *Vice Pres*
Donna Coe, *Principal*
▼ EMP: 10
SALES (est): 1.9MM **Privately Held**
WEB: www.carbonyte.com
SIC: 2851 Paints & paint additives

(P-8630)
CARDINAL INDUSTRIAL FINISHES (PA)
1329 Potrero Ave, South El Monte (91733-3088)
P.O. Box 9296 (91733-0965)
PHONE..............................626 444-9274
Lawrence C Felix, *CEO*
Rosanna Richardson, *Executive*
Patterson Sandoke, *Executive*
Jason Nocero, *Creative Dir*
Steve Lafavre, *Regional Mgr*
◆ EMP: 100 EST: 1952
SQ FT: 50,000
SALES (est): 70.8MM **Privately Held**
WEB: www.cardinalpaint.com
SIC: 2851 Lacquers, varnishes, enamels & other coatings

(P-8631)
CARDINAL PAINT AND POWDER INC
15010 Don Julian Rd, City of Industry (91746-3301)
PHONE..............................626 937-6767
Stanley W Ekstrom, *Branch Mgr*
EMP: 179
SALES (corp-wide): 70MM **Privately Held**
SIC: 2851 Paints & allied products
PA: Cardinal Paint And Powder, Inc.
1900 Aerojet Way
North Las Vegas NV 89030
702 852-2333

(P-8632)
CARDINAL PAINT AND POWDER INC
890 Commercial St, San Jose (95112-1410)
PHONE..............................408 452-8522
Tom Cross, *Manager*
EMP: 20

SALES (corp-wide): 70MM **Privately Held**
WEB: www.cardinalpaint.com
SIC: 2851 Paints & allied products
PA: Cardinal Paint And Powder, Inc.
1900 Aerojet Way
North Las Vegas NV 89030
702 852-2333

(P-8633)
CATALINA INDUSTRIES INC
Also Called: Catalina Paint Stores
8814 Reseda Blvd, Northridge (91324-4039)
PHONE..............................818 772-8888
Bernard Cohn, *Owner*
EMP: 12
SQ FT: 3,050
SALES (corp-wide): 5.2MM **Privately Held**
WEB: www.catalinapaint.com
SIC: 2851 5198 5231 Paints & allied products; paints; paint, glass & wallpaper
PA: Catalina Industries, Inc.
11919 Vose St
North Hollywood CA 91605
818 765-2629

(P-8634)
CDH PAINTING INC
802 Harris St, Eureka (95503-4542)
PHONE..............................707 443-4429
Duane Hagans, *President*
Gina Loya, *Office Mgr*
Jacquee Carlino, *Technology*
Clayton Hagans, *Director*
EMP: 12
SALES (est): 650K **Privately Held**
SIC: 2851 Lacquers, varnishes, enamels & other coatings

(P-8635)
CONDUCTIVE SCIENCE INC
11643 Rverside Dr Ste 115, Lakeside (92040)
PHONE..............................858 699-1837
Tom Judish, *President*
▲ EMP: 10
SALES (est): 1.1MM **Privately Held**
SIC: 2851 Coating, air curing

(P-8636)
CONSOLIDATED COLOR CORPORATION
12316 Carson St, Hawaiian Gardens (90716-1604)
PHONE..............................562 420-7714
Michael J Muldown, *President*
Deborah Muldown, *Vice Pres*
Lidia Cardenas, *Accounting Mgr*
James Muldown, *VP Sales*
EMP: 25
SQ FT: 30,000
SALES (est): 5.2MM **Privately Held**
SIC: 2851 2865 Paints & paint additives; cyclic crudes & intermediates

(P-8637)
CONTINENTAL COATINGS INC
10938 Beech Ave, Fontana (92337-7260)
PHONE..............................909 355-1200
Robert Wang, *President*
Jack Keenan, *Vice Pres*
Joe Seaton, *Vice Pres*
Stephanie Varela, *Mng Member*
Mathilde Mendez, *Director*
▲ EMP: 16 EST: 1976
SQ FT: 20,000
SALES (est): 4.9MM **Privately Held**
WEB: www.continentalcoatings.com
SIC: 2851 Paints & paint additives

(P-8638)
CONTRACT TRANSPORTATION SYS CO
Also Called: Certified Distribution Svcs
12500 Slauson Ave Ste B2, Santa Fe Springs (90670-8618)
PHONE..............................562 696-3262
Chuck Huff, *Branch Mgr*
EMP: 53
SALES (corp-wide): 17.5B **Publicly Held**
WEB: www.ctsoh.net
SIC: 2851 Paints & allied products

HQ: Contract Transportation System Co.
101 W Prospect Ave
Cleveland OH 44115
216 566-2000

(P-8639)
CRAWFORD PRODUCTS COMPANY INC
409 N Park Ave, Montebello (90640-4137)
P.O. Box 4339, Whittier (90607-4339)
PHONE..............................323 721-6429
Deborah L Crawford, *CEO*
EMP: 12 EST: 1993
SALES (est): 2.9MM **Privately Held**
WEB: www.crawfords.com
SIC: 2851 Putty

(P-8640)
D J SIMPSON COMPANY (PA)
Also Called: Simpson Coatings Group, The
401 S Canal St A, South San Francisco (94080-4606)
PHONE..............................650 225-9404
Timothy Simpson, *President*
EMP: 15
SQ FT: 35,000
SALES (est): 5MM **Privately Held**
WEB: www.djsimpson.com
SIC: 2851 Paints & allied products

(P-8641)
DUNCAN ENTERPRISES (HQ)
Also Called: Ilovetocreate A Duncan Entps
5673 E Shields Ave, Fresno (93727-7819)
PHONE..............................559 291-4444
Larry Duncan, *CEO*
Larry Hermansen, *President*
Larry R Duncan, *CEO*
Valerie Marderosian, *Vice Pres*
Bruce Sharp, *Vice Pres*
◆ EMP: 175 EST: 1944
SQ FT: 260,000
SALES (est): 69.8MM
SALES (corp-wide): 49.7MM **Privately Held**
WEB: www.duncancrafts.com
SIC: 2851 3299 3952 3944 Colors in oil, except artists'; ceramic fiber; lead pencils & art goods; games, toys & children's vehicles
PA: Duncan Financial Corporation
5673 E Shields Ave
Fresno CA 93727
559 291-4444

(P-8642)
DURA TECHNOLOGIES INC
2720 S Willow Ave Ste A, Bloomington (92316-3259)
P.O. Box 333 (92316-0333)
PHONE..............................909 877-8477
Douglas L Dennis, *President*
Gina L Dennis, *Vice Pres*
▲ EMP: 150
SQ FT: 14,000
SALES (est): 23.5MM **Privately Held**
SIC: 2851 Paints & allied products

(P-8643)
ENGINEERED COATING TECH INC
2838 E 54th St, Vernon (90058-3632)
PHONE..............................323 588-0260
EMP: 12
SQ FT: 17,000
SALES (est): 1.6MM **Privately Held**
WEB: www.ecoatingtechnology.com
SIC: 2851

(P-8644)
ENGINERED PNT APPLICATIONS LLC
1586 Franklin Ave, Redlands (92373-7102)
PHONE..............................626 737-7400
Ernest Mancilla,
EMP: 12
SALES (est): 2MM **Privately Held**
WEB:
www.engineeredpaintapplications.com
SIC: 2851 3567 Paints & allied products; industrial furnaces & ovens

(P-8645)
ENNIS-FLINT INC
200 2nd St, Bakersfield (93304-3200)
PHONE..............................661 328-0503
Richard Gonzalez, *Branch Mgr*
EMP: 20
SALES (corp-wide): 132.8MM **Privately Held**
WEB: www.ennispaint.com
SIC: 2851 Paints & allied products
PA: Ennis-Flint, Inc.
4161 Piedmont Pkwy # 370
Greensboro NC 27410
800 331-8118

(P-8646)
EPMAR CORPORATION
13210 Barton Cir, Whittier (90605-3254)
PHONE..............................562 946-8781
Joe Matrange, *President*
Christine Rivera, *Accountant*
◆ EMP: 38
SQ FT: 26,000
SALES (est): 14.2MM
SALES (corp-wide): 867.5MM **Publicly Held**
WEB: www.epmar.com
SIC: 2851 2891 2821 3087 Epoxy coatings; polyurethane coatings; adhesives & sealants; plastics materials & resins; custom compound purchased resins
PA: Quaker Chemical Corporation
1 Quaker Park
Conshohocken PA 19428
610 832-4000

(P-8647)
INTEGRATED OPTICAL SVCS CORP
Also Called: Ios Optics
3270 Keller St Ste 109, Santa Clara (95054-2615)
PHONE..............................408 982-9510
Douglas Fitzpatrick, *President*
Elmer Valencia, *Treasurer*
Gener Gatmaitan, *Engineer*
Maria Flores, *QC Mgr*
▲ EMP: 35
SALES (est): 8MM **Privately Held**
WEB: www.ioscorp.net
SIC: 2851 3827 Paints & allied products; prisms, optical

(P-8648)
JANCO CHEMICAL CORPORATION
Also Called: Janco Airless Center
1235 5th St, Berkeley (94710-1395)
PHONE..............................510 527-9770
Glenn A Kjelstrom, *President*
Janice S Kjelstrom, *Vice Pres*
EMP: 13 EST: 1962
SQ FT: 12,000
SALES (est): 2.4MM **Privately Held**
SIC: 2851 5198 Wood stains; paint brushes, rollers, sprayers

(P-8649)
KELLY-MOORE PAINT COMPANY INC (PA)
Also Called: Kelly-Moore Paints
987 Commercial St, San Carlos (94070-4018)
P.O. Box 3016 (94070-1316)
PHONE..............................650 592-8337
Steve De Voe, *Ch of Bd*
Steven Jackson, *CFO*
Steven Devoe, *Vice Pres*
Daniel Englert, *Vice Pres*
Todd Wirdzek, *Vice Pres*
◆ EMP: 250 EST: 1946
SQ FT: 350,000
SALES (est): 720.2MM **Privately Held**
WEB: www.kellymoore.com
SIC: 2851 Paints: oil or alkyd vehicle or water thinned; lacquers, varnishes, enamels & other coatings; removers & cleaners

(P-8650)
KELLY-MOORE PAINT COMPANY INC
Also Called: Kelly-Moore Paints
3954 Decoto Rd, Fremont (94555-3114)
PHONE..............................510 505-9834
EMP: 23

SALES (corp-wide): 720.2MM **Privately Held**
SIC: 2851 Paints: oil or alkyd vehicle or water thinned; lacquers, varnishes, enamels & other coatings; removers & cleaners
PA: Kelly-Moore Paint Company, Inc.
987 Commercial St
San Carlos CA 94070
650 592-8337

(P-8651)
KELLY-MOORE PAINT COMPANY INC
Also Called: Kelly-Moore Paints
1075 Commercial St, San Carlos (94070-4007)
PHONE.....................650 595-0333
Jasjit Valbiel, *Manager*
Joseph P Cristiano, *President*
EMP: 20
SALES (corp-wide): 720.2MM **Privately Held**
WEB: www.kellymoore.com
SIC: 2851 5231 Vinyl coatings, strippable; paints: oil or alkyd vehicle or water thinned; lacquers, varnishes, enamels & other coatings; removers & cleaners; paint
PA: Kelly-Moore Paint Company, Inc.
987 Commercial St
San Carlos CA 94070
650 592-8337

(P-8652)
KOTT INC
27161 Burbank, El Toro (92610-2501)
PHONE.....................949 770-5055
John T Kott, *President*
Dorothy Kott, *Corp Secy*
EMP: 10
SALES (est): 557.4K
SALES (corp-wide): 5.1MM **Privately Held**
WEB: www.kott.com
SIC: 2851 6794 Lacquers, varnishes, enamels & other coatings; franchises, selling or licensing
PA: Kott Koatings Inc
27161 Burbank
El Toro CA 92610
949 770-5055

(P-8653)
LAIRD COATINGS CORPORATION
Also Called: Coatings Resource
15541 Commerce Ln, Huntington Beach (92649-1601)
PHONE.....................714 894-5252
Edwin Laird, *CEO*
Jeff Laird, *President*
▲ EMP: 48
SQ FT: 17,500
SALES (est): 6.2MM **Privately Held**
WEB: www.coatingsresource.com
SIC: 2851 2865 Paints & paint additives; dyes, synthetic organic

(P-8654)
LIFE PAINT COMPANY (PA)
12927 Sunshine Ave, Santa Fe Springs (90670-4732)
P.O. Box 2488 (90670-0488)
PHONE.....................562 944-6391
Ronald Sibbrel, *President*
Fred Benson, *Corp Secy*
Mike De La Vega, *Vice Pres*
▲ EMP: 40
SQ FT: 30,000
SALES (est): 13.2MM **Privately Held**
WEB: www.lifepaint.com
SIC: 2851 2899 2821 Paints & allied products; waterproofing compounds; thermosetting materials

(P-8655)
MADDIEBRIT PRODUCTS LLC
Also Called: Grab Green
537 Constitution Ave B, Camarillo (93012-8571)
PHONE.....................818 483-0096
Michael Edell,
Nicole Breitung, *Marketing Staff*
Drew Edell, *Mktg Coord*
Patricia Spencer,
EMP: 10

SALES (est): 2.4MM **Privately Held**
SIC: 2851 Removers & cleaners

(P-8656)
MASTER POWDER COATING INC
13721 Bora Dr, Santa Fe Springs (90670-5007)
PHONE.....................562 863-4135
Judith Flores, *CEO*
Juan Renteria, *Vice Pres*
Dalila Flores, *VP Opers*
EMP: 37 EST: 2006
SALES (est): 8.6MM **Privately Held**
SIC: 2851 Paints & allied products

(P-8657)
MIRACLE COVER (PA)
20721 Goshawk Ln, Huntington Beach (92646-5529)
P.O. Box 6081 (92615-6081)
PHONE.....................714 842-8863
Paul D Jordan, *President*
Douglas Jordan, *Vice Pres*
Terri Jordan, *Vice Pres*
EMP: 11
SQ FT: 13,000
SALES: 800K **Privately Held**
SIC: 2851 5169 2891 Putty, wood fillers & sealers; chemicals, industrial & heavy; adhesives & sealants

(P-8658)
MONOPOLE INC
4661 Alger St, Los Angeles (90039-1127)
P.O. Box 250534, Glendale (91225-0534)
PHONE.....................818 500-8585
Antoine Abikhalil, *President*
Lawrence Bogert, *Manager*
▲ EMP: 15
SQ FT: 40,000
SALES: 2MM **Privately Held**
WEB: www.monopoleinc.com
SIC: 2851 Paints & allied products

(P-8659)
MOTORSHIELD LLC
Also Called: Motoshieldpro
3364 Garfield Ave, Commerce (90040-3102)
PHONE.....................323 396-9200
Rick Fung,
Maria Ortega, *General Mgr*
EMP: 15 EST: 2016
SALES (est): 1MM **Privately Held**
SIC: 2851 Undercoatings, paint

(P-8660)
MULTICOAT PRODUCTS INC
23331 Antonio Pkwy, Rcho STA Marg (92688-2664)
PHONE.....................949 888-7100
Dave Maietta, *President*
John Dill, *Vice Pres*
Dave Lascano, *Marketing Staff*
Mike Baham, *Manager*
EMP: 15 EST: 1995
SALES (est): 4.6MM **Privately Held**
SIC: 2851 2899 3299 3479 Paints & paint additives; waterproofing compounds; stucco; painting, coating & hot dipping

(P-8661)
PAINT-CHEM INC
Also Called: Transchem Coatings
1680 Miller Ave, Los Angeles (90063-1613)
P.O. Box 151014 (90015-8014)
PHONE.....................213 747-7725
Amir Afshar, *President*
Eugene Golling, *Vice Pres*
Eddie Andrews, *Admin Sec*
EMP: 15
SQ FT: 8,000
SALES (est): 3MM **Privately Held**
SIC: 2851 5198 Coating, air curing; paints

(P-8662)
PERFORMANCE COATINGS INC
360 Lake Mendocino Dr, Ukiah (95482-9497)
P.O. Box 1569 (95482-1569)
PHONE.....................707 462-3023
Barbara Newell, *Ch of Bd*
◆ EMP: 20
SQ FT: 4,300

SALES (est): 7.9MM **Privately Held**
WEB: www.penofin.com
SIC: 2851 Wood stains

(P-8663)
POLY-FIBER INC (PA)
Also Called: Consolidated Aircraft Coatings
4343 Fort Dr, Riverside (92509-6784)
P.O. Box 3129 (92519-3129)
PHONE.....................951 684-4280
Jon Goldenbaum, *President*
Greg Albarin, *General Mgr*
Marlene Gatten, *Admin Sec*
Greg Albarian, *Opers Staff*
EMP: 20
SQ FT: 75,000
SALES: 2.1MM **Privately Held**
WEB: www.polyfiber.com
SIC: 2851 Undercoatings, paint

(P-8664)
PPG INDUSTRIES INC
5750 Imhoff Dr Ste A, Concord (94520-5330)
PHONE.....................925 798-0539
Marlon Medina, *Principal*
EMP: 11
SALES (corp-wide): 15.3B **Publicly Held**
SIC: 2851 Paints & allied products
PA: Ppg Industries, Inc.
1 Ppg Pl
Pittsburgh PA 15272
412 434-3131

(P-8665)
PPG INDUSTRIES INC
10060 Mission Mill Rd, City of Industry (90601-1738)
PHONE.....................562 692-4010
Gerald Roberts, *Manager*
EMP: 15
SALES (corp-wide): 15.3B **Publicly Held**
WEB: www.ppg.com
SIC: 2851 Paints & allied products
PA: Ppg Industries, Inc.
1 Ppg Pl
Pittsburgh PA 15272
412 434-3131

(P-8666)
PPG INDUSTRIES INC
Also Called: PPG 9726
1128 N Highland Ave, Los Angeles (90038-1205)
PHONE.....................310 559-2335
Jim Dabbs, *Manager*
EMP: 24
SALES (corp-wide): 15.3B **Publicly Held**
WEB: www.ppg.com
SIC: 2851 Paints & allied products
PA: Ppg Industries, Inc.
1 Ppg Pl
Pittsburgh PA 15272
412 434-3131

(P-8667)
PPG INDUSTRIES INC
Also Called: PPG 9721
43639 10th St W, Lancaster (93534-4801)
PHONE.....................661 945-7871
Jim Dabbs, *Branch Mgr*
EMP: 24
SALES (corp-wide): 15.3B **Publicly Held**
WEB: www.ppg.com
SIC: 2851 Paints & allied products
PA: Ppg Industries, Inc.
1 Ppg Pl
Pittsburgh PA 15272
412 434-3131

(P-8668)
PPG INDUSTRIES INC
Also Called: PPG 9722
74240 Highway 111, Palm Desert (92260-4138)
PHONE.....................760 340-1762
David Warrez, *Branch Mgr*
EMP: 24
SALES (corp-wide): 15.3B **Publicly Held**
WEB: www.ppg.com
SIC: 2851 Paints & allied products
PA: Ppg Industries, Inc.
1 Ppg Pl
Pittsburgh PA 15272
412 434-3131

(P-8669)
PPG INDUSTRIES INC
Also Called: Industrial Coatings Division
15541 Commerce Ln, Huntington Beach (92649-1601)
PHONE.....................714 894-5252
Jeff Laird, *Manager*
EMP: 30
SALES (corp-wide): 15.3B **Publicly Held**
WEB: www.ppg.com
SIC: 2851 Paints & allied products
PA: Ppg Industries, Inc.
1 Ppg Pl
Pittsburgh PA 15272
412 434-3131

(P-8670)
PPG INDUSTRIES INC
11601 United St, Mojave (93501-7048)
PHONE.....................661 824-4532
Michelle Brown, *Purchasing*
Andrew Soehnlen, *Opers Mgr*
EMP: 24
SALES (corp-wide): 15.3B **Publicly Held**
WEB: www.ppg.com
SIC: 2851 Paints & allied products
PA: Ppg Industries, Inc.
1 Ppg Pl
Pittsburgh PA 15272
412 434-3131

(P-8671)
PRECISION COATINGS INC
1220 4th St, Berkeley (94710-1303)
PHONE.....................510 525-3600
Michael Emmerich, *President*
EMP: 10
SALES (est): 815.6K **Privately Held**
SIC: 2851 Paints & allied products

(P-8672)
PRO LINE PAINT COMPANY
2646 Main St, San Diego (92113-3613)
PHONE.....................619 232-8968
Anthony A Mitchell, *CEO*
▼ EMP: 48
SALES (est): 6.8MM **Privately Held**
SIC: 2851 5198 5231 Paints & allied products; paints; paint

(P-8673)
PRODUCTS/TECHNIQUES INC
Also Called: P T I
3271 S Riverside Ave, Bloomington (92316-3515)
PHONE.....................909 877-3951
Steven Andrews, *President*
Ryan Andrews, *Officer*
Barry Boden, *Vice Pres*
Sean Andrews, *Director*
EMP: 16 EST: 1947
SQ FT: 12,000
SALES (est): 4.5MM **Privately Held**
WEB: www.ptipaint.com
SIC: 2851 Coating, air curing

(P-8674)
PROWEST TECHNOLOGIES INC
Also Called: Procoat
2872 S Santa Fe Ave, San Marcos (92069-6046)
PHONE.....................760 510-9003
Salim Khalfan, *President*
Debbie Walker, *Corp Secy*
EMP: 25
SQ FT: 3,500
SALES: 2.5MM **Privately Held**
WEB: www.daveblanchard.com
SIC: 2851 Paints & allied products

(P-8675)
R & S MANUFACTURING & SUP INC
16616 Garfield Ave, Paramount (90723-5305)
PHONE.....................909 622-5881
Ronald Hoffman, *Principal*
Susan Hoffman, *Admin Sec*
EMP: 18
SQ FT: 20,000
SALES (est): 3.8MM **Privately Held**
SIC: 2851 Colors in oil, except artists'

▲ = Import ▼=Export
◆ =Import/Export

(P-8676)
R J MCGLENNON COMPANY INC (PA)
Also Called: Maclac Co
198 Utah St, San Francisco (94103-4826)
PHONE.............................415 552-0311
Michael McGlennon, *President*
Michael Mc Glennon, *President*
EMP: 22
SQ FT: 30,000
SALES (est): 3.7MM **Privately Held**
WEB: www.maclac.com
SIC: 2851 Lacquer: bases, dopes, thinner; enamels

(P-8677)
RUPERT GIBBON & SPIDER INC
Also Called: Jacquard Products
1147 Healdsburg Ave, Healdsburg (95448-3405)
P.O. Box 425 (95448-0425)
PHONE.............................800 442-0455
Asher Katz, *President*
Devon Scrivner, *Treasurer*
EMP: 35
SQ FT: 24,570
SALES (est): 7.3MM **Privately Held**
SIC: 2851 8742 5169 Paints & allied products; merchandising consultant; waxes, except petroleum

(P-8678)
SCOTCH PAINT CORPORATION
Also Called: Draw Tite
5928 Garfield Ave, Commerce (90040-3607)
PHONE.............................310 329-1259
Charles Mac Harg, *President*
EMP: 12
SALES (est): 3MM **Privately Held**
WEB: www.scotchpaint.com
SIC: 2851 5231 Paints & allied products; paint, glass & wallpaper

(P-8679)
SIERRACIN CORPORATION (HQ)
12780 San Fernando Rd, Sylmar (91342-3796)
PHONE.............................818 741-1656
Barry N Gillespie, *CEO*
Michael H McGarry, *Exec VP*
Viktoras R Sekmakas, *Exec VP*
Frank S Sklarsky, *Exec VP*
David B Navikas, *Senior VP*
▲ EMP: 550 EST: 1952
SQ FT: 287,000
SALES (est): 85.4MM
SALES (corp-wide): 15.3B **Publicly Held**
WEB: www.sierracin.com
SIC: 2851 Paints & allied products
PA: Ppg Industries, Inc.
1 Ppg Pl
Pittsburgh PA 15272
412 434-3131

(P-8680)
SIMPSON COATINGS GROUP INC
401 S Canal St A, South San Francisco (94080-4606)
P.O. Box 2265 (94083-2265)
PHONE.............................650 873-5990
Tim Simpson, *President*
Diane Simpson, *Admin Sec*
EMP: 25
SQ FT: 35,000
SALES (est): 4.6MM
SALES (corp-wide): 5MM **Privately Held**
WEB: www.djsimpson.com
SIC: 2851 Paints & allied products
PA: D J Simpson Company
401 S Canal St A
South San Francisco CA 94080
650 225-9404

(P-8681)
SPECIALIZED MILLING CORP
Also Called: Specialty Finishes
10330 Elm Ave, Fontana (92337-7319)
PHONE.............................909 357-7890
Jack Neems, *President*
Seymour S Neems, *Ch of Bd*
Adele Neems, *Treasurer*
EMP: 18

SQ FT: 11,000
SALES (est): 2.4MM **Privately Held**
SIC: 2851 Paints & allied products

(P-8682)
SPECIALTY COATINGS & CHEM INC
Also Called: Special-T
7360 Varna Ave, North Hollywood (91605-4008)
P.O. Box 32459, Los Angeles (90032-0459)
PHONE.............................818 983-0055
Alaistair Macdonald, *President*
W Daniel Ernt, *Vice Pres*
Larry Wick, *Admin Sec*
▲ EMP: 27 EST: 1964
SQ FT: 15,000
SALES (est): 5.4MM **Privately Held**
SIC: 2851 Plastics base paints & varnishes; enamels; lacquer: bases, dopes, thinner

(P-8683)
STILES PAINT MANUFACTURING INC
21595 Curtis St, Hayward (94545-1307)
PHONE.............................510 887-8868
Khosrow Sohrabi, *President*
Bruce Sohrabi, *Vice Pres*
EMP: 13
SQ FT: 19,000
SALES (est): 3.5MM **Privately Held**
SIC: 2851 Paints & paint additives

(P-8684)
SUPERIOR SNDBLST & COATING
8315 Beech Ave, Fontana (92335-3285)
PHONE.............................909 428-9994
EMP: 10
SQ FT: 10,900
SALES (est): 1.3MM **Privately Held**
SIC: 2851 5088

(P-8685)
TALYARPS CORPORATION
3465 S La Cienega Blvd, Los Angeles (90016-4409)
PHONE.............................310 559-2335
Fax: 310 836-6094
EMP: 25
SQ FT: 25,000
SALES (corp-wide): 33.6MM **Privately Held**
SIC: 2851
PA: Talyarps Corporation
143 Sparks Ave
Pelham NY 10803
914 699-3030

(P-8686)
TEX-COAT LLC
5950 Avalon Blvd, Los Angeles (90003-1310)
P.O. Box 73109 (90003-0109)
PHONE.............................323 233-3111
Stuart M Haines, *Ch of Bd*
David Castaneda, *Technician*
EMP: 20
SALES (corp-wide): 129.5MM **Privately Held**
WEB: www.texcoat.com
SIC: 2851 Paints & paint additives; lacquers, varnishes, enamels & other coatings
HQ: Tex-Coat Llc
2422 E 15th St
Panama City FL 32405
800 454-0340

(P-8687)
TIBBETTS NEWPORT CORPORATION
2337 S Birch St, Santa Ana (92707-3402)
PHONE.............................714 546-6662
Shil Park, *President*
Minah Park, *Admin Sec*
EMP: 12
SQ FT: 25,000
SALES (est): 3.2MM **Privately Held**
SIC: 2851 Paints: oil or alkyd vehicle or water thinned

(P-8688)
TRESCO PAINT CO
21595 Curtis St, Hayward (94545-1307)
PHONE.............................510 887-7254
Khosrow M Sohrabi, *President*
Behrooz Sohrabi, *Vice Pres*
EMP: 12
SQ FT: 18,000
SALES: 800K **Privately Held**
SIC: 2851 Paints & allied products

(P-8689)
TUFF KOTE SYSTEMS INC
7033 Orangethorpe Ave B, Buena Park (90621-3300)
PHONE.............................714 522-7341
William Ritt, *President*
EMP: 15
SQ FT: 2,000
SALES: 750K **Privately Held**
WEB: www.tuffkotesystemsintl.net
SIC: 2851 Paints & allied products

(P-8690)
US BIOSERVICES (PA)
5100 E Hunter Ave, Anaheim (92807-2049)
PHONE.............................800 801-1140
Mike Brunelle, *Principal*
Mike Hernandez, *Director*
EMP: 47
SALES (est): 7.9MM **Privately Held**
SIC: 2851 Paints & allied products

(P-8691)
VINYLVISIONS COMPANY LLC
Also Called: Trim Quick
1233 Enterprise Ct, Corona (92882-7126)
PHONE.............................800 321-8746
John P Halle, *Mng Member*
Helen Halle, *Mng Member*
EMP: 20
SQ FT: 40,000
SALES (est): 6.4MM **Privately Held**
SIC: 2851 Vinyl coatings, strippable

(P-8692)
WALTON INDUSTRIES INC
Also Called: General Coatings
1220 E North Ave, Fresno (93725-1930)
P.O. Box 11127 (93771-1127)
PHONE.............................559 233-6300
Lee Walton, *President*
EMP: 17
SQ FT: 40,000
SALES (est): 3.9MM **Privately Held**
WEB: www.generalcoatings.net
SIC: 2851 3086 Paints & allied products; insulation or cushioning material, foamed plastic

(P-8693)
WEATHERMAN PRODUCTS INC (PA)
Also Called: Rainguard International
21622 Surveyor Cir, Huntington Beach (92646-7068)
PHONE.............................949 515-8800
Claude Florent, *CEO*
Rosa Hernandez, *Opers Staff*
Russell Fowler, *Marketing Staff*
Julia Pineda, *Marketing Staff*
Dianna Gonzales, *Manager*
▲ EMP: 15 EST: 1997
SQ FT: 12,000
SALES (est): 2.8MM **Privately Held**
SIC: 2851 Paints & allied products

(P-8694)
WLS COATINGS INC
1680 Miller Ave, Los Angeles (90063-1613)
P.O. Box 151014 (90015-8014)
PHONE.............................310 538-2155
Walter Standridge, *President*
EMP: 10
SALES (est): 1.3MM **Privately Held**
SIC: 2851 Paints & allied products

(P-8695)
WONDER MARKETING INC
Also Called: Leather Cpr
11601 Wilshire Blvd # 2150, Los Angeles (90025-1757)
PHONE.............................310 235-1469
D Darren Zuzow, *President*
EMP: 40 EST: 1999

SQ FT: 14,000
SALES (est): 6.6MM **Privately Held**
WEB: www.leathercpr.com
SIC: 2851 Removers & cleaners

2861 Gum & Wood

(P-8696)
KINGSFORD PRODUCTS COMPANY LLC (HQ)
1221 Broadway Ste 1300, Oakland (94612-2072)
PHONE.............................510 271-7000
Richard T Conti, *President*
A W Biebl, *President*
Karen Rose, *CFO*
L L Hoover, *Treasurer*
B C Blewett, *Vice Pres*
▲ EMP: 75
SQ FT: 506,000
SALES: 108MM
SALES (corp-wide): 6.2B **Publicly Held**
WEB: www.kingsford.com
SIC: 2861 2099 2035 2033 Charcoal, except activated; dressings, salad: dry mixes; dressings, salad: raw & cooked (except dry mixes); barbecue sauce: packaged in cans, jars, etc.; insecticides, agricultural or household
PA: The Clorox Company
1221 Broadway Ste 1300
Oakland CA 94612
510 271-7000

2865 Cyclic-Crudes, Intermediates, Dyes & Org Pigments

(P-8697)
BIOTIUM INC
46117 Landing Pkwy, Fremont (94538-6407)
PHONE.............................510 265-1027
SEI Mao, *President*
Vivien Chen, *Vice Pres*
Wai-Yee Leung, *Vice Pres*
Mikhail Guzaev, *Research*
Fei Mao, *Research*
▼ EMP: 10
SALES (est): 2.6MM **Privately Held**
WEB: www.biotium.com
SIC: 2865 Dyes, synthetic organic

(P-8698)
CARETEX INC
4581 Firestone Blvd, South Gate (90280-3343)
PHONE.............................323 567-5074
Richard Kang, *President*
EMP: 65 EST: 1987
SQ FT: 30,000
SALES: 6MM **Privately Held**
SIC: 2865 2269 Dyes, synthetic organic; finishing plants

(P-8699)
COLOR SCIENCE INC
Also Called: C S I
1230 E Glenwood Pl, Santa Ana (92707-3000)
PHONE.............................714 434-1033
Jocelyn Eubank, *CEO*
Mark Hoffenberg, *President*
EMP: 15
SQ FT: 9,000
SALES (est): 5.7MM
SALES (corp-wide): 11.1MM **Privately Held**
WEB: www.modifiedplastics.com
SIC: 2865 Color pigments, organic
PA: Modified Plastics, Inc.
1240 E Glenwood Pl
Santa Ana CA 92707
714 546-4667

(P-8700)
DEALZER COM
9250 Reseda Blvd, Northridge (91324-3142)
PHONE.............................818 429-1155
Albert Frajian, *Owner*

PRODUCTS & SVCS

EMP: 10 **EST:** 2008
SALES (est): 1.3MM **Privately Held**
SIC: 2865 Hydroquinones

(P-8701)
HAZTECH SYSTEMS INC
4996 Gold Leaf Dr, Mariposa (95338-8510)
P.O. Box 929 (95338-0929)
PHONE....................209 966-8088
Thomas Archibald, *CEO*
Brenda Archibald, *Admin Sec*
EMP: 20
SALES: 2MM **Privately Held**
WEB: www.hazcat.com
SIC: 2865 Chemical indicators

(P-8702)
PACIFIC VISTA FOODS LLC
2380 Back Nine St, Oceanside
(92056-1701)
PHONE....................760 908-9840
David Roberts, *President*
Jordan Scharg, *Treasurer*
Richard Navarro, *Vice Pres*
EMP: 48
SALES (est): 2.4MM **Privately Held**
SIC: 2865 5963 5142 5143 Acids, coal
tar; direct selling establishments; dairy
products, house-to-house; packaged
frozen goods; ice cream & ices

(P-8703)
PERMALITE PLASTICS CORP
Also Called: Mks Color Composite
3121 E Ana St, Compton (90221-5606)
PHONE....................310 669-9492
Frederic Van Bergh, *President*
Richard Van Bergh, *Vice Pres*
EMP: 30 **EST:** 1946
SQ FT: 16,000
SALES (est): 5.7MM **Privately Held**
WEB: www.permaliteplastics.com
SIC: 2865 2891 Color pigments, organic;
adhesives

**2869 Industrial Organic
Chemicals, NEC**

(P-8704)
ACULON INC
11839 Sorrento Valley Rd # 901, San Diego
(92121-1040)
PHONE....................858 350-9474
Eric L Bruner, *President*
Gerald W Gruber, *CEO*
Christopher Harris, *COO*
EMP: 10
SQ FT: 10,000
SALES (est): 1.5MM **Privately Held**
SIC: 2869 Industrial organic chemicals

(P-8705)
**AEMETIS ADVNCED FELS
KEYES INC**
4209 Jessup Rd, Ceres (95307-9604)
P.O. Box 879, Keyes (95328-0879)
PHONE....................209 632-4511
Eric McAfee, *CEO*
Andy Foster, *COO*
Todd Waltz, *CFO*
Lydia Beebe, *Bd of Directors*
Kelly Shaver, *Relations*
EMP: 47
SALES (est): 15.6MM
SALES (corp-wide): 171.5MM **Publicly
Held**
SIC: 2869 Ethyl alcohol, ethanol
PA: Aemetis, Inc.
   20400 Stevens
   Cupertino CA 95014
   408 213-0940

(P-8706)
**AEROJET ROCKETDYNE DE
INC (HQ)**
8900 De Soto Ave, Canoga Park
(91304-1967)
P.O. Box 7922 (91309-7922)
PHONE....................818 586-1000
Eileen P Drake, *CEO*
Pete Gleszer, *Vice Pres*
Ken Panos, *Vice Pres*
Harlambakis Chris, *Business Dir*
Brad Morris, *Program Mgr*

▲ **EMP:** 199
SALES (est): 642.7MM
SALES (corp-wide): 1.9B **Publicly Held**
SIC: 2869 3724 Rocket engine fuel, or-
ganic; aircraft engines & engine parts
PA: Aerojet Rocketdyne Holdings, Inc.
   222 N Pacific Coast Hwy # 50
   El Segundo CA 90245
   310 252-8100

(P-8707)
**AEROJET ROCKETDYNE DE
INC**
8495 Carla Ln, West Hills (91304-3201)
PHONE....................818 586-9629
EMP: 115
SALES (corp-wide): 1.9B **Publicly Held**
SIC: 2869 3724 Rocket engine fuel, or-
ganic; aircraft engines & engine parts
HQ: Inc Aerojet Rocketdyne Of De
   8900 De Soto Ave
   Canoga Park CA 91304
   818 586-1000

(P-8708)
**AEROJET ROCKETDYNE DE
INC**
9001 Lurline Ave, Chatsworth
(91311-6122)
PHONE....................818 586-1000
Helen Lubin, *Branch Mgr*
EMP: 115
SALES (corp-wide): 1.9B **Publicly Held**
SIC: 2869 3724 Rocket engine fuel, or-
ganic; aircraft engines & engine parts
HQ: Inc Aerojet Rocketdyne Of De
   8900 De Soto Ave
   Canoga Park CA 91304
   818 586-1000

(P-8709)
AKZO NOBEL INC
Also Called: ICI Paints Store
3010 Bristol St, Costa Mesa (92626-3036)
PHONE....................714 966-0934
Art Peraza, *Branch Mgr*
EMP: 34
SALES (corp-wide): 11.3B **Privately Held**
SIC: 2869 Industrial organic chemicals
HQ: Akzo Nobel Inc.
   525 W Van Buren St Fl 16
   Chicago IL 60607
   312 544-7000

(P-8710)
AKZO NOBEL INC
Also Called: ICI Paints Store
735 N Escondido Blvd, Escondido
(92025-1703)
PHONE....................760 743-7374
Carlos Rios, *Branch Mgr*
EMP: 34
SALES (corp-wide): 11.3B **Privately Held**
SIC: 2869 Industrial organic chemicals
HQ: Akzo Nobel Inc.
   525 W Van Buren St Fl 16
   Chicago IL 60607
   312 544-7000

(P-8711)
**ALLIANCE HOSE &
EXTRUSIONS INC**
533 W Collins Ave, Orange (92867-5509)
P.O. Box 1037, Gardena (90249-0037)
PHONE....................714 202-8500
Scott H Franklin, *Vice Pres*
▲ **EMP:** 20
SQ FT: 15,000
SALES (est): 1.3MM
SALES (corp-wide): 5.3MM **Privately
Held**
WEB: www.calgasket.com
SIC: 2869 Silicones
PA: California Gasket And Rubber Corpora-
tion
   533 W Collins Ave
   Orange CA 92867
   310 323-4250

(P-8712)
AMERICAN BIODIESEL INC
Also Called: Community Fuels
809 Snedeker Ave Ste C, Stockton
(95203-4923)
PHONE....................209 466-4823

Chris Young, *Principal*
EMP: 11
SALES (est): 1.6MM
SALES (corp-wide): 19.7MM **Privately
Held**
SIC: 2869 Fuels
PA: American Biodiesel, Inc.
   809c Snedeker Ave
   Stockton CA 95203
   760 942-9306

(P-8713)
AMRICH ENERGY INC
1160 Marsh St Ste 105, San Luis Obispo
(93401-3382)
PHONE....................805 354-0830
Trent J Benedetti, *Principal*
EMP: 12
SALES (est): 2.4MM **Privately Held**
SIC: 2869 Hydraulic fluids, synthetic base

(P-8714)
AMYRIS INC (PA)
5885 Hollis St Ste 100, Emeryville
(94608-2405)
PHONE....................510 450-0761
John Melo, *President*
◆ **EMP:** 277
SQ FT: 136,000
SALES: 63.6MM **Publicly Held**
WEB: www.amyrisbiotech.com
SIC: 2869 Industrial organic chemicals

(P-8715)
**APPLIED SILICONE COMPANY
LLC**
Also Called: Applied Silicone Corporation
1050 Cindy Ln, Carpinteria (93013-2906)
PHONE....................805 525-5657
Ralph Alastair Winn, *President*
Phil Galarnau, *Vice Pres*
▲ **EMP:** 70
SQ FT: 20,000
SALES (est): 13.3MM
SALES (corp-wide): 1.4B **Publicly Held**
SIC: 2869 Silicones
HQ: Nusil Technology Llc
   1050 Cindy Ln
   Carpinteria CA 93013
   805 684-8780

(P-8716)
BASF CATALYSTS LLC
46820 Fremont Blvd, Fremont
(94538-6571)
PHONE....................510 490-2150
Teresa Concreras, *Administration*
EMP: 13
SALES (corp-wide): 71.7B **Privately Held**
SIC: 2869 Industrial organic chemicals
HQ: Basf Catalysts Llc
   33 Wood Ave S
   Iselin NJ 08830
   732 205-5000

(P-8717)
BASF CORPORATION
138 E Meats Ave, Orange (92865-3310)
PHONE....................714 921-1430
John Zomer, *Opers-Prdtn-Mfg*
EMP: 20
SQ FT: 10,000
SALES (corp-wide): 71.7B **Privately Held**
WEB: www.basf.com
SIC: 2869 2821 Industrial organic chemi-
cals; plastics materials & resins
HQ: Basf Corporation
   100 Park Ave
   Florham Park NJ 07932
   973 245-6000

(P-8718)
BASF CORPORATION
38403 Cherry St, Newark (94560-4716)
PHONE....................510 796-9911
Rich Hall, *Manager*
EMP: 12
SALES (corp-wide): 71.7B **Privately Held**
SIC: 2869 Industrial organic chemicals
HQ: Basf Corporation
   100 Park Ave
   Florham Park NJ 07932
   973 245-6000

(P-8719)
BASF ENZYMES LLC (DH)
3550 John Hopkins Ct, San Diego
(92121-1121)
PHONE....................858 431-8520
Matthew Lepore,
Robert Malone,
◆ **EMP:** 12
SALES (est): 290.6K
SALES (corp-wide): 71.7B **Privately Held**
SIC: 2869 Industrial organic chemicals
HQ: Basf Corporation
   100 Park Ave
   Florham Park NJ 07932
   973 245-6000

(P-8720)
**BASF VENTURE CAPITAL AMER
INC**
46820 Fremont Blvd, Fremont
(94538-6571)
PHONE....................510 445-6140
Hans Ulrich Engel, *President*
EMP: 10
SALES (est): 1.1MM
SALES (corp-wide): 71.7B **Privately Held**
SIC: 2869 Industrial organic chemicals
HQ: Basfin Corporation
   100 Park Ave
   Florham Park NJ 07932
   973 245-6000

(P-8721)
BEARS FOR HUMANITY INC
Also Called: Futurama
841 Ocean View Ave, San Mateo
(94401-3139)
PHONE....................866 325-1668
Renju Prathap, *President*
EMP: 50
SQ FT: 10,000
SALES (est): 10MM **Privately Held**
SIC: 2869 Industrial organic chemicals

(P-8722)
BIODICO WESTSIDE LLC
426 Donze Ave, Santa Barbara
(93101-1312)
PHONE....................805 683-8103
Russell Teall,
EMP: 12 **EST:** 2014
SALES (est): 832.8K **Privately Held**
SIC: 2869 Industrial organic chemicals

(P-8723)
BIOTECH ENERGY OF AMERICA
30 Castro Ave, San Rafael (94901-4819)
PHONE....................714 904-7844
Stig Westling, *CEO*
EMP: 10
SALES (est): 561.3K **Privately Held**
SIC: 2869 Industrial organic chemicals

(P-8724)
BIOTIX INC (HQ)
10636 Scripps Summit Ct # 130, San Diego
(92131-3979)
PHONE....................858 875-7696
Paul Nowak, *CEO*
Ron Perkins, *COO*
Tony Altig, *CFO*
Mickie Henshall, *Vice Pres*
Celia Reyes, *Vice Pres*
◆ **EMP:** 45
SALES (est): 5MM
SALES (corp-wide): 20.1MM **Privately
Held**
SIC: 2869 Laboratory chemicals, organic
PA: Biotix Holdings, Inc.
   10636 Scripps Summit Ct # 130
   San Diego CA 92131
   858 875-7696

(P-8725)
**CAL-INDIA FOODS
INTERNATIONAL**
Also Called: Specilty Enzymes Btechnologies
13591 Yorba Ave, Chino (91710-5071)
PHONE....................909 613-1660
Vic Rathi, *President*
Vasant Rathi, *Principal*
▲ **EMP:** 20
SQ FT: 12,000

▲ = Import ▼=Export
◆ =Import/Export

SALES (est): 6.2MM **Privately Held**
WEB: www.specialtyenzymes.com
SIC: 2869 Enzymes

(P-8726)
CALERA CORPORATION
Also Called: Chemetry
11500 Dolan Rd, Moss Landing
(95039-9715)
PHONE..................................831 731-6000
Ryan Gilliam, *CEO*
Jill Aufricht, *CFO*
Bob Snyder, *Security Dir*
EMP: 40 EST: 1985
SALES (est): 13.7MM **Privately Held**
SIC: 2869 Industrial organic chemicals

(P-8727)
CALIFORNIA BIO-PRODUCTEX INC
13220 Crown Ave, Hanford (93230-9413)
PHONE..................................559 582-5308
Leo Wirzbicki, *President*
EMP: 25
SQ FT: 2,500
SALES (est): 4.3MM **Privately Held**
SIC: 2869 2099 Industrial organic chemicals; yeast

(P-8728)
CALYSTA INC (PA)
1140 Obrien Dr Ste B, Menlo Park
(94025-1411)
PHONE..................................650 492-6880
Alan Shaw, *CEO*
Ted Hull, *CFO*
Lynsey Wenger, *CFO*
Craig Barratt, *Vice Pres*
Dennis Leong, *VP Bus Dvlpt*
EMP: 22
SALES (est): 3.4MM **Privately Held**
SIC: 2869 Industrial organic chemicals

(P-8729)
CALZYME LABORATORIES INC (PA)
3443 Miguelito Ct, San Luis Obispo
(93401-7124)
PHONE..................................805 541-5754
Muzaffar Iqbal, *President*
Usman Iqbal, *CFO*
Umer Iqbal, *Vice Pres*
EMP: 14
SQ FT: 18,000
SALES: 3MM **Privately Held**
WEB: www.calzyme.com
SIC: 2869 Enzymes

(P-8730)
CARBON RECYCLING INCORPORATED
Also Called: Carbon Recycling Inernational
7938 Ivanhoe Ave Ste B, La Jolla
(92037-4569)
PHONE..................................619 491-9200
Kim-Chinh Tran, *President*
EMP: 15
SALES (est): 959.4K **Privately Held**
SIC: 2869 Fuels

(P-8731)
CLARIANT CORPORATION
801 W 14th St, Long Beach (90813-1403)
PHONE..................................661 763-5192
Devon Bench, *Manager*
EMP: 40
SALES (corp-wide): 6.6B **Privately Held**
WEB: www.myclariant.com
SIC: 2869 Industrial organic chemicals
HQ: Clariant Corporation
4000 Monroe Rd
Charlotte NC 28205
704 331-7000

(P-8732)
CLARIANT PLAS COATINGS USA LLC
14355 Ramona Ave, Chino (91710-5740)
PHONE..................................909 606-1325
Mike Urbano, *Branch Mgr*
EMP: 18
SALES (corp-wide): 6.6B **Privately Held**
SIC: 2869 Industrial organic chemicals

HQ: Clariant Plastics & Coatings Usa Llc
4000 Monroe Rd
Charlotte NC 28205
704 331-7000

(P-8733)
CORONA PATHOLOGY
4444 W Riverside Dr # 308, Burbank
(91505-4073)
PHONE..................................818 566-1891
Conrad Gorospi, *Principal*
EMP: 13 EST: 2002
SQ FT: 5,000
SALES: 350K **Privately Held**
SIC: 2869 Laboratory chemicals, organic

(P-8734)
COSKATA INC
Also Called: Coskata Energy
3945 Freedom Cir Ste 560, Santa Clara
(95054-1269)
PHONE..................................630 657-5800
William Roe, *President*
David Blair, *CFO*
Wesley J Bolsen, *Chief Mktg Ofcr*
Richard E Tobey, *Vice Pres*
John A Crum, *Principal*
EMP: 12
SALES (est): 4.9MM **Privately Held**
WEB: www.coskata.com
SIC: 2869 Ethyl alcohol, ethanol

(P-8735)
DNA HEALTH INSTITUTE LLC
Also Called: Dna Health Inst Cyrogenic Div
4562 Westinghouse St B, Ventura
(93003-5797)
PHONE..................................805 654-9363
Noel Aguilar,
EMP: 12 EST: 2001
SALES (est): 2.3MM **Privately Held**
WEB: www.dnaskin.com
SIC: 2869 Laboratory chemicals, organic

(P-8736)
EDENIQ INC
2505 N Shirk Rd, Visalia (93291-8605)
PHONE..................................559 302-1777
Brian Thome, *CEO*
CAM Cast, *Vice Pres*
Peter Kilner, *Vice Pres*
Dan Michalopoulos, *Vice Pres*
▲ EMP: 100
SQ FT: 35,000
SALES (est): 23.8MM **Privately Held**
WEB: www.edeniq.com
SIC: 2869 Fuels

(P-8737)
ETHANOL ENERGY SYSTEMS LLC
406 Delta Ave, Isleton (95641)
PHONE..................................916 777-5654
EMP: 10
SALES (est): 700.4K **Privately Held**
SIC: 2869

(P-8738)
FIRMENICH
424 S Atchison St, Anaheim (92805-4045)
PHONE..................................714 535-2871
Adele Naidu, *Vice Pres*
John Flores, *Engineer*
Brian Kirckof, *Engineer*
Dustin Duimstra, *Purch Agent*
Todd Larato, *Safety Mgr*
EMP: 117
SALES (est): 18.9MM **Privately Held**
SIC: 2869 Industrial organic chemicals

(P-8739)
FIRSTELEMENT FUEL INC
2549 Eastbluff Dr 334, Newport Beach
(92660-3500)
PHONE..................................949 274-5701
Shane Stephens, *Administration*
EMP: 12
SALES (corp-wide): 1.7MM **Privately Held**
SIC: 2869 Fuels
PA: Firstelement Fuel Inc.
5151 California Ave # 220
Irvine CA 92617
949 246-0769

(P-8740)
GFP ETHANOL LLC
Also Called: Calgren Renewable Fuels
11704 Road 120, Pixley (93256)
P.O. Box E (93256-1005)
PHONE..................................559 757-3850
Lyle Schlyer, *President*
Sarah Gonzales, *Admin Asst*
Teresa Stevenson, *Accountant*
Tim Morillo, *Plant Mgr*
Jerry Schroeder, *Plant Mgr*
EMP: 34
SALES (est): 10.3MM **Privately Held**
SIC: 2869 2046 Ethyl alcohol, ethanol; corn oil, crude
PA: Sjv Biodiesel, Llc
11704 Road 120
Pixley CA 93256
559 757-3850

(P-8741)
GLOBAL SILICONES INC
49 Industrial Way, Buellton (93427-9565)
PHONE..................................805 686-4500
Philip Galarneau, *President*
Santiago Speceiro, *General Mgr*
Erin Certs, *Manager*
EMP: 10
SALES (est): 1.9MM **Privately Held**
SIC: 2869 Industrial organic chemicals

(P-8742)
HEXION INC
Borden
625 The City Dr S Ste 300, Orange
(92868-4966)
PHONE..................................714 971-0180
Rick Steen, *Branch Mgr*
EMP: 14 **Privately Held**
SIC: 2869 Industrial organic chemicals
HQ: Hexion Inc.
180 E Broad St Fl 26
Columbus OH 43215
614 225-4000

(P-8743)
HOW 2 SAVE FUEL LLC
Also Called: How2savefuel.com
18017 Chtswrth St Ste 166, Granada Hills
(91344-5608)
PHONE..................................818 882-1189
EMP: 10 EST: 2008
SALES (est): 1MM **Privately Held**
SIC: 2869

(P-8744)
INNOVATIVE ORGANICS INC
4905 E Hunter Ave, Anaheim (92807-2058)
PHONE..................................714 701-3900
Robert E Futrell Jr, *President*
Douglas E Ward, *Vice Pres*
EMP: 25
SQ FT: 30,000
SALES: 5.7MM **Privately Held**
SIC: 2869 2899 Industrial organic chemicals; chemical preparations

(P-8745)
INTERNATIONAL ACADEMY OF FIN (PA)
Also Called: Cordova Industries
13177 Foothill Blvd, Sylmar (91342-4830)
P.O. Box 922079 (91392-2079)
PHONE..................................818 361-7724
Sam Cordova, *President*
Steven M Cordova, *President*
Rodrick Cordova, *Exec VP*
Sam Scott Cordova, *Vice Pres*
Steven Schector, *Vice Pres*
EMP: 24
SQ FT: 6,000
SALES: 59MM **Privately Held**
SIC: 2869 3944 2879 Alcohols, industrial: denatured (non-beverage); video game machines, except coin-operated; insecticides, agricultural or household

(P-8746)
JDM PROPERTIES
410 S Golden State Blvd, Turlock
(95380-4959)
PHONE..................................209 632-0616
Joaquin Rose, *President*
EMP: 20
SQ FT: 4,410

SALES (est): 1.5MM **Privately Held**
SIC: 2869 5083 Hydraulic fluids, synthetic base; farm implements

(P-8747)
JOHN B CAMPBELL MD A PROF CORP
9292 Chesapeake Dr # 100, San Diego
(92123-1060)
PHONE..................................858 576-9960
John B Campbell, *President*
John Campbell, *Director*
EMP: 11
SALES (est): 1.2MM **Privately Held**
SIC: 2869 Laboratory chemicals, organic

(P-8748)
JSR MICRO INC (HQ)
Also Called: Materials Innovation
1280 N Mathilda Ave, Sunnyvale
(94089-1213)
PHONE..................................408 543-8800
Eric R Johnson, *President*
Eiichi Kobayashi, *Vice Pres*
Nalini Murdter, *Managing Dir*
Akiko Shiraishi, *Executive Asst*
Doug Pagano, *Admin Sec*
◆ EMP: 140
SQ FT: 12,125
SALES (est): 37MM **Privately Held**
WEB: www.jsrmicro.com
SIC: 2869 2899 Industrial organic chemicals; chemical preparations

(P-8749)
KORE INFRASTRUCTURE LLC
200 N Pacific Coast Hwy # 340, El Segundo (90245-4340)
PHONE..................................310 367-1003
EMP: 10 **Privately Held**
SIC: 2869 Fuels
PA: Kore Infrastructure, Llc
4 High Pine
Glen Cove NY 11542

(P-8750)
LAMB FUELS INC
725 Main St Ste B, Chula Vista
(91911-6168)
PHONE..................................619 216-6940
Gregory Scott Lamb, *CEO*
Rochelle Lamb, *Admin Mgr*
Kezin Parabia, *VP Opers*
▼ EMP: 21
SALES (est): 5.1MM **Privately Held**
WEB: www.lambfuels.com
SIC: 2869 Fuels

(P-8751)
LESLIES ORGANICS LLC
Also Called: Coconut Secret
1297 Dynamic St, Petaluma (94954-1457)
PHONE..................................415 383-9800
Randy Stoler,
Mark Colbert, *General Mgr*
Leslie Caren,
Neena Dolwani, *Manager*
▲ EMP: 15 EST: 2007
SALES (est): 3MM **Privately Held**
SIC: 2869 Sweeteners, synthetic

(P-8752)
MENLO ENERGY LLC
555 California St # 4600, San Francisco
(94104-1503)
PHONE..................................415 762-8200
Gaurav Shah, *Mng Member*
▲ EMP: 20
SQ FT: 34,000
SALES (est): 2.5MM **Privately Held**
SIC: 2869 2911 Glycerin; diesel fuels

(P-8753)
MOLECULE LABS INC
524 Stone Rd Ste A, Benicia (94510-1169)
PHONE..................................925 473-8200
Michael Guasch, *CEO*
Willyumm Ruiz, *Master*
EMP: 50
SALES (est): 1.1MM **Privately Held**
SIC: 2869 Laboratory chemicals, organic

(P-8754)
MOVEEL FUEL LLC
15000 S Avalon Blvd Ste K, Gardena
(90248-2035)
P.O. Box 59118, Los Angeles (90059-0118)
PHONE..........................213 748-1444
Serj Oganesyan, *Mng Member*
EMP: 10 EST: 2009
SALES (est): 2MM **Privately Held**
SIC: 2869 1311 Fuels; crude petroleum &
natural gas production; crude petroleum
production

(P-8755)
NEKTAR THERAPEUTICS AL CORP
455 Mission Bay Blvd S, San Francisco
(94158-2158)
PHONE..........................256 512-9200
Milton Harris, *General Mgr*
EMP: 70 **Publicly Held**
SIC: 2869 Ethylene glycols
HQ: Nektar Therapeutics Al, Corporation
1112 Church St Nw
Huntsville AL 35801

(P-8756)
NEXSTEPPE SEEDS INC
400 E Jamie Ct Ste 202, South San Fran-
cisco (94080-6230)
PHONE..........................650 887-5700
EMP: 35 EST: 2013
SALES (est): 3.4MM **Privately Held**
SIC: 2869

(P-8757)
NEXSUN CORP
3250 Wilshire Blvd # 1410, Los Angeles
(90010-1604)
PHONE..........................213 382-2220
Justin Lee, *Ch of Bd*
David Pyrce, *CEO*
EMP: 25
SALES (est): 3.3MM **Privately Held**
SIC: 2869 Industrial organic chemicals

(P-8758)
NORAC INC (PA)
405 S Motor Ave, Azusa (91702-3232)
PHONE..........................626 334-2907
Wallace McCloskey, *President*
Brian Sanchez, *Lab Dir*
Olive J Mc Closkey, *Principal*
Lee Miller, *Principal*
Jim Scholler, *Principal*
▼ EMP: 258 EST: 1953
SQ FT: 10,000
SALES (est): 66.6MM **Privately Held**
WEB: www.norac.com
SIC: 2869 Industrial organic chemicals

(P-8759)
OPUS 12 INCORPORATED
614 Bancroft Way Ste B, Berkeley
(94710-2224)
Rural Route 820 (94704)
PHONE..........................917 349-3740
Nicholas Flanders, *CEO*
Etosha Cave, *Principal*
Kendra Kuhl, *Principal*
EMP: 13
SQ FT: 1,000
SALES (est): 237.9K **Privately Held**
SIC: 2869 Industrial organic chemicals

(P-8760)
PACIFIC ETHANOL CENTRAL LLC (HQ)
400 Capitol Mall Ste 2060, Sacramento
(95814-4436)
P.O. Box 10, Pekin IL (61555-0010)
PHONE..........................916 403-2123
Neil M Koehler, *President*
EMP: 75
SALES (est): 145.8MM
SALES (corp-wide): 1.5B **Publicly Held**
SIC: 2869 Ethyl alcohol, ethanol
PA: Pacific Ethanol, Inc.
400 Capitol Mall Ste 2060
Sacramento CA 95814
916 403-2123

(P-8761)
PACIFIC ETHANOL WEST LLC
400 Capitol Mall Ste 2060, Sacramento
(95814-4436)
PHONE..........................916 403-2123
Neil M Koehler,
EMP: 150
SALES (est): 16.1MM
SALES (corp-wide): 1.5B **Publicly Held**
SIC: 2869 Ethanolamines
PA: Pacific Ethanol, Inc.
400 Capitol Mall Ste 2060
Sacramento CA 95814
916 403-2123

(P-8762)
PENTA BIOTECH INC
1100 Industrial Rd Ste 4, San Carlos
(94070-4131)
PHONE..........................650 598-9328
John Huang, *President*
EMP: 12
SQ FT: 11,000
SALES: 1MM **Privately Held**
WEB: www.pentabiotech.com
SIC: 2869 Industrial organic chemicals

(P-8763)
PREMIER FUEL DISTRIBUTORS INC
7213 Rosecrans Ave Ste B, Paramount
(90723-7512)
PHONE..........................562 602-1000
Hugo Rodriguez, *CEO*
EMP: 14
SALES (est): 5.8MM **Privately Held**
SIC: 2869 Fuels

(P-8764)
PRIMETECH SILICONES INC
6655 Doolittle Ave, Riverside (92503-1454)
PHONE..........................951 509-6655
Salvador Avalos, *President*
Ophelia Avalos, *Vice Pres*
▲ EMP: 10
SQ FT: 12,000
SALES: 1.5MM **Privately Held**
SIC: 2869 Silicones

(P-8765)
PROPEL BIOFUELS INC (PA)
Also Called: Propel Fuels
1815 19th St, Sacramento (95811-6712)
PHONE..........................800 871-0773
Robert R Elam, *President*
Koichi Kurisu, *COO*
Ken Jibiki, *Info Tech Mgr*
Joanna Woessner, *Project Mgr*
Muang Saeteurn, *Marketing Staff*
EMP: 10 EST: 2006
SQ FT: 3,200
SALES (est): 2.4MM **Privately Held**
SIC: 2869 Fuels

(P-8766)
PROTEMACH INC
Also Called: Golden Farms
7133 Remmet Ave, Canoga Park
(91303-2016)
PHONE..........................310 622-2693
Saed Moshaver, *CEO*
EMP: 11
SQ FT: 8,500
SALES: 1.8MM **Privately Held**
SIC: 2869 2099 Perfumes, flavorings &
food additives; spices, including grinding

(P-8767)
PROVIVI INC (PA)
1701 Colorado Ave, Santa Monica
(90404-3436)
PHONE..........................310 828-2307
Pedro S L Coelho, *CEO*
EMP: 25
SALES (est): 5.3MM **Privately Held**
SIC: 2869 Laboratory chemicals, organic

(P-8768)
PURE ONE ENVIRONMENTAL INC
Also Called: Pure One Business Svc Group
3400 W Warner Ave Ste A, Santa Ana
(92704-5300)
PHONE..........................714 641-1430
James Jordan, *President*

EMP: 10
SALES (est): 1.2MM **Privately Held**
SIC: 2869 8748 5169 Industrial organic
chemicals; environmental consultant; organic chemicals, synthetic

(P-8769)
PUROSIL LLC
1660 Leeson Ln, Corona (92879-2061)
PHONE..........................951 271-3900
EMP: 10
SALES (corp-wide): 126.4MM **Privately Held**
SIC: 2869 Silicones
HQ: Purosil Llc
708 S Temescal St Ste 102
Corona CA 92879

(P-8770)
PUROSIL LLC (HQ)
708 S Temescal St Ste 102, Corona
(92879-2096)
P.O. Box 2467 (92878-2467)
PHONE..........................951 271-3900
Thomas Garrett, *President*
▲ EMP: 65
SQ FT: 5,000
SALES (est): 25MM
SALES (corp-wide): 126.4MM **Privately Held**
SIC: 2869 Silicones
PA: Mcp Industries, Inc.
708 S Temescal St Ste 101
Corona CA 92879
951 736-1881

(P-8771)
RENNOVIA INC
3040 Oakmead Village Dr, Santa Clara
(95051-0808)
PHONE..........................650 804-7400
Robert Wedinger, *CEO*
Thomas Boussie, *Vice Pres*
EMP: 15
SQ FT: 14,000
SALES (est): 4.9MM **Privately Held**
SIC: 2869 8731 Industrial organic chemi-
cals; biotechnical research, commercial

(P-8772)
SAINT-GOBAIN CERAMICS PLAS INC
Innovative Organics Division
4905 E Hunter Ave, Anaheim (92807-2058)
PHONE..........................714 701-3900
Robert E Futrell Jr, *Branch Mgr*
EMP: 30
SALES (corp-wide): 215.9MM **Privately Held**
WEB: www.sgceramics.com
SIC: 2869 2899 Industrial organic chemi-
cals; chemical preparations
HQ: Saint-Gobain Ceramics & Plastics, Inc.
750 E Swedesford Rd
Valley Forge PA 19482

(P-8773)
SCIGEN INC
7041 Marcelle St, Paramount
(90723-4838)
PHONE..........................310 324-6576
Steve Wheeler, *President*
Peer Hashmi, *CFO*
Tim Grant, *Officer*
Lori Wheeler, *Officer*
John Arnzen, *Vice Pres*
EMP: 10
SALES (est): 1.9MM **Privately Held**
SIC: 2869 2833 3089 5169 Laboratory
chemicals, organic; medicinal chemicals;
toilets, portable chemical: plastic; indus-
trial chemicals; automatic chemical ana-
lyzers

(P-8774)
SIERRA NATURAL SCIENCE INC
538 Brunken Ave Ste 2, Salinas
(93901-4372)
PHONE..........................831 757-1702
Kel Lemons, *President*
EMP: 18
SALES (est): 3MM **Privately Held**
SIC: 2869 Polyhydric alcohol esters,
aminos, etc.

(P-8775)
SPECIALIZED PRODUCTS & DESIGN
1428 N Manzanita St, Orange
(92867-3662)
PHONE..........................714 289-1428
Dennis Bergdorf, *CFO*
Deborah Bergdorf, *Corp Secy*
EMP: 12
SQ FT: 6,000
SALES: 1.2MM **Privately Held**
SIC: 2869 3069 Silicones; tubing, rubber

(P-8776)
SPECILTY ENZYMES BTECHNOLOGIES
Also Called: Seb
13591 Yorba Ave, Chino (91710-5071)
PHONE..........................909 613-1660
Vasant Rathi, *Principal*
Shrinivas Dengeti, *Research*
Rajendra Newase, *Prdtn Mgr*
EMP: 16
SALES (est): 3.3MM **Privately Held**
SIC: 2869 Enzymes

(P-8777)
SPOETY CUTS CORPORATION
6510 Wooster Ave, Los Angeles
(90056-2132)
PHONE..........................310 908-1512
Kinney D Marks, *President*
Kinney Marks, *Officer*
EMP: 10
SALES: 15K **Privately Held**
SIC: 2869 Industrial organic chemicals

(P-8778)
STRATOS RENEWABLES CORPORATION
Also Called: A Development Stage Company
9440 Santa Monica Blvd, Beverly Hills
(90210-4653)
PHONE..........................310 402-5901
EMP: 28
SALES (est): 254.8K **Privately Held**
SIC: 2869 0133 Ethyl alcohol, ethanol;
sugarcane & sugar beets

(P-8779)
USL PARALLEL PRODUCTS CAL
12281 Arrow Rte, Rancho Cucamonga
(91739-9601)
PHONE..........................909 980-1200
Gene Kiesel, *CEO*
Ken Reese, *President*
Tim Cusson, *Vice Pres*
Bob Pasma, *Vice Pres*
Jim Russell, *Vice Pres*
▲ EMP: 35
SQ FT: 6,000
SALES: 8.9MM
SALES (corp-wide): 49.8MM **Privately Held**
SIC: 2869 Alcohols, industrial: denatured
(non-beverage)
PA: Parallel Environmental Services Corpo-
ration
401 Industry Rd
Louisville KY 40208
502 471-2444

(P-8780)
UTAK LABORATORIES INC
25020 Avenue Tibbitts, Valencia
(91355-3447)
PHONE..........................661 294-3935
James D Plutchak, *CEO*
EMP: 26
SQ FT: 12,000
SALES: 4MM **Privately Held**
WEB: www.utak.com
SIC: 2869 Industrial organic chemicals

(P-8781)
VERTIMASS LLC
2 Park Plz Ste 700, Irvine (92614-8517)
PHONE..........................949 417-1396
William Shopoff, *Principal*
John Hannon, *COO*
Charles Wyman, *Principal*
EMP: 11
SALES (est): 1MM **Privately Held**
SIC: 2869 Industrial organic chemicals

(P-8782)
VISCON CALIFORNIA LLC
3121 Standard St, Bakersfield
(93308-6242)
PHONE..................................661 327-7061
Michael Porter,
Patrick Porter,
Kelli Terrell, *Assistant*
EMP: 10
SALES (est): 6MM **Privately Held**
WEB: www.visconusa.com
SIC: 2869 Fuels

(P-8783)
VISHAY SILICONIX LLC
2585 Junction Ave, San Jose (95134-1923)
PHONE..................................408 988-8000
Felix Zandman, *Ch of Bd*
Peter G Henrici, *Senior VP*
Joel Abarquez, *Senior Engr*
▲ **EMP:** 700
SALES (est): 98MM
SALES (corp-wide): 3B **Publicly Held**
SIC: 2869 Silicones
HQ: Siliconix Incorporated
2585 Junction Ave
San Jose CA 95134
408 988-8000

(P-8784)
WACKER CHEMICAL
CORPORATION
Also Called: Precision Silicones
13910 Oaks Ave, Chino (91710-7010)
PHONE..................................909 590-8822
Sudipta Das, *Branch Mgr*
Liz Bobo, *Human Res Mgr*
Barbara Hartford, *Production*
EMP: 44
SALES (corp-wide): 5.7B **Privately Held**
WEB:
www.wackerchemicalcorporation.com
SIC: 2869 5169 Silicones; industrial chemicals
HQ: Wacker Chemical Corporation
3301 Sutton Rd
Adrian MI 49221
517 264-8500

(P-8785)
WINNER INDUSTRIAL
CHEMICALS
154 W Foothill Blvd Ste A, Upland
(91786-8702)
PHONE..................................909 887-6228
Detra Jones, *President*
Cornelius Wallace, *CFO*
Carol Redding, *Vice Pres*
EMP: 20
SALES (est): 2.2MM **Privately Held**
SIC: 2869 Industrial organic chemicals

(P-8786)
ZENTIS NORTH AMERICA LLC
16911 S Normandie Ave, Gardena
(90247-5437)
PHONE..................................310 719-2600
David Daneshmayeh, *CEO*
Shelena McClinton, *Human Res Mgr*
▲ **EMP:** 100
SALES (est): 19.4MM
SALES (corp-wide): 789.1MM **Privately Held**
SIC: 2869 2899 2099 2087 Industrial organic chemicals; chemical preparations; food preparations; flavoring extracts & syrups
PA: Zentis Gmbh & Co. Kg
Julicher Str. 177
Aachen 52070
241 476-00

2873 Nitrogenous Fertilizers

(P-8787)
1ST CHOICE FERTILIZER INC
1515 Aurora Dr, San Leandro
(94577-3105)
PHONE..................................800 504-5699
Bright Omoruyi, *Principal*
EMP: 10

SALES: 500K **Privately Held**
SIC: 2873 Fertilizers: natural (organic), except compost

(P-8788)
AGRA TRADING LLC
60 Independence Cir # 203, Chico
(95973-4921)
PHONE..................................530 894-1782
Jon Kim, *Mng Member*
EMP: 12
SQ FT: 1,800
SALES: 12MM **Privately Held**
WEB: www.agratrading.com
SIC: 2873 Fertilizers: natural (organic), except compost

(P-8789)
AIRGAS INC
15116 Canary Ave, La Mirada
(90638-5218)
PHONE..................................714 521-4789
EMP: 10
SALES (corp-wide): 163.9MM **Privately Held**
SIC: 2873
HQ: Airgas, Inc.
259 N Radnor Chester Rd # 100
Radnor PA 19087
610 687-5253

(P-8790)
BOYER INC
105 Thompson Rd, Watsonville (95076)
P.O. Box 82 (95077-0082)
PHONE..................................831 724-0123
Fred Willoughby, *CEO*
▲ **EMP:** 22
SALES (est): 5MM
SALES (corp-wide): 29.4MM **Privately Held**
SIC: 2873 2874 Nitrogenous fertilizers; phosphatic fertilizers
PA: Willoughby Farms, Inc.
261 Coward Rd
Watsonville CA
831 722-7763

(P-8791)
CVR NITROGEN LP (DH)
10877 Wilshire Blvd Fl 10, Los Angeles
(90024-4251)
PHONE..................................310 571-9800
Keith B Forman, *CEO*
John H Diesch, *President*
Jeffrey R Spain, *CFO*
Wilfred Bahl Jr, *Senior VP*
Julie Dawoodjee Cafarella, *Vice Pres*
EMP: 10 **EST:** 2015
SALES: 340.7MM **Publicly Held**
SIC: 2873 Ammonium nitrate, ammonium sulfate

(P-8792)
DR EARTH INC
4021 Devon Ct, Vacaville (95688-8730)
P.O. Box 460, Winters (95694-0460)
PHONE..................................707 448-4676
Milad Shammas, *CEO*
Ray Sidey, *President*
Debra White, *COO*
Tyler Vinyard, *Vice Pres*
▲ **EMP:** 15
SQ FT: 958,320
SALES (est): 2.2MM **Privately Held**
SIC: 2873 5191 Fertilizers: natural (organic), except compost; fertilizer & fertilizer materials

(P-8793)
GRO-POWER INC
15065 Telephone Ave, Chino (91710-9614)
PHONE..................................909 393-3744
Brent Holden, *President*
▼ **EMP:** 25
SALES (est): 5MM **Privately Held**
WEB: www.gropower.com
SIC: 2873 0782 0721 Fertilizers: natural (organic), except compost; lawn & garden services; crop planting & protection

(P-8794)
HYPONEX CORPORATION
Also Called: Scotts- Hyponex
15978 El Prado Rd, Chino (91708-9158)
PHONE..................................909 597-2811

Roclund White, *Branch Mgr*
Kay Scott, *Office Mgr*
EMP: 28
SQ FT: 10,000
SALES (corp-wide): 2.6B **Publicly Held**
SIC: 2873 Plant foods, mixed: from plants making nitrog. fertilizers
HQ: Hyponex Corporation
14111 Scottslawn Rd
Marysville OH 43040
937 644-0011

(P-8795)
HYPONEX CORPORATION
Also Called: Scotts- Hyponex
23390 E Flood Rd, Linden (95236-9488)
P.O. Box 479 (95236-0479)
PHONE..................................209 887-3845
Aaron Teach, *Manager*
EMP: 45
SALES (corp-wide): 2.6B **Publicly Held**
SIC: 2873 Plant foods, mixed: from plants making nitrog. fertilizers
HQ: Hyponex Corporation
14111 Scottslawn Rd
Marysville OH 43040
937 644-0011

(P-8796)
KELLOGG SUPPLY INC
Also Called: Kellogg Garden Product
12686 Locke Rd, Lockeford (95237-9701)
PHONE..................................209 727-3130
Clayton De Bie, *Principal*
Alejandro Frias, *Plant Mgr*
EMP: 50
SALES (corp-wide): 80MM **Privately Held**
WEB: www.kellogggarden.com
SIC: 2873 5191 2875 Nitrogenous fertilizers; fertilizer & fertilizer materials; fertilizers, mixing only
PA: Kellogg Supply, Inc.
350 W Sepulveda Blvd
Carson CA 90745
310 830-2200

(P-8797)
MAR VISTA RESOURCES LLC
745 North Ave, Corcoran (93212-1906)
P.O. Box 218 (93212-0218)
PHONE..................................559 992-4535
Jay Irvine, *President*
Travis Cardoza, *Info Tech Mgr*
Marrs Gist, *Plant Mgr*
Steve Iliff, *Sales Mgr*
Rick Loya, *Sales Staff*
▲ **EMP:** 13
SALES (est): 20MM **Privately Held**
SIC: 2873 Plant foods, mixed: from plants making nitrog. fertilizers

(P-8798)
MINERAL KING MINERALS INC
(PA)
7600 N Ingram Ave Ste 105, Fresno
(93711-5824)
PHONE..................................559 582-9228
EMP: 18
SQ FT: 2,000
SALES (est): 1.5MM **Privately Held**
SIC: 2873

(P-8799)
NAC MFG INC
601 Kettering Dr, Ontario (91761-8153)
PHONE..................................909 472-3033
Stanley Hsiao, *CEO*
Jeff Zhang, *Manager*
EMP: 20 **EST:** 2014
SQ FT: 106,000
SALES (est): 2.6MM **Privately Held**
SIC: 2873 Fertilizers: natural (organic), except compost

(P-8800)
NUTRIEN AG SOLUTIONS INC
2150 Eastman Ave, Oxnard (93030-5168)
P.O. Box 1307 (93032-1307)
PHONE..................................805 488-3646
Mike Dinsley, *Manager*
EMP: 16 **Privately Held**
WEB: www.cropproductionservices.com
SIC: 2873 5261 Fertilizers: natural (organic), except compost; fertilizer

HQ: Nutrien Ag Solutions, Inc.
3005 Rocky Mountain Ave
Loveland CO 80538
970 685-3300

(P-8801)
RED STAR FERTILIZER CO
17132 Hellman Ave, Eastvale
(92880-9724)
PHONE..................................909 597-4801
Donald C Mc Millan, *Ch of Bd*
Paul E Bernhard Jr, *President*
Michael Hughes, *Corp Secy*
EMP: 55
SQ FT: 52,100
SALES (est): 9.4MM **Privately Held**
SIC: 2873 2421 Fertilizers: natural (organic), except compost; sawmills & planing mills, general

(P-8802)
RENTECH NTRGN PASADENA
SPA LLC
10877 Wilshire Blvd # 710, Los Angeles
(90024-4341)
PHONE..................................310 571-9805
EMP: 18
SALES: 334.6MM **Publicly Held**
SIC: 2873 Nitrogenous fertilizers
HQ: Cvr Nitrogen, Lp
10877 Wilshire Blvd Fl 10
Los Angeles CA 90024
310 571-9800

(P-8803)
SCOTTS COMPANY LLC
742 Industrial Way, Shafter (93263-4018)
PHONE..................................661 387-9555
Aaron Leach, *Branch Mgr*
EMP: 17
SALES (corp-wide): 2.6B **Publicly Held**
WEB: www.scottscompany.com
SIC: 2873 Fertilizers: natural (organic), except compost
HQ: The Scotts Company Llc
14111 Scottslawn Rd
Marysville OH 43040
937 644-0011

(P-8804)
SPAWN MATE INC
Also Called: Arroyo Grande Mushroom Farm
4000 Huasna Rd, Arroyo Grande
(93420-6135)
P.O. Box 1551 (93421-1551)
PHONE..................................805 473-7250
Art Lopez, *General Mgr*
EMP: 38
SALES (corp-wide): 22.1MM **Privately Held**
WEB: www.spawnmate.com
SIC: 2873 0182 5148 Fertilizers: natural (organic), except compost; mushrooms grown under cover; vegetables
PA: Spawn Mate, Inc.
260 Westgate Dr
Watsonville CA 95076
831 763-5300

(P-8805)
TI INC
13802 Avenue 352, Visalia (93292-9543)
PHONE..................................559 972-1475
Bryce Iden, *Principal*
EMP: 12 **EST:** 1984
SALES (est): 729K **Privately Held**
SIC: 2873 Plant foods, mixed: from plants making nitrog. fertilizers

(P-8806)
ULTRA GRO LLC
1043 S Granada Dr, Madera (93637-4801)
PHONE..................................559 661-0977
Donald F Parreira,
Steven G Best,
Craig F Fourchy,
EMP: 25
SALES (est): 5.3MM **Privately Held**
SIC: 2873 Fertilizers: natural (organic), except compost

(P-8807)
WESTERN NUTRIENTS
CORPORATION
245 Industrial St, Bakersfield (93307-2703)
PHONE..................................661 327-9604

PRODUCTS & SVCS

Craig Waterman, *President*
Mark Armstrong, *Sales Mgr*
▲ EMP: 20
SQ FT: 6,000
SALES (est): 5MM **Privately Held**
WEB: www.westernnutrientscorp.com
SIC: 2873 Fertilizers: natural (organic), except compost; nitrogen solutions (fertilizer); plant foods, mixed: from plants making nitrog. fertilizers

(P-8808)
WESTERN ORGANICS INC
Gro-Well Brands
4343 Mckinley Ave, Stockton (95206-3906)
PHONE....................209 982-4936
Jesus Redudlo, *Branch Mgr*
EMP: 40
SALES (corp-wide): 59.9MM **Privately Held**
WEB: www.sierraorganics.com
SIC: 2873 5199 Fertilizers: natural (organic), except compost; bark
PA: Western Organics, Inc.
420 E Southern Ave
Tempe AZ 85282
602 792-0275

(P-8809)
WHITTIER FERTILIZER COMPANY
9441 Kruse Rd, Pico Rivera (90660-1492)
PHONE....................562 699-3461
Robert Osborn, *CEO*
Janet Osborn, *Corp Secy*
Jim Osborn, *General Mgr*
▲ EMP: 51
SQ FT: 20,000
SALES (est): 13.6MM **Privately Held**
SIC: 2873 5261 2875 Fertilizers: natural (organic), except compost; garden supplies & tools; fertilizers, mixing only

---

2875 Fertilizers, Mixing Only

(P-8810)
ACTAGRO LLC (PA)
677 W Palmdon Dr Ste 108, Fresno (93704-1094)
P.O. Box 309, Biola (93606-0309)
PHONE....................559 369-2222
Monty Bayer, *CEO*
Greg Crawford, *COO*
Terri West, *CFO*
Casey McDaniel, *Managing Dir*
Brandon Laws, *Technical Staff*
▲ EMP: 31
SQ FT: 7,000
SALES (est): 35.6MM **Privately Held**
WEB: www.actagro.com
SIC: 2875 Fertilizers, mixing only

(P-8811)
BRANDT CONSOLIDATED INC
3654 S Willow Ave, Fresno (93725-9036)
PHONE....................559 499-2100
EMP: 15
SALES (corp-wide): 159MM **Privately Held**
SIC: 2875 5191 Fertilizers, mixing only; farm supplies
PA: Brandt Consolidated, Inc.
2935 S Koke Mill Rd
Springfield IL 62711
217 547-5800

(P-8812)
COLD CREEK COMPOST INC
6000 Potter Valley Rd, Ukiah (95482-9260)
PHONE....................707 485-5966
Martin Mileck, *President*
Mari Mileck, *Admin Sec*
Sam Todd, *Architect*
EMP: 11
SALES (est): 1.6MM **Privately Held**
SIC: 2875 5261 Compost; fertilizer

(P-8813)
JH BIOTECH INC (PA)
4951 Olivas Park Dr, Ventura (93003-7667)
P.O. Box 3538 (93006-3538)
PHONE....................805 650-8933
Hsinhung John Hsu, *President*

◆ EMP: 23
SQ FT: 3,000
SALES (est): 15.5MM **Privately Held**
WEB: www.jhbiotech.com
SIC: 2875 Fertilizers, mixing only

(P-8814)
NUTRIEN AG SOLUTIONS INC
3348 Claus Rd, Modesto (95355-9725)
PHONE....................209 551-1424
Dan Sardella, *Manager*
Richard Baker, *Manager*
David Vermeulen, *Consultant*
EMP: 35
SQ FT: 28,395 **Privately Held**
WEB: www.cropproductionservices.com
SIC: 2875 5261 5191 5999 Fertilizers, mixing only; fertilizer; fertilizer & fertilizer materials; insecticides; insecticides
HQ: Nutrien Ag Solutions, Inc.
3005 Rocky Mountain Ave
Loveland CO 80538
970 685-3300

(P-8815)
TESSENDERLO KERLEY INC
10724 Energy St, Hanford (93230-9518)
PHONE....................559 582-9200
Amos Riley, *Branch Mgr*
EMP: 14 **Privately Held**
SIC: 2875 Fertilizers, mixing only
HQ: Tessenderlo Kerley, Inc.
2255 N 44th St Ste 300
Phoenix AZ 85008
602 889-8300

(P-8816)
TRIAD ENERGY RESOURCES INC
Also Called: Triad Waste Management
204 Kerr Ave, Modesto (95354-3809)
PHONE....................209 527-0607
Mike Daley, *President*
▲ EMP: 20
SALES (est): 3.3MM **Privately Held**
SIC: 2875 Fertilizers, mixing only

(P-8817)
TRUE ORGANIC PRODUCTS INC
20225 W Kamm Ave, Helm (93627)
PHONE....................559 866-3001
EMP: 15
SALES (corp-wide): 5.4MM **Privately Held**
SIC: 2875 Fertilizers, mixing only
PA: True Organic Products, Inc.
20225 W Kamm Ave
Helm CA 93627
559 866-3001

2879 Pesticides & Agricultural Chemicals, NEC

(P-8818)
AMERICAN VANGUARD CORPORATION (PA)
Also Called: Avd
4695 Macarthur Ct, Newport Beach (92660-1882)
PHONE....................949 260-1200
Eric G Wintemute, *Ch of Bd*
Ulrich G Trogele, *COO*
David T Johnson, *CFO*
Scott Baskin, *Bd of Directors*
Lawrence Clark, *Bd of Directors*
◆ EMP: 60
SQ FT: 19,953
SALES: 454.2MM **Publicly Held**
WEB: www.amvac-chemical.com
SIC: 2879 Pesticides, agricultural or household

(P-8819)
AMVAC CHEMICAL CORPORATION (HQ)
4695 Macarthur Ct # 1200, Newport Beach (92660-8859)
PHONE....................323 264-3910
Eric C Wintemute, *President*
Timothy Donnelly, *President*
Bob Trogele, *COO*
David T Johnson, *CFO*

Debra Edwards, *Bd of Directors*
◆ EMP: 36
SQ FT: 152,000
SALES (est): 44.4MM
SALES (corp-wide): 454.2MM **Publicly Held**
SIC: 2879 Pesticides, agricultural or household
PA: American Vanguard Corporation
4695 Macarthur Ct
Newport Beach CA 92660
949 260-1200

(P-8820)
AMVAC CHEMICAL CORPORATION
Also Called: American Vangaurd
4695 Macarthur Ct # 1200, Newport Beach (92660-8859)
PHONE....................949 260-1212
Eric Wintemute, *President*
EMP: 18
SALES (corp-wide): 454.2MM **Publicly Held**
SIC: 2879 Insecticides & pesticides
HQ: Amvac Chemical Corporation
4695 Macarthur Ct # 1200
Newport Beach CA 92660
323 264-3910

(P-8821)
CELLU-CON INC
19994 Meredith Dr, Strathmore (93267-9691)
P.O. Box 185 (93267-0185)
PHONE....................559 568-0190
Duane Hilty, *President*
Carol Hilty, *Vice Pres*
John Yale, *Vice Pres*
EMP: 25
SQ FT: 15,000
SALES (est): 4.1MM **Privately Held**
WEB: www.cellucon.com
SIC: 2879 Soil conditioners

(P-8822)
CERTIS USA LLC
Also Called: Thermo Trilogy
720 5th St, Wasco (93280-1420)
PHONE....................661 758-8471
Michael Hillberry, *Principal*
Mike Allan, *Vice Pres*
Taylor Aguilera, *Regional Mgr*
John Wood, *Regional Mgr*
Bob Wilson, *Engineer*
EMP: 40 **Privately Held**
WEB: www.certisusa.com
SIC: 2879 5191 Pesticides, agricultural or household; insecticides
HQ: Certis U.S.A. L.L.C.
9145 Guilford Rd Ste 175
Columbia MD 21046

(P-8823)
CLOROX INTERNATIONAL COMPANY (HQ)
1221 Broadway Fl 13, Oakland (94612-1837)
P.O. Box 24305 (94623-1305)
PHONE....................510 271-7000
Benno Dorer, *Principal*
Warwick Every-Burns, *President*
Larry Peirof, *CEO*
William F Ausfahl, *Vice Pres*
Edward A Cutter, *Admin Sec*
▼ EMP: 75
SALES (est): 352.3MM
SALES (corp-wide): 6.2B **Publicly Held**
WEB: www.crispins.com
SIC: 2879 2842 Insecticides, agricultural or household; bleaches, household: dry or liquid
PA: The Clorox Company
1221 Broadway Ste 1300
Oakland CA 94612
510 271-7000

(P-8824)
CMR MARKETING AND RES INC
3594 E Wawona Ave, Fresno (93725-9021)
P.O. Box 35000 (93745-5000)
PHONE....................559 499-2100
John Salmonson, *President*
▲ EMP: 30
SQ FT: 70,000

SALES (est): 5.3MM
SALES (corp-wide): 159MM **Privately Held**
WEB: www.montereychemical.com
SIC: 2879 Agricultural chemicals
PA: Brandt Consolidated, Inc.
2935 S Koke Mill Rd
Springfield IL 62711
217 547-5800

(P-8825)
CUSTOM AG FORMULATORS INC (PA)
3430 S Willow Ave, Fresno (93725-9004)
P.O. Box 26104 (93729-6104)
PHONE....................559 435-1052
Gerald Steward, *CEO*
▼ EMP: 52
SALES (est): 17MM **Privately Held**
SIC: 2879 Agricultural chemicals

(P-8826)
DAV TERMITE & PEST INC
2005 Highland Ave, National City (91950-5845)
P.O. Box 390282, San Diego (92149-0282)
PHONE....................619 829-8901
Patricia R Chargualaf, *President*
Ermalene E Chargualaf, *Admin Sec*
EMP: 10
SALES (est): 568.2K **Privately Held**
SIC: 2879 7342 Agricultural chemicals; termite control

(P-8827)
DECCO US POST-HARVEST INC (HQ)
1713 S California Ave, Monrovia (91016-4623)
P.O. Box 120 (91017-0120)
PHONE....................800 221-0925
Francois Girin, *President*
◆ EMP: 50
SALES (est): 16.8MM
SALES (corp-wide): 1.2B **Privately Held**
SIC: 2879 Agricultural chemicals
PA: Upl Limited
Cts No-610, Upl House,
Mumbai MH 40005
227 152-8000

(P-8828)
DUPONT DE NEMOURS INC
2520 Barrington Ct, Hayward (94545-1133)
PHONE....................510 784-9105
Ellen Kullman, *Branch Mgr*
▲ EMP: 11
SALES (corp-wide): 85.9B **Publicly Held**
SIC: 2879 Agricultural chemicals
PA: Dupont De Nemours, Inc.
974 Centre Rd
Wilmington DE 19805
302 774-1000

(P-8829)
GARLIC RESEARCH LABS INC
Also Called: Garlic Valley Farm
624 Ruberta Ave, Glendale (91201-2335)
PHONE....................800 424-7990
William Anderson, *CEO*
Bill Brock, *Shareholder*
Sonja Anderson, *Corp Secy*
▼ EMP: 10
SQ FT: 14,000
SALES (est): 1.4MM **Privately Held**
WEB: www.garlicbarrier.com
SIC: 2879 Insecticides & pesticides; insecticides, agricultural or household

(P-8830)
GROW MORE INC
15600 New Century Dr, Gardena (90248-2129)
PHONE....................310 515-1700
John Atwill II, *CEO*
Debbi Gerber, *Controller*
◆ EMP: 62
SQ FT: 43,560
SALES (est): 17.7MM **Privately Held**
WEB: www.growmore.com
SIC: 2879 2899 2873 2869 Agricultural chemicals; chemical preparations; water treating compounds; nitrogenous fertilizers; industrial organic chemicals; cyclic crudes & intermediates

(P-8831)
HELENA AGRI-ENTERPRISES LLC
12218 11th Ave, Hanford (93230-9523)
P.O. Box 1263 (93232-1263)
PHONE...............................559 582-0291
Steve Dufur, *Manager*
EMP: 25 Privately Held
WEB: www.helenachemical.com
SIC: 2879 5191 Agricultural chemicals;
chemicals, agricultural
HQ: Helena Agri-Enterprises, Llc
255 Schilling Blvd # 300
Collierville TN 38017
901 761-0050

(P-8832)
IMPERIAL COMPOST LLC
1698 Jones St Ste 5, Brawley
(92227-1776)
PHONE...............................760 351-1900
Barbabra Laughrin, *Principal*
EMP: 15
SALES (est): 1.3MM Privately Held
SIC: 2879 Pesticides, agricultural or
household

(P-8833)
MARRONE BIO INNOVATIONS INC (PA)
1540 Drew Ave, Davis (95618-6320)
PHONE...............................530 750-2800
Pamela G Marrone, *CEO*
Linda V Moore, *Exec VP*
Keith J Pitts, *Senior VP*
Amit Vasavada, *Senior VP*
Ron Fisher, *Vice Pres*
▲ **EMP: 103**
SQ FT: 27,300
SALES (est): 21.2MM Publicly Held
WEB: www.marroneorganics.com
SIC: 2879 Agricultural chemicals

(P-8834)
MARY MATAVA
Also Called: Agri Service
3210 Oceanside Blvd, Oceanside (92056)
PHONE...............................760 439-9920
Mary Matava, *Owner*
EMP: 14
SALES (est): 1.3MM Privately Held
SIC: 2879 Soil conditioners

(P-8835)
MONSANTO COMPANY
500 Lucy Brown Rd, San Juan Bautista
(95045-9713)
P.O. Box 183 (95045-0183)
PHONE...............................831 623-7016
EMP: 164
SALES (corp-wide): 45.3B Privately Held
SIC: 2879 Agricultural chemicals
HQ: Monsanto Company
800 N Lindbergh Blvd
Saint Louis MO 63167
314 694-1000

(P-8836)
NATURAL PEST CONTROLS & FIREWD (PA)
Also Called: Npc Firewood
8864 Little Creek Dr, Orangevale
(95662-2125)
PHONE...............................916 726-0855
Jeff Hadden, *Owner*
EMP: 15 EST: 1971
SQ FT: 60,000
SALES (est): 1.4MM Privately Held
WEB: www.natpestco.com
SIC: 2879 Insecticides & pesticides

(P-8837)
NOVARTIS CORPORATION
5300 Chiron Way, Emeryville (94608-2966)
PHONE...............................510 879-9500
EMP: 58
SALES (corp-wide): 51.9B Privately Held
SIC: 2879 0181 2032 2865 Agricultural
chemicals; insecticides, agricultural or
household; pesticides, agricultural or
household; fungicides, herbicides; seeds,
vegetable: growing of; baby foods, including meats: packaged in cans, jars, etc.;
dyes & pigments; drugs acting on the cardiovascular system, except diagnostic

HQ: Novartis Corporation
1 S Ridgedale Ave Ste 1 # 1
East Hanover NJ 07936
212 307-1122

(P-8838)
PAULSEN WHITE OAK LP
3976 Garden Hwy, Nicolaus (95659-9711)
P.O. Box 151 (95659-0151)
PHONE...............................530 656-2201
Carol Thomsen, *General Ptnr*
Lee Ann Hanna, *Partner*
EMP: 12
SQ FT: 1,200
SALES (est): 2MM Privately Held
SIC: 2879 Pesticides, agricultural or
household

(P-8839)
SEMPERVIRENS GROUP
Also Called: Orion Group, The
820 Coventry Rd, Kensington
(94707-1411)
P.O. Box 8104, Berkeley (94707-8104)
PHONE...............................510 847-0801
Christopher Hall, *Owner*
EMP: 11 EST: 1983
SALES (est): 725.2K Privately Held
SIC: 2879 Agricultural chemicals

(P-8840)
SOUTHERN VALLEY CHEMICAL CO
S Derby & Sycamore Rd, Arvin (93203)
P.O. Box 181 (93203-0181)
PHONE...............................661 366-3308
Christopher C Carlson, *CEO*
Russel Carlson, *Corp Secy*
EMP: 11
SQ FT: 13,400
SALES (est): 4.5MM Privately Held
SIC: 2879 Insecticides & pesticides

(P-8841)
TECHNISOIL GLOBAL INC
5660 Westside Rd, Redding (96001-4450)
PHONE...............................530 605-4881
Sean Weaver,
Terry Jensen, *Sales Staff*
James Abner,
EMP: 10
SQ FT: 2,000
SALES (est): 2.2MM Privately Held
SIC: 2879 Soil conditioners

(P-8842)
TRICAL INC
28679 Rd 68, Visalia (93277)
PHONE...............................559 651-0736
Dean Storkan, *President*
EMP: 16
SALES (corp-wide): 29.7MM Privately Held
WEB: www.trical.com
SIC: 2879 Agricultural chemicals
PA: Trical, Inc.
8100 Arroyo Cir
Gilroy CA 95020
831 637-0195

(P-8843)
TRICAL INC (PA)
8100 Arroyo Cir, Gilroy (95020-7305)
P.O. Box 1327, Hollister (95024-1327)
PHONE...............................831 637-0195
Dean Storkan, *CEO*
Hank Maze, *CFO*
Joanne Vargas, *Corp Secy*
Mike Stanghellini, *Research*
Jena Francis, *Marketing Staff*
▲ **EMP: 30**
SQ FT: 6,000
SALES (est): 29.7MM Privately Held
WEB: www.trical.com
SIC: 2879 Agricultural chemicals

(P-8844)
TRICAL INC
8770 Hwy 25, Hollister (95023)
PHONE...............................831 637-0195
Dean Storkan, *CEO*
EMP: 100
SALES (corp-wide): 29.7MM Privately Held
SIC: 2879 Agricultural chemicals

PA: Trical, Inc.
8100 Arroyo Cir
Gilroy CA 95020
831 637-0195

(P-8845)
TRICAL INC
1029 Railroad St, Corona (92882-2416)
PHONE...............................951 737-6960
Joanne Vargas, *Manager*
EMP: 15
SALES (corp-wide): 29.7MM Privately Held
WEB: www.trical.com
SIC: 2879 Agricultural chemicals
PA: Trical, Inc.
8100 Arroyo Cir
Gilroy CA 95020
831 637-0195

(P-8846)
TRICAL INC
1667 Purdy Rd, Mojave (93501-7403)
PHONE...............................661 824-2494
Neil Adkins, *Branch Mgr*
EMP: 20
SALES (corp-wide): 29.7MM Privately Held
SIC: 2879 Agricultural chemicals
PA: Trical, Inc.
8100 Arroyo Cir
Gilroy CA 95020
831 637-0195

(P-8847)
VALENT USA LLC
Also Called: Valent Dublin Laboratories
6560 Trinity Ct, Dublin (94568-2627)
PHONE...............................925 256-2700
Glen Fujie, *Manager*
EMP: 20
SQ FT: 43,000 Privately Held
WEB: www.valent.com
SIC: 2879 Agricultural chemicals
HQ: Valent U.S.A. Llc
1600 Riviera Ave Ste 200
Walnut Creek CA 94596
925 256-2700

(P-8848)
WESTBRIDGE AGRICULTURAL PDTS
1260 Avenida Chelsea, Vista (92081-8315)
PHONE...............................760 599-8855
Christine Koenemann, *CEO*
Tina Koenemann, *President*
Richard Forsyth, *CFO*
Larry Parker, *Vice Pres*
Nicole Friend, *Office Mgr*
▲ **EMP: 15**
SQ FT: 8,000
SALES (est): 4.1MM
SALES (corp-wide): 6.5MM Privately Held
WEB: www.westbridge.com
SIC: 2879 Agricultural chemicals
PA: Westbridge Research Group
1260 Avenida Chelsea
Vista CA 92081
760 599-8855

(P-8849)
WESTBRIDGE RESEARCH GROUP (PA)
1260 Avenida Chelsea, Vista (92081-8315)
PHONE...............................760 599-8855
William Fruehling, *Ch of Bd*
Christine Koenemann, *President*
Tina Koenemann, *CEO*
Richard Forsyth, *CFO*
Andy Hudson, *Director*
EMP: 12
SQ FT: 19,504
SALES (est): 6.5MM Privately Held
SIC: 2879 2873 Agricultural chemicals;
fertilizers: natural (organic), except com-
post

(P-8850)
YARA NORTH AMERICA INC
3961 Channel Dr, West Sacramento
(95691-3431)
PHONE...............................916 375-1109
David Johnson, *Manager*
EMP: 35
SQ FT: 2,000 Privately Held

SIC: 2879 Agricultural chemicals
HQ: Yara North America, Inc
100 N Tampa St Ste 3200
Tampa FL 33602

2891 Adhesives & Sealants

(P-8851)
AC PRODUCTS INC
Also Called: Quaker
9930 Painter Ave, Whittier (90605-2759)
PHONE...............................714 630-7311
Joseph Matrange, *President*
Hugh H Muller, *Exec VP*
Sheldon I Weinstein, *Vice Pres*
◆ **EMP: 35**
SQ FT: 28,000
SALES (est): 11.9MM
SALES (corp-wide): 867.5MM Publicly Held
WEB: www.quakerchem.com
SIC: 2891 2952 8731 Adhesives &
sealants; coating compounds, tar; chemi-
cal laboratory, except testing
PA: Quaker Chemical Corporation
1 Quaker Park
Conshohocken PA 19428
610 832-4000

(P-8852)
ADVANCED CHEMISTRY & TECH INC (HQ)
Also Called: AC Tech
7341 Anaconda Ave, Garden Grove
(92841-2921)
PHONE...............................714 373-8118
Joseph A Muklevicz, *President*
Dean Willard, *CEO*
▲ **EMP: 23**
SALES (est): 5.8MM
SALES (corp-wide): 32.7B Publicly Held
WEB: www.actechaero.com
SIC: 2891 Sealants
PA: 3m Company
3m Center
Saint Paul MN 55144
651 733-1110

(P-8853)
ADVANTAGE ADHESIVES INC
8345 White Oak Ave, Rancho Cucamonga
(91730-3896)
PHONE...............................909 204-4990
Greg Lane, *President*
Jason Rowley, *Technical Staff*
Erika Machado, *Receptionist*
▲ **EMP: 26 EST: 1998**
SQ FT: 25,620
SALES (est): 4.9MM Privately Held
SIC: 2891 Adhesives

(P-8854)
APPLIED PRODUCTS INC
Also Called: Pacific Adhesive
8670 23rd Ave, Sacramento (95826-4904)
PHONE...............................800 274-9801
J Ballmer, *Branch Mgr*
EMP: 11
SALES (corp-wide): 49MM Privately Held
SIC: 2891 5169 Adhesives & sealants; ad-
hesives & sealants
PA: Applied Products, Inc.
6035 Baker Rd
Minnetonka MN 55345
952 933-2224

(P-8855)
AXIOM MATERIALS INC
2320 Pullman St, Santa Ana (92705-5507)
PHONE...............................949 623-4400
John D Lincoln, *CEO*
James Samuel Miele, *CFO*
Jim Miele, *CFO*
Raj Dhawan, *VP Bus Dvlpt*
Legrand Lewis, *Admin Sec*
▲ **EMP: 35**
SQ FT: 15,000
SALES (est): 18.5MM Privately Held
SIC: 2891 2295 Epoxy adhesives; resin or
plastic coated fabrics

(P-8856)
BLAIR ADHESIVE PRODUCTS
11034 Lockport Pl, Santa Fe Springs
(90670-4635)
PHONE...................................562 946-6004
Scott Heger, *President*
EMP: 12
SQ FT: 15,000
SALES (est): 3.4MM **Privately Held**
SIC: 2891 Adhesives, paste; adhesives,
plastic; glue; laminating compounds

(P-8857)
BONDLINE ELCTRNIC ADHSIVE CORP
777 N Pastoria Ave, Sunnyvale
(94085-2918)
PHONE...................................408 830-9200
Neal Olson, *CEO*
Erik V Olson, *President*
EMP: 25
SQ FT: 12,000
SALES (est): 3.6MM **Privately Held**
WEB: www.bondfilm.com
SIC: 2891 Adhesives

(P-8858)
BOSTIK INC
27460 Bostik Ct, Temecula (92590-3698)
PHONE...................................951 296-6425
Ed Lui, *Officer*
Earl Totty, *COO*
John Fels, *Engineer*
EMP: 60
SALES (corp-wide): 98.4MM **Privately Held**
WEB: www.bostik-us.com
SIC: 2891 2899 Adhesives; chemical
preparations
HQ: Bostik, Inc.
11320 W Wtertown Plank Rd
Wauwatosa WI 53226
414 774-2250

(P-8859)
BOYD CORPORATION (DH)
5960 Inglewood Dr Ste 115, Pleasanton
(94588-8611)
PHONE...................................209 236-1111
Mitchell Aiello, *President*
EMP: 31
SALES (est): 798.7MM
SALES (corp-wide): 915.2MM **Privately Held**
SIC: 2891 Adhesives & sealants
HQ: Lti Holdings, Inc.
600 S Mcclure Rd
Modesto CA 95357
209 236-1111

(P-8860)
BOYD CORPORATION
600 S Mcclure Rd, Modesto (95357-0520)
PHONE...................................888 244-6931
EMP: 235
SALES (corp-wide): 915.2MM **Privately Held**
SIC: 2891 Adhesives & sealants
HQ: Boyd Corporation
5960 Inglewood Dr Ste 115
Pleasanton CA 94588
209 236-1111

(P-8861)
BRADLEY TCHNOLOGIES-CALIFORNIA
447 E Rosecrans Ave, Gardena
(90248-2022)
PHONE...................................310 538-0714
Lawrence Stefan, *President*
Rhonda Rocca, *Admin Sec*
EMP: 20
SALES (est): 2.5MM **Privately Held**
SIC: 2891 Adhesives

(P-8862)
CTS CEMENT MANUFACTURING CORP (PA)
12442 Knott St, Garden Grove
(92841-2832)
PHONE...................................714 379-8260
Walter J Hoyle, *CEO*
Sean Casey, *Regional Mgr*
Tommy Fasano, *Regional Mgr*
Louis Priego, *Regional Mgr*

Cody Wann, *District Mgr*
▲ EMP: 45
SQ FT: 14,000
SALES (est): 43MM **Privately Held**
SIC: 2891 Cement, except linoleum & tile

(P-8863)
CTS CEMENT MANUFACTURING CORP
2077 Linda Flora Dr, Los Angeles
(90077-1406)
PHONE...................................310 472-4004
Edward K Rice, *Branch Mgr*
EMP: 17
SALES (corp-wide): 43MM **Privately Held**
SIC: 2891 Cement, except linoleum & tile
PA: Cts Cement Manufacturing Corporation
12442 Knott St
Garden Grove CA 92841
714 379-8260

(P-8864)
CUSTOM BUILDING PRODUCTS INC (DH)
Also Called: C-Cure
7711 Center Ave Ste 500, Huntington
Beach (92647-3076)
PHONE...................................800 272-8786
Don Devine, *CEO*
Brian Ellis, *President*
Thomas R Peck Jr, *President*
Mike Bilek, *COO*
Scott Hanson, *Vice Pres*
◆ EMP: 65 EST: 2005
SQ FT: 15,000
SALES (est): 443.9MM **Privately Held**
WEB: www.custombuildingproducts.com
SIC: 2891 Adhesives & sealants
HQ: The Quikrete Companies Llc
5 Concourse Pkwy Ste 1900
Atlanta GA 30328
404 634-9100

(P-8865)
CUSTOM BUILDING PRODUCTS INC
6511 Salt Lake Ave, Bell (90201-2126)
PHONE...................................323 582-0846
Tom Milan, *Plant Mgr*
Hernandez Mario, *Manager*
John Gallup, *Consultant*
EMP: 75 **Privately Held**
WEB: www.custombuildingproducts.com
SIC: 2891 3273 2899 5032 Adhesives &
sealants; ready-mixed concrete; chemical
preparations; ceramic wall & floor tile
HQ: Custom Building Products, Inc.
7711 Center Ave Ste 500
Huntington Beach CA 92647
800 272-8786

(P-8866)
DAVCO ENTERPRISES INC
Also Called: Design Polymerics
3301 W Segerstrom Ave, Santa Ana
(92704-6402)
PHONE...................................714 432-0600
Lyle R Davis, *President*
Matt Marowitz, *CFO*
Jason Vandriel, *Controller*
Carl Busse, *Regl Sales Mgr*
John Hutchinson, *Manager*
▲ EMP: 13
SQ FT: 15,000
SALES (est): 4.1MM **Privately Held**
WEB: www.designpoly.com
SIC: 2891 Adhesives & sealants

(P-8867)
ELLSWORTH CORPORATION
Also Called: Ellsworth Adhesive Systems
25 Hubble, Irvine (92618-4209)
PHONE...................................949 341-9329
Jim Fisher, *Manager*
Michael McCourt, *Owner*
EMP: 12
SALES (corp-wide): 187.3MM **Privately Held**
WEB: www.ellsworth.com
SIC: 2891 Adhesives
PA: Ellsworth Corporation
W129n10825 Washington Dr
Germantown WI 53022
262 253-8600

(P-8868)
EVK INC
5235 Bandera St, Montclair (91763-4419)
PHONE...................................617 335-3180
Ronald Izen, *President*
EMP: 50 EST: 2014
SQ FT: 30,000
SALES: 5MM **Privately Held**
SIC: 2891 Adhesives, plastic

(P-8869)
GENERAL SEALANTS INC
300 Turnbull Canyon Rd, City of Industry
(91745-1009)
P.O. Box 3855 (91744-0855)
PHONE...................................626 961-0211
Bradley Boyle, *President*
Patricia Boyle, *Owner*
Patrick Boyle, *CFO*
▲ EMP: 120 EST: 1964
SQ FT: 96,000
SALES (est): 35.6MM **Privately Held**
WEB: www.generalsealants.com
SIC: 2891 Adhesives

(P-8870)
GLUESMITH INDUSTRIES
Also Called: Gluesmith, The
801 S Raymond Ave Ste 39, Alhambra
(91803-1545)
PHONE...................................626 282-9390
Gustavo Portillo, *Owner*
Kenny Kimura, *Info Tech Mgr*
EMP: 10
SQ FT: 4,000
SALES (est): 681.9K **Privately Held**
SIC: 2891 5169 Adhesives; adhesives &
sealants

(P-8871)
HB FULLER COMPANY
Also Called: Adhesives Sealants Coatings Div
10500 Industrial Ave, Roseville
(95678-6212)
PHONE...................................916 787-6000
Frank Strasser, *Manager*
EMP: 60
SQ FT: 5,760
SALES (corp-wide): 3B **Publicly Held**
WEB: www.hbfuller.com
SIC: 2891 2851 2821 Adhesives; paints &
allied products; plastics materials & resins
PA: H.B. Fuller Company
1200 Willow Lake Blvd
Saint Paul MN 55110
651 236-5900

(P-8872)
HENKEL ELECTRONIC MTLS LLC
14000 Jamboree Rd, Irvine (92606-1730)
PHONE...................................888 943-6535
Benoit Pouliquen, *Vice Pres*
Paul R Berry, *President*
Alan P Syzdek, *President*
Ruairi Okane, *Manager*
EMP: 170 EST: 2010
SQ FT: 75,000
SALES (est): 1MM
SALES (corp-wide): 22.7B **Privately Held**
SIC: 2891 Adhesives
PA: Henkel Ag & Co. Kgaa
Henkelstr. 67
Dusseldorf 40589
211 797-0

(P-8873)
HENKEL US OPERATIONS CORP
Dexter Electronics Mtls Div
15051 Don Julian Rd, City of Industry
(91746-3302)
P.O. Box 1282, La Puente (91749)
PHONE...................................626 968-6511
Jim Dehart, *Manager*
EMP: 40
SALES (corp-wide): 22.7B **Privately Held**
SIC: 2891 Adhesives
HQ: Henkel Us Operations Corporation
1 Henkel Way
Rocky Hill CT 06067
860 571-5100

(P-8874)
HERNANDEZ ZEFERINO
Also Called: International Seals
1924 E Mcfadden Ave, Santa Ana
(92705-4705)
PHONE...................................714 953-4010
Zeferino Hernandez, *Owner*
EMP: 19
SALES (est): 3.6MM **Privately Held**
WEB: www.international-seals.com
SIC: 2891 Sealants

(P-8875)
INSTANT ASPHALT INC
Also Called: Metacrylics
365 Obata Ct, Gilroy (95020-7036)
PHONE...................................408 280-7733
Mark C Anthenien, *CEO*
Dale Anthenien, *Vice Pres*
Tanesha Santos, *Admin Asst*
Rick Berhorst, *Sales Staff*
Pierce Sinclair, *Consultant*
EMP: 12
SQ FT: 116,305
SALES (est): 6.1MM **Privately Held**
WEB: www.metacrylics.com
SIC: 2891 2952 Adhesives & sealants; as-
phalt felts & coatings; roofing materials;
mastic roofing composition; roofing felts,
cements or coatings

(P-8876)
INTEGRATED POLYMER INDS INC
9741 Irvine Center Dr, Irvine (92618-4324)
PHONE...................................949 788-1050
Ergun Kirlikovali, *President*
Juliana Kirlikovali, *Vice Pres*
EMP: 50
SALES (est): 6.7MM **Privately Held**
SIC: 2891 Adhesives & sealants

(P-8877)
INTERNATIONAL COATINGS CO INC (PA)
13929 166th St, Cerritos (90703-2431)
PHONE...................................562 926-1010
Stephen W Kahane, *CEO*
Herbert A Wells, *Ch of Bd*
Janet Wells, *Treasurer*
Sonja Pulliam, *Office Mgr*
Mario Marquez, *Plant Mgr*
▲ EMP: 40
SQ FT: 50,000
SALES (est): 10.3MM **Privately Held**
WEB: www.iccink.com
SIC: 2891 2899 3555 2893 Adhesives;
ink or writing fluids; printing trades ma-
chinery; printing ink; paints & allied prod-
ucts; plastics materials & resins

(P-8878)
IPS CORPORATION (HQ)
Also Called: Weld-On Adhesives
455 W Victoria St, Compton (90220-6064)
PHONE...................................310 898-3300
Tracy Bilbrough, *CEO*
Will Barton, *CFO*
Gary Rosenfield, *Chief Mktg Ofcr*
Tsetso Stefanov, *Engineer*
Albert Paguio, *Finance Mgr*
◆ EMP: 180 EST: 1953
SQ FT: 22,000
SALES (est): 187.8MM
SALES (corp-wide): 30.9MM **Privately Held**
SIC: 2891 Adhesives, plastic; cement, ex-
cept linoleum & tile

(P-8879)
IPS CORPORATION
Also Called: Weldon Company
17110 S Main St, Gardena (90248-3128)
PHONE...................................310 516-7013
Eduardo Hernandez, *Branch Mgr*
EMP: 55
SALES (corp-wide): 30.9MM **Privately Held**
SIC: 2891 Adhesives
HQ: Ips Corporation
455 W Victoria St
Compton CA 90220
310 898-3300

(P-8880)
MASK-OFF COMPANY INC
345 W Maple Ave, Monrovia (91016-3331)
PHONE..................................626 303-8015
Steven B Sites, *President*
Dimitrianne Wood, *Admin Sec*
Jim Sites, *Director*
▲ **EMP:** 18 **EST:** 1950
SQ FT: 28,160
SALES (est): 4.6MM **Privately Held**
WEB: www.maskoff.com
SIC: 2891 Adhesives

(P-8881)
MITSUBISHI CHEMICAL CRBN FBR
1822 Reynolds Ave, Irvine (92614-5714)
PHONE..................................800 929-5471
Takashi Sasaki, *Vice Pres*
EMP: 110 **Privately Held**
SIC: 2891 5169 Adhesives; chemical additives
HQ: Mitsubishi Chemical Carbon Fiber And Composites, Inc.
5900 88th St
Sacramento CA 95828
-

(P-8882)
OATEY CO
6600 Smith Ave, Newark (94560-4220)
PHONE..................................800 321-9532
David Smith, *Branch Mgr*
EMP: 24
SALES (corp-wide): 470MM **Privately Held**
SIC: 2891 Cement, except linoleum & tile
PA: Oatey Co.
20600 Emerald Pkwy
Cleveland OH 44135
800 203-1155

(P-8883)
PACER TECHNOLOGY (HQ)
Also Called: Super Glue Corporation
3281 E Guasti Rd Ste 260, Ontario (91761-7642)
PHONE..................................909 987-0550
Ronald T Gravette, *Vice Pres*
Ron Gravette, *President*
E T Gravette, *CEO*
Kristine Wright, *CFO*
Steve Burger, *Vice Pres*
◆ **EMP:** 113
SQ FT: 47,700
SALES (est): 37MM
SALES (corp-wide): 19.3MM **Privately Held**
WEB: www.supergluecorp.com
SIC: 2891 3089 3085 Adhesives & sealants; plastic containers, except foam; plastics bottles
PA: Cyan Holding Corporation
9420 Santa Anita Ave
Rancho Cucamonga CA 91730
909 987-0550

(P-8884)
PACER TECHNOLOGY
11201 Jersey Blvd, Rancho Cucamonga (91730-5133)
PHONE..................................909 987-0550
Dale Drymon, *Manager*
EMP: 59
SALES (corp-wide): 19.3MM **Privately Held**
SIC: 2891 Adhesives & sealants
HQ: Pacer Technology
3281 E Guasti Rd Ste 260
Ontario CA 91761
909 987-0550

(P-8885)
PACKAGING SYSTEMS INC
26435 Summit Cir, Santa Clarita (91350-2991)
PHONE..................................661 253-5700
Raymond J Gray, *CEO*
Steve Gray, *President*
Patricia Gray, *Exec VP*
Marie Whitehead, *Accounting Mgr*
Gina Fuss, *QC Mgr*
▼ **EMP:** 42 **EST:** 1976
SQ FT: 25,700

SALES (est): 24.1MM **Privately Held**
WEB: www.pkgsys.net
SIC: 2891 Adhesives & sealants

(P-8886)
PLAS-TECH SEALING TECH LLC
252 Mariah Cir Fl 2, Corona (92879-1751)
PHONE..................................951 737-2228
Chad Miller, *Manager*
Charlotte Miller,
Craig Miller Sr,
Eve Miller,
▲ **EMP:** 35
SQ FT: 16,000
SALES (est): 4.9MM **Privately Held**
WEB: www.plastechsealing.com
SIC: 2891 Sealants

(P-8887)
PRC - DESOTO INTERNATIONAL INC (HQ)
Also Called: PPG Aerospace
24811 Ave Rockefeller, Valencia (91355-3468)
PHONE..................................661 678-4209
Michael H McGarry, *President*
Barry Gillespie, *CEO*
Ralph Dyba, *CFO*
Viktoras R Sekmakas, *Exec VP*
Frank S Sklarsky, *Exec VP*
▲ **EMP:** 320 **EST:** 1945
SQ FT: 200,000
SALES (est): 168.5MM
SALES (corp-wide): 15.3B **Publicly Held**
SIC: 2891 3089 Sealing compounds, synthetic rubber or plastic; adhesives; plastic containers, except foam
PA: Ppg Industries, Inc.
1 Ppg Pl
Pittsburgh PA 15272
412 434-3131

(P-8888)
PRC - DESOTO INTERNATIONAL INC
Also Called: PPG Aerospace
11601 United St, Mojave (93501-7048)
PHONE..................................661 824-4532
Dave Richardson, *Branch Mgr*
EMP: 130
SALES (corp-wide): 15.3B **Publicly Held**
SIC: 2891 Sealing compounds, synthetic rubber or plastic; adhesives
HQ: Prc - Desoto International, Inc.
24811 Ave Rockefeller
Valencia CA 91355
661 678-4209

(P-8889)
QSPAC INDUSTRIES INC (PA)
Also Called: Quality Service Pac Industry
15020 Marquardt Ave, Santa Fe Springs (90670-5704)
PHONE..................................562 407-3868
Jow-Lin Tang, *President*
Wu-Hsiung Chung, *CFO*
Gloria Chang, *Accountant*
Lisa Wang, *Human Res Mgr*
Annie Sung, *Purchasing*
◆ **EMP:** 80
SQ FT: 96,000
SALES (est): 42MM **Privately Held**
SIC: 2891 Adhesives

(P-8890)
RAYNGUARD PROTECTIVE MTLS INC
8280 14th Ave, Sacramento (95826-4719)
PHONE..................................916 454-2560
Gordon Rayner, *President*
Richard Rayner, *Vice Pres*
Twyla Whitson, *Accountant*
Dave Hartman, *Manager*
EMP: 13
SQ FT: 1,200
SALES (est): 8.5MM **Privately Held**
WEB: www.raynguard.com
SIC: 2891 Adhesives & sealants

(P-8891)
RELIABLE PACKAGING SYSTEMS INC
Also Called: Astro Packaging
1300 N Jefferson St, Anaheim (92807-1614)
PHONE..................................714 572-1094
Debra Lynn Dillon, *President*
Debra Dillon, *President*
Ryan Dillon, *Info Tech Mgr*
Ryan Davis, *Mktg Dir*
Herbert Arce, *Sales Staff*
EMP: 17
SQ FT: 5,500
SALES (est): 5.3MM **Privately Held**
WEB: www.astropackaging.com
SIC: 2891 3565 5084 5169 Adhesives & sealants; packaging machinery; packaging machinery & equipment; adhesives & sealants; consulting engineer

(P-8892)
RIVERSIDE LAMINATION CORP
3016 Kansas Ave Bldg 6, Riverside (92507-3456)
PHONE..................................951 682-0100
Theresa Santoro, *CEO*
Steve Hobbs, *Sales Mgr*
EMP: 14 **EST:** 2008
SALES (est): 5.1MM **Privately Held**
SIC: 2891 Laminating compounds

(P-8893)
ROYAL ADHESIVES & SEALANTS LLC
Also Called: Bacon Adhesives
16731 Hale Ave, Irvine (92606-5006)
PHONE..................................949 863-1499
Jeff Swindells, *Branch Mgr*
EMP: 12
SALES (corp-wide): 3B **Publicly Held**
SIC: 2891 2821 Adhesives, plastic; plasticizer/additive based plastic materials
HQ: Royal Adhesives And Sealants Llc
2001 W Washington St
South Bend IN 46628
574 246-5000

(P-8894)
SIGNATURE FLEXIBLE PACKG INC
5519 Jillson St, Commerce (90040-1420)
PHONE..................................323 887-1997
Adrian Backer, *President*
Jeff Sewel, *Vice Pres*
Kelly Redding, *Admin Sec*
Dennis White, *Plant Mgr*
▲ **EMP:** 82
SQ FT: 30,000
SALES (est): 18.9MM **Privately Held**
WEB: www.signatureflexible.com
SIC: 2891 2673 Adhesives & sealants; bags: plastic, laminated & coated

(P-8895)
STIC-ADHESIVE PRODUCTS CO INC
3950 Medford St, Los Angeles (90063-1675)
PHONE..................................323 268-2956
Junho Suh, *President*
Bong Suh, *Info Tech Mgr*
Christy Sandoval, *Manager*
EMP: 150
SQ FT: 75,000
SALES (est): 31.2MM **Privately Held**
WEB: www.sticadhesive.com
SIC: 2891 2851 Adhesives; paints & allied products

(P-8896)
SUPER GLUE CORPORATION
4970 Vanderbilt St, Ontario (91761-2202)
PHONE..................................909 987-0550
Richard Kay, *President*
Jan Baker, *Sales Mgr*
EMP: 10
SALES (corp-wide): 19.3MM **Privately Held**
SIC: 2891 3089 Adhesives & sealants; laminating of plastic
HQ: Pacer Technology
3281 E Guasti Rd Ste 260
Ontario CA 91761
909 987-0550

(P-8897)
TCK USA CORPORATION
2580 Corp Pl Ste F101, Monterey Park (91754)
P.O. Box 1190, Alhambra (91802-1190)
PHONE..................................323 269-2969
Wendy Chen, *President*
Frank Chen, *Vice Pres*
▲ **EMP:** 14
SQ FT: 5,000
SALES (est): 1.7MM **Privately Held**
WEB: www.tckgroup.com
SIC: 2891 Sealing compounds, synthetic rubber or plastic

(P-8898)
TECHNICOTE INC
1141 California Ave, Corona (92881-7233)
PHONE..................................951 372-0627
George Parker, *Manager*
EMP: 50
SQ FT: 2,000
SALES (corp-wide): 78.2MM **Privately Held**
WEB: www.technicote.com
SIC: 2891 2675 Adhesives; die-cut paper & board
PA: Technicote, Inc.
222 Mound Ave
Miamisburg OH 45342
800 358-4448

(P-8899)
TECHPRO SALES & SERVICE INC
3429 Cerritos Ave, Los Alamitos (90720-2107)
P.O. Box 1411 (90720-1411)
PHONE..................................562 594-7878
John D Distefano, *CEO*
EMP: 10 **EST:** 1999
SALES (est): 778K **Privately Held**
SIC: 2891 Sealing compounds, synthetic rubber or plastic

(P-8900)
TUFF - TOE INC
5443 E La Palma Ave, Anaheim (92807-2022)
PHONE..................................714 997-9585
Ryan Pribble, *President*
Victor Vasquez, *VP Opers*
Steve K Hill, *VP Mktg*
▲ **EMP:** 10
SQ FT: 1,800
SALES (est): 2.5MM **Privately Held**
WEB: www.tufftoe.com
SIC: 2891 3949 5091 Adhesives; sporting & athletic goods; sporting & recreation goods

(P-8901)
V HIMARK (USA) INC
Also Called: Cactus Tape
16019 E Foothill Blvd, Irwindale (91702-2813)
PHONE..................................626 305-5766
Charlie Huang, *President*
Cindy Wu, *Sales Mgr*
◆ **EMP:** 10
SQ FT: 12,000
SALES (est): 2.1MM **Privately Held**
WEB: www.vhimarkusa.com
SIC: 2891 Adhesives

(P-8902)
VARNI-LITE COATINGS ASSOCIATES
Also Called: Varni Lite
21595 Curtis St, Hayward (94545-1307)
PHONE..................................510 887-8997
Khosrow Sohrabi, *President*
Behrooz Sohrabi, *Vice Pres*
EMP: 10 **EST:** 1952
SQ FT: 24,000
SALES: 1.2MM **Privately Held**
SIC: 2891 Adhesives

P R O D U C T S & S V C S

2892 Explosives

(P-8903)
ALPHA DYNO NOBEL
Also Called: Alpha Explosives
1682 Sabovich St 30a, Mojave
(93501-1600)
P.O. Box 920 (93502-0920)
PHONE...................661 824-1356
Richard Cross, *Manager*
EMP: 17
SALES (corp-wide): 34MM **Privately Held**
WEB: www.alphaexplosives.com
SIC: 2892 5169 Explosives; explosives
PA: Alpha Dyno Nobel
3400 Nader Rd
Lincoln CA 95648
916 645-3377

(P-8904)
ENERGETIX SOLUTIONS INC
2601 Cherry Ln, Walnut Creek
(94597-2108)
PHONE...................925 926-6412
Alan Broca, *CEO*
Conrad K Wu, *Principal*
EMP: 12
SQ FT: 3,000
SALES (est): 1.8MM **Privately Held**
SIC: 2892 3629 Explosives; blasting machines, electrical

(P-8905)
MP ASSOCIATES INC
Also Called: M P A
6555 Jackson Valley Rd, Ione
(95640-9630)
P.O. Box 546 (95640-0546)
PHONE...................209 274-4715
Thaine Morris, *President*
David Pier, *Treasurer*
Joel Baechle, *Director*
▲ **EMP:** 170
SQ FT: 3,112
SALES (est): 32.7MM **Privately Held**
WEB: www.mpassociates.com
SIC: 2892 2899 Explosives; pyrotechnic ammunition: flares, signals, rockets, etc.

(P-8906)
OWEN OIL TOOLS INC
5001 Standard St, Bakersfield
(93308-4500)
PHONE...................661 637-1380
Frank Isbell, *Manager*
EMP: 34
SALES (corp-wide): 700.8MM **Privately Held**
SIC: 2892 Explosives
HQ: Owen Oil Tools Lp
12001 County Road 1000
Godley TX 76044
817 551-0540

(P-8907)
TELEDYNE RISI INC (HQ)
32727 W Corral Hollow Rd, Tracy (95376)
P.O. Box 359 (95378-0359)
PHONE...................925 456-9700
Al Pichelli, *CEO*
Susan Stowe, *IT/INT Sup*
James Varosh, *Marketing Staff*
EMP: 21
SQ FT: 5,000
SALES: 22MM
SALES (corp-wide): 2.9B **Publicly Held**
WEB: www.teledynereynolds.com
SIC: 2892 Explosives
PA: Teledyne Technologies Inc
1049 Camino Dos Rios
Thousand Oaks CA 91360
805 373-4545

(P-8908)
W A MURPHY INC
26550 National Trails Hwy, Helendale
(92342-9605)
PHONE...................760 245-8711
Sid Perry, *Manager*
EMP: 14
SQ FT: 2,000
SALES (corp-wide): 5.9MM **Privately Held**
WEB: www.murphypowder.com
SIC: 2892 Black powder (explosive)
PA: W. A. Murphy, Inc.
4144 Arden Dr
El Monte CA 91731
626 444-9271

2893 Printing Ink

(P-8909)
AN ENVIRONMENTAL INKS
Also Called: Environmental Inks & Coatings
1920 S Quaker Ridge Pl, Ontario
(91761-8041)
PHONE...................909 930-9656
Paul Holmes, *Regional Mgr*
EMP: 10
SALES (corp-wide): 940.5K **Privately Held**
SIC: 2893 2899 Printing ink; ink or writing fluids
HQ: Environmental Inks And Coatings Canada Ltd.
1 Quality Products Rd
Morganton NC 28655
828 433-1922

(P-8910)
BOMARK INC
601 S 6th Ave, La Puente (91746-3026)
PHONE...................626 968-1666
Herman R Schowe Jr, *Ch of Bd*
H Mark Schowe, *COO*
Kathie Virgil, *CFO*
EMP: 25
SQ FT: 21,000
SALES (est): 5.8MM **Privately Held**
WEB: www.bomarkinks.com
SIC: 2893 Printing ink

(P-8911)
DIVERSFIED NANO SOLUTIONS CORP
10531 4s Commons Dr, San Diego
(92127-3517)
PHONE...................858 924-1017
Srinivasa Deshiikan, *President*
EMP: 50
SQ FT: 1,000
SALES (est): 2MM **Privately Held**
SIC: 2893 Printing ink

(P-8912)
EPIC PRINTING INK CORP
233 Pioneer Pl, Pomona (91768-3255)
PHONE...................909 598-6771
Tim Bradley, *President*
Jeremy Bradley, *Manager*
▼ **EMP:** 15
SQ FT: 7,300
SALES: 3MM
SIC: 2893 2891 2851 Printing ink; laminating compounds; epoxy coatings; polyurethane coatings

(P-8913)
FARBOTECH COLOR INC
Also Called: K & E Printing Ink
1630 Yeager Ave, La Verne (91750-5853)
PHONE...................909 596-9330
Edd Butch, *President*
Fiona Cummings, *Vice Pres*
▲ **EMP:** 15
SQ FT: 15,000
SALES (est): 2.5MM **Privately Held**
SIC: 2893 Printing ink

(P-8914)
FLEXO-TECHNOLOGIES INC
145 Flowerfield Ln, La Habra Heights
(90631-8446)
PHONE...................626 444-2595
Helnut Eric Braun, *President*
EMP: 20 **EST:** 2001
SQ FT: 50,000
SALES: 7MM **Privately Held**
SIC: 2893 8742 Printing ink; management consulting services

(P-8915)
FLINT GROUP US LLC
Also Called: Flint Ink North America Div
650 Tamarack Ave Apt 1502, Brea
(92821-3229)
PHONE...................626 369-6900
Tom Stokes, *Manager*
Brandon Ivey, *Finance Mgr*
Nathan Perry, *Buyer*
EMP: 45
SALES (corp-wide): 177.9K **Privately Held**
WEB: www.flintink.com
SIC: 2893 5085 2899 Printing ink; ink, printers'; ink or writing fluids
HQ: Flint Group Us Llc
17177 N Laurel Park Dr # 300
Livonia MI 48152
734 781-4600

(P-8916)
FLINT GROUP US LLC
14930 Marquardt Ave, Santa Fe Springs
(90670-5129)
P.O. Box 2606 (90670-0606)
PHONE...................562 903-7976
Larry Shanks, *Branch Mgr*
EMP: 19
SALES (corp-wide): 177.9K **Privately Held**
WEB: www.flintink.com
SIC: 2893 Printing ink
HQ: Flint Group Us Llc
17177 N Laurel Park Dr # 300
Livonia MI 48152
734 781-4600

(P-8917)
GANS INK AND SUPPLY CO INC (PA)
1441 Boyd St, Los Angeles (90033-3790)
P.O. Box 33806 (90033-0806)
PHONE...................323 264-2200
Jeffrey Koppelman, *President*
Mike Fanton, *Branch Mgr*
Thomas Debartolo, *Division Mgr*
Liz Koppelman, *Admin Sec*
Chad Koppelman, *Technician*
◆ **EMP:** 50
SQ FT: 28,000
SALES (est): 21.8MM **Privately Held**
WEB: www.gansink.com
SIC: 2893 Printing ink

(P-8918)
GRAPHIC SCIENCES INC
4663 E Guasti Rd Ste B, Ontario
(91761-8196)
PHONE...................909 947-3366
Daniel Ramos, *Branch Mgr*
EMP: 15
SALES (corp-wide): 7.7MM **Privately Held**
SIC: 2893 Printing ink
PA: Graphic Sciences, Inc.
7515 Ne Ambassador Pl L
Portland OR 97220

(P-8919)
HADDADS FINE ARTS INC
3855 E Miraloma Ave, Anaheim
(92806-2124)
PHONE...................714 996-2100
Paula Haddad, *President*
Silvina Bates, *Sales Staff*
EMP: 15
SQ FT: 17,000
SALES (est): 2.6MM **Privately Held**
WEB: www.haddadsfinearts.com
SIC: 2893 Lithographic ink

(P-8920)
INK 2000 CORP
19875 Nordhoff St, Northridge
(91324-3331)
PHONE...................818 882-0168
Sheefang Yu, *President*
Kelvin Yu, *Director*
▲ **EMP:** 10
SQ FT: 5,000
SALES (est): 1.2MM **Privately Held**
WEB: www.ink2000.com
SIC: 2893 Printing ink

(P-8921)
INK MAKERS INC
2121 Yates Ave, Commerce (90040-1911)
PHONE...................323 728-7500
EMP: 15
SQ FT: 15,000
SALES: 1.7MM **Privately Held**
SIC: 2893

(P-8922)
INKJETMADNESSCOM INC
Also Called: Inkgrabber.com
2205 1st St Ste 103, Simi Valley
(93065-1981)
PHONE...................805 583-7755
Keith Ramirez, *President*
Brandon Timar, *Manager*
▲ **EMP:** 16
SALES (est): 3.4MM **Privately Held**
WEB: www.inkjetmadness.com
SIC: 2893 Printing ink

(P-8923)
INX INTERNATIONAL INK CO
Also Called: INX Digital Intl
2125 Williams St, San Leandro
(94577-3224)
PHONE...................510 895-8001
Micol Kranz, *Sales/Mktg Mgr*
EMP: 17 **Privately Held**
SIC: 2893 Printing ink
HQ: Inx International Ink Co.
150 N Martingale Rd # 700
Schaumburg IL 60173
630 382-1800

(P-8924)
INX INTERNATIONAL INK CO
13821 Marquardt Ave, Santa Fe Springs
(90670-5016)
PHONE...................562 404-5664
Elvis Tran, *Manager*
EMP: 12 **Privately Held**
SIC: 2893 2899 Gravure ink; ink or writing fluids
HQ: Inx International Ink Co.
150 N Martingale Rd # 700
Schaumburg IL 60173
630 382-1800

(P-8925)
INX INTERNATIONAL INK CO
1000 Business Park Dr, Dixon
(95620-4310)
PHONE...................707 693-2990
EMP: 12 **Privately Held**
SIC: 2893 Printing ink
HQ: Inx International Ink Co.
150 N Martingale Rd # 700
Schaumburg IL 60173
630 382-1800

(P-8926)
KUPRION INC
4425 Fortran Dr, San Jose (95134-2300)
PHONE...................650 223-1600
Nicholas Antonopoulos, *CEO*
Alfred Zinn, *President*
EMP: 32
SALES (est): 3.2MM **Privately Held**
SIC: 2893 Printing ink

(P-8927)
MERIT PRINTING INK COMPANY
1451 S Lorena St, Los Angeles
(90023-3718)
PHONE...................323 268-1807
Donald W Pettijohn, *President*
Nancy B Pettijohn, *Vice Pres*
EMP: 12 **EST:** 1962
SQ FT: 8,000
SALES (est): 1.5MM **Privately Held**
SIC: 2893 Printing ink

(P-8928)
PROCOLORFLEX INK CORP
3588 Arden Rd, Hayward (94545-3921)
PHONE...................510 293-3033
Jack Donelly, *CEO*
Rick Duarte, *President*
Abraham Cervera, *Manager*
EMP: 12
SALES (est): 2.7MM **Privately Held**
WEB: www.procolorflex.com
SIC: 2893 Printing ink

▲ = Import ▼=Export
◆ =Import/Export

(P-8929)
SELECT OFFICE SYSTEMS INC
1811 W Magnolia Blvd, Burbank
(91506-1725)
P.O. Box 11777 (91510-1777)
PHONE.................................818 861-8320
Andrew Hunter Rouse, *CEO*
EMP: 17
SALES (est): 2.8MM **Privately Held**
SIC: 2893 Printing ink

(P-8930)
SIEGWERK USA INC
871 Cotting Ct Ste H, Vacaville
(95688-9399)
PHONE.................................707 469-7648
Jason Wood, *Manager*
EMP: 29
SALES (corp-wide): 940.5K **Privately Held**
WEB: www.sipana.com
SIC: 2893 Printing ink
HQ: Siegwerk Usa Inc.
3535 Sw 56th St
Des Moines IA 50321
515 471-2100

(P-8931)
SUN CHEMICAL CORPORATION
G P I
120 Mason Cir, Concord (94520-1214)
PHONE.................................925 695-2601
Ted Clinton, *Manager*
EMP: 10 **Privately Held**
WEB: www.sunchemical.com
SIC: 2893 Printing ink
HQ: Sun Chemical Corporation
35 Waterview Blvd Ste 100
Parsippany NJ 07054
973 404-6000

(P-8932)
SUN CHEMICAL CORPORATION
General Printing Ink Division
12963 Park St, Santa Fe Springs
(90670-4083)
PHONE.................................562 946-2327
Paul Stack, *Manager*
Ezequiel Fioriti, *IT/INT Sup*
Grizelda Sullivan, *Controller*
Mike Mena, *Plant Mgr*
EMP: 40 **Privately Held**
WEB: www.sunchemical.com
SIC: 2893 5084 Printing ink; printing trades machinery, equipment & supplies
HQ: Sun Chemical Corporation
35 Waterview Blvd Ste 100
Parsippany NJ 07054
973 404-6000

(P-8933)
SUN CHEMICAL CORPORATION
1599 Factor Ave, San Leandro
(94577-5630)
PHONE.................................510 618-1302
Tom Philis, *Branch Mgr*
Brian Zylka, *Human Resources*
EMP: 25 **Privately Held**
WEB: www.sunchemical.com
SIC: 2893 Printing ink
HQ: Sun Chemical Corporation
35 Waterview Blvd Ste 100
Parsippany NJ 07054
973 404-6000

(P-8934)
TMA LASER GROUP INC
41656 Big Bear Blvd Ste 4, Big Bear City
(92314)
P.O. Box 1628 (92314-1628)
PHONE.................................310 421-0550
Thomas Marcel, *President*
EMP: 10 **EST:** 2011
SQ FT: 1,800
SALES: 1.2MM **Privately Held**
SIC: 2893 Printing ink

(P-8935)
TOYO INK INTERNATIONAL CORP
Also Called: Toyo Ink North America
11190 Valley View St, Cypress
(90630-5231)
PHONE.................................714 899-2377
Horacio Acosta, *Branch Mgr*
Nicole Hernandez, *Admin Asst*

Rachel Belpedio, *Cust Mgr*
EMP: 23 **Privately Held**
WEB: www.toyoink.com
SIC: 2893 5085 2899 Printing ink; industrial supplies; chemical preparations
HQ: Toyo Ink International Corp
1225 N Michael Dr
Wood Dale IL 60191

(P-8936)
UVEXS INCORPORATED
1287 Hammerwood Ave, Sunnyvale
(94089-2231)
P.O. Box 1407, North Bend OR (97459-0089)
PHONE.................................408 734-4402
Brent Puder, *President*
Dorthy Puder, *Shareholder*
Carol Toman, *CPA*
EMP: 14
SQ FT: 13,500
SALES (est): 2.9MM **Privately Held**
WEB: www.uvexs.com
SIC: 2893 5084 Letterpress or offset ink; lithographic ink; screen process ink; printing trades machinery, equipment & supplies

(P-8937)
WESTCOAST INKSOLUTIONS LLC
5928 Garfield Ave, Commerce
(90040-3607)
PHONE.................................323 726-8100
John P Jilek Jr, *Opers Mgr*
Dan Delegge,
EMP: 15
SQ FT: 42,000
SALES: 3.5MM
SALES (corp-wide): 6MM **Privately Held**
WEB: www.inksolutions.com
SIC: 2893 2851 Printing ink; paints & allied products
PA: Ink Solutions, Llc
800 Estes Ave
Elk Grove Village IL 60007
847 593-5200

(P-8938)
WIKOFF COLOR CORPORATION
1329 N Market Blvd # 160, Sacramento
(95834-2960)
PHONE.................................916 928-6965
Geoffrey Peters, *Branch Mgr*
EMP: 10
SALES (corp-wide): 145.1MM **Privately Held**
SIC: 2893 Printing ink
PA: Wikoff Color Corporation
1886 Merritt Rd
Fort Mill SC 29715
803 548-2210

(P-8939)
X TRI INC
8787 Plata Ln Ste 7, Atascadero
(93422-5395)
PHONE.................................805 286-4544
Anthony Foley, *Principal*
Laura Lynn Foley, *Principal*
EMP: 11
SALES (est): 1.7MM **Privately Held**
SIC: 2893 Printing ink

2895 Carbon Black

(P-8940)
ALDILA MATERIALS TECHNOLOGY (DH)
13450 Stowe Dr, Poway (92064-6860)
PHONE.................................858 513-1801
Pete Matthewson, *President*
▼ **EMP:** 33 **EST:** 1997
SALES (est): 21.4MM **Privately Held**
WEB: www.aldila.com
SIC: 2895 Carbon black
HQ: Aldila, Inc.
1945 Kellogg Ave
Carlsbad CA 92008
858 513-1801

2899 Chemical Preparations, NEC

(P-8941)
AMERICAN CONSUMER PRODUCTS LLC
2845 E 26th St, Vernon (90058-8032)
PHONE.................................310 443-3330
David Molayen, *President*
Kam Jahanbigloo, *Vice Pres*
Daryoosh Molayem, *Managing Dir*
◆ **EMP:** 22
SALES (est): 10.3MM
SALES (corp-wide): 37.9MM **Privately Held**
WEB: www.acillc.com
SIC: 2899 2844 2834 Chemical preparations; cosmetic preparations; pharmaceutical preparations
PA: Tabletops Unlimited, Inc.
23000 Avalon Blvd
Carson CA 90745
310 549-6000

(P-8942)
AMERICAN QUALEX INTERNATIONAL
920a Calle Negocio Ste A, San Clemente
(92673-6201)
PHONE.................................949 492-8298
Dan Moothart, *President*
EMP: 10
SALES (est): 770K **Privately Held**
SIC: 2899 Chemical preparations

(P-8943)
AVISTA TECHNOLOGIES INC
140 Bosstick Blvd, San Marcos
(92069-5930)
PHONE.................................760 744-0536
David Walker, *President*
Karen Lindsey, *CFO*
Dan Comstock, *Vice Pres*
Nagham Najeeb, *Engineer*
Naomi Rueth, *Mktg Coord*
▼ **EMP:** 19 **EST:** 1999
SQ FT: 15,500
SALES (est): 5.9MM **Privately Held**
WEB: www.avistatech.com
SIC: 2899 Chemical supplies for foundries; water treating compounds
PA: Avista Technologies (Uk) Ltd.
13 Nasmyth Square
Livingston
131 449-6677

(P-8944)
CADE CORPORATION
609 Deep Valley Dr, Rllng HLS Est
(90274-3629)
PHONE.................................310 539-2508
Norman Angell, *President*
Rozann Stenshoel, *CFO*
Ken Keeth, *Technical Staff*
Tony Dominguez, *Controller*
Natalie Sanchez, *Purch Agent*
EMP: 61
SQ FT: 25,000
SALES: 8MM **Privately Held**
WEB: www.cadeco.com
SIC: 2899 Waterproofing compounds

(P-8945)
CALIFORNIA RESPIRATORY CARE
16055 Ventura Blvd # 715, Encino
(91436-2601)
PHONE.................................818 379-9999
Efy Lavaei, *President*
EMP: 55
SALES (est): 4.1MM **Privately Held**
SIC: 2899 5047 5169 Chemical preparations; medical & hospital equipment; oxygen

(P-8946)
CHEMDIV INC
Also Called: Chemical Diversity Labs
12760 High Bluff Dr # 370, San Diego
(92130-3065)
PHONE.................................858 794-4860
Nikolay P Savchuk, *CEO*
A Ivachtchenko, *Chairman*

Ron Demuth, *Senior VP*
Vadim Bichko, *Vice Pres*
Oleg Korzinov, *Vice Pres*
EMP: 50 **EST:** 1995
SQ FT: 19,000
SALES (est): 16.7MM **Privately Held**
WEB: www.chemdiv.com
SIC: 2899 Chemical preparations

(P-8947)
CHEMICALS INCORPORATED
13560 Colombard Ct, Fontana
(92337-7702)
PHONE.................................951 681-9697
Earl Harper, *CEO*
Herbert N Long, *President*
Anthony Carter, *Vice Pres*
George Burke, *Manager*
Vu Nguyen, *Manager*
▲ **EMP:** 15
SQ FT: 64,000
SALES (est): 3.9MM **Privately Held**
WEB: www.cheminc.com
SIC: 2899 Water treating compounds
PA: Harpure Enterprises, Inc.
13560 Colombard Ct
Fontana CA 92337

(P-8948)
CHEMTREAT INC
Also Called: Trident Technologies
8885 Rehco Rd, San Diego (92121-3261)
PHONE.................................804 935-2000
EMP: 23
SALES (corp-wide): 19.8B **Publicly Held**
SIC: 2899 Water treating compounds
HQ: Chemtreat, Inc.
5640 Cox Rd Ste 300
Glen Allen VA 23060
804 935-2000

(P-8949)
CHEVRON ORONITE COMPANY LLC (DH)
6001 Bollinger Canyon Rd, San Ramon
(94583-5737)
PHONE.................................713 432-2500
Desmond King, *President*
Rich Conway, *CFO*
Andrew Busby, *Design Engr*
Marshall Mahoney, *Engrg Dir*
Frank Oliveri, *Project Mgr*
◆ **EMP:** 50
SALES (est): 340MM
SALES (corp-wide): 166.3B **Publicly Held**
SIC: 2899 2869 1311 2821 Chemical preparations; industrial organic chemicals; crude petroleum & natural gas; polystyrene resins
HQ: Chevron U.S.A. Inc.
6001 Bollinger Canyon Rd D1248
San Ramon CA 94583
925 842-1000

(P-8950)
CHOSEN FOODS LLC (PA)
1747 Hancock St Ste A, San Diego
(92101-1130)
PHONE.................................877 674-2244
Gabriel Perez-Krieb, *Ch of Bd*
Alisa Hilton, *Administration*
Ashley Blackstock, *Accounting Mgr*
Carolina Salas, *Accountant*
Ana Macias, *Controller*
▼ **EMP:** 15
SQ FT: 8,000
SALES (est): 6MM **Privately Held**
SIC: 2899 Essential oils

(P-8951)
CONTRABAND CONTROL SPECIALISTS
Also Called: Zee Consulting
26 H St, Bakersfield (93304-2908)
P.O. Box 2365 (93303-2365)
PHONE.................................661 322-3363
Gary Zvirblis, *President*
Moriah Mendenhall, *Opers Staff*
EMP: 15
SALES (est): 2.2MM **Privately Held**
WEB: www.contrabandcontrol.com
SIC: 2899

PRODUCTS & SVCS

(P-8952)
COPPER HARBOR COMPANY INC
2300 Davis St, San Leandro (94577-2206)
PHONE....................................510 639-4670
Daniel Walters, *President*
EMP: 16 EST: 1997
SQ FT: 18,000
SALES: 2MM **Privately Held**
WEB: www.copperharbor.com
SIC: 2899 2865 2911 Chemical supplies for foundries; solvent naphtha; solvents

(P-8953)
CP KELCO US INC
2025 Harbor Dr, San Diego (92113-2214)
PHONE....................................858 467-6542
Andrew Currie, *Manager*
EMP: 30
SALES (corp-wide): 862.4MM **Privately Held**
WEB: www.cpkelco.com
SIC: 2899 Sizes
HQ: Cp Kelco U.S., Inc.
    3100 Cumberland Blvd Se # 600
    Atlanta GA 30339
    678 247-7300

(P-8954)
CP KELCO US INC
8355 Aero Dr, San Diego (92123-1718)
P.O. Box 23576 (92123)
PHONE....................................858 292-4900
Greg Courney, *Manager*
EMP: 20
SALES (corp-wide): 862.4MM **Privately Held**
WEB: www.cpkelco.com
SIC: 2899 Sizes
HQ: Cp Kelco U.S., Inc.
    3100 Cumberland Blvd Se # 600
    Atlanta GA 30339
    678 247-7300

(P-8955)
CP KELCO US INC
8225 Aero Dr, San Diego (92123-1716)
PHONE....................................858 292-4900
Doug Wilson, *Technology*
Gregory S Faulk, *Technical Staff*
Sharath Golla, *Opers Mgr*
Stefanie Chmura, *Director*
Sarah Wong, *Manager*
EMP: 14 EST: 2016
SALES (est): 1.1MM **Privately Held**
SIC: 2899 Chemical preparations

(P-8956)
CUTWATER SPIRITS LLC
9750 Distribution Ave, San Diego (92121-2310)
PHONE....................................858 672-3848
Guadalupe De La Cruz, *Finance*
EMP: 42
SALES (est): 10.9MM **Privately Held**
SIC: 2899 Distilled water

(P-8957)
DANNIER CHEMICAL INC
2302 Martin Ste 450, Irvine (92612-7401)
PHONE....................................949 221-8660
Daniel Shen, *President*
▲ EMP: 25 EST: 1992
SALES (est): 3.7MM **Privately Held**
WEB: www.dannier.com
SIC: 2899 2869 2833 Chemical preparations; antioxidants, rubber processing: cyclic or acyclic; high purity grade chemicals, organic; laboratory chemicals, organic; organic medicinal chemicals: bulk, uncompounded

(P-8958)
DIAMON FUSION INTL INC
9361 Irvine Blvd, Irvine (92618-1669)
PHONE....................................949 388-8000
Adam Zax, *President*
Russell Slaybaugh, *Vice Pres*
Ana Zax, *Export Mgr*
Syndi Sim, *Marketing Staff*
Dacia Lindner, *Mktg Coord*
EMP: 16
SQ FT: 4,500
SALES (est): 4.3MM **Privately Held**
WEB: www.diamonfusion.com
SIC: 2899 6794 Chemical preparations; patent owners & lessors

(P-8959)
DRYVIT SYSTEMS INC
354 S Acacia St, Woodlake (93286-1644)
PHONE....................................559 564-3591
Dan Smith, *Manager*
EMP: 25
SQ FT: 20,000
SALES (corp-wide): 5.5B **Publicly Held**
WEB: www.dryvitcompanystore.com
SIC: 2899 Chemical preparations
HQ: Dryvit Systems, Inc.
    1 Energy Way
    West Warwick RI 02893
    401 822-4100

(P-8960)
DURA-CHEM INC
18327 Pasadena St, Lake Elsinore (92530-2766)
PHONE....................................951 245-7778
John Hassell, *President*
Allen Bass, *Vice Pres*
Kay Hassell, *Vice Pres*
William Fruscella, *Manager*
EMP: 10 EST: 1977
SQ FT: 6,000
SALES (est): 1.7MM **Privately Held**
WEB: www.thermobond3.com
SIC: 2899 2992 Chemical preparations; lubricating oils

(P-8961)
E W SMITH CHEMICAL CO
4738 Murietta St, Chino (91710-5182)
PHONE....................................909 590-9717
Robert D Cartwright, *President*
Gayle Lewis, *Admin Sec*
EMP: 12
SQ FT: 12,528
SALES (est): 2.2MM **Privately Held**
SIC: 2899 2842 Water treating compounds; specialty cleaning, polishes & sanitation goods

(P-8962)
EKC TECHNOLOGY INC (DH)
Also Called: E K C Technology/Burmar Chem
2520 Barrington Ct, Hayward (94545-1163)
PHONE....................................510 784-9105
Douglas J Holmes, *CEO*
Seng Wui Lim, *President*
John Odom, *President*
Thomas M Connelly Jr, *Exec VP*
David G Bills, *Senior VP*
◆ EMP: 115 EST: 1963
SQ FT: 65,000
SALES (est): 37.4MM
SALES (corp-wide): 30.6B **Publicly Held**
WEB: www.ekctech.com
SIC: 2899 Chemical preparations
HQ: E. I. Du Pont De Nemours And Company
    974 Centre Rd Bldg 735
    Wilmington DE 19805
    302 485-3000

(P-8963)
ENOVA SOLUTIONS INC
3553 Landco Dr Ste B, Bakersfield (93308-6169)
P.O. Box 21988 (93390-1988)
PHONE....................................661 327-2405
Richard Dyer, *President*
Jesse Holman, *Treasurer*
Jodi Hale, *Office Mgr*
Michael Ripley, *Admin Sec*
EMP: 13
SALES (est): 2.7MM **Privately Held**
SIC: 2899 Oil treating compounds

(P-8964)
EUREKA CHEMICAL COMPANY (PA)
234 Lawrence Ave, South San Francisco (94080-6863)
P.O. Box 2205 (94083-2205)
PHONE....................................650 873-5374
Genevieve E Hess, *CEO*
D Tom Stanton, *President*
Jeff Wilson, *Vice Pres*
Marie Oxoby, *Accountant*
◆ EMP: 10
SQ FT: 16,000
SALES (est): 1.4MM **Privately Held**
WEB: www.eurekafluidfilm.com
SIC: 2899 Corrosion preventive lubricant

(P-8965)
EVERSPRING CHEMICAL INC
11577 W Olympic Blvd, Los Angeles (90064-1522)
PHONE....................................310 707-1600
Marvin Lai, *CEO*
▲ EMP: 75
SQ FT: 2,000
SALES (est): 10.2MM **Privately Held**
SIC: 2899 Chemical preparations

(P-8966)
EVONIK CORPORATION
Also Called: Air Products
3305 E 26th St, Vernon (90058-4101)
PHONE....................................323 264-0311
William Ayacha, *Branch Mgr*
EMP: 40
SALES (corp-wide): 2.6B **Privately Held**
WEB: www.airproducts.com
SIC: 2899 2891 2821 Chemical preparations; adhesives & sealants; plastics materials & resins
HQ: Evonik Corporation
    299 Jefferson Rd
    Parsippany NJ 07054
    973 929-8000

(P-8967)
FLAMEMASTER CORPORATION
Also Called: Chemseal
13576 Desmond St, Pacoima (91331-2315)
P.O. Box 4510 (91333-4500)
PHONE....................................818 890-1401
Joseph Mazin, *CEO*
Mary Kay Eason, *Treasurer*
Gary Sokol, *Prdtn Mgr*
▲ EMP: 28
SALES (est): 4.3MM **Privately Held**
WEB: www.flamemaster.com
SIC: 2899 2819 1799 2891 Fire retardant chemicals; industrial inorganic chemicals; coating of metal structures at construction site; sealing compounds, synthetic rubber or plastic

(P-8968)
FUJIFILM ULTRA PURE SLTONS INC (DH)
11225 Commercial Pkwy, Castroville (95012-3205)
PHONE....................................831 632-2120
Christopher Fitzjohn, *President*
Mike Doi, *Treasurer*
Bill Robb, *Vice Pres*
Sherman Stever, *Vice Pres*
Benjamin Carr, *Engineer*
▲ EMP: 20
SALES (est): 21.8MM **Privately Held**
WEB: www.ultrapuresolutions.net
SIC: 2899 Chemical preparations
HQ: Fujifilm Electronic Materials U.S.A., Inc.
    80 Circuit Dr
    North Kingstown RI 02852
    401 522-9499

(P-8969)
GARRATT-CALLAHAN COMPANY (PA)
50 Ingold Rd, Burlingame (94010-2206)
PHONE....................................650 697-5811
Jeffrey L Garratt, *CEO*
Matthew Colvin, *CFO*
Matthew R Garratt, *Exec VP*
Steve Sauer, *Business Mgr*
Reema Rios, *Human Res Mgr*
EMP: 40 EST: 1904
SQ FT: 60,000
SALES (est): 69.4MM **Privately Held**
WEB: www.g-c.com
SIC: 2899 2911 Water treating compounds; oils, lubricating

(P-8970)
GENERAL GRAPHIC CHEMICALS CO
2525 Mandela Pkwy Ste 2, Oakland (94607-1722)
P.O. Box 24472 (94623-1472)
PHONE....................................510 832-4404
Andrew Greenberg, *President*
Bruce Greenberg, *President*
▲ EMP: 17
SQ FT: 14,000
SALES (est): 2.5MM **Privately Held**
WEB: www.generalgraphic.com
SIC: 2899 Chemical preparations

(P-8971)
GGTW LLC
Also Called: South Bay Salt Works
1470 Bay Blvd, Chula Vista (91911-3942)
PHONE....................................619 423-3388
Glenn Warner, *Owner*
Tracy Strahl, *Principal*
▼ EMP: 20
SALES (est): 3.9MM **Privately Held**
SIC: 2899 Salt

(P-8972)
HAIR SYNDICUT
565 N Central Ave, Upland (91786-4241)
PHONE....................................909 946-3200
Cindy Allen, *Owner*
EMP: 15
SALES (est): 1MM **Privately Held**
WEB: www.hairsyndicut.com
SIC: 2899 Chemical preparations

(P-8973)
HEMOSURE INC
5358 Irwindale Ave, Baldwin Park (91706-2086)
PHONE....................................888 436-6787
Dr John Wan, *President*
Sherry Wang, *Human Res Mgr*
EMP: 40
SALES (est): 14.8MM **Privately Held**
WEB: www.whpm.com
SIC: 2899 3841 Chemical preparations; surgical & medical instruments
PA: W.H.P.M. Inc.
    5358 Irwindale Ave
    Irwindale CA 91706
    626 443-8480

(P-8974)
HK ENTERPRISE GROUP INC
Also Called: Hawaii Kai
6540 Lusk Blvd Ste C270, San Diego (92121-2783)
PHONE....................................858 652-4400
George Joseph, *CEO*
EMP: 10
SALES (est): 675.9K **Privately Held**
SIC: 2899 Salt

(P-8975)
HYDRANAUTICS (DH)
401 Jones Rd, Oceanside (92058-1216)
PHONE....................................760 901-2597
Brett Andrews, *CEO*
Upen Bharwada, *COO*
Ellen Class, *Vice Pres*
Michael Concannon, *Vice Pres*
Norio Ikeyama, *Vice Pres*
◆ EMP: 400
SQ FT: 150,000
SALES (est): 120.1MM **Privately Held**
WEB: www.hydranautics.com
SIC: 2899 3589 Chemical preparations; water treatment equipment, industrial
HQ: Nitto Americas, Inc.
    48500 Fremont Blvd
    Fremont CA 94538
    510 445-5400

(P-8976)
HYDRITE CHEMICAL CO
1603 Clancy Ct, Visalia (93291-9253)
PHONE....................................559 651-3450
Steve Reid, *Manager*
EMP: 25
SALES (corp-wide): 686.3MM **Privately Held**
SIC: 2899 Chemical preparations

▲ = Import ▼=Export
◆ =Import/Export

PA: Hydrite Chemical Co.
300 N Patrick Blvd Fl 2
Brookfield WI 53045
262 792-1450

(P-8977)
IL HELTH BUTY NATURAL OILS INC
Also Called: Hbno
322 N Aviador St, Camarillo (93010-8302)
PHONE....................805 384-0473
Josef Demangeat, *CEO*
Marco A Frausto, *Principal*
EMP: 50
SALES (est): 2MM **Privately Held**
SIC: 2899 2836 Essential oils; extracts

(P-8978)
INDEPENDENT INK INC
13700 S Gramac Pl, Gardena (90249)
PHONE....................310 523-4657
Ramesh Sudbraram, *Manager*
EMP: 24
SALES (corp-wide): 3.5MM **Privately Held**
WEB: www.independentink.com
SIC: 2899 Ink or writing fluids
PA: Independent Ink, Inc.
13700 Gramercy Pl
Gardena CA 90249
310 523-4657

(P-8979)
INDIO PRODUCTS INC
Cultural Heritage Candle Co
5331 E Slauson Ave, Commerce (90040-2916)
PHONE....................323 720-9117
Marty Mayer, *Owner*
Olivia Luengas, *Human Res Mgr*
Anna Riva, *Products*
EMP: 33
SALES (corp-wide): 101.8MM **Privately Held**
WEB: www.indioproducts.com
SIC: 2899 3999 5199 5049 Incense; candles; candles; religious supplies
PA: Indio Products, Inc.
12910 Mulberry Dr Unit A
Whittier CA 90602
323 720-1188

(P-8980)
INSULTECH LLC (PA)
3530 W Garry Ave, Santa Ana (92704-6423)
PHONE....................714 384-0506
Lisa Romero, *Mng Member*
Michael Markantonis, *Vice Pres*
Sarah Bantay, *Executive*
Alex Martinez, *Design Engr*
Joe Kersey, *Engineer*
▲ **EMP:** 75
SQ FT: 30,000
SALES (est): 17.3MM **Privately Held**
SIC: 2899 Insulating compounds

(P-8981)
INTEGRITY SUPPORT SERVICES INC
Also Called: Employment Screening Resources
7110 Redwood Blvd Ste C, Novato (94945-4141)
PHONE....................415 898-0044
Lester S Rosen, *President*
Jessica Martelle, *Opers Mgr*
Bruce Guerra, *Opers Staff*
Katie Mahoney, *Opers Staff*
Andrew Church, *Production*
EMP: 10
SALES (est): 2.2MM **Privately Held**
WEB: www.esrcheck.com
SIC: 2899 7323 7375 8742 ; credit reporting services; information retrieval services; human resource consulting services

(P-8982)
K2 PURE SOLUTIONS NOCAL LP
950 Loveridge Rd, Pittsburg (94565-2808)
PHONE....................647 776-0273
Chris McLean, *Partner*
Rosemary Aldrich, *Partner*

Rochelle Aquino, *Partner*
Lella Rosati, *Executive Asst*
EMP: 21
SALES: 4.8MM **Privately Held**
SIC: 2899 Chemical preparations

(P-8983)
KELCO BIO POLYMERS
Also Called: CP Kelco
2025 Harbor Dr, San Diego (92113-2214)
PHONE....................619 595-5000
Diane E Salisbury, *Principal*
Elizabeth Perez, *Administration*
Melinda Robinson, *Business Anlyst*
George Hagedon, *Project Mgr*
Art Casey, *Engineer*
EMP: 21
SALES (est): 3.6MM **Privately Held**
SIC: 2899 Chemical preparations

(P-8984)
KEMIRA WATER SOLUTIONS INC
Also Called: Kemiron Pacific
14000 San Bernardino Ave, Fontana (92335-5258)
PHONE....................909 350-5678
Hailu Mequira, *Manager*
Bryan Johnson, *Manager*
EMP: 23
SALES (corp-wide): 2.9B **Privately Held**
WEB: www.kemiron.com
SIC: 2899 Water treating compounds
HQ: Kemira Water Solutions, Inc.
1000 Parkwood Cir Se # 500
Atlanta GA 30339
770 436-1542

(P-8985)
KIK POOL ADDITIVES INC
5160 E Airport Dr, Ontario (91761-7824)
PHONE....................909 390-9912
John A Christensen, *President*
Brian Patterson, *CFO*
David M Christensen, *Vice Pres*
Debra Schonk, *Vice Pres*
Chet Yoakum, *Vice Pres*
▲ **EMP:** 140 **EST:** 1958
SALES (est): 58.1MM **Privately Held**
WEB: www.kem-tek.com
SIC: 2899 3089 7389 5169 Chemical preparations; plastic hardware & building products; packaging & labeling services; swimming pool & spa chemicals

(P-8986)
KMG CHEMICALS INC
2340 Bert Dr, Hollister (95023-2510)
PHONE....................800 956-7467
Keith Hussinger, *Manager*
EMP: 40
SALES (corp-wide): 590.1MM **Publicly Held**
SIC: 2899 Chemical preparations
HQ: Kmg Chemicals, Inc.
300 Throckmorton St # 1900
Fort Worth TX 76102
817 761-6100

(P-8987)
KMG ELECTRONIC CHEMICALS INC
2340 Bert Dr, Hollister (95023-2510)
PHONE....................831 636-5151
Brad Clark, *Branch Mgr*
Mark Panger, *Executive*
EMP: 11
SALES (corp-wide): 590.1MM **Publicly Held**
SIC: 2899 Chemical preparations
HQ: Kmg Electronic Chemicals, Inc.
300 Throckmorton St # 1900
Fort Worth TX 76102

(P-8988)
LAGUNA COUNTY SANATATION DIST
3500 Black Rd, Santa Maria (93455-5927)
PHONE....................805 934-6282
Mark Moya, *Manager*
EMP: 11
SALES (est): 1.1MM **Privately Held**
SIC: 2899 Water treating compounds

(P-8989)
LG NANOH2O INC
21250 Hawthorne Blvd # 330, Torrance (90503-5541)
PHONE....................424 218-4000
Jeff Green, *CEO*
Doug Barnes, *COO*
John Markovich, *CFO*
Michael Demartino, *Vice Pres*
Nicholas Dyner, *Vice Pres*
▼ **EMP:** 35
SQ FT: 2,000
SALES (est): 7.3MM **Privately Held**
SIC: 2899 Distilled water
PA: Lg Chem, Ltd.
128 Yeoui-Daero, Yeongdeungpo-Gu
Seoul 07336

(P-8990)
LM SCOFIELD COMPANY (DH)
12767 Imperial Hwy, Santa Fe Springs (90670-4711)
PHONE....................323 720-3000
Phillip J Arnold, *President*
Bob Torres, *Regional Mgr*
Janet Dickinson, *Info Tech Dir*
Mike Decandia, *Marketing Staff*
CAM Villar, *Marketing Staff*
◆ **EMP:** 50
SQ FT: 36,000
SALES (est): 23.6MM
SALES (corp-wide): 7.1B **Privately Held**
SIC: 2899 Concrete curing & hardening compounds
HQ: Sika Corporation
201 Polito Ave
Lyndhurst NJ 07071
201 933-8800

(P-8991)
LUBRIZOL ADVANCED MTLS INC
Also Called: LUBRIZOL ADVANCED MATERIALS, INC.
3115 Propeller Dr, Paso Robles (93446-8524)
PHONE....................805 239-1550
Daniel McCornack, *Principal*
EMP: 68
SALES (corp-wide): 225.3B **Publicly Held**
WEB: www.pharma.noveoninc.com
SIC: 2899 Chemical preparations
HQ: Lubrizol Global Management, Inc
9911 Brecksville Rd
Brecksville OH 44141
216 447-5000

(P-8992)
LUBRIZOL CORPORATION
344 Clyde Dr, Walnut Creek (94598-3427)
PHONE....................925 352-4843
Steve Dell'anno, *Manager*
EMP: 15
SALES (corp-wide): 225.3B **Publicly Held**
WEB: www.lubrizol.com
SIC: 2899 Chemical preparations
HQ: The Lubrizol Corporation
29400 Lakeland Blvd
Wickliffe OH 44092
440 943-4200

(P-8993)
LUBRIZOL CORPORATION
30211 Ave D Las Bandras, Rancho Santa Margari (92688)
PHONE....................949 212-1863
EMP: 19
SALES (corp-wide): 182.1B **Publicly Held**
SIC: 2899
HQ: The Lubrizol Corporation
29400 Lakeland Blvd
Wickliffe OH 44092
440 943-4200

(P-8994)
MASTER BUILDERS LLC
Degussa Construction
9060 Haven Ave, Rancho Cucamonga (91730-5405)
PHONE....................909 987-1758
Dave Lougheed, *Manager*
EMP: 21

SALES (corp-wide): 71.7B **Privately Held**
WEB: www.basf-admixtures.com
SIC: 2899 Chemical preparations
HQ: Master Builders, Llc
23700 Chagrin Blvd
Beachwood OH 44122
216 831-5500

(P-8995)
MATSUI INTERNATIONAL CO INC
Also Called: Unimark
1501 W 178th St, Gardena (90248-3203)
PHONE....................310 767-7812
Masa Matsui, *President*
Yoko Gavern, *Asst Admin*
Sayaka Taira, *Human Resources*
Enrique Castillo, *Sales Staff*
Lori Nakawatase, *Sales Staff*
◆ **EMP:** 180
SQ FT: 30,000
SALES (est): 39.1MM **Privately Held**
WEB: www.matsui-color.com
SIC: 2899 Ink or writing fluids
PA: Matsui Shikiso Chemical Co.,Ltd.
64, Sakuradani, Kamikazan, Ya-mashina-Ku
Kyoto KYO 607-8
-

(P-8996)
MC PRODUCTS INC
23331 Antonio Pkwy, Rcho STA Marg (92688-2664)
PHONE....................949 888-7100
Dave Maietta, *President*
EMP: 17
SQ FT: 36,000
SALES (est): 6.2MM **Privately Held**
SIC: 2899 Waterproofing compounds

(P-8997)
MCGRAYEL COMPANY INC
Also Called: Eascare Products USA
5361 S Villa Ave, Fresno (93725-8903)
P.O. Box 12362 (93777-2362)
PHONE....................559 299-7660
Marvin J Rezac Jr, *CEO*
Evangelina Serrano, *President*
Todd Wilson, *Treasurer*
Tiffany Rolofson, *General Mgr*
Joseph Mendez, *Mfg Mgr*
EMP: 25
SQ FT: 10,000
SALES (est): 3.7MM **Privately Held**
WEB: www.mcgrayel.com
SIC: 2899 Water treating compounds

(P-8998)
MEDICAL CHEMICAL CORPORATION
Also Called: M C C
19250 Van Ness Ave, Torrance (90501-1102)
P.O. Box 6217 (90504-0217)
PHONE....................310 787-6800
Emmanuel Didier, *President*
Patrick Braden, *Senior VP*
Kris Kontis, *Vice Pres*
Andy Rocha, *Vice Pres*
Carol Santaloci, *Regl Sales Mgr*
◆ **EMP:** 45 **EST:** 1954
SALES (est): 11.7MM **Privately Held**
WEB: www.med-chem.com
SIC: 2899 2841 Chemical preparations; soap & other detergents

(P-8999)
MICRO-TRACERS INC
1370 Van Dyke Ave, San Francisco (94124-3313)
PHONE....................415 822-1100
David Eisenberg, *President*
Ngaly Frank, *CFO*
Cyrus Frank, *Admin Sec*
MAI Vo, *Mfg Dir*
Daria Gorohova, *Marketing Mgr*
▲ **EMP:** 10
SQ FT: 11,000
SALES (est): 2.1MM **Privately Held**
WEB: www.microtracers.com
SIC: 2899 Chemical preparations

P
R
O
D
U
C
T
S

&

S
V
C
S

(P-9000)
MISSION VALLEY REGIONAL OCCU
5019 Stevenson Blvd, Fremont (94538-2449)
PHONE..............................510 657-1865
Charles Brown, *Principal*
Gordon Sanford, *Principal*
EMP: 45
SALES (est): 2.2MM **Privately Held**
SIC: 2899 Chemical preparations

(P-9001)
MITANN INC (HQ)
Also Called: Zip-Chem Products
400 Jarvis Dr Ste A, Morgan Hill (95037-8106)
PHONE..............................408 782-2500
Dennis Wagner, *President*
Charles Portier, *Vice Pres*
▲ EMP: 24
SQ FT: 50,000
SALES (est): 10.5MM
SALES (corp-wide): 12MM **Privately Held**
WEB: www.zipchem.com
SIC: 2899 5169 2813 Chemical preparations; chemicals & allied products; industrial gases
PA: Andpak, Inc.
    400 Jarvis Dr Ste A
    Morgan Hill CA 95037
    408 776-1072

(P-9002)
MOC PRODUCTS COMPANY INC (PA)
Also Called: Auto Edge Solutions
12306 Montague St, Pacoima (91331-2279)
PHONE..............................818 794-3500
Mark Waco, *CEO*
Dave Waco, *Vice Pres*
Jason Levine, *Executive Asst*
Andrew Bennett, *Admin Asst*
Nati Toledo, *Administration*
▲ EMP: 75
SQ FT: 100,000
SALES (est): 64.6MM **Privately Held**
WEB: www.mocproducts.com
SIC: 2899 7549 5169 Corrosion preventive lubricant; automotive maintenance services; chemicals & allied products

(P-9003)
MORTON SALT INC
7380 Morton Ave, Newark (94560-4200)
P.O. Box 506, Grantsville UT (84029-0506)
PHONE..............................510 797-2281
Jim Oswald, *Manager*
EMP: 13
SALES (corp-wide): 4.6B **Privately Held**
SIC: 2899 Chemical preparations
HQ: Morton Salt, Inc.
    444 W Lake St Ste 3000
    Chicago IL 60606

(P-9004)
NALCO COMPANY LLC
4900 California Ave 420b, Bakersfield (93309-7024)
PHONE..............................661 864-7955
Danny Moreno, *Branch Mgr*
EMP: 17
SALES (corp-wide): 14.6B **Publicly Held**
SIC: 2899 Water treating compounds
HQ: Nalco Company Llc
    1601 W Diehl Rd
    Naperville IL 60563
    630 305-1000

(P-9005)
NALCO COMPANY LLC
1000 Burnett Ave Ste 430, Concord (94520-2091)
PHONE..............................800 798-2247
EMP: 12
SALES (corp-wide): 14.6B **Publicly Held**
WEB: www.nalco.com
SIC: 2899 Corrosion preventive lubricant
HQ: Nalco Company Llc
    1601 W Diehl Rd
    Sugar Land TX 60563
    630 305-1000

(P-9006)
NALCO COMPANY LLC
980 Enchanted Way Ste 203, Simi Valley (93065-0913)
PHONE..............................805 584-9950
Susan Ciciarelli, *Manager*
Cody Moore, *Sales Staff*
David Cuculic, *Manager*
Jeff Alvari, *Accounts Mgr*
Fred Rivers, *Accounts Mgr*
EMP: 12
SALES (corp-wide): 14.6B **Publicly Held**
WEB: www.nalco.com
SIC: 2899 Corrosion preventive lubricant
HQ: Nalco Company Llc
    1601 W Diehl Rd
    Sugar Land TX 60563
    630 305-1000

(P-9007)
NANOSCALE COMBINATORIAL
Also Called: Nanosyn
3100 Central Expy, Santa Clara (95051-0801)
PHONE..............................408 987-2000
Nikolai Sepetov, *President*
Olga Isskova, *Vice Pres*
Jacob Macdonald, *Research*
Olga Miroshnikova, *Research*
David Lonergan, *Director*
EMP: 35
SQ FT: 30,000
SALES (est): 7.5MM **Privately Held**
SIC: 2899 Chemical preparations

(P-9008)
NATIONAL SWEETWATER INC
Also Called: Sweetwater Technologies
43394 Calle De Velardo, Temecula (92592-2625)
PHONE..............................951 303-0999
Debbie CHI-Man Lee, *President*
John W Cornell, *Vice Pres*
▲ EMP: 13
SQ FT: 2,400
SALES (est): 2.2MM **Privately Held**
SIC: 2899 8748 Water treating compounds; business consulting

(P-9009)
NEO TECH AQUA SOLUTIONS INC
3853 Calle Fortunada, San Diego (92123-1824)
PHONE..............................858 571-6590
Stephen Dunham, *President*
George Diefenthal, *COO*
EMP: 15
SQ FT: 6,000
SALES (est): 3.6MM **Privately Held**
WEB: www.uvsciences.com
SIC: 2899 Water treating compounds

(P-9010)
NORTH AMERICAN PETROLEUM
Also Called: Napro
11072 Via El Mercado, Los Alamitos (90720-2812)
P.O. Box 2486 (90720-7486)
PHONE..............................562 598-6671
Melvin Kirschner, *President*
Marilyn K Kirschner, *Treasurer*
Seiichi Okazaki, *Vice Pres*
EMP: 20
SQ FT: 10,000
SALES (est): 2.8MM **Privately Held**
WEB: www.napro.com
SIC: 2899 8661 Oil treating compounds; religious organizations

(P-9011)
NUGENERATION TECHNOLOGIES LLC (PA)
Also Called: Nugentec
1155 Park Ave, Emeryville (94608-3631)
P.O. Box 30428, Stockton (95213-0428)
PHONE..............................707 820-4080
Donato Polignone,
Dino Polignone, *Vice Pres*
Zephyr Mendez, *VP Bus Dvlpt*
Frank Franco, *Technician*
Frank James, *Technology*
◆ EMP: 17 EST: 1997
SQ FT: 11,000

SALES: 7.6MM **Privately Held**
WEB: www.nugentec.com
SIC: 2899 2841 1389 Chemical preparations; soap & other detergents; lease tanks, oil field: erecting, cleaning & repairing; chemically treating wells; oil field services; servicing oil & gas wells

(P-9012)
OCEANS FLAVOR FOODS LLC
4492 Camino De La Plz, San Ysidro (92173-3071)
PHONE..............................619 793-5269
Justin Fisher,
Alan Fisher, *CEO*
EMP: 10
SQ FT: 10,000
SALES: 8MM **Privately Held**
SIC: 2899 Salt

(P-9013)
OUDIMENTARY LLC
43170 Osgood Rd, Fremont (94539-5608)
PHONE..............................510 501-5057
Micah Anderson,
EMP: 11
SALES (est): 1.2MM **Privately Held**
SIC: 2899 Essential oils

(P-9014)
PACIFIC SCIENTIFIC ENERGETIC (HQ)
3601 Union Rd, Hollister (95023-9635)
PHONE..............................831 637-3731
Gregory Scaven, *President*
John Davis, *Vice Pres*
Neal Kerr, *Business Dir*
Will Hunter, *Program Mgr*
Jim Ramsey, *Program Mgr*
EMP: 300
SQ FT: 65,000
SALES: 200MM
SALES (corp-wide): 6.4B **Publicly Held**
WEB: www.psemc.com
SIC: 2899 3489 3483 3699 Igniter grains, boron potassium nitrate; projectors: depth charge, grenade, rocket, etc.; arming & fusing devices for missiles; high-energy particle physics equipment; aircraft armament, except guns; fuses, safety
PA: Fortive Corporation
    6920 Seaway Blvd
    Everett WA 98203
    425 446-5000

(P-9015)
PACIFIC WTRPRFING RSTRTION INC
2845 Pomona Blvd, Pomona (91768-3242)
PHONE..............................909 444-3052
Ronald Bithell, *CEO*
Anthony Bithell, *Vice Pres*
EMP: 32
SALES (est): 6.5MM **Privately Held**
SIC: 2899 7641 Waterproofing compounds; antique furniture repair & restoration

(P-9016)
PHIBRO ANIMAL HEALTH CORP
Phibro-Tech
8851 Dice Rd, Santa Fe Springs (90670-2515)
PHONE..............................562 698-8036
Mark Alling, *Manager*
Suzanne Parsons, *Prdtn Mgr*
Larissa Rider, *Sales Engr*
EMP: 50
SALES (corp-wide): 828MM **Publicly Held**
SIC: 2899 2819 Chemical preparations; industrial inorganic chemicals
HQ: Phibro Animal Health Corporation
    300 Frank W Burr Blvd
    Teaneck NJ 07666
    201 329-7300

(P-9017)
PRESTONE PRODUCTS CORPORATION
Also Called: Kik Custom Products
19500 Mariner Ave, Torrance (90503-1644)
PHONE..............................424 271-4836
Raymond Yu, *Plant Mgr*
EMP: 30

SALES (corp-wide): 3.2MM **Privately Held**
WEB: www.honeywell.com
SIC: 2899 5531 5169 Antifreeze compounds; automotive parts; anti-freeze compounds
HQ: Prestone Products Corporation
    6250 N River Rd Ste 6000
    Rosemont IL 60018
    -

(P-9018)
RADIATOR SPECIALTY COMPANY
Also Called: Highway Safety Control
935 Enterprise Way, NAPA (94558-6209)
PHONE..............................707 252-0122
David Brock, *Manager*
EMP: 30
SALES (corp-wide): 84.8MM **Privately Held**
WEB: www.radiatorspecialty.com
SIC: 2899 3993 3561 3669 Antifreeze compounds; signs & advertising specialties; pumps & pumping equipment; transportation signaling devices
PA: Radiator Specialty Company Inc
    600 Radiator Rd
    Indian Trail NC 28079
    704 688-2302

(P-9019)
RELTON CORPORATION
317 Rolyn Pl, Arcadia (91007-2838)
P.O. Box 60019 (91066-6019)
PHONE..............................800 423-1505
William Kinard, *Chairman*
Craig Kinard, *President*
Wm Craig Kinard, *CEO*
Kevin Kinard, *Treasurer*
Darcey Arena, *Vice Pres*
EMP: 65 EST: 1946
SQ FT: 20,000
SALES (est): 13.5MM **Privately Held**
WEB: www.relton.com
SIC: 2899 3423 3546 2992 Chemical preparations; masons' hand tools; power-driven handtools; lubricating oils & greases

(P-9020)
RICHARD K GOULD INC
Also Called: Sierra Chemical Company
788 Northport Dr, West Sacramento (95691-2145)
PHONE..............................916 371-5943
Robert Gould, *CEO*
Steve Gould, *President*
Karen Silva, *Treasurer* .
EMP: 20
SQ FT: 18,500
SALES (est): 5.2MM **Privately Held**
WEB: www.sierrachemicalcompany.com
SIC: 2899 5999 Oils & essential oils; cleaning equipment & supplies

(P-9021)
RONATEC C2C INC
5651 Palmer Way Ste H, Carlsbad (92010-7244)
P.O. Box 1976, Fallbrook (92088-1976)
PHONE..............................760 476-1890
Shawn J Wetherald, *CEO*
James Wetherald, *Vice Pres*
▼ EMP: 12
SQ FT: 4,500
SALES (est): 7MM **Privately Held**
SIC: 2899 Chemical preparations

(P-9022)
SIGMA-ALDRICH CORPORATION
Also Called: Safc Pharma
6211 El Camino Real, Carlsbad (92009-1604)
PHONE..............................760 710-6213
Tim Quinn, *Manager*
David Backer, *Business Dir*
EMP: 50
SALES (corp-wide): 16.9B **Privately Held**
WEB: www.sigmaaldrich.com
SIC: 2899 Chemical preparations
HQ: Sigma-Aldrich Corporation
    3050 Spruce St
    Saint Louis MO 63103
    314 771-5765

▲ = Import ▼=Export
◆ =Import/Export

(P-9023)
SIKA CORPORATION
12767 Imperial Hwy, Santa Fe Springs
(90670-4711)
PHONE..................................562 941-0231
Jerry Monarch, *Branch Mgr*
Eric Muench, *Vice Pres*
Jon Watson, *QC Dir*
Michael Winge, *Marketing Staff*
EMP: 17
SQ FT: 26,186
SALES (corp-wide): 7.1B **Privately Held**
WEB: www.sikacorp.com
SIC: 2899 Concrete curing & hardening
  compounds
HQ: Sika Corporation
  201 Polito Ave
  Lyndhurst NJ 07071
  201 933-8800

(P-9024)
SKASOL INCORPORATED
1696 W Grand Ave, Oakland (94607-1607)
PHONE..................................510 839-1000
David L Marchman, *President*
Bud Guy, *Vice Pres*
Matt Beauregard, *Accounts Mgr*
Alexander Lechner, *Accounts Mgr*
EMP: 10
SQ FT: 23,000
SALES (est): 1.8MM **Privately Held**
WEB: www.skasol.com
SIC: 2899 Water treating compounds

(P-9025)
SNF HOLDING COMPANY
Also Called: Polypure
4690 Worth St, Los Angeles (90063-1630)
PHONE..................................323 266-4435
Alex Bravo, *General Mgr*
EMP: 13
SQ FT: 15,044 **Privately Held**
WEB: www.snfinc.com
SIC: 2899 Water treating compounds
HQ: Snf Holding Company
  1 Chemical Plant Rd
  Riceboro GA 31323

(P-9026)
**SOUTH ORANGE COUNTY WW
AUTH**
34156 Del Obispo St, Dana Point
(92629-2916)
PHONE..................................949 234-5400
Brian Peck, *Principal*
EMP: 17
SALES (est): 4.1MM **Privately Held**
SIC: 2899 Water treating compounds

(P-9027)
SUEZ WTS USA INC
Also Called: GE Water & Process Tech
3050 Pegasus Dr, Bakersfield
(93308-6817)
PHONE..................................661 393-3035
Anthony Rowe, *Branch Mgr*
EMP: 20
SALES (corp-wide): 94.7MM **Privately
Held**
SIC: 2899 Water treating compounds
HQ: Suez Wts Usa, Inc.
  4636 Somerton Rd
  Trevose PA 19053
  215 355-3300

(P-9028)
TCK MEMBRANE AMERICA INC
3390 E Miraloma Ave, Anaheim
(92806-1911)
PHONE..................................714 678-8832
Kenneth Yoon, *President*
▲ **EMP:** 10
SALES (est): 1.3MM **Privately Held**
SIC: 2899 Vegetable oils, vulcanized or
  sulfurized

(P-9029)
TEH-PARI INTERNATIONAL
Also Called: Auric Blends
334 Ohair Ct Ste B, Santa Rosa
(95407-5706)
P.O. Box 628, Graton (95444-0628)
PHONE..................................707 829-9116
Randy Graves, *President*
Wendy Nicholson, *Admin Sec*

▲ **EMP:** 20
SQ FT: 12,000
SALES: 2.5MM **Privately Held**
WEB: www.auricblends.com
SIC: 2899 Incense

(P-9030)
**TORAY MEMBRANE USA INC
(DH)**
13435 Danielson St, Poway (92064-6825)
PHONE..................................858 218-2360
Steve Cappos, *CEO*
Tak Wakisaka, *Treasurer*
Kimio Kimura, *Vice Pres*
Thomas Wolfe, *Vice Pres*
John Eagleton, *Engineer*
◆ **EMP:** 90
SQ FT: 90,000
SALES (est): 18.9MM **Privately Held**
WEB:
SIC: 2899 Water treating compounds
HQ: Toray Holding (U.S.A.), Inc.
  461 5th Ave Fl 9
  New York NY 10017
  212 697-8150

(P-9031)
TRI SERVICE CO INC
2465 Loma Ave, South El Monte
(91733-1415)
P.O. Box 3513 (91733-0513)
PHONE..................................626 442-3270
Jeff Rein, *CEO*
Elinore Rein, *Corp Secy*
EMP: 11
SQ FT: 8,300
SALES (est): 2.3MM **Privately Held**
SIC: 2899 7699 5084 Water treating com-
  pounds; boiler repair shop; industrial ma-
  chinery & equipment

(P-9032)
TUMELO INC
420 Tesconi Cir Ste B, Santa Rosa
(95401-4681)
PHONE..................................707 523-4411
Scott Maddock, *Principal*
EMP: 25
SALES (est): 1MM **Privately Held**
SIC: 2899 2841 Oils & essential oils; soap
  & other detergents

(P-9033)
UNITED PHARMA LLC
2317 Moore Ave, Fullerton (92833-2510)
PHONE..................................714 738-8999
Bill Wang, *President*
George Koo, *Prdtn Mgr*
▲ **EMP:** 130
SQ FT: 53,000
SALES (est): 45.4MM **Privately Held**
SIC: 2899 Gelatin: edible, technical, photo-
  graphic or pharmaceutical

(P-9034)
US ENVIRONMENTAL
Also Called: Kinetico Quality Water Systems
7085 Jurupa Ave Ste 1, Riverside
(92504-1044)
PHONE..................................951 359-9002
Donald Nalian, *Owner*
Tony Dezember, *Partner*
EMP: 10
SQ FT: 2,975
SALES: 750K **Privately Held**
SIC: 2899 5999 Water treating com-
  pounds; water purification equipment

(P-9035)
VULPINE INC
Also Called: Shape Products
1127 57th Ave, Oakland (94621-4427)
PHONE..................................510 534-1186
Dan Daniel, *President*
Tony Weiler, *Vice Pres*
▲ **EMP:** 14 **EST:** 1979
SQ FT: 22,000
SALES (est): 5MM **Privately Held**
WEB: www.shapeproduct.com
SIC: 2899 5169 Chemical preparations;
  chemicals & allied products

2911 Petroleum Refining

(P-9036)
ACCU-BLEND CORPORATION
364 Malbert St, Perris (92570-8336)
PHONE..................................626 334-7744
Xia Wang, *CEO*
Kenny Wang, *President*
▲ **EMP:** 17
SALES (est): 3.7MM **Privately Held**
WEB: www.accu-blend.com
SIC: 2911 Paraffin wax

(P-9037)
ALON USA LP
Also Called: Alon Asphalt Bakersfield
1201 China Grade Loop, Bakersfield
(93308-9688)
P.O. Box 5655 (93388-5655)
PHONE..................................661 392-3630
Jim Ryan, *Branch Mgr*
EMP: 12
SALES (corp-wide): 10.2B **Publicly Held**
SIC: 2911 Petroleum refining
HQ: Alon Usa, Lp
  12700 Park Central Dr # 1600
  Dallas TX 75251

(P-9038)
**ASBURY GRAPHITE INC
CALIFORNIA**
2855 Franklin Canyon Rd, Rodeo
(94572-2116)
PHONE..................................510 799-3636
Stephen Riddle, *CEO*
Noah Nicoleson, *President*
Sue Rish, *CFO*
◆ **EMP:** 14 **EST:** 1986
SQ FT: 33,000
SALES (est): 37.6MM
SALES (corp-wide): 126.7MM **Privately
Held**
SIC: 2911 3295 2899 Coke, petroleum;
  graphite, natural: ground, pulverized, re-
  fined or blended; fluxes: brazing, solder-
  ing, galvanizing & welding
PA: Asbury Carbons, Inc.
  405 Old Main St
  Asbury NJ 08802
  908 537-2155

(P-9039)
B C SONG INTERNATIONAL INC
Also Called: Bcs International
2509 Technology Dr, Hayward
(94545-4869)
PHONE..................................510 785-8383
Ben C Song, *President*
EMP: 60
SQ FT: 10,000
SALES (est): 6.7MM **Privately Held**
WEB: www.bcsinternational.com
SIC: 2911 2834 Fuel additives; pharma-
  ceutical preparations

(P-9040)
CASTAIC TRUCK STOP INC
31611 Castaic Rd, Castaic (91384-3939)
PHONE..................................661 295-1374
Sarkis Khrimian, *President*
Refe Dimmuck, *Opers Mgr*
EMP: 26
SQ FT: 2,000
SALES (est): 3.9MM **Privately Held**
SIC: 2911 7389 5812 Diesel fuels; flea
  market; American restaurant

(P-9041)
**CHEVRON CAPTAIN COMPANY
LLC (HQ)**
Also Called: Chevron Products Company
6001 Bollinger Canyon Rd, San Ramon
(94583-5737)
PHONE..................................925 842-1000
John S Watson, *Ch of Bd*
Monica Molinar, *Project Mgr*
Gary Workman, *Manager*
◆ **EMP:** 200
SALES (est): 1.2B
SALES (corp-wide): 166.3B **Publicly
Held**
SIC: 2911 Petroleum refining

PA: Chevron Corporation
  6001 Bollinger Canyon Rd
  San Ramon CA 94583
  925 842-1000

(P-9042)
**CHEVRON GLOBAL ENERGY
INC (HQ)**
Also Called: Chevron Global Lubricants
6001 Bollinger Canyon Rd, San Ramon
(94583-5737)
P.O. Box 6046 (94583-0746)
PHONE..................................925 842-1000
Jock D McKenzie, *Ch of Bd*
John S Watson, *Ch of Bd*
Richard J Guiltinan, *CFO*
Malcolm J McAuley, *Treasurer*
Pierre R Breber, *Exec VP*
EMP: 100 **EST:** 1936
SQ FT: 200,000
SALES (est): 1.1B
SALES (corp-wide): 166.3B **Publicly
Held**
SIC: 2911 4731 5172 Petroleum refining;
  freight transportation arrangement; petro-
  leum products
PA: Chevron Corporation
  6001 Bollinger Canyon Rd
  San Ramon CA 94583
  925 842-1000

(P-9043)
**CLEAIRE ADVANCED EMISSION
(PA)**
1001 42nd St, Emeryville (94608-3620)
PHONE..................................510 347-6103
Michael J Doherty, *President*
EMP: 14
SALES (est): 2.3MM **Privately Held**
SIC: 2911 Diesel fuels

(P-9044)
D-1280-X INC
Also Called: Omstar Environmental Products
126 N Marine Ave, Wilmington
(90744-5723)
P.O. Box 6293, San Pedro (90734-6293)
PHONE..................................310 835-6909
Roberta L Skaggs, *CEO*
Richard J Skaggs, *President*
Howard Sargent, *Exec VP*
EMP: 12
SQ FT: 7,500
SALES (est): 1MM **Privately Held**
SIC: 2911 5169 Fuel additives; chemical
  additives

(P-9045)
**DE MENNO-KERDOON TRADING
CO (HQ)**
2000 N Alameda St, Compton
(90222-2702)
PHONE..................................310 537-7100
Jim Ennis, *COO*
Jay Demel, *Vice Pres*
Jim Tice, *Mktg Dir*
N Bonnie Booth, *Manager*
EMP: 149
SQ FT: 60,000
SALES (est): 29.4MM
SALES (corp-wide): 119.4MM **Privately
Held**
SIC: 2911 Oils, fuel
PA: World Oil Marketing Company
  9302 Garfield Ave
  South Gate CA 90280
  562 928-0100

(P-9046)
GLENCORE LTD
Chemoil
2020 Walnut Ave, Long Beach (90806)
PHONE..................................562 427-6611
Ted Christenson, *Manager*
EMP: 30
SALES (corp-wide): 205.4B **Privately
Held**
WEB: www.aimalumni.com
SIC: 2911 Petroleum refining
HQ: Glencore Ltd.
  330 Madison Ave Ste 700
  New York NY 10017
  646 949-2500

(P-9047)
GOLDEN WEST REFINING COMPANY
13116 Imperial Hwy, Santa Fe Springs (90670-4817)
P.O. Box 2128 (90670-0138)
PHONE................................562 921-3581
Ted Orden, *President*
Moshe Sassover, *Senior VP*
EMP: 49
SQ FT: 22,000
SALES (est): 7MM
SALES (corp-wide): 7.3MM **Privately Held**
SIC: 2911 Gasoline
PA: Thrifty Oil Co.
13116 Imperial Hwy
Santa Fe Springs CA 90670
562 921-3581

(P-9048)
INTERNATIONAL GROUP INC
102 Cutting Blvd, Richmond (94804-2126)
PHONE................................510 232-8704
EMP: 12
SALES (corp-wide): 419.3K **Privately Held**
SIC: 2911 Paraffin wax
HQ: The International Group Inc
1007 E Spring St
Titusville PA 16354
814 827-4900

(P-9049)
INTERNATIONAL GROUP INC
102 Cutting Blvd, Richmond (94804-2126)
PHONE................................510 232-8704
Ian King, *Branch Mgr*
EMP: 75
SALES (corp-wide): 419.3K **Privately Held**
SIC: 2911 Paraffin wax; petrolatums, non-medicinal
HQ: International Group, Inc, The
50 Salome Dr
Scarborough ON M1S 2
416 293-4151

(P-9050)
LION TANK LINE INC
5801 Randolph St, Commerce (90040-3415)
PHONE................................323 726-1966
Levon Termandjyan, *President*
EMP: 28
SQ FT: 6,000
SALES (est): 4MM **Privately Held**
SIC: 2911 4213 Diesel fuels; liquid petroleum transport, non-local

(P-9051)
LOS ANGELES REFINING CO
2101 E Pacific Coast Hwy, Wilmington (90744-2914)
PHONE................................310 522-6000
EMP: 15
SALES (est): 2.3MM **Privately Held**
SIC: 2911 Petroleum refining

(P-9052)
M ARGESO & CO INC
2628 River Ave, Rosemead (91770-3302)
PHONE................................626 573-3000
G Douglas Orr, *President*
EMP: 14
SALES (est): 2.9MM **Privately Held**
SIC: 2911 Paraffin wax

(P-9053)
MOLECULUM
3128 Red Hill Ave, Costa Mesa (92626-4525)
PHONE................................714 619-5139
Ivan Krylov, *Regional Mgr*
EMP: 18 EST: 2015
SALES (est): 805.6K **Privately Held**
SIC: 2911 Aromatic chemical products

(P-9054)
NOVVI LLC (PA)
5885 Hollis St Ste 100, Emeryville (94608-2405)
PHONE................................281 488-0833
Jeffrey Brown, *CEO*
Willbe Ho, *Research*

Rachael Butler, *Production*
EMP: 28
SALES (est): 7.9MM **Privately Held**
SIC: 2911 Oils, lubricating

(P-9055)
OBERON FUELS INC (PA)
2159 India St Ste 200, San Diego (92101-1766)
PHONE................................619 255-9361
Ruben S Martin III, *CEO*
Rebecca Boudreaux, *President*
Elliot Hicks, *COO*
Anna Levy, *Project Engr*
John Nagib, *Opers Mgr*
EMP: 20
SALES (est): 1.2MM **Privately Held**
SIC: 2911 Diesel fuels

(P-9056)
ORGANIC INFUSIONS INC (PA)
2390 Las Posas Rd, Camarillo (93010-3479)
PHONE................................805 419-4118
Rose Heart, *President*
▲ EMP: 10
SALES (est): 5MM **Privately Held**
SIC: 2911 2899 Aromatic chemical products; essential oils

(P-9057)
PARAMOUNT PETROLEUM CORP
8835 Somerset Blvd, Paramount (90723-4658)
PHONE................................562 633-4332
Wes Owens, *Branch Mgr*
EMP: 14
SALES (corp-wide): 10.2B **Publicly Held**
SIC: 2911 Petroleum refining
HQ: Paramount Petroleum Corporation
14700 Downey Ave
Paramount CA 90723
562 531-2060

(P-9058)
PARAMOUNT PETROLEUM CORP (DH)
Also Called: Paramount Asphalt
14700 Downey Ave, Paramount (90723-4526)
PHONE................................562 531-2060
W S Lovejoy, *CEO*
Steve S Farkas, *President*
Glenn Clausen, *Vice Pres*
Kathryn Gleeson, *Vice Pres*
Allan Moret, *Vice Pres*
◆ EMP: 155
SQ FT: 6,000
SALES (est): 223.2MM
SALES (corp-wide): 10.2B **Publicly Held**
SIC: 2911 Petroleum refining

(P-9059)
PARAMOUNT PETROLEUM CORP
1201 China Grade Loop, Bakersfield (93308-9688)
P.O. Box 5655 (93388-5655)
PHONE................................661 392-3630
Ron Clark, *Branch Mgr*
EMP: 14
SALES (corp-wide): 10.2B **Publicly Held**
SIC: 2911 Petroleum refining
HQ: Paramount Petroleum Corporation
14700 Downey Ave
Paramount CA 90723
562 531-2060

(P-9060)
PBF ENERGY INC
Also Called: Torrance Refinery
3700 W 190th St, Torrance (90504-5733)
PHONE................................310 212-2800
Pete Trelenberg, *Manager*
EMP: 15
SALES (corp-wide): 27.1B **Publicly Held**
SIC: 2911 5541 Petroleum refining; gasoline service stations
PA: Pbf Energy Inc.
1 Sylvan Way Ste 2
Parsippany NJ 07054
973 455-7500

(P-9061)
PBF ENERGY WESTERN REGION LLC (DH)
111 W Ocean Blvd Ste 1500, Long Beach (90802-7907)
PHONE................................973 455-7500
Thomas J Nimbley, *CEO*
EMP: 354
SALES (est): 47.5MM
SALES (corp-wide): 27.1B **Publicly Held**
SIC: 2911 2992 Petroleum refining; lubricating oils

(P-9062)
PETROIL AMERICAS LIMITED
5651 W Pico Blvd Ste 102, Los Angeles (90019-3874)
P.O. Box 399, Manhattan Beach (90267-0399)
PHONE................................323 931-3720
Thorn Weathersby Jr, *President*
Oscar Weathersby, *Treasurer*
Belinda Weathersby, *Admin Sec*
EMP: 10
SALES (est): 3.2MM **Privately Held**
SIC: 2911 Oils, fuel; greases, lubricating; fuel additives

(P-9063)
REED & GRAHAM INC (PA)
690 Sunol St, San Jose (95126-3751)
P.O. Box 5940 (95150-5940)
PHONE................................408 287-1400
Gerald R Graham Jr, *President*
Gerald R Graham Sr, *Ch of Bd*
Steven Reed Graham, *Senior VP*
David H Pinkham, *General Mgr*
Aldo Branch, *Admin Sec*
▲ EMP: 50
SQ FT: 8,000
SALES (est): 30.2MM **Privately Held**
WEB: www.rginc.com
SIC: 2911 2952 8731 5032 Asphalt or asphaltic materials, made in refineries; road oils; coating compounds, tar; commercial research laboratory; brick, stone & related material

(P-9064)
RHS GAS INC
520 W Pacific Coast Hwy, Long Beach (90806-5237)
PHONE................................310 710-2331
Nathan Sparer, *Principal*
EMP: 10
SALES (est): 450.6K **Privately Held**
SIC: 2911 Solvents

(P-9065)
ROCK ENGINEERED MCHY CO INC
Also Called: Remco
1627 Army Ct Ste 1, Stockton (95206-4100)
PHONE................................925 447-0805
Kevin Cadwalader, *President*
Rich Lustig, *Finance Mgr*
Terrence Costa, *Natl Sales Mgr*
Chalin Luizinho, *Marketing Staff*
Lupe Chin, *Sales Staff*
◆ EMP: 19
SALES (est): 6.6MM **Privately Held**
WEB: www.remcovsi.com
SIC: 2911 5084 Heavy distillates; crushing machinery & equipment

(P-9066)
SAN JOAQUIN REFINING CO INC
3500 Shell St, Bakersfield (93308-5215)
P.O. Box 5576 (93388-5576)
PHONE................................661 327-4257
Kenneth E Fait, *Ch of Bd*
Majid Mojibi, *President*
Dorothy A Gribben, *Admin Sec*
David Pinkston, *IT/INT Sup*
Robert Biehl, *Engineer*
EMP: 130
SQ FT: 15,000
SALES (est): 31MM **Privately Held**
WEB: www.sjr.com
SIC: 2911 Oils, fuel

(P-9067)
SHELL MARTINEZ REFINING CO
Also Called: Shell Martinez Refinery
3485 Pacheco Blvd, Martinez (94553-2120)
P.O. Box 711 (94553-0071)
PHONE................................925 313-3000
Alicia Igarraraz, *General Mgr*
▲ EMP: 900
SALES (est): 149.1MM
SALES (corp-wide): 388.3B **Privately Held**
SIC: 2911 Petroleum refining
HQ: Shell Oil Company
150 N Dairy Ashford Rd A
Houston TX 77079
713 241-6161

(P-9068)
SINCLAIR COMPANIES
4192 N Fresno St, Fresno (93726-4006)
PHONE................................559 228-0913
EMP: 63
SALES (corp-wide): 3.9B **Privately Held**
SIC: 2911 Petroleum refining
PA: The Sinclair Companies
550 E South Temple
Salt Lake City UT 84102
801 524-2700

(P-9069)
SINCLAIR COMPANIES
7760 Crescent Ave, Buena Park (90620-3953)
PHONE................................714 826-5886
EMP: 94
SALES (corp-wide): 3.9B **Privately Held**
SIC: 2911 Petroleum refining
PA: The Sinclair Companies
550 E South Temple
Salt Lake City UT 84102
801 524-2700

(P-9070)
SINCLAIR COMPANIES
5792 N Palm Ave, Fresno (93704-1844)
PHONE................................559 997-3617
EMP: 63
SALES (corp-wide): 3.9B **Privately Held**
SIC: 2911 Petroleum refining
PA: The Sinclair Companies
550 E South Temple
Salt Lake City UT 84102
801 524-2700

(P-9071)
SINCLAIR COMPANIES
1703 W Olive Ave, Fresno (93728-2617)
PHONE................................559 351-1916
EMP: 63
SALES (corp-wide): 3.9B **Privately Held**
SIC: 2911 Petroleum refining
PA: The Sinclair Companies
550 E South Temple
Salt Lake City UT 84102
801 524-2700

(P-9072)
SOUTHERN CALIFORNIA BIODIESEL
Also Called: So California Biodiesel
18760 6th St Ste C, Bloomington (92316-3725)
P.O. Box 1642, Pomona (91769-1642)
PHONE................................951 377-4007
Kenneth Grubaugh, *President*
Daniel Grubaugh, *Vice Pres*
Matthew Grubaugh, *Vice Pres*
Joanne Grubaugh, *Admin Sec*
EMP: 11
SALES (est): 1MM **Privately Held**
SIC: 2911 8748 Diesel fuels; business consulting

(P-9073)
SUN COMPANY SAN BERNARDINO CAL
Also Called: Sun, The
290 N D St Ste 100, San Bernardino (92401-1711)
PHONE................................909 889-9666
Bob Balzer, *Manager*
Daniel Tedford, *Director*
Kimberly Guimarin, *Manager*
EMP: 200

▲ = Import ▼=Export
◆ =Import/Export

SALES (corp-wide): 42MM **Privately Held**
SIC: 2911 2752 Petroleum refining; commercial printing, lithographic
PA: Sun Company Of San Bernardino, California
4030 Georgia Blvd
San Bernardino CA 92407
909 889-9666

(P-9074)
TESORO REFINING & MKTG CO LLC
5905 N Paramount Blvd, Long Beach (90805-3709)
PHONE.................................562 728-2215
EMP: 377 **Publicly Held**
SIC: 2911 5541 Petroleum refining; gasoline service stations
HQ: Tesoro Refining & Marketing Company Llc
19100 Ridgewood Pkwy
San Antonio TX 78259
210 828-8484

(P-9075)
TORCO INTERNATIONAL CORP
1720 S Carlos Ave, Ontario (91761-7920)
PHONE.................................909 980-1495
Ned Tanson, *President*
▼ **EMP:** 12
SQ FT: 30,000
SALES (est): 2.9MM **Privately Held**
WEB: www.torcousa.com
SIC: 2911 Oils, illuminating

(P-9076)
TORRANCE REFINING COMPANY LLC
3700 W 190th St, Torrance (90504-5733)
PHONE.................................310 483-6900
Thomas J Nimbley, *CEO*
EMP: 600
SALES (est): 25.1MM
SALES (corp-wide): 27.1B **Publicly Held**
SIC: 2911 2992 Petroleum refining; lubricating oils
HQ: Pbf Energy Western Region Llc
111 W Ocean Blvd Ste 1500
Long Beach CA 90802
973 455-7500

(P-9077)
TRICOR REFINING LLC
1134 Manor St, Bakersfield (93308-3553)
P.O. Box 5877 (93388-5877)
PHONE.................................661 393-7110
Majid Mojibi, *Mng Member*
Merle Menghini, *Executive*
John Church, *Marketing Mgr*
Don Brookes, *Mng Member*
Kenneth E Fait, *Mng Member*
EMP: 28
SALES (est): 10.8MM **Privately Held**
WEB: www.tricorrefining.com
SIC: 2911 Oils, fuel

(P-9078)
UBI ENERGY CORPORATION
9465 Wilshire Blvd # 300, Beverly Hills (90212-2612)
PHONE.................................310 283-6978
EMP: 200
SALES: 120MM **Privately Held**
SIC: 2911

(P-9079)
ULTRAMAR INC
Also Called: Frost Beacon
2233 Esplanade, Chico (95926-2203)
PHONE.................................530 345-7901
EMP: 12
SALES (corp-wide): 93.9B **Publicly Held**
SIC: 2911
HQ: Ultramar Inc.
1 Valero Way
San Antonio TX 78249
210 345-2000

(P-9080)
ULTRAMAR INC
Also Called: Village Center Ultramar
9508 E Palmdale Blvd, Palmdale (93591-2202)
PHONE.................................661 944-2496
Ken Berglund, *Manager*

EMP: 12
SALES (corp-wide): 117B **Publicly Held**
WEB: www.divi.com
SIC: 2911 Petroleum refining
HQ: Ultramar Inc.
1 Valero Way
San Antonio TX 78249
210 345-2000

(P-9081)
VALERO ENERGY CORPORATION
Also Called: Depot 6, The
17928 Us Highway 18, Apple Valley (92307-2103)
PHONE.................................760 946-3322
Kuldip Randhawa, *Branch Mgr*
Kuldip S Randhawa, *Branch Mgr*
EMP: 30
SALES (corp-wide): 117B **Publicly Held**
SIC: 2911 Petroleum refining
PA: Valero Energy Corporation
1 Valero Way
San Antonio TX 78249
210 345-2000

(P-9082)
VALERO REF COMPANY-CALIFORNIA
3400 E 2nd St, Benicia (94510-1005)
PHONE.................................707 745-7011
Dough Comeau, *Branch Mgr*
Greg Aton, *IT/INT Sup*
Joe Muehlbauer, *Engineer*
Dexter Nigos, *Engineer*
Dave Fry, *Opers Mgr*
EMP: 500
SALES (corp-wide): 117B **Publicly Held**
SIC: 2911 Petroleum refining
HQ: Valero Refining Company-California
1 Valero Way
San Antonio TX 78249
210 345-2000

(P-9083)
VALERO REF COMPANY-CALIFORNIA
2401 E Anaheim St, Wilmington (90744-4009)
PHONE.................................562 491-6754
Mark Thair, *Manager*
EMP: 500
SALES (corp-wide): 117B **Publicly Held**
SIC: 2911 Petroleum refining
HQ: Valero Refining Company-California
1 Valero Way
San Antonio TX 78249
210 345-2000

(P-9084)
VENOCO INC
7979 Hollister Ave, Goleta (93117-2421)
PHONE.................................805 961-2305
EMP: 40
SALES (corp-wide): 224.2MM **Privately Held**
SIC: 2911 5172
HQ: Venoco, Inc.
370 17th St Ste 3900
Denver CO 80202
303 626-8300

(P-9085)
WD-40 COMPANY
Also Called: Hdp Holdings
9715 Businesspark Ave, San Diego (92131-1642)
PHONE.................................619 275-1400
Garry Ridge, *President*
Pete Dumiak, *Vice Pres*
Don Isley, *Vice Pres*
Kevin Nohelty, *Vice Pres*
Wende Oliverio, *Vice Pres*
EMP: 233
SALES (corp-wide): 423.3MM **Publicly Held**
WEB: www.wd40.com
SIC: 2911 Oils, lubricating
PA: Wd-40 Company
9715 Businesspark Ave
San Diego CA 92131
619 275-1400

2951 Paving Mixtures & Blocks

(P-9086)
AJW CONSTRUCTION
966 81st Ave, Oakland (94621-2512)
PHONE.................................510 568-2300
Ed Webster, *Principal*
Oneill Michael, *Vice Pres*
Alfonso Quintor, *Principal*
Juan Quintor, *Principal*
EMP: 42
SALES (est): 9.2MM **Privately Held**
SIC: 2951 Asphalt paving mixtures & blocks

(P-9087)
CALIFORNIA COMMERCIAL ASP CORP (PA)
4211 Ponderosa Ave Ste C, San Diego (92123-1665)
P.O. Box 23420 (92193-3420)
PHONE.................................858 513-0611
Donald Daley Jr, *President*
John Daley, *Principal*
David Hummel, *Principal*
Laura Samaniego, *Asst Controller*
EMP: 10
SALES (est): 4.2MM **Privately Held**
SIC: 2951 Asphalt & asphaltic paving mixtures (not from refineries)

(P-9088)
CALMAT CO (DH)
Also Called: Vulcan Materials
500 N Brand Blvd Ste 500 # 500, Glendale (91203-3319)
PHONE.................................818 553-8821
Tom Hill, *CEO*
James W Smack, *President*
Danny R Shepherd, *COO*
Daniel F Sansone, *CFO*
Barbara Goodrich-Welk, *Vice Pres*
EMP: 150
SQ FT: 40,000
SALES (est): 475.6MM **Publicly Held**
SIC: 2951 1442 1429 3273 Asphalt & asphaltic paving mixtures (not from refineries); construction sand & gravel; igneous rock, crushed & broken-quarrying; ready-mixed concrete; commercial & industrial building operation; land subdividers & developers, residential
HQ: Legacy Vulcan, Llc
1200 Urban Center Dr
Vestavia AL 35242
205 298-3000

(P-9089)
DELTA TRADING LP
Also Called: Crimson Resource Management
17731 Millux Rd, Bakersfield (93311-9714)
PHONE.................................661 834-5560
Mike Purdy, *Partner*
Rob McElroy, *General Mgr*
Ernie Martinez, *Manager*
EMP: 20
SALES (est): 6.8MM **Privately Held**
WEB: www.deltatradinglp.com
SIC: 2951 Asphalt paving mixtures & blocks

(P-9090)
DESERT BLOCK CO INC
11374 Tuxford St, Sun Valley (91352-2636)
PHONE.................................661 824-2624
Bill Fenzel, *President*
William Gapastione, *Vice Pres*
Gary Bedrosian, *Technical Staff*
Brandon Lyons, *Accounts Exec*
EMP: 12
SALES (est): 2.6MM **Privately Held**
SIC: 2951 3272 Concrete, asphaltic (not from refineries); concrete products, precast

(P-9091)
EDGINGTON OIL COMPANY LLC
2400 E Artesia Blvd, Long Beach (90805-1786)
PHONE.................................562 423-1465
Wasyl Kurinij, *President*
T A Novelly, *CEO*
John Hank, *Vice Pres*

Christine Hughes, *Asst Treas*
EMP: 65
SALES (est): 48.3MM
SALES (corp-wide): 10.2B **Publicly Held**
WEB: www.edgoil.com
SIC: 2951 Asphalt paving mixtures & blocks
HQ: Alon Usa Energy, Inc.
12700 Park Central Dr # 1600
Dallas TX 75251

(P-9092)
ESCONDIDO SAND & GRAVEL LLC
500 N Tulip St, Escondido (92025-2533)
P.O. Box 462590 (92046-2590)
PHONE.................................760 432-4690
George Weir, *CEO*
Mark Weir, *Vice Pres*
EMP: 11
SALES (est): 4.5MM **Privately Held**
SIC: 2951 Asphalt paving mixtures & blocks

(P-9093)
GRANITE ROCK CO
365 Blomquist St, Redwood City (94063-2701)
PHONE.................................650 482-3800
Rich Sacher, *Manager*
Stuart Mager, *General Mgr*
EMP: 25
SQ FT: 2,500
SALES (corp-wide): 992MM **Privately Held**
WEB: www.graniterock.com
SIC: 2951 2992 5032 Asphalt & asphaltic paving mixtures (not from refineries); lubricating oils & greases; brick, stone & related material
PA: Granite Rock Co.
350 Technology Dr
Watsonville CA 95076
831 768-2000

(P-9094)
HANSON AGGREGATES LLC
Also Called: Lehigh Hanson
12560 Highway 67, Lakeside (92040-1159)
PHONE.................................858 715-5600
EMP: 15
SALES (corp-wide): 20.6B **Privately Held**
WEB: www.hansonind.com
SIC: 2951 Asphalt paving mixtures & blocks
HQ: Hanson Aggregates Llc
8505 Freport Pkwy Ste 500
Irving TX 75063
469 417-1200

(P-9095)
HUNTMIX INC
Also Called: Calmut Industrial Asphalt
500 N Brand Blvd Ste 500, Glendale (91203-3319)
PHONE.................................818 548-5200
Fax: 323 254-1191
EMP: 165
SQ FT: 70,000
SALES (est): 12MM
SALES (corp-wide): 2.9B **Publicly Held**
SIC: 2951
HQ: Calmat Co.
500 N Brand Blvd Ste 500
Glendale CA 91203
818 553-8821

(P-9096)
LEGACY VULCAN LLC
16001 1/2 E Foothill Blvd, Irwindale (91702)
PHONE.................................626 633-4258
John Sprein, *Branch Mgr*
EMP: 37 **Publicly Held**
WEB: www.vulcanmaterials.com
SIC: 2951 Asphalt paving mixtures & blocks
HQ: Legacy Vulcan, Llc
1200 Urban Center Dr
Vestavia AL 35242
205 298-3000

(P-9097)
LEWIS BARRICADE INC
4000 Westerly Pl Ste 100, Newport Beach (92660-2347)
PHONE..................................661 363-0912
John R Lewis, *President*
Teresa Lewis, *Corp Secy*
EMP: 26 EST: 1998
SQ FT: 20,000
SALES (est): 4.2MM **Privately Held**
WEB: www.flashcoinc.com
SIC: 2951 7353 Concrete, asphaltic (not from refineries); heavy construction equipment rental

(P-9098)
NPG INC (PA)
Also Called: Goldstar Asphalt Products
1354 Jet Way, Perris (92571-7466)
P.O. Box 1515 (92572-1515)
PHONE..................................951 940-0200
Jeff Nelson, *President*
Sharon Nelson, *CFO*
EMP: 56
SQ FT: 6,900
SALES (est): 27.3MM **Privately Held**
WEB: www.goldstarasphalt.com
SIC: 2951 1799 1771 Asphalt & asphaltic paving mixtures (not from refineries); parking lot maintenance; driveway, parking lot & blacktop contractors

(P-9099)
OLDCASTLE APG WEST INC
4202 Gibralter Ct, Stockton (95206-3976)
PHONE..................................209 983-1609
Michelle Tompson, *Manager*
Cy Thomson, *Engineer*
EMP: 12
SALES (corp-wide): 30.6B **Privately Held**
WEB: www.oldcastlestockton.com
SIC: 2951 Asphalt paving mixtures & blocks
HQ: Oldcastle Apg West, Inc.
4720 E Cotton Gin Loop L
Phoenix AZ 85040
602 302-9600

(P-9100)
PARAMOUNT PETROLEUM CORP
10090 Waterman Rd, Elk Grove (95624-4010)
PHONE..................................916 685-9253
John Adams, *General Mgr*
Ed Juno, *Vice Pres*
Wesly Mikes, *Maintence Staff*
EMP: 14
SQ FT: 3,000
SALES (corp-wide): 10.2B **Publicly Held**
SIC: 2951 Asphalt paving mixtures & blocks
HQ: Paramount Petroleum Corporation
14700 Downey Ave
Paramount CA 90723
562 531-2060

(P-9101)
PAVEMENT RECYCLING SYSTEMS INC
Also Called: West Coast Milling
46205 Division St, Lancaster (93535-5908)
PHONE..................................661 948-5599
Steve Ward, *Manager*
EMP: 12
SQ FT: 1,000
SALES (est): 1.6MM
SALES (corp-wide): 126.7MM **Privately Held**
WEB: www.emultech.com
SIC: 2951 1611 Asphalt paving mixtures & blocks; surfacing & paving
PA: Pavement Recycling Systems, Inc.
10240 San Sevaine Way
Jurupa Valley CA 91752
951 682-1091

(P-9102)
PETROCHEM MARKETING
3033 E Washington Blvd, Los Angeles (90023-4219)
PHONE..................................323 526-4084
Mike Burris, *Owner*
EMP: 12

SALES (est): 590K **Privately Held**
SIC: 2951 Asphalt paving mixtures & blocks

(P-9103)
RECYCLED AGGREGATE MTLS CO INC (PA)
Also Called: Ramco
2655 1st St 210, Simi Valley (93065-1547)
PHONE..................................805 522-1646
Dennis L Newman, *President*
EMP: 24
SALES (est): 3.4MM **Privately Held**
SIC: 2951 Concrete, asphaltic (not from refineries)

(P-9104)
REED & GRAHAM INC
26 Light Sky Ct, Sacramento (95828-1016)
PHONE..................................888 381-0800
Bruce Adams, *Branch Mgr*
EMP: 44
SALES (corp-wide): 30.2MM **Privately Held**
WEB: www.rginc.com
SIC: 2951 Paving mixtures
PA: Reed & Graham, Inc.
690 Sunol St
San Jose CA 95126
408 287-1400

(P-9105)
SAN RAFAEL ROCK QUARRY INC
Also Called: Dutra Materials
961 Western Dr, Richmond (94801-3756)
PHONE..................................510 970-7700
Erin Johnson, *Manager*
EMP: 20
SALES (corp-wide): 145.1MM **Privately Held**
SIC: 2951 Asphalt paving mixtures & blocks
HQ: San Rafael Rock Quarry, Inc.
2350 Kerner Blvd Ste 200
San Rafael CA 94901

(P-9106)
SOUTH WESTERN PAVING COMPANY
2250 E Orangethorpe Ave, Fullerton (92831-5329)
PHONE..................................714 577-5750
Kenneth L Nelson, *President*
EMP: 11
SQ FT: 1,800
SALES: 2.3MM **Privately Held**
SIC: 2951 Asphalt paving mixtures & blocks

(P-9107)
VSS EMULTECH INC (HQ)
Also Called: Valley Sleurry Seal Co
7200 Pit Rd, Redding (96001-5352)
PHONE..................................530 243-0111
Wendall Reed, *President*
Mike Heath, *Principal*
Jeff Nowlin, *Manager*
EMP: 15 EST: 1945
SQ FT: 1,000
SALES (est): 8.2MM
SALES (corp-wide): 214.4MM **Privately Held**
WEB: www.emultech.com
SIC: 2951 Asphalt & asphaltic paving mixtures (not from refineries)
PA: Basic Resources Inc
928 12th St Ste 700
Modesto CA 95354
209 521-9771

(P-9108)
VSS EMULTECH INC
3785 Channel Dr, West Sacramento (95691-3421)
P.O. Box 981150 (95798-1150)
PHONE..................................916 371-8480
Doug Stach, *Manager*
EMP: 10
SALES (corp-wide): 214.4MM **Privately Held**
WEB: www.emultech.com
SIC: 2951 Asphalt & asphaltic paving mixtures (not from refineries)

HQ: Vss Emultech Inc
7200 Pit Rd
Redding CA 96001
530 243-0111

2952 Asphalt Felts & Coatings

(P-9109)
ASPHALT PRODUCTS OIL CORP (HQ)
Also Called: Apoc
5903 N Paramount Blvd, Long Beach (90805-3709)
P.O. Box 5248 (90805-0248)
PHONE..................................562 423-6471
Raymond T Hyer Jr, *Ch of Bd*
Bob Hyer, *Vice Pres*
Robert Hyer, *VP Sls/Mktg*
John Athanasion, *Sales Mgr*
Kim Deltiempo, *Sales Mgr*
EMP: 14
SQ FT: 30,000
SALES (est): 2MM
SALES (corp-wide): 270.5MM **Privately Held**
SIC: 2952 Asphalt felts & coatings
PA: Gardner-Gibson, Incorporated
4161 E 7th Ave
Tampa FL 33605
813 248-2101

(P-9110)
BURKE INDUSTRIES INC
Burkeline Roofing
2250 S 10th St, San Jose (95112-4197)
PHONE..................................408 297-3500
John Hurley, *Principal*
EMP: 150
SALES (corp-wide): 720.5MM **Privately Held**
WEB: www.burkeind.com
SIC: 2952 3061 Roofing materials; mechanical rubber goods
HQ: Burke Industries, Inc.
2250 S 10th St
San Jose CA 95112
408 297-3500

(P-9111)
CERTAINTEED CORPORATION
6400 Stevenson Blvd, Fremont (94538-2468)
PHONE..................................510 490-0890
Ed Foster, *Manager*
EMP: 65
SQ FT: 20,000
SALES (corp-wide): 215.9MM **Privately Held**
WEB: www.certainteed.net
SIC: 2952 2951 Asphalt felts & coatings; asphalt paving mixtures & blocks
HQ: Certainteed Llc
20 Moores Rd
Malvern PA 19355
610 893-5000

(P-9112)
FONTANA PAPER MILLS INC
13733 Valley Blvd, Fontana (92335-5268)
P.O. Box 339 (92334-0339)
PHONE..................................909 823-4100
George Thagard III, *President*
Jeff Thagard, *Executive*
Ray G Thagard Jr, *Admin Sec*
Michael Munoz, *Manager*
EMP: 56
SQ FT: 28,000
SALES (est): 18.8MM **Privately Held**
WEB: www.fontanaroof.com
SIC: 2952 2621 Roofing materials; felts, building

(P-9113)
HCO HOLDING I CORPORATION
Also Called: Henry Company
2270 S Castle Harbour Pl, Ontario (91761-5704)
PHONE..................................310 684-5320
Dave Distler, *Branch Mgr*
EMP: 10

SALES (corp-wide): 254.1MM **Privately Held**
SIC: 2952 Roof cement: asphalt, fibrous or plastic
HQ: Hco Holding I Corporation
999 N Pacific Coast Hwy
El Segundo CA 90245

(P-9114)
HCO HOLDING II CORPORATION
999 N Pacific Coast Hwy, El Segundo (90245-2714)
PHONE..................................310 955-9200
Brian C Strauss, *President*
EMP: 90
SALES (est): 46.2MM
SALES (corp-wide): 254.1MM **Privately Held**
SIC: 2952 2821 2891 Roof cement: asphalt, fibrous or plastic; polyurethane resins; sealants
HQ: Hco Holding I Corporation
999 N Pacific Coast Hwy
El Segundo CA 90245

(P-9115)
HENRY COMPANY LLC (HQ)
999 N Pacific Coast Hwy, El Segundo (90245-2714)
PHONE..................................310 955-9200
Frank Ready, *President*
Jason Peel, *CFO*
Mark Longfellow, *Vice Pres*
Christian Nolte, *Vice Pres*
Mehul Patel, *Vice Pres*
◆ EMP: 100
SALES (est): 233.6MM **Publicly Held**
SIC: 2952 2821 2891 Roof cement: asphalt, fibrous or plastic; polyurethane resins; sealants

(P-9116)
HNC PARENT INC (PA)
999 N Pacific Coast Hwy, El Segundo (90245-2714)
PHONE..................................310 955-9200
Rob Newbold, *Principal*
EMP: 100 EST: 2012
SALES (est): 254.1MM **Privately Held**
SIC: 2952 2821 2891 Roof cement: asphalt, fibrous or plastic; polyurethane resins; sealants

(P-9117)
IN-O-VATE INC
Also Called: Inovate Roofing Products
9301 Garfield Ave, South Gate (90280-3804)
PHONE..................................562 806-7515
Bennie Freiborg, *Ch of Bd*
Mark Freiborg, *President*
EMP: 10
SQ FT: 75,160
SALES (est): 2.2MM **Privately Held**
WEB: www.in-o-vate-inc.com
SIC: 2952 Roofing materials

(P-9118)
JAMES HARDIE TRADING CO INC
26300 La Alameda Ste 400, Mission Viejo (92691-8372)
PHONE..................................949 582-2378
Bryon G Borgardt, *President*
EMP: 160
SALES (est): 28.9MM **Privately Held**
SIC: 2952 Siding materials
HQ: James Hardie Transition Co., Inc.
26300 La Alameda Ste 400
Mission Viejo CA 92691
949 348-1800

(P-9119)
LUNDAY-THAGARD COMPANY
9301 Garfield Ave, South Gate (90280-3804)
P.O. Box 1519 (90280-1519)
PHONE..................................562 928-6990
John Todorovich, *Vice Pres*
EMP: 50
SALES (corp-wide): 119.4MM **Privately Held**
SIC: 2952 2951 Roofing materials; asphalt paving mixtures & blocks

HQ: Lunday-Thagard Company
9302 Garfield Ave
South Gate CA 90280
562 928-7000

(P-9120)
MBTECHNOLOGY
188 S Teilman Ave, Fresno (93706-1334)
PHONE...................................559 233-2181
Bahman Behbehani, *President*
Rostam Felfeli, *Vice Pres*
Khogasteh Behbehani, *Admin Sec*
Nina Marini, *Project Mgr*
John Stahl, *Technical Staff*
▲ EMP: 31 EST: 1981
SQ FT: 54,000
SALES (est): 10.8MM **Privately Held**
WEB: www.mbtechnology.com
SIC: 2952 Roofing materials

(P-9121)
**METROTILE MANUFACTURING
LLC**
Also Called: Metro Roof Products
3093 Industry St Ste A, Oceanside
(92054-4895)
PHONE...................................760 435-9842
Patrick Tavaran, *CEO*
◆ EMP: 45
SQ FT: 47,000
SALES (est): 6.9MM **Privately Held**
WEB: www.smartroofs.com
SIC: 2952 Roofing materials
HQ: Headwaters Incorporated
10701 S River Front Pkwy # 300
South Jordan UT 84095

(P-9122)
**MIDWESTERN PIPELINE SVCS
INC (PA)**
160 Klamath Ct, American Canyon
(94503-9700)
PHONE...................................707 557-6633
T Michael Harrison, *President*
John L Poyas, *Senior VP*
Stan Brady, *Vice Pres*
Chris M Harrison, *Vice Pres*
Michael T Wilhite, *Vice Pres*
EMP: 17 EST: 1940
SQ FT: 20,000
SALES (est): 1.9MM **Privately Held**
WEB:
www.midwesternpipelineservices.com
SIC: 2952 1799 Asphalt felts & coatings;
welding on site

(P-9123)
OWENS CORNING SALES LLC
1501 N Tamarind Ave, Compton
(90222-4130)
P.O. Box 5665 (90224-5665)
PHONE...................................310 631-1062
David Randalph, *Branch Mgr*
EMP: 175 **Publicly Held**
WEB: www.owenscorning.com
SIC: 2952 2951 1761 Roofing felts, ce-
ments or coatings; asphalt paving mix-
tures & blocks; roofing, siding & sheet
metal work
HQ: Owens Corning Sales, Llc
1 Owens Corning Pkwy
Toledo OH 43659
419 248-8000

(P-9124)
REP-KOTE PRODUCTS INC
10938 Beech Ave, Fontana (92337-7260)
PHONE...................................909 355-1288
Robert Wang, *President*
EMP: 35
SQ FT: 20,000
SALES (est): 3.4MM **Privately Held**
WEB: www.continentalcoatings.us
SIC: 2952 5084 Asphalt felts & coatings;
water pumps (industrial)

(P-9125)
RGM PRODUCTS INC
Also Called: Ridgeline
3301 Navone Rd, Stockton (95215-9312)
PHONE...................................559 499-2222
Clay Crum, *President*
Gus Freshwater, *Exec VP*
▲ EMP: 400

SALES (est): 49.6MM
SALES (corp-wide): 2.5B **Privately Held**
SIC: 2952 Asphalt felts & coatings
HQ: Elk Premium Building Products, Inc
14911 Quorum Dr Ste 600
Dallas TX 75254
972 851-0400

(P-9126)
TREMCO INCORPORATED
3060 E 44th St, Vernon (90058-2428)
PHONE...................................323 587-3014
Javier Hernandez, *Manager*
EMP: 15
SALES (corp-wide): 5.5B **Publicly Held**
WEB: www.tremcoinc.com
SIC: 2952 Roofing felts, cements or coat-
ings
HQ: Tremco Incorporated
3735 Green Rd
Beachwood OH 44122
216 292-5000

(P-9127)
TROPICAL ASPHALT LLC (PA)
Also Called: Tropical Roofing Products CA
14435 Macaw St, La Mirada (90638-5210)
PHONE...................................714 739-1408
Richard Zegelbone,
EMP: 15
SQ FT: 27,000
SALES (est): 9.7MM **Privately Held**
SIC: 2952 Asphalt felts & coatings

**2992 Lubricating Oils &
Greases**

(P-9128)
**ADELAIDE MARINE SERVICES
LLC**
100 W 35th St Unit Lm, National City
(91950-7925)
PHONE...................................619 852-8722
Angela Putrino, *Mng Member*
EMP: 11
SQ FT: 4,600
SALES: 10MM **Privately Held**
SIC: 2992 Lubricating oils

(P-9129)
AMTECOL INC
Also Called: American Hi-Tech Petro & Chem
810 Wright Ave, Richmond (94804-3640)
PHONE...................................510 235-7979
Susan Wynn, *CEO*
Hoa K Dang, *President*
Truc Huynh, *Vice Pres*
Peter Nguyen, *Vice Pres*
Jack Wynn, *Marketing Mgr*
◆ EMP: 30
SALES (est): 15.4MM **Privately Held**
WEB: www.amtecol.com
SIC: 2992 Lubricating oils

(P-9130)
AOCLSC INC
Also Called: Aocusa
8015 Paramount Blvd, Pico Rivera
(90660-4811)
PHONE...................................813 248-1988
Harry Barkett, *Branch Mgr*
EMP: 150
SALES (corp-wide): 29.2MM **Privately
Held**
SIC: 2992 Lubricating oils
PA: Aoclsc, Inc.
1601 Mcclosky Blvd
Tampa FL 33605
813 248-1988

(P-9131)
AOCLSC INC
Also Called: Aocusa
3365 E Slauson Ave, Vernon (90058-3914)
PHONE...................................562 776-4000
Stephen Milam, *CEO*
EMP: 30
SALES (corp-wide): 29.2MM **Privately
Held**
WEB: www.lsc-online.com
SIC: 2992 Lubricating oils & greases

PA: Aoclsc, Inc.
1601 Mcclosky Blvd
Tampa FL 33605
813 248-1988

(P-9132)
**ARCTIC SILVER
INCORPORATED**
9826 W Legacy Ave, Visalia (93291-9544)
PHONE...................................559 740-0912
Nevin House, *President*
Rochelle Overstreet, *Corp Secy*
Gregg Malm, *Vice Pres*
Terri McCluskey, *Human Res Mgr*
▲ EMP: 12
SQ FT: 3,200
SALES (est): 1.8MM **Privately Held**
WEB: www.arcticsilver.com
SIC: 2992 Lubricating oils & greases

(P-9133)
ARMITE LABORATORIES INC
1560 Superior Ave Ste A4, Costa Mesa
(92627-3676)
PHONE...................................949 646-9035
Josh Walker, *President*
Anders Folkedal, *Treasurer*
▲ EMP: 10 EST: 1923
SQ FT: 7,500
SALES: 2MM **Privately Held**
WEB: www.armitelabs.com
SIC: 2992 2843 2891 5172 Lubricating
oils; penetrants; sealants; petroleum
products; lubricating oils & greases

(P-9134)
BP LUBRICANTS USA INC
Also Called: BP Castrol
801 Wharf St, Richmond (94804-3557)
PHONE...................................510 236-6312
William Walter, *Branch Mgr*
EMP: 40
SQ FT: 17,680
SALES (corp-wide): 298.7B **Privately
Held**
WEB: www.castrolna.com
SIC: 2992 Cutting oils, blending: made
from purchased materials
HQ: Bp Lubricants Usa Inc.
1500 Valley Rd
Wayne NJ 07470
973 633-2200

(P-9135)
CHAMPIONS CHOICE INC
1910 E Via Burton, Anaheim (92806-1228)
PHONE...................................714 635-4491
Adam W Huber, *Ch of Bd*
Al Baudoin, *President*
Melodie Reguero, *Treasurer*
Patrick Huber, *Vice Pres*
Candace Baudoin, *Admin Sec*
EMP: 13
SQ FT: 20,000
SALES (est): 1.6MM **Privately Held**
WEB: www.championschoice.com
SIC: 2992 Lubricating oils

(P-9136)
CHEM ARROW CORP
13643 Live Oak Ln, Irwindale
(91706-1317)
P.O. Box 2366, Baldwin Park (91706-1198)
PHONE...................................626 358-2255
Alphonse Spalding, *Ch of Bd*
Hemith Mitchell, *President*
Alex Klubnikin, *Plant Mgr*
▼ EMP: 25
SQ FT: 36,000
SALES (est): 10.5MM **Privately Held**
WEB: www.chemarrow.com
SIC: 2992 2899 Lubricating oils; rust ar-
resting compounds, animal or vegetable
oil base; fuel tank or engine cleaning
chemicals; metal treating compounds;
rust resisting compounds

(P-9137)
CHEMTOOL INCORPORATED
1300 Goodrich Dr, Tehachapi (93561-1508)
PHONE...................................661 823-7190
Bill Hart, *Manager*
EMP: 30

SALES (corp-wide): 225.3B **Publicly
Held**
WEB: www.chemtool.com
SIC: 2992 2899 5172 Oils & greases,
blending & compounding; chemical
preparations; lubricating oils & greases
HQ: Chemtool Incorporated
801 W Rockton Rd
Rockton IL 61072
815 957-4140

(P-9138)
CHERRY PIT
812 E Monte Vista Ave, Vacaville
(95688-2922)
PHONE...................................707 449-8378
Mike Cherry, *Principal*
EMP: 12
SALES (est): 1.3MM **Privately Held**
SIC: 2992 Lubricating oils & greases

(P-9139)
**DEMENNO/KERDOON
HOLDINGS**
Also Called: D K Environmental
3650 E 26th St, Vernon (90058-4104)
PHONE...................................323 268-3387
Rodney Ananda, *Manager*
EMP: 53
SALES (corp-wide): 119.4MM **Privately
Held**
SIC: 2992 4953 Oils & greases, blending
& compounding; re-refining lubricating oils
& greases; transmission fluid: made from
purchased materials; refuse systems
HQ: Demenno/Kerdoon Holdings
9302 Garfield Ave
South Gate CA 90280
562 231-1550

(P-9140)
**DEMENNO/KERDOON
HOLDINGS (DH)**
Also Called: Demenno-Kerdoon
9302 Garfield Ave, South Gate
(90280-3805)
PHONE...................................562 231-1550
Robert Roth, *Ch of Bd*
Bruce Demenno, *CEO*
Steve Kerdoon, *COO*
Mark Snell, *Principal*
EMP: 67 EST: 1971
SQ FT: 21,000
SALES (est): 25.9MM
SALES (corp-wide): 119.4MM **Privately
Held**
SIC: 2992 2911 Oils & greases, blending
& compounding; re-refining lubricating oils
& greases; transmission fluid: made from
purchased materials; petroleum refining

(P-9141)
**EVERGREEN HOLDINGS INC
(PA)**
18952 Macarthur Blvd # 410, Irvine
(92612-1402)
PHONE...................................949 757-7770
Jacob Voogd, *Ch of Bd*
Gary Colbert, *President*
Jesus Romero, *CFO*
Atam Gossain, *Admin Sec*
▲ EMP: 20
SQ FT: 6,200
SALES (est): 20.6MM **Privately Held**
WEB: www.evergreenoil.com
SIC: 2992 4953 Re-refining lubricating oils
& greases; liquid waste, collection & dis-
posal

(P-9142)
EVERGREEN OIL INC (HQ)
Also Called: Evergreen Environmental Svcs
18025 S Broadway, Gardena (90248-3539)
PHONE...................................949 757-7770
Jake Voogd, *CEO*
Jesus Romero, *CFO*
George Lamont, *Exec VP*
Obert Gwaltney, *VP Opers*
EMP: 23
SALES (est): 48.2MM
SALES (corp-wide): 3.3B **Publicly Held**
WEB: www.evergreenoil.com
SIC: 2992 2911 4953 Lubricating oils &
greases; petroleum refining; refuse sys-
tems

PRODUCTS & SVCS

PA: Clean Harbors, Inc.
42 Longwater Dr
Norwell MA 02061
781 792-5000

(P-9143)
EZ LUBE LLC
532 W Florida Ave, Hemet (92543-4007)
PHONE.................................951 766-1996
Richie Berling, *Manager*
EMP: 638
SALES (corp-wide): 22.5MM **Privately Held**
SIC: 2992 Lubricating oils
PA: Ez Lube, Llc
3540 Howard Way Ste 200
Costa Mesa CA
-

(P-9144)
FLUID LUBRICATION & CHEM CO
18400 S Broadway, Gardena (90248-4633)
PHONE.................................800 826-2415
Christopher L Luther, *CEO*
EMP: 10
SALES (est): 1MM **Privately Held**
SIC: 2992 Lubricating oils

(P-9145)
HUSK-ITT DISTRIBUTORS CORP
Also Called: Huskey Specially Lubricants
1580 Industrial Ave, Norco (92860-2946)
PHONE.................................951 340-4000
Shelby R Huskey, *CEO*
Berlynda Bevacqua, *CFO*
Michael Montgomery, *Vice Pres*
James Spence, *Maintence Staff*
EMP: 18
SQ FT: 30,000
SALES (est): 5.9MM **Privately Held**
WEB: www.huskey.com
SIC: 2992 Oils & greases, blending & compounding

(P-9146)
ILLINOIS TOOL WORKS INC
1050 W 5th St, Azusa (91702-3308)
PHONE.................................847 724-7500
Gerald Miles, *General Mgr*
EMP: 130
SALES (corp-wide): 14.7B **Publicly Held**
SIC: 2992 2899 Lubricating oils; chemical preparations
PA: Illinois Tool Works Inc.
155 Harlem Ave
Glenview IL 60025
847 724-7500

(P-9147)
INTERNATIONAL PETROLEUM PRODUC
Also Called: Ipac
7600 Dublin Blvd Ste 240, Dublin (94568-2908)
PHONE.................................925 556-5530
Brian Cereghino, *CEO*
Jeff Crow, *President*
Alan Krock, *CFO*
Gina Carter, *Controller*
Gordon Dillaman, *Manager*
▲ **EMP:** 10
SQ FT: 7,500
SALES (est): 3.1MM **Privately Held**
WEB: www.ipac-inc.com
SIC: 2992 5172 Lubricating oils & greases; petroleum products

(P-9148)
IPAC INC
7600 Dublin Blvd Ste 240, Dublin (94568-2908)
PHONE.................................925 556-5530
Brian Cereghino, *President*
Neil Olsen, *Project Mgr*
Tammy Tinder, *Natl Sales Mgr*
Jeff Melendez, *Sales Staff*
EMP: 18
SALES: 4.4MM **Privately Held**
SIC: 2992 Lubricating oils & greases

(P-9149)
JONELL OIL CORPORATION
13649 Live Oak Ln, Irwindale (91706-1317)
PHONE.................................626 303-4691

John Tarazi, *CEO*
Helen Tarazi, *President*
EMP: 10
SQ FT: 10,000
SALES: 2MM **Privately Held**
SIC: 2992 Re-refining lubricating oils & greases

(P-9150)
LUBECO INC
6859 Downey Ave, Long Beach (90805-1967)
PHONE.................................562 602-1791
Steven Rossi, *President*
EMP: 45 EST: 1958
SQ FT: 20,000
SALES (est): 7.9MM **Privately Held**
SIC: 2992 2851 Lubricating oils & greases; paints & allied products

(P-9151)
LUCAS OIL PRODUCTS INC (PA)
302 N Sheridan St, Corona (92880-2067)
PHONE.................................951 270-0154
Forrest Lucas, *CEO*
Kevin Asbell, *Vice Pres*
Charlotte Lucas, *Vice Pres*
Robert Patison, *General Mgr*
Dan Robinson, *General Mgr*
◆ **EMP:** 150
SQ FT: 80,000
SALES (est): 100MM **Privately Held**
WEB: www.lucasoil.com
SIC: 2992 5169 Lubricating oils & greases; oil additives

(P-9152)
MACH OIL CORP
17835 Ventura Blvd # 301, Encino (91316-3634)
P.O. Box 261414 (91426-1414)
PHONE.................................818 783-3567
Vahab Aghai, *President*
Amir Sabetin, *CFO*
EMP: 12
SALES (est): 935.7K **Privately Held**
SIC: 2992 Lubricating oils & greases

(P-9153)
PHILLIPS 66 SPECTRUM CORP
Also Called: Red Line Synthetic Oil
6100 Egret Ct, Benicia (94510-1269)
PHONE.................................707 745-6100
Ann M Oglesby, *Principal*
Angela Adams, *Admin Asst*
Timothy Decesaro, *Sales Staff*
Cameron Evans, *Sales Staff*
Roy Howell, *Manager*
EMP: 17
SALES (corp-wide): 28.8MM **Privately Held**
SIC: 2992 Lubricating oils; brake fluid (hydraulic): made from purchased materials; transmission fluid: made from purchased materials
PA: Phillips 66 Spectrum Corporation
3010 Briarpark Dr
Houston TX 77042
281 293-6600

(P-9154)
ROSEMEAD OIL PRODUCTS INC
12402 Los Nietos Rd, Santa Fe Springs (90670-2914)
P.O. Box 2645 (90670-0645)
PHONE.................................562 941-3261
Richard Schoensiegel Jr, *President*
▲ **EMP:** 11
SQ FT: 25,000
SALES (est): 2.9MM
SALES (corp-wide): 3.3B **Publicly Held**
WEB: www.rosemeadoil.com
SIC: 2992 5172 Oils & greases, blending & compounding; lubricating oils & greases
PA: Clean Harbors, Inc.
42 Longwater Dr
Norwell MA 02061
781 792-5000

(P-9155)
SALCO DYNAMIC SOLUTIONS INC (PA)
Also Called: Salco Oil
6248 Surfpoint Cir, Huntington Beach (92648-5590)
PHONE.................................714 374-7500
Lucy George, *CEO*
Scott George, *CFO*
EMP: 35
SALES: 713K **Privately Held**
SIC: 2992 5172 5085 5084 Oils & greases, blending & compounding; petroleum products; industrial supplies; industrial machinery & equipment; machine tools, metal cutting type; machine tool accessories

(P-9156)
SOUTH WEST LUBRICANTS INC
Also Called: Maxima Racing Oils
9266 Abraham Way, Santee (92071-5611)
PHONE.................................619 449-5000
Daniel J Massie, *CEO*
◆ **EMP:** 11
SQ FT: 50,000
SALES (est): 4.4MM **Privately Held**
WEB: www.maximausa.com
SIC: 2992 Lubricating oils

(P-9157)
VAST ENTERPRISES
Also Called: Liquid Packaging
7739 Monroe St, Paramount (90723-5020)
PHONE.................................562 633-3224
Joe Mouren-Laurens, *CEO*
Dean Mouren-Laurens, *Vice Pres*
EMP: 13
SQ FT: 18,000
SALES (est): 3.7MM **Privately Held**
WEB: www.liquidpackagingcompany.com
SIC: 2992 Transmission fluid: made from purchased materials

(P-9158)
W S DODGE OIL CO INC
3710 Fruitland Ave, Maywood (90270-2196)
PHONE.................................323 583-3478
Tom Downs, *President*
David Downs, *Treasurer*
Annemarie Downs, *Vice Pres*
Jim Mather, *Sales Staff*
▲ **EMP:** 17
SQ FT: 12,000
SALES (est): 6MM **Privately Held**
WEB: www.wsdodgeoil.com
SIC: 2992 Cutting oils, blending: made from purchased materials

(P-9159)
WD-40 COMPANY (PA)
9715 Businesspark Ave, San Diego (92131-1642)
PHONE.................................619 275-1400
Garry O Ridge, *President*
Linda A Lang, *Ch of Bd*
Jay W Rembolt, *CFO*
Steven A Brass, *Division Pres*
Michael L Freeman, *Officer*
EMP: 263 EST: 1953
SALES: 423.3MM **Publicly Held**
WEB: www.wd40.com
SIC: 2992 2851 Lubricating oils; removers & cleaners

2999 Products Of Petroleum & Coal, NEC

(P-9160)
LUNDAY-THAGARD COMPANY (HQ)
Also Called: Ltr
9302 Garfield Ave, South Gate (90280-3805)
P.O. Box 1519 (90280-1519)
PHONE.................................562 928-7000
Bernard B Roth, *Ch of Bd*
Robert Roth, *President*
Austin Miller, *COO*
Larry Mori, *Vice Pres*
Steve Roth, *Vice Pres*
EMP: 106

SQ FT: 16,000
SALES (est): 89.9MM
SALES (corp-wide): 119.4MM **Privately Held**
SIC: 2999 2951 2911 Coke; paving blocks; gases & liquefied petroleum gases
PA: World Oil Marketing Company
9302 Garfield Ave
South Gate CA 90280
562 928-0100

(P-9161)
RENTECH INC (PA)
10880 Wilshire Blvd # 1101, Los Angeles (90024-4112)
PHONE.................................310 571-9800
Keith Forman, *President*
Halbert S Washburn, *Ch of Bd*
Keith B Forman, *President*
Paul M Summers, *CFO*
Joseph V Herold, *Senior VP*
EMP: 99
SQ FT: 600
SALES: 150.7MM **Privately Held**
SIC: 2999 2873 6794 Waxes, petroleum: not produced in petroleum refineries; nitrogenous fertilizers; patent buying, licensing, leasing

(P-9162)
WAX RESEARCH INC
Also Called: Globe Rider Distribution
1212 Distribution Way, Vista (92081-8816)
PHONE.................................760 607-0850
John A Dahl, *President*
Cris Dahl, *CFO*
▲ **EMP:** 12
SQ FT: 22,000
SALES (est): 2MM **Privately Held**
WEB: www.stickybumps.com
SIC: 2999 Waxes, petroleum: not produced in petroleum refineries

3011 Tires & Inner Tubes

(P-9163)
AMERICAN GENERAL TOOL GROUP
929 Poinsettia Ave # 101, Vista (92081-8459)
PHONE.................................760 745-7993
Nasreen Godil, *President*
EMP: 40
SALES (est): 6.4MM **Privately Held**
SIC: 3011 3492 3535 3822 Pneumatic tires, all types; control valves, aircraft: hydraulic & pneumatic; control valves, fluid power: hydraulic & pneumatic; pneumatic tube conveyor systems; switches, pneumatic positioning remote

(P-9164)
BAS RECYCLING INC
14050 Day St, Moreno Valley (92553-9106)
PHONE.................................951 214-6590
Ohannes Beudjekian, *Ch of Bd*
Sarkis Beudjeaian, *CEO*
▲ **EMP:** 40
SQ FT: 80,000
SALES (est): 14.7MM **Privately Held**
WEB: www.basrecycling.com
SIC: 3011 Tires, cushion or solid rubber

(P-9165)
BGM INSTALLATION INC
528 E D St, Wilmington (90744-6002)
PHONE.................................310 830-3113
John Battaglia, *Principal*
EMP: 14
SALES (est): 2.3MM **Privately Held**
SIC: 3011 5211 Tires & inner tubes; lumber & other building materials

(P-9166)
CARLSTAR GROUP LLC
1990 S Vintage Ave, Ontario (91761-2819)
PHONE.................................310 816-1015
David Chavez, *Branch Mgr*
EMP: 142
SALES (corp-wide): 1.4B **Privately Held**
SIC: 3011 Industrial tires, pneumatic

▲ = Import ▼=Export
◆ =Import/Export

PA: The Carlstar Group Llc
725 Cool Springs Blvd
Franklin TN 37067
615 503-0220

(P-9167)
CONTINENTAL INTELLIGENT TRANSP
3901 N 1st St, San Jose (95134-1506)
PHONE......................408 391-9008
Seval Oza, *Mng Member*
Eileen Riorden, *Executive Asst*
Tammer Zein-El-Abedien, *Administration*
Tejas Desai,
Seval Oz, *Mng Member*
EMP: 20
SALES (est): 624.1K **Privately Held**
SIC: 3011 Tires & inner tubes

(P-9168)
ITW GLOBAL TIRE REPAIR INC
Also Called: Access Marketing
125 Venture Dr Ste 210, San Luis Obispo
(93401-9105)
PHONE......................805 489-0490
Juan Valls, *CEO*
◆ **EMP:** 71
SQ FT: 20,000
SALES (est): 18.7MM
SALES (corp-wide): 14.7B **Publicly Held**
WEB: www.slime.com
SIC: 3011 2891 Tire & inner tube materials
& related products; adhesives & sealants
PA: Illinois Tool Works Inc.
155 Harlem Ave
Glenview IL 60025
847 724-7500

(P-9169)
SKAT-TRAK INC
654 Avenue K, Calimesa (92320-1115)
P.O. Box 518 (92320-0518)
PHONE......................909 795-2505
Ken Stuart, *President*
Diane Stuart, *Corp Secy*
Glenn Perry, *Purch Agent*
EMP: 115
SQ FT: 3,000
SALES (est): 15.9MM **Privately Held**
WEB: www.skat-trak.com
SIC: 3011 3599 3366 Tires & inner tubes;
propellers, ship & boat: machined; copper
foundries

(P-9170)
TOYO TIRE HLDINGS AMERICAS INC (HQ)
5900 Katella Ave Ste 200a, Cypress
(90630-5019)
PHONE......................562 431-6502
Tomoshige Mizutani, *CEO*
Jeffrey Bootz, *Sales Staff*
▲ **EMP:** 20
SALES (est): 284.7MM **Privately Held**
SIC: 3011 Automobile inner tubes

3021 Rubber & Plastic Footwear

(P-9171)
FOUR STAR DISTRIBUTION
206 Calle Conchita, San Clemente
(92672-5404)
PHONE......................949 369-4420
Markus Bohi, *CEO*
Raul Ries, *President*
Brian Abraham, *Info Tech Dir*
▲ **EMP:** 65
SALES (est): 8MM **Privately Held**
SIC: 3021 Shoes, plastic soles molded to
fabric uppers

(P-9172)
JEVIN ENTERPRISES INC
Also Called: Coast Dance Shoes
11548 Apulia Ct, Porter Ranch
(91326-4400)
P.O. Box 3876, Granada Hills (91394-0876)
PHONE......................818 408-0488
Roxane Agopian, *President*
Harout Agopian, *Treasurer*
▲ **EMP:** 30

SALES (est): 3.5MM **Privately Held**
SIC: 3021 Arctics, rubber or rubber soled
fabric

(P-9173)
JOE MONTANA FOOTWEAR
228 Manhattan Beach Blvd, Manhattan
Beach (90266-5347)
PHONE......................310 318-3100
Robert Greenberg, *CEO*
EMP: 99
SALES (est): 4.4MM **Privately Held**
SIC: 3021 Rubber & plastics footwear

(P-9174)
K-SWISS INC (HQ)
523 W 6th St Ste 534, Los Angeles
(90014-1225)
PHONE......................323 675-2700
Philip Jeong, *Ch of Bd*
Mark Miller, *President*
Barney Waters, *Chief Mktg Ofcr*
Elaine M Molina, *CIO*
Preston Davis, *Sales Staff*
◆ **EMP:** 115
SALES (est): 489.4MM **Privately Held**
WEB: www.kswiss.com
SIC: 3021 Rubber & plastics footwear

(P-9175)
K-SWISS SALES CORP
31248 Oak Crest Dr # 150, Westlake Village (91361-4692)
PHONE......................818 706-5100
Cheryl Kuchinka, *President*
EMP: 242
SALES: 484MM **Privately Held**
WEB: www.kswiss.com
SIC: 3021 Rubber & plastics footwear
HQ: K-Swiss Inc.
523 W 6th St Ste 534
Los Angeles CA 90014
323 675-2700

(P-9176)
NIKE INC
3505 Hayden Ave, Culver City
(90232-2412)
PHONE......................310 736-3800
Michel Melissa, *Branch Mgr*
EMP: 38
SALES (corp-wide): 39.1B **Publicly Held**
SIC: 3021 Rubber & plastics footwear
PA: Nike, Inc.
1 Sw Bowerman Dr
Beaverton OR 97005
503 671-6453

(P-9177)
NIKE INC
222 E Redondo Beach Blvd C, Gardena
(90248-2302)
PHONE......................310 670-6770
Ana Madrid, *Manager*
Thomas Coleman, *Sales Staff*
EMP: 38
SALES (corp-wide): 39.1B **Publicly Held**
WEB: www.nike.com
SIC: 3021 Rubber & plastics footwear
PA: Nike, Inc.
1 Sw Bowerman Dr
Beaverton OR 97005
503 671-6453

(P-9178)
PLS DIABETIC SHOE COMPANY INC
21500 Osborne St, Canoga Park
(91304-1522)
PHONE......................818 734-7080
Ambartsum Kumuryan, *President*
Konstandin Kumuryan, *COO*
▲ **EMP:** 32
SQ FT: 24,031
SALES (est): 4.6MM **Privately Held**
SIC: 3021 Shoes, rubber or plastic molded
to fabric

(P-9179)
PRINCIPLE PLASTICS
1136 W 135th St, Gardena (90247-1919)
P.O. Box 2408 (90247-0408)
PHONE......................310 532-3411
David Hoyt, *President*
Robert Hoyt, *CFO*
▲ **EMP:** 27 EST: 1948

SQ FT: 28,000
SALES (est): 8.3MM **Privately Held**
WEB: www.sloggers.com
SIC: 3021 3949 2519 Galoshes, plastic;
golf equipment; lawn & garden furniture,
except wood & metal

(P-9180)
RECON 1 INC
Also Called: Emergency Preparedness Pdts
4045 Via Pescador, Camarillo
(93012-6830)
PHONE......................805 388-3911
Toll Free:......................888 -
Gary Kalaydjian, *President*
Pete Kalaydjian, *CFO*
◆ **EMP:** 12
SQ FT: 7,000
SALES (est): 2.1MM **Privately Held**
SIC: 3021 5941 Rubber & plastics
footwear; camping equipment

(P-9181)
SKECHERS COLLECTION LLC (HQ)
Also Called: Sketchers
228 Manhattan Beach Blvd, Manhattan
Beach (90266-5347)
PHONE......................310 318-3100
Robert Greenberg, *Mng Member*
Phil Paccione, *Executive*
Jason Kartalis, *Director*
◆ **EMP:** 20
SALES (est): 1.7MM **Publicly Held**
WEB: www.skechers.com
SIC: 3021 5661 Shoes, rubber or plastic
molded to fabric; shoe stores

(P-9182)
SKECHERS USA INC
330 S Sepulveda Blvd, Manhattan Beach
(90266-6828)
PHONE......................310 318-3100
Jeffrey Greenberg, *Vice Pres*
Ryan Rossler, *Vice Pres*
James Beirne, *Director*
Ally Barron, *Manager*
Brian Sanchez, *Manager*
EMP: 25 **Publicly Held**
SIC: 3021 3149 5661 Shoes, rubber or
plastic molded to fabric; athletic shoes,
except rubber or plastic; shoe stores
PA: Skechers U.S.A., Inc.
228 Manhattan Beach Blvd # 200
Manhattan Beach CA 90266

(P-9183)
SKECHERS USA INC II (HQ)
225 S Sepulveda Blvd, Manhattan Beach
(90266-6825)
PHONE......................310 318-3100
Robert Greenburg, *CEO*
Ed Jones, *Business Mgr*
Brian Cross, *Director*
Maria Hernandez, *Manager*
◆ **EMP:** 34
SALES (est): 84.8MM **Publicly Held**
SIC: 3021 5661 Shoes, rubber or plastic
molded to fabric; shoe stores

(P-9184)
SONICSENSORY INC (PA)
1163 Logan St, Los Angeles (90026)
P.O. Box 24, Lake Peekskill NY (10537-0024)
PHONE......................213 336-3747
Susan Paley, *CEO*
Eddie Borjas, *CTO*
EMP: 16
SQ FT: 2,000
SALES (est): 2.8MM **Privately Held**
SIC: 3021 Shoes, rubber or rubber soled
fabric uppers

(P-9185)
SUMMER RIO CORP (PA)
17501 Rowland St, City of Industry
(91748-1115)
PHONE......................626 854-1498
Qing LI, *President*
Lauren Schneider, *Accounts Mgr*
◆ **EMP:** 20

SALES (est): 3.4MM **Privately Held**
WEB: www.summerrio.net
SIC: 3021 Canvas shoes, rubber soled;
shoes, plastic soles molded to fabric uppers; shoes, plastic or plastic molded to
fabric; shoes, rubber or rubber soled fabric uppers

(P-9186)
TOUCHSPORT FOOTWEAR LLC
2969 E Pcf Commerce Dr, E Rncho Dmngz
(90221-5729)
PHONE......................310 763-0208
Peter Liow,
▲ **EMP:** 10
SALES (est): 4.5MM **Privately Held**
SIC: 3021 Sandals, rubber

(P-9187)
VANS INC
796 Northridge Shopg Ctr, Salinas (93906)
PHONE......................831 444-0158
Stephanie Estrada, *Branch Mgr*
EMP: 10
SALES (corp-wide): 13.8MM **Publicly Held**
SIC: 3021 Rubber & plastics footwear
HQ: Vans, Inc.
1588 S Coast Dr
Costa Mesa CA 92626
855 909-8267

(P-9188)
VANS INC
6000 Sepulveda Blvd # 2155, Culver City
(90230-6429)
PHONE......................310 390-7548
EMP: 10
SALES (corp-wide): 13.8MM **Publicly Held**
SIC: 3021 Rubber & plastics footwear
HQ: Vans, Inc.
1588 S Coast Dr
Costa Mesa CA 92626
855 909-8267

(P-9189)
VANS INC
14006 Riverside Dr, Sherman Oaks
(91423-1945)
PHONE......................818 990-1098
Rene Altervain, *Branch Mgr*
EMP: 10
SALES (corp-wide): 13.8MM **Publicly Held**
SIC: 3021 Canvas shoes, rubber soled
HQ: Vans, Inc.
1588 S Coast Dr
Costa Mesa CA 92626
855 909-8267

(P-9190)
VANS INC
1354 Burlingame Ave, Burlingame
(94010-4109)
PHONE......................650 401-3542
Nicole Clough, *Branch Mgr*
EMP: 11
SALES (corp-wide): 13.8MM **Publicly Held**
SIC: 3021 5137 2326 Canvas shoes, rubber soled; women's & children's clothing;
men's & boys' work clothing
HQ: Vans, Inc.
1588 S Coast Dr
Costa Mesa CA 92626
855 909-8267

(P-9191)
VANS INC
5232 E 2nd St, Long Beach (90803-5329)
PHONE......................562 856-1695
Jerry Rodriguez, *General Mgr*
EMP: 10
SALES (corp-wide): 13.8MM **Publicly Held**
SIC: 3021 Canvas shoes, rubber soled
HQ: Vans, Inc.
1588 S Coast Dr
Costa Mesa CA 92626
855 909-8267

P R O D U C T S & S V C S

(P-9192)
VANS INC
3251 20th Ave Ste 237, San Francisco
(94132-1974)
PHONE...................................415 566-3762
Nikki Aclaro, Branch Mgr
EMP: 17
SALES (corp-wide): 13.8MM **Publicly Held**
SIC: **3021** Canvas shoes, rubber soled
HQ: Vans, Inc.
1588 S Coast Dr
Costa Mesa CA 92626
855 909-8267

(P-9193)
VANS INC
13920 Cy Ctr Dr Ste 4035, Chino Hills
(91709)
PHONE...................................909 517-3141
Tyler Tritipo, Branch Mgr
EMP: 10
SALES (corp-wide): 13.8MM **Publicly Held**
SIC: **3021** Canvas shoes, rubber soled
HQ: Vans, Inc.
1588 S Coast Dr
Costa Mesa CA 92626
855 909-8267

(P-9194)
VANS INC (DH)
Also Called: Vans Shoes
1588 S Coast Dr, Costa Mesa
(92626-1533)
PHONE...................................855 909-8267
Arthur I Carver, Senior VP
Scott J Blechman, CFO
Robert L Nagel, Senior VP
Craig E Gosselin, Vice Pres
Doug Paladini, Vice Pres
▲ EMP: 277
SQ FT: 185,000
SALES (est): 291.1MM
SALES (corp-wide): 13.8MM **Publicly Held**
SIC: **3021** 2321 2329 2325 Canvas shoes, rubber soled; protective footwear, rubber or plastic; boots, rubber or rubber soled fabric; men's & boys' sports & polo shirts; polo shirts, men's & boys': made from purchased materials; men's & boys' sportswear & athletic clothing; jackets (suede, leatherette, etc.), sport: men's & boys'; slacks, dress: men's, youths' & boys'; shorts (outerwear): men's, youths' & boys'; hats, caps & millinery; canvas bags
HQ: Vf Outdoor, Llc
2701 Harbor Bay Pkwy
Alameda CA 94502
510 618-3500

(P-9195)
VANS INC
5800 Northgate Dr Ste 44, San Rafael
(94903-6833)
PHONE...................................415 479-1284
George Gray, Branch Mgr
EMP: 10
SALES (corp-wide): 13.8MM **Publicly Held**
SIC: **3021** Canvas shoes, rubber soled
HQ: Vans, Inc.
1588 S Coast Dr
Costa Mesa CA 92626
855 909-8267

(P-9196)
VP FOOTWEAR INC
2536 Loma Ave, South El Monte
(91733-1418)
PHONE...................................626 443-2186
Peter Che, President
▲ EMP: 10
SQ FT: 10,000
SALES (est): 1.2MM **Privately Held**
WEB: www.vpfootwear.com
SIC: **3021** 5139 Rubber & plastics footwear; shoes

3052 Rubber & Plastic Hose & Belting

(P-9197)
BERG-NELSON COMPANY INC
1633 W 17th St, Long Beach (90813-1285)
PHONE...................................562 432-3491
Craig Nelson, President
Ray Dunn, Vice Pres
EMP: 12
SQ FT: 10,000
SALES (est): 1.3MM **Privately Held**
SIC: **3052** 3492 Rubber & plastics hose & beltings; fluid power valves & hose fittings

(P-9198)
GANN PRODUCTS COMPANY INC
9540 Stewart And Gray Rd, Downey
(90241-5590)
PHONE...................................562 862-2337
Larry Gann, President
Lila Gann, Corp Secy
▲ EMP: 10 EST: 1954
SQ FT: 7,000
SALES (est): 2MM **Privately Held**
WEB: www.gannproducts.com
SIC: **3052** 3714 Automobile hose, rubber; motor vehicle body components & frame

(P-9199)
LEWIS-GOETZ AND COMPANY INC
Also Called: Valley Rubber & Gasket
4848 Frontier Way Ste C, Stockton
(95215-8348)
PHONE...................................209 944-0791
Brian Rowland, Manager
Anthony Mattes, Sales Staff
EMP: 11 **Privately Held**
SIC: **3052** 3053 5084 Rubber & plastics hose & beltings; gaskets, packing & sealing devices; industrial machinery & equipment
HQ: Eriks North America, Inc.
650 Washington Rd Ste 500
Pittsburgh PA 15228
800 937-9070

(P-9200)
NAT ARONSON & ASSOCIATES INC
Also Called: Aronson Manufacturing
7640 Gloria Ave Ste J, Van Nuys
(91406-1800)
P.O. Box 7795 (91409-7795)
PHONE...................................818 787-5160
Nathan Aronson, CEO
EMP: 16
SQ FT: 9,200
SALES (est): 2.7MM **Privately Held**
SIC: **3052** Rubber hose

(P-9201)
NORTH AMERICAN FIRE HOSE CORP
Also Called: Nafhc
910 Noble Way, Santa Maria (93454-1506)
P.O. Box 1968 (93456-1968)
PHONE...................................805 922-7076
Michael S Aubuchon, CEO
Virginia Aubuchon, Admin Sec
▲ EMP: 55
SQ FT: 43,000
SALES (est): 13.5MM **Privately Held**
WEB: www.nafhc.com
SIC: **3052** Fire hose, rubber

(P-9202)
OMEGA FIRE INC
441 W Allen Ave Ste 109, San Dimas
(91773-4702)
P.O. Box 4919 (91773-8919)
PHONE...................................818 404-6212
McKenzie Kordabadi, Principal
EMP: 10
SALES (est): 705.9K **Privately Held**
SIC: **3052** 3669 1711 2899 Fire hose, rubber; fire detection systems, electric; fire sprinkler system installation; fire extinguisher charges

---

(P-9203)
PARKER-HANNIFIN CORPORATION
Also Called: Parker Service Center
8460 Kass Dr, Buena Park (90621-3808)
PHONE...................................714 522-8840
Chris Wright, Branch Mgr
EMP: 21
SALES (corp-wide): 14.3B **Publicly Held**
WEB: www.parker.com
SIC: **3052** 3429 Rubber & plastics hose & beltings; manufactured hardware (general)
PA: Parker-Hannifin Corporation
6035 Parkland Blvd
Cleveland OH 44124
216 896-3000

(P-9204)
PRICE RUBBER COMPANY INC
17760 Ideal Pkwy, Manteca (95336-8992)
P.O. Box 100, French Camp (95231-0100)
PHONE...................................209 239-7478
Donna J Sprouse, President
Shurene Rehmke, Vice Pres
Christen A Lewis-Griffin, Admin Sec
EMP: 19
SQ FT: 15,000
SALES (est): 3.4MM **Privately Held**
SIC: **3052** 3053 Rubber & plastics hose & beltings; gaskets, packing & sealing devices

(P-9205)
RALPH L FLORIMONTE
517 Alondra Dr, Huntington Beach
(92648-3768)
PHONE...................................714 960-4470
Ralph Florimonte, CEO
EMP: 18 EST: 2001
SALES (est): 1MM **Privately Held**
SIC: **3052** Vacuum cleaner hose, plastic

(P-9206)
SANI-TECH WEST INC (PA)
1020 Flynn Rd, Camarillo (93012-8705)
PHONE...................................805 389-0400
Richard J Shor, President
Sherry Maxson, Vice Pres
EMP: 80
SQ FT: 27,000
SALES (est): 16.6MM **Privately Held**
WEB: www.sani-techwest.com
SIC: **3052** 3053 Rubber hose; plastic hose; gasket materials

(P-9207)
TE CONNECTIVITY CORPORATION
Also Called: Raychem
6900 Paseo Padre Pkwy, Fremont
(94555-3641)
PHONE...................................650 361-3333
John McGraw, Branch Mgr
EMP: 350
SALES (corp-wide): 13.9B **Privately Held**
WEB: www.raychem.com
SIC: **3052** Plastic hose
HQ: Te Connectivity Corporation
1050 Westlakes Dr
Berwyn PA 19312
610 893-9800

(P-9208)
TECHNICAL HEATERS INC
Also Called: Thermolab
10959 Tuxford St, Sun Valley (91352-2626)
PHONE...................................818 361-7185
Bruce W Jones, President
Linnea Cantu, Bookkeeper
Brock Jones, Sales Mgr
EMP: 18
SQ FT: 35,000
SALES (est): 2.7MM **Privately Held**
WEB: www.techheat.com
SIC: **3052** Plastic hose; heater hose, rubber

(P-9209)
TK PAX INC
Also Called: P A X Industries
1561 Macarthur Blvd, Costa Mesa
(92626-1407)
PHONE...................................714 850-1330
Tom Kawaguchi, President

Randy Tamura, Vice Pres
Armando Martinez, General Mgr
▲ EMP: 30
SQ FT: 30,000
SALES (est): 5.9MM **Privately Held**
WEB: www.paxindustries.com
SIC: **3052** 3053 Rubber hose; plastic hose; gaskets, all materials

(P-9210)
TTI FLOOR CARE NORTH AMER INC
13055 Valley Blvd, Fontana (92335-2603)
PHONE...................................440 996-2802
Ross Verrocchi, Manager
EMP: 450 **Privately Held**
SIC: **3052** 5722 Vacuum cleaner hose, plastic; vacuum cleaners
HQ: Tti Floor Care North America, Inc.
7005 Cochran Rd
Solon OH 44139

(P-9211)
WESTFLEX INC (PA)
Also Called: Western Hose & Gasket
325 W 30th St, National City (91950-7205)
PHONE...................................619 474-7400
Dixon G Legros, President
Paula Legros, CFO
Lorena Vasquez, Sales Staff
Rebecca Strickland,
▲ EMP: 30
SQ FT: 56,000
SALES (est): 6.7MM **Privately Held**
WEB: www.westflex.com
SIC: **3052** 3053 5085 Rubber & plastics hose & beltings; gaskets, packing & sealing devices; gaskets & sealing devices; gasket materials; gaskets, all materials; hose, belting & packing

---

3053 Gaskets, Packing & Sealing Devices

(P-9212)
A & D RUBBER PRODUCTS CO INC (PA)
1438 Bourbon St, Stockton (95204-2404)
PHONE...................................209 941-0100
Dale W Wolford, President
Ann Wolford, Treasurer
▲ EMP: 28
SQ FT: 20,000
SALES (est): 4.2MM **Privately Held**
WEB: www.adrubber.com
SIC: **3053** 5085 2822 5169 Gaskets, packing & sealing devices; industrial supplies; synthetic rubber; synthetic resins; rubber & plastic materials

(P-9213)
A F C HYDRAULIC SEALS
4926 S Boyle Ave, Vernon (90058-3017)
PHONE...................................323 585-9110
Armando Cervantes, President
Felipe Cervantes, Vice Pres
EMP: 10
SQ FT: 7,000
SALES (est): 1.5MM **Privately Held**
SIC: **3053** 5199 Gaskets, all materials; rubber, crude

(P-9214)
ABLE INDUSTRIAL PRODUCTS INC (PA)
2006 S Baker Ave, Ontario (91761-7709)
PHONE...................................909 930-1585
Gilbert J Martinez, CEO
Gloria Martinez, CFO
Jeff Britton, Vice Pres
Debbie Viramontes, Admin Sec
Tracy Rivas, Purchasing
▲ EMP: 30 EST: 1974
SQ FT: 21,120
SALES (est): 9.7MM **Privately Held**
WEB: www.able123.com
SIC: **3053** 3069 5085 Gaskets, all materials; weather strip, sponge rubber; industrial supplies; hose, belting & packing; adhesives, tape & plasters; abrasives

(P-9215)
ADVANCED SEALING (DH)
15500 Blackburn Ave, Norwalk
(90650-6845)
PHONE....................562 802-7782
Don Evans, *President*
Alan Stubblefield, *CFO*
Ann Cullen, *Controller*
▲ **EMP:** 64
SQ FT: 35,000
SALES: 19MM **Privately Held**
WEB: www.advseal.com
SIC: 3053 3965 3052 2992 Gaskets, all
materials; packing materials; fasteners;
heater hose, rubber; lubricating oils; seal-
ing compounds for pipe threads or joints;
industrial valves; automatic regulating &
control valves; pressure valves & regula-
tors, industrial; steam traps
HQ: Eriks North America, Inc.
650 Washington Rd Ste 500
Pittsburgh PA 15228
800 937-9070

(P-9216)
AEROSPACE SEALS &
GASKETS
1478 Davril Cir Ste A, Corona
(92880-6957)
PHONE....................951 256-8380
Amparo Munoz, *Principal*
EMP: 30
SALES: 950K **Privately Held**
SIC: 3053 Gaskets, packing & sealing de-
vices

(P-9217)
AIRSPACE SEAL AND GASKET
CORP
1476 Davril Cir, Corona (92880)
PHONE....................951 256-8380
Herb Menold, *President*
EMP: 26
SALES (est): 1.8MM **Privately Held**
SIC: 3053 Gaskets, packing & sealing de-
vices

(P-9218)
AMERICAN GASKET & DIE
COMPANY
2275 Paragon Dr, San Jose (95131-1307)
PHONE....................408 441-6200
Kenneth J Cesena, *President*
EMP: 10 **EST:** 1976
SQ FT: 10,000
SALES (est): 1.5MM **Privately Held**
SIC: 3053 3554 Gaskets, all materials; die
cutting & stamping machinery, paper con-
verting

(P-9219)
BRYANT RUBBER CORP (PA)
1112 Lomita Blvd, Harbor City
(90710-2205)
PHONE....................310 530-2530
Steven Bryant, *Principal*
William J Bryant, *Shareholder*
Tracy Hunter, *Vice Pres*
Grant McKinley, *Vice Pres*
Steve Rookey, *Vice Pres*
EMP: 37
SQ FT: 60,000
SALES (est): 21.1MM **Privately Held**
WEB: www.bryantrubber.com
SIC: 3053 Gaskets, packing & sealing de-
vices

(P-9220)
BRYANT RUBBER CORP
Also Called: Ingla Rubber Products
1083 W 251st St, Bellflower (90706)
PHONE....................310 530-2530
Jack Klimek, *Branch Mgr*
EMP: 70
SALES (corp-wide): 21.1MM **Privately**
Held
WEB: www.bryantrubber.com
SIC: 3053 3061 Gaskets, packing & seal-
ing devices; mechanical rubber goods
PA: Bryant Rubber Corp.
1112 Lomita Blvd
Harbor City CA 90710
310 530-2530

(P-9221)
CALIBER SEALING SOLUTIONS
INC (PA)
2780 Palisades Dr, Corona (92882-0631)
PHONE....................949 461-0555
Paul Povar, *President*
Jesse Estrada, *Manager*
▲ **EMP:** 15
SALES (est): 1.8MM **Privately Held**
SIC: 3053 Gaskets, packing & sealing de-
vices

(P-9222)
CANNON GASKET INC
7784 Edison Ave, Fontana (92336-3635)
PHONE....................909 355-1547
Billy Jr P Cannon, *President*
Candy Houle, *Admin Sec*
Travis Cannon, *Manager*
▲ **EMP:** 15
SQ FT: 10,000
SALES (est): 3.3MM **Privately Held**
WEB: www.cannongasket.com
SIC: 3053 Gaskets, all materials

(P-9223)
CHAVERS GASKET
CORPORATION
23325 Del Lago Dr, Laguna Hills
(92653-1309)
PHONE....................949 472-8118
Lloyd Chavers, *President*
Gino Roncelli, *Admin Sec*
EMP: 25
SQ FT: 13,000
SALES (est): 4.8MM **Privately Held**
SIC: 3053 Gasket materials; gaskets, all
materials

(P-9224)
CHUS PACKAGING SUPPLIES
INC
10011 Santa Fe Springs Rd, Santa Fe
Springs (90670-2921)
PHONE....................562 944-6411
Pao Chang Chu, *CEO*
Julie Chieh Yu Chu, *President*
▲ **EMP:** 22
SQ FT: 30,000
SALES (est): 9.5MM **Privately Held**
WEB: www.movingpads.com
SIC: 3053 Cup packing, leather

(P-9225)
CIASONS INDUSTRIAL INC
1615 Boyd St, Santa Ana (92705-5103)
PHONE....................714 259-0838
Paul Hsieh, *President*
Samuel Hsieh, *CFO*
Grace S P Hsieh, *Admin Sec*
▲ **EMP:** 30
SQ FT: 25,000
SALES (est): 4.7MM **Privately Held**
WEB: www.ciasons.com
SIC: 3053 3563 Packing: steam engines,
pipe joints, air compressors, etc.; air &
gas compressors

(P-9226)
DAN-LOC GROUP LLC
Also Called: Dan-Loc Bolt & Gasket
20444 Tillman Ave, Carson (90746-3516)
PHONE....................310 538-2822
Rudy Estrada, *Branch Mgr*
EMP: 100
SALES (corp-wide): 57.8MM **Privately**
Held
WEB: www.danloc.com
SIC: 3053 3452 Gaskets & sealing de-
vices; bolts, nuts, rivets & washers
PA: Dan-Loc Group, Llc
725 N Drennan St
Houston TX 77003
713 356-3500

(P-9227)
DAR-KEN INC
Also Called: K & S Enterprises
10515 Rancho Rd, Adelanto (92301-3414)
PHONE....................760 246-4010
Ken Mc Gilp, *Partner*
Darla Mc Gilp, *Partner*
Carl Kessler, *General Mgr*
Raquel Gonzales, *Office Mgr*
EMP: 32

SQ FT: 10,000
SALES (est): 4.2MM **Privately Held**
SIC: 3053 3728 Gaskets, packing & seal-
ing devices; aircraft parts & equipment

(P-9228)
ELASTOMER TECHNOLOGIES
INC
Also Called: Roltec Gasket Manufacturing
255 Glider Cir, Corona (92880-2534)
PHONE....................951 272-5820
Richard O Lester, *CEO*
Randall Lester, *President*
Joan R Lester, *Treasurer*
Randy Lester, *Executive*
EMP: 10
SQ FT: 7,000
SALES (est): 1.3MM **Privately Held**
SIC: 3053 Gasket materials

(P-9229)
FERROTEC (USA)
CORPORATION
Also Called: Ferrotec Temescal
4569 Las Positas Rd Ste C, Livermore
(94551-8865)
PHONE....................925 371-4170
Michael Grivette, *Branch Mgr*
EMP: 50 **Privately Held**
SIC: 3053 Gaskets & sealing devices
HQ: Ferrotec (Usa) Corporation
33 Constitution Dr
Bedford NH 03110
603 472-6800

(P-9230)
FREUDENBERG-NOK GENERAL
PARTNR
Also Called: International Seal Company
2041 E Wilshire Ave, Santa Ana
(92705-4726)
PHONE....................714 834-0602
John Hudspeth, *Manager*
EMP: 150
SQ FT: 28,928
SALES (corp-wide): 11B **Privately Held**
WEB: www.freudenberg-nok.com
SIC: 3053 Gaskets & sealing devices
HQ: Freudenberg-Nok General Partnership
47774 W Anchor Ct
Plymouth MI 48170
734 451-0020

(P-9231)
G F COLE CORPORATION (PA)
21735 S Western Ave, Torrance
(90501-3718)
PHONE....................310 320-0601
Fritz Cole, *President*
Cathy Cole, *Vice Pres*
Elida Rodriguez, *Accountant*
Mike Finn, *Opers Mgr*
▲ **EMP:** 19 **EST:** 1982
SQ FT: 26,000
SALES (est): 3.6MM **Privately Held**
WEB: www.gfcole.com
SIC: 3053 3069 Gaskets, all materials;
hard rubber & molded rubber products

(P-9232)
GASKET MANUFACTURING CO
18001 S Main St, Gardena (90248-3530)
PHONE....................310 217-5600
Maureen E Labor, *CEO*
Dewain R Butler, *Ch of Bd*
Vince Labor, *Vice Pres*
EMP: 33
SQ FT: 66,000
SALES (est): 7.1MM **Privately Held**
WEB: www.gasketmfg.com
SIC: 3053 Gaskets, all materials
PA: Gasket Associates Lp
18001 S Main St
Gardena CA 90248

(P-9233)
GASKET SPECIALTIES INC
Also Called: Rancho Cucamonga Division
8654 Helms Ave, Rancho Cucamonga
(91730-4520)
PHONE....................909 987-4724
Louis Barbee, *Manager*
EMP: 10

SALES (corp-wide): 8.4MM **Privately**
Held
WEB: www.gsimfg.com
SIC: 3053 5085 3452 Gaskets, all materi-
als; industrial supplies; bolts, nuts, rivets
& washers
PA: Gasket Specialties, Inc.
6200 Hollis St
Emeryville CA 94608
510 547-7955

(P-9234)
HAB ENTERPRISES INC
Also Called: Packaging Resource Group
15233 Ventura Blvd # 100, Sherman Oaks
(91403-2200)
PHONE....................310 628-9000
Howard E Mallen, *President*
Chelly Ziegeler, *Vice Pres*
Cheresa Mallen, *Admin Sec*
EMP: 10
SQ FT: 3,000
SALES: 7.1MM **Privately Held**
SIC: 3053 7336 Packing materials; pack-
age design

(P-9235)
HARBOR SEAL INCORPORATED
909 S Myrtle Ave, Monrovia (91016-3426)
PHONE....................626 305-5754
Kunibert Gerhardt, *President*
Karen Edmonds, *Corp Secy*
Marie Gerhardt, *Vice Pres*
EMP: 19
SQ FT: 10,000
SALES: 2MM **Privately Held**
WEB: www.harborsealinc.com
SIC: 3053 Gaskets, packing & sealing de-
vices

(P-9236)
HUTCHINSON SEAL
CORPORATION (DH)
Also Called: National O Rings
11634 Patton Rd, Downey (90241)
PHONE....................248 375-4190
Christian Groche, *President*
Steve Orlowicz, *Data Proc Exec*
Robert Hanson, *VP Engrg*
▲ **EMP:** 430
SQ FT: 125,000
SALES (est): 64MM
SALES (corp-wide): 8.4B **Publicly Held**
SIC: 3053 Gaskets & sealing devices
HQ: Hutchinson Corporation
460 Fuller Ave Ne
Grand Rapids MI 49503
616 459-4541

(P-9237)
INDUSTRIAL GASKET AND SUP
CO
Also Called: Gasketfab Division
23018 Normandie Ave, Torrance
(90502-2691)
P.O. Box 4138 (90510-4138)
PHONE....................310 530-1771
William P Hynes, *President*
Theresa Holmes, *Corp Secy*
Kevin P Treacy, *Vice Pres*
EMP: 23
SQ FT: 11,000
SALES (est): 4.4MM **Privately Held**
SIC: 3053 5085 Gaskets & sealing de-
vices; gaskets; seals, industrial

(P-9238)
INERTECH SUPPLY INC
641 Monterey Pass Rd, Monterey Park
(91754-2418)
PHONE....................626 282-2000
James Huang, *President*
Charlie C Miskell, *Vice Pres*
Bruce Wang, *Vice Pres*
Walter Lee, *Admin Sec*
Jean Okita, *Human Res Mgr*
▲ **EMP:** 75
SQ FT: 14,000
SALES (est): 9.7MM **Privately Held**
WEB: www.inertech.com
SIC: 3053 5085 2891 Gasket materials;
gaskets & sealing devices; gaskets; adhe-
sives & sealants

(P-9239)
J MILLER CO INC
Also Called: Miller Gasket Co
11537 Bradley Ave, San Fernando
(91340-2519)
PHONE..............................818 837-0181
Dennis D Miller, *President*
Elaine Miller, *Corp Secy*
Richard Miller, *General Mgr*
Ryan Young, *Manager*
▲ EMP: 35
SQ FT: 20,000
SALES (est): 6.2MM **Privately Held**
WEB: www.jmillerco.com
SIC: 3053 Gaskets, all materials

(P-9240)
KIRKHILL INC
300 E Cypress St, Brea (92821-4007)
PHONE..............................714 529-4901
Kevin McHenry, *Manager*
EMP: 700
SALES (corp-wide): 3.8B **Publicly Held**
SIC: 3053 3728 2822 Gaskets, packing &
sealing devices; aircraft parts & equip-
ment; synthetic rubber
HQ: Kirkhill Inc.
300 E Cypress St
Brea CA 92821
714 529-4901

(P-9241)
KIRKHILL INC
Also Called: Haskon, Div of
300 E Cypress St, Brea (92821-4007)
PHONE..............................714 529-4901
Michael Harden, *Branch Mgr*
EMP: 700
SALES (corp-wide): 3.8B **Publicly Held**
WEB: www.kirkhill.com
SIC: 3053 3728 2822 Gaskets, packing &
sealing devices; aircraft parts & equip-
ment; synthetic rubber
HQ: Kirkhill Inc.
300 E Cypress St
Brea CA 92821
714 529-4901

(P-9242)
LAMONS GASKET COMPANY
20009 S Rancho Way, Compton
(90220-6318)
PHONE..............................310 886-1133
Joe Medina, *Branch Mgr*
EMP: 18
SALES (corp-wide): 877.1MM **Publicly
Held**
SIC: 3053 5085 Gaskets, all materials;
gaskets
HQ: Lamons Gasket Company
7300 Airport Blvd
Houston TX 77061
713 222-0284

(P-9243)
**MORGAN POLYMER SEALS LLC
(PA)**
2475 A Paseo De Las, San Diego (92154)
PHONE..............................858 679-4946
Kevin Morgan, *President*
Ed Ditz, *Controller*
Mark Conlee, *Sales Staff*
▲ EMP: 22
SQ FT: 33,500
SALES (est): 23.5MM **Privately Held**
SIC: 3053 Gaskets & sealing devices

(P-9244)
PACIFIC DIE CUT INDUSTRIES
3399 Arden Rd, Hayward (94545-3924)
PHONE..............................510 732-8103
Mohammed M Behnam, *CEO*
▲ EMP: 73
SQ FT: 30,000
SALES (est): 16.4MM **Privately Held**
WEB: www.pacificdiecut.com
SIC: 3053 Gaskets & sealing devices

(P-9245)
**PACIFIC STATES FELT MFG CO
INC**
23850 Clawiter Rd Ste 20, Hayward
(94545-1723)
P.O. Box 5024 (94540-5024)
PHONE..............................510 783-2357

Walter L Perscheid Jr, *CEO*
Kristin Gudjohnsen, *General Mgr*
Robert Perscheid, *General Mgr*
EMP: 16
SQ FT: 23,000
SALES (est): 3MM **Privately Held**
WEB: www.pacificstatesfelt.com
SIC: 3053 5085 Gaskets & sealing de-
vices; industrial supplies

(P-9246)
PARCO LLC (PA)
1801 S Archibald Ave, Ontario
(91761-7677)
PHONE..............................909 947-2200
Adam Morrison Burgener, *President*
Louis W Burgener, *Ch of Bd*
Angela L Garcia, *Vice Pres*
Angie Garcia, *Vice Pres*
W Carl Horn, *Vice Pres*
▲ EMP: 122
SQ FT: 154,000
SALES (est): 37.2MM **Privately Held**
WEB: www.parcoinc.com
SIC: 3053 Gaskets, all materials

(P-9247)
PERFORMANCE SEALING INC
Also Called: PSI
1821 Langley Ave, Irvine (92614-5623)
PHONE..............................714 662-5918
Greg Pritchett, *President*
John Schroeder, *Engineer*
Lauren Pritchett, *Human Resources*
EMP: 12
SQ FT: 4,000
SALES (est): 4MM **Privately Held**
WEB: www.psiseal.com
SIC: 3053 Gaskets & sealing devices

(P-9248)
**POLYMER CONCEPTS
TECHNOLOGIES**
13522 Manhasset Rd, Apple Valley
(92308-5790)
P.O. Box 2738 (92307-0052)
PHONE..............................760 240-4999
Rob Girman, *President*
Dean Anderson, *CEO*
Juli Hunzeker, *Info Tech Mgr*
EMP: 15
SQ FT: 3,000
SALES (est): 1.8MM **Privately Held**
WEB: www.polymerconcepts.com
SIC: 3053 Gaskets & sealing devices

(P-9249)
REAL SEAL CO INC
Also Called: Real Seal
1971 Don Lee Pl, Escondido (92029-1141)
PHONE..............................760 743-7263
Patrick Thomas Tobin, *CEO*
Rose Ann Tobin, *Corp Secy*
▲ EMP: 25
SQ FT: 22,000
SALES (est): 4.9MM **Privately Held**
WEB: www.real-seal.com
SIC: 3053 5085 Oil seals, rubber; indus-
trial supplies

(P-9250)
ROETTELE INDUSTRIES
15485 Dupont Ave, Chino (91710-7605)
PHONE..............................909 606-8252
Mark Roettele, *President*
Maurice Roettele, *Ch of Bd*
Randal Roettele, *Treasurer*
Lon Roettele, *Vice Pres*
Maria Landino, *Human Resources*
▲ EMP: 19
SQ FT: 15,000
SALES (est): 3.9MM **Privately Held**
WEB: www.roetteleindustries.com
SIC: 3053 5085 Gaskets, packing & seal-
ing devices; industrial supplies

(P-9251)
**ROMAN GLOBAL RESOURCES
INC**
1027 Calle Trepadora # 2, San Clemente
(92673-6290)
PHONE..............................949 276-4100
Val Roman, *President*
▲ EMP: 10
SQ FT: 3,500

SALES: 2.5MM **Privately Held**
WEB: www.romanseals.com
SIC: 3053 Gaskets, all materials

(P-9252)
RPM PRODUCTS INC (PA)
Also Called: Rubber Plastic & Metal Pdts
30065 Comercio, Rcho STA Marg
(92688-2106)
PHONE..............................949 888-8543
Mark Paolella, *President*
Suzanne Paolella, *Corp Secy*
▲ EMP: 35
SALES (est): 18.2MM **Privately Held**
WEB: www.rpmproducts.com
SIC: 3053 3089 5085 Gaskets & sealing
devices; injection molding of plastics;
molding primary plastic; gaskets & seals

(P-9253)
SCE GASKETS INC
24927 Avenue Tibbitts F, Valencia
(91355-1284)
PHONE..............................661 728-9200
Ryan Hunter, *President*
Aaron Hunter, *Vice Pres*
Caleb Hunter, *Vice Pres*
▼ EMP: 10
SQ FT: 6,000
SALES (est): 1.7MM **Privately Held**
WEB: www.scegaskets.com
SIC: 3053 Gaskets & sealing devices

(P-9254)
SEAL SCIENCE INC (PA)
Also Called: S S I
17131 Daimler St, Irvine (92614-5508)
PHONE..............................949 253-3130
Frederick E Tuliper, *CEO*
Patricia Tuliper, *CFO*
▲ EMP: 68
SQ FT: 25,000
SALES (est): 10.8MM **Privately Held**
WEB: www.sealscience.com
SIC: 3053 3089 3061 Gaskets & sealing
devices; injection molding of plastics; me-
chanical rubber goods

(P-9255)
SEALING CORPORATION
7353 Greenbush Ave B, North Hollywood
(91605-4004)
PHONE..............................818 765-7327
John Patterson, *President*
Adrian Patterson, *Corp Secy*
Barry Lew, *Office Mgr*
▲ EMP: 15
SQ FT: 2,600
SALES (est): 2.5MM **Privately Held**
WEB: www.selcoseal.com
SIC: 3053 Gaskets & sealing devices

(P-9256)
SEWING COLLECTION INC
3113 E 26th St, Vernon (90058-8006)
PHONE..............................323 264-2223
Touraj Tour, *President*
Houshang Tour, *Vice Pres*
▲ EMP: 100
SQ FT: 135,000
SALES (est): 4.2MM **Privately Held**
SIC: 3053 5199 4953 Packing materials;
packaging materials; recycling, waste ma-
terials

(P-9257)
SPIRA MANUFACTURING CORP
650 Jessie St, San Fernando (91340-2233)
PHONE..............................818 764-8222
George M Kunkel, *President*
Michael Kunkel, *General Mgr*
Bonnie Paul, *Admin Sec*
Joseph Sanchez, *Technical Staff*
Ernesto Nunez, *Buyer*
EMP: 30
SQ FT: 15,000
SALES (est): 6.4MM **Privately Held**
WEB: www.spira-emi.com
SIC: 3053 Gaskets, all materials

(P-9258)
**TILLEY MANUFACTURING CO
INC (PA)**
Also Called: Precision Graphics
2734 Spring St, Redwood City
(94063-3524)
P.O. Box 5766 (94063-0766)
PHONE..............................650 365-3598
Owen Conley, *President*
▲ EMP: 24
SQ FT: 35,000
SALES (est): 7.5MM **Privately Held**
WEB: www.tilleymfg.com
SIC: 3053 3411 3634 3312 Gaskets, all
materials; food containers, metal; bever-
age cans, metal: except beer; urns, elec-
tric: household; tool & die steel & alloys;
metal stampings; pressed & blown glass

(P-9259)
WEST COAST GASKET CO
300 Ranger Ave, Brea (92821-6217)
PHONE..............................714 869-0123
Louis Russell, *Principal*
Jean Grey, *CEO*
Angela Steele, *Executive*
Larry Thompson, *General Mgr*
Aaron Kramer, *Sales Mgr*
EMP: 75
SQ FT: 50,000
SALES (est): 16.1MM **Privately Held**
SIC: 3053 3061 3469 5085 Gaskets, all
materials; mechanical rubber goods;
metal stampings; industrial supplies

**3061 Molded, Extruded &
Lathe-Cut Rubber
Mechanical Goods**

(P-9260)
CIANNA MEDICAL INC
6 Journey Ste 125, Aliso Viejo
(92656-5319)
PHONE..............................949 360-0059
Jill Anderson, *President*
Christopher F Serocke, *COO*
Gordon Busenbark, *CFO*
EMP: 10
SALES (est): 13.5MM
SALES (corp-wide): 882.7MM **Publicly
Held**
SIC: 3061 Medical & surgical rubber tubing
(extruded & lathe-cut)
PA: Merit Medical Systems, Inc.
1600 W Merit Pkwy
South Jordan UT 84095
801 253-1600

(P-9261)
CRM CO LLC (PA)
Also Called: C R M
1301 Dove St Ste 940, Newport Beach
(92660-2483)
PHONE..............................949 263-9100
H Barry Takallou, *CEO*
▲ EMP: 44
SALES (est): 9.9MM **Privately Held**
SIC: 3061 Mechanical rubber goods

(P-9262)
CRYSTAL TIPS HOLDINGS
8850 Research Dr, Irvine (92618-4223)
PHONE..............................800 944-3939
Dave Sproat, *CEO*
EMP: 46
SALES (est): 1.4MM **Privately Held**
SIC: 3061 Medical & surgical rubber tubing
(extruded & lathe-cut)

(P-9263)
DYNATECT RO-LAB INC
8830 W Linne Rd, Tracy (95304-9109)
P.O. Box 450 (95378-0450)
PHONE..............................262 786-1500
Henry Wright, *General Mgr*
Marina Wright, *Corp Secy*
John Dodge, *Vice Pres*
▲ EMP: 50 EST: 1971
SQ FT: 65,000

▲ = Import ▼=Export
◆ =Import/Export

SALES (est): 10.1MM
SALES (corp-wide): 1.6B Privately Held
WEB: www.rolabamerican.com
SIC: 3061 3052 3069 3089 Mechanical rubber goods; rubber & plastics hose & beltings; hard rubber & molded rubber products; plastic hardware & building products
HQ: Dynatect Manufacturing, Inc.
2300 S Calhoun Rd
New Berlin WI 53151
262 786-1500

(P-9264)
ICAD INC
345 Potrero Ave, Sunnyvale (94085-4115)
PHONE...................................408 419-2300
Deryl Banks, Branch Mgr
EMP: 69
SALES (corp-wide): 25.6MM Publicly Held
PA: Icad, Inc.
98 Spit Brook Rd Ste 100
Nashua NH 03062
603 882-5200

(P-9265)
J FLYING MANUFACTURING
11000 Brimhall Rd Ste E, Bakersfield (93312-3022)
PHONE...................................805 839-9229
Dennis Walrath, President
Sindy Walrath, Vice Pres
EMP: 20
SALES: 300K Privately Held
SIC: 3061 3599 Mechanical rubber goods; amusement park equipment

(P-9266)
MIKRON PRODUCTS INC
1251 E Belmont St, Ontario (91761-3523)
PHONE...................................909 545-8600
Nicholas Carone, President
Palma Carone, Corp Secy
Ed Duran, Principal
EMP: 100
SQ FT: 20,000
SALES (est): 10.3MM Privately Held
WEB: www.mikronproducts.com
SIC: 3061 Mechanical rubber goods

(P-9267)
PAC-WEST RUBBER PRODUCTS LLC
120 Venture St, San Marcos (92078-4353)
P.O. Box 2733 (92079-2733)
PHONE...................................760 891-0911
Nickolas R Duvall,
Kim P Duvall,
EMP: 12
SQ FT: 6,700
SALES (est): 1.7MM Privately Held
SIC: 3061 Mechanical rubber goods

(P-9268)
PERFORMANCE POLYMER TECH LLC
8801 Washington Blvd # 109, Roseville (95678-6200)
PHONE...................................916 677-1414
Lonnie Wimberly, President
Ken Marshall, COO
Ian Macauley, Vice Pres
Martha Wimberly, Vice Pres
Tony Ochoa, Info Tech Dir
EMP: 35
SQ FT: 37,000
SALES (est): 6MM Privately Held
WEB: www.pptech.com
SIC: 3061 3069 Mechanical rubber goods; molded rubber products

(P-9269)
R & R RUBBER MOLDING INC
2444 Loma Ave, South El Monte (91733-1416)
P.O. Box 3533 (91733-0533)
PHONE...................................626 575-8105
S Castillo III, Vice Pres
Richard Patrick Norman, President
Sixto Castillo III, Vice Pres
Lupe Frausto-Perez,
Antonio Morales, Manager
EMP: 35 EST: 1977

SQ FT: 6,100
SALES (est): 2.9MM Privately Held
WEB: www.rrrubber.com
SIC: 3061 Mechanical rubber goods

(P-9270)
R D RUBBER TECHNOLOGY CORP
12870 Florence Ave, Santa Fe Springs (90670-4540)
PHONE...................................562 941-4800
Walter V Hopkins Jr, President
Rosanne Dukowitz, Exec VP
Andrea Bryan, Office Mgr
Waler Hopkins, CTO
EMP: 27
SQ FT: 15,600
SALES (est): 5MM Privately Held
SIC: 3061 Mechanical rubber goods

(P-9271)
RUBBERCRAFT CORP CAL LTD (DH)
Also Called: Rubber Teck Division
3701 E Conant St, Long Beach (90808-1783)
PHONE...................................562 354-2800
Marc Sanders, CEO
Eric Sanders, CEO
EMP: 238
SQ FT: 40,000
SALES (est): 29.2MM
SALES (corp-wide): 53.9MM Privately Held
WEB: www.rubbercraft.com
SIC: 3061 Appliance rubber goods (mechanical)
HQ: Integrated Polymer Solutions, Inc.
3701 E Conant St
Long Beach CA 90808
562 354-2920

(P-9272)
SANDEE PLASTIC EXTRUSIONS
14932 Gwenchris Ct, Paramount (90723-3423)
PHONE...................................323 979-4020
Thomas Kunkel, President
Matt Andereck,
EMP: 22
SQ FT: 14,000
SALES (est): 6.5MM
SALES (corp-wide): 14.2MM Privately Held
SIC: 3061 Medical & surgical rubber tubing (extruded & lathe-cut)
PA: Sandee Manufacturing Co.
10520 Waveland Ave
Franklin Park IL 60131
847 671-1335

(P-9273)
WESTLAND TECHNOLOGIES INC
107 S Riverside Dr, Modesto (95354-4004)
PHONE...................................800 877-7734
John Grizzard, President
Joe Fleck, Engineer
Yolanda Auld, Human Res Dir
Michael Forrest, Maint Spvr
Benjamin Banta, Director
EMP: 60
SQ FT: 117,000
SALES (est): 26.8MM
SALES (corp-wide): 771.5MM Publicly Held
WEB: www.westlandtech.com
SIC: 3061 3069 Mechanical rubber goods; flooring, rubber: tile or sheet
PA: Esco Technologies Inc.
9900 Clayton Rd Ste A
Saint Louis MO 63124
314 213-7200

┌─────────────────────────────┐
│ **3069 Fabricated Rubber** │
│ **Prdts, NEC**   │
└─────────────────────────────┘

(P-9274)
3-D POLYMERS
13026 S Normandie Ave, Gardena (90249-2126)
PHONE...................................310 324-7694
David Johnson, President
Kathleen Johnson, Corp Secy

EMP: 15
SQ FT: 11,000
SALES (est): 850K Privately Held
WEB: www.3-dpolymers.com
SIC: 3069 3089 3061 Hard rubber & molded rubber products; plastic processing; mechanical rubber goods

(P-9275)
3M COMPANY
1601 S Shamrock Ave, Monrovia (91016-4248)
PHONE...................................626 358-0136
Bob Palmer, Plant Mgr
EMP: 21
SALES (corp-wide): 32.7B Publicly Held
WEB: www.mmm.com
SIC: 3069 Rubber coated fabrics & clothing
PA: 3m Company
3m Center
Saint Paul MN 55144
651 733-1110

(P-9276)
A B BOYD CO (PA)
600 S Mcclure Rd, Modesto (95357-0520)
PHONE...................................209 236-1111
Mitchell Aiello, President
Eric Struik, CFO
Gerardo Sandoval, Maintence Staff
▲ EMP: 24
SQ FT: 100,000
SALES (est): 209.8MM Privately Held
WEB: www.boydcorp.com
SIC: 3069 2822 Hard rubber & molded rubber products; rubber automotive products; synthetic rubber

(P-9277)
ABBA ROLLER LLC (DH)
1351 E Philadelphia St, Ontario (91761-5719)
PHONE...................................909 947-1244
Jeffrey Garvens,
▲ EMP: 20
SQ FT: 4,000
SALES (est): 2.4MM
SALES (corp-wide): 11.1MM Privately Held
SIC: 3069 Roll coverings, rubber
HQ: Electro-Coatings, Inc.
216 Baywood St
Houston TX 77011
713 923-5935

(P-9278)
ACE CALENDERING ENTERPRISES (PA)
Also Called: Midwest Rubber
1311 S Wanamaker Ave, Ontario (91761-2237)
PHONE...................................909 937-1901
Gary Holcomb, CEO
Fred Rodriguez, President
Bob Rich, Vice Pres
EMP: 16
SALES (est): 1.8MM Privately Held
WEB: www.acecalender.com
SIC: 3069 Sheets, hard rubber

(P-9279)
ACUTEK ADHESIVE SPECIALTIES
540 N Oak St, Inglewood (90302-2985)
PHONE...................................310 419-0190
Jerry Muchin, President
Karen Kline, Vice Pres
EMP: 45 EST: 1967
SQ FT: 25,000
SALES (est): 5.9MM Privately Held
WEB: www.acutek.com
SIC: 3069 Medical sundries, rubber

(P-9280)
ALASCO RUBBER & PLASTICS CORP
1250 Enos Ave, Sebastopol (95472-4454)
PHONE...................................707 823-5270
EMP: 17
SALES (est): 982.2K
SALES (corp-wide): 1.8MM Privately Held
SIC: 3069

PA: Alasco Rubber & Plastic Corp
3432 Roberto Ct
San Luis Obispo CA 93401
805 543-3008

(P-9281)
AMES RUBBER MFG CO INC
Also Called: Ames Industrial
4516 Brazil St, Los Angeles (90039-1002)
PHONE...................................818 240-9313
Timothy L Brown, CEO
Pat Brown, Corp Secy
Susie Sandoval, Lab Dir
Maria Lepe, Finance Mgr
Terry Wright, Manager
▲ EMP: 30
SQ FT: 20,000
SALES (est): 5.7MM Privately Held
WEB: www.armcocatalog.com
SIC: 3069 Medical & laboratory rubber sundries & related products; mechanical rubber goods

(P-9282)
APNEA SCIENCES CORPORATION
17 Brownsbury Rd, Laguna Niguel (92677-9382)
PHONE...................................949 226-4421
James Fallon, President
EMP: 17
SALES (est): 1.4MM Privately Held
SIC: 3069 Medical & laboratory rubber sundries & related products

(P-9283)
ARROYO SECO RACQUET CLUB
920 Lohman Ln, South Pasadena (91030-2906)
PHONE...................................323 258-4178
Chandler Thomas, Manager
EMP: 10
SALES (est): 721.5K Privately Held
SIC: 3069 7999 Balls, rubber; tennis courts, outdoor/indoor: non-membership

(P-9284)
ATLAS SPONGE RUBBER COMPANY
114 E Pomona Ave, Monrovia (91016-4638)
PHONE...................................626 359-5391
Tom Johnston, President
Greg Johnston, General Mgr
EMP: 19 EST: 1948
SQ FT: 30,000
SALES: 1.5MM Privately Held
SIC: 3069 Sponge rubber & sponge rubber products; molded rubber products

(P-9285)
ATM PLUS INC
Also Called: Fast Undercar
2232 Verus St Ste F, San Diego (92154-4706)
PHONE...................................619 575-3278
Wally Hussannali, President
EMP: 14
SALES (est): 2.3MM Privately Held
SIC: 3069 Brake linings, rubber

(P-9286)
B CUMMING COMPANY A CORP
9990 Glenoaks Blvd Ste B, Sun Valley (91352-1081)
PHONE...................................818 504-2571
David B Mazer, President
Neftali Martinez, Vice Pres
EMP: 10
SQ FT: 6,500
SALES: 1MM Privately Held
SIC: 3069 Toys, rubber

(P-9287)
BAND-IT RUBBER COMPANY INC
1711 N Delilah St, Corona (92879-1865)
PHONE...................................951 735-5072
Bernard Spangler, President
▲ EMP: 10
SQ FT: 20,000
SALES (est): 1.4MM Privately Held
SIC: 3069 Rubber bands

PRODUCTS & SVCS

(P-9288)
BANDAG LICENSING CORPORATION
2500 E Thompson St, Long Beach (90805-1836)
P.O. Box 140990, Nashville TN (37214-0990)
PHONE..................................562 531-3880
Martin G Carver, *CEO*
EMP: 57
SQ FT: 310,000
SALES (est): 5.8MM **Privately Held**
SIC: 3069 Reclaimed rubber & specialty rubber compounds
HQ: Bridgestone Bandag, Llc
　　2000 Bandag Dr
　　Muscatine IA 52761
　　563 262-2511

(P-9289)
BARGER & ASSOCIATES
Also Called: Advance Fabrication
400 Crown Point Cir, Grass Valley (95945-9089)
PHONE..................................530 271-5424
Michael Barger, *President*
Tiffany Barger, *COO*
EMP: 33
SQ FT: 11,000
SALES (est): 5.3MM **Privately Held**
WEB: www.advancefabrication.com
SIC: 3069 3842 Orthopedic sundries; molded rubber; braces, orthopedic; trusses, orthopedic & surgical

(P-9290)
BURKE INDUSTRIES INC (HQ)
2250 S 10th St, San Jose (95112-4197)
PHONE..................................408 297-3500
Robert Pitman, *President*
Edward Reginelli, *CFO*
Steve Roades, *Vice Pres*
Bob Heathcoate, *Info Tech Mgr*
Dan Garrison, *Technical Mgr*
◆ EMP: 223 EST: 1976
SQ FT: 115,930
SALES (est): 185.4MM
SALES (corp-wide): 720.5MM **Privately Held**
WEB: www.burkeind.com
SIC: 3069 2822 2821 3061 Flooring, rubber: tile or sheet; molded rubber products; polyethylene, chlorosulfonated (hypalon); silicone rubbers; plastics materials & resins; silicone resins; mechanical rubber goods
PA: Mannington Mills Inc.
　　75 Mannington Mills Rd
　　Salem NJ 08079
　　856 935-3000

(P-9291)
CA-WA CORP
1360 W 1st St, Pomona (91766-1305)
PHONE..................................909 868-0630
Jim Sicilia, *CEO*
▲ EMP: 30
SQ FT: 10,000
SALES (est): 1.5MM **Privately Held**
SIC: 3069 Medical & laboratory rubber sundries & related products

(P-9292)
CALIFOAM PRODUCTS INC
10775 Silicon Ave, Montclair (91763-6022)
PHONE..................................909 364-1600
Javier Juarez, *CEO*
▲ EMP: 12
SQ FT: 24,000
SALES (est): 2.1MM **Privately Held**
WEB: www.califoamproducts.com
SIC: 3069 5199 Foam rubber; packaging materials

(P-9293)
CALIFORNIA GASKET AND RBR CORP (PA)
533 W Collins Ave, Orange (92867-5509)
PHONE..................................310 323-4250
Scott H Franklin, *Vice Pres*
EMP: 40 EST: 1942
SQ FT: 51,000
SALES (est): 5.3MM **Privately Held**
WEB: www.calgasket.com
SIC: 3069 3053 3469 3061 Molded rubber products; rubber automotive products; gaskets, packing & sealing devices; metal stampings; appliance rubber goods (mechanical)

(P-9294)
CENTURY RUBBER COMPANY INC
719 Rooster Dr, Bakersfield (93307-9807)
PHONE..................................661 366-7009
Steve Cozzetto, *President*
EMP: 13
SQ FT: 7,500
SALES (est): 2.3MM **Privately Held**
WEB: www.centuryrubber.com
SIC: 3069 Molded rubber products

(P-9295)
CONTINENTAL AMERICAN CORP
Also Called: Pioneer Balloon Co
1333 S Hillward Ave, West Covina (91791-3936)
PHONE..................................626 964-0164
Darlene Todorovich, *Principal*
EMP: 75
SALES (corp-wide): 228.7MM **Privately Held**
WEB: www.qualatex.com
SIC: 3069 2759 5092 Balloons, advertising & toy: rubber; commercial printing; balloons, novelty
PA: Continental American Corporation
　　5000 E 29th St N
　　Wichita KS 67220
　　316 685-2266

(P-9296)
COOPER CROUSE-HINDS LLC
Also Called: Garry Electronics
705 W Ventura Blvd, Camarillo (93010)
PHONE..................................805 484-0543
Alexander M Cutler, *CEO*
EMP: 135 **Privately Held**
SIC: 3069 3678 Hard rubber & molded rubber products; electronic connectors
HQ: Cooper Crouse-Hinds, Llc
　　1201 Wolf St
　　Syracuse NY 13208
　　315 477-7000

(P-9297)
COOPER CROUSE-HINDS LLC
Also Called: Wpi Salem Division
750 W Ventura Blvd, Camarillo (93010-8382)
PHONE..................................805 484-0543
Alexander M Cutler, *Ch of Bd*
EMP: 140 **Privately Held**
SIC: 3069 3678 Hard rubber & molded rubber products; electronic circuits
HQ: Cooper Crouse-Hinds, Llc
　　1201 Wolf St
　　Syracuse NY 13208
　　315 477-7000

(P-9298)
CRICKET COMPANY LLC
68 Leveroni Ct Ste 200, Novato (94949-5769)
PHONE..................................415 475-4150
Wayne Clark, *Mng Member*
Mark Sawyer, *CFO*
Karen Delzell, *Mktg Dir*
▲ EMP: 25
SALES (est): 4.2MM **Privately Held**
WEB: www.cricketco.com
SIC: 3069 Capes, vulcanized rubber or rubberized fabric; brushes, rubber

(P-9299)
CYPRESS SPONGE RUBBER PRODUCTS
Also Called: Rubberite Cypress Sponge Rubbe
301 Goetz Ave, Santa Ana (92707-3707)
PHONE..................................714 546-6464
Barbara Ballou, *President*
Line Hennes, *Administration*
Aaron Brooks, *Plant Mgr*
David Noda, *Sales Associate*
▲ EMP: 12

SQ FT: 25,000
SALES (est): 920K **Privately Held**
WEB: www.cypresssponge.com
SIC: 3069 Sheeting, rubber or rubberized fabric; sponge rubber & sponge rubber products

(P-9300)
DA/PRO RUBBER INC
28635 Braxton Ave, Valencia (91355-4112)
PHONE..................................661 775-6290
Harold Sosner, *Manager*
Thomas Mason, *CFO*
EMP: 100
SQ FT: 31,845
SALES (corp-wide): 69.2MM **Privately Held**
WEB: www.daprorubber.com
SIC: 3069 3061 Molded rubber products; mechanical rubber goods
PA: Da/Pro Rubber, Inc.
　　601 N Poplar Ave
　　Broken Arrow OK 74012
　　918 258-9386

(P-9301)
DEVOLL RUBBER MFG GROUP INC
Also Called: Devoll Rubber Mfg Group
18626 Phantom St, Victorville (92394-7929)
PHONE..................................760 246-0142
John De Voll, *CEO*
Stacy Devoll, *General Mgr*
Amanda De Voll, *Office Mgr*
Amanda D Voll, *Office Mgr*
EMP: 14
SQ FT: 8,000
SALES (est): 2.7MM **Privately Held**
WEB: www.devollrubber.com
SIC: 3069 Medical & laboratory rubber sundries & related products

(P-9302)
DURO FLEX RUBBER PRODUCTS INC
13215 Lakeland Rd, Santa Fe Springs (90670-4522)
PHONE..................................562 946-5533
John A Lozano, *President*
EMP: 11
SQ FT: 6,000
SALES (est): 1.8MM **Privately Held**
WEB: www.duroflexrubber.com
SIC: 3069 Molded rubber products

(P-9303)
DURO ROLLER COMPANY INC
Also Called: Cal State Rubber
13006 Park St, Santa Fe Springs (90670-4098)
PHONE..................................562 944-8856
Maureen Wayda, *President*
Julie Wayda, *Vice Pres*
▲ EMP: 16 EST: 1973
SQ FT: 8,100
SALES (est): 3MM **Privately Held**
WEB: www.duroroller.com
SIC: 3069 3599 Molded rubber products; rubber rolls & roll coverings; machine & other job shop work

(P-9304)
ELITE COMFORT SOLUTIONS LLC
5440 E Francis St, Ontario (91761-3638)
PHONE..................................909 390-6800
EMP: 10
SALES (corp-wide): 4.2B **Publicly Held**
SIC: 3069 Foam rubber
HQ: Elite Comfort Solutions Llc
　　24 Herring Rd
　　Newnan GA 30265
　　828 267-7813

(P-9305)
ENVIRNMNTAL MLDING CNCEPTS LLC
Also Called: E M C
14050 Day St, Moreno Valley (92553-9106)
PHONE..................................951 214-6596
Sarkis Beudjekian, *Mng Member*
Anne Beudjekian,
◆ EMP: 15
SQ FT: 15,000

SALES (est): 2.9MM **Privately Held**
WEB: www.emcmolding.com
SIC: 3069 Reclaimed rubber & specialty rubber compounds

(P-9306)
ESTCO ENTERPRISES INC
1549 Simpson Way, Escondido (92029-1203)
PHONE..................................760 489-8745
Joshua Taylor, *President*
Judith Taylor, *Corp Secy*
EMP: 10 EST: 1970
SQ FT: 10,000
SALES (est): 1.8MM **Privately Held**
WEB: www.estcoenterprises.com
SIC: 3069 Bags, rubber or rubberized fabric

(P-9307)
EVANTEC CORPORATION
Also Called: Evantec Scientific
6120 Valley View St, Buena Park (90620-1030)
PHONE..................................949 632-2811
Ann Nelson, *President*
Evelyn Bogner, *Corp Secy*
Paul Bogner, *Vice Pres*
EMP: 10
SALES (est): 2MM **Privately Held**
WEB: www.evantec.com
SIC: 3069 8742 Linings, vulcanizable rubber; business consultant

(P-9308)
EZ INFLATABLES INC
1410 Vineland Ave, Baldwin Park (91706-5813)
PHONE..................................626 480-9100
Edgar Abraamyan, *President*
▲ EMP: 30 EST: 2007
SQ FT: 12,000
SALES: 1MM **Privately Held**
SIC: 3069 Balloons, advertising & toy: rubber

(P-9309)
FALCON WATERFREE TECH LLC (HQ)
2255 Barry Ave, Los Angeles (90064-1401)
PHONE..................................310 209-7250
James Krug,
Ned Goldsmith, *Vice Pres*
Dimitre Krouchev, *Controller*
Jake Jaskolski, *Sales Mgr*
Andrea Chase, *Marketing Staff*
◆ EMP: 20 EST: 2000
SALES (est): 1.6MM
SALES (corp-wide): 12.1MM **Privately Held**
WEB: www.falconwaterfree.com
SIC: 3069 Pump sleeves, rubber
PA: Management Kingsley Llc Mapleton
　　9952 Santa Monica Blvd
　　Beverly Hills CA 90212
　　310 282-0780

(P-9310)
GAGNE-MULFORD ENTERPRISES
2490 Almond Ave, Concord (94520)
PHONE..................................925 671-7434
John W Mulford, *CEO*
EMP: 19 EST: 2013
SALES (est): 2.3MM **Privately Held**
SIC: 3069 Plumbers' rubber goods

(P-9311)
GIBBS PLASTIC & RUBBER CO
Also Called: Mint Grips
3959 Teal Ct, Benicia (94510-1212)
PHONE..................................707 746-7300
Lee Michels, *Partner*
EMP: 15
SQ FT: 14,000
SALES: 1.2MM **Privately Held**
WEB: www.gibbsrubber.com
SIC: 3069 3061 Molded rubber products; mechanical rubber goods

▲ = Import ▼=Export
◆ =Import/Export

(P-9312)
GOOD-WEST RUBBER CORP (PA)
Also Called: Goodyear Rbr Co Southern Cal
9615 Feron Blvd, Rancho Cucamonga
(91730-4503)
PHONE..........................909 987-1774
Christian Groche, *President*
Fred Ledesma, *Vice Pres*
Harold W Sears, *Vice Pres*
Patrick Sears, *Vice Pres*
Flynn Sears, *Technology*
▲ EMP: 97
SQ FT: 56,000
SALES (est): 21.8MM **Privately Held**
SIC: 3069 3061 5531 Molded rubber
products; liner strips, rubber; mechanical
rubber goods; automotive tires

(P-9313)
GOODWEST RUBBER LININGS INC
Also Called: Goodwest Linings & Coatings
8814 Industrial Ln, Rancho Cucamonga
(91730-4528)
PHONE..........................888 499-0085
Ryan Sears, *President*
Larry Sears, *Corp Secy*
Fred Ledesma, *Vice Pres*
Patrick Sears, *Vice Pres*
EMP: 20
SQ FT: 300,000
SALES (est): 4.7MM **Privately Held**
WEB: www.goodwestlining.com
SIC: 3069 Linings, vulcanizable rubber

(P-9314)
HARBOR PRODUCTS INC
15001 Lakewood Blvd, Paramount
(90723-4513)
PHONE..........................562 633-8184
Bill Deal, *President*
Rudy Santana, *Vice Pres*
Edwin Aceituno, *Mktg Dir*
▲ EMP: 10 EST: 1975
SQ FT: 10,000
SALES: 750K **Privately Held**
SIC: 3069 Custom compounding of rubber
materials

(P-9315)
HEXPOL COMPOUNDING CA INC
Also Called: Mrp Holdings Corp.
491 Wilson Way, City of Industry
(91744-3935)
PHONE..........................626 961-0311
Tracy Garrison, *President*
Ernie Ulmer, *CFO*
David Schlothauer, *Managing Dir*
EMP: 97 EST: 2011
SALES (est): 11.8MM
SALES (corp-wide): 1.5B **Privately Held**
SIC: 3069 Custom compounding of rubber
materials
HQ: Hexpol Holding Ab
Skeppsbron 3
Malmo

(P-9316)
HEXPOL COMPOUNDING LLC
11841 Wakeman St, Santa Fe Springs
(90670-2130)
PHONE..........................562 464-4482
Andrew Wallace, *Manager*
EMP: 25
SALES (corp-wide): 1.5B **Privately Held**
SIC: 3069 Molded rubber products
HQ: Hexpol Compounding Llc
14330 Kinsman Rd
Burton OH 44021
440 834-4644

(P-9317)
HITT COMPANIES
Also Called: Hitt Marking Devices I D Tech
3231 W Macarthur Blvd, Santa Ana
(92704-6801)
PHONE..........................714 979-1405
Harold G Hitt, *President*
Ken Hitt, *Vice Pres*
Heidi Hitt, *Admin Sec*
Tue Truong, *Manager*
▲ EMP: 24
SQ FT: 10,000
SALES (est): 4.7MM **Privately Held**
WEB: www.hittmarking.com
SIC: 3069 3993 5199 Stationers' rubber
sundries; signs & advertising specialties;
badges

(P-9318)
HOLZ RUBBER COMPANY INC
Also Called: Hr
1129 S Sacramento St, Lodi (95240-5701)
PHONE..........................209 368-7171
James R Dryburgh, *President*
David Smith, *President*
Ben Tannler, *Vice Pres*
Stephen McBurnett, *Design Engr*
Ted Cooper, *Engineer*
▲ EMP: 120
SQ FT: 144,000
SALES: 18MM **Privately Held**
WEB: www.holzrubber.com
SIC: 3069 3441 3061 Molded rubber
products; fabricated structural metal; me-
chanical rubber goods

(P-9319)
HOUSTON RUBBER CO INC
12623 Foothill Blvd, Sylmar (91342-5312)
PHONE..........................818 899-1108
Thane Neely, *President*
EMP: 10 EST: 1972
SQ FT: 6,000
SALES: 860K **Privately Held**
SIC: 3069 Molded rubber products

(P-9320)
HUTCHINSON AROSPC & INDUST INC
Also Called: Barry Controls Aerospace
4510 W Vanowen St, Burbank
(91505-1135)
P.O. Box 7710 (91510-7710)
PHONE..........................818 843-1000
Grant Hintze, *CEO*
Arnaud Vaz, *President*
L Garcia, *Admin Asst*
David Sio, *Info Tech Dir*
Ivan Roson, *Project Engr*
EMP: 156
SALES (corp-wide): 8.4B **Publicly Held**
WEB: www.barrycontrols.com
SIC: 3069 Molded rubber products
HQ: Hutchinson Aerospace & Industry, Inc.
82 South St
Hopkinton MA 01748
508 417-7000

(P-9321)
INFLATABLE ENTERPRISES INC
1418 Vineland Ave, Baldwin Park
(91706-5813)
PHONE..........................818 482-6509
Levon Abraamyan, *CEO*
▲ EMP: 11 EST: 2016
SQ FT: 10,000
SALES: 700K **Privately Held**
SIC: 3069 Rubberized fabrics

(P-9322)
INNOCOR WEST LLC
300-310 S Tippecanoe Ave, San
Bernardino (92408)
PHONE..........................909 307-3737
Carol S Eicher, *CEO*
Doug Vaughan, *CFO*
▲ EMP: 21
SQ FT: 150,000
SALES (est): 2.7MM
SALES (corp-wide): 238.1MM **Privately
Held**
WEB: www.advancedinnovations.net
SIC: 3069 5021 Pillows, sponge rubber;
mattresses
HQ: Innocor, Inc.
200 Schulz Dr Ste 2
Red Bank NJ 07701

(P-9323)
INTERNATIONAL RUBBER PDTS INC (PA)
Also Called: Irp
1035 Calle Amanecer, San Clemente
(92673-6260)
PHONE..........................909 947-1244
Rod Trujillo, *CEO*
Casper Zublin Jr, *President*
Rod Trujillo, *CEO*
Susan Perkins, *CFO*
Jose Castro, *Exec VP*
▲ EMP: 97
SQ FT: 45,000
SALES (est): 26.2MM **Privately Held**
WEB: www.wagnerrubber.com
SIC: 3069 Medical & laboratory rubber
sundries & related products

(P-9324)
IOMIC INC
530 Technology Dr Ste 100, Irvine
(92618-1350)
PHONE..........................714 564-1600
Toshihiko Hachiro, *President*
CHI Wu, *Sales Staff*
▲ EMP: 13
SALES (est): 1.6MM **Privately Held**
SIC: 3069 Grips or handles, rubber

(P-9325)
KINSALE HOLDINGS INC (PA)
Also Called: Validant
475 Sansome St Ste 570, San Francisco
(94111-3136)
PHONE..........................415 400-2600
Brian Burns, *CEO*
Kimberly Snyder, *Senior Partner*
John McShane, *Managing Prtnr*
Purvi Chekuri, *Vice Pres*
Bettina Wernimont, *Administration*
EMP: 60
SQ FT: 10,000
SALES (est): 27MM **Privately Held**
SIC: 3069 Druggists' rubber sundries

(P-9326)
KIRKHILL INC
12023 Woodruff Ave, Downey
(90241-5603)
P.O. Box 7012 (90242-7012)
PHONE..........................562 803-1117
Robert L Harold, *Chairman*
Bruce Mekjian, *President*
Mike Brickner, *Vice Pres*
Gary Riopelle, *Principal*
Arlene Hite, *Admin Sec*
EMP: 95
SQ FT: 173,000
SALES (est): 13.5MM **Privately Held**
SIC: 3069 Acid bottles, rubber

(P-9327)
KOR WATER
200 Spectrum Center Dr # 300, Irvine
(92618-5004)
PHONE..........................714 708-7567
Eric Barnes, *CEO*
Paul Schustak, *COO*
Jamie Walker, *Office Mgr*
Shanan Markley, *Opers Staff*
Josh Taft, *Director*
▲ EMP: 12
SALES (est): 1.8MM **Privately Held**
SIC: 3069 Water bottles, rubber

(P-9328)
LEONARDS MOLDED PRODUCTS INC
25031 Anza Dr, Valencia (91355-3414)
PHONE..........................661 253-2227
Randy Smith, *President*
Frank Smith, *Vice Pres*
Marty Kudlac, *General Mgr*
EMP: 25
SQ FT: 5,000
SALES (est): 4.2MM **Privately Held**
SIC: 3069 Molded rubber products

(P-9329)
LINE ONE LABORATORIES INC USA
9600 Lurline Ave, Chatsworth
(91311-5107)
PHONE..........................818 886-2288
Budiman Lee, *President*
Robert Gruber, *Vice Pres*
▲ EMP: 26
SQ FT: 22,000
SALES (est): 4.2MM **Privately Held**
SIC: 3069 5122 Medical & laboratory rub-
ber sundries & related products; medical
rubber goods

(P-9330)
LUSIDA RUBBER PRODUCTS
2540 Corp Pl Ste B103, Alhambra (91803)
PHONE..........................323 446-0280
Wayne Chin, *Principal*
▲ EMP: 15 EST: 2010
SALES (est): 1.2MM **Privately Held**
SIC: 3069 Fabricated rubber products

(P-9331)
MATZ RUBBER CO INC
1209 Chestnut St, Burbank (91506-1626)
PHONE..........................323 849-5170
Phillip Jensen, *President*
Jan Jensen, *Treasurer*
EMP: 25
SQ FT: 12,000
SALES (est): 3.6MM **Privately Held**
WEB: www.matzrubber.com
SIC: 3069 3541 3291 Rubber covered
motor mounting rings (rubber bonded);
machine tools, metal cutting type; abra-
sive products

(P-9332)
MCP INDUSTRIES INC (PA)
Also Called: Mission Rubber Co
708 S Temescal St Ste 101, Corona
(92879-2096)
P.O. Box 1839 (92878-1839)
PHONE..........................951 736-1881
Walter N Garrett, *CEO*
Charlotte Garrett, *Corp Secy*
Owen Garrett, *Vice Pres*
▲ EMP: 15
SQ FT: 100,000
SALES (est): 126.4MM **Privately Held**
WEB: www.missionrubber.com
SIC: 3069 3259 3089 Molded rubber
products; sewer pipe or fittings, clay; in-
jection molding of plastics

(P-9333)
MEDCONX INC
2901 Tasman Dr Ste 211, Santa Clara
(95054-1138)
PHONE..........................408 330-0003
Hal Kent, *President*
William Deihl, *CFO*
EMP: 22
SALES (est): 5.5MM **Privately Held**
SIC: 3069 Medical & laboratory rubber
sundries & related products
PA: Atl Technology, Llc
1335 W 1650 N
Springville UT 84663

(P-9334)
MITCHELL PROCESSING LLC
2778 Pomona Blvd, Pomona (91768-3222)
PHONE..........................909 519-5759
Mark Mitchell,
EMP: 20
SQ FT: 100,000
SALES (est): 774.3K **Privately Held**
SIC: 3069 Custom compounding of rubber
materials

(P-9335)
MITCHELL RUBBER PRODUCTS LLC (PA)
10220 San Sevaine Way, Jurupa Valley
(91752-1100)
PHONE..........................951 681-5655
Theodore C Ballou, *CEO*
Mark Mitchell, *Admin Sec*
▲ EMP: 235
SQ FT: 76,000
SALES (est): 84.4MM **Privately Held**
WEB: www.mitchellrubber.com
SIC: 3069 2891 2822 Mats or matting,
rubber; floor coverings, rubber; rubber au-
tomotive products; custom compounding
of rubber materials; adhesives & sealants;
synthetic rubber

(P-9336)
MITCHELL RUBBER PRODUCTS LLC
Valley Processing
10220 San Sevaine Way, Jurupa Valley
(91752-1100)
PHONE..........................951 681-5655
Jeff Mitchell, *Branch Mgr*

PRODUCTS & SVCS

EMP: 100
SALES (corp-wide): 84.4MM **Privately Held**
WEB: www.mitchellrubber.com
SIC: 3069 8721 3061 Rubber floor coverings, mats & wallcoverings; accounting, auditing & bookkeeping; mechanical rubber goods
PA: Mitchell Rubber Products Llc
　　10220 San Sevaine Way
　　Jurupa Valley CA 91752
　　951 681-5655

(P-9337)
MIZU INC (PA)
2225 Faraday Ave Ste E, Carlsbad (92008-7212)
PHONE...............................307 690-3219
Tim Pogue, *CEO*
Mike Kenney, *Opers Mgr*
▲ EMP: 16
SALES (est): 6.5MM **Privately Held**
SIC: 3069 Water bottles, rubber

(P-9338)
MODUS ADVANCED INC
1575 Greenville Rd, Livermore (94550-9713)
PHONE...............................925 962-5943
Rick Mackirdy, *CEO*
Don E Ulery, *Chairman*
Dave Elliott, *QA Dir*
▲ EMP: 35
SQ FT: 25,000
SALES: 12MM **Privately Held**
WEB: www.westernrubber.com
SIC: 3069 Molded rubber products

(P-9339)
MOMENTUM MANAGEMENT LLC
Also Called: Bushman Products
1206 W Jon St, Torrance (90502-1208)
PHONE...............................310 329-2599
Justin Ross,
Keith Caggiano, *Principal*
Aumann Conde, *Principal*
Jeff Swenson, *Graphic Designe*
Mitchell Robison, *Accountant*
▲ EMP: 15
SALES (est): 2.6MM **Privately Held**
SIC: 3069 Toys, rubber

(P-9340)
MORTAN INDUSTRIES INC
880 Columbia Ave Ste 2, Riverside (92507-2159)
PHONE...............................951 682-2215
John A Mortan, *President*
Frieda Mortan, *Vice Pres*
EMP: 27 EST: 1981
SQ FT: 22,000
SALES (est): 3.6MM **Privately Held**
WEB: www.mortanindustries.com
SIC: 3069 Hard rubber & molded rubber products

(P-9341)
NEBIA INC
375 Alabama St Ste 200, San Francisco (94110-1966)
PHONE...............................203 570-6222
Philip Winter, *CEO*
EMP: 12
SQ FT: 3,700
SALES: 100K **Privately Held**
SIC: 3069 Bath sprays, rubber

(P-9342)
NEW WORLD MANUFACTURING INC
27627 Dutcher Creek Rd, Cloverdale (95425-9753)
P.O. Box 248 (95425-0248)
PHONE...............................707 894-5257
Gerald E Moore, *President*
Rebecca S Moore, *Treasurer*
G James Moore, *Vice Pres*
EMP: 12 EST: 1971
SQ FT: 7,500

SALES: 745.7K **Privately Held**
WEB: www.newworldmfg.com
SIC: 3069 2394 2515 Linings, vulcanizable rubber; liners & covers, fabric: made from purchased materials; air cushions & mattresses, canvas; mattresses, waterbed flotation

(P-9343)
NEWBY RUBBER INC
320 Industrial St, Bakersfield (93307-2706)
PHONE...............................661 327-5137
Kelly Newby, *President*
Lori Newby, *Admin Sec*
▼ EMP: 25
SQ FT: 80,000
SALES (est): 5.3MM **Privately Held**
WEB: www.newbyrubber.com
SIC: 3069 Molded rubber products; hard rubber & molded rubber products

(P-9344)
NEWLINE RUBBER COMPANY
13165 Monterey Hwy # 100, San Martin (95046-9204)
PHONE...............................408 214-0359
Cherie Newland, *President*
Joseph E Newland, *CFO*
John Newland, *Vice Pres*
EMP: 12
SQ FT: 8,000
SALES (est): 1.4MM **Privately Held**
WEB: www.newlinerubber.com
SIC: 3069 Molded rubber products

(P-9345)
NUSIL TECHNOLOGY LLC
2343 Pegasus Dr, Bakersfield (93308-6804)
PHONE...............................661 391-4750
Scott Mraz,
EMP: 75
SALES (corp-wide): 1.4B **Publicly Held**
WEB: www.nusil.com
SIC: 3069 2821 Rubber coated fabrics & clothing; plastics materials & resins
HQ: Nusil Technology Llc
　　1050 Cindy Ln
　　Carpinteria CA 93013
　　805 684-8780

(P-9346)
NUSIL TECHNOLOGY LLC
1150 Mark Ave, Carpinteria (93013-2918)
PHONE...............................805 684-8780
Tom Baningan,
Jacquelyn Heffner, *Prgrmr*
EMP: 95
SALES (corp-wide): 1.4B **Publicly Held**
WEB: www.nusil.com
SIC: 3069 Bags, rubber or rubberized fabric
HQ: Nusil Technology Llc
　　1050 Cindy Ln
　　Carpinteria CA 93013
　　805 684-8780

(P-9347)
ONEILL WETSUITS LLC (PA)
1071 41st Ave, Santa Cruz (95062-4400)
P.O. Box 6300 (95063-6300)
PHONE...............................831 475-7500
Pat O'Neill, *Mng Member*
John Pope, *COO*
Michelle Molfino, *CFO*
Cherry Chu, *Vice Pres*
Patrice Riley, *Executive Asst*
◆ EMP: 70
SQ FT: 14,000
SALES (est): 24.3MM **Privately Held**
WEB: www.oneill.com
SIC: 3069 5091 Wet suits, rubber; watersports equipment & supplies

(P-9348)
P & E RUBBER PROCESSING INC
15380 Lyons Valley Rd, Jamul (91935-3509)
PHONE...............................760 241-2643
Edmundo Bolanos, *President*
Elizabeth Fornwald, *Office Mgr*
EMP: 20
SQ FT: 10,000
SALES (est): 2.4MM **Privately Held**
SIC: 3069 Rubber hardware

(P-9349)
PACIFIC EAGLE USA INC
9707 El Poche St Ste H, South El Monte (91733-3001)
PHONE...............................626 455-0033
Arthur Shih, *President*
▲ EMP: 40
SALES (est): 3.4MM **Privately Held**
SIC: 3069 7389 Wet suits, rubber; barter exchange

(P-9350)
PACIFICTECH MOLDED PDTS INC
22805 Savi Ranch Pkwy F, Yorba Linda (92887-4634)
PHONE...............................714 279-9928
Jane Xu, *President*
Mike Lou, *Project Mgr*
▲ EMP: 18
SALES (est): 2.7MM **Privately Held**
SIC: 3069 Rubber automotive products

(P-9351)
PECA CORPORATION
9707 El Poche St Ste H, El Monte (91733-3001)
PHONE...............................626 452-8873
Arthur T S Shih, *President*
▲ EMP: 38
SQ FT: 6,200
SALES (est): 3.9MM **Privately Held**
SIC: 3069 5941 5091 3949 Wet suits, rubber; fishing equipment; fishing tackle; sporting & athletic goods

(P-9352)
PHOENIX DEVENTURES INC
18655 Madrone Pkwy # 180, Morgan Hill (95037-8101)
PHONE...............................408 782-6240
Jeffrey Christian, *President*
Dacy Coleman, *Opers Staff*
EMP: 47
SQ FT: 30,000
SALES (est): 10MM **Privately Held**
SIC: 3069 Medical & laboratory rubber sundries & related products

(P-9353)
PIERCAN USA INC
160 Bosstick Blvd, San Marcos (92069-5930)
PHONE...............................760 599-4543
Vincent Lucas, *President*
Gean-Christopher Lucas, *Treasurer*
Stan Diniz, *General Mgr*
Antoine Dobrowolski, *General Mgr*
Philippe Bourdon, *VP Opers*
▲ EMP: 19
SQ FT: 16,000
SALES (est): 4.2MM **Privately Held**
WEB: www.latextechnology.com
SIC: 3069 2259 Rug backing compounds, latex; work gloves, knit

(P-9354)
PMR PRECISION MFG & RBR CO INC
1330 Etiwanda Ave, Ontario (91761-8605)
PHONE...............................909 605-7525
Samuel Surh, *President*
George Y Surh, *Executive*
George Surh, *General Mgr*
EMP: 30
SQ FT: 36,800
SALES (est): 5.1MM **Privately Held**
SIC: 3069 2295 Rubberized fabrics; coated fabrics, not rubberized

(P-9355)
POLY-SEAL INDUSTRIES
725 Channing Way, Berkeley (94710-2494)
PHONE...............................510 843-9722
Daniel K Baker, *President*
▼ EMP: 15
SQ FT: 6,250
SALES (est): 2.1MM **Privately Held**
SIC: 3069 Molded rubber products

(P-9356)
POLYMERIC TECHNOLOGY INC
1900 Marina Blvd, San Leandro (94577-3207)
PHONE...............................510 895-6001

Patrick Tool, *CEO*
Roger Castillo, *Mfg Staff*
▲ EMP: 50
SQ FT: 90,000
SALES (est): 11.2MM **Privately Held**
WEB: www.poly-tek.com
SIC: 3069 2821 8731 3061 Molded rubber products; plastics materials & resins; commercial physical research; mechanical rubber goods

(P-9357)
PRO-TECH MATS INDUSTRIES INC
72370 Quarry Trl Ste A, Thousand Palms (92276-6647)
PHONE...............................760 343-3667
Randy Ernst, *President*
EMP: 14
SQ FT: 5,650
SALES (est): 3MM **Privately Held**
SIC: 3069 Medical & laboratory rubber sundries & related products

(P-9358)
PROCO PRODUCTS INC (PA)
2431 Wigwam Dr, Stockton (95205-2430)
P.O. Box 590 (95201-0590)
PHONE...............................209 943-6088
Edward Marchese, *President*
Mike Lassas, *President*
Robert Coffee, *Vice Pres*
Scott Wallace, *Vice Pres*
Michael Lassas, *VP Admin*
◆ EMP: 28
SQ FT: 22,000
SALES (est): 6MM **Privately Held**
WEB: www.procoproducts.com
SIC: 3069 2821 3443 3441 Molded rubber products; polytetrafluoroethylene resins (teflon); pipe, standpipe & culverts; fabricated structural metal

(P-9359)
PROLAB ORTHOTICS INC
575 Airpark Rd, NAPA (94558-7514)
PHONE...............................707 257-4400
Paul Scherer, *CEO*
Aaron Meltzer, *President*
Dan Demars, *Executive*
Toni Smith, *CTO*
Reanne Martinez, *Manager*
EMP: 42
SQ FT: 8,200
SALES (est): 6.7MM **Privately Held**
WEB: www.prolab-usa.com
SIC: 3069 3842 Medical & laboratory rubber sundries & related products; surgical appliances & supplies

(P-9360)
PROMOTONAL DESIGN CONCEPTS INC
Also Called: Creative Inflatables
9872 Rush St, South El Monte (91733-2635)
PHONE...............................626 579-4454
Adam Melendez, *CEO*
Rick Villalpando, *Project Mgr*
◆ EMP: 71
SALES (est): 11.7MM **Privately Held**
WEB: www.creatableinflatables.com
SIC: 3069 7389 5092 2394 Balloons, advertising & toy: rubber; balloons, novelty & toy; toy novelties & amusements; canvas & related products; canvas awnings & canopies; shades, canvas: made from purchased materials

(P-9361)
R & R SERVICES CORPORATION
Also Called: Geolabs Westlake Village
31119 Via Colinas Ste 502, Westlake Village (91362-3941)
PHONE...............................818 889-2562
Ronald Z Shmerling, *President*
Timothy Casey, *Marketing Staff*
Lawain Ross, *Supervisor*
EMP: 25 EST: 1983
SALES (est): 3.7MM **Privately Held**
WEB: www.geolabswv.com
SIC: 3069 8999 8711 Laboratory sundries: cases, covers, funnels, cups, etc.; geological consultant; engineering services

▲ = Import ▼=Export
◆ =Import/Export

(P-9362)
R & S PROCESSING CO INC
15712 Illinois Ave, Paramount
(90723-4113)
P.O. Box 2037 (90723-8037)
PHONE............................562 531-0738
Karen A Kelly, *President*
Anthony J Inga, *Corp Secy*
Linda M Inga, *Vice Pres*
Darlene Rodriguez, *Info Tech Mgr*
EMP: 73 **EST:** 1959
SQ FT: 53,000
SALES (est): 13.4MM **Privately Held**
WEB: www.rsprocessing.com
SIC: 3069 Reclaimed rubber (reworked by
manufacturing processes)

(P-9363)
RELIABLE RUBBER PRODUCTS INC
2600 Yosemite Blvd Ste B, Modesto
(95354-4041)
PHONE............................209 525-9750
Marc Wilkins, *President*
William R Green, *CFO*
▲ **EMP:** 12
SQ FT: 13,000
SALES (est): 1.4MM **Privately Held**
SIC: 3069 Rubber hardware

(P-9364)
RENEE RIVERA HAIR ACCESSORIES
2295 Chestnut St Ste 2, San Francisco
(94123-2654)
PHONE............................415 776-6613
Renee Rivera, *Owner*
EMP: 10
SQ FT: 1,000
SALES (est): 901.5K **Privately Held**
SIC: 3069 Rubber hair accessories

(P-9365)
ROBERT CROWDER & CO INC
901 S Greenwood Ave Ste L, Montebello
(90640-5835)
PHONE............................323 248-7737
Oscar Cardenas, *President*
EMP: 12
SALES (est): 1.4MM **Privately Held**
SIC: 3069 5198 Wallcoverings, rubber;
wallcoverings

(P-9366)
ROGERS CORPORATION
Also Called: Diversified Silicone
13937 Rosecrans Ave, Santa Fe Springs
(90670-5209)
PHONE............................562 404-8942
Brian Lindey, *General Mgr*
Brian Lindey, *Sales Mgr*
Diana Mendoza, *Director*
EMP: 60
SALES (corp-wide): 879MM **Publicly Held**
SIC: 3069 Bags, rubber or rubberized fabric
PA: Rogers Corporation
2225 W Chandler Blvd
Chandler AZ 85224
480 917-6000

(P-9367)
RUBBERITE CORP (PA)
Also Called: Rubberite Cypress Sponge
Rubbe
301 Goetz Ave, Santa Ana (92707-3707)
PHONE............................714 546-6464
Greg Brooks, *President*
Barbara Ballou, *Corp Secy*
Terry Brooks, *Vice Pres*
Dave Chaney, *Plant Mgr*
▲ **EMP:** 15
SQ FT: 52,000
SALES (est): 2.1MM **Privately Held**
SIC: 3069 Molded rubber products

(P-9368)
SANTA FE RUBBER PRODUCTS INC
12306 Washington Blvd, Whittier
(90606-2597)
PHONE............................562 693-2776
William Krames, *President*
Mike Peterman, *Vice Pres*
EMP: 50
SQ FT: 30,000
SALES (est): 8.4MM **Privately Held**
WEB: www.santaferubber.com
SIC: 3069 Molded rubber products

(P-9369)
SATORI SEAL CORPORATION
8455 Utica Ave, Rancho Cucamonga
(91730-3809)
PHONE............................909 987-8234
Anne Acebo, *President*
Dale McGrosky, *Vice Pres*
▲ **EMP:** 10
SQ FT: 10,000
SALES (est): 1.7MM **Privately Held**
WEB: www.satoriseal.com
SIC: 3069 5085 Molded rubber products;
rubber goods, mechanical

(P-9370)
SEAL INNOVATIONS INC
820 S Palm Ave Ste 15, Alhambra
(91803-1544)
PHONE............................626 282-7325
Myrna Galvan, *President*
▲ **EMP:** 10
SALES (est): 1.2MM **Privately Held**
SIC: 3069 Fabricated rubber products

(P-9371)
SGT BOARDRIDERS INC
Also Called: Aleeda Wetsuits
7403 Slater Ave, Huntington Beach
(92647-6228)
PHONE............................714 274-8000
Steve Terry, *President*
EMP: 19
SQ FT: 6,000
SALES: 1.4MM **Privately Held**
SIC: 3069 Wet suits, rubber

(P-9372)
SHERCON INC
18704 S Ferris Pl, Rancho Dominguez
(90220-6400)
PHONE............................800 228-3218
Keith Ennis, *CEO*
EMP: 60
SQ FT: 50,000
SALES: 4.2MM
SALES (corp-wide): 2.9B **Privately Held**
WEB: www.shercon.com
SIC: 3069 3089 2672 Tape, pressure sensitive: rubber; injection molded finished
plastic products; coated & laminated
paper
HQ: Protective Industries, Inc.
2150 Elmwood Ave
Buffalo NY 14207
716 876-9951

(P-9373)
SOUTH BAY CORPORATION
Also Called: Windy Balloon Company
1335 W 134th St, Gardena (90247-1904)
PHONE............................310 532-5353
Ashhad S Khan, *CEO*
Wendy L Khan, *Vice Pres*
Sharon Aeder,
▲ **EMP:** 14
SQ FT: 12,000
SALES (est): 1.4MM **Privately Held**
SIC: 3069 Balloons, advertising & toy: rubber

(P-9374)
STOCKTON RUBBER MFGCOINC
Also Called: SRC
5023 N Flood Rd, Linden (95236-9455)
P.O. Box 639 (95236-0639)
PHONE............................209 887-1172
Earl D Wilson, *CEO*
Ursula Wilson, *Treasurer*
David V Teslaar, *Finance Mgr*
EMP: 28
SQ FT: 7,500
SALES (est): 5.7MM **Privately Held**
SIC: 3069 Medical & laboratory rubber
sundries & related products

(P-9375)
SUMITOMO ELECTRIC INTERCONN
915 Armorlite Dr, San Marcos
(92069-1440)
PHONE............................760 761-0600
Nobuyoshi Fujinama, *President*
Kristin Massaro, *Buyer*
Ruben Soto, *Mfg Mgr*
Tom Kearney, *Sales Staff*
Lisa Lambros, *Sales Staff*
▲ **EMP:** 60
SQ FT: 55,000
SALES (est): 7.1MM **Privately Held**
WEB: www.seipusa.com
SIC: 3069 Tubing, rubber
HQ: Sumitomo Electric Fine Polymer, Inc.
1-950, Asashironishi, Kumatoricho
Sennan-Gun OSK 590-0
-

(P-9376)
TA AEROSPACE CO (DH)
28065 Franklin Pkwy, Valencia
(91355-4117)
PHONE............................661 775-1100
Carol Marinello, *President*
Clare Cole, *Administration*
Harry Hong, *Info Tech Mgr*
Eleno Recio, *Info Tech Mgr*
Ali Sarhang, *Info Tech Mgr*
▲ **EMP:** 250
SQ FT: 100,000
SALES: 243.1MM
SALES (corp-wide): 3.8B **Publicly Held**
WEB: www.kirkhill.com
SIC: 3069 Reclaimed rubber & specialty
rubber compounds
HQ: Esterline Technologies Corp
500 108th Ave Ne Ste 1500
Bellevue WA 98004
425 453-9400

(P-9377)
TALCO FOAM INC (PA)
Also Called: Talco Foam Products
1631 Entp Blvd Ste 30, West Sacramento
(95691)
PHONE............................916 492-8840
Dave Talbot, *Principal*
▲ **EMP:** 15
SQ FT: 30,000
SALES (est): 3.2MM **Privately Held**
SIC: 3069 Foam rubber

(P-9378)
TAPE SERVICE LTD
4510 Carter Ct, Chino (91710-5060)
PHONE............................909 627-8811
Edward Lewis Sr, *President*
Marleen Lewis, *Vice Pres*
EMP: 12
SQ FT: 25,000
SALES (est): 1.7MM **Privately Held**
WEB: www.tapeservice.com
SIC: 3069 7389 5113 Tape, pressure sensitive: rubber; packaging & labeling services; pressure sensitive tape

(P-9379)
TIMEMED LABELING SYSTEMS INC (DH)
27770 N Entrmt Dr Ste 200, Valencia
(91355)
PHONE............................818 897-1111
Cecil Kost, *CEO*
Patrick Singer, *President*
Tracey Carpentier, *COO*
Mark Segal, *CFO*
EMP: 100
SQ FT: 75,000
SALES (est): 11.9MM
SALES (corp-wide): 1.1B **Publicly Held**
SIC: 3069 Tape, pressure sensitive: rubber
HQ: Precision Dynamics Corporation
25124 Sprngfeld Ct Ste 20
Valencia CA 91355
818 897-1111

(P-9380)
TINYINKLINGCOM LLC
Also Called: Matsmatsmats.com
6303 Owensmouth Ave Fl 10, Woodland
Hills (91367-2262)
PHONE............................877 777-6287
Mark Carmer,
▼ **EMP:** 12 **EST:** 2000
SALES (est): 2.4MM **Privately Held**
WEB: www.tinyinkling.com
SIC: 3069 5199 Rubber floor coverings,
mats & wallcoverings; general merchandise, non-durable

(P-9381)
TRAFFIX DEVICES INC
12128 Yucca Rd, Adelanto (92301-2708)
PHONE............................760 246-7171
Dennis Fortner, *Manager*
EMP: 35
SALES (corp-wide): 13MM **Privately Held**
WEB: www.traffixdevices.com
SIC: 3069 Medical & laboratory rubber
sundries & related products
PA: Traffix Devices, Inc.
160 Avenida La Pata
San Clemente CA 92673
949 361-5663

(P-9382)
UROCARE PRODUCTS INC
2735 Melbourne Ave, Pomona
(91767-1931)
PHONE............................909 621-6013
Friedhelm Franke, *CEO*
Raymond Halsey-Franke, *President*
Sylvia Bender, *CFO*
Glenn Franke, *Admin Sec*
▲ **EMP:** 11
SQ FT: 30,000
SALES (est): 2.4MM **Privately Held**
WEB: www.urocare.com
SIC: 3069 3089 Medical & laboratory rubber sundries & related products; injection
molded finished plastic products

(P-9383)
US RUBBER RECYCLING INC
1231 Lincoln St, Colton (92324-3533)
PHONE............................909 825-1200
Rick Snyder, *President*
Jr R Snyder, *Technology*
Stephanie Slater, *Manager*
▲ **EMP:** 22
SQ FT: 30,000
SALES (est): 400K **Privately Held**
SIC: 3069 Acid bottles, rubber

(P-9384)
US RUBBER ROLLER COMPANY INC
1516 7th St, Riverside (92507-4421)
PHONE............................951 682-2221
Jose Uribe, *President*
Lebizia Uribe, *Vice Pres*
Ramie Uribe, *Admin Sec*
EMP: 18
SQ FT: 10,000
SALES: 1.5MM **Privately Held**
SIC: 3069 Medical & laboratory rubber
sundries & related products

(P-9385)
VAL PAK PRODUCTS
20731 Centre Pointe Pkwy, Santa Clarita
(91350-2967)
PHONE............................661 252-0115
Ben Solakian, *Owner*
Ed Navickas, *Sales Mgr*
John Mihranian, *Accounts Exec*
EMP: 14
SQ FT: 33,700
SALES (est): 1.1MM **Privately Held**
SIC: 3069 Chlorinated rubbers, natural

(P-9386)
VIKING RUBBER PRODUCTS INC
2600 Homestead Pl, Compton
(90220-5610)
PHONE............................310 868-5200
Rod Trujillo, *CEO*
Leigh Munsell, *President*
Ricardo Ordonez, *CFO*
EMP: 80

SALES (est): 6.2MM
SALES (corp-wide): 26.2MM **Privately Held**
WEB: www.vikingrubber.com
SIC: **3069** 3061 Custom compounding of rubber materials; mechanical rubber goods
PA: International Rubber Products, Inc.
1035 Calle Amanecer
San Clemente CA 92673
909 947-1244

(P-9387)
VIP RUBBER COMPANY INC (PA)
540 S Cypress St, La Habra (90631-6127)
PHONE..............................714 774-7635
Howard Vipperman, *President*
Bernardyne Vipperman, *Corp Secy*
Steve Gillespie, *Principal*
Claudia Hargett, *Principal*
Maria Mendez, *Principal*
▲ EMP: 120
SQ FT: 58,000
SALES (est): 29.7MM **Privately Held**
WEB: www.plastic-rubber.com
SIC: **3069** 3089 3061 Rubber hardware; sponge rubber & sponge rubber products; plastic hardware & building products; mechanical rubber goods

(P-9388)
WEST AMERICAN RUBBER CO LLC (PA)
Also Called: Warco
1337 W Braden Ct, Orange (92868-1123)
P.O. Box 6146 (92863-6146)
PHONE..............................714 532-3355
Steven Hemstreet, *Mng Member*
Kelvin Baker, *CFO*
Ronald Shaffer, *Vice Pres*
Jim Deleo, *Executive*
Michael Escobedo, *Info Tech Mgr*
▲ EMP: 400
SQ FT: 12,500
SALES (est): 73.4MM **Privately Held**
WEB: www.warco.com
SIC: **3069** 3061 3053 Sheets, hard rubber; mechanical rubber goods; gaskets, all materials

(P-9389)
WEST AMERICAN RUBBER CO LLC
Also Called: Warco
750 N Main St, Orange (92868-1106)
P.O. Box 6146 (92863-6146)
PHONE..............................714 532-3355
Renan Mendez, *Vice Pres*
Kelvin Baker, *CFO*
EMP: 165
SALES (est): 27.1MM
SALES (corp-wide): 73.4MM **Privately Held**
WEB: www.warco.com
SIC: **3069** Sheets, hard rubber
PA: West American Rubber Company Llc
1337 W Braden Ct
Orange CA 92868
714 532-3355

(P-9390)
Y & D RUBBER CORPORATION
1451 S Carlos Ave, Ontario (91761-7676)
PHONE..............................909 517-1683
Trinidad Yepez, *President*
Alma Torres, *Purchasing*
EMP: 12
SQ FT: 15,000
SALES (est): 2.1MM **Privately Held**
SIC: **3069** Custom compounding of rubber materials

3081 Plastic Unsupported Sheet & Film

(P-9391)
ADVANCED MATERIALS ANALYSIS
740 Sierra Vista Ave D, Mountain View (94043-2576)
PHONE..............................650 391-4190
GE Lou, *Officer*

EMP: 10
SALES (est): 1MM **Privately Held**
SIC: **3081** Photographic & X-ray film & sheet

(P-9392)
ARLON GRAPHICS LLC
200 Boysenberry Ln, Placentia (92870-6413)
PHONE..............................714 985-6300
Andrew McNeill, *President*
Andrew Huddlestone, *President*
Rich Trombino, *Vice Pres*
Chad Russell, *VP Sales*
◆ EMP: 150
SALES (est): 56.1MM
SALES (corp-wide): 333.1MM **Privately Held**
SIC: **3081** Vinyl film & sheet
PA: Flexcon Company, Inc.
1 Flexcon Industrial Park
Spencer MA 01562
508 885-8200

(P-9393)
ARVINYL LAMINATES LP
233 N Sherman Ave, Corona (92882-1844)
PHONE..............................951 371-7800
Andy Peters, *Partner*
Linda Foster, *Sales Mgr*
EMP: 33
SALES (est): 11.5MM **Privately Held**
SIC: **3081** Vinyl film & sheet

(P-9394)
AVIATION AND INDUS DEV CORP
Also Called: Crystal Vision Packg Systems
23870 Hawthorne Blvd, Torrance (90505-5908)
PHONE..............................310 373-6057
Donald A Hilmer, *CEO*
Banu Simrose, *CFO*
Patricia Hilmer, *Corp Secy*
Meshia Barton, *Sales Mgr*
Karl Behrens, *Marketing Staff*
▲ EMP: 10
SQ FT: 8,650
SALES (est): 1.6MM **Privately Held**
WEB: www.crystalvisionpkg.com
SIC: **3081** 5162 Packing materials, plastic sheet; plastics film

(P-9395)
BERRY GLOBAL FILMS LLC
14000 Monte Vista Ave, Chino (91710-5537)
PHONE..............................909 517-2872
J Brendan Barba, *President*
Sakar Markar, *QC Dir*
EMP: 200
SQ FT: 63,480 **Publicly Held**
WEB: www.aepinc.com
SIC: **3081** 2673 Polyethylene film; bags: plastic, laminated & coated
HQ: Berry Global Films, Llc
95 Chestnut Ridge Rd
Montvale NJ 07645
201 641-6600

(P-9396)
C & R EXTRUSIONS INC
2618 River Ave, Rosemead (91770-3302)
PHONE..............................626 642-0244
Luis Michel, *President*
EMP: 12
SALES (est): 1.5MM **Privately Held**
SIC: **3081** Plastic film & sheet

(P-9397)
COMMEX CORPORATION
20408 Corsair Blvd, Hayward (94545-1004)
PHONE..............................510 887-4000
Yau CHI Wai, *CEO*
Edward Yau, *President*
▲ EMP: 19
SQ FT: 50,000
SALES (est): 5.3MM
SALES (corp-wide): 3MM **Privately Held**
SIC: **3081** Plastic film & sheet
PA: Yau's International Holding, Inc
20408 Corsair Blvd
Hayward CA 94545
510 887-4000

(P-9398)
COMPASS INNOVATIONS INC
Also Called: Careray USA
2352 Walsh Ave, Santa Clara (95051-1301)
PHONE..............................408 418-3985
Jianqiang Liu, *President*
EMP: 120
SALES (est): 3.7MM **Privately Held**
SIC: **3081** 5047 Photographic & X-ray film & sheet; X-ray film & supplies

(P-9399)
CREATIVE IMPRESSIONS INC
7697 9th St, Buena Park (90621-2898)
PHONE..............................714 521-4441
Marc D Abbott, *President*
▲ EMP: 45
SQ FT: 8,000
SALES (est): 5.7MM **Privately Held**
SIC: **3081** Plastic film & sheet

(P-9400)
DELSTAR HOLDING CORP
9225 Isaac St, Santee (92071-5615)
PHONE..............................619 258-1503
Scott Anglin, *Branch Mgr*
▲ EMP: 26 **Publicly Held**
SIC: **3081** Polypropylene film & sheet
HQ: Delstar Holding Corp.
100 N Point Ctr E Ste 600
Alpharetta GA 30022
800 514-0186

(P-9401)
DELSTAR TECHNOLOGIES INC
Also Called: Swm
1306 Fayette St, El Cajon (92020-1513)
PHONE..............................619 258-1503
Mark Laughlin, *Manager*
EMP: 50 **Publicly Held**
SIC: **3081** Polypropylene film & sheet
HQ: Delstar Technologies, Inc.
601 Industrial Rd
Middletown DE 19709
302 378-8888

(P-9402)
DIALACT CORPORATION
Also Called: Dialex
1111 Elko Dr Ste D, Sunnyvale (94089-2263)
PHONE..............................510 659-8099
Alex Yam, *CEO*
Alex Vainer, *President*
EMP: 13
SQ FT: 8,000
SALES: 1.5MM **Privately Held**
WEB: www.dialact.com
SIC: **3081** Unsupported plastics film & sheet

(P-9403)
DINSMORE & ASSOCIATES INC
1681 Kettering, Irvine (92614-5613)
PHONE..............................714 641-7111
Jason Dinsmore, *CEO*
Erin Dinsmore, *General Mgr*
Nick Dario, *Accounts Mgr*
Philippe Servando, *Accounts Mgr*
▲ EMP: 15
SALES (est): 3.4MM **Privately Held**
WEB: www.dinsmoreinc.com
SIC: **3081** 8711 Film base, cellulose acetate or nitrocellulose plastic; machine tool design

(P-9404)
FLEXCON COMPANY INC
12840 Reservoir St, Chino (91710-2944)
PHONE..............................909 465-0408
David R Trujillo, *Manager*
EMP: 35
SALES (corp-wide): 333.1MM **Privately Held**
WEB: www.flexcon.com
SIC: **3081** 2679 Plastic film & sheet; labels, paper: made from purchased material
PA: Flexcon Company, Inc.
1 Flexcon Industrial Park
Spencer MA 01562
508 885-8200

(P-9405)
GLAD PRODUCTS COMPANY (HQ)
1221 Broadway Ste A, Oakland (94612-1837)
PHONE..............................510 271-7000
William V Stephenson, *Ch of Bd*
Thomas H Rowland, *President*
Donald A De Santis, *CFO*
Joseph B Furey, *Vice Pres*
Lolita Hill, *Admin Asst*
▲ EMP: 150
SQ FT: 40,000
SALES (est): 804.5MM
SALES (corp-wide): 6.2B **Publicly Held**
WEB: www.gladproducts.com
SIC: **3081** 2673 2842 3295 Plastic film & sheet; plastic bags: made from purchased materials; automobile polish; waxes for wood, leather & other materials; cat box litter
PA: The Clorox Company
1221 Broadway Ste 1300
Oakland CA 94612
510 271-7000

(P-9406)
IMPAK CORPORATION
Also Called: Impak Worldwide
13700 S Broadway, Los Angeles (90061-1012)
PHONE..............................323 277-4700
Kevin Cullen, *President*
Edber Aguirre, *General Mgr*
Raymond Torres, *General Mgr*
Jeff Low, *Planning*
Lorraine Rincon, *Info Tech Mgr*
◆ EMP: 15
SQ FT: 12,000
SALES (est): 4.2MM **Privately Held**
WEB: www.sorbentsystems.com
SIC: **3081** Packing materials, plastic sheet

(P-9407)
KW PLASTICS RECYCLING DIVISION
1861 Sunnyside Ct, Bakersfield (93308-6848)
P.O. Box 80418 (93380-0418)
PHONE..............................661 392-0500
John Putman, *General Mgr*
EMP: 60
SALES (corp-wide): 70.7MM **Privately Held**
WEB: www.kwplastics.com
SIC: **3081** 3089 3354 3082 Polypropylene film & sheet; plastic processing; aluminum extruded products; unsupported plastics profile shapes
PA: Kw Plastics
279 Pike County Lake Rd
Troy AL 36079
334 566-1563

(P-9408)
LIFOAM INDUSTRIES LLC
Also Called: Lifoam Mfg
2340 E 52nd St, Vernon (90058-3444)
PHONE..............................323 587-1934
Dennis Bevans, *Branch Mgr*
EMP: 45
SQ FT: 40,000
SALES (corp-wide): 8.6B **Publicly Held**
WEB: www.lifoam.com
SIC: **3081** 3086 Packing materials, plastic sheet; plastics foam products
HQ: Lifoam Industries, Llc
9999 E 121st
Belcamp MD 21017
866 770-3626

(P-9409)
MERCURY PLASTICS INC
Poly Pak Packaging Division
2939 E Washington Blvd, Los Angeles (90023-4218)
PHONE..............................323 264-2400
Benjamin Deutsch, *Branch Mgr*
EMP: 95
SALES (corp-wide): 164.2MM **Privately Held**
SIC: **3081** 2677 Polyethylene film; envelopes

▲ = Import ▼=Export
◆ =Import/Export

PA: Mercury Plastics, Inc.
14825 Salt Lake Ave
City Of Industry CA 91746
626 961-0165

(P-9410)
MERRILLS PACKAGING INC
Also Called: Merrill's Packaging Supply
1529 Rollins Rd, Burlingame (94010-2305)
PHONE.....................................650 259-5959
Kenneth V Merrill, *CEO*
Gabriel King, *Prdtn Mgr*
Andy D Cpp, *Accounts Exec*
◆ EMP: 80
SQ FT: 60,000
SALES (est): 27.5MM **Privately Held**
WEB: www.merrills.com
SIC: 3081 Unsupported plastics film &
sheet

(P-9411)
METRO WORLD PLASTICS INC
344348 Shell St, San Francisco (94102)
PHONE.....................................415 255-8515
Rip Ridley, *President*
EMP: 10
SQ FT: 2,000
SALES (est): 925.3K **Privately Held**
SIC: 3081 Polyethylene film

(P-9412)
MODERN WALL GRAPHICS LLC
2191 W Esplanade Ave, San Jacinto
(92582-3723)
PHONE.....................................760 787-0346
Christa Demartini,
EMP: 25
SQ FT: 4,000
SALES (est): 3.2MM **Privately Held**
WEB: www.wallslicks.com
SIC: 3081 Floor or wall covering, unsup-
ported plastic

(P-9413)
MONTEBELLO PLASTICS LLC
601 W Olympic Blvd, Montebello
(90640-5229)
P.O. Box 789 (90640-0789)
PHONE.....................................323 728-6814
Timothy F Guth,
Evelyn Garcia, *Manager*
EMP: 50
SQ FT: 25,000
SALES (est): 9.3MM **Privately Held**
SIC: 3081 2673 3089 Packing materials,
plastic sheet; trash bags (plastic film):
made from purchased materials; extruded
finished plastic products

(P-9414)
NATIONWIDE PLASTIC PRODUCTS
16809 Gramercy Pl, Gardena
(90247-5205)
PHONE.....................................310 366-7585
Daniel Tai, *President*
John McGee, *CEO*
EMP: 30
SQ FT: 10,000
SALES (est): 2MM **Privately Held**
SIC: 3081 5093 Plastic film & sheet; plas-
tics scrap

(P-9415)
NEXUS CALIFORNIA INC
4551 Brickell Privado St, Ontario
(91761-7828)
PHONE.....................................909 937-1000
Kariman Sholakh, *President*
▲ EMP: 15
SQ FT: 23,512
SALES (est): 3MM **Privately Held**
WEB: www.nexuscalifornia.com
SIC: 3081 2673 Plastic film & sheet; plas-
tic bags: made from purchased materials

(P-9416)
OCEANIA INC
14209 Gannet St, La Mirada (90638-5220)
PHONE.....................................562 926-8886
Tai Leong, *CEO*
Angela Leung, *Vice Pres*
▲ EMP: 30
SALES (est): 5.4MM **Privately Held**
SIC: 3081 Plastic film & sheet

(P-9417)
PROVIDIEN THERMOFORMING INC
Also Called: Specialty Manufacturing, Inc.
6740 Nancy Ridge Dr, San Diego
(92121-2230)
PHONE.....................................858 850-1591
Jeffrey S Goble, *CEO*
Jenny Ames, *President*
Frank Ames Jr, *Admin Sec*
Paul Jazwin, *Manager*
▲ EMP: 48
SQ FT: 25,500
SALES (est): 8.1MM **Privately Held**
SIC: 3081 Unsupported plastics film &
sheet
PA: Providien, Llc
7333 E Dbltree Rnch Rd
Scottsdale AZ 85258
-

(P-9418)
RIDOUT PLASTICS COMPANY
Also Called: Eplastics
5535 Ruffin Rd, San Diego (92123-1397)
PHONE.....................................858 560-1551
Elliot Rabin, *President*
Denise Hogan, *Controller*
▼ EMP: 35
SQ FT: 32,000
SALES (est): 12.8MM **Privately Held**
WEB: www.ridoutplastics.com
SIC: 3081 3082 5162 2541 Unsupported
plastics film & sheet; unsupported plastics
profile shapes; plastics materials & basic
shapes; wood partitions & fixtures

(P-9419)
SAINT-GOBAIN SOLAR GARD LLC (DH)
Also Called: Saint-Gobain Performance Plas
4540 Viewridge Ave, San Diego
(92123-1637)
P.O. Box 2864, Clinton IA (52733-2864)
PHONE.....................................866 300-2674
Steven Messmer, *Mng Member*
Kristen Mallardi, *Human Res Mgr*
M Shawn Puccio,
◆ EMP: 88
SQ FT: 65,000
SALES (est): 61.7MM
SALES (corp-wide): 215.9MM **Privately Held**
SIC: 3081 5162 3479 Plastic film & sheet;
plastics film; coating of metals & formed
products
HQ: Saint-Gobain Performance Plastics
Corporation
31500 Solon Rd
Solon OH 44139
440 836-6900

(P-9420)
SCIENTIFIC SPECIALTIES INC
Also Called: Ssi
1310 Thurman St, Lodi (95240-3145)
PHONE.....................................209 333-2120
Kenneth Hovatter, *Principal*
Cindy Schock, *COO*
Danielle Hovatter, *Design Engr*
Bill Schmierer, *Controller*
Beverly Hutchinson, *Purch Mgr*
◆ EMP: 100
SALES (est): 23.3MM **Privately Held**
WEB: www.scientificspecialties.com
SIC: 3081 Unsupported plastics film &
sheet

(P-9421)
SIMPLEX STRIP DOORS LLC (DH)
Also Called: Simplex Isolation Systems
14500 Miller Ave, Fontana (92336-1696)
PHONE.....................................800 854-7951
Vince Lake, *Vice Pres*
Charlie McKenrick, *Vice Pres*
Shannon Mayfield, *Marketing Staff*
▲ EMP: 30
SQ FT: 28,000
SALES (est): 4.8MM
SALES (corp-wide): 7.9B **Privately Held**
WEB: www.simplexstripdoors.com
SIC: 3081 Vinyl film & sheet

(P-9422)
STOROPACK INC
2210 Junction Ave, San Jose (95131-1210)
PHONE.....................................408 435-1537
Lester Whisnant, *Manager*
Troy Biscardi, *Opers Staff*
Brad Engeman, *Manager*
EMP: 25
SALES (corp-wide): 535.4MM **Privately Held**
WEB: www.storopack.com
SIC: 3081 3086 Packing materials, plastic
sheet; plastics foam products
HQ: Storopack, Inc.
4758 Devitt Dr
West Chester OH 45246
513 874-0314

(P-9423)
TRAFFIC WORKS INC
5720 Soto St, Huntington Park
(90255-2631)
PHONE.....................................323 582-0616
Steve Josephson, *Owner*
Mark Contreras, *CFO*
▲ EMP: 20
SQ FT: 20,000
SALES (est): 3.6MM **Privately Held**
WEB: www.trafficworks.us
SIC: 3081 2678 Packing materials, plastic
sheet; stationery: made from purchased
materials

(P-9424)
TRM MANUFACTURING INC
375 Trrm Cir, Corona (92879-1758)
P.O. Box 77520 (92877-0117)
PHONE.....................................951 256-8550
Ted Moore, *President*
Anaisa Moore, *Vice Pres*
▲ EMP: 200
SQ FT: 200,000
SALES (est): 2.2MM **Privately Held**
WEB: www.trmmfg.com
SIC: 3081 Polyethylene film

(P-9425)
W PLASTICS INC
Also Called: Western Plastics Temecula
2543 41573 Dendy Pkwy, Temecula
(92590)
PHONE.....................................800 442-9727
Michael T F Cunningham, *President*
Thomas C Cunningham, *Treasurer*
Patrick Cunningham, *Vice Pres*
Pamela Long, *Office Mgr*
Henri Lim, *Opers Staff*
◆ EMP: 35
SQ FT: 65,000
SALES (est): 9.2MM **Privately Held**
SIC: 3081 1799 Plastic film & sheet; food
service equipment installation

(P-9426)
WESTERN SUMMIT MFG CORP
Also Called: Southern International Packg
30200 Cartier Dr, Rancho Palos Verdes
(90275-5722)
PHONE.....................................626 333-3333
Donald K Clark, *President*
EMP: 60
SQ FT: 55,000
SALES (est): 7.3MM **Privately Held**
SIC: 3081 2759 2673 Unsupported plas-
tics film & sheet; commercial printing;
bags: plastic, laminated & coated

3082 Plastic Unsupported Profile Shapes

(P-9427)
ALL WEST PLASTICS INC
5451 Argosy Ave, Huntington Beach
(92649-1038)
PHONE.....................................714 894-9922
L Scott Leishman, *President*
EMP: 27
SQ FT: 35,000
SALES (est): 3.9MM **Privately Held**
WEB: www.allwestplastics.com
SIC: 3082 Unsupported plastics profile
shapes

(P-9428)
B GONE BIRD INC (PA)
15375 Barranca Pkwy Ste D, Irvine
(92618-2206)
PHONE.....................................949 387-5662
Bruce Alan Donoho, *CEO*
Julianne Donoho, *President*
◆ EMP: 18
SQ FT: 7,100
SALES (est): 2.9MM **Privately Held**
WEB: www.birdbgone.com
SIC: 3082 Unsupported plastics profile
shapes

(P-9429)
JSN PACKAGING PRODUCTS INC
9700 Jeronimo Rd, Irvine (92618-2019)
PHONE.....................................949 458-0050
Jim Nagel, *President*
James H Nagel Jr, *CEO*
Sandra Nagel, *Treasurer*
EMP: 65
SALES (est): 9.5MM **Privately Held**
SIC: 3082 3089 Tubes, unsupported plas-
tic; caps, plastic

(P-9430)
KELCOURT PLASTICS INC (DH)
Also Called: Kelpac Medical
1000 Calle Recodo, San Clemente
(92673-6225)
PHONE.....................................949 361-0774
Neil Shillingford, *CEO*
Bob Carter, *Controller*
Julio Cueva, *Plant Mgr*
▲ EMP: 80
SQ FT: 20,000
SALES: 20MM
SALES (corp-wide): 7.9B **Privately Held**
WEB: www.kelcourt.com
SIC: 3082 Tubes, unsupported plastic
HQ: Pexco Llc
6470 E Johns Rssng 430
Johns Creek GA 30097
770 777-8540

(P-9431)
KELPAC MEDICAL
2189 Britannia Blvd, San Diego
(92154-8307)
PHONE.....................................619 710-2550
EMP: 58
SALES (corp-wide): 7.9B **Privately Held**
SIC: 3082 Tubes, unsupported plastic
HQ: Kelcourt Plastics, Inc.
1000 Calle Recodo
San Clemente CA 92673
949 361-0774

(P-9432)
MEDICAL EXTRUSION TECH INC (PA)
Also Called: M E T
26608 Pierce Cir Ste A, Murrieta
(92562-1008)
PHONE.....................................951 698-4346
Tom E Bauer, *CEO*
I Rikki Bauer, *Vice Pres*
EMP: 42
SQ FT: 16,645
SALES (est): 9.8MM **Privately Held**
WEB: www.medicalextrusion.com
SIC: 3082 Tubes, unsupported plastic

(P-9433)
POLYMEREX MEDICAL CORP
7358 Trade St, San Diego (92121-2422)
PHONE.....................................858 695-0765
Yan-Ho Shu, *President*
Eileen Hsieh, *Admin Sec*
EMP: 15
SQ FT: 5,200
SALES (est): 2.7MM **Privately Held**
WEB: www.polymerex.com
SIC: 3082 3083 Tubes, unsupported plas-
tic; laminated plastics plate & sheet

(P-9434)
REEVES EXTRUDED PRODUCTS INC
1032 Stockton Ave, Arvin (93203-2330)
PHONE.....................................661 854-5970
Grady Reeves, *CEO*
Sandy Shelton, *Treasurer*

Beverly Palmer, *Admin Sec*
Steve Reeves, *Admin Sec*
EMP: 75 **EST:** 1967
SQ FT: 45,000
SALES (est): 13.1MM **Privately Held**
WEB: www.reeves-extruded.com
SIC: 3082 Unsupported plastics profile shapes

3083 Plastic Laminated Plate & Sheet

(P-9435)
A B C PLASTICS INC
Also Called: A B C Plastic Fabrication,
9132 De Soto Ave, Chatsworth
(91311-4907)
PHONE..........................818 775-0065
Mark Walters, *President*
Ivan Jackovich, *Vice Pres*
Antonio Guerrero, *Prdtn Mgr*
▲ **EMP:** 15
SQ FT: 8,000
SALES (est): 8MM **Privately Held**
WEB: www.abcplastics.com
SIC: 3083 7319 5046 3089 Plastic finished products, laminated; display advertising service; store fixtures; plastic processing

(P-9436)
ACRYLICORE INC
15902 S Broadway, Gardena (90248-2406)
PHONE..........................310 515-4846
Shane Nia, *President*
EMP: 13
SQ FT: 7,500
SALES (est): 2.6MM **Privately Held**
WEB: www.acrylicore.com
SIC: 3083 Plastic finished products, laminated

(P-9437)
ARMORED MOBILITY INC
5610 Scotts Valley Dr B332, Scotts Valley
(95066-3476)
PHONE..........................831 430-9899
Tony Pollace, *CEO*
Mike Berritto, *President*
Joel Bahu, *Vice Pres*
Bill Gazza, *VP Sales*
EMP: 34
SALES: 40.7K **Privately Held**
SIC: 3083 Plastic finished products, laminated

(P-9438)
ENDURAL LLC
1685 Scenic Ave Ste A, Costa Mesa
(92626-1409)
PHONE..........................714 434-6533
James P Burra,
Karmen White, *Accountant*
Susan Williams,
EMP: 15 **EST:** 1961
SALES: 7.5MM **Privately Held**
WEB: www.endural.com
SIC: 3083 Plastic finished products, laminated

(P-9439)
HERITAGE PRODUCTS LLC
20932c Currier Rd Unit C, Walnut
(91789-3019)
PHONE..........................909 839-1866
Ron Bollig, *Mng Member*
Jason Bollig, *Sales Staff*
Dana Bollig, *Mng Member*
EMP: 10
SALES (est): 1.2MM **Privately Held**
SIC: 3083 Plastic finished products, laminated

(P-9440)
INNOVATIVE PLASTICS INC
5502 Buckingham Dr, Huntington Beach
(92649-5701)
PHONE..........................714 891-8800
Gary Elmer, *President*
EMP: 12
SQ FT: 10,500

SALES (est): 1.5MM **Privately Held**
WEB: www.e-surfshop.com
SIC: 3083 5947 3089 Plastic finished products, laminated; gift, novelty & souvenir shop; plastic processing

(P-9441)
JOHNSON LAMINATING COATING INC
20631 Annalee Ave, Carson (90746-3502)
PHONE..........................310 635-4929
Scott Davidson, *President*
Cristina Kovar, *Research*
Ray Cruz, *Graphic Designe*
Beverly Hadley, *Accountant*
Kathy Truver, *Controller*
▲ **EMP:** 75
SQ FT: 50,000
SALES (est): 25.1MM **Privately Held**
WEB: www.johnsonwindowfilms.com
SIC: 3083 3081 2891 1541 Laminated plastic sheets; window sheeting, plastic; unsupported plastics film & sheet; adhesives & sealants; food products manufacturing or packing plant construction; silicones

(P-9442)
LINDSEY DOORS INC
Also Called: Lindsey Mfg
81101 Indio Blvd Ste D16, Indio
(92201-1920)
PHONE..........................760 775-1959
Pierre Letellier, *President*
Katherine Letellier, *Admin Sec*
EMP: 22
SALES (est): 4.2MM **Privately Held**
WEB: www.lindseydoors.com
SIC: 3083 1521 Thermoplastic laminates: rods, tubes, plates & sheet; single-family housing construction

(P-9443)
LITE EXTRUSIONS MANUFACTURING
15025 S Main St, Gardena (90248-1922)
PHONE..........................323 770-4298
Paul Puga, *President*
William Puga, *Corp Secy*
Barbara Puga, *Vice Pres*
Willy Puga, *Sales Executive*
EMP: 30
SQ FT: 23,500
SALES (est): 5MM **Privately Held**
WEB: www.liteextrusions.com
SIC: 3083 Thermoplastic laminates: rods, tubes, plates & sheet

(P-9444)
NELCO PRODUCTS INC (HQ)
1100 E Kimberly Ave, Anaheim
(92801-1101)
PHONE..........................714 879-4293
Margaret M Kendrick, *President*
▲ **EMP:** 105
SALES (est): 22.9MM **Privately Held**
WEB: www.nelcoproducts.com
SIC: 3083 Laminated plastics plate & sheet

(P-9445)
PACIFIC PLASTIC TECHNOLOGY INC
Also Called: P P T
9555 Hyssop Dr, Rancho Cucamonga
(91730-6124)
PHONE..........................909 987-4200
Robert Sawyer Sr, *CEO*
James P Sawyer, *Exec VP*
Robert Sawyer Jr, *Vice Pres*
▲ **EMP:** 50
SALES (est): 10.6MM **Privately Held**
WEB: www.plastictech.com
SIC: 3083 8711 3544 Plastic finished products, laminated; engineering services; special dies, tools, jigs & fixtures

(P-9446)
PARAMOUNT LAMINATES INC
Also Called: Paramount Laminates & Cabinets
15527 Vermont Ave, Paramount
(90723-4295)
PHONE..........................562 531-7580
Dan Neeley, *President*
Wayne De Puy, *President*

Brian Depuy, *CEO*
Sheila De Puy, *Corp Secy*
EMP: 18 **EST:** 1966
SQ FT: 5,000
SALES (est): 1.5MM **Privately Held**
WEB: www.paramountlaminate.com
SIC: 3083 Laminated plastics plate & sheet

(P-9447)
PHILLIPS BROS PLASTICS INC
17831 S Western Ave, Gardena
(90248-3681)
PHONE..........................310 532-8020
James Phillips, *President*
David Phillips, *General Mgr*
Alan Phillips, *VP Prdtn*
EMP: 20 **EST:** 1956
SQ FT: 28,000
SALES (est): 1.2MM **Privately Held**
SIC: 3083 3089 Plastic finished products, laminated; injection molding of plastics

(P-9448)
PLASTIC INNOVATIONS INC
10513 San Sevaine Way, Jurupa Valley
(91752-3286)
PHONE..........................951 361-0251
Chinpan Patel, *CEO*
EMP: 19
SQ FT: 22,000
SALES (est): 3.1MM **Privately Held**
SIC: 3083 Plastic finished products, laminated

(P-9449)
PLASTICS RESEARCH CORPORATION
Also Called: PRC
1400 S Campus Ave, Ontario (91761-4330)
PHONE..........................909 391-9050
Gene Gregory, *CEO*
Robert Black, *President*
Michael Maedel, *Exec VP*
▲ **EMP:** 100
SQ FT: 105,000
SALES (est): 27.5MM **Privately Held**
SIC: 3083 Laminated plastics plate & sheet

(P-9450)
PLASTIFAB INC
Also Called: Plastifab/Leed Plastics
1425 Palomares St, La Verne
(91750-5294)
PHONE..........................909 596-1927
Rick Donnelly, *President*
Jerri Kelly, *Financial Exec*
EMP: 30
SQ FT: 15,000
SALES (est): 4.8MM **Privately Held**
WEB: www.plastifab.biz
SIC: 3083 5162 3089 Laminated plastic sheets; plastics sheets & rods; plastic processing

(P-9451)
PLASTIFAB SAN DIEGO
12145 Paine St, Poway (92064-7124)
PHONE..........................858 679-6600
Philip Staub, *President*
Robert M Lincoln, *Partner*
Mark Weinrich, *Partner*
EMP: 18
SQ FT: 15,000
SALES (est): 3.3MM **Privately Held**
WEB: www.plastifabsd.com
SIC: 3083 5162 3089 Laminated plastic sheets; plastics sheets & rods; plastic processing

(P-9452)
PTM & W INDUSTRIES INC
10640 Painter Ave, Santa Fe Springs
(90670-4092)
PHONE..........................562 946-4511
Charles E Owen, *CEO*
William Ryan, *Vice Pres*
Doug Mayer, *District Mgr*
John Peralta, *District Mgr*
Stacey Nickel, *Administration*
▲ **EMP:** 25
SQ FT: 25,000

SALES (est): 6.6MM **Privately Held**
WEB: www.ptm-w.com
SIC: 3083 2992 2891 2851 Plastic finished products, laminated; lubricating oils & greases; adhesives & sealants; paints & allied products; plastics materials & resins

(P-9453)
REPET INC
14207 Monte Vista Ave, Chino
(91710-5724)
PHONE..........................909 594-5333
Shubin Zhao, *President*
Francisco Hernandez, *Project Mgr*
▲ **EMP:** 145
SALES (est): 33.1MM **Privately Held**
WEB: www.repetusa.com
SIC: 3083 Plastic finished products, laminated

(P-9454)
ROCK WEST COMPOSITES INC (PA)
1602 Precision Park Ln, San Diego
(92173-1346)
PHONE..........................801 566-3402
James P Gormican, *CEO*
EMP: 20
SALES (est): 8.9MM **Privately Held**
WEB: www.rockwestcomposites.com
SIC: 3083 Laminated plastics plate & sheet

(P-9455)
SCHAFFER LABORATORIES INC
Also Called: Western Plastic Products
8441 Monroe Ave, Stanton (90680-2615)
PHONE..........................714 202-1594
▲ **EMP:** 13
SQ FT: 9,000
SALES: 750K **Privately Held**
SIC: 3083 3089

(P-9456)
SPARTECH LLC
14263 Gannet St, La Mirada (90638-5220)
PHONE..........................714 523-2260
Julie A McAlindon, *Manager*
EMP: 14
SALES (corp-wide): 961.3MM **Privately Held**
SIC: 3083 Thermoplastic laminates: rods, tubes, plates & sheet
PA: Spartech Llc
11650 Lkeside Crossing Ct
Saint Louis MO 63146
314 569-7400

(P-9457)
SWISS PRODUCTIONS INC
2801 Golf Course Dr, Ventura
(93003-7610)
PHONE..........................805 654-8379
Kenneth Ray Putman, *CEO*
Joyce Snyder, *CFO*
Joyce C Snyder, *CFO*
Michelle Rogers, *Officer*
Richard G Petrash, *Senior VP*
▲ **EMP:** 46
SQ FT: 25,000
SALES (est): 5.8MM **Privately Held**
WEB: www.swissproductions.com
SIC: 3083 3469 Plastic finished products, laminated; metal stampings

(P-9458)
TURRET PUNCH CO INC
7780 Edison Ave, Fontana (92336-3635)
PHONE..........................909 587-1820
Carol Lang, *CEO*
Steve Lang, *President*
Ken Lutkus, *Technician*
EMP: 10 **EST:** 1972
SQ FT: 15,000
SALES (est): 2.1MM **Privately Held**
WEB: www.goturethane.com
SIC: 3083 3082 Plastic finished products, laminated; unsupported plastics profile shapes

(P-9459)
VCLAD LAMINATES INC
2103 Seaman Ave, South El Monte
(91733-2628)
PHONE..........................626 442-2100
David Thomson, *President*

▲ = Import ▼=Export
◆ =Import/Export

▲ **EMP:** 20
SALES (est): 3.3MM **Privately Held**
WEB: www.vclad.com
SIC: 3083 2434 Laminated plastic sheets; wood kitchen cabinets

(P-9460)
VILLANUEVA PLASTIC COMPANY INC
372 W Tullock St, Rialto (92376-7702)
PHONE..............................909 581-3870
Jose C Villanueva, *President*
EMP: 11
SALES (est): 1.5MM **Privately Held**
SIC: 3083 Plastic finished products, laminated

(P-9461)
WORLD MANUFACTURING INC (PA)
350 Fischer Ave Ste B, Costa Mesa (92626-4508)
PHONE..............................714 662-3539
Michael Robinson, *President*
Alan Katz, *Vice Pres*
◆ **EMP:** 10
SQ FT: 22,000
SALES (est): 1.7MM **Privately Held**
WEB: www.worldmanufacturing.com
SIC: 3083 3081 3993 Plastic finished products, laminated; packing materials, plastic sheet; neon signs

3084 Plastic Pipe

(P-9462)
ADVANCED DRAINAGE SYSTEMS INC
1025 Commerce Dr, Madera (93637-5201)
P.O. Box 1117 (93639-1117)
PHONE..............................559 674-4989
Richard Tartaglia, *Branch Mgr*
EMP: 20
SQ FT: 16,000
SALES (corp-wide): 1.3B **Publicly Held**
WEB: www.ads-pipe.com
SIC: 3084 Plastics pipe
PA: Advanced Drainage Systems, Inc.
4640 Trueman Blvd
Hilliard OH 43026
614 658-0050

(P-9463)
ASSISVIS INC
10780 Mulberry Ave, Fontana (92337-7062)
PHONE..............................909 628-2031
Ken Lam, *President*
EMP: 22
SALES (est): 4.9MM **Privately Held**
SIC: 3084 3089 Plastics pipe; plastic processing

(P-9464)
BEAR INDUSTRIAL HOLDINGS INC
Also Called: Bear Industrial Supply & Mfg
9971 Muirlands Blvd, Irvine (92618-2508)
PHONE..............................562 926-3000
Kevin E Wheeler, *CEO*
EMP: 21
SALES (est): 3.9MM **Privately Held**
WEB: www.bearism.com
SIC: 3084 Plastics pipe

(P-9465)
CHEVRON PHILLIPS CHEM CO LP
Also Called: Performance Pipe Div
6001 Bollinger Canyon Rd, San Ramon (94583-5737)
PHONE..............................909 420-5500
Phil Foley, *Branch Mgr*
EMP: 80
SALES (corp-wide): 8B **Privately Held**
WEB: www.cpchem.com
SIC: 3084 Plastics pipe
HQ: Chevron Phillips Chemical Company Lp
10001 Six Pines Dr
The Woodlands TX 77380
832 813-4100

(P-9466)
GEORG FISCHER HARVEL LLC
7001 Schirra Ct, Bakersfield (93313-2165)
PHONE..............................661 396-0653
EMP: 86
SALES (corp-wide): 4.6B **Privately Held**
SIC: 3084 Plastics pipe
HQ: Georg Fischer Harvel Llc
300 Kuebler Rd
Easton PA 18040
610 252-7355

(P-9467)
HANCOR INC
140 Vineland Rd, Bakersfield (93307-9515)
PHONE..............................661 366-1520
James Tingle, *Manager*
EMP: 60
SALES (corp-wide): 1.3B **Publicly Held**
SIC: 3084 5051 Plastics pipe; pipe & tubing, steel
HQ: Hancor, Inc.
4640 Trueman Blvd
Hilliard OH 43026
614 658-0050

(P-9468)
HUNTER INDUSTRIES INCORPORATED (PA)
1940 Diamond St, San Marcos (92078-5190)
PHONE..............................760 744-5240
Gregory Hunter, *President*
◆ **EMP:** 277
SQ FT: 450,000
SALES (est): 328.9MM **Privately Held**
WEB: www.hunterindustries.com
SIC: 3084 5087 Plastics pipe; sprinkler systems

(P-9469)
IPEX USA LLC
Valor Div of Naco Ind
2395 Maggio Cir, Lodi (95240-8814)
PHONE..............................209 368-7131
Daniel Gruber, *Branch Mgr*
EMP: 11
SQ FT: 8,500
SALES (corp-wide): 7MM **Privately Held**
WEB: www.nacopvc.com
SIC: 3084 Plastics pipe
HQ: Ipex Usa Llc
10100 Rodney St
Pineville NC 28134
704 889-2431

(P-9470)
J-M MANUFACTURING COMPANY INC (PA)
Also Called: JM Eagle
5200 W Century Blvd, Los Angeles (90045-5928)
PHONE..............................800 621-4404
Walter Wang, *CEO*
John MAI, *CFO*
Neal Gordon, *Vice Pres*
David Merritt, *Vice Pres*
Shirley Wang, *Principal*
◆ **EMP:** 150
SQ FT: 24,000
SALES (est): 1B **Privately Held**
SIC: 3084 2821 3491 Plastics pipe; polyvinyl chloride resins (PVC); water works valves

(P-9471)
KAKUICHI AMERICA INC
23540 Telo Ave, Torrance (90505-4013)
PHONE..............................310 539-1590
Yasuo Ogami, *CEO*
Kenichi Tanaka, *Principal*
▲ **EMP:** 100
SQ FT: 110,000
SALES (est): 29.1MM **Privately Held**
SIC: 3084 Plastics pipe
HQ: Kakuichi Co., Ltd.
1415, Midoricho, Tsuruga
Nagano NAG 380-0

(P-9472)
PACIFIC PLASTICS INC
111 S Berry St, Brea (92821-4827)
PHONE..............................714 990-9050
Anayat Raminfar, *President*

Rahim Arian, *Treasurer*
Farhad Bahremand, *Vice Pres*
Rahim Kashanian, *Vice Pres*
Aman Ramin, *Vice Pres*
▲ **EMP:** 71
SQ FT: 32,000
SALES (est): 36.1MM **Privately Held**
SIC: 3084 Plastics pipe

(P-9473)
PRINSCO INC
2839 S Cherry Ave, Fresno (93706-5406)
PHONE..............................559 485-5542
John Hoff, *Branch Mgr*
EMP: 30
SALES (corp-wide): 90.9MM **Privately Held**
WEB: www.prinsco.com
SIC: 3084 Plastics pipe
PA: Prinsco, Inc.
1717 16th St Ne Fl 3
Willmar MN 56201
320 978-4116

(P-9474)
PW EAGLE INC
Also Called: JM Eagle
5200 W Century Blvd Fl 10, Los Angeles (90045-5971)
PHONE..............................800 621-4404
EMP: 267
SALES (corp-wide): 978.3MM **Privately Held**
SIC: 3084
HQ: Pw Eagle, Inc.
5200 W Century Blvd
Los Angeles CA 90045
800 621-4404

(P-9475)
PW EAGLE INC
Also Called: P W Pipe
23711 Rider St, Perris (92570-7114)
PHONE..............................951 657-7400
EMP: 267
SALES (corp-wide): 978.3MM **Privately Held**
SIC: 3084 3644
HQ: Pw Eagle, Inc.
5200 W Century Blvd
Los Angeles CA 90045
800 621-4404

(P-9476)
PW EAGLE INC
Also Called: P W Pipe
3500 Robin Ln, Shingle Springs (95682)
P.O. Box 386 (95682-0386)
PHONE..............................530 677-2286
Fax: 530 677-3642
EMP: 100
SALES (corp-wide): 978.3MM **Privately Held**
SIC: 3084
HQ: Pw Eagle, Inc.
5200 W Century Blvd
Los Angeles CA 90045
800 621-4404

(P-9477)
REHAU INCORPORATED
Also Called: Rehau Constructions
1250 Corona Pointe Ct # 301, Corona (92879-1780)
PHONE..............................951 549-9017
Joe Lepire, *Manager*
Dan Drosu, *Natl Sales Mgr*
EMP: 10 **Privately Held**
WEB: www.rehauna.com
SIC: 3084 3089 Plastics pipe; extruded finished plastic products
PA: Rehau Incorporated
1501 Edwards Ferry Rd Ne
Leesburg VA 20176

(P-9478)
US PIPE FABRICATION LLC
Also Called: Water Works Manufacturing
3387 Plumas Arboga Rd, Marysville (95901)
P.O. Box 2480 (95901-0089)
PHONE..............................530 742-5171
Tom Nascimento, *Vice Pres*
EMP: 35

SALES (corp-wide): 1.4B **Publicly Held**
SIC: 3084 3088 3494 Plastics pipe; plastics plumbing fixtures; valves & pipe fittings
HQ: Us Pipe Fabrication, Llc
2 Chase Corporate Dr # 200
Hoover AL 35244

(P-9479)
VALENCIA PIPE COMPANY
Also Called: Home-Flex
28839 Industry Dr, Valencia (91355-5419)
PHONE..............................661 257-3923
Andrew Dervin, *CEO*
Curt Meyer, *CFO*
Peter Dervin, *Vice Pres*
Uriel Sandoval, *Vice Pres*
Jon Eggly, *Info Tech Dir*
▲ **EMP:** 40 **EST:** 2007
SQ FT: 60,000
SALES: 42.7MM **Privately Held**
SIC: 3084 5074 3479 3312 Plastics pipe; pipes & fittings, plastic; coating or wrapping steel pipe; iron & steel: galvanized, pipes, plates, sheets, etc.

3085 Plastic Bottles

(P-9480)
AMCOR RIGID PACKAGING USA LLC
Also Called: Ball Plastic Container
14270 Ramona Ave, Chino (91710-5738)
PHONE..............................909 517-2700
Curt Crogan, *Branch Mgr*
Cesar Macias, *Buyer*
Edmund Garcia, *Purch Agent*
EMP: 175 **Privately Held**
WEB: www.ball.com
SIC: 3085 3411 Plastics bottles; metal cans
HQ: Amcor Rigid Packaging Usa, Llc
40600 Ann Arbor Rd E # 201
Plymouth MI 48170

(P-9481)
CHI FUNG PLASTICS INC
1000 54th Ave, Oakland (94601-5646)
PHONE..............................510 532-4835
Eric Wu, *President*
EMP: 13
SQ FT: 40,000
SALES (est): 2.2MM **Privately Held**
SIC: 3085 Plastics bottles

(P-9482)
CLASSIC CONTAINERS INC
1700 S Hellman Ave, Ontario (91761-7638)
PHONE..............................909 930-3610
Manny G Hernandez Sr, *CEO*
Manny Hernandez Jr, *Treasurer*
Ernie Hernandez, *Vice Pres*
Maria Hernandez, *Admin Sec*
Kevin Tippitt, *Sales Staff*
EMP: 280
SQ FT: 60,000
SALES (est): 68.1MM **Privately Held**
WEB: www.classiccontainers.com
SIC: 3085 5085 3089 Plastics bottles; industrial supplies; plastic containers, except foam

(P-9483)
CONSOLIDATED CONTAINER CO LLC
Mayfair Plastics
1500 E 223rd St, Carson (90745-4316)
PHONE..............................310 952-8736
Larry Lindsey, *Manager*
Enrique Yanez, *Manager*
EMP: 80
SALES (corp-wide): 14B **Publicly Held**
WEB: www.cccllc.com
SIC: 3085 2656 Plastics bottles; sanitary food containers
HQ: Consolidated Container Company, Llc
2500 Windy Ridge Pkwy Se # 1400
Atlanta GA 30339
678 742-4600

PRODUCTS & SVCS

(P-9484)
CONSOLIDATED CONTAINER CO LLC
Also Called: Reid Plastics
5772 Jurupa St Ste B, Ontario
(91761-3643)
PHONE.............................909 390-6637
Steve Thompson, *Manager*
EMP: 15
SALES (corp-wide): 14B **Publicly Held**
WEB: www.cccllc.com
SIC: **3085** 3556 Plastics bottles; beverage machinery; juice extractors, fruit & vegetable: commercial type
HQ: Consolidated Container Company, Llc
2500 Windy Ridge Pkwy Se # 1400
Atlanta GA 30339
678 742-4600

(P-9485)
CONSOLIDATED CONTAINER CO LLC
1620 Gobel Way, Modesto (95358-5745)
PHONE.............................209 531-9180
Michael Foley, *Principal*
EMP: 87
SALES (corp-wide): 14B **Publicly Held**
WEB: www.cccllc.com
SIC: **3085** 2821 3089 Plastics bottles; polycarbonate resins; plastic containers, except foam
HQ: Consolidated Container Company, Llc
2500 Windy Ridge Pkwy Se # 1400
Atlanta GA 30339
678 742-4600

(P-9486)
GRAHAM PACKAGING CO EUROPE LLC
11555 Arrow Rte, Rancho Cucamonga
(91730-4944)
PHONE.............................909 989-5367
EMP: 147 **Privately Held**
SIC: **3085**
HQ: Graham Packaging Company Europe Llc
2401 Pleasant Valley Rd # 2
York PA 17402
717 849-8500

(P-9487)
LIQUI-BOX CORPORATION
Liqui-Box Division
5772 Jurupa St Ste C, Ontario
(91761-3643)
PHONE.............................909 390-4646
Lou Pershin, *Principal*
EMP: 40
SALES (corp-wide): 377.2MM **Privately Held**
WEB: www.liquibox.com
SIC: **3085** 3089 2656 Plastics bottles; plastic processing; sanitary food containers
PA: Liqui-Box Corporation
901 E Byrd St Ste 1105
Richmond VA 23219
804 325-1400

(P-9488)
MUNCHKIN INC (PA)
7835 Gloria Ave, Van Nuys (91406-1822)
PHONE.............................818 893-5000
Steven B Dunn, *CEO*
Andrew Keimach, *President*
Tom Emrey, *COO*
Jeff Hale, *COO*
Gary Rolfes, *CFO*
▲ EMP: 123
SQ FT: 63,000
SALES (est): 40.7MM **Privately Held**
WEB: www.munchkininc.com
SIC: **3085** 3069 5999 Plastics bottles; teething rings, rubber; bibs, vulcanized rubber or rubberized fabric; infant furnishings & equipment

(P-9489)
NARAYAN CORPORATION
Also Called: Plastic Processing Co
13432 Estrella Ave, Gardena (90248-1513)
PHONE.............................310 719-7330
Harshad Desai, *President*
▲ EMP: 37

SALES (est): 5.5MM **Privately Held**
SIC: **3085** 3089 Plastics bottles; bottle caps, molded plastic

(P-9490)
PLASCOR INC
972 Columbia Ave, Riverside (92507-2140)
PHONE.............................951 328-1010
David Harrigan, *President*
Sean Harrigan, *Manager*
▼ EMP: 135
SQ FT: 50,000
SALES (est): 39.3MM **Privately Held**
SIC: **3085** Plastics bottles

(P-9491)
PLAXICON HOLDING CORPORATION
Also Called: Plaxicon Co
10660 Acacia St, Rancho Cucamonga
(91730-5409)
PHONE.............................909 944-6868
Bill Williams, *CEO*
EMP: 130
SQ FT: 150,000
SALES (est): 13.2MM
SALES (corp-wide): 14.1MM **Privately Held**
WEB: www.liquidcontainer.com
SIC: **3085** 3089 Plastics bottles; plastic containers, except foam
HQ: Graham Packaging Company Europe Llc
2401 Pleasant Valley Rd # 2
York PA 17402

(P-9492)
POLY-TAINER INC (PA)
Also Called: Custom Molded Devices
450 W Los Angeles Ave, Simi Valley
(93065-1646)
PHONE.............................805 526-3424
Paul G Strong, *President*
Julie Williams, *CEO*
Stephanie Strong, *Vice Pres*
Gabriela Llamas, *Human Res Dir*
Johnny Llamas, *Purch Mgr*
▲ EMP: 290 EST: 1970
SQ FT: 95,000
SALES (est): 78.7MM **Privately Held**
WEB: www.polytainer.com
SIC: **3085** Plastics bottles

(P-9493)
PRETIUM PACKAGING LLC
Also Called: Custom Blow Molding
946 S Andreasen Dr, Escondido
(92029-1914)
PHONE.............................760 737-7995
EMP: 170
SALES (corp-wide): 141MM **Privately Held**
SIC: **3085** 2671 Plastics bottles; plastic film, coated or laminated for packaging
HQ: Pretium Packaging, L.L.C.
15450 S Outer Forty Dr St
Chesterfield MO 63017
314 727-8200

(P-9494)
RING CONTAINER TECH LLC
3643 Finch Rd, Modesto (95357-4143)
PHONE.............................209 238-3426
Joel McDonald, *Manager*
Tom Sponder, *Plant Mgr*
EMP: 23
SALES (corp-wide): 292.3MM **Privately Held**
WEB: www.ringcontainer.com
SIC: **3085** 3411 Plastics bottles; food containers, metal
PA: Ring Container Technologies, Llc.
1 Industrial Park
Oakland TN 38060
800 280-7464

(P-9495)
RING CONTAINER TECH LLC
8275 Almeria Ave, Fontana (92335-3280)
PHONE.............................909 350-8416
Fred Miller, *Branch Mgr*
Kevin Devries, *Plant Mgr*
EMP: 40
SQ FT: 60,800

SALES (corp-wide): 292.3MM **Privately Held**
WEB: www.ringcontainer.com
SIC: **3085** 3411 3089 Plastics bottles; food containers, metal; blow molded finished plastic products
PA: Ring Container Technologies, Llc.
1 Industrial Park
Oakland TN 38060
800 280-7464

(P-9496)
TRIPLE DOT CORP
3302 S Susan St, Santa Ana (92704-6841)
PHONE.............................714 241-0888
Tony T Tsai, *President*
Elaine Chang, *Corp Secy*
Jason Tsai, *Vice Pres*
▲ EMP: 36
SQ FT: 35,000
SALES (est): 6.3MM **Privately Held**
WEB: www.triple-dot.com
SIC: **3085** 5085 3089 Plastics bottles; glass bottles; plastic containers, except foam

(P-9497)
US PLASTIC INC
1561 Estridge Ave Ste 102, Riverside
(92507)
PHONE.............................951 300-9360
Kyeong Hee Lee, *President*
▲ EMP: 20
SALES (est): 4.6MM **Privately Held**
SIC: **3085** Plastics bottles

3086 Plastic Foam Prdts

(P-9498)
ABAD FOAM INC
6560 Caballero Blvd, Buena Park
(90620-1130)
PHONE.............................714 994-2223
Abad Chavez, *President*
Cesar Chavez, *COO*
Chris Wertz, *Sales Staff*
▲ EMP: 50
SALES (est): 10MM **Privately Held**
WEB: www.abadfoam.com
SIC: **3086** Plastics foam products

(P-9499)
ADVANCED FOAM INC
1745 W 134th St, Gardena (90249-2015)
PHONE.............................310 515-0728
James Conley, *President*
Susan L Conley, *Admin Sec*
EMP: 38
SQ FT: 17,500
SALES (est): 7.1MM **Privately Held**
WEB: www.advancedfoam.net
SIC: **3086** 3299 Packaging & shipping materials, foamed plastic; ornamental & architectural plaster work

(P-9500)
ADVANCED MATERIALS INC (HQ)
20211 S Susana Rd, Compton
(90221-5725)
PHONE.............................310 537-5444
Fax: 310 763-6869
▲ EMP: 19
SQ FT: 56,000
SALES (est): 2.5MM
SALES (corp-wide): 138.8MM **Publicly Held**
WEB: www.ami4.com
SIC: **3086**
PA: Ufp Technologies, Inc.
100 Hale St
Newburyport MA 01950
978 352-2200

(P-9501)
AGRI CEL INC
401 Road 192, Delano (93215-9598)
PHONE.............................661 792-2107
Louis Pandol, *President*
Jack Pandol, *Vice Pres*
Steve Pandol, *Vice Pres*
▲ EMP: 90
SQ FT: 30,000

SALES (est): 9.1MM **Privately Held**
WEB: www.agri-cel.com
SIC: **3086** Packaging & shipping materials, foamed plastic

(P-9502)
ALLMAN PRODUCTS INC
21251 Deering Ct, Canoga Park
(91304-5016)
P.O. Box 10625 (91309-1625)
PHONE.............................818 715-0093
Allan Allman, *President*
▲ EMP: 20
SQ FT: 8,000
SALES (est): 3MM **Privately Held**
SIC: **3086** Plastics foam products

(P-9503)
AMERICAN POLY-FOAM COMPANY INC
1455 Crocker Ave, Hayward (94544-7032)
P.O. Box 3307 (94540-3307)
PHONE.............................510 786-3626
Steven T Alexakos, *President*
Theresa Andrade, *Human Res Mgr*
Matt Ballock, *Accounts Mgr*
Kevin Finerty, *Accounts Mgr*
▲ EMP: 25
SALES (est): 5MM
SALES (corp-wide): 376.3MM **Privately Held**
SIC: **3086** Packaging & shipping materials, foamed plastic
PA: Future Foam, Inc.
1610 Avenue N
Council Bluffs IA 51501
712 323-9122

(P-9504)
ARCHITECTURAL FOAM PRODUCTS
3237 Santa Rosa Ave, Santa Rosa
(95407-7951)
PHONE.............................707 544-2779
Jose Gaitan, *Owner*
▼ EMP: 12
SALES (est): 953.1K **Privately Held**
SIC: **3086** Insulation or cushioning material, foamed plastic

(P-9505)
ARTISTIC COVERINGS INC
14135 Artesia Blvd, Cerritos (90703-7025)
PHONE.............................562 404-9343
Troy Robinson, *President*
Michelle Robinson, *Vice Pres*
▲ EMP: 30
SQ FT: 24,000
SALES (est): 5.5MM **Privately Held**
WEB: www.artisticcoverings.com
SIC: **3086** 3949 2759 Padding, foamed plastic; track & field athletic equipment; commercial printing

(P-9506)
ASTROFOAM MOLDING COMPANY INC
4117 Calle Tesoro, Camarillo (93012-8760)
PHONE.............................805 482-7276
Anthony Bevan, *Ch of Bd*
Steven Bevan, *President*
Pamela R Bevan, *Corp Secy*
Christopher Bevan, *Vice Pres*
▲ EMP: 18 EST: 1969
SQ FT: 21,000
SALES (est): 2.6MM **Privately Held**
WEB: www.astrofoam.com
SIC: **3086** Plastics foam products

(P-9507)
ATLAS FOAM PRODUCTS
12836 Arroyo St, Sylmar (91342-5304)
PHONE.............................818 837-3626
Jeff Naples, *President*
Sandra Naples, *Admin Sec*
Pamela Lindlief, *Purch Agent*
EMP: 18
SQ FT: 28,000
SALES (est): 3.4MM **Privately Held**
WEB: www.atlasfoam.com
SIC: **3086** Packaging & shipping materials, foamed plastic

▲ = Import ▼=Export
◆ =Import/Export

(P-9508)
BACK SUPPORT SYSTEMS INC
67688 San Andreas St, Desert Hot Springs
(92240-6804)
P.O. Box 961 (92240-0907)
PHONE..................................760 329-1472
Jeffrey A Kalatsky, *President*
Jeffrey Kalatsky, *Manager*
▲ EMP: 17
SQ FT: 9,800
SALES (est): 1.6MM **Privately Held**
WEB: www.backsupportsystems.com
SIC: 3086 5047 Plastics foam products;
therapy equipment

(P-9509)
BOWERS & KELLY PRODUCTS INC
4572 E Eisenhower Cir, Anaheim
(92807-1823)
PHONE..................................714 630-1285
EMP: 26
SALES (est): 3.3MM **Privately Held**
SIC: 3086

(P-9510)
BUD WIL INC
Also Called: B W I
1170 N Red Gum St, Anaheim
(92806-2539)
PHONE..................................714 630-1242
M Charles Williams, *President*
EMP: 30
SQ FT: 22,000
SALES (est): 5MM **Privately Held**
SIC: 3086 Plastics foam products

(P-9511)
CALIFORNIA PERFORMANCE PACKG
Also Called: Pacific Tech Products Ontario
33200 Lewis St, Union City (94587-2202)
PHONE..................................909 390-4422
Randall Lake, *President*
EMP: 400
SALES (est): 34.2MM
SALES (corp-wide): 4MM **Privately Held**
SIC: 3086 Packaging & shipping materials,
foamed plastic
HQ: Great American Industries Inc
300 Plaza Dr
Vestal NY 13850
607 729-9331

(P-9512)
CAPPAC PLASTIC PRODUCTS
5835 S Malt Ave, Commerce (90040-3589)
PHONE..................................323 721-7542
Stephen Peterson, *Owner*
EMP: 20 EST: 1961
SQ FT: 27,000
SALES (est): 1.7MM **Privately Held**
SIC: 3086 2671 Packaging & shipping ma-
terials, foamed plastic; packaging paper &
plastics film, coated & laminated

(P-9513)
CARPENTER CO
Also Called: Carpenter E R Co
7809 Lincoln Ave, Riverside (92504-4442)
P.O. Box 7788 (92513-7788)
PHONE..................................951 354-7550
Jim Nanfeldt, *Manager*
EMP: 480
SALES (corp-wide): 1.8B **Privately Held**
WEB: www.carpenter.com
SIC: 3086 2821 7389 5033 Insulation or
cushioning material, foamed plastic; plas-
tics materials & resins; furniture finishing;
insulation materials
PA: Carpenter Co.
5016 Monument Ave
Richmond VA 23230
804 359-0800

(P-9514)
CLEAN CUT TECHNOLOGIES LLC
1145 N Ocean Cir, Anaheim (92806-1939)
PHONE..................................714 864-3500
Tim Bell, *President*
James Miller, *Engineer*
Dustin Kelekoma, *QC Mgr*
Jeremy Chiong, *Production*
Caroline Nieto, *Sales Staff*

EMP: 100 EST: 2000
SALES (est): 14.3MM
SALES (corp-wide): 2.9B **Privately Held**
WEB: www.cleancuttek.com
SIC: 3086 Packaging & shipping materials,
foamed plastic
HQ: Oliver Products Company
445 6th St Nw
Grand Rapids MI 49504
616 456-7711

(P-9515)
CMD PRODUCTS
Also Called: C M D Products
1130 Conroy Ln Ste 301, Roseville
(95661-4154)
PHONE..................................916 434-0228
David Harris, *President*
▲ EMP: 15
SALES (est): 2.9MM **Privately Held**
WEB: www.cmdproducts.com
SIC: 3086 Plastics foam products

(P-9516)
COLD PACK SYSTEM INC
9020 Activity Rd Ste A, San Diego
(92126-4454)
PHONE..................................858 586-0800
David McKinney, *CEO*
Alice Duong, *Principal*
◆ EMP: 15
SQ FT: 20,000
SALES: 3.5MM
SALES (corp-wide): 133.6K **Privately Held**
WEB: www.coldpacksystem.com
SIC: 3086 2037 Packaging & shipping ma-
terials, foamed plastic; fruits, quick frozen
& cold pack (frozen)
PA: Coldpack
Cold Pack Cold Pack System
Alfortville
153 141-115

(P-9517)
CONSOLIDATED CONTAINER CO LP
Also Called: A Division Continental Can Co
1217 E Saint Gertrude Pl, Santa Ana
(92707-3029)
PHONE..................................714 241-6640
Cesare Calabrese, *Branch Mgr*
Veronica Banuelos, *Purch Mgr*
EMP: 100
SALES (corp-wide): 14B **Publicly Held**
SIC: 3086 3085 Plastics foam products;
plastics bottles
HQ: Consolidated Container Company Lp
2500 Windy Ridge Pkwy Se # 1400
Atlanta GA 30339
678 742-4600

(P-9518)
CORRUGATED AND PACKAGING LLC
951 Poinsettia Ave # 602, Vista
(92081-8464)
PHONE..................................619 559-1564
David Ortiz,
Santiago Fernandez,
Ruben Villegas,
EMP: 205
SALES: 7MM **Privately Held**
SIC: 3086 2653 Packaging & shipping ma-
terials, foamed plastic; corrugated & solid
fiber boxes

(P-9519)
CPD INDUSTRIES
Also Called: Custom Packaging Design
4665 State St, Montclair (91763-6130)
PHONE..................................909 465-5596
Carlos Hurtado, *President*
Sergio Briceno, *CFO*
Jeff Lenhardt, *Accounts Mgr*
EMP: 29
SQ FT: 22,000
SALES (est): 5.2MM **Privately Held**
WEB: www.casefoam.com
SIC: 3086 Packaging & shipping materials,
foamed plastic

(P-9520)
CUSTOM CONVERTING INC
2625 Temple Heights Dr C, Oceanside
(92056-3590)
PHONE..................................760 724-0664
Dan Kloos, *President*
Tresa Gliponeo, *Vice Pres*
Tolu Peters, *General Mgr*
▲ EMP: 15
SQ FT: 21,000
SALES (est): 3.5MM **Privately Held**
WEB: www.customconverting.com
SIC: 3086 Packaging & shipping materials,
foamed plastic

(P-9521)
DART CONTAINER CORP CALIFORNIA (PA)
150 S Maple Ctr, Corona (92880)
PHONE..................................951 735-8115
Robert C Dart, *CEO*
Kevin Fox, *Treasurer*
John Scramling, *Technology*
Richard Bailey, *Engineer*
Roy Moyer, *Engineer*
▲ EMP: 300
SQ FT: 50,000
SALES (est): 89.3MM **Privately Held**
SIC: 3086 Cups & plates, foamed plastic

(P-9522)
DART CONTAINER CORP CALIFORNIA
Also Called: Dart Container Corp Calif
1400 E Victor Rd, Lodi (95240-0833)
PHONE..................................209 333-8088
John Brice, *President*
Linette Burila, *Human Res Mgr*
Connie Castillo, *QC Dir*
Ron Crookham, *Plant Mgr*
EMP: 170
SALES (corp-wide): 89.3MM **Privately Held**
SIC: 3086 Cups & plates, foamed plastic
PA: Dart Container Corporation Of Califor-
nia
150 S Maple Ctr
Corona CA 92880
951 735-8115

(P-9523)
DEPENDABLE PLAS & PATTERN INC
4900 Fulton Dr, Fairfield (94534-1641)
PHONE..................................707 863-4900
Harry Marquez, *President*
Emil Eger, *Vice Pres*
EMP: 50
SQ FT: 50,000
SALES (est): 8.4MM **Privately Held**
SIC: 3086 Plastics foam products

(P-9524)
DIVERSIFIED PACKAGING INC
2221 S Anne St, Santa Ana (92704-4410)
PHONE..................................714 850-9316
David A Hoyt, *President*
Kathleen Hoyt, *Corp Secy*
Donald Hoyt, *Vice Pres*
EMP: 46
SALES (est): 5.2MM **Privately Held**
SIC: 3086 7389 Packaging & shipping ma-
terials, foamed plastic; packaging & label-
ing services

(P-9525)
EDM INTERNATIONAL LOGISTICS
2225 W Commwl Ave Ste 110, Alhambra
(91803)
PHONE..................................626 588-2299
Yijie Wan, *Principal*
▲ EMP: 13
SALES (est): 2.2MM **Privately Held**
SIC: 3086 Packaging & shipping materials,
foamed plastic

(P-9526)
ELITE COMFORT SOLUTIONS LLC
Also Called: Commerce Foam Plant
4542 Dunham St, Commerce
(90040-5415)
P.O. Box 910922, Los Angeles (90091-
0922)
PHONE..................................323 266-0422
Mark Stenger, *Manager*
EMP: 131
SALES (corp-wide): 4.2B **Publicly Held**
SIC: 3086 Insulation or cushioning mate-
rial, foamed plastic
HQ: Elite Comfort Solutions Llc
24 Herring Rd
Newnan GA 30265
828 267-7813

(P-9527)
EPE INDUSTRIES USA INC
Also Called: Epe Industries USA Dallas
17654 Newhope St Ste A, Fountain Valley
(92708-4294)
PHONE..................................800 315-0336
Robbie Seagroves, *Branch Mgr*
EMP: 15 **Privately Held**
SIC: 3086 Carpet & rug cushions, foamed
plastic
HQ: Epe Industries Usa, Inc.
17654 Newhope St Ste A
Fountain Valley CA 92708

(P-9528)
EPE INDUSTRIES USA INC (HQ)
Also Called: Epe USA
17654 Newhope St Ste A, Fountain Valley
(92708-4294)
PHONE..................................800 315-0336
Troy Merrell, *CEO*
Toshio Yanagi, *CFO*
Mohammed Hashmani, *General Mgr*
Darryl Lambert, *General Mgr*
Basilio Vazquez, *General Mgr*
EMP: 18
SALES (est): 54.2MM **Privately Held**
SIC: 3086 Ice chests or coolers (portable),
foamed plastic; packaging & shipping ma-
terials, foamed plastic; padding, foamed
plastic

(P-9529)
FIVE STAR FOOD CONTAINERS INC
250 Eastgate Rd, Barstow (92311-3224)
PHONE..................................626 437-6219
Larry Luc, *President*
▲ EMP: 60
SALES: 30MM **Privately Held**
SIC: 3086 Plastics foam products

(P-9530)
FOAM CONCEPTS INC
4729 E Wesley Dr, Anaheim (92807-1941)
PHONE..................................714 693-1037
Stephen C Ross, *Owner*
▲ EMP: 20
SQ FT: 9,000
SALES (est): 4.4MM **Privately Held**
WEB: www.styro-loc.com
SIC: 3086 Packaging & shipping materials,
foamed plastic

(P-9531)
FOAM FABRICATORS INC
301 9th St Ste B, Modesto (95351-4055)
PHONE..................................209 523-7002
Daniel Schloss, *Manager*
EMP: 17 **Publicly Held**
WEB: www.foamfabricators.com
SIC: 3086 Packaging & shipping materials,
foamed plastic
HQ: Foam Fabricators, Inc.
8722 E San Alberto # 200
Scottsdale AZ 85258
480 607-7330

(P-9532)
FOAM FACTORY INC
17515 S Santa Fe Ave, Compton
(90221-5400)
PHONE..................................310 603-9808
Felipe Alcazar, *President*
▼ EMP: 45

P R O D U C T S   &   S V C S

SQ FT: 40,000
SALES (est): 8.5MM **Privately Held**
WEB: www.foambymail.com
SIC: 3086 3069 5199 5087 Insulation or cushioning material, foamed plastic; foam rubber; foams & rubber; upholsterers' equipment & supplies

(P-9533)
FOAM MOLDERS AND SPECIALTIES (PA)
Also Called: Foam Specialties
11110 Business Cir, Cerritos (90703-5523)
PHONE..............................562 924-7757
Daniel M Doke, *President*
Dan Doke, *President*
Norman Himel, *CFO*
Rory Strammer, *Vice Pres*
Pat Zaremba, *Vice Pres*
▲ EMP: 100
SQ FT: 35,600
SALES (est): 16MM **Privately Held**
WEB: www.foammolders.com
SIC: 3086 3089 Plastics foam products; thermoformed finished plastic products

(P-9534)
FOAM MOLDERS AND SPECIALTIES
20004 State Rd, Cerritos (90703-6495)
PHONE..............................562 924-7757
EMP: 50
SALES (corp-wide): 16MM **Privately Held**
SIC: 3086 Plastics foam products
PA: Foam Molders And Specialties
11110 Business Cir
Cerritos CA 90703
562 924-7757

(P-9535)
FOAM PLASTICS & RBR PDTS CORP
Also Called: Case Club
4765 E Bryson St, Anaheim (92807-1901)
PHONE..............................714 779-0990
Kirk Plehn, *President*
Brent Plehn, *General Mgr*
Darren Plehn, *Sales Staff*
EMP: 15
SQ FT: 10,000
SALES (est): 2.8MM **Privately Held**
SIC: 3086 5099 Plastics foam products; cases, carrying

(P-9536)
FOAM-CRAFT INC
2441 Cypress Way, Fullerton (92831-5103)
PHONE..............................714 459-9971
Bruce Schneider, *President*
Michael Blatt, *Admin Sec*
▲ EMP: 165
SQ FT: 110,000
SALES (est): 27.8MM
SALES (corp-wide): 376.3MM **Privately Held**
SIC: 3086 Plastics foam products
PA: Future Foam, Inc.
1610 Avenue N
Council Bluffs IA 51501
712 323-9122

(P-9537)
FOAMATION INC
11852 Glenoaks Blvd, San Fernando (91340-1804)
PHONE..............................818 837-6613
Joshua Cobb, *President*
Ariana Cobb, *COO*
EMP: 10 EST: 1999
SALES (est): 1.2MM **Privately Held**
WEB: www.foamation.com
SIC: 3086 Plastics foam products

(P-9538)
FOAMEX LP
1400 E Victoria Ave, San Bernardino (92408-2924)
PHONE..............................909 824-8981
Ron Paez, *Manager*
EMP: 47
SALES (corp-wide): 385.3MM **Privately Held**
SIC: 3086 Carpet & rug cushions, foamed plastic

PA: Foamex L.P.
1400 N Providence Rd # 2000
Media PA 19063
610 565-2374

(P-9539)
FOAMORDERCOM INC
3455 Collins Ave, Richmond (94806-2000)
PHONE..............................415 503-1188
Michael Gorham, *President*
◆ EMP: 18
SQ FT: 8,900
SALES (est): 3.4MM **Privately Held**
WEB: www.foamorder.com
SIC: 3086 Insulation or cushioning material, foamed plastic

(P-9540)
FUTURE FOAM INC
2451 Cypress Way, Fullerton (92831-5103)
PHONE..............................714 871-2344
Randall Lake, *Manager*
EMP: 30
SALES (corp-wide): 376.3MM **Privately Held**
SIC: 3086 Insulation or cushioning material, foamed plastic
PA: Future Foam, Inc.
1610 Avenue N
Council Bluffs IA 51501
712 323-9122

(P-9541)
FUTURE FOAM INC
1000 E Grant Line Rd # 100, Tracy (95304-2836)
PHONE..............................209 832-1886
Michael Walsh, *Branch Mgr*
EMP: 42
SALES (corp-wide): 376.3MM **Privately Held**
SIC: 3086 Carpet & rug cushions, foamed plastic; ice chests or coolers (portable), foamed plastic; insulation or cushioning material, foamed plastic
PA: Future Foam, Inc.
1610 Avenue N
Council Bluffs IA 51501
712 323-9122

(P-9542)
FUTURE FOAM INC
2441 Cypress Way, Fullerton (92831-5103)
PHONE..............................714 459-9971
Pedro Cevallos, *Sales Mgr*
EMP: 165
SALES (corp-wide): 376.3MM **Privately Held**
SIC: 3086 Plastics foam products
PA: Future Foam, Inc.
1610 Avenue N
Council Bluffs IA 51501
712 323-9122

(P-9543)
FUTURE FOAM INC
Also Called: Formcraft
2441 Cypress Way, Fullerton (92831-5103)
PHONE..............................714 459-9971
Frank Deleon, *Branch Mgr*
Athena Nicolaou, *General Mgr*
EMP: 42
SALES (corp-wide): 376.3MM **Privately Held**
SIC: 3086 2515 Carpet & rug cushions, foamed plastic; mattresses, containing felt, foam rubber, urethane, etc.
PA: Future Foam, Inc.
1610 Avenue N
Council Bluffs IA 51501
712 323-9122

(P-9544)
FXI INC
Also Called: Foamex
2451 Polvorosa Ave, San Leandro (94577-2237)
P.O. Box 1735 (94577-0809)
PHONE..............................510 357-2600
Bud Silvey, *Manager*
EMP: 100 **Privately Held**
SIC: 3086 Packaging & shipping materials, foamed plastic

HQ: Fxi, Inc.
1400 N Providence Rd # 2000
Media PA 19063

(P-9545)
FXI INC
Also Called: Foamex
2060 N Batavia St, Orange (92865-3102)
PHONE..............................714 637-0110
Mark Stuart, *Branch Mgr*
EMP: 200 **Privately Held**
SIC: 3086 Padding, foamed plastic
HQ: Fxi, Inc.
1400 N Providence Rd # 2000
Media PA 19063

(P-9546)
GLORIANN FARMS INC
11104 W Tracy Blvd, Tracy (95304-9434)
PHONE..............................209 221-7121
Mark Bacchetti, *Branch Mgr*
EMP: 230
SALES (corp-wide): 33.1MM **Privately Held**
WEB: www.pbproduce.com
SIC: 3086 Plastics foam products
PA: Gloriann Farms, Inc.
4598 S Tracy Blvd Ste 160
Tracy CA 95377
209 834-0010

(P-9547)
GOLD VENTURE INC
Also Called: North American Foam & Packg
1050 S State College Blvd, Fullerton (92831-5335)
PHONE..............................909 623-1810
Fax: 909 865-6880
▲ EMP: 150
SQ FT: 95,000
SALES (est): 19.6MM
SALES (corp-wide): 459.1MM **Privately Held**
WEB: www.goldventure.com
SIC: 3086
PA: Future Foam, Inc.
1610 Avenue N
Council Bluffs IA 51501
712 323-9122

(P-9548)
GREEN RUBBER-KENNEDY AG LP (PA)
1310 Dayton St, Salinas (93901-4416)
P.O. Box 7488, Spreckels (93962-7488)
PHONE..............................831 753-6100
John H Green, *Partner*
John T Green, *Partner*
Patricia Green, *Partner*
Mark D Kennedy, *Partner*
Mark Kennedy, *Executive*
◆ EMP: 40
SQ FT: 13,500
SALES (est): 25.2MM **Privately Held**
WEB: www.greenrubber.com
SIC: 3086 3535 5083 5085 Plastics foam products; belt conveyor systems, general industrial use; agricultural machinery & equipment; industrial supplies

(P-9549)
HAPPY2EZ INC
14191 Beach Blvd Ste B, Westminster (92683-4863)
PHONE..............................714 897-6100
Katherine Vu, *CEO*
Thanh Vo, *Principal*
▲ EMP: 14
SALES (est): 1.6MM **Privately Held**
SIC: 3086 5999 Plastics foam products; foam & foam products

(P-9550)
HD CARRY INC
81 Columbia Ste 150, Aliso Viejo (92656-4113)
P.O. Box 218, Lake Forest (92609-0218)
PHONE..............................949 831-6022
Gary W Lantz, *President*
Carol Lantz, *Treasurer*
EMP: 15
SQ FT: 6,000

SALES (est): 2.2MM **Privately Held**
WEB: www.hdcarry.com
SIC: 3086 Packaging & shipping materials, foamed plastic

(P-9551)
HUHTAMAKI INC
4209 Noakes St, Commerce (90023-4024)
PHONE..............................323 269-0151
Mark Pettigrew, *Branch Mgr*
EMP: 450
SALES (corp-wide): 3.5B **Privately Held**
SIC: 3086 3089 2657 2656 Cups & plates, foamed plastic; plastic containers, except foam; folding paperboard boxes; sanitary food containers; disposable plates, cups, napkins & eating utensils; paperboard mills
HQ: Huhtamaki, Inc.
9201 Packaging Dr
De Soto KS 66018
913 583-3025

(P-9552)
INTER PACKING INC
Also Called: Flexy Foam
12315 Colony Ave, Chino (91710-2092)
PHONE..............................909 465-5555
Alfonso Cardenas, *President*
EMP: 20
SQ FT: 10,000
SALES (est): 2.4MM **Privately Held**
WEB: www.flexyfoam.com
SIC: 3086 2653 Padding, foamed plastic; corrugated boxes, partitions, display items, sheets & pad

(P-9553)
K & B FOAM INC
9335 Airway Rd Ste 100, San Diego (92154-7930)
PHONE..............................619 661-1870
Kenji Kasahara, *Ch of Bd*
Yo Kojima, *President*
Masahiro Ieyoshi, *Exec VP*
▲ EMP: 150
SALES (est): 16.7MM **Privately Held**
WEB: www.kbfoam.com
SIC: 3086 Packaging & shipping materials, foamed plastic

(P-9554)
KIVA CONTAINER CORPORATION
Also Called: CP Products
2700 E Regal Park Dr, Anaheim (92806-2417)
PHONE..............................714 630-3850
Claudia England, *CEO*
Norman England, *Treasurer*
Ken England, *Vice Pres*
Tina England, *Admin Sec*
EMP: 12
SQ FT: 14,800
SALES (est): 2.7MM **Privately Held**
WEB: www.cpproducts.net
SIC: 3086 Packaging & shipping materials, foamed plastic

(P-9555)
MARKO FOAM PRODUCTS INC (PA)
2500 White Rd Ste A, Irvine (92614-6276)
PHONE..............................800 862-7561
Donald J Peterson, *Ch of Bd*
Tyson Peterson, *President*
Parker Wayne, *Technician*
Ilir Bordoniqi, *Engineer*
▲ EMP: 30 EST: 1962
SQ FT: 114,000
SALES (est): 16.4MM **Privately Held**
WEB: www.markofoam.com
SIC: 3086 5999 Packaging & shipping materials, foamed plastic; packaging materials: boxes, padding, etc.

(P-9556)
MONSTER CITY STUDIOS
411 S West Ave, Fresno (93706-1320)
PHONE..............................559 498-0540
Dennis Keiser, *Ch of Bd*
Kathy Keiser, *Corp Secy*
Randal Keiser, *Vice Ch Bd*
Andy Anderson, *Art Dir*
Gyl Keiser, *Director*
EMP: 11

SALES (est): 1.4MM **Privately Held**
SIC: 3086 Plastics foam products

(P-9557)
MULTI-LINK INTERNATIONAL CORP
12235 Los Nietos Rd, Santa Fe Springs (90670-2909)
PHONE..................................562 941-5380
SAI Hung Chan, *President*
▼ EMP: 20
SQ FT: 45,000
SALES (est): 3.5MM **Privately Held**
WEB: www.multilinkintl.com
SIC: 3086 Plastics foam products

(P-9558)
NEW IMAGE FOAM PRODUCTS LLC
6835 Power Inn Rd, Sacramento (95828-2401)
P.O. Box 245509 (95824-5509)
PHONE..................................916 388-0741
Dave McDonald,
Wendy King, *Office Mgr*
Christian Kambel, *Sales Staff*
Arnold C Morairty,
EMP: 23
SQ FT: 47,000
SALES (est): 2.8MM **Privately Held**
SIC: 3086 Insulation or cushioning material, foamed plastic

(P-9559)
OCEAN BLUE INC
Also Called: Teamwork Packaging
494 Commercial Rd, San Bernardino (92408-3706)
PHONE..................................909 478-9910
Mehdi Abbas, *President*
▲ EMP: 20
SALES (est): 6.1MM **Privately Held**
SIC: 3086 Packaging & shipping materials, foamed plastic

(P-9560)
PEDNAR PRODUCTS INC (PA)
1823 Enterprise Way, Monrovia (91016-4272)
PHONE..................................626 960-9883
Art Narevsky, *President*
William Hill, *Vice Pres*
Sue Narevsky, *Admin Sec*
Mike Laban, *Project Mgr*
Ryan Sweeney, *Products*
◆ EMP: 10
SQ FT: 5,389
SALES (est): 1.3MM **Privately Held**
WEB: www.pednar.net
SIC: 3086 Plastics foam products

(P-9561)
PMC GLOBAL INC (PA)
12243 Branford St, Sun Valley (91352-1010)
PHONE..................................818 896-1101
Philip E Kamins, *CEO*
Gary E Kamins, *President*
Thian C Cheong, *CFO*
Janette Whitt, *CFO*
Steven G Cohen, *Vice Pres*
◆ EMP: 3800
SALES (est): 2.5B **Privately Held**
WEB: www.pmcglobalinc.com
SIC: 3086 3674 2865 2816 Plastics foam products; semiconductors & related devices; food dyes or colors, synthetic; color pigments; fiberglass insulation; industrial inorganic chemicals

(P-9562)
POMONA QUALITY FOAM LLC
1279 Philadelphia St, Pomona (91766-5536)
PHONE..................................909 628-7844
Michael Clark,
Theodore Clark,
EMP: 67
SQ FT: 70,000
SALES (est): 3MM **Privately Held**
SIC: 3086 Plastics foam products

(P-9563)
PREGIS
159 N San Antonio Ave, Pomona (91767-5635)
PHONE..................................909 469-8100
Don Crites, *Manager*
▲ EMP: 23
SALES (est): 4.2MM
SALES (corp-wide): 3B **Privately Held**
SIC: 3086 Packaging & shipping materials, foamed plastic
PA: Aea Investors Lp
666 5th Ave Fl 36
New York NY 10103
212 644-5900

(P-9564)
QUALITY FOAM PACKAGING INC
31855 Corydon St, Lake Elsinore (92530-8501)
PHONE..................................951 245-4429
Noel A Castellon, *President*
Ruth Castellon, *Corp Secy*
James Barrett, *Vice Pres*
Noel Castellon Jr, *Plant Mgr*
▲ EMP: 25
SQ FT: 56,000
SALES: 9.7MM **Privately Held**
WEB: www.qualitycase.com
SIC: 3086 Packaging & shipping materials, foamed plastic

(P-9565)
QYCELL CORPORATION
600 Etiwanda Ave, Ontario (91761-8635)
PHONE..................................909 390-6644
Grant Kesler, *CEO*
▲ EMP: 25
SQ FT: 45,000
SALES: 14MM **Privately Held**
SIC: 3086 Plastics foam products

(P-9566)
RINCO INTERNATIONAL INC
31056 Genstar Rd, Hayward (94544-7830)
PHONE..................................510 785-1633
Rollin Yi, *President*
▲ EMP: 14 EST: 2006
SALES (est): 3.2MM **Privately Held**
SIC: 3086 Packaging & shipping materials, foamed plastic

(P-9567)
SABRED INTERNATIONAL PACKG INC
3740 Prospect Ave, Yorba Linda (92886-1742)
P.O. Box 566 (92885-0566)
PHONE..................................714 996-2800
Sabrina Sierra, *President*
Edward A Sierra, *Vice Pres*
EMP: 22
SQ FT: 15,000
SALES (est): 3MM **Privately Held**
WEB: www.sabred.com
SIC: 3086 5199 5113 5087 Plastics foam products; packaging materials; corrugated & solid fiber boxes; janitors' supplies

(P-9568)
SEALED AIR CORPORATION
Packaging Products Div
19440 Arenth Ave, City of Industry (91748-1424)
PHONE..................................909 594-1791
Jamie Hall, *Human Resources*
EMP: 75
SALES (corp-wide): 4.7B **Publicly Held**
WEB: www.sealedair.com
SIC: 3086 Packaging & shipping materials, foamed plastic
PA: Sealed Air Corporation
2415 Cascade Pointe Blvd
Charlotte NC 28208
980 221-3235

(P-9569)
SPECIALTY ENTERPRISES CO
Also Called: Seco Industries
6858 E Acco St, Commerce (90040-1902)
PHONE..................................323 726-9721
Charles De Heras, *President*
▲ EMP: 100
SQ FT: 60,000

SALES (est): 20.4MM **Privately Held**
WEB: www.seco-ind.com
SIC: 3086 3565 Plastics foam products; packaging machinery

(P-9570)
STYROTEK INC
345 Road 176, Delano (93215-9471)
P.O. Box 1180 (93216-1180)
PHONE..................................661 725-4957
Martin Caratan, *President*
Dale Arthur, *Corp Secy*
Sanford L Campbell, *Opers Mgr*
Luis Gonzalez, *Manager*
▲ EMP: 110
SQ FT: 18,500
SALES (est): 26.6MM **Privately Held**
WEB: www.styrotek.com
SIC: 3086 Packaging & shipping materials, foamed plastic

(P-9571)
TEMPLOCK ENTERPRISES LLC
1 N Calle Cesar Chavez # 170, Santa Barbara (93103-5621)
PHONE..................................805 962-3100
Brian Scarminach,
▲ EMP: 12
SQ FT: 5,000
SALES (est): 1.5MM **Privately Held**
WEB: www.templock.com
SIC: 3086 Packaging & shipping materials, foamed plastic

(P-9572)
TEMPO PLASTIC CO
1227 N Miller Park Ct, Visalia (93291-9343)
P.O. Box 44, Morro Bay (93443-0044)
PHONE..................................559 651-7711
Douglas B Rogers, *President*
Doug Rogers, *Sales Staff*
▲ EMP: 15
SQ FT: 26,000
SALES: 1.1MM **Privately Held**
WEB: www.tempo-foam.com
SIC: 3086 Packaging & shipping materials, foamed plastic; cups & plates, foamed plastic; ice chests or coolers (portable), foamed plastic

(P-9573)
TOPPER PLASTICS INC
Also Called: Tpi
461 E Front St, Covina (91723-1299)
PHONE..................................626 331-0561
Patricia Beery, *CEO*
Lewis Beery, *CFO*
Susan Beery, *Admin Sec*
EMP: 15
SQ FT: 20,000
SALES (est): 2.2MM **Privately Held**
SIC: 3086 Packaging & shipping materials, foamed plastic

(P-9574)
UFP TECHNOLOGIES INC
20211 S Susana Rd, Compton (90221-5725)
PHONE..................................714 662-0277
Richard Tunila, *Branch Mgr*
Laura Huhn, *Purch Mgr*
Shannon McClure, *Manager*
EMP: 50
SALES (corp-wide): 190.4MM **Publicly Held**
SIC: 3086 Packaging & shipping materials, foamed plastic
PA: Ufp Technologies, Inc.
100 Hale St
Newburyport MA 01950
978 352-2200

(P-9575)
URETHANE MASTERS INC
455 54th St Ste 102, San Diego (92114-2220)
PHONE..................................651 829-1032
Gayle McEnroe, *Mng Member*
EMP: 15
SALES (est): 553.8K **Privately Held**
SIC: 3086 Plastics foam products

(P-9576)
VEFO INC
3202 Factory Dr, Pomona (91768-3903)
PHONE..................................909 598-3856
Roger Voss, *President*
Pat Voss, *Admin Sec*
Elizabeth Hernandez, *Products*
EMP: 20
SQ FT: 11,000
SALES (est): 4.1MM **Privately Held**
WEB: www.vefo-foamshapes.com
SIC: 3086 Plastics foam products

(P-9577)
WALTER N COFFMAN INC
5180 Naranja St, San Diego (92114-3515)
PHONE..................................619 266-2642
Walter N Coffman, *CEO*
EMP: 70
SALES (est): 10.4MM **Privately Held**
SIC: 3086 Cups & plates, foamed plastic

(P-9578)
WARDLEY INDUSTRIAL INC
907 Stokes Ave, Stockton (95215-4027)
P.O. Box 55323 (95205-8823)
PHONE..................................209 932-1088
Jackey Wong, *President*
Ambrose Tam, *Treasurer*
Margaret Wong, *Admin Sec*
▲ EMP: 43
SQ FT: 165,000
SALES (est): 9.4MM **Privately Held**
WEB: www.wardleyfilm.com
SIC: 3086 5084 Packaging & shipping materials, foamed plastic; industrial machinery & equipment

3087 Custom Compounding Of Purchased Plastic Resins

(P-9579)
AUBIN INDUSTRIES INC
23833 S Chrisman Rd, Tracy (95304-8003)
PHONE..................................800 324-0051
Philip Aubin, *President*
Linda Aubin, *Corp Secy*
EMP: 15
SQ FT: 13,000
SALES: 1.3MM **Privately Held**
WEB: www.aubinindustries.com
SIC: 3087 Custom compound purchased resins

3088 Plastic Plumbing Fixtures

(P-9580)
AQUATIC CO
Lasco Bathware
8101 E Kaiser Blvd # 200, Anaheim (92808-2287)
PHONE..................................714 993-1220
Scott Hartman, *Manager*
Mike Seymour, *President*
Paul Van Slyke, *Finance*
Dante San Miguel, *Manager*
EMP: 110
SQ FT: 5,000
SALES (corp-wide): 443.5MM **Privately Held**
SIC: 3088 1711 5211 Shower stalls, fiberglass & plastic; plumbing, heating, air-conditioning contractors; bathroom fixtures, equipment & supplies
HQ: Aquatic Co.
1700 N Delilah St
Corona CA 92879
-

(P-9581)
AQUATIC CO (HQ)
1700 N Delilah St, Corona (92879-1893)
PHONE..................................714 993-1220
Gary Anderson, *CEO*
Craig Nyenhuis, *Plant Mgr*
▲ EMP: 72

SALES (est): 309.6MM
SALES (corp-wide): 443.5MM Privately Held
SIC: **3088** Shower stalls, fiberglass & plastic
PA: The American Bath Group
435 Industrial Rd
Savannah TN 38372
731 925-7656

(P-9582)
AQUATIC INDUSTRIES INC
8101 E Kaiser Blvd # 200, Anaheim (92808-2287)
PHONE......................800 877-2005
Anthony Reading, *CEO*
Margaret Voskamp, *Vice Pres*
Oscar Martinez, *Administration*
EMP: 160
SQ FT: 78,004
SALES (est): 23.9MM Privately Held
SIC: **3088 5999 3949** Plastics plumbing fixtures; hot tub & spa chemicals, equipment & supplies; sporting & athletic goods

(P-9583)
CREATIVE SHOWER DOOR CORP
43652 S Grimmer Blvd, Fremont (94538-6381)
PHONE......................510 623-9000
John Patrick Olmstead, *Owner*
EMP: 11
SALES (est): 1.8MM Privately Held
SIC: **3088** Shower stalls, fiberglass & plastic

(P-9584)
ELMCO & ASSOC (PA)
11225 Trade Center Dr # 100, Rancho Cordova (95742-6267)
PHONE......................916 383-0110
Kirk Kleiner, *Vice Pres*
Bruce Jenkins, *General Mgr*
David Moore, *General Mgr*
Tanya Brady, *Manager*
Richard Martinez, *Accounts Mgr*
EMP: 11
SALES (est): 1.7MM Privately Held
SIC: **3088** Plastics plumbing fixtures

(P-9585)
EUROTECH SHOWERS INC
23552 Commerce Center Dr A, Laguna Hills (92653-1514)
PHONE......................949 716-4099
James Simmons, *President*
EMP: 25
SQ FT: 2,800
SALES (est): 632.6K Privately Held
SIC: **3088** Shower stalls, fiberglass & plastic

(P-9586)
FIBER CARE BATHS INC
9832 Yucca Rd Ste A, Adelanto (92301-2471)
PHONE......................760 246-0019
Harry R Kilpatrick, *CEO*
Kaye Allen, *Controller*
EMP: 275
SQ FT: 6,000
SALES (est): 46.9MM Privately Held
WEB: www.fibercarebaths.com
SIC: **3088** Shower stalls, fiberglass & plastic; tubs (bath, shower & laundry), plastic

(P-9587)
FLORESTONE PRODUCTS CO (PA)
2851 Falcon Dr, Madera (93637-9287)
PHONE......................559 661-4171
Ronald R Flores, *CEO*
Carol Deaver, *Treasurer*
Marcos Robles, *Purch Mgr*
Doug Brown, *Natl Sales Mgr*
▲ EMP: 47
SQ FT: 190,000
SALES (est): 7.7MM Privately Held
WEB: www.florestone.com
SIC: **3088** Shower stalls, fiberglass & plastic; tubs (bath, shower & laundry), plastic

(P-9588)
JACUZZI INC
13925 City Center Dr # 200, Chino Hills (91709-5438)
PHONE......................909 606-1416
Thomas Koos, *President*
Joshua Ebersole, *Finance*
Disa Kenney-Haynes, *Marketing Mgr*
EMP: 23
SALES (est): 3.5MM Privately Held
SIC: **3088** Tubs (bath, shower & laundry), plastic

(P-9589)
JACUZZI PRODUCTS CO (DH)
13925 City Center Dr # 200, Chino Hills (91709-5438)
PHONE......................909 606-1416
Thomas D Koos, *CEO*
Philip Weeks, *President*
▲ EMP: 120
SALES (est): 103.4MM Privately Held
WEB: www.jacuzzico.net
SIC: **3088** Tubs (bath, shower & laundry), plastic; hot tubs, plastic or fiberglass
HQ: Jacuzzi Inc.
14525 Monte Vista Ave
Chino CA 91710
909 606-7733

(P-9590)
JACUZZI PRODUCTS CO
14525 Monte Vista Ave, Chino (91710-5721)
PHONE......................909 548-7732
Jim Barry, *Manager*
EMP: 500 **Privately Held**
WEB: www.jacuzzico.net
SIC: **3088 5091** Tubs (bath, shower & laundry), plastic; fitness equipment & supplies
HQ: Jacuzzi Products Co.
13925 City Center Dr # 200
Chino Hills CA 91709
909 606-1416

(P-9591)
LE ELEGANT BATH INC
Also Called: American Bath Factory
13405 Estelle St, Corona (92879-1877)
PHONE......................951 734-0238
Richard Wheeler, *President*
Debbie Wheeler, *Admin Sec*
◆ EMP: 120
SQ FT: 18,000
SALES (est): 23.1MM Privately Held
WEB: www.americanbathfactory.com
SIC: **3088** Tubs (bath, shower & laundry), plastic

(P-9592)
MITRANI USA CORP
7451 Westcliff Dr, West Hills (91307-5210)
PHONE......................818 888-9994
▲ EMP: 10
SALES (est): 1.1MM Privately Held
WEB: www.mitrani-usa.com
SIC: **3088**

(P-9593)
OUTSOL INC
Also Called: Rinsekit
5910 Sea Lion Pl Ste 120, Carlsbad (92010-6656)
PHONE......................760 415-8060
Chris Crawford, *President*
EMP: 12
SALES (est): 484.2K Privately Held
SIC: **3088** Plastics plumbing fixtures

(P-9594)
PAINTED RHINO INC
14310 Veterans Way, Moreno Valley (92553-9058)
PHONE......................951 656-5524
Ryan Franklin, *President*
▲ EMP: 35 EST: 2007
SQ FT: 25,000
SALES (est): 5.7MM Privately Held
SIC: **3088** Shower stalls, fiberglass & plastic

(P-9595)
PEGGY S LANE INC
Also Called: C M P
2701 Merced St, San Leandro (94577-5601)
PHONE......................510 483-1202
Matt Clementz, *President*
EMP: 100 EST: 1979
SQ FT: 35,000
SALES (est): 21.7MM Privately Held
SIC: **3088 3281 1752 1743** Tubs (bath, shower & laundry), plastic; bathroom fixtures, plastic; cut stone & stone products; floor laying & floor work; terrazzo, tile, marble, mosaic work

(P-9596)
SMITHS ACTION PLASTIC INC (PA)
Also Called: Action Plastics
645 S Santa Fe St, Santa Ana (92705-4143)
PHONE......................714 836-4141
James A Smith, *President*
EMP: 15
SQ FT: 5,000
SALES (est): 9MM Privately Held
SIC: **3088 5063 3089** Plastics plumbing fixtures; electrical fittings & construction materials; plastic processing

(P-9597)
VORTEX WHIRLPOOL SYSTEMS INC
Also Called: Catalina Spas
26035 Jefferson Ave, Murrieta (92562-6983)
PHONE......................951 940-4556
Boyd Cargill, *President*
▲ EMP: 60
SQ FT: 100,000
SALES (est): 14.6MM Privately Held
WEB: www.catalinaspas.com
SIC: **3088** Hot tubs, plastic or fiberglass

(P-9598)
WATKINS MANUFACTURING CORP
1325 Hot Springs Way, Vista (92081-8360)
PHONE......................760 598-6464
EMP: 11
SALES (corp-wide): 8.3B Publicly Held
SIC: **3088** Hot tubs, plastic or fiberglass
HQ: Watkins Manufacturing Corporation
1280 Park Center Dr
Vista CA 92081
760 598-6464

3089 Plastic Prdts

(P-9599)
A & S MOLD & DIE CORP
9705 Eton Ave, Chatsworth (91311-4306)
PHONE......................818 341-5393
Arno Adlhoch, *CEO*
Karen Adlhoch, *Corp Secy*
▲ EMP: 90
SQ FT: 35,000
SALES: 8MM Privately Held
WEB: www.aandsmold.com
SIC: **3089 3544** Injection molding of plastics; special dies, tools, jigs & fixtures

(P-9600)
A&A GLOBAL IMPORTS INC
3359 E 50th St, Vernon (90058-3003)
PHONE......................323 767-5990
David Aryan, *President*
Brian Anav, *COO*
James Bunting, *CFO*
Adam Wolf, *Vice Pres*
Maribel Mora, *Assistant*
▲ EMP: 26
SALES: 27.1MM Privately Held
SIC: **3089** Injection molded finished plastic products

(P-9601)
ACCENT PLASTICS INC (PA)
1925 Elise Cir, Corona (92879-1882)
PHONE......................951 273-7777
Thomas A Pridonoff, *CEO*
Bonnie Pridonoff, *Admin Sec*

Josue Cordon, *Administration*
Denise Parks, *Director*
Paul Stephens, *Manager*
◆ EMP: 78
SQ FT: 56,000
SALES (est): 16.6MM Privately Held
WEB: www.accentplastics.com
SIC: **3089** Injection molding of plastics

(P-9602)
ACCENT PLASTICS INC
1915 Elise Cir, Corona (92879-1882)
PHONE......................951 273-7777
EMP: 20
SALES (corp-wide): 16.6MM Privately Held
SIC: **3089** Injection molding of plastics
PA: Accent Plastics, Inc.
1925 Elise Cir
Corona CA 92879
951 273-7777

(P-9603)
ACCO BRANDS USA LLC
14430 Best Ave, Garden Grove (92841)
PHONE......................562 941-0505
Dennis L Chandler,
EMP: 35
SALES (corp-wide): 1.9B Publicly Held
WEB: www.gbc.com
SIC: **3089 2761 3496 2675** Injection molding of plastics; manifold business forms; clips & fasteners, made from purchased wire; folders, filing, die-cut: made from purchased materials
HQ: Acco Brands Usa Llc
4 Corporate Dr
Lake Zurich IL 60047
800 222-6462

(P-9604)
ACE COMPOSITES INC
1394 Sky Harbor Dr, Olivehurst (95961-7416)
P.O. Box 59 (95961-0059)
PHONE......................530 743-1885
Todd Hambrook, *President*
Noe Lopez, *Vice Pres*
John Pimentel, *Vice Pres*
Mark Phelps, *Admin Sec*
EMP: 55
SQ FT: 40,000
SALES (est): 8.5MM Privately Held
WEB: www.acecomposites.com
SIC: **3089** Plastic & fiberglass tanks

(P-9605)
ACE PRECISION MOLD CO INC
14701 Carmenita Rd, Norwalk (90650-5230)
PHONE......................562 921-8999
Mark S Hyon, *CEO*
EMP: 10
SQ FT: 2,100
SALES (est): 920K Privately Held
SIC: **3089 7699** Injection molding of plastics; industrial tool grinding

(P-9606)
ACORN PLASTICS INC (HQ)
13818 Oaks Ave, Chino (91710-7008)
PHONE......................909 591-8461
Donald Morris, *Ch of Bd*
Kristin E Kahle, *Corp Secy*
William D Morris, *Vice Pres*
EMP: 71
SQ FT: 94,000
SALES (est): 12.2MM
SALES (corp-wide): 85MM Privately Held
WEB: www.whitehallmfg.com
SIC: **3089** Injection molding of plastics
PA: Acorn Engineering Company
15125 Proctor Ave
City Of Industry CA 91746
800 488-8999

(P-9607)
ACORN-GENCON PLASTICS LLC
13818 Oaks Ave, Chino (91710-7008)
PHONE......................909 591-8461
Donald E Morris, *Mng Member*
Jacqueline Morovati, *General Mgr*
Gabby Soria, *Office Mgr*
Pamela Carlton, *Manager*

▲ = Import ▼=Export
◆ =Import/Export

Juan Madrigal, *Supervisor*
▲ **EMP:** 68 **EST:** 2001
SQ FT: 94,000
SALES (est): 12.2MM
SALES (corp-wide): 85MM **Privately Held**
WEB: www.acorn-gencon.com
SIC: 3089 3088 3821 3082 Injection molded finished plastic products; plastics plumbing fixtures; laboratory apparatus & furniture; unsupported plastics profile shapes
HQ: Acorn Plastics, Inc
13818 Oaks Ave
Chino CA 91710
909 591-8461

(P-9608)
ACRYLIC DESIGNS INC
1221 N Barsten Way, Anaheim (92806-1822)
PHONE....................714 630-1370
Mitchell Dedic, *President*
Vickie Dedic, *Vice Pres*
EMP: 10
SQ FT: 8,000
SALES (est): 1.5MM **Privately Held**
WEB: www.acrylicdesigns.com
SIC: 3089 7336 Molding primary plastic; commercial art & graphic design

(P-9609)
ACTION ENTERPRISES INC
Also Called: Actionmold
1911 S Betmor Ln, Anaheim (92805-6703)
PHONE....................714 978-0333
Bill Hall, *CEO*
Steve Burd, *CFO*
EMP: 12
SALES (est): 1.4MM **Privately Held**
SIC: 3089 Injection molding of plastics

(P-9610)
ACTION INNOVATIONS INC
Also Called: Action Mold and Tool Co
1911 S Betmor Ln, Anaheim (92805-6703)
PHONE....................714 978-0333
Bill Hall, *CEO*
Stephen Burd, *President*
EMP: 30
SQ FT: 15,000
SALES (est): 4.8MM **Privately Held**
WEB: www.actionmold.com
SIC: 3089 Injection molding of plastics

(P-9611)
ADVANCED CMPSITE PDTS TECH INC
Also Called: Acpt
15602 Chemical Ln, Huntington Beach (92649-1507)
PHONE....................714 895-5544
James C Leslie II, *President*
Alec Ghasemi, *Program Mgr*
Theada Burgess, *Controller*
Larry Clem, *Mfg Staff*
Clampitt Ryan, *Mktg Dir*
EMP: 45
SQ FT: 25,300
SALES (est): 9.9MM **Privately Held**
WEB: www.acpt.com
SIC: 3089 8748 Hardware, plastic; business consulting

(P-9612)
ADVANCED COMPOSITES ENGRG LLC
Also Called: Advanced Composites Engrg
42245 Sarah Way, Temecula (92590-3463)
PHONE....................951 694-3055
Joe Albertellie,
Meredith Albertellie,
EMP: 10
SQ FT: 8,000
SALES (est): 1MM **Privately Held**
WEB: www.advancedcompositeseng.com
SIC: 3089 2221 Reinforcing mesh, plastic; flat panels, plastic; hardware, plastic; fiberglass fabrics

(P-9613)
ADVANCED THRMLFORMING ENTP INC
Also Called: A T E
3750 Oceanic Way, Oceanside (92056-2650)
PHONE....................760 722-4400
Hai Parson, *President*
Anh Doan, *Shareholder*
David Cox, *Vice Pres*
EMP: 13
SALES (est): 1.8MM **Privately Held**
SIC: 3089 Thermoformed finished plastic products

(P-9614)
AIR LOGISTICS CORPORATION (PA)
Also Called: Field Applied Cmposite Systems
146 Railroad Ave, Monrovia (91016-4642)
PHONE....................626 633-0294
George H Schirtzinger, *CEO*
David Buckley, *Vice Pres*
Franz Worth, *Program Mgr*
George Schirtzinger, *CIO*
Scott Dorgan, *Accounting Mgr*
◆ **EMP:** 20
SALES (est): 4.5MM **Privately Held**
WEB: www.airlog.com
SIC: 3089 3728 Reinforcing mesh, plastic; aircraft parts & equipment

(P-9615)
AJAX - UNTD PTTRNS & MOLDS INC
Also Called: Ajax Custom Manufacturing
34585 7th St, Union City (94587-3673)
PHONE....................510 476-8000
Dana Waldman, *CEO*
Mark REA, *Engineer*
Diana Alvarez, *Human Res Dir*
Ramnik Nijjar, *Production*
Neal Laybhen, *Director*
EMP: 140
SQ FT: 85,000
SALES (est): 1.3MM
SALES (corp-wide): 823.6MM **Publicly Held**
WEB: www.ajaxmfg.com
SIC: 3089 3599 3543 Plastic processing; machine shop, jobbing & repair; foundry patternmaking
PA: Ichor Holdings, Ltd.
3185 Laurelview Ct
Fremont CA 94538
510 897-5200

(P-9616)
AKRA PLASTIC PRODUCTS INC
1504 E Cedar St, Ontario (91761-5761)
PHONE....................909 930-1999
R Wayne Callaway, *President*
Bentley Callaway, *Vice Pres*
Alex Semeczko, *Vice Pres*
EMP: 37
SQ FT: 36,000
SALES (est): 6.6MM **Privately Held**
WEB: www.akraplastics.com
SIC: 3089 Injection molding of plastics; plastic processing

(P-9617)
ALLEN MOLD INC
1100 W Katella Ave Ste N, Orange (92867-3515)
PHONE....................714 538-6517
Clayton Allen, *President*
EMP: 18
SQ FT: 5,800
SALES (est): 3.3MM **Privately Held**
WEB: www.allenmold.com
SIC: 3089 Injection molding of plastics

(P-9618)
ALLTEC INTEGRATED MFG INC
Also Called: New Age Enclosures
2240 S Thornburg St, Santa Maria (93455-1248)
PHONE....................805 595-3500
Randall Dennis, *CEO*
Justin Tomlinson, *Program Mgr*
Don Circosta, *Opers Staff*
Stan Ryland, *Sales Mgr*
▲ **EMP:** 40
SQ FT: 13,500

SALES (est): 9.4MM **Privately Held**
WEB: www.alltecmfg.com
SIC: 3089 2821 Injection molding of plastics; plastics materials & resins

(P-9619)
ALPHENA TECHNOLOGIES
414 Cloverleaf Dr Ste B, Baldwin Park (91706-6507)
PHONE....................626 961-6098
Shirley Chung, *President*
Doug Vanlent, *Director*
▲ **EMP:** 10
SALES (est): 1.3MM **Privately Held**
SIC: 3089 Plastics products

(P-9620)
AMA PLASTICS (PA)
1100 Citrus St, Riverside (92507-1731)
PHONE....................951 734-5600
Mark Atchinson, *CEO*
Patricia Christie, *Business Anlyst*
Taylor Atchison, *Engineer*
Ed Buehler, *Engineer*
Jeff Fontaine, *Engineer*
◆ **EMP:** 393
SQ FT: 92,000
SALES (est): 149.5MM **Privately Held**
WEB: www.amaplastics.com
SIC: 3089 3544 Molding primary plastic; forms (molds), for foundry & plastics working machinery

(P-9621)
AMCOR RIGID PACKAGING USA LLC
14270 Ramona Ave, Chino (91710-5738)
PHONE....................520 746-0737
Dan Meyer, *Branch Mgr*
EMP: 16 **Privately Held**
WEB: www.slpcamericas.com
SIC: 3089 Plastic containers, except foam
HQ: Amcor Rigid Packaging Usa, Llc
40600 Ann Arbor Rd E # 201
Plymouth MI 48170

(P-9622)
AMERICAN APPAREL ACC INC (PA)
10160 Olney St, El Monte (91731-2312)
PHONE....................626 350-3828
Lily Chang, *President*
Steve Bernstein, *Vice Pres*
▲ **EMP:** 21
SQ FT: 5,000
SALES (est): 2MM **Privately Held**
WEB: www.aaahangers.com
SIC: 3089 Injection molding of plastics

(P-9623)
AMERICAN DESIGN INC
1672 Industrial Blvd, Chula Vista (91911-3922)
PHONE....................619 429-1995
Bruce R Jamieson, *President*
Cathy Jamieson, *CFO*
Catherine Jamieson, *Corp Secy*
EMP: 16
SQ FT: 20,000
SALES (est): 2.8MM **Privately Held**
SIC: 3089 Plastic processing

(P-9624)
AMERICAN GARAGE DECOR INC
10883 Thornmint Rd, San Diego (92127-2403)
PHONE....................760 975-9148
David Hill, *CEO*
EMP: 10
SQ FT: 5,000
SALES: 4MM **Privately Held**
SIC: 3089 Injection molded finished plastic products

(P-9625)
AMERICAN INNOTEK INC (PA)
Also Called: Brief Relief
2655 Vsta Pcf Drv Ocnside Oceanside, Oceanside (92056)
PHONE....................760 741-6600
Clarence A Cassidy, *Ch of Bd*
Niki Kopenhaver, *President*
Terry H Cassidy, *Vice Pres*

Pattison Keith, *Controller*
Barbara Smith, *Controller*
◆ **EMP:** 57
SQ FT: 54,000
SALES (est): 10.3MM **Privately Held**
WEB: www.restop.com
SIC: 3089 3431 3088 Plastic containers, except foam; metal sanitary ware; plastics plumbing fixtures

(P-9626)
AMERICAN PLASTIC CARD CO
21550 Oxnard St Ste 300, Woodland Hills (91367-7109)
PHONE....................818 784-4224
Jim Akbar, *President*
James Alexander, *Vice Pres*
Peggy Peterson, *Vice Pres*
Peggy Pedersen, *VP Mktg*
EMP: 120
SQ FT: 50,000
SALES (est): 14.3MM **Privately Held**
WEB: www.apcci.com
SIC: 3089 2759 Identification cards, plastic; commercial printing

(P-9627)
AMERICAN TECHNICAL MOLDING INC
2052 W 11th St, Upland (91786-3509)
PHONE....................909 982-1025
▲ **EMP:** 120
SQ FT: 50,000
SALES (est): 21.8MM
SALES (corp-wide): 368.7MM **Privately Held**
WEB: www.deepdraw.com
SIC: 3089 Injection molding of plastics
HQ: Bandera Acquisition, Llc
2 Hampshire St
Foxborough MA 02035
480 553-6400

(P-9628)
AMERIMADE TECHNOLOGY INC
449 Mountain Vista Pkwy, Livermore (94551-8212)
PHONE....................925 243-9090
Todd Thomas, *President*
James Olivas, *Engineer*
Stephanie Castro, *Purch Mgr*
EMP: 50
SQ FT: 65,000
SALES (est): 9.7MM **Privately Held**
WEB: www.amerimade.com
SIC: 3089 3674 Injection molding of plastics; semiconductors & related devices

(P-9629)
AMFLEX PLASTICS INCORPORATED
4039 Calle Platino Ste G, Oceanside (92056-5827)
PHONE....................760 643-1756
Raul A Castro, *President*
Ana Maria Castro, *CFO*
EMP: 14
SQ FT: 18,000
SALES (est): 3.5MM **Privately Held**
WEB: www.amflex.com
SIC: 3089 Injection molded finished plastic products

(P-9630)
ANAHEIM CUSTOM EXTRUDERS INC
Also Called: Ace
4640 E La Palma Ave, Anaheim (92807-1910)
PHONE....................714 693-8508
William A Czapar, *Ch of Bd*
Chrintina Smith, *Exec VP*
EMP: 48
SQ FT: 26,000
SALES (est): 9.2MM **Privately Held**
WEB: www.acextrusions.com
SIC: 3089 3082 Extruded finished plastic products; unsupported plastics profile shapes

(P-9631)
ANDERSON MOULDS INCORPORATED
3131 E Anita St, Stockton (95205-3904)
PHONE....................209 943-1145

Garry W Anderson, *President*
Victoria Anderson, *Corp Secy*
▲ EMP: 15 EST: 1975
SQ FT: 48,000
SALES (est): 2.4MM **Privately Held**
WEB: www.andersonmoulds.com
SIC: 3089 Injection molding of plastics

(P-9632)
ANNMAR INDUSTRIES INC
990 S Jay Cir, Anaheim (92808-2105)
PHONE..................................714 630-5443
Mark Thornberg, *President*
Julie Thornberg, *Corp Secy*
EMP: 10
SQ FT: 9,160
SALES (est): 1.4MM **Privately Held**
WEB: www.annmarindustries.com
SIC: 3089 3471 3088 Plastic hardware &
building products; plating & polishing;
plastics plumbing fixtures

(P-9633)
ANURA PLASTIC ENGINEERIGN
5050 Rivergrade Rd, Baldwin Park
(91706-1405)
PHONE..................................626 814-9684
Wolfgang Buehler, *CEO*
Anura Welikala, *President*
EMP: 100
SQ FT: 35,000
SALES (est): 8.4MM **Privately Held**
WEB: www.apec-plastics.com
SIC: 3089 Injection molding of plastics

(P-9634)
AP PLASTICS
4025 Garner Rd, Riverside (92501-1043)
PHONE..................................951 782-0705
Gary A Bennett, *Principal*
EMP: 11
SALES (est): 1.6MM **Privately Held**
SIC: 3089 Air mattresses, plastic

(P-9635)
ARC PLASTICS INC
14010 Shoemaker Ave, Norwalk
(90650-4536)
PHONE..................................562 802-3299
Richard Renaudo, *President*
Olga Peralta, *Vice Pres*
EMP: 20
SQ FT: 1,600
SALES (est): 3.7MM **Privately Held**
SIC: 3089 Injection molded finished plastic
products; injection molding of plastics

(P-9636)
**ARCHITECTURAL PLASTICS
INC**
1299 N Mcdowell Blvd, Petaluma
(94954-1133)
PHONE..................................707 765-9898
Pierre Miremont, *President*
Mark Lindlow, *Exec VP*
Keith Kwitchoff, *Supervisor*
▼ EMP: 32
SQ FT: 16,000
SALES (est): 6.8MM **Privately Held**
WEB: www.archplastics.com
SIC: 3089 Injection molding of plastics

(P-9637)
ARGEE MFG CO SAN DIEGO INC
9550 Pathway St, Santee (92071-4169)
PHONE..................................619 449-5050
Robert Goldman, *President*
Ruth Goldman, *Treasurer*
Efi Mizrahi, *General Mgr*
Ali Bafandeh, *Controller*
▲ EMP: 75
SQ FT: 65,000
SALES (est): 16.1MM **Privately Held**
WEB: www.argeecorp.com
SIC: 3089 Plastic hardware & building
products

(P-9638)
ARLON LLC
Arlon Adhesives-Films Division
2811 S Harbor Blvd, Santa Ana
(92704-5805)
P.O. Box 5260 (92704-0260)
PHONE..................................714 540-2811
Elmer Pruim, *President*
EMP: 150

SQ FT: 124,478
SALES (corp-wide): 879MM **Publicly
Held**
WEB: www.arlon.com
SIC: 3089 3081 2672 Plastic hardware &
building products; unsupported plastics
film & sheet; coated & laminated paper
HQ: Arlon Llc
1100 Governor Lea Rd
Bear DE 19701
302 834-2100

(P-9639)
**ARMORCAST PRODUCTS
COMPANY INC**
500 S Dupont Ave, Ontario (91761-1508)
PHONE..................................909 390-1365
Paul Boghossian, *Branch Mgr*
EMP: 40
SALES (corp-wide): 59.3MM **Privately
Held**
SIC: 3089 5092 Plastic processing; toys
PA: Armorcast Products Company, Inc.
9140 Lurline Ave
Chatsworth CA 91311
818 982-3600

(P-9640)
ART SERVICES MELROSE
626 N Almont Dr, West Hollywood
(90069-5608)
PHONE..................................310 247-1452
Jeff Roberts, *President*
Russ Roberts, *Master*
EMP: 14
SALES (est): 1.2MM **Privately Held**
WEB: www.artservicesmelrose.com
SIC: 3089 Plastic processing

(P-9641)
ARTHURMADE PLASTICS INC
Also Called: Kirk Containers
2131 Garfield Ave, Commerce
(90040-1805)
PHONE..................................323 721-7325
Kirk Marounian, *President*
Arthur Marounian, *Vice Pres*
Silva Marounian, *Vice Pres*
EMP: 75
SQ FT: 20,000
SALES (est): 29.2MM **Privately Held**
WEB: www.apikirkcontainers.com
SIC: 3089 Injection molding of plastics

(P-9642)
ARTISTIC PLASTICS INC
725 E Harrison St, Corona (92879-1350)
PHONE..................................951 808-9700
Diane Mixson, *President*
EMP: 10
SALES (est): 1.2MM **Privately Held**
SIC: 3089 Air mattresses, plastic

(P-9643)
ARZ TECH INC
1407 N Batavia St Ste 115, Orange
(92867-3525)
PHONE..................................714 642-9954
Xiaoyuan Zhang, *Principal*
▲ EMP: 14
SALES (est): 2MM **Privately Held**
SIC: 3089 Injection molding of plastics

(P-9644)
ATS PRODUCTS INC (PA)
2785 Goodrick Ave, Richmond
(94801-1109)
PHONE..................................510 234-3173
J Jeffrey Shea, *President*
Perry Mestre, *Engineer*
Mike Park, *Med Doctor*
▲ EMP: 50
SQ FT: 35,000
SALES (est): 15.6MM **Privately Held**
WEB: www.atsduct.com
SIC: 3089 Plastic hardware & building
products

(P-9645)
AVERY PLASTICS INC
4070 Goldfinch St Ste A, San Diego
(92103-1865)
P.O. Box 180486, Coronado (92178-0486)
PHONE..................................619 696-1230
Martin Avery, *President*
Pauline Avery, *CEO*

EMP: 95
SQ FT: 50,000
SALES (est): 11.6MM **Privately Held**
SIC: 3089 Injection molding of plastics

(P-9646)
AXIUM PLASTICS LLC
5701 Clark St, Ontario (91761-3640)
PHONE..................................909 969-0766
Kulwinder Singh, *Manager*
EMP: 58 **Privately Held**
SIC: 3089 Plastic containers, except foam
PA: Axium Plastics, Llc
9005 Smiths Mill Rd
New Albany OH 43054

(P-9647)
AXYGEN INC (HQ)
Also Called: Axygen Scientific
33210 Central Ave, Union City
(94587-2010)
PHONE..................................510 494-8900
Hemant Gupta, *President*
Amit Bansal, *CFO*
Kathy Beuttenmuller, *Manager*
◆ EMP: 45
SQ FT: 33,000
SALES (est): 19.9MM
SALES (corp-wide): 11.2B **Publicly Held**
WEB: www.axygen.com
SIC: 3089 Injection molding of plastics
PA: Corning Incorporated
1 Riverfront Plz
Corning NY 14831
607 974-9000

(P-9648)
B & S PLASTICS INC
Also Called: Waterway Plastics
2200 Sturgis Rd, Oxnard (93030-8978)
PHONE..................................805 981-0262
Bill Spears, *CEO*
Sandy Spears, *Corp Secy*
▲ EMP: 700
SQ FT: 240,000
SALES (est): 228.8MM **Privately Held**
WEB: www.waterwayplastics.com
SIC: 3089 Injection molding of plastics

(P-9649)
B AND P PLASTICS INC
Also Called: Advance Plastics
225 W 30th St, National City (91950-7203)
PHONE..................................619 477-1893
Bruce Browne, *President*
Patricia Browne, *General Mgr*
▲ EMP: 35 EST: 1974
SQ FT: 10,000
SALES (est): 11.5MM **Privately Held**
WEB: www.advanceplastics.com
SIC: 3089 3061 Molding primary plastic;
mechanical rubber goods

(P-9650)
**BACE MANUFACTURING INC
(HQ)**
Also Called: Spm
3125 E Coronado St, Anaheim
(92806-1915)
PHONE..................................714 630-6002
Richard R Harris, *President*
Shannon White, *Vice Pres*
EMP: 700
SQ FT: 200,000
SALES (est): 80.5MM
SALES (corp-wide): 456.1MM **Privately
Held**
WEB: www.spmfremont.com
SIC: 3089 Injection molding of plastics;
molding primary plastic
PA: Medplast Group, Inc.
7865 Northcourt Rd # 100
Houston TX 77040
480 553-6400

(P-9651)
BACE MANUFACTURING INC
Spm/Fremont, CA
45581 Northport Loop W, Fremont
(94538-6462)
PHONE..................................510 657-5800
James W Collins, *Manager*
EMP: 100

SALES (corp-wide): 456.1MM **Privately
Held**
SIC: 3089 3544 Molding primary plastic;
special dies, tools, jigs & fixtures
HQ: Bace Manufacturing, Inc.
3125 E Coronado St
Anaheim CA 92806
714 630-6002

(P-9652)
BALDA C BREWER INC (DH)
Also Called: C Brewer Company
4501 E Wall St, Ontario (91761-8143)
PHONE..................................714 630-6810
Christoph Klaus, *CEO*
Steve Holland, *President*
Harold Hee, *Vice Pres*
Sal Tinajero, *Info Tech Mgr*
Tom Arttus, *Purch Mgr*
▲ EMP: 158 EST: 1968
SQ FT: 60,000
SALES (est): 47.1MM
SALES (corp-wide): 562.9K **Privately
Held**
SIC: 3089 3544 Molding primary plastic;
special dies, tools, jigs & fixtures
HQ: Clere Ag
Schluterstr. 45
Berlin 10707
302 130-0430

(P-9653)
**BARBER-WEBB COMPANY INC
(PA)**
3833 Medford St, Los Angeles
(90063-1997)
PHONE..................................541 488-4821
Donald B Barber Jr, *President*
James Barber, *Exec VP*
James C Barber, *Exec VP*
Wr Greenbecker, *Senior VP*
Brian Barber, *Admin Sec*
▼ EMP: 30
SQ FT: 106,000
SALES (est): 10.6MM **Privately Held**
WEB: www.barber-webb.com
SIC: 3089 Plastic processing

(P-9654)
BARNES PLASTICS INC
18903 Anelo Ave, Gardena (90248-4598)
PHONE..................................310 329-6301
Charles Walker, *CEO*
Scott Piepmeyer, *Vice Pres*
Kathy Choi, *Accounting Mgr*
▲ EMP: 30
SQ FT: 30,000
SALES (est): 5.9MM **Privately Held**
WEB: www.barnesplastics.com
SIC: 3089 Injection molding of plastics

(P-9655)
**BAYVIEW PLASTIC SOLUTIONS
INC**
43651 S Grimmer Blvd, Fremont
(94538-6347)
PHONE..................................510 360-0001
Martin Hernandez, *President*
Terri Hernandez, *General Mgr*
Katie Loux, *Office Mgr*
Nathan Martinez, *Prdtn Mgr*
EMP: 26
SALES (est): 5.5MM **Privately Held**
SIC: 3089 Plastic processing

(P-9656)
BEEMAK PLASTICS LLC
Also Called: Beemak-Idl Display Products
16711 Knott Ave, La Mirada (90638-6013)
PHONE..................................310 886-5880
Howard Topping, *President*
Chris Braun, *President*
Jason Owens, *Executive*
Andrew Marosi, *Design Engr*
Ian Ellis, *Project Mgr*
▲ EMP: 100
SQ FT: 110,000
SALES (est): 23.9MM
SALES (corp-wide): 579.2MM **Privately
Held**
WEB: www.beemak.com
SIC: 3089 Injection molding of plastics
HQ: Deflecto, Llc
7035 E 86th St
Indianapolis IN 46250
317 849-9555

▲ = Import ▼=Export
◆ =Import/Export

(P-9657)
BENT MANUFACTURING CO
BDAA INC
15442 Chemical Ln, Huntington Beach
(92649-1220)
PHONE..........................714 842-0600
Bruce Christopher Bent, *CEO*
EMP: 10
SALES (est): 1.4MM **Privately Held**
SIC: 3089 3499 5093 Blow molded finished plastic products; barricades, metal; barrels & drums

(P-9658)
BERICAP LLC
1671 Champagne Ave Ste B, Ontario
(91761-3650)
PHONE..........................909 390-5518
Steve Buckley,
David Andison, *President*
Hany Shash, *Sr Corp Ofcr*
Carsten Pfromm, *Vice Pres*
Ozgur Akin, *General Mgr*
▲ EMP: 67
SALES (est): 17.9MM
SALES (corp-wide): 533.7K **Privately Held**
WEB: www.bericap.com
SIC: 3089 Injection molded finished plastic products
HQ: Bericap Holding Gmbh
Kirchstr. 5
Budenheim 55257
613 929-020

(P-9659)
BERRY GLOBAL INC
3030 S Susan St, Santa Ana (92704-6435)
PHONE..........................714 751-2920
Martha Harmon, *Manager*
EMP: 14 **Publicly Held**
WEB: www.6sens.com
SIC: 3089 Bottle caps, molded plastic
HQ: Berry Global, Inc.
101 Oakley St
Evansville IN 47710
812 424-2904

(P-9660)
BERRY GLOBAL INC
4875 E Hunter Ave, Anaheim (92807-2005)
PHONE..........................714 777-5200
Don Parodi, *Manager*
Karen Boyer, *Executive*
Alejandro Martinez, *Controller*
Serenity Minucci, *Supervisor*
EMP: 15 **Publicly Held**
SIC: 3089 3081 Bottle caps, molded plastic; unsupported plastics film & sheet
HQ: Berry Global, Inc.
101 Oakley St
Evansville IN 47710
812 424-2904

(P-9661)
BERRY GLOBAL INC
14000 Monte Vista Ave, Chino
(91710-5537)
PHONE..........................909 465-9055
Salama Elsayed, *Branch Mgr*
Brian Arigan, *Purch Agent*
EMP: 200 **Publicly Held**
SIC: 3089 3081 Bottle caps, molded plastic; unsupported plastics film & sheet
HQ: Berry Global, Inc.
101 Oakley St
Evansville IN 47710
812 424-2904

(P-9662)
BERRY GLOBAL INC
13335 Orden Dr, Santa Fe Springs
(90670-6334)
PHONE..........................800 462-3843
Laura Reta, *Branch Mgr*
EMP: 25 **Publicly Held**
WEB: www.6sens.com
SIC: 3089 Plastic containers, except foam
HQ: Berry Global, Inc.
101 Oakley St
Evansville IN 47710
812 424-2904

(P-9663)
BETTER WORLD
MANUFACTURING INC (PA)
Also Called: A Better Trap
3535 N Sabre Dr, Fresno (93727-7817)
PHONE..........................559 291-4276
Richard Alvarado, *President*
Rich Alvarado, *President*
Janie Alvarado, *Vice Pres*
▲ EMP: 10
SQ FT: 25,000
SALES (est): 1.6MM **Privately Held**
WEB: www.jeffry.com
SIC: 3089 Injection molding of plastics

(P-9664)
BEYOND GREEN LLC
2 Rancho Cir, Lake Forest (92630-8325)
PHONE..........................800 983-7221
Vijay Patel, *Mng Member*
EMP: 10
SQ FT: 8,500
SALES (est): 393.6K **Privately Held**
SIC: 3089 Garbage containers, plastic

(P-9665)
BH-TECH INC
7841 Balboa Ave Ste 208, San Diego
(92111-2313)
PHONE..........................858 694-0900
Seung Hoon Han, *CEO*
Woo Hyuk Choi, *CFO*
EMP: 700
SQ FT: 500
SALES: 50MM **Privately Held**
SIC: 3089 Injection molding of plastics

(P-9666)
BLISTERPAK INC
3020 Supply Ave, Commerce (90040-2710)
PHONE..........................323 728-5555
Steven C Mattis, *CEO*
Ric Munoz, *IT/INT Sup*
▲ EMP: 20 EST: 1974
SQ FT: 15,000
SALES (est): 4.6MM **Privately Held**
SIC: 3089 Thermoformed finished plastic products

(P-9667)
BLOW MOLDED PRODUCTS INC
Also Called: Bmp
4720 Felspar St, Riverside (92509-3068)
PHONE..........................951 360-6055
Larry Harden, *CEO*
EMP: 40
SQ FT: 25,000
SALES (est): 10.6MM **Privately Held**
WEB: www.blowmoldedproducts.com
SIC: 3089 Injection molding of plastics

(P-9668)
BOLERO INDS INC A CAL CORP
Also Called: Bolero Plastics
11850 Burke St, Santa Fe Springs
(90670-2536)
PHONE..........................562 693-3000
Daniel Imasdounian, *CEO*
Vasken Imasdounian, *Vice Pres*
Annie Imasdounian, *Admin Sec*
Nova Imasdounian, *Safety Mgr*
EMP: 25 EST: 1975
SQ FT: 19,500
SALES (est): 4.5MM **Privately Held**
WEB: www.boleroplastics.com
SIC: 3089 Injection molding of plastics

(P-9669)
BOMATIC INC (HQ)
Also Called: Bmi
43225 Business Park Dr, Temecula
(92590-3648)
P.O. Box 580 (92593-0580)
PHONE..........................909 947-3900
Kjeld R Hestehave, *President*
Borge Hestehave, *Ch of Bd*
Mary Ann, *CEO*
Kirk Franks, *CFO*
Kresten Hestehave, *Vice Pres*
▲ EMP: 40
SQ FT: 35,000
SALES (est): 23.6MM **Privately Held**
WEB: www.bomatic.com
SIC: 3089 Plastic containers, except foam; injection molding of plastics

PA: Universal Packaging West, Inc.
43225 Business Park Dr
Temecula CA 92590
909 947-3900

(P-9670)
BOMATIC INC
2181 E Francis St, Ontario (91761-7723)
PHONE..........................909 947-3900
Back Melon, *Manager*
EMP: 50
SALES (corp-wide): 23.6MM **Privately Held**
WEB: www.bomatic.com
SIC: 3089 Plastic containers, except foam
HQ: Bomatic Inc.
43225 Business Park Dr
Temecula CA 92590
909 947-3900

(P-9671)
BOTTLEMATE INC
2095 Leo Ave, Commerce (90040-1626)
PHONE..........................323 887-9009
Kai-Win Chuang, *CEO*
Anderson Chuang, *Vice Pres*
MEI-LI Chang, *Admin Sec*
Harry Achekian, *Accounts Exec*
Chen Katherine, *Accounts Exec*
▲ EMP: 25
SQ FT: 25,000
SALES (est): 4.5MM **Privately Held**
WEB: www.bottlemate.com
SIC: 3089 5162 Blow molded finished plastic products; plastics products

(P-9672)
BRADLEY MANUFACTURING CO INC
Also Called: Bradley's Plastic Bag Co
9130 Firestone Blvd, Downey
(90241-5319)
PHONE..........................562 923-5556
Keith Smith, *President*
Richard Lane, *Corp Secy*
EMP: 28
SQ FT: 30,000
SALES (est): 4.9MM **Privately Held**
WEB: www.bradleybag.com
SIC: 3089 3069 3083 2673 Plastic processing; tubing, rubber; laminated plastics plate & sheet; bags: plastic, laminated & coated

(P-9673)
BRAIFORM ENTERPRISES INC
Plaza Plastic
576 N Gilbert St, Fullerton (92833-2549)
PHONE..........................714 526-0257
John Bontiorno, *Manager*
EMP: 100
SQ FT: 54,000 **Privately Held**
SIC: 3089 Clothes hangers, plastic; plastic kitchenware, tableware & houseware
HQ: Braiform Enterprises Incorporated
12 Gerber Rd Ste B
Asheville NC 28803
828 277-6420

(P-9674)
BREWER IRVINE INC
Also Called: Brevet Industries
16661 Jamboree Rd, Irvine (92606-5118)
PHONE..........................949 474-7000
Charles Brewer, *President*
EMP: 65
SQ FT: 59,000
SALES (est): 9.6MM **Privately Held**
WEB: www.brevetind.com
SIC: 3089 Injection molded finished plastic products

(P-9675)
BUILDING COMPONENTS
3148 Abington Dr, Beverly Hills
(90210-1101)
PHONE..........................310 274-6516
Clyde Berkus, *Owner*
EMP: 10
SALES (est): 1MM **Privately Held**
SIC: 3089 Plastic hardware & building products

(P-9676)
BUMBLE BEE PLASTICS INC
10140 Shoemaker Ave, Santa Fe Springs
(90670-3404)
PHONE..........................562 903-0833
EMP: 15
SALES (corp-wide): 1.6MM **Privately Held**
SIC: 3089 Injection molding of plastics
PA: Bee Bumble Plastics Inc
3553 Atlantic Ave 328
Long Beach CA 90807
310 749-1655

(P-9677)
BUMJIN AMERICA INC (PA)
2177 Britannia Blvd # 204, San Diego
(92154-8307)
PHONE..........................619 671-0386
Yong Jin Lee, *President*
Jason Park, *CFO*
Jeong Jae Park, *CFO*
▲ EMP: 14
SQ FT: 200,000
SALES (est): 3.9MM **Privately Held**
WEB: www.ssdplastics.com
SIC: 3089 Air mattresses, plastic; injection molding of plastics

(P-9678)
C & G PLASTICS
Also Called: C & G Mercury Plastics
12729 Foothill Blvd, Sylmar (91342-5314)
PHONE..........................818 837-3773
Greg Leighton, *President*
▲ EMP: 25
SQ FT: 6,000
SALES (est): 1.5MM **Privately Held**
WEB: www.cgplastics.com
SIC: 3089 Injection molding of plastics

(P-9679)
C & R MOLDS INC
2737 Palma Dr, Ventura (93003-7651)
P.O. Box 5644 (93005-0644)
PHONE..........................805 658-7098
Randall Ohnemus, *President*
Marla Ohnemus, *Treasurer*
Randy Ohnemus, *Facilities Mgr*
Steve Ohnemus, *Director*
Tom Alspaugh, *Manager*
▲ EMP: 24
SQ FT: 12,000
SALES (est): 4.7MM **Privately Held**
SIC: 3089 3544 Injection molding of plastics; plastic hardware & building products; special dies, tools, jigs & fixtures

(P-9680)
C & S PLASTICS
12621 Foothill Blvd, Sylmar (91342-5312)
PHONE..........................818 896-2489
Charles E Spears, *President*
Karen Spears, *Admin Sec*
EMP: 15
SQ FT: 6,000
SALES: 2.5MM **Privately Held**
WEB: www.candsplastics.com
SIC: 3089 Injection molding of plastics

(P-9681)
C-PAK INDUSTRIES INC
4925 Hallmark Pkwy, San Bernardino
(92407-1870)
PHONE..........................909 880-6017
Arch Young, *President*
EMP: 28
SQ FT: 25,000
SALES: 2.5MM **Privately Held**
WEB: www.c-pak.net
SIC: 3089 Molding primary plastic

(P-9682)
CAL-MIL PLASTIC PRODUCTS INC (PA)
4079 Calle Platino, Oceanside
(92056-5805)
PHONE..........................800 321-9069
Johnny Callahan, *CEO*
Barney Callahan, *Vice Pres*
Julia Sass, *Marketing Staff*
Dustin Smith,
Gustavo Sanchez, *Director*
◆ EMP: 30
SQ FT: 60,000

SALES (est): 9.1MM **Privately Held**
WEB: www.calmil.com
SIC: 3089 Plastic containers, except foam

(P-9683)
CAL-MOLD INCORPORATED
Also Called: Pierco
3900 Hamner Ave, Eastvale (91752-1017)
PHONE.....................................951 361-6400
Erik Fleming, *President*
Edward T Fleming, *Chairman*
EMP: 220
SQ FT: 170,000
SALES (est): 26.7MM **Privately Held**
WEB: www.mail.tstonramp.com
SIC: 3089 Injection molding of plastics

(P-9684)
CAL-TRON CORPORATION
2290 Dixon Ln, Bishop (93514-8094)
PHONE.....................................760 873-8491
Dan J Pool, *President*
Colleen Pool, *Corp Secy*
EMP: 22 EST: 1963
SQ FT: 24,000
SALES (est): 2MM **Privately Held**
WEB: www.caltroncorp.com
SIC: 3089 Injection molded finished plastic
   products

(P-9685)
CALIFORNIA FLEX
CORPORATION (PA)
Also Called: Cal Flex
1318 1st St, San Fernando (91340-2804)
PHONE.....................................818 361-1169
Clifford A Schroeder, *President*
Jani Schroeder, *Corp Secy*
◆ EMP: 14
SQ FT: 18,500
SALES (est): 4.3MM **Privately Held**
SIC: 3089 Ducting, plastic

(P-9686)
CALIFORNIA PLASTIC CNTRS
INC
2210 E Artesia Blvd, Long Beach
   (90805-1739)
PHONE.....................................562 423-3900
Jeff Vice, *President*
Steve Rockenbach, *CFO*
Gottfried Schmidt, *Admin Sec*
EMP: 15
SQ FT: 20,000
SALES (est): 4MM **Privately Held**
SIC: 3089 Injection molding of plastics

(P-9687)
CALIFORNIA PLASTICS INC
1611 S Rose Ave, Oxnard (93033-2470)
PHONE.....................................805 483-8188
Rene Ribbers, *President*
Rebecca Ribbers, *CFO*
EMP: 12
SALES (est): 1.9MM **Privately Held**
SIC: 3089 Injection molding of plastics

(P-9688)
CALIFORNIA QUALITY PLAS INC
Also Called: Bel-Air Cases
2104 S Cucamonga Ave, Ontario
   (91761-5609)
PHONE.....................................909 930-5667
Erik Calcott, *Branch Mgr*
EMP: 20
SALES (corp-wide): 12.7MM **Privately
Held**
SIC: 3089 Plastic containers, except foam;
   boxes, plastic; flat panels, plastic; thermo-
   formed finished plastic products
PA: California Quality Plastics, Inc.
   2226 S Castle Harbour Pl
   Ontario CA 91761
   909 930-5535

(P-9689)
CAMBRO MANUFACTURING
COMPANY (PA)
5801 Skylab Rd, Huntington Beach
   (92647-2051)
P.O. Box 2000 (92647-2000)
PHONE.....................................714 848-1555
Argyle Campbell, *CEO*
Nick Ditrolio, *Vice Pres*
Chris Fairgrief, *Vice Pres*

Chip Jarvis, *Vice Pres*
Lisa Bowman, *Admin Sec*
◆ EMP: 500 EST: 1951
SQ FT: 300,000
SALES (est): 307.8MM **Privately Held**
WEB: www.cambro.com
SIC: 3089 Trays, plastic; plastic containers,
   except foam

(P-9690)
CAMBRO MANUFACTURING
COMPANY
7601 Clay Ave, Huntington Beach
   (92648-2219)
PHONE.....................................714 848-1555
David Capestro, *Manager*
Oscar Dominguez, *Executive*
Leand Oliver, *Buyer*
Victor Rios, *Supervisor*
EMP: 273
SALES (corp-wide): 307.8MM **Privately
Held**
SIC: 3089 Plastic containers, except foam
PA: Cambro Manufacturing Company Inc
   5801 Skylab Rd
   Huntington Beach CA 92647
   714 848-1555

(P-9691)
CAMBRO MANUFACTURING
COMPANY
5801 Skylab Rd, Huntington Beach
   (92647-2051)
PHONE.....................................714 848-1555
Argyle Campbell, *President*
EMP: 500
SALES (corp-wide): 307.8MM **Privately
Held**
SIC: 3089 Trays, plastic
PA: Cambro Manufacturing Company Inc
   5801 Skylab Rd
   Huntington Beach CA 92647
   714 848-1555

(P-9692)
CANYON PLASTICS INC
28455 Livingston Ave, Valencia
   (91355-4173)
PHONE.....................................800 350-2275
Karshan A Gajera, *CEO*
Steve McNear, *Executive*
Steven Cruz, *VP Sales*
▲ EMP: 78
SQ FT: 110,950
SALES (est): 17.8MM **Privately Held**
WEB: www.canyonplastics.com
SIC: 3089 3544 Plastic containers, except
   foam; injection molding of plastics; forms
   (molds), for foundry & plastics working
   machinery

(P-9693)
CAPCO/PSA
Also Called: California Art Products Co
11125 Vanowen St, North Hollywood
   (91605-6316)
PHONE.....................................818 762-4276
Zaven P Berberian, *President*
EMP: 26 EST: 1967
SQ FT: 18,000
SALES (est): 4.4MM **Privately Held**
SIC: 3089 2821 Planters, plastic; plastic
   containers, except foam; plastics materi-
   als & resins

(P-9694)
CAPTIVE PLASTICS LLC
601 Tesla Dr A, Lathrop (95330-9263)
PHONE.....................................209 858-9188
Jim Campbell, *Branch Mgr*
Bill Ventresca, *Engineer*
EMP: 100 **Publicly Held**
WEB: www.captiveplastics.com
SIC: 3089 Plastic containers, except foam
HQ: Captive Plastics, Llc
   101 Oakley St
   Evansville IN 47710
   812 424-2904

(P-9695)
CARAVAN MANUFACTURING CO
INC
10814 Los Vaqueros Cir, Los Alamitos
   (90720-2516)
PHONE.....................................714 220-9722

Geoffrey Bennett, *President*
Geraldine Bennett, *Treasurer*
Tim Bennett, *Vice Pres*
EMP: 10
SQ FT: 12,500
SALES: 750K **Privately Held**
WEB: www.caravanmfg.com
SIC: 3089 Injection molded finished plastic
   products

(P-9696)
CARPOD INC
12132 Gothic Ave, Granada Hills
   (91344-2819)
PHONE.....................................818 395-8676
Martin Aghajanian, *President*
▲ EMP: 10
SQ FT: 1,000
SALES: 100K **Privately Held**
SIC: 3089 Automotive parts, plastic

(P-9697)
CARR MANAGEMENT INC
22324 Temescal Canyon Rd, Corona
   (92883-4622)
PHONE.....................................951 277-4800
Nick Rende, *Branch Mgr*
EMP: 70 **Privately Held**
SIC: 3089 Stock shapes, plastic
PA: Carr Management, Inc.
   1 Tara Blvd Ste 303
   Nashua NH 03062

(P-9698)
CCI INDUSTRIES INC (PA)
Also Called: Cool Curtain CCI
350 Fischer Ave Ste A, Costa Mesa
   (92626-4508)
PHONE.....................................714 662-3879
Michael Robinson, *President*
▲ EMP: 30
SQ FT: 15,000
SALES (est): 5.1MM **Privately Held**
WEB: www.coolcurtain.com
SIC: 3089 3564 3496 Doors, folding:
   plastic or plastic coated fabric; aircurtains
   (blower); grilles & grillework, woven wire

(P-9699)
CCL TUBE INC (HQ)
2250 E 220th St, Carson (90810-1638)
PHONE.....................................310 635-4444
Andreas Iseli, *CEO*
Susan Wood, *Human Res Mgr*
Dana Barnard, *Materials Mgr*
Sandra Pacay, *Production*
Tim Harrison, *Cust Mgr*
▲ EMP: 200
SQ FT: 300,000
SALES (est): 44.6MM
SALES (corp-wide): 3.9B **Privately Held**
WEB: www.ccltubes.com
SIC: 3089 Injection molded finished plastic
   products
PA: Ccl Industries Inc
   111 Gordon Baker Rd Suite 801
   Toronto ON M2H 3
   800 563-2464

(P-9700)
CECO ENVIRONMENTAL CORP
Also Called: Hee
4222 E La Palma Ave, Anaheim
   (92807-1816)
PHONE.....................................760 530-1409
Jamie Warren, *Branch Mgr*
EMP: 38
SALES (corp-wide): 337.3MM **Publicly
Held**
SIC: 3089 Plastic & fiberglass tanks
PA: Ceco Environmental Corp.
   14651 Dallas Pkwy Ste 50
   Dallas TX 75254
   214 357-6181

(P-9701)
CENTRAL CALIFORNIA CONT
MFG
Also Called: Synder California Container
800 Commerce Dr, Chowchilla
   (93610-9395)
P.O. Box 848 (93610-0848)
PHONE.....................................559 665-7611
Tom O'Connell, *CEO*
Shelli Humphries, *Controller*

EMP: 20
SQ FT: 2,500
SALES (est): 2.5MM **Privately Held**
SIC: 3089 Plastic containers, except foam

(P-9702)
CERTAINTEED CORONA INC
235 Radio Rd, Corona (92879-1725)
PHONE.....................................951 272-1300
Marshall J Stuart, *Ch of Bd*
Kathryn Stuart, *Corp Secy*
EMP: 200
SQ FT: 128,000
SALES (est): 20.9MM
SALES (corp-wide): 215.9MM **Privately
Held**
WEB: www.certainteed.net
SIC: 3089 3442 Doors, folding: plastic or
   plastic coated fabric; windows, plastic;
   metal doors, sash & trim
HQ: Certainteed Llc
   20 Moores Rd
   Malvern PA 19355
   610 893-5000

(P-9703)
CERTIFIED THERMOPLASTICS
LLC
Also Called: Certified Thermoplastics Inc
26381 Ferry Ct, Santa Clarita
   (91350-2998)
PHONE.....................................661 222-3006
Robert Duncan, *President*
▲ EMP: 35
SQ FT: 30,000
SALES (est): 7.2MM
SALES (corp-wide): 629.3MM **Publicly
Held**
WEB: www.ctplastics.com
SIC: 3089 Injection molding of plastics
HQ: Ducommun Labarge Technologies, Inc.
   1601 E Broadway Rd
   Phoenix AZ 85040
   480 998-0733

(P-9704)
CG MOTOR SPORTS INC
5150 Eucalyptus Ave Ste A, Chino
   (91710-9218)
PHONE.....................................909 628-1440
Debbie Law, *President*
▲ EMP: 16
SALES (est): 2.5MM **Privately Held**
SIC: 3089 Automotive parts, plastic

(P-9705)
CHAUHAN INDUSTRIES INC
32 Wood Rd Ste A, Camarillo
   (93010-8399)
PHONE.....................................805 484-1616
Raj Chauhan, *President*
EMP: 16
SQ FT: 6,000
SALES: 1.5MM **Privately Held**
SIC: 3089 Windows, plastic

(P-9706)
CHAWK TECHNOLOGY INTL INC
(PA)
31033 Huntwood Ave, Hayward
   (94544-7007)
PHONE.....................................510 330-5299
Jonathan Chang, *CEO*
▲ EMP: 64
SALES: 11.4MM **Privately Held**
SIC: 3089 Injection molding of plastics

(P-9707)
CHEM-TAINER INDUSTRIES INC
Also Called: Chemtainer Industries
135 E Stanley St, Compton (90220-5604)
PHONE.....................................310 635-5400
George Karathanas, *Opers-Prdtn-Mfg*
EMP: 30
SALES (corp-wide): 46.5MM **Privately
Held**
WEB: www.chemtainer.com
SIC: 3089 2821 Plastic & fiberglass tanks;
   plastics materials & resins
PA: Chem-Tainer Industries Inc.
   361 Neptune Ave
   West Babylon NY 11704
   631 422-8300

▲ = Import ▼=Export
◆ =Import/Export

(P-9708)
CHINA CUSTOM MANUFACTURING LTD
44843 Fremont Blvd, Fremont (94538-6318)
PHONE...................510 979-1920
George Huang, *President*
Robin Lee, *Vice Pres*
▲ EMP: 860
SALES (est): 71.7MM **Privately Held**
WEB: www.ccmfg.com
SIC: 3089 Injection molded finished plastic products; injection molding of plastics

(P-9709)
CHUBBY GORILLA INC (PA)
10425 Slusher Dr, Santa Fe Springs (90670-3750)
PHONE...................844 365-5218
Ibraheim Hamsa Aboabdo, *CEO*
Eyad Aboabdo, *Vice Pres*
EMP: 30
SALES (est): 302.9K **Privately Held**
SIC: 3089 Closures, plastic

(P-9710)
CLEAR-AD INC
Also Called: Brochure Holders 4u
2410 W 3rd St, Santa Ana (92703-3519)
PHONE...................877 899-1002
Juan Diaz, *CEO*
Bruce Kelly, *Vice Pres*
Barbara Snow, *Purch Mgr*
EMP: 30
SQ FT: 17,006
SALES (est): 6MM **Privately Held**
WEB: www.clearad.com
SIC: 3089 3544 3993 3061 Injection molded finished plastic products; forms (molds), for foundry & plastics working machinery; displays & cutouts, window & lobby; medical & surgical rubber tubing (extruded & lathe-cut); advertising specialties

(P-9711)
CMP DISPLAY SYSTEMS INC
23301 Wilmington Ave, Carson (90745-6209)
PHONE...................805 499-3642
William M Hooker, *CEO*
Ken Collin, *President*
Bruce Miller, *Vice Pres*
EMP: 75
SALES (est): 10MM
SALES (corp-wide): 629.3MM **Publicly Held**
WEB: www.cmp-displays.com
SIC: 3089 3823 3812 Plastic processing; industrial instrmnts msrmnt display/control process variable; search & navigation equipment
HQ: Ducommun Labarge Technologies, Inc.
23301 Wilmington Ave
Carson CA 90745
310 513-7200

(P-9712)
COAST TO COAST MFG LLC
Also Called: Fire Windows and Doors
430 Nevada St, Redlands (92373-4244)
P.O. Box 1503, Perris (92572-1503)
PHONE...................909 798-5024
John Seymour, *Mng Member*
EMP: 11
SALES (est): 2.6MM **Privately Held**
WEB: www.coasttocoastmfg.com
SIC: 3089 Windows, plastic

(P-9713)
CODAN US CORPORATION
3511 W Sunflower Ave, Santa Ana (92704-6944)
PHONE...................714 430-1300
Peter Schwark, *Ch of Bd*
Jeff Nielsen, *President*
Bernd J Larsen, *CEO*
Deon Miller, *Vice Pres*
Dawna Ferguson, *Admin Sec*
▲ EMP: 145
SQ FT: 180,000
SALES (est): 26.3MM
SALES (corp-wide): 192.5K **Privately Held**
WEB: www.codanus.com
SIC: 3089 Molding primary plastic

HQ: Codan Medizinische Gerate Gmbh & Co Kg
Stig Husted-Andersen Str. 11
Lensahn 23738
436 351-11

(P-9714)
COLVIN-FRIEDMAN LLC
1311 Commerce St, Petaluma (94954-1426)
PHONE...................707 769-4488
Mitchell Friedman, *President*
Madelyn Helper, *Cust Mgr*
EMP: 25 EST: 1949
SQ FT: 10,000
SALES (est): 4.6MM **Privately Held**
WEB: www.colvin-friedman.com
SIC: 3089 5162 3544 Plastic processing; injection molding of plastics; plastics materials; dies, plastics forming

(P-9715)
COMMERCIAL PATTERNS INC
3162 Baumberg Ave Ste H, Hayward (94545-4434)
PHONE...................510 784-1014
Donald Loobey Sr, *President*
Mildred Loobey, *Treasurer*
Don Loobey Jr, *Vice Pres*
Mark Loobey, *Vice Pres*
EMP: 16
SQ FT: 8,000
SALES (est): 2MM **Privately Held**
WEB: www.commpattern.com
SIC: 3089 2821 Molding primary plastic; polyurethane resins

(P-9716)
CONROY & KNOWLTON INC
320 S Montebello Blvd, Montebello (90640-5112)
PHONE...................323 665-5288
William A Conroy, *President*
Michelle Conroy, *Manager*
EMP: 18 EST: 1946
SQ FT: 17,000
SALES (est): 2MM **Privately Held**
SIC: 3089 Plastic hardware & building products; injection molding of plastics

(P-9717)
CONSOLIDATED CONT HOLDINGS LLC
17851 Railroad St, City of Industry (91748-1118)
PHONE...................626 964-9657
Ric Ibarra, *Manager*
EMP: 50
SALES (corp-wide): 1.6B **Privately Held**
SIC: 3089 Plastic containers, except foam
PA: Consolidated Container Holdings Llc
2500 Windy Ridge Pkwy Se
Atlanta GA 30339
678 742-4600

(P-9718)
CONSOLIDATED CONT HOLDINGS LLC
Also Called: California Plastics
12165 Madera Way, Riverside (92503-4849)
PHONE...................951 340-9390
Steve Thompson, *Manager*
Gabriel Guijosa, *Supervisor*
EMP: 32
SALES (corp-wide): 1.6B **Privately Held**
SIC: 3089 Plastic containers, except foam
PA: Consolidated Container Holdings Llc
2500 Windy Ridge Pkwy Se
Atlanta GA 30339
678 742-4600

(P-9719)
CONSOLIDATED CONTAINER CO LLC
Also Called: Reid Plastics Customer Svcs
1070 Samuelson St, City of Industry (91748-1219)
PHONE...................888 425-7343
Fred Braham, *Principal*
Lidia Raya, *Technician*
Celestino Ramos, *Supervisor*
EMP: 44

SALES (corp-wide): 14B **Publicly Held**
WEB: www.ccclic.com
SIC: 3089 3085 Plastic containers, except foam; plastics bottles
HQ: Consolidated Container Company, Llc
2500 Windy Ridge Pkwy Se # 1400
Atlanta GA 30339
678 742-4600

(P-9720)
CONSOLIDATED CONTAINER CO LLC
4516 Azusa Canyon Rd, Irwindale (91706-2742)
PHONE...................626 856-2100
EMP: 60
SALES (corp-wide): 14B **Publicly Held**
SIC: 3089 Plastic containers, except foam
HQ: Consolidated Container Company, Llc
2500 Windy Ridge Pkwy Se # 1400
Atlanta GA 30339
678 742-4600

(P-9721)
CONSOLIDATED CONTAINER CO LLC
Also Called: Stewart/Walker Company
75 W Valpico Rd, Tracy (95376-9129)
PHONE...................209 820-1700
Fred Branham, *Opers-Prdtn-Mfg*
EMP: 104
SALES (corp-wide): 14B **Publicly Held**
WEB: www.ccclic.com
SIC: 3089 3085 Pallets, plastic; plastics bottles
HQ: Consolidated Container Company, Llc
2500 Windy Ridge Pkwy Se # 1400
Atlanta GA 30339
678 742-4600

(P-9722)
CONSOLIDATED CONTAINER CO LP
Envision Plastics
14312 Central Ave, Chino (91710-5752)
PHONE...................909 590-7334
EMP: 50
SALES (corp-wide): 14B **Publicly Held**
SIC: 3089 Plastic containers, except foam
HQ: Consolidated Container Company Lp
2500 Windy Ridge Pkwy Se # 1400
Atlanta GA 30339
678 742-4600

(P-9723)
CONTAINER COMPONENTS INC (PA)
Also Called: Duraflex
21947 Plummer St, Chatsworth (91311-4002)
P.O. Box 4735 (91313-4735)
PHONE...................818 882-4300
Craig V Taylor, *CEO*
Darlene Taylor, *Admin Sec*
▲ EMP: 49
SQ FT: 23,000
SALES (est): 12.8MM **Privately Held**
SIC: 3089 4731 Plastic containers, except foam; freight forwarding

(P-9724)
CONTAINER OPTIONS INC
1493 E San Bernardino Ave, San Bernardino (92408-2927)
PHONE...................909 478-0045
Patricia Shockey, *CEO*
Charles Shockley, *Office Mgr*
EMP: 18
SQ FT: 43,000
SALES: 5MM **Privately Held**
SIC: 3089 Plastic containers, except foam

(P-9725)
CONTAINER TECHNOLOGY INC (PA)
5454 San Patricio Dr, Santa Barbara (93111-1455)
P.O. Box 60508 (93160-0508)
PHONE...................805 683-5825
Gary Clancy, *President*
EMP: 20

SALES (est): 3.4MM **Privately Held**
WEB: www.containertechnology.com
SIC: 3089 3443 5113 Plastic containers, except foam; tubs, plastic (containers); industrial vessels, tanks & containers; boxes & containers

(P-9726)
COOL-PAK LLC
401 N Rice Ave, Oxnard (93030-7936)
PHONE...................805 981-2434
Niall Kelly,
Ross Bonn, *Project Mgr*
Alicia Aldis, *Purchasing*
Victor Garcia, *Opers Mgr*
Ruben Trevino, *Plant Mgr*
▲ EMP: 85
SQ FT: 124,000
SALES (est): 25.3MM
SALES (corp-wide): 11.6B **Privately Held**
WEB: www.cool-pak.com
SIC: 3089 Plastic containers, except foam
HQ: Bunzl Distribution Usa, Llc
1 Cityplace Dr Ste 200
Saint Louis MO 63141
314 997-5959

(P-9727)
CORD INDUSTRIES INC
541 Industrial Way Ste 2, Fallbrook (92028-2257)
PHONE...................760 728-4590
Donald Conibear, *President*
EMP: 10 EST: 1976
SQ FT: 7,500
SALES (est): 1MM **Privately Held**
SIC: 3089 Injection molding of plastics

(P-9728)
CORNUCOPIA TOOL & PLASTICS INC
448 Sherwood Rd, Paso Robles (93446-3554)
P.O. Box 1915 (93447-1915)
PHONE...................805 238-7660
Larry Horn, *President*
Art Horn, *Vice Pres*
EMP: 47
SQ FT: 20,000
SALES (est): 9.8MM **Privately Held**
WEB: www.cornucopiaplastics.com
SIC: 3089 3544 Injection molding of plastics; industrial molds

(P-9729)
COSMETIC SPECIALTIES INTL LLC
550 E 3rd St, Oxnard (93030-6020)
PHONE...................805 487-6698
Michael J Musso, *President*
Mark Hauptman, *President*
Bruce Bellerose, *COO*
David Paneiko, *CFO*
Lisa Naylor, *Vice Pres*
▲ EMP: 102
SALES (est): 27.3MM
SALES (corp-wide): 4.4MM **Privately Held**
SIC: 3089 Injection molded finished plastic products
PA: Asparron Capital, Llc
1701 W Northwest Hwy # 100
Grapevine TX 76051
817 865-6573

(P-9730)
COUNTRY PLASTICS INC
32501 Road 228, Woodlake (93286-9705)
PHONE...................559 597-2556
Jay D Ayres, *President*
Jenny Ayres, *Corp Secy*
▲ EMP: 17
SQ FT: 3,000
SALES (est): 4.4MM **Privately Held**
WEB: www.countryplastics.net
SIC: 3089 Injection molded finished plastic products; injection molding of plastics

(P-9731)
CPC GROUP INC
Also Called: New Paradise
11223 Rush St Ste I, South El Monte (91733-3566)
PHONE...................626 350-8848
Harry Pan, *President*
▲ EMP: 10

P R O D U C T S & S V C S

SQ FT: 5,000
SALES (est): 1.3MM **Privately Held**
SIC: 3089 Tableware, plastic; novelties, plastic

(P-9732)
CRAFTECH EDM CORPORATION
Also Called: Crafttech
2941 E La Jolla St, Anaheim (92806-1306)
PHONE................................714 630-8117
John Butler, *President*
Peggy Thomas, *CFO*
Alfredo Bonetto, *Senior VP*
John Ayers, *Vice Pres*
Douglas Barker, *Vice Pres*
▲ EMP: 220
SQ FT: 35,000
SALES (est): 69.4MM **Privately Held**
WEB: www.craftechcorp.com
SIC: 3089 3559 Injection molding of plastics; plastics working machinery

(P-9733)
CREATIVE COMPUTER PRODUCTS
Also Called: Creative Plastic Printing
6369 Nncy Rdge Dr Ste 200, San Diego (92121)
PHONE................................858 458-1965
EMP: 15
SQ FT: 3,000
SALES (est): 2.1MM **Privately Held**
WEB: www.creativeplastic.com
SIC: 3089 3577

(P-9734)
CRESCENT PLASTICS INC
Also Called: Servtech Plastics
1711 S California Ave, Monrovia (91016-4623)
PHONE................................626 359-9248
Maqbool Zafar, *CEO*
Ralph Melton, *President*
▲ EMP: 12 EST: 2001
SALES (est): 2.2MM **Privately Held**
WEB: www.servtechplastics.com
SIC: 3089 Injection molding of plastics

(P-9735)
CROWN MFG CO INC
37625 Sycamore St, Newark (94560-3946)
PHONE................................510 742-8800
Aziz Shariat, *CEO*
Hector Pedraza, *Engineer*
Diosa Tenorio, *Manager*
▲ EMP: 40
SQ FT: 60,000
SALES (est): 7.4MM **Privately Held**
WEB: www.crown-plastics.com
SIC: 3089 Injection molding of plastics

(P-9736)
CURBELL PLASTICS INC
1670 Brandywine Ave Ste B, Chula Vista (91911-6071)
PHONE................................619 575-4633
Drew Singer, *Manager*
Rodriquez Monica, *Sales Staff*
EMP: 20
SALES (corp-wide): 216.5MM **Privately Held**
SIC: 3089 Doors, folding: plastic or plastic coated fabric
HQ: Curbell Plastics, Inc.
7 Cobham Dr
Orchard Park NY 14127

(P-9737)
CUSTOM ENGINEERING PLASTICS LP
8558 Miramar Pl, San Diego (92121-2530)
PHONE................................858 452-0961
Sylvia Hammond, *Managing Prtnr*
Jack Hammond, *Partner*
Brock Sinkiewicz, *Opers Mgr*
Michael Getgen, *QC Mgr*
▲ EMP: 18
SQ FT: 11,400
SALES (est): 3.1MM **Privately Held**
WEB: www.cepi.com
SIC: 3089 3544 Injection molding of plastics; forms (molds), for foundry & plastics working machinery

(P-9738)
CUSTOM PLASTIC FORM INC
6868 Farmdale Ave, North Hollywood (91605-6208)
PHONE................................818 765-2229
Artin Hovik Voskanyan, *CEO*
EMP: 10
SALES (est): 1.2MM **Privately Held**
SIC: 3089 Plastic processing

(P-9739)
CUSTOM PLASTICS LLC (PA)
1305 Brooks St, Ontario (91762-3612)
PHONE................................909 984-0200
Ammar Alshash, *Mng Member*
Linn W Derickson, *Principal*
Mary Sue Derickson, *Principal*
▲ EMP: 12
SALES (est): 3MM **Privately Held**
WEB: www.spinwelding.com
SIC: 3089 5812 Injection molding of plastics; eating places

(P-9740)
CYPRESS MANUFACTURING LLC
Also Called: Hitech Plastics and Molds
25620 Rye Canyon Rd Ste B, Valencia (91355-1140)
PHONE................................818 477-2777
Robert Loranger, *Mng Member*
Christine Loranger, *Administration*
Jun Lee, *QC Mgr*
Arian Dart,
◆ EMP: 15
SQ FT: 20,000
SALES (est): 2MM **Privately Held**
SIC: 3089 Injection molding of plastics

(P-9741)
CYTYDEL PLASTICS INC
17813 S Main St Ste 117, Gardena (90248-3542)
PHONE................................310 523-2884
Aeran Lee, *President*
Chang Lee, *Treasurer*
▲ EMP: 20
SQ FT: 10,200
SALES (est): 2.5MM **Privately Held**
WEB: www.cytydel.net
SIC: 3089 Plastic processing

(P-9742)
D & D PLASTICS INCORPORATED
Also Called: Rti
1632 W 139th St, Gardena (90249-3003)
PHONE................................310 515-1934
Donald A Dettman, *President*
David Dettman, *Treasurer*
EMP: 15
SQ FT: 15,000
SALES (est): 2.5MM **Privately Held**
WEB: www.d-dplastics.com
SIC: 3089 Injection molding of plastics

(P-9743)
D & T FIBERGLASS INC
8900 Osage Ave, Sacramento (95828-1124)
P.O. Box 293330 (95829-3330)
PHONE................................916 383-9012
Donald R Stommel, *CEO*
EMP: 37
SQ FT: 35,000
SALES (est): 8.9MM **Privately Held**
WEB: www.dtfiberglass.com
SIC: 3089 Plastic & fiberglass tanks

(P-9744)
D W MACK CO INC
900 W 8th St, Azusa (91702-2216)
P.O. Box 1247, Monrovia (91017-1247)
PHONE................................626 969-1817
Danny J Mack, *President*
Joseph Demarco, *Vice Pres*
Dennis S Mack, *Admin Sec*
▲ EMP: 40 EST: 1979
SALES (est): 7.6MM **Privately Held**
WEB: www.dwmack.com
SIC: 3089 Kits, plastic

(P-9745)
D&W FINE PACK LLC
Also Called: C&M Fine Pack
4162 Georgia Blvd, San Bernardino (92407-1852)
PHONE................................206 767-7777
EMP: 160
SALES (corp-wide): 614.5MM **Privately Held**
SIC: 3089 Plastic containers, except foam
HQ: D&W Fine Pack Llc
777 Mark St
Wood Dale IL 60191
-

(P-9746)
DCO ENVIRONMENTAL & RECYCL LLC
300 Montgomery St Ste 421, San Francisco (94104-1903)
PHONE................................573 204-3844
Claudine Osipow, *Mng Member*
◆ EMP: 16
SALES (est): 3.8MM **Privately Held**
SIC: 3089 Plastic processing
PA: Dco International Trading Inc.
300 Montgomery St Ste 421
San Francisco CA 94104

(P-9747)
DECO PLASTICS INC
9530 Pathway St Ste 105, Santee (92071-4171)
PHONE................................619 448-6843
William H Peck, *President*
Robert Peck, *Vice Pres*
EMP: 19
SALES (est): 1MM **Privately Held**
SIC: 3089 Plastic processing

(P-9748)
DELAMO MANUFACTURING INC
7171 Telegraph Rd, Montebello (90640-6511)
PHONE................................323 936-3566
Fred Morad, *CEO*
EMP: 80 EST: 2008
SQ FT: 120,000
SALES (est): 2MM **Privately Held**
SIC: 3089 Plastic kitchenware, tableware & houseware

(P-9749)
DELFIN DESIGN & MFG INC
15672 Producer Ln, Huntington Beach (92649-1310)
PHONE................................949 888-4644
John M Rief, *President*
Rita Williams, *Corp Secy*
Paul Iverson, *Exec VP*
▲ EMP: 28
SALES (est): 5.9MM **Privately Held**
SIC: 3089 3083 Thermoformed finished plastic products; plastic finished products, laminated

(P-9750)
DELPHON INDUSTRIES LLC (PA)
Also Called: Touchmark
31398 Huntwood Ave, Hayward (94544-7818)
PHONE................................510 576-2220
Jeanne Beacham, *Mng Member*
Diana Morgan, *CFO*
Anthony Lee, *Senior Engr*
Don Moody, *Human Res Dir*
James Garner, *Director*
▲ EMP: 123
SQ FT: 40,000
SALES (est): 25.8MM **Privately Held**
WEB: www.delphon.com
SIC: 3089 Plastic processing

(P-9751)
DELTA YIMIN TECHNOLOGIES INC
Also Called: Delta Pacific Products
33170 Central Ave, Union City (94587-2042)
PHONE................................510 487-4411
Fred Betke, *President*
Richard Ellis, *Vice Pres*
◆ EMP: 48

SQ FT: 34,000
SALES (est): 16.1MM
SALES (corp-wide): 91.5MM **Privately Held**
WEB: www.deltapacificinc.com
SIC: 3089 Injection molded finished plastic products; injection molding of plastics
PA: Westfall Technik, Inc.
7455 Arroyo Crossing Pkwy
Las Vegas NV
480 629-4836

(P-9752)
DEMTECH SERVICES INC
6414 Capitol Ave, Diamond Springs (95619-9393)
PHONE................................530 621-3200
Dave McLaury, *President*
Thomas Metzger, *General Mgr*
Tylene Ebbe, *Executive Asst*
Jeff Loyd, *Purch Agent*
Gus Fauci, *Prdtn Mgr*
▲ EMP: 24
SQ FT: 8,000
SALES (est): 5MM **Privately Held**
WEB: www.demtech.com
SIC: 3089 Thermoformed finished plastic products

(P-9753)
DENALI WATER SOLUTIONS LLC
3031 Franklin Ave, Riverside (92507-3337)
PHONE................................714 799-0801
EMP: 17
SALES (corp-wide): 55.1MM **Privately Held**
SIC: 3089 Plastic & fiberglass tanks
PA: Denali Water Solutions Llc
3308 Bernice Ave
Russellville AR 72802
479 498-0500

(P-9754)
DESIGN OCTAVES
2701 Research Park Dr, Soquel (95073-2090)
PHONE................................831 464-8500
Norman Weiss, *CEO*
Dan McCabe, *Vice Pres*
Nancie Newby, *Office Admin*
Julie Hottel, *Technology*
Eliseo Valencia, *Technology*
EMP: 30 EST: 1979
SQ FT: 21,000
SALES (est): 4.8MM **Privately Held**
WEB: www.designoctaves.com
SIC: 3089 3469 Cases, plastic; metal stampings

(P-9755)
DESIGN WEST TECHNOLOGIES INC
2701 Dow Ave, Tustin (92780-7209)
PHONE................................714 731-0201
Ryan Hur, *President*
Kristofer Nicolas, *Project Engr*
Bob Olson, *Engineer*
Kirk Hayward, *Controller*
Chris Burt, *Director*
▲ EMP: 65
SQ FT: 60,000
SALES (est): 17MM **Privately Held**
SIC: 3089 8711 Injection molded finished plastic products; electrical or electronic engineering

(P-9756)
DESIGNER SASH AND DOOR SYS INC
Also Called: Designer Fashion Door
45899 Via Tornado, Temecula (92590-3359)
PHONE................................951 657-4179
Ross Eberhart, *President*
Kenneth McBride, *Treasurer*
EMP: 91
SQ FT: 20,000
SALES (est): 15.1MM **Privately Held**
SIC: 3089 2431 5211 Windows, plastic; window frames & sash, plastic; doors, folding: plastic or plastic coated fabric; doors, wood; door & window products

(P-9757)
DIMENSIONAL PLASTICS CORP
6565 Crescent Park W # 111, Playa Vista
(90094-2284)
PHONE..............................305 691-5961
Sir Ronald Barnette, *President*
Allen Barnette, *Vice Pres*
◆ **EMP:** 20
SQ FT: 30,000
SALES (est): 3.3MM **Privately Held**
WEB: www.krinklglas.com
SIC: 3089 Molding primary plastic; casting
of plastic; laminating of plastic; synthetic
resin finished products

(P-9758)
**DISPENSING DYNAMICS INTL
INC (PA)**
Also Called: Perrin Craft
1020 Bixby Dr, City of Industry
(91745-1703)
PHONE..............................626 961-3691
Dean Debuhr, *CEO*
Art Brake, *President*
Larry Maccormack, *President*
Chris Sigmon, *President*
Scott Strachan, *COO*
◆ **EMP:** 99
SQ FT: 57,000
SALES (est): 51.9MM **Privately Held**
WEB: www.perrin.com
SIC: 3089 3993 Injection molding of plas-
tics; signs & advertising specialties

(P-9759)
DISTINCTIVE PLASTICS INC
1385 Decision St, Vista (92081-8523)
PHONE..............................760 599-9100
Timothy Curnutt, *President*
Violeta Curnutt, *Vice Pres*
Tina Corson, *Materials Mgr*
▲ **EMP:** 62
SQ FT: 44,500
SALES (est): 13.6MM **Privately Held**
WEB: www.distinctiveplastics.com
SIC: 3089 3312 Injection molding of plas-
tics; tool & die steel

(P-9760)
DIVERSE OPTICS INC
10310 Regis Ct, Rancho Cucamonga
(91730-3055)
PHONE..............................909 593-9330
Erik Fleming, *President*
Letty Dela Cruz, *Sales Engr*
Letty Trevino, *Sales Engr*
Deborah De Melo, *Director*
EMP: 20 **EST:** 1987
SQ FT: 20,000
SALES (est): 4.6MM **Privately Held**
WEB: www.diverseoptics.com
SIC: 3089 3827 Injection molding of plas-
tics; lenses, optical: all types except oph-
thalmic

(P-9761)
DIVERSIFIED PLASTICS INC
Also Called: Pacific Plas Injection Molding
1333 Keystone Way, Vista (92081-8311)
PHONE..............................760 598-5333
Rob Gilman, *General Mgr*
EMP: 30
SALES (corp-wide): 16.7MM **Privately
Held**
SIC: 3089 3544 Injection molding of plas-
tics; industrial molds
PA: Diversified Plastics, Inc.
8617 Xylon Ct
Minneapolis MN 55445
763 424-2525

(P-9762)
DODGE - WASMUND MFG INC
4510 Manning Rd, Pico Rivera
(90660-2191)
PHONE..............................562 692-8104
Gloria Schulz, *President*
Dennis Schulz, *Vice Pres*
▲ **EMP:** 12
SQ FT: 30,000
SALES (est): 1.9MM **Privately Held**
WEB: www.ladylynn.com
SIC: 3089 Plastic hardware & building
products; injection molding of plastics

(P-9763)
DOMINO PLASTICS MFG INC
601 Gateway Ct, Bakersfield (93307-6827)
PHONE..............................661 396-3744
W Thomas Bathe III, *CEO*
Neil Conway, *President*
Mike Zavala, *Sales Staff*
EMP: 21
SQ FT: 16,000
SALES (est): 5.8MM **Privately Held**
WEB: www.dominoplastics.com
SIC: 3089 Billfold inserts, plastic

(P-9764)
DON CONIBEAR
541 Industrial Way Ste 2, Fallbrook
(92028-2257)
PHONE..............................760 728-4590
Don Conibear, *Owner*
EMP: 10
SALES (est): 1MM **Privately Held**
SIC: 3089 Plastic processing

(P-9765)
DOREL JUVENILE GROUP INC
9950 Calabash Ave, Fontana (92335-5210)
PHONE..............................909 428-0295
Carrisa John, *Principal*
EMP: 111
SALES (corp-wide): 2.6B **Privately Held**
WEB: www.coscoproducts.com
SIC: 3089 Plastic kitchenware, tableware &
houseware
HQ: Dorel Juvenile Group, Inc.
2525 State St
Columbus IN 47201
800 457-5276

(P-9766)
DOREL JUVENILE GROUP INC
Also Called: Cosco Home & Office Products
5400 Shea Center Dr, Ontario
(91761-7892)
PHONE..............................909 390-5705
Rick Mc Cook, *Manager*
EMP: 111
SALES (corp-wide): 2.6B **Privately Held**
WEB: www.coscoproducts.com
SIC: 3089 Plastic kitchenware, tableware &
houseware
HQ: Dorel Juvenile Group, Inc.
2525 State St
Columbus IN 47201
800 457-5276

(P-9767)
**DURA PLASTIC PRODUCTS INC
(PA)**
533 E Third St, Beaumont (92223-2715)
P.O. Box 2097 (92223-0997)
PHONE..............................951 845-3161
Kevin L Rost, *CEO*
Ursula Rost, *Shareholder*
Willi K Rost, *Shareholder*
Hardy Rost, *President*
Monica Rost, *CFO*
◆ **EMP:** 100
SQ FT: 150,000
SALES (est): 33.8MM **Privately Held**
WEB: www.duraplastics.com
SIC: 3089 Fittings for pipe, plastic

(P-9768)
**EAGLE MOLD TECHNOLOGIES
INC**
12330 Crosthwaite Cir, Poway
(92064-6823)
PHONE..............................858 530-0888
Ulrich Bark, *President*
Rosemary Bark, *Treasurer*
Dave Bark, *Vice Pres*
David Bark, *Vice Pres*
Gregory Bark, *Vice Pres*
EMP: 20
SQ FT: 10,500
SALES (est): 4.3MM **Privately Held**
WEB: www.eaglemold.com
SIC: 3089 3544 Injection molded finished
plastic products; injection molding of plas-
tics; special dies, tools, jigs & fixtures

(P-9769)
**EAGLE PRODUCTS - PLAST
INDUST**
10811 Fremont Ave, Ontario (91762-3912)
PHONE..............................909 465-1548
Henry Ngo, *President*
Thu Nguyen, *Corp Secy*
EMP: 20
SQ FT: 6,100
SALES (est): 2.2MM **Privately Held**
WEB: www.eagleproducts-inc.com
SIC: 3089 Plastic processing

(P-9770)
EAST LA LAMINATION INC
616 N Hazard Ave, Los Angeles
(90063-3338)
PHONE..............................323 881-9838
Videl Napoles, *President*
EMP: 10 **EST:** 2001
SALES (est): 100K **Privately Held**
SIC: 3089 Laminating of plastic

(P-9771)
ECOPLAST CORPORATION INC
13414 Slover Ave, Fontana (92337-6977)
PHONE..............................909 346-0450
Jose Perez, *President*
EMP: 59
SQ FT: 40,000
SALES (est): 13.2MM **Privately Held**
WEB: www.primelinepolymers.com
SIC: 3089 Plastic containers, except foam

(P-9772)
EDCO PLASTICS INC
2110 E Winston Rd, Anaheim
(92806-5534)
PHONE..............................714 772-1986
Edward A Contreras, *President*
Maria Contreras, *Vice Pres*
▲ **EMP:** 49
SQ FT: 25,000
SALES (est): 9.8MM **Privately Held**
SIC: 3089 Molding primary plastic; injec-
tion molding of plastics

(P-9773)
EDGE PLASTICS INC (PA)
Also Called: O D I
3016 Kansas Ave Bldg 3, Riverside
(92507-3442)
PHONE..............................951 786-4750
Earl David Grimes, *President*
Holly Grimes, *Admin Sec*
Kathy Mascorro, *Accountant*
Ralph Vasquez, *Controller*
▲ **EMP:** 35
SQ FT: 23,000
SALES (est): 6.1MM **Privately Held**
WEB: www.edgeplastics.com
SIC: 3089 5199 5091 Injection molding of
plastics; advertising specialties; bicycle
parts & accessories

(P-9774)
EDRIS PLASTICS MFG INC
4560 Pacific Blvd, Vernon (90058-2208)
PHONE..............................323 581-7000
Hovanes Hovik Issagholian, *CEO*
▲ **EMP:** 26
SQ FT: 27,000
SALES (est): 5.1MM **Privately Held**
WEB: www.edrisplastics.com
SIC: 3089 Injection molding of plastics

(P-9775)
**EE PAULEY PLASTIC
EXTRUSION**
17177 Navajo Rd, Apple Valley
(92307-1046)
PHONE..............................760 240-3737
EMP: 12 **EST:** 2010
SALES (est): 1.8MM **Privately Held**
SIC: 3089 Extruded finished plastic prod-
ucts

(P-9776)
EEP HOLDINGS LLC (PA)
4626 Eucalyptus Ave, Chino (91710-9215)
PHONE..............................909 597-7861
Earl E Payton, *CEO*
EMP: 12

SALES (est): 164.5MM **Privately Held**
SIC: 3089 3544 Molding primary plastic;
special dies, tools, jigs & fixtures

(P-9777)
ELEPHANT FLOWERS LLC
3904 Gibraltar Ave Apt 8, Los Angeles
(90008-1245)
PHONE..............................213 327-6323
Dwon McCarthy,
EMP: 66
SALES (est): 2MM **Privately Held**
SIC: 3089 Flower pots, plastic

(P-9778)
EMPIRE WEST INC
Also Called: Empire West Plastics
9270 Graton Rd, Graton (95444-9375)
P.O. Box 511 (95444-0511)
PHONE..............................707 823-1190
Richard F Yonash, *CEO*
Donna Yonash, *Vice Pres*
Rachel Larman, *Office Admin*
Ritch Foster, *Technology*
Jerome Johnson, *Finance*
EMP: 28
SQ FT: 30,000
SALES (est): 4.9MM **Privately Held**
WEB: www.empirewest.com
SIC: 3089 Thermoformed finished plastic
products

(P-9779)
ENDUREQUEST CORPORATION
1813 Thunderbolt Dr, Porterville
(93257-9300)
PHONE..............................559 783-9220
Kenneth Dewing, *President*
Russell Sarno, *Vice Pres*
▲ **EMP:** 25
SQ FT: 10,000
SALES (est): 4.4MM **Privately Held**
SIC: 3089 Plastic hardware & building
products; injection molding of plastics

(P-9780)
**ENGINEERING MODEL
ASSOCIATES (PA)**
Also Called: Ema
1020 Wallace Way, City of Industry
(91748-1027)
PHONE..............................626 912-7011
John Jay Wanderman, *President*
Leon Katz, *Admin Sec*
EMP: 25
SQ FT: 28,000
SALES (est): 11.8MM **Privately Held**
SIC: 3089 5162 Plastic processing; plas-
tics products

(P-9781)
**ENVIRONMENTAL SAMPLING
SUP INC**
640 143rd Ave, San Leandro (94578-3304)
PHONE..............................510 465-4988
William Levey, *Branch Mgr*
EMP: 12
SALES (corp-wide): 866.9K **Privately
Held**
SIC: 3089 3231 Plastic containers, except
foam; products of purchased glass
HQ: Environmental Sampling Supply, Inc.
4101 Shuffel St Nw
North Canton OH 44720
330 497-9396

(P-9782)
EW TRADING INC
Also Called: Ew Packaging
17510 S Broadway Unit B, Gardena
(90248-3550)
PHONE..............................310 515-9898
Robert Lonas, *CEO*
Yenshan Lou, *CFO*
▲ **EMP:** 12
SQ FT: 15,000
SALES (est): 2.6MM **Privately Held**
WEB: www.ewpackaging.com
SIC: 3089 Plastic containers, except foam

(P-9783)
**EXPRESS SYSTEMS & ENGRG
INC**
41357 Date St, Murrieta (92562-7030)
PHONE..............................951 461-1500

PRODUCTS & SVCS

Mike Arndt, *President*
▲ EMP: 25
SQ FT: 14,000
SALES (est): 2.5MM **Privately Held**
WEB: www.exp-sys.com
SIC: 3089 Injection molding of plastics

(P-9784)
EXTRUMED INC (DH)
Also Called: Vesta
547 Trm Cir, Corona (92879-1768)
PHONE..............................951 547-7400
Phil Estes, *President*
Eric R Schnur, *CEO*
Chris Guglielmi, *CFO*
EMP: 47
SQ FT: 53,000
SALES (est): 18MM
SALES (corp-wide): 225.3B **Publicly Held**
WEB: www.extrumed.com
SIC: 3089 Injection molding of plastics
HQ: Vesta Intermediate Funding, Inc.
　　9900 S 57th St
　　Franklin WI 53132
　　414 423-0550

(P-9785)
FABRICATED EXTRUSION CO LLC (PA)
2331 Hoover Ave, Modesto (95354-3907)
PHONE..............................209 529-9200
Jeffrey S Aichele, *Mng Member*
Allison Aichele, *CFO*
Tom Peot, *Vice Pres*
Jeffrey Aichele, *CTO*
Brian Indelicato, *QA Dir*
EMP: 43
SQ FT: 36,000
SALES (est): 10.5MM **Privately Held**
WEB: www.fabexco.com
SIC: 3089 Extruded finished plastic products

(P-9786)
FABRICMATE SYSTEMS INC
2781 Golf Course Dr A, Ventura (93003-7941)
PHONE..............................805 642-7470
Craig S Lanuza, *President*
Trisha Nieves, *Sales Staff*
▲ EMP: 18 EST: 1995
SQ FT: 16,116
SALES (est): 4.3MM **Privately Held**
WEB: www.fabricmate.com
SIC: 3089 Extruded finished plastic products

(P-9787)
FISCHER MOLD INCORPORATED
393 Meyer Cir, Corona (92879-1078)
PHONE..............................951 279-1140
Robert Fischer, *President*
Eleanor Fischer, *Admin Sec*
▲ EMP: 60
SQ FT: 32,000
SALES (est): 14.1MM **Privately Held**
WEB: www.fischermoldinc.com
SIC: 3089 Injection molding of plastics; special dies, tools, jigs & fixtures

(P-9788)
FIT-LINE INC
Also Called: Flarelink
2901 Tech Ctr, Santa Ana (92705-5657)
PHONE..............................714 549-9091
Ronni Levinson, *CEO*
Frank Hayesc, *Principal*
David Van Hooton, *Principal*
George Alvarado, *Opers Mgr*
▼ EMP: 20
SQ FT: 4,500
SALES (est): 4.1MM **Privately Held**
WEB: www.fit-line.net
SIC: 3089 Fittings for pipe, plastic

(P-9789)
FM PLASTICS
Also Called: FM Industries
9950 Marconi Dr Ste 106, San Diego (92154-7272)
P.O. Box 431498, San Ysidro (92143-1498)
PHONE..............................619 661-5929
Frank Real, *President*
EMP: 38

SQ FT: 5,000
SALES (est): 3.9MM **Privately Held**
SIC: 3089 Trays, plastic

(P-9790)
FOAM FABRICATORS INC
1810 S Santa Fe Ave, Compton (90221-5319)
PHONE..............................310 537-5760
Ted I Florkiewicz, *Opers-Prdtn-Mfg*
EMP: 17 **Publicly Held**
WEB: www.foamfabricators.com
SIC: 3089 3086 Molding primary plastic; plastics foam products
HQ: Foam Fabricators, Inc.
　　8722 E San Alberto # 200
　　Scottsdale AZ 85258
　　480 607-7330

(P-9791)
FOAM INJECTION PLASTICS INC
2548 Grant Ave, San Lorenzo (94580-1810)
PHONE..............................510 317-0218
John Zolkos, *President*
EMP: 11
SALES (est): 1.2MM **Privately Held**
SIC: 3089 Injection molding of plastics

(P-9792)
FORMULA PLASTICS INC
451 Tecate Rd Ste 2b, Tecate (91980)
PHONE..............................866 307-1362
Alexander Mora, *CEO*
Elias Mora, *President*
Joe Mora, *Vice Pres*
Monica Mora, *Vice Pres*
▲ EMP: 500
SQ FT: 20,000
SALES (est): 42.8MM **Privately Held**
WEB: www.formulaplastics.com
SIC: 3089 Injection molding of plastics

(P-9793)
FORTUNE BRANDS WINDOWS INC
Also Called: Simonton Windows
2019 E Monte Vista Ave, Vacaville (95688-3100)
PHONE..............................707 446-7600
Tom Riseili, *General Mgr*
EMP: 101
SALES (corp-wide): 2B **Publicly Held**
WEB: www.simonton.com
SIC: 3089 3442 Window frames & sash, plastic; sash, door or window: metal
HQ: Fortune Brands Windows, Inc
　　3948 Townsfair Way # 200
　　Columbus OH 43219
　　614 532-3500

(P-9794)
FRESCO PLASTICS INC
5680 Carmel Valley Rd, Carmel (93923-9506)
PHONE..............................831 625-9877
Jonathan C Drake,
EMP: 25
SALES (est): 1.9MM **Privately Held**
SIC: 3089 Plastic processing

(P-9795)
FRESNO PRECISION PLASTICS INC (PA)
998 N Temperance Ave, Clovis (93611-8606)
PHONE..............................559 323-9595
Henry Mata, *President*
John Flores III, *Vice Pres*
David Freriks, *Vice Pres*
Tina Carr, *Sales Associate*
EMP: 10
SQ FT: 20,000
SALES (est): 12.3MM **Privately Held**
WEB: www.precisionplastics.ws
SIC: 3089 5162 3993 2821 Thermoformed finished plastic products; plastics sheets & rods; signs & advertising specialties; plastics materials & resins; automotive & apparel trimmings

(P-9796)
FRESNO PRECISION PLASTICS INC
8456 Carbide Ct, Sacramento (95828-5609)
PHONE..............................916 689-5284
David Frericks, *Manager*
EMP: 15
SALES (est): 1.4MM
SALES (corp-wide): 12.3MM **Privately Held**
WEB: www.precisionplastics.ws
SIC: 3089 Injection molding of plastics
PA: Fresno Precision Plastics, Inc.
　　998 N Temperance Ave
　　Clovis CA 93611
　　559 323-9595

(P-9797)
G & D INDUSTRIES INC
1202 E Edna Pl, Covina (91724-2509)
PHONE..............................626 331-1250
Gary Adkins, *President*
Vicki Horton, *Treasurer*
Gregory L Adkins, *Vice Pres*
Cindy Taylor, *Admin Sec*
Mike Boling, *Prgrmr*
EMP: 12
SQ FT: 4,000
SALES (est): 1.9MM **Privately Held**
WEB: www.gdindustries.com
SIC: 3089 Injection molding of plastics

(P-9798)
G B REMANUFACTURING INC
2040 E Cherry Indus Cir, Long Beach (90805-4410)
PHONE..............................562 272-7333
Michael J Kitching, *President*
F William Kitching, *Chairman*
Patricia Kitching, *Treasurer*
Joe Evert, *Engineer*
Lisa Kitching, *Human Resources*
▲ EMP: 70
SQ FT: 26,400
SALES (est): 13.3MM **Privately Held**
WEB: www.gbreman.com
SIC: 3089 Injection molded finished plastic products

(P-9799)
GADIA POLYTHYLENE SUPPLIES INC
21141 Itasca St, Chatsworth (91311-4928)
PHONE..............................818 775-0096
Willy Gadia, *President*
Zinna Gadia, *President*
EMP: 14
SALES (est): 1.9MM **Privately Held**
SIC: 3089 3086 Plastic containers, except foam; plastics foam products

(P-9800)
GARY MANUFACTURING INC
2626 Southport Way Ste E, National City (91950-8754)
PHONE..............................619 429-4479
Brian Smith, *President*
Helen Smith, *Vice Pres*
Kerri Smith, *Opers Staff*
▲ EMP: 30 EST: 1958
SQ FT: 10,000
SALES (est): 5.8MM **Privately Held**
WEB: www.garymanufacturing.com
SIC: 3089 2392 5162 2673 Plastic containers, except foam; napkins, fabric & nonwoven: made from purchased materials; tablecloths: made from purchased materials; plastics materials & basic shapes; bags: plastic, laminated & coated; textile bags; curtains & draperies

(P-9801)
GEIGER PLASTICS INC
16150 S Maple Ave A, Gardena (90248-2837)
PHONE..............................310 327-9926
Charlotte May, *President*
Vangie Ramirez, *Corp Secy*
Michael Kamau, *Prdtn Mgr*
Kent May, *Manager*
EMP: 20
SQ FT: 10,000

SALES (est): 4.3MM **Privately Held**
WEB: www.geigerplastics.com
SIC: 3089 3559 Injection molding of plastics; plastics working machinery

(P-9802)
GEMINI FILM & BAG INC (PA)
Also Called: Gemini Plastics
3574 Fruitland Ave, Maywood (90270-2008)
P.O. Box 806, Atwood (92811-0806)
PHONE..............................323 582-0901
James Fruth, *President*
Brian Kunisch, *CFO*
EMP: 25
SQ FT: 12,000
SALES (est): 3.5MM **Privately Held**
WEB: www.geminiplastics.com
SIC: 3089 8742 Extruded finished plastic products; manufacturing management consultant

(P-9803)
GEO PLASTICS
2200 E 52nd St, Vernon (90058-3446)
PHONE..............................323 277-8106
Michael Abraham Morris, *CEO*
Justin Hunt, *Vice Pres*
Romeo Maglian, *Maint Spvr*
Rita Adams, *Manager*
▲ EMP: 27
SALES (est): 8.6MM **Privately Held**
WEB: www.geoplastics.com
SIC: 3089 Extruded finished plastic products

(P-9804)
GIBRALTAR PLASTIC PDTS CORP
12885 Foothill Blvd, Sylmar (91342-5317)
PHONE..............................818 365-9318
Harvey J Jacobs, *President*
Hilary Gauthier, *General Mgr*
Adam Libarkin, *General Mgr*
Keith Jacobs, *VP Mfg*
EMP: 25
SQ FT: 30,000
SALES (est): 6.1MM **Privately Held**
WEB: www.gibraltarplastic.com
SIC: 3089 Injection molded finished plastic products; cases, plastic

(P-9805)
GILL CORPORATION (PA)
4056 Easy St, El Monte (91731-1054)
PHONE..............................626 443-6094
Stephen E Gill, *President*
Bill Heinze, *CFO*
William Heinze, *CFO*
Gabriel Esparza, *Vice Pres*
Irv Freund, *Vice Pres*
◆ EMP: 236
SQ FT: 390,000
SALES (est): 250.9MM **Privately Held**
WEB: www.mcgillcorp.com
SIC: 3089 3469 3272 2448 Laminating of plastic; panels, building: plastic; honeycombed metal; panels & sections, prefabricated concrete; cargo containers, wood & metal combination; aircraft

(P-9806)
GKM INTERNATIONAL LLC
1725 Burbury Way, San Marcos (92078-0928)
PHONE..............................310 791-7092
EMP: 99
SALES: 500K **Privately Held**
SIC: 3089

(P-9807)
GKN ARSPACE TRNSPRNCY SYSTEMS (DH)
12122 Western Ave, Garden Grove (92841-2915)
PHONE..............................714 893-7531
Hans Buthker, *CEO*
Joakim Anderson, *CEO*
Mike McCann, *CEO*
Will Hoy, *CFO*
Remy Behra, *Senior VP*
▲ EMP: 218
SQ FT: 324,000

SALES (est): 72.8MM
SALES (corp-wide): 11B **Privately Held**
WEB: www.gkntransparencysystems.com
SIC: **3089** 3231 3827 3728 Windows, plastic; windshields, plastic; mirrors, truck & automobile; made from purchased glass; optical instruments & lenses; aircraft parts & equipment; unsupported plastics film & sheet; plastics materials & resins
HQ: Gkn America Corp.
1180 Peachtree St Ne # 2450
Atlanta GA 30309
630 972-9300

(P-9808)
GLOBE PLASTICS INC
13477 12th St, Chino (91710-5206)
PHONE..................................909 464-1520
Nywood Wu, *President*
Clifton Chang, *Vice Pres*
▲ EMP: 20 EST: 1958
SQ FT: 12,000
SALES (est): 4.5MM **Privately Held**
WEB: www.globecomposites.com
SIC: **3089** 3544 Injection molding of plastics; special dies, tools, jigs & fixtures

(P-9809)
GLOVEFIT INTERNATIONAL CORP
4705 N Sonora Ave Ste 108, Fresno (93722-3947)
PHONE..................................559 243-1110
Bill Burgess, *Vice Pres*
▲ EMP: 15
SQ FT: 10,000
SALES (est): 1.7MM **Privately Held**
WEB: www.glovefit.com
SIC: **3089** Work gloves, plastic

(P-9810)
GOLDEN PLASTICS CORPORATION
8465 Baldwin St, Oakland (94621-1924)
PHONE..................................510 569-6465
Ron Pardee, *President*
Stewart Pardee, *President*
Ruth Pardee, *Corp Secy*
Daniel K Pardee, *Vice Pres*
Ronald S Pardee, *Vice Pres*
▲ EMP: 17
SQ FT: 9,500
SALES (est): 2.3MM **Privately Held**
WEB: www.goldenplasticscorp.com
SIC: **3089** Plastic hardware & building products; ducting, plastic; plastic processing

(P-9811)
GOLDMAN GLOBAL GREENFIELD INC
2025 E 48th St, Vernon (90058-2021)
PHONE..................................323 589-3444
Michelle Choi, *President*
▲ EMP: 19
SQ FT: 17,000
SALES (est): 2.2MM **Privately Held**
SIC: **3089** Plastic processing

(P-9812)
GRAHAM PACKAGING COMPANY LP
3300 W Segerstrom Ave, Santa Ana (92704-6403)
PHONE..................................714 979-1835
Paul Wu, *Manager*
Debbi Goyette, *Vice Pres*
Derek Johns, *Prdtn Mgr*
Gerald Fisher, *QC Mgr*
Penny Martin, *Production*
EMP: 60
SQ FT: 127,516
SALES (corp-wide): 14.1MM **Privately Held**
WEB: www.grahampackaging.com
SIC: **3089** Plastic containers, except foam
HQ: Graham Packaging Company, L.P.
700 Indian Springs Dr # 100
Lancaster PA 17601
717 849-8500

(P-9813)
GRAHAM PACKAGING COMPANY LP
9041 Pittsburgh Ave, Rancho Cucamonga (91730-5551)
P.O. Box 1568 (91729-1568)
PHONE..................................909 484-2900
George Plummer, *Manager*
EMP: 35
SALES (corp-wide): 14.1MM **Privately Held**
WEB: www.grahampackaging.com
SIC: **3089** Plastic containers, except foam
HQ: Graham Packaging Company, L.P.
700 Indian Springs Dr # 100
Lancaster PA 17601
717 849-8500

(P-9814)
GRAHAM PACKAGING COMPANY LP
Modesto Plant
513 S Mcclure Rd, Modesto (95357-0520)
PHONE..................................209 578-1112
Kevin Beveris, *Branch Mgr*
Mustafa Al Rawi, *QC Mgr*
Steve Enos, *Manager*
Carmen Fernandez, *Manager*
EMP: 80
SALES (corp-wide): 14.1MM **Privately Held**
WEB: www.grahampackaging.com
SIC: **3089** Plastic containers, except foam
HQ: Graham Packaging Company, L.P.
700 Indian Springs Dr # 100
Lancaster PA 17601
717 849-8500

(P-9815)
GRAND FUSION HOUSEWARES INC (PA)
12 Partridge, Irvine (92604-4519)
PHONE..................................888 614-7263
Hilton Blieden, *President*
EMP: 12
SQ FT: 1,000
SALES: 850.2K **Privately Held**
SIC: **3089** 3083 2869 Kitchenware, plastic; laminated plastic sheets; silicones

(P-9816)
GRAND FUSION HOUSEWARES INC
9375 Customhouse Plz, San Diego (92154-7653)
PHONE..................................909 292-5776
Hilton Blieden, *President*
EMP: 21
SALES (corp-wide): 850.2K **Privately Held**
SIC: **3089** Kitchenware, plastic
PA: Grand Fusion Housewares, Inc
12 Partridge
Irvine CA 92604
888 614-7263

(P-9817)
GRAND PACKAGING PET TECH
513 S Mcclure Rd, Modesto (95357-0520)
PHONE..................................209 578-1112
Steve Enos, *Manager*
EMP: 55
SALES (est): 5.2MM **Privately Held**
SIC: **3089** Plastics products

(P-9818)
GRIFF INDUSTRIES INC
4515 Runway Dr, Lancaster (93536-8530)
PHONE..................................661 728-0111
Michael Griffin, *President*
◆ EMP: 19 EST: 1999
SQ FT: 8,400
SALES (est): 3.8MM **Privately Held**
WEB: www.griffindustries.com
SIC: **3089** Injection molding of plastics

(P-9819)
H N LOCKWOOD INC
880 Sweeney Ave, Redwood City (94063-3024)
PHONE..................................650 366-9557
Daniel A Lockwood, *President*
Raoul Jeanneret, *Office Mgr*
Maggie Moreno, *Office Mgr*
EMP: 30

SQ FT: 1,030
SALES (est): 4.1MM **Privately Held**
WEB: www.hnlockwood.com
SIC: **3089** 2759 Plastic processing; commercial printing

(P-9820)
HAMMERHEAD INDUSTRIES INC
5720 Nicolle St, Ventura (93003-7612)
PHONE..................................805 658-9922
Kenneth S Collin Jr, *President*
John Salentine, *Vice Pres*
Mark Bursek, *Principal*
▲ EMP: 12
SQ FT: 8,000
SALES (est): 2.1MM **Privately Held**
WEB: www.gearkeeper.com
SIC: **3089** Injection molding of plastics

(P-9821)
HENRY PLASTIC MOLDING INC
Also Called: Hpmi
41703 Albrae St, Fremont (94538-3120)
PHONE..................................510 490-7993
Edwin Henry, *CEO*
Edwin L Henry Sr, *Shareholder*
Helen Henry, *Corp Secy*
Linda Henry, *Vice Pres*
Don Kattenhorn, *Engineer*
▲ EMP: 165
SQ FT: 45,000
SALES (est): 32.9MM **Privately Held**
WEB: www.henryplastic.com
SIC: **3089** Injection molding of plastics

(P-9822)
HERMAN ENGINEERING & MFG INC
4501 E Airport Dr Ste B, Ontario (91761-7877)
P.O. Box 418, Oak Harbor OH (43449-0418)
PHONE..................................909 483-1631
Donald B Donisthorpe, *President*
Tiffany Herrmann, *Manager*
▲ EMP: 15
SQ FT: 30,000
SALES (est): 2.4MM **Privately Held**
SIC: **3089** Plastic containers, except foam

(P-9823)
HI-REL PLASTICS & MOLDING CORP
7575 Jurupa Ave, Riverside (92504-1012)
PHONE..................................951 354-0258
Rakesh Bajaria, *CEO*
Dennis Sovalia, *President*
Harry Thummer, *CFO*
Rick Bajria, *Vice Pres*
▲ EMP: 50
SQ FT: 15,000
SALES (est): 8MM **Privately Held**
SIC: **3089** 3549 3599 Injection molded finished plastic products; assembly machines, including robotic; machine shop, jobbing & repair

(P-9824)
HIGH SIERRA PLASTICS
375 Joe Smith Rd, Bishop (93514-8800)
PHONE..................................760 873-5600
Robert W Wilson, *Partner*
EMP: 15
SALES (est): 551.9K **Privately Held**
SIC: **3089** 3544 Blow molded finished plastic products; plastic processing; thermoformed finished plastic products; industrial molds

(P-9825)
HIGHLAND PLASTICS INC
Also Called: Hi-Plas
3650 Dulles Dr, Jurupa Valley (91752-3260)
PHONE..................................951 360-9587
James L Nelson, *Principal*
William B Warren, *CFO*
Yvette Warren, *Technology*
Viginia Warren, *Human Res Dir*
Barry Adams, *Plant Engr*
◆ EMP: 130 EST: 1974
SQ FT: 150,000

SALES (est): 35.3MM **Privately Held**
WEB: www.hiplas.com
SIC: **3089** Injection molding of plastics

(P-9826)
HONOR PLASTICS & MOLDING INC
3270 Pomona Blvd, Pomona (91768-3282)
PHONE..................................909 594-7487
Dinesh Savalia, *CEO*
Ann Campbell, *CFO*
EMP: 48 EST: 2016
SQ FT: 42,000
SALES: 9MM **Privately Held**
SIC: **3089** Injection molding of plastics

(P-9827)
HOOD MANUFACTURING INC
Also Called: Thermobile
2621 S Birch St, Santa Ana (92707-3410)
PHONE..................................714 979-7681
Michael Hood, *President*
Patrica Hood, *Admin Sec*
Michele Rauschenbach, *CIO*
EMP: 60
SQ FT: 24,000
SALES: 5MM **Privately Held**
WEB: www.goodserver.com
SIC: **3089** 3585 Injection molded finished plastic products; refrigeration & heating equipment

(P-9828)
HOOSIER PLSTIC FABRICATION INC
1152 California Ave, Corona (92881-3324)
P.O. Box 78926 (92877-0164)
PHONE..................................951 272-3070
Robert G Simms, *CEO*
Shannon Sims, *Executive*
Shanna Garcia, *General Mgr*
Willie Abundez, *Info Tech Mgr*
Cesar Mier, *Project Mgr*
EMP: 145
SQ FT: 45,000
SALES (est): 39MM **Privately Held**
WEB: www.hoosierplastic.com
SIC: **3089** Plastic processing

(P-9829)
HOPE PLASTIC CO INC
5353 Strohm Ave, North Hollywood (91601-3526)
PHONE..................................818 769-5560
Steven Borden, *President*
Bill Borden, *Treasurer*
Hope Borden, *Admin Sec*
▲ EMP: 20 EST: 1964
SQ FT: 17,000
SALES (est): 3.9MM **Privately Held**
SIC: **3089** Injection molding of plastics

(P-9830)
HOUSEWARES INTERNATIONAL INC
Also Called: American Household Company
1933 S Broadway Ste 867, Los Angeles (90007-4523)
PHONE..................................323 581-3000
Kamyar Solouki, *CEO*
Sean Solouki, *Vice Pres*
Norick Parseh, *Controller*
Sandra Lopez, *Traffic Mgr*
Sandra Cuellar, *Sales Mgr*
◆ EMP: 35
SALES (est): 8.3MM **Privately Held**
WEB: www.housewaresintl.com
SIC: **3089** 5023 Kitchenware, plastic; kitchenware

(P-9831)
HUMANGEAR INC
636 Shrader St, San Francisco (94117-2716)
PHONE..................................415 580-7553
Chris Miksovsky, *President*
▲ EMP: 19
SALES (est): 2.3MM **Privately Held**
SIC: **3089** Tubs, plastic (containers)

(P-9832)
HUSKY INJECTION MOLDING
3505 Cadillac Ave Ste N4, Costa Mesa (92626-1433)
PHONE..................................714 545-8200

Michael Smith, *Manager*
EMP: 14
SQ FT: 6,501
SALES (corp-wide): 1B **Privately Held**
SIC: 3089 Injection molding of plastics
HQ: Husky Injection Molding Systems, Inc.
　　288 North Rd
　　Milton VT 05468
　　802 859-8000

(P-9833)
ICHOR SYSTEMS INC
Also Called: Ajax
34585 7th St, Union City (94587-3673)
PHONE.....................510 476-8000
Tom Rohrs, *Manager*
EMP: 140
SALES (corp-wide): 823.6MM **Publicly Held**
SIC: 3089 3599 3543 Injection molding of plastics; machine shop, jobbing & repair; foundry patternmaking
HQ: Ichor Systems, Inc.
　　3185 Laurelview Ct
　　Fremont CA 94538

(P-9834)
ICORE INTERNATIONAL INC
3780 Flightline Dr, Santa Rosa (95403-1054)
PHONE.....................707 535-2700
Ted Perdue, *CEO*
Arnold Nixon, *CFO*
Mark McGrath, *Vice Pres*
Nancy Huang, *Controller*
Linda Freudenberg, *Human Res Dir*
EMP: 205
SQ FT: 49,000
SALES (est): 68.5MM
SALES (corp-wide): 833.4MM **Privately Held**
WEB: www.icoreintl.com
SIC: 3089 Molding primary plastic
PA: Safran
　　2 Bd Du General Martial Valin
　　Paris 15e Arrondissement 75015
　　140 608-080

(P-9835)
IDEMIA AMERICA CORP
3150 E Ana St, Compton (90221-5607)
PHONE.....................310 884-7900
Eric Daniele, *Director*
Jf Arzel, *Vice Pres*
Antoine Kelman, *Vice Pres*
Didier Labat, *Administration*
Jeremy Berker, *Info Tech Mgr*
EMP: 161
SALES (corp-wide): 4.6B **Privately Held**
WEB: www.oberthurcs.com
SIC: 3089 3083 Identification cards, plastic; plastic finished products, laminated
HQ: Idemia America Corp.
　　296 Concord Rd Ste 300
　　Billerica MA 01821
　　978 215-2400

(P-9836)
IKEGAMI MOLD CORP AMERICA
3570 Camino Del Rio N # 106, San Diego (92108-1747)
PHONE.....................619 858-6855
Masatomo Ikegami, *President*
Yoshiyuki Koga, *Vice Pres*
Jesus Dias, *Production*
▲ **EMP:** 18
SALES (est): 2.6MM **Privately Held**
SIC: 3089 Injection molding of plastics
PA: Ikegami Mold Engineering Co.,Ltd.
　　2-664-8, Toyonodai
　　Kazo STM 349-1

(P-9837)
INCA PLASTICS MOLDING CO INC
948 E Belmont St, Ontario (91761-4549)
PHONE.....................909 923-3235
Howard L Haigh, *President*
▲ **EMP:** 53
SQ FT: 33,000

SALES (est): 10.7MM **Privately Held**
WEB: www.incaplastics.com
SIC: 3089 3714 3544 3443 Injection molding of plastics; motor vehicle parts & accessories; special dies, tools, jigs & fixtures; fabricated plate work (boiler shop)

(P-9838)
INFINITI PLASTIC TECHNOLOGIES
11150 Santa Monica Blvd # 1280, Los Angeles (90025-3380)
PHONE.....................310 618-8288
Saeed Yousefian, *CEO*
Catherine Wu, *Vice Pres*
▲ **EMP:** 19
SQ FT: 100,000
SALES (est): 2.7MM
SALES (corp-wide): 2.7MM **Privately Held**
SIC: 3089 Cases, plastic
PA: Infiniti Media, Inc.
　　11150 Santa Monica Blvd # 1280
　　Los Angeles CA 90025
　　310 618-8288

(P-9839)
INLINE PLASTICS INC
1950 S Baker Ave, Ontario (91761-7755)
PHONE.....................909 923-1033
Kelly Orr, *CEO*
Alfredo Perez, *Vice Pres*
EMP: 25
SQ FT: 21,000
SALES (est): 7MM **Privately Held**
WEB: www.inlineplasticsinc.com
SIC: 3089 Extruded finished plastic products

(P-9840)
INNOVATIVE MOLDING (HQ)
1200 Valley House Dr # 100, Rohnert Park (94928-4902)
PHONE.....................707 238-9250
Grahame W Reid, *CEO*
Lynn Brooks, *CEO*
Alan Williams, *CFO*
Robert T Stenson, *Corp Secy*
Rodger Moody, *Vice Pres*
EMP: 75
SQ FT: 27,000
SALES (est): 20.3MM
SALES (corp-wide): 877.1MM **Publicly Held**
WEB: www.innovativemolding.com
SIC: 3089 Bottle caps, molded plastic; injection molding of plastics
PA: Trimas Corporation
　　38505 Woodward Ave # 200
　　Bloomfield Hills MI 48304
　　248 631-5450

(P-9841)
INNOVTIVE RTTIONAL MOLDING INC
Also Called: IRM
2300 W Pecan Ave, Madera (93637-5056)
PHONE.....................559 673-4764
Daniel Humphries, *President*
Shellie Humphries, *Vice Pres*
EMP: 12
SALES (est): 2.9MM **Privately Held**
SIC: 3089 Molding primary plastic

(P-9842)
INTERNATIONAL LAST MFG CO
Also Called: Salpy
5060 Densmore Ave, Encino (91436-1554)
PHONE.....................818 767-2045
Kevork Kalaidjian, *President*
Salpy Kalaidjian, *Vice Pres*
EMP: 20
SALES: 1MM **Privately Held**
SIC: 3089 3111 3131 5139 Soles, boot or shoe: plastic; sole leather; inner soles, leather; heels, shoe & boot: leather or wood; shoes

(P-9843)
IPARTS INC
Also Called: Ipart Automotive
14975 Hilton Dr, Fontana (92336-2082)
PHONE.....................909 587-6059
Andy Banh, *Office Mgr*
EMP: 10 **EST:** 2013

SALES (est): 688.7K **Privately Held**
SIC: 3089 Automotive parts, plastic

(P-9844)
IPS INDUSTRIES INC
Also Called: Spectrum Bags
12641 166th St, Cerritos (90703-2101)
PHONE.....................562 623-2555
Frank Su, *CEO*
Peter Hii, *CFO*
David Silva, *Exec VP*
Ben Tran, *Exec VP*
Betty Green, *Vice Pres*
◆ **EMP:** 80
SQ FT: 150,000
SALES (est): 30.3MM **Privately Held**
SIC: 3089 3629 Battery cases, plastic or plastic combination; battery chargers, rectifying or nonrotating

(P-9845)
ITOUCHLESS HOUSEWARES PDTS INC
777 Mariners Island Blvd # 125, San Mateo (94404-5008)
PHONE.....................650 578-0578
Fong Chan, *President*
Michael Shek, *Marketing Staff*
▲ **EMP:** 50
SALES (est): 6.8MM **Privately Held**
WEB: www.itouchless.net
SIC: 3089 Plastic kitchenware, tableware & houseware

(P-9846)
J & L CSTM PLSTIC EXTRSONS INC
1532 Santa Anita Ave, South El Monte (91733-3314)
PHONE.....................626 442-0711
Louis Salmon, *President*
Jaime Lizarraga, *Vice Pres*
EMP: 30
SALES (est): 5.1MM **Privately Held**
WEB: www.jlplastic.com
SIC: 3089 Plastic hardware & building products; plastic processing

(P-9847)
J P SPECIALTIES INC
25811 Jefferson Ave, Murrieta (92562-6961)
P.O. Box 1507, Lake Elsinore (92531-1507)
PHONE.....................951 763-7077
David R Poole, *President*
Shannon Poole, *Corp Secy*
Allison Nuno, *Sales Staff*
◆ **EMP:** 10
SQ FT: 6,850
SALES (est): 2MM **Privately Held**
WEB: www.jpspecialties.com
SIC: 3089 3548 5162 5082 Plastic hardware & building products; welding & cutting apparatus & accessories; plastics materials & basic shapes; construction & mining machinery

(P-9848)
JACOBSON PLASTICS INC
1401 Freeman Ave, Long Beach (90804-2518)
PHONE.....................562 433-4911
Jeff Jacobson, *President*
Linda Asher, *Executive*
Anthony Gates, *Director*
▲ **EMP:** 75 **EST:** 1962
SQ FT: 25,000
SALES (est): 13.4MM **Privately Held**
WEB: www.jacobsonplastics.com
SIC: 3089 3544 Injection molding of plastics; special dies, tools, jigs & fixtures

(P-9849)
JAKE STEHELIN ETIENNE
Also Called: Pope
8551 Canoga Ave, Canoga Park (91304-2609)
PHONE.....................818 998-4250
Etienne Stehelin, *Owner*
EMP: 60
SQ FT: 9,700

SALES (est): 5MM **Privately Held**
SIC: 3089 3599 6519 3544 Injection molding of plastics; thermoformed finished plastic products; machine shop, jobbing & repair; real property lessors; special dies, tools, jigs & fixtures

(P-9850)
JARDEN CORPORATION
Also Called: Leslie-Locke
23610 Banning Blvd, Carson (90745-6220)
PHONE.....................800 755-9520
Frank Rodriquez, *Branch Mgr*
EMP: 98
SALES (corp-wide): 8.6B **Publicly Held**
SIC: 3089 2499 3634 Plastic containers, except foam; plastic kitchenware, tableware & houseware; toothpicks, wood; electric housewares & fans; electric household cooking appliances; electric household cooking utensils; personal electrical appliances
HQ: Jarden Llc
　　221 River St
　　Hoboken NJ 07030

(P-9851)
JASON TOOL & ENGINEERING INC
7101 Honold Cir, Garden Grove (92841-1424)
PHONE.....................714 895-5067
Jack Winterswyk, *President*
Curtis H Thompson, *Corp Secy*
▲ **EMP:** 30 **EST:** 1979
SQ FT: 30,000
SALES (est): 5.7MM **Privately Held**
WEB: www.jasontool.com
SIC: 3089 3544 Injection molding of plastics; dies, plastics forming

(P-9852)
JB PLASTICS INC
1921 E Edinger Ave, Santa Ana (92705-4720)
PHONE.....................714 541-8500
Joseph N Chiodo, *President*
Bruce Donoho, *Vice Pres*
EMP: 45
SQ FT: 30,000
SALES (est): 13.5MM **Privately Held**
WEB: www.jb-plastics.com
SIC: 3089 Injection molding of plastics

(P-9853)
JEM-HD CO INC
10030 Via De La Amistad F, San Diego (92154-7299)
PHONE.....................619 710-1443
Jae Man Lee, *CEO*
EMP: 70
SALES (est): 4.5MM **Privately Held**
SIC: 3089 Injection molding of plastics

(P-9854)
JESS HOWARD
Also Called: Plastic Molding Shop, The
2800 Richter Ave, Oroville (95966-5939)
PHONE.....................530 533-3888
Jess Howard, *Owner*
▲ **EMP:** 12
SALES (est): 1.3MM **Privately Held**
SIC: 3089 Injection molding of plastics

(P-9855)
JET PLASTICS (PA)
941 N Eastern Ave, Los Angeles (90063-1307)
PHONE.....................323 268-6706
Lee R Johnson, *President*
Lee Johnson, *President*
Lon Johnson, *Vice Pres*
Lowel Johnson, *Admin Sec*
Linda Huerta, *Manager*
◆ **EMP:** 80 **EST:** 1948
SQ FT: 30,000
SALES (est): 20.1MM **Privately Held**
WEB: www.jetplastics.com
SIC: 3089 Injection molding of plastics

(P-9856)
JG PLASTICS GROUP LLC
335 Fischer Ave, Costa Mesa (92626-4522)
PHONE.....................714 751-4266

▲ = Import ▼=Export
◆ =Import/Export

Dale Balough,
◆ **EMP:** 50
SQ FT: 32,000
SALES (est): 10.4MM **Privately Held**
WEB: www.jgplastics.com
SIC: 3089 3544 Injection molding of plastics; special dies, tools, jigs & fixtures

(P-9857)
JOHN L PERRY STUDIO INC
3000 Paseo Mercado # 102, Oxnard
(93036-7960)
PHONE..............................805 981-9665
John L Perry, *President*
▲ **EMP:** 35
SALES (est): 3.7MM **Privately Held**
WEB: www.johnperry.com
SIC: 3089 Plastic processing

(P-9858)
JOHNSON DOC ENTERPRISES
11933 Vose St, North Hollywood
(91605-5786)
PHONE..............................818 764-1543
Ronald Braverman, *President*
Scott Watkins, *Vice Pres*
Karla Montoya, *Human Res Dir*
James Jackson, *Human Res Mgr*
Wendie Murphy, *Purch Mgr*
◆ **EMP:** 22 **EST:** 1987
SALES (est): 5.3MM **Privately Held**
SIC: 3089 Novelties, plastic

(P-9859)
JS PLASTICS INC (PA)
1283 E Main St Ste 112a, El Cajon
(92021-7211)
P.O. Box 433, Tecate (91980-0433)
PHONE..............................619 672-5972
Jeong Chul Park, *CEO*
Kyon Hee Lee, *President*
▲ **EMP:** 50
SQ FT: 300
SALES (est): 2.7MM **Privately Held**
SIC: 3089 Injection molding of plastics

(P-9860)
JSN INDUSTRIES INC
9700 Jeronimo Rd, Irvine (92618-2019)
PHONE..............................949 458-0050
James H Nagel Jr, *CEO*
Sandra Nagel, *Vice Pres*
EMP: 70
SQ FT: 65,000
SALES (est): 16.8MM **Privately Held**
WEB: www.jsn.com
SIC: 3089 Injection molded finished plastic products

(P-9861)
JUNOPACIFIC INC
2840 Res Pk Dr Ste 160, Soquel (95073)
PHONE..............................831 462-1141
Jeff Wollerman, *Manager*
Somasekhar Krishnamurthy, *Program Mgr*
EMP: 150
SALES (corp-wide): 348.6MM **Privately Held**
SIC: 3089 Injection molding of plastics
HQ: Junopacific, Inc.
1040 Lund Blvd
Anoka MN 55303
763 703-5000

(P-9862)
KEEPCUP LTD
431 Colyton St, Los Angeles (90013-2210)
PHONE..............................310 957-2070
Gregory Lambert, *Administration*
▲ **EMP:** 10
SALES (est): 1.6MM **Privately Held**
SIC: 3089 Tumblers, plastic

(P-9863)
KENNERLEY-SPRATLING INC (PA)
2116 Farallon Dr, San Leandro
(94577-6604)
PHONE..............................510 351-8230
Richard Spratling, *CEO*
Bill Roure, *CFO*
Kevin Ahern, *Vice Pres*
Paul Hoefler, *Principal*
Tom Bridgeman, *General Mgr*
▲ **EMP:** 250
SQ FT: 60,000

SALES (est): 135.2MM **Privately Held**
WEB: www.ksplastic.com
SIC: 3089 3082 Injection molding of plastics; unsupported plastics profile shapes

(P-9864)
KENNERLEY-SPRATLING INC
Also Called: M O S Plastics
2308 Zanker Rd, San Jose (95131-1115)
PHONE..............................408 944-9407
Douglas Cullum, *Principal*
Youhan Khosravi, *Engineer*
Narayan Krishnan, *Senior Buyer*
Yesenia Mendoza, *Warehouse Mgr*
Seyed Tahaei, *Manager*
EMP: 134
SALES (corp-wide): 135.2MM **Privately Held**
WEB: www.ksplastic.com
SIC: 3089 Injection molding of plastics
PA: Kennerley-Spratling, Inc.
2116 Farallon Dr
San Leandro CA 94577
510 351-8230

(P-9865)
KEPNER PLAS FABRICATORS INC
3131 Lomita Blvd, Torrance (90505-5158)
PHONE..............................310 325-3162
Frank Meyers, *CEO*
Meryl Bayley, *Admin Sec*
Jeff Zelin, *Purch Mgr*
Ben Cowart, *Sales Associate*
▲ **EMP:** 26 **EST:** 1960
SQ FT: 50,000
SALES (est): 5.2MM **Privately Held**
WEB: www.kepnerplastics.com
SIC: 3089 Molding primary plastic; plastic processing

(P-9866)
KING PLASTICS INC
840 N Elm St, Orange (92867-7908)
P.O. Box 6229 (92863-6229)
PHONE..............................714 997-7540
Larry E Lathrum, *CEO*
David Marlow, *Maintence Staff*
◆ **EMP:** 96
SQ FT: 100,000
SALES (est): 16MM **Privately Held**
WEB: www.kingplastics.com
SIC: 3089 Plastic kitchenware, tableware & houseware; injection molded finished plastic products

(P-9867)
KIRK API CONTAINERS
2131 Garfield Ave, Commerce
(90040-1805)
PHONE..............................323 278-5400
Arthur Marounian, *Vice Pres*
▼ **EMP:** 34
SALES (est): 8.9MM **Privately Held**
SIC: 3089 Plastic containers, except foam

(P-9868)
KNIGHTSBRIDGE PLASTICS INC
Also Called: K P I
3075 Osgood Ct, Fremont (94539-5612)
PHONE..............................510 249-9722
Jean Nagra, *CEO*
Dave Platt, *President*
Dave Terry, *Treasurer*
Sean Tregear, *Vice Pres*
Saini Kamal, *Mfg Staff*
▲ **EMP:** 58
SQ FT: 19,000
SALES (est): 16.4MM **Privately Held**
WEB: www.kpi.net
SIC: 3089 3423 Injection molding of plastics; hand & edge tools

(P-9869)
KOTONICA INC
3226 N Frederic St, Burbank (91504-1722)
PHONE..............................818 898-0978
Viken Kotoyan, *President*
▲ **EMP:** 15
SQ FT: 10,920
SALES (est): 1.8MM **Privately Held**
SIC: 3089 Injection molded finished plastic products

(P-9870)
KRATOS UNMANNED AERIAL SYSTEMS
Also Called: Composite Engineering, Inc.
5381 Raley Blvd, Sacramento
(95838-1701)
PHONE..............................916 431-7977
Eric M Demarco, *CEO*
Amy Fournier, *President*
Michel M Fournier, *Vice Pres*
Louis Grana, *Vice Pres*
Jeff Herro, *Vice Pres*
▲ **EMP:** 350
SQ FT: 60,000
SALES (est): 74.8MM **Publicly Held**
WEB: www.cei.to
SIC: 3089 Pallets, plastic
PA: Kratos Defense & Security Solutions, Inc.
10680 Treena St Ste 600
San Diego CA 92131

(P-9871)
KURTZ FAMILY CORPORATION
Also Called: Milwright
1450 Industrial Ave, Sebastopol
(95472-4848)
PHONE..............................707 823-1213
Stephen E Kurtz, *President*
EMP: 10
SQ FT: 9,000
SALES (est): 1.7MM **Privately Held**
WEB: www.milwright.net
SIC: 3089 Injection molding of plastics

(P-9872)
L & H MOLD & ENGINEERING INC (PA)
Also Called: L & H Molds
140 Atlantic St, Pomona (91768-3285)
PHONE..............................909 930-1547
Stan Hillary, *CEO*
Steve Hillary, *President*
Brenda Bishop, *Admin Sec*
EMP: 23
SQ FT: 6,000
SALES (est): 3.1MM **Privately Held**
SIC: 3089 Injection molding of plastics

(P-9873)
LABCON NORTH AMERICA
3700 Lakeville Hwy # 200, Petaluma
(94954-7611)
PHONE..............................707 766-2100
James A Happ, *President*
Newman Linda, *COO*
Connie Hansen, *CFO*
Mike Ford, *General Mgr*
Lily Remennik, *Administration*
◆ **EMP:** 200
SQ FT: 120,000
SALES (est): 68.5MM
SALES (corp-wide): 210.3MM **Privately Held**
WEB: www.labcon.com
SIC: 3089 Injection molding of plastics
PA: Helena Laboratories Corporation
1530 Lindbergh Dr
Beaumont TX 77707
409 842-3714

(P-9874)
LANTIC INC
Also Called: Molded Interconnect Industries
27081 Burbank, Foothill Ranch
(92610-2505)
PHONE..............................949 830-9951
Hung Vinh, *President*
Lien Pham, *Shareholder*
Hoi Vinh, *Shareholder*
Huy Vinh, *Shareholder*
Xuan L Cong, *Admin Sec*
▲ **EMP:** 15 **EST:** 1994
SQ FT: 10,700
SALES (est): 1.5MM **Privately Held**
WEB: www.lantic.com
SIC: 3089 Injection molding of plastics

(P-9875)
LEHRER BRLLNPRFKTION WERKS INC (PA)
Also Called: Lbi - USA
20801 Nordhoff St, Chatsworth
(91311-5925)
P.O. Box 3519 (91313-3519)
PHONE..............................818 407-1890
Keith Lehrer, *President*
Julie Walker, *CFO*
Chett Lehrer, *Corp Secy*
Brian Friesz, *CTO*
▲ **EMP:** 23
SQ FT: 38,000
SALES (est): 8.4MM **Privately Held**
SIC: 3089 Cases, plastic

(P-9876)
LEVEL TREK CORP
5670 Schaefer Ave Ste N, Chino
(91710-9021)
P.O. Box 8416, Rowland Heights (91748-0416)
PHONE..............................626 689-4829
Anne Shaw, *Principal*
▲ **EMP:** 11
SALES (est): 1.1MM **Privately Held**
SIC: 3089 Plastics products

(P-9877)
LIDO INDUSTRIES INC
Also Called: Fiberglass Fabricators
456 S Montgomery Way, Orange
(92868-4015)
PHONE..............................714 633-3731
Lisa Burnam, *President*
Cliff E Ryan, *President*
Margaret L Ryan, *Vice Pres*
EMP: 10
SQ FT: 18,000
SALES (est): 1MM **Privately Held**
SIC: 3089 5199 Planters, plastic; pet supplies

(P-9878)
LINER TECHNOLOGIES INC
Also Called: Flexi-Liner
4821 Chino Ave, Chino (91710-5132)
PHONE..............................909 594-6610
Tait Eyre, *President*
Jaye Irsik, *Office Mgr*
Angela Eyre, *Admin Sec*
Saul Jauregui, *Mktg Dir*
Dustin Goff, *Supervisor*
▼ **EMP:** 20
SQ FT: 20,000
SALES (est): 4.3MM **Privately Held**
WEB: www.flexi-liner.com
SIC: 3089 Plastic containers, except foam

(P-9879)
LORITZ & ASSOCIATES INC
Also Called: L & A Plastics
24895 La Palma Ave, Yorba Linda
(92887-5531)
PHONE..............................714 694-0200
Edward F Loritz, *CEO*
Ken Loritz, *President*
Anita Court, *Vice Pres*
◆ **EMP:** 33
SQ FT: 6,000
SALES (est): 8.3MM **Privately Held**
SIC: 3089 Plastic processing

(P-9880)
LORMAC PLASTICS INC (PA)
2225 Meyers Ave, Escondido (92029-1005)
PHONE..............................760 745-9115
Wayne Browning, *CEO*
Ronald Klopf, *President*
Adrienne Klopf, *Vice Pres*
Steve Klopf, *Admin Sec*
Slutsky Paula, *CTO*
▼ **EMP:** 13
SQ FT: 10,000
SALES (est): 1.4MM **Privately Held**
WEB: www.lormac.com
SIC: 3089 Injection molding of plastics

(P-9881)
LUXCO HOLDINGS LLC
6465 Lorena Ave, Jurupa Valley
(91752-2532)
PHONE..............................626 888-7688
Chelsea Morris,
EMP: 10

PRODUCTS & SVCS

SQ FT: 34,650
SALES (est): 591K
SALES (corp-wide): 4.2B **Publicly Held**
SIC: 3089 3429 Hardware, plastic; motor vehicle hardware; aircraft & marine hardware, inc. pulleys & similar items; marine hardware
PA: Leggett & Platt, Incorporated
1 Leggett Rd
Carthage MO 64836
417 358-8131

(P-9882)
M & A PLASTICS INC
11735 Sheldon St, Sun Valley (91352-1580)
PHONE..............................818 768-0479
Guillermo S Morales, *President*
Nancy M Morales, *Treasurer*
EMP: 35
SQ FT: 20,000
SALES (est): 6MM **Privately Held**
WEB: www.maplastics.com
SIC: 3089 Injection molding of plastics

(P-9883)
MACRO PLASTICS INC (DH)
2250 Huntington Dr, Fairfield (94533-9732)
PHONE..............................707 437-1200
Warren Macdonald, *CEO*
Steve Moya, *CFO*
Pamela Whitehead, *Sales Staff*
▲ EMP: 40
SQ FT: 28,000
SALES (est): 39.6MM
SALES (corp-wide): 657.7MM **Privately Held**
SIC: 3089 Injection molding of plastics
HQ: Ipl Inc
140 Rue Commerciale
Saint-Damien-De-Buckland QC G0R 2
418 789-2880

(P-9884)
MAGIC PLASTICS INC
25215 Avenue Stanford, Santa Clarita (91355-3923)
PHONE..............................800 369-0303
John Sarno, *CEO*
Patrick Madormo, *CFO*
Tony Madormo, *Vice Pres*
Nan Sarno, *Admin Sec*
Noe Herrera, *Manager*
▲ EMP: 55
SQ FT: 75,000
SALES (est): 10.4MM **Privately Held**
WEB: www.magicplastics.com
SIC: 3089 Injection molding of plastics

(P-9885)
MANHATTAN COMPONENTS INC
5920 Lakeshore Dr, Cypress (90630-3371)
PHONE..............................714 761-7249
David Hattan, *President*
Dorothy Hattan, *Treasurer*
▲ EMP: 10
SQ FT: 10,987
SALES (est): 1.1MM **Privately Held**
SIC: 3089 Injection molding of plastics

(P-9886)
MASTER PLASTICS INCORPORATED
820 Eubanks Dr Ste I, Vacaville (95688-8837)
PHONE..............................707 451-3168
Ravi Mirchandani, *Principal*
Frank Ortiz, *QC Mgr*
▲ EMP: 25
SQ FT: 35,000
SALES (est): 7.2MM **Privately Held**
SIC: 3089 Injection molding of plastics

(P-9887)
MCNEAL ENTERPRISES INC
2031 Ringwood Ave, San Jose (95131-1703)
PHONE..............................408 922-7290
De Anna McNeal-Mirzadegan, *CEO*
De Anna Mirzadegan, *Vice Pres*
Robert McNeal, *Admin Sec*
EMP: 100 EST: 1976
SQ FT: 62,000

SALES (est): 17.8MM **Privately Held**
WEB: www.mcneal.com
SIC: 3089 3498 3559 Injection molding of plastics; laminating of plastic; thermoformed finished plastic products; closures, plastic; tube fabricating (contract bending & shaping); semiconductor manufacturing machinery

(P-9888)
MDI EAST INC (HQ)
Also Called: Molded Devices
6918 Ed Perkic St, Riverside (92504-1001)
PHONE..............................951 509-6918
Brian P Anderson, *President*
Jason Fairfield, *CFO*
Tobe Allenbrand, *Vice Pres*
EMP: 39 EST: 2009
SALES (est): 9.4MM
SALES (corp-wide): 17.3MM **Privately Held**
SIC: 3089 Molding primary plastic
PA: Molded Devices, Inc.
6918 Ed Perkic St
Riverside CA 92504
480 785-9100

(P-9889)
MEDEGEN LLC (DH)
4501 E Wall St, Ontario (91761-8143)
P.O. Box 515111, Los Angeles (90051-5111)
PHONE..............................909 390-9080
Charles Stroupe, *CEO*
W Mark Dorris,
Paul M Ellis,
Jeffrey S Goble,
Michael E Stanley,
▲ EMP: 50
SQ FT: 3,000
SALES (est): 135.6MM
SALES (corp-wide): 15.9B **Publicly Held**
WEB: www.medegen.com
SIC: 3089 Injection molded finished plastic products

(P-9890)
MEDPLAST GROUP INC
45581 Northport Loop W, Fremont (94538-6462)
PHONE..............................510 657-5800
Linda Amaral, *Branch Mgr*
Gaynell Mays, *Human Res Mgr*
EMP: 225
SALES (corp-wide): 456.1MM **Privately Held**
WEB: www.unitedplasticsgroup.com
SIC: 3089 Injection molded finished plastic products
PA: Medplast Group, Inc.
7865 Northcourt Rd # 100
Houston TX 77040
480 553-6400

(P-9891)
MEDWAY PLASTICS CORPORATION
2250 E Cherry Indus Cir, Long Beach (90805-4414)
PHONE..............................562 630-1175
Thomas Hutchinson Jr, *CEO*
Mary Hutchinson, *CFO*
Gerry Hutchinson, *Vice Pres*
Rick Hutchinson, *Vice Pres*
Sheryl McDaniel, *Vice Pres*
◆ EMP: 196 EST: 1974
SALES (est): 55.5MM **Privately Held**
WEB: www.medwayplastics.com
SIC: 3089 Injection molded finished plastic products; injection molding of plastics

(P-9892)
MEESE INC
Also Called: Meese Obitron Dunn Co
16404 Knott Ave, La Mirada (90638-5760)
PHONE..............................714 739-4005
Toll Free:..............................888 -
Mark McClung, *Manager*
EMP: 30
SQ FT: 54,792
SALES (corp-wide): 119.6MM **Privately Held**
WEB: www.modroto.com
SIC: 3089 Injection molding of plastics

HQ: Meese, Inc.
535 N Midland Ave
Saddle Brook NJ 07663
201 796-4490

(P-9893)
MERLIN-ALLTEC MOLD MAKING INC
15543 Minnesota Ave, Paramount (90723-4118)
PHONE..............................562 529-5050
Ranjiv Goonetilleke, *President*
▲ EMP: 10
SALES (est): 1.6MM **Privately Held**
WEB: www.plasticbus.com
SIC: 3089 3544 Injection molding of plastics; special dies, tools, jigs & fixtures

(P-9894)
MERRICK ENGINEERING INC (PA)
1275 Quarry St, Corona (92879-1707)
PHONE..............................951 737-6040
Abraham M Abdi, *President*
Katina Brown, *CFO*
Katrina Brown, *Officer*
Roy Jorgensen, *Vice Pres*
Shannon Daugherty, *Branch Mgr*
◆ EMP: 250 EST: 1971
SQ FT: 150,000
SALES (est): 88.8MM **Privately Held**
WEB: www.merrickengineering.com
SIC: 3089 Injection molding of plastics

(P-9895)
MICRODYNE PLASTICS INC
1901 E Cooley Dr, Colton (92324-6322)
PHONE..............................909 503-4010
Judy Lopez, *CEO*
Tracey Kimberlin, *Security Dir*
Scott Brown, *Engineer*
Claudia Lopez AP, *Accountant*
Claudia Mendosa, *CPA*
▲ EMP: 100
SQ FT: 33,000
SALES (est): 21.8MM **Privately Held**
WEB: www.microdyneplastics.com
SIC: 3089 Blow molded finished plastic products; injection molding of plastics

(P-9896)
MICROMOLD INC
2100 Iowa Ave, Riverside (92507-2413)
P.O. Box 51118 (92517-2118)
PHONE..............................951 684-7130
Robert Aust, *President*
Ron Peterson, *Vice Pres*
Bill Tischler, *QC Mgr*
Dave Dunn, *Mktg Dir*
EMP: 15
SQ FT: 11,000
SALES (est): 3.8MM **Privately Held**
WEB: www.micromoldinc.com
SIC: 3089 Molding primary plastic; injection molding of plastics

(P-9897)
MILGARD MANUFACTURING INC
Also Called: Milgard Windows
26879 Diaz Rd, Temecula (92590-3470)
PHONE..............................480 763-6000
Cory Hall, *Branch Mgr*
EMP: 14
SALES (corp-wide): 8.3B **Publicly Held**
WEB: www.milgard.com
SIC: 3089 3442 5211 3231 Windows, plastic; sash, door or window: metal; door & window products; products of purchased glass; glass & glazing work; carpentry work
HQ: Milgard Manufacturing Incorporated
1010 54th Ave E
Fife WA 98424
253 922-6030

(P-9898)
MINA PRODUCT DEVELOPMENT INC
3020 Red Hill Ave, Costa Mesa (92626-4524)
PHONE..............................714 966-2150
Babek Khamenian, *President*
Mariel Bobadilla, *Office Mgr*
Jeannine Weber, *Office Admin*
▲ EMP: 10

SQ FT: 12,000
SALES: 1.2MM **Privately Held**
SIC: 3089 Molding primary plastic

(P-9899)
MISSION CUSTOM EXTRUSION INC
10904 Beech Ave, Fontana (92337-7260)
P.O. Box 310302 (92331-0302)
PHONE..............................909 822-1581
Moses Tersaud, *President*
EMP: 42
SQ FT: 23,400
SALES (est): 3.3MM **Privately Held**
SIC: 3089 Awnings, fiberglass & plastic combination

(P-9900)
MISSION PLASTICS INC
1930 S Parco Ave, Ontario (91761-8312)
PHONE..............................909 947-7287
Patrick Dauphinee, *CEO*
Charles Montes, *Corp Secy*
Gabriel Angulo, *Engineer*
Marc Aspiras, *Engineer*
Matthew Dauphinee, *Engineer*
▲ EMP: 120
SQ FT: 20,000
SALES (est): 36.7MM **Privately Held**
WEB: www.missionplastics.com
SIC: 3089 Injection molding of plastics

(P-9901)
MITSUBISHI CHEMICAL ADVNCD MTR
3837 Imperial Way, Stockton (95215-9691)
PHONE..............................209 464-2701
EMP: 22 **Privately Held**
SIC: 3089 Injection molding of plastics
HQ: Mitsubishi Chemical Advanced Materials Inc.
2120 Fairmont Ave
Reading PA 19605
610 320-6600

(P-9902)
MODERN CONCEPTS INC
3121 E Ana St, E Rncho Dmngz (90221-5606)
PHONE..............................310 637-0013
Richard J Warpack, *President*
▲ EMP: 60
SQ FT: 42,000
SALES: 10MM **Privately Held**
SIC: 3089 3087 Coloring & finishing of plastic products; custom compound purchased resins

(P-9903)
MODIFIED PLASTICS INC (PA)
1240 E Glenwood Pl, Santa Ana (92707-3000)
PHONE..............................714 546-4667
Robert Estep, *CEO*
Jocelyn Eubank, *Corp Secy*
Kevin Rodgers, *Sales Mgr*
▲ EMP: 27
SQ FT: 18,000
SALES (est): 11.1MM **Privately Held**
WEB: www.modifiedplastics.com
SIC: 3089 Injection molding of plastics; plastic processing

(P-9904)
MOHAMMAD KHAN
Also Called: M N Enterprises
2606 Imperial Ave, San Diego (92102-4002)
PHONE..............................619 231-1664
Mohammad Khan, *Owner*
EMP: 12
SALES (est): 1MM **Privately Held**
SIC: 3089 5046 Kitchenware, plastic; restaurant equipment & supplies

(P-9905)
MOLDED DEVICES INC (PA)
Also Called: Mdi
6918 Ed Perkic St, Riverside (92504-1001)
PHONE..............................480 785-9100
Brian Anderson, *President*
Jason Fairfield, *CFO*
Chuck Brider, *Vice Pres*
Duane Estes, *Opers Mgr*
▲ EMP: 30 EST: 1963
SQ FT: 26,000

▲ = Import ▼=Export
◆ =Import/Export

SALES (est): 17.3MM **Privately Held**
WEB: www.moldeddevices.com
SIC: 3089 Injection molding of plastics

(P-9906)
MOLDED FIBER GL COMPANIES - W
Also Called: M F G West
9400 Holly Rd, Adelanto (92301-3900)
P.O. Box 370 (92301-0370)
PHONE....................................760 246-4042
Richard Morrison, *CEO*
Dave Denny, *Exec VP*
Jim Sommer, *Vice Pres*
James Enslow, *Engineer*
Jose Cisneros, *Sales Executive*
▲ EMP: 100
SQ FT: 66,000
SALES (est): 21.6MM
SALES (corp-wide): 589.3MM **Privately Held**
WEB: www.moldedfiberglass.com
SIC: 3089 Air mattresses, plastic
PA: Molded Fiber Glass Companies
    2925 Mfg Pl
    Ashtabula OH 44004
    440 997-5851

(P-9907)
MOLDING CORPORATION AMERICA
10349 Norris Ave, Pacoima (91331-2220)
PHONE....................................818 890-7877
Mark Hurley, *CEO*
Sandra Rinder, *Vice Pres*
Dave Crowther, *General Mgr*
▲ EMP: 50
SQ FT: 59,000
SALES (est): 8.3MM **Privately Held**
WEB: www.moldingcorp.com
SIC: 3089 Injection molding of plastics

(P-9908)
MOLDING INTL & ENGRG INC
Also Called: M I E
42136 Avenida Alvarado, Temecula (92590-3400)
PHONE....................................951 296-5010
Bradway B Adams, *CEO*
EMP: 80
SQ FT: 27,000
SALES (est): 8.5MM **Privately Held**
WEB: www.mie.com
SIC: 3089 3544 2821 Injection molded finished plastic products; industrial molds; plastics materials & resins

(P-9909)
MOLDING SOLUTIONS INC (PA)
3225 Regional Pkwy, Santa Rosa (95403-8214)
PHONE....................................707 575-1218
Barbara F Roberts, *President*
EMP: 61
SQ FT: 22,000
SALES (est): 5.5MM **Privately Held**
SIC: 3089 Plastic hardware & building products

(P-9910)
MONCO PRODUCTS INC
7562 Acacia Ave, Garden Grove (92841-4057)
PHONE....................................714 891-2788
Tom Monson, *President*
Jerry Monson, *Vice Pres*
▲ EMP: 50 EST: 1979
SQ FT: 15,000
SALES (est): 6.4MM **Privately Held**
SIC: 3089 Injection molding of plastics

(P-9911)
MORGAN HILL PLASTICS INC
8118 Arroyo Cir, Gilroy (95020-7305)
PHONE....................................408 779-2118
Chet Hudson, *President*
EMP: 20 EST: 1972
SQ FT: 26,000
SALES (est): 2.7MM **Privately Held**
SIC: 3089 Injection molding of plastics; plastic processing

(P-9912)
MORRIS ENTERPRISES INC
16799 Schoenborn St, North Hills (91343-6107)
PHONE....................................818 894-9103
Morris Weinberg, *President*
Benjamin Weinberg, *Vice Pres*
Simon Morrison, *CTO*
EMP: 20 EST: 1959
SQ FT: 5,000
SALES (est): 1.6MM **Privately Held**
SIC: 3089 3676 3674 3577 Blow molded finished plastic products; molding primary plastic; electronic resistors; semiconductors & related devices; computer peripheral equipment

(P-9913)
MOSPLASTICS INC
2308 Zanker Rd, San Jose (95131-1115)
PHONE....................................408 944-9407
Douglas Cullum, *CEO*
Dan Flamen, *Shareholder*
Tom Howard, *Shareholder*
Werner Schultz, *President*
EMP: 134 EST: 1977
SQ FT: 60,000
SALES (est): 17.2MM
SALES (corp-wide): 135.2MM **Privately Held**
WEB: www.mosinc.com
SIC: 3089 Injection molding of plastics
PA: Kennerley-Spratling, Inc.
    2116 Farallon Dr
    San Leandro CA 94577
    510 351-8230

(P-9914)
MOTHER LODE PLAS MOLDING INC
Also Called: Central Plastics and Mfg
1905 N Macarthur Dr # 100, Tracy (95376-2845)
PHONE....................................209 532-5146
Chand Shyani, *President*
Hiren Patel, *Vice Pres*
▲ EMP: 27
SQ FT: 30,000
SALES (est): 3.5MM **Privately Held**
WEB: www.mlplastics.com
SIC: 3089 2671 Injection molding of plastics; thermoplastic coated paper for packaging

(P-9915)
MTECH INC
Also Called: Blackline Manufacturing
1072 Marauder St Ste 210, Chico (95973-9001)
PHONE....................................530 894-5091
Jason Black, *President*
Bernadette Black, *CFO*
Thomas E Black Sr, *Vice Pres*
Tyler Wilson, *Sales Dir*
EMP: 19
SQ FT: 3,000
SALES (est): 1.4MM **Privately Held**
WEB: www.blacklinemfg.com
SIC: 3089 3569 3552 3523 Injection molding of plastics; firefighting apparatus; printing machinery, textile; sprayers & spraying machines, agricultural

(P-9916)
NANKAI ENVIRO-TECH CORPORATION
2320 Paseo De Las America, San Diego (92154-7281)
PHONE....................................619 754-2250
Kan Kaneko, *CEO*
Takayoshi Hirayama, *President*
Hitoshi Nakamura, *Vice Pres*
Minoru Watanaba, *Admin Sec*
▲ EMP: 168
SALES (est): 44.9MM **Privately Held**
SIC: 3089 Molding primary plastic
HQ: Kuroda Electric Co., Ltd.
    5-17-9, Minamioi
    Shinagawa-Ku TKY 140-0

(P-9917)
NATIONAL DIVERSIFIED SALES INC (HQ)
Also Called: Nds
21300 Victory Blvd # 215, Woodland Hills (91367-2525)
P.O. Box 339, Lindsay (93247-0339)
PHONE....................................559 562-9888
Michael Gummeson, *President*
Randall Stott, *CFO*
Cindy Castaneda, *Vice Pres*
John Koehler, *VP Bus Dvlpt*
Consuelo Alarcon, *Admin Asst*
◆ EMP: 200
SQ FT: 5,000
SALES (est): 210.5MM
SALES (corp-wide): 1.2B **Privately Held**
SIC: 3089 Plastic hardware & building products; fittings for pipe, plastic
PA: Norma Group Se
    Edisonstr. 4
    Maintal 63477
    618 140-30

(P-9918)
NATIONAL MEDICAL PRODUCTS INC
57 Parker Unit A, Irvine (92618-1605)
PHONE....................................949 768-1147
Dahyabhai Patel, *President*
Kaushik Patel, *CFO*
Jack Kay, *Research*
Sana Patel, *Sales Mgr*
EMP: 16
SQ FT: 28,630
SALES (est): 2.4MM **Privately Held**
WEB: www.jtip.com
SIC: 3089 Injection molded finished plastic products

(P-9919)
NATIONAL SCIENTIFIC SUP CO INC
260 York Pl, Claremont (91711-4883)
PHONE....................................909 621-4585
EMP: 15
SALES (corp-wide): 5.9MM **Privately Held**
SIC: 3089 Plastic processing
PA: National Scientific Supply Company, Inc.
    240 York Pl
    Claremont CA
    909 621-4585

(P-9920)
NEO PACIFIC HOLDINGS INC
Also Called: Pro-Action Products
14940 Calvert St, Van Nuys (91411-2603)
PHONE....................................818 786-2900
Steve Chan, *President*
▲ EMP: 48
SQ FT: 24,000
SALES (est): 9.5MM **Privately Held**
WEB: www.proactionpd.com
SIC: 3089 Injection molding of plastics

(P-9921)
NEOPLAST INC
1350 Citrus St, Riverside (92507-1625)
PHONE....................................951 300-9300
Richard S Risch, *President*
EMP: 19
SALES (est): 1.9MM **Privately Held**
SIC: 3089 Plastic processing

(P-9922)
NEWELL BRANDS INC
17182 Nevada St, Victorville (92394-7806)
PHONE....................................760 246-2700
EMP: 18
SALES (corp-wide): 8.6B **Publicly Held**
SIC: 3089 Plastic kitchenware, tableware & houseware
PA: Newell Brands Inc.
    221 River St Ste 13
    Hoboken NJ 07030
    201 610-6600

(P-9923)
NEWLIGHT TECHNOLOGIES INC
14382 Astronautics Ln, Huntington Beach (92647-2081)
PHONE....................................714 556-4500

Mark Herrema, *CEO*
Evan Creelman, *COO*
Kenton Kimmel, *CTO*
Dave Henton, *Development*
Wes Coleman, *Human Resources*
EMP: 29
SALES (est): 7.5MM **Privately Held**
SIC: 3089 Plastic processing

(P-9924)
NEWPORT LAMINATES INC
3121 W Central Ave, Santa Ana (92704-5302)
PHONE....................................714 545-8335
Brad A Bollman, *President*
Wendy Bollman, *Vice Pres*
EMP: 40
SQ FT: 24,000
SALES (est): 3.8MM **Privately Held**
SIC: 3089 Fiber, vulcanized

(P-9925)
NEWPORT PLASTIC INC
Also Called: Country Weave
1525 E Edinger Ave, Santa Ana (92705-4907)
PHONE....................................714 549-1955
Kay Hale, *President*
Mike Williams, *COO*
EMP: 20
SALES (est): 2.7MM
SALES (corp-wide): 9.3MM **Privately Held**
SIC: 3089 Injection molding of plastics
PA: Newport Plastics, Llc
    1525 E Edinger Ave
    Santa Ana CA 92705
    800 854-8402

(P-9926)
NEWPORT PLASTICS LLC (PA)
1525 E Edinger Ave, Santa Ana (92705-4907)
PHONE....................................800 854-8402
Shirley Carlisle, *Principal*
Peter Bonin,
Kathleen Steck,
EMP: 25
SQ FT: 8,000
SALES (est): 9.3MM **Privately Held**
SIC: 3089 Injection molding of plastics

(P-9927)
NEWPORT THIN FILM LAB INC
13824 Magnolia Ave, Chino (91710-7027)
PHONE....................................909 591-0276
Scott Powers, *President*
Carrie Powers, *Corp Secy*
Brianne Mitchell, *Executive*
Ever Mata, *Sales Mgr*
EMP: 17
SQ FT: 11,118
SALES (est): 3.4MM **Privately Held**
WEB: www.newportlab.com
SIC: 3089 3827 Lenses, except optical: plastic; optical instruments & lenses

(P-9928)
NISHIBA INDUSTRIES CORPORATION
2360 Marconi Ct, San Diego (92154-7241)
PHONE....................................619 661-8866
Yoshiaki Nishiba, *President*
Claudia Gutierrez, *Technology*
▲ EMP: 650
SQ FT: 2,500
SALES (est): 108.8MM **Privately Held**
WEB: www.nishiba.com
SIC: 3089 3544 5162 Plastic hardware & building products; special dies, tools, jigs & fixtures; plastics materials & basic shapes
PA: Nishiba Industry Co., Ltd.
    5-1274, Hirosawacho
    Kiryu GNM 376-0

(P-9929)
NORCO INJECTION MOLDING INC
Also Called: Norco Plastics
14325 Monte Vista Ave, Chino (91710-5726)
P.O. Box 2528 (91708-2528)
PHONE....................................909 393-4000
Jack Williams, *President*

P R O D U C T S & S V C S

Shellie Binchi, *Cust Mgr*
▲ EMP: 100
SQ FT: 45,000
SALES (est): 14.5MM **Privately Held**
WEB: www.niminc.com
SIC: 3089 3544 Injection molding of plastics; special dies, tools, jigs & fixtures

(P-9930)
NORCO PLASTICS INC
14325 Monte Vista Ave, Chino
(91710-5726)
P.O. Box 2528 (91708-2528)
PHONE..................................909 393-4000
John Williams, *CEO*
Leticia Babcock, *QC Mgr*
Cynthia Breceda, *Assistant*
▲ EMP: 90
SALES (est): 19.8MM **Privately Held**
SIC: 3089 Plastic containers, except foam; injection molding of plastics

(P-9931)
NORTON PACKAGING INC (PA)
Also Called: Norpak
20670 Corsair Blvd, Hayward
(94545-1008)
PHONE..................................510 786-1922
Scott Norton, *Co-President*
Greg Norton, *Co-President*
Mark Norton, *Vice Pres*
Rodney Friensehner, *QC Mgr*
Tom Kenny, *QC Mgr*
◆ EMP: 188
SQ FT: 7,200
SALES (est): 69.3MM **Privately Held**
WEB: www.nortonpackaging.com
SIC: 3089 Food casings, plastic; plastic containers, except foam

(P-9932)
NORTON PACKAGING INC
5800 S Boyle Ave, Vernon (90058-3927)
PHONE..................................323 588-6167
Joe Schrick, *Branch Mgr*
Jin Kim, *Info Tech Mgr*
EMP: 60
SALES (corp-wide): 69.3MM **Privately Held**
WEB: www.nortonpackaging.com
SIC: 3089 5162 Plastic containers, except foam; resins
PA: Norton Packaging, Inc.
20670 Corsair Blvd
Hayward CA 94545
510 786-1922

(P-9933)
NORWESCO INC
13241 11th Ave, Hanford (93230-9591)
PHONE..................................559 585-1668
Tom Smith, *Branch Mgr*
EMP: 14
SALES (corp-wide): 44.1MM **Privately Held**
WEB: www.ncmmolding.com
SIC: 3089 Septic tanks, plastic
PA: Norwesco, Inc.
4365 Steiner St
Saint Bonifacius MN 55375
952 446-1945

(P-9934)
NUBS PLASTICS INC
991 Park Center Dr, Vista (92081-8312)
PHONE..................................760 598-2525
Niyogi Ramolia, *President*
▼ EMP: 30
SQ FT: 13,000
SALES (est): 5.9MM **Privately Held**
WEB: www.progressivemolding.com
SIC: 3089 Injection molding of plastics

(P-9935)
NUCLEUS ENTERPRISES LLC
888 Prospect St Ste 200, La Jolla
(92037-4261)
PHONE..................................619 517-8747
Ernesto Mendiola Otero, *Mng Member*
Albert Armas, *Controller*
Luis Escobedo,
Luis Antonio Rodriguez,
Manuel Mendiola Rios, *Mng Member*
◆ EMP: 51 EST: 2015
SQ FT: 1,200

SALES: 1MM **Privately Held**
SIC: 3089 Injection molding of plastics

(P-9936)
NUCONIC PACKAGING LLC
4889 Loma Vista Ave, Vernon
(90058-3216)
PHONE..................................323 588-9033
Alan Franz, *CEO*
Ally Jacoby, *Office Mgr*
Francisco Diaz, *Opers Staff*
Skip Farber,
Camplastic Packaging,
▲ EMP: 31
SQ FT: 30,000
SALES (est): 11.2MM **Privately Held**
SIC: 3089 4783 Plastic containers, except foam; packing & crating
PA: Carlin Capital Partners, Llc
15760 Ventura Blvd # 700
Encino CA 91436

(P-9937)
NURSERY SUPPLIES INC
534 W Struck Ave, Orange (92867-5522)
PHONE..................................714 538-0251
Dom Lovell, *Manager*
Elvia Ramirez, *Admin Asst*
Mickey Hockenberry, *Buyer*
Rob Barnett, *Maintence Staff*
EMP: 40
SALES (corp-wide): 118.6MM **Privately Held**
WEB: www.nurserysupplies.com
SIC: 3089 Flower pots, plastic
PA: Nursery Supplies, Inc.
1415 Orchard Dr
Chambersburg PA 17201
717 263-7780

(P-9938)
NYPRO INC
Also Called: Nypro Healthcare Baja
505 Main St Rm 107, Chula Vista
(91911-6059)
PHONE..................................619 498-9250
Gregg Lambert, *General Mgr*
Christopher Johnson, *Business Dir*
Jorge Mendez, *IT/INT Sup*
Josh Gikis, *Project Engr*
Michael Butala, *Engineer*
EMP: 75
SALES (corp-wide): 25.2B **Publicly Held**
WEB: www.nypro.com
SIC: 3089 3559 Injection molding of plastics; robots, molding & forming plastics
HQ: Nypro Inc.
101 Union St
Clinton MA 01510
978 365-8100

(P-9939)
NYPRO SAN DIEGO INC
505 Main St, Chula Vista (91911-6075)
PHONE..................................619 482-7033
Gordon Lankton, *CEO*
Ernie Rice, *President*
▼ EMP: 80
SQ FT: 66,000
SALES (est): 23MM
SALES (corp-wide): 25.2B **Publicly Held**
WEB: www.nypro.com
SIC: 3089 Injection molding of plastics
HQ: Nypro Inc.
101 Union St
Clinton MA 01510
978 365-8100

(P-9940)
O K COLOR AMERICA CORPORATION
578 Amapola Ave, Torrance (90501-1472)
PHONE..................................310 320-9343
Osamu Hanatani, *Ch of Bd*
Tadashi Hanatani, *CEO*
Osamu Sakai, *Exec VP*
Shuichiro Wakimoto, *Admin Sec*
▲ EMP: 10
SQ FT: 10,102
SALES (est): 2.1MM **Privately Held**
WEB: www.calsakcolorants.com
SIC: 3089 5169 Injection molded finished plastic products; synthetic resins, rubber & plastic materials

PA: Ok-Kasei Co., Ltd.
1-7-3, Bingomachi, Chuo-Ku
Osaka OSK 541-0

(P-9941)
OCEAN DIVERS USA LLC
Also Called: Odusa
975 Park Center Dr, Vista (92081-8312)
PHONE..................................760 599-6898
Don Weston, *Mng Member*
David Domshteyn, *COO*
Jim Pang Ching,
◆ EMP: 10
SQ FT: 9,000
SALES: 1MM **Privately Held**
WEB: www.odusa.net
SIC: 3089 Plastic processing

(P-9942)
OPTICOLOR INC
15281 Graham St, Huntington Beach
(92649-1108)
PHONE..................................714 893-8839
Daniel Neufeld, *President*
Pamela Young, *General Mgr*
Ron Radmer, *Sales Staff*
▲ EMP: 11
SQ FT: 10,000
SALES (est): 5.1MM **Privately Held**
WEB: www.opticolorinc.com
SIC: 3089 Extruded finished plastic products; plastic processing

(P-9943)
P S C MANUFACTURING INC
Also Called: Plastic Service Center
3424 De La Cruz Blvd, Santa Clara
(95054-2610)
PHONE..................................408 988-5115
Howard Roetken, *President*
Dreena Roetken, *Vice Pres*
EMP: 35
SQ FT: 26,000
SALES (est): 4.9MM **Privately Held**
SIC: 3089 Plastic processing

(P-9944)
PACIFIC MOLDING INC
1390 Dodson Way, Riverside (92507-2003)
P.O. Box 56251 (92517-1151)
PHONE..................................951 683-2100
EMP: 10 EST: 2011
SALES (est): 1.3MM **Privately Held**
SIC: 3089

(P-9945)
PACO PLASTICS & ENGRG INC
8540 Dice Rd, Santa Fe Springs
(90670-2592)
PHONE..................................562 698-0916
Greg K Dowden, *President*
Diana Dowden, *Vice Pres*
Alisha Attella, *Office Mgr*
Joshua Mezin, *QC Mgr*
Sergio Vasquez, *Manager*
EMP: 12
SQ FT: 12,000
SALES (est): 2.2MM **Privately Held**
WEB: www.pacoplastics.com
SIC: 3089 3429 Injection molding of plastics; aircraft hardware

(P-9946)
PACON INC
4249 Puente Ave, Baldwin Park
(91706-3420)
PHONE..................................626 814-4654
Robert M Austin, *CEO*
Michael Austin, *Vice Pres*
Veronica Padilla, *Office Mgr*
Jeff Protzo, *Sales Staff*
◆ EMP: 103
SQ FT: 44,000
SALES (est): 21.2MM **Privately Held**
WEB: www.paconinc.com
SIC: 3089 Extruded finished plastic products

(P-9947)
PACTIV LLC
2024 Norris Rd, Bakersfield (93308-2238)
PHONE..................................661 392-4000
Steve Stewart, *Plant Mgr*
Wayne Schneider, *Admin Asst*
EMP: 300

SALES (corp-wide): 14.1MM **Privately Held**
WEB: www.pactiv.com
SIC: 3089 3086 Kitchenware, plastic; plastics foam products
HQ: Pactiv Llc
1900 W Field Ct
Lake Forest IL 60045
847 482-2000

(P-9948)
PACTIV LLC
12500 Slauson Ave Ste H1, Santa Fe
Springs (90670-8639)
PHONE..................................562 693-1451
Craig Snedden, *Manager*
Gus Gonzalez, *Human Res Dir*
EMP: 94
SALES (corp-wide): 14.1MM **Privately Held**
WEB: www.pactiv.com
SIC: 3089 Plastic containers, except foam
HQ: Pactiv Llc
1900 W Field Ct
Lake Forest IL 60045
847 482-2000

(P-9949)
PACTIV LLC
Also Called: Pactiv Corp
8201 W Elowin Ct, Visalia (93291-9262)
PHONE..................................909 622-1151
Tim Tyler, *Manager*
EMP: 150
SALES (corp-wide): 14.1MM **Privately Held**
WEB: www.pactiv.com
SIC: 3089 Thermoformed finished plastic products
HQ: Pactiv Llc
1900 W Field Ct
Lake Forest IL 60045
847 482-2000

(P-9950)
PAN PACIFIC PLASTICS MFG INC
26551 Danti Ct, Hayward (94545-3917)
PHONE..................................510 785-6888
Ying Wang, *President*
Robert Lin, *CFO*
Mike Tan, *Vice Pres*
Maurice Wang, *Vice Pres*
Michael Gonzalez, *Marketing Staff*
◆ EMP: 44 EST: 1981
SQ FT: 46,080
SALES (est): 6.8MM **Privately Held**
WEB: www.pppmi.com
SIC: 3089 2673 Plastic processing; bags: plastic, laminated & coated

(P-9951)
PANOB CORP
1531 E Cedar St, Ontario (91761-5762)
PHONE..................................909 947-8008
Arthur Graner Thorne, *President*
John Graner Thorne, *Treasurer*
Barbara Thorne, *Admin Sec*
EMP: 50
SQ FT: 12,000
SALES (est): 4.2MM
SALES (corp-wide): 6.8MM **Privately Held**
WEB: www.paramountpanels.com
SIC: 3089 3728 3613 Plastic processing; aircraft parts & equipment; switchgear & switchboard apparatus
PA: Paramount Panels, Inc.
1531 E Cedar St
Ontario CA 91761
909 947-8008

(P-9952)
PARADIGM PACKAGING EAST LLC
Also Called: Paradigm Packaging West
9177 Center Ave, Rancho Cucamonga
(91730-5312)
P.O. Box 10, Upland (91785-0010)
PHONE..................................909 985-2750
Steve Costecki, *Manager*
EMP: 125

▲ = Import ▼=Export
◆ =Import/Export

SALES (corp-wide): 17.2MM **Privately Held**
WEB: www.paradigmpackaging.com
SIC: **3089** Plastic containers, except foam; caps, plastic
HQ: Paradigm Packaging East Llc
141 5th St
Saddle Brook NJ 07663
201 909-3400

(P-9953)
PARAMOUNT PANELS INC (PA)
Also Called: California Plasteck
1531 E Cedar St, Ontario (91761-5762)
PHONE.................................909 947-8008
Arthur G Thorne, *President*
John Thorn, *Vice Pres*
John G Thorne, *Vice Pres*
John Thorne, *Branch Mgr*
Jorge Ramirez, *Engineer*
EMP: 32 **EST:** 1962
SQ FT: 12,000
SALES (est): 6.8MM **Privately Held**
SIC: **3089 3812 3728** Plastic processing; search & navigation equipment; aircraft parts & equipment

(P-9954)
PARAMUNT PLSTIC FBRICATORS INC
Also Called: Paramount Fabricators
11251 Jersey Blvd, Rancho Cucamonga (91730-5147)
PHONE.................................909 987-4757
Peter M Smits, *President*
Rose I Smits, *Vice Pres*
EMP: 17
SQ FT: 60,000
SALES (est): 3.7MM **Privately Held**
WEB: www.paramountfabricators.com
SIC: **3089** Plastic containers, except foam

(P-9955)
PARKER PLASTICS INC
12762 Highway 29, Lower Lake (95457-9872)
P.O. Box 459 (95457-0459)
PHONE.................................707 994-6363
George K Parker, *President*
Jack Parker, *Treasurer*
▲ **EMP:** 25
SQ FT: 3,200
SALES (est): 4.1MM **Privately Held**
SIC: **3089** Injection molding of plastics; thermoformed finished plastic products

(P-9956)
PBY PLASTICS INC
2571 Lindsey Privado Dr, Ontario (91761-3452)
PHONE.................................909 930-6700
Joe Ilmberger, *President*
Janis K Ilmberger, *Treasurer*
Terry Baker, *Vice Pres*
Sam Powers, *Vice Pres*
EMP: 10
SQ FT: 5,000
SALES: 3.5MM **Privately Held**
SIC: **3089** Injection molding of plastics; plastic processing

(P-9957)
PEERLESS INJECTION MOLDING LLC
Also Called: Proplas Technologies
14321 Corp Dr, Garden Grove (92843)
PHONE.................................714 689-1920
Scott Taylor, *President*
▲ **EMP:** 50
SQ FT: 51,112
SALES (est): 12.7MM
SALES (corp-wide): 77.9MM **Privately Held**
WEB: www.peerlessmold.com
SIC: **3089** Injection molding of plastics
PA: Comar, Inc.
201 Laurel Rd Fl 2
Voorhees NJ 08043
856 692-6100

(P-9958)
PENINSULA PACKAGING LLC
2401 Bert Dr Ste A, Hollister (95023-2563)
PHONE.................................831 634-0940
Joe Nash, *Manager*
EMP: 180

SALES (corp-wide): 5.3B **Publicly Held**
SIC: **3089 7389** Plastic containers, except foam; packaging & labeling services
HQ: Peninsula Packaging, Llc
1030 N Anderson Rd
Exeter CA 93221
559 594-6813

(P-9959)
PIGS TAIL USA LLC
925 W Lambert Rd, Brea (92821-2943)
PHONE.................................714 566-0011
Scott Bartlett, *CEO*
Rob Mitchell, *COO*
▲ **EMP:** 12
SALES (est): 2.7MM **Privately Held**
SIC: **3089** Hardware, plastic

(P-9960)
PIONETICS CORPORATION
151 Old County Rd Ste H, San Carlos (94070-6247)
PHONE.................................650 551-0250
Gordon Mitchard, *President*
Steve Tondre, *Opers Staff*
▲ **EMP:** 12 **EST:** 1995
SALES: 1MM **Privately Held**
WEB: www.pionetics.com
SIC: **3089** Extruded finished plastic products

(P-9961)
PITBULL GYM INCORPORATED
Also Called: Art Plates
10782 Edison Ct, Rancho Cucamonga (91730-4845)
PHONE.................................909 980-7960
Gary John Vandenlangenberg, *President*
▲ **EMP:** 15
SQ FT: 10,120
SALES (est): 1.5MM **Privately Held**
WEB: www.fitness-wear-direct.com
SIC: **3089 5072** Bottle caps, molded plastic; hardware

(P-9962)
PITTMAN PRODUCTS INTERNATIONAL
Also Called: Pittman Outdoors
650 S Jefferson St Ste D, Placentia (92870-6640)
PHONE.................................562 926-6660
James Pittman, *CEO*
▲ **EMP:** 15
SALES (est): 1.8MM **Privately Held**
SIC: **3089** Air mattresses, plastic

(P-9963)
PLA-COR INCORPORATED
10207 Buena Vista Ave D, Santee (92071-4482)
P.O. Box 522, Campo (91906-0522)
PHONE.................................619 478-2139
Lewis Hein, *CEO*
Derrell J Weldy, *President*
Michael D Weldy, *Vice Pres*
EMP: 17
SQ FT: 6,000
SALES (est): 2.3MM **Privately Held**
WEB: www.pla-cor.com
SIC: **3089** Plastic hardware & building products

(P-9964)
PLANET PLEXI CORP
2872 Walnut Ave Ste A, Tustin (92780-7003)
PHONE.................................949 206-1183
Bahram Bakhtiar, *Principal*
Padra Pazoki, *Administration*
Brian Kaanehe, *Marketing Staff*
EMP: 12
SALES (est): 2MM **Privately Held**
SIC: **3089** Injection molding of plastics; plastic processing

(P-9965)
PLASCENE INC
1600 Pacific Ave, Oxnard (93033-2746)
PHONE.................................562 695-0240
Hy Duy Tran, *CEO*
▲ **EMP:** 17

SALES (est): 1.4MM
SALES (corp-wide): 1.1MM **Privately Held**
SIC: **3089 5162** Air mattresses, plastic; plastics materials & basic shapes; plastics resins
HQ: Duy Tan Plastics Manufacturing Corporation
298 Ho Hoc Lam Street,
Ho Chi Minh
283 876-2222

(P-9966)
PLASIDYNE ENGINEERING & MFG
3230 E 59th St, Long Beach (90805-4502)
P.O. Box 5578 (90805-0578)
PHONE.................................562 531-0510
Dean C Sutherland, *President*
EMP: 22
SQ FT: 15,000
SALES: 2.3MM **Privately Held**
WEB: www.plasidyne.com
SIC: **3089** Plastic hardware & building products

(P-9967)
PLASMETEX INDUSTRIES
1425 Linda Vista Dr, San Marcos (92078-3806)
PHONE.................................760 744-8300
Adolph Saupe, *President*
▲ **EMP:** 13 **EST:** 1963
SQ FT: 1,000
SALES (est): 1.8MM **Privately Held**
WEB: www.plasmetex.com
SIC: **3089** Injection molding of plastics

(P-9968)
PLASTHEC MOLDING INC
1945 S Grove Ave, Ontario (91761-5616)
PHONE.................................909 947-4267
Hector Carrion, *President*
James Downey, *Vice Pres*
EMP: 84 **EST:** 1978
SQ FT: 34,000
SALES (est): 14.8MM **Privately Held**
WEB: www.plasthec.com
SIC: **3089** Injection molding of plastics

(P-9969)
PLASTIC AND METAL CENTER INC
23162 La Cadena Dr, Laguna Hills (92653-1405)
PHONE.................................949 770-0610
Faramarz Khaladj, *President*
Fred Carr, *Vice Pres*
Denise Khaladj, *Admin Sec*
Jim Aschtiani, *Engineer*
EMP: 25
SQ FT: 20,000
SALES (est): 5.1MM **Privately Held**
WEB: www.plastic-metal.com
SIC: **3089** Injection molding of plastics; thermoformed finished plastic products

(P-9970)
PLASTIC DRESS-UP COMPANY
11077 Rush St, South El Monte (91733-3546)
PHONE.................................626 442-7711
Myron H Funk, *President*
◆ **EMP:** 84
SQ FT: 130,000
SALES (est): 9.8MM **Privately Held**
WEB: www.pdu.com
SIC: **3089** Novelties, plastic

(P-9971)
PLASTIC FABRICATION TECH LLC
2320 E Cherry Indus Cir, Long Beach (90805-4417)
PHONE.................................773 509-1700
Jay Magness Jr, *President*
Mary Hutchinson, *CFO*
EMP: 100
SQ FT: 20,000
SALES (est): 6.4MM **Privately Held**
SIC: **3089** Plastic processing

(P-9972)
PLASTIC PROCESSING CORP
13432 Estrella Ave, Gardena (90248-1513)
PHONE.................................310 719-7330
Dagmer Schulte-Derne, *Ch of Bd*
Steve Rockenbach, *CFO*
▲ **EMP:** 50
SQ FT: 20,000
SALES (est): 4.9MM **Privately Held**
SIC: **3089** Blow molded finished plastic products

(P-9973)
PLASTICS DEVELOPMENT CORP
960 Calle Negocio, San Clemente (92673-6201)
PHONE.................................949 492-0217
Inder Jain, *President*
Vijay Jain, *Corp Secy*
Sanie Jain, *Vice Pres*
▲ **EMP:** 23
SQ FT: 7,000
SALES (est): 4.9MM **Privately Held**
WEB: www.plasticsdev.com
SIC: **3089** Injection molding of plastics

(P-9974)
PLASTICS PLUS TECHNOLOGY INC
1495 Research Dr, Redlands (92374-4584)
PHONE.................................909 747-0555
Kathy Bodor, *President*
Barbara Saber, *Manager*
EMP: 33
SQ FT: 35,000
SALES (est): 8.8MM **Privately Held**
WEB: www.plasticsplus.com
SIC: **3089 3544** Injection molding of plastics; forms (molds), for foundry & plastics working machinery

(P-9975)
PLASTIJECT LLC
14811 Spring Ave, Santa Fe Springs (90670-5109)
PHONE.................................562 926-6705
EMP: 13 **EST:** 1997
SALES (est): 1.5MM **Privately Held**
SIC: **3089**

(P-9976)
PLASTIQUE UNIQUE INC
3383 Livonia Ave, Los Angeles (90034-3127)
PHONE.................................310 839-3968
Christine Galonska, *President*
Lionel Funes, *Vice Pres*
Silvia Totado, *Director*
EMP: 27
SQ FT: 5,000
SALES (est): 3.8MM **Privately Held**
WEB: www.plastiqueuniqueinc.com
SIC: **3089** Injection molding of plastics

(P-9977)
PLASTO TECH INTERNATIONAL INC
4 Autry, Irvine (92618-2708)
PHONE.................................949 458-1880
Ben Khalaj, *President*
Jacqueline Khalaj, *CEO*
▲ **EMP:** 20
SQ FT: 16,530
SALES (est): 4.2MM **Privately Held**
WEB: www.plastotech.com
SIC: **3089 5084 8711 7389** Injection molding of plastics; industrial machinery & equipment; consulting engineer; design, commercial & industrial; plastics sheets & rods

(P-9978)
PLASTPRO 2000 INC (PA)
Also Called: Plastpro Doors
5200 W Century Blvd Fl 9, Los Angeles (90045-5900)
PHONE.................................310 693-8600
Franco An, *CEO*
Shirley Wang, *President*
Johnny MAI, *CFO*
Walter Wang, *Chairman*
Benny Hugo, *Programmer Anys*
◆ **EMP:** 126

SALES (est): 16.9MM **Privately Held**
WEB: www.plastproinc.com
SIC: 3089 Fiberglass doors

(P-9979)
PLASTRUCT INC
1020 Wallace Way, City of Industry
(91748-1027)
PHONE........................626 912-7017
John J Wanderman, *President*
EMP: 57
SQ FT: 28,000
SALES (est): 7.5MM
SALES (corp-wide): 11.8MM **Privately
Held**
WEB: www.plastruct.com
SIC: 3089 5945 3952 Plastic processing;
hobby, toy & game shops; lead pencils &
art goods
PA: Engineering Model Associates Inc
1020 Wallace Way
City Of Industry CA 91748
626 912-7011

(P-9980)
PLEXI FAB INC
1142 E Elm Ave, Fullerton (92831-5024)
PHONE........................714 447-8494
Abol Fazli, *President*
Mike Hall, *President*
Venis Hall, *Vice Pres*
◆ EMP: 17
SQ FT: 20,000
SALES (est): 2.5MM **Privately Held**
WEB: www.plexifab.com
SIC: 3089 Plastic processing

(P-9981)
POLYMER LOGISTICS INC
1725 Sierra Ridge Dr, Riverside
(92507-7133)
PHONE........................951 567-2900
Albert Terrazas, *Branch Mgr*
EMP: 27 **Privately Held**
SIC: 3089 5085 5162 Pallets, plastic;
boxes, crates, etc., other than paper;
plastics materials & basic shapes
PA: Polymer Logistics, Inc.
4630 Woodland Corp Blvd
Tampa FL 33614

(P-9982)
POLYTECH COLOR &
COMPOUNDING
847 S Wanamaker Ave, Ontario
(91761-8152)
PHONE........................909 923-7008
Brian Cockren, *President*
EMP: 13
SALES (est): 1.1MM **Privately Held**
SIC: 3089 5169 Coloring & finishing of
plastic products; synthetic resins, rubber
& plastic materials

(P-9983)
POP PLASTICS ACRYLIC DISP
INC
8211 Orangethorpe Ave, Buena Park
(90621-3811)
PHONE........................714 523-8500
Jeff Dougherty, *President*
David A Lewis, *COO*
Steven K North, *CFO*
▲ EMP: 20
SQ FT: 15,000
SALES (est): 3.1MM **Privately Held**
SIC: 3089 Plates, plastic

(P-9984)
PPP LLC
601 W Olympic Blvd, Montebello
(90640-5229)
P.O. Box 789 (90640-0789)
PHONE........................323 832-9627
Evelyn Garcia, *Mng Member*
Jan Voelkers, *Administration*
Ute Carstens, *Opers Staff*
EMP: 50 EST: 2001
SALES (est): 6.7MM **Privately Held**
WEB: www.ppp.net
SIC: 3089 Injection molding of plastics

(P-9985)
PRE/PLASTICS INC
Also Called: Preplastics
12600 Locksley Ln Ste 100, Auburn
(95602-2070)
PHONE........................530 823-1820
Richard L Miller, *CEO*
Linda Miller, *Corp Secy*
Brian Miller, *Director*
EMP: 30
SQ FT: 20,000
SALES (est): 9.1MM **Privately Held**
WEB: www.preplastics.com
SIC: 3089 Injection molding of plastics

(P-9986)
PRECISE AEROSPACE MFG INC
Also Called: Precise Plastic Products
224 Glider Cir, Corona (92880-2533)
PHONE........................951 898-0500
Ronnie E Harwood, *CEO*
Roxanne Abdi, *President*
Sandy Armas, *Manager*
▲ EMP: 42
SQ FT: 39,000
SALES (est): 13.7MM **Privately Held**
WEB: www.preciseplastic.com
SIC: 3089 3544 Molding primary plastic;
industrial molds

(P-9987)
PRECISION MOLDED PLASTICS
INC
880 W 9th St, Upland (91786-4540)
PHONE........................909 981-9662
David S Vanvoorhis, *CEO*
Brown Ash, *VP Bus Dvlpt*
Ash Brown, *General Mgr*
Pablo Andres, *Technician*
Paul Conlon, *Plant Mgr*
EMP: 11
SQ FT: 8,000
SALES (est): 3.1MM **Privately Held**
WEB: www.precisionmoldedplastics.com
SIC: 3089 Injection molding of plastics

(P-9988)
PRECISION PLASTIC LLC
555 Twin Dolphin Dr, Redwood City
(94065-2129)
PHONE........................510 324-8676
Eric Appelblom, *Mng Member*
Martha Conway, *Principal*
EMP: 175
SALES (est): 9.4MM **Privately Held**
WEB: www.precision-plastics.net
SIC: 3089 Plastic processing

(P-9989)
PREDATOR MOTORSPORTS
INC
1250 Distribution Way, Vista (92081-8816)
PHONE........................760 734-1749
Ryan Wilson, *President*
Dan Wilson, *Vice Pres*
Nyela Wilson, *Controller*
Autumn Conquest, *Human Resources*
Garrett Robbins, *Sales Mgr*
▲ EMP: 15
SQ FT: 15,000
SALES (est): 3.1MM **Privately Held**
WEB: www.predatormotorsports.com
SIC: 3089 3465 Automotive parts, plastic;
body parts, automobile: stamped metal

(P-9990)
PREMIUM PLASTICS MACHINE
INC
15956 Downey Ave, Paramount
(90723-5190)
PHONE........................323 979-3889
David Pennington, *President*
Michael Robert Pennington, *Exec VP*
Suzanne Pennington, *Vice Pres*
▲ EMP: 16 EST: 1976
SQ FT: 6,241
SALES (est): 2.3MM **Privately Held**
SIC: 3089 Molding primary plastic; injec-
tion molding of plastics

(P-9991)
PREPRODUCTION PLASTICS
INC
Also Called: P P I
210 Teller St, Corona (92879-1886)
PHONE........................951 340-9680
Koby Loosen, *President*
Barbara Loosen, *Corp Secy*
Ron Loosen, *Principal*
Paul Rice, *Engineer*
Bert Bruch, *Buyer*
▲ EMP: 50
SQ FT: 45,000
SALES (est): 19.2MM **Privately Held**
WEB: www.ppiplastics.com
SIC: 3089 3544 Molding primary plastic;
forms (molds), for foundry & plastics
working machinery

(P-9992)
PRES-TEK PLASTICS INC (PA)
11060 Tacoma Dr, Rancho Cucamonga
(91730-4857)
PHONE........................909 360-1600
Donna C Pursell, *CEO*
Ron Noggle, *Vice Pres*
Lyndsay Petersen, *Office Mgr*
Ranjeeta Ty, *Project Mgr*
Luis Cardenas, *Engineer*
EMP: 28 EST: 2005
SALES (est): 19.1MM **Privately Held**
SIC: 3089 Injection molding of plastics

(P-9993)
PRINCE LIONHEART INC (PA)
2421 Westgate Rd, Santa Maria
(93455-1075)
PHONE........................805 922-2250
Kelly Griffiths, *CEO*
Debbie Di Nardi, *Vice Pres*
Thomas McConnell, *Vice Pres*
Nicole Maya, *Controller*
Richard Siegel, *Opers Staff*
▲ EMP: 40
SQ FT: 80,000
SALES (est): 9.7MM **Privately Held**
WEB: www.princelionheart.com
SIC: 3089 Injection molding of plastics

(P-9994)
PRINCETON CASE WEST INC
1444 W Mccoy Ln, Santa Maria
(93455-1005)
PHONE........................805 928-8840
Douglas Laggrenm, *President*
Jim Laggren, *Vice Pres*
EMP: 20
SQ FT: 22,000
SALES (est): 3.5MM **Privately Held**
WEB: www.pcwest.net
SIC: 3089 3161 Cases, plastic; luggage

(P-9995)
PRO DESIGN GROUP INC
438 E Alondra Blvd, Gardena
(90248-2902)
PHONE........................310 767-1032
Chris Raab, *President*
Christopher Allen Raab, *President*
Maria Chanlder, *Vice Pres*
▼ EMP: 35
SQ FT: 50,000
SALES (est): 8.9MM **Privately Held**
WEB: www.conceptdisplay.com
SIC: 3089 Plastic kitchenware, tableware &
houseware; plastic processing

(P-9996)
PRODUCT DESIGN
DEVELOPMENTS
15611 Container Ln, Huntington Beach
(92649-1532)
PHONE........................714 898-6895
Steven F Doke, *President*
EMP: 35
SQ FT: 25,000
SALES (est): 5.3MM **Privately Held**
SIC: 3089 4724 Plastic containers, except
foam; travel agencies

(P-9997)
PRODUCTIVITY CALIFORNIA
INC
Also Called: Pro Cal
10533 Sessler St, South Gate
(90280-7251)
PHONE........................562 923-3100
Gary Vollers, *President*
Don Uchiyama, *Admin Sec*
EMP: 70
SQ FT: 100,000
SALES (est): 11.8MM
SALES (corp-wide): 566.7MM **Publicly
Held**
WEB: www.myersind.com
SIC: 3089 Plastic containers, except foam
PA: Myers Industries, Inc.
1293 S Main St
Akron OH 44301
330 253-5592

(P-9998)
PROMEX INTERNATIONAL PLAS
INC
12860 San Fernando Rd D, Sylmar
(91342-3783)
PHONE........................818 367-5352
Gilbert Anguiano, *President*
EMP: 42
SQ FT: 30,000
SALES (est): 6.9MM **Privately Held**
SIC: 3089 Injection molding of plastics

(P-9999)
PROTECTIVE INDUSTRIES INC
Also Called: Caplugs
18704 S Ferris Pl, Rancho Dominguez
(90220-6400)
PHONE........................310 537-2300
Fred Karam, *Branch Mgr*
Melanie Casey, *Marketing Staff*
Paul Dulak, *Supervisor*
EMP: 60
SALES (corp-wide): 2.9B **Privately Held**
WEB: www.mokon.com
SIC: 3089 Plastic containers, except foam
HQ: Protective Industries, Inc.
2150 Elmwood Ave
Buffalo NY 14207
716 876-9951

(P-10000)
PROULX MANUFACTURING INC
Also Called: Universal Products
11433 6th St, Rancho Cucamonga
(91730-6024)
PHONE........................909 980-0662
Richard Proulx, *President*
Raymond E Proulx, *CFO*
Lorraine Proulx, *Admin Sec*
◆ EMP: 45
SALES (est): 9.1MM **Privately Held**
WEB: www.universalproducts.com
SIC: 3089 Plastic hardware & building
products

(P-10001)
PROVIDIEN INJCTION MOLDING
INC
Also Called: Pedi
2731 Loker Ave W, Carlsbad (92010-6601)
PHONE........................760 931-1844
Jeffrey S Goble, *CEO*
Richard D Witchey Jr, *President*
Paul Jazwin, *CFO*
Jim Yee, *Vice Pres*
Louise Witchey, *Admin Sec*
◆ EMP: 74
SQ FT: 50,000
SALES (est): 26.7MM **Privately Held**
WEB: www.pediplastics.com
SIC: 3089 Injection molded finished plastic
products; injection molding of plastics
HQ: Witco Industries, Inc
2731 Loker Ave W
Carlsbad CA

(P-10002)
QUALI-TECH MOLD
5939 Sycamore Ct, Chino (91710-9139)
PHONE........................909 464-8124
Martin Lane, *Owner*
EMP: 10
SQ FT: 6,600

SALES (est): 850K **Privately Held**
SIC: **3089** Injection molding of plastics

(P-10003)
**QUASHNICK TOOL
CORPORATION**
225 N Guild Ave, Lodi (95240-0844)
PHONE..................................209 334-5283
Robert Hampton, *CEO*
Terry Quashnick, *President*
Duane Saville, *Exec VP*
Jinnet Quashnick, *Admin Sec*
EMP: 45
SQ FT: 15,000
SALES (est): 6.8MM **Privately Held**
WEB: www.quashnick.com
SIC: **3089 3544** Injection molding of plastics; industrial molds

(P-10004)
QUIET RIDE SOLUTIONS LLC
1122 S Wilson Way Ste 1, Stockton
(95205-7048)
PHONE..................................209 942-4777
Timothy Cox,
Jacquelyn Cox,
▲ EMP: 12
SQ FT: 6,600
SALES (est): 1.6MM **Privately Held**
WEB: www.quietride.com
SIC: **3089** Automotive parts, plastic

(P-10005)
**R C WESTBURG ENGINEERING
INC**
23302 Vista Grande Dr, Laguna Hills
(92653-1410)
PHONE..................................949 859-4648
Ronald C Westburg, *President*
Eileen Westburg, *Vice Pres*
▲ EMP: 12
SQ FT: 13,000
SALES (est): 750K **Privately Held**
SIC: **3089 3851** Injection molding of plastics; protective eyeware

(P-10006)
RAKAR INCORPORATED
1700 Emerson Ave, Oxnard (93033-1847)
PHONE..................................805 487-2721
Theresa Padilla, *CEO*
Sarah Vibbart, *CFO*
Diego Padilla, *Exec VP*
Jamie Baker, *Office Mgr*
Barbara Mahaney, *Human Res Mgr*
EMP: 48
SQ FT: 28,000
SALES (est): 10.2MM **Privately Held**
SIC: **3089 3544** Injection molding of plastics; forms (molds), for foundry & plastics working machinery

(P-10007)
RAMKO INJECTION INC
3500 Tanya Ave, Hemet (92545-9410)
PHONE..................................951 652-3510
Robert G Andrei, *President*
Davina Gomez, *Purchasing*
Hilda Anguiano, *Sr Project Mgr*
EMP: 100
SALES: 16MM **Privately Held**
SIC: **3089 3364** Blow molded finished plastic products; nonferrous die-castings except aluminum

(P-10008)
RAMTEC ASSOCIATES INC
Also Called: Con-Tech Plastics
3200 E Birch St Ste B, Brea (92821-6287)
PHONE..................................714 996-7477
Ralph Riehl, *President*
Vernon Meurer, *Vice Pres*
▲ EMP: 28
SQ FT: 35,000
SALES (est): 6.7MM **Privately Held**
WEB: www.contechplastics.com
SIC: **3089** Molding primary plastic; injection molding of plastics

(P-10009)
RAPIDWERKS INCORPORATED
1257 Quarry Ln Ste 140, Pleasanton
(94566-8483)
PHONE..................................925 417-0124
Scott Herbert, *President*
EMP: 25

SQ FT: 15,000
SALES: 5MM **Privately Held**
WEB: www.rapidwerks.com
SIC: **3089** Injection molding of plastics

(P-10010)
**RATERMANN MANUFACTURING
INC (PA)**
Also Called: Rmi
601 Pinnacle Pl, Livermore (94550-9705)
PHONE..................................800 264-7793
George Ratermann, *President*
Doug Griffith, *CFO,*
Melissa Adams, *Accounting Mgr*
Shane Page, *Purch Mgr*
Mike Andries, *Marketing Staff*
◆ EMP: 40
SQ FT: 20,000
SALES (est): 18MM **Privately Held**
SIC: **3089 3081 3679** Plastic processing; packing materials, plastic sheet; cryogenic cooling devices for infrared detectors, masers

(P-10011)
REHRIG PACIFIC COMPANY (HQ)
4010 E 26th St, Vernon (90058-4477)
PHONE..................................323 262-5145
William J Rehrig, *President*
Michael J Doka, *Ch of Bd*
James L Drew, *CFO*
Rajesh Luhar, *CFO*
Roger Hsu, *Info Tech Dir*
◆ EMP: 150
SQ FT: 200,000
SALES (est): 527.6MM **Privately Held**
SIC: **3089 2821** Cases, plastic; garbage containers, plastic; molding primary plastic; plasticizer/additive based plastic materials

(P-10012)
**REHRIG PACIFIC HOLDINGS
INC (PA)**
4010 E 26th St, Vernon (90058-4477)
PHONE..................................323 262-5145
William J Rehrig, *CEO*
Michael J Doka, *President*
James L Drew, *CFO*
William Widmann, *Vice Pres*
Muriel Kiser, *Admin Sec*
EMP: 17
SALES (est): 527.6MM **Privately Held**
SIC: **3089 2821** Cases, plastic; garbage containers, plastic; molding primary plastic; plasticizer/additive based plastic materials

(P-10013)
**REINHOLD INDUSTRIES INC
(DH)**
12827 Imperial Hwy, Santa Fe Springs
(90670-4761)
PHONE..................................562 944-3281
Clarence Hightower, *CEO*
Carl Walker, *CFO*
Scott Walker, *Administration*
Rachelle Manganti, *Info Tech Mgr*
Sergio Millan, *Project Engr*
▲ EMP: 145
SQ FT: 130,000
SALES (est): 36.8MM **Publicly Held**
WEB: www.reinhold-ind.com
SIC: **3089 3764 2531** Molding primary plastic; guided missile & space vehicle propulsion unit parts; seats, aircraft

(P-10014)
RENY & CO INC
Also Called: Renymed
4505 Littlejohn St, Baldwin Park
(91706-2239)
PHONE..................................626 962-3078
Steve Raiken, *CEO*
Renee Hamm, *Office Mgr*
Stephanie Clemente-Finley, *Human Res Mgr*
EMP: 18 EST: 1985
SQ FT: 7,000
SALES (est): 6.2MM **Privately Held**
WEB: www.renyco.com
SIC: **3089** Plastic hardware & building products; injection molding of plastics

(P-10015)
REPSCO INC
5300 Claus Rd Ste 3, Modesto
(95357-1665)
P.O. Box 2809, Parker CO (80134-1424)
PHONE..................................303 294-0364
Paul Bennett Jr, *President*
John Shedd, *Shareholder*
Bob Flynn, *Vice Pres*
◆ EMP: 25
SALES (est): 7.8MM **Privately Held**
WEB: www.repsco.com
SIC: **3089** Plastic processing

(P-10016)
RESINART CORPORATION
Also Called: Resinart Plastics
1621 Placentia Ave, Costa Mesa
(92627-4311)
PHONE..................................949 642-3665
Gary Uecker, *President*
Frank Uecker, *Treasurer*
Gene Chandler, *Vice Pres*
EMP: 40
SQ FT: 15,000
SALES (est): 5.5MM **Privately Held**
WEB: www.resinart.com
SIC: **3089** Molding primary plastic; panels, building: plastic

(P-10017)
REYRICH PLASTICS INC
1734 S Vineyard Ave, Ontario
(91761-7746)
PHONE..................................909 484-8444
Sandy Reyes, *President*
Tina Richter, *CFO*
EMP: 11 EST: 2012
SQ FT: 1,000
SALES: 1.2MM **Privately Held**
SIC: **3089** Injection molding of plastics

(P-10018)
RIMNETICS INC
Also Called: R I M
3445 De La Cruz Blvd, Santa Clara
(95054-2110)
PHONE..................................650 969-6590
David L Chew, *President*
Gary Quigley, *Principal*
Marjorie Chew, *Admin Sec*
Al Sanchez, *Production*
Daniel Chew, *Marketing Mgr*
EMP: 46
SQ FT: 20,000
SALES (est): 9.2MM
SALES (corp-wide): 22.9MM **Privately Held**
WEB: www.rimnetics.com
SIC: **3089** Injection molding of plastics
PA: Minimatics, Inc.
3445 De La Cruz Blvd
Santa Clara CA 95054
650 969-5630

(P-10019)
RLS ENTERPRISES
Also Called: Del Craft Plastics
25072 Wilkes Pl, Laguna Hills
(92653-4926)
PHONE..................................714 493-1735
Steve Hjelmstrom, *President*
Lora Crafton-Stogner, *CFO*
EMP: 20
SQ FT: 7,500
SALES: 1MM **Privately Held**
WEB: www.rlsenterprises.com
SIC: **3089 6531** Laminating of plastic; appraiser, real estate

(P-10020)
ROBBINS AUTO TOP LLC
321 Todd Ct, Oxnard (93030-5192)
P.O. Box 5567 (93031-5567)
PHONE..................................805 278-8249
Martin Brown, *President*
Douglas Robbins, *Engineer*
Harry H Lynch, *Mng Member*
▲ EMP: 65
SQ FT: 53,000
SALES (est): 12.4MM **Privately Held**
WEB: www.robbinsautotopco.com
SIC: **3089** Automotive parts, plastic

(P-10021)
RODAK PLASTICS CO INC
31721 Knapp St, Hayward (94544-7827)
PHONE..................................510 471-0898
Charles Romero, *President*
Catherine Helms, *Corp Secy*
Paul Helms, *Vice Pres*
EMP: 12
SQ FT: 13,000
SALES (est): 1.6MM **Privately Held**
WEB: www.islamicdigest.net
SIC: **3089** Injection molding of plastics; plastic processing

(P-10022)
**ROLENN MANUFACTURING INC
(PA)**
2065 Roberta St, Riverside (92507-2644)
PHONE..................................951 682-1185
Thomas J Accatino, *President*
Christie Accatino, *Corp Secy*
Larry Morrison, *Mfg Spvr*
EMP: 20 EST: 1965
SQ FT: 9,000
SALES (est): 6MM **Privately Held**
WEB: www.rolenn.com
SIC: **3089 3599** Injection molding of plastics; molding primary plastic; machine & other job shop work

(P-10023)
**RONCO PLASTICS
INCORPORATED**
15022 Parkway Loop Ste B, Tustin
(92780-6529)
PHONE..................................714 259-1385
Ronald L Pearson, *President*
EMP: 24
SQ FT: 28,000
SALES: 4.1MM **Privately Held**
SIC: **3089** Plastic containers, except foam; septic tanks, plastic

(P-10024)
RONFORD PRODUCTS INC
1116 E 2nd St, Pomona (91766-2114)
PHONE..................................909 622-7446
Carl Higgins, *Manager*
EMP: 28
SALES (corp-wide): 2.1MM **Privately Held**
WEB: www.ronfordproducts.com
SIC: **3089 5093** Plastic processing; plastics scrap
PA: Ronford Products, Inc.
16616 Garfield Ave
Paramount CA 90723
562 408-1081

(P-10025)
ROPAK CORPORATION (DH)
Also Called: Ropak Packaging
10540 Talbert Ave 200w, Fountain Valley
(92708-6027)
PHONE..................................714 845-2845
Greg A Toft, *CEO*
Patrick M Sheller, *Exec VP*
Kyle Cruz, *Director*
Russell Hammond, *Director*
Douglas Stotlar, *Director*
◆ EMP: 35
SQ FT: 12,000
SALES (est): 307.8MM
SALES (corp-wide): 1.2B **Privately Held**
WEB: www.ropakcorp.com
SIC: **3089** Plastic containers, except foam

(P-10026)
ROTATIONAL MOLDING INC
Also Called: R M I
17038 S Figueroa St, Gardena
(90248-3089)
PHONE..................................310 327-5401
Mario Poma, *CEO*
Douglas Russell, *CFO*
Sherri Poma, *Human Res Mgr*
Kyle Poma, *Regl Sales Mgr*
Peter Ramos, *Sales Staff*
EMP: 65
SALES (est): 11.6MM **Privately Held**
SIC: **3089** Plastic containers, except foam; garbage containers, plastic

PRODUCTS & SVCS

(P-10027)
ROTO DYNAMICS INC
1925 N Lime St, Orange (92865-4123)
PHONE.....................714 685-0183
Yogindra Saran, CEO
Rishi Saran, Vice Pres
EMP: 24
SALES (est): 5.6MM Privately Held
SIC: 3089 Plastic containers, except foam;
battery cases, plastic or plastic combina-
tion; boxes, plastic; cases, plastic

(P-10028)
ROTO LITE INC
84701 Avenue 48, Coachella (92236-1201)
PHONE.....................909 923-4353
Sandy Canzone, President
Dan Hammond, Vice Pres
John Hammond, Admin Sec
EMP: 22
SALES (est): 1.1MM Privately Held
WEB: www.rotolite.com
SIC: 3089 0781 Plastic containers, except
foam; landscape services

(P-10029)
ROTO POWER INC
191 Granite St Ste A, Corona
(92879-1286)
PHONE.....................951 751-9850
David Howey, Officer
EMP: 16
SALES (est): 815.4K Privately Held
SIC: 3089 Injection molding of plastics

(P-10030)
ROTO WEST ENTERPRISES INC
15651 Container Ln, Huntington Beach
(92649-1532)
PHONE.....................714 899-2030
EMP: 15
SALES (est): 1.1MM Privately Held
SIC: 3089

(P-10031)
ROYAL INTERPACK MIDWEST INC
475 Palmyrita Ave, Riverside (92507-1812)
PHONE.....................626 675-0637
EMP: 10 EST: 2015
SALES (est): 631.7K Privately Held
SIC: 3089

(P-10032)
ROYAL INTERPACK NORTH AMER INC
475 Palmyrita Ave, Riverside (92507-1812)
PHONE.....................951 787-6925
Radhika Shah, CEO
Tee Komsan, President
Visnau Chawla, Principal
Abu Hossain, Administration
Radhika Chawla, Finance
▲ EMP: 45
SALES (est): 14.6MM Privately Held
SIC: 3089 Thermoformed finished plastic
products

(P-10033)
RPM PLASTIC MOLDING INC
2821 E Miraloma Ave, Anaheim
(92806-1804)
PHONE.....................714 630-9300
Michael Ferik, CEO
Phil Hothan, Admin Sec
▲ EMP: 25
SALES (est): 4.7MM Privately Held
SIC: 3089 Injection molding of plastics

(P-10034)
RSK TOOL INCORPORATED
410 W Carob St, Compton (90220-5213)
PHONE.....................310 537-3302
Ronald Kohagura, President
Mark Kohagura, President
Virginia Kohagura, Vice Pres
EMP: 35
SQ FT: 27,000
SALES (est): 4.7MM Privately Held
WEB: www.rsktool.com
SIC: 3089 Injection molding of plastics

(P-10035)
RUSSELL-STANLEY
Also Called: Russell-Stanley West
9449 Santa Anita Ave, Rancho Cucamonga
(91730-6118)
PHONE.....................909 980-7114
Robert Singleton, President
Daniel Miller, President
▼ EMP: 60
SQ FT: 75,000
SALES (est): 6MM
SALES (corp-wide): 1.2B Privately Held
WEB: www.mausergroup.com
SIC: 3089 Plastic containers, except foam
HQ: Mauser Usa, Llc
35 Cotters Ln Ste C
East Brunswick NJ 08816
732 353-7100

(P-10036)
RYKO PLASTIC PRODUCTS INC
701 E Francis St, Ontario (91761-5514)
PHONE.....................909 773-0050
Melvin Victor Morrow, President
EMP: 10
SQ FT: 42,000
SALES (est): 1.6MM Privately Held
SIC: 3089 Plastic processing

(P-10037)
S C R MOLDING INC
2340 Pomona Rd, Corona (92880-6929)
PHONE.....................951 736-5490
Carl E Thompson, President
Richard H McCray, Vice Pres
Karen Thompson, Admin Sec
EMP: 18
SQ FT: 21,000
SALES (est): 2.5MM Privately Held
WEB: www.scrmolding.com
SIC: 3089 Injection molding of plastics

(P-10038)
S&B INDUSTRY INC
Also Called: Fxp Technologies
105 S Puente St, Brea (92821-3844)
PHONE.....................909 569-4155
Paul H Shiung, President
EMP: 60 Privately Held
SIC: 3089 Injection molded finished plastic
products
HQ: S&B Industry, Inc.
13301 Park Vista Blvd # 100
Fort Worth TX 76177

(P-10039)
SABERT CORPORATION
860 Palmyrita Ave, Riverside (92507-1810)
PHONE.....................951 342-0240
Steve Butler, Manager
Ernesto Cortes, Technical Staff
Timothy Rowles, Technical Staff
EMP: 10
SALES (corp-wide): 215.2MM Privately
Held
WEB: www.sabert.com
SIC: 3089 Dishes, plastic, except foam
PA: Sabert Corporation
2288 Main St
Sayreville NJ 08872
800 722-3781

(P-10040)
SAN DIEGO ACE INC
8490 Mathis Pl, San Diego (92127-6122)
P.O. Box 486, Tecate (91980-0486)
PHONE.....................619 252-3148
Young Moo Kwon, President
▲ EMP: 200 EST: 1992
SQ FT: 2,000
SALES (est): 9.2MM Privately Held
WEB: www.sandiegoace.com
SIC: 3089 Molding primary plastic

(P-10041)
SANDIA PLASTICS INC
Also Called: Ultimate Solutions
15571 Container Ln, Huntington Beach
(92649-1530)
PHONE.....................714 901-8400
William Allan, CEO
Bisson Monty, President
▲ EMP: 31
SQ FT: 2,500

SALES (est): 7MM Privately Held
WEB: www.sandiaplastics.com
SIC: 3089 Injection molded finished plastic
products

(P-10042)
SANTA CLARITA PLASTIC MOLDING
24735 Avenue Rockefeller, Valencia
(91355-3466)
PHONE.....................661 294-2257
Walter Schrey, President
Thomas Schrey, Principal
EMP: 15 EST: 1998
SALES (est): 1.2MM Privately Held
WEB: www.santaclaritaplasticsurgeon.com
SIC: 3089 Plastic processing

(P-10043)
SANTA FE EXTRUDERS INC
15315 Marquardt Ave, Santa Fe Springs
(90670-5709)
P.O. Box 524, Olney IL (62450-0524)
PHONE.....................562 921-8991
Brick Pinckney, President
Jeanne Pinckney, Corp Secy
EMP: 62 EST: 1981
SQ FT: 30,000
SALES (est): 10.6MM Privately Held
WEB: www.sfext.com
SIC: 3089 3083 3081 2673 Extruded fin-
ished plastic products; laminated plastics
plate & sheet; unsupported plastics film &
sheet; bags: plastic, laminated & coated

(P-10044)
SANTA MONICA PLASTICS LLC
1631 Stanford St, Santa Monica
(90404-4113)
PHONE.....................310 403-2849
Eric Warren, Mng Member
EMP: 12 EST: 2011
SALES (est): 1.3MM Privately Held
SIC: 3089 Injection molded finished plastic
products; plastic processing

(P-10045)
SCHAEFER SYSTEMS INTL INC
1250 Thurman St, Lodi (95240-3134)
PHONE.....................209 365-6030
Mark Phillips, Branch Mgr
Shannon Ramirez, Office Admin
EMP: 30
SALES (corp-wide): 1.8B Privately Held
WEB: www.ssimail.net
SIC: 3089 Injection molding of plastics
HQ: Schaefer Systems International, Inc.
10021 Westlake Dr
Charlotte NC 28273
704 944-4500

(P-10046)
SCHOLLE IPN CORPORATION
2500 Cooper Ave, Merced (95348-4312)
PHONE.....................209 384-3100
Marcia Mickle, Manager
EMP: 400
SQ FT: 80,000
SALES (corp-wide): 283.7MM Privately
Held
WEB: www.scholle.com
SIC: 3089 2671 Plastic containers, except
foam; packaging paper & plastics film,
coated & laminated
PA: Scholle Ipn Corporation
200 W North Ave
Northlake IL 60164
708 562-7290

(P-10047)
SCHOLLE IPN PACKAGING INC
2500 Cooper Ave, Merced (95348-4312)
PHONE.....................209 384-3100
Chris Bunggay, Engineer
Eloy Maldonado, Engineer
Eric Zamora, Engineer
EMP: 280
SALES (corp-wide): 283.7MM Privately
Held
SIC: 3089 Plastic processing
HQ: Scholle Ipn Packaging, Inc.
200 W North Ave
Northlake IL 60164

(P-10048)
SCIENTIFIC MOLDING CORP LTD
3250 Brickway Blvd, Santa Rosa
(95403-8235)
PHONE.....................707 303-3041
EMP: 72
SALES (corp-wide): 601.9MM Privately
Held
SIC: 3089
PA: Scientific Molding Corporation, Ltd.
330 Smc Dr
Somerset WI 54025
715 247-3500

(P-10049)
SCOTLAND ENTRY SYSTEMS INC
159 S Beverly Dr, Beverly Hills
(90212-3002)
PHONE.....................818 376-0777
Bejan Souferian, President
CHI Bui, Executive Asst
EMP: 10
SALES (est): 1.9MM Privately Held
WEB: www.scotlandentry.com
SIC: 3089 1731 Fences, gates & acces-
sories: plastic; safety & security special-
ization

(P-10050)
SCRIBNER ENGINEERING INC
11455 Hydraulics Dr, Rancho Cordova
(95742-6870)
PHONE.....................916 638-1515
Richard L Scribner, President
Janet Scribner, Corp Secy
Linda Beisner, General Mgr
EMP: 25
SQ FT: 30,000
SALES (est): 3.5MM Privately Held
SIC: 3089 Injection molding of plastics

(P-10051)
SCRIBNER PLASTICS
11455 Hydraulics Dr, Rancho Cordova
(95742-6870)
PHONE.....................916 638-1515
Rick Scribner, Owner
EMP: 15 EST: 2001
SALES (est): 1.8MM Privately Held
WEB: www.scribnerplastics.com
SIC: 3089 Molding primary plastic; injec-
tion molding of plastics

(P-10052)
SCULPTOR BODY MOLDING (PA)
10817 W Stallion Ranch Rd, Sunland
(91040-3702)
PHONE.....................818 761-3767
Monica Canon Ferguson, Principal
Steve Ferguson, Vice Pres
EMP: 10
SALES (est): 1.6MM Privately Held
SIC: 3089 Molding primary plastic

(P-10053)
SERCO MOLD INC (PA)
Also Called: Serpac Electronic Enclosures
2009 Wright Ave, La Verne (91750-5812)
PHONE.....................626 331-0517
Patricia Ann Serio, CEO
Don Serio Jr, Vice Pres
Lori Clark, Manager
▲ EMP: 45 EST: 1978
SQ FT: 85,000
SALES (est): 4.9MM Privately Held
WEB: www.serpac.com
SIC: 3089 3544 5999 Injection molding of
plastics; industrial molds; electronic parts
& equipment

(P-10054)
SETCO LLC
4875 E Hunter Ave, Anaheim (92807-2005)
PHONE.....................812 424-2904
Patty Harper, Branch Mgr
Richard Hofmann,
EMP: 15 Publicly Held
SIC: 3089 Plastic containers, except foam
HQ: Setco, Llc
101 Oakley St
Evansville IN 47710
812 424-2904

(P-10055)
SF GLOBAL LLC
250 Frank H Ogawa Plz, Oakland
(94612-2010)
PHONE..................................888 536-5593
Raul Hinojosa,
EMP: 10
SALES (est): 1.1MM **Privately Held**
SIC: 3089 Identification cards, plastic

(P-10056)
SIERRACIN/SYLMAR
CORPORATION
Also Called: PPG Aerospace
12780 San Fernando Rd, Sylmar
(91342-3728)
PHONE..................................818 362-6711
Barry Gillespie, *CEO*
▲ **EMP:** 600
SQ FT: 300,000
SALES (est): 150MM
SALES (corp-wide): 15.3B **Publicly Held**
WEB: www.sierracin.com
SIC: 3089 3812 3621 3231 Windshields,
plastic; search & navigation equipment;
motors & generators; products of pur-
chased glass
PA: Ppg Industries, Inc.
1 Ppg Pl
Pittsburgh PA 15272
412 434-3131

(P-10057)
SISTEMA US INC (PA)
775 Southpoint Blvd, Petaluma
(94954-1495)
P.O. Box 5068, Novato (94948-5068)
PHONE..................................707 773-2200
Simon Kirby, *President*
Peter Carter, *CFO*
▲ **EMP:** 30
SQ FT: 42,500
SALES (est): 4.2MM **Privately Held**
WEB: www.typhoonhousewares.com
SIC: 3089 Plastic kitchenware, tableware &
houseware

(P-10058)
SKB CORPORATION (PA)
434 W Levers Pl, Orange (92867-3605)
PHONE..................................714 637-1252
Steven A Kottman, *CEO*
David Sanderson, *Vice Pres*
Don Weber, *VP Mfg*
Will Steven, *Manager*
◆ **EMP:** 350
SALES (est): 72.5MM **Privately Held**
WEB: www.skbcases.com
SIC: 3089 3161 Cases, plastic; luggage

(P-10059)
SMART LLC
Also Called: Smart Wax
14108 S Western Ave, Gardena
(90249-3010)
PHONE..................................310 674-8135
David Knotek, *CEO*
Sergio Galindo, *Vice Pres*
Paul Schneider, *Vice Pres*
Ivan Cabrera, *Purchasing*
Roxana Arredondo, *Production*
▼ **EMP:** 40
SALES (est): 12.9MM **Privately Held**
WEB: www.smartwax.com
SIC: 3089 5013 Automotive parts, plastic;
automotive supplies & parts

(P-10060)
SMITHCO PLASTICS INC (PA)
3330 W Harvard St, Santa Ana
(92704-3920)
PHONE..................................714 545-9107
Stanley L Smith, *President*
Nancy Smith, *Treasurer*
Dan Smith, *Vice Pres*
EMP: 14
SQ FT: 8,500
SALES (est): 1.5MM **Privately Held**
SIC: 3089 Injection molding of plastics;
plastic processing

(P-10061)
SNAPWARE CORPORATION
Also Called: Corningware Corelle & More
3900 Hamner Ave, Eastvale (91752-1017)
PHONE..................................951 361-3100
Kris Malkoski, *CEO*
Ken Tran, *COO*
Grant Hartman, *Vice Pres*
Alex Yuan, *Technology*
Susan R Mercado, *Controller*
◆ **EMP:** 180
SQ FT: 168,345
SALES (est): 48.7MM **Privately Held**
WEB: www.snapware.com
SIC: 3089 Plastic kitchenware, tableware &
houseware
HQ: Corelle Brands Llc
9525 Bryn Mawr Ave
Rosemont IL 60018
847 233-8600

(P-10062)
SNYDER INDUSTRIES LLC
800 Commerce Dr, Chowchilla
(93610-9395)
PHONE..................................559 665-7611
Reyes Morales, *CEO*
EMP: 65
SALES (corp-wide): 4.7B **Privately Held**
SIC: 3089 Pallets, plastic
HQ: Snyder Industries, Llc
6940 O St Ste 100
Lincoln NE 68510
402 467-5221

(P-10063)
SOUTH BAY CSTM PLSTIC
EXTRDERS
2554 Commercial St, San Diego
(92113-1132)
P.O. Box 131195 (92170-1195)
PHONE..................................619 544-0808
Abraham Rafiee, *President*
Hassan Rafiee, *Vice Pres*
EMP: 20
SQ FT: 14,000
SALES (est): 3MM **Privately Held**
WEB: www.southbayplastic.com
SIC: 3089 Plastic containers, except foam

(P-10064)
SPIN PRODUCTS INC
13878 Yorba Ave, Chino (91710-5518)
PHONE..................................909 590-7000
Paul Burlingham, *President*
William Burlingham, *Vice Pres*
Andrea Gutierrez, *Accounting Mgr*
Gonzalo Banuelos, *Prdtn Mgr*
▲ **EMP:** 24
SQ FT: 96,000
SALES (est): 5.8MM **Privately Held**
WEB: www.spinproducts.com
SIC: 3089 Plastic containers, except foam

(P-10065)
SR PLASTICS COMPANY LLC
(PA)
640 Parkridge Ave, Norco (92860-3124)
PHONE..................................951 520-9486
Larry Kaford, *Principal*
Larry Novak,
EMP: 15
SALES (est): 5.2MM **Privately Held**
SIC: 3089 Injection molding of plastics

(P-10066)
SR PLASTICS COMPANY LLC
692 Parkridge Ave, Norco (92860-3124)
PHONE..................................951 479-5394
EMP: 30
SALES (corp-wide): 5.2MM **Privately**
Held
SIC: 3089 Injection molding of plastics
PA: Sr Plastics Company, Llc
640 Parkridge Ave
Norco CA 92860
951 520-9486

(P-10067)
STACK PLASTICS INC
3525 Haven Ave, Menlo Park (94025-1009)
PHONE..................................650 361-8600
Mark Rackley, *President*
Michael Mendonca, *Vice Pres*
David Diaz, *Engineer*
▲ **EMP:** 30
SQ FT: 9,000
SALES (est): 6.9MM **Privately Held**
WEB: www.wcsplastics.com
SIC: 3089 Injection molding of plastics

(P-10068)
STAR PLASTIC DESIGN
25914 President Ave, Harbor City
(90710-3333)
PHONE..................................310 530-7119
Dana Maltun, *President*
Maria Martinez, *Office Mgr*
▲ **EMP:** 60
SQ FT: 25,000
SALES (est): 9.2MM **Privately Held**
WEB: www.starplastic.com
SIC: 3089 Injection molding of plastics

(P-10069)
STAR SANITATION SERVICES
4 Harris Rd, Salinas (93908-8608)
PHONE..................................831 754-6794
Bartley Walker, *Mng Member*
Sheryl Smith,
EMP: 10
SALES (est): 1.8MM **Privately Held**
SIC: 3089 1799 Toilets, portable chemical:
plastic; fence construction

(P-10070)
STAR SHIELD SOLUTIONS LLC
4315 Santa Ana St, Ontario (91761-7872)
PHONE..................................866 662-4477
Gil Stanfill, *Mng Member*
Bryan Cobb, *Opers Staff*
Jim Kwon, *Marketing Staff*
EMP: 60
SALES (est): 1.8MM **Privately Held**
SIC: 3089 7389 Automotive parts, plastic;
financial services

(P-10071)
STEVE LESHNER CLEAR
SYSTEMS
13438 Wyandotte St, North Hollywood
(91605-4012)
PHONE..................................818 764-9223
Steve Leshner, *Owner*
EMP: 11
SQ FT: 5,000
SALES (est): 658K **Privately Held**
SIC: 3089 5211 Injection molding of plas-
tics; closets, interiors & accessories

(P-10072)
STONE CANYON INDUSTRIES
LLC (PA)
1875 Century Park E # 320, Los Angeles
(90067-2539)
PHONE..................................310 570-4869
James H Fordyce, *CEO*
James Fordyce, *Managing Prtnr*
Michael Neumann, *President*
Adam Cohn, *CEO*
Michael Salvator, *COO*
EMP: 53 **EST:** 2014
SALES (est): 1.2B **Privately Held**
SIC: 3089 Plastic containers, except foam

(P-10073)
STRAND ART COMPANY INC
4700 E Hunter Ave, Anaheim (92807-1919)
PHONE..................................714 777-0444
Kevin Strand, *President*
Vicky Strand, *Admin Sec*
▲ **EMP:** 50
SQ FT: 10,480
SALES (est): 7.9MM **Privately Held**
WEB: www.strandart.com
SIC: 3089 Injection molded finished plastic
products

(P-10074)
STRATASYS DIRECT INC (HQ)
Also Called: Stratasys Direct Manufacturing
28309 Avenue Crocker, Valencia
(91355-1251)
PHONE..................................661 295-4400
Joseph Allison, *CEO*
Peter Keller, *CFO*
Tom Smolders, *CFO*
▲ **EMP:** 190
SQ FT: 24,000
SALES (est): 100.1MM
SALES (corp-wide): 179MM **Privately**
Held
WEB: www.solidconcepts.com
SIC: 3089 Plastic processing; casting of
plastic

PA: Stratasys Ltd
1 Holzman Haim
Rehovot 76704
893 143-14

(P-10075)
STUDER CREATIVE PACKAGING
INC
5652 Mountain View Ave, Yorba Linda
(92886-5528)
PHONE..................................818 344-1665
James R Studer, *President*
Chris Studer, *Vice Pres*
Mike Studer, *Vice Pres*
Yvonne E Studer, *Admin Sec*
EMP: 14
SQ FT: 23,000
SALES (est): 1.1MM **Privately Held**
SIC: 3089 Thermoformed finished plastic
products

(P-10076)
SUPERIOR MOLD CO INC
1927 E Francis St, Ontario (91761-7719)
PHONE..................................909 947-7028
Anthony Codet, *CEO*
EMP: 21
SALES (est): 4.5MM **Privately Held**
SIC: 3089 Injection molding of plastics

(P-10077)
SYNTECH DEVELOPMENT &
MFG INC
Also Called: S D M
13948 Mountain Ave, Chino (91710-9018)
PHONE..................................909 465-5554
Harry N Herbert, *CEO*
Bob Hobbs, *President*
Eddie Montelongo, *President*
Ellen Miller, *Administration*
EMP: 25 **EST:** 1998
SQ FT: 11,000
SALES (est): 4.9MM **Privately Held**
WEB: www.sdmplastics.com
SIC: 3089 Injection molding of plastics

(P-10078)
TALCO PLASTICS INC
3270 E 70th St, Long Beach (90805-1821)
PHONE..................................562 630-1224
Ajit Ferera, *Manager*
EMP: 34
SALES (corp-wide): 90.5MM **Privately**
Held
WEB: www.talcoplastics.com
SIC: 3089 4953 Extruded finished plastic
products; recycling, waste materials
PA: Talco Plastics, Inc.
1000 W Rincon St
Corona CA 92880
951 531-2000

(P-10079)
TAMSHELL CORP
237 Glider Cir, Corona (92880-2534)
PHONE..................................951 272-9395
John Hernandez, *President*
Art Pierce, *Vice Pres*
Adam Bolt, *General Mgr*
Michael Hernandez, *General Mgr*
Maricela Giles, *Office Mgr*
EMP: 95
SQ FT: 20,000
SALES (est): 25MM **Privately Held**
WEB: www.tamshell.com
SIC: 3089 Caps, plastic; plastic hardware
& building products; hardware, plastic;
bearings, plastic

(P-10080)
TARAL PLASTICS
34343 Zwissig Way, Union City (94587)
PHONE..................................510 972-6300
▲ **EMP:** 10 **EST:** 2015
SALES (est): 1.4MM **Privately Held**
SIC: 3089 Jars, plastic

(P-10081)
TEKSUN INC
1549 N Poinsettia Pl # 1, Los Angeles
(90046-3662)
PHONE..................................310 479-0794
David Meyer, *President*
EMP: 15
SQ FT: 6,800

PRODUCTS & SVCS

SALES (est): 2.9MM **Privately Held**
WEB: www.teksun.com
SIC: 3089 Plastic processing; injection molded finished plastic products

(P-10082)
TGS MOLDING LLC
Also Called: Tgs Plastic
425 E Parkcenter Cir S, San Bernardino (92408-2872)
P.O. Box 17787, Anaheim (92817-7787)
PHONE..................................909 890-1707
Antoine Semaan, *Mng Member*
Lewis Allen,
Rima Semaan,
EMP: 11
SQ FT: 2,000
SALES (est): 880K **Privately Held**
SIC: 3089 Molding primary plastic

(P-10083)
THERMODYNE INTERNATIONAL LTD
1841 S Business Pkwy, Ontario (91761-8537)
PHONE..................................909 923-9945
Gary S Ackerman, *Ch of Bd*
Scott Ackerman, *CFO*
Josh Ackerman, *Administration*
◆ EMP: 110 EST: 1967
SQ FT: 57,500
SALES (est): 18.9MM **Privately Held**
WEB: www.shokstop.com
SIC: 3089 3694 Plastic containers, except foam; engine electrical equipment

(P-10084)
THREE-D PLASTICS INC
Also Called: Three-D Traffic Works
424 N Varney St, Burbank (91502-1732)
PHONE..................................323 849-1316
Joe Dvoracek, *President*
EMP: 15
SALES (est): 1.7MM
SALES (corp-wide): 9.7MM **Privately Held**
WEB: www.trafficwks.com
SIC: 3089 Injection molded finished plastic products; injection molding of plastics
PA: Three-D Plastics, Inc.
430 N Varney St
Burbank CA 91502
323 849-1316

(P-10085)
THREE-D PLASTICS INC (PA)
Also Called: Three-D Traffics Works
430 N Varney St, Burbank (91502-1732)
PHONE..................................323 849-1316
Frank J Dvoracek, *CEO*
Tim Trumbo, *COO*
Kathleen D Trumbo, *Corp Secy*
Joseph Dvoracek, *Vice Pres*
Jo Dvoracek, *Manager*
EMP: 37
SQ FT: 40,000
SALES (est): 9.7MM **Privately Held**
WEB: www.trafficwks.com
SIC: 3089 Injection molding of plastics

(P-10086)
TIGERS PLASTICS INC
14721 Lull St, Van Nuys (91405-1211)
PHONE..................................818 901-9393
Set Ayrapetyan, *President*
EMP: 10
SALES (est): 1.5MM **Privately Held**
WEB: www.tigersinc.com
SIC: 3089 Boxes, plastic

(P-10087)
TNT PLASTIC MOLDING INC (PA)
725 E Harrison St, Corona (92879-1350)
PHONE..................................951 808-9700
Diane Mixson, *President*
John Chadwick, *CFO*
Doug Chadwick, *Vice Pres*
Lynn Chadwick, *Vice Pres*
R J Jamaica, *Human Res Dir*
▲ EMP: 118
SQ FT: 30,000
SALES (est): 38.5MM **Privately Held**
WEB: www.artisticplastics.com
SIC: 3089 Injection molding of plastics

(P-10088)
TOM YORK ENTERPRISES INC
Also Called: Kal Plastics
2050 E 48th St, Vernon (90058-2022)
PHONE..................................323 581-6194
Tom York, *CEO*
Romeo Castro, *QC Mgr*
EMP: 25
SQ FT: 45,000
SALES (est): 4.1MM **Privately Held**
WEB: www.kal-plastics.com
SIC: 3089 3993 Boxes, plastic; tubs, plastic (containers); thermoformed finished plastic products; signs & advertising specialties

(P-10089)
TOTEX MANUFACTURING INC
3050 Lomita Blvd, Torrance (90505-5103)
PHONE..................................310 326-2028
Tommy Tong, *President*
Jim Sides, *Director*
▲ EMP: 70
SALES (est): 31.5MM **Privately Held**
WEB: www.totexusa.com
SIC: 3089 5063 Battery cases, plastic or plastic combination; batteries, dry cell

(P-10090)
TRANPAK INC
2860 S East Ave, Fresno (93725-1909)
PHONE..................................800 827-2474
Martin Ueland, *President*
Christian Ueland, *COO*
Donna Ueland, *Treasurer*
Lucie Colmenero, *Info Tech Mgr*
Brett Miller, *Sales Staff*
◆ EMP: 21
SQ FT: 80,000
SALES (est): 9.3MM **Privately Held**
WEB: www.tranpak.com
SIC: 3089 Air mattresses, plastic

(P-10091)
TRIAD TOOL & ENGINEERING INC
Also Called: Engineered Plastic Division
1750 Rogers Ave, San Jose (95112-1109)
PHONE..................................408 436-8411
William Bartlett, *President*
David C Bartlett, *Vice Pres*
James S Bartlett, *Vice Pres*
Mildred Carvelho, *Admin Sec*
EMP: 35 EST: 1978
SQ FT: 39,960
SALES (est): 5.5MM **Privately Held**
SIC: 3089 3599 3364 3363 Injection molded finished plastic products; machine shop, jobbing & repair; zinc & zinc-base alloy die-castings; aluminum die-castings

(P-10092)
TRIDENT PRODUCTS INC
1370 W San Marcos Blvd # 120, San Marcos (92078-1601)
PHONE..................................760 510-1160
David Brandt, *President*
Frank Stephan, *CFO*
EMP: 60
SQ FT: 48,000
SALES (est): 5.1MM **Privately Held**
SIC: 3089 Plastic hardware & building products; plastic processing

(P-10093)
TRIM-LOK INC (PA)
6855 Hermosa Cir, Buena Park (90620-1151)
P.O. Box 6180 (90622-6180)
PHONE..................................714 562-0500
Gary Whitener, *President*
Jack Hetherington, *Officer*
Lilia Quintero, *Administration*
Balan Sorin, *Info Tech Mgr*
Raluca Mactavish, *Engineer*
◆ EMP: 180
SQ FT: 57,000
SALES (est): 36.2MM **Privately Held**
WEB: www.trimlok.com
SIC: 3089 Molding primary plastic

(P-10094)
TRU-FORM PLASTICS INC
14600 Hoover St, Westminster (92683-5346)
PHONE..................................310 327-9444

Douglas W Sahm Sr, *CEO*
John D Evans, *COO*
Clauve Hurwicz, *CFO*
Anita Lorber, *Vice Pres*
▲ EMP: 35
SQ FT: 1,000
SALES (est): 7.5MM **Privately Held**
WEB: www.truform.com
SIC: 3089 Pallets, plastic; plastic processing

(P-10095)
TST MOLDING LLC
Also Called: All Ameri Injec Moldi Servi
42322 Avenida Alvarado, Temecula (92590-3445)
PHONE..................................951 296-6200
Terry Voss, *Mng Member*
Tammy Richer, *Accounting Mgr*
Dave Hawley,
EMP: 27
SALES (est): 4MM **Privately Held**
SIC: 3089 Injection molding of plastics

(P-10096)
TTL HOLDINGS LLC (HQ)
4626 Eucalyptus Ave, Chino (91710-9215)
PHONE..................................909 597-7861
Earl E Payton, *Mng Member*
Liz Smith,
Earl Payton, *Mng Member*
EMP: 10
SALES (est): 130.8MM
SALES (corp-wide): 164.5MM **Privately Held**
WEB: www.trendtechnologies.com
SIC: 3089 3544 Molding primary plastic; special dies, tools, jigs & fixtures
PA: Eep Holdings, Llc
4626 Eucalyptus Ave
Chino CA 91710
909 597-7861

(P-10097)
UDECOR INC (PA)
Also Called: Proceilingtiles
8302 Espresso Dr Ste 130, Bakersfield (93312-5688)
PHONE..................................877 550-0600
James Welch, *President*
Robert Welch, *CEO*
Scott Fischer, *Vice Pres*
EMP: 10 EST: 2012
SQ FT: 6,000
SALES (est): 7.4MM **Privately Held**
SIC: 3089 5961 Injection molding of plastics;

(P-10098)
UFO DESIGNS (PA)
5812 Machine Dr, Huntington Beach (92649-1101)
PHONE..................................714 892-4420
Jitendra Patel, *President*
Alfie Patel, *Vice Pres*
EMP: 16
SQ FT: 35,000
SALES (est): 3.8MM **Privately Held**
WEB: www.ufodesign.com
SIC: 3089 Injection molding of plastics

(P-10099)
UFO INC
2110 Belgrave Ave, Huntington Park (90255-2713)
P.O. Box 58192, Los Angeles (90058-0192)
PHONE..................................323 588-5450
Efi Youavian, *President*
Efraim Youavian, *CEO*
Umar Farooq, *Prdtn Mgr*
◆ EMP: 50
SQ FT: 65,000
SALES (est): 14.8MM **Privately Held**
SIC: 3089 2842 5199 Sponges, plastic; specialty cleaning, polishes & sanitation goods; foams & rubber

(P-10100)
UNCKS UNIQUE PLASTICS INC
1215 Brooks St, Ontario (91762-3609)
PHONE..................................909 983-5181
Fax: 909 984-6376
EMP: 16
SALES (est): 1MM **Privately Held**
SIC: 3089 3544

(P-10101)
UPLAND FAB INC
1445 Brooks St Ste L, Ontario (91762-3665)
PHONE..................................909 933-9185
Patsy Sapra, *CEO*
Jackson Sapra, *Shareholder*
Paul Sapra, *CEO*
Steven Sapra, *CFO*
Dawn Lancaster, *Office Mgr*
EMP: 24 EST: 1970
SQ FT: 12,000
SALES (est): 5.4MM **Privately Held**
WEB: www.uplandfab.com
SIC: 3089 Plastic & fiberglass tanks; plastic processing

(P-10102)
URETHANE PRODUCTS CORPORATION
Also Called: U P C
17842 Sampson Ln, Huntington Beach (92647-7147)
PHONE..................................800 913-0062
Kelly Goulis, *CEO*
Elizabeth Thermos, *President*
▲ EMP: 12
SQ FT: 13,000
SALES (est): 2.3MM **Privately Held**
WEB: www.urethaneproducts.com
SIC: 3089 Plastic processing

(P-10103)
URETHANE SCIENCE INC
8357 Standustrial St, Stanton (90680-2617)
PHONE..................................714 828-3210
Roger Evans, *President*
Paula Evans, *President*
EMP: 10 EST: 1981
SQ FT: 4,500
SALES (est): 580.8K **Privately Held**
WEB: www.hdmolding.com
SIC: 3089 3086 Injection molding of plastics; plastics foam products

(P-10104)
US POLYMERS INC (PA)
Also Called: Duramax Building Products
1057 S Vail Ave, Montebello (90640-6019)
PHONE..................................323 728-3023
Viken Ohanesian, *CEO*
Vram Ohanesian, *CFO*
Haigan Ohanesian, *Treasurer*
Jacques Ohanesian, *Vice Pres*
◆ EMP: 100
SQ FT: 70,000
SALES (est): 40.3MM **Privately Held**
WEB: www.uspolymersinc.com
SIC: 3089 3084 Shutters, plastic; plastics pipe

(P-10105)
USA EXTRUDED PLASTICS INC
965 E Discovery Ln, Anaheim (92801-1147)
PHONE..................................714 991-6061
Joseph Florimonte, *President*
Vida Aiona, *Vice Pres*
Linda Florimonte, *Admin Sec*
EMP: 16
SQ FT: 11,000
SALES: 2.5MM **Privately Held**
WEB: www.usaextrudedplastics.com
SIC: 3089 Extruded finished plastic products

(P-10106)
V-T INDUSTRIES INC
16222 Phoebe Ave, La Mirada (90638-5610)
PHONE..................................714 521-2008
EMP: 16
SALES (corp-wide): 197.9MM **Privately Held**
SIC: 3089 3083 4213 2435 Plastic hardware & building products; doors, folding: plastic or plastic coated fabric; plastic finished products, laminated; trucking, except local; hardwood veneer & plywood; wood kitchen cabinets; millwork
PA: V-T Industries Inc.
1000 Industrial Park
Holstein IA 51025
712 368-4381

▲ = Import ▼=Export
◆ =Import/Export

(P-10107)
VALENCIA MOLD
25611 Hercules St, Santa Clarita
(91355-5051)
PHONE....................661 257-0066
Luis Ruiz, *Owner*
EMP: 16
SQ FT: 11,000
SALES (est): 1.8MM Privately Held
SIC: 3089 Injection molding of plastics

(P-10108)
VALLEY DECORATING COMPANY
2829 E Hamilton Ave, Fresno
(93721-3208)
PHONE....................559 495-1100
James Offen, *President*
Rebecca Karmann, *Production*
▼ EMP: 20
SQ FT: 25,000
SALES (est): 4.1MM Privately Held
WEB: www.valleydecorating.com
SIC: 3089 Novelties, plastic

(P-10109)
VAN GRACE QUALITY INJECTION
Also Called: Crystal Tex Shoehorn
9164 Appleby St, Downey (90240-2915)
PHONE....................323 931-5255
EMP: 15
SQ FT: 2,000
SALES (est): 2.2MM Privately Held
SIC: 3089

(P-10110)
VANDERVEER INDUSTRIAL PLAS LLC
515 S Melrose St, Placentia (92870-6337)
PHONE....................714 579-7700
Greg Geiss, *President*
EMP: 35
SQ FT: 29,000
SALES: 10MM Privately Held
WEB: www.vanderveerplastics.com
SIC: 3089 Plastic processing

(P-10111)
VANTAGE ASSOCIATES INC
12333 Los Nietos Rd, Santa Fe Springs
(90670-2911)
PHONE....................562 968-1400
Paul Roy, *CEO*
Eric Clack, *President*
Andrea Alpinieri Glover, *CFO*
EMP: 65
SQ FT: 20,000
SALES (corp-wide): 63.6MM Privately
Held
SIC: 3089 2499 5085 3621 Plastic pro-
cessing; spools, reels & pulleys: wood; in-
dustrial supplies; motors & generators;
aircraft parts & equipment; search & navi-
gation equipment
PA: Vantage Associates Inc.
900 Civic Center Dr
National City CA 91950
619 477-6940

(P-10112)
VIANT MEDICAL LLC
45581 Northport Loop W, Fremont
(94538-6462)
PHONE....................510 657-5800
Bill Tarajos, *Branch Mgr*
EMP: 11
SALES (corp-wide): 368.7MM Privately
Held
SIC: 3089 Injection molding of plastics
HQ: Viant Medical, Llc
2 Hampshire St
Foxborough MA 02035

(P-10113)
VOLEX INC (HQ)
Also Called: Powercords
3110 Coronado Dr, Santa Clara
(95054-3205)
PHONE....................669 444-1740
Christoph Eisenhardt, *CEO*
James Stuart, *President*
Nick Parker, *CFO*
▲ EMP: 30 EST: 1979

SQ FT: 10,000
SALES (est): 417.5MM
SALES (corp-wide): 372.1MM Privately
Held
WEB: www.volex.com
SIC: 3089 Injection molded finished plastic
products
PA: Volex Plc
Holbrook House
Richmond TW10
203 370-8830

(P-10114)
VOLEX INC
511 E San Ysidro Blvd, San Ysidro
(92173-3150)
PHONE....................619 205-4900
EMP: 28
SALES (corp-wide): 372.1MM Privately
Held
SIC: 3089 Injection molded finished plastic
products
HQ: Volex Inc.
3110 Coronado Dr
Santa Clara CA 95054
669 444-1740

(P-10115)
WADDINGTON NORTH AMERICA INC
Also Called: Wna City of Industry
1135 Samuelson St, City of Industry
(91748-1222)
PHONE....................626 913-4022
Mike Evans, *President*
Rodney Harano, *Controller*
Oscar Vasquez, *QC Mgr*
Dennis Juhnke, *Maintence Staff*
EMP: 182
SALES (corp-wide): 2.9B Privately Held
SIC: 3089 Plastic kitchenware, tableware &
houseware
HQ: Waddington North America, Inc.
50 E Rivercenter Blvd # 650
Covington KY 41011

(P-10116)
WATERDOG PRODUCTS INC
1148 Pioneer Way, El Cajon (92020-1925)
PHONE....................619 441-9688
John Harriman, *President*
Klint Dingley, *Vice Pres*
Jayne Harriman, *Vice Pres*
Todd Widegren, *Vice Pres*
▲ EMP: 14
SQ FT: 12,400
SALES (est): 2.1MM Privately Held
WEB: www.waterdogproducts.com
SIC: 3089 Plastic & fiberglass tanks

(P-10117)
WCP INC
Also Called: West Coast Vinyl Windows
17730 Crusader Ave, Cerritos
(90703-2629)
PHONE....................562 653-9797
Charles Neubauer, *President*
▲ EMP: 95
SQ FT: 50,000
SALES (est): 20.4MM Privately Held
SIC: 3089 3211 Windows, plastic; insulat-
ing glass, sealed units

(P-10118)
WESCO ENTERPRISES INC
12681 Corral Pl, Santa Fe Springs
(90670-4748)
PHONE....................562 944-3100
John Song, *President*
▲ EMP: 16
SQ FT: 21,000
SALES (est): 3.4MM Privately Held
WEB: www.kingseal.com
SIC: 3089 3842 2499 Work gloves, plas-
tic; gloves, safety; skewers, wood; tooth-
picks, wood

(P-10119)
WEST COAST PLASTICS INC
10025 Shoemaker Ave, Santa Fe Springs
(90670-3401)
PHONE....................562 777-8024
Javier Franco, *President*
Judith Garcia, *Vice Pres*
Bob Ibanez, *Admin Sec*

EMP: 11
SQ FT: 30,000
SALES (est): 2.4MM Privately Held
WEB: www.wcpi.net
SIC: 3089 Blow molded finished plastic
products

(P-10120)
WEST COAST WINDOWS & DOORS INC
1112 Willow Pass Ct, Concord
(94520-1006)
PHONE....................925 681-1776
Richard Beil,
Kelly Mullins,
EMP: 13
SALES (est): 1.6MM Privately Held
SIC: 3089 5031 5211 7299 Windows,
plastic; doors & windows; windows,
storm: wood or metal; home improvement
& renovation contractor agency

(P-10121)
WEST-BAG INC
1161 Monterey Pass Rd, Monterey Park
(91754-3614)
PHONE....................323 264-0750
Luis Michel, *President*
Sixto Michel, *Vice Pres*
EMP: 30
SQ FT: 12,000
SALES (est): 4.9MM Privately Held
SIC: 3089 5149 Food casings, plastic;
sausage casings

(P-10122)
WESTERN CASE INCORPORATED (PA)
6400 Sycam Canyo Blvd Ste, Riverside
(92507)
PHONE....................951 214-6380
Toll Free:....................877 -
Paul F Queyrel, *CEO*
▲ EMP: 52
SQ FT: 19,000
SALES (est): 7.9MM Privately Held
WEB: www.westerncase.com
SIC: 3089 3544 3444 Cases, plastic; spe-
cial dies, tools, jigs & fixtures; sheet met-
alwork

(P-10123)
WESTLAKE ENGRG ROTO FORM
Also Called: Jaz Products
1041 E Santa Barbara St, Santa Paula
(93060-2820)
P.O. Box 3504, Westlake Village (91359-
0504)
PHONE....................805 525-8800
Wade Zimmerman, *President*
Pat Zimmerman, *Corp Secy*
▲ EMP: 24
SQ FT: 75,000
SALES (est): 3.4MM Privately Held
WEB: www.jazproducts.com
SIC: 3089 Planters, plastic; cases, plastic;
buoys & floats, plastic

(P-10124)
WILLIAM KREYSLER & ASSOC INC
501 Green Island Rd, American Canyon
(94503-9649)
PHONE....................707 552-3500
William Bartley Kreysler, *CEO*
Marie Birgitta, *Opers Staff*
Tim Oliver, *Opers Staff*
Jacque Giuffre, *Art Dir*
Joshua Zabel, *Director*
▼ EMP: 26
SALES (est): 5.4MM Privately Held
WEB: www.kreysler.com
SIC: 3089 Panels, building: plastic

(P-10125)
WINDOW HARDWARE SUPPLY
1717 Kirkham St, Oakland (94607-2214)
PHONE....................510 463-0301
Kevin Kemble, *Principal*
▲ EMP: 12
SALES (est): 1.7MM Privately Held
SIC: 3089 Window frames & sash, plastic

(P-10126)
WING INFLATABLES INC (HQ)
1220 5th St, Arcata (95521-6155)
P.O. Box 279 (95518-0279)
PHONE....................707 826-2887
Andrew Branagh, *CEO*
Mark French, *CFO*
Jake Heimbuch, *Vice Pres*
Mark Lougheed, *Vice Pres*
Lisa Zambas, *Vice Pres*
▲ EMP: 115
SQ FT: 80,000
SALES (est): 23.3MM
SALES (corp-wide): 26.8MM Privately
Held
WEB: www.wing.com
SIC: 3089 Plastic boats & other marine
equipment; life rafts, nonrigid: plastic

(P-10127)
WIREWRIGHT INC
3563 Old Conejo Rd, Newbury Park
(91320-2122)
PHONE....................805 499-9194
Hubert Wright, *President*
EMP: 10
SALES (est): 1MM Privately Held
SIC: 3089 Hardware, plastic

(P-10128)
WNA COMET WEST INC
Also Called: Wna City of Industry
1135 Samuelson St, City of Industry
(91748-1222)
PHONE....................626 913-0724
Mike Evans, *President*
Gabriella Flores, *Principal*
Rodney Harano, *Principal*
Janet Parga, *Principal*
▲ EMP: 230
SALES (est): 68.8MM
SALES (corp-wide): 8.6B Publicly Held
SIC: 3089 Plastic kitchenware, tableware &
houseware
PA: Newell Brands Inc.
221 River St Ste 13
Hoboken NJ 07030
201 610-6600

(P-10129)
WOMBAT PRODUCTS INC
Also Called: Portapaint
1384 Callens Rd Ste B, Ventura
(93003-5808)
PHONE....................805 794-1767
John Lockwood, *CEO*
Alexander Auerbach, *COO*
▲ EMP: 22
SQ FT: 5,000
SALES: 5K Privately Held
SIC: 3089 Pails, plastic; air mattresses,
plastic

(P-10130)
WONDER GRIP USA INC
3070 Bristol St Ste 440, Costa Mesa
(92626-3066)
PHONE....................404 290-2015
Chris Weber, *Office Mgr*
EMP: 15 Privately Held
SIC: 3089 Work gloves, plastic

(P-10131)
WREX PRODUCTS INC CHICO
25 Wrex Ct, Chico (95928-7176)
PHONE....................530 895-3838
Wrex A Howard, *Ch of Bd*
Jim Barnett, *President*
James Barnett, *CEO*
Dennis Rupp, *Engineer*
Paul Rye, *Purch Mgr*
▲ EMP: 66
SQ FT: 70,000
SALES: 17.5MM Privately Held
WEB: www.wrexproducts.com
SIC: 3089 3363 3544 3599 Injection
molding of plastics; aluminum die-cast-
ings; special dies, tools, jigs & fixtures;
machine & other job shop work; sand-
blasting equipment

(P-10132)
WUNDER-MOLD INC
790 Eubanks Dr, Vacaville (95688-9470)
PHONE....................707 448-2349
Richard A Martindale, *CEO*

PRODUCTS & SVCS

William Martindale, *Principal*
Calvin Swesey, *General Mgr*
▲ EMP: 22
SQ FT: 56,000
SALES (est): 4.2MM **Privately Held**
SIC: 3089 Injection molding of plastics; injection molded finished plastic products; plastic processing

(P-10133)
XTIME INC
1400 Bridge Pkwy Ste 200, Redwood City (94065-6130)
PHONE....................................650 508-4300
Neal East, *President*
Jim Doehrman, *CFO*
Russ Kalchik, *Vice Pres*
Warren Webermin, *Vice Pres*
Addy Antiporda, *Administration*
EMP: 32 EST: 1999
SQ FT: 6,000
SALES (est): 8.8MM
SALES (corp-wide): 32.3B **Privately Held**
WEB: www.xtime.com
SIC: 3089 Automotive parts, plastic
HQ: Cox Automotive, Inc.
  6205-A Pchtree Dnwoody Rd
  Atlanta GA 30328
  404 843-5000

(P-10134)
YOGI INVESTMENTS INC
Also Called: Creative Extruded Products
419 Capron Ave, West Covina (91792-2828)
PHONE....................................909 984-5703
Lanraman Patel, *Manager*
Arvind Patel, *Shareholder*
Bhavana Patel, *President*
Ketan Patel, *Treasurer*
Pankaj Patel, *Admin Sec*
EMP: 16
SQ FT: 8,000
SALES: 1MM **Privately Held**
SIC: 3089 Extruded finished plastic products

(P-10135)
ZEPCO
1047 E Palm Ave, Burbank (91501-1412)
PHONE....................................818 848-0880
James Froelich, *Managing Prtnr*
Michael Froelich, *Partner*
EMP: 11
SALES (est): 1.4MM **Privately Held**
WEB: www.bottlehangers.com
SIC: 3089 Injection molding of plastics

3111 Leather Tanning & Finishing

(P-10136)
ANDREW ALEXANDER INC
Also Called: Falltech
1306 S Alameda St, Compton (90221-4803)
PHONE....................................323 752-0066
Michael Dancyger, *President*
Jeff Crosson, *CFO*
▲ EMP: 100
SQ FT: 100,000
SALES (est): 29MM **Privately Held**
WEB: www.falltech.com
SIC: 3111 Harness leather

(P-10137)
DALE CHAVEZ COMPANY INC
35165 La Bonita Donna, Temecula (92592)
P.O. Box 468 (92593-0468)
PHONE....................................951 303-0592
Dale Chavez, *President*
Patricia Chavez, *Vice Pres*
EMP: 10 EST: 1968
SALES (est): 1.3MM **Privately Held**
WEB: www.dalechavezsaddles.com
SIC: 3111 5199 Saddlery leather; leather, leather goods & furs

(P-10138)
HERITAGE LEATHER COMPANY INC
4011 E 52nd St, Maywood (90270-2205)
PHONE....................................323 983-0420
Jose C Munoz, *CEO*

Gustavo Gonzalez, *President*
▲ EMP: 30
SQ FT: 5,000
SALES (est): 4.5MM **Privately Held**
WEB: www.heritageleatherco.com
SIC: 3111 Belting leather

(P-10139)
JISONCASE (USA) LIMITED
9674 Telstar Ave Ste A, El Monte (91731-3022)
PHONE....................................888 233-8880
Hong Chu Deng, *CEO*
EMP: 12 EST: 2012
SALES (est): 1.5MM **Privately Held**
SIC: 3111 Case leather

(P-10140)
LA LA LAND PRODUCTION & DESIGN
2155 E 7th St Ste 300, Los Angeles (90023-1034)
PHONE....................................323 267-8485
Alexander M Zar, *CEO*
EMP: 35
SQ FT: 30,000
SALES: 4MM **Privately Held**
SIC: 3111 Accessory products, leather

(P-10141)
LEATHEROCK INTERNATIONAL INC
5285 Lovelock St, San Diego (92110-4012)
PHONE....................................619 299-7625
Laurence A Bloch, *CEO*
Rahleen Bloch, *Vice Pres*
▲ EMP: 27
SQ FT: 9,600
SALES (est): 4.2MM **Privately Held**
WEB: www.leatherock.com
SIC: 3111 2387 Bag leather; apparel belts

(P-10142)
LINEA PELLE INC (PA)
7107 Valjean Ave, Van Nuys (91406-3917)
PHONE....................................310 231-9950
Wynn Katz, *President*
Mira Katz, *Vice Pres*
Michael Stafford, *Vice Pres*
Maria Salcedo, *Finance*
Kelley Paratore, *Sales Staff*
▲ EMP: 17
SQ FT: 5,000
SALES (est): 2.7MM **Privately Held**
WEB: www.lineapelleinc.com
SIC: 3111 5621 Accessory products, leather; dress shops

(P-10143)
STITCH AND HIDE LLC
4 Bowie Rd, Rolling Hills (90274-5220)
PHONE....................................310 377-6912
Ross James Smith,
EMP: 10
SALES: 3MM **Privately Held**
SIC: 3111 3199 3171 3172 Accessory products, leather; belt laces, leather; handbags, women's; handbags, regardless of material: men's

(P-10144)
SU MANO INC
536 Milton Dr, San Gabriel (91775-2204)
PHONE....................................562 529-8835
Jeffrey Scott Kenney, *CEO*
Virginia Kenney, *Principal*
EMP: 12
SALES (est): 1.1MM **Privately Held**
SIC: 3111 Bookbinders' leather

(P-10145)
T N T AUTO INC
535 Patrice Pl, Gardena (90248-4232)
PHONE....................................310 715-1117
Peter Shum, *President*
EMP: 75 EST: 1995
SALES (est): 5.5MM **Privately Held**
WEB: www.tntauto.com
SIC: 3111 Upholstery leather

(P-10146)
WILDLIFE FUR DRESSING INC
3415 Harold St, Ceres (95307-3614)
PHONE....................................209 538-2901
Armando Navas, *President*

▲ EMP: 17
SQ FT: 10,000
SALES (est): 1.6MM **Privately Held**
WEB: www.wildlifefur.com
SIC: 3111 Leather tanning & finishing

3131 Boot & Shoe Cut Stock & Findings

(P-10147)
CALIFORNIA STAY CO INC
2600 Overland Ave Apt 219, Los Angeles (90064-3252)
PHONE....................................310 839-7236
Louis Saltsman, *President*
Sidney Saltsman, *Treasurer*
Jeffrey Saltsman, *Vice Pres*
Richard Saltsmans, *Vice Pres*
Helen Saltsman, *Admin Sec*
EMP: 10
SQ FT: 10,000
SALES (est): 1MM **Privately Held**
WEB: www.calriv800.com
SIC: 3131 Stays, shoe

(P-10148)
CI MANAGEMENT LLC
2039 Seabrook Ct, Redwood City (94065-8478)
PHONE....................................650 654-8900
Peter E Katz, *Principal*
EMP: 10
SALES (est): 1.2MM **Privately Held**
SIC: 3131 Counters

(P-10149)
COUNTER
21209 Hawthorne Blvd B, Torrance (90503-5535)
PHONE....................................310 406-3300
Danielle Gumbs, *Principal*
EMP: 30 EST: 2010
SALES (est): 2.9MM **Privately Held**
SIC: 3131 Counters

(P-10150)
CYDWOQ INC
2102 Kenmere Ave, Burbank (91504-3413)
PHONE....................................818 848-8307
Rafi Balouzian, *President*
Richard Delamarter, *Shareholder*
Jordyn Dent, *Technology*
◆ EMP: 28
SQ FT: 15,000
SALES (est): 4.5MM **Privately Held**
WEB: www.cydwoq.com
SIC: 3131 3199 Laces, shoe & boot: leather; leather belting & strapping

(P-10151)
INGRERSOLL RAND INDUS REFRIG
13770 Ramona Ave, Chino (91710-5423)
PHONE....................................909 477-2037
Michael Nobile, *Sales Mgr*
EMP: 13 EST: 2011
SALES (est): 1.6MM **Privately Held**
SIC: 3131 Rands

(P-10152)
PROSOUND COMMUNICATIONS INC
Also Called: Xotic Guitars & Effects
233 N Maclay Ave Ste 403, San Fernando (91340-2908)
PHONE....................................818 367-9593
Toshio Horiba, *CEO*
EMP: 10 EST: 2000
SALES (est): 1.3MM **Privately Held**
WEB: www.prosoundcommunications.com
SIC: 3131 7389 Footwear cut stock

(P-10153)
SIMPLE ORTHOTIC SOLUTIONS LLC
9960 Indiana Ave Ste 15, Riverside (92503-5457)
PHONE....................................951 353-8127
Gerardo Espinoza, *Mng Member*
EMP: 11
SQ FT: 4,800
SALES (est): 954.3K **Privately Held**
SIC: 3131 Inner soles, leather

(P-10154)
SOLE SOCIETY GROUP INC
8511 Steller Dr, Culver City (90232-2426)
P.O. Box 5206 (90231-5206)
PHONE....................................310 220-0808
Andy Solomon, *Mng Member*
Talitha Peters,
▲ EMP: 200
SALES (est): 14.8MM **Privately Held**
SIC: 3131 5661 5621 Boot & shoe accessories; men's boots; women's boots; ready-to-wear apparel, women's
HQ: Vcs Group Llc
  411 W Putnam Ave Ste 210
  Greenwich CT 06830
  203 413-6500

(P-10155)
SUNSPORTS LP
7 Holland, Irvine (92618-2506)
PHONE....................................949 273-6202
Jamey Draper, *Partner*
▲ EMP: 200
SQ FT: 85,000
SALES (est): 20.5MM **Privately Held**
WEB: www.sunsportsusa.com
SIC: 3131 2395 Footwear cut stock; embroidery products, except schiffli machine

---

3142 House Slippers

(P-10156)
FREDI & SONS INC
58 Calle Cabrillo, Foothill Ranch (92610-1746)
PHONE....................................818 881-1170
Farrokh Torkzadeh, *President*
▲ EMP: 10
SALES (est): 1.1MM **Privately Held**
WEB: www.frediandsons.com
SIC: 3142 2253 House slippers; lounging robes, knit

3143 Men's Footwear, Exc Athletic

(P-10157)
ALLBIRDS INC
730 Montgomery St, San Francisco (94111-2104)
PHONE....................................888 963-8944
Joseph Zwillinger, *CEO*
Erick Haskell, *President*
Cori Ferdinando, *Manager*
Dario Nieva, *Manager*
McKean Shaw, *Manager*
EMP: 200
SALES (est): 60.9MM **Privately Held**
SIC: 3143 3144 Men's footwear, except athletic; women's footwear, except athletic

(P-10158)
BRAND X HURARCHES
Also Called: Bucate Plata Importing Co
4228 Telegraph Ave, Oakland (94609-2408)
PHONE....................................510 658-9006
Ronn Simpson, *Owner*
EMP: 49
SALES: 1.6MM **Privately Held**
WEB: www.brandxhuaraches.com
SIC: 3143 3144 6512 Boots, dress or casual: men's; women's footwear, except athletic; commercial & industrial building operation

(P-10159)
LANE INTERNATIONAL TRADING INC (PA)
33155 Transit Ave, Union City (94587-2091)
P.O. Box 2223 (94587-7223)
PHONE....................................510 489-7364
Lane Shay, *President*
▲ EMP: 100
SQ FT: 2,500
SALES (est): 6.3MM **Privately Held**
WEB: www.toolboxdesign.com
SIC: 3143 3144 Men's footwear, except athletic; women's footwear, except athletic

---

▲ = Import ▼=Export
◆ =Import/Export

(P-10160)
**PHOENIX FOOTWEAR GROUP
INC (PA)**
2236 Rutherford Rd # 113, Carlsbad
(92008-8836)
PHONE...................................760 602-9688
James R Riedman, *President*
James Clopton, *President*
Dennis Nelson, *CFO*
Bruce Kaplan, *Exec VP*
Larry Stuart Torchin, *Vice Pres*
◆ **EMP:** 52
SQ FT: 21,700
SALES (est): 10MM **Publicly Held**
WEB: www.danielgreenco.com
SIC: 3143 3144 2329 2339 Men's
footwear, except athletic; women's
footwear, except athletic; men's & boys'
sportswear & athletic clothing; sports-
wear, women's

(P-10161)
SHOES FOR CREWS INTL INC
760 Baldwin Park Blvd, City of Industry
(91746-1503)
PHONE...................................561 683-5090
EMP: 25
SALES (corp-wide): 19.9MM **Privately
Held**
SIC: 3143 3144
PA: Shoes For Crews International, Inc.
250 S Australian Ave # 1700
West Palm Beach FL 33401
561 683-5090

(P-10162)
STEVEN MADDEN LTD
6725 Kimball Ave, Chino (91708-9177)
PHONE...................................909 393-7575
Reyn Williams, *Branch Mgr*
EMP: 75 **Publicly Held**
WEB: www.mypinecastle.com
SIC: 3143 3144 3149 5661 Men's
footwear, except athletic; women's
footwear, except athletic; children's
footwear, except athletic; shoe stores;
women's shoes; men's boots; children's
shoes
PA: Steven Madden, Ltd.
5216 Barnett Ave
Long Island City NY 11104

(P-10163)
**STRATEGIC PARTNERS INC
(PA)**
Also Called: Cherokee Uniform
9800 De Soto Ave, Chatsworth
(91311-4411)
PHONE...................................818 671-2100
Michael Singer, *CEO*
Robert Pierpoint, *CFO*
Jim Beyer, *Exec VP*
Joanna Sacramento, *Admin Asst*
Darla Miller, *Administration*
◆ **EMP:** 203
SQ FT: 140,000
SALES (est): 171.1MM **Privately Held**
WEB: www.strategicpartners.net
SIC: 3143 3144 5139 2339 Men's
footwear, except athletic; women's
footwear, except athletic; shoes; women's
& misses' outerwear; uniforms & vest-
ments; sweaters & sweater jackets: men's
& boys'

(P-10164)
VIONIC GROUP LLC
Also Called: Orthaheel
4040 Civic Center Dr # 430, San Rafael
(94903-4150)
PHONE...................................415 526-6932
Chris Gallagher, *CEO*
Connie X Rishwain, *President*
Bruce Campbell, *COO*
Steve Furtado, *CFO*
Tom Nelson, *Bd of Directors*
▲ **EMP:** 84
SQ FT: 16,000
SALES (est): 19.5MM
SALES (corp-wide): 2.8B **Publicly Held**
SIC: 3143 3144 3149 Orthopedic shoes,
men's; orthopedic shoes, women's; ortho-
pedic shoes, children's

PA: Caleres, Inc.
8300 Maryland Ave
Saint Louis MO 63105
314 854-4000

(P-10165)
WOLVERINE WORLD WIDE INC
Also Called: Beaumont DC 52
1020 Prosperity Way, Beaumont
(92223-2624)
PHONE...................................800 253-2184
EMP: 15
SALES (corp-wide): 2.2B **Publicly Held**
SIC: 3143 Men's footwear, except athletic
PA: Wolverine World Wide, Inc.
9341 Courtland Dr Ne
Rockford MI 49351
616 866-5500

3144 Women's Footwear, Exc Athletic

(P-10166)
ALPARGATAS USA INC
Also Called: Havaianas
513 Boccaccio Ave, Venice (90291-4806)
PHONE...................................646 277-7171
Marcio Moura, *CEO*
Afonso Fugiyama, *President*
Michele Kearns, *Marketing Staff*
◆ **EMP:** 30
SALES (est): 7.6MM **Privately Held**
SIC: 3144 Women's footwear, except ath-
letic
PA: Alpargatas S/A
Av. Doutor Cardoso De Melo 1 336
Sao Paulo SP 04548

(P-10167)
CHINECHEREM EZE INC
Also Called: Chinecherem Eze Foundation
13052 Hawthorne, Los Angeles (90001)
PHONE...................................310 806-1807
Chinecherem Eze, *CEO*
EMP: 10
SALES (est): 388.4K **Privately Held**
SIC: 3144 3171 3143 5094 Women's
footwear, except athletic; boots, canvas or
leather: women's; women's handbags &
purses; men's footwear, except athletic;
jewelry & precious stones

(P-10168)
DAVIS SHOE THERAPEUTICS
3921 Judah St, San Francisco
(94122-1120)
PHONE...................................415 661-8705
Arnold Davis, *Owner*
EMP: 11
SQ FT: 3,000
SALES (est): 1MM **Privately Held**
SIC: 3144 3143 Orthopedic shoes,
women's; orthopedic shoes, men's

(P-10169)
EVOLUTION DESIGN LAB INC
Also Called: Jellypop
150 S Los Robles Ave # 100, Pasadena
(91101-2441)
PHONE...................................626 960-8388
Jennet Chow, *CEO*
Pauline Cheng, *Purch Mgr*
▲ **EMP:** 25
SALES (est): 3.5MM **Privately Held**
SIC: 3144 5139 Women's footwear, ex-
cept athletic; shoes

(P-10170)
IMPO INTERNATIONAL LLC
Also Called: Chili's
3510 Black Rd, Santa Maria (93455-5927)
P.O. Box 639 (93456-0639)
PHONE...................................805 922-7753
Laura Ann Hopkins, *Mng Member*
Laura Hopkins, *Vice Pres*
Isabel Ruiz, *Director*
▲ **EMP:** 24
SQ FT: 30,000
SALES (est): 4.4MM **Privately Held**
WEB: www.impo.com
SIC: 3144 Boots, canvas or leather:
women's; dress shoes; women's; san-
dals, women's

(P-10171)
J & A SHOE COMPANY INC
Also Called: Callisto Shoes Rolling Hills
960 Knox St Bldg A, Torrance
(90502-1086)
PHONE...................................310 324-0139
Leah Bizoumis, *President*
Valerie Kats, *Admin Sec*
▲ **EMP:** 108
SQ FT: 14,500
SALES (est): 17.9MM **Privately Held**
SIC: 3144 Women's footwear, except ath-
letic

(P-10172)
MECO-NAG CORPORATION
Also Called: Dezario Shoe Company
7306 Laurel Canyon Blvd, North Hollywood
(91605-3710)
P.O. Box 16565 (91615-6565)
PHONE...................................818 764-2020
Krikor Astourian, *President*
Vicki Astourian, *Vice Pres*
Cruz Martinez, *Admin Sec*
Mike Miller, *QC Mgr*
◆ **EMP:** 60
SQ FT: 10,000
SALES (est): 7.2MM **Privately Held**
SIC: 3144 Women's footwear, except ath-
letic

(P-10173)
MILLENNIAL BRANDS LLC
126 W 9th St, Los Angeles (90015-1500)
PHONE...................................925 230-0617
Catalin Gaitanaru, *Principal*
EMP: 26 **Privately Held**
SIC: 3144 Women's footwear, except ath-
letic
PA: Millennial Brands Llc
2000 Crow Canyon Pl # 300
San Ramon CA 94583

(P-10174)
ONNIK SHOE COMPANY INC
Also Called: Sergio Shoes
11443 Chandler Blvd, North Hollywood
(91601-2617)
P.O. Box 17018 (91615-7018)
PHONE...................................818 506-5353
Vartan Vartanian, *President*
▲ **EMP:** 30
SQ FT: 20,000
SALES (est): 6.3MM **Privately Held**
WEB: www.sergioshoes.com
SIC: 3144 Women's footwear, except ath-
letic

(P-10175)
OPPO ORIGINAL CORP
108 Brea Canyon Rd 118, Walnut
(91789-3086)
P.O. Box 4025, Diamond Bar (91765-0025)
PHONE...................................909 444-3000
Olive Wang, *Chairman*
Jim Wang, *Exec VP*
◆ **EMP:** 13
SQ FT: 12,000
SALES (est): 2.2MM **Privately Held**
SIC: 3144 Dress shoes, women's

(P-10176)
SOUTH CONE INC
Also Called: Reef
5935 Darwin Ct, Carlsbad (92008-7302)
PHONE...................................760 431-2300
Roger Spatz, *CEO*
Mike Jensen, *President*
◆ **EMP:** 120
SQ FT: 37,583
SALES (est): 18.3MM
SALES (corp-wide): 26.3MM **Privately
Held**
WEB: www.vfc.com
SIC: 3144 3143 5139 Women's footwear,
except athletic; men's footwear, except
athletic; shoes
PA: The Rockport Company Llc
1220 Washington St
Newton MA 02465
617 619-5400

(P-10177)
SURGEON WORLDWIDE INC
4000 Broadway Pl, Los Angeles
(90037-1010)
PHONE...................................707 501-7962
Mariko Chambrone, *Vice Pres*
EMP: 27
SALES (est): 904.1K **Privately Held**
SIC: 3144 3143 Women's footwear, ex-
cept athletic; men's footwear, except ath-
letic

(P-10178)
TATIOSSIAN BROS INC
Also Called: Tate Shoes
11144 Penrose St Ste 11, Sun Valley
(91352-5601)
PHONE...................................818 768-3200
John Tatiossian, *President*
Avo Tatiossian, *Treasurer*
Zoohrab Tatiossian, *Vice Pres*
David Tatiossian, *Admin Sec*
▲ **EMP:** 60
SQ FT: 15,000
SALES (est): 7.8MM **Privately Held**
WEB: www.tateshoes.com
SIC: 3144 Women's footwear, except ath-
letic

3149 Footwear, NEC

(P-10179)
FOOT LOCKER RETAIL INC
Also Called: Champs Sports
2059 Newpark Mall Fl 2, Newark
(94560-5249)
PHONE...................................510 797-5750
Arthur Cervantes, *Manager*
EMP: 19
SALES (corp-wide): 7.9B **Publicly Held**
WEB: www.venatorgroup.com
SIC: 3149 5661 Athletic shoes, except
rubber or plastic; footwear, athletic
HQ: Foot Locker Retail, Inc.
330 W 34th St
New York NY 10001
800 991-6815

(P-10180)
KIA INCORPORATED (PA)
Also Called: Kia Group
13880 Stowe Dr Ste B, Poway
(92064-8826)
PHONE...................................858 824-2999
Reza Mohseni, *President*
Tannaz Mohseni, *CFO*
Bano Mohseni, *Vice Pres*
Freddie Alvia, *IT/INT Sup*
▲ **EMP:** 30
SALES (est): 9.2MM **Privately Held**
SIC: 3149 Athletic shoes, except rubber or
plastic

(P-10181)
NELSON SPORTS INC
10528 Pioneer Blvd, Santa Fe Springs
(90670-3704)
PHONE...................................562 944-8081
Young Chu, *President*
Sook Hee Chu, *Admin Sec*
▲ **EMP:** 45
SQ FT: 10,000
SALES (est): 6.4MM **Privately Held**
WEB: www.nelsonsports.com
SIC: 3149 3021 Athletic shoes, except
rubber or plastic; rubber & plastics
footwear

(P-10182)
**SANTA FE FOOTWEAR
CORPORATION**
9988 Santa Fe Springs Rd, Santa Fe
Springs (90670-2946)
PHONE...................................562 941-9689
Joel Tan, *President*
Joel O Tan, *President*
Debby Tio, *CFO*
Micah Gardner, *Controller*
▲ **EMP:** 15
SQ FT: 30,000
SALES (est): 2.4MM **Privately Held**
SIC: 3149 3144 5139 Children's footwear,
except athletic; women's footwear, except
athletic; footwear

PRODUCTS & SVCS

(P-10183)
SKECHERS USA INC (PA)
228 Manhattan Beach Blvd # 200, Manhattan Beach (90266-5356)
PHONE..................310 318-3100
Robert Greenberg, *Ch of Bd*
Michael Greenberg, *President*
David Weinberg, *COO*
John Vandemore, *CFO*
Mark Nason, *Exec VP*
▲ EMP: 80
SQ FT: 188,000
SALES: 4.6B **Publicly Held**
WEB: www.skechers.com
SIC: 3149 3021 Athletic shoes, except rubber or plastic; shoes, rubber or plastic molded to fabric

(P-10184)
SOLE TECHNOLOGY INC (PA)
Also Called: Etnies
26921 Fuerte, Lake Forest (92630-8149)
PHONE..................949 460-2020
Pierre Senizergues, *President*
James Appleby, *Vice Pres*
Don Brown, *Vice Pres*
Jeremiah Badell, *District Mgr*
Mike Manzoori, *CTO*
▲ EMP: 131
SALES (est): 44.7MM **Privately Held**
WEB: www.soletechnology.com
SIC: 3149 5139 Athletic shoes, except rubber or plastic; footwear

(P-10185)
SOLE TECHNOLOGY INC
17300 Slover Ave, Fontana (92337-8000)
PHONE..................949 460-2020
George Almanza, *Manager*
EMP: 11 **Privately Held**
SIC: 3149 Athletic shoes, except rubber or plastic
PA: Sole Technology, Inc.
26921 Fuerte
Lake Forest CA 92630

3161 Luggage

(P-10186)
ACE PRODUCTS ENTERPRISES INC
Also Called: Ace Products Group
3920 Cypress Dr Ste B, Petaluma (94954-7603)
PHONE..................707 765-1500
Allen R Poster, *President*
Charles Kieser, *CFO*
Will Burner, *Admin Asst*
Jesse Grossmann, *Sales Mgr*
Leah Murphy, *Marketing Staff*
▲ EMP: 21
SALES (est): 3.7MM **Privately Held**
WEB: www.aceproducts.com
SIC: 3161 3931 Musical instrument cases; drums, parts & accessories (musical instruments)

(P-10187)
AMERICAN PRIDE INC
12285 Colony Ave, Chino (91710-2096)
PHONE..................909 591-7688
Steve Liang, *President*
▲ EMP: 25
SQ FT: 9,966
SALES (est): 1.9MM **Privately Held**
SIC: 3161 Luggage

(P-10188)
ANVIL CASES INC
1242 E Edna Pl Unit B, Covina (91724-2540)
PHONE..................626 968-4100
Joseph Calzone, *President*
Vincent Calzone, *Vice Pres*
Marge Murphy, *Sales Staff*
▲ EMP: 125
SALES (est): 19.5MM **Privately Held**
WEB: www.anvilcase.com
SIC: 3161 Musical instrument cases; cases, carrying

PA: Calzone, Ltd.
225 Black Rock Ave
Bridgeport CT 06605
203 367-5766

(P-10189)
AR SQUARE
Also Called: Colorado's Bag Manufacture
8757 Lanyard Ct Ste 150, Rancho Cucamonga (91730-0810)
PHONE..................909 985-5995
Eduardo Ramirez, *CEO*
EMP: 10
SQ FT: 5,100
SALES (est): 1.3MM **Privately Held**
SIC: 3161 Attache cases; briefcases; cases, carrying

(P-10190)
BRIDGEPORT PRODUCTS INC
26895 Aliso Creek Rd B, Aliso Viejo (92656-5301)
PHONE..................949 348-8800
Brent Foster, *President*
Jeffery Hahn, *Treasurer*
Timothy Byk, *Vice Pres*
David Scott, *Admin Sec*
Ueli Gallizzi, *CIO*
◆ EMP: 76
SQ FT: 10,000
SALES (est): 9.9MM **Privately Held**
WEB: www.bridgeport-products.com
SIC: 3161 Traveling bags; cases, carrying

(P-10191)
CHUNMA USA INC
Also Called: Chunma America
2000 E 25th St, Vernon (90058-1128)
PHONE..................323 846-0077
Jae Jung, *President*
◆ EMP: 10
SALES (est): 1.4MM **Privately Held**
SIC: 3161 Luggage
PA: Chunma Corporation
53 Hallimmal-Gil, Seongdong-Gu
Seoul 04735
-

(P-10192)
DONY CORP
Also Called: Dony Trading Los Angeles
1065 S Vail Ave, Montebello (90640-6019)
PHONE..................323 725-7697
Ming Yong LI, *President*
Guofan Jiang, *Shareholder*
Lawrence Lee, *Executive*
▲ EMP: 10
SALES (est): 1.6MM **Privately Held**
SIC: 3161 3171 4731 Luggage; women's handbags & purses; freight transportation arrangement

(P-10193)
EAGLE CREEK INC (DH)
Also Called: Eagle Creek Travel Gear
5935 Darwin Ct, Carlsbad (92008-7302)
PHONE..................760 431-6400
Steve Barker, *President*
Bert Fenenga, *CFO*
Dale Penk, *Senior VP*
Ricky Schlesinger, *Senior VP*
◆ EMP: 98 EST: 1975
SQ FT: 93,000
SALES (est): 46.7MM
SALES (corp-wide): 13.8MM **Publicly Held**
WEB: www.eaglecreek.com
SIC: 3161 Traveling bags
HQ: Vf Outdoor, Llc
2701 Harbor Bay Pkwy
Alameda CA 94502
510 618-3500

(P-10194)
ENCORE CASES INC
8818 Lankershim Blvd, Sun Valley (91352-2516)
PHONE..................818 768-8803
Gary A Peterson, *President*
Randy Romero, *Design Engr*
▲ EMP: 27
SQ FT: 20,000
SALES (est): 5.1MM **Privately Held**
WEB: www.encorecases.com
SIC: 3161 Cases, carrying

(P-10195)
G & G QUALITY CASE CO INC
2025 E 25th St, Vernon (90058-1127)
P.O. Box 58541, Los Angeles (90058-0541)
PHONE..................323 233-2482
Efren Guzman, *President*
Ben Germain, *Treasurer*
Brandon Germain, *Software Dev*
▲ EMP: 70
SQ FT: 13,500
SALES (est): 10.3MM **Privately Held**
WEB: www.ggqualitycase.com
SIC: 3161 Musical instrument cases

(P-10196)
HAMMITT INC
2101 Pacific Coast Hwy A, Hermosa Beach (90254-2796)
PHONE..................310 293-3787
Anthony J Drockton, *CEO*
Dan Goldman, *CTO*
Justin Buck, *Sales Dir*
Amanda Hutchinson, *Marketing Staff*
Jenna Gulick, *Internal Med*
▲ EMP: 15
SALES (est): 1.8MM **Privately Held**
SIC: 3161 3171 Traveling bags; women's handbags & purses

(P-10197)
HSIAO & MONTANO INC
Also Called: Odyssey Innovative Designs
809 W Santa Anita Ave, San Gabriel (91776-1016)
PHONE..................626 588-2528
Mario Montano, *CEO*
John Hsiao, *Vice Pres*
Horng Ou, *Webmaster*
Alice Jen, *Controller*
Dave Lopez, *Sales Mgr*
▲ EMP: 50
SALES (est): 9.2MM **Privately Held**
WEB: www.odysseygear.com
SIC: 3161 3648 5084 1751 Musical instrument cases; lighting equipment; woodworking machinery; cabinet & finish carpentry

(P-10198)
LOGISTERRA INC
6190 Fairmount Ave Ste K, San Diego (92120-3428)
PHONE..................619 280-9992
Tan V Nguyen, *President*
Ann Long, *Vice Pres*
EMP: 45
SQ FT: 14,000
SALES: 2.2MM **Privately Held**
WEB: www.rhodiana.com
SIC: 3161 5948 Cases, carrying; luggage & leather goods stores

(P-10199)
M GROUP INC
Also Called: Bamboosa
9808 Venice Blvd Ste 706, Culver City (90232-6827)
PHONE..................843 221-7830
Michael Moore, *President*
Mindy Johnson, *Admin Sec*
EMP: 24
SQ FT: 10,000
SALES (est): 2.8MM **Privately Held**
SIC: 3161 5651 5136 5137 Clothing & apparel carrying cases; family clothing stores; men's & boys' clothing; women's & children's clothing

(P-10200)
OGIO INTERNATIONAL INC
2180 Rutherford Rd, Carlsbad (92008-7328)
PHONE..................801 619-4100
Anthony Palma, *CEO*
Michael Pratt, *President*
▲ EMP: 100
SQ FT: 70,000
SALES (est): 19.3MM
SALES (corp-wide): 1.2B **Publicly Held**
SIC: 3161 2393 Traveling bags; textile bags
PA: Callaway Golf Company
2180 Rutherford Rd
Carlsbad CA 92008
760 931-1771

(P-10201)
ONEIL KG BAGS
Also Called: K G Bags
124 Belvedere St Ste 12, San Rafael (94901-4704)
PHONE..................415 460-0111
Rob O'Neil, *Owner*
Jamie O"neil, *Vice Pres*
EMP: 12
SALES (est): 1.4MM **Privately Held**
WEB: www.kgbags.com
SIC: 3161 Luggage

(P-10202)
PK INDUSTRIES INC
Also Called: International Apparel
1533 Olivella Way, San Diego (92154-7716)
PHONE..................619 428-6382
▲ EMP: 11
SALES (est): 870K **Privately Held**
SIC: 3161

(P-10203)
PMP PRODUCTS INC
Also Called: American Casuals
19827 Hamilton Ave, Torrance (90502-1341)
PHONE..................310 549-5122
Mariah Qian, *President*
EMP: 15
SALES (est): 1MM **Privately Held**
SIC: 3161 2231 Clothing & apparel carrying cases; apparel & outerwear broadwoven fabrics

(P-10204)
RJ SINGER INTERNATIONAL INC
Also Called: Ruben and Sharam
4801 W Jefferson Blvd, Los Angeles (90016-3920)
PHONE..................323 735-1717
Reouben Melamed, *President*
Farshad Melamed, *Vice Pres*
Sam Abassi, *Human Res Mgr*
▲ EMP: 85
SQ FT: 20,000
SALES (est): 8.3MM **Privately Held**
WEB: www.rjsinger.com
SIC: 3161 2335 2393 2353 Cases, carrying; women's, juniors' & misses' dresses; textile bags; hats & caps; T-shirts & tops, women's: made from purchased materials

(P-10205)
SAFCOR INC
Also Called: Landmark Luggage & Gifts
13455 Ventura Blvd 237a, Sherman Oaks (91423-3830)
PHONE..................818 392-8437
EMP: 10 EST: 2011
SALES (est): 750K **Privately Held**
SIC: 3161

(P-10206)
SCOTT WELSHER
Also Called: To Die For
2031 S Lynx Ave, Ontario (91761-8011)
P.O. Box 5323, Orange (92863-5323)
PHONE..................949 574-4000
Scott Welsher, *Owner*
Jason Welsher, *Co-Owner*
EMP: 10 EST: 1999
SQ FT: 1,900
SALES (est): 840.4K **Privately Held**
SIC: 3161 Clothing & apparel carrying cases

(P-10207)
SIERRA AVIATION
3400 E Tahquitz Canyon Wa, Palm Springs (92262-6920)
PHONE..................760 778-2845
Jimmy Witt, *Manager*
EMP: 36
SALES (est): 2.6MM **Privately Held**
SIC: 3161 Luggage

(P-10208)
SIMON OF CALIFORNIA (PA)
9545 Sawyer St, Los Angeles (90035-4105)
PHONE..................310 559-4871
Simon Frank, *Owner*
Simon Blumberg, *President*
▲ EMP: 12

▲ = Import ▼=Export
◆ =Import/Export

SQ FT: 10,000
SALES (est): 1.6MM **Privately Held**
SIC: 3161 3172 Luggage; personal leather
goods; wallets

(P-10209)
SKB CORPORATION
1633 N Leslie Way, Orange (92867-3633)
PHONE.....................714 637-1572
Steven Kottman, *Owner*
EMP: 300
SALES (corp-wide): 72.5MM **Privately
Held**
WEB: www.skbcases.com
SIC: 3161 Cases, carrying
PA: S.K.B. Corporation
434 W Levers Pl
Orange CA 92867
714 637-1252

(P-10210)
SPECULATIVE PRODUCT DESIGN LLC
303 Bryant St, Mountain View
(94041-1552)
PHONE.....................650 462-9086
EMP: 10 **Privately Held**
SIC: 3161
HQ: Speculative Product Design, Llc
177 Bovet Rd Ste 200
San Mateo CA 94402
650 462-2040

(P-10211)
SPECULATIVE PRODUCT DESIGN LLC (DH)
Also Called: Speck Products
177 Bovet Rd Ste 200, San Mateo
(94402-3118)
PHONE.....................650 462-2040
Robert Hales, *President*
Donald Walden, *CFO*
Patrick Palaad, *Opers Staff*
Janelle Raaff, *Opers Staff*
Daniel Moon, *Marketing Staff*
▲ **EMP:** 56
SQ FT: 5,000
SALES: 150MM
SALES (corp-wide): 177.9K **Privately
Held**
WEB: www.speckdesign.com
SIC: 3161 Cases, carrying
HQ: Samsonite Llc
575 West St Ste 110
Mansfield MA 02048
508 851-1400

(P-10212)
TARGUS US LLC
1211 N Miller St, Anaheim (92806-1933)
PHONE.....................714 765-5555
Mikel H Williams, *CEO*
Lea Baltzinger, *Vice Pres*
Andrew Corkill, *Vice Pres*
Demetrius Romanos, *Vice Pres*
Stan Mortensen, *Admin Sec*
EMP: 10
SQ FT: 200,656
SALES (est): 677.3K
SALES (corp-wide): 172.1MM **Privately
Held**
SIC: 3161 Cases, carrying
PA: Targus International Llc
1211 N Miller St
Anaheim CA 92806
714 765-5555

(P-10213)
TRAVELERS CHOICE TRAVELWARE
Also Called: Golden Pacific
2805 S Reservoir St, Pomona
(91766-6526)
PHONE.....................909 529-7688
Roger Yang, *CEO*
▲ **EMP:** 72
SQ FT: 12,000
SALES (est): 13.6MM **Privately Held**
WEB: www.travelerchoice.com
SIC: 3161 Luggage

(P-10214)
TWO GUYS AND ONE LLC
Also Called: Queen Bees
4433 Pacific Blvd, Vernon (90058-2205)
PHONE.....................213 239-0310
Hoon Lee, *Mng Member*
Hojin Ham, *Admin Sec*
EMP: 11 **EST:** 2018
SALES (est): 286.2K **Privately Held**
SIC: 3161 Clothing & apparel carrying
cases

(P-10215)
WALKER/DUNHAM CORP
Also Called: Walker Bags
445 Barneveld Ave, San Francisco
(94124-1501)
PHONE.....................415 821-3070
Eveline Dunham, *President*
Emily Hughes, *Vice Pres*
Marion Dunham, *Asst Sec*
EMP: 15
SQ FT: 10,000
SALES (est): 1.2MM **Privately Held**
SIC: 3161 Cases, carrying

(P-10216)
ZUCA INC
320 S Milpitas Blvd, Milpitas (95035-5421)
PHONE.....................408 377-9822
Bruce Kinnee, *President*
Jim Goldhawk, *CFO*
◆ **EMP:** 20
SALES (est): 3.3MM **Privately Held**
WEB: www.zuca.com
SIC: 3161 5099 Luggage; luggage

3171 Handbags & Purses

(P-10217)
BRIGHTON COLLECTIBLES LLC
180 El Camino Real, Millbrae
(94030-2606)
PHONE.....................650 838-0086
Jerry Kohl, *Branch Mgr*
EMP: 10
SALES (corp-wide): 310.5MM **Privately
Held**
SIC: 3171 Women's handbags & purses
PA: Brighton Collectibles, Llc
14022 Nelson Ave
City Of Industry CA 91746
626 961-9381

(P-10218)
COACH INC
3333 Bristol St Ste 2883, Costa Mesa
(92626-1821)
PHONE.....................949 365-0771
EMP: 15
SALES (corp-wide): 4.1B **Publicly Held**
SIC: 3171
PA: Coach, Inc.
516 W 34th St Bsmt 5
New York NY 10001
212 594-1850

(P-10219)
COACH INC
434 W Hillcrest Dr, Thousand Oaks
(91360-4222)
PHONE.....................805 496-9933
EMP: 15
SALES (corp-wide): 4.1B **Publicly Held**
SIC: 3171
PA: Coach, Inc.
516 W 34th St Bsmt 5
New York NY 10001
212 594-1850

(P-10220)
DREAM PRODUCTS INCORPORATED
9754 Deering Ave, Chatsworth
(91311-4301)
PHONE.....................818 773-4233
Richard Goldman, *CEO*
Linda Denninger, *Vice Pres*
Eneida Sanchez-Aguilar, *Buyer*
Ellen O'Shaunnessy, *Marketing Staff*
Brent Goldman, *Art Dir*
EMP: 22

SALES (est): 3.8MM **Privately Held**
SIC: 3171 3172 Women's handbags &
purses; personal leather goods

(P-10221)
FRANCES MARY ACCESSORIES INC
3732 Mt Diablo Blvd # 260, Lafayette
(94549-3643)
PHONE.....................925 962-2111
Mary Frances Shaffer, *President*
Carolyn Miller, *Office Mgr*
Candee Hart, *Admin Sec*
Amanda Savage, *Graphic Designe*
EMP: 1020
SALES (est): 4MM **Privately Held**
SIC: 3171 Handbags, women's

(P-10222)
GLASER DESIGNS INC
1469 Pacific Ave, San Francisco
(94109-2640)
PHONE.....................415 552-3188
Myron Glaser, *President*
Kari Glaser, *Vice Pres*
EMP: 10
SQ FT: 10,000
SALES (est): 1.8MM **Privately Held**
SIC: 3171 3172 3161 Handbags,
women's; personal leather goods; hand-
bags, regardless of material: men's; cloth-
ing & apparel carrying cases

(P-10223)
GLOBAL UNLIMITED EXPORT LLC
3407 W 6th St Ste 802, Los Angeles
(90020-2582)
PHONE.....................213 365-7051
Joshua Son, *President*
EMP: 11
SALES (est): 448.3K **Privately Held**
SIC: 3171 3999 Women's handbags &
purses; handles, handbag & luggage

(P-10224)
ISABELLE HANDBAGS INC
3155 Bandini Blvd Unit A, Vernon
(90058-4134)
PHONE.....................323 277-9888
Roye Xu, *President*
James Ll, *Vice Pres*
▲ **EMP:** 35
SQ FT: 2,000
SALES (est): 2.9MM **Privately Held**
SIC: 3171 5632 Handbags, women's;
handbags

(P-10225)
PROJECT 1920 INC
Also Called: Senreve
441 Jackson St, San Francisco
(94111-1601)
PHONE.....................415 529-2245
EMP: 16
SALES (corp-wide): 1.2MM **Privately
Held**
SIC: 3171 Women's handbags & purses
PA: Project 1920, Inc.
441 Jackson St
San Francisco CA 94111
415 990-9788

(P-10226)
SBNW LLC (PA)
320 W 31st St, Los Angeles (90007-3806)
PHONE.....................213 234-5122
Jill Ause,
Jason Rimokh,
EMP: 110
SALES (est): 11.5MM **Privately Held**
SIC: 3171 Handbags, women's

(P-10227)
SVEN DESIGN INC
Also Called: Sven Design Handbag Outlet
2301 4th St, Berkeley (94710-2401)
PHONE.....................510 848-7836
Sven Stalman, *President*
Susan Stalman, *Vice Pres*
▲ **EMP:** 18 **EST:** 1970
SQ FT: 3,500

SALES (est): 2.2MM **Privately Held**
SIC: 3171 3149 5948 5661 Women's
handbags & purses; children's footwear,
except athletic; luggage & leather goods
stores; children's shoes; personal leather
goods

(P-10228)
TAPESTRY INC
Also Called: Coach
100 Citadel Dr Ste 709, Commerce
(90040-1641)
PHONE.....................323 725-6792
EMP: 15
SALES (corp-wide): 6B **Publicly Held**
SIC: 3171 Women's handbags & purses
PA: Tapestry, Inc.
10 Hudson Yards
New York NY 10001
212 594-1850

(P-10229)
TAPESTRY INC
28200 Highway 189, Lake Arrowhead
(92352-9700)
PHONE.....................909 337-5207
EMP: 15
SALES (corp-wide): 6B **Publicly Held**
SIC: 3171 Handbags, women's
PA: Tapestry, Inc.
10 Hudson Yards
New York NY 10001
212 594-1850

(P-10230)
URBAN EXPRESSIONS INC
5500 Union Pacific Ave, Commerce
(90022-5139)
PHONE.....................310 593-4574
Arash Vojdani, *President*
Farbod Shakouri, *Vice Pres*
▲ **EMP:** 20
SALES (est): 3.4MM **Privately Held**
SIC: 3171 5137 Handbags, women's;
handbags

3172 Personal Leather Goods

(P-10231)
ALLEGRO PACIFIC CORPORATION
7250 Oxford Way, Commerce
(90040-3643)
PHONE.....................323 724-0101
▲ **EMP:** 16
SALES (est): 2MM **Privately Held**
SIC: 3172

(P-10232)
CASE WORLD CO
301 S Doubleday Ave, Ontario
(91761-1514)
PHONE.....................626 330-1000
Fax: 909 390-5222
EMP: 17
SALES (est): 1.6MM **Privately Held**
WEB: www.caseworld.tv
SIC: 3172

(P-10233)
DEUX LUX INC (PA)
11609 Vanowen St Ste B, North Hollywood
(91605-6170)
PHONE.....................213 746-7040
Sara Naghedi, *President*
Joseph Bautista, *Accountant*
Kelly Cameron, *Production*
Geneva Barr, *Accounts Mgr*
▲ **EMP:** 26
SALES (est): 3.1MM **Privately Held**
SIC: 3172 Handbags, regardless of mate-
rial: men's

(P-10234)
GARYS LEATHER CREATIONS INC
Also Called: Gary's of California
12644 Bradford Pl, Granada Hills
(91344-1510)
PHONE.....................818 831-9977
Steven Matzdorff, *President*
Jeff Matzdorff, *Admin Sec*
EMP: 98

(PA)=Parent Co (HQ)=Headquarters (DH)=Div Headquarters
✪ = New Business established in last 2 years

SQ FT: 45,000
SALES (est): 6.6MM **Privately Held**
SIC: **3172** Wallets; coin purses; key cases;
card cases

(P-10235)
KATZKIN LEATHER INTERIORS INC
6868 W Acco St, Montebello (90640-5441)
PHONE..............................323 725-1243
Brooks Mayberry, *President*
▲ EMP: 15
SALES (est): 2MM **Privately Held**
SIC: **3172** Personal leather goods

(P-10236)
KOLTOV INC (PA)
300 S Lewis Rd Ste A, Camarillo
(93012-6620)
P.O. Box 2922 (93011-2922)
PHONE..............................805 764-0280
Joe Covrigaru, *CEO*
Brett Stone, *President*
Phillip Shieh, *Principal*
▲ EMP: 20
SALES (est): 9MM **Privately Held**
SIC: **3172** 5199 Personal leather goods;
leather, leather goods & furs

(P-10237)
LEATHER PRO INC
Also Called: Turtleback Case
12900 Bradley Ave, Sylmar (91342-3829)
PHONE..............................818 833-8822
Brian Eremita, *President*
Tom Sutter, *Vice Pres*
▲ EMP: 20
SQ FT: 13,000
SALES (est): 3.7MM **Privately Held**
WEB: www.leatherproinc.com
SIC: **3172** Personal leather goods

(P-10238)
LITE LINE FRAME BAGS
535 N Puente St, Brea (92821-2805)
PHONE..............................562 905-3150
Jim Porterfield, *President*
EMP: 20 EST: 2011
SALES (est): 1.3MM **Privately Held**
SIC: **3172** Cases, jewelry

(P-10239)
LOUIS VUITTON US MFG INC
Also Called: Lvusm
321 W Covina Blvd, San Dimas
(91773-2907)
PHONE..............................909 599-2411
Jean Claude Calverone, *Director*
▲ EMP: 10
SQ FT: 100,000
SALES (est): 2.8MM
SALES (corp-wide): 361.7MM **Privately Held**
WEB: www.lvhm.com
SIC: **3172** 3161 Handbags, regardless of
material: men's; wallets; luggage
HQ: Louis Vuitton North America, Inc.
1 E 57th St
New York NY 10022
212 758-8877

(P-10240)
MASCORRO LEATHER INC
1303 S Gerhart Ave, Commerce
(90022-4256)
PHONE..............................323 724-6759
Antonio Mascorro, *President*
Yolanda Mascorro, *Admin Sec*
▲ EMP: 100 EST: 1977
SQ FT: 20,000
SALES (est): 10.6MM **Privately Held**
SIC: **3172** Wallets

(P-10241)
MESKIN KHOSROW KAY
Also Called: Graffeo Leather Collection
661 Laurel St, San Carlos (94070-3111)
PHONE..............................650 595-3090
Khosrow Meskin, *Partner*
EMP: 48
SALES (est): 3.8MM **Privately Held**
SIC: **3172** 5199 5948 3151 Personal
leather goods; leather, leather goods &
furs; leather goods, except luggage &
shoes; leather gloves & mittens; apparel
belts; leather & sheep-lined clothing

(P-10242)
RAIKA INC
13150 Saticoy St, North Hollywood
(91605-3402)
PHONE..............................818 503-5911
Raika Alberts, *President*
Roxanne Nemati, *COO*
Wayne Alberts, *Executive*
▲ EMP: 38
SQ FT: 10,000
SALES (est): 4.7MM **Privately Held**
WEB: www.raikausa.com
SIC: **3172** 5199 Personal leather goods;
leather, leather goods & furs

(P-10243)
RUIZ INDUSTRIES INC
13027 Telfair Ave, Sylmar (91342-3548)
PHONE..............................818 582-6882
Maria Ruiz, *President*
Moises Ruiz, *President*
Maria E Ruiz, *Admin Sec*
EMP: 15 EST: 1976
SQ FT: 5,000
SALES (est): 1.8MM **Privately Held**
SIC: **3172** 2821 Personal leather goods;
vinyl resins

3199 Leather Goods, NEC

(P-10244)
AKER INTERNATIONAL INC
Also Called: Aker Leather Products
2248 Main St Ste 4, Chula Vista
(91911-3932)
PHONE..............................619 423-5182
Kamuran Aker, *CEO*
Laurie Aker, *President*
Levent Aker, *COO*
▲ EMP: 30 EST: 1981
SQ FT: 10,000
SALES (est): 3MM **Privately Held**
SIC: **3199** Holsters, leather; leather belting
& strapping

(P-10245)
ARIAT INTERNATIONAL INC (PA)
3242 Whipple Rd, Union City (94587-1217)
PHONE..............................510 477-7000
Elizabeth Cross, *CEO*
Pankaj Gupta, *CFO*
Liz Bradley, *Vice Pres*
Rial Chew, *Vice Pres*
Sherie Lee, *Vice Pres*
◆ EMP: 200
SALES (est): 145.1MM **Privately Held**
WEB: www.ariat.com
SIC: **3199** 5139 5137 5136 Equestrian
related leather articles; boots, horse;
leather garments; footwear; women's &
children's clothing; men's & boys' clothing

(P-10246)
CUSTOM LEATHERCRAFT MFG LLC (DH)
Also Called: CLC Work Gear
10240 Alameda St, South Gate
(90280-5551)
PHONE..............................323 752-2221
Ron Pickens, *CEO*
Harry Karapetian, *Vice Pres*
Jim Fleming, *Regional Mgr*
Frank Gutierrez, *Project Mgr*
Stefanie Leary, *Accounting Mgr*
◆ EMP: 50
SQ FT: 150,000
SALES (est): 43.7MM
SALES (corp-wide): 1.3B **Privately Held**
SIC: **3199** 2394 Leather belting & strap-
ping; aprons: welders', blacksmiths', etc.:
leather; novelties, leather; canvas & re-
lated products
HQ: Hultafors Group Ab
Hultaforsvagen 21
Hultafors 517 9
337 237-400

(P-10247)
ELEANOR RIGBY LEATHER CO
4660 La Jolla Village Dr # 100, San Diego
(92122-4604)
PHONE..............................619 356-5590
Peter Robinson, *CEO*

▲ EMP: 30 EST: 2011
SQ FT: 2,000
SALES: 900K **Privately Held**
SIC: **3199** Leather garments

(P-10248)
M & L HAIGHT LLC
Also Called: Camp Bow Wow Temecula
42192 Sarah Way, Temecula (92590-3401)
PHONE..............................951 587-2267
Michael Haight, *Mng Member*
Lisa Haight, *Mng Member*
EMP: 22 EST: 2011
SQ FT: 150
SALES: 818K **Privately Held**
SIC: **3199** 0752 Dog furnishings: collars,
leashes, muzzles, etc.: leather; animal
boarding services; boarding services,
kennels

(P-10249)
OCCIDENTAL MANUFACTURING INC
4200 Ross Rd, Sebastopol (95472-2220)
PHONE..............................707 824-2560
Darryl G Thurner, *Owner*
Susan Alberts, *Sales Mgr*
EMP: 48 EST: 1980
SQ FT: 18,000
SALES (est): 16.7MM **Privately Held**
WEB: www.occidentalleather.com
SIC: **3199** Leather garments

(P-10250)
OFF LEAD INC
9751 N Highway 99, Stockton
(95212-1603)
PHONE..............................209 931-6909
John C Weber, *President*
EMP: 11 EST: 2001
SALES (est): 1.2MM **Privately Held**
WEB: www.offlead.com
SIC: **3199** Dog furnishings: collars,
leashes, muzzles, etc.: leather

(P-10251)
R & J LEATHERCRAFT
12155 Magnolia Ave Ste 8d, Riverside
(92503-4903)
PHONE..............................951 688-1685
Ray Hazelwood, *Owner*
EMP: 10
SQ FT: 7,000
SALES (est): 530K **Privately Held**
SIC: **3199** Leather garments

(P-10252)
SAFARILAND LLC
3120 E Mission Blvd, Ontario (91761-2900)
P.O. Box 51478 (91761-0078)
PHONE..............................909 923-7300
Warren B Kanders, *Branch Mgr*
Hope Bianchi-Sjursen, *Marketing Staff*
Scott Carnahan, *Marketing Staff*
Patricia Coppedge, *Sales Staff*
Geoffrey Patti, *Director*
EMP: 354
SALES (corp-wide): 1B **Privately Held**
WEB: www.protecharmored.com
SIC: **3199** 3842 Holsters, leather; bullet-
proof vests
HQ: Safariland, Llc
13386 International Pkwy
Jacksonville FL 32218
904 741-5400

(P-10253)
STIRWORKS INC
2010 Lincoln Ave, Pasadena (91103-1323)
PHONE..............................800 657-2427
Jean-Paul Labrosse, *CEO*
EMP: 23
SALES (est): 4.2MM **Privately Held**
SIC: **3199** Stirrups, wood or metal

(P-10254)
SUNSET LEATHER GROUP
8527 Melrose Ave, West Hollywood
(90069-5114)
PHONE..............................310 388-4898
Olivier Slama, *Principal*
EMP: 30
SALES (est): 2.1MM **Privately Held**
SIC: **3199** Leather garments

(P-10255)
TREND CHASERS LLC
2311 S Santa Fe Ave, Vernon
(90058-1154)
PHONE..............................213 749-2661
Alon Zeltzer,
Deborah Kirkland, *Sales Staff*
EMP: 50 EST: 2010
SALES (est): 5.4MM **Privately Held**
SIC: **3199** Leather garments

(P-10256)
US DUTY GEAR INC
1616 E Francis St Unit Qr, Ontario
(91761-5766)
PHONE..............................909 391-8800
Jose Flores, *President*
Estela Flores, *Vice Pres*
EMP: 22
SALES (est): 196.5K **Privately Held**
SIC: **3199** Aprons: welders', blacksmiths',
etc.: leather

(P-10257)
WHEELSKINS INC
2821 10th St, Berkeley (94710-2710)
PHONE..............................510 841-2128
James Valley, *President*
EMP: 17 EST: 1977
SQ FT: 15,000
SALES (est): 2.2MM **Privately Held**
WEB: www.wheelskins.com
SIC: **3199** 3172 5199 5136 Novelties,
leather; personal leather goods; chamois
leather; gloves, men's & boys'; gloves,
women's & children's

(P-10258)
YATES GEAR INC
2608 Hartnell Ave Ste 6, Redding
(96002-2347)
PHONE..............................530 222-4606
John Yates, *President*
Karen Yates, *Vice Pres*
Blaine Stidham, *Prdtn Mgr*
Brad Colombero, *Sales Staff*
▲ EMP: 55
SALES (est): 9.4MM **Privately Held**
WEB: www.yatesgear.com
SIC: **3199** 3842 Safety belts, leather; per-
sonal safety equipment

3211 Flat Glass

(P-10259)
ABRISA INDUSTRIAL GLASS INC (HQ)
Also Called: Abrisa Glass & Coating
200 Hallock Dr, Santa Paula (93060-9646)
P.O. Box 85055, Chicago IL (60680-0851)
PHONE..............................805 525-4902
Blake Fennell, *CEO*
Bob Miller, *Vice Pres*
Nilda Rohrbach, *Administration*
David Kwan, *Info Tech Dir*
Heather Swartz, *Credit Mgr*
▲ EMP: 90
SQ FT: 93,000
SALES (est): 23.9MM
SALES (corp-wide): 256.5MM **Privately Held**
WEB: www.abrisa.com
SIC: **3211** Strengthened or reinforced
glass; tempered glass
PA: Graham Partners, Inc.
3811 West Chester Pike # 200
Newtown Square PA 19073
610 408-0500

(P-10260)
BUDGET ENTERPRISES INC
Also Called: Solar Art
9301 Research Dr, Irvine (92618-4288)
PHONE..............................949 697-9544
Matthew Darienzo, *CEO*
Jody Johnson, *Administration*
Kirk Lane, *Director*
EMP: 25
SALES (est): 3.4MM **Privately Held**
SIC: **3211** Construction glass

▲ = Import ▼=Export
◆ =Import/Export

(P-10261)
CARDINAL GLASS INDUSTRIES INC
Also Called: Cardinal C G
24100 Cardinal Ave, Moreno Valley (92551-9545)
PHONE..............................951 485-9007
Scott Paisley, *Branch Mgr*
Irene Orona, *COO*
Tracy Cashmer, *Executive*
Jennifer Gregg, *Purch Agent*
EMP: 75
SALES (corp-wide): 1B **Privately Held**
WEB: www.cardinalcorp.com
SIC: **3211** 5039 3229 Flat glass; glass construction materials; pressed & blown glass
PA: Cardinal Glass Industries Inc
   775 Pririe Ctr Dr Ste 200
   Eden Prairie MN 55344
   952 229-2600

(P-10262)
CEVIANS LLC
3128 Red Hill Ave, Costa Mesa (92626-4525)
PHONE..............................714 619-5135
Eric Lemay, *President*
EMP: 55
SALES (est): 16.1MM **Privately Held**
SIC: **3211** Flat glass

(P-10263)
CHAD EMPEY
Also Called: Glass Shop of The North Bay
1329 Scott St Ste G, Petaluma (94954-6557)
PHONE..............................707 762-1900
Chad Empey, *Owner*
EMP: 15
SQ FT: 25,000
SALES: 1.1MM **Privately Held**
SIC: **3211** 3231 Construction glass; mirrored glass

(P-10264)
GLASSWERKS LA INC
Glasswerks SD Division
42005 Zevo Dr, Temecula (92590-3780)
PHONE..............................800 729-1324
Rancy Stiecert, *Branch Mgr*
EMP: 20 **Privately Held**
SIC: **3211** Flat glass
HQ: Glasswerks La, Inc.
   8600 Rheem Ave
   South Gate CA 90280
   888 789-7810

(P-10265)
GUARDIAN INDUSTRIES LLC
Also Called: Guardian-Kingsburg
11535 E Mountain View Ave, Kingsburg (93631-9233)
PHONE..............................559 891-8867
Jeffery Booey, *Manager*
Drew Kirk, *Engineer*
Jay Jayakrishnan, *Maintence Staff*
EMP: 275
SQ FT: 486,000
SALES (corp-wide): 40.6B **Privately Held**
WEB: www.guardian.com
SIC: **3211** 3231 Sheet glass; tempered glass; products of purchased glass
HQ: Guardian Industries, Llc
   2300 Harmon Rd
   Auburn Hills MI 48326
   248 340-1800

(P-10266)
GUARDIAN INDUSTRIES CORP
11535 E Mountain View Ave, Kingsburg (93631-9233)
PHONE..............................559 891-8867
Fax: 714 525-3529
EMP: 60
SALES (corp-wide): 27.6B **Privately Held**
SIC: **3211** 5231
HQ: Guardian Industries Corp.
   2300 Harmon Rd
   Auburn Hills MI 48326
   248 340-1800

(P-10267)
GUARDIAN INDUSTRIES CORP
11535 E Mountain View Ave, Kingsburg (93631-9233)
PHONE..............................559 638-3588
EMP: 90
SALES (corp-wide): 27.6B **Privately Held**
SIC: **3211** 3231
HQ: Guardian Industries Corp.
   2300 Harmon Rd
   Auburn Hills MI 48326
   248 340-1800

(P-10268)
GWLA ACQUISITION CORP (PA)
8600 Rheem Ave, South Gate (90280-3333)
PHONE..............................323 789-7800
Randy Steinberg, *President*
▲ EMP: 11
SALES (est): 74.4MM **Privately Held**
SIC: **3211** 3231 6719 Tempered glass; mirrored glass; investment holding companies, except banks

(P-10269)
HELIOTROPE TECHNOLOGIES INC
850 Marina Village Pkwy, Alameda (94501-1007)
PHONE..............................510 871-3980
Peter Green, *CEO*
Janina Motter, *Engineer*
John Santos, *VP Mfg*
EMP: 22
SALES (est): 3.3MM **Privately Held**
SIC: **3211** Insulating glass, sealed units

(P-10270)
IGS INC
Also Called: Industrial Glass Service
916 E California Ave, Sunnyvale (94085-4505)
PHONE..............................408 733-4621
John R Gracia, *President*
▲ EMP: 15
SQ FT: 15,000
SALES (est): 1.9MM **Privately Held**
SIC: **3211** Optical glass, flat

(P-10271)
LINOLEUM SALES CO INC (PA)
Also Called: Anderson's Carpet & Linoleum
1000 W Grand Ave, Oakland (94607-2933)
PHONE..............................661 327-4053
Don Christophe, *CEO*
Tom Christophe, *President*
Bob Mullarkey, *CFO*
Sheila Anderson, *Vice Pres*
Vince Lopez, *Vice Pres*
EMP: 89 EST: 1954
SQ FT: 3,500
SALES (est): 24.6MM **Privately Held**
WEB: www.andersoncls.com
SIC: **3211** 5713 Flat glass; floor covering stores

(P-10272)
MEDILAND CORPORATION
Also Called: Premium Windows
7027 Motz St, Paramount (90723-4842)
PHONE..............................562 630-9696
Carlos Landazuri, *CEO*
Jose Medina, *Admin Sec*
Kevin Vargas, *Info Tech Mgr*
Julio Varela, *Controller*
Luis Cruz, *Plant Mgr*
▲ EMP: 79
SALES: 9.1MM **Privately Held**
SIC: **3211** 3645 Window glass, clear & colored; garden, patio, walkway & yard lighting fixtures: electric

(P-10273)
POMA GL SPECIALTY WINDOWS INC
Also Called: Afg Insulating Riverside Plant
813 Palmyrita Ave, Riverside (92507-1805)
PHONE..............................951 321-0116
Larry Goins, *Principal*
EMP: 60 **Privately Held**
SIC: **3211** Insulating glass, sealed units

HQ: Poma Glass & Specialty Windows Inc.
   11175 Cicero Dr Ste 400
   Alpharetta GA 30022
   404 446-4200

(P-10274)
SGC INTERNATIONAL INC
6489 Corvette St, Commerce (90040-1702)
PHONE..............................323 318-2998
Xinbo Huang, *President*
James Huang, *Principal*
▲ EMP: 15
SALES (est): 54.7K **Privately Held**
SIC: **3211** 5023 5039 Flat glass; frames & framing, picture & mirror; exterior flat glass: plate or window; interior flat glass: plate or window

(P-10275)
SKYCO SKYLIGHTS INC
401 Goetz Ave, Santa Ana (92707-3709)
PHONE..............................949 629-4090
Ryan Marshall, *CEO*
Robert Marshall, *President*
Gary Ritchie, *Vice Pres*
EMP: 35
SALES (est): 4.8MM **Privately Held**
SIC: **3211** Skylight glass

(P-10276)
SUN VALLEY SKYLIGHTS INC
Also Called: Sun Vlly Skylghts Plus Windws
12884 Pierce St, Pacoima (91331-2524)
PHONE..............................818 686-0032
David Witty, *President*
Abby Witty, *Vice Pres*
Abbi Witty, *Project Mgr*
Larry Davis, *VP Opers*
EMP: 11
SQ FT: 8,350
SALES (est): 1.2MM **Privately Held**
WEB: www.sunvalleyskylights.com
SIC: **3211** 1761 Skylight glass; skylight installation

(P-10277)
SUNDOWN LIQUIDATING CORP (PA)
Also Called: Bristolite
401 Goetz Ave, Santa Ana (92707-3709)
PHONE..............................714 540-8950
Randolph Heartfield, *CEO*
Rick Beets, *President*
Darryl Liyama, *Admin Asst*
Rudy Pavlik, *Research*
Darryl Llyama, *Technology*
▼ EMP: 156 EST: 1970
SQ FT: 100,000
SALES: 32MM **Privately Held**
WEB: www.bristolite.com
SIC: **3211** Skylight glass

(P-10278)
TRANSIT CARE INC
7900 Nelson Rd, Panorama City (91402-6827)
PHONE..............................818 267-3002
William Baldwin, *President*
David Chaimowitz, *CFO*
EMP: 15
SQ FT: 20,000
SALES: 5.2MM **Privately Held**
WEB: www.transitcare.com
SIC: **3211** Strengthened or reinforced glass

(P-10279)
US HORIZON MANUFACTURING INC
Also Called: U.S. Horizon Mfg
28539 Industry Dr, Valencia (91355-5424)
PHONE..............................661 775-1675
Donald E Friest, *CEO*
Garrett A Russell, *President*
▲ EMP: 39 EST: 1998
SQ FT: 44,000
SALES (est): 4.5MM
SALES (corp-wide): 30.6B **Privately Held**
SIC: **3211** 3429 Plate & sheet glass; manufactured hardware (general)
HQ: C. R. Laurence Co., Inc.
   2503 E Vernon Ave
   Vernon CA 90058
   323 588-1281

(P-10280)
VITRO FLAT GLASS LLC
Also Called: Fresno Glass Plant
3333 S Peach Ave, Fresno (93725-9220)
P.O. Box 2748 (93745-2748)
PHONE..............................559 485-4660
Henry Good, *Manager*
EMP: 140 **Privately Held**
WEB: www.ppg.com
SIC: **3211** Window glass, clear & colored
HQ: Vitro Flat Glass Llc
   400 Guys Run Rd
   Cheswick PA 15024
   412 820-8500

(P-10281)
WSGLASS HOLDINGS INC (HQ)
Also Called: Western States Glass
3241 Darby Cmn, Fremont (94539-5601)
P.O. Box 6058 (94538-0658)
PHONE..............................510 623-5000
Michael A Smith, *President*
Michael S Foss, *Vice Pres*
Donald E Post, *Vice Pres*
Jonathan M Witkin, *Vice Pres*
▲ EMP: 33
SQ FT: 107,000
SALES (est): 22.9MM **Privately Held**
WEB: www.westernstatesglass.com
SIC: **3211** 3231 Transparent optical glass, except lenses; insulating glass, sealed units; mirrored glass

---

3221 Glass Containers

(P-10282)
ACME VIAL & GLASS CO
1601 Commerce Way, Paso Robles (93446-3626)
PHONE..............................805 239-2666
Debra C Knowles, *President*
Kay Anderson, *Vice Pres*
Corey Knowles, *General Mgr*
Angel Chairez, *Opers Mgr*
▲ EMP: 25
SALES (est): 3.8MM **Privately Held**
WEB: www.acmevial.com
SIC: **3221** 3231 5113 Vials, glass; products of purchased glass; industrial & personal service paper

(P-10283)
ARDAGH GLASS INC
24441 Avenue 12, Madera (93637-9384)
PHONE..............................559 675-4700
Jaime Navaro, *Manager*
Adan Garcia, *Engineer*
EMP: 34
SALES (corp-wide): 242.1K **Privately Held**
WEB: www.sgcontainers.com
SIC: **3221** 5719 Glass containers; glassware
HQ: Ardagh Glass Inc.
   10194 Crosspoint Blvd
   Indianapolis IN 46256

(P-10284)
ASEPTIC INNOVATIONS INC
4940 E Landon Dr, Anaheim (92807-1971)
PHONE..............................714 584-2110
Noel Calma, *CFO*
EMP: 20 EST: 2016
SQ FT: 37,771
SALES (est): 634.1K **Privately Held**
SIC: **3221** Glass containers

(P-10285)
ASEPTIC TECHNOLOGY LLC
24855 Corbit Pl, Yorba Linda (92887-5543)
PHONE..............................714 694-0168
Joshua Cua,
Julie Hodson, *President*
Noel Calma, *CFO*
EMP: 64 EST: 2013
SQ FT: 59,300
SALES: 7.5MM **Privately Held**
SIC: **3221** Bottles for packing, bottling & canning: glass

(PA)=Parent Co (HQ)=Headquarters (DH)=Div Headquarters
✪ = New Business established in last 2 years
    2020 California
    Manufacturers Register
    421

(P-10286)
CCDA WATERS LLC
2121 E Winston Rd, Anaheim
(92806-5535)
PHONE............................714 991-7031
Jim Peterson,
EMP: 90
SALES (est): 6.7MM **Privately Held**
WEB: www.la.ko.com
SIC: 3221 Water bottles, glass

(P-10287)
CUSTOM PACK INC
11621 Cardinal Cir, Garden Grove
(92843-3814)
PHONE............................714 534-2201
EMP: 16
SALES (est): 659.1K
SALES (corp-wide): 1MM **Privately Held**
SIC: 3221 7389
PA: Custom Pack, Inc.
11661 Cardinal Cir
Garden Grove CA 92843
714 534-5353

(P-10288)
GALLO GLASS COMPANY (HQ)
605 S Santa Cruz Ave, Modesto
(95354-4299)
P.O. Box 1230 (95353-1230)
PHONE............................209 341-3710
Robert J Gallo, *President*
Craig Beck, *Info Tech Mgr*
MO Mashinchi, *Engineer*
Nicky Sabet, *Engineer*
Gordon Stewart, *Engineer*
▲ **EMP:** 1000 **EST:** 1957
SALES (est): 201.2MM
SALES (corp-wide): 2.3B **Privately Held**
SIC: 3221 Glass containers
PA: E. & J. Gallo Winery
600 Yosemite Blvd
Modesto CA 95354
209 341-3111

(P-10289)
**MYERS WINE CNTRY KITCHENS
LLC**
511 Alexis Ct, NAPA (94558-7526)
PHONE............................707 252-9463
Daren Cannels, *President*
Kelly Hull, *COO*
Jill Sheehan, *Vice Pres*
Jack Harkins, *VP Bus Dvlpt*
John McIntosh, *CTO*
▲ **EMP:** 20
SQ FT: 17,000
SALES (est): 3.5MM **Privately Held**
WEB: www.winecountrykitchens.com
SIC: 3221 Bottles for packing, bottling &
canning: glass

(P-10290)
**OWENS-BROCKWAY GLASS
CONT INC**
3600 Alameda Ave, Oakland (94601-3329)
PHONE............................510 436-2000
Rod Detmear, *Manager*
EMP: 100
SALES (corp-wide): 6.8B **Publicly Held**
SIC: 3221 Glass containers
HQ: Owens-Brockway Glass Container Inc.
1 Michael Owens Way
Perrysburg OH 43551
567 336-8449

(P-10291)
OWENS-ILLINOIS INC
14700 W Schulte Rd, Tracy (95377-8628)
PHONE............................209 652-1311
Dana Armagost, *Branch Mgr*
Tubal Monsalve, *Manager*
EMP: 200
SALES (corp-wide): 6.8B **Publicly Held**
SIC: 3221 Glass containers
PA: Owens-Illinois, Inc.
1 Michael Owens Way
Perrysburg OH 43551
567 336-5000

(P-10292)
PACIFIC VIAL MFG INC
2738 Supply Ave, Commerce (90040-2704)
PHONE............................323 721-7004
Steven OH, *Principal*

▲ **EMP:** 40
SQ FT: 30,000
SALES (est): 100MM **Privately Held**
WEB: www.pacificvial.com
SIC: 3221 Vials, glass

(P-10293)
**SAINT GOBAIN CONTAINERS
INC**
2600 Stanford Ct, Fairfield (94533-2767)
PHONE............................707 437-8700
Phil Ringhome, *Principal*
EMP: 10
SALES (est): 1.2MM
SALES (corp-wide): 215.9MM **Privately
Held**
WEB: www.saint-gobain.fr
SIC: 3221 Glass containers
PA: Compagnie De Saint-Gobain
Les Miroirs La Defense 3
Courbevoie 92400
140 880-316

(P-10294)
WORLD WINE BOTTLES LLC
Also Called: World Wine Bottles & Packaging
1370 Trancas St Ste 411, NAPA
(94558-2912)
PHONE............................707 339-2102
Niel Sodell, *President*
Martin Foigelman,
▲ **EMP:** 50
SQ FT: 50,000
SALES (est): 50MM **Privately Held**
SIC: 3221 5182 Bottles for packing, bot-
tling & canning: glass; wine

**3229 Pressed & Blown
Glassware, NEC**

(P-10295)
ALAMILLO RADOLFO
Also Called: Pacific Light Blown Glass
4901 Patata St Ste 404, Cudahy
(90201-5945)
PHONE............................323 773-9614
Radolfo Alamillo, *Owner*
EMP: 12
SQ FT: 4,800
SALES (est): 1.1MM **Privately Held**
WEB: www.pacificlite.com
SIC: 3229 5023 Glassware, art or decora-
tive; lamps: floor, boudoir, desk

(P-10296)
**ALLIANCE FIBER OPTIC PDTS
INC**
275 Gibraltar Dr, Sunnyvale (94089-1312)
PHONE............................408 736-6900
Peter C Chang, *Ch of Bd*
Anita K Ho, *CFO*
David A Hubbard, *Exec VP*
▲ **EMP:** 75
SQ FT: 18,088
SALES (est): 81.1MM
SALES (corp-wide): 11.2B **Publicly Held**
WEB: www.afop.com
SIC: 3229 3661 Fiber optics strands; fiber
optics communications equipment
PA: Corning Incorporated
1 Riverfront Plz
Corning NY 14831
607 974-9000

(P-10297)
AMERICAN QUALEX INC
920 Calle Negocio Ste A, San Clemente
(92673-6207)
PHONE............................949 492-8298
Dan Moothart, *President*
Charles Moothart, *Corp Secy*
Tun Khin, *Safety Mgr*
EMP: 10
SQ FT: 6,000
SALES (est): 1.1MM **Privately Held**
SIC: 3229 Scientific glassware

(P-10298)
ANNIEGLASS INC (PA)
310 Harvest Dr, Watsonville (95076-5103)
P.O. Box 2610 (95077-2610)
PHONE............................831 761-2041
Annie Morhauser, *President*
EMP: 25

SQ FT: 16,000
SALES (est): 3.6MM **Privately Held**
WEB: www.annieglass.com
SIC: 3229 Tableware, glass or glass ce-
ramic

(P-10299)
**ANRITSU INSTRUMENTS
COMPANY**
490 Jarvis Dr, Morgan Hill (95037-2834)
PHONE............................315 797-4449
Takanori Sumi, *President*
Frank Tiernan, *Vice Pres*
Robert Hendersen, *Admin Sec*
EMP: 50
SQ FT: 60,000
SALES (est): 4.7MM **Privately Held**
WEB: www.nettest.com
SIC: 3229 Fiber optics strands
HQ: Anritsu U.S. Holding, Inc.
490 Jarvis Dr
Morgan Hill CA 95037
408 778-2000

(P-10300)
CARLEY INC (PA)
1502 W 228th St, Torrance (90501-5105)
PHONE............................310 325-8474
James A Carley, *President*
Margaret Tsang, *CFO*
Suzy Bush, *Manager*
▲ **EMP:** 300
SQ FT: 14,000
SALES (est): 30MM **Privately Held**
WEB: www.carleylamps.com
SIC: 3229 3646 3641 Lamp parts &
shades, glass; commercial indusl & insti-
tutional electric lighting fixtures; electric
lamps

(P-10301)
CDEQ
9421 Telfair Ave, Sun Valley (91352-1332)
PHONE............................818 767-5143
Chaim Dekel, *President*
EMP: 30 **EST:** 1995
SQ FT: 10,000
SALES (est): 2.8MM **Privately Held**
SIC: 3229 Glassware, art or decorative

(P-10302)
CONNECTIVE SOLUTIONS LLC
14252 Culver Dr Ste A343, Irvine
(92604-0317)
PHONE............................800 241-2792
John Haney, *Mng Member*
Jeff Haney,
EMP: 10
SQ FT: 500
SALES (est): 100K **Privately Held**
WEB: www.connectivesol.com
SIC: 3229 Fiber optics strands

(P-10303)
DESAIS DESIGN CRAFT
408 S Gladys Ave, San Gabriel
(91776-1923)
PHONE............................626 285-3189
Navnit Desai, *President*
Dharmishta Desai, *Admin Sec*
EMP: 10
SQ FT: 9,500
SALES (est): 951.9K **Privately Held**
SIC: 3229 Lamp parts & shades, glass

(P-10304)
DONOCO INDUSTRIES INC
Also Called: Encore Plastics
5642 Research Dr Ste B, Huntington Beach
(92649-1634)
P.O. Box 3208 (92605-3208)
PHONE............................714 893-7889
Richard Harvey, *CEO*
Donald Okada, *CFO*
George West, *Treasurer*
EMP: 25
SQ FT: 12,000
SALES (est): 3.3MM **Privately Held**
WEB: www.encoreplastics.com
SIC: 3229 Tableware, glass or glass ce-
ramic

(P-10305)
**FARLOWS SCNTFIC
GLSSBLWING INC**
Also Called: Farlows Scentific Glassblowing
962 Golden Gate Ter Ste B, Grass Valley
(95945-5972)
PHONE............................530 477-5513
Gary Farlow, *President*
Charolette Farlow, *Vice Pres*
EMP: 25
SQ FT: 5,250
SALES (est): 2.3MM **Privately Held**
WEB: www.farlowsci.com
SIC: 3229 Scientific glassware

(P-10306)
FUJITSU OPTICAL CO
1280 E Arques Ave, Sunnyvale
(94085-5401)
PHONE............................408 746-6000
Hiroto Kodama, *CEO*
EMP: 12
SALES (est): 431.8K **Privately Held**
SIC: 3229 Optical glass
PA: Fujitsu Limited
1-5-2, Higashishimbashi
Minato-Ku TKY 105-0
-

(P-10307)
GLAS WERK INC
29710 Ave De Las Bndra, Rcho STA Marg
(92688-2614)
PHONE............................949 766-1296
Maik Bollhorn, *President*
▲ **EMP:** 26
SQ FT: 6,000
SALES (est): 2MM **Privately Held**
WEB: www.glaswerk.com
SIC: 3229 Scientific glassware

(P-10308)
GW PARTNERS INTERNATIONAL
Also Called: Gw Crystal
8351 Elm Ave Ste 106, Rancho Cuca-
monga (91730-7639)
P.O. Box 1995 (91729-1995)
PHONE............................909 980-1010
Scott Erickson, *President*
▲ **EMP:** 11
SQ FT: 4,200
SALES (est): 1.8MM **Privately Held**
SIC: 3229 Novelty glassware

(P-10309)
H I S C INC
1009 Calle Recodo, San Clemente
(92673-6237)
P.O. Box 457 (92674-0457)
PHONE............................949 492-8968
Robert Depalma, *President*
Roxanne Depalma, *Shareholder*
◆ **EMP:** 10
SQ FT: 6,000
SALES (est): 1.2MM **Privately Held**
WEB: www.floralarranger.com
SIC: 3229 2381 3432 5193 Vases, glass;
gloves, work: woven or knit, made from
purchased materials; lawn hose nozzles
& sprinklers; planters & flower pots; gar-
den tools, hand

(P-10310)
HAUSENWARE KOYO LLC
2111 Laughlin Rd, Windsor (95492-8212)
PHONE............................412 897-3064
Ulrich Honighausen,
Kelley Clayton,
▲ **EMP:** 10 **EST:** 2012
SQ FT: 18,000
SALES (est): 637.1K **Privately Held**
SIC: 3229 Tableware, glass or glass ce-
ramic

(P-10311)
IFIBER OPTIX INC
14450 Chambers Rd, Tustin (92780-6914)
PHONE............................714 665-9796
Sanjeev Jaiswal, *President*
▲ **EMP:** 25
SQ FT: 5,731
SALES (est): 4.5MM **Privately Held**
WEB: www.ifiberoptix.com
SIC: 3229 Fiber optics strands

▲ = Import ▼=Export
◆ =Import/Export

(P-10312)
IMPERIAL ENTERPRISES INC
9666 Owensmouth Ave Ste A, Chatsworth
(91311-8044)
PHONE...................................818 886-5028
Galina Zingerman, *CEO*
Boris Zingerman, *Vice Pres*
Steven Zingerman, *Exec Dir*
Colleen Forbes, *Administration*
Laura Jeffrey, *Human Res Mgr*
▲ EMP: 40
SQ FT: 13,000
SALES (est): 3.7MM **Privately Held**
SIC: 3229 5023 Glassware, art or decora-
tive; home furnishings

(P-10313)
INTEX FORMS INC
1333 Old County Rd, Belmont
(94002-3922)
PHONE...................................650 654-7855
Tom Olson, *Ch of Bd*
EMP: 32
SALES (est): 3.2MM **Privately Held**
SIC: 3229 Glass fiber products

(P-10314)
KIMDURLA INC
Also Called: Edwards Industries
12841 Blmfeld St Unit 104, Studio City
(91604)
PHONE...................................818 504-4041
Milton Friedman, *President*
Norma Friedman, *Vice Pres*
EMP: 28
SALES (est): 3MM **Privately Held**
SIC: 3229 2299 Glassware, art or decora-
tive; yarn, metallic, ceramic or paper
fibers

(P-10315)
**LARSON ELECTRONIC GLASS
INC**
2840 Bay Rd, Redwood City (94063-3503)
P.O. Box 371 (94064-0371)
PHONE...................................650 369-6734
Charles Kraft, *President*
Jill Kraft, *CFO*
▼ EMP: 10 EST: 1954
SQ FT: 10,000
SALES (est): 1.3MM **Privately Held**
SIC: 3229 Glassware, industrial

(P-10316)
LEGACY US LLC
Also Called: Legacy Glass Studios
1800 El Camino Real Ste D, Menlo Park
(94027-4103)
PHONE...................................650 714-9750
Kim Reeves,
Jeff Dalton,
EMP: 10
SQ FT: 3,500
SALES (est): 852.1K **Privately Held**
SIC: 3229 Glassware, industrial

(P-10317)
LEWIS JOHN GLASS STUDIO
10229 Pearmain St, Oakland (94603-3023)
PHONE...................................510 635-4607
John C Lewis, *Owner*
EMP: 12
SQ FT: 17,000
SALES (est): 1.4MM **Privately Held**
WEB: www.johnlewisglass.com
SIC: 3229 5947 Pressed & blown glass;
gift, novelty & souvenir shop

(P-10318)
LIFI LABS INC (PA)
Also Called: Lifx
350 Townsend St Ste 830, San Francisco
(94107-0009)
PHONE...................................650 739-5563
Jake Lawton, *Principal*
EMP: 13
SALES (est): 13.5MM **Privately Held**
SIC: 3229 Bulbs for electric lights

(P-10319)
MEMORY GLASS LLC
325 Rutherford St Ste E, Goleta
(93117-3728)
PHONE...................................805 682-6469
Nicholas Savage,

Kim Price, *VP Sales*
Lena Savage,
Michael Savage,
▲ EMP: 10
SALES (est): 1MM **Privately Held**
SIC: 3229 Art, decorative & novelty glass-
ware

(P-10320)
MODERN CERAMICS MFG INC
2240 Lundy Ave, San Jose (95131-1816)
PHONE...................................408 383-0554
Christina Hoang, *CEO*
Tuan Le, *Purch Agent*
Frank Kramer, *Opers Mgr*
Tim Nishimura, *QC Mgr*
▲ EMP: 20 EST: 1999
SQ FT: 3,087
SALES (est): 6.7MM **Privately Held**
WEB: www.modernceramics.com
SIC: 3229 Tableware, glass or glass ce-
ramic

(P-10321)
**NEPTEC OPTICAL SOLUTIONS
INC**
48603 Warm Springs Blvd, Fremont
(94539-7782)
PHONE...................................510 687-1101
David Cheng, *President*
Eugene Lin, *Vice Pres*
Sylvia Bustamante, *Purch Mgr*
Sharon Lu, *Purch Mgr*
▲ EMP: 25
SALES (est): 950K **Privately Held**
SIC: 3229 Pressed & blown glass

(P-10322)
NEXFON CORPORATION
7172 Regional St, Dublin (94568-2324)
PHONE...................................925 200-2233
Yi Qin, *President*
Dr Charles Qian, *Project Mgr*
▲ EMP: 12
SALES (est): 658.7K **Privately Held**
WEB: www.nexfon.com
SIC: 3229 Fiber optics strands

(P-10323)
OPTIWORKS INC (PA)
47211 Bayside Pkwy, Fremont
(94538-6517)
PHONE...................................510 438-4560
Roger Liang, *CEO*
Annie Kuo, *Vice Pres*
Steve Kuo, *Vice Pres*
Elizabeth Rueda, *Engineer*
Sherry Hsiao, *Accounting Mgr*
EMP: 65
SALES (est): 17.2MM **Privately Held**
WEB: www.optiworks.com
SIC: 3229 Fiber optics strands

(P-10324)
ORBITS LIGHTWAVE INC
41 S Chester Ave, Pasadena (91106-3104)
PHONE...................................626 513-7400
Yaakov Shevy, *CEO*
EMP: 17 EST: 1999
SQ FT: 9,700
SALES (est): 2.1MM **Privately Held**
WEB: www.orbitslightwave.com
SIC: 3229 Fiber optics strands

(P-10325)
**ORIENT & FLUME ART GLASS
CO**
2161 Park Ave, Chico (95928-6702)
P.O. Box 3298 (95927-3298)
PHONE...................................530 893-0373
Douglas Boyd, *President*
John A Powell, *CFO*
EMP: 30
SQ FT: 20,000
SALES (est): 2.9MM **Privately Held**
WEB: www.orientandflume.com
SIC: 3229 8412 Glassware, art or decora-
tive; museums & art galleries

(P-10326)
**PERFORMANCE COMPOSITES
INC**
1418 S Alameda St, Compton
(90221-4802)
PHONE...................................310 328-6661

Francis Hu, *President*
Peter McNicol, *General Mgr*
Eddie Mejia, *Admin Asst*
Susan Tashiro, *Controller*
Adela Gonzalez, *Human Res Mgr*
EMP: 75
SQ FT: 46,000
SALES (est): 8.5MM **Privately Held**
WEB: www.performancecomposites.com
SIC: 3229 3624 3544 Glass fiber prod-
ucts; carbon & graphite products; special
dies, tools, jigs & fixtures

(P-10327)
PLEXUS OPTIX INC
3333 Quality Dr, Rancho Cordova
(95670-7985)
PHONE...................................800 852-7600
James R Lynch, *President*
EMP: 32
SALES (est): 1.1MM
SALES (corp-wide): 8.8MM **Privately
Held**
SIC: 3229 Optical glass
PA: Vsp Optical Group, Inc.
3333 Quality Dr
Rancho Cordova CA 95670
916 851-4682

(P-10328)
**PRECISION GLASS BEVELLING
INC**
Also Called: Rbs Glass Designs
15201 Keswick St Ste A, Van Nuys
(91405-1014)
PHONE...................................818 989-2727
Richard Sloan, *President*
Mike Latzer, *Vice Pres*
▲ EMP: 20
SQ FT: 7,000
SALES (est): 2.1MM **Privately Held**
SIC: 3229 5231 Pressed & blown glass;
glass, leaded or stained

(P-10329)
RANDOM TECHNOLOGIES LLC
2325 3rd St Ste 404, San Francisco
(94107-4304)
PHONE...................................415 255-1267
Amos Gottlieb, *Mng Member*
EMP: 10
SQ FT: 3,600
SALES (est): 1.4MM **Privately Held**
WEB: www.randomtechnologies.com
SIC: 3229 2821 Fiber optics strands; poly-
tetrafluoroethylene resins (teflon)

(P-10330)
SHAMIR INSIGHT INC
9938 Via Pasar, San Diego (92126-4559)
PHONE...................................858 514-8330
Raanan Naftalovich, *CEO*
Joyce Hornaday, *VP Human Res*
Richard Dailey, *VP Sales*
Mary Mulvey, *Marketing Staff*
Jeff Pilkington, *Accounts Exec*
▲ EMP: 77 EST: 1997
SALES (est): 14.5MM
SALES (corp-wide): 1.1MM **Privately
Held**
WEB: www.shamirlens.com
SIC: 3229 Optical glass
HQ: Shamir Optical Industry Ltd
Kibbutz
Shamir 12135
469 477-77

(P-10331)
**SPOTLITE AMERICA
CORPORATION (PA)**
9937 Jefferson Blvd # 110, Culver City
(90232-3529)
PHONE...................................310 829-0200
Halston Mikail, *CEO*
▲ EMP: 22 EST: 2014
SQ FT: 17,000
SALES (est): 24.7MM **Privately Held**
SIC: 3229 3699 Bulbs for electric lights;
electrical equipment & supplies

(P-10332)
VITRICO CORP
Also Called: Firelight Glass
2181 Williams St, San Leandro
(94577-3224)
PHONE...................................510 652-6731

Karen Boss, *CEO*
James Maslach, *President*
EMP: 12
SQ FT: 20,000
SALES (est): 1.7MM **Privately Held**
SIC: 3229 Glassware, art or decorative;
glassware, industrial

(P-10333)
**WEST COAST QUARTZ
CORPORATION (HQ)**
Also Called: W C Q
1000 Corporate Way, Fremont
(94539-6105)
PHONE...................................510 249-2160
Johng S Bae, *CEO*
Dave Lopes, *President*
Howard Cho, *COO*
Tim Mattson, *Info Tech Mgr*
Michele Graff, *Controller*
▲ EMP: 97 EST: 1981
SQ FT: 60,000
SALES (est): 28.8MM **Privately Held**
WEB: www.wcq.com
SIC: 3229 3679 3674 5065 Glassware,
industrial; quartz crystals, for electronic
application; semiconductors & related de-
vices; semiconductor devices

(P-10334)
WOLFRAM INC
1309 Doker Dr Ste B, Modesto
(95351-1603)
PHONE...................................209 238-9610
Steven Alexander, *President*
▲ EMP: 10
SQ FT: 5,000
SALES (est): 1MM **Privately Held**
WEB: www.wolfram.com
SIC: 3229 Lamp parts & shades, glass

(P-10335)
ZEONS INC
291 S Cienega Blvd 102, Beverly Hills
(90211)
PHONE...................................323 302-8299
Naved Jafry, *President*
EMP: 312
SQ FT: 3,500
SALES: 13MM **Privately Held**
SIC: 3229 1629 6211 Insulators, electri-
cal: glass; power plant construction; in-
vestment certificate sales; oil & gas lease
brokers

**3231 Glass Prdts Made Of
Purchased Glass**

(P-10336)
ALAN LEM & CO INC
Also Called: Advance Aqua Tanks
515 W 130th St, Los Angeles (90061-1180)
PHONE...................................310 538-4282
Alan Y Lem, *President*
EMP: 21
SQ FT: 11,000
SALES (est): 2.9MM **Privately Held**
WEB: www.advanceaquatanks.com
SIC: 3231 Aquariums & reflectors, glass

(P-10337)
ANTHONY DOORS INC
Also Called: Anthony International
12812 Arroyo St, Sylmar (91342-5301)
PHONE...................................818 365-9451
Jeff Clark, *Branch Mgr*
EMP: 425
SALES (corp-wide): 6.9B **Publicly Held**
WEB: www.kramerusa.com
SIC: 3231 5078 3585 Doors, glass: made
from purchased glass; tempered glass:
made from purchased glass; glass sheet,
bent: made from purchased glass; display
cases, refrigerated; evaporative con-
densers, heat transfer equipment
HQ: Anthony Doors, Inc.
12391 Montero Ave
Sylmar CA 91342
818 365-9451

PRODUCTS & SVCS

(P-10338)
ATLAS SPECIALTIES CORPORATION (PA)
Also Called: Atlas Shower Door Co
4337 Astoria St, Sacramento (95838-3001)
PHONE....................................503 636-8182
Edwin A Lindquist, *President*
Fred Ferri, *CFO*
Roger Lindquist, *Vice Pres*
EMP: 28 **EST:** 1955
SQ FT: 5,000
SALES (est): 3MM **Privately Held**
SIC: 3231 5039 Doors, glass: made from purchased glass; glass construction materials

(P-10339)
AVALON GLASS & MIRROR COMPANY
642 Alondra Blvd, Carson (90746-1049)
PHONE....................................323 321-8806
Salvador G Gomez, *President*
Randy Seeinberg, *President*
Ed Rosengrant, *Vice Pres*
Ruben Huerta, *Admin Sec*
▲ **EMP:** 100
SQ FT: 100,000
SALES (est): 15.3MM **Privately Held**
WEB: www.avalonmirrorglass.com
SIC: 3231 5023 5231 3211 Mirrored glass; furniture tops; glass: cut, beveled or polished; glassware; mirrors & pictures, framed & unframed; glass; flat glass
PA: Gwla Acquisition Corp.
    8600 Rheem Ave
    South Gate CA 90280

(P-10340)
BANANAFISH PRODUCTIONS INC
1536 W Embassy St, Anaheim (92802-1016)
PHONE....................................714 956-2129
Dan Iman, *President*
Jerry Smith, *Principal*
EMP: 11
SQ FT: 4,500
SALES: 300K **Privately Held**
WEB: www.bananafishproductions.com
SIC: 3231 Ornamental glass: cut, engraved or otherwise decorated

(P-10341)
BERGIN GLASS IMPRESSIONS INC
938 Kaiser Rd, NAPA (94558-6206)
PHONE....................................707 224-0111
Michael Bergin, *Owner*
EMP: 20
SALES (corp-wide): 3.5MM **Privately Held**
WEB: www.berginglass.com
SIC: 3231 Ornamental glass: cut, engraved or otherwise decorated
PA: Bergin Glass Impressions, Inc.
    2511 Napa Vly Ste
    Napa CA 94558
    707 224-0111

(P-10342)
BEVELED EDGE INC
Also Called: Original Glass Design
1740 Junction Ave Ste D, San Jose (95112-1035)
PHONE....................................408 467-9900
Mark Idzal, *President*
▲ **EMP:** 16
SQ FT: 8,500
SALES (est): 1.7MM **Privately Held**
WEB: www.thebevelededge.com
SIC: 3231 Products of purchased glass

(P-10343)
BLOMBERG WINDOWS SYSTEMS
Also Called: Blomberg Glass
1453 Blair Ave, Sacramento (95822-3410)
PHONE....................................916 428-8060
J Philip Collier, *Ch of Bd*
Ralph S Blomberg, *Vice Pres*
EMP: 135
SALES (est): 7.3MM **Privately Held**
SIC: 3231 Doors, glass: made from purchased glass

(P-10344)
CALIFORNIA GLASS BENDING CORP
Also Called: CGB
2100 W 139th St, Gardena (90249-2412)
PHONE....................................310 549-5255
Robert N Green, *CEO*
Kelly Green, *Owner*
EMP: 30
SQ FT: 30,000
SALES (est): 3.7MM **Privately Held**
WEB: www.calglassbending.com
SIC: 3231 Products of purchased glass

(P-10345)
CAMBRIDGE LASER LABORATORIES
853 Brown Rd, Fremont (94539-7090)
PHONE....................................510 651-0110
Brian L Bohan, *President*
Kimberley Darrah, *Admin Sec*
EMP: 10
SQ FT: 8,000
SALES (est): 1.2MM **Privately Held**
WEB: www.cambridgelasers.com
SIC: 3231 Medical & laboratory glassware: made from purchased glass; scientific & technical glassware: from purchased glass

(P-10346)
CARDINAL GLASS INDUSTRIES INC
Also Called: Cardinal Cg Company
1125 E Lanzit Ave, Los Angeles (90059-1559)
PHONE....................................323 319-0070
EMP: 43
SALES (corp-wide): 1B **Privately Held**
SIC: 3231 Products of purchased glass
PA: Cardinal Glass Industries Inc
    775 Pririe Ctr Dr Ste 200
    Eden Prairie MN 55344
    952 229-2600

(P-10347)
CARLOS SHOWER DOORS INC
300 Kentucky St, Bakersfield (93305-4230)
P.O. Box 6009 (93386-6009)
PHONE....................................661 327-5594
Phillip Calvillo, *President*
Loni Amado, *President*
Edward Amado, *Vice Pres*
Steven Amado, *Vice Pres*
Phillip C Calvillo, *Admin Sec*
EMP: 11
SQ FT: 10,000
SALES (est): 907.5K **Privately Held**
WEB: www.carlosshowerdoors.com
SIC: 3231 Doors, glass: made from purchased glass; insulating glass: made from purchased glass

(P-10348)
CORAL REEF AQUARIUM
515 W 130th St, Los Angeles (90061-1180)
PHONE....................................310 538-4282
Alan Y Lem, *Owner*
EMP: 21
SALES (est): 1MM **Privately Held**
SIC: 3231 Ornamental glass: cut, engraved or otherwise decorated

(P-10349)
CUSTOM INDUSTRIES INC
1371 N Miller St, Anaheim (92806-1412)
PHONE....................................714 779-9101
Thomas McAfee, *President*
▲ **EMP:** 21
SALES (est): 3.7MM **Privately Held**
SIC: 3231 Doors, glass: made from purchased glass

(P-10350)
CV WNDOWS DORS RIVERSIDE INC
Also Called: Cv of Riverside
6676 Lance Dr, Riverside (92507-0769)
P.O. Box 802813, Santa Clarita (91380-2813)
PHONE....................................951 784-8766
Kevin Grossman, *CEO*
EMP: 25

SALES (est): 4.5MM **Privately Held**
WEB: www.empireshowerdoors.com
SIC: 3231 3211 3442 2431 Doors, glass: made from purchased glass; window glass, clear & colored; window & door frames; windows & window parts & trim, wood

(P-10351)
D G U TRADING CORPORATION
Also Called: Door & Glass Unique
1999 W Holt Ave, Pomona (91768-3352)
PHONE....................................909 469-1288
Linda Chuang, *President*
▲ **EMP:** 40
SQ FT: 5,000
SALES (est): 3.9MM **Privately Held**
WEB: www.adgu.com
SIC: 3231 5031 5211 Stained glass: made from purchased glass; doors; doors, wood or metal, except storm

(P-10352)
DA-LY GLASS CORP
Also Called: Western Glass Co
1193 W 2nd St, Pomona (91766-1308)
PHONE....................................323 589-5461
William J Dake, *President*
EMP: 30
SQ FT: 25,000
SALES (est): 3MM **Privately Held**
WEB: www.westernglassco.com
SIC: 3231 3281 3211 1411 Laminated glass: made from purchased glass; decorated glassware: chipped, engraved, etched, etc.; cut stone & stone products; flat glass; dimension stone

(P-10353)
DECOR SHOWER DOOR AND GLASS CO
Also Called: Decor Shower Enclosures
1819 Tanen St Ste A, NAPA (94559-1392)
PHONE....................................707 253-0622
Brad Taylor, *President*
EMP: 10
SQ FT: 2,500
SALES: 600K **Privately Held**
SIC: 3231 Doors, glass: made from purchased glass

(P-10354)
DIANE MARKIN INC
112 Penn St, El Segundo (90245-3907)
PHONE....................................310 322-0200
Diane Markin, *President*
▲ **EMP:** 12
SQ FT: 9,000
SALES: 1MM **Privately Held**
WEB: www.dianemarkin.com
SIC: 3231 3861 Art glass: made from purchased glass; printing frames, photographic

(P-10355)
DUO PANE INDUSTRIES
2444 Trevino Way, Fairfield (94534-7524)
PHONE....................................707 426-9696
Dave Crompton, *Owner*
EMP: 15
SQ FT: 15,000
SALES (est): 987.3K **Privately Held**
SIC: 3231 Insulating glass: made from purchased glass

(P-10356)
E & R GLASS CONTRACTORS INC
5369 Brooks St, Montclair (91763-4539)
PHONE....................................909 624-1763
Eric Dryden, *President*
Russ Dryden, *Vice Pres*
EMP: 22
SQ FT: 800
SALES (est): 3.2MM **Privately Held**
WEB: www.eandrglass.com
SIC: 3231 Products of purchased glass

(P-10357)
EMPIRE SHOWER DOORS INC
1217 N Mcdowell Blvd, Petaluma (94954-1112)
PHONE....................................707 773-2898
Roy German, *President*
Marylou German, *Admin Sec*
EMP: 15
SQ FT: 5,000

SALES (est): 2MM **Privately Held**
WEB: www.empireshowerdoors.com
SIC: 3231 5031 1793 Doors, glass: made from purchased glass; doors; glass & glazing work

(P-10358)
FABRICATED GLASS SPC INC
2350 S Watney Way Ste E, Fairfield (94533-6738)
PHONE....................................707 429-6160
Harvey Holtz, *President*
EMP: 17
SALES (corp-wide): 33.9MM **Privately Held**
WEB: www.fabglass.com
SIC: 3231 Mirrored glass
PA: Fabricated Glass Specialties, Inc.
    101 E Rapp Rd
    Talent OR 97540
    541 535-1582

(P-10359)
FIRE AND LIGHT ORIGINALS LP
100 Ericson Ct Ste 100 # 100, Arcata (95521-8932)
P.O. Box 2813, McKinleyville (95519-2813)
PHONE....................................707 825-7500
John McClurg, *Partner*
Gaea Resources, *Partner*
EMP: 18
SALES (est): 2.3MM **Privately Held**
WEB: www.fireandlight.com
SIC: 3231 Products of purchased glass

(P-10360)
FLYLEAF WINDOWS INC
11040 Bollinger Canyon Rd, San Ramon (94582-4969)
PHONE....................................925 344-1181
Billy Alcantara, *President*
EMP: 40
SALES: 500K **Privately Held**
SIC: 3231 3211 Doors, glass: made from purchased glass; window glass, clear & colored

(P-10361)
GAFFOGLIO FMLY MTLCRAFTERS INC (PA)
Also Called: Camera Ready Cars
11161 Slater Ave, Fountain Valley (92708-4921)
PHONE....................................714 444-2000
George Gaffoglio, *CEO*
Ruben Gaffoglio, *President*
Mike Alexander, *COO*
EMP: 109
SQ FT: 94,000
SALES (est): 17.4MM **Privately Held**
WEB: www.metalcrafters.com
SIC: 3231 3711 3365 Mirrors, truck & automobile: made from purchased glass; automobile assembly, including specialty automobiles; aerospace castings, aluminum

(P-10362)
GLASSPLAX
26605 Madison Ave, Murrieta (92562-8909)
PHONE....................................951 677-4800
Steve Tortomasi, *President*
▲ **EMP:** 20
SALES (est): 2.2MM **Privately Held**
WEB: www.glassplax.com
SIC: 3231 5094 Ornamental glass: cut, engraved or otherwise decorated; trophies

(P-10363)
GLASSWERKS LA INC (HQ)
Also Called: Glasswerks Group
8600 Rheem Ave, South Gate (90280-3333)
PHONE....................................888 789-7810
Randy Steinberg, *President*
Edwin Rosengrant, *Vice Pres*
Ruben Huerta, *Admin Sec*
Melina Barz, *Representative*
▲ **EMP:** 280 **EST:** 1949
SQ FT: 100,000

SALES (est): 61.9MM **Privately Held**
SIC: 3231 3211 Mirrored glass; tempered glass: made from purchased glass; furniture tops, glass: cut, beveled or polished; flat glass

(P-10364)
GP MERGER SUB INC
Also Called: Glaspro
9401 Ann St, Santa Fe Springs (90670-2613)
PHONE..............................562 946-7722
Joseph Green, *President*
Bishop McNeill, *Chief Mktg Ofcr*
Stephen Sudeth, *Creative Dir*
Jason Hillman, *Info Tech Dir*
Rafaella Carreno, *Controller*
▲ EMP: 85
SQ FT: 75,000
SALES (est): 17.8MM **Privately Held**
WEB: www.gftc.net
SIC: 3231 Laminated glass: made from purchased glass

(P-10365)
INDUSTRIAL GLASS PRODUCTS INC
4229 Union Pacific Ave, Los Angeles (90023-4016)
PHONE..............................323 526-7125
Esther Ramirez, *President*
▲ EMP: 15
SQ FT: 10,000
SALES: 900K **Privately Held**
WEB: www.industrialglassproducts.com
SIC: 3231 5039 Products of purchased glass; glass construction materials

(P-10366)
INNOVATIVE STRUCTURAL GL INC
Also Called: I S G
40220 Pierce Dr, Three Rivers (93271-9332)
P.O. Box 775 (93271-0775)
PHONE..............................559 561-7000
Manuel Marinos, *CEO*
Cynthia Marinos, *CFO*
Bryan Elkington, *Design Engr*
Julie Gray, *Controller*
▲ EMP: 20
SQ FT: 100,000
SALES (est): 2.6MM **Privately Held**
WEB: www.structuralglass.com
SIC: 3231 Products of purchased glass

(P-10367)
INVENIOS LLC
320 N Nopal St, Santa Barbara (93103-3225)
PHONE..............................805 962-3333
Paul Then, *President*
EMP: 83
SALES (est): 2MM **Privately Held**
SIC: 3231 Products of purchased glass

(P-10368)
J & B MANUFACTURING CORP
Also Called: San Diego Mirror and Window
2780 La Mirada Dr Ste C, Vista (92081-8404)
PHONE..............................760 846-6316
Toll Free:..............................877 -
Daniel Jaoudi, *President*
EMP: 160
SQ FT: 40,000
SALES (est): 16.6MM **Privately Held**
WEB: www.sdmw.com
SIC: 3231 5231 5211 Doors, glass: made from purchased glass; glass; door & window products

(P-10369)
JANEL GLASS COMPANY INC
2960 Marsh St, Los Angeles (90039-2911)
P.O. Box 39849 (90039-0849)
PHONE..............................323 661-8621
Fax: 323 661-8738
EMP: 50
SQ FT: 27,000
SALES (est): 5.4MM **Privately Held**
SIC: 3231

(P-10370)
JS GLASS WHOLESALE
2035 E 37th St, Vernon (90058-1414)
PHONE..............................213 746-5577
Yong Yi, *Owner*
Ashley Hong, *Manager*
EMP: 12
SQ FT: 6,450
SALES (est): 749.2K **Privately Held**
SIC: 3231 Products of purchased glass

(P-10371)
JUDSON STUDIOS INC
200 S Avenue 66, Los Angeles (90042-3632)
PHONE..............................323 255-0131
David Judson, *President*
EMP: 15 EST: 1897
SQ FT: 10,000
SALES (est): 1.5MM **Privately Held**
WEB: www.judsonstudios.com
SIC: 3231 Stained glass: made from purchased glass

(P-10372)
KINESTRAL TECHNOLOGIES INC (PA)
3955 Trust Way, Hayward (94545-3723)
PHONE..............................650 416-5200
Suk Bae Cha, *CEO*
Sam Bergh, *COO*
Thomas Krivas, *Vice Pres*
Susan Alejandrino, *Office Mgr*
Tiffany Davis, *Executive Asst*
▲ EMP: 130
SQ FT: 1,000
SALES (est): 27.4MM **Privately Held**
SIC: 3231 Products of purchased glass

(P-10373)
LARRY MTHVIN INSTALLATIONS INC (HQ)
Also Called: L M I
501 Kettering Dr, Ontario (91761-8150)
PHONE..............................909 563-1700
Larry Methvin, *CEO*
Mary Duran, *Human Resources*
Kim Coburn, *Purchasing*
Steve Phipps, *Sales Staff*
David Dantuono, *Manager*
▲ EMP: 200
SQ FT: 28,000
SALES (est): 58.7MM
SALES (corp-wide): 2.2B **Publicly Held**
SIC: 3231 3431 1751 Doors, glass: made from purchased glass; shower stalls, metal; carpentry work; window & door (prefabricated) installation
PA: Patrick Industries, Inc.
107 W Franklin St
Elkhart IN 46516
574 294-7511

(P-10374)
LARRY MTHVIN INSTALLATIONS INC
Also Called: LMI
128 N Cluff Ave, Lodi (95240-3104)
PHONE..............................209 368-2105
Christy Puerta, *Vice Pres*
EMP: 50
SALES (corp-wide): 2.2B **Publicly Held**
SIC: 3231 3088 Framed mirrors; shower stalls, fiberglass & plastic
HQ: Larry Methvin Installations, Inc.
501 Kettering Dr
Ontario CA 91761
909 563-1700

(P-10375)
LUNDBERG STUDIOS INC
131 Old Coast Rd, Davenport (95017-4007)
PHONE..............................831 423-2532
Rebecca Lundberg, *President*
Donya Scharping, *Office Mgr*
EMP: 20 EST: 1970
SQ FT: 6,000
SALES: 2MM **Privately Held**
SIC: 3231 Art glass: made from purchased glass

(P-10376)
M AND W GLASS
10745 Vernon Ave, Ontario (91762-4040)
PHONE..............................909 517-3585
Florencio Sanchez, *Owner*
EMP: 22
SQ FT: 15,000
SALES (est): 1.9MM **Privately Held**
WEB: www.mandwglass.com
SIC: 3231 Cut & engraved glassware: made from purchased glass

(P-10377)
MADRONE HOSPICE INC
217 W Miner St, Yreka (96097-2919)
PHONE..............................530 842-2547
Judith Mc Quoid, *Branch Mgr*
EMP: 20 **Privately Held**
SIC: 3231 Novelties, glass: fruit, foliage, flowers, animals, etc.
PA: Madrone Hospice Inc
255 Collier Cir
Yreka CA 96097

(P-10378)
MANUFACTURERS/HYLAND LTD
650 Reed St, Santa Clara (95050-3010)
PHONE..............................408 748-1806
James P Hyland, *President*
Mary Jo Hyland, *Admin Sec*
EMP: 12
SQ FT: 3,000
SALES (est): 1MM **Privately Held**
WEB: www.jphc.com
SIC: 3231 3915 8322 4813 Art glass: made from purchased glass; jewelers' materials & lapidary work; individual & family services; telephone communication, except radio;

(P-10379)
MASTERPIECE LEADED WINDOWS
11651 Rverside Dr Ste 143, Lakeside (92040)
P.O. Box 710461, Santee (92072-0461)
PHONE..............................858 391-3344
Joel Debus, *President*
Joy J Debus, *Shareholder*
James Debus, *Senior VP*
Jim Debus, *Vice Pres*
Ellen Grant, *Accounts Mgr*
▲ EMP: 25
SQ FT: 2,000
SALES: 1.7MM **Privately Held**
WEB: www.mpglass.com
SIC: 3231 5023 Leaded glass; window furnishings

(P-10380)
MILGARD MANUFACTURING INC
Also Called: Milgard-Simi Valley
355 E Easy St, Simi Valley (93065-1801)
PHONE..............................805 581-6325
Wayne Ramay, *Branch Mgr*
Cal Mc Clure, *Maintence Staff*
Calvin Mc Clure, *Maintence Staff*
EMP: 232
SALES (corp-wide): 8.3B **Publicly Held**
WEB: www.milgard.com
SIC: 3231 5031 3442 Products of purchased glass; metal doors, sash & trim; metal doors, sash & trim
HQ: Milgard Manufacturing Incorporated
1010 54th Ave E
Fife WA 98424
253 922-6030

(P-10381)
NEWPORT INDUSTRIAL GLASS INC
Also Called: Glass Fabrication and Dist
8610 Central Ave, Stanton (90680-2720)
P.O. Box 127 (90680-0127)
PHONE..............................714 484-7500
Ray Larsen, *Director*
Pilin Chung, *Shareholder*
EMP: 20
SALES (est): 2.7MM **Privately Held**
SIC: 3231 3827 3851 5039 Products of purchased glass; mirrors, optical; lens grinding, except prescription: ophthalmic; protective eyeware; exterior flat glass: plate or window

(P-10382)
OLDCASTLE BUILDINGENVELOPE INC
6850 Stevenson Blvd, Fremont (94538-2484)
PHONE..............................510 651-2292
Barry Adams, *Branch Mgr*
EMP: 63
SALES (corp-wide): 30.6B **Privately Held**
WEB: www.oldcastleglass.com
SIC: 3231 5231 Tempered glass: made from purchased glass; insulating glass: made from purchased glass; glass
HQ: Oldcastle Buildingenvelope, Inc.
5005 Lndn B Jnsn Fwy 10
Dallas TX 75244
214 273-3400

(P-10383)
OLDCASTLE BUILDINGENVELOPE INC
5631 Ferguson Dr, Commerce (90022-5132)
P.O. Box 22243, Los Angeles (90022-0243)
PHONE..............................323 722-2007
Luis Soto, *Principal*
Lee Bradley, *Credit Staff*
Jim Westphal, *Products*
Drew Aycock, *Sales Staff*
Jeff Geier, *Sales Staff*
EMP: 51
SQ FT: 200,000
SALES (corp-wide): 30.6B **Privately Held**
WEB: www.oldcastleglass.com
SIC: 3231 5231 Tempered glass: made from purchased glass; insulating glass: made from purchased glass
HQ: Oldcastle Buildingenvelope, Inc.
5005 Lndn B Jnsn Fwy 10
Dallas TX 75244
214 273-3400

(P-10384)
PACIFIC ARTGLASS CORPORATION
Also Called: Pacific Glass
125 W 157th St, Gardena (90248-2225)
PHONE..............................310 516-7828
John Williams, *President*
▲ EMP: 23
SQ FT: 18,000
SALES (est): 3.4MM **Privately Held**
WEB: www.pacificartglass.com
SIC: 3231 Aquariums & reflectors, glass

(P-10385)
PAI GP INC
Also Called: Pai Enterprises
5914 Crenshaw Blvd, Los Angeles (90043-3030)
PHONE..............................323 549-5355
Robert Johnson, *President*
Michael Woodman, *CFO*
▲ EMP: 77
SQ FT: 4,000
SALES (est): 7.6MM **Privately Held**
WEB: www.paigp.com
SIC: 3231 Products of purchased glass

(P-10386)
PAUL CRIST STUDIOS INC
8317 Secura Way, Santa Fe Springs (90670-2213)
PHONE..............................562 696-9992
Paul Crist, *President*
EMP: 14
SALES (est): 1.2MM **Privately Held**
WEB: www.mosaicshades.com
SIC: 3231 Art glass: made from purchased glass; stained glass: made from purchased glass

(P-10387)
RAYOTEK SCIENTIFIC INC
Also Called: Rayotek Sight Windows
11499 Sorrento Valley Rd, San Diego (92121-1305)
PHONE..............................858 558-3671
William Raggio, *President*
Jessica Yadley, *CFO*
Jay Alegre, *Admin Asst*
James Heimerl, *Engineer*
Matthew Raggio, *Production*
EMP: 51
SQ FT: 30,000

PRODUCTS & SVCS

SALES: 6MM **Privately Held**
WEB: www.rayotek.com
SIC: 3231 8748 Products of purchased glass; business consulting

(P-10388)
RESEARCH & DEV GL PDTS & EQP
Also Called: Research & Dev GL Pdts &
1808 Harmon St, Berkeley (94703-2416)
PHONE....................................510 547-6464
Doug Dobson, *President*
EMP: 12 **EST:** 1967
SQ FT: 10,000
SALES: 800K **Privately Held**
WEB: www.go.to
SIC: 3231 3229 Scientific & technical glassware: from purchased glass; ornamental glass: cut, engraved or otherwise decorated; pressed & blown glass

(P-10389)
SCI-TECH GLASSBLOWING INC
5555 Tech Cir, Moorpark (93021-1795)
P.O. Box 207 (93020-0207)
PHONE....................................805 523-9790
Glenn Gaydick, *Shareholder*
Craig Gaydick, *Shareholder*
EMP: 12
SQ FT: 4,600
SALES (est): 1.4MM **Privately Held**
SIC: 3231 Scientific & technical glassware: from purchased glass

(P-10390)
SHOWERTEK INC
952 School St 219, NAPA (94559-2826)
PHONE....................................707 224-1480
Thomas Christianson, *CEO*
Alison T Christianson, *Vice Pres*
◆ **EMP:** 12
SALES (est): 1.4MM **Privately Held**
WEB: www.showertek.com
SIC: 3231 3651 5063 Mirrored glass; household audio equipment; flashlights

(P-10391)
SREAM INC
12869 Temescal Canyon Rd A, Corona (92883-4021)
PHONE....................................951 245-6999
Jarir Farraj, *CEO*
Steve Rodriguez, *COO*
EMP: 34 **EST:** 2013
SALES (est): 2.8MM **Privately Held**
SIC: 3231 5231 Products of purchased glass; glass

(P-10392)
SUNYEAH GROUP CORP
930 S Wanamaker Ave, Ontario (91761-8151)
PHONE....................................909 218-8490
Xiaodong Shi, *CEO*
EMP: 21
SALES (est): 3.4MM **Privately Held**
SIC: 3231 3429 Doors, glass: made from purchased glass; manufactured hardware (general)

(P-10393)
THERMALSUN GLASS PRODUCTS INC
3950 Brickway Blvd, Santa Rosa (95403-1070)
PHONE....................................707 579-9534
Jeffrey Paul Kloes, *CEO*
▲ **EMP:** 34
SQ FT: 70,000
SALES (est): 6.4MM **Privately Held**
WEB: www.thermalsun.com
SIC: 3231 Insulating glass: made from purchased glass

(P-10394)
TRILOGY GLASS AND PACKG INC
975 Corporate Cntr Pkwy # 120, Santa Rosa (95407-5465)
PHONE....................................707 521-1300
Greg Windisch, *President*
Rick Miron, *CFO*
▲ **EMP:** 31
SQ FT: 24,000

SALES (est): 2.4MM
SALES (corp-wide): 453.7MM **Privately Held**
SIC: 3231 Products of purchased glass
HQ: Tricorbraun Inc.
6 Cityplace Dr Ste 1000
Saint Louis MO 63141
314 569-3633

(P-10395)
TRIVIEW GLASS INDUSTRIES LLC
711 S Stimson Ave, City of Industry (91745-1627)
PHONE....................................626 363-7980
Alexander A Kastaniuk, *CEO*
Elisa Vazquez, *Sales Staff*
Jorge Galvan, *Maintence Staff*
Miguel Barrientos, *Manager*
▲ **EMP:** 99
SALES (est): 20.8MM **Privately Held**
SIC: 3231 Products of purchased glass

(P-10396)
TWED-DELLS INC
Also Called: California Glass & Mirror Div
1900 S Susan St, Santa Ana (92704-3924)
PHONE....................................714 754-6900
Corey M Myer Jr, *President*
Gayle Myer, *Admin Sec*
▲ **EMP:** 38 **EST:** 1980
SQ FT: 45,000
SALES (est): 6.2MM **Privately Held**
WEB: www.tbmglass.com
SIC: 3231 Mirrored glass

(P-10397)
TWIN GLASS INDUSTRIES INC
16880 Joleen Way Ste 2, Morgan Hill (95037-4650)
PHONE....................................408 779-8801
Richard P Lopes, *CEO*
EMP: 10
SQ FT: 7,000
SALES (est): 1.2MM **Privately Held**
WEB: www.twinglass.com
SIC: 3231 Furniture tops, glass: cut, beveled or polished

(P-10398)
ULTRA GLASS
4001 Vista Park Ct Ste 1, Sacramento (95834-2975)
PHONE....................................916 338-3911
Kurtis Ryder, *President*
EMP: 15
SQ FT: 10,000
SALES (est): 4MM **Privately Held**
WEB: www.ultraglass.com
SIC: 3231 Doors, glass: made from purchased glass; insulating glass: made from purchased glass

(P-10399)
USA FIRE GLASS
Also Called: Oc Glass
6789 Quail Hill Pkwy # 613, Irvine (92603-4233)
PHONE....................................949 302-7728
Richard Newman, *CEO*
EMP: 16
SQ FT: 2,800
SALES (est): 820.5K **Privately Held**
WEB: www.usafireglass.com
SIC: 3231 Aquariums & reflectors, glass

(P-10400)
VIEW INC (PA)
Also Called: Soladigm
195 S Milpitas Blvd, Milpitas (95035-5425)
PHONE....................................408 263-9200
RAO Mulpuri, *CEO*
Brian Harrison, *COO*
Walt Lifsey, *COO*
James Fay, *CFO*
Vidul Prakash, *CFO*
▲ **EMP:** 87
SALES (est): 46.3MM **Privately Held**
SIC: 3231 Products of purchased glass

(P-10401)
WARDROBE SPECIALTIES LTD
607 Glass Ln, Modesto (95356-9665)
PHONE....................................209 523-2094
Barbara Lee Stanton, *Partner*
EMP: 15

SQ FT: 5,400
SALES (est): 1.1MM **Privately Held**
SIC: 3231 Doors, glass: made from purchased glass

(P-10402)
ZADRO PRODUCTS INC
14462 Astronautics Ln # 101, Huntington Beach (92647-2077)
PHONE....................................714 892-9200
Zlatko Zadro, *President*
Becky Zadro, *Vice Pres*
◆ **EMP:** 35
SQ FT: 22,000
SALES (est): 5.7MM **Privately Held**
WEB: www.zadroinc.com
SIC: 3231 3641 Mirrored glass; electric lamps

3241 Cement, Hydraulic

(P-10403)
CALPORTLAND COMPANY
Also Called: San Luis Obispo Rdymx Plant
219 Tank Farm Rd, San Luis Obispo (93401-7509)
PHONE....................................805 345-3400
Dan Sampson, *Branch Mgr*
Bruce Mercier, *Exec Dir*
Pat Imhoff, *Technical Mgr*
Binh Phan, *Research*
Martin Dale, *Manager*
EMP: 68 **Privately Held**
SIC: 3241 Cement, hydraulic
HQ: Calportland Company
2025 E Financial Way
Glendora CA 91741
626 852-6200

(P-10404)
CALPORTLAND COMPANY
Also Called: California Portland Cement
9350 Oak Creek Rd, Mojave (93501-7738)
PHONE....................................661 824-2401
Bruce Shaffer, *Branch Mgr*
Carla Martinez, *Administration*
Bill Leonard, *Technology*
Steve Troy, *Engineer*
Carol Deck, *Counsel*
EMP: 130 **Privately Held**
WEB: www.calportland.com
SIC: 3241 5032 5211 Masonry cement; brick, stone & related material; cement
HQ: Calportland Company
2025 E Financial Way
Glendora CA 91741
626 852-6200

(P-10405)
CALPORTLAND COMPANY
695 S Rancho Ave, Colton (92324-3242)
P.O. Box 947 (92324-0947)
PHONE....................................909 825-4260
Mike Robertson, *Branch Mgr*
EMP: 36 **Privately Held**
WEB: www.calportland.com
SIC: 3241 5211 Masonry cement; cement
HQ: Calportland Company
2025 E Financial Way
Glendora CA 91741
626 852-6200

(P-10406)
CALPORTLAND COMPANY
19409 National Trails Hwy, Oro Grande (92368-9705)
PHONE....................................760 245-5321
EMP: 17 **Privately Held**
SIC: 3241 3273 5032 Portland cement; ready-mixed concrete; brick, stone & related material
HQ: Calportland Company
2025 E Financial Way
Glendora CA 91741
626 852-6200

(P-10407)
CALPORTLAND COMPANY
2201 W Washington St # 6, Stockton (95203-2942)
PHONE....................................209 469-0109
Warren Burchett, *Manager*
EMP: 15 **Privately Held**
WEB: www.calportland.com

SIC: 3241 3273 Portland cement; ready-mixed concrete
HQ: Calportland Company
2025 E Financial Way
Glendora CA 91741
626 852-6200

(P-10408)
CALPORTLAND COMPANY (DH)
Also Called: Arizona Portland Cement
2025 E Financial Way, Glendora (91741-4692)
P.O. Box 5025 (91740-0885)
PHONE....................................626 852-6200
Michio Kimura, *Ch of Bd*
James A Repman, *President*
Allen Hamblen, *CEO*
James A Wendoll, *CFO*
Noboru Kasai, *Vice Ch Bd*
▲ **EMP:** 77
SQ FT: 28,000
SALES (est): 182.7MM **Privately Held**
WEB: www.calportland.com
SIC: 3241 3273 5032 Portland cement; ready-mixed concrete; brick, stone & related material
HQ: Taiheiyo Cement U.S.A., Inc.
2025 E Fincl Way Ste 200
Glendora CA 91741
626 852-6200

(P-10409)
CALPORTLAND COMPANY
Also Called: Catalina Pacific Concrete
8981 Bradley Ave, Sun Valley (91352-2602)
PHONE....................................818 767-0508
Alfonso Coss, *Supervisor*
EMP: 31 **Privately Held**
WEB: www.calportland.com
SIC: 3241 3273 Cement, hydraulic; ready-mixed concrete
HQ: Calportland Company
2025 E Financial Way
Glendora CA 91741
626 852-6200

(P-10410)
CEMEX CNSTR MTLS PCF LLC
Also Called: Aggregate -Sunol Quarry
6527 Calaveras Rd, Sunol (94586-9530)
P.O. Box 546 (94586-0546)
PHONE....................................925 862-2201
Rich Biers, *Branch Mgr*
EMP: 12 **Privately Held**
SIC: 3241 Cement, hydraulic
HQ: Cemex Construction Materials Pacific, Llc
1501 Belvedere Rd
West Palm Beach FL 33406
561 833-5555

(P-10411)
HANSON AGGREGATES LLC
3555 E Vineyard Ave, Oxnard (93036)
PHONE....................................805 485-3101
EMP: 65
SALES (corp-wide): 20.6B **Privately Held**
WEB: www.hansonind.com
SIC: 3241 Cement, hydraulic
HQ: Hanson Aggregates Llc
8505 Freport Pkwy Ste 500
Irving TX 75063
469 417-1200

(P-10412)
HANSON AGGREGATES LLC
5785 Mission Center Rd, San Diego (92108-4387)
P.O. Box 639069 (92163-9069)
PHONE....................................619 299-8640
EMP: 25
SALES (corp-wide): 15.6B **Privately Held**
SIC: 3241
HQ: Hanson Aggregates Llc
8505 Freport Pkwy Ste 500
Irving TX 75063
469 417-1200

(P-10413)
HANSON AGGREGATES LLC
9255 Camino Santa Fe, San Diego (92121-6209)
P.O. Box 639069 (92163-9069)
PHONE....................................858 577-2727
Kevin Everly, *Manager*

EMP: 15
SALES (corp-wide): 20.6B Privately Held
WEB: www.hansonind.com
SIC: 3241 Cement, hydraulic
HQ: Hanson Aggregates Llc
    8505 Freport Pkwy Ste 500
    Irving TX 75063
    469 417-1200

(P-10414)
HANSON AGGREGATES LLC
19494 River Rock Rd, Corona
(92881-5094)
P.O. Box 1115 (92878-1115)
PHONE...................................951 371-7625
Rick Sanford, *Manager*
EMP: 30
SALES (corp-wide): 20.6B Privately Held
WEB: www.hansonind.com
SIC: 3241 1442 Cement, hydraulic; con-
    struction sand & gravel
HQ: Hanson Aggregates Llc
    8505 Freport Pkwy Ste 500
    Irving TX 75063
    469 417-1200

(P-10415)
HANSON LEHIGH INC
12667 Alcosta Blvd # 400, San Ramon
(94583-4427)
PHONE...................................925 244-6500
Dan Herrington, *CEO*
EMP: 40
SALES (est): 4.1MM Privately Held
SIC: 3241 Cement, hydraulic

(P-10416)
**HEADWATERS CONSTRUCTION
INC**
Also Called: Louis W Osborn Co.
16005 Phoebe Ave, La Mirada
(90638-5607)
PHONE...................................714 523-1530
Rudy Valverde, *General Mgr*
EMP: 30
SQ FT: 18,000
SALES (est): 3.8MM Privately Held
SIC: 3241 Cement, hydraulic

(P-10417)
**JAMES HARDIE BUILDING PDTS
INC**
26300 La Alameda Ste 400, Mission Viejo
(92691-8372)
PHONE...................................949 348-1800
Louis Gries, *President*
Jason Miele, *Vice Pres*
Bryan Cummings, *Administration*
Jason Fang, *Administration*
Monica Lorey, *Administration*
EMP: 86
SQ FT: 97,250 Privately Held
SIC: 3241 Natural cement
HQ: James Hardie Building Products Inc.
    231 S La Salle St # 2000
    Chicago IL 60604
    312 291-5072

(P-10418)
JETSET CALIFORNIA INC
Also Called: Jet Set California
2150 Edison Ave, San Leandro
(94577-1131)
PHONE...................................510 632-7800
Greg Willener, *President*
EMP: 10
SQ FT: 8,000
SALES (est): 1.1MM Privately Held
WEB: www.jetsetcement.com
SIC: 3241 Masonry cement

(P-10419)
**LATICRETE INTERNATIONAL
INC**
22740 Temescal Canyon Rd, Corona
(92883-4107)
PHONE...................................951 277-1776
Todd Belanger, *General Mgr*
Colby Fradette, *Planning*
Christopher Condeni, *Technical Staff*
Gary Jones, *Technical Staff*
Bill Lange, *Technical Staff*
EMP: 10

SALES (corp-wide): 165MM Privately
Held
WEB: www.laticrete.com
SIC: 3241 Cement, hydraulic
PA: Laticrete International, Inc.
    1 Laticrete Park N
    Bethany CT 06524
    203 393-0010

(P-10420)
**LEHIGH SOUTHWEST CEMENT
CO**
13573 E Tehachapi Blvd, Tehachapi
(93561-8155)
PHONE...................................661 822-4445
Axel Conrads, *General Mgr*
Ron Hibdon, *President*
Michael Rohmaller, *Engineer*
Jaromir Vojtech, *Engineer*
Frank Torres, *Plant Mgr*
EMP: 130
SALES (corp-wide): 20.6B Privately Held
SIC: 3241 3273 2951 1442 Portland ce-
    ment; ready-mixed concrete; asphalt
    paving mixtures & blocks; construction
    sand & gravel
HQ: Lehigh Southwest Cement Company
    2300 Clayton Rd Ste 300
    Concord CA 94520
    972 653-5500

(P-10421)
**LEHIGH SOUTHWEST CEMENT
CO**
24001 Stevens Creek Blvd, Cupertino
(95014-5659)
PHONE...................................408 996-4271
W Lee, *Branch Mgr*
Neil McDermott, *Administration*
Gregg Hilliker, *Electrical Engi*
Richard Beatty, *VP Sales*
Sandra Harris, *Maintence Staff*
EMP: 15
SALES (corp-wide): 20.6B Privately Held
SIC: 3241 2891 5032 5211 Portland ce-
    ment; cement, except linoleum & tile; ce-
    ment; cement
HQ: Lehigh Southwest Cement Company
    2300 Clayton Rd Ste 300
    Concord CA 94520
    972 653-5500

(P-10422)
**LEHIGH SOUTHWEST CEMENT
CO (DH)**
2300 Clayton Rd Ste 300, Concord
(94520-2175)
PHONE...................................972 653-5500
Dan Harrington, *CEO*
Mark Esolen, *Opers Mgr*
Bill Boughton, *VP Sales*
▲ EMP: 15
SQ FT: 10,000
SALES (est): 149.1MM
SALES (corp-wide): 20.6B Privately Held
SIC: 3241 2891 5032 5211 Portland ce-
    ment; masonry cement; pozzolana ce-
    ment; cement, except linoleum & tile;
    cement; cement

(P-10423)
**MITSUBISHI CEMENT
CORPORATION**
5808 State Highway 18, Lucerne Valley
(92356-8179)
PHONE...................................760 248-7373
Jim Russell, *Branch Mgr*
Jerry Wheeler, *Plant Mgr*
Eric Jen, *Terminal Mgr*
EMP: 175
WEB: www.mitsubishicement.com
SIC: 3241 Portland cement
HQ: Mitsubishi Cement Corporation
    151 Cassia Way
    Henderson NV 89014
    702 932-3900

(P-10424)
**MOSS LANDING CEMENT CO
LLC**
7697 Highway 1, Moss Landing
(95039-9697)
PHONE...................................831 731-6000
Brent Constantz,
▲ EMP: 17

SALES (est): 2.6MM Privately Held
SIC: 3241 Masonry cement

(P-10425)
**NATIONAL CEMENT COMPANY
INC (HQ)**
15821 Ventura Blvd # 475, Encino
(91436-2935)
PHONE...................................818 728-5200
James E Rotch, *Ch of Bd*
Denise Taylor, *Finance*
Pragati Kapoor, *Controller*
Enrique Hernandez, *QC Mgr*
Puckett Bill, *Sales Staff*
▲ EMP: 38 EST: 1920
SQ FT: 11,446
SALES (est): 305.8MM
SALES (corp-wide): 484.9MM Privately
Held
SIC: 3241 3273 Portland cement; ready-
    mixed concrete
PA: Vicat
    Tour Manhattan
    Courbevoie 92400
    158 868-686

(P-10426)
NORTH AMERICA PWR & INFRA
19112 Gridley Rd 2001, Cerritos
(90703-6613)
PHONE...................................562 403-4337
Daniel Lu, *President*
Jacob Singh, *Principal*
EMP: 50
SALES (est): 1.3MM Privately Held
SIC: 3241 1611 Natural cement; general
    contractor; highway & street construction

(P-10427)
OLDCASTLE APG WEST INC
10714 Poplar Ave, Fontana (92337-7333)
PHONE...................................909 355-6422
EMP: 40
SALES (corp-wide): 30.6B Privately Held
WEB: www.sierrapavers.com
SIC: 3241 Masonry cement
HQ: Oldcastle Apg West, Inc.
    4720 E Cotton Gin Loop L
    Phoenix AZ 85040
    602 302-9600

(P-10428)
RMC PACIFIC MATERIALS INC
30350 S Tracy Blvd, Tracy (95377-8121)
PHONE...................................209 835-1454
Gordon Brown, *Manager*
EMP: 24 Privately Held
SIC: 3241 3273 1442 Cement, hydraulic;
    ready-mixed concrete; construction sand
    & gravel
HQ: Rmc Pacific Materials, Inc.
    6601 Koll Center Pkwy
    Pleasanton CA 94566
    925 426-8787

(P-10429)
**RMC PACIFIC MATERIALS INC
(DH)**
Also Called: Cemex
6601 Koll Center Pkwy, Pleasanton
(94566-3112)
P.O. Box 5252 (94566-0252)
PHONE...................................925 426-8787
Eric F Woodhouse, *President*
Rodrigo Trevia O, *CFO*
◆ EMP: 200 EST: 1906
SQ FT: 30,000
SALES (est): 81.4MM Privately Held
SIC: 3241 3273 3531 1442 Cement, hy-
    draulic; ready-mixed concrete; asphalt
    plant, including gravel-mix type; sand
    mining; gravel & pebble mining; abrasive
    products
HQ: Rmc Usa, Inc
    920 Memorial City Way
    Houston TX 77024
    713 650-6200

| 3251 Brick & Structural Clay Tile |

(P-10430)
ARTO BRICK VENEER MFGCO
Also Called: Arto Brick and Cal Pavers
15209 S Broadway, Gardena (90248-1823)
PHONE...................................310 768-8500
Arto Alajian, *CEO*
Patrick Blake, *Vice Pres*
Reza Tabarrok, *Opers Staff*
Stephanie Morgan, *Sales Mgr*
EMP: 40
SQ FT: 18,000
SALES (est): 3.2MM Privately Held
WEB: www.artobrick.com
SIC: 3251 Brick & structural clay tile

(P-10431)
**BRICKSCHAIN CNSTR
BLOCKCHAIN**
511 Olive St, Santa Barbara (93101-1609)
PHONE...................................833 274-2572
Bassem Hamdy, *CEO*
EMP: 10
SALES (est): 355.8K Privately Held
SIC: 3251 Structural brick & blocks

(P-10432)
CALSTAR PRODUCTS INC
3945 Freedom Cir Ste 560, Santa Clara
(95054-1269)
PHONE...................................262 752-9131
Joel Rood, *CEO*
Mike Lemberg, *CFO*
EMP: 60
SALES (est): 12MM Privately Held
WEB: www.calstarcement.com
SIC: 3251 Paving brick, clay

(P-10433)
CASTAIC CLAY PRODUCTS LLC
32201 Castaic Lake Dr, Castaic
(91384-4134)
PHONE...................................661 259-3066
Dan Navarro,
Norma Gardner, *Accounting Mgr*
EMP: 95
SALES (est): 6.8MM Privately Held
WEB: www.castaicbrick.com
SIC: 3251 Brick & structural clay tile

(P-10434)
**CLAY CASTAIC
MANUFACTURING CO**
Also Called: Castaic Brick
32201 Castaic Lake Dr, Castaic
(91384-4134)
P.O. Box 8 (91310-0008)
PHONE...................................661 259-3066
Mike Mallow, *CEO*
Annette Mallow, *Treasurer*
Dan Navarro, *Controller*
EMP: 95
SQ FT: 10,000
SALES (est): 11MM Privately Held
SIC: 3251 Brick clay: common face,
    glazed, vitrified or hollow

(P-10435)
PABCO CLAY PRODUCTS LLC
Also Called: Gladding McBean
601 7th St, Lincoln (95648-1828)
PHONE...................................916 645-3341
Bill Padavona, *Branch Mgr*
Gerardo De La Cerda, *Technician*
Patrice Duran, *Engineer*
Joe Parker, *Natl Sales Mgr*
Jamie Farnham, *Sales Mgr*
EMP: 250
SALES (corp-wide): 1.5B Privately Held
SIC: 3251 3253 3259 3269 Ceramic
    glazed brick, clay; ceramic wall & floor
    tile; clay sewer & drainage pipe & tile;
    roofing tile, clay; vases, pottery
HQ: Pabco Clay Products, Llc
    605 Industrial Way
    Dixon CA 95620

(P-10436)
PABCO CLAY PRODUCTS LLC
Also Called: H C Muddox
4875 Bradshaw Rd, Sacramento
(95827-9727)
PHONE.....................................916 859-6320
Greg Morrison, *Branch Mgr*
EMP: 70
SALES (corp-wide): 1.5B **Privately Held**
SIC: 3251 Brick & structural clay tile
HQ: Pabco Clay Products, Llc
605 Industrial Way
Dixon CA 95620

3253 Ceramic Tile

(P-10437)
CALIFORNIA POTTERIES INC
Also Called: California Pot & Tile Works
859 E 60th St, Los Angeles (90001-1014)
PHONE.....................................323 235-4151
John McLean, *President*
EMP: 20
SALES (est): 2.4MM **Privately Held**
SIC: 3253 5032 Ceramic wall & floor tile;
ceramic wall & floor tile

(P-10438)
CONCEPT STUDIO INC
3195 Red Hill Ave Ste G, Costa Mesa
(92626-3430)
PHONE.....................................949 759-0606
Richard Goddard, *President*
Karen Bishop, *Vice Pres*
Carolyn Schneider, *Manager*
▲ **EMP:** 14
SQ FT: 5,000
SALES (est): 1.8MM **Privately Held**
WEB: www.conceptstudioinc.com
SIC: 3253 Ceramic wall & floor tile

(P-10439)
DURAMAR FLOOR INC
Also Called: Duramar Interior Surfaces
2500 White Rd Ste B, Irvine (92614-6276)
PHONE.....................................949 724-8800
Farhad Abdollahi, *President*
Tom Belcher, *Principal*
Nicholas Ounanian, *Principal*
▲ **EMP:** 19
SQ FT: 64,000
SALES (est): 2.9MM **Privately Held**
WEB: www.duramar.com
SIC: 3253 Floor tile, ceramic

(P-10440)
ELYSIUM MOSAICS INC
Also Called: Elysium Ceramics
1180 N Anaheim Blvd, Anaheim
(92801-2502)
PHONE.....................................714 991-7885
Yue Zhou, *CEO*
▲ **EMP:** 17
SALES (est): 3.2MM **Privately Held**
SIC: 3253 Mosaic tile, glazed & unglazed:
ceramic

(P-10441)
FIRE & EARTH CERAMICS
418 Santander Dr, San Ramon
(94583-2143)
PHONE.....................................303 442-0245
Jeff Gaines, *Owner*
Clarence Harrison, *CIO*
EMP: 10
SALES: 500K **Privately Held**
SIC: 3253 Mosaic tile, glazed & unglazed:
ceramic

(P-10442)
GBM MANUFACTURING INC
1188 S Airport Way, Stockton (95205-6933)
PHONE.....................................888 862-8397
Wen Jie Chen, *President*
▲ **EMP:** 12
SQ FT: 30,000
SALES: 2MM **Privately Held**
SIC: 3253 Ceramic wall & floor tile

(P-10443)
GOLDEN STONE GROUP LLC
10862 Garden Grove Blvd, Garden Grove
(92843-1202)
PHONE.....................................714 723-1505
John Nguyen, *President*
EMP: 10
SQ FT: 7,000
SALES (est): 323.4K **Privately Held**
SIC: 3253 Floor tile, ceramic

(P-10444)
JEFFREY COURT INC
620 Parkridge Ave, Norco (92860-3124)
PHONE.....................................951 340-3383
James Lawson, *President*
Frank Toms, *CFO*
Thaddeus Crump, *Project Mgr*
Trey Welch, *Project Mgr*
Carolyn Morgan, *Graphic Designe*
▲ **EMP:** 75
SQ FT: 60,000
SALES (est): 13MM **Privately Held**
SIC: 3253 Ceramic wall & floor tile

(P-10445)
KEN MASON TILE INC
14600 S Western Ave, Gardena
(90249-3306)
PHONE.....................................562 432-7574
Ken Paul, *President*
Glenn Paul, *Vice Pres*
EMP: 30
SQ FT: 7,500
SALES (est): 3.1MM **Privately Held**
WEB: www.kenmasontile.com
SIC: 3253 1743 3272 Mosaic tile, glazed
& unglazed: ceramic; tile installation, ce-
ramic; concrete products

(P-10446)
MALIBU CERAMIC WORKS
903 Fairbanks Ave, Long Beach
(90813-2861)
P.O. Box 1406, Topanga (90290-1406)
PHONE.....................................310 455-2485
Robert Harris, *President*
Matthew Harris, *Opers Staff*
EMP: 20
SALES (est): 2.3MM **Privately Held**
SIC: 3253 Floor tile, ceramic

(P-10447)
**OCEANSIDE GLASSTILE
COMPANY (PA)**
Also Called: Mandala
5858 Edison Pl, Carlsbad (92008-6519)
PHONE.....................................760 929-4000
Sean Gildea, *CEO*
Sean M Gildea, *CEO*
Greg Lehr, *COO*
Miles Bradley, *CFO*
John Marckx, *Exec VP*
◆ **EMP:** 375
SQ FT: 48,000
SALES (est): 107.4MM **Privately Held**
WEB: www.glasstile.com
SIC: 3253 5032 Mosaic tile, glazed &
unglazed: ceramic; tile, clay or other ce-
ramic, excluding refractory

(P-10448)
ORTECH INC
Also Called: Ortech Advanced Ceramics
6760 Folsom Blvd 100, Sacramento
(95819-4626)
PHONE.....................................916 549-9696
Oded Morgenshtern, *President*
▲ **EMP:** 20
SALES (est): 2.6MM **Privately Held**
SIC: 3253 Ceramic wall & floor tile

(P-10449)
**PROGRESSIVE TECHNOLOGY
INC**
4130 Citrus Ave Ste 17, Rocklin
(95677-4006)
PHONE.....................................916 632-6715
Shannon Rogers, *President*
Carol Rogers, *Vice Pres*
EMP: 30
SQ FT: 23,000
SALES (est): 4.8MM **Privately Held**
WEB: www.prgtech.com
SIC: 3253 Ceramic wall & floor tile

(P-10450)
SMD ENTERPRISES INC
Also Called: California Pot & Tile Works
859 E 60th St, Los Angeles (90001-1014)
P.O. Box 1437 (90001-0437)
PHONE.....................................323 235-4151
John R McLean, *President*
EMP: 35
SALES (est): 2.9MM **Privately Held**
SIC: 3253 3269 Floor tile, ceramic; ce-
ramic wall & floor tile; art & ornamental
ware, pottery

(P-10451)
**SONOMA TILEMAKERS INC
(DH)**
7750 Bell Rd, Windsor (95492-8518)
PHONE.....................................707 837-8177
Jon Gray, *President*
Kenneth E Wiedemann, *CEO*
Todd Kukral, *Executive*
Dana Higgins, *Human Res Dir*
Sergio Garcia, *Training Dir*
▲ **EMP:** 59
SQ FT: 22,000
SALES (est): 10.6MM
SALES (corp-wide): 45.5MM **Privately
Held**
WEB: www.sonomatilemakers.com
SIC: 3253 Ceramic wall & floor tile
HQ: United Tile Corp.
750 S Michigan St
Seattle WA 98108
425 251-5290

(P-10452)
**STRATAMET ADVANCED MTLS
CORP**
2718 Prune Ave, Fremont (94539-6780)
PHONE.....................................510 440-1697
EMP: 16
SALES (est): 1.7MM **Privately Held**
SIC: 3253

(P-10453)
SUNTILE INC
Also Called: Morena Tile
32951 Calle Perfecto, San Juan Capistrano
(92675-4705)
PHONE.....................................949 489-8990
Kristy Coulston, *Office Mgr*
EMP: 19
SALES (corp-wide): 3.3MM **Privately
Held**
SIC: 3253 Ceramic wall & floor tile
PA: Suntile Inc
7919 Silverton Ave # 412
San Diego CA 92126
858 695-9700

(P-10454)
SURFACES TILE CRAFT INC
7900 Andasol Ave, Northridge
(91325-4429)
PHONE.....................................818 609-0719
Ricardo Gomez, *CEO*
Yesenia Reynoso, *Admin Sec*
EMP: 15
SALES (est): 1.4MM **Privately Held**
SIC: 3253 Mosaic tile, glazed & unglazed:
ceramic

(P-10455)
SWISSTRAX LLC
82579 Fleming Way Ste A, Indio
(92201-2395)
PHONE.....................................760 347-3330
Randy A Nelson, *CEO*
Jim Miller, *Vice Pres*
◆ **EMP:** 17
SALES (est): 3.8MM **Privately Held**
SIC: 3253 Ceramic wall & floor tile

(P-10456)
TILE ARTISANS INC
4288 State Highway 70, Oroville
(95965-8340)
PHONE.....................................800 601-4199
Dale Marsh, *President*
▲ **EMP:** 10
SQ FT: 16,000
SALES (est): 855.6K **Privately Held**
WEB: www.tileartisans.com
SIC: 3253 Ceramic wall & floor tile

(P-10457)
TILE GUILD INC
2424 E 55th St, Vernon (90058-3506)
PHONE.....................................323 581-3770
Dennis Caffrey, *President*
EMP: 15
SQ FT: 18,000
SALES (est): 1MM **Privately Held**
WEB: www.tileguildinc.com
SIC: 3253 Ceramic wall & floor tile

(P-10458)
WIZARD ENTERPRISE
12605 Daphne Ave, Hawthorne
(90250-3309)
PHONE.....................................323 756-8430
Thomas Meagher, *Partner*
Michael Meagher, *Partner*
EMP: 10
SALES (est): 1.3MM **Privately Held**
SIC: 3253 5092 5032 Ceramic wall &
floor tile; arts & crafts equipment & sup-
plies; ceramic wall & floor tile

3255 Clay Refractories

(P-10459)
B & B REFRACTORIES INC
12121 Los Nietos Rd, Santa Fe Springs
(90670-2907)
PHONE.....................................562 946-4535
John Svet, *President*
Jeanette Svet, *Vice Pres*
▲ **EMP:** 18 EST: 1965
SQ FT: 50,000
SALES (est): 2.2MM **Privately Held**
WEB: www.bbrefractories.com
SIC: 3255 Clay refractories

(P-10460)
HANDCRAFT TILE INC
786 View Dr, Pleasanton (94566-9791)
PHONE.....................................408 262-1140
EMP: 11 EST: 1953
SQ FT: 13,000
SALES (est): 1.3MM **Privately Held**
WEB: www.handcrafttile.com
SIC: 3255

(P-10461)
PROTECH MINERALS INC
17092 S D St, Victorville (92395-3304)
PHONE.....................................760 245-3441
Chul Lim Choe, *President*
Chong Choe, *Vice Pres*
EMP: 10
SQ FT: 3,757
SALES (est): 1.4MM **Privately Held**
SIC: 3255 Tile, clay refractory

3259 Structural Clay Prdts, NEC

(P-10462)
**EAGLE ROOFING PRODUCTS
FLA LLC**
3546 N Riverside Ave, Rialto (92377-3802)
PHONE.....................................909 822-6000
Robert C Burlingame, *Mng Member*
Travis Rozas, *Sales Staff*
Joe H Anderson Jr,
M D Anderson,
Kevin C Burlingame,
EMP: 38
SALES (est): 6.8MM **Privately Held**
SIC: 3259 Roofing tile, clay

(P-10463)
**MARUHACHI CERAMICS
AMERICA INC**
1985 Sampson Ave, Corona (92879-6006)
PHONE.....................................800 736-6221
Yoshihiro Suzuki, *President*
Linda Hanson, *CFO*
Sharon Suzuki, *Executive*
Yoshi Suzuki, *General Mgr*
Thelma Svoboda, *Mktg Dir*
▲ **EMP:** 22
SQ FT: 83,250
SALES (est): 5.3MM **Privately Held**
WEB: www.mca-tile.com
SIC: 3259 Roofing tile, clay

▲ = Import ▼ =Export
◆ =Import/Export

(P-10464)
PABCO BUILDING PRODUCTS LLC
Also Called: Gladding McBean
601 7th St, Lincoln (95648-1828)
P.O. Box 97 (95648-0097)
PHONE..................................916 645-3341
Erik Absalon, General Mgr
EMP: 100
SQ FT: 952
SALES (corp-wide): 1.5B Privately Held
SIC: 3259 Architectural terra cotta; clay
sewer & drainage pipe & tile
HQ: Pabco Building Products, Llc
10600 White Rock Rd # 100
Rancho Cordova CA 95670
510 792-1577

3261 China Plumbing Fixtures & Fittings

(P-10465)
BBK SPECIALTIES INC
24147 Del Monte Dr # 297, Valencia
(91355-3855)
PHONE..................................661 255-2857
EMP: 15
SALES (est): 1.6MM Privately Held
SIC: 3261 3431

(P-10466)
HCP INDUSTRIES INC
415 Otterson Dr Ste 10, Chico
(95928-8239)
P.O. Box 6747 (95927-6747)
PHONE..................................530 899-5591
Norman Hueckel, President
Dixie Hueckel, Corp Secy
EMP: 13
SQ FT: 22,800
SALES (est): 1.4MM Privately Held
WEB: www.hcpindustries.com
SIC: 3261 Soap dishes, vitreous china

(P-10467)
LOTUS HYGIENE SYSTEMS INC
1621 E Saint Andrew Pl, Santa Ana
(92705-4932)
PHONE..................................714 259-8805
Xiang Liu, President
▲ EMP: 20
SQ FT: 10,000
SALES (est): 1.5MM Privately Held
WEB: www.lotusseats.com
SIC: 3261 Vitreous plumbing fixtures

(P-10468)
TUBULAR SPECIALTIES MFG INC
Also Called: T S M
13011 S Spring St, Los Angeles
(90061-1685)
PHONE..................................310 515-4801
Marcia Lynn Hemphill, CEO
L C Huntley, Ch of Bd
Arif Mansuri, Treasurer
Mansuri Arif, Director
▲ EMP: 62 EST: 1966
SQ FT: 38,000
SALES (est): 8.8MM Privately Held
WEB: www.calltsm.com
SIC: 3261 2656 3446 Bathroom acces-
sories/fittings, vitreous china or earthen-
ware; sanitary food containers; railings,
prefabricated metal

3262 China, Table & Kitchen Articles

(P-10469)
SKY ONE INC
Also Called: Vertex China
1793 W 2nd St, Pomona (91766-1253)
PHONE..................................909 622-3333
Hoi Shum, CEO
Gary Dallas, Vice Pres
Ken Joyce, Vice Pres
▲ EMP: 19
SQ FT: 14,000

SALES (est): 3.2MM Privately Held
SIC: 3262 Dishes, commercial or household: vitreous china

3263 Earthenware, Whiteware, Table & Kitchen Articles

(P-10470)
BROMWELL COMPANY (PA)
8605 Santa Monica Blvd, Los Angeles
(90069-4109)
PHONE..................................800 683-2626
Sean Bandawat, President
EMP: 13
SALES (est): 1.9MM Privately Held
SIC: 3263 Semivitreous table & kitchen-
ware

(P-10471)
MASTERS IN METAL INC
131 Lombard St, Oxnard (93030-5161)
PHONE..................................805 988-1992
Wayne R Haddox, President
Dennis Haddox, Vice Pres
▲ EMP: 50
SQ FT: 11,000
SALES (est): 7.1MM Privately Held
WEB: www.mastersinmetal.com
SIC: 3263 3952 Commercial tableware or
kitchen articles, fine earthenware; sizes,
gold & bronze: artists'

(P-10472)
WRENCHWARE INC
2751 Reche Canyon Rd # 104, Colton
(92324-9570)
PHONE..................................951 784-2717
Edwin A Jonas Jr, President
◆ EMP: 10
SALES (est): 855.2K Privately Held
SIC: 3263 Tableware, household & com-
mercial: semivitreous

3264 Porcelain Electrical Splys

(P-10473)
ALTA PROPERTIES INC
Channel Industries
839 Ward Dr, Santa Barbara (93111-2920)
PHONE..................................805 967-0171
EMP: 475
SALES (corp-wide): 197.5MM Privately
Held
SIC: 3264 Porcelain electrical supplies
PA: Alta Properties, Inc.
879 Ward Dr
Santa Barbara CA 93111
805 967-0171

(P-10474)
ALTA PROPERTIES INC (PA)
Also Called: Ctg
879 Ward Dr, Santa Barbara (93111-2920)
P.O. Box 90326 (93190-0326)
PHONE..................................805 967-0171
Robert F Carlson, CEO
Paul J Downey, CFO
Randy Copperman, Vice Pres
Gary Douville, Vice Pres
Mark Shaw, Vice Pres
▲ EMP: 167
SQ FT: 21,000
SALES (est): 197.5MM Privately Held
WEB: www.channeltech.com
SIC: 3264 3699 3823 3679 Porcelain
electrical supplies; underwater sound
equipment; infrared instruments, industrial
process type; transducers, electrical

(P-10475)
COORSTEK INC
Coorstek Sales Fremont
41348 Christy St, Fremont (94538-3115)
PHONE..................................510 492-6600
Doug Coors, Branch Mgr
EMP: 70
SALES (corp-wide): 407.6MM Privately
Held
SIC: 3264 Porcelain electrical supplies

HQ: Coorstek, Inc.
14143 Denver West Pkwy # 400
Lakewood CO 80401
303 271-7000

(P-10476)
COUNTIS INDUSTRIES INC
Also Called: Orbit Industries
12295 Charles Dr, Grass Valley
(95945-9371)
PHONE..................................530 272-8334
EMP: 20 EST: 1956
SQ FT: 10,000
SALES: 10MM Privately Held
WEB: www.countis.com
SIC: 3264 3423

(P-10477)
KOMAG INCORPORATED
1710 Automation Pkwy, San Jose
(95131-1873)
PHONE..................................408 576-2150
Tim Starkey, Principal
Frank Cunanan, Research
EMP: 19
SALES (est): 1.8MM Privately Held
SIC: 3264 Magnets, permanent: ceramic or
ferrite

(P-10478)
LEON ASSEMBLY SOLUTIONS INC
Also Called: Imesa
10650 Scripps Ranch Blvd # 123, San
Diego (92131-2470)
PHONE..................................858 397-2826
Alejandro A Leon, CEO
Rachel Padden, Admin Asst
EMP: 100
SQ FT: 120
SALES: 4.7MM Privately Held
SIC: 3264 7389 Porcelain electrical sup-
plies;

(P-10479)
MAGNET SALES & MFG CO INC (HQ)
Also Called: Integrated Magnetics
11248 Playa Ct, Culver City (90230-6100)
PHONE..................................310 391-7213
Anil Nanji, President
Gary Hooper, CFO
Paul Minamoto, Program Mgr
Will Effertz, IT Executive
Ben Pendleton, Info Tech Mgr
▲ EMP: 75 EST: 1930
SQ FT: 45,000
SALES (est): 39.9MM
SALES (corp-wide): 47.2MM Privately
Held
WEB: www.magnetsales.com
SIC: 3264 3621 Porcelain electrical sup-
plies; servomotors, electric; coils, for elec-
tric motors or generators; torque motors,
electric
PA: Integrated Technologies Group, Inc.
11250 Playa Ct
Culver City CA 90230
310 391-7213

(P-10480)
PACIFIC CERAMICS INC
3524 Bassett St, Santa Clara (95054)
PHONE..................................408 747-4600
Dennis J Fleming, President
EMP: 37
SALES (est): 5.5MM Privately Held
WEB: www.pceramics.com
SIC: 3264 Magnets, permanent: ceramic or
ferrite

(P-10481)
PRECISION FRRITES CERAMICS INC
5432 Production Dr, Huntington Beach
(92649-1525)
PHONE..................................714 901-7622
Myung Sook Hong, CEO
Sung MO Hong, President
Frank Hong, Vice Pres
Ji SOO Lee, Vice Pres
Humberto Macias, Data Proc Exec
EMP: 90
SQ FT: 23,811

SALES (est): 14.4MM Privately Held
WEB: www.semiceramic.com
SIC: 3264 3674 3599 Porcelain electrical
supplies; semiconductors & related devices; machine shop, jobbing & repair

(P-10482)
SAN JOSE DELTA ASSOCIATES INC
482 Sapena Ct, Santa Clara (95054-2442)
PHONE..................................408 727-1448
Scott J Budde, CEO
EMP: 50
SQ FT: 12,500
SALES (est): 6.3MM Privately Held
WEB: www.sanjosedelta.com
SIC: 3264 Magnets, permanent: ceramic or
ferrite; porcelain parts for electrical de-
vices, molded

(P-10483)
SHIP SUPPLY INTERNATIONAL INC
Also Called: Universal Maritime
1215 255th St, Harbor City (90710-2914)
PHONE..................................310 325-3188
Mike Konstantas, CEO
EMP: 10
SALES (est): 1.7MM
SALES (corp-wide): 40.1MM Privately
Held
SIC: 3264 3699 5063 2297 Porcelain
electrical supplies; electrical equipment &
supplies; electrical apparatus & equip-
ment; bonded-fiber fabrics, except felt;
ship furniture
PA: Ship Supply Of Florida, Inc.
19680 Marino Lake Cir # 24
Miromar Lakes FL 33913
305 681-7447

3269 Pottery Prdts, NEC

(P-10484)
ASDAK INTERNATIONAL
Also Called: Oggi Corp
1809 1/2 N Orngethorpe Pa, Anaheim
(92801-1141)
PHONE..................................714 449-0733
Ajit Das, President
Barbara Das, CFO
Paul Williamson, Vice Pres
Stephen Curtis, Natl Sales Mgr
▲ EMP: 12
SQ FT: 29,000
SALES (est): 1.9MM Privately Held
SIC: 3269 Pottery cooking & kitchen arti-
cles

(P-10485)
BERNEY-KARP INC
3350 E 26th St, Vernon (90058-4145)
PHONE..................................323 260-7122
Morry Karp, President
Anna Ramos, Vice Pres
▲ EMP: 74 EST: 1970
SQ FT: 80,000
SALES (est): 8.2MM Privately Held
WEB: www.ceramic-source.com
SIC: 3269 Pottery cooking & kitchen arti-
cles

(P-10486)
CLAY DESIGNS INC
6435 Green Valley Cir # 112, Culver City
(90230-7047)
PHONE..................................562 432-3991
James L Camm, President
▲ EMP: 43
SALES (est): 4.7MM Privately Held
WEB: www.claydesign.com
SIC: 3269 Figures: pottery, china, earthen-
ware & stoneware; stoneware pottery
products

(P-10487)
DEERS MERCHANDISE INC
347 Enterprise Pl, Pomona (91768-3245)
P.O. Box 624, Azusa (91702-0624)
PHONE..................................909 869-8619
Edmond Tong, President
▼ EMP: 16
SQ FT: 86,000

SALES: 11MM **Privately Held**
SIC: 3269 Textile guides, porcelain
PA: Desiree Company Limited
    Rm 74 G/F Peninsula Ctr
    Tsim Sha Tsui East KLN

(P-10488)
GAINEY CERAMICS INC
1200 Arrow Hwy, La Verne (91750-5217)
PHONE...................909 596-4464
Steve Gainey, *CEO*
▲ **EMP:** 150
SQ FT: 75,500
SALES (est): 13.4MM **Privately Held**
WEB: www.gaineyceramics.com
SIC: 3269 Flower pots, red earthenware

(P-10489)
HAGEN-RENAKER INC (PA)
914 W Cienega Ave, San Dimas
(91773-2415)
P.O. Box 427 (91773-0427)
PHONE...................909 599-2341
Susan Renaker Nikas, *President*
Mary Lou Salas, *Treasurer*
EMP: 178
SQ FT: 88,964
SALES (est): 13.8MM **Privately Held**
WEB: www.hagenrenaker.com
SIC: 3269 0181 Figures: pottery, china,
earthenware & stoneware; nursery stock,
growing of

(P-10490)
HEATH CERAMICS LTD
2900 18th St, San Francisco (94110-2005)
PHONE...................415 361-5552
Robin Petravic, *Manager*
EMP: 78
SALES (corp-wide): 20MM **Privately Held**
SIC: 3269 Stoneware pottery products
PA: Heath Ceramics, Ltd.
    400 Gate 5 Rd
    Sausalito CA 94965
    415 332-3732

(P-10491)
JAY GEE SALES
Also Called: We-Cel Creations
703 Arroyo St, San Fernando
(91340-2248)
PHONE...................818 365-1311
Gary S Gelzer, *Owner*
Jerry Gelzer, *Owner*
EMP: 11
SQ FT: 1,200
SALES (est): 662.6K **Privately Held**
SIC: 3269 5945 Vases, pottery; ceramics
supplies

(P-10492)
SANTA BARBARA DESIGN STUDIO (PA)
1600 Pacific Ave, Oxnard (93033-2746)
P.O. Box 6087, Santa Barbara (93160-
6087)
PHONE...................805 966-3883
Raymond Markow, *CEO*
Brenda Ross, *Production*
◆ **EMP:** 70
SQ FT: 2,400
SALES (est): 6.3MM **Privately Held**
WEB:
www.santabarbaraceramicdesign.com
SIC: 3269 5719 Art & ornamental ware,
pottery; pottery

(P-10493)
STEVEN RHOADES CERAMIC DESIGNS
17595 Harvard Ave Ste C, Irvine
(92614-8522)
PHONE...................949 250-1076
Steven Rhoades, *Owner*
▲ **EMP:** 12
SALES (est): 771.5K **Privately Held**
SIC: 3269 5023 Art & ornamental ware,
pottery; pottery

(P-10494)
STONEWARE DESIGN CO
5332 Polis Dr, La Palma (90623-1787)
PHONE...................562 432-8145
Mung Huot Taing, *Owner*

EMP: 15
SQ FT: 30,000
SALES: 450K **Privately Held**
SIC: 3269 Stoneware pottery products

(P-10495)
WEST COAST PORCELAIN INC
133 N Sherman Ave, Corona (92882-1842)
PHONE...................951 278-8680
Jim Hatfield, *President*
Dean Reade, *Vice Pres*
Robert Sloss, *Vice Pres*
EMP: 20
SQ FT: 30,000
SALES (est): 2.2MM **Privately Held**
SIC: 3269 Chemical porcelain

(P-10496)
WORLD TRADITIONS INC
332 Camino De La Luna, Perris
(92571-2992)
PHONE...................951 990-6346
Mariela Molina, *CEO*
EMP: 30
SALES (est): 1.5MM **Privately Held**
SIC: 3269 Pottery products

(P-10497)
YF MANUFACTURE INC
2455 Maple Ave, Pomona (91767-2232)
PHONE...................626 768-0029
Peihua Ninci, *President*
EMP: 15
SALES (est): 453.5K **Privately Held**
SIC: 3269 Pottery products

3271 Concrete Block & Brick

(P-10498)
AIR-VOL BLOCK INC
1 Suburban Rd, San Luis Obispo
(93401-7523)
P.O. Box 931 (93406-0931)
PHONE...................805 543-1314
Robert J Miller, *President*
Richard Ayres, *Vice Pres*
Bryon Avila, *Mfg Mgr*
Gary Abney, *Sales Staff*
Mike Lutzow, *Supervisor*
EMP: 40
SQ FT: 1,400
SALES (est): 8.3MM **Privately Held**
WEB: www.airvolblock.com
SIC: 3271 Blocks, concrete or cinder: stan-
dard

(P-10499)
ANGELUS BLOCK CO INC
4575 E Vineyard Ave, Oxnard
(93036-1009)
PHONE...................805 485-1137
Sonny Foster, *Manager*
Fernando Carrillo, *Engineer*
EMP: 45
SALES (corp-wide): 21.6MM **Privately Held**
WEB: www.angelusblock.com
SIC: 3271 5211 Blocks, concrete or cin-
der: standard; masonry materials & sup-
plies
PA: Angelus Block Co., Inc.
    11374 Tuxford St
    Sun Valley CA 91352
    714 637-8594

(P-10500)
ANGELUS BLOCK CO INC
1705 N Main St, Orange (92865-4116)
PHONE...................714 637-8594
John Suratt, *Manager*
Laurie Kenney, *Manager*
EMP: 51
SQ FT: 21,528
SALES (corp-wide): 21.6MM **Privately Held**
WEB: www.angelusblock.com
SIC: 3271 Blocks, concrete or cinder: stan-
dard
PA: Angelus Block Co., Inc.
    11374 Tuxford St
    Sun Valley CA 91352
    714 637-8594

(P-10501)
APPLIED LIQUID POLYMER
17213 Roseton Ave, Artesia (90701-2645)
PHONE...................562 402-6300
Jon Paul Zentgraf Sr, *Principal*
EMP: 11 **EST:** 2007
SALES (est): 550K **Privately Held**
SIC: 3271 Brick, concrete

(P-10502)
BASALITE BUILDING PRODUCTS LLC
Also Called: Basalite-Tracy
11888 W Linne Rd, Tracy (95377-8102)
PHONE...................209 833-3670
Bryan Langland, *Manager*
Christina Ignacio, *Marketing Staff*
Sandy Holsopple, *Manager*
EMP: 150
SQ FT: 20,000
SALES (corp-wide): 1.5B **Privately Held**
WEB: www.basalite.com
SIC: 3271 1741 Blocks, concrete or cin-
der: standard; masonry & other stonework
HQ: Basalite Building Products, Llc
    2150 Douglas Blvd Ste 260
    Roseville CA 95661
    707 678-1901

(P-10503)
CALSTONE COMPANY
13755 Llagas Ave, San Martin
(95046-9563)
PHONE...................408 686-9627
Joe Young, *Manager*
EMP: 15
SQ FT: 23,262
SALES (corp-wide): 16.3MM **Privately Held**
WEB: www.calstone.com
SIC: 3271 Blocks, concrete or cinder: stan-
dard
PA: Calstone Company
    5787 Obata Way
    Gilroy CA 95020
    408 984-8800

(P-10504)
CALSTONE COMPANY
421 Crystal Way, Galt (95632-8418)
PHONE...................209 745-2981
Ted Schimdt, *Manager*
EMP: 50
SALES (corp-wide): 16.3MM **Privately Held**
WEB: www.calstone.com
SIC: 3271 3272 Blocks, concrete or cin-
der: standard; concrete products
PA: Calstone Company
    5787 Obata Way
    Gilroy CA 95020
    408 984-8800

(P-10505)
CASTLELITE BLOCK LLC (PA)
8615 Robben Rd, Dixon (95620-9608)
PHONE...................707 678-3465
John Espinoza,
EMP: 23
SALES (est): 4.7MM **Privately Held**
WEB: www.castleliteblock.com
SIC: 3271 Blocks, concrete or cinder: stan-
dard

(P-10506)
CEMEX CNSTR MTLS PCF LLC
Also Called: Readymix - Fairfield R/M
1601 Cement Hill Rd, Fairfield
(94533-2659)
PHONE...................707 422-2520
Vince Bush, *Vice Pres*
EMP: 50 **Privately Held**
WEB: www.rinkermaterials.com
SIC: 3271 Blocks, concrete or cinder: stan-
dard
HQ: Cemex Construction Materials Pacific,
Llc
    1501 Belvedere Rd
    West Palm Beach FL 33406
    561 833-5555

(P-10507)
CEMEX CNSTR MTLS PCF LLC
Also Called: Readymix - Tremont R/M
7059 Tremont Rd, Dixon (95620-9609)
PHONE...................707 580-3138

Ed Ozbun, *Manager*
EMP: 12 **Privately Held**
WEB: www.rinkermaterials.com
SIC: 3271 Blocks, concrete or cinder: stan-
dard
HQ: Cemex Construction Materials Pacific,
Llc
    1501 Belvedere Rd
    West Palm Beach FL 33406
    561 833-5555

(P-10508)
EARTHPRO INC
2010 El Camino Real, Santa Clara
(95050-4051)
PHONE...................408 294-1920
EMP: 28
SALES (est): 1.8MM **Privately Held**
SIC: 3271

(P-10509)
GREENSCAPE SOLUTIONS INC
7051 27th St, Riverside (92509-1538)
PHONE...................909 714-8333
Claudia Lanuza, *President*
EMP: 26
SALES (est): 2.2MM **Privately Held**
SIC: 3271 Blocks, concrete: landscape or
retaining wall

(P-10510)
L P MCNEAR BRICK CO INC
Also Called: McNear Brick & Block
1 Mcnear Brickyard Rd, San Rafael
(94901-8310)
P.O. Box 151380 (94915-1380)
PHONE...................415 453-7702
John E McNear, *CEO*
Jeffrey McNear, *President*
Dan Mc Near, *CFO*
Daniel McNear, *CFO*
Daniel M Near, *Treasurer*
◆ **EMP:** 70
SALES (est): 13MM **Privately Held**
WEB: www.mcnear.com
SIC: 3271 3251 Brick, concrete; brick clay:
common face, glazed, vitrified or hollow

(P-10511)
ORCO BLOCK & HARDSCAPE (PA)
11100 Beach Blvd, Stanton (90680-3219)
PHONE...................714 527-2239
Richard J Muth, *CEO*
Eldon La Bossiere, *Office Mgr*
Mary M Muth, *Admin Sec*
Robert Gleason, *Plant Mgr*
Juan Tejeda, *Sales Staff*
EMP: 60
SQ FT: 5,000
SALES (est): 33.4MM **Privately Held**
WEB: www.orco-block.com
SIC: 3271 Architectural concrete: block,
split, fluted, screen, etc.; blocks, concrete
or cinder: standard

(P-10512)
ORCO BLOCK & HARDSCAPE
3501 Oceanside Blvd, Oceanside
(92056-2602)
PHONE...................760 757-1780
EMP: 35
SALES (corp-wide): 33.4MM **Privately Held**
WEB: www.orco-block.com
SIC: 3271 3272 2951 Concrete block &
brick; concrete products, precast; asphalt
paving mixtures & blocks
PA: Orco Block & Hardscape
    11100 Beach Blvd
    Stanton CA 90680
    714 527-2239

(P-10513)
ORCO BLOCK & HARDSCAPE
26380 Palomar Rd, Romoland
(92585-9811)
PHONE...................951 928-3619
Fax: 951 928-3153
EMP: 28
SALES (corp-wide): 33.6MM **Privately Held**
SIC: 3271 3272

▲ = Import ▼=Export
◆ =Import/Export

PA: Orco Block & Hardscape
11100 Beach Blvd
Stanton CA 90680
714 527-2239

(P-10514)
QUINN DEVELOPMENT CO
Also Called: Mission Concrete Products
5787 Obata Way, Gilroy (95020-7018)
PHONE..................................408 842-9320
Charles Quinn Jr, CEO
Patrick Quinn, President
Dawn Quinn, Treasurer
EMP: 12
SQ FT: 36,000
SALES (est): 2.4MM Privately Held
SIC: 3271 Blocks, concrete: landscape or
retaining wall

(P-10515)
RCP BLOCK & BRICK INC (PA)
8240 Broadway, Lemon Grove
(91945-2004)
P.O. Box 579 (91946-0579)
PHONE..................................619 460-9101
Michael Finch, CEO
Eugene M Chubb, Corp Secy
Charles T Finch, Vice Pres
EMP: 57
SQ FT: 4,000
SALES (est): 43.4MM Privately Held
WEB: www.rcpblock.com
SIC: 3271 5211 5032 Blocks, concrete or
cinder: standard; masonry materials &
supplies; concrete building products

(P-10516)
RCP BLOCK & BRICK INC
8755 N Magnolia Ave, Santee
(92071-4594)
PHONE..................................619 448-2240
Randy Scott, Branch Mgr
EMP: 20
SALES (corp-wide): 43.4MM Privately
Held
WEB: www.rcpblock.com
SIC: 3271 5032 5211 Blocks, concrete or
cinder: standard; concrete & cinder block;
lumber & other building materials
PA: Rcp Block & Brick, Inc.
8240 Broadway
Lemon Grove CA 91945
619 460-9101

(P-10517)
RCP BLOCK & BRICK INC
75 N 4th Ave, Chula Vista (91910-1007)
PHONE..................................619 474-1516
Tim Ostrom, Manager
EMP: 24
SALES (corp-wide): 43.4MM Privately
Held
WEB: www.rcpblock.com
SIC: 3271 5032 5211 Blocks, concrete or
cinder: standard; concrete & cinder block;
concrete & cinder block
PA: Rcp Block & Brick, Inc.
8240 Broadway
Lemon Grove CA 91945
619 460-9101

(P-10518)
RCP BLOCK & BRICK INC
577 N Vulcan Ave, Encinitas (92024-2120)
PHONE..................................760 753-1164
Chico Savage, Manager
EMP: 20
SALES (corp-wide): 43.4MM Privately
Held
WEB: www.rcpblock.com
SIC: 3271 5211 Blocks, concrete or cin-
der: standard; lumber & other building
materials
PA: Rcp Block & Brick, Inc.
8240 Broadway
Lemon Grove CA 91945
619 460-9101

(P-10519)
**SOIL RETENTION PRODUCTS
INC (PA)**
1265 Carlsbad Village Dr # 100, Carlsbad
(92008-1972)
PHONE..................................951 928-8477
Jan Jansson, President
Jan Erik Jansson, President

Tabatha Burley, Office Mgr
Nicholle Swearingen, Mktg Coord
Julia Schmid Janson, Manager
▼ EMP: 13
SALES (est): 3.5MM Privately Held
SIC: 3271 Blocks, concrete: landscape or
retaining wall

(P-10520)
**SOIL RETENTION PRODUCTS
INC**
1765 Watson Rd, Romoland (92585)
PHONE..................................951 928-8477
Richard Aydlette, Manager
Niklas Jansson, Engineer
Barbara Oneil, Engineer
Don Wedeking, Sales Staff
EMP: 13
SALES (corp-wide): 3.5MM Privately
Held
SIC: 3271 Blocks, concrete: landscape or
retaining wall
PA: Soil Retention Products, Inc.
1265 Carlsbad Village Dr # 100
Carlsbad CA 92008
951 928-8477

(P-10521)
SUMMIT SERVICES INC
Also Called: PCA Summit Service
1430 Valle Grande, Escondido
(92025-7637)
P.O. Box 270392, San Diego (92198-2392)
PHONE..................................760 737-7630
Peter Atkins, President
▲ EMP: 12
SALES (est): 1.3MM Privately Held
WEB: www.summit-services.com
SIC: 3271 Blocks, concrete: landscape or
retaining wall

(P-10522)
UV LANDSCAPING LLC
Also Called: Landscape Contractor
477 Old Natividad Rd, Salinas
(93906-1407)
P.O. Box 4022 (93912-4022)
PHONE..................................831 275-5296
EMP: 18
SALES (est): 1MM Privately Held
SIC: 3271 0782 4971

(P-10523)
**VALLEY ROCK LNDSCPE
MATERIAL**
4018 Taylor Rd, Loomis (95650-9004)
PHONE..................................916 652-7209
Kurtis D Nixon, President
Don Clark, CFO
Kelly Nixon, Vice Pres
EMP: 20
SQ FT: 300
SALES: 4.1MM Privately Held
SIC: 3271 5261 Blocks, concrete: land-
scape or retaining wall; nurseries & gar-
den centers

(P-10524)
VIGILANT BALLISTICS INC
1055 W 7th St Ph 33, Los Angeles
(90017-2528)
PHONE..................................213 212-3232
Paul Tremaine, President
EMP: 15
SALES (est): 646.6K Privately Held
SIC: 3271 Blocks, concrete or cinder: stan-
dard; blocks, concrete: heat absorbing;
architectural concrete: block, split, fluted,
screen, etc.

(P-10525)
**WESTERN STATES WHOLESALE
INC (PA)**
Also Called: C-Cure
1420 S Bon View Ave, Ontario
(91761-4405)
P.O. Box 3340 (91761-0934)
PHONE..................................909 947-0028
Randall Humphreys, CEO
Donna Humphreys, Treasurer
Robert Humphreys, Vice Pres
Kelli Clavel, Purchasing
▲ EMP: 215
SQ FT: 60,000

SALES (est): 73.1MM Privately Held
WEB: www.wswcorp.com
SIC: 3271 5072 5032 5211 Concrete
block & brick; bolts; drywall materials;
lumber products

3272 Concrete Prdts

(P-10526)
**ACKER STONE INDUSTRIES
INC (HQ)**
13296 Temescal Canyon Rd, Corona
(92883-5299)
PHONE..................................951 674-0047
Giora Ackerstein, Ch of Bd
Anita May, Asst Controller
Ronen Dolberg, Opers Mgr
Ron Ehrler, Sales Mgr
Mike Millard, Sales Mgr
▲ EMP: 50
SQ FT: 14,000
SALES (est): 13.8MM
SALES (corp-wide): 1.1MM Privately
Held
WEB: www.ackerstone.com
SIC: 3272 3271 Concrete products, pre-
cast; paving blocks, concrete; blocks,
concrete: landscape or retaining wall
PA: Ackerstein Zvi Ltd.
103 Medinat Hayehudim
Herzliya 46766
995 966-66

(P-10527)
**AMERICAN ORNAMENTAL
STUDIO**
1 Fairview Pl, Millbrae (94030-1114)
PHONE..................................650 589-0561
Lara Giambastiani, President
EMP: 12
SQ FT: 7,500
SALES (est): 790K Privately Held
SIC: 3272 Precast terrazo or concrete
products

(P-10528)
**AMERON INTERNATIONAL
CORP**
1020 B St, Fillmore (93015-1024)
PHONE..................................425 258-2616
William Miner, Branch Mgr
EMP: 115
SALES (corp-wide): 8.4B Publicly Held
SIC: 3272 Cylinder pipe, prestressed or
pretensioned concrete
HQ: Ameron International Corporation
7909 Parkwood Circle Dr
Houston TX 77036
713 375-3700

(P-10529)
**AMERON INTERNATIONAL
CORP**
Ameron Pole Products & Systems
1020 B St, Fillmore (93015-1024)
PHONE..................................805 524-0223
West Allison, Manager
EMP: 100
SALES (corp-wide): 8.4B Publicly Held
WEB: www.ameron.com
SIC: 3272 3648 3646 3441 Concrete
products, precast; lighting equipment;
commercial indusl & institutional electric
lighting fixtures; fabricated structural
metal; steel pipe & tubes
HQ: Ameron International Corporation
7909 Parkwood Circle Dr
Houston TX 77036
713 375-3700

(P-10530)
ANOZIRA INCORPORATED
2415 San Ramon Vly Blvd, San Ramon
(94583-5381)
PHONE..................................925 771-8400
Brian Haber, President
EMP: 15
SALES (est): 1.1MM Privately Held
SIC: 3272 1611 7389 Paving materials,
prefabricated concrete; highway & street
construction;

(P-10531)
**ARCHITCTURAL FACADES
UNLIMITED**
600 E Luchessa Ave, Gilroy (95020-7068)
PHONE..................................408 846-5350
Mary Alice Kinzler Bracken, CEO
Francis X Bracken, Vice Pres
Robert Bianco, Sales Staff
Maurice Lafayette, Manager
EMP: 75
SQ FT: 35,000
SALES (est): 16.5MM Privately Held
WEB: www.architecturalfacades.com
SIC: 3272 Concrete products, precast

(P-10532)
AUBURN TILE INC
545 W Main St, Ontario (91762-3718)
P.O. Box 10 (91762-8010)
PHONE..................................909 984-2841
Udo Helferich, President
Steve Helferich, Vice Pres
EMP: 17 EST: 1958
SQ FT: 6,000
SALES (est): 1.5MM Privately Held
WEB: www.auburntile.com
SIC: 3272 Roofing tile & slabs, concrete

(P-10533)
AVILAS GARDEN ART (PA)
14608 Merrill Ave, Fontana (92335-4219)
PHONE..................................909 350-4546
Ralph G Avila, Owner
EMP: 121
SQ FT: 7,000
SALES (est): 9.9MM Privately Held
SIC: 3272 5261 5211 5199 Precast ter-
razo or concrete products; lawn orna-
ments; masonry materials & supplies;
statuary

(P-10534)
**BASALITE BUILDING
PRODUCTS LLC (HQ)**
2150 Douglas Blvd Ste 260, Roseville
(95661-3873)
PHONE..................................707 678-1901
Scott Weber, President
Dallas Barrett, CFO
Richard Blickensderfer, Bd of Directors
Alfred Mueller, Bd of Directors
Fredrick Nelson, Bd of Directors
◆ EMP: 37
SALES (est): 201.1MM
SALES (corp-wide): 1.5B Privately Held
WEB: www.basalite.com
SIC: 3272 Concrete products, precast
PA: Pacific Coast Building Products, Inc.
10600 White Rock Rd # 100
Rancho Cordova CA 95670
916 631-6500

(P-10535)
**BASALITE BUILDING
PRODUCTS LLC**
Also Called: Epic Plastics
104 E Turner Rd, Lodi (95240-0673)
PHONE..................................209 333-6161
Dallas Barrett Jr, CFO
Maureen Cleary, Human Res Dir
Navid Rezaei, Plant Mgr
Cindy Rhed, Cust Mgr
EMP: 25
SALES (corp-wide): 1.5B Privately Held
SIC: 3272 Concrete products
HQ: Basalite Building Products, Llc
2150 Douglas Blvd Ste 260
Roseville CA 95661
707 678-1901

(P-10536)
BESCAL INC
Also Called: Bes Concrete Products
10304 W Linne Rd, Tracy (95377-9128)
PHONE..................................209 836-3492
EMP: 48
SALES (est): 6.7MM Privately Held
WEB: www.bescal.com
SIC: 3272

(P-10537)
BLACKS IRRIGATIONS SYSTEMS
Also Called: Black's Irrigation Systems
144 N Chowchilla Blvd, Chowchilla (93610)
P.O. Box 357 (93610-0357)
PHONE......................................559 665-4891
James Black, *President*
Cheryl Black, *Corp Secy*
EMP: 12
SQ FT: 1,500
SALES (est): 1.9MM **Privately Held**
SIC: 3272 Irrigation pipe, concrete

(P-10538)
BOND MANUFACTURING CO INC (PA)
2516 Verne Roberts Cir H3, Antioch (94509-7918)
PHONE......................................925 252-1135
Daryl Merritt, *CEO*
Ronald Merritt, *Ch of Bd*
Cameron Jenkins, *Principal*
Catherine Sulprizio, *Controller*
Harold Jennings, *Clerk*
◆ EMP: 100
SQ FT: 250,000
SALES: 125MM **Privately Held**
WEB: www.bondmfg.com
SIC: 3272 5083 Fireplaces, concrete; lawn & garden machinery & equipment; garden machinery & equipment

(P-10539)
BONSAL AMERICAN INC
16005 Phoebe Ave, La Mirada (90638-5607)
PHONE......................................714 523-1530
Frank Maggio, *Branch Mgr*
EMP: 34
SALES (corp-wide): 30.6B **Privately Held**
WEB: www.bonsalamerican.com
SIC: 3272 1442 3253 2899 Dry mixture concrete; construction sand & gravel; ceramic wall & floor tile; chemical preparations
HQ: Bonsal American, Inc.
625 Griffith Rd Ste 100
Charlotte NC 28217
704 525-1621

(P-10540)
BORAL ROOFING LLC
9508 S Harlan Rd, French Camp (95231-9625)
PHONE......................................209 982-1473
EMP: 49 **Privately Held**
SIC: 3272 Concrete products
HQ: Boral Roofing Llc
7575 Irvine Center Dr # 100
Irvine CA 92618
949 756-1605

(P-10541)
BORAL ROOFING LLC
Also Called: Monier Lifetile
342 Roth Rd, Lathrop (95330-9029)
PHONE......................................209 983-1600
Lewis Garcia, *Opers-Prdtn-Mfg*
EMP: 65
SQ FT: 33,545 **Privately Held**
WEB: www.monierlifetile.com
SIC: 3272 Tile, precast terrazzo or concrete
HQ: Boral Roofing Llc
7575 Irvine Center Dr # 100
Irvine CA 92618
949 756-1605

(P-10542)
BORAL ROOFING LLC
Also Called: Monier Lifetile
3511 N Riverside Ave, Rialto (92377-3803)
PHONE......................................909 822-4407
Kevin O Neil, *Manager*
Bob Hale, *Sales Staff*
EMP: 80 **Privately Held**
WEB: www.monierlifetile.com
SIC: 3272 3251 5032 2952 Roofing tile & slabs, concrete; brick clay: common face, glazed, vitrified or hollow; cinders; asphalt felts & coatings

HQ: Boral Roofing Llc
7575 Irvine Center Dr # 100
Irvine CA 92618
949 756-1605

(P-10543)
BORDER PRECAST INC
615 Us Highway 111, Brawley (92227-2903)
PHONE......................................760 351-1233
EMP: 10
SALES (est): 710K **Privately Held**
SIC: 3272

(P-10544)
BUILDMAT PLUS INVESTMENTS INC
Also Called: Metroll
15435 Arrow Blvd Bldg A, Fontana (92335-1222)
P.O. Box 305, Rancho Cucamonga (91739-0305)
PHONE......................................909 823-7663
Shamsher Kanji, *CEO*
EMP: 12 EST: 2011
SQ FT: 17,000
SALES (est): 3.4MM **Privately Held**
SIC: 3272 Concrete stuctural support & building material

(P-10545)
CALAVERAS MATERIALS INC
1100 Lowe Rd, Hughson (95326-9178)
PHONE......................................209 883-0448
George Lefler, *Manager*
EMP: 11
SALES (corp-wide): 20.6B **Privately Held**
SIC: 3272 Concrete products
HQ: Calaveras Materials Inc.
1100 Lowe Rd
Hughson CA 95326
209 883-0448

(P-10546)
CALIFORNIA CONCRETE PIPE CORP
2960 S Highway 99, Stockton (95215-8047)
PHONE......................................209 466-4212
James B Schack, *Ch of Bd*
Cy Thomson III, *Vice Pres*
Michael Lynch, *Admin Sec*
Robert Quinn, *Asst Sec*
EMP: 19 EST: 1980
SQ FT: 2,440
SALES (est): 1.8MM
SALES (corp-wide): 30.6B **Privately Held**
SIC: 3272 Sewer pipe, concrete
HQ: Oldcastle Infrastructure, Inc.
7000 Cntl Prkaway Ste 800
Atlanta GA 30328
470 602-2000

(P-10547)
CEMEX CNSTR MTLS PCF LLC
Also Called: Shop -Ncal Rmx Fixed Maint Sho
1601 Cement Hill Rd, Fairfield (94533-2659)
PHONE......................................707 422-2520
Graham Dubois, *Principal*
Hector Avalos, *Area Mgr*
John Barrett, *Manager*
EMP: 33 **Privately Held**
SIC: 3272 Concrete products
HQ: Cemex Construction Materials Pacific, Llc
1501 Belvedere Rd
West Palm Beach FL 33406
561 833-5555

(P-10548)
CENTRAL PRECAST CONCRETE INC
Also Called: Western Concrete Products
3500 Boulder St, Pleasanton (94566-4700)
P.O. Box 727 (94566-0868)
PHONE......................................925 417-6854
Don Hmphreys, *President*
Vince Bormolini, *Corp Secy*
Charles Bormolini, *Vice Pres*
EMP: 30
SQ FT: 3,000

SALES (est): 2.6MM
SALES (corp-wide): 1.5B **Publicly Held**
WEB: www.westernconcreteproducts.com
SIC: 3272 1442 Manhole covers or frames, concrete; culvert pipe, concrete; sewer pipe, concrete; construction sand & gravel
PA: U.S. Concrete, Inc.
331 N Main St
Euless TX 76039
817 835-4105

(P-10549)
CHANNEL SYSTEMS INC
74 98th Ave, Oakland (94603-1002)
PHONE......................................510 568-7170
Lauren Bockmiller, *President*
Douglas Bockmiller, *Treasurer*
▲ EMP: 45
SQ FT: 20,000
SALES (est): 4.6MM **Privately Held**
WEB: www.channelsystems.com
SIC: 3272 5031 1542 1541 Building materials, except block or brick: concrete; building materials, interior; nonresidential construction; industrial buildings & warehouses

(P-10550)
CHRISTY VAULT COMPANY (PA)
1000 Collins Ave, Colma (94014-3299)
PHONE......................................650 994-1378
Robert B Christensen, *Ch of Bd*
Gregg Christensen, *Vice Pres*
Hal Wilkes, *Sales Executive*
EMP: 28
SQ FT: 16,500
SALES (est): 3.4MM **Privately Held**
SIC: 3272 Burial vaults, concrete or precast terrazzo; concrete products, precast

(P-10551)
CLARK - PACIFIC CORPORATION
131 Los Angeles St, Irwindale (91706)
PHONE......................................626 962-8751
Ed Wopschall, *Branch Mgr*
EMP: 75
SALES (corp-wide): 229.7MM **Privately Held**
SIC: 3272 Concrete products, precast
PA: Clark - Pacific Corporation
1980 S River Rd
West Sacramento CA 95691
916 371-0305

(P-10552)
CLARK - PACIFIC CORPORATION
13592 Slover Ave, Fontana (92337-6978)
PHONE......................................909 823-1433
Donald Clark, *Owner*
EMP: 120
SALES (corp-wide): 229.7MM **Privately Held**
WEB: www.clarkpacific.com
SIC: 3272 5211 Concrete products, precast; masonry materials & supplies
PA: Clark - Pacific Corporation
1980 S River Rd
West Sacramento CA 95691
916 371-0305

(P-10553)
CLARK - PACIFIC CORPORATION
3478 Buskirk Ave Ste 1039, Pleasant Hill (94523-4344)
PHONE......................................925 746-7176
Wayne Edwards, *Branch Mgr*
EMP: 63
SALES (corp-wide): 229.7MM **Privately Held**
SIC: 3272 Concrete products
PA: Clark - Pacific Corporation
1980 S River Rd
West Sacramento CA 95691
916 371-0305

(P-10554)
CON-FAB CALIFORNIA CORPORATION (PA)
Also Called: Confab
1910 Lathrop Rd, Lathrop (95330-9708)
PHONE......................................209 249-4700

Philip French, *President*
Miaja French, *Shareholder*
Rigo Garcia, *CFO*
Brent Koch, *Chief Engr*
Emily Porter, *HR Admin*
EMP: 20
SQ FT: 2,400
SALES (est): 4.8MM **Privately Held**
WEB: www.confabca.com
SIC: 3272 Concrete products, precast

(P-10555)
COOK CONCRETE PRODUCTS INC
5461 Eastside Rd, Redding (96001-4533)
P.O. Box 720280 (96099-7280)
PHONE......................................530 243-2562
L Edward Shaw, *President*
EMP: 35 EST: 1956
SQ FT: 1,000
SALES (est): 6MM **Privately Held**
WEB: www.cookconcreteproducts.com
SIC: 3272 Concrete products, precast

(P-10556)
CORESLAB STRUCTURES LA INC
150 W Placentia Ave, Perris (92571-3200)
PHONE......................................951 943-9119
Mario Franciosa, *CEO*
Lou Franciosa, *President*
Jorgen Clausen, *Vice Pres*
Robert H Konoske, *Vice Pres*
Robert Konoske, *Vice Pres*
EMP: 200 EST: 1955
SQ FT: 25,000
SALES (est): 38.7MM
SALES (corp-wide): 27.3MM **Privately Held**
SIC: 3272 Concrete products, precast
HQ: Coreslab Holdings U S Inc
332 Jones Rd Suite 1
Stoney Creek ON L8E 5
905 643-0220

(P-10557)
CREATIVE STONE MFG INC (PA)
Also Called: Coronado Stone Products
11191 Calabash Ave, Fontana (92337-7018)
PHONE......................................909 357-8295
Melton Bacon, *President*
Scott Ebersole, *Vice Pres*
Amy Toledo, *Comptroller*
Bob Ratkovic, *Production*
▲ EMP: 180
SQ FT: 10,000
SALES (est): 61.2MM **Privately Held**
WEB: www.arroyo.net
SIC: 3272 Siding, precast stone

(P-10558)
CULTURED STONE CORPORATION (DH)
Hwy 29 & Tower Rd, NAPA (94559)
PHONE......................................707 255-1727
Stephen Nowak, *CEO*
▼ EMP: 739 EST: 1967
SQ FT: 17,000
SALES (est): 34.3MM **Publicly Held**
WEB: www.culturedstone.com
SIC: 3272 3281 Cast stone, concrete; cut stone & stone products
HQ: Owens Corning Sales, Llc
1 Owens Corning Pkwy
Toledo OH 43659
419 248-8000

(P-10559)
DCC GENERAL ENGRG CONTRS INC
2180 Meyers Ave, Escondido (92029-1001)
PHONE......................................760 480-7400
Frank D'Agostini, *President*
Scott Woods, *Vice Pres*
EMP: 75
SQ FT: 2,100
SALES (est): 12.6MM **Privately Held**
SIC: 3272 1771 3531 Concrete products; curb & sidewalk contractors; asphalt plant, including gravel-mix type

(P-10560)
DESIGN INDUSTRIES INC
17918 Brook Dr W, Madera (93638-9624)
P.O. Box 26386, Fresno (93729-6386)
PHONE....................559 675-3535
Robert Cisco, *President*
James Cisco, *Vice Pres*
EMP: 15
SQ FT: 8,283
SALES: 1.7MM **Privately Held**
SIC: 3272 1791 Concrete stuctural sup-
port & building material; concrete rein-
forcement, placing of

(P-10561)
DIVERSITECH CORPORATION
9252 Cassia Rd, Adelanto (92301-3936)
PHONE....................760 246-4200
Nelson Janapha, *Manager*
EMP: 10
SQ FT: 60,000
SALES (corp-wide): 34.6MM **Privately
Held**
SIC: 3272 Concrete products
HQ: Diversitech Corporation
6650 Sugarloaf Pkwy # 100
Duluth GA 30097
678 542-3600

(P-10562)
DIXIETRUSS INC
Also Called: Mission Truss
12538 Vigilante Rd, Lakeside (92040-1112)
PHONE....................619 873-0440
Francisco Hernandez, *CEO*
Erica Chadbourne, *Finance Mgr*
EMP: 10
SALES (est): 1.6MM **Privately Held**
SIC: 3272 Roofing tile & slabs, concrete

(P-10563)
DO IT RIGHT PRODUCTS LLC
(PA)
44321 62nd St W, Lancaster (93536-7533)
PHONE....................661 722-9664
Elana K Sherve, *Principal*
EMP: 11
SALES (est): 2.3MM **Privately Held**
SIC: 3272 Concrete products

(P-10564)
DYNAMIC PRE-CAST CO INC
5300 Sebastopol Rd, Santa Rosa
(95407-6423)
PHONE....................707 573-1110
Guenter Meiburg, *President*
Elaine Meiburg, *Vice Pres*
Sharon Elder, *Finance Mgr*
EMP: 15
SQ FT: 2,500
SALES (est): 3.8MM **Privately Held**
WEB: www.dynamicprecast.com
SIC: 3272 1771 Concrete products, pre-
cast; concrete work

(P-10565)
EDESSA INC
Also Called: Thompson Building Materials
11027 Cherry Ave, Fontana (92337-7118)
PHONE....................909 823-1377
Fax: 909 823-8409
▲ EMP: 23
SALES (est): 4.2MM **Privately Held**
SIC: 3272 5032

(P-10566)
EISEL ENTERPRISES INC
714 Fee Ana St, Placentia (92870-6705)
PHONE....................714 993-1706
Lyle Eisel, *President*
Janis Eisel, *Corp Secy*
Kim Webster, *Vice Pres*
Eric Webster, *General Mgr*
EMP: 35
SQ FT: 4,000
SALES (est): 6.1MM **Privately Held**
SIC: 3272 Meter boxes, concrete

(P-10567)
ELDORADO STONE LLC (DH)
1370 Grand Ave Bldg B, San Marcos
(92078-2404)
P.O. Box 2289 (92079-2289)
PHONE....................800 925-1491
Donald P Newman, *Mng Member*

Cassandra Nestoroff, *Executive Asst*
Brad Yantha, *Database Admin*
Paul Shin, *Business Mgr*
Phil Kennedy, *Controller*
◆ EMP: 50
SALES: 537.6MM **Privately Held**
SIC: 3272 Concrete products, precast

(P-10568)
ELK CORPORATION OF TEXAS
6200 S Zerker Rd, Shafter (93263-9612)
PHONE....................661 391-3900
Gus Freshwater, *Vice Pres*
EMP: 150
SALES (corp-wide): 2.5B **Privately Held**
SIC: 3272 2952 Precast terrazo or con-
crete products; asphalt felts & coatings
HQ: Elk Corporation Of Texas
14911 Quorum Dr Ste 600
Dallas TX 75254

(P-10569)
EMPIRE PRE CAST
19473 Grand Ave, Lake Elsinore
(92530-6341)
PHONE....................951 609-1590
Carol Stahl, *Owner*
EMP: 25 EST: 2000
SALES: 2MM **Privately Held**
SIC: 3272 Precast terrazo or concrete
products

(P-10570)
FARLEY PAVING STONE CO INC
Also Called: Farley Interlocking Pav Stones
75135 Sheryl Ave Ste A, Palm Desert
(92211-5114)
P.O. Box 10946 (92255-0946)
PHONE....................760 773-3960
Shon Farley, *Vice Pres*
Charissa Farley, *President*
Hector Gonzalez, *Vice Pres*
Kimberly Ellis, *Sales Mgr*
EMP: 70
SQ FT: 900
SALES (est): 8.9MM **Privately Held**
SIC: 3272 3531 3281 Paving materials,
prefabricated concrete; pavers; curbing,
paving & walkway stone; paving blocks,
cut stone

(P-10571)
FAST ACCESS INC
Also Called: Elements Archtectural Surfaces
1765 Howard Pl, Redlands (92373-8090)
PHONE....................909 748-1245
Michael Menendez, *CEO*
EMP: 16
SALES (est): 1.3MM **Privately Held**
SIC: 3272 Concrete products

(P-10572)
FIOLAS DEVELOPMENT LLC
Also Called: Fiola Development
5362 Bolsa Ave Ste H, Huntington Beach
(92649-1055)
PHONE....................714 893-7559
John C Fiola, *Mng Member*
Magiee Fiola, *Vice Pres*
EMP: 10
SALES (est): 1MM **Privately Held**
SIC: 3272 Building materials, except block
or brick: concrete

(P-10573)
FIORE STONE INC
19930 Jolora Ave, Corona (92881-4615)
PHONE....................909 424-0221
Bruce Raabe, *President*
EMP: 45
SQ FT: 160,000
SALES (est): 7.6MM **Privately Held**
SIC: 3272 Concrete products, precast

(P-10574)
FLORENCE & NEW ITLN ART CO
INC
27735 Industrial Blvd, Hayward
(94545-4045)
PHONE....................510 785-9674
Mariano Fontana, *CEO*
Gerard Fontana, *CFO*
Marc Fontana, *Vice Pres*
Rick M Moore, *Sales Mgr*
▲ EMP: 40

SQ FT: 30,000
SALES (est): 6.6MM **Privately Held**
WEB: www.florenceartcompany.com
SIC: 3272 Concrete products

(P-10575)
FOAMTEC LLC
4420 Commodity Way Ste A, Shingle
Springs (95682-7250)
PHONE....................916 851-8621
Jeffrey Lemon, *Executive*
◆ EMP: 12
SQ FT: 9,000
SALES: 1.2MM **Privately Held**
SIC: 3272 Building materials, except block
or brick: concrete

(P-10576)
FOLSOM READY MIX INC (PA)
3401 Fitzgerald Rd, Rancho Cordova
(95742-6815)
PHONE....................916 851-8300
Scott Silva, *President*
Randy Barnes, *Vice Pres*
Jon Jackson, *QC Mgr*
Chad Dalbec, *Manager*
EMP: 30
SALES (est): 9.5MM **Privately Held**
WEB: www.folsomreadymix.com
SIC: 3272 3273 Concrete stuctural sup-
port & building material; ready-mixed con-
crete

(P-10577)
FORTERRA PIPE & PRECAST
LLC
7020 Tokay Ave, Sacramento
(95828-2418)
PHONE....................916 379-9695
Drew Black, *Manager*
EMP: 60
SALES (corp-wide): 1.4B **Publicly Held**
SIC: 3272 Pipe, concrete or lined with con-
crete
HQ: Forterra Pipe & Precast, Llc
511 E John Carpenter Fwy
Irving TX 75062
469 458-7973

(P-10578)
FORTERRA PIPE & PRECAST
LLC
Also Called: South Coast Materials Co
9229 Harris Plant Rd, San Diego
(92145-0001)
P.O. Box 639069 (92163-9069)
PHONE....................858 715-5600
Carol Hartwig, *Branch Mgr*
Marvin Howell, *Opers Mgr*
Ian Firth, *Plant Supt*
EMP: 15
SALES (corp-wide): 1.4B **Publicly Held**
WEB: www.hansonplc.com
SIC: 3272 Concrete products
HQ: Forterra Pipe & Precast, Llc
511 E John Carpenter Fwy
Irving TX 75062
469 458-7973

(P-10579)
GC PRODUCTS INC
601 7th St, Lincoln (95648-1828)
PHONE....................916 645-3870
John Coburn, *President*
Michael Coburn, *Vice Pres*
EMP: 43
SQ FT: 4,000
SALES (est): 8.9MM **Privately Held**
SIC: 3272 Concrete products

(P-10580)
GEORGE L THROOP CO
Also Called: Do It Best
444 N Fair Oaks Ave, Pasadena
(91103-3619)
P.O. Box 92405 (91109-2405)
PHONE....................626 796-0285
Jeffrey Throop, *President*
Ann T Comey, *Corp Secy*
George L Throop III, *Vice Pres*
▲ EMP: 32 EST: 1921
SQ FT: 10,500
SALES (est): 10MM **Privately Held**
SIC: 3272 5211 5251 Concrete products;
millwork & lumber; cement; hardware

(P-10581)
GEORGETOWN PRECAST INC
2420 Georgia Slide Rd, Georgetown
(95634-2201)
P.O. Box 65 (95634-0065)
PHONE....................530 333-4404
Ronny R Beam, *President*
EMP: 12 EST: 1974
SQ FT: 2,600
SALES (est): 1.5MM **Privately Held**
SIC: 3272 5039 Septic tanks, con-
crete; tanks, concrete; manhole covers or
frames, concrete; ready-mixed concrete;
septic tanks

(P-10582)
GIANNINI GARDEN ORNAMENTS
INC
225 Shaw Rd, South San Francisco
(94080-6605)
PHONE....................650 873-4493
Piera Giannini, *President*
Alessandro Giannini, *Sales Staff*
Joan Chiorato, *Manager*
▲ EMP: 30
SALES (est): 6.2MM **Privately Held**
WEB: www.gianninigarden.com
SIC: 3272 Concrete products

(P-10583)
HEADWATERS INCORPORATED
1345 Philadelphia St, Pomona
(91766-5564)
PHONE....................909 627-9066
Jim Johnson, *Manager*
Jenna Luvin, *Human Res Dir*
ARA Mardirosian, *Terminal Mgr*
EMP: 15 **Privately Held**
SIC: 3272 Concrete products
HQ: Headwaters Incorporated
10701 S River Front Pkwy # 300
South Jordan UT 84095

(P-10584)
HEITMAN BROOKS II LLC (PA)
Also Called: Brooks Products
1850 S Parco Ave, Ontario (91761-8302)
PHONE....................909 947-7470
Micheal Heitman, *Mng Member*
Frederick C Heitman,
EMP: 14
SQ FT: 25,000
SALES (est): 3.7MM **Privately Held**
WEB: www.brooksproducts.net
SIC: 3272 Concrete products, precast

(P-10585)
HILFIKER PIPE CO
Also Called: Hilfiker Retaining Walls
1902 Hilfiker Ln, Eureka (95503-5711)
PHONE....................707 443-5091
Harold Hilfiker, *President*
Brenda Peterson, *Treasurer*
William K Hilfiker, *Vice Pres*
Brian Stringer, *Vice Pres*
Suzanne Blackburn, *Admin Sec*
EMP: 30 EST: 1900
SQ FT: 14,400
SALES (est): 5.3MM **Privately Held**
WEB: www.hilfiker.com
SIC: 3272 3315 5051 5074 Concrete
products, precast; wall & ceiling squares,
concrete; welded steel wire fabric; pipe &
tubing, steel; pipes & fittings, plastic

(P-10586)
HILLHOLDER BLOCKS BY
MODERN
3239 Bancroft Dr, Spring Valley
(91977-2613)
PHONE....................619 463-6344
Jack Spencer, *President*
Deborah Fehlberg, *Vice Pres*
EMP: 13
SQ FT: 3,890
SALES (est): 1MM **Privately Held**
SIC: 3272 Concrete products, precast

(P-10587)
HYDRO CONDUIT OF TEXAS LP
Also Called: Colton Facilities
1205 S Rancho Ave, Colton (92324-3342)
PHONE....................909 825-1500
Rob Courney, *Branch Mgr*

PRODUCTS & SVCS

EMP: 18 **Privately Held**
WEB: www.prestressservices.com
SIC: 3272 5051 3599 Pipe, concrete or lined with concrete; pipe & tubing, steel; machine shop, jobbing & repair
HQ: Hydro Conduit Of Texas, Lp
6560 Langfield Rd 3-H
Houston TX 77092

(P-10588)
INDEPNDENT FLR TSTG INSPTN INC
2300 Clayton Rd Ste 1240, Concord (94520-2121)
PHONE....................925 676-7682
Lee Eliseian, *President*
EMP: 16
SALES (est): 381.1K **Privately Held**
SIC: 3272 8611 Floor slabs & tiles, precast concrete; business associations

(P-10589)
J & R CONCRETE PRODUCTS INC
440 W Markham St, Perris (92571-8138)
PHONE....................951 943-5855
Raul Ramirez, *President*
EMP: 42
SQ FT: 40,000
SALES (est): 7.5MM **Privately Held**
SIC: 3272 Meter boxes, concrete

(P-10590)
J G TORRES COMPANY OF HAWAII (PA)
825 Independence Ave, Mountain View (94043-2301)
P.O. Box 1270 (94042-1270)
PHONE....................650 967-7219
Jess G Torres, *President*
Jackie Torres Sheehan, *Vice Pres*
EMP: 30
SQ FT: 2,500
SALES (est): 3.9MM **Privately Held**
SIC: 3272 1771 Concrete products, precast; concrete work

(P-10591)
JENSEN ENTERPRISES INC
7210 State Highway 32, Orland (95963-9790)
PHONE....................530 865-4277
Don Jensen, *Branch Mgr*
Barbara Patten, *Office Admin*
EMP: 15
SALES (corp-wide): 186.5MM **Privately Held**
WEB: www.jensenprecast.net
SIC: 3272 5039 Concrete products, precast; septic tanks
PA: Jensen Enterprises, Inc.
825 Steneri Way
Sparks NV 89431
775 352-2700

(P-10592)
JENSEN ENTERPRISES INC
Also Called: Jensen Precast
14221 San Bernardino Ave, Fontana (92335-5232)
PHONE....................909 357-7264
Carol Kohanle, *Manager*
Terry Velarde, *Human Res Mgr*
Peggy Jarman, *Purch Mgr*
Ruben Gallegos, *Safety Mgr*
Pete Banayat, *Sales Staff*
EMP: 300
SALES (corp-wide): 186.5MM **Privately Held**
SIC: 3272 7699 5211 5039 Concrete products, precast; waste cleaning services; masonry materials & supplies; septic tanks; concrete forms, sheet metal
PA: Jensen Enterprises, Inc.
825 Steneri Way
Sparks NV 89431
775 352-2700

(P-10593)
KRISTICH-MONTEREY PIPE CO INC
225 Salinas Rd Ste B, Royal Oaks (95076-5253)
P.O. Box 606, Watsonville (95077-0606)
PHONE....................831 724-4186
Chris Kristich, *President*
EMP: 12
SQ FT: 2,000
SALES (est): 2.1MM **Privately Held**
SIC: 3272 Pipe, concrete or lined with concrete

(P-10594)
KTI INCORPORATED
Also Called: Rialto Concrete Products
3011 N Laurel Ave, Rialto (92377-3725)
PHONE....................909 434-1888
Kenneth D Thompson, *CEO*
Daniel J Deming, *President*
Jerry Cowden, *Vice Pres*
EMP: 100
SQ FT: 400
SALES (est): 29.9MM **Privately Held**
SIC: 3272 Concrete products, precast

(P-10595)
L K LEHMAN TRUCKING
Also Called: A & L Ready-Mix
19333 Industrial Dr, Sonora (95370-9232)
P.O. Box 9 (95370-0009)
PHONE....................209 532-5586
Vince Estosipo, *Manager*
EMP: 26
SALES (corp-wide): 3.2MM **Privately Held**
SIC: 3272 3429 3273 3271 Concrete products, precast; manufactured hardware (general); ready-mixed concrete; concrete block & brick; construction sand & gravel
PA: L. K. Lehman Trucking
19333 Industrial Dr
Sonora CA 95370
209 532-5586

(P-10596)
LEGACY VULCAN LLC
Also Called: Sales Office
16013 E Foothill Blvd, Irwindale (91702-2813)
PHONE....................626 856-6148
Bill Watts, *Ltd Ptnr*
EMP: 15 **Publicly Held**
WEB: www.vulcanmaterials.com
SIC: 3272 Concrete products
HQ: Legacy Vulcan, Llc
1200 Urban Center Dr
Vestavia AL 35242
205 298-3000

(P-10597)
LEGACY VULCAN LLC
Also Called: Gustine Ready Mix
28525 Bambouer Rd, Gustine (95322-9570)
PHONE....................209 854-3088
EMP: 16
SALES (corp-wide): 3.5B **Publicly Held**
SIC: 3272
HQ: Legacy Vulcan, Llc
1200 Urban Center Dr
Vestavia AL 35242
205 298-3000

(P-10598)
LEGACY VULCAN LLC
Also Called: Oceanside Ready Mix
2925 Industry St, Oceanside (92054-4813)
PHONE....................760 439-0624
Al Thrower, *Manager*
EMP: 14 **Publicly Held**
WEB: www.vulcanmaterials.com
SIC: 3272 Concrete products
HQ: Legacy Vulcan, Llc
1200 Urban Center Dr
Vestavia AL 35242
205 298-3000

(P-10599)
LINDSAY TRNSP SOLUTIONS INC (HQ)
Also Called: Barrier Systems Sales & Svc
180 River Rd, Rio Vista (94571-1208)
PHONE....................707 374-6800
Richard W Parod, *CEO*
David B Downing, *President*
Chris Sanders, *COO*
Mark A Roth, *Treasurer*
James Raabe, *Vice Pres*
▲ **EMP:** 79
SQ FT: 45,000
SALES (est): 63.2MM
SALES (corp-wide): 444MM **Publicly Held**
WEB: www.barriersystemsinc.com
SIC: 3272 3559 Concrete products, precast; concrete products machinery
PA: Lindsay Corporation
18135 Burke St Ste 100
Elkhorn NE 68022
402 829-6800

(P-10600)
LITE STONE CONCRETE LLC
12650 Highway 67 Ste B, Lakeside (92040-1132)
PHONE....................619 596-9151
John B Ward III,
Van Hunt, *Plant Mgr*
Edward Van Hunt, *Manager*
EMP: 14
SALES: 1.7MM **Privately Held**
WEB: www.litestoneconcrete.com
SIC: 3272 Concrete products

(P-10601)
MASONRY FIREPLACE INDS LLC
6391 Jurupa Ave, Riverside (92504-1140)
P.O. Box 4338 (92514-4338)
PHONE....................714 542-5397
Willard P Harris,
Liza Reyes, *Office Mgr*
Willard V Harris Jr,
EMP: 10
SALES (est): 1.6MM **Privately Held**
WEB: www.mason-lite.com
SIC: 3272 Concrete products

(P-10602)
MID-STATE CONCRETE PRODUCTS
1625 E Donovan Rd Ste C, Santa Maria (93454-2519)
P.O. Box 219 (93456-0219)
PHONE....................805 928-2855
Ralph Vander Veen, *President*
Pat Vander Veen, *Vice Pres*
Anneke Vander Veen, *General Mgr*
Terri Rogers, *Controller*
Ron Vanderveen, *Opers Staff*
EMP: 23
SQ FT: 2,000
SALES (est): 4.8MM **Privately Held**
WEB: www.midstateconcrete.com
SIC: 3272 Concrete products, precast; covers, catch basin: concrete; manhole covers or frames, concrete; septic tanks, concrete

(P-10603)
MODERN STAIRWAYS INC
3239 Bancroft Dr, Spring Valley (91977-2698)
PHONE....................619 466-1484
Jack Spencer, *President*
Deborah Spencer, *Vice Pres*
EMP: 12 **EST:** 1962
SQ FT: 1,000
SALES (est): 1.2MM **Privately Held**
WEB: www.modernstairways.com
SIC: 3272 Burial vaults, concrete or precast terrazzo; grave markers, concrete; steps, prefabricated concrete

(P-10604)
MS CAST STONE INC
Also Called: Souther Archtctural Cast Stone
235 Via Del Monte, Oceanside (92058-1223)
P.O. Box 1133, Wildomar (92595-1133)
PHONE....................760 754-9697
Marco Souther, *President*

Angela Souther, *Admin Sec*
EMP: 30 **EST:** 2016
SALES (est): 2.3MM **Privately Held**
SIC: 3272 Concrete products

(P-10605)
N V CAST STONE LLC
Also Called: NAPA Valley Cast Stone
1111 Green Island Rd, Vallejo (94503-9639)
PHONE....................707 261-6615
Mark Akey, *Mng Member*
Tom Brown,
Jeff Latreille,
Bill Tough,
EMP: 100
SQ FT: 50,000
SALES (est): 29.6MM **Privately Held**
WEB: www.nvcssystems.com
SIC: 3272 3281 Concrete products, precast; cut stone & stone products

(P-10606)
NEWBASIS WEST LLC
2626 Kansas Ave, Riverside (92507-2600)
PHONE....................951 787-0600
Karl Stockbridge, *CEO*
Jennifer Ewing, *CFO*
Kim Ruiz, *Controller*
◆ **EMP:** 115
SALES (est): 44.7MM **Privately Held**
SIC: 3272 Manhole covers or frames, concrete; tanks, concrete; meter boxes, concrete; concrete products, precast
PA: Echo Rock Ventures, Inc.
370 Hammond Dr
Auburn CA 95603
530 823-9600

(P-10607)
NEWMAN AND SONS INC (PA)
2655 1st St Ste 210, Simi Valley (93065-1578)
PHONE....................805 522-1646
Dennis L Newman, *President*
EMP: 41 **EST:** 1938
SQ FT: 12,500
SALES (est): 3.6MM **Privately Held**
SIC: 3272 Paving materials, prefabricated concrete

(P-10608)
NUCAST INDUSTRIES INC
Also Called: Robbins Precast
23220 Park Canyon Dr, Corona (92883-6006)
PHONE....................951 277-8888
David Minasian, *Principal*
Anthony Minasian, *Principal*
EMP: 14
SQ FT: 5,000
SALES (est): 2.8MM **Privately Held**
SIC: 3272 5211 Concrete products, precast; masonry materials & supplies

(P-10609)
OLDCAST PRECAST (DH)
Also Called: Riverside Foundary
2434 Rubidoux Blvd, Riverside (92509-2144)
PHONE....................951 788-9720
Thomas D Lynch, *Ch of Bd*
John R Waren, *President*
EMP: 35
SQ FT: 7,000
SALES (est): 4.5MM
SALES (corp-wide): 30.6B **Privately Held**
SIC: 3272 3271 Concrete products, precast; concrete block & brick
HQ: Oldcastle Infrastructure, Inc.
7000 Cntl Prkaway Ste 800
Atlanta GA 30328
470 602-2000

(P-10610)
OLDCASTLE INFRASTRUCTURE INC
Also Called: Utility Vault
10650 Hemlock Ave, Fontana (92337-7296)
P.O. Box 310039 (92331-0039)
PHONE....................909 428-3700
Glenn Scheaffer, *Manager*
Adriana Ramirez, *Safety Mgr*
EMP: 162

SALES (corp-wide): 30.6B **Privately Held**
WEB: www.oldcastle-precast.com
SIC: **3272** Concrete products, precast
HQ: Oldcastle Infrastructure, Inc.
 7000 Cntl Prkaway Ste 800
 Atlanta GA 30328
 470 602-2000

(P-10611)
OLDCASTLE INFRASTRUCTURE INC
10441 Vine St, Lakeside (92040-2415)
PHONE.................................619 390-2251
EMP: 49
SALES (corp-wide): 30.6B **Privately Held**
SIC: **3272** Concrete products
HQ: Oldcastle Infrastructure, Inc.
 7000 Cntl Prkaway Ste 800
 Atlanta GA 30328
 470 602-2000

(P-10612)
OLDCASTLE INFRASTRUCTURE INC
Also Called: Utility Vault
3786 Valley Ave, Pleasanton (94566-4766)
P.O. Box 727 (94566-0868)
PHONE.................................925 846-8183
Miles Bennett, *General Mgr*
Mario Lopez, *Project Engr*
Joe Barden, *VP Sales*
Carol Vacchio, *Director*
John Lewis, *Manager*
EMP: 50
SQ FT: 36,000
SALES (corp-wide): 30.6B **Privately Held**
WEB: www.oldcastle-precast.com
SIC: **3272 5211** Concrete products, precast; masonry materials & supplies
HQ: Oldcastle Infrastructure, Inc.
 7000 Cntl Prkaway Ste 800
 Atlanta GA 30328
 470 602-2000

(P-10613)
OLDCASTLE INFRASTRUCTURE INC
Also Called: Utility Vault
10050 Black Mountain Rd, San Diego (92126-4517)
P.O. Box 1590, Fontana (92334)
PHONE.................................858 578-5336
John Scott, *Manager*
Michael Scott, *Mfg Staff*
EMP: 20
SALES (corp-wide): 30.6B **Privately Held**
WEB: www.oldcastle-precast.com
SIC: **3272 5211** Burial vaults, concrete or precast terrazzo; masonry materials & supplies
HQ: Oldcastle Infrastructure, Inc.
 7000 Cntl Prkaway Ste 800
 Atlanta GA 30328
 470 602-2000

(P-10614)
OLDCASTLE INFRASTRUCTURE INC
2960 S Highway 99, Stockton (95215-8047)
P.O. Box 30610 (95213-0610)
PHONE.................................209 235-1173
Cy Thomson, *Manager*
EMP: 50
SALES (corp-wide): 30.6B **Privately Held**
WEB: www.oldcastle-precast.com
SIC: **3272** Pipe, concrete or lined with concrete
HQ: Oldcastle Infrastructure, Inc.
 7000 Cntl Prkaway Ste 800
 Atlanta GA 30328
 470 602-2000

(P-10615)
OLDCASTLE INFRASTRUCTURE INC
Also Called: Old Castle Inclosure Solution
801 S Pine St, Madera (93637-5219)
PHONE.................................559 675-1813
Greg Barner, *Manager*
EMP: 10
SALES (corp-wide): 30.6B **Privately Held**
SIC: **3272** Concrete products

HQ: Oldcastle Infrastructure, Inc.
 7000 Cntl Prkaway Ste 800
 Atlanta GA 30328
 470 602-2000

(P-10616)
OLDCASTLE INFRASTRUCTURE INC
5236 Arboga Rd, Marysville (95901)
PHONE.................................530 742-8368
Sherman Wren, *Manager*
EMP: 35
SALES (corp-wide): 30.6B **Privately Held**
WEB: www.oldcastle-precast.com
SIC: **3272 3644** Concrete products; non-current-carrying wiring services
HQ: Oldcastle Infrastructure, Inc.
 7000 Cntl Prkaway Ste 800
 Atlanta GA 30328
 470 602-2000

(P-10617)
OLDCASTLE INFRASTRUCTURE INC
Also Called: Utility Vault
2512 Harmony Grove Rd, Escondido (92029-2800)
PHONE.................................951 683-8200
John Scott, *Manager*
Volkmer Mark, *Sales Staff*
EMP: 50
SALES (corp-wide): 30.6B **Privately Held**
WEB: www.oldcastle-precast.com
SIC: **3272 3446** Concrete products, precast; pipe, concrete or lined with concrete; open flooring & grating for construction
HQ: Oldcastle Infrastructure, Inc.
 7000 Cntl Prkaway Ste 800
 Atlanta GA 30328
 470 602-2000

(P-10618)
OUTDOOR CREATIONS INC
2270 Barney Rd, Anderson (96007-4305)
P.O. Box 50, Round Mountain (96084-0050)
PHONE.................................530 365-6106
Albert E Puhlman Jr, *President*
EMP: 10
SQ FT: 10,000
SALES (est): 1.9MM **Privately Held**
SIC: **3272** Concrete products, precast

(P-10619)
OVER & OVER READY MIX INC
Also Called: Borges Rock Product
8216 Tujunga Ave, Sun Valley (91352-3932)
P.O. Box 309, Moorpark (93020-0309)
PHONE.................................818 983-1588
Ed Borges, *President*
EMP: 80
SALES (est): 13.4MM **Privately Held**
SIC: **3272 3273** Concrete products; ready-mixed concrete

(P-10620)
PACIFIC INTRLOCK PVNGSTONE INC (PA)
1895 San Felipe Rd, Hollister (95023-2541)
PHONE.................................831 637-9163
Dean Richardt Tonder, *CEO*
John Tonder, *Principal*
Carol Lindgren, *Office Admin*
EMP: 18
SALES (est): 2.6MM **Privately Held**
SIC: **3272** Concrete products, precast

(P-10621)
PACIFIC STONE DESIGN INC
1201 E Wakeham Ave, Santa Ana (92705-4145)
PHONE.................................714 836-5757
Scott Sterling, *President*
Kathy Sterling, *CFO*
EMP: 45 EST: 1996
SQ FT: 40,000
SALES (est): 7.6MM **Privately Held**
WEB: www.pacificstone.net
SIC: **3272** Concrete products, precast

(P-10622)
PARAGON BUILDING PRODUCTS INC (PA)
2191 5th St Ste 111, Norco (92860-1966)
P.O. Box 99 (92860-0099)
PHONE.................................951 549-1155
Jeffrey M Goodman, *President*
Jack Goodman, *CEO*
Richard Goodman, *Corp Secy*
Jeannie Kozinski, *Accounts Mgr*
▲ EMP: 25
SQ FT: 16,500
SALES (est): 29.3MM **Privately Held**
WEB: www.paragonbp.us
SIC: **3272 3271 5032** Dry mixture concrete; concrete block & brick; brick, concrete; paving blocks, concrete; brick, stone & related material

(P-10623)
PIRANHA PIPE & PRECAST INC
16000 Avenue 25, Chowchilla (93610-9353)
P.O. Box 670 (93610-0670)
PHONE.................................559 665-7473
Anita Simpson, *President*
Cortney Baker-Tyler, *Purchasing*
▲ EMP: 28
SALES (est): 6.2MM **Privately Held**
SIC: **3272** Precast terrazo or concrete products

(P-10624)
POLE DANZER
3777 Paseo De Olivos, Fallbrook (92028-8601)
PHONE.................................760 419-9514
Robert Trent, *Owner*
EMP: 10
SALES (est): 727.7K **Privately Held**
SIC: **3272** Poles & posts, concrete

(P-10625)
PORTERVILLE CONCRETE PIPE INC
474 S Main St, Porterville (93257-5324)
P.O. Box 408 (93258-0408)
PHONE.................................559 784-6187
Vincent Jurkovich, *President*
Steve Jurkovich, *Corp Secy*
Nick Jurkovich, *Executive*
EMP: 16
SQ FT: 1,500
SALES (est): 1.9MM **Privately Held**
SIC: **3272** Pipe, concrete or lined with concrete

(P-10626)
PRECAST CON TECH UNLIMITED LLC
Also Called: Ctu Precast
1260 Furneaux Rd, Olivehurst (95961-7415)
PHONE.................................530 749-6501
Rez Moulla,
Todd Whitney, *Officer*
Kevin Steinkraus, *Opers Mgr*
EMP: 80
SQ FT: 160,000
SALES: 13.1MM **Privately Held**
SIC: **3272** Concrete products, precast

(P-10627)
PRECAST INNOVATIONS INC
1670 N Main St, Orange (92867-3405)
PHONE.................................714 921-4060
Chester Valdovinos, *President*
EMP: 28
SQ FT: 20,000
SALES (est): 4.1MM **Privately Held**
SIC: **3272 1791** Concrete products, precast; precast concrete structural framing or panels, placing of

(P-10628)
PRECAST REPAIR
Also Called: Cano Architecture
5494 Morgan St, Ontario (91762-4631)
PHONE.................................909 627-5477
Delfie Cano, *Owner*
Ray Conel, *Co-Owner*
EMP: 20 EST: 1989

SALES (est): 1.8MM **Privately Held**
WEB: www.precastrepair.com
SIC: **3272** Precast terrazo or concrete products

(P-10629)
PRECISION TILE CO
Also Called: Penrose Coping Company
11140 Penrose St, Sun Valley (91352-2724)
P.O. Box 1612, Canyon Country (91386-1612)
PHONE.................................818 767-7673
Brad Rose, *President*
Patricia Rose, *Treasurer*
Wallace Rose, *Vice Pres*
EMP: 12
SQ FT: 4,000
SALES (est): 1.3MM **Privately Held**
SIC: **3272 1743** Copings, concrete; tile installation, ceramic

(P-10630)
PRIME BUILDING MATERIAL INC (PA)
6900 Lankershim Blvd, North Hollywood (91605-6110)
PHONE.................................818 765-6767
Hector Galvan, *CEO*
Mark Soult, *Mfg Mgr*
Kristin Sharp, *Supervisor*
EMP: 50
SALES (est): 10.8MM **Privately Held**
WEB: www.prime3.com
SIC: **3272** Concrete products, precast

(P-10631)
PRIME BUILDING MATERIAL INC
Also Called: Eldorado Stone
7811 Lankershim Blvd, North Hollywood (91605-2523)
PHONE.................................818 503-4242
Alfredo Martinez, *Manager*
EMP: 10 **Privately Held**
SIC: **3272** Concrete products, precast
PA: Prime Building Material, Inc.
 6900 Lankershim Blvd
 North Hollywood CA 91605

(P-10632)
PRIME FORMING & CNSTR SUPS
Also Called: Fitzgerald Formliners
1500a E Chestnut Ave, Santa Ana (92701-6321)
PHONE.................................714 547-6710
Edward Fitzgerald, *President*
Brian Sheehan, *General Mgr*
Mindy Casey, *Sales Mgr*
Eric Lundberg, *Sales Mgr*
Elton Shaw, *Mktg Coord*
EMP: 46
SQ FT: 30,000
SALES (est): 9.7MM **Privately Held**
WEB: www.formliners.com
SIC: **3272** Concrete products

(P-10633)
QUIKRETE CALIFORNIA LLC
Also Called: Quickrete
3940 Temescal Canyon Rd, Corona (92883-5618)
PHONE.................................951 277-3155
John O Winshester, *Mng Member*
EMP: 130
SALES (est): 23.9MM **Privately Held**
SIC: **3272** Concrete products
HQ: The Quikrete Companies Llc
 5 Concourse Pkwy Ste 1900
 Atlanta GA 30328
 404 634-9100

(P-10634)
QUIKRETE COMPANIES INC
Also Called: Quikrete Northern California
14200 Road 284, Porterville (93257-9374)
PHONE.................................559 781-1949
Ron Santiago, *General Mgr*
Alejandro Saldana, *Manager*
EMP: 16 **Privately Held**
WEB: www.quikrete.com
SIC: **3272** Concrete products

HQ: The Quikrete Companies Llc
5 Concourse Pkwy Ste 1900
Atlanta GA 30328
404 634-9100

(P-10635)
QUIKRETE COMPANIES LLC
7705 Wilbur Way, Sacramento
(95828-4929)
PHONE..................510 490-4670
Dennis McGovern, *Branch Mgr*
Robert Hernandez, *Manager*
EMP: 46 Privately Held
SIC: 3272 Dry mixture concrete
HQ: The Quikrete Companies Llc
5 Concourse Pkwy Ste 1900
Atlanta GA 30328
404 634-9100

(P-10636)
QUIKRETE COMPANIES LLC
9265 Camino Santa Fe, San Diego
(92121-2201)
P.O. Box 420931 (92142-0931)
PHONE..................858 549-2371
Pete Samone, *Branch Mgr*
EMP: 39 Privately Held
SIC: 3272 Concrete products
HQ: The Quikrete Companies Llc
5 Concourse Pkwy Ste 1900
Atlanta GA 30328
404 634-9100

(P-10637)
QUIKRETE COMPANIES LLC
Also Called: Quikrete of Atlanta
6950 Stevenson Blvd, Fremont
(94538-2400)
PHONE..................510 490-4670
Steven B Rafael, *Manager*
EMP: 100 Privately Held
WEB: www.quikrete.com
SIC: 3272 5032 Concrete products, pre-
cast; cement
HQ: The Quikrete Companies Llc
5 Concourse Pkwy Ste 1900
Atlanta GA 30328
404 634-9100

(P-10638)
QUIKRETE COMPANIES LLC
Also Called: True Cast Concrete Products
11145 Tuxford St, Sun Valley (91352-2632)
PHONE..................323 875-1367
Greg Gibhel, *Principal*
EMP: 75 Privately Held
WEB: www.quikrete.com
SIC: 3272 3271 5211 Steps, prefabricated
concrete; concrete block & brick; masonry
materials & supplies
HQ: The Quikrete Companies Llc
5 Concourse Pkwy Ste 1900
Atlanta GA 30328
404 634-9100

(P-10639)
**REDWOOD VALLEY GRAVEL
PRODUCTS**
11200 East Rd, Redwood Valley
(95470-6108)
PHONE..................707 485-8585
David Ford, *President*
Melvin Ford, *Vice Pres*
EMP: 13
SQ FT: 1,280
SALES (est): 1.3MM Privately Held
WEB: www.redwoodvalleygravel.com
SIC: 3272 Septic tanks, concrete

(P-10640)
RIVER VALLEY PRECAST INC
14796 Washington Dr, Fontana
(92335-6263)
PHONE..................928 764-3839
Darryl Kerr, *President*
EMP: 20
SALES (est): 2.1MM Privately Held
SIC: 3272 Precast terrazo or concrete
products

(P-10641)
RMR PRODUCTS INC (PA)
11011 Glenoaks Blvd Ste 1, Pacoima
(91331-1634)
PHONE..................818 890-0896
David McKendrick, *CEO*

Jim McKendrick, *President*
EMP: 25
SQ FT: 3,200
SALES (est): 3.2MM Privately Held
SIC: 3272 Chimney caps, concrete

(P-10642)
ROCK SOLID STONE LLC
308 Industrial Way Ste B, Fallbrook
(92028-2356)
PHONE..................760 731-6191
Scott Morel,
Elidio Escobedo, *Partner*
EMP: 15
SALES (est): 2.3MM Privately Held
SIC: 3272 Stone, cast concrete

(P-10643)
**ROMA FABRICATING
CORPORATION**
Also Called: Roma Marble & Tile
2638 S Santa Fe Ave, San Marcos
(92069-5926)
P.O. Box 1231 (92079-1231)
PHONE..................760 727-8040
Pietro Deangelis, *President*
Leo Deangelis, *CFO*
Marco Deangelis, *Vice Pres*
Bruno Deangelis, *Admin Sec*
EMP: 20
SQ FT: 3,500
SALES: 1.6MM Privately Held
SIC: 3272 1743 Precast terrazo or con-
crete products; marble installation, interior

(P-10644)
SAN BENITO SUPPLY (PA)
2984 Monterey Hwy, San Jose
(95111-3155)
PHONE..................831 637-5526
Mark Schipper, *President*
Ted Schipper, *Admin Sec*
EMP: 129
SQ FT: 1,870
SALES (est): 24.1MM Privately Held
WEB: www.sanbenitosupply.com
SIC: 3272 5032 Concrete products; brick,
stone & related material

(P-10645)
**SAN DIEGO PRECAST
CONCRETE INC (HQ)**
Also Called: US Concrete Precast
2735 Cactus Rd, San Diego (92154-8024)
PHONE..................619 240-8000
Douglas McLaughlin, *President*
EMP: 32 EST: 1999
SQ FT: 1,600
SALES (est): 9.5MM
SALES (corp-wide): 1.5B Publicly Held
SIC: 3272 3281 Meter boxes, concrete;
prestressed concrete products; urns, cut
stone
PA: U.S. Concrete, Inc.
331 N Main St
Euless TX 76039
817 835-4105

(P-10646)
SANDMAN INC (PA)
Also Called: Star Concrete
1404 S 7th St, San Jose (95112-5927)
PHONE..................408 947-0669
Gerald Ray Blatt, *CEO*
Nicole Candelaria, *CFO*
Jerry Blatt, *Director*
EMP: 42
SQ FT: 14,000
SALES (est): 17.6MM
**SALES (corp-wide): 18MM Privately
Held**
SIC: 3272 3273 Dry mixture concrete;
ready-mixed concrete

(P-10647)
SANDMAN INC
1510 S 7th St, San Jose (95112-5929)
PHONE..................408 947-0159
EMP: 44
**SALES (corp-wide): 18MM Privately
Held**
SIC: 3272 Building materials, except block
or brick: concrete

PA: Sandman, Inc.
1404 S 7th St
San Jose CA 95112
408 947-0669

(P-10648)
SANDSTONE DESIGNS INC
14828 Calvert St, Van Nuys (91411-2707)
PHONE..................818 787-5005
Mesrop Badalyan, *President*
Jiro J Badalyan, *General Mgr*
▲ **EMP: 20**
SQ FT: 20,000
SALES: 1.1MM Privately Held
SIC: 3272 Concrete products, precast

(P-10649)
**SELVAGE CONCRETE
PRODUCTS**
3309 Sebastopol Rd, Santa Rosa
(95407-6740)
PHONE..................707 542-2762
Bill C Banthrall, *President*
Linda J Banthrall, *Vice Pres*
William Kelley, *General Mgr*
EMP: 12 EST: 1952
SQ FT: 1,112
SALES: 1.3MM Privately Held
WEB: www.selvageconcrete.com
SIC: 3272 Septic tanks, concrete

(P-10650)
SIERRA PRECAST INC
Also Called: U.S. Concrete Precast Group
1 Live Oak Ave, Morgan Hill (95037-9245)
PHONE..................408 779-1000
Eric Scholz, *President*
EMP: 62 EST: 1974
SQ FT: 4,000
SALES (est): 6.8MM
SALES (corp-wide): 1.5B Publicly Held
WEB: www.sierraprecast.com
SIC: 3272 1771 Panels & sections, pre-
fabricated concrete; columns, concrete;
concrete work
PA: U.S. Concrete, Inc.
331 N Main St
Euless TX 76039
817 835-4105

(P-10651)
SISSELL BROS
4322 E 3rd St, Los Angeles (90022-1501)
PHONE..................323 261-0106
John F Foote, *President*
Joan M Foote, *Treasurer*
Dorothy Sissell, *Vice Pres*
EMP: 13
SQ FT: 7,000
SALES (est): 1MM Privately Held
SIC: 3272 Burial vaults, concrete or pre-
cast terrazzo

(P-10652)
**SONOMA CAST STONE
CORPORATION**
133 Copeland St Ste A, Petaluma
(94952-3145)
PHONE..................877 283-2400
James Herwatt, *CEO*
Stephen Rosenblatt, *President*
David Jensen, *Treasurer*
Kris Adriano, *Bookkeeper*
Carl Finney, *Manager*
◆ **EMP: 25 EST: 1997**
SQ FT: 42,000
SALES (est): 4.5MM Privately Held
WEB: www.sonomastone.com
SIC: 3272 Concrete products

(P-10653)
SOUTHER CAST STONE INC
235 Via Del Monte, Oceanside
(92058-1223)
P.O. Box 1133, Wildomar (92595-1133)
PHONE..................760 754-9697
Phillip Souther, *President*
EMP: 20
SQ FT: 7,000
SALES (est): 3.7MM Privately Held
SIC: 3272 Concrete products

(P-10654)
**SOUTHWEST CONCRETE
PRODUCTS**
519 S Benson Ave, Ontario (91762-4002)
PHONE..................909 983-9789
Bob Dzajkich, *President*
Natalie Dzajkich, *Treasurer*
Gary Pollard, *General Mgr*
Eileen Dzajkich, *Admin Sec*
Mike Stenseth, *Engineer*
▲ **EMP: 40**
SQ FT: 25,000
SALES (est): 7MM Privately Held
SIC: 3272 5032 Manhole covers or
frames, concrete; brick, stone & related
material
PA: Taiheyo Kenkou Center Co.,Ltd.
164-2, Rokuchome, Yotsukuramachi
Iwaki FSM 979-0
-

(P-10655)
SPEC FORMLINERS INC
1038 E 4th St, Santa Ana (92701-4751)
PHONE..................714 429-9500
Stephen A Deering, *CEO*
Anthony Zaha, *Vice Pres*
EMP: 26 EST: 1996
SQ FT: 23,000
SALES (est): 8.4MM Privately Held
WEB: www.specformliners.com
SIC: 3272 Concrete products

(P-10656)
STEPSTONE INC (PA)
17025 S Main St, Gardena (90248-3125)
PHONE..................310 327-7474
Gordon S McWilliams, *CEO*
Paul Mitchell, *President*
Kelsy Carrington, *Production*
EMP: 50
SQ FT: 15,000
SALES (est): 10.2MM Privately Held
WEB: www.stepstoneinc.com
SIC: 3272 Concrete products, precast; bur-
ial vaults, concrete or precast terrazzo

(P-10657)
STEPSTONE INC
13238 S Figueroa St, Los Angeles
(90061-1140)
PHONE..................310 327-7474
Kelsy Carrington, *Branch Mgr*
EMP: 40
**SALES (corp-wide): 10.2MM Privately
Held**
WEB: www.stepstoneinc.com
SIC: 3272 Concrete products, precast
PA: Stepstone, Inc.
17025 S Main St
Gardena CA 90248
310 327-7474

(P-10658)
STREUTER TECHNOLOGIES
208 Avenida Fabricante # 200, San
Clemente (92672-7536)
PHONE..................949 369-7630
Bart S Streuter, *President*
Brad Streuter, *Vice Pres*
▲ **EMP: 50**
SQ FT: 13,000
SALES (est): 7.4MM Privately Held
WEB: www.streuter.com
SIC: 3272 3089 5051 Concrete window &
door components, sills & frames; win-
dows, plastic; ferrous metals

(P-10659)
STRUCTURECAST
8261 Mccutchen Rd, Bakersfield
(93311-9407)
PHONE..................661 833-4490
Brent Dezember, *President*
Rick Treatch, *CFO*
Ann Dzember, *Corp Secy*
Glenn McMillan, *Project Mgr*
Michael Shepherd, *Project Mgr*
EMP: 100
SQ FT: 10,000
SALES (est): 15.8MM Privately Held
WEB: www.structurecast.com
SIC: 3272 1791 Precast terrazo or con-
crete products; precast concrete struc-
tural framing or panels, placing of

▲ = Import ▼=Export
◆ =Import/Export

(P-10660)
UNITED MEMORIAL PRODUCTS INC
Also Called: United Memorial/Matthews Intl
4845 Pioneer Blvd, Whittier (90601-1842)
P.O. Box 721 (90608-0721)
PHONE.................................562 699-3578
Joseph Bartolacci, *Owner*
Mac Sharrock, *General Mgr*
▲ **EMP:** 65
SALES (est): 7MM
SALES (corp-wide): 1.5B **Publicly Held**
SIC: 3272 3281 Concrete stuctural support & building material; cut stone & stone products
PA: Matthews International Corporation
2 N Shore Ctr Ste 200
Pittsburgh PA 15212
412 442-8200

(P-10661)
UNIVERSAL PRECAST CONCRETE INC
16538 Clear Creek Rd, Redding
(96001-5111)
P.O. Box 994170 (96099-4170)
PHONE.................................530 243-6477
Paul D'Amico, *CEO*
Gary McCall, *Admin Sec*
◆ **EMP:** 14
SQ FT: 15,000
SALES (est): 3.5MM **Privately Held**
SIC: 3272 Concrete products, precast

(P-10662)
US CONCRETE INC
Also Called: American Concrete Products
1 Live Oak Ave, Morgan Hill (95037-9245)
PHONE.................................408 779-1000
Eric Scholz, *Manager*
EMP: 28
SALES (corp-wide): 1.5B **Publicly Held**
SIC: 3272 Concrete products, precast
PA: U.S. Concrete, Inc.
331 N Main St
Euless TX 76039
817 835-4105

(P-10663)
UTILITY COMPOSITE SOLUTIONS IN (PA)
4600 Pavlov Ave Unit 221, San Diego
(92122-3869)
PHONE.................................858 442-3187
Lyle Dunbar, *President*
Denis Rediker, *COO*
Scott Homes, *Senior VP*
Walt Losch, *Vice Pres*
EMP: 10
SQ FT: 10,000
SALES: 700K **Privately Held**
SIC: 3272 8711 Poles & posts, concrete; engineering services

(P-10664)
W R MEADOWS INC
Also Called: W. R. Meadows Southern Cal
2300 Valley Blvd, Pomona (91768-1168)
P.O. Box 667, Walnut (91788-0667)
PHONE.................................909 469-2606
Michael Knapp, *Branch Mgr*
EMP: 30
SALES (corp-wide): 118.3MM **Privately Held**
WEB: www.wrmeadows.com
SIC: 3272 3444 2899 2891 Concrete products; concrete forms, sheet metal; chemical preparations; adhesives & sealants
PA: W. R. Meadows, Inc.
300 Industrial Dr
Hampshire IL 60140
847 214-2100

(P-10665)
WALTERS & WOLF GLASS COMPANY
41450 Cowbell Rd, Fremont (94538)
PHONE.................................510 226-9800
Jody Vegas, *Branch Mgr*
EMP: 68
SALES (corp-wide): 104.1MM **Privately Held**
SIC: 3272 Precast terrazo or concrete products

PA: Walters & Wolf Glass Company
41450 Boscell Rd
Fremont CA 94538
510 490-1115

(P-10666)
WALTERS & WOLF PRECAST
41450 Boscell Rd, Fremont (94538-3103)
PHONE.................................510 226-9800
Randy A Wolf, *President*
Jeff B Belzer, *CFO*
Doug Frost, *Vice Pres*
Ed Knowles, *Vice Pres*
Juliusz Knuzynksi, *Vice Pres*
▲ **EMP:** 160
SALES (est): 21.7MM **Privately Held**
SIC: 3272 Concrete products, precast

(P-10667)
WATERGUSH INC
440 N Wolfe Rd Ste E252, Sunnyvale
(94085-3869)
PHONE.................................408 524-3074
Antonio Aguilera, *CTO*
EMP: 44
SALES (est): 2.9MM **Privately Held**
SIC: 3272 Fountains, concrete

(P-10668)
WE HALL COMPANY INC
Also Called: Pacific Corrugated Pipe Co
5999 Power Inn Rd, Sacramento
(95824-2318)
PHONE.................................916 383-4891
Rob Roles, *Manager*
EMP: 14
SALES (corp-wide): 16.7MM **Privately Held**
SIC: 3272 Culvert pipe, concrete
PA: W.E. Hall Company, Inc.
471 Old Newport Blvd # 205
Newport Beach CA 92663
949 650-4555

(P-10669)
WILLIS CONSTRUCTION CO INC
2261 San Juan Hwy, San Juan Bautista
(95045-9565)
PHONE.................................831 623-2900
Lawrence M Willis, *CEO*
Mark Hildebrand, *President*
Tom Yezek, *CFO*
Roger Ely, *Vice Pres*
Stacy Jenkins, *Administration*
◆ **EMP:** 120 **EST:** 1976
SQ FT: 4,000
SALES: 30.6MM **Privately Held**
WEB: www.pre-cast.org
SIC: 3272 1791 Concrete products, precast; precast concrete structural framing or panels, placing of

---

3273 Ready-Mixed Concrete

(P-10670)
A & A READY MIXED CONCRETE INC
10250 W Linne Rd, Tracy (95377-9128)
PHONE.................................209 830-5070
Jessey Diaz, *Branch Mgr*
EMP: 18
SALES (corp-wide): 55.9MM **Privately Held**
WEB: www.aareadymix.com
SIC: 3273 Ready-mixed concrete
PA: A & A Ready Mixed Concrete, Inc.
4621 Teller Ave Ste 130
Newport Beach CA 92660
949 253-2800

(P-10671)
A & A READY MIXED CONCRETE INC
Also Called: Associated Ready Mixed Con
134 W Redondo Beach Blvd, Gardena
(90248-2290)
PHONE.................................310 515-0933
Ray Kemp, *Manager*
Anthony Otanez, *Technician*
Joaquin Qualin, *Sales Staff*
EMP: 30

SALES (corp-wide): 55.9MM **Privately Held**
WEB: www.aareadymix.com
SIC: 3273 Ready-mixed concrete
PA: A & A Ready Mixed Concrete, Inc.
4621 Teller Ave Ste 130
Newport Beach CA 92660
949 253-2800

(P-10672)
A & A READY MIXED CONCRETE INC (PA)
4621 Teller Ave Ste 130, Newport Beach
(92660-2165)
PHONE.................................949 253-2800
Kurt Caillier, *President*
Randy Caillier, *Corp Secy*
Michael Krussman, *Vice Pres*
Steve Swearingen, *General Mgr*
Heidi Bright, *Admin Asst*
▲ **EMP:** 45 **EST:** 1956
SQ FT: 8,000
SALES (est): 55.9MM **Privately Held**
WEB: www.aareadymix.com
SIC: 3273 Ready-mixed concrete

(P-10673)
A & A READY MIXED CONCRETE INC
Also Called: A&A Concrete Supply
1201 Market St, Yuba City (95991-3414)
PHONE.................................530 671-1220
Harry Johnston, *Manager*
EMP: 10
SALES (corp-wide): 55.9MM **Privately Held**
WEB: www.aareadymix.com
SIC: 3273 Ready-mixed concrete
PA: A & A Ready Mixed Concrete, Inc.
4621 Teller Ave Ste 130
Newport Beach CA 92660
949 253-2800

(P-10674)
A & A READY MIXED CONCRETE INC
Also Called: A & A Concrete Supply
3578 Esplanade A, Chico (95973-0209)
PHONE.................................530 342-5989
Tim Hostettler, *Manager*
EMP: 20
SQ FT: 20,000
SALES (corp-wide): 55.9MM **Privately Held**
WEB: www.aareadymix.com
SIC: 3273 8611 Ready-mixed concrete; business associations
PA: A & A Ready Mixed Concrete, Inc.
4621 Teller Ave Ste 130
Newport Beach CA 92660
949 253-2800

(P-10675)
A & A READY MIXED CONCRETE INC
3809 Bithell Ln, Suisun City (94585-9644)
PHONE.................................707 399-0682
Bob Perrine, *Branch Mgr*
EMP: 24
SALES (corp-wide): 55.9MM **Privately Held**
SIC: 3273 Ready-mixed concrete
PA: A & A Ready Mixed Concrete, Inc.
4621 Teller Ave Ste 130
Newport Beach CA 92660
949 253-2800

(P-10676)
A & A READY MIXED CONCRETE INC
9645 Washburn Rd, Downey (90241-5614)
PHONE.................................562 923-7281
Jim Lytle, *Manager*
EMP: 15
SALES (corp-wide): 55.9MM **Privately Held**
SIC: 3273 Ready-mixed concrete
PA: A & A Ready Mixed Concrete, Inc.
4621 Teller Ave Ste 130
Newport Beach CA 92660
949 253-2800

(P-10677)
A & A READY MIXED CONCRETE INC
Also Called: A&A Concrete Supply
4035 E Mariposa Rd, Stockton
(95215-8142)
PHONE.................................209 546-1950
Matt Murphy, *General Mgr*
EMP: 25
SALES (corp-wide): 55.9MM **Privately Held**
WEB: www.aareadymix.com
SIC: 3273 Ready-mixed concrete
PA: A & A Ready Mixed Concrete, Inc.
4621 Teller Ave Ste 130
Newport Beach CA 92660
949 253-2800

(P-10678)
A & A READY MIXED CONCRETE INC
25901 Towne Centre Dr, Foothill Ranch
(92610-2462)
PHONE.................................949 580-1844
Steve Fausneaucht, *Plant Mgr*
Brandon Agles, *Technical Staff*
Ron Huff, *Director*
EMP: 15
SALES (corp-wide): 55.9MM **Privately Held**
SIC: 3273 Ready-mixed concrete
PA: A & A Ready Mixed Concrete, Inc.
4621 Teller Ave Ste 130
Newport Beach CA 92660
949 253-2800

(P-10679)
A & A READY MIXED CONCRETE INC
Also Called: A&A Concrete Supply
8272 Berry Ave, Sacramento (95828-1602)
PHONE.................................916 383-3756
Ron Boburn, *Branch Mgr*
EMP: 35
SALES (corp-wide): 55.9MM **Privately Held**
WEB: www.aareadymix.com
SIC: 3273 Ready-mixed concrete
PA: A & A Ready Mixed Concrete, Inc.
4621 Teller Ave Ste 130
Newport Beach CA 92660
949 253-2800

(P-10680)
A TEICHERT & SON INC
Also Called: Teichert Readymix
7466 Pacific Ave, Pleasant Grove
(95668-9708)
PHONE.................................916 991-8170
Dave Bearden, *Division Mgr*
EMP: 40
SALES (corp-wide): 784MM **Privately Held**
SIC: 3273 Ready-mixed concrete
HQ: A. Teichert & Son, Inc.
3500 American River Dr
Sacramento CA 95864

(P-10681)
A TEICHERT & SON INC
Also Called: Teichert Readymix
8609 Jackson Rd, Sacramento
(95826-9731)
PHONE.................................916 386-6974
Dave Bearden, *Division Mgr*
EMP: 40
SALES (corp-wide): 784MM **Privately Held**
SIC: 3273 Ready-mixed concrete
HQ: A. Teichert & Son, Inc.
3500 American River Dr
Sacramento CA 95864

(P-10682)
A TEICHERT & SON INC
Also Called: Teichert Readymix
721 Berry St, Roseville (95678-1307)
PHONE.................................916 783-7132
Dave Bearden, *Division Mgr*
EMP: 40
SALES (corp-wide): 784MM **Privately Held**
SIC: 3273 Ready-mixed concrete

HQ: A. Teichert & Son, Inc.
3500 American River Dr
Sacramento CA 95864

(P-10683)
ALLIANCE READY MIX INC (PA)
915 Sheridan Rd, Arroyo Grande
(93420-5834)
P.O. Box 1163 (93421-1163)
PHONE.................................805 343-0360
Brandt Robertson, *President*
EMP: 20
SALES (est): 5.1MM **Privately Held**
SIC: 3273 Ready-mixed concrete

(P-10684)
ALLIED CONCRETE & SUPPLY CO
440 Mitchell Rd Ste B, Modesto
(95354-3915)
P.O. Box 1022 (95353-1022)
PHONE.................................209 524-3177
Michael G Ruddy Sr, *President*
Martin J Ruddy III, *Treasurer*
James M Ruddy, *Vice Pres*
Martin Ruddy Jr, *Vice Pres*
Sally Ruddy, *Vice Pres*
EMP: 20
SQ FT: 3,500
SALES: 800K **Privately Held**
WEB: www.allied-concrete-supply.com
SIC: 3273 Ready-mixed concrete

(P-10685)
ALLIED CONCRETE RDYMX SVCS LLC
450 Amador St, San Francisco
(94124-1248)
P.O. Box 2104, Alameda (94501-0208)
PHONE.................................415 282-8117
Randy Burgo,
Brad Burgo,
Gary Burgo,
EMP: 11
SALES (est): 3.2MM **Privately Held**
SIC: 3273 Ready-mixed concrete

(P-10686)
ALPHA MATERIALS INC
6170 20th St, Riverside (92509-2031)
PHONE.................................951 788-5150
Brian Oaks, *President*
EMP: 36
SQ FT: 1,200
SALES (est): 6.4MM **Privately Held**
SIC: 3273 Ready-mixed concrete

(P-10687)
AMADOR TRANSIT MIX INC
Also Called: Knife River
12480 Ridge Rd, Sutter Creek
(95685-9673)
P.O. Box 1265, Jackson (95642-1265)
PHONE.................................209 223-0406
Brian Drake, *President*
Brian E Drake, *Vice Pres*
EMP: 35
SALES (est): 4.2MM
SALES (corp-wide): 4.5B **Publicly Held**
WEB: www.fullercontracting.com
SIC: 3273 1611 Ready-mixed concrete;
grading
HQ: Knife River Corporation
1150 W Century Ave
Bismarck ND 58503
701 530-1400

(P-10688)
AMERICAN READY MIX INC
1141 W Graaf Ave, Ridgecrest
(93555-2307)
P.O. Box 1138 (93556-1138)
PHONE.................................760 446-4556
Leroy Ladd, *President*
Donna Ladd, *Vice Pres*
EMP: 15
SQ FT: 500
SALES (est): 1.6MM **Privately Held**
WEB: www.americanreadymix.net
SIC: 3273 Ready-mixed concrete

(P-10689)
ANTHONYS RDYMX & BLDG SUPS INC (PA)
4500 Manhattan Beach Blvd, Lawndale
(90260-2040)
PHONE.................................310 542-9400
Anthony Pagnini, *President*
Rudy Monteza, *CIO*
Tracy Bricker, *Info Tech Mgr*
EMP: 15
SQ FT: 4,000
SALES (est): 1.8MM **Privately Held**
WEB: www.anthonysreadymix.com
SIC: 3273 Ready-mixed concrete

(P-10690)
ANTIOCH BUILDING MATERIALS CO
Also Called: Brentwood Readymix
6823 Brentwood Blvd, Brentwood
(94513-2121)
P.O. Box 870, Antioch (94509-0086)
PHONE.................................925 634-3541
Neil Larson, *Manager*
EMP: 20
SQ FT: 8,538
SALES (corp-wide): 15.2MM **Privately Held**
SIC: 3273 Ready-mixed concrete
PA: Antioch Building Materials, Co.
1375 California Ave
Pittsburg CA 94565
925 432-0171

(P-10691)
ARROW TRANSIT MIX
507 E Avenue L12, Lancaster
(93535-5417)
PHONE.................................661 945-7600
H D Follendore, *President*
Christine Follendore, *Admin Sec*
Charla Anderson, *Bookkeeper*
EMP: 35
SQ FT: 7,200
SALES (est): 7.6MM **Privately Held**
SIC: 3273 Ready-mixed concrete

(P-10692)
ASSOCIATED READY MIX CON INC (PA)
4621 Teller Ave Ste 130, Newport Beach
(92660-2165)
PHONE.................................949 253-2800
Kurt Caillier, *President*
Randy Caillier, *Corp Secy*
Chris Pizano, *Vice Pres*
Bonnie Baker, *Finance*
Harvey Sanders, *Safety Mgr*
EMP: 40
SALES (est): 17.5MM **Privately Held**
SIC: 3273 Ready-mixed concrete

(P-10693)
ASSOCIATED READY MIX CONCRETE
8946 Bradley Ave, Sun Valley
(91352-2601)
PHONE.................................818 504-3100
Tim Sullivan, *Manager*
EMP: 40 **Privately Held**
SIC: 3273 Ready-mixed concrete
PA: Associated Ready Mix Concrete, Inc.
4621 Teller Ave Ste 130
Newport Beach CA 92660

(P-10694)
AZUSA ROCK INC
Also Called: Los Banos Rock and Ready Mix
22101 Sunset Dr, Los Banos (93635)
P.O. Box 1111 (93635-1111)
PHONE.................................209 826-5066
Wayne Stoughton, *Manager*
EMP: 30 **Publicly Held**
SIC: 3273 Ready-mixed concrete
HQ: Azusa Rock, Llc
3901 Fish Canyon Rd
Azusa CA 91702
858 530-9444

(P-10695)
B & B RED-I-MIX CONCRETE INC
Also Called: B & B Services
590 Live Oak Ave, Baldwin Park
(91706-1315)
PHONE.................................626 359-8371
Mike Gatherer, *President*
EMP: 31
SQ FT: 4,400
SALES (est): 2.9MM **Privately Held**
SIC: 3273 Ready-mixed concrete

(P-10696)
BEACON CONCRETE INC
Also Called: Lighthouse Trucking
1597 S Bluff Rd, Montebello (90640-6601)
PHONE.................................323 889-7775
Lou Earlabaugh, *President*
EMP: 27
SALES (est): 3.4MM **Privately Held**
SIC: 3273 Ready-mixed concrete

(P-10697)
BODE CONCRETE LLC
755 Stockton Ave, San Jose (95126-1839)
PHONE.................................415 920-7100
Danvers Boardman, *Mng Member*
Douglas Boardman,
Kathy Boardman,
Randolph Boardman,
EMP: 67
SQ FT: 5,000
SALES (est): 4.8MM
SALES (corp-wide): 1.5B **Publicly Held**
SIC: 3273 Ready-mixed concrete
HQ: Central Concrete Supply Co.Inc.
755 Stockton Ave
San Jose CA 95126
408 293-6272

(P-10698)
BUILDERS CONCRETE INC (DH)
3664 W Ashlan Ave, Fresno (93722-4499)
P.O. Box 9129 (93790-9129)
PHONE.................................559 225-3667
Charlie Wensley, *President*
Don Unmacht, *President*
Dominique Bidet, *Corp Secy*
Rod Gonzales, *Credit Mgr*
Justin Cook, *QC Mgr*
EMP: 50
SQ FT: 2,500
SALES (est): 7.8MM
SALES (corp-wide): 484.9MM **Privately Held**
WEB: www.buildersconcrete.com
SIC: 3273 Ready-mixed concrete
HQ: National Cement Company Of Califor-
nia, Inc.
15821 Ventura Blvd # 475
Encino CA 91436
818 728-5200

(P-10699)
BUILDERS CONCRETE INC NPP
15821 Ventura Blvd Ste 47, Encino
(91436-2915)
PHONE.................................559 229-6643
EMP: 11
SALES (est): 3.7MM **Privately Held**
SIC: 3273 Ready-mixed concrete

(P-10700)
C B CONCRETE CONSTRUCTION
641 University Ave, Los Gatos
(95032-4415)
PHONE.................................408 354-3484
Christopher Bearden, *Principal*
EMP: 10 EST: 2008
SALES (est): 1.2MM **Privately Held**
SIC: 3273 1771 1741 Ready-mixed con-
crete; driveway contractor; masonry &
other stonework

(P-10701)
CAL PORTLAND CEMENT CO
Also Called: Calportland
695 S Rancho Ave, Colton (92324-3242)
PHONE.................................909 423-0436
Allen Hamblen, *CEO*
Kirk McDonald, *Vice Pres*
Deanne Powers, *Accounting Mgr*
Stacie Reynolds, *Purch Agent*
Tom Wilson, *Plant Engr*
EMP: 23

SALES (est): 3.3MM **Privately Held**
SIC: 3273 Ready-mixed concrete

(P-10702)
CALAVERAS MATERIALS INC (DH)
Also Called: CMI
1100 Lowe Rd, Hughson (95326-9178)
P.O. Box 26240, Fresno (93729-6240)
PHONE.................................209 883-0448
David Vickers, *President*
EMP: 20
SQ FT: 8,000
SALES (est): 28.1MM
SALES (corp-wide): 20.6B **Privately Held**
SIC: 3273 5032 3272 2951 Ready-mixed
concrete; sand, construction; gravel; con-
crete products; asphalt paving mixtures &
blocks; construction sand & gravel

(P-10703)
CALPORTLAND COMPANY
Also Called: Catalina Pacific Concrete
1030 W Gladstone St, Azusa (91702-4207)
PHONE.................................626 334-3226
Bill Klawatter, *Manager*
April Avila, *Technology*
EMP: 15 **Privately Held**
WEB: www.calportland.com
SIC: 3273 Ready-mixed concrete
HQ: Calportland Company
2025 E Financial Way
Glendora CA 91741
626 852-6200

(P-10704)
CALPORTLAND COMPANY
590 Live Oak Ave, Irwindale (91706-1315)
PHONE.................................626 691-2596
Wes May, *Branch Mgr*
Zuhair Hasan, *Engineer*
Jack Hompland, *Engineer*
EMP: 68 **Privately Held**
SIC: 3273 Ready-mixed concrete
HQ: Calportland Company
2025 E Financial Way
Glendora CA 91741
626 852-6200

(P-10705)
CATALINA PACIFIC CONCRETE
19030 Normandie Ave, Torrance
(90502-1009)
PHONE.................................310 532-4600
Patrick E Greene, *President*
EMP: 23
SQ FT: 1,500
SALES (est): 2.8MM **Privately Held**
SIC: 3273 Ready-mixed concrete

(P-10706)
CEMEX (PA)
5180 Gldn Fthl Pkwy # 200, El Dorado Hills
(95762-9347)
PHONE.................................916 941-2800
Paul Brittain, *Owner*
EMP: 26
SALES (est): 18.5MM **Privately Held**
SIC: 3273 Ready-mixed concrete

(P-10707)
CEMEX INC
7633 Southfront Rd 250, Livermore
(94551-8204)
PHONE.................................925 606-2200
EMP: 10 **Privately Held**
SIC: 3273 Ready-mixed concrete
HQ: Cemex, Inc.
10100 Katy Fwy Ste 300
Houston TX 77043
713 650-6200

(P-10708)
CEMEX INC
4120 Jurupa St Ste 202, Ontario
(91761-1423)
PHONE.................................909 974-5500
Gilberto Perez, *President*
Gary Clay, *Manager*
EMP: 28 **Privately Held**
SIC: 3273 Ready-mixed concrete
HQ: Cemex, Inc.
10100 Katy Fwy Ste 300
Houston TX 77043
713 650-6200

▲ = Import ▼=Export
◆ =Import/Export

(P-10709)
CEMEX CEMENT INC
9035 Happy Camp Rd, Moorpark
(93021-9726)
P.O. Box 1030 (93020-1030)
PHONE..............................805 529-1355
Tom Powell, *Branch Mgr*
EMP: 50 Privately Held
SIC: 3273 1442 Ready-mixed concrete;
  construction sand & gravel
HQ: Cemex Cement, Inc.
  10100 Katy Fwy Ste 300
  Houston TX 77043
  713 650-6200

(P-10710)
CEMEX CNSTR MTLS PCF LLC
Also Called: Cem - Long Bch Terminal
601 Pier D Ave, Long Beach (90802-6240)
PHONE..............................562 435-0195
Steve Dillion, *Branch Mgr*
EMP: 10 Privately Held
SIC: 3273 Ready-mixed concrete
HQ: Cemex Construction Materials Pacific,
  Llc
  1501 Belvedere Rd
  West Palm Beach FL 33406
  561 833-5555

(P-10711)
CEMEX CNSTR MTLS PCF LLC
3221 N Riverside Ave, Rialto (92377-3823)
PHONE..............................951 377-9657
EMP: 10 Privately Held
SIC: 3273 Ready-mixed concrete
HQ: Cemex Construction Materials Pacific,
  Llc
  1501 Belvedere Rd
  West Palm Beach FL 33406
  561 833-5555

(P-10712)
CEMEX CNSTR MTLS PCF LLC
Also Called: Aggregate -Eliot Quarry
1544 Stanley Blvd, Pleasanton
(94566-6308)
P.O. Box 697 (94566-0866)
PHONE..............................925 846-2824
Gordon Brown, *Branch Mgr*
EMP: 45 Privately Held
SIC: 3273 Ready-mixed concrete
HQ: Cemex Construction Materials Pacific,
  Llc
  1501 Belvedere Rd
  West Palm Beach FL 33406
  561 833-5555

(P-10713)
CEMEX CNSTR MTLS PCF LLC
Also Called: Sierra Rm / Bm
5481 Davidson Rd, El Dorado (95623)
P.O. Box 537 (95623-0537)
PHONE..............................530 626-3590
Susanne Combellack, *Branch Mgr*
EMP: 38 Privately Held
SIC: 3273 Ready-mixed concrete
HQ: Cemex Construction Materials Pacific,
  Llc
  1501 Belvedere Rd
  West Palm Beach FL 33406
  561 833-5555

(P-10714)
CEMEX CNSTR MTLS PCF LLC
Also Called: Readymix -Tracy Rm Dual
30350 S Tracy Blvd, Tracy (95377-8121)
PHONE..............................209 835-1454
Jerry Larson, *Branch Mgr*
Luis Hernandez, *VP Human Res*
EMP: 23 Privately Held
SIC: 3273 Ready-mixed concrete
HQ: Cemex Construction Materials Pacific,
  Llc
  1501 Belvedere Rd
  West Palm Beach FL 33406
  561 833-5555

(P-10715)
CEMEX CNSTR MTLS PCF LLC
Also Called: Aggregate -Patterson Quarry
8705 Camp Far West Rd, Sheridan
(95681-9757)
PHONE..............................916 645-1949
EMP: 38 Privately Held
SIC: 3273 Ready-mixed concrete

HQ: Cemex Construction Materials Pacific,
  Llc
  1501 Belvedere Rd
  West Palm Beach FL 33406
  561 833-5555

(P-10716)
CEMEX CNSTR MTLS PCF LLC
Also Called: Readymix -Orange Rm Dual
1730 N Main St, Orange (92865-4117)
P.O. Box 54423, Los Angeles (90054-0423)
PHONE..............................714 637-9470
James Nelli, *Manager*
EMP: 15 Privately Held
SIC: 3273 Ready-mixed concrete
HQ: Cemex Construction Materials Pacific,
  Llc
  1501 Belvedere Rd
  West Palm Beach FL 33406
  561 833-5555

(P-10717)
CEMEX CNSTR MTLS PCF LLC
Also Called: Aggregate - Lemon Cove Quarry
24325 Lomitas Dr, Woodlake (93286)
PHONE..............................559 597-2397
Pete Locastro, *Branch Mgr*
EMP: 16 Privately Held
SIC: 3273 Ready-mixed concrete
HQ: Cemex Construction Materials Pacific,
  Llc
  1501 Belvedere Rd
  West Palm Beach FL 33406
  561 833-5555

(P-10718)
CEMEX CNSTR MTLS PCF LLC
Also Called: Shop -Bradshaw Maintenance
Sho
9751 Kiefer Blvd, Sacramento
(95827-3828)
PHONE..............................916 364-2470
Ed Ozbun, *Branch Mgr*
EMP: 23 Privately Held
SIC: 3273 Ready-mixed concrete
HQ: Cemex Construction Materials Pacific,
  Llc
  1501 Belvedere Rd
  West Palm Beach FL 33406
  561 833-5555

(P-10719)
CEMEX CNSTR MTLS PCF LLC
Also Called: Readymix -Oakland Rm
333 23rd Ave, Oakland (94606-5303)
PHONE..............................925 858-4344
Ray L Groue, *Branch Mgr*
EMP: 38 Privately Held
SIC: 3273 Ready-mixed concrete
HQ: Cemex Construction Materials Pacific,
  Llc
  1501 Belvedere Rd
  West Palm Beach FL 33406
  561 833-5555

(P-10720)
CEMEX CNSTR MTLS PCF LLC
Also Called: Readymix -Concord Rm Dual
3951 Laura Alice Way, Concord
(94520-8544)
PHONE..............................925 688-1025
Jack Shade, *Manager*
EMP: 20
SQ FT: 2,000 Privately Held
SIC: 3273 Ready-mixed concrete
HQ: Cemex Construction Materials Pacific,
  Llc
  1501 Belvedere Rd
  West Palm Beach FL 33406
  561 833-5555

(P-10721)
CEMEX CNSTR MTLS PCF LLC
Also Called: Cem - Sacramento Terminal
8251 Power Ridge Rd, Sacramento
(95826-4723)
PHONE..............................916 383-0526
EMP: 19 Privately Held
SIC: 3273 Ready-mixed concrete
HQ: Cemex Construction Materials Pacific,
  Llc
  1501 Belvedere Rd
  West Palm Beach FL 33406
  561 833-5555

(P-10722)
CEMEX CNSTR MTLS PCF LLC
Also Called: Readymix - Delano Rm
1100 Garzoli Ave, Delano (93215-9303)
PHONE..............................661 725-1819
Keith Stogle, *Branch Mgr*
EMP: 23 Privately Held
SIC: 3273 Ready-mixed concrete
HQ: Cemex Construction Materials Pacific,
  Llc
  1501 Belvedere Rd
  West Palm Beach FL 33406
  561 833-5555

(P-10723)
CEMEX CNSTR MTLS PCF LLC
Also Called: Readymix -Redlands Rm Dual
8203 Alabama Ave, Highland (92346-4255)
PHONE..............................909 335-3105
Erick Garcia, *Branch Mgr*
EMP: 17 Privately Held
SIC: 3273 Ready-mixed concrete
HQ: Cemex Construction Materials Pacific,
  Llc
  1501 Belvedere Rd
  West Palm Beach FL 33406
  561 833-5555

(P-10724)
CEMEX CNSTR MTLS PCF LLC
Also Called: Readymix -Elk Grove Rm
10286 Waterman Rd, Elk Grove
(95624-9403)
PHONE..............................916 686-8310
Lee Thomson, *Branch Mgr*
EMP: 15 Privately Held
SIC: 3273 Ready-mixed concrete
HQ: Cemex Construction Materials Pacific,
  Llc
  1501 Belvedere Rd
  West Palm Beach FL 33406
  561 833-5555

(P-10725)
CEMEX CNSTR MTLS PCF LLC
Also Called: Readymix - Old River Rm
11638 Old River Rd, Bakersfield
(93311-9798)
PHONE..............................661 396-0510
Keith Stogeell, *General Mgr*
EMP: 30 Privately Held
SIC: 3273 Ready-mixed concrete
HQ: Cemex Construction Materials Pacific,
  Llc
  1501 Belvedere Rd
  West Palm Beach FL 33406
  561 833-5555

(P-10726)
CEMEX CNSTR MTLS PCF LLC
Also Called: Admin - Shafter Admin Office
131 Vultee Ave, Shafter (93263-4049)
PHONE..............................661 746-3423
Scott Ely, *Branch Mgr*
EMP: 23 Privately Held
SIC: 3273 Ready-mixed concrete
HQ: Cemex Construction Materials Pacific,
  Llc
  1501 Belvedere Rd
  West Palm Beach FL 33406
  561 833-5555

(P-10727)
CEMEX CNSTR MTLS PCF LLC
Also Called: Readymix -Newman Rm
3407 W Stuhr Rd, Newman (95360-9774)
PHONE..............................209 862-0182
EMP: 23
SALES (corp-wide): 15.4B Privately Held
SIC: 3273
HQ: Cemex Construction Materials Pacific,
  Llc
  1501 Belvedere Rd
  West Palm Beach FL 33406
  561 833-5555

(P-10728)
CEMEX CNSTR MTLS PCF LLC
Also Called: Aggregate - Cache Creek S&G
30288 Highway 16, Madison (95653)
PHONE..............................530 666-2137
Anthony Russo, *President*
EMP: 22 Privately Held
WEB: www.rinkermaterials.com
SIC: 3273 Ready-mixed concrete

HQ: Cemex Construction Materials Pacific,
  Llc
  1501 Belvedere Rd
  West Palm Beach FL 33406
  561 833-5555

(P-10729)
CEMEX CNSTR MTLS PCF LLC
Also Called: Readymix -Walnut Rm
20903 Currier Rd, Walnut (91789-3020)
PHONE..............................909 594-0105
Gary Garcia, *Branch Mgr*
EMP: 20 Privately Held
SIC: 3273 Ready-mixed concrete
HQ: Cemex Construction Materials Pacific,
  Llc
  1501 Belvedere Rd
  West Palm Beach FL 33406
  561 833-5555

(P-10730)
CEMEX CNSTR MTLS PCF LLC
Also Called: Readymix -Fontana Rm
13200 Santa Ana Ave, Fontana
(92337-8215)
PHONE..............................909 355-8754
Scott Mullins, *Branch Mgr*
EMP: 15 Privately Held
SIC: 3273 Ready-mixed concrete
HQ: Cemex Construction Materials Pacific,
  Llc
  1501 Belvedere Rd
  West Palm Beach FL 33406
  561 833-5555

(P-10731)
CEMEX CNSTR MTLS PCF LLC
Also Called: Readymix -Moorpark Rm
9035 Roseland Ave, Moorpark
(93021-9784)
PHONE..............................805 529-1544
Rudolph Contreras, *Branch Mgr*
EMP: 16 Privately Held
SIC: 3273 Ready-mixed concrete
HQ: Cemex Construction Materials Pacific,
  Llc
  1501 Belvedere Rd
  West Palm Beach FL 33406
  561 833-5555

(P-10732)
CEMEX CNSTR MTLS PCF LLC
Also Called: Readymix -Modesto Rm
318 Beard Ave, Modesto (95354-4025)
PHONE..............................209 524-6322
Jerry Larsen, *Branch Mgr*
EMP: 23 Privately Held
SIC: 3273 Ready-mixed concrete
HQ: Cemex Construction Materials Pacific,
  Llc
  1501 Belvedere Rd
  West Palm Beach FL 33406
  561 833-5555

(P-10733)
CEMEX CNSTR MTLS PCF LLC
Also Called: Readymix -Compton Rm
2722 N Alameda St, Compton
(90222-2302)
P.O. Box 57002, Irvine (92619-7002)
PHONE..............................310 603-9122
Pete Pacheco, *Vice Pres*
EMP: 16 Privately Held
SIC: 3273 Ready-mixed concrete
HQ: Cemex Construction Materials Pacific,
  Llc
  1501 Belvedere Rd
  West Palm Beach FL 33406
  561 833-5555

(P-10734)
CEMEX CNSTR MTLS PCF LLC
Also Called: Readymix -Los Angeles Rm Dual
625 Lamar St, Los Angeles (90031-2512)
PHONE..............................323 221-1828
David Martinez, *Manager*
EMP: 23 Privately Held
SIC: 3273 Ready-mixed concrete
HQ: Cemex Construction Materials Pacific,
  Llc
  1501 Belvedere Rd
  West Palm Beach FL 33406
  561 833-5555

PRODUCTS & SVCS

(P-10735)
CEMEX CNSTR MTLS PCF LLC
Also Called: Readymix -Hollywood Rm Dual
1000 N La Brea Ave, West Hollywood
(90038-2324)
PHONE.................................323 466-4928
Jim Henderson, *Branch Mgr*
EMP: 34 Privately Held
SIC: 3273 Ready-mixed concrete
HQ: Cemex Construction Materials Pacific,
Llc
1501 Belvedere Rd
West Palm Beach FL 33406
561 833-5555

(P-10736)
CEMEX MATERIALS LLC
7059 Tremont Rd, Dixon (95620-9609)
PHONE.................................707 678-4311
Ed Ozbun, *Branch Mgr*
EMP: 27 Privately Held
SIC: 3273 Ready-mixed concrete
HQ: Cemex Materials Llc
1501 Belvedere Rd
West Palm Beach FL 33406
561 833-5555

(P-10737)
CEMEX MATERIALS LLC
401 Wright Ave, Richmond (94804-3508)
PHONE.................................510 234-3616
Karl H Watson Jr, *Branch Mgr*
EMP: 38 Privately Held
SIC: 3273 Ready-mixed concrete
HQ: Cemex Materials Llc
1501 Belvedere Rd
West Palm Beach FL 33406
561 833-5555

(P-10738)
CEMEX MATERIALS LLC
1601 Cement Hill Rd, Fairfield
(94533-2659)
PHONE.................................707 448-7121
Marc Mammola, *Manager*
EMP: 10 Privately Held
WEB: www.rinkermaterials.com
SIC: 3273 Ready-mixed concrete
HQ: Cemex Materials Llc
1501 Belvedere Rd
West Palm Beach FL 33406
561 833-5555

(P-10739)
CEMEX MATERIALS LLC
385 Tower Rd, NAPA (94558)
P.O. Box 3508 (94558-0553)
PHONE.................................707 255-3035
George Kerr, *Manager*
EMP: 25
SQ FT: 30,000 Privately Held
WEB: www.prestressservices.com
SIC: 3273 Ready-mixed concrete
HQ: Cemex Materials Llc
1501 Belvedere Rd
West Palm Beach FL 33406
561 833-5555

(P-10740)
CEMEX MATERIALS LLC
4150 N Brawley Ave, Fresno (93722-3914)
PHONE.................................559 275-2241
EMP: 27 Privately Held
WEB: www.rinkermaterials.com
SIC: 3273 Ready-mixed concrete
HQ: Cemex Materials Llc
1501 Belvedere Rd
West Palm Beach FL 33406
561 833-5555

(P-10741)
CEMEX MATERIALS LLC
1205 S Rancho Ave, Colton (92324-3342)
PHONE.................................909 825-1500
Lindsey Hank, *Manager*
EMP: 22 Privately Held
WEB: www.rinkermaterials.com
SIC: 3273 Ready-mixed concrete
HQ: Cemex Materials Llc
1501 Belvedere Rd
West Palm Beach FL 33406
561 833-5555

(P-10742)
CEMEX USA INC
8731 Orange St, Redlands (92374-1779)
PHONE.................................909 798-1144
EMP: 120
SALES (corp-wide): 15.4B Privately Held
SIC: 3273
HQ: Cemex U.S.A., Inc.
929 Gessner Rd Ste 1900
Houston TX 77024
713 650-6200

(P-10743)
**CENTRAL CONCRETE SUPPLY
COINC (HQ)**
Also Called: Westside Building Materials
755 Stockton Ave, San Jose (95126-1839)
PHONE.................................408 293-6272
William T Albanese, *CEO*
Scott Perrine, *President*
Laurie Cerrito, *Vice Pres*
Jeff Davis, *Vice Pres*
David Perry, *Vice Pres*
EMP: 80
SQ FT: 2,000
SALES (est): 80MM
SALES (corp-wide): 1.5B Publicly Held
SIC: 3273 Ready-mixed concrete
PA: U.S. Concrete, Inc.
331 N Main St
Euless TX 76039
817 835-4105

(P-10744)
CLAY MIX LLC
1003 N Abby St, Fresno (93701-1007)
PHONE.................................559 485-0065
Ritsuko Miyazaki, *Principal*
EMP: 12 EST: 2008
SALES (est): 1.7MM Privately Held
SIC: 3273 Ready-mixed concrete

(P-10745)
CLEARLAKE LAVA INC
Also Called: Point Lakeview Rock & Redi-Mix
13329 Point Lakeview Rd, Lower Lake
(95457-9728)
PHONE.................................707 995-1515
Don Vantelt, *President*
EMP: 15
SALES (corp-wide): 8MM Privately Held
SIC: 3273 5211 Ready-mixed concrete;
cement
PA: Clearlake Lava Inc
14572 E Highway 20
Clearlake Oaks CA 95423
707 998-1115

(P-10746)
CONCRETE INC
749 S Stanislaus St, Stockton
(95206-1570)
P.O. Box 66001 (95206-0901)
PHONE.................................209 830-1962
David Varney, *Branch Mgr*
EMP: 30
SALES (corp-wide): 4.5B Publicly Held
SIC: 3273 Ready-mixed concrete
HQ: Concrete, Inc.
400 S Lincoln St
Stockton CA 95203
209 933-6999

(P-10747)
CONCRETE INC
10260 Waterman Rd, Elk Grove
(95624-9403)
PHONE.................................209 933-6999
Terry Hildestad, *Branch Mgr*
EMP: 10
SALES (corp-wide): 4.5B Publicly Held
SIC: 3273 Ready-mixed concrete
HQ: Concrete, Inc.
400 S Lincoln St
Stockton CA 95203
209 933-6999

(P-10748)
CONCRETE INC (DH)
400 S Lincoln St, Stockton (95203-3312)
P.O. Box 66001 (95206-0901)
PHONE.................................209 933-6999
David C Barney, *CEO*
Terry D Hildestad, *CEO*
Larry Hansen, *CFO*
Mary Ann Johnson, *Vice Pres*

Lester H Loble II, *Admin Sec*
EMP: 55
SALES (est): 14.4MM
SALES (corp-wide): 4.5B Publicly Held
SIC: 3273 5032 Ready-mixed concrete;
brick, stone & related material
HQ: Knife River Corporation
1150 W Century Ave
Bismarck ND 58503
701 530-1400

(P-10749)
CONCRETE READY MIX INC
33 Hillsdale Ave, San Jose (95136-1308)
P.O. Box 50006 (95150-0006)
PHONE.................................408 224-2452
Ron Minnis, *President*
EMP: 35
SALES (est): 5.5MM Privately Held
WEB: www.concretecrm.com
SIC: 3273 Ready-mixed concrete

(P-10750)
**CORONET CONCRETE
PRODUCTS (PA)**
Also Called: Desert Redi Mix
83801 Avenue 45, Indio (92201-3311)
PHONE.................................760 398-2441
James Richert, *CEO*
EMP: 24
SQ FT: 2,000
SALES (est): 5.7MM Privately Held
SIC: 3273 3272 Ready-mixed concrete;
concrete products; manhole covers or
frames, concrete

(P-10751)
CROOKSHANKS SALES CO INC
Also Called: CSC Ranch
2375 Dairy Ave, Corcoran (93212-3503)
P.O. Box 338 (93212-0338)
PHONE.................................559 992-5077
Jason Proctor, *President*
Donna Proctor, *President*
Morris Proctor, *Treasurer*
Dorothy Crookshanks, *Vice Pres*
Laura Snodgrass, *Admin Sec*
EMP: 50
SQ FT: 2,500
SALES (est): 6.4MM Privately Held
SIC: 3273 0191 3275 Ready-mixed con-
crete; general farms, primarily crop; agri-
cultural gypsum

(P-10752)
**DENNIE MANNING CONCRETE
INC**
Also Called: D & K Concrete Co
15815 Arrow Blvd, Fontana (92335-3245)
PHONE.................................909 823-7521
Steve Mogan, *President*
Denise Manning, *Treasurer*
L G Manning, *Vice Pres*
EMP: 13 EST: 1923
SQ FT: 1,000
SALES (est): 3MM Privately Held
SIC: 3273 Ready-mixed concrete

(P-10753)
DIVERSIFIED MINERALS INC
Also Called: Dmi Ready Mix
1100 Mountain View Ave F, Oxnard
(93030-7213)
PHONE.................................805 247-1069
James W Price, *President*
Sharron Price, *Corp Secy*
▲ **EMP: 44**
SQ FT: 44,482
SALES (est): 16MM Privately Held
SIC: 3273 4013 3531 3241 Ready-mixed
concrete; railroad terminals; bituminous,
cement & concrete related products &
equipment; pozzolana cement

(P-10754)
E-Z HAUL READY MIX INC
Also Called: Star Building Products
1538 N Blackstone Ave, Fresno
(93703-3612)
PHONE.................................559 233-6603
Calvin Coley, *President*
Pat Coley, *Treasurer*
Donald Crawford, *Vice Pres*
EMP: 30
SQ FT: 1,500

SALES (est): 5.2MM Privately Held
SIC: 3273 5211 Ready-mixed concrete;
cement

(P-10755)
ELITE READY-MIX LLC
6790 Bradshaw Rd, Sacramento
(95829-9303)
PHONE.................................916 366-4627
Dominic Sposeto,
Mike Camello, *Business Mgr*
Braxton Edwards, *Opers Mgr*
EMP: 35
SALES (est): 8.1MM Privately Held
SIC: 3273 Ready-mixed concrete

(P-10756)
**FAR WEST EQUIPMENT
RENTALS**
649 7th St, Lincoln (95648-1828)
PHONE.................................916 645-2929
Jeff Drennor, *President*
EMP: 15
SALES (est): 1.1MM Privately Held
SIC: 3273 Ready-mixed concrete

(P-10757)
**FEATHER RIVER CONCRETE
PRODUCT**
675 State Box Rd, Oroville (95965-5885)
PHONE.................................530 532-7915
EMP: 10
**SALES (corp-wide): 4.6MM Privately
Held**
SIC: 3273
PA: Feather River Concrete Product
1295 State Highway 99
Gridley CA 95948
530 846-5842

(P-10758)
FOLSOM READY MIX INC
19291 Latona Rd, Anderson (96007-9405)
PHONE.................................530 365-0191
Brian Phillippen, *Vice Pres*
EMP: 17
**SALES (corp-wide): 9.5MM Privately
Held**
SIC: 3273 Ready-mixed concrete
PA: Folsom Ready Mix, Inc.
3401 Fitzgerald Rd
Rancho Cordova CA 95742
916 851-8300

(P-10759)
FOOTHILL READY MIX INC
11415 State Highway 99w, Red Bluff
(96080-7716)
PHONE.................................530 527-2565
Kevin Brunnemer, *President*
Cathy Brunnemer, *Admin Sec*
EMP: 20 EST: 1979
SQ FT: 1,000
SALES (est): 3.3MM Privately Held
SIC: 3273 Ready-mixed concrete

(P-10760)
FRONTIER CONCRETE INC
717 Mercantile St, Vista (92083-5919)
P.O. Box 3800 (92085-3800)
PHONE.................................760 724-4483
Mike Williams, *President*
EMP: 10
SALES (est): 1.7MM Privately Held
SIC: 3273 Ready-mixed concrete

(P-10761)
GARY BALE REDI-MIX CON INC
16131 Construction Cir W, Irvine
(92606-4410)
PHONE.................................949 786-9441
Kyle Goerlitz, *CEO*
Carol Beck, *Controller*
EMP: 80
SALES (est): 26.7MM Privately Held
SIC: 3273 Ready-mixed concrete

(P-10762)
GIBBEL BROS INC
Also Called: True Cast Concrete Products
11145 Tuxford St, Sun Valley (91352-2632)
PHONE.................................323 875-1367
Gregory Gibbel, *President*
EMP: 50 EST: 1965
SQ FT: 1,500

▲ = Import ▼=Export
◆ =Import/Export

SALES (est): 5.5MM **Privately Held**
SIC: **3273** 3271 Ready-mixed concrete;
blocks, concrete or cinder: standard

(P-10763)
GIBSON AND SCHAEFER INC (PA)
1126 Rock Wood Rd, Heber (92249)
P.O. Box 1539 (92249-1539)
PHONE..................................619 352-3535
Don Gibson, *President*
Maria Schaefer, *Treasurer*
P M Schaefer, *Vice Pres*
Rhoberta Gibson, *Admin Sec*
EMP: 50
SQ FT: 1,440
SALES: 8MM **Privately Held**
SIC: **3273** 5032 Ready-mixed concrete;
gravel

(P-10764)
GOLDEN EMPIRE CONCRETE CO
8211 Gosford Rd, Bakersfield (93313-9663)
P.O. Box 25000 (93390-5000)
PHONE..................................661 325-6833
Damin Banducci, *Principal*
EMP: 10 EST: 1988
SALES (est): 2.6MM
SALES (corp-wide): 484.9MM **Privately Held**
SIC: **3273** Ready-mixed concrete
PA: Vicat
Tour Manhattan
Courbevoie 92400
158 868-686

(P-10765)
GRANITE ROCK CO
Also Called: Pavex Construction Co
1755 Del Monte Blvd, Seaside (93955-3603)
PHONE..................................831 392-3700
Mike Chernetsky, *Branch Mgr*
Mike Chernetzkor, *Sales Staff*
Willie Diaz, *Accounts Mgr*
EMP: 35
SALES (corp-wide): 992MM **Privately Held**
WEB: www.graniterock.com
SIC: **3273** 5032 Ready-mixed concrete;
brick, stone & related material; sand, construction; stone, crushed or broken
PA: Granite Rock Co.
350 Technology Dr
Watsonville CA 95076
831 768-2000

(P-10766)
HANFORD READY-MIX INC
9800 Kent St, Elk Grove (95624-9483)
PHONE..................................916 405-1918
Preston Hanford Jr, *CEO*
Diane Hanford-Butz, *Vice Pres*
EMP: 22
SQ FT: 3,500
SALES (est): 4.4MM **Privately Held**
SIC: **3273** Ready-mixed concrete

(P-10767)
HANFORD SAND & GRAVEL INC
9800 Kent St, Elk Grove (95624-9483)
PHONE..................................916 782-9150
Preston Hanford III, *President*
Diane Hanford-Butz, *Corp Secy*
Jacqueline Hanford, *Vice Pres*
EMP: 11
SALES (est): 1.9MM **Privately Held**
SIC: **3273** Ready-mixed concrete

(P-10768)
HANSON AGGREGATES LLC
13550 Live Oak Ln, Irwindale (91706-1318)
PHONE..................................626 358-1811
Carol Smith, *Principal*
EMP: 30
SALES (corp-wide): 20.6B **Privately Held**
WEB: www.hansonind.com
SIC: **3273** 5032 Ready-mixed concrete;
stone, crushed or broken; sand, construction; gravel

HQ: Hanson Aggregates Llc
8505 Freport Pkwy Ste 500
Irving TX 75063
469 417-1200

(P-10769)
HANSON AGGRGTES MD-PACIFIC INC
Also Called: Lehigh Hanson
180 Atascadero Rd, Morro Bay (93442-1515)
P.O. Box 71, San Luis Obispo (93406-0071)
PHONE..................................805 928-3764
John Newhaul, *Manager*
EMP: 11
SALES (corp-wide): 20.6B **Privately Held**
SIC: **3273** 1442 Ready-mixed concrete;
construction sand & gravel
HQ: Hanson Aggregates Mid-Pacific, Inc.
12667 Alcosta Blvd # 400
San Ramon CA

(P-10770)
HANSON LEHIGH INC
3000 Executive Pkwy # 240, San Ramon (94583-2300)
PHONE..................................972 653-5603
Blake Hall, *Branch Mgr*
Erich Borjas, *Technology*
Kenneth Moore, *Regl Sales Mgr*
EMP: 30
SALES (corp-wide): 20.6B **Privately Held**
SIC: **3273** Ready-mixed concrete
HQ: Hanson Lehigh Inc
300 E John Carpenter Fwy
Irving TX 75062

(P-10771)
HI-GRADE MATERIALS CO
6500 E Avenue T, Littlerock (93543-1722)
P.O. Box 1050 (93543-1050)
PHONE..................................661 533-3100
Rod Elderton, *Manager*
EMP: 32
SALES (corp-wide): 53.1MM **Privately Held**
SIC: **3273** Ready-mixed concrete
HQ: Hi-Grade Materials Co.
17671 Bear Valley Rd
Hesperia CA
760 244-9325

(P-10772)
HOLLIDAY ROCK TRUCKING INC (PA)
1401 N Benson Ave, Upland (91786-2166)
PHONE..................................909 982-1553
Frederick N Holliday, *President*
Penny Holliday, *President*
Ronald Chambers, *Vice Pres*
John Holliday, *Vice Pres*
EMP: 60
SQ FT: 2,000
SALES (est): 7.9MM **Privately Held**
SIC: **3273** 4212 Ready-mixed concrete;
local trucking, without storage

(P-10773)
HOLLISTER LANDSCAPE SUPPLY INC (HQ)
520 Crazy Horse Canyon Rd A, Salinas (93907-9224)
PHONE..................................831 443-8644
Barbara A Chapin, *President*
Sharon Holmes, *Admin Sec*
Janet Snodderly, *Manager*
EMP: 10
SQ FT: 1,500
SALES (est): 6.3MM **Privately Held**
SIC: **3273** 5032 Ready-mixed concrete;
aggregate

(P-10774)
J F SHEA CO INC
Also Called: Shasta Ready Mix
17400 Clear Creek Rd, Redding (96001-5113)
PHONE..................................530 246-2200
Jim McCowen, *Principal*
EMP: 35
SALES (corp-wide): 2.2B **Privately Held**
SIC: **3273** Ready-mixed concrete

PA: J. F. Shea Co., Inc.
655 Brea Canyon Rd
Walnut CA 91789
909 594-9500

(P-10775)
J P GUNITE INC
9458 New Colt Ct, El Cajon (92021-2323)
PHONE..................................619 938-0228
Juan Padilla, *President*
EMP: 20
SALES (est): 3.4MM **Privately Held**
SIC: **3273** Ready-mixed concrete

(P-10776)
KEN ANDERSON
Also Called: Cen Cal Rock & Ready Mix
904 Frontage Rd, Ripon (95366)
PHONE..................................209 604-8579
Ken Anderson, *Owner*
EMP: 25
SALES (est): 1.5MM **Privately Held**
SIC: **3273** 5191 Ready-mixed concrete;
farm supplies

(P-10777)
KYLES ROCK & REDI-MIX INC
1221 San Simeon Dr, Roseville (95661-5364)
PHONE..................................916 681-4848
Kyle Rosburg, *CEO*
Patti Rosburg, *CFO*
EMP: 40
SQ FT: 1,700
SALES (est): 5.3MM **Privately Held**
SIC: **3273** Ready-mixed concrete

(P-10778)
LAS ANIMAS CON & BLDG SUP INC
146 Encinal St, Santa Cruz (95060-2111)
P.O. Box 507 (95061-0507)
PHONE..................................831 425-4084
Scott French, *President*
EMP: 20
SALES (est): 6MM **Privately Held**
SIC: **3273** Ready-mixed concrete

(P-10779)
LEBATA INC
Also Called: A & A Ready Mix Concrete
4621 Teller Ave Ste 130, Newport Beach (92660-2165)
PHONE..................................949 253-2800
Kurt Caillier, *President*
Don Baillie, *Plant Mgr*
EMP: 30
SALES (est): 5MM **Privately Held**
SIC: **3273** Ready-mixed concrete

(P-10780)
LEES CONCRETE MATERIALS INC
200 S Pine St, Madera (93637-5206)
P.O. Box 509 (93639-0509)
PHONE..................................559 486-2440
Tom Da Silva, *President*
Deidre Da Silva, *Treasurer*
EMP: 19 EST: 1963
SQ FT: 7,000
SALES (est): 4.8MM **Privately Held**
SIC: **3273** Ready-mixed concrete

(P-10781)
LEGACY VULCAN LLC
Also Called: Durbin Rock Plant
13000 Los Angeles St, Irwindale (91706-2240)
PHONE..................................626 856-6150
Danny Robinson, *Manager*
EMP: 20 **Publicly Held**
WEB: www.vulcanmaterials.com
SIC: **3273** Ready-mixed concrete
HQ: Legacy Vulcan, Llc
1200 Urban Center Dr
Vestavia AL 35242
205 298-3000

(P-10782)
LEGACY VULCAN LLC
Also Called: Saticoy Rock Asphalt and Rdymx
6029 E Vineyard Ave, Oxnard (93036-1042)
PHONE..................................805 647-1161
Robert Dryden, *Branch Mgr*

EMP: 26 **Publicly Held**
WEB: www.vulcanmaterials.com
SIC: **3273** Ready-mixed concrete
HQ: Legacy Vulcan, Llc
1200 Urban Center Dr
Vestavia AL 35242
205 298-3000

(P-10783)
LEGACY VULCAN LLC
Also Called: Palmdale Rock and Asphalt
6851 E Avenue T, Littlerock (93543-1705)
PHONE..................................661 533-2127
Cindy Figueroa, *Safety Mgr*
EMP: 22 **Publicly Held**
WEB: www.vulcanmaterials.com
SIC: **3273** Ready-mixed concrete
HQ: Legacy Vulcan, Llc
1200 Urban Center Dr
Vestavia AL 35242
205 298-3000

(P-10784)
LEGACY VULCAN LLC
Also Called: Bakersfield Yard Asp & Rdymx
8517 E Panama Ln, Bakersfield (93307-9400)
P.O. Box 22800 (93390-2800)
PHONE..................................661 835-4800
Gene Weslo, *Manager*
Tony Smith, *Sales Staff*
EMP: 75 **Publicly Held**
WEB: www.vulcanmaterials.com
SIC: **3273** 2951 Ready-mixed concrete;
asphalt paving mixtures & blocks
HQ: Legacy Vulcan, Llc
1200 Urban Center Dr
Vestavia AL 35242
205 298-3000

(P-10785)
LEGACY VULCAN LLC
Also Called: Western Division
20350 Highland Ave, Rialto (92377)
PHONE..................................909 875-5180
Darol Charlson, *Manager*
EMP: 30 **Publicly Held**
WEB: www.vulcanmaterials.com
SIC: **3273** Ready-mixed concrete
HQ: Legacy Vulcan, Llc
1200 Urban Center Dr
Vestavia AL 35242
205 298-3000

(P-10786)
LEGACY VULCAN LLC
Also Called: San Emidio Quarry
Hwy W 166 Of Old Rver Rd, Bakersfield (93313)
PHONE..................................661 858-2673
Dan Bectel, *General Mgr*
EMP: 30 **Publicly Held**
WEB: www.vulcanmaterials.com
SIC: **3273** Ready-mixed concrete
HQ: Legacy Vulcan, Llc
1200 Urban Center Dr
Vestavia AL 35242
205 298-3000

(P-10787)
LEGACY VULCAN LLC
11599 Old Friant Rd, Fresno (93730-1214)
PHONE..................................559 434-1202
Frank Costa, *Manager*
Michael Ingram, *Accountant*
EMP: 60 **Publicly Held**
WEB: www.vulcanmaterials.com
SIC: **3273** Ready-mixed concrete
HQ: Legacy Vulcan, Llc
1200 Urban Center Dr
Vestavia AL 35242
205 298-3000

(P-10788)
LEGACY VULCAN LLC
13900 Lang Station Rd, Canyon Country (91387-2213)
PHONE..................................661 252-1010
Frank Parra, *Manager*
EMP: 25 **Publicly Held**
WEB: www.vulcanmaterials.com
SIC: **3273** Ready-mixed concrete
HQ: Legacy Vulcan, Llc
1200 Urban Center Dr
Vestavia AL 35242
205 298-3000

(P-10789)
LEGACY VULCAN LLC
Also Called: Triangle Rock Products
11501 Florin Rd, Sacramento
(95830-9499)
PHONE..................................916 682-0850
Robert Fine, *Manager*
EMP: 18 Publicly Held
WEB: www.vulcanmaterials.com
SIC: 3273 Ready-mixed concrete
HQ: Legacy Vulcan, Llc
1200 Urban Center Dr
Vestavia AL 35242
205 298-3000

(P-10790)
LEGACY VULCAN LLC
365 N Canyon Pkwy, Livermore (94551)
PHONE..................................925 373-1802
Don Kahler, *Branch Mgr*
EMP: 26 Publicly Held
WEB: www.vulcanmaterials.com
SIC: 3273 Ready-mixed concrete
HQ: Legacy Vulcan, Llc
1200 Urban Center Dr
Vestavia AL 35242
205 298-3000

(P-10791)
LEGACY VULCAN LLC
7107 E Avenue T, Littlerock (93543-1703)
PHONE..................................661 533-2125
Lorene Harrigan, *Manager*
EMP: 26 Publicly Held
WEB: www.vulcanmaterials.com
SIC: 3273 Ready-mixed concrete
HQ: Legacy Vulcan, Llc
1200 Urban Center Dr
Vestavia AL 35242
205 298-3000

(P-10792)
LEGACY VULCAN LLC
Also Called: Sun Valley Rock and Asphalt
11401 Tuxford St, Sun Valley (91352-2639)
PHONE..................................818 983-0146
Jim Dean, *Branch Mgr*
EMP: 26
SQ FT: 16,945 Publicly Held
WEB: www.vulcanmaterials.com
SIC: 3273 Ready-mixed concrete
HQ: Legacy Vulcan, Llc
1200 Urban Center Dr
Vestavia AL 35242
205 298-3000

(P-10793)
LEHIGH SOUTHWEST CEMENT CO
15390 Wonderland Blvd, Redding
(96003-8526)
PHONE..................................530 275-1581
James Ellison, *Opers-Prdtn-Mfg*
Joe Baudizzon, *Project Engr*
EMP: 115
SALES (corp-wide): 20.6B Privately Held
SIC: 3273 3241 Ready-mixed concrete;
cement, hydraulic
HQ: Lehigh Southwest Cement Company
2300 Clayton Rd Ste 300
Concord CA 94520
972 653-5500

(P-10794)
LEHIGH SOUTHWEST CEMENT CO
2201 W Washington St, Stockton
(95203-2942)
PHONE..................................209 465-2624
Steve Olivas, *Manager*
EMP: 15
SALES (corp-wide): 20.6B Privately Held
SIC: 3273 Ready-mixed concrete
HQ: Lehigh Southwest Cement Company
2300 Clayton Rd Ste 300
Concord CA 94520
972 653-5500

(P-10795)
LIVINGSTONS CONCRETE SVC INC (PA)
5416 Roseville Rd, North Highlands
(95660-5097)
PHONE..................................916 334-4313
Patricia Henley, *President*

Edith Livingston, *Corp Secy*
Ted Henley, *Vice Pres*
Larry Livingston, *Principal*
Michael Livingston, *Principal*
EMP: 24
SALES (est): 13.7MM Privately Held
WEB: www.livingstonsconcrete.com
SIC: 3273 Ready-mixed concrete

(P-10796)
LIVINGSTONS CONCRETE SVC INC
Also Called: Plant 1
5416 Roseville Rd, North Highlands
(95660-5097)
PHONE..................................916 334-4313
Terry Regan, *Branch Mgr*
EMP: 27
SALES (corp-wide): 13.7MM Privately Held
WEB: www.livingstonsconcrete.com
SIC: 3273 Ready-mixed concrete
PA: Livingston's Concrete Service, Inc.
5416 Roseville Rd
North Highlands CA 95660
916 334-4313

(P-10797)
LIVINGSTONS CONCRETE SVC INC
Also Called: Plant 3
2915 Lesvos Ct, Lincoln (95648-9341)
PHONE..................................916 334-4313
Bill Redden, *Branch Mgr*
EMP: 24
SALES (corp-wide): 13.7MM Privately Held
WEB: www.livingstonsconcrete.com
SIC: 3273 Ready-mixed concrete
PA: Livingston's Concrete Service, Inc.
5416 Roseville Rd
North Highlands CA 95660
916 334-4313

(P-10798)
LYNCH READY MIX CONCRETE CO
Also Called: Mission Ready Mix
11011 Azahar St Ste 4, Ventura
(93004-1944)
PHONE..................................805 647-2817
Robert A Lynch, *President*
Laverne Lynch, *Vice Pres*
EMP: 12
SQ FT: 500
SALES (est): 2.4MM Privately Held
WEB: www.missionreadymix.com
SIC: 3273 Ready-mixed concrete

(P-10799)
M B I READY-MIX L L C
44 Central St, Colfax (95713-9006)
PHONE..................................530 346-2432
Paul Manuel, *Principal*
Kellye Manuel,
Matthew Melugin,
James Milhous,
Gary Smith,
EMP: 20
SALES (est): 1.7MM Privately Held
SIC: 3273 Ready-mixed concrete

(P-10800)
MATHEWS READY MIX LLC
Also Called: Mathews Readymix
249 Lamon St, Yuba City (95991-4200)
P.O. Box 749, Marysville (95901-0020)
PHONE..................................530 671-2400
Lee Cooper, *Manager*
EMP: 20
SALES (corp-wide): 1.3B Publicly Held
WEB: www.eaglematerials.com
SIC: 3273 Ready-mixed concrete
HQ: Mathews Ready Mix Llc
4711 Hammonton Rd
Marysville CA 95901
530 749-6525

(P-10801)
MATHEWS READYMIX INC
1619 Skyway, Chico (95928)
PHONE..................................530 893-8856
Chad Christee, *Branch Mgr*
EMP: 12
SQ FT: 4,780

SALES (est): 1MM Privately Held
SIC: 3273 Ready-mixed concrete

(P-10802)
METRO READY MIX
1635 James Rd, Bakersfield (93308-9749)
P.O. Box 80487 (93380-0487)
PHONE..................................661 829-7851
Corky Graviss, *Owner*
EMP: 11
SALES (est): 1.4MM Privately Held
SIC: 3273 Ready-mixed concrete

(P-10803)
MIX GARDEN INC
1083 Vine St, Healdsburg (95448-4830)
PHONE..................................707 433-4327
Michael J Kopetsky, *Principal*
EMP: 10
SALES (est): 1MM Privately Held
SIC: 3273 Ready-mixed concrete

(P-10804)
NATIONAL CEMENT CO CAL INC
Also Called: Lebec - Ncc CA Cement Company
5 Miles East Of I 5 Ofc H, Lebec (93243)
PHONE..................................661 248-6733
Gerardo Valds, *Branch Mgr*
EMP: 14
SALES (corp-wide): 484.9MM Privately Held
SIC: 3273 Ready-mixed concrete
HQ: National Cement Company Of California, Inc.
15821 Ventura Blvd # 475
Encino CA 91436
818 728-5200

(P-10805)
NATIONAL CEMENT CO CAL INC (DH)
15821 Ventura Blvd # 475, Encino
(91436-2935)
PHONE..................................818 728-5200
Steven Weiss, *President*
Pragati Kapoor, *CFO*
Dominique Bidet, *Treasurer*
▲ **EMP: 34**
SQ FT: 12,000
SALES (est): 68MM
SALES (corp-wide): 484.9MM Privately Held
SIC: 3273 3241 Ready-mixed concrete;
cement, hydraulic
HQ: National Cement Company, Inc.
15821 Ventura Blvd # 475
Encino CA 91436
818 728-5200

(P-10806)
NATIONAL READY MIXED CON CO
4549 Brazil St, Los Angeles (90039-1001)
PHONE..................................323 245-5539
Bob McFarlane, *Branch Mgr*
EMP: 11
SALES (corp-wide): 484.9MM Privately Held
SIC: 3273 Ready-mixed concrete
HQ: National Ready Mixed Concrete Co
15821 Ventura Blvd # 475
Encino CA 91436
818 728-5200

(P-10807)
NATIONAL READY MIXED CON CO
6969 Deering Ave, Canoga Park
(91303-2171)
PHONE..................................818 884-0893
Mike Randolph, *Manager*
EMP: 11
SALES (corp-wide): 484.9MM Privately Held
SIC: 3273 Ready-mixed concrete
HQ: National Ready Mixed Concrete Co
15821 Ventura Blvd # 475
Encino CA 91436
818 728-5200

(P-10808)
NATIONAL READY MIXED CON CO (DH)
15821 Ventura Blvd # 475, Encino
(91436-4778)
PHONE..................................818 728-5200
Tim Toland, *CEO*
Don Unmacht, *Vice Pres*
Helen Giampietro, *Transportation*
▲ **EMP: 20**
SQ FT: 40,000
SALES (est): 32.4MM
SALES (corp-wide): 484.9MM Privately Held
SIC: 3273 Ready-mixed concrete
HQ: National Cement Company Of California, Inc.
15821 Ventura Blvd # 475
Encino CA 91436
818 728-5200

(P-10809)
NATIONAL READY MIXED CON CO
11725 Artesia Blvd, Artesia (90701-3850)
PHONE..................................562 865-6211
Sher Cowan, *Branch Mgr*
Sam Hild, *General Mgr*
EMP: 11
SALES (corp-wide): 484.9MM Privately Held
SIC: 3273 Ready-mixed concrete
HQ: National Ready Mixed Concrete Co
15821 Ventura Blvd # 475
Encino CA 91436
818 728-5200

(P-10810)
NAVAJO CONCRETE INC
Also Called: Navajo Rock & Block
2484 Ramada Dr, Paso Robles
(93446-3949)
P.O. Box 117, Templeton (93465-0117)
PHONE..................................805 238-0955
Fax: 805 238-0140
EMP: 15
SQ FT: 144
SALES (est): 1.8MM Privately Held
SIC: 3273

(P-10811)
NORCAL RECYCLED ROCK AGGREGATE (PA)
291a Shell Ln, Willits (95490-4520)
P.O. Box 2088, Ukiah (95482-2088)
PHONE..................................707 459-9636
Frank Dutra, *President*
EMP: 11
SALES (est): 1.7MM Privately Held
SIC: 3273 Ready-mixed concrete

(P-10812)
P & L CONCRETE PRODUCTS INC
1900 Roosevelt Ave, Escalon
(95320-1763)
PHONE..................................209 838-1448
Jeff Francis, *President*
Arlene Francis, *Vice Pres*
EMP: 22
SQ FT: 1,500
SALES (est): 4.3MM Privately Held
WEB: www.plconcrete.net
SIC: 3273 Ready-mixed concrete

(P-10813)
PACIFIC AGGREGATES INC
28251 Lake St, Lake Elsinore
(92530-1635)
PHONE..................................951 245-2460
Kai Chin, *CEO*
Dale Kline, *Vice Pres*
Kim Chan, *Controller*
Mike Garcia, *Prdtn Mgr*
▲ **EMP: 75**
SQ FT: 1,000
SALES (est): 12.6MM
SALES (corp-wide): 893.5MM Privately Held
WEB: www.castlecooke.net
SIC: 3273 Ready-mixed concrete
PA: Castle & Cooke, Inc.
1 Dole Dr
Westlake Village CA 91362

▲ = Import ▼=Export
◆ =Import/Export

(P-10814)
PLEASANTON READY MIX CONCRETE
Also Called: Pleasanton Readymix Concrete
3400 Boulder St, Pleasanton (94566-4769)
P.O. Box 879 (94566-0874)
PHONE.................................925 846-3226
Albert Riebli, *President*
John Santos, *Treasurer*
EMP: 15
SQ FT: 1,000
SALES (est): 4MM **Privately Held**
SIC: 3273 Ready-mixed concrete

(P-10815)
PUENTE READY MIX INC (PA)
209 N California Ave, City of Industry
(91744-4324)
P.O. Box 3345 (91744-0345)
PHONE..................................626 968-0711
Mark Keuning, *Ch of Bd*
Ronald A Biang, *President*
Rick Dachman, *Vice Pres*
Kevin Keuning, *Vice Pres*
Marcia Biang, *Admin Sec*
EMP: 23 **EST:** 1949
SQ FT: 5,000
SALES (est): 4.3MM **Privately Held**
SIC: 3273 Ready-mixed concrete

(P-10816)
RANCHO READY MIX
28251 Lake St, Lake Elsinore
(92530-1635)
PHONE.................................951 674-0488
William Summers, *President*
Mal Gatherer, *Corp Secy*
EMP: 50
SQ FT: 1,000
SALES (est): 12MM **Privately Held**
SIC: 3273 Ready-mixed concrete

(P-10817)
RC READYMIX CO INC
1227 Greenville Rd, Livermore
(94550-9299)
PHONE.................................925 449-7785
Rob Costa, *President*
Rob C0sta, *President*
EMP: 24 **EST:** 1998
SALES (est): 4.9MM **Privately Held**
SIC: 3273 Ready-mixed concrete

(P-10818)
RIGHT AWAY CONCRETE PMPG INC
401 Kennedy St, Oakland (94606-5321)
PHONE.................................510 536-1900
David Filipek, *Manager*
Jose Chacon, *Supervisor*
EMP: 30
SQ FT: 3,328
SALES (corp-wide): 1.5B **Publicly Held**
SIC: 3273 1771 Ready-mixed concrete;
concrete pumping
HQ: Right Away Concrete Pumping, Inc.
725 Julie Ann Way
Oakland CA 94621
-

(P-10819)
RMC PACIFIC MATERIALS INC
1544 Stanley Blvd, Pleasanton
(94566-6308)
P.O. Box 249 (94566-0836)
PHONE.................................925 846-2824
Rich Bier, *Plant Mgr*
Steve Powers, *Branch Mgr*
EMP: 42 **Privately Held**
SIC: 3273 3241 1442 Ready-mixed con-
crete; cement, hydraulic; construction
sand & gravel
HQ: Rmc Pacific Materials, Inc.
6601 Koll Center Pkwy
Pleasanton CA 94566
925 426-8787

(P-10820)
ROBAR ENTERPRISES INC (PA)
17671 Bear Valley Rd, Hesperia
(92345-4902)
PHONE.................................760 244-5456
Jonathan D Hove, *CEO*
Al Calvanico, *CFO*
Robert E Hove, *Chairman*

Sean McGill, *Branch Mgr*
Sherrie Short, *Admin Asst*
EMP: 150 **EST:** 1981
SQ FT: 26,000
SALES (est): 53.1MM **Privately Held**
WEB: www.robarenterprises.com
SIC: 3273 5051 3441 Ready-mixed con-
crete; steel; building components, struc-
tural steel

(P-10821)
ROBERTSONS DISTRIBUTORS INC
1990 N Hargrave St, Banning
(92220-7000)
PHONE.................................951 849-4766
Bill Lambert, *Manager*
EMP: 12
SALES (corp-wide): 3.7MM **Privately
Held**
WEB: www.robertsonshomedecor.com
SIC: 3273 Ready-mixed concrete
PA: Robertsons Distributors, Inc
18217 Parthenia St
Northridge CA 91325
818 701-0168

(P-10822)
ROBERTSONS RDY MIX LTD A CAL
2975 Hwy 18, Lake Arrowhead (92352)
P.O. Box 3600, Corona (92878-3600)
PHONE.................................909 337-7577
Carl Moore, *Manager*
EMP: 10 **Privately Held**
WEB: www.rrmca.com
SIC: 3273 Ready-mixed concrete
HQ: Robertson's Ready Mix, Ltd., A Califor-
nia Limited Partnership
200 S Main St Ste 200 # 200
Corona CA 92882
951 493-6500

(P-10823)
ROBERTSONS RDY MIX LTD A CAL
12203 Violet Rd, Adelanto (92301-2714)
PHONE.................................760 246-4000
Jim Konoske, *Manager*
EMP: 10 **Privately Held**
WEB: www.rrmca.com
SIC: 3273 5211 Ready-mixed con-
crete; cement; concrete pumping
HQ: Robertson's Ready Mix, Ltd., A Califor-
nia Limited Partnership
200 S Main St Ste 200 # 200
Corona CA 92882
951 493-6500

(P-10824)
ROBERTSONS READY MIX LTD (HQ)
200 S Main St Ste 200 # 200, Corona
(92882-2212)
P.O. Box 3600 (92878-3600)
PHONE.................................951 493-6500
Jon Troesh, *Partner*
Don Rubidoux, *General Mgr*
David Ruiz, *Info Tech Mgr*
Anthony Lunetta, *Software Dev*
Darrin Dragna, *Sales Staff*
▲ **EMP:** 85
SQ FT: 22,008
SALES (est): 616.7MM **Privately Held**
WEB: www.rrmca.com
SIC: 3273 3531 5032 2951 Ready-mixed
concrete; bituminous, cement & concrete
related products & equipment; asphalt
plant, including gravel-mix type; concrete
plants; asphalt mixture; paving mixtures;
concrete mixtures; asphalt paving mix-
tures & blocks; construction sand & gravel

(P-10825)
ROBERTSONS READY MIX LTD
2470 Pomona Blvd, Pomona (91768-3276)
PHONE.................................909 623-9185
Dan Hawley, *Area Spvr*
EMP: 30 **Privately Held**
WEB: www.rrmca.com
SIC: 3273 Ready-mixed concrete

HQ: Robertson's Ready Mix, Ltd., A California Limited Partnership
200 S Main St Ste 200 # 200
Corona CA 92882
951 493-6500

(P-10826)
ROBERTSONS READY MIX LTD
200 S Main St Ste 200 # 200, Corona
(92882-2212)
PHONE.................................800 834-7557
Robert Burmeister, *President*
EMP: 20 **Privately Held**
SIC: 3273 Ready-mixed concrete
HQ: Robertson's Ready Mix, Ltd., A Califor-
nia Limited Partnership
200 S Main St Ste 200 # 200
Corona CA 92882
951 493-6500

(P-10827)
ROBERTSONS READY MIX LTD
27401 3rd St, Highland (92346-4242)
PHONE.................................909 425-2930
Dennis Troesh, *President*
EMP: 28 **Privately Held**
SIC: 3273 Ready-mixed concrete
HQ: Robertson's Ready Mix, Ltd., A Califor-
nia Limited Partnership
200 S Main St Ste 200 # 200
Corona CA 92882
951 493-6500

(P-10828)
SERVICE ROCK PRODUCTS CORP
2820 E Main St, Barstow (92311-5882)
PHONE.................................760 252-1615
Vince Bommarito, *Manager*
EMP: 35 **Privately Held**
WEB: www.servicerock.com
SIC: 3273 Ready-mixed concrete
HQ: Service Rock Products Corporation
151 Cassia Way
Henderson NV 89014
702 798-0568

(P-10829)
SERVICE ROCK PRODUCTS CORP
7900 Moss Ave, California City
(93505-4311)
P.O. Box 3600, Corona (92878-3600)
PHONE.................................760 373-9140
Clark Monier, *Branch Mgr*
EMP: 30 **Privately Held**
WEB: www.servicerock.com
SIC: 3273 Ready-mixed concrete
HQ: Service Rock Products Corporation
151 Cassia Way
Henderson NV 89014
702 798-0568

(P-10830)
SERVICE ROCK PRODUCTS CORP
200 S Main St Ste 200 # 200, Corona
(92882-2212)
PHONE.................................760 245-7997
Alex Delgado, *Branch Mgr*
EMP: 12 **Privately Held**
WEB: www.servicerock.com
SIC: 3273 Ready-mixed concrete
HQ: Service Rock Products Corporation
151 Cassia Way
Henderson NV 89014
702 798-0568

(P-10831)
SERVICE ROCK PRODUCTS CORP
2157 W Inyokern Rd, Ridgecrest
(93555-8538)
PHONE.................................760 446-2606
George Vernaci, *Manager*
EMP: 51 **Privately Held**
WEB: www.servicerock.com
SIC: 3273 Ready-mixed concrete
HQ: Service Rock Products Corporation
151 Cassia Way
Henderson NV 89014
702 798-0568

(P-10832)
SERVICE ROCK PRODUCTS CORP
37790 75th St E, Palmdale (93552-4200)
PHONE.................................661 533-3443
Ron Pinion, *Manager*
EMP: 30 **Privately Held**
WEB: www.servicerock.com
SIC: 3273 5032 1442 Ready-mixed con-
crete; stone, crushed or broken; construc-
tion sand & gravel
HQ: Service Rock Products Corporation
151 Cassia Way
Henderson NV 89014
702 798-0568

(P-10833)
SHAMROCK MATERIALS INC (PA)
181 Lynch Creek Way # 201, Petaluma
(94954-2388)
P.O. Box 751300 (94975-1300)
PHONE.................................707 781-9000
Eugene B Ceccotti, *CEO*
Robert Bowen, *CFO*
Jeff Nehmens, *Vice Pres*
Tom Hunt, *Opers Mgr*
Joe Enes, *Manager*
▲ **EMP:** 25 **EST:** 1945
SQ FT: 5,000
SALES (est): 30.3MM **Privately Held**
WEB: www.shamrockmat.com
SIC: 3273 5211 Ready-mixed concrete;
lumber & other building materials

(P-10834)
SHAMROCK MATERIALS INC
Also Called: Shamrock Materials of Cotati
8150 Gravenstein Hwy, Cotati
(94931-4127)
PHONE.................................707 792-4695
Jorge Barjas, *Manager*
EMP: 15
SALES (corp-wide): 30.3MM **Privately
Held**
WEB: www.shamrockmat.com
SIC: 3273 Ready-mixed concrete
PA: Shamrock Materials, Inc.
181 Lynch Creek Way # 201
Petaluma CA 94954
707 781-9000

(P-10835)
SHAMROCK MATERIALS INC
Also Called: Shamrock Fireplace
548 Du Bois St, San Rafael (94901-3964)
P.O. Box 751300, Petaluma (94975-1300)
PHONE.................................415 455-1575
Mike Isetta, *Manager*
John Zimmerman, *Mktg Dir*
EMP: 29
SALES (corp-wide): 30.3MM **Privately
Held**
WEB: www.shamrockmat.com
SIC: 3273 Ready-mixed concrete
PA: Shamrock Materials, Inc.
181 Lynch Creek Way # 201
Petaluma CA 94954
707 781-9000

(P-10836)
SHAMROCK MATERIALS OF NOVATO
7552 Redwood Blvd, Novato (94945-2425)
P.O. Box 808044, Petaluma (94975-8044)
PHONE.................................415 892-1571
Eugene B Ceccotti, *CEO*
EMP: 15
SALES (est): 1.6MM
SALES (corp-wide): 30.3MM **Privately
Held**
WEB: www.shamrockmat.com
SIC: 3273 Ready-mixed concrete
PA: Shamrock Materials, Inc.
181 Lynch Creek Way # 201
Petaluma CA 94954
707 781-9000

(P-10837)
SIERRA-TAHOE READY MIX INC
1526 Emerald Bay Rd, South Lake Tahoe
(96150-6112)
PHONE.................................530 541-1877
Donald Wallace, *President*
William Santos, *Treasurer*

PRODUCTS & SVCS

EMP: 22
SQ FT: 2,000
SALES (est): 18.8MM **Privately Held**
SIC: 3273 Ready-mixed concrete

(P-10838)
SOUSA READY MIX LLC
Also Called: Siskiyou County Family Plng R
100 Upton Rd, Mount Shasta (96067-9169)
P.O. Box 157 (96067-0157)
PHONE..................................530 926-4485
Gregory Juell, *Mng Member*
EMP: 15 **EST:** 1976
SQ FT: 1,200
SALES: 1.7MM **Privately Held**
SIC: 3273 Ready-mixed concrete

(P-10839)
**SOUTH VALLEY MATERIALS
INC (DH)**
7673 N Ingram Ave Ste 101, Fresno
(93711-5854)
P.O. Box 26240 (93729-6240)
PHONE..................................559 277-7060
James G Brown, *President*
EMP: 60
SQ FT: 6,000
SALES (est): 9MM
SALES (corp-wide): 20.6B **Privately Held**
SIC: 3273 Ready-mixed concrete

(P-10840)
**SOUTH VALLEY MATERIALS
INC**
7761 Hanford Armona Rd, Hanford
(93230-9343)
P.O. Box 26240, Fresno (93729-6240)
PHONE..................................559 582-0532
David Vickers, *Branch Mgr*
EMP: 36
SALES (corp-wide): 20.6B **Privately Held**
SIC: 3273 Ready-mixed concrete
HQ: South Valley Materials, Inc.
7673 N Ingram Ave Ste 101
Fresno CA 93711
559 277-7060

(P-10841)
**SPRAGUES ROCK AND SAND
COMPANY (PA)**
Also Called: Spragues Ready Mix
230 Longden Ave, Irwindale (91706-1328)
PHONE..................................626 445-2125
Carole Cotter, *Ch of Bd*
Michael Toland, *President*
Jerry Anctil, *CFO*
Gerald Anctil, *Treasurer*
Juli Paez, *Corp Secy*
EMP: 22 **EST:** 1953
SQ FT: 2,100
SALES (est): 7.2MM **Privately Held**
SIC: 3273 Ready-mixed concrete

(P-10842)
**SPRAGUES ROCK AND SAND
COMPANY**
Also Called: Spragues Ready Mix Concrete
5400 Bennett Rd, Simi Valley (93063-5135)
PHONE..................................805 522-7010
Michael Toland, *Manager*
EMP: 15
SALES (est): 1.6MM
SALES (corp-wide): 7.2MM **Privately Held**
SIC: 3273 Ready-mixed concrete
PA: Spragues' Rock And Sand Company
230 Longden Ave
Irwindale CA 91706
626 445-2125

(P-10843)
**STANDARD CONCRETE
PRODUCTS (HQ)**
Also Called: Associated Ready Mix Concrete
13550 Live Oak Ln, Baldwin Park
(91706-1318)
P.O. Box 15326, Santa Ana (92735-0326)
PHONE..................................310 829-4537
David Hummel, *President*
Brian Serra, *Vice Pres*
EMP: 20
SQ FT: 2,400

SALES (est): 13.1MM
SALES (corp-wide): 55.9MM **Privately
Held**
WEB: www.standard-concrete.com
SIC: 3273 Ready-mixed concrete
PA: A & A Ready Mixed Concrete, Inc.
4621 Teller Ave Ste 130
Newport Beach CA 92660
949 253-2800

(P-10844)
STATE READY MIX INC
3127 Los Angeles Ave, Oxnard
(93036-1010)
PHONE..................................805 647-2817
Robert Lynch, *President*
EMP: 30
SALES (corp-wide): 5.8MM **Privately
Held**
WEB: www.statereadymix.com
SIC: 3273 Ready-mixed concrete
PA: State Ready Mix, Inc.
1011 Azahar St Ste 1
Ventura CA 93004
805 647-2817

(P-10845)
STATE READY MIX INC (PA)
1011 Azahar St Ste 1, Ventura (93004)
PHONE..................................805 647-2817
Russell Cochran, *CEO*
Robert A Lynch, *President*
EMP: 40
SALES (est): 5.8MM **Privately Held**
WEB: www.statereadymix.com
SIC: 3273 Ready-mixed concrete

(P-10846)
STEVE ROCK & READY MIX
5044 Osgood Way, Fair Oaks
(95628-5272)
P.O. Box 1764 (95628-1764)
PHONE..................................916 966-1600
Steve Boblitt, *Owner*
EMP: 10
SALES: 950K **Privately Held**
SIC: 3273 4212 5211 Ready-mixed con-
crete; local trucking, without storage; con-
crete & cinder block

(P-10847)
**SUPERIOR READY MIX
CONCRETE LP**
Also Called: Srm Contracting & Paving
7192 Mission Gorge Rd, San Diego
(92120-1131)
PHONE..................................619 265-0955
Brent Cooper, *Branch Mgr*
EMP: 50
SALES (corp-wide): 205.2MM **Privately
Held**
WEB: www.superiorrm.com
SIC: 3273 Ready-mixed concrete
PA: Superior Ready Mix Concrete L.P.
1508 Mission Rd
Escondido CA 92029
760 745-0556

(P-10848)
**SUPERIOR READY MIX
CONCRETE LP**
Also Called: Canyon Rock & Asphalt
7500 Mission Gorge Rd, San Diego
(92120-1304)
PHONE..................................619 265-0296
Tracy Mall, *Manager*
EMP: 45
SALES (corp-wide): 205.2MM **Privately
Held**
WEB: www.superiorrm.com
SIC: 3273 Ready-mixed concrete
PA: Superior Ready Mix Concrete L.P.
1508 Mission Rd
Escondido CA 92029
760 745-0556

(P-10849)
**SUPERIOR READY MIX
CONCRETE LP**
802 E Main St, El Centro (92243-9474)
P.O. Box 400 (92244-0400)
PHONE..................................760 352-4341
Donald Lee, *Branch Mgr*
EMP: 30

SALES (corp-wide): 205.2MM **Privately
Held**
SIC: 3273 Ready-mixed concrete
PA: Superior Ready Mix Concrete L.P.
1508 Mission Rd
Escondido CA 92029
760 745-0556

(P-10850)
**SUPERIOR READY MIX
CONCRETE LP**
Also Called: American Ready Mix
1508 W Mission St, Escondido (92029)
PHONE..................................760 728-1128
Greg Sage, *Manager*
EMP: 15
SALES (corp-wide): 205.2MM **Privately
Held**
WEB: www.superiorrm.com
SIC: 3273 1442 Ready-mixed concrete;
construction sand & gravel
PA: Superior Ready Mix Concrete L.P.
1508 Mission Rd
Escondido CA 92029
760 745-0556

(P-10851)
**SUPERIOR READY MIX
CONCRETE LP**
24635 Temescal Canyon Rd, Corona
(92883-5422)
PHONE..................................951 277-3553
Justine Moss, *Branch Mgr*
EMP: 45
SALES (corp-wide): 205.2MM **Privately
Held**
WEB: www.superiorrm.com
SIC: 3273 Ready-mixed concrete
PA: Superior Ready Mix Concrete L.P.
1508 Mission Rd
Escondido CA 92029
760 745-0556

(P-10852)
**SUPERIOR READY MIX
CONCRETE LP (PA)**
Also Called: Southland Ready Mix Concrete
1508 Mission Rd, Escondido (92029-1194)
PHONE..................................760 745-0556
Donald Lee, *Partner*
Paul Brouwer, *Technical Mgr*
Richard Brouwer, *Opers Mgr*
John Knieff, *Sales Staff*
Dennis Spicuzza, *Sales Staff*
EMP: 50
SQ FT: 3,000
SALES (est): 205.2MM **Privately Held**
WEB: www.superiorrm.com
SIC: 3273 1611 5032 Ready-mixed con-
crete; surfacing & paving; gravel; sand,
construction

(P-10853)
**SUPERIOR READY MIX
CONCRETE LP**
Also Called: Hemet Ready Mix
1130 N State St, Hemet (92543-1510)
PHONE..................................951 658-9225
Wayne Heckerman, *Principal*
EMP: 40
SALES (corp-wide): 205.2MM **Privately
Held**
WEB: www.superiorrm.com
SIC: 3273 5211 Ready-mixed concrete;
masonry materials & supplies
PA: Superior Ready Mix Concrete L.P.
1508 Mission Rd
Escondido CA 92029
760 745-0556

(P-10854)
**SUPERIOR READY MIX
CONCRETE LP**
Also Called: TTT Concrete
12494 Highway 67, Lakeside (92040-1133)
PHONE..................................619 443-7510
Jerry Anderson, *Manager*
EMP: 40
SQ FT: 3,200
SALES (corp-wide): 205.2MM **Privately
Held**
WEB: www.superiorrm.com
SIC: 3273 Ready-mixed concrete

PA: Superior Ready Mix Concrete L.P.
1508 Mission Rd
Escondido CA 92029
760 745-0556

(P-10855)
**SUPERIOR READY MIX
CONCRETE LP**
72270 Varner Rd, Thousand Palms
(92276-3341)
PHONE..................................760 343-3418
Mark Higgins, *Manager*
EMP: 30
SALES (corp-wide): 205.2MM **Privately
Held**
WEB: www.superiorrm.com
SIC: 3273 Ready-mixed concrete
PA: Superior Ready Mix Concrete L.P.
1508 Mission Rd
Escondido CA 92029
760 745-0556

(P-10856)
TEICHERT INC (PA)
3500 American River Dr, Sacramento
(95864-5802)
P.O. Box 15002 (95851-0002)
PHONE..................................916 484-3011
Judson T Riggs, *President*
Louis V Riggs, *Ch of Bd*
Narendra M Pathipati, *CFO*
Clark Hulbert, *Vice Pres*
Anne S Haslam, *Admin Sec*
▲ **EMP:** 213 **EST:** 1887
SALES (est): 784MM **Privately Held**
WEB: www.teichert.com
SIC: 3273 5032 1611 1442 Ready-mixed
concrete; brick, stone & related material;
highway & street construction; construc-
tion sand & gravel; single-family housing
construction; air ducts, sheet metal

(P-10857)
TROESH READYMIX INC
2280 Hutton Rd, Nipomo (93444-9448)
PHONE..................................805 928-3764
Steve Troesh, *President*
Renee Troesh, *Vice Pres*
EMP: 70
SALES (est): 8.7MM **Privately Held**
SIC: 3273 Ready-mixed concrete

(P-10858)
US CONCRETE INC
Also Called: Westside Concrete Materials
755 Stockton Ave, San Jose (95126-1839)
PHONE..................................408 947-8606
Dave Perry, *Branch Mgr*
EMP: 13
SALES (corp-wide): 1.5B **Publicly Held**
SIC: 3273 Ready-mixed concrete
PA: U.S. Concrete, Inc.
331 N Main St
Euless TX 76039
817 835-4105

(P-10859)
VIKING READY MIX CO INC
Also Called: Glendale Ready-Mixed Concrete
4549 Brazil St, Los Angeles (90039-1001)
PHONE..................................818 243-4243
Joe Perez, *Branch Mgr*
Jason Colley, *Plant Mgr*
EMP: 24
SALES (corp-wide): 484.9MM **Privately
Held**
SIC: 3273 Ready-mixed concrete
HQ: Viking Ready Mix Co., Inc.
3664 W Ashlan Ave
Fresno CA 93722
559 225-3667

(P-10860)
VIKING READY MIX CO INC
4988 Firestone Blvd, South Gate
(90280-3544)
PHONE..................................323 564-1866
Gary Hill, *Manager*
EMP: 21
SALES (corp-wide): 484.9MM **Privately
Held**
SIC: 3273 Ready-mixed concrete
HQ: Viking Ready Mix Co., Inc.
3664 W Ashlan Ave
Fresno CA 93722
559 225-3667

▲ = Import ▼=Export
◆ =Import/Export

(P-10861)
VIKING READY MIX CO INC
1641 Tollhouse, Clovis (93611)
P.O. Box 9129, Fresno (93790-9129)
PHONE.................................559 225-3667
Charlie Wensley, *Manager*
EMP: 21
SQ FT: 5,984
SALES (corp-wide): 484.9MM **Privately Held**
SIC: 3273 Ready-mixed concrete
HQ: Viking Ready Mix Co., Inc.
 3664 W Ashlan Ave
 Fresno CA 93722
 559 225-3667

(P-10862)
VIKING READY MIX CO INC
12100 11th Ave, Hanford (93230-9523)
PHONE.................................559 344-7931
Don Unmacht, *Manager*
EMP: 15
SALES (corp-wide): 484.9MM **Privately Held**
SIC: 3273 Ready-mixed concrete
HQ: Viking Ready Mix Co., Inc.
 3664 W Ashlan Ave
 Fresno CA 93722
 559 225-3667

(P-10863)
VIKING READY MIX CO INC
11725 Artesia Blvd, Artesia (90701-3850)
PHONE.................................562 865-6211
Sher Cowan, *Manager*
EMP: 20
SQ FT: 2,151
SALES (corp-wide): 484.9MM **Privately Held**
SIC: 3273 Ready-mixed concrete
HQ: Viking Ready Mix Co., Inc.
 3664 W Ashlan Ave
 Fresno CA 93722
 559 225-3667

(P-10864)
VIKING READY MIX CO INC
15203 Oxnard St, Van Nuys (91411-2617)
PHONE.................................818 786-2210
Richard Vowman, *Manager*
EMP: 20
SALES (corp-wide): 484.9MM **Privately Held**
SIC: 3273 Ready-mixed concrete
HQ: Viking Ready Mix Co., Inc.
 3664 W Ashlan Ave
 Fresno CA 93722
 559 225-3667

(P-10865)
VIKING READY MIX CO INC
Also Called: Skyline Concrete
9010 Norris Ave, Sun Valley (91352-2617)
PHONE.................................818 768-0050
Michael Randauf, *Manager*
EMP: 30
SALES (corp-wide): 484.9MM **Privately Held**
SIC: 3273 Ready-mixed concrete
HQ: Viking Ready Mix Co., Inc.
 3664 W Ashlan Ave
 Fresno CA 93722
 559 225-3667

(P-10866)
VIKING READY MIX CO INC
Also Called: National Ready Mix
2620 Buena Vista St, Duarte (91010-3338)
PHONE.................................626 303-7755
Sergio Dalenduela, *Manager*
EMP: 32
SALES (corp-wide): 484.9MM **Privately Held**
SIC: 3273 5211 Ready-mixed concrete; cement
HQ: Viking Ready Mix Co., Inc.
 3664 W Ashlan Ave
 Fresno CA 93722
 559 225-3667

(P-10867)
VIKING READY MIX CO INC
Also Called: Skyline Concrete
6969 Deering Ave, Canoga Park (91303-2171)
PHONE.................................818 884-0893

Mike Randolph, *Manager*
EMP: 20
SALES (corp-wide): 484.9MM **Privately Held**
SIC: 3273 Ready-mixed concrete
HQ: Viking Ready Mix Co., Inc.
 3664 W Ashlan Ave
 Fresno CA 93722
 559 225-3667

(P-10868)
VULCAN MATERIALS CO
849 W Washington Ave, Escondido (92025-1634)
PHONE.................................760 737-3486
A F Gerstell, *President*
EMP: 50
SALES (est): 5.2MM **Publicly Held**
WEB: www.calmat.com
SIC: 3273 Ready-mixed concrete
HQ: Calmat Co.
 500 N Brand Blvd Ste 500 # 500
 Glendale CA 91203
 818 553-8821

(P-10869)
VULCAN MATERIALS COMPANY
7522 Pso De La Fnte Nrte, San Diego (92154-5704)
PHONE.................................619 661-1088
EMP: 19 **Publicly Held**
SIC: 3273 Ready-mixed concrete
PA: Vulcan Materials Company
 1200 Urban Center Dr
 Vestavia AL 35242

(P-10870)
VULCAN MATERIALS COMPANY
16005 E Foothill Blvd, Irwindale (91702-2813)
PHONE.................................626 334-4913
Mitchell Clark, *Manager*
Jay Carter, *Sales Staff*
Rosemary Luna, *Sales Staff*
EMP: 13 **Publicly Held**
SIC: 3273 Ready-mixed concrete
PA: Vulcan Materials Company
 1200 Urban Center Dr
 Vestavia AL 35242

(P-10871)
VULCAN MATERIALS COMPANY
500 N Brand Blvd Ste 500 # 500, Glendale (91203-3319)
PHONE.................................818 241-7356
Tom Cathey, *Sales Staff*
EMP: 16 **Publicly Held**
SIC: 3273 Ready-mixed concrete
PA: Vulcan Materials Company
 1200 Urban Center Dr
 Vestavia AL 35242

(P-10872)
WERNER CORPORATION
Also Called: Foster Sand & Gravel
25050 Maitri Rd, Corona (92883-5105)
PHONE.................................951 277-4586
Mark Miller, *Manager*
EMP: 15
SALES (corp-wide): 8.6MM **Privately Held**
SIC: 3273 Ready-mixed concrete
PA: Werner Corporation
 25555 Maitri Rd
 Corona CA 92883
 951 277-3900

(P-10873)
WESTERN READY MIX CONCRETE CO (PA)
Gyle Rd, Willows (95988)
P.O. Box 770 (95988-0770)
PHONE.................................530 934-2185
James B Hill, *President*
EMP: 35
SQ FT: 1,000
SALES (est): 4.8MM **Privately Held**
SIC: 3273 5211 Ready-mixed concrete; sand & gravel

(P-10874)
YREKA TRANSIT MIX CONCRETE
126 Schantz Rd, Yreka (96097-9556)
PHONE.................................530 842-4351
Darren Rose, *President*
EMP: 12
SQ FT: 2,300
SALES: 1MM **Privately Held**
SIC: 3273 Ready-mixed concrete

3274 Lime

(P-10875)
LHOIST NORTH AMERICA ARIZ INC
Also Called: Industry Terminal Us31
14931 Salt Lake Ave, City of Industry (91746-3115)
PHONE.................................626 336-4578
Emilio Asence, *Terminal Mgr*
Antoine Riguelle, *Vice Pres*
Laurent Yvon, *Vice Pres*
Didier Lesueur, *Research*
Greg Littleton, *Plant Mgr*
EMP: 10
SQ FT: 80,529
SALES (corp-wide): 2.6MM **Privately Held**
SIC: 3274 5032 Lime; lime building products
HQ: Lhoist North America Of Arizona, Inc.
 5600 Clearfork Main St
 Fort Worth TX 76109
 817 732-8164

3275 Gypsum Prdts

(P-10876)
FLANNERY INC (PA)
300 Parkside Dr, San Fernando (91340-3035)
PHONE.................................818 837-7585
Barry A Rutherford, *President*
EMP: 10
SQ FT: 21,000
SALES (est): 2.1MM **Privately Held**
WEB: www.flannerytrim.com
SIC: 3275 5072 Plaster & plasterboard, gypsum; miscellaneous fasteners

(P-10877)
GEORGIA-PACIFIC LLC
801 Minaker Dr, Antioch (94509-2134)
P.O. Box 460 (94509-0511)
PHONE.................................925 757-2870
Kurt Betty, *Opers-Prdtn-Mfg*
EMP: 105
SALES (corp-wide): 40.6B **Privately Held**
WEB: www.gp.com
SIC: 3275 Wallboard, gypsum
HQ: Georgia-Pacific Llc
 133 Peachtree St Nw
 Atlanta GA 30303
 404 652-4000

(P-10878)
GEORGIA-PACIFIC LLC
1401 W Pier D St, Long Beach (90802-1025)
P.O. Box 337350, North Las Vegas NV (89033-7350)
PHONE.................................562 435-7094
Scott Mc Donald, *Sales Mgr*
Jimmie Kingston, *Principal*
EMP: 20
SALES (corp-wide): 40.6B **Privately Held**
WEB: www.gp.com
SIC: 3275 Wallboard, gypsum
HQ: Georgia-Pacific Llc
 133 Peachtree St Nw
 Atlanta GA 30303
 404 652-4000

(P-10879)
HACKER INDUSTRIES INC (PA)
1600 Newport Dr 275, Newport Beach (92660)
P.O. Box 5918 (92662-5918)
PHONE.................................949 729-3101
Wesley D Hacker, *President*
Kerry V Hacker, *Vice Pres*

Christina Eater, *Marketing Staff*
Christy Desalvo, *Sales Staff*
Carlos Martinez, *Manager*
▲ **EMP:** 11
SALES: 2.9MM **Privately Held**
WEB: www.hackerindustries.com
SIC: 3275 Cement, keene's

(P-10880)
NEW NGC INC
1850 Pier B St, Long Beach (90813-2604)
P.O. Box 1888 (90801-1888)
PHONE.................................562 435-4465
Tim Fout, *Manager*
EMP: 120
SALES (corp-wide): 723.5MM **Privately Held**
WEB: www.natgyp.com
SIC: 3275 Gypsum products
HQ: New Ngc, Inc.
 2001 Rexford Rd
 Charlotte NC 28211
 -

(P-10881)
PABCO BUILDING PRODUCTS LLC
Also Called: Pabco Gypsum
37851 Cherry St, Newark (94560-4348)
P.O. Box 405 (94560-0405)
PHONE.................................510 792-9555
Charlie Coleman, *Manager*
EMP: 90
SALES (corp-wide): 1.5B **Privately Held**
SIC: 3275 Gypsum products
HQ: Pabco Building Products, Llc
 10600 White Rock Rd # 100
 Rancho Cordova CA 95670
 510 792-1577

(P-10882)
PABCO BUILDING PRODUCTS LLC
37849 Cherry St, Newark (94560-4348)
PHONE.................................510 792-1577
Ryan Lucchetti, *President*
EMP: 20
SALES (corp-wide): 1.5B **Privately Held**
SIC: 3275 3251 3259 Gypsum products; brick clay: common face, glazed, vitrified or hollow; architectural terra cotta
HQ: Pabco Building Products, Llc
 10600 White Rock Rd # 100
 Rancho Cordova CA 95670
 510 792-1577

(P-10883)
PABCO BUILDING PRODUCTS LLC (HQ)
10600 White Rock Rd # 100, Rancho Cordova (95670-6293)
PHONE.................................510 792-1577
Ryan Lucchetti, *President*
Brian Hobdy, *CFO*
Jack Haarlander, *Bd of Directors*
Alfred Mueller, *Bd of Directors*
Larry Solari, *Bd of Directors*
▲ **EMP:** 20
SALES (est): 211.6MM
SALES (corp-wide): 1.5B **Privately Held**
SIC: 3275 3251 3259 Gypsum products; brick clay: common face, glazed, vitrified or hollow; architectural terra cotta
PA: Pacific Coast Building Products, Inc.
 10600 White Rock Rd # 100
 Rancho Cordova CA 95670
 916 631-6500

(P-10884)
PABCO BUILDING PRODUCTS LLC
Also Called: Pabco Paper
4460 Pacific Blvd, Vernon (90058-2206)
PHONE.................................323 581-6113
Mike Willoughby, *Branch Mgr*
Kristin Martin, *Associate*
EMP: 75
SALES (corp-wide): 1.5B **Privately Held**
SIC: 3275 Gypsum products
HQ: Pabco Building Products, Llc
 10600 White Rock Rd # 100
 Rancho Cordova CA 95670
 510 792-1577

PRODUCTS & SVCS

(P-10885)
PACIFIC COAST SUPPLY LLC
Also Called: Pacific Supply
30158 Road 68, Visalia (93291-9586)
P.O. Box 1429 (93279-1429)
PHONE..................559 651-2185
Kevin Viera, *Branch Mgr*
EMP: 25
SALES (corp-wide): 1.5B **Privately Held**
SIC: 3275 3272 2952 5211 Wallboard, gypsum; concrete products; asphalt felts & coatings; lumber & other building materials
HQ: Pacific Coast Supply, Llc
4290 Roseville Rd
North Highlands CA 95660
916 971-2301

(P-10886)
UNITED STATES GYPSUM COMPANY
3810 Evan Hewes Hwy, Imperial (92251-9529)
P.O. Box 2450, El Centro (92244-2450)
PHONE..................760 358-3200
George Keelan, *Finance*
EMP: 300
SALES (corp-wide): 8.2B **Privately Held**
WEB: www.usg.com
SIC: 3275 Gypsum products
HQ: United States Gypsum Company
550 W Adams St Ste 1300
Chicago IL 60661
312 606-4000

3281 Cut Stone Prdts

(P-10887)
AMERICAN MARBLE & GRANITE CO (PA)
4084 Whittier Blvd, Los Angeles (90023-2527)
P.O. Box 23156 (90023-0156)
PHONE..................323 268-7979
John Vega, *President*
EMP: 14 EST: 1894
SQ FT: 600
SALES (est): 2.1MM **Privately Held**
SIC: 3281 5999 Tombstones, cut stone (not finishing or lettering only); tombstones

(P-10888)
AMERICAN MARBLE & ONYX CO INC
10321 S La Cienega Blvd, Los Angeles (90045-6109)
PHONE..................323 776-0900
Frederick Gherardi, *President*
Susan Gibbs, *Treasurer*
Steve Gherardi, *Vice Pres*
▲ EMP: 20
SQ FT: 30,000
SALES (est): 2.3MM **Privately Held**
WEB: www.amocmarble.com
SIC: 3281 1743 Marble, building: cut & shaped; marble installation, interior

(P-10889)
ANDREA ZEE CORPORATION
Also Called: Marble Palace
711 S San Joaquin St, Stockton (95203-3727)
PHONE..................209 462-1700
Ravi K Sharma, *President*
Christine George, *Vice Pres*
EMP: 16
SALES (est): 980K **Privately Held**
SIC: 3281 5023 Marble, building: cut & shaped; floor coverings

(P-10890)
ART CRAFT STATUARY INC
10441 Edes Ave, Oakland (94603-3015)
PHONE..................510 633-1411
Alipio Fabbri, *President*
Ivana Fabbri, *Vice Pres*
EMP: 40
SQ FT: 43,000
SALES: 2MM **Privately Held**
WEB: www.artcraftstatuary.com
SIC: 3281 3272 Cut stone & stone products; concrete products

(P-10891)
BARRYS CULTURED MARBLE INC
866 Teal Dr, Benicia (94510-1249)
PHONE..................707 745-3444
Barry Martin, *President*
Carole Martin, *Vice Pres*
EMP: 11
SALES (est): 1MM **Privately Held**
SIC: 3281 5211 1799 Cut stone & stone products; bathroom fixtures, equipment & supplies; counter top installation

(P-10892)
BEST MARBLE CO
2446 Teagarden St, San Leandro (94577-4336)
PHONE..................510 614-0155
Dwight Hammack, *Owner*
EMP: 25
SALES (est): 2.4MM **Privately Held**
SIC: 3281 2821 Marble, building: cut & shaped; granite, cut & shaped; plastics materials & resins

(P-10893)
BEST-WAY MARBLE & TILE CO INC
Also Called: Best Way Marble
5037 Telegraph Rd, Los Angeles (90022-4922)
PHONE..................323 266-6794
Shelley Herrera, *President*
Eddie Escarrega, *Project Mgr*
Carlos Vidaurri, *Supervisor*
◆ EMP: 28
SQ FT: 16,000
SALES (est): 3.2MM **Privately Held**
WEB: www.bestwaymarble.com
SIC: 3281 1743 Table tops, marble; marble installation, interior

(P-10894)
BETTY STILLWELL
Also Called: Baja Onyx & Marble Intl
524 W Calle Primera # 1004, San Ysidro (92173-2836)
PHONE..................619 428-2001
Bettye Stilwell, *Owner*
EMP: 55 EST: 1968
SQ FT: 700
SALES (est): 3.3MM **Privately Held**
SIC: 3281 1743 Furniture, cut stone; building stone products; terrazzo, tile, marble, mosaic work

(P-10895)
CARNEVALE & LOHR INC
6521 Clara St, Bell Gardens (90201-5634)
PHONE..................562 927-8311
Louie Carnevale, *CEO*
David Carnevale, *Principal*
Michael Carnevale, *Principal*
Edmund B Lohr IV, *Principal*
▲ EMP: 26
SALES (est): 3.6MM **Privately Held**
SIC: 3281 1741 Cut stone & stone products; marble masonry, exterior construction

(P-10896)
CENTRAL MARBLE SUPPLY INC
Also Called: Marble Works of San Diego
3754 Main St Ste B, San Diego (92113-3834)
PHONE..................619 595-1800
Charlene Butler, *President*
Michael Butler, *President*
EMP: 15
SQ FT: 5,000
SALES: 1MM **Privately Held**
WEB: www.marbleworkssandiego.com
SIC: 3281 1743 Marble, building: cut & shaped; marble installation, interior

(P-10897)
COAST FLAGSTONE CO
1810 Colorado Ave, Santa Monica (90404-3412)
PHONE..................310 829-4010
Timothy Wang, *Owner*
EMP: 70 EST: 2010
SALES (est): 4MM **Privately Held**
SIC: 3281 Flagstones

(P-10898)
COLD SPRING GRANITE COMPANY
Raymond Granite Div
36772 Road 606, Raymond (93653-9703)
PHONE..................559 689-3257
John Mansfield, *President*
EMP: 40
SQ FT: 4,000
SALES (corp-wide): 317MM **Privately Held**
WEB: www.granitemountainstonedesign.com
SIC: 3281 1411 5032 Granite, cut & shaped; granite, dimension-quarrying; brick, stone & related material
PA: Cold Spring Granite Company Inc
17482 Granite West Rd
Cold Spring MN 56320
320 685-3621

(P-10899)
COLD SPRING GRANITE COMPANY
802 W Pinedale Ave # 102, Fresno (93711-5771)
PHONE..................559 438-2100
Julio Orozco, *Branch Mgr*
EMP: 22
SALES (corp-wide): 317MM **Privately Held**
SIC: 3281 Dimension stone for buildings
PA: Cold Spring Granite Company Inc
17482 Granite West Rd
Cold Spring MN 56320
320 685-3621

(P-10900)
COLOR SKY INC
14439 Joanbridge St, Baldwin Park (91706-1747)
PHONE..................626 338-8565
Yuehua Zhao, *CEO*
Kuanghao Tseng,
EMP: 11
SALES: 452K **Privately Held**
SIC: 3281 Cut stone & stone products

(P-10901)
CORTIMA CO
83778 Avenue 45, Indio (92201-3310)
PHONE..................760 347-5535
Franz P Jevne III, *President*
EMP: 20
SQ FT: 23,000
SALES (est): 2.3MM **Privately Held**
WEB: www.cortima.com
SIC: 3281 Marble, building: cut & shaped; granite, cut & shaped

(P-10902)
DAVIS STONE INC
519 Venture St, Escondido (92029-1213)
PHONE..................760 745-7881
Ken Davis, *President*
Denise Davis, *CFO*
▲ EMP: 26
SQ FT: 9,000
SALES: 2.6MM **Privately Held**
WEB: www.davisstone.com
SIC: 3281 Table tops, marble

(P-10903)
DEJAGERS INC
45846 Flower St, Indio (92201-4606)
PHONE..................760 775-4755
Gordon Dejager, *President*
Darryl Williams, *Vice Pres*
EMP: 25
SALES (est): 2.2MM **Privately Held**
SIC: 3281 Granite, cut & shaped

(P-10904)
DEMILLE MARBLE & GRANITE INC
72091 Woburn Ct Ste D, Thousand Palms (92276-2317)
PHONE..................760 341-7525
Mark Demille, *President*
EMP: 30
SALES (est): 3.6MM **Privately Held**
WEB: www.demillemarble.com
SIC: 3281 1741 Marble, building: cut & shaped; marble masonry, exterior construction

(P-10905)
EMPORIUM DI SANARREY CORP
Also Called: Pietri Bersage Store Design
631 S East St, Anaheim (92805-4842)
P.O. Box 6219, Fullerton (92834-6219)
PHONE..................714 780-5474
Helenee Cruz, *Principal*
Clemente Cruz, *President*
EMP: 10
SALES: 526K **Privately Held**
SIC: 3281 Cut stone & stone products

(P-10906)
FOREMOST INTERIORS INC
2318 Gold River Rd, Rancho Cordova (95670-4413)
PHONE..................916 635-1423
Randall Mertes, *President*
Rose Mertes, *Admin Sec*
EMP: 30
SQ FT: 10,000
SALES (est): 4MM **Privately Held**
WEB: www.foremostinteriors.com
SIC: 3281 2434 1751 Marble, building: cut & shaped; wood kitchen cabinets; carpentry work

(P-10907)
GGF MARBLE & SUPPLY INC
1375 Franquette Ave Ste F, Concord (94520-7932)
PHONE..................925 676-8385
Gaspare Giorgio Fundaro, *President*
Gregory Markeil,
Vince Rizzuto,
◆ EMP: 15
SQ FT: 2,500
SALES (est): 1MM **Privately Held**
SIC: 3281 Furniture, cut stone

(P-10908)
GREEK MARBLE INC
1600 N San Fernando Rd, Los Angeles (90065-1262)
PHONE..................323 221-6624
Levon Gorlekian, *President*
▲ EMP: 10
SQ FT: 9,000
SALES: 900K **Privately Held**
SIC: 3281 Marble, building: cut & shaped; granite, cut & shaped

(P-10909)
HALABI INC (PA)
Also Called: Duracite
2100 Huntington Dr, Fairfield (94533-9731)
PHONE..................707 402-1600
Fadi M Halabi, *CEO*
George Marino, *CFO*
Lenna Geist, *Human Res Dir*
EMP: 137
SQ FT: 66,000
SALES (est): 102.8MM **Privately Held**
WEB: www.duracite.com
SIC: 3281 1799 Cut stone & stone products; counter top installation

(P-10910)
HANSON AGGRGTES MD-PACIFIC INC
Pine Hollow To Kaiser Rd, Clayton (94517)
P.O. Box 279 (94517-0279)
PHONE..................925 672-4955
Dave Autsen, *Manager*
EMP: 10
SALES (corp-wide): 20.6B **Privately Held**
SIC: 3281 3531 Cut stone & stone products; aggregate spreaders
HQ: Hanson Aggregates Mid-Pacific, Inc.
12667 Alcosta Blvd # 400
San Ramon CA

(P-10911)
HONOR LIFE MEDALLIONS
Also Called: Hlm
955 Park Center Dr, Vista (92081-8312)
PHONE..................760 727-8581
Randy Scott Willis, *CEO*
Roderick Geis, *COO*
July Willis, *Office Mgr*
Edelia Willis, *Admin Sec*
Mark Heddy, *Sales Mgr*
EMP: 12

▲ = Import ▼=Export
◆ =Import/Export

SALES (est): 684.6K
SALES (corp-wide): 10.1MM **Privately Held**
WEB: www.rayzist.com
SIC: **3281** Altars, cut stone
PA: Rayzist Photomask, Inc.
955 Park Center Dr
Vista CA 92081
760 727-8561

(P-10912)
KAMMERER ENTERPRISES INC
Also Called: American Marble
1280 N Melrose Dr, Vista (92083-3469)
PHONE..............................760 560-0550
William S Kammerer, *CEO*
Bill Kammerer, *President*
Karl Miethke, *Vice Pres*
▲ EMP: 100
SALES (est): 15.2MM **Privately Held**
WEB: www.amarble.com
SIC: **3281** Curbing, granite or stone

(P-10913)
L&S STONE LLC (DH)
Also Called: L & S Stone and Fireplace Shop
1370 Grand Ave Ste B, San Marcos
(92078-2404)
PHONE..............................760 736-3232
Chuck Baer, *President*
◆ EMP: 50
SQ FT: 35,000
SALES (est): 7.8MM **Privately Held**
WEB: www.lsfireplace.com
SIC: **3281** Cut stone & stone products
HQ: Eldorado Stone Llc
1370 Grand Ave Bldg B
San Marcos CA 92078
800 925-1491

(P-10914)
MARBLE CITY COMPANY INC
611 Taylor Way Ste 6, San Carlos
(94070-6305)
PHONE..............................650 802-8189
Andrei Gourji, *President*
Sarah Vilotti, *Business Dir*
▲ EMP: 12
SQ FT: 8,000
SALES (est): 1.6MM **Privately Held**
WEB: www.marblecityca.com
SIC: **3281** Table tops, marble

(P-10915)
MARBLE SHOP INC (PA)
180 Bliss Ave, Pittsburg (94565-4977)
PHONE..............................925 439-6910
Barbara Gutridge, *President*
EMP: 25
SQ FT: 7,800
SALES (est): 3.2MM **Privately Held**
SIC: **3281** Marble, building: cut & shaped;
granite, cut & shaped

(P-10916)
MOVA STONE INC
4361 Pell Dr Ste 100, Sacramento
(95838-2581)
PHONE..............................916 922-2080
Vasily Moskalets, *President*
EMP: 24
SQ FT: 11,000
SALES (est): 2.2MM **Privately Held**
SIC: **3281** Curbing, granite or stone

(P-10917)
MULHERIN MONUMENTAL INC
1000 S 2nd St, El Centro (92243-3448)
PHONE..............................760 353-7717
Joe Mulherin, *President*
Yolanda Mulherin, *Corp Secy*
EMP: 12
SALES: 1MM **Privately Held**
SIC: **3281** Monument or burial stone, cut &
shaped

(P-10918)
PAUL MERRILL COMPANY INC
350 W Central Ave # 141, Brea
(92821-3006)
PHONE..............................562 691-1871
Paul Merrill, *President*
Marlene Merrill, *Admin Sec*
EMP: 14
SALES (est): 1.1MM **Privately Held**
SIC: **3281** Granite, cut & shaped

(P-10919)
PAVESTONE LLC
27600 County Road 90, Winters
(95694-9003)
PHONE..............................530 795-4400
Wes May, *Manager*
Brad Hayes, *Plant Mgr*
Jeannie Del Toro, *Transptn Dir*
EMP: 50 **Privately Held**
WEB: www.pavestone.com
SIC: **3281** Paving blocks, cut stone
HQ: Pavestone, Llc
5 Concourse Pkwy Ste 1900
Atlanta GA 30328
404 926-3167

(P-10920)
PERMECO
1970 Walker St, La Verne (91750-5144)
P.O. Box 337 (91750-0337)
PHONE..............................909 599-9600
Mark Carson, *President*
Linn Childress, *Vice Pres*
▲ EMP: 12
SQ FT: 15,600
SALES (est): 2MM **Privately Held**
SIC: **3281** Granite, cut & shaped; marble,
building: cut & shaped

(P-10921)
PRECISION GRANITE USA INC
Also Called: Precision Granite Company
174 N Aspan Ave, Azusa (91702-4224)
P.O. Box 427, Whittier (90608-0427)
PHONE..............................562 696-8328
John De Leon, *President*
▲ EMP: 24
SQ FT: 11,904
SALES (est): 400K **Privately Held**
SIC: **3281** Granite, cut & shaped

(P-10922)
PRIME SURFACES INC
25111 Normandie Ave, Harbor City
(90710-2407)
P.O. Box 821 (90710-0821)
PHONE..............................310 448-2292
Chad M Benner, *President*
EMP: 10
SQ FT: 9,600
SALES (est): 1.1MM **Privately Held**
SIC: **3281** 5211 Cut stone & stone prod-
ucts; counter tops

(P-10923)
PROVENCE STONE
1040 Varian St, San Carlos (94070-5315)
PHONE..............................650 631-5600
Motaz Elias, *President*
▲ EMP: 11
SALES (est): 2MM **Privately Held**
WEB: www.provencestone.com
SIC: **3281** Marble, building: cut & shaped

(P-10924)
PYRAMID GRANITE & METALS INC
660 Superior St, Escondido (92029-1330)
PHONE..............................760 745-6309
Philip M Hoadley, *President*
Linda Forrest, *Vice Pres*
EMP: 24
SQ FT: 5,000
SALES (est): 2MM **Privately Held**
WEB: www.pyramidgranite.com
SIC: **3281** Granite, cut & shaped

(P-10925)
QORTSTONE INC
Also Called: Qrtstone
7733 Lemona Ave, Van Nuys (91405-1137)
PHONE..............................877 899-7678
Ani Vartabetian, *CEO*
Mina Marvavi, *Office Mgr*
▲ EMP: 11
SALES (est): 72.6K **Privately Held**
SIC: **3281** Cut stone & stone products

(P-10926)
QUALITY MARBLE & GRANITE INC
25 Hegenberger Pl, Oakland (94621-1301)
PHONE..............................510 635-0228
Byron Ho, *CEO*
Wennie Ho, *President*

EMP: 11
SALES (est): 1.5MM **Privately Held**
SIC: **3281** Cut stone & stone products

(P-10927)
RCS CUSTOM STONEWORKS
3280 Vine St Ste 201, Riverside
(92507-2610)
PHONE..............................714 309-0620
Anthony Beber, *Owner*
EMP: 12
SALES (est): 800K **Privately Held**
SIC: **3281** Granite, cut & shaped; marble,
building: cut & shaped

(P-10928)
REGAL CULTURED MARBLE INC
1239 E Franklin Ave, Pomona
(91766-5450)
P.O. Box 780534, Maspeth NY (11378-
0534)
PHONE..............................909 802-2388
Phillip K Black, *President*
David Sklar, *Vice Pres*
EMP: 50 EST: 1968
SQ FT: 12,000
SALES (est): 3.6MM **Privately Held**
SIC: **3281** 2821 Bathroom fixtures, cut
stone; plastics materials & resins

(P-10929)
RUGGERI MARBLE AND GRANITE INC
16001 S San Pedro St C, Gardena
(90248-2543)
PHONE..............................310 513-2155
Andre Ruggeri, *President*
Robert Ruggeri, *Treasurer*
Giovanna F MWC, *Office Mgr*
▲ EMP: 80
SQ FT: 6,650
SALES (est): 11.2MM **Privately Held**
WEB: www.ruggerimarble.com
SIC: **3281** 5032 Marble, building: cut &
shaped; granite, cut & shaped; ceramic
wall & floor tile

(P-10930)
SHARCAR ENTERPRISES INC
Also Called: Custom Marble & Onyx
201 Winmoore Way, Modesto
(95358-5743)
P.O. Box 581710 (95358-0030)
PHONE..............................209 531-2200
Carl Schenewark, *President*
Daryl Schenewark, *Treasurer*
Sharon Schenewark, *Admin Sec*
EMP: 70
SQ FT: 10,000
SALES (est): 9MM **Privately Held**
SIC: **3281** 1799 Bathroom fixtures, cut
stone; counter top installation

(P-10931)
SINOSOURCE INTL CO INC
230 Adrian Rd, Millbrae (94030-3103)
PHONE..............................650 697-6668
Ken Jiang, *President*
▲ EMP: 15
SALES (est): 2MM **Privately Held**
SIC: **3281** Urns, cut stone

(P-10932)
SOUTH BAY MARBLE INC (PA)
15745 E Alta Vista Way, San Jose
(95127-1736)
PHONE..............................650 594-4251
Bob Sutton, *President*
▲ EMP: 19 EST: 1978
SALES (est): 2.7MM **Privately Held**
SIC: **3281** Marble, building: cut & shaped;
building stone products; granite, cut &
shaped

(P-10933)
STANDRIDGE GRANITE CORPORATION
9437 Santa Fe Springs Rd, Santa Fe
Springs (90670-2684)
PHONE..............................562 946-6334
Deborah Deleon, *President*
Steven Piel, *Plant Mgr*
EMP: 30 EST: 1965
SQ FT: 24,000

SALES (est): 3.9MM **Privately Held**
WEB: www.standridgegranite.com
SIC: **3281** 1411 Granite, cut & shaped; di-
mension stone

(P-10934)
STONE MERCHANTS LLC
889 Linda Flora Dr, Los Angeles
(90049-1628)
PHONE..............................310 471-1815
Yogesh Anand, *CEO*
▲ EMP: 60 EST: 2008
SALES (est): 3.3MM **Privately Held**
SIC: **3281** Cut stone & stone products

(P-10935)
SUN MARBLE INC
Also Called: Sun Marble/Home Express
1300 Norman Ave, Santa Clara
(95054-2056)
PHONE..............................510 783-9900
Gloria You, *CEO*
Wen Lin Sheu, *President*
▲ EMP: 24
SQ FT: 7,000
SALES (est): 3.1MM **Privately Held**
SIC: **3281** Granite, cut & shaped; house-
hold articles, except furniture: cut stone

(P-10936)
SUPERIOR STONE PRODUCTS INC
923 E Arlee Pl, Anaheim (92805-5645)
PHONE..............................714 635-7775
Costandi Awadalla, *President*
EMP: 15 EST: 2014
SALES (est): 1.4MM **Privately Held**
SIC: **3281** Cut stone & stone products

(P-10937)
VENTURA GL INC
12595 Foothill Blvd, Sylmar (91342-5310)
PHONE..............................818 890-1886
John Ventura, *President*
EMP: 15
SQ FT: 8,000
SALES (est): 2MM **Privately Held**
SIC: **3281** 5032 Marble, building: cut &
shaped; marble building stone

(P-10938)
VETERANS EMPLOYMENT AGENCY INC
3906 Ginko Way, Sacramento
(95834-3833)
PHONE..............................650 245-0599
Irvin Goodwin, *CEO*
EMP: 12
SALES (est): 796.1K **Privately Held**
SIC: **3281** Cut stone & stone products

3291 Abrasive Prdts

(P-10939)
ABRASIVE WHEELS INC
17841 E Valley Blvd, City of Industry
(91744-5733)
PHONE..............................626 935-8800
Isidro Topete, *President*
EMP: 10
SQ FT: 10,000
SALES (est): 1.1MM **Privately Held**
WEB: www.abrasivewheels.com
SIC: **3291** 5085 Wheels, abrasive; abra-
sives

(P-10940)
ARROW ABRASIVE COMPANY INC
12033 1/2 Regentview Ave, Downey
(90241-5517)
PHONE..............................562 869-2282
Alan Bates, *President*
Linda Bates, *Treasurer*
Michael Bates, *Vice Pres*
EMP: 11
SQ FT: 5,000
SALES: 700K **Privately Held**
SIC: **3291** Wheels, grinding: artificial

(P-10941)
BUFF AND SHINE MFG INC
2139 E Del Amo Blvd, Rancho Dominguez
(90220-6301)
PHONE.................................310 886-5111
Richard Umbrell, *President*
Elizabeth Umbrell, *Vice Pres*
▲ EMP: 40
SQ FT: 25,792
SALES (est): 9.6MM **Privately Held**
WEB: www.buffandshine.com
SIC: 3291 Buffing or polishing wheels,
abrasive or nonabrasive

(P-10942)
CAPITOL STEEL PRODUCTS
Also Called: Ruben Ortiz
6331 Power Inn Rd Ste B, Sacramento
(95824-2353)
PHONE.................................916 383-3368
Ruben Ortiz, *General Mgr*
Bud Lindau, *Owner*
EMP: 11
SALES (est): 1.3MM **Privately Held**
SIC: 3291 Abrasive metal & steel products

(P-10943)
CARBIDE PRODUCTS CO INC
22711 S Western Ave, Torrance
(90501-4994)
PHONE.................................310 320-7910
Arthur E Johnson, *President*
Irene W Johnson, *Corp Secy*
Gary Johnson, *Vice Pres*
EMP: 10 EST: 1954
SQ FT: 4,000
SALES (est): 940K **Privately Held**
SIC: 3291 Tungsten carbide abrasive

(P-10944)
COLUMBIA STONE PRODUCTS
663 S Rancho Santa Fe Rd, San Marcos
(92078-3973)
PHONE.................................760 737-3215
Faruk Delener, *Principal*
▲ EMP: 12
SALES (est): 1.2MM **Privately Held**
SIC: 3291 Silicon carbide abrasive

(P-10945)
CRATEX MANUFACTURING CO INC
328 Encinitas Blvd # 200, Encinitas
(92024-8704)
PHONE.................................760 942-2877
Allen Mc Casland, *Chairman*
Ricker Mc Casland, *President*
Barbara Mc Casland, *Admin Sec*
Cheryl Abbott, *Human Res Mgr*
Ron Liesch, *Sales Staff*
▲ EMP: 75
SQ FT: 5,875
SALES (est): 12.1MM **Privately Held**
WEB: www.cratex.com
SIC: 3291 Wheels, grinding: artificial; abrasive buffs, bricks, cloth, paper, stones, etc.

(P-10946)
FALCON ABRASIVE MANUFACTURING
5490 Brooks St, Montclair (91763-4520)
P.O. Box 713, Walnut (91788-0713)
PHONE.................................909 598-3078
Steve De La Torre, *President*
Rosemarie De Latorre, *Corp Secy*
▼ EMP: 17
SQ FT: 6,900
SALES (est): 2.2MM **Privately Held**
WEB: www.falconabrasive.com
SIC: 3291 5085 Wheels, abrasive; industrial supplies

(P-10947)
JASON INCORPORATED
Jackson Lea Division
13006 Philadelphia St # 305, Whittier
(90601-4210)
PHONE.................................562 921-9821
Ron Locher, *Vice Pres*
EMP: 33
SQ FT: 30,000

SALES (corp-wide): 612.9MM **Publicly Held**
WEB: www.jasoninc.com
SIC: 3291 2273 3599 Buffing or polishing wheels, abrasive or nonabrasive; automobile floor coverings, except rubber or plastic; custom machinery
HQ: Jason Incorporated
833 E Michigan St Ste 900
Milwaukee WI 53202
414 277-9300

(P-10948)
JET ABRASIVES INC
Also Called: Jet & Western Abrasives
1891 E Miraloma Ave, Placentia
(92870-6707)
P.O. Box 58567, Los Angeles (90058-0567)
PHONE.................................323 588-1245
Barry Rothstein, *President*
Joy Demain, *Shareholder*
EMP: 33
SQ FT: 36,000
SALES (est): 3.3MM **Privately Held**
WEB: www.gritbiz.com
SIC: 3291 Abrasive products

(P-10949)
MAGNUM ABRASIVES INC
758 S Allen St, San Bernardino
(92408-2210)
PHONE.................................909 890-1100
Manuel Acuna, *President*
Richard Frenkel, *Vice Pres*
▲ EMP: 20
SQ FT: 13,400
SALES (est): 2.6MM **Privately Held**
WEB: www.magnumabrasives.com
SIC: 3291 5085 Abrasive products; abrasives

(P-10950)
MAVERICK ABRASIVES CORPORATION
4340 E Miraloma Ave, Anaheim
(92807-1886)
PHONE.................................714 854-9531
Rami Aryan, *President*
Gregory Becker, *Manager*
◆ EMP: 60
SQ FT: 15,000
SALES (est): 6.6MM **Privately Held**
WEB: www.maverickabrasives.com
SIC: 3291 Abrasive products

(P-10951)
MK TOOL AND ABRASIVE INC
4710 S Eastern Ave, Los Angeles
(90040-2913)
PHONE.................................562 776-8818
Olinda Kapila, *President*
Rajiv Kapila, *Vice Pres*
Pete Barton, *Sales Staff*
▲ EMP: 14
SQ FT: 15,000
SALES (est): 1.8MM **Privately Held**
SIC: 3291 3541 5251 Synthetic abrasives; abrasive buffs, bricks, cloth, paper, stones, etc.; machine tools, metal cutting type; builders' hardware

(P-10952)
PAC-COM INTERNATIONAL
13564 Larwin Cir, Santa Fe Springs
(90670-5031)
PHONE.................................562 903-3900
Sang Park, *President*
▲ EMP: 13
SALES (est): 1.3MM **Privately Held**
SIC: 3291 Abrasive products

(P-10953)
PEARLMAN ENTERPRISES INC (DH)
6210 Garfield Ave, Commerce
(90040-3613)
PHONE.................................800 969-5561
Daniel Davidenko, *CEO*
Eric Aguirre, *CFO*
John Waterworth, *CFO*
EMP: 215

SALES (est): 56.2MM
SALES (corp-wide): 12.8MM **Privately Held**
SIC: 3291 3843 3991 3421 Wheels, abrasive; abrasive points, wheels & disks, dental; brushes, household or industrial; razor blades & razors; fabricated structural metal
HQ: Pearlman Holdings, Inc.
3950 Steve Reynolds Blvd
Norcross GA 30093
800 458-6222

(P-10954)
SIMPSON MANUFACTURING CO INC
5151 S Airport Way, Stockton
(95206-3991)
PHONE.................................209 234-7775
David McDonald, *Manager*
Cory Peach, *Sr Software Eng*
Nancy Karr, *Credit Staff*
Ahmet Ogut, *Prdtn Mgr*
EMP: 350
SALES (corp-wide): 1B **Publicly Held**
SIC: 3291 Metallic abrasive
PA: Simpson Manufacturing Co., Inc.
5956 W Las Positas Blvd
Pleasanton CA 94588
925 560-9000

(P-10955)
SUPREME ABRASIVES
Also Called: Continental Machine Tool Co
1021 Fuller St, Santa Ana (92701-4212)
PHONE.................................949 250-8644
William W Taylor, *CEO*
Robert Longman, *Vice Pres*
▲ EMP: 19 EST: 1958
SQ FT: 20,000
SALES (est): 2.3MM **Privately Held**
SIC: 3291 Wheels, abrasive

(P-10956)
TECHNIFEX PRODUCTS LLC
25261 Rye Canyon Rd, Valencia
(91355-1203)
PHONE.................................661 294-3800
Montgomery C Lunde, *CEO*
Rockne J Hall, *Chairman*
Joe Ortiz, *Vice Pres*
Jim Sharits, *Vice Pres*
Sherry Ferguson, *Controller*
▲ EMP: 25
SALES (est): 4.3MM **Privately Held**
WEB: www.sensorytheatersystems.com
SIC: 3291 Steel wool

(P-10957)
TYFLONG INTERNATIONAL INC
606 Pena Dr, Davis (95618-7720)
P.O. Box 4208 (95617-4208)
PHONE.................................530 746-3001
Manyu LI, *President*
Sarah Liu, *CFO*
Martin Arata, *Vice Pres*
▲ EMP: 10
SQ FT: 8,000
SALES: 3MM **Privately Held**
WEB: www.tyflong.com
SIC: 3291 Abrasive products

(P-10958)
VIBRA FINISH CO (PA)
Also Called: Vibrahone
2220 Shasta Way, Simi Valley
(93065-1831)
PHONE.................................805 578-0033
Haskel Hall, *President*
Jerry Rindal, *Vice Pres*
▲ EMP: 20 EST: 1924
SQ FT: 41,000
SALES (est): 4MM **Privately Held**
WEB: www.vibrafinish.com
SIC: 3291 Abrasive products

(P-10959)
WESTERN ABRASIVES INC
4383 Fruitland Ave, Vernon (90058-3119)
PHONE.................................323 588-1245
EMP: 16
SQ FT: 36,000
SALES: 2MM **Privately Held**
SIC: 3291

(P-10960)
YEAGER ENTERPRISES CORP
Also Called: Pasco
7100 Village Dr, Buena Park (90621-2261)
PHONE.................................714 994-2040
Joseph O'Mera, *CEO*
David M Yeager, *President*
Joan F Yeager, *Vice Pres*
▲ EMP: 81
SQ FT: 55,000
SALES (est): 11.5MM **Privately Held**
SIC: 3291 Abrasive products

3292 Asbestos products

(P-10961)
FRANCO AMERICAN CORPORATION
Also Called: Franco American Textile
1051 Monterey Pass Rd, Monterey Park
(91754-3612)
PHONE.................................323 268-2345
Roland Jones, *President*
▲ EMP: 18
SALES (est): 2.6MM **Privately Held**
SIC: 3292 Asbestos textiles, except insulating material

(P-10962)
H2 ENVIRONMENTAL
13122 6th St, Chino (91710-4105)
PHONE.................................909 628-0369
Amy Disantiago, *Owner*
EMP: 14
SALES (est): 2.2MM **Privately Held**
SIC: 3292 1799 Asbestos products; asbestos removal & encapsulation

(P-10963)
LAMART CORPORATION
Also Called: Orcon Aerospace
2600 Central Ave Ste E, Union City
(94587-3187)
P.O. Box 2936, Douglas GA (31534-2936)
PHONE.................................510 489-8100
EMP: 110
SALES (corp-wide): 93.3MM **Privately Held**
SIC: 3292 3559 Blankets, insulating for aircraft asbestos; bag seaming & closing machines (sewing machinery)
PA: Lamart Corporation
16 Richmond St
Clifton NJ 07011
973 772-6262

(P-10964)
THERMOSTATIC INDUSTRIES INC
Also Called: T M O
9654 Hermosa Ave, Rancho Cucamonga
(91730-5812)
PHONE.................................323 277-0900
Alan M Goldman, *CEO*
Sanford Lathrop Jr, *President*
▲ EMP: 30
SQ FT: 1,500
SALES (est): 4.9MM **Privately Held**
WEB: www.thermostatic.com
SIC: 3292 Pipe covering (heat insulating material), except felt; asbestos textiles, except insulating material

3295 Minerals & Earths: Ground Or Treated

(P-10965)
3M COMPANY
18750 Minnesota Rd, Corona
(92881-4313)
PHONE.................................951 737-3441
Flees Peter, *Branch Mgr*
Michael Eskew, *Director*
Peter Flees, *Manager*
EMP: 150
SALES (corp-wide): 32.7B **Publicly Held**
WEB: www.mmm.com
SIC: 3295 2952 Roofing granules; asphalt felts & coatings

▲ = Import ▼=Export
◆ =Import/Export

PA: 3m Company
3m Center
Saint Paul MN 55144
651 733-1110

(P-10966)
A&M PRODUCTS MANUFACTURING CO (HQ)
1221 Broadway Ste 51, Oakland
(94612-1837)
PHONE...................510 271-7000
Lawrence Peiros, *Principal*
▲ EMP: 37
SALES (est): 11.7MM
SALES (corp-wide): 6.2B **Publicly Held**
SIC: 3295 Minerals, ground or treated
PA: The Clorox Company
1221 Broadway Ste 1300
Oakland CA 94612
510 271-7000

(P-10967)
ALGER ALTERNATIVE ENERGY LLC
1536 Jones St, Brawley (92227-1700)
PHONE...................317 493-5289
Harold Leonard Alger II, *President*
EMP: 11
SALES (corp-wide): 1.3MM **Privately Held**
SIC: 3295 Minerals, ground or treated
PA: Alger Alternative Energy Llc
7362 Remcon Cir
El Paso TX 79912
915 317-8447

(P-10968)
AZTEC PERLITE COMPANY INC
1518 Simpson Way, Escondido
(92029-1205)
PHONE...................760 741-1733
Domenic Di Nardo, *President*
Anna Di Nardo, *Owner*
Matt Goecker, *Manager*
EMP: 15
SQ FT: 5,000
SALES (est): 2.2MM **Privately Held**
SIC: 3295 Perlite, aggregate or expanded

(P-10969)
CLAY LAGUNA CO (HQ)
14400 Lomitas Ave, City of Industry
(91746-3018)
PHONE...................626 330-0631
Jonathan W Brooks, *Principal*
Laurie Brooks, *Corp Secy*
Jon Pacini, *Manager*
◆ EMP: 127
SQ FT: 110,000
SALES (est): 20.6MM
SALES (corp-wide): 9.5MM **Privately Held**
SIC: 3295 5032 Clay, ground or otherwise treated; tile & clay products
PA: Jon Brooks, Inc.
14400 Lomitas Ave
City Of Industry CA 91746
626 330-0631

(P-10970)
DESICCARE INC
3400 Pomona Blvd, Pomona (91768-3236)
PHONE...................909 444-8272
Shaneen Aros, *CFO*
Jack Schrader, *Vice Pres*
David Wells, *QC Mgr*
Michael McClure, *Sales Staff*
EMP: 20 **Privately Held**
SIC: 3295 Desiccants, clay: activated
PA: Desiccare, Inc.
3930 W Windmill Ln # 100
Las Vegas NV 89139

(P-10971)
GEO DRILLING FLUIDS INC
Also Called: Imco
7268 Frasinetti Rd, Sacramento
(95828-3717)
PHONE...................916 383-2811
Eric Sruck, *Systems Mgr*
EMP: 21
SQ FT: 5,000

SALES (corp-wide): 66.3MM **Privately Held**
WEB: www.clayimco.com
SIC: 3295 5945 Clay for petroleum refining, chemically processed; barite, ground or otherwise treated; ceramics supplies
PA: Geo Drilling Fluids, Inc.
1431 Union Ave
Bakersfield CA 93305
661 325-5919

(P-10972)
ISP GRANULE PRODUCTS INC
1900 Hwy 104, Ione (95640)
PHONE...................209 274-2930
Sunil Kumar, *President*
EMP: 100
SALES (est): 8.6MM
SALES (corp-wide): 86.2MM **Privately Held**
SIC: 3295 Roofing granules
HQ: Isp Minerals Llc
34 Charles St
Hagerstown MD 21740

(P-10973)
JOHN CRANE INC
Also Called: Crane, John
12760 Florence Ave, Santa Fe Springs
(90670-3906)
PHONE...................562 802-2555
Dave Bretfch, *General Mgr*
Gary Cannon, *Mfg Spvr*
EMP: 35
SALES (corp-wide): 4.1B **Privately Held**
WEB: www.johncrane.com
SIC: 3295 3541 3053 Minerals, ground or treated; lapping machines; gaskets, packing & sealing devices
HQ: John Crane Inc.
227 W Monroe St Ste 1800
Chicago IL 60606
312 605-7800

(P-10974)
JON BROOKS INC (PA)
Also Called: Laguna Clay Company
14400 Lomitas Ave, City of Industry
(91746-3018)
PHONE...................626 330-0631
Jon Brooks, *President*
Laurie Brooks, *Corp Secy*
◆ EMP: 103
SQ FT: 117,000
SALES (est): 9.5MM **Privately Held**
SIC: 3295 5085 Clay, ground or otherwise treated; refractory material

(P-10975)
PARATECH INC
15940 Minnesota Ave, Paramount
(90723-4914)
P.O. Box 718 (90723-0718)
PHONE...................562 633-2045
Steven F Park, *President*
EMP: 20
SQ FT: 17,300
SALES (est): 2.3MM **Privately Held**
WEB: www.paratech.com
SIC: 3295 Steatite, ground or otherwise treated

(P-10976)
RDM MULTI-ENTERPRISES INC
20428 Belshire Ave, Lakewood
(90715-1604)
PHONE...................562 924-1820
Evelyn Difrancesco, *CEO*
Ronald Difrancesco, *Vice Pres*
EMP: 12
SALES (est): 962K **Privately Held**
SIC: 3295 3291 Roofing granules; metallic abrasive

(P-10977)
SGL TECHNIC LLC (DH)
Also Called: Inc Polycarbon
28176 Avenue Stanford, Valencia
(91355-1119)
PHONE...................661 257-0500
Ken Mamon, *President*
Brian Green, *Vice Pres*
Kathy Vanschoonhoven, *Administration*
Robert Cruse, *Research*
Jay Tumuluri, *Controller*

▲ EMP: 62 EST: 1967
SQ FT: 130,000
SALES (est): 15.2MM
SALES (corp-wide): 1.2B **Privately Held**
WEB: www.polycarbon.com
SIC: 3295 3624 Graphite, natural: ground, pulverized, refined or blended; carbon & graphite products
HQ: Sgl Carbon, Llc
10715 David Taylor Dr # 460
Charlotte NC 28262
704 593-5100

(P-10978)
SPECIALTY GRANULES LLC
1900 State Hwy 104, Ione (95640)
P.O. Box 400 (95640-0400)
PHONE...................209 274-5323
George Dias, *Plant Mgr*
Steve Contreras, *Maintence Staff*
EMP: 50
SALES (corp-wide): 86.2MM **Privately Held**
SIC: 3295 Roofing granules
PA: Specialty Granules Llc
13424 Pa Ave Ste 303
Hagerstown MD 21742
301 733-4000

3296 Mineral Wool

(P-10979)
ACOUSTICAL INTERIORS INC (PA)
123 Princeton Ave, El Granada (94018)
PHONE...................650 728-9441
Janet McLurg, *Exec VP*
Josh Murphy, *Manager*
EMP: 10
SALES (est): 1.6MM **Privately Held**
WEB: www.acousticalinteriors.com
SIC: 3296 1742 Acoustical board & tile, mineral wool; acoustical & ceiling work

(P-10980)
C A SCHROEDER INC (PA)
Also Called: Casco Mfg
1318 1st St, San Fernando (91340-2804)
PHONE...................818 365-9561
Susan A Knudsen, *CEO*
Clifford A Schroeder, *President*
Bill Griffith, *General Mgr*
Alf Knudsen, *Sales Mgr*
Robert Voorhees, *Sales Staff*
EMP: 42
SQ FT: 18,500
SALES (est): 7.1MM **Privately Held**
WEB: www.cal-flex.com
SIC: 3296 3585 3444 3433 Fiberglass insulation; refrigeration & heating equipment; sheet metalwork; heating equipment, except electric

(P-10981)
CERTAINTEED CORPORATION
17775 Avenue 23 1/2, Chowchilla
(93610-9758)
PHONE...................559 665-4831
James Vicary, *Manager*
Glenn Abraham, *Opers-Prdtn-Mfg*
EMP: 400
SALES (corp-wide): 215.9MM **Privately Held**
WEB: www.certainteed.net
SIC: 3296 5033 Fiberglass insulation; insulation materials
HQ: Certainteed Llc
20 Moores Rd
Malvern PA 19355
610 893-5000

(P-10982)
CONSOLIDATED FIBRGLS PDTS CO
Also Called: Conglas
3801 Standard St, Bakersfield
(93308-5230)
PHONE...................661 323-6026
Daron J Thomas, *CEO*
Jack Pfeffer, *Vice Ch Bd*
Mike Lewis, *Opers Staff*
EMP: 60
SQ FT: 20,000

SALES (est): 9.2MM **Privately Held**
WEB: www.conglas.com
SIC: 3296 Fiberglass insulation

(P-10983)
INSULFAB INC
4725 Calle Alto, Camarillo (93012-8538)
PHONE...................805 482-2751
Sieg Borck, *President*
William Brown, *Corp Secy*
Ernest Sieger, *Vice Pres*
Rachael Greathouse, *Manager*
Candice Simpkins, *Manager*
EMP: 58
SQ FT: 23,000
SALES (est): 4.2MM **Privately Held**
SIC: 3296 Insulation: rock wool, slag & silica minerals

(P-10984)
JOHNS MANVILLE CORPORATION
5916 County Road 49, Willows
(95988-9703)
PHONE...................530 934-6243
Tom Lowe, *Branch Mgr*
Dave Elmer, *Technical Staff*
Felix Chavez, *Engineer*
Susan Cleland, *Buyer*
Dave Quackenbush, *Purch Agent*
EMP: 340
SALES (corp-wide): 225.3B **Publicly Held**
WEB: www.jm.com
SIC: 3296 Fiberglass insulation
HQ: Johns Manville Corporation
717 17th St Ste 800
Denver CO 80202
303 978-2000

(P-10985)
JOHNS MANVILLE CORPORATION
4301 Firestone Blvd, South Gate
(90280-3318)
PHONE...................323 568-2220
Rudi Bianchi, *Manager*
Jose Romo, *Technician*
Rafael Cabral, *Safety Mgr*
Lowell Gentry, *Supervisor*
EMP: 60
SALES (corp-wide): 225.3B **Publicly Held**
WEB: www.jm.com
SIC: 3296 Mineral wool
HQ: Johns Manville Corporation
717 17th St Ste 800
Denver CO 80202
303 978-2000

(P-10986)
KAINALU BLUE INC
4675 North Ave, Oceanside (92056-3511)
PHONE...................760 806-6400
Robin Gray, *President*
Scott Wester, *Vice Pres*
Morgan Castellanos, *Human Res Mgr*
EMP: 30
SQ FT: 30,000
SALES (est): 5.2MM **Privately Held**
WEB: www.lamvin.com
SIC: 3296 3275 Acoustical board & tile, mineral wool; gypsum products

(P-10987)
KNAUF INSULATION INC
3100 Ashby Rd, Shasta Lake (96019-9136)
PHONE...................530 275-9665
Bill Taylor, *Branch Mgr*
Randy Turner, *Plant Engr*
Iain James, *Manager*
Travis Parker, *Manager*
EMP: 150
SALES (corp-wide): 8.2B **Privately Held**
WEB: www.knaufusa.com
SIC: 3296 Mineral wool
HQ: Knauf Insulation, Inc.
1 Knauf Dr
Shelbyville IN 46176
317 398-4434

PRODUCTS & SVCS

(P-10988)
LAMART CALIFORNIA INC
33428 Alvarado Niles Rd, Union City
(94587-3110)
P.O. Box 1648, Clifton NJ (07015-1648)
PHONE...................................973 772-6262
Steven Hirsh, *President*
Graeme Silbert, *CFO*
EMP: 20 EST: 2016
SALES (est): 767.3K
SALES (corp-wide): 93.3MM **Privately
Held**
SIC: 3296 Fiberglass insulation
PA: Lamart Corporation
   16 Richmond St
   Clifton NJ 07011
   973 772-6262

(P-10989)
**UNITED STATES MINERAL PDTS
CO**
Also Called: Isolatek International
4062 Georgia Blvd, San Bernardino
(92407-1847)
PHONE...................................909 473-6993
Adrienne Bowen, *Branch Mgr*
Russell Harvey, *District Mgr*
Kyle Sheffer, *Plant Mgr*
Stanley Warenda, *Manager*
EMP: 70
SALES (corp-wide): 48.6MM **Privately
Held**
SIC: 3296 Mineral wool insulation products
PA: United States Mineral Products Com-
   pany Inc
   41 Furnace St
   Stanhope NJ 07874
   973 347-1200

(P-10990)
UPF CORPORATION
3747 Standard St, Bakersfield
(93308-5228)
PHONE...................................661 323-8227
Jack Pfeffer, *President*
Mike Rushing, *Supervisor*
▼ EMP: 35
SALES (est): 5.9MM **Privately Held**
WEB: www.upf-usa.com
SIC: 3296 Fiberglass insulation

3297 Nonclay Refractories

(P-10991)
COORSTEK VISTA INC
2065 Thibodo Rd, Vista (92081-7988)
PHONE...................................760 542-7065
John K Coors, *CEO*
Richard Palicka, *President*
▲ EMP: 101
SQ FT: 106,000
SALES (est): 11MM
SALES (corp-wide): 407.6MM **Privately
Held**
WEB: www.coorstek.com
SIC: 3297 Nonclay refractories
HQ: Coorstek, Inc.
   14143 Denver West Pkwy # 400
   Lakewood CO 80401
   303 271-7000

(P-10992)
HEATSHIELD PRODUCTS INC
938 S Andreasen Dr Ste C, Escondido
(92029-1920)
P.O. Box 462500 (92046-2500)
PHONE...................................760 751-0441
Bruce Heye, *Partner*
Stephen J Heye, *Partner*
EMP: 20
SQ FT: 500
SALES (est): 2.5MM **Privately Held**
SIC: 3297 High temperature mortar, non-
clay

(P-10993)
SIMONS BRICK CORPORATION
4301 Firestone Blvd, South Gate
(90280-3318)
PHONE...................................951 279-1000
John Williams, *President*
EMP: 20
SQ FT: 24,000

SALES (est): 2MM
SALES (corp-wide): 1.5B **Privately Held**
WEB: www.simonsbrick.com
SIC: 3297 5211 Brick refractories; brick
HQ: Basalite Building Products, Llc
   2150 Douglas Blvd Ste 260
   Roseville CA 95661
   707 678-1901

**3299 Nonmetallic Mineral
Prdts, NEC**

(P-10994)
A S BATLE COMPANY
Also Called: Www.asbworkshop.com
224 Mississippi St, San Francisco
(94107-2529)
PHONE...................................415 864-3300
Delia Batle, *Partner*
Agelio Batle, *Partner*
▲ EMP: 10
SALES: 400K **Privately Held**
WEB: www.asbworkshop.com
SIC: 3299 5712 Architectural sculptures:
gypsum, clay, papier mache, etc.; custom
made furniture, except cabinets

(P-10995)
ALS GARDEN ART INC (PA)
311 W Citrus St, Colton (92324-1412)
PHONE...................................909 424-0221
Donald Bracci, *President*
EMP: 290 EST: 1949
SQ FT: 305,000
SALES (est): 17MM **Privately Held**
WEB: www.alsgardenart.com
SIC: 3299 3272 Statuary: gypsum, clay,
papier mache, metal, etc.; concrete prod-
ucts

(P-10996)
**APPROVED NETWORKS INC
(PA)**
Also Called: Approved Optics
6 Orchard Ste 150, Lake Forest
(92630-8352)
PHONE...................................800 590-9535
Thomas Horton, *Managing Dir*
Kurt Dumteman, *COO*
Ron Beale, *CFO*
Anthony Daraby, *Engineer*
Denise Ryan, *Opers Staff*
EMP: 54 EST: 2010
SQ FT: 9,500
SALES: 123MM **Privately Held**
SIC: 3299 Art goods: plaster of paris, pa-
pier mache & scagliola

(P-10997)
**ATTILAS BYSHORE ART STUDIO
LLC**
2207 Quesada Ave, San Francisco
(94124-1921)
PHONE...................................415 282-2815
Attila Tivadar, *Mng Member*
▲ EMP: 11
SQ FT: 4,058
SALES: 1MM **Privately Held**
WEB: www.attilastudio.com
SIC: 3299 Statuary: gypsum, clay, papier
mache, metal, etc.

(P-10998)
**BLUE EAGLE STUCCO
PRODUCTS**
1407 N Clark St, Fresno (93703-3615)
PHONE...................................559 485-4100
Tom Graves, *Owner*
EMP: 12
SALES (est): 1.1MM **Privately Held**
SIC: 3299 Stucco

(P-10999)
**BMI PRODUCTS NORTHERN
CAL INC**
990 Ames Ave, Milpitas (95035-6303)
PHONE...................................408 293-4008
Arnold Germann, *CEO*
▲ EMP: 11
SQ FT: 22,000

SALES (est): 2.7MM
SALES (corp-wide): 215.9MM **Privately
Held**
WEB: www.bmi-products.com
SIC: 3299 5091 Stucco; watersports
equipment & supplies; golf & skiing equip-
ment & supplies
HQ: Schenker-Winkler Holding Ag
   C/O Sanitas Troesch Ag
   Bern BE 3018

(P-11000)
BRANDELLI ARTS INC
1250 Shaws Flat Rd, Sonora (95370-5433)
PHONE...................................714 537-0969
Robert Brandelli, *President*
Aurora Brandelli, *Vice Pres*
EMP: 46
SALES (est): 3.2MM **Privately Held**
WEB: www.brandelliarts.com
SIC: 3299 3272 Statuary: gypsum, clay,
papier mache, metal, etc.; concrete prod-
ucts

(P-11001)
BURLINGAME INDUSTRIES INC
Also Called: Eagle Roofing Products Co
2352 N Locust Ave, Rialto (92377-5000)
PHONE...................................909 355-7000
Robert Burlingame, *President*
John Campbell, *Sales Staff*
Hawk Kinney, *Sales Staff*
Elven Whitchurch, *Cust Mgr*
EMP: 200
SQ FT: 76,704
SALES (corp-wide): 81.5MM **Privately
Held**
SIC: 3299 3272 2952 Tile, sand lime;
concrete products; asphalt felts & coat-
ings
PA: Burlingame Industries, Incorporated
   3546 N Riverside Ave
   Rialto CA 92377
   909 355-7000

(P-11002)
CAL COAST STUCCO
10932 Tuxford St, Sun Valley (91352-2625)
PHONE...................................818 767-0115
Michael D Masino, *Principal*
Roger Gackenbach, *Vice Pres*
Debi Negrette, *Controller*
Ellen Hardin, *Bookkeeper*
Hugo Navarro, *Superintendent*
▲ EMP: 13
SALES (est): 2MM **Privately Held**
SIC: 3299 Stucco

(P-11003)
CERADYNE INC (HQ)
1922 Barranca Pkwy, Irvine (92606-4826)
PHONE...................................949 862-9600
Joel P Moskowitz, *CEO*
Mike Lipscombe, *President*
Jerrold J Pellizzon, *CFO*
Thomas A Cole, *Vice Pres*
Peter Hartl, *Vice Pres*
◆ EMP: 277
SQ FT: 99,000
SALES (est): 628.6MM
SALES (corp-wide): 32.7B **Publicly Held**
WEB: www.ceradyne.com
SIC: 3299 3671 Ceramic fiber; cathode
ray tubes, including rebuilt
PA: 3m Company
   3m Center
   Saint Paul MN 55144
   651 733-1110

(P-11004)
CERADYNE INC
17466 Daimler St, Irvine (92614-5514)
PHONE...................................949 756-0642
Joel Moskowitz, *Branch Mgr*
EMP: 11
SQ FT: 33,965
SALES (corp-wide): 32.7B **Publicly Held**
WEB: www.ceradyne.com
SIC: 3299 3264 Ceramic fiber; porcelain
electrical supplies
HQ: Ceradyne, Inc.
   1922 Barranca Pkwy
   Irvine CA 92606
   949 862-9600

(P-11005)
**CHINA MASTER USA ENTRMT
CO**
17890 Castleton St # 230, City of Industry
(91748-1756)
PHONE...................................626 810-9372
Richard Wang, *Mng Member*
EMP: 12
SALES (est): 689.8K **Privately Held**
WEB: www.chinamasterusa.com
SIC: 3299 Ceramic fiber

(P-11006)
DOUGLAS & STURGESS INC
1023 Factory St, Richmond (94801-2161)
PHONE...................................510 235-8411
Arthur Cordisco, *Manager*
EMP: 10
SQ FT: 10,250
SALES (corp-wide): 1.1MM **Privately
Held**
WEB: www.artstuf.com
SIC: 3299 Art goods: plaster of paris, pa-
pier mache & scagliola
PA: Douglas & Sturgess, Inc
   730 Bryant St
   San Francisco CA 94107
   415 896-6283

(P-11007)
**FOUNDRY SERVICE & SUPPLIES
INC**
2029 S Parco Ave, Ontario (91761-5700)
PHONE...................................909 284-5000
Curt Parnell, *CEO*
Joel Leathers, *Vice Pres*
Dave Quayle, *Sales Staff*
▲ EMP: 24
SQ FT: 40,000
SALES (est): 4.5MM **Privately Held**
WEB: www.foundryservice.com
SIC: 3299 Art goods: plaster of paris, pa-
pier mache & scagliola

(P-11008)
J P WEAVER & COMPANY INC
941 Air Way, Glendale (91201-3001)
PHONE...................................818 500-1740
Lenna Tyler Kast, *President*
Domonique Blizzard, *Admin Asst*
Angela Isayan, *Manager*
EMP: 15
SQ FT: 10,000
SALES (est): 1.2MM **Privately Held**
WEB: www.jpweaver.com
SIC: 3299 2431 Moldings, architectural:
plaster of paris; millwork

(P-11009)
LOMELIS STATUARY INC (PA)
Also Called: Lomeli's Gardens
11921 E Brandt Rd, Lockeford
(95237-9708)
P.O. Box 1356 (95237-1356)
PHONE...................................209 367-1131
Doris Lomeli, *President*
Adriana Lomeli, *Treasurer*
Carlos Lomeli, *Admin Sec*
Elsa Lomeli, *Admin Sec*
EMP: 25
SQ FT: 28,000
SALES (est): 2.2MM **Privately Held**
WEB: www.lomelis-statuary.com
SIC: 3299 5021 5261 Statuary: gypsum,
clay, papier mache, metal, etc.; outdoor &
lawn furniture; nurseries & garden centers

(P-11010)
MAXFORD TECHNOLOGY LLC
2225 Calle De Luna, Santa Clara
(95054-1002)
PHONE...................................408 855-8288
Jonathan Chan,
▲ EMP: 16
SQ FT: 22,000
SALES (est): 14.5MM **Privately Held**
WEB: www.maxfordtech.com
SIC: 3299 Non-metallic mineral statuary &
other decorative products

(P-11011)
MERLEX STUCCO INC
Also Called: Merlex Stucco Mfg
2911 N Orange Olive Rd, Orange
(92865-1699)
PHONE..............................877 547-8822
Steve Combs, *President*
◆ EMP: 35 EST: 1963
SQ FT: 30,000
SALES (est): 6.8MM **Privately Held**
WEB: www.merlex.com
SIC: 3299 Stucco

(P-11012)
**MONTEREY FOAM COMPANY
INC**
1716 Stone Ave Ste A, San Jose
(95125-1308)
P.O. Box 28565 (95159-8365)
PHONE..............................408 279-6756
Mitchell Dougherty, *President*
David Anderson, *Admin Sec*
EMP: 10
SALES (est): 860K **Privately Held**
SIC: 3299 Ornamental & architectural plaster work

(P-11013)
**MORGAN TECHNICAL
CERAMICS INC**
2425 Whipple Rd, Hayward (94544-7807)
PHONE..............................510 491-1100
Mark Robertshaw, *CEO*
Andrew Hosty, *COO*
Kevin Dangerfield, *CFO*
Andrew Shilston, *Chairman*
Henry Rodriguez, *Engineer*
EMP: 18 EST: 1991
SALES (est): 2.7MM **Privately Held**
SIC: 3299 Ceramic fiber

(P-11014)
MOTOART LLC
21809 S Western Ave, Torrance
(90501-3724)
PHONE..............................310 375-4531
David Hall,
Mike Rudden, *Partner*
Donovan Fell,
EMP: 10
SQ FT: 1,400
SALES (est): 1.7MM **Privately Held**
WEB: www.motoart.com
SIC: 3299 Architectural sculptures: gypsum, clay, papier mache, etc.

(P-11015)
OMEGA PRODUCTS CORP (HQ)
Also Called: Omega Products International
8111 Fruitridge Rd, Sacramento
(95826-4759)
P.O. Box 77220, Corona (92877-0107)
PHONE..............................916 635-3335
Kenneth R Thompson, *CEO*
Lutz Lamparter, *COO*
Todd Martin, *Vice Pres*
Sam Shen, *Purch Mgr*
Christine Camponovo, *Sales Staff*
▲ EMP: 60
SQ FT: 11,000
SALES (est): 34MM
SALES (corp-wide): 77.9MM **Privately Held**
WEB: www.omega-products.com
SIC: 3299 2899 Stucco; chemical preparations
PA: Opal Service, Inc.
282 S Anita Dr
Orange CA 92868
714 935-0900

(P-11016)
OMEGA PRODUCTS CORP
282 S Anita Dr Fl 3, Orange (92868-3308)
P.O. Box 1149 (92856-0149)
PHONE..............................714 935-0900
Todd Martin, *Manager*
EMP: 32
SALES (corp-wide): 77.9MM **Privately Held**
WEB: www.omega-products.com
SIC: 3299 Stucco

HQ: Omega Products Corp.
8111 Fruitridge Rd
Sacramento CA 95826
916 635-3335

(P-11017)
OPAL SERVICE INC (PA)
282 S Anita Dr, Orange (92868-3308)
P.O. Box 1149 (92856-0149)
PHONE..............................714 935-0900
Kenneth R Thompson, *CEO*
Dylan Budd, *Sales Staff*
▲ EMP: 30
SQ FT: 1,200
SALES (est): 77.9MM **Privately Held**
SIC: 3299 5031 5211 Stucco; doors & windows; lumber & other building materials

(P-11018)
PAREX USA INC (DH)
4125 E La Palma Ave # 250, Anaheim
(92807-1869)
PHONE..............................714 778-2266
Rodrigo Lacerda, *President*
Bret McClanahan, *District Mgr*
Jason Whitlock, *District Mgr*
Dannie Castro, *Info Tech Mgr*
Tina Cannedy, *Technical Staff*
◆ EMP: 30 EST: 1926
SALES (est): 134.6MM
SALES (corp-wide): 2.6MM **Privately Held**
WEB: www.parexlahabra.com
SIC: 3299 5031 Stucco; building materials, interior
HQ: Parexgroup Participations Sas
19 Place De La Resistance
Issy Les Moulineaux 92130
141 172-000

(P-11019)
PAREX USA INC
11290 Vallejo Ct, French Camp
(95231-9771)
PHONE..............................209 983-8002
Steve Horn, *Manager*
EMP: 20
SALES (corp-wide): 2.6MM **Privately Held**
WEB: www.parexlahabra.com
SIC: 3299 2851 Stucco; paints & allied products
HQ: Parex Usa, Inc.
4125 E La Palma Ave # 250
Anaheim CA 92807
714 778-2266

(P-11020)
**RICHARD MACDONALD
STUDIOS INC (PA)**
Also Called: Mac Donald, Richard Galleries
16 Lower Ragsdale Dr, Monterey
(93940-5728)
PHONE..............................831 655-0424
Richard Mac Donald Jr, *President*
Edrees Rohina, *Technology*
▲ EMP: 14
SALES (est): 2.9MM **Privately Held**
WEB: www.dawsoncolefineart.com
SIC: 3299 Architectural sculptures: gypsum, clay, papier mache, etc.

(P-11021)
SMALL PRECISION TOOLS INC
Also Called: Wire Bonding Tools
1330 Clegg St, Petaluma (94954-1127)
PHONE..............................707 765-4545
Peter Glutz, *President*
Joe Gracia, *CFO*
Yanling Geng, *Vice Pres*
Mary Ong, *Vice Pres*
Kevin Hepp, *Info Tech Mgr*
▲ EMP: 94
SQ FT: 25,000
SALES (est): 13.8MM
SALES (corp-wide): 27.3MM **Privately Held**
WEB: www.smallprecisiontools.com
SIC: 3299 Ceramic fiber
PA: Spt Roth Ag
Werkstrasse 28
Lyss BE 3250
323 878-080

(P-11022)
VANDORN PLASTERING
657 Lincoln Rd Ste D, Yuba City
(95991-6671)
PHONE..............................530 671-2748
EMP: 10 EST: 2007
SALES (est): 823.7K **Privately Held**
SIC: 3299 1771 1742

(P-11023)
WASTWEET STUDIO INC
962 Adams St, Albany (94706-2022)
PHONE..............................206 369-9060
EMP: 10
SALES (est): 722.3K **Privately Held**
SIC: 3299 Architectural sculptures: gypsum, clay, papier mache, etc.

**3312 Blast Furnaces, Coke
Ovens, Steel & Rolling Mills**

(P-11024)
ALTEMP ALLOYS INC
330 W Taft Ave, Orange (92865-4222)
PHONE..............................714 279-0249
Connie Mayhill, *CEO*
EMP: 15
SQ FT: 25,000
SALES (est): 4.5MM **Privately Held**
WEB: www.altempalloys.com
SIC: 3312 Wire products, steel or iron

(P-11025)
**AMERICAN BLAST SYSTEMS
INC**
Also Called: Blast Structures
16182 Gothard St Ste H, Huntington Beach
(92647-3642)
PHONE..............................949 244-6859
Kassie Stratton, *Manager*
EMP: 25
SALES (corp-wide): 4.7MM **Privately Held**
SIC: 3312 Blast furnace & related products
PA: American Blast Systems, Inc.
3101 Villa Way
Newport Beach CA 92663
949 244-6859

(P-11026)
**AMERICAN PLANT SERVICES
INC (PA)**
6242 N Paramount Blvd, Long Beach
(90805-3714)
P.O. Box 727 (90801-0727)
PHONE..............................562 630-1773
George M Bragg, *President*
Mary-Ann Pool, *Treasurer*
EMP: 51
SALES (est): 8.9MM **Privately Held**
SIC: 3312 Blast furnaces & steel mills

(P-11027)
**ARTSONS MANUFACTURING
COMPANY**
11121 Garfield Ave, South Gate
(90280-7505)
PHONE..............................323 773-3469
Jeffery A Winders, *CEO*
Jeffrey A Winders, *CEO*
Steve Winders, *CFO*
Art L Winders, *Vice Pres*
▲ EMP: 28
SALES (est): 6.7MM **Privately Held**
SIC: 3312 Wire products, steel or iron

(P-11028)
**ATI FLAT RLLED PDTS HLDNGS
LLC**
8570 Mercury Ln, Pico Rivera
(90660-3796)
PHONE..............................562 654-3900
W D Lieser, *Branch Mgr*
EMP: 10 **Publicly Held**
WEB: www.alleghenyludlum.com
SIC: 3312 Sheet or strip, steel, cold-rolled: own hot-rolled; stainless steel

HQ: Ati Flat Rolled Products Holdings, Llc
1000 Six Ppg Pl
Pittsburgh PA 15222
412 394-3047

(P-11029)
BAMBACIGNO STEEL COMPANY
4930 Mchenry Ave, Modesto (95356-9669)
PHONE..............................209 524-9681
Mary Bambacigno, *CEO*
Bill Boughton, *Vice Pres*
Sheila Arnold, *Admin Sec*
Nicole Kochman, *Accountant*
EMP: 48 EST: 1955
SQ FT: 51,440
SALES (est): 11.1MM **Privately Held**
WEB: www.bambacigno.com
SIC: 3312 Structural shapes & pilings, steel

(P-11030)
BROWN-PACIFIC INC
Also Called: B P W
13639 Bora Dr, Santa Fe Springs
(90670-5010)
PHONE..............................562 921-3471
Ron R Nagele, *CEO*
Emmanuel Pak, *Exec VP*
Claudia Nagele, *Vice Pres*
Kenneth Brown, *Principal*
Cale Carter, *Engineer*
EMP: 32
SQ FT: 35,000
SALES (est): 12.4MM **Privately Held**
WEB: www.brownpacific.com
SIC: 3312 3355 3357 3356 Bar, rod & wire products; wire, aluminum: made in rolling mills; bars, rolled, aluminum; nonferrous wiredrawing & insulating; nonferrous rolling & drawing; cold finishing of steel shapes; steel wire & related products

(P-11031)
**CALIFORNIA AMFORGE
CORPORATION**
750 N Vernon Ave, Azusa (91702-2231)
PHONE..............................626 334-4931
William Taylor, *Branch Mgr*
Paula Romero, *Purch Dir*
EMP: 100
SQ FT: 20,000
SALES (corp-wide): 20.7MM **Privately Held**
WEB: www.cal-amforge.com
SIC: 3312 3462 Forgings, iron & steel; iron & steel forgings
PA: California Amforge Corporation
750 N Vernon Ave
Azusa CA 91702
626 334-4931

(P-11032)
**CALIFORNIA STEEL INDS INC
(PA)**
Also Called: Si
14000 San Bernardino Ave, Fontana
(92335-5259)
P.O. Box 5080 (92334-5080)
PHONE..............................909 350-6300
Marcelo Botelho, *President*
Hiroshi Adachi, *Ch of Bd*
Tadaaki Yamaguchi, *Ch of Bd*
Ricardo Bernardes, *Exec VP*
Brett Guge, *Exec VP*
▲ EMP: 277
SALES (est): 241.5MM **Privately Held**
WEB: www.californiasteel.com
SIC: 3312 3317 Slabs, steel; plate, sheet & strip, except coated products; pipes, wrought: welded, lock joint or heavy riveted

(P-11033)
CALIFORNIA STEEL INDS INC
1 California Steel Way, Fontana (92335)
PHONE..............................909 350-6300
Kyle Schulty, *Branch Mgr*
Howard Taylor, *Supervisor*
Mario Villa, *Supervisor*
EMP: 548

SALES (corp-wide): 241.5MM **Privately Held**
SIC: 3312 3317 Slabs, steel; plate, sheet & strip, except coated products; pipes, wrought: welded, lock joint or heavy riveted
PA: California Steel Industries, Inc.
14000 San Bernardino Ave
Fontana CA 92335
909 350-6300

(P-11034)
CALIFORNIA STL STAIR RAIL MFR
587 Carnegie St, Manteca (95337-6102)
PHONE..................................209 824-1785
Richard G Lee, *President*
Dave Geserick, *CFO*
EMP: 30 EST: 1997
SQ FT: 30,000
SALES (est): 6.9MM **Privately Held**
WEB: www.calstair.com
SIC: 3312 Rails, steel or iron; structural shapes & pilings, steel

(P-11035)
CARPENTER TECHNOLOGY CORP
Also Called: Carpenter Specialty Alloys
8250 Milliken Ave, Rancho Cucamonga (91730-3927)
PHONE..................................909 476-4000
Sean Bell, *Manager*
EMP: 33
SALES (corp-wide): 2.3B **Publicly Held**
SIC: 3312 Stainless steel
PA: Carpenter Technology Corporation
1735 Market St Fl 15
Philadelphia PA 19103
610 208-2000

(P-11036)
CARTER HOLT HARVEY HOLDINGS
1230 Railroad St, Corona (92882-1837)
PHONE..................................951 272-8180
John Miller, *President*
EMP: 53
SQ FT: 60,000
SALES (est): 4.3MM **Privately Held**
WEB: www.chh.com
SIC: 3312 Blast furnaces & steel mills
HQ: Carter Holt Harvey Limited
173 Captain Springs Road
Auckland 1061

(P-11037)
CHAPALA IRON & MANUFACTURING
1301 Callens Rd, Ventura (93003-5602)
PHONE..................................805 654-9803
Patrick Davis, *Owner*
EMP: 15
SQ FT: 3,600
SALES (est): 2MM **Privately Held**
SIC: 3312 3446 Blast furnaces & steel mills; architectural metalwork

(P-11038)
CITY INDUSTRIAL TOOL & DIE (PA)
25524 Frampton Ave, Harbor City (90710-2907)
PHONE..................................310 530-1234
Steve Kuljis, *President*
Eileen Kuljis, *Admin Sec*
EMP: 12
SQ FT: 5,000
SALES (est): 895.2K **Privately Held**
SIC: 3312 3469 3444 3544 Tool & die steel & alloys; metal stampings; sheet metalwork; special dies, tools, jigs & fixtures

(P-11039)
COAST CUTTERS CO INC
2500 Royale Pl, Fullerton (92833-1526)
PHONE..................................626 444-2965
Bill Dunlap, *President*
Bonnie Dunlap, *Treasurer*
Steve Dunlap, *Vice Pres*
John Merritt, *Vice Pres*
Laurie Smith, *Office Mgr*
EMP: 10

SQ FT: 6,500
SALES: 700K **Privately Held**
SIC: 3312 5072 Tool & die steel; power tools & accessories

(P-11040)
COMMERCIAL METALS COMPANY
12451 Arrow Rte, Etiwanda (91739-9601)
PHONE..................................909 899-9993
Chris Lloyd, *Branch Mgr*
David Hansen, *Sales Mgr*
EMP: 10
SALES (corp-wide): 5.8B **Publicly Held**
SIC: 3312 Blast furnaces & steel mills
PA: Commercial Metals Company
6565 N Macarthur Blvd # 800
Irving TX 75039
214 689-4300

(P-11041)
DESIGN SHAPES IN STEEL INC
10315 Rush St, South El Monte (91733-3341)
PHONE..................................626 579-2032
Peter Costruba II, *President*
EMP: 20 EST: 1979
SQ FT: 10,000
SALES: 2MM **Privately Held**
SIC: 3312 3446 3444 Primary finished or semifinished shapes; architectural metalwork; sheet metalwork

(P-11042)
DIETRICH INDUSTRIES INC
2525 S Airport Way, Stockton (95206-3521)
PHONE..................................209 547-9066
Randy Rose, *Manager*
EMP: 56
SALES (corp-wide): 3.7B **Publicly Held**
WEB: www.dietrichmetalframing.com
SIC: 3312 Blast furnaces & steel mills
HQ: Dietrich Industries, Inc.
200 W Old Wilson Bridge Rd
Worthington OH 43085
800 873-2604

(P-11043)
EASYFLEX INC
Also Called: Easy Flex
7423 Doig Dr, Garden Grove (92841-1807)
PHONE..................................888 577-8999
Sunmin Kim OH, *President*
Hun Kim, *General Mgr*
Joseph Lee, *Sales Mgr*
◆ EMP: 25
SQ FT: 30,000
SALES (est): 8.7MM **Privately Held**
SIC: 3312 Stainless steel

(P-11044)
FLOW DYNAMICS INC
1215 E Acacia St Ste 104, Ontario (91761-4003)
PHONE..................................909 930-5522
John McCarthy, *President*
Philip Espinoza, *Vice Pres*
Gabriel Burciaga, *Sales Staff*
Tammy McCarthy, *Manager*
EMP: 16
SQ FT: 2,222
SALES (est): 4.4MM **Privately Held**
SIC: 3312 Stainless steel

(P-11045)
GONDOLA SKATE MVG SYSTEMS INC (PA)
9941 Prospect Ave, Santee (92071-4318)
PHONE..................................619 222-6487
Frank C Cozza, *CEO*
Sharmin Self, *Administration*
EMP: 13
SQ FT: 2,000
SALES: 4MM **Privately Held**
WEB: www.gondolaskate.com
SIC: 3312 Locomotive wheels, rolled

(P-11046)
GRAND METALS INC
Also Called: Select Fabrications
325 N Cota St, Corona (92880-2014)
PHONE..................................310 327-5554
Kevin Malloy, *President*
Thomas Malloy, *Ch of Bd*
EMP: 11

SQ FT: 18,000
SALES (est): 2.1MM **Privately Held**
SIC: 3312 Structural shapes & pilings, steel

(P-11047)
HARDY FRAMES INC
Also Called: My Tech USA
250 Klug Cir, Corona (92880-5409)
PHONE..................................951 245-9525
Clifford Grant, *Branch Mgr*
EMP: 100
SALES (corp-wide): 1.9MM **Privately Held**
SIC: 3312 Stainless steel
PA: Hardy Frames, Inc.
1732 Palma Dr Ste 200
Ventura CA 93003
805 477-0793

(P-11048)
HERRICK CORPORATION
Stockton Steel
3003 E Hammer Ln, Stockton (95212-2801)
P.O. Box 8429 (95208-0429)
PHONE..................................209 956-4751
Tom Juano, *Manager*
Karen Griffin, *Administration*
EMP: 186
SALES (corp-wide): 221.8MM **Privately Held**
SIC: 3312 3441 Structural shapes & pilings, steel; fabricated structural metal
PA: The Herrick Corporation
3003 E Hammer Ln
Stockton CA 95212
209 956-4751

(P-11049)
HOLT TOOL & MACHINE INC
2909 Middlefield Rd, Redwood City (94063-3328)
PHONE..................................650 364-2547
Leo Hoenighausen, *President*
Ulrich Hoenighausen, *CFO*
Karen Garcia, *Technology*
Remus Regnelala, *Mfg Mgr*
EMP: 21
SQ FT: 12,000
SALES (est): 5.7MM **Privately Held**
SIC: 3312 3469 7692 3544 Tool & die steel & alloys; metal stampings; welding repair; special dies, tools, jigs & fixtures

(P-11050)
INTERNATIONAL MFG TECH INC (DH)
Also Called: Nassco
2798 Harbor Dr, San Diego (92113-3650)
PHONE..................................619 544-7741
Willam J Cuddy, *CEO*
James C Scott, *President*
William J Cuddy, *Manager*
Jaime De Chico, *Assistant*
▲ EMP: 24
SALES (est): 24.8MM
SALES (corp-wide): 36.1B **Publicly Held**
SIC: 3312 3731 Structural & rail mill products; shipbuilding & repairing
HQ: Nassco Holdings Incorporated
2798 Harbor Dr
San Diego CA 92113
619 544-3400

(P-11051)
INTERSTATE REBAR INC
2457 N Ventura Ave Ste L, Ventura (93001-0345)
P.O. Box 670, Oak View (93022-0670)
PHONE..................................805 643-6892
Ronald Moore, *President*
EMP: 10
SALES (est): 1.7MM **Privately Held**
SIC: 3312 Plate, sheet & strip, except coated products; tool & die steel & alloys

(P-11052)
JOSEPH MCCRINK
Also Called: Kva Stainless
2802 Luciernaga St, Carlsbad (92009-5926)
PHONE..................................760 489-1500
Joe Mc Crink, *Vice Pres*
Douglas Gore, *Principal*
EMP: 16

SALES (est): 2.7MM **Privately Held**
SIC: 3312 Stainless steel

(P-11053)
KEN-WOR CORP
Also Called: Parcor
13962 Enterprise Dr, Garden Grove (92843-4021)
PHONE..................................714 554-6210
Steve Worrell, *President*
Ken Upton, *Treasurer*
EMP: 38
SQ FT: 10,000
SALES (est): 3MM **Privately Held**
SIC: 3312 3444 Stainless steel; sheet metalwork

(P-11054)
LAMAR TOOL AND DIE CASTING INC
4230 Technology Dr, Modesto (95356-9484)
PHONE..................................209 545-5525
Larry Snoreen, *President*
Margie Snoreen, *Treasurer*
Brian Kolsters, *Vice Pres*
Carol Lemmons, *Human Resources*
Craig Feaga, *Safety Mgr*
▲ EMP: 41
SQ FT: 20,000
SALES (est): 5.5MM **Privately Held**
WEB: www.lamartooldie.com
SIC: 3312 3463 3364 Tool & die steel & alloys; nonferrous forgings; nonferrous die-castings except aluminum

(P-11055)
LINCOLN IRON WORKS
507 7th St, Santa Monica (90402-2707)
PHONE..................................310 684-2543
EMP: 22 EST: 2012
SALES (est): 2.1MM **Privately Held**
SIC: 3312

(P-11056)
MAC PRODUCTS INC
Also Called: Mac Performance Exhaust
43214 Black Deer Loop # 113, Temecula (92590-3428)
PHONE..................................951 296-3077
Mack Jones Sr, *President*
Mack Jones Jr, *Corp Secy*
▲ EMP: 52
SQ FT: 56,000
SALES (est): 10.2MM **Privately Held**
WEB: www.macperformance.com
SIC: 3312 3751 3714 Tubes, steel & iron; motorcycles, bicycles & parts; motor vehicle parts & accessories

(P-11057)
MIKES METAL WORKS INC
3552 Fowler Canyon Rd, Jamul (91935-1602)
PHONE..................................619 440-8804
Mike Hancock, *President*
JD Hudson, *Manager*
EMP: 18
SQ FT: 6,000
SALES (est): 4.1MM **Privately Held**
WEB: www.mikesmetalworksinc.com
SIC: 3312 Stainless steel

(P-11058)
NORTHLAND PROCESS PIPING INC
400 E St, Lemoore (93245-2616)
PHONE..................................559 925-9724
Cal Bredek, *Supervisor*
EMP: 100
SALES (corp-wide): 30.2MM **Privately Held**
SIC: 3312 Stainless steel
PA: Northland Process Piping, Inc.
1662 320th Ave
Isle MN 56342
320 679-2119

(P-11059)
PACIFIC TOLL PROCESSING INC
Also Called: P T P
24724 Wilmington Ave, Carson (90745-6127)
PHONE..................................310 952-4992

▲ = Import ▼=Export
◆ =Import/Export

Anthony J Camasta, *CEO*
Mark Proner, *Exec VP*
EMP: 40
SQ FT: 101,000
SALES (est): 11.6MM **Privately Held**
WEB: www.pacifictoll.com
SIC: 3312 4785 Structural & rail mill products; toll road operation

(P-11060)
PRECISION WIRE PRODUCTS INC
Also Called: Lcl Pacific
11215 Wilmington Ave, Los Angeles (90059-1299)
PHONE.....................323 569-8165
Frank Vega, *Branch Mgr*
EMP: 25
SALES (corp-wide): 42.4MM **Privately Held**
WEB: www.precisionwireproducts.com
SIC: 3312 Wire products, steel or iron
PA: Precision Wire Products, Inc.
6150 Sheila St
Commerce CA 90040
323 890-9100

(P-11061)
PRICE INDUSTRIES INC
Also Called: International Iron Products
10883 Thornmint Rd, San Diego (92127-2403)
PHONE.....................858 673-4451
Kenneth Alan Price, *President*
Joe Cyr, *COO*
Terry Isbell, *Vice Pres*
Barbara Price, *Admin Sec*
Tracey Minnick, *Administration*
EMP: 75
SQ FT: 4,000
SALES (est): 17.8MM **Privately Held**
WEB: www.intliron.com
SIC: 3312 3441 1791 5072 Structural & rail mill products; fabricated structural metal; structural steel erection; bolts, nuts & screws

(P-11062)
QUALITY CRAFT MOLD INC
6424 Woodward Dr, Magalia (95954-8709)
PHONE.....................530 873-7790
Chris Moritz, *President*
EMP: 10
SQ FT: 4,200
SALES (est): 1.3MM **Privately Held**
WEB: www.qualitycraftinc.com
SIC: 3312 Tool & die steel & alloys

(P-11063)
R S R STEEL FABRICATION INC
11040 I Ave, Hesperia (92345-5214)
PHONE.....................760 244-2210
Hector Grijalva, *President*
Ruth Grijalva, *Vice Pres*
EMP: 28
SQ FT: 12,000
SALES (est): 6.1MM **Privately Held**
SIC: 3312 Structural shapes & pilings, steel

(P-11064)
REDLINE PRCISION MACHINING INC
907 E Francis St, Ontario (91761-5631)
PHONE.....................909 483-1273
Jon Bouch, *CEO*
Cheryl Bouch, *Admin Sec*
EMP: 15 **EST:** 1997
SQ FT: 10,000
SALES (est): 2MM **Privately Held**
SIC: 3312 Tool & die steel & alloys

(P-11065)
RELIABLE MILL SUPPLY CO
1550 Millview Rd, Ukiah (95482-3341)
P.O. Box 269 (95482-0269)
PHONE.....................707 462-1458
Norman E Johnson Jr, *President*
Harold Johnson, *Vice Pres*
Bow Johnson, *Admin Sec*
EMP: 10
SQ FT: 27,000
SALES (est): 2.3MM **Privately Held**
SIC: 3312 5051 5085 Blast furnaces & steel mills; metals service centers & offices; mill supplies

(P-11066)
RHINO MANUFACTURING GROUP INC
14440 Meadowrun St, San Diego (92129-3328)
PHONE.....................866 624-8844
Heather Mordhorst, *CEO*
Aimee Gaede, *COO*
▲ **EMP:** 12
SALES (est): 1.9MM **Privately Held**
WEB: www.rhinomfg.net
SIC: 3312 1771 5051 5085 Stainless steel; concrete work; steel; rubber goods, mechanical; foams & rubber; rubber, crude

(P-11067)
RTM PRODUCTS INC
13120 Arctic Cir, Santa Fe Springs (90670-5508)
PHONE.....................562 926-2400
Robert M Thierjung, *Principal*
EMP: 23
SALES (est): 4.6MM **Privately Held**
SIC: 3312 Tool & die steel & alloys; tool & die steel

(P-11068)
SEARING INDUSTRIES INC
8901 Arrow Rte, Rancho Cucamonga (91730-4410)
P.O. Box 3059 (91729-3059)
PHONE.....................909 948-3030
Lee Searing, *President*
Steve Abbey, *Exec VP*
Margaret Cantu, *Exec VP*
Mmargaret Cantu, *Vice Pres*
Annie Wood, *Office Mgr*
◆ **EMP:** 120
SQ FT: 265,000
SALES (est): 51.2MM **Privately Held**
WEB: www.searingindustries.com
SIC: 3312 3317 Tubes, steel & iron; hot-rolled iron & steel products; steel pipe & tubes

(P-11069)
SIMEC USA CORPORATION
Also Called: Pacific Steel
1700 Cleveland Ave Ste B, National City (91950-4215)
PHONE.....................619 474-7081
Sergio Vigil Gonzalez, *CEO*
Sandy Mendez, *Persnl Mgr*
EMP: 20
SQ FT: 1,000
SALES (est): 3.8MM **Privately Held**
SIC: 3312 Bars, iron: made in steel mills; structural shapes & pilings, steel
HQ: Simec International 6, S.A. De C.V.
Av. Lazaro Cardenas No. 601 Edificio A-3 Piso 4
Guadalajara JAL. 44470

(P-11070)
SIMSOLVE
310 Elizabeth Ln, Corona (92880-2504)
PHONE.....................951 898-6880
Dennis Anderson, *President*
EMP: 10
SALES (est): 897.6K **Privately Held**
SIC: 3312 Rails, steel or iron

(P-11071)
SMITH BROS STRL STL PDTS INC
Also Called: Smith Bros Cstm Met Fbrication
1535 Potrero Ave, South El Monte (91733-3016)
PHONE.....................626 350-1872
Christopher Smith, *President*
Chris Smith, *President*
Reginald Smith, *Vice Pres*
EMP: 15 **EST:** 1976
SQ FT: 30,000
SALES (est): 2.4MM **Privately Held**
SIC: 3312 Structural shapes & pilings, steel

(P-11072)
SOUTHERN CAL GOLD PDTS INC
2350 Santiago Ct, Oxnard (93030-7932)
P.O. Box 1933, Camarillo (93011-1933)
PHONE.....................805 988-0777
Glenn Harris, *CEO*
Gina Harris, *Treasurer*
EMP: 10
SALES (est): 2.2MM **Privately Held**
SIC: 3312 Armor plate

(P-11073)
STAR STAINLESS SCREW CO
30150 Ahern Ave, Union City (94587-1202)
PHONE.....................510 489-6569
Tim Roberto, *Manager*
EMP: 15
SALES (corp-wide): 100.9MM **Privately Held**
SIC: 3312 5072 Stainless steel; hardware
PA: Star Stainless Screw Co.
30 W End Rd
Totowa NJ 07512
973 256-2300

(P-11074)
STATE PIPE & SUPPLY INC
Westcoast Pipe Lining Division
2180 N Locust Ave, Rialto (92377-4166)
PHONE.....................909 356-5670
Kenneth Walker, *Manager*
EMP: 50 **Privately Held**
WEB: www.statepipe.com
SIC: 3312 Blast furnaces & steel mills
HQ: State Pipe & Supply, Inc.
183 S Cedar Ave
Rialto CA 92376
909 877-9999

(P-11075)
STRADA WHEELS INC
560 S Magnolia Ave, Ontario (91762-4011)
PHONE.....................626 336-1634
Enrico Aiello, *President*
Joyce Aiello, *Vice Pres*
Maria Yneguez, *General Mgr*
▲ **EMP:** 14
SALES (est): 2.9MM **Privately Held**
SIC: 3312 5014 Wheels; tires & tubes

(P-11076)
STRESSTEEL INC
Also Called: Sas Stressteel
47375 Fremont Blvd, Fremont (94538-6521)
PHONE.....................888 284-8752
Michael A Pagano, *CEO*
Dion Gray, *CFO*
Tom Pavlovic, *Engineer*
▲ **EMP:** 11
SALES (est): 2.2MM **Privately Held**
SIC: 3312 8711 Bar, rod & wire products; engineering services

(P-11077)
TAMCO (DH)
Also Called: Gerdau Rancho Cucamonga
12459 Arrow Rte, Rancho Cucamonga (91739-9807)
PHONE.....................909 899-0660
Chia Yuan Wang, *CEO*
Vilmar Babot, *CFO*
Harley Scardoelli, *Admin Sec*
◆ **EMP:** 62
SQ FT: 150,000
SALES (est): 51.3MM
SALES (corp-wide): 5.8B **Publicly Held**
WEB: www.tamcosteel.com
SIC: 3312 Blast furnaces & steel mills
HQ: Cmc Steel Us, Llc
6565 N Macarthur Blvd
Irving TX 75039
214 689-4300

(P-11078)
TREE ISLAND WIRE (USA) INC (DH)
Also Called: TI Wire
3880 Valley Blvd, Walnut (91789-1515)
P.O. Box 90100, San Bernardino (92427-1100)
PHONE.....................909 594-7511
Amar S Doman, *Ch of Bd*
Dale R Maclean, *CEO*

Nancy Davies, *CFO*
Stephen Ogden, *Vice Pres*
▲ **EMP:** 250
SALES (est): 125.8MM
SALES (corp-wide): 178.3MM **Privately Held**
SIC: 3312 Blast furnaces & steel mills
HQ: Tree Island Industries Ltd
3933 Boundary Rd
Richmond BC V6V 1
604 524-3744

(P-11079)
USS-PSCO INDS A CAL JINT VENTR (PA)
900 Loveridge Rd, Pittsburg (94565-2808)
P.O. Box 471 (94565-0471)
PHONE.....................800 877-7672
Michael Piekut, *Manager*
Sungwon Shin, *Vice Pres*
Alan Jones, *Admin Asst*
Young Sohn, *Tech/Comp Coord*
Randy Sanders, *Software Dev*
▲ **EMP:** 759
SQ FT: 100,000
SALES (est): 648.9MM **Privately Held**
WEB: www.ussposco.com
SIC: 3312 Sheet or strip, steel, cold-rolled: own hot-rolled; tinplate; iron & steel: galvanized, pipes, plates, sheets, etc.

(P-11080)
WAYNE TOOL & DIE CO
15853 Olden St, Sylmar (91342-1249)
PHONE.....................818 364-1611
Kenneth E Ruggles, *President*
EMP: 50
SQ FT: 1,200
SALES (est): 4.4MM **Privately Held**
SIC: 3312 Tool & die steel

(P-11081)
WEISER IRON INC
64 Sundance Dr, Pomona (91766-4894)
PHONE.....................909 429-4600
David Metoyer, *President*
Carmela Metoyer, *Corp Secy*
EMP: 47
SALES (est): 9.9MM **Privately Held**
WEB: www.weiseriron.com
SIC: 3312 Structural shapes & pilings, steel

(P-11082)
WHEEL AND TIRE CLUB INC
Also Called: Discounted Wheel Warehouse
1301 Burton St, Fullerton (92831-5212)
PHONE.....................714 422-3505
Naeem Niamat, *President*
◆ **EMP:** 35
SQ FT: 42,000
SALES (est): 18MM **Privately Held**
SIC: 3312 Locomotive wheels, rolled

> **3313 Electrometallurgical Prdts**

(P-11083)
R D MATHIS COMPANY
2840 Gundry Ave, Signal Hill (90755-1813)
P.O. Box 92916, Long Beach (90809-2916)
PHONE.....................562 426-7049
Robert Lumley, *President*
Barbara Bennett, *Treasurer*
Kirk Bennett, *Vice Pres*
EMP: 25 **EST:** 1963
SQ FT: 10,000
SALES (est): 5.4MM **Privately Held**
WEB: www.rdmathis.com
SIC: 3313 8711 3567 3443 Molybdenum silicon, not made in blast furnaces; engineering services; industrial furnaces & ovens; fabricated plate work (boiler shop); fabricated structural metal

(P-11084)
TUNGSTEN HEAVY POWDER INC (PA)
Also Called: Tungsten Heavy Powder & Parts
6170 Cornerstone Ct E # 310, San Diego (92121-3767)
PHONE.....................858 693-6100
Joseph Sery, *CEO*
Oscar Cruz, *COO*

PRODUCTS & SVCS

Chris Witt, *CFO*
Karina Erali, *Office Mgr*
Gil Sery, *CTO*
▲ **EMP:** 60
SQ FT: 10,000
SALES: 39.2MM **Privately Held**
WEB: www.tungstenheavypowder.com
SIC: 3313 Tungsten carbide powder

3315 Steel Wire Drawing & Nails & Spikes

(P-11085)
BULLZEYE MFG
13625 Clements Rd, Lodi (95240-9754)
P.O. Box 187, Linden (95236-0187)
PHONE..................................209 482-5626
Brian Gideon, *Mng Member*
EMP: 15 EST: 2010
SALES (est): 936.9K **Privately Held**
SIC: 3315 Steel wire & related products

(P-11086)
CARLISLE INTERCONNECT TECH INC
Thermax
4200 Garner Rd, Riverside (92501-1003)
PHONE..................................951 788-0252
John Berlin, *Branch Mgr*
Teresa Tovar, *Administration*
Jonathan Busch, *Project Mgr*
Thai Tran, *Engineer*
Kevin Dyer, *Production*
EMP: 20
SALES (corp-wide): 4.4B **Publicly Held**
SIC: 3315 2241 3496 Steel wire & related products; narrow fabric mills; miscellaneous fabricated wire products
HQ: Carlisle Interconnect Technologies, Inc.
100 Tensolite Dr
Saint Augustine FL 32092

(P-11087)
D & D TECHNOLOGIES USA INC
17531 Metzler Ln, Huntington Beach (92647-6242)
PHONE..................................949 852-5140
▼ **EMP:** 29
SALES: 12MM **Privately Held**
SIC: 3315
HQ: D & D Technologies Pty. Limited
U6 4 Aquatic Dr
Frenchs Forest NSW 2086

(P-11088)
DAVIS WIRE CORPORATION (HQ)
5555 Irwindale Ave, Irwindale (91706-2046)
PHONE..................................626 969-7651
Jim Baske, *President*
Emily Heisley, *Ch of Bd*
Hak Kim, *CFO*
▲ **EMP:** 150
SQ FT: 265,000
SALES (est): 86.7MM **Privately Held**
WEB: www.daviswire.com
SIC: 3315 Wire, ferrous/iron; wire products, ferrous/iron: made in wiredrawing plants

(P-11089)
DAYTON SUPERIOR CORPORATION
6001 20th St, Riverside (92509-2030)
PHONE..................................951 782-9517
Jeffrey Bokn, *Branch Mgr*
EMP: 65
SALES (corp-wide): 43B **Publicly Held**
SIC: 3315 Steel wire & related products
HQ: Dayton Superior Corporation
1125 Byers Rd
Miamisburg OH 45342
937 866-0711

(P-11090)
DAYTON SUPERIOR CORPORATION
562 W Santa Ana Ave, Bloomington (92316-2914)
PHONE..................................909 820-0112

John Ciccerelli, *President*
EMP: 40
SALES (corp-wide): 43B **Publicly Held**
SIC: 3315 Steel wire & related products
HQ: Dayton Superior Corporation
1125 Byers Rd
Miamisburg OH 45342
937 866-0711

(P-11091)
DHL WIRE PRODUCTS
Also Called: Chandler Wire Products
2325 1st St, La Verne (91750-5532)
PHONE..................................909 596-2909
Debra Oehmke, *Principal*
EMP: 10
SALES (est): 631.8K **Privately Held**
SIC: 3315 Steel wire & related products

(P-11092)
DOOR SERVICE COMPANY
Also Called: Patton Door and Gate
680 S Williams Rd, Palm Springs (92264-1549)
PHONE..................................760 320-0788
Fax: 760 323-9553
EMP: 15 EST: 2007
SALES (est): 1.2MM **Privately Held**
SIC: 3315 1751

(P-11093)
FENCER ENTERPRISES LLC
Also Called: Wireman Fence Products
3469 Fitzgerald Rd, Rancho Cordova (95742-6815)
PHONE..................................916 635-1700
Lisa Leonard Hilbers, *Mng Member*
EMP: 12
SALES (est): 2.3MM **Privately Held**
WEB: www.wiremanfence.com
SIC: 3315 Chain link fencing; fence gates posts & fittings: steel

(P-11094)
HALSTEEL INC (DH)
4190 Santa Ana St Ste A, Ontario (91761-1527)
P.O. Box 90100, San Bernardino (92427-1100)
PHONE..................................909 937-1001
Rebecca Kalis, *President*
Donald Halstead, *Treasurer*
Ed Halstead, *Vice Pres*
EMP: 20
SQ FT: 100,000
SALES: 5.4MM
SALES (corp-wide): 178.3MM **Privately Held**
WEB: www.halsteel.com
SIC: 3315 5051 Nails, steel: wire or cut; staples, steel: wire or cut; nails
HQ: Tree Island Industries Ltd
3933 Boundary Rd
Richmond BC V6V 1
604 524-3744

(P-11095)
HAMROCK INC
12521 Los Nietos Rd, Santa Fe Springs (90670-2915)
PHONE..................................562 944-0255
Stephen R Hamrock, *Principal*
Jerry Hamrock, *Vice Pres*
Marty Hamrock, *Purchasing*
▲ **EMP:** 250
SQ FT: 169,000
SALES (est): 49MM **Privately Held**
WEB: www.hamrock.com
SIC: 3315 2542 3496 3317 Wire & fabricated wire products; racks, merchandise display or storage: except wood; miscellaneous fabricated wire products; steel pipe & tubes

(P-11096)
HANGERS RANDY WEST COAST CTR
Also Called: Manetti Group
5350 Zambrano St, Commerce (90040-3036)
PHONE..................................323 728-2253
Gabrino Bonuelos, *Manager*
Mario Sebastrano, *Manager*
▲ **EMP:** 18
SALES (est): 2.8MM **Privately Held**
SIC: 3315 Hangers (garment), wire

(P-11097)
HOGAN CO INC
2741 S Lilac Ave, Bloomington (92316-3213)
PHONE..................................909 421-0245
Kraig B Hogan, *President*
◆ **EMP:** 20
SQ FT: 9,150
SALES (est): 5.3MM **Privately Held**
SIC: 3315 3531 Spikes, steel: wire or cut; bituminous, cement & concrete related products & equipment

(P-11098)
INWESCO INCORPORATED (PA)
746 N Coney Ave, Azusa (91702-2239)
PHONE..................................626 334-7115
David L Morris, *CEO*
Jeremy Acheson, *Vice Pres*
EMP: 65
SQ FT: 30,000
SALES: 25MM **Privately Held**
WEB: www.inwesco.com
SIC: 3315 Steel wire & related products

(P-11099)
IZURIETA FENCE COMPANY INC
3000 Gilroy St, Los Angeles (90039-2819)
PHONE..................................323 661-4759
Peter Izurieta, *Owner*
EMP: 10
SALES (est): 1.5MM **Privately Held**
SIC: 3315 1799 Chain link fencing; fence construction

(P-11100)
MASTER-HALCO INC
8008 Church Ave, Highland (92346-4318)
PHONE..................................909 350-4740
Paul Stites, *Branch Mgr*
EMP: 50 **Privately Held**
WEB: www.fenceonline.com
SIC: 3315 4226 7692 3496 Fence gates posts & fittings: steel; special warehousing & storage; welding repair; miscellaneous fabricated wire products; metal stampings
HQ: Master-Halco, Inc.
3010 Lbj Fwy Ste 800
Dallas TX 75234
972 714-7300

(P-11101)
MERCHANTS METALS LLC
6466 Mission Blvd, Riverside (92509-4128)
PHONE..................................951 686-1888
Rob Sisco, *Manager*
EMP: 12
SQ FT: 8,750
SALES (corp-wide): 2.9B **Privately Held**
SIC: 3315 3496 Fence gates posts & fittings: steel; miscellaneous fabricated wire products
HQ: Merchants Metals Llc
211 Perimeter Center Pkwy
Atlanta GA 30346
770 741-0306

(P-11102)
MK MAGNETICS INC
17030 Muskrat Ave, Adelanto (92301-2258)
PHONE..................................760 246-6373
Magne Stangenes, *President*
John Stangenes, *Vice Pres*
Jay Runge, *Admin Sec*
Bryce E Kelchner, *Info Tech Dir*
Lori Tice, *Purch Agent*
▲ **EMP:** 53
SQ FT: 45,000
SALES (est): 11.1MM
SALES (corp-wide): 19.3MM **Privately Held**
WEB: www.mkmagnetics.com
SIC: 3315 Steel wire & related products
PA: Stangenes Industries, Inc.
1052 E Meadow Cir
Palo Alto CA 94303
650 855-9926

(P-11103)
NEW PRODUCT INTEGRATION SOLUTN
Also Called: Npi Solutions
685 Jarvis Dr Ste A, Morgan Hill (95037-2813)
PHONE..................................408 944-9178
Kevin R Andersen, *President*
Dawn Casterson, *CFO*
Cindy E Chambers, *Controller*
▲ **EMP:** 65
SQ FT: 15,000
SALES (est): 25.9MM **Privately Held**
WEB: www.npisolutions.com
SIC: 3315 Cable, steel: insulated or armored

(P-11104)
PRO DETENTION INC
Also Called: Viking Products
2238 N Glassell St Ste E, Orange (92865-2742)
PHONE..................................714 881-3680
Mike Peterson, *CEO*
▲ **EMP:** 70
SALES: 8MM **Privately Held**
SIC: 3315 Wire & fabricated wire products

(P-11105)
ROBERT P MARTIN COMPANY
Also Called: Bob Martin Co
2209 Seaman Ave, South El Monte (91733-2630)
PHONE..................................323 686-2220
Robert P Martin Jr, *CEO*
Naomi Martin, *President*
EMP: 14
SQ FT: 14,000
SALES (est): 1.7MM **Privately Held**
SIC: 3315 3357 Wire & fabricated wire products; nonferrous wiredrawing & insulating

(P-11106)
SAC VALLEY ORNAMENTAL IR OUTL
8540 Thys Ct, Sacramento (95828-1007)
P.O. Box 277127 (95827-7127)
PHONE..................................916 383-6340
Mark Eveleth, *President*
EMP: 10
SALES (est): 689K **Privately Held**
SIC: 3315 1791 Fence gates posts & fittings: steel; structural steel erection

(P-11107)
SAFELAND INDUSTRIAL SUPPLY INC (PA)
10278 Birtcher Dr, Jurupa Valley (91752-1827)
PHONE..................................909 786-1967
Lijun Zhang, *President*
▲ **EMP:** 16
SALES (est): 2.5MM **Privately Held**
SIC: 3315 3312 Steel wire & related products; stainless steel

(P-11108)
SILICON VALLEY MFG INC
6520 Central Ave, Newark (94560-3933)
PHONE..................................510 791-9450
Mark Serpa, *Principal*
EMP: 24 EST: 2007
SALES: 5MM **Privately Held**
SIC: 3315 Steel wire & related products

(P-11109)
SOFT FLEX CO
22678 Broadway, Sonoma (95476-8217)
P.O. Box 80 (95476-0080)
PHONE..................................707 938-3539
Scott Clark, *Partner*
Mike Sherman, *Partner*
EMP: 20
SQ FT: 2,500
SALES (est): 3.8MM **Privately Held**
WEB: www.softflextm.com
SIC: 3315 3915 Steel wire & related products; jewelry parts, unassembled

▲ = Import ▼=Export
◆ =Import/Export

(P-11110)
SUN POWER SECURITY GATES INC
438 Tyler Rd, Merced (95341-8807)
P.O. Box 2044 (95344-0044)
PHONE..............................209 722-3990
Robert Osborn, *President*
Gene Felling, *Vice Pres*
Dusty Major, *General Mgr*
EMP: 17
SQ FT: 3,500
SALES (est): 2MM **Privately Held**
WEB: www.sun-power.com
SIC: 3315 3677 Fence gates posts & fittings: steel; transformers power supply, electronic type

(P-11111)
TREE ISLAND WIRE (USA) INC
Industrial Alloys
13470 Philadelphia Ave, Fontana (92337-7700)
PHONE..............................909 594-7511
Rebecca Kalis, *Branch Mgr*
EMP: 90
SALES (corp-wide): 178.3MM **Privately Held**
SIC: 3315 Wire, steel: insulated or armored
HQ: Tree Island Wire (Usa), Inc.
3880 Valley Blvd
Walnut CA 91789

(P-11112)
TREE ISLAND WIRE (USA) INC
K-Lath
3880 W Valley Blvd, Pomona (91769)
PHONE..............................909 595-6617
Ken Stufford, *Manager*
EMP: 256
SALES (corp-wide): 178.3MM **Privately Held**
SIC: 3315 Wire, steel: insulated or armored
HQ: Tree Island Wire (Usa), Inc.
3880 Valley Blvd
Walnut CA 91789

(P-11113)
TREE ISLAND WIRE (USA) INC
12459 Arrow Rte, Rancho Cucamonga (91739-9807)
PHONE..............................800 255-6974
Krish Singh, *Branch Mgr*
Dean Patterson, *General Mgr*
Brendan Moloney, *Sales Dir*
EMP: 75
SALES (est): 271.9K **Privately Held**
SIC: 3315 Wire & fabricated wire products

(P-11114)
US HANGER COMPANY LLC
17501 S Denver Ave, Gardena (90248-3410)
PHONE..............................310 323-8030
Gene Livshin, *Mng Member*
▲ EMP: 47
SALES (est): 7.2MM **Privately Held**
SIC: 3315 5199 Hangers (garment), wire; clothes hangers

(P-11115)
WAVENET INC (PA)
707 E Sepulveda Blvd, Carson (90745-6032)
PHONE..............................310 885-4200
Yihong Jang, *President*
Kevin Chang, *COO*
▲ EMP: 20
SQ FT: 29,000
SALES (est): 2.9MM **Privately Held**
SIC: 3315 Wire & fabricated wire products

(P-11116)
WIRETECH INC (PA)
6440 Canning St, Commerce (90040-3122)
PHONE..............................323 722-4933
William Hillpot, *President*
Martin Valenzuela, *Manager*
Brett Brown, *Accounts Mgr*
▲ EMP: 87
SALES (est): 33.3MM **Privately Held**
WEB: www.wiretech.com
SIC: 3315 Steel wire & related products

3316 Cold Rolled Steel Sheet, Strip & Bars

(P-11117)
ARROW STEEL PRODUCTS INC
13171 Santa Ana Ave, Fontana (92337-6949)
PHONE..............................909 349-1032
Gerald Baldanado, *President*
EMP: 10
SQ FT: 22,000
SALES (est): 1MM **Privately Held**
SIC: 3316 Cold-rolled strip or wire

(P-11118)
CALSTRIP INDUSTRIES INC (PA)
3030 Dulles Dr, Jurupa Valley (91752-3240)
PHONE..............................323 726-1345
Thomas B Nelis, *Chairman*
Jon Nelis, *CEO*
EMP: 40 EST: 1939
SQ FT: 135,000
SALES: 160MM **Privately Held**
WEB: www.calstripsteel.com
SIC: 3316 Strip steel, cold-rolled: from purchased hot-rolled

(P-11119)
KIP STEEL INC
1650 Valley Ln, Fullerton (92833-1718)
PHONE..............................714 461-1051
EMP: 23
SALES (corp-wide): 2.1MM **Privately Held**
SIC: 3316 Cold finishing of steel shapes
PA: Kip Steel, Inc.
21314 Twisted Willow Ln
Katy TX 77450
714 461-1051

(P-11120)
NEXCOIL STEEL LLC
1265 Shaw Rd, Stockton (95215-4020)
PHONE..............................209 900-1919
Gary Stein, *Principal*
Robert Elkington, *Principal*
Fred Morrison, *Principal*
EMP: 17
SALES (est): 755.2K **Privately Held**
SIC: 3316 Bars, steel, cold finished, from purchased hot-rolled

(P-11121)
REMINGTON ROLL FORMING INC
2445 Chico Ave, El Monte (91733-1612)
P.O. Box 9325 (91733-0979)
PHONE..............................626 350-5196
Thomas Henry, *President*
EMP: 15
SQ FT: 25,000
SALES (est): 2.3MM **Privately Held**
SIC: 3316 Cold finishing of steel shapes

(P-11122)
WE HALL COMPANY INC (PA)
Also Called: Pacific Corrugated Pipe Co
471 Old Newport Blvd # 205, Newport Beach (92663-4243)
P.O. Box 15010 (92659-5010)
PHONE..............................949 650-4555
J K Leason, *CEO*
Jim Andre, *President*
EMP: 12
SQ FT: 3,000
SALES (est): 16.7MM **Privately Held**
WEB: www.pcpipe.com
SIC: 3316 Cold finishing of steel shapes

3317 Steel Pipe & Tubes

(P-11123)
CHARMAN MANUFACTURING INC
5681 S Downey Rd, Vernon (90058-3719)
PHONE..............................213 489-7000
Shahab Namvar, *President*
Shawn Namvar, *President*
Ezra Namvar, *Vice Pres*

David Namvar, *Purchasing*
▲ EMP: 25
SALES (est): 5.2MM **Privately Held**
SIC: 3317 Steel pipe & tubes

(P-11124)
COLTRIN INC
4466 Worth St, Los Angeles (90063-2538)
PHONE..............................323 266-6872
Carlos Vega, *President*
Janet Shanley, *Manager*
Luis Vega, *Manager*
EMP: 10
SALES (est): 1.6MM **Privately Held**
SIC: 3317 Steel pipe & tubes

(P-11125)
CONTECH ENGNERED SOLUTIONS INC
950 S Coast Dr Ste 145, Costa Mesa (92626-7833)
PHONE..............................714 281-7883
EMP: 1288
SALES (corp-wide): 119.2MM **Privately Held**
SIC: 3317 Steel pipe & tubes
PA: Contech Engineered Solutions Inc.
9025 Ctr Pinte Dr Ste 400
West Chester OH 45069
513 645-7000

(P-11126)
CRITERION AUTOMATION INC
1722 Production Cir, Riverside (92509-1717)
PHONE..............................951 683-2400
Chris Carda, *President*
Brad Laeger, *Vice Pres*
Dave Cappuccilli, *Marketing Staff*
Christopher J Carda, *Marketing Staff*
EMP: 13
SALES (est): 3.2MM **Privately Held**
WEB: www.criterionautomation.com
SIC: 3317 5719 Steel pipe & tubes; metalware

(P-11127)
HANNIBAL INDUSTRIES INC (PA)
3851 S Santa Fe Ave, Vernon (90058-1712)
PHONE..............................323 513-1200
Blanton Bartlett, *President*
Heidy Moon, *CFO*
Steve Rogers, *Vice Pres*
David Thang, *Administration*
Raquel McFarland, *Office Spvr*
◆ EMP: 214
SQ FT: 285,000
SALES (est): 60.2MM **Privately Held**
WEB: www.hannibalindustries.com
SIC: 3317 Tubes, seamless steel

(P-11128)
IMPERIAL PIPE SERVICES LLC
12375 Brown Ave, Riverside (92509-1868)
PHONE..............................951 682-3307
Leonard Shapiro,
Bob Raber,
Steve Teller,
Henry Atilano, *Manager*
EMP: 21
SALES (est): 13MM
SALES (corp-wide): 72.3MM **Privately Held**
WEB: www.sandhillmgmt.com
SIC: 3317 Steel pipe & tubes
PA: Shapco Inc.
1666 20th St Ste 100
Santa Monica CA 90404
310 264-1666

(P-11129)
K-TUBE CORPORATION
Also Called: K Tube Technologies
13400 Kirkham Way Frnt, Poway (92064-7167)
PHONE..............................858 513-9229
Greg May, *CEO*
Laurie Montanez, *Admin Asst*
Carl Lindberg, *Info Tech Mgr*
Houman Esmaeilpour, *Technician*
Tim Krewson, *Technician*
EMP: 100
SQ FT: 75,000

SALES (est): 29.5MM
SALES (corp-wide): 1.3B **Privately Held**
WEB: www.ktube.com
SIC: 3317 Tubing, mechanical or hypodermic sizes: cold drawn stainless
PA: Cook Group Incorporated
750 N Daniels Way
Bloomington IN 47404
812 339-2235

(P-11130)
MARUICHI AMERICAN CORPORATION
11529 Greenstone Ave, Santa Fe Springs (90670-4622)
PHONE..............................562 903-8600
Wataru Cho Morita, *President*
Teruo Horikawa, *Ch of Bd*
Yasunori Yoshimura, *CEO*
Tak Ishihara, *Exec VP*
Mike Ishikawa, *Exec VP*
▲ EMP: 85
SQ FT: 240,000
SALES (est): 63MM **Privately Held**
WEB: www.macsfs.com
SIC: 3317 Pipes, seamless steel; tubes, seamless steel
PA: Maruichi Steel Tube Ltd.
5-1-60, Namba, Chuo-Ku
Osaka OSK 542-0

(P-11131)
MASKELL RIGGING & EQUIPMENT (PA)
Also Called: Maskell Fusion Tech Services
6650 Doolittle Ave, Riverside (92503-1432)
PHONE..............................951 900-7460
Salma Bushala, *CEO*
Mitch Price, *VP Opers*
Reed Olive, *Manager*
Jeff Silveira, *Manager*
▼ EMP: 15
SQ FT: 9,000
SALES (est): 4.9MM **Privately Held**
SIC: 3317 7353 1799 1796 Steel pipe & tubes; heavy construction equipment rental; rigging & scaffolding; machine moving & rigging; hand tools; power tools & accessories

(P-11132)
NORTHWEST PIPE COMPANY
12351 Rancho Rd, Adelanto (92301-2711)
PHONE..............................760 246-3191
Charles Koenig, *Vice Pres*
EMP: 300
SALES (corp-wide): 172.1MM **Publicly Held**
WEB: www.nwpipe.com
SIC: 3317 3321 Pipes, wrought: welded, lock joint or heavy riveted; gray & ductile iron foundries
PA: Northwest Pipe Company
201 Ne Park Plaza Dr # 100
Vancouver WA 98684
360 397-6250

(P-11133)
PRIMUS PIPE AND TUBE INC (DH)
5855 Obispo Ave, Long Beach (90805-3715)
PHONE..............................562 808-8000
Tommy Grahn, *President*
Scott Templeton, *Exec VP*
Karl Almond, *Vice Pres*
Domenick Di Giallonardo, *Vice Pres*
Roy Harrison, *Vice Pres*
▲ EMP: 100
SQ FT: 120,000
SALES (est): 65.9MM **Privately Held**
SIC: 3317 Steel pipe & tubes
HQ: Ta Chen International, Inc.
5855 Obispo Ave
Long Beach CA 90805
562 808-8000

(P-11134)
ROSCOE MOSS MANUFACTURING CO (PA)
Also Called: Roscoe Moss Company
4360 Worth St, Los Angeles (90063-2536)
P.O. Box 31064 (90031-0064)
PHONE..............................323 261-4185

Roscoe Moss Jr, *Ch of Bd*
Robert A Vanvaler, *President*
Tony Creque, *CFO*
Luis Ramirez, *CFO*
George E Moss, *Vice Ch Bd*
▼ **EMP:** 90 **EST:** 1913
SQ FT: 20,000
SALES (est): 22.5MM **Privately Held**
WEB: www.roscoemoss.com
SIC: 3317 Well casing, wrought: welded,
lock joint or heavy riveted; tubes,
wrought: welded or lock joint

(P-11135)
**ROSCOE MOSS
MANUFACTURING CO**
4360 Worth St, Los Angeles (90063-2536)
P.O. Box 31064 (90031-0064)
PHONE.....................323 263-4111
Roscoe Moss Jr, *Ch of Bd*
Robert V Valer, *President*
George E Moss, *Vice Ch Bd*
EMP: 80
SQ FT: 20,000
SALES (est): 4.5MM
SALES (corp-wide): 22.5MM **Privately
Held**
WEB: www.roscoemoss.com
SIC: 3317 Steel pipe & tubes
PA: Roscoe Moss Manufacturing Company
4360 Worth St
Los Angeles CA 90063
323 261-4185

(P-11136)
SUPERIOR TECH INC
Also Called: Superior Technologies
13850 Benson Ave, Chino (91710-7005)
PHONE.....................909 364-2300
Peter Chifo, *Principal*
EMP: 16
SALES (est): 2.9MM **Privately Held**
WEB: www.superior-tech.net
SIC: 3317 Tubes, wrought: welded or lock
joint

(P-11137)
TUBE ONE INDUSTRIES INC
4055 Garner Rd, Riverside (92501-1043)
PHONE.....................951 300-2998
Kimber Liu, *CEO*
Susan Liu, *Vice Pres*
Richard Liu, *Regl Sales Mgr*
Patrick Liu, *Manager*
▲ **EMP:** 15
SQ FT: 46,000
SALES (est): 3.4MM **Privately Held**
SIC: 3317 Steel pipe & tubes

(P-11138)
VALLEY METALS LLC
Also Called: Leggett & Platt 0768
13125 Gregg St, Poway (92064-7122)
P.O. Box 85402, San Diego (92186-5402)
PHONE.....................858 513-1300
Kirk Nelson, *Mng Member*
EMP: 40 **EST:** 1946
SQ FT: 47,700
SALES (est): 11.4MM
SALES (corp-wide): 4.2B **Publicly Held**
WEB: www.valleymetals.com
SIC: 3317 Tubes, wrought: welded or lock
joint
HQ: Western Pneumatic Tube Company,
Llc
835 6th St S
Kirkland WA 98033
425 822-8271

(P-11139)
VEST INC
6023 Alcoa Ave, Vernon (90058-3954)
P.O. Box 58827, Los Angeles (90058-0827)
PHONE.....................800 421-6370
Kenji Morita, *CEO*
Iwaki Sugimoto, *President*
Hide Yamada, *President*
Sam Fukazawa, *CFO*
▲ **EMP:** 77
SQ FT: 312,000
SALES (est): 828.9K **Privately Held**
WEB: www.vestinc.com
SIC: 3317 3547 Tubes, wrought: welded
or lock joint; rolling mill machinery

HQ: Shoji Jfe Trade America Inc
301 E Ocean Blvd Ste 1750
Long Beach CA 90802
562 637-3500

3321 Gray Iron Foundries

(P-11140)
**ALHAMBRA FOUNDRY
COMPANY LTD**
Also Called: Afco
1147 S Meridian Ave, Alhambra
(91803-1218)
P.O. Box 469 (91802-0469)
PHONE.....................626 289-4294
Arzhang Baghkhanian, *CEO*
James Wright, *Vice Pres*
Mike Smalski, *General Mgr*
▲ **EMP:** 46
SQ FT: 48,370
SALES: 8MM **Privately Held**
WEB: www.alhambrafoundry.com
SIC: 3321 3312 5051 Gray iron castings;
structural shapes & pilings, steel; iron &
steel (ferrous) products

(P-11141)
EJ USA INC
2020 W 14th St, Long Beach (90813-1042)
PHONE.....................562 528-0258
Aess Illes, *Branch Mgr*
EMP: 12 **Privately Held**
SIC: 3321 Manhole covers, metal
HQ: Ej Usa, Inc.
301 Spring St
East Jordan MI 49727
800 874-4100

(P-11142)
FOX HILLS INDUSTRIES
5831 Research Dr, Huntington Beach
(92649-1385)
PHONE.....................714 893-1940
John Burk, *President*
Doug Reichard, *President*
Raj Mittal, *Vice Pres*
Frank Reilly, *Vice Pres*
Steve Pashkutz, *General Mgr*
▲ **EMP:** 25
SQ FT: 20,000
SALES (est): 6.1MM **Privately Held**
SIC: 3321 3366 3365 3322 Ductile iron
castings; castings (except die): brass; alu-
minum foundries; malleable iron foundries

(P-11143)
GLOBE IRON FOUNDRY INC
5649 Randolph St, Commerce
(90040-3489)
PHONE.....................323 723-8983
John M Pratto, *President*
Othon Garcia, *CFO*
John Pratto Jr, *Vice Pres*
Jeff Pratto, *VP Sales*
Mike Gaston, *Maintence Staff*
EMP: 64
SQ FT: 58,000
SALES (est): 13.3MM **Privately Held**
WEB: www.globeiron.com
SIC: 3321 3543 3369 Gray iron castings;
ductile iron castings; industrial patterns;
nonferrous foundries

(P-11144)
JDH PACIFIC INC (PA)
14821 Artesia Blvd, La Mirada
(90638-6006)
PHONE.....................562 926-8088
Donald Hu, *President*
Jon Elgas, *Opers Mgr*
▲ **EMP:** 30
SQ FT: 103,000
SALES (est): 33.4MM **Privately Held**
SIC: 3321 3324 3599 3462 Gray iron
castings; commercial investment cast-
ings, ferrous; crankshafts & camshafts,
machining; iron & steel forgings; machin-
ery forgings, ferrous

(P-11145)
LODI IRON WORKS INC (PA)
Also Called: Galt Steel Foundry
820 S Sacramento St, Lodi (95240-4710)
P.O. Box 1150 (95241-1150)
PHONE.....................209 368-5395
Kevin Van Steenberge, *President*
Michael Van Steenberge, *Vice Pres*
Michael Vansteenberg, *Purch Mgr*
Mike Van Steenberge, *VP Mfg*
Gwen Krenecki, *Director*
EMP: 46 **EST:** 1943
SQ FT: 11,000
SALES (est): 13.4MM **Privately Held**
WEB: www.lodiiron.com
SIC: 3321 3312 Gray iron castings; stain-
less steel

(P-11146)
LODI IRON WORKS INC
Also Called: Galt Steel Foundry
609 W Amador St, Galt (95632)
PHONE.....................209 368-5395
Ken Degrammont, *Manager*
Kevin Van Steenberge, *President*
EMP: 10
SALES (corp-wide): 13.4MM **Privately
Held**
WEB: www.lodiiron.com
SIC: 3321 3312 Gray & ductile iron
foundries; stainless steel
PA: Lodi Iron Works, Inc.
820 S Sacramento St
Lodi CA 95240
209 368-5395

(P-11147)
MCWANE INC (PA)
Also Called: AB & I Foundry
7825 San Leandro St, Oakland
(94621-2515)
PHONE.....................510 632-3467
Allan Boscacci, *President*
Clifford Wixson, *Ch of Bd*
John Callagy, *CFO*
Kevin McCullough, *Vice Pres*
Patricia Boscacci, *Admin Sec*
▲ **EMP:** 195 **EST:** 1906
SQ FT: 150,000
SALES (est): 41.2MM **Privately Held**
WEB: www.abifoundry.com
SIC: 3321 3494 Soil pipe & fittings: cast
iron; gray iron castings; valves & pipe fit-
tings

(P-11148)
RIDGE FOUNDRY INC
Also Called: Ridge Cast Metals
1554 Doolittle Dr, San Leandro
(94577-2271)
PHONE.....................510 352-0551
Norman Stamm, *President*
EMP: 20 **EST:** 1956
SQ FT: 25,000
SALES (est): 3.5MM **Privately Held**
SIC: 3321 3325 3369 3365 Gray iron
castings; ductile iron castings; steel
foundries; nonferrous foundries; alu-
minum foundries; malleable iron foundries

(P-11149)
THOMPSON GUNDRILLING INC
13840 Saticoy St, Van Nuys (91402-6582)
PHONE.....................323 873-4045
Michael Thompson, *President*
Virginia Ramsey, *CFO*
Robert Thompson, *Director*
EMP: 39 **EST:** 1973
SQ FT: 32,000
SALES (est): 3.4MM **Privately Held**
WEB: www.thompsongundrilling.com
SIC: 3321 Gray & ductile iron foundries

3322 Malleable Iron Foundries

(P-11150)
COVERT IRON WORKS
7821 Otis S Ave, Huntington Park (90255)
PHONE.....................323 560-2792
Fax: 323 560-8351
EMP: 19 **EST:** 1923
SQ FT: 20,000

SALES (est): 2.2MM **Privately Held**
WEB: www.covertironworks.com
SIC: 3322 3321

(P-11151)
**STEVEN HANDELMAN STUDIOS
(PA)**
Also Called: Handelman, Steven Studios
716 N Milpas St, Santa Barbara
(93103-3029)
PHONE.....................805 884-9070
Steven Handelman, *Owner*
EMP: 35 **EST:** 1973
SALES (est): 4.4MM **Privately Held**
WEB: www.stevenhandelmanstudios.com
SIC: 3322 Malleable iron foundries

3324 Steel Investment Foundries

(P-11152)
**ALIGN AEROSPACE HOLDING
INC (DH)**
21123 Nordhoff St, Chatsworth
(91311-5816)
PHONE.....................818 727-7800
Jerome De Truchis, *President*
You Lei, *COO*
Pan Linwu, *CFO*
Chen Hongliang, *Exec VP*
Christopher Eckenrode, *Manager*
EMP: 12
SALES (est): 118.3MM
SALES (corp-wide): 43.3B **Privately Held**
SIC: 3324 Aerospace investment castings,
ferrous
HQ: Zhuhai Zhenye Supply Chain Manage-
ment Co., Ltd.
Inside Of Airchina Area, Jiuzhou
Boulevard
Zhuhai 51901
756 323-3222

(P-11153)
**ARCONIC GLOBAL FAS & RINGS
INC**
Arconic Fastening Systems
800 S State College Blvd, Fullerton
(92831-5334)
PHONE.....................714 871-1550
Craig Brown, *Manager*
EMP: 100
SALES (corp-wide): 14B **Publicly Held**
SIC: 3324 3365 Aerospace investment
castings, ferrous; aerospace castings,
aluminum
HQ: Arconic Global Fasteners & Rings, Inc.
3990a Heritage Oak Ct
Simi Valley CA 93063
805 527-3600

(P-11154)
CAST PARTS INC (DH)
Also Called: Cpp-Pomona
4200 Valley Blvd, Walnut (91789-1408)
PHONE.....................909 595-2252
Steve Clodfelter, *President*
Ali Ghavami, *COO*
EMP: 185
SQ FT: 300,000
SALES (est): 59.5MM
SALES (corp-wide): 6.9B **Privately Held**
WEB: www.castparts.com
SIC: 3324 3365 Steel investment
foundries; aluminum foundries
HQ: Consolidated Precision Products Corp.
1621 Euclid Ave Ste 1850
Cleveland OH 44115
216 453-4800

(P-11155)
CAST PARTS INC
Also Called: Cpp-City of Industry
16800 Chestnut St, City of Industry
(91748-1017)
PHONE.....................626 937-3444
David Atwood, *Branch Mgr*
John Grace, *Engineer*
Karen Beckashley, *Manager*
EMP: 160
SALES (corp-wide): 6.9B **Privately Held**
SIC: 3324 Aerospace investment castings,
ferrous

▲ = Import ▼=Export
◆ =Import/Export

HQ: Cast Parts, Inc.
4200 Valley Blvd
Walnut CA 91789
909 595-2252

(P-11156)
CIRCOR AEROSPACE PDTS GROUP
2301 Wardlow Cir, Corona (92880-2801)
PHONE..................................951 270-6200
Scott Buckhout, *President*
Pritesh Patel, *Info Tech Dir*
EMP: 300
SALES (est): 17.8MM
SALES (corp-wide): 1.1B **Publicly Held**
SIC: 3324 Aerospace investment castings, ferrous
PA: Circor International, Inc.
30 Corporate Dr Ste 200
Burlington MA 01803
781 270-1200

(P-11157)
CONSOLIDATED FOUNDRIES INC
Also Called: C P P
4200 W Valley Blvd, Pomona (91769)
PHONE..................................909 595-2252
Steve Clodfelter, *President*
German Rangel, *Vice Pres*
Mike Decker, *Info Tech Dir*
Hoang Nguyen, *Info Tech Mgr*
Todd Lallier, *Engineer*
▲ **EMP:** 44
SALES (est): 13.6MM **Privately Held**
SIC: 3324 Aerospace investment castings, ferrous

(P-11158)
INITIUM AEROSPACE LLC
4255 Ruffin Rd Ste 100, San Diego (92123-1247)
PHONE..................................818 324-3684
Etienne Boisseau, *CEO*
Adam Boettner, *Manager*
EMP: 17
SQ FT: 2,500
SALES (est): 883.9K **Privately Held**
SIC: 3324 3369 3365 3812 Aerospace investment castings, ferrous; aerospace castings, nonferrous: except aluminum; aerospace castings, aluminum; aircraft/aerospace flight instruments & guidance systems

(P-11159)
KRALLCAST INC
16205 Ward Way, City of Industry (91745-1715)
PHONE..................................626 333-0678
Anthony Krallman, *President*
EMP: 10
SQ FT: 12,000
SALES (est): 1.3MM **Privately Held**
WEB: www.krallcast.com
SIC: 3324 Commercial investment castings, ferrous

(P-11160)
LISI AEROSPACE NORTH AMER INC
2602 Skypark Dr, Torrance (90505-5314)
PHONE..................................310 326-8110
Christian Darville, *CEO*
Ken Pham, *Purch Agent*
◆ **EMP:** 900 EST: 2009
SALES (est): 100MM
SALES (corp-wide): 177.9K **Privately Held**
SIC: 3324 Aerospace investment castings, ferrous
HQ: Hi-Shear Corporation
2600 Skypark Dr
Torrance CA 90505
310 784-4025

(P-11161)
MCDANIEL INC
10807 Monte Vista Ave, Montclair (91763-6113)
PHONE..................................909 591-8353
Timothy McDaniel, *President*
Shelly McDaniel, *Vice Pres*
Dave Davidson, *Supervisor*
EMP: 16 EST: 1997

SALES (est): 5MM **Privately Held**
SIC: 3324 Steel investment foundries

(P-11162)
MILLER CASTINGS INC (PA)
2503 Pacific Park Dr, Whittier (90601-1680)
PHONE..................................562 695-0461
Ralph Miller, *President*
Hadi Khandehroo, *CEO*
Bahman Khandehroo, *Engineer*
Debora Monterroso, *Purchasing*
Mariya Servin-Lopez, *Purchasing*
▲ **EMP:** 96
SQ FT: 40,000
SALES (est): 76.1MM **Privately Held**
WEB: www.millercastings.com
SIC: 3324 Steel investment foundries

(P-11163)
MILLER CASTINGS INC
12251 Coast Dr, Whittier (90601-1608)
PHONE..................................562 695-0461
EMP: 10
SALES (corp-wide): 76.1MM **Privately Held**
SIC: 3324 Steel investment foundries
PA: Miller Castings, Inc.
2503 Pacific Park Dr
Whittier CA 90601
562 695-0461

(P-11164)
NET SHAPES INC
1336 E Francis St Ste B, Ontario (91761-5723)
PHONE..................................909 947-3231
Joseph S Cannone, *President*
Patricia Schwent, *CFO*
Cordy Champan, *QA Dir*
Sonia Narvaez, *Sales Staff*
EMP: 120
SQ FT: 43,500
SALES (est): 25.6MM **Privately Held**
WEB: www.netshapes.com
SIC: 3324 Steel investment foundries

(P-11165)
PAC-RANCHO INC (DH)
11000 Jersey Blvd, Rancho Cucamonga (91730-5103)
PHONE..................................909 987-4721
Steve Clodfelter, *President*
Ali Ghavami, *Vice Pres*
EMP: 180
SQ FT: 55,000
SALES: 18.5MM
SALES (corp-wide): 6.9B **Privately Held**
SIC: 3324 3354 3369 Commercial investment castings, ferrous; aluminum extruded products; nonferrous foundries
HQ: Consolidated Precision Products Corp.
1621 Euclid Ave Ste 1850
Cleveland OH 44115
216 453-4800

(P-11166)
PACIFIC COMPOSITES INC
221 Calle Pintoresco, San Clemente (92672-7505)
PHONE..................................949 498-8600
EMP: 12
SQ FT: 12,000
SALES: 1.5MM **Privately Held**
SIC: 3324

(P-11167)
REED MANUFACTURING INC
Also Called: American Casting Co
51 Fallon Rd, Hollister (95023-9401)
PHONE..................................831 637-5641
John Reed, *President*
Simeon Bauer, *Vice Pres*
Chris St John, *Vice Pres*
Jeff Ferrara, *Engineer*
Oliver Hayes, *Engineer*
EMP: 35
SQ FT: 7,200
SALES (est): 8.6MM **Privately Held**
WEB: www.americancastingco.com
SIC: 3324 Commercial investment castings, ferrous

(P-11168)
SIERRA TECHNICAL SERVICES INC
Also Called: STS
101 Commercial Way Unit D, Tehachapi (93561-1427)
PHONE..................................661 823-1092
Roger Hayes, *President*
Debra Hayes, *Vice Pres*
EMP: 15
SQ FT: 7,000
SALES: 1.8MM **Privately Held**
SIC: 3324 8711 Aerospace investment castings, ferrous; engineering services

3325 Steel Foundries, NEC

(P-11169)
CALIFORNIA ELECTRIC STEEL
250 Monte Verda, Angels Camp (95222)
P.O. Box 817 (95222-0817)
PHONE..................................209 736-0465
Norman Stamm, *President*
Lorne Whittle, *President*
Joanne Whittle, *Corp Secy*
Donna Stamm, *Vice Pres*
EMP: 24 EST: 1854
SQ FT: 10,000
SALES (est): 5.4MM **Privately Held**
SIC: 3325 Alloy steel castings, except investment

(P-11170)
DAMERON ALLOY FOUNDRIES (PA)
6330 Gateway Dr Ste B, Cypress (90630-4836)
PHONE..................................310 631-5165
John W Dameron, *President*
Augustin Huerta, *Exec VP*
Joseph De Julio, *Vice Pres*
Christina Dameron, *Admin Mgr*
▲ **EMP:** 100 EST: 1946
SQ FT: 5,000
SALES (est): 22.1MM **Privately Held**
WEB: www.dameron.net
SIC: 3325 3324 Steel foundries; commercial investment castings, ferrous

(P-11171)
LIQUIDMETAL TECHNOLOGIES INC (PA)
20321 Valencia Cir, Lake Forest (92630-8159)
PHONE..................................949 635-2100
Lugee LI, *Ch of Bd*
Bruce Bromage, *COO*
Abdi Mahamedi, *Vice Ch Bd*
Bryce Van, *VP Finance*
Christina Martinez, *Supervisor*
▲ **EMP:** 28
SQ FT: 41,000
SALES: 532K **Publicly Held**
SIC: 3325 Alloy steel castings, except investment

(P-11172)
METAL CAST INC
Also Called: Metalcast
2002 W Chestnut Ave, Santa Ana (92703-4341)
P.O. Box 3099 (92703-0099)
PHONE..................................714 285-9792
Rigoberto Urquiza, *President*
EMP: 20
SQ FT: 12,000
SALES (est): 3.3MM **Privately Held**
SIC: 3325 Alloy steel castings, except investment

(P-11173)
TUSCO CASTING CORPORATION
934 E Victor Rd, Lodi (95240-0722)
P.O. Box 537 (95241-0537)
PHONE..................................209 368-5137
Kevin Steiger, *President*
Tanen Steiger, *Vice Pres*
EMP: 20 EST: 1965
SQ FT: 20,000

SALES (est): 3.7MM **Privately Held**
SIC: 3325 3365 3322 Alloy steel castings, except investment; aluminum foundries; malleable iron foundries

(P-11174)
WEST COAST FOUNDRY LLC (HQ)
2450 E 53rd St, Huntington Park (90255)
PHONE..................................323 583-1421
Michael Bargani, *President*
John Heine, *CFO*
Toni Banuelos, *Manager*
▲ **EMP:** 20
SQ FT: 18,000
SALES (est): 10.6MM
SALES (corp-wide): 178.1MM **Privately Held**
SIC: 3325 Alloy steel castings, except investment
PA: Speyside Equity Fund I Lp
430 E 86th St
New York NY 10028
212 994-0308

(P-11175)
WEST COAST STEEL & PROC LLC (PA)
Also Called: Steelco USA
3534 Philadelphia St, Chino (91710-2088)
PHONE..................................909 393-8405
Erik Gamm,
EMP: 75
SALES (est): 22.1MM **Privately Held**
SIC: 3325 Steel foundries

3331 Primary Smelting & Refining Of Copper

(P-11176)
CORRPRO COMPANIES INC
10260 Matern Pl, Santa Fe Springs (90670-3248)
PHONE..................................562 944-1636
Randy Galinski, *Principal*
EMP: 21
SALES (corp-wide): 1.3B **Publicly Held**
WEB: www.corrpro.com
SIC: 3331 1799 Cathodes (primary), copper; corrosion control installation
HQ: Corrpro Companies, Inc.
1055 W Smith Rd
Medina OH 44256
330 723-5082

3334 Primary Production Of Aluminum

(P-11177)
ADVANCED PATTERN & MOLD
1720 S Balboa Ave, Ontario (91761-7773)
PHONE..................................909 930-3444
Dan Hilger, *Partner*
Chris Vanderhagen, *Partner*
EMP: 15
SQ FT: 10,400
SALES (est): 2.3MM **Privately Held**
WEB: www.advancedpattern.com
SIC: 3334 Primary aluminum

(P-11178)
ARCONIC INC
Also Called: Alcoa
1300 Rancho Conejo Blvd, Newbury Park (91320-1405)
PHONE..................................805 262-4230
EMP: 427
SALES (corp-wide): 14B **Publicly Held**
SIC: 3334 Primary aluminum
PA: Arconic Inc.
201 Isabella St Ste 200
New York NY 15212
412 553-1950

(P-11179)
ARCONIC INC
Also Called: Alcoa
800 S State College Blvd, Fullerton (92831-5334)
PHONE..................................714 871-1550
Ui Choi, *Branch Mgr*
Patti Sherwood, *Sr Software Eng*

Genevieve Retamosa, *Engineer*
Bernie Rios, *Engineer*
Cory Littlefield, *Buyer*
EMP: 427
SALES (corp-wide): 14B **Publicly Held**
SIC: 3334 Primary aluminum
PA: Arconic Inc.
201 Isabella St Ste 200
Pittsburgh PA 15212
412 553-1950

(P-11180)
ARCONIC INC
Also Called: Alcoa
801 S Placentia Ave, Fullerton
(92831-5153)
PHONE.....................714 278-8981
EMP: 427
SALES (corp-wide): 14B **Publicly Held**
SIC: 3334 Primary aluminum
PA: Arconic Inc.
201 Isabella St Ste 200
New York NY 15212
412 553-1950

(P-11181)
ARCONIC INC
Also Called: Alcoa
3016 Lomita Blvd, Torrance (90505-5103)
PHONE.....................212 836-2674
Quan Tran, *Marketing Staff*
Angela Isley, *Manager*
EMP: 427
SALES (corp-wide): 14B **Publicly Held**
SIC: 3334 Primary aluminum
PA: Arconic Inc.
201 Isabella St Ste 200
New York NY 15212
412 553-1950

(P-11182)
ARCONIC INC
Also Called: Alcoa
12975 Bradley Ave, Sylmar (91342-3830)
PHONE.....................818 367-2261
James Costello, *President*
Natanael Orellana, *Engineer*
EMP: 427
SALES (corp-wide): 14B **Publicly Held**
SIC: 3334 Primary aluminum
PA: Arconic Inc.
201 Isabella St Ste 200
New York NY 15212
412 553-1950

(P-11183)
GAMMA ALLOYS INC
28128 Livingston Ave, Valencia
(91355-4115)
PHONE.....................661 294-5291
Mark Sommer,
Ken Polak,
Al Sommer,
Kris Sommer,
EMP: 10
SALES: 1.5MM **Privately Held**
SIC: 3334 Primary aluminum

(P-11184)
KAISER ALUMINUM
CORPORATION (PA)
27422 Portola Pkwy # 350, Foothill Ranch
(92610-2837)
PHONE.....................949 614-1740
Jack A Hockema, *Ch of Bd*
Keith A Harvey, *President*
Neal E West, *CFO*
Courtney Lynn, *Treasurer*
Holly Duckworth, *Officer*
▼ **EMP:** 60
SQ FT: 36,000
SALES: 1.5B **Publicly Held**
WEB: www.kaiseral.com
SIC: 3334 3353 3354 3355 Primary aluminum; aluminum sheet, plate & foil; aluminum rod & bar; bars, extruded, aluminum; rods, extruded, aluminum; wire, aluminum: made in rolling mills; cable, aluminum: made in rolling mills

(P-11185)
MAURICE & MAURICE ENGRG
INC
17579 Mesa St Ste B4, Hesperia
(92345-8308)
P.O. Box 403682 (92340-3682)
PHONE.....................760 949-5151
Jennifer Thomas, *CEO*
Aron Maurice, *Treasurer*
Jennifer Maurice, *Admin Sec*
EMP: 27 EST: 1973
SQ FT: 22,000
SALES: 2MM **Privately Held**
WEB: www.mauricemawer.com
SIC: 3334 Primary aluminum

(P-11186)
PRL ALUMINUM INC
14760 Don Julian Rd, City of Industry
(91746-3107)
PHONE.....................626 968-7507
Roberto Landeros, *CEO*
Aamer Javaid, *Info Tech Dir*
David Olague, *Sales Staff*
EMP: 100
SALES (est): 21.8MM
SALES (corp-wide): 79MM **Privately Held**
SIC: 3334 Primary aluminum
PA: Prl Glass Systems, Inc.
13644 Nelson Ave
City Of Industry CA 91746
626 961-5890

3339 Primary Nonferrous Metals, NEC

(P-11187)
A D S GOLD INC
3843 E Eagle Dr, Anaheim (92807-1705)
PHONE.....................714 632-1888
Patrick Joe Lopez, *CEO*
EMP: 14
SQ FT: 8,600
SALES (est): 2.9MM **Privately Held**
WEB: www.adsgold.com
SIC: 3339 Precious metals

(P-11188)
ARGEN CORPORATION (PA)
Also Called: Jelenko
5855 Oberlin Dr, San Diego (92121-3706)
PHONE.....................858 455-7900
Anton Woolf, *CEO*
Lou Azzara, *President*
Jackie Woolf, *President*
Jay Lowy, *COO*
Neil Wainstein, *CFO*
▲ **EMP:** 203
SQ FT: 39,609
SALES (est): 63.3MM **Privately Held**
WEB: www.argen.com
SIC: 3339 3843 Precious metals; dental equipment & supplies

(P-11189)
COMMODITY RESOURCE
ENVMTL INC
Also Called: Commodity Rsource Enviromental
11847 United St, Mojave (93501-7047)
PHONE.....................661 824-2416
Mike Kelsey, *General Mgr*
Michael Kelsey, *Plant Mgr*
EMP: 44
SALES (est): 6MM
SALES (corp-wide): 7.9MM **Privately Held**
SIC: 3339 3341 Precious metals; secondary nonferrous metals
PA: Commodity Resource & Environmental, Inc.
116 E Prospect Ave
Burbank CA 91502
818 843-2811

(P-11190)
FOREM MANUFACTURING INC
Also Called: Forem Metal
844 66th Ave, Oakland (94621-3716)
PHONE.....................510 577-9500
EMP: 12

SALES (est): 1.1MM **Privately Held**
SIC: 3339

(P-11191)
IRA GOLD GROUP LLC
9107 Wilshire Blvd # 450, Beverly Hills
(90210-5531)
PHONE.....................800 984-6008
Robert Smith, *Partner*
EMP: 10
SALES: 15MM **Privately Held**
SIC: 3339 Precious metals

(P-11192)
J & B REFINING INC
Also Called: J & B Enterprises
1650 Russell Ave, Santa Clara
(95054-2031)
PHONE.....................408 988-7900
Ken Epsman, *President*
Javier Espinosa, *Accounts Mgr*
EMP: 10 EST: 1973
SQ FT: 22,000
SALES (est): 1.7MM **Privately Held**
WEB: www.jandb.com
SIC: 3339 Precious metals

(P-11193)
NL INDUSTRIES INC
Also Called: Axel Johnson Metals
403 Ryder St, Vallejo (94590-7269)
PHONE.....................707 552-4850
Howard Harcker, *Vice Pres*
EMP: 40
SALES (corp-wide): 118.2MM **Publicly Held**
SIC: 3339 3341 Titanium metal, sponge & granules; secondary nonferrous metals
PA: N L Industries, Inc.
5430 Lbj Fwy Ste 1700
Dallas TX 75240
972 233-1700

(P-11194)
PCC ROLLMET INC
1822 Deere Ave, Irvine (92606-4817)
PHONE.....................949 221-5333
Ken Buck, *President*
Mark Donegan, *Ch of Bd*
Shawn Hagel, *CFO*
EMI Donis, *Vice Pres*
EMP: 70
SALES (est): 21.4MM
SALES (corp-wide): 225.3B **Publicly Held**
SIC: 3339 Nickel refining (primary)
HQ: Precision Castparts Corp.
4650 Sw Mcdam Ave Ste 300
Portland OR 97239
503 946-4800

(P-11195)
SUPERIOR QUARTZ INC
Also Called: Silica Engineering Group
3370 Edward Ave, Santa Clara
(95054-2309)
PHONE.....................408 844-9663
Nermin Aganbegovic, *President*
EMP: 15
SQ FT: 13,000
SALES: 6.4MM **Privately Held**
WEB: www.silicaeng.com
SIC: 3339 3679 3264 Silicon, pure; quartz crystals, for electronic application; magnets, permanent: ceramic or ferrite

(P-11196)
WESTERN MESQUITE MINES
INC
6502 E Us Highway 78, Brawley
(92227-9306)
PHONE.....................928 341-4653
Randall Oliphant, *Chairman*
Cory Atiyeh, *President*
Robert Gallagher, *CEO*
W Hanson P Geo, *Vice Pres*
Penny Brian, *Admin Sec*
EMP: 20
SALES (est): 14MM
SALES (corp-wide): 30.1MM **Privately Held**
SIC: 3339 Gold refining (primary)
PA: Equinox Gold Corp
700 West Pender St Suite 1501
Vancouver BC V6C 1
604 558-0560

3341 Secondary Smelting & Refining Of Nonferrous Metals

(P-11197)
ALL METALS INC (PA)
Also Called: Ecs Refining
705 Reed St, Santa Clara (95050-3942)
PHONE.....................408 200-7000
James L Taggart, *President*
Kenneth Taggart, *Vice Pres*
Ken Taggart, *Program Mgr*
Jim Nelson, *General Mgr*
Kent Taggart, *General Mgr*
▲ **EMP:** 20 EST: 1980
SQ FT: 24,000
SALES (est): 11.5MM **Privately Held**
WEB: www.allmetals.com
SIC: 3341 4953 3339 Secondary precious metals; tin smelting & refining (secondary); lead smelting & refining (secondary); silver recovery from used photographic film; refuse systems; primary nonferrous metals

(P-11198)
CUSTOM ALLOY SALES INC
(PA)
Also Called: Custom Alloy Light Metals
13191 Crssrds Pkwy N, City of Industry
(91746)
PHONE.....................626 369-3641
Brandon Cox, *CEO*
Kenneth J Cox, *President*
Tim Chisum, *CFO*
Nicholas Drakos, *Vice Pres*
Angel Vega, *Director*
◆ **EMP:** 80
SALES (est): 150MM **Privately Held**
WEB: www.customingot.com
SIC: 3341 5051 Aluminum smelting & refining (secondary); zinc

(P-11199)
DAVID H FELL & CO INC (PA)
6009 Bandini Blvd, Los Angeles
(90040-2967)
PHONE.....................323 722-9992
Larry Fell, *CEO*
Lawrence Fell, *President*
Sondra Fell, *Treasurer*
Ed Wegener, *Vice Pres*
▼ **EMP:** 24
SQ FT: 18,000
SALES (est): 4.5MM **Privately Held**
WEB: www.dhfco.com
SIC: 3341 5094 Secondary precious metals; bullion, precious metals

(P-11200)
ESPERER HOLDINGS INC (PA)
3820 State St, Santa Barbara
(93105-3182)
PHONE.....................805 880-4220
D Stephen Sorensen, *CEO*
Julie Danley, *Director*
EMP: 20 EST: 2011
SALES (est): 3.8MM **Privately Held**
SIC: 3341 3911 Secondary precious metals; jewelry, precious metal; medals, precious or semiprecious metal

(P-11201)
GEMINI INDUSTRIES INC
2311 Pullman St, Santa Ana (92705-5585)
PHONE.....................949 250-4011
M Elguindy, *CEO*
Melinda Munoz, *CFO*
Munib Razzaq, *Vice Pres*
Melissa Jones, *Executive*
Diana Keiffer, *Admin Sec*
▲ **EMP:** 75
SQ FT: 150,000
SALES (est): 17.8MM **Privately Held**
SIC: 3341 Secondary precious metals; platinum group metals, smelting & refining (secondary)

▲ = Import ▼=Export
◆ =Import/Export

(P-11202)
GPS METALS LAB INC
12396 World Trade Dr, San Diego
(92128-3786)
PHONE..............................858 433-6125
Christian Galvis, *Principal*
Miguel Palomino, *President*
EMP: 30
SALES (est): 1.5MM Privately Held
SIC: 3341 5051 5093 3339 Secondary precious metals; recovery & refining of nonferrous metals; nonferrous metal sheets, bars, rods, etc.; nonferrous metals scrap; precious metals

(P-11203)
HERAEUS PRCOUS MTLS N AMER LLC (DH)
15524 Carmenita Rd, Santa Fe Springs
(90670-5610)
PHONE..............................562 921-7464
Roland Gerner, *Mng Member*
Nicole Taylor, *Research*
Ryan Christiansen, *Accountant*
Henry MA, *Sales Mgr*
Karin Butfiloski, *Sales Staff*
▲ EMP: 200
SQ FT: 71,000
SALES (est): 72.8MM
SALES (corp-wide): 355.8K Privately Held
WEB: www.heraeusca.com
SIC: 3341 2899 Gold smelting & refining (secondary); silver smelting & refining (secondary); platinum group metals, smelting & refining (secondary); chemical preparations; salt
HQ: Heraeus Holding Gesellschaft Mit Beschrankter Haftung
Heraeusstr. 12-14
Hanau 63450
618 135-0

(P-11204)
MATTHEY JOHNSON INC
Also Called: Noble Metals
12205 World Trade Dr, San Diego
(92128-3766)
P.O. Box Orld Trade (92128)
PHONE..............................858 716-2400
Steve Hill, *Branch Mgr*
Edward H Ravert, *Vice Pres*
Chris Craft, *Info Tech Dir*
Maria Kurtz, *Info Tech Mgr*
Praus Lee, *IT/INT Sup*
EMP: 139
SALES (corp-wide): 13.8B Privately Held
SIC: 3341 Secondary nonferrous metals
HQ: Johnson Matthey Inc.
435 Devon Park Dr Ste 600
Wayne PA 19087
610 971-3000

(P-11205)
METECH RECYCLING INC
6200 Engle Way, Gilroy (95020-7012)
PHONE..............................408 848-3050
Tom Richards, *Branch Mgr*
EMP: 30
SQ FT: 40,000
SALES (corp-wide): 62.7MM Privately Held
SIC: 3341 3339 Secondary nonferrous metals; primary nonferrous metals
HQ: Metech Recycling, Inc.
6200 Engle Way
Gilroy CA 95020
408 763-9887

(P-11206)
ON-GARD METALS INC
8638 Cleta St, Downey (90241-5201)
PHONE..............................562 622-9057
Dick Gard, *President*
EMP: 12
SQ FT: 6,000
SALES (est): 1.1MM Privately Held
SIC: 3341 Aluminum smelting & refining (secondary)

(P-11207)
PROCESS MATERIALS INC
5625 Brisa St Ste B, Livermore
(94550-2526)
PHONE..............................925 245-9626
Barry Nudelman, *President*

Lori Nudelman, *CFO*
Adam Nudelman, *Manager*
▲ EMP: 13
SQ FT: 18,000
SALES (est): 2.4MM Privately Held
WEB: www.processmaterials.com
SIC: 3341 Secondary nonferrous metals

(P-11208)
QUEMETCO WEST LLC (DH)
720 S 7th Ave, City of Industry
(91746-3124)
PHONE..............................626 330-2294
Robert E Finn, *Mng Member*
George Cummins,
Peter King,
▲ EMP: 19
SALES (est): 2MM
SALES (corp-wide): 276.4MM Privately Held
SIC: 3341 Lead smelting & refining (secondary)
HQ: Rsr Corporation
2777 N Stemmons Fwy # 2000
Dallas TX 75207
214 631-6070

(P-11209)
TEXAS TST INC
13428 Benson Ave, Chino (91710-5258)
PHONE..............................951 685-2155
Andrew G Stein, *CEO*
Robert Stein, *President*
◆ EMP: 50
SALES (est): 9.5MM
SALES (corp-wide): 64.6MM Privately Held
SIC: 3341 Aluminum smelting & refining (secondary)
PA: Tst, Inc.
13428 Benson Ave
Chino CA 91710
951 737-3169

(P-11210)
THOROCK METALS INC
1213 S Pacific Coast Hwy, Redondo Beach
(90277-4905)
PHONE..............................310 537-1597
Holly Kadota, *President*
Holly M Kadota, *President*
Craig Mock, *CFO*
Jeff Mock, *Exec VP*
EMP: 25 EST: 1968
SQ FT: 50,000
SALES (est): 4.7MM Privately Held
WEB: www.thorockmetals.com
SIC: 3341 Aluminum smelting & refining (secondary)

(P-11211)
TST INC
Alpase
13428 Benson Ave, Chino (91710-5258)
PHONE..............................951 727-3169
Andrew G Stein, *CEO*
EMP: 40
SALES (corp-wide): 64.6MM Privately Held
SIC: 3341 Aluminum smelting & refining (secondary)
PA: Tst, Inc.
13428 Benson Ave
Chino CA 91710
951 737-3169

(P-11212)
TST INC (PA)
Also Called: Alpase
13428 Benson Ave, Chino (91710-5258)
PHONE..............................951 737-3169
Andrew G Stein, *CEO*
Robert A Stein, *Ch of Bd*
Greg Levine, *Vice Pres*
Lorenzo Rojas, *Controller*
◆ EMP: 260
SQ FT: 123,000
SALES (est): 64.6MM Privately Held
WEB: www.tst-inc.com
SIC: 3341 5093 Aluminum smelting & refining (secondary); metal scrap & waste materials

---

3351 Rolling, Drawing & Extruding Of Copper

(P-11213)
C F W RESEARCH & DEV CO
Also Called: Cfw Precision Metal Components
338 S 4th St, Grover Beach (93433-1999)
P.O. Box 446 (93483-0446)
PHONE..............................805 489-8750
Michael A Greenelsh, *President*
Kathryn Greenelsh, *Corp Secy*
Harlan Silva, *Vice Pres*
EMP: 16
SQ FT: 10,000
SALES (est): 4.3MM
SALES (corp-wide): 11MM Privately Held
WEB: www.cfwpmc.com
SIC: 3351 Wire, copper & copper alloy
PA: California Fine Wire Co.
338 S 4th St
Grover Beach CA 93433
805 489-5144

(P-11214)
CTS FABRICATION USA INC
11220 Pyrites Way Ste 300, Gold River
(95670-6334)
PHONE..............................916 852-6303
Gary Stanley, *President*
Terry Stanley, *Shareholder*
Mary Stanley, *Admin Sec*
▲ EMP: 10
SALES (est): 1.7MM Privately Held
WEB: www.ctsflange.com
SIC: 3351 Copper pipe

3353 Aluminum Sheet, Plate & Foil

(P-11215)
AMERICAN ALUPACK INDS LLC
1201 N Rice Ave Unit B, Oxnard
(93030-7964)
PHONE..............................805 485-1500
Manny Thakkar, *CEO*
Mita Thakkar, *President*
Irma H Thakkar, *Director*
◆ EMP: 35
SQ FT: 60,000
SALES (est): 17MM Privately Held
SIC: 3353 Foil, aluminum

(P-11216)
EURAMAX HOLDINGS INC
Also Called: Amerimax
1411 N Daly St, Anaheim (92806-1503)
PHONE..............................714 563-8260
Steve Bringers, *Manager*
EMP: 12
SALES (corp-wide): 840.5MM Privately Held
SIC: 3353 5051 Coils, sheet aluminum; aluminum bars, rods, ingots, sheets, pipes, plates, etc.
PA: Omnimax Holdings, Inc.
303 Research Dr Ste 400
Norcross GA 30092
770 449-7066

(P-11217)
GOLDEN STATE ASSEMBLY INC
47823 Westinghouse Dr, Fremont
(94539-7437)
P.O. Box 611913, San Jose (95161-1913)
PHONE..............................510 226-8155
Yesenia Castillo, *CEO*
Cesar E Madrueno, *President*
Nancy Martinez, *Accounting Mgr*
Vicente Madrueno, *Production*
EMP: 200
SALES (est): 19MM Privately Held
SIC: 3353 3569 3312 3679 Aluminum sheet & strip; assembly machines, nonmetalworking; wire products, steel or iron; harness assemblies for electronic use: wire or cable; aluminum wire & cable

(P-11218)
ITW SEMISYSTEMS INC
625 Wool Creek Dr Ste G, San Jose
(95112-2622)
PHONE..............................408 350-0244
EMP: 30
SALES (est): 3.7MM
SALES (corp-wide): 41MM Privately Held
WEB: www.mdc-vacuum.com
SIC: 3353
PA: Mdc Vacuum Products, Llc
30962 Santana St
Hayward CA 94544
510 265-3500

(P-11219)
KAISER ALUMINUM FAB PDTS LLC (HQ)
Also Called: Kafp
27422 Portola Pkwy # 200, Foothill Ranch
(92610-2831)
PHONE..............................949 614-1740
Jack A Hockema, *President*
Joseph P Bellino, *CFO*
John M Donnan, *Vice Pres*
Rebecca Harris, *Planning*
Andrew Kolman, *Engineer*
◆ EMP: 2200
SALES (est): 767.4MM
SALES (corp-wide): 1.5B Publicly Held
WEB: www.kaisertwd.com
SIC: 3353 3334 3354 3355 Aluminum sheet, plate & foil; primary aluminum; aluminum rod & bar; wire, aluminum: made in rolling mills
PA: Kaiser Aluminum Corporation
27422 Portola Pkwy # 350
Foothill Ranch CA 92610
949 614-1740

(P-11220)
KAISER ALUMINUM INVESTMENTS CO (HQ)
Also Called: Kaic
27422 Portola Pkwy # 350, Foothill Ranch
(92610-2837)
PHONE..............................949 614-1740
Jack A Hockema, *President*
Joseph P Bellino, *CFO*
Daniel J Rinkenberger, *Treasurer*
John M Donnan, *Vice Pres*
EMP: 200
SALES (est): 211.3MM
SALES (corp-wide): 1.5B Publicly Held
SIC: 3353 3334 3354 3355 Aluminum sheet, plate & foil; primary aluminum; aluminum rod & bar; wire, aluminum: made in rolling mills
PA: Kaiser Aluminum Corporation
27422 Portola Pkwy # 350
Foothill Ranch CA 92610
949 614-1740

(P-11221)
MATERIAL SCIENCES CORPORATION
Also Called: MSC-La
3730 Capitol Ave, City of Industry
(90601-1731)
PHONE..............................562 699-4550
Patrick Murley, *CEO*
EMP: 45
SALES (corp-wide): 131.2MM Privately Held
SIC: 3353 Aluminum sheet, plate & foil
PA: Material Sciences Corporation
6855 Commerce Blvd
Canton MI 48187
734 207-4444

(P-11222)
MAVERICK ENTERPRISES INC
751 E Gobbi St, Ukiah (95482-6205)
PHONE..............................707 463-5591
Steve Otterbeck, *President*
Mike Benetti, *COO*
Jon Henderson, *Exec VP*
Kevin Forster, *Vice Pres*
Fred Koeppel, *Vice Pres*
▲ EMP: 105
SQ FT: 30,000
SALES (est): 31.4MM Privately Held
WEB: www.maverickcaps.com
SIC: 3353 Foil, aluminum

PA: Pcm Companies, Llc
2150 Dodd Rd
Mendota Heights MN 55120
-

(P-11223)
SOUTHWIRE INC (HQ)
Also Called: Electrical Products Division
11695 Pacific Ave, Fontana (92337-8225)
PHONE....................................310 884-8500
Mark Kaminski, *COO*
EMP: 15
SQ FT: 210,000
SALES (est): 83.2MM
SALES (corp-wide): 2.2B **Privately Held**
WEB: www.alflex.com
SIC: 3353 3644 3315 Coils, sheet aluminum; electric conduits & fittings; cable, steel: insulated or armored
PA: Southwire Company, Llc
1 Southwire Dr
Carrollton GA 30119
770 832-4242

(P-11224)
TCI TEXARKANA INC (DH)
5855 Obispo Ave, Long Beach (90805-3715)
PHONE....................................562 808-8000
Johnny Hsieh, *CEO*
James Chang, *Vice Pres*
Andrew Chang, *Controller*
EMP: 12
SALES (est): 10.3MM **Privately Held**
SIC: 3353 Coils, sheet aluminum
HQ: Ta Chen International, Inc.
5855 Obispo Ave
Long Beach CA 90805
562 808-8000

(P-11225)
TECHNICAL ANODIZE
1142 Price Ave, Pomona (91767-5838)
PHONE....................................909 865-9034
Fernando Salazar, *Partner*
Emilio Mendez, *Partner*
EMP: 13
SALES (est): 1.9MM **Privately Held**
SIC: 3353 3471 2796 Plates, aluminum; sand blasting of metal parts; electrotype plates

---
3354 Aluminum Extruded Prdts

(P-11226)
BUILDIT ENGINEERING CO INC
3074 N Lima St, Burbank (91504-2012)
PHONE....................................818 244-6666
Barry Alberts, *President*
Pat Alberts, *Treasurer*
Scott Alberts, *Vice Pres*
▲ **EMP:** 12
SQ FT: 8,000
SALES (est): 1.8MM **Privately Held**
WEB: www.builditengineering.com
SIC: 3354 3312 8711 Aluminum extruded products; stainless steel; engineering services

(P-11227)
CASELLA ALUMINUM EXTRUSIONS
Also Called: C A E
824 N Todd Ave, Azusa (91702-2228)
PHONE....................................714 961-8322
EMP: 12
SQ FT: 8,000
SALES (est): 1.5MM **Privately Held**
SIC: 3354

(P-11228)
COLUMBIA ALUMINUM PRODUCTS LLC
2565 Sampson Ave, Corona (92879-7109)
PHONE....................................323 728-7361
Drew D Mumford, *Owner*
Grant Palenske, *Vice Pres*
▲ **EMP:** 70
SQ FT: 60,000
SALES (est): 22.5MM **Privately Held**
WEB:
www.columbiaaluminumproductsllc.com
SIC: 3354 Aluminum extruded products

(P-11229)
FRY REGLET CORPORATION (PA)
14013 Marquardt Ave, Santa Fe Springs (90670-5018)
P.O. Box 665, La Mirada (90637-0665)
PHONE....................................800 237-9773
Stephen Reed, *CEO*
Avon M Hall, *President*
James Tuttle, *CFO*
EMP: 200 **EST:** 1945
SQ FT: 20,000
SALES (est): 96.8MM **Privately Held**
WEB: www.fryreglet.com
SIC: 3354 Aluminum extruded products

(P-11230)
GEMINI ALUMINUM CORPORATION
3255 Pomona Blvd, Pomona (91768-3291)
P.O. Box 1462, Sandpoint ID (83864-0866)
PHONE....................................909 595-7403
Alan J Hardy, *President*
Healani Hardy, *Admin Sec*
EMP: 30 **EST:** 1976
SQ FT: 10,000
SALES (est): 9.6MM **Privately Held**
SIC: 3354 Aluminum rod & bar

(P-11231)
GLOBAL TRUSS AMERICA LLC
4295 Charter St, Vernon (90058-2520)
PHONE....................................323 415-6225
Charles Davies, *Mng Member*
Kenneth Kahn, *General Mgr*
◆ **EMP:** 55
SQ FT: 60,000
SALES (est): 16MM **Privately Held**
WEB: www.globaltruss.com
SIC: 3354 Aluminum extruded products

(P-11232)
HASTINGS IRRIGATION PIPE CO
17619 Road 24, Madera (93638-9645)
PHONE....................................559 675-1200
Geryanne Hansen, *Manager*
EMP: 14
SQ FT: 22,000
SALES (corp-wide): 35MM **Privately Held**
WEB: www.hipco-ne.com
SIC: 3354 Pipe, extruded, aluminum
PA: Hastings Irrigation Pipe Co.
1801 E South St
Hastings NE 68901
402 463-6633

(P-11233)
HYDRO EXTRUDER LLC
18111 Railroad St, City of Industry (91748-1216)
PHONE....................................626 964-3411
Matt Zundel, *Sales Dir*
EMP: 300
SALES (corp-wide): 18.9B **Privately Held**
SIC: 3354 Aluminum extruded products
HQ: Hydro Extruder, Llc
Airport Offc Park
Moon Township PA 15108

(P-11234)
KAISER ALUMINUM CORPORATION
6250 Bandini Blvd, Commerce (90040-3168)
PHONE....................................323 726-8011
D F Smith, *Manager*
Sean O'Brien, *Project Mgr*
Jordan Marcelo, *Accountant*
Stephen Law, *Director*
Raul Reyes, *Manager*
EMP: 22
SALES (corp-wide): 1.5B **Publicly Held**
SIC: 3354 Aluminum extruded products
PA: Kaiser Aluminum Corporation
27422 Portola Pkwy # 350
Foothill Ranch CA 92610
949 614-1740

(P-11235)
KAISER ALUMINUM FAB PDTS LLC
6250 Bandini Blvd, Commerce (90040-3168)
PHONE....................................323 722-7151
D F Smith, *Branch Mgr*
EMP: 150
SALES (corp-wide): 1.5B **Publicly Held**
WEB: www.kaisertwd.com
SIC: 3354 Aluminum extruded products
HQ: Kaiser Aluminum Fabricated Products, Llc
27422 Portola Pkwy # 200
Foothill Ranch CA 92610

(P-11236)
LUXFER INC
1995 3rd St, Riverside (92507-3483)
PHONE....................................951 684-5110
Brian McGuire, *Manager*
Jeff Riddell, *Human Res Mgr*
EMP: 178
SALES (corp-wide): 487.9MM **Privately Held**
WEB: www.luxfer-ecare.com
SIC: 3354 3728 Aluminum extruded products; aircraft parts & equipment
HQ: Luxfer Inc.
3016 Kansas Ave Bldg 1
Riverside CA 92507
951 684-5110

(P-11237)
MAGELLAN INTERNATIONAL CORP
Also Called: Magerack
4453 Enterprise St, Fremont (94538-6306)
PHONE....................................510 656-6661
Jason Xie, *President*
▲ **EMP:** 10
SQ FT: 3,000
SALES (est): 5MM **Privately Held**
WEB: www.magellancorp.com
SIC: 3354 7389 Shapes, extruded aluminum; translation services

(P-11238)
MERIT ALUMINUM INC (PA)
2480 Railroad St, Corona (92880-5418)
PHONE....................................951 735-1770
Michael Rapport, *President*
Evan Rapport, *Vice Pres*
Vincent Lee, *Human Res Mgr*
▲ **EMP:** 100
SQ FT: 58,000
SALES (est): 43.6MM **Privately Held**
WEB: www.frontier-aluminum.com
SIC: 3354 Aluminum extruded products

(P-11239)
MICRO TRIM INC
3613 W Macarthur Blvd # 605, Santa Ana (92704-6846)
PHONE....................................714 241-7046
Robert Catena, *President*
Jodi Catena, *Treasurer*
Stefanie Catena, *Vice Pres*
Ryan Preciado, *Office Mgr*
Lori Peterson, *Marketing Mgr*
EMP: 12
SQ FT: 4,500
SALES (est): 1.3MM **Privately Held**
WEB: www.microtrim.com
SIC: 3354 Aluminum extruded products

(P-11240)
MOBILE DESIGNS INC
4650 Caterpillar Rd, Redding (96003-1416)
PHONE....................................530 244-1050
William Marsh, *President*
▼ **EMP:** 13
SALES (est): 2.2MM **Privately Held**
WEB: www.mobiledesigns.com
SIC: 3354 Aluminum extruded products

(P-11241)
NEAL FEAY COMPANY
Also Called: Troy Metal Products
133 S La Patera Ln, Goleta (93117-3291)
PHONE....................................805 967-4521
Neal C Rasmussen, *CEO*
N J Rasmussen, *Corp Secy*
Alex Rasmussen, *Vice Pres*

Alan Owens, *Executive*
Fernando Ayala, *Prgrmr*
EMP: 60 **EST:** 1944
SQ FT: 50,000
SALES (est): 14.4MM **Privately Held**
WEB: www.nealfeay.com
SIC: 3354 3469 Tube, extruded or drawn, aluminum; electronic enclosures, stamped or pressed metal

(P-11242)
PARAMOUNT EXTRUSIONS COMPANY (PA)
6833 Rosecrans Ave, Paramount (90723-3152)
P.O. Box 847 (90723-0847)
PHONE....................................562 634-3291
Charles E Munson, *CEO*
Leslie C Munson, *President*
Frank Fry, *Vice Pres*
Gary Munson, *Admin Sec*
▲ **EMP:** 30
SQ FT: 2,000
SALES (est): 6MM **Privately Held**
WEB: www.paramountextrusions.com
SIC: 3354 3312 Aluminum extruded products; blast furnaces & steel mills

(P-11243)
PARAMOUNT EXTRUSIONS COMPANY
6833 Rosecrans Ave Ste A, Paramount (90723-3152)
P.O. Box 847 (90723-0847)
PHONE....................................562 634-3291
Les Munson, *President*
EMP: 24
SALES (est): 2.9MM
SALES (corp-wide): 6MM **Privately Held**
WEB: www.paramountextrusions.com
SIC: 3354 Aluminum extruded products
PA: Paramount Extrusions Company
6833 Rosecrans Ave
Paramount CA 90723
562 634-3291

(P-11244)
SAPA EXTRUSIONS INC
2821 E Philadelphia St A, Ontario (91761-8522)
PHONE....................................909 947-7682
EMP: 166
SALES (corp-wide): 80MM **Privately Held**
SIC: 3354
HQ: Sapa Extrusions, Inc.
9600 Bryn Mawr Ave # 250
Rosemont IL 60018
412 299-2286

(P-11245)
SIERRA ALUMINUM COMPANY (HQ)
2345 Fleetwood Dr, Riverside (92509-2426)
PHONE....................................951 781-7800
Edward A Harris, *CEO*
Ed Harris, *COO*
Tim Lara, *Vice Pres*
Shayne Seever, *Vice Pres*
Patrick Knight, *Administration*
▲ **EMP:** 24
SQ FT: 62,000
SALES (est): 10.7MM
SALES (corp-wide): 1.8B **Privately Held**
WEB: www.sierraaluminum.com
SIC: 3354 Aluminum extruded products
PA: Samuel, Son & Co., Limited
2360 Dixie Rd
Mississauga ON L4Y 1
905 279-5460

(P-11246)
SUN VALLEY PRODUCTS INC
Also Called: Sun Valley Extrusion
4640 Sperry St, Los Angeles (90039-1018)
PHONE....................................818 247-8350
Kerry Dodge, *Branch Mgr*
EMP: 35
SALES (corp-wide): 5.8MM **Privately Held**
WEB: www.sunvalleyextrusion.com
SIC: 3354 Aluminum extruded products

HQ: Sun Valley Products, Inc.
4626 Sperry St
Los Angeles CA 90039
818 247-8350

(P-11247)
SUN VALLEY PRODUCTS INC (HQ)
4626 Sperry St, Los Angeles (90039-1018)
PHONE.................................818 247-8350
Jennifer K Hillman, *President*
Rosanne M Kusar, *Ch of Bd*
Angelica K Clark, *Treasurer*
EMP: 60 EST: 1960
SQ FT: 64,980
SALES (est): 9MM
SALES (corp-wide): 5.8MM **Privately Held**
WEB: www.sunvalleyextrusion.com
SIC: 3354 Aluminum extruded products
PA: Darfield Industries Inc
4626 Sperry St
Los Angeles CA 90039
818 247-8350

(P-11248)
SUPERIOR METAL SHAPES INC
4730 Eucalyptus Ave, Chino (91710-9255)
PHONE.................................909 947-3455
David A Stockton, *President*
Yasushi Shimabukuro, *Consultant*
EMP: 40
SQ FT: 64,000
SALES: 7MM **Privately Held**
SIC: 3354 Shapes, extruded aluminum

(P-11249)
TRULITE GL ALUM SOLUTIONS LLC
19430 San Jose Ave, City of Industry (91748-1421)
PHONE.................................800 877-8439
Elizabeth Hemsing, *Manager*
Elizabeth Ruiz, *Human Res Mgr*
Luis Cervera, *Production*
Lien Waivers, *Products*
Beau Hadley, *Sales Staff*
EMP: 16 **Privately Held**
SIC: 3354 Aluminum extruded products
PA: Trulite Glass & Aluminum Solutions, Llc
403 Westpark Ct Ste 201
Peachtree City GA 30269

(P-11250)
UNIVERSAL ALLOY CORPORATION
Also Called: Alu Menziken
2871 E John Ball Way, Anaheim (92806-2497)
PHONE.................................714 630-7200
Nancy Newmeyer, *Branch Mgr*
Tim Myers, *President*
EMP: 300
SALES (corp-wide): 1.4B **Privately Held**
WEB: www.menzaero.com
SIC: 3354 Shapes, extruded aluminum
HQ: Universal Alloy Corporation
180 Lamar Haley Pkwy
Canton GA 30114
888 479-7230

(P-11251)
UNIVERSAL MLDING EXTRUSION INC (DH)
Also Called: Umex
9151 Imperial Hwy, Downey (90242-2808)
PHONE.................................562 401-1015
Dominick L Baione, *CEO*
Sonia Prines, *Sales Staff*
Jesse Lara, *Manager*
▼ EMP: 45
SALES (est): 49.1MM **Privately Held**
WEB: www.umextrude.com
SIC: 3354 Aluminum extruded products
HQ: Universal Molding Company
9151 Imperial Hwy
Downey CA 90242
310 886-1750

(P-11252)
US POLYMERS INC
5910 Bandini Blvd, Commerce (90040-2963)
PHONE.................................323 727-6888

Vram Ohanesiam, *Manager*
EMP: 37
SALES (corp-wide): 40.3MM **Privately Held**
WEB: www.uspolymersinc.com
SIC: 3354 5719 Aluminum extruded products; window furnishings
PA: U.S. Polymers, Inc.
1057 S Vail Ave
Montebello CA 90640
323 728-3023

(P-11253)
VISION SYSTEMS INC
11322 Woodside Ave N, Santee (92071-4728)
PHONE.................................619 258-7300
Fred W Witte, *President*
James Schlereth, *Vice Pres*
Denise Fletcher, *Administration*
Michelle Murray, *Administration*
Whitey Rishel, *Purch Mgr*
▲ EMP: 60
SQ FT: 32,000
SALES (est): 34.1MM **Privately Held**
WEB: www.visionsystems.org
SIC: 3354 3442 Aluminum extruded products; window & door frames

(P-11254)
VISTA METALS CORP (PA)
13425 Whittram Ave, Fontana (92335-2999)
PHONE.................................909 823-4278
Andrew Primack, *CEO*
Raymond Alpert, *Corp Secy*
Steve Chevlin, *Exec VP*
Robert Praefke, *Exec VP*
Ket Tran, *Admin Asst*
◆ EMP: 239 EST: 1968
SQ FT: 17,000
SALES (est): 68.5MM **Privately Held**
SIC: 3354 3341 Aluminum extruded products; aluminum smelting & refining (secondary)

3355 Aluminum Rolling & Drawing, NEC

(P-11255)
ARCADIA INC
2324 Del Monte St, West Sacramento (95691-3807)
PHONE.................................916 375-1478
Eddy Sala, *Branch Mgr*
EMP: 20
SALES (corp-wide): 124.6MM **Privately Held**
WEB: www.arcadiaincorporated.com
SIC: 3355 Extrusion ingot, aluminum: made in rolling mills
PA: Arcadia, Inc.
2301 E Vernon Ave
Vernon CA 90058
323 269-7300

(P-11256)
ARCADIA INC (PA)
Also Called: Arcadia Norcal
2301 E Vernon Ave, Vernon (90058-8052)
PHONE.................................323 269-7300
James Schladen, *CEO*
Khan Chow, *CFO*
Henry Nguyen, *Executive*
Neal Anderson, *Division Mgr*
Mark Knutson, *General Mgr*
▲ EMP: 250
SQ FT: 50,000
SALES (est): 124.6MM **Privately Held**
WEB: www.arcadiaincorporated.com
SIC: 3355 Extrusion ingot, aluminum: made in rolling mills

(P-11257)
CST POWER AND CONSTRUCTION INC (HQ)
879 W 190th St Ste 1100, Gardena (90248-4205)
PHONE.................................310 523-2322
Walter G Mitchell, *Ch of Bd*
Charles E Miller, *President*
Joseph Schmidt, *CEO*
◆ EMP: 70 EST: 1964

SALES (est): 19MM
SALES (corp-wide): 353.7MM **Privately Held**
SIC: 3355 3569 3448 3444 Structural shapes, rolled, aluminum; filter elements, fluid, hydraulic line; prefabricated metal buildings; sheet metalwork; fabricated structural metal

(P-11258)
DURALUM PRODUCTS INC (PA)
8269 Alpine Ave, Sacramento (95826-4708)
P.O. Box 1061, Fair Oaks (95628-1061)
PHONE.................................916 452-7021
William Anson, *CEO*
Bill Anson, *President*
Cheryl L Anson, *Corp Secy*
Ron Cull, *Manager*
Brian Quinn, *Manager*
EMP: 14 EST: 1962
SQ FT: 40,000
SALES (est): 8.9MM **Privately Held**
WEB: www.duralum.com
SIC: 3355 Aluminum rolling & drawing

(P-11259)
DURALUM PRODUCTS INC
2485 Railroad St, Corona (92880-5419)
PHONE.................................951 736-4500
Ron Cull, *Manager*
EMP: 15
SALES (corp-wide): 8.9MM **Privately Held**
WEB: www.duralum.com
SIC: 3355 Aluminum rolling & drawing
PA: Duralum Products, Inc.
8269 Alpine Ave
Sacramento CA 95826
916 452-7021

(P-11260)
GEO A DIACK INC
1250 S Johnson Dr, City of Industry (91745-2481)
PHONE.................................626 961-2491
Thomas Gonzalez, *President*
Consuelo Diack, *Vice Pres*
Tom Gonzalez, *Warehouse Mgr*
EMP: 32
SQ FT: 30,000
SALES (est): 4.7MM **Privately Held**
WEB: www.showcasesbydiack.com
SIC: 3355 Aluminum rolling & drawing

(P-11261)
INTERSTATE STEEL CENTER CO
7001 S Alameda St, Los Angeles (90001-2204)
PHONE.................................323 583-0855
Leon Banks, *President*
William Korth, *Admin Sec*
EMP: 50
SQ FT: 53,000
SALES (est): 5.8MM **Privately Held**
SIC: 3355 3312 Coils, wire aluminum: made in rolling mills; blast furnaces & steel mills

(P-11262)
JAYCO HAWAII CALIFORNIA
1468 66th St, Emeryville (94608-1014)
PHONE.................................510 601-9916
John Delay, *President*
EMP: 10
SALES (est): 1.3MM **Privately Held**
SIC: 3355 Rails, rolled & drawn, aluminum

(P-11263)
METALS USA BUILDING PDTS LP (DH)
955 Columbia St, Brea (92821-2923)
PHONE.................................713 946-9000
Charles Canning, *Partner*
Robert McPherson, *Partner*
▲ EMP: 700
SQ FT: 60,000
SALES (est): 300.4MM
SALES (corp-wide): 11.5B **Publicly Held**
WEB: www.gerardusa.com
SIC: 3355 5031 1542 Structural shapes, rolled, aluminum; building materials, exterior; commercial & office buildings, renovation & repair

HQ: Metals Usa, Inc.
4901 Nw 17th Way Ste 405
Fort Lauderdale FL 33309
954 202-4000

(P-11264)
METALS USA BUILDING PDTS LP
1951 S Parco Ave Ste C, Ontario (91761-8315)
PHONE.................................800 325-1305
Steve Brang, *Manager*
EMP: 45
SALES (corp-wide): 11.5B **Publicly Held**
WEB: www.gerardusa.com
SIC: 3355 Structural shapes, rolled, aluminum
HQ: Metals Usa Building Products Lp
955 Columbia St
Brea CA 92821
713 946-9000

(P-11265)
METALS USA BUILDING PDTS LP
11340 White Rock Rd Ste B, Rancho Cordova (95742-6606)
PHONE.................................916 635-2245
EMP: 25
SALES (corp-wide): 9.2B **Publicly Held**
SIC: 3355
HQ: Metals Usa Building Products Lp
2440 Albright Dr
Houston TX 92821
713 946-9000

(P-11266)
METALS USA BUILDING PDTS LP
955 Columbia St, Brea (92821-2923)
PHONE.................................714 529-0407
Fred Seal, *General Mgr*
EMP: 30
SALES (corp-wide): 11.5B **Publicly Held**
WEB: www.gerardusa.com
SIC: 3355 Structural shapes, rolled, aluminum
HQ: Metals Usa Building Products Lp
955 Columbia St
Brea CA 92821
713 946-9000

(P-11267)
QLC MANUFACTURING LLC
462 Vista Way, Milpitas (95035-5406)
PHONE.................................408 221-8550
Dung Nguyen, *Mng Member*
EMP: 11
SALES (est): 1.3MM **Privately Held**
SIC: 3355 Aluminum rolling & drawing

(P-11268)
SOUTHERN ALUM FINSHG CO INC
Also Called: Saf West
4356 Caterpillar Rd, Redding (96003-1422)
PHONE.................................530 244-7518
Sam Heier, *Branch Mgr*
EMP: 90
SALES (corp-wide): 50.2MM **Privately Held**
SIC: 3355 Structural shapes, rolled, aluminum
PA: Southern Aluminum Finishing Company, Inc.
1581 Huber St Nw
Atlanta GA 30318
404 355-1560

(P-11269)
WERNER SYSTEMS INC
Also Called: Woodbridge Glass
14321 Myford Rd, Tustin (92780-7022)
PHONE.................................714 838-4444
Virgina Siciliani, *CEO*
Vito Siciliani, *Director*
▲ EMP: 20
SQ FT: 58,000
SALES (est): 6.1MM **Privately Held**
WEB: www.wernerengineering.com
SIC: 3355 Aluminum rolling & drawing

3356 Rolling, Drawing-Extruding Of Nonferrous Metals

(P-11270)
DYNAMET INCORPORATED
16052 Beach Blvd Ste 221, Huntington Beach (92647-3855)
PHONE..................714 375-3150
Tom Proteau, *Manager*
EMP: 25
SALES (corp-wide): 2.3B **Publicly Held**
WEB: www.dynamet.com
SIC: 3356 Titanium & titanium alloy bars, sheets, strip, etc.
HQ: Dynamet Incorporated
195 Museum Rd
Washington PA 15301
724 228-1000

(P-11271)
FLASHCO MANUFACTURING INC (PA)
150 Todd Rd Ste 400, Santa Rosa (95407-8101)
PHONE..................707 824-4448
Gregory J Morrow, *CEO*
▲ EMP: 30
SQ FT: 7,500
SALES (est): 6.7MM **Privately Held**
WEB: www.flashcomfg.com
SIC: 3356 Lead & lead alloy bars, pipe, plates, shapes, etc.

(P-11272)
GRANDIS METALS INTL CORP
Also Called: Grandis Titanium
29752 Ave De Las Bndra, Rcho STA Marg (92688-2615)
PHONE..................949 459-2621
Vasily T Semeniuta, *President*
Igor Krjenitski, *Vice Pres*
Theodore Semeniuta, *Vice Pres*
◆ EMP: 12
SALES (est): 1.6MM **Privately Held**
SIC: 3356 Titanium

(P-11273)
HI TECH SOLDER
700 Monroe Way, Placentia (92870-6308)
PHONE..................714 572-1200
Jose Salas, *Partner*
Hector Salas, *Partner*
EMP: 10
SALES (est): 870K **Privately Held**
SIC: 3356 Solder: wire, bar, acid core, & rosin core

(P-11274)
INTERSPACE BATTERY INC (PA)
2009 W San Bernardino Rd, West Covina (91790-1006)
PHONE..................626 813-1234
Paul Godber, *Ch of Bd*
Donald W Godber, *President*
Scott Hollett, *Maintence Staff*
EMP: 12
SQ FT: 36,000
SALES (est): 3.4MM **Privately Held**
SIC: 3356 3691 Battery metal; storage batteries

(P-11275)
JOAOS A TIN FISH BAR & EATERY
2750 Dewey Rd, San Diego (92106-6142)
PHONE..................619 794-2192
Mike Alves, *Owner*
EMP: 30
SALES (est): 2.7MM **Privately Held**
SIC: 3356 Tin

(P-11276)
MS2 TECHNOLOGIES LLC
2448 E 25th St, Vernon (90058-1209)
PHONE..................310 277-4110
Larry Kay,
Cindy Flame,
EMP: 10
SALES: 2.5MM **Privately Held**
SIC: 3356 Nonferrous rolling & drawing

(P-11277)
NEW CNTURY MTALS SOUTHEAST INC
Also Called: Rti Los Angeles
15723 Shoemaker Ave, Norwalk (90650-6863)
PHONE..................562 356-6804
Marie T Batz, *Admin Sec*
EMP: 14
SALES (est): 2.4MM
SALES (corp-wide): 14B **Publicly Held**
SIC: 3356 Titanium; titanium & titanium alloy bars, sheets, strip, etc.; titanium & titanium alloy: rolling, drawing or extruding
HQ: Rmi Titanium Company, Llc
1000 Warren Ave
Niles OH 44446
330 652-9952

(P-11278)
OCEANIA INTERNATIONAL LLC
Also Called: Stanford Advanced Materials
23661 Birtcher Dr, Lake Forest (92630-1770)
PHONE..................949 407-8904
Alexander Chen, *Mng Member*
Arnie Pell, *Vice Pres*
Alex Chen,
▲ EMP: 40 EST: 2012
SALES (est): 9.9MM **Privately Held**
SIC: 3356 3313 Titanium & titanium alloy bars, sheets, strip, etc.; zirconium & zirconium alloy bars, sheets, strip, etc.; ferromolybdenum; ferrosilicon, not made in blast furnaces; ferrotungsten

(P-11279)
P KAY METAL INC (PA)
Also Called: P K Metal
2448 E 25th St, Los Angeles (90058-1209)
PHONE..................323 585-5058
Larry Kay, *President*
Sharon Kay, *Treasurer*
Cindy Flame, *Admin Sec*
▲ EMP: 45
SQ FT: 25,000
SALES (est): 58.5MM **Privately Held**
WEB: www.pkaymetal.com
SIC: 3356 Lead & lead alloy bars, pipe, plates, shapes, etc.

(P-11280)
TITANIUM METALS CORPORATION
Also Called: Timet
403 Ryder St, Vallejo (94590-7269)
PHONE..................707 552-4850
David Madsen, *Principal*
Doug McCoy, *Opers Mgr*
EMP: 98
SALES (corp-wide): 225.3B **Publicly Held**
SIC: 3356 3366 3313 Titanium; titanium & titanium alloy bars, sheets, strip, etc.; castings (except die); electrometallurgical products
HQ: Titanium Metals Corporation
4832 Richmond Rd Ste 100
Warrensville Heights OH 44128
610 968-1300

(P-11281)
UMC ACQUISITION CORP (PA)
Also Called: Universal Molding Company
9151 Imperial Hwy, Downey (90242-2808)
PHONE..................562 940-0300
Dominick L Baione, *Ch of Bd*
Edward L Koch III, *President*
Lon Thompson, *Programmer Anys*
Lionel N Pailhas, *Manager*
EMP: 50
SQ FT: 62,000
SALES (est): 55.1MM **Privately Held**
SIC: 3356 3354 3471 3479 Nonferrous rolling & drawing; aluminum extruded products; anodizing (plating) of metals or formed products; aluminum coating of metal products

(P-11282)
UNIVERSAL MOLDING COMPANY (HQ)
9151 Imperial Hwy, Downey (90242-2808)
PHONE..................310 886-1750
Dominick L Baione, *Ch of Bd*

Carol Hansen, *Exec VP*
Joe Sokol, *Info Tech Mgr*
Lon Thompson, *Programmer Anys*
Jerry Moore, *Opers Mgr*
EMP: 160
SQ FT: 62,000
SALES (est): 54MM **Privately Held**
WEB: www.universalmold.com
SIC: 3356 3354 3448 3471 Nonferrous rolling & drawing; aluminum extruded products; screen enclosures; anodizing (plating) of metals or formed products; aluminum coating of metal products; sheet metalwork

(P-11283)
VSMPO TIRUS US
2850 E Cedar St, Ontario (91761-8514)
PHONE..................909 230-9020
Dave Richardson, *Owner*
Cheryl King, *Accountant*
◆ EMP: 45
SALES (est): 6.3MM
SALES (corp-wide): 43.1K **Privately Held**
SIC: 3356 Titanium
HQ: Vsmpo-Tirus, U.S., Inc.
1745 Shea Center Dr # 330
Highlands Ranch CO 80129
720 746-1023

(P-11284)
VSMPO-TIRUS US INC
Also Called: West Coast Service Center
2850 E Cedar St, Ontario (91761-8514)
PHONE..................909 230-9020
Dave Richardson, *Manager*
EMP: 20
SALES (corp-wide): 43.1K **Privately Held**
WEB: www.vsmpo-tirus.com
SIC: 3356 Titanium
HQ: Vsmpo-Tirus, U.S., Inc.
1745 Shea Center Dr # 330
Highlands Ranch CO 80129
720 746-1023

3357 Nonferrous Wire Drawing

(P-11285)
ALPHA WIRE CORPORATION
Also Called: Coast Custom Cable
1048 E Burgrove St, Carson (90746-3514)
PHONE..................310 639-9473
Michael Dugar, *Branch Mgr*
EMP: 750
SALES (corp-wide): 225.8MM **Privately Held**
SIC: 3357 3699 Coaxial cable, nonferrous; electrical equipment & supplies
PA: Alpha Wire Corporation
711 Lidgerwood Ave
Elizabeth NJ 07202
908 925-8000

(P-11286)
ARIA TECHNOLOGIES INC
102 Wright Brothers Ave, Livermore (94551-9240)
PHONE..................925 292-1616
Paula McGuinness, *CEO*
Joe McGuinness, *President*
Dave Dickens, *Vice Pres*
▲ EMP: 20
SQ FT: 15,000
SALES (est): 5.6MM **Privately Held**
WEB: www.ariatech.com
SIC: 3357 Communication wire

(P-11287)
BEE WIRE & CABLE INC
2850 E Spruce St, Ontario (91761-8550)
PHONE..................909 923-5800
Arjan Bera, *President*
Kiran Kaneria, *Treasurer*
Nalin Kaneria, *Admin Sec*
▲ EMP: 26
SQ FT: 34,400
SALES (est): 6.3MM **Privately Held**
WEB: www.beeflex.com
SIC: 3357 Building wire & cable, nonferrous

(P-11288)
BELDEN INC
47823 Westinghouse Dr, Fremont (94539-7437)
PHONE..................510 438-9071
Dhrupad Trevidi, *President*
Steve Trunkett, *Sales Staff*
EMP: 10
SALES (corp-wide): 2.5B **Publicly Held**
SIC: 3357 Nonferrous wiredrawing & insulating
PA: Belden Inc.
1 N Brentwood Blvd Fl 15
Saint Louis MO 63105
314 854-8000

(P-11289)
BLAKE WIRE & CABLE CORP
16134 Runnymede St, Van Nuys (91406-2912)
PHONE..................818 781-8300
Robert Weiner, *President*
Victor Weiner, *Vice Pres*
EMP: 12
SQ FT: 5,500
SALES (est): 3.3MM **Privately Held**
WEB: www.blakewire.com
SIC: 3357 5051 Nonferrous wiredrawing & insulating; wire

(P-11290)
BRIDGEWAVE COMMUNICATIONS INC
17034 Camino San Bernardo, San Diego (92127-5708)
PHONE..................408 567-6900
Amir Makleff, *President*
John Keating, *CFO*
Pamela Valentine, *Vice Pres*
Thu Nguyen, *Engineer*
Carol Lee, *Finance*
▲ EMP: 25
SALES (est): 6.4MM **Privately Held**
WEB: www.bridgewave.com
SIC: 3357 3229 Communication wire; pressed & blown glass

(P-11291)
BROADATA COMMUNICATIONS INC
2545 W 237th St Ste K, Torrance (90505-5229)
PHONE..................310 530-1416
Freddie Lin, *President*
Patty Shaw, *CFO*
Gary Fong, *Design Engr*
Daniel Laconsay, *Controller*
◆ EMP: 19 EST: 2000
SQ FT: 10,000
SALES: 13.2MM **Privately Held**
WEB: www.bcifiber.com
SIC: 3357 3663 Fiber optic cable (insulated); television broadcasting & communications equipment

(P-11292)
CALIFORNIA INSULATED WIRE &
3050 N California St, Burbank (91504-2004)
PHONE..................818 569-4930
Bill Boyd, *President*
Lois Boyd, *Corp Secy*
Bruce Boyd, *Vice Pres*
Micheal Boyd, *Vice Pres*
EMP: 60
SQ FT: 26,000
SALES (est): 16.2MM **Privately Held**
SIC: 3357 Communication wire; fiber optic cable (insulated)

(P-11293)
CALMONT ENGINEERING & ELEC (PA)
Also Called: Calmont Wire & Cable
420 E Alton Ave, Santa Ana (92707-4278)
PHONE..................714 549-0336
Barbara Monteleone, *President*
Blanche F Chilcote, *Corp Secy*
Ignacio Espinoza, *Planning*
Hung Tran, *Engineer*
Lisa Ashcraft, *Sales Staff*
EMP: 37 EST: 1970
SQ FT: 24,000

▲ = Import ▼=Export
◆ =Import/Export

SALES: 4.5MM **Privately Held**
WEB: www.calmont.com
SIC: 3357 3061 Nonferrous wiredrawing &
insulating; medical & surgical rubber tubing (extruded & lathe-cut)

(P-11294)
CARMEN ABATO ENTERPRISES
11258 Monarch St Ste G, Garden Grove
(92841-1436)
PHONE................................714 895-1887
David Abato, *President*
Jolin Abato, *Treasurer*
EMP: 11
SQ FT: 6,500
SALES: 1MM **Privately Held**
SIC: 3357 7629 5065 Communication
wire; electrical measuring instrument re-
pair & calibration; electronic parts

(P-11295)
**CENTURUM INFORMATION
TECH INC**
4250 Pacific Hwy Ste 105, San Diego
(92110-3219)
PHONE................................619 224-1100
Brad Geiger, *Manager*
EMP: 50
SALES (corp-wide): 57.1MM **Privately
Held**
SIC: 3357 Shipboard cable, nonferrous
HQ: Centurum Information Technology, Inc.
651 Route 73 N Ste 107
Marlton NJ 08053
856 751-1111

(P-11296)
CENTURY WIRE & CABLE INC
7400 E Slauson Ave, Commerce
(90040-3300)
PHONE................................213 236-8879
David Lifschitz, *CEO*
Galen Ho'o, *President*
Saleem Baakza, *Vice Pres*
Anthony Batista, *Vice Pres*
Carl Tom, *VP Mktg*
EMP: 100
SALES (est): 12.2MM
SALES (corp-wide): 84.8MM **Privately
Held**
WEB: www.centurywire.com
SIC: 3357 5063 Nonferrous wiredrawing &
insulating; electrical apparatus & equip-
ment
HQ: Gehr Industries, Inc.
7400 E Slauson Ave
Commerce CA 90040
323 728-5558

(P-11297)
CFKBA INC (PA)
150 Jefferson Dr, Menlo Park (94025-1115)
PHONE................................650 847-3900
Richard Johns, *Ch of Bd*
Laurent Mayer, *Vice Pres*
Wendell Jesseman, *Admin Sec*
Gail Goulette, *Purchasing*
◆ EMP: 63
SQ FT: 43,000
SALES (est): 5.8MM **Privately Held**
WEB: www.baycable.com
SIC: 3357 5063 Nonferrous wiredrawing &
insulating; wire & cable

(P-11298)
COAST 2 COAST CABLES LLC
3162 E La Palma Ave Ste D, Anaheim
(92806-2810)
PHONE................................714 666-1062
Lynn Swearingen, *Mng Member*
Ronald Benadom,
EMP: 17
SQ FT: 14,040
SALES: 2.3MM **Privately Held**
SIC: 3357 Nonferrous wiredrawing & insu-
lating

(P-11299)
DACON SYSTEMS INC
1891 N Delilah St, Corona (92879-1800)
PHONE................................951 735-2100
Drexel Daniels, *President*
Mark Daniels, *CEO*
▲ EMP: 10
SQ FT: 14,000

SALES (est): 1.7MM **Privately Held**
WEB: www.daconsys.com
SIC: 3357 Communication wire; automotive wire & cable, except ignition sets:
nonferrous; building wire & cable, nonferrous

(P-11300)
DACON SYSTEMS INC
Also Called: Victor Wire & Cable
12915 S Spring St, Los Angeles
(90061-1631)
PHONE................................310 842-9933
Robert Smith, *General Mgr*
Mark Daniels, *President*
EMP: 10
SALES (est): 594.7K **Privately Held**
SIC: 3357 5051 Nonferrous wiredrawing &
insulating; metals service centers & of-
fices

(P-11301)
DICAR INC
1285 Alma Ct, San Jose (95112-5943)
P.O. Box 1653, Morgan Hill (95038-1653)
PHONE................................408 295-1106
Edward Garcia, *CEO*
Ed Garcia, *President*
Diana M Garcia, *CFO*
Carol Garcia, *Vice Pres*
EMP: 26
SQ FT: 9,900
SALES (est): 6.4MM **Privately Held**
WEB: www.dicarinc.com
SIC: 3357 3599 3089 3679 Coaxial
cable, nonferrous; communication wire;
machine & other job shop work; blow
molded finished plastic products; harness
assemblies for electronic use: wire or
cable

(P-11302)
FALMAT INC
Also Called: C B S
1873 Diamond St, San Marcos
(92078-5128)
PHONE................................800 848-4257
Lewis Brian Falk, *CEO*
Shannon Baroni, *Corp Secy*
Donald Falk, *Vice Pres*
Alan Palmer, *Executive*
Brian Falk, *General Mgr*
▲ EMP: 175
SQ FT: 40,000
SALES (est): 57.3MM **Privately Held**
WEB: www.falmat.com
SIC: 3357 5063 Nonferrous wiredrawing &
insulating; wire & cable

(P-11303)
FIBEROPTIC SYSTEMS INC
60 Moreland Rd Ste A, Simi Valley
(93065-1643)
PHONE................................805 579-6600
Sanford S Stark, *President*
Kathy Hanau, *CFO*
EMP: 29
SQ FT: 14,000
SALES (est): 6.6MM **Privately Held**
WEB: www.fiberopticsystems.com
SIC: 3357 3229 Fiber optic cable (insu-
lated); fiber optics strands

(P-11304)
**FORWARD INTEGRATION
TECHNOLOGY**
444 Nelo St, Santa Clara (95054-2144)
PHONE................................408 988-3330
Mitra Vakili, *President*
Ray Vakili, *General Mgr*
EMP: 15
SQ FT: 5,000
SALES: 500K **Privately Held**
SIC: 3357 7373 Nonferrous wiredrawing &
insulating; systems integration services

(P-11305)
GEHR INDUSTRIES INC (HQ)
7400 E Slauson Ave, Commerce
(90040-3300)
PHONE................................323 728-5558
David Lifschitz, *CEO*
Galen Ho'o, *President*
Mark Goldman, *COO*
Carl Rosenthal, *Exec VP*
Saleem Baakza, *Vice Pres*

▲ EMP: 150 EST: 1965
SQ FT: 260,000
SALES (est): 69.7MM
SALES (corp-wide): 84.8MM **Privately
Held**
SIC: 3357 5063 5072 5085 Nonferrous
wiredrawing & insulating; electrical appa-
ratus & equipment; hardware; industrial
supplies
PA: The Gehr Group Inc
7400 E Slauson Ave
Commerce CA 90040
323 728-5558

(P-11306)
GLOBAL MFG SOLUTIONS LLC
2100 E Valencia Dr Ste D, Fullerton
(92831-4811)
PHONE................................562 356-3222
Mike Lin, *Mng Member*
Tom Liu, *General Mgr*
Eugene Tsai,
▲ EMP: 20
SQ FT: 10,000
SALES (est): 3.4MM **Privately Held**
WEB: www.gocables.com
SIC: 3357 Communication wire

(P-11307)
JUDD WIRE INC
870 Los Vallecitos Blvd, San Marcos
(92069-1479)
PHONE................................760 744-7720
Hiro Sugiyama, *Branch Mgr*
Kenji Tamura, *Engineer*
EMP: 11
SQ FT: 105,000 **Privately Held**
WEB: www.juddwire.com
SIC: 3357 3315 Communication wire;
steel wire & related products
HQ: Judd Wire Inc.
124 Turnpike Rd
Turners Falls MA 01376
413 863-9402

(P-11308)
LOGICO LLC
6020 Progressive Ave # 900, San Diego
(92154-6639)
PHONE................................619 600-5198
Shimi Porat, *Mng Member*
EMP: 10
SALES (est): 120.9K **Privately Held**
SIC: 3357 5063 Automotive wire & cable,
except ignition sets: nonferrous; control &
signal wire & cable, including coaxial

(P-11309)
MX ELECTRONICS MFG INC
Also Called: Interconnect Solutions
1651 E Saint Andrew Pl, Santa Ana
(92705-4932)
PHONE................................714 258-0200
Lawrence Reusing, *President*
Mike Anderson, *CFO*
◆ EMP: 58
SQ FT: 40,000
SALES (est): 15.2MM
SALES (corp-wide): 35.7MM **Privately
Held**
WEB: www.isiconnect.com
SIC: 3357 Aluminum wire & cable
PA: Experts En Memoire Internationale Inc,
Les
2321 Rue Cohen
Saint-Laurent QC H4R 2
514 333-5010

(P-11310)
NEPTEC OS INC
Also Called: Neptec Optical Solutions
48603 Warm Springs Blvd, Fremont
(94539-7782)
PHONE................................510 687-1101
David Cheng, *President*
Lan Ni, *CFO*
Chaoyu Yue, *Vice Pres*
EMP: 25 EST: 2008
SALES: 500K **Privately Held**
WEB: www.neptecos.com
SIC: 3357 Fiber optic cable (insulated)

(P-11311)
**NEW ENGLAND INTERCONNECT
SYSTE**
Also Called: Nei Systems
46840 Lakeview Blvd, Fremont
(94538-6543)
PHONE................................603 355-3515
Harry Avonti, *General Mgr*
EMP: 300
SALES (est): 32.8MM
SALES (corp-wide): 75MM **Privately
Held**
WEB: www.neisystems.com
SIC: 3357 3643 Nonferrous wiredrawing &
insulating; current-carrying wiring devices
HQ: New England Wire Technologies Cor-
poration
130 N Main St
Lisbon NH 03585
603 838-6624

(P-11312)
OKONITE COMPANY
2900 Skyway Dr, Santa Maria
(93455-1897)
PHONE................................805 922-6682
Rick Flory, *Branch Mgr*
Robin O'Sullivan, *Vice Pres*
Elbert Bustle, *Plant Engr*
Tom Petty, *Maintence Staff*
Mario Castellanos, *Manager*
EMP: 150
SQ FT: 10,000
SALES (corp-wide): 407MM **Privately
Held**
WEB: www.okonite.com
SIC: 3357 Nonferrous wiredrawing & insu-
lating
PA: The Okonite Company Inc
102 Hilltop Rd
Ramsey NJ 07446
201 825-0300

(P-11313)
OPTICOMM CORP
2015 Chestnut St, Alhambra (91803-1542)
PHONE................................626 293-3400
David Caidar, *President*
Allon Caider, *Vice Pres*
EMP: 23
SQ FT: 15,000
SALES (est): 2.7MM
SALES (corp-wide): 85.6MM **Publicly
Held**
WEB: www.opticomm.com
SIC: 3357 8748 Fiber optic cable (insu-
lated); telecommunications consultant
PA: Emcore Corporation
2015 Chestnut St
Alhambra CA 91803
626 293-3400

(P-11314)
**PRECISION FIBER PRODUCTS
INC**
Also Called: Pfp
142 N Milpitas Blvd # 298, Milpitas
(95035-4401)
PHONE................................408 946-4040
Ray Pierce, *President*
Amanda Jensen, *Accounting Mgr*
◆ EMP: 10
SALES (est): 1.6MM **Privately Held**
WEB: www.precisionfiberproducts.com
SIC: 3357 Fiber optic cable (insulated)

(P-11315)
PRIME WIRE & CABLE INC (HQ)
280 Machlin Ct Fl 2, Walnut (91789-3026)
PHONE................................888 445-9955
Juhng-Shyu Shieh, *CEO*
Joe Ferlauto, *President*
Jerzy Marcinkowsky, *Engineer*
Greer Huang, *Controller*
Robin Fernandez, *Art Dir*
▲ EMP: 50
SQ FT: 150,000
SALES (est): 74.4MM **Privately Held**
WEB: www.primewirecable.com
SIC: 3357 Building wire & cable, nonfer-
rous

PRODUCTS & SVCS

(P-11316)
QPC FIBER OPTIC LLC
27612 El Lazo, Laguna Niguel
(92677-3913)
PHONE...............................949 361-8855
Steven J Wilkes, *President*
David Olsen, *CFO*
EMP: 28
SQ FT: 1,400
SALES: 2.5MM **Privately Held**
WEB: www.qpcfiber.com
SIC: 3357 Fiber optic cable (insulated)

(P-11317)
RF PRECISION CABLES INC
1600 S Anaheim Blvd Ste A, Anaheim
(92805-6231)
PHONE...............................714 772-7567
Sabry El Masry, *President*
David Rivers, *Vice Pres*
▲ EMP: 11
SQ FT: 1,700
SALES: 1MM **Privately Held**
WEB: www.rfprecisioncables.com
SIC: 3357 3679 Coaxial cable, nonferrous;
microwave components

(P-11318)
SOUTH BAY CABLE CORP (PA)
54125 Maranatha Dr, Idyllwild (92549)
P.O. Box 67 (92549-0067)
PHONE...............................951 659-2183
Gordon W Brown Sr, *CEO*
Joyce Brown, *Corp Secy*
EMP: 75
SQ FT: 80,000
SALES (est): 14.6MM **Privately Held**
WEB: www.southbaycable.com
SIC: 3357 Nonferrous wiredrawing & insu-
lating

(P-11319)
SOUTH BAY CABLE CORP
42033 Rio Nedo, Temecula (92590-3705)
P.O. Box 67, Idyllwild (92549-0067)
PHONE...............................951 296-9900
Gordon Brown, *President*
EMP: 15
SALES (corp-wide): 14.6MM **Privately
Held**
WEB: www.southbaycable.com
SIC: 3357 Nonferrous wiredrawing & insu-
lating
PA: South Bay Cable Corp.
54125 Maranatha Dr
Idyllwild CA 92549
951 659-2183

(P-11320)
**STANDARD WIRE & CABLE CO
(PA)**
Also Called: AMERICAN WIRE SALES
2050 E Vista Bella Way, Rancho
Dominguez (90220-6109)
P.O. Box 9054, Compton (90224-9054)
PHONE...............................310 609-1811
Russell J Skrable, *President*
Dick Hampikian, *Ch of Bd*
◆ EMP: 40
SQ FT: 45,000
SALES: 11.6MM **Privately Held**
WEB: www.standard-wire.com
SIC: 3357 5063 Coaxial cable, nonferrous;
wire & cable; electronic wire & cable;
power wire & cable

(P-11321)
SUPERIOR ESSEX INC
5250 Ontario Mills Pkwy # 300, Ontario
(91764-5131)
PHONE...............................909 481-4804
Victor Alegria, *Branch Mgr*
EMP: 10 **Privately Held**
SIC: 3357 Nonferrous wiredrawing & insu-
lating
HQ: Superior Essex Inc.
6120 Powers Ferry Rd # 150
Atlanta GA 30339
770 657-6000

(P-11322)
TAG-CONNECT LLC
433 Airport Blvd Ste 425, Burlingame
(94010-2014)
PHONE...............................877 244-4156
Neil Sherman, *Principal*

EMP: 12
SALES (est): 1.4MM **Privately Held**
SIC: 3357 Coaxial cable, nonferrous

(P-11323)
**TE CONNECTIVITY
CORPORATION**
501 Oakside Ave Side, Redwood City
(94063-3800)
PHONE...............................650 361-3333
Batu Berkok, *Plant Mgr*
EMP: 10
SALES (corp-wide): 13.9B **Privately Held**
WEB: www.raychem.com
SIC: 3357 Automotive wire & cable, except
ignition sets: nonferrous
HQ: Te Connectivity Corporation
1050 Westlakes Dr
Berwyn PA 19312
610 893-9800

(P-11324)
**TYCO INTERNATIONAL MGT CO
LLC**
300 Constitution Dr, Menlo Park
(94025-1140)
PHONE...............................650 361-3333
Don Wood, *Principal*
EMP: 300 **Privately Held**
SIC: 3357 Communication wire
HQ: Tyco International Management Com-
pany, Llc
9 Roszel Rd Ste 2
Princeton NJ 08540
609 720-4200

(P-11325)
VICTOR WIRE AND CABLE LLC
12915 S Spring St, Los Angeles
(90061-1631)
PHONE...............................310 842-9933
Robert Smith, *Sales Executive*
EMP: 11
SQ FT: 20,000
SALES (est): 2.1MM **Privately Held**
WEB: www.victorwire.com
SIC: 3357 Nonferrous wiredrawing & insu-
lating

(P-11326)
**WINTRONICS INTERNATIONAL
INC**
Also Called: Winstronics
3817 Spinnaker Ct, Fremont (94538-6537)
PHONE...............................510 226-7588
Ben Yueh, *President*
▲ EMP: 25
SQ FT: 12,000
SALES (est): 9.5MM **Privately Held**
WEB: www.winsusa.com
SIC: 3357 Communication wire

(P-11327)
**WIRE TECHNOLOGY
CORPORATION**
9527 Laurel St, Los Angeles (90002-2653)
P.O. Box 1608, South Gate (90280-1608)
PHONE...............................310 635-6935
Rachel Mendoza, *President*
Darlene Delange, *Vice Pres*
Robert Mendoza, *Principal*
EMP: 25 EST: 1970
SQ FT: 4,000
SALES (est): 5.5MM **Privately Held**
WEB: www.wiretechnology.com
SIC: 3357 Nonferrous wiredrawing & insu-
lating

3363 Aluminum Die

(P-11328)
A & B DIE CASTING CO INC
900 Alfred Nobel Dr, Hercules
(94547-1814)
PHONE...............................877 708-0009
Bernard E Dathe, *President*
Stephen Dathe, *COO*
Robert Dathe, *Corp Secy*
Alex Hantke, *Vice Pres*
George Donatello, *Info Tech Mgr*
EMP: 35
SQ FT: 19,000

SALES (est): 23K **Privately Held**
SIC: 3363 3364 Aluminum die-castings;
zinc & zinc-base alloy die-castings

(P-11329)
AEROTEC ALLOYS INC
10632 Alondra Blvd, Norwalk (90650-5301)
PHONE...............................562 809-1378
Robert W Franklin, *CEO*
Mitchell Frahm, *Vice Pres*
Shery Franklin, *Vice Pres*
EMP: 50
SQ FT: 18,000
SALES (est): 14.1MM **Privately Held**
WEB: www.aerotecalloys.com
SIC: 3363 3312 3365 3325 Aluminum
die-castings; blast furnaces & steel mills;
aluminum foundries; steel foundries

(P-11330)
ALLOY DIE CASTING CO
Also Called: Alloy De Casting Co
6550 Caballero Blvd, Buena Park
(90620-1130)
PHONE...............................714 521-9800
Eric Sanders, *President*
EMP: 350 EST: 1939
SQ FT: 55,000
SALES (est): 93.5MM **Privately Held**
WEB: www.alloydie.com
SIC: 3363 Aluminum die-castings

(P-11331)
ALPHACAST FOUNDRY INC
826 S Santa Fe Ave, Los Angeles
(90021-1725)
PHONE...............................213 624-7156
Luis Rangel, *President*
EMP: 10
SQ FT: 6,800
SALES (est): 1.7MM **Privately Held**
SIC: 3363 Aluminum die-castings

(P-11332)
**ALUMINUM DIE CASTING CO
INC**
10775 San Sevaine Way, Jurupa Valley
(91752-1146)
PHONE...............................951 681-3900
Steve Bennett, *CEO*
James Bennett, *Shareholder*
Rudy Bennett, *Vice Pres*
Carolyn Hibbs,
Paul Spencer, *Art Dir*
EMP: 65 EST: 1950
SQ FT: 31,000
SALES (est): 16.6MM **Privately Held**
WEB: www.adc3900.com
SIC: 3363 3364 Aluminum die-castings;
nonferrous die-castings except aluminum

(P-11333)
ARROW DIECASTING INC
4031 Goodwin Ave, Los Angeles
(90039-1197)
PHONE...............................323 245-8439
Kirk Harris, *President*
Lynn Harris, *Vice Pres*
EMP: 10 EST: 1955
SQ FT: 7,400
SALES: 1MM **Privately Held**
SIC: 3363 3364 Aluminum die-castings;
zinc & zinc-base alloy die-castings

(P-11334)
COOLING SOURCE INC
2021 Las Positas Ct # 101, Livermore
(94551-7311)
PHONE...............................925 292-1293
Michel Gelinas, *President*
Wayne Finger, *Regl Sales Mgr*
Jason Shrider, *Sales Staff*
▲ EMP: 118 EST: 2009
SQ FT: 4,000
SALES (est): 23.4MM **Privately Held**
SIC: 3363 3354 3325 3469 Aluminum
die-castings; shapes, extruded aluminum;
alloy steel castings, except investment;
metal stampings

(P-11335)
**EAST BAY BRASS FOUNDRY
INC**
1200 Chesley Ave, Richmond
(94801-2144)
PHONE...............................510 233-7171

Milton G Stewart, *President*
Teresa K Stewart, *Admin Sec*
EMP: 20
SQ FT: 16,700
SALES (est): 1.8MM **Privately Held**
WEB: www.eastbaybrass.com
SIC: 3363 3364 3366 3369 Aluminum
die-castings; brass & bronze die-castings;
bronze foundry; nonferrous foundries; alu-
minum foundries

(P-11336)
EDELBROCK FOUNDRY CORP
1320 S Buena Vista St, San Jacinto
(92583-4665)
PHONE...............................951 654-6677
Otis Victor Edelbrock, *President*
Nancy Edelbrock, *Treasurer*
Ronald L Webb, *Exec VP*
Aristedes Seles, *Vice Pres*
Samantha Alpirez, *Admin Sec*
EMP: 691
SQ FT: 75,000
SALES (est): 91.5MM **Privately Held**
WEB: www.edelbrock.com
SIC: 3363 3365 3325 Aluminum die-cast-
ings; aluminum foundries; steel foundries
HQ: Edelbrock, Llc
2700 California St
Torrance CA 90503
310 781-2222

(P-11337)
**HYATT DIE CAST ENGRG CORP -
S**
12250 Industry St, Garden Grove
(92841-2816)
PHONE...............................714 622-2131
Mike Senter, *Branch Mgr*
Garry Slate, *Purchasing*
EMP: 23
SALES (corp-wide): 26.8MM **Privately
Held**
SIC: 3363 Aluminum die-castings
PA: Hyatt Die Cast And Engineering Corpo-
ration - South
4656 Lincoln Ave
Cypress CA 90630
714 826-7550

(P-11338)
**HYATT DIE CAST ENGRG CORP -
S**
Also Called: Hyatt Die Casting
1250 Kifer Rd, Sunnyvale (94086-5304)
PHONE...............................408 523-7000
Kul Dhanota, *Branch Mgr*
EMP: 40
SALES (corp-wide): 26.8MM **Privately
Held**
WEB: www.hyattdiecast.com
SIC: 3363 Aluminum die-castings
PA: Hyatt Die Cast And Engineering Corpo-
ration - South
4656 Lincoln Ave
Cypress CA 90630
714 826-7550

(P-11339)
ICSN INC
521 Princeland Ct, Corona (92879-1383)
PHONE...............................951 687-2305
Kevin Ko, *President*
Derek Kiyabu, *Project Mgr*
Renee Lee, *Accounting Mgr*
Michelle Macias, *Manager*
▲ EMP: 14
SALES (est): 1.9MM **Privately Held**
SIC: 3363 Aluminum die-castings

(P-11340)
**KEARNEYS ALUMINUM
FOUNDRY INC (PA)**
2660 S Dearing Ave, Fresno (93725-2104)
P.O. Box 2926 (93745-2926)
PHONE...............................559 233-2591
Victor T Kearney Sr, *CEO*
Gary A Kearney, *President*
Michael Kearney, *President*
William Kearney, *President*
Robert Kearney Jr, *Vice Pres*
▲ EMP: 20
SQ FT: 80,000
SALES (est): 3.4MM **Privately Held**
SIC: 3363 Aluminum die-castings

▲ = Import ▼=Export
◆ =Import/Export

(P-11341)
KENWALT DIE CASTING CORP
Also Called: Kenwait Die Casting Company
8719 Bradley Ave, Sun Valley
(91352-2799)
PHONE..................818 768-5800
Ken Zaucha Sr, *President*
Rose Zaucha, *Shareholder*
Gabby Cheherlian, *Admin Asst*
Justin Robertson, *Sales Associate*
▼ EMP: 25
SQ FT: 20,000
SALES (est): 6.2MM **Privately Held**
WEB: www.kenwalt.com
SIC: 3363 Aluminum die-castings

(P-11342)
MAGNESIUM ALLOY PRODUCTS CO LP
2420 N Alameda St, Compton
(90222-2895)
PHONE..................323 636-2276
Richard Killen, *Partner*
James Long, *Partner*
EMP: 50
SALES: 4.5MM **Privately Held**
SIC: 3363 Aluminum die-castings

(P-11343)
PACIFIC DIE CASTING CORP
6155 S Eastern Ave, Commerce
(90040-3401)
PHONE..................323 725-1308
Jeff Orlandini, *Vice Pres*
Sonny Yun, *Shareholder*
▲ EMP: 150
SQ FT: 8,000
SALES (est): 23.1MM **Privately Held**
SIC: 3363 Aluminum die-castings

(P-11344)
PENINSULA LIGHT METALS LLC (HQ)
875 W 8th St, Azusa (91702-2247)
PHONE..................626 765-4856
Steve Frediani,
◆ EMP: 10
SQ FT: 5,000
SALES (est): 1.7MM **Privately Held**
WEB: www.peninsula-lm.com
SIC: 3363 Aluminum die-castings

(P-11345)
PERFORMANCE ALUMINUM PRODUCTS
520 S Palmetto Ave, Ontario (91762-4121)
PHONE..................909 391-4131
John Reed, *President*
▲ EMP: 20
SALES (est): 3.4MM **Privately Held**
WEB: www.performancealuminum.com
SIC: 3363 Aluminum die-castings

(P-11346)
PIONEER DIECASTERS INC
4209 Chevy Chase Dr, Los Angeles
(90039-1294)
PHONE..................323 245-6561
Carl H Spahr, *President*
Gretchen Perry, *Admin Sec*
EMP: 17
SQ FT: 18,000
SALES: 1.8MM **Privately Held**
SIC: 3363 3364 5051 Aluminum die-castings; zinc & zinc-base alloy die-castings; aluminum bars, rods, ingots, sheets, pipes, plates, etc.

(P-11347)
SAN JOSE DIE CASTING CORP
600 Business Park Dr # 100, Lincoln
(95648-9364)
PHONE..................408 262-6500
Everett Callaghan, *President*
Leonid Kirshon, *Vice Pres*
Mark Callaghan, *Engineer*
▲ EMP: 27
SALES (est): 6.1MM **Privately Held**
WEB: www.sjdiecasting.com
SIC: 3363 3364 3599 3441 Aluminum die-castings; zinc & zinc-base alloy die-castings; machine shop, jobbing & repair; fabricated structural metal; nonferrous foundries

(P-11348)
SEA SHIELD MARINE PRODUCTS
Also Called: American Zinc Enterprises
20832 Currier Rd, Walnut (91789-3017)
PHONE..................909 594-2507
Wendell Walter Godwin, *CEO*
Shelley Lopez, *CFO*
Alicia Vongoeben, *Administration*
▲ EMP: 45
SQ FT: 25,000
SALES: 5MM **Privately Held**
WEB: www.diecastofamerica.com
SIC: 3363 3364 Aluminum die-castings; magnesium & magnesium-base alloy die-castings; zinc & zinc-base alloy die-castings

(P-11349)
SKS DIE CAST & MACHINING INC (PA)
1849 Oak St, Alameda (94501-1412)
PHONE..................510 523-2541
Sean Keating, *CEO*
Jerome W Keating, *President*
Menelos J Moore, *Treasurer*
Leonore Keating, *Admin Sec*
Jesusa Fusade, *Asst Treas*
▲ EMP: 44
SQ FT: 50,000
SALES (est): 9.1MM **Privately Held**
WEB: www.sksdiecasting.com
SIC: 3363 3845 Aluminum die-castings; electromedical equipment

(P-11350)
VENUS ALLOYS INC (PA)
1415 S Allec St, Anaheim (92805-6306)
PHONE..................714 635-8800
E K Venugopal, *President*
Kousalya Venugopal, *Admin Sec*
EMP: 24
SQ FT: 20,000
SALES: 60K **Privately Held**
SIC: 3363 3364 Aluminum die-castings; brass & bronze die-castings

---

3364 Nonferrous Die Castings, Exc Aluminum

(P-11351)
ALCAST MFG INC
2910 Fisk Ln, Redondo Beach
(90278-5437)
PHONE..................310 542-3581
EMP: 30
SALES (corp-wide): 7.3MM **Privately Held**
SIC: 3364 3363 Brass & bronze die-castings; aluminum die-castings
PA: Alcast Mfg, Inc.
7355 E Slauson Ave
Commerce CA 90040
310 542-3581

(P-11352)
AMERICAN DIE CASTING INC
14576 Fontlee Ln, Fontana (92335-2599)
PHONE..................909 356-7768
Walter Mueller, *President*
Marjorie Mueller, *Treasurer*
Jeffrey Mueller, *Vice Pres*
Janet Sorensen, *Office Mgr*
EMP: 50
SQ FT: 20,000
SALES: 7MM **Privately Held**
SIC: 3364 3363 Zinc & zinc-base alloy die-castings; brass & bronze die-castings; lead & zinc die-castings; aluminum die-castings

(P-11353)
CALIFORNIA DIE CASTING INC
1820 S Grove Ave, Ontario (91761-5613)
PHONE..................909 947-9947
Dan C Lane, *President*
Roy Herring, *Corp Secy*
Jerry C Holland, *Vice Pres*
EMP: 49
SQ FT: 3,000

SALES (est): 8.6MM **Privately Held**
WEB: www.caldiecast.com
SIC: 3364 3363 Nonferrous die-castings except aluminum; aluminum die-castings

(P-11354)
CUSTOM DESIGN IRON WORKS INC
9182 Kelvin Ave, Chatsworth (91311-5901)
PHONE..................818 700-9182
Shaia Schuchmacher, *President*
Beverly Schuchmacher, *Vice Pres*
EMP: 13
SQ FT: 4,980
SALES (est): 2.4MM **Privately Held**
SIC: 3364 1799 Nonferrous die-castings except aluminum; ornamental metal work

(P-11355)
DEL MAR INDUSTRIES (PA)
Also Called: Del Mar Die Casting Co
12901 S Western Ave, Gardena
(90249-1917)
P.O. Box 881, Venice (90294-0881)
PHONE..................323 321-0600
D R Taylor, *CEO*
Susan Davis, *Shareholder*
Louis A Cuhrt, *CFO*
Judith Taylor, *Admin Sec*
EMP: 100 EST: 1968
SQ FT: 68,000
SALES (est): 13.4MM **Privately Held**
WEB: www.delmarindustries.com
SIC: 3364 Zinc & zinc-base alloy die-castings; magnesium & magnesium-base alloy die-castings

(P-11356)
DEL MAR INDUSTRIES
Gardena Plating Co
12901 S Western Ave, Gardena
(90249-1917)
PHONE..................310 327-2634
Fax: 310 327-2904
EMP: 25 **Privately Held**
SIC: 3364 3471
PA: Del Mar Industries
12901 S Western Ave
Gardena CA 90249
323 321-0600

(P-11357)
DYNACAST LLC
25952 Commercentre Dr, Lake Forest
(92630-8815)
PHONE..................949 707-1211
John Hess, *Branch Mgr*
Thinh Pho, *Exec VP*
Paula Hernandez, *Human Res Mgr*
Chris Mitchell, *Opers Mgr*
Dan Feinberg, *Sales Engr*
EMP: 140
SALES (corp-wide): 1.2B **Privately Held**
SIC: 3364 Nonferrous die-castings except aluminum
HQ: Dynacast, Llc
14045 Ballantyne Cor Ste
Charlotte NC 28277
704 927-2790

(P-11358)
FTG AEROSPACE INC (DH)
20740 Marilla St, Chatsworth (91311-4407)
PHONE..................818 407-4024
Michael Labrador, *President*
▼ EMP: 42
SQ FT: 13,000
SALES: 21MM
SALES (corp-wide): 84.2MM **Privately Held**
SIC: 3364 Nonferrous die-castings except aluminum
HQ: Firan Technology Group (Usa) Corporation
20750 Marilla St
Chatsworth CA 91311
818 407-4024

(P-11359)
PRESSURE CAST PRODUCTS CORP
4210 E 12th St, Oakland (94601-4411)
PHONE..................510 532-7310
Willis Mc Neil, *President*
Vikki Cantwell, *General Mgr*
Jean Mc Neil, *Admin Sec*

▲ EMP: 45
SQ FT: 30,000
SALES (est): 7.9MM **Privately Held**
WEB: www.pressurecastproducts.com
SIC: 3364 3363 Zinc & zinc-base alloy die-castings; aluminum die-castings

(P-11360)
PROTECH MATERIALS INC
20919 Cabot Blvd, Hayward (94545-1155)
PHONE..................510 887-5870
MEI Zhang, *President*
Larry Liu, *Vice Pres*
Jacques Matteau, *VP Bus Dvlpt*
▲ EMP: 16
SQ FT: 7,100
SALES (est): 3.6MM **Privately Held**
SIC: 3364 3443 Nonferrous die-castings except aluminum; high vacuum coaters, metal plate

(P-11361)
VERTECHS ENTERPRISES INC (PA)
1071 Industrial Pl, El Cajon (92020-3107)
PHONE..................858 578-3900
Geosef Straza, *CEO*
George C Straza, *Admin Sec*
Todd Elliott, *Opers Staff*
▲ EMP: 63
SALES (est): 16.3MM **Privately Held**
SIC: 3364 3724 3544 Copper & copper alloy die-castings; aircraft engines & engine parts; die sets for metal stamping (presses)

3365 Aluminum Foundries

(P-11362)
ADM WORKS LLC
1343 E Wilshire Ave, Santa Ana
(92705-4420)
PHONE..................714 245-0536
Jimmy Garcia, *Mng Member*
Javier Valbibieso,
EMP: 23
SALES (est): 5MM **Privately Held**
SIC: 3365 7389 8711 Aerospace castings, aluminum; design services; engineering services

(P-11363)
AEROL CO INC (PA)
19560 S Rancho Way, Rancho Dominguez
(90220-6038)
PHONE..................310 762-2660
Frederick M Seibert, *CEO*
Ron Olivier, *General Mgr*
Long Nguyen, *Engineer*
Fe Lorma Rivera, *Controller*
Keih Dufaul, *Sales Staff*
▲ EMP: 36
SQ FT: 45,000
SALES (est): 5.1MM **Privately Held**
SIC: 3365 2821 3714 3728 Aluminum foundries; plastics materials & resins; motor vehicle parts & accessories; wheels, aircraft; manufactured hardware (general); industrial trucks & tractors

(P-11364)
AIRCRAFT FOUNDRY CO INC
Also Called: Afco
5316 Pacific Blvd, Huntington Park
(90255-2596)
PHONE..................323 587-3171
Ronald Caliva, *President*
Don Caliva, *Treasurer*
Ken Caliva, *Vice Pres*
Glenn Caliva, *Admin Sec*
EMP: 18 EST: 1942
SQ FT: 16,000
SALES: 500K **Privately Held**
WEB: www.aircraftfoundry.com
SIC: 3365 Aluminum & aluminum-based alloy castings

(P-11365)
ALCAST MFG INC (PA)
7355 E Slauson Ave, Commerce
(90040-3626)
PHONE..................310 542-3581
Kiwon Ban, *CEO*
SOO Ban, *Treasurer*

Steve Portner, *General Mgr*
Lily Martinez, *Admin Sec*
Johnna Schulz, *Mfg Staff*
▲ EMP: 25
SALES (est): 7.3MM **Privately Held**
WEB: www.alcast.com
SIC: 3365 3366 3544 3369 Aluminum
foundries; brass foundry; special dies,
tools, jigs & fixtures; nonferrous foundries;
nonferrous die-castings except aluminum;
fabricated structural metal

(P-11366)
ALUMISTAR INC
Also Called: Pacific Cast Products
12711 Imperial Hwy, Santa Fe Springs
(90670-4711)
PHONE..............................562 633-6673
Peter Lake, *President*
▲ EMP: 26
SQ FT: 20,000
SALES (est): 4.5MM **Privately Held**
WEB: www.alumistar.com
SIC: 3365 Aluminum & aluminum-based
alloy castings

(P-11367)
ANGELUS ALUMINUM FOUNDRY CO
3479 E Pico Blvd, Los Angeles
(90023-3084)
PHONE..............................323 268-0145
Edward E Vena, *President*
Henry L Vena, *Vice Pres*
Judy Vena, *Admin Sec*
EMP: 11 **EST:** 1953
SQ FT: 12,800
SALES (est): 1.4MM **Privately Held**
SIC: 3365 Aluminum & aluminum-based
alloy castings

(P-11368)
BUDDY BAR CASTING CORPORATION
10801 Sessler St, South Gate
(90280-7222)
PHONE..............................562 861-9664
Edward W Barksdale Sr, *Principal*
Bill Fell, *President*
Ty Barksdale, *Corp Secy*
John Fell, *Vice Pres*
Mike McKeen, *Vice Pres*
▲ EMP: 80 **EST:** 1953
SQ FT: 25,000
SALES (est): 18.1MM **Privately Held**
WEB: www.buddybarcasting.com
SIC: 3365 Aluminum & aluminum-based
alloy castings

(P-11369)
CALIDAD INC
1730 S Balboa Ave, Ontario (91761-7773)
PHONE..............................909 947-3937
Don Cornell, *President*
Daniel Garcia, *Vice Pres*
Rito Garcia, *Administration*
Blake Orlando, *Engineer*
EMP: 30
SQ FT: 10,000
SALES (est): 6.1MM **Privately Held**
WEB: www.calidadinc.com
SIC: 3365 3324 Aluminum foundries; steel
investment foundries

(P-11370)
CHOICE FOODSERVICES INC
Also Called: Children's Choice
569 San Ramon Valley Blvd, Danville
(94526-4024)
PHONE..............................925 837-0104
Justin Gagnon, *President*
Ryan Mariopti, *CFO*
Karen Heller, *Business Dir*
Elicia Berry, *Sales Staff*
Keith Cosbey, *Director*
▲ EMP: 80
SALES (est): 23.1MM **Privately Held**
SIC: 3365 5049 Cooking/kitchen utensils,
cast aluminum; school supplies

(P-11371)
CONSOLDTED PRECISION PDTS CORP
Also Called: Cpp Cudahy
8333 Wilcox Ave, Cudahy (90201-5919)
P.O. Box 1099 (90201-7099)
PHONE..............................323 773-2363
Steve Gallardo, *Branch Mgr*
EMP: 130
SALES (corp-wide): 6.9B **Privately Held**
SIC: 3365 3324 Aluminum foundries; steel
investment foundries
HQ: Consolidated Precision Products Corp.
1621 Euclid Ave Ste 1850
Cleveland OH 44115
216 453-4800

(P-11372)
CONSOLDTED PRECISION PDTS CORP
705 Industrial Way, Port Hueneme
(93041-3505)
PHONE..............................805 488-6451
Al Bannister, *Facilities Mgr*
EMP: 190
SALES (corp-wide): 6.9B **Privately Held**
SIC: 3365 Aluminum foundries
HQ: Consolidated Precision Products Corp.
1621 Euclid Ave Ste 1850
Cleveland OH 44115
216 453-4800

(P-11373)
CRAFTECH METAL FORMING INC
24100 Water Ave Ste B, Perris
(92570-6738)
PHONE..............................951 940-6444
Richard L Shaw, *President*
EMP: 50
SQ FT: 26,000
SALES (est): 10.7MM **Privately Held**
WEB: www.craftechmetal.com
SIC: 3365 Aerospace castings, aluminum

(P-11374)
CYGNET AEROSPACE CORP
1971 Fearn Ave, Los Osos (93402-2517)
P.O. Box 6603 (93412-6603)
PHONE..............................805 528-2376
Christopher Szarek, *President*
Rose Garza, *Bd of Directors*
EMP: 10
SALES (est): 580K **Privately Held**
WEB: www.cygnet-aero.com
SIC: 3365 5088 Aerospace castings, alu-
minum; transportation equipment & sup-
plies

(P-11375)
CYTEC ENGINEERED MATERIALS INC
1440 N Kraemer Blvd, Anaheim
(92806-1404)
PHONE..............................714 632-1174
Ron Martin, *Branch Mgr*
EMP: 125
SQ FT: 135,055
SALES (corp-wide): 12.8MM **Privately Held**
WEB: www.cytecengineeredmaterials.com
SIC: 3365 2891 2851 2823 Aerospace
castings, aluminum; adhesives &
sealants; paints & allied products; cellu-
losic manmade fibers
HQ: Cytec Engineered Materials Inc.
2085 E Tech Cir Ste 200
Tempe AZ 85284

(P-11376)
DC PARTNERS INC (PA)
Also Called: Soligen 2006
19329 Bryant St, Northridge (91324-4114)
PHONE..............................714 558-9444
Yehoram Uziel, *President*
Alecia Wagner, *Principal*
EMP: 32
SALES (est): 3.4MM **Privately Held**
WEB: www.soligen2006.com
SIC: 3365 3599 Aluminum foundries; ma-
chine & other job shop work

(P-11377)
DC PARTNERS INC
Also Called: Soligen 2006
19408 Londelius St, Northridge
(91324-3511)
PHONE..............................818 718-1221
Gary Kanegis, *Principal*
Chick Lewis, *Opers Staff*
David Hadley, *Director*
Patrick J Lavelle, *Director*
EMP: 25
SALES (corp-wide): 3.4MM **Privately Held**
WEB: www.soligen2006.com
SIC: 3365 Aluminum foundries
PA: Dc Partners, Inc.
19329 Bryant St
Northridge CA 91324
714 558-9444

(P-11378)
DOWELL ALUMINUM FOUNDRY INC
11342 Hartland St, North Hollywood
(91605-6387)
PHONE..............................323 877-9645
Lynn F Dompe, *President*
EMP: 19 **EST:** 1954
SQ FT: 17,000
SALES (est): 3.7MM **Privately Held**
SIC: 3365 3369 Aluminum foundries; non-
ferrous foundries

(P-11379)
DWA ALMINUM COMPOSITES USA INC
21100 Superior St, Chatsworth
(91311-4308)
PHONE..............................818 998-1504
Mark R Van Den Bergh, *CEO*
Gary Wolfe, *COO*
J J Shah, *CFO*
Neel Shah, *Project Mgr*
EMP: 20
SQ FT: 40,000
SALES (est): 5MM **Privately Held**
SIC: 3365 Aluminum & aluminum-based
alloy castings

(P-11380)
EMPLOYEE OWNED PACIFIC CAST PR
Also Called: Aluminum Casting Company
12711 Imperial Hwy, Santa Fe Springs
(90670-4711)
PHONE..............................562 633-6673
Alex B Hall, *President*
EMP: 30
SQ FT: 18,000
SALES (est): 3.9MM **Privately Held**
SIC: 3365 Aluminum & aluminum-based
alloy castings

(P-11381)
FONTANA FOUNDRY CORPORATION
8306 Cherry Ave, Fontana (92335-3026)
PHONE..............................909 822-6128
Jeffrey Ritz, *President*
Susan Ritz, *CFO*
EMP: 25
SQ FT: 11,500
SALES (est): 5MM **Privately Held**
WEB: www.fontanafoundry.com
SIC: 3365 Aluminum & aluminum-based
alloy castings

(P-11382)
GENERAL FOUNDRY SERVICE CORP
1390 Business Center Pl, San Leandro
(94577-2212)
PHONE..............................510 297-5040
Edward J Ritelli Jr, *CEO*
Edward J Ritelli Sr, *President*
Steve Bybee, *Manager*
Albert Gonzalez, *Manager*
EMP: 70
SQ FT: 15,200

SALES (est): 14.6MM **Privately Held**
WEB: www.genfoundry.com
SIC: 3365 3543 3369 3324 Aluminum &
aluminum-based alloy castings; machinery castings, aluminum; industrial patterns; nonferrous foundries; steel
investment foundries

(P-11383)
INTERORBITAL SYSTEMS
1394 Barnes St Bldg 7, Mojave
(93501-1673)
P.O. Box 662 (93502-0662)
PHONE..............................661 824-1662
Randa Milliron, *CEO*
Roderick Milliron, *President*
EMP: 12
SQ FT: 6,000
SALES (est): 150K **Privately Held**
WEB: www.interorbital.com
SIC: 3365 3764 Aerospace castings, alu-
minum; guided missile & space vehicle
propulsion unit parts; propulsion units for
guided missiles & space vehicles

(P-11384)
LYNWOOD PATTERN SERVICE INC
2528 E 127th St, Compton (90222-1514)
P.O. Box 536, Lynwood (90262-0536)
PHONE..............................310 631-2225
Jose Alvarez, *President*
Benjamen Alvarez, *Vice Pres*
Benjamin Alvarez, *Manager*
Jason Alvarez, *Manager*
EMP: 15
SQ FT: 4,000
SALES (est): 2MM **Privately Held**
SIC: 3365 3543 Aluminum & aluminum-
based alloy castings; foundry patternmak-
ing

(P-11385)
MAGPARTS (DH)
Also Called: Cpp-Azusa
1545 W Roosevelt St, Azusa (91702-3281)
PHONE..............................626 334-7897
Richard H Emerson, *President*
L Scott Mac Donald, *Vice Pres*
Ellen E Skatvold, *Admin Sec*
Ivan Gastelum, *Technician*
Stephen A Mac Donald, *Site Mgr*
EMP: 73
SQ FT: 100,000
SALES (est): 19.8MM
SALES (corp-wide): 6.9B **Privately Held**
WEB: www.magparts.com
SIC: 3365 3369 Aluminum & aluminum-
based alloy castings; magnesium &
magnes.-base alloy castings, exc. die-
casting
HQ: Consolidated Precision Products Corp.
1621 Euclid Ave Ste 1850
Cleveland OH 44115
216 453-4800

(P-11386)
OASIS ALLOY WHEELS INC
Also Called: Oasis Metal Works
400 S Lemon St, Anaheim (92805-3816)
PHONE..............................714 533-3286
EMP: 13
SQ FT: 10,000
SALES: 2MM **Privately Held**
WEB: www.oasiswheels.com
SIC: 3365

(P-11387)
PAC FOUNDRIES INC
Also Called: Prime Alloy Steel Casting
705 Industrial Way, Port Hueneme
(93041-3505)
PHONE..............................805 986-1308
Steve Clodfelter, *President*
EMP: 229
SALES (est): 37.2MM
SALES (corp-wide): 6.9B **Privately Held**
WEB: www.pacificalloy.com
SIC: 3365 Aerospace castings, aluminum
HQ: Consolidated Precision Products Corp.
1621 Euclid Ave Ste 1850
Cleveland OH 44115
216 453-4800

▲ = Import ▼=Export
◆ =Import/Export

(P-11388)
RELATIVITY SPACE INC
8701 Aviation Blvd, Inglewood
(90301-2003)
PHONE....................................424 393-4309
Tim Ellis, *CEO*
Alexander Kwan, *Vice Pres*
Jordan Noone, *CTO*
EMP: 10
SQ FT: 10,000
SALES: 500K **Privately Held**
SIC: 3365 Aerospace castings, aluminum

(P-11389)
SONFARREL AEROSPACE LLC
3010 E La Jolla St, Anaheim (92806-1310)
PHONE....................................714 630-7280
Jeffrey Greer,
Ken Anderson,
EMP: 96
SALES (est): 175.3K **Privately Held**
SIC: 3365 Aerospace castings, aluminum

(P-11390)
TRILORE TECHNOLOGIES INC
3000 Danville Blvd 525f, Alamo
(94507-1574)
PHONE....................................925 295-0734
John Collins, *CEO*
Pritam Dhaliwal, *CFO*
Jason Pearson, *Vice Pres*
EMP: 30
SQ FT: 24,000
SALES (est): 5.1MM **Privately Held**
WEB: www.trilore.com
SIC: 3365 Aluminum foundries

(P-11391)
VAN BRUNT FOUNDRY INC
5136 Chakemco St, South Gate
(90280-6443)
PHONE....................................323 569-2832
Richard Ledesma, *President*
EMP: 12 **EST:** 1963
SQ FT: 10,000
SALES (est): 1.3MM **Privately Held**
SIC: 3365 Aluminum & aluminum-based
    alloy castings

3366 Copper Foundries

(P-11392)
ACME CASTINGS INC
6009 Santa Fe Ave, Huntington Park
(90255-2723)
PHONE....................................323 583-3129
Lee Lewis, *President*
Ruth Lewis, *Corp Secy*
EMP: 40 **EST:** 1963
SQ FT: 25,000
SALES (est): 6.3MM **Privately Held**
WEB: www.acme-castings.com
SIC: 3366 3325 3365 3322 Copper
    foundries; alloy steel castings, except in-
    vestment; aluminum foundries; malleable
    iron foundries

(P-11393)
**AMERICAN FINE ARTS
FOUNDRY LLC**
2520 N Ontario St Ste A, Burbank
(91504-4708)
PHONE....................................818 848-7593
Brett Barney,
Chris Delling, *Mktg Dir*
Angel Meza, *Sales Staff*
EMP: 25 **EST:** 1981
SQ FT: 3,000
SALES (est): 4.1MM **Privately Held**
WEB: www.afafoundry.com
SIC: 3366 3544 Castings (except die):
    bronze; forms (molds), for foundry & plas-
    tics working machinery

(P-11394)
ART BRONZE INC
11275 San Fernando Rd, San Fernando
(91340-3422)
PHONE....................................818 897-2222
Ian G Killips, *CEO*
EMP: 29
SQ FT: 11,400

SALES: 1.8MM **Privately Held**
SIC: 3366 3312 Bronze foundry; stainless
    steel

(P-11395)
**ASI/SILICA MACHINERY LLC
(PA)**
6404 Independence Ave, Woodland Hills
(91367-2607)
PHONE....................................818 920-1962
Ed Connor,
Patrick Tomlinson, *Engineer*
Wendy Amberg, *Purch Agent*
Dr Frank Dabby,
Fred Golob,
EMP: 23 **EST:** 1997
SQ FT: 11,000
SALES (est): 5.4MM **Privately Held**
WEB: www.asisilica.com
SIC: 3366 Machinery castings: brass

(P-11396)
E R METALS INC
Also Called: Heritage Bronze
14407 Main St, Hesperia (92345-4617)
PHONE....................................760 948-2309
Robert Escoto Sr, *President*
Robert Escoto Jr, *Corp Secy*
EMP: 13 **EST:** 1963
SALES (est): 1.5MM **Privately Held**
WEB: www.heritagebronze.com
SIC: 3366 3363 Copper foundries; alu-
    minum die-castings

(P-11397)
**FLEETWOOD CONTINENTAL
INC**
19451 S Susana Rd, Compton
(90221-5713)
PHONE....................................310 609-1477
David J Forster, *President*
▲ **EMP:** 75
SQ FT: 5,000
SALES (est): 16.3MM **Privately Held**
WEB: www.fleetcon.com
SIC: 3366 3823 3561 3523 Castings (ex-
    cept die): bronze; turbine flow meters, in-
    dustrial process type; pumps & pumping
    equipment; farm machinery & equipment

(P-11398)
**FRESNO VALVES & CASTINGS
INC (PA)**
7736 E Springfield Ave, Selma
(93662-9408)
P.O. Box 40 (93662-0040)
PHONE....................................559 834-2511
Jeffery T Showalter, *CEO*
John E Showalter, *President*
Jeffrey T Showalter, *CEO*
Kevin Follansbee, *CFO*
Denise Cano, *Human Res Mgr*
▲ **EMP:** 200
SALES (est): 56.2MM **Privately Held**
WEB: www.fresnovalves.com
SIC: 3366 3494 3523 3491 Brass
    foundry; pipe fittings; sprinkler systems,
    field; irrigation equipment, self-propelled;
    industrial valves

(P-11399)
**GALAXY DIE & ENGINEERING
INC**
Also Called: Galaxy Bearing Company
24910 Avenue Tibbitts, Valencia
(91355-3426)
PHONE....................................661 775-9301
Jawahar Saini, *President*
Hamid Baig, *Shareholder*
Sooltan Ali Bhoy, *Shareholder*
Malkiat Saini, *Shareholder*
Elizabeth Krueger, *General Mgr*
EMP: 40
SQ FT: 30,000
SALES: 3.2MM **Privately Held**
WEB: www.galaxybearing.com
SIC: 3366 3575 Bushings & bearings;
    computer terminals

(P-11400)
GASSER-OLDS INC
1800 Highland Ave, Manhattan Beach
(90266-4525)
P.O. Box 58286, Los Angeles (90058-0286)
PHONE....................................323 583-9031

Richard J Efurd, *Vice Pres*
John W Efurd III, *Vice Pres*
EMP: 25
SALES (est): 4.7MM **Privately Held**
WEB: www.gasserolds.com
SIC: 3366 5099 3369 3365 Brass
    foundry; bronze foundry; castings (except
    die): brass; monuments & grave markers;
    nonferrous foundries; aluminum foundries

(P-11401)
**MAGNESIUM ALLOY PDTS CO
INC**
2420 N Alameda St, Compton
(90222-2895)
P.O. Box 4668 (90224-4668)
PHONE....................................310 605-1440
J W Long, *President*
M B Long, *Admin Sec*
EMP: 46 **EST:** 1945
SQ FT: 90,000
SALES (est): 11.3MM **Privately Held**
SIC: 3366 Copper foundries

(P-11402)
MARTIN BRASS FOUNDRY
22427 Bear Creek Dr N, Murrieta
(92562-3088)
PHONE....................................951 698-7041
Roland L Martin, *President*
Glen Martin, *Vice Pres*
John W Martin, *Admin Sec*
EMP: 55
SQ FT: 20,000
SALES (est): 6.3MM **Privately Held**
WEB: www.martinbrass.com
SIC: 3366 Brass foundry; bronze foundry

(P-11403)
**MATTHEWS INTERNATIONAL
CORP**
442 W Esplanade Ave 105, San Jacinto
(92583-5006)
PHONE....................................951 537-6615
Rocky Thornton, *Manager*
EMP: 25
SALES (corp-wide): 1.6B **Publicly Held**
SIC: 3366 Copper foundries
PA: Matthews International Corporation
    2 N Shore Ctr Ste 200
    Pittsburgh PA 15212
    412 442-8200

(P-11404)
MONTCLAIR BRONZE INC (PA)
5621 State St, Montclair (91763-6241)
P.O. Box 2009 (91763-0509)
PHONE....................................909 986-2664
Dan Griffiths, *CEO*
Wayne Freeberg, *President*
Dan Griffiths, *CEO*
Thomas Freeberg, *Admin Sec*
Magdi Abdellatif, *Sales Engr*
EMP: 30
SQ FT: 8,000
SALES (est): 4.5MM **Privately Held**
SIC: 3366 3599 Bronze foundry; machine
    shop, jobbing & repair

(P-11405)
POINTECH
Hunters Point Shpyd, San Francisco
(94124)
P.O. Box 884234 (94188-4234)
PHONE....................................415 822-8704
Eric Swenson, *Owner*
EMP: 20
SALES (est): 3.6MM **Privately Held**
WEB: www.pointech.net
SIC: 3366 Copper foundries

(P-11406)
SIERRA SCULPTURE INC
Also Called: Van Howd Studios
13333 New Airport Rd, Auburn
(95602-7419)
P.O. Box 7197 (95604-7197)
PHONE....................................530 887-1581
Douglas Van Howd, *President*
Nancy Van Howd, *Executive*
Holly Thomasson, *Sales Staff*
EMP: 11
SQ FT: 6,000
SALES (est): 1.3MM **Privately Held**
SIC: 3366 Bronze foundry

3369 Nonferrous Foundries: Castings, NEC

(P-11407)
AIRBOLT INDUSTRIES INC
25334 Stanford Ave Unit B, Valencia
(91355)
PHONE....................................818 767-5600
Melissa Ramirez, *President*
Oscar Ramirez, *CEO*
EMP: 11
SQ FT: 7,000
SALES (est): 1.5MM **Privately Held**
SIC: 3369 3365 Aerospace castings, non-
    ferrous: except aluminum; aerospace
    castings, aluminum

(P-11408)
**ALLIEDSIGNAL AROSPC SVC
CORP (HQ)**
Also Called: Allied Signal Aerospace
2525 W 190th St, Torrance (90504-6002)
PHONE....................................310 323-9500
Bernd F Kessler, *President*
James V Gelly, *Treasurer*
Mary Beth Orson, *Vice Pres*
Lois H Fuchs, *Asst Treas*
David A Cohen, *Asst Sec*
EMP: 44 **EST:** 2003
SALES (est): 23.4MM
SALES (corp-wide): 41.8B **Publicly Held**
SIC: 3369 3822 3812 3769 Nonferrous
    foundries; auto controls regulating residntl
    & coml environmt & applncs; search &
    navigation equipment; guided missile &
    space vehicle parts & auxiliary equip-
    ment; fabricated plate work (boiler shop)
PA: Honeywell International Inc.
    300 S Tryon St
    Charlotte NC 28202
    973 455-2000

(P-11409)
**AURORA CASTING & ENGRG
INC**
1790 E Lemonwood Dr, Santa Paula
(93060-9510)
PHONE....................................805 933-2761
John Carlos Penrose, *CEO*
Lizet Nava, *Cust Mgr*
EMP: 65
SQ FT: 25,000
SALES (est): 14MM **Privately Held**
SIC: 3369 Nonferrous foundries

(P-11410)
B & G AEROSPACE METALS
1801 Railroad St, Corona (92880-2512)
P.O. Box 2767, Fallbrook (92088-2767)
PHONE....................................951 738-8133
John Bowling, *President*
Vince Bowling, *Vice Pres*
EMP: 25
SQ FT: 20,000
SALES (est): 2.1MM **Privately Held**
SIC: 3369 Nonferrous foundries

(P-11411)
**CAST-RITE INTERNATIONAL
INC (PA)**
515 E Airline Way, Gardena (90248-2501)
PHONE....................................310 532-2080
Donald E Dehaan, *CEO*
Howard Watkins, *CFO*
Wynn Chapman, *Vice Pres*
▲ **EMP:** 90
SQ FT: 59,330
SALES (est): 29MM **Privately Held**
SIC: 3369 Zinc & zinc-base alloy castings,
    except die-castings

(P-11412)
CPP-PORT HUENEME
705 Industrial Way, Port Hueneme
(93041-3505)
PHONE....................................805 488-6451
Steve Clodfelter, *Owner*
EMP: 230
SQ FT: 12,770

SALES (est): 24MM
SALES (corp-wide): 6.9B **Privately Held**
WEB: www.cfi-pac.com
SIC: 3369 Castings, except die-castings,
precision
HQ: Consolidated Precision Products Corp.
1621 Euclid Ave Ste 1850
Cleveland OH 44115
216 453-4800

(P-11413)
DECCO CASTINGS INC
1596 Pioneer Way, El Cajon (92020-1673)
PHONE..................................619 444-9437
Carl Decina, *President*
Kit Kesinger, *QC Mgr*
EMP: 45
SQ FT: 20,000
SALES (est): 15.4MM **Privately Held**
WEB: www.deccocastings.com
SIC: 3369 3365 3325 Nonferrous
foundries; aluminum foundries; steel
foundries

(P-11414)
DELT INDUSTRIES INC
90 W Easy St Ste 2, Simi Valley
(93065-6206)
P.O. Box 940067 (93094-0067)
PHONE..................................805 579-0213
Estelle Lee, *President*
Jerry Martin, *Vice Pres*
Debra Schultz, *Admin Sec*
EMP: 18
SQ FT: 10,000
SALES (est): 3.8MM **Privately Held**
SIC: 3369 5088 Nonferrous foundries;
transportation equipment & supplies

(P-11415)
EXCELITY
Also Called: Solara Engineering
11127 Dora St, Sun Valley (91352-3339)
PHONE..................................818 767-1000
Shaun Tan, *President*
EMP: 50
SALES (est): 9.5MM **Privately Held**
SIC: 3369 3812 Aerospace castings, non-
ferrous: except aluminum; acceleration in-
dicators & systems components,
aerospace

(P-11416)
FENICO PRECISION CASTINGS
INC
7805 Madison St, Paramount
(90723-4220)
PHONE..................................562 634-5000
Don Tomeo, *President*
Sherry Tomeo, *CFO*
Sonny Tran, *Engineer*
Gary Gunning, *Prdtn Mgr*
▲ EMP: 75
SQ FT: 20,000
SALES (est): 14.8MM **Privately Held**
SIC: 3369 3366 3324 3322 Machinery
castings, nonferrous: ex. alum., copper,
die, etc.; copper foundries; steel invest-
ment foundries; malleable iron foundries

(P-11417)
FS - PRECISION TECH CO LLC
3025 E Victoria St, Compton (90221-5616)
PHONE..................................310 638-0595
Juan Molina, *Exec VP*
Betty Ruffalo, *Info Tech Mgr*
Brad Moore, *Engineer*
Estela Moreno, *Engineer*
Israel M Sanchez,
▲ EMP: 100
SALES (est): 23.9MM **Privately Held**
WEB: www.fs-precision.com
SIC: 3369 Titanium castings, except die-
casting
PA: Fs-Elliott Company, Inc.
5710 Mellon Rd
Export PA 15632

(P-11418)
IMPRO INDUSTRIES USA INC
(DH)
21660 Copley Dr Ste 100, Diamond Bar
(91765-4174)
PHONE..................................909 396-6525
Hui INA Wang, *CEO*

Julia Chang, *Treasurer*
Ann C Conder, *Purch Mgr*
James Chen, *Purchasing*
◆ EMP: 10
SALES: 167MM **Privately Held**
SIC: 3369 5051 Castings, except die-cast-
ings, precision; castings, rough: iron or
steel

(P-11419)
PANKL AEROSPACE SYSTEMS
16615 Edwards Rd, Cerritos (90703-2437)
PHONE..................................562 207-6300
Horst Rieger, *CEO*
Harry Glieder, *President*
Josef Blazicek, *Chairman*
Alexander Aigner, *Technical Staff*
Juergen Fisher, *Engineer*
EMP: 75
SQ FT: 63,040
SALES (est): 20.7MM
SALES (corp-wide): 1.7B **Privately Held**
SIC: 3369 3724 Aerospace castings, non-
ferrous: except aluminum; aircraft engines
& engine parts
HQ: Pankl Holdings, Inc.
1902 Mcgaw Ave
Irvine CA 92614

(P-11420)
PCC STRUCTURALS INC
Also Called: PCC Structurals-San Leandro
414 Hester St, San Leandro (94577-1024)
PHONE..................................510 568-6400
Craig Milton, *Branch Mgr*
David Pagan, *Engineer*
Laura Norberg, *Accountant*
Taylor Schaack, *Facilities Mgr*
Greg Lawless, *Manager*
EMP: 180
SALES (corp-wide): 225.3B **Publicly
Held**
SIC: 3369 Nonferrous foundries
HQ: Pcc Structurals, Inc.
4600 Se Harney Dr
Portland OR 97206
503 777-3881

(P-11421)
PRIME ALLOY STEEL CASTINGS
INC
717 Industrial Way, Port Hueneme
(93041-3505)
PHONE..................................805 488-6451
Steve Clodfelter, *CEO*
Ali Ghavami, *COO*
Michael Dyar, *CFO*
William Fanner, *Vice Pres*
EMP: 140
SQ FT: 12,000
SALES (est): 14.4MM
SALES (corp-wide): 6.9B **Privately Held**
WEB: www.pacfoundries.com
SIC: 3369 Castings, except die-castings,
precision
HQ: Consolidated Precision Products Corp.
1621 Euclid Ave Ste 1850
Cleveland OH 44115
216 453-4800

(P-11422)
RADIAN THERMAL PRODUCTS
INC
Also Called: Radian Heat Sinks
2160 Walsh Ave, Santa Clara
(95050-2512)
PHONE..................................408 988-6200
Gerald L McIntyre, *Chairman*
Mong Hu, *CEO*
Kevin Pinheiro, *Engineer*
Abhinav Sharma, *Engineer*
Alejandro Valle, *Engineer*
▲ EMP: 54
SQ FT: 26,500
SALES (est): 13.7MM **Privately Held**
SIC: 3369 Castings, except die-castings,
precision

(P-11423)
SANTA ROSA LEAD PRODUCTS
INC
33 S University St, Healdsburg
(95448-4021)
PHONE..................................707 431-1477
Jeremy Winter, *General Mgr*

EMP: 27 EST: 1973
SQ FT: 6,100
SALES (est): 5.6MM
SALES (corp-wide): 110.2MM **Privately
Held**
SIC: 3369 3444 Lead castings, except die-
castings; sheet metalwork
PA: Metalico, Inc.
135 Dermody St
Cranford NJ 07016
908 497-9610

(P-11424)
SYNERTECH PM INC
11711 Monarch St, Garden Grove
(92841-1830)
PHONE..................................714 898-9151
Charles Barre, *CEO*
Kristen Barre, *President*
Victor Samarov, *Vice Pres*
Catherine Crawford, *Admin Asst*
▲ EMP: 17
SQ FT: 20,000
SALES (est): 3.4MM **Privately Held**
WEB: www.synertechpm.com
SIC: 3369 Aerospace castings, nonferrous:
except aluminum

(P-11425)
TECHNI-CAST CORP
11220 Garfield Ave, South Gate
(90280-7586)
PHONE..................................562 923-4585
Bryn Jhan Van Hiel II, *President*
Donald Van Hiel, *Vice Pres*
Lynne Van Hiel, *Vice Pres*
Elaine M Kay, *Admin Sec*
▲ EMP: 80
SQ FT: 60,000
SALES (est): 20.3MM **Privately Held**
WEB: www.techni-cast.com
SIC: 3369 3599 3364 3325 Lead, zinc &
white metal; machinery castings, nonfer-
rous: ex. alum., copper, die, etc.; machine
shop, jobbing & repair; nonferrous die-
castings except aluminum; steel foundries

(P-11426)
UNITED CASTINGS INC
5154 F St, Chino (91710-5161)
P.O. Box 2689 (91708-2689)
PHONE..................................909 627-7645
Albert Lewis, *President*
Doris Lewis, *Corp Secy*
▲ EMP: 11
SQ FT: 6,000
SALES (est): 1.7MM
SALES (corp-wide): 9.3MM **Privately
Held**
WEB: www.uncastings.com
SIC: 3369 Castings, except die-castings,
precision
PA: Glass Incorporated International
14055 Laurelwood Pl
Covina CA 91724
909 628-4212

3398 Metal Heat Treating

(P-11427)
ABRASIVE FINISHING CO
Also Called: Afco
14920 S Main St, Gardena (90248-1921)
PHONE..................................310 323-7175
William Swanson, *President*
EMP: 32 EST: 1957
SQ FT: 2,600
SALES (est): 5MM **Privately Held**
WEB: www.abrasivefinishing.com
SIC: 3398 3471 Shot peening (treating
steel to reduce fatigue); plating & polish-
ing

(P-11428)
ACCURATE STEEL TREATING
INC
10008 Miller Way, South Gate
(90280-5496)
PHONE..................................562 927-6528
Ronald Loyns, *President*
Mike Bastin, *Vice Pres*
EMP: 38
SQ FT: 10,000

SALES (est): 8.7MM **Privately Held**
WEB: www.accuratesteeltreating.com
SIC: 3398 Metal heat treating

(P-11429)
ADB INDUSTRIES
Also Called: Subsidy of Be Aerospace
1400 Manhattan Ave, Fullerton
(92831-5222)
PHONE..................................310 679-9193
Brian Dietz, *President*
EMP: 90
SQ FT: 50,000
SALES (est): 9.7MM
SALES (corp-wide): 66.5B **Publicly Held**
WEB: www.adbco.com
SIC: 3398 8711 7692 3444 Brazing
(hardening) of metal; engineering serv-
ices; welding repair; sheet metalwork
HQ: Tsi Group, Inc.
94 Tide Mill Rd
Hampton NH 03842

(P-11430)
AEROCRAFT HEAT TREATING
CO INC
15701 Minnesota Ave, Paramount
(90723-4120)
PHONE..................................562 674-2400
David W Dickson, *CEO*
Robert Lyddon, *Vice Pres*
EMP: 57 EST: 1947
SQ FT: 18,000
SALES (est): 14.2MM
SALES (corp-wide): 225.3B **Publicly
Held**
WEB: www.aerocraft-ht.com
SIC: 3398 Metal heat treating
HQ: Precision Castparts Corp.
4650 Sw Mcdam Ave Ste 300
Portland OR 97239
503 946-4800

(P-11431)
AL-MAG HEAT TREAT
9735 Alpaca St, South El Monte
(91733-3028)
PHONE..................................626 442-8570
Don Dees, *President*
EMP: 13
SQ FT: 12,000
SALES (est): 1.1MM **Privately Held**
SIC: 3398 Metal heat treating

(P-11432)
AREMAC HEAT TREATING INC
330 S 9th Ave, City of Industry
(91746-3311)
P.O. Box 90068 (91715-0068)
PHONE..................................626 333-3898
B E Kopaskie, *President*
Bernard E Kopaskie, *President*
D R Butler, *Vice Pres*
Jan Kopaskie, *Admin Sec*
Steve Allensworth, *Sales Mgr*
EMP: 38 EST: 1967
SQ FT: 14,000
SALES (est): 9.8MM **Privately Held**
SIC: 3398 Metal heat treating

(P-11433)
ASTRO ALUMINUM TREATING
CO INC
11040 Palmer Ave, South Gate
(90280-7497)
PHONE..................................562 923-4344
Mark R Dickson, *President*
Alex Gaxiola, *Planning*
Miguel Nuevano, *MIS Staff*
Mike Burns, *Controller*
David Zambrano, *Safety Mgr*
EMP: 90 EST: 1977
SQ FT: 4,800
SALES (est): 23.1MM **Privately Held**
WEB: www.astroaluminum.com
SIC: 3398 Metal heat treating

(P-11434)
BODYCOTE IMT INC
Also Called: Alum-A-Therm
7474 Garden Grove Blvd, Westminster
(92683-2227)
PHONE..................................714 893-6561
Jeff Monty, *Branch Mgr*
EMP: 55

▲ = Import ▼=Export
◆ =Import/Export

SALES (corp-wide): 935.8MM **Privately Held**
SIC: 3398 Metal heat treating
HQ: Bodycote Imt, Inc.
155 River St
Andover MA 01810
978 470-0876

(P-11435)
BODYCOTE THERMAL PROC INC
2900 S Sunol Dr, Vernon (90058-4315)
PHONE....................................323 264-0111
Chris Hall, *Branch Mgr*
Oscar Ortiz, *Manager*
EMP: 10
SALES (corp-wide): 935.8MM **Privately Held**
SIC: 3398 Metal heat treating
HQ: Bodycote Thermal Processing, Inc.
12700 Park Central Dr # 700
Dallas TX 75251
214 904-2420

(P-11436)
BODYCOTE THERMAL PROC INC
515 W Apra St Ste A, Compton (90220-5502)
PHONE....................................310 604-8000
Jose Catano, *Branch Mgr*
Tracy Glende, *President*
Jose Salcedo, *Supervisor*
EMP: 21
SALES (corp-wide): 935.8MM **Privately Held**
SIC: 3398 Metal heat treating
HQ: Bodycote Thermal Processing, Inc.
12700 Park Central Dr # 700
Dallas TX 75251
214 904-2420

(P-11437)
BODYCOTE THERMAL PROC INC
7474 Garden Grove Blvd, Westminster (92683-2227)
PHONE....................................714 893-6561
Manuel Granillo, *Branch Mgr*
EMP: 80
SQ FT: 7,369
SALES (corp-wide): 935.8MM **Privately Held**
SIC: 3398 Metal heat treating
HQ: Bodycote Thermal Processing, Inc.
12700 Park Central Dr # 700
Dallas TX 75251
214 904-2420

(P-11438)
BODYCOTE THERMAL PROC INC
11845 Burke St, Santa Fe Springs (90670-2537)
PHONE....................................562 693-3135
Paul Dymond, *Branch Mgr*
EMP: 26
SALES (corp-wide): 935.8MM **Privately Held**
SIC: 3398 Brazing (hardening) of metal
HQ: Bodycote Thermal Processing, Inc.
12700 Park Central Dr # 700
Dallas TX 75251
214 904-2420

(P-11439)
BODYCOTE THERMAL PROC INC
4240 Technology Dr, Fremont (94538-6337)
PHONE....................................510 492-4200
Paul Dymond, *Manager*
EMP: 25
SALES (corp-wide): 935.8MM **Privately Held**
SIC: 3398 Metal heat treating
HQ: Bodycote Thermal Processing, Inc.
12700 Park Central Dr # 700
Dallas TX 75251
214 904-2420

(P-11440)
BODYCOTE THERMAL PROC INC
9921 Romandel Ave, Santa Fe Springs (90670-3441)
PHONE....................................562 946-1717
Manuel Granillo, *Principal*
EMP: 31
SALES (corp-wide): 935.8MM **Privately Held**
SIC: 3398 Metal heat treating
HQ: Bodycote Thermal Processing, Inc.
12700 Park Central Dr # 700
Dallas TX 75251
214 904-2420

(P-11441)
BODYCOTE USA INC
2900 S Sunol Dr, Vernon (90058-4315)
PHONE....................................323 264-0111
EMP: 10
SQ FT: 31,717
SALES (corp-wide): 935.8MM **Privately Held**
SIC: 3398 Metal heat treating
HQ: Bodycote Usa, Inc.
12700 Park Central Dr # 700
Dallas TX 75251
214 904-2420

(P-11442)
BURBANK STEEL TREATING INC
415 S Varney St, Burbank (91502-2194)
PHONE....................................818 842-0975
Mildred Bennett, *Ch of Bd*
Larry Bennett, *President*
Kenneth Bennett, *Vice Pres*
EMP: 45 EST: 1969
SQ FT: 16,000
SALES (est): 8.8MM **Privately Held**
WEB: www.burbanksteel.com
SIC: 3398 Metal heat treating

(P-11443)
BYINGTON STEEL TREATING INC (PA)
1225 Memorex Dr, Santa Clara (95050-2888)
PHONE....................................408 727-6630
Kathryn Byington, *CEO*
Clyde D Byington, *President*
Sean Byington, *COO*
Catherine A Byington, *Vice Pres*
Don Judson, *Vice Pres*
EMP: 22
SQ FT: 25,000
SALES (est): 3.6MM **Privately Held**
WEB: www.byingtonsteel.com
SIC: 3398 Tempering of metal

(P-11444)
CALSTRIP STEEL CORPORATION (HQ)
3030 Dulles Dr, Jurupa Valley (91752-3240)
PHONE....................................323 838-2097
Thomas B Nelis, *President*
Douglas Clark, *Vice Pres*
Diane England, *Administration*
▲ EMP: 77
SQ FT: 190,000
SALES (est): 18.6MM
SALES (corp-wide): 160MM **Privately Held**
WEB: www.calstripsteel.com
SIC: 3398 3316 Metal heat treating; strip steel, cold-rolled: from purchased hot-rolled
PA: Calstrip Industries, Inc.
3030 Dulles Dr
Jurupa Valley CA 91752
323 726-1345

(P-11445)
CERTIFIED METAL CRAFT INC
877 Vernon Way, El Cajon (92020-1940)
PHONE....................................619 593-3636
John C Wiederkehr, *President*
Mark Wiederkehr, *Vice Pres*
Tianne Wiederkehr, *Office Mgr*
Berger Steve, *QC Mgr*
Pam Cash, *Representative*
EMP: 30
SQ FT: 29,500

SALES (est): 7.8MM **Privately Held**
WEB: www.certifiedmetalcraft.com
SIC: 3398 Brazing (hardening) of metal; tempering of metal

(P-11446)
CITY STEEL HEAT TREATING INC
1221 W Struck Ave, Orange (92867-3531)
PHONE....................................562 789-7373
Samuel Boyer, *President*
EMP: 15
SALES (est): 1.8MM **Privately Held**
SIC: 3398 Metal heat treating

(P-11447)
COAST HEAT TREATING CO
1767 Industrial Way, Los Angeles (90023-4394)
PHONE....................................323 263-6944
Frank Garcia, *President*
EMP: 36
SQ FT: 10,000
SALES: 1.5MM **Privately Held**
SIC: 3398 Metal heat treating

(P-11448)
CONTINENTAL HEAT TREATING INC
10643 Norwalk Blvd, Santa Fe Springs (90670-3821)
PHONE....................................562 944-8808
James Stull, *President*
Dennis Hugie, *Principal*
Don Lowman, *Principal*
Ken Nelson, *Principal*
Shaun Radford, *General Mgr*
EMP: 62
SQ FT: 20,000
SALES (est): 16MM **Privately Held**
SIC: 3398 Metal heat treating

(P-11449)
COOK INDUCTION HEATING CO INC
4925 Slauson Ave, Maywood (90270-3094)
P.O. Box 430 (90270-0430)
PHONE....................................323 560-1327
Keith Doolittle, *CEO*
Richard Egkan, *Vice Pres*
EMP: 21
SQ FT: 24,500
SALES (est): 4.4MM **Privately Held**
SIC: 3398 3728 Metal heat treating; aircraft assemblies, subassemblies & parts

(P-11450)
DIVERSFIED MTLLRGICAL SVCS INC
Also Called: Varco Heat Treating
12101 Industry St, Garden Grove (92841-2813)
P.O. Box 5500 (92846-0500)
PHONE....................................714 895-7777
Don A Gay, *President*
Winston E Mote, *Vice Pres*
EMP: 35
SQ FT: 28,000
SALES (est): 7.9MM **Privately Held**
WEB: www.varcoheat.com
SIC: 3398 4924 3479 Metal heat treating; natural gas distribution; coating of metals & formed products

(P-11451)
GARNER HEAT TREAT INC
10001 Denny St, Oakland (94603-3090)
PHONE....................................510 568-0587
Alvenia Garner, *President*
EMP: 10
SQ FT: 12,000
SALES (est): 1.5MM **Privately Held**
SIC: 3398 Metal heat treating

(P-11452)
H P APPLICATIONS
4727 E 49th St, Vernon (90058-2703)
PHONE....................................323 585-2894
Gustavo Perez, *President*
EMP: 12
SALES (est): 1MM **Privately Held**
SIC: 3398 Metal heat treating

(P-11453)
HI TECH HEAT TREATING INC
331 W 168th St, Gardena (90248-2732)
PHONE....................................310 532-3705
Alastair Oldfield, *President*
EMP: 16
SALES: 1.1MM **Privately Held**
SIC: 3398 Metal heat treating

(P-11454)
INTERNTONAL METALLURGICAL SVCS
Also Called: Scarrott Metallurgical Co
6371 Arizona Cir, Los Angeles (90045-1201)
PHONE....................................310 645-7300
Dave Scarrott, *President*
Ralph Jones, *Vice Pres*
Jose Catano, *General Mgr*
Laura Farrell, *Accounting Mgr*
Navid Khalilian, *Manager*
EMP: 19
SQ FT: 8,000
SALES (est): 4.5MM **Privately Held**
WEB: www.scarrott.com
SIC: 3398 Brazing (hardening) of metal

(P-11455)
KPI SERVICES INC
Also Called: Kittyhawk Products
11651 Monarch St, Garden Grove (92841-1816)
PHONE....................................714 895-5024
Charles Barre, *CEO*
Dennis Poor, *President*
Lois Barre, *Corp Secy*
Steve Belloise, *Vice Pres*
Dee Dee Poor, *Vice Pres*
▲ EMP: 35 EST: 1995
SQ FT: 12,500
SALES (est): 11.9MM **Privately Held**
WEB: www.kittyhawkinc.com
SIC: 3398 Metal heat treating

(P-11456)
METAL IMPROVEMENT COMPANY LLC
2588 Industry Way A, Lynwood (90262-4015)
PHONE....................................323 585-2168
Amando Yanez, *Manager*
Marilu Romero, *Human Res Dir*
Tom Weber, *Plant Engr*
EMP: 50
SQ FT: 28,260
SALES (corp-wide): 2.4B **Publicly Held**
WEB: www.mic-houston.com
SIC: 3398 Shot peening (treating steel to reduce fatigue)
HQ: Metal Improvement Company, Llc
80 E Rte 4 Ste 310
Paramus NJ 07652
201 843-7800

(P-11457)
METAL IMPROVEMENT COMPANY LLC
E/M Coatings Solutions
6940 Farmdale Ave, North Hollywood (91605-6210)
PHONE....................................818 983-1952
Brent Taylor, *Branch Mgr*
EMP: 85
SALES (corp-wide): 2.4B **Publicly Held**
WEB: www.curtisswright.com
SIC: 3398 Shot peening (treating steel to reduce fatigue)
HQ: Metal Improvement Company, Llc
80 E Rte 4 Ste 310
Paramus NJ 07652
201 843-7800

(P-11458)
METAL IMPROVEMENT COMPANY LLC
Also Called: Para Tech Coating
35 Argonaut Ste A1, Laguna Hills (92656-4151)
PHONE....................................949 855-8010
Bill Gleason, *Manager*
Patricia Langraphi, *QC Mgr*
Rick Segarra, *Manager*
EMP: 30

SALES (corp-wide): 2.4B **Publicly Held**
SIC: 3398 Shot peening (treating steel to reduce fatigue)
HQ: Metal Improvement Company, Llc
80 E Rte 4 Ste 310
Paramus NJ 07652
201 843-7800

(P-11459)
METAL IMPROVEMENT COMPANY LLC
E/M Coatings Services
20751 Superior St, Chatsworth (91311-4416)
PHONE.................................818 407-6280
Brent Taylor, *Branch Mgr*
EMP: 96
SALES (corp-wide): 2.4B **Publicly Held**
SIC: 3398 Shot peening (treating steel to reduce fatigue)
HQ: Metal Improvement Company, Llc
80 E Rte 4 Ste 310
Paramus NJ 07652
201 843-7800

(P-11460)
METAL IMPROVEMENT COMPANY LLC
7655 Longard Rd Bldg A, Livermore (94551-8208)
PHONE.................................925 960-1090
Jim McManus, *Manager*
Marissa Skog, *Manager*
EMP: 40
SALES (corp-wide): 2.4B **Publicly Held**
WEB: www.mic-houston.com
SIC: 3398 Shot peening (treating steel to reduce fatigue)
HQ: Metal Improvement Company, Llc
80 E Rte 4 Ste 310
Paramus NJ 07652
201 843-7800

(P-11461)
METAL IMPROVEMENT COMPANY LLC
2151 S Hathaway St, Santa Ana (92705-5247)
PHONE.................................714 546-4160
Joe Wheaton, *Manager*
EMP: 18
SALES (corp-wide): 2.4B **Publicly Held**
WEB: www.mic-houston.com
SIC: 3398 Shot peening (treating steel to reduce fatigue)
HQ: Metal Improvement Company, Llc
80 E Rte 4 Ste 310
Paramus NJ 07652
201 843-7800

(P-11462)
METAL IMPROVEMENT COMPANY LLC
2588a Industry Way, Lynwood (90262-4015)
PHONE.................................323 563-1533
Amando Yanez, *Manager*
EMP: 17
SALES (corp-wide): 2.4B **Publicly Held**
WEB: www.mic-houston.com
SIC: 3398 Shot peening (treating steel to reduce fatigue)
HQ: Metal Improvement Company, Llc
80 E Rte 4 Ste 310
Paramus NJ 07652
201 843-7800

(P-11463)
METAL PRODUCTS ENGINEERING
3050 Leonis Blvd, Vernon (90058-2914)
PHONE.................................323 581-8121
Luppe R Luppen, *Ch of Bd*
Paula Luppen, *Corp Secy*
EMP: 24 EST: 1997
SQ FT: 40,000
SALES (est): 1.8MM
SALES (corp-wide): 2.4MM **Privately Held**
WEB: www.metalproductseng.com
SIC: 3398 3469 3578 3596 Metal heat treating; metal stampings; change making machines; scales & balances, except laboratory

PA: Luppen Holdings, Inc.
3050 Leonis Blvd
Vernon CA 90058
323 581-8121

(P-11464)
NEWTON HEAT TREATING COMPANY
19235 E Walnut Dr N, City of Industry (91748-1494)
P.O. Box 8010, Rowland Heights (91748-0010)
PHONE.................................626 964-6528
Greg Newton, *President*
Linda Malcor, *Admin Sec*
Miguel Zaragoza, *QC Mgr*
EMP: 71
SQ FT: 1,900
SALES: 4MM **Privately Held**
WEB: www.newtonheattreating.com
SIC: 3398 8734 3444 Metal heat treating; X-ray inspection service, industrial; sheet metalwork

(P-11465)
PEEN-RITE INC
11662 Sheldon St, Sun Valley (91352-1597)
PHONE.................................818 767-3676
Bill Swanson, *President*
Richard Bluth, *Vice Pres*
Tillie Bluth, *Admin Sec*
EMP: 16 EST: 1965
SQ FT: 13,000
SALES (est): 3.2MM **Privately Held**
WEB: www.peenrite.com
SIC: 3398 Shot peening (treating steel to reduce fatigue)

(P-11466)
PROTECH THERMAL SERVICES
1954 Tandem, Norco (92860-3607)
PHONE.................................951 272-5808
Brian Grier, *President*
Nathan Smith, *Principal*
Carolyn Dearborn, *Accountant*
Keith Grier, *Sales Staff*
Shawn Ince, *Sales Staff*
EMP: 33
SQ FT: 4,000
SALES (est): 9.1MM **Privately Held**
SIC: 3398 Metal heat treating

(P-11467)
QUALITY HEAT TREATING INC
3305 Burton Ave, Burbank (91504-3199)
PHONE.................................818 840-8212
James G Stull, *President*
EMP: 34
SQ FT: 20,000
SALES (est): 6.9MM **Privately Held**
WEB: www.qualityht.com
SIC: 3398 3471 Metal heat treating; sand blasting of metal parts

(P-11468)
SOLAR ATMOSPHERES INC
8606 Live Oak Ave, Fontana (92335-3172)
PHONE.................................909 217-7400
Amy Blanes, *Branch Mgr*
Steve Lodge, *Manager*
EMP: 24
SALES (corp-wide): 25.4MM **Privately Held**
WEB: www.solaratm.com
SIC: 3398 Annealing of metal
PA: Solar Atmospheres, Inc.
1969 Clearview Rd
Souderton PA 18964
215 721-1502

(P-11469)
SUPERHEAT FGH SERVICES INC
1333 Willow Pass Rd, Concord (94520-7930)
PHONE.................................925 808-6711
Brad Hennig, *Branch Mgr*
EMP: 18
SALES (corp-wide): 65.3MM **Privately Held**
SIC: 3398 Metal heat treating
PA: Superheat Fgh Services, Inc.
313 Garnet Dr
New Lenox IL 60451
708 478-0205

(P-11470)
SUPREME STEEL TREATING INC
2466 Seaman Ave, El Monte (91733-1926)
PHONE.................................626 350-5865
Neal Begerow, *President*
Irene Jimenez, *Executive*
EMP: 23
SQ FT: 5,400
SALES (est): 4.2MM **Privately Held**
WEB: www.supremesteeltreating.com
SIC: 3398 Metal heat treating

(P-11471)
TEAM INC
Also Called: Team Industrial Services
2580 W 237th St, Torrance (90505-5217)
PHONE.................................310 514-2312
Bill Pigeon, *Manager*
Chuck Morissette, *Comp Spec*
Cassandra Barraza, *Technician*
Brian Boucher, *Opers Mgr*
Thomas Yeager, *Opers Mgr*
EMP: 60
SALES (corp-wide): 1.2B **Publicly Held**
SIC: 3398 3567 Metal heat treating; heating units & devices, industrial: electric; fuel-fired furnaces & ovens
HQ: Team, Inc.
5095 Paris St
Denver CO 80239

(P-11472)
THERMAL-VAC TECHNOLOGY INC
1221 W Struck Ave, Orange (92867-3531)
PHONE.................................714 997-2601
Steve Driscol, *CEO*
Aaron Anderson, *President*
Ely Enriquez, *Buyer*
Ashley Staack, *Sales Staff*
EMP: 41
SQ FT: 26,800
SALES (est): 13.3MM **Privately Held**
WEB: www.thermal-vac.com
SIC: 3398 Brazing (hardening) of metal

(P-11473)
THERMO PRODUCTS INC
Also Called: Thermcore
13185 Nevada City Ave, Grass Valley (95945-9568)
PHONE.................................909 888-2882
Larry Nameche, *President*
David Wade, *CEO*
Maria Wade, *Admin Sec*
▲ EMP: 55
SQ FT: 235,000
SALES (est): 6.7MM **Privately Held**
WEB: www.thermcore.com
SIC: 3398 Metal heat treating

(P-11474)
TRI-J METAL HEAT TREATING CO (PA)
327 E Commercial St, Pomona (91767-5505)
PHONE.................................909 622-9999
Debra Cramer, *Admin Sec*
Albert W James Jr, *President*
Robert L James, *Vice Pres*
Lena James, *Admin Sec*
▲ EMP: 19 EST: 1976
SQ FT: 17,500
SALES (est): 2.9MM **Privately Held**
SIC: 3398 Annealing of metal

(P-11475)
TRIUMPH GROUP INC
2136 S Hathaway St, Santa Ana (92705-5248)
PHONE.................................714 546-9842
Jeffry D Frisby, *CEO*
Leslie Zimmer, *Vice Pres*
Christyne Contreras, *Purch Agent*
Darin McCoy, *QC Mgr*
Renato Torres, *Director*
EMP: 350 **Publicly Held**
SIC: 3398 3479 3471 8734 Shot peening (treating steel to reduce fatigue); coating of metals & formed products; electroplating & plating; metallurgical testing laboratory

PA: Triumph Group, Inc.
899 Cassatt Rd Ste 210
Berwyn PA 19312

(P-11476)
VALLEY METAL TREATING INC
355 S East End Ave, Pomona (91766-2312)
PHONE.................................909 623-6316
James G Stull, *President*
EMP: 38
SQ FT: 8,000
SALES (est): 7.5MM **Privately Held**
WEB: www.valleymt.net
SIC: 3398 Metal heat treating

3399 Primary Metal Prdts, NEC

(P-11477)
ALINABAL INC
Lamsco West
29101 The Old Rd, Valencia (91355-1014)
PHONE.................................661 877-9356
Glad Baldwin, *General Mgr*
Ralph Hernandez, *Production*
EMP: 25
SALES (corp-wide): 57MM **Privately Held**
WEB: www.dacoinstrument.com
SIC: 3399 3469 Laminating steel; stamping metal for the trade
HQ: Alinabal, Inc.
28 Woodmont Rd
Milford CT 06460
203 877-3241

(P-11478)
HAI ADVNCED MTL SPCIALISTS INC
Also Called: H A I
1688 Sierra Madre Cir, Placentia (92870-6628)
PHONE.................................714 414-0575
Daren J Gansert, *President*
Debra Gansert, *Vice Pres*
Debbie Gansert, *General Mgr*
▲ EMP: 15
SQ FT: 10,000
SALES (est): 3.7MM **Privately Held**
WEB: www.haiams.com
SIC: 3399 Powder, metal

(P-11479)
LEE FASTENERS INC
3327 San Gabriel Blvd H, Rosemead (91770-2584)
PHONE.................................626 287-6848
Michael Hua, *President*
▲ EMP: 10
SALES (est): 1.2MM **Privately Held**
WEB: www.leefasteners.com
SIC: 3399 Metal fasteners

(P-11480)
MELLING TOOL RUSH METALS LLC
Also Called: Melling Sintered Metals
16100 S Figueroa St, Gardena (90248-2617)
PHONE.................................580 725-3295
Mark Melling, *CEO*
▲ EMP: 65
SQ FT: 48,000
SALES: 8MM
SALES (corp-wide): 265MM **Privately Held**
WEB: www.cloyes.com
SIC: 3399 Powder, metal
PA: Melling Tool Co.
2620 Saradan Dr
Jackson MI 49202
517 787-8172

(P-11481)
MICRO SURFACE ENGR INC (PA)
Also Called: Ball TEC
1550 E Slauson Ave, Los Angeles (90011-5099)
P.O. Box 58611 (90011)
PHONE.................................323 582-7348
Eugene A Gleason Jr, *President*
Eugene A Gleason III, *Corp Secy*

▲ = Import ▼=Export
◆ =Import/Export

Helen Gleason, *Vice Pres*
Patricia Johnson, *Finance Dir*
Tony Velazquez, *Prdtn Mgr*
EMP: 35 **EST:** 1952
SQ FT: 46,000
SALES (est): 5.7MM **Privately Held**
WEB: www.precisionballs.com
SIC: 3399 Steel balls

(P-11482)
PARMATECH CORPORATION
2221 Pine View Way, Petaluma
(94954-5688)
PHONE......................707 778-2266
Peter Frost, *CEO*
Caryn E Mitchell, *Treasurer*
Bryan Mc Bride, *General Mgr*
Kai Lee, *Engineer*
▲ **EMP:** 75
SQ FT: 22,000
SALES (est): 22.6MM
SALES (corp-wide): 77.1MM **Privately Held**
WEB: www.parmatech.com
SIC: 3399 Powder, metal
PA: Atw Companies, Inc.
125 Metro Center Blvd # 3001
Warwick RI 02886
401 244-1002

(P-11483)
PERRY TOOL & RESEARCH INC
3415 Enterprise Ave, Hayward
(94545-3284)
PHONE......................510 782-9226
Kenneth Fasselman, *CEO*
Ken F Fusselman, *Manager*
EMP: 35 **EST:** 1962
SQ FT: 13,000
SALES (est): 7.9MM **Privately Held**
WEB: www.perrytool.com
SIC: 3399 Powder, metal

(P-11484)
PRECISION PWDRED MET PARTS INC
145 Atlantic St, Pomona (91768-3286)
PHONE......................909 595-5656
Maurice Bridgman, *President*
David Connelly, *Corp Secy*
Andy Pirkle, *CIO*
Quan Nguyen, *Chief Engr*
▲ **EMP:** 48
SQ FT: 25,000
SALES (est): 16.1MM **Privately Held**
WEB: www.precisionpm.com
SIC: 3399 Powder, metal

(P-11485)
SCAFCO CORPORATION
2443 Foundry Park Ave, Fresno
(93706-4531)
PHONE......................559 256-9911
Larry Stone, *President*
EMP: 18
SALES (corp-wide): 160.5MM **Privately Held**
SIC: 3399 Iron ore recovery from open hearth slag
PA: Scafco Corporation
2800 E Main Ave
Spokane WA 99202
509 343-9000

(P-11486)
SENJU COMTEK CORP
1171 N 4th St Ste 80, San Jose
(95112-4968)
PHONE......................408 792-3830
Ryoichi Suzuki, *Branch Mgr*
Hiro Ota, *Info Tech Mgr*
EMP: 15 **Privately Held**
WEB: www.senjucomtek.com
SIC: 3399 Paste, metal
HQ: Senju Comtek Corp.
2989 San Ysidro Way
Santa Clara CA 95051

(P-11487)
SENJU COMTEK CORP (HQ)
2989 San Ysidro Way, Santa Clara
(95051-0604)
PHONE......................408 963-5300
Masato Shimamura, *CEO*
Derek Daily, *General Mgr*

◆ **EMP:** 11
SALES (est): 7.6MM **Privately Held**
WEB: www.senjucomtek.com
SIC: 3399 Paste, metal

(P-11488)
SIMPSON MANUFACTURING CO INC (PA)
5956 W Las Positas Blvd, Pleasanton
(94588-8540)
PHONE......................925 560-9000
Karen Colonias, *CEO*
Peter N Louras Jr, *Ch of Bd*
Brian J Magstadt, *CFO*
Michael Bless, *Bd of Directors*
Celeste Ford, *Bd of Directors*
EMP: 150
SALES: 1B **Publicly Held**
WEB: www.simpsonmfg.com
SIC: 3399 3441 Metal fasteners; building components, structural steel

(P-11489)
UNITED METAL PRODUCTS INC
Also Called: Ump
234 N Sherman Ave, Corona (92882-1843)
PHONE......................951 739-9535
Bernie Smokowski, *President*
Jacqueline Lowery, *Corp Secy*
Patricia Smokowski, *Vice Pres*
Jim Murphy, *General Mgr*
Ryan Jones, *Sales Staff*
EMP: 14
SALES (est): 2.5MM **Privately Held**
WEB: www.unitedmetalproducts.com
SIC: 3399 Metal fasteners

(P-11490)
VALIMET INC (PA)
431 Sperry Rd, Stockton (95206-3907)
P.O. Box 31690 (95213-1690)
PHONE......................209 444-1600
Kurt F Leopold, *CEO*
George Campbell, *President*
Michaela Leopold, *Admin Sec*
Autumn Hatten, *Admin Asst*
Matt Hendon, *Technician*
EMP: 58 **EST:** 1957
SQ FT: 200,000
SALES (est): 26.4MM **Privately Held**
WEB: www.valimet.com
SIC: 3399 Powder, metal

(P-11491)
VAST NATIONAL INC
Also Called: De Anza Muffler Service
4480 Main St A, Riverside (92501-4144)
PHONE......................951 788-7030
Fershteh Bavadi, *CEO*
EMP: 12
SALES (est): 2.2MM **Privately Held**
SIC: 3399 Nails: aluminum, brass or other nonferrous metal or wire

---
3411 Metal Cans

(P-11492)
AMERICAN PRODUCTION CO INC
Also Called: Super Chef
2734 Spring St, Redwood City
(94063-3524)
P.O. Box 5766 (94063-0766)
PHONE......................650 368-5334
Owen Conley, *President*
EMP: 69
SQ FT: 35,000
SALES (est): 7.3MM
SALES (corp-wide): 7.5MM **Privately Held**
WEB: www.tilleymfg.com
SIC: 3411 2656 3412 Food & beverage containers; sanitary food containers; metal barrels, drums & pails
PA: Tilley Manufacturing Co, Inc
2734 Spring St
Redwood City CA 94063
650 365-3598

(P-11493)
BALL CORPORATION
Also Called: Metal Fd Hhld Pdts Pckging Div
300 Greger St, Oakdale (95361-8613)
PHONE......................209 848-6500

Michael Wright, *Branch Mgr*
Dave Miller, *President*
EMP: 260
SALES (corp-wide): 11.6B **Publicly Held**
WEB: www.ball.com
SIC: 3411 Metal cans
PA: Ball Corporation
10 Longs Peak Dr
Broomfield CO 80021
303 469-3131

(P-11494)
BALL METAL BEVERAGE CONT CORP
Ball Metal Beverage Cont Div
2400 Huntington Dr, Fairfield (94533-9734)
PHONE......................707 437-7516
David R Trujillo, *Branch Mgr*
EMP: 172
SQ FT: 115,000
SALES (corp-wide): 11.6B **Publicly Held**
SIC: 3411 Metal cans
HQ: Ball Metal Beverage Container Corp.
9300 W 108th Cir
Westminster CO 80021
-

(P-11495)
BWAY CORPORATION
11440 Pacific Ave, Fontana (92337-8226)
PHONE......................951 361-4100
Mark Klug, *Manager*
Louie Arriaga, *Manager*
EMP: 30
SALES (corp-wide): 1.2B **Privately Held**
WEB: www.bwaycorp.com
SIC: 3411 3499 Metal cans; ammunition boxes, metal
HQ: Bway Corporation
375 Northridge Rd Ste 600
Atlanta GA 30350

(P-11496)
JOSEPH COMPANY INTERNATIONAL
1711 Langley Ave, Irvine (92614-5679)
PHONE......................949 474-2200
Mitchell J Joseph, *President*
▲ **EMP:** 20
SQ FT: 18,000
SALES (est): 3.8MM **Privately Held**
SIC: 3411 Food & beverage containers

(P-11497)
KLEAN KANTEEN INC
3960 Morrow Ln, Chico (95928-8912)
PHONE......................530 592-4552
James Osgood, *CEO*
Darrell Cresswell, *President*
Jeff Cresswell, *COO*
Kevin Welch, *Info Tech Mgr*
Vicki Hightower, *Controller*
▲ **EMP:** 79 **EST:** 1976
SQ FT: 5,000
SALES: 31MM **Privately Held**
WEB: www.justjumpit.com
SIC: 3411 Food containers, metal

(P-11498)
MAT MAT
21029 Itasca St, Chatsworth (91311-4924)
PHONE......................818 678-9392
Fernando Roblesgio, *President*
EMP: 10
SALES (est): 716K **Privately Held**
SIC: 3411 Can lids & ends, metal

(P-11499)
METAL CONTAINER CORPORATION
7155 Central Ave, Riverside (92504-1400)
PHONE......................951 354-0444
Bob Parker, *Branch Mgr*
Wes Novian, *Opers Staff*
EMP: 200
SALES (corp-wide): 1.5B **Privately Held**
SIC: 3411 Can lids & ends, metal
HQ: Metal Container Corporation
3636 S Geyer Rd Ste 100
Saint Louis MO 63127
314 577-2000

(P-11500)
METAL CONTAINER CORPORATION
10980 Inland Ave, Jurupa Valley
(91752-1127)
PHONE......................951 360-4500
Otto Sosapavon, *Principal*
EMP: 171
SALES (corp-wide): 1.5B **Privately Held**
SIC: 3411 Aluminum cans
HQ: Metal Container Corporation
3636 S Geyer Rd Ste 100
Saint Louis MO 63127
314 577-2000

(P-11501)
PACIFIC BRIDGE PACKAGING INC
103 Exchange Pl, Pomona (91768-4307)
PHONE......................909 598-1988
Peter Chang, *CEO*
William Hsu, *General Mgr*
▲ **EMP:** 10
SQ FT: 10,000
SALES (est): 121.8K **Privately Held**
SIC: 3411 3499 3221 3085 Metal cans; aerosol valves, metal; bottles for packing, bottling & canning: glass; plastics bottles

(P-11502)
SILGAN CONTAINERS CORPORATION (DH)
21600 Oxnard St Ste 1600, Woodland Hills
(91367-3609)
PHONE......................818 348-3700
Anthony J Allott, *CEO*
Thomas J Snyder, *Ch of Bd*
James D Beam, *President*
R Phillip Silver, *Vice Ch Bd*
Frank W Hogan III, *Senior VP*
◆ **EMP:** 100
SALES (est): 444.9MM
SALES (corp-wide): 4.4B **Publicly Held**
SIC: 3411 Food containers, metal
HQ: Silgan Containers Llc
21600 Oxnard St Ste 1600
Woodland Hills CA 91367
818 710-3700

(P-11503)
SILGAN CONTAINERS LLC (HQ)
21600 Oxnard St Ste 1600, Woodland Hills
(91367-5082)
PHONE......................818 710-3700
Thomas Snyder, *Mng Member*
Ron Ford, *CFO*
Richard Brewer, *Senior VP*
Daniel Carson, *Senior VP*
Michael Beninato, *Vice Pres*
◆ **EMP:** 100
SALES (est): 1.9B
SALES (corp-wide): 4.4B **Publicly Held**
WEB: www.silgancontainers.com
SIC: 3411 Food containers, metal
PA: Silgan Holdings Inc.
4 Landmark Sq Ste 400
Stamford CT 06901
203 975-7110

(P-11504)
SILGAN CONTAINERS MFG CORP
4000 Yosemite Blvd, Modesto
(95357-1580)
PHONE......................209 521-6469
William Jennings, *Bd of Directors*
Merlyn Hodges, *Admin Mgr*
EMP: 82
SALES (corp-wide): 4.4B **Publicly Held**
SIC: 3411 Metal cans
HQ: Silgan Containers Manufacturing Corporation
21600 Oxnard St Ste 1600
Woodland Hills CA 91367

(P-11505)
SILGAN CONTAINERS MFG CORP
2200 Wilbur Ave, Antioch (94509-8506)
PHONE......................925 778-8000
Arnold Naimark, *Branch Mgr*
EMP: 30

PRODUCTS & SVCS

SALES (corp-wide): 4.4B **Publicly Held**
WEB: www.silgancontainers.com
SIC: 3411 Metal cans
HQ: Silgan Containers Manufacturing Corporation
21600 Oxnard St Ste 1600
Woodland Hills CA 91367

(P-11506)
SILGAN CONTAINERS MFG CORP
3250 Patterson Rd, Riverbank
(95367-2938)
PHONE..................................209 869-3601
Gary Miller, *Branch Mgr*
EMP: 45
SQ FT: 200,000
SALES (corp-wide): 4.4B **Publicly Held**
WEB: www.silgancontainers.com
SIC: 3411 Metal cans
HQ: Silgan Containers Manufacturing Corporation
21600 Oxnard St Ste 1600
Woodland Hills CA 91367

(P-11507)
SILGAN CONTAINERS MFG CORP (DH)
21600 Oxnard St Ste 1600, Woodland Hills
(91367-5082)
PHONE..................................818 710-3700
Thomas Snyder, *Principal*
EMP: 277
SALES (est): 345.2MM
SALES (corp-wide): 4.4B **Publicly Held**
SIC: 3411 Metal cans
HQ: Silgan Containers Llc
21600 Oxnard St Ste 1600
Woodland Hills CA 91367
818 710-3700

3412 Metal Barrels, Drums, Kegs & Pails

(P-11508)
B STEPHEN COOPERAGE INC
10746 Vernon Ave, Ontario (91762-4039)
P.O. Box 9537 (91762-9537)
PHONE..................................909 591-2929
Toll Free:............................877 -
Mike Stephen, *CEO*
Ben Stephen, *President*
EMP: 15
SQ FT: 174,240
SALES (est): 1.2MM **Privately Held**
SIC: 3412 Metal barrels, drums & pails

(P-11509)
GREIF INC
8250 Almeria Ave, Fontana (92335-3279)
PHONE..................................909 350-2112
Andy Wade, *Manager*
Daniel Gunsett, *Bd of Directors*
Robert Diaz, *Purchasing*
Amanda Wade, *Plant Mgr*
Jim Boswell, *Maintence Staff*
EMP: 25
SQ FT: 73,320
SALES (corp-wide): 3.8B **Publicly Held**
WEB: www.greif.com
SIC: 3412 2674 2655 2449 Drums, shipping: metal; bags: uncoated paper & multiwall; fiber cans, drums & similar products; wood containers
PA: Greif, Inc.
425 Winter Rd
Delaware OH 43015
740 549-6000

(P-11510)
MYERS CONTAINER LLC
21508 Ferrero B, Walnut (91789-5216)
PHONE..................................800 406-9377
Manuel Vasquez,
EMP: 25
SALES (corp-wide): 30.5MM **Privately Held**
WEB: www.myerscontainer.com
SIC: 3412 Metal barrels, drums & pails

HQ: Myers Container, Llc
8435 Ne Killingsworth St
Portland OR 97220
-

3421 Cutlery

(P-11511)
ARCH FOODS INC
610 85th Ave, Oakland (94621-1223)
PHONE..................................510 868-6000
EMP: 30 **Privately Held**
SIC: 3421 5149 Cutlery; dried or canned foods
PA: Arch Foods Inc
25817 Clawiter Rd
Hayward CA 94545

(P-11512)
ARCH FOODS INC (PA)
25817 Clawiter Rd, Hayward (94545-3217)
P.O. Box 2355, Clovis (93613-2355)
PHONE..................................510 331-8352
Jeff Lim, *CEO*
Ida Maria, *Manager*
▼ **EMP:** 50
SQ FT: 2,000
SALES (est): 4MM **Privately Held**
WEB: www.archfoods.com
SIC: 3421 5149 Cutlery; dried or canned foods

(P-11513)
ASIAS FINEST
407 Camino Del Rio S, San Diego
(92108-3502)
PHONE..................................619 297-0800
EMP: 14
SALES (est): 894.1K **Privately Held**
SIC: 3421 Table & food cutlery, including butchers'

(P-11514)
EDGEWELL PER CARE BRANDS LLC
599 S Barranca Ave, Covina (91723-2777)
PHONE..................................949 466-0131
EMP: 360
SALES (corp-wide): 2.2B **Publicly Held**
WEB: www.eveready.com
SIC: 3421 Razor blades & razors
HQ: Edgewell Personal Care Brands, Llc
6 Research Dr
Shelton CT 06484
203 944-5500

(P-11515)
GILLETTE COMPANY
19900 Macarthur Blvd, Irvine (92612-2445)
PHONE..................................949 851-2222
Charles Kiernan, *President*
EMP: 10
SALES (corp-wide): 67.6B **Publicly Held**
WEB: www.gillette.com
SIC: 3421 2844 3951 2899 Razor blades & razors; toilet preparations; pens & mechanical pencils; correction fluid
HQ: The Gillette Company
1 Gillette Park
Boston MA 02127
617 421-7000

(P-11516)
NEPTUNE TRADING INC
4021 Greystone Dr, Ontario (91761-3100)
PHONE..................................909 923-0236
Margaret Lu, *President*
Michael Lu, *Vice Pres*
Nicholas Sanchez, *Creative Dir*
▲ **EMP:** 11
SQ FT: 38,000
SALES (est): 3.6MM **Privately Held**
SIC: 3421 5092 5072 Knife blades & blanks; toy novelties & amusements; cutlery

(P-11517)
PRESSED RIGHT LLC
23615 El Toro Rd, Lake Forest
(92630-4707)
PHONE..................................866 257-5774
Robert Szutz, *Managing Dir*
EMP: 16

SALES (est): 2.6MM **Privately Held**
SIC: 3421 Table & food cutlery, including butchers'

(P-11518)
SIERRA FOODS INC
13352 Imperial Hwy, Santa Fe Springs
(90670-4819)
PHONE..................................562 802-3500
EMP: 13
SALES (corp-wide): 10.3MM **Privately Held**
SIC: 3421 Table & food cutlery, including butchers'
PA: Sierra Foods, Inc.
23300 Cinema Dr
Santa Clarita CA 91355
661 254-1025

(P-11519)
SOORAKSAN SOOJEBI
4003 Wilshire Blvd Ste I, Los Angeles
(90010-3431)
PHONE..................................213 389-2818
EMP: 11 EST: 2010
SALES: 600K **Privately Held**
SIC: 3421

3423 Hand & Edge Tools

(P-11520)
ADVANCED CUTTING TOOLS INC
17741 Metzler Ln, Huntington Beach
(92647-6246)
PHONE..................................714 842-9376
Stjepan Herceg, *President*
Maria Nelson, *Vice Pres*
EMP: 30
SQ FT: 10,200
SALES (est): 4.3MM **Privately Held**
SIC: 3423 3545 5251 Hand & edge tools; machine tool accessories; tools

(P-11521)
AVANT ENTERPRISES INC (PA)
18457 Railroad St, City of Industry
(91748-1233)
PHONE..................................866 300-3311
Jianwei Zhang, *CEO*
▲ **EMP:** 21
SALES (est): 3MM **Privately Held**
SIC: 3423 Tools or equipment for use with sporting arms

(P-11522)
BRITISH AMERICAN TL & DIE LLC
2273 E Via Burton, Anaheim (92806-1222)
PHONE..................................714 776-8995
Graham Butler, *CEO*
EMP: 175
SALES: 21MM **Privately Held**
SIC: 3423 Cutting dies, except metal cutting

(P-11523)
CALIFORNIA FLEXRAKE CORP
9620 Gidley St, Temple City (91780-4215)
PHONE..................................626 443-4026
John P McGuire, *President*
▲ **EMP:** 25
SALES (est): 6.3MM **Privately Held**
WEB: www.flexrake.com
SIC: 3423 Garden & farm tools, including shovels

(P-11524)
CARBIDE COMPANY LLC
Also Called: Monster Tool Company
2470 Ash St Ste 1, Vista (92081-8461)
P.O. Box 1749, San Marcos (92079-1749)
PHONE..................................760 477-1000
Pamela Rae Brossman, *Mng Member*
Mark Dalhover, *Mfg Dir*
Pam Brossman,
Josh Lynberg,
◆ **EMP:** 100
SQ FT: 30,000
SALES: 22MM **Privately Held**
SIC: 3423 Hand & edge tools

(P-11525)
CATALINA TEMPERING INC (PA)
1125 E Lanzit Ave, Los Angeles
(90059-1559)
PHONE..................................323 789-7800
Randy Steinberg, *President*
EMP: 31
SALES (est): 9.7MM **Privately Held**
WEB: www.catalinatempering.com
SIC: 3423 Cutters, glass

(P-11526)
CRAFTSMAN CUTTING DIES INC (PA)
Also Called: Ccd
2273 E Via Burton, Anaheim (92806-1222)
PHONE..................................714 776-8995
Thomas Hughes, *President*
Cathy Ong-Chan, *Treasurer*
Ronald Ong, *Vice Pres*
▲ **EMP:** 25
SQ FT: 11,000
SALES (est): 2.7MM **Privately Held**
SIC: 3423 3544 Cutting dies, except metal cutting; special dies, tools, jigs & fixtures

(P-11527)
DURSTON MANUFACTURING COMPANY
Also Called: Vim Tools
1395 Palomares St, La Verne
(91750-5241)
P.O. Box 340 (91750-0340)
PHONE..................................909 593-1506
Donovan Norton, *CEO*
James Maloney, *President*
Mary Dills, *Accounting Mgr*
▲ **EMP:** 18 EST: 1946
SQ FT: 29,000
SALES (est): 3.6MM **Privately Held**
WEB: www.vimtools.com
SIC: 3423 Mechanics' hand tools

(P-11528)
EQH LIMITED INC
5440 Mcconnell Ave, Los Angeles
(90066-7037)
PHONE..................................310 736-4130
Eric Golden, *President*
EMP: 27
SALES (est): 3.4MM **Privately Held**
WEB: www.equipoisinc.com
SIC: 3423 3523 Tools or equipment for use with sporting arms; planting, haying, harvesting & processing machinery

(P-11529)
FLEX-MATE INC
Also Called: D & G Manufacturing
1855 E 29th St Ste E, Signal Hill
(90755-1919)
PHONE..................................562 426-7169
Theresa Gleason, *President*
EMP: 12
SQ FT: 6,000
SALES (est): 1.8MM **Privately Held**
SIC: 3423 Hand & edge tools

(P-11530)
GARDEN PALS INC
1300 Valley Vista Dr # 209, Diamond Bar
(91765-3940)
PHONE..................................909 605-0200
WEI Chun Hsu, *CEO*
Robert Deal, *COO*
▲ **EMP:** 20
SALES (est): 487MM **Privately Held**
WEB: www.gardenpals.com
SIC: 3423 Garden & farm tools, including shovels
PA: Formosa Tools Co., Ltd.
No. 22, Yanhai Rd., Sec. 2
Fushing Hsiang CHA 50645

(P-11531)
HALEX CORPORATION (HQ)
4200 Santa Ana St Ste A, Ontario
(91761-1539)
PHONE..................................909 629-6219
Mark Chichak, *President*
▲ **EMP:** 43

▲ = Import ▼=Export
◆ =Import/Export

SALES (est): 38.1MM
SALES (corp-wide): 1.1B **Publicly Held**
WEB: www.halexcorp.com
SIC: 3423 Carpet layers' hand tools
PA: Gcp Applied Technologies Inc.
  62 Whittemore Ave
  Cambridge MA 02140
  617 876-1400

(P-11532)
KAL-CAMERON MANUFACTURING (HQ)
Also Called: Pro American Premium Tools
4265 Puente Ave, Baldwin Park
(91706-3420)
PHONE..................................626 338-7308
John Toshima, *Ch of Bd*
EMP: 100
SQ FT: 32,000
SALES (est): 10.8MM
SALES (corp-wide): 23.1MM **Privately Held**
SIC: 3423 Mechanics' hand tools
PA: American Kal Enterprises, Inc.
  4265 Puente Ave
  Baldwin Park CA 91706
  626 338-7308

(P-11533)
KEMPER ENTERPRISES INC
13595 12th St, Chino (91710-5208)
P.O. Box 696 (91708-0696)
PHONE..................................909 627-6191
Herbert H Stampfl, *President*
Librado Cortez, *Admin Sec*
Richard Harrison, *Info Tech Mgr*
Dolores Maufras, *Sales Mgr*
Debbie Biessener, *Manager*
▲ EMP: 30
SQ FT: 30,000
SALES (est): 6.2MM **Privately Held**
WEB: www.kemperdolls.com
SIC: 3423 Hand & edge tools

(P-11534)
LARIN CORP
5651 Schaefer Ave, Chino (91710-9048)
PHONE..................................909 464-0605
Shouyun Zhang, *President*
▲ EMP: 20
SQ FT: 50,000
SALES (est): 4MM **Privately Held**
WEB: www.larincorp.com
SIC: 3423 Jacks: lifting, screw or ratchet
(hand tools)

(P-11535)
LEITCH & CO INC
Also Called: Intertool Innovative Tooling
1607 Abram Ct, San Leandro
(94577-3226)
PHONE..................................510 483-2323
Fax: 510 483-2391
▼ EMP: 10
SALES (est): 1.4MM **Privately Held**
WEB: www.leitchco.com
SIC: 3423 5085 5251

(P-11536)
MORGAN MANUFACTURING INC
521 2nd St, Petaluma (94952-5121)
P.O. Box 737 (94953-0737)
PHONE..................................707 763-6848
Carl T Palmgren, *President*
Lillian Raposo, *Vice Pres*
Mary Kinney, *Marketing Mgr*
EMP: 15
SALES (est): 2.8MM **Privately Held**
WEB: www.morganmfg.com
SIC: 3423 3499 Hand & edge tools; stabilizing bars (cargo), metal

(P-11537)
NUPLA LLC
11912 Sheldon St, Sun Valley
(91352-1509)
PHONE..................................818 768-6800
Ronald Ortiz,
▲ EMP: 120
SQ FT: 160,000
SALES (est): 21.7MM
SALES (corp-wide): 24.3MM **Privately Held**
WEB: www.nuplacorp.com
SIC: 3423 3089 Hand & edge tools; handles, brush or tool: plastic

PA: Saunders Midwest Llc
  29 E Madison St Ste 900
  Chicago IL 60602
  312 372-3690

(P-11538)
OMEGA TECHNOLOGIES INC
31125 Via Colinas Ste 905, Westlake Village (91362-3972)
PHONE..................................818 264-7970
John Bland Schoolland, *President*
◆ EMP: 13
SQ FT: 3,800
SALES: 4.2MM **Privately Held**
WEB: www.omegatec.com
SIC: 3423 5072 5085 Hand & edge tools; hardware; industrial supplies

(P-11539)
PACIFIC HANDY CUTTER INC
Also Called: PHC
17819 Gillette Ave, Irvine (92614-6501)
PHONE..................................714 662-1033
Mark Marinovich, *CEO*
▲ EMP: 35
SQ FT: 16,000
SALES (est): 8.7MM
SALES (corp-wide): 169.9MM **Privately Held**
SIC: 3423 3421 Hand & edge tools; cutlery
HQ: Phc Sharp Holdings, Inc
  17819 Gillette Ave
  Irvine CA 92614
  714 662-1033

(P-11540)
PRECISION JEWELRY TOOLS & SUPS
1555 Alum Rock Ave, San Jose
(95116-2426)
PHONE..................................408 251-7990
Robert Persekian, *President*
EMP: 20
SQ FT: 12,000
SALES: 2MM **Privately Held**
WEB: www.percisiondisplays.com
SIC: 3423 Jewelers' hand tools

(P-11541)
PRODUCTS ENGINEERING CORP (PA)
Also Called: PEC Tool
2645 Maricopa St, Torrance (90503-5144)
PHONE..................................310 787-4500
Richard A Luboviski, *CEO*
Bernard Brooks, *Treasurer*
Julie Hood, *Vice Pres*
Sandy Luboviski, *Vice Pres*
Sandra Molioo, *Human Res Dir*
▲ EMP: 60 EST: 1960
SQ FT: 68,000
SALES: 4.5MM **Privately Held**
WEB: www.pectools.com
SIC: 3423 Hand & edge tools

(P-11542)
QUADRTECH CORPORATION
Also Called: Studex
521 W Rosecrans Ave, Gardena
(90248-1514)
PHONE..................................310 523-1697
Vladimir Reil, *President*
Christie Arana, *Admin Asst*
Frank Kabacic, *Purch Mgr*
▲ EMP: 185
SALES (est): 24.9MM **Privately Held**
WEB: www.quadrtech.com
SIC: 3423 3915 Jewelers' materials & lapidary work; jewelers' hand tools

(P-11543)
SCHLEY PRODUCTS INC
5350 E Hunter Ave, Anaheim (92807-2053)
PHONE..................................714 693-7666
Paul Schley, *President*
Chad Schley, *Vice Pres*
Mark Schley, *Vice Pres*
Rich Lomanto, *General Mgr*
Todd Haner, *Manager*
▲ EMP: 11
SQ FT: 10,000
SALES (est): 2.2MM **Privately Held**
WEB: www.sptool.com
SIC: 3423 Mechanics' hand tools

(P-11544)
SHARP PROFILES LLC
828 W Cienega Ave, San Dimas
(91773-2489)
PHONE..................................760 246-9446
EMP: 15
SALES (est): 3.8MM **Privately Held**
SIC: 3423

(P-11545)
STANLEY ACCESS TECH LLC
4230 E Airport Dr Ste 107, Ontario
(91761-3702)
PHONE..................................909 628-9272
John Rapisarda, *Manager*
EMP: 225
SALES (corp-wide): 13.9B **Publicly Held**
WEB: www.stanleyworks.com
SIC: 3423 Hand & edge tools
HQ: Stanley Access Technologies Llc
  65 Scott Swamp Rd
  Farmington CT 06032

(P-11546)
STANLEY ACCESS TECH LLC
1312 Dupont Ct, Manteca (95336-6004)
PHONE..................................209 221-4066
Brian Sheppard, *Manager*
EMP: 225
SALES (corp-wide): 13.9B **Publicly Held**
WEB: www.stanleyworks.com
SIC: 3423 Hand & edge tools
HQ: Stanley Access Technologies Llc
  65 Scott Swamp Rd
  Farmington CT 06032

(P-11547)
SUPERCLOSET
Also Called: Kind Led Grow Lights
3555 Airway Dr, Santa Rosa (95403-1605)
P.O. Box 6105 (95406-0105)
PHONE..................................831 588-7829
Kip Lewis Andersen, *CEO*
Rory Kagan, *CEO*
Nicholas Schweitzer, *COO*
Stacey Martin, *Human Res Mgr*
▲ EMP: 20
SQ FT: 18,000
SALES (est): 3.3MM **Privately Held**
SIC: 3423 5261 Garden & farm tools, including shovels; lawn & garden equipment

(P-11548)
TOUGHBUILT INDUSTRIES INC (PA)
25371 Cmmrcntre Dr Dte 20 200 Dte, Lake Forest (92630)
PHONE..................................949 528-3100
Michael Panosian, *Ch of Bd*
Zareh Kachatoorian, *COO*
Zareh Khachatoorian, *COO*
Manu Ohri, *CFO*
Joshua Keeler, *Vice Pres*
EMP: 13 EST: 2012
SQ FT: 8,300
SALES: 15.2MM **Publicly Held**
SIC: 3423 3429 3069 Hand & edge tools; manufactured hardware (general); kneeling pads, rubber

(P-11549)
TRONEX TECHNOLOGY INCORPORATED
2860 Cordelia Rd Ste 230, Fairfield
(94534-1808)
PHONE..................................707 426-2550
Arne Salvesen, *President*
Karin Salvesen, *Vice Pres*
Nina Blaicher, *Sales Staff*
EMP: 20
SQ FT: 4,000
SALES (est): 3.2MM **Privately Held**
WEB: www.tronextools.com
SIC: 3423 5049 Screw drivers, pliers, chisels, etc. (hand tools); precision tools

(P-11550)
UNDERGROUND AUTOWERKS INC (PA)
106 E 17th St, National City (91950-4512)
PHONE..................................619 336-9000
Andrew Castellanos, *Principal*

EMP: 11
SALES (est): 1.4MM **Privately Held**
SIC: 3423 Mechanics' hand tools

3425 Hand Saws & Saw Blades

(P-11551)
DIAMOND K2
23911 Garnier St Ste C, Torrance
(90505-7523)
P.O. Box 346 (90508-0346)
PHONE..................................310 539-6116
Les Kuzmick, *Ch of Bd*
Richard Kirby, *President*
EMP: 21
SQ FT: 7,600
SALES (est): 4MM **Privately Held**
SIC: 3425 3531 5082 Saw blades & handsaws; construction machinery; concrete processing equipment

(P-11552)
FANNO SAW WORKS
224 W 8th Ave, Chico (95926-3242)
P.O. Box 628 (95927-0628)
PHONE..................................530 895-1762
Robert A Fanno, *President*
▲ EMP: 10
SQ FT: 8,000
SALES (est): 1.6MM **Privately Held**
SIC: 3425 Saw blades & handsaws

(P-11553)
HI-LINE INDUSTRIAL SAW AND SUP
179 Business Center Dr, Corona
(92880-1757)
PHONE..................................714 921-1600
William Johnston, *President*
Diane Y Johnston, *Vice Pres*
EMP: 11
SALES: 3MM **Privately Held**
SIC: 3425 5072 Saw blades & handsaws; saw blades

(P-11554)
NORDIC SAW & TOOL MFRS
2114 Divanian Dr, Turlock (95382-9680)
P.O. Box 1128 (95381-1128)
PHONE..................................209 634-9015
Dewey Larson, *President*
EMP: 30
SQ FT: 11,000
SALES (est): 2.6MM **Privately Held**
WEB: www.nordicsaw.com
SIC: 3425 3421 3545 Saw blades & handsaws; knives: butchers', hunting, pocket, etc.; bits for use on lathes, planers, shapers, etc.

(P-11555)
SAWBIRD INC (PA)
Also Called: Cal Saw Canada
721 Brannan St, San Francisco
(94103-4927)
PHONE..................................415 861-0644
Warren M Bird, *President*
Ben Joseph, *Vice Pres*
Benson L Joseph, *Vice Pres*
Hazel E Bird, *Admin Sec*
▲ EMP: 20
SQ FT: 17,500
SALES (est): 3.3MM **Privately Held**
WEB: www.calsaw.com
SIC: 3425 3423 7699 Saw blades for hand or power saws; knives, agricultural or industrial; knife, saw & tool sharpening & repair

(P-11556)
WESTERN SAW MANUFACTURERS INC
3200 Camino Del Sol, Oxnard
(93030-8998)
PHONE..................................805 981-0999
Kevin Baron, *CEO*
Kraig Baron, *President*
Frank Baron, *CEO*
Nancy Pounds, *Corp Secy*
Anthony Baratta, *Chief Engr*
▲ EMP: 50
SQ FT: 70,000

SALES: 11MM **Privately Held**
WEB: www.westernsaw.com
SIC: 3425 3546 Saw blades & handsaws; power-driven handtools

3429 Hardware, NEC

(P-11557)
ACCURIDE INTERNATIONAL INC (PA)
12311 Shoemaker Ave, Santa Fe Springs (90670-4721)
PHONE..................562 903-0200
Scott E Jordan, *CEO*
Jeffrey Dunlap, *CFO*
Jerome Barr, *Principal*
Corey Westra, *Engineer*
Chris Lu, *Analyst*
▲ **EMP:** 47
SALES (est): 482.6MM **Privately Held**
WEB: www.accuride.com
SIC: 3429 Manufactured hardware (general)

(P-11558)
ACTRON MANUFACTURING INC
1841 Railroad St, Corona (92880-2512)
PHONE..................951 371-0885
Frank Rechberg, *CEO*
Dow Rechberg, *Corp Secy*
EMP: 93
SQ FT: 30,000
SALES (est): 20.1MM **Privately Held**
WEB: www.actronmfginc.com
SIC: 3429 Aircraft hardware

(P-11559)
AIRWORTHY CABIN SOLUTIONS LLC
1560 S Harris Ct, Anaheim (92806-5931)
PHONE..................714 901-0660
Joe Gerber,
EMP: 18
SALES (est): 783.1K
SALES (corp-wide): 51.4MM **Privately Held**
SIC: 3429 Aircraft hardware
PA: Airworthy Aerospace Industries, Inc.
2020 Oneil Rd
Hudson WI 54016
715 386-0969

(P-11560)
ALARIN AIRCRAFT HINGE INC
Also Called: Commerce
6231 Randolph St, Commerce (90040-3514)
PHONE..................323 725-1666
Gregory A Sanders, *President*
EMP: 25
SQ FT: 11,000
SALES (est): 5MM **Privately Held**
WEB: www.alarin.com
SIC: 3429 3728 Aircraft hardware; aircraft parts & equipment

(P-11561)
ALVIN D TROYER AND ASSOCIATES
310 Shaw Rd Ste F, South San Francisco (94080-6615)
PHONE..................650 574-0167
Gary Troyer, *President*
Dan Troyer, *Vice Pres*
EMP: 11
SALES (est): 790K **Privately Held**
SIC: 3429 Door locks, bolts & checks

(P-11562)
AMERICAN EMPEROR INC
888 Doolittle Dr, San Leandro (94577-1020)
PHONE..................713 478-5973
Wai Ming Ng, *CEO*
EMP: 17
SALES (est): 5.4MM **Privately Held**
SIC: 3429 Furniture builders' & other household hardware

(P-11563)
ARCMATE MANUFACTURING CORP
911 S Andreasen Dr, Escondido (92029-1934)
PHONE..................760 489-1140
Bob Traber, *CEO*
Robert Traber, *President*
▲ **EMP:** 12
SQ FT: 6,650
SALES (est): 1.3MM **Privately Held**
WEB: www.arcmate.com
SIC: 3429 5072 5251 Manufactured hardware (general); hand tools; tools, hand

(P-11564)
ASCO SINTERING CO
2750 Garfield Ave, Commerce (90040-2610)
P.O. Box 911157 (90091-1157)
PHONE..................323 725-3550
Neil Moore, *CEO*
Robert Lebrun, *CFO*
Ian Harris, *Plant Mgr*
▲ **EMP:** 33 **EST:** 1971
SQ FT: 69,000
SALES: 9MM **Privately Held**
WEB: www.ascosintering.com
SIC: 3429 3714 Manufactured hardware (general); motor vehicle parts & accessories

(P-11565)
AUTOMOTIVE RACING PRODUCTS INC (PA)
Also Called: A R P
1863 Eastman Ave, Ventura (93003-8084)
PHONE..................805 339-2200
Gary Holzapfel, *CEO*
Mike Holzapfel, *President*
Kelly Schau, *CFO*
Robert Florine, *Exec VP*
Robert Flourin, *Vice Pres*
▲ **EMP:** 65
SQ FT: 10,000
SALES (est): 29.6MM **Privately Held**
WEB: www.arp-bolts.com
SIC: 3429 3714 3452 Manufactured hardware (general); motor vehicle parts & accessories; bolts, nuts, rivets & washers

(P-11566)
AUTOMOTIVE RACING PRODUCTS INC
Also Called: A R P
1760 E Lemonwood Dr, Santa Paula (93060-9510)
PHONE..................805 525-1497
Michael Holzapsel, *Branch Mgr*
Chris Raschke, *Sales Dir*
EMP: 60
SALES (est): 9MM
SALES (corp-wide): 29.6MM **Privately Held**
WEB: www.arp-bolts.com
SIC: 3429 Manufactured hardware (general)
PA: Automotive Racing Products, Inc.
1863 Eastman Ave
Ventura CA 93003
805 339-2200

(P-11567)
AVIBANK MFG INC
Avk Industrial Products
25323 Rye Canyon Rd, Valencia (91355-1205)
PHONE..................661 257-2329
James M Wolpert, *General Mgr*
EMP: 85
SQ FT: 23,000
SALES (corp-wide): 225.3B **Publicly Held**
SIC: 3429 3541 3452 Manufactured hardware (general); machine tools, metal cutting type; bolts, nuts, rivets & washers
HQ: Avibank Mfg., Inc.
11500 Sherman Way
North Hollywood CA 91605
818 392-2100

(P-11568)
B & B SPECIALTIES INC (PA)
4321 E La Palma Ave, Anaheim (92807-1887)
PHONE..................714 985-3000
Bruce Borchardt, *President*
Thomas Rutan, *VP Bus Dvlpt*
Marianne Bardsley, *Controller*
Max Mendia, *Mfg Mgr*
Stephen Read, *Sales Staff*
▲ **EMP:** 190
SQ FT: 40,000
SALES (est): 40.3MM **Privately Held**
WEB: www.bbspecialties.com
SIC: 3429 3452 Metal fasteners; bolts, nuts, rivets & washers

(P-11569)
BAIER MARINE COMPANY INC
2920 Airway Ave, Costa Mesa (92626-6008)
PHONE..................800 455-3917
Mark Smith, *President*
Danielle Rockmaker, *Sales Mgr*
Felice Lineberry, *Manager*
◆ **EMP:** 20
SALES: 1,000K **Privately Held**
WEB: www.baiermarine.com
SIC: 3429 Manufactured hardware (general)

(P-11570)
BALDWIN HARDWARE CORPORATION (DH)
Also Called: Baldwin Brass
19701 Da Vinci, Foothill Ranch (92610-2622)
PHONE..................949 672-4000
David R Lumley, *CEO*
▲ **EMP:** 816 **EST:** 1944
SQ FT: 300,000
SALES (est): 107.8MM
SALES (corp-wide): 3.1B **Publicly Held**
SIC: 3429 Builders' hardware; locks or lock sets; cabinet hardware
HQ: Spectrum Brands, Inc.
3001 Deming Way
Middleton WI 53562
608 275-3340

(P-11571)
BATON LOCK & HARDWARE CO INC
Also Called: Baton Security
14275 Commerce Dr, Garden Grove (92843-4944)
PHONE..................714 265-3636
Hwei Ying Chen, *President*
Fong Shiang Hsu, *President*
Sharron Hsu, *Vice Pres*
WEI Hsu, *Vice Pres*
▲ **EMP:** 24
SQ FT: 15,025
SALES (est): 3.1MM **Privately Held**
WEB: www.batonlockusa.com
SIC: 3429 Keys, locks & related hardware; locks or lock sets

(P-11572)
BAUER INDUSTRIES (PA)
Also Called: Sports Rack Vehicle Outfitters
708 Alhambra Blvd Ste 2, Sacramento (95816-3851)
PHONE..................916 648-9200
Greg Bauer, *President*
John Bauer, *Vice Pres*
Tom Mollerus, *Vice Pres*
Chris Luyet, *General Mgr*
▲ **EMP:** 11
SQ FT: 2,500
SALES (est): 15.6MM **Privately Held**
WEB: www.bauerworld.com
SIC: 3429 5013 5531 5961 Motor vehicle hardware; automotive supplies & parts; automotive accessories; automotive supplies & equipment, mail order

(P-11573)
BEYOND SEATING INC
2120 Edwards Ave, South El Monte (91733-2038)
PHONE..................323 633-5359
Ruth Hernandez, *President*
Eric Hernandez, *Vice Pres*
EMP: 10

SALES: 1MM **Privately Held**
SIC: 3429 Furniture hardware

(P-11574)
BULDOOR LLC
647 Camino De Los, San Clemente (92673)
PHONE..................877 388-1366
Luis Morales, *Mng Member*
▲ **EMP:** 10
SQ FT: 20,000
SALES: 4MM **Privately Held**
SIC: 3429 5072 Manufactured hardware (general); hardware

(P-11575)
C-FAB
932 W 17th St, Costa Mesa (92627-4403)
P.O. Box 6177, Laguna Niguel (92607-6177)
PHONE..................949 646-2616
Steve Degroote, *Owner*
EMP: 25
SQ FT: 7,000
SALES: 1.2MM **Privately Held**
WEB: www.cfab.com
SIC: 3429 Marine hardware

(P-11576)
CAL-JUNE INC (PA)
Also Called: Jim-Buoy
5238 Vineland Ave, North Hollywood (91601-3221)
P.O. Box 9551 (91609-1551)
PHONE..................323 877-4164
James H Robertson, *President*
Jennifer D Jacobson, *President*
Andrea Robertson, *Vice Pres*
Melini Robertson, *Vice Pres*
▼ **EMP:** 48 **EST:** 1966
SQ FT: 3,000
SALES (est): 9.3MM **Privately Held**
WEB: www.jimbuoy.com
SIC: 3429 Marine hardware

(P-11577)
CALIFORNIA SCREW PRODUCTS CORP
14957 Gwenchris Ct, Paramount (90723-3423)
P.O. Box 228 (90723-0228)
PHONE..................562 633-6626
Larry Valeriano, *CEO*
Pio Granados, *Engineer*
Letitia Serrano, *Human Res Dir*
Vikki Errett, *Purchasing*
Jerry Dominguez, *Opers Mgr*
EMP: 108
SQ FT: 20,000
SALES (est): 14.7MM **Privately Held**
WEB: www.calscrew.net
SIC: 3429 3452 Metal fasteners; bolts, nuts, rivets & washers

(P-11578)
CALMEX FIREPLACE EQUIPMENT MFG
Also Called: Calmex Fireplace Equip Mfg
13629 Talc St, Santa Fe Springs (90670-5113)
PHONE..................716 645-2901
Maria Hirshal, *President*
Rosa Franco, *Vice Pres*
EMP: 15
SQ FT: 15,000
SALES: 2MM **Privately Held**
WEB: www.calmexfireplaces.com
SIC: 3429 Fireplace equipment, hardware: andirons, grates, screens

(P-11579)
CIRCOR AEROSPACE INC
Also Called: Circor Aerospace Machining Ctr
15148 Bledsoe St, Sylmar (91342-3807)
PHONE..................951 270-6200
Steve Alford, *Branch Mgr*
EMP: 91
SALES (corp-wide): 1.1B **Publicly Held**
SIC: 3429 3599 3451 3497 Manufactured hardware (general); machine & other job shop work; machine shop, jobbing & repair; screw machine products; metal foil & leaf; aircraft parts & equipment

HQ: Circor Aerospace, Inc.
2301 Wardlow Cir
Corona CA 92880

(P-11580)
CRAIN CUTTER COMPANY INC
1155 Wrigley Way, Milpitas (95035-5426)
PHONE..............................408 946-6100
Millard Crain Jr, *CEO*
Jennifer Crain, *Shareholder*
Lance Crain, *Shareholder*
Judy Escobedo, *Office Mgr*
Lou Pinon, *Manager*
▲ EMP: 87
SQ FT: 110,000
SALES (est): 20.8MM **Privately Held**
WEB: www.craintools.com
SIC: 3429 3545 Manufactured hardware
(general); machine tool accessories

(P-11581)
CRD MFG INC
1539 W Orange Grove Ave A, Orange
(92868-1110)
PHONE..............................714 871-3300
Timothy Carroll, *CEO*
EMP: 18
SALES (est): 3.5MM **Privately Held**
SIC: 3429 3699 Motor vehicle hardware;
welding machines & equipment, ultra-
sonic

(P-11582)
CREMAX U S A CORPORATION
Also Called: Icy Dock USA
11740 Clark St, Arcadia (91006-5805)
PHONE..............................626 956-8800
Jeff Fung, *Branch Mgr*
EMP: 10 **Privately Held**
SIC: 3429 Manufactured hardware (gen-
eral)
PA: Cremax Tech Co., Ltd.
2f, 18, Lane 609, Chung Hsin Rd.,
Sec. 5,
New Taipei City TAP 24159
-

(P-11583)
CUSTOM HARDWARE MFG INC
2112 E 4th St Ste 228g, Santa Ana
(92705-3840)
PHONE..............................714 547-7440
▲ EMP: 45
SQ FT: 4,500
SALES: 3.4MM **Privately Held**
WEB: www.chmi.com
SIC: 3429

(P-11584)
**D & D TECHNOLOGIES (USA)
INC**
17531 Metzler Ln, Huntington Beach
(92647-6242)
PHONE..............................714 677-1300
David Calabria, *CEO*
Richard Woodbeck, *Business Mgr*
▲ EMP: 12
SQ FT: 12,000
SALES (est): 3.5MM **Privately Held**
WEB: www.ddtechusa.com
SIC: 3429 Manufactured hardware (gen-
eral)
HQ: D & D Technologies Pty. Limited
U 6 4 Aquatic Dr
Frenchs Forest NSW 2086

(P-11585)
DARNELL CORPORATION
17915 Railroad St, City of Industry
(91748-1113)
PHONE..............................626 912-1688
Brent Bargar, *President*
EMP: 52
SALES (est): 8.5MM **Privately Held**
SIC: 3429 Manufactured hardware (gen-
eral)

(P-11586)
DARNELL-ROSE INC
1205 Via Roma, Colton (92324-3909)
PHONE..............................626 912-1688
John Posen, *Principal*
Robbie McCullah, *Vice Pres*
EMP: 11

SALES (est): 2.4MM **Privately Held**
SIC: 3429 Aircraft & marine hardware, inc.
pulleys & similar items

(P-11587)
DOVAL INDUSTRIES INC
Also Called: Doval Industries Co
3961 N Mission Rd, Los Angeles
(90031-2931)
PHONE..............................323 226-0335
Cruz Sandoval, *CEO*
▲ EMP: 65
SALES (est): 9.6MM **Privately Held**
SIC: 3429 5072 2759 Keys, locks & re-
lated hardware; hardware; screen printing

(P-11588)
EDDIE MOTORSPORTS
11479 6th St, Rancho Cucamonga
(91730-6024)
PHONE..............................909 581-7398
Frank E Borges, *Owner*
▲ EMP: 10
SQ FT: 26,000
SALES (est): 100K **Privately Held**
SIC: 3429 Aircraft & marine hardware, inc.
pulleys & similar items

(P-11589)
EUROPEAN SERVICES GROUP
Also Called: Topslide International
5062 Caspian Cir, Huntington Beach
(92649-1210)
PHONE..............................714 898-0595
Gus P Frousiakis, *President*
John Frousiakis, *Vice Pres*
◆ EMP: 14
SALES (est): 1.6MM **Privately Held**
WEB: www.topslide.com
SIC: 3429 Furniture builders' & other
household hardware

(P-11590)
FXC CORPORATION (PA)
3050 Red Hill Ave, Costa Mesa
(92626-4524)
PHONE..............................714 556-7400
Irene Chevrier, *CEO*
Densmore Kelly, *Human Resources*
Michael Urban, *Materials Mgr*
EMP: 21
SQ FT: 26,000
SALES (est): 14.7MM **Privately Held**
WEB: www.fxcguardian.com
SIC: 3429 2399 Parachute hardware;
parachutes

(P-11591)
**GARDNER FAMILY LTD
PARTNERSHIP**
Also Called: HMC Display
300 Commerce Dr, Madera (93637-5215)
PHONE..............................559 675-8149
Curtis K Gardner,
Christine G Gardner, *Manager*
▲ EMP: 25 EST: 1967
SQ FT: 45,000
SALES (est): 4.9MM **Privately Held**
SIC: 3429 Manufactured hardware (gen-
eral)

(P-11592)
**GARHAUER MARINE
CORPORATION**
1062 W 9th St, Upland (91786-5726)
PHONE..............................909 985-9993
William Felgenhauer, *President*
Mary Felgenhauer, *Admin Sec*
EMP: 33 EST: 1971
SQ FT: 10,000
SALES (est): 5MM **Privately Held**
WEB: www.garhauermarine.com
SIC: 3429 Marine hardware

(P-11593)
HARTWELL CORPORATION (DH)
Also Called: Hasco
900 Richfield Rd, Placentia (92870-6788)
PHONE..............................714 993-4200
Dain Miller, *President*
Justin Reinach, *Info Tech Mgr*
Kristina Arney, *Project Leader*
Emilio Cariaga, *Design Engr*
Adam Villareal, *Enginr/R&D Asst*
▲ EMP: 200
SQ FT: 134,000

SALES (est): 214.2MM
SALES (corp-wide): 3.8B **Publicly Held**
WEB: www.hartwellcorp.com
SIC: 3429 Aircraft hardware
HQ: Mckechnie Aerospace Investments,
Inc.
20 Pacifica Ste 200
Irvine CA
859 887-6200

(P-11594)
HEARTHCO INC
5781 Pleasant Valley Rd, El Dorado
(95623-4200)
PHONE..............................530 622-3877
Dan Zacher, *President*
Laurene Zacher, *CFO*
Paul Amador, *Sales Mgr*
EMP: 25 EST: 2001
SALES (est): 4.3MM **Privately Held**
WEB: www.heartco.com
SIC: 3429 Fireplace equipment, hardware:
andirons, grates, screens

(P-11595)
HI-SHEAR CORPORATION
2600 Skypark Dr, Torrance (90505-5373)
PHONE..............................310 326-8110
Kurt Weideman, *Manager*
EMP: 25
SALES (corp-wide): 177.9K **Privately
Held**
WEB: www.hi-shear.com
SIC: 3429 3452 Manufactured hardware
(general); bolts, nuts, rivets & washers
HQ: Hi-Shear Corporation
2600 Skypark Dr
Torrance CA 90505
310 784-4025

(P-11596)
HODGE PRODUCTS INC
Also Called: Www.masterlocks.com
7365 Mission Gorge Rd F, San Diego
(92120-1274)
P.O. Box 1326, El Cajon (92022-1326)
PHONE..............................619 444-3147
Anthony Hodge, *President*
Allan Hodge, *Treasurer*
▲ EMP: 25
SALES (est): 10MM **Privately Held**
WEB: www.hpionline.com
SIC: 3429 5099 Locks or lock sets; locks
& lock sets

(P-11597)
**HOLLYWOOD BED SPRING MFG
INC**
5959 Corvette St, Commerce
(90040-1601)
PHONE..............................323 887-9500
Larry Harrow, *CEO*
Jason Harrow, *President*
Andrea Harrow, *Admin Sec*
◆ EMP: 90 EST: 1945
SQ FT: 55,000
SALES (est): 22MM **Privately Held**
WEB: www.hollywoodbed.com
SIC: 3429 2515 2511 2514 Manufactured
hardware (general); mattresses & bed-
springs; wood household furniture; frames
for box springs or bedsprings: metal

(P-11598)
**HOLLYWOOD ENGINEERING
INC**
Also Called: Hollywood Bike Racks
12812 S Spring St, Los Angeles
(90061-1620)
PHONE..............................310 516-8600
Neil Nusbaum, *President*
Andre Levy, *Vice Pres*
▲ EMP: 10 EST: 1973
SQ FT: 35,000
SALES (est): 4MM **Privately Held**
WEB: www.hollywoodracks.com
SIC: 3429 3496 Bicycle racks, automotive;
miscellaneous fabricated wire products

(P-11599)
INTELLIGENT ENERGY INC
1731 Tech Dr Ste 755, San Jose (95110)
PHONE..............................562 997-3600
Henri Winand, *President*
Larry Frost, *Corp Secy*
Hazen Burford, *Vice Pres*

Julian Hughes, *Vice Pres*
EMP: 30
SQ FT: 9,600
SALES (est): 5.6MM
SALES (corp-wide): 4.4MM **Privately
Held**
WEB: www.intelligent-energy.com
SIC: 3429 3694 Bicycle racks, automotive;
alternators, automotive
PA: Intelligent Energy Limited
Charnwood Building
Loughborough LEICS LE11
150 927-1271

(P-11600)
JAMES P MCNAIR CO INC
Also Called: Valma Properties
2236 Irving St, San Francisco
(94122-1619)
P.O. Box 22072 (94122-0072)
PHONE..............................415 681-2200
Lydia McNair, *President*
Linda Idiart, *Treasurer*
Michael James Mc Nair, *Vice Pres*
Rhonda Bouyea, *Admin Sec*
EMP: 10
SQ FT: 2,200
SALES (est): 1.1MM **Privately Held**
SIC: 3429 6512 6514 Locks or lock sets;
nonresidential building operators; dwelling
operators, except apartments

(P-11601)
**JONATHAN ENGNRED
SLUTIONS CORP (PA)**
250 Commerce Ste 100, Irvine
(92602-1341)
PHONE..............................714 665-4400
Paul Salazar, *CEO*
Michael Berneth, *President*
Eric Hersom, *Officer*
Les Van Kanten, *Admin Sec*
Bob Bryson, *Technology*
▲ EMP: 44 EST: 1954
SQ FT: 120,000
SALES (est): 79.9MM **Privately Held**
WEB: www.jonathanengr.com
SIC: 3429 3562 Manufactured hardware
(general); ball bearings & parts

(P-11602)
K & W MANUFACTURING CO INC
23107 Temescal Canyon Rd, Corona
(92883-6001)
PHONE..............................951 277-3300
Gerald W Keck, *President*
Denise Jure, *Vice Pres*
Carolyn Keck, *Admin Sec*
EMP: 16
SQ FT: 15,000
SALES: 400K **Privately Held**
WEB: www.k-and-w-mfg.com
SIC: 3429 3631 Fireplace equipment,
hardware: andirons, grates, screens; bar-
becues, grills & braziers (outdoor cook-
ing)

(P-11603)
KL-MEGLA AMERICA LLC
2221 Celsius Ave Ste A, Oxnard
(93030-7258)
PHONE..............................818 334-5311
Peter Reinecke, *CEO*
Julie Maddox, *Office Mgr*
Lawrence Glasner, *Mng Member*
▲ EMP: 20 EST: 2008
SALES (est): 3MM **Privately Held**
SIC: 3429 Manufactured hardware (gen-
eral)

(P-11604)
KLINKY MANUFACTURING CO
4000 W Magnolia Blvd D, Burbank
(91505-2827)
PHONE..............................818 766-6256
Dee Maser, *President*
▲ EMP: 10
SALES (est): 688.9K **Privately Held**
SIC: 3429 Keys, locks & related hardware

(P-11605)
LIGHT COMPOSITE CORPORATION
Also Called: Forespar
22322 Gilberto, Rcho STA Marg (92688-2102)
PHONE.............................949 858-8820
Robert R Foresman, *President*
Marilyn Holst, *Treasurer*
Juin Foresman, *Principal*
▲ EMP: 60
SALES (est): 5.8MM **Privately Held**
SIC: 3429 Marine hardware

(P-11606)
LOCK AMERICA INC
Also Called: Mr Lock
9168 Stellar Ct, Corona (92883-4923)
PHONE.............................951 277-5180
Ming Shiao, *President*
Frank Minnella, *CEO*
Watson Visuwan, *Vice Pres*
Candice Smith, *Technology*
Ronny Ramsay, *Consultant*
▲ EMP: 19
SQ FT: 11,500
SALES (est): 3.2MM **Privately Held**
WEB: www.laigroup.com
SIC: 3429 5099 Keys, locks & related hardware; locks & lock sets

(P-11607)
MAC ENGINEERING & COMPONENTS
5122 Calle Del Sol, Santa Clara (95054-1009)
PHONE.............................408 286-3030
Chris Cardaman, *Owner*
EMP: 12
SALES (est): 1.7MM **Privately Held**
SIC: 3429 5085 Builders' hardware; fasteners, industrial: nuts, bolts, screws, etc.

(P-11608)
MARIN USA
265 Bel Marin Keys Blvd, Novato (94949-5724)
PHONE.............................415 382-6000
Matt Vanenkevort, *CEO*
▲ EMP: 20
SALES (est): 1.7MM **Privately Held**
SIC: 3429 Bicycle racks, automotive

(P-11609)
MCDANIEL MANUFACTURING INC
6180 Enterprise Dr Ste D, Diamond Springs (95619-9471)
PHONE.............................530 626-6336
John McDaniel, *President*
Nora McDaniel, *Corp Secy*
EMP: 15
SALES (est): 2.3MM **Privately Held**
WEB: www.mcdanielmfg.com
SIC: 3429 3443 3089 Manufactured hardware (general); stills, pressure: metal plate; hardware, plastic

(P-11610)
MCMAHON STEEL COMPANY INC
1880 Nirvana Ave, Chula Vista (91911-6118)
PHONE.............................619 671-9700
Derek J McMahon, *President*
Kevin McMahon, *Vice Pres*
Robert Smith, *Engineer*
Cynthia Dealba, *Human Res Dir*
EMP: 120
SQ FT: 14,300
SALES (est): 32.6MM **Privately Held**
WEB: www.mcmahonsteel.com
SIC: 3429 1791 3441 Manufactured hardware (general); structural steel erection; fabricated structural metal

(P-11611)
MID-WEST WHOLESALE HARDWARE CO
Also Called: Banner Solutions
1274 N Grove St, Anaheim (92806-2113)
PHONE.............................714 630-4751
Terry Olson, *Branch Mgr*
EMP: 22

SALES (corp-wide): 27.8MM **Privately Held**
SIC: 3429 5072 Manufactured hardware (general); hardware
PA: Mid-West Wholesale Hardware Co Inc
1000 Century Dr
Kansas City MO 64120
816 245-1142

(P-11612)
MOELLER MFG & SUP LLC
Also Called: Moeller Mfg & Sup Inc
805 E Cerritos Ave, Anaheim (92805-6328)
PHONE.............................714 999-5551
Stevens Chevillotte, *President*
Peter George, *CEO*
Debbie Comstock, *Director*
EMP: 45 EST: 1978
SALES: 14MM
SALES (corp-wide): 167.6MM **Privately Held**
WEB: www.moellermfg.com
SIC: 3429 3452 Aircraft hardware; washers, metal
PA: Consolidated Aerospace Manufacturing, Llc
1425 S Acacia Ave
Fullerton CA 92831
714 989-2797

(P-11613)
MONADNOCK COMPANY
Also Called: Lisi Aerospace
16728 Gale Ave, City of Industry (91745-1803)
PHONE.............................626 964-6581
Christian Darville, *CEO*
Michael Reyes, *Vice Pres*
Rebeca Macias, *Administration*
Curtis Kerr, *Planning*
Kelly Schreiber, *Analyst*
▼ EMP: 190 EST: 1987
SQ FT: 90,000
SALES (est): 50MM
SALES (corp-wide): 177.9K **Privately Held**
WEB: www.monadnock.com
SIC: 3429 Aircraft hardware; metal fasteners
HQ: Hi-Shear Corporation
2600 Skypark Dr
Torrance CA 90505
310 784-4025

(P-11614)
MONOGRAM AEROSPACE FAS INC (HQ)
3423 Garfield Ave, Commerce (90040-3103)
PHONE.............................323 722-4760
David Adler, *President*
Michelle Mullin, *Sales Mgr*
▲ EMP: 136
SQ FT: 97,500
SALES (est): 46.3MM
SALES (corp-wide): 877.1MM **Publicly Held**
WEB: www.monogramaerospace.com
SIC: 3429 3452 Manufactured hardware (general); bolts, metal
PA: Trimas Corporation
38505 Woodward Ave # 200
Bloomfield Hills MI 48304
248 631-5450

(P-11615)
MOORE TOOL CO
16701 Chestnut St Ste 8, Hesperia (92345-6114)
PHONE.............................760 949-4142
Cliff Moore, *Owner*
EMP: 21
SQ FT: 12,000
SALES (est): 2MM **Privately Held**
SIC: 3429 5072 Motor vehicle hardware; miscellaneous fasteners

(P-11616)
NUSET INC
1364 Marion Ct, City of Industry (91745-2418)
PHONE.............................626 246-1668
Caron Ng, *Vice Chairman*
Melissa Lee, *Officer*
EMP: 20

SALES (est): 745.5K **Privately Held**
SIC: 3429 Keys, locks & related hardware

(P-11617)
ORION ORNAMENTAL IRON INC
6918 Tujunga Ave, North Hollywood (91605-6212)
PHONE.............................818 752-0688
Sunil Patel, *CEO*
Atul Patel, *President*
Ben Oru, *Technology*
Jaleen Jong, *Sales Executive*
▲ EMP: 40
SQ FT: 30,000
SALES (est): 5.3MM **Privately Held**
WEB: www.ironartbyorion.com
SIC: 3429 Builders' hardware

(P-11618)
PACIFIC LOCK COMPANY (PA)
25605 Hercules St, Valencia (91355-5051)
PHONE.............................661 294-3707
Gregory B Waugh, *President*
Patty Yang, *CFO*
Joshua Fleagane, *Vice Pres*
▲ EMP: 29
SQ FT: 18,000
SALES (est): 3.1MM **Privately Held**
WEB: www.paclock.com
SIC: 3429 3699 5099 Keys & key blanks; security devices; locks & lock sets

(P-11619)
PAU HANA GROUP LLC
Also Called: Kjl Fasteners
94601 State Rte 70, Chilcoot (96105)
P.O. Box 201 (96105-0201)
PHONE.............................530 993-6800
Kristine L J Lock, *Mng Member*
Raymond W Lock,
EMP: 12
SQ FT: 5,000
SALES (est): 2.5MM **Privately Held**
WEB: www.kjlfast.com
SIC: 3429 Manufactured hardware (general)

(P-11620)
PECOWOOD INC
7707 Alondra Blvd, Paramount (90723-5003)
PHONE.............................562 633-2538
EMP: 12
SQ FT: 8,000
SALES (est): 1.6MM **Privately Held**
SIC: 3429

(P-11621)
R C PRODUCTS CORP
22322 Gilberto, Rcho STA Marg (92688-2102)
PHONE.............................949 858-8820
Robert R Foresman, *President*
Marilyn Holst, *Admin Sec*
EMP: 60
SQ FT: 40,000
SALES (est): 3.8MM
SALES (corp-wide): 9.2MM **Privately Held**
WEB: www.forespar.com
SIC: 3429 Marine hardware
PA: Forespar Products Corp.
22322 Gilberto
Rcho Sta Marg CA 92688
949 858-8820

(P-11622)
RAILMAKERS INC
864 W 18th St, Costa Mesa (92627-4411)
PHONE.............................949 642-6506
John Hawley, *President*
David C Hawley, *Corp Secy*
EMP: 12
SQ FT: 10,000
SALES (est): 1.7MM **Privately Held**
WEB: www.railmakers.com
SIC: 3429 Marine hardware

(P-11623)
REVERSICA DESIGN INC
1900 Commercial Way Ste A, Santa Cruz (95065-1844)
PHONE.............................831 459-9033
EMP: 10
SALES (est): 580K **Privately Held**
SIC: 3429

(P-11624)
RPC LEGACY INC
Also Called: Terry Hinge & Hardware
14600 Arminta St, Van Nuys (91402-5902)
PHONE.............................818 787-9000
Authur William, *Branch Mgr*
EMP: 75
SALES (corp-wide): 16.1MM **Privately Held**
WEB: www.rockfordprocess.com
SIC: 3429 Manufactured hardware (general)
PA: Rpc Legacy, Inc.
2020 7th St
Rockford IL 61104
815 966-2000

(P-11625)
SATURN FASTENERS INC
425 S Varney St, Burbank (91502-2193)
PHONE.............................818 973-1807
Raymond D Barker Jr, *President*
Laura Elaine Barker, *Chairman*
Valentin Espinoza, *Planning*
Ken Biddle, *Plant Mgr*
▲ EMP: 112
SQ FT: 38,000
SALES (est): 16.8MM
SALES (corp-wide): 30.9MM **Privately Held**
WEB: www.saturnfasteners.com
SIC: 3429 5085 5072 3452 Metal fasteners; industrial supplies; bolts, nuts & screws; bolts, nuts, rivets & washers
HQ: Acument Global Technologies, Inc.
6125 18 Mile Rd
Sterling Heights MI 48314
586 254-3900

(P-11626)
SCHLAGE LOCK COMPANY LLC
2297 Niels Bohr Ct # 209, San Diego (92154-7928)
PHONE.............................619 671-0276
Rosa Cardenas, *Manager*
EMP: 20 **Privately Held**
SIC: 3429 Locks or lock sets
HQ: Schlage Lock Company Llc
11819 N Penn St
Carmel IN 46032
317 810-3700

(P-11627)
SECURITY DOOR CONTROLS (PA)
801 Avenida Acaso, Camarillo (93012-8726)
P.O. Box 3670 (93011-3670)
PHONE.............................805 494-0622
David A Geringer, *President*
Arthur V Geringer, *Ch of Bd*
Gloria Marchand, *Treasurer*
Richard Geringer, *Vice Pres*
Shane Geringer, *Vice Pres*
◆ EMP: 50
SQ FT: 19,000
SALES (est): 13.1MM **Privately Held**
WEB: www.sdcsecurity.com
SIC: 3429 Door locks, bolts & checks

(P-11628)
SOLID-SCOPE MACHINING CO INC
17925 Adria Maru Ln, Carson (90746-1401)
PHONE.............................310 523-2366
Patsy Rhinehart, *President*
Robert Rhinehart, *Vice Pres*
EMP: 16
SQ FT: 6,000
SALES (est): 3.1MM **Privately Held**
WEB: www.solid-scope.com
SIC: 3429 3728 Aircraft hardware; aircraft parts & equipment

(P-11629)
SPECIALTY APARTMENT SUPPLY INC
3991 E Miraloma Ave, Anaheim (92806-6201)
P.O. Box 6110 (92816-0110)
PHONE.............................714 630-2275
Elisa Gen, *CEO*
EMP: 11

▲ = Import ▼=Export
◆ =Import/Export

SALES (est): 1.7MM **Privately Held**
SIC: 3429 Furniture builders' & other
household hardware

(P-11630)
SPEP ACQUISITION CORP (PA)
Also Called: Sierra Pacific Engrg & Pdts
4041 Via Oro Ave, Long Beach
(90810-1458)
P.O. Box 5246, Carson (90749-5246)
PHONE..................................310 608-0693
David Mochalski, *CEO*
Shaffiq Rahim, *CFO*
Larry Mirick, *Chairman*
Jhonny Cuyuch, *Engineer*
Maggie Zhang, *Controller*
◆ EMP: 70
SQ FT: 48,300
SALES (est): 18.4MM **Privately Held**
WEB: www.SPEP.com
SIC: 3429 8711 5072 Manufactured hard-
ware (general); engineering services;
hardware

(P-11631)
STAR DIE CASTING INC
12209 Slauson Ave, Santa Fe Springs
(90670-2605)
PHONE..................................562 698-0627
Jer Ming Yu, *President*
MEI H Yu, *Treasurer*
Mark Chen, *QC Mgr*
▲ EMP: 80
SQ FT: 13,290
SALES (est): 9.4MM **Privately Held**
SIC: 3429 3364 3544 Builders' hardware;
nonferrous die-castings except aluminum;
special dies & tools

(P-11632)
STAR ONE INVESTMENTS LLC
1304 Buttercup Ct, Roseville (95661-5459)
PHONE..................................916 858-1178
Danny Walrath,
EMP: 15
SALES (est): 3MM **Privately Held**
SIC: 3429 Manufactured hardware (gen-
eral)

(P-11633)
STORUS CORPORATION (PA)
3266 Buskirk Ave, Pleasant Hill
(94523-4315)
PHONE..................................925 322-8700
Scott Kaminski, *President*
David Kaminski, *Vice Pres*
▲ EMP: 10
SALES (est): 733K **Privately Held**
WEB: www.storus.com
SIC: 3429 Builders' hardware

(P-11634)
SYNERGETIC TECH GROUP INC
1712 Earhart, La Verne (91750-5826)
PHONE..................................909 305-4711
Kevin E Jones, *CEO*
EMP: 10
SQ FT: 2,400
SALES (est): 2MM **Privately Held**
SIC: 3429 3821 5065 Aircraft hardware;
worktables, laboratory; electronic parts &
equipment

(P-11635)
T G SCHMEISER CO INC
Also Called: Schmeiser Farm Equipment
3160 E California Ave, Fresno
(93702-4108)
P.O. Box 1047 (93714-1047)
PHONE..................................559 486-4569
Andrew W Cummings, *CEO*
Andrew Wcummings, *CEO*
Shirley Cummings, *Corp Secy*
Olga Pirogova, *Engineer*
Dave Vanvleet, *Opers Mgr*
▼ EMP: 35
SQ FT: 36,000
SALES (est): 6MM **Privately Held**
WEB: www.tgschmeiser.com
SIC: 3429 3523 Manufactured hardware
(general); soil preparation machinery, ex-
cept turf & grounds

(P-11636)
TOMORROWS HEIRLOOMS INC
Also Called: Stone Manufacturing Company
1636 W 135th St, Gardena (90249-2506)
P.O. Box 1325 (90249-0325)
PHONE..................................310 323-6720
Amit V Patel, *President*
Sumi Patel, *Treasurer*
Kumar V Patel, *Vice Pres*
EMP: 26
SQ FT: 22,000
SALES (est): 4.5MM **Privately Held**
WEB: www.stonemfg.com
SIC: 3429 Fireplace equipment, hardware:
andirons, grates, screens

(P-11637)
TOP LINE MFG INC
7032 Alondra Blvd, Paramount
(90723-3926)
P.O. Box 739 (90723-0739)
PHONE..................................562 633-0605
Anne Graffy, *CEO*
Bill Watermen, *Officer*
Salim Khan, *Bookkeeper*
Tom Graffy, *Plant Mgr*
▲ EMP: 29
SQ FT: 20,000
SALES (est): 5.9MM **Privately Held**
WEB: www.toplinemfg.com
SIC: 3429 Motor vehicle hardware; bicycle
racks, automotive; luggage racks, car top

(P-11638)
TRIANGLE BRASS MFG CO INC (PA)
Also Called: Trimco
1351 Rocky Point Dr, Oceanside
(92056-5864)
P.O. Box 23277, Los Angeles (90023-0277)
PHONE..................................323 262-4191
Martin Simon, *President*
Adam Matusz, *COO*
Gloria Simon, *Vice Pres*
Tanisha St Onge, *Accountant*
▲ EMP: 70
SQ FT: 45,000
SALES (est): 12.5MM **Privately Held**
WEB: www.trimcobbw.com
SIC: 3429 Door opening & closing devices,
except electrical

(P-11639)
TUL INC
663 Brea Canyon Rd Ste 6, Walnut
(91789-3045)
PHONE..................................909 444-0577
Ted Chen, *President*
▲ EMP: 100
SALES (est): 9MM **Privately Held**
SIC: 3429 Manufactured hardware (gen-
eral)

(P-11640)
UMPCO INC
7100 Lampson Ave, Garden Grove
(92841-3914)
P.O. Box 5158 (92846-0158)
PHONE..................................714 897-3531
Dan Miller, *CEO*
EMP: 75
SQ FT: 60,000
SALES (est): 18.7MM **Privately Held**
WEB: www.umpco.com
SIC: 3429 Clamps, metal

(P-11641)
VIT PRODUCTS INC
2063 Wineridge Pl, Escondido
(92029-1931)
PHONE..................................760 480-6702
Don Pagano, *President*
Arthur Arns, *Ch of Bd*
EMP: 36
SQ FT: 24,000
SALES (est): 6.9MM **Privately Held**
WEB: www.vitproducts.com
SIC: 3429 2295 Clamps, couplings, noz-
zles & other metal hose fittings; coated
fabrics, not rubberized

(P-11642)
WESTERN HARDWARE COMPANY
161 Commerce Way, Walnut (91789-2719)
PHONE..................................909 595-6201
Gayle E Pacheco, *President*
▲ EMP: 12
SALES (est): 1.7MM **Privately Held**
SIC: 3429 Manufactured hardware (gen-
eral)

(P-11643)
WINDLINE MARINE
14601 S Broadway, Gardena (90248-1811)
PHONE..................................310 516-9812
Robert Barbour, *Ch of Bd*
Glenn Smith, *President*
Steven Jason Ruiz, *CFO*
Irma Limon, *Admin Sec*
Jason Ruiz, *Info Tech Dir*
EMP: 184
SQ FT: 50,000
SALES (est): 25.7MM **Privately Held**
SIC: 3429 Marine hardware

(P-11644)
YOUNG ENGINEERS INC
25841 Commercentre Dr, Lake Forest
(92630-8812)
P.O. Box 278 (92609-0278)
PHONE..................................949 581-9411
Miki Young, *President*
Pat Wells, *President*
Richard Switzer, *Engineer*
Terry Litwinski, *Sales Staff*
Joseph Aquino, *Maint Spvr*
EMP: 65
SQ FT: 26,000
SALES (est): 14.5MM **Privately Held**
WEB: www.youngengineers.com
SIC: 3429 Aircraft hardware

(P-11645)
YOUNGDALE MANUFACTURING CORP
1216 Liberty Way Ste B, Vista
(92081-8369)
P.O. Box 3209 (92085-3209)
PHONE..................................760 727-0644
Peter Youngdale, *Ch of Bd*
Joseph Carrick, *President*
Christine Carrick, *Vice Pres*
Susan Youngdale, *VP Finance*
Nidia Ferrer, *Sales Executive*
▲ EMP: 20 EST: 1964
SQ FT: 25,000
SALES (est): 4MM **Privately Held**
SIC: 3429 Cabinet hardware

**3431 Enameled Iron & Metal
Sanitary Ware**

(P-11646)
ALTMANS PRODUCTS LLC (HQ)
7136 Kittyhawk Ave Apt 4, Los Angeles
(90045-2137)
PHONE..................................310 559-4093
Edgardo Flores, *CEO*
▲ EMP: 38
SQ FT: 1,300
SALES (est): 7.9MM **Privately Held**
WEB: www.altmansproducts.com
SIC: 3431 Sinks: enameled iron, cast iron
or pressed metal

(P-11647)
HYDRO SYSTEMS INC (PA)
29132 Avenue Paine, Valencia
(91355-5402)
PHONE..................................661 775-0686
Scott G Steinhardt, *President*
Larry Burroughs, *Vice Pres*
Dave Ortwein, *Vice Pres*
Debbie Steinhardt, *Vice Pres*
Ashley Steinhardt, *Human Res Mgr*
EMP: 96
SQ FT: 90,000
SALES (est): 17.8MM **Privately Held**
WEB: www.hydrosystem.com
SIC: 3431 3432 3088 Bathtubs: enam-
eled iron, cast iron or pressed metal;
plumbing fixture fittings & trim; plastics
plumbing fixtures

(P-11648)
KOHLER CO
701 S Arrowhead Ave, San Bernardino
(92408-2004)
PHONE..................................909 890-4291
Gary Mayfield, *Branch Mgr*
EMP: 48
SALES (corp-wide): 7.7B **Privately Held**
SIC: 3431 Plumbing fixtures: enameled
iron cast iron or pressed metal
PA: Kohler Co.
444 Highland Dr
Kohler WI 53044
920 457-4441

(P-11649)
MAG AEROSPACE INDUSTRIES INC
Also Called: Monogram Systems
1500 Glenn Curtiss St, Carson
(90746-4012)
P.O. Box 11189 (90749-1189)
PHONE..................................310 631-3800
Sebastien Weber, *President*
Tim Birbeck, *Vice Pres*
Mike Nieves, *Vice Pres*
James Durso, *Executive*
Gil Lenhard, *Executive*
◆ EMP: 350
SQ FT: 150,000
SALES (est): 164.4MM
SALES (corp-wide): 833.4MM **Privately
Held**
SIC: 3431 3728 Plumbing fixtures: enam-
eled iron cast iron or pressed metal;
portable chemical toilets, metal; aircraft
parts & equipment
PA: Safran
2 Bd Du General Martial Valin
Paris 15e Arrondissement 75015
140 608-080

(P-11650)
SEACHROME CORPORATION
1906 E Dominguez St, Long Beach
(90810-1002)
PHONE..................................310 427-8010
Sam C Longo Jr, *CEO*
Sam C Longo Sr, *Corp Secy*
Diane Stevens, *Info Tech Mgr*
Jan Phan, *Human Res Mgr*
Daniel Sowinski, *Inv Control Mgr*
▲ EMP: 112
SQ FT: 50,000
SALES (est): 25.9MM **Privately Held**
WEB: www.seachrome.com
SIC: 3431 5072 3842 3429 Bathroom fix-
tures, including sinks; builders' hardware;
surgical appliances & supplies; manufac-
tured hardware (general)

**3432 Plumbing Fixture
Fittings & Trim, Brass**

(P-11651)
A & C TRADE CONSULTANTS INC
Also Called: A & C Imports & Exports
1 Edwards Ct Ste 101, Burlingame
(94010-2428)
PHONE..................................650 375-7000
Sharon H Hsu, *President*
Sharon Hsu, *President*
▲ EMP: 10
SQ FT: 20,000
SALES: 4MM **Privately Held**
WEB: www.actradesf.com
SIC: 3432 5734 Plumbing fixture fittings &
trim; magnetic disks

(P-11652)
ACORNVAC INC
Also Called: Acorn Vac
13818 Oaks Ave, Chino (91710-7008)
PHONE..................................909 902-1141
Donald E Morris, *CEO*
Neil Levers, *Design Engr*
Tom Zinn, *Engrg Dir*
Carlos Galeazzi, *Engineer*
Craig Johnson, *Natl Sales Mgr*
EMP: 20

PRODUCTS & SVCS

SALES: 11.2MM
SALES (corp-wide): 85MM **Privately Held**
SIC: 3432 Plastic plumbing fixture fittings, assembly
PA: Acorn Engineering Company
　　15125 Proctor Ave
　　City Of Industry CA 91746
　　800 488-8999

(P-11653)
ALL-AMERICAN MFG CO
2201 E 51st St, Vernon (90058-2814)
PHONE.......................323 581-6293
John F Norton, *President*
▲ **EMP:** 25
SQ FT: 20,000
SALES (est): 4.5MM **Privately Held**
WEB: www.aamfgco.com
SIC: 3432 3469 Plumbing fixture fittings & trim; stamping metal for the trade

(P-11654)
AMERICAN BRASS & ALUM FNDRY CO
2060 Garfield Ave, Commerce (90040-1804)
P.O. Box 80304, Los Angeles (90040)
PHONE.......................800 545-9988
Tony Orapallo Jr, *President*
Robert A Orapallo, *Vice Pres*
◆ **EMP:** 20
SQ FT: 15,000
SALES (est): 2.3MM **Privately Held**
WEB: www.abainc.net
SIC: 3432 Plumbers' brass goods: drain cocks, faucets, spigots, etc.; plastic plumbing fixture fittings, assembly

(P-11655)
AMERISINK INC (PA)
835 Fremont Ave, San Leandro (94577-5713)
PHONE.......................510 667-9998
Wilson Qi, *President*
◆ **EMP:** 15
SQ FT: 20,900
SALES (est): 2.1MM **Privately Held**
SIC: 3432 Plumbing fixture fittings & trim

(P-11656)
AQUEST INC
4120 Pine Meadows Way, Pebble Beach (93953-3021)
PHONE.......................831 622-9296
Bruce Oliver, *CEO*
Robert J Brecha, *President*
Neil Oliver, *President*
Betty Oliver, *Admin Sec*
▲ **EMP:** 25
SQ FT: 13,000
SALES (est): 3.2MM **Privately Held**
WEB: www.aquestinc.com
SIC: 3432 Faucets & spigots, metal & plastic

(P-11657)
ARROWHEAD BRASS & PLUMBING LLC
4900 Valley Blvd, Los Angeles (90032-3317)
PHONE.......................323 221-9137
Fred Schneider, *CEO*
Jeff Layton, *Vice Pres*
Jose Berumen, *Maint Spvr*
▲ **EMP:** 80
SQ FT: 35,000
SALES (est): 18.9MM **Privately Held**
SIC: 3432 Faucets & spigots, metal & plastic

(P-11658)
BRADLEY CORP
5556 Ontario Mills Pkwy, Ontario (91764-5117)
PHONE.......................909 481-7255
Ron Schamb, *Branch Mgr*
EMP: 12
SALES (corp-wide): 165.9MM **Privately Held**
WEB: www.bradleycorp.com
SIC: 3432 Plumbing fixture fittings & trim
PA: Bradley Corporation
　　W142n9101 Fountain Blvd
　　Menomonee Falls WI 53051
　　262 251-6000

(P-11659)
BRASSTECH INC (HQ)
Also Called: Newport Brass
2001 Carnegie Ave, Santa Ana (92705-5531)
PHONE.......................949 417-5207
John V Halso, *CEO*
◆ **EMP:** 155
SQ FT: 70,000
SALES (est): 76.7MM
SALES (corp-wide): 8.3B **Publicly Held**
WEB: www.newportbrass.com
SIC: 3432 Plumbing fixture fittings & trim
PA: Masco Corporation
　　17450 College Pkwy
　　Livonia MI 48152
　　313 274-7400

(P-11660)
CALIFORNIA FAUCETS INC
5231 Argosy Ave, Huntington Beach (92649-1015)
PHONE.......................657 400-1639
Blas Ramierez, *Branch Mgr*
EMP: 19
SALES (corp-wide): 17.7MM **Privately Held**
WEB: www.calfaucets.com
SIC: 3432 Faucets & spigots, metal & plastic
PA: California Faucets, Inc.
　　5271 Argosy Ave
　　Huntington Beach CA 92649
　　714 890-0450

(P-11661)
CALIFORNIA FAUCETS INC (PA)
5271 Argosy Ave, Huntington Beach (92649-1015)
PHONE.......................714 890-0450
Jeff Silverstein, *CEO*
Sonia Silverstein, *Corp Secy*
Melissa Shaia-Egle, *Executive Asst*
Bridget Ratzlaff, *Admin Asst*
Gabriele Head, *Administration*
◆ **EMP:** 75
SALES (est): 17.7MM **Privately Held**
WEB: www.calfaucets.com
SIC: 3432 Faucets & spigots, metal & plastic

(P-11662)
CENTRAL VLY ASSEMBLY PACKG INC
5515 E Lamona Ave 103, Fresno (93727-2226)
PHONE.......................559 486-4260
Nate Perry, *CEO*
John Perry, *COO*
EMP: 24
SALES (est): 3.5MM **Privately Held**
SIC: 3432 3565 3089 3824 Plastic plumbing fixture fittings, assembly; bag opening, filling & closing machines; vacuum packaging machinery; blister or bubble formed packaging, plastic; linear counters

(P-11663)
CHAMPION-ARROWHEAD LLC
5147 Alhambra Ave, Los Angeles (90032-3413)
PHONE.......................323 221-9137
Jim Shearer, *Mng Member*
Joe Rella, *Sales Staff*
▲ **EMP:** 99 **EST:** 1936
SQ FT: 4,000
SALES (est): 1.2MM **Privately Held**
WEB: www.arrowheadbrass.com
SIC: 3432 Plumbing fixture fittings & trim

(P-11664)
CISCOS SHOP
2911 E Miraloma Ave # 17, Anaheim (92806-1838)
PHONE.......................657 230-9158
Francisco Chavez, *Partner*
EMP: 10
SALES (est): 1.3MM **Privately Held**
SIC: 3432 Plumbing fixture fittings & trim

(P-11665)
COLLICUTT ENERGY SERVICES INC
12349 Hawkins St, Santa Fe Springs (90670-3366)
PHONE.......................562 944-4413
Toll Free:.......................866 -
Tim Rahman, *Branch Mgr*
EMP: 25
SQ FT: 77,000
SALES (corp-wide): 33.5MM **Privately Held**
SIC: 3432 Plumbing fixture fittings & trim
HQ: Collicutt Energy Services Inc.
　　940 Riverside Pkwy Ste 80
　　West Sacramento CA 95605
　　-

(P-11666)
COLUMBIA SANITARY PRODUCTS
Also Called: Columbia Products Co
1622 Browning, Irvine (92606-4809)
PHONE.......................949 474-0777
Dorothy Lazier, *CEO*
Paul Escalera, *President*
▲ **EMP:** 20
SQ FT: 20,000
SALES (est): 10MM **Privately Held**
WEB: www.columbiasinks.com
SIC: 3432 Plumbing fixture fittings & trim

(P-11667)
FISHER MANUFACTURING CO INC (PA)
1900 S O St, Tulare (93274-6850)
P.O. Box 60 (93275-0060)
PHONE.......................559 685-5200
Ray Fisher Jr, *President*
Kay Fisher, *Shareholder*
Karen Lauterbach, *Shareholder*
Kathleen Sebahar, *Shareholder*
Steve Sebahar, *Vice Pres*
◆ **EMP:** 38
SQ FT: 50,000
SALES (est): 4MM **Privately Held**
WEB: www.fisher-mfg.com
SIC: 3432 Plumbers' brass goods: drain cocks, faucets, spigots, etc.

(P-11668)
FLUIDMASTER INC (PA)
30800 Rancho Viejo Rd, San Juan Capistrano (92675-1564)
PHONE.......................949 728-2000
Robert Anderson Schoepe, *CEO*
Michael Draves, *President*
Terry Bland, *CFO*
Robert Connell, *Exec VP*
Jeff Peterson, *Regional Mgr*
◆ **EMP:** 400 **EST:** 1957
SALES (est): 213.3MM **Privately Held**
WEB: www.fluidmaster.com
SIC: 3432 3089 Plumbing fixture fittings & trim; injection molding of plastics

(P-11669)
G T WATER PRODUCTS INC
5239 N Commerce Ave, Moorpark (93021-1763)
PHONE.......................805 529-2900
George Tash, *President*
Russell Reasner, *Vice Pres*
Steve Schmitt, *Vice Pres*
Julie Shipley, *Vice Pres*
Debra Tash, *Vice Pres*
▲ **EMP:** 17
SQ FT: 20,000
SALES (est): 4.1MM **Privately Held**
WEB: www.gtwaterproducts.com
SIC: 3432 Plumbing fixture fittings & trim

(P-11670)
GMS LANDSCAPES INC
207 Camino Leon, Camarillo (93012-8635)
PHONE.......................805 402-3925
Sarah Corbin, *President*
EMP: 85
SALES (est): 2.6MM **Privately Held**
SIC: 3432 0781 Plumbing fixture fittings & trim; landscape services

(P-11671)
HIRSCH PIPE & SUPPLY CO INC
31920 Del Obispo St # 275, San Juan Capistrano (92675-3192)
PHONE.......................949 487-7009
Bill Glockner, *Branch Mgr*
EMP: 18
SALES (corp-wide): 158MM **Privately Held**
SIC: 3432 5074 5251 Plumbing fixture fittings & trim; plumbing fittings & supplies; pumps & pumping equipment
PA: Hirsch Pipe & Supply Co., Inc.
　　15025 Oxnard St Ste 100
　　Van Nuys CA 91411
　　818 756-0900

(P-11672)
MASCO CORPORATION
19914 Via Baron Way, Rancho Dominguez (90220)
PHONE.......................313 274-7400
EMP: 94
SALES (corp-wide): 8.3B **Publicly Held**
SIC: 3432 2434 Faucets & spigots, metal & plastic; vanities, bathroom: wood
PA: Masco Corporation
　　17450 College Pkwy
　　Livonia MI 48152
　　313 274-7400

(P-11673)
MCP INDUSTRIES INC
Also Called: Mission Rubber
1660 Leeson Ln, Corona (92879-2061)
PHONE.......................951 736-1313
Charlotte Garrett, *Admin Sec*
EMP: 50
SALES (corp-wide): 126.4MM **Privately Held**
WEB: www.missionrubber.com
SIC: 3432 Plumbing fixture fittings & trim
PA: Mcp Industries, Inc.
　　708 S Temescal St Ste 101
　　Corona CA 92879
　　951 736-1881

(P-11674)
MUIRSIS INC
2841 Saturn St Ste J, Brea (92821-6226)
PHONE.......................714 579-1555
Allen Yeh, *President*
Ralph Bedolla, *Opers Staff*
▲ **EMP:** 10
SALES (est): 950.9K **Privately Held**
SIC: 3432 Plumbing fixture fittings & trim

(P-11675)
PIPE GUARD INC
10723 Sherman Way, Sun Valley (91352-5155)
PHONE.......................818 765-2424
Peter Zamkochyan, *President*
EMP: 20
SALES (est): 975.3K **Privately Held**
SIC: 3432 Plumbing fixture fittings & trim

(P-11676)
PLUMBING PRODUCTS INC
Also Called: Trim To Trade
77551 El Duna Ct Ste I, Palm Desert (92211-4147)
PHONE.......................760 343-3306
Gary Yavitz, *President*
Jessie Yavitz, *Corp Secy*
▲ **EMP:** 15 **EST:** 1947
SQ FT: 36,000
SALES (est): 2.3MM **Privately Held**
WEB: www.plumbingproducts.com
SIC: 3432 3431 Plumbers' brass goods: drain cocks, faucets, spigots, etc.; bathroom fixtures, including sinks

(P-11677)
PRICE PFISTER INC
Also Called: Pfister Faucets
19701 Da Vinci, Foothill Ranch (92610-2622)
PHONE.......................949 672-4003
James M Loree, *President*
Craig A Douglas, *Treasurer*
Bruce Beatt, *Admin Sec*
EMP: 32
SALES (est): 9.2MM
SALES (corp-wide): 3.1B **Publicly Held**
SIC: 3432 Plumbing fixture fittings & trim

HQ: Spectrum Brands Legacy, Inc.
3001 Deming Way
Middleton WI 53562

(P-11678)
PRICE PFISTER INC (DH)
Also Called: Price Pfister Brass Mfg
19701 Da Vinci, Lake Forest (92610-2622)
PHONE.................................949 672-4000
Gregory John Gluchowski, *CEO*
▲ EMP: 800
SQ FT: 127,612
SALES (est): 128.8MM
SALES (corp-wide): 3.1B **Publicly Held**
SIC: 3432 Faucets & spigots, metal & plastic; plumbers' brass goods: drain cocks, faucets, spigots, etc.
HQ: Spectrum Brands, Inc.
3001 Deming Way
Middleton WI 53562
608 275-3340

(P-11679)
RAIN BIRD CORPORATION
Also Called: Rain Bird Golf Division
970 W Sierra Madre Ave, Azusa
(91702-1873)
PHONE.................................626 812-3400
Matt Circle, *Manager*
Dave Evans, *Principal*
EMP: 30
SALES (corp-wide): 86.7MM **Privately Held**
WEB: www.rainbird.com
SIC: 3432 3494 3433 Plumbing fixture fittings & trim; valves & pipe fittings; heating equipment, except electric
PA: Rain Bird Corporation
970 W Sierra Madre Ave
Azusa CA 91702
626 812-3400

(P-11680)
RSS MANUFACTURING
1261 Logan Ave, Costa Mesa
(92626-4004)
PHONE.................................714 361-4800
Geoffrey Escalette, *Owner*
▲ EMP: 14 EST: 2010
SALES (est): 2.2MM **Privately Held**
SIC: 3432 Faucets & spigots, metal & plastic; plumbers' brass goods: drain cocks, faucets, spigots, etc.

(P-11681)
SANTEC INC
3501 Challenger St Fl 2, Torrance
(90503-1697)
PHONE.................................310 542-0063
Nicolas Chen, *CEO*
James S Chen, *Principal*
Charles Silva, *Director*
▲ EMP: 50
SQ FT: 32,000
SALES (est): 9.6MM **Privately Held**
SIC: 3432 Faucets & spigots, metal & plastic

(P-11682)
STRUCTURES UNLIMITED
7671 Arlington Ave, Riverside
(92503-1407)
PHONE.................................951 688-6300
Jim Bean, *President*
EMP: 10
SALES (est): 1MM **Privately Held**
SIC: 3432 Plumbing fixture fittings & trim

(P-11683)
SUNRISE SPECIALTY COMPANY
61 Skyway Ln, Oakland (94619-3627)
PHONE.................................510 729-7277
Robert Weinstein, *CEO*
Malcolm Smith, *Ch of Bd*
◆ EMP: 13
SQ FT: 100,000
SALES (est): 2.8MM **Privately Held**
WEB: www.sunrisespecialty.com
SIC: 3432 Plumbers' brass goods: drain cocks, faucets, spigots, etc.

(P-11684)
TBS IRRIGATION PRODUCTS INC
8787 Olive Ln Bldg 3, Santee
(92071-4137)
PHONE.................................619 579-0520
Michael J Folkman, *President*
Neil Faulkman, *Corp Secy*
William Butson, *Vice Pres*
EMP: 20
SQ FT: 25,000
SALES (est): 5MM **Privately Held**
SIC: 3432 3523 3088 Lawn hose nozzles & sprinklers; farm machinery & equipment; plastics plumbing fixtures

(P-11685)
TRIPOS INDUSTRIES INC
Also Called: Tripus Industries
2448 Glendower Ave, Los Angeles
(90027-1111)
PHONE.................................323 669-0488
SA Young Hong, *President*
EMP: 25
SQ FT: 6,500
SALES (est): 2.2MM **Privately Held**
SIC: 3432 Plumbing fixture fittings & trim

(P-11686)
VALADONS PLUMBING SERVICE INC
315 Coleshill St, Bakersfield (93312-7046)
P.O. Box 20748 (93390-0748)
PHONE.................................661 201-1460
EMP: 11
SALES (est): 2.3MM **Privately Held**
SIC: 3432

(P-11687)
WATERLESS CO INC
1050 Joshua Way, Vista (92081-7807)
PHONE.................................760 727-7723
Klaus Reichardt, *President*
Lisa Saenz Brown, *Vice Pres*
▲ EMP: 10
SQ FT: 30,000
SALES (est): 1.8MM **Privately Held**
WEB: www.waterless.com
SIC: 3432 Plastic plumbing fixture fittings, assembly

(P-11688)
WATERSTONE LLC
Also Called: Waterstone Faucets
41180 Raintree Ct, Murrieta (92562-7020)
P.O. Box 1240, Temecula (92593-1240)
PHONE.................................951 304-0520
Christopher G Kuran, *Mng Member*
Steve Kliewer, *Vice Pres*
Debbie Culver, *Technical Staff*
Julie Colio, *Human Res Mgr*
Pam Donnelly, *Purchasing*
▲ EMP: 210
SQ FT: 42,000
SALES (est): 13MM **Privately Held**
SIC: 3432 Faucets & spigots, metal & plastic

3433 Heating Eqpt

(P-11689)
ADVANCED CONSERVATION TECHNOLO
Also Called: Act Inc Dmand Kontrols Systems
3176 Pullman St Ste 119, Costa Mesa
(92626-3317)
PHONE.................................714 668-1200
Larry Acker, *CEO*
Donna-Marie Acker, *President*
Kristine Parker, *Vice Pres*
Tina Cook, *Purch Mgr*
EMP: 16
SQ FT: 7,000
SALES (est): 3MM **Privately Held**
WEB: www.gothotwater.com
SIC: 3433 Boilers, low-pressure heating: steam or hot water

(P-11690)
BENCHMARK THERMAL CORPORATION
13185 Nevada City Ave, Grass Valley
(95945-9568)
PHONE.................................530 477-5011
Vincent Palmieri, *CEO*
Gil Mathew, *President*
Laralee Hannah, *Admin Sec*
EMP: 52
SQ FT: 20,000
SALES (est): 11MM **Privately Held**
WEB: www.benchmarkthermal.com
SIC: 3433 Heating equipment, except electric

(P-11691)
BIOTHERM HYDRONIC INC
Also Called: True Leaf Technologies
476 Primero Ct, Cotati (94931-3014)
P.O. Box 750967, Petaluma (94975-0967)
PHONE.................................707 794-9660
Jim K Rearden, *CEO*
Michael G Muchow, *CFO*
Thad Humphrey, *Engineer*
Joel Rechin, *Sales Staff*
▲ EMP: 15
SQ FT: 10,000
SALES (est): 4.1MM **Privately Held**
WEB: www.trueleaf.net
SIC: 3433 Heating equipment, except electric

(P-11692)
BROAN-NUTONE LLC
622 Emery Rd, Tecate (91980)
P.O. Box 1910 (91980-1910)
PHONE.................................262 673-8795
Joel Fletcher, *Mng Member*
Almon C Hall,
EMP: 227
SALES (est): 50.3MM
SALES (corp-wide): 11B **Privately Held**
SIC: 3433 3564 Solar heaters & collectors; ventilating fans: industrial or commercial
HQ: Nortek, Inc.
8000 Phoenix Pkwy
O Fallon MO 63368
636 561-7300

(P-11693)
CAPITAL COOKING EQUIPMENT
13211 Florence Ave, Santa Fe Springs
(90670-4509)
PHONE.................................562 903-1168
Surjit Kalsi, *Co-COB*
Roberto Bernal, *Co-COB*
Alejandro Bernal, *Exec VP*
Raul Chita, *Exec VP*
Porfiro Guzman, *Exec VP*
▲ EMP: 47
SQ FT: 7,000
SALES (est): 9.2MM **Privately Held**
WEB: www.capital-cooking.com
SIC: 3433 3631 Stoves, wood & coal burning; gas ranges, domestic

(P-11694)
COEN COMPANY INC (DH)
951 Mariners Island Blvd, San Mateo
(94404-1558)
PHONE.................................650 522-2100
Earl W Schnell, *President*
Steve Londerville, *Executive*
Samantha Jones, *Administration*
Mey Saephan, *Administration*
Vladimir Lifshits, *Technical Mgr*
◆ EMP: 40 EST: 1912
SALES (est): 16.6MM
SALES (corp-wide): 40.6B **Privately Held**
WEB: www.coen.com
SIC: 3433 3823 Burners, furnaces, boilers & stokers; combustion control instruments
HQ: Koch Engineered Solutions, Llc
4111 E 37th St N
Wichita KS 67220
316 828-8515

(P-11695)
ENDEPO INC
2100 Geng Rd Ste 210, Palo Alto
(94303-3307)
PHONE.................................707 428-3245
Egemen Seymen, *CEO*
Scott Sullivan, *COO*

EMP: 12
SALES (est): 80.8K **Privately Held**
SIC: 3433 5074 Solar heaters & collectors; heating equipment & panels, solar

(P-11696)
FAFCO INC (PA)
435 Otterson Dr, Chico (95928-8207)
PHONE.................................530 332-2100
Freeman A Ford, *Ch of Bd*
Robert C Leckinger, *CEO*
Nancy I Garvin, *CFO*
Phil Delnegro, *Vice Pres*
Jeff Monian, *Info Tech Mgr*
◆ EMP: 48
SQ FT: 57,500
SALES (est): 8.3MM **Privately Held**
WEB: www.fafco.com
SIC: 3433 Heaters, swimming pool: oil or gas

(P-11697)
GC AERO INC
21143 Hawth Blvd Ste 136, Torrance
(90503)
PHONE.................................310 539-7600
Jim Cowherd, *President*
▲ EMP: 15
SQ FT: 11,500
SALES (est): 2.3MM **Privately Held**
WEB: www.gcaero.com
SIC: 3433 3674 3822 3672 Heating equipment, except electric; integrated circuits, semiconductor networks, etc.; temperature controls, automatic; printed circuit boards

(P-11698)
GREENVOLTS INC
19200 Stevens Creek Blvd # 200, Cupertino (95014-2530)
PHONE.................................415 963-4030
EMP: 90
SALES (est): 14.5MM **Privately Held**
WEB: www.greenvolts.com
SIC: 3433 Solar heaters & collectors

(P-11699)
HEATEFLEX CORPORATION
Also Called: Safna A Division of Heateflex
405 E Santa Clara St, Arcadia
(91006-7227)
PHONE.................................626 599-8566
Jorge Ramirez, *President*
Cathy Zhou, *Controller*
Patricia Nhan, *Sales Staff*
EMP: 38
SALES (est): 10.2MM **Privately Held**
WEB: www.heateflex.com
SIC: 3433 3823 3559 3443 Heating equipment, except electric; industrial instrmnt msrmnt display/control process variable; ammunition & explosives, loading machinery; buoys, metal; assembly machines, non-metalworking

(P-11700)
INDUSTRIAL MANUFACTURING INC
10110 Norwalk Blvd, Santa Fe Springs
(90670-3326)
P.O. Box 3163 (90670-0163)
PHONE.................................562 941-5888
Eddie Cerda, *President*
EMP: 14
SQ FT: 15,700
SALES (est): 1MM **Privately Held**
SIC: 3433 Radiators, except electric

(P-11701)
INFRARED DYNAMICS INC
3830 Prospect Ave, Yorba Linda
(92886-1742)
PHONE.................................714 572-4050
Robert Cowan, *President*
▲ EMP: 32 EST: 1959
SQ FT: 23,500
SALES (est): 6.4MM **Privately Held**
WEB: www.infradyne.com
SIC: 3433 5075 Heating equipment, except electric; warm air heating equipment & supplies

(P-11702)
INNOVATIVE COMBUSTION TECH (PA)
Also Called: S.T. Johnson Company
5160 Fulton Dr, Fairfield (94534-1639)
PHONE..................................510 652-6000
Antonio De La O, *President*
Todd Cole, *Executive*
Barbara Florio, *Admin Sec*
Scott Krahn, *Engineer*
Bob Nickeson, *Engineer*
▼ EMP: 16 EST: 1903
SALES (est): 8.5MM **Privately Held**
WEB: www.stjohnson.com
SIC: 3433 Gas-oil burners, combination

(P-11703)
IRONRIDGE INC (HQ)
28357 Industrial Blvd, Hayward
(94545-4428)
PHONE..................................800 227-9523
Rich Tiu, *CEO*
William Kim, *Ch of Bd*
Corey Geiger, *COO*
Jim Clark, *CFO*
David Briggs, *Vice Pres*
▲ EMP: 50
SQ FT: 10,000
SALES (est): 26.8MM
SALES (corp-wide): 47.2MM **Privately Held**
WEB: www.2seas.com
SIC: 3433 5074 Solar heaters & collectors; heating equipment & panels, solar
PA: Esdec, Inc.
976 Brady Ave Nw Ste 100
Atlanta GA 30318
404 512-0716

(P-11704)
MANTA SOLAR CORPORATION
5420 Fulton St, San Francisco
(94121-3535)
PHONE..................................928 853-6216
Carlos Kronen, *CEO*
EMP: 10
SALES (est): 708.1K **Privately Held**
SIC: 3433 Solar heaters & collectors

(P-11705)
MANUFACTURERS COML FIN LLC
Also Called: Benchmark Thermal
13185 Nevada City Ave, Grass Valley
(95945-9568)
PHONE..................................530 477-5011
Michael Kayman,
Roger Ruttenberg, *Vice Pres*
Eric Doan, *Accountant*
EMP: 40
SQ FT: 8,000
SALES (est): 1.3MM **Privately Held**
SIC: 3433 Room & wall heaters, including radiators

(P-11706)
PYRON SOLAR III LLC
1216 Liberty Way Ste A, Vista
(92081-8369)
P.O. Box 5427, Bakersfield (93388-5427)
PHONE..................................760 599-5100
Stanley W Ellis, *CEO*
Stephanie Rosenthal, *President*
Duncan Earl, *CTO*
Joe Bentley, *Chief Engr*
EMP: 10
SQ FT: 8,000
SALES (est): 1MM **Privately Held**
SIC: 3433 Solar heaters & collectors
PA: Ellis Energy Investments, Inc.
1400 Norris Rd
Bakersfield CA 93308

(P-11707)
R E DILLARD 1 LLC
300 California St Fl 7, San Francisco
(94104-1415)
PHONE..................................415 675-1500
Greg Wilson, *Director*
EMP: 99
SALES (est): 5.3MM **Privately Held**
SIC: 3433 Solar heaters & collectors

(P-11708)
RASMUSSEN IRON WORKS INC
12028 Philadelphia St, Whittier
(90601-3925)
PHONE..................................562 696-8718
Theodore Rasmussen, *President*
Irene Rasmussen, *Vice Pres*
Rett Rasmussen, *Vice Pres*
T E Rasmussen, *Vice Pres*
Ray Vazla, *Vice Pres*
▲ EMP: 53 EST: 1907
SQ FT: 40,000
SALES (est): 10.3MM **Privately Held**
WEB: www.bbqislands.com
SIC: 3433 Logs, gas fireplace

(P-11709)
RAYPAK INC (DH)
2151 Eastman Ave, Oxnard (93030-5194)
PHONE..................................805 278-5300
Kevin McDonald, *Vice Pres*
Mike Inlow, *Acting CFO*
Brian McDonald, *Officer*
Rich Corcoran, *Vice Pres*
Bob Morgan, *General Mgr*
▲ EMP: 320
SQ FT: 250,000
SALES (est): 117.9MM **Privately Held**
WEB: www.raypak.com
SIC: 3433 Heaters, swimming pool: oil or gas
HQ: Rheem Manufacturing Company Inc
1100 Abernathy Rd # 1700
Atlanta GA 30328
770 351-3000

(P-11710)
RE TRANQUILLITY 8 LLC
300 California St Fl 7, San Francisco
(94104-1415)
PHONE..................................415 675-1500
Yumin Liu, *President*
Helen Kang Shin, *Vice Pres*
EMP: 86
SALES (est): 3.4MM
SALES (corp-wide): 3.7B **Privately Held**
SIC: 3433 Solar heaters & collectors
HQ: Recurrent Energy Development Holdings, Llc
3000 Oak Rd Ste 300
Walnut Creek CA 94597
415 675-1500

(P-11711)
RETECH SYSTEMS LLC
100 Henry Station Rd, Ukiah (95482-2116)
PHONE..................................707 462-6522
Earl Good, *President*
James Goltz, *Executive*
Parm Bassi, *Program Mgr*
Jerry Camotta, *Program Mgr*
Brian Flinn, *Program Mgr*
◆ EMP: 120
SALES (est): 51MM
SALES (corp-wide): 73.6MM **Privately Held**
WEB: www.retechsystemsllc.com
SIC: 3433 Burners, furnaces, boilers & stokers
PA: Seco Warwick S A
Ul. Sobieskiego 8
Swiebodzin 66-20
486 838-2050

(P-11712)
SCHEU MANUFACTURING CO (PA)
297 Stowell St, Upland (91786-6624)
P.O. Box 250 (91785-0250)
PHONE..................................909 982-8933
Leland C Scheu, *Ch of Bd*
Daniel N League Jr, *Shareholder*
Allyn Scheu, *President*
▲ EMP: 15
SQ FT: 7,000
SALES (est): 7.1MM **Privately Held**
SIC: 3433 Space heaters, except electric

(P-11713)
SILICON ENERGY LLC (PA)
9 Cushing Ste 200, Irvine (92618-4227)
PHONE..................................360 618-6500
Gary Shaver, *Mng Member*
▲ EMP: 18
SQ FT: 26,000

SALES (est): 2.6MM **Privately Held**
SIC: 3433 Solar heaters & collectors

(P-11714)
SMA AMERICA PRODUCTION LLC
6020 West Oaks Blvd # 300, Rocklin
(95765-5472)
PHONE..................................720 347-6000
Pierre Pascal Urbon,
Ravi Dodballapur, *Technical Staff*
Scott Ellenburg, *Analyst*
Chris Mahoney, *Sales Engr*
Laura Stetser, *Marketing Staff*
◆ EMP: 200 EST: 2009
SQ FT: 150,000
SALES (est): 80.3MM
SALES (corp-wide): 871.1MM **Privately Held**
SIC: 3433 Solar heaters & collectors
HQ: Sma Solar Technology America Llc
6020 West Oaks Blvd
Rocklin CA 95765
916 625-0870

(P-11715)
SOLAR INDUSTRIES INC
731 N Market Blvd Ste J, Sacramento
(95834-1211)
PHONE..................................916 567-9650
Kerry Bradford, *Manager*
EMP: 25
SALES (corp-wide): 87.1MM **Privately Held**
SIC: 3433 Solar heaters & collectors
PA: Solar Industries, Inc.
4940 S Alvernon Way
Tucson AZ 85706
520 790-8989

(P-11716)
SOLARRESERVE LLC (PA)
520 Broadway Fl 6, Santa Monica
(90401-2420)
PHONE..................................310 315-2200
Tom Georgis, *CEO*
Kevin Smith, *CEO*
Tim Rosenzweig, *CFO*
Alistair Jessop, *Senior VP*
Stephen Mullennix, *Senior VP*
EMP: 20
SALES (est): 6.5MM **Privately Held**
SIC: 3433 1711 4911 Solar heaters & collectors; solar energy contractor; electric services

(P-11717)
SOLARROOFSCOM INC
5840 Gibbons Dr Ste H, Carmichael
(95608-6903)
PHONE..................................916 481-7200
Albert C Rich, *President*
Susan Rich, *CEO*
Chris McKay, *Parts Mgr*
EMP: 11
SQ FT: 8,000
SALES (est): 576K **Privately Held**
WEB: www.solarroofs.com
SIC: 3433 Solar heaters & collectors

(P-11718)
SPI SOLAR INC (PA)
4677 Old Ironsides Dr, Santa Clara
(95054-1809)
PHONE..................................408 919-8000
Xiaofeng Peng, *CEO*
Stan Luboda, *Vice Pres*
EMP: 19
SALES (est): 91.6MM **Privately Held**
WEB: www.solarpowerinc.net
SIC: 3433 Solar heaters & collectors

(P-11719)
ST JOHNSON COMPANY LLC
5160 Fulton Dr, Fairfield (94534-1639)
PHONE..................................510 652-6000
Antonio De La O, *President*
Barbara Florio, *CFO*
EMP: 40
SALES (est): 5.2MM
SALES (corp-wide): 8.5MM **Privately Held**
SIC: 3433 Heating equipment, except electric

PA: Innovative Combustion Technologies
Inc
5160 Fulton Dr
Fairfield CA 94534
510 652-6000

(P-11720)
SUNEARTH INC
8425 Almeria Ave, Fontana (92335-3288)
PHONE..................................909 434-3100
Brian Gold, *CEO*
Richard R Reed, *CFO*
Adam Chrisman, *Admin Sec*
◆ EMP: 45
SQ FT: 17,000
SALES (est): 10.5MM
SALES (corp-wide): 18.5MM **Privately Held**
WEB: www.sunearthinc.com
SIC: 3433 Solar heaters & collectors
PA: The Solaray Corporation
761 Ahua St
Honolulu HI 96819
808 523-0711

(P-11721)
SUNSTREAM TECHNOLOGY INC
749 Azure Hills Dr, Simi Valley
(93065-5522)
PHONE..................................720 502-4446
John Anderson, *CEO*
Howard Wolin, *COO*
Daryl Overholt, *CFO*
EMP: 53
SALES (est): 6.3MM **Privately Held**
SIC: 3433 Solar heaters & collectors

(P-11722)
SUNTECH AMERICA INC (PA)
Also Called: Suntech Power
2721 Shattuck Ave, Berkeley (94705-1008)
PHONE..................................415 882-9922
Zhengrong Shi, *CEO*
John Lefebvre, *President*
David King, *CFO*
▲ EMP: 16
SALES (est): 2.8MM **Privately Held**
WEB: www.suntech-power.com
SIC: 3433 Solar heaters & collectors

(P-11723)
SUNWATER SOLAR INC
865 Marina Bay Pkwy # 39, Richmond
(94804-6426)
P.O. Box 688, Novato (94948-0688)
PHONE..................................650 739-5297
EMP: 12
SQ FT: 2,000
SALES (est): 1.7MM **Privately Held**
SIC: 3433

(P-11724)
WAX BOX FIRELOG CORPORATION
Also Called: Cleanflame
1791 State Highway 99, Gridley
(95948-2209)
PHONE..................................530 846-2200
Kory H Hamman, *CEO*
Howard Hamman, *CFO*
Brian Hamman, *Vice Pres*
▲ EMP: 42
SQ FT: 50,000
SALES: 3.5MM **Privately Held**
SIC: 3433 Logs, gas fireplace

(P-11725)
WISE SOLAR INC
4401 Atlantic Ave Ste 200, Long Beach
(90807-2264)
PHONE..................................888 406-7879
Andrew Thorry, *President*
Jeff Meyers, *President*
Michael Santoyo, *President*
EMP: 10
SALES (est): 1.3MM **Privately Held**
SIC: 3433 Solar heaters & collectors

▲ = Import ▼=Export
◆ =Import/Export

3441 Fabricated Structural Steel

(P-11726)
101 VERTICAL FABRICATION INC
10255 Beech Ave, Fontana (92335-6356)
PHONE...................................909 428-6000
Dustin J Nabor, *President*
Fidel J Nabor, *Ch of Bd*
Paul Kwon, *CFO*
Richard Berg, *Vice Pres*
Jim O'Shea, *Comptroller*
EMP: 27
SQ FT: 48,000
SALES: 2.4MM
SALES (corp-wide): 17.9MM **Privately Held**
WEB: www.101pipe.com
SIC: 3441 Fabricated structural metal
PA: 101 Pipe & Casing, Inc.
30300 Agoura Rd Ste 240
Agoura Hills CA 91301
818 707-9101

(P-11727)
3 D STUDIOS
800 51st Ave, Oakland (94601-5627)
PHONE...................................510 535-1809
Fax: 510 535-1534
EMP: 14
SQ FT: 5,000
SALES (est): 1.2MM **Privately Held**
WEB: www.3dstudios.net
SIC: 3441

(P-11728)
A & A FABRICATION & POLSG CORP
12031 Philadelphia St, Whittier (90601-3926)
PHONE...................................562 696-0441
Amanda Henderson, *President*
Edward Henderson, *Controller*
EMP: 16
SQ FT: 14,000
SALES: 1.8MM **Privately Held**
SIC: 3441 Fabricated structural metal

(P-11729)
A M T METAL FABRICATORS INC
211 Parr Blvd, Richmond (94801-1119)
PHONE...................................510 236-1414
Michael R Turpen, *President*
Cheryl Turpen, *CFO*
EMP: 20
SQ FT: 12,000
SALES (est): 5.5MM **Privately Held**
WEB: www.amtmetals.com
SIC: 3441 Building components, structural steel

(P-11730)
ABRAHAM STEEL FABRICATION INC
2741 Mcmillan Ave Ste B, San Luis Obispo (93401-6796)
PHONE...................................805 544-8610
David Rivas, *President*
EMP: 10
SQ FT: 7,200
SALES (est): 1.6MM **Privately Held**
WEB: www.abrahamsteel.com
SIC: 3441 3446 3713 Building components, structural steel; architectural metalwork; truck beds

(P-11731)
ABSOLUTE MACHINING
20622 Superior St Unit 4, Chatsworth (91311-4432)
PHONE...................................818 709-7367
Tim Ohanlon, *Owner*
EMP: 15 **EST:** 1996
SALES (est): 502.5K **Privately Held**
SIC: 3441 Fabricated structural metal

(P-11732)
ACCELERATED CNSTR & MET LLC
2955 Farrar Ave, Modesto (95354-4118)
PHONE...................................209 846-7998
Bruce Elliott,

Dave Raybourn,
EMP: 10 **EST:** 2013
SALES: 858.2K **Privately Held**
SIC: 3441 1622 1771 Fabricated structural metal; bridge, tunnel & elevated highway; concrete work

(P-11733)
ACCURATE METAL PRODUCTS INC
4276 Campbell St, Riverside (92509-2617)
PHONE...................................951 360-3594
Elanor Quintero, *President*
Tony Schmidt, *Admin Sec*
EMP: 15
SALES (est): 1.4MM **Privately Held**
SIC: 3441 Fabricated structural metal

(P-11734)
ADTEK INC
1460 Ellerd Dr, Turlock (95380-5749)
PHONE...................................209 634-0300
Bob Zinzenoul, *Principal*
Tom Ady, *Senior VP*
Mike Spence, *Prgrmr*
EMP: 30
SALES (est): 6.6MM **Privately Held**
SIC: 3441 Building components, structural steel

(P-11735)
ADVANCED LGS LLC
11905 Regentview Ave, Downey (90241-5515)
PHONE...................................818 652-4252
Alex Youssef, *Principal*
EMP: 12
SALES: 3MM **Privately Held**
SIC: 3441 Building components, structural steel

(P-11736)
ADVANCED METAL FORMING INC
2618 National Ave, San Diego (92113-3693)
P.O. Box 13530 (92170-3530)
PHONE...................................619 239-9437
Jacqueline Beavan, *President*
Charles Teahan, *Vice Pres*
EMP: 10 **EST:** 1966
SQ FT: 1,800
SALES (est): 1.2MM **Privately Held**
WEB: www.advancedmetalforming.com
SIC: 3441 Fabricated structural metal

(P-11737)
AEROFAB CORPORATION
4001 E Leaverton Ct, Anaheim (92807-1610)
PHONE...................................714 635-0902
Matthew Owen, *President*
George Robinson, *Vice Pres*
EMP: 17
SQ FT: 10,000
SALES: 3.5MM **Privately Held**
SIC: 3441 Fabricated structural metal

(P-11738)
AFAKORI INC
Also Called: AAF Steel Structural
29390 Hunco Way, Lake Elsinore (92530-2757)
PHONE...................................949 859-4277
Amir A Fakori, *President*
Luz Marina Agreda, *Admin Sec*
▲ **EMP:** 20
SQ FT: 15,000
SALES: 2.2MM **Privately Held**
WEB: www.afakoriwelding.com
SIC: 3441 Building components, structural steel

(P-11739)
AG MACHINING INC
609 Science Dr, Moorpark (93021-2005)
PHONE...................................805 531-9555
Angel Garcia, *President*
Bryan Garcia, *Vice Pres*
Eddie Garcia, *Vice Pres*
▲ **EMP:** 85
SQ FT: 117,000

SALES: 15.4MM **Privately Held**
WEB: www.agmachininginc.com
SIC: 3441 3444 Fabricated structural metal; sheet metalwork; metal housings, enclosures, casings & other containers; pipe, sheet metal; restaurant sheet metalwork

(P-11740)
AHLBORN STRUCTURAL STEEL INC
1230 Century Ct, Santa Rosa (95403-1042)
PHONE...................................707 573-0742
Thomas Ahlborn, *CEO*
Lance Ballenger, *Vice Pres*
Cathy Ahlborn, *Admin Sec*
EMP: 34
SALES (est): 8.3MM **Privately Held**
WEB: www.ahlbornstructural.com
SIC: 3441 Fabricated structural metal

(P-11741)
ALL WEST FABRICATORS INC
44875 Fremont Blvd, Fremont (94538-6318)
PHONE...................................510 623-1200
Gary J Lee, *President*
Keith Lee, *Vice Pres*
EMP: 40
SALES (est): 4.5MM **Privately Held**
SIC: 3441 Fabricated structural metal for bridges

(P-11742)
AMAZING STEEL COMPANY
Also Called: Mitchellamazing
4564 Mission Blvd, Montclair (91763-6106)
PHONE...................................909 590-0393
Jim Mitchell, *President*
EMP: 20
SQ FT: 25,000
SALES (est): 2.5MM **Privately Held**
SIC: 3441 7692 7699 Fabricated structural metal; welding repair; hydraulic equipment repair

(P-11743)
AMERICAN STEEL MASTERS INC
15050 Proctor Ave, City of Industry (91746-3305)
PHONE...................................626 333-3375
Jose Luis Hernandez, *President*
EMP: 21
SALES (est): 4.5MM **Privately Held**
SIC: 3441 Fabricated structural metal

(P-11744)
ASC PROFILES LLC
Also Called: AEP Span
10905 Beech Ave, Fontana (92337-7295)
PHONE...................................909 823-0401
Steve Balding, *Manager*
Renee Roman, *Sales Staff*
Janice Wheelock, *Manager*
EMP: 150
SQ FT: 71,842 **Privately Held**
WEB: www.ascpacific.com
SIC: 3441 3448 Fabricated structural metal; prefabricated metal buildings
HQ: Asc Profiles Llc
2110 Enterprise Blvd
West Sacramento CA 95691
916 376-2800

(P-11745)
ASSOCIATED REBAR INC
1095 Madison Ln, Salinas (93907-1815)
P.O. Box 10212 (93912-7212)
PHONE...................................831 758-1820
Chris Bartlebaugh, *President*
Alfredo Garcia, *Corp Secy*
EMP: 20
SQ FT: 1,500
SALES (est): 4.6MM **Privately Held**
SIC: 3441 Fabricated structural metal

(P-11746)
AZTEC TECHNOLOGY CORPORATION (PA)
Also Called: Aztec Containers
2550 S Santa Fe Ave, Vista (92084-8098)
PHONE...................................760 727-2300
Brian Hyndman, *CEO*

Michael Hyndman, *Treasurer*
Catherine Hyndman, *Vice Pres*
Theresa Gualtieri, *General Mgr*
Steven Hyndman, *Admin Sec*
EMP: 20
SQ FT: 3,000
SALES: 9.5MM **Privately Held**
WEB: www.azteccontainer.com
SIC: 3441 Fabricated structural metal

(P-11747)
BAY CITY MARINE INC (PA)
1625 Cleveland Ave, National City (91950-4212)
PHONE...................................619 477-3991
Michelle Ralph, *President*
Paul Ralph, *COO*
David Lloyd, *Treasurer*
Steve Johnston, *Vice Pres*
Fred Hays, *General Mgr*
EMP: 25
SQ FT: 11,000
SALES (est): 4.8MM **Privately Held**
WEB: www.baycitymarine.com
SIC: 3441 3731 7699 Fabricated structural metal; military ships, building & repairing; boat repair

(P-11748)
BIG VALLEY METALS
620 Houston St Ste 1, West Sacramento (95691-2255)
P.O. Box 934 (95691-0934)
PHONE...................................916 372-2383
J Robert Vela, *Owner*
EMP: 13
SALES (est): 2.1MM **Privately Held**
SIC: 3441 Fabricated structural metal

(P-11749)
BILL WILLIAMS WELDING CO
1735 Santa Fe Ave, Long Beach (90813-1292)
PHONE...................................562 432-5421
Martha Williams-Hermon, *President*
EMP: 25 **EST:** 1945
SQ FT: 30,000
SALES: 2.1MM **Privately Held**
SIC: 3441 7692 Fabricated structural metal; automotive welding

(P-11750)
BOBS IRON INC
740 Kevin Ct, Oakland (94621-4040)
PHONE...................................510 567-8983
Robert Smith, *President*
EMP: 20
SQ FT: 9,500
SALES: 2MM **Privately Held**
SIC: 3441 Fabricated structural metal

(P-11751)
BOYD CORPORATION (PA)
Also Called: Boyd Construction
5832 Ohio St, Yorba Linda (92886-5323)
P.O. Box 6012, Anaheim (92816-0012)
PHONE...................................714 533-2375
Mitch Aiello, *President*
EMP: 12 **EST:** 1980
SALES (est): 11.3MM **Privately Held**
WEB: www.boydcompanies.com
SIC: 3441 2891 Fabricated structural metal; adhesives

(P-11752)
BRUNTON ENTERPRISES INC
Also Called: Plas-Tal Manufacturing Co
8815 Sorensen Ave, Santa Fe Springs (90670-2636)
PHONE...................................562 945-0013
Sean P Brunton, *CEO*
John W Brunton Jr, *President*
John Brunton, *Vice Pres*
Patrick Scott, *Network Mgr*
Dennis Donnatin, *Project Mgr*
EMP: 125 **EST:** 1947
SQ FT: 45,000
SALES: 43.7MM **Privately Held**
WEB: www.plas-tal.com
SIC: 3441 Fabricated structural metal

(P-11753)
C A BUCHEN CORP
9231 Glenoaks Blvd, Sun Valley (91352-2688)
PHONE...................................818 767-5408

John Oster, *CEO*
Ryan Chapman, *Vice Pres*
EMP: 25
SQ FT: 22,500
SALES: 6.6MM **Privately Held**
WEB: www.cabuchen.com
SIC: 3441 1791 3312 Fabricated structural metal; structural steel erection; iron & steel: galvanized, pipes, plates, sheets, etc.

(P-11754)
C AND R SALES INC
Also Called: Kretzschmar Steel
3750 S Riverside Ave, Colton (92324-3329)
PHONE.....................951 686-6864
Tim Kretzschmar, *President*
EMP: 19
SQ FT: 1,800
SALES (est): 5.4MM **Privately Held**
SIC: 3441 Fabricated structural metal

(P-11755)
CAC FABRICATION INC
9710 Owensmouth Ave Ste C, Chatsworth (91311-8077)
PHONE.....................818 882-2626
David Agins, *President*
EMP: 12
SQ FT: 5,000
SALES: 1MM **Privately Held**
WEB: www.cacfab.com
SIC: 3441 Fabricated structural metal

(P-11756)
CALCON STEEL CONSTRUCTION
Also Called: Hamilton Iron Works
1226 W 196th St, Torrance (90502-1101)
PHONE.....................310 768-8094
Sung Nam, *President*
Hannah Nam, *Admin Sec*
EMP: 20
SQ FT: 50,000
SALES (est): 3.7MM **Privately Held**
SIC: 3441 Fabricated structural metal

(P-11757)
CALCRAFT CORPORATION
Also Called: Calcraft Company
1426 S Willow Ave, Rialto (92376-7720)
PHONE.....................909 879-2900
Daniel Steven Ensman, *President*
Dan Ensman, *Executive*
Sergio Garcia, *Principal*
EMP: 15
SQ FT: 30,000
SALES (est): 4.4MM **Privately Held**
SIC: 3441 Fabricated structural metal

(P-11758)
CAMPBELL CERTIFIED INC (PA)
1629 Ord Way, Oceanside (92056-3599)
PHONE.....................760 722-9353
Mark Anthony Campbell, *CEO*
Lauralee Campbell, *Administration*
EMP: 49
SQ FT: 45,000
SALES (est): 10MM **Privately Held**
WEB: www.campbellwelding.com
SIC: 3441 Fabricated structural metal

(P-11759)
CANYON STEEL FABRICATORS INC
8314 Sultana Ave, Fontana (92335-3265)
PHONE.....................951 683-2352
Thomas J Baggett, *President*
Ray Magnon, *Vice Pres*
Doug Magnon, *Admin Sec*
EMP: 22
SALES (est): 4.9MM **Privately Held**
SIC: 3441 Fabricated structural metal

(P-11760)
CAPITOL IRON WORKS INC
7009 Power Inn Rd, Sacramento (95828-2498)
PHONE.....................916 381-1554
Daniel D Howard, *President*
Steve Hartzell, *President*
Diana Howard, *Corp Secy*
Ruben Reyes, *Project Mgr*
EMP: 20
SQ FT: 3,000

SALES: 2.2MM **Privately Held**
WEB: www.capitolironworks.com
SIC: 3441 Fabricated structural metal

(P-11761)
CAPITOL STEEL FABRICATORS INC
3565 Greenwood Ave, Commerce (90040-3305)
PHONE.....................323 721-5460
James Moreland, *President*
Eric Jonkey, *Shareholder*
Janice Moreland, *Vice Pres*
Carol Chavez, *Office Mgr*
Justin Smith, *Production*
EMP: 25
SQ FT: 10,000
SALES (est): 6.9MM **Privately Held**
WEB: www.capitolsteel.com
SIC: 3441 Fabricated structural metal

(P-11762)
CARLYLE GLASGOW WLDG SVCS INC
4747 E State St Ste A, Ontario (91762-3924)
P.O. Box 1194, Brea (92822-1194)
PHONE.....................909 902-1814
Carlyle F Glasgow, *President*
Katrina Glasgow, *Vice Pres*
EMP: 12
SALES (est): 1.8MM **Privately Held**
WEB: www.carlylegwelding.com
SIC: 3441 Fabricated structural metal

(P-11763)
CARROLL METAL WORKS INC
740 W 16th St, National City (91950-4205)
PHONE.....................619 477-9125
Pat Carroll, *President*
EMP: 95
SQ FT: 11,500
SALES (est): 18.7MM **Privately Held**
SIC: 3441 Fabricated structural metal

(P-11764)
CENTRAL VALLEY MACHINING INC
5820 E Harvard Ave, Fresno (93727-1373)
PHONE.....................559 291-7749
Long MAI, *President*
Peter MAI, *Vice Pres*
EMP: 20
SQ FT: 5,000
SALES: 1.2MM **Privately Held**
SIC: 3441 Fabricated structural metal

(P-11765)
CH INDUSTRIAL TECHNOLOGY INC
3160 E California Ave, Fresno (93702-4108)
PHONE.....................559 485-8011
Cameron Williams, *President*
Jeremiah Burleson, *Admin Sec*
▲ **EMP:** 13
SQ FT: 17,000
SALES: 139.6K **Privately Held**
SIC: 3441 3479 Fabricated structural metal; painting of metal products

(P-11766)
CHRIS FRENCH METAL INC
2500 Union St, Oakland (94607-2462)
PHONE.....................510 238-9339
Chris French, *President*
EMP: 10
SALES (est): 2.3MM **Privately Held**
SIC: 3441 Fabricated structural metal

(P-11767)
CK STEEL INC
19826 S Alameda St, Compton (90221-6211)
PHONE.....................310 638-0855
Chin Kim, *President*
EMP: 13
SALES (est): 2.2MM **Privately Held**
SIC: 3441 Fabricated structural metal

(P-11768)
COAST AEROSPACE MFG INC
950 Richfield Rd, Placentia (92870-6732)
PHONE.....................714 893-8066
Louis Ponce, *President*

David Rodriguez, *President*
Steven Castillo, *Vice Pres*
Frank Fleck, *Vice Pres*
Emma Balibalos, *Office Mgr*
EMP: 43
SALES (est): 9.8MM **Privately Held**
WEB: www.coastaerospace.com
SIC: 3441 3544 3559 5063 Fabricated structural metal; special dies & tools; semiconductor manufacturing machinery; wire & cable; machine tool design

(P-11769)
COLUMBIA STEEL INC
2175 N Linden Ave, Rialto (92377-4445)
PHONE.....................909 874-8840
Gustavo Waldemar Theisen, *CEO*
Charmaine Helenihi, *CFO*
William Young, *Chairman*
Mike Loop, *Exec VP*
Luis Theisen, *Vice Pres*
EMP: 75 **EST:** 1975
SQ FT: 63,384
SALES (est): 35.7MM **Publicly Held**
WEB: www.columbiasteelinc.com
SIC: 3441 Building components, structural steel
PA: American Tower Corporation
116 Huntington Ave # 1100
Boston MA 02116
-

(P-11770)
COMMERCIAL SHEET METAL WORKS
Also Called: CSM Metal Fabricating & Engrg
1800 S San Pedro St, Los Angeles (90015-3711)
PHONE.....................213 748-7321
Jack L Gardener, *President*
Dave Hodges, *Sales Mgr*
Tommy Campos, *Sales Staff*
Tyler Brown, *Director*
▲ **EMP:** 27 **EST:** 1916
SQ FT: 22,000
SALES (est): 11.5MM **Privately Held**
WEB: www.csmworks.com
SIC: 3441 Fabricated structural metal

(P-11771)
COMPLETE METAL FABRICATION INC
596 E Main St, El Centro (92243-9471)
P.O. Box 1529 (92244-1529)
PHONE.....................760 353-0260
Jesse Ray Riddle, *CEO*
EMP: 19
SALES (est): 4.3MM **Privately Held**
SIC: 3441 Fabricated structural metal

(P-11772)
CONSTEEL INDUSTRIAL INC
15435 Woodcrest Dr, Whittier (90604-3236)
PHONE.....................562 806-4575
Luis Lagarica, *CEO*
Maria Torres, *CFO*
Russ Lambert, *Admin Sec*
Frankie Alamintos, *Director*
Robert Geronca, *Director*
EMP: 27
SALES: 8.2MM **Privately Held**
SIC: 3441 Fabricated structural metal

(P-11773)
CONXTECH INC
24493 Clawiter Rd, Hayward (94545-2219)
PHONE.....................510 264-9112
Nicholas Chase, *Project Mgr*
EMP: 110
SALES (corp-wide): 34.6MM **Privately Held**
SIC: 3441 Building components, structural steel
PA: Conxtech, Inc.
6701 Koll Center Pkwy
Pleasanton CA 94566
510 264-9111

(P-11774)
CONXTECH INC (PA)
6701 Koll Center Pkwy, Pleasanton (94566-8061)
PHONE.....................510 264-9111
Robert J Simmons, *President*
Mike Martini, *CFO*

Raymond G Kitasoe, *Vice Pres*
Tj Simmons, *Vice Pres*
Kelly Luttrell, *VP Bus Dvlpt*
◆ **EMP:** 40
SQ FT: 100,000
SALES (est): 34.6MM **Privately Held**
WEB: www.conxtech.com
SIC: 3441 Building components, structural steel

(P-11775)
CORCORAN SAWTELLE ROSPRIM INC
Also Called: Sawtelle & Rosprim Machine Sp
542 Otis Ave, Corcoran (93212-1823)
PHONE.....................559 992-2117
Terry Kwast, *President*
EMP: 30
SQ FT: 35,000
SALES (est): 6.8MM **Privately Held**
SIC: 3441 3599 Fabricated structural metal; machine shop, jobbing & repair

(P-11776)
COVINA WELDING & SHTMTL INC
473 E Front St, Covina (91723-1205)
P.O. Box 5039 (91723-5039)
PHONE.....................626 332-6293
Larry Evans, *President*
Miguel A Ayala, *Vice Pres*
EMP: 17 **EST:** 1944
SQ FT: 13,000
SALES (est): 2.7MM **Privately Held**
SIC: 3441 Fabricated structural metal

(P-11777)
CUSTOM SOURCE DESIGN INC
15642 Dupont Ave Ste A, Chino (91710-7616)
PHONE.....................909 597-5221
Christopher Montoya, *President*
▲ **EMP:** 12 **EST:** 2014
SALES: 2MM **Privately Held**
SIC: 3441 Fabricated structural metal

(P-11778)
CUSTOM STEEL FABRICATION INC
Also Called: C & J Industries
11966 Rivera Rd, Santa Fe Springs (90670-2232)
PHONE.....................562 907-2777
John Toscano, *President*
Carole Toscano, *CEO*
EMP: 17
SQ FT: 3,400
SALES (est): 2.6MM **Privately Held**
SIC: 3441 Fabricated structural metal

(P-11779)
CW INDUSTRIES
1735 Santa Fe Ave, Long Beach (90813-1242)
PHONE.....................562 432-5421
Craig Wildvank, *Principal*
EMP: 12
SALES (est): 2MM **Privately Held**
SIC: 3441 3548 5084 Building components, structural steel; welding apparatus; oil refining machinery, equipment & supplies

(P-11780)
D & M STEEL INC
13020 Pierce St, Pacoima (91331-2528)
PHONE.....................818 896-2070
Michael Atia, *President*
David Dagni, *Vice Pres*
EMP: 37
SQ FT: 16,500
SALES (est): 9.6MM **Privately Held**
SIC: 3441 Fabricated structural metal

(P-11781)
D D WIRE CO INC (PA)
4335 Temple City Blvd, Temple City (91780-4229)
PHONE.....................626 442-0459
Wes Berry, *President*
James Howe, *COO*
David Berry, *CFO*
Dorsey Wire, *Principal*
Elizabeth D Berry, *Admin Sec*
EMP: 22

▲ = Import ▼=Export
◆ =Import/Export

SQ FT: 24,000
SALES (est): 4.6MM **Privately Held**
WEB: www.ddwire.com
SIC: 3441 3469 Fabricated structural metal; stamping metal for the trade

(P-11782)
D D WIRE CO INC
4942 Encinita Ave, Temple City (91780-3705)
PHONE..........................626 285-0298
Wesley Berry, *Manager*
Dorsey Wire, *Owner*
EMP: 15
SALES (corp-wide): 4.6MM **Privately Held**
WEB: www.ddwire.com
SIC: 3441 3469 Fabricated structural metal; metal stampings
PA: D. D. Wire Co., Inc.
4335 Temple City Blvd
Temple City CA 91780
626 442-0459

(P-11783)
DAVISON IRON WORKS INC
8845 Elder Creek Rd Ste A, Sacramento (95828-1835)
PHONE..........................916 381-2121
Andrew Peszynski, *President*
Candy Holland, *Vice Pres*
EMP: 50
SQ FT: 3,500
SALES (est): 12.7MM **Privately Held**
WEB: www.davisoniron.com
SIC: 3441 Fabricated structural metal

(P-11784)
DELTA REBAR SERVICES INC
2410 Bates Ave, Concord (94520-1206)
PHONE..........................925 798-4220
Dan Yust, *President*
EMP: 12
SQ FT: 700
SALES (est): 2.1MM **Privately Held**
SIC: 3441 Fabricated structural metal

(P-11785)
DIVERSIFIED HANGAR COMPANY
5905 Monterey Rd, Paso Robles (93446-7670)
PHONE..........................805 239-8229
Bryan Watson, *Owner*
EMP: 10
SQ FT: 10,000
SALES (est): 640K **Privately Held**
SIC: 3441 Building components, structural steel

(P-11786)
DONALD H BINKLEY
Also Called: D & D Engineering
2901 Commerce Way, Turlock (95380-9471)
PHONE..........................209 664-9792
Donald H Binkley, *Owner*
EMP: 17
SALES (est): 2.3MM **Privately Held**
SIC: 3441 3599 Fabricated structural metal; machine shop, jobbing & repair

(P-11787)
EAGLE IRON FABRICATION INC
Also Called: Eagle Iron Works
100 Medburn St Ste A, Concord (94520-1123)
PHONE..........................925 686-9510
Vic Griffith, *Partner*
Jim Pola, *Vice Pres*
EMP: 10
SQ FT: 5,500
SALES (est): 1.4MM **Privately Held**
WEB: www.eagleironworks.net
SIC: 3441 Fabricated structural metal

(P-11788)
EMERALD STEEL INC
727 66th Ave, Oakland (94621-3713)
PHONE..........................510 553-1386
Brian Earley, *President*
Tricia Lawson, *Manager*
EMP: 10
SALES (est): 2.4MM **Privately Held**
SIC: 3441 Fabricated structural metal

(P-11789)
EW CORPRTION INDUS FABRICATORS (PA)
1002 E Main St, El Centro (92243)
P.O. Box 2189 (92244-2189)
PHONE..........................760 337-0020
Tiberio R Esparza, *President*
◆ **EMP:** 80 **EST:** 1973
SQ FT: 100,000
SALES (est): 12.3MM **Privately Held**
WEB: www.ewcorporation.com
SIC: 3441 Fabricated structural metal

(P-11790)
FABCO STEEL FABRICATION INC
14688 San Bernardino Ave, Fontana (92335-5319)
P.O. Box 8636, Alta Loma (91701-0636)
PHONE..........................909 350-1535
John E Schick, *President*
Rich Schick, *CFO*
Doug Schick, *Vice Pres*
EMP: 35 **EST:** 1979
SQ FT: 30,000
SALES (est): 11MM **Privately Held**
WEB: www.fabcosteel.com
SIC: 3441 Fabricated structural metal

(P-11791)
FABRICATION TECH INDS INC
2200 Haffley Ave, National City (91950-6418)
P.O. Box 1447 (91951-1447)
PHONE..........................619 477-4141
Joey Houshar, *Ch of Bd*
Martha Houshar, *Admin Sec*
▲ **EMP:** 75
SQ FT: 50,000
SALES (est): 19.4MM **Privately Held**
WEB: www.ftisd.com
SIC: 3441 Fabricated structural metal

(P-11792)
FALCON IRON
775 Wakefield Ct, Oakdale (95361-7761)
PHONE..........................209 845-8229
Bruce Leverett, *Owner*
EMP: 10
SALES (est): 1.7MM **Privately Held**
SIC: 3441 Fabricated structural metal

(P-11793)
FERROSAUR INC
Also Called: Industrial Welding
4821 Mountain Lakes Blvd, Redding (96003-1454)
PHONE..........................530 246-7843
Thomas Largent, *Vice Pres*
Thomas R Largent, *CEO*
EMP: 13
SQ FT: 33,000
SALES (est): 3.1MM **Privately Held**
SIC: 3441 7692 2298 5932 Fabricated structural metal; welding repair; rope, except asbestos & wire; building materials, secondhand

(P-11794)
FIFE METAL FABRICATING INC
4191 Eastside Rd, Redding (96001-3884)
PHONE..........................530 243-4696
Doyle Fife Jr, *President*
Joanne Fife, *Corp Secy*
EMP: 17 **EST:** 1965
SQ FT: 10,000
SALES (est): 3.7MM **Privately Held**
SIC: 3441 3446 Building components, structural steel; architectural metalwork

(P-11795)
FLORIAN INDUSTRIES INC
151 Industrial Way, Brisbane (94005-1003)
PHONE..........................415 330-9000
Chuck Lutz, *President*
EMP: 15
SQ FT: 2,000
SALES: 2MM **Privately Held**
SIC: 3441 Fabricated structural metal

(P-11796)
FOSS MARITIME COMPANY
49 W Pier D St, Long Beach (90802)
PHONE..........................562 437-6098
Wendall Koi, *Principal*

EMP: 10
SALES (corp-wide): 1.9B **Privately Held**
SIC: 3441 Boat & barge sections, prefabricated metal
HQ: Foss Maritime Company, Llc.
450 Alaskan Way S Ste 706
Seattle WA 98104
206 281-3800

(P-11797)
FREEBERG INDUS FBRICATION CORP
2874 Progress Pl, Escondido (92029-1516)
PHONE..........................760 737-7614
Marc Brown, *President*
James R St John, *CEO*
EMP: 85
SQ FT: 128,000
SALES (est): 22.9MM **Privately Held**
WEB: www.freeberg.com
SIC: 3441 3444 Fabricated structural metal; sheet metalwork

(P-11798)
FRESNO FAB-TECH INC
1035 K St, Sanger (93657-3383)
PHONE..........................559 875-9800
Chris Kisling, *President*
EMP: 40
SQ FT: 35,000
SALES (est): 10.7MM **Privately Held**
SIC: 3441 Fabricated structural metal

(P-11799)
G2 METAL FAB
6954 Preston Ave, Livermore (94551-9545)
PHONE..........................925 443-7903
Orlando Gutierrez, *President*
Nohora Gutierrez, *Vice Pres*
EMP: 24 **EST:** 2007
SALES (est): 9.1MM **Privately Held**
SIC: 3441 Fabricated structural metal

(P-11800)
GAMMELL INDUSTRIES INC
7535 Jackson St, Paramount (90723-4909)
PHONE..........................562 634-6653
James Ruffner, *President*
Roy Gammell, *Vice Pres*
EMP: 10
SQ FT: 13,000
SALES (est): 968K **Privately Held**
SIC: 3441 Fabricated structural metal

(P-11801)
GAYLE MANUFACTURING CO INC (PA)
1455 E Kentucky Ave, Woodland (95776-6121)
P.O. Box 1365 (95776-1365)
PHONE..........................530 662-0284
Gary Glenn, *President*
James Deblasio, *CFO*
David Deblasio, *Vice Pres*
Christopher Mahler, *Vice Pres*
Nelson Vieira, *Vice Pres*
EMP: 142
SQ FT: 72,000
SALES (est): 82.7MM **Privately Held**
SIC: 3441 Fabricated structural metal

(P-11802)
GENERAL STEEL FABRICATORS INC
12179 Branford St Ste B, Sun Valley (91352-5733)
PHONE..........................818 897-1300
Mehrad Maleki, *President*
EMP: 15
SALES (est): 555.1K **Privately Held**
SIC: 3441 Fabricated structural metal

(P-11803)
GERLINGER FNDRY MCH WORKS INC (PA)
1527 Sacramento St, Redding (96001-1914)
P.O. Box 992195 (96099-2195)
PHONE..........................530 243-1053
Fred Gerlinger, *CEO*
Jo Gerlinger, *CFO*
Tim Gerlinger, *Vice Pres*
EMP: 55
SQ FT: 45,000

SALES (est): 22.4MM **Privately Held**
WEB: www.gerlinger.com
SIC: 3441 3494 7692 5051 Fabricated structural metal; valves & pipe fittings; welding repair; steel

(P-11804)
GLAZIER STEEL INC
650 Sandoval Way, Hayward (94544-7129)
PHONE..........................510 471-5300
Craig Glazier, *CEO*
Harold Glazier, *President*
Austin Nunez, *Project Mgr*
EMP: 75 **EST:** 1982
SQ FT: 26,897
SALES (est): 24.4MM **Privately Held**
SIC: 3441 Fabricated structural metal

(P-11805)
GOLDEN STATE STEEL & STAIR INC (PA)
479 Mason St, Vacaville (95688-4540)
P.O. Box 5203 (95696-5203)
PHONE..........................707 455-0400
Joan Baker, *President*
Fred Baker, *CFO*
EMP: 20
SQ FT: 3,500
SALES (est): 4.7MM **Privately Held**
WEB: www.gsssinc.com
SIC: 3441 Fabricated structural metal

(P-11806)
GRATING PACIFIC INC (PA)
3651 Sausalito St, Los Alamitos (90720-2436)
PHONE..........................562 598-4314
Ronald S Robertson, *President*
Jeffrey Robertson, *Vice Pres*
Stacy Henry, *Office Mgr*
David Scheuerlein, *Sales Mgr*
▲ **EMP:** 20
SQ FT: 40,000
SALES (est): 20.8MM **Privately Held**
SIC: 3441 3446 Fabricated structural metal; architectural metalwork

(P-11807)
HERRICK CORPORATION (PA)
Also Called: San Bernandina Steel
3003 E Hammer Ln, Stockton (95212-2801)
P.O. Box 8429 (95208-0429)
PHONE..........................209 956-4751
David H Dornsife, *CEO*
Doug Griffin, *President*
Peter Abila, *CFO*
Richard Gonsalves, *Project Mgr*
Troy Cox, *Controller*
▲ **EMP:** 50
SALES (est): 221.8MM **Privately Held**
SIC: 3441 Fabricated structural metal

(P-11808)
HITECH METAL FABRICATION CORP
Also Called: H M F
1705 S Claudina Way, Anaheim (92805-6544)
PHONE..........................714 635-3505
Ba V Nguyen, *President*
Matthew Vu, *Vice Pres*
Lucia Coronel, *Admin Mgr*
Norman Pham, *Purch Agent*
EMP: 60
SQ FT: 42,850
SALES (est): 13.6MM **Privately Held**
SIC: 3441 Fabricated structural metal

(P-11809)
HOMESTEAD SHEET METAL
9031 Memory Ln, Spring Valley (91977-2152)
PHONE..........................619 469-4373
George Tomlanovich, *President*
Chuck Highfill, *Corp Secy*
EMP: 20
SQ FT: 5,625
SALES (est): 4.8MM **Privately Held**
WEB: www.homesteadsheetmetal.com
SIC: 3441 Fabricated structural metal

(P-11810)
INDUSTRIAL MACHINE & MFG CO
Also Called: Immco
2626 Seaman Ave, El Monte (91733-1930)
PHONE..................................626 444-0181
Diane Teresa, *President*
Ron Teresa, *Corp Secy*
David Teresa, *Vice Pres*
Mark Teresa, *Vice Pres*
EMP: 15 EST: 1959
SQ FT: 5,500
SALES (est): 866.3K **Privately Held**
WEB: www.immcohandtrucks.com
SIC: 3441 3569 3537 Fabricated structural metal; assembly machines, non-metalworking; industrial trucks & tractors

(P-11811)
INNOVATION ALLEY LLC
5473 E Hedges Ave, Fresno (93727-2252)
PHONE..................................559 453-6974
Donald Ripley, *President*
EMP: 12
SALES: 1.5MM **Privately Held**
SIC: 3441 Fabricated structural metal

(P-11812)
INTEGRAL ENGRG FABRICATION INC
520 Hofgaarden St, City of Industry (91744-5529)
PHONE..................................626 369-0958
John Zheng, *CEO*
Son T Nguyen, *Admin Sec*
EMP: 25
SQ FT: 20,000
SALES (est): 5.3MM **Privately Held**
WEB: www.integral-ef.com
SIC: 3441 Fabricated structural metal

(P-11813)
IRON DOG FABRICATION INC
3450 Regional Pkwy Ste E, Santa Rosa (95403-8247)
PHONE..................................707 579-7831
Duncan Woods, *President*
Cynthia Woods, *Corp Secy*
EMP: 17
SQ FT: 18,000
SALES (est): 4.3MM **Privately Held**
SIC: 3441 7692 1791 Building components, structural steel; welding repair; structural steel erection

(P-11814)
J AND D STL FBRICATION REPR LP
2360 Westgate Rd, Santa Maria (93455-1046)
P.O. Box 5487 (93456-5487)
PHONE..................................805 928-9674
Joe Trevino, *Partner*
David Cox, *Partner*
Yvonne Miller, *Manager*
EMP: 17
SQ FT: 12,500
SALES: 185.3K **Privately Held**
SIC: 3441 Fabricated structural metal

(P-11815)
JAANN INC
225 W 15th St, National City (91950-4407)
PHONE..................................619 336-0584
Jesus Lavin, *President*
EMP: 10
SALES (est): 1MM **Privately Held**
SIC: 3441 Fabricated structural metal

(P-11816)
JAMAC STEEL INC
533 E Belmont St, Ontario (91761-3352)
P.O. Box 3877 (91761-0983)
PHONE..................................909 983-7592
William J McKernan, *CEO*
Maggie Mc Kernan, *Vice Pres*
EMP: 24
SALES (est): 6.2MM **Privately Held**
SIC: 3441 Fabricated structural metal

(P-11817)
JC METAL SPECIALISTS INC
238 Michelle Ct, South San Francisco (94080-6201)
PHONE..................................650 827-1618

Jeffrey Chan, *Branch Mgr*
EMP: 11
SALES (corp-wide): 4.2MM **Privately Held**
SIC: 3441 Building components, structural steel
PA: J.C. Metal Specialists, Inc.
220 Michelle Ct
San Francisco CA 94124
415 822-3878

(P-11818)
JC METAL SPECIALISTS INC (PA)
220 Michelle Ct, San Francisco (94124)
PHONE..................................415 822-3878
Judy Chan, *President*
Jeffrey Chan, *CFO*
Kent Ouyang, *CFO*
EMP: 20
SQ FT: 7,500
SALES (est): 4.2MM **Privately Held**
SIC: 3441 Building components, structural steel

(P-11819)
JCI METAL PRODUCTS (PA)
6540 Federal Blvd, Lemon Grove (91945-1311)
PHONE..................................619 229-8206
Marcel Becker, *CEO*
Mark Withers, *President*
Lorey Topham, *CFO*
Rich Bartlett, *Vice Pres*
Jeremy Vaughan, *CIO*
EMP: 57
SQ FT: 21,000
SALES (est): 9.2MM **Privately Held**
SIC: 3441 1761 Fabricated structural metal for ships; architectural sheet metal work

(P-11820)
JLP MANUFACTURING INC
5609 Arrow Hwy Ste D, Montclair (91763-1677)
PHONE..................................909 931-7797
John L Parry, *President*
EMP: 12 EST: 2008
SALES (est): 1.9MM **Privately Held**
SIC: 3441 Fabricated structural metal

(P-11821)
JOHASEE REBAR INC
18059 Rosedale Hwy, Bakersfield (93314-8684)
PHONE..................................661 589-0972
Mike Hill Sr, *CEO*
Michael Hill Jr, *COO*
Tamara L Chapman, *CFO*
Hill Michael, *Vice Pres*
Joe Harrison, *Director*
EMP: 47
SALES (est): 18.2MM
SALES (corp-wide): 3.4MM **Privately Held**
WEB: www.johaseerebar.com
SIC: 3441 1791 Fabricated structural metal; concrete reinforcement, placing of
PA: Lms Holdings (Ab) Ltd
7452 132 St
Surrey BC V3W 4
604 598-9930

(P-11822)
K SHORT INC
126 W Walnut Ave, Monrovia (91016-3444)
PHONE..................................626 358-8511
Karl G Short, *President*
Margaret Short, *Vice Pres*
EMP: 10
SQ FT: 11,000
SALES (est): 1.5MM **Privately Held**
SIC: 3441 Fabricated structural metal

(P-11823)
KASCO FAB INC
4529 S Chestnut Ave Lowr, Fresno (93725-9244)
PHONE..................................559 442-1018
Hidemi Kimura, *CEO*
Ken Kimura, *Vice Pres*
EMP: 75
SQ FT: 200,000

SALES (est): 14.5MM **Privately Held**
SIC: 3441 3449 Building components, structural steel; miscellaneous metalwork

(P-11824)
KC METAL PRODUCTS INC (PA)
Also Called: Kc Metals
1960 Hartog Dr, San Jose (95131-2212)
PHONE..................................408 436-8754
Robert J Daugherty, *President*
Sandra Daugherty, *Admin Sec*
EMP: 72
SQ FT: 60,000
SALES (est): 11.2MM **Privately Held**
WEB: www.kcmetals.com
SIC: 3441 3429 Fabricated structural metal; manufactured hardware (general)

(P-11825)
KSU CORPORATION
3 Emmy Ln, Ladera Ranch (92694-1521)
PHONE..................................951 409-7055
Luz Marina Agreda, *CEO*
EMP: 15
SALES (est): 688.2K **Privately Held**
SIC: 3441 Building components, structural steel

(P-11826)
LEES IMPERIAL WELDING INC
3300 Edison Way, Fremont (94538-6150)
PHONE..................................510 657-4900
Gary Lee, *CEO*
Keith Lee, *Vice Pres*
EMP: 150
SQ FT: 59,000
SALES (est): 43MM **Privately Held**
SIC: 3441 Fabricated structural metal

(P-11827)
LEEWAY IRON WORKS INC
565 Estabrook St, San Leandro (94577-3511)
PHONE..................................510 357-8637
John Louis, *President*
Audrey Louis, *Office Mgr*
EMP: 10 EST: 1963
SQ FT: 5,200
SALES (est): 798.6K **Privately Held**
SIC: 3441 1799 Fabricated structural metal; ornamental metal work

(P-11828)
LEHMANS MANUFACTURING CO INC
4960 E Jensen Ave, Fresno (93725-1897)
PHONE..................................559 486-1700
Adam Lehman Jr, *Ch of Bd*
Kenneth Lehman, *President*
Joyce Lehman, *Corp Secy*
Sharon Ramirez, *Office Mgr*
EMP: 15 EST: 1946
SQ FT: 36,000
SALES (est): 4.3MM **Privately Held**
WEB: www.lehmansmfg.com
SIC: 3441 Fabricated structural metal

(P-11829)
LEVEL 23 FAB
2117 S Anne St, Santa Ana (92704-4408)
PHONE..................................714 979-2323
EMP: 15
SALES (est): 3MM **Privately Held**
SIC: 3441 Fabricated structural metal

(P-11830)
M AND M STAMPING CORP
13821 Oaks Ave, Chino (91710-7009)
PHONE..................................909 590-2704
Juan Uribe Sr, *President*
Juan Uribe Jr, *Vice Pres*
EMP: 15
SQ FT: 8,000
SALES: 2MM **Privately Held**
SIC: 3441 3444 Fabricated structural metal; sheet metalwork

(P-11831)
M W REID WELDING INC
Also Called: South Bay Welding
781 Oconner St, El Cajon (92020-1644)
PHONE..................................619 401-5880
Bruce A Reid, *President*
Susan Reid, *Corp Secy*
Timothy Fair, *Vice Pres*
Timothy Hill, *Vice Pres*

EMP: 78 EST: 1965
SQ FT: 25,000
SALES: 16.3MM **Privately Held**
WEB: www.southbaywelding.com
SIC: 3441 Fabricated structural metal

(P-11832)
MADISON INC OF OKLAHOMA
18000 Studebaker Rd, Cerritos (90703-2679)
PHONE..................................918 224-6990
John Samuel Frey, *President*
Barbara Cruncleton, *Corp Secy*
Robert E Hansen, *Vice Pres*
EMP: 67 EST: 1946
SALES (est): 23.8MM
SALES (corp-wide): 129.4MM **Privately Held**
SIC: 3441 1541 3448 3444 Fabricated structural metal; prefabricated building erection, industrial; prefabricated metal buildings; sheet metalwork
PA: John S. Frey Enterprises
1900 E 64th St
Los Angeles CA 90001
323 583-4061

(P-11833)
MADISON INDUSTRIES INC ARIZONA
18000 Studebaker Rd # 305, Cerritos (90703-2679)
PHONE..................................602 252-3083
John S Frey, *President*
Barbara A Cruncleton, *Corp Secy*
Robert E Hanson, *Vice Pres*
EMP: 20 EST: 1947
SQ FT: 4,000
SALES (est): 4.5MM
SALES (corp-wide): 129.4MM **Privately Held**
SIC: 3441 3448 Building components, structural steel; prefabricated metal buildings
PA: John S. Frey Enterprises
1900 E 64th St
Los Angeles CA 90001
323 583-4061

(P-11834)
MADRUGA IRON WORKS INC
305 Gandy Dancer Dr, Tracy (95377-9083)
PHONE..................................209 832-7003
Joseph Raymond Madruga, *CEO*
Elizabeth Betsy Madruga, *President*
Raymond M Madruga, *President*
Betsy M Weber, *Vice Pres*
EMP: 45
SQ FT: 50,000
SALES (est): 18.8MM **Privately Held**
WEB: www.madrugaironworks.com
SIC: 3441 3599 Fabricated structural metal; machine shop, jobbing & repair

(P-11835)
MAH KUO
Also Called: Ksm Structural Steel
377 El Dorado Dr, Daly City (94015-2124)
PHONE..................................805 766-2309
Kuo Mah, *Owner*
EMP: 11
SALES (est): 1.7MM **Privately Held**
SIC: 3441 Fabricated structural metal

(P-11836)
MANCIAS STEEL COMPANY INC
519 Horning St, San Jose (95112-2913)
PHONE..................................408 295-5096
Lupe Mancias Jr, *President*
Rick Mancias, *Vice Pres*
Elizabeth Frausto, *Technology*
EMP: 12
SQ FT: 12,000
SALES (est): 2MM **Privately Held**
WEB: www.manciassteel.com
SIC: 3441 Fabricated structural metal

(P-11837)
MARIN MANUFACTURING INC
195 Mill St, San Rafael (94901-4020)
PHONE..................................415 453-1825
Daniel G Seright, *President*
Richard A Simanek, *Corp Secy*
EMP: 12
SQ FT: 12,000

▲ = Import ▼=Export
◆ =Import/Export

SALES: 199.9K **Privately Held**
SIC: 3441 3599 7692 Building components, structural steel; machine shop, jobbing & repair; welding repair

(P-11838)
MAYA STEELS FABRICATION INC
301 E Compton Blvd, Gardena (90248-2015)
PHONE..................................310 532-8830
Meir Amsalam, *CEO*
Yechiel Yogev, *CEO*
Yogev Yechiel, *Treasurer*
Sara Haddad, *Vice Pres*
Angie Martires, *Human Res Mgr*
EMP: 64 **EST:** 1982
SQ FT: 65,000
SALES (est): 26.6MM **Privately Held**
WEB: www.mayasteel.com
SIC: 3441 Building components, structural steel

(P-11839)
MCCAIN MANUFACTURING INC
2633 Progress St, Vista (92081-8402)
PHONE..................................760 295-9290
Jeffrey Lynn McCain, *CEO*
EMP: 61
SALES (est): 60.4K **Privately Held**
SIC: 3441 Fabricated structural metal

(P-11840)
MCWHIRTER STEEL INC
42211 7th St E, Lancaster (93535-5400)
PHONE..................................661 951-8998
David McWhirter, *President*
Angela McWhirter, *CFO*
Nathan McWhirter, *Director*
EMP: 15
SQ FT: 21,000
SALES: 4MM **Privately Held**
WEB: www.dandddweldinginc.com
SIC: 3441 1791 Fabricated structural metal; structural steel erection; iron work, structural

(P-11841)
METAL FABRICATION AND ART LLC
3499 E 15th St, Los Angeles (90023-3833)
PHONE..................................323 980-9595
Landon Ryan, *President*
EMP: 10
SALES (est): 2.3MM **Privately Held**
SIC: 3441 Fabricated structural metal

(P-11842)
METAL SUPPLY LLC
11810 Center St, South Gate (90280-7832)
PHONE..................................562 634-9940
Dion Genchi, *President*
Bruce E Hubert, *Owner*
Nicole Hefner, *President*
Deann Jenki, *General Mgr*
Barbara Hubert, *Admin Sec*
▼ **EMP:** 63
SQ FT: 50,000
SALES (est): 9.6MM **Privately Held**
WEB: www.metalsupply.com
SIC: 3441 5051 Fabricated structural metal; iron & steel (ferrous) products; aluminum bars, rods, ingots, sheets, pipes, plates, etc.

(P-11843)
METALS USA BUILDING PDTS LP
6450a Caballero Blvd, Buena Park (90620-1128)
PHONE..................................714 522-7852
Tom Bush, *Branch Mgr*
EMP: 70
SALES (corp-wide): 11.5B **Publicly Held**
WEB: www.gerardusa.com
SIC: 3441 3444 Fabricated structural metal; sheet metalwork
HQ: Metals Usa Building Products Lp
955 Columbia St
Brea CA 92821
713 946-9000

(P-11844)
METALSET INC
1200 Hensley St, Richmond (94801-1900)
PHONE..................................510 233-9998
Wesley Sillineri, *Principal*
Wes Sillineri, *President*
Shaun McMahon, *Project Mgr*
Dave Alvarez, *Mfg Staff*
Chris Peacock, *Director*
EMP: 22
SALES (est): 6.1MM **Privately Held**
SIC: 3441 Fabricated structural metal

(P-11845)
MILLERS FAB & WELD CORP
6100 Industrial Ave, Riverside (92504-1120)
PHONE..................................951 359-3100
James Miller, *President*
EMP: 21 **EST:** 1964
SQ FT: 2,100
SALES: 2.5MM **Privately Held**
SIC: 3441 Fabricated structural metal

(P-11846)
MITCHELL FABRICATION
Also Called: Amazing Steel
4564 Mission Blvd, Montclair (91763-6106)
PHONE..................................909 590-0393
Jim Mitchell, *President*
▲ **EMP:** 30
SQ FT: 35,000
SALES (est): 7.1MM **Privately Held**
SIC: 3441 Fabricated structural metal

(P-11847)
MJM EXPERT PIPE FBRCATION WLDG
3404 Wrenwood St, Bakersfield (93309-9331)
PHONE..................................661 330-8698
Michael J Martin, *Owner*
EMP: 20
SALES: 500K **Privately Held**
SIC: 3441 Fabricated structural metal

(P-11848)
MONSTER ROUTE INC
3559 Haven Ave Ste A, Menlo Park (94025-1009)
PHONE..................................650 368-1628
SAI M Chiang, *President*
▲ **EMP:** 12
SQ FT: 2,500
SALES (est): 3.1MM **Privately Held**
SIC: 3441 Fabricated structural metal

(P-11849)
MONTEREY BAY REBAR INC (PA)
547 Airport Blvd, Watsonville (95076-2003)
PHONE..................................831 724-3013
Raoul Ortiz, *President*
Enrique Regalado, *Office Mgr*
EMP: 13 **EST:** 2000
SALES: 2MM **Privately Held**
SIC: 3441 Fabricated structural metal

(P-11850)
MUHLHAUSER ENTERPRISES INC (PA)
Also Called: Muhlhauser Steel
25825 Adams Ave, Murrieta (92562-0601)
P.O. Box 159, Bloomington (92316-0159)
PHONE..................................909 877-2792
William C Muhlhauser, *President*
Gisela Muhlhauser, *Corp Secy*
EMP: 30 **EST:** 1961
SALES (est): 6MM **Privately Held**
SIC: 3441 1791 Building components, structural steel; structural steel erection

(P-11851)
MUHLHAUSER STEEL INC
25825 Adams Ave, Murrieta (92562-0601)
P.O. Box 159, Bloomington (92316-0159)
PHONE..................................909 877-2792
William Muhlhauser, *President*
Zigfried Muhlhauser, *Senior VP*
EMP: 20
SALES (est): 2MM
SALES (corp-wide): 6MM **Privately Held**
WEB: www.msisteel.com
SIC: 3441 1791 Building components, structural steel; structural steel erection

PA: Muhlhauser Enterprises, Inc.
25825 Adams Ave
Murrieta CA 92562
909 877-2792

(P-11852)
MYWI FABRICATORS INC
2115-2119 Edwards Ave, South El Monte (91733)
PHONE..................................626 279-6994
Henry Yue, *President*
Jeanne Yue, *Admin Sec*
EMP: 18
SQ FT: 5,000
SALES (est): 4.1MM **Privately Held**
WEB: www.mywifabricators.com
SIC: 3441 Fabricated structural metal

(P-11853)
NATIONAL METAL FABRICATORS
28435 Century St, Hayward (94545-4862)
P.O. Box 56478 (94545-6478)
PHONE..................................510 887-6231
Steven L Kint, *CEO*
Gayle Kint, *Treasurer*
Mark Nickles, *Vice Pres*
Mike Wieber, *Vice Pres*
EMP: 25
SQ FT: 26,000
SALES (est): 5.5MM **Privately Held**
WEB: www.nationalmetalfabricators.com
SIC: 3441 Fabricated structural metal

(P-11854)
OC WATERJET
2280 N Batavia St, Orange (92865-3106)
PHONE..................................714 685-0851
David Gaulke, *Principal*
EMP: 10
SALES (est): 570K **Privately Held**
SIC: 3441 Boat & barge sections, prefabricated metal

(P-11855)
OLSON AND CO STEEL
3488 W Ashlan Ave, Fresno (93722-4443)
PHONE..................................559 224-7811
Del Stephens, *Branch Mgr*
Robert Moretti, *Chief Engr*
Steve Rivera, *Safety Mgr*
Henry Mendez, *Sr Project Mgr*
EMP: 100
SALES (est): 16.4MM
SALES (corp-wide): 68.4MM **Privately Held**
WEB: www.olsonsteel.com
SIC: 3441 3446 Building components, structural steel; architectural metalwork
PA: Olson And Co. Steel
1941 Davis St
San Leandro CA 94577
510 489-4680

(P-11856)
P S R IRON WORKS
Also Called: Republic Iron Works
10819 Michael Hunt Dr, El Monte (91733-3423)
P.O. Box 3251 (91733-0251)
PHONE..................................626 442-3360
Eric P Robles, *CEO*
EMP: 10 **EST:** 1937
SQ FT: 30,000
SALES (est): 1.2MM **Privately Held**
SIC: 3441 Fabricated structural metal

(P-11857)
PACIFIC COAST FABRICATORS INC
14375 Telephone Ave, Chino (91710-5777)
PHONE..................................909 627-3833
Michael Scheck, *President*
Anthony Caruso, *Admin Sec*
EMP: 10
SALES (est): 744.5K **Privately Held**
SIC: 3441 Fabricated structural metal

(P-11858)
PACIFIC COAST IRONWORKS INC
8831 Miner St, Los Angeles (90002-1835)
PHONE..................................323 585-1320
Andrew Larkin Jr, *President*
Ron David, *Treasurer*

Max Gonzalez, *Vice Pres*
Mike Larkin, *Vice Pres*
EMP: 15
SQ FT: 22,000
SALES (est): 3.3MM **Privately Held**
SIC: 3441 Fabricated structural metal

(P-11859)
PACIFIC MARITIME INDS CORP
Also Called: P M I
1790 Dornoch Ct, San Diego (92154-7206)
PHONE..................................619 575-8141
John Atkinson, *CEO*
Elvia Andrade, *General Mgr*
Phu Vu, *Engineer*
Heydi Herrera, *Assistant*
▲ **EMP:** 110 **EST:** 1995
SQ FT: 38,000
SALES (est): 37.9MM **Privately Held**
WEB: www.pacmaritime.com
SIC: 3441 Fabricated structural metal

(P-11860)
PACIFIC STEEL FABRICATORS INC
8275 San Leandro St, Oakland (94621-1901)
PHONE..................................209 464-9474
Andres Estrada, *President*
Alfonso Beas, *Vice Pres*
Miguel Beas, *Vice Pres*
Oscar Ortiz, *Vice Pres*
EMP: 36
SQ FT: 80,000
SALES: 4MM **Privately Held**
SIC: 3441 Building components, structural steel

(P-11861)
PARAMOUNT ROLL FORMING CO INC
12120 Florence Ave, Santa Fe Springs (90670-4434)
PHONE..................................562 944-6151
Kenneth Moscrip, *Ch of Bd*
Myrtle Moscrip, *Corp Secy*
▲ **EMP:** 23
SQ FT: 15,000
SALES (est): 5.4MM **Privately Held**
WEB: www.paramount-roll.com
SIC: 3441 Fabricated structural metal

(P-11862)
PARK STEEL CO INC
515 E Pine St, Compton (90222-2817)
P.O. Box 4787 (90224-4787)
PHONE..................................310 638-6101
Gregory M Park, *President*
Sally O Park, *Treasurer*
Randy Park, *Admin Sec*
EMP: 18
SQ FT: 70,000
SALES (est): 4.3MM **Privately Held**
SIC: 3441 1791 Bridge sections, prefabricated highway; concrete reinforcement, placing of

(P-11863)
PERPETUAL MOTION GROUP INC
11939 Sherman Rd, North Hollywood (91605-3717)
PHONE..................................818 982-4300
Joe Rando, *Principal*
EMP: 100
SQ FT: 55,000
SALES (est): 5.8MM **Privately Held**
SIC: 3441 Fabricated structural metal

(P-11864)
PLACER WATERWORKS INC
1325 Furneaux Rd, Plumas Lake (95961-7485)
PHONE..................................530 742-9675
Karl Kern, *President*
Sheila Kern, *Vice Pres*
EMP: 20
SQ FT: 10,500
SALES (est): 5.8MM **Privately Held**
WEB: www.placerwaterworks.com
SIC: 3441 Fabricated structural metal

PRODUCTS & SVCS

(P-11865)
PRECISION LASER TEK
285 Industrial Way, Woodland
(95776-6012)
PHONE....................530 661-3580
Richard Correll, *Owner*
Angele Correll, *Agent*
EMP: 30
SALES (est): 216K **Privately Held**
WEB: www.westatesfire.com
SIC: 3441 3711 Fabricated structural
metal; motor vehicles & car bodies

(P-11866)
PRECISION METAL CRAFTS
16920 Gridley Pl, Cerritos (90703-1740)
PHONE....................562 468-7080
Coleman Conard III, *Owner*
EMP: 18
SQ FT: 24,100
SALES (est): 3MM **Privately Held**
SIC: 3441 Fabricated structural metal

(P-11867)
PRECISION WELDING INC
241 Enterprise Pkwy, Lancaster
(93534-7201)
PHONE....................661 729-3436
David R Jones, *President*
David Jones, *President*
EMP: 23
SQ FT: 10,000
SALES (est): 5.7MM **Privately Held**
SIC: 3441 1799 Fabricated structural
metal; welding on site

(P-11868)
**PREMIER STEEL STRUCTURES
INC**
13345 Estelle St, Corona (92879-1881)
PHONE....................951 356-6655
Armando Rodarte, *President*
EMP: 30 EST: 2016
SALES (est): 5.5MM **Privately Held**
SIC: 3441 Fabricated structural metal

(P-11869)
R & I INDUSTRIES INC
2910 S Archibald Ave A, Ontario
(91761-7323)
PHONE....................909 923-7747
William Franklin Rowan Sr, *CEO*
Ardith Rowan, *Treasurer*
William Franklin Rowan Jr, *Vice Pres*
Elena Tellez, *Administration*
Scott Rowan, *Engineer*
EMP: 40 EST: 1978
SQ FT: 12,000
SALES (est): 10.9MM **Privately Held**
WEB: www.rimetal.com
SIC: 3441 Building components, structural
steel

(P-11870)
R & R FABRICATIONS INC
13438 Lambert Rd, Whittier (90605-2454)
PHONE....................562 693-0500
Rodney Galan, *President*
EMP: 10
SALES (est): 1MM **Privately Held**
SIC: 3441 Fabricated structural metal

(P-11871)
R & R METAL FABRICATORS
14846 Ramona Blvd, Baldwin Park
(91706-3436)
PHONE....................626 960-6400
Martha Rodriguez, *Manager*
EMP: 10
SALES (est): 1.3MM **Privately Held**
SIC: 3441 Fabricated structural metal

(P-11872)
RAMP ENGINEERING INC
6850 Walthall Way, Paramount
(90723-2028)
PHONE....................562 531-8030
Mark Scott, *CEO*
Robert C Scott, *Ch of Bd*
Lisa Scott, *CFO*
Nathan Scott, *Software Dev*
EMP: 16
SQ FT: 12,000

SALES (est): 4.2MM **Privately Held**
WEB: www.rampengineering.com
SIC: 3441 Fabricated structural metal

(P-11873)
RICHARDSON STEEL INC
9102 Harness St Ste A, Spring Valley
(91977-3924)
PHONE....................619 697-5892
John Richardson, *President*
Lance Richardson, *COO*
Natalie N Lautner, *CFO*
EMP: 32
SQ FT: 5,000
SALES (est): 8.2MM **Privately Held**
SIC: 3441 Fabricated structural metal

(P-11874)
RND CONTRACTORS INC
14796 Jurupa Ave Ste A, Fontana
(92337-7232)
PHONE....................909 429-8500
Nancy Sauter, *President*
EMP: 40
SALES (est): 12.5MM **Privately Held**
SIC: 3441 Fabricated structural metal

(P-11875)
**ROBECKS WLDG &
FABRICATION INC**
1150 Mabury Rd Ste 1, San Jose
(95133-1031)
PHONE....................408 287-0202
Armon Robeck, *President*
Laurie Morado, *Corp Secy*
Ronald Robeck, *Vice Pres*
EMP: 22
SQ FT: 6,000
SALES (est): 4.7MM **Privately Held**
SIC: 3441 7692 Fabricated structural
metal; welding repair

(P-11876)
ROBERT J ALANDT & SONS
Also Called: Central Cal Metals
4692 N Brawley Ave, Fresno (93722-3921)
PHONE....................559 275-1391
Frank Alandt, *President*
Joseph Alandt, *Corp Secy*
Robert Alandt, *Vice Pres*
EMP: 45 EST: 1950
SQ FT: 50,000
SALES (est): 11MM **Privately Held**
SIC: 3441 Fabricated structural metal

(P-11877)
ROSE METAL PRODUCTS INC
Also Called: R M P
1754 Tech Dr Ste 100, San Jose (95110)
P.O. Box 3238, Springfield MO (65808-
3238)
PHONE....................417 865-1676
Wiley P Buchanan, *President*
James Skinner, *Vice Pres*
Mark T Wickizer, *Vice Pres*
Andrew Rouse, *Design Engr*
Bruce Darnell, *Technology*
EMP: 62 EST: 1960
SQ FT: 88,675
SALES (est): 17.8MM **Privately Held**
WEB: www.rosemetalproducts.com
SIC: 3441 5051 Fabricated structural
metal; sheets, metal

(P-11878)
**SCHROEDER IRON
CORPORATION**
8417 Beech Ave, Fontana (92335-1200)
PHONE....................909 428-6471
Linda Schroeder, *President*
Jason Hampton, *Project Mgr*
EMP: 30
SQ FT: 23,000
SALES (est): 9MM **Privately Held**
WEB: www.schroederiron.com
SIC: 3441 Building components, structural
steel

(P-11879)
**SCRAPE CERTIFIED WELDING
INC**
2525 Old Highway 395, Fallbrook
(92028-8794)
PHONE....................760 728-1308
Jeff D Scrape, *President*

EMP: 91
SALES: 14.7MM **Privately Held**
SIC: 3441 Fabricated structural metal

(P-11880)
**SIERRA METAL FABRICATORS
INC**
Also Called: Sierra Metalk Fabricators
529 Searls Ave, Nevada City (95959-3003)
P.O. Box 1359 (95959-1359)
PHONE....................530 265-4591
Jason White, *President*
Steve Sears, *Supervisor*
EMP: 30 EST: 1974
SQ FT: 30,000
SALES (est): 6.6MM **Privately Held**
WEB: www.sierrametal.com
SIC: 3441 Fabricated structural metal

(P-11881)
SMB INDUSTRIES INC (PA)
Also Called: Metal Works Supply
550 Georgia Pacific Way, Oroville
(95965-9638)
PHONE....................530 534-6266
Sean Pierce, *President*
Mike Phulps, *Treasurer*
Dave Brewton, *Project Mgr*
EMP: 68
SQ FT: 45,000
SALES: 216K **Privately Held**
SIC: 3441 Expansion joints (structural
shapes), iron or steel

(P-11882)
SPARTAN INC
3030 M St, Bakersfield (93301-2137)
PHONE....................661 327-1205
John Wood, *President*
Louis Stern, *CEO*
Tami Black, *CFO*
Teresa Wood, *Treasurer*
John D Clemmey, *Vice Pres*
▼ EMP: 65
SQ FT: 125,000
SALES (est): 14.8MM **Privately Held**
SIC: 3441 8711 Fabricated structural
metal; engineering services

(P-11883)
SPEC IRON INC
7244 Varna Ave, North Hollywood
(91605-4102)
PHONE....................818 765-4070
Razmik Pouladian, *President*
EMP: 10
SQ FT: 4,000
SALES (est): 1.3MM **Privately Held**
SIC: 3441 Fabricated structural metal

(P-11884)
SS METAL FABRICATORS
2501 S Birch St, Santa Ana (92707-3408)
PHONE....................949 631-4272
Kim Harding, *Owner*
EMP: 12
SALES (est): 2MM **Privately Held**
SIC: 3441 Fabricated structural metal

(P-11885)
**STAINLESS PROCESS SYSTEMS
INC**
1650 Beacon Pl, Oxnard (93033-2433)
PHONE....................805 483-7100
Mark Hayman, *President*
EMP: 14 EST: 2007
SQ FT: 27,126
SALES: 2.6MM **Privately Held**
SIC: 3441 Fabricated structural metal

(P-11886)
STL FABRICATION INC
10207 Elm Ave, Fontana (92335-6322)
PHONE....................909 823-5033
Ruben Ramirez, *Principal*
EMP: 10
SALES (est): 2.4MM **Privately Held**
SIC: 3441 Building components, structural
steel

(P-11887)
STO-KAR ENTERPRISES
1112 Arroyo St Ste 2, San Fernando
(91340-1850)
PHONE....................818 886-5600

Maureen Stone, *President*
EMP: 20
SQ FT: 5,000
SALES (est): 3.3MM **Privately Held**
SIC: 3441 Fabricated structural metal

(P-11888)
STRETCH-RUN INC
Also Called: Pleasanton Steel Supply
6621 Brisa St, Livermore (94550-2505)
PHONE....................925 606-1599
Gil Badilla, *President*
EMP: 11
SQ FT: 5,500
SALES (est): 1.9MM **Privately Held**
SIC: 3441 5051 3799 2833 Building com-
ponents, structural steel; steel; wheelbar-
rows; vitamins, natural or synthetic: bulk,
uncompounded

(P-11889)
SUBURBAN STEEL INC (PA)
706 W California Ave, Fresno
(93706-3599)
PHONE....................559 268-6281
Stan J Cavalla, *President*
Ron Cavalla, *Vice Pres*
Jerry Wood, *Manager*
EMP: 40
SQ FT: 12,000
SALES (est): 9MM **Privately Held**
SIC: 3441 3446 Building components,
structural steel; railings, bannisters,
guards, etc.: made from metal pipe

(P-11890)
SUMMIT INDUSTRIES INC
Also Called: Jardine Performance Products
1280 Graphite Dr, Corona (92881-3308)
PHONE....................951 739-5900
Rick May, *Manager*
EMP: 40
SALES (corp-wide): 15.2MM **Privately
Held**
WEB: www.jardineproducts.com
SIC: 3441 Fabricated structural metal
PA: Summit Industries Inc.
    1220 Railroad St
    Corona CA
    951 371-1744

(P-11891)
**SUPERIOR PIPE FABRICATORS
INC**
10211 S Alameda St, Los Angeles
(90002-3837)
PHONE....................323 569-6500
Robert E Moehlman, *President*
EMP: 10
SQ FT: 64,000
SALES: 1MM **Privately Held**
WEB: www.superiorpipefab.com
SIC: 3441 Fabricated structural metal

(P-11892)
SURI STEEL INC
5851 Towne Ave, Los Angeles
(90003-1323)
PHONE....................323 224-3166
Marco Cartin, *President*
Suyi Campos, *Executive Asst*
EMP: 12
SALES: 500K **Privately Held**
SIC: 3441 Building components, structural
steel

(P-11893)
SVM MACHINING INC
6520 Central Ave, Newark (94560-3933)
PHONE....................510 791-9450
Mark Serpa, *President*
EMP: 30
SQ FT: 21,000
SALES (est): 6.5MM **Privately Held**
WEB: www.svmfg.com
SIC: 3441 Building components, structural
steel

(P-11894)
**T M INDUSTRIES
INCORPORATED**
1085 Di Giulio Ave, Santa Clara
(95050-2805)
PHONE....................408 736-5202
Nicholas F Hayes, *President*
Dayle V Hayes, *Vice Pres*

▲ = Import ▼=Export
◆ =Import/Export

▼ **EMP:** 12
SQ FT: 18,000
SALES (est): 1.9MM **Privately Held**
WEB: www.tmindustriesinc.com
SIC: 3441 Fabricated structural metal

(P-11895)
T&S MANUFACTURING TECH LLC
Also Called: Atech Manufacturing
1530 Oakland Rd Ste 120, San Jose
(95112-1241)
PHONE....................408 441-0285
Tony Tolani,
Shalini Tolani,
EMP: 20
SQ FT: 6,000
SALES (est): 5.5MM **Privately Held**
SIC: 3441 3999 Fabricated structural
metal; atomizers, toiletry

(P-11896)
TAN SET CORPORATION
Also Called: Specialty Metal Fabrication
1 S Fairview Ave, Goleta (93117-3364)
PHONE....................805 967-4567
Tanis M Hammond, *President*
Seth Hammond, *Vice Pres*
EMP: 12
SQ FT: 15,000
SALES (est): 1MM **Privately Held**
SIC: 3441 Fabricated structural metal

(P-11897)
TARDIF SHEET METAL & AC
412 N Santa Fe St, Santa Ana
(92701-4907)
PHONE....................714 547-7135
Michael J Tardif, *President*
Mercedes Tardif, *Vice Pres*
EMP: 10 **EST:** 1956
SQ FT: 15,000
SALES (est): 900K **Privately Held**
SIC: 3441 1761 1711 Fabricated struc-
tural metal; sheet metalwork; warm air
heating & air conditioning contractor

(P-11898)
TERMINAL MANUFACTURING CO LLC
Also Called: T M C
707 Gilman St, Berkeley (94710-1312)
PHONE....................510 526-3071
Steve Millinger, *Mng Member*
Kristen Hatch, *Technology*
Isaac Viscarra, *Engineer*
Richard Robison,
EMP: 30
SQ FT: 30,000
SALES (est): 8.3MM **Privately Held**
SIC: 3441 Fabricated structural metal

(P-11899)
TITAN METAL FABRICATORS INC (PA)
352 Balboa Cir, Camarillo (93012-8644)
PHONE....................805 487-5050
Steve Muscarella, *President*
Tom Muscarella, *Vice Pres*
Larry Haubner, *Business Mgr*
▲ **EMP:** 69 **EST:** 1998
SQ FT: 15,000
SALES (est): 31.2MM **Privately Held**
WEB: www.titanmf.com
SIC: 3441 Fabricated structural metal

(P-11900)
TOBIN STEEL COMPANY INC
817 E Santa Ana Blvd, Santa Ana
(92701-3909)
P.O. Box 717 (92702-0717)
PHONE....................714 541-2268
Linda A Robin, *CEO*
Carl Tobin, *President*
Jim Tobin, *Vice Pres*
Steve Tobin, *Vice Pres*
Linda Tobin, *Controller*
EMP: 65
SQ FT: 20,000
SALES (est): 19.2MM **Privately Held**
WEB: www.tobinsteel.com
SIC: 3441 Building components, structural
steel

(P-11901)
TOLAR MANUFACTURING CO INC
258 Mariah Cir, Corona (92879-1751)
PHONE....................951 808-0081
Gary Tolar, *President*
Rhonda Tolar, *Vice Pres*
Carlos Garcia, *Engineer*
▲ **EMP:** 40
SQ FT: 22,000
SALES (est): 16.2MM **Privately Held**
WEB: www.tolarmfg.com
SIC: 3441 3599 3448 Fabricated struc-
tural metal; machine shop, jobbing & re-
pair; prefabricated metal buildings

(P-11902)
TRANS BAY STEEL CORPORATION (PA)
2801 Giant Rd Ste H, San Pablo
(94806-2275)
PHONE....................510 277-3756
William Kavicky, *President*
William H Kroplin, *Vice Pres*
EMP: 50
SALES (est): 7.2MM **Privately Held**
SIC: 3441 Fabricated structural metal

(P-11903)
TRINITY STEEL CORPORATION
Also Called: Con Sol Enterprises
918 Mission Rock Rd B1, Santa Paula
(93060-9107)
PHONE....................805 648-3486
Patrick Barrett, *President*
Craig Brown, *Vice Pres*
Matthew Brown, *Manager*
EMP: 10
SALES (est): 1.5MM **Privately Held**
SIC: 3441 Fabricated structural metal

(P-11904)
TRUSSWORKS INTERNATIONAL INC
2850 E Coronado St, Anaheim
(92806-2503)
PHONE....................714 630-2772
Michael Farrell, *President*
Ali Shantyaei, *Vice Pres*
Pam Tudor, *Executive*
Steven Pugh, *Controller*
EMP: 60 **EST:** 2007
SQ FT: 60,000
SALES (est): 19.1MM **Privately Held**
SIC: 3441 3446 1791 Fabricated struc-
tural metal; architectural metalwork;
stairs, fire escapes, balconies, railings &
ladders; fences, gates, posts & flagpoles;
stairs, staircases, stair treads; prefabri-
cated metal; building front installation
metal

(P-11905)
UNISTRUT INTERNATIONAL CORP
1679 Atlantic St, Union City (94587-2048)
PHONE....................510 476-1200
Tim Kipper, *Manager*
EMP: 10 **Publicly Held**
WEB: www.unistrutconstruction.com
SIC: 3441 Fabricated structural metal
HQ: Unistrut International Corporation
16100 Lathrop Ave
Harvey IL 60426
800 882-5543

(P-11906)
UNIVERSAL CELL SITE SVCS INC
2428 Research Dr, Livermore
(94550-3850)
PHONE....................925 447-4500
Jeremy L King, *President*
EMP: 40
SQ FT: 15,000
SALES: 4MM **Privately Held**
SIC: 3441 Tower sections, radio & televi-
sion transmission

(P-11907)
UNIVERSAL STEEL SERVICES INC
5034 Heintz St, Baldwin Park
(91706-1816)
P.O. Box 2428, Irwindale (91706-1232)
PHONE....................626 960-1455
Ramon T Lopez, *CEO*
Meira Carrasco, *Manager*
EMP: 12
SALES (est): 2.5MM **Privately Held**
SIC: 3441 Building components, structural
steel

(P-11908)
US TOWER CORP
1099 W Ropes Ave, Woodlake
(93286-1806)
PHONE....................559 564-6000
Everett Cook, *Manager*
Ron Stephens, *Creative Dir*
Shana Sawyer, *General Mgr*
Jan Wilson, *Planning*
Teng Yang, *IT/INT Sup*
EMP: 52
SALES (corp-wide): 19.1MM **Privately
Held**
WEB: www.ustower.com
SIC: 3441 Tower sections, radio & televi-
sion transmission
PA: Us Tower Corp.
702 E North St
Lincoln KS 67455
785 524-9966

(P-11909)
V & F FABRICATION COMPANY INC
13902 Seaboard Cir, Garden Grove
(92843-3910)
PHONE....................714 265-0630
Vinh Nguyen, *President*
Vinh Van Nguyen, *CEO*
Bao Truong, *General Mgr*
Sen Truong, *Admin Sec*
Yvonne Nguyen, *Buyer*
▲ **EMP:** 35
SALES (est): 8.5MM **Privately Held**
SIC: 3441 3599 3769 3444 Fabricated
structural metal; machine shop, jobbing &
repair; guided missile & space vehicle
parts & auxiliary equipment; sheet metal-
work

(P-11910)
VALMONT INDUSTRIES INC
4116 Whiteside St, Los Angeles
(90063-1619)
PHONE....................323 264-6660
Sandy Valencia, *Branch Mgr*
Barry Ruffalo, *Exec VP*
Charles Aguilar, *General Mgr*
Irma Taddi, *Office Mgr*
Shadava Schneider, *Administration*
EMP: 69
SALES (corp-wide): 2.7B **Publicly Held**
SIC: 3441 Fabricated structural metal
PA: Valmont Industries, Inc.
1 Valmont Plz Ste 500
Omaha NE 68154
402 963-1000

(P-11911)
VALMONT INDUSTRIES INC
Also Called: Valmont Newmark
3970 Lenwood Rd, Barstow (92311-9408)
PHONE....................760 253-3070
Glyde Reeves, *Manager*
EMP: 10
SALES (corp-wide): 2.7B **Publicly Held**
WEB: www.valmont.com
SIC: 3441 Fabricated structural metal
PA: Valmont Industries, Inc.
1 Valmont Plz Ste 500
Omaha NE 68154
402 963-1000

(P-11912)
VIRGIL WALKER INC
Also Called: Auton Motorized Systems
24856 Avenue Rockefeller, Valencia
(91355-3467)
P.O. Box 801960, Santa Clarita (91380-
1960)
PHONE....................661 797-4101

Arthur Walker, *CEO*
EMP: 15
SALES (est): 1.2MM **Privately Held**
SIC: 3441 Fabricated structural metal

(P-11913)
VORTEX ENGINEERING LLC
9425 Wheatlands Ct, Santee (92071-2831)
PHONE....................619 258-9660
Andrew Dumke, *Mng Member*
EMP: 12
SQ FT: 12,777
SALES (est): 1.7MM **Privately Held**
SIC: 3441 3443 3444 3449 Fabricated
structural metal; fabricated plate work
(boiler shop); sheet metalwork; miscella-
neous metalwork

(P-11914)
VSC INCORPORATED (PA)
Also Called: VULCAN STEEL COMPANY
2038 S Sycamore Ave, Bloomington
(92316-2463)
P.O. Box 386 (92316-0386)
PHONE....................909 877-0975
Davis H Hopper, *CEO*
Connie Gonzales, *Manager*
EMP: 10 **EST:** 1963
SQ FT: 2,000
SALES: 6.7MM **Privately Held**
SIC: 3441 Building components, structural
steel

(P-11915)
WADCO INDUSTRIES INC
Also Called: Wadco Steel Sales
2625 S Willow Ave, Bloomington
(92316-3258)
PHONE....................909 874-5400
David D Scheibel, *CEO*
Salvador Arratia, *President*
Scott Brown, *Treasurer*
Anthony Salazar, *Vice Pres*
Richard Warren, *General Mgr*
EMP: 47
SQ FT: 50,000
SALES (est): 9.5MM **Privately Held**
WEB: www.wadco.com
SIC: 3441 5051 Building components,
structural steel; steel

(P-11916)
WADE METAL PRODUCTS
1818 Los Angeles St, Fresno (93721-3113)
PHONE....................559 237-9233
Marian Esquibel, *CEO*
Curtis Esquibel, *CFO*
EMP: 15
SQ FT: 12,000
SALES (est): 3.8MM **Privately Held**
SIC: 3441 Fabricated structural metal

(P-11917)
WELDWAY INC
521 Hi Tech Pkwy, Oakdale (95361-9395)
PHONE....................209 847-8083
Mike Sala, *President*
Steve Brooks, *Corp Secy*
EMP: 35
SQ FT: 4,500
SALES (est): 7.1MM **Privately Held**
WEB: www.weldwayinc.com
SIC: 3441 Fabricated structural metal

(P-11918)
WESTAR METAL FABRICATION INC
1926 Potrero Ave, South El Monte
(91733-3025)
PHONE....................626 350-0718
Uoqi Lee, *President*
▲ **EMP:** 10
SALES (est): 1.4MM **Privately Held**
WEB: www.westarmetal.com
SIC: 3441 Fabricated structural metal

(P-11919)
WESTCO IRON WORKS INC (PA)
5828 S Naylor Rd, Livermore (94551-8308)
PHONE....................925 961-9152
Mark Shoermsser, *President*
Scott Hofstede, *CFO*
Brad Thompson, *Vice Pres*
John Winger, *Vice Pres*
EMP: 90

PRODUCTS & SVCS

SALES (est): 33.3MM **Privately Held**
WEB: www.westcoironworks.com
SIC: **3441** Fabricated structural metal

(P-11920)
WESTECH METAL FABRICATION INC
3420 E St, San Diego (92102-3336)
PHONE...................................619 702-9353
Jeff Bjelland, *President*
Mike Bjelland, *Vice Pres*
EMP: 11
SQ FT: 18,000
SALES (est): 1.6MM **Privately Held**
WEB: www.westechmetalfab.com
SIC: **3441 7692 3446** Welding repair;
stairs, fire escapes, balconies, railings &
ladders; railings, bannisters, guards, etc.:
made from metal pipe; ornamental metal-
work; fabricated structural metal for ships

(P-11921)
WESTERN BAY SHEET METAL INC
1410 Hill St, El Cajon (92020-5749)
PHONE...................................619 233-1753
James Lozano, *President*
Helena Lopez, *Corp Secy*
Roy Lozano, *Vice Pres*
Rob Hoffman, *Superintendent*
▲ EMP: 45 EST: 1981
SQ FT: 9,800
SALES (est): 17.6MM **Privately Held**
WEB: www.westernbay.net
SIC: **3441 3444** Fabricated structural
metal; sheet metalwork

(P-11922)
WOODLAND WELDING WORKS
1955 E Main St, Woodland (95776-6202)
P.O. Box 1194 (95776-1194)
PHONE...................................530 666-5531
Felix Franco, *President*
Maribel Santiago, *Office Mgr*
Sara Franco, *Admin Sec*
Ray Stemler, *Project Mgr*
EMP: 12
SQ FT: 18,000
SALES (est): 2.6MM **Privately Held**
WEB: www.woodlandwelding.com
SIC: **3441** Fabricated structural metal

(P-11923)
YUBA CITY STEEL PRODUCTS CO
532 Crestmont Ave, Yuba City
(95991-6209)
PHONE...................................530 673-4554
Clinton L West, *Ch of Bd*
Robert Zellner, *President*
▼ EMP: 30 EST: 1944
SQ FT: 81,000
SALES (est): 7.7MM **Privately Held**
WEB: www.ycsteel.com
SIC: **3441** Fabricated structural metal

(P-11924)
ZETH ENGINEERING INC
11929 Pepperwood St, Victorville
(92392-1213)
PHONE...................................310 930-9100
Hans Tadeja, *President*
EMP: 15 EST: 2011
SALES: 1MM **Privately Held**
SIC: **3441** Building components, structural
steel

3442 Metal Doors, Sash, Frames, Molding & Trim

(P-11925)
A & A CUSTOM SHUTTERS
10465 San Fernando Rd # 8, Pacoima
(91331-2602)
PHONE...................................818 383-1819
Aaron Lopez, *President*
EMP: 10
SALES (est): 910K **Privately Held**
SIC: **3442** Shutters, door or window: metal

(P-11926)
ACCENT INDUSTRIES INC (PA)
Also Called: Accent Awnings
1600 E Saint Gertrude Pl, Santa Ana
(92705-5312)
PHONE...................................714 708-1389
Karl Desmarais, *CEO*
▲ EMP: 30
SQ FT: 26,000
SALES (est): 3MM **Privately Held**
WEB: www.accentawnings.com
SIC: **3442 3444 2394 5999** Shutters,
door or window: metal; awnings &
canopies; canvas & related products;
awnings

(P-11927)
ACTIVE WINDOW PRODUCTS
Also Called: Z Industries
5431 W San Fernando Rd, Los Angeles
(90039-1088)
P.O. Box 39125 (90039-0125)
PHONE...................................323 245-5185
Michael Schoenfeld, *President*
Rosa Castro, *Treasurer*
▲ EMP: 53
SQ FT: 96,000
SALES (est): 10.4MM **Privately Held**
SIC: **3442** Storm doors or windows, metal

(P-11928)
ADVANCE OVERHEAD DOOR INC
15829 Stagg St, Van Nuys (91406-1969)
PHONE...................................818 781-5590
Leland S Groshong, *President*
Don Henderson, *Treasurer*
Marguerite Groshong, *Admin Sec*
EMP: 37 EST: 1956
SQ FT: 25,000
SALES (est): 4.6MM **Privately Held**
SIC: **3442 2431** Garage doors, overhead:
metal; garage doors, overhead: wood

(P-11929)
ADVANCED ARCHITECTURAL FRAMES
Also Called: Advance Architectural
17102 Newhope St, Fountain Valley
(92708-8223)
PHONE...................................424 209-6018
EMP: 33
SQ FT: 4,000
SALES: 6.4MM **Privately Held**
SIC: **3442 5211**

(P-11930)
ALUMATHERM INCORPORATED
1717 Kirkham St, Oakland (94607-2214)
PHONE...................................510 832-2819
Kevin Smith, *President*
EMP: 10 EST: 1954
SQ FT: 22,000
SALES (est): 1.1MM **Privately Held**
SIC: **3442** Casements, aluminum; screens,
window, metal

(P-11931)
ARCADIA INC
2323 Firestone Blvd, South Gate
(90280-2684)
PHONE...................................310 665-0490
EMP: 40
SALES (corp-wide): 124.6MM **Privately
Held**
SIC: **3442** Window & door frames
PA: Arcadia, Inc.
2301 E Vernon Ave
Vernon CA 90058
323 269-7300

(P-11932)
ARCHITECTURAL BLOMBERG LLC
Also Called: Blomberg Window Systems
1453 Blair Ave, Sacramento (95822-3410)
P.O. Box 22485 (95822-0485)
PHONE...................................916 428-8060
Jeremy Drucker, *Mng Member*
EMP: 32
SALES: 84MM **Privately Held**
SIC: **3442** Window & door frames

(P-11933)
B & B DOORS AND WINDOWS INC
11455 Ilex Ave, San Fernando
(91340-3430)
PHONE...................................818 837-8480
Jeffrey C Brothers, *CEO*
Lori Brothers, *Treasurer*
EMP: 20
SQ FT: 7,200
SALES (est): 2.5MM **Privately Held**
SIC: **3442 5031** Window & door frames;
doors & windows

(P-11934)
BAYFAB METALS INC
870 Doolittle Dr, San Leandro
(94577-1079)
PHONE...................................510 568-8950
Susan Miranda, *President*
EMP: 20
SQ FT: 21,000
SALES (est): 4.4MM **Privately Held**
WEB: www.bayfabmetals.com
SIC: **3442 3444 3446 3499** Metal doors,
sash & trim; metal housings, enclosures,
casings & other containers; louvers, venti-
lating; shims, metal; name plates: except
engraved, etched, etc.: metal

(P-11935)
BAYSIDE SHUTTERS
Also Called: Southwest Shutter Shaque
1464 N Batavia St, Orange (92867-3505)
PHONE...................................714 628-9994
John Bussjaeger, *Owner*
▲ EMP: 10 EST: 1989
SQ FT: 5,000
SALES (est): 846.4K **Privately Held**
WEB: www.baysideshutters.com
SIC: **3442** Metal doors, sash & trim

(P-11936)
BELCO CABINETS INC
1109 Black Diamond Way, Lodi
(95240-0746)
PHONE...................................209 334-5437
Roy Belanger, *President*
EMP: 15 EST: 1978
SQ FT: 21,000
SALES: 2.3MM **Privately Held**
SIC: **3442 2434** Metal doors; wood kitchen
cabinets

(P-11937)
BEST ROLL-UP DOOR INC
13202 Arctic Cir, Santa Fe Springs
(90670-5510)
PHONE...................................562 802-2233
Edward Choi, *President*
▲ EMP: 20
SQ FT: 15,000
SALES (est): 4MM **Privately Held**
SIC: **3442** Rolling doors for industrial build-
ings or warehouses, metal

(P-11938)
BLOMBERG BUILDING MATERIALS (PA)
Also Called: Blomberg Window Systems
1453 Blair Ave, Sacramento (95822-3410)
PHONE...................................916 428-8060
J Philip Collier, *CEO*
Bud Warren, *Executive*
EMP: 100
SALES (est): 13.6MM **Privately Held**
WEB: www.blombergwindowsystems.com
SIC: **3442** Metal doors, sash & trim

(P-11939)
BLUM CONSTRUCTION CO INC
Also Called: European Rolling Shutters
404 Umbarger Rd Ste A, San Jose
(95111-2083)
PHONE...................................408 629-3740
Helmut Blum, *President*
Renate Blum, *Vice Pres*
▲ EMP: 15
SQ FT: 10,500
SALES (est): 2.8MM **Privately Held**
WEB: www.ers-shading.com
SIC: **3442 3444 1751 1799** Shutters,
door or window: metal; awnings &
canopies; window & door installation &
erection; awning installation

(P-11940)
BONELLI ENTERPRISES
Also Called: Bonelli Windows and Doors
330 Corey Way, South San Francisco
(94080-6709)
PHONE...................................650 873-3222
David J Bonelli, *President*
Mara Bonelli, *Admin Sec*
EMP: 25
SQ FT: 25,000
SALES (est): 5MM
SALES (corp-wide): 1.7B **Privately Held**
WEB: www.bonelli.com
SIC: **3442 1751** Window & door frames;
screen & storm doors & windows; window
& door (prefabricated) installation
PA: Pella Corporation
102 Main St
Pella IA 50219
641 621-1000

(P-11941)
CLEAR VIEW LLC
1650 Las Plumas Ave Ste A, San Jose
(95133-1657)
PHONE...................................408 271-2734
Daniel Lezotte,
Andrew Lezotte, *Mng Member*
EMP: 15
SALES (est): 1.5MM **Privately Held**
SIC: **3442 5084** Screen doors, metal; in-
dustrial machinery & equipment

(P-11942)
COLUMBIA HOLDING CORP
14400 S San Pedro St, Gardena
(90248-2027)
PHONE...................................310 327-4107
Daryl McCollend, *Ch of Bd*
Lawrence Goodman, *President*
▲ EMP: 300
SQ FT: 100,000
SALES (est): 23.8MM **Privately Held**
SIC: **3442 2431 2439** Metal doors, sash &
trim; millwork; structural wood members

(P-11943)
CR LAURENCE CO INC
Columbia Manufacturing Corp
14400 S San Pedro St, Gardena
(90248-2027)
PHONE...................................310 327-9300
Andrew Spooner, *Vice Pres*
EMP: 14
SALES (corp-wide): 30.6B **Privately Held**
SIC: **3442** Screen doors, metal
HQ: C. R. Laurence Co., Inc.
2503 E Vernon Ave
Vernon CA 90058
323 588-1281

(P-11944)
DC SHADES & SHUTTERS AWNINGS
2370 Thunderbird Dr, Thousand Oaks
(91362-3236)
PHONE...................................818 597-9705
David Chadida, *Owner*
EMP: 10
SALES (est): 300K **Privately Held**
SIC: **3442 5719** Shutters, door or window:
metal; window furnishings

(P-11945)
DECRATEK INC
2875 Executive Pl, Escondido
(92029-1524)
PHONE...................................760 747-1706
Richard Smerud, *President*
EMP: 30
SQ FT: 25,000
SALES (est): 3.9MM **Privately Held**
WEB: www.decratek.com
SIC: **3442** Window & door frames

(P-11946)
DESIGNLINE WINDOWS & DOORS INC
5674 El Camino Real Ste K, Carlsbad
(92008-7130)
PHONE...................................760 931-9422
Harry Norman McCurry, *President*
Norman McCurry, *President*
Dennis Alba, *Vice Pres*
Bob Ross, *Vice Pres*

EMP: 20
SALES (est): 2MM **Privately Held**
SIC: 3442 Window & door frames

(P-11947)
DIABLO MOLDING & TRIM COMPANY
5600 Sunol Blvd Ste C, Pleasanton (94566-8802)
P.O. Box 2190, Dublin (94568-0218)
PHONE..................................925 417-0663
Alex Blumin, *President*
EMP: 22
SALES (est): 3.4MM **Privately Held**
WEB: www.diablomolding.com
SIC: 3442 Molding, trim & stripping

(P-11948)
DOOR COMPONENTS INC
Also Called: DCI Hollow Metal On Demand
7980 Redwood Ave, Fontana (92336-1638)
PHONE..................................909 770-5700
Robert Briggs, *President*
Ronald Green, *Vice Pres*
Cindi Bowen, *Info Tech Mgr*
Bill Rogers, *Engineer*
Michael Ruch, *Engineer*
EMP: 200
SQ FT: 45,000
SALES (est): 42.2MM **Privately Held**
WEB: www.doorcomponents.com
SIC: 3442 Metal doors; sash, door or window: metal

(P-11949)
EAST BAY GLASS COMPANY INC
Also Called: Jal-Vue Window Company
601 50th Ave, Oakland (94601-5003)
PHONE..................................510 834-2535
Neda Ahmed, *President*
Adel M Ali, *Vice Pres*
Miguel Aviles, *Opers Mgr*
Miguel A Aviles, *Manager*
▲ EMP: 11
SALES: 2.5MM **Privately Held**
SIC: 3442 1793 1542 Window & door frames; glass & glazing work; commercial & office building contractors

(P-11950)
EDEY MANUFACTURING CO INC
Also Called: Edey Door
2159 E 92nd St, Los Angeles (90002-2509)
PHONE..................................323 566-6151
Fax: 323 566-0262
EMP: 21
SQ FT: 54,000
SALES (est): 1.3MM **Privately Held**
WEB: www.edeydoors.com
SIC: 3442

(P-11951)
ELEGANCE ENTRIES INC
Also Called: Elegance Entries and Windows
1130 N Kraemer Blvd Ste G, Anaheim (92806-1918)
PHONE..................................714 632-3667
Fred W Polivka, *CEO*
Brian Polivka, *Treasurer*
Tracy Polivka, *Admin Sec*
EMP: 18
SQ FT: 5,300
SALES (est): 2.7MM **Privately Held**
WEB: www.eleganceentries.com
SIC: 3442 Window & door frames; door & window products

(P-11952)
ELIZABETH SHUTTERS INC
525 S Rancho Ave, Colton (92324-3240)
PHONE..................................909 825-1531
Dean Frost, *CEO*
Maren Frost, *CFO*
Maggie Castaneda, *Accountant*
EMP: 45
SQ FT: 51,000
SALES (est): 6.7MM **Privately Held**
WEB: www.elizabethshutters.com
SIC: 3442 5023 5211 2431 Shutters, door or window: metal; window furnishings; door & window products; millwork

(P-11953)
EUROLINE STEEL WINDOWS
Also Called: Euroline Steel Windows & Doors
22600 Savi Ranch Pkwy E, Yorba Linda (92887-4616)
PHONE..................................877 590-2741
Elyas Balta, *CEO*
Melanie Caswell, *Senior Buyer*
▲ EMP: 20
SALES (est): 3.7MM **Privately Held**
SIC: 3442 Window & door frames

(P-11954)
FANBOYS WINDOW FACTORY INC (PA)
10750 Saint Louis Dr, El Monte (91731-2028)
PHONE..................................626 280-8787
Lili Bell, *CEO*
Jeff Bell, *COO*
EMP: 21
SQ FT: 10,000
SALES: 2MM **Privately Held**
SIC: 3442 Window & door frames

(P-11955)
FORDERER CORNICE WORKS
3364 Arden Rd, Hayward (94545-3923)
PHONE..................................415 431-4100
Fax: 510 783-6646
EMP: 10 EST: 1875
SQ FT: 1,000
SALES (est): 2MM **Privately Held**
SIC: 3442 5031 3429 2431

(P-11956)
GILWIN COMPANY
2354 Lapham Dr, Modesto (95354-3912)
PHONE..................................209 522-9775
Donald P Miller, *President*
Wanda SAI, *Office Mgr*
Gilwin Story, *Opers Staff*
EMP: 23
SQ FT: 27,000
SALES (est): 2.6MM **Privately Held**
SIC: 3442 Window & door frames; casements, aluminum

(P-11957)
GRANDESIGN DECOR INC
1727 N 1st St, San Jose (95112-4510)
PHONE..................................408 436-9969
Gail Hung, *President*
EMP: 25
SALES (est): 3.1MM **Privately Held**
WEB: www.gdecor.com
SIC: 3442 Window & door frames

(P-11958)
HRH DOOR CORP
Also Called: Wayne - Dalton Sacramento
830 Prosessor Ln, Sacramento (95834)
PHONE..................................916 928-0600
Jim Lawrence, *Principal*
EMP: 30
SALES (corp-wide): 600.8MM **Privately Held**
WEB: www.waynedalton.com
SIC: 3442 2431 Metal doors, sash & trim; millwork
PA: Hrh Door Corp.
   1 Door Dr
   Mount Hope OH 44660
   850 208-3400

(P-11959)
J T WALKER INDUSTRIES INC
Also Called: Rite Screen
9322 Hyssop Dr, Rancho Cucamonga (91730-6103)
PHONE..................................909 481-1909
Dan Harvey, *President*
EMP: 50
SQ FT: 36,929
SALES (corp-wide): 1.1B **Privately Held**
SIC: 3442 Screen & storm doors & windows
PA: J. T. Walker Industries, Inc.
   1310 N Hercules Ave Ste A
   Clearwater FL 33765
   727 461-0501

(P-11960)
JANUS INTERNATIONAL GROUP LLC
2535 W La Palma Ave, Anaheim (92801-2612)
PHONE..................................714 503-6120
David Curtis, *Principal*
Archer Shannon, *Sales Associate*
Wilson Michael, *Manager*
Tanner Julie, *Assistant*
EMP: 30
SALES (corp-wide): 240.3MM **Privately Held**
SIC: 3442 Metal doors
PA: Janus International Group, Llc
   135 Janus Intl Blvd
   Temple GA 30179
   770 562-2850

(P-11961)
JOANKA INC
Also Called: M & A Custom Doors
25510 Frampton Ave, Harbor City (90710-2907)
PHONE..................................310 326-8940
Manuel A Valenzuela, *President*
EMP: 13
SQ FT: 4,640
SALES (est): 994K **Privately Held**
SIC: 3442 Window & door frames

(P-11962)
K K MOLDS INC
926 Western Ave Ste D, Glendale (91201-2390)
PHONE..................................818 548-8988
Frank Kan, *President*
Man Yee Kan, *Admin Sec*
▲ EMP: 10
SALES: 1.3MM **Privately Held**
SIC: 3442 Moldings & trim, except automobile: metal

(P-11963)
L & L LOUVERS INC
12355 Doherty St, Riverside (92503-4842)
PHONE..................................951 735-9300
Terry Green, *President*
Robert Hammond, *Vice Pres*
EMP: 24
SQ FT: 11,000
SALES (est): 3.6MM **Privately Held**
WEB: www.louver1.com
SIC: 3442 Louvers, shutters, jalousies & similar items

(P-11964)
LAWRENCE ROLL UP DOORS INC (PA)
4525 Littlejohn St, Baldwin Park (91706-2239)
PHONE..................................626 962-4163
Paul Weston Freberg, *CEO*
Steve Hahn, *Manager*
▲ EMP: 35 EST: 1925
SQ FT: 35,000
SALES (est): 17.9MM **Privately Held**
WEB: www.lawrencedoors.com
SIC: 3442 3446 Rolling doors for industrial buildings or warehouses, metal; architectural metalwork

(P-11965)
LAWRENCE ROLL UP DOORS INC
11035 Stranwood Ave, Mission Hills (91345-1416)
PHONE..................................818 837-1963
Paul Lawrence, *President*
EMP: 10
SALES (corp-wide): 17.9MM **Privately Held**
WEB: www.lawrencedoors.com
SIC: 3442 Rolling doors for industrial buildings or warehouses, metal
PA: Lawrence Roll Up Doors, Inc.
   4525 Littlejohn St
   Baldwin Park CA 91706
   626 962-4163

(P-11966)
LAWRENCE ROLL UP DOORS INC
1406 Virginia Ave Ste 10, Baldwin Park (91706-5805)
PHONE..................................626 338-6041
Robert Lee, *Manager*
EMP: 10
SALES (corp-wide): 17.9MM **Privately Held**
SIC: 3442 Rolling doors for industrial buildings or warehouses, metal
PA: Lawrence Roll Up Doors, Inc.
   4525 Littlejohn St
   Baldwin Park CA 91706
   626 962-4163

(P-11967)
M N M MANUFACTURING INC
3019 E Harcourt St, Compton (90221-5503)
PHONE..................................310 898-1099
Matt Klein, *President*
Elizabeth Klein, *Vice Pres*
Suzanne Figueroa, *Executive*
Marlene Klein, *Admin Sec*
EMP: 60
SQ FT: 24,000
SALES (est): 8MM **Privately Held**
WEB: www.mnmmfg.com
SIC: 3442 Sash, door or window: metal

(P-11968)
MAKO OVERHEAD DOOR INC
5618 E La Palma Ave, Anaheim (92807-2110)
PHONE..................................714 998-0122
Mike McCall, *President*
EMP: 12
SALES: 2MM **Privately Held**
SIC: 3442 Garage doors, overhead: metal; jalousies, metal

(P-11969)
METAL MANUFACTURING CO INC
2240 Evergreen St, Sacramento (95815-3281)
PHONE..................................916 922-3484
Jerry Guest, *President*
Troy Smith, *Treasurer*
Henry Baum, *Admin Sec*
EMP: 20
SQ FT: 19,000
SALES: 2MM **Privately Held**
SIC: 3442 Metal doors; window & door frames

(P-11970)
METAL TITE PRODUCTS (PA)
Also Called: Krieger Speciality Products
4880 Gregg Rd, Pico Rivera (90660-2107)
PHONE..................................562 695-0645
Robert J McCluney, *President*
Charles Mc Cluney, *Shareholder*
James Mc Cluney, *Shareholder*
A W Mc Cluney, *Ch of Bd*
William Mc Cluney, *Executive*
EMP: 58
SQ FT: 39,000
SALES (est): 10.8MM **Privately Held**
WEB: www.kriegersteel.com
SIC: 3442 1751 Metal doors; window & door frames; window & door (prefabricated) installation

(P-11971)
MILGARD MANUFACTURING INC
Also Called: Milgard Windows
6050 88th St, Sacramento (95828-1119)
PHONE..................................916 387-0700
Bert Dimauro, *Branch Mgr*
EMP: 186
SALES (corp-wide): 8.3B **Publicly Held**
SIC: 3442 Window & door frames
HQ: Milgard Manufacturing Incorporated
   1010 54th Ave E
   Fife WA 98424
   253 922-6030

PRODUCTS & SVCS

(P-11972)
MILLWORKS ETC INC
Also Called: Steel Works Etc
2586 Calcite Cir, Newbury Park
(91320-1203)
PHONE.....................................805 499-3400
Robin W Shattuck, *CEO*
Beverly Buswell, *Controller*
Christine Bohannan, *Manager*
Mike Starkey, *Manager*
◆ EMP: 25
SALES (est): 4.5MM **Privately Held**
SIC: 3442 Window & door frames

(P-11973)
MULTIQUIP INDUSTRIES CORP
22605 La Palma Ave # 507, Yorba Linda
(92887-6713)
PHONE.....................................888 996-7267
Daniel Burgess, *President*
EMP: 17 EST: 2012
SALES (est): 2.9MM **Privately Held**
SIC: 3442 3537 Rolling doors for industrial
buildings or warehouses, metal; loading
docks: portable, adjustable & hydraulic

(P-11974)
OMNIMAX INTERNATIONAL INC
Also Called: Alumax Building Products
28921 Us Highway 74, Sun City
(92585-9675)
PHONE.....................................951 928-1000
Mitchell B Lewis, *CEO*
EMP: 106
SALES (corp-wide): 840.5MM **Privately Held**
WEB: www.amerimaxbp.com
SIC: 3442 3444 5999 Casements, alu-
minum; sheet metalwork; awnings
HQ: Omnimax International, Inc.
30 Technology Pkwy S # 400
Peachtree Corners GA 30092

(P-11975)
PRECISE IRON DOORS INC
12331 Foothill Blvd, Sylmar (91342-6003)
PHONE.....................................818 338-6269
EMP: 20
SALES (est): 2.5MM **Privately Held**
SIC: 3442 5031 5999 Metal doors; metal
doors, sash & trim; miscellaneous retail
stores

(P-11976)
R & S AUTOMATION INC
283 W Bonita Ave, Pomona (91767-1848)
PHONE.....................................800 962-3111
Jerry Bradfield, *Manager*
Brad Goepner, *Manager*
EMP: 12
SALES (corp-wide): 3MM **Privately Held**
WEB: www.doorsbyrns.com
SIC: 3442 3446 5031 5063 Metal doors;
grillwork, ornamental metal; doors; door
frames, all materials; motor controls,
starters & relays: electric; door & window
repair
PA: R & S Automation, Inc.
2041 W Avenue 140th
San Leandro CA 94577
510 357-4110

(P-11977)
R & S MANUFACTURING INC (HQ)
Also Called: R & S Rolling Door Products
33955 7th St, Union City (94587-3521)
P.O. Box 2737 (94587-7737)
PHONE.....................................510 429-1788
Gordon J Ong, *President*
James Greaves, *Treasurer*
Ray Zarodney, *Admin Sec*
Robert R Smith, *Director*
▲ EMP: 43 EST: 1979
SQ FT: 36,136
SALES (est): 8MM
SALES (corp-wide): 6MM **Privately Held**
SIC: 3442 3231 Rolling doors for industrial
buildings or warehouses, metal; louvers,
shutters, jalousies & similar items; prod-
ucts of purchased glass
PA: R & S Erection, Incorporated
2057 W Avenue 140th
San Leandro CA 94577
510 483-3710

(P-11978)
R & S MFG SOUTHERN CAL INC
Also Called: R & S Mfg
283 W Bonita Ave, Pomona (91767-1848)
PHONE.....................................909 596-2090
Ray Rodney, *CEO*
EMP: 14
SQ FT: 15,000
SALES (est): 3MM
SALES (corp-wide): 6MM **Privately Held**
SIC: 3442 5031 Rolling doors for industrial
buildings or warehouses, metal; doors &
windows
HQ: R & S Manufacturing, Inc.
33955 7th St
Union City CA 94587
510 429-1788

(P-11979)
R & S OVERHEAD DOOR OF SO CAL
Also Called: Door Doctor
1617 N Orangethorpe Way, Anaheim
(92801-1228)
PHONE.....................................714 680-0600
David Fowler, *President*
EMP: 25
SALES (est): 3.2MM **Privately Held**
SIC: 3442 7699 1731 3446 Rolling doors
for industrial buildings or warehouses,
metal; door & window repair; access con-
trol systems specialization; gates, orna-
mental metal

(P-11980)
R LANG COMPANY
Also Called: Truframe
8240 W Doe Ave, Visalia (93291-9263)
P.O. Box 7960 (93290-7960)
PHONE.....................................559 651-0701
Richard A Lang, *President*
Judith D Lang, *Corp Secy*
Heather Simon, *HR Admin*
◆ EMP: 75 EST: 1967
SALES (est): 14.6MM **Privately Held**
WEB: www.rollaway.com
SIC: 3442 3444 3211 5031 Screen
doors, metal; window & door frames; sky-
lights, sheet metal; flat glass; windows

(P-11981)
SAN JOAQUIN WINDOW INC (PA)
Also Called: ATI Windows
1455 Columbia Ave, Riverside
(92507-2013)
PHONE.....................................909 946-3697
Stephen Schwartz, *CEO*
Daniel Schwartz, *President*
Won Yang, *Manager*
EMP: 61
SQ FT: 190,000
SALES (est): 14.2MM **Privately Held**
SIC: 3442 5211 Metal doors, sash & trim;
door & window products

(P-11982)
SCREEN SHOP INC
601 Hamline St, San Jose (95110-1192)
PHONE.....................................408 295-7384
John V Salamida, *President*
Sue Green, *Vice Pres*
Sue Greene, *Admin Asst*
EMP: 10
SQ FT: 2,200
SALES (est): 2MM **Privately Held**
WEB: www.thescreenshop.com
SIC: 3442 2431 5211 Screen & storm
doors & windows; screens, window,
metal; screen doors, metal; window
screens, wood frame; doors, wood; door
& window products; doors, storm: wood or
metal; windows, storm: wood or metal

(P-11983)
SECURITY METAL PRODUCTS CORP (DH)
5678 Concours, Ontario (91764-5394)
PHONE.....................................310 641-6690
Chris Holloway, *CEO*
EMP: 28
SALES (est): 5.1MM
SALES (corp-wide): 9.3B **Privately Held**
SIC: 3442 Metal doors

HQ: Assa, Inc.
110 Sargent Dr
New Haven CT 06511
203 624-5225

(P-11984)
SOLATUBE INTERNATIONAL INC (PA)
2210 Oak Ridge Way, Vista (92081-8341)
PHONE.....................................888 765-2882
David W Rillie, *CEO*
Jennifer Delaney, *Executive Asst*
Nathalie Lavoie, *Credit Staff*
Phyllis Wallace, *Hum Res Coord*
Joshua Hernandez, *Human Res Mgr*
◆ EMP: 100
SQ FT: 105,000
SALES (est): 24.8MM **Privately Held**
WEB: www.solatube.com
SIC: 3442 Metal doors, sash & trim

(P-11985)
STILES CUSTOM METAL INC
1885 Kinser Rd, Ceres (95307-4606)
PHONE.....................................209 538-3667
David Stiles, *President*
Jim Ludlow, *CFO*
Steve Stiles, *Vice Pres*
Adam Hale, *Project Mgr*
Jerry Grant, *Chief Engr*
EMP: 87
SQ FT: 56,000
SALES (est): 17.4MM **Privately Held**
WEB: www.stilesdoor.com
SIC: 3442 Metal doors; window & door
frames

(P-11986)
TJE COMPANY
Also Called: Onyx Shutters
18343 Gale Ave, City of Industry
(91748-1201)
PHONE.....................................909 869-7777
Sylvia Lee, *CEO*
Philip Kim, *Vice Pres*
◆ EMP: 19 EST: 2007
SALES (est): 3.4MM **Privately Held**
SIC: 3442 Shutters, door or window: metal

(P-11987)
TMP LLC
Also Called: Titan Metal Products
3011 Academy Way, Sacramento
(95815-1540)
PHONE.....................................916 920-2555
Glen Harelson, *President*
Flora Harelson, *Treasurer*
EMP: 23 EST: 1977
SQ FT: 18,000
SALES (est): 5.7MM **Privately Held**
WEB: www.titanmetalproducts.com
SIC: 3442 Metal doors; window & door
frames; sash, door or window: metal;
moldings & trim, except automobile: metal

(P-11988)
TORRANCE STEEL WINDOW CO INC
1819 Abalone Ave, Torrance (90501-3704)
PHONE.....................................310 328-9181
Dong K Lim, *President*
▲ EMP: 45
SQ FT: 32,000
SALES (est): 8.6MM **Privately Held**
WEB: www.torrancesteelwindow.com
SIC: 3442 Window & door frames

(P-11989)
WONDER METALS CORPORATION
4351 Caterpillar Rd, Redding (96003-1494)
PHONE.....................................530 241-3251
Viki Cubbage, *President*
Brandon Long, *Project Mgr*
EMP: 14
SQ FT: 38,000
SALES (est): 2.8MM **Privately Held**
WEB: www.wondermetals.com
SIC: 3442 Louvers, shutters, jalousies &
similar items

3443 Fabricated Plate Work

(P-11990)
ACD LLC (DH)
Also Called: A C D
2321 Pullman St, Santa Ana (92705-5512)
PHONE.....................................949 261-7533
James Estes,
Richard S Young, *Executive*
Leo Arreola, *General Mgr*
Erica Jehling, *General Mgr*
Julieta Manzo, *Admin Asst*
◆ EMP: 117
SQ FT: 52,000
SALES: 39.6MM **Privately Held**
WEB: www.acdcom.com
SIC: 3443 3559 Cryogenic tanks, for liq-
uids & gases; cryogenic machinery, in-
dustrial
HQ: Cryogenic Industries, Inc.
27710 Jefferson Ave # 301
Temecula CA 92590
951 677-2081

(P-11991)
AERO-CLAS HEAT TRAN PROD INC
1677 Curtiss Ct, La Verne (91750-5848)
PHONE.....................................909 596-1630
Paul Saurenman, *CEO*
EMP: 15
SALES (est): 3.2MM **Privately Held**
SIC: 3443 Heat exchangers: coolers (after,
inter), condensers, etc.

(P-11992)
ALPHA TECHNOLOGIES GROUP INC (PA)
11990 San Vicente Blvd # 350, Los Angeles
(90049-6608)
PHONE.....................................310 566-4005
Lawrence Butler, *Ch of Bd*
Robert C Streiter, *President*
James J Polakiewicz, *CFO*
Steve E Chupik, *Vice Pres*
EMP: 337
SALES (est): 30.4MM **Publicly Held**
WEB: www.nationalne.com
SIC: 3443 Fabricated plate work (boiler
shop)

(P-11993)
APPLIED SYSTEMS LLC
6666 Box Sprng Blvd Rvrsi Riverside,
Riverside (92507)
PHONE.....................................951 842-6300
Chris Phillips,
EMP: 10
SALES (est): 454.3K **Privately Held**
SIC: 3443 Industrial vessels, tanks & con-
tainers

(P-11994)
B H TANK WORKS INC
1919 N San Fernando Rd, Los Angeles
(90065-1228)
PHONE.....................................323 221-1579
Fax: 323 221-6559
EMP: 17
SALES (est): 1.9MM **Privately Held**
WEB: www.bhtank.com
SIC: 3443

(P-11995)
BA HOLDINGS (DH)
3016 Kansas Ave Bldg 1, Riverside
(92507-3445)
PHONE.....................................951 684-5110
John S Rhodes, *CEO*
EMP: 30
SALES (est): 127.7MM
SALES (corp-wide): 487.9MM **Privately Held**
SIC: 3443 3728 Cylinders, pressure: metal
plate; aircraft parts & equipment

(P-11996)
BENICIA FABRICATION & MCH INC
101 E Channel Rd, Benicia (94510-1155)
PHONE.....................................707 745-8111
Thomas D Cepernich, *CEO*
Dennis Michael Rose, *President*

▲ = Import ▼=Export
◆ =Import/Export

Steven Rose, *Exec VP*
Robert Mattsson, *Engineer*
Janet Saladino, *Controller*
EMP: 150
SQ FT: 80,000
SALES (est): 41.4MM **Privately Held**
WEB: www.beniciafab.com
SIC: 3443 3599 Fabricated plate work (boiler shop); machine shop, jobbing & repair

(P-11997)
BLACOH FLUID CONTROLS INC (PA)
601 Columbia Ave Ste D, Riverside (92507-2149)
PHONE..............................951 342-3100
Andrew Yeghnazar, *President*
Gary Cornell, *President*
John Eoff, *Vice Pres*
Dianna Vise, *Vice Pres*
Jennifer Wingfield, *Info Tech Mgr*
EMP: 12 **EST:** 1977
SQ FT: 11,000
SALES (est): 2.5MM **Privately Held**
WEB: www.blacoh.com
SIC: 3443 Fabricated plate work (boiler shop)

(P-11998)
BREEZAIRE PRODUCTS CO
8610 Production Ave Ste A, San Diego (92121-2278)
PHONE..............................858 566-7465
Ronald Brown, *President*
▼ **EMP:** 10 **EST:** 1978
SQ FT: 1,200
SALES (est): 1.7MM **Privately Held**
WEB: www.breezaire.com
SIC: 3443 3585 Economizers (boilers); beer dispensing equipment

(P-11999)
CALIENTE SYSTEMS INC
6821 Central Ave, Newark (94560-3938)
PHONE..............................510 790-0300
Rajan Barma, *CEO*
John Hughes, *Treasurer*
EMP: 91
SQ FT: 10,000
SALES (est): 7.9MM **Privately Held**
WEB: www.calientesystems.net
SIC: 3443 3567 3433 Heat exchangers, plate type; industrial furnaces & ovens; heating equipment, except electric

(P-12000)
CATALINA CYLINDERS INC (PA)
7300 Anaconda Ave, Garden Grove (92841-2930)
PHONE..............................714 890-0999
Gregory Keeler, *CEO*
Roark Keeler, *CFO*
Richard Hill, *Vice Pres*
Tom Newell, *General Mgr*
David Silva, *Sales Staff*
EMP: 29
SALES (est): 22.9MM
SALES (corp-wide): 24.4MM **Privately Held**
SIC: 3443 3491 Fabricated plate work (boiler shop); compressed gas cylinder valves

(P-12001)
CENTRAL VALLEY TANK OF CAL
4752 E Carmen Ave, Fresno (93703-4501)
PHONE..............................559 456-3500
Kathy Tackett, *President*
EMP: 16
SALES (est): 3.9MM **Privately Held**
SIC: 3443 Boiler shop products: boilers, smokestacks, steel tanks

(P-12002)
CERTIFIED STAINLESS SVC INC
Also Called: Westmark
441 Business Park Way, Atwater (95301-9499)
PHONE..............................209 356-3300
Chris Portmann, *Branch Mgr*
EMP: 15

SALES (corp-wide): 37.2MM **Privately Held**
SIC: 3443 3569 Tanks for tank trucks, metal plate; firefighting apparatus & related equipment
PA: Certified Stainless Service Inc.
2704 Railroad Ave
Ceres CA 95307
209 537-4747

(P-12003)
CERTIFIED STAINLESS SVC INC (PA)
Also Called: West-Mark
2704 Railroad Ave, Ceres (95307-4600)
P.O. Box 100 (95307-0100)
PHONE..............................209 537-4747
Grant Smith, *President*
Dale Steeley, *Partner*
Jack Smith, *Shareholder*
William Doughty, *CFO*
Scott Vincent, *Corp Secy*
▲ **EMP:** 180
SQ FT: 64,000
SALES (est): 58.7MM **Privately Held**
WEB: www.west-mark.com
SIC: 3443 3715 7538 Tanks for tank trucks, metal plate; truck trailers; general truck repair

(P-12004)
CERTIFIED STAINLESS SVC INC
Also Called: West-Mark
581 Industry Way, Atwater (95301-9457)
P.O. Box 100, Ceres (95307-0100)
PHONE..............................209 537-4747
Grant Smith, *Branch Mgr*
Heather Silveira, *Manager*
EMP: 50
SALES (corp-wide): 37.2MM **Privately Held**
WEB: www.west-mark.com
SIC: 3443 3569 Tanks for tank trucks, metal plate; firefighting apparatus & related equipment
PA: Certified Stainless Service Inc.
2704 Railroad Ave
Ceres CA 95307
209 537-4747

(P-12005)
CHART INC
46441 Landing Pkwy, Fremont (94538-6496)
PHONE..............................408 371-3303
Daniel Sullivan, *Branch Mgr*
EMP: 21 **Publicly Held**
SIC: 3443 Fabricated plate work (boiler shop)
HQ: Chart Inc.
407 7th St Nw
New Prague MN 56071
952 758-4484

(P-12006)
CJI PROCESS SYSTEMS INC
Also Called: Lee Ray Sandblasting
12000 Clark St, Santa Fe Springs (90670-3709)
PHONE..............................562 777-0614
Archie Cholakian, *President*
John Cholakian, *Vice Pres*
▼ **EMP:** 70
SQ FT: 35,000
SALES (est): 25.5MM **Privately Held**
WEB: www.cjiprocesssystems.com
SIC: 3443 3441 3444 Tanks, lined: metal plate; fabricated structural metal; sheet metalwork

(P-12007)
CMT SHEET METAL
22732 Granite Way Ste C, Laguna Hills (92653-1263)
PHONE..............................949 679-9868
Wes Hinze, *CEO*
Wes Hinze Jr, *President*
Gayle Hinze, *Admin Sec*
EMP: 15
SALES (est): 3.4MM **Privately Held**
SIC: 3443 Boiler & boiler shop work

(P-12008)
COMPUTRUS INC
250 Klug Cir, Corona (92880-5409)
PHONE..............................951 245-9103

William Turnbull, *President*
Scott R Carroll, *Vice Pres*
EMP: 40
SALES (est): 6.5MM
SALES (corp-wide): 225.3B **Publicly Held**
WEB: www.computrus.com
SIC: 3443 Truss plates, metal
HQ: Mitek Industries, Inc.
16023 Swinly Rdg
Chesterfield MO 63017
314 434-1200

(P-12009)
CONSOLIDATED FABRICATORS CORP (PA)
Also Called: CF
14620 Arminta St, Van Nuys (91402-5902)
PHONE..............................818 901-1005
Michael J Melideo, *CEO*
Jeff Lombardi, *President*
Brian A Atwater, *COO*
Kerry Holmes, *Vice Pres*
Robert Cardenas, *Engineer*
▲ **EMP:** 110 **EST:** 1974
SQ FT: 150,000
SALES (est): 106.8MM **Privately Held**
WEB: www.con-fab.com
SIC: 3443 5051 3444 Dumpsters, garbage; steel; studs & joists, sheet metal

(P-12010)
CONTAINMENT CONSULTANTS INC
Also Called: Ideal Envmtl Pdts & Svcs
110 Old Gilroy St, Gilroy (95020-6948)
P.O. Box 307 (95021-0307)
PHONE..............................408 848-6998
Anne Anderson, *President*
EMP: 16
SQ FT: 14,000
SALES (est): 3.5MM **Privately Held**
WEB: www.chem-stor.com
SIC: 3443 8748 Tanks, standard or custom fabricated: metal plate; environmental consultant

(P-12011)
CONTAINMENT SOLUTIONS INC
2600 Pegasus Dr, Bakersfield (93308-6809)
PHONE..............................661 399-9556
Joe Wiegand, *Manager*
Valerie Austin, *Human Res Mgr*
Dorrie Melville, *Manager*
EMP: 100 **Privately Held**
WEB: www.containmentsolutions.com
SIC: 3443 Industrial vessels, tanks & containers
HQ: Containment Solutions, Inc.
333 N Rivershire Dr # 190
Conroe TX 77304

(P-12012)
CONTECH ENGNERED SOLUTIONS LLC
2245 Canyon Creek Rd, Redding (96001-3727)
PHONE..............................530 243-1207
Jerry Burton, *Manager*
EMP: 20 **Privately Held**
SIC: 3443 3444 Fabricated plate work (boiler shop); sheet metalwork
HQ: Contech Engineered Solutions Llc
9025 Centre Pointe Dr # 400
West Chester OH 45069
513 645-7000

(P-12013)
COOK AND COOK INCORPORATED
Also Called: Royal Welding & Fabricating
1000 E Elm Ave, Fullerton (92831-5022)
PHONE..............................714 680-6669
Wallace F Cook, *President*
Patricia Cook, *Vice Pres*
Seyung Kim, *Executive*
Veronica Covarrubias, *Human Resources*
EMP: 30 **EST:** 1967
SQ FT: 30,000

SALES (est): 6.8MM **Privately Held**
WEB: www.royalwelding.com
SIC: 3443 3599 3444 Industrial vessels, tanks & containers; amusement park equipment; sheet metalwork

(P-12014)
CROSNO CONSTRUCTION INC
819 Sheridan Rd, Arroyo Grande (93420-5833)
PHONE..............................805 343-7437
Wade Crosno, *President*
Jaime Crosno, *CFO*
Brian Terberg, *Engineer*
EMP: 48
SQ FT: 5,000
SALES (est): 19.9MM **Privately Held**
SIC: 3443 Fabricated plate work (boiler shop)

(P-12015)
DAVIS GREGG ENTERPRISES INC
8525 Roland Acres Dr, Santee (92071-4453)
PHONE..............................619 449-4250
Davis Gregg, *President*
Mary Gregg, *Vice Pres*
▲ **EMP:** 14
SQ FT: 4,800
SALES (est): 1.2MM **Privately Held**
SIC: 3443 Tanks, standard or custom fabricated: metal plate

(P-12016)
DESIGN FORM INC
8250 Electric Ave, Stanton (90680-2640)
PHONE..............................714 952-3700
Glenn Baldwin, *CEO*
EMP: 11
SQ FT: 7,000
SALES: 1.2MM **Privately Held**
WEB: www.designform.com
SIC: 3443 Tanks, standard or custom fabricated: metal plate

(P-12017)
DUNWEIZER MACHINE INC
Also Called: Dunweizer Mch & Fabrication
8338 Allport Ave, Santa Fe Springs (90670-2108)
P.O. Box 3046 (90670-0046)
PHONE..............................562 698-7787
Dennis Schweizer, *President*
Jim Van Eperen, *Marketing Staff*
EMP: 19
SQ FT: 20,000
SALES (est): 3.7MM **Privately Held**
SIC: 3443 3599 Fabricated plate work (boiler shop); machine shop, jobbing & repair

(P-12018)
EDGE ELECTRONICS CORPORATION
Also Called: Mc Intyre Coil
14670 Wicks Blvd, San Leandro (94577-6716)
PHONE..............................510 614-7988
Dennis T Wong, *President*
William Schwartz, *Vice Pres*
EMP: 25
SQ FT: 20,300
SALES (est): 4.3MM **Privately Held**
SIC: 3443 Heat exchangers, plate type

(P-12019)
HARSCO CORPORATION
Also Called: Harsco Distribution Center
5580 Cherry Ave, Long Beach (90805-5504)
PHONE..............................909 444-2527
Ron Eickelman, *Branch Mgr*
EMP: 15
SALES (corp-wide): 1.7B **Publicly Held**
WEB: www.harsco.com
SIC: 3443 Fabricated plate work (boiler shop)
PA: Harsco Corporation
350 Poplar Church Rd
Camp Hill PA 17011
717 763-7064

PRODUCTS & SVCS

(P-12020)
HAYDEN PRODUCTS LLC
Also Called: Hayden Industrial Products
1393 E San Bernardino Ave, San
Bernardino (92408-2964)
PHONE..............................951 736-2600
Harold Lehon, *Mng Member*
Peter Camenzind, *Co-Owner*
James Neitz, *President*
Loper Greg, *Info Tech Mgr*
Brian Cheser, *IT/INT Sup*
▲ EMP: 80
SQ FT: 55,000
SALES (est): 29.4MM **Privately Held**
WEB: www.haydenindustrial.com
SIC: 3443 Heat exchangers, condensers &
components

(P-12021)
HYUNDAI TRANSLEAD (HQ)
8880 Rio San Diego Dr # 600, San Diego
(92108-1634)
PHONE..............................619 574-1500
Bong Jae Lee, *CEO*
Glen Harney, *COO*
Sb Yoon, *CFO*
Adam Hill, *Vice Pres*
Jae Jung, *General Mgr*
▲ EMP: 87
SALES (est): 867.3MM **Privately Held**
WEB: www.translead.com
SIC: 3443 3715 3412 Industrial vessels,
tanks & containers; semitrailers for truck
tractors; metal barrels, drums & pails

(P-12022)
**ITW BLDING CMPONENTS
GROUP INC**
Also Called: ITW Alpine
8801 Folsom Blvd Ste 107, Sacramento
(95826-3249)
PHONE..............................916 387-0116
Sally Thomas, *Sales/Mktg Mgr*
EMP: 30
SALES (corp-wide): 14.7B **Publicly Held**
WEB: www.alpineengineeredproducts.com
SIC: 3443 3469 Truss plates, metal;
stamping metal for the trade
HQ: Itw Building Components Group, Inc.
13389 Lakefront Dr
Earth City MO 63045
314 344-9121

(P-12023)
JOHANSING IRON WORKS INC
849 Jackson St, Benicia (94510-2907)
P.O. Box 847 (94510-0847)
PHONE..............................707 361-8190
Thomas Johansing, *President*
EMP: 10
SQ FT: 20,000
SALES: 1.4MM **Privately Held**
WEB: www.johansing.com
SIC: 3443 Heat exchangers, plate type;
vessels, process or storage (from boiler
shops): metal plate

(P-12024)
KEESEE TANK COMPANY
Also Called: Advance Pacific Tank
721 S Melrose St, Placentia (92870-6307)
PHONE..............................714 528-1814
Kenneth Keesee, *Owner*
EMP: 10
SQ FT: 60,000
SALES (est): 1.7MM **Privately Held**
SIC: 3443 Fabricated plate work (boiler
shop)

(P-12025)
KSM VACUUM PRODUCTS INC
1959 Concourse Dr, San Jose
(95131-1708)
PHONE..............................408 514-2400
Yun Ho Kim, *CEO*
Robert Snowden, *Principal*
▲ EMP: 14
SALES (est): 2.8MM **Privately Held**
SIC: 3443 High vacuum coaters, metal
plate

(P-12026)
LA VILLETA DE SONOMA
23000 Arnold Dr, Sonoma (95476-9208)
PHONE..............................707 939-9392
Leon Mardo, *Owner*

▲ EMP: 22
SALES (est): 1.8MM **Privately Held**
WEB: www.lavilleta.com
SIC: 3443 Annealing boxes, pots, or cov-
ers

(P-12027)
**LUXFER-GTM TECHNOLOGIES
LLC (PA)**
1619 Shattuck Ave, Berkeley (94709-1611)
PHONE..............................415 856-0570
Michael Koonce, *President*
Dan Jones, *Mfg Dir*
Tim Tiger, *Sales Staff*
EMP: 20 EST: 2012
SQ FT: 1,700
SALES: 3.6MM **Privately Held**
SIC: 3443 Tanks for tank trucks, metal
plate

(P-12028)
M-5 STEEL MFG INC (PA)
1450 Mirasol St, Los Angeles
(90023-3148)
PHONE..............................323 263-9383
Douglas A Linkon, *CEO*
Henry Casas, *Info Tech Mgr*
▲ EMP: 50
SQ FT: 100,000
SALES (est): 11.5MM **Privately Held**
SIC: 3443 3444 Fabricated plate work
(boiler shop); gutters, sheet metal

(P-12029)
MCKENNA BOILER WORKS INC
1510 N Spring St, Los Angeles
(90012-1925)
PHONE..............................323 221-1171
Richard R Smith, *President*
James F Smith, *Treasurer*
EMP: 15
SQ FT: 14,000
SALES (est): 3.5MM **Privately Held**
SIC: 3443 7699 Boilers: industrial, power,
or marine; boiler repair shop

(P-12030)
MELCO STEEL INC
1100 W Foothill Blvd, Azusa (91702-2818)
PHONE..............................626 334-7875
Michel Kashou, *President*
Joann Reese, *Treasurer*
Mazin Kashou, *Vice Pres*
EMP: 30 EST: 1971
SQ FT: 25,500
SALES (est): 7.6MM **Privately Held**
SIC: 3443 Vessels, process or storage
(from boiler shops): metal plate; auto-
claves, industrial

(P-12031)
**MODERN CUSTOM
FABRICATION**
2421 E California Ave, Fresno
(93721-3301)
P.O. Box 11925 (93775-1925)
PHONE..............................559 264-4741
James E Jones, *CEO*
James W Gray, *Vice Pres*
John W Jones, *Principal*
Barbara Nix, *Human Res Mgr*
Ramon Colmenero, *Purch Agent*
EMP: 35 EST: 2001
SALES (est): 10.3MM
SALES (corp-wide): 126.3MM **Privately
Held**
WEB: www.modweldco.com
SIC: 3443 Fabricated plate work (boiler
shop)
PA: Modern Welding Company, Inc.
2880 New Hartford Rd
Owensboro KY 42303
270 685-4400

(P-12032)
MOSIER BROS
19580 Avenue 344, Woodlake (93286)
PHONE..............................559 564-3304
Mark Taylor, *President*
C Joanne Taylor, *Admin Sec*
Byron Taylor, *Director*
EMP: 10 EST: 1963
SQ FT: 5,000
SALES (est): 1.8MM **Privately Held**
SIC: 3443 Tanks, lined: metal plate

(P-12033)
**NATIONWIDE BOILER
INCORPORATED (PA)**
42400 Christy St, Fremont (94538-3141)
PHONE..............................510 490-7100
Larry Day, *President*
James Hermerding, *Vice Pres*
Michele Tomas, *Vice Pres*
Farheen Mobeen, *Admin Asst*
Anthony Difede, *VP Finance*
◆ EMP: 51 EST: 1967
SQ FT: 35,000
SALES: 29.2MM **Privately Held**
WEB: www.nationwideboiler.com
SIC: 3443 Fabricated plate work (boiler
shop)

(P-12034)
NWPC LLC
Also Called: Nothwest Pipe Company
10100 W Linne Rd, Tracy (95377-9128)
PHONE..............................209 836-5050
Scott Montross, *CEO*
EMP: 75
SALES: 39MM
SALES (corp-wide): 172.1MM **Publicly
Held**
SIC: 3443 3317 Fabricated plate work
(boiler shop); steel pipe & tubes
PA: Northwest Pipe Company
201 Ne Park Plaza Dr # 100
Vancouver WA 98684
360 397-6250

(P-12035)
P-W WESTERN INC
9415 Kruse Rd, Pico Rivera (90660-1430)
PHONE..............................562 463-9055
Timothy Place, *CEO*
Emilia Gonzales, *Finance*
EMP: 65
SQ FT: 60,000
SALES (est): 10MM
SALES (corp-wide): 21.2MM **Privately
Held**
WEB: www.pwtray.com
SIC: 3443 Cable trays, metal plate
HQ: P-W Industries Inc
9415 Kruse Rd
Pico Rivera CA 90660
562 463-9055

(P-12036)
**PACIFIC STEAM EQUIPMENT
INC**
Also Called: P S E Boilers
11748 Slauson Ave, Santa Fe Springs
(90670-2227)
PHONE..............................562 906-9292
William S Shanahan MD, *President*
Shin Duk Kang, *Vice Pres*
▲ EMP: 25 EST: 1954
SQ FT: 22,500
SALES (est): 5MM **Privately Held**
WEB: www.pacificsteam.com
SIC: 3443 5074 3582 2841 Tanks, stan-
dard or custom fabricated: metal plate;
boilers: industrial, power, or marine;
plumbing & hydronic heating supplies;
steam fittings; commercial laundry equip-
ment; soap & other detergents

(P-12037)
PACIFIC TANK & CNSTR INC
17995 E Highway 46, Shandon
(93461-9636)
PHONE..............................805 237-2929
Tom Yanaga, *Manager*
EMP: 30
SALES (est): 4.3MM **Privately Held**
WEB: www.pacifictank.net
SIC: 3443 Fabricated plate work (boiler
shop)
PA: Pacific Tank & Construction, Inc.
31551 Avnida Los Cerritos
San Juan Capistrano CA 92675

(P-12038)
**PALMDALE HEAT TREATING
INC**
38834 17th St E, Palmdale (93550-3915)
PHONE..............................661 274-8604
Jon Fishel, *President*
Janette Gorman, *Treasurer*

Catherine Battaglia, *Corp Secy*
James Rodgers, *Vice Pres*
EMP: 15
SQ FT: 5,000
SALES (est): 2MM **Privately Held**
SIC: 3443 Fabricated plate work (boiler
shop)

(P-12039)
**PARKER-HANNIFIN
CORPORATION**
Hydraulic Accumulator Division
14087 Borate St, Santa Fe Springs
(90670-5336)
PHONE..............................562 404-1938
Mark Gagnon, *Branch Mgr*
EMP: 20
SALES (corp-wide): 14.3B **Publicly Held**
WEB: www.parker.com
SIC: 3443 3052 2822 Fabricated plate
work (boiler shop); rubber & plastics hose
& beltings; synthetic rubber
PA: Parker-Hannifin Corporation
6035 Parkland Blvd
Cleveland OH 44124
216 896-3000

(P-12040)
PERRIS SKYVENTURE
Also Called: Perris Wind Tunnel
2093 Goetz Rd, Perris (92570-9315)
PHONE..............................951 940-4290
Ben Conatser, *President*
Diane Conatser, *Vice Pres*
Pat Conatser, *Manager*
EMP: 15
SQ FT: 1,788
SALES (est): 2.1MM **Privately Held**
WEB: www.perrisskyventure.com
SIC: 3443 Wind tunnels

(P-12041)
POLARGY INC
1148 Sonora Ct, Sunnyvale (94086-5308)
PHONE..............................408 752-0186
Cary Frame, *President*
Denise Banning, *Regl Sales Mgr*
EMP: 30
SALES (est): 6.5MM **Privately Held**
SIC: 3443 3585 Reactor containment ves-
sels, metal plate; parts for heating, cool-
ing & refrigerating equipment

(P-12042)
PREMIERE RECYCLE CO
348 Phelan Ave, San Jose (95112-4103)
PHONE..............................408 297-7910
Robert Hill, *President*
EMP: 50
SALES (est): 6.2MM **Privately Held**
WEB: www.premierrecycle.com
SIC: 3443 4953 4212 Dumpsters,
garbage; garbage: collecting, destroying
& processing; local trucking, without stor-
age

(P-12043)
**PROTEC ARISAWA AMERICA
INC**
2455 Ash St, Vista (92081-8424)
PHONE..............................760 599-4800
Shinichi Miura, *President*
◆ EMP: 50
SALES (est): 15.7MM **Privately Held**
SIC: 3443 Process vessels, industrial:
metal plate

(P-12044)
**QUALITY VESSEL
ENGINEERING INC**
8515 Chetle Ave, Santa Fe Springs
(90670-2205)
PHONE..............................562 696-2100
John Gill, *President*
EMP: 15
SALES (est): 2.7MM **Privately Held**
WEB: www.howardfab.com
SIC: 3443 Cylinders, pressure: metal plate

(P-12045)
RECON SERVICES INC
2255 Via Cerro, Jurupa Valley
(92509-2412)
P.O. Box 60816, Irvine (92602-6027)
PHONE..............................951 682-1400

▲ = Import ▼=Export
◆ =Import/Export

EMP: 15
SQ FT: 15,000
SALES (est): 3MM **Privately Held**
SIC: 3443 Industrial vessels, tanks & containers

(P-12046)
RILEYS TANKS/D&J SERVICE
3261 S Elm Ave, Fresno (93706-5622)
PHONE..................................559 237-1403
Joseph V Riley, *Co-Owner*
Ramona J Riley, *Co-Owner*
EMP: 12
SQ FT: 10,000
SALES (est): 1.3MM **Privately Held**
WEB: www.rileystanks.com
SIC: 3443 Gas holders, metal plate; water tanks, metal plate

(P-12047)
ROY E HANSON JR MFG (PA)
Also Called: Hanson Tank
1600 E Washington Blvd, Los Angeles (90021-3123)
P.O. Box 30507 (90030-0507)
PHONE..................................213 747-7514
Jonathan Goss, *CEO*
Roy E Hanson Jr, *Shareholder*
Johnathan Goss, *CEO*
Thys Dorenbosch, *Treasurer*
Cliff Jones, *Vice Pres*
▼ EMP: 82
SQ FT: 55,000
SALES (est): 12.3MM **Privately Held**
WEB: www.hansontank.com
SIC: 3443 Fuel tanks (oil, gas, etc.): metal plate

(P-12048)
S & H WELDING INC
8604 Elder Creek Rd, Sacramento (95828-1803)
PHONE..................................916 386-8921
John Jones, *President*
EMP: 15
SQ FT: 10,000
SALES (est): 3.3MM **Privately Held**
WEB: www.calottery.com
SIC: 3443 Fabricated plate work (boiler shop)

(P-12049)
S BRAVO SYSTEMS INC
Also Called: Bravo Support
2929 Vail Ave, Commerce (90040-2615)
PHONE..................................323 888-4133
Paola Bravo Recendez, *CEO*
Gracie Kurt, *Safety Dir*
Keith Pearson, *Opers Mgr*
Micah Nelson, *Natl Sales Mgr*
Trent Caster, *Regl Sales Mgr*
▲ EMP: 26
SQ FT: 40,000
SALES (est): 10.4MM **Privately Held**
WEB: www.sbravo.com
SIC: 3443 Containers, shipping (bombs, etc.): metal plate

(P-12050)
SAN-I-PAK PACIFIC INC
23355 S Bird Rd, Tracy (95304-9339)
P.O. Box 1183 (95378-1183)
PHONE..................................209 836-2310
John L Hall, *President*
Wilburn Hall, *Vice Pres*
Steve Hilliker, *Planning*
EMP: 50
SQ FT: 25,000
SALES (est): 9.9MM **Privately Held**
WEB: www.sanipak.com
SIC: 3443 Sterilizing chambers, metal plate

(P-12051)
SID E PARKER BOILER MFG CO INC
Also Called: Parker Boiler Co
5930 Bandini Blvd, Commerce (90040-2903)
PHONE..................................323 727-9800
Sid D Danenhauer, *Ch of Bd*
Ed Marchak, *CFO*
Greg G Danenhauer, *Vice Pres*
Bob Barnes, *Purch Mgr*
Allan Cuilty, *Plant Mgr*
◆ EMP: 66

SQ FT: 80,000
SALES: 15MM **Privately Held**
WEB: www.parkerboiler.com
SIC: 3443 3433 Boilers: industrial, power, or marine; heating equipment, except electric

(P-12052)
SMS INDUSTRIAL INC
Also Called: Winery Services Group
1628 N Main St, Salinas (93906-5102)
PHONE..................................831 337-4271
Orlando T Michelon, *Principal*
Corinne White, *President*
Lonny White, *General Mgr*
EMP: 13
SQ FT: 2,100
SALES (est): 3.1MM **Privately Held**
WEB: www.summitmechanicalsystems.com
SIC: 3443 Tanks, standard or custom fabricated: metal plate

(P-12053)
SOUTH GATE ENGINEERING LLC
13477 Yorba Ave, Chino (91710-5055)
PHONE..................................909 628-2779
Peter Morin,
Greg Alba, *Analyst*
Carlos Tapia, *Maintence Staff*
William Paolino, *Mng Member*
EMP: 115 EST: 1947
SALES (est): 32.7MM **Privately Held**
WEB: www.southgateengineering.com
SIC: 3443 Vessels, process or storage (from boiler shops): metal plate; heat exchangers: coolers (after, inter), condensers, etc.

(P-12054)
SPX COOLING TECHNOLOGIES INC
Recold Division
550 Mercury Ln, Brea (92821-4830)
PHONE..................................714 529-6080
Doug Vickers, *Manager*
EMP: 40
SALES (corp-wide): 1.5B **Publicly Held**
WEB: www.cts.spx.com
SIC: 3443 Fabricated plate work (boiler shop)
HQ: Spx Cooling Technologies, Inc.
7401 W 129th St
Overland Park KS 66213
913 664-7400

(P-12055)
SPX CORPORATION
17815 Newhope St Ste M, Fountain Valley (92708-5426)
PHONE..................................714 434-2576
EMP: 99
SALES (corp-wide): 1.4B **Publicly Held**
SIC: 3443
PA: Spx Corporation
13320a Balntyn Corp Pl
Charlotte NC 28277
980 474-3700

(P-12056)
SPX CORPORATION
1515 S Harris Ct, Anaheim (92806-5932)
PHONE..................................714 634-3855
EMP: 12
SALES (corp-wide): 1.4B **Publicly Held**
SIC: 3443
PA: Spx Corporation
13320a Balntyn Corp Pl
Charlotte NC 28277
980 474-3700

(P-12057)
STEEL STRUCTURES INC
28777 Avenue 15 1/2, Madera (93638-2316)
PHONE..................................559 673-8021
Daniel Riley, *President*
Tracy Riley, *Vice Pres*
EMP: 22
SQ FT: 44,000
SALES: 5MM **Privately Held**
WEB: www.steelstructuresinc.com
SIC: 3443 Tanks, standard or custom fabricated: metal plate

(P-12058)
STEEL UNLIMITED INC
Also Called: Sui Companies
3200 Myers St, Riverside (92503-5530)
PHONE..................................909 873-1222
Mike Frabotta, *President*
David Sunde, *Vice Pres*
Eric C Carpenter, *Data Proc Staff*
Sheridan Sunde, *Personnel Assit*
Alex Amaya, *Marketing Staff*
▲ EMP: 75 EST: 1996
SQ FT: 142,000
SALES (est): 30.4MM **Privately Held**
WEB: www.steelunlimited.com
SIC: 3443 Plate work for the metalworking trade

(P-12059)
STRUCTURAL COMPOSITES INDS LLC (DH)
Also Called: SCI
336 Enterprise Pl, Pomona (91768-3244)
PHONE..................................909 594-7777
Ken Miller, *Mng Member*
Bruce Riser, *Finance*
◆ EMP: 40
SALES (est): 21.6MM
SALES (corp-wide): 3.7B **Publicly Held**
WEB: www.scicomposites.com
SIC: 3443 Tanks, lined: metal plate
HQ: Worthington Cylinder Corporation
200 W Old Wlson Bridge Rd
Worthington OH 43085
614 840-3210

(P-12060)
SUPERIOR STORAGE TANK INC
14700 Industry Cir, La Mirada (90638-5817)
PHONE..................................714 226-1914
Griff Williams, *CEO*
Rob Henderson, *COO*
EMP: 15
SALES (est): 3.4MM **Privately Held**
SIC: 3443 7692 Fuel tanks (oil, gas, etc.): metal plate; welding repair

(P-12061)
SUPERIOR TANK CO INC (PA)
Also Called: Stci
9500 Lucas Ranch Rd, Rancho Cucamonga (91730-5724)
PHONE..................................909 912-0580
Jesus Eric Marquez, *President*
Lewis A Marquez, *Treasurer*
Michael Anderson, *Branch Mgr*
Huel L Gulf, *Branch Mgr*
George Marquez, *Admin Sec*
◆ EMP: 50
SQ FT: 53,392
SALES: 32.7MM **Privately Held**
SIC: 3443 3494 1791 1794 Fuel tanks (oil, gas, etc.): metal plate; water tanks, metal plate; valves & pipe fittings; structural steel erection; excavation work

(P-12062)
TAIT & ASSOCIATES INC
2131 S Dupont Dr, Anaheim (92806-6102)
PHONE..................................714 560-8222
Jim Streipz, *Branch Mgr*
Jacob Vandervis, *Vice Pres*
EMP: 100
SALES (corp-wide): 39.8MM **Privately Held**
SIC: 3443 Fuel tanks (oil, gas, etc.): metal plate
PA: Tait & Associates, Inc.
701 Parkcenter Dr
Santa Ana CA 92705
866 584-0283

(P-12063)
THERMAL EQUIPMENT CORPORATION
Also Called: TEC
2030 E University Dr, Compton (90220-6410)
PHONE..................................310 328-6600
Nancy Huffman, *President*
Mike Courtney, *Project Mgr*
▼ EMP: 45
SQ FT: 45,000

SALES (est): 13MM **Privately Held**
WEB: www.thermalequipment.com
SIC: 3443 3821 2842 Autoclaves, industrial; process vessels, industrial: metal plate; vessels, process or storage (from boiler shops): metal plate; laboratory apparatus & furniture; specialty cleaning, polishes & sanitation goods
PA: Km3 Holdings Company Inc
2030 E University Dr
Rancho Dominguez CA
310 328-6600

(P-12064)
THERMALLY ENGINEERED MANUFACTU
Also Called: T E M P
543 W 135th St, Gardena (90248-1505)
PHONE..................................310 523-9934
Robert Greenwood, *President*
Binh Vinh, *Vice Pres*
▲ EMP: 27
SQ FT: 50,000
SALES: 4.4MM **Privately Held**
WEB: www.temp.com
SIC: 3443 Heat exchangers, condensers & components

(P-12065)
THOMPSON TANK INC
8029 Phlox St, Downey (90241-4816)
P.O. Box 790, Lakewood (90714-0790)
PHONE..................................562 869-7711
David B Thompson, *President*
Robert I Grue, *Treasurer*
EMP: 19
SQ FT: 225,000
SALES (est): 4.7MM **Privately Held**
WEB: www.thompsontank.com
SIC: 3443 7699 3715 3713 Tanks, standard or custom fabricated: metal plate; tank repair & cleaning services; truck trailers; truck & bus bodies

(P-12066)
UNIVERSAL DEFENSE
412 Cucamonga Ave, Claremont (91711-5019)
P.O. Box 1372 (91711-1372)
PHONE..................................909 626-4178
Christine A Sayegh, *Principal*
EMP: 20
SALES (est): 1.7MM **Privately Held**
SIC: 3443 Fabricated plate work (boiler shop)

(P-12067)
VENDING SECURITY PRODUCTS
770 Newton Way, Costa Mesa (92627-4277)
PHONE..................................949 646-1474
Bruce Jenks, *President*
▲ EMP: 10
SQ FT: 3,000
SALES (est): 1.5MM **Privately Held**
SIC: 3443 Metal parts

(P-12068)
WAGNER PLATE WORKS WEST INC (PA)
Also Called: P V T Supply
14015 Garfield Ave, Paramount (90723-2137)
PHONE..................................562 531-6050
Jack Brian Purtell, *President*
EMP: 25
SQ FT: 60,000
SALES (est): 6MM **Privately Held**
WEB: www.pvtpvt.com
SIC: 3443 5051 Tanks, lined: metal plate; pipe & tubing, steel

(P-12069)
WATERCREST INC
4850 E Airport Dr, Ontario (91761-7818)
PHONE..................................909 390-3944
Jeremiah B Robins, *CEO*
Gary F Johnson, *President*
▲ EMP: 51
SQ FT: 29,000
SALES (est): 7MM **Privately Held**
SIC: 3443 Heat exchangers, condensers & components

PRODUCTS & SVCS

(P-12070)
WESTERN COMBUSTION ENGRG INC
640 E Realty St, Carson (90745-6016)
P.O. Box 5331, San Pedro (90733-5331)
PHONE..........................310 834-9389
Marcia L Paul, *CEO*
Christian R Paul, *President*
EMP: 12 EST: 1977
SQ FT: 10,000
SALES (est): 2.7MM **Privately Held**
WEB: www.westerncombustion.com
SIC: 3443 7699 3567 Heat exchangers: coolers (after, inter), condensers, etc.; boiler & heating repair services; industrial furnaces & ovens

(P-12071)
WORTHINGTON CYLINDER CORP
336 Enterprise Pl, Pomona (91768-3244)
PHONE..........................909 594-7777
Maria Matchell, *Sales Staff*
EMP: 191
SALES (corp-wide): 3.7B **Publicly Held**
SIC: 3443 Cylinders, pressure: metal plate
HQ: Worthington Cylinder Corporation
200 W Old Wilson Bridge Rd
Worthington OH 43085
614 840-3210

(P-12072)
XCHANGER MANUFACTURING CORP
Also Called: Wiegmann & Rose
263 S Vasco Rd, Livermore (94551-9203)
P.O. Box 4187, Oakland (94614-4187)
PHONE..........................510 632-8828
Scott E Logan, *President*
Shirley Teason, *Finance Dir*
EMP: 21
SQ FT: 80,000
SALES (est): 4MM **Privately Held**
WEB: www.wiegmannandrose.com
SIC: 3443 Heat exchangers: coolers (after, inter), condensers, etc.

(P-12073)
XTREME MANUFACTURING LLC
1775 Park St Ste 82, Selma (93662-3659)
PHONE..........................559 891-2978
Jose Vallejo, *Branch Mgr*
Mark Kroeker, *Engineer*
EMP: 21
SALES (corp-wide): 60.8MM **Privately Held**
SIC: 3443 Metal parts
PA: Xtreme Manufacturing, Llc
1401 Mineral Ave
Las Vegas NV 89106
702 851-3701

3444 Sheet Metal Work

(P-12074)
101 ROOFING & SHEET METAL CO
1390 Wallace Ave, San Francisco (94124-3316)
PHONE..........................415 695-0101
Christie Chung, *Owner*
EMP: 11
SALES (est): 620K **Privately Held**
SIC: 3444 1761 Sheet metalwork; roofing contractor

(P-12075)
253 INC
245 E Harris Ave, South San Francisco (94080-6807)
PHONE..........................650 737-5670
Michael Calleja, *CEO*
EMP: 10
SALES (est): 950K **Privately Held**
SIC: 3444 Sheet metalwork

(P-12076)
5H SHEET METAL FABRICATION INC
1826 W Business Center Dr, Orange (92867-7904)
PHONE..........................714 633-7544
Hoa Nguyen, *CEO*

Helena Nguyen, *CFO*
Hoa Thi Nguyen, *Admin Sec*
EMP: 15
SQ FT: 10,000
SALES (est): 2.3MM **Privately Held**
SIC: 3444 Sheet metalwork

(P-12077)
A & G INDUSTRIES INC
341 Enterprise St, San Marcos (92078-4339)
PHONE..........................760 891-0323
Roger B Souders, *CEO*
Nate Souders, *Buyer*
EMP: 13
SQ FT: 6,000
SALES (est): 2.4MM **Privately Held**
SIC: 3444 Sheet metal specialties, not stamped

(P-12078)
A & J PRECISION SHEETMETAL INC
1161 N 4th St, San Jose (95112-4945)
PHONE..........................408 885-9134
Amrik Atwal, *CEO*
Jagtar Atwal, *President*
Suki Atwal, *Vice Pres*
▲ EMP: 52
SQ FT: 1,600
SALES (est): 10.6MM **Privately Held**
WEB: www.ajsheetmetal.com
SIC: 3444 Sheet metalwork

(P-12079)
A & M SCULPTURED METALS LLC
Also Called: A & M Sculpture Lighting
1781 N Indiana St, Los Angeles (90063-2523)
PHONE..........................323 263-2221
Jerry Orlandini,
EMP: 30
SQ FT: 10,000
SALES (est): 5MM **Privately Held**
SIC: 3444 Sheet metalwork

(P-12080)
A H K ELECTRONIC SHTMTL INC
875 Jarvis Dr Ste 120, Morgan Hill (95037-2887)
PHONE..........................408 778-3901
Vinai Kumar, *President*
Farid Ghantous, *COO*
Paul Pace, *Accounts Exec*
EMP: 20
SQ FT: 30,000
SALES (est): 3.9MM **Privately Held**
WEB: www.ahksheetmetal.com
SIC: 3444 Sheet metal specialties, not stamped

(P-12081)
A R S MECHANICAL
1205 N 5th St Frnt Frnt, San Jose (95112-4443)
PHONE..........................408 288-8822
Henry Lee, *President*
Connie Wong, *President*
Elayne Christian, *Office Mgr*
Deen Shareef, *Manager*
Brandon Blackmon, *Accounts Exec*
EMP: 12
SALES: 1MM **Privately Held**
SIC: 3444 1711 Metal ventilating equipment; hoods, range: sheet metal; plumbing, heating, air-conditioning contractors

(P-12082)
A-1 METAL PRODUCTS INC
2707 Supply Ave, Commerce (90040-2703)
PHONE..........................323 721-3334
Jerry Calsbeek, *President*
Patricia Calsbeek, *Corp Secy*
EMP: 24 EST: 1952
SQ FT: 40,000
SALES (est): 5MM **Privately Held**
WEB: www.a1metalproducts.com
SIC: 3444 Sheet metal specialties, not stamped

(P-12083)
ABLE SHEET METAL INC (PA)
614 N Ford Blvd, Los Angeles (90022-1195)
PHONE..........................323 269-2181

Dmitri Triphon, *CEO*
Ingrid Anderson, *Office Mgr*
Sharon Cohn, *Technology*
Jess Grandy, *Opers Staff*
Sharon Cofsky Cohn, *Manager*
▲ EMP: 40
SQ FT: 25,000
SALES: 6MM **Privately Held**
SIC: 3444 Sheet metal specialties, not stamped

(P-12084)
ACCURATE HEATING & COOLING INC
Also Called: Tru-Fit Manufacturing
3515 Yosemite Ave, Lathrop (95330-9748)
PHONE..........................209 858-4125
Joan Kauffman, *President*
Melvin Kauffman, *Shareholder*
Jill Brandenburg, *Corp Secy*
Janet Murray, *Manager*
EMP: 23
SQ FT: 30,000
SALES (est): 5MM **Privately Held**
WEB: www.deltaac.com
SIC: 3444 Ducts, sheet metal

(P-12085)
ADAMS-CAMPBELL COMPANY LTD
15323 Proctor Ave, City of Industry (91745-1022)
P.O. Box 3867 (91744-0867)
PHONE..........................626 330-3425
Bob Ludlam, *General Mgr*
EMP: 25
SALES (corp-wide): 12MM **Privately Held**
WEB: www.adamscampbell.com
SIC: 3444 Sheet metalwork
PA: Adams-Campbell Company Ltd
15343 Proctor Ave
City Of Industry CA 91745
626 330-3425

(P-12086)
ADVANCED METAL MFG INC
49 Strathearn Pl, Simi Valley (93065-1653)
PHONE..........................805 322-4161
Scott Stewart, *CEO*
Gina Stewart, *Controller*
▲ EMP: 23
SALES (est): 4.4MM **Privately Held**
SIC: 3444 Sheet metalwork

(P-12087)
ADVANCED METAL WORKS INC
1560 H St, Fresno (93721-1616)
PHONE..........................559 237-2332
Preston Cross, *President*
Graydon William Cross, *Manager*
EMP: 11
SALES (est): 1.6MM **Privately Held**
WEB: www.fourcsmetal.com
SIC: 3444 Awnings & canopies

(P-12088)
ADVANCED MFG & DEV INC
Also Called: Metalfx
200 N Lenore Ave, Willits (95490-3209)
PHONE..........................707 459-9451
Gordon Short, *President*
▲ EMP: 128
SQ FT: 65,000
SALES (est): 19.6MM **Privately Held**
WEB: www.metalfx.com
SIC: 3444 2541 3469 3567 Housings for business machines, sheet metal; cabinets, except refrigerated: show, display, etc.: wood; metal stampings; industrial furnaces & ovens; coin-operated amusement machines; boxes, wood

(P-12089)
AERO BENDING COMPANY
560 Auto Center Dr Ste A, Palmdale (93551-4485)
PHONE..........................661 948-2363
Robert Burns, *President*
EMP: 30
SQ FT: 26,000
SALES (est): 8.4MM **Privately Held**
WEB: www.aerobendingco.co
SIC: 3444 5088 Sheet metalwork; aircraft engines & engine parts

(P-12090)
AERO PRECISION ENGINEERING INC
11300 Hindry Ave, Los Angeles (90045-6228)
PHONE..........................310 642-9747
Sherry L Martinez, *President*
John Segotta, *Prgrmr*
Tom Segotta, *Exec Sec*
EMP: 45
SQ FT: 55,000
SALES (est): 8.7MM **Privately Held**
WEB: www.aeroprecisioneng.com
SIC: 3444 3599 Sheet metal specialties, not stamped; machine shop, jobbing & repair

(P-12091)
AF GOMES INC
901 Commercial St Ste 140, San Jose (95112-1441)
PHONE..........................408 453-7300
Albert Gomes, *President*
Fern Gomes, *COO*
Ashley Taylor, *Opers Staff*
EMP: 25
SQ FT: 1,100
SALES (est): 4.1MM **Privately Held**
SIC: 3444 Sheet metalwork

(P-12092)
AIR TRANSPORT MANUFACTURING
2629 Foothill Blvd, La Crescenta (91214-3511)
PHONE..........................818 504-3300
Kirn Kessen, *President*
John Callahan, *Vice Pres*
Richard Norris, *Admin Sec*
EMP: 10
SQ FT: 18,000
SALES (est): 750K **Privately Held**
SIC: 3444 Sheet metalwork

(P-12093)
AIRCRAFT STAMPING COMPANY INC
1285 Paseo Alicia, San Dimas (91773-4407)
PHONE..........................323 283-1239
Michael Nolan, *President*
Linda Nolan, *Shareholder*
EMP: 30
SQ FT: 17,900
SALES (est): 3.8MM **Privately Held**
WEB: www.aircraftstamping.com
SIC: 3444 3469 Sheet metal specialties, not stamped; metal stampings

(P-12094)
AIRTRONICS METAL PRODUCTS INC (PA)
140 San Pedro Ave, Morgan Hill (95037-5123)
PHONE..........................408 977-7800
Jeff Burke, *CEO*
John Richardson, *Ch of Bd*
James Ellis, *Vice Pres*
Fermin Rodriguez, *Vice Pres*
Kyle O'Leary, *CIO*
▲ EMP: 139
SQ FT: 55,000
SALES (est): 37.4MM **Privately Held**
WEB: www.airtronics.com
SIC: 3444 3479 Sheet metalwork; painting, coating & hot dipping

(P-12095)
AKAS MANUFACTURING CORPORATION
Also Called: Labtronix
3200 Investment Blvd, Hayward (94545-3807)
PHONE..........................510 786-3200
Santosh Sud, *President*
Artie Sud, *Vice Pres*
EMP: 25
SQ FT: 60,000
SALES (est): 3.2MM **Privately Held**
WEB: www.labtronix.com
SIC: 3444 3441 Sheet metalwork; fabricated structural metal

(P-12096)
ALCO ENGRG & TOOLING CORP
Also Called: Alco Metal Fab
3001 Oak St, Santa Ana (92707-4235)
PHONE..................714 556-6060
Frank Vallefuoco, *President*
Angelo D'Eramo, *Corp Secy*
Tom Hare, *Vice Pres*
Arnold Casado, *Purchasing*
EMP: 40 **EST:** 1944
SQ FT: 32,000
SALES (est): 8.7MM **Privately Held**
SIC: 3444 Sheet metal specialties, not stamped

(P-12097)
ALL METAL FABRICATION
617 S Raymond Ave, Pasadena (91105-3219)
PHONE..................626 449-6191
Rick Meone, *Owner*
EMP: 10 **EST:** 1998
SQ FT: 1,500
SALES (est): 879.4K **Privately Held**
SIC: 3444 Sheet metalwork

(P-12098)
ALL SPEC SHEET METAL INC
547 Bliss Ave, Pittsburg (94565-5001)
PHONE..................925 427-4900
Dwayne Jones, *President*
Dennis Jones, *Vice Pres*
EMP: 12
SALES (est): 1.6MM **Privately Held**
SIC: 3444 1761 Sheet metalwork; sheet metalwork

(P-12099)
ALL-WAYS METAL INC
401 E Alondra Blvd, Gardena (90248-2901)
PHONE..................310 217-1177
Shirley Pickens, *President*
Scott Pickens, *Vice Pres*
Jesse Gutierrez, *QC Mgr*
EMP: 30
SQ FT: 29,000
SALES (est): 7.1MM **Privately Held**
WEB: www.allwaysmetal.com
SIC: 3444 Sheet metal specialties, not stamped

(P-12100)
ALLIANCE METAL PRODUCTS INC
20844 Plummer St, Chatsworth (91311-5004)
PHONE..................818 709-1204
Dan L Rowlett Jr, *CEO*
EMP: 212
SQ FT: 2,000
SALES (est): 726K **Privately Held**
SIC: 3444 Sheet metal specialties, not stamped

(P-12101)
ALPHA PRODUCTIONS INCORPORATED
5830 W Jefferson Blvd, Los Angeles (90016-3109)
PHONE..................310 559-1364
Missak Azirian, *President*
John Forker, *VP Sales*
Cliff Gimbert, *Manager*
▲ **EMP:** 25
SQ FT: 25,000
SALES (est): 3.8MM **Privately Held**
WEB: www.alphaawning.com
SIC: 3444 Awnings, sheet metal

(P-12102)
AMD INTERNATIONAL TECH LLC
Also Called: International Rite-Way Pdts
1725 S Campus Ave, Ontario (91761-4346)
PHONE..................909 985-8300
Ravinder Joshi,
Lou Pattengell, *General Mgr*
EMP: 25
SQ FT: 17,000
SALES (est): 2.6MM **Privately Held**
SIC: 3444 1761 Sheet metal specialties, not stamped; sheet metalwork

(P-12103)
AMERICAN AEROSPACE PDTS INC
1720 S Santa Fe St, Santa Ana (92705-4813)
PHONE..................714 662-7620
Syed Ahsun, *President*
EMP: 15
SQ FT: 10,000
SALES (est): 725.9K **Privately Held**
SIC: 3444 3728 5072 Sheet metalwork; aircraft parts & equipment; hardware

(P-12104)
AMERICAN AIRCRAFT PRODUCTS INC
Also Called: A A P
15411 S Broadway, Gardena (90248-2207)
PHONE..................310 532-7434
Gerald R Tupper, *President*
EMP: 67
SQ FT: 54,000
SALES (est): 16.7MM **Privately Held**
WEB: www.americanaircraft.com
SIC: 3444 3599 Sheet metalwork; machine shop, jobbing & repair

(P-12105)
AMERICAN COFFEE URN MFG CO INC
Also Called: A C U Precision Sheet Metal
5178 Western Way, Perris (92571-7422)
PHONE..................951 943-1495
Jeff Johs, *President*
Andy Johs, *Vice Pres*
EMP: 13
SQ FT: 9,280
SALES (est): 2MM **Privately Held**
SIC: 3444 Sheet metalwork

(P-12106)
AMERICAN METAL PROCESSING
390 Front St, El Cajon (92020-4206)
PHONE..................619 444-6171
EMP: 30
SQ FT: 15,000
SALES (est): 4MM **Privately Held**
SIC: 3444

(P-12107)
AMERICAN RANGE CORPORATION
13592 Desmond St, Pacoima (91331-2315)
PHONE..................818 897-0808
Shane Demirjian, *President*
Mourad Demirjian, *Vice Pres*
Richard Lenning, *Vice Pres*
Jose Guevara, *General Mgr*
Nairi Lakhouian, *Engineer*
◆ **EMP:** 120
SQ FT: 125,000
SALES (est): 26.9MM **Privately Held**
WEB: www.americanrange.com
SIC: 3444 3631 Hoods, range: sheet metal; household cooking equipment

(P-12108)
AMERICAN SHEET METAL INC
1430 N Daly St, Anaheim (92806-1502)
PHONE..................714 780-0155
Eli Choueiry, *President*
EMP: 11
SQ FT: 5,588
SALES (est): 2.1MM **Privately Held**
SIC: 3444 Sheet metal specialties, not stamped

(P-12109)
ANDRUS SHEET METAL INC
Also Called: Seaport Stainless
5021 Seaport Ave, Richmond (94804-4638)
PHONE..................510 232-8687
Ray Doving, *President*
Linda Doving, *Vice Pres*
Ryan Doving, *Vice Pres*
Lisa Cook, *Office Mgr*
Larry Camilleri, *Plant Mgr*
EMP: 30 **EST:** 1977
SQ FT: 14,000
SALES (est): 6.9MM **Privately Held**
WEB: www.seaportstainless.com
SIC: 3444 Restaurant sheet metalwork

(P-12110)
ANGELS SHEET METAL INC
Also Called: Distinctive Metals By Angel S
320 N Main St, Angels Camp (95222-9206)
PHONE..................209 736-0911
Jerri Mills, *President*
EMP: 10
SALES (corp-wide): 4.3MM **Privately Held**
SIC: 3444 Sheet metalwork
PA: Angel's Sheet Metal, Inc.
2502 Gun Club Rd
Angels Camp CA 95222
209 736-0911

(P-12111)
ANGELUS SHEET METAL MFG CO
Also Called: Angelus Sheet Metal & Plbg Sup
1355 Carroll Ave, Los Angeles (90026-5109)
PHONE..................323 221-4191
Ronald S Coutin, *President*
Leonard Coutin, *Manager*
EMP: 13 **EST:** 1932
SALES (est): 1.1MM **Privately Held**
SIC: 3444 Sheet metalwork

(P-12112)
ANOROC PRECISION SHTMTL INC
19122 S Santa Fe Ave, Compton (90221-5910)
PHONE..................310 515-6015
Roxanne Zavala, *CEO*
Pete Corona, *Vice Pres*
Peter Corona, *Vice Pres*
EMP: 25 **EST:** 1978
SQ FT: 15,000
SALES (est): 4.5MM **Privately Held**
WEB: www.anoroc.com
SIC: 3444 Sheet metal specialties, not stamped

(P-12113)
AP PRECISION METALS INC
1215 30th St, San Diego (92154-3477)
PHONE..................619 628-0003
Lane A Litke, *CEO*
Susan D Miller, *Treasurer*
Susan Miller, *Treasurer*
Victor B Miller, *Vice Pres*
Dustin Campbell, *General Mgr*
EMP: 11
SALES (est): 2MM **Privately Held**
WEB: www.apprecision.com
SIC: 3444 Sheet metalwork

(P-12114)
ARRK PRODUCT DEV GROUP USA INC
1949 Palomar Oaks Way A, Carlsbad (92011-1312)
PHONE..................858 552-1587
Carlos Herrera, *President*
Koji Tsujino, *CEO*
Takuya Kasai, *CFO*
▲ **EMP:** 145
SALES (est): 28MM **Privately Held**
SIC: 3444 Sheet metalwork
HQ: Arrk Corporation
2-2-9, Minamihommachi, Chuo-Ku
Osaka OSK 541-0
-

(P-12115)
ARTHUR P LAMARRE & SONS INC
1918 Paulson Rd Ste 101, Turlock (95380-8738)
P.O. Box 2704 (95381-2704)
PHONE..................209 667-6557
Arthur Lamarre Jr, *President*
Steven Lamarre, *CFO*
Kevin Lamarre, *Vice Pres*
David Lamarre, *Admin Sec*
EMP: 10
SQ FT: 7,500
SALES (est): 1MM **Privately Held**
SIC: 3444 Ducts, sheet metal

(P-12116)
ARTISTIC WELDING INC
Also Called: Precision Sheet Metal
505 E Gardena Blvd, Gardena (90248-2915)
PHONE..................310 515-4922
George R Sandoval, *President*
Mary Sandoval, *Admin Sec*
EMP: 65 **EST:** 1974
SQ FT: 85,000
SALES (est): 11.2MM **Privately Held**
WEB: www.artistic-welding.com
SIC: 3444 Sheet metalwork

(P-12117)
ASCENT TECHNOLOGY INC
838 Jury Ct, San Jose (95112-2815)
PHONE..................408 213-1080
Mark S Fanelli, *President*
Joy Kan, *Human Res Mgr*
Jeff Cherenoff, *VP Sales*
▲ **EMP:** 35
SALES (est): 4.5MM **Privately Held**
WEB: www.ascenttech.com
SIC: 3444 3364 Sheet metalwork; nonferrous die-castings except aluminum

(P-12118)
ASM CONSTRUCTION INC
Also Called: American Sheet Metal
1947 John Towers Ave, El Cajon (92020-1117)
PHONE..................619 449-1966
Robert Burner, *President*
Ron Burner Jr, *CFO*
EMP: 41
SQ FT: 9,000
SALES (est): 9.2MM **Privately Held**
WEB: www.americansm.com
SIC: 3444 Sheet metalwork

(P-12119)
ASM PRECISION INC
613 Martin Ave Ste 106, Rohnert Park (94928-2000)
PHONE..................707 584-7950
Mario R Felciano, *President*
Jay Sandoval, *Vice Pres*
EMP: 15 **EST:** 2007
SQ FT: 9,000
SALES (est): 4MM **Privately Held**
SIC: 3444 Sheet metal specialties, not stamped

(P-12120)
ATLAS SHEET METAL INC
19 Musick, Irvine (92618-1638)
PHONE..................949 600-8787
James M Odlum, *President*
Raelene Pace, *CFO*
EMP: 17
SQ FT: 5,500
SALES (est): 3.5MM **Privately Held**
WEB: www.atlassheetmetal.net
SIC: 3444 Sheet metalwork

(P-12121)
AXIAL INDUSTRIES INC
1991 Senter Rd, San Jose (95112-2631)
PHONE..................408 977-7800
Buddy G Rogers Jr, *CEO*
Michael Nevin, *Principal*
EMP: 145
SQ FT: 42,000
SALES (est): 13.6MM
SALES (corp-wide): 37.4MM **Privately Held**
WEB: www.axialind.com
SIC: 3444 Sheet metal specialties, not stamped
PA: Airtronics Metal Products, Inc.
140 San Pedro Ave
Morgan Hill CA 95037
408 977-7800

(P-12122)
AYMAR ENGINEERING
9434 Abraham Way, Santee (92071-5835)
PHONE..................619 562-1121
Wayne Aymar, *Owner*
EMP: 14
SQ FT: 13,000
SALES (est): 2.2MM **Privately Held**
WEB: www.aymarengineering.com
SIC: 3444 3469 Sheet metal specialties, not stamped; metal stampings

PRODUCTS & SVCS

(P-12123)
AZACHOROK CONTRACT SVCS LLC
320 Grand Cypress Ave # 502, Palmdale (93551-3622)
PHONE....................................661 951-6566
Loren Peterson,
EMP: 14
SQ FT: 12,000
SALES (est): 2.5MM **Privately Held**
WEB: www.accuratemachineco.com
SIC: 3444 3663 Sheet metalwork; airborne radio communications equipment; carrier equipment, radio communications

(P-12124)
B & CAWNINGS INC
Also Called: B & C Industries
3082 E Miraloma Ave, Anaheim (92806-1810)
PHONE....................................714 632-3303
CHI Le, Chairman
Buu Pham, President
Jeff Pham, Vice Pres
Chris Walker, Vice Pres
Matthew Walker, Vice Pres
▲ EMP: 30
SQ FT: 7,000
SALES: 4.2MM **Privately Held**
WEB: www.bcawnings.com
SIC: 3444 Awnings, sheet metal

(P-12125)
B & G METAL INC
9408 Gidley St, Temple City (91780-4211)
PHONE....................................626 444-8566
Bob Ellingsworth, President
EMP: 12
SALES (est): 935.9K **Privately Held**
WEB: www.bgsminc.com
SIC: 3444 Sheet metalwork

(P-12126)
B METAL FABRICATION INC
318 S Maple Ave, South San Francisco (94080-6306)
PHONE....................................650 615-7705
Robert Steinebel, CEO
Berthold Steinebel, President
Brigitte Steinebel, Officer
Barbara Blundell, Vice Pres
Bob Foster, Vice Pres
EMP: 30
SQ FT: 14,000
SALES (est): 6MM **Privately Held**
WEB: www.bmetalfabrication.com
SIC: 3444 Sheet metal specialties, not stamped

(P-12127)
BARZILLAI MANUFACTURING CO
1410 S Cucamonga Ave, Ontario (91761-4509)
PHONE....................................909 947-4200
Ray Richmond, President
Garrett Zopf, Treasurer
EMP: 17
SQ FT: 5,200
SALES (est): 2.2MM **Privately Held**
SIC: 3444 Sheet metalwork

(P-12128)
BASMAT INC (PA)
Also Called: McStarlite
1531 240th St, Harbor City (90710-1308)
PHONE....................................310 325-2063
John W Basso, CEO
John Allen Basso, President
Henry Matadlu, President
Tim Benfer, COO
Simon Menezies, General Mgr
▲ EMP: 100
SQ FT: 42,000
SALES (est): 20.7MM **Privately Held**
WEB: www.mcstarlite.com
SIC: 3444 Sheet metalwork

(P-12129)
BAY CITIES TIN SHOP INC
Also Called: Bay Cities Metal Products
301 E Alondra Blvd, Gardena (90248-2809)
PHONE....................................310 660-0351
Henry Kamberg, CEO

Gary Mugford, President
Debra Childress, Vice Pres
Guillermo Patino, Opers Mgr
EMP: 43
SALES (est): 9.1MM **Privately Held**
WEB: www.baycitiesmetalproducts.com
SIC: 3444 Sheet metal specialties, not stamped

(P-12130)
BELLAMA CSTM MET FBRCATORS INC
Also Called: B C M
3129 Main St, Chula Vista (91911-5705)
PHONE....................................619 585-3351
Michael Bellama, President
Randy Bellama, Treasurer
Don Bellama, Vice Pres
Robert Page, Vice Pres
Jo Ann Bellama, Admin Sec
EMP: 10
SQ FT: 10,000
SALES (est): 1.4MM **Privately Held**
SIC: 3444 Sheet metalwork

(P-12131)
BEND-TEK INC
2205 S Yale St, Santa Ana (92704-4426)
PHONE....................................714 210-8966
Melinda Nguyen, CEO
Eric Tran, CFO
Mac Le, Officer
EMP: 100
SQ FT: 7,000
SALES (est): 10MM **Privately Held**
WEB: www.bendtekinc.com
SIC: 3444 Pipe, sheet metal

(P-12132)
BMB METAL PRODUCTS CORPORATION
Also Called: B M B
11460 Elks Cir, Rancho Cordova (95742-7332)
PHONE....................................916 631-9120
Jerry Mc Donald, President
Jerry Donald, Vice Pres
Jolene Harlos,
EMP: 24 EST: 1966
SQ FT: 23,000
SALES (est): 6.3MM **Privately Held**
WEB: www.bmbcorp.com
SIC: 3444 Sheet metalwork

(P-12133)
BOOZAK INC
Also Called: K Squared Metals
508 Chaney St Ste A, Lake Elsinore (92530-2797)
PHONE....................................951 245-6045
Kevin Kluzak, President
Kevin Booth, Vice Pres
EMP: 45
SALES (est): 5.8MM **Privately Held**
WEB: www.boozak.com
SIC: 3444 Sheet metalwork

(P-12134)
BORGA STL BLDNGS CMPONENTS INC
300 W Peach St, Fowler (93625-2530)
P.O. Box 35 (93625-0035)
PHONE....................................559 834-5375
Ronald Heskett, CEO
Scott Boatwright, Controller
Amila Roberts, Human Resources
Pete Garza, Opers Mgr
EMP: 35
SQ FT: 90,000
SALES (est): 10MM **Privately Held**
SIC: 3444 3448 3446 Metal housings, enclosures, casings & other containers; buildings, portable: prefabricated metal; railings, prefabricated metal

(P-12135)
BOTNER MANUFACTURING INC
900 Aladdin Ave, San Leandro (94577-4308)
PHONE....................................510 569-2943
Donn Botner, President
▲ EMP: 10
SQ FT: 45,000

SALES (est): 3.6MM **Privately Held**
SIC: 3444 3441 Sheet metalwork; fabricated structural metal

(P-12136)
BRADY SHEET METAL INC
320 N Victory Blvd, Burbank (91502-1840)
PHONE....................................818 846-4043
Steve Drugan, President
Craig Brady, Vice Pres
EMP: 10 EST: 1933
SQ FT: 5,000
SALES (est): 1.5MM **Privately Held**
SIC: 3444 Sheet metalwork

(P-12137)
BT SHEET METAL INC
1031 Calle Trepadora D, San Clemente (92673-6289)
PHONE....................................949 481-5715
Brad Tetherton, President
Kelli Lambert, Office Mgr
EMP: 12
SQ FT: 5,000
SALES (est): 1.3MM **Privately Held**
SIC: 3444 Sheet metalwork

(P-12138)
BURLINGAME HTG VENTILATION INC
821 Malcolm Rd, Burlingame (94010-1406)
PHONE....................................650 697-9142
Douglass Ulrich, CEO
Fred Ulrich, President
Patricia Ann Ulrich, Corp Secy
EMP: 15
SQ FT: 3,000
SALES (est): 2.6MM **Privately Held**
SIC: 3444 1711 Sheet metalwork; heating & air conditioning contractors

(P-12139)
BUXCON SHEETMETAL INC
11222 Woodside Ave N, Santee (92071-4716)
PHONE....................................619 937-0001
Richard Buxton, President
Thomas Buxton, CFO
Larry Henry, Admin Sec
EMP: 15
SQ FT: 18,138
SALES (est): 5.7MM **Privately Held**
SIC: 3444 Sheet metalwork

(P-12140)
C & J METAL PRODUCTS INC
6323 Alondra Blvd, Paramount (90723-3750)
PHONE....................................562 634-3101
Roy L Chapman, President
Isabelle Chapman, Corp Secy
▲ EMP: 40 EST: 1946
SQ FT: 37,000
SALES (est): 6.9MM **Privately Held**
WEB: www.cjmetals.com
SIC: 3444 Ventilators, sheet metal

(P-12141)
C&J FAB CENTER INC
Also Called: Gardena Sheet Metal
1415 W 135th St, Gardena (90249-2232)
PHONE....................................310 323-0970
Charlie Rim, President
EMP: 10
SQ FT: 12,000
SALES (est): 1.3MM **Privately Held**
SIC: 3444 Sheet metalwork

(P-12142)
C&O MANUFACTURING COMPANY INC
9640 Beverly Rd, Pico Rivera (90660-2137)
PHONE....................................562 692-7525
Cesar Gonzalez, President
Oscar Valdez, Vice Pres
EMP: 67
SQ FT: 22,000
SALES (est): 11.9MM **Privately Held**
WEB: www.cnomfg.com
SIC: 3444 Sheet metal specialties, not stamped

(P-12143)
CAL PAC SHEET METAL INC
2720 S Main St Ste B, Santa Ana (92707-3404)
PHONE....................................714 979-2733
Marushkah Kurtz, CEO
Collin Cumbee, CFO
Bob Catalano, Vice Pres
Carolyn Miller, Principal
Craig Faucher, Project Mgr
EMP: 40
SQ FT: 5,000
SALES (est): 8MM **Privately Held**
WEB: www.calpacsheetmetal.com
SIC: 3444 Sheet metal specialties, not stamped

(P-12144)
CALIFORNIA EXPANDED MET PDTS (PA)
Also Called: Cemco
13191 Crosrds Pkwy N 32, City of Industry (91746)
PHONE....................................626 369-3564
Raymond E Poliquin, CEO
Richard Poliquin, President
Tom Porter, Exec VP
Manuel Luna, Manager
◆ EMP: 68 EST: 1982
SQ FT: 40,000
SALES (est): 73.8MM **Privately Held**
SIC: 3444 Sheet metalwork

(P-12145)
CALIFORNIA HYDROFORMING CO INC
850 Lawson St, City of Industry (91748-1103)
PHONE....................................626 912-0036
David Bonafede, President
David Wickey, Vice Pres
EMP: 15 EST: 1956
SQ FT: 17,500
SALES (est): 3.1MM **Privately Held**
WEB: www.cal-hydro.com
SIC: 3444 3469 Sheet metalwork; stamping metal for the trade

(P-12146)
CALIFORNIA METAL GROUP INC
Also Called: B C Lighting
1205 S Alameda St, Compton (90220-4803)
PHONE....................................310 609-1400
Benjamin Castellanos, President
EMP: 12
SQ FT: 7,200
SALES: 1MM **Privately Held**
SIC: 3444 3441 Sheet metalwork; fabricated structural metal

(P-12147)
CALIFORNIA PANEL SYSTEMS LLP
1020 N Marshall Ave, El Cajon (92020-1829)
PHONE....................................619 562-7010
Joe Isom, President
Karl J Isom, Partner
EMP: 20
SALES (est): 1.1MM **Privately Held**
SIC: 3444 Sheet metalwork

(P-12148)
CALIFORNIA PRECISION PDTS INC
Also Called: Cppi
6790 Flanders Dr, San Diego (92121-2902)
PHONE....................................858 638-7300
Joe Bean, CEO
EMP: 80
SQ FT: 50,000
SALES (est): 16.2MM **Privately Held**
WEB: www.calprec.com
SIC: 3444 Sheet metal specialties, not stamped

(P-12149)
CAMPBELL & LOFTIN INC
Also Called: Superior Sheet Metal
1560 N Missile Way, Anaheim (92801-1223)
PHONE....................................714 871-1950
Sue Loftin, President
Sue Loften, President

▲ = Import ▼=Export
◆ =Import/Export

Casey Crowder, *Vice Pres*
EMP: 10
SQ FT: 15,000
SALES (est): 2MM **Privately Held**
SIC: 3444 Elbows, for air ducts, stovepipes, etc.: sheet metal

(P-12150)
CAPTIVE-AIRE SYSTEMS INC
2510 Cloudcrest Way, Riverside (92507-3027)
PHONE....................................951 231-5102
EMP: 13
SALES (corp-wide): 389.2MM **Privately Held**
SIC: 3444 Restaurant sheet metalwork
PA: Captive-Aire Systems, Inc.
4641 Paragon Park Rd # 104
Raleigh NC 27616
919 882-2410

(P-12151)
CAPTIVE-AIRE SYSTEMS INC
6856 Lockheed Dr, Redding (96002-9769)
PHONE....................................530 351-7150
Csaba Sikur, *Branch Mgr*
EMP: 140
SALES (corp-wide): 389.2MM **Privately Held**
WEB: www.captiveaire.com
SIC: 3444 Metal ventilating equipment
PA: Captive-Aire Systems, Inc.
4641 Paragon Park Rd # 104
Raleigh NC 27616
919 882-2410

(P-12152)
CARDINAL SHEET METAL INC
3184 Durahart St, Riverside (92507-3449)
PHONE....................................951 788-8800
Penny Seyler, *President*
Bruce Seyler, *Vice Pres*
Johny Riteveld, *Admin Sec*
EMP: 10
SQ FT: 9,000
SALES (est): 1.5MM **Privately Held**
SIC: 3444 Roof deck, sheet metal; siding, sheet metal

(P-12153)
CARSON VALLEY INC
13215 Barton Cir, Whittier (90605-3255)
PHONE....................................562 906-0062
Mark Priestley, *President*
Carmen Priestley, *Vice Pres*
Gary Lemay, *Foreman/Supr*
EMP: 11
SQ FT: 6,500
SALES (est): 1.1MM **Privately Held**
WEB: www.carsonvalley.com
SIC: 3444 Pipe, sheet metal

(P-12154)
CARTEL INDUSTRIES LLC
17152 Armstrong Ave, Irvine (92614-5718)
PHONE....................................949 474-3200
William Penick,
Vickie Chukiat, *Controller*
Kirby Unfried, *QC Mgr*
Andy Van Der Roest, *Opers Staff*
Gant Penick,
▲ **EMP:** 49
SQ FT: 30,000
SALES (est): 13.3MM **Privately Held**
WEB: www.cartelind.com
SIC: 3444 Sheet metal specialties, not stamped

(P-12155)
CG MANUFACTURING INC
Also Called: K-Bros
21021 Osborne St, Canoga Park (91304-1744)
PHONE....................................818 886-1191
George Thomas, *President*
EMP: 11
SQ FT: 15,000
SALES (est): 195.1K **Privately Held**
WEB: www.k-bros.com
SIC: 3444 Sheet metalwork

(P-12156)
CIRCLEMASTER INC
7777 Alvarado Rd Ste 320, La Mesa (91942-8247)
PHONE....................................858 578-3900

Neville T Henkel Jr, *President*
EMP: 10
SQ FT: 4,000
SALES (est): 920K **Privately Held**
WEB: www.circlemaster.net
SIC: 3444 Sheet metalwork

(P-12157)
CLARKWESTERN DIETRICH BUILDING
Also Called: Clarkdietrich Building Systems
6510 General Rd, Riverside (92509-0103)
PHONE....................................951 360-3500
Clark Dietrich, *Owner*
Reymundo Rangel, *Programmer Anys*
EMP: 16 **Privately Held**
SIC: 3444 8711 3081 Studs & joists, sheet metal; engineering services; vinyl film & sheet
HQ: Clarkwestern Dietrich Building Systems Llc
9050 Cntre Pnte Dr Ste 40
West Chester OH 45069

(P-12158)
COAST SHEET METAL INC
990 W 17th St, Costa Mesa (92627-4403)
PHONE....................................949 645-2224
Wayne Chambers, *President*
Marna Chambers, *Vice Pres*
EMP: 35 **EST:** 1960
SQ FT: 3,800
SALES (est): 5.8MM **Privately Held**
WEB: www.coastsheetmetal.com
SIC: 3444 Sheet metal specialties, not stamped

(P-12159)
COMCO SHEET METAL COMPANY
237 Southbrook Pl, Clayton (94517-1035)
PHONE....................................510 832-6433
Armand Butticci III, *President*
Maria Butticci, *Corp Secy*
EMP: 12
SQ FT: 13,000
SALES (est): 1.8MM **Privately Held**
SIC: 3444 Restaurant sheet metalwork

(P-12160)
COMPUTER METAL PRODUCTS CORP
Also Called: Vline Industries
370 E Easy St, Simi Valley (93065-1802)
PHONE....................................805 520-6966
Jim Visage, *President*
Angel Angeles, *COO*
Karen Bender, *CFO*
Keith Murphy, *Prdtn Mgr*
Chris Visage, *Sales Mgr*
EMP: 90
SQ FT: 25,000
SALES (est): 18MM **Privately Held**
WEB: www.computermetal.com
SIC: 3444 Sheet metalwork

(P-12161)
CONCISE FABRICATORS INC
7550 Panasonic Way, San Diego (92154-8207)
PHONE....................................520 746-3226
James Dean Johnson, *President*
Bill Maples, *CFO*
Cynthia Whitby, *Materials Mgr*
▼ **EMP:** 50
SQ FT: 120,000
SALES (est): 14.4MM **Privately Held**
SIC: 3444 Sheet metalwork
PA: Blackbird Management Group, Llc
240 E Illinois St # 2004
Chicago IL 60611

(P-12162)
CONTRACT METAL PRODUCTS INC
45535 Northport Loop W Fl Flr 1, Fremont (94538)
PHONE....................................510 979-4811
John Young, *President*
Matt Bostaph, *Safety Mgr*
EMP: 30 **EST:** 1974
SQ FT: 80,000

SALES (est): 6.2MM **Privately Held**
WEB: www.contractmetals.com
SIC: 3444 3599 7692 Sheet metal specialties, not stamped; machine shop, jobbing & repair; welding repair

(P-12163)
COPP INDUSTRIAL MFG INC
2837 Metropolitan Pl, Pomona (91767-1897)
PHONE....................................909 593-7448
Larry R Marvin, *CEO*
Brian Hershman, *President*
Chris Marvin, *Planning*
Rick Rose, *Prdtn Mgr*
EMP: 21
SQ FT: 15,000
SALES (est): 4.5MM **Privately Held**
WEB: www.coppmfg.com
SIC: 3444 Sheet metalwork

(P-12164)
CORTEC PRECISION SHTMTL INC (PA)
2231 Will Wool Dr, San Jose (95112-2628)
PHONE....................................408 278-8540
Mike Corrales, *Vice Pres*
John Corrales, *President*
Richard Corrales, *Vice Pres*
Armando Miranda, *Technology*
MAI Nguyen, *Accountant*
EMP: 153
SQ FT: 78,000
SALES (est): 21.5MM **Privately Held**
SIC: 3444 Sheet metal specialties, not stamped

(P-12165)
COY INDUSTRIES INC
Also Called: E R C Company
2970 E Maria St, E Rncho Dmngz (90221-5802)
PHONE....................................310 603-2970
Michael Coy, *President*
James Patrick Coy, *Corp Secy*
Ramiro Espitia, *Engineer*
Edna Lockwood, *Human Res Dir*
Thomas Gazzillo, *QC Mgr*
EMP: 95 **EST:** 1972
SQ FT: 50,000
SALES (est): 5.8MM **Privately Held**
WEB: www.ercco.com
SIC: 3444 3469 Sheet metal specialties, not stamped; metal stampings

(P-12166)
CPC FABRICATION INC
2904 Oak St, Santa Ana (92707-3723)
PHONE....................................714 549-2426
Thomas Baker, *CEO*
Stacey Sarver, *Office Mgr*
Lyn Baker, *Admin Sec*
Jonathan Edwards, *Director*
EMP: 31
SQ FT: 15,000
SALES (est): 6.4MM **Privately Held**
WEB: www.cpcfab.com
SIC: 3444 Sheet metal specialties, not stamped

(P-12167)
CREATIVE MFG SOLUTIONS
18400 Sutter Blvd, Morgan Hill (95037-2819)
PHONE....................................408 327-0600
Tim Patrick Herlihy, *President*
Tammy Herlihy, *CFO*
Jorge Magana, *Prgrmr*
Israel Ruiz, *Buyer*
EMP: 22
SQ FT: 12,000
SALES (est): 5.9MM **Privately Held**
SIC: 3444 Sheet metal specialties, not stamped

(P-12168)
CROWN PRODUCTS INC
Also Called: Crown Steel
177 Newport Dr Ste A, San Marcos (92069-1470)
PHONE....................................760 471-1188
David J Carr, *President*
EMP: 22 **EST:** 1969
SQ FT: 20,000

SALES (est): 4.6MM **Privately Held**
SIC: 3444 3589 Sheet metalwork; commercial cooking & foodwarming equipment

(P-12169)
D & B PRECISION SHTMTL INC
693 Hi Tech Pkwy, Oakdale (95361-9372)
PHONE....................................209 848-3030
Loretta Ballard, *President*
Wes Ballard, *Vice Pres*
Jorge Ayala, *QC Mgr*
EMP: 12
SQ FT: 10,000
SALES (est): 3.1MM **Privately Held**
SIC: 3444 Sheet metalwork

(P-12170)
D&A METAL FABRICATION INC
16129 Runnymede St, Van Nuys (91406-2913)
PHONE....................................818 780-8231
Jenny Anastasiu, *Office Mgr*
Anca Morgan, *Vice Pres*
EMP: 16
SALES (est): 748.1K **Privately Held**
SIC: 3444 Sheet metalwork

(P-12171)
DAAZE INC
Also Called: C & H Metal Products
1714 S Grove Ave Ste B, Ontario (91761-4550)
PHONE....................................626 442-4961
Octavio Hurtado, *Principal*
Jeanet Alvarez, *Vice Pres*
Octavio Hurtado III, *Admin Sec*
EMP: 15
SQ FT: 28,000
SALES (est): 2.4MM **Privately Held**
WEB: www.chmetals.com
SIC: 3444 Sheet metalwork

(P-12172)
DALE BRISCO INC
2132 S Temperance Ave, Fowler (93625-9760)
PHONE....................................559 834-5926
Jamie Brisco, *President*
Cheryl Brisco, *Office Mgr*
EMP: 17
SQ FT: 50,000
SALES: 1MM **Privately Held**
WEB: www.dalebriscoinc.com
SIC: 3444 Pipe, sheet metal; ducts, sheet metal; flues & pipes, stove or furnace: sheet metal; pile shells, sheet metal

(P-12173)
DANRICH WELDING COINC
7001 Jackson St, Paramount (90723-4834)
PHONE....................................562 634-4811
Richard Schenk, *President*
Julie Lippincott, *Office Mgr*
EMP: 12 **EST:** 1970
SQ FT: 10,800
SALES (est): 1.8MM **Privately Held**
WEB: www.danrichwelding.com
SIC: 3444 7692 Sheet metalwork; welding repair

(P-12174)
DAVE ANNALA
Also Called: Weld Design
1628 E Wilshire Ave, Santa Ana (92705-4505)
PHONE....................................714 541-8383
Dave Annala, *Owner*
EMP: 10
SQ FT: 6,000
SALES: 899K **Privately Held**
SIC: 3444 7692 Sheet metalwork; welding repair

(P-12175)
DAVE WHIPPLE SHEET METAL INC
1077 N Cuyamaca St, El Cajon (92020-1803)
PHONE....................................619 562-6962
Dave Whipple Sr, *President*
Carol Whipple, *Treasurer*
Stacie Rigg, *Office Mgr*
EMP: 34
SQ FT: 9,000

SALES (est): 7.2MM **Privately Held**
WEB: www.whipplesm.com
SIC: **3444** Sheet metalwork

(P-12176)
DECK WEST INC
1900 Sanguinetti Ln, Stockton
(95205-3403)
PHONE............................209 939-9700
Patty Shipman, *CEO*
Cliff Heard, *Project Mgr*
EMP: 11
SQ FT: 26,000
SALES (est): 1.5MM **Privately Held**
WEB: www.deckwest.com
SIC: **3444** Metal roofing & roof drainage
   equipment; metal flooring & siding

(P-12177)
DECRA ROOFING SYSTEMS INC
(DH)
1230 Railroad St, Corona (92882-1837)
PHONE............................951 272-8180
Willard C Hudson Jr, *President*
Chad Colton, *Vice Pres*
Matt Albrecht, *Regional Mgr*
Tanya Salas, *Administration*
Chris Tang, *MIS Mgr*
▲ EMP: 70
SQ FT: 60,000
SALES (est): 29.6MM **Privately Held**
SIC: **3444** Metal roofing & roof drainage
   equipment
HQ: Fletcher Building Holdings Usa, Inc.
   1230 Railroad St
   Corona CA 92882
   951 272-8180

(P-12178)
DELAFOIL HOLDINGS INC (PA)
18500 Von Karman Ave # 450, Irvine
(92612-0504)
PHONE............................949 752-4580
Drew Adams, *Managing Dir*
EMP: 310
SALES (est): 17.1MM **Privately Held**
WEB: www.stonecreekcapital.com
SIC: **3444** Radiator shields or enclosures,
   sheet metal

(P-12179)
DELANEY MANUFACTURING
INC
6810 Downing Ave, Bakersfield
(93308-5810)
PHONE............................661 587-6681
Bill McBride, *Principal*
EMP: 14 EST: 2008
SQ FT: 50,000
SALES (est): 2.5MM **Privately Held**
SIC: **3444** Sheet metalwork

(P-12180)
DELTA FABRICATION INC
9600 De Soto Ave, Chatsworth
(91311-5012)
PHONE............................818 407-4000
Chava Ostrowsky, *CEO*
Joe Ostrowsky, *President*
EMP: 90
SQ FT: 20,000
SALES (est): 17.1MM **Privately Held**
SIC: **3444** Sheet metalwork

(P-12181)
DEPENDABLE PRECISION MFG
INC
1111 S Stockton St Ste A, Lodi
(95240-5933)
PHONE............................209 369-1055
Clifford L McBride, *President*
EMP: 17
SQ FT: 30,000
SALES (est): 2.3MM **Privately Held**
SIC: **3444** Sheet metal specialties, not
   stamped

(P-12182)
DEROSA ENTERPRISES INC
Also Called: PSI
15935 Spring Oaks Rd # 1, El Cajon
(92021-2648)
PHONE............................760 743-5500
Gabriel De Rosa, *President*
Matt De Rosa, *General Mgr*

Watt De Rosa, *General Mgr*
Manny Rivera, *Safety Dir*
EMP: 40
SQ FT: 13,000
SALES (est): 6.6MM **Privately Held**
WEB: www.psimfg.com
SIC: **3444** Sheet metal specialties, not
   stamped

(P-12183)
DEVINCENZI METAL PRODUCTS
INC
1809 Castenada Dr, Burlingame
(94010-5716)
PHONE............................650 692-5800
Robert C Devincenzi, *CEO*
Janice Samuelson, *Corp Secy*
Steven Devincenzi, *Vice Pres*
▲ EMP: 75 EST: 1978
SQ FT: 90,000
SALES (est): 18.5MM **Privately Held**
WEB: www.devmetal.com
SIC: **3444** Sheet metal specialties, not
   stamped

(P-12184)
DIMIC STEEL TECH INC
145 N 8th Ave, Upland (91786-5402)
PHONE............................909 946-6767
Miles Dimic, *President*
Anna Dimic, *CFO*
Marija Goodale, *Officer*
▲ EMP: 24 EST: 1973
SQ FT: 45,000
SALES (est): 6.8MM **Privately Held**
WEB: www.dimicsheetmetal.com
SIC: **3444** Sheet metal specialties, not
   stamped

(P-12185)
DIRECT SURPLUS SALES INC
Also Called: Surplus Ctys Fbrction Mfg Wldg
4801 Feather River Blvd # 3, Oroville
(95965-9690)
PHONE............................530 533-9999
Walter Seidenglanz, *Manager*
EMP: 10
SALES (corp-wide): 3.7MM **Privately**
Held
WEB: www.hwy70.net
SIC: **3444** Metal housings, enclosures,
   casings & other containers
PA: Direct Surplus Sales Inc
   4514 Pacific Heights Rd
   Oroville CA 95965
   530 534-9956

(P-12186)
DOKA USA LTD
Also Called: Conesco Industries
6901 Central Ave, Riverside (92504-1407)
PHONE............................951 509-0023
Peter Franceschina, *Principal*
Sharon Abbott, *Opers Mgr*
Nick Jung, *Opers Staff*
EMP: 13
SALES (corp-wide): 1.7B **Privately Held**
SIC: **3444** Concrete forms, sheet metal
HQ: Doka Usa Ltd.
   214 Gates Rd
   Little Ferry NJ 07643
   201 641-6500

(P-12187)
DUR-RED PRODUCTS
4900 Cecilia St, Cudahy (90201-5993)
PHONE............................323 771-9000
Russell Smith, *President*
Linda Harrison, *Corp Secy*
EMP: 50
SQ FT: 135,000
SALES (est): 8.5MM **Privately Held**
WEB: www.dur-red.com
SIC: **3444** 3446 Sheet metalwork; archi-
   tectural metalwork

(P-12188)
DURAVENT INC (DH)
Also Called: M&G Duravent, Inc.
877 Cotting Ct, Vacaville (95688-9354)
PHONE............................800 835-4429
Simon Davis, *CEO*
◆ EMP: 350

SALES (est): 99.8MM
SALES (corp-wide): 154.5MM **Privately**
Held
SIC: **3444** Metal ventilating equipment
HQ: M & G Group Europe B.V.
   Dr. A.F. Philipsweg 39
   Assen 9403
   503 139-944

(P-12189)
E & S PRECISION SHEETMETAL
MFG
19298 Mclane St, North Palm Springs
(92258)
P.O. Box 581136 (92258-1136)
PHONE............................760 329-1607
Steve Egresits, *President*
Margit R Egresits, *Corp Secy*
EMP: 18
SQ FT: 10,000
SALES (est): 2.8MM **Privately Held**
SIC: **3444** Sheet metal specialties, not
   stamped

(P-12190)
E-M MANUFACTURING INC
1290 Dupont Ct, Manteca (95336-6003)
P.O. Box 397, Half Moon Bay (94019-0397)
PHONE............................209 825-1800
Jody Elliot, *President*
Mike Elliot, *Corp Secy*
EMP: 19
SQ FT: 15,500
SALES (est): 36.7K **Privately Held**
SIC: **3444** Sheet metal specialties, not
   stamped; metal housings, enclosures,
   casings & other containers

(P-12191)
ECB CORP
Also Called: Omni Duct Systems
1650 Parkway Blvd, West Sacramento
(95691-5020)
PHONE............................916 492-8900
Lou Yuhas, *Branch Mgr*
Samuel Jew, *Controller*
Steve Pedroza, *Sales Mgr*
EMP: 40
SALES (est): 3.9MM
SALES (corp-wide): 48.8MM **Privately**
Held
WEB: www.omniduct.com
SIC: **3444** Ducts, sheet metal
PA: Ecb Corp.
   6400 Artesia Blvd
   Buena Park CA 90620
   714 385-8900

(P-12192)
ECLIPSE METAL FABRICATION
INC
2901 Spring St, Redwood City
(94063-3935)
PHONE............................650 298-8731
Joe Anaya, *President*
Eduardo Molina, *CFO*
Eduardo Melina, *Treasurer*
Al Cuevas, *Financial Exec*
EMP: 50
SQ FT: 15,000
SALES (est): 12.4MM **Privately Held**
WEB: www.eclipsemf.com
SIC: **3444** Sheet metalwork

(P-12193)
EDWARDS SHEET METAL
SUPPLY INC
7810 Burnet Ave, Van Nuys (91405-1009)
PHONE............................818 785-8600
Edward Der-Mesropian, *President*
Jacqueline Der-Mesropian, *Corp Secy*
EMP: 25
SQ FT: 20,000
SALES (est): 4.3MM **Privately Held**
SIC: **3444** Booths, spray: prefabricated
   sheet metal

(P-12194)
ELITE E/M INC
340 Martin Ave, Santa Clara (95050-3112)
PHONE............................408 988-3505
Igor Brovarny, *President*
EMP: 32
SQ FT: 12,300

SALES (est): 5.1MM **Privately Held**
WEB: www.eliteem.com
SIC: **3444** 3559 3599 3542 Forming machine work, sheet metal; semiconductor
   manufacturing machinery; machine &
   other job shop work; presses: forming,
   stamping, punching, sizing (machine
   tools); design, commercial & industrial;
   mechanical engineering

(P-12195)
EMPIRE SHEET METAL INC
1215 S Bon View Ave, Ontario
(91761-4402)
PHONE............................909 923-2927
Martin Layman, *President*
EMP: 14
SALES (est): 2.7MM **Privately Held**
SIC: **3444** Sheet metalwork

(P-12196)
EMTEC ENGINEERING
16840 Joleen Way Ste F1, Morgan Hill
(95037-4606)
PHONE............................408 779-5800
Edward R Ruminski, *President*
EMP: 19
SQ FT: 16,000
SALES (est): 4.2MM **Privately Held**
SIC: **3444** 3599 3469 Sheet metalwork;
   machine shop, jobbing & repair; metal
   stampings

(P-12197)
ENCORE INDUSTRIES
597 Brennan St, San Jose (95131-1202)
PHONE............................408 416-0501
Gary Vogel, *CEO*
Tom Fitzgerald, *Treasurer*
Gordon Tigue, *Vice Pres*
▲ EMP: 50
SALES (est): 11.8MM **Privately Held**
SIC: **3444** 3441 Sheet metalwork; fabri-
   cated structural metal

(P-12198)
EQUIPMENT DESIGN & MFG INC
119 Explorer St, Pomona (91768-3278)
PHONE............................909 594-2229
Rick Clewett, *CEO*
Steve Clewett, *Vice Pres*
Ryan Clewett, *Admin Sec*
Jack Cave, *Engineer*
Ellie Huckins, *Purchasing*
EMP: 55 EST: 1976
SQ FT: 27,400
SALES: 6.5MM **Privately Held**
WEB: www.equipmentdesign.net
SIC: **3444** Sheet metalwork

(P-12199)
ESM AEROSPACE INC
1203 W Isabel St, Burbank (91506-1407)
PHONE............................818 841-3653
Jerome Flament, *President*
Rina Flament, *Admin Sec*
EMP: 25
SQ FT: 8,900
SALES: 2.9MM **Privately Held**
SIC: **3444** Casings, sheet metal

(P-12200)
ESPANA METAL CRAFT INC
7600 Ventura Canyon Ave, Van Nuys
(91402-6372)
PHONE............................818 988-4988
Salvador J Espana, *President*
Catalina Espana, *Owner*
EMP: 18
SQ FT: 7,300
SALES (est): 3.3MM **Privately Held**
WEB: www.espanametal.com
SIC: **3444** Sheet metalwork

(P-12201)
EUGENIOS SHEET METAL INC
2151 Maple Privado, Ontario (91761-7603)
PHONE............................909 923-2002
Eugenio M Lozano, *President*
EMP: 18
SQ FT: 10,000
SALES (est): 3.8MM **Privately Held**
WEB: www.eugeniossheetmetal.com
SIC: **3444** Sheet metalwork

▲ = Import ▼=Export
◆ =Import/Export

(P-12202)
EVERT HANCOCK INCORPORATED
Also Called: Amfab
1809 N National St, Anaheim (92801-1016)
PHONE..................714 870-0376
Greg Evert, *President*
Scott Evert, *General Mgr*
EMP: 10
SQ FT: 10,000
SALES: 90K Privately Held
SIC: 3444 Sheet metal specialties, not stamped

(P-12203)
EXCEL SHEET METAL INC (PA)
Also Called: Excel Bridge Manufacturing Co.
12001 Shoemaker Ave, Santa Fe Springs (90670-4718)
PHONE..................562 944-0701
Craig E Vasquez, *CEO*
Jeffrey Vasquez, *Vice Pres*
Ignacio Saldana, *Plant Mgr*
Ken Longino, *Prdtn Mgr*
Chad Vasquez, *Marketing Staff*
▼ EMP: 60
SQ FT: 16,000
SALES (est): 10MM Privately Held
WEB: www.excelbridge.com
SIC: 3444 1622 Sheet metalwork; bridge construction

(P-12204)
EXECUTIVE TOOL INC
1220 N Richfield Rd, Anaheim (92807-1812)
PHONE..................714 996-1276
Vahan Bandoian, *President*
Doris Bandoian, *Treasurer*
Charles R Cook, *Vice Pres*
EMP: 28 EST: 1971
SQ FT: 20,000
SALES (est): 4.5MM Privately Held
SIC: 3444 3599 Sheet metalwork; machine shop, jobbing & repair

(P-12205)
EXHAUST CENTER INC
Also Called: Eci Fuel Systems
1794 W 11th St, Upland (91786-3504)
PHONE..................951 685-8602
Greg S Mitchell, *CEO*
Robert Mitchell, *CFO*
Cesar Martinez, *Supervisor*
EMP: 15
SQ FT: 15,000
SALES (est): 3.9MM Privately Held
WEB: www.ecifuelsystems.com
SIC: 3444 Sheet metalwork

(P-12206)
EXPRESS SHEET METAL PRODUCT
10131 Flora Vista St, Bellflower (90706-4804)
PHONE..................562 925-9340
Ramon Castaneda, *President*
Emma Lara, *Office Mgr*
EMP: 16
SQ FT: 6,000
SALES (est): 2.3MM Privately Held
SIC: 3444 Sheet metalwork

(P-12207)
F T B & SON INC
11551 Markon Dr, Garden Grove (92841-1808)
PHONE..................714 891-8003
Frank Taylor Brown, *CEO*
Kathy M Ayers, *CFO*
EMP: 23 EST: 1972
SQ FT: 37,000
SALES (est): 4.6MM Privately Held
WEB: www.ftbson.com
SIC: 3444 Ducts, sheet metal

(P-12208)
FAB TRON
1358 N Jefferson St, Anaheim (92807-1614)
PHONE..................714 996-4270
William Hayes, *Partner*
Robert Hayes, *Partner*
EMP: 10
SQ FT: 17,000
SALES (est): 1.6MM Privately Held
WEB: www.fabtron.com
SIC: 3444 3441 Sheet metalwork; fabricated structural metal

(P-12209)
FABRICATION NETWORK INC
Also Called: Fabnet
5410 E La Palma Ave, Anaheim (92807-2023)
PHONE..................714 393-5282
Robert F Denham, *President*
Donald V Eide, *CFO*
EMP: 75
SQ FT: 45,000
SALES (est): 7.5MM Privately Held
WEB: www.fabnetonline.com
SIC: 3444 3599 Metal housings, enclosures, casings & other containers; forming machine work, sheet metal; machine shop, jobbing & repair

(P-12210)
FABRITEC PRECISION INC (PA)
1060 Reno Ave, Modesto (95351-1233)
P.O. Box 32370, San Jose (95152-2370)
PHONE..................209 529-8504
Jack Taek Bong Kim, *President*
Hester Lou-Kim, *Corp Secy*
EMP: 15 EST: 1997
SQ FT: 16,800
SALES (est): 1.9MM Privately Held
WEB: www.fabpi.com
SIC: 3444 Sheet metalwork

(P-12211)
FABTRONIC INC
5026 Calmview Ave, Baldwin Park (91706-1899)
PHONE..................626 962-3293
Carlos Duarte, *President*
David Thompson, *Vice Pres*
▼ EMP: 20
SQ FT: 26,000
SALES (est): 2MM Privately Held
SIC: 3444 3829 Sheet metal specialties, not stamped; fare registers for street cars, buses, etc.

(P-12212)
FLETCHER BLDG HOLDINGS USA INC (DH)
1230 Railroad St, Corona (92882-1837)
PHONE..................951 272-8180
Willard Hudson, *President*
Steve Jones, *CFO*
John Miller, *Vice Pres*
Shanna Amsbry, *Administration*
Cindy Reyes, *Accountant*
◆ EMP: 70
SQ FT: 60,000
SALES (est): 29.8MM Privately Held
SIC: 3444 Metal roofing & roof drainage equipment

(P-12213)
FLEXTRONICS INTL PA INC
677 Gibraltar Dr, Milpitas (95035-6335)
PHONE..................408 577-2489
Tim Griffin, *Director*
EMP: 11
SALES (corp-wide): 26.2B Privately Held
SIC: 3444 Sheet metalwork
HQ: Flextronics International Pa, Inc.
847 Gibraltar Dr
Milpitas CA 95035
408 576-7000

(P-12214)
FORCE FABRICATION INC
2233 Statham Blvd, Oxnard (93033-3913)
PHONE..................805 754-2235
Justin Gamble, *Vice Pres*
Isabella Gamble, *President*
Anne Davis, *CFO*
EMP: 10
SALES: 500K Privately Held
SIC: 3444 Pipe, sheet metal

(P-12215)
FORTERRA PIPE & PRECAST LLC
30781 San Diego St, Shafter (93263-9764)
PHONE..................661 746-3527
Deloras Thornberg, *Principal*
EMP: 15

SALES (corp-wide): 1.4B Publicly Held
SIC: 3444 3531 Sheet metalwork; asphalt plant, including gravel-mix type
HQ: Forterra Pipe & Precast, Llc
511 E John Carpenter Fwy
Irving TX 75062
469 458-7973

(P-12216)
FOUR SEASONS RESTAURANT EQP
412 Jenks Cir, Corona (92880-2506)
PHONE..................951 278-9100
Larry Kaye, *President*
EMP: 29
SQ FT: 19,000
SALES (est): 4.5MM Privately Held
SIC: 3444 Restaurant sheet metalwork

(P-12217)
FUNKTION USA
3465 Ann Dr, Carlsbad (92008-2002)
PHONE..................760 473-4171
John Bandimere, *Owner*
EMP: 10
SALES (est): 899.9K Privately Held
WEB: www.functionusa.com
SIC: 3444 7319 Sheet metalwork; display advertising service

(P-12218)
GAINES MANUFACTURING INC
12200 Kirkham Rd, Poway (92064-6806)
PHONE..................858 486-7100
Ted Gaines, *Owner*
EMP: 40
SQ FT: 23,000
SALES (est): 6.5MM Privately Held
WEB: www.gainesmfg.com
SIC: 3444 Mail (post office) collection or storage boxes, sheet metal

(P-12219)
GARD INC
Also Called: Reliable Sheet Metal Works
524 E Walnut Ave, Fullerton (92832-2540)
PHONE..................714 738-5891
Arthur Schade, *President*
Dan Schade, *Corp Secy*
Arthur Schade Jr, *Vice Pres*
EMP: 20
SQ FT: 12,000
SALES (est): 3.9MM Privately Held
SIC: 3444 Sheet metal specialties, not stamped

(P-12220)
GCM MEDICAL & OEM INC
Also Called: Global Contract Manufacturing
1350 Atlantic St, Union City (94587-2004)
PHONE..................510 475-0404
Seanus Meaghr, *President*
Brandon Miller, *Technician*
Maria Martinez, *Purch Agent*
Rafael Ojeda, *Mfg Mgr*
Andre Finney, *Opers Staff*
◆ EMP: 78 EST: 1983
SQ FT: 80,000
SALES (est): 32.7MM Privately Held
WEB: www.globalcontractmanufacturing.com
SIC: 3444 3541 Sheet metalwork; machine tools, metal cutting type

(P-12221)
GENERAL FORMING CORPORATION
2413 Moreton St, Torrance (90505-5395)
PHONE..................310 326-0624
Charles E Vegher, *CEO*
Joanne Vegher, *Vice Pres*
Efrain Partida, *Prgrmr*
Tim Wall, *Purch Mgr*
EMP: 47
SQ FT: 18,000
SALES (est): 9.3MM Privately Held
SIC: 3444 3812 3769 Sheet metal specialties, not stamped; search & navigation equipment; guided missile & space vehicle parts & auxiliary equipment

(P-12222)
GEORGE HOOD INC
890 Faulstich Ct, San Jose (95112-1361)
PHONE..................408 295-6507
Charles Crow, *Controller*

Katy Laubach, *President*
EMP: 34 EST: 2014
SALES (est): 1.8MM Privately Held
SIC: 3444 Roof deck, sheet metal

(P-12223)
GERARD ROOF PRODUCTS LLC (DH)
Also Called: Gerard Roofing Technologies
721 Monroe Way, Placentia (92870-6309)
PHONE..................714 529-0407
Donald P Newman, *Mng Member*
EMP: 30
SALES (est): 4.6MM Privately Held
SIC: 3444 Sheet metalwork

(P-12224)
GKN AEROSPACE CAMARILLO INC
4680 Calle Carga, Camarillo (93012-8559)
PHONE..................805 383-6684
Richard Oldfield, *CEO*
David Lind, *President*
Bernd Hermann, *CFO*
▲ EMP: 19
SQ FT: 25,000
SALES (est): 7.3MM
SALES (corp-wide): 11B Privately Held
WEB: www.sheetsmfg.com
SIC: 3444 Sheet metalwork
HQ: Gkn Limited
Po Box 4128
Redditch WORCS
152 751-7715

(P-12225)
GRAYD-A PRCSION MET FBRICATORS
13233 Florence Ave, Santa Fe Springs (90670-4509)
PHONE..................562 944-8951
William Gray Jr, *President*
Jo Dell Gray, *Corp Secy*
William Gray III, *Vice Pres*
EMP: 20
SQ FT: 17,500
SALES (est): 4.2MM Privately Held
WEB: www.grayd-a.com
SIC: 3444 Sheet metal specialties, not stamped

(P-12226)
GRAYSIX COMPANY
2427 4th St, Berkeley (94710-2488)
PHONE..................510 845-5936
Robert Gray, *President*
EMP: 24 EST: 1946
SQ FT: 16,000
SALES (est): 3.8MM Privately Held
SIC: 3444 3469 Housings for business machines, sheet metal; metal stampings

(P-12227)
GROUP MANUFACTURING SERVICES (PA)
1928 Hartog Dr, San Jose (95131-2212)
PHONE..................408 436-1040
Curtis Molyneaux, *President*
Patti Thatcher, *CFO*
Jay Garrett, *Sales Staff*
Dave Molyneaux, *Sales Staff*
Mike Tool, *Manager*
EMP: 80
SQ FT: 30,000
SALES (est): 15.4MM Privately Held
WEB: www.groupmanufacturing.com
SIC: 3444 Ducts, sheet metal

(P-12228)
GROUP MANUFACTURING SERVICES
2751 Merc Dr Ste 900, Rancho Cordova (95742)
PHONE..................916 858-3270
Jerry Myrick, *Manager*
EMP: 13
SALES (corp-wide): 15.4MM Privately Held
WEB: www.groupmanufacturing.com
SIC: 3444 Sheet metal specialties, not stamped
PA: Group Manufacturing Services Inc
1928 Hartog Dr
San Jose CA 95131
408 436-1040

(P-12229)
GUTTERGLOVE INC
8860 Industrial Ave # 140, Roseville
(95678-6204)
P.O. Box 3326, Rocklin (95677-8468)
PHONE..................................916 624-5000
Matt Smith, *CEO*
Catherine Austin, *Executive*
Robert Lenney, *Director*
▲ **EMP:** 54
SQ FT: 43,000
SALES: 11MM **Privately Held**
SIC: 3444 Gutters, sheet metal

(P-12230)
HAIMETAL DUCT INC
625 Arroyo St, San Fernando
(91340-2219)
PHONE..................................818 768-2315
Rouben Hovsepian, *President*
EMP: 16
SQ FT: 10,000
SALES: 2.2MM **Privately Held**
SIC: 3444 Ducts, sheet metal; ventilators,
sheet metal

(P-12231)
HALLMARK METALS INC
600 W Foothill Blvd, Glendora
(91741-2403)
PHONE..................................626 335-1263
Joseph Allen Zerucha, *CEO*
Scott Schoenick, *President*
Marina Carmona, *Treasurer*
David Peifer, *Vice Pres*
Candice Schoenick, *Vice Pres*
EMP: 28 **EST:** 1959
SQ FT: 23,000
SALES (est): 6.5MM **Privately Held**
WEB: www.hallmarkmetals.com
SIC: 3444 3469 Sheet metalwork; ma-
chine parts, stamped or pressed metal

(P-12232)
HAMILTON METALCRAFT INC
848 N Fair Oaks Ave, Pasadena
(91103-3046)
PHONE..................................626 795-4811
Sandra Stahler, *President*
EMP: 25 **EST:** 1966
SQ FT: 10,000
SALES (est): 4.4MM **Privately Held**
WEB: www.hamiltonmetal.com
SIC: 3444 Casings, sheet metal

(P-12233)
HARDCRAFT INDUSTRIES INC
Also Called: Peninsula Metal Fabrication
2221 Ringwood Ave, San Jose
(95131-1736)
PHONE..................................408 432-8340
Andrew Brandt Kwiram, *President*
Melissa Eakin,
Larry Quinnell, *Director*
EMP: 52
SALES (est): 2.6MM **Privately Held**
SIC: 3444 Forming machine work, sheet
metal

(P-12234)
HARRIS PRECISION
Also Called: Harris Precision Sheet Metal
161 Lost Lake Ln, Campbell (95008-6615)
PHONE..................................408 866-4160
Barry B Harris, *Owner*
EMP: 13
SQ FT: 2,000
SALES (est): 1.1MM **Privately Held**
SIC: 3444 Sheet metal specialties, not
stamped

(P-12235)
HENRY LI
Also Called: Central Machine & Sheet Metal
1020 Rock Ave, San Jose (95131-1610)
PHONE..................................408 944-9100
Henry LI, *Owner*
EMP: 10
SALES (est): 1.2MM **Privately Held**
SIC: 3444 Sheet metalwork

(P-12236)
HI-CRAFT METAL PRODUCTS
606 W 184th St, Gardena (90248-4282)
PHONE..................................310 323-6949
Bill Gerich, *CEO*

Jennifer Gerich, *Shareholder*
Ted Gerich, *Shareholder*
Liz Gallagher, *Corp Secy*
Edward P Gerich, *Vice Pres*
EMP: 20 **EST:** 1948
SQ FT: 11,000
SALES (est): 4.4MM **Privately Held**
WEB: www.hicraftmetal.com
SIC: 3444 3469 Sheet metal specialties,
not stamped; metal stampings

(P-12237)
**HILL MANUFACTURING
COMPANY LLC**
3363 Edward Ave, Santa Clara
(95054-2334)
PHONE..................................408 988-4744
J Douglas Wickham,
Barbara A Wickham, *CFO*
EMP: 46
SQ FT: 24,500
SALES (est): 9.2MM **Privately Held**
WEB: www.hill-mfg.com
SIC: 3444 Sheet metal specialties, not
stamped

(P-12238)
HOLZINGER INDUS SHTMTL INC
12440 Mccann Dr, Santa Fe Springs
(90670-3335)
PHONE..................................562 944-6337
Frank Alverez, *President*
EMP: 12
SQ FT: 9,000
SALES: 1MM **Privately Held**
SIC: 3444 Sheet metalwork

(P-12239)
HP PRECISION INC
288 Navajo St, San Marcos (92078-2423)
PHONE..................................760 752-9377
Bradley S Hayes, *President*
Tho Phan, *COO*
EMP: 23
SALES (est): 4.5MM **Privately Held**
WEB: www.hppmf.com
SIC: 3444 Sheet metalwork

(P-12240)
HSI MECHANICAL INC
1013 N Emerald Ave, Modesto
(95351-2851)
PHONE..................................209 408-0183
Tim Scott, *Principal*
Preston Stephens, *President*
Brent Holloway, *Vice Pres*
EMP: 21
SQ FT: 4,000
SALES (est): 1.2MM **Privately Held**
SIC: 3444 Sheet metalwork

(P-12241)
HUB CONSTRUCTION SPC INC
Also Called: Hub Construction Speciality
5310 San Fernando Rd, Glendale
(91203-2407)
PHONE..................................909 379-2100
Dean Oveton, *Branch Mgr*
EMP: 100
SALES (corp-wide): 35.1MM **Privately
Held**
SIC: 3444 Concrete forms, sheet metal
PA: Hub Construction Specialties, Inc.
379 S I St
San Bernardino CA 92410
909 889-0161

(P-12242)
I & A INC
Also Called: Peninsula Metal Fabrication
2221 Ringwood Ave, San Jose
(95131-1736)
PHONE..................................408 432-8340
Anthony Davis, *President*
Heather Jevens, *CFO*
Ishbel Davis, *Vice Pres*
Ian Davis, *Principal*
EMP: 41
SQ FT: 48,000
SALES (est): 7.4MM **Privately Held**
WEB: www.pmf.com
SIC: 3444 Sheet metal specialties, not
stamped

(P-12243)
IMPAKT HOLDINGS LLC
490 Gianni St, Santa Clara (95054-2413)
PHONE..................................650 692-5800
Dan Rubin, *CEO*
Daniel Yang, *COO*
Kirk Johnson, *CFO*
EMP: 14
SALES (est): 2.8MM **Privately Held**
SIC: 3444 Sheet metalwork

(P-12244)
**INFINITY KITCHEN PRODUCTS
INC**
Also Called: Infinity Stainless Products
7750 Scout Ave, Bell Gardens
(90201-4942)
PHONE..................................562 806-5771
Serafin Valdez, *President*
Victor Valdez, *Director*
EMP: 15
SQ FT: 25,000
SALES (est): 3.1MM **Privately Held**
WEB: www.infinitystainless.com
SIC: 3444 Restaurant sheet metalwork

(P-12245)
**INLAND MARINE INDUSTRIES
INC**
Also Called: Inland Metal Technologies
3245 Depot Rd, Hayward (94545-2709)
PHONE..................................510 785-8555
Jennifer Sutton, *President*
Mike Berg, *Manager*
◆ **EMP:** 180
SALES: 41MM **Privately Held**
WEB: www.inlandmetal.com
SIC: 3444 Sheet metalwork

(P-12246)
**INNOVATIVE DESIGN AND
SHEET ME**
Also Called: Innovative Emergency Equipment
616 Mrlbrugh Ave Unit S-1, Riverside
(92507)
PHONE..................................951 222-2270
EMP: 16 **EST:** 2015
SALES (est): 99.4K **Privately Held**
SIC: 3444 3699 3647 3641 Forming machine work, sheet metal; skylights, sheet
metal; trouble lights; dome lights, automotive; flasher lights, automotive; pilot lights,
radio

(P-12247)
INTEGRITY SHEET METAL INC
319 Mcarthur Way Ste 1, Upland
(91786-5669)
PHONE..................................909 608-0449
William Hicks, *President*
EMP: 10
SALES (est): 1.7MM **Privately Held**
SIC: 3444 Sheet metalwork

(P-12248)
INTERLOCK INDUSTRIES INC
Also Called: Middle Sales
1326 Paddock Pl, Woodland (95776-5919)
PHONE..................................530 668-5690
Dwight Isaac, *Manager*
EMP: 56
SALES (corp-wide): 390.6MM **Privately
Held**
WEB: www.metalsales.us.com
SIC: 3444 Roof deck, sheet metal
PA: Interlock Industries, Inc.
545 S 3rd St Ste 310
Louisville KY 40202
502 569-2007

(P-12249)
INTERNATIONAL WEST INC
Also Called: Continental Industries
1025 N Armando St, Anaheim
(92806-2606)
PHONE..................................714 632-9190
Jeffery Aaron Hayden, *President*
Tami Hayden, *CFO*
EMP: 56
SQ FT: 8,500
SALES (est): 12.5MM **Privately Held**
WEB: www.continental-ind.net
SIC: 3444 Sheet metalwork

(P-12250)
INVENTIVE RESOURCES INC
Also Called: Iri
5038 Salida Blvd, Salida (95368-9403)
P.O. Box 1316 (95368-1316)
PHONE..................................209 545-1663
John A Paoluccio, *CEO*
John J Paoluccio, *President*
Dorene Paoluccio, *CFO*
EMP: 10
SQ FT: 3,313
SALES (est): 597.2K **Privately Held**
WEB: www.biocoal.net
SIC: 3444 8731 3826 Ducts, sheet metal;
commercial research laboratory; environ-
mental testing equipment

(P-12251)
J & L METAL PRODUCTS
1121 Railroad St Ste 103, Corona
(92882-8219)
PHONE..................................951 278-0100
James C Ciarletta, *President*
Jay Ciarletta, *Treasurer*
EMP: 19
SALES (est): 3.8MM **Privately Held**
SIC: 3444 Sheet metal specialties, not
stamped

(P-12252)
JAUBIN SALES & MFG CORP
Also Called: J Sheet Metal
2006 E Gladwick St, Compton
(90220-6202)
PHONE..................................310 631-8647
Marie Jaubin, *President*
EMP: 12
SQ FT: 10,000
SALES (est): 990K **Privately Held**
WEB: www.jsheetmetal.com
SIC: 3444 Sheet metal specialties, not
stamped

(P-12253)
JBW PRECISION INC
2650 Lavery Ct, Newbury Park
(91320-1581)
PHONE..................................805 499-1973
David Ogden, *President*
Dawn Spalding, *Corp Secy*
Jack Ogden, *Vice Pres*
Rhonda Ogden, *Marketing Mgr*
EMP: 23 **EST:** 1969
SQ FT: 2,500
SALES (est): 4.9MM **Privately Held**
WEB: www.jbwprecision.com
SIC: 3444 Forming machine work, sheet
metal

(P-12254)
JEFFREY FABRICATION LLC
Also Called: C & J Metal Prducts
6323 Alondra Blvd, Paramount
(90723-3750)
PHONE..................................562 634-3101
Lilly Chang, *Mng Member*
EMP: 50
SALES (est): 7MM **Privately Held**
SIC: 3444 Sheet metalwork

(P-12255)
JIM JAMES ENTERPRISES INC
9148 Jordan Ave, Chatsworth
(91311-5707)
PHONE..................................818 772-8595
Irene Hagle, *President*
Chris H Hagle, *Purch Mgr*
EMP: 10 **EST:** 1974
SQ FT: 10,000
SALES (est): 1MM **Privately Held**
SIC: 3444 Sheet metal specialties, not
stamped

(P-12256)
**JOHNSON INDUSTRIAL SHEET
METAL**
2131 Barstow St, Sacramento
(95815-3628)
P.O. Box 15859 (95852-0859)
PHONE..................................916 927-8244
Curtis Johnson, *President*
Donna Johnson, *Vice Pres*
EMP: 10
SQ FT: 8,000

SALES (est): 1.7MM **Privately Held**
WEB: www.johnson-ind.com
SIC: 3444 Sheet metal specialties, not
stamped

(P-12257)
JRI INC
Also Called: John Russo Industrial Metal
38021 Cherry St, Newark (94560-4524)
PHONE..................................510 494-5300
Ralph Colet, *President*
EMP: 24
SQ FT: 170,000
SALES (est): 4.1MM **Privately Held**
SIC: 3444 Sheet metalwork

(P-12258)
K & E MANUFACTURING INC
1966 Freeman Ave, Signal Hill
(90755-1241)
PHONE..................................562 494-7570
Ernesto Sandoval, *President*
EMP: 16
SQ FT: 15,000
SALES (est): 1.3MM **Privately Held**
SIC: 3444 Sheet metalwork

(P-12259)
K C SHEETMETAL INC
943 Berryessa Rd Ste B3, San Jose
(95133-1007)
PHONE..................................408 441-6620
Phil Casey, *Owner*
EMP: 10
SQ FT: 7,700
SALES (est): 590K **Privately Held**
SIC: 3444 Sheet metalwork

(P-12260)
KARGO MASTER INC
11261 Trade Center Dr, Rancho Cordova
(95742-6223)
PHONE..................................916 638-8703
John Hancock, *President*
David Lewis, *Vice Pres*
Erika Hubert, *General Mgr*
Nick Wendell, *Engineer*
Terri Aquino, *Accountant*
EMP: 40
SALES: 9MM **Privately Held**
WEB: www.kargomaster.com
SIC: 3444 Sheet metalwork

(P-12261)
**KB SHEETMETAL FABRICATION
INC**
17371 Mount Wynne Cir B, Fountain Valley
(92708-4107)
PHONE..................................714 979-1780
Cong Nguyen, *President*
Tung Vo, *Vice Pres*
EMP: 25
SQ FT: 12,000
SALES (est): 4.3MM **Privately Held**
SIC: 3444 3441 Sheet metalwork; fabri-
cated structural metal

(P-12262)
KEITH E ARCHAMBEAU SR INC
Also Called: American Precision Sheet Metal
20615 Plummer St, Chatsworth
(91311-5112)
PHONE..................................818 718-6110
Keith Archambeau Jr, *President*
John Wetlsch, *Vice Pres*
EMP: 20
SQ FT: 10,000
SALES (est): 4.1MM **Privately Held**
SIC: 3444 Sheet metal specialties, not
stamped

(P-12263)
**L & T PRECISION
CORPORATION**
12105 Kirkham Rd, Poway (92064-6870)
PHONE..................................858 513-7874
Loc Nguyen, *President*
Son Le, *COO*
Tho Nguyen, *Vice Pres*
Tien D Nguyen, *Principal*
Tien Nguyen, *Admin Sec*
EMP: 110
SQ FT: 48,000

SALES (est): 32.1MM **Privately Held**
WEB: www.laptalo.com
SIC: 3444 3599 Sheet metal specialties,
not stamped; machine & other job shop
work

(P-12264)
LAPTALO ENTERPRISES INC
Also Called: J L Precision Sheet Metal
2360 Zanker Rd, San Jose (95131-1115)
PHONE..................................408 727-6633
Jakov Laptalo, *CEO*
Michael Laptalo, *President*
Tony Grizelj, *Vice Pres*
Todd Morey, *Vice Pres*
Slavko Laptalo, *Admin Sec*
EMP: 100
SQ FT: 60,000
SALES (est): 34.6MM **Privately Held**
SIC: 3444 Sheet metal specialties, not
stamped

(P-12265)
LARA MANUFACTURING INC
Also Called: M & J Precision
16235 Vineyard Blvd, Morgan Hill
(95037-7123)
PHONE..................................408 778-0811
Mark A Lara, *President*
Mark Lara, *President*
John Lara, *Vice Pres*
EMP: 20
SQ FT: 20,000
SALES (est): 278.1K **Privately Held**
SIC: 3444 Sheet metalwork

(P-12266)
LEVMAR INC
Also Called: Concord Sheet Metal
1666 Willow Pass Rd, Pittsburg
(94565-1702)
PHONE..................................925 680-8723
Mark Riley, *President*
EMP: 15
SALES (est): 2MM **Privately Held**
SIC: 3444 Sheet metalwork

(P-12267)
**LOR-VAN MANUFACTURING
LLC**
3307 Edward Ave, Santa Clara
(95054-2341)
PHONE..................................408 980-1045
Christopher Girardot,
Ismelda Lopez, *Engineer*
Lorena Lopez,
EMP: 28
SQ FT: 6,400
SALES (est): 5.8MM **Privately Held**
WEB: www.lor-vanmfg.com
SIC: 3444 3699 Sheet metal specialties,
not stamped; laser welding, drilling & cut-
ting equipment

(P-12268)
**LUCIO FAMILY ENTERPRISES
INC**
Also Called: Compactor Management Com-
pany
2150 Prune Ave, Fremont (94539-6730)
PHONE..................................510 623-2323
Sandra Lucio, *President*
David Lucio, *CFO*
EMP: 26
SALES (est): 5.9MM **Privately Held**
WEB: www.compactormc.com
SIC: 3444 4953 Bins, prefabricated sheet
metal; recycling, waste materials

(P-12269)
LUNAS SHEET METAL INC
3125 Molinaro St Ste 102, Santa Clara
(95054-2433)
PHONE..................................408 492-1260
Antonio Luna, *President*
Lupe Luna, *CFO*
EMP: 15
SQ FT: 10,000
SALES (est): 2.9MM **Privately Held**
SIC: 3444 Sheet metalwork

(P-12270)
LYNAM INDUSTRIES INC
13050 Santa Ana Ave, Fontana
(92337-6948)
PHONE..................................951 360-1919

Troy Lindstrom, *President*
Vince Lozano, *Engineer*
Ito Dennis, *Opers Mgr*
Aniceto Jimenez, *Opers Staff*
Greg Traeger P E, *Director*
▲ EMP: 85
SQ FT: 39,000
SALES (est): 25MM **Privately Held**
WEB: www.lynamindustries.com
SIC: 3444 Sheet metal specialties, not
stamped

(P-12271)
LYNX ENTERPRISES INC
724 E Grant Line Rd Ste B, Tracy
(95304-2800)
PHONE..................................209 833-3400
Vance R Anderson, *President*
Keith J Anderson, *CFO*
Keith Anderson, *CFO*
Carlos Aldona, *Admin Sec*
Rosalinda Orta, *Purchasing*
▲ EMP: 60
SQ FT: 52,000
SALES: 13.5MM **Privately Held**
WEB: www.fleetwoodrv.com
SIC: 3444 3446 3443 3441 Sheet metal-
work; architectural metalwork; fabricated
plate work (boiler shop); fabricated struc-
tural metal

(P-12272)
**M C I MANUFACTURING INC
(PA)**
1020 Rock Ave, San Jose (95131-1610)
PHONE..................................408 456-2700
Henry LI, *President*
EMP: 45
SQ FT: 22,000
SALES: 5MM **Privately Held**
WEB: www.mcimfg.com
SIC: 3444 Metal housings, enclosures,
casings & other containers

(P-12273)
M&L METALS INC
25362 Cypress Ave, Hayward
(94544-2208)
PHONE..................................510 732-1745
Mike Lowe, *President*
Greg Pirrone, *Opers Staff*
EMP: 11
SQ FT: 6,000
SALES: 1.1MM **Privately Held**
SIC: 3444 Sheet metalwork

(P-12274)
M-T METAL FABRICATIONS INC
536 Lewelling Blvd Ste A, San Leandro
(94579-1845)
PHONE..................................510 357-5262
Ross Bigler, *President*
Justin Bigler, *Vice Pres*
Sandy Ferreira, *General Mgr*
EMP: 14
SQ FT: 12,900
SALES (est): 2MM **Privately Held**
SIC: 3444 Sheet metal specialties, not
stamped

(P-12275)
MAC CAL COMPANY
Also Called: Mac Cal Manufacturing
1737 Junction Ave, San Jose (95112-1010)
PHONE..................................408 441-1435
Michael Hall, *President*
Renee Hall, *CEO*
Cathy McDonald, *CFO*
Darryl Payne, *Executive*
Bob Duncan, *General Mgr*
EMP: 80
SALES (est): 18.7MM **Privately Held**
WEB: www.maccal.com
SIC: 3444 3479 7336 Sheet metal spe-
cialties, not stamped; housings for busi-
ness machines, sheet metal; name
plates: engraved, etched, etc.; silk screen
design

(P-12276)
MAG HIGH TECH
14718 Arminta St, Panorama City
(91402-5904)
PHONE..................................818 786-8366
Jerry Rothlisberger, *Owner*
Korena Rothlisberger, *Admin Sec*

EMP: 12
SALES (est): 1MM **Privately Held**
SIC: 3444 Forming machine work, sheet
metal

(P-12277)
**MARINE & REST FABRICATORS
INC**
3768 Dalbergia St, San Diego
(92113-3815)
PHONE..................................619 232-7267
Carlos Velazquez, *President*
EMP: 44
SQ FT: 7,600
SALES (est): 8.4MM **Privately Held**
SIC: 3444 3731 Restaurant sheet metal-
work; military ships, building & repairing

(P-12278)
MASS PRECISION INC
46555 Landing Pkwy, Fremont
(94538-6421)
PHONE..................................408 954-0200
Greg Kraus, *Manager*
EMP: 125
SALES (corp-wide): 69.3MM **Privately
Held**
SIC: 3444 3599 Sheet metalwork; ma-
chine shop, jobbing & repair
PA: Mass Precision, Inc.
2110 Oakland Rd
San Jose CA 95131
408 954-0200

(P-12279)
MASS PRECISION INC (PA)
Also Called: Machining and Frame Division
2110 Oakland Rd, San Jose (95131-1565)
PHONE..................................408 954-0200
Al Stucky Jr, *President*
W Ray Allen, *CFO*
Brandi Weaver, *Executive Asst*
Jeff Stimson, *Engineer*
John Garrett, *Buyer*
▲ EMP: 420
SQ FT: 200,000
SALES (est): 69.3MM **Privately Held**
WEB: www.massprecision.com
SIC: 3444 3599 Sheet metal specialties,
not stamped; machine shop, jobbing & re-
pair

(P-12280)
MASTER ENTERPRISES INC
Also Called: A B C Restaurant Equipment Co
2025 Lee Ave, South El Monte
(91733-2505)
PHONE..................................626 442-1821
Brian Kim Lien, *CEO*
Wen Lin, *Treasurer*
Thanh Quach, *Admin Sec*
EMP: 20
SQ FT: 20,000
SALES (est): 3.5MM **Privately Held**
WEB: www.masel.net
SIC: 3444 5087 Restaurant sheet metal-
work; restaurant supplies

(P-12281)
MASTER FAB INC
9210 Stellar Ct, Corona (92883-4906)
PHONE..................................951 277-4772
Kenneth Scheel, *President*
Troy Jackson, *Admin Sec*
EMP: 16 EST: 1980
SQ FT: 11,000
SALES (est): 3.6MM **Privately Held**
SIC: 3444 Sheet metalwork

(P-12282)
**MASTER METAL PRODUCTS
COMPANY**
495 Emory St, San Jose (95110-1999)
PHONE..................................408 275-1210
Lee A Henderson, *President*
EMP: 12 EST: 1942
SQ FT: 18,000
SALES (est): 2.3MM **Privately Held**
SIC: 3444 Sheet metal specialties, not
stamped

(P-12283)
MATERIAL SUPPLY INC (PA)
Also Called: MSI Hvac
11700 Industry Ave, Fontana (92337-6934)
PHONE..................................951 801-5004

Dion Quinn, *CEO*
Jon Dautrich, *Vice Pres*
Robert Hascall, *Vice Pres*
EMP: 170
SQ FT: 80,000
SALES (est): 108.7MM **Privately Held**
WEB: www.msihvac.com
SIC: 3444 5075 7623 1711 Metal venti-
lating equipment; warm air heating & air
conditioning; air filters; ventilating equip-
ment & supplies; air conditioning repair;
heating & air conditioning contractors

(P-12284)
**MATTHEWS MANUFACTURING
INC**
3301 E 14th St, Los Angeles (90023-3801)
PHONE..........................323 980-4373
Benyamin Mikhael-Ford, *President*
Fiyodor Mikhael-Ford, *Corp Secy*
Fred Mikhael-Ford, *Vice Pres*
EMP: 27
SQ FT: 20,000
SALES (est): 34K **Privately Held**
SIC: 3444 3599 Sheet metalwork; ma-
chine shop, jobbing & repair

(P-12285)
**MAXIMUM QUALITY METAL
PDTS INC**
Also Called: Max Q
1017 E Acacia St, Ontario (91761-4554)
PHONE..........................909 902-5018
John Kim, *President*
Paul Kim, *Admin Sec*
EMP: 20
SQ FT: 10,000
SALES (est): 4.9MM **Privately Held**
SIC: 3444 Sheet metalwork

(P-12286)
MAYONI ENTERPRISES
10320 Glenoaks Blvd, Pacoima
(91331-1699)
PHONE..........................818 896-0026
Isaac Benyehuda, *CEO*
Isaac Glazer, *Vice Pres*
EMP: 60
SQ FT: 17,000
SALES (est): 3MM **Privately Held**
SIC: 3444 3581 Sheet metal specialties,
not stamped; automatic vending ma-
chines

(P-12287)
MCMILLIN MFG CORP
Also Called: McMillin Wire Products
40 E Verdugo Ave, Burbank (91502-1931)
PHONE..........................323 981-8585
Bruce Goodman, *President*
EMP: 57
SQ FT: 42,000
SALES (est): 6.8MM **Privately Held**
SIC: 3444 3496 3441 3315 Sheet metal-
work; miscellaneous fabricated wire prod-
ucts; fabricated structural metal; steel
wire & related products

(P-12288)
**MEADOWS SHEET METAL AND
AC INC**
Also Called: Meadows Mechanical
333 Crown Vista Dr, Gardena
(90248-1705)
PHONE..........................310 615-1125
Madonna Rose, *CEO*
Dennis Johnson, *CFO*
Thomas Nolan, *Exec VP*
Jack Malisani, *Vice Pres*
Jonathan Estrada, *Foreman/Supr*
EMP: 50 EST: 1949
SQ FT: 5,000
SALES (est): 21.7MM **Privately Held**
SIC: 3444 1711 Sheet metalwork; heating
& air conditioning contractors

(P-12289)
**MELROSE METAL PRODUCTS
INC**
44533 S Grimmer Blvd, Fremont
(94538-6309)
PHONE..........................510 657-8771
Mitchell A Hoppe, *CEO*
Harry Hoppe, *Shareholder*
Shirley Hoppe, *Vice Pres*

EMP: 20
SQ FT: 40,000
SALES (est): 6.8MM **Privately Held**
WEB: www.gomelrose.com
SIC: 3444 Sheet metal specialties, not
stamped; ventilators, sheet metal; booths,
spray; prefabricated sheet metal; cowls or
scoops, air (ship ventilators): sheet metal

(P-12290)
**MERIDIAN RAPID DEF GROUP
LLC**
177 E Colo Blvd Ste 200, Pasadena
(91105)
PHONE..........................720 616-7795
Peter Whitford, *CEO*
Eric Alms, *President*
James Miller, *Vice Pres*
Karen Ewald, *Administration*
Akshat Agrawal, *Engineer*
EMP: 10
SALES (est): 1.1MM **Privately Held**
SIC: 3444 Sheet metalwork

(P-12291)
METAL ENGINEERING INC
1642 S Sacramento Ave, Ontario
(91761-8052)
PHONE..........................626 334-1819
Arthur A Valenzuela, *President*
Wendy Linares, *Admin Asst*
Petra Markoski, *Opers Staff*
EMP: 23
SQ FT: 14,000
SALES (est): 2.7MM **Privately Held**
SIC: 3444 1761 Awnings & canopies;
sheet metalwork

(P-12292)
METAL ENGINEERING & MFG
1031b W Kirkwall Rd, Azusa (91702-5127)
PHONE..........................626 334-5271
Petra Markoski, *Owner*
EMP: 12
SALES (est): 1.1MM **Privately Held**
WEB: www.metaleng.com
SIC: 3444 Sheet metalwork

(P-12293)
**METAL FINISHING SOLUTIONS
INC**
870 Comstock St, Santa Clara
(95054-3404)
PHONE..........................408 988-8642
Tony Grizelj, *Principal*
Joe Kulic, *General Mgr*
EMP: 10
SALES (est): 1.4MM **Privately Held**
SIC: 3444 Sheet metalwork

(P-12294)
METAL MASTER INC
4611 Overland Ave, San Diego
(92123-1233)
PHONE..........................858 292-8880
Benito Garrido, *President*
Dianne Yeaman, *CFO*
Donald Wagner, *Vice Pres*
Ricky Ruiz, *Purchasing*
Wendi Lane, *Asst Mgr*
EMP: 41
SQ FT: 30,000
SALES (est): 9.7MM **Privately Held**
WEB: www.metalmasterinc.com
SIC: 3444 3541 Sheet metalwork; metal
housings, enclosures, casings & other
containers; milling machines

(P-12295)
**METAL SALES
MANUFACTURING CORP**
14213 Whittram Ave, Fontana
(92335-3045)
P.O. Box 8922, Rancho Cucamonga
(91701-0922)
PHONE..........................909 829-8618
Kevin Fitzgerald, *Manager*
EMP: 10
SALES (corp-wide): 390.6MM **Privately
Held**
SIC: 3444 1761 Metal roofing & roof
drainage equipment; roofing contractor

HQ: Metal Sales Manufacturing Corporation
545 S 3rd St Ste 200
Louisville KY 40202
502 855-4300

(P-12296)
**METAL-FAB SERVICES
INDUSTRIES**
2500 E Miraloma Way, Anaheim
(92806-1608)
PHONE..........................714 630-7771
Carlos Mondragon, *CEO*
▲ **EMP:** 49
SQ FT: 28,000
SALES (est): 10.4MM **Privately Held**
SIC: 3444 Sheet metal specialties, not
stamped

(P-12297)
METALPRO INDUSTRIES INC
28064 Avenue Stanford H, Santa Clarita
(91355-1158)
PHONE..........................661 294-0764
Robert Theberge, *President*
Edmundo Gomez, *Treasurer*
Mark Theberge, *Vice Pres*
Mary Badberg, *Office Mgr*
Arlan Sams, *Admin Sec*
EMP: 40
SQ FT: 13,000
SALES (est): 6.5MM **Privately Held**
WEB: www.metalproindustries.net
SIC: 3444 Sheet metal specialties, not
stamped

(P-12298)
METALS DIRECT INC
6771 Eastside Rd, Redding (96001-5059)
PHONE..........................530 605-1931
Dale Williams, *President*
Terry Williams, *Vice Pres*
EMP: 29
SALES (est): 3.1MM **Privately Held**
SIC: 3444 5082 1761 5039 Siding, sheet
metal; contractors' materials; roofing, sid-
ing & sheet metal work; metal buildings;
agricultural building contractors

(P-12299)
**MEYERS SHEET METAL BOX
INC**
138 W Harris Ave, South San Francisco
(94080-6009)
PHONE..........................650 873-8889
James H C Liang, *President*
Chung Lai Liang, *Corp Secy*
EMP: 12
SQ FT: 7,500
SALES (est): 1.7MM **Privately Held**
SIC: 3444 Sheet metalwork

(P-12300)
**MICROFAB MANUFACTURING
INC**
Also Called: Microfab Mfg Shtmtl Pdts
220 Distribution St, San Marcos
(92078-4358)
PHONE..........................760 744-7240
Scott Dillard, *Owner*
Nancy Dillard, *Vice Pres*
EMP: 16
SQ FT: 10,252
SALES (est): 1.1MM **Privately Held**
WEB: www.microfabmfg.com
SIC: 3444 Sheet metal specialties, not
stamped

(P-12301)
MICROFORM PRECISION LLC
4244 S Market Ct Ste A, Sacramento
(95834-1243)
PHONE..........................916 419-0580
Timothy E Rice, *Mng Member*
Tim Rice, *Data Proc Staff*
Brian Cook, *Engineer*
Bryan Wallace, *Buyer*
▲ **EMP:** 55 EST: 1981
SQ FT: 42,000
SALES (est): 12.7MM **Privately Held**
WEB: www.mform.com
SIC: 3444 Sheet metal specialties, not
stamped

(P-12302)
**MIKES SHEET METAL
PRODUCTS**
Also Called: Uniproducts
3315 Elkhorn Blvd, North Highlands
(95660-3112)
PHONE..........................916 348-3800
Michael R Meredith, *President*
Ginny Meredith, *Vice Pres*
EMP: 25
SQ FT: 10,000
SALES (est): 4.4MM **Privately Held**
SIC: 3444 Ducts, sheet metal

(P-12303)
**MILESTONE AV TECHNOLOGIES
LLC**
11150 Inland Ave Ste A, Jurupa Valley
(91752-1164)
PHONE..........................800 266-7225
Keith Blackwell, *Branch Mgr*
EMP: 15
SALES (corp-wide): 21.2MM **Privately
Held**
WEB: www.middleatlantic.com
SIC: 3444 Sheet metalwork
HQ: Legrand Av Inc.
6436 City West Pkwy
Eden Prairie MN 55344
866 977-3901

(P-12304)
MILLENNIUM METALCRAFT INC
3201 Osgood Cmn, Fremont (94539-5029)
PHONE..........................510 657-4700
Kenneth Watson, *President*
Gwendolyn Watson, *CFO*
EMP: 30
SQ FT: 8,100
SALES (est): 4MM **Privately Held**
SIC: 3444 Sheet metal specialties, not
stamped

(P-12305)
MMIX TECHNOLOGIES
Also Called: Countywide Metal
1348 Pioneer Way, El Cajon (92020-1626)
P.O. Box 12794 (92022-2794)
PHONE..........................619 631-6644
Emmaneul J Carlos, *CEO*
Emmanuel J Carlos, *President*
EMP: 10
SALES (est): 1.5MM **Privately Held**
SIC: 3444 Forming machine work, sheet
metal

(P-12306)
MMP SHEET METAL INC
501 Commercial Way, La Habra
(90631-6170)
PHONE..........................562 691-1055
Frank Varanelli, *President*
Mike Varanelli, *Vice Pres*
EMP: 30 EST: 1977
SQ FT: 8,500
SALES (est): 5.1MM **Privately Held**
SIC: 3444 Sheet metal specialties, not
stamped

(P-12307)
**MODERN-AIRE VENTILATING
INC**
Also Called: Modern Aire Ventilating
7319 Lankershim Blvd, North Hollywood
(91605-3895)
PHONE..........................818 765-9870
Steven Herman, *President*
Robert Delmazo, *VP Sales*
Patrick Hartman, *Manager*
EMP: 20
SQ FT: 20,000
SALES (est): 3.3MM **Privately Held**
WEB: www.modernaire.com
SIC: 3444 3645 Hoods, range: sheet
metal; residential lighting fixtures

(P-12308)
**MODULAR METAL
FABRICATORS INC**
24600 Nandina Ave, Moreno Valley
(92551-9537)
PHONE..........................951 242-3154
E E Gearing, *CEO*
Don Gearing, *President*
John Wingate, *Treasurer*

Mike Beam, *Exec VP*
Pat Geary, *Director*
▲ **EMP:** 130
SQ FT: 200,000
SALES (est): 25.2MM **Privately Held**
SIC: 3444 Pipe, sheet metal; ducts, sheet
metal

(P-12309)
MONACO SHEET METAL
Also Called: Sun Sheet Metal
5131 Santa Fe St Ste A, San Diego
(92109-1612)
PHONE..............................858 272-0297
Troy Monaco, *President*
Douglas Tracy, *Business Mgr*
EMP: 10
SQ FT: 12,048
SALES (est): 1MM **Privately Held**
SIC: 3444 Sheet metalwork

(P-12310)
MONTEREY MECHANICAL CO
Also Called: Contra Costa Metal Fabricators
1126 Landini Ln, Concord (94520-3704)
PHONE..............................925 689-6670
Todd Monday, *Manager*
EMP: 10
SALES (corp-wide): 75MM **Privately
Held**
WEB: www.montmech.com
SIC: 3444 1761 Sheet metalwork; sheet
metalwork
  PA: Monterey Mechanical Co.
     8275 San Leandro St
     Oakland CA 94621
     510 632-3173

(P-12311)
MORTS CUSTOM SHEETMETAL
18121 Clear Creek Rd, Redding
(96001-5233)
PHONE..............................530 241-7013
David Cox, *Owner*
Jeannine Cox, *Co-Owner*
EMP: 10
SQ FT: 2,000
SALES: 900K **Privately Held**
SIC: 3444 Sheet metalwork

(P-12312)
NEW CAL METALS INC
Also Called: Artesian Home Products
3495 Swetzer Rd, Granite Bay (95746)
P.O. Box 1126, Loomis (95650-1126)
PHONE..............................916 652-7424
Larry Dumm, *President*
Slate Bryer, *Shareholder*
Chris Tataschiore, *Vice Pres*
▲ **EMP:** 15 **EST:** 2008
SQ FT: 15,000
SALES (est): 2.6MM **Privately Held**
SIC: 3444 Metal ventilating equipment

(P-12313)
NEW GREENSCREEN INCORPORATED
Impac International
11445 Pacific Ave, Fontana (92337-8227)
PHONE..............................951 685-9660
Kory Lavoy, *Division Mgr*
EMP: 50 **Privately Held**
SIC: 3444 3315 Housings for business
machines, sheet metal; steel wire & re-
lated products
  PA: New Greenscreen, Incorporated
     5500 Jurupa St
     Ontario CA 91761

(P-12314)
NOLL/NORWESCO LLC
1320 Performance Dr, Stockton
(95206-4925)
PHONE..............................209 234-1600
Gary Henry, *Mng Member*
Alex MAI, *Info Tech Dir*
EMP: 130
SALES (est): 21.7MM
SALES (corp-wide): 1B **Publicly Held**
SIC: 3444 Sheet metalwork
  PA: Gibraltar Industries, Inc.
     3556 Lake Shore Rd # 100
     Buffalo NY 14219
     716 826-6500

(P-12315)
NOR-CAL METAL FABRICATORS
1121 3rd St, Oakland (94607-2509)
PHONE..............................510 350-0121
Robert C Hall, *Ch of Bd*
Michael Tran, *President*
Rick Turner, *Info Tech Mgr*
Troy Nickles, *Mfg Staff*
Craig Macdonald, *Director*
▲ **EMP:** 51 **EST:** 1960
SQ FT: 100,000
SALES (est): 14MM **Privately Held**
SIC: 3444 3661 Sheet metal specialties,
not stamped; telephone & telegraph ap-
paratus

(P-12316)
NORTH VALLEY RAIN GUTTERS
27 Freight Ln Ste C, Chico (95973-8962)
PHONE..............................530 894-3347
Michael Gaston, *Owner*
EMP: 12
SQ FT: 3,000
SALES (est): 1.1MM **Privately Held**
SIC: 3444 1761 Gutters, sheet metal;
downspouts, sheet metal; gutter & down-
spout contractor

(P-12317)
OC METALS INC
2720 S Main St Ste B, Santa Ana
(92707-3404)
PHONE..............................714 668-0783
Marushkah Kurtz, *CEO*
Mari Kurtz, *President*
Brent Catalano, *Sales Staff*
EMP: 20
SQ FT: 23,000
SALES (est): 5.2MM **Privately Held**
SIC: 3444 Sheet metalwork

(P-12318)
ONETO MANUFACTURING COMPANY
146 S Maple Ave, South San Francisco
(94080-6302)
PHONE..............................650 875-1710
Jack Liberatore, *President*
Barbara L Liberatore, *Vice Pres*
Robert Liberatore, *Admin Sec*
EMP: 16
SQ FT: 20,000
SALES (est): 2.5MM **Privately Held**
SIC: 3444 Sheet metal specialties, not
stamped

(P-12319)
ORTRONICS INC
Also Called: Electrorack
1443 S Sunkist St, Anaheim (92806-5626)
PHONE..............................714 776-5420
Mark Panico, *President*
James Laperriere, *Treasurer*
Robert Julian, *Vice Pres*
Valerie Alsante, *Admin Sec*
Maria Flammer, *Buyer*
▲ **EMP:** 120
SQ FT: 50,000
SALES (est): 25.8MM
SALES (corp-wide): 21.2MM **Privately
Held**
WEB: www.electrorack.com
SIC: 3444 3679 Sheet metalwork; power
supplies, all types: static
  HQ: Legrand Holding, Inc.
     60 Woodlawn St
     West Hartford CT 06110
     860 233-6251

(P-12320)
OXNARD PRCSION FABRICATION INC
Also Called: O P F
2200 Teal Club Rd, Oxnard (93030-8640)
PHONE..............................805 985-0447
David Garza, *President*
Robert Valles, *Vice Pres*
EMP: 30
SQ FT: 107,000
SALES (est): 6.2MM **Privately Held**
WEB: www.opfinc.com
SIC: 3444 3469 3443 Sheet metal spe-
cialties, not stamped; metal stampings;
fabricated plate work (boiler shop)

(P-12321)
P A S U INC
1891 Nirvana Ave, Chula Vista
(91911-6117)
PHONE..............................619 421-1151
Donald R Palumbo, *President*
▲ **EMP:** 115 **EST:** 1979
SQ FT: 100,000
SALES (est): 17.1MM **Privately Held**
WEB: www.gceindustries.com
SIC: 3444 3825 Sheet metalwork; test
equipment for electronic & electrical cir-
cuits

(P-12322)
P T INDUSTRIES INC
3220 Industry Dr, Signal Hill (90755-4014)
PHONE..............................562 961-3431
Kim Nguyen, *President*
Thuy Nguyen, *Admin Sec*
EMP: 19
SQ FT: 19,000
SALES (est): 3.7MM **Privately Held**
SIC: 3444 Sheet metalwork

(P-12323)
PACIFIC AWARD METALS INC (HQ)
1450 Virginia Ave, Baldwin Park
(91706-5819)
PHONE..............................626 814-4410
Brian J Lipke, *CEO*
W Brent Taylor, *President*
Frank Fulford, *VP Sales*
Brent Taylor, *Manager*
EMP: 100
SQ FT: 110,000
SALES (est): 57.9MM
SALES (corp-wide): 1B **Publicly Held**
WEB: www.awardmetals.com
SIC: 3444 3312 Sheet metalwork; blast
furnaces & steel mills
  PA: Gibraltar Industries, Inc.
     3556 Lake Shore Rd # 100
     Buffalo NY 14219
     716 826-6500

(P-12324)
PACIFIC AWARD METALS INC
13169 Slover Ave, Fontana (92337-6923)
PHONE..............................626 814-4410
EMP: 50
SALES (corp-wide): 1B **Publicly Held**
SIC: 3444 3312 Sheet metalwork; blast
furnaces & steel mills
  HQ: Pacific Award Metals, Inc.
     1450 Virginia Ave
     Baldwin Park CA 91706
     626 814-4410

(P-12325)
PACIFIC DUCT INC
5499 Brooks St, Montclair (91763-4563)
PHONE..............................909 635-1335
Riad M Wahid, *President*
Brad Smead, *Opers Mgr*
George Bobo, *Supervisor*
▲ **EMP:** 30
SQ FT: 15,000
SALES (est): 6.4MM **Privately Held**
WEB: www.pacificduct.com
SIC: 3444 5075 5039 Metal ventilating
equipment; warm air heating & air condi-
tioning; air ducts, sheet metal

(P-12326)
PACIFIC MODERN HOMES INC
9723 Railroad St, Elk Grove (95624-2456)
P.O. Box 670 (95759-0670)
PHONE..............................916 685-9514
Anthony Colbert, *President*
Anthony B Colbert, *President*
Chris J Fellersen, *Senior VP*
Kenneth S Rader, *Vice Pres*
▼ **EMP:** 20
SQ FT: 3,800
SALES (est): 3.1MM **Privately Held**
WEB: www.pmhi.com
SIC: 3444 5031 Metal roofing & roof
drainage equipment; building materials,
exterior; building materials, interior

(P-12327)
PACIFIC SHEET METAL INC
Also Called: Pacific Metal Fab & Design
497 S Pine St, Madera (93637-5213)
PHONE..............................559 661-4044
Michael Hayes, *President*
EMP: 10
SQ FT: 8,000
SALES (est): 1.7MM **Privately Held**
SIC: 3444 Sheet metal specialties, not
stamped

(P-12328)
PALEX METALS INC
3601 Thomas Rd, Santa Clara
(95054-2040)
PHONE..............................408 496-6111
Donald J Russo, *President*
John Jameson, *CFO*
Mary Magda Russo, *Vice Pres*
EMP: 45 **EST:** 1973
SALES (est): 7MM **Privately Held**
WEB: www.palexmetals.com
SIC: 3444 Sheet metal specialties, not
stamped

(P-12329)
PCI INDUSTRIES INC
6501 Potello St, Commerce (90040)
PHONE..............................323 728-0004
Greg Skilley, *Vice Pres*
EMP: 100
SALES (corp-wide): 48.2MM **Privately
Held**
SIC: 3444 3564 Metal ventilating equip-
ment; filters, air: furnaces, air conditioning
equipment, etc.
  PA: Pci Industries, Inc.
     5101 Blue Mound Rd
     Fort Worth TX 76106
     817 509-2300

(P-12330)
PEGA PRECISION INC
18800 Adams Ct, Morgan Hill
(95037-2816)
PHONE..............................408 776-3700
Lewis H Fast, *President*
Aaron Fast, *Vice Pres*
EMP: 20
SQ FT: 30,000
SALES (est): 4.2MM **Privately Held**
WEB: www.precisionpega.com
SIC: 3444 3599 Housings for business
machines, sheet metal; machine shop,
jobbing & repair

(P-12331)
PENFIELD PRODUCTS INC
Also Called: Custom Home Accessories
11300 Trade Center Dr A, Rancho Cordova
(95742-6329)
PHONE..............................916 635-0231
Jeffrey Feldman, *CEO*
EMP: 22 **EST:** 2013
SQ FT: 18,000
SALES: 5MM **Privately Held**
SIC: 3444 5999 Mail (post office) collec-
tion or storage boxes, sheet metal; tro-
phies & plaques

(P-12332)
PERI FORMWORK SYSTEMS INC
15369 Valencia Ave, Fontana
(92335-3268)
PHONE..............................909 356-5797
Gustavo Berringer, *Systems Staff*
Andrea Casas, *Manager*
EMP: 24
SALES (corp-wide): 1.7B **Privately Held**
WEB: www.peri-usa.com
SIC: 3444 Concrete forms, sheet metal
  HQ: Peri Formwork Systems, Inc.
     7135 Dorsey Run Rd
     Elkridge MD 21075
     410 712-7225

(P-12333)
PETERSON SHEET METAL INC
Also Called: Peterson Sheetmetal
12925 Alcosta Blvd Ste 2, San Ramon
(94583-1341)
PHONE..............................925 830-1766
Carl Peterson, *President*
Darlene Peterson, *Vice Pres*

EMP: 13
SQ FT: 3,200
SALES (est) 1.6MM **Privately Held**
SIC: **3444** Sheet metalwork

(P-12334)
PINNACLE MANUFACTURING CORP
17680 Butterfield Blvd # 100, Morgan Hill (95037-3173)
PHONE...................................408 778-6100
Philip Stolzman, *President*
Luis Sapien, *Engineer*
Kristen Mullen, *Manager*
▲ EMP: 35
SALES (est): 8.9MM **Privately Held**
SIC: **3444** Sheet metalwork

(P-12335)
PINNACLE PRECISION SHTMTL CORP (PA)
5410 E La Palma Ave, Anaheim (92807-2023)
PHONE...................................714 777-3129
David Oddo, *President*
Paul Oddo, *Shareholder*
Brian McLaughlin, *Vice Pres*
EMP: 185
SALES (est): 37MM **Privately Held**
SIC: **3444** Sheet metalwork

(P-12336)
PINNACLE PRECISION SHTMTL CORP
Fabnet
5410 E La Palma Ave, Anaheim (92807-2023)
PHONE...................................714 777-3129
Robert F Denham, *Branch Mgr*
EMP: 75
SALES (corp-wide): 37MM **Privately Held**
SIC: **3444** 3599 Metal housings, enclosures, casings & other containers; forming machine work, sheet metal; machine shop, jobbing & repair
PA: Pinnacle Precision Sheet Metal Corporation
5410 E La Palma Ave
Anaheim CA 92807
714 777-3129

(P-12337)
PNA CONSTRUCTION TECH INC
301 Espee St Ste E, Bakersfield (93301-2659)
PHONE...................................661 326-1700
Matt Wilen, *Principal*
EMP: 35
SALES (corp-wide): 9.9MM **Privately Held**
SIC: **3444** Concrete forms, sheet metal
PA: P.N.A. Construction Technologies, Inc.
1349 W Bryn Mawr Ave
Itasca IL 60143
770 668-9500

(P-12338)
PRECISE INDUSTRIES INC
610 Neptune Ave, Brea (92821-2909)
PHONE...................................714 482-2333
Terry D Wells, *President*
Jose Quintana, *Program Mgr*
Robert L Wells, *Admin Sec*
Dave Trubey, *Info Tech Dir*
Jan Van Der Kolk, *Prgrmr*
▲ EMP: 120
SQ FT: 78,000
SALES (est): 29.5MM **Privately Held**
WEB: www.preciseind.com
SIC: **3444** 3679 3599 Sheet metalwork; electronic circuits; machine & other job shop work

(P-12339)
PRECISION STEEL PRODUCTS INC
Also Called: Steel Products International
13124 Avalon Blvd, Los Angeles (90061-2738)
PHONE...................................310 523-2002
Raul De Latorre, *President*
Deborah De Latorre, *Admin Sec*
EMP: 22
SQ FT: 24,000

SALES (est): 3.4MM **Privately Held**
WEB: www.steelproducts.biz
SIC: **3444** 3441 Sheet metalwork; fabricated structural metal

(P-12340)
PRISM AEROSPACE
3087 12th St, Riverside (92507-4904)
PHONE...................................951 582-2850
Eng Tan, *CEO*
Peng Tan, *President*
EMP: 50
SQ FT: 100,000
SALES (est): 11.9MM **Privately Held**
SIC: **3444** 3812 Forming machine work, sheet metal; aircraft/aerospace flight instruments & guidance systems; acceleration indicators & systems components, aerospace

(P-12341)
PRO METAL PRODUCTS
25559 Jesmond Dene Rd, Escondido (92026-8602)
P.O. Box 687, Temecula (92593-0687)
PHONE...................................760 480-0212
Fred West, *Owner*
EMP: 14
SQ FT: 12,000
SALES (est): 1.6MM **Privately Held**
SIC: **3444** Sheet metalwork

(P-12342)
PRO-TEK MANUFACTURING INC
4849 Southfront Rd, Livermore (94551-9482)
PHONE...................................925 454-8100
Steven M Krider, *President*
Sargon Alkurge, *Vice Pres*
Daniel McKenzie, *Vice Pres*
Rita Levina, *Accountant*
David Gerhard, *Manager*
▲ EMP: 49
SQ FT: 35,240
SALES (est): 11.5MM **Privately Held**
WEB: www.protekmfg.com
SIC: **3444** 3449 Sheet metalwork; miscellaneous metalwork

(P-12343)
PROMPT PRECISION METALS INC
1649 E Whitmore Ave, Ceres (95307-7203)
PHONE...................................209 531-1210
Don Widdifield, *President*
Joan Widdifield, *Admin Sec*
EMP: 65
SQ FT: 70,000
SALES (est): 11.8MM **Privately Held**
WEB: www.promptprecision.com
SIC: **3444** Sheet metal specialties, not stamped

(P-12344)
PWP MANUFACTURING LLC
1325 Norman Ave, Santa Clara (95054-2027)
PHONE...................................408 748-0120
Kimberly Reed,
Kim Reed, *Vice Pres*
Michael Reed,
EMP: 25
SQ FT: 18,000
SALES (est): 4.7MM **Privately Held**
SIC: **3444** 3315 Sheet metal specialties, not stamped; wire products, ferrous/iron; made in wiredrawing plants

(P-12345)
QUALITY FABRICATION INC (PA)
9631 Irondale Ave, Chatsworth (91311-5009)
PHONE...................................818 407-5015
Pradeep Kumar, *CEO*
John Rajaranam, *Project Leader*
▲ EMP: 74
SALES (est): 12.7MM **Privately Held**
WEB: www.quality-fab.com
SIC: **3444** Sheet metal specialties, not stamped

(P-12346)
QUALITY METAL FABRICATION LLC
2350 Wilbur Way, Auburn (95602-9500)
PHONE...................................530 887-7388
Thomas Neithercutt, *Mng Member*
EMP: 27
SQ FT: 12,000
SALES (est): 4.8MM **Privately Held**
WEB: www.qualitymetalfabrication.com
SIC: **3444** 1799 Sheet metalwork; welding on site

(P-12347)
R & R DUCTWORK LLC
12820 Lakeland Rd, Santa Fe Springs (90670-4515)
PHONE...................................562 944-9660
Brian Klebowski, *Mng Member*
EMP: 18
SQ FT: 14,000
SALES (est): 1.5MM **Privately Held**
SIC: **3444** Ducts, sheet metal

(P-12348)
R & V SHEET METAL INC
3197 Grapevine St, Mira Loma (91752-3501)
PHONE...................................951 361-9455
Ricardo Rico, *President*
EMP: 12
SALES (est): 1.3MM **Privately Held**
SIC: **3444** Sheet metalwork

(P-12349)
RADIATION PROTECTION & SPC INC
1531 W Orangewood Ave, Orange (92868-2006)
PHONE...................................714 771-7702
John Jory, *President*
EMP: 15
SALES (est): 3MM **Privately Held**
SIC: **3444** Radiator shields or enclosures, sheet metal

(P-12350)
RAMDA METAL SPECIALTIES INC
13012 Crenshaw Blvd, Gardena (90249-1544)
PHONE...................................310 538-2136
Daniel Guevara, *CEO*
EMP: 25
SQ FT: 25,000
SALES (est): 2.5MM **Privately Held**
WEB: www.ramda.com
SIC: **3444** Metal housings, enclosures, casings & other containers

(P-12351)
RAYCO BURIAL PRODUCTS INC
Also Called: Rayco B Products
1601 Raymond Ave, Monrovia (91016-4690)
PHONE...................................626 357-1996
Geza Dala, *President*
Valerie Dala, *Treasurer*
Ilene Sakamoto, *Vice Pres*
Martin Dala, *Admin Sec*
EMP: 30 EST: 1961
SQ FT: 20,000
SALES (est): 4.2MM **Privately Held**
SIC: **3444** Sheet metal specialties, not stamped

(P-12352)
RECOATING-WEST INC (PA)
Also Called: Rwi
4170 Douglas Blvd Ste 120, Granite Bay (95746-9703)
PHONE...................................916 652-8290
Brian Hope, *President*
Ian Cameron, *CFO*
Cheryl Poderzay, *Office Mgr*
Glenn Shafto, *Analyst*
Pavel Proshak, *Foreman/Supr*
▲ EMP: 35
SQ FT: 41,000
SALES (est): 5.9MM **Privately Held**
WEB: www.recoatingwest.com
SIC: **3444** Sheet metalwork

(P-12353)
REDDING METAL CRAFTERS INC
3871 Rancho Rd, Redding (96002-9328)
PHONE...................................530 222-4400
Robert Robinson III, *President*
Barbara Robinson, *Corp Secy*
Gregory Robinson, *Vice Pres*
EMP: 11
SQ FT: 10,000
SALES (est): 1.3MM **Privately Held**
SIC: **3444** Restaurant sheet metalwork

(P-12354)
RIGOS EQUIPMENT MFG LLC
Also Called: Rigos Sheet Metal
14501 Joanbridge St, Baldwin Park (91706-1749)
PHONE...................................626 813-6621
Yury Anguiano,
EMP: 23
SQ FT: 3,600
SALES (est): 4MM **Privately Held**
SIC: **3444** Sheet metalwork

(P-12355)
ROBERT F CHAPMAN INC
43100 Exchange Pl, Lancaster (93535-4524)
PHONE...................................661 940-9482
Tim Mitchell, *CEO*
John H Mitchell, *President*
Paulette Mitchell, *Admin Sec*
Mario Lua, *Business Mgr*
EMP: 53
SQ FT: 62,000
SALES (est): 11.7MM **Privately Held**
WEB: www.robertfchapman.com
SIC: **3444** 3549 Sheet metalwork; metalworking machinery

(P-12356)
ROMLA CO
Also Called: Romla Ventilator Co
9668 Heinrich Hertz Dr D, San Diego (92154-7919)
PHONE...................................619 946-1224
Ronald W Haneline, *CEO*
Bob Haneline, *Vice Pres*
Robert Haneline, *Vice Pres*
Jesse Soto, *Purchasing*
Vicky Gadea, *Buyer*
▲ EMP: 33 EST: 1945
SQ FT: 18,000
SALES (est): 8.2MM **Privately Held**
WEB: www.romla.com
SIC: **3444** Metal ventilating equipment

(P-12357)
RON NUNES ENTERPRISES LLC
7703 Las Positas Rd, Livermore (94551-8205)
PHONE...................................925 371-0220
Ron Nunes, *President*
Mark Timm, *Marketing Staff*
EMP: 15
SQ FT: 28,000
SALES (est): 2.7MM **Privately Held**
WEB: www.ronnunes.com
SIC: **3444** 7692 3443 3441 Sheet metal specialties, not stamped; welding repair; fabricated plate work (boiler shop); fabricated structural metal

(P-12358)
RONALD F OGLETREE INC
Also Called: Ogletree's
935 Vintage Ave, Saint Helena (94574-1400)
PHONE...................................707 963-3537
Ronald Ogletree, *President*
Matthew CIA, *Vice Pres*
Jennifer Elkins, *Info Tech Mgr*
EMP: 45 EST: 1946
SQ FT: 22,500
SALES (est): 8.5MM **Privately Held**
WEB: www.ogletreecorp.com
SIC: **3444** 3441 1791 Sheet metal specialties, not stamped; fabricated structural metal; structural steel erection

▲ = Import ▼=Export
◆ =Import/Export

(P-12359)
ROYAL MANUFACTURING INDS INC
600 W Warner Ave, Santa Ana (92707-3347)
PHONE...................714 668-9199
Robert Rieck, *President*
EMP: 14
SQ FT: 9,000
SALES (est): 2.2MM **Privately Held**
WEB: www.royalmfgind.com
SIC: 3444 Sheet metalwork

(P-12360)
ROYALITE MFG INC (PA)
1055 Terminal Way, San Carlos (94070-3226)
PHONE...................650 637-1440
Robert Amarillas, *President*
Dez Farnady, *General Mgr*
▼ EMP: 14
SALES (est): 1.8MM **Privately Held**
WEB: www.royalite-mfg.com
SIC: 3444 3446 Skylights, sheet metal; ladders, for permanent installation: metal

(P-12361)
RUSS INTERNATIONAL INC
1658 W 132nd St, Gardena (90249-2006)
PHONE...................310 329-7121
Randy Carter, *CEO*
Edmond Russ, *Chairman*
Joshua Bettencourt, *Technology*
▲ EMP: 22 EST: 1952
SQ FT: 20,000
SALES (est): 4.2MM **Privately Held**
WEB: www.russ-international.com
SIC: 3444 Sheet metal specialties, not stamped

(P-12362)
S & L CONTRACTING
900 W Kern Ave Ste 900 # 900, Mc Farland (93250-1815)
PHONE...................661 371-6379
Sergio Tindeo, *President*
EMP: 50
SALES (est): 2.6MM **Privately Held**
SIC: 3444 Sheet metalwork

(P-12363)
SA SERVING LINES INC
Also Called: G A Systems
226 W Carleton Ave, Orange (92867-3608)
PHONE...................714 848-7529
Steve Aderson, *CEO*
Pat Devalle, *CFO*
Virginia Anderson, *Corp Secy*
EMP: 19
SALES (est): 3MM **Privately Held**
SIC: 3444 Metal housings, enclosures, casings & other containers

(P-12364)
SABRIN CORPORATION
Also Called: Astronics Company
2836 E Walnut St, Pasadena (91107-3755)
PHONE...................626 792-3813
Josef Wrablicz, *President*
▲ EMP: 19 EST: 1961
SQ FT: 8,000
SALES (est): 3.5MM **Privately Held**
SIC: 3444 Forming machine work, sheet metal

(P-12365)
SAE ENGINEERING INC
365 Reed St, Santa Clara (95050-3107)
PHONE...................408 492-1784
Benjamin Yates, *Chairman*
Alan Pats, *President*
James Millich, *Vice Pres*
Joanna Yates, *Vice Pres*
▲ EMP: 40
SQ FT: 30,000
SALES (est): 8.1MM
SALES (corp-wide): 48.6MM **Privately Held**
SIC: 3444 3599 Sheet metalwork; machine shop, jobbing & repair
PA: Hilby-Yates, Inc.
282 Brokaw Rd
Santa Clara CA 95050
408 988-0700

(P-12366)
SAL J ACSTA SHEETMETAL MFG INC
Also Called: Acosta Sheet Metal Mfg Co
930 Remillard Ct, San Jose (95122-2625)
PHONE...................408 275-6370
Sal J Acosta, *CEO*
Anthony Morales, *CFO*
Randy Acosta, *Treasurer*
Sandi Acosta, *Vice Pres*
Michelle Acosta, *Admin Sec*
▲ EMP: 65
SQ FT: 118,000
SALES (est): 16.2MM **Privately Held**
WEB: www.acostallc.com
SIC: 3444 Sheet metal specialties, not stamped

(P-12367)
SAN DEGO PRCSION MACHINING INC
9375 Ruffin Ct, San Diego (92123-5304)
PHONE...................858 499-0379
William Matteson, *CEO*
Jason Matteson, *Vice Pres*
Jim Fox, *Sales Mgr*
EMP: 50 EST: 1971
SQ FT: 23,000
SALES (est): 10.2MM **Privately Held**
WEB: www.sdpm.com
SIC: 3444 3599 3312 Sheet metalwork; machine shop, jobbing & repair; stainless steel

(P-12368)
SAXTON INDUSTRIAL INC
1736 Standard Ave, Glendale (91201-2010)
PHONE...................818 265-0702
Ben Abadian, *President*
Marjan Abadian, *Vice Pres*
▲ EMP: 18
SQ FT: 33,000
SALES: 2MM **Privately Held**
WEB: www.saxtonindustrial.com
SIC: 3444 3499 3724 Sheet metalwork; trophies, metal, except silver; aircraft engines & engine parts

(P-12369)
SCREEN TECH INC
4754 Bennett Dr, Livermore (94551-4800)
PHONE...................408 885-9750
Stevan S Robertson, *Principal*
Marsha Robertson, *Vice Pres*
Tony Phan, *Senior Engr*
Tanya Graves, *Human Res Dir*
Matt Larson, *Opers Mgr*
▲ EMP: 60
SQ FT: 52,000
SALES (est): 13.4MM **Privately Held**
WEB: www.screentechinc.com
SIC: 3444 Sheet metal specialties, not stamped

(P-12370)
SE-GI PRODUCTS INC
20521 Teresita Way, Lake Forest (92630-8142)
PHONE...................951 737-8320
◆ EMP: 21
SALES (est): 4MM **Privately Held**
SIC: 3444

(P-12371)
SEGUNDO METAL PRODUCTS INC
Also Called: Advantage Metal Products
7855 Southfront Rd, Livermore (94551-8230)
PHONE...................925 667-2009
Mike Segundo, *President*
Phil Segundo, *Executive*
▲ EMP: 80
SQ FT: 60,000
SALES (est): 16.2MM **Privately Held**
WEB: www.advantagemetal.com
SIC: 3444 Sheet metalwork

(P-12372)
SHAFER METAL STAKE (PA)
25176 Avenue 5 1/2, Madera (93637-9586)
PHONE...................559 674-9487
Merwyn E Shafer, *Owner*
EMP: 14 EST: 1979

SQ FT: 1,300
SALES: 2MM **Privately Held**
SIC: 3444 Sheet metalwork

(P-12373)
SHEET METAL PROTOTYPE INC
19420 Londelius St, Northridge (91324-3511)
PHONE...................818 772-2715
Jane E Lamborn, *President*
EMP: 11
SQ FT: 7,500
SALES (est): 1.5MM **Privately Held**
SIC: 3444 Sheet metal specialties, not stamped

(P-12374)
SHEET METAL SERVICE
2310 E Orangethorpe Ave, Anaheim (92806-1231)
PHONE...................714 446-0196
Miguel Nunez, *President*
EMP: 18
SQ FT: 10,000
SALES (est): 4.1MM **Privately Held**
SIC: 3444 Sheet metalwork

(P-12375)
SHEET METAL SPECIALIST LLC
11698 Warm Springs Rd, Riverside (92505-5862)
PHONE...................951 351-6828
Michael Uranga,
Sandy Sligar,
EMP: 38
SQ FT: 18,000
SALES (est): 6.2MM **Privately Held**
SIC: 3444 Sheet metal specialties, not stamped

(P-12376)
SHEET MTAL FABRICATION SUP INC
2020 Railroad Dr, Sacramento (95815-3515)
PHONE...................916 641-6884
Cipriano Espinor, *President*
John Espinor, *Vice Pres*
Cheree Batchelor, *Office Admin*
Mark Johnston, *Sales Staff*
Rick Espinor, *Manager*
EMP: 80
SQ FT: 14,000
SALES (est): 12.6MM **Privately Held**
SIC: 3444 Ducts, sheet metal

(P-12377)
SHEETMETAL ENGINEERING
1780 Voyager Ave, Simi Valley (93063-3301)
PHONE...................805 306-0390
Kenneth Chamberlain, *President*
Kathy Chou, *CFO*
David Reed, *Vice Pres*
Dave L Reed, *Technology*
EMP: 25
SQ FT: 21,000
SALES (est): 4.2MM **Privately Held**
WEB: www.sheetmetaleng.com
SIC: 3444 1799 Sheet metal specialties, not stamped; welding on site

(P-12378)
SHOWERDOORDIRECT LLC
20100 Normandie Ave, Torrance (90502-1211)
PHONE...................310 327-8060
Adam Slutske,
▲ EMP: 51
SALES (est): 5.2MM
SALES (corp-wide): 11.8MM **Privately Held**
SIC: 3444 Bins, prefabricated sheet metal; radiator shields or enclosures, sheet metal
PA: Century Shower Door Co., Inc.
20100 Normandie Ave
Torrance CA 90502
310 327-8060

(P-12379)
SMS FABRICATIONS INC
11698 Warm Springs Rd, Riverside (92505-5862)
PHONE...................951 351-6828
Michael A Uranga, *CEO*

Sandy Sligar, *President*
Scott Sligar, *Vice Pres*
EMP: 36
SALES (est): 7.4MM **Privately Held**
SIC: 3444 Sheet metalwork

(P-12380)
SOMAR CORPORATION
13006 Halldale Ave, Gardena (90249-2118)
PHONE...................310 329-1446
Martin Torres, *President*
Ramona Torres, *Office Mgr*
EMP: 16
SQ FT: 32,000
SALES (est): 2.7MM **Privately Held**
SIC: 3444 3353 Sheet metalwork; aluminum sheet, plate & foil

(P-12381)
SONOMA METAL PRODUCTS INC
601 Aviation Blvd, Santa Rosa (95403-1025)
PHONE...................707 484-9876
Brian K Herndon, *President*
Wanda Dunbar, *Shareholder*
Sharon Herndon, *Treasurer*
Don Dunbar, *Admin Sec*
EMP: 62
SQ FT: 54,000
SALES: 5.7MM **Privately Held**
SIC: 3444 3496 2522 Housings for business machines, sheet metal; miscellaneous fabricated wire products; office furniture, except wood

(P-12382)
SOUTH BAY DIVERSFD SYSTEMS INC
Also Called: U S Fabrications
1841 National Ave, Hayward (94545-1707)
PHONE...................510 784-3094
Thomas S Waller, *President*
▲ EMP: 15
SALES (est): 3.3MM **Privately Held**
WEB: www.usfabrications.com
SIC: 3444 Sheet metalwork

(P-12383)
SPACESONICS INCORPORATED
Also Called: Paysonic
30300 Union City Blvd, Union City (94587-1514)
PHONE...................650 610-0999
Ignacio C Palomarez, *President*
Elizabeth Palomarez, *Treasurer*
Hortencia Villanuedo, *Admin Sec*
Carlos Palomarez, *Info Tech Dir*
Diane Palomarez, *Info Tech Mgr*
▲ EMP: 90
SQ FT: 55,000
SALES (est): 23.9MM **Privately Held**
WEB: www.spacesonic.com
SIC: 3444 Metal housings, enclosures, casings & other containers

(P-12384)
SPAN-O-MATIC INC
825 Columbia St, Brea (92821-2917)
PHONE...................714 256-4700
Wolfgang Arnold, *President*
Erik A Arnold, *CEO*
Lynda Arnold, *CFO*
Carl Arnold, *Vice Pres*
Frank Mann, *Engineer*
EMP: 40 EST: 1972
SQ FT: 50,000
SALES (est): 8.4MM **Privately Held**
WEB: www.spanomatic.com
SIC: 3444 Sheet metalwork

(P-12385)
SPEC-BUILT SYSTEMS INC
2150 Michael Faraday Dr, San Diego (92154-7903)
PHONE...................619 661-8100
Randy Eifler, *President*
EMP: 75
SQ FT: 25,000
SALES (est): 22.4MM **Privately Held**
WEB: www.specbuilt.com
SIC: 3444 Sheet metalwork

PRODUCTS & SVCS

(P-12386)
SPECIALTY FABRICATIONS INC
2674 Westhills Ct, Simi Valley
(93065-6234)
PHONE....................805 579-9730
Mark Zimmerman, *President*
Randy Zimmerman, *Corp Secy*
EMP: 49 **EST:** 1978
SQ FT: 80,000
SALES (est): 11.8MM **Privately Held**
WEB: www.specfabinc.com
SIC: 3444 3599 Sheet metalwork; machine & other job shop work

(P-12387)
SPRAY ENCLOSURE TECHNOLOGIES
Also Called: Spray Tech
1427 N Linden Ave, Rialto (92376-8601)
PHONE....................909 419-7011
Tyler Rand, *President*
▲ **EMP:** 30
SQ FT: 59,000
SALES (est): 7.4MM **Privately Held**
WEB: www.mercuryairmakeup.com
SIC: 3444 Booths, spray: prefabricated sheet metal

(P-12388)
STEELDYNE INDUSTRIES
Also Called: ABC Sheet Metal
2871 E La Cresta Ave, Anaheim
(92806-1817)
PHONE....................714 630-6200
Jeff Duveneck, *President*
Richard Duveneck, *Vice Pres*
Zachary Pihl, *Engineer*
EMP: 40
SQ FT: 20,000
SALES (est): 11.8MM **Privately Held**
WEB: www.abcsheetmetal.com
SIC: 3444 Sheet metalwork

(P-12389)
STEELER INC
2901 Orange Grove Ave, North Highlands
(95660-5703)
PHONE....................916 483-3600
Kirk Bache, *Manager*
EMP: 10
SALES (corp-wide): 41.7MM **Privately Held**
WEB: www.steeler.com
SIC: 3444 5072 Studs & joists, sheet metal; builders' hardware; miscellaneous fasteners
PA: Steeler, Inc.
10023 Martin Luther King
Seattle WA 98178
206 725-8500

(P-12390)
STEIN INDUSTRIES INC (PA)
4005 Artesia Ave, Fullerton (92833-2519)
PHONE....................714 522-4560
Rudi Steinhilber, *CEO*
Theodore Steinhilber, *President*
Dave Spivy, *CFO*
EMP: 37 **EST:** 1982
SQ FT: 30,800
SALES (est): 4.6MM **Privately Held**
WEB: www..steinindustries.com
SIC: 3444 2599 Sheet metalwork; work benches, factory

(P-12391)
STOLL METALCRAFT INC
24808 Anza Dr, Valencia (91355-1258)
PHONE....................661 295-0401
Gunter Stoll, *President*
Frank Meacham, *Program Mgr*
EMP: 105
SQ FT: 45,000
SALES (est): 24.8MM **Privately Held**
WEB: www.stoll-metalcraft.com
SIC: 3444 Sheet metal specialties, not stamped

(P-12392)
STRETCH FORMING CORPORATION
Also Called: Sfc
804 S Redlands Ave, Perris (92570-2478)
PHONE....................951 443-0911
Brian D Geary, *CEO*

Jim Lowther, *General Mgr*
Jose Corvorubbias, *Info Tech Mgr*
▲ **EMP:** 105
SQ FT: 97,000
SALES: 14.2MM **Privately Held**
SIC: 3444 Sheet metalwork

(P-12393)
SUN SHEETMETAL SOLUTIONS INC
3565 Charter Park Dr, San Jose
(95136-1346)
P.O. Box 731244 (95173-1244)
PHONE....................408 445-8047
Chau Nguyen, *President*
Rebecca Trinhle, *CFO*
Tom Nguyen, *Vice Pres*
Vince Blecha, *Sales Mgr*
Kevin Trinhle, *Accounts Mgr*
EMP: 20 **EST:** 2000
SQ FT: 10,000
SALES (est): 4.6MM **Privately Held**
WEB: www.sunsheetmetals.com
SIC: 3444 3552 Sheet metal specialties, not stamped; fabric forming machinery & equipment

(P-12394)
SUPERIOR DUCT FABRICATION INC
1683 Mount Vernon Ave, Pomona
(91768-3300)
PHONE....................909 620-8565
Mike Hilgert, *CEO*
Kerry Bootke, *Vice Pres*
Steve Pedroza, *Opers Mgr*
Rita Olivarria, *Manager*
◆ **EMP:** 107
SQ FT: 3,900
SALES (est): 33.5MM **Privately Held**
WEB: www.sdfab.com
SIC: 3444 Ducts, sheet metal

(P-12395)
SUPERIOR METAL FABRICATORS
4768 Felspar St, Riverside (92509-3038)
PHONE....................951 360-2474
Ron Didonanto, *President*
Dave Anderson, *Vice Pres*
EMP: 12
SQ FT: 10,000
SALES (est): 1.3MM **Privately Held**
SIC: 3444 Sheet metalwork

(P-12396)
SUPERIOR METALS INC
838 Jury Ct Ste B, San Jose (95112-2815)
PHONE....................408 938-3488
Hugo Navarez, *President*
EMP: 15
SQ FT: 7,000
SALES (est): 1.9MM **Privately Held**
SIC: 3444 Sheet metalwork

(P-12397)
SWIFT FAB
515 E Alondra Blvd, Gardena
(90248-2903)
PHONE....................310 366-7295
Robert Senter, *Owner*
EMP: 17
SQ FT: 6,000
SALES (est): 2.1MM **Privately Held**
WEB: www.swiftfab.com
SIC: 3444 Sheet metal specialties, not stamped

(P-12398)
SWIFT-COR PRECISION INC
344 W 157th St, Gardena (90248-2135)
PHONE....................310 354-1207
Sam Longo Jr, *President*
Tony Serge, *CFO*
EMP: 62
SQ FT: 100,000
SALES (est): 8.8MM **Privately Held**
WEB: www.swiftcor.com
SIC: 3444 Sheet metalwork

(P-12399)
T & F SHEET METALS FAB
15607 New Century Dr, Gardena
(90248-2128)
PHONE....................310 516-8548

Thomas Medina, *President*
Hector Medina, *Vice Pres*
EMP: 32
SQ FT: 9,800
SALES: 3.5MM **Privately Held**
SIC: 3444 Sheet metalwork

(P-12400)
TALINS COMPANY
17800 S Main St Ste 121, Gardena
(90248-3511)
PHONE....................310 378-3715
George Talbott, *Owner*
EMP: 15 **EST:** 1977
SQ FT: 3,200
SALES (est): 1.6MM **Privately Held**
SIC: 3444 Sheet metalwork

(P-12401)
TAYLOR WINGS INC
3720 Omec Cir, Rancho Cordova
(95742-7303)
PHONE....................916 851-9464
Terry Taylor, *President*
EMP: 25
SQ FT: 11,700
SALES (est): 5.3MM **Privately Held**
WEB: www.taylorwings.com
SIC: 3444 Sheet metalwork

(P-12402)
TED RIECK ENTERPRISES INC
Also Called: Royal Metal
1228 S Wright St, Santa Ana (92705-4507)
PHONE....................714 542-4763
Ted Rieck, *President*
Penny Rieck, *Vice Pres*
EMP: 14
SQ FT: 9,000
SALES: 1.5MM **Privately Held**
SIC: 3444 Sheet metalwork

(P-12403)
TEE -N -JAY MANUFACTURING INC
9145 Glenoaks Blvd, Sun Valley
(91352-2612)
PHONE....................818 504-2961
Jeff Berns, *President*
Tamara Berns, *Corp Secy*
Sandi Hollingsworth, *Office Mgr*
EMP: 20
SQ FT: 10,187
SALES (est): 3MM **Privately Held**
WEB: www.tee-n-jay.com
SIC: 3444 Sheet metalwork

(P-12404)
TEOHC CALIFORNIA INC
1320 Performance Dr, Stockton
(95206-4925)
PHONE....................209 234-1600
Nicholas L Saakvitne, *CEO*
Gary Henry, *President*
Jim Willis, *CFO*
Mark J Comfort, *Vice Pres*
Bruce Couturier, *Vice Pres*
EMP: 350 **EST:** 1943
SQ FT: 350,000
SALES (est): 31.7MM
SALES (corp-wide): 1B **Publicly Held**
WEB: www.gibraltar1.com
SIC: 3444 3479 Furnace casings, sheet metal; gutters, sheet metal; galvanizing of iron, steel or end-formed products
PA: Gibraltar Industries, Inc.
3556 Lake Shore Rd # 100
Buffalo NY 14219
716 826-6500

(P-12405)
TFC MANUFACTURING INC
4001 Watson Plaza Dr, Lakewood
(90712-4034)
PHONE....................562 426-9559
Majid Shahbazi, *President*
Hamid Sharifat, *Vice Pres*
EMP: 81
SQ FT: 28,500
SALES (est): 21.7MM **Privately Held**
WEB: www.tfcmfg.com
SIC: 3444 Sheet metalwork

(P-12406)
THERMA LLC
1601 Las Plumas Ave, San Jose
(95133-1613)
PHONE....................408 347-3400
Joseph Parisi, *CEO*
Mike Fisher, *COO*
Nicki Parisi, *CFO*
Kent Beasterfield, *Administration*
Manh Phan, *Administration*
▲ **EMP:** 1200
SALES (est): 228.8MM
SALES (corp-wide): 325.9MM **Privately Held**
WEB: www.therma.com
SIC: 3444 3448 Sheet metalwork; prefabricated metal components
PA: Therma Holdings Llc
1601 Las Plumas Ave
San Jose CA 95133
408 347-3400

(P-12407)
THOMAS E DAVIS INC
Also Called: Tedco
6736 Preston Ave Ste A, Livermore
(94551-8521)
P.O. Box 2376 (94551-2376)
PHONE....................925 373-1373
Cynthia Davis, *President*
Michael Davis, *President*
Jennifer J Hunt, *CFO*
EMP: 10
SQ FT: 12,000
SALES (est): 1.2MM **Privately Held**
WEB: www.tedcosheetmetal.com
SIC: 3444 Sheet metal specialties, not stamped

(P-12408)
TJ COMPOSITES INC
Also Called: Martin Enterprises
7231 Boulder Ave, Highland (92346-3313)
PHONE....................951 928-8713
Thomas M Jones, *President*
EMP: 30
SQ FT: 2,000
SALES (est): 11.4MM **Privately Held**
SIC: 3444 Metal housings, enclosures, casings & other containers

(P-12409)
TN SHEET METAL INC
18385 Bandilier Cir, Fountain Valley
(92708-7001)
PHONE....................714 593-0100
Thony Quang Nguyen, *CEO*
▲ **EMP:** 19 **EST:** 2001
SQ FT: 12,035
SALES (est): 4.3MM **Privately Held**
SIC: 3444 Ducts, sheet metal

(P-12410)
TREND TECHNOLOGIES LLC (DH)
4626 Eucalyptus Ave, Chino (91710-9215)
P.O. Box 515001, Los Angeles (90051-5001)
PHONE....................909 597-7861
Earl Payton, *Mng Member*
Jeffrey Stump, *Vice Pres*
Barb Raftree, *Admin Asst*
Liz Perez, *Administration*
Cesar Lemus, *Prgrmr*
▲ **EMP:** 200
SQ FT: 125,000
SALES (est): 130.8MM
SALES (corp-wide): 164.5MM **Privately Held**
SIC: 3444 3469 3499 3089 Metal housings, enclosures, casings & other containers; electronic enclosures, stamped or pressed metal; aquarium accessories, metal; injection molding of plastics
HQ: Ttl Holdings, Llc
4626 Eucalyptus Ave
Chino CA 91710
909 597-7861

(P-12411)
TRI FAB ASSOCIATES INC
48351 Lakeview Blvd, Fremont
(94538-6533)
PHONE....................510 651-7628
Ronald A Brochu, *President*
Joseph R Santosuosso, *CEO*

▲ = Import ▼=Export
◆ =Import/Export

Judy Archer, *Controller*
Richard Petrarca, *Controller*
Michael Taft, *QC Mgr*
EMP: 90
SQ FT: 35,000
SALES (est): 18.5MM **Privately Held**
WEB: www.trifab.com
SIC: 3444 Sheet metal specialties, not stamped

(P-12412)
TRI PRECISION SHEETMETAL INC
845 N Elm St, Orange (92867-7909)
PHONE....................714 632-8838
Ross Morrow, *President*
Rob Morrow, *CFO*
EMP: 40
SALES (est): 8.8MM **Privately Held**
WEB: www.triprecision.com
SIC: 3444 Housings for business machines, sheet metal; sheet metal specialties, not stamped

(P-12413)
TRIO METAL STAMPING INC
15318 Proctor Ave, City of Industry (91745-1023)
PHONE....................626 336-1228
Damian Rickard, *CEO*
Rudy Hernandez, *COO*
Georgia Boris, *Corp Secy*
Cindy Hansen, *Purch Mgr*
EMP: 53
SQ FT: 75,000
SALES (est): 8MM **Privately Held**
WEB: www.triometalstamping.com
SIC: 3444 3469 Sheet metalwork; stamping metal for the trade

(P-12414)
TRU-DUCT INC
2500 Swetwater Sprng Blvd, Spring Valley (91978-2007)
PHONE....................619 660-3858
Drew E Miles, *CEO*
EMP: 45
SQ FT: 14,400
SALES (est): 11.3MM **Privately Held**
SIC: 3444 Ducts, sheet metal

(P-12415)
UNITED DURALUME PRODUCTS INC
350 S Raymond Ave, Fullerton (92831-4689)
PHONE....................714 773-4011
Mike Winston Adams, *CEO*
EMP: 15
SQ FT: 128,600
SALES (est): 3.2MM **Privately Held**
SIC: 3444 1521 Awnings & canopies; patio & deck construction & repair

(P-12416)
UNITED FABRICATION INC
1250 Avenida Acaso Ste C, Camarillo (93012-8729)
PHONE....................805 482-2354
John Osgood, *President*
Philip Amanta, *President*
EMP: 15
SQ FT: 11,000
SALES (est): 2MM **Privately Held**
SIC: 3444 2514 Metal ventilating equipment; cabinets, radio & television: metal

(P-12417)
UNITED MECH MET FBRICATORS INC
Also Called: Umec
33353 Lewis St, Union City (94587-2205)
PHONE....................510 537-4744
Gina Wang, *CEO*
Barry Brescia, *Vice Chairman*
Camille Alcayde, *Manager*
Albert Sevilla, *Manager*
EMP: 50
SALES (est): 14.2MM **Privately Held**
WEB: www.umec.net
SIC: 3444 3443 3556 Sheet metalwork; fabricated plate work (boiler shop); food products machinery

(P-12418)
UNITED SHEETMETAL INC
44153 S Grimmer Blvd, Fremont (94538-6350)
PHONE....................510 257-1858
Chung Yuan Tsai, *CEO*
Peggy Loo, *CFO*
▲ **EMP:** 11
SALES (est): 2.2MM **Privately Held**
WEB: www.unitedsheetmetal.com
SIC: 3444 Sheet metal specialties, not stamped
PA: Cheng Fwa Industrial Co., Ltd.
5f, 252, Sec. 2, New Taipei Blvd.,
New Taipei City TAP 24158
-

(P-12419)
US PRECISION SHEET METAL INC
Also Called: U S Precision Manufacturing
4020 Garner Rd, Riverside (92501-1006)
PHONE....................951 276-2611
Amanda Hawkins, *CEO*
Ray Mayo, *President*
Sal Giulano, *Vice Pres*
EMP: 68 **EST:** 1981
SQ FT: 25,000
SALES (est): 13.3MM **Privately Held**
WEB: www.usprecision.net
SIC: 3444 Sheet metal specialties, not stamped

(P-12420)
USK MANUFACTURING INC
720 Zwissig Way, Union City (94587-3602)
PHONE....................510 471-7555
Moon Do Kim, *CEO*
Jina Kim, *Vice Pres*
Cindy Fong, *Principal*
▲ **EMP:** 45
SQ FT: 85,000
SALES: 5MM **Privately Held**
WEB: www.uskmfg.com
SIC: 3444 Sheet metalwork

(P-12421)
VALLEY PRECISION METAL PRODUCT
Also Called: Valley Engravers
27771 Avenue Hopkins, Santa Clarita (91355-1223)
PHONE....................661 607-0100
Toll Free:....................888 -
Howard R Vermillion Jr, *President*
EMP: 30
SQ FT: 15,000
SALES (est): 4.3MM
SALES (corp-wide): 5.3MM **Privately Held**
WEB: www.valleyprecisionmetal.com
SIC: 3444 3599 Sheet metalwork; machine shop, jobbing & repair
PA: Valley Precision Metal Products, Inc.
27771 Avenue Hopkins
Valencia CA 91355
661 607-0100

(P-12422)
VANGUARD FABRICATION CORP
14578 Hawthorne Ave, Fontana (92335-2507)
PHONE....................909 355-0832
Bill Tully, *President*
EMP: 12
SQ FT: 7,000
SALES (est): 2MM **Privately Held**
SIC: 3444 Sheet metalwork

(P-12423)
VERCO DECKING INC
8333 Lime Ave, Fontana (92335)
P.O. Box 3487 (92334-3487)
PHONE....................909 822-8079
Mike Decasas, *Opers-Prdtn-Mfg*
EMP: 15
SALES (corp-wide): 25B **Publicly Held**
SIC: 3444 Siding, sheet metal
HQ: Verco Decking, Inc.
4340 N 42nd Ave
Phoenix AZ 85019
602 272-1347

(P-12424)
VERCO DECKING INC
607 Wilbur Ave, Antioch (94509-7502)
P.O. Box 1259 (94509-0125)
PHONE....................925 778-2102
Tim Ferrier, *Manager*
EMP: 15
SQ FT: 49,914
SALES (corp-wide): 25B **Publicly Held**
SIC: 3444 3441 Roof deck, sheet metal; fabricated structural metal
HQ: Verco Decking, Inc.
4340 N 42nd Ave
Phoenix AZ 85019
602 272-1347

(P-12425)
VERSAFAB CORP (PA)
15919 S Broadway, Gardena (90248-2489)
PHONE....................800 421-1822
Edward Penfold Jr, *Ch of Bd*
Joe Flynn, *President*
Sylvia Franco, *QC Mgr*
Debbie Wilson, *Manager*
EMP: 43 **EST:** 1982
SQ FT: 35,000
SALES (est): 10.2MM **Privately Held**
WEB: www.versafabcorp.com
SIC: 3444 3465 3496 3469 Sheet metalwork; moldings or trim, automobile: stamped metal; miscellaneous fabricated wire products; metal stampings

(P-12426)
VERSAFORM CORPORATION
1377 Specialty Dr, Vista (92081-8521)
PHONE....................760 599-0961
Ronals S Saks, *President*
EMP: 73
SQ FT: 24,000
SALES (est): 11.1MM **Privately Held**
WEB: www.lmiaerospace.com
SIC: 3444 3549 3398 Forming machine work, sheet metal; sheet metal specialties, not stamped; metalworking machinery; metal heat treating
HQ: Lmi Aerospace, Inc.
411 Fountain Lakes Blvd
Saint Charles MO 63301
636 946-6525

(P-12427)
VIVER CO INC
Also Called: Viver Sheet Metal
1934 W 144th St, Gardena (90249-2928)
PHONE....................310 327-4578
Victor Loya, *Owner*
EMP: 10
SQ FT: 5,000
SALES (est): 1MM **Privately Held**
SIC: 3444 Ducts, sheet metal

(P-12428)
VIVID INC
1250 Memorex Dr, Santa Clara (95050-2812)
P.O. Box 700125, San Jose (95170-0125)
PHONE....................408 982-9101
John Comeau, *President*
Walt Pena, *Vice Pres*
Keith Lough, *Project Mgr*
Thomas Nguyen, *Project Mgr*
▲ **EMP:** 53
SQ FT: 38,800
SALES (est): 10.3MM **Privately Held**
WEB: www.vividinc.com
SIC: 3444 Sheet metalwork

(P-12429)
VTS SHEETMETAL SPECIALIST CO
1041 N Grove St, Anaheim (92806-2015)
PHONE....................714 237-1420
Tom Bonnett, *President*
SA H Vo, *Admin Sec*
EMP: 31
SQ FT: 21,300
SALES: 3.4MM **Privately Held**
WEB: www.vtsfab.com
SIC: 3444 Metal housings, enclosures, casings & other containers

(P-12430)
W A CALL MANUFACTURING CO INC
1710 Rogers Ave, San Jose (95112-1189)
PHONE....................408 436-1450
W A Pat Call Jr, *President*
Justin Pourroy, *Vice Pres*
EMP: 15 **EST:** 1950
SQ FT: 36,250
SALES (est): 2.9MM **Privately Held**
SIC: 3444 5075 Metal ventilating equipment; warm air heating & air conditioning

(P-12431)
W E HALL CO
Also Called: Pacific Corrugated Pipe
13680 Slover Ave, Fontana (92337-6951)
PHONE....................909 829-4235
Sandee Knuckey, *Manager*
EMP: 12
SALES (corp-wide): 16.7MM **Privately Held**
SIC: 3444 3449 5051 3312 Culverts, sheet metal; miscellaneous metalwork; pipe & tubing, steel; blast furnaces & steel mills
PA: W.E. Hall Company, Inc.
471 Old Newport Blvd # 205
Newport Beach CA 92663
949 650-4555

(P-12432)
WENCON DEVELOPMENT INC
Also Called: Quick Mount Pv
2700 Mitchell Dr Ste 2, Walnut Creek (94598-1602)
PHONE....................925 478-8269
Claudia Wentworth, *President*
Jeff Spies, *President*
Sam Cast, *Vice Pres*
Ben Kuttesch, *Engineer*
Cynthia Johnston, *Controller*
▲ **EMP:** 88
SQ FT: 1,700
SALES (est): 18.9MM
SALES (corp-wide): 47.2MM **Privately Held**
SIC: 3444 Awnings & canopies
PA: Esdec, Inc.
976 Brady Ave Nw Ste 100
Atlanta GA 30318
404 512-0716

(P-12433)
WEST COAST CUSTOM SHEET METAL
9045 Glenoaks Blvd, Sun Valley (91352-2040)
PHONE....................818 252-7500
George Vartan, *President*
EMP: 19
SQ FT: 8,500
SALES (est): 2.7MM **Privately Held**
SIC: 3444 Sheet metalwork

(P-12434)
WEST COAST FAB INC
700 S 32nd St, Richmond (94804-4106)
PHONE....................510 529-0177
Thomas Nelson, *President*
Scott Shelby, *QC Mgr*
EMP: 15
SQ FT: 18,000
SALES (est): 3.7MM **Privately Held**
WEB: www.westcoastfabinc.com
SIC: 3444 Sheet metal specialties, not stamped

(P-12435)
WESTERN SHEET METALS INC
190 E Harrison St Ste B, Corona (92879-1377)
PHONE....................951 272-3600
Albert Rivera, *President*
Matt Rola, *General Mgr*
EMP: 11
SALES (est): 12.9K **Privately Held**
WEB: www.westernsheetmetal.com
SIC: 3444 Sheet metalwork

(P-12436)
WESTFAB MANUFACTURING INC
3370 Keller St, Santa Clara (95054-2612)
PHONE....................408 727-0550

PRODUCTS & SVCS

Akbar Soleimanieh, *President*
Homeira Lotfi, *CFO*
EMP: 45
SQ FT: 22,000
SALES: 5MM **Privately Held**
WEB: www.westfab.com
SIC: 3444 Sheet metalwork

(P-12437)
WILL-MANN INC
225 E Santa Fe Ave, Fullerton
(92832-1917)
P.O. Box 976 (92836-0976)
PHONE..............................714 870-0350
Manfred Frischmuth, *President*
Sabina Andrassy, *Treasurer*
Lore Frischmuth, *Vice Pres*
Tracy Herget, *Manager*
EMP: 40
SQ FT: 30,000
SALES (est): 8.2MM **Privately Held**
WEB: www.will-mann.com
SIC: 3444 7692 3471 Sheet metal specialties, not stamped; welding repair; plating & polishing

(P-12438)
WINBO USA INC
2120 California Ave Ste 2, Corona
(92881-3301)
PHONE..............................951 738-9978
Eddie Cheung, *President*
▲ **EMP:** 40
SALES (est): 592.6K **Privately Held**
SIC: 3444 Machine guards, sheet metal

(P-12439)
Y2K PRECISION SHEETMETAL INC
3831 E La Palma Ave, Anaheim
(92807-1721)
PHONE..............................714 632-3901
Hoang Ha, *President*
EMP: 10
SALES (est): 1.4MM **Privately Held**
WEB: www.y2ksheetmetal.com
SIC: 3444 Sheet metalwork

3446 Architectural & Ornamental Metal Work

(P-12440)
A AND M ORNAMENTAL IRON & WLDG
1611 Railroad St, Corona (92880-2503)
PHONE..............................951 734-6730
Michael J Tallick, *Owner*
EMP: 14
SQ FT: 4,000
SALES (est): 2MM **Privately Held**
SIC: 3446 Architectural metalwork

(P-12441)
A/C FOLDING GATES
1374 E 9th St, Pomona (91766-3831)
PHONE..............................909 629-3026
Clifton G Adams, *Owner*
EMP: 13
SQ FT: 16,000
SALES (est): 970K **Privately Held**
SIC: 3446 1799 Gates, ornamental metal; fence construction

(P-12442)
ABLE IRON WORKS
222 Hershey St, Pomona (91767-5810)
PHONE..............................909 397-5300
Stephen Holmes, *CEO*
Robert Pittenger, *Director*
EMP: 20
SQ FT: 12,000
SALES: 10MM **Privately Held**
WEB: www.ableironwork.com
SIC: 3446 Architectural metalwork

(P-12443)
ABS MANUFACTURERS INC
519 Horning St, San Jose (95112-2913)
PHONE..............................408 295-5984
Rick Mancias, *President*
Lupe Mancias Jr, *Vice Pres*
EMP: 17
SQ FT: 4,000

SALES (est): 2.6MM **Privately Held**
WEB: www.classof72.com
SIC: 3446 Ornamental metalwork

(P-12444)
ACCESS PROFESSIONAL INC
Also Called: Access Professional Systems
1955 Cordell Ct Ste 104, El Cajon
(92020-0901)
PHONE..............................858 571-4444
Russell Scheppmann, *President*
Krista Terrel, *Office Mgr*
Al Jenkins, *Manager*
EMP: 18
SALES (est): 4.9MM **Privately Held**
SIC: 3446 7521 1731 Fences, gates, posts & flagpoles; automobile parking; voice, data & video wiring contractor

(P-12445)
ACE IRON INC
929 Howard St, Marina Del Rey
(90292-5518)
PHONE..............................510 324-3300
Aejaz Sareshwala, *President*
EMP: 145
SQ FT: 60,000
SALES (est): 16.5MM **Privately Held**
WEB: www.aceiron.com
SIC: 3446 3441 1791 Fences or posts, ornamental iron or steel; building components, structural steel; structural steel erection

(P-12446)
ACTIANCE INC
1400 Seaport Blvd, Redwood City
(94063-5594)
PHONE..............................650 631-6300
EMP: 42
SALES (est): 10.3MM **Privately Held**
SIC: 3446

(P-12447)
ADF INCORPORATED
Also Called: Able Design and Fabrication
1550 W Mahalo Pl, Rancho Dominguez
(90220-5422)
PHONE..............................310 669-9700
Lou Mannick, *President*
Duc Luu, *Info Tech Dir*
Brian Webster, *Engineer*
Mercedes Chavez, *Human Res Mgr*
Mayra Herrera, *Purch Mgr*
EMP: 30
SQ FT: 23,000
SALES (est): 7.5MM **Privately Held**
WEB: www.able-design.com
SIC: 3446 Partitions & supports/studs, including accoustical systems

(P-12448)
ALABAMA METAL INDUSTRIES CORP
Also Called: Amico Fontana
11093 Beech Ave, Fontana (92337-7268)
P.O. Box 310353 (92331-0353)
PHONE..............................909 350-9280
Lilly Mc Donalds, *Branch Mgr*
Susan Esquibel, *Office Mgr*
EMP: 45
SALES (corp-wide): 1B **Publicly Held**
WEB: www.amico-online.com
SIC: 3446 Open flooring & grating for construction
HQ: Alabama Metal Industries Corporation
3245 Fayette Ave
Birmingham AL 35208
205 787-2611

(P-12449)
AMERICAN STEEL & STAIRWAYS INC
8525 Forest St Ste A, Gilroy (95020-3797)
PHONE..............................408 848-2992
Martin Vollrath, *President*
Margit Vollrath, *Corp Secy*
Nancy Vollrath, *General Mgr*
EMP: 33
SQ FT: 18,000
SALES (est): 8.3MM **Privately Held**
WEB:
www.americansteelandstairways.com
SIC: 3446 3441 Ornamental metalwork; fabricated structural metal

(P-12450)
AMEX MANUFACTURING INC
2307 Avenida Costa Este, San Diego
(92154-6275)
PHONE..............................619 391-7412
Yong H Kim, *CEO*
Nick Espinoza, *Purch Mgr*
Alex Kim, *Accounts Mgr*
▲ **EMP:** 12
SALES (est): 9.5MM **Privately Held**
SIC: 3446 3448 3444 Architectural metalwork; prefabricated metal buildings; sheet metalwork

(P-12451)
ARBOR FENCE INC
22725 8th St E Ste C, Sonoma
(95476-2829)
PHONE..............................707 938-3133
Ronald Wooden, *President*
EMP: 22
SALES (est): 4MM **Privately Held**
WEB: www.arborfence.com
SIC: 3446 3315 2499 5211 Fences, gates, posts & flagpoles; chain link fencing; fencing, wood; fencing; security devices

(P-12452)
ARCHITECTURAL ENTERPRISES INC
Also Called: Hi-Tech Iron Works
5821 Randolph St, Commerce
(90040-3415)
PHONE..............................323 268-4000
Tom Lee, *President*
John S Lee, *Treasurer*
Alma Gutierrez, *Admin Sec*
EMP: 40
SQ FT: 20,000
SALES (est): 3.3MM **Privately Held**
SIC: 3446 Fences or posts, ornamental iron or steel; gates, ornamental metal

(P-12453)
ATR TECHNOLOGIES INCORPORATED
Also Called: Aluminum Tube Railings
805 Towne Center Dr, Pomona
(91767-5901)
PHONE..............................909 399-9724
Donald Terry, *President*
Debbie Terry, *Partner*
Dave C Terry, *Treasurer*
Debra L Terry, *Admin Sec*
▼ **EMP:** 15
SQ FT: 15,800
SALES (est): 1.5MM **Privately Held**
WEB: www.atrtechnologies.com
SIC: 3446 Architectural metalwork

(P-12454)
AZTECA ORNAMENTAL METALS
Also Called: Azteca Ornamental Iron Works
2738 Stingle Ave, Rosemead (91770-3329)
PHONE..............................626 280-2822
Ricardo Gomez, *Owner*
Magdaleno Gomez Sr,
EMP: 12 EST: 1966
SALES (est): 1.1MM **Privately Held**
SIC: 3446 Fences or posts, ornamental iron or steel

(P-12455)
BAY ORNAMENTAL IRON INC
757 Newton Way, Costa Mesa
(92627-4277)
PHONE..............................949 548-1015
Fax: 949 423-0084
EMP: 24
SQ FT: 4,000
SALES (est): 3.5MM **Privately Held**
WEB: www.bayornamentaliron.com
SIC: 3446

(P-12456)
BLACKLION ENTERPRISES INC (PA)
1731 Bonita Vista Dr, San Bernardino
(92404-2107)
PHONE..............................951 328-0400
Bryan Decarvalho, *CEO*
EMP: 12
SQ FT: 18,000

SALES: 1.1MM **Privately Held**
SIC: 3446 Architectural metalwork

(P-12457)
BRADFIELD MANUFACTURING INC
2633 E Mardi Gras Ave, Anaheim
(92806-3243)
PHONE..............................714 543-8348
Gerry L Bradfield, *President*
Nola Read, *Treasurer*
Roderick S Bradfield, *Vice Pres*
EMP: 18
SQ FT: 12,000
SALES (est): 1.5MM **Privately Held**
WEB: www.bradfieldstairs.com
SIC: 3446 Stairs, staircases, stair treads: prefabricated metal

(P-12458)
BRODHEAD GRATING PRODUCTS LLC
3651 Sausalito St, Los Alamitos
(90720-2436)
PHONE..............................562 598-4314
Ronald Robertson,
Ron Robertson,
EMP: 12
SQ FT: 20,000
SALES (est): 1.2MM **Privately Held**
SIC: 3446 Open flooring & grating for construction

(P-12459)
BRODHEAD STEEL PRODUCTS CO (PA)
7550 Alpine Rd, La Honda (94020-9785)
PHONE..............................650 871-8251
David R Brodhead, *President*
Joy Asdoorian, *Corp Secy*
EMP: 30 EST: 1945
SQ FT: 2,500
SALES (est): 3.5MM **Privately Held**
SIC: 3446 1791 Open flooring & grating for construction; concrete reinforcement, placing of

(P-12460)
CANTERBURY DESIGNS INC
Also Called: Canterbury International
6195 Maywood Ave, Huntington Park
(90255-3213)
PHONE..............................323 936-7111
Larry Snyder, *President*
Laura Snyder, *Vice Pres*
John Flanton, *Mfg Staff*
▲ **EMP:** 20 EST: 1964
SALES (est): 3.7MM **Privately Held**
WEB: www.compvillage.com
SIC: 3446 3873 Architectural metalwork; clocks, assembly of

(P-12461)
CHALLENGER ORNAMENTAL IR WORKS
437 W Palmer Ave, Glendale (91204-2407)
PHONE..............................818 507-7030
Nerses Espanosian, *President*
EMP: 14
SQ FT: 6,500
SALES (est): 1MM **Privately Held**
SIC: 3446 Architectural metalwork; gates, ornamental metal; railings, prefabricated metal; grillwork, ornamental metal

(P-12462)
CLARK STEEL FABRICATORS INC
12610 Vigilante Rd, Lakeside (92040-1113)
P.O. Box 1370 (92040-0910)
PHONE..............................619 390-1502
Kimberley L Clark, *President*
Kevin B Clark, *Vice Pres*
Steve Dickerson, *Executive*
Kevin Clark, *General Mgr*
Tarah Miinch, *Office Admin*
EMP: 45 EST: 1977
SQ FT: 12,500
SALES: 10.9MM **Privately Held**
WEB: www.clarksteelfab.com
SIC: 3446 3441 Architectural metalwork; fabricated structural metal

(P-12463)
COLUMBIA FABRICATING CO INC
5079 Gloria Ave, Encino (91436-1553)
PHONE..................................818 247-4220
Joseph Goldberg, *CEO*
Dalia Goldberg, *CFO*
EMP: 50
SQ FT: 19,000
SALES (est): 9.6MM **Privately Held**
SIC: 3446 Architectural metalwork

(P-12464)
CRABTREE GLASS COMPANY INC
13203 Sherman Way, North Hollywood (91605-4649)
PHONE..................................818 765-1840
Jerry Otworth, *CEO*
EMP: 10
SQ FT: 1,553
SALES (est): 1.7MM **Privately Held**
WEB: www.crabtreeglass.com
SIC: 3446 1793 Architectural metalwork;
glass & glazing work

(P-12465)
CRANEVEYOR CORP
13730 Central Ave, Chino (91710-5503)
PHONE..................................909 627-6801
Mike Williams, *Branch Mgr*
EMP: 20
SALES (corp-wide): 27MM **Privately Held**
SIC: 3446 3536 Railings, bannisters,
guards, etc.: made from metal pipe;
hoists, cranes & monorails
PA: Craneveyor Corp.
1524 Potrero Ave
El Monte CA 91733
626 442-1524

(P-12466)
CURRAN ENGINEERING COMPANY INC
28727 Industry Dr, Valencia (91355-5414)
P.O. Box 26, Castaic (91310-0026)
PHONE..................................800 643-6353
Douglas M Curran, *CEO*
Patrick Curran, *President*
EMP: 20 EST: 1947
SQ FT: 20,000
SALES (est): 3.7MM **Privately Held**
WEB: www.curranengineering.com
SIC: 3446 5399 Architectural metalwork;
Army-Navy goods

(P-12467)
CUSTOM METAL WORKS
2233 W 2nd St, Santa Ana (92703-3511)
PHONE..................................714 953-5481
Fax: 714 953-5494
EMP: 10
SQ FT: 4,000
SALES: 400K **Privately Held**
SIC: 3446

(P-12468)
DELTA IRONWORKS INC
15420 Meridian Rd, Salinas (93907-8788)
P.O. Box 10580 (93912-7580)
PHONE..................................831 663-1190
Salomon M Dominguez, *CEO*
EMP: 15
SQ FT: 9,000
SALES (est): 2.7MM **Privately Held**
SIC: 3446 3441 Architectural metalwork;
fabricated structural metal

(P-12469)
DENNISON INC
Also Called: Maxxon Company
17901 Railroad St, City of Industry (91748-1113)
PHONE..................................626 965-8917
Dennis MA, *President*
▲ EMP: 47
SQ FT: 26,000
SALES: 16MM **Privately Held**
WEB: www.maxxonusa.com
SIC: 3446 Architectural metalwork

(P-12470)
DEVINCNZI ARCHTCTURAL PDTS INC
1717 Adrian Rd, Burlingame (94010-2104)
PHONE..................................650 692-5800
Robert Devincenzi, *President*
Janice Devincenzi-Samuelson, *Treasurer*
William Galvin, *Vice Pres*
Steven Devincenzi, *Admin Sec*
EMP: 14 EST: 1982
SQ FT: 11,000
SALES (est): 3MM **Privately Held**
SIC: 3446 Architectural metalwork

(P-12471)
ECLIPSE DESIGN INC
427 Corona Rd, Petaluma (94954-1406)
P.O. Box 750727 (94975-0727)
PHONE..................................707 763-3104
Russ Williams, *Owner*
EMP: 10
SALES (est): 1.4MM **Privately Held**
WEB: www.eclipsedesigngp.com
SIC: 3446 Ornamental metalwork

(P-12472)
EUROCRAFT ARCHTECTURAL MET INC
5619 Watcher St, Bell Gardens (90201-1632)
PHONE..................................323 771-1323
John Fechter, *President*
David Sawez, *General Mgr*
Kris Debruyne, *Prdtn Mgr*
EMP: 30
SQ FT: 30,000
SALES (est): 5.4MM **Privately Held**
WEB: www.eurocraftmetal.com
SIC: 3446 Architectural metalwork

(P-12473)
FABLE INC
595 Quarry Rd, San Carlos (94070-6222)
PHONE..................................650 598-9616
James Guaspari, *President*
A J Guaspari, *Vice Pres*
EMP: 10
SQ FT: 21,000
SALES (est): 1.3MM **Privately Held**
WEB: www.fableinc.com
SIC: 3446 Ornamental metalwork

(P-12474)
FABRICOR PRODUCTS INC
Also Called: Fabricor Stamping
22512 Curtis Pl, California City (93505-6009)
PHONE..................................760 373-8292
Roy S Waisman, *President*
EMP: 10
SQ FT: 9,000
SALES (est): 805.2K **Privately Held**
WEB: www.fabricorproducts.com
SIC: 3446 3469 Lamp posts, metal; metal
stampings

(P-12475)
FENCE FACTORY
Perimeter Security Systems
1482 Callens Rd, Ventura (93003-5605)
PHONE..................................805 644-5482
Phillip Mumma, *Sales/Mktg Mgr*
EMP: 10
SALES (corp-wide): 29.9MM **Privately Held**
WEB: www.fencefactory.com
SIC: 3446 Gates, ornamental metal
HQ: Fence Factory
2419 Palma Dr
Ventura CA 93003
805 644-7207

(P-12476)
GLENDALE IRON
Also Called: Glendale Stl & Orna Ironworks
4208 Chevy Chase Dr, Los Angeles (90039-1225)
PHONE..................................818 247-1098
Henry Ostray, *Owner*
Robert Ostray, *Manager*
EMP: 10
SALES: 630K **Privately Held**
SIC: 3446 Architectural metalwork

(P-12477)
GOLD COAST IRONWORKS
531 Montgomery Ave, Oxnard (93036-1066)
P.O. Box 1453, Oak View (93022-1453)
PHONE..................................805 485-6921
Richard Gill McFerron, *CEO*
Joanne McFerron, *Treasurer*
Riichard McFerron, *Administration*
Michael McFerron, *Project Mgr*
Adam Bennett, *Project Engr*
EMP: 15
SQ FT: 3,200
SALES (est): 2.5MM **Privately Held**
WEB: www.gcironworks.com
SIC: 3446 Architectural metalwork

(P-12478)
GREGORY PATTERSON
Also Called: Ccoi Gate & Fence
1741 Shelton Dr, Hollister (95023-9245)
P.O. Box 669, Aromas (95004-0669)
PHONE..................................831 636-1015
Gregory Patterson, *Owner*
Kate Deegan, *Sales Staff*
EMP: 20
SQ FT: 3,000
SALES (est): 3.1MM **Privately Held**
SIC: 3446 Fences or posts, ornamental
iron or steel; gates, ornamental metal

(P-12479)
H & M WROUGHT IRON FACTORY
2560 Main St Ste A, Chula Vista (91911-4665)
PHONE..................................619 427-5682
Hector Huerta, *Owner*
EMP: 12 EST: 1980
SQ FT: 3,500
SALES (est): 1.3MM **Privately Held**
SIC: 3446 Architectural metalwork

(P-12480)
HART & COOLEY INC
1121 Annadale Ave, Sanger (93657-3247)
P.O. Box 127 (93657-0127)
PHONE..................................559 875-1212
David Daniels, *Manager*
EMP: 50 **Privately Held**
SIC: 3446 Grillwork, ornamental metal
HQ: Hart & Cooley, Inc.
5030 Corp Exch Blvd Se
Grand Rapids MI 49512
616 656-8200

(P-12481)
INFINITY ACCESS PLUS INC
12945 Sherman Way Ste 8, North Hollywood (91605-7308)
PHONE..................................818 270-8172
Kirby Gray, *President*
EMP: 10
SALES (est): 1MM **Privately Held**
SIC: 3446 Fences, gates, posts & flagpoles

(P-12482)
IRON MASTER
759 Arroyo St Ste D, San Fernando (91340-2277)
P.O. Box 260, North Hollywood (91603-0260)
PHONE..................................818 361-4060
Sandor Czene, *Owner*
Scott Bush, *Sales Engr*
EMP: 15 EST: 1978
SQ FT: 12,650
SALES: 1MM **Privately Held**
SIC: 3446 3441 Architectural metalwork;
fabricated structural metal

(P-12483)
IRON SHIELD INC
5926 Agnes Ave, Temple City (91780-2217)
PHONE..................................626 287-4568
J Chou, *Manager*
EMP: 10 EST: 1990
SALES: 120K **Privately Held**
SIC: 3446 Gates, ornamental metal

(P-12484)
J TALLEY CORPORATION (PA)
Also Called: Talley Metal Fabrication
989 W 7th St, San Jacinto (92582-3813)
P.O. Box 850 (92581-0850)
PHONE..................................951 654-2123
Joe Brown Talley, *CEO*
Eloy Ochoa, *Foreman/Supr*
Rick Hammond, *Manager*
Margie Mayer, *Manager*
EMP: 40 EST: 1963
SQ FT: 13,400
SALES (est): 8.2MM **Privately Held**
WEB: www.talleymetal.com
SIC: 3446 3444 Railings, prefabricated
metal; sheet metalwork

(P-12485)
JANSEN ORNAMENTAL SUPPLY CO
10926 Schmidt Rd, El Monte (91733-2708)
PHONE..................................626 442-0271
Mike Jansen, *CEO*
Harry Jansen, *President*
John Jansen, *Admin Sec*
▲ EMP: 30 EST: 1960
SQ FT: 22,000
SALES (est): 6.7MM **Privately Held**
WEB: www.jansensupply.com
SIC: 3446 Architectural metalwork

(P-12486)
JMI STEEL INC
8983 San Fernando Rd, Sun Valley (91352-1410)
PHONE..................................818 768-3955
Martin J Blaha, *President*
EMP: 21
SQ FT: 11,000
SALES (est): 4.3MM **Privately Held**
SIC: 3446 Fences or posts, ornamental
iron or steel

(P-12487)
JONES IRON WORKS
2658 Griffith Park Blvd, Los Angeles (90039-2520)
PHONE..................................323 386-2368
EMP: 15 EST: 2013
SQ FT: 5,000
SALES (est): 890K **Privately Held**
SIC: 3446

(P-12488)
K & J WIRE PRODUCTS CORP
1220 N Lance Ln, Anaheim (92806-1812)
PHONE..................................714 816-0360
Klaus Borutzki, *President*
Barbara Borutzki, *Corp Secy*
EMP: 28
SQ FT: 21,000
SALES (est): 2.8MM **Privately Held**
WEB: www.kajwire.com
SIC: 3446 3496 3315 Architectural
metalwork; miscellaneous fabricated wire
products; store fixtures & display equipment; wire & fabricated wire products

(P-12489)
KAWNEER COMPANY INC
Also Called: Brite Vue Div
7200 W Doe Ave, Visalia (93291-9296)
PHONE..................................559 651-4000
Norris McElroy, *Branch Mgr*
Gary Durham, *Engineer*
Lee Bawanan, *Manager*
EMP: 250
SQ FT: 200,000
SALES (corp-wide): 14B **Publicly Held**
WEB: www.kawneer.com
SIC: 3446 Architectural metalwork
HQ: Kawneer Company, Inc.
555 Guthridge Ct
Norcross GA 30092
770 449-5555

(P-12490)
KESCLO FINANCIAL INC
Also Called: Air Distribution Products
150 W 6th St Ste 205, San Pedro (90731-3300)
PHONE..................................800 322-8676
Charles Close, *President*
Mike Kessler, *Vice Pres*
▲ EMP: 36

PRODUCTS & SVCS

SALES (est): 2.3MM **Privately Held**
SIC: **3446** Registers (air), metal

(P-12491)
L & H IRON INC
Also Called: Lartech
1049 Felipe Ave, San Jose (95122-2602)
PHONE...................................408 287-8797
Kirk Larson, *President*
EMP: 11
SALES (est): 810K **Privately Held**
SIC: **3446** 3441 Fabricated structural
metal; stairs, staircases, stair treads: pre-
fabricated metal

(P-12492)
LAVI INDUSTRIES (PA)
27810 Avenue Hopkins, Valencia
(91355-3409)
PHONE...................................877 275-5284
Gavriel Lavi, *President*
Yariv Blumkine, *COO*
Susan Lavi, *Vice Pres*
Ashlee Wyss, *Executive*
Shawna Kessler, *Program Mgr*
◆ EMP: 80
SQ FT: 80,000
SALES (est): 15.8MM **Privately Held**
SIC: **3446** Architectural metalwork

(P-12493)
LINDBLADE METALWORKS INC
Also Called: Lindblade Metal Works
14355 Macaw St, La Mirada (90638-5208)
PHONE...................................714 670-7172
Vernon Lindblade, *CEO*
Marilyn Lindblade, *Vice Pres*
Tim Hostetler, *Sales Associate*
EMP: 20 EST: 1973
SQ FT: 16,250
SALES (est): 5.4MM **Privately Held**
WEB: www.lindblademetalworks.com
SIC: **3446** Architectural metalwork

(P-12494)
LNI CUSTOM MANUFACTURING INC
15542 Broadway Center St, Gardena
(90248-2137)
PHONE...................................310 978-2000
Scott Blakely, *CEO*
EMP: 50
SALES (est): 12.8MM **Privately Held**
WEB: www.lnisigns.com
SIC: **3446** 5046 Architectural metalwork;
neon signs

(P-12495)
LUR INC
Also Called: Lumar Metals
599 S East End Ave, Pomona
(91766-2302)
PHONE...................................909 623-4999
Marlene Racca, *President*
Cindy Rowland, *Office Mgr*
EMP: 15
SQ FT: 10,000
SALES (est): 3.2MM **Privately Held**
WEB: www.lumarmetals.com
SIC: **3446** Architectural metalwork

(P-12496)
M C METAL INC
1347 Donner Ave, San Francisco
(94124-3612)
PHONE...................................415 822-2288
Jeffrey Mark, *President*
EMP: 17
SALES (est): 3.8MM **Privately Held**
SIC: **3446** Architectural metalwork

(P-12497)
MAS METALS INC
32410 Central Ave, Union City
(94587-2007)
PHONE...................................510 259-1426
Mitzon Altana, *President*
EMP: 12
SALES (est): 2.6MM **Privately Held**
SIC: **3446** Architectural metalwork

(P-12498)
MASTER METAL WORKS INC
Also Called: Mmw Operation
1805 Potrero Ave, South El Monte
(91733-3022)
PHONE...................................626 444-8818
Susan Barnard, *President*
Brian Elliott, *Vice Pres*
EMP: 27
SQ FT: 18,000
SALES (est): 6.5MM **Privately Held**
WEB: www.mastermetalworks.com
SIC: **3446** 3444 Architectural metalwork;
sheet metal specialties, not stamped

(P-12499)
METAL X DIRECT INC
1555 Mesa Verde Dr E 11g, Costa Mesa
(92626-5112)
PHONE...................................949 336-0055
Sean Lancona, *President*
EMP: 14
SALES (est): 1MM **Privately Held**
SIC: **3446** 3441 Architectural metalwork;
building components, structural steel

(P-12500)
MODERN METAL INSTALLATIONS
4400 Shady Oak Way, Fair Oaks
(95628-5727)
PHONE...................................916 316-0997
Richard Sharon, *Owner*
EMP: 10 EST: 2001
SALES (est): 750K **Privately Held**
SIC: **3446** Architectural metalwork

(P-12501)
MOZ DESIGNS INC
711 Kevin Ct, Oakland (94621-4039)
PHONE...................................510 632-0853
Murry Sandford, *CEO*
Herbert M Sandford III, *Vice Pres*
Tripp Sanford, *Vice Pres*
Graham Carlisle, *Project Mgr*
Noliwe Alexander, *Controller*
◆ EMP: 25
SQ FT: 10,000
SALES (est): 4.8MM **Privately Held**
WEB: www.mozdesigns.com
SIC: **3446** Architectural metalwork

(P-12502)
OLSON AND CO STEEL (PA)
1941 Davis St, San Leandro (94577-1262)
PHONE...................................510 489-4680
David Olson, *CEO*
Dylan Olson, *President*
Thomas Fluehr, *COO*
Kevin Cullen, *CFO*
Tom Stavropoulos, *Project Mgr*
▲ EMP: 225
SQ FT: 130,000
SALES (est): 68.4MM **Privately Held**
WEB: www.olsonsteel.com
SIC: **3446** 3441 Architectural metalwork;
fabricated structural metal

(P-12503)
RAMI DESIGNS INC
24 Hammond Ste E, Irvine (92618-1680)
PHONE...................................949 588-8288
Ron Taybi, *President*
EMP: 19
SQ FT: 6,000
SALES: 6MM **Privately Held**
SIC: **3446** 3299 3229 Architectural metal-
work; architectural sculptures: gypsum,
clay, papier mache, etc.; glass furnishings
& accessories

(P-12504)
RICHARD SANCHEZ
Also Called: Rincon Ironworks
531 Montgomery Ave, Oxnard
(93036-1066)
PHONE...................................805 455-2904
Rick Sanchez, *Owner*
▲ EMP: 14
SQ FT: 5,000
SALES (est): 376.9K **Privately Held**
SIC: **3446** Architectural metalwork

(P-12505)
ROYAL STALL
1865 Industrial Way, Sanger (93657-9501)
P.O. Box 568 (93657-0568)
PHONE...................................559 875-8100
Richard Funston, *Owner*
Kay Funston, *Co-Owner*
EMP: 11
SQ FT: 8,000
SALES: 1MM **Privately Held**
WEB: www.royalstall.com
SIC: **3446** 3448 Fences, gates, posts &
flagpoles; farm & utility buildings

(P-12506)
SANIE MANUFACTURING COMPANY
2600 S Yale St, Santa Ana (92704-5228)
PHONE...................................714 751-7700
Mendi Haidarali, *President*
Mohammad Haidari, *Vice Pres*
Tony Azadi, *Manager*
EMP: 18 EST: 1981
SQ FT: 8,900
SALES (est): 5.2MM **Privately Held**
WEB: www.saniemfg.com
SIC: **3446** Fences or posts, ornamental
iron or steel

(P-12507)
SAPPHIRE MANUFACTURING INC
505 Porter Way, Placentia (92870-6454)
PHONE...................................714 401-3117
Hector Garibay, *CEO*
Cheryl Kaye, *Sales Executive*
EMP: 20
SQ FT: 25,000
SALES: 3MM **Privately Held**
SIC: **3446** 7371 Fences or posts, orna-
mental iron or steel; computer software
development & applications

(P-12508)
SECURITY CONTRACTOR SVCS INC
Also Called: S C S
5311 Jackson St, North Highlands
(95660-5004)
PHONE...................................916 338-4800
Basil Lobaugh, *Manager*
Larry Marshall, *Asst Controller*
EMP: 26
SALES (corp-wide): 37.6MM **Privately Held**
WEB: www.scsfence.com
SIC: **3446** 5211 Fences or posts, orna-
mental iron or steel; lumber & other build-
ing materials
PA: Security Contractor Services, Inc.
5339 Jackson St
North Highlands CA 95660
916 338-4200

(P-12509)
SONOMA ACCESS CTRL SYSTEMS INC
21600 8th St E, Sonoma (95476-2821)
PHONE...................................707 935-3458
David Nisenson, *President*
Paula Nisenson, *Vice Pres*
EMP: 25
SQ FT: 8,000
SALES (est): 3.8MM **Privately Held**
WEB: www.access-control-systems.net
SIC: **3446** 1799 Gates, ornamental metal;
fence construction

(P-12510)
SPECIAL IRON SECURITY SYSTEMS
2030 Rosemead Blvd, El Monte
(91733-1518)
PHONE...................................626 443-7877
Ricky McKeyne, *President*
EMP: 10
SQ FT: 15,000
SALES (est): 1MM **Privately Held**
SIC: **3446** 1799 Fences, gates, posts &
flagpoles; fence construction

(P-12511)
STEVE ZAPPETINI & SON INC
885 Penny Royal Ln, San Rafael
(94903-4303)
PHONE...................................415 454-2511
David J Zappetini, *President*
Russell Zappetini, *President*
David Zappetini, *Corp Secy*
EMP: 28
SQ FT: 10,000
SALES (est): 4.1MM **Privately Held**
SIC: **3446** 3713 7692 Railings, bannis-
ters, guards, etc.: made from metal pipe;
stairs, staircases, stair treads: prefabri-
cated metal; grillwork, ornamental metal;
truck bodies (motor vehicles); welding re-
pair

(P-12512)
SURCO PRODUCTS INC
14001 S Main St, Los Angeles
(90061-2196)
PHONE...................................310 323-2520
Ludwig Surkin, *President*
Uri Surkin, *Vice Pres*
Amir Surkin, *Cust Mgr*
▲ EMP: 15 EST: 1971
SQ FT: 20,000
SALES (est): 2.5MM **Privately Held**
SIC: **3446** 3429 Ladders, for permanent
installation: metal; luggage racks, car top

(P-12513)
TAJIMA USA DISSOLVING CORP
Also Called: Tajima /Crl
2503 E Vernon Ave, Vernon (90058-1826)
PHONE...................................323 588-1281
Bernard P Harris, *Ch of Bd*
EMP: 12
SALES (est): 1.2MM
SALES (corp-wide): 30.6B **Privately Held**
WEB: www.tajimacorpusa.com
SIC: **3446** Architectural metalwork
HQ: C. R. Laurence Co., Inc.
2503 E Vernon Ave
Vernon CA 90058
323 588-1281

(P-12514)
TECHNIBUILDERS IRON INC
1049 Felipe Ave, San Jose (95122-2602)
PHONE...................................408 287-8797
Roy S Larson, *President*
EMP: 34
SQ FT: 7,200
SALES (est): 5.5MM **Privately Held**
SIC: **3446** Ornamental metalwork

(P-12515)
THORNTON STEEL & IR WORKS INC
1323 S State College Pkwy, Anaheim
(92806-5242)
PHONE...................................714 491-8800
Ken Thornton, *CEO*
Steven Braseny, *President*
Richard Salcedo, *Vice Pres*
EMP: 20
SQ FT: 12,200
SALES (est): 3.3MM **Privately Held**
WEB: www.thorntonsteelironworks.com
SIC: **3446** Architectural metalwork

(P-12516)
TJS METAL MANUFACTURING INC
10847 Drury Ln, Lynwood (90262-1833)
PHONE...................................310 604-1545
Jose Antonio Gallegos, *CEO*
EMP: 26 EST: 1999
SQ FT: 30,000
SALES (est): 8.4MM **Privately Held**
SIC: **3446** Architectural metalwork

(P-12517)
TRI-STATE STAIRWAY CORP
706 W California Ave, Fresno
(93706-3502)
PHONE...................................559 268-0875
Ron Cavella, *President*
Sharry Cavella, *Corp Secy*
Stan Cavella, *Vice Pres*
EMP: 40
SQ FT: 1,000

▲ = Import ▼=Export
◆ =Import/Export

SALES (est): 5.1MM
SALES (corp-wide): 9MM **Privately Held**
WEB: www.travcorps.com
SIC: 3446 3272 Railings, bannisters,
  guards, etc.: made from metal pipe; con-
  crete products, precast
PA: Suburban Steel, Inc.
  706 W California Ave
  Fresno CA 93706
  559 268-6281

(P-12518)
V I P IRONWORKS INC
8319 Hindry Ave, Los Angeles
(90045-3205)
PHONE..............................310 216-2890
Hector Guiterrez, *President*
EMP: 10
SQ FT: 5,109
SALES (est): 1.7MM **Privately Held**
SIC: 3446 5051 Architectural metalwork;
  iron & steel (ferrous) products

(P-12519)
VALLEY STAIRWAY INC
5684 E Shields Ave, Fresno (93727-7818)
P.O. Box 245, Clovis (93613-0245)
PHONE..............................559 299-0151
Jerry De George, *President*
Anthony De George Jr, *Corp Secy*
EMP: 16 EST: 1957
SQ FT: 29,464
SALES (est): 2.9MM **Privately Held**
WEB: www.valleystairwayinc.com
SIC: 3446 Stairs, staircases, stair treads:
  prefabricated metal

(P-12520)
WASHINGTON ORNA IR WORKS INC
Production Steel
17913 S Main St, Gardena (90248-3520)
PHONE..............................310 327-8660
Luke Welsh, *Manager*
Eric Welsh, *Project Mgr*
Johnathan Power, *Marketing Mgr*
EMP: 20
SALES (corp-wide): 24.6MM **Privately Held**
WEB: www.washingtoniron.com
SIC: 3446 1542 Architectural metalwork;
  nonresidential construction
PA: Washington Ornamental Iron Works
  Inc.
  17926 S Broadway
  Gardena CA 90248
  310 327-8660

(P-12521)
WEIS/ROBART PARTITIONS INC
Also Called: Michigan Metal Partitions
3501 E La Palma Ave, Anaheim
(92806-2117)
PHONE..............................714 666-0822
John R Penner, *President*
Eleanor Penner, *Treasurer*
Beverly Booms, *Vice Pres*
Sarah Michener, *Vice Pres*
Donald Harms, *Admin Sec*
EMP: 15
SQ FT: 8,000
SALES (est): 2MM **Privately Held**
WEB: www.weisrobart.com
SIC: 3446 Partitions, ornamental metal

(P-12522)
WEST CAST ARCHITECTURAL SHTMTL
Also Called: West Coast Asm
2215 Oakland Rd, San Jose (95131-1416)
PHONE..............................408 776-2700
Mark Yeager, *CEO*
Paul Deharo, *Shareholder*
Randi Stefani, *Office Mgr*
EMP: 10 EST: 2012
SALES (est): 2.7MM **Privately Held**
SIC: 3446 Architectural metalwork

(P-12523)
WESTERN SQUARE INDUSTRIES INC
1621 N Brdwy, Stockton (95205)
PHONE..............................209 944-0921
Trygue Mikkelsen, *President*
David Bowyer, *Manager*

▲ EMP: 40
SQ FT: 44,000
SALES (est): 10.5MM **Privately Held**
SIC: 3446 2542 2514 3441 Fences or
  posts, ornamental iron or steel; gates, ornamental metal; racks, merchandise display or storage: except wood; tables,
  household: metal; fabricated structural
  metal

(P-12524)
WROUGHT IRON FENCING & SUPPLY
1370 La Mirada Dr, San Marcos
(92078-2443)
PHONE..............................760 591-3110
Thomas W Barrett, *President*
Tom Barrett, *President*
EMP: 35
SALES (est): 4.7MM **Privately Held**
WEB:
www.wroughtironfencingandsupply.com
SIC: 3446 Fences, gates, posts & flag-
  poles

3448 Prefabricated Metal Buildings & Cmpnts

(P-12525)
ACORN ENGINEERING COMPANY (PA)
Also Called: Morris Group International
15125 Proctor Ave, City of Industry
(91746-3327)
P.O. Box 3527 (91744-0527)
PHONE..............................800 488-8999
Donald E Morris, *President*
Charles C Fredricks, *Treasurer*
Kathryn Morris, *Treasurer*
Keith Marshall, *Exec VP*
Vince Conti, *Vice Pres*
◆ EMP: 702 EST: 1955
SQ FT: 120,000
SALES: 85MM **Privately Held**
WEB: www.whitehallmfg.com
SIC: 3448 3431 3442 Buildings, portable:
  prefabricated metal; plumbing fixtures:
  enameled iron cast iron or pressed metal;
  metal doors

(P-12526)
AFC FINISHING SYSTEMS
250 Airport Pkwy, Oroville (95965-9249)
PHONE..............................530 533-8907
Carl Lee Hagan, *President*
Nicky Trevino, *Vice Pres*
Michelle Carr, *Accountant*
Justin Hagan, *Plant Mgr*
Chris Funk, *Sales Mgr*
EMP: 35
SQ FT: 56,000
SALES (est): 9.8MM **Privately Held**
WEB: www.afc-ca.com
SIC: 3448 3446 3441 Prefabricated metal
  buildings; sheet metalwork; fabricated
  structural metal

(P-12527)
ALLIED CONTAINER SYSTEMS INC
Also Called: ACS
511 Wilbur Ave Ste B4, Antioch
(94509-7563)
PHONE..............................925 944-7600
Brian Horsfall, *Ch of Bd*
Robbin Kilgore, *Officer*
Susan Horsfall, *Vice Pres*
Jennifer Lamar, *Vice Pres*
Quinton Miller, *General Mgr*
▼ EMP: 140
SQ FT: 20,000
SALES (est): 28.4MM **Privately Held**
WEB: www.alliedcontainer.com
SIC: 3448 8748 3559 Prefabricated metal
  buildings; environmental consultant;
  chemical machinery & equipment

(P-12528)
ALLIED MDULAR BLDG SYSTEMS INC (PA)
642 W Nicolas Ave, Orange (92868-1316)
PHONE..............................714 516-1188
Fred Ketcho, *CEO*

Kevin Peithman, *President*
Richard Navarro, *Treasurer*
Raj Singh, *Vice Pres*
Cathy Peithman, *Admin Sec*
EMP: 38
SQ FT: 35,000
SALES (est): 9.1MM **Privately Held**
WEB: www.alliedmodular.com
SIC: 3448 Prefabricated metal buildings

(P-12529)
ALUMAWALL INC
1701 S 7th St Ste 9, San Jose
(95112-6000)
PHONE..............................408 275-7165
David M Warda, *President*
Lori Warda, *President*
Steven Aguilar, *Technology*
Dagmar Van Fleet, *Controller*
EMP: 65
SQ FT: 50,000
SALES (est): 17.1MM **Privately Held**
WEB: www.alumawall.com
SIC: 3448 Prefabricated metal components

(P-12530)
AMERICAN CARPORTS INC (PA)
1415 Clay St, Colusa (95932-2064)
PHONE..............................866 730-9865
Primo Castillo, *President*
Milton Castillo, *President*
Venani Torres, *Corp Secy*
EMP: 11
SQ FT: 500,000
SALES (est): 3.7MM **Privately Held**
SIC: 3448 Garages, portable: prefabricated
  metal; carports: prefabricated metal

(P-12531)
AMERICORE INC
19705 August Ave, Hilmar (95324-9302)
P.O. Box 1353 (95324-1353)
PHONE..............................209 632-5679
Ryan Marques Cunha, *President*
EMP: 47 EST: 2007
SALES (est): 13.2MM **Privately Held**
SIC: 3448 3699 3841 Prefabricated metal
  buildings; electrical welding equipment;
  diagnostic apparatus, medical

(P-12532)
ASC PROFILES LLC
5001 Bailey Loop, McClellan (95652-2530)
PHONE..............................916 376-2899
Richard Stewart, *Branch Mgr*
EMP: 33 **Privately Held**
SIC: 3448 Prefabricated metal buildings
HQ: Asc Profiles Llc
  2110 Enterprise Blvd
  West Sacramento CA 95691
  916 376-2800

(P-12533)
BARNS AND BUILDINGS INC
23100 Baxter Rd, Wildomar (92595-9699)
P.O. Box 1555 (92595-1555)
PHONE..............................951 678-4571
Russell Greer, *CEO*
Barret Hilzer, *COO*
EMP: 80
SQ FT: 40,000
SALES (est): 7.6MM **Privately Held**
SIC: 3448 1541 5083 Prefabricated metal
  components; steel building construction;
  livestock equipment

(P-12534)
BARNS BY HARRAHS
3489 S 99w, Corning (96021-9736)
PHONE..............................530 824-4611
Toll Free:..............................888 -
Dave Harrah, *Partner*
Dennis Harrah, *Partner*
EMP: 12
SALES (est): 1.5MM **Privately Held**
WEB: www.barnsbyharrahs.com
SIC: 3448 Farm & utility buildings

(P-12535)
BLUESCOPE BUILDINGS N AMER INC
Also Called: Butler Manufacturing
7440 W Doe Ave, Visalia (93291-9296)
P.O. Box 1590 (93279-1590)
PHONE..............................559 651-5300
Juan Carlos Garcia, *Branch Mgr*

EMP: 200 **Privately Held**
SIC: 3448 Prefabricated metal buildings
HQ: Bluescope Buildings North America,
  Inc.
  1540 Genessee St
  Kansas City MO 64102
  -

(P-12536)
CA-TE LP
Also Called: California Technology
33230 La Colina Dr, Springville
(93265-9617)
PHONE..............................559 539-1530
Guy Minter, *Partner*
EMP: 10
SALES (est): 1.2MM **Privately Held**
SIC: 3448 Prefabricated metal components

(P-12537)
CALIFORNIA EXPANDED MET PDTS
Also Called: Cemco
1001a Pttsburg Antoch Hwy, Pittsburg
(94565-4199)
PHONE..............................925 473-9340
Ned Martin, *Manager*
EMP: 40
SALES (corp-wide): 73.8MM **Privately Held**
SIC: 3448 3449 3444 3441 Prefabricated
  metal buildings; miscellaneous metal-
  work; sheet metalwork; fabricated struc-
  tural metal
PA: California Expanded Metal Products
  Company
  13191 Crosrds Pkwy N 32
  City Of Industry CA 91746
  626 369-3564

(P-12538)
CALIFORNIA RAMP WORKS INC
273 N Benson Ave, Upland (91786-5614)
PHONE..............................909 949-1601
Brian Moore, *President*
Joseph M Ciaglia Jr, *Director*
Sara Kindig, *Manager*
EMP: 25
SALES (est): 4.7MM **Privately Held**
SIC: 3448 Ramps: prefabricated metal

(P-12539)
CBC STEEL BUILDINGS LLC
1700 E Louise Ave, Lathrop (95330-9795)
P.O. Box 1009 (95330-1009)
PHONE..............................209 858-2425
Steve Campbell, *President*
EMP: 120
SQ FT: 105,000
SALES (est): 36.7MM
SALES (corp-wide): 25B **Publicly Held**
WEB: www.cbcsteelbuildings.com
SIC: 3448 Prefabricated metal buildings
PA: Nucor Corporation
  1915 Rexford Rd Ste 400
  Charlotte NC 28211
  704 366-7000

(P-12540)
CLAMSHELL STRUCTURES INC
Also Called: Clamshell Buildings
1101 Maulhardt Ave, Oxnard (93030-7995)
PHONE..............................805 988-1340
Gregory J Mangan, *CEO*
Michael R Kane, *Vice Pres*
Michael Kane, *VP Engrg*
Dean Daddario, *Analyst*
EMP: 15
SQ FT: 46,000
SALES (est): 5.2MM
SALES (corp-wide): 1MM **Privately Held**
WEB: www.clamshell.com
SIC: 3448 Prefabricated metal buildings
PA: Clamshell Holdings, Inc.
  1101 Maulhardt Ave
  Oxnard CA 93030
  805 988-1340

(P-12541)
CRATE MODULAR INC
3025 E Dominguez St, Carson
(90810-1437)
PHONE..............................310 405-0829
Lisa Sharp, *CEO*
Moises Bada, *Treasurer*
Natasaha Deski, *Vice Pres*

(PA)=Parent Co (HQ)=Headquarters (DH)=Div Headquarters
✪ = New Business established in last 2 years

3448 - Prefabricated Metal Buildings & Cmpnts County (P-12542)

PRODUCTS & SERVICES SECTION

EMP: 99
SALES (est): 3.2MM **Privately Held**
SIC: 3448 Prefabricated metal buildings

(P-12542)
DURACOLD REFRIGERATION MFG LLC
1551 S Primrose Ave, Monrovia
(91016-4542)
PHONE..................................626 358-1710
Harold Monsher, *General Ptnr*
Ben Monsher, *Partner*
EMP: 22 EST: 1996
SQ FT: 25,000
SALES (est): 4.2MM **Privately Held**
SIC: 3448 3585 Prefabricated metal components; refrigeration & heating equipment

(P-12543)
EMERALD KINGDOM GREENHOUSE LLC
104 Masonic Ln, Weaverville (96093)
PHONE..................................530 215-5670
Kate Brown,
▲ EMP: 30
SALES (est): 5.5MM **Privately Held**
SIC: 3448 5191 Greenhouses: prefabricated metal; greenhouse equipment & supplies

(P-12544)
ENVIROPLEX INC
4777 Carpenter Rd, Stockton
(95215-8106)
PHONE..................................209 466-8000
Glenn Owens, *President*
Sharon Castello, *Administration*
John Kozler, *Project Mgr*
Gaylene Givens, *Business Mgr*
EMP: 60
SQ FT: 102,000
SALES (est): 10.6MM
SALES (corp-wide): 498.3MM **Publicly Held**
WEB: www.enviroplexinc.com
SIC: 3448 Buildings, portable: prefabricated metal
PA: Mcgrath Rentcorp
5700 Las Positas Rd
Livermore CA 94551
925 606-9200

(P-12545)
FCP INC
23100 Baxter Rd, Wildomar (92595-9699)
P.O. Box 1555 (92595-1555)
PHONE..................................951 678-4571
Russell J Greer, *CEO*
Mike Regan, *Division Mgr*
Stuart Wilson, *Opers Mgr*
Kathy Cvelbar, *Consultant*
EMP: 100
SQ FT: 200,000
SALES: 15MM **Privately Held**
SIC: 3448 1541 Prefabricated metal components; steel building construction

(P-12546)
FCP INC
4125 Market St Ste 14, Ventura
(93003-5643)
P.O. Box 1217, Carpinteria (93014-1217)
PHONE..................................805 684-1117
Barryet Hilzer, *President*
Mike Regan, *Division Mgr*
EMP: 46
SALES (corp-wide): 15MM **Privately Held**
WEB: www.fcp.net
SIC: 3448 1541 Prefabricated metal components; steel building construction
PA: Fcp, Inc.
23100 Baxter Rd
Wildomar CA 92595
951 678-4571

(P-12547)
GCN SUPPLY LLC
9070 Bridgeport Pl, Rancho Cucamonga
(91730-5530)
PHONE..................................909 643-4603
Gustavo Chona Sr, *Mng Member*
EMP: 50 EST: 2015

SALES: 10MM **Privately Held**
SIC: 3448 2671 Prefabricated metal buildings; plastic film, coated or laminated for packaging

(P-12548)
GRO-TECH SYSTEMS INC
17282 Cattle Dr, Rough and Ready
(95975-9761)
PHONE..................................530 432-7012
Scott Patrick Stephan, *CEO*
EMP: 14
SALES (est): 4.4MM **Privately Held**
SIC: 3448 Greenhouses: prefabricated metal

(P-12549)
H ROBERTS CONSTRUCTION
2165 W Gaylord St, Long Beach
(90813-1033)
PHONE..................................562 590-4825
Kathleen F Roberts, *President*
Ethel Curamen, *Office Mgr*
Ken Kenedy, *Opers Mgr*
EMP: 51 EST: 1988
SQ FT: 1,100
SALES: 8.2MM **Privately Held**
SIC: 3448 Buildings, portable: prefabricated metal

(P-12550)
INTERSTATE CARPORTS CORP
1280 S Buena Vista St A, San Jacinto
(92583-4603)
PHONE..................................951 654-1750
Robert Aguilar, *President*
EMP: 11
SQ FT: 4,800
SALES: 2.5MM **Privately Held**
SIC: 3448 Buildings, portable: prefabricated metal

(P-12551)
JOHN L CONLEY INC
Also Called: Conley's Mfg & Sales
4344 Mission Blvd, Montclair (91763-6017)
PHONE..................................909 627-0981
John L Conley, *CEO*
Tom Conley, *President*
Dean Conley, *Vice Pres*
Howard Davis, *Vice Pres*
Russ Jorgenson, *Technical Staff*
◆ EMP: 75 EST: 1946
SALES (est): 20.6MM **Privately Held**
WEB: www.conleys.com
SIC: 3448 3441 Greenhouses: prefabricated metal; buildings, portable: prefabricated metal; fabricated structural metal

(P-12552)
JTS MODULAR INC
7001 Mcdivitt Dr Ste B, Bakersfield
(93313-2030)
P.O. Box 41765 (93384-1765)
PHONE..................................661 835-9270
Dene Hurlbert, *President*
Phillip Engler, *Vice Pres*
Lee Hawkins, *Vice Pres*
John Hurlbert, *Vice Pres*
EMP: 50
SQ FT: 4,000
SALES (est): 14.2MM **Privately Held**
SIC: 3448 Prefabricated metal buildings

(P-12553)
KINGSPAN INSULATED PANELS INC
Kingspan API
2000 Morgan Rd, Modesto (95358-9407)
PHONE..................................209 531-9091
Russell Shiels, *President*
Donal Curtin, *Director*
EMP: 90 **Privately Held**
SIC: 3448 Prefabricated metal buildings
HQ: Kingspan Insulated Panels Inc.
726 Summerhill Dr
Deland FL 32724
386 626-6789

(P-12554)
KRAEMER & CO MFG INC
3778 County Road 99w, Orland
(95963-9785)
PHONE..................................530 865-7982
Ben Kraemer, *President*
Nancy Kraemer, *Treasurer*

Gerald Kraemer, *Admin Sec*
EMP: 15
SQ FT: 6,900
SALES (est): 3.5MM **Privately Held**
WEB: www.kcomfg.com
SIC: 3448 3523 3441 3412 Farm & utility buildings; farm machinery & equipment; elevators, farm; fabricated structural metal; metal barrels, drums & pails

(P-12555)
M & K BUILDERS INC
3212 Bixby Way, Stockton (95209-1590)
P.O. Box 690727 (95269-0727)
PHONE..................................209 478-7531
Jerry Kaufman, *President*
Kevin Kauffman, *Admin Sec*
Matt Kaufman, *Admin Sec*
EMP: 13
SALES: 500K **Privately Held**
SIC: 3448 Buildings, portable: prefabricated metal

(P-12556)
MADERA CARPORTS INC
17462 Baldwin St, Madera (93638-9418)
PHONE..................................559 662-1815
Jose L Madera, *President*
Daisy Kraus, *Manager*
EMP: 12
SQ FT: 625
SALES (est): 2.4MM **Privately Held**
SIC: 3448 Carports: prefabricated metal

(P-12557)
MADISON INDUSTRIES (HQ)
18000 Studebaker Rd # 305, Cerritos
(90703-2681)
PHONE..................................323 583-4061
John Frey Jr, *President*
John Samuel Frey, *President*
Jacob Torres, *Engineer*
Grace Lee, *Controller*
Sam Frey, *Sales Staff*
EMP: 35
SQ FT: 24,000
SALES (est): 11MM
SALES (corp-wide): 129.4MM **Privately Held**
SIC: 3448 3441 1542 Prefabricated metal buildings; fabricated structural metal; non-residential construction
PA: John S. Frey Enterprises
1900 E 64th St
Los Angeles CA 90001
323 583-4061

(P-12558)
MCELROY METAL MILL INC
17031 Koala Rd, Adelanto (92301-2246)
PHONE..................................760 246-5545
Pete Nadler, *Business Mgr*
Joe Corban, *Manager*
EMP: 35
SQ FT: 37,700
SALES (corp-wide): 373.4MM **Privately Held**
WEB: www.mcelroymetal.com
SIC: 3448 Prefabricated metal components
PA: Mcelroy Metal Mill, Inc.
1500 Hamilton Rd
Bossier City LA 71111
318 747-8000

(P-12559)
MCGRATH RENTCORP
Also Called: Mobile Management
11450 Mission Blvd, Jurupa Valley
(91752-1015)
PHONE..................................951 360-6600
Thomas Sanders, *Manager*
Brett Turley, *General Mgr*
EMP: 110
SALES (corp-wide): 498.3MM **Publicly Held**
SIC: 3448 7519 Prefabricated metal buildings; trailer rental
PA: Mcgrath Rentcorp
5700 Las Positas Rd
Livermore CA 94551
925 606-9200

(P-12560)
MOBILE MINI INC
44580 Old Warm Sprng Blvd, Fremont
(94538-6152)
PHONE..................................510 252-9326
Andrew Lemen, *Manager*
EMP: 10
SALES (corp-wide): 593.2MM **Publicly Held**
SIC: 3448 3441 3412 7359 Buildings, portable: prefabricated metal; fabricated structural metal; metal barrels, drums & pails; equipment rental & leasing
PA: Mobile Mini, Inc.
4646 E Van Buren St # 400
Phoenix AZ 85008
480 894-6311

(P-12561)
MOBILE MINI INC
16351 Mckinley Ave, Lathrop (95330-8702)
PHONE..................................209 858-9300
Lora Kirsten, *Branch Mgr*
EMP: 40
SALES (corp-wide): 593.2MM **Publicly Held**
WEB: www.mobilemini.com
SIC: 3448 Buildings, portable: prefabricated metal
PA: Mobile Mini, Inc.
4646 E Van Buren St # 400
Phoenix AZ 85008
480 894-6311

(P-12562)
MOBILE MINI INC
42207 3rd St E, Lancaster (93535-5314)
P.O. Box 1538, Rialto (92377-1538)
PHONE..................................909 356-1690
Craig Nelson, *General Mgr*
Robin Pace, *Human Res Mgr*
EMP: 150
SALES (corp-wide): 593.2MM **Publicly Held**
WEB: www.mobilemini.com
SIC: 3448 Buildings, portable: prefabricated metal
PA: Mobile Mini, Inc.
4646 E Van Buren St # 400
Phoenix AZ 85008
480 894-6311

(P-12563)
MOBILE MINI INC
Also Called: Mobile Mini Storage
12345 Crosthwaite Cir, Poway
(92064-6817)
PHONE..................................858 578-9222
Dennis D'Assis, *Branch Mgr*
EMP: 25
SALES (corp-wide): 593.2MM **Publicly Held**
WEB: www.mobilemini.com
SIC: 3448 3441 3412 7359 Buildings, portable: prefabricated metal; fabricated structural metal; drums; shipping: metal; shipping container leasing
PA: Mobile Mini, Inc.
4646 E Van Buren St # 400
Phoenix AZ 85008
480 894-6311

(P-12564)
MORIN CORP
Also Called: Morin West
10707 Commerce Way, Fontana
(92337-8216)
PHONE..................................909 428-3747
Ilhan Eser, *Vice Pres*
Alysha Lenard, *Sales Executive*
EMP: 30 **Privately Held**
SIC: 3448 Prefabricated metal buildings
HQ: Morin Corporation
685 Middle St
Bristol CT 06010
860 584-0900

(P-12565)
MORRIS GROUP INTERNATIONAL (PA)
15125 Proctor Ave, City of Industry
(91746-3327)
P.O. Box 3527 (91744-0527)
PHONE..................................626 336-4561
Donald E Morris, *President*
Ann Luong, *Vice Pres*

2020 California
Manufacturers Register

▲ = Import ▼=Export
◆ =Import/Export

Mike Polis, *Vice Pres*
Charles White, *Vice Pres*
Jim Widmer, *Vice Pres*
EMP: 12
SALES (est): 1.4MM **Privately Held**
SIC: 3448 3431 3842 3442 Buildings, portable: prefabricated metal; plumbing fixtures: enameled iron cast iron or pressed metal; grafts, artificial: for surgery; metal doors

(P-12566)
NCI GROUP INC
Also Called: Metal Coaters
9123 Center Ave, Rancho Cucamonga (91730-5312)
PHONE.............................909 987-4681
Colin Lally, *Branch Mgr*
Darrell Bancroft, *Office Mgr*
Kathy Delaney, *Human Res Dir*
Colleen Shelton, *Safety Mgr*
Luis Pasillas, *Plant Mgr*
EMP: 75
SALES (corp-wide): 2B **Publicly Held**
SIC: 3448 3446 Prefabricated metal buildings; prefabricated metal components; architectural metalwork
HQ: Nci Group, Inc.
10943 N Sam Huston Pkwy W
Houston TX 77064
281 897-7788

(P-12567)
NCI GROUP INC
Also Called: Metal Building Components Mbci
550 Industry Way, Atwater (95301-9457)
P.O. Box 793 (95301-0793)
PHONE.............................209 357-1000
Bill Jones, *Manager*
Danny Saldana, *Plant Mgr*
EMP: 125
SALES (corp-wide): 2B **Publicly Held**
SIC: 3448 Prefabricated metal buildings; prefabricated metal components
HQ: Nci Group, Inc.
10943 N Sam Huston Pkwy W
Houston TX 77064
281 897-7788

(P-12568)
ORANGE COUNTY ERECTORS INC
517 E La Palma Ave, Anaheim (92801-2536)
PHONE.............................714 502-8455
Richard Lewis, *CEO*
Sandra Lewis, *Senior VP*
Kevin Heynen, *Project Mgr*
David Pineda, *Project Mgr*
Bryan Jurgenson, *Human Res Mgr*
EMP: 50 **EST:** 1975
SQ FT: 80,000
SALES (est): 17.2MM **Privately Held**
WEB: www.ocerectors.com
SIC: 3448 3441 1791 Buildings, portable: prefabricated metal; fabricated structural metal; structural steel erection

(P-12569)
PACIFIC METAL BUILDINGS INC
270 Old Highway 99, Maxwell (95955)
P.O. Box 485 (95955-0485)
PHONE.............................530 438-2777
Eusebio Castillo, *CEO*
EMP: 19 **EST:** 2010
SALES (est): 3.3MM **Privately Held**
SIC: 3448 Prefabricated metal buildings

(P-12570)
PRE-INSULATED METAL TECH INC (HQ)
Also Called: All Weather Insulated Panels
929 Aldridge Rd, Vacaville (95688-9282)
PHONE.............................707 359-2280
William H Lowery, *President*
Michael T Lowery, *Vice Pres*
Nicholas McInturf, *Technician*
Cesar Belmonte, *Project Mgr*
Nathan Gates, *Project Mgr*
▲ **EMP:** 50
SQ FT: 96,000
SALES (est): 15.3MM **Privately Held**
SIC: 3448 Panels for prefabricated metal buildings

(P-12571)
PROGRESSIVE MARKETING PDTS INC
2620 Palisades Dr, Corona (92882-0631)
PHONE.............................714 888-1700
Leonard Dozier, *CEO*
Kathy Bent, *CFO*
Richard Pierro, *Co-CEO*
Tiffany Dozier, *Exec VP*
Sam Malik, *Exec VP*
▲ **EMP:** 80
SQ FT: 47,000
SALES (est): 21.3MM **Privately Held**
WEB: www.premiermounts.com
SIC: 3448 Prefabricated metal buildings

(P-12572)
QUICK DECK INC
15390 Byron Hwy, Byron (94514)
P.O. Box 537 (94514-0537)
PHONE.............................704 888-0327
Fred A Wagner III, *President*
Graham L Scott, *Vice Pres*
Lauren Wintz, *Opers Staff*
EMP: 10
SQ FT: 2,500
SALES (est): 1.4MM **Privately Held**
SIC: 3448 3537 7352 Ramps: prefabricated metal; platforms, cargo; medical equipment rental

(P-12573)
ROBERTSON-CECO II CORPORATION
Also Called: Star Building Systems
12101 E Brandt Rd, Lockeford (95237-9550)
PHONE.............................209 727-5504
Greg Lewis, *Manager*
EMP: 120
SQ FT: 7,000
SALES (corp-wide): 2B **Publicly Held**
WEB: www.robertsonceco.com
SIC: 3448 Buildings, portable: prefabricated metal
HQ: Robertson-Ceco Ii Corporation
10943 N Sam Huston Pkwy W
Houston TX 77064

(P-12574)
SOLO STEEL ERECTORS INC
762 Portal Dr, Chico (95973-1230)
PHONE.............................530 893-2293
Shawn M Bentley, *President*
Shawn Bentley, *President*
Jason Baldridge, *Treasurer*
Nikolas Radtke, *Admin Sec*
EMP: 12
SALES: 1.9MM **Privately Held**
SIC: 3448 1521 Prefabricated metal buildings; single-family housing construction

(P-12575)
STELL INDUSTRIES INC
Also Called: C-Thru Sunrooms
1477 Davril Cir, Corona (92880-6957)
PHONE.............................951 369-8777
Gary P Stell Jr, *CEO*
Jason S Albany, *President*
Mike Leigh, *President*
EMP: 50 **EST:** 1947
SQ FT: 5,000
SALES (est): 11.3MM **Privately Held**
WEB: www.c-thru.com
SIC: 3448 Sunrooms, prefabricated metal

(P-12576)
T M P SERVICES INC (PA)
2929 Kansas Ave, Riverside (92507-2639)
PHONE.............................951 213-3900
Prentiss Tarver Jr, *Shareholder*
Shari Taylor, *President*
Pete Tarver, *Treasurer*
EMP: 25
SQ FT: 32,000
SALES: 6MM **Privately Held**
WEB: www.tmpservices.com
SIC: 3448 Ramps: prefabricated metal

(P-12577)
TIFFANY STRUCTURES
13162 Hwy 8 Bus Spc 205, El Cajon (92021)
PHONE.............................619 905-9684

Raymond Tiffany, *Owner*
Julia Tiffany, *Co-Owner*
EMP: 25
SQ FT: 1,100
SALES (est): 2.5MM **Privately Held**
SIC: 3448 Prefabricated metal components

(P-12578)
TOLCO INCORPORATED
Also Called: Viking Fabrication
6480 Box Springs Blvd, Riverside (92507-0744)
PHONE.............................951 656-3111
Patrick Shaughnessy, *Principal*
Chris Sharp, *Opers Mgr*
EMP: 30
SALES (est): 3.7MM **Privately Held**
SIC: 3448 Prefabricated metal buildings

(P-12579)
TONY BORGES
Also Called: Component Hsing Systems U S A
8685 Bowers Ave, South Gate (90280-3317)
PHONE.............................310 962-8700
Tony Borges, *Owner*
EMP: 22
SQ FT: 40,000
SALES: 5MM **Privately Held**
SIC: 3448 Buildings, portable: prefabricated metal

(P-12580)
UNITED CARPORTS LLC
7280 Sycamore Canyon Blvd # 1, Riverside (92508-2316)
PHONE.............................800 757-6742
Ryan Spates, *CEO*
Garrett Spates, *Vice Pres*
EMP: 18
SQ FT: 5,000
SALES: 3.3MM **Privately Held**
SIC: 3448 Prefabricated metal buildings

(P-12581)
WESTERN METAL SUPPLY CO INC
2115 E Valley Pkwy Ste E, Escondido (92027-2703)
PHONE.............................760 233-7800
Abel Caballero, *President*
Scott Tanner, *Admin Sec*
EMP: 15
SALES: 3.2MM **Privately Held**
SIC: 3448 Prefabricated metal buildings

3449 Misc Structural Metal Work

(P-12582)
3G REBAR INC
6400 Price Way, Bakersfield (93308-5119)
PHONE.............................661 588-0294
John M Dean, *President*
EMP: 15
SQ FT: 5,600
SALES: 3.5MM **Privately Held**
SIC: 3449 Bars, concrete reinforcing: fabricated steel

(P-12583)
ACME SCREW PRODUCTS INC
7950 S Alameda St, Huntington Park (90255-6697)
PHONE.............................323 581-8611
Richard Matthews, *President*
Cynthia Matthews, *Admin Sec*
EMP: 25 **EST:** 1942
SQ FT: 13,500
SALES (est): 4.5MM **Privately Held**
SIC: 3449 Miscellaneous metalwork

(P-12584)
AMC MACHINING INC
1540 Commerce Way, Paso Robles (93446-3524)
P.O. Box 665 (93447-0665)
PHONE.............................805 238-5452
Alex Camp, *President*
Nicole Prizmich, *Manager*
EMP: 21
SQ FT: 10,000

SALES: 4MM **Privately Held**
SIC: 3449 Miscellaneous metalwork

(P-12585)
BACKSTAGE EQUIPMENT INC
Also Called: Backstage Studio Equip
8052 Lankershim Blvd, North Hollywood (91605-1609)
PHONE.............................818 504-6026
Cary Griffith, *President*
EMP: 13
SQ FT: 9,801
SALES (est): 2.6MM **Privately Held**
WEB: www.backstageweb.com
SIC: 3449 3646 Miscellaneous metalwork; commercial indusl & institutional electric lighting fixtures

(P-12586)
BONNER METAL PROCESSING LLC
6052 Industrial Way Ste A, Livermore (94551-9711)
PHONE.............................925 455-3833
Robert Bonner,
Renato Garofani,
Long Hoang,
EMP: 34
SQ FT: 15,000
SALES (est): 5.2MM **Privately Held**
SIC: 3449 Miscellaneous metalwork

(P-12587)
CALIFORNIA STEEL PRODUCTS
10851 Drury Ln, Lynwood (90262-1833)
PHONE.............................310 603-5645
Enrique Garcia, *President*
Ricardo Moctezuma, *Vice Pres*
Faranak Zanj, *Human Resources*
EMP: 12
SALES (est): 2.1MM **Privately Held**
SIC: 3449 3452 3312 Miscellaneous metalwork; bolts, metal; rods, iron & steel: made in steel mills

(P-12588)
CUSTOM FABRICATED METALS LLC
14580 Manzanita Dr, Fontana (92335-5377)
PHONE.............................909 822-8828
Dan Vartan, *Mng Member*
Dave Macias,
EMP: 10 **EST:** 1997
SQ FT: 15,000
SALES (est): 1.9MM **Privately Held**
WEB: www.cfm2000.com
SIC: 3449 Miscellaneous metalwork

(P-12589)
DB BUILDING FASTENERS INC (PA)
Also Called: Db Building Fasteners
5555 E Gibralter, Ontario (91764-5121)
P.O. Box 4407, Rancho Cucamonga (91729-4407)
PHONE.............................909 581-6740
Brent Dooley, *President*
Andrew Cohn, *Corp Secy*
John Dooley III, *Vice Pres*
Marco Ramos, *Sales Staff*
Danny Cintron, *Warehouse Mgr*
▲ **EMP:** 20
SALES (est): 5.4MM **Privately Held**
WEB: www.selfdrillers.com
SIC: 3449 Miscellaneous metalwork

(P-12590)
FYFE CO LLC (HQ)
4995 Murphy Canyon Rd # 110, San Diego (92123-4365)
PHONE.............................858 444-2970
Edward Fyfe,
Julio Sanchez, *Project Engr*
Reymundo Ortiz, *Engineer*
Tommy Jimenez, *Business Mgr*
David A Morris,
EMP: 17
SQ FT: 6,000
SALES (est): 4.4MM
SALES (corp-wide): 1.3B **Publicly Held**
WEB: www.fyfeco.com
SIC: 3449 Bars, concrete reinforcing: fabricated steel

PA: Aegion Corporation
17988 Edison Ave
Chesterfield MO 63005
636 530-8000

(P-12591)
H WAYNE LEWIS INC
Also Called: Amber Steel Co.
312 S Willow Ave, Rialto (92376-6313)
P.O. Box 900 (92377-0900)
PHONE.......................909 874-2213
H Wayne Lewis, *CEO*
Kriss Lewis, *COO*
Janet Lewis, *Treasurer*
Dan Bergen, *Vice Pres*
Shannon Gonzalez, *Financial Exec*
EMP: 40 EST: 1983
SQ FT: 8,100
SALES (est): 14.7MM **Privately Held**
WEB: www.ambersteel.net
SIC: 3449 Bars, concrete reinforcing: fabricated steel

(P-12592)
INNOVATIVE METAL INDS INC
Also Called: Southwest Data Products
1330 Riverview Dr, San Bernardino
(92408-2944)
PHONE.......................909 796-6200
Kelly Brodhagan, *Principal*
▲ EMP: 100
SQ FT: 150,000
SALES (est): 20.5MM **Privately Held**
SIC: 3449 Curtain wall, metal

(P-12593)
JR DANIELS COMMERCIAL BLDRS
Also Called: Innovative Steel Structures
907 Maze Blvd, Modesto (95351-1851)
PHONE.......................209 545-6040
James R Daniels, *President*
EMP: 60
SQ FT: 1,900
SALES (est): 8.3MM **Privately Held**
SIC: 3449 Bars, concrete reinforcing: fabricated steel

(P-12594)
LMS REINFORCING STEEL USA LP (PA)
18059 Rosedale Hwy, Bakersfield
(93314-8684)
PHONE.......................604 598-9930
Norm Streu, *President*
Janice Comeau, *CFO*
Mike Schutz, *Vice Pres*
EMP: 17
SALES: 15MM **Privately Held**
SIC: 3449 Bars, concrete reinforcing: fabricated steel

(P-12595)
LUSTRE-CAL NAMEPLATE CORP
715 S Guild Ave, Lodi (95240-3153)
P.O. Box 439 (95241-0439)
PHONE.......................209 370-1600
Clydene Hohenrieder, *CEO*
Joseph Hohenrieder, *President*
Heather Chartrand, *COO*
▲ EMP: 65
SQ FT: 50,000
SALES (est): 14.5MM **Privately Held**
WEB: www.lustrecal.com
SIC: 3449 Miscellaneous metalwork

(P-12596)
NI INDUSTRIES INC
7300 E Slauson Ave, Commerce
(90040-3627)
PHONE.......................309 283-3355
David Adler, *President*
Brian McGuire, *President*
Anil Shanehg, *Vice Pres*
▲ EMP: 25
SQ FT: 30,000
SALES (est): 3.4MM
SALES (corp-wide): 877.1MM **Publicly Held**
WEB: www.niindustries.com
SIC: 3449 Miscellaneous metalwork

PA: Trimas Corporation
38505 Woodward Ave # 200
Bloomfield Hills MI 48304
248 631-5450

(P-12597)
PACIFIC INTERNATIONAL STL CORP
2889 Navone Rd, Stockton (95215-9324)
PHONE.......................209 931-0900
James H Lewis, *President*
Carol Lewis, *Corp Secy*
EMP: 25 EST: 1956
SQ FT: 3,500
SALES (est): 3.7MM **Privately Held**
WEB: www.pacificinternational.com
SIC: 3449 5051 Miscellaneous metalwork; steel

(P-12598)
PACIFIC STEEL GROUP (PA)
Also Called: Psg
4805 Murphy Canyon Rd, San Diego
(92123-4324)
PHONE.......................858 251-1100
Eric Benson, *Principal*
John Scurlock, *President*
Monica Kamoss, *CFO*
EMP: 87
SQ FT: 26,000
SALES (est): 147.6MM **Privately Held**
SIC: 3449 Bars, concrete reinforcing: fabricated steel

(P-12599)
PACIFIC STEEL GROUP
2301 Napa Vallejo Hwy, NAPA
(94558-6242)
PHONE.......................707 669-3136
Alfredo Gonzalez, *Branch Mgr*
EMP: 21
SALES (corp-wide): 147.6MM **Privately Held**
SIC: 3449 Bars, concrete reinforcing: fabricated steel
PA: Pacific Steel Group
4805 Murphy Canyon Rd
San Diego CA 92123
858 251-1100

(P-12600)
PACIFIC WEST FOREST PRODUCTS
13434 Browns Valley Dr, Chico
(95973-9322)
P.O. Box 2082 (95927-2082)
PHONE.......................530 899-7313
Keith Lindquist, *President*
Kevin Linquist, *Vice Pres*
▲ EMP: 16
SQ FT: 37,000
SALES (est): 3.2MM **Privately Held**
SIC: 3449 5031 Custom roll formed products; lumber: rough, dressed & finished

(P-12601)
PSCMB REPAIRS INC
Also Called: Quality Industry Repair
12145 Slauson Ave, Santa Fe Springs
(90670-2603)
PHONE.......................626 448-7778
Stephany Castellanos, *CEO*
EMP: 40
SALES (est): 6.3MM **Privately Held**
SIC: 3449 Miscellaneous metalwork

(P-12602)
QUALITY STEEL FABRICATORS INC
13275 Gregg St, Poway (92064-7120)
PHONE.......................858 748-8400
Bryan J Miller, *President*
Cheryl Wolf, *Controller*
EMP: 20
SALES (est): 4.3MM **Privately Held**
SIC: 3449 Bars, concrete reinforcing: fabricated steel

(P-12603)
SACRAMENTO REBAR INC (PA)
5072 Hillsdale Cir # 200, El Dorado Hills
(95762-5753)
PHONE.......................916 447-9700
Stanley Rhodes, *CEO*
Janet Rhodes, *CFO*

EMP: 44
SQ FT: 5,000
SALES (est): 10.1MM **Privately Held**
WEB: www.sacramentorebar.com
SIC: 3449 Bars, concrete reinforcing: fabricated steel

(P-12604)
SHIRLEE INDUSTRIES INC
13985 Sycamore Way, Chino (91710-7017)
PHONE.......................909 590-4120
Tom Shaw, *President*
Jeff Shaw, *Vice Pres*
EMP: 12
SQ FT: 35,000
SALES (est): 2.2MM **Privately Held**
WEB: www.shirleeindustries.com
SIC: 3449 3444 Miscellaneous metalwork; sheet metalwork

(P-12605)
SIMPSON STRONG-TIE COMPANY INC (HQ)
5956 W Las Positas Blvd, Pleasanton
(94588-8540)
P.O. Box 10789 (94588-0789)
PHONE.......................925 560-9000
Karen Colonias, *CEO*
Phillip Kingsfather, *President*
Terry Kingsfather, *President*
Jacinta Pister, *Senior VP*
Michael Herbert, *Vice Pres*
▲ EMP: 150 EST: 1914
SQ FT: 89,000
SALES (est): 482.4MM
SALES (corp-wide): 1B **Publicly Held**
SIC: 3449 2891 Joists, fabricated bar; adhesives
PA: Simpson Manufacturing Co., Inc.
5956 W Las Positas Blvd
Pleasanton CA 94588
925 560-9000

(P-12606)
SIMPSON STRONG-TIE COMPANY INC
5151 S Airport Way, Stockton
(95206-3991)
PHONE.......................209 234-7775
Bruce Lewis, *Branch Mgr*
Megan Jones, *Administration*
Phillip Hui, *Technician*
Tim Koss, *Project Mgr*
Jeff Barraclough, *Technical Staff*
EMP: 100
SALES (corp-wide): 1B **Publicly Held**
SIC: 3449 3444 3441 Joists, fabricated bar; sheet metalwork; fabricated structural metal
HQ: Simpson Strong-Tie Company Inc.
5956 W Las Positas Blvd
Pleasanton CA 94588
925 560-9000

(P-12607)
SIMPSON STRONG-TIE INTL INC (DH)
5956 W Las Positas Blvd, Pleasanton
(94588-8540)
P.O. Box 10789 (94588-0789)
PHONE.......................925 560-9000
Karen Colonias, *CEO*
▲ EMP: 100
SQ FT: 89,000
SALES (est): 22.9MM
SALES (corp-wide): 1B **Publicly Held**
SIC: 3449 Joists, fabricated bar
HQ: Simpson Strong-Tie Company Inc.
5956 W Las Positas Blvd
Pleasanton CA 94588
925 560-9000

(P-12608)
SOLHER IRON
1555 Galvez Ave Ste 400, San Francisco
(94124-1707)
PHONE.......................415 822-9900
Martin Solorzano, *Owner*
Juan Solorzano, *Office Mgr*
EMP: 12
SALES (est): 2.5MM **Privately Held**
WEB: www.solheriron.com
SIC: 3449 Bars, concrete reinforcing: fabricated steel

(P-12609)
SRSS LLC
1400 Airport Blvd, Santa Rosa
(95403-1023)
PHONE.......................707 544-7777
Mark Ferronato, *Manager*
Danny Cotta, *Prdtn Mgr*
Nathan Williams, *Prdtn Mgr*
Rodney Ferronato, *Manager*
EMP: 14
SALES (est): 2.4MM **Privately Held**
SIC: 3449 Bars, concrete reinforcing: fabricated steel

(P-12610)
TRI STAR METALS INC
8749 Pedrick Rd, Dixon (95620-9604)
PHONE.......................707 678-1140
Robert Clouse, *President*
Barbara Delaney, *Vice Pres*
Andrew Delaney, *Director*
Aaron Moynihan, *Director*
EMP: 10 EST: 1966
SQ FT: 11,200
SALES (est): 1.6MM **Privately Held**
WEB: www.dixonymachine.com
SIC: 3449 Miscellaneous metalwork

(P-12611)
UNITED MISC & ORNA STL INC
Also Called: Umo Steel
4700 Horner St, Union City (94587-2531)
PHONE.......................510 429-8755
Juan M Romero, *President*
Jose Barrera, *Vice Pres*
Jose G Romero, *Principal*
EMP: 48
SALES (est): 2.7MM **Privately Held**
WEB: www.umosteelinc.com
SIC: 3449 Bars, concrete reinforcing: fabricated steel

(P-12612)
VISTA STEEL CO INC (PA)
6100 Francis Botello Rd C, Goleta
(93117-3259)
PHONE.......................805 964-4732
Maria Di Maggio, *President*
EMP: 50 EST: 1969
SQ FT: 600
SALES (est): 7.9MM **Privately Held**
SIC: 3449 Bars, concrete reinforcing: fabricated steel

(P-12613)
WESTCO INDUSTRIES INC
Also Called: Corbell Products
2625 S Willow Ave, Bloomington
(92316-3258)
PHONE.......................909 874-8700
David Schibel, *President*
Erick Maravilla, *Info Tech Mgr*
▲ EMP: 25
SQ FT: 25,000
SALES (est): 5.2MM **Privately Held**
SIC: 3449 Bars, concrete reinforcing: fabricated steel

3451 Screw Machine Prdts

(P-12614)
ABEL AUTOMATICS INC
Also Called: Abel Reels
165 N Aviador St, Camarillo (93010-8484)
PHONE.......................805 484-8789
David C Dragoo, *CEO*
Margie Hanley, *Office Mgr*
▲ EMP: 30
SQ FT: 16,000
SALES: 3MM **Privately Held**
SIC: 3451 3949 Screw machine products; reels, fishing

(P-12615)
ACCU-SWISS INC (PA)
544 Armstrong Way, Oakdale
(95361-9367)
PHONE.......................209 847-1016
Sohel Sareshwala, *President*
Asfiya Sareshwala, *Corp Secy*
Ali Gabajiwala, *Engineer*
EMP: 19
SQ FT: 10,000

▲ = Import ▼=Export
◆ =Import/Export

SALES (est): 4MM **Privately Held**
WEB: www.accuswissinc.com
SIC: 3451 8711 Screw machine products; engineering services

(P-12616)
AD-DE-PRO INC
8276 Phlox St, Downey (90241-4883)
P.O. Box 807 (90241-0807)
PHONE..................................562 862-1915
Tom Burdett, *President*
Beverly Mathis, *Corp Secy*
EMP: 16 EST: 1965
SQ FT: 5,000
SALES (est): 1.3MM **Privately Held**
SIC: 3451 Screw machine products

(P-12617)
ALGER PRECISION MACHINING LLC
724 S Bon View Ave, Ontario (91761-1913)
PHONE..................................909 986-4591
Duane Femrite, *Principal*
▲ EMP: 160
SQ FT: 35,000
SALES (est): 44MM **Privately Held**
WEB: www.alger1.com
SIC: 3451 Screw machine products

(P-12618)
ALPHA OMEGA SWISS INC
23305 La Palma Ave, Yorba Linda (92887-4773)
PHONE..................................714 692-8009
Dale La Rock, *President*
Randy L Jones, *Vice Pres*
Robert Palmer, *General Mgr*
EMP: 30
SQ FT: 15,500
SALES (est): 3.3MM **Privately Held**
WEB: www.alphaomegaswiss.com
SIC: 3451 3599 Screw machine products; machine shop, jobbing & repair

(P-12619)
ALVA MANUFACTURING INC
236 E Orangethorpe Ave, Placentia (92870-6442)
PHONE..................................714 237-0925
Tam V Nguyen, *Principal*
Grant McKinley, *COO*
Sarah Naguib, *Admin Asst*
Aryan Ghomi, *Project Engr*
MAI Truong, *Engineer*
EMP: 24
SQ FT: 15,000
SALES (est): 1.5MM **Privately Held**
SIC: 3451 3452 3728 3599 Screw machine products; bolts, nuts, rivets & washers; aircraft parts & equipment; machine & other job shop work; machine shop, jobbing & repair

(P-12620)
ANWRIGHT CORPORATION
10225 Glenoaks Blvd, Pacoima (91331-1605)
P.O. Box 330940 (91333-0940)
PHONE..................................818 896-2465
Lloyd Anderson, *President*
David Richardson, *Vice Pres*
Elva Guadiana, *Bookkeeper*
EMP: 48
SQ FT: 15,000
SALES (est): 2.4MM **Privately Held**
WEB: www.anwright.com
SIC: 3451 3599 Screw machine products; machine shop, jobbing & repair

(P-12621)
ATHANOR GROUP INC
921 E California St, Ontario (91761-1918)
PHONE..................................909 467-1205
Duane L Femrite, *President*
Richard Krause, *Vice Pres*
EMP: 165 EST: 1958
SQ FT: 35,600
SALES (est): 11.3MM **Privately Held**
SIC: 3451 Screw machine products

(P-12622)
ATLAS SCREW MACHINE PDTS CO
560 Natoma St, San Francisco (94103-2885)
PHONE..................................415 621-6737

John Stadlberger, *President*
Mike Boitano, *Vice Pres*
EMP: 10 EST: 1956
SQ FT: 2,500
SALES (est): 1.2MM **Privately Held**
WEB: www.atlasscrew.com
SIC: 3451 Screw machine products

(P-12623)
BALDA HK PLASTICS INC
Also Called: H K Prcision Turning Machining
3229 Roymar Rd, Oceanside (92058-1311)
PHONE..................................760 757-1100
Dan Wannigen, *Manager*
EMP: 60
SQ FT: 9,808
SALES (corp-wide): 562.9K **Privately Held**
WEB: www.hkplasticseng.com
SIC: 3451 3544 3089 Screw machine products; special dies & tools; injection molded finished plastic products
HQ: Balda Hk Plastics Inc.
1825 Corporate Ctr
Oceanside CA 92056
760 757-1200

(P-12624)
BTM-BEARTECH MANUFACTURING
910 S Placentia Ave Ste A, Placentia (92870-8001)
P.O. Box 10422, Santa Ana (92711-0422)
PHONE..................................714 550-1700
Rick E Fobear, *President*
James Thomas, *Mng Member*
EMP: 10
SQ FT: 7,000
SALES: 684.5K
SALES (corp-wide): 4.7MM **Privately Held**
WEB: www.beartechmfg.com
SIC: 3451 3452 3599 Screw machine products; bolts, nuts, rivets & washers; machine & other job shop work; machine shop, jobbing & repair
PA: Beartech Alloys, Inc.
910 S Placentia Ave Ste A
Placentia CA 92870
714 550-1700

(P-12625)
COLUMBIA SCREW PRODUCTS INC
2901 Halladay St, Santa Ana (92705-5622)
PHONE..................................714 549-1171
William E Gorham, *President*
Dolores Gorham, *Treasurer*
Candy Gorham, *Manager*
EMP: 15 EST: 1954
SQ FT: 4,000
SALES: 800K **Privately Held**
WEB: www.columbiascrew.com
SIC: 3451 Screw machine products

(P-12626)
CRELLIN MACHINE COMPANY
Also Called: BT Screw Products
114 W Elmyra St, Los Angeles (90012-1819)
PHONE..................................323 225-8101
Richard Kirkendall, *President*
EMP: 45
SQ FT: 22,000
SALES (est): 6.3MM **Privately Held**
WEB: www.btcrellin.com
SIC: 3451 3541 Screw machine products; machine tools, metal cutting type

(P-12627)
CUSTOM MFG LLC
12946 Los Nietos Rd, Santa Fe Springs (90670-3020)
PHONE..................................562 944-0245
Walter Mason, *Owner*
David McKenery, *Accounting Mgr*
Laura McKenery,
EMP: 10 EST: 1974
SQ FT: 5,000
SALES (est): 567.8K **Privately Held**
SIC: 3451 Screw machine products

(P-12628)
CUTTING EDGE MACHINING INC (PA)
1331 Old County Rd Ste A, Belmont (94002-3968)
PHONE..................................408 738-8677
Jack Corey, *CEO*
Gloria L Corey, *Corp Secy*
EMP: 25
SALES (est): 6.8MM **Privately Held**
WEB: www.cemnv.com
SIC: 3451 Screw machine products

(P-12629)
DESIGNED METAL CONNECTIONS INC (DH)
Also Called: Permaswage USA
14800 S Figueroa St, Gardena (90248-1719)
PHONE..................................310 323-6200
Thomas McDonnell, *Vice Pres*
▲ EMP: 500
SQ FT: 175,000
SALES (est): 194MM
SALES (corp-wide): 225.3B **Publicly Held**
SIC: 3451 Screw machine products
HQ: Precision Castparts Corp.
4650 Sw Mcdam Ave Ste 300
Portland OR 97239
503 946-4800

(P-12630)
EDWARD KOEHN CO INC
820 Folger Ave, Berkeley (94710-2817)
PHONE..................................510 843-0821
Paul Koehn, *President*
Beatrice Koehn, *Treasurer*
EMP: 10 EST: 1942
SQ FT: 4,500
SALES (est): 1.1MM **Privately Held**
SIC: 3451 Screw machine products

(P-12631)
FASTENER INNOVATION TECH INC
Also Called: F I T
19300 S Susana Rd, Compton (90221-5711)
PHONE..................................310 538-1111
Larry Valeriano, *CEO*
EMP: 100
SQ FT: 65,000
SALES: 20.6MM **Privately Held**
WEB: www.fitfastener.com
SIC: 3451 3728 3452 3429 Screw machine products; aircraft parts & equipment; bolts, nuts, rivets & washers; manufactured hardware (general)

(P-12632)
GLENCO MANUFACTURING COMPANY
707 S Hope Ave, Ontario (91761-1826)
PHONE..................................909 984-3348
Fax: 909 988-5970
EMP: 50
SQ FT: 15,027
SALES (est): 8.8MM **Privately Held**
WEB: www.glencomfg.com
SIC: 3451

(P-12633)
GT PRECISION INC
Also Called: Alard Machine Products
1629 W 132nd St, Gardena (90249-2005)
PHONE..................................310 323-4374
Gregg Thompson, *CEO*
Andrew Lozano, *Planning*
Jose Zaragoza, *Info Tech Mgr*
Greg Granja, *Controller*
Eduardo Solano, *Maint Spvr*
▲ EMP: 107
SQ FT: 11,700
SALES (est): 20.9MM **Privately Held**
WEB: www.alardmachine.com
SIC: 3451 Screw machine products

(P-12634)
H&M PRECISION MACHINING
Also Called: H & M Precision Machining
504 Robert Ave, Santa Clara (95050-2955)
PHONE..................................408 982-9184
Jane Harvey, *President*
EMP: 11

SQ FT: 8,000
SALES (est): 1.7MM **Privately Held**
SIC: 3451 3469 Screw machine products; machine parts, stamped or pressed metal

(P-12635)
HTS-ENGINEERING INC
4079 Oceanside Blvd Ste J, Oceanside (92056-5810)
PHONE..................................760 631-2070
Chris Dubreuil, *CEO*
Angela Robertson, *Manager*
EMP: 15
SQ FT: 7,700
SALES (est): 2.2MM **Privately Held**
WEB: www.hts-engineering.com
SIC: 3451 Screw machine products

(P-12636)
IRL-MEX MANUFACTURING COMPANY
Also Called: Union Swiss Manufacturing Co
1436 Flower St, Glendale (91201-2422)
PHONE..................................818 246-7211
Mathew Graham, *President*
Victor Paquini, *Vice Pres*
Alastair Rippon, *Opers Staff*
EMP: 10
SQ FT: 3,500
SALES (est): 2MM **Privately Held**
WEB: www.unionswiss.com
SIC: 3451 Screw machine products

(P-12637)
JUNE PRECISION MFG INC
Also Called: Tri-State Manufacturing
22276 Chestnut Ln, Lake Forest (92630-4303)
PHONE..................................949 855-9121
David Oldfield, *President*
EMP: 10
SALES: 950K **Privately Held**
SIC: 3451 Screw machine products

(P-12638)
L & S MACHINE INC
Also Called: L&S Machine Enterprises
711 W 17th St Ste H2, Costa Mesa (92627-4347)
PHONE..................................562 924-9007
Keith Longerot, *President*
EMP: 15
SQ FT: 12,500
SALES (est): 1MM **Privately Held**
WEB: www.lsmachine.com
SIC: 3451 Screw machine products

(P-12639)
M & R ENGINEERING CO
227 E Meats Ave, Orange (92865-3311)
PHONE..................................714 991-8480
Natalia Sephton, *President*
Maureen Derseweh, *General Mgr*
EMP: 15 EST: 1973
SQ FT: 32,000
SALES (est): 3.7MM **Privately Held**
WEB: www.m-reng.com
SIC: 3451 3541 Screw machine products; lathes

(P-12640)
MARS ENGINEERING COMPANY INC
Also Called: Vin-Max
699 Montague St, San Leandro (94577-4323)
PHONE..................................510 483-0541
Manny Ambrosio, *President*
Christy Ambrosio, *Corp Secy*
EMP: 35
SQ FT: 15,000
SALES (est): 6.9MM **Privately Held**
WEB: www.marseng.com
SIC: 3451 Screw machine products

(P-12641)
MERCED SCREW PRODUCTS INC
1861 Grogan Ave, Merced (95341-6432)
PHONE..................................209 723-7706
Steve Centivich, *President*
EMP: 40
SQ FT: 17,000
SALES (est): 7.4MM **Privately Held**
SIC: 3451 Screw machine products

PRODUCTS & SVCS

(P-12642)
NORSCO INC
1816 Ackley Cir, Oakdale (95361-9446)
PHONE.....................209 845-2327
Greg Siekierski, *President*
EMP: 10
SALES (est): 1.1MM **Privately Held**
WEB: www.norscoinc.com
SIC: 3451 Screw machine products

(P-12643)
ONYX INDUSTRIES INC (PA)
Also Called: Quad R Tech
1227 254th St, Harbor City (90710-2912)
PHONE.....................310 539-8830
Vladimir Reil, *CEO*
▲ EMP: 100
SQ FT: 30,000
SALES (est): 21MM **Privately Held**
SIC: 3451 Screw machine products

(P-12644)
ONYX INDUSTRIES INC
521 W Rosecrans Ave, Gardena
(90248-1514)
PHONE.....................310 851-6161
Siamak Maghoul, *Branch Mgr*
EMP: 20
SALES (corp-wide): 21MM **Privately Held**
SIC: 3451 Screw machine products
PA: Onyx Industries Inc
1227 254th St
Harbor City CA 90710
310 539-8830

(P-12645)
PACIFIC SCREW PRODUCTS INC
Also Called: Rollin J. Lobaugh
1331 Old County Rd Ste C, Belmont
(94002-3968)
PHONE.....................650 583-9682
Jack Corey, *President*
Gloria Corey, *Corp Secy*
EMP: 52
SQ FT: 24,000
SALES (est): 9.2MM **Privately Held**
WEB: www.rjlobaugh.com
SIC: 3451 Screw machine products

(P-12646)
PENCOM ACCURACY INC
Also Called: Accuracy Screw Machine Pdts
1300 Industrial Rd Ste 21, San Carlos
(94070-4141)
PHONE.....................510 785-5022
Bill Gardiner, *President*
Deborah Gardiner, *Vice Pres*
EMP: 52
SQ FT: 8,000
SALES (est): 6.7MM
SALES (corp-wide): 148.3MM **Privately Held**
WEB: www.pencomsf.com
SIC: 3451 Screw machine products
PA: Peninsula Components, Inc.
1300 Industrial Rd Ste 21
San Carlos CA 94070
650 593-3288

(P-12647)
PRECISION TECHNOLOGY AND MFG
3147 Durahart St, Riverside (92507-3463)
PHONE.....................951 788-0252
Jose Pompa, *President*
Lorraine Pagones, *Corp Secy*
Juan Pompa, *Vice Pres*
EMP: 43
SQ FT: 9,000
SALES (est): 5.8MM **Privately Held**
WEB: www.pretechm.com
SIC: 3451 3643 Screw machine products;
contacts, electrical

(P-12648)
PRICE MANUFACTURING CO INC
372 N Smith Ave, Corona (92880-6971)
PHONE.....................951 371-5660
Robert P Schiffmacher, *CEO*
Ively Schiffmacher, *Corp Secy*
EMP: 32
SQ FT: 15,600

SALES (est): 6.9MM **Privately Held**
WEB: www.pricemfg.com
SIC: 3451 Screw machine products

(P-12649)
R & R MACHINE PRODUCTS INC
760 W Mill St, San Bernardino
(92410-3348)
PHONE.....................909 885-7500
Eric Reiser, *President*
Belinda Reiser, *Corp Secy*
Karl Reiser, *Vice Pres*
EMP: 13
SQ FT: 5,000
SALES (est): 1MM **Privately Held**
WEB: www.grscrew.com
SIC: 3451 3643 Screw machine products;
electric connectors; contacts, electrical

(P-12650)
SIERRA SWISS & MACHINE INC
12854 Earhart Ave Ste 103, Auburn
(95602-9015)
P.O. Box 2797, Grass Valley (95945-2797)
PHONE.....................530 346-1110
EMP: 13
SQ FT: 3,000
SALES (est): 1.6MM **Privately Held**
SIC: 3451

(P-12651)
SORENSON ENGINEERING INC (PA)
32032 Dunlap Blvd, Yucaipa (92399-1767)
PHONE.....................909 795-2434
David L Sorenson, *President*
Paul Sewell, *Principal*
Robert Lunderville, *Research*
Grant Feenstra, *Engineer*
Phil Kim, *Engineer*
▲ EMP: 170 EST: 1956
SQ FT: 61,000
SALES (est): 36.2MM **Privately Held**
WEB: www.sorensoneng.com
SIC: 3451 Screw machine products

(P-12652)
SWISS-MICRON INC
22361 Gilberto Ste A, Rcho STA Marg
(92688-2103)
PHONE.....................949 589-0430
Kurt Sollberger, *CEO*
Beverley Sollberger, *Vice Pres*
Casey Colliflower, *Purch Mgr*
Alan McManus, *Prdtn Mgr*
EMP: 53
SQ FT: 16,000
SALES: 7MM **Privately Held**
WEB: www.swissmicron.com
SIC: 3451 Screw machine products

(P-12653)
SWISS-TECH MACHINING LLC
10564 Industrial Ave, Roseville
(95678-6223)
PHONE.....................916 797-6010
Pete Kummli,
EMP: 25
SQ FT: 20,000
SALES (est): 4.1MM **Privately Held**
WEB: www.stmachining.com
SIC: 3451 Screw machine products

(P-12654)
T L MACHINE INC
14272 Commerce Dr, Garden Grove
(92843-4942)
PHONE.....................714 554-4154
Thanh X Ly, *President*
Thanh Ly, *President*
Quynh Nguyen, *Executive*
Tuyen Hoang, *General Mgr*
Tuyen Ly, *Admin Sec*
▲ EMP: 90
SQ FT: 39,126
SALES (est): 22.3MM **Privately Held**
WEB: www.tlmachine.com
SIC: 3451 3561 3593 3728 Screw ma-
chine products; pumps & pumping equip-
ment; fluid power cylinders & actuators;
aircraft parts & equipment; aircraft; guided
missiles & space vehicles

(P-12655)
THOMAS T BERNSTEIN
1160 Daveric Dr, Pasadena (91107-1740)
PHONE.....................626 351-0570
Thomas T Bernstein, *Owner*
EMP: 40
SALES (est): 1.5MM **Privately Held**
SIC: 3451 Screw machine products

(P-12656)
TRIUMPH PRECISION PRODUCTS
Also Called: TP Products
13636 Vaughn St Ste A, San Fernando
(91340-3052)
PHONE.....................818 897-4700
Victor Linares, *President*
Javier Cervantes, *Vice Pres*
Jesus Cervantes, *Admin Sec*
EMP: 17
SQ FT: 19,500
SALES (est): 2.3MM **Privately Held**
WEB: www.tpproducts.com
SIC: 3451 Screw machine products

(P-12657)
UNIVERSAL SCREW PRODUCTS INC
20421 Earl St, Torrance (90503-2414)
P.O. Box 14241 (90503-8241)
PHONE.....................310 371-1170
Ken Shank, *President*
Michael Flannigan, *Admin Sec*
EMP: 20
SQ FT: 6,000
SALES (est): 3.7MM **Privately Held**
SIC: 3451 Screw machine products

(P-12658)
V M P INC
24830 Avenue Tibbitts, Valencia
(91355-3404)
PHONE.....................661 294-9934
Betty Schreiner, *President*
Steve Schreiner, *Treasurer*
Robert Schreiner Jr, *Vice Pres*
Suzanne St George, *Admin Sec*
▲ EMP: 16
SQ FT: 25,000
SALES (est): 3.1MM **Privately Held**
WEB: www.vmpinc.com
SIC: 3451 Screw machine products

(P-12659)
WARD AUTOMATIC MACHINE PDTS
1265 Goodrick Dr Ste E, Tehachapi
(93561-1562)
PHONE.....................661 822-7543
Ralph Ward, *President*
Bess Ward, *Treasurer*
EMP: 10
SQ FT: 7,500
SALES: 1MM **Privately Held**
WEB: www.wardautomatic.com
SIC: 3451 Screw machine products

(P-12660)
WESTERN SCREW PRODUCTS INC
11770 Slauson Ave, Santa Fe Springs
(90670-2269)
PHONE.....................562 698-5793
Lester P Kovats, *President*
William Doolittle, *Corp Secy*
Margaret K Doolittle, *Vice Pres*
Steve Kovats, *Vice Pres*
Tony Moore, *General Mgr*
EMP: 50 EST: 1940
SQ FT: 30,000
SALES (est): 8.9MM **Privately Held**
WEB: www.westernscrew.com
SIC: 3451 Screw machine products

(P-12661)
WYATT PRECISION MACHINE INC
3301 E 59th St, Long Beach (90805-4503)
PHONE.....................562 634-0524
Dennis Allison, *President*
Allen Harmon, *Vice Pres*
Paul Layton, *Vice Pres*
EMP: 47
SQ FT: 14,000

SALES (est): 8.5MM **Privately Held**
WEB: www.wyattprecisionmachine.com
SIC: 3451 Screw machine products

(P-12662)
ZENITH SCREW PRODUCTS INC
10910 Painter Ave, Santa Fe Springs
(90670-4552)
P.O. Box 2747 (90670-0747)
PHONE.....................562 941-0281
Kenneth Miller, *President*
Donald S Miller, *Ch of Bd*
Connie Miller, *Treasurer*
Keith L Miller, *Vice Pres*
EMP: 20
SQ FT: 7,000
SALES (est): 1.3MM **Privately Held**
WEB: www.zspinc.com
SIC: 3451 Screw machine products

3452 Bolts, Nuts, Screws, Rivets & Washers

(P-12663)
3-V FASTENER CO INC
320 Reed Cir, Corona (92879-1349)
PHONE.....................951 734-4391
Mark Gordon, *CEO*
Robert Cantillo, *Supervisor*
EMP: 56
SQ FT: 18,500
SALES (est): 12.8MM
SALES (corp-wide): 167.6MM **Privately Held**
WEB: www.3vfasteners.com
SIC: 3452 Bolts, metal; nuts, metal;
screws, metal
PA: Consolidated Aerospace Manufactur-
ing, Llc
1425 S Acacia Ave
Fullerton CA 92831
714 989-2797

(P-12664)
A J FASTENERS INC
Also Called: Pacific Hardware Sales
2800 E Miraloma Ave, Anaheim
(92806-1803)
PHONE.....................714 630-1556
Lawrence Roa, *President*
▲ EMP: 20 EST: 1975
SQ FT: 15,000
SALES (est): 3.2MM **Privately Held**
WEB: www.ajfasteners.com
SIC: 3452 5072 3469 Screws, metal;
screws; metal stampings

(P-12665)
ANILLO INDUSTRIES INC (PA)
2090 N Glassell St, Orange (92865-3306)
P.O. Box 5586 (92863-5586)
PHONE.....................714 637-7000
Kurt Hilton Koch, *President*
Mark Koch, *Vice Pres*
EMP: 28
SQ FT: 80,000
SALES (est): 5.6MM **Privately Held**
WEB: www.anilloinc.com
SIC: 3452 3325 3499 3429 Washers;
bushings, cast steel: except investment;
shims, metal; manufactured hardware
(general)

(P-12666)
B&B HARDWARE INC
Also Called: Sealtight Technology
5370 Hollister Ave Ste 2, Santa Barbara
(93111-2399)
P.O. Box 60840 (93160-0840)
PHONE.....................805 683-6700
Larry Bogatz, *President*
Diana Bogatz, *Vice Pres*
▲ EMP: 28
SQ FT: 4,000
SALES (est): 4.1MM **Privately Held**
WEB: www.sealtightfastener.com
SIC: 3452 5085 Bolts, nuts, rivets & wash-
ers; industrial supplies

▲ = Import ▼=Export
◆ =Import/Export

(P-12667)
BAY STANDARD MANUFACTURING INC (PA)
Also Called: Bsmi
24485 Marsh Creek Rd, Brentwood (94513-4319)
P.O. Box 801 (94513-0801)
PHONE...................................925 634-1181
Gary W Landgraf, *CEO*
Gregory Iverson, *President*
Karen Landgraf, *Vice Pres*
Mark Heaney, *Sales Mgr*
Alison Watts, *Property Mgr*
◆ EMP: 50
SQ FT: 25,000
SALES (est): 13.2MM **Privately Held**
WEB: www.baystandard.com
SIC: 3452 5072 Bolts, metal; bolts

(P-12668)
BLUE CIRCLE CORP
7520 Monroe St, Paramount (90723-4922)
PHONE...................................562 531-2711
Ronald E Anderson, *President*
Chris Anderson, *Vice Pres*
Jeffrey Anderson, *Vice Pres*
Walda Anderson, *Admin Sec*
EMP: 15
SQ FT: 13,000
SALES (est): 1.4MM **Privately Held**
SIC: 3452 3365 Bolts, metal; aluminum & aluminum-based alloy castings

(P-12669)
BRILES AEROSPACE INC
1559 W 135th St, Gardena (90249-2219)
PHONE...................................310 701-2087
Michael P Briles, *President*
EMP: 12
SQ FT: 22,000
SALES: 900K **Privately Held**
SIC: 3452 Bolts, nuts, rivets & washers

(P-12670)
BUTLER INC
1600 W 166th St, Gardena (90247-4704)
PHONE...................................310 323-3114
John Hollern, *President*
Cynthia Hollern, *Vice Pres*
Tod Polidori, *QC Mgr*
EMP: 14
SQ FT: 10,000
SALES (est): 2.6MM **Privately Held**
SIC: 3452 Bolts, metal

(P-12671)
C B S FASTENERS INC
1345 N Brasher St, Anaheim (92807-2046)
PHONE...................................714 779-6368
Gerald Bozarth, *President*
Vic Luna, *Plant Mgr*
EMP: 39 EST: 1974
SQ FT: 10,400
SALES (est): 6.8MM **Privately Held**
WEB: www.cbsfasteners.com
SIC: 3452 Screws, metal

(P-12672)
CONCRETEACCESSORIESCOM
130 N Gilbert St, Fullerton (92833-2505)
PHONE...................................714 871-9434
Vasken Kassarjian, *President*
▲ EMP: 15
SALES: 3MM **Privately Held**
SIC: 3452 Bolts, nuts, rivets & washers

(P-12673)
CONKLIN & CONKLIN INCORPORATED
34201 7th St, Union City (94587-3655)
PHONE...................................510 489-5500
James Edward Conklin, *President*
Barbara Conklin, *Vice Pres*
▲ EMP: 30
SQ FT: 23,000
SALES (est): 4.5MM **Privately Held**
SIC: 3452 Bolts, nuts, rivets & washers

(P-12674)
CONSTRUCTION TL & THREADING CO
8476 Garfield Ave, Bell Gardens (90201-6125)
PHONE...................................562 927-1326
James T Pokracki, *President*

Rita Pokracki, *Corp Secy*
EMP: 16
SQ FT: 8,800
SALES (est): 2.4MM **Privately Held**
WEB: www.constructiontool.com
SIC: 3452 Bolts, nuts, rivets & washers

(P-12675)
DOUBLECO INCORPORATED
Also Called: R & D Fasteners
9444 9th St, Rancho Cucamonga (91730-4509)
P.O. Box 250, Upland (91785-0250)
PHONE...................................909 481-0799
Craig Scheu, *President*
Leland Scheu, *Sr Corp Ofcr*
Ryan McCaffrey, *General Mgr*
EMP: 100
SQ FT: 30,000
SALES (est): 28.4MM **Privately Held**
WEB: www.rdfast.com
SIC: 3452 5072 Bolts, metal; bolts

(P-12676)
DUPREE INC
Also Called: Stake Fastener
14395 Ramona Ave, Chino (91710-5740)
P.O. Box 1797 (91708-1797)
PHONE...................................909 597-4889
Jim Pon, *President*
James D Dupree, *Vice Pres*
▲ EMP: 31 EST: 1958
SQ FT: 60,000
SALES (est): 6.1MM **Privately Held**
WEB: www.dupreeinc.com
SIC: 3452 6512 Bolts, metal; gate hooks; commercial & industrial building operation

(P-12677)
FASTENER DEPOT INC
6166 Enterprise Dr Ste A, Diamond Springs (95619-9440)
PHONE...................................530 621-3070
Mildred Navalance, *President*
EMP: 10
SALES (est): 1.9MM **Privately Held**
SIC: 3452 Bolts, nuts, rivets & washers

(P-12678)
FEDERAL MANUFACTURING CORP
9825 De Soto Ave, Chatsworth (91311-4412)
PHONE...................................818 341-9825
Helen Rainey, *President*
Arthur Rainey, *President*
Paul Rainey, *Vice Pres*
Sharon Carlson, *Manager*
EMP: 42
SQ FT: 36,000
SALES (est): 8MM **Privately Held**
WEB: www.federalmanufacturing.com
SIC: 3452 3812 3462 3429 Bolts, metal; search & navigation equipment; iron & steel forgings; manufactured hardware (general)

(P-12679)
GOLDEN BOLT LLC
9361 Canoga Ave, Chatsworth (91311-5879)
PHONE...................................818 626-8261
Crystal Crook,
EMP: 12
SALES (est): 2.4MM **Privately Held**
SIC: 3452 Bolts, metal

(P-12680)
HI-SHEAR CORPORATION (DH)
2600 Skypark Dr, Torrance (90505-5373)
PHONE...................................310 784-4025
Christian Darville, *CEO*
Raymond Thornton, *Engineer*
▲ EMP: 600 EST: 1943
SQ FT: 180,000
SALES (est): 247.7MM
SALES (corp-wide): 177.9K **Privately Held**
WEB: www.hi-shear.com
SIC: 3452 3429 Bolts, nuts, rivets & washers; aircraft hardware
HQ: Lisi Aerospace
42 A 52
Paris 12e Arrondissement 75012
140 198-200

(P-12681)
HUCK INTERNATIONAL INC
Also Called: Arconic Fastening Systems
900 E Watson Center Rd, Carson (90745-4201)
PHONE...................................310 830-8200
Jim Dawn, *Manager*
Hojat Boojani, *Engineer*
Brad Warezak, *Director*
EMP: 203
SALES (corp-wide): 14B **Publicly Held**
WEB: www.huck.com
SIC: 3452 Nuts, metal
HQ: Huck International, Inc.
3724 E Columbia St
Tucson AZ 85714
520 519-7400

(P-12682)
IDEAL FASTENERS INC
3850 E Miraloma Ave, Anaheim (92806-2127)
PHONE...................................714 630-7840
George Hennes, *President*
Lawrence McBride, *Treasurer*
David Boehm, *Vice Pres*
Christine Sumner, *Controller*
Dave Aguilera, *Foreman/Supr*
EMP: 50 EST: 1969
SQ FT: 35,500
SALES (est): 9.9MM **Privately Held**
WEB: www.idealfasteners.com
SIC: 3452 Screws, metal

(P-12683)
INSTRUMENT BEARING FACTORY USA
19360 Rinaldi St, Northridge (91326-1607)
PHONE...................................818 989-5052
Dorothy Heller, *President*
EMP: 50
SQ FT: 30,000
SALES (est): 2.6MM **Privately Held**
SIC: 3452 5085 Bolts, metal; industrial supplies

(P-12684)
JW MANUFACTURING INC
Also Called: Arconic Fstening Systems Rings
12989 Bradley Ave, Sylmar (91342)
PHONE...................................805 498-4594
Jacob Wood, *President*
▲ EMP: 60
SQ FT: 40,000
SALES (est): 7.7MM **Privately Held**
SIC: 3452 5072 Nuts, metal; bolts, nuts & screws

(P-12685)
KINGFA GLOBAL INC
1910 S Archibald Ave D, Ontario (91761-8501)
PHONE...................................909 212-5413
Xiaojun Gao, *CEO*
Norm Matthias, *Accounts Exec*
EMP: 11
SALES (est): 1.4MM
SALES (corp-wide): 1MM **Privately Held**
SIC: 3452 5961 Bolts, nuts, rivets & washers; tools & hardware, mail order
PA: Wuxi Zhuocheng Mechanical Components Co., Ltd.
Building 6, Liando U-Valley 2, Beitang District
Wuxi 21410
510 823-5066

(P-12686)
MS AEROSPACE INC
13928 Balboa Blvd, Sylmar (91342-1086)
PHONE...................................818 833-9095
Michel Szostak, *CEO*
Jerome Taieb, *CFO*
Jim Cole, *Vice Pres*
Ken Robinson, *Vice Pres*
Michelle Szostak, *VP Bus Dvlpt*
EMP: 302
SALES (est): 95.8MM **Privately Held**
WEB: www.msaerospace.com
SIC: 3452 3728 Bolts, nuts, rivets & washers; aircraft parts & equipment

(P-12687)
ND INDUSTRIES INC
Also Called: N D Industries
13929 Dinard Ave, Santa Fe Springs (90670-4920)
PHONE...................................562 926-3321
Tim Marzano, *Opers-Prdtn-Mfg*
Scot Wickham, *Vice Pres*
David Palmquist, *Assistant*
EMP: 40
SALES (corp-wide): 81.5MM **Privately Held**
WEB: www.ndindustries.com
SIC: 3452 2891 5072 Bolts, nuts, rivets & washers; adhesives & sealants; screws
PA: Nd Industries, Inc.
1000 N Crooks Rd
Clawson MI 48017
248 288-0000

(P-12688)
NELSON STUD WELDING INC
20621 Valley Blvd Ste B, Walnut (91789-2748)
PHONE...................................909 468-2105
Steven J Whitham, *President*
EMP: 10
SALES (corp-wide): 13.9B **Publicly Held**
SIC: 3452 Bolts, nuts, rivets & washers
HQ: Nelson Stud Welding, Inc.
7900 W Ridge Rd
Elyria OH 44035
440 329-0400

(P-12689)
NYLOK LLC
Also Called: Nylok Western Fastener
313 N Euclid Way, Anaheim (92801-6738)
PHONE...................................714 635-3993
Scott Plantiga, *Manager*
EMP: 45
SALES (corp-wide): 18MM **Privately Held**
SIC: 3452 Bolts, nuts, rivets & washers
PA: Nylok, Llc
15260 Hallmark Ct
Macomb MI 48042
586 786-0100

(P-12690)
POWER FASTENERS INC
650 E 60th St, Los Angeles (90001-1012)
P.O. Box 512056 (90051-0056)
PHONE...................................323 232-4362
Patrick Harrington, *President*
▲ EMP: 30
SQ FT: 35,000
SALES (est): 5.1MM **Privately Held**
WEB: www.powerfasteners.com
SIC: 3452 3448 Bolts, nuts, rivets & washers; prefabricated metal components

(P-12691)
RISCO INC
390 Risco Cir, Beaumont (92223-2676)
PHONE...................................951 769-2899
Joseph A Frainee II, *CEO*
Cynthia R Frainee, *Vice Pres*
Michael Wilcox, *Opers Staff*
EMP: 30 EST: 1964
SQ FT: 30,000
SALES: 3MM **Privately Held**
WEB: www.risco-fasteners.com
SIC: 3452 Bolts, metal; rivets, metal

(P-12692)
SCHRILLO COMPANY LLC
16750 Schoenborn St, North Hills (91343-6192)
PHONE...................................818 894-8241
Edward Schrillo, *Mng Member*
Donna Talamantez, *Treasurer*
Anthony Schrillo, *Exec VP*
Jeri Nowlen, *Admin Sec*
Monica Rivera, *Purchasing*
▲ EMP: 40
SQ FT: 60,000
SALES (est): 9.3MM **Privately Held**
WEB: www.schrillo.com
SIC: 3452 Screws, metal

(P-12693)
SPS TECHNOLOGIES LLC
Also Called: Pb Fasteners
1700 W 132nd St, Gardena (90249-2008)
PHONE...................................310 323-6222

Sandra Calderon, *VP Human Res*
EMP: 260
SALES (corp-wide): 225.3B **Publicly Held**
SIC: 3452 Screws, metal
HQ: Sps Technologies, Llc
301 Highland Ave
Jenkintown PA 19046
215 572-3000

(P-12694)
SPS TECHNOLOGIES LLC
Air Industries
12570 Knott St, Garden Grove (92841-3932)
PHONE...................714 892-5571
Michael Wu, *Controller*
Tim Che, *Info Tech Dir*
Toby Oberholtzer, *Plant Mgr*
Horacio Padilla, *Foreman/Supr*
Edward Park, *Director*
EMP: 50
SALES (corp-wide): 225.3B **Publicly Held**
WEB: www.spst.com
SIC: 3452 Bolts, metal
HQ: Sps Technologies, Llc
301 Highland Ave
Jenkintown PA 19046
215 572-3000

(P-12695)
STUD WELDING SYSTEMS INC
15306 Proctor Ave, City of Industry (91745-1023)
PHONE...................626 330-7434
Gary Edward, *CEO*
EMP: 20
SALES (est): 3.3MM **Privately Held**
WEB: www.sws4studs.com
SIC: 3452 3548 Rivets, metal; welding apparatus

(P-12696)
SUNLAND AEROSPACE FASTENERS
12920 Pierce St, Pacoima (91331-2526)
PHONE...................818 485-8929
Jack Wilson, *CEO*
EMP: 14
SQ FT: 11,000
SALES: 1.1MM **Privately Held**
SIC: 3452 Bolts, nuts, rivets & washers

(P-12697)
TWIST TITE MFG INC
13344 Cambridge St, Santa Fe Springs (90670-4904)
PHONE...................562 229-0990
Spiro Aykias, *CEO*
Martha Leonard, *Admin Mgr*
EMP: 32
SQ FT: 18,200
SALES (est): 6.1MM **Privately Held**
WEB: www.twisttitemfg.com
SIC: 3452 Bolts, nuts, rivets & washers

(P-12698)
U-C COMPONENTS INC (PA)
18700 Adams Ct, Morgan Hill (95037-2804)
P.O. Box 430 (95038-0430)
PHONE...................408 782-1929
Nancy Anderson, *President*
EMP: 23
SQ FT: 16,000
SALES: 5MM **Privately Held**
WEB: www.uccomponents.com
SIC: 3452 Screws, metal; washers, metal

(P-12699)
VALLEY-TODECO INC (DH)
Also Called: Arconic Fastening Systems
12975 Bradley Ave, Sylmar (91342-3852)
PHONE...................800 992-4444
Jim Cotello, *President*
▲ EMP: 36
SQ FT: 105,000
SALES (est): 16.5MM
SALES (corp-wide): 14B **Publicly Held**
SIC: 3452 5085 Bolts, nuts, rivets & washers; fasteners, industrial: nuts, bolts, screws, etc.

HQ: Arconic Global Fasteners & Rings, Inc.
3990a Heritage Oak Ct
Simi Valley CA 93063
805 527-3600

3462 Iron & Steel Forgings

(P-12700)
A-1 ORNAMENTAL IRONWORKS INC
4637 E White Ave, Fresno (93702-1623)
PHONE...................559 251-1447
Alfredo Arreguin, *President*
EMP: 10
SQ FT: 1,080
SALES (est): 748K **Privately Held**
SIC: 3462 3446 Ornamental metal forgings, ferrous; architectural metalwork

(P-12701)
ADVANCED STRUCTURAL TECH INC
Also Called: Asa
950 Richmond Ave, Oxnard (93030-7212)
PHONE...................805 204-9133
Robert Melsness, *President*
Doug Jone, *General Mgr*
Kevin Black, *Engineer*
April Pence, *Engineer*
Dawn Fowler, *Human Res Mgr*
▼ EMP: 135
SALES (est): 33MM **Privately Held**
SIC: 3462 Aircraft forgings, ferrous

(P-12702)
AJAX FORGE COMPANY (PA)
1956 E 48th St, Vernon (90058-2006)
PHONE...................323 582-6307
Fred Goble, *President*
Steve Mc Elrath, *Shareholder*
Carol Mc Neal, *Controller*
EMP: 20
SQ FT: 10,000
SALES (est): 3.3MM **Privately Held**
SIC: 3462 Iron & steel forgings

(P-12703)
AJAX FORGE COMPANY
1960 E 48th St, Vernon (90058-2006)
PHONE...................323 582-6307
Fred Goble, *Manager*
EMP: 20
SQ FT: 22,443
SALES (corp-wide): 3.3MM **Privately Held**
SIC: 3462 Iron & steel forgings
PA: Ajax Forge Company
1956 E 48th St
Vernon CA 90058
323 582-6307

(P-12704)
BAY EQUIPMENT CO INC
44221 S Grimmer Blvd, Fremont (94538-6309)
PHONE...................510 226-8800
Pat Pecoraro, *President*
Gerry Pecoraro, *Vice Pres*
EMP: 12
SQ FT: 18,000
SALES (est): 2.3MM **Privately Held**
WEB: www.bayequipmentco.com
SIC: 3462 5082 Construction or mining equipment forgings, ferrous; scaffolding

(P-12705)
BERKELEY FORGE & TOOL INC
1331 Eastshore Hwy, Berkeley (94710-1320)
PHONE...................510 525-5117
Peter Bierwith, *President*
Paul Bierwith, *Shareholder*
Robert Bierwith, *Corp Secy*
Ed Hinckley, *Vice Pres*
Michael Meidow, *Vice Pres*
▲ EMP: 80
SQ FT: 50,000
SALES (est): 23.1MM **Privately Held**
WEB: www.berkforge.com
SIC: 3462 Construction or mining equipment forgings, ferrous

(P-12706)
COULTER FORGE TECHNOLOGY INC
Also Called: Coulter Steel and Forge
1494 67th St, Emeryville (94608-1016)
P.O. Box 8008 (94662-0901)
PHONE...................510 420-3500
Peter Bierwith, *President*
Robert Bierwith, *Vice Pres*
Wayne Lehnert, *General Mgr*
Cola Chan, *Asst Controller*
John Martin, *QC Mgr*
▲ EMP: 18
SQ FT: 20,000
SALES (est): 4.1MM **Privately Held**
WEB: www.coulter-forge.com
SIC: 3462 Iron & steel forgings

(P-12707)
ESCO INDUSTRIES INC
1755 Iowa Ave Bldg A, Riverside (92507-0525)
P.O. Box 52568 (92517-3568)
PHONE...................951 782-2130
Chung Ll Lin, *President*
▲ EMP: 15
SALES (est): 47.1MM **Privately Held**
SIC: 3462 Automotive & internal combustion engine forgings

(P-12708)
FIRTH RIXSON INC
11711 Arrow Rte, Rancho Cucamonga (91730-4902)
PHONE...................909 483-2200
EMP: 21
SALES (corp-wide): 23.9B **Publicly Held**
SIC: 3462
HQ: Firth Rixson, Inc.
1616 Harvard Ave 53
Newburgh Heights OH 44105
860 760-1040

(P-12709)
FORGED METALS INC
Also Called: Arconic Fstening Systems Rings
10685 Beech Ave, Fontana (92337-7212)
PHONE...................909 350-9260
◆ EMP: 200
SQ FT: 4,800
SALES (est): 88.3MM
SALES (corp-wide): 14B **Publicly Held**
SIC: 3462 Iron & steel forgings
PA: Arconic Inc.
201 Isabella St Ste 200
New York NY 15212
412 553-1950

(P-12710)
G & N RUBICON GEAR INC
225 Citation Cir, Corona (92880-2523)
PHONE...................951 356-3800
Cheryl A Edwards, *Ch of Bd*
Ryan B Edwards, *President*
Frank Salazar, *Admin Sec*
Marshall Alvarado, *Manager*
Andrew Weston, *Manager*
EMP: 68
SQ FT: 25,000
SALES: 10MM **Privately Held**
SIC: 3462 Gears, forged steel

(P-12711)
JAZ DISTRIBUTION INC
8485 Artesia Blvd Ste B, Buena Park (90621-4195)
PHONE...................714 521-3888
Tavis Tan, *President*
Mark Uchinao, *Vice Pres*
▲ EMP: 16
SALES: 5.8MM **Privately Held**
WEB: www.jazalloy.com
SIC: 3462 5013 Railroad wheels, axles, frogs or other equipment: forged; automotive supplies & parts

(P-12712)
KIMS WELDING AND IRON WORKS
Also Called: Kim's Fence
2331 E Orangethorpe Ave, Fullerton (92831-5330)
PHONE...................714 680-7700
David S Kim, *President*
EMP: 20

SQ FT: 5,000
SALES (est): 2.2MM **Privately Held**
SIC: 3462 1799 Ornamental metal forgings, ferrous; welding on site

(P-12713)
LUFKIN INDUSTRIES LLC
Also Called: Gear Division
3901 Fanucchi Way, Shafter (93263-9539)
PHONE...................661 746-0792
EMP: 11
SALES (corp-wide): 121.6B **Publicly Held**
SIC: 3462 Gears, forged steel
HQ: Lufkin Industries, Llc
601 S Raguet St
Lufkin TX 75904
936 634-2211

(P-12714)
MATTCO FORGE INC (PA)
16443 Minnesota Ave, Paramount (90723-4985)
PHONE...................562 634-8635
Denis B Brady, *CEO*
John Lindbeck, *President*
Daniel Fitzgerald, *Vice Pres*
Andrew Fite, *Controller*
Mark Haupert, *QC Mgr*
▲ EMP: 53
SQ FT: 150,000
SALES (est): 13.9MM **Privately Held**
WEB: www.mattcoforge.com
SIC: 3462 Iron & steel forgings

(P-12715)
NEWMAN FLANGE & FITTING CO
1649 L St, Newman (95360-1048)
P.O. Box 905 (95360-0905)
PHONE...................209 862-2977
Samuel Liebelt, *President*
Penny Mello, *Chairman*
Helmut Liebelt, *Treasurer*
▲ EMP: 70 EST: 1974
SQ FT: 1,800
SALES: 14.6MM **Privately Held**
SIC: 3462 Flange, valve & pipe fitting forgings, ferrous

(P-12716)
PACIFIC FORGE INC
10641 Etiwanda Ave, Fontana (92337-6991)
PHONE...................909 390-0701
Leland Boren, *Chairman*
Ronald D Browne, *President*
Jacqueline Dyer, *Vice Pres*
Scott Bryant, *Buyer*
Debby Croulet, *Safety Dir*
EMP: 55
SQ FT: 34,816
SALES: 20MM
SALES (corp-wide): 312.9MM **Privately Held**
WEB: www.pacificforge.com
SIC: 3462 3463 Iron & steel forgings; nonferrous forgings
PA: Avis Industrial Corporation
1909 S Main St
Upland IN 46989
765 998-8100

(P-12717)
PERFORMANCE FORGED PRODUCTS
7401 Telegraph Rd, Montebello (90640-6515)
PHONE...................323 722-3460
James Gilliland, *President*
Frank Andrus, *Shareholder*
Lois Gilliland, *Treasurer*
Christopher Ambrosini, *Engineer*
EMP: 20
SQ FT: 20,000
SALES (est): 5.8MM **Privately Held**
SIC: 3462 Automotive & internal combustion engine forgings

(P-12718)
PRECISION METAL PRODUCTS INC (HQ)
850 W Bradley Ave, El Cajon (92020-1277)
PHONE...................619 448-2711
Randy L Greely, *CEO*

Ross Worthington, *General Mgr*
Walter Love, *Manager*
▲ **EMP:** 138 **EST:** 1963
SQ FT: 92,000
SALES (est): 23.4MM
SALES (corp-wide): 260.7MM **Privately Held**
WEB: www.pmp-elcajon.com
SIC: 3462 Iron & steel forgings
PA: Hbd Industries Inc
5200 Upper Metro
Dublin OH 43017
614 526-7000

(P-12719)
PREMCO FORGE INC
5200 Tweedy Blvd, South Gate (90280-5397)
PHONE..................................323 564-6666
Brian James Patrick, *President*
Randall Roschnafsky, *Sales Mgr*
EMP: 10
SQ FT: 16,000
SALES (est): 2MM **Privately Held**
SIC: 3462 Iron & steel forgings

(P-12720)
PREMIER GEAR & MACHINING INC
2360 Pomona Rd, Corona (92880-6929)
P.O. Box 2799 (92878-2799)
PHONE..................................951 278-5505
Steve Golden, *President*
Huy Nguyen, *Treasurer*
EMP: 25
SQ FT: 21,000
SALES (est): 5.8MM **Privately Held**
WEB: www.premiergearinc.com
SIC: 3462 3599 Iron & steel forgings; machine shop, jobbing & repair

(P-12721)
PRESS FORGE COMPANY
7700 Jackson St, Paramount (90723-5073)
P.O. Box 1432 (90723-1432)
PHONE..................................562 531-4962
Jeffrey M Carlton, *CEO*
Michael Buxton, *President*
Mike Buxton, *President*
▲ **EMP:** 80
SQ FT: 32,726
SALES (est): 21MM
SALES (corp-wide): 225.3B **Publicly Held**
SIC: 3462 Iron & steel forgings
HQ: Precision Castparts Corp.
4650 Sw Mcdam Ave Ste 300
Portland OR 97239
503 946-4800

(P-12722)
SCODAN SYSTEMS INC
12373 Barringer St, South El Monte (91733-4141)
PHONE..................................626 444-1020
Eric Yang, *President*
Hector Pinedo, *Vice Pres*
EMP: 13
SQ FT: 10,000
SALES (est): 2.5MM **Privately Held**
SIC: 3462 Automotive & internal combustion engine forgings

(P-12723)
TIMKEN GEARS & SERVICES INC
Also Called: Philadelphia Gear
12935 Imperial Hwy, Santa Fe Springs (90670-4715)
PHONE..................................310 605-2600
Tony Tartaglio, *Branch Mgr*
Richard Brossia, *Manager*
EMP: 26
SALES (corp-wide): 3.5B **Publicly Held**
WEB: www.philagear.com
SIC: 3462 Gear & chain forgings; gears, forged steel; anchors, forged
HQ: Timken Gears & Services Inc.
901 E 8th Ave Ste 100
King Of Prussia PA 19406

(P-12724)
TURBO INTERNATIONAL
2151 Las Palmas Dr Ste E, Carlsbad (92011-1575)
PHONE..................................760 476-1444
Seth Carks, *CEO*
Alex Jimenez, *Accounts Mgr*
▲ **EMP:** 17
SALES (est): 3.1MM **Privately Held**
SIC: 3462 Automotive forgings, ferrous: crankshaft, engine, axle, etc.

(P-12725)
VALLEY FORGE ACQUISITION CORP
444 S Motor Ave, Azusa (91702-3231)
PHONE..................................626 969-8701
Michael K Holmes, *President*
Michael Holmes, *President*
EMP: 15
SQ FT: 37,000
SALES (est): 2.9MM
SALES (corp-wide): 68.2MM **Privately Held**
SIC: 3462 Iron & steel forgings
PA: Tuffli Company Incorporated
2780 Skypark Dr Ste 460
Torrance CA 90505
310 326-5500

(P-12726)
VI-STAR GEAR CO INC
7312 Jefferson St, Paramount (90723-4094)
PHONE..................................323 774-3750
Thomas R Redfield, *President*
Chris Redfield, *Vice Pres*
EMP: 30
SQ FT: 12,000
SALES (est): 4.8MM **Privately Held**
SIC: 3462 3728 Iron & steel forgings; gears, aircraft power transmission

(P-12727)
VOSSLOH SIGNALING USA INC
Also Called: J Manufacturing
12799 Loma Rica Dr, Grass Valley (95945-9552)
P.O. Box 600 (95945-0600)
PHONE..................................530 272-8194
Normand Frenette, *CEO*
▲ **EMP:** 24
SQ FT: 20,000
SALES (est): 5.7MM
SALES (corp-wide): 990.2MM **Privately Held**
WEB: www.jmirail.com
SIC: 3462 Railroad wheels, axles, frogs or other equipment; forged
HQ: Vossloh Track Material, Inc.
5662a Leesport Ave
Reading PA 19605
610 926-5400

3463 Nonferrous Forgings

(P-12728)
ALUM-ALLOY CO INC
603 S Hope Ave, Ontario (91761-1824)
PHONE..................................909 986-0410
David Howell, *CEO*
Clark Howell, *President*
Marilyn Howell, *Corp Secy*
Michelle Howell, *Office Mgr*
EMP: 40
SQ FT: 20,000
SALES (est): 5.6MM **Privately Held**
SIC: 3463 3365 Aluminum forgings; aluminum foundries

(P-12729)
ALUMINUM PRECISION PDTS INC
1001 Mcwane Blvd, Oxnard (93033-9016)
PHONE..................................805 488-4401
Richard Hayes, *Branch Mgr*
Jennifer Meyers, *General Mgr*
Jeff Hall, *Maintence Staff*
EMP: 125
SQ FT: 15,000
SALES (corp-wide): 212MM **Privately Held**
SIC: 3463 Aluminum forgings

PA: Aluminum Precision Products, Inc.
3333 W Warner Ave
Santa Ana CA 92704
714 546-8125

(P-12730)
ALUMINUM PRECISION PDTS INC
Also Called: Jigmasters Tool & Gauge
502 E Alton Ave, Santa Ana (92707-4244)
PHONE..................................714 549-4075
William Peacock, *Manager*
EMP: 100
SALES (corp-wide): 212MM **Privately Held**
WEB: www.aluminumprecision.com
SIC: 3463 7389 3599 Aluminum forgings; grinding, precision: commercial or industrial; machine shop, jobbing & repair
PA: Aluminum Precision Products, Inc.
3333 W Warner Ave
Santa Ana CA 92704
714 546-8125

(P-12731)
CONTINENTAL FORGE COMPANY (PA)
412 E El Segundo Blvd, Compton (90222-2317)
PHONE..................................310 603-1014
Margaret A Haueisen, *President*
Jesus Romero, *Prgrmr*
Marion Turner, *Maintence Staff*
Sallye Singleton, *Manager*
EMP: 85 **EST:** 1969
SQ FT: 27,000
SALES (est): 18.5MM **Privately Held**
WEB: www.cforge.com
SIC: 3463 Aluminum forgings

(P-12732)
INDEPENDENT FORGE COMPANY
692 N Batavia St, Orange (92868-1221)
PHONE..................................714 997-7337
Rosemary Ruiz, *President*
Joe Ramirez, *Vice Pres*
Gloria Lopez, *Admin Sec*
Patricia Taoipu, *Analyst*
▲ **EMP:** 40
SQ FT: 11,900
SALES (est): 7.2MM **Privately Held**
WEB: www.independentforge.com
SIC: 3463 Aluminum forgings

(P-12733)
LINDSEY MANUFACTURING CO
Also Called: Lindsey International Co.
760 N Georgia Ave, Azusa (91702-2249)
P.O. Box 877 (91702-0877)
PHONE..................................626 969-3471
Keith E Lindsey, *President*
Frederick Findley, *CFO*
Saul Silva, *CFO*
Lela Lindsey, *Admin Sec*
Arthur Sierra, *IT Specialist*
▲ **EMP:** 110 **EST:** 1947
SQ FT: 60,000
SALES (est): 44.8MM **Privately Held**
WEB: www.lindsey-usa.com
SIC: 3463 3644 Pole line hardware forgings, nonferrous; noncurrent-carrying wiring services

(P-12734)
LUXFER INC
Superform USA
6825 Jurupa Ave, Riverside (92504-1039)
PHONE..................................951 351-4100
Michael Reynolds, *Vice Pres*
EMP: 38
SALES (corp-wide): 487.9MM **Privately Held**
WEB: www.luxfer-ecare.com
SIC: 3463 Aluminum forgings
HQ: Luxfer Inc.
3016 Kansas Ave Bldg 1
Riverside CA 92507
951 684-5110

(P-12735)
QUALITY ALUMINUM FORGE LLC (HQ)
793 N Cypress St, Orange (92867-6605)
PHONE..................................714 639-8191

Michael S Lipscomb,
Ismael Calvillo, *Administration*
Brian Pam, *Info Tech Dir*
Kevin Vu, *Info Tech Dir*
Maria Avendano, *Info Tech Mgr*
EMP: 68 **EST:** 2011
SALES (est): 39.1MM
SALES (corp-wide): 111.2MM **Publicly Held**
SIC: 3463 Aluminum forgings
PA: Sifco Industries, Inc.
970 E 64th St
Cleveland OH 44103
216 881-8600

(P-12736)
SIERRA ALLOYS COMPANY
5467 Ayon Ave, Irwindale (91706-2044)
PHONE..................................626 969-6711
Craig Culaciati, *CEO*
Jeff Augustyn, *Exec VP*
Ed Brennan, *Vice Pres*
▲ **EMP:** 52 **EST:** 1974
SQ FT: 75,000
SALES (est): 17.8MM **Privately Held**
WEB: www.sierraalloys.com
SIC: 3463 3494 3312 Nonferrous forgings; valves & pipe fittings; blast furnaces & steel mills

(P-12737)
SUPERFORM USA INCORPORATED
6825 Jurupa Ave, Riverside (92504-1039)
P.O. Box 5375 (92517-5375)
PHONE..................................951 351-4100
Michael Reynolds, *Vice Pres*
▼ **EMP:** 29
SQ FT: 25,000
SALES (est): 205.3K
SALES (corp-wide): 487.9MM **Privately Held**
SIC: 3463 Aluminum forgings
HQ: Luxfer Inc.
3016 Kansas Ave Bldg 1
Riverside CA 92507
951 684-5110

(P-12738)
TURBINE ENG CMPNENTS TECH CORP
Also Called: Tech Powers
8839 Pioneer Blvd, Santa Fe Springs (90670-2007)
P.O. Box 2966 (90670-0966)
PHONE..................................562 908-0200
Ronald L Patlian, *Branch Mgr*
Long Truong, *Prgrmr*
Melissa Roberts, *Materials Mgr*
George Florez, *Marketing Staff*
Barry Lakin, *Manager*
EMP: 105 **Privately Held**
WEB: www.tectcorp.com
SIC: 3463 3599 Engine or turbine forgings, nonferrous; machine shop, jobbing & repair
HQ: Turbine Engine Components Technologies Corporation
334 Beechwood Rd Ste 303
Fort Mitchell KY 41017
859 426-0090

(P-12739)
WJB BEARINGS INC
535 Brea Canyon Rd, City of Industry (91789-3001)
PHONE..................................909 598-6238
John Jun Jiang, *CEO*
▲ **EMP:** 25
SQ FT: 30,000
SALES (est): 5.5MM **Privately Held**
SIC: 3463 5085 Bearing & bearing race forgings, nonferrous; bearings

3465 Automotive Stampings

(P-12740)
AC AIR TECHNOLOGY INC
13832 Magnolia Ave, Chino (91710-7027)
PHONE..................................855 884-7222
Anthony Yu Chan, *CEO*
EMP: 11 **EST:** 2012

P R O D U C T S & S V C S

SALES (est): 85.8K **Privately Held**
SIC: 3465 Body parts, automobile:
stamped metal

(P-12741)
APOLLO METAL SPINNING CO INC
15315 Illinois Ave, Paramount
(90723-4108)
PHONE....................................562 634-5141
George Di Matteo, *President*
Josephine Di Matteo, *Corp Secy*
EMP: 15
SQ FT: 4,650
SALES: 1.2MM **Privately Held**
SIC: 3465 3469 5015 Hub caps, automo-
bile: stamped metal; spinning metal for
the trade; automotive parts & supplies,
used

(P-12742)
BECS PACIFIC LTD
19456 Colombo St Ste B, Bakersfield
(93308-9847)
PHONE....................................661 397-9400
Christopher Bramall, *Branch Mgr*
EMP: 15
SALES (corp-wide): 17.4MM **Privately Held**
SIC: 3465 Body parts, automobile:
stamped metal
PA: Becs Pacific Ltd
2825 Pellissier Pl
City Of Industry CA 90601
562 908-6890

(P-12743)
C W MOSS AUTO PARTS INC
402 W Chapman Ave, Orange
(92866-1308)
PHONE....................................714 639-3083
Derek Looney, *President*
EMP: 10
SQ FT: 15,108
SALES (est): 1.5MM **Privately Held**
WEB: www.cwmoss.com
SIC: 3465 5531 Body parts, automobile:
stamped metal; automotive parts

(P-12744)
CARR PATTERN CO INC
27419 Via Industria, Temecula
(92590-3752)
PHONE....................................951 719-1068
Jeff Carr, *CEO*
Jeff A Carr, *CEO*
EMP: 10 EST: 1945
SALES (est): 217.3K **Privately Held**
WEB: www.carr.com
SIC: 3465 5051 Body parts, automobile:
stamped metal; metals service centers &
offices

(P-12745)
KYOHO MANUFACTURING CALIFORNIA
Also Called: Khmca
809 Walker Ave, Oakland (94610-2018)
PHONE....................................209 941-6200
Shigenori Hamada, *President*
Bill Borten, *Vice Pres*
▲ EMP: 168
SALES (est): 17.5MM **Privately Held**
SIC: 3465 Automotive stampings
HQ: Kyoho Machine Works,Ltd.
6, Toyotacho
Toyota AIC 471-0

(P-12746)
MARINE FENDERS INTL INC
909 Mahar Ave, Wilmington (90744-3828)
PHONE....................................310 834-7037
Gerald Thermos, *President*
◆ EMP: 25
SQ FT: 22,000
SALES (est): 8.1MM **Privately Held**
WEB: www.marinefendersintl.com
SIC: 3465 Fenders, automobile: stamped
or pressed metal

(P-12747)
ROOTLIEB INC
815 S Soderquist Rd, Turlock
(95380-5723)
P.O. Box 1810 (95381-1810)
PHONE....................................209 632-2203
Thomas H Rootlieb, *President*
EMP: 13
SQ FT: 25,000
SALES (est): 1.6MM **Privately Held**
WEB: www.rootlieb.com
SIC: 3465 Fenders, automobile: stamped
or pressed metal; body parts, automobile:
stamped metal

(P-12748)
SALEEN AUTOMOTIVE INC (PA)
2735 Wardlow Rd, Corona (92882-2869)
PHONE....................................800 888-8945
Steve Saleen, *Ch of Bd*
Amy Boylan, *President*
David Fiene, *CFO*
EMP: 22
SALES: 13.7MM **Publicly Held**
SIC: 3465 3711 Body parts, automobile:
stamped metal; automobile assembly, in-
cluding specialty automobiles; automobile
bodies, passenger car, not including en-
gine, etc.

(P-12749)
SEYMOUR LEVINGER & CO
Also Called: Spectre Performance
1455 Citrus St, Riverside (92507-1603)
PHONE....................................909 673-9800
Amir Rosenbaum, *CEO*
Mike Morrow, *VP Sales*
▲ EMP: 40
SQ FT: 16,000
SALES (est): 5.8MM **Privately Held**
WEB: www.spectreperformance.com
SIC: 3465 Body parts, automobile:
stamped metal

(P-12750)
T-REX TRUCK PRODUCTS INC
Also Called: T-Rex Grilles
2365 Railroad St, Corona (92880-5411)
PHONE....................................800 287-5900
Behrouz Mizban, *President*
Tom Ameduri, *Sales Staff*
▼ EMP: 55
SQ FT: 45,000
SALES (est): 11.3MM **Privately Held**
SIC: 3465 Automotive stampings

(P-12751)
TROY SHEET METAL WORKS INC
Also Called: Troy Products
1024 S Vail Ave, Montebello (90640-6020)
PHONE....................................323 720-4100
Carl Moses Kahalewai, *CEO*
Paul Alvarado, *Shareholder*
Marci Norkin, *Shareholder*
Carol Stewart, *Shareholder*
Rigo Guadiana, *CFO*
EMP: 33 EST: 1930
SQ FT: 16,000
SALES (est): 9.4MM **Privately Held**
WEB: www.troyproducts.com
SIC: 3465 3444 3714 3564 Automotive
stampings; sheet metalwork; motor vehi-
cle parts & accessories; blowers & fans

3466 Crowns & Closures

(P-12752)
RIEKE CORPORATION
1200 Valley House Dr # 100, Rohnert Park
(94928-4934)
PHONE....................................707 238-9250
Rohnert Park, *Branch Mgr*
EMP: 180
SALES (corp-wide): 877.1MM **Publicly Held**
SIC: 3466 Closures, stamped metal
HQ: Rieke Corporation
500 W 7th St
Auburn IN 46706
260 925-3700

3469 Metal Stampings, NEC

(P-12753)
4X DEVELOPMENT INC
2650 E 28th St, Signal Hill (90755-2202)
PHONE....................................562 424-2225
Alex Horeczko, *President*
Scott Dudek, *Vice Pres*
EMP: 10
SQ FT: 11,000
SALES: 3MM **Privately Held**
WEB: www.extremesupply.com
SIC: 3469 Helmets, steel

(P-12754)
A & F METAL PRODUCTS
520 Farnel Rd Ste L, Santa Maria
(93458-4993)
PHONE....................................805 346-2040
Art Andrade, *Owner*
EMP: 10
SALES: 850K **Privately Held**
SIC: 3469 Metal stampings

(P-12755)
A & J MANUFACTURING COMPANY
70 Icon, Foothill Ranch (92610-3000)
PHONE....................................714 544-9570
Ada Gentry, *Ch of Bd*
Pam Woodward, *Treasurer*
Janice Lyerly, *Vice Pres*
Ian Amstedter, *Info Tech Dir*
Mike Gates, *Engineer*
EMP: 32
SQ FT: 40,000
SALES (est): 6.6MM **Privately Held**
WEB: www.aj-racks.com
SIC: 3469 Electronic enclosures, stamped
or pressed metal

(P-12756)
A-W ENGINEERING COMPANY INC
8528 Dice Rd, Santa Fe Springs
(90670-2590)
PHONE....................................562 945-1041
Guy Hansen, *President*
Anthony Giangrande, *Corp Secy*
EMP: 36 EST: 1965
SQ FT: 38,000
SALES (est): 8.9MM **Privately Held**
WEB: www.aw-eng.com
SIC: 3469 3544 Stamping metal for the
trade; special dies & tools

(P-12757)
AAA STAMPING INC
1630 Shearwater St, Ontario (91761-5710)
P.O. Box 4027 (91761-1001)
PHONE....................................909 947-4151
Tom Hendrickson, *President*
Sal Chico, *Vice Pres*
EMP: 20
SQ FT: 15,100
SALES (est): 3.5MM **Privately Held**
SIC: 3469 Stamping metal for the trade

(P-12758)
AARON DUTT ENTERPRISES INC
Also Called: Bowers Machining
1140 N Kraemer Blvd Ste M, Anaheim
(92806-1919)
PHONE....................................714 632-7035
Ajaya Kumar Dutt, *President*
Jiwan Dutt, *Vice Pres*
EMP: 10
SQ FT: 4,000
SALES: 730K **Privately Held**
SIC: 3469 8711 Machine parts, stamped
or pressed metal; engineering services

(P-12759)
ACRONTOS MANUFACTURING INC
Also Called: Al Industries
1641 E Saint Gertrude Pl, Santa Ana
(92705-5311)
PHONE....................................714 850-9133
Ngoc V Hoang, *President*
EMP: 30
SQ FT: 22,000

SALES (est): 6.1MM **Privately Held**
WEB: www.alindustries.com
SIC: 3469 3599 3441 Metal stampings;
machine & other job shop work; fabricated structural metal

(P-12760)
ACTION STAMPING INC
517 S Glendora Ave, Glendora
(91741-6212)
P.O. Box 778 (91740-0778)
PHONE....................................626 914-7466
Henry Reynolds, *CEO*
Terry Reynolds, *President*
Mike Chavez, *Opers Mgr*
▲ EMP: 42
SQ FT: 55,000
SALES (est): 7.6MM **Privately Held**
SIC: 3469 Stamping metal for the trade

(P-12761)
ADVANCED HONEYCOMB TECH
1015 Linda Vista Dr Ste C, San Marcos
(92078-2609)
PHONE....................................760 744-3200
Richard Greven, *President*
Rick Greven, *Vice Pres*
Money Greven, *Admin Sec*
EMP: 25
SQ FT: 10,000
SALES: 3.5MM **Privately Held**
WEB: www.ahtinc.com
SIC: 3469 2679 Honeycombed metal;
honeycomb core & board: made from pur-
chased material

(P-12762)
ALCO TECH INC
Also Called: Crome Gallery
12750 Raymer St Unit 2, North Hollywood
(91605-4227)
PHONE....................................818 503-9209
Ben Tavakkoli, *President*
EMP: 11
SALES (est): 133.1K **Privately Held**
SIC: 3469 3479 7692 4581 Metal stamp-
ings; painting, coating & hot dipping;
welding repair; aircraft maintenance & re-
pair services

(P-12763)
ALL NEW STAMPING CO
10801 Lower Azusa Rd, El Monte
(91731-1307)
P.O. Box 5948 (91734-1948)
PHONE....................................626 443-8813
Donald Schuil, *President*
Robert Larson, *Corp Secy*
EMP: 150 EST: 1962
SQ FT: 40,000
SALES: 13MM **Privately Held**
WEB: www.allnewstamping.com
SIC: 3469 3441 3444 Stamping metal for
the trade; fabricated structural metal;
sheet metal specialties, not stamped

(P-12764)
ALPINE INDUSTRIES
5820 Serrano Dr, Mount Shasta
(96067-9127)
P.O. Box 277 (96067-0277)
PHONE....................................530 926-2460
David Webb, *Owner*
EMP: 13
SALES (est): 803.5K **Privately Held**
SIC: 3469 Metal stampings

(P-12765)
AMITY WASHER & STAMPING CO
10926 Painter Ave, Santa Fe Springs
(90670-4529)
PHONE....................................562 941-1259
James M Mc Ginley, *President*
Nancy Wilson, *Admin Sec*
EMP: 25
SQ FT: 15,000
SALES (est): 2.6MM **Privately Held**
WEB: www.amity.com
SIC: 3469 3544 Metal stampings; special
dies, tools, jigs & fixtures

(P-12766)
APT METAL FABRICATORS INC
11164 Bradley Ave, Pacoima (91331-2405)
PHONE....................................818 896-7478

▲ = Import ▼=Export
◆ =Import/Export

Dennis M Vigo, *President*
Susan Vigo, *Corp Secy*
Monica Lovato, *Office Mgr*
Monica Gutierrez, *Site Mgr*
Tom Cekalovich, *Plant Mgr*
▼ **EMP:** 26 **EST:** 1975
SQ FT: 18,000
SALES (est): 6.4MM **Privately Held**
WEB: www.aptmetal.com
SIC: 3469 Stamping metal for the trade

(P-12767)
ASCENT MANUFACTURING LLC
2545 W Via Palma, Anaheim (92801-2624)
PHONE................................714 540-6414
Travis Mullen, *CEO*
David Kramer, *VP Sales*
EMP: 34
SQ FT: 17,000
SALES (est): 3.9MM **Privately Held**
WEB: www.ascentmfg.com
SIC: 3469 1796 Machine parts, stamped
or pressed metal; machinery installation

(P-12768)
B-J MACHINE INC
1763 N Batavia St, Orange (92865-4103)
PHONE................................714 685-0712
Larry T Vu, *President*
EMP: 10 **EST:** 1998
SQ FT: 6,000
SALES (est): 1.2MM **Privately Held**
SIC: 3469 Machine parts, stamped or
pressed metal

(P-12769)
BANDEL MFG INC
4459 Alger St, Los Angeles (90039-1292)
PHONE................................818 246-7493
Ed Finley, *President*
Chester Carlson, *Exec VP*
EMP: 23 **EST:** 1947
SQ FT: 15,000
SALES (est): 4.9MM **Privately Held**
WEB: www.bandel.com
SIC: 3469 Stamping metal for the trade

(P-12770)
BERTOLIN ENGINEERING CORP
485 Robert Ave, Santa Clara (95050-2918)
PHONE................................408 988-0166
Frank Bertolin, *President*
EMP: 13
SQ FT: 5,000
SALES (est): 1.6MM **Privately Held**
SIC: 3469 8711 Automobile license tags,
stamped metal; mechanical engineering

(P-12771)
BINDER METAL PRODUCTS INC
14909 S Broadway, Gardena (90248-1817)
P.O. Box 2306 (90247-0306)
PHONE................................626 602-3824
Steve Binder, *President*
Ana Weber, *CFO*
Jerry Shain, *Vice Pres*
Olivia Gutierrez, *Human Res Mgr*
Melissa Loera, *Human Res Mgr*
▲ **EMP:** 75 **EST:** 1925
SQ FT: 35,000
SALES (est): 20.8MM **Privately Held**
WEB: www.bindermetal.com
SIC: 3469 Metal stampings

(P-12772)
BLOOMERS METAL STAMPINGS INC
28615 Braxton Ave, Valencia (91355-4112)
PHONE................................661 257-2955
Matt Holland, *CEO*
Perry Bloomer, *President*
Ella H Bloomer, *CFO*
EMP: 30
SQ FT: 25,000
SALES (est): 5.6MM **Privately Held**
WEB: www.bloomersmetal.com
SIC: 3469 Stamping metal for the trade

(P-12773)
BOX MASTER
17000 Sierra Hwy, Canyon Country
(91351-1615)
PHONE................................661 298-2666
Linda Neville, *Owner*
EMP: 25

SALES (est): 1.6MM **Privately Held**
WEB: www.boxmaster.com
SIC: 3469 Boxes: tool, lunch, mail, etc.:
stamped metal

(P-12774)
BRAXTON CARIBBEAN MFG CO INC
2641 Walnut Ave, Tustin (92780-7005)
PHONE................................714 508-3570
Thomas Ordway, *President*
Robert Dionne, *Principal*
Joesph Triano, *Principal*
EMP: 62
SALES (est): 9.6MM **Privately Held**
WEB: www.braxtonca.com
SIC: 3469 Metal stampings

(P-12775)
BRICE TOOL & STAMPING
1170 N Van Horne Way, Anaheim
(92806-2506)
PHONE................................714 630-6400
Russel Brice, *President*
EMP: 15 **EST:** 1956
SQ FT: 10,000
SALES (est): 2.2MM **Privately Held**
WEB: www.bricetool.com
SIC: 3469 3544 Stamping metal for the
trade; dies, steel rule

(P-12776)
C&C METAL FORM & TOOLING INC
Also Called: Promag
10654 Garfield Ave, South Gate
(90280-7334)
PHONE................................562 861-9554
Chris Chiang, *President*
Mike Ballard, *General Mgr*
Drew Kelley, *Marketing Staff*
Kristina Kessler, *Sales Staff*
Payton Schachtell, *Sales Staff*
EMP: 25
SALES (est): 3.2MM **Privately Held**
WEB: www.promagindustries.com
SIC: 3469 5941 3482 7389 Stamping
metal for the trade; sporting goods & bicy-
cle shops; small arms ammunition; design
services

(P-12777)
CABRAC INC
13250 Paxton St, Pacoima (91331-2356)
PHONE................................818 834-0177
Hans Kaufmann, *President*
Sue Kaufmann, *Executive*
EMP: 20 **EST:** 1973
SQ FT: 20,000
SALES (est): 3.4MM **Privately Held**
WEB: www.cabrac.com
SIC: 3469 Electronic enclosures, stamped
or pressed metal

(P-12778)
CALFABCO (PA)
Also Called: Mr Washerman
1432 Chico Ave, South El Monte
(91733-2936)
PHONE................................323 265-1205
Boris Elbaum, *President*
Jerry Garcia, *Asst Mgr*
EMP: 15 **EST:** 1966
SQ FT: 6,000
SALES (est): 2.6MM **Privately Held**
SIC: 3469 Stamping metal for the trade

(P-12779)
CAMISASCA AUTOMOTIVE MFG INC
20341 Hermana Cir, Lake Forest
(92630-8701)
PHONE................................949 452-0195
Henry Camisasca, *CEO*
EMP: 20
SALES (corp-wide): 5.2MM **Privately Held**
SIC: 3469 Automobile license tags,
stamped metal
PA: Camisasca Automotive Manufacturing,
Inc.
20352 Hermana Cir
Lake Forest CA 92630
949 452-0195

(P-12780)
CAMISASCA AUTOMOTIVE MFG INC (PA)
20352 Hermana Cir, Lake Forest
(92630-8701)
PHONE................................949 452-0195
Henry Camisasca, *CEO*
Georgann Camisasca, *CFO*
Gabriel Mejia, *Manager*
▲ **EMP:** 20
SQ FT: 16,000
SALES (est): 5.2MM **Privately Held**
WEB: www.camincusa.com
SIC: 3469 Automobile license tags,
stamped metal

(P-12781)
CARAN PRECISION ENGRG MFG CORP
Spiveco
2830 Orbiter St, Brea (92821-6224)
PHONE................................714 447-5400
Raymond Sheeks, *President*
EMP: 90
SALES (corp-wide): 24.6MM **Privately Held**
WEB: www.caranprecision.com
SIC: 3469 3599 Metal stampings; machine
& other job shop work
PA: Caran Precision Engineering & Manu-
facturing Corp.
2830 Orbiter St
Brea CA 92821
714 447-5400

(P-12782)
CARSONS INC
Also Called: Carson's Coatings
550 Industrial Dr Ste 200, Galt
(95632-1647)
PHONE................................209 745-2387
Duane Carson, *President*
Terry Carson, *Vice Pres*
▲ **EMP:** 20
SQ FT: 53,000
SALES (est): 3MM **Privately Held**
WEB: www.carsonscoatings.com
SIC: 3469 Architectural panels or parts,
porcelain enameled

(P-12783)
CHEEK ENGINEERING & STAMPING
1732 Mcgaw Ave, Irvine (92614-5732)
PHONE................................714 832-9480
Chris Huff, *President*
Julia Huff, *Vice Pres*
EMP: 10
SQ FT: 25,000
SALES (est): 1.3MM **Privately Held**
WEB: www.cheekengineering.com
SIC: 3469 Stamping metal for the trade

(P-12784)
CIMRMAAN IVO
Also Called: Deft Precision Machining
7550 Trade St, San Diego (92121-2412)
PHONE................................858 693-1536
Ivo Cimrmaan, *Owner*
EMP: 11
SQ FT: 4,000
SALES (est): 1.2MM **Privately Held**
SIC: 3469 Machine parts, stamped or
pressed metal

(P-12785)
CKD INDUSTRIES INC
501 E Jamie Ave, La Habra (90631-6842)
PHONE................................714 871-5600
Rolf Hess, *President*
Rose Hess, *Vice Pres*
EMP: 12
SQ FT: 15,000
SALES: 1MM **Privately Held**
SIC: 3469 8711 3544 Metal stampings;
designing: ship, boat, machine & product;
special dies & tools

(P-12786)
COMMERCIAL METAL FORMING INC
341 W Collins Ave, Orange (92867-5505)
PHONE................................714 532-6321
William Kowal, *President*
Donald E Washdewicz, *Vice Pres*

Phil Smith, *Engineer*
Marie Votino, *Buyer*
Kymberli Wagner, *Buyer*
▲ **EMP:** 25
SALES (est): 11.9MM **Privately Held**
SIC: 3469 Metal stampings

(P-12787)
CONSOLIDATED FABRICATORS CORP
901 Simmerhorn Rd, Galt (95632-8501)
PHONE................................209 745-4604
Laurance Beralino, *Manager*
EMP: 80
SALES (corp-wide): 106.8MM **Privately Held**
WEB: www.con-fab.com
SIC: 3469 Metal stampings
PA: Consolidated Fabricators Corporation
14620 Arminta St
Van Nuys CA 91402
818 901-1005

(P-12788)
CONTEXT ENGINEERING CO
Also Called: Sidco Labelling Systems
1043 Di Giulio Ave, Santa Clara
(95050-2805)
PHONE................................408 748-9112
David Clemson, *President*
Martin Clemson, *Vice Pres*
Lucy Del Real, *General Mgr*
Maral Panossian, *General Mgr*
Mary Clemson, *Admin Sec*
▲ **EMP:** 25
SQ FT: 4,500
SALES (est): 3.2MM **Privately Held**
WEB: www.contextengineering.com
SIC: 3469 5131 5084 Electronic enclo-
sures, stamped or pressed metal; labels;
industrial machinery & equipment

(P-12789)
CRENSHAW DIE AND MFG CORP
7432 Prince Dr, Huntington Beach
(92647-4553)
PHONE................................949 475-5505
James V Ireland, *CEO*
Dale Congelliere, *President*
Sharon Piers, *CFO*
Jim Miller, *Vice Pres*
David Umana, *Purch Mgr*
EMP: 55
SQ FT: 38,000
SALES (est): 12.2MM **Privately Held**
WEB: www.crenshawdiemfg.com
SIC: 3469 Stamping metal for the trade

(P-12790)
CYGNET STAMPNG & FABRICTNG INC
916 Western Ave, Glendale (91201)
PHONE................................818 240-7574
Ron Ernst, *Manager*
Scott McGrath, *Vice Pres*
EMP: 10
SALES (corp-wide): 4.6MM **Privately Held**
SIC: 3469 Stamping metal for the trade
PA: Cygnet Stamping And Fabricating, Inc.,
A Swan Technologies Corporation
613 Justin Ave
Glendale CA 91201
818 240-7574

(P-12791)
CYGNET STAMPNG & FABRICTNG INC (PA)
613 Justin Ave, Glendale (91201-2326)
PHONE................................818 240-7574
Marko Swan, *President*
E Michael Swan, *Vice Pres*
John Swan, *Vice Pres*
EMP: 30
SQ FT: 28,000
SALES (est): 4.6MM **Privately Held**
SIC: 3469 Stamping metal for the trade

(P-12792)
DECCO GRAPHICS INC
24411 Frampton Ave, Harbor City
(90710-2107)
PHONE................................310 534-2861
Harry B Line, *President*
Alex Pitones,

PRODUCTS & SVCS

Phil Kielty, *Cust Mgr*
EMP: 43
SQ FT: 5,000
SALES (est): 8.2MM **Privately Held**
SIC: 3469 2759 Stamping metal for the trade; commercial printing

(P-12793)
DIAMOND PERFORATED METALS INC
Also Called: Amico - Diamond Perforated
7300 W Sunnyview Ave, Visalia (93291-9605)
PHONE..........................559 651-1889
Brian Lipke, *CEO*
Guy Anderson, *Vice Pres*
Joe Smith, *Vice Pres*
Stephen Seitz, *Sales Staff*
EMP: 78
SQ FT: 80,000
SALES (est): 27.1MM
SALES (corp-wide): 1B **Publicly Held**
WEB: www.diamondperf.com
SIC: 3469 Perforated metal, stamped
PA: Gibraltar Industries, Inc.
3556 Lake Shore Rd # 100
Buffalo NY 14219
716 826-6500

(P-12794)
DIE-NAMIC FABRICATION INC
378 E Orange Show Rd, San Bernardino (92408-2414)
PHONE..........................909 350-2870
C Anthony Esposito, *CEO*
Louise A Uphus, *Corp Secy*
Genelle J Esposito, *Vice Pres*
EMP: 10
SQ FT: 20,000
SALES (est): 1.9MM **Privately Held**
WEB: www.die-namicfab.com
SIC: 3469 3441 Metal stampings; fabricated structural metal

(P-12795)
DIVERSIFIED TOOL & DIE
2585 Birch St, Vista (92081-8433)
PHONE..........................760 598-9100
Ernst Wilms, *CEO*
Rosa Wilms, *Partner*
Ernesto Rabino, *Engineer*
EMP: 30
SQ FT: 33,000
SALES (est): 4.6MM **Privately Held**
WEB: www.stamping.com
SIC: 3469 3544 Stamping metal for the trade; special dies & tools

(P-12796)
E2E MFG LLC
7139 Koll Center Pkwy, Pleasanton (94566-3120)
PHONE..........................925 862-2057
Igonni Fajardo,
Humera Nawaz, *Program Mgr*
Christine Luna, *Office Mgr*
Dennis Custodio, *Engineer*
Raja Maruthu, *Engineer*
▲ **EMP:** 46
SQ FT: 11,238
SALES (est): 9.3MM **Privately Held**
WEB: www.fourte.com
SIC: 3469 Metal stampings

(P-12797)
EAGLEWARE MANUFACTURING CO INC
12683 Corral Pl, Santa Fe Springs (90670-4748)
PHONE..........................562 320-3100
Brett L Gross, *President*
Eric Gross, *Vice Pres*
▲ **EMP:** 32
SQ FT: 130,000
SALES (est): 5.6MM **Privately Held**
SIC: 3469 3421 Stamping metal for the trade; household cooking & kitchen utensils, metal; cooking ware, except porcelain enamelled; cutlery

(P-12798)
EBSCO PRODUCTIONS INC
1040 N Las Palmas Ave 1, Los Angeles (90038-2409)
PHONE..........................323 960-2599
Scott A Stone, *President*

EMP: 50
SALES (est): 3.9MM **Privately Held**
SIC: 3469 Radio or television chassis, stamped metal

(P-12799)
ELIXIR INDUSTRIES
24800 Chrisanta Dr # 100, Mission Viejo (92691-4833)
PHONE..........................949 860-5000
EMP: 10
SQ FT: 57,707
SALES (corp-wide): 28.3MM **Privately Held**
SIC: 3469 3714 3441
PA: Elixir Industries
24800 Chrisanta Dr # 210
Mission Viejo CA 92691
949 860-5000

(P-12800)
ERC CONCEPTS CO INC
1255 Birchwood Dr, Sunnyvale (94089-2206)
P.O. Box 62019 (94088-2019)
PHONE..........................408 734-5345
Felix Oramas, *President*
Reina Oramas, *Vice Pres*
EMP: 35
SQ FT: 17,000
SALES (est): 7.4MM **Privately Held**
WEB: www.erc-concepts.com
SIC: 3469 Machine parts, stamped or pressed metal

(P-12801)
EXACT CNC INDUSTRIES INC
20640 Bahama St, Chatsworth (91311-6118)
PHONE..........................818 527-1908
Harout H Neksalyan, *CEO*
EMP: 10
SALES (est): 1.1MM **Privately Held**
SIC: 3469 Machine parts, stamped or pressed metal

(P-12802)
EXCEL INDUSTRIES INC
Also Called: Accu-Tek
1601 Fremont Ct, Ontario (91761-8309)
PHONE..........................909 947-4867
William Kohout, *President*
EMP: 21 **EST:** 1975
SALES (est): 3.6MM **Privately Held**
WEB: www.accu-tekfirearms.com
SIC: 3469 3484 3542 3496 Metal stampings; small arms; machine tools, metal forming type; miscellaneous fabricated wire products

(P-12803)
FALLBROOK INDUSTRIES INC
Also Called: Standish Precision Products
323 Industrial Way Ste 1, Fallbrook (92028-2357)
PHONE..........................760 728-7229
Michael Standish, *President*
Dennis Standish, *Vice Pres*
Emily Standish, *Opers Mgr*
William Howard, *Prdtn Mgr*
▲ **EMP:** 20
SQ FT: 15,000
SALES (est): 3.7MM **Privately Held**
WEB: www.standishproducts.com
SIC: 3469 Machine parts, stamped or pressed metal

(P-12804)
FORM & FUSION MFG INC
11251 Trade Center Dr, Rancho Cordova (95742-6223)
PHONE..........................916 638-8576
Greg Bryant, *Manager*
EMP: 10
SALES (corp-wide): 4.4MM **Privately Held**
SIC: 3469 Metal stampings
PA: Form & Fusion Mfg., Inc.
11261 Trade Center Dr
Rancho Cordova CA 95742
916 638-8576

(P-12805)
FORM & FUSION MFG INC (PA)
Also Called: Urgent Upfits
11261 Trade Center Dr, Rancho Cordova (95742-6223)
PHONE..........................916 638-8576
John Hancock, *President*
Dave Lewis, *Shareholder*
Stacey Silva, *Production*
EMP: 27
SQ FT: 40,000
SALES: 4.4MM **Privately Held**
SIC: 3469 3465 Metal stampings; automotive stampings

(P-12806)
GALAXY MANUFACTURING INC
3200 Bassett St, Santa Clara (95054-2701)
P.O. Box 1153 (95052-1153)
PHONE..........................408 654-4583
EMP: 11
SQ FT: 5,000
SALES (est): 1.7MM **Privately Held**
WEB: www.galaxymfg.net
SIC: 3469

(P-12807)
GERGAY AND ASSOCIATES
78 Delmar St, San Francisco (94117-4006)
PHONE..........................415 431-4163
George Gergay, *Partner*
Andrea Gergay, *Partner*
Nicole Gergay, *Partner*
Peter Gergay, *Partner*
EMP: 49
SALES: 5MM **Privately Held**
SIC: 3469 Porcelain enameled products & utensils

(P-12808)
GLOBAL PCCI (GPC) (PA)
2465 Campus Dr Ste 100, Irvine (92612-1502)
PHONE..........................757 637-9000
Sherri Bovino, *Partner*
Robert W Urban,
EMP: 120
SQ FT: 10,000
SALES (est): 21.2MM **Privately Held**
SIC: 3469 4499 Metal stampings; salvaging, distressed vessels & cargoes

(P-12809)
GRASS MANUFACTURING CO INC
2850 Bay Rd, Redwood City (94063-3503)
PHONE..........................650 366-2556
Eric Grass, *President*
Cheryl Grass, *Office Mgr*
Bonnie Grass, *Admin Sec*
Jennifer Grass, *Bookkeeper*
EMP: 10
SQ FT: 8,000
SALES (est): 1.1MM **Privately Held**
WEB: www.grassmfg.com
SIC: 3469 Stamping metal for the trade

(P-12810)
GRIMCO INC
13454 Imperial Hwy, Santa Fe Springs (90670-4820)
PHONE..........................562 449-4964
Marty Meisner, *Branch Mgr*
EMP: 24
SALES (corp-wide): 97.5MM **Privately Held**
SIC: 3469 2759 3429 Patterns on metal; screen printing; manufactured hardware (general)
PA: Grimco, Inc.
11745 Sppngton Brracks Rd
Saint Louis MO 63127
636 305-0088

(P-12811)
HANMAR LLC (PA)
Also Called: Metalite Manufacturing
11441 Bradley Ave, Pacoima (91331-2304)
PHONE..........................818 240-0170
Hannes Michael Schachtner, *CEO*
Jan Schacatner, *CFO*
Tony Mayer, *Office Mgr*
Sisi Hall, *Senior Buyer*
Joey Sauceda, *QC Mgr*
EMP: 42 **EST:** 1969
SQ FT: 25,000

SALES (est): 8.9MM **Privately Held**
SIC: 3469 Spinning metal for the trade; stamping metal for the trade

(P-12812)
HARTWELL CORPORATION
9810 6th St, Rancho Cucamonga (91730-5795)
PHONE..........................909 987-4616
Finmon Elliot, *Branch Mgr*
David Gwilt, *Info Tech Dir*
Greg Lada, *Sales Engr*
Mike Strain, *Maint Spvr*
EMP: 62
SQ FT: 101,495
SALES (corp-wide): 3.8B **Publicly Held**
WEB: www.hartwellcorp.com
SIC: 3469 3429 Metal stampings; manufactured hardware (general)
HQ: Hartwell Corporation
900 Richfield Rd
Placentia CA 92870
714 993-4200

(P-12813)
HESTAN SMART COOKING INC
1 Meyer Plz, Vallejo (94590-5925)
PHONE..........................773 710-1538
Stanley Cheng, *CEO*
EMP: 10
SALES (est): 400.4K **Privately Held**
SIC: 3469 5046 Cooking ware, except porcelain enamelled; cooking equipment, commercial
PA: Meyer International Holdings Limited
C/O: Vistra (Bvi) Limited
Road Town

(P-12814)
HI TECH HONEYCOMB INC
9355 Ruffin Ct, San Diego (92123-5304)
PHONE..........................858 974-1600
Joao J Costa, *CEO*
Selma Costa, *President*
John J Costa, *CEO*
Michael Corbosiero, *Officer*
John Costa, *Vice Pres*
EMP: 136
SQ FT: 20,000
SALES (est): 33.8MM **Privately Held**
WEB: www.hthoneycomb.com
SIC: 3469 Honeycombed metal

(P-12815)
HI-TEMP INSULATION INC
4700 Calle Alto, Camarillo (93012-8489)
PHONE..........................805 484-2774
Sieg Borck, *CEO*
Diane Humphrey, *Vice Pres*
Donna Porter, *Executive*
David Blake, *CIO*
Kathleen Creamer, *Info Tech Mgr*
▲ **EMP:** 310 **EST:** 1964
SQ FT: 100,000
SALES: 74.7MM **Privately Held**
WEB: www.hi-tempinsulation.com
SIC: 3469 3296 Spinning metal for the trade; fiberglass insulation

(P-12816)
HOME PARADISE LLC
Also Called: Cabinet Home
905 Westminster Ave G, Alhambra (91803-1211)
PHONE..........................626 284-9999
Jian Q Chen, *President*
▲ **EMP:** 13
SALES (est): 2.4MM **Privately Held**
SIC: 3469 1799 Kitchen fixtures & equipment, porcelain enameled; kitchen fixtures & equipment: metal, except cast aluminum; kitchen & bathroom remodeling

(P-12817)
HOUSTON BAZZ CO
Also Called: Bazz Houston Co
12700 Western Ave, Garden Grove (92841-4017)
PHONE..........................714 898-2666
Javier Castro, *President*
Chester O Houston, *Corp Secy*
Cecilia Rodriguez, *Technical Staff*
▲ **EMP:** 85
SQ FT: 50,000

▲ = Import ▼=Export
◆ =Import/Export

SALES (est): 21.3MM **Privately Held**
WEB: www.bazz-houston.com
SIC: 3469 3495 3493 Machine parts, stamped or pressed metal; mechanical springs, precision; steel springs, except wire

(P-12818)
HSG MANUFACTURING INC
13346 Monte Vista Ave, Chino (91710-5147)
PHONE..................................909 902-5915
Gill Singh, *President*
Hadasen Singh, *Principal*
▲ EMP: 12
SQ FT: 8,000
SALES (est): 7MM **Privately Held**
WEB: www.hsgmanufacturing.com
SIC: 3469 Machine parts, stamped or pressed metal

(P-12819)
HUGIN COMPONENTS INC
Also Called: H C I
4231 Pacific St Ste 23, Rocklin (95677-2135)
PHONE..................................916 652-1070
Steve Katonis, *President*
Sharon Katonis, *Vice Pres*
EMP: 15
SQ FT: 18,000
SALES (est): 2.4MM **Privately Held**
WEB: www.hugincomponents.com
SIC: 3469 Electronic enclosures, stamped or pressed metal

(P-12820)
IMPERIAL CAL PRODUCTS INC
425 Apollo St, Brea (92821-3110)
PHONE..................................714 990-9100
Shari Bittel, *President*
Kathy Flentye, *Vice Pres*
Janet Dirisio, *Manager*
▲ EMP: 35
SQ FT: 35,000
SALES (est): 3.8MM **Privately Held**
WEB: www.imperialhoods.com
SIC: 3469 Kitchen fixtures & equipment: metal, except cast aluminum

(P-12821)
INFINITY STAMPS INC
Also Called: Branding Irons Unlimited
8577 Canoga Ave, Canoga Park (91304-2609)
PHONE..................................818 576-1188
Billie Eglick, *President*
Oren Eglick, *General Mgr*
EMP: 10
SQ FT: 4,500
SALES (est): 1.8MM **Privately Held**
WEB: www.infinitystamps.com
SIC: 3469 Stamping metal for the trade

(P-12822)
INNOVATIVE STAMPING INC
Also Called: Innovative Systems
2068 E Gladwick St, Compton (90220-6202)
P.O. Box 5327 (90224-5327)
PHONE..................................310 537-6996
Gerald L Czaban, *President*
Kim Stevenson, *Vice Pres*
▼ EMP: 32 EST: 1976
SQ FT: 128,000
SALES (est): 6MM **Privately Held**
WEB: www.innovative-sys.com
SIC: 3469 Metal stampings

(P-12823)
INTERPLEX NASCAL INC
15777 Gateway Cir, Tustin (92780-6470)
PHONE..................................714 505-2900
Jim Martellotti, *President*
John Fili, *General Mgr*
Susan Smith, *Senior Buyer*
▲ EMP: 79 EST: 1969
SQ FT: 33,000
SALES (est): 13.9MM **Privately Held**
WEB: www.interplexchina.com
SIC: 3469 Stamping metal for the trade
HQ: Interplex Industries, Inc.
231 Ferris Ave
Rumford RI 02916
718 961-6212

(P-12824)
INTRI-PLEX TECHNOLOGIES INC (HQ)
751 S Kellogg Ave, Goleta (93117-3832)
PHONE..................................805 683-3414
Lawney J Falloon, *CEO*
Lawrence Ellis, *CFO*
John Sullivan, *Vice Pres*
Bob Tench, *Opers Staff*
Anvita Chitnis, *Supervisor*
▲ EMP: 126
SQ FT: 46,000
SALES (est): 21.6MM **Privately Held**
SIC: 3469 Stamping metal for the trade
PA: Ipt Holding Inc
751 S Kellogg Ave
Goleta CA 93117
805 683-3414

(P-12825)
J-MARK MANUFACTURING INC
Also Called: J-Mark Company
2480 Coral St, Vista (92081-8430)
PHONE..................................760 727-6956
Mark Baker, *President*
Debbie Baker, *Treasurer*
Dale Jackson, *Vice Pres*
Carol Jackson, *Admin Sec*
Steve Tugwell, *Prdtn Mgr*
EMP: 22
SQ FT: 24,000
SALES (est): 3.5MM **Privately Held**
SIC: 3469 3599 Electronic enclosures, stamped or pressed metal; machine shop, jobbing & repair

(P-12826)
JAY MANUFACTURING CORP
Also Called: Jay Mfg
7425 Fulton Ave, North Hollywood (91605-4116)
PHONE..................................818 255-0500
Michael Jordan, *President*
Marna Jordan, *Treasurer*
Katheryn Jordan, *Admin Sec*
EMP: 10 EST: 1944
SQ FT: 16,000
SALES (est): 1.7MM **Privately Held**
WEB: www.jaymfg.com
SIC: 3469 Stamping metal for the trade

(P-12827)
JB INDUSTRIES CORP
Also Called: J B I
451 Commercial Way, La Habra (90631-6168)
P.O. Box 17365, Anaheim (92817-7365)
PHONE..................................562 691-2105
Jaime Borja, *President*
Jim Borja Jr, *CFO*
Mercedes Borja, *Vice Pres*
EMP: 12
SQ FT: 10,000
SALES (est): 2.6MM **Privately Held**
SIC: 3469 3599 Machine parts, or pressed metal; machine shop, jobbing & repair

(P-12828)
KAGA (USA) INC
2620 S Susan St, Santa Ana (92704-5816)
PHONE..................................714 540-2697
Masaaki Nozaki, *President*
Fumio Shiina, *Treasurer*
Takashi Nozaki, *Vice Pres*
Nobuharu Nozaki, *Admin Sec*
Asami Fujioka, *Accountant*
▲ EMP: 30
SQ FT: 38,400
SALES (est): 6.3MM **Privately Held**
WEB: www.kagainc.com
SIC: 3469 Electronic enclosures, stamped or pressed metal
PA: Kaga,Inc.
140, Ni, Ota, Tsubatamachi
Kahoku-Gun ISH 929-0

(P-12829)
KATLAN INDUSTRIES INC
Also Called: Leejay Industries
3202 Blume Dr, Los Alamitos (90720-4813)
PHONE..................................562 618-0940
Lance Schumacher, *President*
Rebecca Schumacher, *Vice Pres*
EMP: 10

SQ FT: 12,000
SALES: 600K **Privately Held**
SIC: 3469 3429 Machine parts, stamped or pressed metal; cabinet hardware

(P-12830)
KB DELTA INC
Also Called: KB Delta Comprsr Valve Parts
3340 Fujita St, Torrance (90505-4017)
PHONE..................................310 530-1539
Boris Giourof, *CEO*
Katarina Giourof, *Vice Pres*
Cynthia Vasquez, *Sales Mgr*
Mauricio Rodriguez, *Manager*
▼ EMP: 37
SQ FT: 5,500
SALES (est): 7MM **Privately Held**
WEB: www.kbdelta.com
SIC: 3469 5085 7699 Machine parts, stamped or pressed metal; industrial supplies; compressor repair

(P-12831)
KELLY TOOL & MFGCOINC
433 S Palm Ave, Alhambra (91803-1422)
PHONE..................................626 289-7962
Labron H Burdette, *President*
EMP: 10 EST: 1957
SQ FT: 12,000
SALES (est): 1.4MM **Privately Held**
SIC: 3469 3541 Stamping metal for the trade; machine tools, metal cutting type; machine tool replacement & repair parts, metal cutting types

(P-12832)
KING PRECISION INC
111 Harrison Ct, Santa Cruz (95062-1125)
PHONE..................................831 426-2704
Dallas King, *President*
Richard King, *Senior VP*
EMP: 27 EST: 1999
SQ FT: 8,000
SALES (est): 4MM **Privately Held**
WEB: www.kingprecision.com
SIC: 3469 7692 3829 3827 Machine parts, stamped or pressed metal; welding repair; measuring & controlling devices; optical instruments & lenses; guided missile & space vehicle parts & auxiliary equipment

(P-12833)
KINGS CRATING INC
Also Called: Reyes Machining
1364 Pioneer Way, El Cajon (92020-1626)
PHONE..................................619 590-2631
EMP: 30
SQ FT: 30,000
SALES (est): 1.9MM **Privately Held**
WEB: www.reyesmfg.com
SIC: 3469
PA: King's Crating, Inc.
1364 Pioneer Way
El Cajon CA 92020

(P-12834)
KITCHEN EQUIPMENT MFG CO INC
Also Called: Kemco
2102 Maple Privado, Ontario (91761-7602)
PHONE..................................909 923-3153
David Rodriguez, *President*
EMP: 40
SQ FT: 15,000
SALES (est): 7.6MM **Privately Held**
SIC: 3469 3431 Kitchen fixtures & equipment, porcelain enameled; metal sanitary ware

(P-12835)
KITCOR CORPORATION
9959 Glenoaks Blvd, Sun Valley (91352-1085)
PHONE..................................323 875-2820
Kent Kitchen, *Principal*
Alice Kitchen, *Treasurer*
Bob Kitchen, *Vice Pres*
Jim Kitchen, *Vice Pres*
Kimberly Schulman, *Office Mgr*
EMP: 35 EST: 1943
SQ FT: 42,000

SALES (est): 8.5MM **Privately Held**
WEB: www.kitcor.com
SIC: 3469 Kitchen fixtures & equipment: metal, except cast aluminum

(P-12836)
KOPYKAKE ENTERPRISES INC (PA)
Also Called: Mayer Baking Co
3699 W 240th St, Torrance (90505-6002)
PHONE..................................310 373-8906
Gerald G Mayer, *President*
Greg Mayer, *Vice Pres*
Rick Mayer, *Vice Pres*
Gary A Newland, *Plant Mgr*
David Good, *Mktg Dir*
◆ EMP: 19 EST: 1970
SQ FT: 22,000
SALES (est): 6.5MM **Privately Held**
WEB: www.kopykake.com
SIC: 3469 2051 Kitchen fixtures & equipment: metal, except cast aluminum; bakery: wholesale or wholesale/retail combined

(P-12837)
LARRY SPUN PRODUCTS INC
1533 S Downey Rd, Los Angeles (90023-4042)
PHONE..................................323 881-6300
Hilario F Hurtado, *CEO*
EMP: 49
SQ FT: 6,000
SALES (est): 8.3MM **Privately Held**
SIC: 3469 Spinning metal for the trade

(P-12838)
LOCK-RIDGE TOOL COMPANY INC
2000 Pomona Blvd, Pomona (91768-3323)
PHONE..................................909 865-8309
Keith Clark, *President*
Penney Clark, *Corp Secy*
Ashford Clark, *Vice Pres*
▲ EMP: 52
SQ FT: 21,000
SALES (est): 9.4MM **Privately Held**
WEB: www.lockridgetool.com
SIC: 3469 Stamping metal for the trade

(P-12839)
LUPPEN HOLDINGS INC (PA)
Also Called: Metal Products Engineering
3050 Leonis Blvd, Vernon (90058-2914)
PHONE..................................323 581-8121
Luppe R Luppen, *Ch of Bd*
Paula Luppen, *Treasurer*
Ray Woodmansee, *Vice Pres*
▲ EMP: 24 EST: 1940
SQ FT: 40,000
SALES (est): 2.4MM **Privately Held**
WEB: www.metalproductseng.com
SIC: 3469 3578 3596 Stamping metal for the trade; change making machines; scales & balances, except laboratory

(P-12840)
M L Z INC
Also Called: Spun Products
1800 W 9th St, Long Beach (90813-2614)
PHONE..................................562 436-3540
Larry Weber, *President*
Linda Weber, *Admin Sec*
EMP: 10
SQ FT: 4,000
SALES (est): 1.1MM **Privately Held**
WEB: www.spunproducts.com
SIC: 3469 Spinning metal for the trade

(P-12841)
MC WILLIAM & SON INC
Also Called: California Tool & Die
421 S Irwindale Ave, Azusa (91702-3217)
PHONE..................................626 969-1821
Dan McWilliam, *President*
Dana Matejka, *Treasurer*
EMP: 19
SQ FT: 26,000
SALES (est): 4.2MM **Privately Held**
WEB: www.californiatool-die.com
SIC: 3469 3544 Stamping metal for the trade; special dies, tools, jigs & fixtures

(P-12842)
MCINTIRE TOOL DIE & MACHINE (PA)
Also Called: Omega Tool Die & Machine
308 S Mountain View Ave, San Bernardino
(92408-1415)
PHONE............................909 888-0440
Barbara McIntire, *President*
Chester L McIntire, *Shareholder*
Jane Kingsley, *Treasurer*
EMP: 12
SQ FT: 13,500
SALES (est): 2.3MM **Privately Held**
WEB: www.omegatool-usa.com
SIC: 3469 Metal stampings

(P-12843)
METALITE MANUFACTURING COMPANY
Also Called: Metalite Mfg Companys
11441 Bradley Ave, Pacoima (91331-2304)
PHONE............................818 890-2802
Hanness Schachtner, *CEO*
Jan Schacatner, *CFO*
Bud Van Netta, *Marketing Staff*
Leonard Alvidrez, *Manager*
EMP: 39 EST: 1923
SQ FT: 58,000
SALES (est): 8.9MM **Privately Held**
SIC: 3469 Stamping metal for the trade
PA: Hanmar, Llc
    11441 Bradley Ave
    Pacoima CA 91331
    818 240-0170

(P-12844)
METCO MANUFACTURING INC
Also Called: Metco Fourslide Manufacturing
17540 S Denver Ave, Gardena
(90248-3411)
PHONE............................310 516-6547
Jack Bishop, *President*
Dana Beisel, *Vice Pres*
Darryl Scholl, *Vice Pres*
Shirley Bishop, *Admin Sec*
EMP: 29
SQ FT: 11,200
SALES (est): 6.1MM **Privately Held**
WEB: www.metcofourslide.com
SIC: 3469 Stamping metal for the trade

(P-12845)
MEYER COOKWARE INDUSTRIES INC
1 Meyer Plz, Vallejo (94590-5925)
PHONE............................707 551-2800
Stanley Cheng, *Ch of Bd*
EMP: 50
SALES (est): 11MM **Privately Held**
WEB: www.meyer.com
SIC: 3469 Cooking ware, except porcelain
enamelled
HQ: Meyer Corporation, U.S.
    1 Meyer Plz
    Vallejo CA 94590
    707 551-2800

(P-12846)
MEYER CORPORATION US (HQ)
Also Called: Meyer Wines
1 Meyer Plz, Vallejo (94590-5925)
PHONE............................707 551-2800
Stanley Kin Sui Cheng, *CEO*
Ed Blackman, *COO*
Barry Minehart, *Branch Mgr*
Christopher Banning, *Director*
◆ EMP: 80
SQ FT: 180,000
SALES (est): 86.7MM **Privately Held**
WEB: www.meyer.com
SIC: 3469 3631 5023 Cooking ware, ex-
cept porcelain enamelled; household
cooking equipment; kitchenware

(P-12847)
MICRO MATRIX SYSTEMS (PA)
Also Called: M M S
1899 Salem Ct, Claremont (91711-2638)
PHONE............................909 626-8544
Grant P Zarbock, *CEO*
Kerry Zarbock, *Vice Pres*
Kimberly Henderson, *Human Res Mgr*
▲ EMP: 25

SALES (est): 4.1MM **Privately Held**
WEB: www.mmsys.biz
SIC: 3469 Stamping metal for the trade

(P-12848)
NANOPRECISION PRODUCTS INC
802 Calle Plano, Camarillo (93012-8557)
PHONE............................310 597-4991
Michael K Barnoski, *CEO*
Shawn Matsuda, *Technical Staff*
Meirong Shi, *Technical Staff*
Ren Yang, *Engineer*
Jim Goell, *Marketing Staff*
EMP: 25
SALES (est): 6.7MM **Privately Held**
SIC: 3469 3721 Stamping metal for the
trade; research & development on aircraft
by the manufacturer

(P-12849)
NATIONAL METAL STAMPINGS INC
42110 8th St E, Lancaster (93535-5444)
PHONE............................661 945-1157
William T Bloomer, *President*
Madeleine J Bloomer, *Corp Secy*
Bill Bloomer, *General Mgr*
John Doyle, *General Mgr*
▲ EMP: 70
SQ FT: 20,000
SALES (est): 13.2MM **Privately Held**
WEB: www.nationalmetal.com
SIC: 3469 Stamping metal for the trade

(P-12850)
NEW GORDON INDUSTRIES LLC
13750 Rosecrans Ave, Santa Fe Springs
(90670-5027)
PHONE............................562 483-7378
Steven Lazar, *President*
Daniel Laskaris, *General Mgr*
Michelle Scott, *Accountant*
Lisa Wheeler, *QC Mgr*
EMP: 22
SQ FT: 22,000
SALES (est): 4.9MM **Privately Held**
WEB: www.ngica.com
SIC: 3469 Stamping metal for the trade

(P-12851)
ORANGE METAL SPINNING AND STAM
2601 Orange Ave, Santa Ana (92707-3724)
P.O. Box 80070, Rcho STA Marg (92688-
0070)
PHONE............................714 754-0770
Mario Haber, *President*
Enrique Haber, *Vice Pres*
Elsa Haber, *Admin Sec*
EMP: 13
SQ FT: 10,000
SALES (est): 1.2MM **Privately Held**
SIC: 3469 Spinning metal for the trade

(P-12852)
P P MFG CO INC
13130 Arctic Cir, Santa Fe Springs
(90670-5508)
PHONE............................562 921-3640
Ronald Burr, *President*
Glenn Burr, *Treasurer*
EMP: 14
SQ FT: 10,000
SALES (est): 1.4MM **Privately Held**
SIC: 3469 3544 Stamping metal for the
trade; special dies & tools

(P-12853)
PACIFIC METAL STAMPINGS INC
28415 Witherspoon Pkwy, Valencia
(91355-4174)
PHONE............................661 257-7656
Brian Schlotfelt, *CEO*
Scott Schlotfelt, *Vice Pres*
Karen Robinson, *Accounts Mgr*
▲ EMP: 30
SQ FT: 21,000
SALES (est): 6.3MM **Privately Held**
WEB: www.pacificmetalstampings.com
SIC: 3469 Stamping metal for the trade

(P-12854)
PACIFIC PRECISION METALS INC
Also Called: Tubing Seal Cap Co
1100 E Orangethorpe Ave, Anaheim
(92801-1161)
P.O. Box 51481, Ontario (91761-0081)
PHONE............................951 226-1500
Ajay N Thakkar, *President*
EMP: 130
SQ FT: 2,063
SALES (est): 27.5MM **Privately Held**
SIC: 3469 3429 2599 8711 Stamping
metal for the trade; door locks, bolts &
checks; locks or lock sets; cabinets, fac-
tory; machine tool design; metal house-
hold furniture
PA: Triyar Sv, Llc
    10850 Wilshire Blvd
    Los Angeles CA 90024

(P-12855)
PERIDOT CORPORATION
1072 Serpentine Ln, Pleasanton
(94566-4731)
PHONE............................925 461-8830
Patrick Pickerell, *President*
Debra Van Sickle, *Vice Pres*
Debra Vansickle, *Vice Pres*
Marisol Palomares, *Administration*
Jojo Garcia, *Purch Mgr*
EMP: 60
SQ FT: 30,000
SALES (est): 12.6MM **Privately Held**
WEB: www.peridotcorp.com
SIC: 3469 Metal stampings

(P-12856)
PERRINS REGISTRATION OFFICE
17727 Chatsworth St, Granada Hills
(91344-5604)
PHONE............................818 832-1332
Cynthia Perrin, *Principal*
EMP: 10
SALES (est): 854.1K **Privately Held**
SIC: 3469 Automobile license tags,
stamped metal

(P-12857)
PLATESCAN INC
20101 Sw Birch St Ste 250, Newport Beach
(92660-1770)
PHONE............................949 851-1600
Robert Pinzler, *Vice Pres*
EMP: 23
SALES: 950K **Privately Held**
SIC: 3469 Automobile license tags,
stamped metal

(P-12858)
PRECISION RESOURCE INC
Also Called: Precision Resource Cal Div
5803 Engineer Dr, Huntington Beach
(92649-1127)
PHONE............................714 891-4439
Robert Fitzgerald, *Principal*
EMP: 275
SQ FT: 27,000
SALES (corp-wide): 260.1MM **Privately
Held**
WEB: www.precisionresource.com
SIC: 3469 3544 Stamping metal for the
trade; special dies, tools, jigs & fixtures
PA: Precision Resource, Inc.
    25 Forest Pkwy
    Shelton CT 06484
    203 925-0012

(P-12859)
PRECISION STAMPG SOLUTIONS INC
500 Egan Ave, Beaumont (92223-2191)
PHONE............................951 845-1174
Clay T Barnes, *CEO*
EMP: 50
SALES: 11MM **Privately Held**
SIC: 3469 Metal stampings

(P-12860)
PRICE-LEHO CO INC
3841 Mission Oaks Blvd, Camarillo
(93012-5099)
PHONE............................805 482-8967

Theresa Leho, *Chairman*
Robert Leho, *President*
EMP: 10
SQ FT: 12,800
SALES: 250K **Privately Held**
SIC: 3469 3544 Metal stampings; special
dies & tools

(P-12861)
PROFESSIONAL FINISHING SYSTEMS
Also Called: Pfs
12341 Gladstone Ave, Sylmar
(91342-5319)
PHONE............................818 365-8888
Vern Coley, *CEO*
Pat Ramnarine, *Vice Pres*
EMP: 17
SQ FT: 14,000
SALES (est): 3.1MM **Privately Held**
WEB: www.profinishing.com
SIC: 3469 5084 3471 Machine parts,
stamped or pressed metal; machine tools
& metalworking machinery; plating & pol-
ishing

(P-12862)
PROFORMANCE MANUFACTURING INC
1922 Elise Cir, Corona (92879-1882)
PHONE............................951 279-1230
Robert Morales, *President*
Tim Borth, *Technical Staff*
EMP: 20
SQ FT: 21,000
SALES (est): 3.9MM **Privately Held**
WEB: www.proformancemfg.com
SIC: 3469 3599 3451 3312 Machine
parts, stamped or pressed metal; ma-
chine & other job shop work; screw ma-
chine products; blast furnaces & steel
mills; special dies, tools, jigs & fixtures

(P-12863)
PROTO LAMINATIONS INC
13666 Bora Dr, Santa Fe Springs
(90670-5006)
PHONE............................562 926-4777
Mark R Rippy, *President*
Tina L Rippy, *Corp Secy*
EMP: 12
SQ FT: 11,000
SALES (est): 1.9MM **Privately Held**
WEB: www.protolam.com
SIC: 3469 Machine parts, stamped or
pressed metal

(P-12864)
PROTOTYPE & SHORT-RUN SVCS INC
Also Called: Pass
1310 W Collins Ave, Orange (92867-5415)
PHONE............................714 449-9661
Jack Mc Devitt, *President*
Lorene Schmdt, *Office Mgr*
Doug Eschen, *Admin Asst*
Florence Lulu Montoya, *Manager*
EMP: 25
SQ FT: 6,700
SALES: 8MM **Privately Held**
WEB: www.prototype-shortrun.com
SIC: 3469 Stamping metal for the trade

(P-12865)
QUALITY METAL SPINNING AND
4047 Transport St, Palo Alto (94303-4914)
PHONE............................650 858-2491
Joseph Czisch Jr, *President*
Xenia Czisch, *Vice Pres*
EMP: 30
SQ FT: 34,000
SALES (est): 6.8MM **Privately Held**
WEB: www.qmsshields.com
SIC: 3469 3599 Stamping metal for the
trade; machine shop, jobbing & repair

(P-12866)
R & R STAMPING FOUR SLIDE CORP
2440 Railroad St, Corona (92880-5418)
PHONE............................909 595-6444
David A Janes Jr, *President*
EMP: 60 EST: 1988
SQ FT: 65,000

▲ = Import ▼=Export
◆ =Import/Export

SALES (est): 5.2MM **Privately Held**
WEB: www.cmemetal.com
SIC: 3469 3444 Stamping metal for the trade; sheet metalwork

(P-12867)
R ZAMORA INC
Also Called: Tecxel
2826 La Mirada Dr Ste D, Vista
(92081-8445)
PHONE.....................760 597-1130
Reggie Zamora, *President*
EMP: 21
SQ FT: 10,000
SALES: 2.5MM **Privately Held**
WEB: www.tecxel.com
SIC: 3469 Machine parts, stamped or pressed metal

(P-12868)
RAGO & SON INC
1029 51st Ave, Oakland (94601-5653)
P.O. Box 7309 (94601-0309)
PHONE.....................510 536-5700
Dominic Anthony Rago, *CEO*
Dominic Rago, *President*
Deborah Rago, *Corp Secy*
Gerald Accardo Jr, *Vice Pres*
Gerald Accardo Sr, *Vice Pres*
EMP: 80 EST: 1969
SQ FT: 38,000
SALES (est): 20.2MM **Privately Held**
WEB: www.rago-son.com
SIC: 3469 Stamping metal for the trade

(P-12869)
RSR METAL SPINNING INC
850 E Edna Pl, Covina (91723-1410)
PHONE.....................626 814-2339
Russell Spencer, *President*
Jenny Spencer, *Admin Sec*
EMP: 15
SQ FT: 6,800
SALES (est): 2.2MM **Privately Held**
WEB: www.rsrmetalspinning.com
SIC: 3469 Spinning metal for the trade

(P-12870)
SCHUBERTH NORTH AMERICA LLC
33 Journey Ste 200, Aliso Viejo
(92656-5345)
PHONE.....................949 215-0893
Randy Northrup,
Doreena Daniel, *Controller*
EMP: 15
SQ FT: 2,000
SALES (est): 6.3MM
SALES (corp-wide): 775.7K **Privately Held**
SIC: 3469 Helmets, steel
HQ: Schuberth Gmbh
Stegelitzer Str. 12
Magdeburg 39126
391 810-60

(P-12871)
SERRA MANUFACTURING CORP (PA)
3039 E Las Hermanas St, Compton
(90221-5575)
PHONE.....................310 537-4560
Kris Hernandez, *CEO*
John Hernandez, *President*
Maria Cerda, *Opers Staff*
EMP: 48
SQ FT: 23,916
SALES: 7MM **Privately Held**
WEB: www.serramfg.com
SIC: 3469 Stamping metal for the trade

(P-12872)
SESSA MANUFACTURING & WELDING
2932 Golf Course Dr, Ventura
(93003-7689)
PHONE.....................805 644-2284
Michael J Sessa, *CEO*
Lea Sessa, *Shareholder*
EMP: 40 EST: 1980
SQ FT: 15,500
SALES (est): 7.7MM **Privately Held**
WEB: www.sessamfg.com
SIC: 3469 Stamping metal for the trade

(P-12873)
SKM INDUSTRIES INC
Also Called: Job Shop Managers
28966 Hancock Pkwy, Valencia
(91355-1069)
PHONE.....................661 294-8373
Sanjeev Kapoor, *President*
▼ EMP: 14
SQ FT: 4,300
SALES (est): 3.1MM **Privately Held**
WEB: www.skmproducts.com
SIC: 3469 Machine parts, stamped or pressed metal

(P-12874)
SOUTHWEST GREENE INTL INC
Also Called: Greene Group
4055 Calle Platino # 200, Oceanside
(92056-5861)
PHONE.....................760 639-4960
Alexis Willingham, *President*
Steve James, *Engineer*
▲ EMP: 105
SQ FT: 80,000
SALES (est): 20.8MM **Privately Held**
SIC: 3469 Metal stampings

(P-12875)
SPECIALTY FINANCE INC
Also Called: David Engineering & Mfg
1230 Quarry St, Corona (92879-1708)
P.O. Box 77035 (92877-0101)
PHONE.....................951 735-5200
Mike David, *CEO*
Michael David, *President*
Sarah Caoile, *Technology*
EMP: 30
SALES: 5MM **Privately Held**
SIC: 3469 3544 Metal stampings; special dies & tools

(P-12876)
SPECIALTY INTERNATIONAL INC
11144 Penrose St Ste 11, Sun Valley
(91352-5601)
PHONE.....................818 768-8810
Anthony J Magnone, *President*
Jack McConnell, *Vice Pres*
▲ EMP: 100
SALES (est): 15.7MM **Privately Held**
WEB: www.specialtyinternational.com
SIC: 3469 Metal stampings

(P-12877)
STEICO INDUSTRIES INC
1814 Ord Way, Oceanside (92056-1502)
PHONE.....................760 438-8015
Troy Steiner, *CEO*
Ron Case, *Vice Pres*
Debbie Wolcott, *Controller*
▲ EMP: 230
SQ FT: 52,000
SALES: 36.8MM
SALES (corp-wide): 1.3B **Privately Held**
WEB: www.steicoindustries.com
SIC: 3469 5051 Metal stampings; metals service centers & offices
HQ: Senior Operations Llc
300 E Devon Ave
Bartlett IL 60103
630 372-3500

(P-12878)
STRATUS COML COOKING EQP INC
1760 W 1st St, Irwindale (91702-3259)
PHONE.....................626 969-7041
Robert Spenuzza, *CEO*
EMP: 11
SALES (est): 1.4MM **Privately Held**
SIC: 3469 Kitchen fixtures & equipment: metal, except cast aluminum

(P-12879)
SUNSTONE COMPONENTS GROUP INC (HQ)
Also Called: Sun Stone Sales
42136 Avenida Alvarado, Temecula
(92590-3400)
PHONE.....................951 296-5010
Bradway B Adams, *CEO*
David Bernard, *CFO*
EMP: 30

SALES (est): 8MM
SALES (corp-wide): 39.6MM **Privately Held**
WEB: www.sss-i.com
SIC: 3469 Metal stampings
PA: Pancon Corporation
350 Revolutionary Dr
East Taunton MA 02718
781 297-6000

(P-12880)
TEAM MANUFACTURING INC
2625 Homestead Pl, Rancho Dominguez
(90220-5610)
PHONE.....................310 639-0251
Ed Ellis, *CEO*
James Cheatham, *Vice Pres*
Luis Almanza, *Manager*
▲ EMP: 50
SQ FT: 34,000
SALES (est): 6.8MM **Privately Held**
WEB: www.teammfg.com
SIC: 3469 3544 Stamping metal for the trade; die sets for metal stamping (presses)

(P-12881)
TECHNLOGY KNWLDGABLE MACHINING
Also Called: Tekma
1920 Kona Dr, Compton (90220-5417)
PHONE.....................310 608-7756
Phong Ly, *President*
Hoa Ly, *Treasurer*
EMP: 10
SQ FT: 10,000
SALES: 650K **Privately Held**
SIC: 3469 Machine parts, stamped or pressed metal

(P-12882)
TOOLANDER ENGINEERING INC
1110 Via Callejon, San Clemente
(92673-6230)
PHONE.....................949 498-8339
Fred Kutzmarski, *President*
Harry F Kutzmarski, *Shareholder*
Steve Kutzmarski, *Vice Pres*
EMP: 10
SQ FT: 10,000
SALES (est): 950K **Privately Held**
SIC: 3469 3544 Stamping metal for the trade; special dies & tools

(P-12883)
TOP NOTCH MANUFACTURING INC
1488 Pioneer Way Ste 17, El Cajon
(92020-1633)
PHONE.....................619 588-2033
Peter Vickonoff, *President*
Patricia Santore, *CFO*
Jason Janik, *General Mgr*
EMP: 11
SQ FT: 6,000
SALES (est): 880K **Privately Held**
SIC: 3469 3444 Machine parts, stamped or pressed metal; sheet metalwork

(P-12884)
TRAVIS MIKE INC
Also Called: Mt
2420 Celsius Ave Ste D, Oxnard
(93030-5160)
PHONE.....................805 201-3363
Travis Frazier, *CEO*
Mike Brabante, *Principal*
▲ EMP: 10
SALES (est): 2MM **Privately Held**
SIC: 3469 Machine parts, stamped or pressed metal

(P-12885)
TRU-FORM INDUSTRIES INC (PA)
Also Called: Tru Form Industries
14511 Anson Ave, Santa Fe Springs
(90670-5393)
PHONE.....................562 802-2041
Vernon M Hildebrandt, *CEO*
Vern Hildebrandt, *MIS Mgr*
Mark Tiedeman, *Sales Executive*
▲ EMP: 70
SQ FT: 50,000

SALES (est): 13.8MM **Privately Held**
WEB: www.tru-form.com
SIC: 3469 3496 3429 Metal stampings; clips & fasteners, made from purchased wire; manufactured hardware (general)

(P-12886)
TUNG TAI GROUP
1726 Rogers Ave, San Jose (95112-1109)
PHONE.....................408 573-8681
Toll Free:.....................877 -
Joseph Chen, *President*
◆ EMP: 12
SALES (est): 2.6MM **Privately Held**
SIC: 3469 5093 Metal stampings; metal scrap & waste materials

(P-12887)
VANGUARD TOOL & MFG CO INC
Also Called: Vanguard Tool & Manufacturing
8388 Utica Ave, Rancho Cucamonga
(91730-3849)
PHONE.....................909 980-9392
Robert A Scudder, *President*
Connie Scudder, *Vice Pres*
EMP: 49
SQ FT: 47,000
SALES (est): 9.5MM **Privately Held**
SIC: 3469 Stamping metal for the trade

(P-12888)
VERDUGO TOOL & ENGRG CO INC
20600 Superior St, Chatsworth
(91311-4414)
PHONE.....................818 998-1101
Kevin Gresiak, *President*
Johny Abarca, *Manager*
Arminda Aguayo, *Manager*
EMP: 17
SQ FT: 15,000
SALES (est): 3.6MM **Privately Held**
WEB: www.verdugotool.com
SIC: 3469 3544 Metal stampings; special dies & tools

(P-12889)
WALKER SPRING & STAMPING CORP
1555 S Vintage Ave, Ontario (91761-3655)
PHONE.....................909 390-4300
Lang Walker, *Ch of Bd*
Bruce Walker, *President*
Carmen Prieto, *CFO*
Randy Walker, *Vice Pres*
James D Walker Jr, *VP Mfg*
▲ EMP: 110 EST: 1954
SQ FT: 108,000
SALES (est): 28MM **Privately Held**
WEB: www.walkercorp.com
SIC: 3469 3495 Stamping metal for the trade; precision springs

(P-12890)
WEST COAST MANUFACTURING INC
1822 Western Ave, Stanton (90680)
PHONE.....................714 897-4221
Patrick Hundley, *President*
Minerva Hundley, *Vice Pres*
Ann Marie Lind, *Manager*
▲ EMP: 26
SQ FT: 8,000
SALES (est): 5.6MM **Privately Held**
WEB: www.westcoastmfg.com
SIC: 3469 Machine parts, stamped or pressed metal

(P-12891)
WEST COAST METAL STAMPING INC
550 W Crowther Ave, Placentia
(92870-6312)
PHONE.....................714 792-0322
Jerome R Reinhart, *President*
Dan A Totoiu, *Vice Pres*
EMP: 32
SQ FT: 58,000
SALES: 5MM **Privately Held**
WEB: www.bjtooldie.com
SIC: 3469 Metal stampings

PRODUCTS & SVCS

(P-12892)
WESTERN METAL SPINNING & MFG
Also Called: Western Metal Spinning Farming
5055 Western Way, Perris (92571-7420)
PHONE..............................951 657-0711
David Domanske, *President*
EMP: 10 EST: 1945
SQ FT: 20,000
SALES (est): 1.9MM **Privately Held**
WEB: www.kissaviation.com
SIC: 3469 3411 Spinning metal for the trade; metal cans

(P-12893)
WILLIAMS METAL BLANKING DIES
16222 Minnesota Ave, Paramount (90723-4916)
PHONE..............................562 634-4592
Verle Williams, *President*
Fred Harmon, *Vice Pres*
EMP: 12
SQ FT: 10,000
SALES: 810.2K **Privately Held**
SIC: 3469 3544 Stamping metal for the trade; special dies & tools

---

3471 Electroplating, Plating, Polishing, Anodizing & Coloring

---

(P-12894)
A & D PLATING INC
2265 Micro Pl Ste A, Escondido (92029-1011)
PHONE..............................760 480-4580
Antonio Medina, *President*
EMP: 11
SQ FT: 2,400
SALES: 550K **Privately Held**
SIC: 3471 Electroplating of metals or formed products; plating of metals or formed products

(P-12895)
A & E ANODIZING INC
652 Charles St Ste A, San Jose (95112-1433)
PHONE..............................408 297-5910
Edwardo Ibanez, *President*
Angelica Ibanez, *CFO*
Laura Santiesteban, *Manager*
EMP: 15
SALES (est): 1.6MM **Privately Held**
SIC: 3471 Anodizing (plating) of metals or formed products

(P-12896)
A&A METAL FINISHING ENTPS LLC
8290 Alpine Ave, Sacramento (95826-4748)
PHONE..............................916 442-1063
Anthony R Nole, *Vice Pres*
Nancy M Casale, *Admin Sec*
EMP: 20
SALES (est): 1.9MM **Privately Held**
SIC: 3471 Electroplating of metals or formed products

(P-12897)
A-H PLATING INC
28079 Avenue Stanford, Valencia (91355-1104)
PHONE..............................818 845-6243
John Waschack, *President*
EMP: 65
SALES (est): 5MM
SALES (corp-wide): 30MM **Privately Held**
WEB: www.sunvairoverhaul.com
SIC: 3471 Plating of metals or formed products
HQ: Sunvair, Inc.
   29145 The Old Rd
   Valencia CA 91355
   661 294-3777

(P-12898)
AAA PLATING & INSPECTION INC
424 E Dixon St, Compton (90222-1420)
PHONE..............................323 979-8930
Gerald Wahlin, *CEO*
Charles Schwan, *Corp Secy*
Marie Reed, *Human Res Mgr*
Bill Cox, *Production*
Gregg Halligan, *Sales Staff*
EMP: 95
SQ FT: 50,000
SALES (est): 15.1MM **Privately Held**
WEB: www.aaaplating.com
SIC: 3471 8734 Anodizing (plating) of metals or formed products; metallurgical testing laboratory

(P-12899)
ABLE METAL PLATING INC
932 86th Ave, Oakland (94621-1642)
P.O. Box 43480 (94624-0480)
PHONE..............................510 569-6539
Jose Vasquez, *President*
Rafael De La Paz, *Vice Pres*
Elizabeth Vasquez, *Vice Pres*
EMP: 20
SQ FT: 7,500
SALES: 1MM **Privately Held**
SIC: 3471 Electroplating of metals or formed products

(P-12900)
ACCUCROME PLATING CO INC
115 W 154th St, Gardena (90248-2201)
PHONE..............................310 327-8268
Armen Maghtessian, *President*
EMP: 10
SQ FT: 1,800
SALES (est): 896.8K **Privately Held**
SIC: 3471 Chromium plating of metals or formed products; cleaning, polishing & finishing

(P-12901)
ACCURATE ANODIZING INC
1801 W El Segundo Blvd, Compton (90222-1026)
P.O. Box 5207 (90224-5207)
PHONE..............................310 637-0349
Thomas P Oakes, *President*
John Oakes, *Corp Secy*
Laura Oakes, *Exec VP*
EMP: 10
SQ FT: 8,000
SALES (est): 1.1MM **Privately Held**
SIC: 3471 Anodizing (plating) of metals or formed products; plating of metals or formed products

(P-12902)
ACCURATE PLATING COMPANY
2811 Alcazar St, Los Angeles (90033-1108)
P.O. Box 33348 (90033-0348)
PHONE..............................323 268-8567
Dennis Orr, *President*
Rigo Rodriguez, *Vice Pres*
EMP: 30 EST: 1949
SQ FT: 18,000
SALES (est): 3.6MM **Privately Held**
WEB: www.accurateplating.com
SIC: 3471 Electroplating of metals or formed products

(P-12903)
ACTIVE PLATING INC
1411 E Pomona St, Santa Ana (92705-4802)
PHONE..............................714 547-0356
Keith Korta, *President*
EMP: 25
SQ FT: 6,000
SALES (est): 3.3MM **Privately Held**
SIC: 3471 Electroplating of metals or formed products; plating of metals or formed products

(P-12904)
ADHARA INC (PA)
9465 Customhouse Plz H1, San Diego (92154-7632)
PHONE..............................619 661-9901
Enrique Mereles, *President*
EMP: 10

SALES (est): 1.6MM **Privately Held**
WEB: www.adhara.net
SIC: 3471 Plating & polishing

(P-12905)
ADVANCED METAL FINISHING LLC
Also Called: AMF
2130 March Rd, Roseville (95747-9308)
PHONE..............................530 888-7772
Mischelle Von Rembov,
EMP: 20
SQ FT: 4,500
SALES (est): 3.5MM **Privately Held**
SIC: 3471 Finishing, metals or formed products

(P-12906)
ADVANCED SURFACE FINISHING INC
1181 N 4th St Ste 50, San Jose (95112-4962)
PHONE..............................408 275-9718
Salah Hamed, *President*
Jose Diaz, *Vice Pres*
EMP: 10
SQ FT: 17,000
SALES: 1.5MM **Privately Held**
SIC: 3471 Plating of metals or formed products

(P-12907)
ADVANCED TECH PLATING
1061 N Grove St, Anaheim (92806-2015)
PHONE..............................714 630-7093
Meliton Gomez, *President*
EMP: 30
SQ FT: 9,706
SALES (est): 2.6MM **Privately Held**
SIC: 3471 Plating of metals or formed products

(P-12908)
AERO MANUFACTURING & PLTG CO
Also Called: Automation Plating
927 Thompson Ave, Glendale (91201-2011)
PHONE..............................818 241-2844
William Wiggins, *Chairman*
Peter Wiggins, *Chairman*
EMP: 50 EST: 1958
SQ FT: 65,000
SALES (est): 4MM **Privately Held**
WEB: www.apczinc.com
SIC: 3471 Plating of metals or formed products

(P-12909)
AERODYNAMIC PLATING CO
13620 S Saint Andrews Pl, Gardena (90249-2480)
PHONE..............................310 329-7959
Joe Reynoso Jr, *President*
Joe Reynoso Sr, *Treasurer*
EMP: 60 EST: 1967
SQ FT: 5,500
SALES (est): 5.7MM **Privately Held**
SIC: 3471 Anodizing (plating) of metals or formed products; electroplating of metals or formed products

(P-12910)
AGUILAR WILLIAMS INC
Also Called: Tool & Jig Plating Co
7635 Baldwin Pl, Whittier (90602-1024)
PHONE..............................562 693-2736
Jesus Aguilar, *President*
Michael Williams, *Treasurer*
Leonor Oropeza, *Admin Sec*
EMP: 13
SALES: 720K **Privately Held**
SIC: 3471 Chromium plating of metals or formed products

(P-12911)
AI INDUSTRIES LLC (PA)
1725 E Byshore Rd Ste 101, Redwood City (94063)
PHONE..............................650 366-4099
Shannon Lew,
Bob Mosko, *Human Res Mgr*
EMP: 79
SQ FT: 27,000

SALES (est): 19.4MM **Privately Held**
WEB: www.aiindustries.com
SIC: 3471 3479 Anodizing (plating) of metals or formed products; coating of metals & formed products

(P-12912)
ALCO PLATING CORP (PA)
Also Called: Modern Plating
1400 Long Beach Ave, Los Angeles (90021-2794)
PHONE..............................213 749-7561
E Edward Manzetti, *President*
Emil Edward Manzetti, *President*
David Manzetti, *Vice Pres*
▲ EMP: 110
SQ FT: 65,000
SALES (est): 10.5MM **Privately Held**
SIC: 3471 Electroplating of metals or formed products

(P-12913)
ALERT PLATING COMPANY
9939 Glenoaks Blvd, Sun Valley (91352-1023)
PHONE..............................818 771-9304
David La Liberte, *President*
Maurice La Liberte, *Ch of Bd*
Ed Lee, *Treasurer*
Shirley La Liberte, *Admin Sec*
EMP: 45
SQ FT: 22,000
SALES (est): 6.8MM **Privately Held**
SIC: 3471 Finishing, metals or formed products; plating of metals or formed products

(P-12914)
ALL METALS PROC SAN DIEGO INC
Also Called: AMC
8401 Standustrial St, Stanton (90680-2688)
PHONE..............................714 828-8238
Kevin Fairfax, *Vice Pres*
EMP: 120
SQ FT: 27,000
SALES (est): 16.2MM **Privately Held**
WEB: www.drilube.com
SIC: 3471 3479 8734 Electroplating of metals or formed products; enameling, including porcelain, of metal products; painting of metal products; X-ray inspection service, industrial; metallurgical testing laboratory

(P-12915)
ALLBLACK CO INC
13090 Park St, Santa Fe Springs (90670-4032)
PHONE..............................562 946-2955
Juan F Guerrero, *President*
Lorena Guerrero, *Corp Secy*
▲ EMP: 39
SQ FT: 12,000
SALES (est): 3.3MM **Privately Held**
SIC: 3471 Electroplating of metals or formed products

(P-12916)
ALLEN INDUSTRIAL INC
960 S Hathaway St, Banning (92220-6302)
P.O. Box 776 (92220-0006)
PHONE..............................951 849-4966
David Dohoda, *Owner*
EMP: 10
SALES (est): 1MM **Privately Held**
SIC: 3471 7699 Plating of metals or formed products; industrial machinery & equipment repair

(P-12917)
ALLIANCE CHEMICAL & ENVMTL
Also Called: Alliance Finishing and Mfg
1721 Ives Ave, Oxnard (93033-1866)
PHONE..............................805 385-3330
Mark Hyman, *President*
Heather Hyman, *Vice Pres*
EMP: 16
SQ FT: 15,600
SALES (est): 2.6MM **Privately Held**
WEB: www.starkart.com
SIC: 3471 Plating & polishing

▲ = Import ▼=Export
◆ =Import/Export

(P-12918)
ALLOY TECH ELECTROPOLISHING
2220 S Huron Dr, Santa Ana (92704-4947)
PHONE..................................714 434-6604
Ursula Zagner, *CEO*
George Zagner, *Vice Pres*
EMP: 10
SQ FT: 10,000
SALES (est): 1.2MM **Privately Held**
WEB: www.atep.com
SIC: 3471 Cleaning, polishing & finishing

(P-12919)
ALM CHROME
654 Young St, Santa Ana (92705-5633)
PHONE..................................714 545-3540
Lanberto Morales, *Owner*
EMP: 50
SALES (est): 3.2MM **Privately Held**
SIC: 3471 Electroplating of metals or
  formed products

(P-12920)
ALPHA POLISHING CORPORATION (PA)
Also Called: General Plating
1313 Mirasol St, Los Angeles
(90023-3108)
PHONE..................................323 263-7593
Alan Olick, *President*
Trinidad Gonzales, *Vice Pres*
EMP: 60
SQ FT: 7,500
SALES (est): 10.5MM **Privately Held**
WEB: www.generalplating.com
SIC: 3471 3911 Plating of metals or
  formed products; polishing, metals or
  formed products; pins (jewelry), precious
  metal

(P-12921)
ALPHACOAT FINISHING LLC
9350 Cabot Dr, San Diego (92126-4311)
PHONE..................................949 748-7796
Ravinder Joshi,
Vaishali Joshi,
EMP: 28 EST: 2017
SALES: 1.7MM **Privately Held**
SIC: 3471 Plating of metals or formed
  products

(P-12922)
ALUMFLAM NORTH AMERICA
16604 Edwards Rd, Cerritos (90703-2438)
PHONE..................................562 926-9520
Carl Lorentzen, *Principal*
Zac Monroe, *Project Mgr*
Edith Loera, *Engineer*
EMP: 20
SALES (est): 1.4MM **Privately Held**
SIC: 3471 Coloring & finishing of aluminum
  or formed products

(P-12923)
ALUMIN-ART PLATING CO INC
803 W State St, Ontario (91762-4130)
PHONE..................................909 983-1866
David Rudy, *President*
Barbara Newman, *Treasurer*
Joyce Clements, *Vice Pres*
Isaac Rudy, *Safety Mgr*
Jerry Newman, *Manager*
EMP: 30 EST: 1961
SQ FT: 6,500
SALES (est): 1.5MM **Privately Held**
SIC: 3471 Electroplating of metals or
  formed products

(P-12924)
ALUMINUM COATING TECH INC
Also Called: A.C.T.
8290 Alpine Ave, Sacramento
(95826-4748)
PHONE..................................916 442-1063
Steven S Hickey, *CEO*
EMP: 20
SALES (est): 1.6MM **Privately Held**
SIC: 3471 Plating of metals or formed
  products

(P-12925)
AMEX PLATING INCORPORATED
3333 Woodward Ave, Santa Clara
(95054-2628)
PHONE..........................408 986-8222
Jose Rodriguez, *President*
Sylvia D Rodriguez, *CEO*
Rebeca Rodriguez, *Vice Pres*
EMP: 30
SQ FT: 10,850
SALES (est): 3.6MM **Privately Held**
SIC: 3471 Finishing, metals or formed
  products; anodizing (plating) of metals or
  formed products

(P-12926)
ANADITE CAL RESTORATION TR
Also Called: Metal Finishing Division
10647 Garfield Ave, South Gate
(90280-7391)
P.O. Box 1399 (90280-1399)
PHONE..................................562 861-2205
Margie Gutierrez, *Branch Mgr*
EMP: 46
SALES (corp-wide): 4.2MM **Privately
Held**
WEB: www.anadite.com
SIC: 3471 Finishing, metals or formed
  products
PA: Anadite California Restoration Trust
  711 W Hurst Blvd
  Hurst TX 76053
  817 282-9171

(P-12927)
ANAPLEX CORPORATION
15547 Garfield Ave, Paramount
(90723-4033)
PHONE..................................714 522-4481
Carmen Campbell, *CEO*
Bernie Kerper, *President*
Julio Valdivieso, *Bd of Directors*
EMP: 48 EST: 1962
SQ FT: 38,000
SALES (est): 5.9MM **Privately Held**
SIC: 3471 Plating of metals or formed
  products; finishing, metals or formed
  products

(P-12928)
ANOCOTE
7550 Trade St, San Diego (92121-2412)
PHONE..................................858 566-1015
Romy Cimarmann, *President*
EMP: 12
SQ FT: 1,100
SALES (est): 994K **Privately Held**
SIC: 3471 Coloring & finishing of aluminum
  or formed products

(P-12929)
ANODIZING INDUSTRIES INC
5222 Alhambra Ave, Los Angeles
(90032-3403)
P.O. Box 32459 (90032-0459)
PHONE..................................323 227-4916
Eugene J Golling, *President*
Amir Afshar, *Vice Pres*
▲ **EMP:** 30
SQ FT: 8,000
SALES (est): 4.6MM **Privately Held**
WEB: www.anodizingindusries.com
SIC: 3471 3479 2396 Anodizing (plating)
  of metals or formed products; cleaning,
  polishing & finishing; painting of metal
  products; automotive & apparel trimmings

(P-12930)
ANODYNE INC
2230 S Susan St, Santa Ana (92704-4493)
PHONE..................................714 549-3321
Ralph Adams, *President*
Patti Kientz, *Vice Pres*
Gary Fox, *Director*
Sue Grace, *Accounts Mgr*
EMP: 49 EST: 1960
SQ FT: 30,000
SALES (est): 6.1MM **Privately Held**
SIC: 3471 8734 Anodizing (plating) of met-
  als or formed products; testing laborato-
  ries

(P-12931)
APPLIED ANODIZE INC
622 Charcot Ave Ste D, San Jose
(95131-2205)
PHONE..................................408 435-9191
Jose Muguerza, *President*
EMP: 55 EST: 1978
SQ FT: 14,000
SALES (est): 5MM **Privately Held**
SIC: 3471 Coloring & finishing of aluminum
  or formed products; finishing, metals or
  formed products; plating of metals or
  formed products

(P-12932)
AQUARIAN COATINGS CORP
1140 N Tustin Ave, Anaheim (92807-1778)
PHONE..................................714 632-0230
Ronald Marquez, *President*
Rose Marquez, *Vice Pres*
EMP: 37 EST: 1974
SQ FT: 20,000
SALES (est): 3.3MM **Privately Held**
SIC: 3471 Electroplating of metals or
  formed products

(P-12933)
ARA TECHNOLOGY
1286 Anvilwood Ave, Sunnyvale
(94089-2203)
PHONE..................................408 734-8131
Mardig Chakalian, *President*
Haig Chakalian, *Vice Pres*
EMP: 20 EST: 1977
SQ FT: 10,000
SALES (est): 1.9MM **Privately Held**
SIC: 3471 Plating of metals or formed
  products

(P-12934)
ARTISTIC PLTG & MET FINSHG INC
2801 E Miraloma Ave, Anaheim
(92806-1804)
PHONE..................................619 661-1691
Kipton Kahler, *President*
EMP: 100
SQ FT: 44,573
SALES (est): 10.2MM **Privately Held**
SIC: 3471 Chromium plating of metals or
  formed products

(P-12935)
ARTURO CAMPOS
Also Called: A&A Plating
796 Palmyrita Ave Ste B, Riverside
(92507-1824)
PHONE..................................951 300-2111
Arturo Campos, *Owner*
▼ **EMP:** 12 EST: 2007
SQ FT: 3,680
SALES (est): 882.5K **Privately Held**
SIC: 3471 Plating of metals or formed
  products

(P-12936)
ASSOCIATED PLATING COMPANY
Also Called: A P C
9636 Ann St, Santa Fe Springs
(90670-2902)
PHONE..................................562 946-5525
Michael Evans, *President*
Jon Shulkin, *Shareholder*
Diane Crane, *Vice Pres*
Randy Roth, *Plant Engr*
Theresa Flores,
▲ **EMP:** 42 EST: 1952
SQ FT: 18,000
SALES (est): 4.8MM **Privately Held**
WEB: www.associatedplating.com
SIC: 3471 Finishing, metals or formed
  products; electroplating of metals or
  formed products

(P-12937)
ASTRO CHROME AND POLSG CORP
8136 Lankershim Blvd, North Hollywood
(91605-1611)
PHONE..................................818 781-1463
Jesse Gonzalez, *President*
Eazi Tamen, *General Mgr*
EMP: 23
SQ FT: 3,000

SALES (est): 1.7MM **Privately Held**
SIC: 3471 Plating of metals or formed
  products

(P-12938)
ATMF INC
Also Called: Ano-Tech Metal Finishing
807 Lincoln Ave, Clovis (93612-2245)
PHONE..................................559 299-6836
Carol Downs, *CEO*
Kelly S Downs, *President*
Gregory Ott, *Vice Pres*
Rich Tuman, *Purch Mgr*
Brett Hunter, *Plant Mgr*
EMP: 30
SQ FT: 8,000
SALES (est): 5.1MM **Privately Held**
WEB: www.atmf.com
SIC: 3471 Anodizing (plating) of metals or
  formed products; coloring & finishing of
  aluminum or formed products

(P-12939)
AUTOMATION PLATING CORPORATION
927 Thompson Ave, Glendale
(91201-2011)
PHONE..................................323 245-4951
William D Wiggins, *Co-COB*
Peter K Wiggins, *CEO*
Pat Kinzy, *COO*
Marcia Mitchell, *CFO*
Edward Lee, *Admin Sec*
EMP: 40
SQ FT: 65,000
SALES (est): 6.1MM **Privately Held**
SIC: 3471 Plating of metals or formed
  products

(P-12940)
B & C PLATING CO
1507 S Sunol Dr, Los Angeles
(90023-4031)
PHONE..................................323 263-6757
Dick Patel, *President*
Suresh Sheth, *Admin Sec*
EMP: 22
SQ FT: 10,000
SALES (est): 2.3MM **Privately Held**
WEB: www.bandcplating.com
SIC: 3471 2899 Plating of metals or
  formed products; chemical preparations

(P-12941)
BARRY AVENUE PLATING CO INC
2210 Barry Ave, Los Angeles (90064-1488)
PHONE..................................310 478-0078
Chuck Kearsley, *President*
Charles B Kearsley IV, *President*
Ken Kearsley, *Vice Pres*
Kenneth F Kearsley, *Vice Pres*
Timothy Dearn, *Opers Mgr*
▼ **EMP:** 88
SQ FT: 26,000
SALES: 16.7MM **Privately Held**
SIC: 3471 Plating of metals or formed
  products

(P-12942)
BHC INDUSTRIES INC
239 E Greenleaf Blvd, Compton
(90220-4913)
PHONE..................................310 632-2000
Gary Barken, *President*
EMP: 25 EST: 2000
SQ FT: 20,000
SALES (est): 3.8MM **Privately Held**
SIC: 3471 Chromium plating of metals or
  formed products

(P-12943)
BLACK OXIDE INDUSTRIES INC
1745 N Orangethorpe Park, Anaheim
(92801-1139)
PHONE..................................714 870-9610
Pete Mata, *President*
Evelyn Mata, *Corp Secy*
Edward Mata, *Vice Pres*
EMP: 35 EST: 1974
SALES (est): 5MM **Privately Held**
WEB: www.blackoxideindustries.com
SIC: 3471 3479 Electroplating & plating;
  coating of metals & formed products

(P-12944)
BLACK OXIDE SERVICE INC
Also Called: Bos
1070 Linda Vista Dr Ste A, San Marcos
(92078-2653)
PHONE....................................760 744-8692
Leopold Slivnik, *President*
Monica Slivnik, *Opers Staff*
EMP: 10
SQ FT: 1,250
SALES (est): 1.2MM **Privately Held**
WEB: www.blackoxideservice.com
SIC: 3471 5169 Plating of metals or
formed products; chemicals & allied products

(P-12945)
BLAIRS METAL POLSG PLTG CO INC
17760 Crusader Ave, Cerritos
(90703-2629)
PHONE....................................562 860-7106
Keith W Blair, *CEO*
Keith Blair, *Vice Pres*
EMP: 13 **EST:** 1950
SQ FT: 10,000
SALES (est): 1MM **Privately Held**
SIC: 3471 Polishing, metals or formed
products

(P-12946)
BOBBYS METAL FINISHING
12423 Gladstone Ave # 25, Sylmar
(91342-5341)
PHONE....................................818 837-1928
Roberto Montenegro, *Principal*
EMP: 10
SALES (est): 807.7K **Privately Held**
SIC: 3471 Polishing, metals or formed
products

(P-12947)
BODYCOTE THERMAL PROC INC
3370 Benedict Way, Huntington Park
(90255-4517)
PHONE....................................323 583-1231
Chris Hall, *Branch Mgr*
EMP: 87
SQ FT: 16,694
SALES (corp-wide): 935.8MM **Privately Held**
SIC: 3471 3398 Plating & polishing; metal
heat treating
HQ: Bodycote Thermal Processing, Inc.
12700 Park Central Dr # 700
Dallas TX 75251
214 904-2420

(P-12948)
BONNER PROCESSING INC
6052 Industrial Way Ste A, Livermore
(94551-9711)
PHONE....................................925 455-3833
Robert Bonner, *President*
EMP: 40
SQ FT: 19,500
SALES (est): 3.8MM **Privately Held**
SIC: 3471 Tumbling (cleaning & polishing)
of machine parts

(P-12949)
BOWMAN PLATING CO INC
2631 E 126th St, Compton (90222-1599)
P.O. Box 5205 (90224-5205)
PHONE....................................310 639-4343
Mac Esfandi, *President*
John Esfandi, *Shareholder*
Cyrus Gipoor, *Shareholder*
Massoud Akhavi, *Officer*
Brad Simpson, *Vice Pres*
EMP: 150 **EST:** 1952
SALES (est): 21.7MM **Privately Held**
WEB: www.bowmanplating.com
SIC: 3471 Plating of metals or formed
products

(P-12950)
BRITE PLATING CO INC
1313 Mirasol St, Los Angeles
(90023-3108)
PHONE....................................323 263-7593
Alan Olick, *CEO*
Kashiam Patel, *Vice Pres*
EMP: 71

SQ FT: 60,000
SALES (est): 7.5MM **Privately Held**
SIC: 3471 Plating of metals or formed
products

(P-12951)
BRONZE-WAY PLATING CORPORATION (PA)
3301 E 14th St, Los Angeles (90023-3893)
PHONE....................................323 266-6933
Sarkis Mikhael-Fard, *President*
Benjamin Mikhael-Fard, *Vice Pres*
Fiyodor Mikhael-Fard, *Vice Pres*
Fred Mikhael-Fard, *Vice Pres*
EMP: 44 **EST:** 1956
SQ FT: 27,000
SALES (est): 3.2MM **Privately Held**
SIC: 3471 Electroplating of metals or
formed products

(P-12952)
BUDS POLISHING & METAL FINSHG
1156 N Kraemer Pl, Anaheim (92806-1922)
PHONE....................................714 632-0121
Forrest Graybill, *President*
EMP: 15
SALES (est): 1.7MM **Privately Held**
SIC: 3471 Polishing, metals or formed
products

(P-12953)
BURBANK PLATING SERVICE CORP
13561 Desmond St, Pacoima
(91331-2394)
PHONE....................................818 899-1157
Robert Scheer, *President*
Andy Scheer, *Vice Pres*
Midge Churchill, *Bookkeeper*
▲ **EMP:** 15 **EST:** 1965
SQ FT: 20,000
SALES (est): 1.2MM **Privately Held**
SIC: 3471 Plating of metals or formed
products

(P-12954)
BURLINGTON ENGINEERING INC
220 W Grove Ave, Orange (92865-3204)
PHONE....................................714 921-4045
Karen Corbell, *President*
David Corbell, *Vice Pres*
EMP: 21
SQ FT: 18,000
SALES (est): 2.2MM **Privately Held**
WEB: www.burlingtoneng.com
SIC: 3471 3398 Plating & polishing; metal
heat treating

(P-12955)
BUSH POLISHING & CHROME
2236 W 2nd St, Santa Ana (92703-3511)
PHONE....................................714 537-7440
David L Bush Sr, *Owner*
Chris Hefferon, *Opers Dir*
EMP: 12
SALES (est): 1MM **Privately Held**
WEB: www.bushpolishingandchrome.com
SIC: 3471 Finishing, metals or formed
products

(P-12956)
C C M D INC
Also Called: Hytech Processing
700 Centinela Ave, Inglewood
(90302-2414)
PHONE....................................310 673-5532
Michael S Graves, *President*
Odette Graves, *CFO*
EMP: 15
SQ FT: 7,000
SALES: 850K **Privately Held**
WEB: www.hytechprocessing.com
SIC: 3471 Finishing, metals or formed
products

(P-12957)
C P AUTO PRODUCTS INC
3901 Medford St, Los Angeles
(90063-1608)
P.O. Box 63915 (90063-0915)
PHONE....................................323 266-3850
Tom Longo, *President*
▲ **EMP:** 50

SQ FT: 100,000
SALES (est): 4.9MM **Privately Held**
WEB: www.derale.com
SIC: 3471 3714 3564 Plating of metals or
formed products; motor vehicle parts &
accessories; blowers & fans

(P-12958)
CADILLAC PLATING INC
1147 W Struck Ave, Orange (92867-3529)
PHONE....................................714 639-0342
Adan Ibarra, *President*
Lupe Ibarra, *Treasurer*
Alfred Ibarra, *Assistant VP*
EMP: 18 **EST:** 1972
SQ FT: 6,000
SALES (est): 2.2MM **Privately Held**
SIC: 3471 Plating of metals or formed
products; electroplating of metals or
formed products

(P-12959)
CAL-AURUM INDUSTRIES
15632 Container Ln, Huntington Beach
(92649-1533)
PHONE....................................714 898-0996
Paul A Ginder, *President*
Chuck Tygard, *Vice Pres*
Allen Witbeck, *Vice Pres*
Vern Marken, *Controller*
Mark Deitelbaum, *Manager*
EMP: 35 **EST:** 1971
SQ FT: 25,000
SALES (est): 5.9MM **Privately Held**
WEB: www.cal-aurum.com
SIC: 3471 Plating of metals or formed
products

(P-12960)
CAL-TRON PLATING INC
11919 Rivera Rd, Santa Fe Springs
(90670-2209)
PHONE....................................562 945-1181
Carl Troncale Jr, *CEO*
Carl Troncale Sr, *Ch of Bd*
EMP: 45
SQ FT: 15,000
SALES: 3.5MM **Privately Held**
SIC: 3471 Electroplating of metals or
formed products; polishing, metals or
formed products

(P-12961)
CALIFORNIA METAL PROCESSING CO
1518 W Slauson Ave # 1530, Los Angeles
(90047-1230)
PHONE....................................323 753-2247
Terry Andersen, *Partner*
Merry Anderson, *Ltd Ptnr*
Robert Gates, *Ltd Ptnr*
Thelma Gates, *Ltd Ptnr*
EMP: 21
SQ FT: 10,800
SALES (est): 1.8MM **Privately Held**
SIC: 3471 8734 Plating of metals or
formed products; testing laboratories

(P-12962)
CALIFORNIA TECHNICAL PLTG CORP
11533 Bradley Ave, San Fernando
(91340-2519)
PHONE....................................818 365-8205
David Anzures Sr, *President*
Sandra Anzures, *Corp Secy*
Brett Lpio, *General Mgr*
EMP: 45
SQ FT: 26,000
SALES: 5.1MM **Privately Held**
WEB: www.caltechplating.com
SIC: 3471 Plating of metals or formed
products; cleaning & descaling metal
products; chromium plating of metals or
formed products

(P-12963)
CARTER PLATING INC
1842 N Keystone St, Burbank
(91504-3417)
PHONE....................................818 842-1325
Val T Romney Sr, *President*
Earlene Romney, *Vice Pres*
EMP: 11 **EST:** 1953
SQ FT: 2,400

SALES (est): 1.1MM **Privately Held**
SIC: 3471 Plating of metals or formed
products

(P-12964)
CEMCOAT INC
4928 W Jefferson Blvd, Los Angeles
(90016-3923)
PHONE....................................323 733-0125
Farzaneh Aalam, *President*
Mike Aalam, *Vice Pres*
EMP: 20
SQ FT: 14,500
SALES (est): 2.3MM **Privately Held**
SIC: 3471 Plating of metals or formed
products

(P-12965)
CERTIFIED STEEL TREATING CORP
2454 E 58th St, Vernon (90058-3592)
PHONE....................................323 583-8711
Janice Davis, *President*
Pauline Nicolls, *Shareholder*
Dante Germano, *CFO*
Jeff Davis, *General Mgr*
Chuck Groves, *General Mgr*
EMP: 42
SQ FT: 30,000
SALES: 7.5MM **Privately Held**
WEB: www.certifiedsteeltreat.com
SIC: 3471 3398 Sand blasting of metal
parts; annealing of metal

(P-12966)
CHICO METAL FINISHING INC
3151 Richter Ave, Oroville (95966-5918)
PHONE....................................530 534-7308
Tom Cosf, *President*
Jim Marry, *General Mgr*
EMP: 10
SQ FT: 7,500
SALES (est): 936.5K **Privately Held**
SIC: 3471 Plating of metals or formed
products

(P-12967)
CHROMAL PLATING COMPANY
Also Called: Chromal Plating & Grinding
1748 Workman St, Los Angeles
(90031-3395)
PHONE....................................323 222-0119
Ethel Bokelman, *President*
Robin Osborn, *CFO*
Robin Ospoin, *CFO*
Robin Bokelman, *Corp Secy*
Ray F Bokelman Jr, *Vice Pres*
EMP: 28
SQ FT: 20,625
SALES (est): 4.2MM **Privately Held**
WEB: www.chromal.com
SIC: 3471 3999 Electroplating of metals or
formed products; custom pulverizing &
grinding of plastic materials

(P-12968)
CLASSIC COMPONENTS INC (PA)
Also Called: South Bay Chrome
3420 W Fordham Ave, Santa Ana
(92704-4422)
PHONE....................................714 619-5690
Bernard R Glass, *President*
Gary Glass, *Admin Sec*
EMP: 10
SQ FT: 17,000
SALES (est): 2.6MM **Privately Held**
WEB: www.chromeplating.com
SIC: 3471 Electroplating of metals or
formed products

(P-12969)
CLASSIC COMPONENTS INC
Also Called: South Bay Chrme/Chrome Effects
7651 Whitney Dr, Huntington Beach
(92647-3033)
PHONE....................................714 619-5690
Gary Glass, *Manager*
EMP: 22
SALES (corp-wide): 2.6MM **Privately Held**
WEB: www.chromeplating.com
SIC: 3471 Chromium plating of metals or
formed products

▲ = Import ▼=Export
◆ =Import/Export

PA: Classic Components Inc.
3420 W Fordham Ave
Santa Ana CA 92704
714 619-5690

(P-12970)
CLEAN SCIENCES INC
301 Whitney Pl, Fremont (94539-7665)
PHONE.................................510 440-8660
Jonathan Kaye, *President*
Snehal Patel, *Technician*
Dave Mortenson, *Director*
EMP: 12
SALES (est): 1.8MM **Privately Held**
WEB: www.cleansciences.com
SIC: 3471 Cleaning & descaling metal products

(P-12971)
COAST PLATING INC
417 W 164th St, Gardena (90248-2726)
PHONE.................................323 770-0240
Jose Solorzano, *Branch Mgr*
EMP: 15
SQ FT: 18,000
SALES (corp-wide): 8.6MM **Privately Held**
SIC: 3471 Plating of metals or formed products; anodizing (plating) of metals or formed products
PA: Coast Plating, Inc.
128 W 154th St
Gardena CA 90248
323 770-0240

(P-12972)
COAST TO COAST MET FINSHG CORP
401 S Raymond Ave, Alhambra (91803-1532)
PHONE.................................626 282-2122
Gildardo Bernal, *President*
Bill Maier, *Principal*
David Bernal, *Admin Sec*
EMP: 25
SQ FT: 20,000
SALES (est): 3.7MM **Privately Held**
SIC: 3471 3646 3645 Finishing, metals or formed products; commercial indusl & institutional electric lighting fixtures; residential lighting fixtures

(P-12973)
COASTLINE METAL FINISHING CORP
7061 Patterson Dr, Garden Grove (92841-1414)
PHONE.................................714 895-9099
Tracy Glende, *CEO*
Jamie Mitchell, *CFO*
Matthew Alty, *Vice Pres*
Rosa Vazquez, *Supervisor*
EMP: 83
SQ FT: 18,600
SALES (est): 9.3MM **Privately Held**
WEB: www.coastlinemetalfinishing.com
SIC: 3471 Finishing, metals or formed products; electroplating & plating; anodizing (plating) of metals or formed products

(P-12974)
COLORCARDS 960
6224 Via Regla, San Diego (92122-3921)
PHONE.................................858 535-9311
Robert Munroe, *Partner*
Duane R Churchwell, *Partner*
EMP: 46
SALES (est): 1.7MM **Privately Held**
SIC: 3471 3999 Coloring & finishing of aluminum or formed products; manufacturing industries

(P-12975)
COMMERCIAL SAND BLAST COMPANY
Also Called: Gcm Coating
2678 E 26th St, Vernon (90058-1218)
P.O. Box 58184, Los Angeles (90058-0184)
PHONE.................................323 581-8672
Fax: 323 589-2121
EMP: 11
SQ FT: 5,200
SALES (est): 1.4MM **Privately Held**
WEB: www.commercialsandblast.com
SIC: 3471 3479

(P-12976)
COMPONENT SURFACES INC
11880 Cmnty Rd Ste 380, Poway (92064)
PHONE.................................858 513-3656
David Sheilds, *President*
EMP: 15
SQ FT: 1,000
SALES: 350K **Privately Held**
SIC: 3471 Plating of metals or formed products

(P-12977)
CONNECTOR PLATING CORP
327 W 132nd St, Los Angeles (90061-1105)
PHONE.................................310 323-1622
Dale S Chung, *President*
EMP: 10
SQ FT: 12,000
SALES (est): 1.3MM **Privately Held**
SIC: 3471 Plating of metals or formed products

(P-12978)
CONNELL PROCESSING INC
3094 N Avon St, Burbank (91504-2003)
PHONE.................................818 845-7661
Stephen Lee, *President*
David Augustine, *Vice Pres*
EMP: 27
SQ FT: 25,000
SALES: 3.5MM **Privately Held**
WEB: www.connellprocessing.com
SIC: 3471 Finishing, metals or formed products; electroplating of metals or formed products

(P-12979)
CONTINUOUS COATING CORP (PA)
Also Called: Clinch-On Cornerbead Company
520 W Grove Ave, Orange (92865-3210)
PHONE.................................714 637-4642
Ralph M Scott, *President*
Kenneth N Harel, *Corp Secy*
Grace Meda, *Plant Mgr*
Kenneth Harel, *Manager*
EMP: 85
SQ FT: 84,000
SALES (est): 14.5MM **Privately Held**
WEB: www.clinchon.com
SIC: 3471 3444 7389 Electroplating of metals or formed products; sheet metal specialties, not stamped; metal slitting & shearing

(P-12980)
CRISOL METAL FINISHING
444 E Gardena Blvd C, Gardena (90248-2914)
PHONE.................................310 516-1165
Sebastian Carlo, *Owner*
EMP: 12
SALES (est): 1.4MM **Privately Held**
SIC: 3471 Plating of metals or formed products

(P-12981)
CSL OPERATING LLC
Also Called: C S L
529 Aldo Ave, Santa Clara (95054-2263)
PHONE.................................408 727-0893
Mahesh Naik, *President*
Kavita Patel, *Human Res Mgr*
Tim Mickael, *Manager*
▲ EMP: 55
SQ FT: 16,000
SALES (est): 7.5MM **Privately Held**
SIC: 3471 Anodizing (plating) of metals or formed products; cleaning & descaling metal products; electroplating of metals or formed products; cleaning, polishing & finishing

(P-12982)
DANCO ANODIZING INC (PA)
Also Called: Danco Metal Surfacing
44 La Porte St, Arcadia (91006-2827)
P.O. Box 660727, (91066-0727)
PHONE.................................626 445-3303
Sherri Vivian Scherer, *President*
David Tatge, *Treasurer*
George Saunders, *QC Mgr*
Lavaughn Daniel, *Marketing Mgr*
EMP: 40 EST: 1971
SQ FT: 10,000

SALES: 13.3MM **Privately Held**
WEB: www.danco.net
SIC: 3471 Anodizing (plating) of metals or formed products

(P-12983)
DANCO ANODIZING INC
1750 E Monticello Ct, Ontario (91761-7740)
PHONE.................................909 923-0562
Joe Galvan, *Manager*
Krista Panneton, *Office Mgr*
Tony Defries, *Info Tech Dir*
EMP: 20
SALES (corp-wide): 13.3MM **Privately Held**
WEB: www.danco.net
SIC: 3471 Anodizing (plating) of metals or formed products
PA: Danco Anodizing, Inc.
44 La Porte St
Arcadia CA 91006
626 445-3303

(P-12984)
DECORE PLATING COMPANY INC
434 W 164th St, Gardena (90248-2727)
PHONE.................................310 324-6755
Don Argo, *President*
Diana Argo, *Vice Pres*
EMP: 10 EST: 1962
SQ FT: 7,128
SALES (est): 1MM **Privately Held**
SIC: 3471 Plating & polishing

(P-12985)
DILLON AIRCRAFT DEBURRING
11771 Sheldon St, Sun Valley (91352-1506)
PHONE.................................818 768-0801
Pedro Dillon, *President*
Consuelo Dillon, *Treasurer*
Alejandra Dillon, *Vice Pres*
EMP: 20
SQ FT: 4,000
SALES (est): 1.7MM **Privately Held**
SIC: 3471 Cleaning, polishing & finishing

(P-12986)
DIMAD ENTERPRISES INC (PA)
Also Called: Dimad Metal Finishing
44 La Porte St, Arcadia (91006-2827)
P.O. Box 660727 (91066-0727)
PHONE.................................626 445-3303
Bruce P Merwin, *President*
David Tatge, *Treasurer*
EMP: 13 EST: 1974
SQ FT: 2,000
SALES: 1.5MM **Privately Held**
SIC: 3471 Plating of metals or formed products

(P-12987)
DU-ALL ANODIZING CORPORATION
730 Chestnut St, San Jose (95110-1803)
PHONE.................................408 275-6694
Edward Marchand, *President*
Greg Marchand, *President*
Tony Evins, *Vice Pres*
EMP: 18
SALES (est): 1.1MM **Privately Held**
SIC: 3471 Anodizing (plating) of metals or formed products

(P-12988)
DU-ALL ANODIZING INC
730 Chestnut St, San Jose (95110-1803)
PHONE.................................408 275-6694
Gregrey Marchand, *President*
Tony Athens, *Vice Pres*
EMP: 20
SQ FT: 10,000
SALES (est): 1.7MM **Privately Held**
WEB: www.duallanodizing.com
SIC: 3471 6531 Anodizing (plating) of metals or formed products; finishing, metals or formed products; real estate agents & managers

(P-12989)
DUNHAM METAL PROCESSING CO
936 N Parker St, Orange (92867-5580)
P.O. Box 3736 (92857-0736)
PHONE.................................714 532-5551
Charles H Dunham, *Owner*
EMP: 40
SALES (est): 3.1MM **Privately Held**
SIC: 3471 2396 3341 Anodizing (plating) of metals or formed products; plating of metals or formed products; automotive & apparel trimmings; secondary nonferrous metals

(P-12990)
E F T FAST QUALITY SERVICE
2328 S Susan St, Santa Ana (92704-4421)
PHONE.................................714 751-1487
Michael Carnarius, *President*
Francis Ang, *President*
Ernesto Melecia, *Vice Pres*
Eiko Senaca, *Principal*
EMP: 10
SALES (est): 1.4MM **Privately Held**
SIC: 3471 Plating & polishing

(P-12991)
E M E INC
Also Called: Electro Machine & Engrg Co
500 E Pine St, Compton (90222-2818)
P.O. Box 4998 (90224-4998)
PHONE.................................310 639-1621
Wesley Turnbow, *CEO*
Steven Turnbow, *President*
Randy Turnbow, *Chairman*
Ricardo Osorio, *Opers Mgr*
EMP: 125
SQ FT: 65,000
SALES: 8.8MM **Privately Held**
WEB: www.emeplating.com
SIC: 3471 2899 Anodizing (plating) of metals or formed products; chemical preparations

(P-12992)
EL MONTE PLATING COMPANY
11409 Stewart St, El Monte (91731-2748)
PHONE.................................626 448-3607
Darrel Jensen, *Owner*
EMP: 16
SQ FT: 5,000
SALES (est): 870K **Privately Held**
SIC: 3471 Plating of metals or formed products; polishing, metals or formed products

(P-12993)
ELECTRO PLATING SPECIALTIES
2436 American Ave, Hayward (94545-1810)
PHONE.................................510 786-1881
Mary L Hall, *President*
Debbie McPeek, *Executive*
EMP: 32
SQ FT: 10,000
SALES (est): 3.7MM **Privately Held**
WEB: www.eps-plating.com
SIC: 3471 Electroplating of metals or formed products

(P-12994)
ELECTROCHEM SOLUTIONS INC
32500 Central Ave, Union City (94587-2032)
PHONE.................................510 476-1840
David Rossiter, *CEO*
Frank Ruano, *Opers Mgr*
Janet Nielsen, *Sales Mgr*
EMP: 14
SALES (est): 1.3MM **Privately Held**
SIC: 3471 Electroplating of metals or formed products

(P-12995)
ELECTROCHEM SOLUTIONS LLC
32500 Central Ave, Union City (94587-2032)
PHONE.................................510 476-1840
David Rossiter, *President*
Scott Sammons, *Cust Mgr*
EMP: 62

PRODUCTS & SVCS

SQ FT: 21,315
SALES (est): 6.1MM **Privately Held**
SIC: 3471 Electroplating of metals or formed products

(P-12996)
ELECTRODE TECHNOLOGIES INC
Also Called: Reid Metal Finishing
3110 W Harvard St Ste 14, Santa Ana (92704-3940)
PHONE.................714 549-3771
Tim A Grandcolas, *President*
Ivan Padron, *Admin Sec*
▲ **EMP:** 40
SQ FT: 10,000
SALES (est): 5.7MM **Privately Held**
SIC: 3471 Finishing, metals or formed products

(P-12997)
ELECTROLIZING INC
1947 Hooper Ave, Los Angeles (90011-1354)
P.O. Box 11900 (90011-0900)
PHONE.................213 749-7876
Susan B Grant, *President*
Jack Morgan, *Vice Pres*
EMP: 26 **EST:** 1947
SQ FT: 10,000
SALES (est): 3.5MM **Privately Held**
SIC: 3471 Electroplating of metals or formed products

(P-12998)
ELECTROLURGY INC (PA)
1121 Duryea Ave, Irvine (92614-5519)
PHONE.................949 250-4494
Eron G Eklund, *President*
June Eklund, *Ch of Bd*
Sean Eklund, *Vice Pres*
EMP: 48
SQ FT: 25,000
SALES (est): 14.1MM **Privately Held**
WEB: www.electrolurgy.com
SIC: 3471 3429 Electroplating of metals or formed products; anodizing (plating) of metals or formed products; polishing, metals or formed products; marine hardware

(P-12999)
ELECTROMATIC INC
7351 Radford Ave, North Hollywood (91605-3715)
PHONE.................818 765-3236
Norman Francis, *Branch Mgr*
EMP: 10
SQ FT: 7,351
SALES (corp-wide): 3.1MM **Privately Held**
WEB: www.electromatic.com
SIC: 3471 Polishing, metals or formed products
PA: Electromatic Inc
789 S Kellogg Ave
Goleta CA 93117
805 964-9880

(P-13000)
ELECTROMATIC INC (PA)
789 S Kellogg Ave, Goleta (93117-3884)
PHONE.................805 964-9880
Mary F Wilk, *President*
Wyman Winn, *Vice Pres*
Diana Wilk, *Admin Sec*
EMP: 10
SQ FT: 18,000
SALES (est): 3.1MM **Privately Held**
WEB: www.electromatic.com
SIC: 3471 Polishing, metals or formed products

(P-13001)
ELECTROMATIC INC
14025 Stage Rd, Santa Fe Springs (90670-5225)
PHONE.................562 623-9993
Diego Alvizo, *Manager*
EMP: 15
SALES (corp-wide): 3.1MM **Privately Held**
WEB: www.electromatic.com
SIC: 3471 Polishing, metals or formed products

PA: Electromatic Inc
789 S Kellogg Ave
Goleta CA 93117
805 964-9880

(P-13002)
ELECTRON PLATING III INC
13932 Enterprise Dr, Garden Grove (92843-4021)
PHONE.................714 554-2210
Jose Luis Padilla Sr, *President*
Luis Padilla Sr, *President*
EMP: 32
SQ FT: 10,000
SALES (est): 3.8MM **Privately Held**
SIC: 3471 Electroplating of metals or formed products; plating of metals or formed products

(P-13003)
ELECTRONIC CHROME GRINDING CO
9128 Dice Rd, Santa Fe Springs (90670-2545)
PHONE.................562 946-6671
Philip Reed, *President*
Jeannette Goble, *Corp Secy*
Dale Reed, *Vice Pres*
Mike Reed, *Vice Pres*
Debbie Scheibel, *Controller*
EMP: 22
SQ FT: 55,000
SALES (est): 3.2MM **Privately Held**
SIC: 3471 3599 Electroplating of metals or formed products; machine shop, jobbing & repair

(P-13004)
ELECTRONIC PRECISION SPC INC
545 Mercury Ln, Brea (92821-4831)
PHONE.................714 256-8950
Henry Brown, *President*
Ashley Rodriguez, *Office Mgr*
Eddie Sabala,
EMP: 34
SQ FT: 4,000
SALES (est): 5.4MM **Privately Held**
WEB: www.elecprec.com
SIC: 3471 Electroplating of metals or formed products

(P-13005)
ELITE METAL FINISHING LLC (PA)
540 Spectrum Cir, Oxnard (93030-8988)
PHONE.................805 983-4320
Joe Hansen, *President*
Joel Clemons, *General Mgr*
Marilyn Hansen, *Purch Mgr*
George Hansen,
EMP: 47 **EST:** 2001
SQ FT: 55,000
SALES: 3.3MM **Privately Held**
WEB: www.elitemetalfinishing.com
SIC: 3471 8734 Plating of metals or formed products; testing laboratories; metallurgical testing laboratory

(P-13006)
ELITE METAL FINISHING LLC
3430 Galaxy Pl, Oxnard (93030-8984)
PHONE.................805 983-4320
EMP: 88
SALES (corp-wide): 3.3MM **Privately Held**
SIC: 3471 Plating of metals or formed products
PA: Elite Metal Finishing, Llc
540 Spectrum Cir
Oxnard CA 93030
805 983-4320

(P-13007)
ETCHED MEDIA CORPORATION
101 Gilman Ave, Campbell (95008-3005)
PHONE.................408 374-6895
Elias Antoun, *President*
Farid Ghantous, *Vice Pres*
Jane Strang, *Buyer*
Kenny Vo, *Production*
▲ **EMP:** 32 **EST:** 1980
SQ FT: 15,000

PA: Electromatic Inc
789 S Kellogg Ave
Goleta CA 93117
805 964-9880

SALES (est): 5.1MM **Privately Held**
WEB: www.etchedmedia.com
SIC: 3471 3479 3993 2396 Decorative plating & finishing of formed products; name plates: engraved, etched, etc.; signs & advertising specialties; automotive & apparel trimmings

(P-13008)
F & H PLATING LLC
12023 Vose St Ste A, North Hollywood (91605-5775)
PHONE.................818 765-1221
Ron Bernal,
Randy Bernal,
EMP: 10
SQ FT: 5,000
SALES (est): 770K **Privately Held**
SIC: 3471 Plating of metals or formed products

(P-13009)
FINE QUALITY METAL FINSHG INC
1640 Daisy Ave, Long Beach (90813-1525)
PHONE.................562 983-7425
Edna Bolour, *President*
Cy Gipoor, *Shareholder*
Manoucher Esfandi, *Treasurer*
EMP: 15
SQ FT: 6,000
SALES (est): 1.9MM **Privately Held**
WEB: www.finequalitymetalfinishing.com
SIC: 3471 Plating of metals or formed products

(P-13010)
FLORENCE INTERNATIONAL COMPANY
Also Called: Dixon Hard Chrome
11645 Pendleton St, Sun Valley (91352-2502)
PHONE.................818 767-9650
Ronald Dixon, *President*
Donald Dixon, *Vice Pres*
Lawrence Dixon, *Vice Pres*
EMP: 45
SQ FT: 15,000
SALES (est): 5MM **Privately Held**
SIC: 3471 8734 Plating of metals or formed products; chromium plating of metals or formed products; testing laboratories

(P-13011)
FOUR-D METAL FINISHING INC
1065 Memorex Dr, Santa Clara (95050-2809)
PHONE.................408 730-5722
Peter Deguara, *President*
Melissa Wurfer, *Manager*
EMP: 30
SQ FT: 11,000
SALES (est): 3.7MM **Privately Held**
WEB: www.aanddstudios.com
SIC: 3471 Electroplating of metals or formed products

(P-13012)
GCG CORPORATION
Also Called: Gcg Precision Metal Finishing
608 Ruberta Ave, Glendale (91201-2335)
PHONE.................818 247-8508
Eugene Cockran, *President*
Gene Cockran, *Vice Pres*
EMP: 12
SQ FT: 13,000
SALES (est): 1.2MM **Privately Held**
SIC: 3471 Plating of metals or formed products

(P-13013)
GEM ENTERPRISES LLC
300 N Andreasen Dr, Escondido (92029-1317)
PHONE.................760 746-6616
Jason Guthrie,
Rick Guthrie,
Russ Guthrie,
EMP: 25
SQ FT: 5,300
SALES: 1MM **Privately Held**
SIC: 3471 Plating & polishing

(P-13014)
GEORGE INDUSTRIES
4116 Whiteside St, Los Angeles (90063-1619)
PHONE.................323 264-6660
Jeff Briggs, *President*
EMP: 380
SQ FT: 38,200
SALES (est): 34.7MM
SALES (corp-wide): 2.7B **Publicly Held**
WEB: www.valmont.com
SIC: 3471 3479 Anodizing (plating) of metals or formed products; cleaning & descaling metal products; plating of metals or formed products; aluminum coating of metal products
PA: Valmont Industries, Inc.
1 Valmont Plz Ste 500
Omaha NE 68154
402 963-1000

(P-13015)
GLOBAL PLATING INC
44620 S Grimmer Blvd, Fremont (94538-6386)
PHONE.................510 659-8764
Douglas Brothers, *President*
Charles Liggett, *Opers Staff*
EMP: 35
SQ FT: 23,000
SALES: 2.9MM **Privately Held**
SIC: 3471 Plating of metals or formed products; finishing, metals or formed products; electroplating of metals or formed products

(P-13016)
GRANATH & GRANATH INC
Also Called: Sonic Plating Company
1930 W Rosecrans Ave, Gardena (90249-2930)
P.O. Box 5387 (90249-5387)
PHONE.................310 327-5740
Richard E Granath Jr, *President*
Richard E Granath Sr, *Vice Pres*
Tina Mc Vey, *Admin Sec*
EMP: 22 **EST:** 1964
SQ FT: 40,000
SALES (est): 2.5MM **Privately Held**
SIC: 3471 Anodizing (plating) of metals or formed products; plating of metals or formed products

(P-13017)
GRAYBILLS METAL POLISHING INC
1212 E Puente Ave, West Covina (91790-1358)
PHONE.................626 967-5742
EMP: 10
SQ FT: 10,000
SALES: 467K **Privately Held**
SIC: 3471

(P-13018)
GSP ACQUISITION CORPORATION
Also Called: Gardena Specialized Processing
19745 Lassen St, Chatsworth (91311-5646)
PHONE.................310 532-9430
Michael Palatas, *President*
EMP: 42
SQ FT: 10,000
SALES: 1.1MM **Privately Held**
SIC: 3471 Finishing, metals or formed products

(P-13019)
GSP METAL FINISHING INC
16520 S Figueroa St, Gardena (90248-2625)
PHONE.................818 744-1328
Mike Palatas, *Vice Pres*
EMP: 35
SALES: 3MM **Privately Held**
SIC: 3471 Plating & polishing

(P-13020)
HAMMON PLATING CORPORATION
890 Commercial St, Palo Alto (94303-4905)
PHONE.................650 494-2691
Tom Wooten, *President*

▲ = Import ▼=Export
◆ =Import/Export

Glen Phinney, *Corp Secy*
Michelle Hammel, *Accounting Mgr*
Dil Jeer, *QC Mgr*
Phillip Kelman, *Opers Staff*
EMP: 35
SQ FT: 5,000
SALES (est): 5.1MM **Privately Held**
WEB: www.hammonplating.com
SIC: 3471 Electroplating of metals or
   formed products; plating of metals or
   formed products

(P-13021)
HANE & HANE INC
Also Called: University Plating Co
650 University Ave, San Jose (95110-1828)
PHONE.................................408 292-2140
Carter Hane, *President*
EMP: 20 **EST:** 1958
SQ FT: 700
SALES (est): 2.1MM **Privately Held**
SIC: 3471 Electroplating of metals or
   formed products

(P-13022)
HAROS ANODIZING SPECIALIST
630 Walsh Ave, Santa Clara (95050-2600)
PHONE.................................408 980-0892
Espanisalo Haro, *Owner*
EMP: 10
SQ FT: 2,500
SALES (est): 1MM **Privately Held**
SIC: 3471 Anodizing (plating) of metals or
   formed products

(P-13023)
HENRYS METAL POLISHING WORKS
9856 Rush St, South El Monte
(91733-2635)
PHONE.................................323 263-9701
Danny Reese, *President*
EMP: 13 **EST:** 1952
SALES (est): 1.6MM **Privately Held**
SIC: 3471 Polishing, metals or formed
   products

(P-13024)
HIGHTOWER PLATING & MFG CO
Also Called: Hightower Metals
2090 N Glassell St, Orange (92865-3306)
P.O. Box 5586 (92863-5586)
PHONE.................................714 637-9110
Kurt Koch, *President*
Mark Koch, *Vice Pres*
EMP: 50
SQ FT: 8,000
SALES (est): 5.6MM **Privately Held**
SIC: 3471 Plating of metals or formed
   products

(P-13025)
HIXSON METAL FINISHING
829 Production Pl, Newport Beach
(92663-2809)
PHONE.................................800 900-9798
Carl Blazik, *Principal*
Douglas Greene, *President*
Tina Matinpour, *Executive Asst*
Tom Riha, *Project Mgr*
Greg Gannon, *Plant Mgr*
EMP: 85
SQ FT: 38,000
SALES (est): 15.7MM **Privately Held**
WEB: www.hixsonmetalfinishing.com
SIC: 3471 Finishing, metals or formed
   products

(P-13026)
HUMBERTO MURILLO INC
Also Called: Data Electronic Services
410 Nantucket Pl, Santa Ana (92703-3545)
PHONE.................................714 541-2628
Humberto Murillo, *President*
EMP: 45 **EST:** 1994
SALES: 4MM **Privately Held**
SIC: 3471 Electroplating of metals or
   formed products

(P-13027)
HY-TECH PLATING INC
1011 American St, San Carlos
(94070-5303)
PHONE.................................650 593-4566
Wendell Wessbecher, *President*

Joel Osias, *Exec VP*
EMP: 22
SALES (est): 2.1MM **Privately Held**
SIC: 3471 Finishing, metals or formed
   products; plating of metals or formed
   products

(P-13028)
INDUSTRIAL METAL FINISHING
1941 Petra Ln, Placentia (92870-6749)
PHONE.................................714 628-8808
Robert E Hayden, *President*
EMP: 19
SQ FT: 12,000
SALES (est): 2.4MM **Privately Held**
WEB: www.indmetfin.com
SIC: 3471 Finishing, metals or
   formed products; shot peening (treating
   steel to reduce fatigue)

(P-13029)
INDUSTRIAL ZINC PLATING CORP
Also Called: Industrial Plating Co
7217 San Luis St, Carlsbad (92011-4622)
P.O. Box 9518, Long Beach (90810-0518)
PHONE.................................760 918-6877
EMP: 25
SQ FT: 45,000
SALES: 2MM **Privately Held**
SIC: 3471

(P-13030)
INTA TECHNOLOGIES CORPORATION
2281 Calle De Luna, Santa Clara
(95054-1023)
PHONE.................................408 748-9955
Mina Doshi, *President*
Pia Gronvaldt, *Planning*
Francis Honey, *Engineer*
Jerry Walias, *Engineer*
Nina Doshi, *Controller*
EMP: 23
SQ FT: 15,000
SALES (est): 3.9MM **Privately Held**
WEB: www.intatech.com
SIC: 3471 2891 Electroplating of metals or
   formed products; sealants

(P-13031)
INTEGRATED MFG TECH INC (DH)
Also Called: IMT International
45473 Warm Springs Blvd, Fremont
(94539-6104)
PHONE.................................408 934-5879
Andy Loung, *CEO*
Kay Tan, *CFO*
▲ **EMP:** 13 **EST:** 1980
SQ FT: 21,000
SALES: 10MM
SALES (corp-wide): 78.2MM **Privately Held**
SIC: 3471 3599 Polishing, metals or
   formed products; machine shop, jobbing
   & repair
HQ: Asl International Trading, Inc.
   1477 N Milpitas Blvd
   Milpitas CA 95035
   510 659-9770

(P-13032)
INTERNTIONAL PHOTO PLATES CORP
Also Called: Nanofilm
2641 Townsgate Rd Ste 100, Westlake Village (91361-2724)
PHONE.................................805 496-5031
Valdis Sneberg, *President*
Dale Burow, *Vice Pres*
Araceli White-Davis, *Vice Pres*
Maria Flores, *Executive*
Dorothy Cesari, *Admin Sec*
▲ **EMP:** 37
SQ FT: 8,000
SALES (est): 4.7MM **Privately Held**
WEB: www.nanofilm.com
SIC: 3471 2796 Plating & polishing;
   platemaking services

(P-13033)
J P TURGEON & SONS INC
7758 Scout Ave, Bell (90201-4942)
PHONE.................................323 773-3105

David E Turgeon, *President*
Robert L Turgeon, *Treasurer*
Joseph Phillip Turgeon Jr, *Vice Pres*
Charles D Turgeon, *Admin Sec*
▲ **EMP:** 25
SQ FT: 9,200
SALES (est): 1.8MM **Privately Held**
SIC: 3471 Polishing, metals or formed
   products; buffing for the trade

(P-13034)
JD PROCESSING INC
2220 Cape Cod Way, Santa Ana
(92703-3563)
PHONE.................................714 972-8161
Thomas Scimeca, *CEO*
Luis Magana, *Planning*
Gonzalo Magana, *Prdtn Mgr*
EMP: 50
SALES (est): 276.4K **Privately Held**
SIC: 3471 3559 Anodizing (plating) of met-
   als or formed products; anodizing equip-
   ment

(P-13035)
KANETIC LTD LLC
Also Called: Kane Aerospace
7000 Merrill Ave, Chino (91710-9091)
PHONE.................................505 228-5692
Jana Spruce, *President*
John Spruce, *CEO*
EMP: 10 **EST:** 2016
SALES (est): 373.2K **Privately Held**
SIC: 3471 3429 Plating & polishing; metal
   fasteners

(P-13036)
KEN HOFFMANN INC
Also Called: Palm Springs Plating
345 Del Sol Rd, Palm Springs
(92262-1607)
P.O. Box 4488 (92263-4488)
PHONE.................................760 325-6012
Ken Hoffmann, *President*
EMP: 20
SQ FT: 4,200
SALES (est): 3.1MM **Privately Held**
WEB: www.psplating.com
SIC: 3471 Electroplating of metals or
   formed products

(P-13037)
KRYLER CORP
Also Called: Pacific Grinding
1217 E Ash Ave, Fullerton (92831-5019)
PHONE.................................714 871-9611
Chet Krygier Jr, *President*
Phyllis Krygier, *Admin Sec*
EMP: 30
SQ FT: 900
SALES (est): 3.8MM **Privately Held**
WEB: www.krylercorp.com
SIC: 3471 Chromium plating of metals or
   formed products

(P-13038)
L N L ANODIZING INC
9900 Glenoaks Blvd Ste 3, Sun Valley
(91352-1061)
PHONE.................................818 768-9224
George Larry Sentena, *President*
EMP: 21
SQ FT: 6,000
SALES (est): 1.5MM **Privately Held**
WEB: www.lnlanodizing.com
SIC: 3471 Anodizing (plating) of metals or
   formed products

(P-13039)
LA HABRA PLATING CO INC
900 S Cypress St, La Habra (90631-6887)
PHONE.................................562 694-2704
Sylvester Roblea, *President*
Maria Robles, *QC Mgr*
EMP: 10 **EST:** 1972
SQ FT: 6,800
SALES: 740K **Privately Held**
WEB: www.lahabraplating.com
SIC: 3471 Plating of metals or formed
   products

(P-13040)
LAKIN INDUSTRIES INC (PA)
Also Called: A & G Electropolish
18330 Ward St, Fountain Valley
(92708-6853)
PHONE.................................714 968-6438
Gary Lakin, *CEO*
EMP: 12
SQ FT: 6,200
SALES (est): 2.4MM **Privately Held**
SIC: 3471 Electroplating & plating; polish-
   ing, metals or formed products

(P-13041)
LEOS METAL POLISHING
Also Called: Leos Metal Polishing Works
10980 Alameda St, Lynwood (90262-1722)
PHONE.................................310 635-5257
Tranquelino Leos, *Owner*
Tranquilino Leos, *Owner*
EMP: 15
SQ FT: 1,250
SALES: 900K **Privately Held**
SIC: 3471 Polishing, metals or formed
   products

(P-13042)
LORTZ & SON MFG CO
Also Called: Lortz Manufacturing
4042 Patton Way, Bakersfield
(93308-5030)
PHONE.................................281 241-9418
Nathan C Lortz, *President*
Steven E Fisher, *Shareholder*
Nathan Lortz, *General Mgr*
Mike Miller, *General Mgr*
Karen Lortz, *Admin Sec*
EMP: 130 **EST:** 1939
SQ FT: 50,000
SALES (est): 14MM **Privately Held**
WEB: www.lortz.com
SIC: 3471 3443 7692 3441 Plating & pol-
   ishing; fabricated plate work (boiler shop);
   welding repair; fabricated structural metal

(P-13043)
M & G CUSTOM POLISHING
8356 Standustrial St, Stanton
(90680-2618)
PHONE.................................714 995-0261
Martin Ayala, *Partner*
Gerardo Ayala, *Partner*
EMP: 13
SQ FT: 1,500
SALES (est): 1.1MM **Privately Held**
SIC: 3471 Polishing, metals or formed
   products

(P-13044)
M & R PLATING CORPORATION
12375 Montague St, Arleta (91331-2214)
PHONE.................................818 896-2700
Andres Rauda, *CEO*
EMP: 17 **EST:** 1976
SQ FT: 11,000
SALES (est): 2.2MM **Privately Held**
WEB: www.m-rplatingcorp.com
SIC: 3471 Plating of metals or formed
   products

(P-13045)
M P C INDUSTRIAL PRODUCTS INC
Also Called: M P C Industries
2150 Mcgaw Ave, Irvine (92614-0912)
PHONE.................................949 863-0106
Paul F Queyrel, *Chairman*
John A Spencer, *CFO*
▲ **EMP:** 30 **EST:** 1952
SQ FT: 55,000
SALES (est): 4.8MM **Privately Held**
SIC: 3471 3541 Polishing, metals or
   formed products; grinding, polishing, buff-
   ing, lapping & honing machines

(P-13046)
MAIN STEEL LLC
3100 Jefferson St, Riverside (92504-4339)
PHONE.................................951 789-3010
Mike Folley, *Branch Mgr*
EMP: 52
SALES (corp-wide): 1.8B **Privately Held**
SIC: 3471 Polishing, metals or formed
   products; buffing for the trade

(PA)=Parent Co (HQ)=Headquarters (DH)=Div Headquarters
✪ = New Business established in last 2 years

2020 California
Manufacturers Register

531

P R O D U C T S   &   S V C S

HQ: Main Steel, Llc
2200 Pratt Blvd
Elk Grove Village IL 60007
847 916-1220

(P-13047)
MAKPLATE LLC
5780 Obata Way, Gilroy (95020-7092)
PHONE....................................408 842-7572
Naaim Ali Yahya,
Linh Ngo, *Engineer*
Yusuf Zhumkhawala PHD,
EMP: 12
SQ FT: 5,000
SALES (est): 1MM **Privately Held**
WEB: www.makplate.com
SIC: 3471 Gold plating

(P-13048)
MENCARINI & JARWIN INC
Also Called: Chrome Craft
5950 88th St, Sacramento (95828-1109)
PHONE....................................916 383-1660
Philip B Jarwin, *Ch of Bd*
Lillian J Jarwin, *President*
Judith Marrs, *Admin Sec*
EMP: 16 **EST:** 1963
SQ FT: 46,000
SALES: 2MM **Privately Held**
SIC: 3471 Chromium plating of metals or
formed products

(P-13049)
METAL CHEM INC
21514 Nordhoff St, Chatsworth
(91311-5822)
PHONE....................................818 727-9951
Carlos Pongo, *President*
EMP: 30
SALES (est): 3.5MM **Privately Held**
SIC: 3471 3443 Plating of metals or
formed products; fabricated plate work
(boiler shop)

(P-13050)
METAL PREPARATIONS
1000 E Ocean Blvd # 416, Long Beach
(90802-8510)
PHONE....................................213 628-5176
Jeff Savage, *President*
Jason Savage, *Vice Pres*
EMP: 25
SQ FT: 32,000
SALES (est): 2.5MM **Privately Held**
WEB: www.metalpreparations.com
SIC: 3471 Cleaning & descaling metal
products; polishing, metals or formed
products

(P-13051)
METAL SURFACES INC
6060 Shull St, Bell Gardens (90201-6297)
P.O. Box 5001 (90202-5001)
PHONE....................................562 927-1331
Charles K Bell, *CEO*
Sam Bell, *COO*
Lala Khachatrian, *Engineer*
Nel Wallace, *Human Res Mgr*
Theresa Bell, *Purchasing*
EMP: 150
SQ FT: 85,000
SALES (est): 22.3MM **Privately Held**
WEB: www.metalsurfaces.com
SIC: 3471 Electroplating of metals or
formed products

(P-13052)
MILNERS ANODIZING
3330 Mcmaude Pl, Santa Rosa
(95407-8120)
PHONE....................................707 584-1188
Terry Burson, *Owner*
Claire Burson, *Co-Owner*
Michael Marian, *Vice Pres*
EMP: 15
SQ FT: 7,200
SALES (est): 891K **Privately Held**
WEB: www.milnersanodizing.com
SIC: 3471 Anodizing (plating) of metals or
formed products

(P-13053)
MODESTO PLTG & POWDR COATING
436 Mitchell Rd Ste D, Modesto
(95354-3932)
P.O. Box 576095 (95357-6095)
PHONE....................................209 526-2696
Tom Sutter, *President*
Rex Sutter, *Vice Pres*
EMP: 10 **EST:** 1968
SALES (est): 1.3MM **Privately Held**
WEB: www.modestoplating.com
SIC: 3471 5169 Chromium plating of met-
als or formed products; chemicals & allied
products

(P-13054)
MONTOYA & JARAMILLO INC
Also Called: Swift Metal Finishing
1161 Richard Ave, Santa Clara
(95050-2843)
PHONE....................................408 727-5776
Robert Montoya Jr, *President*
Dyanne Castro, *Treasurer*
EMP: 19 **EST:** 1963
SQ FT: 6,000
SALES (est): 1.3MM **Privately Held**
SIC: 3471 Electroplating of metals or
formed products

(P-13055)
MORRELLS ELECTRO PLATING INC
Also Called: Morrell's Metal Finishing
432 E Euclid Ave, Compton (90222-2899)
P.O. Box 3085 (90223-3085)
PHONE....................................310 639-1024
Cyrus Gipoor, *President*
EMP: 30 **EST:** 1948
SQ FT: 20,000
SALES (est): 5.1MM **Privately Held**
WEB: www.morrellsplating.com
SIC: 3471 Anodizing (plating) of metals or
formed products

(P-13056)
MULTICHROME COMPANY INC (PA)
Also Called: Microplate
1013 W Hillcrest Blvd, Inglewood
(90301-2019)
PHONE....................................310 216-1086
Steven A Peterman, *President*
EMP: 31 **EST:** 1962
SQ FT: 5,000
SALES (est): 3MM **Privately Held**
WEB: www.multiplate.com
SIC: 3471 Electroplating of metals or
formed products

(P-13057)
NASMYTH TMF INC
29102 Hancock Pkwy, Valencia
(91355-1066)
PHONE....................................818 954-9504
Peter Smith, *CEO*
Chris Sosa, *General Mgr*
EMP: 54
SQ FT: 10,000
SALES (est): 6.2MM **Privately Held**
SIC: 3471 3479 Anodizing (plating) of met-
als or formed products; coating of metals
& formed products
PA: Nasmyth Group Limited
Nasmyth House
Coventry W MIDLANDS CV7 9
-

(P-13058)
NECLEC
5945 E Harvard Ave, Fresno (93727-8621)
PHONE....................................559 797-0103
Rod Bandy, *President*
EMP: 32
SQ FT: 9,955
SALES (est): 1.8MM **Privately Held**
SIC: 3471 Chromium plating of metals or
formed products

(P-13059)
NEUTRON PLATING INC
2993 E Blue Star St, Anaheim
(92806-2511)
PHONE....................................714 632-9241
Manuel Zavala, *President*

Glafira Zavala, *Treasurer*
Manuel Zavala Jr, *Vice Pres*
Sylvia Cassillas, *Admin Sec*
EMP: 70
SQ FT: 16,000
SALES (est): 5.8MM **Privately Held**
WEB: www.gepower.com
SIC: 3471 Electroplating of metals or
formed products; anodizing (plating) of
metals or formed products

(P-13060)
NEUTRONIC STAMPING & PLATING
100 Business Center Dr, Corona (92880)
PHONE....................................714 964-8900
Nicholas Ravlich, *CFO*
Robert Soltero, *Opers Mgr*
Eve Shute, *Sales Staff*
EMP: 30
SQ FT: 27,000
SALES (est): 4.4MM **Privately Held**
WEB: www.neutronicstamping.com
SIC: 3471 3469 Plating & polishing; metal
stampings

(P-13061)
NEW AGE METAL FINISHING LLC
2169 N Pleasant Ave, Fresno
(93705-4730)
PHONE....................................559 498-8585
Michael Zelinski,
EMP: 26
SQ FT: 5,000
SALES (est): 2.9MM **Privately Held**
SIC: 3471 Plating of metals or formed
products

(P-13062)
NORMANDY REFINISHERS INC
355 S Rosemead Blvd, Pasadena
(91107-4955)
PHONE....................................626 792-9202
Gregory Sarkisian, *President*
Doris Sarkisian, *Vice Pres*
EMP: 22
SQ FT: 2,000
SALES (est): 1.7MM **Privately Held**
SIC: 3471 3431 Decorative plating & fin-
ishing of formed products; bathroom fix-
tures, including sinks

(P-13063)
NORTH COUNTY POLISHING
220 S Hale Ave Ste A, Escondido
(92029-1719)
PHONE....................................760 480-0847
Michael Meziere, *Partner*
David Meziere, *Partner*
Don Meziere, *Partner*
EMP: 28
SQ FT: 1,200
SALES (est): 140K **Privately Held**
SIC: 3471 Polishing, metals or formed
products

(P-13064)
OMNI METAL FINISHING INC (PA)
11665 Coley River Cir, Fountain Valley
(92708-4279)
PHONE....................................714 231-3716
Victor M Salazar, *President*
Victor Loyola, *CFO*
Filiberto Hernandez, *Treasurer*
Ramiro Salazar, *Admin Sec*
Vijay Merchant, *Engineer*
EMP: 100
SQ FT: 34,000
SALES (est): 20.6MM **Privately Held**
WEB: www.omnimetal.com
SIC: 3471 Plating of metals or formed
products

(P-13065)
OPTI-FORMS INC
42310 Winchester Rd, Temecula
(92590-4810)
PHONE....................................951 296-1300
Ralph C Dawson, *CEO*
Clint Tinker, *Chairman*
Kevin Thompson, *Exec VP*
Robert Brunson, *Vice Pres*
EMP: 52
SQ FT: 61,000

SALES (est): 7.4MM **Privately Held**
WEB: www.optiforms.com
SIC: 3471 3827 Plating of metals or
formed products; optical instruments &
lenses

(P-13066)
ORANGE COUNTY PLATING COINC
940 N Parker St 960, Orange
(92867-5581)
PHONE....................................714 532-4610
Lawrence J Honikel, *President*
Jeanne T Honikel, *Corp Secy*
Daniel L Honikel, *Vice Pres*
EMP: 50
SQ FT: 12,000
SALES (est): 5MM **Privately Held**
WEB: www.ocplating.com
SIC: 3471 Electroplating of metals or
formed products

(P-13067)
ORDWAY METAL POLISHING
1901 N San Fernando Rd, Los Angeles
(90065-1281)
PHONE....................................323 225-3373
Jim Pratt, *Owner*
EMP: 20
SQ FT: 4,000
SALES (est): 1MM **Privately Held**
SIC: 3471 Polishing, metals or formed
products

(P-13068)
P K SELECTIVE METAL PLTG INC
415 Mathew St, Santa Clara (95050-3105)
PHONE....................................408 988-1910
Peter Kellett, *President*
EMP: 16
SQ FT: 21,000
SALES (est): 1.5MM **Privately Held**
WEB: www.pkselective.com
SIC: 3471 Anodizing (plating) of metals or
formed products; plating of metals or
formed products

(P-13069)
PENTRATE METAL PROCESSING
3517 E Olympic Blvd, Los Angeles
(90023-3976)
PHONE....................................323 269-2121
John J Grana, *President*
Nick Grana, *Corp Secy*
Vincent Grana, *Vice Pres*
EMP: 30 **EST:** 1945
SQ FT: 18,000
SALES (est): 4MM **Privately Held**
WEB: www.pentrate.com
SIC: 3471 Electroplating of metals or
formed products; plating of metals or
formed products

(P-13070)
PG IMTECH OF CALIFORNIA LLC
8424 Secura Way, Santa Fe Springs
(90670-2216)
PHONE....................................562 945-8943
Chuck Wolitski,
Fred Mose,
EMP: 11
SQ FT: 6,450
SALES (est): 333.9K **Privately Held**
SIC: 3471 Anodizing (plating) of metals or
formed products

(P-13071)
PLASMA RGGEDIZED SOLUTIONS INC
5452 Business Dr, Huntington Beach
(92649-1226)
PHONE....................................714 893-6063
Bob Marla, *Branch Mgr*
EMP: 25
SALES (corp-wide): 16.3MM **Privately
Held**
WEB: www.plasmasystems.com
SIC: 3471 3479 Electroplating & plating;
coating of metals & formed products

▲ = Import ▼=Export
◆ =Import/Export

PA: Plasma Ruggedized Solutions, Inc.
2284 Ringwood Ave Ste A
San Jose CA 95131
408 954-8405

(P-13072)
PLATERONICS PROCESSING INC
9164 Independence Ave, Chatsworth
(91311-5902)
PHONE...................................818 341-2191
Joseph Roter, *President*
Lee F Roter, *Corp Secy*
Marvin Roter, *Vice Pres*
EMP: 35
SQ FT: 6,500
SALES (est): 3MM **Privately Held**
WEB: www.plateronics.com
SIC: 3471 5051 Finishing, metals or
formed products; metals service centers
& offices

(P-13073)
PLATRON COMPANY WEST
26260 Eden Landing Rd, Hayward
(94545-3717)
PHONE...................................510 781-5588
Tim Martin, *Partner*
Bruce Garratt, *Partner*
James White, *Prdtn Mgr*
EMP: 17
SALES (est): 2.3MM **Privately Held**
WEB: www.platron.com
SIC: 3471 Plating & polishing

(P-13074)
PRECIOUS METALS PLATING CO INC
2635 Orange Ave, Santa Ana (92707-3738)
PHONE...................................714 546-6271
Chad Wayne Bird, *President*
Nell Lester, *General Mgr*
Betty Bird, *Admin Sec*
EMP: 15 **EST:** 1957
SQ FT: 6,500
SALES (est): 3.6MM **Privately Held**
WEB: www.pmplating.com
SIC: 3471 Electroplating of metals or
formed products

(P-13075)
PRECISION ANODIZING & PLTG INC
Also Called: P A P
1601 N Miller St, Anaheim (92806-1469)
PHONE...................................714 996-1601
Jose A Salazar, *CEO*
Kim Hayner, *Human Res Mgr*
Jordan Salazar, *Purchasing*
Imelda Isidoro, *Exec Sec*
Julie Gutierrez, *Manager*
EMP: 89 **EST:** 1971
SQ FT: 44,000
SALES (est): 13.2MM **Privately Held**
WEB: www.anodizing-plating.com
SIC: 3471 Electroplating of metals or
formed products

(P-13076)
PREMIER METAL PROCESSING INC
971 Vernon Way, El Cajon (92020-1832)
PHONE...................................760 415-9027
Mohammed Shamsi, *President*
EMP: 10
SQ FT: 13,000
SALES (est): 975.5K **Privately Held**
SIC: 3471 Plating of metals or formed
products; electroplating & plating; anodiz-
ing (plating) of metals or formed products;
electroplating of metals or formed prod-
ucts

(P-13077)
PRIDE METAL POLISHING INC
10822 Saint Louis Dr, El Monte
(91731-2030)
PHONE...................................626 350-1326
Rod Lowell, *President*
EMP: 19
SQ FT: 15,000
SALES (est): 1.9MM **Privately Held**
WEB: www.pridepolishing.com
SIC: 3471 Polishing, metals or formed
products

(P-13078)
PRIME PLATING AEROSPACE INC
11321 Goss St, Sun Valley (91352-3206)
P.O. Box 1843 (91353-1843)
PHONE...................................818 768-9100
Fred Schmidt, *President*
EMP: 12 **EST:** 2012
SALES (est): 641.6K **Privately Held**
SIC: 3471 Electroplating of metals or
formed products; plating of metals or
formed products

(P-13079)
PROCESS STAINLESS LAB INC (PA)
Also Called: Advance Elctro Polishing
1280 Memorex Dr, Santa Clara
(95050-2812)
PHONE...................................408 980-0535
Clay Hudson, *Owner*
David Hays, *Co-Owner*
Hector I Valdez, *General Mgr*
Lou Moore, *Bookkeeper*
David Diller, *Accounts Mgr*
EMP: 27
SQ FT: 8,000
SALES (est): 3.2MM **Privately Held**
WEB: www.pslinc.com
SIC: 3471 Polishing, metals or formed
products

(P-13080)
PRODIGY SURFACE TECH INC
Also Called: Arrhenius
807 Aldo Ave Ste 103, Santa Clara
(95054-2254)
PHONE...................................408 492-9390
John Shaw, *President*
Mark Danitschek, *President*
Randy Souza, *Sales Staff*
Sheila Tosado, *Cust Mgr*
EMP: 38
SQ FT: 14,500
SALES (est): 4.8MM **Privately Held**
WEB: www.prodigysurfacetech.com
SIC: 3471 Electroplating of metals or
formed products; plating of metals or
formed products

(P-13081)
PROFESSIONAL FINISHING INC
770 Market Ave, Richmond (94801-1303)
PHONE...................................510 233-7629
Ricardo E Gomez, *President*
Pauline Ochoa, *Manager*
EMP: 60
SQ FT: 18,000
SALES (est): 7.6MM **Privately Held**
WEB: www.profinn.com
SIC: 3471 Plating & polishing

(P-13082)
PURUS INTERNATIONAL INC
82860 Avenue 45, Indio (92201-2396)
PHONE...................................760 775-4500
Dennis K Baldwin, *President*
Eric Bookland, *Vice Pres*
◆ **EMP:** 19
SQ FT: 3,000
SALES (est): 5MM **Privately Held**
WEB: www.purusint.com
SIC: 3471 Cleaning, polishing & finishing

(P-13083)
QUAKER CITY PLATING
Also Called: Quaker City Plating & Silvrsm
11729 Washington Blvd, Whittier
(90606-2498)
P.O. Box 2406 (90610-2406)
PHONE...................................562 945-3721
Michael Crain, *Managing Prtnr*
Angelo Dirado, *Managing Prtnr*
▲ **EMP:** 220
SQ FT: 48,000
SALES (est): 58.8MM **Privately Held**
WEB: www.quakercityplating.com
SIC: 3471 Plating of metals or formed
products

(P-13084)
QUALITY CONTROL PLATING INC
4425 E Airport Dr Ste 113, Ontario
(91761-7815)
PHONE...................................909 605-0206
Jay J Singh, *Vice Pres*
Mona Singh, *President*
EMP: 22
SQ FT: 3,500
SALES (est): 2.1MM **Privately Held**
SIC: 3471 Plating of metals or formed
products

(P-13085)
R L ANODIZING
Also Called: R L Anodizing & Plating
11331 Penrose St, Sun Valley
(91352-3109)
PHONE...................................818 252-3804
Raymond Lane, *Owner*
EMP: 15
SALES (est): 920K **Privately Held**
SIC: 3471 Anodizing (plating) of metals or
formed products

(P-13086)
RD METAL POLISHING INC
244 Pioneer Pl, Pomona (91768-3275)
PHONE...................................909 594-8393
Ron Delgado Jr, *President*
Ranulfo M Delgado Sr, *Vice Pres*
EMP: 38
SQ FT: 11,000
SALES (est): 3MM **Privately Held**
SIC: 3471 Polishing, metals or formed
products

(P-13087)
REAL PLATING INC
1245 W 2nd St, Pomona (91766-1310)
PHONE...................................909 623-2304
Juan Real, *CEO*
EMP: 25 **EST:** 2007
SQ FT: 5,264
SALES (est): 2MM **Privately Held**
SIC: 3471 Plating of metals or formed
products

(P-13088)
RON KEHL ENGINEERING
384 Umbarger Rd Ste B, San Jose
(95111-2079)
PHONE...................................408 629-6632
Ron Kehl, *Owner*
▲ **EMP:** 12
SQ FT: 6,000
SALES (est): 877.2K **Privately Held**
SIC: 3471 3599 8711 Polishing, metals or
formed products; machine & other job
shop work; industrial engineers

(P-13089)
ROSE MANUFACTURING GROUP INC
Also Called: Elite Metal Finishing
2525 Jason Ct Ste 102, Oceanside
(92056-3000)
PHONE...................................760 407-0232
Dan Rose, *President*
EMP: 14
SQ FT: 3,300
SALES (est): 1.8MM **Privately Held**
SIC: 3471 Plating of metals or formed
products; sand blasting of metal parts

(P-13090)
ROSENKRANZ ENTERPRISES INC
Also Called: A & B Sandblast Co
2447 E 54th St, Los Angeles (90058-3503)
PHONE...................................323 583-9021
Lance Rosenkranz, *President*
EMP: 15
SQ FT: 40,000
SALES (est): 1.3MM **Privately Held**
SIC: 3471 Sand blasting of metal parts

(P-13091)
S & K PLATING INC
2727 N Compton Ave, Compton
(90222-1097)
PHONE...................................310 632-7141
Mardig Tchakalian, *President*
EMP: 25

SQ FT: 7,500
SALES (est): 2.6MM **Privately Held**
SIC: 3471 Electroplating of metals or
formed products

(P-13092)
SAFE PLATING INC
18001 Railroad St, City of Industry
(91748-1215)
PHONE...................................626 810-1872
Magdy Seif, *President*
Mario Gomez, *Executive*
Cielo Gamboa, *IT/INT Sup*
Cielo Paguio, *Manager*
Ekram Seif, *Manager*
EMP: 58
SQ FT: 35,000
SALES (est): 7.6MM **Privately Held**
WEB: www.safeplating.com
SIC: 3471 Gold plating; electroplating of
metals or formed products

(P-13093)
SAL RODRIGUEZ
Also Called: Quality Plating
1680 Almaden Expy Ste I, San Jose
(95125-1324)
PHONE...................................408 993-8091
Sal Rodriguez, *Owner*
EMP: 10
SALES (est): 625.9K **Privately Held**
SIC: 3471 Plating of metals or formed
products

(P-13094)
SANFORD METAL PROCESSING CO
990 Obrien Dr, Menlo Park (94025-1407)
PHONE...................................650 327-5172
Martha Gonzalez, *Principal*
EMP: 10
SQ FT: 7,500
SALES (est): 1.5MM **Privately Held**
SIC: 3471 Plating of metals or formed
products; anodizing (plating) of metals or
formed products

(P-13095)
SANTA ANA PLATING CORP (PA)
1726 E Rosslynn Ave, Fullerton
(92831-5111)
PHONE...................................310 923-8305
Tony Kakuk, *President*
Michael F Gustin, *Owner*
EMP: 55
SQ FT: 17,100
SALES (est): 5.6MM **Privately Held**
SIC: 3471 Finishing, metals or formed
products; plating of metals or formed
products

(P-13096)
SANTA CLARA PLATING CO INC
1773 Grant St, Santa Clara (95050-3974)
PHONE...................................408 727-9315
Thomas L Coss, *President*
Wendy Coss, *Shareholder*
EMP: 85
SQ FT: 13,000
SALES (est): 9.3MM **Privately Held**
WEB: www.scpci.com
SIC: 3471 Electroplating of metals or
formed products

(P-13097)
SANTOSHI CORPORATION
Also Called: Alum-A-Coat
2439 Seaman Ave, El Monte (91733-1936)
PHONE...................................626 444-7118
Hershad Shah, *President*
Raksha Shah, *Vice Pres*
Greg Hart, *Executive*
EMP: 33
SQ FT: 15,000
SALES (est): 6.2MM **Privately Held**
SIC: 3471 Coloring & finishing of aluminum
or formed products; electroplating of met-
als or formed products

(P-13098)
SCHMIDT INDUSTRIES INC
Also Called: Prime Plating
11321 Goss St, Sun Valley (91352-3206)
P.O. Box 1843 (91353-1843)
PHONE...................................818 768-9100
Fred Schmidt, *President*

EMP: 90
SQ FT: 30,000
SALES (est): 12.4MM **Privately Held**
SIC: 3471 Anodizing (plating) of metals or
formed products

(P-13099)
SEMANO INC
31757 Knapp St, Hayward (94544-7827)
PHONE.....................................510 489-2360
Frank Largusa, *President*
Terry Dillon, *Corp Secy*
Hans Sellge, *Vice Pres*
Rick Randall, *Controller*
Shanti Raikar, *Safety Mgr*
▲ EMP: 35
SQ FT: 13,000
SALES (est): 5.7MM **Privately Held**
SIC: 3471 Electroplating of metals or
formed products

(P-13100)
SHEFFIELD PLATERS INC
9850 Waples St, San Diego (92121-2921)
PHONE.....................................858 546-8484
Dale Watkins Jr, *President*
Shelley Watkins, *Shareholder*
Mark Watkins, *Exec VP*
Vincent Noonan, *Business Dir*
Jennifer McCown, *QC Mgr*
EMP: 45 EST: 1966
SQ FT: 20,000
SALES (est): 6.5MM **Privately Held**
WEB: www.sheffieldplaters.com
SIC: 3471 Plating of metals or formed
products

(P-13101)
SIZE CONTROL PLATING CO
13349 Temple Ave, La Puente
(91746-1580)
PHONE.....................................626 369-3014
Ron Todden, *President*
EMP: 11 EST: 1958
SQ FT: 8,800
SALES: 700K **Privately Held**
WEB: www.sizecontrol.net
SIC: 3471 8734 Electroplating of metals or
formed products; product testing laborato-
ries

(P-13102)
SJ VALLEY PLATING INC
491 Perry Ct, Santa Clara (95054-2624)
PHONE.....................................408 988-5502
Jeff Adams, *President*
Michele Adams, *Admin Sec*
Rosalino Hernandez, *Manager*
EMP: 12
SQ FT: 10,000
SALES (est): 1MM **Privately Held**
SIC: 3471 Chromium plating of metals or
formed products; plating of metals or
formed products

(P-13103)
SOUTHWEST PLATING CO INC
1344 W Slauson Ave, Los Angeles
(90044-2897)
PHONE.....................................323 753-3781
Gus Brigantino, *Owner*
EMP: 15
SALES (est): 1.8MM **Privately Held**
SIC: 3471 Chromium plating of metals or
formed products

(P-13104)
**SPECTRUM PLATING COMPANY
INC**
202 W 140th St, Los Angeles (90061-1006)
PHONE.....................................310 533-0748
Mary McMeans, *CEO*
Jesus Diaz, *Corp Secy*
Donna Martinez, *Vice Pres*
Scott McLean, *Maintence Staff*
Pat Gonzales, *Manager*
EMP: 25
SQ FT: 60,000
SALES (est): 4.2MM **Privately Held**
WEB: www.spectrumplating.com
SIC: 3471 Electroplating of metals or
formed products

(P-13105)
**STABILE PLATING COMPANY
INC**
1150 E Edna Pl, Covina (91724-2592)
PHONE.....................................626 339-9091
David Crest, *President*
Eric Crest, *Vice Pres*
Steven Crest, *Vice Pres*
Stephanie Esqueda, *Office Mgr*
EMP: 22 EST: 1959
SQ FT: 6,000
SALES (est): 1.5MM **Privately Held**
WEB: www.stableplating.com
SIC: 3471 3444 3353 Plating of metals or
formed products; sheet metalwork; alu-
minum sheet, plate & foil

(P-13106)
STAINLESS MICRO-POLISH INC
1286 N Grove St, Anaheim (92806-2113)
PHONE.....................................714 632-8903
Robert Maculsay, *President*
Elizabeth Maculsay, *Treasurer*
Michael Gierut, *General Mgr*
EMP: 15 EST: 1979
SQ FT: 10,000
SALES (est): 2MM **Privately Held**
WEB: www.stainlessmicropolish.com
SIC: 3471 Polishing, metals or formed
products

(P-13107)
**STANDARD METAL PRODUCTS
INC**
1541 W 132nd St, Gardena (90249-2107)
P.O. Box 7636, Torrance (90504-9036)
PHONE.....................................310 532-9861
Danny Corrales Jr, *CEO*
Dan Corrales Sr, *Treasurer*
Jo Ann Stanley, *Bookkeeper*
EMP: 35 EST: 1972
SQ FT: 24,000
SALES (est): 3.9MM **Privately Held**
WEB: www.sheet-metal.com
SIC: 3471 3444 Cleaning, polishing & fin-
ishing; sheet metalwork

(P-13108)
STAR FINISHES INC
40429 Brickyard Dr, Madera (93636-9515)
PHONE.....................................559 261-1076
Doug Hagen, *President*
EMP: 15
SQ FT: 7,760
SALES: 800K **Privately Held**
WEB: www.starfinishes.com
SIC: 3471 Finishing, metals or formed
products

(P-13109)
STUART-DEAN CO INC
14731 Franklin Ave Ste L, Tustin
(92780-7221)
PHONE.....................................714 544-4460
Steven Materazzo, *Manager*
EMP: 16
SALES (corp-wide): 65.4MM **Privately
Held**
WEB: www.mail.stuartdean.com
SIC: 3471 Polishing, metals or formed
products
PA: Stuart-Dean Co. Inc.
450 Fashion Ave Ste 3800
New York NY 10123
212 273-6900

(P-13110)
**SUPERIOR CONNECTOR
PLATING INC**
Also Called: Superior Plating
1901 E Cerritos Ave, Anaheim
(92805-6427)
PHONE.....................................714 774-1174
Juan Martin, *President*
Andrew Miller, *Officer*
EMP: 22
SQ FT: 7,500
SALES (est): 1.6MM **Privately Held**
SIC: 3471 Electroplating of metals or
formed products

(P-13111)
**SUPERIOR METAL FINISHING
INC**
1733 W 134th St, Gardena (90249-2015)
PHONE.....................................310 464-8010
William Leffingwell Sr, *President*
Duane O'Reilly, *Corp Secy*
EMP: 14
SQ FT: 5,290
SALES (est): 1.4MM **Privately Held**
WEB: www.superiormetalfinishing.com
SIC: 3471 Finishing, metals or formed
products

(P-13112)
SUPERIOR PLATING INC
9001 Glenoaks Blvd, Sun Valley
(91352-2040)
PHONE.....................................818 252-1088
EMP: 35
SALES (est): 2.7MM **Privately Held**
SIC: 3471

(P-13113)
SUPERIOR PROCESSING
1115 Las Brisas Pl, Placentia (92870-6644)
PHONE.....................................714 524-8525
Michael P Mc Guire, *President*
EMP: 10
SQ FT: 7,500
SALES: 1MM **Privately Held**
WEB: www.superior-processing.com
SIC: 3471 Electroplating of metals or
formed products; gold plating

(P-13114)
SURFACING SOLUTIONS INC
27637 Commerce Center Dr, Temecula
(92590-2521)
PHONE.....................................951 699-0035
Tiffany Halverson, *President*
Shawn Halverson, *Vice Pres*
Keith Cantillon, *Contractor*
EMP: 16
SQ FT: 5,000
SALES (est): 2.3MM **Privately Held**
SIC: 3471 Decorative plating & finishing of
formed products

(P-13115)
**SYMCOAT METAL PROCESSING
INC**
7887 Dunbrook Rd Ste C, San Diego
(92126-4382)
PHONE.....................................858 451-3313
Sylvia Twiggs, *President*
Michelle Kanganis, *Vice Pres*
EMP: 27
SQ FT: 12,000
SALES (est): 2.9MM **Privately Held**
WEB: www.symcoat.net
SIC: 3471 3341 Finishing, metals or
formed products; secondary nonferrous
metals

(P-13116)
TECHNIC INC
1170 N Hawk Cir, Anaheim (92807-1789)
PHONE.....................................714 632-0200
Mike Chicos, *Opers-Prdtn-Mfg*
Jeff Cannis, *Technical Mgr*
Maria Coe, *Human Res Mgr*
Mike Cortes, *Safety Mgr*
EMP: 30
SALES (corp-wide): 125.5MM **Privately
Held**
WEB: www.technic.com
SIC: 3471 2899 3678 3672 Plating of
metals or formed products; plating com-
pounds; electronic connectors; printed cir-
cuit boards; precious metals;
semiconductor devices
PA: Technic, Inc.
47 Molter St
Cranston RI 02910
401 781-6100

(P-13117)
**THERMIONICS LABORATORY
INC**
Thermionics Metal Proc Inc
3118 Depot Rd, Hayward (94545-2708)
PHONE.....................................510 786-0680
Al Nielsen, *Manager*
EMP: 75

SQ FT: 1,300
SALES (corp-wide): 12MM **Privately
Held**
WEB: www.thermionicscorp.com
SIC: 3471 8711 7342 Cleaning & descal-
ing metal products; engineering services;
disinfecting & pest control services
HQ: Thermionics Laboratory, Inc.
3118 Depot Rd
Hayward CA 94545
510 538-3304

(P-13118)
TMW CORPORATION
Also Called: Aero Chrome Plating
14647 Arminta St, Panorama City
(91402-5901)
PHONE.....................................818 374-1074
Moheb Mansour, *Vice Pres*
Michael R Tawadros, *Opers Mgr*
EMP: 42
SALES (est): 5.4MM
SALES (corp-wide): 10.5MM **Privately
Held**
SIC: 3471 Electroplating of metals or
formed products
PA: T.M.W. Corporation
15148 Bledsoe St
Sylmar CA
818 362-5665

(P-13119)
TRIDENT PLATING INC
10046 Romandel Ave, Santa Fe Springs
(90670-3424)
PHONE.....................................562 906-2556
Maty Rodriguez, *President*
Ian Holmber, *Corp Secy*
Juan Carlos Rodriguez, *Vice Pres*
EMP: 28
SQ FT: 18,197
SALES: 2MM **Privately Held**
SIC: 3471 Gold plating; electroplating of
metals or formed products

(P-13120)
TRIUMPH PROCESSING INC
Also Called: Valence Lynwood
2605 Industry Way, Lynwood (90262-4007)
PHONE.....................................323 563-1338
Peter Labarbera, *CEO*
Richard C III, *CEO*
Eric Purinton, *Safety Mgr*
EMP: 103 EST: 1968
SQ FT: 140,000
SALES: 18.1MM
SALES (corp-wide): 103MM **Privately
Held**
WEB: www.dvindustries.com
SIC: 3471 3398 3356 Anodizing (plating)
of metals or formed products; finishing,
metals or formed products; polishing,
metals or formed products; metal heat
treating; nonferrous rolling & drawing
PA: Valence Surface Technologies Llc
1790 Hughes Landing Blvd
The Woodlands TX 77380
855 370-5920

(P-13121)
U M S INC
Also Called: A C Plating
317 Mount Vernon Ave, Bakersfield
(93307-2743)
PHONE.....................................661 324-5454
Robert D McBride, *President*
Tori McBride, *Office Mgr*
EMP: 22 EST: 1968
SQ FT: 15,000
SALES (est): 2.4MM **Privately Held**
WEB: www.acplating.com
SIC: 3471 Plating of metals or formed
products

(P-13122)
**U S CHROME CORP
CALIFORNIA**
1480 Canal Ave, Long Beach (90813-1244)
PHONE.....................................562 437-2825
Nick R Stahenoli, *Manager*
EMP: 17
SQ FT: 4,800

SALES (corp-wide): 28.5MM **Privately Held**
WEB: www.uschromeofca.com
SIC: 3471 Chromium plating of metals or formed products
HQ: U S Chrome Corporation Of California
175 Garfield Ave
Stratford CT
203 378-9622

(P-13123)
ULTRA-PURE METAL FINISHING
1764 N Case St, Orange (92865-4212)
PHONE................................714 637-3150
David Juarez, *President*
Nina Juarez, *Vice Pres*
EMP: 17
SQ FT: 11,160
SALES (est): 1.9MM **Privately Held**
SIC: 3471 Electroplating of metals or formed products

(P-13124)
ULTRAMET
12173 Montague St, Pacoima (91331-2210)
PHONE................................818 899-0236
Andrew Duffy, *CEO*
James Kaplan, *Shareholder*
Richard B Kaplan, *Shareholder*
Walter Abrams, *Admin Sec*
Pysa Davis, *Admin Asst*
▲ EMP: 79
SQ FT: 43,000
SALES (est): 16.2MM **Privately Held**
WEB: www.ultramet.com
SIC: 3471 8731 Electroplating & plating; commercial physical research

(P-13125)
UNIVERSAL METAL PLATING
704 S Taylor Ave, Montebello (90640-5562)
PHONE................................626 969-7932
Guadalupe Martinez, *Partner*
EMP: 15
SALES (corp-wide): 1.8MM **Privately Held**
SIC: 3471 Chromium plating of metals or formed products
PA: Universal Metal Plating
1526 W 1st St
Irwindale CA 91702
626 969-7931

(P-13126)
V & M PLATING CO
14024 Avalon Blvd, Los Angeles (90061-2692)
PHONE................................310 532-5633
Anthony Babiak, *President*
Timothy Babiak, *Vice Pres*
▲ EMP: 19
SQ FT: 7,500
SALES (est): 1.4MM **Privately Held**
WEB: www.vmplating.com
SIC: 3471 Chromium plating of metals or formed products; electroplating of metals or formed products

(P-13127)
VALLEY CHROME PLATING INC
Also Called: Wing Master
1028 Hoblitt Ave, Clovis (93612-2805)
P.O. Box 189 (93613-0189)
PHONE................................559 298-8094
Thomas A Lucas, *CEO*
Ray Lucas, *President*
Catherine L Booey, *Corp Secy*
Greg Lucas, *Vice Pres*
Matthew Lucas, *Vice Pres*
▲ EMP: 70
SQ FT: 30,000
SALES (est): 13.8MM **Privately Held**
WEB: www.valleychrome.com
SIC: 3471 3714 Plating of metals or formed products; bumpers & bumperettes, motor vehicle

(P-13128)
VIRGIL M STUTZMAN INC
Also Called: Stutzman Plating
5045 Exposition Blvd, Los Angeles (90016-3913)
P.O. Box 78457 (90016-0457)
PHONE................................323 732-9146
Virgil M Stutzman, *President*

Joseph C Stutzman, *Treasurer*
James D Stutzman, *Vice Pres*
EMP: 50 EST: 1967
SQ FT: 4,000
SALES (est): 5.4MM **Privately Held**
WEB: www.stutzmanplating.com
SIC: 3471 5051 3369 3364 Electroplating of metals or formed products; metals service centers & offices; nonferrous foundries; nonferrous die-castings except aluminum

(P-13129)
WE FIVE-R CORPORATION
Also Called: Bank C Plating Co
1507 S Sunol Dr, Los Angeles (90023-4031)
PHONE................................323 263-6757
Dick Patel, *President*
◆ EMP: 18 EST: 1950
SQ FT: 8,000
SALES (est): 1.2MM **Privately Held**
SIC: 3471 Plating of metals or formed products

(P-13130)
WEST VALLEY PLATING INC
21061 Superior St Ste A, Chatsworth (91311-4330)
PHONE................................818 709-1684
Josephina Campos, *President*
EMP: 15
SALES (est): 2.1MM **Privately Held**
SIC: 3471 Plating of metals or formed products; electroplating of metals or formed products

---

3479 Coating & Engraving, NEC

(P-13131)
A & R POWDER COATING INC
1198 N Grove St Ste B, Anaheim (92806-2136)
PHONE................................714 630-0709
Jack Rainwater, *President*
Everett Ryan, *President*
EMP: 12
SQ FT: 5,500
SALES: 900K **Privately Held**
SIC: 3479 Coating of metals & formed products

(P-13132)
A-1 ENGRAVING CO INC
8225 Phlox St, Downey (90241-4880)
PHONE................................562 861-2216
Jack E Young, *President*
Grace Young, *Corp Secy*
Don Schram, *Vice Pres*
EMP: 12
SQ FT: 22,900
SALES (est): 1.2MM **Privately Held**
SIC: 3479 Engraving jewelry silverware, or metal; etching & engraving

(P-13133)
ABACUS POWDER COATING
1829 Tyler Ave, South El Monte (91733-3617)
PHONE................................626 443-7556
Esther Davidoff, *President*
EMP: 25
SALES (est): 3MM **Privately Held**
WEB: www.abacuspowder.com
SIC: 3479 Coating of metals & formed products

(P-13134)
ACCURATE DIAL & NAMEPLATE INC (PA)
329 Mira Loma Ave, Glendale (91204-2912)
PHONE................................323 245-9181
Jerry D Childs, *President*
David V Howarth, *CEO*
Erin Dyer, *Vice Pres*
Robert Childs, *Senior Buyer*
Barb Menzel, *Marketing Mgr*
EMP: 12

SALES (est): 3.5MM **Privately Held**
SIC: 3479 3613 2759 1721 Name plates: engraved, etched, etc.; control panels, electric; commercial printing; painting & paper hanging; signs & advertising specialties

(P-13135)
ADFA INCORPORATED
Also Called: A&A Jewelry Supply
319 W 6th St, Los Angeles (90014-1703)
PHONE................................213 627-8004
Robert Adem, *President*
Naim Farah, *Vice Pres*
Danny Farah, *General Mgr*
▲ EMP: 45
SALES (est): 3.4MM **Privately Held**
SIC: 3479 3548 3172 Engraving jewelry silverware, or metal; electric welding equipment; cases, jewelry

(P-13136)
ADVANCE FINISHING
11645 S Broadway, Los Angeles (90061-1834)
PHONE................................323 754-2889
Ramon Verdin, *Owner*
EMP: 18 EST: 1981
SQ FT: 10,000
SALES: 1MM **Privately Held**
SIC: 3479 Painting of metal products

(P-13137)
ADVANCED INDUS COATINGS INC
950 Industrial Dr, Stockton (95206-3927)
PHONE................................209 234-2700
Toll Free:................................877 -
Ronald Cymanski, *President*
David Arney, *COO*
Marianne Arney, *Corp Secy*
Steve Hockett, *Vice Pres*
EMP: 53
SQ FT: 48,000
SALES (est): 7MM **Privately Held**
WEB: www.aic-coatings.com
SIC: 3479 Coating of metals & formed products

(P-13138)
AERO POWDER COATING INC
710 Monterey Pass Rd, Monterey Park (91754-3607)
PHONE................................323 264-6405
Phillip Kontos, *President*
EMP: 39
SQ FT: 27,000
SALES (est): 3.3MM **Privately Held**
SIC: 3479 Coating of metals & formed products

(P-13139)
AIRCOAT INC
13405 S Broadway, Los Angeles (90061-1127)
PHONE................................310 527-2258
Francisco Ramirez, *President*
EMP: 15
SQ FT: 20,000
SALES: 900K **Privately Held**
SIC: 3479 Painting of metal products; painting, coating & hot dipping

(P-13140)
ALL SOURCE COATINGS INC
10625 Scripps Ranch Blvd D, San Diego (92131-1012)
PHONE................................858 586-0903
Jerry Zumbro, *President*
Emily Pinkston, *Office Mgr*
Sarah Kindt, *Admin Asst*
EMP: 21
SQ FT: 2,000
SALES: 980K **Privately Held**
SIC: 3479 1721 Aluminum coating of metal products; painting & paper hanging; commercial painting

(P-13141)
AMERICAN ETCHING & MFG
13730 Desmond St, Pacoima (91331-2706)
PHONE................................323 875-3910
Gary Kipka, *President*
Frances D Torre, *Officer*
EMP: 45

SQ FT: 20,000
SALES (est): 5.7MM **Privately Held**
WEB: www.aemetch.com
SIC: 3479 Etching on metals

(P-13142)
ANDREWS POWDER COATING INC
10138 Canoga Ave, Chatsworth (91311-3005)
PHONE................................818 700-1030
Scott Andrews, *President*
Tc Carter, *Sales Staff*
EMP: 28 EST: 1991
SALES (est): 3.6MM **Privately Held**
SIC: 3479 Coating of metals & formed products

(P-13143)
APPLIED COATINGS & LININGS
3224 Rosemead Blvd, El Monte (91731-2807)
PHONE................................626 280-6354
James Horton, *President*
Ed Horton, *Treasurer*
EMP: 24
SQ FT: 150,000
SALES (est): 2.7MM **Privately Held**
WEB: www.appliedcoatings.com
SIC: 3479 3471 Coating of metals & formed products; coating or wrapping steel pipe; plating & polishing

(P-13144)
APPLIED POWDERCOAT INC
3101 Camino Del Sol, Oxnard (93030-8999)
PHONE................................805 981-1991
Victor Anselmo, *President*
J Michael Hagan, *Ch of Bd*
Deborah Anselmo, *Manager*
EMP: 32
SQ FT: 30,000
SALES (est): 5.2MM **Privately Held**
WEB: www.appliedpowder.com
SIC: 3479 Coating of metals & formed products

(P-13145)
ATLAS GALVANIZING LLC
2639 Leonis Blvd, Vernon (90058-2203)
PHONE................................323 587-6247
Victor Bruno Jr,
Patricia New,
EMP: 36 EST: 1936
SQ FT: 20,000
SALES (est): 5.2MM **Privately Held**
WEB: www.atlasgalvanizing.com
SIC: 3479 Galvanizing of iron, steel or end-formed products

(P-13146)
B & B ENAMELING INC
17591 Sampson Ln, Huntington Beach (92647-7722)
PHONE................................714 848-0044
Jay V Bogert, *President*
EMP: 10
SQ FT: 7,000
SALES (est): 1.2MM **Privately Held**
SIC: 3479 Enameling, including porcelain, of metal products; coating of metals & formed products

(P-13147)
B & C PAINTING SOLUTIONS INC
107 Val Dervin Pkwy, Stockton (95206-4001)
PHONE................................209 982-0422
Gary Maggard, *CEO*
Gloria Garay, *Office Mgr*
EMP: 28
SQ FT: 40,000
SALES (est): 3.8MM **Privately Held**
WEB: www.bcpaintingsolutions.com
SIC: 3479 Coating of metals & formed products

(P-13148)
B R & F SPRAY INC
3380 De La Cruz Blvd, Santa Clara (95054-2608)
PHONE................................408 988-7582
Ronald Grainger, *President*
Florence Grainger, *Corp Secy*

EMP: 10
SQ FT: 14,000
SALES (est): 1.2MM Privately Held
WEB: www.brf-spray.com
SIC: 3479 3471 Painting of metal products; plating & polishing

(P-13149)
BELL POWDER COATING INC
4747 Mcgrath St, Ventura (93003-6495)
P.O. Box 7117 (93006-7117)
PHONE...........................805 658-2233
Carl Bell, *President*
Judith Bell, *Vice Pres*
EMP: 15
SQ FT: 16,500
SALES (est): 1.5MM Privately Held
SIC: 3479 Aluminum coating of metal products; coating of metals & formed products

(P-13150)
BJS&T ENTERPRISES INC
Also Called: San Diego Powder Coating
1702 N Magnolia Ave # 101, El Cajon (92020-1287)
PHONE...........................619 448-7795
Bob Johnson, *President*
Stephen Johnson, *Vice Pres*
Philip Johnson, *General Mgr*
Michelle Simmons, *General Mgr*
Teri Howe, *Accounting Mgr*
EMP: 15
SQ FT: 7,000
SALES (est): 2.3MM Privately Held
SIC: 3479 Coating of metals & formed products

(P-13151)
BRIGHT SHARK POWDER COATING
4530 Schaefer Ave, Chino (91710-5539)
PHONE...........................909 591-1385
Rosalva Garcia, *Partner*
EMP: 14
SQ FT: 9,600
SALES (est): 2.3MM Privately Held
SIC: 3479 Coating of metals & formed products

(P-13152)
CAL NOR POWDER COATING INC
265 E Clay St, Ukiah (95482-4915)
PHONE...........................707 462-0217
Robert Loucks, *CEO*
EMP: 10
SQ FT: 30,000
SALES (est): 740K Privately Held
SIC: 3479 Painting of metal products; coating of metals & formed products

(P-13153)
CALIFORNIA ETCHING INC
1952 Iroquois St, NAPA (94559-1328)
PHONE...........................707 224-9966
Tim L Arnold, *President*
EMP: 10
SALES (est): 1.2MM Privately Held
WEB: www.californiaetching.com
SIC: 3479 Etching & engraving

(P-13154)
CALSPRAY INC
1905 Bay Rd, East Palo Alto (94303-1394)
PHONE...........................650 325-0096
John Garcia, *President*
EMP: 14 EST: 1966
SQ FT: 10,000
SALES (est): 1MM Privately Held
SIC: 3479 Painting of metal products

(P-13155)
CALWEST GALVANIZING CORP
2226 E Dominguez St, Carson (90810-1086)
PHONE...........................310 549-2200
Toll Free:...........................888 -
Isaac Malbonado, *General Mgr*
Isaac Maldonado, *Asst Mgr*
▲ EMP: 70
SQ FT: 20,000

SALES (est): 8.2MM
SALES (corp-wide): 2.7B Publicly Held
WEB: www.calwestgalvanizing.com
SIC: 3479 3317 Galvanizing of iron, steel or end-formed products; steel pipe & tubes
PA: Valmont Industries, Inc.
1 Valmont Plz Ste 500
Omaha NE 68154
402 963-1000

(P-13156)
CANAY MANUFACTURING INC
Also Called: Powder Coating Plus
26140 Avenue Hall, Valencia (91355-4808)
PHONE...........................661 295-0205
Earl T Bayless, *President*
Micah Turner, *Sales Staff*
EMP: 14 EST: 1995
SALES (est): 1.7MM Privately Held
SIC: 3479 Coating of metals & formed products

(P-13157)
CERTIFIED ENAMELING INC
3342 Emery St, Los Angeles (90023-3810)
PHONE...........................323 264-4403
Glenn Ziegel, *President*
Zulma Castellon, *Production*
EMP: 95 EST: 1953
SQ FT: 50,000
SALES (est): 14.1MM Privately Held
WEB: www.certifiedenameling.com
SIC: 3479 Coating of metals & formed products

(P-13158)
CLASS A POWDERCOAT INC
7506 Henrietta Dr, Sacramento (95822-5145)
PHONE...........................916 681-7474
Klay Stubbs, *President*
Kirk Stubbs, *Vice Pres*
EMP: 25
SALES (est): 3.6MM Privately Held
SIC: 3479 3471 Painting of metal products; sand blasting of metal parts

(P-13159)
COATING SERVICES GROUP LLC
Also Called: Csg
11649 Rverside Dr Ste 139, Lakeside (92040)
PHONE...........................619 596-7444
Hans Sleeuwenhoek, *CEO*
Jeff Grant, *President*
EMP: 10
SQ FT: 5,500
SALES: 1MM Privately Held
SIC: 3479 Etching & engraving

(P-13160)
COATINGS BY SANDBERG INC
856 N Commerce St, Orange (92867-7900)
PHONE...........................714 538-0888
Nona Sandberg, *President*
Gerald Sandberg, *Admin Sec*
EMP: 14 EST: 1997
SQ FT: 12,000
SALES (est): 1.6MM Privately Held
WEB: www.cbs-dichroic.com
SIC: 3479 Coating of metals & formed products

(P-13161)
COLOR TEC INDUSTRIAL FINISHING
11231 Ilex Ave, Pacoima (91331-2725)
PHONE...........................818 897-2669
Michael Cabral, *Owner*
EMP: 20
SQ FT: 6,000
SALES (est): 1.7MM Privately Held
SIC: 3479 Coating of metals & formed products

(P-13162)
CREST COATING INC
1361 S Allec St, Anaheim (92805-6304)
PHONE...........................714 635-7090
Michael D Erickson, *CEO*
Bonnie George, *Vice Pres*
Kristina Palmer-Brick, *Purchasing*
Louie Munet, *Buyer*

Andrew Starritt, *Opers Mgr*
▲ EMP: 60 EST: 1968
SQ FT: 55,000
SALES (est): 9.5MM Privately Held
WEB: www.crestcoating.com
SIC: 3479 Coating of metals & formed products

(P-13163)
CUSTOM ENAMELERS INC
18340 Mount Baldy Cir, Fountain Valley (92708-6181)
PHONE...........................714 540-7884
Ronald Folmer, *President*
Janet Folmer, *Treasurer*
Daryl Folmer, *Vice Pres*
EMP: 30 EST: 1957
SQ FT: 27,000
SALES (est): 3.5MM Privately Held
SIC: 3479 Enameling, including porcelain, of metal products; coating of metals & formed products

(P-13164)
DENMAC INDUSTRIES INC
7616 Rosecrans Ave, Paramount (90723-2508)
P.O. Box 2144 (90723-8144)
PHONE...........................562 634-2714
Mark Plechot, *President*
Maurice Plechot, *CFO*
James Campangna, *Vice Pres*
▲ EMP: 40
SQ FT: 20,000
SALES (est): 5.7MM Privately Held
WEB: www.denmac-ind.com
SIC: 3479 Coating of metals & formed products

(P-13165)
DOUG TRIM SUB CONTRACTOR
32010 Alaga Ave, Pearblossom (93553-3465)
PHONE...........................661 944-2884
Doug Trim, *Principal*
EMP: 12
SALES (est): 560K Privately Held
SIC: 3479 1721 Painting, coating & hot dipping; painting & paper hanging

(P-13166)
DRYWIRED DEFENSE LLC
9606 Santa Monica Blvd # 4, Beverly Hills (90210-4427)
PHONE...........................310 684-3891
Alex Nesic, *Vice Pres*
Samantha Gonzalez, *Pub Rel Dir*
EMP: 20 EST: 2012
SQ FT: 4,000
SALES (est): 1.9MM Privately Held
SIC: 3479 3672 Coating electrodes; coating, rust preventive; printed circuit boards

(P-13167)
DURA COAT PRODUCTS INC (PA)
5361 Via Ricardo, Riverside (92509-2414)
PHONE...........................951 341-6500
Myung K Hong, *CEO*
Suzanne Faust, *CFO*
Dan Knight, *Vice Pres*
Lorrie Y Hong, *Admin Sec*
Sue Javier, *Accountant*
◆ EMP: 64
SQ FT: 29,000
SALES (est): 72.9MM Privately Held
SIC: 3479 2851 Aluminum coating of metal products; coating of metals & formed products; paints & allied products

(P-13168)
E-FAB INC
1075 Richard Ave, Santa Clara (95050-2815)
P.O. Box 239 (95052-0239)
PHONE...........................408 727-5218
James W Scales, *President*
Carol Spicker, *CFO*
Jerry Banks, *Vice Pres*
Ed Hinson, *General Mgr*
EMP: 22
SQ FT: 4,000
SALES (est): 2MM Privately Held
WEB: www.e-fab.com
SIC: 3479 Etching & engraving

(P-13169)
ECP POWDER COATING
Also Called: El Cajon Plating
1835 John Towers Ave A, El Cajon (92020-1145)
PHONE...........................619 448-3932
Scott Rasmussen, *President*
Diane Rasmussen, *Admin Sec*
EMP: 11
SQ FT: 7,400
SALES (est): 1.4MM Privately Held
SIC: 3479 Coating of metals & formed products; painting, coating & hot dipping

(P-13170)
EEMUS MANUFACTURING CORP
11111 Rush St, South El Monte (91733-3548)
PHONE...........................626 443-8841
Gitte Simionian, *President*
Richard Mitchell, *Vice Pres*
Art Arteaga, *Principal*
EMP: 14
SQ FT: 20,000
SALES (est): 1.5MM Privately Held
SIC: 3479 Etching on metals

(P-13171)
ELECTRO METAL FINISHING CORP (PA)
1194 N Grove St, Anaheim (92806-2109)
PHONE...........................714 630-8940
Tony Vargas, *President*
EMP: 17
SQ FT: 11,900
SALES (est): 1.6MM Privately Held
WEB: www.electrometalfinish.com
SIC: 3479 Painting of metal products

(P-13172)
ELECTRO STAR INDUS COATING INC
Also Called: Electro Star Powder Coatings
1945 Airport Blvd, Red Bluff (96080-4518)
PHONE...........................530 527-5400
Baron A Pierce, *President*
Susan Pierce, *CFO*
EMP: 15 EST: 1979
SQ FT: 4,000
SALES (est): 1.4MM Privately Held
WEB: www.electrostar.net
SIC: 3479 Coating of metals & formed products

(P-13173)
ELECTRO TECH COATINGS INC
836 Rancheros Dr Ste A, San Marcos (92069-7035)
PHONE...........................760 746-0292
Adam P Mitchell, *President*
Linda Mitchell, *CFO*
Allen L Mitchell, *Vice Pres*
Denise Mitchell, *Admin Sec*
EMP: 20
SQ FT: 13,000
SALES: 1MM Privately Held
WEB: www.electrotechcoatings.com
SIC: 3479 3471 Coating of metals & formed products; sand blasting of metal parts

(P-13174)
ENGINEERED APPLICATION LLC
4727 E 49th St, Vernon (90058-2703)
PHONE...........................323 585-2894
Gil Hestmark,
EMP: 16
SALES (est): 2.2MM Privately Held
WEB: www.engineeredapps.com
SIC: 3479 Coating of metals & formed products

(P-13175)
ETS EXPRESS INC (PA)
420 Lombard St, Oxnard (93030-5100)
PHONE...........................805 278-7771
Sharon Eyal, *President*
Taly Eyal, *CFO*
Gabriel Marcial, *CFO*
Derek Hansen, *Vice Pres*
Hunter Larson, *Graphic Designe*
▲ EMP: 35
SQ FT: 40,000

SALES (est): 14MM **Privately Held**
WEB: www.etsexpress.com
SIC: 3479 3231 Etching & engraving; cut & engraved glassware; made from purchased glass

(P-13176)
EXCLUSIVE POWDER COATINGS INC
24922 Anza Dr Ste C, Valencia (91355-1230)
P.O. Box 803307, Santa Clarita (91380-3307)
PHONE..................................661 294-9812
Mark Kier, *CEO*
▲ **EMP:** 11
SQ FT: 8,500
SALES (est): 1.7MM **Privately Held**
SIC: 3479 Coating of metals & formed products

(P-13177)
EXPERT COATINGS & GRAPHICS LLC
1570 S Lewis St, Anaheim (92805-6423)
PHONE..................................714 476-2086
Sandra Day, *CEO*
EMP: 12
SALES (est): 1.8MM **Privately Held**
SIC: 3479 Painting, coating & hot dipping

(P-13178)
FLAME-SPRAY INC
4674 Alvarado Canyon Rd, San Diego (92120-4304)
PHONE..................................619 283-2007
Larry Suhl, *President*
Pam Scalzo, *Shareholder*
Darrel Suhl, *Vice Pres*
Roxy Suhl, *Office Mgr*
▲ **EMP:** 20 **EST:** 1969
SQ FT: 20,000
SALES (est): 3.3MM **Privately Held**
WEB: www.flamesprayinc.com
SIC: 3479 Coating of metals & formed products

(P-13179)
FLETCHER COATING CO
426 W Fletcher Ave, Orange (92865-2612)
PHONE..................................714 637-4763
Kurtis Breeding, *CEO*
▲ **EMP:** 50
SQ FT: 37,500
SALES (est): 5.5MM **Privately Held**
WEB: www.fletcherkote.com
SIC: 3479 Coating of metals & formed products

(P-13180)
FUSION COATINGS INC
6589 Las Positas Rd, Livermore (94551-5157)
PHONE..................................925 443-8083
Paul Fleury, *President*
Julie Fleury, *Co-Owner*
EMP: 15
SQ FT: 7,000
SALES (est): 1MM **Privately Held**
WEB: www.fusioncoatings.com
SIC: 3479 Coating of metals & formed products

(P-13181)
FVO SOLUTIONS INC
Also Called: FOOTHILL VOCATIONAL OPPORTUNIT
789 N Fair Oaks Ave, Pasadena (91103-3045)
PHONE..................................626 449-0218
William C Murphy, *CEO*
Gretchen Reed, *Chairman*
▲ **EMP:** 75
SQ FT: 24,000
SALES: 2MM **Privately Held**
WEB: www.foothillvoc.org
SIC: 3479 3999 Coating of metals & formed products; gold stamping, except books

(P-13182)
GB INDUSTRIAL SPRAY INC
1140 Bessemer Ave Ste 1, Manteca (95337-6108)
PHONE..................................209 825-7176
Gary L Beauchamp, *CEO*

SALES (est): 1.5MM **Privately Held**
SIC: 3479 Painting of metal products

(P-13183)
GEBE ELECTRONIC SERVICES INC
4112 W Jefferson Blvd, Los Angeles (90016-4125)
PHONE..................................323 731-2439
R O Fergus Sr, *President*
R O Fergus Jr, *Treasurer*
Gregory Fergus, *Vice Pres*
EMP: 25
SQ FT: 10,500
SALES (est): 1MM **Privately Held**
SIC: 3479 Bonderizing of metal or metal products; coating of metals & formed products

(P-13184)
GEMTECH INDS GOOD EARTH MFG
Also Called: Gemtech International
2737 S Garnsey St, Santa Ana (92707-3340)
P.O. Box 15506 (92735-0506)
PHONE..................................714 848-2517
Shig Shiwota, *President*
Maya Shiwota, *Vice Pres*
David Shiwota, *Managing Dir*
▲ **EMP:** 24
SQ FT: 10,500
SALES (est): 3MM **Privately Held**
WEB: www.gemtechpowder.com
SIC: 3479 Coating of metals & formed products

(P-13185)
GENERAL COATINGS MFG CORP
1220 E North Ave, Fresno (93725-1930)
PHONE..................................559 495-4004
Laxmi C Gupta, *CEO*
Nutan Thapa, *Principal*
EMP: 10
SALES (est): 801.2K
SALES (corp-wide): 25.4MM **Privately Held**
SIC: 3479 Coating of metals & formed products; coating of metals with plastic or resins; coating of metals with silicon; coating or wrapping steel pipe
PA: American Polymers Corp.
14722 Spring Ave
Santa Fe Springs CA 90670
562 802-8834

(P-13186)
GILBERT SPRAY COAT INC
300 Laurelwood Rd, Santa Clara (95054-2311)
PHONE..................................408 988-0747
Todd McLean, *President*
Lisa McLean, *Vice Pres*
EMP: 20 **EST:** 1939
SQ FT: 5,000
SALES (est): 2MM **Privately Held**
WEB: www.gilbertspray.com
SIC: 3479 Painting of metal products; painting, coating & hot dipping

(P-13187)
GRAND-WAY FABRI-GRAPHIC INC
22550 Lamplight Pl, Santa Clarita (91350-5729)
PHONE..................................818 206-8560
Marlene Kane, *President*
EMP: 20
SQ FT: 10,500
SALES (est): 2MM **Privately Held**
SIC: 3479 Etching & engraving; painting of metal products

(P-13188)
GUERNSEY COATING LABORATORY
1788 Goodyear Ave, Ventura (93003-8080)
PHONE..................................805 642-1508
Peter Guernsey, *Owner*
Robert Mendenhall, *Sales Staff*
EMP: 12
SQ FT: 9,000

SALES (est): 1.2MM **Privately Held**
WEB: www.gclinc.com
SIC: 3479 Coating of metals & formed products

(P-13189)
HALEY INDUS CTINGS LININGS INC
2919 Tanager Ave, Commerce (90040-2723)
PHONE..................................323 588-8086
Yvonne P Haley, *President*
EMP: 21
SALES (est): 3.3MM **Privately Held**
SIC: 3479 1771 Coating of metals & formed products; flooring contractor

(P-13190)
HIGH-TECH COATINGS INC
1724 S Santa Fe St, Santa Ana (92705-4813)
PHONE..................................714 547-2122
Dan C Hilton, *Owner*
Sharon Hilton, *Human Res Mgr*
EMP: 15
SQ FT: 8,500
SALES (est): 1.7MM **Privately Held**
SIC: 3479 Coating of metals & formed products

(P-13191)
HUES METAL FINISHING INC
977 Linda Vista Dr, San Marcos (92078-2611)
PHONE..................................760 744-5566
Dolour S Smith-Wormald, *CEO*
Gregg L Wormald, *President*
EMP: 17
SQ FT: 11,000
SALES: 700K **Privately Held**
WEB: www.huesinc.com
SIC: 3479 Painting of metal products

(P-13192)
INLAND POWDER COATING CORP
Also Called: Prs Industries
1656 S Bon View Ave Ste F, Ontario (91761-4419)
P.O. Box 3427 (91761-0943)
PHONE..................................909 947-1122
David Paul Flatten, *President*
Debbie Flatten, *Treasurer*
EMP: 104
SQ FT: 83,000
SALES (est): 15.3MM **Privately Held**
WEB: www.inlandpowder.com
SIC: 3479 3471 Coating of metals & formed products; sand blasting of metal parts

(P-13193)
INNOVATIVE TECHNOLOGY INC
1501 Cook Pl, Goleta (93117-3123)
P.O. Box 60007, Santa Barbara (93160-0007)
PHONE..................................805 571-8384
Howard Gabel, *President*
Ralph Tapphorn, *Vice Pres*
EMP: 10
SQ FT: 4,000
SALES (est): 1.2MM **Privately Held**
WEB: www.inovati.com
SIC: 3479 3399 Coating of metals & formed products; powder, metal

(P-13194)
ISLAND POWDER COATING
1830 Tyler Ave, South El Monte (91733-3618)
PHONE..................................626 279-2460
Joe Graham, *Owner*
EMP: 30
SALES (est): 5.3MM **Privately Held**
SIC: 3479 Coating of metals & formed products

(P-13195)
ITALIX COMPANY INC
120 Mast St Ste A, Morgan Hill (95037-5154)
PHONE..................................408 988-2487
Robert L Armanasco, *President*
Frank Fantino, *CEO*
Trisha Coyoca, *Info Tech Mgr*
Jeff Zweers, *Engineer*

EMP: 19
SQ FT: 8,000
SALES (est): 2.9MM **Privately Held**
WEB: www.italix.com
SIC: 3479 3471 Etching, photochemical; finishing, metals or formed products

(P-13196)
KENNEDY NAME PLATE CO INC
4501 Pacific Blvd, Vernon (90058-2207)
PHONE..................................323 585-0121
William J Kennedy Jr, *President*
Mike Kennedy, *Vice Pres*
EMP: 25
SQ FT: 36,000
SALES: 3MM **Privately Held**
WEB: www.knpco.com
SIC: 3479 7336 3993 3444 Name plates: engraved, etched, etc.; silk screen design; signs & advertising specialties; sheet metalwork; coated & laminated paper; packaging paper & plastics film, coated & laminated

(P-13197)
KENS SPRAY EQUIPMENT INC (DH)
Also Called: Alloy Processing
1900 W Walnut St, Compton (90220-5019)
PHONE..................................310 635-9995
Joseph I Snowden, *Principal*
Brian Leibl, *President*
Sandra Jeglum, *Corp Secy*
EMP: 53
SQ FT: 37,000
SALES (est): 24.7MM
SALES (corp-wide): 225.3B **Publicly Held**
WEB: www.alloyprocessing.com
SIC: 3479 Painting of metal products
HQ: Precision Castparts Corp.
4650 Sw Mcdam Ave Ste 300
Portland OR 97239
503 946-4800

(P-13198)
KION TECHNOLOGY INC
2190 Oakland Rd, San Jose (95131-1571)
PHONE..................................408 435-3008
Moto Hayashi, *President*
Shirley Chau, *Admin Sec*
EMP: 15
SQ FT: 8,000
SALES (est): 1.7MM **Privately Held**
WEB: www.kiontechnology.com
SIC: 3479 Coating of metals & formed products

(P-13199)
LEONS POWDER COATING
834 49th Ave, Oakland (94601-5136)
PHONE..................................510 437-9224
Jose Pelayo, *Owner*
EMP: 13
SALES (est): 1.3MM **Privately Held**
SIC: 3479 Coating of metals with plastic or resins; painting, coating & hot dipping

(P-13200)
LICENSE FRAME INC
Also Called: Baron & Baron
15462 Electronic Ln, Huntington Beach (92649-1334)
PHONE..................................714 903-7550
Catherine Baron, *President*
Peter Baron, *Vice Pres*
▲ **EMP:** 25
SALES (est): 2.1MM **Privately Held**
WEB: www.licenseframe.com
SIC: 3479 Engraving jewelry silverware, or metal

(P-13201)
LINABOND INC
1161 Avenida Acaso, Camarillo (93012-8720)
PHONE..................................805 484-7373
Richard Bertram, *President*
German Gilli, *Vice Pres*
Georgia Dreifus, *Admin Sec*
▲ **EMP:** 12
SQ FT: 23,000
SALES (est): 1.6MM **Privately Held**
WEB: www.linabond.com
SIC: 3479 Coating of metals with plastic or resins

PRODUCTS & SVCS

(P-13202)
LOS ANGELES GALVANIZING CO
2518 E 53rd St, Huntington Park
(90255-2505)
PHONE...................................323 583-2263
Lance Michael Rosenkranz, *CEO*
Jamie Rosenkranz, *Vice Pres*
Lance Rosenkranz, *Vice Pres*
Tim Rosenkranz, *Vice Pres*
EMP: 58 EST: 1932
SQ FT: 26,000
SALES (est): 8.7MM **Privately Held**
WEB: www.lagalvanizing.com
SIC: 3479 Galvanizing of iron, steel or end-formed products

(P-13203)
LUSTER COTE INC
10841 Business Dr, Fontana (92337-8235)
PHONE...................................909 355-9995
Jan Niblett, *President*
EMP: 14
SQ FT: 29,000
SALES: 1.1MM **Privately Held**
SIC: 3479 3444 Coating of metals & formed products; awnings, sheet metal

(P-13204)
MABEL BAAS INC
Also Called: Royal Coatings
3960 Royal Ave, Simi Valley (93063-3380)
PHONE...................................805 520-8075
Marilyn Teperson, *President*
EMP: 50
SALES (est): 7.1MM **Privately Held**
WEB: www.royalcoatings.com
SIC: 3479 Coating of metals & formed products; painting, coating & hot dipping

(P-13205)
MELROSE NAMEPLATE LABEL CO INC (PA)
26575 Corporate Ave, Hayward
(94545-3920)
PHONE...................................510 732-3100
Chris Somers, *President*
Kathy Brenner, *Admin Sec*
▼ EMP: 30
SQ FT: 33,000
SALES (est): 6.2MM **Privately Held**
WEB: www.melrose-nl.com
SIC: 3479 3993 3643 3355 Name plates: engraved, etched, etc.; signs & advertising specialties; current-carrying wiring devices; aluminum rolling & drawing; laminated plastics plate & sheet; coated & laminated paper

(P-13206)
MERCURY METAL DIE & LETTER CO (PA)
Also Called: Hts Division
600 3rd St Ste A, Lake Elsinore
(92530-2748)
P.O. Box 86 (92531-0086)
PHONE...................................951 674-8717
Hugh Mosbacher, *President*
Kristin Lulak, *Manager*
▲ EMP: 15
SQ FT: 10,000
SALES (est): 2MM **Privately Held**
WEB: www.mercurymarking.com
SIC: 3479 3953 3544 Engraving jewelry silverware, or metal; marking devices; diamond dies, metalworking

(P-13207)
METAL COATERS CALIFORNIA INC
Also Called: Metal Coaters System
9123 Center Ave, Rancho Cucamonga
(91730-5312)
PHONE...................................909 987-4681
Norman C Chambers, *CEO*
Dick Klein, *President*
EMP: 75
SALES (est): 11.4MM
SALES (corp-wide): 2B **Publicly Held**
SIC: 3479 Painting of metal products
PA: Cornerstone Building Brands, Inc.
5020 Weston Pkwy Ste 400
Cary NC 27513
888 975-9436

(P-13208)
MOORE QUALITY GALVANIZING INC
3001 Falcon Dr, Madera (93637-8601)
P.O. Box 420 (93639-0420)
PHONE...................................559 673-2822
Thomas E Moore, *President*
Kellie Moore, *Corp Secy*
Marie Moore, *Vice Pres*
EMP: 30
SQ FT: 11,000
SALES (est): 4.6MM **Privately Held**
WEB: www.mooregalvanizing.com
SIC: 3479 Galvanizing of iron, steel or end-formed products

(P-13209)
MOORE QUALITY GALVANIZING LP
3001 Falcon Dr, Madera (93637-8601)
P.O. Box 420 (93639-0420)
PHONE...................................559 673-2822
Marie Moore, *General Ptnr*
Kellie Moore, *Partner*
EMP: 28
SQ FT: 18,000
SALES: 6MM **Privately Held**
SIC: 3479 Galvanizing of iron, steel or end-formed products

(P-13210)
NANOFLOWX LLC
3364 Garfield Ave, Commerce
(90040-3102)
PHONE...................................323 396-9200
Yu Ting Huang, *Mng Member*
EMP: 25 EST: 2015
SALES: 4MM **Privately Held**
SIC: 3479 Aluminum coating of metal products

(P-13211)
NEWPORT METAL FINISHING INC
Also Called: Brass Tech
3230 S Standard Ave, Santa Ana
(92705-5630)
PHONE...................................714 556-8411
Ron Foy, *President*
EMP: 70
SQ FT: 10,000
SALES (est): 6.1MM **Privately Held**
SIC: 3479 3471 Painting, coating & hot dipping; plating & polishing

(P-13212)
NORM HARBOLDT
Also Called: Primo Sandblasting
17592 Gothard St, Huntington Beach
(92647-6214)
PHONE...................................714 596-4242
Norm Harboldt, *President*
EMP: 20
SQ FT: 10,000
SALES: 900K **Privately Held**
SIC: 3479 Coating of metals & formed products

(P-13213)
NU TEC POWDERCOATING
2990 E Blue Star St, Anaheim
(92806-2511)
PHONE...................................714 632-5045
Joseph Kent, *Owner*
EMP: 11
SQ FT: 6,500
SALES (est): 861.4K **Privately Held**
SIC: 3479 Painting of metal products; coating of metals & formed products

(P-13214)
OLYMPIC COATINGS
2200 Micro Pl, Escondido (92029-1010)
PHONE...................................760 745-3322
Joel Johnson, *Owner*
EMP: 25
SQ FT: 4,500
SALES (est): 2.4MM **Privately Held**
WEB: www.olycoatings.com
SIC: 3479 Coating of metals & formed products

(P-13215)
OPTICAL COATING LABORATORY LLC (HQ)
Also Called: Ocli
2789 Northpoint Pkwy, Santa Rosa
(95407-7397)
PHONE...................................707 545-6440
Fred Van Milligen, *President*
Pat Higgins, *Vice Pres*
Shawn Cullen, *General Mgr*
Marina Nedeltcheva, *Admin Asst*
Scott Martin, *Manager*
EMP: 400
SQ FT: 490,000
SALES (est): 131MM
SALES (corp-wide): 1.1B **Publicly Held**
WEB: www.ocli.com
SIC: 3479 3577 3827 Coating of metals & formed products; computer peripheral equipment; optical instruments & lenses
PA: Viavi Solutions Inc.
6001 America Center Dr # 6
San Jose CA 95002
408 404-3600

(P-13216)
OUR POWDER COATING INC
Also Called: Stretch Film Center
10103 Freeman Ave, Santa Fe Springs
(90670-3407)
P.O. Box 3007, Whittier (90605-0007)
PHONE...................................562 946-0525
Mehdi Kohnechi, *President*
EMP: 10
SQ FT: 30,000
SALES (est): 1.2MM **Privately Held**
WEB: www.ourpowdercoating.com
SIC: 3479 Coating of metals & formed products

(P-13217)
PAC POWDER INC
Also Called: Pacific Powder Coating
148 S G St Ste 9, Arcata (95521-6690)
PHONE...................................707 826-1630
Ken Stevenson, *President*
Patti Lohr, *Admin Sec*
EMP: 10
SQ FT: 55,000
SALES (est): 1.2MM **Privately Held**
SIC: 3479 3441 Coating of metals & formed products; fabricated structural metal

(P-13218)
PACIFIC GALVANIZING INC
715 46th Ave, Oakland (94601-5096)
PHONE...................................510 261-7331
William Branagh, *President*
EMP: 25
SQ FT: 16,000
SALES: 3.7MM
SALES (corp-wide): 16.5MM **Privately Held**
WEB: www.branagh.com
SIC: 3479 Galvanizing of iron, steel or end-formed products
PA: Branagh Inc.
750 Kevin Ct
Oakland CA 94621
510 638-6455

(P-13219)
PACIFIC METAL FINISHING INC
440 Sherwood Rd, Paso Robles
(93446-3554)
PHONE...................................805 237-8886
Riaz Mohammad, *President*
EMP: 10
SQ FT: 12,000
SALES (est): 1.2MM **Privately Held**
SIC: 3479 Coating of metals & formed products

(P-13220)
PACIFIC POWDER COATING INC
8637 23rd Ave, Sacramento (95826-4903)
PHONE...................................916 381-1154
Jeffrey M Rochester, *President*
Gabriel Ayala, *Prdtn Mgr*
▲ EMP: 30
SQ FT: 40,000

SALES: 6.3MM **Privately Held**
WEB: www.pacpowder.com
SIC: 3479 3449 Coating of metals & formed products; miscellaneous metalwork

(P-13221)
PAINT SPECIALISTS INC
8629 Bradley Ave, Sun Valley
(91352-3303)
P.O. Box 1124 (91353-1124)
PHONE...................................818 771-0552
Mike Kim, *President*
EMP: 25
SQ FT: 15,000
SALES (est): 2.3MM **Privately Held**
SIC: 3479 Coating of metals & formed products; painting of metal products

(P-13222)
PEARSON ENGINEERING CORP
Also Called: Vaga Industries
2505 Loma Ave, South El Monte
(91733-1417)
PHONE...................................626 442-7436
Colleen Trost, *President*
EMP: 15
SQ FT: 10,000
SALES (est): 2.2MM **Privately Held**
WEB: www.vaga.com
SIC: 3479 Etching, photochemical

(P-13223)
PERFORMANCE POWDER INC
2940 E La Jolla St Ste A, Anaheim
(92806-1349)
PHONE...................................714 632-0600
Kevin Aaberg, *President*
Robert Goldberg, *Vice Pres*
EMP: 29
SALES (est): 3.6MM **Privately Held**
WEB: www.powdercoatz.com
SIC: 3479 Coating of metals & formed products; painting of metal products

(P-13224)
PGM METAL FINISHING
409 W Blueridge Ave, Orange
(92865-4203)
P.O. Box 4026 (92863-4026)
PHONE...................................714 282-9193
David Hill, *President*
EMP: 15
SQ FT: 4,800
SALES (est): 1.1MM **Privately Held**
SIC: 3479 Painting of metal products

(P-13225)
PLASMA RGGEDIZED SOLUTIONS INC (PA)
2284 Ringwood Ave Ste A, San Jose
(95131-1722)
PHONE...................................408 954-8405
Jim Stameson, *CEO*
Evan Persky, *CFO*
EMP: 68
SALES (est): 16.3MM **Privately Held**
WEB: www.plasmasystems.com
SIC: 3479 Coating of metals & formed products

(P-13226)
PLASMA TECHNOLOGY INCORPORATED (PA)
Also Called: P T I
1754 Crenshaw Blvd, Torrance
(90501-3384)
PHONE...................................310 320-3373
Robert Donald Dowell, *CEO*
Satish Dixit, *Vice Pres*
Diane Parkhurst, *Admin Asst*
Rich Peterson, *Info Tech Dir*
Ryan Saruwatari, *Technology*
▲ EMP: 73 EST: 1984
SQ FT: 40,000
SALES (est): 17.4MM **Privately Held**
SIC: 3479 Coating of metals & formed products

(P-13227)
PORTER POWDER COATING INC
510 S Rose St, Anaheim (92805-4751)
PHONE...................................714 956-2010
Jerry D Porter, *President*

▲ = Import ▼ =Export
◆ =Import/Export

Eugene Gonzalez, *Vice Pres*
EMP: 10 **EST:** 1996
SQ FT: 12,497
SALES (est): 1MM **Privately Held**
WEB: www.porterpowder.com
SIC: 3479 Coating of metals & formed products

(P-13228)
POWDER COATING USA INC
440 Sherwood Rd, Paso Robles (93446-3554)
PHONE..................................805 237-8886
John C Wright Jr, *President*
EMP: 11 **EST:** 2013
SALES (est): 1.3MM **Privately Held**
SIC: 3479 Coating of metals & formed products

(P-13229)
POWDERCOAT SERVICES LLC
1747 W Lincoln Ave Ste K, Anaheim (92801-6770)
PHONE..................................714 533-2251
Ravi RAO, *President*
Annalee Binswanger, *Office Mgr*
▲ **EMP:** 38
SQ FT: 75,000
SALES (est): 9.5MM **Privately Held**
WEB: www.powdercoatservices.com
SIC: 3479 7211 Coating of metals & formed products; power laundries, family & commercial
PA: Meridian General Capital Fund Ii, L.P.
46 Peninsula Ctr
Rllng Hls Est CA 90274
310 818-4500

(P-13230)
PREMIER COATINGS INC
Also Called: Premier Finishing
7910 Longe St, Stockton (95206-3933)
PHONE..................................209 982-5585
Craig M Walters, *President*
Thom Foulks, *Vice Pres*
Wendy Foulks, *Admin Sec*
EMP: 75
SQ FT: 30,000
SALES (est): 11.4MM **Privately Held**
SIC: 3479 Hot dip coating of metals or formed products

(P-13231)
PRIMO POWDER COATING & SNDBLST
17592 Gothard St, Huntington Beach (92647-6214)
PHONE..................................714 596-4242
Daniel Regan, *Owner*
EMP: 10
SALES (est): 882.9K **Privately Held**
SIC: 3479 Coating of metals & formed products

(P-13232)
PVD COATINGS II LLC
5271 Argosy Ave, Huntington Beach (92649-1015)
PHONE..................................714 899-4892
Red Silversterstein, *Mng Member*
EMP: 18
SALES (est): 364.3K **Privately Held**
WEB: www.pvdcoatings.net
SIC: 3479 Coating of metals & formed products

(P-13233)
PYRAMID POWDER COATING INC
12251 Montague St, Pacoima (91331-2212)
PHONE..................................818 768-5898
Quasim Riaz, *President*
EMP: 25
SQ FT: 9,000
SALES (est): 2.5MM **Privately Held**
WEB: www.ppcoating.com
SIC: 3479 Coating of metals & formed products

(P-13234)
QUALITY PAINTING CO
19136 San Jose Ave, Rowland Heights (91748-1415)
PHONE..................................626 964-2529
Louise J Merkel, *President*

Ronald Merkel, *Treasurer*
James H Merkel, *Vice Pres*
EMP: 21
SQ FT: 15,000
SALES: 600K **Privately Held**
SIC: 3479 Coating of metals with plastic or resins; painting of metal products; varnishing of metal products

(P-13235)
QUALITY POWDER COATING LLC
Also Called: Quality Coating
7373 Atoll Ave Ste B, North Hollywood (91605-4108)
PHONE..................................818 982-8322
Nazim Khan,
Hasmukh Bhakta,
Shivie Dillon,
EMP: 16
SQ FT: 20,000
SALES (est): 1.7MM **Privately Held**
WEB: www.qualitycoating.com
SIC: 3479 Coating of metals & formed products; painting, coating & hot dipping

(P-13236)
RELIABLE POWDER COATINGS LLC
1577 Factor Ave, San Leandro (94577-5615)
PHONE..................................510 895-5551
Shawn Taylor,
EMP: 14
SQ FT: 32,000
SALES: 1.8MM **Privately Held**
SIC: 3479 Coating of metals & formed products

(P-13237)
RGF ENTERPRISES INC
220 Citation Cir, Corona (92880-2522)
PHONE..................................951 734-6922
Rodney G Fisher, *President*
EMP: 26
SQ FT: 15,000
SALES (est): 3.2MM **Privately Held**
SIC: 3479 Coating of metals & formed products

(P-13238)
RTS POWDER COATING INC (PA)
15121 Sierra Bonita Ln, Chino (91710-8904)
PHONE..................................909 393-5404
Donald D Reed Sr, *President*
Richard C Schleicher, *Manager*
EMP: 20
SQ FT: 8,100
SALES: 1.1MM **Privately Held**
WEB: www.ddrjrii.com
SIC: 3479 Coating of metals & formed products

(P-13239)
S B I F INC
Also Called: Santa Barbara Indus Finshg
873 S Kellogg Ave, Goleta (93117-3805)
PHONE..................................805 683-1711
Shelby See Jr, *President*
Rochelle See, *Corp Secy*
EMP: 15 **EST:** 1971
SQ FT: 6,750
SALES (est): 1.7MM **Privately Held**
WEB: www.sbifin.com
SIC: 3479 7336 Painting of metal products; silk screen design

(P-13240)
S C COATINGS CORPORATION
41745 Elm St Ste 101, Murrieta (92562-1405)
PHONE..................................951 461-9777
Michael Podratz, *President*
Victor Lopez, *Vice Pres*
Michaela Zavala, *Manager*
EMP: 48
SQ FT: 2,000
SALES: 7.3MM **Privately Held**
SIC: 3479 Coating of metals with silicon

(P-13241)
SAN DEGO PRTECTIVE COATING INC
9344 Wheatlands Rd Ste A, Santee (92071-5643)
P.O. Box 713130 (92072-3130)
PHONE..................................619 448-7795
Robert Johnson, *President*
Steve Johnson, *Vice Pres*
Theresa Johnson, *Admin Sec*
EMP: 17
SALES (est): 1MM **Privately Held**
WEB: www.sandiegopowdercoating.com
SIC: 3479 Coating of metals & formed products

(P-13242)
SCIENTIFIC METAL FINISHING
3180 Molinaro St, Santa Clara (95054-2425)
PHONE..................................408 970-9011
Theodore G Otto III, *President*
Kathleen Otto, *CFO*
Carolyn Silberman, *Manager*
EMP: 40
SQ FT: 18,000
SALES (est): 5.1MM **Privately Held**
WEB: www.scientificmetal.com
SIC: 3479 2851 Coating of metals & formed products; paints & allied products

(P-13243)
SCIENTIFIC SPRAY FINISHES INC
315 S Richman Ave, Fullerton (92832-2195)
PHONE..................................714 871-5541
Carlos A Lopez, *President*
Sharon Lopez, *Corp Secy*
EMP: 35 **EST:** 1964
SQ FT: 15,000
SALES (est): 1.5MM **Privately Held**
SIC: 3479 3399 Coating of metals & formed products; powder, metal

(P-13244)
SDC TECHNOLOGIES INC (DH)
45 Parker Ste 100, Irvine (92618-1658)
PHONE..................................714 939-8300
Antonios Grigoriou, *CEO*
Richard Chang, *Vice Pres*
John Quinn, *Vice Pres*
Elise Loprieno, *Admin Asst*
Tracy Mummert, *Technician*
▲ **EMP:** 25
SQ FT: 16,800
SALES (est): 15.1MM **Privately Held**
SIC: 3479 2851 Coating of metals with plastic or resins; paints & allied products
HQ: Mitsui Chemicals America, Inc.
800 Westchester Ave N607
Rye Brook NY 10573
914 253-0777

(P-13245)
SHAWCOR PIPE PROTECTION LLC
14000 San Bernardino Ave, Fontana (92335-5258)
P.O. Box 1317 (92334-1317)
PHONE..................................909 357-9002
Heath Legg, *Manager*
EMP: 10
SALES (corp-wide): 1.6B **Privately Held**
WEB: www.bredero-shaw.com
SIC: 3479 2891 Coating or wrapping steel pipe; adhesives & sealants
HQ: Shawcor Pipe Protection Llc
5875 N Sam Houston Pkwy W # 200
Houston TX 77086

(P-13246)
SHMAZE INDUSTRIES INC
Also Called: Shmaze Custom Coatings
20792 Canada Rd, Lake Forest (92630-6732)
PHONE..................................949 583-1448
Michael Shamassian, *President*
Joanne Shamassian, *Treasurer*
Craig Rysavy, *Opers Staff*
EMP: 50
SQ FT: 21,500

SALES (est): 6.3MM **Privately Held**
WEB: www.shmaze.com
SIC: 3479 Coating of metals with plastic or resins

(P-13247)
SLICKOTE
Also Called: Paint Chem
730 University Ave, Burbank (91504-3925)
PHONE..................................818 749-3066
Eddie Andrews, *General Mgr*
EMP: 15
SALES (est): 1.1MM **Privately Held**
WEB: www.slickote.com
SIC: 3479 Coating of metals & formed products

(P-13248)
SOCCO PLASTIC COATING COMPANY
11251 Jersey Blvd, Rancho Cucamonga (91730-5147)
PHONE..................................909 987-4753
Peter M Smits Jr, *President*
Rose Smits, *Vice Pres*
EMP: 25
SQ FT: 60,000
SALES (est): 3.3MM **Privately Held**
WEB: www.soccoplastics.com
SIC: 3479 3444 3088 2851 Coating of metals with plastic or resins; sheet metalwork; plastics plumbing fixtures; paints & allied products

(P-13249)
SPECIALTY COATING SYSTEMS INC
4435 E Airport Dr Ste 100, Ontario (91761-7816)
PHONE..................................909 390-8818
Steven Frease, *Branch Mgr*
EMP: 30 **Privately Held**
SIC: 3479 Painting, coating & hot dipping
HQ: Specialty Coating Systems, Inc.
7645 Woodland Dr
Indianapolis IN 46278

(P-13250)
SPECILIZED CRMIC POWDR COATING
Also Called: Specialized Coating
5862 Research Dr, Huntington Beach (92649-1348)
PHONE..................................714 901-2628
Lee Crecelius, *President*
EMP: 12
SALES (est): 1.1MM **Privately Held**
WEB: www.specializedcoating.com
SIC: 3479 Chasing on metals

(P-13251)
SPRAYLINE ENTERPRISES INC
10774 Grand Ave, Ontario (91762-4007)
PHONE..................................909 627-8411
Phil Merenda, *President*
Russ Guthrie, *Treasurer*
Candy Merenda, *Vice Pres*
Darlene Guthrie, *Principal*
EMP: 20
SQ FT: 9,000
SALES: 500K **Privately Held**
SIC: 3479 Painting of metal products

(P-13252)
SPRAYTRONICS INC
6001 Butler Ln Ste 204, Scotts Valley (95066-3548)
PHONE..................................408 988-3636
EMP: 20
SQ FT: 30,000
SALES (est): 1.9MM **Privately Held**
SIC: 3479

(P-13253)
ST PIERRE GONZALEZ ENTERPRISES
419 E La Palma Ave, Anaheim (92801-2534)
PHONE..................................714 491-2191
Jose Gonzalez, *President*
EMP: 30
SALES (est): 1.7MM **Privately Held**
SIC: 3479 Painting, coating & hot dipping

(P-13254)
STEELSCAPE INC
11200 Arrow Rte, Rancho Cucamonga
(91730-4805)
PHONE...........................909 987-4711
Ron Hurst, *Branch Mgr*
Nouh Anies, *Engineer*
Brenda Eubanks, *HR Admin*
Jeff Sanders, *Director*
Gomez Steven, *Manager*
EMP: 17
SALES (corp-wide): 192.8MM **Privately Held**
WEB: www.steelscape.com
SIC: 3479 Coating of metals & formed products
PA: Steelscape, Llc
222 W Kalama River Rd
Kalama WA 98625
360 673-8200

(P-13255)
SUB-ONE TECHNOLOGY INC
161 S Vasco Rd Ste L, Livermore
(94551-5130)
PHONE...........................925 924-1020
Dore Rosenblum, *President*
▼ EMP: 12
SQ FT: 19,315
SALES (est): 2.3MM
SALES (corp-wide): 20.1B **Publicly Held**
WEB: www.sub-one.com
SIC: 3479 Coating of metals & formed products
PA: Aecom
1999 Avenue Of The Stars # 2600
Los Angeles CA 90067
213 593-8000

(P-13256)
SUNDIAL INDUSTRIES INC
Also Called: Powder Painting By Sundial
8421 Telfair Ave, Sun Valley (91352-3926)
PHONE...........................818 767-4477
Toll Free:...........................866 -
Hasu Bhakta, *President*
Naseen Khan, *Corp Secy*
Gurtreet Riaz, *Vice Pres*
▲ EMP: 30
SQ FT: 13,000
SALES (est): 5.1MM **Privately Held**
SIC: 3479 Coating of metals & formed products

(P-13257)
SUNDIAL POWDER COATINGS INC
Also Called: Bottle Coatings
8421 Telfair Ave, Sun Valley (91352-3926)
PHONE...........................818 767-4477
Hasu Bhakta, *CEO*
EMP: 25
SALES (est): 3.4MM **Privately Held**
WEB: www.sundialpowdercoatings.com
SIC: 3479 Coating of metals with plastic or resins; coating of metals & formed products

(P-13258)
SURFACE MDFICATION SYSTEMS INC
12917 Park St, Santa Fe Springs
(90670-4045)
PHONE...........................562 946-7472
Rajan Bamola, *President*
Larry V Gilpin, *Vice Pres*
Thomas Ewell, *Engineer*
Karla Cano, *Director*
EMP: 10
SQ FT: 12,000
SALES (est): 1.3MM **Privately Held**
WEB: www.surfacemodificationsystems.com
SIC: 3479 Coating of metals & formed products

(P-13259)
THERM-O-NAMEL INC
2780 M L King Jr Blvd, Lynwood (90262)
PHONE...........................310 631-7866
Grant Kinsman, *President*
Colleen Kinsman, *Corp Secy*
Byron Kinsman, *Vice Pres*
Sylvia Kinsman, *Vice Pres*
EMP: 15 EST: 1950
SQ FT: 15,000
SALES (est): 1.8MM **Privately Held**
WEB: www.therm-o-namel.com
SIC: 3479 3555 2851 2759 Painting of metal products; coating of metals & formed products; printing trades machinery; paints & allied products; commercial printing; automotive & apparel trimmings

(P-13260)
TIODIZE CO INC (PA)
5858 Engineer Dr, Huntington Beach
(92649-1166)
PHONE...........................714 898-4377
Thomas R Adams, *CEO*
Lynnette Cubbin, *Purch Mgr*
Tom Moore, *Purchasing*
Felix Delacruz, *Opers Mgr*
Wade Friedrichs, *Marketing Staff*
EMP: 65 EST: 1966
SQ FT: 26,000
SALES (est): 9.9MM **Privately Held**
SIC: 3479 Coating of metals & formed products

(P-13261)
TIODIZE CO INC
Tiodize Company
5858 Engineer Dr, Huntington Beach
(92649-1166)
PHONE...........................248 348-6050
Mark Miller, *General Mgr*
EMP: 10
SALES (corp-wide): 9.9MM **Privately Held**
WEB: www.tiodize.com
SIC: 3479 Coating of metals & formed products
PA: Tiodize Co., Inc.
5858 Engineer Dr
Huntington Beach CA 92649
714 898-4377

(P-13262)
ULTIMATE METAL FINISHING CORP
6150 Sheila St, Commerce (90040-2407)
PHONE...........................323 890-9100
John Ondrasik, *President*
James M Sales, *General Mgr*
EMP: 12
SQ FT: 4,800
SALES (est): 943.4K
SALES (corp-wide): 42.4MM **Privately Held**
WEB: www.precisionwireproducts.com
SIC: 3479 Coating of metals & formed products
PA: Precision Wire Products, Inc.
6150 Sheila St
Commerce CA 90040
323 890-9100

(P-13263)
UNITED WESTERN ENTERPRISES INC
Also Called: Uwe
850 Flynn Rd Ste 200, Camarillo
(93012-8783)
PHONE...........................805 389-1077
Gerald Williams, *President*
Mike Lynch, *Vice Pres*
Charles Boone, *Opers Mgr*
Rigo Flores, *Prdtn Mgr*
John Garcia, *Opers-Prdtn-Mfg*
EMP: 29 EST: 1969
SQ FT: 21,000
SALES (est): 3.9MM **Privately Held**
WEB: www.uweinc.com
SIC: 3479 Etching, photochemical

(P-13264)
VACMET INC
8740 Hellman Ave, Rancho Cucamonga
(91730-4418)
P.O. Box 3526 (91729-3526)
PHONE...........................909 948-9344
Carl Grindle, *CEO*
Gladys Marroquin, *Treasurer*
EMP: 49
SALES (est): 3.5MM **Privately Held**
SIC: 3479 Coating of metals with plastic or resins

(P-13265)
VAIDER INC
Also Called: Vaider Manufacturing
553 Martin Ave Ste 1, Rohnert Park
(94928-2091)
PHONE...........................707 584-3655
John Follenvaider, *President*
Shane Follenvaider, *Vice Pres*
Janine Follenvaider, *Admin Sec*
EMP: 10
SQ FT: 9,000
SALES: 800K **Privately Held**
WEB: www.vaidermfg.com
SIC: 3479 Coating of metals & formed products

(P-13266)
VISTA COATINGS INC
Also Called: Vista Powder Coatings
1440 6th St, Manhattan Beach
(90266-6344)
PHONE...........................310 635-7697
Mike Acuna, *President*
EMP: 20
SQ FT: 10,000
SALES: 1MM **Privately Held**
SIC: 3479 Painting of metal products

(P-13267)
WESTERN EDGE INC
37957 Sierra Hwy, Palmdale (93550-5375)
PHONE...........................661 947-3900
Kris E Johnson, *Owner*
EMP: 13
SALES (est): 1.3MM **Privately Held**
SIC: 3479 Painting of metal products

(P-13268)
WILSENERGY LLC
42440 Winchester Rd, Temecula
(92590-2504)
P.O. Box 1085, Murrieta (92564-1085)
PHONE...........................951 676-7700
Shanyn Wilson,
Steve Wilson,
EMP: 10 EST: 2011
SQ FT: 5,700
SALES: 1MM **Privately Held**
SIC: 3479 5065 Painting of metal products; coils, electronic

(P-13269)
WM J MATSON COMPANY
213 N Olive St, Ventura (93001-2515)
PHONE...........................805 684-9410
William J Matson, *President*
Ann Matson, *Vice Pres*
EMP: 15
SQ FT: 5,000
SALES (est): 750K **Privately Held**
SIC: 3479 Coating of metals & formed products

3482 Small Arms

(P-13270)
H3 HIGH SECURITY SOLUTIONS LLC
434 1/2 Palos Verdes Blvd, Redondo Beach
(90277-6514)
PHONE...........................310 373-2319
Bazzel Baz, *Principal*
EMP: 25
SALES (est): 2MM **Privately Held**
SIC: 3482 Small arms ammunition

3483 Ammunition, Large

(P-13271)
FIELD TIME TARGET TRAINING LLC
Also Called: Ft3 Tactical
8230 Electric Ave, Stanton (90680-2640)
PHONE...........................714 677-2841
Michael R Kaplan, *President*
EMP: 24 EST: 2010
SALES (est): 1.9MM **Privately Held**
SIC: 3483 7999 Ammunition, except for small arms; shooting range operation

(P-13272)
REYNOLDS SYSTEMS INC
18649 State Highway 175, Middletown
(95461)
P.O. Box 1229 (95461-1229)
PHONE...........................707 928-5244
Richard Reynolds, *CEO*
Rosa Leon, *Supervisor*
EMP: 10 EST: 1962
SQ FT: 6,000
SALES (est): 2.5MM **Privately Held**
WEB: www.reynoldssystems.com
SIC: 3483 Ammunition, except for small arms

(P-13273)
URUHU HIGHLANDS LTD
14360 Valerio St Apt 311, Van Nuys
(91405-1463)
PHONE...........................424 213-9725
Nicholas Kasule, *Principal*
EMP: 10
SALES (est): 399.4K **Privately Held**
SIC: 3483 7389 Ammunition, except for small arms;

3484 Small Arms

(P-13274)
ALLIANT TCHSYSTEMS OPRTONS LLC
151 Martinvale Ln Ste 150, San Jose
(95119-1455)
PHONE...........................408 513-3271
EMP: 10 **Publicly Held**
SIC: 3484 Small arms
HQ: Alliant Techsystems Operations Llc
601 Carlson Pkwy Ste 600
Minnetonka MN 55305
-

(P-13275)
ENTREPRISE ARMS INC
Also Called: Enterprise Arms
15509 Arrow Hwy, Irwindale (91706-2002)
PHONE...........................626 962-4692
Walter Chow, *CEO*
Howard Chow, *President*
EMP: 30
SQ FT: 15,000
SALES (est): 4.4MM **Privately Held**
WEB: www.entreprise.com
SIC: 3484 3949 Small arms; sporting & athletic goods

(P-13276)
PHOENIX ARMS
4231 E Brickell St, Ontario (91761-1512)
PHONE...........................909 937-6900
Dave Brazeau, *Owner*
▲ EMP: 20
SALES (est): 2.5MM **Privately Held**
SIC: 3484 Guns (firearms) or gun parts, 30 mm. & below

(P-13277)
SAI INDUSTRIES
Also Called: Standard Armament
631 Allen Ave, Glendale (91201-2013)
PHONE...........................818 842-6144
Curtis Correll, *CEO*
Gary Correll, *President*
Marcene Correll, *Vice Pres*
Cathy Joens, *Admin Sec*
Lars Nilsson, *Controller*
◆ EMP: 40 EST: 1950
SQ FT: 24,000
SALES: 5MM **Privately Held**
WEB: www.standardarmament.com
SIC: 3484 Guns (firearms) or gun parts, 30 mm. & below

(P-13278)
TACTICOMBAT INC
11640 Mcbean Dr, El Monte (91732-1105)
PHONE...........................626 315-4433
Daisy Chan, *President*
Tik Yan TSE, *CEO*
EMP: 11
SQ FT: 2,500
SALES (est): 1MM **Privately Held**
SIC: 3484 3949 Small arms; sporting & athletic goods

▲ = Import ▼=Export
◆ =Import/Export

(P-13279)
TENCATE ADVANCED ARMOR USA INC (DH)
120 Cremona Dr Ste 130, Goleta (93117-3159)
PHONE..............................805 845-4085
Joseph Dobriski, *President*
David Kapp, *Vice Pres*
EMP: 21
SALES (est): 275K
SALES (corp-wide): 1.2B **Privately Held**
SIC: 3484 Small arms
HQ: Tencate Advanced Armour Holding B.V.
G Van Der Muelenweg 3
Nijverdal
546 544-911

(P-13280)
ZEV TECHNOLOGIES INC (PA)
Also Called: Glockworx
1051 Yarnell Pl, Oxnard (93033-2453)
PHONE..............................805 486-5800
Matthew Ridenour, *CEO*
Alec Wolf, *President*
Roe Wolf, *Admin Sec*
Andrew Harding, *Sales Associate*
Ives Lopez, *Sales Staff*
EMP: 18
SALES (est): 5.3MM **Privately Held**
SIC: 3484 Guns (firearms) or gun parts, 30 mm. & below

3489 Ordnance & Access, NEC

(P-13281)
ARMTEC DEFENSE PRODUCTS CO (DH)
85901 Avenue 53, Coachella (92236-2607)
PHONE..............................760 398-0143
Robert W Cremin, *CEO*
Ron Di Felice, *Manager*
◆ **EMP:** 330
SQ FT: 108,000
SALES (est): 78.5MM
SALES (corp-wide): 3.8B **Publicly Held**
SIC: 3489 Artillery or artillery parts, over 30 mm.
HQ: Esterline Technologies Corp
500 108th Ave Ne Ste 1500
Bellevue WA 98004
425 453-9400

(P-13282)
IO2 TECHNOLOGY LLC
310 Shaw Rd Ste G, South San Francisco (94080-6615)
PHONE..............................650 308-4216
Jay Fields,
EMP: 10
SALES (est): 670.4K **Privately Held**
SIC: 3489 Projectors: depth charge, grenade, rocket, etc.

(P-13283)
NETWORKS ELECTRONIC CO LLC
9750 De Soto Ave, Chatsworth (91311-4409)
PHONE..............................818 341-0440
Tamara M Christen, *Mng Member*
Andrew Campany, *Engineer*
Terry Soroor, *Engineer*
Lucy Lopez, *Manager*
▼ **EMP:** 26
SQ FT: 25,000
SALES: 6.2MM **Privately Held**
SIC: 3489 Ordnance & accessories

(P-13284)
ROBERTS RESEARCH LABORATORY
23150 Kashiwa Ct, Torrance (90505-4027)
PHONE..............................310 320-7310
David Roberts, *President*
A L Roberts, *President*
Kathryn Roberts, *Treasurer*
David E Roberts, *Vice Pres*
EMP: 15 EST: 1964
SQ FT: 10,000

SALES (est): 2.4MM **Privately Held**
SIC: 3489 8731 Ordnance & accessories; commercial research laboratory

(P-13285)
VECTOR LAUNCH INC
100 Century Center Ct # 400, San Jose (95112-4535)
PHONE..............................888 346-7778
EMP: 146
SALES (corp-wide): 6.9MM **Privately Held**
SIC: 3489 Rocket launchers
PA: Vector Launch Inc.
350 S Toole Ave
Tucson AZ 85701
888 346-7778

3491 Industrial Valves

(P-13286)
A & G INSTR SVC & CALIBRATION
1227 N Tustin Ave, Anaheim (92807-1616)
PHONE..............................714 630-7400
Bill Arnould, *President*
Humberto Mexia, *Vice Pres*
EMP: 17
SQ FT: 4,100
SALES (est): 3.1MM **Privately Held**
WEB: www.a-and-g.com
SIC: 3491 7699 Process control regulator valves; professional instrument repair services

(P-13287)
ADVANCED PROCESS SERVICES INC
4350 E Washington Blvd, Commerce (90023-4410)
PHONE..............................323 278-6530
Somjit Burdi, *CEO*
Thomas Burdi, *Vice Pres*
EMP: 20
SALES (est): 4.9MM **Privately Held**
WEB: www.advprocserv.com
SIC: 3491 Process control regulator valves

(P-13288)
AQUASYN LLC
9525 Owensmouth Ave Ste E, Chatsworth (91311-8006)
PHONE..............................818 350-0423
Dean Richards, *Branch Mgr*
Vincent Mitchell, *Business Mgr*
Chris Belieu, *Sales Staff*
Patricia Hall, *Cust Mgr*
Ferdinand Alora, *Manager*
EMP: 18
SALES (corp-wide): 15MM **Privately Held**
SIC: 3491 Industrial valves
PA: Aquasyn, Llc
1771 South Sutro Ter
Carson City NV 89706
818 350-0423

(P-13289)
ASCO AUTOMATIC SWITCH
Also Called: Asco Automatic Switch Co
333 City Blvd W Ste 2140, Orange (92868-2966)
PHONE..............................714 937-0811
Sam Ladva, *Manager*
Mark Hallenbeck, *Principal*
Scott Cameron, *Manager*
EMP: 10
SALES (est): 758.4K **Privately Held**
SIC: 3491 Industrial valves

(P-13290)
AUTOMATIC SWITCH COMPANY
120 S Chaparral Ct # 200, Anaheim (92808-2237)
PHONE..............................714 283-4000
Jeremy Lass, *Manager*
EMP: 13
SALES (corp-wide): 17.4B **Publicly Held**
WEB: www.ascoval.com
SIC: 3491 Solenoid valves
HQ: Automatic Switch Company
50-60 Hanover Rd
Florham Park NJ 07932
973 966-2000

(P-13291)
AUTOMATION & ENTERTAINMENT INC (PA)
25870 Soquel San Jose Rd, Los Gatos (95033-9235)
PHONE..............................408 353-4223
Paul Wilkinson, *CEO*
EMP: 13 EST: 2011
SALES (est): 4.1MM **Privately Held**
SIC: 3491 Automatic regulating & control valves

(P-13292)
AVALCO INC
2029 Verdugo Blvd Ste 710, Montrose (91020-1626)
PHONE..............................310 676-3057
Alexander Armond, *CEO*
▲ **EMP:** 12
SQ FT: 10,000
SALES: 1.5MM **Privately Held**
SIC: 3491 Industrial valves

(P-13293)
BAILEY VALVE INC
264 W Fallbrook Ave # 105, Fresno (93711-5807)
PHONE..............................559 434-2838
Eric Brewer, *President*
John Edward, *Vice Pres*
▲ **EMP:** 35
SQ FT: 3,500
SALES (est): 10.6MM **Privately Held**
WEB: www.baileyvalve.com
SIC: 3491 Industrial valves

(P-13294)
BARBEE VALVE & SUPPLY INC (HQ)
745 Main St, Anaheim (92805)
PHONE..............................619 585-8484
Timothy Wilkinson, *CEO*
EMP: 12 EST: 1959
SALES (est): 2.1MM
SALES (corp-wide): 17MM **Privately Held**
WEB: www.selcoproducts.com
SIC: 3491 5085 Industrial valves; valves & fittings
PA: Sel Sales, Inc.
8780 Technology Way
Reno NV 89521
775 674-5100

(P-13295)
BERMINGHAM CONTROLS INC A (PA)
11144 Business Cir, Cerritos (90703-5523)
PHONE..............................562 860-0463
Gregory Gass, *President*
Edwin Bonner, *CFO*
Kevin Mulholland, *Vice Pres*
EMP: 37
SQ FT: 20,000
SALES: 15MM **Privately Held**
WEB: www.bermingham.com
SIC: 3491 3823 5084 Industrial valves; industrial instrmnts msrmnt display/control process variable; industrial machinery & equipment

(P-13296)
CASTOR ENGINEERING INC
450 Commercial Way, La Habra (90631-6167)
P.O. Box 3808 (90632-3808)
PHONE..............................562 690-4036
Lawrence Bailey, *President*
Amber L Bailey, *Vice Pres*
Amber Bailey, *Vice Pres*
▼ **EMP:** 10
SQ FT: 6,500
SALES: 1MM **Privately Held**
SIC: 3491 Industrial valves

(P-13297)
CHLADNI & JARIWALA INC
Also Called: Baja Products
1120 E Locust St, Ontario (91761-4537)
PHONE..............................909 947-5227
Buck Jariwala, *President*
George Chladni, *Vice Pres*
▲ **EMP:** 25
SQ FT: 1,000

SALES (est): 3.8MM **Privately Held**
WEB: www.rkvalve.com
SIC: 3491 3053 3086 Industrial valves; gaskets, all materials; oil seals, rubber; insulation or cushioning material, foamed plastic

(P-13298)
CIRCOR AEROSPACE INC (HQ)
Also Called: Circle Seal Controls
2301 Wardlow Cir, Corona (92880-2801)
P.O. Box 2824, Spartanburg SC (29304-2824)
PHONE..............................951 270-6200
Scott Buckhout, *CEO*
Carl Nasca, *President*
Renuka Ayer, *Vice Pres*
Steve Cartolano, *Vice Pres*
Christopher Celtruda, *Vice Pres*
▲ **EMP:** 245
SQ FT: 100,000
SALES (est): 80.4MM
SALES (corp-wide): 1.1B **Publicly Held**
WEB: www.circleseal.com
SIC: 3491 3494 3769 5085 Pressure valves & regulators, industrial; plumbing & heating valves; guided missile & space vehicle parts & auxiliary equipment; seals, industrial
PA: Circor International, Inc.
30 Corporate Dr Ste 200
Burlington MA 01803
781 270-1200

(P-13299)
COMPONENTS FOR AUTOMATION INC (PA)
Also Called: Gc Valves
1737 Lee St, Simi Valley (93065-3652)
PHONE..............................805 582-0065
Victoria Janousek, *President*
James Janousek, *Managing Dir*
Sara Shunkwiler, *Office Mgr*
Chuck Grinston, *Manager*
Paul Janousek, *Manager*
▲ **EMP:** 10
SQ FT: 2,400
SALES (est): 3.1MM **Privately Held**
WEB: www.cfa-inc.com
SIC: 3491 5085 Solenoid valves; valves & fittings

(P-13300)
CONTROL COMPONENTS INC (DH)
Also Called: IMI CCI
22591 Avenida Empresa, Rcho STA Marg (92688-2012)
PHONE..............................949 858-1877
Charles Merrimon, *President*
Sukhjit Purcaval, *CFO*
Gary Song, *Senior Engr*
Geoff Caflisch, *Regl Sales Mgr*
George Friedrichs, *Manager*
◆ **EMP:** 365
SQ FT: 75,000
SALES (est): 176.4MM
SALES (corp-wide): 2.4B **Privately Held**
WEB: www.ccivalve.com
SIC: 3491 Process control regulator valves
HQ: Imi Americas Inc.
5400 S Delaware St
Littleton CO 80120
763 488-5400

(P-13301)
CURTISS-WRIGHT CORPORATION
Also Called: Defense Solutions
28965 Avenue Penn, Santa Clarita (91355-4185)
PHONE..............................661 257-4430
Val Zarov, *General Mgr*
Jesse Richardson, *IT/INT Sup*
Brenin Steinhart, *Contract Mgr*
Mario Garcia, *Buyer*
EMP: 21
SALES (corp-wide): 2.4B **Publicly Held**
SIC: 3491 Industrial valves
PA: Curtiss-Wright Corporation
130 Harbour Place Dr # 300
Davidson NC 28036
704 869-4600

(P-13302)
CURTISS-WRIGHT FLOW CONTROL
Also Called: Collins Technologies
38 Executive Park Ste 350, Irvine
(92614-6745)
PHONE..................................949 271-7500
Glenn Roberts, *Manager*
EMP: 89
SALES (corp-wide): 2.4B **Publicly Held**
SIC: 3491 Industrial valves
HQ: Curtiss-Wright Flow Control Service,
　　Llc
　　1966 Broadhollow Rd Ste E
　　Farmingdale NY 11735
　　631 293-3800

(P-13303)
CURTISS-WRIGHT FLOW CONTROL
Penny & Giles
28965 Avenue Penn, Valencia
(91355-4185)
PHONE..................................626 851-3100
Neal Handler, *Branch Mgr*
EMP: 160
SALES (corp-wide): 2.4B **Publicly Held**
SIC: 3491 Industrial valves
HQ: Curtiss-Wright Flow Control Service,
　　Llc
　　1966 Broadhollow Rd Ste E
　　Farmingdale NY 11735
　　631 293-3800

(P-13304)
END-EFFECTORS INC
1230 Coleman Ave, Santa Clara
(95050-4338)
P.O. Box 242 (95052-0242)
PHONE..................................408 727-0100
Frank J Ardezzone, *President*
EMP: 10
SALES (est): 828.8K **Privately Held**
WEB: www.fjaind.com
SIC: 3491 3621 Automatic regulating &
　　control valves; torque motors, electric

(P-13305)
FCKINGSTON CO
Also Called: Storm Manufacturing
23201 Normandie Ave, Torrance
(90501-5050)
PHONE..................................310 326-8287
Joe Taormina, *President*
Michelle Allen, *Administration*
Rick Ward, *Information Mgr*
Joe Bui, *Engineer*
Connie Hobbs, *Sales Staff*
▲ EMP: 70
SQ FT: 32,500
SALES (est): 10.1MM **Privately Held**
WEB: www.fckingston.com
SIC: 3491 3494 Industrial valves; plumb-
　　ing & heating valves

(P-13306)
FLOW N CONTROL INC
4452 Ocean View Blvd # 201, Montrose
(91020-1287)
PHONE..................................818 330-7425
Rick Jesmok, *Principal*
Catherine Jones, *Materials Mgr*
EMP: 11 EST: 2014
SALES (est): 1.4MM **Privately Held**
SIC: 3491 Industrial valves

(P-13307)
HUDSON VALVE CO INC
5630 District Blvd # 108, Bakersfield
(93313-2109)
PHONE..................................661 831-6208
EMP: 20
SQ FT: 3,027
SALES (est): 1.9MM **Privately Held**
SIC: 3491

(P-13308)
INTERNTNAL PLYMR SOLUTIONS INC
Also Called: Ipolymer
5 Studebaker, Irvine (92618-2013)
PHONE..................................949 458-3731
Patrick P Lee, *CEO*
Michael Siino, *President*
Richard Ryan, *CFO*

Mark O'Donnell, *Treasurer*
Dan Foulds, *Engineer*
EMP: 33
SQ FT: 18,000
SALES (est): 8.3MM **Privately Held**
WEB: www.becomfg.com
SIC: 3491 3674 Industrial valves; semi-
　　conductors & related devices

(P-13309)
JAMES JONES COMPANY
1470 S Vintage Ave, Ontario (91761-3646)
PHONE..................................909 418-2558
Jerry Schnelzer, *General Mgr*
Terry Martinez, *Office Mgr*
◆ EMP: 141
SQ FT: 68,000
SALES (est): 22.4MM
SALES (corp-wide): 916MM **Publicly Held**
WEB: www.jamesjones.com
SIC: 3491 3494 Fire hydrant valves; pipe
　　fittings
HQ: Mueller Group, Llc
　　1200 Abernathy Rd
　　Atlanta GA 30328
　　770 206-4200

(P-13310)
LEEMCO INC (PA)
360 S Mount Vernon Ave, Colton
(92324-3912)
PHONE..................................909 422-0088
Ali Marandi, *President*
Allen Marandi, *Vice Pres*
Bill B Becker, *General Mgr*
Rob Whaling, *Sales Staff*
Tony Garner, *Manager*
◆ EMP: 11 EST: 1969
SALES (est): 1.3MM **Privately Held**
WEB: www.leemco.com
SIC: 3491 Gas valves & parts, industrial

(P-13311)
LITTLE FIREFIGHTER CORPORATION
Also Called: Firefighter Gas Safety Pdts
204 S Center St, Santa Ana (92703-4302)
PHONE..................................714 834-0410
Tod Minato, *President*
EMP: 16
SQ FT: 8,000
SALES (est): 3.4MM **Privately Held**
WEB: www.littlefirefighter.com
SIC: 3491 Gas valves & parts, industrial

(P-13312)
LUBRICATION SCIENTIFICS INC
Also Called: All Technology Machine
17651 Armstrong Ave, Irvine (92614-5727)
PHONE..................................714 557-0664
Richard T Hanley, *President*
Adam Rinderer, *Opers Mgr*
EMP: 15
SQ FT: 6,000
SALES (est): 3.9MM **Privately Held**
WEB: www.lubesci.com
SIC: 3491 Industrial valves

(P-13313)
MDC VACUUM PRODUCTS LLC
23874b Cabot Blvd, Hayward
(94545-1661)
PHONE..................................510 265-3500
EMP: 61
SALES (corp-wide): 41MM **Privately Held**
SIC: 3491 Industrial valves
PA: Mdc Vacuum Products, Llc
　　30962 Santana St
　　Hayward CA 94544
　　510 265-3500

(P-13314)
MEGGITT NORTH HOLLYWOOD INC (HQ)
Also Called: Meggitt Control Systems
12838 Saticoy St, North Hollywood
(91605-3505)
PHONE..................................818 765-8160
Dennis Hutton, *CEO*
Derek Aitken, *Info Tech Dir*
Mary Rustia, *Info Tech Mgr*
Jason Garcia, *Project Engr*
Max Lang, *Engineer*
▲ EMP: 230

SQ FT: 10,000
SALES (est): 102.7MM
SALES (corp-wide): 2.6B **Privately Held**
WEB: www.whittakercontrols.com
SIC: 3491 Industrial valves
PA: Meggitt Plc
　　Atlantic House, Aviation Park West
　　Christchurch BH23
　　120 259-7597

(P-13315)
METREX VALVE CORP
505 S Vermont Ave, Glendora
(91741-6206)
PHONE..................................626 335-4027
Doug Jorgensen, *President*
Scott Burson, *President*
Walter E Jorgensen, *President*
Andrea Jorgensen, *Corp Secy*
Alfred Doug Jorgensen, *Vice Pres*
▲ EMP: 25 EST: 1940
SQ FT: 25,000
SALES (est): 5.2MM **Privately Held**
WEB: www.metrexvalve.com
SIC: 3491 Industrial valves

(P-13316)
MICRO MATIC USA INC
19791 Bahama St, Northridge
(91324-3350)
PHONE..................................818 882-8012
Peter J Muzzonigro, *President*
Jeff Crowell, *Opers Staff*
Michael Godwin, *Sales Mgr*
Mike Godwin, *Sales Mgr*
Steve Bradt, *Sales Staff*
EMP: 21
SALES (corp-wide): 260MM **Privately Held**
SIC: 3491 5087 3585 Industrial valves;
　　liquor dispensing equipment & systems;
　　soda fountain & beverage dispensing
　　equipment & parts
HQ: Micro Matic Usa, Inc.
　　2386 Simon Ct
　　Brooksville FL 34604
　　352 544-1081

(P-13317)
PACIFIC SEISMIC PRODUCTS INC
233 E Avenue H8, Lancaster (93535-1821)
PHONE..................................661 942-4499
Etsuko Ikegaya, *President*
Shigeko I Aramaki, *Corp Secy*
EMP: 24
SQ FT: 10,000
SALES (est): 2.6MM **Privately Held**
SIC: 3491 Industrial valves

(P-13318)
PACIFIC VALVES
Also Called: Crane Co
3201 Walnut Ave, Signal Hill (90755-5225)
PHONE..................................562 426-2531
Anthony Duncan, *Principal*
Mark Controls Corporation, *Owner*
Bradley Ellis, *Vice Pres*
▲ EMP: 78
SQ FT: 128,128
SALES (est): 933.3K **Privately Held**
SIC: 3491 Industrial valves

(P-13319)
QVE INC
7829 Industry Ave, Pico Rivera
(90660-4305)
PHONE..................................626 961-0114
Harold Fortner, *President*
EMP: 21
SALES (est): 1.7MM **Privately Held**
SIC: 3491 3443 Industrial valves; space
　　simulation chambers, metal plate

(P-13320)
RHINO VALVE USA INC
5833 Pembroke Ave, Bakersfield
(93308-4020)
PHONE..................................661 587-0220
Mark D Norman, *President*
Deborah Lockhart, *CFO*
Andy Bush, *Vice Pres*
Lee Patterson, *General Mgr*
▲ EMP: 10
SQ FT: 6,800

SALES (est): 2.1MM **Privately Held**
SIC: 3491 Industrial valves

(P-13321)
SIZTO TECH CORPORATION
892 Commercial St, Palo Alto
(94303-4905)
PHONE..................................650 856-8833
Chung Sizto, *President*
Kevin I Bdbc, *Opers Staff*
EMP: 12 EST: 2015
SALES (est): 1.9MM **Privately Held**
SIC: 3491 Industrial valves

(P-13322)
SOUTHERN CAL VALVE MGT CO INC
13209 Barton Cir Ste C, Whittier
(90605-3290)
P.O. Box 813, Norwalk (90651-0813)
PHONE..................................562 404-2246
Southern California, *Principal*
James Bullard, *Manager*
Harlie Bourque, *Clerk*
EMP: 13 EST: 2012
SALES (est): 2MM **Privately Held**
SIC: 3491 Industrial valves

(P-13323)
STORM MANUFACTURING GROUP INC
23201 Normandie Ave, Torrance
(90501-5050)
PHONE..................................310 326-8287
Dale Philippi, *CEO*
Russell Kneipp, *President*
Bob Straw, *Vice Pres*
Rick Ward, *Vice Pres*
Georgia S Claessens, *Admin Sec*
▲ EMP: 74
SQ FT: 41,936
SALES (est): 13.8MM
SALES (corp-wide): 75.9MM **Privately Held**
WEB: www.storm-manufacturing.com
SIC: 3491 3494 Industrial valves; sprinkler
　　systems, field
PA: Storm Industries, Inc.
　　23223 Normandie Ave
　　Torrance CA 90501
　　310 534-5232

(P-13324)
VAT INCORPORATED
655 River Oaks Pkwy, San Jose
(95134-1907)
PHONE..................................408 813-2700
Tom Murphy, *Branch Mgr*
EMP: 20
SALES (corp-wide): 702.4MM **Privately Held**
SIC: 3491 Industrial valves
HQ: Vat Incorporated
　　655 River Oaks Pkwy
　　San Jose CA 95134
　　781 935-1446

3492 Fluid Power Valves & Hose Fittings

(P-13325)
CONTROL ENTERPRISES INC
Also Called: C E I
40124 Highway 49, Oakhurst (93644-8826)
PHONE..................................559 683-2044
Deborah Hill-Gossett, *President*
Ken Gossett, *Vice Pres*
EMP: 10
SQ FT: 5,800
SALES (est): 761.7K **Privately Held**
WEB: www.ceivalve.com
SIC: 3492 Fluid power valves & hose fit-
　　tings

(P-13326)
CRANE CO
13105 Saticoy St, North Hollywood
(91605-3403)
PHONE..................................310 403-2820
EMP: 32
SALES (corp-wide): 3.3B **Publicly Held**
SIC: 3492 Control valves, fluid power: hy-
　　draulic & pneumatic

▲ = Import ▼=Export
◆ =Import/Export

PA: Crane Co.
   100 1st Stamford Pl # 300
   Stamford CT 06902
   203 363-7300

(P-13327)
DIAMOND-U PRODUCTS INC
Also Called: C P Products
515 W Cowles St, Long Beach
(90813-1567)
PHONE..........................562 436-8245
Dominic Picarelli, *CEO*
Margarita Castellanos, *Manager*
Irma Mireles, *Manager*
▲ EMP: 10
SQ FT: 20,000
SALES (est): 1.9MM **Privately Held**
WEB: www.diamondu.com
SIC: 3492 Hose & tube fittings & assemblies, hydraulic/pneumatic

(P-13328)
ELECTROFILM MFG CO LLC
Also Called: Hartzell Aerospace
28150 Industry Dr, Valencia (91355-4100)
PHONE..........................661 257-2242
Daniel L Oconnell,
James W Brown III,
Joseph W Brown,
Matthew Jesch,
David Schmidt,
EMP: 80
SQ FT: 43,000
SALES (est): 22.2MM
SALES (corp-wide): 2.7B **Publicly Held**
WEB: www.ef-heaters.com
SIC: 3492 3728 3812 Control valves, aircraft: hydraulic & pneumatic; aircraft body & wing assemblies & parts; aircraft assemblies, subassemblies & parts; aircraft power transmission equipment; aircraft propellers & associated equipment; acceleration indicators & systems components, aerospace
HQ: Itt Aerospace Controls Llc
   28150 Industry Dr
   Valencia CA 91355
   315 568-7258

(P-13329)
FABER ENTERPRISES INC
14800 S Figueroa St, Gardena
(90248-1719)
PHONE..........................310 323-6200
Kevin M Stein, *CEO*
Esther Faber, *Ch of Bd*
Ronald E Spencer, *President*
Marilyn Spencer, *Corp Secy*
Loretta Appel, *Vice Pres*
EMP: 110
SALES (est): 20.3MM **Privately Held**
WEB: www.faberent.com
SIC: 3492 Control valves, aircraft: hydraulic & pneumatic

(P-13330)
FUJIKIN OF AMERICA INC (HQ)
454 Kato Ter, Fremont (94539-8332)
PHONE..........................408 980-8269
Hiroshi Ogawa, *CEO*
Masayuki Hida, *Managing Dir*
Katsuko Kiuchi, *Accounting Mgr*
Mohamed Saleem, *Controller*
Stella Chen, *Sales Staff*
▲ EMP: 22
SQ FT: 5,000
SALES (est): 13.3MM **Privately Held**
SIC: 3492 Control valves, fluid power: hydraulic & pneumatic

(P-13331)
INDUSTRIAL TUBE COMPANY LLC
28150 Industry Dr, Valencia (91355-4100)
PHONE..........................661 295-4000
Farrokh Batliwala,
Daniel L Oconnell,
EMP: 99
SQ FT: 28,000

SALES (est): 33.2MM
SALES (corp-wide): 2.7B **Publicly Held**
WEB: www.industrialtube.net
SIC: 3492 3728 3812 Control valves, aircraft: hydraulic & pneumatic; aircraft body & wing assemblies & parts; aircraft assemblies, subassemblies & parts; aircraft power transmission equipment; aircraft propellers & associated equipment; acceleration indicators & systems components, aerospace
HQ: Itt Aerospace Controls Llc
   28150 Industry Dr
   Valencia CA 91355
   315 568-7258

(P-13332)
MARTIN AEROSPACE CORPORATION
Also Called: Martin Company, The
11150 Tennessee Ave 1b, Los Angeles
(90064-1814)
PHONE..........................310 231-0055
C B Martin, *President*
EMP: 10 EST: 1983
SQ FT: 5,060
SALES (est): 1.4MM **Privately Held**
SIC: 3492 Hose & tube fittings & assemblies, hydraulic/pneumatic

(P-13333)
S&H MELKES INC
9928 Hayward Way, South El Monte
(91733-3114)
PHONE..........................626 448-5062
David Fisher, *President*
Dao Ha, *Vice Pres*
EMP: 20
SALES (est): 2.3MM **Privately Held**
SIC: 3492 3728 Fluid power valves & hose fittings; aircraft parts & equipment

(P-13334)
WESTFIELD HYDRAULICS INC
13834 Del Sur St, San Fernando
(91340-3440)
PHONE..........................818 896-6414
Robert Schacht, *CEO*
Frank Davis, *Director*
Kenneth Starbird, *Director*
Jack Umbarger, *Director*
EMP: 15
SQ FT: 10,500
SALES (est): 1.8MM **Privately Held**
SIC: 3492 Control valves, fluid power: hydraulic & pneumatic

3493 Steel Springs, Except Wire

(P-13335)
AMERICAN SPRING INC
321 W 135th St, Los Angeles (90061-1001)
PHONE..........................310 324-2181
Ty Kehlenbec, *President*
▲ EMP: 16
SQ FT: 25,000
SALES (est): 3.5MM **Privately Held**
SIC: 3493 3446 Coiled flat springs; acoustical suspension systems, metal

(P-13336)
ARGO SPRING MFG CO INC
13930 Shoemaker Ave, Norwalk
(90650-4597)
PHONE..........................800 252-2740
Gene Fox, *President*
Kay Greathouse, *Corp Secy*
Michael Fox, *Vice Pres*
▲ EMP: 55 EST: 1966
SQ FT: 20,000
SALES (est): 11MM **Privately Held**
WEB: www.argospring.com
SIC: 3493 3495 3469 3599 Coiled flat springs; wire springs; stamping metal for the trade; custom machinery; springs; miscellaneous fabricated wire products

(P-13337)
EIBACH SPRINGS INC
264 Mariah Cir, Corona (92879-1706)
PHONE..........................951 256-8300
Greg Cooley, *President*
Sieglinde Eibach, *Corp Secy*

Gary Peek, *Vice Pres*
Rosalia Martinez, *Sales Mgr*
Mark Krumme, *Marketing Staff*
◆ EMP: 60
SQ FT: 52,000
SALES (est): 17.2MM
SALES (corp-wide): 549.8K **Privately Held**
SIC: 3493 Steel springs, except wire
HQ: Heinrich Eibach Gmbh
   Am Lennedamm 1
   Finnentrop 57413
   272 151-10

(P-13338)
JUENGERMANN INC
Also Called: Spring Industries
1899 Palma Dr Ste A, Ventura
(93003-5739)
PHONE..........................805 644-7165
Peter Juengermann, *President*
Erich Juengermann, *Admin Sec*
EMP: 40
SQ FT: 21,600
SALES (est): 8MM **Privately Held**
WEB: www.springind.com
SIC: 3493 3495 Steel springs, except wire; wire springs

(P-13339)
MATTHEW WARREN INC
Also Called: Helical Products
901 W Mccoy Ln, Santa Maria
(93455-1109)
P.O. Box 1069 (93456-1069)
PHONE..........................805 928-3851
Leroy McChesney, *Branch Mgr*
EMP: 30
SALES (corp-wide): 185.9MM **Privately Held**
SIC: 3493 Helical springs, hot wound: railroad equipment etc.; hot wound springs, except wire; cold formed springs; coiled flat springs
HQ: Matthew Warren, Inc.
   9501 Tech Blvd Ste 401
   Rosemont IL 60018
   847 349-5760

(P-13340)
MATTHEW WARREN INC
Also Called: Century Spring
5959 Triumph St, Commerce (90040-1609)
PHONE..........................800 237-5225
Bill Cook, *Principal*
Crystal Wiemals, *Admin Asst*
Ayda Mashhadchi, *Engineer*
Gordon Braid, *QC Mgr*
EMP: 75
SALES (corp-wide): 185.9MM **Privately Held**
SIC: 3493 Coiled flat springs; cold formed springs; helical springs, hot wound: railroad equipment etc.; hot wound springs, except wire
HQ: Matthew Warren, Inc.
   9501 Tech Blvd Ste 401
   Rosemont IL 60018
   847 349-5760

(P-13341)
OHARA METAL PRODUCTS
4949 Fulton Dr Ste E, Fairfield
(94534-1648)
PHONE..........................707 863-9090
Tim Ives, *President*
Irene O'Hara, *CEO*
Robin Ives, *CFO*
Kathleen O'Hara,
EMP: 30
SQ FT: 20,000
SALES (est): 5.4MM **Privately Held**
WEB: www.oharamfg.com
SIC: 3493 3721 5051 5085 Steel springs, except wire; helicopters; metals service centers & offices; industrial supplies

(P-13342)
SCHELLINGER SPRING INC
8477 Utica Ave, Rancho Cucamonga
(91730-3809)
PHONE..........................909 373-0799
Dean Schellinger, *President*
EMP: 18
SQ FT: 12,000

SALES (est): 3MM **Privately Held**
WEB: www.schellingerspring.com
SIC: 3493 Steel springs, except wire

(P-13343)
SUPERSPRINGS INTERNATIONAL
505 Maple St, Carpinteria (93013-2070)
PHONE..........................805 745-5553
Mike Visser, *President*
Gerry Lamberti, *CEO*
Robbie Overby, *Mktg Dir*
Pat Curry, *Manager*
EMP: 11
SALES (est): 1.6MM **Privately Held**
WEB: www.supersprings.com
SIC: 3493 Automobile springs

3494 Valves & Pipe Fittings, NEC

(P-13344)
ALLAN AIRCRAFT SUPPLY CO LLC
11643 Vanowen St, North Hollywood
(91605-6128)
PHONE..........................818 765-4992
Robert Kahmann, *Mng Member*
Bob Kahmann, *General Mgr*
Mary Katz, *Controller*
Maria Flores, *Marketing Staff*
Kris Kahmann, *Manager*
EMP: 45 EST: 1952
SQ FT: 30,000
SALES (est): 10MM **Privately Held**
WEB: www.allanaircraft.com
SIC: 3494 Pipe fittings

(P-13345)
AMERON INTERNATIONAL CORP
Ameron Concrete & Steel Pipe
10100 W Linne Rd, Tracy (95377-9128)
PHONE..........................209 836-5050
Lynn Pindar, *Branch Mgr*
EMP: 102
SALES (corp-wide): 8.4B **Publicly Held**
WEB: www.ameron.com
SIC: 3494 3317 3272 Pipe fittings; steel pipe & tubes; concrete products
HQ: Ameron International Corporation
   7909 Parkwood Circle Dr
   Houston TX 77036
   713 375-3700

(P-13346)
ANCO INTERNATIONAL INC
19851 Cajon Blvd, San Bernardino
(92407-1828)
PHONE..........................909 887-2521
Marjorie A Nielsen, *President*
EMP: 36 EST: 1978
SQ FT: 13,500
SALES (est): 7.5MM **Privately Held**
WEB: www.ancointernational.com
SIC: 3494 3599 3492 Valves & pipe fittings; machine shop, jobbing & repair; fluid power valves & hose fittings

(P-13347)
BACKFLOW APPARATUS & VALVE
Also Called: Bavco
20435 S Susana Rd, Long Beach
(90810-1136)
PHONE..........................310 639-5231
James C Purzycki, *CEO*
Brad Stancampiano, *Exec VP*
Bob Purzycki, *Vice Pres*
EMP: 25
SQ FT: 10,000
SALES: 6MM **Privately Held**
WEB: www.bavco.com
SIC: 3494 Plumbing & heating valves

(P-13348)
BERMAD INC (PA)
Also Called: Bermad Control Valves
3816 S Willow Ave Ste 101, Fresno
(93725-9241)
PHONE..........................877 577-4283
Nadav Yakir, *President*
Giora Cameron, *Marketing Staff*

PRODUCTS & SVCS

Yiftah Enav, *Marketing Staff*
▲ **EMP:** 35
SQ FT: 10,000
SALES (est): 7.8MM **Privately Held**
SIC: 3494 Sprinkler systems, field

(P-13349)
BRASSCRAFT
MANUFACTURING CO
Also Called: Brasscraft Corona
215 N Smith Ave, Corona (92880-1741)
PHONE..........................951 735-4375
Val Perillo, *Branch Mgr*
EMP: 94
SALES (corp-wide): 8.3B **Publicly Held**
WEB: www.brasscraft.com
SIC: 3494 3432 5074 Valves & pipe fit-
   tings; plumbing fixture fittings & trim;
   plumbing fittings & supplies
   HQ: Brasscraft Manufacturing Company
      39600 Orchard Hill Pl
      Novi MI 48375
      248 305-6000

(P-13350)
DIE CRAFT STAMPING INC
Also Called: Gorlitz Sewer and Drain
10132 Norwalk Blvd, Santa Fe Springs
(90670-3326)
PHONE..........................562 944-2395
Gerd Kruger, *President*
Edward A Dzwonkowski, *Agent*
▲ **EMP:** 28
SQ FT: 20,000
SALES (est): 2.9MM **Privately Held**
WEB: www.gorlitz.com
SIC: 3494 Couplings, except pressure &
   soil pipe

(P-13351)
DRAGON VALVES INC (PA)
13457 Excelsior Dr, Norwalk (90650-5235)
PHONE..........................562 921-6605
Christopher Bond, *President*
Daniel Rios, *Prdtn Mgr*
Judy Kimura, *Sales Staff*
Robert Bond, *Accounts Mgr*
▲ **EMP:** 20
SALES: 5MM **Privately Held**
WEB: www.dragonvalves.com
SIC: 3494 Valves & pipe fittings

(P-13352)
EVALVE INC
4045 Campbell Ave, Menlo Park
(94025-1006)
PHONE..........................650 330-8100
Ferolyn T Powell, *President*
Doug Hughes, *CFO*
Sean Cleary, *Senior VP*
Bunty Banerjee, *Vice Pres*
Jonathan D Feuchtwang, *Vice Pres*
EMP: 91
SQ FT: 38,000
SALES (est): 11.9MM
SALES (corp-wide): 30.5B **Publicly Held**
WEB: www.evalveinc.com
SIC: 3494 Valves & pipe fittings
   PA: Abbott Laboratories
      100 Abbott Park Rd
      Abbott Park IL 60064
      224 667-6100

(P-13353)
FEDERAL INDUSTRIES INC
Also Called: FI
645 Hawaii St, El Segundo (90245-4814)
PHONE..........................310 297-4040
AVI Wacht, *President*
Asher Bartov, *CEO*
EMP: 15
SALES (est): 3.4MM **Privately Held**
SIC: 3494 3728 Valves & pipe fittings; air-
   craft parts & equipment

(P-13354)
G-G DISTRIBUTION & DEV CO
INC
Also Called: G/G Industries
28545 Livingston Ave, Valencia
(91355-4166)
PHONE..........................661 257-5700
John Gedney, *President*
Richard Greenberg, *CFO*
Mary Ellen, *Admin Sec*
▲ **EMP:** 120

SQ FT: 175,000
SALES (est): 20.5MM **Privately Held**
WEB: www.ggind.com
SIC: 3494 3088 Plumbing & heating
   valves; plastics plumbing fixtures

(P-13355)
GALT PIPE COMPANY
Also Called: Pvc Pipe Fttngs Irrgation Pdts
321 Elm Ave, Galt (95632-1511)
PHONE..........................209 745-2936
Anne Steenblock, *President*
Ann Steenblock, *President*
Dennis Swinney, *CFO*
Alberta Barquist, *Corp Secy*
EMP: 12
SQ FT: 9,000
SALES (est): 2MM **Privately Held**
WEB: www.galtpipe.com
SIC: 3494 Pipe fittings

(P-13356)
GRISWOLD CONTROLS LLC
(PA)
2803 Barranca Pkwy, Irvine (92606-5177)
P.O. Box 19612 (92623-9612)
PHONE..........................949 559-6000
Brooks Sherman, *CEO*
Doris Meyers, *Admin Sec*
Stefan Tuineag, *Engineer*
Karen Longo, *Accountant*
Larry Abts, *Controller*
▲ **EMP:** 130 **EST:** 1960
SQ FT: 60,000
SALES (est): 39.3MM **Privately Held**
SIC: 3494 3491 Valves & pipe fittings; in-
   dustrial valves

(P-13357)
HYDRO FITTING MFG CORP
733 E Edna Pl, Covina (91723-1409)
P.O. Box 1558 (91722-0558)
PHONE..........................626 967-5151
Seth Schwartz, *President*
Carol Lynn, *Human Resources*
EMP: 45 **EST:** 1962
SQ FT: 16,500
SALES (est): 10MM **Privately Held**
WEB: www.hydrofitting.com
SIC: 3494 Valves & pipe fittings

(P-13358)
JIXING (USA) INC
11094 Brentwood Dr, Rancho Cucamonga
(91730-6803)
PHONE..........................626 261-9539
Ye Pang, *Administration*
EMP: 12 **EST:** 2003
SALES (est): 1.8MM **Privately Held**
SIC: 3494 Pipe fittings

(P-13359)
MILLS IRON WORKS
14834 S Maple Ave, Gardena
(90248-1936)
PHONE..........................323 321-6520
Jeffrey Griffith, *CEO*
Kenneth E Berger, *President*
EMP: 75
SQ FT: 48,000
SALES (est): 18.2MM **Privately Held**
WEB: www.millsiron.com
SIC: 3494 Pipe fittings

(P-13360)
MORRILL INDUSTRIES INC
24754 E River Rd, Escalon (95320-8601)
PHONE..........................209 838-2550
Ken Morrill, *President*
Wayne Morrill, *CFO*
Diane Cordray, *Admin Sec*
Bob Morrill, *Prdtn Mgr*
▲ **EMP:** 55
SALES (est): 11.8MM **Privately Held**
WEB: www.morrill-industries.net
SIC: 3494 Sprinkler systems, field

(P-13361)
NOR-CAL PRODUCTS INC (DH)
1967 S Oregon St, Yreka (96097-3462)
P.O. Box 518 (96097-0518)
PHONE..........................530 842-4457
Tom Deany, *President*
David Stone, *CFO*
Monica Coupens, *General Mgr*
Eric Edin, *Engineer*

Jeff Hadley, *Engineer*
▲ **EMP:** 140
SQ FT: 57,000
SALES (est): 43.7MM
SALES (corp-wide): 603.5MM **Privately**
Held
WEB: www.nor-calproducts.com
SIC: 3494 Valves & pipe fittings

(P-13362)
RAIN BIRD CORPORATION (PA)
970 W Sierra Madre Ave, Azusa
(91702-1873)
PHONE..........................626 812-3400
Anthony W La Fetra, *President*
Mike Donoghue, *Vice Pres*
Mike McBride, *Executive*
Bret Ramsey, *Regional Mgr*
Heidi Hanson, *Admin Asst*
▲ **EMP:** 125 **EST:** 1946
SALES (est): 86.7MM **Privately Held**
WEB: www.rainbird.com
SIC: 3494 3432 3523 Sprinkler systems,
   field; lawn hose nozzles & sprinklers; farm
   machinery & equipment

(P-13363)
SPS TECHNOLOGIES LLC
Airdrome Precision Components
14800 S Figueroa St, Gardena
(90248-1719)
P.O. Box 1867, Long Beach (90801-1867)
PHONE..........................562 426-9411
Ben Needleman, *Controller*
EMP: 65
SALES (corp-wide): 225.3B **Publicly**
Held
SIC: 3494 Valves & pipe fittings
   HQ: Sps Technologies, Llc
      301 Highland Ave
      Jenkintown PA 19046
      215 572-3000

(P-13364)
STRAIGHTLINE MECHANICAL
INC
1051 E 6th St, Santa Ana (92701-4752)
PHONE..........................714 204-0940
Jacob Flora, *President*
EMP: 10 **EST:** 2009
SALES (est): 660K **Privately Held**
SIC: 3494 Pipe fittings

(P-13365)
VACCO INDUSTRIES (DH)
10350 Vacco St, South El Monte
(91733-3399)
PHONE..........................626 443-7121
Antonio E Gonzalez, *CEO*
Colon Gardner, *Vice Pres*
Robert Mc Creadie, *Vice Pres*
Steve Morey, *Program Mgr*
Eddie Yang, *Program Mgr*
EMP: 250
SALES (est): 50.3MM
SALES (corp-wide): 771.5MM **Publicly**
Held
WEB: www.vacco.com
SIC: 3494 3492 3728 Valves & pipe fit-
   tings; fluid power valves & hose fittings;
   aircraft parts & equipment
   HQ: Esco Technologies Holding Llc
      9900 Clayton Rd Ste A
      Saint Louis MO 63124
      314 213-7200

(P-13366)
VALLEY PIPE & SUPPLY INC
1801 Santa Clara St, Fresno (93721-2865)
P.O. Box 551 (93709-0551)
PHONE..........................559 233-0321
Mitchell Long, *CEO*
Charles Long, *CFO*
Charles C Long, *Treasurer*
Gary Hanson, *Sales Staff*
▲ **EMP:** 32
SQ FT: 20,000
SALES (est): 7.8MM **Privately Held**
SIC: 3494 5051 5085 5074 Valves & pipe
   fittings; pipe & tubing, steel; valves & fit-
   tings; pipes & tubing, plastic; plumbing &
   heating valves; farm machinery & equip-
   ment

(P-13367)
VALTERRA PRODUCTS LLC
(PA)
15230 San Fernando, Mission Hills
(91345)
PHONE..........................818 898-1671
Dennis Lunder, *Principal*
Harvey Hal, *CFO*
George Grengs, *Principal*
▲ **EMP:** 20
SQ FT: 50,000
SALES (est): 50MM **Privately Held**
WEB: www.valterra.com
SIC: 3494 3088 3949 3432 Valves & pipe
   fittings; plastics plumbing fixtures; skate-
   boards; plumbing fixture fittings & trim

(P-13368)
WILLIAMS MANUFACTURING
COMPANY
12727 Foothill Blvd, Sylmar (91342-5314)
PHONE..........................818 898-2272
Oscar Pineda, *President*
Tammy Delrais, *Director*
Paul Williams, *Manager*
EMP: 12 **EST:** 1974
SQ FT: 7,400
SALES: 500K **Privately Held**
SIC: 3494 Pipe fittings

3495 Wire Springs

(P-13369)
AARD INDUSTRIES INC
Also Called: Aard Spring & Stamping
42075 Avenida Alvarado, Temecula
(92590-3486)
PHONE..........................951 296-0844
William Verstegen, *President*
EMP: 22
SQ FT: 5,000
SALES (est): 4.1MM **Privately Held**
WEB: www.aard.com
SIC: 3495 3469 Wire springs; metal
   stampings

(P-13370)
ADVANCED PRECISION SPRING
1754 Junction Ave Ste A, San Jose
(95112-1037)
PHONE..........................408 436-6595
John Nguyen, *President*
Tom Nguyen, *Vice Pres*
EMP: 15
SQ FT: 6,000
SALES: 3MM **Privately Held**
WEB: www.apspring.com
SIC: 3495 3469 Precision springs; metal
   stampings

(P-13371)
ADVANEX AMERICAS INC (HQ)
5780 Cerritos Ave, Cypress (90630-4741)
PHONE..........................714 995-4519
Kiyoshi Kato, *Ch of Bd*
Yuichi Kato, *President*
James F Grueser, *Exec VP*
Jake Iliopoulos, *Engineer*
Ricardo Villarreal, *Engineer*
▲ **EMP:** 92 **EST:** 1966
SQ FT: 52,000
SALES (est): 24.1MM **Privately Held**
WEB: www.katospring.com
SIC: 3495 Wire springs

(P-13372)
ALFONSO JARAMILLO
Also Called: Acxess Spring
2225 E Cooley Dr, Colton (92324-6324)
PHONE..........................951 276-2777
Alfonso Jaramillo, *Owner*
EMP: 12
SQ FT: 2,500
SALES: 400K **Privately Held**
WEB: www.acxesspring.com
SIC: 3495 Wire springs

(P-13373)
AMERICAN PRECISION SPRING
1513 Arbuckle Ct, Santa Clara
(95054-3401)
PHONE..........................408 986-1020
Kathleen Chu, *President*
Mike Remily, *Vice Pres*

▲ = Import ▼=Export
◆ =Import/Export

Tuan Nguyen, *Opers Mgr*
EMP: 23 **EST:** 1979
SQ FT: 1,500
SALES (est): 4.5MM **Privately Held**
WEB: www.americanprecspring.com
SIC: 3495 Mechanical springs, precision

(P-13374)
ATLAS SPRING MFGCORP
10635 Santa Monica Blvd, Los Angeles (90025-8300)
PHONE.................................310 532-6200
Melvin Bayer, *President*
Stan Grietzer, *Corp Secy*
Jeff Miller, *Vice Pres*
Mary Ann Lamascus, *General Mgr*
EMP: 140
SQ FT: 100,000
SALES (est): 12.9MM **Privately Held**
SIC: 3495 Upholstery springs, unassembled

(P-13375)
BAL SEAL ENGINEERING INC (PA)
19650 Pauling, Foothill Ranch (92610-2610)
PHONE.................................949 460-2100
Richard Dawson, *CEO*
Hugh Cook, *President*
Peter J Balsells, *Chairman*
Jacques Naviaux, *Chairman*
Sean McCarthy, *Officer*
▲ **EMP:** 270 **EST:** 1959
SQ FT: 325,000
SALES (est): 96.7MM **Privately Held**
WEB: www.balseal.com
SIC: 3495 3053 Wire springs; gaskets & sealing devices

(P-13376)
BETTS COMPANY (PA)
Also Called: Betts Spring Manufacturing
2843 S Maple Ave, Fresno (93725-2217)
PHONE.................................559 498-3304
William M Betts IV, *Ch of Bd*
Bill Betts, *President*
Donald Devany, *Vice Pres*
Marcie Hernandez, *Manager*
▲ **EMP:** 75
SQ FT: 7,500
SALES (est): 77.4MM **Privately Held**
WEB: www.bettspring.com
SIC: 3495 3493 Wire springs; instrument springs, precision; mechanical springs, precision; automobile springs

(P-13377)
BETTS COMPANY
Also Called: Betts Truck Parts
10771 Almond Ave Ste B, Fontana (92337-7165)
PHONE.................................909 427-9988
Dan Paul, *Manager*
Phil Picco, *Branch Mgr*
EMP: 17
SALES (corp-wide): 77.4MM **Privately Held**
WEB: www.bettspring.com
SIC: 3495 3493 Wire springs; instrument springs, precision; mechanical springs, precision; automobile springs
PA: Betts Company
2843 S Maple Ave
Fresno CA 93725
559 498-3304

(P-13378)
C & M SPRING & ENGINEERING CO
5244 Las Flores Dr, Chino (91710-9610)
P.O. Box 2559 (91708-2559)
PHONE.................................909 597-2030
Paul Lockhart, *President*
EMP: 26
SQ FT: 15,000
SALES (est): 4.7MM **Privately Held**
WEB: www.cmspring.com
SIC: 3495 3496 Mechanical springs, precision; miscellaneous fabricated wire products

(P-13379)
CLIO INC
Also Called: B&B Spring Co
12981 166th St, Cerritos (90703-2104)
PHONE.................................562 926-3724
Jerome M Johnson, *President*
Reva J Johnson, *CEO*
Imelda Cardenas, *Sales Staff*
EMP: 28
SQ FT: 2,000
SALES (est): 4.8MM **Privately Held**
SIC: 3495 3679 Wire springs; transducers, electrical

(P-13380)
DIVERSIFIED SPRING TECH
9233 Santa Fe Springs Rd, Santa Fe Springs (90670-2617)
PHONE.................................562 944-4049
Leo Hernandez, *President*
Olga Hernandez, *Vice Pres*
EMP: 11
SQ FT: 4,000
SALES: 350K **Privately Held**
WEB: www.diversifiedspring.com
SIC: 3495 3316 5085 Precision springs; clock springs, precision; instrument springs, precision; mechanical springs, precision; cold-rolled strip or wire; springs

(P-13381)
FOREMOST SPRING COMPANY INC
Also Called: Foremost Spring & Mfg
11876 Burke St, Santa Fe Springs (90670-2536)
PHONE.................................562 923-0791
Forrest Gardner, *President*
Christine Brown, *Vice Pres*
Jesus Silva, *Admin Sec*
EMP: 15
SQ FT: 20,000
SALES (est): 1.6MM **Privately Held**
WEB: www.foremostspring.com
SIC: 3495 3469 3493 Mechanical springs, precision; stamping metal for the trade; steel springs, except wire

(P-13382)
NEWCOMB SPRING CORP
Also Called: Newcomb Spring of California
8380 Cerritos Ave, Stanton (90680-2514)
PHONE.................................714 995-5341
Robert Guard, *Manager*
Rick Guard, *Plant Mgr*
EMP: 30
SALES (corp-wide): 71.2MM **Privately Held**
WEB: www.newcombspring.com
SIC: 3495 3469 5085 Wire springs; stamping metal for the trade; springs
PA: Spring Newcomb Corp
5408 Panola Indus Blvd
Decatur GA 30035
770 981-2803

(P-13383)
ORLANDO SPRING CORP
5341 Argosy Ave, Huntington Beach (92649-1036)
PHONE.................................562 594-8411
Frank Mauro, *President*
Zachary Fischer, *CEO*
Robert Dominguez, *Engineer*
Jenna Gibson, *Sales Staff*
EMP: 40
SQ FT: 20,000
SALES (est): 8.5MM **Privately Held**
SIC: 3495 Wire springs

(P-13384)
PENINSULA SPRING CORPORATION
6750 Silacci Way, Gilroy (95020-7035)
P.O. Box 1782 (95021-1782)
PHONE.................................408 848-3361
Joe Kilmer, *President*
Muriel Kilmer, *Vice Pres*
Laura Hampel, *Office Mgr*
EMP: 18
SQ FT: 10,000

SALES: 1.3MM **Privately Held**
WEB: www.peninsulaspring.com
SIC: 3495 3444 3498 3496 Precision springs; forming machine work, sheet metal; fabricated pipe & fittings; miscellaneous fabricated wire products

(P-13385)
PRAXIS MUSICAL INSTRUMENT INC
19122 S Vermont Ave, Gardena (90248-4413)
PHONE.................................714 532-6655
Jong Ho Park, *Principal*
◆ **EMP:** 10 **EST:** 2010
SALES (est): 1.2MM **Privately Held**
SIC: 3495 Instrument springs, precision

(P-13386)
PRECISION COIL SPRING COMPANY
10107 Rose Ave, El Monte (91731-1898)
PHONE.................................626 444-0561
Albert H Goering, *CEO*
Bert Goering, *President*
Cheryl Hyland, *VP Accounting*
Steve Belling, *QC Mgr*
Don Adkins, *VP Sales*
EMP: 100
SQ FT: 45,000
SALES (est): 25.6MM **Privately Held**
WEB: www.pcspring.com
SIC: 3495 Wire springs

(P-13387)
REV CO SPRING MFANUFACTURING
9915 Alburtis Ave, Santa Fe Springs (90670-3209)
PHONE.................................562 949-1958
Evelyn Valles, *President*
Vicky Garcia, *Corp Secy*
Rudy Valles, *Vice Pres*
EMP: 12
SQ FT: 6,000
SALES (est): 750K **Privately Held**
SIC: 3495 Precision springs

(P-13388)
SPRING DELGAU INC
Also Called: Delgau Spring
322 N Garfield Ave, Corona (92882-1826)
PHONE.................................951 371-1000
Bernard Delgau, *President*
EMP: 10 **EST:** 1978
SQ FT: 7,800
SALES (est): 1.7MM **Privately Held**
WEB: www.delgauspring.com
SIC: 3495 Wire springs

(P-13389)
STECHER ENTERPRISES INC
Also Called: C&F WIRE PRODUCTS
8536 Central Ave, Stanton (90680-2718)
PHONE.................................714 484-6900
Fred Stecher, *Director*
Tammy Stecher, *President*
Carol Stecher, *Vice Pres*
EMP: 15
SQ FT: 10,000
SALES (est): 1.7MM **Privately Held**
WEB: www.cfwireproducts.com
SIC: 3495 Instrument springs, precision

(P-13390)
SUPERIOR SPRING COMPANY
1260 S Talt Ave, Anaheim (92806-5533)
PHONE.................................714 490-0881
Robert De Long Jr, *President*
Marilyn Spearman, *CFO*
Tom Pruett, *General Mgr*
Bob Delong, *Project Mgr*
John Wake, *Director*
EMP: 25 **EST:** 1958
SQ FT: 17,000
SALES (est): 5.3MM **Privately Held**
WEB: www.superiorspring.com
SIC: 3495 Wire springs

(P-13391)
TRICOSS INC
Also Called: Tri County Spring & Stamping
4450 Dupont Ct Ste A, Ventura (93003-7790)
PHONE.................................805 644-4107

Karl Schlosser, *President*
Ingrid Boehm, *Admin Sec*
▼ **EMP:** 10
SQ FT: 7,800
SALES: 500K **Privately Held**
WEB: www.tricossinc.com
SIC: 3495 3469 3496 Wire springs; metal stampings; wire cloth & woven wire products

(P-13392)
UNITED PRECISION CORP
20810 Plummer St, Chatsworth (91311-5004)
PHONE.................................818 576-9540
Robert Stanley Hawrylo, *CEO*
David Hawrylo, *Engineer*
EMP: 11 **EST:** 2014
SQ FT: 7,500
SALES (est): 1.3MM **Privately Held**
SIC: 3495 Precision springs; instrument springs, precision

3496 Misc Fabricated Wire Prdts

(P-13393)
ACCURATE WIRE & DISPLAY INC
Also Called: Kersting Library Products
3600 Oak Cliff Dr, Fallbrook (92028-9413)
PHONE.................................310 532-7821
▲ **EMP:** 50
SALES (est): 4.4MM **Privately Held**
SIC: 3496 2514 2517 7319

(P-13394)
AMERICAN WIRE INC
784 S Lugo Ave, San Bernardino (92408-2236)
PHONE.................................909 884-9990
Bian Bie Liem, *CEO*
▲ **EMP:** 19
SQ FT: 12,000
SALES (est): 4MM **Privately Held**
WEB: www.americanwirecorp.com
SIC: 3496 Mesh, made from purchased wire

(P-13395)
ANAHEIM WIRE PRODUCTS INC (PA)
1009 E Vermont Ave, Anaheim (92805-5618)
PHONE.................................714 563-8300
Michael Lewis, *President*
▲ **EMP:** 20
SQ FT: 14,000
SALES (est): 4MM **Privately Held**
WEB: www.anaheimwire.com
SIC: 3496 Miscellaneous fabricated wire products

(P-13396)
AUTOMOTIVE ELECTRONICS SVCS
Also Called: Aeswave.com
5465 E Hedges Ave, Fresno (93727-2279)
PHONE.................................559 292-7851
Jorge Menchu, *President*
Carlos Menchu, *Executive*
▲ **EMP:** 13
SALES (est): 2.8MM **Privately Held**
WEB: www.aeswave.com
SIC: 3496 7373 Cable, uninsulated wire: made from purchased wire; systems software development services

(P-13397)
BILL WOOD LATHING
12188 Central Ave Pmb 621, Chino (91710-2420)
PHONE.................................909 628-1733
William Wood, *Owner*
Deborah Long, *Manager*
EMP: 25
SALES (est): 1.8MM **Privately Held**
SIC: 3496 Lath, woven wire

(P-13398)
BLACKTALON INDUSTRIES INC
481 Technology Way, NAPA (94558-7571)
P.O. Box 300 (94559-0300)
PHONE..............................707 256-1812
Brent Morgan, *President*
EMP: 13
SALES (est): 1.6MM **Privately Held**
SIC: 3496 7382 Fencing, made from purchased wire; burglar alarm maintenance & monitoring

(P-13399)
CABLE MOORE INC (PA)
4700 Coliseum Way, Oakland (94601-5008)
P.O. Box 4067 (94614-4067)
PHONE..............................510 436-8000
Sandra Moore, *CEO*
Gregory Moore, *Corp Secy*
Roy Guzman, *Sales Staff*
Greg Moore, *Sales Staff*
Tere T Oconnor, *Program Dir*
▲ **EMP:** 40
SQ FT: 12,500
SALES (est): 11MM **Privately Held**
WEB: www.cablemoore.com
SIC: 3496 Wire chain

(P-13400)
CABLESTRAND CORP
Also Called: Cable Strand
2660 Signal Pkwy, Long Beach (90755-2205)
PHONE..............................562 595-4527
Allan Weiss, *President*
Paul Weiss, *Chairman*
Karen Weiss, *Vice Pres*
▲ **EMP:** 10
SQ FT: 16,000
SALES (est): 1.6MM **Privately Held**
SIC: 3496 Cable, uninsulated wire: made from purchased wire

(P-13401)
CALIFORNIA WIRE PRODUCTS CORP
Also Called: Cal-Monarch
1316 Railroad St, Corona (92882-1840)
PHONE..............................951 371-7730
John G Frei, *CEO*
Samuel A Agajanian, *President*
Francis Estaris, *CFO*
Sam Agajanian, *Principal*
Darren Murray, *Sales Executive*
▲ **EMP:** 30 **EST:** 1948
SQ FT: 34,000
SALES (est): 7.5MM **Privately Held**
WEB: www.cawire.com
SIC: 3496 2542 Screening, woven wire: made from purchased wire; partitions for floor attachment, prefabricated: except wood

(P-13402)
CARPENTER GROUP
112 Bgley St Crnr Of Rlro Corner Of Railro, Vallejo (94592)
PHONE..............................707 562-3543
Dane Oliver, *Branch Mgr*
EMP: 17
SALES (corp-wide): 27.9MM **Privately Held**
WEB: www.carpenterrigging.com
SIC: 3496 Miscellaneous fabricated wire products
PA: The Carpenter Group
222 Napoleon St
San Francisco CA 94124
415 285-1954

(P-13403)
CARPENTER GROUP
Also Called: Cableco
13100 Firestone Blvd, Santa Fe Springs (90670-5517)
PHONE..............................562 942-8076
Ray Stys, *Branch Mgr*
Sue Yoder, *Vice Pres*
Greg Bailey, *Train & Dev Mgr*
Tom Draper, *Sales Mgr*
EMP: 10

SALES (corp-wide): 27.9MM **Privately Held**
WEB: www.carpenterrigging.com
SIC: 3496 2394 Cable, uninsulated wire: made from purchased wire; liners & covers, fabric: made from purchased materials
PA: The Carpenter Group
222 Napoleon St
San Francisco CA 94124
415 285-1954

(P-13404)
CIRCLE W ENTERPRISES INC
Also Called: Wirenetics Co
27737 Avenue Hopkins, Valencia (91355-1223)
PHONE..............................661 257-2400
Howard Weiss, *CEO*
Michael Weiss, *President*
Phyllis G Weiss, *CEO*
Mark Lee, *Vice Pres*
▲ **EMP:** 50
SQ FT: 65,000
SALES (est): 14.1MM
SALES (corp-wide): 32MM **Privately Held**
WEB: www.wireandcable.com
SIC: 3496 Miscellaneous fabricated wire products
PA: Whitmor Plastic Wire And Cable Corp.
27737 Avenue Hopkins
Santa Clarita CA 91355
661 257-2400

(P-13405)
CLOSETMAID LLC
5150 Edison Ave Ste C, Chino (91710-5786)
PHONE..............................909 590-4444
Ken Graper, *Branch Mgr*
EMP: 15
SALES (corp-wide): 1.9B **Publicly Held**
WEB: www.closetmaidmail.com
SIC: 3496 Miscellaneous fabricated wire products
HQ: Closetmaid Llc
650 Sw 27th Ave
Ocala FL 34471
352 401-6000

(P-13406)
COVE FOUR-SLIDE STAMPING CORP (PA)
Also Called: Cove West Division
355 S Hale Ave, Fullerton (92831)
PHONE..............................516 379-4232
Barry Jaffe, *Principal*
Marjorie R Jaffee, *Admin Sec*
◆ **EMP:** 125 **EST:** 1960
SQ FT: 50,000
SALES (est): 14.2MM **Privately Held**
SIC: 3496 3469 Miscellaneous fabricated wire products; metal stampings

(P-13407)
COVE FOUR-SLIDE STAMPING CORP
Cove West
335 S Hale Ave, Fullerton (92831-4805)
PHONE..............................714 525-2930
Augustine Ruiz, *Branch Mgr*
EMP: 40
SALES (est): 4.5MM
SALES (corp-wide): 14.2MM **Privately Held**
SIC: 3496 3452 3315 Miscellaneous fabricated wire products; bolts, nuts, rivets & washers; wire & fabricated wire products
PA: Cove Four-Slide & Stamping Corp.
355 S Hale Ave
Fullerton CA 92831
516 379-4232

(P-13408)
CUSTOM WIRE PRODUCTS
7580 North Ave, Lemon Grove (91945-1699)
PHONE..............................619 469-2328
Fax: 619 469-4809
EMP: 12
SQ FT: 9,000
SALES (est): 910K **Privately Held**
WEB: www.custom-wire.com
SIC: 3496

(P-13409)
DAHLHAUSER MANUFACTURING CO
1855 Russell Ave, Santa Clara (95054-2035)
PHONE..............................408 988-3717
Dan Dahlhauser, *President*
EMP: 20 **EST:** 1966
SQ FT: 22,000
SALES: 2MM **Privately Held**
SIC: 3496 Wire fasteners

(P-13410)
EJAY FILTRATION INC
3036 Durahart St, Riverside (92507-3446)
P.O. Box 5268 (92517-5268)
PHONE..............................951 683-0805
Jerry Green, *CEO*
Cheryl Young, *President*
Bob Rostig, *Vice Pres*
Jennifer Hall, *General Mgr*
Kavin McNabb, *QA Dir*
EMP: 33
SQ FT: 14,000
SALES (est): 4.8MM **Privately Held**
WEB: www.ejayfiltration.com
SIC: 3496 Mesh, made from purchased wire

(P-13411)
FEATHER FARM INC
1181 4th Ave, NAPA (94559-3617)
PHONE..............................707 255-8833
Jim Brown, *President*
Arlyta Brown, *Vice Pres*
▲ **EMP:** 14
SQ FT: 20,000
SALES (est): 2.1MM **Privately Held**
WEB: www.featherfarm.com
SIC: 3496 0752 Cages, wire; breeding services, pet & animal specialties (not horses)

(P-13412)
FEENEY INC
2603 Union St, Oakland (94607-2423)
PHONE..............................510 893-9473
Grissell Ralston, *CEO*
Katrina Ralston, *President*
Steven Imbrenda, *CFO*
Richard Ralston, *Principal*
Lilibeth Castro, *Human Res Mgr*
▼ **EMP:** 48 **EST:** 1948
SQ FT: 29,000
SALES (est): 11.9MM **Privately Held**
SIC: 3496 Miscellaneous fabricated wire products

(P-13413)
FENCE FACTORY
2650 El Camino Real, Atascadero (93422-1915)
PHONE..............................805 462-1362
Jay Foster, *Manager*
EMP: 12
SALES (corp-wide): 29.9MM **Privately Held**
WEB: www.fencefactory.com
SIC: 3496 5039 3446 Fencing, made from purchased wire; wire fence, gates & accessories; architectural metalwork
HQ: Fence Factory
2419 Palma Dr
Ventura CA 93003
805 644-7207

(P-13414)
FITTINGS THAT FIT INC
4628 Mission Blvd, Montclair (91763-6135)
PHONE..............................909 248-2808
Eric C Wang, *President*
▲ **EMP:** 15
SALES (est): 2.3MM **Privately Held**
WEB: www.ffi-ftf.com
SIC: 3496 Fencing, made from purchased wire

(P-13415)
GROSSI FABRICATION INC
3200 Tully Rd, Hughson (95326-9816)
P.O. Box 937 (95326-0937)
PHONE..............................209 883-2817
Larry Grossi, *President*
Shanon Grossi, *Vice Pres*
EMP: 20

SALES (est): 4.4MM **Privately Held**
SIC: 3496 Netting, woven wire: made from purchased wire

(P-13416)
INNOVIVE LLC (PA)
10019 Waples Ct, San Diego (92121-2962)
PHONE..............................858 309-6620
Dee Conger, *CEO*
Samuel Lujan, *Project Engr*
Leroy Jenson, *Engineer*
Stacy Ho, *Accountant*
Jeremy Jenson, *QC Mgr*
▲ **EMP:** 40
SQ FT: 50,000
SALES (est): 11.3MM **Privately Held**
WEB: www.innoviveinc.com
SIC: 3496 Cages, wire

(P-13417)
INTAKE SCREENS INC
8417 River Rd, Sacramento (95832-9710)
PHONE..............................916 665-2727
Russell Berry, *President*
Russell M Berry III, *Vice Pres*
Judy McAvoy, *Office Mgr*
Ronaele Berry, *Admin Sec*
Jacob Chapin, *Design Engr*
EMP: 15
SQ FT: 3,300
SALES (est): 3.7MM **Privately Held**
WEB: www.intakescreensinc.com
SIC: 3496 Screening, woven wire: made from purchased wire

(P-13418)
INTERMETRO INDUSTRIES CORP
9420 Santa Anita Ave, Rancho Cucamonga (91730-6117)
PHONE..............................909 987-4731
John Skuchas, *Branch Mgr*
EMP: 28
SQ FT: 56,000
SALES (corp-wide): 106.4K **Privately Held**
WEB: www.metro.com
SIC: 3496 2542 Miscellaneous fabricated wire products; partitions & fixtures, except wood
HQ: Intermetro Industries Corporation
651 N Washington St
Wilkes Barre PA 18705
570 825-2741

(P-13419)
K I O KABLES INC
Also Called: Kio Kables
2525 W 10th St, Antioch (94509-1374)
PHONE..............................925 778-7500
Bruce Scott, *President*
EMP: 18
SQ FT: 1,500
SALES (est): 2.6MM **Privately Held**
SIC: 3496 Cable, uninsulated wire: made from purchased wire

(P-13420)
K METAL PRODUCTS INC
Also Called: Benchmark Engineering Div of
11935 Baker Pl, Santa Fe Springs (90670-2551)
PHONE..............................562 693-5425
EMP: 200
SQ FT: 54,000
SALES: 12.5MM **Privately Held**
SIC: 3496 3444 2542 3498

(P-13421)
KEVIN WHALEY
Also Called: Whaley, Kevin Enterprises
9565 Pathway St, Santee (92071-4184)
PHONE..............................619 596-4000
Kevin M Whaley, *Owner*
▼ **EMP:** 25
SQ FT: 24,000
SALES (est): 3.4MM **Privately Held**
SIC: 3496 Cages, wire

(P-13422)
MERCHANTS METALS LLC
6829 Mccomber St, Sacramento (95828-2515)
PHONE..............................916 381-8243
Sara Uyeno, *Manager*
Wendy Mattern, *Sales Staff*

▲ = Import ▼=Export
◆ =Import/Export

EMP: 10
SALES (corp-wide): 2.9B **Privately Held**
SIC: 3496 Miscellaneous fabricated wire products
HQ: Merchants Metals Llc
211 Perimeter Center Pkwy
Atlanta GA 30346
770 741-0306

(P-13423)
MISSION HILLS RADIO/TV INC
Also Called: Mission Hill Audio Video
9474 Chesapeake Dr # 906, San Diego
(92123-1047)
PHONE..................858 277-1100
Jerry Van Wey, *President*
EMP: 10
SQ FT: 5,500
SALES (est): 91.8K **Privately Held**
SIC: 3496 Miscellaneous fabricated wire products

(P-13424)
MIWA INC
5733 San Leandro St Ofc, Oakland
(94621-4426)
PHONE..................510 261-5999
Thomas Yan, *President*
Sandra Yan, *Vice Pres*
▲ **EMP:** 25
SQ FT: 45,000
SALES (est): 2.4MM **Privately Held**
WEB: www.miwafuton.com
SIC: 3496 2512 2511 5719 Mats & matting; couches, sofas & davenports: upholstered on wood frames; screens, privacy: wood; lighting, lamps & accessories

(P-13425)
PACIFIC WIRE PRODUCTS INC
10725 Vanowen St, North Hollywood
(91605-6402)
PHONE..................818 755-6400
Charles L Swick, *President*
Rafael Martinez, *VP Sales*
EMP: 25
SQ FT: 28,000
SALES (est): 3MM **Privately Held**
WEB: www.pacificwire.com
SIC: 3496 Miscellaneous fabricated wire products

(P-13426)
PHIFER INCORPORATED
Also Called: Phifer Western
14408 Nelson Ave, City of Industry
(91744-3513)
PHONE..................626 968-0438
Joel Hartig, *Manager*
EMP: 12
SQ FT: 23,182
SALES (corp-wide): 418MM **Privately Held**
WEB: www.phifer.com
SIC: 3496 Miscellaneous fabricated wire products
PA: Phifer Incorporated
4400 Kauloosa Ave
Tuscaloosa AL 35401
205 345-2120

(P-13427)
PRECISION WIRE PRODUCTS INC (PA)
6150 Sheila St, Commerce (90040-2407)
PHONE..................323 890-9100
Vladimir John Ondrasik Jr, *Principal*
V John Ondrasik, *President*
Crystal McLaughlin, *Safety Dir*
Alex Ramirez, *Maintence Staff*
▲ **EMP:** 200
SQ FT: 200,000
SALES (est): 42.4MM **Privately Held**
WEB: www.precisionwireproducts.com
SIC: 3496 Grocery carts, made from purchased wire

(P-13428)
PREFERRED WIRE PRODUCTS INC
401 N Minnewawa Ave, Clovis
(93611-9194)
PHONE..................559 324-0140
Bradley Actis, *President*
Robert Actis, *Vice Pres*
▲ **EMP:** 10

SALES (est): 1.6MM **Privately Held**
SIC: 3496 Miscellaneous fabricated wire products

(P-13429)
PS INTL INC
655 Vineland Ave, City of Industry
(91746-1912)
PHONE..................626 333-8168
▲ **EMP:** 10
SALES (est): 783.9K **Privately Held**
SIC: 3496 Cages, wire

(P-13430)
R & B WIRE PRODUCTS INC
2902 W Garry Ave, Santa Ana
(92704-6510)
PHONE..................714 549-3355
Richard G Rawlins, *President*
Keys Mike, *General Mgr*
Pedro Contreras, *Technology*
Steve Votaw, *Purch Mgr*
Noah Graham, *Marketing Staff*
◆ **EMP:** 35 **EST:** 1948
SQ FT: 20,000
SALES (est): 10.4MM **Privately Held**
WEB: www.rbwire.com
SIC: 3496 Miscellaneous fabricated wire products

(P-13431)
RAMPONE INDUSTRIES LLC
14235 Commerce Dr, Garden Grove
(92843-4944)
PHONE..................949 581-8701
Horacio Rampone,
▲ **EMP:** 30
SQ FT: 20,000
SALES (est): 6.3MM **Privately Held**
WEB: www.ramponewire.com
SIC: 3496 Miscellaneous fabricated wire products

(P-13432)
RAPID MANUFACTURING A (PA)
8080 E Crystal Dr, Anaheim (92807-2524)
PHONE..................714 974-2432
Joseph Lang, *Partner*
Adriana Dominguez, *Program Mgr*
Roman Pitsil, *Program Mgr*
Jorge Sanchez, *Admin Asst*
Bengie Gonzalez, *Technology*
EMP: 180
SQ FT: 19,500
SALES (est): 49.6MM **Privately Held**
WEB: www.rapidmfg.com
SIC: 3496 Miscellaneous fabricated wire products

(P-13433)
RFC WIRE FORMS INC
525 Brooks St, Ontario (91762-3702)
PHONE..................909 467-0559
Donald C Kemby, *CEO*
Christine Kemby, *Admin Sec*
Amber Magana, *Admin Asst*
Marya Black, *Sales Executive*
Bob Orr, *Sales Mgr*
▲ **EMP:** 70
SQ FT: 29,000
SALES (est): 13.9MM **Privately Held**
WEB: www.rfcwireforms.com
SIC: 3496 Miscellaneous fabricated wire products

(P-13434)
ROCATEQ NORTH AMERICA
4155 Blackhwk Lasas Cir, Danville (94506)
PHONE..................925 648-7794
Linda Downs, *Exec Dir*
▲ **EMP:** 15
SALES (est): 2.4MM **Privately Held**
SIC: 3496 Grocery carts, made from purchased wire

(P-13435)
RPS INC
20331 Corisco St, Chatsworth (91311)
PHONE..................818 350-8088
Travis Miller, *President*
EMP: 25 **EST:** 2017
SQ FT: 1,000
SALES (est): 1MM **Privately Held**
SIC: 3496 7389 Miscellaneous fabricated wire products; design services

(P-13436)
SPECIALTY STEEL PRODUCTS INC
Also Called: California Cage Co
1202 Piper Ranch Rd, San Diego
(92154-7714)
PHONE..................619 671-0720
Gilberto Gallardo, *CEO*
EMP: 10
SALES (est): 2.4MM **Privately Held**
WEB: www.ssp-inc.net
SIC: 3496 Cages, wire

(P-13437)
SYNERGISTIC RESEARCH INC
1736 E Borchard Ave, Santa Ana
(92705-4605)
PHONE..................949 642-2800
Theodore Denney III, *President*
▲ **EMP:** 15
SALES (est): 2.5MM **Privately Held**
WEB: www.synergisticresearch.com
SIC: 3496 Cable, uninsulated wire: made from purchased wire

(P-13438)
SYSTEMS WIRE & CABLE LIMITED
1165 N Stanford Ave, Los Angeles
(90059-3516)
PHONE..................310 532-7870
Ueli Burkhardt, *CEO*
Robert Gaisford, *Vice Pres*
Jennifer Harman, *Office Mgr*
Pete Burkhardt, *Admin Sec*
EMP: 13
SQ FT: 15,000
SALES (est): 2.9MM **Privately Held**
WEB: www.systemswire.com
SIC: 3496 Cable, uninsulated wire: made from purchased wire

(P-13439)
T AND T INDUSTRIES INC (PA)
1835 Dawns Way Ste A, Fullerton
(92831-5301)
PHONE..................714 284-6555
John Vaughn, *President*
John Mayberry, *Officer*
▲ **EMP:** 63 **EST:** 1943
SQ FT: 10,000
SALES (est): 14.1MM **Privately Held**
SIC: 3496 Clips & fasteners, made from purchased wire

(P-13440)
TOP-SHELF FIXTURES LLC
5263 Schaefer Ave, Chino (91710-5554)
P.O. Box 2470 (91708-2470)
PHONE..................909 627-7423
Alonso Munoz, *Mng Member*
Dennis Poudel, *Vice Pres*
Olivia Norris, *Executive Asst*
Juan Verduzco, *Project Mgr*
Rosie Mendoza, *Accountant*
EMP: 95
SQ FT: 90,000
SALES (est): 21.2MM **Privately Held**
WEB: www.topshelffixtures.com
SIC: 3496 Miscellaneous fabricated wire products

(P-13441)
UNIVERSAL WIRE INC
1705 S Campus Ave, Ontario (91761-4346)
PHONE..................626 285-2288
Mahesh Vaghasia, *President*
Himat Desai, *CFO*
Rashmikant Vaghasia, *Vice Pres*
Parshottam Lakhani, *Admin Sec*
▲ **EMP:** 14 **EST:** 1958
SQ FT: 15,000
SALES (est): 2.8MM **Privately Held**
WEB: www.universalwireinc.com
SIC: 3496 Miscellaneous fabricated wire products

(P-13442)
US RIGGING SUPPLY CORP
1600 E Mcfadden Ave, Santa Ana
(92705-4310)
PHONE..................714 545-7444
Richard T Walker, *CEO*
Andre Mendoza, *General Mgr*
Joyce Sandstyke, *Human Res Mgr*

Paul Ottone, *Opers Staff*
Eddie Arias, *Sales Staff*
◆ **EMP:** 50
SQ FT: 20,000
SALES (est): 11MM **Privately Held**
WEB: www.usrigging.com
SIC: 3496 5051 Miscellaneous fabricated wire products; rope, wire (not insulated)

(P-13443)
VOLK ENTERPRISES INC
618 S Kilroy Rd, Turlock (95380-9531)
PHONE..................209 632-3826
Anthony Volks, *Manager*
EMP: 60 **Privately Held**
SIC: 3496 3089 Miscellaneous fabricated wire products; plastic processing
PA: Volk Enterprises, Inc.
1335 Ridgeland Pkwy # 120
Alpharetta GA 30004

(P-13444)
WALKER CORPORATION
1555 S Vintage Ave, Ontario (91761-3655)
P.O. Box 2146, Bakersfield (93303-2146)
PHONE..................909 390-4300
Randall Walker, *Vice Pres*
EMP: 35 **EST:** 2015
SALES (est): 7.9MM **Privately Held**
SIC: 3496 Miscellaneous fabricated wire products

(P-13445)
WESTERN WIRE WORKS INC
7923 Cartilla Ave, Rancho Cucamonga
(91730-3069)
PHONE..................909 483-1186
Zanley I Galton, *President*
EMP: 13
SALES (corp-wide): 33.6MM **Privately Held**
SIC: 3496 Woven wire products
PA: Western Wire Works, Inc.
3950 Nw Saint Helens Rd
Portland OR 97210
503 445-0319

(P-13446)
WHITMOR PLSTIC WIRE CABLE CORP (PA)
Also Called: Whitmor Wire and Cable
27737 Avenue Hopkins, Santa Clarita
(91355-1223)
PHONE..................661 257-2400
Michael Weiss, *President*
Mark Lee, *Vice Pres*
Stella Reaza, *Principal*
Jeff Siebert, *VP Mfg*
Cole McCaslin, *Sales Staff*
▼ **EMP:** 92 **EST:** 1959
SQ FT: 50,000
SALES (est): 32MM **Privately Held**
WEB: www.wireandcable.com
SIC: 3496 5063 3357 Cable, uninsulated wire: made from purchased wire; electrical apparatus & equipment; nonferrous wiredrawing & insulating

(P-13447)
WHITMOR PLSTIC WIRE CABLE CORP
Also Called: Whitmor Wirenetics
28420 Stanford Ave, Valencia (91355)
PHONE..................661 257-2400
Jeff Siebert, *Vice Pres*
EMP: 40
SALES (est): 5MM
SALES (corp-wide): 32MM **Privately Held**
SIC: 3496 5063 Cable, uninsulated wire: made from purchased wire; electrical apparatus & equipment
PA: Whitmor Plastic Wire And Cable Corp.
27737 Avenue Hopkins
Santa Clarita CA 91355
661 257-2400

(P-13448)
WYREFAB INC
15711 S Broadway, Gardena (90248-2401)
P.O. Box 3767 (90247-7467)
PHONE..................310 523-2147
Charles Nick, *President*
John P Massey, *Corp Secy*
Johnathan Massey, *Production*

PRODUCTS & SVCS

Victor Henriquez, *Supervisor*
EMP: 42 **EST:** 1948
SQ FT: 55,000
SALES (est): 7.9MM **Privately Held**
WEB: www.wyrefab.com
SIC: 3496 Miscellaneous fabricated wire
products

(P-13449)
Z B WIRE WORKS INC
1139 Brooks St, Ontario (91762-3607)
PHONE.....................909 391-0995
Guadalupe Zamarripa, *President*
Carmen Zamarripa, *Shareholder*
Jose Zamarripa, *Shareholder*
Alvaro Zammaripa, *Shareholder*
Paul Zammarripa, *Shareholder*
EMP: 10
SQ FT: 10,000
SALES (est): 1.7MM **Privately Held**
WEB: www.zbwireworks.com
SIC: 3496 Miscellaneous fabricated wire
products

3497 Metal Foil & Leaf

(P-13450)
AAMSTAMP MACHINE COMPANY LLC
38960 Trade Center Dr B, Palmdale
(93551-3662)
PHONE.....................661 272-0500
Gordon Starr, *Mng Member*
Ron Johnson, *Opers Mgr*
Matthew Starr,
EMP: 10
SQ FT: 10,000
SALES: 1.2MM **Privately Held**
WEB: www.aamstamp.com
SIC: 3497 Metal foil & leaf

(P-13451)
FRM USA LLC
Also Called: Framing Fabrics International
6001 Santa Monica Blvd, Los Angeles
(90038-1807)
PHONE.....................323 469-9006
Chaim Neuberg, *CEO*
Larry Neuberg, *Principal*
EMP: 50
SQ FT: 15,000
SALES (est): 4.3MM **Privately Held**
WEB: www.framingfabrics.com
SIC: 3497 Metal foil & leaf

(P-13452)
MATERION BRUSH INC
Also Called: Brush Wellman
44036 S Grimmer Blvd, Fremont
(94538-6346)
PHONE.....................510 623-1500
Edward Hefter, *Managing Dir*
Priscilla Adkins, *Info Tech Dir*
EMP: 40
SQ FT: 50,000
SALES (corp-wide): 1.2B **Publicly Held**
WEB: www.brushwellman.com
SIC: 3497 3442 3699 3444 Metal foil &
leaf; window & door frames; electrical
equipment & supplies; sheet metalwork;
engineering services
HQ: Materion Brush Inc.
6070 Parkland Blvd Ste 1
Mayfield Heights OH 44124
216 486-4200

(P-13453)
NORTH PACIFIC INTERNATIONAL
5944 Sycamore Ct, Chino (91710-9138)
PHONE.....................909 628-2224
Tsugio Imai, *President*
▲ **EMP:** 10
SQ FT: 13,000
SALES (est): 3MM **Privately Held**
WEB: www.npcfoil.com
SIC: 3497 2396 Metal foil & leaf; fabric
printing & stamping

3498 Fabricated Pipe & Pipe Fittings

(P-13454)
ACCURATE TUBE BENDING INC
37770 Timber St, Newark (94560-4443)
P.O. Box 990, Fremont (94537-0990)
PHONE.....................510 790-6500
Jon Morrow, *President*
EMP: 33
SQ FT: 28,000
SALES (est): 6.2MM **Privately Held**
WEB: www.atbending.com
SIC: 3498 Tube fabricating (contract bend-
ing & shaping)

(P-13455)
AEROFIT LLC
1425 S Acacia Ave, Fullerton (92831-5317)
PHONE.....................714 521-5060
Jordan A Law, *Managing Prtnr*
David A Werner, *Partner*
▲ **EMP:** 150
SQ FT: 67,000
SALES (est): 46.2MM
SALES (corp-wide): 167.6MM **Privately
Held**
WEB: www.aerofit.net
SIC: 3498 Pipe fittings, fabricated from
purchased pipe
PA: Consolidated Aerospace Manufactur-
ing, Llc
1425 S Acacia Ave
Fullerton CA 92831
714 989-2797

(P-13456)
AL & KRLA PIPE FABRICATORS INC
Also Called: Pipe Fabricators International
8047 Wing Ave, El Cajon (92020-1245)
PHONE.....................619 448-0060
Alvaro Mena, *President*
EMP: 12
SALES: 450K **Privately Held**
SIC: 3498 Fabricated pipe & fittings

(P-13457)
AMERIFLEX INC
2390 Railroad St, Corona (92880-5410)
PHONE.....................951 737-5557
John Bagnuolo, *CEO*
Chester Kwasniak, *CFO*
▲ **EMP:** 76
SQ FT: 32,000
SALES (est): 18.3MM
SALES (corp-wide): 185.9MM **Privately
Held**
WEB: www.ameriflex.net
SIC: 3498 3494 3674 Fabricated pipe &
fittings; valves & pipe fittings; semicon-
ductors & related devices
HQ: Mw Industries, Inc.
9501 Tech Blvd Ste 401
Rosemont IL 60018
847 349-5760

(P-13458)
ANVIL INTERNATIONAL LLC
551 N Loop Dr, Ontario (91761-8629)
PHONE.....................909 418-3233
Gwyn Lundy, *Credit Mgr*
EMP: 12 **Privately Held**
WEB: www.anvilint.com
SIC: 3498 3321 3317 Fabricated pipe &
fittings; gray & ductile iron foundries; steel
pipe & tubes
HQ: Anvil International, Llc
2 Holland Way
Exeter NH 03833
603 418-2800

(P-13459)
B F MC GILLA INC
Also Called: Advance Pipe Bending & Fabg
Co
2020 E Slauson Ave, Huntington Park
(90255-2726)
PHONE.....................323 581-8288
Gary McCray, *President*
Peter Bowman, *Corp Secy*
Malcolm Field, *Vice Pres*
EMP: 20 **EST:** 1976
SQ FT: 4,100

SALES (est): 3.3MM **Privately Held**
WEB: www.advancepipebending.com
SIC: 3498 Tube fabricating (contract bend-
ing & shaping)

(P-13460)
BAKER COUPLING COMPANY INC
2929 S Santa Fe Ave, Vernon
(90058-1425)
PHONE.....................323 583-3444
Ramendra Satyarthi, *President*
▲ **EMP:** 35
SQ FT: 65,000
SALES (est): 7.9MM **Privately Held**
WEB: www.bdssoftware.com
SIC: 3498 Couplings, pipe: fabricated from
purchased pipe; pipe fittings, fabricated
from purchased pipe

(P-13461)
BASSANI MANUFACTURING
Also Called: Bassani Exhaust
2900 E La Jolla St, Anaheim (92806-1305)
PHONE.....................714 630-1821
Darryl Bassani, *President*
Becky Bassani, *Corp Secy*
Kurt Gordon, *Manager*
▲ **EMP:** 46 **EST:** 1969
SQ FT: 20,791
SALES (est): 9.9MM **Privately Held**
WEB: www.bassani.com
SIC: 3498 3599 Fabricated pipe & fittings;
machine shop, jobbing & repair

(P-13462)
CAL PIPE MANUFACTURING INC (PA)
Also Called: Calpipe Security Bollards
19440 S Dminguez Hills Dr, Compton
(90220-6417)
PHONE.....................562 803-4388
Dan Markus, *President*
Sheri Caine-Markus, *Vice Pres*
▲ **EMP:** 45
SQ FT: 125,000
SALES (est): 9.5MM **Privately Held**
WEB: www.calpipe.com
SIC: 3498 Tube fabricating (contract bend-
ing & shaping)

(P-13463)
CALIFORNIA PIPE FABRICATORS
7277 Chevron Way, Dixon (95620-9772)
PHONE.....................707 678-3069
Dennis A Rinearson, *President*
Brenda Rinearson, *Vice Pres*
EMP: 35
SQ FT: 4,800
SALES: 7MM **Privately Held**
SIC: 3498 Fabricated pipe & fittings

(P-13464)
COTT TECHNOLOGIES INC
14923 Proctor Ave, La Puente
(91746-3206)
PHONE.....................626 961-3399
Gilbert L Decardenas, *President*
George C Salmas, *Vice Pres*
EMP: 11
SALES (est): 1.4MM **Privately Held**
WEB: www.cotttechnologies.com
SIC: 3498 Piping systems for pulp paper &
chemical industries

(P-13465)
CRYOWORKS INC
3309 Grapevine St, Mira Loma
(91752-3503)
PHONE.....................951 360-0920
Timothy L Mast, *President*
Tamara Sipos, *CFO*
Donna J Mast, *Vice Pres*
EMP: 30
SALES: 5.9MM **Privately Held**
SIC: 3498 1711 Fabricated pipe & fittings;
plumbing contractors

(P-13466)
CUSTOM PIPE & FABRICATION INC (HQ)
10560 Fern Ave, Stanton (90680-2648)
P.O. Box 978 (90680-0978)
PHONE.....................800 553-3058

Danny Daniel, *CEO*
Leonard Shapiro, *Treasurer*
Tara Kirkland, *Sales Staff*
Jerry Witkow, *Asst Sec*
Rosa Gonzalez, *Supervisor*
▲ **EMP:** 60
SQ FT: 8,000
SALES: 72.5MM
SALES (corp-wide): 72.3MM **Privately
Held**
WEB: www.custompipe.com
SIC: 3498 Tube fabricating (contract bend-
ing & shaping)
PA: Shapco Inc.
1666 20th St Ste 100
Santa Monica CA 90404
310 264-1666

(P-13467)
EDMUND A GRAY CO (PA)
2277 E 15th St, Los Angeles (90021-2852)
PHONE.....................213 625-0376
Lawrence Gray Jr, *CEO*
Patricia Gray, *Treasurer*
Lawrence Gray III, *Vice Pres*
Anna Ramos, *Finance Mgr*
Alma Corral, *Finance*
▲ **EMP:** 71
SQ FT: 50,000
SALES (est): 17.5MM **Privately Held**
WEB: www.eagray.com
SIC: 3498 Pipe fittings, fabricated from
purchased pipe

(P-13468)
ELECTROLURGY INC
Also Called: Electrolurgy Manufacturing
1217 E Normandy Pl, Santa Ana
(92705-4135)
PHONE.....................714 641-7488
Sean Eklund, *Owner*
Lisa Arangua, *Controller*
Nina White, *Purchasing*
EMP: 35
SALES (corp-wide): 14.1MM **Privately
Held**
WEB: www.electrolurgy.com
SIC: 3498 Tube fabricating (contract bend-
ing & shaping)
PA: Electrolurgy, Inc.
1121 Duryea Ave
Irvine CA 92614
949 250-4494

(P-13469)
EXPRESS PIPE & SUPPLY CO LLC (DH)
Also Called: Expressions Home Gallery
1235 S Lewis St, Santa Monica (90404)
PHONE.....................310 204-7238
Greg Boiko, *President*
EMP: 36
SALES (est): 61.8MM **Privately Held**
SIC: 3498 5074 Pipe fittings, fabricated
from purchased pipe; plumbing & hy-
dronic heating supplies
HQ: Morsco Supply, Llc
15850 Dallas Pkwy Fl 2
Dallas TX 75248
877 709-2227

(P-13470)
FLEXIBLE METAL INC (HQ)
Also Called: FMI
1685 Brandywine Ave, Chula Vista
(91911-6020)
PHONE.....................678 280-0127
Donald R Heye, *CEO*
◆ **EMP:** 70
SALES (est): 40.2MM
SALES (corp-wide): 96.5MM **Privately
Held**
WEB: www.flexiblemetal.com
SIC: 3498 Fabricated pipe & fittings
PA: Hyspan Precision Products, Inc.
1685 Brandywine Ave
Chula Vista CA 91911
619 421-1355

(P-13471)
FLO-MAC INC
1846 E 60th St, Los Angeles (90001-1420)
P.O. Box 1078, Huntington Park (90255-
1078)
PHONE.....................323 583-8751
Larry Smith, *President*

▲ = Import ▼=Export
◆ =Import/Export

Mark Smith, *Treasurer*
Scott Crane, *Vice Pres*
EMP: 21 **EST:** 1974
SQ FT: 14,000
SALES (est): 4.7MM **Privately Held**
WEB: www.flo-mac.com
SIC: 3498 Pipe fittings, fabricated from purchased pipe

(P-13472)
ILCO INDUSTRIES INC
1308 W Mahalo Pl, Compton (90220-5418)
PHONE..................................310 631-8655
Elias Awad, *President*
EMP: 35
SQ FT: 23,000
SALES (est): 7.1MM **Privately Held**
WEB: www.ilcoind.com
SIC: 3498 3492 Manifolds, pipe: fabricated from purchased pipe; pipe fittings, fabricated from purchased pipe; pipe sections fabricated from purchased pipe; tube fabricating (contract bending & shaping); hose & tube fittings & assemblies, hydraulic/pneumatic

(P-13473)
JIFCO INC (PA)
Also Called: Jifco Fabaricated Piping
571 Exchange Ct, Livermore (94550-2400)
P.O. Box 589 (94551-0589)
PHONE..................................925 449-4665
Jay Forni Jr, *President*
Kevin Krausgrill, *Executive*
Kerry Thach, *Project Mgr*
Monica Spina Forni, *Director*
Jeffrey Hill, *Director*
EMP: 60
SALES (est): 17.4MM **Privately Held**
WEB: www.jifco.com
SIC: 3498 Tube fabricating (contract bending & shaping)

(P-13474)
KAISER ENTERPRISES INC
Also Called: Insight Mfg Services
798 Murphys Creek Rd, Murphys (95247-9562)
P.O. Box 2609 (95247-2609)
PHONE..................................209 728-2091
Loretta Dietz Kaiser, *President*
Herman Kaiser, *COO*
Jonelle Lewis, *Human Resources*
Suzanne Lewis, *Purchasing*
EMP: 75
SQ FT: 6,900
SALES: 15MM **Privately Held**
SIC: 3498 Coils, pipe: fabricated from purchased pipe

(P-13475)
LEVCO FAB INC
10757 Fremont Ave, Ontario (91762-3910)
PHONE..................................909 465-0840
Ben Levacy, *President*
Gail Levacy, *CFO*
EMP: 11
SQ FT: 6,000
SALES (est): 1.9MM **Privately Held**
SIC: 3498 Fabricated pipe & fittings

(P-13476)
MARINE & INDUSTRIAL SERVICES
2391 W 10th St, Antioch (94509-1366)
PHONE..................................925 757-8791
Thomas M Hannaford, *President*
Janell Mollenhauer, *Accounting Mgr*
Kyle Hannaford, *Manager*
John Cherry, *Superintendent*
EMP: 16
SQ FT: 21,000
SALES (est): 3.7MM **Privately Held**
SIC: 3498 Pipe fittings, fabricated from purchased pipe

(P-13477)
MD STAINLESS SERVICES
8241 Phlox St, Downey (90241-4841)
PHONE..................................562 904-7022
Marvin Davis, *President*
Sunshine Olsen, *Treasurer*
Ralph Gallardo, *General Mgr*
Clay Guinaldo, *Purch Mgr*
EMP: 20
SQ FT: 15,000

SALES (est): 6MM **Privately Held**
WEB: www.mdstainless.com
SIC: 3498 1711 Fabricated pipe & fittings; process piping contractor

(P-13478)
ONE-WAY MANUFACTURING INC
1195 N Osprey Cir, Anaheim (92807-1709)
PHONE..................................714 630-8833
Sue Huang, *CEO*
Ike Huang, *COO*
EMP: 23
SQ FT: 19,400
SALES (est): 5.1MM **Privately Held**
WEB: www.onewaymfg.com
SIC: 3498 3599 1541 7692 Tube fabricating (contract bending & shaping); machine & other job shop work; truck & automobile assembly plant construction; welding repair; mechanical engineering; fluxes: brazing, soldering, galvanizing & welding

(P-13479)
PERFORMANCE TUBE BENDING INC
5462 Diaz St, Baldwin Park (91706-2026)
PHONE..................................626 939-9000
Jaime R Renella, *President*
▲ **EMP:** 17
SALES (est): 3.1MM **Privately Held**
SIC: 3498 Tube fabricating (contract bending & shaping)

(P-13480)
PERNSTNER SONS FABRICATION INC
712 W Harding Rd, Turlock (95380-9743)
PHONE..................................209 345-2430
Jesse J Pernsteiner, *President*
EMP: 14
SALES: 120K **Privately Held**
SIC: 3498 Fabricated pipe & fittings

(P-13481)
PIPE FABRICATING & SUPPLY CO (PA)
1235 N Kraemer Blvd, Anaheim (92806-1921)
PHONE..................................714 630-5200
Fred E Simmons, *CEO*
Jerry Eagle, *Vice Pres*
John M Eagle, *Vice Pres*
Ernie Simmons, *Vice Pres*
▲ **EMP:** 100 **EST:** 1945
SQ FT: 90,000
SALES: 11.2MM **Privately Held**
WEB: www.pipefab.com
SIC: 3498 Tube fabricating (contract bending & shaping)

(P-13482)
PRECISION TUBE BENDING
13626 Talc St, Santa Fe Springs (90670-5173)
PHONE..................................562 921-6723
Diane M Williams, *CEO*
Charles Thomas, *Mfg Staff*
Philip Stephen, *Sales Staff*
John Phipps, *Director*
Bonnie Mayo, *Manager*
EMP: 98
SQ FT: 60,000
SALES (est): 29.1MM **Privately Held**
WEB: www.precision-tube-bending.com
SIC: 3498 Tube fabricating (contract bending & shaping)

(P-13483)
RIGHT MANUFACTURING LLC
7949 Stromesa Ct Ste G, San Diego (92126-6338)
PHONE..................................858 566-7002
Greg Lyon,
Byrd Lh, *Mfg Mgr*
▲ **EMP:** 30 **EST:** 1971
SQ FT: 15,000
SALES (est): 6.6MM **Privately Held**
SIC: 3498 3444 Tube fabricating (contract bending & shaping); sheet metalwork

(P-13484)
RUSSELL FABRICATION CORP
Also Called: American Fabrication
4940 Gilmore Ave, Bakersfield (93308-6150)
PHONE..................................661 861-8495
Kevin Russell, *President*
EMP: 45
SALES (est): 9.9MM **Privately Held**
SIC: 3498 3444 Fabricated pipe & fittings; sheet metalwork

(P-13485)
SAN FRANCISCO PIPE &
Also Called: SF Tube
23099 Connecticut St, Hayward (94545-1605)
PHONE..................................510 785-9148
Rafael M Nunez, *CEO*
Ray Yamanaka, *General Mgr*
Steven Yamanaka, *QC Mgr*
EMP: 46
SALES (est): 9.3MM **Privately Held**
WEB: www.sfpipetube.com
SIC: 3498 Tube fabricating (contract bending & shaping)

(P-13486)
SUPERIOR TUBE PIPE BNDING FBCO
Also Called: Superior Tbeppe Bnding Fbrctn
2407 Industrial Pkwy W, Hayward (94545-5007)
PHONE..................................510 782-9311
Jon T Morrow Jr, *President*
EMP: 50 **EST:** 1965
SQ FT: 22,000
SALES (est): 6.5MM **Privately Held**
SIC: 3498 Tube fabricating (contract bending & shaping); pipe sections fabricated from purchased pipe

(P-13487)
TRINITY PROCESS SOLUTIONS INC
4740 E Bryson St, Anaheim (92807-1901)
PHONE..................................714 701-1112
Jack Brunner, *President*
Candace Brunner, *Vice Pres*
EMP: 20
SQ FT: 13,000
SALES: 3.9MM **Privately Held**
WEB: www.trinityprocesssolutions.com
SIC: 3498 3317 8711 Fabricated pipe & fittings; welded pipe & tubes; engineering services

(P-13488)
TRYMAX
5900 E Lerdo Hwy, Shafter (93263-4023)
PHONE..................................661 391-1572
Jim Garner, *Owner*
Wayne Hicks, *Principal*
▲ **EMP:** 11 **EST:** 2010
SALES (est): 1.3MM **Privately Held**
SIC: 3498 Fabricated pipe & fittings

(P-13489)
TUBE BENDING LLC
4747 Citrus Dr, Pico Rivera (90660-2034)
PHONE..................................562 692-5829
Richard Alvarez,
Beatrice Alvarez,
EMP: 12 **EST:** 2004
SQ FT: 6,460
SALES (est): 1.3MM **Privately Held**
SIC: 3498 Tube fabricating (contract bending & shaping)

(P-13490)
U S WEATHERFORD L P
19468 Creek Rd, Bakersfield (93314-8451)
PHONE..................................661 746-1391
Geary Colvin, *Branch Mgr*
EMP: 18 **Privately Held**
SIC: 3498 3533 Fabricated pipe & fittings; oil field machinery & equipment
HQ: U S Weatherford L P
179 Weatherford Dr
Schriever LA 70395
985 493-6100

(P-13491)
WEATHERFORD INTERNATIONAL LLC
201 Hallock Dr, Santa Paula (93060-9647)
PHONE..................................805 933-0200
EMP: 51 **Privately Held**
SIC: 3498 3533 Fabricated pipe & fittings; oil & gas field machinery
HQ: Weatherford International, Llc
2000 Saint James Pl
Houston TX 77056
713 693-4000

(P-13492)
WESSEX INDUSTRIES INC
8619 Red Oak St, Rancho Cucamonga (91730-4820)
PHONE..................................562 944-5760
Archie Castillo, *President*
Linne A Castillo, *CFO*
Edward Mojica, *Vice Pres*
EMP: 25
SQ FT: 30,000
SALES (est): 6.3MM **Privately Held**
WEB: www.wessexindustriesinc.com
SIC: 3498 8742 Pipe fittings, fabricated from purchased pipe; pipe sections fabricated from purchased pipe; management consulting services

---

3499 Fabricated Metal Prdts, NEC

(P-13493)
A-L-L MAGNETICS
Also Called: Magnet Source Tm, The
2831 E Via Martens, Anaheim (92806-1751)
PHONE..................................714 632-1754
John E Nellessen, *CEO*
Edith Johnson, *Sales Mgr*
Rosemary Kute, *Sales Staff*
▲ **EMP:** 11
SQ FT: 14,000
SALES (est): 2.4MM **Privately Held**
WEB: www.allmagnetics.com
SIC: 3499 5945 5943 5199 Magnets, permanent: metallic; arts & crafts supplies; school supplies; advertising specialties

(P-13494)
AG SPRAYING
5815 S Calaveras Ave, Tranquillity (93668-9709)
P.O. Box 686 (93668-0686)
PHONE..................................559 698-9507
Nino W Carvalho, *Owner*
EMP: 10
SALES (est): 250K **Privately Held**
SIC: 3499 Nozzles, spray: aerosol, paint or insecticide

(P-13495)
ALPHA MAGNETICS INC
23453 Bernhardt St, Hayward (94545-1622)
PHONE..................................510 732-6698
Ken Wadsworth, *President*
▲ **EMP:** 10 **EST:** 1972
SQ FT: 20,000
SALES (est): 1.8MM **Privately Held**
WEB: www.alphamag.com
SIC: 3499 Magnets, permanent: metallic

(P-13496)
AMERICAN SECURITY PRODUCTS CO
Also Called: Amsec
11925 Pacific Ave, Fontana (92337-8231)
P.O. Box 317001 (92331-7001)
PHONE..................................951 685-9680
Dave Lazier, *CEO*
Tom Cassutt, *CFO*
Thomas Cassutt, *Bd of Directors*
Tony Maniaci, *Vice Pres*
Robert Sallee, *Vice Pres*
◆ **EMP:** 220
SQ FT: 150,000
SALES (est): 49.1MM **Privately Held**
SIC: 3499 1731 Safes & vaults, metal; safety & security specialization

PRODUCTS & SVCS

(P-13497)
ANACROWN INC
Also Called: Lantor
25835 Narbonne Ave # 250, Lomita
(90717-3074)
PHONE....................................310 530-1165
Victor A Jauch, *President*
Kefeng Xu, *Sales Staff*
▲ EMP: 12
SQ FT: 18,000
SALES: 859.5K **Privately Held**
WEB: www.anacrown.com
SIC: 3499 5992 Novelties & giftware, including trophies; florists

(P-13498)
ANDERSON BROS ARTISTIC IRON CO
310 Elizabeth Ln, Corona (92880-2504)
PHONE....................................951 898-6880
Dennis Anderson, *President*
Dale Anderson, *Vice Pres*
EMP: 10
SQ FT: 10,000
SALES (est): 1.4MM **Privately Held**
SIC: 3499 1791 Ironing boards, metal; iron work, structural

(P-13499)
ARTISAN HOUSE INC
8238 Lankershim Blvd, North Hollywood
(91605-1613)
PHONE....................................818 767-7476
Dennis Damore, *Branch Mgr*
EMP: 30
SALES (corp-wide): 2.7MM **Privately Held**
PA: Artisan House, Inc.
3750 Cohasset St
Burbank CA 91505
818 565-5030

(P-13500)
ARVI MANUFACTURING INC
1256 Birchwood Dr Ste B, Sunnyvale
(94089-2205)
PHONE....................................408 734-4776
Harold Kirksey, *CEO*
Rita Kirksey, *CFO*
▲ EMP: 11
SQ FT: 5,000
SALES: 1.4MM **Privately Held**
WEB: www.arvi.net
SIC: 3499 Machine bases, metal

(P-13501)
BARRICADE CO & TRAFFIC SUP INC (PA)
Also Called: T B C
3963 Santa Rosa Ave, Santa Rosa
(95407-8274)
PHONE....................................707 523-2350
Jennifer R Pitts, *President*
Robert F Pitts, *Admin Sec*
EMP: 17
SQ FT: 21,000
SALES (est): 5.4MM **Privately Held**
WEB: www.barri-cade.com
SIC: 3499 Barricades, metal

(P-13502)
BEY-BERK INTERNATIONAL (PA)
9145 Deering Ave, Chatsworth
(91311-5802)
PHONE....................................818 773-7534
Kurken Y Berksanlar, *President*
Serop Beylerian, *Vice Pres*
◆ EMP: 24
SQ FT: 19,800
SALES (est): 3.9MM **Privately Held**
SIC: 3499 3873 Novelties & giftware, including trophies; clocks, assembly of

(P-13503)
BISHOP-WISECARVER CORPORATION (PA)
2104 Martin Way, Pittsburg (94565-5027)
PHONE....................................925 439-8272
Pamela Kan, *CEO*
Ali Jabbari, *President*
Shelley Galvin, *Treasurer*
Scott McClintock, *Vice Pres*
Kelly Walden, *Vice Pres*
▲ EMP: 55

SQ FT: 80,000
SALES (est): 14.4MM **Privately Held**
WEB: www.bwc.com
SIC: 3499 5085 3823 Machine bases, metal; bearings; industrial instrmnts msrmnt display/control process variable

(P-13504)
BULLET GUARD CORPORATION
3963 Commerce Dr, West Sacramento
(95691-2168)
PHONE....................................800 233-5632
Sharon Durst, *CEO*
Karlin Lynch, *President*
Marcia Lynch, *Corp Secy*
Sheila Lane, *Sales Mgr*
EMP: 14
SQ FT: 36,000
SALES (est): 4.1MM **Privately Held**
WEB: www.bulletguard.com
SIC: 3499 5099 1796 3316 Fire- or burglary-resistive products; safety equipment & supplies; installing building equipment; cold finishing of steel shapes; blast furnaces & steel mills; products of purchased glass

(P-13505)
CAL-WELD INC
4308 Solar Way, Fremont (94538-6335)
PHONE....................................510 226-0100
Maurice Carson, *President*
EMP: 116
SALES (est): 49.1MM
SALES (corp-wide): 823.6MM **Publicly Held**
SIC: 3499 Aerosol valves, metal
HQ: Ichor Holdings, Llc
9660 Sw Herman Rd
Tualatin OR 97062
503 625-2251

(P-13506)
CALIFORNIA COMPACTOR SVC INC
17000 Sierra Hwy, Canyon Country
(91351-1615)
PHONE....................................661 298-5556
Linda Nevill, *Principal*
EMP: 15 EST: 2014
SALES (est): 1.2MM **Privately Held**
SIC: 3499 Bank chests, metal

(P-13507)
CALRAM LLC
829 Via Alondra, Camarillo (93012-8046)
PHONE....................................805 987-6205
Dwayne Perkar, *CEO*
EMP: 10
SQ FT: 25,000
SALES (est): 627.6K
SALES (corp-wide): 2.3B **Publicly Held**
WEB: www.calraminc.com
SIC: 3499 Novelties & specialties, metal
PA: Carpenter Technology Corporation
1735 Market St Fl 15
Philadelphia PA 19103
610 208-2000

(P-13508)
CAPSTAN CALIFORNIA INC (PA)
16100 S Figueroa St, Gardena
(90248-2617)
PHONE....................................310 366-5999
Mark Paullin, *CEO*
Bonita Gonzales, *CFO*
▲ EMP: 500
SALES (est): 83MM **Privately Held**
WEB: www.capstanatlantic.com
SIC: 3499 Friction material, made from powdered metal

(P-13509)
CHATSWORTH PRODUCTS INC (PA)
Also Called: C P I
29899 Agoura Rd Ste 120, Agoura Hills
(91301-2493)
PHONE....................................818 735-6100
Larry Renaud, *President*
Tom Jorgenson, *CFO*
Larry Varblow, *Corp Secy*
Ted Behrens, *Exec VP*
Wesley Gass, *Vice Pres*
◆ EMP: 25
SQ FT: 16,000

SALES (est): 107.3MM **Privately Held**
WEB: www.chatsworth.com
SIC: 3499 2542 Machine bases, metal; partitions & fixtures, except wood

(P-13510)
CHATSWORTH PRODUCTS INC
9353 Winnetka Ave, Chatsworth
(91311-6033)
PHONE....................................818 882-8595
Michael Custer, *Manager*
Josue Garcia, *Engineer*
EMP: 177
SQ FT: 68,634
SALES (corp-wide): 107.3MM **Privately Held**
WEB: www.chatsworth.com
SIC: 3499 2542 Machine bases, metal; partitions & fixtures, except wood
PA: Chatsworth Products, Inc.
29899 Agoura Rd Ste 120
Agoura Hills CA 91301
818 735-6100

(P-13511)
CORK POPS
7 Commercial Blvd Ste 3, Novato
(94949-6106)
PHONE....................................415 884-6000
William Federighi, *President*
Linda Bridges, *Vice Pres*
Susan Federighi, *Admin Sec*
Susan Poti, *Controller*
◆ EMP: 10
SQ FT: 17,000
SALES (est): 1.6MM **Privately Held**
WEB: www.corkpops.com
SIC: 3499 Novelties & specialties, metal

(P-13512)
CRAFTED METALS INC
9220 Birch St, Spring Valley (91977-4111)
PHONE....................................619 464-1090
John Wheeler, *President*
Vivian Wheeler, *Vice Pres*
EMP: 10
SQ FT: 10,000
SALES (est): 1.9MM **Privately Held**
WEB: www.craftedmetals.com
SIC: 3499 Metal ladders

(P-13513)
DEC FABRICATORS INC
16916 Gridley Pl, Cerritos (90703-1740)
PHONE....................................562 403-3626
William Befort, *President*
EMP: 18
SQ FT: 20,000
SALES (est): 3.3MM **Privately Held**
WEB: www.decfabricators.com
SIC: 3499 2434 Furniture parts, metal; wood kitchen cabinets

(P-13514)
DIVERSE MCHNNG FBRICATION LLC
Also Called: Component Finishing
3620 Cincinnati Ave Ste A, Rocklin
(95765-1203)
P.O. Box 348327, Sacramento (95834-8327)
PHONE....................................916 672-6591
Wade F Gadberry,
Wade Gadberry,
EMP: 13
SQ FT: 5,000
SALES: 398.4K **Privately Held**
WEB: www.componentfinishing.com
SIC: 3499 Ammunition boxes, metal

(P-13515)
DO IT AMERICAN MFG COMPANY LLC
137 Vander St, Corona (92880-1752)
PHONE....................................951 254-9204
Moises Vasquez, *Mng Member*
Jon Armstrong, *VP Opers*
Kathy Armstrong, *Marketing Mgr*
John Armstrong,
Alicia Macias,
EMP: 16
SQ FT: 20,000
SALES (est): 4.4MM **Privately Held**
SIC: 3499 3545 8711 Machine bases, metal; machine tool accessories; engineering services

(P-13516)
DOT BLUE SAFES CORPORATION
2707 N Garey Ave, Pomona (91767-1809)
PHONE....................................909 445-8888
Berge Jalakian, *CEO*
Kevin Trimble, *Director*
▲ EMP: 42
SQ FT: 90,000
SALES (est): 15.4MM **Privately Held**
SIC: 3499 8741 Safes & vaults, metal; management services

(P-13517)
DSTYLE INC
Also Called: Allan Copley Designs
3451 Main St Ste 108, Chula Vista
(91911-5894)
PHONE....................................619 662-0560
Roberto Besquin, *Manager*
Lonnie Nicholson, *Vice Pres*
▲ EMP: 10
SQ FT: 40,000
SALES (est): 2.2MM
SALES (corp-wide): 768MM **Publicly Held**
SIC: 3499 5021 Furniture parts, metal; furniture
PA: Kimball International, Inc.
1600 Royal St
Jasper IN 47546
812 482-1600

(P-13518)
DUST COLLECTOR SERVICES INC
1280 N Sunshine Way, Anaheim
(92806-1746)
PHONE....................................714 237-1690
Timothy Schlentz, *President*
Gregory Schlentz, *Vice Pres*
Jannie Schlentz, *Vice Pres*
Jeff Schlentz, *Vice Pres*
Greg Schlentz, *Sales Staff*
EMP: 20
SQ FT: 10,000
SALES (est): 3.9MM **Privately Held**
WEB: www.dustcollectorservices.com
SIC: 3499 Aerosol valves, metal

(P-13519)
ECOOLTHING CORP
Also Called: Cool Things
1321 E Saint Gertrude Pl A, Santa Ana
(92705-5241)
P.O. Box 6022, Irvine (92616-6022)
PHONE....................................714 368-4791
Connie Wang, *President*
Linda Wang, *Vice Pres*
▲ EMP: 50
SQ FT: 10,000
SALES: 12.8MM **Privately Held**
SIC: 3499 5199 Novelties & giftware, including trophies; gifts & novelties

(P-13520)
ENERGY ABSORPTION SYSTEMS INC
3617 Cincinnati Ave, Rocklin (95765-1202)
PHONE....................................916 645-8181
Barry Stephens, *Manager*
EMP: 150
SQ FT: 22,968
SALES (corp-wide): 2.5B **Publicly Held**
WEB: www.energyabsorption.com
SIC: 3499 3842 3669 3823 Barricades, metal; surgical appliances & supplies; transportation signaling devices; absorption analyzers: infrared, X-ray, etc.: industrial
HQ: Energy Absorption Systems, Inc.
70 W Madison St Ste 2350
Chicago IL 60602
312 467-6750

(P-13521)
EVANS INDUSTRIES INC
Darnell-Rose Div
17915 Railroad St, City of Industry
(91748-1113)
PHONE....................................626 912-1688
Bob Batistic, *Manager*
Rick Chichester, *Chief Mktg Ofcr*
Brent Bargar, *Vice Pres*
Kelly Grimshaw, *Office Mgr*

▲ = Import ▼=Export
◆ =Import/Export

EMP: 120
SALES (corp-wide): 43.7MM **Privately Held**
WEB: www.eiihq.com
SIC: 3499 5072 Wheels: wheelbarrow, stroller, etc.: disc, stamped metal; casters & glides
HQ: Evans Industries, Inc.
    200 Renaissance Ctr # 3150
    Detroit MI 48243
    313 259-2266

(P-13522)
EXECUTIVE SAFE AND SEC CORP
Also Called: Amphion
10722 Edison Ct, Rancho Cucamonga (91730-4845)
PHONE..................909 947-7020
Scott C Denton, *President*
Robyn Denton, *COO*
Paig Parish, *Vice Pres*
Jason Velez, *Project Mgr*
◆ **EMP:** 30 **EST:** 1999
SQ FT: 11,000
SALES (est): 7.8MM **Privately Held**
WEB: www.amphion.biz
SIC: 3499 5072 7382 5099 Safes & vaults, metal; security devices, locks; confinement surveillance systems maintenance & monitoring; locks & lock sets

(P-13523)
HY JO MFG IMPORTS CORP
7615 Siempre Viva Rd B, San Diego (92154-6217)
PHONE..................619 671-1018
John Benator, *CEO*
EMP: 25
SALES (est): 2.6MM **Privately Held**
SIC: 3499 Picture frames, metal

(P-13524)
HYSPAN PRECISION PRODUCTS INC
1683 Brandywine Ave, Chula Vista (91911)
PHONE..................619 421-1355
Bertha Mercado, *Controller*
EMP: 99
SQ FT: 60,000
SALES (est): 3.9MM **Privately Held**
SIC: 3499 Reels, cable: metal

(P-13525)
ICM INSTALLATIONS INC
1180 N Ftn Way Unit B, Anaheim (92806)
PHONE..................714 751-4026
Andrew Luketic, *President*
EMP: 10
SALES (est): 780K **Privately Held**
SIC: 3499 Aerosol valves, metal

(P-13526)
INNOVATIVE METAL PRODUCTS INC
2443 Cades Way Ste 200, Vista (92081-7885)
PHONE..................760 734-1010
Scott Whitney, *CEO*
EMP: 24 **EST:** 2006
SALES (est): 4.7MM **Privately Held**
SIC: 3499 Metal household articles

(P-13527)
J & J PRODUCTS INC
Also Called: J & J Co
9134 Independence Ave, Chatsworth (91311-5902)
PHONE..................818 998-4250
Peter Hauber, *President*
David Kline, *Controller*
Connie Dickinson, *Manager*
Gabi Girard, *Manager*
EMP: 16
SQ FT: 6,400
SALES (est): 2MM **Privately Held**
WEB: www.jandjproducts.com
SIC: 3499 5091 3089 Ammunition boxes, metal; hunting equipment & supplies; plastic processing

(P-13528)
LA PROPOINT INC
10870 La Tuna Canyon Rd, Sun Valley (91352-2009)
PHONE..................818 767-6800
Mark Riddlesperger, *President*
James Hartman, *Vice Pres*
Brad Powers, *Technical Mgr*
Rob Stevens, *Project Mgr*
Mark Youngs, *Project Mgr*
◆ **EMP:** 30
SQ FT: 28,000
SALES: 4.2MM **Privately Held**
WEB: www.lapropoint.com
SIC: 3499 3449 Metal household articles; miscellaneous metalwork

(P-13529)
LAMER STREET KREATIONS CORP
14589 Rancho Vista Dr, Fontana (92335-4299)
PHONE..................909 305-4824
Aaron Riskin, *President*
Van Syverud, *Vice Pres*
EMP: 12
SALES: 3MM **Privately Held**
SIC: 3499 8711 Fire- or burglary-resistive products; engineering services

(P-13530)
LINDSAY/BARNETT INCORPORATED
Also Called: Gallery
2194 Edison Ave Ste H, San Leandro (94577-1130)
PHONE..................510 483-6300
Christie B Jordan, *President*
EMP: 11
SQ FT: 25,000
SALES (est): 2.2MM **Privately Held**
WEB: www.galleryinc.com
SIC: 3499 3231 Novelties & giftware, including trophies; products of purchased glass

(P-13531)
MAGNETIC COMPONENT ENGRG INC (PA)
Also Called: M C E
2830 Lomita Blvd, Torrance (90505-5101)
PHONE..................310 784-3100
Linda Montgomerie, *CEO*
Slava Trosman, *Prgrmr*
Van C Le, *QC Mgr*
▲ **EMP:** 93
SQ FT: 50,000
SALES (est): 13.3MM **Privately Held**
WEB: www.mceproducts.com
SIC: 3499 3677 Magnets, permanent: metallic; electronic coils, transformers & other inductors

(P-13532)
MATERIAL CONTROL INC
Also Called: Cotterman Company
6901 District Blvd Ste A, Bakersfield (93313-2071)
PHONE..................661 617-6033
Tony Ortiz, *Branch Mgr*
EMP: 32
SALES (corp-wide): 82.6MM **Privately Held**
WEB: www.cotterman.com
SIC: 3499 Metal ladders
PA: Material Control Inc.
    130 Seltzer Rd
    Croswell MI 48422
    630 892-4274

(P-13533)
MESA SAFE COMPANY INC
337 W Freedom Ave, Orange (92865-2647)
P.O. Box 52282, Irvine (92619-2282)
PHONE..................714 202-8000
George L Vicente, *President*
Chris Nakao, *Vice Pres*
Pam Perry, *Office Mgr*
Mary Croinin, *Admin Sec*
◆ **EMP:** 40
SQ FT: 75,000

SALES (est): 5.8MM **Privately Held**
WEB: www.mesasafe.com
SIC: 3499 5044 Safes & vaults, metal; vaults & safes

(P-13534)
MICHAEL D WILSON INC
Also Called: Strathmore Ladder
19774 Orange Belt Dr, Strathmore (93267)
P.O. Box 307 (93267-0307)
PHONE..................559 568-1115
Michael D Wilson, *President*
Gary Wilson, *Treasurer*
Jeanie Wilson, *Vice Pres*
Wendi Lopez, *Accounts Exec*
EMP: 12
SQ FT: 7,800
SALES (est): 2.3MM **Privately Held**
WEB: www.citrusladder.com
SIC: 3499 Ladders, portable: metal

(P-13535)
NIBCO INC
1375 Sampson Ave, Corona (92879-1748)
PHONE..................951 737-5599
Steve Malm, *Manager*
EMP: 212
SALES (corp-wide): 683.3MM **Privately Held**
WEB: www.nibco.com
SIC: 3499 Strapping, metal
PA: Nibco Inc.
    1516 Middlebury St
    Elkhart IN 46516
    574 295-3000

(P-13536)
OLDCASTLE INFRASTRUCTURE INC
Also Called: Utility Vault
801 S Pine St, Madera (93637-5219)
PHONE..................559 674-8093
William Wood, *Manager*
EMP: 20
SQ FT: 8,000
SALES (corp-wide): 30.6B **Privately Held**
WEB: www.oldcastle-precast.com
SIC: 3499 1799 3444 3443 Safes & vaults, metal; welding on site; sheet metalwork; fabricated plate work (boiler shop)
HQ: Oldcastle Infrastructure, Inc.
    7000 Cntl Prkaway Ste 800
    Atlanta GA 30328
    470 602-2000

(P-13537)
PAPPALECCO
3650 5th Ave Ste 104, San Diego (92103-4243)
PHONE..................619 906-5566
Francesco Bucci, *Branch Mgr*
EMP: 19 **Privately Held**
SIC: 3499 Ice cream freezers, household, nonelectric: metal
PA: Pappalecco
    1602 State St
    San Diego CA 92101

(P-13538)
PEREZ SEVERINO
Also Called: Alannas Engineer Manufacturing
9710 Owensmouth Ave Lbby, Chatsworth (91311-8074)
PHONE..................818 701-1522
Severiano Perez, *Owner*
EMP: 15
SALES (est): 2.5MM **Privately Held**
SIC: 3499 8711 Machine bases, metal; engineering services

(P-13539)
PREMIER BARRICADES
28441 Felix Valdez Ave, Temecula (92590-1843)
PHONE..................877 345-9700
Conor J Loushin, *President*
EMP: 10
SALES (est): 1.7MM **Privately Held**
SIC: 3499 Barricades, metal
PA: Boston Barricade Company Inc.
    1151 19th St
    Vero Beach FL 32960

(P-13540)
PSM INDUSTRIES INC (PA)
14000 Avalon Blvd, Los Angeles (90061-2636)
PHONE..................888 663-8256
Craig Paullin, *CEO*
Mary Sherrill, *Treasurer*
Susan Paullin, *Admin Sec*
Carolina Arriaga, *Engineer*
Greg Jones, *Engineer*
▲ **EMP:** 89 **EST:** 1956
SALES (est): 22.9MM **Privately Held**
WEB: www.pacificsintered.com
SIC: 3499 Friction material, made from powdered metal

(P-13541)
QUADRANT SOLUTIONS INC
Also Called: Quadrant Technology
561 Monterey Rd, Morgan Hill (95037-9269)
PHONE..................408 463-9451
Chris Moore, *Principal*
EMP: 14
SALES (est): 2.4MM **Privately Held**
SIC: 3499 Magnets, permanent: metallic
PA: Quadrant Solutions Incorporated
    12500 Plantside Dr
    Louisville KY 40299

(P-13542)
QUALITY MAGNETICS CORPORATION
18025 Adria Maru Ln, Carson (90746-1403)
P.O. Box 1238, Desert Hot Springs (92240-0947)
PHONE..................310 632-1941
William K Buckley, *CEO*
Chante Buckley, *CFO*
▲ **EMP:** 18
SQ FT: 27,000
SALES (est): 3.9MM **Privately Held**
WEB: www.qmcnet.com
SIC: 3499 3299 Magnets, permanent: metallic; ceramic fiber

(P-13543)
R & K INDUSTRIAL PRODUCTS CO
Also Called: R&K Industrial Wheels
1945 7th St, Richmond (94801-1639)
PHONE..................510 234-7212
Jorge Ramirez, *President*
Jason Petrovski, *Controller*
EMP: 30
SQ FT: 48,000
SALES (est): 5.7MM **Privately Held**
WEB: www.rkwheels.com
SIC: 3499 Wheels: wheelbarrow, stroller, etc.: disc, stamped metal

(P-13544)
SCHOTT MAGNETICS
1401 Air Wing Rd, San Diego (92154-7705)
PHONE..................619 661-7510
Rob Rossi, *Owner*
▲ **EMP:** 16
SALES (est): 1.4MM **Privately Held**
SIC: 3499 Magnetic shields, metal

(P-13545)
SCHUMAN ENTERPRISES INC
Also Called: Js Manufacturing
1621 Ord Way, Oceanside (92056-3599)
PHONE..................760 940-1322
Joel J Schuman, *President*
Danielle Schuman, *Office Mgr*
EMP: 10 **EST:** 2010
SALES (est): 2.1MM **Privately Held**
SIC: 3499 Novelties & specialties, metal

(P-13546)
SIERRA SAFETY COMPANY
215 Taylor Rd, Newcastle (95658-9601)
PHONE..................916 663-2026
Daniel L Robinson, *President*
EMP: 14
SQ FT: 6,000
SALES (est): 4MM **Privately Held**
WEB: www.sierrasafetyco.com
SIC: 3499 Barricades, metal

PRODUCTS & SVCS

(P-13547)
SPORTSMEN STEEL SAFE FABG CO (PA)
Also Called: Sportsman Steel Gun Safe
6311 N Paramount Blvd, Long Beach
(90805-3301)
PHONE....................562 984-0244
Kevin Hand, *CEO*
Chris Cude, *CFO*
▲ EMP: 22
SQ FT: 30,000
SALES (est): 3.4MM **Privately Held**
SIC: 3499 5999 Safes & vaults, metal;
safety supplies & equipment

(P-13548)
STOKES LADDERS INC
4545 Renfro Dr, Kelseyville (95451)
P.O. Box 445 (95451-0445)
PHONE....................707 279-4306
Jerry Hook, *President*
Karen Hook, *Vice Pres*
Kirk Sills, *Manager*
EMP: 10
SQ FT: 3,600
SALES (est): 1.1MM **Privately Held**
WEB: www.stokesladders.com
SIC: 3499 Ladders, portable: metal

(P-13549)
STRYKER ENTERPRISES INC
Also Called: Recognition Products Mfg
1358 E San Fernando St, San Jose
(95116-2329)
PHONE....................408 295-6300
William J Stryker Jr, *President*
Dennis Woodmansee, *Graphic Designe*
Becky Ryalls, *Accounts Exec*
▲ EMP: 22 EST: 1948
SQ FT: 12,000
SALES (est): 3.9MM **Privately Held**
WEB: www.plaque.com
SIC: 3499 Trophies, metal, except silver

(P-13550)
STURDY GUN SAFE MANUFACTRUING
Also Called: Sturdy Safe
2030 S Sarah St, Fresno (93721-3316)
PHONE....................559 485-8361
Terry Pratt, *Owner*
▲ EMP: 11
SQ FT: 15,000
SALES: 400K **Privately Held**
SIC: 3499 Safes & vaults, metal

(P-13551)
TDA MAGNETICS LLC
1175 W Victoria St, Rancho Dominguez
(90220-5813)
PHONE....................424 213-1585
Tracy Moon, *President*
Jeff Calvert, *Opers Mgr*
EMP: 13 EST: 2015
SALES (est): 996K **Privately Held**
SIC: 3499 Magnets, permanent: metallic

(P-13552)
TRIDUS INTERNATIONAL INC
Also Called: Tridus Magnetics and Assemblie
1145 W Victoria St, Compton (90220-5813)
PHONE....................310 884-3200
Bong Duk Lee, *Ch of Bd*
Hang Up Moon, *President*
Young Ha, *Admin Sec*
Doris Driscoll, *Accountant*
Alma Espinoza, *Purchasing*
▲ EMP: 10
SQ FT: 3,000
SALES (est): 1.9MM **Privately Held**
WEB: www.tridus.com
SIC: 3499 5084 Magnets, permanent:
metallic; industrial machinery & equip-
ment

(P-13553)
UNISORB INC
101 N Indian Hill Blvd C2-201, Claremont
(91711-4670)
PHONE....................626 793-1000
Peter Moore, *Branch Mgr*
EMP: 14
SALES (corp-wide): 5.4MM **Privately
Held**
SIC: 3499 Machine bases, metal

HQ: Unisorb Inc.
4117 Felters Rd Ste A
Michigan Center MI 49254
-

(P-13554)
WATER STUDIO INC
5681 Selmaraine Dr, Culver City
(90230-6119)
PHONE....................310 313-5553
Sean C So, *President*
Sean So, *Principal*
EMP: 12
SQ FT: 8,000
SALES (est): 2.8MM **Privately Held**
SIC: 3499 Fountains (except drinking),
metal

(P-13555)
WATERFOUNTAINSCOM INC
13870 Riverside Dr, Apple Valley
(92307-5989)
PHONE....................760 946-0525
Gary E Jackson, *President*
▲ EMP: 10
SALES (est): 1.1MM **Privately Held**
WEB: www.waterfountains.com
SIC: 3499 Fountains (except drinking),
metal

(P-13556)
WERNER CO
1810 Grogan Ave, Merced (95341-6404)
PHONE....................209 383-3989
Saied Djavadi, *Branch Mgr*
EMP: 10 **Privately Held**
SIC: 3499 Ladders, portable: metal
HQ: Werner Co
93 Werner Rd
Greenville PA 16125
-

(P-13557)
WESTERN FAB INC
Also Called: WESTERN FABRICATORS
9823 E Ave, Hesperia (92345-6280)
PHONE....................760 949-1441
Bryon Porter, *President*
Mandi Porter, *Corp Secy*
EMP: 15
SQ FT: 4,800
SALES (est): 3.5MM **Privately Held**
SIC: 3499 Welding tips, heat resistant:
metal

(P-13558)
WOODSIDE INVESTMENT INC
Also Called: Michael and Company
12405 E Brandt Rd, Lockeford
(95237-9571)
P.O. Box 1100 (95237-1100)
PHONE....................209 787-8040
Jung Kamburov, *Principal*
Dennis Wood, *President*
Erica I Zuiga, *Accounting Mgr*
EMP: 70 EST: 1991
SQ FT: 50,000
SALES (est): 15.1MM **Privately Held**
WEB: www.michaelandcofabricators.com
SIC: 3499 Aerosol valves, metal

3511 Steam, Gas & Hydraulic Turbines &

(P-13559)
ALTURDYNE POWER SYSTEMS INC
1405 N Johnson Ave, El Cajon
(92020-1615)
PHONE....................619 343-3204
Frank Verbeke, *President*
Andy Park, *Manager*
EMP: 30
SQ FT: 3,000
SALES: 6.5MM **Privately Held**
SIC: 3511 1731 Gas turbine generator set
units, complete; electric power systems
contractors

(P-13560)
ARCTURUS MARINE SYSTEMS
Also Called: American Bow Thruster
517a Martin Ave, Rohnert Park
(94928-2048)
PHONE....................707 586-3155
D Milo Hallerberg, *CEO*
Marit Barca, *Master*
David Catterson, *Manager*
▲ EMP: 53
SQ FT: 12,000
SALES (est): 13.4MM **Privately Held**
SIC: 3511 Hydraulic turbines

(P-13561)
BABCOCK & WILCOX COMPANY
Also Called: Babcock and Wilcox
710 Airpark Rd, NAPA (94558-7518)
PHONE....................707 259-1122
David Pavlik, *General Mgr*
Jonathan Graham, *Officer*
Jasmine Harvey, *Officer*
Nik Carter, *Vice Pres*
Pete Goumas, *Vice Pres*
EMP: 25
SALES (corp-wide): 1B **Publicly Held**
SIC: 3511 Turbines & turbine generator
sets
HQ: The Babcock & Wilcox Company
20 S Van Buren Ave
Barberton OH 44203
330 753-4511

(P-13562)
BAE SYSTEMS CONTROLS INC
5140 W Goldleaf Cir G100, Los Angeles
(90056-1666)
PHONE....................323 642-5000
Mike Reader, *Prgrmr*
Stephanie Carrera, *Accounting Dir*
EMP: 135
SALES (corp-wide): 21.6B **Privately Held**
WEB: www.baesystemscontrols.com
SIC: 3511 3721 3812 Turbines &
turbine generator sets; aircraft; search &
navigation equipment; aircraft parts &
equipment
HQ: Bae Systems Controls Inc.
1098 Clark St
Endicott NY 13760
607 770-2000

(P-13563)
CAPSTONE TURBINE CORPORATION (PA)
16640 Stagg St, Van Nuys (91406-1630)
PHONE....................818 734-5300
Darren R Jamison, *President*
Holly A Van Deursen, *Ch of Bd*
Jayme L Brooks, *CFO*
Gary Mayo, *Bd of Directors*
James D Crouse, *Exec VP*
◆ EMP: 153
SQ FT: 79,000
SALES: 83.4MM **Publicly Held**
WEB: www.capstoneturbine.com
SIC: 3511 Turbines & turbine generator
sets

(P-13564)
CATERPILLAR PWR GNRTN SYS
2200 Pacific Hwy, San Diego (92101-1745)
PHONE....................858 694-6629
Ennodio Ramos,
Justin Waldron, *Admin Sec*
Luke Harvey, *Project Mgr*
John Sawyer, *Technology*
Jim Hill, *Engineer*
EMP: 44
SALES (est): 1.1MM
SALES (corp-wide): 54.7B **Publicly Held**
SIC: 3511 Gas turbine generator set units,
complete
PA: Caterpillar Inc.
510 Lake Cook Rd Ste 100
Deerfield IL 60015
224 551-4000

(P-13565)
CLIPPER WINDPOWER PLC
6305 Carpinteria Ave # 300, Carpinteria
(93013-2968)
PHONE....................805 690-3275
Mauricio Quintana,
Michael Keane,
EMP: 740

SALES (est): 77.2MM **Privately Held**
SIC: 3511 Turbines & turbine generator
sets

(P-13566)
COMBUSTION PARTS INC
Also Called: C P I
1770 Gillespie Way # 111, El Cajon
(92020-1087)
PHONE....................858 759-3320
Lori Jenks, *President*
Brent Katsakos, *Vice Pres*
Markus Ito, *Vice Pres*
Tom Huppert, *Finance*
Nikki Petracca, *Personnel*
▼ EMP: 28 EST: 2001
SQ FT: 10,000
SALES (est): 6.2MM **Privately Held**
WEB: www.combustionparts.com
SIC: 3511 3499 Turbines & turbine gener-
ator sets & parts; gas turbines, mechani-
cal drive; welding tips, heat resistant:
metal

(P-13567)
ENER-CORE POWER INC (HQ)
30100 Town Center Dr O, Laguna Niguel
(92677-2064)
PHONE....................949 428-3300
Alain Castro, *CEO*
James Reiman, *Bd of Directors*
Bennet Tchaikovsky, *Bd of Directors*
Douglas Demaret, *Vice Pres*
Douglas Hamrin, *Vice Pres*
EMP: 15
SALES (est): 9.1MM **Publicly Held**
SIC: 3511 Turbines & turbine generator
sets
PA: Ener-Core, Inc.
30100 Town Center Dr
Laguna Niguel CA 92677
949 732-4400

(P-13568)
ENERGENT CORPORATION
1831 Carnegie Ave, Santa Ana
(92705-5528)
PHONE....................949 885-0365
Lance G Hays, *President*
Eufemio Guzman, *Engineer*
EMP: 13
SALES (est): 3.2MM **Privately Held**
SIC: 3511 Turbines & turbine generator
sets

(P-13569)
GALAXY ENERGY SYSTEMS INC
362 N Palm Canyon Dr, Palm Springs
(92262-5668)
PHONE....................760 778-4254
Hans Petermann, *President*
Bill Ost, *Treasurer*
EMP: 10
SALES: 5.5MM **Privately Held**
SIC: 3511 Gas turbines, mechanical drive

(P-13570)
GE WIND ENERGY LLC
13681 Chantico Rd, Tehachapi
(93561-8188)
PHONE....................661 823-6423
Gerlad Turk, *Manager*
EMP: 238
SALES (corp-wide): 121.6B **Publicly
Held**
SIC: 3511 Turbines & turbine generator
sets
HQ: Ge Wind Energy, Llc
13000 Jameson Rd
Tehachapi CA 93561

(P-13571)
GENERAL ELECTRIC COMPANY
26226 Antelope Rd, Romoland
(92585-8739)
P.O. Box 1240 (92585-0240)
PHONE....................951 928-2829
Jim McNaughton, *Branch Mgr*
Ben Kling, *Maintence Staff*
EMP: 500
SALES (corp-wide): 121.6B **Publicly
Held**
SIC: 3511 Turbines & turbine generator
sets

▲ = Import ▼=Export
◆ =Import/Export

PA: General Electric Company
41 Farnsworth St
Boston MA 02210
617 443-3000

(P-13572)
J H P & ASSOCIATES INC
28005 Smyth Dr, Valencia (91355-4023)
PHONE..................................661 799-5888
John Zhang, *Vice Pres*
C Y Zou, *Chairman*
▲ **EMP:** 20
SQ FT: 3,000
SALES (est): 2MM **Privately Held**
WEB: www.jhptech.com
SIC: 3511 3823 3679 3498 Turbines &
turbine generator set units, complete;
pressure gauges, dial & digital; harness
assemblies for electronic use: wire or
cable; manifolds, pipe: fabricated from
purchased pipe; thermometers & temper-
ature sensors

(P-13573)
LA TURBINE (PA)
28557 Industry Dr, Valencia (91355-5424)
PHONE..................................661 294-8290
John Maskaluk, *CEO*
Danny Mascari, *President*
Dominique Maskaluk, *CFO*
Julie Stalmans, *Executive Asst*
Chasen Murphy, *Technician*
▼ **EMP:** 72
SQ FT: 90,000
SALES (est): 24.5MM **Privately Held**
WEB: www.laturbine.com
SIC: 3511 Turbines & turbine generator
sets & parts

(P-13574)
NATEL ENERGY INC
2401 Monarch St, Alameda (94501-7513)
PHONE..................................510 342-5269
Gia Schneider, *CEO*
Abe Schneider, *President*
Dana Nguyen, *Office Mgr*
Dorothy Payne, *Office Mgr*
Peder Aune, *Engineer*
EMP: 14
SALES (est): 3.5MM **Privately Held**
SIC: 3511 Hydraulic turbines

(P-13575)
**SOLAR TURBINES
INCORPORATED (HQ)**
2200 Pacific Hwy, San Diego (92101-1773)
P.O. Box 85376 (92186-5376)
PHONE..................................619 544-5000
Thomas Pellette, *President*
C K Scott-Stanfel, *CFO*
Daniel Boylan, *Treasurer*
P F Browning, *Vice Pres*
D W Esbeck, *Vice Pres*
◆ **EMP:** 3890
SQ FT: 1,080,000
SALES (est): 1.9B
SALES (corp-wide): 54.7B **Publicly Held**
WEB: www.esolar.cat.com
SIC: 3511 Gas turbine generator set units,
complete
PA: Caterpillar Inc.
510 Lake Cook Rd Ste 100
Deerfield IL 60015
224 551-4000

(P-13576)
**SOLAR TURBINES
INCORPORATED**
9250a Sky Park Ct, San Diego
(92123-4302)
PHONE..................................858 715-2060
Betty Ribau, *Project Mgr*
Michael Rhoades, *Engineer*
R Akemann, *Architect*
Joseph Erth, *Manager*
EMP: 175
SQ FT: 60,155
SALES (corp-wide): 54.7B **Publicly Held**
WEB: www.esolar.cat.com
SIC: 3511 Gas turbine generator set units,
complete
HQ: Solar Turbines Incorporated
2200 Pacific Hwy
San Diego CA 92101
619 544-5000

(P-13577)
**SOLAR TURBINES
INCORPORATED**
18 Morgan Ste 100, Irvine (92618-2074)
PHONE..................................949 450-0870
Julie Martin, *Manager*
Kristina Brewer, *Engineer*
EMP: 10
SALES (corp-wide): 54.7B **Publicly Held**
WEB: www.esolar.cat.com
SIC: 3511 Gas turbine generator set units,
complete
HQ: Solar Turbines Incorporated
2200 Pacific Hwy
San Diego CA 92101
619 544-5000

(P-13578)
SOLAR TURBINES INTL CO (DH)
2200 Pacific Hwy, San Diego (92101-1773)
P.O. Box 85376 (92186-5376)
PHONE..................................619 544-5000
Thomas Pellette, *CEO*
Steve Gosslin, *President*
Greg Barr, *Vice Pres*
D W Esbeck, *Vice Pres*
D M Lehmann, *Vice Pres*
EMP: 20 **EST:** 1977
SALES (est): 58.9MM
SALES (corp-wide): 54.7B **Publicly Held**
SIC: 3511 Gas turbine generator set units,
complete
HQ: Solar Turbines Incorporated
2200 Pacific Hwy
San Diego CA 92101
619 544-5000

(P-13579)
SOLAR TURBINES INTL CO
9330 Sky Park Ct, San Diego
(92123-4304)
PHONE..................................858 694-1616
Steve Gosslin, *President*
Srinivas Samavedam, *Info Tech Mgr*
Jeremy Hummel, *Technician*
Neil Cassan, *Project Mgr*
Chelsey Beckerman, *Engineer*
EMP: 23
SALES (corp-wide): 54.7B **Publicly Held**
SIC: 3511 Gas turbine generator set units,
complete
HQ: Solar Turbines International Co Inc
2200 Pacific Hwy
San Diego CA 92101
619 544-5000

(P-13580)
SOLTECH SOLAR INC
1836 Commercenter Cir, San Bernardino
(92408-3430)
PHONE..................................909 890-2282
EMP: 10
SALES (est): 690K **Privately Held**
SIC: 3511

(P-13581)
**UNIVERSAL TURBO
TECHNOLOGY**
1120 E Elm Ave, Fullerton (92831-5024)
PHONE..................................714 600-9585
Marius Paul, *Principal*
EMP: 86
SALES (est): 4.3MM **Privately Held**
SIC: 3511 Turbines & turbine generator
sets

(P-13582)
WEPOWER LLC
32 Journey Ste 250, Aliso Viejo
(92656-5329)
PHONE..................................866 385-9463
Marvin Winkler, *Mng Member*
Howard Makler, *President*
Thomas Schiff,
Kevin B Donovan, *Director*
▲ **EMP:** 15
SALES (est): 1.8MM **Privately Held**
SIC: 3511 Turbines & turbine generator set
units, complete

**3519 Internal Combustion
Engines, NEC**

(P-13583)
AGILITY FUEL SYSTEMS LLC
3335 Susan St Ste 100, Costa Mesa
(92626-1647)
PHONE..................................256 831-6155
Tom Russell, *Branch Mgr*
EMP: 11
SALES (corp-wide): 282.1MM **Privately
Held**
SIC: 3519 Diesel, semi-diesel or duel-fuel
engines, including marine
HQ: Agility Fuel Systems, Llc
1815 Carnegie Ave
Santa Ana CA 92705

(P-13584)
BOOSTPOWER USA INC
2560 Calcite Cir, Newbury Park
(91320-1203)
PHONE..................................805 376-6077
Alexi Sahagian, *President*
EMP: 12
SALES (est): 2.4MM **Privately Held**
WEB: www.boostpower.com
SIC: 3519 7699 Marine engines; marine
engine repair

(P-13585)
CUMMINS PACIFIC LLC
5150 Boyd Rd, Arcata (95521-4449)
PHONE..................................707 822-7392
April Farris, *Branch Mgr*
EMP: 13
SALES (corp-wide): 23.7B **Publicly Held**
WEB: www.cleaire.com
SIC: 3519 Internal combustion engines
HQ: Cummins Pacific, Llc
1939 Deere Ave
Irvine CA 92606

(P-13586)
CUMMINS PACIFIC LLC
5125 Caterpillar Rd, Redding (96003-2049)
PHONE..................................530 244-6898
Mike Goodwin, *Branch Mgr*
Ed James, *Sales Staff*
EMP: 13
SALES (corp-wide): 23.7B **Publicly Held**
WEB: www.cleaire.com
SIC: 3519 Internal combustion engines
HQ: Cummins Pacific, Llc
1939 Deere Ave
Irvine CA 92606

(P-13587)
CUMMINS PACIFIC LLC
875 Riverside Pkwy, West Sacramento
(95605-1502)
PHONE..................................916 371-0630
Mike Goodwin, *Branch Mgr*
EMP: 47
SALES (corp-wide): 23.7B **Publicly Held**
WEB: www.cleaire.com
SIC: 3519 5063 7629 Diesel engine re-
building; generators; generator repair
HQ: Cummins Pacific, Llc
1939 Deere Ave
Irvine CA 92606

(P-13588)
CUMMINS PACIFIC LLC
9520 Stewart And Gray Rd, Downey
(90241-5559)
PHONE..................................866 934-4373
Susan Morales, *Principal*
EMP: 40
SALES (corp-wide): 23.7B **Publicly Held**
SIC: 3519 Internal combustion engines
HQ: Cummins Pacific, Llc
1939 Deere Ave
Irvine CA 92606

(P-13589)
CUMMINS PACIFIC LLC
3061 S Riverside Ave, Bloomington
(92316-3527)
PHONE..................................909 877-0433
Brandon Daste, *Principal*
EMP: 50
SALES (corp-wide): 23.7B **Publicly Held**
SIC: 3519 Internal combustion engines
HQ: Cummins Pacific, Llc
1939 Deere Ave
Irvine CA 92606

(P-13590)
CUMMINS PACIFIC LLC
5333 N Cornelia Ave, Fresno (93722-6403)
PHONE..................................559 277-6760
Joseph Ayerza Suzanne, *Principal*
Tim Blythe, *Manager*
EMP: 65
SALES (corp-wide): 23.7B **Publicly Held**
WEB: www.cleaire.com
SIC: 3519 Internal combustion engines
HQ: Cummins Pacific, Llc
1939 Deere Ave
Irvine CA 92606

(P-13591)
CUMMINS PACIFIC LLC
4601 E Brundage Ln, Bakersfield
(93307-2311)
PHONE..................................661 325-9404
Robert Bickie, *Branch Mgr*
EMP: 50
SALES (corp-wide): 23.7B **Publicly Held**
WEB: www.cleaire.com
SIC: 3519 Diesel engine rebuilding
HQ: Cummins Pacific, Llc
1939 Deere Ave
Irvine CA 92606

(P-13592)
CUMMINS PACIFIC LLC (HQ)
1939 Deere Ave, Irvine (92606-4818)
PHONE..................................949 253-6000
Mark Yragui, *President*
Sharon Hennings, *Accounting Mgr*
Ron Kick, *Sales Staff*
Linda Ward, *Receptionist*
Maxim Gyryluk, *Accounts Exec*
▲ **EMP:** 85
SALES (est): 89.3MM
SALES (corp-wide): 23.7B **Publicly Held**
WEB: www.ccpionline.com
SIC: 3519 5063 7538 Internal combustion
engines; generators; general automotive
repair shops
PA: Cummins Inc.
500 Jackson St
Columbus IN 47201
812 377-5000

(P-13593)
CUMMINS PACIFIC LLC
310 N Johnson Ave, El Cajon (92020-3114)
PHONE..................................619 593-3093
Steve Gallant, *Branch Mgr*
EMP: 25
SALES (corp-wide): 23.7B **Publicly Held**
WEB: www.ccpionline.com
SIC: 3519 Internal combustion engines
HQ: Cummins Pacific, Llc
1939 Deere Ave
Irvine CA 92606

(P-13594)
CUMMINS PACIFIC LLC
3958 Transport St, Ventura (93003-5128)
PHONE..................................805 644-7281
Dan Elliott, *Manager*
EMP: 25
SALES (corp-wide): 23.7B **Publicly Held**
WEB: www.ccpionline.com
SIC: 3519 5063 Internal combustion en-
gines; generators
HQ: Cummins Pacific, Llc
1939 Deere Ave
Irvine CA 92606

(P-13595)
DETROIT DIESEL CORPORATION
10645 Studebaker Rd Fl 2, Downey
(90241-3173)
PHONE.................................562 929-7016
Glen Nutting, *Vice Pres*
EMP: 15
SALES (corp-wide): 191.6B **Privately Held**
WEB: www.detroitdeisel.com
SIC: 3519 Engines, diesel & semi-diesel or dual-fuel; diesel, semi-diesel or duel-fuel engines, including marine
HQ: Detroit Diesel Corporation
13400 W Outer Dr
Detroit MI 48239
313 592-5000

(P-13596)
GALE BANKS ENGINEERING
Also Called: Banks Power Products
546 S Duggan Ave, Azusa (91702-5136)
PHONE.................................626 969-9600
Gale C Banks III, *President*
Vicki L Banks, *Vice Pres*
▲ **EMP:** 195
SQ FT: 121,000
SALES (est): 69.1MM **Privately Held**
WEB: www.getpower.com
SIC: 3519 3714 Parts & accessories, internal combustion engines; motor vehicle parts & accessories

(P-13597)
HIGH TECH MACHINE SHOP S-CORP
15149 Boyle Ave, Fontana (92337-7209)
PHONE.................................909 356-5437
Susie Sanchez, *Owner*
Elias Sanchez, *Co-Owner*
EMP: 13 **EST:** 2015
SALES (est): 1.6MM **Privately Held**
SIC: 3519 Diesel engine rebuilding

(P-13598)
RACING BEAT INC
4789 E Wesley Dr, Anaheim (92807-1941)
PHONE.................................714 779-8677
James Mederer, *President*
▲ **EMP:** 20
SQ FT: 7,500
SALES (est): 3.3MM **Privately Held**
WEB: www.racingbeat.com
SIC: 3519 Parts & accessories, internal combustion engines

(P-13599)
SOUTHWEST PRODUCTS CORPORATION
2875 Cherry Ave, Signal Hill (90755-1908)
PHONE.................................360 887-7400
Jason Hair, *Branch Mgr*
Holly Boranian, *Finance Mgr*
EMP: 15
SALES (corp-wide): 18.1MM **Privately Held**
SIC: 3519 Diesel engine rebuilding
HQ: Southwest Products Corporation
11690 N 132nd Ave
Surprise AZ 85379
306 887-7400

(P-13600)
TRACY INDUSTRIES INC
Also Called: Genuine Parts Distributors
3200 E Guasti Rd Ste 100, Ontario
(91761-8661)
P.O. Box 1260 (91762)
PHONE.................................562 692-9034
Timothy Engvall, *CEO*
Erma Jean Tracy, *Vice Pres*
David Rosenberger, *Admin Sec*
▲ **EMP:** 172
SALES: 142MM **Privately Held**
SIC: 3519 7538 Internal combustion engines; engine rebuilding: automotive

(P-13601)
TRANSONIC COMBUSTION INC
461 Calle San Pablo, Camarillo
(93012-8506)
PHONE.................................805 465-5145
Wolfgang Bullmer, *President*
Timothy Noonan, *CFO*

Mike Cheiky, *CTO*
EMP: 40
SALES (est): 7.1MM **Privately Held**
WEB: www.tscombustion.com
SIC: 3519 Internal combustion engines

(P-13602)
UNITED STATES DEPT OF NAVY
Also Called: Vfa 122 Power Plants
Vfa 122 Hanger 5, Lemoore (93246-0001)
PHONE.................................559 998-2488
Patrick Cleary,
EMP: 600 **Publicly Held**
SIC: 3519 9711 Jet propulsion engines; Navy;
HQ: United States Department Of The Navy
1200 Navy Pentagon
Washington DC 20350

(P-13603)
VALLEY POWER SYSTEMS INC (PA)
Also Called: John Deere Authorized Dealer
425 S Hacienda Blvd, City of Industry
(91745-1123)
PHONE.................................626 333-1243
Hampton Clark Lee, *Ch of Bd*
Michael Barnett, *President*
Robert K Humphryes, *CFO*
Richard Kickliter, *Vice Pres*
Bruce Noble, *Vice Pres*
▲ **EMP:** 100
SQ FT: 49,000
SALES (est): 181.2MM **Privately Held**
WEB: www.valleypowersystems.com
SIC: 3519 5082 Marine engines; construction & mining machinery

3523 Farm Machinery &

(P-13604)
AG RAY INC
Also Called: Injection Molding
20400 N Kennefick Rd, Acampo
(95220-9708)
P.O. Box 1708, Woodbridge (95258-1708)
PHONE.................................209 334-1999
Rose Rogan, *President*
EMP: 12
SALES: 966K **Privately Held**
SIC: 3523 3089 Cabs, tractors & agricultural machinery; injection molded finished plastic products

(P-13605)
AGRIFIM IRRIGATION PDTS INC
Also Called: Nds
2855 S East Ave, Fresno (93725-1908)
PHONE.................................559 443-6680
Rael Sacks, *President*
▲ **EMP:** 15
SQ FT: 15,200
SALES (est): 2.9MM
SALES (corp-wide): 1.2B **Privately Held**
WEB: www.agrifimusa.com
SIC: 3523 Farm machinery & equipment
HQ: National Diversified Sales, Inc.
21300 Victory Blvd # 215
Woodland Hills CA 91367
559 562-9888

(P-13606)
AIR-O FAN PRODUCTS CORPORATION (PA)
Also Called: Air O Fan
507 E Dinuba Ave, Reedley (93654-3531)
PHONE.................................559 638-6546
Larry E Davis, *CEO*
Byre Davis, *President*
Ruby Davis, *Corp Secy*
Larry Davis, *Vice Pres*
David Lincoln, *Vice Pres*
◆ **EMP:** 13 **EST:** 1945
SQ FT: 2,000
SALES (est): 8.1MM **Privately Held**
SIC: 3523 Fertilizing machinery, farm; dusters, mechanical: agricultural

(P-13607)
ALBERS MFG CO INC (PA)
Also Called: Albers Dairy Equipment. Inc
14323 Albers Way, Chino (91710-1134)
PHONE.................................909 597-5537

Teo Albers Jr, *President*
◆ **EMP:** 21
SQ FT: 10,000
SALES (est): 6.4MM **Privately Held**
WEB: www.albersdairyequipment.com
SIC: 3523 Barn stanchions & standards

(P-13608)
AMARILLO WIND MACHINE LLC
20513 Avenue 256, Exeter (93221-9656)
P.O. Box 96809, Chicago IL (60693-6809)
PHONE.................................559 592-4256
Steven Chaloupka, *President*
EMP: 18
SQ FT: 12,000
SALES: 8.3MM
SALES (corp-wide): 225.3B **Publicly Held**
WEB: www.amarillogear.com
SIC: 3523 7699 Farm machinery & equipment; agricultural equipment repair services
HQ: Amarillo Gear Company Llc
2401 W Sundown Ln
Amarillo TX 79118
806 622-1273

(P-13609)
AMERICAN INTERNATIONAL MFG CO
Also Called: Aim Mail Centers
1230 Fortna Ave, Woodland (95776-5905)
PHONE.................................530 666-2446
John Bridges, *CEO*
David Neilson, *President*
Chistophre Neilson, *Principal*
Shelley Marten, *Administration*
Shelby Sachs, *Foreman/Supr*
EMP: 29
SQ FT: 23,000
SALES (est): 8.6MM **Privately Held**
WEB: www.aimfab.com
SIC: 3523 3556 Farm machinery & equipment; food products machinery

(P-13610)
AQUANEERING INC
7960 Stromesa Ct, San Diego
(92126-4329)
PHONE.................................858 578-2028
Mark Francis, *President*
Wendy Porter-Francis, *Vice Pres*
Brendan C Delbos, *Sales Staff*
Bill Kilgore, *Sales Staff*
Kendra Minkler, *Sales Staff*
EMP: 30
SQ FT: 5,100
SALES (est): 8.7MM **Privately Held**
WEB: www.aquaneer.com
SIC: 3523 Farm machinery & equipment

(P-13611)
AWETA-AUTOLINE INC (PA)
4516 E Citron, Fresno (93725-9861)
PHONE.................................559 244-8340
Jeanluc Delcasse, *CEO*
▲ **EMP:** 45
SQ FT: 20,000
SALES (est): 6.2MM **Privately Held**
WEB: www.autolinesorters.com
SIC: 3523 Grading, cleaning, sorting machines, fruit, grain, vegetable

(P-13612)
B W IMPLEMENT CO
288 W Front St, Buttonwillow (93206)
P.O. Box 758 (93206-0758)
PHONE.................................661 764-5254
John C Blair, *President*
Julien Parsons, *Treasurer*
Alene Parsons, *Admin Sec*
EMP: 22
SQ FT: 85,000
SALES (est): 4.3MM **Privately Held**
WEB: www.bwimp.com
SIC: 3523 5083 5999 Tractors, farm; farm implements; farm machinery

(P-13613)
BIG TEX TRAILER MFG INC
1425 E Sixth St, Beaumont (92223-2505)
PHONE.................................951 845-5344
John Armstrong, *General Mgr*
EMP: 15

SALES (corp-wide): 15.3B **Privately Held**
WEB: www.big-tex.com
SIC: 3523 5013 Farm machinery & equipment; motor vehicle supplies & new parts
HQ: Big Tex Trailer Manufacturing, Inc.
950 Interstate Hwy 30 E
Mount Pleasant TX 75455
903 575-0300

(P-13614)
BRAZEAU THOROUGHBRED FARMS LP
30500 State St, Hemet (92543-9258)
PHONE.................................951 925-8957
Nadine Anderson, *Manager*
Paul Brazeau, *Vice Pres*
EMP: 17
SALES (est): 1MM **Privately Held**
SIC: 3523 0291 0752 Harvesters, fruit, vegetable, tobacco, etc.; animal specialty farm, general; boarding services, horses: racing & non-racing

(P-13615)
BRITZ FERTILIZERS INC
12498 11th Ave, Hanford (93230-9523)
PHONE.................................559 582-0942
Keith Roberts, *Manager*
EMP: 30
SALES (corp-wide): 297.6MM **Privately Held**
WEB: www.britzinc.com
SIC: 3523 2873 Spreaders, fertilizer; nitrogenous fertilizers
HQ: Britz Fertilizers Inc.
3265 W Figarden Dr
Fresno CA 93711
559 448-8000

(P-13616)
BROCKS TRAILERS INC
6901 E Brundage Ln, Bakersfield
(93307-3057)
PHONE.................................661 363-5038
Matthew E Brock, *President*
Amanda Shannon, *Marketing Staff*
EMP: 35
SALES (est): 5.7MM **Privately Held**
WEB: www.brockstrailersinc.com
SIC: 3523 5013 7539 5511 Trailers & wagons, farm; trailer parts & accessories; trailer repair; trucks, tractors & trailers: new & used; utility trailers; welding on site

(P-13617)
CAL-COAST DAIRY SYSTEMS INC
424 S Tegner Rd, Turlock (95380-9406)
P.O. Box 737 (95381-0737)
PHONE.................................209 634-9026
Lon Baptista, *President*
Lori Baptista, *Vice Pres*
Stacy Souza, *Office Mgr*
EMP: 30
SQ FT: 16,000
SALES (est): 6.8MM **Privately Held**
WEB: www.calcoastinc.com
SIC: 3523 1542 8711 5083 Dairy equipment (farm); agricultural building contractors; structural engineering; dairy machinery & equipment; residential construction; fabricated plate work (boiler shop)

(P-13618)
CALIFORNIA FARM EQUIPMENT MAG
17045 S Central Vly Hwy, Shafter
(93263-2704)
P.O. Box 1597 (93263-1597)
PHONE.................................661 589-0435
Andrew Cummings, *President*
EMP: 14
SALES (est): 709.4K **Privately Held**
SIC: 3523 Balers, farm: hay, straw, cotton, etc.

(P-13619)
CHERRY VALLEY SHEET METAL
39638 Avenida Sonrisa, Cherry Valley
(92223-4399)
PHONE.................................951 845-1578
Peter Schaeffer, *Partner*
Tony Schmidt, *Partner*
EMP: 10 **EST:** 1960

▲ = Import ▼=Export
◆ =Import/Export

SQ FT: 10,000
SALES (est): 760K **Privately Held**
SIC: **3523** Poultry brooders, feeders & waterers

(P-13620)
COE ORCHARD EQUIPMENT INC
3453 Riviera Rd, Live Oak (95953-9713)
PHONE.....................530 695-5121
Lyman Coe, *CEO*
Lois A Coe, *CFO*
▲ EMP: 100
SQ FT: 45,000
SALES (est): 8.6MM **Privately Held**
WEB: www.coeshakers.com
SIC: **3523** Harvesters, fruit, vegetable, tobacco, etc.

(P-13621)
CUSTOM EQUIPMENT COINC
90 Rock Creek Rd Ste 9, Copperopolis (95228-9251)
PHONE.....................209 785-9891
Craig D Robinson, *President*
Christie Robinson, *Admin Sec*
EMP: 10
SQ FT: 20,000
SALES (est): 1.4MM **Privately Held**
SIC: **3523** 7699 Farm machinery & equipment; farm machinery repair

(P-13622)
D & M MANUFACTURING
5400 S Villa Ave, Fresno (93725-9798)
PHONE.....................559 834-4668
Judy Tolentino, *Owner*
EMP: 18 EST: 1987
SQ FT: 10,000
SALES (est): 769.1K **Privately Held**
SIC: **3523** Fertilizing, spraying, dusting & irrigation machinery

(P-13623)
DALES WELDING INC
Also Called: Dale's Welding & Fabrication
1112 Abbott St A, Salinas (93901-4598)
PHONE.....................831 424-6583
Dale Scheff, *President*
Peggy Scheff, *Corp Secy*
Jeff Scheff, *General Mgr*
EMP: 13
SQ FT: 11,250
SALES: 1MM **Privately Held**
SIC: **3523** 7692 Farm machinery & equipment; welding repair

(P-13624)
DIG CORPORATION
1210 Activity Dr, Vista (92081-8510)
PHONE.....................760 727-0914
David Levy, *President*
Kevin Yakely, *Info Tech Mgr*
Craig Beal, *Engineer*
Racquell Bibens, *Controller*
Anna Woods, *Purch Mgr*
▲ EMP: 84
SQ FT: 45,000
SALES (est): 24.2MM **Privately Held**
WEB: www.digcorp.com
SIC: **3523** Irrigation equipment, self-propelled

(P-13625)
DKP INC
275 N Marks Ave, Fresno (93706-1102)
PHONE.....................559 266-2695
Douglas R King, *President*
EMP: 45
SQ FT: 12,000
SALES (est): 4.5MM
SALES (corp-wide): 5.9MM **Privately Held**
SIC: **3523** Cotton pickers & strippers
PA: R. M. King Company
315 N Marks Ave
Fresno CA
559 266-0258

(P-13626)
DOMRIES ENTERPRISES INC
12281 Road 29, Madera (93638-8332)
PHONE.....................559 485-4306
Candyce L Domries, *CEO*
Lorraine Domries, *Treasurer*
▲ EMP: 35 EST: 1924

SQ FT: 65,000
SALES (est): 8.6MM **Privately Held**
SIC: **3523** 5084 Soil preparation machinery, except turf & grounds; fertilizing, spraying, dusting & irrigation machinery; industrial machinery & equipment

(P-13627)
DOUBLE K INDUSTRIES INC
9711 Mason Ave, Chatsworth (91311-5208)
PHONE.....................818 772-2887
Greg Crisp, *CEO*
Cresencio Lomeli, *Prdtn Mgr*
Fritz Waltjen, *Facilities Mgr*
Michael Beavers,
Valerie Crisp, *Director*
▲ EMP: 24
SALES (est): 6.2MM **Privately Held**
SIC: **3523** Farm machinery & equipment

(P-13628)
DOWDYS SALES AND SERVICES
15185 Avenue 224, Tulare (93274-9305)
PHONE.....................559 688-6973
Brad Dowdy, *President*
Melinda Dowdy, *Corp Secy*
Chris Ince, *Parts Mgr*
EMP: 15
SALES (est): 3.4MM **Privately Held**
WEB: www.dowdys.com
SIC: **3523** Farm machinery & equipment

(P-13629)
DURAND-WAYLAND MACHINERY INC (PA)
1041 E Dinuba Ave, Reedley (93654-3578)
PHONE.....................559 591-6904
Fred A Durand III, *President*
Bill Leverett, *Treasurer*
John Seay, *Vice Pres*
Robert Soria, *Administration*
EMP: 50
SQ FT: 70,000
SALES (est): 8.9MM **Privately Held**
SIC: **3523** 5084 Sprayers & spraying machines, agricultural; industrial machinery & equipment

(P-13630)
E D KILBY MFG & FARMING
Also Called: Kilby Mfg & Farming
286 W Evans Reimer Rd, Gridley (95948-9536)
PHONE.....................530 846-5625
Edward Kilby, *President*
Donna Low Kilby, *Treasurer*
Raymond Pantaleoni, *Vice Pres*
EMP: 25
SQ FT: 10,000
SALES (est): 396.3K **Privately Held**
SIC: **3523** Harvesters, fruit, vegetable, tobacco, etc.

(P-13631)
EARTHOLOGYTECH LLC
928 F Ave, Coronado (92118-2510)
PHONE.....................619 435-5296
Christopher Giglio,
▲ EMP: 20
SQ FT: 1,200
SALES: 300K **Privately Held**
SIC: **3523** Turf & grounds equipment

(P-13632)
EXETER MERCANTILE COMPANY
258 E Pine St, Exeter (93221-1750)
P.O. Box 67 (93221-0067)
PHONE.....................559 592-2121
Robert G Schelling, *President*
Sidney Schelling Jr, *Corp Secy*
Brian Schelling, *Vice Pres*
Staci Smith, *Office Mgr*
Bryan Helin, *Materials Mgr*
▲ EMP: 19
SQ FT: 22,000
SALES (est): 4.8MM **Privately Held**
WEB: www.exetermercantile.com
SIC: **3523** 3537 5072 Tractors, farm; industrial trucks & tractors; hardware

(P-13633)
FLORY INDUSTRIES
4737 Toomes Rd, Salida (95368)
P.O. Box 908 (95368-0908)
PHONE.....................209 545-1167

Howard Flory, *CEO*
Rodney Flory, *Treasurer*
Marlin Flory, *Vice Pres*
Norman Flory, *Admin Sec*
EMP: 75 EST: 1904
SQ FT: 12,000
SALES (est): 36.1MM **Privately Held**
WEB: www.floryindustries.com
SIC: **3523** 5083 3441 0173 Harvesters, fruit, vegetable, tobacco, etc.; farm equipment parts & supplies; fabricated structural metal; tree nuts

(P-13634)
GREENBROZ INC
955 Vernon Way, El Cajon (92020-1832)
PHONE.....................844 379-8746
Cullen Raichart, *CEO*
Lise Bernard, *Sales Staff*
EMP: 16
SQ FT: 7,000
SALES: 3.1MM **Privately Held**
SIC: **3523** Farm machinery & equipment

(P-13635)
HYDROPOINT DATA SYSTEMS INC
1720 Corporate Cir, Petaluma (94954-6924)
PHONE.....................707 769-9696
Chris Spain, *CEO*
Paul Ciandrini, *President*
Mardi Diamond, *Vice Pres*
Chris Manchuck, *Vice Pres*
Ben Slick, *Vice Pres*
▲ EMP: 50
SQ FT: 18,000
SALES (est): 13.3MM **Privately Held**
WEB: www.hydropoint.com
SIC: **3523** Irrigation equipment, self-propelled

(P-13636)
INVELOP INC
Also Called: Double K Industries
9711 Mason Ave, Chatsworth (91311-5208)
PHONE.....................818 772-2887
Gregory S Crisp, *President*
Grant Parrinello, *Engineer*
◆ EMP: 40
SQ FT: 20,700
SALES (est): 6.5MM **Privately Held**
SIC: **3523** 3999 3841 Clippers, for animal use: hand or electric; pet supplies; veterinarians' instruments & apparatus

(P-13637)
IRRITEC USA INC
1420 N Irritec Way, Fresno (93703-4432)
PHONE.....................559 275-8825
Daniel W Eisenberg, *Principal*
Ed Powers, *Sales Mgr*
Fernando Mejorada, *Sales Staff*
◆ EMP: 19
SALES (est): 6.3MM **Privately Held**
SIC: **3523** Irrigation equipment, self-propelled

(P-13638)
J & L IRRIGATION COMPANY INC
4264 W Jensen Ave, Fresno (93706-9049)
PHONE.....................559 237-2181
Lu Dwyer, *President*
Ziv Ronen, *Manager*
EMP: 10
SQ FT: 10,000
SALES (est): 1.9MM **Privately Held**
SIC: **3523** Irrigation equipment, self-propelled

(P-13639)
JACKRABBIT (PA)
Also Called: Dakota AG Welding
471 Industrial Ave, Ripon (95366-2768)
PHONE.....................209 599-6118
Bill Kirkendall, *CEO*
▲ EMP: 82
SQ FT: 15,000
SALES (est): 31.2MM **Privately Held**
WEB: www.jackrabbit.bz
SIC: **3523** Harvesters, fruit, vegetable, tobacco, etc.

(P-13640)
JAIN IRRIGATION INC
2851 E Florence Ave, Fresno (93721-3407)
P.O. Box 71447, Salt Lake City UT (84171-0447)
PHONE.....................559 485-7171
Elizabeth Maxwell, *Branch Mgr*
Ilan Keren, *General Mgr*
Scott Kraus, *VP Finance*
Chawarn Khongsub, *Sales Mgr*
Mike Burch, *Sales Staff*
EMP: 150
SALES (corp-wide): 65.4MM **Privately Held**
WEB: www.aquariusbrands.com
SIC: **3523** 4971 3999 Irrigation equipment, self-propelled; irrigation systems; atomizers; toiletry
PA: Jain Irrigation Holdings Corporation
6975 S Union Park Ctr # 600
Midvale UT 84047
909 395-5200

(P-13641)
JOHNSON FARM MACHINERY CO INC
Also Called: Johnson Manufacturing
38574 Kentucky Ave, Woodland (95695-5835)
P.O. Box 1237 (95776-1237)
PHONE.....................530 662-1788
Kirk David Friedman, *CEO*
EMP: 10
SQ FT: 33,000
SALES (est): 2.9MM **Privately Held**
WEB: www.jfmco.com
SIC: **3523** Trailers & wagons, farm

(P-13642)
KAMPER FABRICATION INC
20107 N Ripon Rd, Ripon (95366-9758)
P.O. Box 177 (95366-0177)
PHONE.....................209 599-7137
Richard Kamper, *President*
Brenda Kamper, *Corp Secy*
EMP: 23
SQ FT: 24,800
SALES (est): 4.2MM **Privately Held**
SIC: **3523** Farm machinery & equipment

(P-13643)
KINGSBURG CULTIVATOR INC
40190 Road 36, Kingsburg (93631-9621)
PHONE.....................559 897-3662
Clint Erling, *President*
Allen Scheidt, *Vice Pres*
EMP: 17 EST: 1954
SQ FT: 1,400
SALES (est): 3.9MM **Privately Held**
WEB: www.kci-mfg.com
SIC: **3523** Harvesters, fruit, vegetable, tobacco, etc.

(P-13644)
KIRBY MANUFACTURING INC (PA)
484 S St 59, Merced (95341-6541)
P.O. Box 989 (95341-0989)
PHONE.....................209 723-0778
Richard M Kirby, *President*
William T Kirby, *Treasurer*
Madeleine Kirby Davenport, *Vice Pres*
Kelly Sellers, *Admin Sec*
Jonthan Garcia, *Purch Mgr*
▼ EMP: 68
SQ FT: 45,000
SALES (est): 15.4MM **Privately Held**
WEB: www.kirbymfg.com
SIC: **3523** Cattle feeding, handling & watering equipment; haying machines: mowers, rakes, stackers, etc.

(P-13645)
KIRBY MANUFACTURING INC
Also Called: Kirby-Tulare Manufacturing
1478 N J St, Tulare (93274-1308)
PHONE.....................559 686-1571
Tom Day, *Branch Mgr*
EMP: 12
SALES (corp-wide): 15.4MM **Privately Held**
WEB: www.kirbymfg.com
SIC: **3523** Cattle feeding, handling & watering equipment

(PA)=Parent Co (HQ)=Headquarters (DH)=Div Headquarters
✿ = New Business established in last 2 years

PRODUCTS & SVCS

PA: Kirby Manufacturing, Inc.
484 S St 59
Merced CA 95341
209 723-0778

(P-13646)
KUBOTA TRACTOR CORPORATION
1175 S Guild Ave, Lodi (95240-3154)
PHONE..................................209 334-9910
Rex Young, *Manager*
Brad Preston, *Regl Sales Mgr*
EMP: 19 Privately Held
WEB: www.kubota.com
SIC: 3523 5082 5083 Tractors, farm; construction & mining machinery; tractors, agricultural
HQ: Kubota Tractor Corporation
1000 Kubota Dr
Grapevine TX 76051
817 756-1171

(P-13647)
LAIRD MFG LLC (PA)
Also Called: Laird Manufacturing
531 S State Highway 59, Merced (95341-6925)
P.O. Box 1053 (95341-1053)
PHONE..................................209 722-4145
Lee Cansler,
Isaac Isakow, *General Mgr*
David Landry, *Administration*
Steve Lemos, *Sales Staff*
Issac Isako,
◆ **EMP: 40 EST:** 1937
SQ FT: 15,000
SALES (est): 10.8MM Privately Held
WEB: www.lairdmfg.com
SIC: 3523 7692 Cattle feeding, handling & watering equipment; welding repair

(P-13648)
LAIRD MFG LLC
1130 Stuart Dr, Merced (95341-6424)
PHONE..................................209 349-8918
Martin Friedman, *Manager*
EMP: 13
SALES (corp-wide): 10.8MM Privately Held
SIC: 3523 Cattle feeding, handling & watering equipment
PA: Laird Mfg., Llc
531 S State Highway 59
Merced CA 95341
209 722-4145

(P-13649)
LIMITED ACCESS UNLIMITED INC
Also Called: Pacific Drilling Co.
5220 Anna Ave Ste A, San Diego (92110-4019)
PHONE..................................619 294-3682
Tod Clark, *CEO*
Craig Roberts, *Vice Pres*
EMP: 16
SALES (est): 2.8MM Privately Held
WEB: www.pacdrill.com
SIC: 3523 1781 Soil sampling machines; water well drilling

(P-13650)
MEDIFARM SO CAL INC
2040 Main St Ste 225, Irvine (92614-8219)
PHONE..................................855 447-6967
Derek Peterson, *Ch of Bd*
Kenneth Vande Vrede, *COO*
Michael James, *CFO*
Michael A Nahass, *Corp Secy*
EMP: 41 EST: 2017
SALES (est): 1.4MM Publicly Held
SIC: 3523 Farm machinery & equipment
PA: Terra Tech Corp.
2040 Main St Ste 225
Irvine CA 92614

(P-13651)
MYTREX INC
4070 N Palm St Ste 707, Fullerton (92835-1036)
PHONE..................................949 800-9725
Ashley Myung Hee Lee, *President*
Helen J Chuang, *CFO*
EMP: 12
SQ FT: 10,000

SALES: 100K Privately Held
SIC: 3523 Peanut combines, diggers, packers & threshers

(P-13652)
NIKKEL IRON WORKS CORPORATION
17045 S Central Vly Hwy, Shafter (93263-2704)
P.O. Box 1597 (93263-1597)
PHONE..................................661 746-4904
Andrew Cummings, *President*
Shirley Cummings, *Treasurer*
Karl Almquist, *General Mgr*
EMP: 17 EST: 1924
SQ FT: 26,000
SALES (est): 3.8MM Privately Held
WEB: www.nikkelironworks.com
SIC: 3523 Farm machinery & equipment

(P-13653)
NYX INDUSTRIES INC
Also Called: Salco Products
9452 Resenda Ave, Fontana (92335-2541)
PHONE..................................909 937-3923
Gabriel Hermida, *CEO*
Cindy Chavez, *President*
▲ **EMP:** 13
SALES: 2.5MM Privately Held
SIC: 3523 Irrigation equipment, self-propelled

(P-13654)
OLSON IRRIGATION SYSTEMS
Also Called: Olson Industrial Systems
10910 Wheatlands Ave A, Santee (92071-2867)
P.O. Box 711570 (92072-1570)
PHONE..................................619 562-3100
Donald Olson, *President*
Kathleen Baldwin, *Treasurer*
▲ **EMP: 28 EST:** 1976
SQ FT: 17,000
SALES (est): 6.9MM
SALES (corp-wide): 1.3B Publicly Held
WEB: www.olsonirrigation.com
SIC: 3523 Sprayers & spraying machines, agricultural
HQ: Evoqua Water Technologies Llc
210 6th Ave Ste 3300
Pittsburgh PA 15222
724 772-0044

(P-13655)
ORCHARD MACHINERY CORPORATION (PA)
Also Called: Orchard Harvest
2700 Colusa Hwy, Yuba City (95993-8927)
PHONE..................................530 673-2822
Don Mayo, *CEO*
Brian Anderson, *Vice Pres*
Greg Kriss, *Vice Pres*
Joe Martinez, *Vice Pres*
Tom Thomas, *Vice Pres*
▲ **EMP:** 60
SQ FT: 70,000
SALES (est): 20.2MM
SALES (corp-wide): 19.6MM Privately Held
WEB: www.shakermaker.com
SIC: 3523 Shakers, tree: nuts, fruits, etc.

(P-13656)
OXBO INTERNATIONAL CORPORATION
10825 W Goshen Ave, Visalia (93291-8759)
PHONE..................................559 897-7012
Rick Radon, *Branch Mgr*
EMP: 12
SALES (corp-wide): 51.4MM Privately Held
WEB: www.oxbocorp.com
SIC: 3523 Farm machinery & equipment
HQ: Oxbo International Corporation
7275 Batavia Byron Rd
Byron NY 14422
585 548-2665

(P-13657)
PELLENC AMERICA INC (DH)
3171 Guerneville Rd, Santa Rosa (95401-4028)
PHONE..................................707 568-7286
Marc Paisnel, *President*

Corinne Remy, *Division Mgr*
J L Guigues, *Director*
Roger Pellenc, *Director*
J P Pettavino, *Director*
▲ **EMP: 24 EST:** 1996
SQ FT: 50,000
SALES (est): 9.9MM
SALES (corp-wide): 2.6MM Privately Held
SIC: 3523 Farm machinery & equipment
HQ: Pellenc
Quartier Notre Dames Des Anges
Pertuis 84120
490 088-086

(P-13658)
PERRYS CUSTOM CHOPPING
21365 Williams Ave, Hilmar (95324-9602)
PHONE..................................209 667-8777
Jeff Perry, *Principal*
EMP: 15
SALES (est): 3MM Privately Held
SIC: 3523 Harvesters, fruit, vegetable, tobacco, etc.

(P-13659)
PINNACLE AGRICULTURE DIST INC
Also Called: Performance AG
1100 S Madera Ave, Kerman (93630-9139)
PHONE..................................559 842-4601
Raymond Maul, *Branch Mgr*
Jeanne G Lloyd, *Vice Pres*
EMP: 18
SALES (corp-wide): 1B Privately Held
SIC: 3523 5191 Sprayers & spraying machines, agricultural; fertilizer & fertilizer materials; feed
HQ: Pinnacle Agriculture Distribution, Inc.
1880 Fall River Dr Ste 100
Loveland CO 80538
970 800-4300

(P-13660)
PRODUCE AVAILABLE INC (PA)
Also Called: Valley Spuds of Oxnard
910 Commercial Ave, Oxnard (93030-7232)
PHONE..................................805 483-5292
Helmut Brinkmann, *President*
Marlene C Kaiser, *Vice Pres*
Regina Dergan, *Sales Mgr*
Lisa Brinkmann, *Sales Staff*
Roger Ramirez, *Sales Staff*
EMP: 57
SQ FT: 20,000
SALES (est): 13.2MM Privately Held
WEB: www.produceavailable.com
SIC: 3523 Potato diggers, harvesters & planters

(P-13661)
RAINDRIP INC
2250 Agate Ct, Simi Valley (93065-1842)
P.O. Box 339, Lindsay (93247-0339)
PHONE..................................818 710-4023
Barry N Hanish, *President*
Jim Whittle, *CFO*
Ruth Mehra, *Admin Sec*
EMP: 50
SQ FT: 31,000
SALES (est): 5.4MM
SALES (corp-wide): 1.2B Privately Held
WEB: www.raindrip.com
SIC: 3523 Irrigation equipment, self-propelled
HQ: National Diversified Sales, Inc.
21300 Victory Blvd # 215
Woodland Hills CA 91367
559 562-9888

(P-13662)
RAMSAY HIGHLANDER INC
Also Called: Highlander Harvesting Aid
45 Gonzales River Rd, Gonzales (93926)
PHONE..................................831 675-3453
Frank Maconachy, *President*
Michele Maconachy, *Corp Secy*
Chris Garnett, *Vice Pres*
David Offerdahl, *Vice Pres*
Scott Harland, *Director*
▲ **EMP:** 38
SQ FT: 34,000

SALES (est): 10.1MM Privately Held
WEB: www.harvestingaid.com
SIC: 3523 5999 7692 7699 Farm machinery & equipment; farm machinery; welding repair; hydraulic equipment repair

(P-13663)
RANCH SYSTEMS LLC
37 Commercial Blvd # 101, Novato (94949-6112)
PHONE..................................415 884-2770
Jacob Christfort,
Leslie Orr, *Production*
Thomas Christfort, *Marketing Staff*
Hylon Kaufmann, *Marketing Staff*
Jill Lear, *Sales Staff*
EMP: 10
SQ FT: 3,600
SALES (est): 2.4MM Privately Held
SIC: 3523 Irrigation equipment, self-propelled

(P-13664)
RANDELL EQUIPTMENT & MFG
Also Called: Randell Equipment & Mfg
1408 S Lexington St, Delano (93215-9783)
PHONE..................................661 725-6380
Lee Brown, *Vice Pres*
▼ **EMP: 28 EST:** 1980
SALES (est): 4.5MM Privately Held
WEB: www.randellequipment.com
SIC: 3523 Sprayers & spraying machines, agricultural

(P-13665)
REN CORPORATION
2201 Francisco Dr, El Dorado Hills (95762-3713)
PHONE..................................916 739-2000
Andrew Furia, *CEO*
EMP: 10 EST: 2014
SQ FT: 10,000
SALES: 1MM Privately Held
SIC: 3523 Grading, cleaning, sorting machines, fruit, grain, vegetable

(P-13666)
RJ BOUDREAU INC
Also Called: Rjb
1641 Princeton Ave Ste 6, Modesto (95350-5759)
PHONE..................................209 480-3172
Ron Boudreau, *President*
EMP: 12
SQ FT: 5,000
SALES: 1MM Privately Held
WEB: www.rjb-brand.com
SIC: 3523 3561 Dairy equipment (farm); pumps & pumping equipment

(P-13667)
RUSSELL KC & SON
375 E Paige Ave, Tulare (93274-8902)
PHONE..................................559 686-3236
EMP: 20
SQ FT: 17,100
SALES (est): 3.1MM Privately Held
SIC: 3523 Dairy equipment (farm)

(P-13668)
SAN JOAQUIN EQUIPMENT LLC
2413 Crows Landing Rd, Modesto (95358-6109)
PHONE..................................209 538-3831
Tim Stokes, *Manager*
Brandon Manrique, *Manager*
EMP: 36
SALES (est): 2MM
SALES (corp-wide): 4.3MM Privately Held
SIC: 3523 Farm machinery & equipment
PA: Belkorp Industries Inc
1508 Broadway W Suite 900
Vancouver BC V6J 1
604 688-8533

(P-13669)
SCAFCO CORPORATION
Also Called: Scafco Steel Stud Mfg
4301 Jetway Ct, North Highlands (95660-5701)
PHONE..................................916 624-7700
Miguel Da Costa, *Branch Mgr*
Justo Fegurgur, *Branch Mgr*
EMP: 36

▲ = Import ▼=Export
◆ =Import/Export

SALES (corp-wide): 160.5MM **Privately Held**
WEB: www.scafco.com
SIC: 3523 Farm machinery & equipment
PA: Scafco Corporation
2800 E Main Ave
Spokane WA 99202
509 343-9000

(P-13670)
SIGNATURE CONTROL SYSTEMS INC
16485 Laguna Canyon Rd # 130, Irvine (92618-3848)
PHONE.............................949 580-3640
Brian Smith, *President*
Jane Smith, *Vice Pres*
Tim Troast, *General Mgr*
▼ **EMP:** 100 **EST:** 2000
SQ FT: 7,000
SALES (est): 23MM **Privately Held**
WEB: www.signaturecontrolsystems.com
SIC: 3523 Irrigation equipment, self-propelled

(P-13671)
SIMPLY COUNTRY INC
10110 Harvest Ln, Rough and Ready (95975-9783)
PHONE.............................530 615-0565
EMP: 15 **EST:** 2011
SQ FT: 6,800
SALES (est): 1.2MM **Privately Held**
SIC: 3523

(P-13672)
SPECIALIZED DAIRY SERVICE INC
Also Called: S D S
1710 E Philadelphia St, Ontario (91761-7705)
PHONE.............................909 923-3420
Joe T Trujillo, *President*
Joe Trujillo, *Vice Pres*
EMP: 22
SQ FT: 25,000
SALES (est): 6.8MM **Privately Held**
SIC: 3523 3556 5083 Dairy equipment (farm); dairy & milk machinery; dairy machinery & equipment

(P-13673)
STORM INDUSTRIES INC (PA)
23223 Normandie Ave, Torrance (90501-5050)
PHONE.............................310 534-5232
Dale R Philippi, *CEO*
Guy E Marge, *Ch of Bd*
Georgia Claessens, *Treasurer*
Michael Hammond, *Vice Pres*
Elizabeth McGovern, *Vice Pres*
▲ **EMP:** 100
SALES (est): 75.9MM **Privately Held**
WEB: www.stormanagement.com
SIC: 3523 6552 Irrigation equipment, self-propelled; subdividers & developers

(P-13674)
TERRA TECH CORP (PA)
2040 Main St Ste 225, Irvine (92614-8219)
PHONE.............................855 447-6967
Derek Peterson, *Ch of Bd*
Kenneth Vande Vrede, *COO*
Michael James, *CFO*
Michael A Nahass, *Corp Secy*
EMP: 33
SALES: 31.3MM **Publicly Held**
SIC: 3523 Farm machinery & equipment

(P-13675)
TORO COMPANY
1588 N Marshall Ave, El Cajon (92020-1523)
PHONE.............................619 562-2950
Timothy Young, *Manager*
EMP: 91
SQ FT: 86,578
SALES (corp-wide): 2.6B **Publicly Held**
WEB: www.toro.com
SIC: 3523 Irrigation equipment, self-propelled
PA: The Toro Company
8111 Lyndale Ave S
Bloomington MN 55420
952 888-8801

(P-13676)
TORO COMPANY
5825 Jasmine St, Riverside (92504-1183)
P.O. Box 489 (92502-0489)
PHONE.............................951 688-9221
Kendrick Melrose, *Manager*
EMP: 74
SALES (corp-wide): 2.6B **Publicly Held**
WEB: www.toro.com
SIC: 3523 Irrigation equipment, self-propelled
PA: The Toro Company
8111 Lyndale Ave S
Bloomington MN 55420
952 888-8801

(P-13677)
TORO COMPANY
70221 Dinah Shore Dr, Rancho Mirage (92270-1314)
PHONE.............................760 321-8396
Robert Wells, *Manager*
EMP: 100
SALES (corp-wide): 2.6B **Publicly Held**
WEB: www.toro.com
SIC: 3523 3524 Fertilizing, spraying, dusting & irrigation machinery; lawn & garden mowers & accessories
PA: The Toro Company
8111 Lyndale Ave S
Bloomington MN 55420
952 888-8801

(P-13678)
VAL PLASTIC USA L L C
4570 Eucalyptus Ave Ste C, Chino (91710-9200)
PHONE.............................909 390-9600
Dablu Kundu, *General Mgr*
▲ **EMP:** 15
SQ FT: 11,000
SALES (est): 2.8MM **Privately Held**
SIC: 3523 Fertilizing, spraying, dusting & irrigation machinery

(P-13679)
VALLEY FABRICATION INC
1056 Pellet Ave, Salinas (93901-4539)
P.O. Box 3618 (93912-3618)
PHONE.............................831 757-5151
George Glen Heffington, *CEO*
Peter De Groot, *Vice Pres*
Jason Tracy, *Project Engr*
Drew Bartholow, *Engineer*
Tyler Brandt, *Purch Mgr*
▲ **EMP:** 60
SQ FT: 86,000
SALES (est): 14.4MM **Privately Held**
WEB: www.valleyfabricationinc.com
SIC: 3523 7699 5013 Farm machinery & equipment; farm machinery repair; truck parts & accessories

(P-13680)
VIERRA BROS FARMS LLC
Also Called: Vierra Bros Dairy
6960 Crane Rd, Oakdale (95361-8017)
PHONE.............................209 247-3468
David Vierra,
Manuel J Vierra,
EMP: 10
SALES (est): 612.3K **Privately Held**
SIC: 3523 0191 Spreaders, fertilizer; general farms, primarily crop

(P-13681)
W THREE CO
1679 River Dr D, Brawley (92227-1747)
P.O. Box 1110 (92227-1110)
PHONE.............................760 344-5841
Gary Williams, *Partner*
Jerry Williams, *Partner*
EMP: 20
SQ FT: 15,000
SALES (est): 2.6MM **Privately Held**
SIC: 3523 5083 Harvesters, fruit, vegetable, tobacco, etc.; agricultural machinery & equipment

(P-13682)
WARREN & BAERG MFG INC
39950 Road 108, Dinuba (93618-9518)
PHONE.............................559 591-6790
Robert L Baerg, *Chairman*
Randy R Baerg, *President*
Louis Garcia, *Engineer*

▲ **EMP:** 20
SQ FT: 15,000
SALES (est): 5.8MM **Privately Held**
SIC: 3523 Planting, haying, harvesting & processing machinery

(P-13683)
WASCO HARDFACING CO
2660 S East Ave, Fresno (93706-5408)
P.O. Box 2395 (93745-2395)
PHONE.............................559 485-5860
Robin R Messick, *CEO*
▲ **EMP:** 60
SQ FT: 20,000
SALES (est): 13.6MM **Privately Held**
SIC: 3523 Farm machinery & equipment

(P-13684)
WEATHER TEC CORP
5645 E Clinton Ave, Fresno (93727-1308)
PHONE.............................559 291-5555
Nick Sterling Rogers, *CEO*
William H Rogers, *President*
Judith Rogers, *Corp Secy*
▲ **EMP:** 12
SQ FT: 40,000
SALES (est): 3.2MM **Privately Held**
WEB: www.weathertec.com
SIC: 3523 3494 Farm machinery & equipment; sprinkler systems, field

(P-13685)
WEISS-MCNAIR LLC (DH)
100 Loren Ave, Chico (95928-7450)
PHONE.............................530 891-6214
Larry Demmer, *President*
Glenn Stanley, *President*
Sinath Chiem, *Engineer*
Josh Gertsch, *Engineer*
Patti Patheal, *Human Res Mgr*
▲ **EMP:** 80 **EST:** 1974
SQ FT: 32,000
SALES (est): 17.3MM **Privately Held**
WEB: www.weissram.com
SIC: 3523 Farm machinery & equipment
HQ: Gould Paper Corporation
11 Madison Ave
New York NY 10010
212 301-0000

(P-13686)
WELDCRAFT INDUSTRIES
18794 Avenue 96, Terra Bella (93270-9630)
P.O. Box 11104 (93270-1104)
PHONE.............................559 784-4322
Gerald R Micke, *President*
Dixie L Micke, *Vice Pres*
EMP: 15
SALES (est): 3.6MM **Privately Held**
SIC: 3523 5191 Harvesters, fruit, vegetable, tobacco, etc.; farm supplies

(P-13687)
WILBUR-ELLIS COMPANY LLC
2903 S Cedar Ave, Fresno (93725-2324)
P.O. Box 1286 (93715-1286)
PHONE.............................559 442-1220
Doug Hudson, *General Mgr*
EMP: 57
SALES (corp-wide): 2.7B **Privately Held**
WEB: www.wilbur-ellis.com
SIC: 3523 Farm machinery & equipment
HQ: Wilbur-Ellis Company Llc
345 California St Fl 27
San Francisco CA 94104
415 772-4000

(P-13688)
WILCOX BROTHERS INC
Also Called: Wilcox AG Products
14180 State Highway 160, Walnut Grove (95690-9741)
P.O. Box 70 (95690-0070)
PHONE.............................916 776-1784
Alan Wilcox, *President*
Bruce Wilcox, *Vice Pres*
▲ **EMP:** 57
SQ FT: 10,800
SALES (est): 16.7MM **Privately Held**
SIC: 3523 Farm machinery & equipment

3524 Garden, Lawn Tractors & Eqpt

(P-13689)
GRAND PACIFIC FIRE PROTECTION
13100 Red Corral Dr, Corona (92883-6312)
PHONE.............................951 226-8304
Dave Boecking, *President*
EMP: 10
SALES: 654K **Privately Held**
SIC: 3524 Lawn & garden equipment

(P-13690)
MANUTECH MFG & DIST
2080 Sunset Dr, Pacific Grove (93950-3729)
P.O. Box 51295 (93950-6295)
PHONE.............................831 655-8794
Angelo Villucci, *Owner*
Kevin Vilucci, *Co-Owner*
EMP: 11
SQ FT: 5,000
SALES (est): 1.3MM **Privately Held**
WEB: www.manutech.com
SIC: 3524 Blowers & vacuums, lawn

(P-13691)
MC LANE MANUFACTURING INC
6814 Foster Bridge Blvd, Bell Gardens (90201-2032)
PHONE.............................562 633-8158
Elmer E Malchow, *Ch of Bd*
Olivia Osorio, *Treasurer*
Ronald Mc Lane, *Vice Pres*
▲ **EMP:** 65 **EST:** 1942
SALES (est): 12.5MM **Privately Held**
WEB: www.mclanemower.com
SIC: 3524 Lawnmowers, residential: hand or power; edgers, lawn

(P-13692)
POWER - TRIM CO
6060 Phyllis Dr, Cypress (90630-5243)
PHONE.............................714 523-8560
James O Dykes, *CEO*
Philip Shearer, *Vice Pres*
Barbara Dykes, *Admin Sec*
▼ **EMP:** 15
SALES (est): 6.5MM **Privately Held**
WEB: www.powertrim.com
SIC: 3524 5083 Edgers, lawn; lawn & garden machinery & equipment

(P-13693)
R & R MAINTENANCE GROUP
1255 Treat Blvd Ste 300, Walnut Creek (94597-7965)
PHONE.............................707 863-0328
Ruben Maturin, *Principal*
EMP: 12
SALES: 180K **Privately Held**
SIC: 3524 Lawn & garden equipment

(P-13694)
ROTARY CORP
3359 E North Ave Ste 102, Fresno (93725-2641)
PHONE.............................559 445-1108
Ed Nelson, *President*
EMP: 10
SALES (est): 1.3MM **Privately Held**
SIC: 3524 Lawn & garden equipment

(P-13695)
SCOTTS TEMECULA OPERATIONS LLC (DH)
42375 Remington Ave, Temecula (92590-2512)
PHONE.............................951 719-1700
Jim Hagedorn, *CEO*
Barry Sanders, *President*
Ken Bowers, *Engineer*
Luis Talavera, *Engineer*
Bob Bawcombe, *Opers Staff*
▲ **EMP:** 25 **EST:** 1953
SQ FT: 400,000
SALES (est): 29.6MM
SALES (corp-wide): 2.6B **Publicly Held**
SIC: 3524 Lawn & garden equipment

PRODUCTS & SVCS

HQ: The Scotts Company Llc
14111 Scottslawn Rd
Marysville OH 43040
937 644-0011

(P-13696)
SONOMA PLANT WORKS INC
Also Called: Monster Gardens
235 Classic Ct, Rohnert Park (94928-1620)
PHONE..........................707 588-8002
Ryan Bonelli, *CEO*
Heather Lott, *Vice Pres*
Chris Buchanan, *Marketing Staff*
Nick Ramponi, *Sales Staff*
▲ EMP: 10
SALES (est): 1.6MM **Privately Held**
SIC: 3524 Lawn & garden equipment

(P-13697)
SPRAYING DEVICES INC
Also Called: S D I
447 E Caldwell Ave, Visalia (93277-7609)
P.O. Box 3107 (93278-3107)
PHONE..........................559 734-5555
William S Bennet II, *President*
Denise Bennett, *Vice Pres*
EMP: 17 EST: 1982
SQ FT: 16,000
SALES (est): 4.3MM **Privately Held**
WEB: www.sprayingdevices.com
SIC: 3524 Lawn & garden equipment

(P-13698)
SPYDER MANUFACTURING INC
545 Porter Way, Placentia (92870-6454)
PHONE..........................714 528-8010
Gary J Monnig, *President*
Marc J Paquet, *Corp Secy*
Jules P Paquet, *Vice Pres*
Matthew Monnig, *Prdtn Mgr*
Alicia Parra, *Manager*
▲ EMP: 13
SQ FT: 11,000
SALES (est): 3.4MM **Privately Held**
WEB: www.spyder-mfg.com
SIC: 3524 Lawn & garden equipment

(P-13699)
TRU-CUT INC
141 E 157th St, Gardena (90248-2508)
PHONE..........................310 630-0422
Nabi Merchant, *CEO*
▲ EMP: 35
SQ FT: 28,620
SALES (est): 7.3MM **Privately Held**
SIC: 3524 5083 Lawn & garden mowers &
accessories; lawnmowers, residential:
hand or power; edgers, lawn; lawn & gar-
den machinery & equipment; lawn ma-
chinery & equipment

(P-13700)
WESTERN CACTUS GROWERS INC
1860 Monte Vista Dr, Vista (92084-7124)
P.O. Box 2018 (92085-2018)
PHONE..........................760 726-1710
Thomas Hans Britsch, *CEO*
Margaret Britsch, *Vice Pres*
▲ EMP: 25
SQ FT: 6,000
SALES (est): 4.1MM **Privately Held**
SIC: 3524 0181 Lawn & garden equip-
ment; florists' greens & flowers

3531 Construction Machinery & Eqpt

(P-13701)
ADEL PARK LLC
1432 Edinger Ave Ste 120, Tustin
(92780-6293)
PHONE..........................213 321-2030
Adel Park, *Principal*
EMP: 15
SALES (est): 1.5MM **Privately Held**
SIC: 3531 Concrete plants

(P-13702)
AGRICULTURAL MANUFACTURING
4106 S Cedar Ave, Fresno (93725-2703)
PHONE..........................559 485-1662
David Sprott, *President*

▲ EMP: 10
SQ FT: 6,000
SALES: 1.5MM **Privately Held**
WEB: www.agmanco.com
SIC: 3531 Aggregate spreaders

(P-13703)
ALTEC INDUSTRIES INC
1450 N 1st St, Dixon (95620-9798)
PHONE..........................707 678-0800
Adam Baxandall, *Branch Mgr*
Spencer Owen, *Technical Staff*
Mark Quiambao, *Sales Staff*
EMP: 15
SALES (corp-wide): 764.3MM **Privately
Held**
SIC: 3531 Construction machinery
HQ: Altec Industries, Inc.
210 Inverness Center Dr
Birmingham AL 35242
205 991-7733

(P-13704)
ALTEC INDUSTRIES INC
325 Industrial Way, Dixon (95620-9763)
PHONE..........................707 678-0800
James Pitts, *Manager*
Debbie Muhl, *Executive*
Mark Clare, *Associate Dir*
James Pitts, *Office Mgr*
James C Pitts, *MIS Dir*
EMP: 60
SQ FT: 17,664
SALES (corp-wide): 764.3MM **Privately
Held**
WEB: www.altec.com
SIC: 3531 3536 3713 3537 Derricks, ex-
cept oil & gas field; aerial work platforms:
hydraulic/elec. truck/carrier mounted;
cranes, overhead traveling; truck bodies
(motor vehicles); industrial trucks & trac-
tors; conveyors & conveying equipment
HQ: Altec Industries, Inc.
210 Inverness Center Dr
Birmingham AL 35242
205 991-7733

(P-13705)
AMERICAN COMPACTION EQP INC
Also Called: Compaction American
29380 Hunco Way, Lake Elsinore
(92530-2757)
PHONE..........................949 661-2921
Richard S Anderson, *CEO*
Monty Ihde, *President*
Kelly Ihde, *Treasurer*
Darryl Kanell, *Vice Pres*
Mike Shoemaker, *Vice Pres*
▲ EMP: 24
SQ FT: 8,500
SALES (est): 9.2MM **Privately Held**
WEB: www.acewheels.com
SIC: 3531 7353 Soil compactors: vibra-
tory; heavy construction equipment rental
HQ: Cascade Corporation
2201 Ne 201st Ave
Fairview OR 97024
503 669-6300

(P-13706)
AUTOBAHN CONSTRUCTION INC
933 N Batavia St Ste A, Orange
(92867-5590)
PHONE..........................714 769-7025
Ali Solehjou, *President*
EMP: 11
SALES: 1.2MM **Privately Held**
WEB: www.autobahnconstruction.com
SIC: 3531 Road construction & mainte-
nance machinery

(P-13707)
B C H MANUFACTURING CO INC
10012 Denny St, Oakland (94603-3004)
PHONE..........................510 569-6586
Barbara Barton, *President*
Lois Crowell, *Shareholder*
James E Crowell, *Corp Secy*
James M Barton, *Vice Pres*
EMP: 10
SQ FT: 10,000

SALES: 1.4MM **Privately Held**
SIC: 3531 1081 3444 Railroad related
equipment; metal mining services; forming machine work, sheet metal

(P-13708)
BDM ENGINEERING INC
1031 S Linwood Ave, Santa Ana
(92705-4323)
P.O. Box 3087, Tustin (92781-3087)
PHONE..........................714 558-6129
Barlowe D Moonilal, *President*
▼ EMP: 20
SQ FT: 20,000
SALES (est): 4.8MM **Privately Held**
WEB: www.bdm-engineering.com
SIC: 3531 Construction machinery

(P-13709)
BINDEL BROS GRADING &
1104 Madison Ln, Salinas (93907-1818)
PHONE..........................831 754-1490
William C Bindel, *President*
Bob Bindel, *Vice Pres*
EMP: 12
SQ FT: 2,000
SALES (est): 1.9MM **Privately Held**
SIC: 3531 1794 Buckets, excavating:
clamshell, concrete, dragline, etc.;
forestry related equipment; excavation &
grading, building construction

(P-13710)
BLACK DIAMOND BLADE COMPANY (PA)
Also Called: Cutting Edge Supply
234 E O St, Colton (92324-3466)
PHONE..........................800 949-9014
John Brenner, *CEO*
Franklin J Brenner Sr, *President*
Hoby Brenner, *Treasurer*
Franklin Brennerc, *Admin Sec*
▲ EMP: 45 EST: 1950
SQ FT: 16,000
SALES (est): 35.1MM **Privately Held**
WEB: www.cuttingedgesupply.com
SIC: 3531 Blades for graders, scrapers,
dozers & snow plows; road construction &
maintenance machinery

(P-13711)
BLASTRAC NA
5220 Gaines St, San Diego (92110-2623)
PHONE..........................800 256-3440
Lenore Lipoufski, *Principal*
▲ EMP: 11
SALES (est): 690K **Privately Held**
SIC: 3531 Construction machinery

(P-13712)
BRENT ENGINEERING INC
81 Shield, Irvine (92618-5212)
PHONE..........................949 679-5630
Ron Burek, *President*
EMP: 15
SALES (est): 3.7MM **Privately Held**
WEB: www.brentengineering.com
SIC: 3531 Road construction & mainte-
nance machinery

(P-13713)
CAL VSTA EROSION CTRL PDTS LLC
459 Country Rd 99w 99 W, Arbuckle
(95912)
PHONE..........................530 476-0706
Renee Shadinger, *CEO*
Bryan Shadinger, *President*
John Shadinger, *CFO*
Maggie Shadinger, *Controller*
EMP: 35
SALES: 2.9MM **Privately Held**
WEB: www.calvistaerosion.com
SIC: 3531 Construction machinery

(P-13714)
CALIFORNIA MFG & ENGRG CO LLC
1401 S Madera Ave, Kerman (93630-9139)
PHONE..........................559 842-1500
Frank Shanahan,
Karen Emery,
Richard Spencer,
▲ EMP: 130

SALES (est): 15.7MM **Privately Held**
WEB: www.dfmfg.com
SIC: 3531 Construction machinery

(P-13715)
CALIFORNIA STONE COATING
37911 Von Euw Cmn, Fremont
(94536-3963)
PHONE..........................510 284-2554
Kevin Farrer, *Owner*
EMP: 15
SALES (est): 2.1MM **Privately Held**
SIC: 3531 Roofing equipment

(P-13716)
CAMLEVER INC
954 S East End Ave, Pomona
(91766-3837)
PHONE..........................909 629-9669
John Z Harris, *President*
Vanessa Rolden, *Admin Sec*
EMP: 12 EST: 1965
SQ FT: 2,500
SALES (est): 2.5MM **Privately Held**
SIC: 3531 3799 3312 Construction ma-
chinery; wheelbarrows; blast furnaces &
steel mills

(P-13717)
CARON COMPACTOR CO
1204 Ullrey Ave, Escalon (95320-8618)
PHONE..........................800 448-8236
James O Caron, *CEO*
Judith S Caron, *Vice Pres*
Mark Stapp, *Sales Mgr*
Joe Kelley, *Sales Staff*
▲ EMP: 25 EST: 1969
SQ FT: 18,000
SALES (est): 6.2MM **Privately Held**
WEB: www.caroncompactor.com
SIC: 3531 3441 Construction machinery
attachments; fabricated structural metal

(P-13718)
CASTLE & COOKE INC
Pacific Aggregates
28251 Lake St, Lake Elsinore
(92530-1635)
PHONE..........................951 245-2460
Mike Garcia, *Manager*
EMP: 80
SALES (corp-wide): 893.5MM **Privately
Held**
SIC: 3531 Mixers, concrete
PA: Castle & Cooke, Inc.
1 Dole Dr
Westlake Village CA 91362

(P-13719)
CATERPILLAR INC
17364 Hawthorne Blvd, Torrance
(90504-1033)
PHONE..........................310 921-9811
Jerry Meza, *Branch Mgr*
EMP: 16
SALES (corp-wide): 54.7B **Publicly Held**
SIC: 3531 Construction machinery
PA: Caterpillar Inc.
510 Lake Cook Rd Ste 100
Deerfield IL 60015
224 551-4000

(P-13720)
CATERPILLAR INC
5101 E Airport Dr, Ontario (91761-7825)
PHONE..........................909 390-9035
Jason Baumann, *Branch Mgr*
EMP: 385
SALES (corp-wide): 54.7B **Publicly Held**
SIC: 3531 3519 3511 Construction ma-
chinery; engines, diesel & semi-diesel or
dual-fuel; gas turbine generator set units,
complete
PA: Caterpillar Inc.
510 Lake Cook Rd Ste 100
Deerfield IL 60015
224 551-4000

(P-13721)
CAVOTEC INET US INC
5665 Corporate Ave, Cypress
(90630-4727)
PHONE..........................714 947-0005
Mike Larkin, *President*
Dorothy Chen, *CFO*

▼ EMP: 70
SALES: 24MM
SALES (corp-wide): 223.6MM **Privately Held**
WEB: www.inetas.com
SIC: 3531 Airport construction machinery
HQ: Cavotec Us Holdings, Inc.
5665 Corporate Ave
Cypress CA 90630
714 545-7900

(P-13722)
CLEASBY MANUFACTURING CO INC (PA)
1414 Bancroft Ave, San Francisco (94124-3603)
P.O. Box 24132 (94124-0132)
PHONE................................415 822-6565
Leslie John Cleasby, *President*
John Cleasby, *President*
EMP: 20
SQ FT: 21,000
SALES: 5MM **Privately Held**
SIC: 3531 5033 Roofing equipment; roofing & siding materials

(P-13723)
COUNTY OF LOS ANGELES
Also Called: Public Works, Dept of
14959 Proctor Ave, La Puente (91746-3206)
PHONE................................626 968-3312
Mike Lee, *Manager*
EMP: 20 **Privately Held**
WEB: www.co.la.ca.us
SIC: 3531 9111 Road construction & maintenance machinery; bituminous batching plants; executive offices
PA: County Of Los Angeles
500 W Temple St Ste 437
Los Angeles CA 90012
213 974-1101

(P-13724)
COUNTY OF LOS ANGELES
Also Called: Public Works, Dept of
3637 Winter Canyon Rd, Malibu (90265-4834)
PHONE................................310 456-8014
Mark Sanchez, *Manager*
EMP: 16 **Privately Held**
WEB: www.co.la.ca.us
SIC: 3531 9621 Graders, road (construction machinery); regulation, administration of transportation
PA: County Of Los Angeles
500 W Temple St Ste 437
Los Angeles CA 90012
213 974-1101

(P-13725)
CUSTOM BUILDING PRODUCTS INC
3525 Zephyr Ct, Stockton (95206-4210)
PHONE................................209 983-8322
EMP: 40 **Privately Held**
WEB: www.custombuildingproducts.com
SIC: 3531 Concrete grouting equipment
HQ: Custom Building Products, Inc.
7711 Center Ave Ste 500
Huntington Beach CA 92647
800 272-8786

(P-13726)
DAVE HUMPHREY ENTERPRISES INC
Also Called: Noble Concrete Plants
145 Gandy Dancer Dr, Tracy (95377-8911)
PHONE................................209 835-2222
Scott Humphrey, *CEO*
David G Humphrey, *President*
Heidi Herbert, *Corp Secy*
Bonnie Doyle, *Accountant*
▲ EMP: 13
SQ FT: 1,000
SALES (est): 4.2MM **Privately Held**
WEB: www.dhenoble.com
SIC: 3531 Batching plants, for aggregate concrete & bulk cement

(P-13727)
EAGLE ROCK INCORPORATED
40029 La Grange Rd, Junction City (96048)
PHONE................................530 623-4444

Larry E Yingling, *President*
David W Yingling, *Vice Pres*
EMP: 15 **EST:** 1980
SQ FT: 720
SALES (est): 2.9MM **Privately Held**
SIC: 3531 2951 1423 Rock crushing machinery, portable; capstans; ship; asphalt & asphaltic paving mixtures (not from refineries); crushed & broken granite

(P-13728)
ENDEAVOR HOMES INC
655 Cal Oak Rd, Oroville (95965-9621)
P.O. Box 1947 (95965-1947)
PHONE................................530 534-0300
Del Fleener, *President*
Shonie Schufeldt, *Treasurer*
William Wicklas, *Vice Pres*
EMP: 20
SALES (est): 6.4MM **Privately Held**
WEB: www.endeavorhomes.com
SIC: 3531 2439 Construction machinery; trusses, wooden roof

(P-13729)
GATOR MACHINERY COMPANY
11020 Cherry Ave, Fontana (92337-7119)
PHONE................................909 823-1688
Charles Wu, *President*
Shirley Wu, *Admin Sec*
Gloria Huang, *Controller*
Ernie Gallegos, *Sales Mgr*
◆ EMP: 11
SALES (est): 3MM **Privately Held**
WEB: www.gatormachinery.com
SIC: 3531 Rock crushing machinery, portable

(P-13730)
GLOBAL POLISHING SOLUTIONS LLC (HQ)
Also Called: Diamatic Management Services
5220 Gaines St, San Diego (92110-2623)
PHONE................................619 295-5505
Stephen Klugherz, *President*
Brian McKinley, *CEO*
John Rittean, *Vice Pres*
Rebecca Salvatierra, *Vice Pres*
Brian Downey, *Controller*
▲ EMP: 30
SALES: 25MM
SALES (corp-wide): 44.5MM **Privately Held**
SIC: 3531 5082 Surfacers, concrete grinding; concrete processing equipment
PA: Blastrac Global, Inc.
222 Greystone Rd
Evergreen CO 80439
405 478-3440

(P-13731)
GLOBAL PRECISION MANUFACTURING
38 Hollins Dr, Santa Cruz (95060-1815)
PHONE................................831 239-9469
Edwin Taylor, *Owner*
Ed Taylor, *Engineer*
EMP: 10
SALES (est): 749.6K **Privately Held**
SIC: 3531 3444 Construction machinery; sheet metalwork

(P-13732)
GREENFORM LLC
12900 Prairie Ave, Hawthorne (90250-5306)
PHONE................................310 331-1665
Felix Schneider, *Principal*
▲ EMP: 10
SALES (est): 960.8K **Privately Held**
SIC: 3531 Bituminous, cement & concrete related products & equipment

(P-13733)
GROUND HOG INC
1470 Victoria Ct, San Bernardino (92408-2831)
P.O. Box 290 (92402-0290)
PHONE................................909 478-5700
Edward Carlson, *President*
Jack Carlson, *Corp Secy*
▼ EMP: 25 **EST:** 1948
SQ FT: 52,000

SALES (est): 6.8MM **Privately Held**
WEB: www.groundhoginc.com
SIC: 3531 Posthole diggers, powered; entrenching machines

(P-13734)
GUNTERT ZMMERMAN CONST DIV INC
222 E 4th St, Ripon (95366-2761)
PHONE................................209 599-0066
Ronald M Guntert Jr, *CEO*
Denise Guntert, *Vice Pres*
Mary Frampton, *Executive Asst*
Iovtcho Delev, *Engineer*
Jeremy Henley, *Engineer*
▲ EMP: 50 **EST:** 1942
SQ FT: 10,000
SALES (est): 23.1MM **Privately Held**
SIC: 3531 3599 Pavers; machine & other job shop work

(P-13735)
H & L TOOTH COMPANY (PA)
1540 S Greenwood Ave, Montebello (90640-6536)
P.O. Box 48, Owasso OK (74055-0048)
PHONE................................323 721-5146
Richard L Launder, *Ch of Bd*
Brian L Launder, *Vice Pres*
▲ EMP: 85 **EST:** 1931
SQ FT: 220,000
SALES (est): 13.2MM **Privately Held**
SIC: 3531 Bucket or scarifier teeth; construction machinery attachments

(P-13736)
HIROK INC
Also Called: Spitzlift
5644 Kearny Mesa Rd Ste H, San Diego (92111-1311)
P.O. Box 3423, Ramona (92065-0959)
PHONE................................619 713-5066
Michael Spitsbergen, *CEO*
Mark Spitsbergen, *Vice Pres*
EMP: 20
SQ FT: 2,500
SALES (est): 4.5MM **Privately Held**
WEB: www.hirok.com
SIC: 3531 Construction machinery

(P-13737)
KENCO ENGINEERING INC
2155 Pfe Rd, Roseville (95747-9765)
P.O. Box 1467 (95678-8467)
PHONE................................916 782-8494
David Lutz, *President*
Donald Lutz, *Vice Pres*
EMP: 30
SQ FT: 25,000
SALES (est): 7.7MM **Privately Held**
WEB: www.kencoengineering.com
SIC: 3531 5082 Construction machinery attachments; general construction machinery & equipment

(P-13738)
MIXMOR INC
3131 Casitas Ave, Los Angeles (90039-2499)
PHONE................................323 664-1941
Michael K McNamara, *CEO*
Ann B Mc Namara, *Corp Secy*
David Ojeda, *Engineer*
William Preston, *Sales Mgr*
EMP: 19 **EST:** 1935
SQ FT: 17,000
SALES (est): 6.6MM **Privately Held**
WEB: www.mixmor.com
SIC: 3531 Construction machinery

(P-13739)
ORBOT
3275 Corporate Vw, Vista (92081-8528)
PHONE................................760 295-2100
Derek Wilson, *CFO*
EMP: 11
SALES (est): 2.5MM **Privately Held**
SIC: 3531 Construction machinery

(P-13740)
PAUL A EVANS INC
1215 Audubon Rd, Mount Shasta (96067-9006)
P.O. Box 940 (96067-0940)
PHONE................................530 859-2505
Paul A Evans, *President*

EMP: 15
SALES (est): 1.1MM **Privately Held**
SIC: 3531 Buckets, excavating: clamshell, concrete, dragline, etc.

(P-13741)
PETER PUGGER MANUFACTURING
3661 Christy Ln, Ukiah (95482-3088)
PHONE................................707 463-1333
Randolph C Wood, *CEO*
Jared Paz, *General Mgr*
▲ EMP: 11
SQ FT: 15,000
SALES (est): 3.3MM **Privately Held**
WEB: www.peterpugger.com
SIC: 3531 Mixers: ore, plaster, slag, sand, mortar, etc.

(P-13742)
QUIK MFG CO
Also Called: Q M C
18071 Mount Washington St, Fountain Valley (92708-6118)
PHONE................................714 754-0337
Dannielle Schmidt, *Ch of Bd*
Steve Schmidt, *President*
George Hunter, *Production*
EMP: 28
SQ FT: 25,000
SALES (est): 1.2MM **Privately Held**
WEB: www.qmccranes.com
SIC: 3531 Cranes

(P-13743)
R E ATCKISON CO INC
1801 W Gladstone St, Azusa (91702-3206)
PHONE................................626 334-0266
Edwards J Atckison, *President*
Roger Atckison, *Treasurer*
EMP: 11
SQ FT: 2,000
SALES (est): 2.7MM **Privately Held**
SIC: 3531 Aerial work platforms: hydraulic/elec. truck/carrier mounted

(P-13744)
REGINA F BARAJAS
Also Called: C and R Pavers
629 Fern St, Escondido (92027-2105)
PHONE................................760 500-0809
Regina F Barajas, *Owner*
Regina Barajas, *Contractor*
EMP: 10 **EST:** 2010
SALES: 900K **Privately Held**
SIC: 3531 Pavers

(P-13745)
SANDWOOD ENTERPRISES
Also Called: Orange County Sandbagger
2424 N Batavia St, Orange (92865-2004)
PHONE................................714 637-2000
Jason Vos, *President*
Angie Vos, *Corp Secy*
EMP: 12
SQ FT: 1,440
SALES (est): 3.7MM **Privately Held**
WEB: www.ocsandbagger.com
SIC: 3531 1795 4212 Asphalt plant, including gravel-mix type; wrecking & demolition work; local trucking, without storage

(P-13746)
SANTA ROSA LEAD PRODUCTS LLC (PA)
33 S University St, Healdsburg (95448-4021)
PHONE................................800 916-5323
EMP: 17
SALES (est): 3.5MM **Privately Held**
SIC: 3531 Roofing equipment

(P-13747)
SCHAMAS MFG COINC
6356 N Irwindale Ave, Irwindale (91702-3210)
PHONE................................626 334-6870
William Schaeffler, *President*
Ralph Mason, *Vice Pres*
EMP: 15
SQ FT: 5,000
SALES (est): 2.4MM **Privately Held**
SIC: 3531 5084 Construction machinery; materials handling machinery

(P-13748)
SILO CITY INC
1401 S Union Ave, Bakersfield
(93307-4141)
PHONE..................................661 387-0179
Michael Clift, *CEO*
▲ EMP: 24
SQ FT: 174,240
SALES (est): 7.4MM **Privately Held**
SIC: 3531 Bituminous, cement & concrete
related products & equipment

(P-13749)
SNL GROUP INC
9818 Holton Way, Redding (96003-9546)
PHONE..................................530 222-5048
Eric Stephens, *Vice Pres*
Tim Lewis, *Principal*
Cynthia Stephens, *Admin Sec*
EMP: 13
SQ FT: 5,000
SALES (est): 3.7MM **Privately Held**
SIC: 3531 Plows: construction, excavating
& grading

(P-13750)
**TANFIELD ENGRG SYSTEMS US
INC**
Also Called: Upright
2686 S Maple Ave, Fresno (93725-2108)
PHONE..................................559 443-6602
Roy Stanley, *President*
Charles Brooks, *CFO*
Doug King, *General Mgr*
David Sternweis, *Controller*
Darren Kell, *Director*
EMP: 15
SQ FT: 67,727
SALES (est): 3.8MM **Privately Held**
SIC: 3531 Aerial work platforms: hy-
draulic/elec. truck/carrier mounted
PA: Tanfield Group Plc
Sandgate House
Newcastle-Upon-Tyne

(P-13751)
TINK INC
2361 Durham Dayton Hwy, Durham
(95938-9604)
PHONE..................................530 895-0897
Robert J Du Bose, *CEO*
Dan M Du Bose, *Vice Pres*
Dan D Bose, *VP Finance*
Rosie Birmingham, *Controller*
Paul Reed, *Sales Staff*
EMP: 40
SQ FT: 53,000
SALES (est): 12.4MM **Privately Held**
SIC: 3531 3444 Construction machinery;
sheet metalwork

(P-13752)
**TNT INDUSTRIAL
CONTRACTORS INC (PA)**
3800 Happy Ln, Sacramento (95827-9721)
PHONE..................................916 395-8400
Josh Twist, *CEO*
Mark Andrews, *Project Mgr*
John Morrill, *Project Mgr*
Dave Richter, *Sr Project Mgr*
EMP: 36
SQ FT: 4,000
SALES: 16.1MM **Privately Held**
WEB: www.tntindustrial.com
SIC: 3531 Construction machinery

(P-13753)
**TRIO ENGINEERED PRODUCTS
INC (HQ)**
505 W Foothill Blvd, Azusa (91702-2345)
PHONE..................................626 851-3966
Michael Francis Burke, *CEO*
Eugene Xue, *Vice Pres*
◆ EMP: 29
SALES (est): 7.4MM
SALES (corp-wide): 3.1B **Privately Held**
WEB: www.trioproducts.com
SIC: 3531 Construction machinery attach-
ments; aggregate spreaders
PA: Weir Group Plc(The)
1 West Regent Street
Glasgow G2 1R
141 637-7111

(P-13754)
TUSCANY PAVERS INC
241 S Twin Oaks Valley Rd, San Marcos
(92078-4330)
PHONE..................................866 596-4092
Daniel Winfield, *Principal*
Mary Ann Erdos, *CFO*
EMP: 11
SALES (est): 1.8MM **Privately Held**
SIC: 3531 Pavers

(P-13755)
US SAWS INC (PA)
Also Called: U S Saw & Blades
3702 W Central Ave, Santa Ana
(92704-5832)
PHONE..................................860 668-2402
Bruce Root, *CEO*
C W Duncan, *President*
Bill Glynn, *Vice Pres*
Helen Duncan, *Sales Staff*
▲ EMP: 18
SQ FT: 4,000
SALES: 7MM **Privately Held**
WEB: www.ussaws.com
SIC: 3531 5082 Blades for graders, scrap-
ers, dozers & snow plows; road construc-
tion & maintenance machinery

(P-13756)
**VOLVO CONSTRUCTION EQP &
SVCS**
22099 Knabe Rd, Corona (92883-7111)
PHONE..................................951 277-7620
Mike Franks, *Principal*
EMP: 26
SALES (est): 31.1MM
SALES (corp-wide): 43.4B **Privately Held**
SIC: 3531 Construction machinery
HQ: Saba Holding Company, Llc
312 Volvo Way
Shippensburg PA 17257
717 532-9181

(P-13757)
WESTERN EQUIPMENT MFG INC
Also Called: Western Equipment Mfg
1160 Olympic Dr, Corona (92881-3390)
PHONE..................................951 284-2000
Kenneth R Thompson, *CEO*
William Weihl, *President*
▲ EMP: 19
SALES (est): 5.1MM **Privately Held**
SIC: 3531 Finishers & spreaders (con-
struction equipment)

3532 Mining Machinery & Eqpt

(P-13758)
**AUTOMATED PACKG SYSTEMS
INC**
10440 Ontiveros Pl Ste 1, Santa Fe Springs
(90670-7335)
PHONE..................................562 941-1476
Bernie Lerner, *President*
Chris Houin, *Engineer*
EMP: 12
SALES (corp-wide): 216MM **Privately
Held**
WEB: www.autobag.com
SIC: 3532 5113 3565 2671 Mining ma-
chinery; industrial & personal service
paper; packaging machinery; packaging
paper & plastics film, coated & laminated;
packaging materials
PA: Automated Packaging Systems Inc.
10175 Philipp Pkwy
Streetsboro OH 44241
330 528-2000

(P-13759)
**POLYALLOYS INJECTED
METALS INC**
14000 Avalon Blvd, Los Angeles
(90061-2636)
PHONE..................................310 715-9800
Craig Paulin, *CEO*
Eden Ines, *Controller*
EMP: 75

SALES (est): 7.7MM
SALES (corp-wide): 22.9MM **Privately
Held**
SIC: 3532 Amalgamators (metallurgical or
mining machinery)
PA: Psm Industries, Inc.
14000 Avalon Blvd
Los Angeles CA 90061
888 663-8256

(P-13760)
REED INTERNATIONAL (HQ)
Also Called: Saunco Air Technologies
13024 Lake Rd, Hickman (95323-9667)
P.O. Box 178 (95323-0178)
PHONE..................................209 874-2357
Wendell Reed, *President*
Kevin Clark, *Project Engr*
▼ EMP: 20 EST: 1973
SALES (est): 3.1MM
SALES (corp-wide): 214.4MM **Privately
Held**
WEB: www.saunco.com
SIC: 3532 5531 3564 3444 Mining ma-
chinery; automotive & home supply
stores; blowers & fans; sheet metalwork
PA: Basic Resources Inc
928 12th St Ste 700
Modesto CA 95354
209 521-9771

(P-13761)
**SPAULDING EQUIPMENT
COMPANY (PA)**
Also Called: Spaulding Crusher Parts
75 Paseo Adelanto, Perris (92570-9343)
P.O. Box 1807 (92572-1807)
PHONE..................................951 943-4531
George E Spaulding, *Ch of Bd*
James Michael Spaulding, *President*
Fred Stemrich, *Corp Secy*
Norman Vetter, *Vice Pres*
◆ EMP: 47
SALES (est): 10.2MM **Privately Held**
SIC: 3532 5082 7699 Mineral beneficia-
tion equipment; mineral beneficiation ma-
chinery; industrial machinery & equipment
repair

(P-13762)
WEBER DRILLING CO INC
401 Hindry Ave, Inglewood (90301-2015)
PHONE..................................310 670-7708
Marlene Wood, *President*
Ronald Wood, *Vice Pres*
EMP: 25
SQ FT: 7,000
SALES (est): 4.6MM **Privately Held**
SIC: 3532 Drills & drilling equipment, min-
ing (except oil & gas)

3533 Oil Field Machinery & Eqpt

(P-13763)
AERA ENERGY LLC
29010 Shell Rd, Coalinga (93210-9235)
PHONE..................................559 935-7418
Kevin Peck, *Branch Mgr*
EMP: 25
SALES (corp-wide): 388.3B **Privately
Held**
WEB: www.aeraenergy.com
SIC: 3533 1311 Oil & gas drilling rigs &
equipment; crude petroleum & natural gas
production
HQ: Aera Energy Llc
10000 Ming Ave
Bakersfield CA 93311
661 665-5000

(P-13764)
**AMR INDUSTRIES
ENTERPRISES INC**
2131 19th Ave Ste 203, San Francisco
(94116-1868)
PHONE..................................415 860-5566
Kristo Regjo, *CEO*
EMP: 23
SALES (est): 5.1MM **Privately Held**
SIC: 3533 Oil & gas field machinery

(P-13765)
AQUEOS CORPORATION
2550 Eastman Ave, Ventura (93003-7714)
PHONE..................................805 676-4330
Theodore Roche, *Branch Mgr*
Jason Kleinschmidt, *Technician*
William Kim, *Supervisor*
Jason Thach, *Supervisor*
Steve Webster, *Supervisor*
EMP: 52
SALES (corp-wide): 32.9MM **Privately
Held**
SIC: 3533 Oil & gas field machinery
PA: Aqueos Corporation
418 Chapala St Ste E&F
Santa Barbara CA 93101
805 364-0570

(P-13766)
AQUEOS CORPORATION (PA)
418 Chapala St Ste E&F, Santa Barbara
(93101-8054)
PHONE..................................805 364-0570
Theodore Roche IV, *President*
Bradley Parro, *CFO*
Travis Detke, *Vice Pres*
Michael Pfau, *Admin Sec*
Curtis Sampson, *Project Leader*
EMP: 104
SQ FT: 23,000
SALES (est): 32.9MM **Privately Held**
WEB: www.divecon.com
SIC: 3533 Oil & gas field machinery

(P-13767)
**BAKER HUGHES A GE
COMPANY LLC**
6117 Schirra Ct, Bakersfield (93313-2167)
PHONE..................................661 834-9654
Joe Howard, *Branch Mgr*
Aaron Bowser, *Opers Staff*
EMP: 87
SALES (corp-wide): 22.8B **Privately Held**
WEB: www.bakerhughes.com
SIC: 3533 Oil & gas field machinery
PA: Baker Hughes, A Ge Company Llc
17021 Aldine Westfield Rd
Houston TX 77073
713 439-8600

(P-13768)
**CAMERON INTERNATIONAL
CORP**
4315 Yeager Way, Bakersfield
(93313-2018)
PHONE..................................661 323-8183
Keith Smith, *District Mgr*
EMP: 10 **Publicly Held**
SIC: 3533 5084 Oil field machinery &
equipment; drilling equipment, excluding
bits
HQ: Cameron International Corporation
4646 W Sam Houston Pkwy N
Houston TX 77041

(P-13769)
**CAMERON INTERNATIONAL
CORP**
535 Getty Ct Ste A, Benicia (94510-1179)
PHONE..................................707 752-8800
EMP: 49 **Publicly Held**
SIC: 3533 Oil field machinery & equipment
HQ: Cameron International Corporation
4646 W Sam Houston Pkwy N
Houston TX 77041

(P-13770)
**CAMERON INTERNATIONAL
CORP**
Also Called: Cooper Cameron Valves
562 River Park Dr, Redding (96003-5381)
PHONE..................................530 242-6965
EMP: 56
SALES (corp-wide): 10.3B **Publicly Held**
SIC: 3533
PA: Cameron International Corporation
1333 West Loop S Ste 1700
Houston TX 77041
713 513-3300

▲ = Import ▼=Export
◆ =Import/Export

(P-13771)
CAMERON WEST COAST (PA)
9452 Resenda Ave, Fontana (92335-2541)
PHONE....................................909 355-8995
Charles Jerry Funderburk, *President*
Garry Stevens, *Vice Pres*
▲ EMP: 10
SQ FT: 14,000
SALES (est): 1.2MM **Privately Held**
WEB: www.elcoinc.com
SIC: 3533 7353 Oil field machinery &
equipment; oil field equipment, rental or
leasing

(P-13772)
CONTROL SYSTEMS INTL INC
1 Sterling, Irvine (92618-2517)
PHONE....................................949 238-4150
Rob Lewis, *General Mgr*
EMP: 34
SALES (corp-wide): 12.6B **Privately Held**
SIC: 3533 Oil & gas field machinery
HQ: Control Systems International, Inc.
8040 Nieman Rd
Shawnee Mission KS 66214
913 599-5010

(P-13773)
DAWSON ENTERPRISES (PA)
Also Called: Cavins Oil Well Tools
2853 Cherry Ave, Signal Hill (90755-1908)
P.O. Box 6039, Long Beach (90806-0039)
PHONE....................................562 424-8564
James M Dawson, *CEO*
Harry Dawson, *President*
Jim Moore, *Executive*
Kirk Moore, *Regional Mgr*
Charles Palmer, *General Mgr*
◆ EMP: 36
SQ FT: 19,000
SALES (est): 9.7MM **Privately Held**
WEB: www.cavins.com
SIC: 3533 7359 Bits, oil & gas field tools:
rock; garage facility & tool rental

(P-13774)
**DOWNHOLE STABILIZATION
INC**
3515 Thomas Way, Bakersfield
(93308-6215)
P.O. Box 2467 (93303-2467)
PHONE....................................661 631-1044
Jim Calanchini, *President*
Diane Calanchini, *Corp Secy*
Jacob Banducci, *Vice Pres*
Joe Calanchini, *Vice Pres*
Mike Jarboe, *Vice Pres*
▲ EMP: 38
SQ FT: 8,800
SALES (est): 11MM **Privately Held**
WEB: www.downholedrillingtools.com
SIC: 3533 5082 3599 1389 Drilling tools
for gas, oil or water wells; construction &
mining machinery; wellpoints (drilling
equipment); amusement park equipment;
machine shop, jobbing & repair; construc-
tion, repair & dismantling services; oil field
services

(P-13775)
FARLEY MACHINE INC
1600 S Union Ave, Bakersfield
(93307-4146)
PHONE....................................661 397-4987
Paul J Farley, *President*
Winney Farley, *Corp Secy*
J B Rogers, *Vice Pres*
EMP: 13
SQ FT: 1,400
SALES (est): 2.5MM **Privately Held**
WEB: www.farley.rwisp.com
SIC: 3533 Oil field machinery & equipment;
water well drilling equipment

(P-13776)
FMC TECHNOLOGIES INC
621 Burning Tree Rd, Fullerton
(92833-1448)
PHONE....................................714 872-5574
Rose Folli, *Principal*
EMP: 15
SALES (corp-wide): 12.6B **Privately Held**
SIC: 3533 Oil field machinery & equipment

HQ: Fmc Technologies, Inc.
11740 Katy Fwy Enrgy Twr
Houston TX 77079
281 591-4000

(P-13777)
FTT HOLDINGS INC
3020 Old Ranch Pkwy, Seal Beach
(90740-2765)
PHONE....................................562 430-6262
Bryan Livingston, *President*
James Leonetti, *CFO*
David Haas, *Exec VP*
EMP: 12
SALES (est): 1.7MM **Privately Held**
SIC: 3533 Oil field machinery & equipment

(P-13778)
**GLOBAL ELASTOMERIC PDTS
INC**
5551 District Blvd, Bakersfield
(93313-2126)
PHONE....................................661 831-5380
Phil W Embury, *President*
Sandy Embury, *Vice Pres*
Jim Pickering, *Safety Mgr*
Tom Pelle, *QC Mgr*
Zachary Ellis, *Sales Staff*
▲ EMP: 55
SQ FT: 20,000
SALES (est): 12.3MM **Privately Held**
WEB: www.globaleee.com
SIC: 3533 5084 Oil & gas field machinery;
oil refining machinery, equipment & sup-
plies; oil well machinery, equipment &
supplies

(P-13779)
HARBISON-FISCHER INC
200 Carver St, Shafter (93263-4008)
PHONE....................................661 399-0628
EMP: 31
SALES (corp-wide): 1.2B **Publicly Held**
SIC: 3533 Oil field machinery & equipment
HQ: Harbison-Fischer, Inc.
901 N Crowley Rd
Crowley TX 76036
817 297-2211

(P-13780)
HYDRIL COMPANY
3237 Patton Way, Bakersfield
(93308-5717)
PHONE....................................661 588-9332
Ken Steinke, *Branch Mgr*
EMP: 343
SALES (corp-wide): 183.7K **Privately
Held**
SIC: 3533 Oil field machinery & equipment
HQ: Hydril Company
302 Mccarty St
Houston TX 77029

(P-13781)
HYDRIL USA DISTRIBUTION LLC
3237 Patton Way, Bakersfield
(93308-5717)
PHONE....................................661 588-9332
Baryy Park, *Manager*
EMP: 12
SALES (corp-wide): 121.6B **Publicly
Held**
WEB: www.hydril.com
SIC: 3533 1389 Oil & gas field machinery;
oil field services
HQ: Hydril Usa Distribution Llc
3300 N Sam Houston Pkwy E
Houston TX 77032
281 449-2000

(P-13782)
KBA ENGINEERING LLC
2157 Mohawk St, Bakersfield
(93308-6020)
P.O. Box 1200 (93302-1200)
PHONE....................................661 323-0487
Richard C Jones, *Mng Member*
Mark Smith, *Human Res Dir*
Chris Ryan, *Purch Mgr*
Cyndee Jenkins, *Purch Agent*
Brad O'Rear,
EMP: 95
SQ FT: 45,000

SALES (est): 19.6MM **Privately Held**
WEB: www.kbaeng.com
SIC: 3533 3462 Oil & gas field machinery;
gear & chain forgings

(P-13783)
KMT INTERNATIONAL INC
344 De Leon Ave, Fremont (94539-5705)
PHONE....................................510 713-1400
Boris Melamed, *President*
Eugene Kravets, *Vice Pres*
Yakov Reznikov, *Director*
▼ EMP: 42
SQ FT: 10,000
SALES (est): 14MM **Privately Held**
SIC: 3533 Gas field machinery & equip-
ment

(P-13784)
**LASALLE INTL HLDINGS GROUP
INC**
9667 Owensmouth Ave, Chatsworth
(91311-4819)
P.O. Box 7396, Northridge (91327-7396)
PHONE....................................818 233-8000
Pierre Yenokian, *President*
Jan Papazian, *CFO*
Alana Yenokian, *Admin Sec*
◆ EMP: 40
SQ FT: 70,000
SALES (est): 5.5MM **Privately Held**
SIC: 3533 5047 1382 Oil & gas field ma-
chinery; medical & hospital equipment; oil
& gas exploration services; geological ex-
ploration, oil & gas field

(P-13785)
**NATIONAL OILWELL VARCO
INC**
Also Called: Nov
1701 W Sequoia Ave, Orange
(92868-1015)
PHONE....................................714 978-1900
Francisco Arellano, *Branch Mgr*
Carlos Garcia, *Opers Staff*
EMP: 24
SALES (corp-wide): 8.4B **Publicly Held**
SIC: 3533 Oil & gas drilling rigs & equip-
ment
PA: National Oilwell Varco, Inc.
7909 Parkwood Circle Dr
Houston TX 77036
713 346-7500

(P-13786)
**NATIONAL OILWELL VARCO
INC**
220 Weakley St, Calexico (92231-9684)
PHONE....................................760 357-0970
EMP: 24
SALES (corp-wide): 8.4B **Publicly Held**
SIC: 3533 Oil & gas field machinery
PA: National Oilwell Varco, Inc.
7909 Parkwood Circle Dr
Houston TX 77036
713 346-7500

(P-13787)
**NATIONAL OILWELL VARCO
INC**
759 N Eckhoff St, Orange (92868-1005)
P.O. Box 6626 (92863-6626)
PHONE....................................714 978-1900
Owen Unruh, *Principal*
Prakash Mehta, *Engineer*
Hassan Parseyan, *Engineer*
Mario Jimenez, *Manager*
Glenn Miller, *Manager*
EMP: 50
SALES (corp-wide): 8.4B **Publicly Held**
WEB: www.natoil.com
SIC: 3533 Oil field machinery & equipment
PA: National Oilwell Varco, Inc.
7909 Parkwood Circle Dr
Houston TX 77036
713 346-7500

(P-13788)
**NATIONAL OILWELL VARCO
INC**
Also Called: Nov Orange Warehouse
752 N Poplar St, Orange (92868-1014)
PHONE....................................714 978-1900
Pete Miller, *President*
EMP: 23

SALES (corp-wide): 8.4B **Publicly Held**
SIC: 3533 Oil field machinery & equipment
PA: National Oilwell Varco, Inc.
7909 Parkwood Circle Dr
Houston TX 77036
713 346-7500

(P-13789)
**OIL COUNTRY
MANUFACTURING**
300 W Stanley Ave, Ventura (93001-1395)
PHONE....................................805 643-1200
Ed Patterson III, *General Mgr*
Robert M Nelson, *Vice Pres*
Dorothy Bacchilega, *Exec Dir*
Michael Lettini, *Consultant*
◆ EMP: 130
SQ FT: 100,000
SALES (est): 24.1MM **Privately Held**
SIC: 3533 5084 Oil field machinery &
equipment; industrial machinery & equip-
ment

(P-13790)
**SEABOARD INTERNATIONAL
INC**
Also Called: Weir Seaboard
3912 Gilmore Ave, Bakersfield
(93308-6214)
PHONE....................................661 325-5026
Rex Duhn, *Branch Mgr*
EMP: 97
SALES (corp-wide): 3.1B **Privately Held**
SIC: 3533 Oil & gas field machinery
HQ: Seaboard International Inc.
13815 South Fwy
Houston TX 77047
713 644-3535

(P-13791)
**SOUTH COAST SCREEN AND
CASING**
19112 S Santa Fe Ave, Compton
(90221-5910)
PHONE....................................310 632-3200
Tyson Scimo, *CEO*
EMP: 19
SALES (est): 4.7MM **Privately Held**
SIC: 3533 Oil & gas drilling rigs & equip-
ment; drill rigs

(P-13792)
TECHNIPFMC US HOLDINGS INC
5200 Northspur Ct, Bakersfield
(93308-6185)
PHONE....................................661 283-1069
Lee McHorse, *Branch Mgr*
EMP: 15
SALES (corp-wide): 12.6B **Privately Held**
SIC: 3533 Oil & gas field machinery
HQ: Fmc Technologies, Inc.
11740 Katy Fwy Enrgy Twr
Houston TX 77079
281 591-4000

(P-13793)
TECHNIPFMC US HOLDINGS INC
810 Manley Dr, San Gabriel (91776-2327)
PHONE....................................310 328-1236
Russell Lew, *Branch Mgr*
Caleb Salankey, *Manager*
EMP: 18
SALES (corp-wide): 12.6B **Privately Held**
SIC: 3533 Oil & gas field machinery
HQ: Fmc Technologies, Inc.
11740 Katy Fwy Enrgy Twr
Houston TX 77079
281 591-4000

(P-13794)
TECHNIPFMC US HOLDINGS INC
260 Cousteau Pl, Davis (95618-5490)
PHONE....................................530 753-6718
John T Gremp, *Ch of Bd*
Jessica King, *President*
John Destiny, *Executive*
Tyler Mickelson, *Regional Mgr*
Mary Lanham, *Executive Asst*
EMP: 28
SALES (corp-wide): 12.6B **Privately Held**
SIC: 3533 Oil & gas field machinery
HQ: Fmc Technologies, Inc.
11740 Katy Fwy Enrgy Twr
Houston TX 77079
281 591-4000

P
R
O
D
U
C
T
S

&

S
V
C
S

(P-13795)
TEXAS BOOM COMPANY INC
2433 Sagebrush Ct, La Jolla (92037-7036)
PHONE..........................281 441-2002
Sourena Fakhimi, *President*
EMP: 10
SALES (est): 1.3MM Privately Held
WEB: www.texasboom.com
SIC: 3533 8748 Oil & gas field machinery;
environmental consultant

(P-13796)
WEATHERFORD
INTERNATIONAL LLC
3356 Lime Ave, Long Beach (90755-4612)
PHONE.......................562 595-0931
Gary Kennedy, *Branch Mgr*
Tracie Breedlove, *Manager*
EMP: 16 Privately Held
WEB: www.weatherford.com
SIC: 3533 Oil & gas field machinery
HQ: Weatherford International, Llc
2000 Saint James Pl
Houston TX 77056
713 693-4000

(P-13797)
WWT INTERNATIONAL INC
1150 N Tustin Ave, Anaheim (92807-1735)
PHONE.......................714 632-0810
Bruce Moore, *Director*
Lee Culwell, *Technology*
EMP: 13
SALES (corp-wide): 11.6MM Privately
Held
SIC: 3533 1389 Oil & gas field machinery;
oil field services
PA: Wwt International, Inc.
9758 Whithorn Dr
Houston TX 77095
281 345-8019

3534 Elevators & Moving Stairways

(P-13798)
ELEVATOR INDUSTRIES INC
110 Main Ave, Sacramento (95838-2015)
PHONE.......................916 921-1495
Guy Buckman, *President*
Jason Buckman, *Vice Pres*
▲ EMP: 16 EST: 2013
SQ FT: 1,500
SALES (est): 482.9K Privately Held
SIC: 3534 7699 Elevators & equipment;
elevators: inspection, service & repair

(P-13799)
ELEVATOR RESEARCH & MFG
CO
1417 Elwood St, Los Angeles
(90021-2812)
PHONE.......................213 746-1914
Frank Edward Park, *President*
Lynn Park, *Vice Pres*
David Alvarez, *General Mgr*
Rogers Barnet, *General Mgr*
Clive Mann, *General Mgr*
EMP: 96 EST: 1964
SQ FT: 5,000
SALES (est): 18.5MM
SALES (corp-wide): 69.5MM Privately
Held
WEB: www.elevatorresearch.com
SIC: 3534 Elevators & equipment
PA: Dewhurst Plc
Unit 9-11
Feltham MIDDX TW13
208 744-8200

(P-13800)
GAL MANUFACTURING CO LLC
Also Called: Bore-Max
3380 Gilman Rd, El Monte (91732-3201)
PHONE.......................626 443-8616
Bret Sturm, *Branch Mgr*
EMP: 14
SALES (corp-wide): 8B Privately Held
SIC: 3534 Elevators & equipment
HQ: G.A.L. Manufacturing Company, Llc
50 E 153rd St
Bronx NY 10451
718 292-9000

(P-13801)
GMS ELEVATOR SERVICES INC
401 Borrego Ct, San Dimas (91773-2971)
PHONE.......................909 599-3904
G Matthew Simpkins, *President*
Nate Simpkins, *General Mgr*
Pamela Simpkins, *Admin Sec*
Shea Nolan, *Project Mgr*
Chris Kongelka, *Sales Mgr*
EMP: 35
SQ FT: 4,000
SALES (est): 9.5MM Privately Held
SIC: 3534 1796 Elevators & equipment;
elevator installation & conversion

(P-13802)
HKA ELEVATOR CONSULTING
INC
23211 S Pointe Dr Ste 101, Laguna Hills
(92653-1478)
PHONE.......................949 348-9711
Daryl Anderson, *President*
EMP: 10
SQ FT: 3,500
SALES: 3MM Privately Held
WEB: www.hkaconsulting.com
SIC: 3534 Elevators & moving stairways

(P-13803)
INTERNACIONAL DE
ELEVADORES SA
9475 Nicola Tesla Ct, San Diego
(92154-7613)
PHONE.......................619 955-6180
EMP: 10 Privately Held
SIC: 3534

(P-13804)
KINEMATICS RESEARCH LTD
(PA)
55 Mitchell Blvd Ste 16, San Rafael
(94903-2010)
PHONE.......................707 763-9993
David Green, *Partner*
EMP: 15
SALES: 500K Privately Held
SIC: 3534 Elevators & equipment

(P-13805)
NEXT LEVEL ELEVATOR INC
2199 N Batavia St Ste S, Orange
(92865-3107)
PHONE.......................888 959-6010
Jevon Hadley, *President*
EMP: 11
SALES (est): 766K Privately Held
SIC: 3534 Elevators & equipment

(P-13806)
NIDEC MOTOR CORPORATION
Also Called: McE
11380 White Rock Rd, Rancho Cordova
(95742-6522)
PHONE.......................916 463-9200
David Adcock, *Administration*
Daniel Jones, *Research*
Jim Kitz, *Technical Staff*
Jeffrey Counts, *Engineer*
Hani Hallak, *Engineer*
EMP: 400 Privately Held
SIC: 3534 3613 Elevators & equipment;
switchgear & switchboard apparatus
HQ: Nidec Motor Corporation
8050 West Florissant Ave
Saint Louis MO 63136

(P-13807)
POWERLIFT DUMBWAITERS
INC
2444 Georgia Slide Rd, Georgetown
(95634-2201)
P.O. Box 4390 (95634-4390)
PHONE.......................800 409-5438
John B Reite, *President*
Brian Schmit, *Sales Staff*
◆ EMP: 26
SQ FT: 7,500
SALES (est): 5.7MM Privately Held
WEB: www.dumbwaiters.com
SIC: 3534 Dumbwaiters

(P-13808)
SAN FRANCISCO ELEV SVCS
INC
6517 Sierra Ln, Dublin (94568-2798)
PHONE.......................925 829-5400
Donovan McKeever, *President*
Brian McLemore, *Sales Mgr*
EMP: 50
SALES (est): 2.4MM Privately Held
SIC: 3534 Stair elevators, motor powered

(P-13809)
SCHINDLER ELEVATOR
CORPORATION
555 Mccormick St, San Leandro
(94577-1107)
PHONE.......................510 382-2075
Dennis Devos, *Manager*
David Stanley, *District Mgr*
Alex Capiato, *General Mgr*
EMP: 30
SALES (corp-wide): 10.9B Privately Held
WEB: www.us.schindler.com
SIC: 3534 1796 7699 Elevators & equip-
ment; elevator installation & conversion;
elevators: inspection, service & repair
HQ: Schindler Elevator Corporation
20 Whippany Rd
Morristown NJ 07960
973 397-6500

(P-13810)
TL SHIELD & ASSOCIATES INC
Also Called: Inclinator of California
1030 Arroyo St, San Fernando
(91340-1822)
P.O. Box 6845, Thousand Oaks (91359-
6845)
PHONE.......................818 509-8228
Thomas Louis Shield, *President*
Greg Sawyer, *Area Mgr*
Ron Woodward, *Administration*
Evelyn Southworth, *Info Tech Mgr*
EMP: 35
SQ FT: 2,000
SALES (est): 12.2MM Privately Held
WEB: www.tlshield.com
SIC: 3534 1796 Elevators & equipment;
elevator installation & conversion

(P-13811)
WINTER & BAIN
MANUFACTURING (PA)
1417 Elwood St, Los Angeles
(90021-2812)
PHONE.......................213 749-3568
Henry Spencer, *Owner*
Henry W Spencer, *President*
Tom Oliver, *General Mgr*
EMP: 16
SQ FT: 8,000
SALES (est): 2.4MM Privately Held
SIC: 3534 Elevators & moving stairways

(P-13812)
WINTER & BAIN
MANUFACTURING
1410 Elwood St, Los Angeles
(90021-2813)
PHONE.......................213 749-3561
Fax: 213 749-0208
EMP: 11
SQ FT: 9,000
SALES (est): 2.5MM Privately Held
SIC: 3534 5084

3535 Conveyors & Eqpt

(P-13813)
AIR TUBE TRANSFER SYSTEMS
INC
Also Called: A T T
715 N Cypress St, Orange (92867-6605)
PHONE.......................714 363-0700
Rick Blodgett, *President*
Frankie Green, *Financial Analy*
EMP: 25
SQ FT: 10,000

SALES (est): 5.4MM Privately Held
WEB: www.attsystems.com
SIC: 3535 1796 7699 3494 Pneumatic
tube conveyor systems; machinery installation; industrial equipment services;
valves & pipe fittings

(P-13814)
AMERICAN ULTRAVIOLET WEST
INC
Also Called: Lesco
23555 Telo Ave, Torrance (90505-4012)
PHONE.......................310 784-2930
Meredith C Stines, *President*
▲ EMP: 21
SQ FT: 22,775
SALES (est): 6.3MM Privately Held
WEB: www.lescouv.com
SIC: 3535 5065 Conveyors & conveying
equipment; electronic parts

(P-13815)
APEX CONVEYOR CORP
41674 Corning Pl, Murrieta (92562-7023)
P.O. Box 812 (92564-0812)
PHONE.......................951 304-7808
Dave Hill,
Barbara Hill,
EMP: 25
SQ FT: 19,000
SALES (est): 5.5MM Privately Held
WEB: www.apexconveyor.com
SIC: 3535 Conveyors & conveying equip-
ment

(P-13816)
APEX CONVEYOR SYSTEMS
INC
41674 Corning Pl, Murrieta (92562-7023)
PHONE.......................951 304-7808
Greg King, *President*
Wenda King, *Admin Sec*
EMP: 14 EST: 2015
SQ FT: 15,000
SALES (est): 1.3MM Privately Held
SIC: 3535 Belt conveyor systems, general
industrial use

(P-13817)
CASE AUTOMATION
CORPORATION
208 Jason Ct, Corona (92879-6101)
PHONE.......................951 493-6666
Don Nielsen, *President*
EMP: 12
SQ FT: 15,000
SALES: 1.2MM Privately Held
WEB: www.caseautomation.com
SIC: 3535 5084 Conveyors & conveying
equipment; industrial machinery & equip-
ment

(P-13818)
CLOUDMINDS TECHNOLOGY
INC
4500 Great America Pkwy # 2, Santa Clara
(95054-1283)
PHONE.......................650 391-6817
Bill Huang, *CEO*
Robert Zhang, *President*
Karl Frederick Rauscher, *Chairman*
Qiang LI, *Vice Pres*
Robert Chen, *Director*
EMP: 10
SALES (est): 984.9K
SALES (corp-wide): 1.1MM Privately
Held
SIC: 3535 Robotic conveyors
PA: Beijing Cloudmind Technology Co., Ltd.
Room 601-602,4a
Block,Baiziwan,Chaoyang District.
Beijing 10002

(P-13819)
CONVEYOR MFG & SVC INC
771 Marylind Ave, Claremont (91711-3531)
PHONE.......................909 621-0406
Jesus Dehorta, *President*
Josefina Dehorta, *Corp Secy*
EMP: 15
SQ FT: 30,000

▲ = Import ▼=Export
◆ =Import/Export

SALES (est): 4.5MM **Privately Held**
WEB: www.conveyormfg.com
SIC: **3535** Conveyors & conveying equipment

(P-13820)
D & B SUPPLY CORP
Also Called: Air Link International
1189 N Grove St Ste A, Anaheim
(92806-2138)
PHONE..............................714 632-3020
Frank Marchette, *CEO*
Cynthia Marchette, *Admin Sec*
▲ EMP: 13
SQ FT: 10,700
SALES (est): 4.1MM **Privately Held**
WEB: www.airlinkint.com
SIC: **3535** Pneumatic tube conveyor systems

(P-13821)
DAIRY CONVEYOR CORP
15212 Connector Ln, Huntington Beach
(92649-1118)
PHONE..............................714 891-0883
Gary Frintenburge, *President*
EMP: 20
SALES (corp-wide): 26.8MM **Privately Held**
SIC: **3535 7699 5084** Conveyors & conveying equipment; industrial machinery & equipment repair; materials handling machinery
PA: Dairy Conveyor Corp.
38 Mount Ebo Rd S
Brewster NY 10509
845 278-7878

(P-13822)
DEAMCO CORPORATION
6520 E Washington Blvd, Commerce
(90040-1822)
PHONE..............................323 890-1190
Armen Hovannesian, *President*
Nick Kanian, *Principal*
▲ EMP: 55
SQ FT: 55,000
SALES (est): 17.5MM **Privately Held**
WEB: www.deamco.com
SIC: **3535** Conveyors & conveying equipment

(P-13823)
E-SOLUTION INC
4081 E La Palma Ave Ste J, Anaheim
(92807-1701)
PHONE..............................714 589-2012
Byung Seek Ahn, *CEO*
Steve Gwon, *CFO*
▲ EMP: 10 EST: 2013
SALES (est): 1.1MM **Privately Held**
SIC: **3535** Robotic conveyors

(P-13824)
FLO STOR ENGINEERING INC (PA)
Also Called: Flostor
21371 Cabot Blvd, Hayward (94545-1650)
PHONE..............................510 887-7179
Robert Weeks, *Owner*
John Andrews, *Project Mgr*
Sam Weeks, *Project Mgr*
John Jackson, *Sales Engr*
Alicia Capps,
▼ EMP: 30
SALES (est): 4.9MM **Privately Held**
WEB: www.flostor.com
SIC: **3535** Conveyors & conveying equipment

(P-13825)
HECO PACIFIC MANUFACTURING
1510 Pacific St, Union City (94587-2099)
PHONE..............................510 487-1155
Malik A Alarab, *President*
Allan M Alarab, *Admin Sec*
Allan Alarab, *Sales Executive*
▼ EMP: 25
SQ FT: 34,000
SALES (est): 11.5MM **Privately Held**
WEB: www.hecopacific.com
SIC: **3535 3536 3531** Conveyors & conveying equipment; cranes, overhead traveling; construction machinery

(P-13826)
INGALLS CONVEYORS INC
1005 W Olympic Blvd, Montebello
(90640-5121)
PHONE..............................323 837-9900
Toll Free:..............................888 -
Maged Labib Nakla, *CEO*
Steve Ingalls, *President*
Colleen Ingalls, *Admin Sec*
EMP: 21
SQ FT: 174,000
SALES (est): 4.3MM **Privately Held**
WEB: www.ingallsconveyors.com
SIC: **3535 8711** Conveyors & conveying equipment; consulting engineer

(P-13827)
INTELLIGRATED SYSTEMS INC
5903 Christie Ave, Emeryville
(94608-1925)
PHONE..............................510 263-2300
Susan Porter, *Manager*
EMP: 264
SALES (corp-wide): 41.8B **Publicly Held**
SIC: **3535 5084 7371** Conveyors & conveying equipment; industrial machinery & equipment; computer software development
HQ: Intelligrated Systems, Inc.
7901 Innovation Way
Mason OH 45040
866 936-7300

(P-13828)
INTELLIGRATED SYSTEMS INC
3721 Douglas Blvd Ste 345, Roseville
(95661-4254)
PHONE..............................916 772-6800
Susan Porter, *Manager*
EMP: 264
SALES (corp-wide): 41.8B **Publicly Held**
SIC: **3535 5084 7371** Conveyors & conveying equipment; industrial machinery & equipment; computer software development
HQ: Intelligrated Systems, Inc.
7901 Innovation Way
Mason OH 45040
866 936-7300

(P-13829)
NEXT LEVEL WAREHOUSE SOLUTIONS
555 Display Way, Sacramento
(95838-3371)
PHONE..............................916 922-7225
Jim Edmondson, *President*
Tom Weaver, *Sales Staff*
EMP: 10
SQ FT: 20,000
SALES (est): 1.9MM **Privately Held**
WEB: www.nextlevelwhse.com
SIC: **3535 3537** Conveyors & conveying equipment; platforms, stands, tables, pallets & similar equipment; lift trucks, industrial: fork, platform, straddle, etc.

(P-13830)
OMRON ROBOTICS SAFETY TECH INC (DH)
Also Called: Omron Adept Technologies, Inc.
4550 Norris Canyon Rd # 150, San Ramon
(94583-1369)
PHONE..............................925 245-3400
Rob Cain, *President*
Joachim Melis, *President*
Seth Halio, *CFO*
Deron Jackson, *CTO*
Joyce Tang, *Project Mgr*
▲ EMP: 170
SQ FT: 57,000
SALES (est): 46.3MM **Privately Held**
WEB: www.adept.com
SIC: **3535 7372** Robotic conveyors; prepackaged software; operating systems computer software
HQ: Omron Management Center Of America, Inc.
2895 Greenspoint Pkwy
Hoffman Estates IL 60169
224 520-7650

(P-13831)
PRIDE CONVEYANCE SYSTEMS INC
Also Called: P C S
1781 Shelton Dr, Hollister (95023-9404)
PHONE..............................831 637-1787
Shannon Pride, *President*
Pat Jordon, *Vice Pres*
Ruben Padilla, *Vice Pres*
Bill Stewart, *Vice Pres*
Mike Zgragen, *Vice Pres*
◆ EMP: 75
SQ FT: 36,000
SALES (est): 34.8MM **Privately Held**
WEB: www.prideconveyance.com
SIC: **3535** Conveyors & conveying equipment

(P-13832)
RALPHS-PUGH CO INC
3931 Oregon St, Benicia (94510-1101)
PHONE..............................707 745-6222
William G Pugh, *CEO*
Deborah Pugh, *Treasurer*
Tom Anderson, *Vice Pres*
Derrick Shelton, *Natl Sales Mgr*
Cara Pfister, *Manager*
EMP: 65 EST: 1912
SQ FT: 36,000
SALES (est): 21.9MM **Privately Held**
WEB: www.ralphs-pugh.com
SIC: **3535** Conveyors & conveying equipment

(P-13833)
SARDEE CORPORATION CALIFORNIA
2731 E Myrtle St, Stockton (95205-4793)
PHONE..............................209 466-1526
Steve Sarovich, *President*
Dolores Sarovich, *Corp Secy*
Alan Bassett, *Vice Pres*
Alex Graham, *Vice Pres*
EMP: 40
SQ FT: 20,000
SALES (est): 8.1MM **Privately Held**
SIC: **3535** Conveyors & conveying equipment

(P-13834)
SCREW CONVEYOR PACIFIC CORP
7807 W Doe Ave, Visalia (93291-9275)
PHONE..............................559 651-2131
Randy Smith, *Principal*
EMP: 20
SALES (corp-wide): 20.5MM **Privately Held**
WEB: www.screwconveyor.com
SIC: **3535** Conveyors & conveying equipment
PA: Screw Conveyor Pacific Corp
700 Hoffman St
Hammond IN 46327
219 931-1450

(P-13835)
SDI INDUSTRIES INC (PA)
13000 Pierce St, Pacoima (91331-2528)
PHONE..............................818 890-6002
Krish Nathan, *CEO*
Mark Conrad, *CFO*
Bob Jackson, *Vice Pres*
Merlin Van Gelderen, *Engineer*
Parviz Jarrahzadeh, *Accounting Mgr*
▲ EMP: 150
SQ FT: 80,000
SALES (est): 40.6MM **Privately Held**
WEB: www.sdiindustries.com
SIC: **3535 3537 8748 8711** Conveyors & conveying equipment; industrial trucks & tractors; business consulting; engineering services; machinery installation

(P-13836)
SMART MACHINES INC
46702 Bayside Pkwy, Fremont
(94538-6582)
PHONE..............................510 661-5000
K C Janac, *President*
Sharon Andres, *Controller*
EMP: 29
SQ FT: 15,258

SALES (est): 4.7MM
SALES (corp-wide): 631.5MM **Publicly Held**
SIC: **3535** Robotic conveyors
PA: Brooks Automation, Inc.
15 Elizabeth Dr
Chelmsford MA 01824
978 262-2400

(P-13837)
SMP ROBOTICS SYSTEMS CORP
851 Burlway Rd Ste 216, Burlingame
(94010-1709)
PHONE..............................415 572-2316
Leo Ryzhenko, *CEO*
EMP: 55 EST: 2014
SQ FT: 350
SALES (est): 4.8MM **Privately Held**
SIC: **3535** Robotic conveyors

(P-13838)
STOCKTON TRI-INDUSTRIES INC
2141 E Anderson St, Stockton
(95205-7010)
P.O. Box 6097 (95206-0097)
PHONE..............................209 948-9701
Fred Wells, *President*
Harrison Freddie Wells, *CEO*
Ray Smith, *Corp Secy*
Jeff Yon, *Accounts Mgr*
EMP: 65
SQ FT: 32,000
SALES (est): 22.3MM **Privately Held**
WEB: www.stocktontri.com
SIC: **3535 3599** Conveyors & conveying equipment; machine shop, jobbing & repair

(P-13839)
TERRA NOVA TECHNOLOGIES INC
10770 Rockvill St, Santee (92071)
PHONE..............................619 596-7400
Ronald Kelly, *President*
Bobby McClinton, *Project Mgr*
Daniel Johnson, *Production*
EMP: 80
SQ FT: 8,366
SALES (est): 3MM
SALES (corp-wide): 4.9MM **Privately Held**
SIC: **3535 8742** Conveyors & conveying equipment; management consulting services
HQ: Cementation Usa Inc.
11075 S State St
Sandy UT 84070
-

(P-13840)
TIG/M LLC
9160 Jordan Ave, Chatsworth
(91311-5707)
PHONE..............................818 709-8500
Alvaro Villa, *CEO*
Brad Read, *President*
David Hall, *CFO*
Polly Chellew, *Project Mgr*
Bradley Read,
EMP: 30
SQ FT: 2,000
SALES: 1.5MM **Privately Held**
SIC: **3535** Trolley conveyors

(P-13841)
WHEELER & REEDER INC
3334 Montrose Ave, La Crescenta
(91214-3341)
PHONE..............................323 268-4163
Chandler Young, *President*
EMP: 10 EST: 1943
SQ FT: 9,000
SALES (est): 1.1MM **Privately Held**
SIC: **3535 3444 5084** Conveyors & conveying equipment; sheet metalwork; conveyor systems

(P-13842)

WOOD MINERALS CONVEYORS INC
Also Called: Terra Nova Technologies, Inc.
10770 Rockville St Ste A, Santee
(92071-8505)
PHONE........................619 596-7400
Ronald Kelly, *President*
◆ **EMP:** 80
SQ FT: 8,366
SALES (est): 40.1MM
SALES (corp-wide): 10B **Privately Held**
WEB: www.tntinc.com
SIC: 3535 8742 Conveyors & conveying equipment; management consulting services; industrial & labor consulting services
HQ: Amec Foster Wheeler Limited
4th Floor Old Change House
Knutsford EC4V
207 429-7500

3536 Hoists, Cranes & Monorails

(P-13843)

AGE LOGISTICS CORPORATION
426 E Duarte Rd, Monrovia (91016-4603)
PHONE........................626 243-5253
Yehuda Fishman, *CEO*
Roger N McMullin, *CEO*
Jim Sameth, *COO*
Daniel Fishman, *Principal*
Erica Fishman, *Principal*
EMP: 10
SQ FT: 101,000
SALES (est): 2.1MM **Privately Held**
WEB: www.agelogistics.com
SIC: 3536 Hoists

(P-13844)

CARPENTER GROUP (PA)
Also Called: Cable-Cisco
222 Napoleon St, San Francisco
(94124-1017)
PHONE........................415 285-1954
Bernard L Martin, *CEO*
Frank Joost, *Vice Pres*
Patty Oliverio, *Admin Sec*
Ralph Key, *Info Tech Dir*
▲ **EMP:** 33
SQ FT: 26,000
SALES (est): 27.9MM **Privately Held**
WEB: www.carpenterrigging.com
SIC: 3536 2394 5085 3496 Hoists; liners & covers, fabric: made from purchased materials; industrial supplies; cable, uninsulated wire: made from purchased wire

(P-13845)

CRANEVEYOR CORP (PA)
1524 Potrero Ave, El Monte (91733-3017)
P.O. Box 3727 (91733-0727)
PHONE........................626 442-1524
Frank Gaetano Trimboli, *CEO*
Greg Bischoff, *President*
Thomas Saunders, *CFO*
Tim Chavez, *Vice Pres*
Kristen Badar, *Info Tech Mgr*
▲ **EMP:** 90
SQ FT: 47,320
SALES: 27MM **Privately Held**
SIC: 3536 3446 Cranes, overhead traveling; monorail systems; railings, bannisters, guards, etc.: made from metal pipe

(P-13846)

DEMAG CRANES & COMPONENTS CORP
Also Called: Material Handling Division
13290 Sabre Blvd, Victorville (92394-7943)
PHONE........................909 880-8800
Michael Perera, *Manager*
EMP: 22
SALES (corp-wide): 3.6B **Privately Held**
WEB: www.demag-us.com
SIC: 3536 7389 5999 5084 Hoists; cranes & monorail systems; crane & aerial lift service; engine & motor equipment & supplies; hoists; construction machinery; installing building equipment
HQ: Demag Cranes & Components Corp.
6675 Parkland Blvd # 200
Solon OH 44139
440 248-2400

(P-13847)

HARRINGTON HOISTS INC
2341 Pomona Rincon Rd # 103, Corona
(92880-6937)
PHONE........................717 665-2000
Bill Erkenbrak, *Branch Mgr*
EMP: 10 **Privately Held**
WEB: www.harringtonhoists.com
SIC: 3536 Hoists, cranes & monorails
HQ: Harrington Hoists, Inc.
401 W End Ave
Manheim PA 17545

(P-13848)

KONECRANES INC
2900 E Belle Ter Bldg A, Bakersfield
(93307-6925)
PHONE........................661 397-9700
EMP: 26
SALES (corp-wide): 3.6B **Privately Held**
SIC: 3536 Hoists, cranes & monorails
HQ: Konecranes, Inc.
4401 Gateway Blvd
Springfield OH 45502

(P-13849)

KONECRANES INC
Also Called: Crane Pro Services
5637 Blaribera St, Livermore (94550)
PHONE........................925 273-0140
Christie Elder, *Manager*
EMP: 14
SALES (corp-wide): 3.6B **Privately Held**
SIC: 3536 Cranes, industrial plant
HQ: Konecranes, Inc.
4401 Gateway Blvd
Springfield OH 45502

(P-13850)

MOBILE EQUIPMENT COMPANY
Also Called: Mobile Equipment Appraisers
3610 Gilmore Ave, Bakersfield
(93308-6208)
PHONE........................661 327-8476
Evelyn Stanfill, *President*
Felecia Stanfill, *Corp Secy*
Paul J Faulconer, *Vice Pres*
Gary Stanfill, *General Mgr*
EMP: 20
SQ FT: 18,580
SALES (est): 4.6MM **Privately Held**
WEB: www.mobile-equipment.com
SIC: 3536 8748 3559 Cranes, overhead traveling; safety training service; automotive related machinery

(P-13851)

SHEEDY DRAYAGE CO
Also Called: Sheedy Hoist
34301 7th St, Union City (94587-3653)
PHONE........................510 441-7300
James Butler, *Branch Mgr*
EMP: 10
SALES (corp-wide): 24.9MM **Privately Held**
WEB: www.sheedycrane.com
SIC: 3536 7389 5211 Hoists; crane & aerial lift service; lumber & other building materials
PA: Sheedy Drayage Co.
1215 Michigan St
San Francisco CA 94107
415 648-7171

(P-13852)

TRADEMARK HOIST INC
Also Called: Trademark Hoist & Crane
1369 Ridgeway St, Pomona (91768-2701)
PHONE........................909 455-0801
Mike Mendoza, *President*
Frank Carletello, *Vice Pres*
John Carletello, *Admin Sec*
Isabel Mirabal, *Manager*
EMP: 20
SQ FT: 4,400
SALES (est): 6.2MM **Privately Held**
WEB: www.trademark-hoist.com
SIC: 3536 Hoists, cranes & monorails

(P-13853)

WESTMONT INDUSTRIES (PA)
10805 Painter Ave Uppr, Santa Fe Springs
(90670-4541)
PHONE........................562 944-6137
Diane Henderson, *President*
David Chetwood, *CFO*
Tiffany Tran, *CTO*
Raymond Tan, *IT/INT Sup*
Jody Hamlow, *Human Res Mgr*
▼ **EMP:** 60
SALES (est): 23.6MM **Privately Held**
WEB: www.westmont.com
SIC: 3536 3533 Cranes, industrial plant; oil & gas field machinery

3537 Indl Trucks, Tractors, Trailers & Stackers

(P-13854)

ABOVE ALL CO FOREARM FORKLIFT
Also Called: A.A.C. Forearm Forklift
14832 Arrow Hwy, Baldwin Park
(91706-1823)
PHONE........................626 962-2990
Mark Lopreiato, *President*
David Correa, *Manager*
Jose Rosales, *Representative*
EMP: 30
SQ FT: 15,000
SALES: 4MM **Privately Held**
SIC: 3537 Lift trucks, industrial: fork, platform, straddle, etc.

(P-13855)

ACTIVE ID LLC
845 Embedded Way, San Jose
(95138-1085)
PHONE........................408 782-3900
George Khalil, *EMP:* 10
SALES (est): 411.2K **Privately Held**
SIC: 3537 Platforms, cargo

(P-13856)

ANCRA INTERNATIONAL LLC (HQ)
601 S Vincent Ave, Azusa (91702-5102)
PHONE........................626 765-4800
Steve Frediani, *CEO*
Nelson Fong, *CFO*
David Nalbandian, *Executive*
John Czarnecki, *Regional Mgr*
Chris Zenke, *Info Tech Dir*
▲ **EMP:** 130
SALES (est): 72.6MM **Privately Held**
WEB: www.ancra-llc.com
SIC: 3537 Lift trucks, industrial: fork, platform, straddle, etc.; loading docks: portable, adjustable & hydraulic

(P-13857)

ANSONS TRANSPORTATION INC
438 E Shaw Ave Ste 434, Fresno
(93710-7602)
PHONE........................559 892-1867
Kimberly Rodriguez, *President*
EMP: 25
SALES: 2.6MM **Privately Held**
SIC: 3537 Trucks, tractors, loaders, carriers & similar equipment

(P-13858)

ANTHONY WELDED PRODUCTS INC (PA)
1447 S Lexington St, Delano (93215-9700)
P.O. Box 299, Simi Valley (93062-0299)
PHONE........................661 721-7211
Frank S Salvucci Sr, *Chairman*
Elsie Salvucci, *President*
EMP: 20
SQ FT: 25,000
SALES (est): 9.2MM **Privately Held**
WEB: www.anthonycarts.com
SIC: 3537 3444 3443 Dollies (hand or power trucks), industrial except mining; sheet metalwork; fabricated plate work (boiler shop)

(P-13859)

BEST INDUSTRIAL SUPPLY
9711 Rush St, South El Monte
(91733-1730)
PHONE........................626 279-5090
James Nickleson, *Partner*
Mike Burgi, *Partner*
EMP: 12
SALES (est): 2.5MM **Privately Held**
WEB: www.bestindustrialsupply.com
SIC: 3537 Forklift trucks

(P-13860)

BISHAMON INDUSTRIES CORP
5651 E Francis St, Ontario (91761-3601)
PHONE........................909 390-0055
Wataru Sugiura, *President*
Robert Clark, *Vice Pres*
Robert Stone, *Vice Pres*
Carl Campbell, *Opers Staff*
Eduardo Lucio, *Regl Sales Mgr*
▲ **EMP:** 45 **EST:** 1986
SQ FT: 77,000
SALES: 10MM **Privately Held**
WEB: www.bishamon.com
SIC: 3537 Lift trucks, industrial: fork, platform, straddle, etc.

(P-13861)

CIMC REEFER TRAILER INC (PA)
22101 Alessandro Blvd, Moreno Valley
(92553-8215)
PHONE........................951 218-1414
Xiaoyi Wang, *CEO*
▲ **EMP:** 16
SALES (est): 8.3MM **Privately Held**
SIC: 3537 Truck trailers, used in plants, docks, terminals, etc.

(P-13862)

CORONADO EQUIPMENT SALES
2275 La Crosse Ave # 210, Colton
(92324-4464)
PHONE........................877 830-7447
David B Coronado, *President*
Donna Coronado, *Vice Pres*
EMP: 11
SALES (est): 2.4MM **Privately Held**
SIC: 3537 3429 Forklift trucks; clamps, metal

(P-13863)

CRANEWORKS SOUTHWEST INC
1312 E Barham Dr, San Marcos
(92078-4503)
PHONE........................760 735-9793
Marise Williams, *Office Mgr*
EMP: 20
SALES (est): 4.9MM **Privately Held**
SIC: 3537 7353 Cranes, industrial truck; cranes & aerial lift equipment, rental or leasing

(P-13864)

CROWN EQUIPMENT CORPORATION
1355 E Fntana Ave Ste 102, Fresno
(93725)
P.O. Box 641173, Cincinnati OH (45264-1173)
PHONE........................559 585-8000
Keith Heinke, *General Mgr*
EMP: 24
SALES (corp-wide): 3.4B **Privately Held**
SIC: 3537 Forklift trucks
PA: Crown Equipment Corporation
44 S Washington St
New Bremen OH 45869
419 629-2311

(P-13865)

CROWN EQUIPMENT CORPORATION
Also Called: Crown Lift Trucks
1300 Palomares St, La Verne
(91750-5232)
PHONE........................626 968-0556
Kevin McCarthy, *Manager*
EMP: 58
SQ FT: 28,000
SALES (corp-wide): 3.4B **Privately Held**
SIC: 3537 Lift trucks, industrial: fork, platform, straddle, etc.

PA: Crown Equipment Corporation
44 S Washington St
New Bremen OH 45869
419 629-2311

(P-13866)
CROWN EQUIPMENT CORPORATION
Also Called: Crown Lift Trucks
4250 Greystone Dr, Ontario (91761-3104)
PHONE.................................909 923-8357
Mike Lammers, *Manager*
EMP: 139
SALES (corp-wide): 3.4B **Privately Held**
SIC: 3537 Lift trucks, industrial: fork, platform, straddle, etc.
PA: Crown Equipment Corporation
44 S Washington St
New Bremen OH 45869
419 629-2311

(P-13867)
CROWN EQUIPMENT CORPORATION
Also Called: Crown Lift Trucks
1400 Crocker Ave, Hayward (94544-7031)
PHONE.................................510 471-7272
Scott Walter, *Manager*
EMP: 45
SALES (corp-wide): 3.4B **Privately Held**
SIC: 3537 Lift trucks, industrial: fork, platform, straddle, etc.
PA: Crown Equipment Corporation
44 S Washington St
New Bremen OH 45869
419 629-2311

(P-13868)
CROWN EQUIPMENT CORPORATION
Also Called: Crown Lift Trucks
1420 Enterprise Blvd, West Sacramento (95691-3485)
PHONE.................................916 373-8980
Ron Bensman, *Manager*
EMP: 44
SALES (corp-wide): 3.4B **Privately Held**
SIC: 3537 Lift trucks, industrial: fork, platform, straddle, etc.
PA: Crown Equipment Corporation
44 S Washington St
New Bremen OH 45869
419 629-2311

(P-13869)
CROWN EQUIPMENT CORPORATION
Also Called: Crown Lift Trucks
4061 Via Oro Ave, Long Beach (90810-1458)
PHONE.................................310 952-6600
Tom Labrador, *Branch Mgr*
EMP: 64
SALES (corp-wide): 3.4B **Privately Held**
SIC: 3537 Lift trucks, industrial: fork, platform, straddle, etc.
PA: Crown Equipment Corporation
44 S Washington St
New Bremen OH 45869
419 629-2311

(P-13870)
DARRELL ZBROWSKI
Also Called: Dz Tranz Group
8465 Vassar Ave, Canoga Park (91304-2508)
PHONE.................................818 324-5961
Darrell Zbrowski, *Owner*
EMP: 90 EST: 2013
SALES: 15.3MM **Privately Held**
SIC: 3537 Trucks: freight, baggage, etc.: industrial, except mining

(P-13871)
DAYTON SUPERIOR CORPORATION
Also Called: American Highway Technology
5300 Claus Rd Ste 7, Modesto (95357-1665)
PHONE.................................209 869-1201
Wesley Tilton, *Manager*
EMP: 25

SALES (corp-wide): 43B **Publicly Held**
WEB: www.daytonsuperior.com
SIC: 3537 Loading docks: portable, adjustable & hydraulic
HQ: Dayton Superior Corporation
1125 Byers Rd
Miamisburg OH 45342
937 866-0711

(P-13872)
FREMONT PACKAGE EXPRESS
734 Still Breeze Way, Sacramento (95831-5544)
PHONE.................................916 541-1812
Terrence Wong, *Owner*
EMP: 15
SALES: 800K **Privately Held**
SIC: 3537 Trucks: freight, baggage, etc.: industrial, except mining

(P-13873)
GOLDEN GATE FREIGHTLINER INC
Also Called: Golden Gate Truck Center
2727 E Central Ave, Fresno (93725-2425)
P.O. Box 12346 (93777-2346)
PHONE.................................559 486-4310
EMP: 150
SALES (corp-wide): 195.4MM **Privately Held**
WEB: www.goldengatetruckcenter.com
SIC: 3537 5511 Trucks: freight, baggage, etc.: industrial, except mining; new & used car dealers
HQ: Golden Gate Freightliner, Inc.
8200 Baldwin St
Oakland CA 94621
559 486-4310

(P-13874)
GOLDEN VALLEY & ASSOCIATES INC
Also Called: Cal Central Catering Trailers
3511 Finch Rd A, Modesto (95357-4143)
PHONE.................................209 549-1549
Estafani Ochoa, *CEO*
Estefani Ochoa, *Administration*
EMP: 22
SQ FT: 30,000
SALES: 3.6MM **Privately Held**
SIC: 3537 Aircraft engine cradles

(P-13875)
HYDRAULIC SHOP INC
2753 S Vista Ave, Bloomington (92316-3269)
PHONE.................................909 875-9336
Christopher O Kirk, *President*
EMP: 20
SQ FT: 4,500
SALES: 4.8MM **Privately Held**
SIC: 3537 Industrial trucks & tractors

(P-13876)
INDUSTRIAL DESIGN PRODUCTS
2700 Pomona Blvd, Pomona (91768-3222)
PHONE.................................909 468-0693
Richard Fleischhacker Jr, *President*
Jose Pizarro, *Exec VP*
EMP: 12
SQ FT: 14,000
SALES (est): 2.1MM **Privately Held**
WEB: www.idp-inc.com
SIC: 3537 5084 2542 Platforms, stands, tables, pallets & similar equipment; materials handling machinery; pallet racks: except wood

(P-13877)
J&S GOODWIN INC (HQ)
5753 E Sta Ana Cyn G355, Anaheim (92807-3230)
PHONE.................................714 956-4040
Arthur J Goodwin, *CEO*
Mark McGregor, *CFO*
Adam Navarro, *General Mgr*
Sharon Goodwin, *Admin Sec*
Thomas Deredec, *Info Tech Mgr*
◆ EMP: 80
SQ FT: 3,000

SALES (est): 40.6MM
SALES (corp-wide): 6B **Publicly Held**
SIC: 3537 5088 5084 Trucks, tractors, loaders, carriers & similar equipment; golf carts; materials handling machinery
PA: Polaris Inc.
2100 Highway 55
Medina MN 55340
763 542-0500

(P-13878)
JE THOMSON & COMPANY LLC
Also Called: Carousel USA
15206 Ceres Ave, Fontana (92335-4311)
PHONE.................................626 334-7190
John Thomson,
▲ EMP: 15
SALES (est): 4.4MM **Privately Held**
SIC: 3537 3535 Tables, lift: hydraulic; trolley conveyors; bulk handling conveyor systems; robotic conveyors

(P-13879)
KARRIOR ELECTRIC VEHICLES INC
Also Called: Karrior Indus Elc Vehicles
570 W 184th St, Gardena (90248-4202)
PHONE.................................310 515-7600
George Kettel, *President*
EMP: 11
SQ FT: 12,000
SALES (est): 1.2MM **Privately Held**
SIC: 3537 7629 Industrial trucks & tractors; electrical equipment repair services

(P-13880)
KEY MATERIAL HANDLING INC
4790 Alamo St, Simi Valley (93063-1837)
PHONE.................................805 520-6007
Richard Galbraith, *President*
Kimberly Galbraith, *Corp Secy*
John Galbraith, *Vice Pres*
▲ EMP: 12
SQ FT: 2,000
SALES (est): 1.6MM **Privately Held**
WEB: www.keymaterial.com
SIC: 3537 4953 5084 5021 Platforms, stands, tables, pallets & similar equipment; trucks, tractors, loaders, carriers & similar equipment; hazardous waste collection & disposal; conveyor systems; shelving

(P-13881)
LATOURETTE LIFT SERVICES
4368 Bandini Blvd, Vernon (90058-4323)
P.O. Box 58163, Los Angeles (90058-0163)
PHONE.................................323 262-9111
Edward Latourette, *Owner*
Scott Henningsen, *General Mgr*
EMP: 15
SALES (est): 1.4MM **Privately Held**
SIC: 3537 Lift trucks, industrial: fork, platform, straddle, etc.

(P-13882)
MACS LIFT GATE INC
2715 Seaboard Ln, Long Beach (90805-3751)
PHONE.................................562 634-5962
Richard Mac Donald, *General Mgr*
EMP: 19
SALES (corp-wide): 3.1MM **Privately Held**
SIC: 3537 5531 3999 Lift trucks, industrial: fork, platform, straddle, etc.; truck equipment & parts; wheelchair lifts
PA: Mac's Lift Gate, Inc.
2801 E South St
Long Beach CA 90805
562 634-5962

(P-13883)
MARDIAN EQUIPMENT CO INC
10168 Channel Rd, Lakeside (92040-1704)
PHONE.................................619 938-8071
George Wheeler, *Manager*
EMP: 25
SALES (corp-wide): 10MM **Privately Held**
SIC: 3537 7353 Cranes, industrial truck; heavy construction equipment rental
PA: Mardian Equipment Co., Inc.
221 S 35th Ave
Phoenix AZ 85009
602 272-2671

(P-13884)
MECHANIZED ENGINEERING SYSTEMS
Also Called: Mensi
737 E 223rd St, Carson (90745-4111)
P.O. Box 17278, Anaheim (92817-7278)
PHONE.................................310 830-9763
Ernest J Stramotas, *President*
EMP: 10
SQ FT: 8,000
SALES: 2MM **Privately Held**
WEB: www.mensilift.com
SIC: 3537 5049 Containers (metal), air cargo; engineers' equipment & supplies

(P-13885)
NOR CAL TRUCK SALES & MFG
Also Called: Nor Car Truck Sales
200 Industrial Way, Benicia (94510-1191)
PHONE.................................925 787-9735
David Jenkins, *Owner*
EMP: 15
SALES: 3.5MM **Privately Held**
SIC: 3537 5511 Trucks, tractors, loaders, carriers & similar equipment; trucks, tractors & trailers: new & used

(P-13886)
OFF DOCK USA INC
22700 S Alameda St, Carson (90810-1909)
PHONE.................................310 522-4400
Michael R Sullivan, *President*
John Burke, *Vice Pres*
EMP: 16
SALES (est): 4.2MM **Privately Held**
SIC: 3537 Containers (metal), air cargo

(P-13887)
PAPE MATERIAL HANDLING INC
2600 Peck Rd, City of Industry (90601-1620)
P.O. Box 60007 (91716-0007)
PHONE.................................562 692-9311
Steve Smith, *Manager*
Jordan Pape, *President*
Chris Wetle, *President*
William Mc Kinley, *Div Sub Head*
EMP: 100
SALES (corp-wide): 640.9MM **Privately Held**
WEB: www.johnson-machinery.com
SIC: 3537 5084 Forklift trucks; industrial machinery & equipment
HQ: Pape' Material Handling, Inc.
355 Goodpasture Island Rd
Eugene OR 97401
541 683-5073

(P-13888)
POWER PT INC
9292 Nancy St, Cypress (90630-3318)
PHONE.................................714 826-7407
Tyson Paulis, *Branch Mgr*
EMP: 11
SALES (corp-wide): 2.4MM **Privately Held**
SIC: 3537 Platforms, stands, tables, pallets & similar equipment
PA: Power Pt Inc
23120 Oleander Ave
Perris CA 92570
951 490-4149

(P-13889)
PRECISION FORKLIFT
15389 Avenue 288, Visalia (93292-9670)
PHONE.................................559 805-5487
Beth Flynt, *Principal*
EMP: 11
SALES (est): 1.5MM **Privately Held**
SIC: 3537 Forklift trucks

(P-13890)
QUALITY LIFT AND EQUIPMENT INC
10845 Norwalk Blvd, Santa Fe Springs (90670-3825)
P.O. Box 2581 (90670-0581)
PHONE.................................562 903-2131
John Andrews, *CEO*
◆ EMP: 10
SQ FT: 3,000

SALES: 1.2MM **Privately Held**
WEB: www.2ndshiftlift.com
SIC: 3537 7699 Forklift trucks; industrial truck repair

(P-13891)
SHRED-TECH USA LLC
1100 S Grove Ave, Ontario (91761-4572)
PHONE..............................909 923-2783
Robert L Dibenedetto,
EMP: 50
SQ FT: 64,000
SALES (est): 5.1MM **Privately Held**
SIC: 3537 Industrial trucks & tractors

(P-13892)
SOUTHERN CALIFORNIA MTL HDLG
168 E Freedom Ave, Anaheim (92801-1004)
PHONE..............................714 773-9630
Ron Walter, *Manager*
EMP: 35 **Privately Held**
WEB: www.scmh.com
SIC: 3537 Forklift trucks
HQ: Southern California Material Handling Inc
12393 Slauson Ave
Whittier CA 90606
562 949-1006

(P-13893)
STROPPINI ENTERPRISES
2546 Mercantile Dr Ste A, Rancho Cordova (95742-8203)
PHONE..............................916 635-8181
Gilbert Stroppini, *Owner*
▲ **EMP:** 17
SQ FT: 12,000
SALES (est): 3.1MM **Privately Held**
SIC: 3537 Platforms, stands, tables, pallets & similar equipment; tables, lift: hydraulic

(P-13894)
SUPERIOR TRAILER WORKS
13700 Slover Ave, Fontana (92337-7067)
PHONE..............................909 350-0185
Jack N Pocock, *CEO*
Jay Pocock, *Corp Secy*
▲ **EMP:** 50
SQ FT: 4,000
SALES (est): 17.2MM **Privately Held**
WEB: www.superiortrailerworks.com
SIC: 3537 7539 Industrial trucks & tractors; trailer repair

(P-13895)
TAYLOR-DUNN MANUFACTURING CO (DH)
2114 W Ball Rd, Anaheim (92804-5498)
PHONE..............................714 956-4040
Keith Simon, *CEO*
Sandy Carlson, *Human Res Mgr*
Winter Lussier, *Human Resources*
Cambria Jenkins, *Buyer*
Bill Manning, *Sales Mgr*
◆ **EMP:** 100 **EST:** 1949
SQ FT: 145,000
SALES (est): 44.8MM
SALES (corp-wide): 6B **Publicly Held**
WEB: www.taylor-dunn.com
SIC: 3537 Trucks, tractors, loaders, carriers & similar equipment
HQ: Polaris Sales Inc.
2100 Highway 55
Hamel MN 55340
763 542-0500

(P-13896)
WALTCO LIFT CORP
227 E Compton Blvd, Gardena (90248-1909)
PHONE..............................323 321-4131
Marshall Walker, *Branch Mgr*
EMP: 69
SALES (corp-wide): 3.7B **Privately Held**
SIC: 3537 3714 Industrial trucks & tractors; motor vehicle parts & accessories
HQ: Waltco Lift Corp.
285 Northeast Ave
Tallmadge OH 44278
330 633-9191

(P-13897)
WIGGINS LIFT CO INC
2571 Cortez St, Oxnard (93036-1642)
P.O. Box 5187 (93031-5187)
PHONE..............................805 485-7821
Hattie Wiggins, *Ch of Bd*
Michael M Wiggins, *President*
Michelle Mc Dowell, *Treasurer*
Paul Hurbace, *Vice Pres*
Jack Mc Dowell, *Vice Pres*
◆ **EMP:** 50 **EST:** 1951
SQ FT: 55,000
SALES (est): 31.2MM **Privately Held**
SIC: 3537 Forklift trucks

(P-13898)
WIN-HOLT EQUIPMENT CORP
2717 N Towne Ave, Pomona (91767-2263)
PHONE..............................909 625-2624
Michael O'Brien, *Manager*
EMP: 15
SQ FT: 36,000
SALES (corp-wide): 83.1MM **Privately Held**
WEB: www.winholt.com
SIC: 3537 Industrial trucks & tractors
PA: Win-Holt Equipment Corp.
20 Crossways Park Dr N # 205
Woodbury NY 11797
516 222-0335

3541 Machine Tools: Cutting

(P-13899)
ACCEL MANUFACTURING INC
1709 Grant St, Santa Clara (95050-3939)
PHONE..............................408 727-5883
Loc Pham, *President*
EMP: 15
SALES (est): 3.6MM **Privately Held**
SIC: 3541 Machine tool replacement & repair parts, metal cutting types

(P-13900)
ACS CO LTD
6341 San Ignacio Ave, San Jose (95119-1202)
PHONE..............................408 981-7162
Jae Hoon Jung, *Managing Dir*
Leah Blendheim, *Admin Sec*
EMP: 125
SALES (est): 10MM **Privately Held**
SIC: 3541 Machine tools, metal cutting type

(P-13901)
AEROSPACE AND COML TOOLING INC
Also Called: A C T
1866 S Lake Pl, Ontario (91761-5788)
PHONE..............................909 930-5780
Oscar Borello, *President*
EMP: 16
SQ FT: 20,000
SALES (est): 3.5MM **Privately Held**
SIC: 3541 Machine tools, metal cutting type

(P-13902)
AEROSPACE TOOL GRINDING
14020 Shoemaker Ave, Norwalk (90650-4536)
P.O. Box 1536 (90651-1536)
PHONE..............................562 802-3339
Alonzo Burgos, *President*
Azzie Burgos, *Vice Pres*
EMP: 15
SALES (est): 1.1MM **Privately Held**
SIC: 3541 5251 Machine tools, metal cutting type; tools

(P-13903)
AKIRA SEIKI U S A INC
255 Capitol St, Livermore (94551-5210)
PHONE..............................925 443-1200
Alan Kludjian, *President*
▲ **EMP:** 17
SALES (est): 2.6MM **Privately Held**
WEB: www.akira-seiki.com
SIC: 3541 Machine tools, metal cutting type

(P-13904)
BERNHARDT & BERNHARDT INC
Also Called: Protool Co
14771 Myford Rd Ste D, Tustin (92780-7206)
PHONE..............................714 544-0708
Norbert Bernhardt, *President*
Jeffrey Wichert, *Facilities Mgr*
EMP: 15 **EST:** 1974
SQ FT: 4,600
SALES: 1MM **Privately Held**
SIC: 3541 Numerically controlled metal cutting machine tools

(P-13905)
CERATIZIT LOS ANGELES LLC
1401 W Walnut St, Rancho Dominguez (90220-5012)
PHONE..............................310 464-8050
Mark Nunez, *President*
Salvador Nunez, *Vice Pres*
Carmen Nunez, *Admin Sec*
▲ **EMP:** 85
SQ FT: 46,000
SALES: 18.9MM **Privately Held**
WEB: www.bestcarbide.com
SIC: 3541 Machine tools, metal cutting type

(P-13906)
CREMACH TECH INC (PA)
Also Called: Creative Machine Technology
369 Meyer Cir, Corona (92879-1078)
PHONE..............................951 735-3194
Mike McNeeley, *CEO*
Jae Wan Choi, *Vice Pres*
Joseph Howard, *Program Mgr*
Stephen OH, *Technology*
Steve Wolford, *Engineer*
EMP: 71
SQ FT: 34,000
SALES: 13MM **Privately Held**
WEB: www.cmtus.com
SIC: 3541 8711 Machine tools, metal cutting type; designing: ship, boat, machine & product

(P-13907)
CREMACH TECH INC
Also Called: Creative Machine Technology
400 E Parkridge Ave, Corona (92879-6618)
PHONE..............................951 735-3194
Mike McNeeley, *Branch Mgr*
EMP: 29 **Privately Held**
SIC: 3541 Machine tools, metal cutting type
PA: Cremach Tech, Inc.
369 Meyer Cir
Corona CA 92879

(P-13908)
CTD MACHINES INC
7355 E Slauson Ave, Commerce (90040-3626)
PHONE..............................213 689-4455
Kiwon Ban, *General Mgr*
Thomas Orlando, *President*
Ellen Orlando, *Corp Secy*
Seymour Lehrer, *Vice Pres*
Shirley Lehrer, *Vice Pres*
EMP: 18
SALES (est): 3.8MM **Privately Held**
WEB: www.ctdsaw.com
SIC: 3541 Cutoff machines (metalworking machinery)

(P-13909)
D G INDUSTRIES
226 Viking Ave, Brea (92821-3818)
PHONE..............................714 990-3787
David Gillanders, *President*
▲ **EMP:** 13
SQ FT: 5,500
SALES (est): 2.2MM **Privately Held**
WEB: www.dgindustries.com
SIC: 3541 Screw machines, automatic

(P-13910)
DAC INTERNATIONAL INC (PA)
Also Called: D A C
6390 Rose Ln, Carpinteria (93013-2998)
PHONE..............................805 684-8307
Kenneth R Payne, *President*
▲ **EMP:** 34

SQ FT: 17,500
SALES: 10MM **Privately Held**
WEB: www.dac-intl.com
SIC: 3541 Machine tools, metal cutting type

(P-13911)
DANAIR INC (PA)
1150 E Acequia Ave, Visalia (93292-6557)
P.O. Box 2577, Elko NV (89803-2577)
PHONE..............................559 734-1961
Mark Hayward, *President*
Dan Scilagyi, *Shareholder*
James Martin, *Corp Secy*
EMP: 10
SQ FT: 7,500
SALES: 3MM **Privately Held**
WEB: www.danairinc.com
SIC: 3541 Centering machines

(P-13912)
DELTA LATH & PLASTER INC
Also Called: Wash System and Dry Wall Works
5451 Whse Way Ste 105, Sacramento (95826)
PHONE..............................916 383-6756
Kevin Nelson, *President*
EMP: 20 **EST:** 2011
SALES (est): 2MM **Privately Held**
SIC: 3541 7299 Lathes; home improvement & renovation contractor agency

(P-13913)
DEVELOPMENT ASSOC CONTRLS
Also Called: D A C
6390 Rose Ln, Carpinteria (93013-2922)
PHONE..............................805 684-8307
Edward W Vernon, *President*
EMP: 43 **EST:** 1994
SALES (est): 5.3MM
SALES (corp-wide): 1.4MM **Privately Held**
WEB: www.dacvision.com
SIC: 3541 Lathes, metal cutting & polishing
HQ: Dac Vision Incorporated
3630 W Miller Rd Ste 350
Garland TX 75041
972 677-2700

(P-13914)
DMG MORI MANUFACTURING USA INC (HQ)
Also Called: DTL Research & Technical Ctr
3805 Faraday Ave, Davis (95618-7773)
PHONE..............................530 746-7400
Adam Hansel, *President*
Hiroshi Takami, *Treasurer*
Zach Piner, *Vice Pres*
Natsuo Okada, *Admin Sec*
▲ **EMP:** 26
SALES (est): 24.1MM **Privately Held**
SIC: 3541 Machine tools, metal cutting type

(P-13915)
DMG MORI USA INC
5740 Warland Dr, Cypress (90630-5030)
PHONE..............................562 430-3800
Shuji Yamashita, *Manager*
Brandon Bebault, *Engineer*
Koji Kato, *Opers Staff*
Daniel Amendola, *Manager*
EMP: 12 **Privately Held**
SIC: 3541 5084 Machine tools, metal cutting type; machine tools & accessories
HQ: Dmg Mori Usa, Inc.
2400 Huntington Blvd
Hoffman Estates IL 60192
847 593-5400

(P-13916)
DOLLAR SHAVE CLUB INC (HQ)
13335 Maxella Ave, Marina Del Rey (90292-5619)
PHONE..............................310 975-8528
Michael Dubin, *CEO*
Danny Miles, *Officer*
David Kujda, *Vice Pres*
Janet Song, *Vice Pres*
Gloria Synn, *Vice Pres*
EMP: 48 **EST:** 2011

▲ = Import ▼ = Export
◆ = Import/Export

SALES (est): 29.9MM
SALES (corp-wide): 58.3B **Privately Held**
SIC: **3541** 3991 2844 Shaving machines (metalworking); shaving brushes; shaving preparations
PA: Unilever N.V.
Weena 455
Rotterdam
102 174-000

(P-13917)
DORINGER MANUFACTURING CO INC
13400 Estrella Ave, Gardena (90248-1513)
PHONE..............................310 366-7766
William Bailey, *President*
Lisa Pomeroy, *Treasurer*
EMP: 15
SQ FT: 50,000
SALES: 6MM **Privately Held**
WEB: www.doringer.com
SIC: **3541** Machine tools, metal cutting type
PA: Cold Saws Of America, Inc
13400 Estrella Ave
Gardena CA
310 366-7766

(P-13918)
DOWNEY GRINDING CO
12323 Bellflower Blvd, Downey (90242-2829)
P.O. Box 583 (90241-0583)
PHONE..............................562 803-5556
Larry Sequeira, *President*
Darla Sequeira, *Corp Secy*
Steve Shailer, *Info Tech Mgr*
▲ EMP: 50
SQ FT: 27,000
SALES (est): 7.9MM **Privately Held**
WEB: www.downeygrinding.com
SIC: **3541** 3599 Machine tools, metal cutting type; machine shop, jobbing & repair

(P-13919)
DR DBURR INC
12943 S Budlong Ave, Gardena (90247-1511)
PHONE..............................310 323-6900
Arturo Alvarez, *Owner*
Jess Alvarez, *Manager*
EMP: 15
SQ FT: 3,500
SALES: 500K **Privately Held**
WEB: www.drdburr.com
SIC: **3541** 3471 Deburring machines; cleaning, polishing & finishing

(P-13920)
ENSIGN US DRLG CAL INC (HQ)
7001 Charity Ave, Bakersfield (93308-5824)
PHONE..............................661 589-0111
Selby Porter, *President*
Mike Gray, *CFO*
Sandy Bullman, *Accounting Dir*
EMP: 64
SALES (est): 10.4MM
SALES (corp-wide): 876.6MM **Privately Held**
SIC: **3541** Drilling & boring machines
PA: Ensign Energy Services Inc
400 5 Ave Sw Suite 1000
Calgary AB T2P 0
403 262-1361

(P-13921)
G & L TOOLING INC
14526 Carmenita Rd, Norwalk (90650)
PHONE..............................562 802-2857
EMP: 12 EST: 1978
SQ FT: 15,000
SALES: 1MM **Privately Held**
SIC: **3541**

(P-13922)
GNB CORPORATION
Also Called: GNB Vacuum Excellence Defined
3200 Dwight Rd Ste 100, Elk Grove (95758-6461)
PHONE..............................916 233-3543
Kenneth W Harrison, *President*
Donald A Bendix, *Corp Secy*
Klaus Rindt, *Vice Pres*
Amy Long, *Human Resources*

▲ EMP: 60
SQ FT: 62,500
SALES (est): 20.7MM **Privately Held**
WEB: www.gnbvalves.com
SIC: **3541** Machine tools, metal cutting type; industrial valves
HQ: Ellison Technologies, Inc.
9912 Pioneer Blvd
Santa Fe Springs CA 90670
562 949-8311

(P-13923)
GODDARD ROTARY TOOL CO INC
525 Opper St, Escondido (92029-1019)
PHONE..............................760 743-6717
Raymond J Goddard, *President*
Gary Goddard, *Vice Pres*
EMP: 11
SQ FT: 10,000
SALES: 478K **Privately Held**
SIC: **3541** Machine tools, metal cutting type

(P-13924)
I & I DEBURRING INC
14504 Carmenita Rd Ste A, Norwalk (90650-5290)
PHONE..............................562 802-0058
Gary Wollum, *President*
Gary Klema, *Principal*
EMP: 19
SQ FT: 4,300
SALES (est): 2.2MM **Privately Held**
WEB: www.i-i-deburring.com
SIC: **3541** Machine tools, metal cutting type

(P-13925)
J C GRINDING (PA)
Also Called: J C Machining
10923 Painter Ave, Santa Fe Springs (90670-4528)
PHONE..............................562 944-3025
Paul Caringella, *Owner*
EMP: 12 EST: 1975
SQ FT: 10,000
SALES (est): 2.2MM **Privately Held**
SIC: **3541** Machine tools, metal cutting type

(P-13926)
JCR AIRCRAFT DEBURRING LLC
Also Called: Jcr Deburring
221 Foundation Ave, La Habra (90631-6812)
PHONE..............................714 870-4427
Juan Carlos Ruiz, *Mng Member*
Omar Ruiz,
EMP: 38
SALES (est): 8.2MM **Privately Held**
SIC: **3541** 3471 Deburring machines; plating & polishing

(P-13927)
JWC CARBIDE INC
33700 Calle Vis, Temecula (92592-9189)
PHONE..............................714 540-8870
Fax: 714 668-8600
EMP: 14
SQ FT: 5,900
SALES: 2.2MM **Privately Held**
WEB: www.jwccarbide.com
SIC: **3541**

(P-13928)
K-V ENGINEERING INC
2411 W 1st St, Santa Ana (92703-3509)
PHONE..............................714 229-9977
Khanh G Vu, *President*
Christie Vu, *CFO*
Duong Vu, *Treasurer*
Hien Delo, *Program Mgr*
EMP: 30
SQ FT: 22,000
SALES (est): 7.4MM **Privately Held**
SIC: **3541** 3542 Milling machines; machine tools, metal forming type; punching & shearing machines; press brakes; riveting machines

(P-13929)
LEAN MANUFACTURING GROUP LLC
29170 Avenue Penn, Valencia (91355-5420)
PHONE..............................661 702-9400
Kimberly Prezioso, *Managing Prtnr*
Patricia Sapien, *Admin Asst*
EMP: 10
SALES (est): 1.8MM **Privately Held**
SIC: **3541** Machine tools, metal cutting type

(P-13930)
LEITZ TOOLING SYSTEMS LP
1145 Orange Show Rd, San Bernardino (92408-2803)
PHONE..............................909 799-8494
Holger Nagel, *Manager*
EMP: 11
SALES (corp-wide): 3.4MM **Privately Held**
SIC: **3541** Machine tools, metal cutting type
PA: Leitz Tooling Systems Lp
4301 East Paris Ave Se
Grand Rapids MI 49512
800 253-6070

(P-13931)
LIBOON GROUP INC
Also Called: Velox Cnc
1746 W Katella Ave Ste 6, Orange (92867-3431)
PHONE..............................714 639-3639
Ronald Liboon, *Principal*
Curtis Peterson, *COO*
▲ EMP: 11 EST: 2011
SQ FT: 8,000
SALES (est): 385K **Privately Held**
SIC: **3541** 7389 Milling machines; design, commercial & industrial

(P-13932)
LISI MEDICAL JEROPA INC (DH)
950 Borra Pl, Escondido (92029-2011)
PHONE..............................760 432-9785
Christian Darville, *CEO*
Richard Warren, *General Mgr*
Crystal Schaffer, *Engineer*
Gregg Senger, *Engineer*
Herve Legrand, *Business Mgr*
▲ EMP: 70
SALES (est): 68.3MM
SALES (corp-wide): 177.9K **Privately Held**
WEB: www.jeropa.com
SIC: **3541** Machine tools, metal cutting type
HQ: Hi-Shear Corporation
2600 Skypark Dr
Torrance CA 90505
310 784-4025

(P-13933)
MELFRED BORZALL INC
2712 Airpark Dr, Santa Maria (93455-1418)
PHONE..............................805 614-4344
Dick Melsheimer, *Principal*
Eric Melsheimer, *Chief Engr*
Jose Mierzejewski, *Production*
▲ EMP: 40
SQ FT: 30,000
SALES (est): 8.5MM **Privately Held**
SIC: **3541** Machine tools, metal cutting type

(P-13934)
METLSAW SYSTEMS INC
2950 Bay Vista Ct, Benicia (94510-1123)
PHONE..............................707 746-6200
Lisa Kvech, *CEO*
Jim Kelly, *Sales Dir*
▲ EMP: 21
SQ FT: 30,000
SALES (est): 6.7MM
SALES (corp-wide): 1B **Privately Held**
WEB: www.metlsaw.com
SIC: **3541** Saws & sawing machines
HQ: Indel, Inc.
10 Indel Ave
Rancocas NJ 08073
609 267-9000

(P-13935)
METRIC MACHINING (PA)
Also Called: Master Machine Products
3263 Trade Center Dr, Riverside (92507-3432)
PHONE..............................909 947-9222
David Parker, *Principal*
Joan Parker, *Treasurer*
Tim Keleher, *CTO*
Bill Stahlke, *Engineer*
Magdalena Lopez, *Controller*
▲ EMP: 50
SQ FT: 45,000
SALES: 7MM **Privately Held**
SIC: **3541** Machine tools, metal cutting type

(P-13936)
MONARCH PRECISION DEBURRING
1514 E Edinger Ave Ste C, Santa Ana (92705-4918)
PHONE..............................714 258-0342
Russ Little, *President*
EMP: 15
SQ FT: 6,100
SALES (est): 2.4MM **Privately Held**
SIC: **3541** Machine tools, metal cutting type

(P-13937)
NEW CENTURY MACHINE TOOLS INC
9641 Santa Fe Springs Rd, Santa Fe Springs (90670-2917)
PHONE..............................562 906-8455
EMP: 15
SQ FT: 35,000
SALES (est): 1.7MM **Privately Held**
SIC: **3541**

(P-13938)
PAPCO SCREW PRODUCTS INC
Also Called: Papco Parts
9410 De Soto Ave Ste A, Chatsworth (91311-4993)
PHONE..............................818 341-2266
Norman J Grencius, *President*
EMP: 13
SQ FT: 6,000
SALES (est): 2.4MM **Privately Held**
WEB: www.papcoparts.com
SIC: **3541** 3451 Screw machines, automatic; screw machine products

(P-13939)
PAUL DOSIER ASSOCIATES INC
913 Chicago Ave, Placentia (92870-1713)
PHONE..............................714 556-7075
David A Dosier, *President*
EMP: 13
SQ FT: 7,500
SALES: 730K **Privately Held**
SIC: **3541** 3599 Machine tool replacement & repair parts, metal cutting types; machine & other job shop work

(P-13940)
PRECISION DEBURRING SERVICES
4440 Manning Rd, Pico Rivera (90660-2164)
PHONE..............................562 944-4497
Darren Smith, *President*
▲ EMP: 80
SALES (est): 5.8MM **Privately Held**
SIC: **3541** Machine tools, metal cutting type

(P-13941)
PRECON INC
Also Called: Precon Gage
3131 E La Palma Ave, Anaheim (92806-2895)
PHONE..............................714 630-7632
James Von Zabern, *President*
Audrey Von Zabern, *Treasurer*
EMP: 20
SQ FT: 10,500

PRODUCTS & SVCS

SALES (est): 2.9MM **Privately Held**
WEB: www.precon-inc.com
SIC: **3541** 3545 3823 3471 Deburring machines; saws & sawing machines; grinding machines, metalworking; gauges (machine tool accessories); industrial instrmnts msrmnt display/control process variable; plating & polishing

(P-13942)
PRODUCTION SAW
9790 Glenoaks Blvd Ste 8, Sun Valley (91352-1055)
P.O. Box 1341 (91353-1341)
PHONE..................................818 765-6100
EMP: 10
SALES (est): 845.8K **Privately Held**
SIC: **3541** 7812

(P-13943)
REPUBLIC MACHINERY CO INC (PA)
Also Called: Lagun Engineering Solutions
800 Sprucelake Dr, Harbor City (90710-1607)
PHONE..................................310 518-1100
Vivian Bezic, *CEO*
Joseph Bezic, *President*
Gary Trapani, *Technical Staff*
Fernando Martinez, *Business Mgr*
Nicole Bezic, *Controller*
▲ EMP: 30
SQ FT: 30,000
SALES (est): 6.9MM **Privately Held**
SIC: **3541** 3542 3549 3545 Drilling & boring machines; arbor presses; extruding machines (machine tools); metal; metalworking machinery; machine knives, metalworking; drilling machine attachments & accessories

(P-13944)
RH STRASBAUGH (PA)
825 Buckley Rd, San Luis Obispo (93401-8192)
PHONE..................................805 541-6424
Alan Strasbaugh, *President*
Allan Paterson, *President*
Eric Jacobson, *Vice Pres*
Bill Kalenian, *Vice Pres*
John Sterbonic, *Info Tech Mgr*
EMP: 82
SQ FT: 135,000
SALES (est): 14MM **Publicly Held**
SIC: **3541** 3559 5065 Grinding, polishing, buffing, lapping & honing machines; grinding machines, metalworking; semiconductor manufacturing machinery; electronic parts & equipment

(P-13945)
ROBB-JACK CORPORATION (PA)
3300 Nicolaus Rd Ste 1, Lincoln (95648-9574)
PHONE..................................916 645-6045
David Baker, *President*
Steve Handrop, *Exec VP*
Patrick Barroga, *Engineer*
Khadidja Norris, *VP Mfg*
Meghan Gardner, *Mktg Coord*
EMP: 82
SQ FT: 42,000
SALES (est): 15.7MM **Privately Held**
WEB: www.robbjack.com
SIC: **3541** Machine tools, metal cutting type

(P-13946)
RYTAN INC
1648 W 134th St, Gardena (90249-2014)
PHONE..................................310 328-6553
Carol J Silbaugh, *CEO*
▲ EMP: 18
SQ FT: 20,400
SALES (est): 3MM **Privately Held**
WEB: www.rytan.com
SIC: **3541** Keysetting machines

(P-13947)
S L FUSCO INC (PA)
1966 E Via Arado, Rancho Dominguez (90220-6100)
P.O. Box 5924, Compton (90224-5924)
PHONE..................................310 868-1010
Jerald C Rosin, *CEO*

Eric Rosin, *President*
Arlene Rosin, *Vice Pres*
Linda Navarro, *Division Mgr*
Dolores Aguayo, *Accounting Mgr*
▲ EMP: 45
SQ FT: 40,000
SALES (est): 44.9MM **Privately Held**
WEB: www.slfusco.com
SIC: **3541** Machine tools, metal cutting type

(P-13948)
S S SCHAFFER CO INC
Also Called: Steel Services Co
5637 District Blvd, Vernon (90058-5518)
PHONE..................................323 560-1430
Steven Schaffer Jr, *President*
Marcia Schaffer, *Treasurer*
Caroline Sallenbach, *Vice Pres*
William Salenbach, *Admin Sec*
EMP: 15 EST: 1940
SQ FT: 30,000
SALES (est): 2.9MM **Privately Held**
SIC: **3541** Grinding machines, metalworking

(P-13949)
SAAVY INC
707 W Whittier Blvd, Montebello (90640-4709)
PHONE..................................323 728-2137
Anie Piliguian, *President*
▲ EMP: 12
SALES (est): 1.7MM **Privately Held**
SIC: **3541** Buffing & polishing machines

(P-13950)
SAF-T-KUT LLC
2652 Dow Ave, Tustin (92780-7208)
PHONE..................................657 210-4426
Dan Tsujioka, *Mng Member*
Emmett Ebner,
EMP: 25
SQ FT: 1,000
SALES (est): 100K **Privately Held**
SIC: **3541** 5072 Pipe cutting & threading machines; hardware

(P-13951)
SHERLINE PRODUCTS INCORPORATED
3235 Executive Rdg, Vista (92081-8527)
PHONE..................................760 727-5181
Joe Martin, *President*
Karl W Rohlin III, *CEO*
Charla Papp, *CFO*
Kat Powell, *Sales Staff*
▲ EMP: 30 EST: 1973
SQ FT: 65,000
SALES (est): 6.5MM **Privately Held**
WEB: www.sherline.com
SIC: **3541** 3545 Lathes, metal cutting & polishing; machine tool accessories

(P-13952)
SOUTHERN CALIFORNIA CARBIDE
12216 Thatcher Ct, Poway (92064-6876)
PHONE..................................858 513-7777
Harjeet Singh, *President*
Satanm Singh, *Vice Pres*
EMP: 20
SQ FT: 10,000
SALES (est): 1.8MM **Privately Held**
SIC: **3541** 3545 Machine tools, metal cutting type; machine tool accessories

(P-13953)
SOUTHWESTERN INDUSTRIES INC (PA)
2615 Homestead Pl, Rancho Dominguez (90220-5610)
P.O. Box 9066, Compton (90224-9066)
PHONE..................................310 608-4422
Richard Leonhard, *CEO*
Stephen Pinto, *President*
Bruce Meredith, *Executive*
Michael McGarry, *Regional Mgr*
Fred Foscalina, *Sr Software Eng*
▲ EMP: 70 EST: 1953
SALES (est): 28.6MM **Privately Held**
SIC: **3541** Machine tools, metal cutting type

(P-13954)
SUPERTEC MACHINERY INC
Also Called: St Supertec
6435 Alondra Blvd, Paramount (90723-3758)
PHONE..................................562 220-1675
Randy Oscar Chu, *CEO*
George Shih, *President*
Rafael Vasquez, *Regl Sales Mgr*
Don Staggenborg, *Sales Mgr*
▲ EMP: 15
SQ FT: 8,420
SALES (est): 3.1MM **Privately Held**
WEB: www.supertecusa.com
SIC: **3541** 3542 7389 Grinding, polishing, buffing, lapping & honing machines; grinding machines, metalworking; machine tools, metal forming type; grinding, precision: commercial or industrial

(P-13955)
TAURUS PRODUCTS INC
67 W Easy St Ste 118, Simi Valley (93065-6203)
PHONE..................................805 584-1555
Arthur P Burgos, *Manager*
EMP: 23
SALES (corp-wide): 4.2MM **Privately Held**
SIC: **3541** Machine tools, metal cutting type
PA: Taurus Products, Inc.
230 Wetstone Dr
Thousand Oaks CA 91362
805 584-1555

(P-13956)
TESCO PRODUCTS
25601 Avenue Stanford, Santa Clarita (91355-1103)
PHONE..................................661 257-0153
Mark Terry, *CEO*
EMP: 12
SQ FT: 2,500
SALES (est): 300K **Privately Held**
WEB: www.tescoproducts.com
SIC: **3541** 5032 Grinding, polishing, buffing, lapping & honing machines; brick, stone & related material

(P-13957)
TJ AEROSPACE INC
12601 Monarch St, Garden Grove (92841-3918)
PHONE..................................714 891-3564
Tien N Dang, *CEO*
EMP: 23
SQ FT: 6,000
SALES (est): 7MM **Privately Held**
SIC: **3541** Machine tools, metal cutting type

(P-13958)
TOOL MAKERS INTERNATIONAL INC
Also Called: T M I
3390 Woodward Ave, Santa Clara (95054-2629)
P.O. Box 4840 (95056-4840)
PHONE..................................408 980-8888
Patrick Chronis, *President*
EMP: 13 EST: 1961
SQ FT: 22,000
SALES (est): 2.6MM **Privately Held**
WEB: www.toolmakersintl.com
SIC: **3541** Machine tools, metal cutting type

(P-13959)
TREAT MANUFACTURING INC
Also Called: Cameron Micro Drill Presses
19401 Rawhide Rd, Sonora (95370-9416)
PHONE..................................209 532-2220
Lonnie Leo Treat, *President*
Anita Treat, *Principal*
▲ EMP: 14
SQ FT: 16,000
SALES (est): 2.7MM **Privately Held**
WEB: www.cameronmicrodrillpress.com
SIC: **3541** 3559 3589 3545 Drill presses; glass making machinery: blowing, molding, forming, etc.; water filters & softeners, household type; machine tool accessories; machine tools, metal forming type

(P-13960)
US UNION TOOL INC (HQ)
1260 N Fee Ana St, Anaheim (92807-1817)
PHONE..................................714 521-6242
Hideo Hirano, *President*
Robert Smallwood, *President*
Sherry Smith, *Database Admin*
John McCandlish, *Manager*
▲ EMP: 45
SQ FT: 44,000
SALES (est): 121.5MM **Privately Held**
WEB: www.usuniontool.com
SIC: **3541** Machine tools, metal cutting type

(P-13961)
VALLEY CUTTING SYSTEM INC
1455 N Belmont Rd, Exeter (93221-9669)
P.O. Box 607, Three Rivers (93271-0607)
PHONE..................................559 684-1229
▲ EMP: 35
SALES (est): 3.4MM **Privately Held**
SIC: **3541** Cutoff machines (metalworking machinery)

(P-13962)
WESTERN FIBER CO INC
4234a Sandrini Rd, Arvin (93203-9200)
P.O. Box 22665, Bakersfield (93390-2665)
PHONE..................................661 854-5556
John Scarrone, *President*
▲ EMP: 40
SALES (est): 5.8MM **Privately Held**
SIC: **3541** Electrical discharge erosion machines

3542 Machine Tools: Forming

(P-13963)
3DEO INC
14000 Van Ness Ave Ste C, Gardena (90249-2942)
PHONE..................................844 496-3825
Matthew Petros, *CEO*
Matthew Sand, *President*
EMP: 11
SQ FT: 13,000
SALES (est): 133.9K **Privately Held**
SIC: **3542** Robots for metal forming: pressing, extruding, etc.

(P-13964)
ADDITION MFG TECH CA INC
1391 Specialty Dr Ste A, Vista (92081-8521)
PHONE..................................760 597-5220
Phillippe Jaubert, *President*
Francois Patanchon, *Vice Pres*
Bob Wolbrink, *Sales Staff*
▲ EMP: 35
SQ FT: 23,432
SALES (est): 9.3MM
SALES (corp-wide): 9.6MM **Privately Held**
WEB: www.eatonleonard.com
SIC: **3542** Bending machines
PA: Addition Manufacturing Technologies Llc
1637 Kingsview Dr
Lebanon OH 45036
513 228-7000

(P-13965)
AIR FRAME FORMING INC
15717 Colorado Ave, Paramount (90723-4210)
PHONE..................................562 663-1662
Carolina Abad, *President*
EMP: 10
SQ FT: 10,000
SALES (est): 902.6K **Privately Held**
SIC: **3542** Machine tools, metal forming type

(P-13966)
AMBRIT INDUSTRIES INC
432 Magnolia Ave, Glendale (91204-2406)
PHONE..................................818 243-1224
Paul Yaussi, *President*
Louis A Yaussi, *Corp Secy*
Michelle Taylor, *Manager*
EMP: 38 EST: 1946
SQ FT: 9,184

SALES (est): 5.6MM **Privately Held**
SIC: **3542** 3363 Die casting machines; aluminum die-castings

(P-13967)
AMERICAN PNEUMATIC TOOLS INC
Also Called: APT
1000 S Grand Ave, Santa Ana (92705-4122)
PHONE.................................562 204-1555
Kim Eads, *President*
Dan O Brien, *CFO*
▲ EMP: 16
SQ FT: 15,000
SALES (est): 3.3MM **Privately Held**
WEB: www.apt-tools.com
SIC: **3542** 3541 3546 3532 Machine tools, metal forming type; machine tools, metal cutting type; power-driven hand-tools; mining machinery; hand & edge tools

(P-13968)
AMERICAN PRECISION HYDRAULICS
5601 Research Dr, Huntington Beach (92649-1620)
PHONE.................................714 903-8610
Susan Smith, *President*
Steve Smith, *Vice Pres*
Leroy Miller, *Opers Mgr*
Judith Spirtos, *QC Mgr*
EMP: 23 EST: 1996
SQ FT: 6,500
SALES (est): 3.5MM **Privately Held**
SIC: **3542** Presses: hydraulic & pneumatic, mechanical & manual

(P-13969)
AUTOMOTIVE ENGINEERED PDTS INC
7149 Mission Gorge Rd, San Diego (92120-1100)
PHONE.................................619 229-7797
James J Bittle, *CFO*
Craig White, *Admin Sec*
EMP: 57
SQ FT: 10,000
SALES (est): 7.5MM **Privately Held**
WEB: www.jbaracingengines.com
SIC: **3542** 3714 Headers; motor vehicle parts & accessories

(P-13970)
BORDEN MANUFACTURING
3314 Pacific Trl, Cottonwood (96022)
PHONE.................................530 347-6642
Ralph Borden, *Partner*
Karen Borden, *Partner*
EMP: 45
SQ FT: 7,200
SALES (est): 7.7MM **Privately Held**
SIC: **3542** Stretching machines

(P-13971)
BROTHERS MACHINE & TOOL INC
11095 Inland Ave, Jurupa Valley (91752-1155)
PHONE.................................951 361-9454
Jose E Razo, *President*
EMP: 20
SALES (est): 2.8MM **Privately Held**
SIC: **3542** Machine tools, metal forming type
PA: Brothers Machine & Tool, Inc.
11098 Inland Ave
Jurupa Valley CA 91752

(P-13972)
BROTHERS MACHINE & TOOL INC (PA)
11098 Inland Ave, Jurupa Valley (91752-1154)
PHONE.................................951 361-2909
Jose E Razzo, *President*
Jose L Razzo, *Treasurer*
Jose F Razzo, *Vice Pres*
EMP: 15
SALES: 2MM **Privately Held**
SIC: **3542** Machine tools, metal forming type

(P-13973)
CARANDO TECHNOLOGIES INC
345 N Harrison St, Stockton (95203-2801)
P.O. Box 1167 (95201-1167)
PHONE.................................209 948-6500
Sidney A Scheutz, *CEO*
Laura Keir, *CFO*
Shannon Crawford, *Office Mgr*
Larry Renzi, *Electrical Engi*
▼ EMP: 25
SQ FT: 35,000
SALES (est): 6.4MM **Privately Held**
WEB: www.carando.net
SIC: **3542** 3548 3599 Machine tools, metal forming type; welding apparatus; custom machinery; machine shop, jobbing & repair

(P-13974)
CIRCLE INDUSTRIAL MFG CORP
Also Called: Cim
2727 N Slater Ave, Compton (90222)
PHONE.................................310 638-5101
Debra Cosio, *Branch Mgr*
EMP: 15
SALES (corp-wide): 5.1MM **Privately Held**
WEB: www.circleindustrial.com
SIC: **3542** Sheet metalworking machines
PA: Circle Industrial Mfg. Corporation
1613 W El Segundo Blvd
Compton CA 90222
310 638-5101

(P-13975)
COASTAL DIE CUTTING INC
7100 Convoy Ct, San Diego (92111-1019)
PHONE.................................619 677-3180
Kevin Otsuka, *President*
Mary Jenkins, *CFO*
EMP: 17
SALES (est): 2.3MM **Privately Held**
SIC: **3542** 7389 3544 Die casting & extruding machines; packaging & labeling services; dies & die holders for metal cutting, forming, die casting

(P-13976)
H & N TOOL & DIE CO INC
201 Jason Ct Ste B, Corona (92879-7100)
PHONE.................................951 372-9071
Tom Nassen, *President*
Rick Nassen, *Treasurer*
Jim Nassen, *Vice Pres*
▼ EMP: 10
SQ FT: 8,000
SALES (est): 1MM **Privately Held**
WEB: www.hnspringnstamping.com
SIC: **3542** 3495 3469 Presses: forming, stamping, punching, sizing (machine tools); wire springs; machine parts, stamped or pressed metal

(P-13977)
HORN MACHINE TOOLS INC
Also Called: H M T
40455 Brickyard Dr # 101, Madera (93636-9516)
PHONE.................................559 431-4131
Kent Horn, *President*
Lee Sanchez, *Sales Staff*
William Winn, *Sales Staff*
▲ EMP: 32 EST: 1996
SALES (est): 7.9MM **Privately Held**
SIC: **3542** 5084 Bending machines; industrial machinery & equipment

(P-13978)
HYPRESS TECHNOLOGIES INC
340 Hearst Dr, Oxnard (93030-5174)
PHONE.................................805 485-4060
John W Keefer, *President*
EMP: 18
SQ FT: 9,100
SALES (est): 1.8MM **Privately Held**
SIC: **3542** Presses: hydraulic & pneumatic, mechanical & manual

(P-13979)
INTERNATIONAL FORMING TECH INC
2331 Sturgis Rd, Oxnard (93030-8934)
PHONE.................................805 278-8060
Siggy Rivalta, *President*
EMP: 40

SALES (est): 5.5MM **Privately Held**
SIC: **3542** Machine tools, metal forming type

(P-13980)
LIP HING METAL INC
738 Phillips, Rowland Heights (91748-1146)
PHONE.................................714 871-9220
Ronald Chow, *Principal*
▲ EMP: 10
SALES (est): 1.3MM **Privately Held**
SIC: **3542** Arbor presses

(P-13981)
LOUIS LEVIN & SON INC
13550 Larwin Cir, Santa Fe Springs (90670-5031)
PHONE.................................562 802-8066
Dale Waite, *President*
EMP: 11
SQ FT: 6,500
SALES (est): 1.8MM **Privately Held**
WEB: www.levinlathe.com
SIC: **3542** Machine tools, metal forming type

(P-13982)
MAGNETIC METALS CORPORATION
2475 W La Palma Ave, Anaheim (92801-2610)
PHONE.................................714 828-4625
Linda Cannon, *Branch Mgr*
EMP: 40
SQ FT: 50,000
SALES (corp-wide): 1B **Privately Held**
WEB: www.magmet.com
SIC: **3542** Magnetic forming machines
HQ: Magnetic Metals Corporation
1900 Hayes Ave
Camden NJ 08105
856 964-7842

(P-13983)
MATHY MACHINE INC
9315 Wheatlands Rd, Santee (92071-2860)
PHONE.................................619 448-0404
Jay Mathy, *President*
Paul Carpenter, *General Mgr*
Bryan Mathy, *Engineer*
EMP: 30 EST: 1979
SQ FT: 14,000
SALES (est): 6.2MM **Privately Held**
WEB: www.mathymachine.com
SIC: **3542** Machine tools, metal forming type

(P-13984)
MEDLIN RAMPS
14903 Marquardt Ave, Santa Fe Springs (90670-5128)
PHONE.................................562 229-1991
Mark Medlin, *Principal*
Pat Crowder, *General Mgr*
▲ EMP: 12
SQ FT: 10,000
SALES (est): 2.5MM **Privately Held**
SIC: **3542** 5084 Machine tools, metal forming type; materials handling machinery

(P-13985)
MJC ENGINEERING AND TECH INC
15401 Assembly Ln, Huntington Beach (92649-1329)
PHONE.................................714 890-0618
Carl Lorentzen, *President*
Bernd Hermann, *CFO*
Gro Jensen, *CFO*
Per Carlson, *Vice Pres*
Percy Carlson, *Vice Pres*
▲ EMP: 18
SQ FT: 10,000
SALES (est): 7.2MM **Privately Held**
WEB: www.mjcengineering.com
SIC: **3542** Spinning machines, metal

(P-13986)
MORAN TOOLS
2515 Bella Vista Dr, Vista (92084-7841)
P.O. Box 1141 (92085-1141)
PHONE.................................760 801-3570
Max Moran, *Owner*

EMP: 20
SALES (est): 2.6MM **Privately Held**
SIC: **3542** Machine tools, metal forming type

(P-13987)
NOLL INC
390 Buckley Rd Frnt, San Luis Obispo (93401-8164)
PHONE.................................805 543-3602
John M Noll, *President*
Andrew Levy, *Engineer*
EMP: 10 EST: 1958
SQ FT: 12,500
SALES (est): 1MM **Privately Held**
WEB: www.nollinc.com
SIC: **3542** 3498 Thread rolling machines; fabricated pipe & fittings

(P-13988)
NUGIER PRESS COMPANY INC
Also Called: Nugier Hydraulics
18031 La Salle Ave, Gardena (90248-3606)
PHONE.................................310 515-6025
Gary Livick, *President*
EMP: 17
SALES (est): 732K **Privately Held**
WEB: www.nugier.com
SIC: **3542** 5084 Presses: hydraulic & pneumatic, mechanical & manual; industrial machinery & equipment

(P-13989)
PHANTOM TOOL & DIE CO
23535 Us Highway 18, Apple Valley (92307-4345)
PHONE.................................760 240-4249
Jack Probert, *Owner*
EMP: 10
SQ FT: 14,500
SALES: 150K **Privately Held**
SIC: **3542** Headers

(P-13990)
PHI
Also Called: PHI Hydraulics
14955 Salt Lake Ave E, City of Industry (91746-3133)
PHONE.................................626 968-9680
Yuriy Rakhlin, *President*
Jim Voigt, *Engineer*
▼ EMP: 25
SQ FT: 25,930
SALES: 3.5MM **Privately Held**
WEB: www.tulipcorp.com
SIC: **3542** 3549 Presses: hydraulic & pneumatic, mechanical & manual; metalworking machinery

(P-13991)
PRECISION FASTENER TOOLING
11530 Western Ave, Stanton (90680-3490)
PHONE.................................714 898-8558
Charles Boyles, *President*
James Azevedo, *Vice Pres*
EMP: 19 EST: 1981
SQ FT: 10,000
SALES (est): 3.2MM **Privately Held**
SIC: **3542** 3544 Bulldozers (metalworking machinery); special dies, tools, jigs & fixtures

(P-13992)
PRECISION FORMING GROUP LLC
511 Commercial Way, La Habra (90631-6170)
PHONE.................................562 501-1985
Mario Diaz, *Mng Member*
EMP: 15 EST: 2013
SALES (est): 1.1MM **Privately Held**
SIC: **3542** Metal deposit forming machines

(P-13993)
RAY CHINN CONSTRUCTION INC
424 24th St, Bakersfield (93301-4104)
PHONE.................................661 327-2731
Raymond Dean Chinn, *President*
EMP: 35
SALES (est): 5.3MM **Privately Held**
SIC: **3542** Mechanical (pneumatic or hydraulic) metal forming machines

(P-13994)
SHARP INDUSTRIES INC (PA)
3501 Challenger St Fl 2, Torrance
(90503-1697)
PHONE...........................310 370-5990
James Chen, *Ch of Bd*
Nicholas Chen, *CEO*
George Lee, *Senior VP*
Roger Lee, *Vice Pres*
▲ EMP: 25
SQ FT: 40,000
SALES (est): 6.2MM **Privately Held**
WEB: www.sharp-industries.com
SIC: 3542 Arbor presses

(P-13995)
SUTHERLAND PRESSES
22561 Carbon Mesa Rd, Malibu
(90265-5018)
PHONE...........................310 453-6981
Mark D Sutherland, *CEO*
Jack Wilson, *Engineer*
▲ EMP: 12
SQ FT: 10,500
SALES (est): 2.5MM **Privately Held**
WEB: www.sutherlandpresses.com
SIC: 3542 Presses: forming, stamping,
punching, sizing (machine tools); presses:
hydraulic & pneumatic, mechanical &
manual

(P-13996)
TRI A MACHINE INC
7221 Garden Grove Blvd Ab, Garden Grove
(92841-4218)
PHONE...........................714 408-8907
Anthony Nguyen, *President*
Trisha Nguyen, *Treasurer*
Luan Nguyen, *Admin Sec*
EMP: 15
SALES: 700K **Privately Held**
SIC: 3542 3541 Spinning lathes; chemical
milling machines; electrochemical milling
machines; turret lathes

(P-13997)
UNIVERSAL PUNCH CORP
4001 W Macarthur Blvd, Santa Ana
(92704-6307)
P.O. Box 26879 (92799-6879)
PHONE...........................714 556-4488
Kenneth L Williams, *President*
Joan Williams, *CFO*
Kevin Williams, *Vice Pres*
▲ EMP: 55
SQ FT: 52,000
SALES (est): 11.5MM **Privately Held**
WEB: www.universalpunch.com
SIC: 3542 3545 3544 3452 Punching &
shearing machines; machine tool acces-
sories; special dies, tools, jigs & fixtures;
bolts, nuts, rivets & washers

(P-13998)
US INDUSTRIAL TOOL & SUP CO
Also Called: Usit Co
14083 S Normandie Ave, Gardena
(90249-2614)
PHONE...........................310 464-8400
Keith Rowland, *CEO*
▲ EMP: 47 EST: 1955
SQ FT: 35,000
SALES (est): 8.9MM **Privately Held**
WEB: www.ustool.com
SIC: 3542 3546 Machine tools, metal
forming type; power-driven handtools

(P-13999)
WEST COAST-ACCUDYNE INC
Also Called: Accudyne Engineering & Eqp
7180 Scout Ave, Bell (90201-3202)
P.O. Box 2159 (90202-2159)
PHONE...........................562 927-2546
George F Schofhauser, *President*
Jill Wigney, *Corp Secy*
Kurt Anderegg, *Vice Pres*
▲ EMP: 20 EST: 1954
SALES (est): 6.2MM **Privately Held**
WEB: www.accudyneeng.com
SIC: 3542 5084 Presses: forming, stamp-
ing, punching, sizing (machine tools); ma-
chine tools & accessories

(P-14000)
XY CORP INC
Also Called: E P S Products
1258 Montalvo Way Ste A, Palm Springs
(92262-5441)
PHONE...........................760 323-0333
Jerry Good, *President*
Greg Good, *Vice Pres*
Jerry Andre, *Engineer*
EMP: 15
SQ FT: 14,000
SALES (est): 3MM **Privately Held**
WEB: www.xydroid.com
SIC: 3542 3299 Presses: hydraulic &
pneumatic, mechanical & manual; orna-
mental & architectural plaster work

3543 Industrial Patterns

(P-14001)
CENTURY PATTERN CO INC
15526 Domart Ave, Norwalk (90650-5314)
PHONE...........................562 402-1707
Min Ho Yang, *President*
EMP: 10 EST: 1976
SALES: 800K **Privately Held**
SIC: 3543 Industrial patterns

(P-14002)
HP CORE CO INC
1843 E 58th Pl, Los Angeles (90001-1415)
PHONE...........................323 582-1688
Ken Catalfo, *President*
Charles Catalfo, *Vice Pres*
EMP: 18 EST: 1964
SQ FT: 12,000
SALES (est): 998.2K **Privately Held**
SIC: 3543 Foundry cores

(P-14003)
R H PATTERN
10700 Jersey Blvd Ste 590, Rancho Cuca-
monga (91730-5124)
PHONE...........................909 484-9141
Robert Hansen, *President*
EMP: 47
SALES (est): 6.1MM **Privately Held**
SIC: 3543 Industrial patterns

(P-14004)
SWISS PATTERN CORP
2611 S Yale St, Santa Ana (92704-5227)
PHONE...........................714 545-8040
Daniel Dick, *President*
EMP: 11
SQ FT: 8,000
SALES (est): 1.7MM **Privately Held**
SIC: 3543 Industrial patterns

(P-14005)
TECHSHOP SAN JOSE LLC
300 S 2nd St, San Jose (95113-2711)
PHONE...........................408 916-4144
Mark Hatch, *CEO*
Emily Elhoffer, *President*
EMP: 17
SALES (est): 1.8MM **Privately Held**
SIC: 3543 3599 Industrial patterns; ma-
chine & other job shop work

3544 Dies, Tools, Jigs, Fixtures & Indl Molds

(P-14006)
A B G INSTRUMENTS & ENGRG
604 30th St, Paso Robles (93446-1293)
PHONE...........................805 238-6262
William Andrasko, *Owner*
EMP: 10
SQ FT: 4,500
SALES (est): 917.6K **Privately Held**
SIC: 3544 Special dies, tools, jigs & fix-
tures

(P-14007)
ACE CLEARWATER ENTERPRISES INC
1614 Kona Dr, Compton (90220-5412)
PHONE...........................310 538-5380
James D Dodson, *Branch Mgr*
EMP: 12

SALES (corp-wide): 42.8MM **Privately Held**
WEB: www.aceclearwater.com
SIC: 3544 3728 3769 Special dies, tools,
jigs & fixtures; aircraft parts & equipment;
guided missile & space vehicle parts &
auxiliary equipment
PA: Ace Clearwater Enterprises, Inc.
19815 Magellan Dr
Torrance CA 90502
310 323-2140

(P-14008)
ADVANCED ENVIROMENTAL
2420 W Carson St, Torrance (90501-3145)
PHONE...........................310 782-9400
Raymond Castro, *Owner*
EMP: 11
SALES (est): 652.8K **Privately Held**
SIC: 3544 5031 Industrial molds; molding,
all materials

(P-14009)
ADVANCED MACHINING TOOLING INC
Also Called: C S C
13535 Danielson St, Poway (92064-6868)
PHONE...........................858 486-9050
Terry A Deane, *CEO*
Tony Cerda, *President*
Jodi Deane, *CFO*
Roxanne Gondek, *Controller*
EMP: 46
SQ FT: 31,000
SALES (est): 10.4MM **Privately Held**
WEB: www.amtmfg.com
SIC: 3544 3599 Special dies, tools, jigs &
fixtures; machine shop, jobbing & repair

(P-14010)
ADVANCED MOLD TECHNOLOGY INC
1560 Moonstone, Brea (92821-2876)
PHONE...........................714 990-0144
Dana Mitchell, *President*
◆ EMP: 19
SQ FT: 8,800
SALES (est): 4.4MM **Privately Held**
WEB: www.advancedmold.com
SIC: 3544 Industrial molds

(P-14011)
ALCO MANUFACTURING INC
207 E Alton Ave, Santa Ana (92707-4416)
PHONE...........................714 549-5007
Frank Reuland, *President*
Ingrid Reuland, *Corp Secy*
EMP: 15 EST: 1980
SQ FT: 11,000
SALES (est): 2.8MM **Privately Held**
WEB: www.alcomanufacturinginc.com
SIC: 3544 3469 3444 Special dies &
tools; stamping metal for the trade; sheet
metalwork

(P-14012)
AMBRIT ENGINEERING CORPORATION
2640 Halladay St, Santa Ana (92705-5649)
PHONE...........................714 557-1074
Terrence Saul, *CEO*
John F Mattimoe, *President*
Thomas W Vickers, *Corp Secy*
Lisa Jane, *Executive Asst*
Mark Wright, *Engineer*
▲ EMP: 65
SQ FT: 32,000
SALES (est): 19.9MM **Privately Held**
WEB: www.ambritengineering.com
SIC: 3544 Forms (molds), for foundry &
plastics working machinery

(P-14013)
AMERICAN DIE & ROLLFORMING
3495 Swetzer Rd, Loomis (95650-9581)
PHONE...........................916 652-7667
Christopher Tatasciore, *President*
Slate Bryer, *Vice Pres*
Larry Dumm, *Admin Sec*
▲ EMP: 10
SALES (est): 1.7MM **Privately Held**
SIC: 3544 Special dies & tools

(P-14014)
AMERICAN INDUSTRIAL CORP
Also Called: Universe Industries
1624 N Orangethorpe Way, Anaheim
(92801-1227)
PHONE...........................714 680-4763
Cirilo Nunez, *President*
Perle Nunez, *Ch of Bd*
EMP: 10
SQ FT: 7,000
SALES (est): 1.5MM **Privately Held**
SIC: 3544 3599 3469 3541 Special dies,
tools, jigs & fixtures; machine & other job
shop work; metal stampings; machine
tools, metal cutting type; machine tool ac-
cessories; ball & roller bearings

(P-14015)
AMERICAN PLASTIC PRODUCTS INC
9243 Glenoaks Blvd, Sun Valley
(91352-2614)
PHONE...........................818 504-1073
Roupen Yegavian, *President*
Varosh Petrosian, *Vice Pres*
▲ EMP: 75
SQ FT: 35,000
SALES (est): 9.3MM **Privately Held**
WEB: www.americanelectro.com
SIC: 3544 Industrial molds

(P-14016)
AMTEC HUMAN CAPITAL INC
21661 Audubon Way, El Toro (92630-5752)
PHONE...........................949 472-0396
Arvie Martin, *Branch Mgr*
EMP: 29
SALES (corp-wide): 5.9MM **Privately Held**
SIC: 3544 Industrial molds
PA: Amtec Human Capital, Inc.
5877 Pine Ave Ste 100
Chino Hills CA
714 993-1900

(P-14017)
ART MOLD DIE CASTING INC
11872 Sheldon St, Sun Valley
(91352-1507)
PHONE...........................818 767-6464
Leo Benavides, *President*
Arman Sarkissian, *Vice Pres*
EMP: 25
SQ FT: 14,000
SALES (est): 3.7MM **Privately Held**
WEB: www.artmoldinc.com
SIC: 3544 3369 3363 Industrial molds;
nonferrous foundries; aluminum die-cast-
ings

(P-14018)
ATS TOOL INC
Also Called: Ats Workholding
30222 Esperanza, Rcho STA Marg
(92688-2121)
PHONE...........................949 888-1744
William Murphy, *President*
Sean Murphy, *Vice Pres*
Tim Schneider, *Vice Pres*
▲ EMP: 20
SALES (est): 3.6MM **Privately Held**
SIC: 3544 Jigs & fixtures

(P-14019)
AVIS ROTO DIE CO
1560 N San Fernando Rd, Los Angeles
(90065-1225)
P.O. Box 65617 (90065-0617)
PHONE...........................323 255-7070
Avetis Iskanian, *CEO*
Mike Keoshgerian, *Vice Pres*
Ron Lee, *Principal*
Hasmink Iskanian, *Administration*
Gary Keshishian, *CTO*
EMP: 30
SQ FT: 32,000
SALES (est): 5.2MM **Privately Held**
WEB: www.avisrd.com
SIC: 3544 Paper cutting dies

(P-14020)
B & R MOLD INC
4564 E Los Angeles Ave C, Simi Valley
(93063-3428)
PHONE...........................805 526-8665
Brent Robinson, *President*

▲ = Import ▼=Export
◆ =Import/Export

Stephen Yamani, *Executive*
EMP: 12
SALES (est): 1.6MM **Privately Held**
WEB: www.brmold.com
SIC: 3544 Industrial molds

(P-14021)
BARROT CORPORATION
1881 Kaiser Ave, Irvine (92614-5707)
PHONE.................................949 852-1640
Jesus Barrot, *President*
Robert Barrot, *Treasurer*
Carlos Barrot, *Vice Pres*
James Barrot, *Admin Sec*
EMP: 22
SQ FT: 15,000
SALES (est): 4.2MM **Privately Held**
WEB: www.barrotcorp.com
SIC: 3544 3769 Special dies & tools;
guided missile & space vehicle parts &
auxiliary equipment

(P-14022)
BENDA TOOL & MODEL WORKS INC
Also Called: A & B Diecasting
900 Alfred Nobel Dr, Hercules
(94547-1814)
PHONE.................................510 741-3170
Robert Dathe, *President*
Stephen Dathe, *CEO*
Judy Newsome, *COO*
Ben Dathe, *Vice Pres*
Steve Dathe, *Vice Pres*
▲ **EMP:** 35 **EST:** 1946
SQ FT: 60,000
SALES (est): 8.9MM **Privately Held**
WEB: www.bendatool.com
SIC: 3544 Dies, steel rule; industrial molds

(P-14023)
BERNMAN MOLD AND ENGINEERING
1219 S Bon View Ave, Ontario
(91761-4402)
PHONE.................................909 930-3844
Manuel J Solario, *President*
EMP: 10
SQ FT: 2,600
SALES (est): 1MM **Privately Held**
SIC: 3544 Industrial molds

(P-14024)
BUCY DIE CASTING
633 S Glenwood Pl, Burbank (91506-2891)
PHONE.................................818 843-5044
Thomas L Bucy Jr, *President*
Ricardo Cruz, *CFO*
Thomas Bucy Sr, *Vice Pres*
Janell R Bucy, *Admin Sec*
EMP: 13
SQ FT: 6,000
SALES (est): 1.9MM **Privately Held**
WEB: www.bucycast.com
SIC: 3544 Dies & die holders for metal cutting, forming, die casting

(P-14025)
C & H MOLDING INCORPORATED
11160 Thurston Ln, Jurupa Valley
(91752-1426)
PHONE.................................951 361-5030
Hugh W Fitzell, *President*
Sarah Fitzell, *Corp Secy*
EMP: 20
SALES (est): 3MM **Privately Held**
SIC: 3544 Forms (molds), for foundry &
plastics working machinery

(P-14026)
C & L TOOL AND DIE INC
8684 Avenida De La Fuente # 12, San
Diego (92154-6220)
PHONE.................................619 270-8385
Ernesto Islas, *President*
Esperanza Islas, *Corp Secy*
EMP: 10
SQ FT: 1,000
SALES (est): 1MM **Privately Held**
SIC: 3544 Special dies & tools

(P-14027)
CACO-PACIFIC CORPORATION (PA)
813 N Cummings Rd, Covina
(91724-2597)
PHONE.................................626 331-3361
Robert G Hoffmann, *President*
Manfred Hoffman, *Ch of Bd*
Thom Williams, *Admin Sec*
▲ **EMP:** 142
SQ FT: 45,000
SALES (est): 19.1MM **Privately Held**
SIC: 3544 Industrial molds

(P-14028)
CAL NOR DESIGN INC (PA)
14126 Washington Ave, San Leandro
(94578-3325)
P.O. Box 2756, Dublin (94568-0275)
PHONE.................................925 829-7722
William Simon, *President*
EMP: 19
SQ FT: 4,000
SALES (est): 1.9MM **Privately Held**
SIC: 3544 Paper cutting dies

(P-14029)
CAL WEST CONSTRUCTION INC
4670 N Wilson Ave, Fresno (93704-3037)
PHONE.................................559 217-3306
EMP: 10
SALES (est): 584K **Privately Held**
SIC: 3544 Industrial molds

(P-14030)
CAST-RITE CORPORATION
515 E Airline Way, Gardena (90248-2593)
PHONE.................................310 532-2080
Donald De Haan, *President*
Howard Watkins, *CFO*
Wynn Chapman, *Vice Pres*
Donald Dehaan, *General Mgr*
Marcela Toro, *Human Res Mgr*
▲ **EMP:** 98
SQ FT: 74,712
SALES (est): 19.4MM
SALES (corp-wide): 29MM **Privately Held**
WEB: www.cast-rite.com
SIC: 3544 3471 3363 Special dies &
tools; plating & polishing; aluminum die-
· castings
PA: Cast-Rite International, Inc.
515 E Airline Way
Gardena CA 90248
310 532-2080

(P-14031)
CHARLES MEISNER INC
201 Sierra Pl Ste A, Upland (91786-5668)
PHONE.................................909 946-8216
Charles Meisner, *President*
Carol Meisner, *Corp Secy*
Tara Meisner, *Purchasing*
EMP: 25 **EST:** 1972
SQ FT: 19,000
SALES (est): 5.5MM **Privately Held**
SIC: 3544 3599 Special dies & tools; ma-
chine shop, jobbing & repair

(P-14032)
CHIP-MAKERS TOOLING SUPPLY INC
7352 Whittier Ave, Whittier (90602-1131)
PHONE.................................562 698-5840
Stephen Smith, *CEO*
Paul Hartman, *President*
Patty Rivera, *Treasurer*
EMP: 17
SQ FT: 10,000
SALES (est): 2.9MM **Privately Held**
WEB: www.chip-makers.com
SIC: 3544 Special dies & tools

(P-14033)
CJ ENTERPRISES
Also Called: Precision Enterprises
11530 Western Ave, Stanton (90680-3435)
PHONE.................................714 898-8558
Chuck Boyles, *Partner*
EMP: 25
SALES (est): 2.4MM **Privately Held**
SIC: 3544 Special dies, tools, jigs & fix-
tures

(P-14034)
CLAMA PRODUCTS INC
1993 Ritchey St, Santa Ana (92705-5100)
PHONE.................................714 258-8606
Hector Sandino, *President*
EMP: 17
SQ FT: 6,000
SALES (est): 1.2MM **Privately Held**
WEB: www.clamaproducts.com
SIC: 3544 3089 Industrial molds; injection
molding of plastics

(P-14035)
COLBRIT MANUFACTURING CO INC
9666 Owensmouth Ave Ste G, Chatsworth
(91311-8050)
PHONE.................................818 709-3608
Gerardo Cruz, *President*
Marina Cruz, *Vice Pres*
▲ **EMP:** 30
SQ FT: 6,000
SALES (est): 5.2MM **Privately Held**
WEB: www.colbrit.com
SIC: 3544 Special dies & tools

(P-14036)
COMPUTED TOOL & ENGINEERING
2910 E Ricker Way, Anaheim (92806-2526)
PHONE.................................714 630-3911
Oscar Torres, *President*
Isabel Torres, *Admin Sec*
EMP: 16
SQ FT: 8,825
SALES (est): 3.2MM **Privately Held**
WEB: www.computedtool.com
SIC: 3544 Special dies & tools

(P-14037)
COMPUTER PLASTICS
1914 National Ave, Hayward (94545-1784)
PHONE.................................510 785-3600
Wayne L Harshbarger, *President*
EMP: 21 **EST:** 1969
SQ FT: 12,700
SALES (est): 3.4MM **Privately Held**
WEB: www.4cpi.com
SIC: 3544 3089 Special dies & tools;
molding primary plastic

(P-14038)
CONCRETE MOLD CORPORATION
Also Called: Besser Company
2121 E Del Amo Blvd, Compton
(90220-6301)
PHONE.................................310 537-5171
Bradley Gardner, *President*
EMP: 35 **EST:** 1960
SQ FT: 30,000
SALES (est): 6.2MM
SALES (corp-wide): 243.4MM **Privately Held**
SIC: 3544 Industrial molds
PA: Besser Company
801 Johnson St
Alpena MI 49707
989 354-4111

(P-14039)
CUSTOM TOOLING & STAMPING OF O
Also Called: Custom Tooling & Automation
1182 N Knollwood Cir, Anaheim
(92801-1307)
PHONE.................................714 979-6782
Robert Kaeton, *President*
EMP: 10 **EST:** 1974
SALES (est): 1.4MM **Privately Held**
SIC: 3544 Special dies & tools

(P-14040)
DAUNTLESS INDUSTRIES INC
Also Called: Dauntless Molds
806 N Grand Ave, Covina (91724-2418)
PHONE.................................626 966-4494
George R Payton, *President*
Norm Holt, *General Mgr*
EMP: 25
SQ FT: 15,000
SALES (est): 5.6MM **Privately Held**
WEB: www.dauntlessmolds.com
SIC: 3544 Forms (molds), for foundry &
plastics working machinery

(P-14041)
DECREVEL INCORPORATED
1836 Soscol Ave, NAPA (94559-1349)
PHONE.................................707 258-8065
P James Decrevel Sr, *President*
Sara Decrevel, *CFO*
EMP: 11
SQ FT: 4,500
SALES (est): 1.5MM **Privately Held**
WEB: www.decrevel.com
SIC: 3544 2752 Special dies & tools; die
sets for metal stamping (presses); com-
mercial printing, lithographic

(P-14042)
DIAMOND INJECTION MOLDS INC
4365 E Lowell St Ste E, Ontario
(91761-2226)
PHONE.................................909 390-2260
Mark Spangler, *President*
Geri Spangler, *Admin Sec*
▲ **EMP:** 14
SQ FT: 10,000
SALES (est): 2.3MM **Privately Held**
WEB: www.diamondmolds.com
SIC: 3544 Industrial molds

(P-14043)
DIE CRAFT ENGINEERING & MFG CO
Also Called: Diecraft
11975 Florence Ave, Santa Fe Springs
(90670-4404)
PHONE.................................562 777-8809
Stepan Manoukian, *President*
EMP: 10
SQ FT: 12,000
SALES (est): 1.5MM **Privately Held**
WEB: www.diecraft.com
SIC: 3544 Special dies, tools, jigs & fix-
tures

(P-14044)
DIE SHOP
7302 Adams St, Paramount (90723-4008)
PHONE.................................562 630-4400
Hector Ramirez, *Owner*
▲ **EMP:** 15
SQ FT: 4,000
SALES (est): 968K **Privately Held**
SIC: 3544 Special dies & tools

(P-14045)
DIVERSIFIED MFG TECH INC
Also Called: Dmt
931 S Via Rodeo, Placentia (92870-6780)
PHONE.................................714 577-7000
Michael McMillian, *CEO*
EMP: 12 **EST:** 2011
SALES: 2MM **Privately Held**
SIC: 3544 3089 Industrial molds; injection
molding of plastics

(P-14046)
DL TOOL AND MFG CO INC
11828 Glenoaks Blvd, San Fernando
(91340-1804)
PHONE.................................818 837-3451
Don A Verity, *President*
Lynne Verity, *Vice Pres*
EMP: 10
SQ FT: 10,500
SALES (est): 1.4MM **Privately Held**
SIC: 3544 Die sets for metal stamping
(presses)

(P-14047)
EDRO ENGINEERING INC (DH)
20500 Carrey Rd, Walnut (91789-2417)
PHONE.................................909 594-5751
Eric Henn, *President*
Laurinda Diaz, *Shareholder*
Guy Recendez, *COO*
Dave Delgato, *Officer*
Michael Guscott, *Vice Pres*
◆ **EMP:** 85
SQ FT: 60,000
SALES: 22.3MM
SALES (corp-wide): 15.3B **Privately Held**
WEB: www.edro.com
SIC: 3544 3599 Special dies & tools; ma-
chine shop, jobbing & repair

PRODUCTS & SVCS

HQ: Voestalpine High Performance Metals
Corporation
2505 Millennium Dr
Elgin IL 60124
877 992-8764

(P-14048)
EDRO SPECIALTY STEELS INC
20500 Carrey Rd, Walnut (91789-2417)
PHONE.................................800 368-3376
Terry Henn, *President*
Kevin Ewing, *CFO*
Bryan Thompson, *Prdtn Mgr*
Ivgen Simsek, *Sales Mgr*
▲ EMP: 11
SALES (est): 1.5MM **Privately Held**
SIC: 3544 Special dies & tools

(P-14049)
ENNIS INC
1600 S Claudina Way, Anaheim
(92805-6541)
PHONE.................................714 765-0400
Perry Shokouhi, *Branch Mgr*
EMP: 250
SALES (corp-wide): 400.7MM **Publicly
Held**
WEB: www.ennis.com
SIC: 3544 Special dies, tools, jigs & fix-
tures
PA: Ennis, Inc.
2441 Presidential Pkwy
Midlothian TX 76065
972 775-9801

(P-14050)
**ENSTROM MOLD &
ENGINEERING INC**
235 Trade St, San Marcos (92078-4373)
PHONE.................................760 744-1880
Fred Enstrom, *President*
Greg Metzger, *Vice Pres*
Janice Enstrom, *Admin Sec*
EMP: 17
SQ FT: 12,500
SALES: 3.5MM **Privately Held**
WEB: www.enstrommold.com
SIC: 3544 3089 Industrial molds; plastic
processing

(P-14051)
**FAIRWAY INJECTION MOLDS
INC**
20109 Paseo Del Prado, Walnut
(91789-2665)
PHONE.................................909 595-2201
Brian Jones, *Managing Dir*
Perry Morgan, *CEO*
Ken Sowski, *Design Engr*
Oscar Fabela, *Technical Staff*
Enrique Barra, *Project Engr*
▲ EMP: 54
SQ FT: 31,147
SALES: 16MM **Privately Held**
WEB: www.fairwaymolds.com
SIC: 3544 Industrial molds

(P-14052)
FELIX TOOL & ENGINEERING
14535 Bessemer St, Van Nuys
(91411-2804)
PHONE.................................818 994-9401
John Felix, *President*
EMP: 23
SQ FT: 6,000
SALES (est): 2.5MM **Privately Held**
WEB: www.felixtool.com
SIC: 3544 3469 Special dies, tools, jigs &
fixtures; metal stampings

(P-14053)
FLOTRON INC
2630 Progress St, Vista (92081-8412)
PHONE.................................760 727-2700
Danny K Horrell, *President*
EMP: 24
SQ FT: 25,000
SALES: 3.5MM **Privately Held**
WEB: www.flotron.com
SIC: 3544 Special dies & tools

(P-14054)
FUSION PRODUCT MFG INC
440 Industrial Rd, Tecate (91980)
PHONE.................................619 819-5521
Adalberto L Ramirez, *President*

Simon Ramirez, *Treasurer*
Jose Ramirez, *Admin Sec*
Arturo Mendez, *Project Mgr*
▼ EMP: 72
SQ FT: 36,000
SALES (est): 2.9MM **Privately Held**
SIC: 3544 Forms (molds), for foundry &
plastics working machinery

(P-14055)
FUTURE MOLDS INC
10349 Regis Ct, Rancho Cucamonga
(91730-3055)
PHONE.................................909 989-7398
Tony R Parsons, *President*
Bruce Lutz, *Vice Pres*
EMP: 10
SQ FT: 11,000
SALES (est): 1.2MM **Privately Held**
SIC: 3544 Industrial molds

(P-14056)
G B MOLD & TOOL DESIGN
640 Giguere Ct, San Jose (95133-1737)
PHONE.................................408 254-3871
George Bunea, *Owner*
EMP: 10
SQ FT: 1,400
SALES (est): 782.8K **Privately Held**
SIC: 3544 Industrial molds

(P-14057)
G E SHELL CORE CO
8346 Salt Lake Ave, Cudahy (90201-5817)
P.O. Box 1099, Bell Gardens (90201-7099)
PHONE.................................323 773-4242
Raul Rivera, *General Mgr*
EMP: 30
SALES (est): 2.7MM
SALES (corp-wide): 6.9B **Privately Held**
SIC: 3544 Industrial molds
HQ: Consolidated Precision Products Corp.
1621 Euclid Ave Ste 1850
Cleveland OH 44115
216 453-4800

(P-14058)
GEMINI MFG & ENGRG INC
1020 E Vermont Ave, Anaheim
(92805-5617)
PHONE.................................714 999-0010
Sandra Lowry, *President*
David Lowry, *Treasurer*
Mike Clavin, *Prdtn Mgr*
EMP: 20
SQ FT: 40,000
SALES (est): 8.4MM **Privately Held**
WEB: www.geminimfg.com
SIC: 3544 3599 Subpresses, metalwork-
ing; machine shop, jobbing & repair

(P-14059)
GMS MOLDS (PA)
729 E 223rd St, Carson (90745-4111)
PHONE.................................310 684-1168
Bradley Gardner, *Owner*
EMP: 10
SALES (est): 2.4MM **Privately Held**
SIC: 3544 Industrial molds

(P-14060)
GRUBER SYSTEMS INC
29083 The Old Rd, Valencia (91355-1083)
PHONE.................................661 257-0464
John Hoskinson, *Ch of Bd*
Katherine Pavard, *President*
Jim Thiessen, *President*
Diana Arima, *Treasurer*
Steve Miller, *Vice Pres*
◆ EMP: 45
SQ FT: 100,000
SALES (est): 13.5MM **Privately Held**
WEB: www.gruber-systems.com
SIC: 3544 3842 3531 3537 Industrial
molds; whirlpool baths, hydrotherapy
equipment; construction machinery; in-
dustrial trucks & tractors

(P-14061)
**HAYES MANUFACTURING SVCS
LLC**
1178 Sonora Ct, Sunnyvale (94086-5308)
PHONE.................................408 730-5035
Matthew Hayes, *President*
Dolores Valdez, *Personnel*
Maria Villanueva, *Purch Agent*

Doloris V Longoria, *Manager*
EMP: 27
SQ FT: 22,000
SALES (est): 5.1MM
SALES (corp-wide): 5.4MM **Privately
Held**
WEB: www.hayesms.com
SIC: 3544 3089 Industrial molds; plastic
processing
PA: Core Industrial Partners, Llc
200 N La Salle St # 2360
Chicago IL 60601
312 566-4880

(P-14062)
**HUGHES BROS AIRCRAFTERS
INC**
11010 Garfield Pl, South Gate
(90280-7512)
PHONE.................................323 773-4541
Susan Hughes, *President*
James P Hughes, *Vice Pres*
Michael Hall, *General Mgr*
Gerry Imes, *QC Mgr*
Francisco Morales, *Manager*
EMP: 43
SQ FT: 15,000
SALES (est): 8.1MM **Privately Held**
WEB: www.hbai.com
SIC: 3544 3449 3444 Die sets for metal
stamping (presses); plastering acces-
sories, metal; sheet metalwork

(P-14063)
**IDEA TOOLING & ENGINEERING
INC**
13915 S Main St, Los Angeles
(90061-2151)
PHONE.................................310 608-7488
Peter Janner, *President*
Inga Janner, *Treasurer*
Monica Janner, *Vice Pres*
Moe Sumbulan, *Vice Pres*
▲ EMP: 56 EST: 1973
SALES (est): 8.8MM **Privately Held**
WEB: www.ite-plastics.com
SIC: 3544 3061 Special dies & tools;
forms (molds), for foundry & plastics
working machinery; mechanical rubber
goods

(P-14064)
INDUSTRIAL TOOL AND DIE INC
1330 E Saint Gertrude Pl, Santa Ana
(92705-5222)
PHONE.................................714 549-1686
Joseph W Adlesh, *President*
EMP: 10 EST: 1967
SQ FT: 3,500
SALES: 1.3MM **Privately Held**
SIC: 3544 Special dies & tools

(P-14065)
JW MOLDING INC
2523 Calcite Cir, Newbury Park
(91320-1204)
PHONE.................................805 499-2682
Ralf Wolters, *President*
Bridgette Wolters, *Admin Sec*
EMP: 15
SQ FT: 16,000
SALES (est): 3.7MM **Privately Held**
WEB: www.jwmolding.com
SIC: 3544 3089 Forms (molds), for
foundry & plastics working machinery; in-
jection molding of plastics

(P-14066)
KAMASHIAN ENGINEERING INC
9128 Rose St, Bellflower (90706-6420)
PHONE.................................562 920-9692
Jerry A Kamashian, *President*
David Cox, *Shareholder*
Harut Avetisyan, *Engineer*
EMP: 10
SQ FT: 4,000
SALES (est): 1.6MM **Privately Held**
WEB: www.kamashian.com
SIC: 3544 Special dies & tools

(P-14067)
**KECK & SCHMIDT TOOL & DIE
INC**
2610 Troy Ave, El Monte (91733-1492)
PHONE.................................626 579-3890

Dieter J Keck, *President*
Tisgisela Keck, *Treasurer*
Sandy Worssold, *Admin Sec*
EMP: 12
SQ FT: 10,500
SALES: 3MM **Privately Held**
WEB: www.keckandschmidt.com
SIC: 3544 3469 Special dies & tools;
metal stampings

(P-14068)
**KINGSON MOLD & MACHINE
INC**
1350 Titan Way, Brea (92821-3707)
PHONE.................................714 871-0221
Gregory S Rex, *CEO*
EMP: 36
SQ FT: 8,500
SALES: 3.7MM **Privately Held**
WEB: www.kingsonmold.com
SIC: 3544 5031 Industrial molds; molding,
all materials

(P-14069)
KIPE MOLDS INC
340 E Crowther Ave, Placentia
(92870-6419)
PHONE.................................714 572-9576
George B Kipe Jr, *President*
Rebbeca L Kipe, *Treasurer*
Brint Kipe, *General Mgr*
George B Kipe Sr, *Admin Sec*
Dana King, *Manager*
EMP: 15 EST: 1970
SQ FT: 15,000
SALES: 3.3MM **Privately Held**
WEB: www.kipemolds.com
SIC: 3544 Industrial molds

(P-14070)
LEE MACHINE PRODUCTS
Also Called: Pneumatic Tube Carrier
2030 Central Ave, Duarte (91010-2913)
PHONE.................................626 301-4105
Thomas Young, *President*
Steve Young, *General Mgr*
EMP: 14 EST: 1965
SQ FT: 7,100
SALES: 8.2MM **Privately Held**
WEB: www.leemachine.com
SIC: 3544 3535 3949 7699 Special dies,
tools, jigs & fixtures; pneumatic tube con-
veyor systems; tennis equipment & sup-
plies; industrial machinery & equipment
repair

(P-14071)
LEO MOLDS
125 W Victoria St, Gardena (90248-3522)
PHONE.................................562 714-4807
Adhemar Paolini, *Owner*
EMP: 12
SQ FT: 6,000
SALES (est): 906.5K **Privately Held**
SIC: 3544 Industrial molds

(P-14072)
M I T INC
Also Called: Morin Industrial Technology
15202 Pipeline Ln, Huntington Beach
(92649-1136)
PHONE.................................714 899-6066
Rene Morin, *President*
EMP: 15
SQ FT: 12,000
SALES (est): 2.7MM **Privately Held**
WEB: www.m-i-s.com
SIC: 3544 Forms (molds), for foundry &
plastics working machinery

(P-14073)
MACDONALD CARBIDE CO
4510 Littlejohn St, Baldwin Park
(91706-2298)
PHONE.................................626 960-4034
Amy Mac Donald, *President*
◆ EMP: 20
SQ FT: 11,140
SALES (est): 3.7MM **Privately Held**
WEB: www.macdonaldcarbide.com
SIC: 3544 3545 Special dies & tools; ma-
chine tool accessories

▲ = Import ▼=Export
◆ =Import/Export

(P-14074)
MAGOR MOLD LLC
420 S Lone Hill Ave, San Dimas
(91773-4600)
PHONE..................909 592-5729
Wolfgang Buhler, *President*
Martin Schottli, *Director*
Dan Agnew, *Manager*
Steve Iiams, *Manager*
▲ **EMP:** 68 **EST:** 1967
SQ FT: 15,000
SALES (est): 12.3MM
SALES (corp-wide): 41.7MM **Privately Held**
WEB: www.magormold.com
SIC: 3544 Industrial molds
PA: Cgs Management Ag
Huobstrasse 14
PfAffikon SZ 8808
554 161-640

(P-14075)
MASTER WASHER STAMPING SVC CO
80899 Camino San Lucas, Indio
(92203-7468)
PHONE..................323 722-0969
William Scallon, *President*
Betty Reina, *Vice Pres*
EMP: 12
SALES: 3MM **Privately Held**
SIC: 3544 3469 Die sets for metal stamping (presses); metal stampings

(P-14076)
MECTEC MOLDS INC
1525 Howard Access Rd D, Upland
(91786-2574)
PHONE..................909 981-3636
T J Wilder, *CEO*
Kristine Wilder, *Admin Sec*
EMP: 10
SQ FT: 4,800
SALES (est): 907.5K **Privately Held**
WEB: www.mectec-molds.com
SIC: 3544 Industrial molds

(P-14077)
METRIC DESIGN & MANUFACTURING
217 E Hacienda Ave, Campbell
(95008-6616)
PHONE..................408 378-4544
Gunther Unruh, *President*
Nguyet Unruh, *Admin Sec*
EMP: 11
SQ FT: 10,000
SALES (est): 1.4MM **Privately Held**
SIC: 3544 7389 3599 Special dies & tools; grinding, precision: commercial or industrial; machine shop, jobbing & repair

(P-14078)
MJOLNIR INDUSTRIES LLC
Also Called: D & M Precision
5701 Perkins Rd, Oxnard (93033-9014)
PHONE..................805 488-3550
Jeffrey Ballard, *Mng Member*
EMP: 12
SQ FT: 14,000
SALES: 1.3MM **Privately Held**
SIC: 3544 3599 Special dies, tools, jigs & fixtures; machine shop, jobbing & repair

(P-14079)
MOLD MASTERS INC
Also Called: Construction Masters
715 Ruberta Ave, Glendale (91201-2336)
PHONE..................323 999-2599
Austin Reid, *President*
EMP: 10
SALES (est): 950K **Privately Held**
SIC: 3544 Industrial molds

(P-14080)
MOLD USA
322 Culver Blve Apt 6, Playa Del Rey
(90293)
PHONE..................310 823-6653
Jaclyn Resnick, *Principal*
EMP: 10
SALES (est): 653.7K **Privately Held**
SIC: 3544 Industrial molds

(P-14081)
MOREAU WETZEL ENGINEERING CO
24424 Main St Ste 604, Carson
(90745-6394)
PHONE..................310 830-5479
Fax: 310 830-5487
EMP: 10 **EST:** 1952
SQ FT: 9,000
SALES: 750K **Privately Held**
SIC: 3544 3599

(P-14082)
MR MOLD & ENGINEERING CORP
2700 E Imperial Hwy Ste C, Brea
(92821-6711)
PHONE..................714 996-5511
Richard Finnie II, *President*
Marilyn Finnie, *Vice Pres*
Ashley Cupp, *Office Mgr*
Ricardo Rodriguez, *Purchasing*
Brian Geisel, *Opers Mgr*
EMP: 31
SQ FT: 14,000
SALES: 4.2MM **Privately Held**
WEB: www.mrmold.com
SIC: 3544 Special dies & tools; jigs & fixtures

(P-14083)
N S CERAMIC MOLDING CO
1336 E Francis St Unit 1, Ontario
(91761-5723)
PHONE..................909 947-3231
James Cannone, *President*
Joanne Ashworth, *Vice Pres*
Jean Mary Zimman, *Vice Pres*
EMP: 45
SQ FT: 8,500
SALES (est): 4.4MM **Privately Held**
SIC: 3544 Industrial molds

(P-14084)
NEVILLE INDUSTRIES INC
Also Called: B & H Tool Company
285 Pawnee St Ste D, San Marcos
(92078-2458)
PHONE..................760 471-8949
Peter Neville, *President*
EMP: 10
SQ FT: 5,000
SALES (est): 900K **Privately Held**
WEB: www.bhtool.com
SIC: 3544 Dies, plastics forming

(P-14085)
NIRON INC
20541 Earlgate St, Walnut (91789-2909)
PHONE..................909 598-1526
Glen Nieberle, *President*
Cheryl Nieberle, *Admin Sec*
EMP: 40
SQ FT: 17,000
SALES (est): 5MM **Privately Held**
WEB: www.niron.com
SIC: 3544 3089 Industrial molds; injection molding of plastics

(P-14086)
OCEANSIDE PLASTIC ENTERPRISES
3038 Industry St Ste 108, Oceanside
(92054-4871)
PHONE..................760 433-0779
Axel Mnich Jr, *President*
EMP: 10
SALES (est): 1.1MM **Privately Held**
SIC: 3544 Industrial molds

(P-14087)
OLIPHANT TOOL COMPANY
15652 Chemical Ln, Huntington Beach
(92649-1507)
PHONE..................714 903-6336
William Oliphant, *Owner*
EMP: 35
SQ FT: 12,000
SALES (est): 3MM **Privately Held**
SIC: 3544 7699 Special dies & tools; industrial tool grinding

(P-14088)
PACE PUNCHES INC
297 Goddard, Irvine (92618-4604)
PHONE..................949 428-2750
Edward W Pepper, *President*
▲ **EMP:** 55
SQ FT: 30,000
SALES (est): 9.7MM **Privately Held**
WEB: www.pacepunches.com
SIC: 3544 Punches, forming & stamping

(P-14089)
PACIFIC DIE CAST INC
15980 Bloomfield Ave, Cerritos
(90703-2155)
PHONE..................562 407-1390
J R Edens, *President*
▲ **EMP:** 12
SALES (est): 1.7MM **Privately Held**
SIC: 3544 Special dies & tools

(P-14090)
PACIFIC DIE SERVICES INC
7626 Baldwin Pl, Whittier (90602-1001)
PHONE..................562 907-4463
Eric Syndinos, *President*
EMP: 12
SQ FT: 5,000
SALES (est): 1.5MM **Privately Held**
SIC: 3544 Dies, steel rule

(P-14091)
PACIFIC SOUTHWEST MOLDS
12307 Woodruff Ave, Downey
(90241-5609)
PHONE..................562 803-9811
Manuel Cabral, *Owner*
Emanuel Cabral, *Partner*
Terry Duerr, *Partner*
EMP: 12
SQ FT: 6,000
SALES (est): 400K **Privately Held**
WEB: www.pacificsouthwestmolds.com
SIC: 3544 Industrial molds

(P-14092)
PDC LLC
Also Called: Precision Diecut
4675 Vinita Ct, Chino (91710-5731)
PHONE..................626 334-5000
Steve Gasparelli, *Mng Member*
Jane Gray, *Finance Mgr*
Patti L W McGlasson,
EMP: 20
SQ FT: 11,000
SALES (est): 5MM **Privately Held**
SIC: 3544 Special dies, tools, jigs & fixtures

(P-14093)
PLASTIKON INDUSTRIES INC (PA)
688 Sandoval Way, Hayward (94544-7129)
PHONE..................510 400-1010
Fred Soofer, *President*
Fereydoon Soofer, *CEO*
Paul Gutwald, *CFO*
Michele Shaw, *Officer*
Peter F Petri, *Vice Pres*
▲ **EMP:** 252 **EST:** 2010
SQ FT: 90,000
SALES (est): 118.9MM **Privately Held**
WEB: www.plastikon.com
SIC: 3544 3089 Special dies, tools, jigs & fixtures; injection molded finished plastic products

(P-14094)
POPE PLASTICS INC
9134 Independence Ave, Chatsworth
(91311-5902)
PHONE..................818 701-1850
EMP: 40
SQ FT: 30,000
SALES (est): 6.5MM **Privately Held**
SIC: 3544

(P-14095)
PRECISION FORGING DIES INC
10710 Sessler St, South Gate
(90280-7221)
PHONE..................562 861-1878
Dan Kloss, *President*
Edmond Kloss, *General Mgr*
EMP: 27

SALES (est): 5.4MM **Privately Held**
SIC: 3544 Special dies & tools

(P-14096)
PRESTIGE MOLD INCORPORATED
11040 Tacoma Dr, Rancho Cucamonga
(91730-4857)
PHONE..................909 980-6600
Donna C Pursell, *CEO*
Donna Koebel, *CFO*
Lance Spangler, *Vice Pres*
Shawn Pecore, *CIO*
John Anderson, *Engineer*
▲ **EMP:** 60
SQ FT: 28,500
SALES (est): 12.3MM
SALES (corp-wide): 19.1MM **Privately Held**
SIC: 3544 Industrial molds
PA: Pres-Tek Plastics, Inc.
11060 Tacoma Dr
Rancho Cucamonga CA 91730
909 360-1600

(P-14097)
PRO MOLD INC
415 Grumman Dr, Riverside (92508-9453)
PHONE..................951 776-0555
Ronald L Fields, *President*
Ed Bickel, *Vice Pres*
Randy Herr, *Vice Pres*
EMP: 11
SQ FT: 10,000
SALES (est): 1.3MM **Privately Held**
SIC: 3544 3089 Forms (molds), for foundry & plastics working machinery; injection molding of plastics

(P-14098)
PRODUCT SLINGSHOT INC
Also Called: Forecast 3d
2221 Rutherford Rd, Carlsbad
(92008-8815)
PHONE..................760 929-9380
Corey Douglas Weber, *President*
Brittany Dunn, *Exec VP*
Donovan Weber, *Vice Pres*
Ken Burns, *Project Mgr*
Matt Nebo, *Project Mgr*
EMP: 96
SQ FT: 28,000
SALES (est): 38.2MM **Privately Held**
WEB: www.forecast3d.com
SIC: 3544 3082 3089 3555 Industrial molds; unsupported plastics profile shapes; casting of plastic; coloring & finishing of plastic products; injection molded finished plastic products; printing trades machinery

(P-14099)
PUNCH PRESS PRODUCTS INC
Also Called: Auto Trend Products
2035 E 51st St, Vernon (90058-2818)
PHONE..................323 581-7151
Delmo Molinari, *Chairman*
CJ Matiszik, *President*
▲ **EMP:** 67
SQ FT: 150,000
SALES (est): 15.3MM **Privately Held**
WEB: www.punch-press.com
SIC: 3544 3469 3471 Special dies & tools; metal stampings; plating & polishing

(P-14100)
PYRAMID MOLD & TOOL
10155 Sharon Cir, Rancho Cucamonga
(91730-5300)
PHONE..................909 476-2555
Stephen M Hoare, *President*
Brandan Heyes, *Admin Sec*
EMP: 42
SQ FT: 30,300
SALES: 6MM **Privately Held**
WEB: www.pyramidmold.com
SIC: 3544 Industrial molds

(P-14101)
ROTO-DIE COMPANY INC
Also Called: Rotometrics
712 N Valley St Ste B, Anaheim
(92801-3828)
PHONE..................714 991-8701
Dick Townsend, *Manager*
EMP: 13

PRODUCTS & SVCS

SALES (corp-wide): 190.8MM **Privately
Held**
WEB: www.rotometrics.com
SIC: 3544 Special dies & tools
PA: Roto-Die Company, Inc.
800 Howerton Ln
Eureka MO 63025
636 587-3600

(P-14102)
S AND S CARBIDE TOOL INC
2830 Via Orange Way Ste D, Spring Valley
(91978-1743)
PHONE...................................619 670-5214
Dennis Strong, *President*
Gary Stewart, *Vice Pres*
EMP: 25
SQ FT: 6,000
SALES (est): 4.5MM **Privately Held**
SIC: 3544 Special dies, tools, jigs & fix-
tures

(P-14103)
SANTA FE ENTERPRISES INC
Also Called: SFE
11654 Pike St, Santa Fe Springs
(90670-2938)
PHONE...................................562 692-7596
David Warner, *President*
Bob Becker, *Vice Pres*
EMP: 27
SQ FT: 20,000
SALES (est): 5.8MM **Privately Held**
SIC: 3544 Special dies & tools

(P-14104)
SCHREY & SONS MOLD CO INC
24735 Avenue Rockefeller, Valencia
(91355-3466)
PHONE...................................661 294-2260
Walter Schrey, *President*
Gertrude Schrey, *Corp Secy*
Thomas Schrey, *Vice Pres*
William Schrey, *Vice Pres*
James Otec, *Design Engr*
EMP: 35
SQ FT: 53,000
SALES (est): 6.5MM **Privately Held**
WEB: www.schrey.com
SIC: 3544 Industrial molds; special dies &
tools

(P-14105)
SOUTH COAST MOLD INC
1852 Mcgaw Ave, Irvine (92614-5734)
PHONE...................................949 253-2000
Paul Novak, *Principal*
Diane Novak, *Principal*
EMP: 10
SALES (est): 839.6K **Privately Held**
WEB: www.southcoastmold.com
SIC: 3544 Industrial molds

(P-14106)
STAINLESS INDUSTRIAL
COMPANIES
11111 Santa Monica Blvd # 1120, Los Ange-
les (90025-3333)
PHONE...................................310 575-9400
Anthony Pritzker, *President*
▲ **EMP:** 100 **EST:** 1998
SALES: 32.3MM
SALES (corp-wide): 225.3B **Publicly
Held**
SIC: 3544 Special dies & tools
HQ: The Marmon Group Llc
181 W Madison St Ste 2600
Chicago IL 60602

(P-14107)
SUPERIOR JIG INC
1540 N Orangethorpe Way, Anaheim
(92801-1289)
PHONE...................................714 525-4777
John Morrissey, *President*
Tracy Reed, *Corp Secy*
Reed Tracy, *Admin Sec*
EMP: 22
SQ FT: 14,000
SALES: 5.1MM **Privately Held**
WEB: www.sji.net
SIC: 3544 3599 Special dies & tools; jigs
& fixtures; machine shop, jobbing & repair

(P-14108)
T & S DIE CUTTING
13301 Alondra Blvd Ste A, Santa Fe
Springs (90670-5563)
PHONE...................................562 802-1731
James Good, *Owner*
Gilda Sanchez, *General Mgr*
EMP: 12
SQ FT: 16,000
SALES: 1.7MM **Privately Held**
SIC: 3544 Dies, steel rule

(P-14109)
T I B INC
Also Called: B.T.i Tool Engineering
9525 Pathway St, Santee (92071-4170)
PHONE...................................619 562-3071
James W Jim Barnhill, *President*
Chris Barnhill, *Vice Pres*
James T Todd Barnhill, *Vice Pres*
EMP: 18
SQ FT: 1,000
SALES (est): 3.4MM **Privately Held**
WEB: www.bti-tool.com
SIC: 3544 Jigs & fixtures; die sets for metal
stamping (presses)

(P-14110)
TARPIN CORPORATION
Also Called: Western Forge Die
5361 Business Dr, Huntington Beach
(92649-1223)
PHONE...................................714 891-6944
Harold Jermakian, *President*
EMP: 35
SALES (est): 5.2MM **Privately Held**
WEB: www.westernforgedie.com
SIC: 3544 Dies, steel rule; special dies &
tools

(P-14111)
TASCO MOLDS INC
6260 Prescott Ct, Chino (91710-7111)
PHONE...................................909 613-1926
Paul S Faris, *President*
EMP: 13
SALES: 1MM **Privately Held**
SIC: 3544 Forms (molds), for foundry &
plastics working machinery

(P-14112)
THUNDERBIRD INDUSTRIES INC
695 W Terrace Dr, San Dimas
(91773-2917)
PHONE...................................909 394-1633
Donald Serio, *President*
EMP: 25
SQ FT: 20,000
SALES (est): 3.3MM **Privately Held**
SIC: 3544 3089 Industrial molds; injection
molding of plastics

(P-14113)
TMK MANUFACTURING
2110 Oakland Rd, San Jose (95131-1565)
PHONE...................................408 732-3200
EMP: 60
SQ FT: 15,700
SALES (est): 3.3MM **Privately Held**
SIC: 3544 3599 3469

(P-14114)
TOOLS & PRODUCTION INC
466 W Arrow Hwy Ste C, San Dimas
(91773-2940)
PHONE...................................626 286-0213
Michael Lamberti, *President*
▲ **EMP:** 20 **EST:** 1955
SQ FT: 10,000
SALES (est): 3.5MM **Privately Held**
WEB: www.toolsandproduction.com
SIC: 3544 Special dies & tools; punches,
forming & stamping

(P-14115)
TOTALLY RADICAL ASSOCIATES
INC
Also Called: Tra Medical
1025 Ortega Way Ste A, Placentia
(92870-7174)
PHONE...................................714 630-2740
James Pontillo, *President*
EMP: 15
SQ FT: 8,300

SALES (est): 1.6MM **Privately Held**
WEB: www.tra-medical.com
SIC: 3544 Industrial molds

(P-14116)
TRIO TOOL & DIE CO (PA)
3340 W El Segundo Blvd, Hawthorne
(90250-4892)
PHONE...................................310 644-4431
John Arroues, *President*
Armstrong Dennis, *Manager*
EMP: 18 **EST:** 1954
SQ FT: 9,200
SALES (est): 3.8MM **Privately Held**
WEB: www.triotoolanddie.com
SIC: 3544 Dies & die holders for metal cut-
ting, forming, die casting; special dies &
tools

(P-14117)
UNITED CALIFORNIA
CORPORATION
12200 Woodruff Ave, Downey
(90241-5608)
P.O. Box 4250 (90241-1250)
PHONE...................................562 803-1521
Dale L Bethke, *President*
Billie Huckins, *Admin Sec*
Erma Parrish, *Accounting Mgr*
EMP: 200
SQ FT: 85,000
SALES (est): 22.9MM **Privately Held**
SIC: 3544 Special dies & tools

(P-14118)
UPM INC
Also Called: Universal Plastic Mold
13245 Los Angeles St, Baldwin Park
(91706-2295)
PHONE...................................626 962-4001
Jason Dowling, *CEO*
Steve Dowling, *President*
Don Ashleigh, *Vice Pres*
Jeanette Garcia, *Human Res Dir*
Cinthya Guevara, *Purch Mgr*
◆ **EMP:** 290
SQ FT: 100,000
SALES (est): 79.7MM **Privately Held**
SIC: 3544 3089 Forms (molds), for
foundry & plastics working machinery; in-
jection molding of plastics

(P-14119)
US DIES INC (PA)
1992 Rockefeller Dr # 300, Ceres
(95307-7274)
PHONE...................................209 664-1402
Thomas Mason, *President*
Diana L Mason, *Corp Secy*
Ken Thomas, *Vice Pres*
EMP: 23 **EST:** 1971
SQ FT: 21,000
SALES (est): 4.2MM **Privately Held**
WEB: www.pwcdies.com
SIC: 3544 Dies, steel rule

(P-14120)
US STEEL RULE DIES INC
Also Called: M D D
40 E Verdugo Ave, Burbank (91502-1931)
PHONE...................................562 921-0690
David Reynolds, *President*
EMP: 35
SALES (est): 5MM **Privately Held**
SIC: 3544 Special dies & tools

(P-14121)
VALCO PLANER WORKS INC
Also Called: Valco Precision Works
6131 Maywood Ave, Huntington Park
(90255-3213)
PHONE...................................323 582-6355
Leonel F Valerio, *President*
Carlos Valerio, *Corp Secy*
Leonel G Valerio Jr, *Vice Pres*
Leslie Valerio, *Purchasing*
▼ **EMP:** 25 **EST:** 1953
SQ FT: 10,000
SALES (est): 4.9MM **Privately Held**
WEB: www.valcoplaner.com
SIC: 3544 3545 Special dies, tools, jigs &
fixtures; machine tool accessories

(P-14122)
VALLEY MFG & ENGRG INC
9105 De Garmo Ave, Sun Valley
(91352-2608)
PHONE...................................818 504-6085
Keith Gross, *President*
May Cahme, *Vice Pres*
EMP: 10 **EST:** 1974
SQ FT: 35,000
SALES (est): 1.5MM **Privately Held**
SIC: 3544 3089 Industrial molds; in-
jection molded finished plastic products;
laminated plastics plate & sheet

(P-14123)
VELCO TOOL & DIE INC
20431 Barents Sea Cir, Lake Forest
(92630-8807)
PHONE...................................949 855-6638
Jose M Velez, *President*
EMP: 10
SQ FT: 5,350
SALES (est): 2.2MM **Privately Held**
WEB: www.velco.net
SIC: 3544 Dies & die holders for metal cut-
ting, forming, die casting

(P-14124)
WAGNER DIE SUPPLY (PA)
2041 Elm Ct, Ontario (91761-7619)
PHONE...................................909 947-3044
Ellsworth Knutson, *President*
John Knutson, *Treasurer*
Mike Knutson, *Vice Pres*
Tom Knutson, *Admin Sec*
▲ **EMP:** 36
SALES (est): 8MM **Privately Held**
SIC: 3544 Dies, steel rule; special dies &
tools

(P-14125)
WEST RAPCO ENVIRONMENTAL
SVCS
Also Called: Rapco-West Asbestos
23852 Pacific Coast Hwy # 941, Malibu
(90265-4876)
PHONE...................................310 450-3335
Steven Amici, *President*
EMP: 30
SQ FT: 2,500
SALES (est): 3.1MM **Privately Held**
SIC: 3544 Industrial molds

(P-14126)
WRIGHT ENGINEERED
PLASTICS INC
3681 N Laughlin Rd, Santa Rosa
(95403-1027)
PHONE...................................707 575-1218
Barbara F Roberts, *CEO*
Larry McKinney, *CIO*
Karrie Bertsch, *Engineer*
Matt Calahan, *QC Mgr*
Bill Walker, *Maintence Staff*
◆ **EMP:** 61
SQ FT: 25,000
SALES: 13.2MM
SALES (corp-wide): 5.5MM **Privately
Held**
WEB: www.wepmolding.com
SIC: 3544 3089 Special dies, tools, jigs &
fixtures; plastic hardware & building prod-
ucts
PA: Molding Solutions Inc
3225 Regional Pkwy
Santa Rosa CA 95403
707 575-1218

(P-14127)
YORK ENGINEERING
7575 Jurupa Ave, Riverside (92504-1012)
PHONE...................................323 256-0439
Phillip Shin, *Owner*
EMP: 11
SALES (est): 1.2MM **Privately Held**
WEB: www.yorkengineering.com
SIC: 3544 Special dies, tools, jigs & fix-
tures

▲ = Import ▼=Export
◆ =Import/Export

3545 Machine Tool Access

(P-14128)
ADTECH TOOL ENGRG CORPORATIONS
13620 Cimarron Ave, Gardena (90249-2459)
PHONE..................310 515-1717
James Lee, *President*
EMP: 13
SQ FT: 11,024
SALES (est): 1.8MM **Privately Held**
SIC: 3545 Collets (machine tool accessories)

(P-14129)
AMERICAN QUALITY TOOLS INC
12650 Magnolia Ave Ste B, Riverside (92503-4690)
PHONE..................951 280-4700
Mukesh Aghi, *President*
Rakesh Aghi, *Vice Pres*
Bertha Najera, *Human Res Mgr*
Patrick Davis, *Sales Staff*
▲ **EMP:** 45
SQ FT: 22,000
SALES (est): 8.6MM **Privately Held**
WEB: www.aqtools.com
SIC: 3545 Cutting tools for machine tools

(P-14130)
AMO CORPORATION
9580 Oak Avenue Pkwy # 9, Folsom (95630-1888)
PHONE..................916 791-2001
Alton Werner, *President*
EMP: 10
SALES (est): 998.7K
SALES (corp-wide): 72K **Privately Held**
SIC: 3545 Machine tool accessories
HQ: Amo Automatisierung MeBtechnik
Optik Gmbh
Nofing 4
St. Peter Am Hart 4963
772 265-8560

(P-14131)
AMP III LLC
Also Called: Advanced Machine Programming
465 Woodview Ave, Morgan Hill (95037-2800)
PHONE..................408 779-2927
Kent Rounds,
EMP: 65
SALES (est): 5.2MM **Privately Held**
SIC: 3545 Precision tools, machinists'

(P-14132)
AMPERTECH INC
636 S State College Blvd, Fullerton (92831-5138)
PHONE..................714 523-4068
Jenny Wang, *President*
Kirby Ku, *Vice Pres*
▲ **EMP:** 50 **EST:** 2000
SQ FT: 4,000
SALES: 4MM **Privately Held**
WEB: www.ampertech.com
SIC: 3545 3679 Machine tool accessories; electronic circuits

(P-14133)
APX TECHNOLOGY CORPORATION
Also Called: Apx Manufacturing
14831 Myford Rd, Tustin (92780-7279)
PHONE..................714 838-8501
Luong Nguyen, *Principal*
Dean Jensen, *Opers Staff*
EMP: 10
SALES (est): 52.8K **Privately Held**
SIC: 3545 Threading tools (machine tool accessories)

(P-14134)
ASI TOOLING LLC
1780 La Costa Meadows Dr # 103, San Marcos (92078-9101)
PHONE..................760 744-2520
Melissa Theriault,
Richard Theriault, *Mng Member*
EMP: 12 **EST:** 2008

SALES (est): 1.9MM **Privately Held**
SIC: 3545 Cutting tools for machine tools

(P-14135)
ATS WORKHOLDING INC
Also Called: Ats Systems
30222 Esperanza, Rcho STA Marg (92688-2121)
PHONE..................800 321-1833
Charles A Goad, *CEO*
Wu Robert, *CFO*
Ken Erkenbrack, *Vice Pres*
Carlos Hernandez, *Principal*
Jeff Toegel, *Regional Mgr*
▲ **EMP:** 67
SQ FT: 22,840
SALES (est): 30MM **Privately Held**
WEB: www.atsworkholding.com
SIC: 3545 Milling machine attachments (machine tool accessories)

(P-14136)
BARKER-CANOGA INC
Also Called: J B Manufacturing Co
16528 Koala Rd Ste A, Adelanto (92301-3966)
PHONE..................760 246-4777
John Barker, *CEO*
Yvonne Barker, *President*
Mike Barker, *Treasurer*
EMP: 10 **EST:** 1965
SQ FT: 8,000
SALES (est): 880K **Privately Held**
SIC: 3545 Honing heads

(P-14137)
BARRANCA HOLDINGS LTD
Also Called: Barranca Diamond Products
22815 Frampton Ave, Torrance (90501-5034)
PHONE..................310 523-5867
Brian Delahaut, *President*
▲ **EMP:** 12 **EST:** 1998
SALES (est): 1.4MM
SALES (corp-wide): 47.1MM **Privately Held**
WEB: www.barrancadiamond.com
SIC: 3545 Diamond cutting tools for turning, boring, burnishing, etc.
PA: Diamond Mk Products Inc
1315 Storm Pkwy
Torrance CA 90501
310 539-5221

(P-14138)
BEAM DYNAMICS INC
5100 Patrick Henry Dr, Santa Clara (95054-1112)
PHONE..................408 764-4805
Mathew Bye, *President*
Jon Maroney, *Vice Pres*
Blaine Boloich, *Director*
EMP: 12
SQ FT: 4,200
SALES (est): 1.1MM
SALES (corp-wide): 1.7B **Publicly Held**
WEB: www.beamdynamics.com
SIC: 3545 Machine tool accessories
PA: Coherent, Inc.
5100 Patrick Henry Dr
Santa Clara CA 95054
408 764-4000

(P-14139)
BENEN MANUFACTURING LLC
2266 Trade Zone Blvd, San Jose (95131-1801)
PHONE..................408 573-7252
Giang Thi Tran, *Mng Member*
EMP: 10 **EST:** 2011
SALES (est): 1.8MM **Privately Held**
SIC: 3545 Measuring tools & machines, machinists' metalworking type

(P-14140)
BLAHA OLDRIH
Also Called: Quality Machining
114 10th St, Ramona (92065-2103)
PHONE..................760 789-9791
Oldrih Blaha, *Partner*
Melita Blaha, *Partner*
EMP: 10
SQ FT: 3,100
SALES (est): 1.4MM **Privately Held**
SIC: 3545 3599 Machine tool accessories; machine shop, jobbing & repair

(P-14141)
BROACH MASTERS INC
1605 Industrial Dr, Auburn (95603-9018)
PHONE..................530 885-1939
Mark Vian, *President*
Elizabeth Vian, *Vice Pres*
EMP: 27
SALES (est): 5MM **Privately Held**
SIC: 3545 3599 Precision tools, machinists'; machine shop, jobbing & repair

(P-14142)
C & GTOOL INC
3247 Back Cir, Sacramento (95821-1710)
PHONE..................916 614-9114
Daniel Crowninshield, *President*
EMP: 11
SALES (est): 16.2MM **Privately Held**
SIC: 3545 Precision tools, machinists'

(P-14143)
CALIFORNIA REAMER COMPANY INC
12747 Los Nietos Rd, Santa Fe Springs (90670-3007)
PHONE..................562 946-6377
David J Neptune, *President*
EMP: 11
SQ FT: 5,500
SALES (est): 1.3MM **Privately Held**
SIC: 3545 Reamers, machine tool

(P-14144)
CAMPBELL ENGINEERING INC
20412 Barents Sea Cir, Lake Forest (92630-8807)
PHONE..................949 859-3306
James Campbell, *President*
Carolyn Campbell, *Principal*
EMP: 24 **EST:** 1994
SQ FT: 3,800
SALES: 2MM **Privately Held**
SIC: 3545 3541 Precision measuring tools; lathes, metal cutting & polishing

(P-14145)
CARBRO CORPORATION
15724 Condon Ave, Lawndale (90260-2531)
P.O. Box 278 (90260-0278)
PHONE..................310 643-8400
Ed Plano, *President*
Jay Rosenbluth, *Treasurer*
Anders Plano, *General Mgr*
Ingela Jussen, *Office Mgr*
Willie Jussen, *Purchasing*
EMP: 40
SQ FT: 14,500
SALES (est): 6MM **Privately Held**
SIC: 3545 End mills; files, machine tool; reamers, machine tool

(P-14146)
CNC FACTORY CORPORATION
4021 W Chandler Ave, Santa Ana (92704-5201)
PHONE..................714 581-5999
Chris Corrales, *CEO*
EMP: 12
SALES (est): 1.2MM **Privately Held**
SIC: 3545 Milling machine attachments (machine tool accessories)

(P-14147)
COASTAL CNTING INDUS SCALE INC
Also Called: Actionpac Scales & Automation
1621 Fiske Pl, Oxnard (93033-1862)
PHONE..................805 486-5754
John W Dishion, *CEO*
Betz Thompson, *Office Mgr*
Edgar Hernandez, *Marketing Staff*
Amelia Dishion, *Corp Comm Staff*
Roberto Santos, *Manager*
▲ **EMP:** 14 **EST:** 1982
SQ FT: 11,000
SALES (est): 4.8MM **Privately Held**
WEB: www.actionpacscales.com
SIC: 3545 Machine tool accessories

(P-14148)
CONCEPT PART SOLUTIONS INC
2047 Zanker Rd, San Jose (95131-2107)
PHONE..................408 748-1244

Richard L Diehl, *CEO*
Bruce Dickson, *Managing Dir*
Ikuko Kato, *Sales Dir*
Christina Forest, *Director*
Alan Beardsworth, *Manager*
EMP: 44
SALES (est): 10.5MM **Privately Held**
SIC: 3545 Machine tool accessories

(P-14149)
COORSTEK INC
4544 Mcgrath St, Ventura (93003-6492)
PHONE..................805 644-5583
EMP: 100
SALES (corp-wide): 829.3MM **Privately Held**
SIC: 3545
HQ: Coorstek, Inc.
14143 Denver Ste 400
Golden CO 80401
303 271-7000

(P-14150)
COORSTEK INC
Coorstek Ventura
4544 Mcgrath St, Ventura (93003-6492)
PHONE..................805 644-5583
Dan Luzi, *Manager*
George Forsman, *Office Mgr*
Tedd Allen, *Info Tech Dir*
David Montoya, *Engineer*
Jose Mendez, *Sales Engr*
EMP: 200
SALES (corp-wide): 407.6MM **Privately Held**
SIC: 3545 Machine tool accessories
HQ: Coorstek, Inc.
14143 Denver West Pkwy # 400
Lakewood CO 80401
303 271-7000

(P-14151)
COPLAN & COPLAN INC
Also Called: Speedpress Sign Supply
2270 Camino Vida Roble H, Carlsbad (92011-1503)
PHONE..................760 268-0583
Jacob Coplan, *CEO*
Noah Coplan, *Vice Pres*
Pamela D Tuck, *Executive*
Mike Salgado, *Purch Agent*
Marita Coplan, *Mktg Dir*
◆ **EMP:** 20
SQ FT: 14,000
SALES (est): 3.9MM **Privately Held**
WEB: www.speedpress.com
SIC: 3545 Tools & accessories for machine tools

(P-14152)
CRAIG TOOLS INC
142 Lomita St, El Segundo (90245-4113)
PHONE..................310 322-0614
William B Cleveland, *President*
Don Tripler, *Exec VP*
Arnulfo Garcia, *Purch Agent*
Alex La Torre, *Manager*
▼ **EMP:** 37 **EST:** 1958
SQ FT: 13,000
SALES (est): 7.1MM **Privately Held**
WEB: www.craigtools.com
SIC: 3545 Precision tools, machinists'

(P-14153)
DEWEYL TOOL CO INC
959 Transport Way, Petaluma (94954-1474)
PHONE..................707 765-5779
William Cline, *President*
Susan Blow, *Vice Pres*
Linda Cline, *Vice Pres*
David Pasfield, *Sales Dir*
EMP: 35
SQ FT: 20,000
SALES (est): 6MM **Privately Held**
WEB: www.deweyl.com
SIC: 3545 Machine tool attachments & accessories

(P-14154)
DIAMOTEC INC
22104 S Vt Ave Ste 104, Torrance (90502-2156)
PHONE..................310 539-4994
Varoujan Kundakjian, *President*
Alex Kundakjian, *Vice Pres*

Rod Shahinian, *Vice Pres*
Houry Abacyan, *Admin Sec*
EMP: 12
SALES: 2.3MM **Privately Held**
WEB: www.diamotec.com
SIC: 3545 Tools & accessories for machine tools

(P-14155)
DIGITAL TECHNOLOGY LAB CORP
Also Called: DTL Mori Seiki
3805 Faraday Ave, Davis (95618-7773)
PHONE..........................530 746-7400
Zach Piner, *President*
Hiroshi Takami, *Treasurer*
Adam Hansel, *Vice Pres*
Natsuo Okada, *Admin Sec*
▲ **EMP:** 55
SALES (est) 9MM **Privately Held**
SIC: 3545 Machine tool accessories
HQ: Dmg Mori Usa, Inc.
2400 Huntington Blvd
Hoffman Estates IL 60192
847 593-5400

(P-14156)
DRILLING & TRENCHING SUP INC (PA)
Also Called: Drilling World
1458 Mariani Ct, Tracy (95376-2825)
PHONE..........................510 895-1650
David Wellington Moran, *CEO*
Sandy Clark, *Office Mgr*
Erin B Moran, *Admin Sec*
Dianne Gonzales, *Manager*
◆ **EMP:** 17
SQ FT: 52,000
SALES (est): 9.2MM **Privately Held**
WEB: www.drillingworld.com
SIC: 3545 Drilling machine attachments & accessories

(P-14157)
DYNATEX INTERNATIONAL
5577 Skylane Blvd, Santa Rosa (95403-1048)
PHONE..........................707 542-4227
Kate Henry, *CEO*
John Tyler, *President*
Leanne Sarcy, *CFO*
Leanne Sarasy, *Vice Pres*
Melanie Jones-Carter, *Purchasing*
EMP: 21 **EST:** 1958
SQ FT: 15,000
SALES (est): 4MM **Privately Held**
SIC: 3545 Cutting tools for machine tools

(P-14158)
ELCON PRECISION LLC
1009 Timothy Dr, San Jose (95133-1043)
PHONE..........................408 292-7800
Dan Brumlik, *Chairman*
Pater Smith, *President*
Jamie Howton, *Mng Member*
EMP: 23
SALES (est): 5MM **Privately Held**
SIC: 3545 Precision tools, machinists'

(P-14159)
FAY AND QRTRMINE MCHINING CORP
Also Called: Fay & Quartermaine Machining
2745 Seaman Ave, El Monte (91733-1935)
PHONE..........................323 686-0224
David Cary, *President*
Yolanda Benitez, *Office Mgr*
EMP: 10
SQ FT: 8,000
SALES (est): 1.6MM **Privately Held**
SIC: 3545 Precision tools, machinists'

(P-14160)
FREEFORM RESEARCH & DEV
Also Called: Sling-Light
1539 Monrovia Ave Ste 23, Newport Beach (92663-2853)
PHONE..........................949 646-3217
Stephen B Wheeler, *President*
Nova Wheeler, *Vice Pres*
EMP: 10
SALES (est): 1MM **Privately Held**
WEB: www.slinglight.com
SIC: 3545 Drilling machine attachments & accessories

(P-14161)
FRT OF AMERICA LLC
1101 S Winchester Blvd, San Jose (95128-3901)
PHONE..........................408 261-2632
Thomas Fries,
EMP: 11
SALES (est): 1.2MM
SALES (corp-wide): 7.4MM **Privately Held**
SIC: 3545 Measuring tools & machines, machinists' metalworking type
PA: Fries Research & Technology Gmbh
Friedrich-Ebert-Str. 75
Bergisch Gladbach 51429
220 484-2430

(P-14162)
GAGE WAFCO CO INC
16625 Gramercy Pl, Gardena (90247-5201)
PHONE..........................310 532-3106
EMP: 12
SQ FT: 3,000
SALES (est): 1.5MM **Privately Held**
SIC: 3545

(P-14163)
GANG YAN DIAMOND PRODUCTS INC
4620 Mission Blvd, Montclair (91763-6135)
PHONE..........................909 590-2255
Xianpu Shen, *President*
Paul Shen, *Vice Pres*
▲ **EMP:** 16
SALES (est): 2.9MM **Privately Held**
SIC: 3545 Diamond cutting tools for turning, boring, burnishing, etc.

(P-14164)
GENIUS TOOLS AMERICAS CORP (PA)
1440 E Cedar St, Ontario (91761-8300)
PHONE..........................909 230-9588
Edward Chou, *President*
Andrew Hwang, *Vice Pres*
▲ **EMP:** 25
SALES (est): 3.9MM **Privately Held**
WEB: www.geniustoolsusa.com
SIC: 3545 Tools & accessories for machine tools

(P-14165)
HEXAGON METROLOGY INC
7 Orchard Ste 102, Lake Forest (92630-8334)
PHONE..........................949 916-4490
Thomas Weinert, *Principal*
EMP: 50
SALES (corp-wide): 4.3B **Privately Held**
SIC: 3545 3823 Precision measuring tools; industrial instrmnts msrmnt display/control process variable
HQ: Hexagon Metrology, Inc.
250 Circuit Dr
North Kingstown RI 02852
401 886-2000

(P-14166)
KEEN-KUT PRODUCTS INC
Also Called: N W D T
3190 Diablo Ave, Hayward (94545-2702)
PHONE..........................510 785-5168
Frank Lenner, *President*
Diana Lenner, *Vice Pres*
EMP: 10
SQ FT: 8,000
SALES (est): 1.5MM **Privately Held**
WEB: www.keenkut.com
SIC: 3545 Diamond cutting tools for turning, boring, burnishing, etc.

(P-14167)
KEMPTON MACHINE WORKS INC
4070 E Leaverton Ct, Anaheim (92807-1610)
PHONE..........................714 990-0596
Greg Kempton, *President*
EMP: 12
SQ FT: 14,000
SALES (est): 1.4MM **Privately Held**
SIC: 3545 3599 Tools & accessories for machine tools; machine shop, jobbing & repair

(P-14168)
LOCK-N-STITCH INC
1015 S Soderquist Rd, Turlock (95380-5726)
PHONE..........................209 632-2345
Gary J Reed, *CEO*
Louise Reed, *President*
Brandi Rollins, *Treasurer*
Arthur Reyes, *Human Res Mgr*
Arno Oja, *Mfg Mgr*
▲ **EMP:** 42
SQ FT: 33,000
SALES: 4.9MM
SALES (corp-wide): 5.9B **Privately Held**
WEB: www.locknstitch.com
SIC: 3545 Threading tools (machine tool accessories)
PA: Wartsila Oyj Abp
Hiililaiturinkuja 2
Helsinki 00180
107 090-000

(P-14169)
MAKINO INC
17800 Newhope St Ste K, Fountain Valley (92708-5429)
PHONE..........................714 444-4334
Jonathan Haye, *Branch Mgr*
EMP: 20 **Privately Held**
SIC: 3545 Tools & accessories for machine tools
HQ: Makino Inc.
7680 Innovation Way
Mason OH 45040
513 573-7200

(P-14170)
MARSHALL GENUINE PRODUCTS LLC
Also Called: Mgp Caliper Covers
616 Marsat Ct, Chula Vista (91911-4646)
PHONE..........................619 754-4099
Michael Barland, *Mng Member*
Rick Cucjen, *Controller*
EMP: 18
SQ FT: 14,500
SALES: 2.5MM **Privately Held**
SIC: 3545 Calipers & dividers

(P-14171)
MERCURY BROACH COMPANY INC
2546 Seaman Ave, El Monte (91733-1986)
PHONE..........................626 443-5904
Mark Eberlein, *President*
EMP: 14 **EST:** 1961
SQ FT: 7,000
SALES (est): 2.2MM **Privately Held**
SIC: 3545 Broaches (machine tool accessories)

(P-14172)
MEYCO MACHINE AND TOOL INC
11579 Martens River Cir, Fountain Valley (92708-4201)
P.O. Box 9659 (92728-9659)
PHONE..........................714 435-1546
Manuel Gomez, *CEO*
Victor Salazar, *Vice Pres*
Lorena Estrada, *Principal*
Max Gomez, *Principal*
Edith Martinez, *Principal*
EMP: 38
SQ FT: 12,500
SALES: 4.2MM **Privately Held**
WEB: www.meycomachine.com
SIC: 3545 Tools & accessories for machine tools

(P-14173)
MICRO TOOL & MANUFACTURING INC
6494 Federal Blvd, Lemon Grove (91945-1376)
PHONE..........................619 582-2884
Fae Galea, *President*
Michael H Galea, *Corp Secy*
Charles Galea, *Vice Pres*
John Galea, *Assistant VP*
Steve J Galea, *Assistant VP*
EMP: 22
SQ FT: 10,000

SALES: 5MM **Privately Held**
SIC: 3545 3544 Precision tools, machinists'; jigs: inspection, gauging & checking; die sets for metal stamping (presses)

(P-14174)
MIST INCORPORATED
9006 Fullbright Ave, Chatsworth (91311-6125)
PHONE..........................818 678-5619
Ken Perlis, *Vice Pres*
Steve Miller, *President*
Scott Febles, *General Mgr*
▲ **EMP:** 20 **EST:** 2000
SQ FT: 14,000
SALES (est): 4MM **Privately Held**
WEB: www.mist-tools.com
SIC: 3545 5085 Cutting tools for machine tools; tools

(P-14175)
MKKR INC
Also Called: Matko
430 E Parkcenter Cir N, San Bernardino (92408-2869)
P.O. Box 8891, Redlands (92375-2091)
PHONE..........................909 890-5994
Matthew Curtis, *President*
Rowena Rivera-Curtis, *Vice Pres*
EMP: 11
SQ FT: 23,500
SALES (est): 1.5MM **Privately Held**
WEB: www.matko.com
SIC: 3545 Scales, measuring (machinists' precision tools)

(P-14176)
MUELLER GAGES COMPANY
318 Agostino Rd, San Gabriel (91776-2505)
P.O. Box 310 (91778-0310)
PHONE..........................626 287-2911
Rhett Mueller, *President*
Sandra Mueller, *Admin Sec*
EMP: 13 **EST:** 1949
SQ FT: 10,500
SALES: 1.3MM **Privately Held**
WEB: www.mueller-gages.com
SIC: 3545 Precision tools, machinists'

(P-14177)
NATIONAL DIAMOND LAB CAL
4650 Alger St, Los Angeles (90039-1192)
PHONE..........................818 240-5770
Jerry Howard, *CEO*
Mary Pettet, *Office Mgr*
◆ **EMP:** 11 **EST:** 1945
SQ FT: 10,000
SALES: 1.8MM **Privately Held**
WEB: www.diamondtooling.com
SIC: 3545 Precision measuring tools

(P-14178)
O AND Y PRECISION INC
312 Piercy Rd, San Jose (95138-1401)
PHONE..........................408 362-1333
Majid Yahyaie, *CEO*
Robbie Oyar,
EMP: 12
SQ FT: 3,000
SALES (est): 1.3MM **Privately Held**
SIC: 3545 Machine tool accessories

(P-14179)
OMEGA DIAMOND INC
10125 Ophir Rd, Newcastle (95658-9504)
PHONE..........................916 652-8122
Samuel Devai, *President*
Roneily Devai, *Admin Sec*
▲ **EMP:** 17
SQ FT: 3,000
SALES (est): 3.2MM **Privately Held**
WEB: www.omegadiamond.com
SIC: 3545 Diamond cutting tools for turning, boring, burnishing, etc.

(P-14180)
PELAGIC PRESSURE SYSTEMS CORP
2002 Davis St, San Leandro (94577-1211)
PHONE..........................510 569-3100
Michael Hollis, *CEO*
▲ **EMP:** 75 **EST:** 1979
SQ FT: 74,000

▲ = Import ▼=Export
◆ =Import/Export

SALES (est): 16.5MM **Privately Held**
WEB: www.pelagicnet.com
SIC: 3545 Gauges (machine tool acces-
sories)
HQ: Aqua-Lung America, Inc.
2340 Cousteau Ct
Vista CA 92081
760 597-5000

(P-14181)
PENHALL DIAMOND PRODUCTS INC
Also Called: Norton Company
1345 S Acacia Ave, Fullerton (92831-5315)
PHONE.................................714 776-0937
Dave Dodd, *General Mgr*
▲ EMP: 76
SQ FT: 30,000
SALES: 7.6MM
SALES (corp-wide): 215.9MM **Privately Held**
WEB: www.sgabrasives.com
SIC: 3545 Diamond cutting tools for turn-
ing, boring, burnishing, etc.; diamond
dressing & wheel crushing attachments
HQ: Saint-Gobain Abrasives, Inc.
1 New Bond St
Worcester MA 01606
508 795-5000

(P-14182)
PENNOYER-DODGE CO
6650 San Fernando Rd, Glendale
(91201-1745)
P.O. Box 5105 (91221-1017)
PHONE.................................818 547-2100
Hazel Dodge, *President*
Karen Dodge, *Admin Sec*
EMP: 40
SALES: 4.5MM **Privately Held**
WEB: www.pdgage.com
SIC: 3545 8734 5084 3643 Gauges (ma-
chine tool accessories); precision tools,
machinists'; calibration & certification; in-
struments & control equipment; current-
carrying wiring devices; special dies,
tools, jigs & fixtures

(P-14183)
PICO CRIMPING TOOLS CO
Also Called: Pico Corporation
444 Constitution Ave, Camarillo
(93012-8504)
PHONE.................................805 388-5510
Shelley Green, *Ch of Bd*
Shelly Green, *Ch of Bd*
Mark Green, *Vice Pres*
EMP: 10 EST: 1955
SQ FT: 10,000
SALES (est): 1.1MM **Privately Held**
WEB: www.picotools.com
SIC: 3545 Machine tool accessories

(P-14184)
PIONEER BROACH COMPANY (PA)
6434 Telegraph Rd, Commerce
(90040-2593)
PHONE.................................323 728-1263
Gary M Ezor, *CEO*
Robert Ezor, *Vice Pres*
Karin Ezor, *Admin Sec*
▲ EMP: 55
SQ FT: 22,000
SALES (est): 9.2MM **Privately Held**
WEB: www.pioneerbroach.com
SIC: 3545 3599 3541 Broaches (machine
tool accessories); machine shop, jobbing
& repair; machine tools, metal cutting type

(P-14185)
PRECISION AEROSPACE & TECH INC
2320 E Orangethorpe Ave A, Anaheim
(92806-1223)
PHONE.................................714 656-1620
EMP: 24
SQ FT: 50,000
SALES: 2.5MM
SALES (corp-wide): 8.7MM **Publicly Held**
WEB: www.eranengineering.com
SIC: 3545 Precision tools, machinists'
PA: M Line Holdings, Inc.
2214 Avalon St
Costa Mesa CA 92627
714 630-6253

(P-14186)
PRECISION CUTTING TOOLS INC
13701 Excelsior Dr, Santa Fe Springs
(90670-5104)
PHONE.................................562 921-7898
Audrey Sheth, *CEO*
▲ EMP: 30
SQ FT: 20,000
SALES (est): 5.9MM **Privately Held**
WEB: www.pctcutters.com
SIC: 3545 3541 Cutting tools for machine
tools; drilling machine tools (metal cutting)

(P-14187)
PRO TOOL SERVICES INC
1704 Sunnyside Ct, Bakersfield
(93308-6859)
P.O. Box 80235 (93380-0235)
PHONE.................................661 393-9222
Ron Jacobs, *President*
Mark Gardener, *Corp Secy*
Jaime Pena, *Foreman/Supr*
EMP: 30
SQ FT: 4,000
SALES (est): 6.4MM **Privately Held**
SIC: 3545 Tools & accessories for machine
tools

(P-14188)
PROGRESSIVE TOOL & DIE INC
17016 S Broadway, Gardena (90248-3114)
PHONE.................................310 327-0569
Peter Martin, *President*
Sandra Martin, *Admin Sec*
EMP: 10
SQ FT: 6,100
SALES (est): 1.7MM **Privately Held**
SIC: 3545 7389 Precision tools, machin-
ists'; grinding, precision: commercial or in-
dustrial

(P-14189)
QUALITY GRINDING CO INC
6800 Caballero Blvd, Buena Park
(90620-1136)
P.O. Box 5968 (90622-5968)
PHONE.................................714 228-2100
Cornel Feceu, *President*
EMP: 16 EST: 1946
SQ FT: 29,000
SALES (est): 2.7MM **Privately Held**
WEB: www.qualitygrinding.net
SIC: 3545 3599 Precision tools, machin-
ists'; machine shop, jobbing & repair

(P-14190)
RAFCO-BRICKFORM LLC (PA)
Also Called: Rafco Products Brickform
11061 Jersey Blvd, Rancho Cucamonga
(91730-5135)
PHONE.................................909 484-3399
Robert Freis, *Mng Member*
Mark Harrington, *Sales Staff*
Matt Bissantti, *Mng Member*
Shawn Russell, *Manager*
Stanley Zawadzki, *Manager*
▲ EMP: 72 EST: 1973
SQ FT: 79,000
SALES (est): 17.7MM **Privately Held**
SIC: 3545 5169 Machine tool accessories;
adhesives, chemical

(P-14191)
SCIENTIFIC CUTTING TOOLS INC
110 W Easy St, Simi Valley (93065-1689)
PHONE.................................805 584-9495
Dale Christopher, *President*
Prudence Kenzie, *CFO*
Gary Christopher, *Vice Pres*
Jan Kaye, *Vice Pres*
Jeff Kaye, *General Mgr*
EMP: 37
SQ FT: 25,000
SALES (est): 6.8MM **Privately Held**
WEB: www.sct-usa.com
SIC: 3545 Machine tool accessories

(P-14192)
SETCO SALES COMPANY
5572 Buckingham Dr, Huntington Beach
(92649-1158)
PHONE.................................714 372-3730
Jeff Clark, *Branch Mgr*

EMP: 10
SALES (corp-wide): 323.1MM **Privately Held**
SIC: 3545 7694 Machine tool accessories;
armature rewinding shops
HQ: Setco Sales Company
5880 Hillside Ave
Cincinnati OH 45233
513 941-5110

(P-14193)
SEV-CAL TOOL INC
3231 Halladay St, Santa Ana (92705-5628)
PHONE.................................714 549-3347
James F Severance, *President*
William E Severance, *Corp Secy*
Naomi Severance, *Vice Pres*
EMP: 20
SALES (est): 3.1MM **Privately Held**
SIC: 3545 3541 3423 Cutting tools for
machine tools; machine tools, metal cut-
ting type; hand & edge tools

(P-14194)
SHARP-RITE TOOL INC
8443 Whirlaway St, Alta Loma
(91701-1324)
PHONE.................................909 948-1234
Gary Kropik, *President*
Raeann Kropik, *Vice Pres*
EMP: 15
SQ FT: 5,000
SALES: 2.5MM **Privately Held**
SIC: 3545 Cutting tools for machine tools

(P-14195)
SMTCL USA INC
21127 Commerce Point Dr, Walnut
(91789-3054)
PHONE.................................626 667-1192
Jianming Zhao, *CEO*
Dan Barbera, *President*
Richard Ormrod, *President*
▲ EMP: 15 EST: 2009
SALES (est): 3.9MM
SALES (corp-wide): 45.4MM **Privately Held**
SIC: 3545 Machine tool attachments & ac-
cessories
PA: Shenyang Machine Tool Imp & Exp
Co.,Ltd
No.1,17a ,Kaifa Road ,Shenyang Eco-
nomic & Technological Developm
Shenyang 11014
242 519-1530

(P-14196)
SOUTHLAND MANUFACTURING INC
Also Called: Southland Enterprises
210 Market Pl, Escondido (92029-1354)
PHONE.................................760 745-7913
Diana Young, *President*
Ruth E Young, *President*
Donald L Young, *Chairman*
Diana Guminsky, *Corp Secy*
Bracken Garritson, *General Mgr*
EMP: 15
SQ FT: 4,000
SALES (est): 2.6MM **Privately Held**
WEB: www.southlandent.com
SIC: 3545 Tool holders

(P-14197)
SOUTHLAND TOOL MFG INC
1430 N Hundley St, Anaheim (92806-1322)
PHONE.................................714 632-8198
David Pryor, *President*
▲ EMP: 16
SALES (est): 3MM **Privately Held**
SIC: 3545 Machine tool accessories

(P-14198)
STADCO (PA)
Also Called: Standard Tool & Die Co
107 S Avenue 20, Los Angeles
(90031-1709)
PHONE.................................323 227-8888
Doug Paletz, *President*
Bob Parsi, *COO*
Bret Matta, *Vice Pres*
Karen Abbott, *Accounting Mgr*
Wally Marimac, *Maint Spvr*
EMP: 140
SQ FT: 15,000

SALES (est): 35.4MM **Privately Held**
SIC: 3545 3599 Precision tools, machinists'; machine shop, jobbing & repair

(P-14199)
STEP TOOLS UNLIMITED INC
Also Called: Destiny Tool
3233 De La Cruz Blvd C, Santa Clara
(95054-2604)
PHONE.................................408 988-8898
Guy Calamia, *President*
Nettie Calamia, *Corp Secy*
EMP: 15
SQ FT: 6,000
SALES (est): 3.5MM **Privately Held**
WEB: www.destinytool.com
SIC: 3545 Cutting tools for machine tools

(P-14200)
STEWART TOOL COMPANY
3647 Omec Cir, Rancho Cordova
(95742-7302)
PHONE.................................916 635-8321
Mark Richard Stewart, *CEO*
Craig Harrington, *Corp Secy*
Dave Hassemeyer, *Admin Sec*
EMP: 55
SQ FT: 22,000
SALES (est): 15.9MM **Privately Held**
WEB: www.stewarttool.com
SIC: 3545 3544 7692 Precision tools, ma-
chinists'; jigs & fixtures; special dies &
tools; welding repair

(P-14201)
SYGMA INC
13168 Flores St, Santa Fe Springs
(90670-4023)
PHONE.................................562 906-8880
Jimmy Fung, *CEO*
▼ EMP: 15
SQ FT: 10,000
SALES (est): 1.4MM **Privately Held**
SIC: 3545 Machine tool accessories

(P-14202)
TLC MACHINING INCORPORATED
Also Called: US Machining
2571 Chant Ct, San Jose (95122-1004)
PHONE.................................408 321-9002
EMP: 35
SQ FT: 5,000
SALES (est): 4.5MM **Privately Held**
SIC: 3545

(P-14203)
TMK MANUFACTURING INC
Also Called: Aaron Bennett
386 Laurelwood Rd, Santa Clara
(95054-2311)
PHONE.................................408 844-8289
Aaron Bennett, *President*
Israel Sanchez, *Vice Pres*
EMP: 20
SALES: 2MM **Privately Held**
WEB: www.tmk-inc.com
SIC: 3545 Precision tools, machinists'

(P-14204)
TOSCO - TOOL SPECIALTY COMPANY
1011 E Slauson Ave, Los Angeles
(90011-5296)
P.O. Box 512157 (90051-0157)
PHONE.................................323 232-3561
Jerry Tetzlaff, *President*
Ted Tetzlaff, *Vice Pres*
▲ EMP: 25
SQ FT: 19,500
SALES: 3.3MM **Privately Held**
WEB: www.toolspecialty.com
SIC: 3545 Cutting tools for machine tools

(P-14205)
TT MACHINE CORP
11651 Anabel Ave, Garden Grove
(92843-3708)
PHONE.................................714 534-5288
Al Tran, *Manager*
EMP: 20
SALES (est): 4.4MM **Privately Held**
SIC: 3545 Machine tool accessories

PRODUCTS & SVCS

(P-14206)
TURNHAM CORPORATION (PA)
Also Called: Blake Manufacturing Co
15312 Proctor Ave, City of Industry
(91745-1023)
PHONE...................................626 330-0415
John R Turnham, *President*
▲ EMP: 17
SQ FT: 7,500
SALES (est): 2.6MM **Privately Held**
WEB: www.blakemanufacturing.com
SIC: 3545 3599 Machine tool accessories;
machine shop, jobbing & repair

(P-14207)
TURNHAM CORPORATION
Also Called: Blake Manufacturing
15310 Proctor Ave, City of Industry
(91745-1023)
PHONE...................................626 968-6481
John Turnham, *Branch Mgr*
EMP: 10
SALES (corp-wide): 2.6MM **Privately Held**
WEB: www.blakemanufacturing.com
SIC: 3545 3728 3599 Machine tool accessories; aircraft assemblies, subassemblies & parts; machine shop, jobbing & repair
PA: Turnham Corporation
    15312 Proctor Ave
    City Of Industry CA 91745
    626 330-0415

(P-14208)
UNITED DRILL BUSHING CORP
Also Called: United California
12200 Woodruff Ave, Downey
(90241-5608)
P.O. Box 4250 (90241-1250)
PHONE...................................562 803-1521
Dale L Bethke, *President*
Billie Huckins, *Admin Sec*
EMP: 150 EST: 1964
SQ FT: 80,000
SALES (est): 23.5MM **Privately Held**
WEB: www.ucc-udb.com
SIC: 3545 3544 Drill bushings (drilling jig);
drilling machine attachments & accessories; tools & accessories for machine
tools; special dies, tools, jigs & fixtures

(P-14209)
VERTEX DIAMOND TOOL COMPANY
940 W Cienega Ave, San Dimas
(91773-2454)
PHONE...................................909 599-1129
Tony Pontone, *CEO*
Loretta Pontone Houchin, *President*
Kenneth Houchin, *Vice Pres*
EMP: 51
SQ FT: 13,000
SALES (est): 3MM **Privately Held**
WEB: www.vertexdiamondtool.com
SIC: 3545 Diamond cutting tools for turning, boring, burnishing, etc.

(P-14210)
VIKING PRODUCTS INC
20 Doppler, Irvine (92618-4306)
PHONE...................................949 379-5100
Marc Kaplan, *CEO*
EMP: 40
SQ FT: 12,000
SALES (est): 8.7MM **Privately Held**
SIC: 3545 Precision measuring tools

(P-14211)
WESTERN GAGE CORPORATION
3316 Maya Linda Ste A, Camarillo
(93012-8776)
PHONE...................................805 445-1410
Donald E Moors, *President*
Nanette Moors, *Corp Sec*
Sharon Garcia, *Executive*
Steve Harrington, *Engineer*
Don Brown, *Site Mgr*
EMP: 24
SQ FT: 22,000
SALES (est): 5.8MM **Privately Held**
WEB: www.westerngage.com
SIC: 3545 Gauges (machine tool accessories)

(P-14212)
WETMORE TOOL AND ENGRG CO
Also Called: Wetmore Cutting Tools
5091 G St, Chino (91710-5141)
PHONE...................................909 364-1000
Jerome David, *CEO*
Phil Kurtz, *President*
Keith Rowland, *Exec VP*
Ted Shill, *Planning*
Rosie Ortiz, *Human Res Mgr*
▲ EMP: 75
SQ FT: 32,000
SALES (est): 15.3MM
SALES (corp-wide): 11.1B **Privately Held**
WEB: www.hpwetmore.com
SIC: 3545 5084 3544 3541 Cutting tools
for machine tools; industrial machinery &
equipment; special dies, tools, jigs & fixtures; machine tools, metal cutting type;
bolts, nuts, rivets & washers
HQ: Dormer Pramet Ab
    Linjegatan 9
    Halmstad 302 5
    351 652-00

(P-14213)
XCELIRON CORP
9540 Vassar Ave, Chatsworth
(91311-4141)
PHONE...................................818 700-8404
Richard Diorio, *President*
Randy Jones, *Vice Pres*
EMP: 10
SQ FT: 10,600
SALES (est): 1.3MM **Privately Held**
WEB: www.xceliron.com
SIC: 3545 3471 Cutting tools for machine
tools; plating of metals or formed products

(P-14214)
YILLIK PRECISION INDUSTRIES
1621 S Cucamonga Ave, Ontario
(91761-4514)
PHONE...................................909 947-2785
Ray Yillik, *President*
Doris Yillik, *Corp Secy*
Paul Filko, *Vice Pres*
EMP: 55
SQ FT: 14,000
SALES (est): 7.7MM
SALES (corp-wide): 22.9MM **Privately Held**
WEB: www.yillik.com
SIC: 3545 3568 3366 Drill bushings
(drilling jig); power transmission equipment; copper foundries
PA: Psm Industries, Inc.
    14000 Avalon Blvd
    Los Angeles CA 90061
    888 663-8256

3546 Power Hand Tools

(P-14215)
BLACK & DECKER (US) INC
Also Called: Dewalt Service Center 148
9020 Alondra Blvd, Bellflower
(90706-4206)
PHONE...................................562 925-7551
Fax: 562 925-2561
EMP: 14
SALES (corp-wide): 11.4B **Publicly Held**
SIC: 3546
HQ: Black & Decker (U.S.) Inc.
    1000 Stanley Dr
    New Britain CT 06053
    860 225-5111

(P-14216)
BLACK & DECKER CORPORATION
3949 E Guasti Rd Ste A, Ontario
(91761-1549)
PHONE...................................909 390-5548
EMP: 15
SALES (corp-wide): 11B **Publicly Held**
SIC: 3546
HQ: The Black & Decker Corporation
    701 E Joppa Rd
    Towson MD 21286
    410 716-3900

(P-14217)
BOLTTECH MANNINGS INC
16926 Keegan Ave, Carson (90746-1322)
PHONE...................................310 604-9500
Michael Zastera, *Manager*
EMP: 57
SALES (corp-wide): 462.1MM **Privately Held**
SIC: 3546 Power-driven handtools
HQ: Bolttech Mannings, Inc.
    501 Mosside Blvd
    North Versailles PA 15137
    724 872-4873

(P-14218)
BOLTTECH MANNINGS INC
475 Industrial Way, Benicia (94510-1119)
PHONE...................................707 751-0157
Peter Smith, *Branch Mgr*
EMP: 57
SALES (corp-wide): 462.1MM **Privately Held**
SIC: 3546 Power-driven handtools
HQ: Bolttech Mannings, Inc.
    501 Mosside Blvd
    North Versailles PA 15137
    724 872-4873

(P-14219)
CHURCHILL AEROSPACE LLC
5091 G St, Chino (91710-5141)
PHONE...................................909 266-3116
Keith Rowland,
EMP: 157
SALES: 22.2MM **Privately Held**
SIC: 3546 Power-driven handtools

(P-14220)
DIAMOND TECH INCORPORATED
4347 Pacific St, Rocklin (95677-2117)
P.O. Box 756 (95677-0756)
PHONE...................................916 624-1118
Sean Ward, *President*
Maureen Ward, *Admin Sec*
Ingo Pfeiffer, *Research*
Anne Gregory, *Agent*
▲ EMP: 10
SQ FT: 9,000
SALES (est): 1.8MM **Privately Held**
WEB: www.dtiinnovations.com
SIC: 3546 Drills & drilling tools; saws &
sawing equipment

(P-14221)
GEORGE JUE MFG CO INC
Also Called: Paramont Metal & Supply Co
8140 Rosecrans Ave, Paramount
(90723-2794)
PHONE...................................562 634-8181
Vincent Jue, *CEO*
George Jue, *President*
Elenor Sylva, *Admin Sec*
Rocky Chernow, *Sales Mgr*
▲ EMP: 60
SQ FT: 80,000
SALES (est): 15.8MM **Privately Held**
WEB: www.champion-equipment.com
SIC: 3546 Drills & drilling tools

(P-14222)
GRANBERG PUMP AND METER LTD
Also Called: Granberg International
1051 Los Medanos St, Pittsburg
(94565-2561)
PHONE...................................707 562-2099
Erik Granberg, *President*
John Mahley, *General Mgr*
Brian Mohr, *Project Mgr*
Lindsey Granberg, *Marketing Mgr*
Ben Hawkins, *Sales Mgr*
◆ EMP: 19
SQ FT: 9,000
SALES: 1.8MM **Privately Held**
WEB: www.granberg.com
SIC: 3546 Power-driven handtools

(P-14223)
HEAD FIRST PRODUCTIONS INC
Also Called: Headfirst Products
14848 Northam St, La Mirada
(90638-5747)
PHONE...................................714 522-3311

Bill Thompson, *President*
▲ EMP: 15
SQ FT: 2,000
SALES (est): 1.9MM **Privately Held**
SIC: 3546 3496 5085 Power-driven handtools; miscellaneous fabricated wire products; fasteners, industrial: nuts, bolts,
screws, etc.

(P-14224)
MEISEI CORPORATION
948 Tourmaline Dr, Newbury Park
(91320-1206)
PHONE...................................805 497-2626
Akio Fukunaga, *President*
Fumio Fukunaga, *Vice Pres*
EMP: 11
SALES (est): 2.1MM **Privately Held**
SIC: 3546 Power-driven handtools

(P-14225)
MK DIAMOND PRODUCTS INC (PA)
1315 Storm Pkwy, Torrance (90501-5041)
PHONE...................................310 539-5221
Robert J Delahaut, *President*
Brian Delahaut, *Vice Pres*
Steve Nichols, *Sales Staff*
Travis Deckert, *Warehouse Mgr*
◆ EMP: 200
SQ FT: 35,000
SALES (est): 47.1MM **Privately Held**
WEB: www.mkdiamond.com
SIC: 3546 3425 Saws & sawing equipment; saw blades & handsaws

(P-14226)
ROBERT BOSCH TOOL CORPORATION
302 E 3rd St 31-1812, Calexico
(92231-2760)
P.O. Box 2837 (92232-2837)
PHONE...................................760 357-5603
Ian Morris, *Manager*
EMP: 186
SALES (corp-wide): 294.8MM **Privately Held**
WEB: www.vermontamerican.com
SIC: 3546 Power-driven handtools
HQ: Robert Bosch Tool Corporation
    1800 W Central Rd
    Mount Prospect IL 60056

(P-14227)
SEESCAN INC (PA)
Also Called: Seektech
3855 Ruffin Rd, San Diego (92123-1813)
PHONE...................................858 244-3300
Mark Olsson, *President*
John Chew, *Vice Pres*
Kira Olsson, *Comms Mgr*
Erik Hawley, *Info Tech Dir*
Ryan Bulger, *Software Engr*
▲ EMP: 180
SQ FT: 63,641
SALES (est): 31.6MM **Privately Held**
WEB: www.seektechinc.com
SIC: 3546 Power-driven handtools

(P-14228)
SHG HOLDINGS CORP (PA)
Also Called: Zephyr Tool Group
201 Hindry Ave, Inglewood (90301-1519)
PHONE...................................310 410-4907
Bernard J Kersulis, *President*
EMP: 100
SQ FT: 53,000
SALES (est): 10.1MM **Privately Held**
SIC: 3546 Power-driven handtools

(P-14229)
THE BLACK & DECKER INC
19701 Da Vinci, El Toro (92610-2622)
PHONE...................................949 672-4000
Chris Metz, *Manager*
Scott Eddington, *Manager*
Todd Soderberg, *Manager*
EMP: 450
SALES (corp-wide): 13.9B **Publicly Held**
WEB: www.blackanddecker.com
SIC: 3546 3553 Power-driven handtools;
woodworking machinery

▲ = Import ▼=Export
◆ =Import/Export

HQ: The Black & Decker Corporation
701 E Joppa Rd
Towson MD 21286
410 716-3900

(P-14230)
ZEPHYR MANUFACTURING CO INC
Also Called: Zephyr Tool Group
201 Hindry Ave, Inglewood (90301-1519)
PHONE..................................310 410-4907
Ray Chin, *VP Finance*
Robert Szanter, *Finance*
Tom Houstan, *VP Mfg*
Earl Houston, *VP Sales*
Douglas Carpenter, *Sales Associate*
▲ EMP: 100
SQ FT: 60,000
SALES (est): 20.5MM **Privately Held**
SIC: 3546 3545 3423 Power-driven hand-
tools; machine tool accessories; hand &
edge tools
PA: Shg Holdings Corp
201 Hindry Ave
Inglewood CA 90301

(P-14231)
ZIRCON CORPORATION (PA)
1580 Dell Ave, Campbell (95008-6918)
PHONE..................................408 866-8600
John Stauss, *President*
Charles J Stauss, *Ch of Bd*
John R Stauss, *President*
Robert Wyler, *Admin Sec*
Steve Schwarzenbach, *Electrical Engi*
▲ EMP: 45
SQ FT: 6,000
SALES (est): 18.5MM **Privately Held**
WEB: www.zircon.com
SIC: 3546 Power-driven handtools

3547 Rolling Mill Machinery & Eqpt

(P-14232)
GEORGE L KOVACS
Also Called: Gerson's Machinery Co
1810 W Business Center Dr, Orange
(92867-7904)
PHONE..................................714 538-8026
George L Kovacs, *Owner*
EMP: 25
SQ FT: 12,000
SALES (est): 2.2MM **Privately Held**
WEB: www.gersons.com
SIC: 3547 3542 Rolling mill machinery;
machine tools, metal forming type

(P-14233)
JOHN LIST CORPORATION
Also Called: Protocast
9732 Cozycroft Ave, Chatsworth
(91311-4498)
PHONE..................................818 882-7848
John List, *President*
Susan List, *Vice Pres*
EMP: 47 EST: 1966
SQ FT: 16,000
SALES (est): 9MM **Privately Held**
WEB: www.protocastjlc.com
SIC: 3547 3365 3369 3366 Ferrous &
nonferrous mill equipment, auxiliary; alu-
minum & aluminum-based alloy castings;
nonferrous foundries; copper foundries

(P-14234)
OLD COUNTRY MILLWORK INC
Also Called: O C M
5855 Hooper Ave, Los Angeles
(90001-1280)
PHONE..................................323 234-2940
Gerard J Kilgallon, *CEO*
Patrick Macdougall, *CFO*
▲ EMP: 38
SQ FT: 36,000
SALES (est): 11.5MM **Privately Held**
WEB: www.e-ocm.com
SIC: 3547 3479 Rolling mill machinery;
painting, coating & hot dipping

(P-14235)
ROBINSON ENGINEERING CORP
3575 Grapevine St, Jurupa Valley
(91752-3505)
PHONE..................................951 361-8000
Peter Robinson, *President*
Zora Robinson, *Vice Pres*
EMP: 14
SQ FT: 20,000
SALES: 1.2MM **Privately Held**
SIC: 3547 Rolling mill machinery

3548 Welding Apparatus

(P-14236)
AMADA MIYACHI AMERICA INC (HQ)
1820 S Myrtle Ave, Monrovia (91016-4833)
PHONE..................................626 303-5676
David Fawcett, *President*
Barbara Kuntz, *Chief Mktg Ofcr*
David Cielinski, *Vice Pres*
James Malloy, *Vice Pres*
Kunio Minejima, *Vice Pres*
◆ EMP: 165
SQ FT: 70,000
SALES (est): 42MM **Privately Held**
WEB: www.miyachiunitek.com
SIC: 3548 3699 3829 Soldering equip-
ment, except hand soldering irons; laser
welding, drilling & cutting equipment;
measuring & controlling devices

(P-14237)
AMERICA MOUNTAIN WLDG INDS INC
1613 Chelsea Rd Ste 208, San Marino
(91108-2419)
PHONE..................................626 698-8066
Hong Kang, *CEO*
EMP: 10
SALES: 2MM **Privately Held**
SIC: 3548 Welding apparatus

(P-14238)
ARC MACHINES INC (HQ)
Also Called: A M I
14320 Arminta St, Panorama City
(91402-6869)
PHONE..................................818 896-9556
Douglas B Solomon, *Vice Pres*
Fidel Gumayagay, *Design Engr*
Dick Meyer, *Engineer*
Greg Fridlyand, *Analyst*
Gayane Aroutiounian, *Accountant*
▲ EMP: 100
SQ FT: 96,000
SALES (est): 47.3MM
SALES (corp-wide): 3.6B **Publicly Held**
WEB: www.arcmachines.com
SIC: 3548 3621 3566 Welding & cutting
apparatus & accessories; motors & gen-
erators; speed changers, drives & gears
PA: Colfax Corporation
420 Natl Bus Pkwy Ste 500
Annapolis Junction MD 20701
301 323-9000

(P-14239)
CREATIVE PATHWAYS INC
20815 Higgins Ct, Torrance (90501-1830)
PHONE..................................310 530-1965
Timothy Rohrberg, *President*
Patrica Rohrberg, *Admin Sec*
Patti Rohrberg, *Administration*
Pamela Whitwell, *Controller*
EMP: 35
SQ FT: 29,000
SALES: 4MM **Privately Held**
WEB: www.creativepathways.com
SIC: 3548 Welding & cutting apparatus &
accessories

(P-14240)
DIAMOND GROUND PRODUCTS INC
2651 Lavery Ct, Newbury Park
(91320-1502)
PHONE..................................805 498-3837
James C Elizarraz, *President*
▲ EMP: 30
SQ FT: 40,000

SALES (est): 5.9MM **Privately Held**
WEB: www.diamondground.com
SIC: 3548 Electrodes, electric welding;
welding & cutting apparatus & accessories

(P-14241)
DIAMOND WELD INDUSTRIES INC
63 W North Ave, Fresno (93706-5516)
PHONE..................................559 268-9999
Nachhatar Dhaliwal, *President*
Jassy Dhaliwal, *CFO*
Gille Dhaliwal, *Vice Pres*
Balbir Dhaliwal, *Admin Sec*
▲ EMP: 10
SQ FT: 15,000
SALES (est): 1.8MM **Privately Held**
SIC: 3548 Welding apparatus

(P-14242)
JANDA COMPANY INC
226 N Sherman Ave Ste A, Corona
(92882-7122)
PHONE..................................951 734-1935
Janet White, *CEO*
Sheryl Dreiling, *Vice Pres*
Rick Goodman, *Mktg Dir*
Jack Fornelli, *Sales Engr*
Rick Gainer, *Sales Staff*
EMP: 20
SQ FT: 299,000
SALES (est): 4.5MM **Privately Held**
WEB: www.jandawelders.com
SIC: 3548 Spot welding apparatus, electric

(P-14243)
KUTON WELDING INC
11380 Luddington St, Sun Valley
(91352-3106)
PHONE..................................818 771-0964
Minh That Ton, *President*
EMP: 14
SALES (est): 1.1MM **Privately Held**
SIC: 3548 1799 Welding & cutting appara-
tus & accessories; welding on site

(P-14244)
LODESTONE LLC
Also Called: Weldstone Portable Welders
4769 E Wesley Dr, Anaheim (92807-1941)
PHONE..................................714 970-0900
Richard H Barden,
Patricia Walck,
EMP: 16
SALES: 950K **Privately Held**
WEB: www.weldstone.net
SIC: 3548 8742 Welding apparatus; man-
agement consulting services

(P-14245)
LONGEVITY GLOBAL INC
23591 Foley St, Hayward (94545-1676)
PHONE..................................877 566-4462
Simon Katz, *CEO*
▲ EMP: 20
SQ FT: 7,000
SALES (est): 2.5MM **Privately Held**
SIC: 3548 3545 3541 3699 Welding ap-
paratus; machine tool accessories; ma-
chine tools, metal cutting type; welding
machines & equipment, ultrasonic; metal-
working machinery

(P-14246)
M K PRODUCTS INC
Also Called: Mk Manufacturing
16882 Armstrong Ave, Irvine (92606-4975)
PHONE..................................949 798-1425
Chris Westlake, *President*
Joe Lapaglia, *CFO*
Joseph J Lapaglia, *CFO*
Barbara Pierce, *Admin Sec*
Stacy Urias, *Administration*
▲ EMP: 81
SQ FT: 80,000
SALES (est): 18.5MM **Privately Held**
WEB: www.mkprod.com
SIC: 3548 Electric welding equipment

(P-14247)
MAITLEN & BENSON INC
Also Called: Wypo
1395 Obispo Ave, Long Beach
(90804-2509)
P.O. Box 4146 (90804-0146)
PHONE..................................562 597-2200
Kem Gallagher, *President*
Gary Ghio, *Shareholder*
Debbie Wilder, *Corp Secy*
EMP: 30
SQ FT: 5,000
SALES (est): 4MM **Privately Held**
WEB: www.wypo.com
SIC: 3548 3499 Welding & cutting appara-
tus & accessories; welding tips, heat re-
sistant: metal

(P-14248)
MILLER ELECTRIC MFG CO
2523 Ellington Ct, Simi Valley
(93063-5322)
PHONE..................................805 520-7494
C Breeden, *Branch Mgr*
EMP: 207
SALES (corp-wide): 14.7B **Publicly Held**
SIC: 3548 Welding apparatus
HQ: Miller Electric Mfg. Llc
1635 W Spencer St
Appleton WI 54914
920 734-9821

(P-14249)
ONEX RF AUTOMATION INC
1824 Flower Ave, Duarte (91010-2931)
PHONE..................................626 358-6639
Onik Bogosyan, *President*
EMP: 12 EST: 1991
SALES (est): 3.1MM **Privately Held**
SIC: 3548 Welding apparatus

(P-14250)
PERKINS
Also Called: Perkins Family Restaurant
7312 Varna Ave Ste A, North Hollywood
(91605-4008)
PHONE..................................818 764-9293
EMP: 21
SALES (est): 1.4MM **Privately Held**
SIC: 3548

(P-14251)
PRAXAIR INC
1950 Loveridge Rd, Pittsburg (94565-4113)
PHONE..................................925 427-1950
John Bellicci, *Branch Mgr*
John Billecci, *Human Res Mgr*
EMP: 20 **Privately Held**
SIC: 3548 2813 Welding apparatus; indus-
trial gases
HQ: Praxair, Inc.
10 Riverview Dr
Danbury CT 06810
203 837-2000

(P-14252)
SEAL SEAT CO
9160 Norwalk Blvd, Santa Fe Springs
(90670-2534)
PHONE..................................626 923-2504
EMP: 11
SALES (est): 1.4MM **Privately Held**
SIC: 3548 Welding apparatus

(P-14253)
SENSBEY INC (PA)
833 Mahler Rd Ste 3, Burlingame
(94010-1609)
PHONE..................................650 697-2032
Katsuhiro Enokawa, *President*
Hiro Ito, *Vice Pres*
EMP: 15
SQ FT: 22,000
SALES (est): 1.5MM **Privately Held**
WEB: www.sensbey.com
SIC: 3548 3634 3822 Soldering equip-
ment, except hand soldering irons; heat-
ing units, for electric appliances; built-in
thermostats, filled system & bimetal types

(P-14254)
SIKAMA INTERNATIONAL INC
118 E Gutierrez St, Santa Barbara
(93101-2314)
P.O. Box 40298 (93140-0298)
PHONE..................................805 962-1000

Sigurd R Wathne, *President*
Mariellen Wathne, *Treasurer*
Kail S Wathne, *Vice Pres*
Kail Wathne, *Vice Pres*
Phillip Skeen, *Sales Mgr*
EMP: 13 EST: 1982
SQ FT: 9,300
SALES: 2MM **Privately Held**
WEB: www.sikama.com
SIC: 3548 Soldering equipment, except hand soldering irons

(P-14255)
SSCO MANUFACTURING INC
Also Called: ARC Products
1245 30th St, San Diego (92154-3477)
PHONE................................619 628-1022
Victor B Miller, *President*
Susan D Miller, *Treasurer*
Lane A Litke, *Vice Pres*
EMP: 35
SQ FT: 21,000
SALES (est): 7.9MM
SALES (corp-wide): 3B **Publicly Held**
WEB: www.arc-products.com
SIC: 3548 5085 7629 7699 Electric welding equipment; welding supplies; circuit board repair; welding equipment repair
PA: Lincoln Electric Holdings, Inc.
22801 Saint Clair Ave
Cleveland OH 44117
216 481-8100

(P-14256)
SUPER WELDING SOUTHERN CAL INC
609 Anita St, Chula Vista (91911-4619)
PHONE................................619 239-8003
Roberto Victoria, *President*
Manuel Victoria, *Officer*
Amelia Victoria, *Vice Pres*
EMP: 20
SQ FT: 54,577
SALES: 2MM **Privately Held**
SIC: 3548 1799 Arc welding generators, alternating current & direct current; welding on site

(P-14257)
TECHNICAL DEVICES COMPANY
560 Alaska Ave, Torrance (90503-3904)
PHONE................................310 618-8437
Douglas N Winther, *CEO*
Rey Malazo, *CFO*
EMP: 48 EST: 1977
SQ FT: 35,000
SALES (est): 6.2MM
SALES (corp-wide): 9.2MM **Privately Held**
WEB: www.technicaldev.com
SIC: 3548 3471 3544 3423 Soldering equipment, except hand soldering irons; cleaning, polishing & finishing; special dies & tools; hand & edge tools
PA: Winther Technologies, Inc.
560 Alaska Ave
Torrance CA 90503
310 618-8437

(P-14258)
VERIDIAM INC (DH)
1717 N Cuyamaca St, El Cajon (92020-1110)
PHONE................................619 448-1000
Chuck Passarelli, *CEO*
Kevin S Beaver, *CFO*
Thomas Cresante, *Principal*
▲ **EMP:** 141
SQ FT: 250,000
SALES (est): 79.8MM **Privately Held**
WEB: www.veridiam.com
SIC: 3548 3545 3317 Welding apparatus; machine tool accessories; steel pipe & tubes
HQ: Whi Capital Partners
191 N Wacker Dr Ste 1500
Chicago IL 60606
312 621-0590

(P-14259)
WHITE INDUSTRIAL CORPORATION
Also Called: Pdr-America
3869 Dividend Dr Ste 1, Shingle Springs (95682-7252)
PHONE................................530 676-6262

Dave White, *President*
Sharon White, *Admin Sec*
Larry Hartman, *Opers Mgr*
▲ **EMP:** 11
SQ FT: 5,200
SALES (est): 2.2MM **Privately Held**
WEB: www.pdr-america.com
SIC: 3548 Welding apparatus

(P-14260)
WINTHER TECHNOLOGIES INC (PA)
Also Called: Technical Devices
560 Alaska Ave, Torrance (90503-3904)
PHONE................................310 618-8437
Douglas N Winther, *President*
Julio Trinidad, *Plant Mgr*
▲ **EMP:** 46
SQ FT: 32,000
SALES (est): 9.2MM **Privately Held**
SIC: 3548 3544 3542 3471 Soldering equipment, except hand soldering irons; special dies & tools; machine tools, metal forming type; cleaning & descaling metal products

3549 Metalworking Machinery, NEC

(P-14261)
5-STARS ENGINEERING ASSOC INC
3393 De La Cruz Blvd, Santa Clara (95054-2633)
PHONE................................408 380-4849
Efrain Ojeda, *CEO*
Luis Vargas, *Vice Pres*
EMP: 26
SQ FT: 46,000
SALES (est): 4.5MM **Privately Held**
SIC: 3549 Assembly machines, including robotic

(P-14262)
ADAPT AUTOMATION INC
1661 Palm St Ste A, Santa Ana (92701-5190)
PHONE................................714 662-4454
Case Van Mechelen, *Principal*
Case V Mechelen, *CEO*
Tia V Mechelen, *Corp Secy*
Peter Smit, *Vice Pres*
EMP: 34
SQ FT: 50,000
SALES (est): 9.1MM **Privately Held**
SIC: 3549 Assembly machines, including robotic

(P-14263)
ASSEMBLY AUTOMATION INDUSTRIES
1849 Business Center Dr, Duarte (91010-2902)
PHONE................................626 303-2777
Francis E Frost, *CEO*
Elizabeth Frost, *Corp Secy*
Jill Chastain, *Manager*
EMP: 35
SQ FT: 10,000
SALES (est): 7.7MM **Privately Held**
WEB: www.assemblyauto.com
SIC: 3549 Metalworking machinery

(P-14264)
BMCI INC
Also Called: Bergandi Machinery Company
1689 S Parco Ave, Ontario (91761-8308)
P.O. Box 3790 (91761-0977)
PHONE................................951 361-8000
Scott Barsotti, *President*
Gary Costanzo, *COO*
Jose Garcia, *Vice Pres*
▼ **EMP:** 45
SQ FT: 45,000
SALES (est): 10MM **Privately Held**
WEB: www.bergandi.com
SIC: 3549 3548 Wiredrawing & fabricating machinery & equipment, ex. die; welding apparatus

(P-14265)
DOT HAIZOL COM
Also Called: Haizol Global
500 S Kraemer Blvd # 205, Brea (92821-6761)
PHONE................................657 258-9027
Owen Sun, *Owner*
EMP: 11
SALES (est): 1.1MM **Privately Held**
SIC: 3549 Metalworking machinery

(P-14266)
EUBANKS ENGINEERING CO (PA)
1921 S Quaker Ridge Pl, Ontario (91761-8041)
P.O. Box 8490, Rancho Cucamonga (91701-0490)
PHONE................................909 483-2456
David C Eubanks, *Principal*
Maria Sanders, *General Mgr*
EMP: 30 EST: 1951
SQ FT: 34,000
SALES (est): 5.6MM **Privately Held**
WEB: www.eubanks.com
SIC: 3549 3825 Wiredrawing & fabricating machinery & equipment, ex. die; test equipment for electronic & electrical circuits

(P-14267)
GANESH INDUSTRIES LLC
20869 Plummer St, Chatsworth (91311-5005)
PHONE................................818 349-9166
Harvinder Singh, *President*
▲ **EMP:** 10
SQ FT: 20,000
SALES (est): 797.3K **Privately Held**
SIC: 3549 Metalworking machinery

(P-14268)
GOLDEN STATE ENGINEERING INC
15338 Garfield Ave, Paramount (90723-4092)
PHONE................................562 634-3125
Alexandra Rostovski, *CEO*
Eugenio Rostovski, *President*
Mary Saguini, *CEO*
Tom Scroggin, *Vice Pres*
EMP: 120
SQ FT: 65,000
SALES (est): 28.4MM **Privately Held**
WEB: www.goldenstateeng.com
SIC: 3549 3541 3451 8711 Metalworking machinery; grinding, polishing, buffing, lapping & honing machines; screw machine products; engineering services; bolts, nuts, rivets & washers

(P-14269)
GOLNEX INC
4259 Aplicella Ct, Manteca (95337-8480)
PHONE................................510 490-6003
Michael Wang, *President*
◆ **EMP:** 20
SALES: 2MM **Privately Held**
WEB: www.golnex.com
SIC: 3549 5085 Screw driving machines; industrial supplies

(P-14270)
H P SOLUTIONS INC
Also Called: H F Johnston Mfg Co
2475 Ash St, Vista (92081-8424)
PHONE................................760 727-2880
Bradley Hayes, *President*
EMP: 45
SQ FT: 40,327
SALES (est): 6.6MM
SALES (corp-wide): 2.2B **Publicly Held**
SIC: 3549 Metalworking machinery
PA: Nordson Corporation
28601 Clemens Rd
Westlake OH 44145
440 892-1580

(P-14271)
HAEGER INCORPORATED (DH)
811 Wakefield Dr, Oakdale (95361-7792)
PHONE................................209 848-4000
Alan Phillips, *CEO*
Wouter Kleizen, *President*
Joe Sommers, *Engineer*

Gena Beck, *Human Res Mgr*
Rod Hagon, *Mktg Dir*
▲ **EMP:** 24
SQ FT: 36,000
SALES (est): 3.7MM **Privately Held**
WEB: www.haeger.com
SIC: 3549 Metalworking machinery
HQ: Phillips Corporation
7390 Coca Cola Dr Ste 200
Hanover MD 21076
410 564-2900

(P-14272)
LAVANG TECH PRCSION SHEET MTLS
14480 Hoover St, Westminster (92683-5319)
PHONE................................714 901-2782
Andy Fan, *Owner*
Andy Pham, *Vice Pres*
Kenny Tran, *General Mgr*
Andy Vu, *General Mgr*
EMP: 13
SQ FT: 10,700
SALES (est): 1.5MM **Privately Held**
WEB: www.lavang-tech.com
SIC: 3549 Metalworking machinery

(P-14273)
LIP HING METAL MFG AMER INC
738 Phillips, Rowland Heights (91748-1146)
PHONE................................626 810-8204
Ronald Chow, *President*
▲ **EMP:** 10
SQ FT: 15,000
SALES (est): 1.9MM **Privately Held**
SIC: 3549 Metalworking machinery

(P-14274)
LTD TECH INC
2630 Lavery Ct Ste B, Newbury Park (91320-1534)
PHONE................................805 480-1886
Lonny Deboisblanc, *President*
Bonnie D Boisblanc, *CFO*
Bonnie Deboisblanc, *CFO*
Eli Zegarra, *Manager*
▲ **EMP:** 16 EST: 2002
SQ FT: 5,000
SALES (est): 2.5MM **Privately Held**
WEB: www.ltdtechnology.com
SIC: 3549 Assembly machines, including robotic

(P-14275)
LTI BOYD
600 S Mcclure Rd, Modesto (95357-0520)
PHONE................................800 554-0200
Mitch Aiello, *President*
Kurt Wetzel, *CFO*
▲ **EMP:** 766
SALES (est): 68.3MM **Privately Held**
SIC: 3549 3053 8711 Metalworking machinery; gaskets, packing & sealing devices; industrial engineers
PA: Sentinel Capital Partners Llc
330 Madison Ave Fl 27
New York NY 10017

(P-14276)
NEATO ROBOTICS INC (HQ)
8100 Jarvis Ave Ste 100, Newark (94560-1192)
PHONE................................510 795-1351
Giacomo Marini, *CEO*
Thomas Nedder, *CEO*
Bruce McAllister, *CFO*
Nancy Nunziati, *Vice Pres*
Aron Cooperman, *Program Mgr*
◆ **EMP:** 71 EST: 2005
SQ FT: 13,000
SALES (est): 27.3MM
SALES (corp-wide): 3.1B **Privately Held**
SIC: 3549 3524 Assembly machines, including robotic; blowers & vacuums, lawn
PA: Vorwerk & Co. Kg
Muhlenweg 17-37
Wuppertal 42275
202 564-0

▲ = Import ▼=Export
◆ =Import/Export

(P-14277)
POSITRONICS INCORPORATED
173 Spring St Ste 120, Pleasanton
(94566-9401)
PHONE..................................925 931-0211
Howard Miles, *President*
Vincent Leung, *Vice Pres*
Radoslaw Szambelan, *Sr Software Eng*
Michel Theunissen, *Sr Software Eng*
John Thoits, *Software Engr*
EMP: 14
SQ FT: 2,200
SALES (est): 1.6MM **Privately Held**
WEB: www.posincorp.com
SIC: 3549 Assembly machines, including
robotic

(P-14278)
**PRODUCTION ASSMBLY
SYSTEMS INC**
12568 Kirkham Ct, Poway (92064-8899)
PHONE..................................858 748-6700
Charles D Ross, *President*
EMP: 22
SQ FT: 12,000
SALES (est): 4.9MM **Privately Held**
WEB: www.production-systems.com
SIC: 3549 Assembly machines, including
robotic

(P-14279)
QUARTET MECHANICS INC
4055 Clipper Ct, Fremont (94538-6540)
PHONE..................................510 490-1886
Henry Walter, *Principal*
EMP: 12
SALES (est): 2MM **Privately Held**
SIC: 3549 Assembly machines, including
robotic

(P-14280)
ROYAL SYSTEMS GROUP
18301 Napa St, Northridge (91325-3617)
PHONE..................................818 717-5010
Royal E Bush, *President*
EMP: 12
SALES (est): 2.4MM **Privately Held**
SIC: 3549 Metalworking machinery

(P-14281)
SAKE ROBOTICS
570 El Camino Real 150-3, Redwood City
(94063-1200)
PHONE..................................650 207-4021
Paul Ekas, *Principal*
EMP: 10
SALES (est): 769.1K **Privately Held**
SIC: 3549 Assembly machines, including
robotic

(P-14282)
**SUITABLE TECHNOLOGIES INC
(PA)**
921 E Charleston Rd, Palo Alto
(94303-4903)
PHONE..................................650 294-3170
Scott Wendell Hassan, *CEO*
David Lundmark, *COO*
Bo Preising, *Officer*
Milan Bhalala, *Vice Pres*
Sacha Zyto, *Sr Software Eng*
▲ EMP: 15
SALES (est): 4.3MM **Privately Held**
SIC: 3549 Assembly machines, including
robotic

(P-14283)
TELEDYNE INSTRUMENTS INC
Also Called: Teledyne Seabotix
14020 Stowe Dr, Poway (92064-6846)
PHONE..................................619 239-5959
EMP: 68
SALES (corp-wide): 2.9B **Publicly Held**
SIC: 3549 Propeller straightening presses
HQ: Teledyne Instruments, Inc.
1049 Camino Dos Rios
Thousand Oaks CA 91360
805 373-4545

(P-14284)
TUBE FORM SOLUTIONS LLC
Also Called: Eaton Leonard Tooling
43218 Bus Pk Dr Ste 202, Temecula
(92590-3601)
PHONE..................................760 599-5001

Jeff Jacobs,
EMP: 10
SALES (corp-wide): 18.4MM **Privately
Held**
SIC: 3549 3545 Metalworking machinery;
tools & accessories for machine tools
PA: Tube Form Solutions, Llc
435 Roske Dr
Elkhart IN 46516
574 295-5041

(P-14285)
UBTECH ROBOTICS CORP
767 S Alameda St, Los Angeles
(90021-1660)
PHONE..................................213 261-7153
John Rhee, *CEO*
EMP: 30
SALES: 10MM
SALES (corp-wide): 52MM **Privately
Held**
SIC: 3549 Assembly machines, including
robotic
PA: Ubtech Robotics Corp Ltd.
Floor 16,22, Building C1, Nanshan
Zhiyuan, No. 1001, Xueyuan Ave
Shenzhen 51810
755 834-7442

(P-14286)
WALLNER EXPAC INC (PA)
Also Called: W T E
1274 S Slater Cir, Ontario (91761-1522)
PHONE..................................909 481-8800
Sophia Wallner, *Ch of Bd*
Michael Wallner, *CEO*
Paul Wallner, *Vice Pres*
Susie Harney, *Purch Mgr*
◆ EMP: 55
SALES (est): 24MM **Privately Held**
WEB: www.expac.com
SIC: 3549 3542 Metalworking machinery;
machine tools, metal forming type

3552 Textile Machinery

(P-14287)
AUTOMETRIX INC
12098 Charles Dr, Grass Valley
(95945-8418)
PHONE..................................530 477-5065
John Palmer, *President*
John Yates, *Vice Pres*
Jeanna Zangara, *Office Mgr*
Jordan Hughes, *Technician*
True Pham, *Marketing Staff*
EMP: 18
SQ FT: 11,000
SALES (est): 5.3MM **Privately Held**
WEB: www.autometrix.com
SIC: 3552 Textile machinery

(P-14288)
DILCO INDUSTRIAL INC
205 E Bristol Ln, Orange (92865-2715)
PHONE..................................714 998-5266
Jay R Dille, *President*
Jay R Dille Jr, *Vice Pres*
Jay Dille, *Vice Pres*
Tina Dille, *Admin Sec*
Wil Palacios, *Prdtn Mgr*
EMP: 15
SQ FT: 6,000
SALES (est): 3.4MM **Privately Held**
SIC: 3552 3993 Silk screens for textile in-
dustry; signs & advertising specialties

(P-14289)
EVERPAC
Also Called: Eveready Pacific Corp
1499 Palmyrita Ave, Riverside
(92507-1600)
PHONE..................................951 774-3274
William R Johnson Jr, *President*
EMP: 54
SALES (est): 3.9MM
SALES (corp-wide): 205.9MM **Privately
Held**
WEB: www.johnson-machinery.com
SIC: 3552 Textile machinery
PA: Johnson Machinery Co.
800 E La Cadena Dr
Riverside CA 92507
951 686-4560

(P-14290)
**P&Y T-SHRTS SILK SCREENING
INC**
Also Called: American Printworks
2126 E 52nd St, Vernon (90058-3448)
P.O. Box 58742, Los Angeles (90058-0742)
PHONE..................................323 585-4604
Yossi Zaga, *President*
Linda Bates, *VP Opers*
EMP: 100
SQ FT: 35,000
SALES (est): 15.8MM **Privately Held**
WEB: www.hraco.com
SIC: 3552 5136 Silk screens for textile in-
dustry; shirts, men's & boys'

(P-14291)
PALACE TEXTILE INC
Also Called: Palace Textiles
8453 Terradell St, Pico Rivera
(90660-5042)
PHONE..................................323 587-7756
▲ EMP: 52
SQ FT: 26,000
SALES (est): 3.5MM **Privately Held**
SIC: 3552 2391 2211

(P-14292)
**PORTABLE SPNDLE REPR
SPCIALIST**
Also Called: Al's Machine Shop
10803 Fremont Ave Ste A, Ontario
(91762-3901)
PHONE..................................909 591-7220
Mark Twogood, *President*
Miguel Ramirez, *Vice Pres*
EMP: 15
SALES (est): 1.8MM **Privately Held**
SIC: 3552 Spindles, textile

(P-14293)
**STITCH CITY INDUSTRIES INC
(PA)**
Also Called: Garmentprinter.com
11823 Slauson Ave Ste 31, Santa Fe
Springs (90670-6525)
PHONE..................................562 408-6144
Fernando Padilla, *CEO*
Destiny Isenberg, *Marketing Mgr*
Arnold Gil, *Sales Staff*
EMP: 10
SQ FT: 2,000
SALES (est): 1.8MM **Privately Held**
SIC: 3552 7219 2396 Embroidery ma-
chines; garment making, alteration & re-
pair; printing & embossing on plastics
fabric articles

(P-14294)
SURFACE ENGINEERING SPC
919 Hamlin Ct, Sunnyvale (94089-1402)
PHONE..................................408 734-8810
Richard Peattie, *President*
Jane Peattie, *Vice Pres*
Brett Courtney, *Engineer*
David Rich, *Engineer*
EMP: 20 EST: 1976
SQ FT: 18,000
SALES (est): 5.8MM **Privately Held**
WEB: www.surfeng.com
SIC: 3552 7389 Spindles, textile; grinding,
precision: commercial or industrial

(P-14295)
TAJIMA USA INC
19925 S Susana Rd, Compton
(90221-5726)
PHONE..................................310 604-8200
Ron Krasnitz, *President*
▲ EMP: 25
SQ FT: 25,000
SALES (est): 3MM **Privately Held**
WEB: www.tajima.com
SIC: 3552 Embroidery machines
PA: Tajima Industries Ltd.
3-19-22, Shirakabe, Higashi-Ku
Nagoya AIC 461-0

(P-14296)
VERSICOLOR INC
Also Called: Versicolor Screenprinting
934 Calle Negocio Ste E, San Clemente
(92673-6210)
PHONE..................................949 361-9698

Mark Feiner, *President*
Sheila Feiner, *Admin Sec*
Cameron Cogan, *Prdtn Mgr*
EMP: 10
SQ FT: 10,000
SALES (est): 950K **Privately Held**
WEB: www.versicolorinc.com
SIC: 3552 2759 Silk screens for textile in-
dustry; screen printing

3553 Woodworking

(P-14297)
A-1 PLASTICS INCORPORATED
618 W Bradley Ave, El Cajon (92020-1214)
PHONE..................................619 444-9442
James Blakemore Jr, *CEO*
Mary R Blakemore, *Treasurer*
EMP: 12
SQ FT: 25,000
SALES: 2.1MM **Privately Held**
SIC: 3553 Cabinet makers' machinery

(P-14298)
KVAL INC
Also Called: Kval Machinery Co
825 Petaluma Blvd S, Petaluma
(94952-5134)
PHONE..................................707 762-4363
Gerald Kvalheim, *CEO*
Andrew M Kvalheim, *Treasurer*
Dave Kvalheim, *Vice Pres*
Mark Kvalheim, *Vice Pres*
Mark Smith, *Vice Pres*
▲ EMP: 125
SALES (est): 34.6MM **Privately Held**
WEB: www.kvalinc.com
SIC: 3553 5084 Woodworking machinery;
industrial machinery & equipment

(P-14299)
**PROFESSIONAL MCHY GROUP
INC**
1885 N Macarthur Dr, Tracy (95376-2820)
PHONE..................................209 832-0100
Kirk Gass, *President*
David Hegger, *Vice Pres*
EMP: 10
SQ FT: 18,000
SALES (est): 2.5MM **Privately Held**
WEB: www.professionalmachinery.com
SIC: 3553 Woodworking machinery

(P-14300)
VOORWOOD COMPANY
Also Called: Turbosand
2350 Barney Rd, Anderson (96007-4306)
PHONE..................................530 365-3311
Adam Britton, *CEO*
Larry Ackernecht, *Vice Pres*
Steve Shifflet, *Admin Sec*
Daniel Warfield, *Engineer*
Carole Corley, *Bookkeeper*
▼ EMP: 30
SQ FT: 60,000
SALES (est): 8.3MM **Privately Held**
WEB: www.turbosand.com
SIC: 3553 Woodworking machinery

(P-14301)
**WANESHEAR TECHNOLOGIES
LLC**
3471 N State St, Ukiah (95482-3080)
PHONE..................................707 462-4761
▼ EMP: 35
SALES: 2.5MM **Privately Held**
SIC: 3553

(P-14302)
WESTERN MOTOR WORKS INC
8332 Osage Ave, Los Angeles
(90045-4401)
PHONE..................................310 382-6896
Hamid Baher, *President*
EMP: 14
SALES (est): 1.9MM **Privately Held**
SIC: 3553 Woodworking machinery

PRODUCTS & SVCS

3554 Paper Inds Machinery

(P-14303)
ADVANCED LASER DIES INC
9629 Beverly Rd, Pico Rivera
(90660-2136)
PHONE.................................562 949-0081
Leo Denlea, *President*
Lisa Denlea, *Vice Pres*
Jerry Zinn, *Office Mgr*
EMP: 10
SQ FT: 5,200
SALES (est): 2MM **Privately Held**
WEB: www.advancedlaserdies.com
SIC: 3554 7373 Die cutting & stamping machinery, paper converting; computer-aided design (CAD) systems service

(P-14304)
CTRA INDUSTRIAL MACHINE
11817 Slauson Ave, Santa Fe Springs
(90670-2219)
PHONE.................................562 698-5188
Jeannine Aviles, *President*
EMP: 11
SQ FT: 8,142
SALES (est): 2.2MM **Privately Held**
SIC: 3554 Folding machines, paper

(P-14305)
ELLISON EDUCATIONAL EQP INC (PA)
Also Called: Sizzix
25862 Commercentre Dr, Lake Forest
(92630-8877)
PHONE.................................949 598-8822
Richard Birse, *CEO*
Kristin Highberg, *CEO*
Roxanne Tran, *Vice Pres*
▲ **EMP:** 60
SQ FT: 132,000
SALES (est): 22.9MM **Privately Held**
WEB: www.ellison.com
SIC: 3554 Cutting machines, paper

(P-14306)
G G C INC (PA)
Also Called: Enterprise Company
2624 Rousselle St, Santa Ana
(92707-3729)
PHONE.................................714 835-6530
Daniel C Gould, *CEO*
Orval Gould, *President*
John Drissen, *Corp Secy*
John A Gould, *Vice Pres*
▲ **EMP:** 44
SQ FT: 18,000
SALES (est): 7MM **Privately Held**
WEB: www.enterpriseco.com
SIC: 3554 3535 3523 3421 Paper industries machinery; conveyors & conveying equipment; farm machinery & equipment; cutlery

(P-14307)
G G C INC
Also Called: Enterprise Co
2624 Rousselle St, Santa Ana
(92707-3729)
PHONE.................................714 835-0551
Orbal Gould, *Manager*
EMP: 47
SALES (corp-wide): 7MM **Privately Held**
WEB: www.enterpriseco.com
SIC: 3554 7699 Paper industries machinery; industrial equipment services
PA: G G C, Inc.
　　2624 Rousselle St
　　Santa Ana CA 92707
　　714 835-6530

(P-14308)
GATSBY INC
2106 Ringwood Ave, San Jose
(95131-1715)
PHONE.................................408 573-8890
Vanvi Luong, *CEO*
Deanna Luong, *Principal*
▲ **EMP:** 10
SALES (est): 952.8K **Privately Held**
SIC: 3554 3542 3089 Fourdrinier machines, paper manufacturing; die casting machines; injection molding of plastics

(P-14309)
GEO M MARTIN COMPANY (PA)
1250 67th St, Emeryville (94608-1121)
PHONE.................................510 652-2200
Merrill D Martin, *CEO*
Robert A Morgan, *President*
Lillian Martin, *CFO*
George R Martin, *Exec VP*
Daniel J D'Angelo, *Vice Pres*
▲ **EMP:** 100
SQ FT: 50,000
SALES (est): 13.8MM **Privately Held**
WEB: www.geomartin.com
SIC: 3554 Corrugating machines, paper

(P-14310)
GEORGE M MARTIN CO
910 Folger Ave, Berkeley (94710-2820)
PHONE.................................510 652-2200
George Martin, *Principal*
George R Martin, *Principal*
EMP: 10
SALES (est): 1.6MM **Privately Held**
SIC: 3554 Paper industries machinery

(P-14311)
MOEN INDUSTRIES
10330 Pioneer Blvd # 235, Santa Fe
Springs (90670-6012)
PHONE.................................562 946-6381
Carl Moen, *President*
Lenard Moen, *Shareholder*
Bob Storms, *Director*
▲ **EMP:** 43
SQ FT: 38,400
SALES (est): 6.1MM
SALES (corp-wide): 53.9MM **Privately Held**
SIC: 3554 5084 3565 Box making machines, paper; industrial machinery & equipment; packaging machinery
PA: R. A. Pearson Company
　　8120 W Sunset Hwy
　　Spokane WA 99224
　　509 838-6226

(P-14312)
PREZANT COMPANY
Also Called: A A Prezant Discount Rbr Bands
940 S Amphlett Blvd, San Mateo
(94402-1801)
PHONE.................................650 342-7413
Shel M Prezant, *President*
Terri R Prezant, *Vice Pres*
EMP: 15
SQ FT: 18,000
SALES (est): 1.8MM **Privately Held**
SIC: 3554 2674 2671 3069 Fourdrinier machines, paper manufacturing; paper bags: made from purchased materials; plastic film, coated or laminated for packaging; rubber bands; plastic bags: made from purchased materials

3555 Printing Trades Machinery & Eqpt

(P-14313)
AMERICAN THERMOFORM CORP (PA)
1758 Brackett St, La Verne (91750-5855)
PHONE.................................909 593-6711
Gary S Nunnelly, *President*
Ruth Haggen, *Vice Pres*
Patrick Nunnelly, *Sales Mgr*
◆ **EMP:** 10 **EST:** 1961
SQ FT: 13,000
SALES (est): 1.7MM **Privately Held**
WEB: www.americanthermoform.com
SIC: 3555 Printing trades machinery

(P-14314)
ANAJET LLC
1100 Valencia Ave, Tustin (92780-6428)
PHONE.................................714 662-3200
Chase Roh, *President*
Juan Manzano, *Regional Mgr*
Chuck Northcutt, *Business Mgr*
Brandon Ebrahim, *Finance Mgr*
Heriberto Corona, *Opers Mgr*
▲ **EMP:** 20
SALES (est): 11.2MM **Privately Held**
SIC: 3555 Printing trades machinery

(P-14315)
APPLIED MANUFACTURING TECH INC
Also Called: Amtec
1464 N Hundley St Anaheim, Anaheim
(92806)
PHONE.................................714 630-9530
Hadi Lalani, *President*
▲ **EMP:** 11
SQ FT: 3,500
SALES (est): 3.1MM **Privately Held**
SIC: 3555 3542 3842 Printing trades machinery; marking machines; welders' hoods

(P-14316)
ASPE INC
42295 Avnida Alvrado Unit, Temecula
(92590)
PHONE.................................951 296-2595
Alexander Szyszko, *CEO*
Thomas Szyszko, *Vice Pres*
Mark Dito, *Sales Staff*
Matt Yeazel, *Sales Staff*
▲ **EMP:** 15
SALES (est): 2MM **Privately Held**
SIC: 3555 Printing trades machinery

(P-14317)
BAY CLASSIFIEDS INC
Also Called: Classified Flea Market
433 Hegenberger Rd # 205, Oakland
(94621-1448)
PHONE.................................510 636-1867
Steve Marini, *President*
EMP: 25
SALES (est): 2.8MM **Privately Held**
WEB: www.bayclassifieds.com
SIC: 3555 2711 Mats, advertising & newspaper; newspapers

(P-14318)
CAL PLATE (PA)
17110 Jersey Ave, Artesia (90701-2694)
PHONE.................................562 403-3000
Richard Borelli, *President*
EMP: 75 **EST:** 1966
SQ FT: 33,000
SALES (est): 23.1MM **Privately Held**
WEB: www.calplate.com
SIC: 3555 3423 3544 Printing plates; cutting dies, except metal cutting; special dies, tools, jigs & fixtures

(P-14319)
CONTAINER GRAPHICS CORP
1137 Graphics Dr, Modesto (95351-1501)
PHONE.................................209 577-0181
Brian Bennett, *Manager*
EMP: 60
SALES (corp-wide): 3MM **Privately Held**
WEB: www.containergraphics.com
SIC: 3555 Printing trades machinery
PA: Container Graphics Corp.
　　114 Ednbrgh S Dr Ste 104
　　Cary NC 27511
　　919 481-4200

(P-14320)
EXECUTIVE BUS SOLUTIONS INC
21356 Nordhoff St Ste 108, Chatsworth
(91311-6917)
PHONE.................................805 499-3290
Mohamad K Nassar, *CEO*
Tarek Nassar, *Financial Analy*
Jamie Royland, *Manager*
EMP: 12
SALES (est): 1.8MM **Privately Held**
SIC: 3555 Copy holders, printers'

(P-14321)
FISHER GRAPHIC INDS A CAL CORP
1137 Graphics Dr, Modesto (95351-1501)
PHONE.................................209 577-0181
Phillip Saunders, *President*
EMP: 400
SQ FT: 36,000
SALES (est): 2.7MM
SALES (corp-wide): 3MM **Privately Held**
WEB: www.containergraphics.com
SIC: 3555 2796 Printing plates; platemaking services

PA: Container Graphics Corp.
　　114 Ednbrgh S Dr Ste 104
　　Cary NC 27511
　　919 481-4200

(P-14322)
FOOT IMPRINT INC
15373 Proctor Ave, City of Industry
(91745-1022)
PHONE.................................626 991-4430
CHI Du, *President*
EMP: 50
SALES (est): 2MM **Privately Held**
SIC: 3555 Printing presses

(P-14323)
FORMALLOY TECHNOLOGIES INC
2810 Via Orange Way Ste A, Spring Valley
(91978-1741)
PHONE.................................619 377-9101
Melanie Lang,
Jeffrey Riemann,
EMP: 10
SALES (est): 227.3K **Privately Held**
SIC: 3555 8711 7372 3559 Printing trades machinery; mechanical engineering; prepackaged software; metal finishing equipment for plating, etc.

(P-14324)
HARRIS & BRUNO MACHINE CO INC (PA)
Also Called: Harris & Bruno International
8555 Washington Blvd, Roseville
(95678-5901)
PHONE.................................916 781-7676
Nick Bruno, *CEO*
Jackie Cabral, *Technical Staff*
Sean Tobler, *Technical Staff*
Jeremy N Dixon, *Electrical Engi*
Bryan Ball, *Engineer*
▲ **EMP:** 64 **EST:** 1944
SQ FT: 45,000
SALES (est): 26.2MM **Privately Held**
WEB: www.harris-bruno.com
SIC: 3555 Printing trades machinery

(P-14325)
HEIDELBERG INSTRUMENTS INC
2539 W 237th St Ste A, Torrance
(90505-5239)
PHONE.................................310 212-5071
Christian Bach, *President*
Gisela La Bella, *Officer*
EMP: 10
SALES: 1.5MM
SALES (corp-wide): 2.6B **Privately Held**
WEB: www.heidelberg-instruments.com
SIC: 3555 5084 Printing trades machinery; instruments & control equipment
HQ: Heidelberg Instruments Mikrotechnik
　　Gmbh
　　Tullastr. 2
　　Heidelberg 69126
　　622 134-300

(P-14326)
IKONG E-COMMERCE INC
385 S Lemon Ave Ste E429, Walnut
(91789-2727)
PHONE.................................888 556-1522
EMP: 10
SALES (est): 421.5K **Privately Held**
SIC: 3555

(P-14327)
IMPERIAL RUBBER PRODUCTS INC
5691 Gates St, Chino (91710-7603)
PHONE.................................909 393-0528
Ronald Hill, *CEO*
Bob Schwartz, *President*
Steve Huff, *Vice Pres*
▲ **EMP:** 35
SQ FT: 20,000
SALES (est): 8.9MM **Privately Held**
WEB: www.imprub.com
SIC: 3555 Printing trades machinery

▲ = Import ▼=Export
◆ =Import/Export

(P-14328)
K C PHOTO ENGRAVING COMPANY
712 Arrow Grand Cir, Covina (91722-2147)
PHONE..................................626 795-4127
Dan Curley, *President*
Sondra Slykhuis, *Corp Secy*
Steve Curley, *Vice Pres*
Jeff Curley, *Accountant*
Sheri Busbee, *Bookkeeper*
EMP: 12 EST: 1963
SQ FT: 23,000
SALES (est): 4.3MM **Privately Held**
WEB: www.kcpe.net
SIC: 3555 2796 2791 Plates, offset; pho-
toengraving plates, linecuts or halftones;
typesetting

(P-14329)
KERNING DATA SYSTEMS INC
9301 Jordan Ave Ste 102, Chatsworth
(91311-5863)
PHONE..................................818 882-8712
Quentin Leef, *President*
EMP: 13
SALES (est): 2.4MM **Privately Held**
WEB: www.kerningdata.com
SIC: 3555 1731 Printing trades machinery;
computer installation

(P-14330)
LITH-O-ROLL CORPORATION
9521 Telstar Ave, El Monte (91731-2994)
P.O. Box 5328 (91734-1328)
PHONE..................................626 579-0340
Rita Sepe, *President*
Jeff Espett, *Vice Pres*
Chris Murray, *Marketing Staff*
Edward Gump, *Manager*
EMP: 50
SQ FT: 30,000
SALES (est): 10.3MM **Privately Held**
SIC: 3555 Printing trades machinery

(P-14331)
MACDERMID PRTG SOLUTIONS LLC
260 S Pacific St, San Marcos
(92078-2461)
PHONE..................................760 510-6277
Lori Chapman, *Branch Mgr*
EMP: 76
SALES (corp-wide): 1.9B **Publicly Held**
SIC: 3555 Printing plates
HQ: Macdermid Graphics Solutions, Llc
5210 Phillip Lee Dr Sw
Atlanta GA 30336

(P-14332)
OCE DSPLAY GRPHICS SYSTEMS INC
2811 Orchard Pkwy, San Jose
(95134-2013)
PHONE..................................773 714-8500
▼ EMP: 100
SALES (est): 34.5K
SALES (corp-wide): 30.7B **Privately Held**
SIC: 3555 3577
HQ: Oce Holding B.V.
Sint Urbanusweg 43
Venlo 5914
773 592-222

(P-14333)
ONE TOUCH SOLUTIONS INC
Also Called: One Touch Office Technology
370 Amapola Ave Ste 106, Torrance
(90501-7241)
PHONE..................................310 320-6868
William Rees, *CEO*
Jayson Beasley, *COO*
Mark Stratton, *CFO*
Arvin Gungap, *Executive*
Breanna Rees, *Sales Staff*
EMP: 15
SQ FT: 5,182
SALES (est): 6.1MM **Privately Held**
SIC: 3555 Printing trades machinery

(P-14334)
PACIFIC BARCODE INC
27531 Enterprise Cir W 201c, Temecula
(92590-4888)
PHONE..................................951 587-8717

Michael Meadors, *President*
Michelle Meadors, *Vice Pres*
Buckley Ross, *Opers Mgr*
Phil Peretz, *Sales Mgr*
Sandi Mathews, *Sales Staff*
EMP: 15 EST: 1999
SQ FT: 8,600
SALES (est): 4.2MM **Privately Held**
WEB: www.pacificbarcode.com
SIC: 3555 2759 3565 3577 Printing
trades machinery; commercial printing; la-
beling machines, industrial; bar code
(magnetic ink) printers

(P-14335)
PAMARCO GLOBAL GRAPHICS INC
Also Called: Pamarco Western
6907 Marlin Cir, La Palma (90623-1018)
PHONE..................................714 739-0700
Richard Shields, *Manager*
EMP: 29 **Privately Held**
SIC: 3555 Printing trades machinery
HQ: Pamarco Global Graphics, Inc.
235 E 11th Ave
Roselle NJ 07203
908 241-1200

(P-14336)
PARA PLATE & PLASTICS CO INC
15910 Shoemaker Ave, Cerritos
(90703-2200)
PHONE..................................562 404-3434
Shane Pearson, *President*
Robert J Clapp, *President*
John Greenamyer, *Treasurer*
Steve Binnard, *Vice Pres*
Barbara Kishiyama, *Controller*
EMP: 27 EST: 1945
SQ FT: 17,000
SALES (est): 3MM **Privately Held**
SIC: 3555 7336 2796 Printing plates;
commercial art & graphic design;
platemaking services

(P-14337)
PHOTOSTONE LLC
Also Called: Stone Impressions
8495 Redwood Creek Ln, San Diego
(92126-1068)
PHONE..................................858 274-3400
Gregory Smith,
Gregory T Smith,
Melinda Smith,
EMP: 10
SALES (est): 1.8MM **Privately Held**
WEB: www.photostone.com
SIC: 3555 Lithographic stones

(P-14338)
PIC MANUFACTURING INC
410 Sherwood Rd, Paso Robles
(93446-3554)
P.O. Box 665 (93447-0665)
PHONE..................................805 238-5451
Michael D Camp, *President*
EMP: 16 EST: 1962
SQ FT: 9,000
SALES (est): 2.4MM **Privately Held**
SIC: 3555 Printing trade parts & attach-
ments

(P-14339)
QUINTEL CORPORATION
685 Jarvis Dr Ste A, Morgan Hill
(95037-2813)
PHONE..................................408 776-5190
Jeffrey C Lane, *President*
Howard Green, *Chief Mktg Ofcr*
Robert Borawski, *Admin Sec*
Keith Radousky, *CTO*
EMP: 20 EST: 1978
SQ FT: 12,500
SALES (est): 3.3MM **Privately Held**
WEB: www.quintelcorp.com
SIC: 3555 Printing trades machinery

(P-14340)
RIMA ENTERPRISES INC
Also Called: Rima-System
5340 Argosy Ave, Huntington Beach
(92649-1037)
PHONE..................................714 893-4534
Horst K Steinhart, *CEO*
John Kipp, *Technical Mgr*

Jeff Schwarz, *Engineer*
Venu Sunkara, *Opers Staff*
Rema Sheth, *Director*
▲ EMP: 62
SQ FT: 50,000
SALES (est): 12.3MM **Privately Held**
WEB: www.rimasystem.com
SIC: 3555 Bookbinding machinery

(P-14341)
THISTLE ROLLER CO INC
209 Van Norman Rd, Montebello
(90640-5393)
PHONE..................................323 685-5322
Lizbeth Karpynec, *CEO*
Eric Karpynetz, *Vice Pres*
Luis Lopez, *Safety Mgr*
▲ EMP: 35
SQ FT: 45,000
SALES (est): 9.3MM **Privately Held**
SIC: 3555 3312 2796 Printing trades ma-
chinery; blast furnaces & steel mills;
platemaking services

(P-14342)
XEROX INTERNATIONAL PARTNERS (DH)
Also Called: Fuji Xerox
3174 Porter Dr, Palo Alto (94304-1212)
PHONE..................................408 953-2700
Sunil Gupta, *Partner*
▲ EMP: 50
SALES (est): 15.1MM
SALES (corp-wide): 405.1MM **Publicly Held**
WEB: www.xerox.com
SIC: 3555 Leads, printers'
HQ: Xerox Corporation
201 Merritt 7
Norwalk CT 06851
203 968-3000

┌─────────────────────────────┐
│ **3556 Food Prdts Machinery** │
└─────────────────────────────┘

(P-14343)
ALUMINUM PROS INC
Also Called: Malco Manufacturing
13917 S Main St, Los Angeles
(90061-2151)
PHONE..................................310 366-7696
Fax: 310 366-7694
EMP: 12 EST: 2011
SALES (est): 970K **Privately Held**
SIC: 3556

(P-14344)
APEX BREWING SUPPLY
3237 Rippey Rd Ste 600, Loomis
(95650-7662)
PHONE..................................916 250-7950
Joseph Fredrickson, *President*
▲ EMP: 10
SQ FT: 15,000
SALES (est): 4MM **Privately Held**
SIC: 3556 Food products machinery

(P-14345)
ATLAS PACIFIC ENGINEERING CO
Also Called: Sinclair Systems
3115 S Willow Ave, Fresno (93725-9349)
PHONE..................................559 233-4500
Don Freeman, *Principal*
Liliana Castillo, *Relations*
EMP: 60
SALES (corp-wide): 93.8MM **Privately Held**
WEB: www.atlaspacific.com
SIC: 3556 Food products machinery
HQ: Atlas Pacific Engineering Company
1 Atlas Ave
Pueblo CO 81001
719 948-3040

(P-14346)
ATLAS PACIFIC ENGINEERING CO
4500 N Star Way, Modesto (95356-9534)
PHONE..................................209 574-9884
Regina Webster, *Principal*
EMP: 44

SALES (corp-wide): 93.8MM **Privately Held**
WEB: www.atlaspacific.com
SIC: 3556 5046 Food products machinery;
commercial equipment
HQ: Atlas Pacific Engineering Company
1 Atlas Ave
Pueblo CO 81001
719 948-3040

(P-14347)
AVALON MFG CO INCOIRPORATED
509 Bateman Cir, Corona (92880-2012)
PHONE..................................951 340-0280
Bill Enger, *President*
Troy Enger, *Vice Pres*
Kyle Enger, *Engineer*
EMP: 14 EST: 1976
SQ FT: 19,277
SALES (est): 3.2MM **Privately Held**
WEB: www.enger.com
SIC: 3556 Bakery machinery
PA: Enger, Inc.
509 Bateman Cir
Corona CA 92880

(P-14348)
BHOGART LLC
1919 Monterey Hwy Ste 80, San Jose
(95112-6147)
PHONE..................................855 553-3887
Kimberly Schaefer, *Partner*
Kevin Dolan, *Partner*
Thomas Lynch, *CEO*
David Schaefer, *CTO*
EMP: 38
SALES (est): 7.7MM **Privately Held**
SIC: 3556 Smokers, food processing
equipment

(P-14349)
BILLINGTON WELDING & MFG INC
Also Called: Bwm
1442 N Emerald Ave, Modesto
(95351-1115)
P.O. Box 4460 (95352-4460)
PHONE..................................209 526-0846
Timothy Ryan Billington, *CEO*
Francis Billington, *President*
EMP: 60
SQ FT: 26,000
SALES (est): 13.8MM **Privately Held**
WEB: www.hopkinsbwm.com
SIC: 3556 3535 Food products machinery;
conveyors & conveying equipment

(P-14350)
BIOSYNTHETIC TECHNOLOGIES LLC (HQ)
Also Called: Lubrigreen
2 Park Plz Ste 200, Irvine (92614-8569)
P.O. Box 856, Malta MT (59538-0856)
PHONE..................................949 390-5910
Allen Barbieri,
Bruce Marley, *Vice Pres*
Peter Harker, *Info Tech Dir*
Travis Thompson, *Research*
Michael Rabbass, *Broker*
EMP: 13
SQ FT: 4,800
SALES (est): 1.5MM
SALES (corp-wide): 3.5B **Publicly Held**
WEB: www.peaksandprairies.com
SIC: 3556 Oilseed crushing & extracting
machinery
PA: Calumet Specialty Products Partners
Lp
2780 Wtrfront Pkwy E Dr S
Indianapolis IN 46214
317 328-5660

(P-14351)
BLENTECH CORPORATION
2899 Dowd Dr, Santa Rosa (95407-7897)
PHONE..................................707 523-5949
Darrell Horn, *President*
Gina Muelrath, *President*
Daniel Voit, *COO*
Joseph Yarnall, *Exec VP*
Sandy Louke, *Admin Asst*
▲ EMP: 60
SQ FT: 27,000

P R O D U C T S & S V C S

SALES (est): 18.6MM **Privately Held**
WEB: www.blentech.com
SIC: **3556** Mixers, commercial, food; meat processing machinery; poultry processing machinery; pasta machinery

(P-14352)
BLUE NALU INC
Also Called: Bluenalu
6197 Cornerstone Ct E, San Diego (92121-4718)
PHONE..................................858 703-8703
Henry Louis Cooperhouse, *CEO*
Chris Somogyi, *Chairman*
EMP: 12
SALES (est): 2.5MM **Privately Held**
SIC: **3556** Fish & shellfish processing machinery

(P-14353)
CAPNA FABRICATION
Also Called: Capna Systems
15148 Bledsoe St, Sylmar (91342-3807)
PHONE..................................888 416-6777
Vitaly Mekk, *CEO*
Gene Galyuk, *CTO*
EMP: 30
SALES (est): 5.8MM **Privately Held**
SIC: **3556** Oilseed crushing & extracting machinery

(P-14354)
CASA HERRERA INC (PA)
2655 Pine St, Pomona (91767-2115)
PHONE..................................909 392-3930
Michael L Herrera, *CEO*
Alfred J Herrera, *President*
Ronald L Meade, *President*
Susan A Herrera, *Treasurer*
Frank J Herrera, *Exec VP*
◆ EMP: 136 EST: 1970
SQ FT: 100,000
SALES (est): 23.9MM **Privately Held**
WEB: www.casaherrera.com
SIC: **3556** Food products machinery

(P-14355)
CHOOLJIAN & SONS INC
Also Called: Del Ray Packaging
Del Rey Ave, Del Rey (93616)
P.O. Box 160 (93616-0160)
PHONE..................................559 888-2031
Gerald Chooljian, *Corp Secy*
EMP: 60
SQ FT: 1,152
SALES (corp-wide): 29.1MM **Privately Held**
SIC: **3556** Dehydrating equipment, food processing
PA: Chooljian & Sons, Inc.
5287 S Del Rey Ave
Del Rey CA 93616
559 888-2031

(P-14356)
COMMERCIAL MANUFACTURING
2432 S Railroad Ave, Fresno (93706-5108)
P.O. Box 947 (93714-0947)
PHONE..................................559 237-1855
Larry Hagopian, *President*
Charles Uju, *CIO*
Michael Tarver, *Engineer*
EMP: 45
SQ FT: 45,000
SALES (est): 11.3MM **Privately Held**
WEB: www.commercialmfg.com
SIC: **3556** Food products machinery

(P-14357)
CRIVELLER CALIFORNIA CORP
185 Grant Ave, Healdsburg (95448-9539)
PHONE..................................707 431-2211
Bruno Criveller, *President*
Mario Creveller, *Vice Pres*
Robert Begin, *Sales Staff*
Aaron Belluomini, *Accounts Exec*
▲ EMP: 15
SALES: 5MM **Privately Held**
SIC: **3556** Brewers' & maltsters' machinery

(P-14358)
CURRIE MACHINERY CO INC
1731 Cabana Dr, San Jose (95125-5504)
P.O. Box 192, Santa Clara (95052-0192)
PHONE..................................408 727-0422

SALES (est): 14.9MM **Privately Held**
Donald W Currie, *President*
Patrick Bradley, *Vice Pres*
EMP: 100 EST: 1919
SALES (est): 1.5MM **Privately Held**
WEB: www.currie.net
SIC: **3556** 5084 3537 3535 Food products machinery; industrial machinery & equipment; industrial trucks & tractors; conveyors & conveying equipment; farm machinery & equipment

(P-14359)
DALE GROVE CORPORATION
Also Called: Gdc
1501 Stone Creek Dr, San Jose (95132-1933)
PHONE..................................408 251-7220
Stephanie Mattos, *CEO*
John R Mattos, *Vice Pres*
Ruth Howell, *Bookkeeper*
EMP: 36
SQ FT: 28,000
SALES (est): 5.9MM **Privately Held**
WEB: www.grovedale.com
SIC: **3556** 3535 3429 Food products machinery; conveyors & conveying equipment; manufactured hardware (general)

(P-14360)
EMILIOMITI LLC
2129 Harrison St, San Francisco (94110-1321)
PHONE..................................415 621-1171
Emilio Mitidieri, *Mng Member*
Reama Barclay, *Manager*
▲ EMP: 13 EST: 1979
SQ FT: 5,000
SALES (est): 2MM **Privately Held**
SIC: **3556** Pasta machinery

(P-14361)
FOOD EQUIPMENT MFG CO
Also Called: Femco
175 Mitchell Rd, Hollister (95023-9603)
P.O. Box 257 (95024-0257)
PHONE..................................831 637-1624
Sal Felice, *President*
Elizabeth Felice, *Treasurer*
EMP: 12
SQ FT: 2,800
SALES (est): 2.3MM **Privately Held**
SIC: **3556** Food products machinery

(P-14362)
FOOD MAKERS BAKERY EQP INC
16019 Adelante St, Irwindale (91702-3255)
PHONE..................................626 358-1343
Tom Fowler, *Principal*
Linda Fowler, *Admin Sec*
Garry Garcia, *Sales Mgr*
▲ EMP: 40
SQ FT: 51,000
SALES (est): 11MM **Privately Held**
WEB: www.foodmakersequipment.com
SIC: **3556** Bakery machinery

(P-14363)
FOODTOOLS CONSOLIDATED INC (PA)
315 Laguna St, Santa Barbara (93101-1716)
PHONE..................................805 962-8383
Martin Grano, *Ch of Bd*
Matt Browne, *Vice Pres*
Doug Petrovich, *Vice Pres*
Tashia Honcharenko, *Office Mgr*
Ilan Amzallag, *Technology*
◆ EMP: 48
SQ FT: 8,500
SALES (est): 11.1MM **Privately Held**
WEB: www.foodtools.com
SIC: **3556** 2679 Slicers, commercial, food; paper products, converted

(P-14364)
FOTIS AND SON IMPORTS INC
15451 Electronic Ln, Huntington Beach (92649-1333)
PHONE..................................714 894-9022
Peter Georgatsos, *President*
Laura Georgatsos, *Corp Secy*
Russ Hillas, *Exec VP*
Eleni Hillas, *Principal*
▲ EMP: 50
SQ FT: 34,000

SALES (est): 14.9MM **Privately Held**
WEB: www.greekfoodandwine.com
SIC: **3556** Food products machinery

(P-14365)
FPEC CORPORATION A CAL CORP (PA)
Also Called: Food Processing Equipment Co
13623 Pumice St, Santa Fe Springs (90670-5105)
PHONE..................................562 802-3727
Alan Davison, *CEO*
Ethel Davison, *Corp Secy*
Tom Kearney, *Controller*
Margo Blunk, *Human Res Mgr*
Sean Davison, *Marketing Staff*
EMP: 18
SQ FT: 18,000
SALES (est): 9.9MM **Privately Held**
WEB: www.fpec.com
SIC: **3556** Food products machinery

(P-14366)
G & I ISLAS INDUSTRIES INC (PA)
Also Called: G & I Industries
12860 Schabarum Ave, Baldwin Park (91706-6801)
P.O. Box 1262 (91706-7262)
PHONE..................................626 960-5020
Gonzalo R Islas, *CEO*
Sara Islas, *Vice Pres*
▲ EMP: 27
SQ FT: 12,500
SALES (est): 5.4MM **Privately Held**
SIC: **3556** 5084 Bakery machinery; food industry machinery

(P-14367)
GENERIC MANUFACTURING CORP
27455 Bostik Ct, Temecula (92590-3698)
PHONE..................................951 296-2838
Lonnie Belt, *President*
EMP: 10
SQ FT: 20,000
SALES (est): 1.9MM **Privately Held**
SIC: **3556** Food products machinery

(P-14368)
GERARD H TANZI INC
Also Called: Industrial Machining Co
22555 Sawmill Flat Rd, Columbia (95310)
P.O. Box 1159 (95310-1159)
PHONE..................................209 532-0855
Gerard H Tanzi, *President*
EMP: 10
SQ FT: 2,000
SALES (est): 1.4MM **Privately Held**
SIC: **3556** 3724 Smokers, food processing equipment; aircraft engines & engine parts

(P-14369)
GOLDEN PACIFIC SEAFOODS INC
700 S Raymond Ave, Fullerton (92831-5233)
PHONE..................................714 589-8888
Tony Zavala, *President*
EMP: 65
SALES: 10MM **Privately Held**
SIC: **3556** Meat, poultry & seafood processing machinery

(P-14370)
HACKETT INDUSTRIES INC
Also Called: West Star Industries
4445 E Fremont St, Stockton (95215-4007)
PHONE..................................209 955-8220
Michelle E Focke, *CEO*
Richard Hackett, *President*
Mark Lathrop, *CFO*
Carolyn Hackett, *Admin Sec*
EMP: 43
SQ FT: 90,000
SALES (est): 8.8MM **Privately Held**
SIC: **3556** 3444 3431 Food products machinery; sheet metalwork; metal sanitary ware

(P-14371)
HAYWARD GORDON US INC
9351 Industrial Way, Adelanto (92301-3932)
PHONE..................................760 246-3430
EMP: 42
SALES (corp-wide): 41.9MM **Privately Held**
SIC: **3556** Cutting, chopping, grinding, mixing & similar machinery; mixers, feed, except agricultural
HQ: Hayward Gordon Us, Inc.
1541 S 92nd Pl
Seattle WA 98108
206 767-5660

(P-14372)
HEPHAESTUS INNOVATIONS
2661 W Bch St Ste 3b Suit, Watsonville (95076)
PHONE..................................831 254-8555
Jessica Garcia, *President*
EMP: 12
SALES (est): 714K **Privately Held**
SIC: **3556** Dehydrating equipment, food processing

(P-14373)
HUD INDUSTRIES
2104 W Rosecrans Ave, Gardena (90249-2990)
PHONE..................................310 327-7110
Pete Breum Jr, *President*
Rhonda Breum, *Office Mgr*
EMP: 13
SQ FT: 20,000
SALES (est): 2MM **Privately Held**
SIC: **3556** Food products machinery

(P-14374)
ICE LINK LLC
954 N Batavia St, Orange (92867-5589)
PHONE..................................714 771-6580
Eric Berge, *Mng Member*
Mary Palomino, *Executive*
EMP: 12
SALES (est): 1.5MM **Privately Held**
SIC: **3556** Food products machinery

(P-14375)
INTERSTATE MEAT CO INC
Also Called: Sterling Pacific Meat Co.
6114 Scott Way, Commerce (90040-3518)
PHONE..................................323 838-9400
James T Asher, *President*
Luis Munoz, *Vice Pres*
EMP: 16
SALES (est): 3.4MM **Privately Held**
SIC: **3556** Meat processing machinery

(P-14376)
J C FORD COMPANY
Also Called: JC Ford
901 S Leslie St, La Habra (90631-6841)
PHONE..................................714 871-7361
Scott D Ruhe, *CEO*
Orlando Hurtado, *Engineer*
Jane Baker, *Controller*
Robert Meyer, *VP Sales*
Kyle Armstrong, *Sales Mgr*
◆ EMP: 95
SQ FT: 80,000
SALES (est): 41.5MM **Privately Held**
WEB: www.jcford.com
SIC: **3556** Food products machinery
PA: Ruhe Corporation
901 S Leslie St
La Habra CA 90631

(P-14377)
JOHN BEAN TECHNOLOGIES CORP
Also Called: Jbt Food Tech Madera
2300 W Industrial Ave, Madera (93637-5210)
PHONE..................................559 661-3200
Eric Madsen, *Branch Mgr*
Nemesio Boquiren, *Engineer*
William Bayliss, *Business Mgr*
Brian Reed, *Marketing Staff*
EMP: 165 **Publicly Held**
SIC: **3556** Food products machinery

▲ = Import ▼=Export
◆ =Import/Export

PA: John Bean Technologies Corporation
70 W Madison St Ste 4400
Chicago IL 60602

(P-14378)
JOHN BEAN TECHNOLOGIES CORP
1660 Iowa Ave Ste 100, Riverside
(92507-0501)
P.O. Box 5710 (92517-5710)
PHONE...............................951 222-2300
Thomas Brickweg, *Principal*
Bill Williams, *Mfg Staff*
EMP: 50 **Publicly Held**
SIC: 3556 3542 3523 Dairy & milk machinery; nail heading machines; dairy equipment (farm)
PA: John Bean Technologies Corporation
70 W Madison St Ste 4400
Chicago IL 60602

(P-14379)
JOHN BEAN TECHNOLOGIES CORP
9829 W Legacy Ave, Visalia (93291-9544)
PHONE...............................559 651-8300
Billy Wofferd, *Branch Mgr*
Dana Dillard, *Manager*
EMP: 108 **Publicly Held**
SIC: 3556 Food products machinery
PA: John Bean Technologies Corporation
70 W Madison St Ste 4400
Chicago IL 60602

(P-14380)
JUICEBOT & CO LLC
999 Corporate Dr Ste 100, Ladera Ranch
(92694-2149)
PHONE...............................651 270-8860
Kamal Mohammand, *Mng Member*
EMP: 10
SALES (est): 421.5K **Privately Held**
SIC: 3556 2037 Juice extractors, fruit & vegetable: commercial type; fruit juices

(P-14381)
JUICY WHIP INC
1668 Curtiss Ct, La Verne (91750-5848)
PHONE...............................909 392-7500
Gus Stratton, *President*
▲ **EMP:** 28
SQ FT: 23,000
SALES (est): 7.2MM **Privately Held**
WEB: www.juicywhip.com
SIC: 3556 2033 Beverage machinery; fruit juices: fresh

(P-14382)
LAWRENCE EQUIPMENT INC (PA)
2034 Peck Rd, El Monte (91733-3727)
PHONE...............................626 442-2894
John Lawrence, *CEO*
Jack Kirkpatrick, *Shareholder*
Linda Lawrence, *Vice Pres*
Glenn Shelton, *Vice Pres*
Karen Foster, *Info Tech Dir*
▲ **EMP:** 200
SQ FT: 50,000
SALES (est): 98.3MM **Privately Held**
WEB: www.lawrenceequipment.com
SIC: 3556 Flour mill machinery

(P-14383)
MACHINE BUILDING SPECIALTIES
Also Called: Conveyor Concepts
1977 Blake Ave, Los Angeles (90039-3832)
PHONE...............................323 666-8289
Charles Conaway, *Ch of Bd*
Dennis James Conaway, *President*
Sharon Conaway, *Treasurer*
Sandra Conaway, *Admin Sec*
EMP: 25 **EST:** 1960
SQ FT: 17,000
SALES (est): 5.5MM **Privately Held**
SIC: 3556 3535 Bakery machinery; belt conveyor systems, general industrial use

(P-14384)
MARTIN ENGINEERING CO INC
5454 2nd St, Irwindale (91706-2000)
PHONE...............................626 960-5153
Jonathan Martin, *President*
Joanne Hughes, *Manager*
EMP: 15 **EST:** 1960
SQ FT: 10,000
SALES: 3MM **Privately Held**
SIC: 3556 Food products machinery

(P-14385)
MEAT PACKERS BUTCHERS SUP INC
Also Called: Mpbs Industries
2820 E Washington Blvd, Los Angeles (90023-4274)
PHONE...............................323 268-8514
Jimmy Jin, *CEO*
Shaofa Jin, *Ch of Bd*
Maricel Salvacion, *Webmaster*
Pat Ward, *Regl Sales Mgr*
▲ **EMP:** 17
SQ FT: 16,000
SALES (est): 4.1MM **Privately Held**
WEB: www.mpbs.com
SIC: 3556 Food products machinery

(P-14386)
MIGHTY SOY INC
1227 S Eastern Ave, Los Angeles (90022-4809)
PHONE...............................323 266-6969
Maung Myint, *President*
Gin Yee Lee, *Vice Pres*
EMP: 14 **EST:** 1980
SQ FT: 8,000
SALES: 485.9K **Privately Held**
SIC: 3556 2099 2075 Smokers, food processing equipment; food preparations; soybean oil mills

(P-14387)
MONTEREY COAST BREWING LLC
165 Main St, Salinas (93901-3403)
PHONE...............................831 758-2337
Charles Lloyd,
Lucy Lloyd,
EMP: 12
SALES (est): 1.5MM **Privately Held**
SIC: 3556 Brewers' & maltsters' machinery

(P-14388)
NATIONAL BAND SAW COMPANY
1055 W Avenue L12, Lancaster (93534-7045)
PHONE...............................661 294-9552
Harley Frank, *President*
Norman Frank, *Ch of Bd*
▲ **EMP:** 17
SQ FT: 12,000
SALES (est): 3.8MM **Privately Held**
WEB: www.nbsparts.com
SIC: 3556 Meat processing machinery

(P-14389)
O H I COMPANY
820 S Pershing Ave, Stockton (95206-1176)
P.O. Box 622 (95201-0622)
PHONE...............................209 466-8921
Thomas W Hubbard, *CEO*
Ben Wallace, *Vice Pres*
▲ **EMP:** 26 **EST:** 1970
SQ FT: 40,000
SALES (est): 8.1MM **Privately Held**
WEB: www.ohicompany.com
SIC: 3556 3443 Food products machinery; fabricated plate work (boiler shop)

(P-14390)
PACIFIC PACKAGING MCHY LLC
Also Called: Pack West Machinery
200 River Rd, Corona (92880-1435)
PHONE...............................951 393-2200
Gerald Carpino, *CEO*
Jerry Carpino, *President*
Mario Bele, *Project Mgr*
Tiffany Flowers, *Engineer*
Ann Tau, *Bookkeeper*
▲ **EMP:** 25 **EST:** 1962
SQ FT: 30,000

SALES (est): 3.6MM
SALES (corp-wide): 587.9MM **Privately Held**
WEB: www.pacificpak.com
SIC: 3556 3565 Food products machinery; packaging machinery
PA: Pro Mach, Inc.
50 E Rivercntr Blvd 180
Covington KY 41011
513 831-8778

(P-14391)
PACKERS MANUFACTURING INC
4212 W Hemlock Ave, Visalia (93277-6902)
PHONE...............................559 732-4886
Dwight Plumley, *President*
Teddy A Plumley, *Treasurer*
EMP: 24
SQ FT: 22,250
SALES (est): 3.8MM **Privately Held**
SIC: 3556 7699 Packing house machinery; industrial machinery & equipment repair

(P-14392)
PHANTOM CARRIAGE BREWERY
18525 S Main St, Gardena (90248-4611)
PHONE...............................310 538-5834
Jack Wignot, *CEO*
Martin Seab, *General Mgr*
EMP: 25
SALES (est): 2.3MM **Privately Held**
SIC: 3556 Brewers' & maltsters' machinery

(P-14393)
POTENTIAL DESIGN INC
4185 E Jefferson Ave, Fresno (93725-9707)
P.O. Box 69, Fowler (93625-0069)
PHONE...............................559 834-5361
William Tjerrild, *President*
Jim J Tjerrild, *CFO*
▼ **EMP:** 17
SQ FT: 20,000
SALES (est): 9.1MM **Privately Held**
WEB: www.lonesomegeorge.com
SIC: 3556 Packing house machinery

(P-14394)
PURATOS CORPORATION
Also Called: Puratos West Coast
18831 S Laurel Park Rd, Compton (90220-6004)
PHONE...............................310 632-1361
Carlos Figuerido, *Manager*
EMP: 30
SALES (corp-wide): 30.1MM **Privately Held**
WEB: www.puratos.com
SIC: 3556 7699 5046 2041 Bakery machinery; restaurant equipment repair; bakery equipment & supplies; flour & other grain mill products
HQ: Puratos Corporation
1660 Suckle Hwy
Pennsauken NJ 08110

(P-14395)
RBM CONVEYOR SYSTEMS INC
1570 W Mission Blvd, Pomona (91766-1247)
PHONE...............................909 620-1333
Roobik Kureghian, *President*
Armine Kureghian, *Treasurer*
Emin Kureghian, *Sales Executive*
▲ **EMP:** 20
SQ FT: 40,000
SALES (est): 6.7MM **Privately Held**
WEB: www.rbmcsi.com
SIC: 3556 8711 3537 3535 Food products machinery; engineering services; industrial trucks & tractors; conveyors & conveying equipment

(P-14396)
REXNORD INDUSTRIES LLC
Also Called: Industrial Components Div
2175 Union Pl, Simi Valley (93065-1661)
PHONE...............................805 583-5514
Dave Kleinhaus, *Manager*
EMP: 152 **Publicly Held**

SIC: 3556 3568 Food products machinery; couplings, shaft: rigid, flexible, universal joint, etc.
HQ: Rexnord Industries, Llc
247 W Freshwater Way # 200
Milwaukee WI 53204
414 643-3000

(P-14397)
RIPON MFG CO
Also Called: RMC
652 S Stockton Ave, Ripon (95366-2798)
PHONE...............................209 599-2148
Glenn Navarro, *President*
Ursula Navarro, *Corp Secy*
EMP: 20
SQ FT: 45,000
SALES (est): 5.7MM **Privately Held**
WEB: www.riponmfgco
SIC: 3556 3535 Food products machinery; conveyors & conveying equipment

(P-14398)
RMJV LP
Also Called: Fresh Creative Foods
3285 Corporate Vw, Vista (92081-8528)
PHONE...............................503 526-5752
Diana Robertson, *Partner*
Jorge Villalobos, *General Mgr*
Justin Grizzle, *Administration*
Blair Capen, *Research*
Patricia Duenas, *Human Res Mgr*
EMP: 300
SQ FT: 35,000
SALES (est): 100.3MM
SALES (corp-wide): 1.6B **Privately Held**
SIC: 3556 Food products machinery
PA: Reser's Fine Foods, Inc.
15570 Sw Jenkins Rd
Beaverton OR 97006
503 643-6431

(P-14399)
SC BEVERAGE INC
2300 Peck Rd, City of Industry (90601-1601)
PHONE...............................562 463-8918
Gilbert Ortega, *President*
Christopher Munguia, *Vice Pres*
EMP: 20
SALES (est): 3MM **Privately Held**
WEB: www.scbeverage.com
SIC: 3556 Brewers' & maltsters' machinery

(P-14400)
SHAVER SPECIALTY COINC
20608 Earl St, Torrance (90503-3009)
PHONE...............................310 370-6941
George Shaver, *President*
Ronald Shaver, *Vice Pres*
▲ **EMP:** 22 **EST:** 1937
SQ FT: 20,000
SALES (est): 3.6MM **Privately Held**
WEB: www.shaverengines.com
SIC: 3556 3599 Choppers, commercial, food; machine shop, jobbing & repair

(P-14401)
SPX FLOW US LLC
26561 Rancho Pkwy S, Lake Forest (92630-8301)
PHONE...............................949 455-8150
Brian Ahern, *Manager*
EMP: 67
SALES (corp-wide): 2B **Publicly Held**
SIC: 3556 Food products machinery
HQ: Spx Flow Us, Llc
135 Mount Read Blvd
Rochester NY 14611
585 436-5550

(P-14402)
STAINLESS WORKS MFG INC
225 Salinas Rd Bldg 5a, Royal Oaks (95076-5253)
PHONE...............................831 728-5097
Jose Medina, *Owner*
EMP: 22 **EST:** 2002
SALES: 3MM **Privately Held**
WEB: www.stainlessworksmfg.com
SIC: 3556 Food products machinery

P R O D U C T S   &   S V C S

(P-14403)
STALFAB
131 Algen Ln, Watsonville (95076-8624)
P.O. Box 780 (95077-0780)
PHONE..................................831 786-1600
Eric Buksa, *Owner*
EMP: 12
SQ FT: 5,000
SALES (est): 1.6MM **Privately Held**
SIC: 3556 Food products machinery

(P-14404)
SUPERIOR FOOD MACHINERY INC
8311 Sorensen Ave, Santa Fe Springs
(90670-2125)
PHONE..................................562 949-0396
Danny Reyes, *President*
Polo Reyes, *President*
Marc Reyes, *Vice Pres*
EMP: 23
SQ FT: 14,000
SALES (est): 5.5MM **Privately Held**
WEB: www.superiorinc.com
SIC: 3556 Food products machinery

(P-14405)
TETRA PAK PROCESSING EQUIP
1408 W Main St Ste E, Ripon
(95366-3013)
PHONE..................................209 599-4634
Brad Clark, *Branch Mgr*
EMP: 88
SALES (corp-wide): 6.2B **Privately Held**
WEB: www.tetrapak.com
SIC: 3556 Food products machinery
HQ: Tetra Pak Processing Equipment Inc.
801 Kingsley St S
Winsted MN 55395

(P-14406)
TOMRA SORTING INC (DH)
Also Called: Best USA
875 Embarcadero Dr, West Sacramento
(95605-1503)
PHONE..................................720 870-2240
Bert Van Der Auwera, *CEO*
Paul Berghmans, *President*
Eddy De Reyes, *Vice Pres*
Johan Peeters, *Vice Pres*
Marc Ryman, *Vice Pres*
▲ **EMP:** 91
SQ FT: 6,000
SALES (est): 22.4MM
SALES (corp-wide): 1B **Privately Held**
WEB: www.bestusa.com
SIC: 3556 Food products machinery
HQ: Tomra Sorting Nv
Romeinse Straat 20
Leuven 3001
164 085-80

(P-14407)
TPI MARKETING LLC
Also Called: Twin Peaks Ingredients
14985 Hilton Dr, Fontana (92336-2082)
P.O. Box 1745, Rancho Cucamonga
(91729-1745)
PHONE..................................302 703-0283
Kyle Boen, *Mng Member*
Trevor Boen,
EMP: 10
SQ FT: 10,000
SALES: 2MM **Privately Held**
SIC: 3556 5499 5149 Food products machinery; vitamin food stores; health foods

(P-14408)
TRIPLE E MANUFACTURING INC
Also Called: Ernst Mfg
2121 S Union Ave, Bakersfield
(93307-4155)
P.O. Box 70155 (93387-0155)
PHONE..................................661 831-7553
Martin W Etcheverry, *President*
Rick Etcheverry, *Treasurer*
EMP: 25
SQ FT: 40,000
SALES (est): 4.2MM **Privately Held**
SIC: 3556 3565 Packing house machinery; packaging machinery

(P-14409)
UNIMARK INTERNATIONAL INC
22601 Allview Ter, Laguna Beach
(92651-1547)
PHONE..................................949 497-1235
Richard Ness, *President*
EMP: 12
SQ FT: 5,000
SALES (est): 1.3MM **Privately Held**
SIC: 3556 5149 Food products machinery; groceries & related products

(P-14410)
UNITED BAKERY EQUIPMENT CO INC
Also Called: Hartman Slices Division
19216 S Laurel Park Rd, Compton
(90220-6008)
PHONE..................................310 635-8121
Loren Schieler, *Manager*
Paul Bastasch, *Vice Pres*
Anita Nunez, *Office Mgr*
Michael Bastasch, *Engineer*
EMP: 40
SQ FT: 63,089
SALES (corp-wide): 31MM **Privately Held**
SIC: 3556 5046 Slicers, commercial, food; bakery equipment & supplies
PA: United Bakery Equipment Company. Inc.
19216 S Laurel Park Rd
Rancho Dominguez CA 90220
310 635-8121

(P-14411)
VALLEY PACKLINE SOLUTIONS
5259 Avenue 408, Reedley (93654-9131)
PHONE..................................559 638-7821
Jim Parra, *Principal*
EMP: 30
SALES (est): 8.7MM **Privately Held**
SIC: 3556 Dehydrating equipment, food processing

(P-14412)
VERSACO MANUFACTURING INC
550 E Luchessa Ave, Gilroy (95020-7068)
PHONE..................................408 848-2880
Alan R Owens, *President*
John K Ishizuka, *Vice Pres*
EMP: 15
SQ FT: 30,000
SALES (est): 3.2MM **Privately Held**
SIC: 3556 3661 3312 3537 Food products machinery; telephone & telegraph apparatus; structural & rail mill products; industrial trucks & tractors

(P-14413)
VISTAN CORPORATION
Ashlock Company
855 Montague St, San Leandro
(94577-4327)
P.O. Box 1676 (94577-0398)
PHONE..................................510 351-0560
Sheryl Sullivan, *Branch Mgr*
Ted Hubbard, *Engineer*
Marilyn Perkins, *Purch Agent*
EMP: 13
SQ FT: 11,345
SALES (corp-wide): 21.8MM **Privately Held**
WEB: www.sloughcreek.com
SIC: 3556 7359 Food products machinery; equipment rental & leasing
PA: Vistan Corporation
3870 Halfway Rd
The Plains VA 20198
540 253-5540

(P-14414)
WILLIAM BOUNDS LTD
23625 Madison St, Torrance (90505-6004)
P.O. Box 1547 (90505-0547)
PHONE..................................310 375-0505
Helen Bounds, *President*
Sharon Bounds, *Vice Pres*
Rick Fouse, *Manager*
▲ **EMP:** 30
SQ FT: 18,000

SALES (est): 6.1MM **Privately Held**
WEB: www.wmboundsltd.com
SIC: 3556 8733 Food products machinery; noncommercial research organizations

(P-14415)
WILLIE BYLSMA
Also Called: W & J Dairy
10217 Atlas Ct, Oakdale (95361-7776)
PHONE..................................209 847-3362
Willie Bylsma, *Owner*
Jolene C Bylsma, *Principal*
EMP: 18
SALES: 500K **Privately Held**
SIC: 3556 Dairy & milk machinery

3559 Special Ind Machinery, NEC

(P-14416)
AC PHOTONICS INC
2701 Northwestern Pkwy, Santa Clara
(95051-0947)
PHONE..................................408 986-9838
Yongjian Wang, *President*
Zuhong Qu, *Vice Pres*
Tony Cortez, *Business Mgr*
Marcella Jiang, *Sales Staff*
▲ **EMP:** 24
SQ FT: 10,000
SALES (est): 16.2MM **Privately Held**
WEB: www.acphotonics.com
SIC: 3559 Fiber optics strand coating machinery

(P-14417)
ACME CRYOGENICS INC
Also Called: Cryogenic Experts
531 Sandy Cir, Oxnard (93036-0971)
PHONE..................................805 981-4500
Robert Worcester Jr, *Branch Mgr*
EMP: 30
SALES (corp-wide): 39.6MM **Privately Held**
SIC: 3559 Cryogenic machinery, industrial
PA: Acme Cryogenics, Inc.
2801 Mitchell Ave
Allentown PA 18103
610 966-4488

(P-14418)
ADCON LAB INC
6110 Running Springs Rd, San Jose
(95135-2209)
PHONE..................................408 531-9187
Raymond Jin, *President*
◆ **EMP:** 20
SALES: 2MM **Privately Held**
WEB: www.adconlab.com
SIC: 3559 Semiconductor manufacturing machinery

(P-14419)
ADCOTECH CORPORATION
1980 Tarob Ct, Milpitas (95035-6824)
PHONE..................................408 943-9999
Ron B Stillman, *President*
EMP: 93
SALES (est): 4.3MM
SALES (corp-wide): 1.1B **Publicly Held**
SIC: 3559 Electron tube making machinery
HQ: Jdsu Acterna Holdings Llc
1 Milestone Center Ct
Germantown MD 20876
240 404-1550

(P-14420)
ADVANCED INDUSTRIAL CERAMICS
2449 Zanker Rd, San Jose (95131-1116)
PHONE..................................408 955-9990
Chau Nguyen, *Owner*
EMP: 25
SQ FT: 7,500
SALES (est): 7MM **Privately Held**
SIC: 3559 3674 Semiconductor manufacturing machinery; stud bases or mounts for semiconductor devices

(P-14421)
ALTAIR TECHNOLOGIES INC
41970 Christy St, Fremont (94538-3160)
PHONE..................................650 508-8700
Chris Ferrari, *CEO*

Chris Wallace, *CFO*
Christopher Ferrari, *Engineer*
▼ **EMP:** 30
SALES (est): 8.2MM **Privately Held**
WEB: www.altairusa.com
SIC: 3559 7692 Electronic component making machinery; brazing

(P-14422)
AMERGENCE TECHNOLOGY INC
295 Brea Canyon Rd, Walnut
(91789-3049)
PHONE..................................909 859-8400
Shavonne Tran, *President*
▲ **EMP:** 29
SQ FT: 40,000
SALES (est): 4MM **Privately Held**
SIC: 3559 Recycling machinery

(P-14423)
APERIA TECHNOLOGIES INC
1616 Rollins Rd, Burlingame (94010-2302)
PHONE..................................415 494-9624
Joshua Carter, *CEO*
Bryan Duggan, *Vice Pres*
Josue Rojas, *Software Dev*
Brandon Haws, *Technical Staff*
Lucas Cooter, *Engineer*
▲ **EMP:** 33
SALES (est): 10.5MM **Privately Held**
SIC: 3559 Automotive maintenance equipment

(P-14424)
APPLIED MATERIALS INC (PA)
3050 Bowers Ave, Santa Clara
(95054-3298)
P.O. Box 58039 (95052-8039)
PHONE..................................408 727-5555
Gary E Dickerson, *President*
Thomas J Iannotti, *Ch of Bd*
Daniel J Durn, *CFO*
Ginetto Addiego, *Senior VP*
Steve Ghanayem, *Senior VP*
▲ **EMP:** 800
SALES: 17.2B **Publicly Held**
WEB: www.appliedmaterials.com
SIC: 3559 3674 Semiconductor manufacturing machinery; semiconductors & related devices

(P-14425)
APPLIED MATERIALS INC
9000 Foothills Blvd, Roseville
(95747-4411)
PHONE..................................916 786-3900
Scott Ribordy, *Principal*
EMP: 10
SALES (corp-wide): 17.2B **Publicly Held**
WEB: www.appliedmaterials.com
SIC: 3559 Semiconductor manufacturing machinery
PA: Applied Materials, Inc.
3050 Bowers Ave
Santa Clara CA 95054
408 727-5555

(P-14426)
APPLIED MATERIALS INC
974 E Arques Ave, Sunnyvale
(94085-4520)
PHONE..................................408 727-5555
James Morgan, *Branch Mgr*
Gill Lee, *CTO*
Walters Shen, *Info Tech Mgr*
Dave Dunne, *Software Engr*
Naveen Makwana, *Software Engr*
EMP: 48
SALES (corp-wide): 17.2B **Publicly Held**
WEB: www.appliedmaterials.com
SIC: 3559 Semiconductor manufacturing machinery
PA: Applied Materials, Inc.
3050 Bowers Ave
Santa Clara CA 95054
408 727-5555

(P-14427)
ARSYS INC
Also Called: Ellexar
1428 S Grand Ave, Santa Ana
(92705-4400)
PHONE..................................714 654-7681
Allan Emami, *President*
EMP: 10

▲ = Import ▼=Export
◆ =Import/Export

SQ FT: 2,100
SALES: 350K **Privately Held**
SIC: 3559 Electronic component making machinery

(P-14428)
AUTOMATION TECHNICAL SVCS INC
10459 Roselle St Ste C, San Diego (92121-1527)
PHONE..................................619 302-6970
Kelvin Wiley, *President*
EMP: 10
SALES (est): 1.8MM **Privately Held**
SIC: 3559 Semiconductor manufacturing machinery

(P-14429)
AUTOTECHBIZCOM INC
23551 Commerce Center Dr l, Laguna Hills (92653-1513)
PHONE..................................949 245-7033
EMP: 13
SQ FT: 1,500
SALES: 2.2MM **Privately Held**
SIC: 3559 7359

(P-14430)
AVANZATO TECHNOLOGY CORP
5335 Mcconnell Ave, Los Angeles (90066-7025)
PHONE..................................312 509-0506
Carissa Davino, *CEO*
Jeremy Green, *Director*
EMP: 20
SALES (est): 821.2K **Privately Held**
SIC: 3559 5065 Electronic component making machinery; electronic parts

(P-14431)
BARKENS HARDCHROME INC
239 E Greenleaf Blvd, Compton (90220-4913)
PHONE..................................310 632-2000
Gary Barken, *CEO*
Carol Barken, *Vice Pres*
Ken Ames, *Manager*
EMP: 25
SQ FT: 60,000
SALES (est): 6.8MM **Privately Held**
WEB: www.barkenshardchrome.com
SIC: 3559 5082 Metal finishing equipment for plating, etc.; oil field equipment

(P-14432)
BELOVAC LLC
435 E Lincoln St Ste A, Banning (92220-6012)
PHONE..................................951 427-4299
Jeff Bell, *Owner*
EMP: 18
SALES (est): 3.8MM **Privately Held**
SIC: 3559 Plastics working machinery

(P-14433)
BENDPAK INC
1645 E Lemonwood Dr, Santa Paula (93060-9651)
PHONE..................................805 933-9970
Donald Ray Henthorn, *President*
Jeffery Kritzer, *Senior VP*
Ryan Delapp, *Sales Staff*
Abraham Viveros,
Antonio Barrios, *Clerk*
◆ EMP: 150
SQ FT: 30,000
SALES: 69.8MM **Privately Held**
WEB: www.bendpak.com
SIC: 3559 Automotive related machinery; automotive maintenance equipment; industrial trucks & tractors

(P-14434)
BIJAN RAD INC
Also Called: Sysparc
16125 Cantlay St, Van Nuys (91406-3416)
PHONE..................................818 902-1606
Bijan RAD, *CEO*
◆ EMP: 25
SQ FT: 9,000
SALES (est): 2.6MM **Privately Held**
SIC: 3559 1731 Parking facility equipment & supplies; access control systems specialization

(P-14435)
BOOM INDUSTRIAL INC
167 University Pkwy, Pomona (91768-4301)
PHONE..................................909 495-3555
Huiwen Chen, *CEO*
EMP: 60
SALES (est): 2.5MM **Privately Held**
SIC: 3559 3069 Rubber working machinery, including tires; rubber automotive products; castings, rubber

(P-14436)
BROOKS AUTOMATION INC
13915 Danielson St # 103, Poway (92064-8884)
P.O. Box 231280, San Diego (92193-1280)
PHONE..................................858 527-7000
Emil Erickson, *CFO*
Dean Knox, *Project Mgr*
David Mort, *Prdtn Mgr*
Tara Dripps, *Mktg Coord*
EMP: 12
SALES (corp-wide): 631.5MM **Publicly Held**
SIC: 3559 Semiconductor manufacturing machinery
PA: Brooks Automation, Inc.
15 Elizabeth Dr
Chelmsford MA 01824
978 262-2400

(P-14437)
C & D SEMICONDUCTOR SVCS INC (PA)
Also Called: C&D Precision Machining
2031 Concourse Dr, San Jose (95131-1727)
PHONE..................................408 383-1888
Dong Van Nguyen, *CEO*
Brad Avrit, *Vice Pres*
Dong Nguyen, *Vice Pres*
Tien Nguyen, *Vice Pres*
Thanh Truong, *Design Engr*
◆ EMP: 50
SQ FT: 3,600
SALES (est): 11.1MM **Privately Held**
WEB: www.cdsemi.com
SIC: 3559 Semiconductor manufacturing machinery

(P-14438)
CHA INDUSTRIES INC
Also Called: Cha Vacuum Technology
4201 Business Center Dr, Fremont (94538-6357)
PHONE..................................510 683-8554
Stephen Kaplan, *President*
Sharon Krawiecki, *Treasurer*
Stephen Dipietro, *Admin Sec*
Charles Hester, *Technician*
Steve Kaplan, *Technical Staff*
▼ EMP: 25
SQ FT: 39,000
SALES: 5.8MM **Privately Held**
WEB: www.chaindustries.com
SIC: 3559 Semiconductor manufacturing machinery

(P-14439)
CHEMICAL SAFETY TECHNOLOGY INC
Also Called: C S T I
2461 Autumnvale Dr, San Jose (95131-1802)
PHONE..................................408 263-0984
Lincoln Bejan, *President*
Jackie Bejan, *Vice Pres*
Quan Nguyen, *Electrical Engi*
EMP: 26
SQ FT: 14,000
SALES (est): 6MM **Privately Held**
WEB: www.kemsafe.com
SIC: 3559 Refinery, chemical processing & similar machinery

(P-14440)
CLEANPARTSET INC
3530 Bassett St, Santa Clara (95054-2704)
PHONE..................................408 886-3300
Patrick Bogart, *CEO*
Joreg Hohnloser, *President*
Lisa Peddy, *CFO*
Ken Pelan, *CFO*
Bernard Adams, *Principal*

▲ EMP: 24
SQ FT: 35,000
SALES (est): 3.5MM
SALES (corp-wide): 14.1MM **Privately Held**
WEB: www.tosohset.com
SIC: 3559 Semiconductor manufacturing machinery
HQ: Cleanpart International, Inc
631 International Pkwy
Richardson TX 75081

(P-14441)
COLD JET LLC
10281 Trademark St Ste A, Rancho Cucamonga (91730-5846)
PHONE..................................513 831-3211
Steve Schick, *Manager*
EMP: 10
SALES (corp-wide): 65MM **Privately Held**
WEB: www.coldjet.com
SIC: 3559 Cryogenic machinery, industrial
PA: Cold Jet, Llc
455 Wards Corner Rd # 100
Loveland OH 45140
513 831-3211

(P-14442)
COSMODYNE LLC
3010 Old Ranch Pkwy # 300, Seal Beach (90740-2750)
PHONE..................................562 795-5990
George Papagelis,
Frank Andrews, *President*
Sean Jones, *Project Mgr*
George Win, *Project Mgr*
Irina Dean, *Research*
◆ EMP: 50
SQ FT: 125,000
SALES (est): 15.6MM **Privately Held**
SIC: 3559 Smelting & refining machinery & equipment
HQ: Cryogenic Industries, Inc.
27710 Jefferson Ave # 301
Temecula CA 92590
951 677-2081

(P-14443)
CP MANUFACTURING INC (HQ)
6795 Calle De Linea, San Diego (92154-8017)
PHONE..................................619 477-3175
Robert M Davis, *President*
Ruth Davis, *Ch of Bd*
Michael W Howard, *COO*
Theodora Davis Inman, *Vice Pres*
John O Willis, *Vice Pres*
▲ EMP: 104 EST: 1977
SQ FT: 60,572
SALES (est): 27.4MM
SALES (corp-wide): 113.6MM **Privately Held**
WEB: www.cpmfg.com
SIC: 3559 Recycling machinery
PA: Ims Recycling Services, Inc.
2697 Main St
San Diego CA 92113
619 231-2521

(P-14444)
CROSSING AUTOMATION INC (HQ)
46702 Bayside Pkwy, Fremont (94538-6582)
PHONE..................................510 661-5000
Robert B Macknight Kkk, *President*
Mark D Morelli, *President*
Stephen S Schwartz, *CEO*
Lindon G Robertson, *Exec VP*
David C Gray, *Senior VP*
▲ EMP: 34
SQ FT: 5,500
SALES (est): 59.1MM
SALES (corp-wide): 631.5MM **Publicly Held**
WEB: www.crossinginc.com
SIC: 3559 Semiconductor manufacturing machinery
PA: Brooks Automation, Inc.
15 Elizabeth Dr
Chelmsford MA 01824
978 262-2400

(P-14445)
CRYOGENIC MACHINERY CORP
7306 Greenbush Ave, North Hollywood (91605-4096)
PHONE..................................818 765-6688
Peter Fritz, *President*
Adrian Unger, *Treasurer*
EMP: 12
SQ FT: 10,000
SALES (est): 2.7MM **Privately Held**
WEB: www.cryomach.com
SIC: 3559 7699 Cryogenic machinery, industrial; industrial machinery & equipment repair

(P-14446)
CRYOPORT SYSTEMS INC (HQ)
17305 Daimler St, Irvine (92614-5510)
PHONE..................................949 540-7204
Jerrell W Shelton, *President*
Bret Bollinger, *Officer*
Dee Kelly, *Vice Pres*
Ly Le, *Accountant*
Kirk Randall, *Sales Dir*
EMP: 15
SQ FT: 28,000
SALES: 2.8MM
SALES (corp-wide): 19.6MM **Publicly Held**
WEB: www.cryoport.com
SIC: 3559 Cryogenic machinery, industrial
PA: Cryoport, Inc.
17305 Daimler St
Irvine CA 92614
949 470-2300

(P-14447)
CRYOQUIP LLC (DH)
25720 Jefferson Ave, Murrieta (92562-6929)
PHONE..................................951 677-2060
Patrick Billman, *President*
Rebecca Jerkins, *Administration*
Eric Fales, *Design Engr*
Cheryl Marchello, *Technology*
Ted Ban, *Engineer*
◆ EMP: 12
SQ FT: 110
SALES (est): 3.5MM **Privately Held**
SIC: 3559 8711 Cryogenic machinery, industrial; engineering services
HQ: Cryogenic Industries, Inc.
27710 Jefferson Ave # 301
Temecula CA 92590
951 677-2081

(P-14448)
CRYST MARK INC A SWAN TECHNO C
Also Called: Crystal Mark
613 Justin Ave, Glendale (91201-2326)
PHONE..................................818 240-7520
John Swan, *President*
E Michael Swan, *Vice Pres*
Marko S Swan, *Vice Pres*
Pauline Swan, *Asst Sec*
Diana Galvez, *Assistant*
EMP: 40
SQ FT: 18,000
SALES (est): 9.6MM **Privately Held**
WEB: www.crystalmarkinc.com
SIC: 3559 3471 Semiconductor manufacturing machinery; screening equipment, electric; sand blasting of metal parts

(P-14449)
CUSTOM METAL FINISHING CORP
17804 S Western Ave, Gardena (90248-3620)
P.O. Box 368 (90248-0368)
PHONE..................................310 532-5075
David Alverez, *President*
Larry Alvarez, *Shareholder*
Victor Alvarez, *Shareholder*
Kelly Alverez, *Treasurer*
Lilly Alvarez, *Vice Pres*
EMP: 40
SQ FT: 7,500
SALES (est): 5.6MM **Privately Held**
WEB: www.custommetalfinishing.com
SIC: 3559 3471 Metal finishing equipment for plating, etc.; plating & polishing

PRODUCTS & SVCS

(P-14450)
CUSTOPHARM INC (PA)
Also Called: Leucadia Pharmaceuticals
2325 Camino Vida Roble A, Carlsbad
(92011-1567)
PHONE.....................760 683-0901
William Larkins, *CEO*
Dave McCleary, *Vice Pres*
EMP: 17
SALES (est): 4.6MM **Privately Held**
SIC: 3559 8071 Chemical machinery &
equipment; medical laboratories

(P-14451)
DATA PHYSICS CORPORATION
9031 Polsa Ct, Corona (92883)
PHONE.....................408 216-8443
Kevin McIntosh, *Manager*
EMP: 25
SALES (corp-wide): 13.9MM **Privately
Held**
SIC: 3559
PA: Data Physics Corporation
2480 N 1st St Ste 100
San Jose CA 95131
408 437-0100

(P-14452)
DISHCRAFT ROBOTICS INC
611 Taylor Way Ste 1, San Carlos
(94070-6305)
PHONE.....................415 595-9671
EMP: 10
SALES (est): 1.9MM **Privately Held**
SIC: 3559 8733 Special industry machin-
ery; research institute

(P-14453)
DURON INCORPORATED
4633 Camden Dr, Corona Del Mar
(92625-3104)
PHONE.....................949 721-0900
Paul P Duron, *President*
EMP: 10
SALES (est): 954K **Privately Held**
SIC: 3559 8711 Cryogenic machinery, in-
dustrial; consulting engineer

(P-14454)
**DYNALINEAR TECHNOLOGIES
INC**
51 E Campbell Ave 108b, Campbell
(95008-2988)
PHONE.....................408 376-5090
Gl Young Lee, *President*
EMP: 10
SALES: 1.2MM **Privately Held**
WEB: www.dynalinear.com
SIC: 3559 Semiconductor manufacturing
machinery

(P-14455)
EAGLE VALLEY GINNING LLC
27480 S Bennett Rd, Firebaugh
(93622-9405)
PHONE.....................209 826-5002
Aaron Barcellos,
John F Bennett,
Timothy R Hall,
EMP: 26
SALES (est): 2.6MM **Privately Held**
SIC: 3559 Cotton ginning machinery

(P-14456)
EBS PRODUCTS
5082 Bolsa Ave Ste 112, Huntington Beach
(92649-1046)
P.O. Box 11060, Westminster (92685-
1060)
PHONE.....................714 896-6700
Peter C Hollub, *President*
Janice Walters, *Office Mgr*
Manuel Rendon, *Opers Mgr*
EMP: 12
SALES (est): 1.6MM **Privately Held**
SIC: 3559 Automotive related machinery

(P-14457)
EKSO BIONICS INC (PA)
1414 Harbour Way S # 1201, Richmond
(94804-3628)
PHONE.....................510 984-1761
Eythor Bender, *CEO*
Nathan Harding, *COO*
Max Scheder- Biesehin, *CFO*

Brandon Frees, *Vice Pres*
Bianca Momand, *Vice Pres*
EMP: 74
SALES (est): 16.1MM **Privately Held**
WEB: www.berkeleyexoworks.com
SIC: 3559 Cryogenic machinery, industrial

(P-14458)
**ELITE SERVICE EXPERTS INC
(PA)**
725 Del Paso Rd, Sacramento
(95834-1106)
PHONE.....................916 275-3956
Roy Hill, *President*
EMP: 10
SALES (est): 1MM **Privately Held**
SIC: 3559 Parking facility equipment &
supplies

(P-14459)
ENERGY RECOVERY INC (PA)
1717 Doolittle Dr, San Leandro
(94577-2231)
PHONE.....................510 483-7370
Chris Gannon, *President*
Hans Peter Michelet, *Ch of Bd*
Chris M Gannon, *President*
Josh Ballard, *CFO*
Alexander Buehler, *Bd of Directors*
▲ EMP: 114
SQ FT: 170,000
SALES: 61MM **Publicly Held**
SIC: 3559 Desalination equipment

(P-14460)
ENVIROKINETICS INC (PA)
101 S Milliken Ave, Ontario (91761-7836)
PHONE.....................909 621-7599
Henry Seal, *President*
Long Le, *Vice Pres*
EMP: 15
SQ FT: 6,000
SALES (est): 5.8MM **Privately Held**
SIC: 3559 Petroleum refinery equipment

(P-14461)
**EPOCH INTERNATIONAL ENTPS
INC**
46583 Fremont Blvd, Fremont
(94538-6409)
PHONE.....................510 556-1225
Foad Ghalili, *President*
Monireh Meshgin, *CFO*
Ladon Ghalili, *General Mgr*
Mandy Shi, *Engineer*
Betty Su, *Engineer*
▲ EMP: 180
SQ FT: 5,550
SALES (est): 38.7MM **Privately Held**
WEB: www.epoch-int.com
SIC: 3559 Electronic component making
machinery

(P-14462)
**ESPACE ENTERPRISES TECH
INC**
Also Called: E Enterprise Tech
3010 N 1st St, San Jose (95134-2023)
PHONE.....................408 844-8176
Esther Hutchinson, *President*
Phan Pham, *Founder*
Pham Phan, *Vice Pres*
EMP: 12
SQ FT: 7,000
SALES (est): 4MM **Privately Held**
WEB: www.e-enterprisetech.com
SIC: 3559 Semiconductor manufacturing
machinery

(P-14463)
**EXCELLON ACQUISITION LLC
(HQ)**
Also Called: Excellon Automation Co
20001 S Rancho Way, Compton
(90220-6318)
PHONE.....................310 668-7700
Bailey Su,
Danny Hernandez, *Electrical Engi*
Warren Wong, *Business Mgr*
Barbara Tilk, *Buyer*
EMP: 38
SQ FT: 35,000

SALES (est): 10.9MM
SALES (corp-wide): 1.8MM **Privately
Held**
WEB: www.excellon.com
SIC: 3559 Semiconductor manufacturing
machinery

(P-14464)
**EXPERT SEMICONDUCTOR
TECH INC**
Also Called: Expertech
10 Victor Sq Ste 100, Scotts Valley
(95066-3562)
P.O. Box 66508 (95067-6508)
PHONE.....................831 439-9300
Jonathan George, *President*
Mark Cooper, *Vice Pres*
Martin Henig, *Mfg Dir*
Ralph Mason, *Sales Staff*
EMP: 25
SQ FT: 40,000
SALES (est): 6.3MM **Privately Held**
WEB: www.exper-tech.com
SIC: 3559 Semiconductor manufacturing
machinery

(P-14465)
**FANUC AMERICA
CORPORATION**
Also Called: Fanuc Robotics West
25951 Commercentre Dr, Lake Forest
(92630-8805)
PHONE.....................949 595-2700
Mike Hollingsworth, *Manager*
Robert Crawford, *District Mgr*
James Farmer, *District Mgr*
Peter Fitzgerald, *General Mgr*
Florin Stef, *Design Engr*
EMP: 30 **Privately Held**
WEB: www.fanucrobotics.com
SIC: 3559 3548 3569 Metal finishing
equipment for plating, etc.; electric weld-
ing equipment; robots, assembly line: in-
dustrial & commercial
HQ: Fanuc America Corporation
3900 W Hamlin Rd
Rochester Hills MI 48309
248 377-7000

(P-14466)
FC MANAGEMENT SERVICES
Also Called: PC Recycle
2001 Anchor Ct Ste B, Newbury Park
(91320-1616)
PHONE.....................805 499-0050
Fulton Connor, *President*
EMP: 21
SALES (est): 2.5MM **Privately Held**
SIC: 3559 Electronic component making
machinery

(P-14467)
**FLIGHT MICROWAVE
CORPORATION**
410 S Douglas St, El Segundo
(90245-4628)
PHONE.....................310 607-9819
Rolf Kich, *President*
Mike Callas, *CFO*
Mark Van Alstyne, *Vice Pres*
Richard Bennett, *Director*
EMP: 30
SQ FT: 8,000
SALES (est): 5.7MM **Privately Held**
WEB: www.flightmicrowave.com
SIC: 3559 Electronic component making
machinery

(P-14468)
**FLIR MOTION CTRL SYSTEMS
INC**
6769 Hollister Ave, Goleta (93117-3001)
PHONE.....................650 692-3900
Philip Kahn, *President*
David Gaw, *Vice Pres*
▼ EMP: 26
SQ FT: 6,000
SALES (est): 2.8MM
SALES (corp-wide): 1.7B **Publicly Held**
WEB: www.dperception.com
SIC: 3559 3541 Semiconductor manufac-
turing machinery; robots for drilling, cut-
ting, grinding, polishing, etc.

PA: Flir Systems, Inc.
27700 Sw Parkway Ave
Wilsonville OR 97070
503 498-3547

(P-14469)
FUZETRON INC
Also Called: Creative Industries
2111 Paseo Grande, El Cajon
(92019-3854)
PHONE.....................619 244-5141
▲ EMP: 15
SQ FT: 8,000
SALES (est): 1.1MM **Privately Held**
WEB: www.creativewheels.com
SIC: 3559 8732

(P-14470)
**GARAGE EQUIPMENT SUPPLY
INC**
646 Flinn Ave Ste A, Moorpark
(93021-1895)
PHONE.....................805 530-0027
Danette Henthorn, *CEO*
Gary Henthorn, *President*
Mike Oconnell, *Empl Benefits*
▲ EMP: 15
SQ FT: 25,000
SALES (est): 14.4MM **Privately Held**
WEB: www.gesusa.com
SIC: 3559 Automotive maintenance equip-
ment

(P-14471)
GEI INC
Also Called: GALAXY ENTERPRISES IN-
TERNATION
301 E Arrow Hwy Ste 108, San Dimas
(91773-3364)
PHONE.....................909 592-2234
Vincent Chung, *President*
Wally Rogozinski, *Officer*
▲ EMP: 10
SQ FT: 5,000
SALES (est): 1.5MM **Privately Held**
WEB: www.gei-inc.com
SIC: 3559 Electronic component making
machinery

(P-14472)
GLASTAR CORPORATION
8425 Canoga Ave, Canoga Park
(91304-2607)
PHONE.....................818 341-0301
Lorie Mitchell, *President*
George Lopez, *Buyer*
EMP: 20
SQ FT: 14,000
SALES (est): 4.3MM **Privately Held**
WEB: www.glastar.com
SIC: 3559 3563 3231 Glass making ma-
chinery: blowing, molding, forming, etc.;
spraying & dusting equipment; products
of purchased glass

(P-14473)
**GLOBALFOUNDRIES US INC
(DH)**
Also Called: Global Foundries
2600 Great America Way, Santa Clara
(95054-1169)
PHONE.....................408 462-3900
Thomas Caulfield, *CEO*
Dr John Goldsberry, *CFO*
Louis Lupin, *Officer*
Jeff Worth, *Officer*
Daniel Durn, *Exec VP*
▲ EMP: 277
SALES (est): 1.3B **Privately Held**
SIC: 3559 3825 5065 Semiconductor
manufacturing machinery; semiconductor
test equipment; semiconductor devices
HQ: Mamoura Diversified Global Holding
P.J.S.C
Near Muroor (4th) Rd & Mohamed
Mamoura A, Bin Khalifa (15th) Str
Abu Dhabi
241 358-45

(P-14474)
**GREENVITY COMMUNICATIONS
INC (PA)**
2150 Trade Zone Blvd, San Jose
(95131-1730)
PHONE.....................408 935-9358

▲ = Import ▼=Export
◆ =Import/Export

Hung Nguyen, *CEO*
Edward Inyoung Cho, *Vice Pres*
Jayesh Desai, *Vice Pres*
John Tero, *Vice Pres*
Nanci Vogtli, *Vice Pres*
EMP: 21 **EST:** 2010
SQ FT: 10,000
SALES: 20MM **Privately Held**
SIC: 3559 3674 Semiconductor manufacturing machinery; semiconductors & related devices

(P-14475)
HANTRONIX INC
10080 Bubb Rd, Cupertino (95014-4132)
PHONE....................408 252-1100
Wayne Choi, *CEO*
Latha Ravi, *Purchasing*
Jaime Lim, *Sales Staff*
Richard Choi, *Manager*
Max Mun, *Manager*
▲ **EMP:** 22
SQ FT: 10,000
SALES: 26.3MM **Privately Held**
WEB: www.hantronix.com
SIC: 3559 5065 5577 Electronic component making machinery; electronic parts & equipment; computer peripheral equipment

(P-14476)
I3 NANOTEC LLC
Also Called: Ctg
5040 Commercial Cir Ste A, Concord (94520-1250)
PHONE....................510 594-2299
Jim Wile, *President*
John Bluhm, *Vice Pres*
Steven McCormick, *Vice Pres*
Manish Goel,
EMP: 10
SALES (est): 1.5MM **Privately Held**
SIC: 3559 Recycling machinery

(P-14477)
IMTEC ACCULINE LLC
Also Called: Intelligent Quartz Solutions
49036 Milmont Dr, Fremont (94538-7301)
PHONE....................510 770-1800
Paul V Mendes, *Mng Member*
Richard Faria, *Controller*
Emily Xiang, *Senior Buyer*
Lynn Culver, *Manager*
Henry Szczyglewski, *Manager*
▲ **EMP:** 24
SQ FT: 27,000
SALES (est): 6MM **Privately Held**
WEB: www.imtecacculine.com
SIC: 3559 Semiconductor manufacturing machinery

(P-14478)
INDUSTRIAL DYNAMICS CO LTD (PA)
Also Called: Filtec
3100 Fujita St, Torrance (90505-4007)
P.O. Box 2945 (90509-2945)
PHONE....................310 325-5633
David Storey, *President*
Nick Newman, *Officer*
Steve M Calhoun, *Principal*
Ken Hudson, *Telecom Exec*
David Petersen, *Software Dev*
▲ **EMP:** 216 **EST:** 1960
SQ FT: 155,000
SALES (est): 38.4MM **Privately Held**
WEB: www.pcbdriller.com
SIC: 3559 3829 Screening equipment, electric; measuring & controlling devices

(P-14479)
INDUSTRIAL TOOLS INC
1111 S Rose Ave, Oxnard (93033-2499)
PHONE 805 483-1111
Donald O Murphy, *President*
John E Anderson, *Ch of Bd*
Kay Nolan, *CFO*
Michael Moffatt, *Technology*
Tony Lewis, *Engineer*
EMP: 50 **EST:** 1961
SQ FT: 65,000

SALES (est): 11.4MM **Privately Held**
WEB: www.indtools.com
SIC: 3559 3545 3544 3541 Semiconductor manufacturing machinery; machine tool accessories; special dies, tools, jigs & fixtures; machine tools, metal cutting type

(P-14480)
INTEVAC INC (PA)
3560 Bassett St, Santa Clara (95054-2704)
PHONE....................408 986-9888
David S Dury, *Ch of Bd*
Wendell T Blonigan, *President*
Richard Lavine, *President*
James Moniz, *CFO*
Andres Brugal, *Exec VP*
▲ **EMP:** 196
SQ FT: 169,583
SALES: 95.1MM **Publicly Held**
SIC: 3559 Semiconductor manufacturing machinery

(P-14481)
INTEVAC INC
Intevac Fabrication Center
3560 Bassett St, Santa Clara (95054-2704)
PHONE....................408 986-9888
Don Cordoni, *Manager*
EMP: 20
SALES (corp-wide): 95.1MM **Publicly Held**
SIC: 3559 3674 Semiconductor manufacturing machinery; semiconductors & related devices
PA: Intevac, Inc.
3560 Bassett St
Santa Clara CA 95054
408 986-9888

(P-14482)
JACKS TECHNOLOGIES & INDS INC
Also Called: J T I
225 N Palomares St, Pomona (91767-5549)
PHONE....................909 865-2595
David Jacks, *President*
Randy Walston, *Vice Pres*
▲ **EMP:** 10
SQ FT: 4,000
SALES (est): 2MM **Privately Held**
WEB: www.zeph.com
SIC: 3559 Electronic component making machinery

(P-14483)
JASPER DISPLAY CORP
2952 Bunker Hill Ln # 110, Santa Clara (95054-1103)
PHONE....................408 831-5788
Kenneth Tai, *CEO*
Terrence Poon, *Vice Pres*
Kaushik Sheth, *General Mgr*
Jack McGwire, *CIO*
Robert Savage, *Software Engr*
EMP: 20 **EST:** 2009
SALES (est): 860.9K **Privately Held**
SIC: 3559 Electronic component making machinery
PA: Jasper Display Corp.
7f-16, 81, Shui Li Rd.,
Hsinchu City 30059

(P-14484)
JGM AUTOMOTIVE TOOLING INC
Also Called: Motec USA
5355 Industrial Dr, Huntington Beach (92649-1516)
PHONE....................714 895-7001
James Munn, *CEO*
EMP: 24
SQ FT: 8,000
SALES (est): 4.7MM **Privately Held**
SIC: 3559 5531 Automotive maintenance equipment; automobile & truck equipment & parts

(P-14485)
JOHNSON MARBLE MACHINERY INC
7325 Varna Ave, North Hollywood (91605-4009)
PHONE....................818 764-6186

Mark Brandtner, *Regional Mgr*
Ted Johnson, *President*
Jean May Johnson, *Vice Pres*
▲ **EMP:** 10
SQ FT: 20,000
SALES (est): 4MM **Privately Held**
SIC: 3559 5084 5032 Stone working machinery; industrial machinery & equipment; marble building stone

(P-14486)
K V R INVESTMENT GROUP INC
Also Called: Pacific Plating
12113 Branford St, Sun Valley (91352-5710)
PHONE....................818 896-1102
Rakesh Bajaria, *President*
Benny Kadhrota, *Treasurer*
Ken Pansuria, *Vice Pres*
Harry Thummar, *Vice Pres*
EMP: 60 **EST:** 1997
SALES (est): 9.2MM **Privately Held**
SIC: 3559 3471 Metal finishing equipment for plating, etc.; plating & polishing

(P-14487)
KEYSSA SYSTEMS INC
655 Campbell Technology P, Campbell (95008-5060)
PHONE....................408 637-2300
Eric Almgren, *CEO*
John McAdoo, *CFO*
Mariel Van Tatenhove, *Vice Pres*
EMP: 10 **EST:** 2015
SALES (est): 271.4K **Privately Held**
SIC: 3559 5065 Semiconductor manufacturing machinery; semiconductor devices

(P-14488)
LAM RESEARCH CORPORATION
3724 Dawn Cir, Union City (94587-2626)
PHONE....................510 572-2186
Stephen Truong, *Principal*
EMP: 72
SALES (corp-wide): 9.6B **Publicly Held**
SIC: 3559 Semiconductor manufacturing machinery
PA: Lam Research Corporation
4650 Cushing Pkwy
Fremont CA 94538
510 572-0200

(P-14489)
LAM RESEARCH CORPORATION
46555 Landing Pkwy, Fremont (94538-6421)
PHONE....................510 572-3200
James Bagley, *Branch Mgr*
Rick Gottscho, *Exec VP*
Thad Nicholson, *Engineer*
Steve Koniniec, *Opers Staff*
EMP: 86
SALES (corp-wide): 9.6B **Publicly Held**
WEB: www.lamrc.com
SIC: 3559 Semiconductor manufacturing machinery
PA: Lam Research Corporation
4650 Cushing Pkwy
Fremont CA 94538
510 572-0200

(P-14490)
LAM RESEARCH INTL HOLDG CO (HQ)
4650 Cushing Pkwy, Fremont (94538-6401)
PHONE....................510 572-0200
Douglas Bettinger, *CFO*
Reyleene Hunt, *Prgrmr*
Daniel Cocciardi, *Engineer*
Sean Larsen, *Engineer*
Chin-Yi Liu, *Engineer*
EMP: 15
SALES (est): 5.7MM
SALES (corp-wide): 9.6B **Publicly Held**
SIC: 3559 Semiconductor manufacturing machinery
PA: Lam Research Corporation
4650 Cushing Pkwy
Fremont CA 94538
510 572-0200

(P-14491)
LEGACY SYSTEMS INCORPORATED
4160 Technology Dr Ste E, Fremont (94538-6360)
PHONE....................510 651-2312
Robert Matthews, *President*
Dipak Dutta, *Vice Pres*
EMP: 10
SALES (est): 1.6MM **Privately Held**
SIC: 3559 Chemical machinery & equipment

(P-14492)
LILY POND PRODUCTS
Also Called: Campbell Pump Co
351 W Cromwell Ave # 105, Fresno (93711-6115)
P.O. Box 939, Sanger (93657-0939)
PHONE....................559 431-5203
Fred Campbell, *Owner*
EMP: 10
SQ FT: 2,000
SALES (est): 701.9K **Privately Held**
WEB: www.lilypond.com
SIC: 3559 3561 Clay working & tempering machines; pumps & pumping equipment

(P-14493)
LYTEN INC
933 Kifer Rd Ste B, Sunnyvale (94086-5208)
PHONE....................650 400-5635
Daniel Cook, *CEO*
Scott Mobley, *COO*
William Wraith, *Chairman*
Dean Witter, *Principal*
EMP: 10
SALES (est): 1.5MM **Privately Held**
SIC: 3559 Chemical machinery & equipment

(P-14494)
MARKETING BUS ADVANTAGE INC
1940 Olivera Rd Ste E, Concord (94520-5484)
PHONE....................925 933-3637
Rachel A Browne, *CEO*
Merrick Browne, *Vice Pres*
EMP: 10
SQ FT: 10,000
SALES: 670K **Privately Held**
SIC: 3559 Automotive maintenance equipment

(P-14495)
MEEDER EQUIPMENT COMPANY (PA)
Also Called: Ransome Manufacturing
3495 S Maple Ave, Fresno (93725-2494)
P.O. Box 12446 (93777-2446)
PHONE....................559 485-0979
Jeffrey D Vertz, *President*
Jeffrey Vertz, *President*
James Moe, *Corp Secy*
Shawn Huffman, *Vice Pres*
Wane Morgan, *Vice Pres*
▲ **EMP:** 45
SQ FT: 13,000
SALES: 24MM **Privately Held**
WEB: www.ransomemfg.com
SIC: 3559 5084 3714 8711 Refinery, chemical processing & similar machinery; industrial machinery & equipment; propane conversion equipment; propane conversion equipment, motor vehicle; building construction consultant

(P-14496)
MEGA MACHINERY INC
6688 Doolittle Ave, Riverside (92503-1432)
PHONE....................951 300-9300
Richard Risch, *President*
Roger Blaney, *Vice Pres*
EMP: 15
SQ FT: 20,000
SALES (est): 3.8MM **Privately Held**
WEB: www.mega.biz
SIC: 3559 Plastics working machinery

(P-14497)
MERITEK ELECTRONICS CORP (PA)
5160 Rivergrade Rd, Baldwin Park (91706-1406)
PHONE..................................626 373-1728
Pa-Shih Oliver Su, *CEO*
Annie Lien, *Program Mgr*
Su Oliver, *Administration*
◆ EMP: 75
SQ FT: 60,000
SALES (est): 16.5MM **Privately Held**
WEB: www.meritekusa.com
SIC: 3559 5065 Electronic component making machinery; electronic parts

(P-14498)
MICROBAR INC
45473 Warm Springs Blvd, Fremont (94539-6104)
PHONE..................................510 659-9770
EMP: 295
SQ FT: 50,000
SALES (est): 29.8MM **Privately Held**
SIC: 3559

(P-14499)
MMR TECHNOLOGIES INC (PA)
41 Daggett Dr, San Jose (95134-2109)
PHONE..................................650 962-9620
William Little, *CEO*
Maria Reeves, *Admin Asst*
Jessica Jordan, *Administration*
Debra Hoon, *Controller*
EMP: 16
SQ FT: 6,700
SALES (est): 2.5MM **Privately Held**
SIC: 3559 Cryogenic machinery, industrial

(P-14500)
MOORE EPITAXIAL INC
Also Called: Moore Technologies
1422 Harding Ave, Tracy (95376-3319)
PHONE..................................209 833-0100
Gary Moore, *President*
Tim Brown, *Vice Pres*
▲ EMP: 30
SQ FT: 22,000
SALES (est): 5.9MM **Privately Held**
WEB: www.mooretech.com
SIC: 3559 3674 Semiconductor manufacturing machinery; wafers (semiconductor devices)

(P-14501)
MOREHOUSE-COWLES LLC
Also Called: Epworth Morehouse Cowles
13930 Magnolia Ave, Chino (91710-7029)
PHONE..................................909 627-7222
Michael E Pfau,
EMP: 25
SALES (est): 5.9MM
SALES (corp-wide): 1.4B **Publicly Held**
WEB: www.morehousecowles.com
SIC: 3559 Chemical machinery & equipment
HQ: Nusil Technology Llc
　　1050 Cindy Ln
　　Carpinteria CA 93013
　　805 684-8780

(P-14502)
MPJ RECYCLING LLC
2100 21st St Ste B, Sacramento (95818-1762)
PHONE..................................916 761-5740
Maryann Hodgson, *CEO*
John Hodgson,
EMP: 10
SQ FT: 100
SALES (est): 1.1MM **Privately Held**
WEB: www.mpjrecycling.com
SIC: 3559 Recycling machinery

(P-14503)
MT SYSTEMS INC
Also Called: Micro Tech Systems
49040 Milmont Dr, Fremont (94538-7301)
PHONE..................................510 651-5277
Thomas Mike Vukosav, *President*
Kelly Vukosav, *Manager*
▼ EMP: 17 EST: 2000
SQ FT: 16,000

SALES (est): 6MM **Privately Held**
WEB: www.macrotron2.com
SIC: 3559 Semiconductor manufacturing machinery

(P-14504)
MULTIBEAM CORPORATION
3951 Burton Dr, Santa Clara (95054-1583)
PHONE..................................408 980-1800
Dr David K Lam, *Ch of Bd*
Lynn Barringer, *President*
Tom Rigoli, *Vice Pres*
EMP: 35
SALES (est): 5.9MM **Privately Held**
SIC: 3559 Semiconductor manufacturing machinery

(P-14505)
N-TEK INC
Also Called: Ntek
823 Kifer Rd, Sunnyvale (94086-5204)
P.O. Box 71001 (94086-0976)
PHONE..................................408 735-8442
Zoltran Albert, *Owner*
Zoltan Albert, *Owner*
EMP: 30
SALES (est): 1.7MM **Privately Held**
SIC: 3559 3674 Semiconductor manufacturing machinery; semiconductors & related devices

(P-14506)
NEODORA LLC
Also Called: Espe Machine Work / Ver Mfg
1545 Berger Dr, San Jose (95112-2704)
PHONE..................................650 283-3319
Madhumathi Rupakukla,
EMP: 20 EST: 2014
SQ FT: 12,000
SALES (est): 1.5MM **Privately Held**
SIC: 3559 Sewing machines & hat & zipper making machinery

(P-14507)
NEW LOGIC RESEARCH INC
5040 Commercial Cir Ste A, Concord (94520-1250)
PHONE..................................510 655-7305
Gregory Johnson, *CEO*
Dr J Brad Culkin, *President*
Julie Vukuvojac, *CFO*
Chip Johnson, *Vice Pres*
Suzanne Meade, *Office Mgr*
◆ EMP: 90
SQ FT: 44,000
SALES (est): 17.6MM **Privately Held**
WEB: www.newlogicresearch.com
SIC: 3559 Chemical machinery & equipment

(P-14508)
NORCHEM CORPORATION (PA)
5649 Alhambra Ave, Los Angeles (90032-3107)
PHONE..................................323 221-0221
Gevork Minissian, *CEO*
Kevin Minissian, *Vice Pres*
Leo Gastelum, *Director*
Houri Minissian, *Asst Mgr*
▲ EMP: 55
SQ FT: 50,000
SALES (est): 11.8MM **Privately Held**
SIC: 3559 2842 2841 Chemical machinery & equipment; laundry cleaning preparations; soap & other detergents

(P-14509)
NURO INC
1300 Terra Bella Ave # 100, Mountain View (94043-1850)
PHONE..................................650 476-2687
David Ferguson, *CEO*
Jiajun Zhu, *Principal*
EMP: 12 EST: 2017
SALES (est): 2.1MM **Privately Held**
SIC: 3559 Robots, molding & forming plastics

(P-14510)
OZONE SAFE FOOD INC
31500 Grape St, Lake Elsinore (92532-9709)
P.O. Box 580490, North Palm Springs (92258-0490)
PHONE..................................951 228-2151
Mark Taggatz, *President*

Sherry Wilson, *Office Mgr*
EMP: 10
SALES (est): 16.1K **Privately Held**
WEB: www.ozonesafefoods.com
SIC: 3559 Ozone machines

(P-14511)
P & L SPECIALTIES
1650 Almar Pkwy, Santa Rosa (95403-8253)
PHONE..................................707 573-3141
Edwin Barr, *President*
Lisa Hyde, *Vice Pres*
Kevin Young, *Sales Staff*
▲ EMP: 15
SQ FT: 15,000
SALES (est): 4.4MM **Privately Held**
WEB: www.pnlspecialties.com
SIC: 3559 3556 Recycling machinery; beverage machinery

(P-14512)
PACIFIC GINNING COMPANY LLC
33370 W Nebraska Ave, Cantua Creek (93608)
PHONE..................................559 829-9446
Matt Toste,
EMP: 23
SALES (est): 2.1MM **Privately Held**
SIC: 3559 Cotton ginning machinery

(P-14513)
PALOMAR TECHNOLOGIES INC (PA)
2728 Loker Ave W, Carlsbad (92010-6603)
PHONE..................................760 931-3600
Bruce Hueners, *CEO*
Carl Hempel, *CFO*
Matt Clements, *Sr Software Eng*
Shawn Rivera, *Info Tech Mgr*
Evan Hueners, *Technology*
EMP: 79
SQ FT: 40,000
SALES (est): 20.7MM **Privately Held**
WEB: www.palomartechnologies.com
SIC: 3559 Semiconductor manufacturing machinery

(P-14514)
PARKER-HANNIFIN CORPORATION
Water Purification
2630 E El Presidio St, Carson (90810-1115)
PHONE..................................310 608-5600
Brian Hook, *Manager*
EMP: 200
SALES (corp-wide): 14.3B **Publicly Held**
WEB: www.parker.com
SIC: 3559 Desalination equipment
PA: Parker-Hannifin Corporation
　　6035 Parkland Blvd
　　Cleveland OH 44124
　　216 896-3000

(P-14515)
PEABODY ENGINEERING & SUP INC
13435 Estelle St, Corona (92879-1877)
PHONE..................................951 734-7711
Mark Peabody, *CEO*
Larry Peabody, *President*
Cheryl Peabody, *General Mgr*
Candice Brown, *Accountant*
Ruth Noordwal, *Editor*
◆ EMP: 25 EST: 1952
SQ FT: 32,400
SALES (est): 7.2MM **Privately Held**
WEB: www.etanks.com
SIC: 3559 5084 Chemical machinery & equipment; industrial machinery & equipment

(P-14516)
PERCEPTIMED INC
365 San Antonio Rd, Mountain View (94040-1213)
PHONE..................................650 941-7000
Frank Starn, *CEO*
Alan Jacobs, *President*
Hamutal Anavi Russo, *CFO*
Sheila Wallace, *Admin Sec*
Jackie Gratto, *Engineer*
EMP: 27

SALES: 1.9MM **Privately Held**
SIC: 3559 Pharmaceutical machinery

(P-14517)
PERSYS ENGINEERING INC
815 Swift St, Santa Cruz (95060-5851)
PHONE..................................831 471-9300
Gideon Drimer, *CEO*
Ofer Molad, *President*
Oz Drimer, *COO*
Mike Pitts, *Prdtn Mgr*
Armando Avalos, *Manager*
▲ EMP: 23
SQ FT: 12,000
SALES (est): 4.9MM **Privately Held**
WEB: www.persyseng.com
SIC: 3559 8711 7699 Semiconductor manufacturing machinery; engineering services; industrial equipment cleaning

(P-14518)
PHILLIPS 66 CO CARBON GROUP
2555 Willow Rd, Arroyo Grande (93420-5731)
PHONE..................................805 489-4050
EMP: 16
SALES (est): 2.6MM **Privately Held**
SIC: 3559 Petroleum refinery equipment

(P-14519)
PICOTRACK
309 Laurelwood Rd Ste 21, Santa Clara (95054-2313)
PHONE..................................408 988-7000
Thu Doan, *Partner*
Soang Nguyen, *Partner*
EMP: 10
SALES (est): 1.8MM **Privately Held**
SIC: 3559 Semiconductor manufacturing machinery

(P-14520)
PRECISION EUROPEAN INC
11594 Coley River Cir, Fountain Valley (92708-4219)
PHONE..................................714 241-9657
Detlef Herrmann, *President*
Tanja Herrmann, *Vice Pres*
Dave Juergens, *Admin Sec*
▲ EMP: 13
SQ FT: 8,000
SALES: 1.5MM **Privately Held**
WEB: www.peius.com
SIC: 3559 7538 Automotive maintenance equipment; general automotive repair shops

(P-14521)
PROLINE CONCRETE TOOLS INC
2664 Vista Pacific Dr, Oceanside (92056-3514)
PHONE..................................760 758-7240
Jeff Irwin, *CEO*
Paul Sowa, *CFO*
Nan Di Givanni, *Manager*
▼ EMP: 27
SALES (est): 6.2MM **Privately Held**
WEB: www.prolineconcretetools.com
SIC: 3559 Concrete products machinery

(P-14522)
PUROTECS INC
6678 Owens Dr Ste 104, Pleasanton (94588-3324)
PHONE..................................925 215-0380
Ken Stevens, *Principal*
Kevin Shuster, *Technical Staff*
EMP: 10 EST: 2012
SALES (est): 1.7MM **Privately Held**
SIC: 3559 Chemical machinery & equipment

(P-14523)
QONTROL DEVICES INC
167 Mason Way Ste A7, City of Industry (91746-2338)
PHONE..................................626 968-4268
Show Jow, *CEO*
Charles Jow, *President*
Terry Dowell, *Project Mgr*
Vinh Ly, *Project Mgr*
Calvin Son, *Sales Staff*
▲ EMP: 10
SQ FT: 30,000

▲ = Import ▼=Export
◆ =Import/Export

SALES (est): 1.6MM **Privately Held**
WEB: www.qontroldevices.com
SIC: 3559

(P-14524)
QUALITY MACHINING & DESIGN INC
2857 Aiello Dr, San Jose (95111-2155)
PHONE..............................408 224-7976
Ryszard Ott, *President*
EMP: 30
SQ FT: 23,000
SALES: 7.8MM **Privately Held**
WEB: www.qualitymd.com
SIC: 3559 3365 Semiconductor manufacturing machinery; aerospace castings, aluminum

(P-14525)
RAPID ANODIZING LLC
1216 W Slauson Ave, Los Angeles (90044-2822)
PHONE..............................323 753-5255
Jonathan Minter, *CEO*
Florence Fratello, *Administration*
Jake Minter, *Administration*
EMP: 10
SALES (est): 718.5K **Privately Held**
SIC: 3559 Refinery, chemical processing & similar machinery

(P-14526)
RCH ASSOCIATES INC
349 Earhart Way, Livermore (94551-9509)
PHONE..............................510 657-7846
Robert C Hoelsch, *President*
Chris Guiver, *Info Tech Dir*
Matthew Furlo, *Engineer*
Isidro Trujillo, *Prdtn Mgr*
EMP: 14
SALES (est): 3.1MM **Privately Held**
SIC: 3559 Semiconductor manufacturing machinery

(P-14527)
REDLINE DETECTION LLC
828 W Taft Ave, Orange (92865-4232)
PHONE..............................714 451-1411
Zachary Parker, *Principal*
Alex Parker, *Vice Pres*
Gene Stauffer, *General Mgr*
Evelyn Sandoval, *Accountant*
▲ EMP: 10
SQ FT: 6,500
SALES (est): 2.1MM **Privately Held**
WEB: www.redlinedetection.com
SIC: 3559 Automotive maintenance equipment

(P-14528)
RICHARD VEECK
9966 Golf Link Rd, Hilmar (95324-9306)
PHONE..............................209 667-0872
Richard Veeck, *Owner*
Jaince Veeck, *Treasurer*
EMP: 15
SALES (est): 943.3K **Privately Held**
SIC: 3559 Recycling machinery

(P-14529)
RICK PALENSHUS
Also Called: Pro Coat Powder Coating
560 3rd St, Lake Elsinore (92530-2729)
PHONE..............................951 245-2100
Rick Palenshus, *Owner*
EMP: 18
SQ FT: 18,000
SALES (est): 3MM **Privately Held**
WEB: www.procoatpowdercoating.com
SIC: 3559 Metal finishing equipment for plating, etc.

(P-14530)
RITE TRACK EQUIPMENT SVCS INC
2151 Otoole Ave Ste 40, San Jose (95131-1330)
PHONE..............................408 432-0131
EMP: 15 **Privately Held**
SIC: 3559
PA: Rite Track Equipment Services, Inc.
8655 Rite Track Way
West Chester OH 45069

(P-14531)
RUBICON EXPRESS (PA)
Also Called: Rubicon Manufacturing
3290 Monier Cir Ste 100, Rancho Cordova (95742-7368)
PHONE..............................916 858-8575
Ryan Wallace, *President*
EMP: 10
SQ FT: 30,000
SALES (est): 3.4MM **Privately Held**
WEB: www.rubiconexpress.com
SIC: 3559 5013 Automotive related machinery; motor vehicle supplies & new parts

(P-14532)
RUCKER & KOLLS INC (HQ)
Also Called: Rucker & Knolls
1064 Yosemite Dr, Milpitas (95035-5410)
PHONE..............................408 934-9875
Arlen Chou, *President*
Hsun Chou, *Director*
EMP: 27
SQ FT: 6,000
SALES (est): 3.2MM
SALES (corp-wide): 13.3MM **Privately Held**
WEB: www.ruckerkolls.com
SIC: 3559 3825 Semiconductor manufacturing machinery; instruments to measure electricity
PA: Eico, Inc.
1054 Yosemite Dr
Milpitas CA 95035
408 945-9898

(P-14533)
RXSAFE LLC
2453 Cades Way Bldg A, Vista (92081-7858)
PHONE..............................760 593-7161
William Holmes, *CEO*
Keith Butler, *COO*
David Wilkinson, *CFO*
Brian Kichler, *Vice Pres*
Michael James, *CTO*
EMP: 58
SALES (est): 10.4MM **Privately Held**
SIC: 3559 Pharmaceutical machinery

(P-14534)
SAFETY-KLEEN SYSTEMS INC
3561 S Maple Ave, Fresno (93725-2415)
PHONE..............................559 486-1960
Allan Calandra, *Manager*
EMP: 18
SQ FT: 2,000
SALES (corp-wide): 3.3B **Publicly Held**
SIC: 3559 7359 5172 4212 Degreasing machines, automotive & industrial; equipment rental & leasing; petroleum products; hazardous waste transport; solvents recovery service; industrial supplies
HQ: Safety-Kleen Systems, Inc.
2600 N Central Expy # 400
Richardson TX 75080
972 265-2000

(P-14535)
SANDVIK THERMAL PROCESS INC
19500 Nugget Blvd, Sonora (95370-9248)
PHONE..............................209 533-1990
James T Johnson, *CEO*
Eric Anderson, *Design Engr*
Bradley Blackmore, *Design Engr*
Frank Figoni, *Finance*
Sue Westgate, *Human Res Dir*
▲ EMP: 75 EST: 1981
SQ FT: 100,000
SALES (est): 19.8MM
SALES (corp-wide): 11.1B **Privately Held**
SIC: 3559 Semiconductor manufacturing machinery
HQ: Sandvik, Inc.
17-02 Nevins Rd
Fair Lawn NJ 07410
201 794-5000

(P-14536)
SANTUR CORPORATION (HQ)
40931 Encyclopedia Cir, Fremont (94538-2436)
PHONE..............................510 933-4100
Paul Meissner, *President*
George W Laplante, *CFO*

Bardia Pezeshki, *CTO*
Sabeur Siala, *VP Engrg*
Richard Wilmer, *VP Opers*
EMP: 28
SQ FT: 20,000
SALES (est): 4.5MM **Publicly Held**
WEB: www.santurcorp.com
SIC: 3559 Electronic component making machinery

(P-14537)
SEMICONDUCTOR EQUIPMENT CORP
Also Called: SEC
5154 Goldman Ave, Moorpark (93021-1760)
PHONE..............................805 529-2293
Donald I Moore, *CEO*
Richard Folsom, *Treasurer*
Chris Ryding, *Sr Software Eng*
Mickey Omori, *Technical Staff*
Suzy Tritenbach, *Sales Staff*
▲ EMP: 16
SQ FT: 12,500
SALES (est): 3.4MM **Privately Held**
WEB: www.semicorp.com
SIC: 3559 Semiconductor manufacturing machinery

(P-14538)
SPT MICROTECHNOLOGIES USA INC
1150 Ringwood Ct, San Jose (95131-1726)
PHONE..............................408 571-1400
Vivek RAO, *COO*
Seiichi Ogino, *President*
Takayoshi Kikuchi, *Treasurer*
Andy Bavin, *General Mgr*
Masayoshi Tanaka, *Admin Sec*
EMP: 43
SQ FT: 28,000
SALES (est): 6.6MM **Privately Held**
SIC: 3559 Semiconductor manufacturing machinery

(P-14539)
STARCO ENTERPRISES INC (PA)
Also Called: Four Star Chemical
3137 E 26th St, Vernon (90058-8006)
PHONE..............................323 266-7111
Jerry Ulrich, *CEO*
William Edwards, *CFO*
Ross Sklar, *Co-CEO*
Darin Brown, *VP Opers*
▲ EMP: 75
SQ FT: 25,000
SALES (est): 19.6MM **Privately Held**
WEB: www.fourstarchemical.com
SIC: 3559 5169 5191 Degreasing machines, automotive & industrial; specialty cleaning & sanitation preparations; farm supplies

(P-14540)
SUPERIOR AUTOMATION INC
47770 Westinghouse Dr, Fremont (94539-7475)
PHONE..............................408 227-4898
Sean Kessinger, *President*
Donald Brosio, *Officer*
Kevin Johnson, *Vice Pres*
Lance Faure, *Engineer*
Roger Kessinger, *Director*
EMP: 12
SQ FT: 11,000
SALES (est): 3.3MM **Privately Held**
WEB: www.superiorautomation.com
SIC: 3559 Semiconductor manufacturing machinery

(P-14541)
SUSS MICROTEC INC (HQ)
220 Klug Cir, Corona (92880-5409)
PHONE..............................408 940-0300
Frank Averdung, *President*
Franz Richter, *Ch of Bd*
Stefan Schneidewind, *Ch of Bd*
Wilfried Bair, *President*
Peter Szafir, *President*
EMP: 130
SQ FT: 37,000

SALES (est): 16.7MM
SALES (corp-wide): 233.4MM **Privately Held**
SIC: 3559 3825 3674 Semiconductor manufacturing machinery; instruments to measure electricity; semiconductors & related devices
PA: SUss Microtec Se
SchleiBheimer Str. 90
Garching B. Munchen 85748
893 200-70

(P-14542)
SUVOLTA INC
130 Knowles Dr Ste D, Los Gatos (95032-1832)
PHONE..............................408 866-4125
Bruce McWilliams, *President*
Louis Parrillo, *COO*
Leslie Wilkinson, *Director*
EMP: 21
SALES (est): 3.7MM **Privately Held**
SIC: 3559 Semiconductor manufacturing machinery

(P-14543)
T ULTRA EQUIPMENT COMPANY INC
41980 Christy St, Fremont (94538-3161)
PHONE..............................510 440-3900
John Flaagan, *President*
James Flaagan, *Engineer*
Christine Groves, *Controller*
Jesus Ortiz, *Prdtn Mgr*
◆ EMP: 12
SQ FT: 9,408
SALES: 3MM **Privately Held**
WEB: www.ultrat.com
SIC: 3559 7699 Semiconductor manufacturing machinery; industrial machinery & equipment repair

(P-14544)
TEMECULA QUALITY PLATING INC
43095 Black Deer Loop, Temecula (92590-3413)
PHONE..............................951 296-9875
Duc Vo, *President*
Dat Vo, *Vice Pres*
EMP: 18 EST: 2011
SQ FT: 10,000
SALES: 1.3MM **Privately Held**
SIC: 3559 Metal finishing equipment for plating, etc.

(P-14545)
TEXON USA INC
48438 Milmont Dr, Fremont (94538-7326)
PHONE..............................510 256-7210
Hyuncheol Han, *CEO*
EMP: 10
SALES (est): 1.8MM **Privately Held**
SIC: 3559 5065 Special industry machinery; electronic parts & equipment

(P-14546)
TRADEMARK PLASTICS INC
807 Palmyrita Ave, Riverside (92507-1805)
PHONE..............................909 941-8810
Erin Carty, *CEO*
Carolyn Carty, *President*
Phil Estrada, *Executive*
Robby Sinor, *Project Engr*
▲ EMP: 150
SQ FT: 100,000
SALES (est): 76.6MM **Privately Held**
WEB: www.trademarkplastics.com
SIC: 3559 3089 Plastics working machinery; injection molding of plastics

(P-14547)
TRI-C MANUFACTURING INC
517 Houston St, West Sacramento (95691-2213)
PHONE..............................916 371-1700
Lilburn Clyde Lamar, *President*
EMP: 20 EST: 1969
SALES (est): 3.9MM
SALES (corp-wide): 4.2MM **Privately Held**
SIC: 3559 Rubber working machinery, including tires

PA: Tri-C Machine Corporation
520 Harbor Blvd
West Sacramento CA 95691
916 371-8090

(P-14548)
TRIO-TECH INTERNATIONAL (PA)
16139 Wyandotte St, Van Nuys
(91406-3423)
PHONE.....................818 787-7000
Siew Wai Yong, *President*
A Charles Wilson, *Ch of Bd*
Victor H M Ting, *CFO*
Hwee Poh Lim, *Vice Pres*
S K Soon, *Vice Pres*
EMP: 10
SQ FT: 5,200
SALES: 39.2MM **Publicly Held**
WEB: www.triotech.com
SIC: 3559 3825 5084 3533 Semiconductor manufacturing machinery; semiconductor test equipment; instruments & control equipment; oil & gas field machinery; real estate leasing & rentals

(P-14549)
ULTRA TEC MANUFACTURING INC
1025 E Chestnut Ave, Santa Ana
(92701-6425)
PHONE.....................714 542-0608
Joseph I Rubin, *President*
Robert Rubin, *Vice Pres*
EMP: 15
SQ FT: 7,000
SALES (est): 2.9MM **Privately Held**
WEB: www.ultratecusa.com
SIC: 3559 3541 Synthetic filament extruding machines; grinding, polishing, buffing, lapping & honing machines

(P-14550)
ULTRATECH INC (HQ)
3050 Zanker Rd, San Jose (95134-2126)
PHONE.....................408 321-8835
Arthur W Zafiropoulo, *President*
Masoud Safa, *Vice Pres*
Calvin Wang, *Vice Pres*
Simon Chua, *General Mgr*
David Lee, *General Mgr*
EMP: 176
SQ FT: 100,000
SALES: 194MM
SALES (corp-wide): 542MM **Publicly Held**
SIC: 3559 Semiconductor manufacturing machinery
PA: Veeco Instruments Inc.
1 Terminal Dr
Plainview NY 11803
516 677-0200

(P-14551)
ULTRON SYSTEMS INC
5105 Maureen Ln, Moorpark (93021-1783)
PHONE.....................805 529-1485
Aki Egerer, *President*
Aaron Chan, *Vice Pres*
▲ **EMP:** 17
SQ FT: 8,000
SALES (est): 3.9MM **Privately Held**
WEB: www.ultronsystems.com
SIC: 3559 Semiconductor manufacturing machinery

(P-14552)
VA-TRAN SYSTEMS INC
677 Anita St Ste A, Chula Vista
(91911-4661)
PHONE.....................619 423-4555
James E Sloan, *President*
Chris Sloan, *Vice Pres*
▲ **EMP:** 10
SQ FT: 5,000
SALES (est): 1MM **Privately Held**
WEB: www.vatran.com
SIC: 3559 Cryogenic machinery, industrial

(P-14553)
VIZUALOGIC LLC
1493 E Bentley Dr, Corona (92879-5102)
PHONE.....................407 509-3421
Malek Tawil,
Janis Patterson,
EMP: 200

SQ FT: 3,000
SALES: 20MM **Privately Held**
SIC: 3559 Automotive related machinery

(P-14554)
WALCO INC
9017 Arrow Rte, Rancho Cucamonga
(91730-4412)
PHONE.....................909 483-3333
James Wilkinson, *CEO*
Mary Martin, *Opers Mgr*
EMP: 26
SALES (est): 6MM **Privately Held**
SIC: 3559 Ammunition & explosives, loading machinery

(P-14555)
WESLAN SYSTEMS INC
1244 Commerce Ave, Woodland
(95776-5902)
PHONE.....................530 668-3304
Richard Weston, *President*
Belma Weston, *CFO*
Larry Davis, *MIS Staff*
EMP: 12
SQ FT: 15,000
SALES: 3MM **Privately Held**
WEB: www.weslan.com
SIC: 3559 Semiconductor manufacturing machinery

(P-14556)
WEST COAST CRYOGENICS INC
Also Called: West Coast Cryogenics Services
503 W Larch Rd Ste K, Tracy
(95304-1670)
PHONE.....................800 657-0545
Danny Silveira, *President*
Krystal Silveria, *Vice Pres*
Pam Coelho, *Manager*
Anita Hollingsworth, *Manager*
EMP: 24
SALES (est): 2.2MM **Privately Held**
SIC: 3559 Cryogenic machinery, industrial

3561 Pumps & Pumping

(P-14557)
ADVANCED RESULTS COMPANY INC
18760 Afton Ave, Saratoga (95070-4653)
PHONE.....................408 986-0123
Arkady Dorf, *President*
Jamie Wang, *Admin Sec*
EMP: 15
SQ FT: 2,200
SALES (est): 1.6MM **Privately Held**
SIC: 3561 Industrial pumps & parts

(P-14558)
AGGREGATE MINING PRODUCTS LLC
21780 Temescal Canyon Rd, Corona
(92883-5669)
PHONE.....................951 277-1267
Bill Medina,
Frank Smith,
EMP: 12
SALES (est): 1.9MM **Privately Held**
SIC: 3561 Pump jacks & other pumping equipment

(P-14559)
AQUASTAR POOL PRODUCTS INC
Also Called: Aquastar Pool Productions
2340 Palma Dr Ste 104, Ventura
(93003-8091)
PHONE.....................877 768-2717
Olaf Mjelde, *CEO*
Sarah Reimer, *Admin Sec*
Chris Freihaut, *Sales Staff*
▲ **EMP:** 16
SALES (est): 4MM **Privately Held**
SIC: 3561 Pumps; domestic: water or sump

(P-14560)
AQUATEC INTERNATIONAL INC
Also Called: Aquatec Water Systems
17422 Pullman St, Irvine (92614-5527)
PHONE.....................949 225-2200

Bryan Hausner, *CEO*
Sami Levi, *CFO*
Ivar Schoenmeyr, *Corp Secy*
Isak Levi, *Vice Pres*
Vasko Rizof, *Info Tech Mgr*
▲ **EMP:** 95
SQ FT: 30,000
SALES (est): 28.9MM **Privately Held**
SIC: 3561 Pumps & pumping equipment

(P-14561)
BESTWAY HYDRAULICS CO INC
1518 S Santa Fe Ave, Compton
(90221-4919)
PHONE.....................310 639-2507
Ehud Nahir, *President*
Alona Nahir, *Treasurer*
EMP: 35
SQ FT: 7,000
SALES (est): 2.5MM **Privately Held**
WEB: www.bestwayhydraulics.com
SIC: 3561 5084 Cylinders, pump; industrial machinery & equipment

(P-14562)
BORIN MANUFACTURING INC
5741 Buckingham Pkwy B, Culver City
(90230-6520)
PHONE.....................310 822-1000
Frank William Borin, *CEO*
Gregg Steele, *Vice Pres*
Julian Portela, *Technician*
EMP: 40
SALES (est): 9MM **Privately Held**
WEB: www.borin.com
SIC: 3561 3443 3317 3494 Pumps & pumping equipment; fabricated plate work (boiler shop); steel pipe & tubes; valves & pipe fittings; telephone & telegraph apparatus; oil & gas field machinery

(P-14563)
CASCADE PUMP COMPANY
10107 Norwalk Blvd, Santa Fe Springs
(90670-3354)
P.O. Box 2767 (90670-0767)
PHONE.....................562 946-1414
T W Summerfield, *CEO*
John Summerfield, *CFO*
Brian Summerfield, *Engineer*
Scott Summerfield, *Human Res Dir*
John Gay, *Purch Mgr*
EMP: 60
SQ FT: 120,000
SALES (est): 29.5MM **Privately Held**
WEB: www.cascadepump.com
SIC: 3561 3594 Pumps, domestic: water or sump; fluid power pumps & motors

(P-14564)
COASTAL PRODUCTS COMPANY INC
2157 Mohawk St, Bakersfield
(93308-6020)
P.O. Box 1200 (93302-1200)
PHONE.....................661 323-0487
Dorothy Jones, *President*
Richard Jones, *General Mgr*
Marc Pasquini, *General Mgr*
Susan Privett, *Sales Staff*
EMP: 14
SQ FT: 2,500
SALES (est): 1.6MM **Privately Held**
SIC: 3561 Pumps & pumping equipment

(P-14565)
CRYOGNIC INDS SVC CMPANIES LLC (DH)
Also Called: Cryoatlanta
1851 Kaiser Ave, Irvine (92614-5707)
PHONE.....................949 261-7533
Jim Eftes, *CEO*
EMP: 12 **EST:** 2012
SQ FT: 2,500
SALES (est): 7.5MM **Privately Held**
SIC: 3561 Industrial pumps & parts
HQ: Acd, Llc
2321 Pullman St
Santa Ana CA 92705
949 261-7533

(P-14566)
CRYOSTAR USA LLC
13117 Meyer Rd, Whittier (90605-3555)
PHONE.....................562 903-1290
Jose Moreno,

Mark Sutton, *General Mgr*
Bruno Brethes, *Technical Staff*
Edra Ivora, *CPA*
Sean Hardy, *Sales Mgr*
▲ **EMP:** 42
SALES (est): 10MM **Privately Held**
SIC: 3561 Pump jacks & other pumping equipment
HQ: Cryostar Sas
2 Rue De L Industrie
Hesingue 68220
389 702-727

(P-14567)
CURLIN MEDICAL INC (HQ)
15662 Commerce Ln, Huntington Beach
(92649-1604)
PHONE.....................714 897-9301
Martin Berarei, *President*
▲ **EMP:** 10
SALES (est): 5.9MM
SALES (corp-wide): 2.9B **Publicly Held**
WEB: www.curlinmedical.com
SIC: 3561 Pumps & pumping equipment
PA: Moog Inc.
400 Jamison Rd
Elma NY 14059
716 805-2604

(P-14568)
DISCFLO CORPORATION
Also Called: Disc Pumps
10850 Hartley Rd, Santee (92071-2802)
PHONE.....................619 596-3181
Max Gurth, *CEO*
Arlene Bermio, *Controller*
Xochitl Aguirre, *Opers Mgr*
◆ **EMP:** 35
SQ FT: 50,000
SALES (est): 10.5MM **Privately Held**
WEB: www.discflo.com
SIC: 3561 Industrial pumps & parts

(P-14569)
DUONETICS
Also Called: Polynetics
809 E Parkridge Ave # 102, Corona
(92879-6610)
PHONE.....................951 808-4903
Robert Pernice, *President*
Charles Pernice, *Vice Pres*
Charles A Pernice, *Vice Pres*
EMP: 10
SQ FT: 7,000
SALES (est): 2.4MM **Privately Held**
WEB: www.duonetics.com
SIC: 3561 3599 3728 Industrial pumps & parts; machine & other job shop work; dynetric balancing stands, aircraft

(P-14570)
ELLIOTT COMPANY
51 Main Ave, Sacramento (95838-2014)
PHONE.....................916 920-5451
Evertt Hylton, *Branch Mgr*
EMP: 85 **Privately Held**
SIC: 3561 Pumps & pumping equipment
HQ: Elliott Company
901 N 4th St
Jeannette PA 15644
724 527-2811

(P-14571)
FLOW CONTROL LLC
17942 Cowan, Irvine (92614-6026)
PHONE.....................949 608-3900
Sonia Hollies, *Mng Member*
EMP: 10 **Publicly Held**
SIC: 3561 Pumps, domestic: water or sump
HQ: Flow Control Llc
1 International Dr
Rye Brook NY 10573
914 323-5700

(P-14572)
FLOWSERVE CORPORATION
2300 E Vernon Ave Stop 76, Vernon
(90058-1609)
PHONE.....................323 584-1890
Rick Soldo, *Branch Mgr*
Jama Meyer, *General Mgr*
Gary Mignacca, *General Mgr*
Hrishikesh Gadre, *Research*
Rhett Butler, *Technical Staff*
EMP: 342

▲ = Import ▼=Export
◆ =Import/Export

SALES (corp-wide): 3.8B **Publicly Held**
SIC: 3561 Pumps & pumping equipment
PA: Flowserve Corporation
5215 N Ocnnor Blvd Ste 23 Connor
Irving TX 75039
972 443-6500

(P-14573)
FLOWSERVE CORPORATION
1909 E Cashdan St, Compton
(90220-6422)
PHONE..................................310 667-4220
Dan Lattimore, *Manager*
Paul Bender, *Project Mgr*
Don Arrasmith, *Engineer*
Gerardo Galvan, *Engineer*
Justin Schultz, *Engineer*
EMP: 50
SALES (corp-wide): 3.8B **Publicly Held**
SIC: 3561 Industrial pumps & parts
PA: Flowserve Corporation
5215 N Ocnnor Blvd Ste 23 Connor
Irving TX 75039
972 443-6500

(P-14574)
FLOWSERVE CORPORATION
6077 Egret Ct, Benicia (94510-1205)
PHONE..................................707 745-4710
Keith Slothers, *Manager*
John Ireland, *Engineer*
Jim Dobson, *Sales Staff*
EMP: 18
SALES (corp-wide): 3.8B **Publicly Held**
SIC: 3561 Industrial pumps & parts
PA: Flowserve Corporation
5215 N Ocnnor Blvd Ste 23 Connor
Irving TX 75039
972 443-6500

(P-14575)
FLOWSERVE CORPORATION
27455 Tierra Alta Way C, Temecula
(92590-3498)
PHONE..................................951 296-2464
Paul Cortenbach, *Branch Mgr*
Jeannie Del Monte, *Engineer*
Steve Rose, *Manager*
EMP: 200
SALES (corp-wide): 3.8B **Publicly Held**
SIC: 3561 3053 Industrial pumps & parts;
gaskets, packing & sealing devices
PA: Flowserve Corporation
5215 N Ocnnor Blvd Ste 23 Connor
Irving TX 75039
972 443-6500

(P-14576)
GOULDS PUMPS
3951 Capitol Ave, City of Industry
(90601-1734)
PHONE..................................562 949-2113
Mike Suess, *Manager*
▲ **EMP:** 22
SALES (est): 4.8MM **Privately Held**
SIC: 3561 Pumps & pumping equipment

(P-14577)
GRISWOLD PUMP COMPANY
22069 Van Buren St, Grand Terrace
(92313-5607)
PHONE..................................909 422-1700
Dale Pavlovich, *President*
Michael Boul, *Vice Pres*
Dave Spitzer, *Vice Pres*
Edward Vaughn, *Vice Pres*
▲ **EMP:** 25
SQ FT: 25,000
SALES (est): 6MM
SALES (corp-wide): 6.9B **Publicly Held**
WEB: www.griswoldpump.com
SIC: 3561 5084 Industrial pumps & parts;
industrial machinery & equipment
HQ: Wilden Pump And Engineering Llc
22069 Van Buren St
Grand Terrace CA 92313
909 422-1700

(P-14578)
GROVER SMITH MFG CORP
Also Called: Grover Manufacturing
620 S Vail Ave, Montebello (90640-4952)
P.O. Box 986 (90640-0986)
PHONE..................................323 724-3444
Marilyn Schirmer, *President*
W Michael Meeker, *Ch of Bd*

Lino Paras, *Treasurer*
Michael Meyer, *Manager*
EMP: 30
SQ FT: 65,000
SALES (est): 7.1MM **Privately Held**
WEB: www.grovermfg.com
SIC: 3561 3569 Pumps & pumping equip-
ment; lubrication equipment, industrial

(P-14579)
GRUNDFOS CBS INC
Also Called: Paco Pumps By Grundfos
25568 Seaboard Ln, Hayward
(94545-3210)
PHONE..................................510 512-1300
Steve Wilson, *Branch Mgr*
EMP: 18
SALES (corp-wide): 4.1B **Privately Held**
WEB: www.us.grundfos.com
SIC: 3561 Pumps & pumping equipment
HQ: Grundfos Cbs Inc.
902 Koomey Rd
Brookshire TX 77423
281 994-2700

(P-14580)
HARBISON-FISCHER INC
2801 Pegasus Dr, Bakersfield
(93308-6818)
PHONE..................................661 387-0166
Tom Demos, *Branch Mgr*
EMP: 20
SALES (corp-wide): 1.2B **Publicly Held**
WEB: www.hfpumps.com
SIC: 3561 Industrial pumps & parts
HQ: Harbison-Fischer, Inc.
901 N Crowley Rd
Crowley TX 76036
817 297-2211

(P-14581)
HASKEL INTERNATIONAL LLC (HQ)
100 E Graham Pl, Burbank (91502-2076)
PHONE..................................818 843-4000
Chris Krieps, *CEO*
Roy Todd, *Planning*
Gerry Levasseur, *Information Mgr*
Steve Quigley, *Engineer*
Froilan Tolentino, *Engineer*
▲ **EMP:** 125
SQ FT: 78,000
SALES (est): 76.9MM
SALES (corp-wide): 382.5MM **Privately Held**
WEB: www.haskel.com
SIC: 3561 3594 5084 5085 Pumps &
pumping equipment; fluid power pumps;
hydraulic systems equipment & supplies;
hose, belting & packing; valves, pistons &
fittings; electrical equipment & supplies
PA: Accudyne Industries, Llc
2728 N Harwood St Ste 200
Dallas TX 75201
469 518-4777

(P-14582)
HI-FLO CORP
5161 E El Cedral St, Long Beach
(90815-3903)
PHONE..................................562 468-0800
Alfred Brunella, *President*
Rick Brizendine, *Admin Sec*
EMP: 15
SQ FT: 5,000
SALES (est): 2.1MM **Privately Held**
WEB: www.hiflocorp.com
SIC: 3561 Pumps, oil well & field

(P-14583)
HP WATER SYSTEMS INC
9338 W Whites Bridge Ave, Fresno
(93706-9515)
PHONE..................................559 268-4751
Hollis Priest Jr, *President*
Joyce Priest, *Admin Sec*
EMP: 30
SQ FT: 3,000
SALES (est): 11.4MM **Privately Held**
SIC: 3561 1781 Pumps & pumping equip-
ment; water well drilling

(P-14584)
HYDRAFORCE INCORPORATED
7383 Orangewood Dr, Riverside
(92504-1027)
PHONE..................................951 689-3987
Javier Soto, *CEO*
Ricardo Michel, *Manager*
EMP: 14 **EST:** 1990
SQ FT: 4,000
SALES (est): 1.6MM **Privately Held**
SIC: 3561 Cylinders, pump

(P-14585)
HYDRAULIC TECHNOLOGY INC
3833 Cincinnati Ave, Rocklin (95765-1302)
PHONE..................................916 645-3317
Daniel Stokes, *President*
Catherine Stokes, *Admin Sec*
EMP: 10 **EST:** 1966
SQ FT: 10,400
SALES (est): 2.1MM **Privately Held**
WEB: www.hydraulictechnology.com
SIC: 3561 3823 Pumps & pumping equip-
ment; pressure measurement instru-
ments, industrial

(P-14586)
ITT LLC
3878 S Willow Ave Ste 104, Fresno
(93725-9015)
PHONE..................................559 265-4730
Jeff Barrow, *Manager*
EMP: 15
SALES (corp-wide): 2.7B **Publicly Held**
WEB: www.ittind.com
SIC: 3561 Pumps & pumping equipment
HQ: Itt Llc
1133 Westchester Ave N-100
White Plains NY 10604
914 641-2000

(P-14587)
ITT WATER & WASTEWATER USA INC
790 Chadbourne Rd Ste A, Fairfield
(94534-9617)
PHONE..................................707 422-9894
Larry Kuehner, *Branch Mgr*
EMP: 20
SQ FT: 15,400 **Publicly Held**
WEB: www.flygtus.com
SIC: 3561 Pumps & pumping equipment
HQ: Itt Water & Wastewater U.S.A., Inc.
1 Greenwich Pl Ste 2
Shelton CT 06484
262 548-8181

(P-14588)
KEENE ENGINEERING INC (PA)
Also Called: Keene Industries
20201 Bahama St, Chatsworth
(91311-6204)
PHONE..................................818 485-2681
Jerry Keene, *CEO*
Tina Ngo Shin, *CFO*
Patrick O Keene, *Corp Secy*
Mark A Keene, *Vice Pres*
John Hartman, *Sales Staff*
▼ **EMP:** 10 **EST:** 1957
SQ FT: 22,000
SALES (est): 8MM **Privately Held**
WEB: www.keeneengineering.com
SIC: 3561 3531 Pumps & pumping equip-
ment; dredging machinery

(P-14589)
LOS ANGLES PUMP VALVE PDTS INC
Also Called: Los Angeles Brass Products
2528 E 57th St, Huntington Park
(90255-2521)
P.O. Box 2007 (90255-1307)
PHONE..................................323 277-7788
Santos J Pinto, *President*
Phil Pinto, *Vice Pres*
EMP: 20
SQ FT: 11,000
SALES (est): 4.1MM **Privately Held**
SIC: 3561 Pump jacks & other pumping
equipment

(P-14590)
MESSER LLC
Boc Edwards Systems Chemistry
2041 Mission College Blvd, Santa Clara
(95054)
PHONE..................................408 496-1177
Tom Haren, *Manager*
EMP: 80
SQ FT: 30,000
SALES (corp-wide): 1.4B **Privately Held**
SIC: 3561 Pumps & pumping equipment
HQ: Messer Llc
200 Somerset Corp Blvd # 7000
Bridgewater NJ 08807
908 464-8100

(P-14591)
MJW INC
Also Called: American Lab and Systems
1328 W Slauson Ave, Los Angeles
(90044-2824)
PHONE..................................323 778-8900
Mike Curry, *President*
Linda Curry, *Vice Pres*
Shane Curry, *General Mgr*
EMP: 65
SQ FT: 30,000
SALES (est): 13.5MM **Privately Held**
WEB: www.hydraulicsmall.com
SIC: 3561 Industrial pumps & parts

(P-14592)
N Z PUMP CO INC
Also Called: New Zealand Pump Company
801 S Palm Ave, Alhambra (91803-1426)
PHONE..................................626 458-8023
Claire Jenkinson Johns, *Principal*
James Maines, *Vice Chairman*
▲ **EMP:** 18
SALES (est): 4MM **Privately Held**
SIC: 3561 Industrial pumps & parts

(P-14593)
PENGUIN PUMPS INCORPORATED
Also Called: Filter Pump Industries
7932 Ajay Dr, Sun Valley (91352-5315)
PHONE..................................818 504-2391
Jerome S Hollander, *President*
Sonya E Hollander, *Corp Secy*
Mitchell A Hollander, *Vice Pres*
▲ **EMP:** 50
SQ FT: 20,000
SALES (est): 16.6MM **Privately Held**
WEB: www.filterpump.com
SIC: 3561 3569 Pumps & pumping equip-
ment; filters, general line: industrial

(P-14594)
PEP WEST INC
Also Called: Pentair Technical Products
7328 Trade St, San Diego (92121-3435)
PHONE..................................800 525-4682
Beth Wozniak, *CEO*
Bill Biancaniello, *President*
Michael Meyer, *Treasurer*
Randall Hogan, *Bd of Directors*
Judy Carle, *Vice Pres*
▲ **EMP:** 800
SALES (est): 155.7MM **Privately Held**
WEB: www.pentair.com
SIC: 3561 Pumps & pumping equipment

(P-14595)
POLARIS E-COMMERCE INC
1941 E Occidental St, Santa Ana
(92705-5115)
PHONE..................................714 907-0582
Insoo Hwang, *CEO*
▲ **EMP:** 25 **EST:** 2010
SALES (est): 3.8MM **Privately Held**
SIC: 3561 Industrial pumps & parts

(P-14596)
PROVAC SALES INC
3131 Soquel Dr Ste A, Soquel
(95073-2098)
PHONE..................................831 462-8900
Paul Flood, *CEO*
EMP: 23
SALES: 2.6MM **Privately Held**
WEB: www.provac.com
SIC: 3561 5084 Pumps & pumping equip-
ment; pumps & pumping equipment

PRODUCTS & SVCS

(PA)=Parent Co (HQ)=Headquarters (DH)=Div Headquarters
✿ = New Business established in last 2 years

(P-14597)
REED LLC
Also Called: Reed Manufacturing
13822 Oaks Ave, Chino (91710-7008)
PHONE...................................909 287-2100
James W Shea, President
Cliff KAO, Vice Pres
Ivan Ward, Materials Mgr
◆ EMP: 40 EST: 1957
SQ FT: 69,000
SALES (est): 11.4MM Privately Held
WEB: www.reedmfg.com
SIC: 3561 3531 Pumps & pumping equipment; bituminous, cement & concrete related products & equipment

(P-14598)
SMITH PRECISION PRODUCTS CO
Also Called: Smith Pumps
1299 Lawrence Dr, Newbury Park (91320-1306)
P.O. Box 276 (91319-0276)
PHONE...................................805 498-6616
Walter W Smith, President
Warren Smith, Treasurer
Karen Bolyard, Controller
John Ives, Sales Executive
▲ EMP: 21
SQ FT: 16,000
SALES: 2.4MM Privately Held
WEB: www.smithpumps.com
SIC: 3561 Industrial pumps & parts

(P-14599)
SULZER PUMP SOLUTIONS US INC
1650 Bell Ave Ste 140, Sacramento (95838-2869)
PHONE...................................916 925-8508
Dale Gretzinger, Manager
EMP: 20
SALES (corp-wide): 16.1MM Privately Held
WEB: www.absgroup.com
SIC: 3561 Pumps & pumping equipment
PA: Sulzer Pump Solutions (Us) Inc.
140 Pond View Dr
Meriden CT 06450
203 238-2700

(P-14600)
TOMIKO INC
Also Called: American Industrial Pump
1615 W 10th St, Antioch (94509-1363)
P.O. Box 8056, Pittsburg (94565-8056)
PHONE...................................925 754-5694
Michael Gianni, CEO
Enrique Pallado, Corp Secy
Tom Fox, Director
▲ EMP: 13
SALES (est): 3.5MM Privately Held
SIC: 3561 Industrial pumps & parts

(P-14601)
TOTAL PROCESS SOLUTIONS LLC
1400 Norris Rd, Bakersfield (93308-2232)
PHONE...................................661 829-7910
Eddie L Rice, Mng Member
Stan Ellis, Mng Member
Travis Ellis, Mng Member
Joey L Taylor, Mng Member
EMP: 30
SALES (est): 9.4MM Privately Held
SIC: 3561 3563 Cylinders, pump; air & gas compressors including vacuum pumps

(P-14602)
TR ENGINEERING INC
1350 Green Hills Rd 10, Scotts Valley (95066-4986)
PHONE...................................831 430-9920
Robert J Romero, President
Jill Koering-Romero, Vice Pres
Tarek Lutfi, Software Dev
EMP: 10 EST: 1982
SQ FT: 8,800
SALES: 1MM Privately Held
WEB: www.trengineering.com
SIC: 3561 3491 Pumps & pumping equipment; industrial valves

(P-14603)
TRILLIUM PUMPS USA INC (DH)
Also Called: Floway Pumps
2494 S Railroad Ave, Fresno (93706-5109)
P.O. Box 164 (93707-0164)
PHONE...................................559 442-4000
John Kavalam, President
Eric Smith, Area Mgr
Vern Avakian, Info Tech Dir
Richard Debarry, Software Dev
Keith Hart, Project Mgr
◆ EMP: 130 EST: 1932
SQ FT: 128,000
SALES (est): 40.3MM Privately Held
SIC: 3561 Industrial pumps & parts
HQ: First Reserve Corporation, L.L.C.
290 Harbor Dr Fl 1
Stamford CT 06902
203 661-6601

(P-14604)
WESTCOAST ROTOR INC
119 W 154th St, Gardena (90248-2201)
PHONE...................................310 327-5050
Vehan Mahdessian, President
Krikor Mahdessian, CFO
▲ EMP: 21
SQ FT: 15,625
SALES (est): 4.4MM Privately Held
WEB: www.westcoastrotor.com
SIC: 3561 Industrial pumps & parts

(P-14605)
WILDEN PUMP AND ENGRG LLC (DH)
22069 Van Buren St, Grand Terrace (92313-5651)
PHONE...................................909 422-1700
Denny L Buskirk, Mng Member
Rance James, Info Tech Dir
Linda Anderson, Purch Dir
Kathy Manley, Purch Mgr
Daniel Anderson,
◆ EMP: 295 EST: 1956
SQ FT: 153,000
SALES (est): 66.7MM
SALES (corp-wide): 6.9B Publicly Held
WEB: www.wildenpump.com
SIC: 3561 Industrial pumps & parts
HQ: Canada Organization & Development Llc
3005 Highland Pkwy
Downers Grove IL 60515
630 743-2563

(P-14606)
XYLEM INC
3878 S Willow Ave, Fresno (93725-9015)
PHONE...................................559 265-4731
John Morales, Manager
▲ EMP: 13
SALES (est): 2.8MM Privately Held
SIC: 3561 Pumps & pumping equipment

(P-14607)
ZILIFT INC
3600 Pegasus Dr Unit 7, Bakersfield (93308-7089)
PHONE...................................661 369-8579
EMP: 12
SALES (est): 1.8MM Privately Held
SIC: 3561 Pumps & pumping equipment
HQ: Zilift Limited
Unit A
Aberdeen AB23
-

3562 Ball & Roller Bearings

(P-14608)
AMERICAN METAL BEARING COMPANY
7191 Acacia Ave, Garden Grove (92841-5297)
PHONE...................................714 892-5527
Alfred A Anawati, CEO
Jim Demaio, Corp Secy
Michael Litton, Vice Pres
Tom Nguyen, Design Engr
Matthew Ghiassi, QC Mgr
▲ EMP: 21 EST: 1921
SQ FT: 40,000

SALES (est): 5.9MM
SALES (corp-wide): 21.9MM Privately Held
WEB: www.ambco.net
SIC: 3562 7699 3568 Ball bearings & parts; roller bearings & parts; rebabbitting; power transmission equipment
PA: Marisco, Ltd.
91-607 Malakole St
Kapolei HI 96707
808 682-1333

(P-14609)
CLEAN WAVE MANAGEMENT INC
Also Called: Impact Bearing
1291 Puerta Del Sol, San Clemente (92673-6310)
PHONE...................................949 361-5356
Richard D Kay Jr, CEO
Stanley Truong, QC Mgr
Michael Bartlett, Manager
Michael J Bartlett, Manager
◆ EMP: 30
SQ FT: 20,000
SALES (est): 5.7MM Privately Held
SIC: 3562 Ball bearings & parts

(P-14610)
INDUSTRIAL TCTNICS BRINGS CORP (DH)
18301 S Santa Fe Ave, E Rncho Dmngz (90221-5519)
PHONE...................................310 537-3750
Michael J Hartnett, CEO
Malek Machta, Senior Engr
Ricardo Perez, Manager
EMP: 71
SQ FT: 70,000
SALES (est): 27.5MM
SALES (corp-wide): 702.5MM Publicly Held
SIC: 3562 5085 Roller bearings & parts; bearings
HQ: Roller Bearing Company Of America, Inc.
102 Willenbrock Rd
Oxford CT 06478
203 267-7001

(P-14611)
LINMARR ASSOCIATES INC
8 Hammond Ste 108, Irvine (92618-1601)
PHONE...................................949 215-5466
Sharon A Hoffman, Owner
William K Hoffman II, Vice Pres
Brynne McGovern, Sales Staff
Nancy Piper, Manager
EMP: 10
SQ FT: 5,500
SALES (est): 14.5MM Privately Held
WEB: www.linmarr.com
SIC: 3562 5063 5065 Ball & roller bearings; switches, except electronic; capacitors, electronic

(P-14612)
NOMA BEARING CORPORATION
1555 W Rosecrans Ave, Gardena (90249-3027)
PHONE...................................310 329-1800
Toshi Noma, President
Kevin Tanaka, Vice Pres
▲ EMP: 10
SQ FT: 15,000
SALES (est): 2.4MM Privately Held
SIC: 3562 Ball bearings & parts

(P-14613)
NSK PRECISION AMERICA INC
Also Called: NSK Prec Amer Santa Fe Springs
13921 Bettencourt St, Cerritos (90703-1011)
PHONE...................................562 968-1000
Philip Jennings, Manager
EMP: 12 Privately Held
SIC: 3562 Ball & roller bearings
HQ: Nsk Precision America, Inc.
3450 Bearing Dr
Franklin IN 46131
317 738-5000

(P-14614)
SCHAEFFLER GROUP USA INC
34700 Pacific Coast Hwy # 203, Capistrano Beach (92624-1349)
PHONE...................................949 234-9799
Rich Peterson, Branch Mgr
Kevin Marx, Manager
EMP: 342
SALES (corp-wide): 68.1B Privately Held
SIC: 3562 Ball & roller bearings
HQ: Schaeffler Group Usa Inc.
308 Springhill Farm Rd
Fort Mill SC 29715
803 548-8500

(P-14615)
SHEPHARD CASTERS
4451 Eucalyptus Ave, Chino (91710-9702)
PHONE...................................909 393-0597
David Onsurez, Principal
▲ EMP: 11 EST: 2009
SALES (est): 1.9MM Privately Held
SIC: 3562 5072 Casters; casters & glides

(P-14616)
SPECIALTY MOTIONS INC
5480 Smokey Mountain Way, Yorba Linda (92887-4247)
PHONE...................................951 735-8722
Thomas Corey, CEO
Dorothy Corey, CFO
EMP: 20
SQ FT: 13,000
SALES (est): 5.3MM Privately Held
WEB: www.smi4motion.com
SIC: 3562 5085 Ball & roller bearings; bearings

(P-14617)
TIMKEN COMPANY
4422 Corporate Center Dr, Los Alamitos (90720-2539)
PHONE...................................714 484-2400
Alma Cruz, Info Tech Dir
Ciprian Boscaiu, Engineer
Doug Howland, Controller
Ed Esmaeili, Buyer
Peter Nguyen, Manager
EMP: 277
SALES (corp-wide): 3.5B Publicly Held
SIC: 3562 Ball & roller bearings
PA: The Timken Company
4500 Mount Pleasant St Nw
North Canton OH 44720
234 262-3000

(P-14618)
U S BEARINGS
5001b Commerce Dr, Baldwin Park (91706-1424)
PHONE...................................626 358-0181
Michael Harnett, President
EMP: 20
SALES (est): 1.5MM
SALES (corp-wide): 702.5MM Publicly Held
SIC: 3562 Ball & roller bearings
HQ: Roller Bearing Company Of America, Inc.
102 Willenbrock Rd
Oxford CT 06478
203 267-7001

(P-14619)
UNITED STATES BALL CORPORATION
Also Called: Express Machining
15919 Phoebe Ave, La Mirada (90638-5628)
PHONE...................................714 521-6500
Tony Armas, President
Philip Armas, Vice Pres
EMP: 10
SALES (est): 2.6MM Privately Held
WEB: www.usball.com
SIC: 3562 Ball bearings & parts

(P-14620)
WEARTECH INTERNATIONAL INC (HQ)
1177 N Grove St, Anaheim (92806-2110)
PHONE...................................714 683-2430
George D Blankenship, CEO
Michael G Konieczny, Treasurer
Thomas Christie, Vice Pres

▲ = Import ▼=Export
◆ =Import/Export

Keith Konieczny, *Executive*
Ruckie Balendran, *Office Mgr*
▲ EMP: 40
SQ FT: 30,000
SALES (est): 12MM
SALES (corp-wide): 3B **Publicly Held**
WEB: www.weartech.net
SIC: 3562 3313 3548 3496 Ball bearings
& parts; alloys, additive, except copper:
not made in blast furnaces; welding appa-
ratus; miscellaneous fabricated wire prod-
ucts; electrical or electronic engineering
PA: Lincoln Electric Holdings, Inc.
22801 Saint Clair Ave
Cleveland OH 44117
216 481-8100

3563 Air & Gas

(P-14621)
APOLLO SPRAYERS INTL INC
1030 Joshua Way, Vista (92081-7807)
PHONE.................................760 727-8300
John A Darroch, *President*
Bill Boxer, *Senior VP*
John B Darroch Sr, *Vice Pres*
Beth Darroch, *Director*
▲ EMP: 11
SALES (est): 2.2MM **Privately Held**
WEB: www.hvlp.com
SIC: 3563 5198 Spraying outfits: metals,
paints & chemicals (compressor); paint
brushes, rollers, sprayers

(P-14622)
**ATLAS COPCO COMPRESSORS
LLC**
6094 Stewart Ave, Fremont (94538-3152)
PHONE.................................510 413-5200
Mark Kaebnick, *Mng Member*
Tim McNickle, *Mktg Dir*
Rawleigh Hedrick, *Sales Mgr*
Mark Kiser, *Sales Engr*
Kashmir Uppal, *Manager*
EMP: 17
SALES (corp-wide): 10.5B **Privately Held**
WEB: www.atlascopco.com
SIC: 3563 Air & gas compressors
HQ: Atlas Copco Compressors Llc
300 Technology Center Way # 5
Rock Hill SC 29730
866 472-1015

(P-14623)
**ATLAS COPCO COMPRESSORS
LLC**
12827 Telegraph Rd, Santa Fe Springs
(90670-4007)
PHONE.................................866 545-4999
Bengt Kvarnback, *Branch Mgr*
EMP: 35
SALES (corp-wide): 10.5B **Privately Held**
WEB: www.atlascopco.com
SIC: 3563 Air & gas compressors
HQ: Atlas Copco Compressors Llc
300 Technology Center Way # 5
Rock Hill SC 29730
866 472-1015

(P-14624)
**ATLAS COPCO COMPRESSORS
LLC**
48434 Milmont Dr, Fremont (94538-7326)
PHONE.................................510 413-5200
Howard Chantell, *Manager*
EMP: 19
SALES (corp-wide): 10.5B **Privately Held**
SIC: 3563 Air & gas compressors
HQ: Atlas Copco Compressors Llc
300 Technology Center Way # 5
Rock Hill SC 29730
866 472-1015

(P-14625)
**C M AUTOMOTIVE SYSTEMS
INC (PA)**
120 Commerce Way, Walnut (91789-2714)
PHONE.................................909 869-7912
Chander Mittal, *President*
Jack Ambegaokar, *Chief Engr*
Kamlesh Dave, *Supervisor*
▲ EMP: 24
SQ FT: 20,370

SALES: 5.7MM **Privately Held**
WEB: www.cmautomotive.com
SIC: 3563 Air & gas compressors

(P-14626)
COMPRESSED AIR CONCEPTS
16207 Carmenita Rd, Cerritos
(90703-2212)
PHONE.................................310 537-1350
Mark Hana, *Owner*
EMP: 25
SALES (est): 2MM **Privately Held**
SIC: 3563 Air & gas compressors

(P-14627)
COMPUVAC INDUSTRIES INC
18381 Mount Langley St, Fountain Valley
(92708-6904)
PHONE.................................949 574-5085
David Donnelly, *President*
Jean Yoo, *Office Mgr*
▲ EMP: 16
SQ FT: 13,000
SALES (est): 4.2MM **Privately Held**
WEB: www.compuvacind.com
SIC: 3563 Vacuum (air extraction) sys-
tems, industrial

(P-14628)
DRESSER-RAND COMPANY
18502 Dominguez Hill Dr, Rancho
Dominguez (90220-6415)
PHONE.................................310 223-0600
Bob Lundeen, *Manager*
EMP: 32
SALES (corp-wide): 95B **Privately Held**
WEB: www.dresser-rand.com
SIC: 3563 Air & gas compressors
HQ: Dresser-Rand Company
500 Paul Clark Dr
Olean NY 14760
716 375-3000

(P-14629)
DRESSER-RAND LLC
Also Called: Dresser-Rand Sales
5159 Commercial Cir Ste D, Concord
(94520-8582)
PHONE.................................925 356-5700
Bob Lundeen, *Principal*
Mark Davis, *Accounts Mgr*
EMP: 31
SALES (corp-wide): 95B **Privately Held**
SIC: 3563 Air & gas compressors
HQ: Dresser-Rand Llc
1200 W Sam Houston Pkwy N
Houston TX 77043
713 354-6100

(P-14630)
**EBARA TECHNOLOGIES INC
(DH)**
51 Main Ave, Sacramento (95838-2014)
PHONE.................................916 920-5451
Nasao Asami, *Ch of Bd*
Mitsuhiko Shirakashi, *President*
Tadashi Urata, *President*
Naoki Ando, *CEO*
Masumi Shionuma, *Corp Secy*
▲ EMP: 100
SQ FT: 160,000
SALES (est): 86.7MM **Privately Held**
WEB: www.ebaratech.com
SIC: 3563 Vacuum pumps, except labora-
tory

(P-14631)
GS MANUFACTURING
985 W 18th St, Costa Mesa (92627-4541)
PHONE.................................949 642-1500
Gary L Smith, *CEO*
EMP: 10
SALES (est): 1.1MM **Privately Held**
SIC: 3563 Spraying & dusting equipment

(P-14632)
**HUNTINGTON MECHANICAL
LABS INC**
Also Called: Huntington Mechanical Labs
13355 Nevada City Ave, Grass Valley
(95945-9091)
PHONE.................................530 273-9533
Ronald Scott Hooper, *CEO*
Ron Hooper, *President*
Kyle Lind, *Engineer*
Tami Isaacson, *Accounting Mgr*

EMP: 36
SQ FT: 45,000
SALES (est): 9.8MM **Privately Held**
WEB: www.huntvac.com
SIC: 3563 Vacuum pumps, except labora-
tory; vacuum (air extraction) systems, in-
dustrial

(P-14633)
**KOBELCO COMPRESSORS
AMER INC**
301 N Smith Ave, Corona (92880-1742)
PHONE.................................951 739-3030
EMP: 75 **Privately Held**
SIC: 3563 Air & gas compressors
HQ: Kobelco Compressors America, Inc.
1450 W Rincon St
Corona CA 92880
951 739-3030

(P-14634)
**KOBELCO COMPRESSORS
AMER INC (DH)**
1450 W Rincon St, Corona (92880-9205)
PHONE.................................951 739-3030
Makoto Motoyoshi, *President*
Baishali Chatterjee, *Electrical Engi*
Daisuke Morita, *Sales Mgr*
◆ EMP: 260
SALES (est): 88.3MM **Privately Held**
WEB: www.kobelcoedti.com
SIC: 3563 Air & gas compressors including
vacuum pumps
HQ: Kobe Steel Usa Holdings Inc.
535 Madison Ave Fl 5
New York NY 10022
212 751-9400

(P-14635)
MAX SMT CORP
Also Called: Omxie
5675 Kimball Ct, Chino (91710-9121)
PHONE.................................877 589-9422
Shirlei Bi, *President*
◆ EMP: 10
SQ FT: 12,000
SALES: 40K **Privately Held**
SIC: 3563 Air & gas compressors

(P-14636)
NU VENTURE DIVING CO
Also Called: Nuvair
1600 Beacon Pl, Oxnard (93033-2433)
PHONE.................................805 815-4044
Glenn A Huebner, *CEO*
Janet Huebner, *CFO*
◆ EMP: 28
SQ FT: 27,000
SALES (est): 4.5MM **Privately Held**
WEB: www.nuvair.com
SIC: 3563 Air & gas compressors

(P-14637)
**PACIFIC TCHNICAL EQP ENGRG
INC**
Also Called: Pacific Tek
1298 N Blue Gum St, Anaheim
(92806-2413)
PHONE.................................714 835-3088
Kirk Preston, *CEO*
Dan Skorcz, *President*
EMP: 10
SQ FT: 10,400
SALES (est): 2.6MM **Privately Held**
WEB: www.pacific-tek.com
SIC: 3563 Vacuum (air extraction) sys-
tems, industrial

(P-14638)
POOLE VENTURA INC
Also Called: P V I
321 Bernoulli Cir, Oxnard (93030-5164)
P.O. Box 5023 (93031-5023)
PHONE.................................805 981-1784
Henry Poole Jr, *President*
Nader Jamshidi, *Vice Pres*
Aaron Dingus, *Engineer*
EMP: 12
SQ FT: 10,000
SALES (est): 2.7MM **Privately Held**
WEB: www.pvisystemtech.com
SIC: 3563 Vacuum (air extraction) sys-
tems, industrial

(P-14639)
PTB SALES INC (PA)
1361 Mountain View Cir, Azusa
(91702-1649)
PHONE.................................626 334-0500
Patrick T Blackwell, *CEO*
John Norton, *Vice Pres*
Brendan Riley, *Vice Pres*
Dean Scarborough, *Admin Sec*
James Grimm, *Engineer*
▲ EMP: 33
SQ FT: 16,000
SALES (est): 5.1MM **Privately Held**
WEB: www.ptbsales.com
SIC: 3563 3679 Vacuum (air extraction)
systems, industrial; power supplies, all
types: static

(P-14640)
**RHINO LININGS CORPORATION
(PA)**
9747 Businesspark Ave, San Diego
(92131-1661)
PHONE.................................858 450-0441
Pierre Gagnon, *President*
◆ EMP: 65
SQ FT: 20,000
SALES (est): 42MM **Privately Held**
WEB: www.rhinolatino.com
SIC: 3563 3559 Air & gas compressors;
automotive related machinery

(P-14641)
SPRAYLINE MANUFACTURING
10110 Greenleaf Ave, Santa Fe Springs
(90670-3416)
PHONE.................................562 941-5313
Brady Wilson, *Owner*
EMP: 10 EST: 1997
SALES (est): 1.7MM **Privately Held**
WEB: www.sprayline.com
SIC: 3563 Spraying & dusting equipment

(P-14642)
TAYLOR INVESTMENTS LLC
Also Called: Global Precision Manufacturing
13355 Nevada City Ave, Grass Valley
(95945-9091)
PHONE.................................530 273-4135
Edwin Taylor, *President*
Ronald Hooper, *Vice Pres*
EMP: 34
SALES (est): 1.4MM **Privately Held**
SIC: 3563 Air & gas compressors

3564 Blowers & Fans

(P-14643)
ADVANTEC MFS INC
Also Called: Micro Filtration Systems
6723 Sierra Ct Ste A, Dublin (94568-2689)
PHONE.................................925 479-0625
Yoshioki Matsuo, *President*
Katsuhiro Shiotani, *Vice Pres*
Kazuo Matsumura, *Admin Sec*
Debby Leglu, *Sales Staff*
Yuji Hokari, *Director*
▲ EMP: 13
SQ FT: 10,000
SALES (est): 3.1MM **Privately Held**
SIC: 3564 Air purification equipment; fil-
ters, air; furnaces, air conditioning equip-
ment, etc.
HQ: Toyo Roshi Kaisha, Ltd.
1-18-10, Otowa
Bunkyo-Ku TKY 112-0

(P-14644)
**ADWEST TECHNOLOGIES INC
(HQ)**
4222 E La Palma Ave, Anaheim
(92807-1816)
PHONE.................................714 632-8595
Brian Cannon, *Vice Pres*
Craig Bayer, *President*
Maryann Erickson, *Vice Pres*
Richard Whitford, *Vice Pres*
EMP: 35
SQ FT: 23,500

SALES (est): 7.8MM
SALES (corp-wide): 337.3MM **Publicly Held**
WEB: www.adwestusa.com
SIC: 3564 3585 3826 Air purification equipment; heating equipment, complete; thermal analysis instruments, laboratory type
PA: Ceco Environmental Corp.
  14651 Dallas Pkwy Ste 50
  Dallas TX 75254
  214 357-6181

(P-14645)
AIR BLAST INC
2050 Pepper St, Alhambra (91801-3162)
P.O. Box 367, San Gabriel (91778-0367)
PHONE....................626 576-0144
Carl Von Wolffradt, *President*
Patty Von Wolffradt, *Corp Secy*
Judy Doland, *Opers Staff*
EMP: 11
SQ FT: 4,100
SALES (est): 2.3MM **Privately Held**
WEB: www.airblastinc.com
SIC: 3564 Turbo-blowers, industrial; blowing fans: industrial or commercial

(P-14646)
AIR FACTORS INC
4771 Arroyo Vis Ste D, Livermore (94551-4847)
PHONE....................925 579-0040
Robert Browning, *President*
EMP: 12
SALES (est): 1.3MM **Privately Held**
WEB: www.airfactors.com
SIC: 3564 Blowers & fans

(P-14647)
AIRGARD INC (PA)
1755 Mccarthy Blvd, Milpitas (95035-7416)
PHONE....................408 573-0701
Dan White, *President*
Dyana Chargin, *CFO*
Martin Johnson, *CFO*
Mark Johnsgard, *Officer*
Kevin McGinnis, *Vice Pres*
▲ **EMP:** 23
SALES (est): 6.2MM **Privately Held**
WEB: www.airgard.com
SIC: 3564 Air purification equipment

(P-14648)
AMERICAN METAL FILTER COMPANY
611 Marsat Ct, Chula Vista (91911-4648)
PHONE....................619 628-1917
Valentine C Deilgat, *President*
Michele Carter, *Technology*
EMP: 17
SALES: 1.7MM **Privately Held**
WEB: www.amfco.com
SIC: 3564 Filters, air: furnaces, air conditioning equipment, etc.

(P-14649)
ATLAS COPCO MAFI-TRENCH CO LLC (DH)
3037 Industrial Pkwy, Santa Maria (93455-1807)
PHONE....................805 352-0112
James T Reilly, *President*
Peter Wagner, *Ch of Bd*
◆ **EMP:** 208
SQ FT: 90,000
SALES (est): 75.6MM
SALES (corp-wide): 10.5B **Privately Held**
WEB: www.mafi-trench.com
SIC: 3564 3533 8744 Turbo-blowers, industrial; oil & gas field machinery; facilities support services
HQ: Atlas Copco North America Llc
  6 Century Dr Ste 310
  Parsippany NJ 07054
  973 397-3400

(P-14650)
CALIFORNIA TURBO INC
10721 Business Dr, Fontana (92337-8252)
PHONE....................909 854-2800
Arthur May, *President*
Ram Iyer, *General Mgr*
Larry Ford, *Prdtn Mgr*
Cameron Young, *Sales Mgr*
▲ **EMP:** 10

SQ FT: 18,000
SALES (est): 2.3MM **Privately Held**
WEB: www.californiaturbo.com
SIC: 3564 Ventilating fans: industrial or commercial

(P-14651)
CAMFIL USA INC
500 Industrial Ave, Corcoran (93212-9629)
PHONE....................559 992-5118
Fausto Chavez, *Branch Mgr*
Monique Viellette, *Manager*
EMP: 64
SALES (corp-wide): 921.6MM **Privately Held**
SIC: 3564 Dust or fume collecting equipment, industrial
HQ: Camfil Usa, Inc.
  1 N Corporate Dr
  Riverdale NJ 07457
  973 616-7300

(P-14652)
CENTRAL BLOWER CO
211 S 7th Ave, City of Industry (91746-3288)
PHONE....................626 330-3182
David Roger Petersen, *President*
Mary Petersen, *Shareholder*
Eleanor Petersen, *Vice Pres*
EMP: 20
SQ FT: 24,000
SALES (est): 5.3MM **Privately Held**
WEB: www.centralblower.com
SIC: 3564 Exhaust fans: industrial or commercial; blowing fans: industrial or commercial

(P-14653)
CLARCOR AIR FILTRATION PDTS
1295 E Ontario Ave # 102, Corona (92881-6653)
PHONE....................951 272-1850
Larry Johnson, *Branch Mgr*
Maria Monteon, *Human Res Dir*
EMP: 66
SALES (corp-wide): 14.3B **Publicly Held**
WEB: www.airguard.com
SIC: 3564 Air cleaning systems
HQ: Clarcor Air Filtration Products, Inc
  100 River Ridge Cir
  Jeffersonville IN 47130
  502 969-2304

(P-14654)
CLOUDBURST INC
707 E Hueneme Rd, Oxnard (93033-8654)
PHONE....................805 986-4125
Michael Davis, *CEO*
▲ **EMP:** 30
SQ FT: 7,000
SALES (est): 6.6MM **Privately Held**
WEB: www.cloudburst.com
SIC: 3564 3585 Blowing fans: industrial or commercial; refrigeration & heating equipment

(P-14655)
ECW TECHNOLOGY INC
609 Deep Valley Dr, Rllng HLS Est (90274-3629)
PHONE....................310 373-0082
REA-Tiing Liu, *President*
Wen Bow, *CFO*
EMP: 15
SQ FT: 3,000
SALES (est): 1.8MM **Privately Held**
WEB: www.ecwtechnology.com
SIC: 3564 5169 Air purification equipment; chemicals, industrial & heavy

(P-14656)
ENVION LLC
14724 Ventura Blvd Fl 200, Sherman Oaks (91403-3514)
PHONE....................818 217-2500
Craig Shandler,
▲ **EMP:** 100
SQ FT: 36,000
SALES: 17.8MM
SALES (corp-wide): 20MM **Privately Held**
WEB: www.ionicpro.com
SIC: 3564 Air purification equipment

PA: Sylmark Inc.
  7821 Orion Ave Ste 200
  Van Nuys CA 91406
  818 217-2000

(P-14657)
ENVIROCARE INTERNATIONAL INC
507 Green Island Rd, American Canyon (94503-9649)
PHONE....................707 638-6800
John Tate III, *President*
Russell Helfond, *COO*
Satbir Ahluwalia, *Vice Pres*
Lisa Helfond, *Vice Pres*
Brian Higgins, *CTO*
EMP: 22
SQ FT: 10,000
SALES (est): 6.1MM **Privately Held**
SIC: 3564 Air cleaning systems; air purification equipment; dust or fume collecting equipment, industrial; precipitators, electrostatic

(P-14658)
EURAMCO SAFETY INC
Also Called: Ram Centrifical Products
2746 Via Orange Way, Spring Valley (91978-1744)
PHONE....................619 670-9590
Wayne Allen, *President*
Zach Allen, *Vice Pres*
Scott Carroll, *Engineer*
Dirk Davidson, *Controller*
Terry Singleton, *Marketing Mgr*
▲ **EMP:** 16
SQ FT: 15,000
SALES (est): 5.6MM **Privately Held**
WEB: www.euramcosafety.com
SIC: 3564 3429 Blowers & fans; marine hardware

(P-14659)
EXODUST COLLECTORS LLC
7045 Jackson St, Paramount (90723-4834)
PHONE....................562 808-0842
Daniel Meyers,
EMP: 10
SALES (est): 446.2K **Privately Held**
SIC: 3564 Purification & dust collection equipment

(P-14660)
FILTRATION GROUP LLC
498 Aviation Blvd, Santa Rosa (95403-1069)
PHONE....................707 525-8633
Dean Kerstetter, *Director*
Estella Prado, *Human Res Mgr*
Alison Huber, *Plant Mgr*
EMP: 80
SALES (corp-wide): 320.9MM **Privately Held**
WEB: www.filtrationgroup.com
SIC: 3564 Filters, air: furnaces, air conditioning equipment, etc.
PA: Filtration Group Llc
  912 E Washington St Ste 1
  Joliet IL 60433
  815 726-4600

(P-14661)
GREENHECK FAN CORPORATION
170 Cyber Ct, Rocklin (95765-1205)
PHONE....................916 626-3400
Mike Venturi, *Manager*
Tim Kilgore, *Managing Dir*
EMP: 120
SALES (corp-wide): 1.2B **Privately Held**
WEB: www.greenheck.com
SIC: 3564 Blowers & fans
PA: Greenheck Fan Corporation
  1100 Greenheck Dr
  Schofield WI 54476
  715 359-6171

(P-14662)
HOCKIN DIVERSFD HOLDINGS INC
Also Called: Sonic Dry Clean
1672 Main St Ste E362, Ramona (92065-5257)
PHONE....................760 787-0510
John Hockins, *President*

▼ **EMP:** 10
SALES (est): 2MM **Privately Held**
SIC: 3564 Air cleaning systems

(P-14663)
INFICOLD INC
14654 Placida Ct, Saratoga (95070-5740)
PHONE....................408 464-8007
Himanshu Pokharna, *CEO*
CA Sharma, *Manager*
EMP: 10 **EST:** 2015
SALES (est): 653.3K **Privately Held**
SIC: 3564 3585 Filters, air: furnaces, air conditioning equipment, etc.; compressors for refrigeration & air conditioning equipment

(P-14664)
INTERTEX LLC
Also Called: Intertex, Inc.
550 S Ayon Ave, Azusa (91702-5121)
PHONE....................626 385-3300
Edward Demirdjian, *President*
Greg Aghamanoukian, *President*
Fred Yang, *Director*
◆ **EMP:** 25
SALES (est): 27MM **Privately Held**
WEB: www.b-air.com
SIC: 3564 Blowers & fans
HQ: Lasko Products, Llc
  820 Lincoln Ave
  West Chester PA 19380
  610 692-7400

(P-14665)
IQAIR NORTH AMERICA INC
14351 Firestone Blvd, La Mirada (90638-5527)
PHONE....................877 715-4247
Glory Z Dolphin, *CEO*
Frank Hammes, *President*
▲ **EMP:** 48
SQ FT: 40,000
SALES (est): 13.9MM
SALES (corp-wide): 331.2K **Privately Held**
WEB: www.iqair.com
SIC: 3564 8742 5999 Air cleaning systems; materials mgmt. (purchasing, handling, inventory) consultant; air purification equipment
PA: Icleen Entwicklungs- Und Vertriebsanstalt Fur Umweltprodukte
  C/O Jgt Treuunternehmen Reg.
  Vaduz
  -

(P-14666)
JETAIR TECHNOLOGIES LLC
1756 Eastman Ave Ste 100, Ventura (93003-5756)
PHONE....................805 654-7000
William Anderson, *Mng Member*
Kevin Beyer, *Mng Member*
Dan Snyder, *Mng Member*
▲ **EMP:** 19
SQ FT: 6,000
SALES (est): 5.6MM **Privately Held**
WEB: www.jetairtech.com
SIC: 3564 Turbo-blowers, industrial

(P-14667)
KIRK A SCHLIGER
Also Called: Bear Label Machines
11240 Pyrites Way, Gold River (95670-4481)
PHONE....................916 638-8433
Fax: 916 638-8209
EMP: 10
SALES (est): 1.4MM **Privately Held**
WEB: www.bearlabelmachine.com
SIC: 3564

(P-14668)
M D H BURNER & BOILER CO INC
12106 Center St, South Gate (90280-8046)
PHONE....................562 630-2875
Mauro Donate, *CEO*
EMP: 18
SQ FT: 5,000
SALES (est): 5.8MM **Privately Held**
SIC: 3564 7699 3443 3433 Air purification equipment; boiler repair shop; fabricated plate work (boiler shop); heating equipment, except electric

(P-14669)
MACROAIR TECHNOLOGIES INC (PA)
Also Called: Macro Air Technologies
794 S Allen St, San Bernardino
(92408-2210)
PHONE...................................909 890-2270
Edward Boyd, *CEO*
Eric Fronk, *CFO*
Jaylin Krell, *Vice Pres*
Renee Spindle, *Admin Mgr*
Christina Bierly, *Accountant*
◆ **EMP:** 45
SQ FT: 15,000
SALES (est): 20.2MM **Privately Held**
SIC: 3564 Ventilating fans: industrial or
commercial

(P-14670)
MARS AIR SYSTEMS LLC
14716 S Broadway, Gardena (90248-1814)
PHONE...................................310 532-1555
EMP: 75 **EST:** 2009
SALES (est): 7.2MM **Privately Held**
SIC: 3564

(P-14671)
MEGGITT AIRDYNAMICS INC (DH)
2616 Research Dr, Corona (92882-6978)
PHONE...................................951 734-0070
Lloyd Oshiro, *President*
EMP: 31
SQ FT: 90,000
SALES (est): 10.8MM
SALES (corp-wide): 2.6B **Privately Held**
SIC: 3564 3563 Ventilating fans: industrial
or commercial; air & gas compressors

(P-14672)
OPTIMIZATION CORPORATION
Also Called: McIntyre Industries
14680 Wicks Blvd, San Leandro
(94577-6716)
PHONE...................................510 614-5890
John-Paul Farsight, *CEO*
EMP: 13
SQ FT: 30,000
SALES (est): 2MM **Privately Held**
WEB: www.mcintyresg.com
SIC: 3564 Air purification equipment

(P-14673)
POLLUTION CONTROL SPECIALISTS
1354 Ritchey St, Santa Ana (92705-4727)
PHONE...................................949 474-0137
Steve Fleischman, *President*
EMP: 22
SALES (est): 4.2MM **Privately Held**
SIC: 3564 Air cleaning systems

(P-14674)
PUROLATOR PDTS A FILTRATION CO
Also Called: Air Filter Sales
20671 Corsair Blvd, Hayward
(94545-1007)
PHONE...................................510 785-4800
Dave Lowinski, *Manager*
EMP: 10
SALES (corp-wide): 14.3B **Publicly Held**
WEB: www.afss.net
SIC: 3564 Filters, air: furnaces, air condi-
tioning equipment, etc.
HQ: Purolator Products Air Filtration Com-
pany
100 River Ridge Cir
Jeffersonville IN 47130
866 925-2247

(P-14675)
QC MANUFACTURING INC
26040 Ynez Rd, Temecula (92591-6033)
PHONE...................................951 325-6340
Dane Stevenson, *President*
Ted Greenman, *Executive*
Mj Stroder, *Executive*
Chris Bell, *Marketing Mgr*
▲ **EMP:** 65
SALES (est): 16.6MM **Privately Held**
SIC: 3564 Blowers & fans

(P-14676)
RAM CENTRIFUGAL PRODUCTS INC
2746 Via Orange Way, Spring Valley
(91978-1744)
PHONE...................................619 670-9590
Wayne Allen, *President*
Gary Clemons, *Manager*
EMP: 10 **EST:** 1970
SALES: 3MM **Privately Held**
SIC: 3564 3429 Blowers & fans; marine
hardware

(P-14677)
ROTRON INCORPORATED
Ametek Rotron
474 Raleigh Ave, El Cajon (92020-3138)
PHONE...................................619 593-7400
Fred Taylor, *Manager*
EMP: 12
SALES (corp-wide): 4.8B **Publicly Held**
WEB: www.rotronmilaero.com
SIC: 3564 Blowers & fans
HQ: Rotron Incorporated
55 Hasbrouck Ln
Woodstock NY 12498
845 679-2401

(P-14678)
SONIC AIR SYSTEMS INC
1050 Beacon St, Brea (92821-2938)
PHONE...................................714 255-0124
Dan Vanderpyl, *CEO*
Terry Riley, *Vice Pres*
▲ **EMP:** 40
SQ FT: 50,000
SALES (est): 11.9MM **Privately Held**
WEB: www.sonicairsystems.com
SIC: 3564 Blowers & fans

(P-14679)
STANDARD FILTER CORPORATION (PA)
5928 Balfour Ct, Carlsbad (92008-7304)
PHONE...................................866 443-3615
Tobey Wiik, *President*
◆ **EMP:** 40
SQ FT: 30,000
SALES (est): 5.1MM **Privately Held**
WEB: www.standardfilter.com
SIC: 3564 5199 Filters, air: furnaces, air
conditioning equipment, etc.; felt

(P-14680)
SUNON INC (PA)
Also Called: Eme Fan & Motor
1075 W Lambert Rd Ste A, Brea
(92821-2944)
PHONE...................................714 255-0208
Yin Su Hong, *CEO*
▲ **EMP:** 32
SQ FT: 22,000
SALES (est): 4.8MM **Privately Held**
WEB: www.sunonusa.com
SIC: 3564 Blowers & fans

(P-14681)
SUPERIOR FILTRATION PDTS LLC
3401 Etiwanda Ave 811b, Jurupa Valley
(91752-1128)
PHONE...................................951 681-1700
Julie Haight, *Manager*
EMP: 13
SALES (corp-wide): 18.4MM **Privately Held**
SIC: 3564 Blowers & fans
PA: Superior Filtration Products, Llc
160 N 400 W
North Salt Lake UT 84054
801 621-5200

(P-14682)
TEMPEST TECHNOLOGY CORPORATION
4708 N Blythe Ave, Fresno (93722-3930)
PHONE...................................559 277-7577
Leroy B Coffman III, *President*
Joseph Schanda, *COO*
Dannette Dunn, *Controller*
Bruce Mahlmann, *Buyer*
Curt Johnson, *Sales Staff*
▲ **EMP:** 25
SQ FT: 22,000

SALES (est): 7MM **Privately Held**
SIC: 3564 Ventilating fans: industrial or
commercial

(P-14683)
TERRA UNIVERSAL INC
800 S Raymond Ave, Fullerton
(92831-5234)
PHONE...................................714 526-0100
G H Sadaghiani, *CEO*
Kayvon Sadaghiani, *Sales Engr*
Tim Beckmann, *Marketing Staff*
Steve Matsumoto, *Manager*
▲ **EMP:** 195 **EST:** 1975
SQ FT: 88,000
SALES (est): 73.6MM **Privately Held**
WEB: www.desiccator.com
SIC: 3564 3567 3569 3572 Purification &
dust collection equipment; air purification
equipment; filters, air: furnaces, air condi-
tioning equipment, etc.; ventilating fans:
industrial or commercial; heating units &
devices, industrial: electric; filters; com-
puter storage devices; refrigeration equipment, complete; clean room supplies

(P-14684)
TRI-DIM FILTER CORPORATION
15271 Fairfield Ranch Rd # 150, Chino Hills
(91709-8865)
PHONE...................................626 333-9428
Stephen Murphy, *Site Mgr*
EMP: 11
SALES (corp-wide): 4.5B **Privately Held**
SIC: 3564 Filters, air: furnaces, air condi-
tioning equipment, etc.
HQ: Tri-Dim Filter Corporation
93 Industrial Dr
Louisa VA 23093
540 967-2600

(P-14685)
TRI-DIM FILTER CORPORATION
15271 Fairfield Ranch Rd # 150, Chino Hills
(91709-8865)
PHONE...................................626 826-5893
Scott Breckenridge, *Manager*
Karla Harrison, *Export Mgr*
Louis Flores, *Consultant*
EMP: 30
SALES (corp-wide): 4.5B **Privately Held**
WEB: www.tridim.com
SIC: 3564 Filters, air: furnaces, air condi-
tioning equipment, etc.
HQ: Tri-Dim Filter Corporation
93 Industrial Dr
Louisa VA 23093
540 967-2600

(P-14686)
US TOYO FAN CORPORATION (HQ)
16025 Arrow Hwy Ste F, Irwindale
(91706-2063)
P.O. Box 1941, Burbank (91507-1941)
PHONE...................................626 338-1111
William Jacobs, *President*
Arnold Weisman, *Corp Secy*
Robert Rosenthal, *Vice Pres*
▲ **EMP:** 19
SQ FT: 10,000
SALES (est): 7.6MM
SALES (corp-wide): 66.3MM **Privately Held**
WEB: www.ustoyofan.com
SIC: 3564 Blowers & fans
PA: Desco Industries, Inc.
3651 Walnut Ave
Chino CA 91710
909 627-8178

(P-14687)
VENTUREDYNE LTD
Climet Instruments Company
1320 W Colton Ave, Redlands
(92374-2864)
P.O. Box 1760 (92373-0543)
PHONE...................................909 793-2788
Ray Felbinger, *Manager*
Jim Strachan, *General Mgr*
Rosalinda Saavedra, *Administration*
John R Grater, *Data Proc Staff*
Tony Orr, *Senior Engr*
EMP: 65

SALES (corp-wide): 146.4MM **Privately Held**
SIC: 3564 3829 3825 3823 Blowing fans:
industrial or commercial; measuring &
controlling devices; instruments to measure electricity; industrial instrmnts msrmnt
display/control process variable; relays &
industrial controls
PA: Venturedyne, Ltd.
600 College Ave
Pewaukee WI 53072
262 691-9900

(P-14688)
VORTECH ENGINEERING INC
1650 Pacific Ave, Oxnard (93033-2746)
PHONE...................................805 247-0226
Jim Middlebrook, *CEO*
Randolf Riley, *President*
▲ **EMP:** 42
SALES (est): 12MM **Privately Held**
WEB: www.vortechsuperchargers.com
SIC: 3564 Blowing fans: industrial or com-
mercial

(P-14689)
WEMS INC (PA)
Also Called: Wems Electronics
4650 W Rosecrans Ave, Hawthorne
(90250-6898)
P.O. Box 528 (90251-0528)
PHONE...................................310 644-0251
Ronald Hood, *CEO*
Carroll Whitney, *President*
Mel Hughes, *Vice Pres*
Gina Simons, *Executive Asst*
Charles Wilson, *Admin Sec*
EMP: 84
SQ FT: 78,000
SALES (est): 17.6MM **Privately Held**
WEB: www.wems.com
SIC: 3564 3612 6513 Blowers & fans;
transformers, except electric; apartment
building operators

(P-14690)
WHIPPLE INDUSTRIES INC
3292 N Weber Ave, Fresno (93722-4942)
PHONE...................................559 442-1261
Arthur Whipple, *CEO*
Sherry Anderson, *Admin Sec*
▲ **EMP:** 15
SQ FT: 5,258
SALES (est): 4.6MM **Privately Held**
WEB: www.whipplesuperchargers.com
SIC: 3564 3732 3724 3714 Turbo-blow-
ers, industrial; boat building & repairing;
aircraft engines & engine parts; motor ve-
hicle parts & accessories

(P-14691)
XCELAERO CORPORATION
4540 Broad St Ste 120, San Luis Obispo
(93401-8729)
PHONE...................................805 547-2660
Dennis Pfister, *President*
Molly Attala, *CFO*
Pat Lawless, *Vice Pres*
Chellatta Balan, *CTO*
Frank Kock, *Design Engr*
EMP: 16
SQ FT: 7,500
SALES (est): 3.1MM **Privately Held**
SIC: 3564 Ventilating fans: industrial or
commercial

3565 Packaging Machinery

(P-14692)
7 U P RC BOTTLING COMPANY
Also Called: 7-Up
1300 W Taft Ave, Orange (92865-4127)
PHONE...................................714 974-8560
Chuck Shanely, *President*
EMP: 60
SALES (est): 8MM **Privately Held**
SIC: 3565 2086 Bottling machinery: filling,
capping, labeling; bottled & canned soft
drinks

(P-14693)
ACCU-SEAL SENCORPWHITE INC
225 Bingham Dr Ste B, San Marcos (92069-1418)
PHONE...................................760 591-9800
Lesly Jensen, *President*
Katie McLintock, *Human Resources*
EMP: 19
SQ FT: 14,000
SALES (est): 7.6MM
SALES (corp-wide): 500MM **Privately Held**
WEB: www.accu-seal.com
SIC: 3565 Packaging machinery
HQ: Sencorpwhite, Inc.
400 Kidds Hill Rd
Hyannis MA 02601
508 771-9400

(P-14694)
ACCUTEK PACKAGING EQUIPMENT CO (PA)
Also Called: Kiss Packaging Systems
2980 Scott St, Vista (92081-8321)
PHONE...................................760 734-4177
Edward Chocholek, *Principal*
Darren Chocholek, *Vice Pres*
Drake Chocholek, *Vice Pres*
Drew Chocholek, *Vice Pres*
Jim Starks, *Senior Engr*
◆ **EMP:** 49
SALES (est): 15.6MM **Privately Held**
WEB: www.accutekpackaging.com
SIC: 3565 Packaging machinery

(P-14695)
ADCO MANUFACTURING
2170 Academy Ave, Sanger (93657-3795)
PHONE...................................559 875-5563
Kate King, *President*
Glen Long, *COO*
Frank Hoffman, *Vice Pres*
Maureen Say, *Manager*
◆ **EMP:** 150
SQ FT: 75,000
SALES (est): 57.8MM **Privately Held**
WEB: www.adcomfg.com
SIC: 3565 Carton packing machines

(P-14696)
AVP TECHNOLOGY LLC
4140 Business Center Dr, Fremont (94538-6354)
PHONE...................................510 683-0157
Hugh Chau, *CEO*
Lalaine Cortez, *President*
Lam Vo, *Design Engr*
Lynn Chau,
▲ **EMP:** 45
SQ FT: 4,000
SALES (est): 4.9MM **Privately Held**
WEB: www.avptechnology.com
SIC: 3565 Vacuum packaging machinery

(P-14697)
B & H MANUFACTURING CO INC (PA)
Also Called: B & H Labeling Systems
3461 Roeding Rd, Ceres (95307-9442)
P.O. Box 247 (95307-0247)
PHONE...................................209 537-5785
Roman M Eckols, *CEO*
Calvin E Bright, *Ch of Bd*
Lyn E Bright, *President*
Marjorie Bright, *Corp Secy*
Bob Adamson, *Vice Pres*
◆ **EMP:** 117
SQ FT: 65,000
SALES (est): 25.2MM **Privately Held**
WEB: www.bhlabeling.com
SIC: 3565 Labeling machines, industrial

(P-14698)
BELCO PACKAGING SYSTEMS INC
910 S Mountain Ave, Monrovia (91016-3641)
PHONE...................................626 357-9566
Helen V Misik, *CEO*
A Michael Misik, *President*
▲ **EMP:** 25 **EST:** 1959
SQ FT: 35,000

SALES (est): 9.1MM **Privately Held**
WEB: www.belcomedical.com
SIC: 3565 Packing & wrapping machinery

(P-14699)
BLC WC INC
Also Called: Imperial System
2900 Faber St, Union City (94587-1228)
PHONE...................................510 489-5400
John Kramer, *Branch Mgr*
EMP: 35
SALES (corp-wide): 16.2MM **Privately Held**
WEB: www.bestlabel.com
SIC: 3565 2679 3953 2672 Labeling machines, industrial; labels, paper: made from purchased material; marking devices; coated & laminated paper
PA: Blc Wc, Inc.
13260 Moore St
Cerritos CA 90703
562 926-1452

(P-14700)
BLICK INDUSTRIES LLC
2245 Laguna Canyon Rd, Laguna Beach (92651-1141)
PHONE...................................949 499-5026
Beverly Wesley, *Mng Member*
Klint Olsen, *Sales Mgr*
Dan Wacholder,
▼ **EMP:** 10
SQ FT: 750
SALES (est): 2.2MM **Privately Held**
SIC: 3565 Vacuum packaging machinery

(P-14701)
BOYD & BOYD INDUSTRIES (PA)
3500 Chester Ave, Bakersfield (93301-1630)
PHONE...................................661 631-8400
Jerry Boyd, *Owner*
◆ **EMP:** 17
SQ FT: 30,000
SALES: 1MM **Privately Held**
SIC: 3565 5084 3535 Packaging machinery; packaging machinery & equipment; unit handling conveying systems

(P-14702)
CAN LINES ENGINEERING INC (PA)
Also Called: C L E
9839 Downey Norwalk Rd, Downey (90241-5596)
PHONE...................................562 861-2996
Donald Koplien, *CEO*
Keenan Koplien, *President*
Erik Koplien, *Vice Pres*
Darwin Smock, *Research*
Tim Jolly, *Director*
EMP: 100 **EST:** 1960
SQ FT: 40,000
SALES (est): 18.9MM **Privately Held**
SIC: 3565 3556 Canning machinery, food; bottling machinery: filling, capping, labeling; food products machinery

(P-14703)
COLIMATIC USA INC
9272 Jeronimo Rd Ste 115, Irvine (92618-1914)
PHONE...................................949 600-6440
Franceso Libretti, *President*
Larry Lachowski, *Manager*
▲ **EMP:** 11
SALES (est): 1.7MM **Privately Held**
SIC: 3565 Packaging machinery

(P-14704)
CORASIA CORP
363 Fairview Way, Milpitas (95035-3024)
PHONE...................................408 321-8508
Chen Chin Hsien, *President*
▲ **EMP:** 10
SALES (est): 1.4MM **Privately Held**
SIC: 3565 Packaging machinery

(P-14705)
CVC TECHNOLOGIES INC
10861 Business Dr, Fontana (92337-8235)
PHONE...................................909 355-0311
Sheng Hui Yang, *CEO*
K Joe Yang, *President*
▲ **EMP:** 21
SQ FT: 29,000

SALES (est): 6.5MM **Privately Held**
WEB: www.cvcusa.com
SIC: 3565 Labeling machines, industrial
PA: Cvc Technologies Inc.
No. 190, Gongye 9th Rd.,
Taichung City 41280
-

(P-14706)
ELLISON BINER
2685 S Melrose Dr, Vista (92081-8783)
PHONE...................................760 598-6500
Edward Chocholek, *President*
Drake Chochok, *Info Tech Dir*
EMP: 55
SALES (est): 6.4MM **Privately Held**
SIC: 3565 Packaging machinery

(P-14707)
FOOD MACHINERY SALES INC
Also Called: Serpa Packaging Solutions
7020 W Sunnyview Ave, Visalia (93291-9639)
PHONE...................................559 651-2339
Fernando M Serpa, *President*
Joseph Scalia, *CFO*
Manuela Parreira, *Admin Sec*
Juan Ramirez, *Project Mgr*
Jason Wolf, *Technical Staff*
◆ **EMP:** 100
SQ FT: 62,000
SALES (est): 20.6MM **Privately Held**
WEB: www.fmsmfg.com
SIC: 3565 Carton packing machines

(P-14708)
GOLDEN W PPR CONVERTING CORP (PA)
Also Called: G W
2480 Grant Ave, San Lorenzo (94580-1808)
PHONE...................................510 317-0646
Shirley Hooi, *President*
David Hooi, *Vice Pres*
Henry Hooi, *Principal*
Kevin Miller, *Technology*
Dave Hool, *Opers Staff*
▼ **EMP:** 129
SQ FT: 42,000
SALES (est): 27.5MM **Privately Held**
WEB: www.goldenwestpaper.com
SIC: 3565 2657 Carton packing machines; folding paperboard boxes

(P-14709)
HANNAN PRODUCTS CORP (PA)
220 N Smith Ave, Corona (92880-1740)
PHONE...................................951 735-1587
Henry H Jenkins, *President*
Nancy P Jenkins, *Shareholder*
Lawrence Jenkins, *Vice Pres*
Alfred Ramos, *Vice Pres*
Elena Nicklaus, *Office Mgr*
EMP: 16
SQ FT: 36,000
SALES (est): 3.4MM **Privately Held**
SIC: 3565 3053 3554 3549 Packaging machinery; packing materials; paper industries machinery; cutting & slitting machinery

(P-14710)
HASCO FABRICATION INC
13370 Monte Vista Ave, Chino (91710-5147)
P.O. Box 519 (91708-0519)
PHONE...................................909 627-0326
Fred R Haskin, *President*
Thomas Haskin, *Treasurer*
Thomas R Haskin, *Corp Secy*
Steven F Haskin, *Vice Pres*
EMP: 10
SQ FT: 12,000
SALES (est): 2MM **Privately Held**
SIC: 3565 3535 Canning machinery, food; belt conveyor systems, general industrial use

(P-14711)
HIS INDUSTRIES INC
Also Called: Phoenix Engineering
1202 W Shelley Ct, Orange (92868-1239)
PHONE...................................562 407-0512
Lynn Worthington, *President*
▲ **EMP:** 20
SQ FT: 6,000

SALES (est): 1.6MM **Privately Held**
SIC: 3565 Packaging machinery

(P-14712)
JACKSAM CORPORATION
Also Called: JACKSAM CORP BLACKOUT
30191 Avenida De Las, Rancho Santa Margari (92688)
PHONE...................................800 605-3580
Mark Adams, *President*
Michael Sakala, *CFO*
David Hall, *Exec VP*
Malachi Bodine, *Project Mgr*
David Franklin, *Senior Engr*
EMP: 25 **EST:** 1989
SQ FT: 4,000
SALES: 6.6MM **Privately Held**
SIC: 3565 Bottling machinery: filling, capping, labeling

(P-14713)
KLIPPENSTEIN CORPORATION
5399 S Villa Ave, Fresno (93725-8903)
PHONE...................................559 834-4258
Kenneth Ray Klippenstein, *CEO*
Wendy Klippenstein, *Corp Secy*
Jason Reimer, *Master*
▲ **EMP:** 25 **EST:** 1979
SQ FT: 13,000
SALES (est): 4.2MM **Privately Held**
WEB: www.klippenstein.com
SIC: 3565 Packaging machinery

(P-14714)
KODIAK CARTONERS INC
Also Called: Ywd Cartoners
2550 S East Ave Ste 101, Fresno (93706-5121)
PHONE...................................559 266-4844
Casandra Tanney, *President*
EMP: 50
SALES (est): 8.1MM **Privately Held**
SIC: 3565 Packing & wrapping machinery

(P-14715)
LANE WINPAK INC (HQ)
998 S Sierra Way, San Bernardino (92408-2122)
PHONE...................................909 386-1762
Bruce J Berry, *CEO*
Ted Torrens, *President*
M G Johnston, *CFO*
Olivier Muggli, *Vice Pres*
Sue Iiams, *Executive*
▲ **EMP:** 70
SQ FT: 45,000
SALES (est): 9.8MM
SALES (corp-wide): 889.6MM **Privately Held**
WEB: www.wipak.com
SIC: 3565 Packaging machinery
PA: Winpak Ltd
100 Saulteaux Cres
Winnipeg MB R3J 3
204 889-1015

(P-14716)
M & O PERRY INDUSTRIES INC
412 N Smith Ave, Corona (92880-6903)
PHONE...................................951 734-9838
Phillip Osterhaus, *CEO*
Jesse Nhem, *Electrical Engi*
Cheng Lee, *Engineer*
Betty Hampton, *Purch Agent*
Detlef Teubert, *Marketing Staff*
▲ **EMP:** 40
SQ FT: 20,000
SALES (est): 10.4MM **Privately Held**
WEB: www.moperry.com
SIC: 3565 8711 7629 5084 Packaging machinery; engineering services; electrical repair shops; conveyor systems

(P-14717)
MAF INDUSTRIES INC (HQ)
36470 Highway 99, Traver (93673)
P.O. Box 218 (93673-0218)
PHONE...................................559 897-2905
Thomas Blanc, *President*
Philippe Blanc, *Vice Pres*
Florian Best, *Department Mgr*
Raul Mejia, *Admin Sec*
Christophe Kumsta, *Research*
◆ **EMP:** 80
SQ FT: 30,000

▲ = Import ▼=Export
◆ =Import/Export

SALES (est): 23.1MM **Privately Held**
WEB: www.mafindustries.com
SIC: **3565** 5084 Packing & wrapping machinery; food industry machinery

(P-14718)
MFG PACKAGING PRODUCTS
3200 Enterprise St, Brea (92821-6238)
PHONE.................................714 984-2300
Fax: 714 984-2350
EMP: 10
SALES (est): 1MM **Privately Held**
SIC: **3565**

(P-14719)
NAFM LLC
Also Called: Nafm Engineering Service
1521 Pomona Rd Ste A, Corona
(92880-6925)
PHONE.................................951 738-1114
John Yamosaki, *Mng Member*
Jacek K Zdzienicki, *Vice Pres*
Kay Yamasaki,
▲ EMP: 10
SQ FT: 25,000
SALES (est): 2.3MM **Privately Held**
SIC: **3565** Packaging machinery

(P-14720)
P R P MULTISOURCE INC
3836 Wacker Dr, Jurupa Valley
(91752-1147)
PHONE.................................951 681-6100
Phil Woss, *President*
Kurt Fisch, *Treasurer*
Daniel Landeros, *Buyer*
▲ EMP: 20
SQ FT: 25,000
SALES (est): 4.9MM **Privately Held**
SIC: **3565** 5084 Vacuum packaging machinery; packaging machinery & equipment

(P-14721)
PACKAGING AIDS CORPORATION (PA)
Also Called: P A C
25 Tiburon St, San Rafael (94901-4721)
P.O. Box 9144 (94912-9144)
PHONE.................................415 454-4868
Serge Berguig, *President*
Mark Goldman, *COO*
Adam Greenlief, *General Mgr*
Greg Quinn, *General Mgr*
Shawn Thurston, *Controller*
▲ EMP: 35
SQ FT: 27,000
SALES (est): 6.5MM **Privately Held**
WEB: www.packagingaids.com
SIC: **3565** 5084 Bag opening, filling & closing machines; industrial machinery & equipment

(P-14722)
PACKLINE TECHNOLOGIES INC
5929 Avenue 408, Dinuba (93618-9791)
P.O. Box 636, Kingsburg (93631-0636)
PHONE.................................559 591-3150
Lorin R Reed, *President*
Ken Nikkel, *Sales Engr*
Brent Willems, *Sales Staff*
EMP: 30
SALES (est): 9.3MM **Privately Held**
SIC: **3565** 5084 Packaging machinery; packaging machinery & equipment

(P-14723)
PNEUMATIC SCALE CORPORATION
Also Called: Pneumatic Scale Angelus
2811 E Philadelphia St B, Ontario
(91761-8538)
PHONE.................................909 527-7600
Bob Chopman, *CEO*
Michelle Woodyard, *Analyst*
EMP: 10
SALES (corp-wide): 3B **Privately Held**
SIC: **3565** Packaging machinery
HQ: Pneumatic Scale Corporation
10 Ascot Pkwy
Cuyahoga Falls OH 44223
330 923-0491

(P-14724)
PRO PACK SYSTEMS INC
1354 Dayton St Ste A, Salinas
(93901-4426)
P.O. Box 903, Monterey (93942-0903)
PHONE.................................831 771-1300
David Paul Zurlinden, *CEO*
Judy Zurlinden, *Vice Pres*
EMP: 12
SQ FT: 10,500
SALES (est): 2.8MM **Privately Held**
SIC: **3565** Carton packing machines

(P-14725)
PROMARKSVAC CORPORATION
1915 E Acacia St, Ontario (91761-7921)
PHONE.................................909 923-3888
Mohsin Syed, *President*
▲ EMP: 12 EST: 2009
SQ FT: 24,000
SALES (est): 2.5MM **Privately Held**
SIC: **3565** Packaging machinery

(P-14726)
SARDEE INDUSTRIES INC
2731 E Myrtle St, Stockton (95205-4718)
PHONE.................................209 466-1526
Alan Basset, *Branch Mgr*
EMP: 26
SALES (corp-wide): 13.5MM **Privately Held**
WEB: www.sardee.com
SIC: **3565** 3536 Packaging machinery; hoists, cranes & monorails
PA: Sardee Industries, Inc.
5100 Academy Dr Ste 400
Lisle IL 60532
630 824-4200

(P-14727)
SHRINK WRAP PROS LLC
275 E Hillcrest Dr Ste 16, Thousand Oaks
(91360-5827)
PHONE.................................805 207-9050
Cheryl Key, *President*
Chris Key,
Craig Key,
EMP: 10
SALES (est): 1.4MM **Privately Held**
SIC: **3565** 5084 2392 Packaging machinery; processing & packaging equipment; slipcovers: made of fabric, plastic etc.

(P-14728)
SYSTEMS TECHNOLOGY INC
Also Called: Delaware Systems Technology
1350 Riverview Dr, San Bernardino
(92408-2944)
PHONE.................................909 799-9950
David R Landon, *CEO*
John G Stjohn, *CEO*
Allyn Peterson, *Engineer*
Grace Howard, *Purchasing*
▲ EMP: 65
SQ FT: 43,000
SALES (est): 18.9MM **Privately Held**
WEB: www.systems-technology-inc.com
SIC: **3565** Packing & wrapping machinery

(P-14729)
TERRY B LOWE
Also Called: Data Scale
42430 Blacow Rd, Fremont (94539-5621)
PHONE.................................510 651-7350
Terry B Lowe, *Owner*
▲ EMP: 10 EST: 1974
SQ FT: 6,000
SALES (est): 1.5MM **Privately Held**
WEB: www.datascale.com
SIC: **3565** Packaging machinery

(P-14730)
THIELE TECHNOLOGIES INC
1949 E Manning Ave, Reedley
(93654-9462)
PHONE.................................559 638-8484
Ed Suarez, *Manager*
Mark Reimer, *Engineer*
Stephen Waters, *Controller*
Kelly Abell, *Clerk*
EMP: 257
SALES (corp-wide): 3B **Privately Held**
SIC: **3565** Packaging machinery

HQ: Thiele Technologies, Inc.
315 27th Ave Ne
Minneapolis MN 55418
612 782-1200

(P-14731)
TRANSFER ENGINEERING & MFG INC
1100 La Avenida St Ste A, Mountain View
(94043-1453)
PHONE.................................510 651-3000
Michael Ackert, *President*
Jorg A Kaminsky, *CFO*
EMP: 25
SALES (est): 5.8MM **Privately Held**
WEB: www.transferengineering.com
SIC: **3565** Vacuum packaging machinery

(P-14732)
UNITED BAKERY EQUIPMENT CO INC (PA)
Also Called: Hartman Slicer Div
19216 S Laurel Park Rd, Rancho
Dominguez (90220-6008)
PHONE.................................310 635-8121
Larry Brown, *CEO*
Randy Hanson, *Engineer*
Johny Tusi, *Engineer*
Stephanie Neuerburg, *Accountant*
Bob Plourde, *Human Res Mgr*
◆ EMP: 100 EST: 1966
SALES (est): 31MM **Privately Held**
SIC: **3565** 3556 Packaging machinery; bakery machinery

(P-14733)
VERICOOL INC
7066 Las Positas Rd Ste C, Livermore
(94551-5134)
PHONE.................................925 337-0808
Darrell Jobe, *CEO*
EMP: 28
SALES (est): 9MM **Privately Held**
SIC: **3565** Packaging machinery

(P-14734)
VISTECH MFG SOLUTIONS LLC (PA)
Also Called: Vis Tech
1156 Scenic Dr Ste 120, Modesto
(95350-6100)
PHONE.................................209 544-9333
John Jacinto, *Mng Member*
Tim Martin, *Engineer*
Lane Simpson,
Jose Zamora, *Director*
▲ EMP: 23
SQ FT: 32,500
SALES (est): 58.3MM **Privately Held**
SIC: **3565** Packaging machinery

(P-14735)
W E PLEMONS MCHY SVCS INC
13479 E Industrial Dr, Parlier (93648-9678)
P.O. Box 787 (93648-0787)
PHONE.................................559 646-6630
William Plemons, *President*
John Robinson, *Shareholder*
Edward Baskette, *CFO*
Olivia Kozera, *Vice Pres*
Jeff Winters, *Vice Pres*
▲ EMP: 25
SQ FT: 30,000
SALES (est): 9MM **Privately Held**
WEB: www.weplemons.com
SIC: **3565** 7699 Packaging machinery; industrial machinery & equipment repair

(P-14736)
W J ELLISON CO INC
Also Called: Pack West Machinery Co
200 River Rd, Corona (92880-1435)
PHONE.................................626 814-4766
William J Ellison, *President*
Janice K Ellison, *Vice Pres*
EMP: 24
SQ FT: 20,000
SALES (est): 6.7MM **Privately Held**
SIC: **3565** Packaging machinery

(P-14737)
WILD HORSE INDUSTRIAL CORP
Also Called: Simplex Filler Co
640 Airpark Rd Ste A, NAPA (94558-7569)
PHONE.................................707 265-6801
G Donald Murray III, *President*
Edna Murray, *CFO*
Jonathan Fuller, *Plant Mgr*
Piper Quinones, *Marketing Staff*
EMP: 15
SQ FT: 15,500
SALES (est): 2MM **Privately Held**
WEB: www.simplexfiller.com
SIC: **3565** Packaging machinery

3566 Speed Changers, Drives & Gears

(P-14738)
AMERICAN CHAIN & GEAR COMPANY
3370 Paseo Halcon, San Clemente
(92672-3523)
P.O. Box 58722, Los Angeles (90058-0722)
PHONE.................................323 581-9131
John Kyle, *President*
EMP: 13
SQ FT: 26,000
SALES (est): 2.3MM **Privately Held**
SIC: **3566** 3568 5063 Gears, power transmission, except automotive; sprockets (power transmission equipment); power transmission equipment, electric

(P-14739)
AMERICAN PRECISION GEAR CO
365 Foster City Blvd, Foster City
(94404-1104)
PHONE.................................650 627-8060
Steve W Lefczik, *President*
EMP: 20
SQ FT: 22,000
SALES (est): 6.1MM **Privately Held**
WEB: www.amgear.com
SIC: **3566** Gears, power transmission, except automotive

(P-14740)
CLARKE ENGINEERING INC
8058 Lankershim Blvd, North Hollywood
(91605-1609)
PHONE.................................818 768-0690
Roger D Clarke, *President*
Lee V Mason, *Vice Pres*
Lee Mason, *Vice Pres*
EMP: 12
SQ FT: 5,500
SALES (est): 2.5MM **Privately Held**
WEB: www.clarkgear.com
SIC: **3566** Gears, power transmission, except automotive

(P-14741)
HECO INC
Also Called: Pascal Systems
2350 Del Monte St, West Sacramento
(95691-3807)
P.O. Box 1388 (95691-1388)
PHONE.................................916 372-5411
Michael H Jacobs, *President*
Allen Rasmussen, *Vice Pres*
Darryl Fine, *Manager*
▲ EMP: 13 EST: 1975
SQ FT: 10,000
SALES: 6.5MM **Privately Held**
WEB: www.hecogear.com
SIC: **3566** Speed changers (power transmission equipment), except auto

(P-14742)
INTRA AEROSPACE LLC
10671 Civic Center Dr, Rancho Cucamonga
(91730-3804)
PHONE.................................909 476-0343
Robert Sayig, *Principal*
EMP: 35
SALES (est): 6.2MM **Privately Held**
SIC: **3566** Speed changers, drives & gears

(P-14743)
JETCO TORQUE TOOLS LLC
835 Meridian St, Duarte (91010-3587)
PHONE..................................626 359-2881
Bradley Jenkins, *Mng Member*
EMP: 10 EST: 2015
SALES: 1.5MM **Privately Held**
SIC: 3566 3621 Torque converters, except automotive; torque motors, electric

(P-14744)
MARPLES GEARS INC
808 W Santa Anita Ave, San Gabriel (91776-1017)
PHONE..................................626 570-1744
James A Phillips IV, *CEO*
Jeff Goff, *General Mgr*
EMP: 23
SQ FT: 5,000
SALES: 3.9MM **Privately Held**
WEB: www.marplesgears.com
SIC: 3566 Speed changers, drives & gears

(P-14745)
MARTIN SPROCKET & GEAR INC
1199 Vine St, Sacramento (95811-0426)
PHONE..................................916 441-7172
Steve Delay, *Branch Mgr*
Scott McNeil, *Safety Mgr*
EMP: 50
SQ FT: 100,000
SALES (corp-wide): 456MM **Privately Held**
SIC: 3566 3535 3534 3462 Gears, power transmission, except automotive; conveyors & conveying equipment; elevators & moving stairways; iron & steel forgings; hand & edge tools; sprockets (power transmission equipment)
PA: Martin Sprocket & Gear, Inc.
3100 Sprocket Dr
Arlington TX 76015
817 258-3000

(P-14746)
MARTIN SPROCKET & GEAR INC
5920 Triangle Dr, Commerce (90040-3688)
PHONE..................................323 728-8117
Gus Diaz, *Manager*
EMP: 12
SQ FT: 8,500
SALES (corp-wide): 456MM **Privately Held**
SIC: 3566 5085 3568 Gears, power transmission, except automotive; sprockets; power transmission equipment
PA: Martin Sprocket & Gear, Inc.
3100 Sprocket Dr
Arlington TX 76015
817 258-3000

(P-14747)
QUALITY GEARS INC
Also Called: Associated Gear
12139 Slauson Ave, Santa Fe Springs (90670-2603)
PHONE..................................562 921-9938
Stephany Castellanos, *President*
Bill Guillermo Castellanos, *Vice Pres*
Stephanie Castellanos, *Manager*
EMP: 12 EST: 2011
SALES: 100K **Privately Held**
SIC: 3566 Gears, power transmission, except automotive

(P-14748)
REXNORD LLC
3690 Jurupa St, Ontario (91761-2910)
PHONE..................................909 467-8102
EMP: 197 **Publicly Held**
SIC: 3566 Speed changers, drives & gears
HQ: Rexnord Llc
3001 W Canal St
Milwaukee WI 53208
414 342-3131

(P-14749)
SEW-EURODRIVE INC
30599 San Antonio St, Hayward (94544-7101)
PHONE..................................510 487-3560
Marvin Leeper, *Branch Mgr*
John McNamee, *Manager*

Darwin Tindan, *Manager*
EMP: 44
SALES (corp-wide): 3.4B **Privately Held**
WEB: www.seweurodrive.com
SIC: 3566 Speed changers, drives & gears
HQ: Sew-Eurodrive, Inc.
1295 Old Spartanburg Hwy
Lyman SC 29365
864 439-7537

(P-14750)
SOLAR TURBINES INCORPORATED
2200 Pacific Hwy, San Diego (92101-1773)
PHONE..................................619 544-5352
EMP: 50
SQ FT: 45,000
SALES (corp-wide): 54.7B **Publicly Held**
WEB: www.esolar.cat.com
SIC: 3566 3462 Gears, power transmission, except automotive; iron & steel forgings
HQ: Solar Turbines Incorporated
2200 Pacific Hwy
San Diego CA 92101
619 544-5000

(P-14751)
US GEAR & PUMPS
1249 S Diamond Bar Blvd # 325, Diamond Bar (91765-4122)
PHONE..................................909 525-3026
Eony Clark, *Owner*
EMP: 20
SALES (est): 1.4MM **Privately Held**
SIC: 3566 Speed changers, drives & gears

3567 Indl Process Furnaces & Ovens

(P-14752)
ALLEN MORGAN
Also Called: Tsi/Protherm
1233 W Collins Ave, Orange (92867-5412)
PHONE..................................714 538-7492
Allen Morgan, *Owner*
EMP: 12
SQ FT: 3,000
SALES (est): 2.1MM **Privately Held**
WEB: www.allenmorgan.com
SIC: 3567 Heating units & devices, industrial: electric

(P-14753)
AMARK INDUSTRIES INC (PA)
600 W Esplanade Ave, San Jacinto (92583-4903)
PHONE..................................951 654-7351
Pepper Renshaw, *President*
Gordon Moss, *CFO*
EMP: 122 EST: 1961
SALES (est): 14MM **Privately Held**
WEB: www.amarkindustries.com
SIC: 3567 Industrial furnaces & ovens

(P-14754)
AMERICAN INDUCTION TECH INC
310 N Palm St Ste B, Brea (92821-2867)
P.O. Box 292 (92822-0292)
PHONE..................................714 456-1122
Apolinar Rosas, *President*
▲ EMP: 13
SALES (est): 2.4MM **Privately Held**
SIC: 3567 Induction heating equipment

(P-14755)
ASC PROCESS SYSTEMS INC
28402 Livingston Ave, Valencia (91355-4172)
PHONE..................................818 833-0088
David C Mason, *President*
◆ EMP: 250
SQ FT: 41,000
SALES: 55.9MM **Privately Held**
WEB: www.aschome.com
SIC: 3567 3585 3563 7378 Industrial furnaces & ovens; heating & air conditioning combination units; vacuum pumps, except laboratory; computer peripheral equipment repair & maintenance; fabricated plate work (boiler shop)

(P-14756)
BAKER FURNACE INC
2680 Orbiter St, Brea (92821-6265)
PHONE..................................714 223-7262
Ernest E Bacon, *President*
Diane Bacon, *Treasurer*
Sergio Luevano, *Engineer*
▼ EMP: 19
SQ FT: 25,000
SALES (est): 5.8MM
SALES (corp-wide): 95.3MM **Privately Held**
WEB: www.bakerfurnace.com
SIC: 3567 Heating units & devices, industrial: electric
HQ: Tps, Llc
2821 Old Route 15
New Columbia PA 17856
570 538-7200

(P-14757)
CIRCLE INDUSTRIAL MFG CORP (PA)
Also Called: Cim Services
1613 W El Segundo Blvd, Compton (90222-1024)
PHONE..................................310 638-5101
Ronald M La Forest, *President*
Karen La Forest, *Treasurer*
John La Forest, *Vice Pres*
EMP: 23
SQ FT: 3,500
SALES (est): 5.1MM **Privately Held**
WEB: www.circleindustrial.com
SIC: 3567 3542 3535 3444 Industrial furnaces & ovens; sheet metalworking machines; conveyors & conveying equipment; sheet metalwork

(P-14758)
CONCEPTS & METHODS CO INC
Also Called: Camco Furnace
1017 Bransten Rd, San Carlos (94070-4020)
PHONE..................................650 593-1064
Anthony Barulich, *President*
Kay Barulich, *Corp Secy*
EMP: 10
SQ FT: 12,000
SALES (est): 4.4MM **Privately Held**
WEB: www.camcoequipment.com
SIC: 3567 Vacuum furnaces & ovens

(P-14759)
DICK FARRELL INDUSTRIES INC
Also Called: D.F. Industries
5071 Lindsay Ct, Chino (91710-5757)
PHONE..................................909 613-9424
Timothy Farrell, *Principal*
Richard Farrell, *Vice Pres*
Lisa Van Den Berg, *Admin Sec*
▲ EMP: 17
SQ FT: 25,000
SALES (est): 4.8MM **Privately Held**
WEB: www.dfindustries.com
SIC: 3567 3312 7699 Industrial furnaces & ovens; ferroalloys, produced in blast furnaces; industrial machinery & equipment repair

(P-14760)
DS FIBERTECH CORP
Also Called: Interntonal Thermoproducts Div
11015 Mission Park Ct, Santee (92071-5601)
PHONE..................................619 562-7001
Duong Minh Nguyen, *CEO*
Son Dinh Nguyen, *President*
Eric Ulrich, *Vice Pres*
Minh Nguyen, *Human Res Mgr*
Andrew Dill, *Sales Engr*
▲ EMP: 45
SQ FT: 14,000
SALES (est): 10.7MM **Privately Held**
WEB: www.itp-dsf.com
SIC: 3567 Heating units & devices, industrial: electric

(P-14761)
ENERGY RECONNAISSANCE INC
Also Called: California Heating Equipment
1270 N Red Gum St, Anaheim (92806-1820)
PHONE..................................714 630-4491
John Tittelsitz, *President*
EMP: 10
SALES: 2MM **Privately Held**
SIC: 3567 Electrical furnaces, ovens & heating devices, exc. induction

(P-14762)
FLUIDIX INC (PA)
1422 Mammoth Tav Rd C6, Mammoth Lakes (93546)
P.O. Box 1807 (93546-1807)
PHONE..................................760 935-2016
Kent A Rianda, *President*
EMP: 11
SALES (est): 1MM **Privately Held**
WEB: www.thetroutfly.com
SIC: 3567 Heating units & devices, industrial: electric

(P-14763)
HEATER DESIGNS INC
2211 S Vista Ave, Bloomington (92316-2921)
PHONE..................................909 421-0971
James Fan, *Chairman*
Tom Odendahl, *President*
EMP: 30
SQ FT: 14,500
SALES (est): 5.6MM **Privately Held**
WEB: www.heaterdesigns.net
SIC: 3567 Heating units & devices, industrial: electric

(P-14764)
INDUCTION TECHNOLOGY CORP
22060 Bear Valley Rd, Apple Valley (92308-7209)
PHONE..................................760 246-7333
Micahel T Dicken, *President*
Michael T Dicken, *President*
Marilyn Dicken, *Admin Sec*
Adam Estrada, *Engineer*
Tom Van Norman, *Controller*
EMP: 21 EST: 1979
SQ FT: 25,000
SALES (est): 6.3MM **Privately Held**
WEB: www.inductiontech.com
SIC: 3567 7699 Induction heating equipment; industrial machinery & equipment repair

(P-14765)
INDUSTRIAL FURNACE & INSUL INC
2090 S Hellman Ave, Ontario (91761-8018)
PHONE..................................909 947-2449
Gobind Panjabi, *President*
Michael O'Rourke, *Vice Pres*
▲ EMP: 12
SQ FT: 10,200
SALES (est): 2.6MM **Privately Held**
WEB: www.indfurn.com
SIC: 3567 Ceramic kilns & furnaces

(P-14766)
INDUSTRIAL PROCESS EQP INC
Also Called: I P E
1700 Industrial Ave, Norco (92860-2949)
PHONE..................................714 447-0171
Michael J Waggoner, *CEO*
James Waggoner, *President*
Cody Waggoner, *Manager*
▼ EMP: 16
SQ FT: 30,220
SALES (est): 6.5MM **Privately Held**
SIC: 3567 Industrial furnaces & ovens

(P-14767)
JHAWAR INDUSTRIES LLC
Also Called: G-M Enterprises
525 Klug Cir, Corona (92880-5452)
PHONE..................................951 340-4646
Suresh Jhawar, *CEO*
Paul Warg, *CFO*
Veena Jhawar, *Exec VP*
John Kemper, *Controller*
▼ EMP: 41 EST: 1975

▲ = Import ▼=Export
◆ =Import/Export

SQ FT: 50,000
SALES: 20MM **Privately Held**
WEB: www.gmenterprises.com
SIC: 3567 Vacuum furnaces & ovens

(P-14768)
L C MILLER COMPANY
717 Monterey Pass Rd, Monterey Park
(91754-3606)
PHONE..................................323 268-3611
Dolores Naimy, *President*
Dave Vito, *COO*
Victor De Lucia, *Vice Pres*
EMP: 27
SQ FT: 14,000
SALES (est): 4.8MM **Privately Held**
WEB: www.lcmiller.com
SIC: 3567 3546 3625 3398 Heating units
& devices, industrial: electric; saws &
sawing equipment; industrial electrical re-
lays & switches; metal heat treating

(P-14769)
LOCHABER CORNWALL INC
(PA)
Also Called: Furnace Pros
675 N Eckhoff St Ste D, Orange
(92868-1000)
PHONE..................................714 935-0302
James Clark, *President*
Katherine Clark, *Treasurer*
EMP: 13
SALES (est): 1.9MM **Privately Held**
SIC: 3567 Electrical furnaces, ovens &
heating devices, exc. induction

(P-14770)
MESSANA INC
Also Called: Messana Radiant Cooling
4105 Soquel Dr Ste B, Soquel
(95073-2116)
PHONE..................................855 729-6244
Alessandro Arnulfo, *CEO*
Dan McDunn, *Sales Staff*
Francesco Marchesi, *Director*
▲ EMP: 15
SQ FT: 2,500
SALES (est): 1.4MM **Privately Held**
SIC: 3567 Radiant heating systems, indus-
trial process

(P-14771)
MODULAR PROCESS TECH
CORP
1675 Walsh Ave Ste E, Santa Clara
(95050-2626)
PHONE..................................408 325-8640
EMP: 12
SQ FT: 3,300
SALES (est): 1.7MM **Privately Held**
WEB: www.modularpro.com
SIC: 3567 3559

(P-14772)
PACIFIC KILN INSULATIONS INC
14370 Veterans Way, Moreno Valley
(92553-9058)
PHONE..................................951 697-4422
Joel Fritz, *President*
▲ EMP: 12 EST: 1978
SQ FT: 10,000
SALES (est): 3.4MM **Privately Held**
SIC: 3567 Fuel-fired furnaces & ovens

(P-14773)
PRIME HEAT INCORPORATED
1844 Friendship Dr Ste A, El Cajon
(92020-1115)
PHONE..................................619 449-6623
Herb Boekamp, *President*
▲ EMP: 18
SQ FT: 20,500
SALES (est): 4.7MM **Privately Held**
SIC: 3567 Heating units & devices, indus-
trial: electric

(P-14774)
RAMA CORPORATION
600 W Esplanade Ave, San Jacinto
(92583-4999)
PHONE..................................951 654-7351
Peggy Renshaw, *President*
Marilyn Renshaw, *Vice Pres*
EMP: 45 EST: 1947
SQ FT: 25,000

SALES: 2MM
SALES (corp-wide): 14MM **Privately**
Held
WEB: www.amarkindustries.com
SIC: 3567 3634 Heating units & devices,
industrial: electric; electric housewares &
fans
PA: Amark Industries Inc
600 W Esplanade Ave
San Jacinto CA 92583
951 654-7351

(P-14775)
SCHMID THERMAL SYSTEMS
INC
200 Westridge Dr, Watsonville
(95076-4172)
PHONE..................................831 763-0113
Thomas Stewart, *CEO*
William Daley, *Admin Sec*
Chuck Attema, *Engineer*
Debbie Kertai, *Senior Buyer*
Greg Michel, *Manager*
◆ EMP: 110
SQ FT: 34,000
SALES: 25.7MM
SALES (corp-wide): 355.8K **Privately**
Held
WEB: www.sierratherm.com
SIC: 3567 3559 3674 Electrical furnaces,
ovens & heating devices, exc. induction;
broom making machinery; semiconduc-
tors & related devices
HQ: Gebr. Schmid Gmbh
Robert-Bosch-Str. 32-36
Freudenstadt 72250
744 153-80

(P-14776)
THERMTRONIX CORPORATION
(PA)
17129 Muskrat Ave, Adelanto
(92301-2260)
P.O. Box 100 (92301-0100)
PHONE..................................760 246-4500
Robert Nealon, *President*
Deborah Nealon, *Admin Sec*
▲ EMP: 25
SQ FT: 12,000
SALES (est): 6.1MM **Privately Held**
WEB: www.thermtronix.com
SIC: 3567 Metal melting furnaces, indus-
trial: electric

(P-14777)
TP SOLAR INC
Also Called: Tpsi
16310 Downey Ave, Paramount
(90723-5500)
PHONE..................................562 808-2171
Alex Rey, *President*
Peter Ragay, *Vice Pres*
▼ EMP: 26
SQ FT: 4,000
SALES: 3.2MM **Privately Held**
SIC: 3567 Industrial furnaces & ovens

(P-14778)
W P KEITH CO INC
8323 Loch Lomond Dr, Pico Rivera
(90660-2588)
PHONE..................................562 948-3636
Carol N Keith, *CEO*
Wendell P Keith Jr, *President*
Bernd Matzer, *Engineer*
Charlie Birks, *Sales Mgr*
▲ EMP: 25 EST: 1954
SQ FT: 19,200
SALES (est): 7.8MM **Privately Held**
WEB: www.keithkilns.com
SIC: 3567 Kilns; metal melting furnaces,
industrial: fuel-fired; metal melting fur-
naces, industrial: electric

(P-14779)
WARMBOARD INC
8035 Soquel Dr Ste 41a, Aptos
(95003-3948)
PHONE..................................831 685-9276
Terry Alberg, *President*
Mark Florez, *Manager*
EMP: 20
SQ FT: 1,250

SALES (est): 6.2MM **Privately Held**
WEB: www.warmboard.com
SIC: 3567 Radiant heating systems, indus-
trial process

3568 Mechanical Power
Transmission Eqpt, NEC

(P-14780)
ANACO INC
1001 El Camino Ave, Corona (92879-1756)
PHONE..................................951 372-2732
Leon Nolen III, *President*
Karina N Barajas, *Vice Pres*
Jack Dunaway, *Technical Staff*
Tina Velasquez, *Human Res Mgr*
Larry Fuscher, *Safety Mgr*
▲ EMP: 140
SALES (est): 41.3MM
SALES (corp-wide): 1.2B **Privately Held**
WEB: www.mcwane.com
SIC: 3568 Couplings, shaft: rigid, flexible,
universal joint, etc.
PA: Mcwane, Inc.
2900 Highway 280 S # 300
Birmingham AL 35223
205 414-3100

(P-14781)
ATR SALES INC
Also Called: Atra-Flex
110 E Garry Ave, Santa Ana (92707-4201)
PHONE..................................714 432-8411
Jerry Hauck, *CEO*
Tom Arutunian, *Shareholder*
Raymond Hoyt, *Corp Secy*
Darin Martinez, *Vice Pres*
EMP: 26
SQ FT: 12,000
SALES: 10MM **Privately Held**
WEB: www.atra-flex.com
SIC: 3568 Couplings, shaft: rigid, flexible,
universal joint, etc.

(P-14782)
BALL SCREWS & ACTUATORS
CO INC (HQ)
Also Called: B S A
48767 Kato Rd, Fremont (94538-7313)
PHONE..................................510 770-5932
Steve Randazzo, *President*
▲ EMP: 73
SQ FT: 30,000
SALES (est): 10.4MM
SALES (corp-wide): 19.8B **Publicly Held**
SIC: 3568 3625 3593 3562 Power trans-
mission equipment; actuators, industrial;
fluid power cylinders & actuators; ball &
roller bearings; bolts, nuts, rivets & wash-
ers
PA: Danaher Corporation
2200 Penn Ave Nw Ste 800w
Washington DC 20037
202 828-0850

(P-14783)
GEMINI BIO PRODUCTS
930 Riverside Pkwy Ste 50, Broderick
(95605-1511)
PHONE..................................916 471-3540
EMP: 14
SALES (est): 289.6K **Privately Held**
SIC: 3568

(P-14784)
HYSPAN PRECISION PRODUCTS
INC (PA)
1685 Brandywine Ave, Chula Vista
(91911-6097)
PHONE..................................619 421-1355
Donald R Heye, *President*
Eric Barnes, *CFO*
Phillip Ensz, *CFO*
Zoltan Takarich, *Info Tech Mgr*
Walsh Tom, *Engineer*
◆ EMP: 100
SQ FT: 54,000
SALES (est): 96.5MM **Privately Held**
WEB: www.hyspan.com
SIC: 3568 3496 3441 Ball joints, except
aircraft & automotive; woven wire prod-
ucts; expansion joints (structural shapes),
iron or steel

(P-14785)
INDU-ELECTRIC NORTH AMER
INC (PA)
27756 Avenue Hopkins, Valencia
(91355-1222)
PHONE..................................310 578-2144
Martin Gerber, *CEO*
▲ EMP: 49
SQ FT: 11,000
SALES (est): 13.9MM **Privately Held**
WEB: www.induelectric.com
SIC: 3568 5063 Power transmission
equipment; power transmission equip-
ment, electric

(P-14786)
INDUSTRIAL SPROCKETS
GEARS INC
13650 Rosecrans Ave, Santa Fe Springs
(90670-5025)
PHONE..................................323 233-7221
Max R Patridge, *CEO*
Mark Partridge, *Treasurer*
Monty Patridge, *Vice Pres*
Connie Patridge-Eason, *Admin Sec*
EMP: 21
SQ FT: 18,000
SALES (est): 5MM **Privately Held**
SIC: 3568 3566 3462 Drives, chains &
sprockets; sprockets (power transmission
equipment); drives, high speed industrial,
except hydrostatic; iron & steel forgings

(P-14787)
KLA TENCOR
Also Called: Air Bearing Technology
2260 American Ave Ste 1, Hayward
(94545-1815)
PHONE..................................510 887-2647
Art Cormier, *Principal*
Roger Peters, *Principal*
Jeff Rhoton, *Principal*
EMP: 25
SALES (est): 2.3MM **Privately Held**
WEB: www.airbearingtechnology.com
SIC: 3568 3545 Bearings, bushings &
blocks; machine tool accessories

(P-14788)
LAUNCHPOINT TECHNOLOGIES
INC
Also Called: Magnetic Moments
5735 Hollister Ave Ste B, Goleta
(93117-6410)
PHONE..................................805 683-9659
Brad E Paden, *President*
Diana Hadjes, *CFO*
Dave Paden, *Vice Pres*
Mike Ricci, *Vice Pres*
Alvin R Paden, *Admin Sec*
EMP: 15
SQ FT: 5,000
SALES (est): 4.3MM **Privately Held**
WEB: www.launchpnt.com
SIC: 3568 Bearings, plain

(P-14789)
PRECISION BABBITT CO INC
1007 S Whitemarsh Ave, Compton
(90220-4439)
PHONE..................................562 531-9173
Michael Machala, *President*
EMP: 12
SQ FT: 3,200
SALES (est): 2.5MM **Privately Held**
WEB: www.precisionbabbitt.com
SIC: 3568 7699 Bearings, plain; rebabbit-
ting

(P-14790)
REMANFCTURED CONVERTER
MBL LLC
Also Called: Remanufactured Converter MBL
582 N Batavia St, Orange (92868-1219)
PHONE..................................714 744-8988
Desmond Tan,
Jeronimo Bustillos,
Gustavo Magana,
EMP: 15
SQ FT: 7,000
SALES (est): 2.9MM **Privately Held**
SIC: 3568 Chain, power transmission

(P-14791)
RNOVATE INC
Also Called: Rnc
834 S Broadway, Los Angeles
(90014-3501)
PHONE.....................213 489-1617
John Parros, CEO
▲ EMP: 32
SQ FT: 20,000
SALES (est): 8.3MM Privately Held
SIC: 3568 Belting, chain

3569 Indl Machinery & Eqpt, NEC

(P-14792)
A&D FIRE SPRINKLERS INC
1601 W Orangewood Ave, Orange
(92868-2008)
PHONE.....................714 634-3923
Andrew Otero, CEO
Ronald Devito, Project Mgr
EMP: 15 Privately Held
SIC: 3569 Sprinkler systems, fire: automatic
PA: A&D Fire Sprinklers, Inc.
7130 Convoy Ct
San Diego CA 92111

(P-14793)
AEROSPACE FACILITIES GROUP INC
1590 Raleys Ct Ste 30, West Sacramento
(95691-3488)
PHONE.....................702 513-8336
Julie Robinson, President
Ji Chang, Principal
EMP: 18
SQ FT: 20,000
SALES (est): 759.7K Privately Held
SIC: 3569 1721 3812 Assembly machines, non-metalworking; aircraft painting; air traffic control systems & equipment, electronic

(P-14794)
AKM FIRE INC
18322 Oxnard St, Tarzana (91356-1502)
PHONE.....................818 343-8208
Yaakov Azran, President
Mary Azran, Admin Sec
EMP: 24
SALES: 1.5MM Privately Held
SIC: 3569 1711 Sprinkler systems, fire: automatic; fire sprinkler system installation

(P-14795)
AVX FILTERS CORPORATION
11144 Penrose St Ste 7, Sun Valley
(91352-2756)
PHONE.....................818 767-6770
John Gilbertson, President
Juan Arvizu, Engineer
Linda Shoemack, Human Res Mgr
Jody Jeppson, Cust Mgr
Bill Gerbing, Manager
▲ EMP: 90
SQ FT: 25,000
SALES (est): 18.2MM Publicly Held
WEB: www.avxcorp.com
SIC: 3569 3675 Filters; electronic capacitors
HQ: Avx Corporation
1 Avx Blvd
Fountain Inn SC 29644
864 967-2150

(P-14796)
BARON USA LLC
350 Baron Cir, Woodland (95776)
PHONE.....................931 528-8476
Derek L Baranowski, President
Diana M Baranowski, Admin Sec
EMP: 24
SQ FT: 28,000
SALES (est): 6.5MM Privately Held
WEB: www.baronusa.com
SIC: 3569 3567 Filters, general line: industrial; vacuum furnaces & ovens

(P-14797)
BAY AREA INDUS FILTRATION INC
6355 Coliseum Way, Oakland
(94621-3719)
P.O. Box 2071, San Leandro (94577-0207)
PHONE.....................510 562-6373
Thomas S Schneider, President
Diana E Schneider, Vice Pres
Debbie Oliver, Admin Mgr
EMP: 24
SALES (est): 5.8MM Privately Held
SIC: 3569 5085 3564 2674 Filters, general line: industrial; filters, industrial; blowers & fans; bags: uncoated paper & multiwall

(P-14798)
BEAM ON TECHNOLOGY CORPORATION
317 Brokaw Rd, Santa Clara (95050-4335)
PHONE.....................408 982-0161
Rajoo Venkat, President
EMP: 27
SALES (est): 6.8MM Privately Held
WEB: www.beamon.com
SIC: 3569 3544 3543 Assembly machines, non-metalworking; special dies, tools, jigs & fixtures; industrial patterns

(P-14799)
BORETT AUTOMATION TECHNOLOGIES
3824 Bowsprit Cir, Westlake Village
(91361-3814)
PHONE.....................818 597-8664
Richard Boring, Partner
A W Charret, Partner
EMP: 14
SQ FT: 3,400
SALES (est): 1.7MM Privately Held
SIC: 3569 5084 Robots, assembly line: industrial & commercial; conveyor systems

(P-14800)
CAPSTONE FIRE MANAGEMENT INC (PA)
2240 Auto Park Way, Escondido
(92029-1249)
PHONE.....................760 839-2290
Jerry Dusa, President
Christopher Dusa, Vice Pres
Matthew Dusa, Vice Pres
Chris Dusa, Marketing Staff
Ed McOrmond, Chief
EMP: 31 EST: 1989
SALES (est): 4.2MM Privately Held
WEB: www.fire-stop.com
SIC: 3569 Firefighting apparatus & related equipment

(P-14801)
CAPTIVE OCEAN REEF ENTERPRISES
Also Called: Ecosystem Aquarium
34135 Moongate Ct, Dana Point
(92629-2671)
PHONE.....................949 581-8888
Leng Sy, President
▲ EMP: 10
SQ FT: 10,800
SALES (est): 900K Privately Held
WEB: www.ecosystemaquarium.com
SIC: 3569 Filters

(P-14802)
CHAD INDUSTRIES INCORPORATED
1565 S Sinclair St, Anaheim (92806-5934)
PHONE.....................714 938-0080
Scott W Klimczak, President
Wayne Rapp, Admin Sec
▲ EMP: 40
SQ FT: 31,000
SALES (est): 8.9MM Privately Held
WEB: www.chadindustries.com
SIC: 3569 Robots, assembly line: industrial & commercial

(P-14803)
CLAYTON MANUFACTURING COMPANY (PA)
Also Called: Clayton Industries
17477 Hurley St, City of Industry
(91744-5106)
PHONE.....................626 443-9381
John Clayton, President
Alexander Smirnoff, CFO
Boyd A Calvin, Senior VP
Allen L Cluer, Vice Pres
Phyllis Nielson, Vice Pres
▲ EMP: 147 EST: 1930
SQ FT: 215,000
SALES (est): 109.8MM Privately Held
WEB: www.claytonindustries.com
SIC: 3569 3829 3511 Generators: steam, liquid oxygen or nitrogen; dynamometer instruments; turbines & turbine generator sets

(P-14804)
CLAYTON MANUFACTURING INC (HQ)
17477 Hurley St, City of Industry
(91744-5106)
PHONE.....................626 443-9381
William Clayton Jr, CEO
John Clayton, President
Boyd A Calvin, Treasurer
Allen L Cluer, Vice Pres
Tim Pressley, Manager
▼ EMP: 80 EST: 1930
SQ FT: 215,000
SALES (est): 17.1MM
SALES (corp-wide): 109.8MM Privately Held
SIC: 3569 3829 Generators: steam, liquid oxygen or nitrogen; dynamometer instruments
PA: Clayton Manufacturing Company
17477 Hurley St
City Of Industry CA 91744
626 443-9381

(P-14805)
CLOUD COMPANY (PA)
4855 Morabito Pl, San Luis Obispo
(93401-8748)
PHONE.....................805 549-8093
James H Rucker, Ch of Bd
David L Rucker, President
Karen Rucker, Admin Sec
Seanah Muindi, Data Proc Staff
EMP: 25
SQ FT: 7,000
SALES (est): 3.3MM Privately Held
WEB: www.cloudinc.com
SIC: 3569 Liquid automation machinery & equipment

(P-14806)
CODE-IN-MOTION LLC
232 Avenida Fabricante # 103, San Clemente (92672-7553)
PHONE.....................949 361-2633
Jovan Zivkovic,
Mani Arbabi, Administration
Wally Popovich, Purch Mgr
Hubert Schroeder, VP Sales
Dan Popovich,
EMP: 15
SQ FT: 13,000
SALES (est): 2.2MM Privately Held
WEB: www.code-in-motion.com
SIC: 3569 3565 Robots, assembly line: industrial & commercial; labeling machines, industrial

(P-14807)
DELTA DESIGN INC (HQ)
12367 Crosthwaite Cir, Poway
(92064-6817)
PHONE.....................858 848-8000
Samer Aabbani, President
James A Donahue, President
Jeff Jose, CFO
Charles A Schwan, Chairman
James McFarlane, Senior VP
▲ EMP: 400 EST: 1957
SQ FT: 334,000
SALES (est): 12.2MM
SALES (corp-wide): 451.7MM Publicly Held
SIC: 3569 3825 3674 Testing chambers for altitude, temperature, ordnance, power; test equipment for electronic & electrical circuits; semiconductors & related devices
PA: Cohu, Inc.
12367 Crosthwaite Cir
Poway CA 92064
858 848-8100

(P-14808)
DELTA TAU DATA SYSTEMS INC CAL (HQ)
Also Called: Omron Delta Tau
21314 Lassen St, Chatsworth
(91311-4254)
PHONE.....................818 998-2095
Yasuto Ikuta, President
Tamara Dimitri, Treasurer
Dominic Dimitri, Vice Pres
Ronnie Rostamian, QA Dir
John Prout, Technology
EMP: 130
SQ FT: 140,000
SALES (est): 39.1MM Privately Held
WEB: www.deltatau.com
SIC: 3569 7372 3625 3577 Robots, assembly line: industrial & commercial; prepackaged software; relays & industrial controls; computer peripheral equipment

(P-14809)
DELTA TAU INTERNATIONAL INC
21314 Lassen St, Chatsworth
(91311-4254)
PHONE.....................818 998-2095
Yasuto Ikuta, President
EMP: 14
SQ FT: 35,000
SALES (est): 1.8MM Privately Held
WEB: www.deltatau.com
SIC: 3569 Robots, assembly line: industrial & commercial
HQ: Delta Tau Data Systems Inc Of California
21314 Lassen St
Chatsworth CA 91311
818 998-2095

(P-14810)
DESCHNER CORPORATION
3211 W Harvard St, Santa Ana
(92704-3976)
PHONE.....................714 557-1261
Joe Alessi, President
Toby Ryan, CEO
Frank Solis, CFO
EMP: 35
SQ FT: 21,600
SALES (est): 8MM Privately Held
WEB: www.deschner.com
SIC: 3569 3594 Liquid automation machinery & equipment; fluid power pumps & motors

(P-14811)
EDEN EQUIPMENT COMPANY INC
5670 Wilshire Blvd # 1400, Los Angeles
(90036-5612)
PHONE.....................909 629-2217
Joe Kovach, President
Branden Crowe, Opers Mgr
◆ EMP: 15 EST: 1982
SQ FT: 10,000
SALES (est): 3.8MM Privately Held
WEB: www.edenequipment.com
SIC: 3569 Filters, general line: industrial; filters

(P-14812)
EKLAVYA LLC
Also Called: Nexus Automation
2021 Las Positas Ct # 141, Livermore
(94551-7304)
PHONE.....................925 443-3296
Sandeep Patel,
Vinita Chaturvedi, Chief Mktg Ofcr
EMP: 10
SQ FT: 4,000

▲ = Import ▼=Export
◆ =Import/Export

SALES (est): 1.9MM **Privately Held**
SIC: 3569 3559 3565 5084 Robots, assembly line: industrial & commercial; pharmaceutical machinery; semiconductor manufacturing machinery; packaging machinery; labeling machines, industrial; industrial machinery & equipment; machine shop, jobbing & repair

(P-14813)
ENTEGRIS GP INC
4175 Santa Fe Rd, San Luis Obispo (93401-8159)
PHONE.....................805 541-9299
Bertrand Loy, *President*
◆ EMP: 130
SQ FT: 50,000
SALES (est): 66.8MM
SALES (corp-wide): 1.5B **Publicly Held**
WEB: www.puregastechnologies.com
SIC: 3569 Gas producers, generators & other gas related equipment
PA: Entegris, Inc.
129 Concord Rd
Billerica MA 01821
978 436-6500

(P-14814)
FILBUR MANUFACTURING LLC
Also Called: Filbur Pool & Spa Filtration
20 Centerpointe Dr # 110, La Palma (90623-2558)
PHONE.....................714 228-6000
Ching-Hsiung Lin, *Mng Member*
Bruce Stump, *Vice Pres*
Christopher Corpus, *Info Tech Mgr*
Guadalupe Carillo, *Accounting Mgr*
Merced Pereda-Osorio, *Asst Controller*
▲ EMP: 42 EST: 1996
SQ FT: 93,000
SALES (est): 12.8MM **Privately Held**
WEB: www.filburmfg.com
SIC: 3569 Filters

(P-14815)
FIREBLAST GLOBAL INC
545 Monica Cir, Corona (92880-5447)
PHONE.....................951 277-8319
Richard Egelin, *CEO*
EMP: 25
SALES (est): 8.5MM **Privately Held**
WEB: www.fireblast.com
SIC: 3569 8711 Firefighting apparatus; engineering services

(P-14816)
FIREQUICK PRODUCTS INC
1137 Red Rock Inyokern Rd, Inyokern (93527)
P.O. Box 910 (93527-0910)
PHONE.....................760 371-4279
Beth J Sumners, *President*
Bill Sumners, *Vice Pres*
EMP: 15
SALES: 2.5MM **Privately Held**
WEB: www.firequick.com
SIC: 3569 Firefighting apparatus & related equipment

(P-14817)
FIRST RESPONDER FIRE
Also Called: 1st Responder Fire Protection
19146 Stare St, Northridge (91324-1266)
PHONE.....................562 842-6602
John Flores, *President*
EMP: 11
SALES: 2.6MM **Privately Held**
SIC: 3569 7389 1711 1799 Sprinkler systems, fire: automatic; ; fire sprinkler system installation; irrigation sprinkler system installation; coating, caulking & weather, water & fireproofing; repairing fire damage, single-family houses

(P-14818)
FJA INDUSTRIES INC
1230 Coleman Ave, Santa Clara (95050-4338)
P.O. Box 242 (95052-0242)
PHONE.....................408 727-0100
Frank J Ardezzone, *CEO*
▲ EMP: 14
SQ FT: 10,000
SALES: 600K **Privately Held**
SIC: 3569 Robots, assembly line: industrial & commercial

(P-14819)
FLAME GARD INC
6825 E Washington Blvd, Los Angeles (90040-1905)
PHONE.....................323 888-8707
Lawrence Capalbo, *President*
Thomas E Capalbo, *CFO*
Gary Barros, *VP Sales*
EMP: 67
SQ FT: 12,000
SALES (est): 7MM
SALES (corp-wide): 30MM **Privately Held**
WEB: www.flamegard.com
SIC: 3569 3444 Filters; sheet metalwork
PA: Taylor Freezers Of Southern California, Inc.
6825 E Washington Blvd
Commerce CA 90040
323 889-8700

(P-14820)
FLYERS ENERGY LLC
444 Yolanda Ave Ste A, Santa Rosa (95404-8090)
PHONE.....................707 546-0766
EMP: 70
SALES (corp-wide): 263.9MM **Privately Held**
SIC: 3569 5172 Lubrication equipment, industrial; lubricating oils & greases
PA: Flyers Energy, Llc
2360 Lindbergh St
Auburn CA 95602
530 885-0401

(P-14821)
GENERON IGS INC
Also Called: M G Generon
992 Arcy Ln Bldg 992, Pittsburg (94565)
P.O. Box 271 (94565-0015)
PHONE.....................925 431-1030
Karen Skala, *Manager*
EMP: 25
SALES (corp-wide): 35MM **Privately Held**
WEB: www.generon-ca.com
SIC: 3569 2813 3081 Separators for steam, gas, vapor or air (machinery); industrial gases; unsupported plastics film & sheet
HQ: Generon Igs, Inc.
16250 State Highway 249
Houston TX 77086
713 937-5200

(P-14822)
GLASMAN SHIM & STAMPING INC
226 N Sherman Ave Ste B, Corona (92882-7122)
PHONE.....................951 278-8197
Larry Glasman Jr, *CEO*
EMP: 10
SQ FT: 4,320
SALES (est): 1.6MM **Privately Held**
WEB: www.bolsanwestinc.com
SIC: 3569 Surveillance ovens for aging & testing powder

(P-14823)
GUSMER ENTERPRISES INC
Also Called: Cellulo Co Division
81 M St, Fresno (93721-3215)
PHONE.....................908 301-1811
Fred Mazanec, *Opers Mgr*
Orlando Gomez, *Info Tech Dir*
EMP: 75
SQ FT: 18,644
SALES (corp-wide): 34MM **Privately Held**
WEB: www.gusmerenterprises.com
SIC: 3569 Filters, general line: industrial
PA: Gusmer Enterprises, Inc.
1165 Globe Ave
Mountainside NJ 07092
908 301-1811

(P-14824)
HARTWICK COMBUSTION TECH INC
9426 Stewart And Gray Rd, Downey (90241-5351)
PHONE.....................562 922-8300
Peter Hartwick, *President*

Andrea Hartwick, *Corp Secy*
EMP: 10
SALES: 800K **Privately Held**
SIC: 3569 Cremating ovens

(P-14825)
HONEYBEE ROBOTICS LTD
398 W Washington Blvd, Pasadena (91103-2000)
PHONE.....................510 207-4555
Stephen Gorvan, *Branch Mgr*
EMP: 11
SALES (corp-wide): 196.2MM **Privately Held**
SIC: 3569 Filters
HQ: Honeybee Robotics, Ltd.
Suit Bldg 128
Brooklyn NY 11205
212 966-0661

(P-14826)
HYDRO-LOGIC PURIFICATION
370 Encinal St Ste 150, Santa Cruz (95060-2182)
PHONE.....................888 426-5644
Rich Gellert, *CEO*
EMP: 12
SQ FT: 2,500
SALES (est): 1.9MM **Privately Held**
SIC: 3569 Filters

(P-14827)
IMERYS PERLITE USA INC
1450 Simpson Way, Escondido (92029-1311)
P.O. Box 462908 (92046-2908)
PHONE.....................760 745-5900
Darin Jackman, *Manager*
EMP: 10
SQ FT: 13,288
SALES (corp-wide): 3MM **Privately Held**
WEB: www.worldminerals.com
SIC: 3569 Filters, general line: industrial
HQ: Imerys Perlite Usa, Inc.
1732 N 1st St Ste 450
San Jose CA 95112

(P-14828)
INDUSTRIAL EQP SOLUTIONS INC
Also Called: I E S
301 N Smith Ave, Corona (92880-1742)
PHONE.....................951 272-9540
Mohammad A Gauhar, *CEO*
Awais A Gauhar, *President*
Minhaj Khan, *Project Engr*
▲ EMP: 15
SQ FT: 7,000
SALES (est): 9.1MM **Privately Held**
WEB: www.ies-corp.com
SIC: 3569 Filters

(P-14829)
INDUSTRIAL FIRE SPRNKLR CO INC
3845 Imperial Ave, San Diego (92113-1702)
PHONE.....................619 266-6030
L David Sandage, *President*
Holly Kay, *Accounts Mgr*
EMP: 35
SALES (est): 8.4MM **Privately Held**
WEB: www.industrialfiresprinkler.com
SIC: 3569 1731 Sprinkler systems, fire: automatic; fire detection & burglar alarm systems specialization

(P-14830)
INVIA ROBOTICS INC (PA)
5701 Lindero Canyon Rd 3-100, Westlake Village (91362-6487)
PHONE.....................818 597-1680
Lior Elazary, *CEO*
Dan Parks, *COO*
Kristen Moore, *Chief Mktg Ofcr*
Corwin Carson, *Officer*
Randolph Voorhies, *CTO*
EMP: 10
SQ FT: 2,400
SALES: 2MM **Privately Held**
SIC: 3569 Robots, assembly line: industrial & commercial

(P-14831)
J R SCHNEIDER CO INC
849 Jackson St, Benicia (94510-2994)
PHONE.....................707 745-0404
Bernice Schneider, *Ch of Bd*
J Stephen Schneider, *President*
Donna C Block, *CEO*
Chris Canada, *CFO*
Andy Ricketts, *Technical Staff*
◆ EMP: 13
SQ FT: 100,000
SALES (est): 3.5MM **Privately Held**
WEB: www.jrschneider.com
SIC: 3569 3471 3443 Filters, general line: industrial; plating & polishing; fabricated plate work (boiler shop)

(P-14832)
JEREMYWELL INTERNATIONAL INC
14 Vanderbilt, Irvine (92618-2010)
PHONE.....................949 588-6888
Stephanie Chang, *Principal*
Tom Tetrick, *General Mgr*
▲ EMP: 11 EST: 2013
SALES (est): 1.1MM **Privately Held**
SIC: 3569 General industrial machinery
PA: Hangzhou Fuhua Co., Ltd.
181, Fengqi Road
Hangzhou

(P-14833)
KINGS WAY SALES AND MKTG LLC
6680 Lockheed Dr, Redding (96002-9014)
PHONE.....................530 722-0272
David Mahrt, *Mng Member*
Charlin Mahrt,
David M Mahrt, *Mng Member*
EMP: 14
SQ FT: 4,500
SALES (est): 2.4MM **Privately Held**
SIC: 3569 Firefighting apparatus

(P-14834)
KNIGHT LLC (HQ)
15340 Barranca Pkwy, Irvine (92618-2215)
PHONE.....................949 595-4800
George Noa, *President*
Rob Goodyear, *Managing Prtnr*
Richard Yanez, *Vice Pres*
Rick Yanez, *Vice Pres*
Chris March, *Regl Sales Mgr*
▲ EMP: 100 EST: 1972
SQ FT: 46,000
SALES (est): 18.6MM
SALES (corp-wide): 2.4B **Publicly Held**
WEB: www.knightequip.com
SIC: 3569 3582 3589 Liquid automation machinery & equipment; commercial laundry equipment; dishwashing machines, commercial
PA: Idex Corporation
1925 W Field Ct Ste 200
Lake Forest IL 60045
847 498-7070

(P-14835)
LUBRICATION SCIENTICS LLC
17651 Armstrong Ave, Irvine (92614-5727)
PHONE.....................714 557-0664
Richard Hanley, *Mng Member*
James Schoen, *Marketing Mgr*
EMP: 48
SALES (est): 6.6MM **Privately Held**
SIC: 3569 Lubricating equipment

(P-14836)
MAHMOOD IZADI INC
Also Called: Solatron Enterprises
3115 Lomita Blvd, Torrance (90505-5108)
PHONE.....................310 325-0463
Mahmood Izadi, *President*
EMP: 14
SQ FT: 9,500
SALES: 850K **Privately Held**
WEB: www.solatron.com
SIC: 3569 Assembly machines, non-metalworking; testing chambers for altitude, temperature, ordnance, power

(P-14837)
MATICIAN INC
430 Sherman Ave Ste 100, Palo Alto
(94306-1852)
PHONE..................650 504-9181
Navneet Dalal, *Principal*
EMP: 11
SQ FT: 2,000
SALES (est): 1.5MM **Privately Held**
SIC: 3569 Robots, assembly line: industrial
& commercial

(P-14838)
MILLENNIUM AUTOMATION
1300 Fulton Pl, Fremont (94539-7990)
PHONE..................510 683-5942
Paul Adams, *President*
Jim Miller, *Treasurer*
David Miller, *Vice Pres*
Michael Mock, *Executive*
Gerald Fedor, *Admin Sec*
EMP: 16 EST: 1997
SQ FT: 5,500
SALES (est): 3.6MM
SALES (corp-wide): 988.5K **Privately
Held**
SIC: 3569 5084 Liquid automation ma-
chinery & equipment; robots, industrial
HQ: Marposs Spa
Via Saliceto 13
Bentivoglio BO 40010
051 899-111

(P-14839)
MYERS MIXERS LLC
8376 Salt Lake Ave, Cudahy (90201-5817)
PHONE..................323 560-4723
Gary Myers,
Cary Buller,
EMP: 41
SALES (est): 9.7MM **Privately Held**
SIC: 3569 Centrifuges, industrial

(P-14840)
NATIONAL FILTER MEDIA CORP
17130 Muskrat Ave Ste B, Adelanto
(92301-2473)
PHONE..................760 246-4551
EMP: 52
SALES (corp-wide): 658.7MM **Privately
Held**
SIC: 3569
HQ: The National Filter Media Corporation
691 N 400 W
Salt Lake City UT 84103
801 363-6736

(P-14841)
ONEX ENTERPRISES CORPORATION
Also Called: Onex Automation
1824 Flower Ave, Duarte (91010-2931)
PHONE..................626 358-6639
Onik Bogosyan, *President*
Edwin Thomassien, *CFO*
▲ EMP: 12
SALES (est): 1.3MM **Privately Held**
WEB: www.onexautomation.com
SIC: 3569 5084 Robots, assembly line: in-
dustrial & commercial; robots, industrial

(P-14842)
PACIFIC CONSOLIDATED INDS LLC
Also Called: PCI
12201 Magnolia Ave, Riverside
(92503-4820)
PHONE..................951 479-0860
Bob Eng, *Mng Member*
Tarik Naheiri, *President*
Paul Stevens, *CFO*
Soeren Schmitz, *Vice Pres*
Terry Wheaton, *General Mgr*
◆ EMP: 77
SQ FT: 85,000
SALES (est): 31.1MM
SALES (corp-wide): 11.3MM **Privately
Held**
WEB: www.pci-intl.com
SIC: 3569 1382 Gas separators (machin-
ery); oil & gas exploration services
PA: Pci Holding Company, Inc.
12201 Magnolia Ave
Riverside CA 92503
951 479-0860

(P-14843)
PALL CORPORATION
4116 Sorrento Valley Blvd, San Diego
(92121-1407)
PHONE..................858 455-7264
Richard Mc Donald, *General Mgr*
Raul Casillas, *Mfg Spvr*
Levar Kelly, *Manager*
EMP: 70
SALES (corp-wide): 19.8B **Publicly Held**
WEB: www.pall.com
SIC: 3569 Filters
HQ: Pall Corporation
25 Harbor Park Dr
Port Washington NY 11050
516 484-5400

(P-14844)
PALL CORPORATION
1630 W Industrial Park St, Covina
(91722-3419)
PHONE..................626 339-7388
Robert Wicke, *Senior VP*
EMP: 364
SALES (corp-wide): 19.8B **Publicly Held**
SIC: 3569 Filters
HQ: Pall Corporation
25 Harbor Park Dr
Port Washington NY 11050
516 484-5400

(P-14845)
PARKER-HANNIFIN CORPORATION
Racor Division
3400 Finch Rd, Modesto (95354-4125)
P.O. Box 3208 (95353-3208)
PHONE..................209 521-7860
Brian Hook, *Branch Mgr*
Leeanne McInerny, *Executive Asst*
Roberto Jimenez, *Technician*
Monty Dhimmar, *Engineer*
Chris Van Lewen, *Engineer*
EMP: 700
SALES (corp-wide): 14.3B **Publicly Held**
WEB: www.parker.com
SIC: 3569 3561 3714 3564 Filters, gen-
eral line: industrial; pumps & pumping
equipment; motor vehicle parts & acces-
sories; blowers & fans
PA: Parker-Hannifin Corporation
6035 Parkland Blvd
Cleveland OH 44124
216 896-3000

(P-14846)
PARKER-HANNIFIN CORPORATION
Also Called: Process Advanced Filtration
2340 Eastman Ave, Oxnard (93030-5178)
PHONE..................805 604-3400
Aaron Zell, *Branch Mgr*
EMP: 187
SALES (corp-wide): 14.3B **Publicly Held**
WEB: www.parker.com
SIC: 3569 Filters
PA: Parker-Hannifin Corporation
6035 Parkland Blvd
Cleveland OH 44124
216 896-3000

(P-14847)
PC VAUGHAN MFG CORP
Also Called: Rostar Filters
1278 Mercantile St, Oxnard (93030-7522)
PHONE..................805 278-2555
Jeff Starin, *President*
EMP: 141 EST: 1981
SQ FT: 40,000
SALES (est): 5.5MM **Privately Held**
SIC: 3569 Filters

(P-14848)
PCI HOLDING COMPANY INC (PA)
12201 Magnolia Ave, Riverside
(92503-4820)
PHONE..................951 479-0860
Bob Eng, *CEO*
Tarik Naheiri, *President*
Gary Swiniarski, *Sales Dir*
EMP: 103
SALES (est): 11.3MM **Privately Held**
SIC: 3569 1382 Gas separators (machin-
ery); oil & gas exploration services

(P-14849)
PECOFACET (US) INC
Also Called: Clarcor Industrial Air
8314 Tiogawoods Dr, Sacramento
(95828-5048)
PHONE..................916 689-2328
Lori Radman, *Principal*
EMP: 12
SALES (corp-wide): 14.3B **Publicly Held**
SIC: 3569 3823 Filters, general line: in-
dustrial; separators for steam, gas, vapor
or air (machinery); flow instruments, in-
dustrial process type
HQ: Pecofacet (Us), Inc.
118 Washington Ave
Mineral Wells TX 76067
940 325-2575

(P-14850)
PIPELINE PRODUCTS INC
1650 Linda Vista Dr # 110, San Marcos
(92078-3810)
PHONE..................760 744-8907
Scott Higley, *President*
EMP: 17
SQ FT: 20,000
SALES (est): 4.8MM **Privately Held**
WEB: www.pipelineproducts.com
SIC: 3569 Filter elements, fluid, hydraulic
line

(P-14851)
PISTON HYDRAULIC SYSTEM INC
11614 Mcbean Dr, El Monte (91732-1105)
PHONE..................626 350-0100
Roobik Keshishian, *President*
Edwin Thomassian, *Vice Pres*
EMP: 10
SQ FT: 4,600
SALES (est): 820K **Privately Held**
SIC: 3569 8742 5084 Assembly ma-
chines, non-metalworking; robots, assem-
bly line: industrial & commercial;
automation & robotics consultant; con-
veyor systems

(P-14852)
POLLEY INC (PA)
Also Called: Kelco Sales & Engineering
11936 Front St, Norwalk (90650-2911)
P.O. Box 305 (90651-0305)
PHONE..................562 868-9861
Tracy Polley, *President*
Martin Blake, *Office Mgr*
Bill Mincher, *Sales Staff*
Francis Kelly, *Manager*
▲ EMP: 20 EST: 1950
SQ FT: 24,000
SALES (est): 3.3MM **Privately Held**
WEB: www.kelcosales.com
SIC: 3569 Blast cleaning equipment, dust-
less

(P-14853)
PUROLATOR ADVANCED FILTRATION
8314 Tiogawoods Dr, Sacramento
(95828-5048)
PHONE..................916 689-2328
Norm Johnson, *President*
EMP: 30
SQ FT: 40,000
SALES (est): 5.5MM
SALES (corp-wide): 14.3B **Publicly Held**
WEB: www.filterproducts.com
SIC: 3569 Filters
HQ: Clarcor Inc.
840 Crescent Centre Dr # 600
Franklin TN 37067
615 771-3100

(P-14854)
REC INC
Also Called: Ridgeline Engineering Company
2442 Cades Way, Vista (92081-7830)
PHONE..................760 727-8006
Patrick Falley, *President*
Anthony Moreau, *Vice Pres*
EMP: 10
SQ FT: 13,500
SALES (est): 2.6MM **Privately Held**
WEB: www.rec.com
SIC: 3569 Liquid automation machinery &
equipment

(P-14855)
RESCUE 42 INC
370 Ryan Ave Ste 120, Chico
(95973-9530)
P.O. Box 1242 (95927-1242)
PHONE..................530 891-3473
Tim Oconnell, *President*
EMP: 15
SALES (est): 3.9MM **Privately Held**
WEB: www.rescue42.com
SIC: 3569 Firefighting apparatus & related
equipment

(P-14856)
SEPARATION ENGINEERING INC
931 S Andreasen Dr Ste A, Escondido
(92029-1959)
PHONE..................760 489-0101
Charles E Hull, *President*
▲ EMP: 30
SQ FT: 20,000
SALES (est): 7.5MM **Privately Held**
SIC: 3569 Filters, general line: industrial

(P-14857)
SIEMENS INDUSTRY INC
5375 S Boyle Ave, Vernon (90058-3923)
PHONE..................323 277-1500
Ken Oldmixon, *Manager*
EMP: 33
SALES (corp-wide): 95B **Privately Held**
SIC: 3569 Filters
HQ: Siemens Industry, Inc.
1000 Deerfield Pkwy
Buffalo Grove IL 60089
847 215-1000

(P-14858)
SIEMENS INDUSTRY INC
1441 E Washington Blvd, Los Angeles
(90021-3039)
PHONE..................724 772-1237
Aaron Boles, *Branch Mgr*
Jim Christian, *Senior Mgr*
Tracey Williamson, *Manager*
EMP: 33
SALES (corp-wide): 95B **Privately Held**
SIC: 3569 Filters
HQ: Siemens Industry, Inc.
1000 Deerfield Pkwy
Buffalo Grove IL 60089
847 215-1000

(P-14859)
SOLARON POOL HEATING INC (PA)
3460 Business Dr Ste 100, Sacramento
(95820-2167)
PHONE..................916 858-8146
Ron Harveck, *CEO*
EMP: 10
SALES (est): 2.4MM **Privately Held**
SIC: 3569 Heaters, swimming pool: electric

(P-14860)
SP3 DIAMOND TECHNOLOGIES INC
1605 Wyatt Dr, Santa Clara (95054-1587)
PHONE..................877 773-9940
EMP: 15
SALES (est): 2.4MM
SALES (corp-wide): 7.8MM **Privately
Held**
SIC: 3569
PA: Sp3, Inc.
1605 Wyatt Dr
Santa Clara CA 95054
408 492-0630

(P-14861)
SPINTEK FILTRATION INC
10863 Portal Dr, Los Alamitos
(90720-2508)
PHONE..................714 236-9190
William A Greene, *CEO*
Patricia Kirk, *Vice Pres*
Donna Aubrey, *Office Mgr*
Jason D Gilmour, *Engineer*
Justin Rodriguez, *Marketing Staff*
◆ EMP: 15
SQ FT: 3,000
SALES (est): 4.3MM **Privately Held**
SIC: 3569 3069 8711 Filters & strainers,
pipeline; roofing, membrane rubber; engi-
neering services

(P-14862)
STEARNS PRODUCT DEV CORP (PA)
Also Called: Doughpro
20281 Harvill Ave, Perris (92570-7235)
PHONE..................................951 657-0379
Steven Raio, *President*
Kim Kitchin, *Technical Mgr*
Leslie Gamester, *Human Res Mgr*
Eddie Martinez, *Purch Mgr*
Charles Wieland, *VP Mfg*
▲ EMP: 91
SQ FT: 50,000
SALES: 12MM **Privately Held**
SIC: 3569 3444 Assembly machines, non-metalworking; sheet metalwork

(P-14863)
SUPPRESS FIRE ATMTC SPRINKLERS
363 Cliffwood Park St G, Brea
(92821-4106)
PHONE..................................714 671-5939
Oscar Delatorre, *President*
EMP: 10
SQ FT: 1,500
SALES (est): 850K **Privately Held**
SIC: 3569 Firefighting apparatus & related equipment

(P-14864)
SYNERGY OIL LLC
1201 Dove St Ste 475, Newport Beach
(92660-2812)
P.O. Box 993, Okmulgee OK (74447-0993)
PHONE..................................888 333-1933
Robert Falco, *Mng Member*
EMP: 30 EST: 2009
SQ FT: 4,000
SALES: 2.5MM **Privately Held**
SIC: 3569 5172 Gas producers, generators & other gas related equipment; fuel oil

(P-14865)
TRINET CONSTRUCTION INC
3934 Geary Blvd, San Francisco
(94118-3219)
PHONE..................................415 695-7814
Nora Mary Hickey, *President*
William Hickey, *Vice Pres*
Abhishek Shrivastava, *Sr Software Eng*
EMP: 12
SALES (est): 5.5MM **Privately Held**
SIC: 3569 Firefighting apparatus & related equipment; firefighting apparatus

(P-14866)
TWIN DESIGN CO LLC
18458 Carlwyn Dr, Castro Valley
(94546-2030)
PHONE..................................510 329-4991
Zachary Hollis,
EMP: 10
SALES (est): 446.2K **Privately Held**
SIC: 3569 Robots, assembly line: industrial & commercial

(P-14867)
TYCO FIRE PRODUCTS LP
Also Called: Tyco Fire Protection Products
6952 Preston Ave, Livermore (94551-9545)
PHONE..................................925 687-6957
EMP: 200 **Privately Held**
SIC: 3569 Sprinkler systems, fire: automatic; generators: steam, liquid oxygen or nitrogen
HQ: Tyco Fire Products Lp
    1400 Pennbrook Pkwy
    Lansdale PA 19446
    215 362-0700

(P-14868)
TYCO SIMPLEXGRINNELL
3077 Wiljan Ct Ste B, Santa Rosa
(95407-5764)
PHONE..................................707 578-3212
Mark Watson, *District Mgr*
EMP: 40
SQ FT: 1,200
SALES (corp-wide): 1.3B **Privately Held**
SIC: 3569 1711 3498 3669 Sprinkler systems, fire: automatic; fire sprinkler system installation; pipe fittings, fabricated from purchased pipe; smoke detectors

PA: Tyco Simplexgrinnell
    1501 Nw 51st St
    Boca Raton FL 33431
    561 988-3658

(P-14869)
VERTEX INDUSTRIAL INC
Also Called: Vertex Water Products
5138 Brooks St, Montclair (91763-4800)
PHONE..................................909 626-2100
Jean Voznick, *Ch of Bd*
Henry P Voznick, *President*
Hal Voznick, *Vice Pres*
Steven Voznick, *Vice Pres*
Steve Murphy, *Sales Staff*
▲ EMP: 10
SQ FT: 15,000
SALES (est): 1.9MM **Privately Held**
WEB: www.vertexwater.com
SIC: 3569 5074 Filters; water purification equipment

(P-14870)
WASSER FILTRATION INC (PA)
Also Called: Pacific Press
1215 N Fee Ana St, Anaheim (92807-1804)
PHONE..................................714 982-5600
Sean Duby, *President*
▲ EMP: 80
SQ FT: 20,000
SALES (est): 18.4MM **Privately Held**
WEB: www.pacpress.com
SIC: 3569 5084 Filters, general line: industrial; filters & strainers, pipeline; industrial machinery & equipment

(P-14871)
WATER FILTER EXCHANGE INC
980 Kirkton Pl, Glendale (91207-1550)
PHONE..................................818 808-2541
Mireille Chividian, *CEO*
EMP: 14
SQ FT: 5,000
SALES: 10MM **Privately Held**
SIC: 3569 Filters

(P-14872)
WEST BOND INC (PA)
1551 S Harris Ct, Anaheim (92806-5932)
PHONE..................................714 978-1551
John C Price, *President*
Gary Phillips, *Vice Pres*
Phyllis Eppig, *Admin Sec*
Lorri Witters, *Sales Mgr*
Matt Ritchie, *Sales Staff*
▼ EMP: 47 EST: 1966
SQ FT: 38,000
SALES (est): 7.1MM **Privately Held**
WEB: www.westbond.com
SIC: 3569 Assembly machines, non-metalworking

(P-14873)
WOMACK INTERNATIONAL INC
3855 Cypress Dr Ste H, Petaluma
(94954-5690)
PHONE..................................707 763-1800
Thomas Womack, *President*
Michael Oakes, *Vice Pres*
Jef Templeton, *Engineer*
▼ EMP: 20 EST: 1980
SQ FT: 130,000
SALES (est): 3.6MM **Privately Held**
SIC: 3569 Filter elements, fluid, hydraulic line

(P-14874)
YASKAWA AMERICA INC
1701 Kaiser Ave, Irvine (92614-5705)
PHONE..................................949 263-2640
Frank Bibas, *Branch Mgr*
EMP: 14 **Privately Held**
WEB: www.motoman.com
SIC: 3569 Robots, assembly line: industrial & commercial
HQ: Yaskawa America, Inc.
    2121 Norman Dr
    Waukegan IL 60085
    847 887-7000

3571 Electronic Computers

(P-14875)
3D SYSTEMS INC
16550 W Bernardo Dr # 5, San Diego
(92127-1870)
PHONE..................................803 280-7777
EMP: 10 **Publicly Held**
SIC: 3571 Electronic computers
HQ: 3d Systems, Inc.
    333 Three D Systems Cir
    Rock Hill SC 29730
    803 326-3900

(P-14876)
3PAR INC (HQ)
4209 Technology Dr, Fremont
(94538-6339)
PHONE..................................510 445-1046
David C Scott, *President*
Adriel G Lares, *CFO*
Alastair A Short, *Vice Pres*
Ashok Singhal PHD, *CTO*
Kevin Minh Lam, *Technology*
EMP: 188
SQ FT: 263,000
SALES (est): 57.5MM
SALES (corp-wide): 30.8B **Publicly Held**
WEB: www.pardata.com
SIC: 3571 2542 Electronic computers; partitions & fixtures, except wood
PA: Hewlett Packard Enterprise Company
    6280 America Center Dr
    San Jose CA 95002
    650 687-5817

(P-14877)
A S A ENGINEERING INC
Also Called: Micro Express
8 Hammond Ste 105, Irvine (92618-1601)
PHONE..................................949 460-9911
Art Afshar, *President*
K C Shabak, *Vice Pres*
◆ EMP: 35
SQ FT: 2,000
SALES (est): 4.4MM **Privately Held**
WEB: www.microexpress.net
SIC: 3571 5963 Personal computers (microcomputers); direct selling establishments

(P-14878)
ACCURATE ALWAYS INC
127 Ocean Ave, Half Moon Bay
(94019-4042)
PHONE..................................650 728-9428
Yousef Shemisa, *CEO*
Kate Haley, *Chief Mktg Ofcr*
Kate Shemisa, *Chief Mktg Ofcr*
EMP: 25
SQ FT: 3,500
SALES: 3.1MM **Privately Held**
WEB: www.accuratealways.com
SIC: 3571 Electronic computers

(P-14879)
ACME PORTABLE MACHINES INC
1330 Mountain View Cir, Azusa
(91702-1648)
PHONE..................................626 610-1888
James Cheng, *President*
Henry Chandra, *General Mgr*
Myles Kelvin, *General Mgr*
Chih Kuo, *Mktg Dir*
Henry Truong, *Manager*
▲ EMP: 30
SQ FT: 12,200
SALES (est): 7.3MM **Privately Held**
WEB: www.acmeportable.com
SIC: 3571 Electronic computers

(P-14880)
ADEGBESAN ADEFEMI
Also Called: Femi Data Telecommunication
1525 254th St, Harbor City (90710-2716)
PHONE..................................310 663-0789
Adefemi Adegbesan, *Owner*
EMP: 43
SALES: 100K **Privately Held**
SIC: 3571 Electronic computers

(P-14881)
ADVANCED KEYBOARD TECH INC
Also Called: Akt
2501 Golden Hill Rd # 200, Paso Robles
(93446-6391)
PHONE..................................805 237-2055
Joel Stark, *President*
Jeffrey C Stark, *Vice Pres*
EMP: 11
SQ FT: 2,000
SALES (est): 1.5MM **Privately Held**
SIC: 3571 Electronic computers

(P-14882)
AECHELON TECHNOLOGY INC (PA)
888 Brannan St Ste 210, San Francisco
(94103-4930)
PHONE..................................415 255-0120
Nacho Sanz-Pastor, *CEO*
Chris Blumenthal, *COO*
Bruce Johnson, *COO*
Luis Barcena, *Exec VP*
David Morgan, *Technology*
▲ EMP: 46 EST: 1998
SQ FT: 40,000
SALES (est): 18.4MM **Privately Held**
WEB: www.aechelon.com
SIC: 3571 Electronic computers

(P-14883)
AFFORDABLE GOODS
131 Cognac Cir, Sacramento (95835-2035)
PHONE..................................916 514-1049
Swarn Katyal, *Owner*
Vandana Katyal, *Owner*
EMP: 14
SALES: 575K **Privately Held**
SIC: 3571 5941 Electronic computers; sporting goods & bicycle shops

(P-14884)
ALERATEC INC
9851 Owensmouth Ave, Chatsworth
(91311-3802)
PHONE..................................818 678-6900
Perry Solomon, *CEO*
Allen Rosenthal, *CFO*
Kellie Chai, *Office Mgr*
▲ EMP: 24
SQ FT: 5,000
SALES (est): 4.6MM **Privately Held**
WEB: www.aleratec.com
SIC: 3571 Computers, digital, analog or hybrid

(P-14885)
ALLHEALTH INC
515 S Figueroa St # 1300, Los Angeles
(90071-3301)
PHONE..................................213 538-0762
John R Cochran, *CEO*
EMP: 250 EST: 1998
SALES (est): 22.4MM **Privately Held**
SIC: 3571 7381 Electronic computers; security guard service

(P-14886)
ALPHA RESEARCH & TECH INC
Also Called: Art
5175 Hillsdale Cir # 100, El Dorado Hills
(95762-5776)
PHONE..................................916 431-9340
Deann Kerr, *President*
Mark Eggers, *Info Tech Mgr*
John Pleines, *Technology*
Nathan Brizzee, *Engineer*
Steve Totah, *Engineer*
EMP: 73
SQ FT: 22,000
SALES (est): 18.1MM **Privately Held**
WEB: www.artruggedsystems.com
SIC: 3571 Electronic computers

(P-14887)
AMERICAN CRCUIT CARD RETAINERS
2310 E Orangethorpe Ave, Anaheim
(92806-1231)
PHONE..................................714 738-6194
Dan Morales, *President*
Miguel D Nunez, *CFO*
EMP: 10
SQ FT: 3,000

SALES (est): 732K **Privately Held**
SIC: **3571** Electronic computers

(P-14888)
AMERICAN RELIANCE INC
Also Called: Amrel
12941 Ramona Blvd Ste F, Baldwin Park
(91706-3756)
PHONE.....................................626 443-6818
Edward Chen, *CEO*
Shelly Chen, *Admin Sec*
▲ **EMP:** 45
SQ FT: 72,000
SALES: 21.1MM **Privately Held**
WEB: www.amrel.com
SIC: **3571** Electronic computers

(P-14889)
AMPRO ADLINK TECHNOLOGY INC
Also Called: Ampro Computers, Inc.
5215 Hellyer Ave Ste 110, San Jose
(95138-1007)
PHONE.....................................408 360-0200
Elizabeth Campbell, *CEO*
Mark Peterson, *Ch of Bd*
Joanne M Williams, *President*
Charles M Frank, *CFO*
Len Backus, *Vice Pres*
▲ **EMP:** 65
SQ FT: 25,000
SALES (est): 15.2MM **Privately Held**
WEB: www.ampro.com
SIC: **3571** Electronic computers
PA: Adlink Technology Inc.
9f, No. 166, Jian Yi Rd.
New Taipei City TAP 23511

(P-14890)
AMTEK ELECTRONIC INC
Also Called: Manufacturers Import & Export
1150 N 5th St, San Jose (95112-4415)
PHONE.....................................408 971-8787
Kathryn Yuen, *President*
John Yuen, *Vice Pres*
T C Yuen, *Vice Pres*
EMP: 35
SQ FT: 22,000
SALES: 2.5MM **Privately Held**
SIC: **3571** 3679 3577 Electronic computers; power supplies, all types: static; computer peripheral equipment

(P-14891)
APPLE TREE INTERNATIONAL CORP
10700 Business Dr Ste 200, Fontana
(92337-8201)
PHONE.....................................626 679-7025
Min Xiao, *CEO*
EMP: 11
SQ FT: 170,000
SALES (est): 202.7K **Privately Held**
SIC: **3571** Electronic computers

(P-14892)
BOLD DATA TECHNOLOGY INC
Also Called: Crown Micro
47540 Seabridge Dr, Fremont
(94538-6547)
PHONE.....................................510 490-8296
Eugene Kiang, *President*
Marco Yee, *CFO*
Winston Xia, *Exec VP*
Bonnie Silva, *Administration*
Lai Tsui, *Human Res Mgr*
▲ **EMP:** 45
SQ FT: 50,000
SALES (est): 34.5MM **Privately Held**
WEB: www.boldata.com
SIC: **3571** 3577 3674 Personal computers (microcomputers); computer peripheral equipment; computer logic modules

(P-14893)
BORSOS ENGINEERING INC
5924 Balfour Ct Ste 102, Carlsbad
(92008-7378)
PHONE.....................................760 930-0296
Steven D Borso, *President*
EMP: 25
SQ FT: 5,600
SALES (est): 4.1MM **Privately Held**
SIC: **3571** Electronic computers

(P-14894)
BULL HN INFO SYSTEMS INC
6077 Bristol Pkwy, Culver City
(90230-6601)
PHONE.....................................310 337-3600
Tom Skelly, *Branch Mgr*
EMP: 20
SALES (corp-wide): 166.6MM **Privately Held**
SIC: **3571** 3577 7378 7373 Mainframe computers; computer peripheral equipment; computer & data processing equipment repair/maintenance; computer peripheral equipment repair & maintenance; systems integration services
HQ: Bull Hn Information Systems Inc.
285 Billerica Rd Ste 200
Chelmsford MA 01824
978 294-6000

(P-14895)
CEMTROL INC
3035 E La Jolla St, Anaheim (92806-1303)
PHONE.....................................714 666-6606
Sharon Paz, *President*
Marie Penton, *CEO*
Samuel Paz, *Engineer*
EMP: 15
SALES: 3.3MM **Privately Held**
SIC: **3571** Electronic computers

(P-14896)
CENTENT COMPANY
3879 S Main St, Santa Ana (92707-5787)
PHONE.....................................714 979-6491
August Freimanis, *Partner*
Mariss Freimanis, *Partner*
Luke Freimanis, *General Mgr*
EMP: 20 EST: 1972
SQ FT: 2,500
SALES (est): 2.8MM **Privately Held**
WEB: www.centent.com
SIC: **3571** 5063 Computers, digital, analog or hybrid; electrical apparatus & equipment

(P-14897)
COASTAL PVA OPCO LLC
2929 Grandview St, Placerville
(95667-4635)
PHONE.....................................530 406-3303
Joseph P Binkley,
Jeff Miller, *CFO*
EMP: 15
SALES (est): 780.5K **Privately Held**
SIC: **3571** Electronic computers

(P-14898)
COBALT ROBOTICS INC
4019 Transport St Ste De, Palo Alto
(94303-4914)
PHONE.....................................650 781-3626
Travis Deyle, *CEO*
EMP: 60
SALES (est): 181.3K **Privately Held**
SIC: **3571** Electronic computers

(P-14899)
COLFAX INTERNATIONAL
2805 Bowers Ave Ste 230, Santa Clara
(95051-0971)
PHONE.....................................408 730-2275
Gautam Shah, *CEO*
Barbara Karvonen, *COO*
▼ **EMP:** 32
SALES: 10.1MM **Privately Held**
WEB: www.colfax-intl.com
SIC: **3571** Electronic computers

(P-14900)
COMPUTER ACCESS TECH CORP
3385 Scott Blvd, Santa Clara (95054-3115)
PHONE.....................................408 727-6600
Fax: 408 727-6622
EMP: 67
SQ FT: 14,000
SALES (est): 6.1MM
SALES (corp-wide): 2.1B **Publicly Held**
SIC: **3571** 7371 3577
HQ: Teledyne Lecroy, Inc.
700 Chestnut Ridge Rd
Chestnut Ridge NY 10977
845 425-2000

(P-14901)
CONTINUOUS COMPUTING CORP
Also Called: Ccpu
10431 Wtridge Cir Ste 110, San Diego
(92121)
PHONE.....................................858 882-8800
Mike Dagenais, *CEO*
Ron Pyles, *President*
Bob Wise, *President*
Erez Barnavon, *CFO*
Robert Cagle, *Vice Pres*
EMP: 22
SQ FT: 48,000
SALES (est): 7.6MM
SALES (corp-wide): 133.7MM **Privately Held**
WEB: www.ccpu.com
SIC: **3571** 3661 4812 5045 Computers, digital, analog or hybrid; telephone & telegraph apparatus; radio telephone communication; computers, peripherals & software; computer integrated systems design
PA: Radisys Corporation
5435 Ne Dawson Creek Dr
Hillsboro OR 97124
503 615-1100

(P-14902)
CYBERNET MANUFACTURING INC
5 Holland Ste 201, Irvine (92618-2574)
PHONE.....................................949 600-8000
Pouran Shoaee, *CEO*
Jeff Salem, *Purch Dir*
Tim Dalke, *Natl Sales Mgr*
Joe Divino, *VP Mktg*
Tina Jo Wentz, *Marketing Staff*
◆ **EMP:** 720
SALES (est): 117.8MM **Privately Held**
WEB: www.cybernetman.com
SIC: **3571** 3577 Electronic computers; computer peripheral equipment

(P-14903)
DELL INC
Also Called: Enterprise Solutions Group
5450 Great America Pkwy, Santa Clara
(95054-3644)
PHONE.....................................408 206-5466
Nariman Teymourian, *Exec Dir*
Tj Paganini, *Executive Asst*
Mike Chow, *Engineer*
EMP: 11
SALES (corp-wide): 90.6B **Publicly Held**
SIC: **3571** Electronic computers
HQ: Dell Inc.
1 Dell Way
Round Rock TX 78682
800 289-3355

(P-14904)
EDGE SOLUTIONS CONSULTING INC (PA)
2801 Townsgate Rd Ste 111, Westlake Village (91361-3028)
P.O. Box 661480, Arcadia (91066-1480)
PHONE.....................................818 591-3500
Marti R Hedge, *President*
Robert Hedge, *Vice Pres*
Kathy Valencia, *Principal*
Kailee Holt, *Business Anlyst*
Sean Thomas, *Accounts Exec*
EMP: 28
SQ FT: 600
SALES (est): 10.2MM **Privately Held**
SIC: **3571** Mainframe computers

(P-14905)
ELECTRONIC COOLING SOLUTIONS
2344 Walsh Ave Ste B, Santa Clara
(95051-1327)
PHONE.....................................408 738-8331
William Maltz, *President*
EMP: 15 EST: 2009
SALES (est): 2.4MM **Privately Held**
SIC: **3571** Electronic computers

(P-14906)
ELECTRONIC SYSTEMS INNOVATION
Also Called: Esi
5777 W Century Blvd # 1225, Los Angeles
(90045-5600)
PHONE.....................................310 645-8400
Eli Cohen, *President*
EMP: 15
SALES (est): 1.9MM **Privately Held**
SIC: **3571** Electronic computers

(P-14907)
ELMA ELECTRONIC INC (HQ)
44350 S Grimmer Blvd, Fremont
(94538-6385)
PHONE.....................................510 656-3400
Fred Ruegg, *CEO*
Klaus Montoya, *Partner*
Dominique Ruegg, *Partner*
Kanwar Singh, *Partner*
Shan Morgan, *President*
▲ **EMP:** 150
SQ FT: 100,000
SALES: 70.5K
SALES (corp-wide): 146.8MM **Privately Held**
SIC: **3571** 3575 3577 Electronic computers; computer terminals; computer peripheral equipment
PA: Elma Electronic Ag
Hofstrasse 93
Wetzikon ZH 8620
449 334-111

(P-14908)
EMC CORPORATION
2201 Dupont Dr Ste 500, Irvine
(92612-7520)
PHONE.....................................949 794-9999
Leonnard Iventosch, *Manager*
Evelyn Wilbur, *Associate*
EMP: 85
SALES (corp-wide): 90.6B **Publicly Held**
WEB: www.emc.com
SIC: **3571** 5045 Electronic computers; computers, peripherals & software
HQ: Emc Corporation
176 South St
Hopkinton MA 01748
508 435-1000

(P-14909)
ENDACE USA LIMITED
99 Almaden Blvd Ste 555, San Jose
(95113-1600)
PHONE.....................................877 764-5411
Stuart Wilson, *CEO*
Andrew Harsant, *CFO*
EMP: 19
SQ FT: 1,072
SALES: 12MM
SALES (corp-wide): 1MM **Privately Held**
SIC: **3571** Personal computers (microcomputers)
HQ: Endace Limited
Level 1, Building C
Auckland 1051
988 740-87

(P-14910)
EXPORTECH WORLDWIDE LLC
Also Called: Imagictech
14310 Burning Tree Dr, Victorville
(92395-4368)
PHONE.....................................909 278-9477
Carlos A Colin,
EMP: 10
SALES: 60K **Privately Held**
SIC: **3571** Electronic computers

(P-14911)
GARNER HOLT PRODUCTIONS INC
1255 Research Dr, Redlands (92374-4541)
PHONE.....................................909 799-3030
Garner L Holt, *President*
Andrew Garner, *Partner*
Michelle Berg, *Vice Pres*
Victor Martin, *Project Mgr*
Lloyd Ball, *Engineer*
EMP: 50
SQ FT: 50,000

SALES: 9.6MM **Privately Held**
WEB: www.garnerholt.com
SIC: 3571 Electronic computers

(P-14912)
GATEWAY INC (DH)
7565 Irvine Center Dr # 150, Irvine
(92618-4933)
PHONE..............................949 471-7000
Ed Coleman, *CEO*
Bradly Shaw, *President*
John Goldsberry, *CFO*
Craig Calle, *Treasurer*
Michael R Tyler, *Senior VP*
▲ EMP: 250
SQ FT: 98,000
SALES (est): 331MM **Privately Held**
WEB: www.gateway.com
SIC: 3571 3577 Personal computers (microcomputers); computer peripheral equipment

(P-14913)
GATEWAY US RETAIL INC
7565 Irvine Center Dr, Irvine (92618-4918)
PHONE..............................949 471-7000
Wayne R Inouye, *President*
Brian Firestone, *Exec VP*
▲ EMP: 134 EST: 1998
SQ FT: 147,000
SALES (est): 10.5MM **Privately Held**
WEB: www.emachines.com
SIC: 3571 3577 5045 Electronic computers; computer peripheral equipment; computers, peripherals & software
HQ: Gateway, Inc.
7565 Irvine Center Dr # 150
Irvine CA 92618
949 471-7000

(P-14914)
GENERAL DYNMICS MSSION SYSTEMS
5922 Roseville Rd, Sacramento
(95842-4030)
PHONE..............................916 339-3852
EMP: 151
SALES (corp-wide): 36.1B **Publicly Held**
SIC: 3571 Electronic computers
HQ: General Dynamics Mission Systems, Inc.
12450 Fair Lakes Cir # 200
Fairfax VA 22033
703 263-2800

(P-14915)
GENESIS COMPUTER SYSTEMS INC
4055 E La Palma Ave Ste C, Anaheim
(92807-1750)
PHONE..............................714 632-3648
Awaiz Akram, *President*
Shawn Dewan, *Vice Pres*
Sam Patel, *Purch Agent*
EMP: 31
SQ FT: 3,500
SALES (est): 6.6MM **Privately Held**
SIC: 3571 Electronic computers

(P-14916)
HP INC (PA)
1501 Page Mill Rd, Palo Alto (94304-1126)
P.O. Box 10301 (94303-0890)
PHONE..............................650 857-1501
Dion J Weisler, *President*
Alex Cho, *President*
Enrique Lores, *President*
Steve Fieler, *CFO*
Todd Gustafson, *Vice Pres*
EMP: 2500 EST: 1939
SALES: 58.4B **Publicly Held**
SIC: 3571 7372 3861 3577 Personal computers (microcomputers); minicomputers; prepackaged software; cameras, still & motion picture (all types); diazotype (whiteprint) reproduction machines & equipment; printers, computer; optical scanning devices; computer storage devices; computer terminals

(P-14917)
HP INC
481 Cottonwood Dr, Milpitas (95035)
PHONE..............................650 857-1501
Shengwu Luo, *Branch Mgr*
EMP: 1001

SALES (corp-wide): 58.4B **Publicly Held**
SIC: 3571 Personal computers (microcomputers)
PA: Hp, Inc.
1501 Page Mill Rd
Palo Alto CA 94304
650 857-1501

(P-14918)
HP INC
1501 Page Mill Rd, Palo Alto (94304-1126)
PHONE..............................650 857-4946
Richard D Lampman, *Senior VP*
EMP: 3000
SALES (corp-wide): 58.4B **Publicly Held**
SIC: 3571 Personal computers (microcomputers)
PA: Hp, Inc.
1501 Page Mill Rd
Palo Alto CA 94304
650 857-1501

(P-14919)
HP INC
130 Lytton Ave, Palo Alto (94301-1065)
PHONE..............................650 857-1501
Mark S Manasse, *Principal*
Daniel Palmans, *Technical Staff*
EMP: 80
SALES (corp-wide): 58.4B **Publicly Held**
SIC: 3571 Personal computers (microcomputers)
PA: Hp, Inc.
1501 Page Mill Rd
Palo Alto CA 94304
650 857-1501

(P-14920)
HP INC
3495 Deer Creek Rd, Palo Alto
(94304-1316)
P.O. Box 10301 (94303-0890)
PHONE..............................650 857-1501
Deidre Hoehn, *Branch Mgr*
EMP: 25
SALES (corp-wide): 58.4B **Publicly Held**
SIC: 3571 Personal computers (microcomputers)
PA: Hp, Inc.
1501 Page Mill Rd
Palo Alto CA 94304
650 857-1501

(P-14921)
HP INC
303 2nd St Ste S500, San Francisco
(94107-1373)
PHONE..............................415 979-3700
Ben Nelson, *General Mgr*
Chuck Zelanis, *Program Mgr*
Jennifer Kwan, *Marketing Staff*
Jeff Dahncke, *Corp Comm Staff*
Sarah Acosta, *Manager*
EMP: 70
SALES (corp-wide): 58.4B **Publicly Held**
SIC: 3571 Personal computers (microcomputers)
PA: Hp, Inc.
1501 Page Mill Rd
Palo Alto CA 94304
650 857-1501

(P-14922)
HPI FEDERAL LLC (HQ)
1501 Page Mill Rd, Palo Alto (94304-1126)
PHONE..............................650 857-1501
Mark T Prather, *President*
Todd Wallace, *Mfg Staff*
Dave Block, *Senior Mgr*
EMP: 14
SALES (est): 1.8MM
SALES (corp-wide): 58.4B **Publicly Held**
SIC: 3571 Personal computers (microcomputers)
PA: Hp, Inc.
1501 Page Mill Rd
Palo Alto CA 94304
650 857-1501

(P-14923)
INDUSTRIAL CPU SYSTEMS INTL
Also Called: Icpu
2225 S Grand Ave, Santa Ana
(92705-5235)
P.O. Box 93445, Los Angeles (90093-0445)
PHONE..............................714 957-2815
Mehrdad Ayati, *President*
Mehran Ayali, *Exec Dir*
EMP: 15
SQ FT: 7,000
SALES (est): 1.4MM **Privately Held**
WEB: www.icpu.com
SIC: 3571 Electronic computers; computer software systems analysis & design, custom

(P-14924)
INNOWI INC
3240 Scott Blvd, Santa Clara (95054-3011)
PHONE..............................408 609-9404
Zia Hasnain, *CEO*
Asis REO, *President*
Saisel Seed, *CIO*
Saad Ahmed, *Engineer*
EMP: 40 EST: 2014
SALES (est): 2.1MM **Privately Held**
SIC: 3571 Electronic computers

(P-14925)
INSPUR SYSTEMS INC (HQ)
47451 Fremont Blvd, Fremont
(94538-6504)
PHONE..............................800 697-5893
Ziliang Leon Zheng, *President*
Meng Zhu, *CFO*
Ian Dillon, *Executive*
Kelvin KAO, *Executive*
Zhiqiang LI, *General Mgr*
▲ EMP: 50
SALES: 410MM
SALES (corp-wide): 28.2MM **Privately Held**
SIC: 3571 Electronic computers
PA: Inspur Group Co., Ltd.
4f,North Floor No.5 Building,Langchao Technology Park, No.1036,L
Jinan 25009
531 851-0600

(P-14926)
INTERNATIONAL BUS MCHS CORP
Also Called: IBM
6033 W Century Blvd # 610, Los Angeles
(90045-6410)
PHONE..............................310 412-8699
Danny Brennan, *Administration*
Dorin Popa, *IT/INT Sup*
Lee Armstrong, *Manager*
Joe Raby, *Manager*
EMP: 923
SALES (corp-wide): 79.5B **Publicly Held**
WEB: www.ibm.com
SIC: 3571 Minicomputers
PA: International Business Machines Corporation
1 New Orchard Rd Ste 1 # 1
Armonk NY 10504
914 499-1900

(P-14927)
INTERNATIONAL BUS MCHS CORP
IBM
600 Anton Blvd Ste 400, Costa Mesa
(92626-7677)
PHONE..............................714 472-2237
Jim Steele, *General Mgr*
EMP: 750
SALES (corp-wide): 79.5B **Publicly Held**
WEB: www.ibm.com
SIC: 3571 5045 1731 Computers, digital, analog or hybrid; computers; computer installation
PA: International Business Machines Corporation
1 New Orchard Rd Ste 1 # 1
Armonk NY 10504
914 499-1900

(P-14928)
IPARIS LLC
10120 Wexted Way, Elk Grove
(95757-5501)
PHONE..............................866 293-2872
Jacque Ojadidi,
EMP: 10
SQ FT: 3,900
SALES: 2MM **Privately Held**
SIC: 3571 2741 Electronic computers;

(P-14929)
JAF INTERNATIONAL INC
2917 Bayview Dr, Fremont (94538-6520)
PHONE..............................510 656-1718
Yi Zhao, *CEO*
Sherry Shi, *General Mgr*
Joy Yan, *General Mgr*
Candice Han, *Accounting Mgr*
Phuong Truong, *Accounting Mgr*
▲ EMP: 12 EST: 2008
SQ FT: 12,000
SALES (est): 3.7MM **Privately Held**
SIC: 3571 8748 Electronic computers; business consulting

(P-14930)
JETNEXUS LLC
3201 Great America Pkwy, Santa Clara
(95054)
PHONE..............................800 568-9921
Greg Howett, *Mng Member*
EMP: 50 EST: 2002
SQ FT: 200
SALES (est): 3.2MM **Privately Held**
SIC: 3571 Electronic computers

(P-14931)
JOINT TECHNOLOGIES LIMITED
5120 E La Palma Ave # 205, Anaheim
(92807-2091)
PHONE..............................949 361-1158
Nigel Cheatle, *CEO*
Pamela Higbie, *Admin Sec*
EMP: 10
SQ FT: 4,500
SALES (est): 1.6MM **Privately Held**
WEB: www.jointtech.com
SIC: 3571 7371 Personal computers (microcomputers); computer software systems analysis & design, custom

(P-14932)
KASER CORPORATION
39969 Paseo Padre Pkwy, Fremont
(94538-2975)
PHONE..............................510 657-9002
Steve Hung, *President*
Manny Tang, *Vice Pres*
▲ EMP: 15
SALES (est): 2.2MM **Privately Held**
WEB: www.kasercorp.com
SIC: 3571 Electronic computers

(P-14933)
KONTRON AMERICA INC
9477 Waples St Ste 150, San Diego
(92121-2937)
PHONE..............................800 822-7522
John Goode Jr, *President*
Thomas Sparrvik, *COO*
Ken Lowe, *CFO*
Jim St John, *Engineer*
Jessica Summers, *Consultant*
▲ EMP: 75
SQ FT: 40,000
SALES (est): 11.1MM
SALES (corp-wide): 1.1B **Privately Held**
WEB: www.aplabs.com
SIC: 3571 7373 Electronic computers; computer integrated systems design
HQ: Kontron S&T Ag
Lise-Meitner-Str. 3-5
Augsburg 86156
821 408-60

(P-14934)
KONTRON AMERICA INCORPORATED (DH)
9477 Waples St Ste 150, San Diego
(92121-2937)
PHONE..............................858 677-0877
Kevin Rhoads, *CEO*
Stefan Milnov, *President*
Fran Moore, *Vice Pres*
Jenette Carlson, *Program Mgr*

Debra Downey, *Administration*
▲ **EMP:** 163
SQ FT: 140,000
SALES (est): 76.5MM
SALES (corp-wide): 1.1B **Privately Held**
WEB: www.kontron.com
SIC: 3571 3577 Electronic computers;
　computer peripheral equipment
HQ: Kontron S&T Ag
　　Lise-Meitner-Str. 3-5
　　Augsburg 86156
　　821 408-60

(P-14935)
KUNA SYSTEMS CORPORATION
883 Sneath Ln Ste 222, San Bruno
(94066-2413)
PHONE..................................650 263-8257
Saiway Fu, *CEO*
Haomiao Huang, *Vice Pres*
EMP: 12 **EST:** 2012
SQ FT: 1,500
SALES (est): 659.4K **Privately Held**
SIC: 3571 Computers, digital, analog or
　hybrid

(P-14936)
L3 TECHNOLOGIES INC
Also Called: Winchester Electronics Div
9795 Bus Park Dr Ste K, Sacramento
(95827-1708)
PHONE..................................916 363-6581
Herbert Russell, *Branch Mgr*
EMP: 55
SALES (corp-wide): 6.8B **Publicly Held**
SIC: 3571 Personal computers (microcom-
　puters)
HQ: L3 Technologies, Inc.
　　600 3rd Ave Fl 34
　　New York NY 10016
　　212 697-1111

(P-14937)
LD SMART INC
Also Called: Link Depot
15350 Stafford St, La Puente (91744-4420)
PHONE..................................626 581-8887
Benny Sun, *President*
▲ **EMP:** 12
SALES (est): 2.5MM **Privately Held**
WEB: www.link-depot.com
SIC: 3571 Electronic computers

(P-14938)
M2 MARKETPLACE INC
2555 W 190th St 201, Torrance
(90504-6002)
PHONE..................................310 354-3600
Sam Khulusi, *President*
EMP: 14
SALES (est): 3.7MM **Publicly Held**
WEB: www.onsale.com
SIC: 3571 Electronic computers
HQ: Pcm, Inc.
　　1940 E Mariposa Ave
　　El Segundo CA 90245
　　310 354-5600

(P-14939)
MAGNELL ASSOCIATE INC
Also Called: Newegg.com
17708 Rowland St, City of Industry
(91748-1119)
PHONE..................................626 271-1320
Fred Chang, *President*
EMP: 13
SALES (corp-wide): 2B **Privately Held**
SIC: 3571 5961 5045 Personal comput-
　ers (microcomputers); computers & pe-
　ripheral equipment, mail order;
　computers, peripherals & software
HQ: Magnell Associate, Inc.
　　17560 Rowland St
　　City Of Industry CA 91748
　　626 271-9700

(P-14940)
MC2 SABTECH HOLDINGS INC
Also Called: Ixi Technology
22705 Savi Ranch Pkwy, Yorba Linda
(92887-4604)
PHONE..................................714 221-5000
Michael Carter, *CEO*
Thomas Bell, *CFO*
Jin Qiao, *Engineer*
Karen Thomas Gibson, *Accountant*

Janet Pippins, *Marketing Staff*
EMP: 40
SQ FT: 40,000
SALES (est): 15.3MM **Privately Held**
WEB: www.sabtech.com
SIC: 3571 3672 Electronic computers;
　printed circuit boards

(P-14941)
MCUBE INC (PA)
2570 N 1st St Ste 300, San Jose
(95131-1018)
PHONE..................................408 637-5503
Ben Lee, *CEO*
Sanjay Bhandari, *Vice Pres*
Evie Kuo, *Admin Asst*
Jacob LI, *Sr Consultant*
EMP: 24
SALES (est): 7.8MM **Privately Held**
SIC: 3571 Personal computers (microcom-
　puters)

(P-14942)
MEDIATEK USA INC (PA)
2840 Junction Ave, San Jose (95134-1922)
PHONE..................................408 526-1899
Ming-Kai Tsai, *Ch of Bd*
Jyh-Jer Cho, *Vice Chairman*
Ching-Jiang Hsieh, *President*
David Ku, *CFO*
Cheng-Te Chuang, *Senior VP*
▲ **EMP:** 102 **EST:** 1997
SALES (est): 75.8MM **Privately Held**
SIC: 3571 3674 Electronic computers;
　semiconductors & related devices

(P-14943)
MEDIATEK USA INC
96 Corporate Park Ste 300, Irvine
(92606-3107)
PHONE..................................408 526-1899
EMP: 11
SALES (corp-wide): 75.8MM **Privately
Held**
SIC: 3571 3674 Electronic computers;
　semiconductors & related devices
PA: Mediatek Usa Inc.
　　2840 Junction Ave
　　San Jose CA 95134
　　408 526-1899

(P-14944)
MELROSE MAC INC
2400 W Olive Ave, Burbank (91506-2630)
PHONE..................................818 840-8466
Sean Nasseri, *Branch Mgr*
EMP: 13
SALES (corp-wide): 12.2MM **Privately
Held**
WEB: www.melrosemac.com
SIC: 3571 5045 5734 8748 Electronic
　computers; computers, peripherals & soft-
　ware; computer & software stores; busi-
　ness consulting
PA: Melrose Mac, Inc.
　　6614 Melrose Ave
　　Los Angeles CA 90038
　　323 937-4600

(P-14945)
MERCURY SYSTEMS - TRSTED MSSIO (HQ)
Also Called: Mercury Systems - Trsted Mssio
47200 Bayside Pkwy, Fremont
(94538-6567)
PHONE..................................510 252-0870
Mark Aslett, *President*
Dennis Smith, *President*
Didier Mc Thibaud, *COO*
Michael D Ruppert, *CFO*
Christopher C Cambria, *Exec VP*
EMP: 65
SQ FT: 54,000
SALES (est): 25.1MM
SALES (corp-wide): 654.7MM **Publicly
Held**
SIC: 3571 Electronic computers
PA: Mercury Systems, Inc.
　　50 Minuteman Rd
　　Andover MA 01810
　　978 256-1300

(P-14946)
MICILE INC
1225 S Shamrock Ave, Monrovia
(91016-4244)
PHONE..................................626 381-9974
Naresh Menon, *CEO*
Jim Axtelle, *Project Mgr*
EMP: 15
SALES (est): 1.1MM **Privately Held**
SIC: 3571 Minicomputers

(P-14947)
MICRO/SYS INC
3730 Park Pl, Montrose (91020-1623)
PHONE..................................818 244-4600
Susan Wooley, *President*
James K Finster, *Vice Pres*
Jeannette Klein, *Technology*
Alex Ayala, *Electrical Engi*
Jeannette Finster, *Supervisor*
EMP: 30
SALES (est): 6MM **Privately Held**
WEB: www.embeddedsys.com
SIC: 3571 3674 Electronic computers;
　semiconductors & related devices

(P-14948)
MIDERN COMPUTER INC
Also Called: Sager Computers
18005 Cortney Ct, City of Industry
(91748-1203)
PHONE..................................626 964-8682
Shooing Song Yuan, *President*
T Y Lee, *Vice Pres*
Frank Chu, *General Mgr*
Jim Hung, *Webmaster*
Tim LI, *Engineer*
▲ **EMP:** 40
SQ FT: 10,000
SALES (est): 11.4MM **Privately Held**
WEB: www.sager-midern.com
SIC: 3571 Personal computers (microcom-
　puters)

(P-14949)
MILDEF INC (PA)
630 W Lambert Rd, Brea (92821-3139)
PHONE..................................703 224-8835
Magnus Pyk, *President*
Wendy Cheng, *Manager*
EMP: 10
SQ FT: 5,000
SALES (est): 6MM **Privately Held**
SIC: 3571 Electronic computers

(P-14950)
MINTRONIX INC
6090 Cielo Vista Ct, Camarillo
(93012-8210)
PHONE..................................805 482-1298
Robert Lee, *President*
Yaoling Lee, *Controller*
▲ **EMP:** 15
SQ FT: 10,000
SALES (est): 7MM **Privately Held**
WEB: www.mintronix.com
SIC: 3571 Electronic computers

(P-14951)
MITAC USA INC (DH)
Also Called: Mio Technology
47988 Fremont Blvd, Fremont
(94538-6507)
PHONE..................................510 661-2800
Billy Ho, *President*
Matthew Miau, *Chairman*
EMP: 27
SALES (est): 10.2MM **Privately Held**
WEB: www.mitacusa.com
SIC: 3571 Electronic computers

(P-14952)
MITXPC INC
Also Called: Mitxpc Embedded Sys Solutions
45437 Warm Springs Blvd, Fremont
(94539-6104)
PHONE..................................510 226-6883
Eric Pang, *CEO*
John Ho, *Sales Mgr*
▲ **EMP:** 13
SQ FT: 10,000
SALES (est): 1MM **Privately Held**
SIC: 3571 8731 Computers, digital, analog
　or hybrid; computer (hardware) develop-
　ment

(P-14953)
MOCKINGBIRD NETWORKS
10040 Bubb Rd, Cupertino (95014-4132)
PHONE..................................408 342-5300
Pong Lim, *CEO*
Ken Murray, *President*
John Chun, *COO*
Steve Y Kim, *Principal*
Alex Finch, *Finance*
EMP: 80
SQ FT: 8,000
SALES (est): 7.9MM **Privately Held**
WEB: www.mockingbirdnetworks.com
SIC: 3571 3672 3577 Electronic comput-
　ers; printed circuit boards; computer pe-
　ripheral equipment

(P-14954)
MULFAT LLC
15835 Monte St Ste 103, Sylmar
(91342-7673)
PHONE..................................818 367-0149
Daniel Mulcahey, *Principal*
EMP: 20 **EST:** 2010
SALES (est): 1.4MM **Privately Held**
SIC: 3571 Electronic computers

(P-14955)
MYRICOM INC
3871 E Colo Blvd Ste 101, Pasadena
(91107)
PHONE..................................626 821-5555
Nanette Boden, *President*
Robert Henigson, *Ch of Bd*
Rick Patton, *CFO*
Mike McPherson, *Vice Pres*
John Hagerman, *Marketing Staff*
▲ **EMP:** 45
SQ FT: 17,000
SALES (est): 10.2MM **Privately Held**
WEB: www.myri.com
SIC: 3571 Electronic computers

(P-14956)
NIXSYS INC
34 Mauchly Ste B, Irvine (92618-2357)
PHONE..................................714 435-9610
Nicolas Szczedrin, *President*
Andrew Martinovich, *Opers Mgr*
Brandon Lang, *Cust Mgr*
▲ **EMP:** 10
SALES (est): 2.6MM **Privately Held**
WEB: www.nixsys.com
SIC: 3571 7379 Electronic computers;
　computer related consulting services

(P-14957)
OMNICELL INC
725 Sycamore Dr, Milpitas (95035-7411)
PHONE..................................408 907-8868
EMP: 10 **Publicly Held**
SIC: 3571 Electronic computers
PA: Omnicell, Inc.
　　590 E Middlefield Rd
　　Mountain View CA 94043

(P-14958)
OMNICELL INC (PA)
590 E Middlefield Rd, Mountain View
(94043-4008)
PHONE..................................650 251-6100
Randall A Lipps, *Ch of Bd*
J Christopher Drew, *President*
Robin G Seim, *President*
Peter J Kuipers, *CFO*
Scott Seidelmann, *Ch Credit Ofcr*
▲ **EMP:** 273
SQ FT: 99,900
SALES: 787.3MM **Publicly Held**
WEB: www.omnicell.com
SIC: 3571 Electronic computers

(P-14959)
ORACLE AMERICA INC (HQ)
Also Called: Sun Microsystems
500 Oracle Pkwy, Redwood City
(94065-1677)
PHONE..................................650 506-7000
Jeffrey O Henley, *Chairman*
Jeffrey Henley, *Vice Chairman*
Safra A Catz, *President*
Mark V Hurd, *President*
Kevin Melia, *CFO*
▲ **EMP:** 3500

▲ = Import ▼=Export
◆ =Import/Export

SALES (est): 9.6B
SALES (corp-wide): 39.5B **Publicly Held**
WEB: www.oracle.com
SIC: 3571 7379 7373 7372 Minicomputers; computer related consulting services; systems integration services; operating systems computer software; microprocessors
PA: Oracle Corporation
500 Oracle Pkwy
Redwood City CA 94065
650 506-7000

(P-14960)
PARALLAX INCORPORATED
Also Called: Parallax Research
599 Menlo Dr Ste 100, Rocklin (95765-3725)
PHONE....................916 624-8333
Charles Gracey III, *President*
Charles Gracey II, *Treasurer*
Carolyn Montzingo, *General Mgr*
Mary Beth Gracey, *Controller*
▲ **EMP:** 33
SQ FT: 11,000
SALES (est): 8.6MM **Privately Held**
WEB: www.parallax.com
SIC: 3571 5045 3577 Minicomputers; computers, peripherals & software; computer peripheral equipment

(P-14961)
PIRANHA EMS INC
2681 Zanker Rd, San Jose (95134-2137)
PHONE....................408 520-3963
Roger Malmrose, *CEO*
Richard Walkup, *Exec VP*
EMP: 35
SALES (est): 8.2MM **Privately Held**
SIC: 3571 Electronic computers

(P-14962)
POLYWELL COMPANY INC
Also Called: Polywell Computers
1461 San Mateo Ave Ste 1, South San Francisco (94080-6553)
PHONE....................650 583-7222
Chin Lo, *CEO*
Alexis Lam, *Executive*
Samuel Yu, *Technician*
Ava Lo, *Finance*
Kham Senava, *Mktg Dir*
▲ **EMP:** 40
SQ FT: 20,000
SALES (est): 16.9MM **Privately Held**
WEB: www.polywell.com
SIC: 3571 Personal computers (microcomputers)

(P-14963)
PREMIO INC (PA)
918 Radecki Ct, City of Industry (91748-1132)
PHONE....................626 839-3100
Crystal Tsao, *President*
Kevin Wu, *Exec VP*
Wai Lee, *Executive*
Ken Szeto, *General Mgr*
Robert Lu, *Technical Staff*
▲ **EMP:** 120
SQ FT: 140,000
SALES (est): 43MM **Privately Held**
WEB: www.premioinc.com
SIC: 3571 7373 7378 Personal computers (microcomputers); computer integrated systems design; computer maintenance & repair

(P-14964)
PROBE-LOGIC INC
1885 Lundy Ave Ste 101, San Jose (95131-1887)
PHONE....................408 416-0777
Hon Cheng, *CEO*
Luis Morales, *Sales Mgr*
Ken Chen, *Manager*
EMP: 92
SQ FT: 15,000
SALES (est): 17.1MM **Privately Held**
WEB: www.probelogic.com
SIC: 3571 Electronic computers

(P-14965)
PSITECH INC
18368 Bandilier Cir, Fountain Valley (92708-7001)
PHONE....................714 964-7818
John T Kerr, *Ch of Bd*
John S Kerr, *Shareholder*
EMP: 12
SQ FT: 6,000
SALES (est): 2.3MM **Privately Held**
WEB: www.psitech.com
SIC: 3571 3577 Personal computers (microcomputers); computer peripheral equipment

(P-14966)
QANTEL TECHNOLOGIES INC
3506 Breakwater Ct, Hayward (94545-3611)
PHONE....................510 731-2080
Michael Galvin, *President*
Christy Garrelts, *Regional Mgr*
Mary Olague, *Administration*
Woody Smith, *Software Engr*
Steven Wong, *Senior Engr*
EMP: 42
SQ FT: 12,000
SALES (est): 8.4MM **Privately Held**
WEB: www.qantel.com
SIC: 3571 7371 Electronic computers; computer software development

(P-14967)
RAPT TOUCH INC
1875 S Grant St Ste 925, San Mateo (94402-7036)
PHONE....................415 994-1537
Mark Anderson, *CEO*
EMP: 12
SALES (est): 1MM **Privately Held**
SIC: 3571 Electronic computers

(P-14968)
RAYTHEON COMPANY
26 Castilian Dr, Goleta (93117-5565)
PHONE....................805 562-2730
Robert Martinez, *Principal*
EMP: 18
SALES (corp-wide): 27B **Publicly Held**
SIC: 3571 Computers, digital, analog or hybrid
PA: Raytheon Company
870 Winter St
Waltham MA 02451
781 522-3000

(P-14969)
ROSEWILL INC
17708 Rowland St, City of Industry (91748-1119)
PHONE....................626 271-1420
Fred Chang, *CEO*
Rick Quiroga, *Treasurer*
Lee Cheng, *Admin Sec*
Devin Rose, *Manager*
Hip Lee, *Asst Sec*
▲ **EMP:** 22
SALES (est): 3.9MM
SALES (corp-wide): 2B **Privately Held**
SIC: 3571 5045 Electronic computers; computers, peripherals & software
HQ: Magnell Associate, Inc.
17560 Rowland St
City Of Industry CA 91748
626 271-9700

(P-14970)
RUGGED SYSTEMS INC
Also Called: Core Systems
13000 Danielson St Ste Q, Poway (92064-6827)
PHONE....................858 391-1006
Chris O Brien, *CEO*
Chris Alan Schaffner, *President*
EMP: 156
SQ FT: 63,000
SALES (est): 24.2MM **Privately Held**
WEB: www.coresystemsusa.com
SIC: 3571 7373 Electronic computers; computer integrated systems design

(P-14971)
S E P E INC
Also Called: Fax Star
245 Fischer Ave Ste C4, Costa Mesa (92626-4538)
PHONE....................714 241-7373
Michel J Remion, *President*
Patty King, *Admin Sec*
EMP: 20
SQ FT: 5,000
SALES (est): 3MM **Privately Held**
WEB: www.faxstar.com
SIC: 3571 7371 4822 Electronic computers; computer software development; facsimile transmission services

(P-14972)
SERVERS DIRECT LLC
20480 Business Pkwy, Walnut (91789-2938)
PHONE....................800 576-7931
Andy Juang, *CEO*
Howard Gilles, *CFO*
EMP: 140
SALES (est): 2.1MM **Privately Held**
WEB: www.equuscs.com
SIC: 3571 Mainframe computers
PA: Equus Computer Systems, Inc.
7725 Washington Ave S
Edina MN 55439

(P-14973)
SHASTA ELECTRONIC MFG SVCS INC
Also Called: Shasta Ems
525 E Brokaw Rd, San Jose (95112-1004)
PHONE....................408 436-1267
Vinh Nguyen, *President*
Rang Nguyen, *Vice Pres*
EMP: 20
SQ FT: 11,000
SALES (est): 4.7MM **Privately Held**
WEB: www.shastaems.com
SIC: 3571 Electronic computers

(P-14974)
SHUGART CORPORATION (PA)
Also Called: Interntnal Assmbly Specialists
25 Brookline, Aliso Viejo (92656-1461)
PHONE....................949 488-8779
Dennis Narlinger, *President*
Steve Alvey, *CFO*
Israel Rodriguez, *Manager*
EMP: 110
SQ FT: 2,500
SALES (est): 18.4MM **Privately Held**
WEB: www.ias-shugart.com
SIC: 3571 Computers, digital, analog or hybrid

(P-14975)
SIGMA MFG & LOGISTICS LLC
10050 Fthlls Blvd Ste 100, Roseville (95747)
PHONE....................916 781-3052
Ushadevi Chenna,
Sara Feeney, *Personnel*
Tanuja Chenna,
Venkatasubbanna Chenna,
EMP: 20
SQ FT: 35,000
SALES (est): 3.5MM **Privately Held**
SIC: 3571 Computers, digital, analog or hybrid

(P-14976)
SIPIX IMAGING INC (DH)
47428 Fremont Blvd, Fremont (94538-6503)
PHONE....................510 743-2928
Felix Ho, *President*
Ching-Shon Ho, *CEO*
Mr Simon Nip, *CFO*
Ms Lynne C Garone, *Vice Pres*
▲ **EMP:** 40
SQ FT: 33,000
SALES (est): 7.3MM **Privately Held**
WEB: www.sipix.com
SIC: 3571 7371 Computers, digital, analog or hybrid; custom computer programming services

(P-14977)
SOLAR REGION INC
Also Called: Sumas Media
1314 John Reed Ct, City of Industry (91745-2406)
PHONE....................909 595-8500
Julie Shen, *President*
Alphonse Wu, *Vice Pres*
▲ **EMP:** 10
SALES (est): 2MM **Privately Held**
WEB: www.solarregion.net
SIC: 3571 5521 3823 Electronic computers; used car dealers; industrial instrmnts msrmnt display/control process variable

(P-14978)
SOLARFLARE COMMUNICATIONS INC (PA)
7505 Irvine Center Dr, Irvine (92618-2991)
PHONE....................949 581-6830
Russell Stern, *President*
David Parry, *President*
Mary Jane Abalos, *CFO*
John Graham, *Vice Pres*
Jim Icuss, *Surgery Dir*
EMP: 97
SQ FT: 22,097
SALES (est): 46.2MM **Privately Held**
WEB: www.solarflare.com
SIC: 3571 Electronic computers

(P-14979)
SONY CORPORATION OF AMERICA (PA)
16530 Via Esprillo Mz7190, San Diego (92127-1898)
PHONE....................212 833-8000
Karen E Kelso, *Vice Pres*
Jennifer Clark, *Vice Pres*
Don Vietti, *Vice Pres*
Sachiko Davis, *Planning*
Tom Sawyer, *Info Tech Dir*
EMP: 22
SALES (est): 1MM **Privately Held**
SIC: 3571 Computers, digital, analog or hybrid

(P-14980)
SUMICOM-USA
1729 Little Orchard St, San Jose (95125-1055)
PHONE....................408 385-2046
William Carey, *President*
EMP: 12
SALES (est): 865.7K **Privately Held**
SIC: 3571 Electronic computers

(P-14981)
SUPER MICRO COMPUTER INC (PA)
980 Rock Ave, San Jose (95131-1615)
PHONE....................408 503-8000
Charles Liang, *Ch of Bd*
David Weigand, *Ch Credit Ofcr*
Don Clegg, *Senior VP*
George KAO, *Senior VP*
Sara Liu, *Senior VP*
▲ **EMP:** 742
SQ FT: 1,197,000
SALES (est): 1.3B **Publicly Held**
WEB: www.supermicro.com
SIC: 3571 3572 7372 Electronic computers; computer storage devices; prepackaged software

(P-14982)
SYNERGY MICROSYSTEMS INC (DH)
28965 Avenue Penn, Valencia (91355-4185)
PHONE....................858 452-0020
Chris Wiltsey, *Director*
EMP: 70
SALES (est): 6.7MM
SALES (corp-wide): 2.4B **Publicly Held**
WEB: www.synergymicro.com
SIC: 3571 Computers, digital, analog or hybrid
HQ: Curtiss-Wright Controls, Inc.
15801 Brixham Hill Ave # 200
Charlotte NC 28277
704 869-4600

(P-14983)
SYNNEX CORPORATION
6551 W Schulte Rd Ste 100, Tracy
(95377-8130)
PHONE...............................510 656-3333
Simon Leung, *Branch Mgr*
Curtis Martin, *Opers Mgr*
EMP: 15
SALES (corp-wide): 20B **Publicly Held**
SIC: **3571** Personal computers (microcomputers)
PA: Synnex Corporation
44201 Nobel Dr
Fremont CA 94538
510 656-3333

(P-14984)
TANGENT COMPUTER INC
45800 Northport Loop W, Fremont
(94538-6413)
PHONE...............................650 342-9388
Doug Monsour, *President*
EMP: 80
SALES (est): 6MM
SALES (corp-wide): 33.2MM **Privately Held**
SIC: **3571** Personal computers (microcomputers)
PA: Tangent Computer, Inc.
191 Airport Blvd
Burlingame CA 94010
888 683-2881

(P-14985)
TANGENT COMPUTER INC (PA)
Also Called: Tanget Fastnet
191 Airport Blvd, Burlingame (94010-2006)
PHONE...............................888 683-2881
Douglas James Monsour, *CEO*
Ron Perkes, *President*
Maher Zabaneh, *Vice Pres*
Alex Kucich, *Info Tech Dir*
Chris Lee, *Engineer*
EMP: 100
SQ FT: 80,000
SALES (est): 33.2MM **Privately Held**
SIC: **3571 5734** Personal computers (microcomputers); computer & software stores

(P-14986)
TARACOM CORPORATION
1220 Memorex Dr, Santa Clara
(95050-2845)
PHONE...............................408 691-6655
Farhad Haghighi, *CEO*
EMP: 15
SALES: 2.5MM **Privately Held**
SIC: **3571** Electronic computers

(P-14987)
TERADATA OPERATIONS INC (HQ)
17095 Via Del Campo, San Diego
(92127-1711)
PHONE...............................937 242-4030
Victor Lund, *President*
James Ballard, *Partner*
John Emanuel, *President*
Oliver Ratzesberger, *COO*
Mark Culhane, *CFO*
EMP: 100
SALES (est): 357.2MM **Publicly Held**
SIC: **3571 7379** Electronic computers; computer related consulting services

(P-14988)
THOUSANDSHORES INC
37707 Cherry St, Newark (94560-4347)
PHONE...............................510 477-0249
Ding He, *CEO*
Zhi Liu, *President*
Sam Liu, *Vice Pres*
◆ EMP: 19
SALES (est): 3.5MM **Privately Held**
SIC: **3571 5999** Electronic computers; mobile telephones & equipment

(P-14989)
TOSHIBA AMER INFO SYSTEMS INC
2 Musick, Irvine (92618-1631)
P.O. Box 19724 (92623-9724)
PHONE...............................949 587-6378
Dick Walker, *Project Mgr*

EMP: 85 **Privately Held**
WEB: www.toshiba-components.com
SIC: **3571** Electronic computers
HQ: Toshiba America Information Systems, Inc.
1251 Ave Of The Amrcas St
New York NY 10020
949 583-3000

(P-14990)
TOUCHPINT ELCTRNIC SLTIONS LLC
38372 Innovation Ct # 306, Murrieta
(92563-2616)
PHONE...............................951 734-8083
EMP: 10
SQ FT: 10,000
SALES (est): 680K **Privately Held**
SIC: **3571**

(P-14991)
TRANSLATTICE INC (PA)
3398 Londonderry Dr, Santa Clara
(95050-6619)
PHONE...............................408 749-8478
Frank Huerta, *CEO*
Michael Lyle, *President*
EMP: 20
SQ FT: 4,197
SALES (est): 2.5MM **Privately Held**
SIC: **3571** Electronic computers

(P-14992)
TREX ENTERPRISES CORPORATION (PA)
Also Called: Ophthonix
10455 Pacific Center Ct, San Diego
(92121-4339)
PHONE...............................858 646-5300
Dr Kenneth Y Tang, *Ch of Bd*
EMP: 70
SQ FT: 90,000
SALES (est): 26.8MM **Privately Held**
WEB: www.trexenterprises.com
SIC: **3571** Electronic computers

(P-14993)
TRI MAP INTERNATIONAL INC
119 Val Dervin Pkwy Ste 5, Stockton
(95206-4000)
PHONE...............................209 234-0100
Howard Jensen, *CEO*
Lee Jensen, *President*
Laura Jensen, *CFO*
David Jensen, *Exec VP*
Jim Ridgwell, *Vice Pres*
EMP: 13
SQ FT: 36,000
SALES (est): 4.1MM **Privately Held**
WEB: www.trimapintl.com
SIC: **3571** Personal computers (microcomputers)

(P-14994)
UNITEK TECHNOLOGY INC
10211 Bellegrave Ave, Mira Loma
(91752-1919)
PHONE...............................909 930-5700
Yubo Ho, *President*
EMP: 15
SQ FT: 21,000
SALES (est): 3.7MM **Privately Held**
SIC: **3571 5734** Electronic computers; computer & software stores

(P-14995)
VMC HOLDINGS GROUP CORP
9667 Owensmouth Ave # 202, Chatsworth
(91311-4818)
P.O. Box 7396, Northridge (91327-7396)
PHONE...............................818 993-1466
Pierre Yenokian, *President*
Chris Geudo, *CFO*
Dorothy Yenokian, *Vice Pres*
EMP: 49
SQ FT: 8,500
SALES (est): 6.1MM **Privately Held**
WEB: www.vmcholdings.com
SIC: **3571** Electronic computers

(P-14996)
VOICEBOARD CORPORATION
473 Post St, Camarillo (93010-8553)
PHONE...............................805 389-3100
Greg Peacock, *President*
EMP: 12

SQ FT: 10,000
SALES (est): 1.3MM **Privately Held**
WEB: www.voiceboard.com
SIC: **3571** Electronic computers

(P-14997)
VOLTEDGE LLC
1701 Quail St Ste 600, Newport Beach
(92660-2757)
PHONE...............................949 877-8900
Chris Richards,
EMP: 15 EST: 2018
SALES (est): 3.3MM **Privately Held**
SIC: **3571 1531** Electronic computers;

(P-14998)
WIZELINE INC (PA)
456 Montgomery St # 2200, San Francisco
(94104-1255)
PHONE...............................415 373-6365
Bismarck Lepe, *CEO*
Anthony Conte, *CFO*
Daniele Lasher, *Executive Asst*
Ericka Veliz, *Executive Asst*
Kelly Flowers, *Sales Staff*
EMP: 47
SALES (est): 24.8MM **Privately Held**
SIC: **3571** Computers, digital, analog or hybrid

(P-14999)
XMULTIPLE TECHNOLOGIES (PA)
Also Called: Xmultiple/Xrjax
543 Country Club Dr B-128, Simi Valley
(93065-0637)
PHONE...............................805 579-1100
Alan Pocrass, *CEO*
Jeremy Chiu, *President*
Luke Flowers, *Vice Pres*
Emrich Kollar, *Vice Pres*
Drew Storberg, *Vice Pres*
▲ EMP: 13
SALES (est): 4.1MM **Privately Held**
SIC: **3571 3663 3661 3577** Electronic computers; multiplex equipment; telephone & telegraph apparatus; computer peripheral equipment

---

3572 Computer Storage Devices

(P-15000)
ABERDEEN LLC
9808 Alburtis Ave, Santa Fe Springs
(90670-3208)
PHONE...............................562 903-1500
Menahem M Ovadya, *Mng Member*
Jack Tateel, *Exec VP*
Charles Stevens, *Mktg Dir*
Suhua Deng,
Tracy Gardner,
▲ EMP: 48
SALES (est): 24.6MM **Privately Held**
WEB: www.aberdeeninc.com
SIC: **3572 3571** Computer storage devices; electronic computers

(P-15001)
ADVANCED HPC INC
8228 Mercury Ct Ste 100, San Diego
(92111-1232)
PHONE...............................858 716-8262
Toni Falcone, *President*
Jeff Tomlinson, *Vice Pres*
Joe Lipman, *General Mgr*
Adam Jundt, *Engineer*
EMP: 15
SALES: 18MM **Privately Held**
SIC: **3572 3571** Computer storage devices; electronic computers

(P-15002)
ALLSTAR MICROELECTRONICS INC
Also Called: Allstarshop.com
30191 Avendia De Las, Rancho Santa Margari (92688)
PHONE...............................949 546-0888
Ming-Chyi Chiang, *President*
EMP: 18
SQ FT: 12,843

SALES (est): 4.7MM **Privately Held**
WEB: www.allstarshop.com
SIC: **3572** Computer storage devices

(P-15003)
AMCAN USA LLC
8970 Crestmar Pt, San Diego
(92121-3222)
PHONE...............................858 587-1032
Nils Forsmann,
▲ EMP: 15
SALES (est): 2.5MM **Privately Held**
SIC: **3572** Computer tape drives & components

(P-15004)
AMPEX DATA SYSTEMS CORPORATION (HQ)
26460 Corporate Ave, Hayward
(94545-3914)
PHONE...............................650 367-2011
Gary Thom, *President*
Mike Bevington, *Sr Software Eng*
Tushar Malwankar, *Design Engr*
Charles Curran, *Business Mgr*
Downing Don, *Business Mgr*
▲ EMP: 58
SQ FT: 15,661
SALES (est): 15.6MM
SALES (corp-wide): 22MM **Privately Held**
WEB: www.ampexdata.com
SIC: **3572** Computer storage devices
PA: Delta Information Systems, Inc.
747 Dresher Rd Ste 100
Horsham PA 19044
215 657-5270

(P-15005)
APPLIED MICRO CIRCUITS CORP
Amcc
455 W Maude Ave, Sunnyvale
(94085-3540)
PHONE...............................408 523-1000
Faye Pairman, *Branch Mgr*
EMP: 42 **Publicly Held**
WEB: www.amcc.com
SIC: **3572 8731 3613 3577** Computer auxiliary storage units; computer (hardware) development; switchgear & switchboard apparatus; computer peripheral equipment
HQ: Applied Micro Circuits Corp
4555 Great America Pkwy # 601
Santa Clara CA 95054
408 542-8600

(P-15006)
APPRO INTERNATIONAL INC (DH)
Also Called: Cray Cluster Solutions
220 Devcon Dr, San Jose (95112-4210)
PHONE...............................408 941-8100
Daniel Kim, *President*
James Yi, *CFO*
Steve Lyness, *Vice Pres*
Giri Chukkapalli, *CTO*
Anthony Kenisky, *Sales Staff*
▲ EMP: 41
SQ FT: 40,000
SALES (est): 9.4MM
SALES (corp-wide): 30.8B **Publicly Held**
WEB: www.appro.com
SIC: **3572 3577 3571** Computer storage devices; computer peripheral equipment; electronic computers
HQ: Cray Inc.
901 5th Ave Ste 1000
Seattle WA 98164
206 701-2000

(P-15007)
ATP ELECTRONICS INC
2590 N 1st St Ste 150, San Jose
(95131-1049)
PHONE...............................408 732-5000
Jeffray W Hsieh, *CEO*
Dean Chang, *Ch of Bd*
Danny Lin, *General Mgr*
Winnie Chan, *Human Res Dir*
Hollie Lee, *Sales Mgr*
▲ EMP: 23
SQ FT: 10,000

▲ = Import ▼=Export
◆ =Import/Export

SALES (est): 7.8MM **Privately Held**
WEB: www.atpinc.com
SIC: 3572 Computer storage devices
PA: Atp Electronics Taiwan Inc.
    10f, No. 185, Tiding Blvd., Sec. 2
    Taipei City TAP 11493
    -

(P-15008)
BITMICRO NETWORKS INC (PA)
47929 Fremont Blvd, Fremont
(94538-6508)
PHONE....................................510 743-3124
David Shapowal, *CEO*
Dave Shapowal, *COO*
Stephen Uriarte, *Exec VP*
Gary Kohli, *Vice Pres*
Bharadwaj Pudipeddi, *Vice Pres*
EMP: 16
SQ FT: 14,000
SALES: 10MM **Privately Held**
WEB: www.bitmicro.com
SIC: 3572 Computer disk & drum drives &
    components; computer tape drives &
    components

(P-15009)
BNL TECHNOLOGIES INC
Also Called: Fantom Drives
20525 Manhattan Pl, Torrance
(90501-1825)
PHONE....................................310 320-7272
Behzad Eshghieh, *CEO*
Hamid Khorsand, *Ch of Bd*
Nasser Ahdout, *CFO*
Monica Vicencio, *Info Tech Dir*
Tony Tan, *Technology*
▲ EMP: 26 EST: 1998
SALES (est): 9.4MM **Privately Held**
WEB: www.fantomdrives.com
SIC: 3572 Computer storage devices

(P-15010)
CALDIGIT INC
1941 E Miraloma Ave Ste B, Placentia
(92870-6770)
PHONE....................................714 572-6668
PO Hung Chen, *CEO*
▲ EMP: 15
SALES (est): 3MM **Privately Held**
SIC: 3572 Disk drives, computer; magnetic
    storage devices, computer

(P-15011)
CAPSA SOLUTIONS LLC
14000 S Broadway, Los Angeles
(90061-1018)
PHONE....................................800 437-6633
Jeff Strickler, *CFO*
EMP: 40
SALES (corp-wide): 169.9MM **Privately
Held**
SIC: 3572 Computer storage devices
HQ: Capsa Solutions Llc
    4253 Ne 189th Ave
    Portland OR 97230
    503 766-2324

(P-15012)
CELEROS CORP
559 Clyde Ave Ste 220, Mountain View
(94043-2270)
PHONE....................................650 325-6900
Hossein Alaee, *CEO*
EMP: 20
SQ FT: 7,000
SALES (est): 2.7MM **Privately Held**
WEB: www.celeros.com
SIC: 3572 Computer storage devices

(P-15013)
**CENTON ELECTRONICS INC
(PA)**
27412 Aliso Viejo Pkwy, Aliso Viejo
(92656-3371)
PHONE....................................949 855-9111
Jennifer Miscione, *CEO*
Gene Miscione, *President*
Janet Miscione, *Vice Pres*
Paul Tinsley, *Sales Mgr*
Laura Miscione, *Sales Staff*
▲ EMP: 60
SQ FT: 20,000

SALES (est): 17.7MM **Privately Held**
WEB: www.centon.com
SIC: 3572 5734 7379 Computer storage
    devices; computer software & acces-
    sories; computer related consulting serv-
    ices

(P-15014)
CERTANCE LLC (HQ)
Also Called: Quantum Corporation
141 Innovation Dr, Irvine (92617-3211)
PHONE....................................949 856-7800
Howard L Matthews, *President*
Donald L Waite, *Chairman*
Enrique Lopez-Pineda, *Engineer*
Roy Owen, *Senior Engr*
Mary J Randles, *Marketing Staff*
EMP: 300
SALES (est): 74MM
SALES (corp-wide): 402.6MM **Privately
Held**
WEB: www.quantum.com
SIC: 3572 Computer tape drives & compo-
    nents
PA: Quantum Corporation
    224 Airport Pkwy Ste 550
    San Jose CA 95110
    408 944-4000

(P-15015)
CHENBRO MICOM (USA) INC
2800 Jurupa St, Ontario (91761-2903)
PHONE....................................909 937-0100
MEI CHI Chen, *President*
▲ EMP: 20 EST: 1983
SALES (est): 5.8MM **Privately Held**
SIC: 3572 Computer storage devices
PA: Chenbro Micom Co., Ltd.
    15f, 150, Chien 1st Rd.,
    New Taipei City TAP 23511
    -

(P-15016)
CLOUD ENGINES INC
77 Geary St Ste 500, San Francisco
(94108-5703)
PHONE....................................415 738-8076
Daniel Putterman, *President*
Gregory Smith, *CFO*
Jed Putterman, *Exec VP*
Brad Dietrich, *CTO*
EMP: 45
SALES (est): 6.4MM **Privately Held**
SIC: 3572 Computer storage devices

(P-15017)
CMS PRODUCTS INC
12 Mauchly Ste E, Irvine (92618-2398)
P.O. Box 2789, Capistrano Beach (92624-
0789)
PHONE....................................714 424-5520
Kenneth Burke, *President*
Ronald C Harrell, *Shareholder*
Jim Sedin, *Shareholder*
Mark Balce, *Vice Pres*
Terry O'Neill, *Vice Pres*
▲ EMP: 40
SQ FT: 30,000
SALES (est): 8MM **Privately Held**
WEB: www.cmsstorage.com
SIC: 3572 3577 7379 Computer storage
    devices; computer peripheral equipment;
    data processing consultant

(P-15018)
COMPUCASE CORPORATION
Also Called: Orion Tech
16720 Chestnut St Ste C, City of Industry
(91748-1038)
PHONE....................................626 336-6588
Doung Fu Hsu, *President*
Aaron Tao, *COO*
Phillip Liu, *Manager*
▲ EMP: 1500
SQ FT: 30,000
SALES (est): 165.7MM **Privately Held**
WEB: www.compucaseusa.com
SIC: 3572 Computer storage devices
PA: Compucase Enterprise Co., Ltd.
    225, Lane 54, Anhe Rd., Sec. 2,
    Tainan City 70967

(P-15019)
CORAID INC (PA)
255 Shoreline Dr Ste 650, Redwood City
(94065-1431)
PHONE....................................650 517-9300
Dave Kresse, *CEO*
Audrey Maclean, *Ch of Bd*
Stewart Grierson, *CFO*
Glenn Neufeld, *Foreman/Supr*
Bantley Coile, *Deputy Dir*
EMP: 91
SALES (est): 21.6MM **Privately Held**
WEB: www.coraid.com
SIC: 3572 Computer storage devices

(P-15020)
**DATADIRECT NETWORKS INC
(PA)**
Also Called: D D N
9351 Deering Ave, Chatsworth
(91311-5858)
PHONE....................................818 700-7600
Alex Bouzari, *CEO*
Gordon Manning, *President*
Ian Angelo, *CFO*
Camellia Ngo, *Officer*
Bret Weber, *Exec VP*
▲ EMP: 120
SQ FT: 50,000
SALES (est): 251.7MM **Privately Held**
WEB: www.datadirectnet.com
SIC: 3572 7374 Computer auxiliary stor-
    age units; data processing service

(P-15021)
DSSD INC
4025 Bohannon Dr, Menlo Park
(94025-1004)
PHONE....................................775 773-8665
William Moore, *President*
Andreas Bechtolsheim, *Director*
EMP: 11
SQ FT: 7,500
SALES (est): 6.8MM **Privately Held**
SIC: 3572 Computer storage devices

(P-15022)
DUALCOR TECHNOLOGIES INC
1 Embarcadero Ctr Ste 500, San Francisco
(94111-3610)
PHONE....................................831 684-2457
Tim Glass, *CEO*
Rob Howe, *President*
Bryan T Cupps, *CTO*
EMP: 25
SQ FT: 12,000
SALES (est): 1.9MM **Privately Held**
WEB: www.dualcor.com
SIC: 3572 Computer storage devices

(P-15023)
DURA MICRO INC
Also Called: Acom Data
901 E Cedar St, Ontario (91761-5572)
P.O. Box 5499, Diamond Bar (91765-7499)
PHONE....................................909 947-4590
Titus Wu, *President*
▲ EMP: 46
SQ FT: 46,000
SALES (est): 6.5MM **Privately Held**
WEB: www.acomdata.com
SIC: 3572 3577 Computer storage de-
    vices; computer peripheral equipment

(P-15024)
EMC CORPORATION
6701 Koll Center Pkwy # 150, Pleasanton
(94566-8061)
PHONE....................................925 948-9000
Rich Napolitano, *Principal*
EMP: 75
SALES (corp-wide): 90.6B **Publicly Held**
SIC: 3572 Computer storage devices
HQ: Emc Corporation
    176 South St
    Hopkinton MA 01748
    508 435-1000

(P-15025)
EMC CORPORATION
Also Called: Cloudscaling Group
455 Market St Fl 4, San Francisco
(94105-2486)
PHONE....................................877 636-8589
Michael Grant, *Principal*
Inna Kats, *Executive Asst*

EMP: 40
SALES (corp-wide): 90.6B **Publicly Held**
SIC: 3572 Computer storage devices
HQ: Emc Corporation
    176 South St
    Hopkinton MA 01748
    508 435-1000

(P-15026)
EMC CORPORATION
6801 Koll Center Pkwy, Pleasanton
(94566-7047)
PHONE....................................925 600-6800
Kelly Campos, *Branch Mgr*
Casey Dumlao, *Business Anlyst*
Jonas Irwin, *Research*
Michael Ottati, *Engineer*
Jeff Smith, *Sales Staff*
EMP: 65
SALES (corp-wide): 90.6B **Publicly Held**
SIC: 3572 Computer storage devices
HQ: Emc Corporation
    176 South St
    Hopkinton MA 01748
    508 435-1000

(P-15027)
EP HOLDINGS INC
Also Called: Ep Memory
30442 Esperanza, Rcho STA Marg
(92688-2144)
PHONE....................................949 713-4600
Eric Krantz, *CEO*
EMP: 20
SALES (est): 16.2MM **Privately Held**
SIC: 3572 Computer storage devices

(P-15028)
**FORTASA MEMORY SYSTEMS
INC**
1670 S Amphlett Blvd, San Mateo
(94402-2510)
PHONE....................................888 367-8588
Tatyana Nakhimovsky, *President*
Samuel Nakhimovsky, *General Mgr*
▼ EMP: 12
SQ FT: 1,500
SALES (est): 1.7MM **Privately Held**
SIC: 3572 Computer storage devices

(P-15029)
FORTEMEDIA INC
Also Called: Fortemedia China
4051 Burton Dr, Santa Clara (95054-1585)
PHONE....................................408 716-8011
May Ip, *Manager*
EMP: 65
SALES (corp-wide): 10.3MM **Privately
Held**
WEB: www.fortemedia.com
SIC: 3572 Computer disk & drum drives &
    components
PA: Fortemedia, Inc.
    4051 Burton Dr
    Santa Clara CA 95054
    408 716-8028

(P-15030)
FORTEMEDIA INC
19050 Pruneridge Ave, Cupertino (95014)
PHONE....................................408 716-8028
Minghua Chu, *Manager*
EMP: 65
SALES (corp-wide): 10.3MM **Privately
Held**
WEB: www.fortemedia.com
SIC: 3572 Computer disk & drum drives &
    components
PA: Fortemedia, Inc.
    4051 Burton Dr
    Santa Clara CA 95054
    408 716-8028

(P-15031)
GIGAMEM LLC
18375 Bandilier Cir, Fountain Valley
(92708-7001)
PHONE....................................949 461-9999
Keller J Lee, *Mng Member*
▲ EMP: 15
SQ FT: 9,500
SALES (est): 2.2MM
SALES (corp-wide): 18.9MM **Privately
Held**
WEB: www.gigaram.com
SIC: 3572 Computer storage devices

PRODUCTS & SVCS

PA: Memoryten, Inc.
2995 Mead Ave
Santa Clara CA 95051
408 516-4141

(P-15032)
GLOBALSCALE TECHNOLOGIES INC
1200 N Van Buren St Ste D, Anaheim
(92807-1638)
PHONE...................714 632-9239
Richard Cheng, *President*
Bryan Cheng, *Sales Mgr*
John Meng, *Director*
▲ **EMP:** 11
SALES (est): 2.3MM **Privately Held**
SIC: 3572 Computer storage devices

(P-15033)
GLOBALVISION SYSTEMS INC
9401 Oakdale Ave Ste 100, Chatsworth
(91311-6512)
PHONE...................888 227-7967
Oliver Song, *CEO*
Scott Grant, *Manager*
EMP: 18
SALES (est): 3.3MM **Privately Held**
SIC: 3572 Computer disk & drum drives &
components

(P-15034)
GOHARDDRIVE INC
Also Called: Goharddrive.com
137 S 8th Ave Ste E, La Puente
(91746-3247)
PHONE...................626 593-9927
Yee Wey Tan, *President*
▲ **EMP:** 12 **EST:** 2011
SALES (est): 19.9MM **Privately Held**
SIC: 3572 Disk drives, computer

(P-15035)
GST INC
3419 Via Lido Ste 164, Newport Beach
(92663-3908)
PHONE...................949 510-1142
David Breisacher, *CEO*
▼ **EMP:** 51
SQ FT: 10,000
SALES (est): 5.5MM **Privately Held**
WEB: www.gstinc.com
SIC: 3572 Computer storage devices

(P-15036)
H CO COMPUTER PRODUCTS (PA)
Also Called: Thinkcp Technologies
16812 Hale Ave, Irvine (92606-5021)
PHONE...................949 833-3222
Ali Hojreh, *CEO*
Mark Hojreh, *CFO*
Bryon Strachan, *Division Mgr*
Saed Hojreh, *Admin Sec*
Mohammad Hojreh, *Director*
◆ **EMP:** 26
SQ FT: 15,600
SALES (est): 5.7MM **Privately Held**
WEB: www.thinkcp.com
SIC: 3572 3577 Computer storage de-
vices; computer peripheral equipment

(P-15037)
HEADWAY TECHNOLOGIES INC
463 S Milpitas Blvd, Milpitas (95035-5438)
PHONE...................408 935-1020
Nabil Arnaout, *Branch Mgr*
Brenda Baltazar, *Administration*
Tony Nguyen, *Engineer*
Zunde Yang, *Engineer*
Yukinori Ikegawa, *Senior Engr*
EMP: 10 **Privately Held**
SIC: 3572 Computer disk & drum drives &
components
HQ: Headway Technologies, Inc.
682 S Hillview Dr
Milpitas CA 95035
408 934-5300

(P-15038)
HEADWAY TECHNOLOGIES INC (HQ)
682 S Hillview Dr, Milpitas (95035-5457)
PHONE...................408 934-5300
Mao-Min Chen, *President*
Thomas Surran, *CFO*

Gary Pester, *Vice Pres*
Pai-Kang Wang, *Vice Pres*
Casey Moore, *Admin Asst*
▲ **EMP:** 200
SALES (est): 309.7MM **Privately Held**
WEB: www.headway.com
SIC: 3572 Magnetic storage devices, com-
puter

(P-15039)
HEADWAY TECHNOLOGIES INC
497 S Hillview Dr, Milpitas (95035-7702)
PHONE...................408 934-5300
Yoshiro Nakagawa, *VP Opers*
EMP: 200 **Privately Held**
SIC: 3572 Computer storage devices
HQ: Headway Technologies, Inc.
682 S Hillview Dr
Milpitas CA 95035
408 934-5300

(P-15040)
HGST INC
Also Called: Skyera
5601 Great Oaks Pkwy, San Jose
(95119-1003)
PHONE...................408 418-4148
EMP: 160
SALES (corp-wide): 16.5B **Publicly Held**
SIC: 3572 Computer storage devices
HQ: Hgst, Inc.
5601 Great Oaks Pkwy
San Jose CA 95119
408 717-6000

(P-15041)
HGST INC
951 Sandisk Dr, Milpitas (95035-7933)
PHONE...................408 801-2394
Michael Ray, *Principal*
Ulrich Hansen, *Vice Pres*
Craig Taylor, *Sales Staff*
EMP: 10
SALES (corp-wide): 16.5B **Publicly Held**
SIC: 3572 Computer storage devices
HQ: Hgst, Inc.
5601 Great Oaks Pkwy
San Jose CA 95119
408 717-6000

(P-15042)
HGST INC (DH)
5601 Great Oaks Pkwy, San Jose
(95119-1003)
PHONE...................408 717-6000
John Coyne, *CEO*
Stephen Milligan, *President*
Douglas A Gross, *COO*
Michael A Murray, *CFO*
Dean Amini, *Vice Pres*
▲ **EMP:** 17
SALES (est): 700.6MM
SALES (corp-wide): 16.5B **Publicly Held**
WEB: www.hitachigst.com
SIC: 3572 Computer storage devices

(P-15043)
HIGHPOINT TECHNOLOGIES INC
41650 Christy St, Fremont (94538-3114)
PHONE...................408 942-5800
Michael Whang, *President*
Yuan-Lang Chang, *CFO*
Tao Xiong, *Engineer*
From Yu, *Engineer*
Corey Baker, *Manager*
▲ **EMP:** 12
SQ FT: 14,500
SALES (est): 2.5MM **Privately Held**
SIC: 3572 8731 Computer disk & drum
drives & components; computer (hard-
ware) development

(P-15044)
HITACHI VANTARA CORPORATION (DH)
2535 Augustine Dr, Santa Clara
(95054-3003)
PHONE...................408 970-1000
Jack Domme, *President*
Minoru Kosuge, *Ch of Bd*
Brian Householder, *President*
Catriona Fallon, *CFO*
Rick Martig, *CFO*
▲ **EMP:** 450 **EST:** 1979
SQ FT: 250,000

SALES (est): 2B **Privately Held**
WEB: www.hds.com
SIC: 3572 Computer storage devices
HQ: Hitachi Vantara
2845 Lafayette St
Santa Clara CA 95050
408 970-1000

(P-15045)
I-TECH COMPANY LTD LBLTY CO
42978 Osgood Rd, Fremont (94539-5627)
PHONE...................510 226-9226
Alan Chung, *CEO*
Rong Lee, *Engineer*
▲ **EMP:** 10
SALES (est): 1.6MM **Privately Held**
WEB: www.i-techcompany.com
SIC: 3572 3577 Computer storage de-
vices; computer peripheral equipment

(P-15046)
I/OMAGIC CORPORATION (PA)
20512 Crescent Bay Dr, Lake Forest
(92630-8847)
PHONE...................949 707-4800
Tony Shahbaz, *Ch of Bd*
Mary St George, *Treasurer*
Paula Lecossois, *Marketing Staff*
▲ **EMP:** 30
SQ FT: 52,000 **Privately Held**
WEB: www.iomagic.com
SIC: 3572 3651 Computer storage de-
vices; home entertainment equipment,
electronic

(P-15047)
IN WIN DEVELOPMENT USA INC
188 Brea Canyon Rd, Walnut
(91789-3086)
PHONE...................909 348-0588
Wen Hsien Lai, *President*
Paul Hao, *Vice Pres*
▲ **EMP:** 20 **EST:** 1989
SQ FT: 50,000
SALES (est): 3.8MM **Privately Held**
SIC: 3572 Computer tape drives & compo-
nents
PA: In Win Development Inc.
57, Lane 350, Nan Shang Rd.,
Taoyuan City TAY 33392

(P-15048)
INNOVATIVE DIVERSFD TECH INC
Also Called: Disk Faktory
18062 Irvine Blvd Ste 304, Tustin
(92780-3329)
PHONE...................949 455-1701
EMP: 28
SQ FT: 7,800
SALES (est): 4.4MM **Privately Held**
WEB: www.burncd.com
SIC: 3572 7371

(P-15049)
INTELLIGENT STORAGE SOLUTION
2073 Otoole Ave, San Jose (95131-1303)
PHONE...................408 428-0105
Dat Do, *President*
Ian Wallace, *Engineer*
Mark Wallace, *Rector*
▲ **EMP:** 200
SALES (est): 24.7MM **Privately Held**
SIC: 3572 Computer disk & drum drives &
components

(P-15050)
IOSAFE INC
10600 Industrial Ave # 120, Roseville
(95678-6210)
PHONE...................888 984-6723
Robb Moore, *CEO*
Christine Davis, *CFO*
Andrea Moore, *Treasurer*
Matt Eargis, *VP Sales*
Chris Wilson, *Sales Mgr*
▲ **EMP:** 18
SQ FT: 20,000
SALES (est): 5.5MM **Privately Held**
WEB: www.iosafe.com
SIC: 3572 Computer storage devices

(P-15051)
JMR ELECTRONICS INC
Also Called: J M R Components
8968 Fullbright Ave, Chatsworth
(91311-6123)
PHONE...................818 993-4801
Josef Rabinovitz, *President*
Judy Schoen, *CFO*
Mirit Rabinovitz, *Corp Secy*
Teresa Torres, *Vice Pres*
David Rosenthal, *Engineer*
▲ **EMP:** 22 **EST:** 1982
SQ FT: 24,000
SALES (est): 7.5MM **Privately Held**
SIC: 3572 Computer storage devices

(P-15052)
LGARDE INC
15181 Woodlawn Ave, Tustin (92780-6487)
PHONE...................714 259-0771
Gayle D Bilyeu, *Ch of Bd*
Constantine Cassapakis, *President*
Alan R Hirasuna, *Treasurer*
Gordon Veal, *Admin Sec*
Carlos Rios, *Mfg Staff*
EMP: 24 **EST:** 1971
SQ FT: 19,000
SALES (est): 5.4MM **Privately Held**
WEB: www.lgarde.com
SIC: 3572 8731 2822 3769 Tape
recorders for computers; engineering lab-
oratory, except testing; acrylic rubbers,
polyacrylate; guided missile & space vehi-
cle parts & auxiliary equipment; radio &
TV communications equipment

(P-15053)
LOOKER DATA SCIENCES INC (PA)
101 Church St Fl 4, Santa Cruz
(95060-3963)
PHONE...................831 244-0340
Frank Bien, *CEO*
Lloyd Tabb, *Ch of Bd*
Jen Grant, *Chief Mktg Ofcr*
Nick Caldwell, *Officer*
Ryan Gurney, *Officer*
EMP: 60
SALES (est): 17.1MM **Privately Held**
SIC: 3572 Computer tape drives & compo-
nents

(P-15054)
MARANTI NETWORKS INC
1452 N Vasco Rd, Livermore (94551-9213)
PHONE...................408 834-4000
Debbie Miller, *President*
Kuldeep Sandhu, *Security Dir*
Santosh Lolayekar, *CTO*
Harish Nayak, *VP Mktg*
EMP: 78
SQ FT: 20,000
SALES: 2MM **Privately Held**
SIC: 3572 Computer storage devices

(P-15055)
MAXTOR CORPORATION (DH)
4575 Scotts Valley Dr, Scotts Valley
(95066-4517)
PHONE...................831 438-6550
▲ **EMP:** 100
SALES (est): 418.7MM **Privately Held**
WEB: www.maxtor.com
SIC: 3572
HQ: Seagate Technology (Us) Holdings, Inc
920 Disc Dr
Scotts Valley CA 95014
831 438-6550

(P-15056)
MEMORY EXPERTS INTL USA INC (HQ)
1651 E Saint Andrew Pl, Santa Ana
(92705-4932)
PHONE...................714 258-3000
Guadulupe Reusing, *Ch of Bd*
Lawrence Reusing, *President*
Gerard Reusing, *CEO*
Rino Lampasona, *Vice Pres*
Julian Reusing, *Vice Pres*
▲ **EMP:** 32
SQ FT: 40,000

▲ = Import ▼=Export
◆ =Import/Export

SALES: 15MM
SALES (corp-wide): 35.7MM **Privately Held**
WEB: www.memoryexpertsinc.com/
SIC: 3572 3577 Computer storage devices; computer peripheral equipment
PA: Experts En Memoire Internationale Inc, Les
   2321 Rue Cohen
   Saint-Laurent QC H4R 2
   514 333-5010

(P-15057)
MGM DATA INC
155 W Wash Blvd 105los, Los Angeles (90015-3552)
PHONE..............................213 747-3282
Juan Salazar, *CEO*
EMP: 12 **EST:** 2014
SALES (est): 1.4MM **Privately Held**
SIC: 3572 7374 7389 4226 Computer auxiliary storage units; data processing & preparation; document & office record destruction; document & office records storage

(P-15058)
MICRON CONSUMER PDTS GROUP INC (HQ)
540 Alder Dr, Fremont (94538)
PHONE..............................669 226-3000
Gerald Pittman, *President*
Vincent Nguyen, *Vice Pres*
EMP: 11 **EST:** 2000
SALES (est): 2.5MM
SALES (corp-wide): 23.4B **Publicly Held**
SIC: 3572 Computer storage devices
PA: Micron Technology, Inc.
   8000 S Federal Way
   Boise ID 83716
   208 368-4000

(P-15059)
MITAC INFORMATION SYSTEMS CORP (DH)
39889 Eureka Dr, Newark (94560-4811)
PHONE..............................510 284-3000
Charlotte Chou, *President*
Billy Ho, *President*
Karen Soong, *CFO*
Matthew Miau, *Chairman*
Fred Towns, *Vice Pres*
▲ **EMP:** 103
SQ FT: 240,000
SALES (est): 39.6MM **Privately Held**
WEB: www.mitac.com
SIC: 3572 Computer storage devices

(P-15060)
MTI TECHNOLOGY CORPORATION (PA)
15461 Red Hill Ave # 200, Tustin (92780-7314)
PHONE..............................949 251-1101
EMP: 200
SQ FT: 25,000
SALES (est): 54.8MM **Privately Held**
WEB: www.mti.com
SIC: 3572 3571 7372 3674

(P-15061)
NETAPP INC (PA)
1395 Crossman Ave, Sunnyvale (94089-1114)
PHONE..............................408 822-6000
George Kurian, *President*
Ronald J Pasek, *CFO*
Matthew K Fawcett, *Ch Credit Ofcr*
Brad R Anderson, *Exec VP*
Henri Richard, *Exec VP*
▲ **EMP:** 1600
SQ FT: 700,000
SALES: 6.1B **Publicly Held**
WEB: www.netapp.com
SIC: 3572 7373 7372 Computer storage devices; computer integrated systems design; systems software development services; computer system selling services; prepackaged software

(P-15062)
NEXSAN TECHNOLOGIES INC (DH)
325 E Hillcrest Dr # 150, Thousand Oaks (91360-7799)
PHONE..............................408 724-9809
Philip Black, *CEO*
Gene Spies, *CFO*
George Symons, *Officer*
James R Molenda, *Admin Sec*
Sachin Patel, *Engineer*
▲ **EMP:** 40
SALES (est): 33.3MM
SALES (corp-wide): 41MM **Privately Held**
WEB: www.nexsan.com
SIC: 3572 Computer storage devices
HQ: Nexsan Corporation
   900 E Hamilton Ave # 230
   Campbell CA 95008
   408 724-9809

(P-15063)
NEXSAN TECHNOLOGIES INC
302 Enterprise St, Escondido (92029-1235)
PHONE..............................760 745-3550
Fax: 760 745-3503
EMP: 25 **Publicly Held**
SIC: 3572
HQ: Nexsan Technologies Incorporated
   900 E Hamilton Ave # 230
   Campbell CA 91360
   408 724-9809

(P-15064)
NFLASH INC
23142 Alcalde Dr Ste A, Laguna Hills (92653-1448)
PHONE..............................949 678-9411
Nathan Litinski, *Branch Mgr*
EMP: 19
SALES (corp-wide): 3MM **Privately Held**
SIC: 3572 Magnetic storage devices, computer
PA: Nflash, Inc.
   3080 Kenneth St
   Santa Clara CA 95054
   408 350-0341

(P-15065)
NGD SYSTEMS INC
355 Goddard Ste 200, Irvine (92618-4642)
PHONE..............................949 870-9148
Mohammad Nader Salessi, *CEO*
Al Talavera, *CFO*
Eli Tiomkin, *VP Business*
EMP: 30
SALES (est): 243.2K **Privately Held**
SIC: 3572 Computer storage devices

(P-15066)
NIMBLE STORAGE INC (HQ)
211 River Oaks Pkwy, San Jose (95134-1913)
PHONE..............................408 432-9600
Suresh Vasudevan, *CEO*
Brad Floyd, *Partner*
Harry Lutz, *Partner*
Anup Singh, *CFO*
Janet Matsuda, *Chief Mktg Ofcr*
▲ **EMP:** 204
SQ FT: 165,000
SALES: 402.6MM
SALES (corp-wide): 30.8B **Publicly Held**
SIC: 3572 Computer storage devices
PA: Hewlett Packard Enterprise Company
   6280 America Center Dr
   San Jose CA 95002
   650 687-5817

(P-15067)
NIMBUS DATA INC
5151 California Ave # 100, Irvine (92617-3205)
PHONE..............................650 276-4500
Thomas Isakovich, *CEO*
◆ **EMP:** 50
SALES (est): 10.8MM **Privately Held**
WEB: www.nimbusdata.com
SIC: 3572 Computer storage devices

(P-15068)
NWE TECHNOLOGY INC
1688 Richard Ave, Santa Clara (95050-2844)
PHONE..............................408 919-6100
S C Huang, *President*
▲ **EMP:** 150
SQ FT: 63,000
SALES (est): 19.5MM **Privately Held**
WEB: www.nwetechnology.com
SIC: 3572 Computer disk & drum drives & components

(P-15069)
ORYX ADVANCED MATERIALS INC (PA)
46458 Fremont Blvd, Fremont (94538-6469)
PHONE..............................510 249-1158
Victor Tan, *CEO*
Kwei-San Teng, *Vice Pres*
Diana Lai, *Office Admin*
Tan Geok San, *Director*
▲ **EMP:** 35
SQ FT: 7,000
SALES (est): 5.7MM **Privately Held**
WEB: www.oam-inc.com
SIC: 3572 Disk drives, computer

(P-15070)
OVERLAND STORAGE INC (HQ)
Also Called: S3d Acquisition II Company
4542 Ruffner St Ste 250, San Diego (92111-2267)
PHONE..............................858 571-5555
Eric L Kelly, *CEO*
Kurt L Kalbfleisch, *CFO*
Carol Dixon, *Vice Pres*
David Ochser, *Vice Pres*
Graham Paterson, *Vice Pres*
▲ **EMP:** 87
SQ FT: 51,000
SALES: 105.8MM
SALES (corp-wide): 1.1MM **Privately Held**
WEB: www.overlanddata.com
SIC: 3572 7372 Computer storage devices; prepackaged software
PA: Sphere 3d Inc
   240 Matheson Blvd E
   Mississauga ON L4Z 1
   416 749-5999

(P-15071)
OZMO INC
Also Called: Ozmo Devices
1600 Technology Dr, San Jose (95110-1382)
PHONE..............................650 515-3524
Bill McLean, *CEO*
Jon Edney, *Vice Pres*
Jon Ewanich, *Vice Pres*
Mike Schwartz, *Vice Pres*
EMP: 24 **EST:** 2004
SALES (est): 3.5MM **Privately Held**
SIC: 3572 Computer disk & drum drives & components

(P-15072)
PACIFIC ALLIANCE CAPITAL INC
Also Called: Wct/Pac Data
27141 Aliso Creek Rd # 225, Aliso Viejo (92656-3360)
PHONE..............................949 360-1796
Rick Crane, *CEO*
Susan Holloway, *Shareholder*
David Holloway, *Vice Pres*
Josh Moore, *Principal*
EMP: 12 **EST:** 2000
SQ FT: 28,000
SALES (est): 5.7MM **Privately Held**
WEB: www.pacdata.com
SIC: 3572 Computer storage devices

(P-15073)
PHILIPS & LITE-ON DIGITAL (DH)
Also Called: P L D S
726 S Hillview Dr, Milpitas (95035-5455)
PHONE..............................510 687-1800
Harlie Pseng, *President*
Charlie Pseng, *President*
Armando Abella, *CFO*
Walker Su, *Admin Sec*
▲ **EMP:** 50
SQ FT: 17,088

SALES (est): 35MM
SALES (corp-wide): 20.8B **Privately Held**
WEB: www.liteonit.com
SIC: 3572 Disk drives, computer

(P-15074)
PI-CORAL INC
600 California St Fl 6, San Francisco (94108-2733)
PHONE..............................408 516-5150
Donpaul Stephens, *CEO*
Johnson Agogbua, *President*
Mary Martis, *Executive Asst*
EMP: 80
SQ FT: 15,000
SALES: 1MM **Privately Held**
SIC: 3572 Computer storage devices

(P-15075)
POSTVISION INC
Also Called: Archion
2120 Foothill Blvd # 111, La Verne (91750-2941)
PHONE..............................818 840-0777
Mark Bianchi, *CEO*
Reuben Lima, *COO*
Daniel Stern, *Exec VP*
James A Tucci, *CTO*
EMP: 15
SQ FT: 6,000
SALES (est): 2.9MM **Privately Held**
WEB: www.archion.com
SIC: 3572 Computer storage devices

(P-15076)
PSSC LABS
20432 N Sea Cir, Lake Forest (92630-8806)
PHONE..............................949 380-7288
Janice Lesser, *President*
Larry Lesser, *Vice Pres*
Harrison Angus, *Executive*
Kurtis Henderson, *Comp Tech*
Alex Lesser, *Director*
▲ **EMP:** 15
SQ FT: 2,500
SALES (est): 18MM **Privately Held**
WEB: www.pssclabs.com
SIC: 3572 5734 Computer storage devices; computer & software stores

(P-15077)
PURE STORAGE INC (PA)
650 Castro St Ste 400, Mountain View (94041-2081)
PHONE..............................800 379-7873
Charles H Giancarlo, *CEO*
David Hatfield, *President*
Paul Mountford, *COO*
Robson Grieve, *Chief Mktg Ofcr*
Joseph Pinto, *Officer*
▲ **EMP:** 277
SALES: 1.3B **Publicly Held**
SIC: 3572 7372 Computer storage devices; prepackaged software

(P-15078)
QUALSTAR CORPORATION (PA)
1267 Flynn Rd, Camarillo (93012-8013)
PHONE..............................805 583-7744
Steven N Bronson, *President*
David J Wolenski, *Ch of Bd*
Louann L Negrete, *CFO*
Nick Yarymovych, *Bd of Directors*
Yvonne Ramos, *Admin Asst*
EMP: 20
SQ FT: 15,160
SALES: 12.2MM **Publicly Held**
WEB: www.qualstar.com
SIC: 3572 3695 Tape storage units, computer; magnetic & optical recording media

(P-15079)
QUANTUM CORPORATION (PA)
224 Airport Pkwy Ste 550, San Jose (95110-1097)
PHONE..............................408 944-4000
James J Lerner, *Ch of Bd*
J Michael Dodson, *CFO*
Regan Macpherson, *Officer*
Elizabeth King, *Officer*
Lewis Moorehead, *Officer*
▲ **EMP:** 314
SALES: 402.6MM **Privately Held**
WEB: www.quantum.com
SIC: 3572 Tape storage units, computer

PRODUCTS & SVCS

(P-15080)
QUANTUM CORPORATION
Also Called: New Quantum Living
1441 Melanie Ln, Arcadia (91007-7908)
PHONE..................................213 248-2481
EMP: 110
SALES (corp-wide): 402.6MM **Privately Held**
SIC: 3572 Computer storage devices
PA: Quantum Corporation
　224 Airport Pkwy Ste 550
　San Jose CA 95110
　408 944-4000

(P-15081)
QUANTUM CORPORATION
141 Innovation Dr, Irvine (92617-3211)
PHONE..................................949 856-7800
Lisa Ewbank, *Branch Mgr*
Bob O'Brien, *Manager*
EMP: 90
SALES (corp-wide): 402.6MM **Privately Held**
WEB: www.quantum.com
SIC: 3572 Computer storage devices
PA: Quantum Corporation
　224 Airport Pkwy Ste 550
　San Jose CA 95110
　408 944-4000

(P-15082)
QUANTUM DYNASTY
Also Called: Urban Empire
5934 Rancho Mission Rd # 118, San Diego (92108-2578)
PHONE..................................347 469-1047
Milton Symister, *President*
David Symister, *Vice Pres*
EMP: 10
SALES (est): 1.2MM **Privately Held**
SIC: 3572 Computer storage devices

(P-15083)
QUANTUM PERFORMANCE DEVELOPMEN
32537 Jean Dr, Union City (94587-5017)
PHONE..................................510 870-6381
EMP: 13
SALES (est): 2.3MM **Privately Held**
SIC: 3572

(P-15084)
RADIAN MEMORY SYSTEMS INC
5010 N Pkwy Ste 205, Calabasas (91302)
PHONE..................................818 222-4080
Michael Jadon, *CEO*
Yossi Goldfill, *Software Engr*
Brian Dexheimer, *Director*
Ted Samford, *Director*
EMP: 26 EST: 2011
SALES: 10MM **Privately Held**
SIC: 3572 Computer storage devices

(P-15085)
RANK TECHNOLOGY CORP
1190 Miraloma Way Ste Q, Sunnyvale (94085-4607)
PHONE..................................408 737-1488
Fred Barez, *President*
Henry Barez, *Vice Pres*
EMP: 29
SQ FT: 6,000
SALES (est): 5.1MM **Privately Held**
SIC: 3572 Computer storage devices

(P-15086)
SACHS & ASSOCIATES INC
1230 Rosecrans Ave # 408, Manhattan Beach (90266-2436)
PHONE..................................310 356-7911
Greg T Sachs, *President*
EMP: 10
SALES (est): 1MM **Privately Held**
SIC: 3572 .7379 Computer storage devices;

(P-15087)
SALE 121 CORP (PA)
1467 68th Ave, Sacramento (95822-4728)
P.O. Box 190969, Brooklyn NY (11219-0969)
PHONE..................................888 233-7667
Mohammad Naz, *Principal*
EMP: 99

SQ FT: 3,500
SALES (est): 3.5MM **Privately Held**
SIC: 3572 8748 7373 Disk drives, computer; systems engineering consultant, ex. computer or professional; systems software development services; office computer automation systems integration; turnkey vendors, computer systems

(P-15088)
SANDISK LLC
1101 Sandisk Dr Bldg 5, Milpitas (95035-7936)
PHONE..................................408 801-2928
Michael Marks, *Principal*
Francis Jang, *Sr Software Eng*
Aman Joshi, *Manager*
EMP: 10
SALES (corp-wide): 16.5B **Publicly Held**
SIC: 3572 Computer storage devices
HQ: Sandisk Llc
　951 Sandisk Dr
　Milpitas CA 95035
　408 801-1000

(P-15089)
SANDISK LLC (DH)
Also Called: Western Digital
951 Sandisk Dr, Milpitas (95035-7933)
PHONE..................................408 801-1000
Sanjay Mehrotra, *President*
Michael Marks, *Ch of Bd*
Judy Bruner, *CFO*
John Joy, *Treasurer*
Sumit Sadana, *Exec VP*
▲ EMP: 141
SQ FT: 589,000
SALES (est): 1.9B
SALES (corp-wide): 16.5B **Publicly Held**
WEB: www.sdcard.com
SIC: 3572 Computer storage devices

(P-15090)
SANDISK LLC
Also Called: Ess Division
630 Alder Dr Ste 202, Milpitas (95035-7435)
PHONE..................................408 321-0320
Greg Goles, *Manager*
EMP: 80
SALES (corp-wide): 16.5B **Publicly Held**
SIC: 3572 Computer storage devices
HQ: Sandisk Llc
　951 Sandisk Dr
　Milpitas CA 95035
　408 801-1000

(P-15091)
SAP AG
3410 Hillview Ave, Palo Alto (94304-1395)
PHONE..................................650 849-4000
John Schwarz, *CEO*
Shane Paladin, *Partner*
Lori Mitchell-Keller, *Senior VP*
Claudius Link, *Vice Pres*
David Osborne, *Vice Pres*
EMP: 167
SALES (est): 17.1MM **Privately Held**
SIC: 3572 Computer storage devices

(P-15092)
SCALITY INC
555 California St # 3050, San Francisco (94104-1546)
PHONE..................................650 356-8500
Jerome Lecat, *President*
Erwan Menard, *COO*
Philippe Mechanick, *CFO*
Paul Turner, *Chief Mktg Ofcr*
Hiromasa Ebi, *Vice Pres*
EMP: 45 EST: 2010
SALES (est): 12.2MM
SALES (corp-wide): 16.4MM **Privately Held**
SIC: 3572 Computer storage devices
PA: Scality
　11 Rue Tronchet
　Paris 8e Arrondissement 75008
　142 948-470

(P-15093)
SEAGATE SYSTEMS (US) INC (DH)
Also Called: Xyratex
46831 Lakeview Blvd, Fremont (94538-6552)
PHONE..................................510 687-5200
Steve J Luczo, *Principal*
Ernest Sampias, *CEO*
Richard Pearce, *CFO*
Ken Claffey, *Senior VP*
Todd Gresham, *Senior VP*
▲ EMP: 70
SALES (est): 48.9MM **Privately Held**
SIC: 3572 Disk drives, computer
HQ: Seagate Technology Llc
　10200 S De Anza Blvd
　Cupertino CA 95014
　408 658-1000

(P-15094)
SEAGATE TECHNOLOGY LLC
10042 Wolf Rd, Grass Valley (95949-8192)
PHONE..................................530 410-6594
Martin Furuhjelm, *Principal*
EMP: 240 **Privately Held**
SIC: 3572 Computer storage devices
HQ: Seagate Technology Llc
　10200 S De Anza Blvd
　Cupertino CA 95014
　408 658-1000

(P-15095)
SEAGATE TECHNOLOGY LLC (DH)
10200 S De Anza Blvd, Cupertino (95014-3029)
P.O. Box 4030 (95015-4030)
PHONE..................................408 658-1000
Stephen J Luczo, *President*
Terry Cunningham, *President*
Robert Whitemore, *COO*
Robert Whitmore, *COO*
David A Wickershm, *COO*
▲ EMP: 3000
SQ FT: 383,000
SALES (est): 7.1B **Privately Held**
SIC: 3572 Computer storage devices
HQ: Seagate Technology (Us) Holdings, Inc.
　10200 S De Anza Blvd
　Cupertino CA 95014
　831 438-6550

(P-15096)
SEAGATE TECHNOLOGY LLC
Also Called: Seagate Systems
47488 Kato Rd, Fremont (94538-7319)
PHONE..................................510 624-3728
James Smith, *Manager*
Nelson Gines, *Engineer*
Mark Wojtasiak, *Marketing Staff*
Shail Khiyara, *Products*
EMP: 37 **Privately Held**
SIC: 3572 Computer storage devices
HQ: Seagate Technology Llc
　10200 S De Anza Blvd
　Cupertino CA 95014
　408 658-1000

(P-15097)
SEAGATE TECHNOLOGY LLC
10200 S De Anza Blvd, Cupertino (95014-3029)
PHONE..................................405 324-4799
Alan Shugart, *Branch Mgr*
Fred Zellinger, *Administration*
Brian Schutz, *Business Anlyst*
Gangadhar Moganti, *Analyst*
Candy Pritchard, *Director*
EMP: 11 **Privately Held**
SIC: 3572 Disk drives, computer
HQ: Seagate Technology Llc
　10200 S De Anza Blvd
　Cupertino CA 95014
　408 658-1000

(P-15098)
SEAGATE US LLC
10200 S De Anza Blvd, Cupertino (95014-3029)
PHONE..................................408 658-1000
Stephen J Luczo, *CEO*
EMP: 10

SALES (est): 1.9MM **Privately Held**
SIC: 3572 Magnetic storage devices, computer
PA: Seagate Technology Public Limited Company
　38/39 Fitzwilliam Square West
　Dublin 2

(P-15099)
SHAXON INDUSTRIES INC
4852 E La Palma Ave, Anaheim (92807-1911)
PHONE..................................714 779-1140
Benjamin S Wang, *CEO*
Gilbert Wang, *President*
Thien Cao, *Purch Mgr*
Rick Trask, *Sales Mgr*
Tam Le, *Sales Staff*
▲ EMP: 70
SQ FT: 30,000
SALES (est): 17.1MM **Privately Held**
WEB: www.shaxon.com
SIC: 3572 5045 3678 3661 Computer storage devices; computers & accessories, personal & home entertainment; electronic connectors; telephone & telegraph apparatus; pressed & blown glass

(P-15100)
SHOP4TECHCOM
Also Called: Leda Multimedia
13745 Seminole Dr, Chino (91710-5515)
PHONE..................................909 248-2725
Danny Wang, *President*
Dennis Nguyen, *Info Tech Dir*
Camie Chou, *Manager*
EMP: 45
SQ FT: 25,500
SALES (est): 5.9MM **Privately Held**
SIC: 3572 5731 Computer tape drives & components; video recorders, players, disc players & accessories
PA: Plc Multimedia, Inc.
　1226 E Lexington Ave
　Pomona CA 91766
　909 248-2680

(P-15101)
SILICON TECH INC
Also Called: Silicontech
3009 Daimler St, Santa Ana (92705-5812)
PHONE..................................949 476-1130
Manouch Moshayedi, *CEO*
Mark Moshayedi, *President*
Mike Moshayedi, *President*
EMP: 150
SALES (est): 7.7MM
SALES (corp-wide): 16.5B **Publicly Held**
SIC: 3572 Computer storage devices
HQ: Stec, Inc.
　3355 Michelson Dr Ste 100
　Irvine CA 92612
　415 222-9996

(P-15102)
SMART STORAGE SYSTEMS INC (DH)
39672 Eureka Dr, Newark (94560-4805)
PHONE..................................510 623-1231
Iain Mackenzie, *CEO*
Alan Marten, *President*
Ann T Nguyen, *CFO*
▲ EMP: 15 EST: 1985
SALES (est): 6.4MM
SALES (corp-wide): 16.5B **Publicly Held**
SIC: 3572 5045 Computer storage devices; computers, peripherals & software
HQ: Sandisk Llc
　951 Sandisk Dr
　Milpitas CA 95035
　408 801-1000

(P-15103)
SOLID DATA SYSTEMS INC
3542 Bassett St, Santa Clara (95054-2704)
P.O. Box 320095, Los Gatos (95032-0101)
PHONE..................................408 845-5700
EMP: 15
SQ FT: 3,500
SALES (est): 2.4MM **Privately Held**
WEB: www.soliddata.com
SIC: 3572

(P-15104)
STEC INC (HQ)
3355 Michelson Dr Ste 100, Irvine
(92612-5694)
PHONE....................415 222-9996
Stephen D Milligan, *President*
Faheem Hayat, *President*
▲ EMP: 340
SQ FT: 73,100
SALES (est): 70.3MM
SALES (corp-wide): 16.5B **Publicly Held**
WEB: www.stec-inc.com
SIC: 3572 3674 3577 Computer storage
devices; semiconductors & related de-
vices; computer peripheral equipment
PA: Western Digital Corporation
5601 Great Oaks Pkwy
San Jose CA 95119
408 717-6000

(P-15105)
SYNAPSENSE CORPORATION
340 Palladio Pkwy Ste 530, Folsom
(95630-8833)
PHONE....................916 294-0110
Bart Tichelman, *President*
Dr Raju Pandey, *CTO*
EMP: 11
SALES (est): 2.4MM
SALES (corp-wide): 1.2B **Privately Held**
SIC: 3572 Computer storage devices
PA: Panduit Corp.
18900 Panduit Dr
Tinley Park IL 60487
708 532-1800

(P-15106)
SYPRIS DATA SYSTEMS INC
(HQ)
160 Via Verde, San Dimas (91773-3901)
PHONE....................909 962-9400
Darrell Robertson, *President*
▲ EMP: 50 EST: 1957
SQ FT: 30,000
SALES (est): 178.6MM
SALES (corp-wide): 87.9MM **Publicly
Held**
SIC: 3572 3651 Computer tape drives &
components; tape recorders: cassette,
cartridge or reel: household use
PA: Sypris Solutions, Inc.
101 Bullitt Ln Ste 450
Louisville KY 40222
502 329-2000

(P-15107)
SYSTEMS UPGRADE INC
806 Avenida Pico Ste I, San Clemente
(92673-5693)
PHONE....................949 429-8900
Deborah Allen, *President*
Robert Allen, *Vice Pres*
EMP: 12
SQ FT: 2,500
SALES (est): 2MM **Privately Held**
WEB: www.systemupgrade.com
SIC: 3572 Disk drives, computer

(P-15108)
TEKRAM USA INC
14228 Albers Way, Chino (91710-6940)
PHONE....................714 961-0800
Woon Yei Kou, *President*
Kenny Ngo, *Manager*
▲ EMP: 10
SALES (est): 1.3MM **Privately Held**
SIC: 3572 Computer storage devices

(P-15109)
TERADATA CORPORATION (PA)
17095 Via Del Campo, San Diego
(92127-1711)
PHONE....................866 548-8348
Oliver Ratzesberger, *President*
William Stavropoulos, *Bd of Directors*
Eric Tom, *Officer*
Suzanne Zoumaras, *Officer*
Robert Fair, *Exec VP*
EMP: 277
SALES: 2.1B **Publicly Held**
WEB: www.teradata.com
SIC: 3572 7372 7371 3571 Computer
storage devices; disk drives, computer;
prepackaged software; application com-
puter software; software programming ap-
plications; mainframe computers

(P-15110)
TOTAL PHASE INC
2350 Mission College Blvd # 1100, Santa
Clara (95054-1532)
PHONE....................408 850-6500
Gil Ben-Dov, *CEO*
Annie Lu, *Technical Staff*
EMP: 16
SQ FT: 7,300
SALES (est): 1.3MM **Privately Held**
SIC: 3572 Computer storage devices

(P-15111)
TYPEHAUS INC
2262 Rutherford Rd # 103, Carlsbad
(92008-8818)
PHONE....................760 334-3555
Nicole Gasperoni, *President*
EMP: 15
SALES: 10MM **Privately Held**
SIC: 3572 Computer storage devices

(P-15112)
US CRITICAL LLC (PA)
Also Called: US Critical
6 Orchard Ste 150, Lake Forest
(92630-8352)
PHONE....................949 916-9326
Thomas Horton, *Director*
John Lightman, *CEO*
Kurt Dunteman, *Vice Pres*
Angela Lunt, *Opers Mgr*
EMP: 24
SQ FT: 12,000
SALES (est): 64.1MM **Privately Held**
WEB: www.uscritical.com
SIC: 3572 Computer disk & drum drives &
components

(P-15113)
US CRITICAL LLC
25422 Trabuco Rd 320, Lake Forest
(92630-2791)
PHONE....................800 884-8945
Thomas Horton, *Director*
EMP: 41
SALES (corp-wide): 64.1MM **Privately
Held**
SIC: 3572 Computer disk & drum drives &
components
PA: U.S. Critical, Llc
6 Orchard Ste 150
Lake Forest CA 92630
949 916-9326

(P-15114)
WESTERN DIGITAL
CORPORATION (PA)
5601 Great Oaks Pkwy, San Jose
(95119-1003)
PHONE....................408 717-6000
Matthew E Massengill, *Ch of Bd*
Michael D Cordano, *President*
Srinivasan Sivaram, *President*
Stephen D Milligan, *CEO*
Robert K Eulau, *CFO*
▲ EMP: 1158 EST: 1970
SQ FT: 2,750,000
SALES: 16.5B **Publicly Held**
WEB: www.wdc.com
SIC: 3572 Disk drives, computer

(P-15115)
WESTERN DIGITAL TECH INC
(HQ)
Also Called: WD
5601 Great Oaks Pkwy, San Jose
(95119-1003)
PHONE....................949 672-7000
Stephen D Milligan, *CEO*
John F Coyne, *President*
John Sawyer, *President*
Michael D Cordano, *COO*
Olivier C Leonetti, *CFO*
▲ EMP: 4300
SQ FT: 257,000
SALES (est): 4.5B
SALES (corp-wide): 16.5B **Publicly Held**
WEB: www.wdc.com
SIC: 3572 Disk drives, computer
PA: Western Digital Corporation
5601 Great Oaks Pkwy
San Jose CA 95119
408 717-6000

(P-15116)
ZADARA STORAGE INC
9245 Research Drv Irvine, Irvine (92618)
PHONE....................949 251-0360
Nelson Nahum, *CEO*
Nir Ben Zvi, *COO*
Scott Hebert, *Officer*
Yair Hershko, *Vice Pres*
Doug Jury, *Vice Pres*
▲ EMP: 42
SQ FT: 11,000
SALES (est): 9.7MM **Privately Held**
SIC: 3572 Computer storage devices

3575 Computer Terminals

(P-15117)
ACCO BRANDS USA LLC
Kensington Computer Pdts Group
1500 Fashion Island Blvd # 300, San Mateo
(94404-1597)
PHONE....................650 572-2700
Patty Coffee, *Branch Mgr*
Bill De Meulenaere, *Vice Pres*
John Angeles, *Program Mgr*
David Miller, *Accountant*
Michael Zhang, *Sales Mgr*
EMP: 100
SALES (corp-wide): 1.9B **Publicly Held**
WEB: www.accobrands.com
SIC: 3575 Keyboards, computer, office ma-
chine
HQ: Acco Brands Usa Llc
4 Corporate Dr
Lake Zurich IL 60047
800 222-6462

(P-15118)
ADVANCED DIGITAL RESEARCH
INC
1813 E Dyer Rd Ste 410, Santa Ana
(92705-5731)
PHONE....................949 252-1055
Dennis Childs, *President*
Robert Lasnik, *Vice Pres*
EMP: 10
SQ FT: 1,000
SALES (est): 1.2MM **Privately Held**
WEB: www.adrco.com
SIC: 3575 Computer terminals, monitors &
components

(P-15119)
AG NEOVO TECHNOLOGY
CORP
2362 Qume Dr Ste A, San Jose
(95131-1841)
PHONE....................408 321-8210
Phillip Chang, *President*
Judy Sun, *Finance Mgr*
Tristram Borgmann, *Sales Executive*
David Meng, *Sales Dir*
Curtis Liu, *Sales Mgr*
▲ EMP: 18 EST: 1999
SALES (est): 3.6MM **Privately Held**
WEB: www.neovo-usa.com
SIC: 3575 Computer terminals, monitors &
components
PA: Associated Industries China, Inc.
5f-1, No. 3-1, Park St.
Taipei City TAP 11503
-

(P-15120)
BARCO INC
1421 Mccarthy Blvd, Milpitas (95035-7433)
PHONE....................510 490-1005
EMP: 15
SALES (corp-wide): 771.7MM **Privately
Held**
SIC: 3575 3577 Computer terminals, mon-
itors & components; computer peripheral
equipment
HQ: Barco, Inc.
3059 Premiere Pkwy # 400
Duluth GA 30097
678 475-8000

(P-15121)
CYBERNETIC MICRO SYSTEMS
INC
3000 La Honda Rd, San Gregorio
(94074-9839)
P.O. Box 3000 (94074-3000)
PHONE....................650 726-3000
Edwin E Klingman, *President*
Karen Moty, *Treasurer*
EMP: 11
SQ FT: 6,960
SALES (est): 1.4MM **Privately Held**
WEB: www.controlchips.com
SIC: 3575 7371 Computer terminals, mon-
itors & components; computer software
development

(P-15122)
DIAMANTI INC
111 N Market St Ste 800, San Jose
(95113-1102)
PHONE....................408 645-5111
Tom Barton, *CEO*
Karthik Govindhasamy, *COO*
Mark Balch, *Vice Pres*
Arvind Gupta, *Technical Staff*
EMP: 41
SALES: 9.6MM **Privately Held**
SIC: 3575 Keyboards, computer, office ma-
chine

(P-15123)
HPE GOVERNMENT LLC
46600 Landing Pkwy, Fremont
(94538-6420)
PHONE....................916 435-9200
Pamela Jensen, *Branch Mgr*
EMP: 100
SALES (corp-wide): 30.8B **Publicly Held**
SIC: 3575 3572 7371 7378 Computer
terminals; computer storage devices; custom computer programming services;
computer maintenance & repair; electronic computers
HQ: Hpe Government, Llc.
420 Natl Bus Pkwy Ste 180
Annapolis Junction MD 20701
301 572-1980

(P-15124)
IMC NETWORKS CORP (PA)
25531 Commercentre Dr, Lake Forest
(92630-8873)
PHONE....................949 465-3000
Jerry Roby, *Ch of Bd*
Michael Dailey, *President*
▲ EMP: 32
SQ FT: 35,000
SALES (est): 7.2MM **Privately Held**
WEB: www.imcnetworks.com
SIC: 3575 3577 Computer terminals, mon-
itors & components; computer peripheral
equipment

(P-15125)
INFORMER COMPUTER
SYSTEMS
12711 Western Ave, Garden Grove
(92841-4016)
PHONE....................714 899-2049
EMP: 10
SQ FT: 14,000
SALES (est): 1.7MM **Privately Held**
WEB: www.informer911.com
SIC: 3575

(P-15126)
JUPITER SYSTEMS LLC
Also Called: Infocus Jupiter
31015 Huntwood Ave, Hayward
(94544-7007)
PHONE....................510 675-1000
Jack Klingelhofer, *Ch of Bd*
Eric Wogsberg, *President*
Bob Worthington, *CFO*
Robert Worthington, *CFO*
Daniel Lecour, *Vice Pres*
▲ EMP: 65
SQ FT: 33,000
SALES (est): 15.2MM **Privately Held**
WEB: www.jupiter.com
SIC: 3575 Computer terminals

HQ: Infocus Corporation
13190 Sw 68th Pkwy # 200
Portland OR 97223
503 207-4700

(P-15127)
KEY SOURCE INTERNATIONAL (PA)
7711 Oakport St, Oakland (94621-2026)
PHONE..................................510 562-5000
Robert A D Schwartz, *President*
Thil Brunl, *Vice Pres*
Phil Bruno, *Vice Pres*
Kelly Chen, *Executive*
Paul Schwartz, *CTO*
▲ EMP: 10
SALES (est): 2MM **Privately Held**
WEB: www.ksikeyboards.com
SIC: 3575 3993 2671 Keyboards, computer, office machine; signs & advertising specialties; packaging paper & plastics film, coated & laminated

(P-15128)
LANSTREETCOM
Also Called: Tricir Technologies
17050 Evergreen Pl, City of Industry
(91745-1819)
PHONE..................................626 964-2000
Michael Jen, *President*
EMP: 20
SALES: 8MM **Privately Held**
WEB: www.lanstreet.com
SIC: 3575 Computer terminals, monitors & components

(P-15129)
LIKOM CASEWORKS USA INC (DH)
17890 Castleton St # 309, City of Industry
(91748-6789)
P.O. Box 370070, El Paso TX (79937-0070)
PHONE..................................210 587-7824
Kim Ming Chow, *CEO*
◆ EMP: 26 EST: 1999
SALES (est): 12.8MM
SALES (corp-wide): 355.1MM **Privately Held**
SIC: 3575 3469 Computer terminals, monitors & components; metal stampings
HQ: Likom Caseworks Sdn. Bhd.
19401-1 Jalan Ttc 12
Melaka MLC 75260
633 456-66

(P-15130)
MOTOROLA SOLUTIONS INC
6001 Shellmound St Fl 4th, Emeryville
(94608-1968)
PHONE..................................510 420-7400
EMP: 26
SALES (corp-wide): 5.7B **Publicly Held**
SIC: 3575
PA: Motorola Solutions, Inc.
1303 E Algonquin Rd
Schaumburg IL 60661
847 576-5000

(P-15131)
N-SYNCH TECHNOLOGIES
30100 Town Center Dr 0-204, Laguna
Niguel (92677-2064)
PHONE..................................949 218-7761
Tim Burke, *President*
Annamaria Burke, *Admin Sec*
EMP: 11
SQ FT: 11,000
SALES (est): 1.5MM **Privately Held**
WEB: www.n-synch.com
SIC: 3575 5045 Computer terminals, monitors & components; computer software

(P-15132)
OCP GROUP INC
7130 Engineer Rd, San Diego
(92111-1422)
PHONE..................................858 279-7400
Neil Gleason, *President*
Tracy Sommer, *CEO*
Stan Walker, *Controller*
Leo Sanchez, *Purchasing*
Treacy Sommer, *Director*
▲ EMP: 22

SALES (est): 5.6MM **Privately Held**
SIC: 3575 5051 7549 Computer terminals, monitors & components; cable, wire; automotive maintenance services

(P-15133)
R G B DISPLAY CORPORATION
22525 Kingston Ln, Grass Valley
(95949-7706)
PHONE..................................530 268-2222
Lori Mc Laughlin, *President*
Michelle Hilger, *CFO*
Joan Mc Laughlin, *Corp Secy*
Mike Newman, *Engineer*
EMP: 12 EST: 1978
SQ FT: 14,000
SALES (est): 2.9MM **Privately Held**
WEB: www.rgbdisplay.com
SIC: 3575 Computer terminals, monitors & components

(P-15134)
SGB ENTERPRISES INC
24844 Anza Dr Ste A, Valencia
(91355-1286)
PHONE..................................661 294-8306
Joseph Padula, *President*
Chuck Burkholder, *CFO*
Marvin Beiter, *General Mgr*
Tom Coleman, *Chief Engr*
EMP: 22
SQ FT: 9,600
SALES (est): 7.3MM **Privately Held**
WEB: www.sgbent.com
SIC: 3575 5999 3728 3699 Cathode ray tube (CRT), computer terminal; training materials, electronic; aircraft training equipment; flight simulators (training aids), electronic

(P-15135)
SMK MANUFACTURING INC
1055 Tierra Del Rey Ste H, Chula Vista
(91910-7875)
PHONE..................................619 216-6400
Tetsuya Nakamura, *CEO*
Mathoru Hurukawa, *CFO*
Naomasa Miyata, *Vice Pres*
▲ EMP: 50
SQ FT: 14,688
SALES (est): 22.7MM **Privately Held**
SIC: 3575 Keyboards, computer, office machine
HQ: Smk Electronics Corporation Usa
1055 Tierra Del Rey Ste H
Chula Vista CA 91910
619 216-6400

(P-15136)
TAICOM INTERNATIONAL INC
4241 Business Center Dr A, Fremont
(94538-6302)
PHONE..................................510 656-9200
David Chou, *President*
EMP: 10
SALES (est): 78.5K **Privately Held**
WEB: www.taicom.com
SIC: 3575 7371 Keyboards, computer, office machine; computer software development

(P-15137)
TRANSPARENT PRODUCTS INC
28064 Avenue Stanford E, Valencia
(91355-1160)
PHONE..................................661 294-9787
Fred Bonyadian, *President*
John McVay, *President*
Brenda Captol, *Manager*
▲ EMP: 50
SQ FT: 18,000
SALES (est): 15.3MM **Privately Held**
WEB: www.touchpage.com
SIC: 3575 7371 Computer terminals, monitors & components; computer software systems analysis & design, custom

(P-15138)
WIDE USA CORPORATION
2210 E Winston Rd, Anaheim
(92806-5536)
PHONE..................................714 300-0540
Is Kang, *President*
Hyo Sung Lee, *Exec VP*
▲ EMP: 30
SQ FT: 8,700

SALES: 550K **Privately Held**
SIC: 3575 Computer terminals, monitors & components

3577 Computer Peripheral Eqpt, NEC

(P-15139)
3DCONNEXION INC
6505 Kaiser Dr, Fremont (94555-3614)
PHONE..................................510 713-6000
Rory Dooley, *President*
James V McCanna, *CFO*
Lew Epstein, *Vice Pres*
Niraj Swarup, *Vice Pres*
EMP: 71 EST: 2001
SALES (est): 5.4MM
SALES (corp-wide): 2.7B **Privately Held**
WEB: www.3dconnexion.com
SIC: 3577 5045 Computer peripheral equipment; computers & accessories, personal & home entertainment
HQ: Logitech Inc.
7700 Gateway Blvd
Newark CA 94560
510 795-8500

(P-15140)
ACCES I/O PRODUCTS INC
10623 Roselle St, San Diego (92121-1506)
PHONE..................................858 550-9559
John Persidok, *President*
Michael Pendleton, *Info Tech Mgr*
Roland Samson, *Design Engr*
Ellen Jing, *Accounting Mgr*
Stacy Mason, *Prdtn Mgr*
EMP: 17
SQ FT: 9,447
SALES (est): 6.2MM **Privately Held**
WEB: www.accesio.com
SIC: 3577 Computer peripheral equipment

(P-15141)
ACCURITE TECHNOLOGIES INC
15732 Los Gatos Blvd, Los Gatos
(95032-2504)
PHONE..................................408 395-7100
EMP: 10
SALES (est): 1.3MM **Privately Held**
WEB: www.accurite.com
SIC: 3577

(P-15142)
ACECAD INC
791 Foam St Ste 200, Monterey
(93940-1031)
P.O. Box 1071 (93942-1071)
PHONE..................................831 655-1900
Todd Waldman, *President*
Megan Connolly, *Mktg Dir*
▲ EMP: 12
SQ FT: 4,500
SALES (est): 1.5MM **Privately Held**
SIC: 3577 5045 Computer peripheral equipment; computers, peripherals & software

(P-15143)
ACER AMERICAN HOLDINGS CORP (DH)
333 W San Carlos St # 1500, San Jose
(95110-2726)
PHONE..................................408 533-7700
Emmanuel Fromont, *CEO*
J T Wang, *CEO*
Jon Chandler, *Telecomm Mgr*
Richard Hayden, *Sales Staff*
EMP: 14
SQ FT: 232,000
SALES (est): 329.2MM **Privately Held**
SIC: 3577 3571 Computer peripheral equipment; electronic computers

(P-15144)
ACTIVEWIRE INC
1799 Silacci Dr, Campbell (95008-5130)
P.O. Box 60280, Palo Alto (94306-0280)
PHONE..................................650 465-4000
Mato Hatori, *Branch Mgr*
EMP: 14
SALES (corp-wide): 1.2MM **Privately Held**
SIC: 3577 Computer peripheral equipment

PA: Activewire, Inc.
895 Commercial St Ste 700
Palo Alto CA 94303
650 969-4000

(P-15145)
ACUANT INC (HQ)
Also Called: Card Scanning Solutions
6080 Center Dr Ste 850, Los Angeles
(90045-9229)
PHONE..................................213 867-2621
Yossi Zekri, *President*
Jacob Obrien, *Partner*
Robert Taylor, *Partner*
Bruce Ackerman, *Exec VP*
Iuval Hatzav, *Exec VP*
▲ EMP: 25
SALES (est): 4.3MM
SALES (corp-wide): 30MM **Privately Held**
SIC: 3577 Optical scanning devices
PA: Audax Management Company, Llc
101 Huntington Ave Fl 23
Boston MA 02199
617 859-1500

(P-15146)
ADD-ON COMPUTER PERIPHERAL INC
15775 Gateway Cir, Tustin (92780-6470)
PHONE..................................949 546-8200
James Patton, *CEO*
Matthew McCormick, *Vice Pres*
Kim Couch, *Purchasing*
Denise Gonzalez, *Opers Staff*
Brent Loomis,
▲ EMP: 130
SQ FT: 11,000
SALES (est): 17.1MM **Privately Held**
WEB: www.addoncomputer.com
SIC: 3577 5045 Computer peripheral equipment; computers, peripherals & software

(P-15147)
ADDICE INC (PA)
19977 Harrison Ave, City of Industry
(91789-2848)
PHONE..................................626 617-7779
Hsing Yueh Chang, *CEO*
▲ EMP: 10
SALES (est): 3.4MM **Privately Held**
SIC: 3577 Computer output to microfilm units

(P-15148)
ADVANCE MODULAR TECHNOLOGY INC
Also Called: A M T
2075 Bering Dr Ste C, San Jose
(95131-2011)
PHONE..................................408 453-9880
Crispian SOO, *President*
Pauline SOO, *Vice Pres*
▲ EMP: 14
SALES (est): 3.5MM **Privately Held**
WEB: www.amchip.com
SIC: 3577 Computer peripheral equipment

(P-15149)
ALCATEL-LUCENT USA INC
2361 Rosecrans Ave # 150, El Segundo
(90245-4916)
PHONE..................................310 297-2620
Marty Sanders, *Principal*
EMP: 12
SALES (corp-wide): 25.8B **Privately Held**
WEB: www.lucent.com
SIC: 3577 Computer peripheral equipment
HQ: Nokia Of America Corporation
600 Mountain Ave Ste 700
New Providence NJ 07974

(P-15150)
ALLEN SARAH &
Also Called: Lightprint Labs
560 Crestlake Dr, San Francisco
(94132-1325)
PHONE..................................415 242-0906
Sarah Allen, *Partner*
Michele Henrion, *Partner*
EMP: 20
SALES (est): 1.9MM **Privately Held**
SIC: 3577 Graphic displays, except graphic terminals

▲ = Import ▼=Export
◆ =Import/Export

(P-15151)
ALLIED TELESIS INC
468 S Abbott Ave, Milpitas (95035-5258)
PHONE..................................408 519-6700
Takayoshi Oshima, *Branch Mgr*
EMP: 70 **Privately Held**
SIC: **3577** Computer peripheral equipment
HQ: Allied Telesis, Inc.
19800 North Creek Pkwy # 100
Bothell WA 98011
408 519-8700

(P-15152)
ALLIED TELESIS INC
3041 Orchard Pkwy, San Jose
(95134-2017)
PHONE..................................408 519-8700
Mike Dunbar, *President*
Benny Barbero, *Engineer*
Craig Van Hook, *Engineer*
Luis Melo, *Senior Engr*
Bob Blazek, *Analyst*
EMP: 34 **Privately Held**
SIC: **3577** Computer peripheral equipment
HQ: Allied Telesis, Inc.
19800 North Creek Pkwy # 100
Bothell WA 98011
408 519-8700

(P-15153)
ALLIED TELESIS INC
3041 Orchard Pkwy, San Jose
(95134-2017)
PHONE..................................408 519-8700
Taki Oshima, *Manager*
Debbie Villanueva, *Partner*
Sultan Cochinwala, *Vice Pres*
Lisa Rosetta, *Vice Pres*
Lisa Thompson, *Vice Pres*
EMP: 20 **Privately Held**
WEB: www.alliedtelesyn.com
SIC: **3577** Computer peripheral equipment
HQ: Allied Telesis, Inc.
19800 North Creek Pkwy # 100
Bothell WA 98011
408 519-8700

(P-15154)
AMAG TECHNOLOGY INC (DH)
20701 Manhattan Pl, Torrance
(90501-1829)
PHONE..................................310 518-2380
Matt Barnette, *Ch of Bd*
N Keith Whitelock, *Ch of Bd*
Robert A Sawyer Jr, *President*
Robert Causee, *CFO*
Gary Thorington-Jones, *Treasurer*
▲ EMP: 50
SQ FT: 24,000
SALES (est): 12.3MM **Privately Held**
WEB: www.amagaccess.com
SIC: **3577** Decoders, computer peripheral
equipment
HQ: G4s Technology Limited
Challenge House
Tewkesbury GLOS GL20
168 429-9400

(P-15155)
ANOVA MICROSYSTEMS INC
173 Santa Rita Ct, Los Altos (94022-1096)
PHONE..................................408 941-1888
Raymond S Chuang, *CEO*
Palm Nyu, *Shareholder*
Chao Huang, *Vice Pres*
Yukon Cherng, *Admin Sec*
Wayne Lu, *Controller*
◆ EMP: 10
SALES (est): 2.2MM **Privately Held**
WEB: www.anova.com
SIC: **3577** 5045 Computer peripheral
equipment; computers & accessories,
personal & home entertainment

(P-15156)
ANTEC INC
47681 Lakeview Blvd, Fremont
(94538-6544)
PHONE..................................510 770-1200
Yih Chung Andrew Lee, *CEO*
Lisa Lin, *Vice Pres*
▲ EMP: 50
SQ FT: 34,000
SALES (est): 10.7MM **Privately Held**
WEB: www.antec-inc.com
SIC: **3577** Computer peripheral equipment

(P-15157)
AOT ELECTRONICS INC
Also Called: Orbit Systems
23172 Alcalde Dr Ste E, Laguna Hills
(92653-1452)
PHONE..................................949 600-6335
Omar Turbi, *President*
Renee Laviolette, *CFO*
◆ EMP: 42
SQ FT: 40,000
SALES (est): 5.6MM **Privately Held**
WEB: www.aotelectronics.com
SIC: **3577** 5065 Printers & plotters; com-
munication equipment; electronic parts

(P-15158)
APRICORN
12191 Kirkham Rd, Poway (92064-6870)
PHONE..................................858 513-2000
Paul Brown, *President*
Michael Gordon, *Vice Pres*
▲ EMP: 29
SQ FT: 21,000
SALES (est): 8.5MM **Privately Held**
WEB: www.apricorn.com
SIC: **3577** 5734 Computer peripheral
equipment; computer & software stores

(P-15159)
ARIES RESEARCH INC
Also Called: Aries Solutions
46750 Fremont Blvd # 107, Fremont
(94538-6573)
P.O. Box 1112, Alamo (94507-7112)
PHONE..................................925 818-1078
Lawrence T Kou, *CEO*
Ilain Kou, *President*
J Bar Houston, *Engineer*
EMP: 11
SQ FT: 8,600
SALES (est): 2.6MM **Privately Held**
SIC: **3577** 3571 Computer peripheral
equipment; electronic computers

(P-15160)
ARUBA NETWORKS INC (HQ)
Also Called: Aruba Networks Cafe
3333 Scott Blvd, Santa Clara (95054-3103)
PHONE..................................408 227-4500
Rishi Varma, *President*
Catherine A Lesjak, *CFO*
Victoria Miranda, *Administration*
Joey Gerodias, *IT/INT Sup*
Lauren Winkelman, *Technology*
EMP: 270
SALES (est): 630.5MM
SALES (corp-wide): 30.8B **Publicly Held**
WEB: www.arubanetworks.com
SIC: **3577** 3663 7371 Computer periph-
eral equipment; mobile communication
equipment; computer software develop-
ment
PA: Hewlett Packard Enterprise Company
6280 America Center Dr
San Jose CA 95002
650 687-5817

(P-15161)
**ASANTE TECHNOLOGIES INC
(PA)**
2223 Oakland Rd, San Jose (95131-1402)
PHONE..................................408 435-8388
Jeff Yuan-Kai Lin, *President*
David Kichar, *COO*
Y C Wang, *Exec VP*
Albert LI, *General Mgr*
Brian Lewis, *Engineer*
EMP: 29
SQ FT: 7,000
SALES (est): 3.3MM **Privately Held**
WEB: www.asante.com
SIC: **3577** Computer peripheral equipment

(P-15162)
ASANTE TECHNOLOGIES INC
673 S Milpitas Blvd # 100, Milpitas
(95035-5446)
PHONE..................................408 435-8388
Carmen Lopez Mngr, *Branch Mgr*
EMP: 16
SALES (corp-wide): 3.3MM **Privately
Held**
SIC: **3577** Computer peripheral equipment

PA: Asante Technologies, Inc.
2223 Oakland Rd
San Jose CA 95131
408 435-8388

(P-15163)
ASANTE TECHNOLOGIES INC
47341 Bayside Pkwy, Fremont
(94538-6574)
PHONE..................................408 435-8388
EMP: 23
SALES (corp-wide): 3.3MM **Privately
Held**
SIC: **3577** Computer peripheral equipment
PA: Asante Technologies, Inc.
2223 Oakland Rd
San Jose CA 95131
408 435-8388

(P-15164)
**AVERMEDIA TECHNOLOGIES
INC**
4038 Clipper Ct, Fremont (94538-6540)
PHONE..................................510 403-0006
Michael Cooke, *President*
▲ EMP: 15
SALES (est): 2.3MM **Privately Held**
SIC: **3577** Computer peripheral equipment
PA: Avermedia Technologies, Inc.
135, Jian 1st Rd.,
New Taipei City TAP 23585

(P-15165)
BAJASYS LLC
9923 Via De La Amistad # 105, San Diego
(92154-7215)
PHONE..................................619 661-0748
Jose Ramirez,
▲ EMP: 13
SALES (est): 1.7MM **Privately Held**
SIC: **3577** Printers, computer

(P-15166)
BARRACUDA NETWORKS INC
5225 Hellyer Ave Ste 150, San Jose
(95138-1088)
PHONE..................................408 342-5400
William D Jenkins Jr, *President*
EMP: 10
SALES (corp-wide): 44.8MM **Privately
Held**
SIC: **3577** Computer peripheral equipment
HQ: Barracuda Networks, Inc.
3175 Winchester Blvd
Campbell CA 95008
408 342-5400

(P-15167)
BDR INDUSTRIES INC
Also Called: Rnd Enterprises
9700 Owensmouth Ave Lbby, Chatsworth
(91311-8073)
PHONE..................................818 341-2112
Scott Riddle, *Branch Mgr*
EMP: 20
SALES (corp-wide): 21.7MM **Privately
Held**
WEB: www.rndcable.com
SIC: **3577** Computer peripheral equipment
PA: B.D.R. Industries, Inc.
820 E Avenue L12
Lancaster CA 93535
661 940-8554

(P-15168)
BERING TECHNOLOGY INC
1608 W Campbell Ave 328, Campbell
(95008-1535)
PHONE..................................408 364-6500
Leung C Lok, *President*
Stephen Sun, *Admin Sec*
Roland F Aquino, *Engineer*
EMP: 45
SALES (est): 6.3MM **Privately Held**
WEB: www.bering.com
SIC: **3577** Computer peripheral equipment

(P-15169)
BEST DATA PRODUCTS INC
Also Called: Diamond Multimedia
21541 Blythe St, Canoga Park
(91304-4910)
PHONE..................................818 534-1414
Bruce Zaman, *President*
Shirley Zaman, *CFO*

Jonh Macalino, *Controller*
▲ EMP: 85
SALES (est): 20.8MM **Privately Held**
WEB: www.bestdata.com
SIC: **3577** Computer peripheral equipment

(P-15170)
BESTEK MANUFACTURING INC
675 Sycamore Dr, Milpitas (95035-7430)
PHONE..................................408 321-8834
Frank Dang, *President*
Tyler Dang, *Director*
EMP: 40
SQ FT: 8,000
SALES (est): 10.3MM **Privately Held**
WEB: www.bestekmfg.com
SIC: **3577** 3679 3672 Computer periph-
eral equipment; harness assemblies for
electronic use: wire or cable; printed cir-
cuit boards

(P-15171)
BIOMETRIC SOLUTIONS LLC
41829 Albrae St Unit 110, Fremont
(94538-3144)
PHONE..................................408 625-7763
Danny Thakkar, *Manager*
EMP: 10
SALES: 60K **Privately Held**
SIC: **3577** Computer peripheral equipment

(P-15172)
BIXOLON AMERICA INC
13705 Cimarron Ave, Gardena
(90249-2463)
PHONE..................................858 764-4580
Chan Young Hwang, *CEO*
Yon H Son, *President*
David Roberts, *Senior VP*
Rosa Jeong, *Accounting Mgr*
Juan Salinas, *Sales Dir*
▲ EMP: 18
SQ FT: 26,000
SALES (est): 3.1MM **Privately Held**
SIC: **3577** Printers, computer
PA: Bixolon Co.,Ltd.
20 Pangyoyeok-Ro 241beon-Gil, Bun-
dang-Gu
Seongnam 13494

(P-15173)
BLACK DIAMOND VIDEO INC
503 Canal Blvd, Richmond (94804-3517)
PHONE..................................510 439-4500
Peter Metcalf, *CEO*
David Martell, *Controller*
▲ EMP: 90
SQ FT: 30,000
SALES: 25MM **Privately Held**
WEB: www.blackdiamondvideo.com
SIC: **3577** 3679 Computer peripheral
equipment; electronic switches
HQ: Steris Corporation
5960 Heisley Rd
Mentor OH 44060
440 354-2600

(P-15174)
BLASTRONIX INC
999 W Highway 4, Murphys (95247)
PHONE..................................209 795-0738
David A Barnes, *President*
Rebecca Barnes, *Vice Pres*
A C Barnes, *Director*
EMP: 10
SQ FT: 2,500
SALES (est): 2.5MM **Privately Held**
WEB: www.blastronix.com
SIC: **3577** 8711 Input/output equipment,
computer; engineering services

(P-15175)
BLUE CEDAR NETWORKS INC
325 Pacific Ave Fl 1, San Francisco
(94111-1711)
PHONE..................................415 329-0401
John Aisien, *CEO*
Jeanne Angelo-Pardo, *CFO*
Chris Ford, *Officer*
EMP: 36 **EST**: 2016
SQ FT: 8,000
SALES (est): 2.3MM **Privately Held**
SIC: **3577** Computer peripheral equipment

PRODUCTS & SVCS

(P-15176)
BO-SHERREL CORPORATION
3340 Tree Swallow Pl, Fremont
(94555-1330)
PHONE..................510 744-3525
Fax: 510 792-0416
EMP: 13 EST: 1976
SQ FT: 2,000
SALES (est): 1.1MM Privately Held
SIC: 3577

(P-15177)
BRAVO COMMUNICATIONS INC
3463 Meadowlands Ln, San Jose
(95135-1645)
PHONE..................408 297-8700
Dennis L Mozingo, President
EMP: 29
SQ FT: 4,000
SALES (est): 3.9MM Privately Held
WEB: www.bravobravo.com
SIC: 3577 3612 Computer peripheral
equipment; transformers, except electric

(P-15178)
**BROCADE CMMNCTIONS
SYSTEMS LLC (DH)**
130 Holger Way, San Jose (95134-1376)
PHONE..................408 333-8000
Hock E Tan, President
Matt Wineberg, Partner
Thomas H Krause Jr, CFO
Jean Samuel Furter, Treasurer
Bimal Tripathi, Surgery Dir
EMP: 800
SQ FT: 562,000
SALES: 2.3B
SALES (corp-wide): 20.8B Publicly Held
WEB: www.brocade.com
SIC: 3577 4813 Computer peripheral
equipment;
HQ: Lsi Corporation
1320 Ridder Park Dr
San Jose CA 95131
408 433-8000

(P-15179)
BRUKER CORPORATION
1717 Dell Ave, Campbell (95008-6904)
PHONE..................408 376-4040
Ingo Schmitz, Senior Engr
EMP: 30
SALES (corp-wide): 1.9B Publicly Held
SIC: 3577 8734 8731 Computer periph-
eral equipment; testing laboratories; com-
mercial physical research
PA: Bruker Corporation
40 Manning Rd
Billerica MA 01821
978 663-3660

(P-15180)
C ENTERPRISES INC
Also Called: C Enterprises, L.P.
2445 Cades Way, Vista (92081-7831)
PHONE..................760 599-5111
Brian Tauber, President
Steven Yamasaki, COO
Bonnie Purtill, Office Admin
Arne Jensen, Mfg Staff
EMP: 64
SQ FT: 36,000
SALES (est): 16.8MM
SALES (corp-wide): 50.2MM Publicly
Held
WEB: www.centerprises.com
SIC: 3577 5045 3357 3229 Computer
peripheral equipment; computers & ac-
cessories, personal & home entertain-
ment; nonferrous wiredrawing &
insulating; pressed & blown glass
PA: Rf Industries, Ltd.
7610 Miramar Rd Ste 6000
San Diego CA 92126
858 549-6340

(P-15181)
**CABLE DEVICES
INCORPORATED (HQ)**
Also Called: Cable Exchange
3008 S Croddy Way, Santa Ana
(92704-6305)
PHONE..................714 554-4370
Marvin S Edwards, CEO
Mark Olson, CFO

Frank B Wyatt, Admin Sec
Yvette Gonzalez, Engineer
Brad Smith, Engineer
▲ EMP: 150
SQ FT: 24,516
SALES: 30MM Publicly Held
WEB: www.4cablex.com
SIC: 3577 Computer peripheral equipment

(P-15182)
CALIFORNIA DIGITAL INC (PA)
6 Saddleback Rd, Rolling Hills
(90274-5141)
P.O. Box 3399, Torrance (90510-3399)
PHONE..................310 217-0500
Terry Reiter, President
Floyd Pothoven, Vice Pres
Wade Wood, Vice Pres
EMP: 82
SQ FT: 30,000
SALES (est): 10MM Privately Held
SIC: 3577 3571 3699 Computer periph-
eral equipment; mainframe computers;
electrical equipment & supplies

(P-15183)
**CALIFORNIA SURVEYING &
DRAFTIN**
411 Russell Ave, Santa Rosa (95403-2219)
PHONE..................707 293-9449
EMP: 17
SALES (corp-wide): 29.7MM Privately
Held
SIC: 3577 5049 Computer peripheral
equipment; surveyors' instruments
PA: California Surveying & Drafting Supply
Inc.
4733 Auburn Blvd
Sacramento CA 95841
916 344-0232

(P-15184)
**CALIFORNIA SURVEYING &
DRAFTIN (PA)**
Also Called: CSDS
4733 Auburn Blvd, Sacramento
(95841-3601)
PHONE..................916 344-0232
Bruce Gandelman, CEO
Mike Woodel, Vice Pres
Dan Soldavini, Principal
EMP: 49
SQ FT: 17,500
SALES: 29.7MM Privately Held
SIC: 3577 7353 3993 5082 Printers &
plotters; heavy construction equipment
rental; displays & cutouts, window &
lobby; general construction machinery &
equipment; printers, computer; drafting
supplies

(P-15185)
CARBON INC
1089 Mills Way, Redwood City
(94063-3119)
PHONE..................650 285-6307
Joseph M Desimone, CEO
Elisa De Martel, CFO
Dara Treseder, Chief Mktg Ofcr
Paul Dilaura, Vice Pres
Heather Miksch, Vice Pres
EMP: 210
SQ FT: 87,000
SALES (est): 1.2MM Privately Held
SIC: 3577 Computer peripheral equipment

(P-15186)
CARDLOGIX
16 Hughes Ste 100, Irvine (92618-1948)
PHONE..................949 380-1312
Walter Lim, Ch of Bd
Bruce Ross, President
Ken Indorf, Vice Pres
Arthur Krause, Vice Pres
Nguyen Anthony, Info Tech Mgr
▲ EMP: 19
SQ FT: 6,000
SALES (est): 4.7MM Privately Held
WEB: www.cardlogic.com
SIC: 3577 3089 Computer peripheral
equipment; panels, building: plastic

(P-15187)
CD ALEXANDER LLC
2802 Willis St, Santa Ana (92705-5714)
P.O. Box 15101 (92735-0101)
PHONE..................949 250-3306
Anthony Gonzalez,
Agustin Hernandez,
EMP: 27
SQ FT: 19,000
SALES (est): 6.5MM Privately Held
WEB: www.cdalexander.com
SIC: 3577 3444 Computer peripheral
equipment; sheet metalwork

(P-15188)
CDC DATA LLC
9735 Lurline Ave, Chatsworth
(91311-4404)
PHONE..................818 350-5070
Joe Varraveto, Mng Member
Ron Ginther, Engineer
▲ EMP: 10
SALES (est): 1.6MM Privately Held
SIC: 3577 Optical scanning devices

(P-15189)
CIPHERTEX LLC
Also Called: Ciphertex Data Security
9301 Jordan Ave Ste 105a, Chatsworth
(91311-5863)
PHONE..................818 773-8989
Jerry Kaner, CEO
Paul Espinosa, Info Tech Dir
Brad Maryman,
Stan Stahl,
▲ EMP: 18
SALES (est): 3.8MM Privately Held
SIC: 3577 3572 Computer peripheral
equipment; computer storage devices

(P-15190)
CISCO SYSTEMS INC
325 E Tasman Dr, San Jose (95134-1405)
PHONE..................408 526-7939
EMP: 691
SALES (corp-wide): 51.9B Publicly Held
SIC: 3577 Data conversion equipment,
media-to-media: computer
PA: Cisco Systems, Inc.
170 W Tasman Dr
San Jose CA 95134
408 526-4000

(P-15191)
CISCO SYSTEMS INC
771 Alder Dr, Milpitas (95035-7927)
PHONE..................408 570-9149
Bill Slime, Manager
Girish Sherikar, Partner
Monica McCarthy, Executive
Himani Mahajan, Sr Software Eng
Hop Le, Software Engr
EMP: 691
SALES (corp-wide): 51.9B Publicly Held
WEB: www.cisco.com
SIC: 3577 7379 Data conversion equip-
ment, media-to-media: computer;
PA: Cisco Systems, Inc.
170 W Tasman Dr
San Jose CA 95134
408 526-4000

(P-15192)
CISCO SYSTEMS INC
500 Terry A Francois Blvd, San Francisco
(94158-2354)
PHONE..................415 837-6261
EMP: 12
SALES (corp-wide): 48B Publicly Held
SIC: 3577
PA: Cisco Systems, Inc.
170 W Tasman Dr
San Jose CA 95134
408 526-4000

(P-15193)
CISCO SYSTEMS INC
3500 Hyland Ave, Costa Mesa
(92626-1469)
PHONE..................714 434-2100
Vu Tran, Director
EMP: 10
SALES (corp-wide): 51.9B Publicly Held
SIC: 3577 Data conversion equipment,
media-to-media: computer

PA: Cisco Systems, Inc.
170 W Tasman Dr
San Jose CA 95134
408 526-4000

(P-15194)
CISCO SYSTEMS INC
121 Theory, Irvine (92617-3209)
PHONE..................408 526-4000
J Pocock, Exec VP
Bob Shutack, Partner
Eric Stevens, Program Mgr
Julie Ivask, Software Dev
Kalyana Karunanidhi, Software Engr
EMP: 691
SALES (corp-wide): 51.9B Publicly Held
SIC: 3577 Data conversion equipment,
media-to-media: computer
PA: Cisco Systems, Inc.
170 W Tasman Dr
San Jose CA 95134
408 526-4000

(P-15195)
CISCO SYSTEMS INC
11 Great Oaks Blvd, San Jose
(95119-1242)
PHONE..................408 225-5248
Kiran Keerthi, Software Engr
Anna Talis, Director
EMP: 678
SALES (corp-wide): 51.9B Publicly Held
SIC: 3577 Data conversion equipment,
media-to-media: computer
PA: Cisco Systems, Inc.
170 W Tasman Dr
San Jose CA 95134
408 526-4000

(P-15196)
CISCO SYSTEMS INC
510 Mccarthy Blvd, Milpitas (95035-7908)
PHONE..................408 526-4000
Helder Antunes, Principal
John Vincent, Administration
Feng Gao, Sr Software Eng
Mallikarjun Jangam, Software Engr
Malini Vijayamohan, Software Engr
EMP: 691
SALES (corp-wide): 51.9B Publicly Held
SIC: 3577 7379 Data conversion equip-
ment, media-to-media: computer;
PA: Cisco Systems, Inc.
170 W Tasman Dr
San Jose CA 95134
408 526-4000

(P-15197)
CISCO SYSTEMS INC
3650 Cisco Way Bldg 17, San Jose
(95134-2205)
PHONE..................408 526-6698
Anthony Perry, Software Engr
Rene Gonzales, Manager
EMP: 649
SALES (corp-wide): 51.9B Publicly Held
SIC: 3577 Computer peripheral equipment
PA: Cisco Systems, Inc.
170 W Tasman Dr
San Jose CA 95134
408 526-4000

(P-15198)
CISCO SYSTEMS INC
4460 Rosewood Dr Ste 100, Pleasanton
(94588-3082)
PHONE..................925 223-1006
Kevin Hodges, Branch Mgr
Yuyang Cao, Software Engr
Eric Ludvigson, Engrg Dir
Michael Dougherty, Technical Staff
Dmitry Kovalev, Engineer
EMP: 691
SALES (corp-wide): 51.9B Publicly Held
WEB: www.cisco.com
SIC: 3577 Data conversion equipment,
media-to-media: computer
PA: Cisco Systems, Inc.
170 W Tasman Dr
San Jose CA 95134
408 526-4000

(P-15199)
CISCO SYSTEMS INC (PA)
170 W Tasman Dr, San Jose (95134-1706)
PHONE..................408 526-4000

Charles H Robbins, *Ch of Bd*
Kelly A Kramer, *CFO*
Stella Low, *Ch Credit Ofcr*
Gerri Elliott, *Chief Mktg Ofcr*
Mark Chandler,
EMP: 700
SALES: 51.9B **Publicly Held**
WEB: www.cisco.com
SIC: 3577 7379 Data conversion equip-
  ment, media-to-media: computer;

(P-15200)
CISCO SYSTEMS INC
3600 Cisco Way, San Jose (95134-2205)
PHONE.....................408 434-1903
John Eira, *Branch Mgr*
Navdeep Johar, *Executive*
Susie Harrison, *Program Mgr*
Denice Rodriguez, *Administration*
Joe Chen, *Software Engr*
EMP: 691
SALES (corp-wide): 51.9B **Publicly Held**
WEB: www.cisco.com
SIC: 3577 Data conversion equipment,
  media-to-media: computer
PA: Cisco Systems, Inc.
  170 W Tasman Dr
  San Jose CA 95134
  408 526-4000

(P-15201)
CISCO SYSTEMS INC
110 W Tasman Dr, San Jose (95134-1700)
PHONE.....................408 424-4050
David Holland, *Manager*
M Christian Mitchell, *Bd of Directors*
Michael Bouchard, *Program Mgr*
Sanjay Purandare, *Program Mgr*
Lin Shen, *Software Dev*
EMP: 7200
SQ FT: 147,000
SALES (corp-wide): 51.9B **Publicly Held**
WEB: www.cisco.com
SIC: 3577 Data conversion equipment,
  media-to-media: computer
PA: Cisco Systems, Inc.
  170 W Tasman Dr
  San Jose CA 95134
  408 526-4000

(P-15202)
CISCO SYSTEMS INC
3700 Cisco Way, San Jose (95134-2206)
PHONE.....................408 526-5999
John T Chambers, *Branch Mgr*
Joe Zhou, *Technical Staff*
EMP: 691
SALES (corp-wide): 51.9B **Publicly Held**
SIC: 3577 Data conversion equipment,
  media-to-media: computer
PA: Cisco Systems, Inc.
  170 W Tasman Dr
  San Jose CA 95134
  408 526-4000

(P-15203)
CISCO TECHNOLOGY INC (HQ)
170 W Tasman Dr, San Jose (95134-1706)
PHONE.....................408 526-4000
Evan Sloves, *CEO*
Marc Briceno, *Vice Pres*
Tony Cox, *Business Dir*
Maria G Cazzaniga, *Admin Asst*
Justin Corlett, *Business Mgr*
EMP: 10
SALES (est): 5MM
SALES (corp-wide): 51.9B **Publicly Held**
SIC: 3577 7379 Data conversion equip-
  ment, media-to-media: computer;
PA: Cisco Systems, Inc.
  170 W Tasman Dr
  San Jose CA 95134
  408 526-4000

(P-15204)
CLICKSCANSHARE INC
3631 Mt Diablo Blvd Ste C, Lafayette
(94549-3788)
PHONE.....................925 283-1400
Eva Dias, *Branch Mgr*
EMP: 30
SALES (corp-wide): 4.1MM **Privately
Held**
SIC: 3577 Data conversion equipment,
  media-to-media: computer

PA: Clickscanshare, Inc.
  8055 Clairemont Mesa Blvd # 101
  San Diego CA 92111
  619 461-5880

(P-15205)
CLICKSCANSHARE INC (PA)
8055 Clairemont Mesa Blvd # 101, San
Diego (92111-1620)
PHONE.....................619 461-5880
Troy Philip Langley, *Principal*
Nick Scalzo, *General Mgr*
Rose Zhao, *Senior Mgr*
Dawn Togami, *Associate*
EMP: 11
SALES (est): 4.1MM **Privately Held**
SIC: 3577 Data conversion equipment,
  media-to-media: computer

(P-15206)
CONVERGENT MANUFACTURING TECH
966 Shulman Ave, Santa Clara
(95050-2822)
PHONE.....................408 987-2770
Kevin C Lettire, *President*
EMP: 12
SQ FT: 5,000
SALES: 4.9MM **Privately Held**
WEB: www.cmt-mtc.com
SIC: 3577 Computer peripheral equipment

(P-15207)
CONVERGING SYSTEMS INC
32420 Nautilus Dr Ste 100, Pls Vrds Pnsl
(90275-6002)
PHONE.....................310 544-2628
Craig Douglass, *President*
EMP: 12
SALES (est): 3MM **Privately Held**
WEB: www.convergingsystems.com
SIC: 3577 3679 Computer peripheral
  equipment; video triggers, except remote
  control TV devices

(P-15208)
CORSAIR COMPONENTS INC (PA)
47100 Bayside Pkwy, Fremont
(94538-6563)
PHONE.....................510 657-8747
Andrew J Paul, *President*
Ronald Van Veen, *Vice Pres*
Jonathan Kuan, *Manager*
EMP: 250
SQ FT: 44,000
SALES (est): 940MM **Privately Held**
SIC: 3577 Computer peripheral equipment

(P-15209)
CPACKET NETWORKS INC
Also Called: Cwr Labs
  2130 Gold St 200, San Jose (95002-3700)
  P.O. Box 430, Alviso (95002-0430)
PHONE.....................650 969-9500
Rony Kay, *CEO*
Brendan O'Flaherty, *Vice Pres*
Juneed Ahamed, *Sr Software Eng*
Jason Blanchard, *Software Engr*
Justin Carr, *Software Engr*
EMP: 22
SALES (est): 7.5MM **Privately Held**
WEB: www.cwrlabs.com
SIC: 3577 Computer peripheral equipment

(P-15210)
CREAFORM USA INC
2031 Main St, Irvine (92614-6509)
PHONE.....................855 939-4446
Martin D Chader, *Manager*
EMP: 10
SALES (est): 1.6MM
SALES (corp-wide): 4.8B **Publicly Held**
SIC: 3577 Optical scanning devices
PA: Ametek, Inc.
  1100 Cassatt Rd
  Berwyn PA 19312
  610 647-2121

(P-15211)
CRITICAL IO LLC
36 Executive Park Ste 150, Irvine
(92614-4715)
PHONE.....................949 553-2200
John Staub, *Mng Member*
Ron Godshalk, *Vice Pres*

Greg Bolstad, *Info Tech Mgr*
Erich Fischer,
Ken Neeld,
EMP: 13
SQ FT: 2,500
SALES (est): 2.8MM **Privately Held**
WEB: www.criticalio.com
SIC: 3577 5045 Computer peripheral
  equipment; computer software

(P-15212)
CS SYSTEMS INC
Also Called: Cs Electronics
  16781 Noyes Ave, Irvine (92606-5123)
PHONE.....................949 475-9100
Christian Schwartz, *President*
Rebecca Martin, *CFO*
Gayle Schwartz, *CFO*
Ray Club, *Administration*
Tim Kiler, *Technical Staff*
▲ **EMP:** 25
SQ FT: 33,200
SALES (est): 5.5MM **Privately Held**
WEB: www.cselex.com
SIC: 3577 3677 Computer peripheral
  equipment; coil windings, electronic

(P-15213)
CYBERDATA CORPORATION
3 Justin Ct, Monterey (93940-5733)
PHONE.....................831 373-2601
Phil Lembo, *President*
▲ **EMP:** 33
SQ FT: 30,000
SALES (est): 6.8MM **Privately Held**
WEB: www.cyberdata.net
SIC: 3577 7379 Computer peripheral
  equipment; computer related consulting
  services

(P-15214)
DELPHI DISPLAY SYSTEMS INC
3550 Hyland Ave, Costa Mesa
(92626-1438)
PHONE.....................714 825-3400
Ken Neeld, *CEO*
Michael Deson, *CEO*
David Skinner, *Vice Pres*
Anita Maldonado, *Accountant*
John Richter, *Manager*
▲ **EMP:** 55 **EST:** 1997
SQ FT: 10,000
SALES (est): 13.9MM **Privately Held**
WEB: www.delphidisplaysystems.com
SIC: 3577 Computer peripheral equipment

(P-15215)
DIGITAL CHECK TECHNOLOGIES INC
10231 Trademark St Ste A, Rancho Cuca-
monga (91730-5821)
PHONE.....................909 204-4638
Thomas P Anderson, *President*
Tom Anderson Jr, *Treasurer*
Glenn Embury, *Vice Pres*
John Gainer, *Admin Sec*
◆ **EMP:** 48
SQ FT: 14,000
SALES (est): 6.5MM **Privately Held**
WEB: www.digitalcheck.com
SIC: 3577 3861 Computer peripheral
  equipment; cameras & related equipment
PA: Digital Check Corp.
  630 Dundee Rd Ste 210
  Northbrook IL 60062

(P-15216)
DIVERSIFIED NANO CORPORATION (PA)
16885 W Bernardo Dr # 275, San Diego
(92127-1618)
PHONE.....................858 673-0387
James Danforth, *President*
▲ **EMP:** 10
SALES (est): 1.4MM **Privately Held**
SIC: 3577 Computer peripheral equipment

(P-15217)
DOCUMENT CAPTURE TECH INC (PA)
41332 Christy St, Fremont (94538-3115)
PHONE.....................408 436-9888
Michael J Campbell, *President*
Richard Dietl, *Ch of Bd*

M Carolyn Ellis, *CFO*
Edward M Straw, *Vice Ch Bd*
Karl Etzel, *Chief Mktg Ofcr*
▲ **EMP:** 25
SQ FT: 32,000
SALES: 17.3MM **Privately Held**
WEB: www.sysviewtech.com
SIC: 3577 Optical scanning devices

(P-15218)
DOUBLESIGHT DISPLAYS INC
2882 Walnut Ave Ste A, Tustin
(92780-7004)
PHONE.....................949 253-1535
Kang Lee, *President*
Dario Dellamaggiore, *General Mgr*
Don Ryu, *Manager*
▲ **EMP:** 10
SQ FT: 2,000
SALES: 2.8MM **Privately Held**
WEB: www.doublesight.com
SIC: 3577 Graphic displays, except
  graphic terminals

(P-15219)
DSS NETWORKS INC
24462 Redlen St, Lake Forest
(92630-3848)
PHONE.....................949 981-3473
Anita Svay, *CEO*
Jerry Marcinko, *President*
Sam Svay, *Vice Pres*
EMP: 15 **EST:** 2000
SQ FT: 4,000
SALES (est): 2MM **Privately Held**
WEB: www.dssnetworks.com
SIC: 3577 Computer peripheral equipment

(P-15220)
E SEEK INC
9471 Ridgehaven Ct Ste E, San Diego
(92123-4357)
PHONE.....................714 832-7980
Larry H Anderson, *President*
Ken Waters, *CEO*
Ali Lebaschi, *Vice Pres*
EMP: 10
SALES (est): 1.1MM **Privately Held**
SIC: 3577 Bar code (magnetic ink) printers

(P-15221)
EFAXCOM (DH)
Also Called: Jetfax
  6922 Hollywood Blvd Fl 5, Los Angeles
  (90028-6125)
PHONE.....................323 817-3207
Ronald Brown, *President*
John H Harris, *Vice Pres*
Gary P Kapner, *Vice Pres*
Dan Gallo, *Risk Mgmt Dir*
Rebecca Conley, *Sales Staff*
EMP: 80
SALES (est): 11MM
SALES (corp-wide): 1.2B **Publicly Held**
WEB: www.efax.com
SIC: 3577 Computer peripheral equipment

(P-15222)
EFAXCOM
Also Called: J2 Global Communications
  5385 Hollister Ave # 208, Santa Barbara
  (93111-2389)
PHONE.....................805 692-0064
Stephen Zendjahas, *Manager*
EMP: 30
SALES (corp-wide): 1.2B **Publicly Held**
WEB: www.efax.com
SIC: 3577 Computer peripheral equipment
HQ: Efax.Com
  6922 Hollywood Blvd Fl 5
  Los Angeles CA 90028
  323 817-3207

(P-15223)
ELECTRONIC RESOURCES NETWORK
Also Called: Tern
  1950 5th St, Davis (95616-4018)
PHONE.....................530 758-0180
Tom Tang, *President*
Ning Lu, *CFO*
Ziqiang Tang, *Vice Pres*
Justin Polanich, *Engineer*
EMP: 15
SQ FT: 6,000

SALES (est): 2.6MM **Privately Held**
WEB: www.tern.com
SIC: 3577 5045 3679 Computer peripheral equipment; computer peripheral equipment; electronic circuits

(P-15224)
EPICOR SOFTWARE CORPORATION
17320 Red Hill Ave # 250, Irvine (92614-5669)
PHONE.....................949 585-4000
Mark Nyquist, *Director*
Bill Wilson, *Vice Pres*
Kevin Torbett, *Sr Software Eng*
Jan Miller, *Technical Staff*
Beth Price, *Marketing Mgr*
EMP: 100 **Publicly Held**
SIC: 3577 5045 Computer peripheral equipment; computers, peripherals & software
HQ: Epicor Software Corporation
804 Las Cimas Pkwy # 200
Austin TX 78746

(P-15225)
EPSON AMERICA INC (DH)
Also Called: Seiko Epson
3840 Kilroy Airport Way, Long Beach (90806-2452)
P.O. Box 93012 (90809-3012)
PHONE.....................800 463-7766
John Lang, *President*
John D Lang, *President*
Agustin Chacon, *Vice Pres*
Mike Isgrig, *Vice Pres*
Genevieve Walker, *Vice Pres*
◆ **EMP:** 510 **EST:** 1975
SQ FT: 163,000
SALES (est): 260.3MM **Privately Held**
WEB: www.presentersonline.com
SIC: 3577 Computer peripheral equipment

(P-15226)
ERICSSON INC
620 Newport Center Dr # 11, Newport Beach (92660-6420)
PHONE.....................949 721-6604
Lucia Garcia, *Branch Mgr*
EMP: 65
SALES (corp-wide): 23.4B **Privately Held**
WEB: www.ericsson.com/us-ca
SIC: 3577 Computer peripheral equipment
HQ: Ericsson Inc.
6300 Legacy Dr
Plano TX 75024
972 583-0000

(P-15227)
EVEREST NETWORKS INC
205 Ravendale Dr, Mountain View (94043-5216)
PHONE.....................408 300-9236
Simon Wright, *CEO*
EMP: 24
SALES (est): 1.4MM **Privately Held**
SIC: 3577 Computer peripheral equipment

(P-15228)
FIRETIDE INC (DH)
2105 S Bascom Ave Ste 220, Campbell (95008-3292)
PHONE.....................408 399-7771
Corry S Hong, *President*
Gordon Lowe, *Partner*
▲ **EMP:** 19
SQ FT: 30,000
SALES (est): 6.8MM
SALES (corp-wide): 508.4MM **Privately Held**
SIC: 3577 3825 4899 Computer peripheral equipment; network analyzers; communication signal enhancement network system
HQ: Unicom Systems Inc.
15535 San Fernando
Mission Hills CA 91345
818 838-0606

(P-15229)
FLEXTRONICS INTL USA INC
927 Gibraltar Dr, Milpitas (95035-6336)
PHONE.....................510 814-7000
EMP: 14

SALES (corp-wide): 26.2B **Privately Held**
SIC: 3577 Graphic displays, except graphic terminals
HQ: Flextronics International Usa, Inc.
6201 America Center Dr
San Jose CA 95002

(P-15230)
FORESEESON CUSTOM DISPLAYS INC (PA)
2210 E Winston Rd, Anaheim (92806-5536)
PHONE.....................714 300-0540
Insik Kang, *President*
Marie Kim, *General Mgr*
Robert Contreras, *Project Mgr*
Robert Tran, *Technology*
Angela Morgan, *Sales Mgr*
▲ **EMP:** 21
SQ FT: 8,000
SALES (est): 4.2MM **Privately Held**
WEB: www.foreseesonusa.com
SIC: 3577 Computer peripheral equipment

(P-15231)
FORTINET INC (PA)
899 Kifer Rd, Sunnyvale (94086-5205)
PHONE.....................408 235-7700
Ken Xie, *Ch of Bd*
Michael Xie, *President*
Keith Jensen, *CFO*
Patrick Chiu, *Vice Pres*
Hemant Jain, *Vice Pres*
▲ **EMP:** 277 **EST:** 2000
SQ FT: 162,000
SALES: 1.8B **Publicly Held**
WEB: www.fortinet.com
SIC: 3577 Computer peripheral equipment

(P-15232)
FUJIFILM DIMATIX INC (HQ)
2250 Martin Ave, Santa Clara (95050-2704)
PHONE.....................408 565-9150
Martin Schoeppler, *President*
Darren Imai, *Vice Pres*
Elizabeth Chabot, *Project Mgr*
Darrell Etter, *Project Mgr*
Laura Doherty, *Technology*
◆ **EMP:** 230
SQ FT: 125,000
SALES (est): 61.9MM **Privately Held**
WEB: www.dimatix.com
SIC: 3577 Printers, computer; readers, sorters or inscribers, magnetic ink

(P-15233)
GDCA INC
1799 Portola Ave Ste 1, Livermore (94551-7947)
PHONE.....................925 456-9900
Ethan Plotkin, *CEO*
Arlin Niernberger, *Engineer*
Kip Kingsland, *Director*
Kaye Porter, *Director*
Corinne Weber, *Director*
EMP: 38
SQ FT: 6,000
SALES (est): 11.1MM **Privately Held**
WEB: www.gdca.com
SIC: 3577 3571 Computer peripheral equipment; electronic computers

(P-15234)
GENOVATION INCORPRATED
17741 Mitchell N, Irvine (92614-6028)
PHONE.....................949 833-3355
Manouchehr Rahimzadeh, *President*
Jeanette Miyata, *Controller*
Barbara Sthrome, *Purch Agent*
▲ **EMP:** 10
SQ FT: 20,000
SALES (est): 2.3MM **Privately Held**
WEB: www.genovation.com
SIC: 3577 7371 Input/output equipment, computer; custom computer programming services

(P-15235)
GIZMAC ACCESSORIES LLC
4025 Spencer St Ste 102, Torrance (90503-2499)
PHONE.....................310 320-5563
Timothy Cave,
▲ **EMP:** 14

SALES (est): 2.4MM **Privately Held**
WEB: www.gizmac.com
SIC: 3577 Computer peripheral equipment

(P-15236)
GOSUB 60
1334 3rd Street Promenade # 309, Santa Monica (90401-1378)
PHONE.....................310 394-4760
Josh Hartwell, *President*
Paul Bolten, *Vice Pres*
EMP: 10
SQ FT: 1,000
SALES (est): 1.3MM **Privately Held**
WEB: www.gosub60.com
SIC: 3577 Computer peripheral equipment

(P-15237)
HALL RESEARCH TECHNOLOGIES LLC (PA)
1163 Warner Ave, Tustin (92780-6458)
PHONE.....................714 641-6607
Ali Haghjoo, *CEO*
Lisa Nguyen, *Exec VP*
Linda Lee, *Accounting Mgr*
Wayne Childs, *Business Mgr*
Coy Veith, *Business Mgr*
◆ **EMP:** 17
SQ FT: 18,200
SALES (est): 9.8MM **Privately Held**
WEB: www.hallresearch.com
SIC: 3577 Computer peripheral equipment

(P-15238)
HANAPS ENTERPRISES
Also Called: Digital Storm
865 Jarvis Dr, Morgan Hill (95037-2858)
PHONE.....................669 235-3810
Paramjit Chana, *CEO*
Surnderjit Chana, *Vice Pres*
Thanh Phan, *General Mgr*
▲ **EMP:** 70
SALES (est): 29.1MM **Privately Held**
SIC: 3577 7379 Computer peripheral equipment; computer related maintenance services

(P-15239)
HUNTER DIGITAL LTD
Also Called: Europian Investment
11999 San Vicente Blvd, Los Angeles (90049-5131)
PHONE.....................310 471-5852
Aaron H Sones, *President*
EMP: 15
SALES (est): 1.6MM **Privately Held**
SIC: 3577 Computer peripheral equipment

(P-15240)
IDENTIV INC (PA)
2201 Walnut Ave Ste 100, Fremont (94538-2334)
PHONE.....................949 250-8888
Steven Humphreys, *CEO*
James E Ousley, *Ch of Bd*
Steven Finney, *CFO*
Sandra Wallach, *CFO*
Phil Montgomery, *Chief Mktg Ofcr*
EMP: 305
SQ FT: 10,935
SALES: 78.1MM **Publicly Held**
WEB: www.scmmicro.com
SIC: 3577 7372 Computer peripheral equipment; prepackaged software

(P-15241)
IMAGING TECHNOLOGIES
15175 Innovation Dr, San Diego (92128-3401)
PHONE.....................858 487-8944
Brian Bonar, *President*
EMP: 10
SALES (est): 1.9MM
SALES (corp-wide): 3.3MM **Publicly Held**
WEB: www.dalrada.com
SIC: 3577 Printers, computer
PA: Dalrada Financial Corporation
11956 Bernardo Plaza Dr
San Diego CA 92128
877 325-7232

(P-15242)
IMMERSION CORPORATION (PA)
50 Rio Robles, San Jose (95134-1806)
PHONE.....................408 467-1900
Carl Schlachte, *CEO*

Tom Lacey, *CEO*
Nancy Erba, *CFO*
David Sugishita, *Bd of Directors*
Todd Conroy, *Senior VP*
EMP: 82
SQ FT: 42,000
SALES: 110.9MM **Publicly Held**
SIC: 3577 7371 Computer peripheral equipment; computer software development & applications

(P-15243)
INCAL TECHNOLOGY INC
46420 Fremont Blvd, Fremont (94538-6469)
PHONE.....................510 657-8405
Cary Caywood, *CEO*
Bruce Simikowski, *Vice Pres*
Naveed Syed, *Design Engr*
Hank Pedersen, *Technology*
Lillian Bledsaw, *Human Res Mgr*
EMP: 25
SQ FT: 7,500
SALES (est): 5.7MM **Privately Held**
SIC: 3577 Computer peripheral equipment

(P-15244)
INCIPIO TECHNOLOGIES INC (PA)
Also Called: Incipio Group
3347 Michelson Dr Ste 100, Irvine (92612-0661)
PHONE.....................949 250-4929
Brian Stech, *CEO*
Steve Finney, *CFO*
Rusty Everett, *Exec VP*
Jeff Buhrman, *Vice Pres*
Christine Burke, *Vice Pres*
◆ **EMP:** 80
SALES (est): 47.6MM **Privately Held**
SIC: 3577 Computer peripheral equipment

(P-15245)
INDUSTRIAL ELECTRONIC ENGINEER
Also Called: Iee
7723 Kester Ave, Van Nuys (91405-1105)
PHONE.....................818 787-0311
Thomas Whinfrey, *President*
Steve Motter, *President*
Elena Valderrama, *CFO*
Donald G Gumpertz, *Chairman*
Michael Tubbs, *Vice Pres*
▲ **EMP:** 100 **EST:** 1947
SQ FT: 131,000
SALES (est): 54.4MM **Privately Held**
SIC: 3577 3575 Graphic displays, except graphic terminals; keyboards, computer, office machine

(P-15246)
INFINEON TECH AMERICAS CORP
Interntnal Rctfier/Hexget Amer
41915 Business Park Dr, Temecula (92590-3637)
PHONE.....................951 375-6008
Marc Rougee, *Branch Mgr*
Javier Solis, *President*
Dale Suddon, *Treasurer*
Marti Jarsey, *Pharmacy Dir*
Travis Miller, *Network Mgr*
EMP: 710
SALES (corp-wide): 8.7B **Privately Held**
WEB: www.irf.com
SIC: 3577 3674 Computer peripheral equipment; semiconductor circuit networks
HQ: Infineon Technologies Americas Corp.
101 N Pacific Coast Hwy
El Segundo CA 90245
310 726-8000

(P-15247)
INNOVATIVE TECH & ENGRG INC
Also Called: Innov8v
2691 Richter Ave Ste 124, Irvine (92606-5124)
PHONE.....................949 955-2501
Hassan Siddiqi, *President*
EMP: 12
SQ FT: 2,200

▲ = Import ▼=Export
◆ =Import/Export

SALES (est): 1.3MM **Privately Held**
SIC: **3577** 5961 1731 5999 Computer peripheral equipment; computers & peripheral equipment, mail order; safety & security specialization; audio-visual equipment & supplies

(P-15248)
INPUT/OUTPUT TECHNOLOGY INC
28415 Industry Dr Ste 520, Valencia (91355-4161)
PHONE..................................661 257-1000
Ted Drapala, *President*
EMP: 20
SALES (est): 3.3MM **Privately Held**
WEB: www.iotechnology.com
SIC: **3577** 3823 Input/output equipment, computer; industrial instrmnts msrmnt display/control process variable

(P-15249)
INSTRUMENTATION TECH SYSTEMS
Also Called: Its
19360 Business Center Dr, Northridge (91324-3547)
PHONE..................................818 886-2034
Paul Hightower, *CEO*
Don C Janess, *Vice Pres*
▼ EMP: 12
SQ FT: 8,200
SALES (est): 2.2MM **Privately Held**
WEB: www.itsamerica.com
SIC: **3577** Encoders, computer peripheral equipment

(P-15250)
INTEL AMERICAS INC (HQ)
2200 Mission College Blvd, Santa Clara (95054-1549)
PHONE..................................408 765-8080
Craig R Barrett, *CEO*
Chris Bartos, *Engineer*
Thomas Pieser, *Business Mgr*
Balaji Srinivasan, *Manager*
▲ EMP: 54
SALES (est): 12.1MM
SALES (corp-wide): 70.8B **Publicly Held**
SIC: **3577** Computer peripheral equipment
PA: Intel Corporation
2200 Mission College Blvd
Santa Clara CA 95054
408 765-8080

(P-15251)
INTEL CORPORATION
3065 Bowers Ave, Santa Clara (95054-3293)
PHONE..................................408 765-2508
Andrew S Grove, *CEO*
Drupad Perumandla, *Sr Software Eng*
Nour Bouziane, *Engineer*
Akhilesh Kumar, *Engineer*
Sharad Tripathi, *Engineer*
EMP: 17
SQ FT: 78,336
SALES (corp-wide): 70.8B **Publicly Held**
WEB: www.intel.com
SIC: **3577** Computer peripheral equipment
PA: Intel Corporation
2200 Mission College Blvd
Santa Clara CA 95054
408 765-8080

(P-15252)
INTEL CORPORATION (PA)
2200 Mission College Blvd, Santa Clara (95054-1549)
P.O. Box 58119 (95052-8119)
PHONE..................................408 765-8080
Robert H Swan, *CEO*
Andy D Bryant, *Ch of Bd*
Venkata S M Renduchintala, *President*
George S Davis, *CFO*
Claire Dixon, *Ch Credit Ofcr*
◆ EMP: 277
SALES: 70.8B **Publicly Held**
WEB: www.intel.com
SIC: **3577** 7372 3674 Computer peripheral equipment; prepackaged software; application computer software; microprocessors

(P-15253)
INTEL CORPORATION
2300 Mission College Blvd, Santa Clara (95054)
PHONE..................................408 425-8398
Ziya MA, *Manager*
EMP: 200
SALES (corp-wide): 70.8B **Publicly Held**
SIC: **3577** Computer peripheral equipment
PA: Intel Corporation
2200 Mission College Blvd
Santa Clara CA 95054
408 765-8080

(P-15254)
INTEL CORPORATION
101 Innovation Dr, San Jose (95134-1941)
PHONE..................................408 544-7000
Dan McNamara, *Branch Mgr*
Vincent Hu, *Vice Pres*
Kevin Lyman, *Vice Pres*
David Moore, *Vice Pres*
Dermot Hargaden, *General Mgr*
EMP: 3000
SALES (corp-wide): 70.8B **Publicly Held**
SIC: **3577** Computer peripheral equipment
PA: Intel Corporation
2200 Mission College Blvd
Santa Clara CA 95054
408 765-8080

(P-15255)
INTEL CORPORATION
2200 Mission College Blvd, Santa Clara (95054-1549)
PHONE..................................503 696-8080
David Ryan, *Branch Mgr*
Nikhil Talpallikar, *Software Engr*
EMP: 200
SALES (corp-wide): 70.8B **Publicly Held**
WEB: www.intel.com
SIC: **3577** Computer peripheral equipment
PA: Intel Corporation
2200 Mission College Blvd
Santa Clara CA 95054
408 765-8080

(P-15256)
INTEL NETWORK SYSTEMS INC
12220 Scrps Summit Dr # 300, San Diego (92131-3698)
PHONE..................................858 877-4652
Seth Deyo, *Branch Mgr*
Ted Taylor, *Vice Pres*
Siddharth Verma, *Technical Staff*
Vamsee Boda, *Engineer*
Scott Cyphers, *Engineer*
EMP: 13
SALES (corp-wide): 70.8B **Publicly Held**
SIC: **3577** Computer peripheral equipment
HQ: Intel Network Systems Inc
77 Reed Rd
Hudson MA 01749
978 553-4000

(P-15257)
INTELLIGENT PERIPHERALS
1123 Judah St, San Francisco (94122-1902)
PHONE..................................415 564-4366
Tennyson Lee, *Owner*
EMP: 12
SALES (est): 1MM **Privately Held**
SIC: **3577** Printers & plotters

(P-15258)
INTERNET MACHINES CORPORATION (PA)
30501 Agoura Rd Ste 203, Agoura Hills (91301-4389)
PHONE..................................818 575-2100
Christopher Hoogenboom, *CEO*
Frank Knuettel II, *CFO*
Chris Haywood, *Vice Pres*
Johann Wilmot, *Executive*
Tracey Ciccone, *Planning*
EMP: 70
SQ FT: 18,500
SALES (est): 6.7MM **Privately Held**
WEB: www.internetmachines.com
SIC: **3577** Computer peripheral equipment

(P-15259)
ISIGN SOLUTIONS INC (PA)
2033 Gateway Pl Ste 659, San Jose (95110-3709)
PHONE..................................650 802-7888
Philip S Sassower, *Ch of Bd*
Michael Engmann, *Ch of Bd*
Andrea Goren, *CFO*
Will Melton, *Administration*
Craig Hutchinson, *Info Tech Dir*
EMP: 10
SQ FT: 2,400
SALES: 917K **Publicly Held**
WEB: www.cic.com
SIC: **3577** 7372 Computer peripheral equipment; prepackaged software

(P-15260)
ITUNER NETWORKS CORPORATION
47801 Fremont Blvd, Fremont (94538-6506)
PHONE..................................510 226-6033
Andrei Bulucea, *President*
Raluca Neacsu, *Vice Pres*
▲ EMP: 15
SALES (est): 3.2MM **Privately Held**
WEB: www.ituner.com
SIC: **3577** 5961 5045 Computer peripheral equipment; computers & peripheral equipment, mail order; computer peripheral equipment

(P-15261)
JUNIPER NETWORKS INC (PA)
1133 Innovation Way, Sunnyvale (94089-1228)
PHONE..................................408 745-2000
Rami Rahim, *CEO*
Brian Martin, *Senior VP*
Thomas A Austin, *Vice Pres*
EMP: 300
SALES: 4.6B **Publicly Held**
WEB: www.juniper.net
SIC: **3577** 7372 Computer peripheral equipment; prepackaged software

(P-15262)
JUNIPER NETWORKS (US) INC
1133 Innovation Way, Sunnyvale (94089-1228)
PHONE..................................408 745-2000
Rami Rahim, *CEO*
Scott Kriens, *Ch of Bd*
Rami Rahim, *CEO*
Robert M Calderoni, *Bd of Directors*
Rahul Merchant, *Bd of Directors*
EMP: 8100
SALES (est): 228.8MM **Publicly Held**
WEB: www.juniper.net
SIC: **3577** Computer peripheral equipment
PA: Juniper Networks, Inc.
1133 Innovation Way
Sunnyvale CA 94089

(P-15263)
KELLER ENTERTAINMENT GROUP INC
1093 Broxton Ave Ste 246, Los Angeles (90024-2831)
PHONE..................................310 443-2226
Max Keller, *Ch of Bd*
Micheline Keller, *President*
David Joseph Keller, *Exec VP*
EMP: 10
SQ FT: 12,000
SALES (est): 1.6MM **Privately Held**
WEB: www.kellerentertainment.com
SIC: **3577** 7922 Computer peripheral equipment; television program, including commercial producers

(P-15264)
KELLY COMPUTER SYSTEMS INC
1060 La Avenida St, Mountain View (94043-1422)
PHONE..................................650 960-1010
Larry Kelly, *President*
Tim Kelly, *Vice Pres*
Lawrence Kelly, *Sales Executive*
EMP: 25
SQ FT: 20,000

SALES (est): 3.3MM **Privately Held**
SIC: **3577** 7371 7373 Computer peripheral equipment; computer software development; systems integration services

(P-15265)
KEMEERA INCORPORATED
Also Called: Oakland Production Center
315 Jefferson St, Oakland (94607-3537)
PHONE..................................510 281-9000
Michelle Malia Mihevc, *CEO*
EMP: 16
SALES (corp-wide): 27.7MM **Privately Held**
SIC: **3577** Printers, computer
PA: Kemeera Incorporated
620 3rd St
Oakland CA 94607
510 281-9000

(P-15266)
KINGSTON DIGITAL INC (DH)
17600 Newhope St, Fountain Valley (92708-4220)
PHONE..................................714 435-2600
John Tu, *President*
David Sun, *Principal*
▲ EMP: 21
SALES (est): 17.5MM **Privately Held**
WEB: www.kingston.com
SIC: **3577** Computer peripheral equipment
HQ: Kingston Technology Company, Inc.
17600 Newhope St
Fountain Valley CA 92708
714 435-2600

(P-15267)
KINGSTON TECHNOLOGY CORP (PA)
17600 Newhope St, Fountain Valley (92708-4298)
PHONE..................................714 445-3495
John Tu, *CEO*
David Hu, *Vice Pres*
David Sun, *Principal*
Christopher McIntosh, *Administration*
Kevin Chiu, *Planning*
▲ EMP: 500
SALES (est): 1.2B **Privately Held**
SIC: **3577** Computer peripheral equipment

(P-15268)
KURDEX CORPORATION
343 Gibraltar Dr, Sunnyvale (94089-1327)
PHONE..................................408 734-8181
Bijan Pourmand, *President*
Mehrdad Pourmand, *Exec VP*
Christina Williams, *Purchasing*
▲ EMP: 11
SQ FT: 21,000
SALES (est): 3.5MM **Privately Held**
WEB: www.kurdex.com
SIC: **3577** Computer peripheral equipment

(P-15269)
L&H ENTERPRISES
2111 Montgomery Ave, Cardiff By The Sea (92007-1817)
PHONE..................................760 230-2275
Mark Laine,
EMP: 10
SALES (est): 1.2MM **Privately Held**
SIC: **3577** 8731 7373 Computer peripheral equipment; computer (hardware) development; computer integrated systems design

(P-15270)
LANTRONIX INC (PA)
7535 Irvine Center Dr, Irvine (92618-2962)
PHONE..................................949 453-3990
Paul H Pickle, *President*
Bernhard Bruscha, *Ch of Bd*
Jeremy R Whitaker, *CFO*
Kevin M Yoder, *Vice Pres*
Mohammed F Hakam, *VP Engrg*
▲ EMP: 120
SQ FT: 27,000
SALES: 46.8MM **Publicly Held**
WEB: www.lantronix.com
SIC: **3577** Data conversion equipment, media-to-media: computer

PRODUCTS & SVCS

(P-15271)
LASERGRAPHICS INC
Also Called: Lasergraphics General Business
20 Ada, Irvine (92618-2303)
PHONE.....................949 753-8282
Mihai Demetrescu PHD, *President*
David Boyd, *CFO*
Stefan Demetrescu, *Senior VP*
Stefan Demetrescu PHD, *Senior VP*
▲ EMP: 40
SQ FT: 20,000
SALES (est): 7MM **Privately Held**
WEB: www.lasergraphics.com
SIC: 3577 7371 3823 Graphic displays,
except graphic terminals; custom com-
puter programming services; industrial in-
strmnts msrmnt display/control process
variable

(P-15272)
LEICA GEOSYSTEMS HDS LLC
5000 Executive Pkwy # 500, San Ramon
(94583-4210)
PHONE.....................925 790-2300
Kem Mooyman, *Manager*
EMP: 72
SQ FT: 25,000
SALES (est): 14MM
SALES (corp-wide): 4.3B **Privately Held**
WEB: www.hds.leica-geosystems.com
SIC: 3577 Optical scanning devices
HQ: Leica Geosystems Ag
Heinrich-Wild-Strasse 201
Heerbrugg SG 9435
717 273-131

(P-15273)
LEIDOS INC
4025 Hancock St Ste 210, San Diego
(92110-5167)
PHONE.....................619 524-2581
Daniel Shrum, *Branch Mgr*
EMP: 28
SALES (corp-wide): 10.1B **Publicly Held**
WEB: www.saic.com
SIC: 3577 Computer peripheral equipment
HQ: Leidos, Inc.
11951 Freedom Dr Ste 500
Reston VA 20190
571 526-6000

(P-15274)
LEXMARK INTERNATIONAL INC
575 Anton Blvd Fl 3, Costa Mesa
(92626-7169)
PHONE.....................714 641-1007
EMP: 35
SALES (corp-wide): 2.5B **Privately Held**
SIC: 3577
PA: Lexmark International, Inc.
740 W New Circle Rd
Lexington KY 40511
859 232-2000

(P-15275)
**LITE ON TECHNOLOGY INTL INC
(HQ)**
720 S Hillview Dr, Milpitas (95035-5455)
PHONE.....................408 945-0222
Kung Soong, *Principal*
Paul Lin, *Vice Chairman*
Joseph Chen, *Vice Pres*
Daisy Young, *Principal*
Tom Soong, *General Mgr*
▲ EMP: 30
SALES (est): 2.9MM **Privately Held**
WEB: www.liteontc.com
SIC: 3577 3572 Computer peripheral
equipment; computer storage devices

(P-15276)
LOGICUBE INC (PA)
19755 Nordhoff Pl, Chatsworth
(91311-6606)
PHONE.....................888 494-8832
Farid Emrani, *President*
Jack M Schuster, *Ch of Bd*
Jeffrey Schuster, *CFO*
Chris Hernandez, *Opers Staff*
▲ EMP: 25
SALES: 8.5MM **Privately Held**
SIC: 3577 Computer peripheral equipment

(P-15277)
LOGITECH INC
3 Jenner Ste 180, Irvine (92618-3835)
PHONE.....................510 795-8500
Darrell Bracken, *Branch Mgr*
Dennis Perez, *Analyst*
Jessica Amortegui, *Director*
Jennifer Treopaldo, *Director*
Tanvi Shah, *Manager*
EMP: 43
SALES (corp-wide): 2.7B **Privately Held**
SIC: 3577 Computer peripheral equipment
HQ: Logitech Inc.
7700 Gateway Blvd
Newark CA 94560
510 795-8500

(P-15278)
LOGITECH INC (HQ)
7700 Gateway Blvd, Newark (94560-1046)
PHONE.....................510 795-8500
Bracken P Darrell, *President*
Guerrino De Luca, *Ch of Bd*
Madhuri Peesapati, *Top Exec*
Michele Hermann, *Vice Pres*
Denis Pavillard, *Vice Pres*
◆ EMP: 276 EST: 1982
SQ FT: 295,560
SALES (est): 1.6B
SALES (corp-wide): 2.7B **Privately Held**
WEB: www.logitech.com
SIC: 3577 Input/output equipment, com-
puter
PA: Logitech International S.A.
Les Chatagnis
Apples VD
218 635-511

(P-15279)
LYNN PRODUCTS INC
Also Called: Pureformance Cables
2645 W 237th St, Torrance (90505-5269)
PHONE.....................310 530-5966
Hsinyu Lin, *President*
Chun MEI Shei, *Treasurer*
Eric Tseng, *Vice Pres*
Chih Tseng, *General Mgr*
Chen Huei Tseng, *Admin Sec*
▲ EMP: 1000
SQ FT: 35,000
SALES (est): 146.3MM **Privately Held**
WEB: www.lynnprod.com
SIC: 3577 3357 Computer peripheral
equipment; fiber optic cable (insulated)

(P-15280)
MACHINABLES INC
Also Called: Twindom
1101 Cowper St, Berkeley (94702-1813)
PHONE.....................415 216-9467
David Ryan Pastewka, *CEO*
Will Brevno, *COO*
Richard Berwick, *Treasurer*
Peter Pastewka, *Principal*
EMP: 12
SQ FT: 5,600
SALES: 250K **Privately Held**
SIC: 3577 7374 7699 Optical scanning
devices; optical scanning data service; in-
dustrial equipment services

(P-15281)
MAGTEK INC (PA)
1710 Apollo Ct, Seal Beach (90740-5617)
PHONE.....................562 546-6400
Ann Marle Hart, *President*
Sam Kamel, *President*
Louis E Struett, *Exec VP*
Roger Applewhite, *Vice Pres*
Brian Davis, *Vice Pres*
▲ EMP: 200
SQ FT: 48,000
SALES (est): 63.4MM **Privately Held**
WEB: www.magtek.com
SIC: 3577 3674 Readers, sorters or in-
scribers, magnetic ink; encoders, com-
puter peripheral equipment;
semiconductors & related devices

(P-15282)
MAKEIT INC
612 S Marengo Ave, Alhambra
(91803-1615)
PHONE.....................626 470-7938
Salomo Murtonen, *CEO*
Shelley Sun, *President*

Russell Singer, *Development*
EMP: 10
SQ FT: 1,900
SALES: 350K **Privately Held**
SIC: 3577 5045 Computer peripheral
equipment; computer peripheral equip-
ment; accounting machines using ma-
chine readable programs

(P-15283)
MARBURG TECHNOLOGY INC
Also Called: Glide-Write
304 Turquoise St, Milpitas (95035-5431)
PHONE.....................408 262-8400
Francis Burga, *CEO*
Mohammad Ebrahimi, *CFO*
Francis Guevara, *Vice Pres*
Lee Nguyen, *Engineer*
▲ EMP: 245
SALES (est): 33.4MM **Privately Held**
SIC: 3577 Disk & diskette equipment, ex-
cept drives

(P-15284)
**MARWAY POWER SYSTEMS INC
(PA)**
Also Called: Marway Power Solutions
1721 S Grand Ave, Santa Ana
(92705-4808)
P.O. Box 30118 (92735-8118)
PHONE.....................714 917-6200
Dan Richter, *President*
Mario Manriquez, *President*
Kevin Jacobs, *CFO*
Van Dang, *MIS Mgr*
Tim Bishop, *Technical Staff*
◆ EMP: 43
SQ FT: 33,400
SALES (est): 10.7MM **Privately Held**
WEB: www.marway.com
SIC: 3577 8711 Computer peripheral
equipment; engineering services

(P-15285)
MEGA FORCE CORPORATION
Also Called: Megaforce
2035 Otoole Ave, San Jose (95131-1301)
PHONE.....................408 956-9989
Stanley Trenh, *President*
EMP: 45
SQ FT: 15,000
SALES (est): 12MM **Privately Held**
WEB: www.megaforcecorp.com
SIC: 3577 Computer peripheral equipment

(P-15286)
MEMJET LABELS INC (DH)
10920 Via Frontera # 120, San Diego
(92127-1730)
PHONE.....................858 673-3300
Len Lauer, *CEO*
Maureen Brock, *President*
Gail Partain, *President*
Bent Serritslev, *Senior VP*
Scott Leger, *Vice Pres*
▲ EMP: 12
SALES (est): 1.6MM **Privately Held**
SIC: 3577 3555 Printers, computer; print-
ing trades machinery

(P-15287)
MEMJET LABELS INC
10918 Technology Pl, San Diego
(92127-1874)
PHONE.....................858 798-3061
EMP: 24
SALES (est): 2.6MM **Privately Held**
SIC: 3577

(P-15288)
**METROMEDIA TECHNOLOGIES
INC**
19401 S Vt Ave Ste E100, Torrance
(90502-4429)
PHONE.....................818 552-6500
Paul Havig, *Branch Mgr*
EMP: 39
SALES (corp-wide): 63.7MM **Privately
Held**
WEB: www.mmt.com
SIC: 3577 Graphic displays, except
graphic terminals
PA: Metromedia Technologies, Inc.
810 7th Ave Fl 29
New York NY 10019
212 273-2100

(P-15289)
MICRO CONNECTORS INC
2700 Mccone Ave, Hayward (94545-1615)
PHONE.....................510 266-0299
Charlie Lin, *President*
▲ EMP: 29
SALES (est): 8MM **Privately Held**
WEB: www.microconnectors.com
SIC: 3577 Computer peripheral equipment

(P-15290)
MICROSOFT CORPORATION
680 Vaqueros Ave, Sunnyvale
(94085-3523)
PHONE.....................650 693-4000
Luis Salazar, *Branch Mgr*
EMP: 180
SALES (corp-wide): 125.8B **Publicly
Held**
WEB: www.microsoft.com
SIC: 3577 Computer peripheral equipment
PA: Microsoft Corporation
1 Microsoft Way
Redmond WA 98052
425 882-8080

(P-15291)
MITAC INFORMATION SYSTEMS
39889 Eureka Dr, Newark (94560-4811)
PHONE.....................510 668-3679
EMP: 50 **Privately Held**
SIC: 3577
HQ: Mitac Information Systems Corp.
44131 Nobel Dr
Fremont CA 94560
510 668-3679

(P-15292)
MOTION ENGINEERING INC (HQ)
Also Called: M E I
33 S La Patera Ln, Santa Barbara
(93117-3214)
PHONE.....................805 696-1200
Robert Steele, *CTO*
EMP: 60
SQ FT: 21,000
SALES (est): 4.7MM
SALES (corp-wide): 19.8B **Publicly Held**
WEB: www.synqnet.org
SIC: 3577 8711 3823 Computer periph-
eral equipment; engineering services; in-
dustrial instrmnts msrmnt display/control
process variable
PA: Danaher Corporation
2200 Penn Ave Nw Ste 800w
Washington DC 20037
202 828-0850

(P-15293)
MOXA AMERICAS INC
601 Valencia Ave Ste 100, Brea
(92823-6357)
PHONE.....................714 528-6777
Tein Shun, *CEO*
Ben Chen, *President*
Frank Hou, *General Mgr*
Harry Liu, *General Mgr*
Graham Lin, *Info Tech Mgr*
▲ EMP: 50
SQ FT: 8,000
SALES (est): 18.2MM **Privately Held**
WEB: www.moxausa.com
SIC: 3577 Input/output equipment, com-
puter
HQ: Moxa Inc.
4f, 135, Lane 235, Pao Chiao Rd.,
New Taipei City TAP 23145

(P-15294)
MPD HOLDINGS INC
Also Called: Mousepad Designs
16200 Commerce Way, Cerritos
(90703-2324)
PHONE.....................562 777-1051
Glenn M Boghosian, *President*
◆ EMP: 34
SALES (est): 7.5MM **Privately Held**
SIC: 3577 Computer peripheral equipment

(P-15295)
NEWNEX TECHNOLOGY CORP
3041 Olcott St, Santa Clara (95054-3222)
PHONE.....................408 986-9988
Sam Liu, *President*
Jean Tang, *CFO*

▲ = Import ▼=Export
◆ =Import/Export

▲ **EMP:** 11
SQ FT: 3,800
SALES (est): 2.3MM **Privately Held**
WEB: www.newnex.com
SIC: 3577 Computer peripheral equipment

(P-15296)
NEWPACKET WIRELESS CORPORATION
1600 Wyatt Dr Ste 10, Santa Clara
(95054-1525)
PHONE..................................408 747-1003
Sanjay Gidwani, *President*
EMP: 10 **EST:** 2014
SALES (est): 751.9K **Privately Held**
SIC: 3577 Computer peripheral equipment

(P-15297)
NEXSYS ELECTRONICS INC (PA)
Also Called: Medweb
70 Zoe St Ste 100, San Francisco
(94107-1753)
PHONE..................................415 541-9980
Peter Killcommons, *President*
Angie Fong, *Executive*
Cindy Newlove, *Administration*
Ralph Peragine, *Administration*
Dave Cundiff, *Engineer*
EMP: 14
SQ FT: 2,700
SALES (est): 4.7MM **Privately Held**
WEB: www.nexsys.com
SIC: 3577 4813 Computer peripheral equipment;

(P-15298)
OLEA KIOSKS INC
13845 Artesia Blvd, Cerritos (90703-9000)
PHONE..................................562 924-2644
Rene Olea, *President*
Andy Koeck, *Vice Pres*
Shauna Olea, *Administration*
Craig Bennett, *Engineer*
Craig Keefner, *Manager*
▲ **EMP:** 63
SQ FT: 50,000
SALES: 13MM **Privately Held**
WEB: www.olea.com
SIC: 3577 Computer peripheral equipment

(P-15299)
OMNIPRINT INC
1923 E Deere Ave, Santa Ana
(92705-5715)
PHONE..................................949 833-0080
Fardin Mostafavi, *President*
▲ **EMP:** 24
SQ FT: 22,000
SALES: 8MM **Privately Held**
SIC: 3577 5045 Printers & plotters; printers, computer

(P-15300)
OMNITRON SYSTEMS TECH INC
38 Tesla, Irvine (92618-4603)
PHONE..................................949 250-6510
Arie Goldberg, *CEO*
Heidi Cairns, *Vice Pres*
Greg Scott, *Manager*
EMP: 75
SQ FT: 15,000
SALES (est): 15.1MM **Privately Held**
WEB: www.omnitron-systems.com
SIC: 3577 Data conversion equipment, media-to-media: computer

(P-15301)
ONE STOP SYSTEMS INC (PA)
Also Called: Oss
2235 Entp St Ste 110, Escondido (92029)
PHONE..................................760 745-9883
Steve Cooper, *Ch of Bd*
John W Morrison Jr, *CFO*
Randy Jones, *Bd of Directors*
Kenneth Potashner, *Bd of Directors*
Charity N Duarte, *Vice Pres*
EMP: 75
SQ FT: 17,911
SALES: 37MM **Publicly Held**
WEB: www.onestopsystems.com
SIC: 3577 Computer peripheral equipment

(P-15302)
ONE STOP SYSTEMS INC
Also Called: Magma
2235 Entp St Ste 110, Escondido (92029)
PHONE..................................858 530-2511
Timothy Miller, *Principal*
EMP: 30
SALES (corp-wide): 37MM **Publicly Held**
SIC: 3577 Computer peripheral equipment
PA: One Stop Systems, Inc.
2235 Entp St Ste 110
Escondido CA 92029
760 745-9883

(P-15303)
OPTIBASE INC (HQ)
931 Benecia Ave, Sunnyvale (94085-2805)
P.O. Box 448, Mountain View (94042-0448)
PHONE..................................800 451-5101
Shlomo Wyler, *CEO*
Michael Chorpash, *President*
Yakir Ben-Naim, *CFO*
EMP: 27
SQ FT: 15,000
SALES (est): 11.7MM
SALES (corp-wide): 3.8MM **Privately Held**
SIC: 3577 Computer peripheral equipment
PA: Optibase Ltd.
8 Hamanofim
Herzliya 46725
737 073-700

(P-15304)
OPTIMA TECHNOLOGY CORPORATION
17062 Murphy Ave, Irvine (92614-5914)
PHONE..................................949 253-5768
Barry Eisler, *Branch Mgr*
EMP: 343
SALES (corp-wide): 17.5MM **Privately Held**
SIC: 3577 Computer peripheral equipment
PA: Optima Technology Corporation
2222 Michelson Dr # 1830
Irvine CA
949 476-0515

(P-15305)
PALO ALTO NETWORKS INC (PA)
3000 Tannery Way, Santa Clara
(95054-2832)
PHONE..................................408 753-4000
Nikesh Arora, *Ch of Bd*
Todd McNeal, *Partner*
Cristina Salmastlian, *Partner*
Amit Singh, *President*
Kathleen Bonanno, *CFO*
EMP: 500
SQ FT: 941,000
SALES: 2.9B **Publicly Held**
WEB: www.paloaltonetworks.com
SIC: 3577 7371 Computer peripheral equipment; computer software development & applications

(P-15306)
PANO LOGIC INC
1100 La Avenida St Ste A, Mountain View
(94043-1453)
PHONE..................................650 743-1773
John Kish, *President*
Parmeet S Chaddha, *Exec VP*
Aly Orady, *CTO*
Nils Bunger, *VP Engrg*
▲ **EMP:** 72
SQ FT: 11,800
SALES (est): 11.1MM **Privately Held**
WEB: www.attodevices.com
SIC: 3577 Computer peripheral equipment

(P-15307)
PHOTO SCIENCES INCORPORATED (PA)
2542 W 237th St, Torrance (90505-5217)
PHONE..................................310 634-1500
Kyle Stogsdill, *CEO*
L J Stogsdill, *Chairman*
Wade Walsh, *Treasurer*
Jeff Platts, *Vice Pres*
Maurice Muehle,
EMP: 34 **EST:** 1972
SQ FT: 35,000

SALES: 6MM **Privately Held**
WEB: www.photo-science.com
SIC: 3577 7335 Computer output to microfilm units; still & slide file production

(P-15308)
PLUSTEK TECHNOLOGY INC
9830 Norwalk Blvd Ste 155, Santa Fe
Springs (90670-6107)
PHONE..................................562 777-1888
Karen Ku, *President*
▲ **EMP:** 13
SQ FT: 15,000
SALES (est): 2.7MM **Privately Held**
SIC: 3577 Optical scanning devices

(P-15309)
PRINCETON TECHNOLOGY INC
1691 Browning, Irvine (92606-4808)
PHONE..................................949 851-7776
Nasir Javed, *CEO*
▲ **EMP:** 30
SQ FT: 14,000
SALES (est): 7.1MM **Privately Held**
WEB: www.princetonusa.com
SIC: 3577 5045 3674 Computer peripheral equipment; computers, peripherals & software; semiconductors & related devices

(P-15310)
PRINTRONIX LLC (PA)
6440 Oak Cyn Ste 200, Irvine
(92618-5209)
PHONE..................................714 368-2300
Werner Heid, *CEO*
Sean Irby, *Vice Pres*
Bill Matthewes, *Vice Pres*
Said Salazar, *Technician*
Marjon Farzadpour, *Human Resources*
▲ **EMP:** 108
SQ FT: 84,580
SALES (est): 48.2MM **Privately Held**
WEB: www.printronix.com
SIC: 3577 Printers, computer

(P-15311)
PRINTRONIX HOLDING CORP
6440 Oak Cyn Ste 200, Irvine
(92618-5209)
PHONE..................................714 368-2300
Werner Heid, *CEO*
EMP: 135
SALES (est): 5.9MM **Privately Held**
SIC: 3577 6719 Printers, computer; investment holding companies, except banks

(P-15312)
PRINTWORX INC
195 Aviation Way Ste 201, Watsonville
(95076-2059)
PHONE..................................831 722-7147
James B Riches, *Ch of Bd*
David Willmon, *President*
EMP: 17
SQ FT: 15,000
SALES (est): 3.2MM **Privately Held**
WEB: www.printworx.net
SIC: 3577 5112 7378 3861 Printers, computer; computer & photocopying supplies; computer & data processing equipment repair/maintenance; photographic equipment & supplies; commercial printing

(P-15313)
PROPHECY TECHNOLOGY LLC
Also Called: Maxus Group
339 Cheryl Ln, Walnut (91789-3003)
PHONE..................................909 598-7998
Juanito Pangalilingan,
▲ **EMP:** 30
SALES (est): 3.8MM **Privately Held**
SIC: 3577 Computer peripheral equipment

(P-15314)
PUREDEPTH INC (PA)
303 Twin Dolphin Dr Fl 6, Redwood City
(94065-1497)
PHONE..................................408 394-9146
Darryl S K Singh, *CEO*
Andy L Wood, *Ch of Bd*
Michael Laycock, *CFO*
EMP: 12
SQ FT: 1,983

SALES (est): 1.1MM **Privately Held**
WEB: www.puredepth.com
SIC: 3577 Graphic displays, except graphic terminals

(P-15315)
R B S INC
31941 La Subida Dr, Trabuco Canyon
(92679-3406)
PHONE..................................949 766-2924
Bob Ball, *President*
EMP: 19
SALES (est): 1.4MM **Privately Held**
SIC: 3577 Printers, computer

(P-15316)
R-QUEST TECHNOLOGIES LLC
4710 Oak Hill Rd, Placerville (95667-9104)
PHONE..................................530 621-9916
Larry Robertson, *President*
EMP: 12
SQ FT: 3,500
SALES (est): 2MM **Privately Held**
SIC: 3577 Disk & diskette equipment, except drives

(P-15317)
RANCHO TECHNOLOGY INC
10783 Bell Ct, Rancho Cucamonga
(91730-4834)
PHONE..................................909 987-3966
Hari Gupta, *President*
John Fobel Jr, *Vice Pres*
EMP: 15
SALES (est): 2.1MM **Privately Held**
SIC: 3577 5045 Computer peripheral equipment; computers, peripherals & software

(P-15318)
RECORTEC INC
2231 Fortune Dr Ste A, San Jose
(95131-1871)
PHONE..................................408 928-1488
Dr Lester H Lee, *President*
Eldon Corl, *Vice Pres*
▲ **EMP:** 13
SQ FT: 24,000
SALES (est): 2.1MM **Privately Held**
WEB: www.recortec.com
SIC: 3577 3571 Computer peripheral equipment; electronic computers

(P-15319)
REDLINE SOLUTIONS INC
3350 Scott Blvd Bldg 5, Santa Clara
(95054-3108)
PHONE..................................408 562-1700
Todd N Baggett, *President*
Tina Natividad, *Administration*
Adrian Down, *Mktg Dir*
Greg Emery, *Sales Staff*
Anthony Mattos, *Manager*
EMP: 18
SQ FT: 4,000
SALES (est): 4.5MM **Privately Held**
WEB: www.redlinesolutions.com
SIC: 3577 Bar code (magnetic ink) printers

(P-15320)
REVERA INCORPORATED
3090 Oakmead Village Dr, Santa Clara
(95051-0862)
PHONE..................................408 510-7400
Glyn Davies, *President*
Timothy Welch, *CFO*
Jim Pouquette, *Vice Pres*
Dave Reed, *CTO*
Jeff Fanton, *Engineer*
▲ **EMP:** 40
SQ FT: 20,000
SALES: 9.9MM
SALES (corp-wide): 67.7MM **Privately Held**
WEB: www.revera.com
SIC: 3577 Optical scanning devices
PA: Nova Measuring Instruments Ltd
Rehovot
Rehovot
732 295-600

(P-15321)
RGB SPECTRUM
950 Marina Village Pkwy, Alameda
(94501-1047)
PHONE..................................510 814-7000

PRODUCTS & SVCS

Robert Marcus, *CEO*
Scott Norder, *Senior VP*
Jed Deame, *Vice Pres*
Tony Spica, *Vice Pres*
Jason Tirado, *Vice Pres*
▲ **EMP:** 81
SQ FT: 27,326
SALES (est): 21.7MM **Privately Held**
WEB: www.rgb.com
SIC: 3577 5731 3679 Graphic displays,
except graphic terminals; video cameras,
recorders & accessories; recording &
playback apparatus, including phono-
graph

(P-15322)
RGB SYSTEMS INC (PA)
Also Called: Extron Electronics
1025 E Ball Rd Ste 100, Anaheim
(92805-5957)
PHONE.............................714 491-1500
Andrew C Edwards, *President*
Ivan Perez, *Vice Pres*
Ron Tucci, *Vice Pres*
Mike Scofield, *Admin Mgr*
Angelica Del Toro, *Administration*
◆ **EMP:** 185
SQ FT: 160,000
SALES (est): 82.4MM **Privately Held**
SIC: 3577 Computer output to microfilm
units

(P-15323)
**RICOH PRTG SYSTEMS AMER
INC (HQ)**
2390 Ward Ave Ste A, Simi Valley
(93065-1897)
PHONE.............................805 578-4000
Osamu Namikawa, *President*
Hiroyuki Kajiyama, *President*
Greg Grant, *Treasurer*
Neil Rapoport, *Vice Pres*
Leonard Stone, *Vice Pres*
▲ **EMP:** 400
SQ FT: 97,400
SALES (est): 109.3MM **Privately Held**
WEB: www.hitachi-printingsolutions.us
SIC: 3577 3861 3955 Printers, computer;
toners, prepared photographic (not made
in chemical plants); developers, photo-
graphic (not made in chemical plants); rib-
bons, inked: typewriter, adding machine,
register, etc.

(P-15324)
ROUCHON INDUSTRIES INC
Also Called: Swiftech
3729 San Gabriel River Pk, Pico Rivera
(90660-1457)
PHONE.............................310 763-0336
Gabriel Rouchon, *President*
▲ **EMP:** 12
SQ FT: 5,000
SALES (est): 2.7MM **Privately Held**
WEB: www.swiftech.com
SIC: 3577 Computer peripheral equipment

(P-15325)
**RUGGED INFO TECH EQP CORP
(PA)**
Also Called: Ritec
25 E Easy St, Simi Valley (93065-7707)
PHONE.............................805 577-9710
Carl C Stella, *President*
Harry P Alteri, *Senior VP*
Christopher Alteri, *Program Mgr*
Roger Lazer, *Admin Sec*
Shelton Leung, *Electrical Engi*
◆ **EMP:** 41
SQ FT: 25,000
SALES: 12MM **Privately Held**
WEB: www.ritecrugged.com
SIC: 3577 Computer peripheral equipment

(P-15326)
**SAMSUNG SDI AMERICA INC
(HQ)**
665 Clyde Ave, Mountain View
(94043-2235)
PHONE.............................408 544-4470
Kikwon Yoon, *CEO*
Young Joon Gil, *President*
Duck Yun Kim, *President*
Ik Hyeon Kim, *CFO*
Hyun Park, *Bd of Directors*
▼ **EMP:** 14

SALES (est): 17.3MM **Privately Held**
SIC: 3577 5045 Computer peripheral
equipment; computer peripheral equipment

(P-15327)
SEAGRA TECHNOLOGY INC
816 W Ahwanee Ave, Sunnyvale
(94085-1409)
PHONE.............................408 230-8706
EMP: 27 **Privately Held**
SIC: 3577 Computer peripheral equipment
PA: Seagra Technology Inc.
14252 Culver Dr
Irvine CA 92604
-

(P-15328)
SEAGRA TECHNOLOGY INC (PA)
14252 Culver Dr, Irvine (92604-0317)
PHONE.............................949 419-6796
Atul Talati, *President*
Timothy Lipsky, *CEO*
Tim Lipsky, *CTO*
▲ **EMP:** 11
SQ FT: 1,200
SALES: 500K **Privately Held**
SIC: 3577 Computer peripheral equipment

(P-15329)
SECUGEN CORPORATION
2065 Martin Ave Ste 108, Santa Clara
(95050-2707)
PHONE.............................408 834-7712
Won Lee, *President*
▲ **EMP:** 30
SALES (est): 5.8MM **Privately Held**
SIC: 3577 Computer peripheral equipment
PA: Pivotec Corporation
Rm 502 5/F
Seongnam

(P-15330)
SEGMENTIO INC
100 California St Ste 700, San Francisco
(94111-4512)
PHONE.............................844 611-0621
Peter Kristian Reinhardt, *President*
Sandra Smith, *CFO*
Laylee Asgari, *Office Mgr*
Mandy Adkins, *Admin Asst*
Andrey Bulgakov, *Software Engr*
EMP: 13
SALES (est): 784.6K **Privately Held**
SIC: 3577 Data conversion equipment,
media-to-media: computer

(P-15331)
**SEMTEK INNVTIVE SOLUTIONS
CORP**
12777 High Bludd Dr 225, San Diego
(92130)
PHONE.............................858 436-2270
John Sarkisian, *Ch of Bd*
Patrick Hazel, *President*
▲ **EMP:** 22
SQ FT: 10,000
SALES (est): 4.1MM **Privately Held**
WEB: www.semtek.com
SIC: 3577 Readers, sorters or inscribers,
magnetic ink

(P-15332)
SENSATA TECHNOLOGIES INC
Also Called: BEI Industrial Encoders
1461 Lawrence Dr, Thousand Oaks
(91320-1303)
PHONE.............................805 716-0322
Glenn Avolio, *Sales Mgr*
Rene Garcia, *Engineer*
Doug McGuire, *Engr R&D*
Mary Trumbo, *Regl Sales Mgr*
Tim Coronado, *Manager*
EMP: 70
SALES (corp-wide): 3.5B **Privately Held**
SIC: 3577 3827 3663 Optical scanning
devices; optical instruments & lenses;
radio & TV communications equipment
HQ: Sensata Technologies, Inc.
529 Pleasant St
Attleboro MA 02703
508 236-3800

(P-15333)
SHARKRACK INC
23842 Cabot Blvd, Hayward (94545-1661)
PHONE.............................510 477-7900
EMP: 10
SQ FT: 15,000
SALES: 4.2MM **Privately Held**
WEB: www.sharkrack.com
SIC: 3577

(P-15334)
SHARPDOTS LLC
Also Called: Sharp Dots.com
3733 San Gabriel Rver Pkw, Pico Rivera
(90660-1458)
PHONE.............................626 599-9696
John Tan,
EMP: 12
SALES (est): 1.9MM **Privately Held**
WEB: www.sharpdots.com
SIC: 3577 Printers, computer

(P-15335)
**SILICON GRAPHICS INTL CORP
(HQ)**
940 N Mccarthy Blvd, Milpitas
(95035-5128)
PHONE.............................669 900-8000
Jorge L Titinger, *CEO*
Cassio Conceicao, *COO*
Mack Asrat, *CFO*
Eng Lim Goh, *Senior VP*
Peter E Hilliard, *Senior VP*
▲ **EMP:** 222
SALES: 532.9MM
SALES (corp-wide): 30.8B **Publicly Held**
WEB: www.sgi.com
SIC: 3577 7371 Computer peripheral
equipment; computer software develop-
ment & applications
PA: Hewlett Packard Enterprise Company
6280 America Center Dr
San Jose CA 95002
650 687-5817

(P-15336)
SKYMICRO INC
2060 E Ave Arboles 344, Thousand Oaks
(91362-1361)
PHONE.............................805 491-8935
Rudy Lopez, *President*
▲ **EMP:** 20
SALES (est): 2.8MM **Privately Held**
WEB: www.skymicro.com
SIC: 3577 Computer peripheral equipment

(P-15337)
SOLFLOWER COMPUTER INC
3337 Kifer Rd, Santa Clara (95051-0719)
PHONE.............................408 733-8100
Kim Vu, *President*
Janet Doan, *Vice Pres*
EMP: 15
SQ FT: 8,000
SALES (est): 3MM **Privately Held**
WEB: www.solflower.com
SIC: 3577 Computer peripheral equipment

(P-15338)
SONY ELECTRONICS INC
Also Called: Sony Broadcast Products
1730 N 1st St, San Jose (95112-4642)
PHONE.............................408 352-4000
Elizabeth Boukis, *Manager*
EMP: 38 **Privately Held**
SIC: 3577 3571 8731 8711 Computer pe-
ripheral equipment; electronic computers;
commercial physical research; engineer-
ing services
HQ: Sony Electronics Inc.
16535 Via Esprillo Bldg 1
San Diego CA 92127
858 942-2400

(P-15339)
SP CONTROLS INC
930 Linden Ave, South San Francisco
(94080-1754)
PHONE.............................650 392-7880
Paul Anson Brown, *CEO*
Gary Arcudi, *Exec VP*
Tim McGrew, *Technical Staff*
Diane Peter, *Opers Mgr*
Lisa Roberts, *Marketing Staff*
▲ **EMP:** 15
SQ FT: 5,000

SALES (est): 3.1MM **Privately Held**
WEB: www.spcontrols.com
SIC: 3577 Computer peripheral equipment

(P-15340)
SPYRUS INC (PA)
103 Bonaventura Dr, San Jose
(95134-2106)
PHONE.............................408 392-9131
Sue Pontius, *CEO*
Tom Dickens, *COO*
Ed Almojuela, *Treasurer*
Steve Kadash, *Vice Pres*
EMP: 40
SQ FT: 15,000
SALES (est): 7.6MM **Privately Held**
WEB: www.spyrus.com
SIC: 3577 7371 7372 Computer periph-
eral equipment; computer software devel-
opment; prepackaged software

(P-15341)
**SURFACE MOUNT TECH
CENTRE**
Also Called: Smt Centre
431 Kato Ter, Fremont (94539-8333)
PHONE.............................408 935-9548
Gary Walker, *Manager*
EMP: 350
SALES (corp-wide): 216.1MM **Privately
Held**
SIC: 3577 3672 Computer peripheral
equipment; printed circuit boards
HQ: Smtc Manufacturing Corporation Of
Canada
7050 Woodbine Ave Suite 300
Markham ON L3R 4
905 479-1810

(P-15342)
SYMBOL TECHNOLOGIES LLC
208 Channing Way, Alameda (94502-6452)
PHONE.............................510 684-2974
EMP: 140
SALES (corp-wide): 4.2B **Publicly Held**
SIC: 3577 Computer peripheral equipment
HQ: Symbol Technologies, Llc
1 Zebra Plz
Holtsville NY 11742
631 737-6851

(P-15343)
SYNAPTICS INCORPORATED
1109 Mckay Dr, San Jose (95131-1706)
PHONE.............................408 904-1100
EMP: 10
SALES (corp-wide): 1.6B **Publicly Held**
SIC: 3577 7372 Computer peripheral
equipment; prepackaged software
PA: Synaptics Incorporated
1251 Mckay Dr
San Jose CA 95131
408 904-1100

(P-15344)
**SYNAPTICS INCORPORATED
(PA)**
1251 Mckay Dr, San Jose (95131-1709)
PHONE.............................408 904-1100
Michael Hurlston, *President*
Francis F Lee, *Ch of Bd*
EMP: 272
SQ FT: 213,000
SALES: 1.6B **Publicly Held**
WEB: www.synaptics.com
SIC: 3577 7372 Computer peripheral
equipment; application computer software

(P-15345)
**SYNCHRONIZED
TECHNOLOGIES INC**
Also Called: Synchrotech
7536 Tyrone Ave, Van Nuys (91405-1447)
PHONE.............................213 368-3760
Eric Hartouni, *President*
John Melikian, *Treasurer*
▲ **EMP:** 15
SALES (est): 2.7MM **Privately Held**
WEB: www.synchrotech.com
SIC: 3577 Computer peripheral equipment

▲ = Import ▼=Export
◆ =Import/Export

(P-15346)
T S MICROTECH INC
17109 Gale Ave, City of Industry
(91745-1810)
PHONE..................................626 839-8998
Steve Heung, *President*
▲ EMP: 10
SQ FT: 7,000
SALES (est): 1.8MM **Privately Held**
WEB: www.fancard.com
SIC: 3577 Computer peripheral equipment

(P-15347)
TELEPATHY INC
1202 Kifer Rd, Sunnyvale (94086-5304)
PHONE..................................408 306-8421
EMP: 25 EST: 2013
SQ FT: 600
SALES (est): 2.5MM **Privately Held**
SIC: 3577

(P-15348)
TELESYNERGY RESEARCH USA INC
40101 Spady St, Fremont (94538-2981)
PHONE..................................408 200-9879
Hsueh-CHI Chin, *President*
EMP: 15 EST: 1993
SALES (est): 1.8MM **Privately Held**
WEB: www.telesynergy.com
SIC: 3577 Computer peripheral equipment

(P-15349)
TERARECON INC (PA)
4000 E 3rd Ave Ste 200, Foster City
(94404-4825)
PHONE..................................650 372-1100
Jeff Sorenson, *President*
Jeffery Sorenson, *President*
Tiecheng Zhao, *Senior VP*
Dianne Oseto, *Admin Sec*
Jeffrey Sorenson, *VP Mktg*
▲ EMP: 80
SQ FT: 11,000
SALES (est): 50.4MM **Privately Held**
WEB: www.terarecon.com
SIC: 3577 5734 Computer peripheral
equipment; computer peripheral equip-
ment

(P-15350)
TONER2PRINT INC
9450 7th St Ste J, Rancho Cucamonga
(91730-5679)
PHONE..................................909 972-9656
Angel Granados, *CEO*
EMP: 10 EST: 2010
SQ FT: 1,100
SALES: 1.4MM **Privately Held**
SIC: 3577 2893 3955 Computer periph-
eral equipment; screen process ink; print
cartridges for laser & other computer
printers

(P-15351)
TOPAZ SYSTEMS INC (PA)
875 Patriot Dr Ste A, Moorpark
(93021-3351)
PHONE..................................805 520-8282
Anthony Zank, *President*
Tom Jacques, *Electrical Engi*
Josh Burkett, *Engineer*
George Vargas, *Engineer*
Priesz Daniel, *Sales Executive*
▲ EMP: 40
SQ FT: 16,000
SALES (est): 10.9MM **Privately Held**
WEB: www.topazsystems.com
SIC: 3577 7371 Graphic displays, except
graphic terminals; custom computer pro-
gramming services

(P-15352)
TOTALTHERMALIMAGINGCOM
8341 La Mesa Blvd, La Mesa
(91942-0217)
PHONE..................................619 303-5884
Britt Midgette, *Principal*
EMP: 10
SALES (est): 1MM **Privately Held**
SIC: 3577 Bar code (magnetic ink) printers

(P-15353)
TOYE CORPORATION
9230 Deering Ave, Chatsworth
(91311-5803)
P.O. Box 3997 (91313-3997)
PHONE..................................818 882-4000
Gordon Morris, *President*
Robert Morrow, *Consultant*
▲ EMP: 12
SQ FT: 5,000
SALES (est): 1.2MM **Privately Held**
WEB: www.toyecorp.com
SIC: 3577 Computer peripheral equipment

(P-15354)
TRANSPARENT DEVICES INC
Also Called: Cybertouch
853 Lawrence Dr, Newbury Park
(91320-2232)
PHONE..................................805 499-5000
Abraham Gohari, *President*
Sergio Loera, *Production*
Dina De Falco, *Manager*
Jennifer Shoemaker, *Manager*
EMP: 20 EST: 1982
SQ FT: 25,000
SALES (est): 4.6MM **Privately Held**
WEB: www.cybertouch.com
SIC: 3577 Graphic displays, except
graphic terminals

(P-15355)
TRI-NET TECHNOLOGY INC
21709 Ferrero, Walnut (91789-5209)
PHONE..................................909 598-8818
Tom Chung, *President*
Lisa Chung, *CFO*
Akinori Ogawa, *Vice Pres*
Cynthia Hsu, *Finance*
Eric Chung, *Sales Staff*
▲ EMP: 100
SQ FT: 35,000
SALES (est): 18.4MM **Privately Held**
SIC: 3577 3571 Computer peripheral
equipment; electronic computers

(P-15356)
TURN-LUCKILY INTERNATIONAL INC
Also Called: Total Technologies
9710 Research Dr, Irvine (92618-4327)
PHONE..................................949 465-0200
George Huang, *President*
Vivien KAO, *Technology*
Nancy Tran, *Technology*
Brian McLeod, *VP Sales*
▲ EMP: 13
SQ FT: 16,000
SALES (est): 2.8MM **Privately Held**
WEB: www.total-technologies.com
SIC: 3577 Computer peripheral equipment

(P-15357)
ULTERA SYSTEMS INC
28241 Crown Valley Pkwy F115, Laguna
Niguel (92677-4441)
PHONE..................................949 367-8800
MO Nourmohamadian, *President*
Cindy Karch, *CFO*
EMP: 17
SQ FT: 6,500
SALES: 5.2MM **Privately Held**
WEB: www.ultera.com
SIC: 3577 Key-tape equipment, except
drives

(P-15358)
UNITED TOTE COMPANY
4205 Ponderosa Ave, San Diego
(92123-1525)
PHONE..................................858 279-4250
Scott Pfennighausen, *Engr R&D*
Roger Villarreal, *Senior Engr*
EMP: 20
SALES (corp-wide): 1B **Publicly Held**
SIC: 3577 7378 Computer peripheral
equipment; computer peripheral equip-
ment repair & maintenance
HQ: United Tote Company
700 Central Ave
Louisville KY 40208

(P-15359)
US COMPUTERS INC
Also Called: U S Technical Institute
181 W Orangethorpe Ave C, Placentia
(92870-6931)
PHONE..................................714 528-0514
Uzma Sheikh, *President*
Saleem Sheikh, *Vice Pres*
EMP: 12
SQ FT: 3,500
SALES: 3MM **Privately Held**
SIC: 3577 8249 Computer peripheral
equipment; vocational schools

(P-15360)
USI MANUFACTURING SERVICES INC
1255 E Arques Ave, Sunnyvale
(94085-4701)
PHONE..................................408 636-9600
Betsy Santiago, *Executive Asst*
Rylane Goncalez, *Analyst*
Cherine Lyle, *Human Res Mgr*
Hillary Plank, *Manager*
EMP: 64
SALES (est): 39.7K **Privately Held**
WEB: www.usica.com
SIC: 3577 Computer peripheral equipment

(P-15361)
VERIFONE INC
10590 W Ocean Air Dr # 250, San Diego
(92130-4679)
PHONE..................................858 436-2270
John Sarkisian, *Branch Mgr*
EMP: 22
SALES (corp-wide): 183MM **Privately Held**
SIC: 3577 Readers, sorters or inscribers,
magnetic ink
HQ: Verifone, Inc.
88 W Plumeria Dr
San Jose CA 95134
408 232-7800

(P-15362)
VIA MECHANICS (USA) INC (DH)
Also Called: Hitachi Via Mechanics USA Inc
150 Charcot Ave Ste C, San Jose
(95131-1130)
PHONE..................................408 392-9650
Noboru Matsuoka, *CEO*
Ted Saito, *Treasurer*
◆ EMP: 12
SQ FT: 8,000
SALES: 14.1MM **Privately Held**
WEB: www.hitachi-via-usa.com
SIC: 3577 Computer peripheral equipment

(P-15363)
VISIONEER INC (HQ)
5673 Gibraltar Dr Ste 150, Pleasanton
(94588-8569)
PHONE..................................925 251-6300
J Larry Smart, *Ch of Bd*
Walt Thinsen, *President*
Greg Elder, *CFO*
John C Dexter, *Vice Pres*
Jeremy Smith, *Technology*
▲ EMP: 50 EST: 1994
SQ FT: 15,000
SALES (est): 10.3MM **Privately Held**
WEB: www.visioneer.com
SIC: 3577 Computer peripheral equipment

(P-15364)
VUZE INC
489 S El Camino Real, San Mateo
(94402-1727)
PHONE..................................650 963-4750
Gilles Bianrosa, *CEO*
EMP: 30
SQ FT: 10,000
SALES (est): 3.2MM **Privately Held**
WEB: www.azureus-inc.com
SIC: 3577 Data conversion equipment,
media-to-media: computer

(P-15365)
WESTERN TELEMATIC INC
5 Sterling, Irvine (92618-2517)
PHONE..................................949 586-9950
Daniel Morrison, *CEO*
Herbert Hoover III, *Ch of Bd*
Everett Sykes, *Vice Pres*
Manda Graves, *Sales Staff*

▲ EMP: 50 EST: 1964
SQ FT: 24,000
SALES (est): 12.7MM **Privately Held**
WEB: www.wti.com
SIC: 3577 5065 Computer peripheral
equipment; electronic parts & equipment

(P-15366)
WILLIAM HO
Also Called: MBA Electronics
40760 Encyclopedia Cir, Fremont
(94538-2473)
PHONE..................................510 226-9089
William Ho, *Owner*
EMP: 15
SQ FT: 21,000
SALES (est): 2.2MM **Privately Held**
WEB: www.mbaelectronics.com
SIC: 3577 Computer peripheral equipment

(P-15367)
WINTEC INDUSTRIES INC (PA)
8674 Thornton Ave, Newark (94560-3330)
PHONE..................................510 953-7440
Sanjay Bonde, *CEO*
Jennifer Chen, *Vice Pres*
Eric Wang, *Principal*
Kong Chen Chen, *Admin Sec*
Ann Varghese, *Administration*
▲ EMP: 100
SQ FT: 85,000
SALES (est): 81.6MM **Privately Held**
SIC: 3577 3674 3572 Computer periph-
eral equipment; semiconductors & related
devices; computer storage devices

(P-15368)
ZEBRA TECHNOLOGIES CORPORATION
1440 Innovative Dr # 100, San Diego
(92154-6631)
PHONE..................................619 661-5465
Mark Wallace, *Branch Mgr*
Dennis Slattery, *Engineer*
Mike Stgermain, *Engineer*
Victor Molina, *Senior Mgr*
Timothy Wong, *Senior Mgr*
EMP: 400
SALES (corp-wide): 4.2B **Publicly Held**
SIC: 3577 Bar code (magnetic ink) printers
PA: Zebra Technologies Corporation
3 Overlook Pt
Lincolnshire IL 60069
847 634-6700

(P-15369)
ZEBRA TECHNOLOGIES CORPORATION
Also Called: Eltron International
30601 Agoura Rd, Agoura Hills
(91301-2150)
PHONE..................................805 579-1800
Don Skinner, *Branch Mgr*
Warren Myers, *Program Mgr*
Chuck Heiberger, *Info Tech Mgr*
Edward Dacey, *Software Engr*
Mike Millman, *VP Engrg*
EMP: 400
SALES (corp-wide): 4.2B **Publicly Held**
WEB: www.zebra.com
SIC: 3577 Bar code (magnetic ink) printers
PA: Zebra Technologies Corporation
3 Overlook Pt
Lincolnshire IL 60069
847 634-6700

(P-15370)
ZEBRA TECHNOLOGIES INTL LLC
2940 N 1st St, San Jose (95134-2021)
PHONE..................................408 473-8500
Jill Stelfox, *Manager*
Farrar Pittman, *Partner*
Keith Bosse, *Office Admin*
Teresa Bauer, *Admin Asst*
Jim Hesse, *Business Anlyst*
EMP: 17
SALES (corp-wide): 4.2B **Publicly Held**
SIC: 3577 Computer peripheral equipment
HQ: Zebra Technologies International, Llc
3 Overlook Pt
Lincolnshire IL 60069
847 634-6700

3578 Calculating & Accounting Eqpt

(P-15371)
ASTERES INC (PA)
4110 Sorrento Valley Blvd, San Diego (92121-1429)
PHONE...............................858 777-8600
Linda Pinney, *CEO*
Marc Thorstenson, *President*
Chris Juetten, *Senior VP*
Martin Bridges, *Vice Pres*
Valerie Gionis, *Vice Pres*
▲ **EMP:** 29
SALES (est): 4.7MM **Privately Held**
WEB: www.asteres.com
SIC: 3578 Cash registers

(P-15372)
AT SYSTEMS TECHNOLOGIES INC
301 N Lake Ave Ste 600, Pasadena (91101-5129)
PHONE...............................317 591-2616
John Sims, *President*
Ronald Lambert, *Shareholder*
Thomas Wantz, *Treasurer*
Rex A Townsend, *Admin Sec*
Patricia Sims, *Asst Treas*
EMP: 35
SALES (est): 5.4MM
SALES (corp-wide): 1.5MM **Privately Held**
WEB: www.autovend.com
SIC: 3578 Coin counters; change making machines
HQ: Garda Cl Technical Services, Inc.
700 S Federal Hwy Ste 300
Boca Raton FL 33432

(P-15373)
CAR ENTERPRISES INC
13100 Main St, Hesperia (92345-4625)
PHONE...............................760 947-6411
Sam Anabi, *President*
EMP: 14
SALES (corp-wide): 132MM **Privately Held**
SIC: 3578 Automatic teller machines (ATM)
PA: C.A.R Enterprises, Inc.
1450 N Benson Ave Unit A
Upland CA 91786
909 932-9242

(P-15374)
COMMUNITY MERCH SOLUTIONS LLC
Also Called: CMS
27201 Puerta Real Ste 120, Mission Viejo (92691-8555)
PHONE...............................877 956-9258
EMP: 35
SALES: 2.9MM **Privately Held**
SIC: 3578

(P-15375)
KOBUS BUSINESS SYSTEMS LLC
Also Called: Kobus Harmse
254 N Alta Ave, Dinuba (93618-1548)
P.O. Box 330 (93618-0330)
PHONE...............................559 595-1915
Kobus Harmse,
EMP: 12
SQ FT: 1,800
SALES: 1.5MM **Privately Held**
SIC: 3578 Calculating & accounting equipment

(P-15376)
PAYMENTMAX PROCESSING INC
600 Hampshire Rd Ste 120, Westlake Village (91361-2584)
P.O. Box 3847, Thousand Oaks (91359-0847)
PHONE...............................805 557-1692
Tony Shap, *President*
EMP: 60
SALES (est): 6.3MM **Privately Held**
SIC: 3578 Point-of-sale devices

(P-15377)
POS PORTAL INC (HQ)
180 Promenade Cir Ste 215, Sacramento (95834-2940)
PHONE...............................530 695-3005
Mike Baur, *CEO*
Kevin Nguyen, *Partner*
Scott Agatep, *COO*
Gus Constancio, *Vice Pres*
Evamarie K Ghiggeri, *Vice Pres*
▲ **EMP:** 28
SQ FT: 12,500
SALES (est): 14.1MM **Publicly Held**
WEB: www.posportal.com
SIC: 3578 3699 Point-of-sale devices; security control equipment & systems

(P-15378)
SIERRA NATIONAL CORPORATION
5140 Alzeda Dr, La Mesa (91941-5725)
PHONE...............................619 258-8200
Fred C Forbes, *President*
Gary Wadsworth, *Vice Pres*
EMP: 40
SQ FT: 5,000
SALES (est): 5MM **Privately Held**
WEB: www.sierranational.com
SIC: 3578 7374 Point-of-sale devices; data processing service

(P-15379)
SUZHOU SOUTH
18351 Colima Rd Ste 82, Rowland Heights (91748-2791)
PHONE...............................626 322-0101
Joel Wynne, *Director*
EMP: 300 EST: 2017
SALES: 16MM **Privately Held**
SIC: 3578 Banking machines

(P-15380)
VERIFONE INC (DH)
88 W Plumeria Dr, San Jose (95134-2134)
PHONE...............................408 232-7800
Paul Galant, *CEO*
Marc Rothman, *CFO*
Katrekia Gambrell, *Treasurer*
Alok Bhanot, *Exec VP*
Albert Liu, *Exec VP*
◆ **EMP:** 190 EST: 1981
SALES (est): 383.5MM
SALES (corp-wide): 183MM **Privately Held**
SIC: 3578 7372 3577 3575 Point-of-sale devices; operating systems computer software; application computer software; computer peripheral equipment; printers, computer; computer terminals; engineering services; current-carrying wiring devices
HQ: Verifone Systems, Inc.
88 W Plumeria Dr
San Jose CA 95134
408 232-7800

(P-15381)
VERIFONE INC
2455 Augustine Dr, Santa Clara (95054)
PHONE...............................408 232-7800
Gene Hodges, *Branch Mgr*
EMP: 155
SALES (corp-wide): 183MM **Privately Held**
SIC: 3578 Point-of-sale devices
HQ: Verifone, Inc.
88 W Plumeria Dr
San Jose CA 95134
408 232-7800

(P-15382)
VERIFONE SYSTEMS INC (HQ)
88 W Plumeria Dr, San Jose (95134-2134)
PHONE...............................408 232-7800
Mike Pulli, *CEO*
Marc E Rothman, *CFO*
Marc Rothman, *CFO*
Vin D'Agostino, *Exec VP*
Albert Liu, *Exec VP*
▲ **EMP:** 92
SALES (est): 1.5B
SALES (corp-wide): 183MM **Privately Held**
SIC: 3578 7372 Point-of-sale devices; operating systems computer software; application computer software

PA: Vertex Holdco, Inc.
88 W Plumeria Dr
San Jose CA 95134
408 232-7800

3579 Office Machines, NEC

(P-15383)
INTELMAIL USA INC
9965 Horn Rd Ste D, Sacramento (95827-1995)
PHONE...............................916 361-9300
Heros Dilanchian, *President*
Cindy Ferrario, *Corp Secy*
Bow Smith, *General Mgr*
▲ **EMP:** 13
SQ FT: 14,000
SALES: 4MM **Privately Held**
SIC: 3579 Mailing machines

(P-15384)
LYNDE-ORDWAY COMPANY INC
3308 W Warner Ave, Santa Ana (92704-5395)
P.O. Box 8709, Fountain Valley (92728-8709)
PHONE...............................714 957-1311
Thomas Ordway, *President*
Penny Ordway, *Admin Sec*
EMP: 18 EST: 1925
SQ FT: 30,000
SALES (est): 3.6MM **Privately Held**
WEB: www.lynde-ordway.com
SIC: 3579 5999 5044 7359 Paper handling machines; coin wrapping machines; business machines & equipment; office equipment; equipment rental & leasing; industrial equipment services

(P-15385)
OLA CORPORATE SERVICES INC
6404 Wilshire Blvd # 525, Los Angeles (90048-5503)
PHONE...............................323 655-1005
Ola Boykin, *CEO*
Mamon Boykin, *CFO*
EMP: 11 EST: 2000
SQ FT: 850
SALES: 177.9K **Privately Held**
SIC: 3579 7389 Typing & word processing machines; translation services

(P-15386)
OUTDOOR GALORE INC
5010 Young St, Bakersfield (93311-9899)
PHONE...............................661 831-8662
Timothy Scott Clark, *Administration*
EMP: 16
SALES (corp-wide): 2.7MM **Privately Held**
SIC: 3579 Mailing, letter handling & addressing machines
PA: Outdoor Galore, Inc.
6801 White Ln Ste A1
Bakersfield CA 93309
661 831-8662

(P-15387)
PARKER POWIS INC
2929 5th St, Berkeley (94710-2736)
PHONE...............................510 848-2463
Kevin Parker, *President*
Charles Marino, *COO*
Tony Cheng, *CFO*
Julie Banados, *Administration*
Sacramento Gonzalez, *Technical Staff*
▲ **EMP:** 75
SQ FT: 54,000
SALES (est): 15MM **Privately Held**
WEB: www.powis.com
SIC: 3579 Binding machines, plastic & adhesive

(P-15388)
PITNEY BOWES INC
25531 Commercentre Dr # 110, Lake Forest (92630-8874)
PHONE...............................949 855-7844
Olaf Jeziorek, *Branch Mgr*
Al Dettlings, *Principal*
EMP: 60

SALES (corp-wide): 3.5B **Publicly Held**
SIC: 3579 7359 Postage meters; business machine & electronic equipment rental services
PA: Pitney Bowes Inc.
3001 Summer St Ste 3
Stamford CT 06905
203 356-5000

(P-15389)
PITNEY BOWES INC
71 Park Ln, Brisbane (94005-1309)
PHONE...............................415 330-9423
Tom Smith, *Manager*
Patrick Sawchuk, *Project Mgr*
Jim Peterson, *Manager*
EMP: 33
SALES (corp-wide): 3.5B **Publicly Held**
SIC: 3579 7359 Postage meters; business machine & electronic equipment rental services
PA: Pitney Bowes Inc.
3001 Summer St Ste 3
Stamford CT 06905
203 356-5000

(P-15390)
PITNEY BOWES INC
11355 W Olympic Blvd Fl 2, Los Angeles (90064-1656)
PHONE...............................310 312-4288
Diane Poynter, *Branch Mgr*
EMP: 42
SALES (corp-wide): 3.5B **Publicly Held**
SIC: 3579 7359 Postage meters; business machine & electronic equipment rental services
PA: Pitney Bowes Inc.
3001 Summer St Ste 3
Stamford CT 06905
203 356-5000

(P-15391)
RESINA
27455 Bostik Ct, Temecula (92590-3698)
PHONE...............................951 296-6585
Loonie Beltes, *President*
EMP: 15
SALES (est): 1.2MM **Privately Held**
SIC: 3579 Office machines

(P-15392)
RICOH ELECTRONICS INC
17482 Pullman St, Irvine (92614-5527)
PHONE...............................714 259-1220
Paul Bakonyi, *Manager*
EMP: 300
SQ FT: 49,359 **Privately Held**
WEB: www.ricohelectronicsinc.com
SIC: 3579 3571 Mailing, letter handling & addressing machines; typing & word processing machines; paper handling machines; electronic computers
HQ: Ricoh Electronics, Inc.
1100 Valencia Ave
Tustin CA 92780
714 566-2500

(P-15393)
WHITTIER MAILING PRODUCTS INC (PA)
13019 Park St, Santa Fe Springs (90670-4005)
PHONE...............................562 464-3000
Richard A Casford, *President*
Luis Contreras, *Vice Pres*
EMP: 42
SQ FT: 5,000
SALES (est): 6.1MM **Privately Held**
WEB: www.traytag.com
SIC: 3579 Mailing, letter handling & addressing machines

(P-15394)
Y NISSIM INC
Also Called: Shear Tech
23509 Spires St, Canoga Park (91304-5241)
PHONE...............................818 718-9024
Yosi Nissim, *President*
Ariela Nissim, *Vice Pres*
EMP: 10
SALES (est): 1.6MM **Privately Held**
WEB: www.sheartech.net
SIC: 3579 Check writing, endorsing or signing machines

▲ = Import ▼=Export
◆ =Import/Export

3581 Automatic Vending Machines

(P-15395)
AQUA PRODUCTS INC
6860 Oran Cir Ste 6351, Buena Park
(90621-3304)
P.O. Box 5930 (90622-5930)
PHONE.......................714 670-0691
Daniel Suh, *President*
Miguel Bonaparte, *Executive*
◆ **EMP:** 30
SQ FT: 5,100
SALES (est): 3.9MM **Privately Held**
WEB: www.watervending.com
SIC: 3581 Automatic vending machines

(P-15396)
BVP DESIGNS INC
21354 Nordhoff St Ste 101, Chatsworth
(91311-6910)
PHONE.......................818 280-2900
Benjiman Grill, *President*
Shimon Grill, *Vice Pres*
EMP: 19
SALES: 2MM **Privately Held**
SIC: 3581 Automatic vending machines

(P-15397)
CARACAL ENTERPRISES LLC
Also Called: Ventek International
1260 Holm Rd Ste A, Petaluma
(94954-7152)
PHONE.......................707 773-3373
Gary Catt, *President*
Bill Paulin, *CFO*
Carol Kresse, *Controller*
▲ **EMP:** 30
SALES: 5.3MM **Privately Held**
SIC: 3581 Automatic vending machines

(P-15398)
GW SERVICES LLC (DH)
1385 Park Center Dr, Vista (92081-8338)
PHONE.......................760 560-1111
Brian McInerney, *President*
Steven D Stringer, *CFO*
EMP: 37
SALES (est): 7.9MM
SALES (corp-wide): 286MM **Publicly Held**
SIC: 3581 Automatic vending machines
HQ: Primo Water Operations, Inc.
101 N Cherry St Ste 501
Winston Salem NC 27101
336 331-4000

(P-15399)
NUTRITION WITHOUT BORDERS LLC
Also Called: H.U.M.A.N. Healthy Vending
4641 Leahy St, Culver City (90232-3515)
PHONE.......................310 845-7745
Sean Kelly,
Andrew Mackensen,
▼ **EMP:** 15
SQ FT: 10,000
SALES (est): 3.3MM **Privately Held**
SIC: 3581 5122 Automatic vending machines; vitamins & minerals

(P-15400)
OAK MANUFACTURING COMPANY INC
2850 E Vernon Ave, Vernon (90058-1804)
P.O. Box 58201, Los Angeles (90058-0201)
PHONE.......................323 581-8087
James Hinton, *President*
EMP: 14
SQ FT: 12,000
SALES (est): 2.3MM **Privately Held**
WEB: www.oakmfg.com
SIC: 3581 Automatic vending machines

(P-15401)
PANTRY RETAIL INC
3095 Kerner Blvd Ste N, San Rafael
(94901-5420)
PHONE.......................415 234-3574
Russ Cohn, *CEO*
Alex Yancher, *COO*
Arnold Lee, *CFO*

EMP: 15
SALES (est): 3.1MM **Privately Held**
SIC: 3581 Automatic vending machines

3582 Commercial Laundry, Dry Clean & Pressing Mchs

(P-15402)
AMERICAN CLEANER AND LAUNDRY
Also Called: American Linen Rental
2230 S Depot St Ste D, Santa Maria
(93455-1205)
PHONE.......................805 925-1571
Chris Consorti, *Shareholder*
Steve Consorti, *Consultant*
EMP: 37
SALES (est): 1.3MM **Privately Held**
SIC: 3582 Commercial laundry equipment

(P-15403)
CONSOLIDATED LAUNDRY LLC
Also Called: Consolidated Laundry Machinery
211 Erie St, Pomona (91768-3328)
P.O. Box 2985 (91769-2985)
PHONE.......................323 232-2417
Jason Farber,
Martin Pharis, *President*
Gabriel Camacho, *Opers Mgr*
John Alvarez, *Director*
EMP: 26
SQ FT: 20,000
SALES: 5MM **Privately Held**
SIC: 3582 Commercial laundry equipment

(P-15404)
DENIM-TECH LLC
2300 E 52nd St, Vernon (90058-3444)
PHONE.......................323 277-8998
Toyoo Tashiro, *Mng Member*
Duane Dunbar, *General Mgr*
Ken Nguyen, *Graphic Designe*
Miki Imada,
▲ **EMP:** 100
SQ FT: 50,000
SALES: 19.8MM **Privately Held**
SIC: 3582 Commercial laundry equipment

(P-15405)
NEWBOLD CLEANERS
4211 Arden Way Ste A, Sacramento
(95864-3037)
PHONE.......................916 481-1130
Kil Cho, *CEO*
Shawn Cho, *Vice Pres*
EMP: 15
SALES (est): 900K **Privately Held**
SIC: 3582 Commercial laundry equipment

3585 Air Conditioning & Heating Eqpt

(P-15406)
ACCO ENGINEERED SYSTEMS INC
3121 N Sillect Ave # 104, Bakersfield
(93308-6364)
PHONE.......................661 631-1975
EMP: 14
SALES (corp-wide): 777.3MM **Privately Held**
SIC: 3585 Air conditioning equipment, complete
PA: Acco Engineered Systems, Inc.
888 E Walnut St
Pasadena CA 91101
818 244-6571

(P-15407)
ACE HEATERS LLC
130 Klug Cir, Corona (92880-5424)
PHONE.......................951 738-2230
William Newbauer III, *President*
EMP: 20
SQ FT: 40,000

SALES: 3MM
SALES (corp-wide): 9.1MM **Privately Held**
SIC: 3585 3443 Heating equipment, complete; boiler & boiler shop work; boiler shop products: boilers, smokestacks, steel tanks; industrial vessels, tanks & containers
PA: Heh Holdings Llc
45 Seymour St
Stratford CT

(P-15408)
ADVANCED AEROSPACE
10781 Forbes Ave, Garden Grove
(92843-4977)
PHONE.......................714 265-6200
Steve Flowers, *President*
Joe St Amand, *Controller*
EMP: 200
SALES (est): 14.9MM **Privately Held**
SIC: 3585 Refrigeration equipment, complete

(P-15409)
AIR SOLUTIONS LLC
37310 Cedar Blvd Ste J, Newark
(94560-4156)
PHONE.......................510 573-6474
Armando Mota, *Mng Member*
EMP: 10
SALES (est): 2.2MM **Privately Held**
SIC: 3585 3822 Refrigeration & heating equipment; thermostats & other environmental sensors

(P-15410)
ALLIANCE AIR PRODUCTS LLC
Also Called: Especializados Del Aire
2285 Michael Faraday Dr, San Diego
(92154-7926)
PHONE.......................619 428-9688
Thomas R Sieber, *Mng Member*
John Searsi,
John Staples,
EMP: 113
SQ FT: 3,300
SALES (est): 25MM **Privately Held**
SIC: 3585 Air conditioning units, complete: domestic or industrial

(P-15411)
ANTHONY DOORS INC (DH)
Also Called: Anthony International
12391 Montero Ave, Sylmar (91342-5370)
PHONE.......................818 365-9451
Jeffrey Clark, *CEO*
David Lautenschaelger, *CFO*
Craig Little, *Senior VP*
Jason Kozakis, *Vice Pres*
Michael Murth, *Vice Pres*
◆ **EMP:** 850
SQ FT: 350,000
SALES (est): 627.6MM
SALES (corp-wide): 6.9B **Publicly Held**
WEB: www.kramerusa.net
SIC: 3585 Refrigeration & heating equipment
HQ: Dover Printing & Identification, Inc.
3005 Highland Pkwy # 200
Downers Grove IL 60515
630 541-1540

(P-15412)
AQUA LOGIC INC
9558 Camino Ruiz, San Diego
(92126-4435)
PHONE.......................858 292-4773
Douglas Russell, *President*
Maralin Russell, *Vice Pres*
Curtis Epps, *Engineer*
Constantino Dimaano, *Purch Agent*
▼ **EMP:** 20
SQ FT: 20,000
SALES (est): 6.1MM **Privately Held**
WEB: www.aqualogicinc.com
SIC: 3585 Refrigeration & heating equipment

(P-15413)
ARI INDUSTRIES INC
Also Called: Airdyne Refrigeration
17018 Edwards Rd, Cerritos (90703-2422)
PHONE.......................714 993-3700
R Tony Bedi, *President*

Ruth Lee Bedi, *Vice Pres*
Ruth Bedi, *Vice Pres*
Ruth Lee, *Vice Pres*
Gary Altiero, *Project Mgr*
EMP: 80
SQ FT: 20,000
SALES (est): 17.9MM **Privately Held**
WEB: www.airdyne.com
SIC: 3585 Refrigeration equipment, complete

(P-15414)
AVIATE ENTERPRISES INC
5844 Price Ave, McClellan (95652-2407)
PHONE.......................916 993-4000
Timothy P Devine, *CEO*
EMP: 27
SQ FT: 3,700
SALES (est): 570.9K **Privately Held**
SIC: 3585 3843 5599 3629 Refrigeration & heating equipment; dental equipment & supplies; golf cart, powered; electronic generation equipment; medical & hospital equipment

(P-15415)
BALTIMORE AIRCOIL COMPANY INC
B A C
15341 Road 28 1/2, Madera (93638-2395)
P.O. Box 960 (93639-0960)
PHONE.......................559 673-9231
Han Yen, *Branch Mgr*
Javier Garcia, *IT Executive*
Kevin Deliman, *Business Mgr*
Victoria Jackson, *Human Res Mgr*
Glen McCaskill, *Materials Mgr*
EMP: 150
SQ FT: 45,000
SALES (corp-wide): 2.4B **Privately Held**
WEB: www.baltimoreaircoil.com
SIC: 3585 Condensers, refrigeration; refrigeration equipment, complete
HQ: Baltimore Aircoil Company, Inc.
7600 Dorsey Run Rd
Jessup MD 20794
410 799-6200

(P-15416)
BIGFOGG INC (PA)
42095 Zevo Dr Ste A2, Temecula
(92590-3747)
PHONE.......................951 587-2460
Christopher Miehl, *President*
Chris Miehl, *President*
EMP: 18
SQ FT: 4,000
SALES: 1.5MM **Privately Held**
WEB: www.bigfogg.com
SIC: 3585 Air conditioning condensers & condensing units

(P-15417)
BROOKS AUTOMATION INC
Also Called: Brooks Polycold Systems
46702 Bayside Pkwy, Fremont
(94538-6582)
PHONE.......................510 498-8745
Steve Michaud, *Branch Mgr*
EMP: 67
SALES (corp-wide): 631.5MM **Publicly Held**
SIC: 3585 3679 Refrigeration & heating equipment; electronic circuits
PA: Brooks Automation, Inc.
15 Elizabeth Dr
Chelmsford MA 01824
978 262-2400

(P-15418)
CALIFRNIA INDUS RFRGN MCHS INC
3197 Cornerstone Dr, Mira Loma
(91752-1028)
PHONE.......................951 361-0040
Shahnaz Ghelani, *Corp Secy*
Rahim Ghelani, *President*
Mansoor Ghelani, *Vice Pres*
EMP: 15

SALES (est): 3.7MM **Privately Held**
WEB: www.caindustrial.com
SIC: **3585** 5075 1711 1731 Air conditioning equipment, complete; compressors for refrigeration & air conditioning equipment; compressors, air conditioning; heating & air conditioning contractors; general electrical contractor

(P-15419)
COMMERCIAL DISPLAY SYSTEMS LLC
Also Called: C D S
17341 Sierra Hwy, Canyon Country (91351-1625)
PHONE...................................818 361-8160
Fernando Calderon,
Nick Beswick, *Technology*
Robert Enriquez, *Technology*
Duane Beswick,
John T Karnes, *Mng Member*
EMP: 30
SQ FT: 17,000
SALES (est): 7MM **Privately Held**
SIC: **3585** Refrigeration & heating equipment

(P-15420)
COMPU AIRE INC
8167 Byron Rd, Whittier (90606-2615)
PHONE...................................562 945-8971
Balbir Narang, *President*
Robert Narang, *Vice Pres*
Mahendra Ahir, *Engineer*
▲ EMP: 150
SQ FT: 75,000
SALES (est): 31.1MM **Privately Held**
WEB: www.compu-aire.com
SIC: **3585** Air conditioning units, complete: domestic or industrial

(P-15421)
COOLTEC REFRIGERATION CORP
1250 E Franklin Ave B, Pomona (91766-5449)
P.O. Box 1150 (91769-1150)
PHONE...................................909 865-2229
Paul Bedi, *CEO*
George Share, *Corp Secy*
Katherine Sanchez, *Office Mgr*
EMP: 22
SQ FT: 50,000
SALES (est): 6.3MM **Privately Held**
WEB: www.cooltecrefrigeration.com
SIC: **3585** Refrigeration equipment, complete

(P-15422)
CUSTOM MECHANICAL SYSTEMS LLC
1830 Embarcadero Ste 103, Oakland (94606-5230)
PHONE...................................510 347-5500
Daniel Hyman, *Mng Member*
Mark Parry, *COO*
EMP: 11 EST: 2008
SQ FT: 7,400
SALES (est): 2MM **Privately Held**
SIC: **3585** Refrigeration & heating equipment

(P-15423)
DATA AIRE INC (HQ)
230 W Blueridge Ave, Orange (92865-4225)
PHONE...................................800 347-2473
Duncan Moffatt, *President*
Edward J Altieri, *Corp Secy*
▲ EMP: 101
SALES (est): 36.4MM
SALES (corp-wide): 379MM **Privately Held**
WEB: www.dataaire.com
SIC: **3585** Air conditioning units, complete: domestic or industrial
PA: Construction Specialties Inc.
3 Werner Way Ste 100
Lebanon NJ 08833
908 236-0800

(P-15424)
DIVERSIFIED PANELS SYSTEMS INC
Also Called: Diversified Construction
2345 Statham Blvd, Oxnard (93033-3911)
PHONE...................................805 487-9241
Richard C Bell, *CEO*
▲ EMP: 10
SALES (est): 6MM **Privately Held**
WEB: www.dpspanels.com
SIC: **3585** 5064 Lockers, refrigerated; refrigerators & freezers

(P-15425)
DUKERS APPLIANCE CO USA LTD (DH)
2488 Peck Rd, Whittier (90601-1604)
PHONE...................................562 568-4060
Yongfei Lai, *CEO*
Christopher Lee, *Admin Sec*
EMP: 10
SQ FT: 50,000
SALES (est): 3MM **Privately Held**
SIC: **3585** Refrigeration equipment, complete
HQ: Guangzhou Boaosi Appliance Co., Ltd.
No.5, Luogang Industrial Zone, Xinshi Rd., Xinke, Xinshi Town, B
Guangzhou 51043
206 263-0702

(P-15426)
DURO DYNE WEST CORP
10837 Commerce Way Ste D, Fontana (92337-8202)
PHONE...................................562 926-1774
Randall S Hinden, *President*
Bernard Hinden, *Director*
▲ EMP: 290 EST: 1961
SALES (est): 30.8MM
SALES (corp-wide): 122.1MM **Privately Held**
SIC: **3585** 3444 Air conditioning units, complete: domestic or industrial; sheet metalwork
PA: Dyne Duro National Corp
81 Spence St
Bay Shore NY 11706
631 249-9000

(P-15427)
ELCO RFRGN SOLUTIONS LLC
Also Called: Kulthorn North America
2554 Commercial St, San Diego (92113-1132)
PHONE...................................619 255-5251
Dean Rafiee, *Mng Member*
EMP: 5000 EST: 2014
SALES (est): 228.8MM **Privately Held**
SIC: **3585** Compressors for refrigeration & air conditioning equipment
PA: Kulthorn Kirby Public Company Limited
126 Soi Chalong Krung 31, Chalong Krung Road
Lat Krabang 10520

(P-15428)
ENERGY LABS INC (DH)
Also Called: E L I
1695 Cactus Rd, San Diego (92154-8102)
PHONE...................................619 671-0100
Ray Irani, *President*
Miguel Reyes, *COO*
James Domholt, *Vice Pres*
Ward Hotze, *Vice Pres*
Bob Leclercq, *Executive*
▲ EMP: 400
SQ FT: 150,000
SALES (est): 201.9MM
SALES (corp-wide): 2.9B **Privately Held**
WEB: www.energylabs.com
SIC: **3585** Heating & air conditioning combination units
HQ: Vertiv Corporation
1050 Dearborn Dr
Columbus OH 43085
614 888-0246

(P-15429)
ENLINK GEOENERGY SERVICES INC
2630 Homestead Pl, Rancho Dominguez (90220-5610)
PHONE...................................424 242-1200
Mark Mizrahi, *President*
Howard Johnson, *CIO*
EMP: 46
SQ FT: 12,000
SALES (est): 6.6MM **Privately Held**
WEB: www.enlinkgeoenergy.com
SIC: **3585** Heat pumps, electric

(P-15430)
ENVIRO-INTERCEPT INC
7327 Varna Ave Unit 5, North Hollywood (91605-4183)
PHONE...................................818 982-6063
Fred Bonamici, *President*
Jim Watt, *Shareholder*
Carlos Alverado, *Vice Pres*
EMP: 12
SQ FT: 11,500
SALES (est): 1.7MM **Privately Held**
SIC: **3585** Refrigeration & heating equipment

(P-15431)
EVAPCO INC
Also Called: Evapco West
1900 W Almond Ave, Madera (93637-5208)
PHONE...................................559 673-2207
Steve Levake, *Manager*
John McCann, *Maint Spvr*
EMP: 150
SQ FT: 88,250
SALES (corp-wide): 382.7MM **Privately Held**
WEB: www.evapco.com
SIC: **3585** Air conditioning units, complete: domestic or industrial; refrigeration equipment, complete
PA: Evapco, Inc.
5151 Allendale Ln
Taneytown MD 21787
410 756-2600

(P-15432)
EVERIDGE INC
Also Called: Thermalrite
8886 White Oak Ave, Rancho Cucamonga (91730-5106)
PHONE...................................909 605-6419
Chris Kahler, *Branch Mgr*
EMP: 50 **Privately Held**
WEB: www.thermalrite.com
SIC: **3585** Refrigeration & heating equipment
PA: Everidge, Inc.
15600 37th Ave N Ste 100
Plymouth MN 55446

(P-15433)
FLUID INDUSTRIAL MFG INC
374 S Milpitas Blvd, Milpitas (95035-5421)
PHONE...................................408 782-9900
Kerry Kirchenbauer, *President*
EMP: 23
SALES (est): 4.5MM **Privately Held**
WEB: www.fluidindmfg.com
SIC: **3585** Refrigeration equipment, complete

(P-15434)
HUSSMANN CORPORATION
13770 Ramona Ave, Chino (91710-5423)
P.O. Box 5133 (91708-5133)
PHONE...................................909 590-4910
Mike Gleason, *General Mgr*
Jorge Marquez, *Human Res Mgr*
Nancy McElwee Taylor, *Manager*
EMP: 350 **Privately Held**
WEB: www.hussmann.com
SIC: **3585** 7623 Refrigeration & heating equipment; refrigeration service & repair
HQ: Hussmann Corporation
12999 St Charles Rock Rd
Bridgeton MO 63044
314 291-2000

(P-15435)
J P LAMBORN CO (PA)
Also Called: J P L
3663 E Wawona Ave, Fresno (93725-9236)
PHONE...................................559 650-2120
John P Lamborn Jr, *CEO*
Pam Lamborn, *Admin Sec*
Chad Ward, *Technology*
Deeane Eltrich, *Accountant*
Olga Valeriano, *Accountant*

◆ EMP: 167 EST: 1961
SQ FT: 125,000
SALES (est): 64.4MM **Privately Held**
WEB: www.jplflex.com
SIC: **3585** Heating & air conditioning combination units

(P-15436)
JENKINS BEVERAGE INC
3630 51st Ave Ste D, Sacramento (95823-1053)
PHONE...................................916 686-1800
George C Jenkins, *President*
EMP: 10
SALES (est): 1.8MM **Privately Held**
WEB: www.jbev.com
SIC: **3585** Refrigeration & heating equipment

(P-15437)
KOCH FILTER CORPORATION
10290 Birtcher Dr, Jurupa Valley (91752-1827)
PHONE...................................951 361-9017
Dan Campbell, *General Mgr*
EMP: 15 **Privately Held**
WEB: www.kochfilter.com
SIC: **3585** Refrigeration & heating equipment
HQ: Koch Filter Corporation
8401 Air Commerce Dr
Louisville KY 40219
502 634-4796

(P-15438)
KOOLFOG INC (PA)
31290 Plantation Dr, Thousand Palms (92276-6604)
PHONE...................................760 321-9203
Bryan Roe, *President*
EMP: 11
SQ FT: 4,000
SALES (est): 3.1MM **Privately Held**
WEB: www.koolfog.com
SIC: **3585** 7819 Humidifiers & dehumidifiers; visual effects production

(P-15439)
LENNOX
4000 Hamner Ave, Eastvale (91752-1022)
PHONE...................................800 953-6669
EMP: 14
SALES (est): 2.3MM **Privately Held**
SIC: **3585** Refrigeration & heating equipment

(P-15440)
LENNOX INDUSTRIES INC
2221 Eastman Ave, Oxnard (93030-5185)
PHONE...................................805 288-8200
Genero De Leon, *Branch Mgr*
EMP: 148
SALES (corp-wide): 3.8B **Publicly Held**
SIC: **3585** Furnaces, warm air: electric; air conditioning units, complete: domestic or industrial
HQ: Lennox Industries Inc.
2100 Lake Park Blvd
Richardson TX 75080
972 497-5000

(P-15441)
LMW ENTERPRISES LLC
Also Called: Lrc Coil Company
12309 Telegraph Rd, Santa Fe Springs (90670-3309)
PHONE...................................562 944-1969
Michael Williams, *General Mgr*
George Aburto,
Linda Williams,
Chester Schaffer, *Mng Member*
▲ EMP: 35 EST: 2010
SQ FT: 35,000
SALES (est): 7.5MM **Privately Held**
WEB: www.lrccoil.com
SIC: **3585** Refrigeration equipment, complete; condensers, refrigeration; evaporative condensers, heat transfer equipment

(P-15442)
MARELLI NORTH AMERICA INC
9 Holland, Irvine (92618-2580)
PHONE...................................949 855-8050
Reid Armstrong, *Vice Pres*
EMP: 150 **Publicly Held**
WEB: www.ckna.com

▲ = Import ▼=Export
◆ =Import/Export

SIC: 3585 Air conditioning, motor vehicle
HQ: Marelli North America, Inc.
1 Calsonic Way
Shelbyville TN 37160
931 684-4490

(P-15443)
MARSAL PACKAGING & RFRGN
931 S Cypress St, La Habra (90631-6833)
PHONE................................714 812-6775
Salvatore Titone, *Principal*
Sal Titone, *President*
EMP: 16
SALES (est): 1.2MM **Privately Held**
SIC: 3585 Refrigeration equipment, complete

(P-15444)
MEE INDUSTRIES INC (PA)
16021 Adelante St, Irwindale (91702-3255)
PHONE................................626 359-4550
Thomas Rupert Mee III, *CEO*
Darcy Sloane, *President*
Berklie Oscarson, *Project Mgr*
Inna Romanova, *Project Mgr*
Lily Ward, *VP Finance*
▲ EMP: 10 EST: 1969
SQ FT: 26,000
SALES (est): 13.6MM **Privately Held**
WEB: www.meefog.com
SIC: 3585 0711 Humidifying equipment, except portable; soil preparation services

(P-15445)
MESTEK INC
Also Called: Anemostat Products
1220 E Watson Center Rd, Carson (90745-4206)
PHONE................................310 835-7500
Chang Hung, *Plant Mgr*
Blanca Olvera, *Executive*
Hari Thacker, *Controller*
EMP: 200
SALES (corp-wide): 629.1MM **Privately Held**
SIC: 3585 3549 3542 3354 Heating equipment, complete; metalworking machinery; punching, shearing & bending machines; shapes, extruded aluminum; mainframe computers; manufactured hardware (general)
PA: Mestek, Inc.
260 N Elm St
Westfield MA 01085
470 898-4533

(P-15446)
MICRO MATIC USA INC
19761 Bahama St 19791, Northridge (91324-3304)
PHONE................................818 701-9765
Torben Toffpegaard, *President*
Jim Motush, *CFO*
Brett Kresge, *Analyst*
Pamela Baldwin, *Human Res Mgr*
Mark Stirett, *Regl Sales Mgr*
EMP: 20
SALES (corp-wide): 260MM **Privately Held**
SIC: 3585 Refrigeration & heating equipment
HQ: Micro Matic Usa, Inc.
2386 Simon Ct
Brooksville FL 34604
352 544-1081

(P-15447)
MYDAX INC
12260 Shale Ridge Ln # 4, Auburn (95602-8400)
PHONE................................530 888-6662
Richard S Frankel, *CEO*
Thomas Spesick, *Vice Pres*
Kurt Graversgaard, *Engineer*
EMP: 19
SQ FT: 15,000
SALES: 2.5MM **Privately Held**
WEB: www.mydax.com
SIC: 3585 Refrigeration equipment, complete

(P-15448)
PROAIR LLC
12151 Madera Way, Riverside (92503-4849)
PHONE................................909 930-6224

Kevin McCarty, *Branch Mgr*
EMP: 10
SALES (corp-wide): 52.4MM **Privately Held**
SIC: 3585 5075 Air conditioning, motor vehicle; automotive air conditioners
HQ: Proair, Llc
6630 E State Highway 114
Haslet TX 76052
817 636-2308

(P-15449)
R E MICHEL COMPANY LLC
Also Called: R E Michel
155 W Victoria St, Long Beach (90805-2162)
PHONE................................310 885-9820
EMP: 18
SALES (corp-wide): 898.2MM **Privately Held**
SIC: 3585 Refrigeration equipment, complete
PA: R. E. Michel Company, Llc
1 Re Michel Dr
Glen Burnie MD 21060
410 760-4000

(P-15450)
R-COLD INC
1221 S G St, Perris (92570-2477)
PHONE................................951 436-5476
Michael Mulcahy, *President*
Ernest Gaston, *CFO*
Chris Stewart, *Purchasing*
Bernie Cold, *Foreman/Supr*
Joshua Elder, *Sales Staff*
EMP: 65
SQ FT: 28,000
SALES (est): 16.1MM **Privately Held**
WEB: www.r-cold.com
SIC: 3585 1541 Refrigeration & heating equipment; industrial buildings & warehouses

(P-15451)
RAHN INDUSTRIES INCORPORATED (PA)
2630 Pacific Park Dr, Whittier (90601-1611)
PHONE................................562 908-0680
John Hancock, *President*
Jeff Meier, *Vice Pres*
Claudia Maytum, *Admin Sec*
Valerie Warwick, *Manager*
▲ EMP: 60
SQ FT: 25,000
SALES (est): 14.8MM **Privately Held**
WEB: www.rahnindustries.com
SIC: 3585 Refrigeration & heating equipment

(P-15452)
REFRIGERATOR MANUFACTURERS LLC
Also Called: Airdyne Refrigeration
17018 Edwards Rd, Cerritos (90703-2422)
PHONE................................562 926-2006
Tony Bedi, *President*
EMP: 47
SALES (est): 6.8MM **Privately Held**
SIC: 3585 Condensers, refrigeration

(P-15453)
TAYLOR COML FOODSERVICE INC
Tyler Refrigeration
221 S Berry St, Brea (92821-4829)
PHONE................................714 255-7200
Phil Herman, *Controller*
EMP: 40
SQ FT: 55,605
SALES (corp-wide): 2.7B **Publicly Held**
WEB: www.ccr.carrier.com
SIC: 3585 Cabinets, show & display, refrigerated
HQ: Taylor Commercial Foodservice Inc.
750 N Blackhawk Blvd
Rockton IL 61072
815 624-8333

(P-15454)
TEAM AIR INC (PA)
Also Called: Team Air Conditioning Eqp
12771 Brown Ave, Riverside (92509-1831)
PHONE................................909 823-1957
Thirusenthil Nathan, *President*

Oliver Corbala, *Vice Pres*
EMP: 35
SALES (est): 12.3MM **Privately Held**
SIC: 3585 Air conditioning equipment, complete

(P-15455)
THREE STAR RFRGN ENGRG INC
Also Called: Kool Star
21720 S Wilmington Ave # 309, Long Beach (90810-1641)
PHONE................................310 327-9090
James Pak, *President*
William So, *CFO*
Kyung Lee, *Admin Sec*
◆ EMP: 50
SQ FT: 68,000
SALES (est): 6.4MM **Privately Held**
WEB: www.koolstar.com
SIC: 3585 4222 Air conditioning condensers & condensing units; condensers, refrigeration; refrigerated warehousing & storage

(P-15456)
TRANE US INC
1601 S De Anza Blvd 235, Cupertino (95014-5347)
PHONE................................408 257-5212
Melvin Davis, *Vice Pres*
Jimmy Carter, *Area Mgr*
Heidi Everly, *Office Mgr*
Darrell Leahy, *Technology*
Erick Hanson, *Technical Staff*
EMP: 15 **Privately Held**
SIC: 3585 Refrigeration & heating equipment
HQ: Trane U.S. Inc.
3600 Pammel Creek Rd
La Crosse WI 54601
608 787-2000

(P-15457)
TRANE US INC
310 Soquel Way, Sunnyvale (94085-4101)
PHONE................................408 481-3600
Don Druyanoff, *Manager*
EMP: 150 **Privately Held**
SIC: 3585 Refrigeration & heating equipment
HQ: Trane U.S. Inc.
3600 Pammel Creek Rd
La Crosse WI 54601
608 787-2000

(P-15458)
TRANE US INC
Also Called: Southern California Trane
3253 E Imperial Hwy, Brea (92821-6722)
PHONE................................626 913-7123
John Clark, *Branch Mgr*
EMP: 100 **Privately Held**
SIC: 3585 Heating & air conditioning combination units
HQ: Trane U.S. Inc.
3600 Pammel Creek Rd
La Crosse WI 54601
608 787-2000

(P-15459)
TRANE US INC
20450 E Walnut Dr N, Walnut (91789-2921)
PHONE................................626 913-7913
Terry Goins, *Area Mgr*
Tyler Clemmer, *District Mgr*
Ray Fraire, *Technician*
Angela Puent, *Project Mgr*
Paul Robertson, *Project Mgr*
EMP: 23 **Privately Held**
SIC: 3585 Refrigeration & heating equipment
HQ: Trane U.S. Inc.
3600 Pammel Creek Rd
La Crosse WI 54601
608 787-2000

(P-15460)
TRANE US INC
2222 Kansas Ave Ste C, Riverside (92507-2635)
PHONE................................951 801-6020
EMP: 62 **Privately Held**
SIC: 3585 Refrigeration & heating equipment

HQ: Trane U.S. Inc.
3600 Pammel Creek Rd
La Crosse WI 54601
608 787-2000

(P-15461)
TRANE US INC
890 Service St Ste A, San Jose (95112-1374)
PHONE................................408 437-0390
EMP: 62 **Privately Held**
SIC: 3585 Refrigeration & heating equipment
HQ: Trane U.S. Inc.
3600 Pammel Creek Rd
La Crosse WI 54601
608 787-2000

(P-15462)
TRANE US INC
1930 E Carson St Ste 101, Carson (90810-1246)
PHONE................................310 971-4555
EMP: 62 **Privately Held**
SIC: 3585 Refrigeration & heating equipment
HQ: Trane U.S. Inc.
3600 Pammel Creek Rd
La Crosse WI 54601
608 787-2000

(P-15463)
TRANE US INC
3565 Corporate Ct Fl 1, San Diego (92123-2415)
PHONE................................858 292-0833
Tyler Clemmer, *Branch Mgr*
Lauren Stephens, *Marketing Staff*
EMP: 50 **Privately Held**
SIC: 3585 Refrigeration & heating equipment
HQ: Trane U.S. Inc.
3600 Pammel Creek Rd
La Crosse WI 54601
608 787-2000

(P-15464)
TRANE US INC
3026 N Bus Park Ave # 104, Fresno (93727-8647)
PHONE................................559 271-4625
Tyler Clemment, *Manager*
Cindy Taft, *Project Mgr*
EMP: 20 **Privately Held**
SIC: 3585 Refrigeration & heating equipment
HQ: Trane U.S. Inc.
3600 Pammel Creek Rd
La Crosse WI 54601
608 787-2000

(P-15465)
TRMC SALE CORPORATION
4215 E Airport Dr, Ontario (91761-1565)
PHONE................................800 290-7073
Joshua Klein, *President*
EMP: 56
SQ FT: 50,000
SALES: 5MM **Privately Held**
SIC: 3585 Room coolers, portable

(P-15466)
TRUMED SYSTEMS INCORPORATED
4350 Executive Dr Ste 120, San Diego (92121-2140)
PHONE................................844 878-6331
Jesper Jensen, *President*
Peter Dickstein, *Vice Pres*
Jim Martindale, *Vice Pres*
Thomas Netzer, *General Mgr*
Joe Milkovits, *CTO*
EMP: 24
SQ FT: 2,000
SALES: 1MM **Privately Held**
SIC: 3585 5078 Refrigeration & heating equipment; commercial refrigeration equipment

(P-15467)
TURBO COIL INC
1532 Sinaloa Ave, Pasadena (91104-2744)
PHONE................................626 644-6254
Hector Delgadillo, *CEO*
EMP: 12
SQ FT: 2,000

PRODUCTS & SVCS

SALES (est): 1.1MM **Privately Held**
SIC: **3585** Compressors for refrigeration & air conditioning equipment

(P-15468)
TURBO REFRIGERATION SYSTEMS
1740 Evergreen St, Duarte (91010-2845)
PHONE..............................626 599-9777
Hector Delgadillo, *CEO*
Jose Carbajal, *Principal*
Roberta Delgadillo, *Principal*
EMP: 26
SQ FT: 4,000
SALES (est): 1.5MM **Privately Held**
SIC: **3585** Condensers, refrigeration

(P-15469)
UTILITY REFRIGERATOR
12160 Sherman Way, North Hollywood (91605-5501)
P.O. Box 570782, Tarzana (91357-0782)
PHONE..............................818 764-6200
Michael Michrowski, *President*
▲ EMP: 15
SALES (est): 2.5MM **Privately Held**
SIC: **3585** Parts for heating, cooling & refrigerating equipment

(P-15470)
VEGE-MIST INC
Also Called: Alco Designs
407 E Redondo Beach Blvd, Gardena (90248-2312)
PHONE..............................310 353-2300
Samuel Cohen, *CEO*
Liz Luna, *General Mgr*
Dick Warden, *Sales Staff*
▲ EMP: 24
SQ FT: 8,000
SALES (est): 8.7MM **Privately Held**
WEB: www.alcodesigns.com
SIC: **3585** 2541 5074 Humidifying equipment, except portable; store & office display cases & fixtures; water purification equipment

(P-15471)
VENSTAR INC (PA)
9250 Owensmouth Ave, Chatsworth (91311-5853)
PHONE..............................818 341-8760
Steve Dushane, *President*
▲ EMP: 15
SALES (est): 3.8MM **Privately Held**
WEB: www.venstarusa.com
SIC: **3585** Refrigeration & heating equipment

(P-15472)
VINOTHEQUE WINE CELLARS
1738 E Alpine Ave, Stockton (95205-2505)
PHONE..............................209 466-9463
Thomas R Schneider, *CEO*
Franklin Pfaller-Martin, *Prdtn Mgr*
Manuel Keo, *Sales Mgr*
Lannette Johnson, *Manager*
Adam Eigenberger, *Accounts Exec*
▼ EMP: 16 EST: 1999
SQ FT: 30,000
SALES (est): 5.5MM **Privately Held**
WEB: www.vinotheque.com
SIC: **3585** Refrigeration equipment, complete

(P-15473)
WESTAIRE ENGINEERING INC
5820 S Alameda St, Vernon (90058-3432)
PHONE..............................323 587-3347
Vazgen Galadjian, *President*
Shane Bekian, *Vice Pres*
Kevin Galadjian, *Vice Pres*
Arabyan Hovhannes, *Chief Engr*
▲ EMP: 15
SQ FT: 50,000
SALES (est): 1.7MM **Privately Held**
SIC: **3585** 5075 Air conditioning units, complete: domestic or industrial; ventilating equipment & supplies

(P-15474)
WHITES HVAC SERVICES INC
131 E Knotts St, Nipomo (93444-9423)
P.O. Box 365 (93444-0365)
PHONE..............................805 801-0167
Mike White, *President*

Georgia White, *CFO*
EMP: 11
SALES: 300K **Privately Held**
SIC: **3585** 7389 Heating & air conditioning combination units;

(P-15475)
WILLIAMS FURNACE CO (HQ)
Also Called: Williams Comfort Products
250 W Laurel St, Colton (92324-1435)
PHONE..............................562 450-3602
Michael Markowich, *President*
Joseph Sum, *Treasurer*
Ruth Ann Davis, *Vice Pres*
James Gidwitz, *Vice Pres*
Aaron Smith, *Vice Pres*
▲ EMP: 173
SQ FT: 400,000
SALES (est): 36.2MM
SALES (corp-wide): 163.9MM **Publicly Held**
SIC: **3585** 3433 Refrigeration & heating equipment; heating equipment, except electric
PA: Continental Materials Corporation
440 S La Salle St # 3100
Chicago IL 60605
312 541-7200

(P-15476)
ZTECH
11481 Sunrise Gold Cir # 1, Rancho Cordova (95742-6545)
PHONE..............................916 635-6784
Michael Kuhlmann, *Owner*
EMP: 15
SQ FT: 9,000
SALES (est): 940K **Privately Held**
WEB: www.resconsys.com
SIC: **3585** 5075 Parts for heating, cooling & refrigerating equipment; ventilating equipment & supplies

3589 Service Ind Machines, NEC

(P-15477)
AATECH
6666 Box Springs Blvd, Riverside (92507-0726)
PHONE..............................909 854-3200
Jerry McAuley, *President*
Darlene McAuley, *Vice Pres*
EMP: 22
SALES (est): 7.1MM **Privately Held**
WEB: www.aatechwater.com
SIC: **3589** Water treatment equipment, industrial

(P-15478)
ACM RESEARCH INC
42307 Osgood Rd Ste I, Fremont (94539-5062)
PHONE..............................510 445-3700
David H Wang, *Ch of Bd*
Min Xu, *CFO*
Lisa Feng, *Officer*
Mark McKechnie, *VP Finance*
EMP: 187
SALES: 74.6MM **Privately Held**
SIC: **3589** Commercial cleaning equipment

(P-15479)
ADS WATER INC
12 N Altadena Dr, Pasadena (91107-3345)
PHONE..............................415 448-6266
Adam Stein, *CEO*
EMP: 10 EST: 2014
SQ FT: 5,000
SALES: 8MM **Privately Held**
SIC: **3589** Water treatment equipment, industrial
PA: Advantageous Systems Llc
525 S Hewitt St
Los Angeles CA 90013

(P-15480)
ADVANCED UV INC
16350 Manning Way, Cerritos (90703-2224)
PHONE..............................562 407-0299
Kiyomitsu Kevin Toma, *CEO*
Kiyo Toma, *Business Anlyst*

▲ EMP: 42 EST: 1996
SQ FT: 30,000
SALES (est): 10.7MM **Privately Held**
WEB: www.advanceduv.com
SIC: **3589** Water purification equipment, household type; water treatment equipment, industrial

(P-15481)
AMIAD USA INC
Also Called: Amiad Filtration Systems
1251 Maulhardt Ave, Oxnard (93030-7990)
P.O. Box 5547 (93031-5547)
PHONE..............................805 988-3323
Tom Akehurst, *President*
Issac Orlans, *Shareholder*
Wendy Paul, *Opers Staff*
Matt Aguiar, *Regl Sales Mgr*
Cosmo Kinsey, *Regl Sales Mgr*
▲ EMP: 35
SQ FT: 30,000
SALES (est): 7.6MM
SALES (corp-wide): 31.9MM **Privately Held**
WEB: www.amiadusa.com
SIC: **3589** Water treatment equipment, industrial
PA: Amiad Water Systems Ltd
Kibbutz
Amiad 12335
469 095-00

(P-15482)
APPLIED MEMBRANES INC
Also Called: Wateranywhere
2450 Business Park Dr, Vista (92081-8847)
PHONE..............................760 727-3711
Gulshan K Dhawan, *CEO*
◆ EMP: 100
SQ FT: 55,000
SALES (est): 32.7MM **Privately Held**
WEB: www.appliedmembranes.com
SIC: **3589** 5074 Water purification equipment, household type; water heaters & purification equipment

(P-15483)
AQUA MAN INC (PA)
Also Called: Aqua Man Service
2568 Turquoise Cir, Newbury Park (91320-1211)
P.O. Box 3906, Westlake Village (91359-0906)
PHONE..............................805 499-5707
Ray Hinton Sr, *President*
EMP: 10
SQ FT: 20,000
SALES (est): 1.7MM **Privately Held**
SIC: **3589** Water purification equipment, household type

(P-15484)
AQUAFINE CORPORATION (HQ)
29010 Avenue Paine, Valencia (91355-4198)
PHONE..............................661 257-4770
Roberta Veloz, *Chairman*
Michael Murphy, *President*
Jiawei Zhang, *Manager*
◆ EMP: 75
SQ FT: 100,000
SALES (est): 12.6MM
SALES (corp-wide): 19.8B **Publicly Held**
SIC: **3589** Water treatment equipment, industrial
PA: Danaher Corporation
2200 Penn Ave Nw Ste 800w
Washington DC 20037
202 828-0850

(P-15485)
AQUEOUS TECHNOLOGIES CORP
1678 N Maple St, Corona (92880-1706)
PHONE..............................909 944-7771
Michael Konrad, *CEO*
Cameron Heckman, *Accounting Mgr*
▲ EMP: 23
SQ FT: 15,000
SALES (est): 5.8MM **Privately Held**
WEB: www.aqueoustech.com
SIC: **3589** 3829 5084 7699 High pressure cleaning equipment; physical property testing equipment; cleaning equipment, high pressure, sand or steam; industrial machinery & equipment repair

(P-15486)
AQUEOUS VETS
288 Jasmine Way, Danville (94506-4747)
PHONE..............................951 764-9384
Robert G Craw, *President*
Charles Wells, *Vice Pres*
Rob Craw, *VP Bus Dvlpt*
Sarah Johnson, *General Mgr*
Chris Perry, *Mfg Staff*
EMP: 10
SALES (est): 2.1MM **Privately Held**
SIC: **3589** Sewage & water treatment equipment

(P-15487)
AUTO WASH CONCEPTS INC
11769 Telegraph Rd, Santa Fe Springs (90670-3657)
PHONE..............................562 948-2575
Douglas Wagner, *President*
Mimi Wagner, *Vice Pres*
EMP: 12
SQ FT: 5,400
SALES (est): 2.1MM **Privately Held**
SIC: **3589** 5087 Car washing machinery; carwash equipment & supplies

(P-15488)
AXEON WATER TECHNOLOGIES
40980 County Center Dr # 110, Temecula (92591-6002)
PHONE..............................760 723-5417
Augustin R Pavel, *President*
Cristhian Paez, *Technician*
Vallari Dalvi, *Engineer*
Ryan Balogh, *Buyer*
Trish Caudillo, *Opers Mgr*
◆ EMP: 85
SQ FT: 47,000
SALES (est): 15.8MM **Privately Held**
WEB: www.roultratec.com
SIC: **3589** 5999 Water filters & softeners, household type; water purification equipment, household type; water purification equipment

(P-15489)
B&W CUSTOM RESTAURANT EQP
541 E Jamie Ave, La Habra (90631-6842)
PHONE..............................714 578-0332
Nathan Bojorquez, *President*
EMP: 20
SALES (est): 5MM **Privately Held**
WEB: www.bwcustom.com
SIC: **3589** 8711 2599 Cooking equipment, commercial; industrial engineers; carts, restaurant equipment

(P-15490)
BAKER FILTRATION
Also Called: Baker Tanks
2700 California Ave, Pittsburg (94565-4100)
PHONE..............................925 252-2400
Mehrzad Emanual, *President*
EMP: 22
SALES (est): 3.7MM **Privately Held**
SIC: **3589** 5074 Water treatment equipment, industrial; water purification equipment

(P-15491)
BARHENA INC
Also Called: Adamation
1085 Bixby Dr, Hacienda Heights (91745-1704)
PHONE..............................888 383-8800
EMP: 25 EST: 1957
SQ FT: 45,000
SALES (est): 2.7MM **Privately Held**
WEB: www.adamationinc.com
SIC: **3589** 3952
PA: Flow Grinding Corp.
70 Conn St
Woburn MA 01801

(P-15492)
BAUER INTERNATIONAL CORP
9251 Irvine Blvd, Irvine (92618-1645)
PHONE..............................714 259-9800
Ernesto Cartojano, *CEO*
EMP: 10

▲ = Import ▼=Export
◆ =Import/Export

SALES (est): 1.7MM **Privately Held**
SIC: **3589** Water treatment equipment, industrial

(P-15493)
BLUE DESERT INTERNATIONAL INC
Also Called: Hydro Quip
510 N Sheridan St Ste A, Corona
(92880-2024)
PHONE....................................951 273-7575
Christopher W Kuttig, *President*
Frank Briese, *Vice Pres*
Mike Staab, *Info Tech Mgr*
▲ EMP: 80
SQ FT: 31,000
SALES (est): 16.6MM **Privately Held**
WEB: www.hydroquip.com
SIC: **3589** Swimming pool filter & water conditioning systems

(P-15494)
CENTRAL COAST WATER AUTHORITY
5250 Annlope Rd, Cholame (93461)
P.O. Box 505, Shandon (93461-0505)
PHONE....................................805 463-2122
Darin Dargatc, *Manager*
EMP: 13 **Privately Held**
WEB: www.ccwa.com
SIC: **3589** 9511 Sewage & water treatment equipment; air, water & solid waste management
PA: Central Coast Water Authority
255 Industrial Way
Buellton CA 93427

(P-15495)
CHEMICAL METHODS ASSOC LLC (DH)
Also Called: CMA Dish Machines
12700 Knott St, Garden Grove
(92841-3938)
PHONE....................................714 898-8781
Fred G Palmer, *President*
Nancy Guzman, *General Mgr*
Candy Wagers, *Executive Asst*
Joseph Nudel, *Design Engr*
Sherry Owen, *Purch Agent*
▲ EMP: 55
SQ FT: 50,000
SALES (est): 15.2MM
SALES (corp-wide): 106.4K **Privately Held**
WEB: www.cmadishmachines.com
SIC: **3589** Dishwashing machines, commercial
HQ: Ali Group North America Corporation
101 Corporate Woods Pkwy
Vernon Hills IL 60061
847 215-6565

(P-15496)
CHEMICAL TECHNOLOGIES INTL INC
Also Called: CTI
2747 Merc Dr Ste 200, Rancho Cordova
(95742)
P.O. Box 968 (95741-0968)
PHONE....................................916 638-1315
Clint Townsend, *CEO*
Risa Townsend, *Corp Secy*
Diane Corey, *Human Resources*
Chad Townsend, *Plant Mgr*
April Weister, *Manager*
▲ EMP: 18
SQ FT: 50,000
SALES (est): 3.8MM **Privately Held**
SIC: **3589** 2842 Commercial cleaning equipment; cleaning or polishing preparations

(P-15497)
CITY OF DELANO
Also Called: Delano Waste Water Treatment
1107 Lytle Ave, Delano (93215-9389)
PHONE....................................661 721-3352
Bill Hylton, *Manager*
EMP: 35 **Privately Held**
SIC: **3589** Water treatment equipment, industrial

PA: City Of Delano
1015 11th Ave
Delano CA 93215
661 721-3300

(P-15498)
CITY OF RIVERSIDE
Also Called: Water Treatment Plant
5950 Acorn St, Riverside (92504-1036)
PHONE....................................951 351-6140
Richard Pallante, *General Mgr*
EMP: 100 **Privately Held**
SIC: **3589** 9111 Water treatment equipment, industrial; mayors' offices
PA: City Of Riverside
3900 Main St Fl 7
Riverside CA 92522
951 826-5311

(P-15499)
CLARITY H2O LLC
752 Pomelo Dr, Vista (92081-6307)
PHONE....................................619 993-4780
Peter Petersen, *CEO*
D Edward McGawley, *COO*
EMP: 12
SQ FT: 25,000
SALES: 3MM **Privately Held**
SIC: **3589** Water treatment equipment, industrial

(P-15500)
CLEAN WATER TECHNOLOGY INC (HQ)
Also Called: CWT
151 W 135th St, Los Angeles (90061-1645)
PHONE....................................310 380-4648
Ariel Lechter, *CEO*
Abe Lu, *General Mgr*
Gerald Friedman, *Admin Sec*
Jason Hicks, *Sales Staff*
▲ EMP: 51 EST: 1996
SQ FT: 30,000
SALES (est): 14MM
SALES (corp-wide): 223.5MM **Privately Held**
WEB: www.cleanwatertech.com
SIC: **3589** Water treatment equipment, industrial
PA: Marvin Engineering Co., Inc.
261 W Beach Ave
Inglewood CA 90302
310 674-5030

(P-15501)
CLEAR WATER CORPORATION INC
7848 San Fernando Rd B, Sun Valley
(91352-4367)
PHONE....................................818 765-8293
Yarvin Gilboa, *President*
EMP: 12
SALES (est): 2.2MM **Privately Held**
SIC: **3589** Water treatment equipment, industrial

(P-15502)
CM BREWING TECHNOLOGIES LLC
Also Called: Ss Brewtech
13681 Newport Ave 8-261, Tustin
(92780-4689)
PHONE....................................888 391-9990
Mitchell Thomson, *CEO*
Michael Fabian, *COO*
Jake Kucera, *Officer*
Curt Kucera, *CTO*
EMP: 15
SALES (est): 12MM
SALES (corp-wide): 2.7B **Publicly Held**
SIC: **3589** 5046 Coffee brewing equipment; coffee brewing equipment & supplies
PA: The Middleby Corporation
1400 Toastmaster Dr
Elgin IL 60120
847 741-3300

(P-15503)
COMCO INC
2151 N Lincoln St, Burbank (91504-3392)
PHONE....................................818 333-8500
Colin Weightman, *President*
Anders Pineiro, *Info Tech Mgr*
Sally Salazar, *Opers Mgr*

Ozzy Cuellar, *Production*
EMP: 36
SQ FT: 12,500
SALES (est): 8.9MM **Privately Held**
WEB: www.microabrasive.com
SIC: **3589** 3291 Sandblasting equipment; abrasive products

(P-15504)
COMPASS WATER SOLUTIONS INC (PA)
15542 Mosher Ave, Tustin (92780-6425)
PHONE....................................949 222-5777
Thomas Farshler, *CEO*
Bill Tidmore, *CFO*
Jade Trieu, *Accountant*
Trent Nieto, *Regl Sales Mgr*
Ricky Sheppard, *Sales Staff*
▲ EMP: 50
SQ FT: 3,000
SALES (est): 12.3MM **Privately Held**
WEB: www.cworldwater.com
SIC: **3589** Water treatment equipment, industrial

(P-15505)
COOK KING INC
15120 Desman Rd, La Mirada
(90638-5737)
PHONE....................................714 739-0502
R C Miller, *President*
Glenna Miller, *Vice Pres*
EMP: 20
SQ FT: 15,000
SALES (est): 2.1MM **Privately Held**
SIC: **3589** Cooking equipment, commercial

(P-15506)
DE NORA WATER TECHNOLOGIES INC
1230 Rosecrans Ave # 300, Manhattan Beach (90266-2477)
PHONE....................................310 618-9700
Marwan Nesicolaci, *Vice Pres*
Wayne De Freest, *Purch Agent*
EMP: 100 **Privately Held**
SIC: **3589** Water treatment equipment, industrial
HQ: De Nora Water Technologies, Inc.
3000 Advance Ln
Colmar PA 18915
215 997-4000

(P-15507)
DEL OZONE HOLDING COMPANY INC
Also Called: Del Industries
3580 Sueldo St, San Luis Obispo
(93401-7338)
P.O. Box 4509 (93403-4509)
PHONE....................................805 541-1601
Mike Hawkins, *President*
Rick Totah, *CFO*
Frank Martin, *Engineer*
Dana Nelson, *Sales Associate*
Jeff Jones, *Sales Staff*
◆ EMP: 42
SALES (est): 10.6MM
SALES (corp-wide): 79.1MM **Privately Held**
WEB: www.delozone.com
SIC: **3589** 7389 8422 6719 Water purification equipment, household type; swimming pool & hot tub service & maintenance; water softener service; aquariums & zoological gardens; investment holding companies, except banks
PA: Custom Molded Products, Llc
36 Herring Rd
Newnan GA 30265
770 632-7112

(P-15508)
DYNAMIC COOKING SYSTEMS INC
Also Called: Fisher & Paykel
695 Town Center Dr # 180, Costa Mesa
(92626-1924)
PHONE....................................714 372-7000
Laurence Mawhinney, *CEO*
Jeff Elder, *CFO*
Scott Davies, *Chief Mktg Ofcr*
Esau Ramirez, *Executive*
Richard Berki, *Regional Mgr*
▲ EMP: 700

SQ FT: 140,000
SALES (est): 143.9MM
SALES (corp-wide): 7.8K **Privately Held**
WEB: www.dcsappliances.com
SIC: **3589** Cooking equipment, commercial
HQ: Fisher & Paykel Appliances Usa Holdings Inc.
695 Town Center Dr # 180
Costa Mesa CA 92626
888 936-7872

(P-15509)
ENAQUA
1350 Specialty Dr Ste D, Vista
(92081-8565)
PHONE....................................760 599-2644
Manoj Kumar Jhawar, *CEO*
Mark Maki, *President*
Rudra Mishra, *CFO*
Rick McIntyre, *Manager*
▲ EMP: 30
SQ FT: 26,000
SALES (est): 7.5MM
SALES (corp-wide): 4.1B **Privately Held**
WEB: www.enaqua.com
SIC: **3589** Water purification equipment, household type
HQ: Grundfos Ab
Lunnagardsgatan 6
Molndal 431 9
771 322-300

(P-15510)
ENGINEERED FOOD SYSTEMS
2490 Anselmo Dr, Corona (92879-8089)
P.O. Box 28321, Anaheim (92809-0144)
PHONE....................................714 921-9913
Martin Olguin, *President*
Irma Olguin, *CFO*
▲ EMP: 25
SQ FT: 18,000
SALES (est): 5.9MM **Privately Held**
SIC: **3589** 5084 Food warming equipment, commercial; food product manufacturing machinery

(P-15511)
ERG TRANSIT SYSTEMS (USA) INC
1800 Sutter St Ste 900, Concord
(94520-2536)
PHONE....................................925 686-8233
Steve Gallagher, *President*
Richard Long, *CFO*
James Carroll, *Treasurer*
Min WEI, *Exec VP*
Larry Weissbach, *Vice Pres*
EMP: 115
SQ FT: 14,474
SALES (est): 16.6MM **Privately Held**
SIC: **3589** Servicing machines, except dry cleaning, laundry: coin-oper.

(P-15512)
EVOQUA WATER TECHNOLOGIES
960 Ames Ave, Milpitas (95035-6303)
PHONE....................................408 586-9745
Bill Johnson, *Manager*
EMP: 13
SALES (est): 2.8MM **Privately Held**
SIC: **3589** Water treatment equipment, industrial

(P-15513)
EVOQUA WATER TECHNOLOGIES LLC
199 Harris Ave Ste 1, Sacramento
(95838-5012)
PHONE....................................916 564-1222
Steve Elliot, *Principal*
EMP: 13
SALES (corp-wide): 1.3B **Publicly Held**
SIC: **3589** Water treatment equipment, industrial
HQ: Evoqua Water Technologies Llc
210 6th Ave Ste 3300
Pittsburgh PA 15222
724 772-0044

(P-15514)
FILTRONICS INC
3726 E Miraloma Ave, Anaheim
(92806-2107)
PHONE....................................714 630-5040

William R Hoyer, *President*
EMP: 12
SALES (est): 2.7MM **Privately Held**
WEB: www.filtronics.com
SIC: 3589 Water purification equipment, household type; water treatment equipment, industrial

(P-15515)
G A SYSTEMS INC
226 W Carleton Ave, Orange (92867-3608)
PHONE..........................714 848-7529
Steven Anderson, *President*
Larry Wange, *Natl Sales Mgr*
EMP: 15 **EST:** 1968
SQ FT: 19,400
SALES (est): 3.2MM **Privately Held**
WEB: www.speedeeserv.com
SIC: 3589 Commercial cooking & food-warming equipment

(P-15516)
GET
Also Called: Vita Science Health Products
2030 W 17th St, Long Beach (90813-1012)
PHONE..........................562 989-5400
Fax: 562 983-7717
EMP: 15
SQ FT: 28,000
SALES (est): 2.4MM **Privately Held**
WEB: www.get-inc.com
SIC: 3589

(P-15517)
GORLITZ SEWER & DRAIN INC
10132 Norwalk Blvd, Santa Fe Springs (90670-3326)
PHONE..........................562 944-3060
James Kruger, *CEO*
Gerd Kruger, *President*
Elba Kruger, *Vice Pres*
▲ **EMP:** 30
SQ FT: 33,300
SALES (est): 6.7MM **Privately Held**
SIC: 3589 Sewer cleaning equipment, power

(P-15518)
H2O ENGINEERING INC
189 Granada Dr, San Luis Obispo (93401-7316)
PHONE..........................805 542-9253
Charles Robert Moncrief III, *CEO*
Chris Nosti, *Engineer*
Cody George, *VP Sales*
Chris Heyde, *Cust Mgr*
Erik Barker, *Supervisor*
EMP: 15
SQ FT: 8,000
SALES (est): 4.3MM **Privately Held**
SIC: 3589 8744 Water treatment equipment, industrial;

(P-15519)
HANNAH INDUSTRIES INC
Also Called: South Coast Water
401 S Santa Fe St, Santa Ana (92705-4139)
P.O. Box 247, Orange (92856-6247)
PHONE..........................714 939-7873
Roy Hall, *President*
Hayley Jackson, *Manager*
Kevin Kouns, *Manager*
Cristina Lomeli, *Manager*
EMP: 15
SQ FT: 15,000
SALES (est): 4.3MM **Privately Held**
WEB: www.hannahbean.com
SIC: 3589 5074 Water treatment equipment, industrial; water purification equipment

(P-15520)
HORIZON INTERNATIONAL LTD
Also Called: Hydrokleen Systems
1480 W Westfield Ave, Porterville (93257-1100)
PHONE..........................559 781-4640
Gordon Woods, *General Mgr*
Peggy Milford, *Principal*
▼ **EMP:** 15
SALES (est): 2MM **Privately Held**
WEB: www.hydrokleensystems.com
SIC: 3589 Swimming pool filter & water conditioning systems

(P-15521)
HRUBY ORBITAL SYSTEMS INC
Also Called: Hos
3275 Corporate Vw, Vista (92081-8528)
PHONE..........................760 936-8054
Jeffrey Thomas Hruby, *CEO*
◆ **EMP:** 10
SALES (est): 4.4MM **Privately Held**
SIC: 3589 Commercial cleaning equipment

(P-15522)
HYDROCOMPONENTS & TECH INC
Also Called: Hydro Components and Tech Inc
1175 Park Center Dr Ste H, Vista (92081-8303)
PHONE..........................760 598-0189
Robert Williamson, *President*
Elizabeth Pierce, *Corp Secy*
John Snyder, *Vice Pres*
▲ **EMP:** 15
SQ FT: 5,500
SALES (est): 2.3MM **Privately Held**
WEB: www.hcti.com
SIC: 3589 Water treatment equipment, industrial

(P-15523)
ILLINOIS TOOL WORKS INC
Stero
3200 Lakeville Hwy, Petaluma (94954-5903)
PHONE..........................800 762-7600
Terry Goodfellow, *Director*
EMP: 65
SALES (corp-wide): 14.7B **Publicly Held**
SIC: 3589 3443 Dishwashing machines, commercial; fabricated plate work (boiler shop)
PA: Illinois Tool Works Inc.
155 Harlem Ave
Glenview IL 60025
847 724-7500

(P-15524)
IMPERIAL MANUFACTURING CO
Also Called: Imperial Coml Cooking Eqp
1128 Sherborn St, Corona (92879-2089)
PHONE..........................951 281-1830
Peter Spenuzza, *President*
EMP: 170
SALES (est): 15.5MM **Privately Held**
SIC: 3589 Cooking equipment, commercial

(P-15525)
INNOVATIVE CONTROL SYSTEMS INC
20992 Bake Pkwy Ste 106, Lake Forest (92630-2170)
PHONE..........................610 881-8061
Cindy Penchishen, *Branch Mgr*
EMP: 20 **Privately Held**
SIC: 3589 Car washing machinery
PA: Innovative Control Systems, Inc.
1349 Jacobsburg Rd
Wind Gap PA 18091

(P-15526)
INTEGRATED AQUA SYSTEMS INC
1235 Activity Dr Ste A, Vista (92081-8562)
PHONE..........................760 745-2201
Sam Courtland, *CEO*
Jeff Richards, *Professor*
Jon Schoeneck, *Manager*
▲ **EMP:** 11
SALES: 950K **Privately Held**
WEB: www.integrated-aqua.com
SIC: 3589 Water treatment equipment, industrial

(P-15527)
INTEGRITY MUNICPL SYSTEMS LLC
13135 Danielson St # 204, Poway (92064-8874)
PHONE..........................858 486-1620
Roop Jain,
Kingston Leung, *Engineer*
Conar Marcos, *Buyer*
Jim Pike,
Georgios Ioannou, *Director*
◆ **EMP:** 16

SALES (est): 3.8MM **Privately Held**
SIC: 3589 1629 8711 Water treatment equipment, industrial; waste water & sewage treatment plant construction; engineering services

(P-15528)
J F DUNCAN INDUSTRIES INC (PA)
Also Called: Duray
9301 Stewart And Gray Rd, Downey (90241-5315)
PHONE..........................562 862-4269
Johnny F Wong, *CEO*
▲ **EMP:** 100
SALES (est): 31.9MM **Privately Held**
WEB: www.duray.org
SIC: 3589 Cooking equipment, commercial

(P-15529)
J L WINGERT COMPANY
11800 Monarch St, Garden Grove (92841-2113)
P.O. Box 6207 (92846-6207)
PHONE..........................714 379-5519
Tommy Thomas, *CEO*
Reeve Thomas, *Principal*
Robert Anderson, *Sales Staff*
EMP: 65
SQ FT: 16,000
SALES (est): 15.4MM **Privately Held**
WEB: www.jlwingert.com
SIC: 3589 5084 Water treatment equipment, industrial; industrial machinery & equipment

(P-15530)
JACUZZI INC (DH)
Also Called: Jacuzzi Outdoor Products
14525 Monte Vista Ave, Chino (91710-5721)
PHONE..........................909 606-7733
Thomas Koos, *CEO*
Roy A Jacuzzi, *Ch of Bd*
Donald C Devine, *President*
Paul Van Slyke, *VP Finance*
◆ **EMP:** 110 **EST:** 1979
SQ FT: 30,000
SALES (est): 541.5MM **Privately Held**
WEB: www.jacuzzi.com
SIC: 3589 3088 Swimming pool filter & water conditioning systems; hot tubs, plastic or fiberglass
HQ: Jacuzzi Brands Llc
13925 City Center Dr # 200
Chino Hills CA 91709
909 606-1416

(P-15531)
JWC ENVIRONMENTAL LLC
Also Called: Disposable Waste System
2600 S Garnsey St, Santa Ana (92707-3339)
PHONE..........................714 662-5829
Steve Glomb, *CFO*
Saretta Brown, *Vice Pres*
Greg Queen, *Vice Pres*
Jeremy Smith, *Vice Pres*
Robert Pepper, *Managing Dir*
EMP: 75
SQ FT: 45,637
SALES (corp-wide): 3.3B **Privately Held**
WEB: www.jwce.com
SIC: 3589 Sewage treatment equipment
HQ: Jwc Environmental Inc.
2850 Redhill Ave Ste 125
Santa Ana CA 92705
949 833-3888

(P-15532)
K2 PURE SOLUTIONS LP
950 Loveridge Rd, Pittsburg (94565-2808)
PHONE..........................925 203-1196
Richard Anthony, *Plant Mgr*
EMP: 60
SALES (corp-wide): 5.8MM **Privately Held**
SIC: 3589 Water purification equipment, household type
PA: K2 Pure Solutions, L.P.
3515 Massillon Rd Ste 290
Uniontown OH 44685
925 526-8112

(P-15533)
KATCHALL FLTRATION SYSTEMS LLC
263 W Fourth St, Beaumont (92223-2609)
PHONE..........................866 528-2425
Kip Searcy, *Sales Staff*
EMP: 10
SALES (est): 1.4MM **Privately Held**
SIC: 3589 Water filters & softeners, household type

(P-15534)
KELLERMYER BERGENSONS SVCS LLC (PA)
1959 Avenida Plaza Real, Oceanside (92056-6024)
PHONE..........................760 631-5111
Mark Minasian, *CEO*
Zulfiqar Rashid, *President*
Aj Long, *CFO*
Vicki Bernholz, *Officer*
Nathaniel Shaw, *Officer*
EMP: 10
SALES: 61.7MM **Privately Held**
SIC: 3589 Commercial cleaning equipment

(P-15535)
LAS COLINAS
600 S Jefferson St Ste M, Placentia (92870-6634)
PHONE..........................714 528-8100
C Christine Licata, *President*
Catharine Christine Licata, *President*
Anthony Licata, *CFO*
EMP: 15
SALES (est): 3.3MM **Privately Held**
SIC: 3589 1711 Asbestos removal equipment; plumbing contractors

(P-15536)
LIFESOURCE WATER SYSTEMS INC (PA)
523 S Fair Oaks Ave, Pasadena (91105-2605)
PHONE..........................626 792-9996
B J Wright, *President*
Jay Wright, *General Mgr*
Michelle Aragon, *Admin Asst*
Amy Wilson, *Graphic Designe*
Umesh Malhotra, *Controller*
EMP: 22
SQ FT: 10,000
SALES (est): 10.6MM **Privately Held**
WEB: www.lifesourcewater.com
SIC: 3589 5074 Water purification equipment, household type; water filters & softeners, household type; plumbing & hydronic heating supplies

(P-15537)
LOPEZ WATER TREATMENT PLANT
2845 Lopez Dr, Arroyo Grande (93420-4998)
PHONE..........................805 473-7152
Ron Coleman, *Superintendent*
EMP: 11
SALES (est): 916.4K **Privately Held**
SIC: 3589 4952 Water treatment equipment, industrial; sewerage systems

(P-15538)
MAR COR PURIFICATION INC
6351 Orangethorpe Ave, Buena Park (90620-1340)
PHONE..........................800 633-3080
Sean West, *Principal*
EMP: 22
SALES (est): 2.5MM **Privately Held**
SIC: 3589 Water treatment equipment, industrial

(P-15539)
MAZZEI INJECTOR COMPANY LLC
500 Rooster Dr, Bakersfield (93307-9555)
PHONE..........................661 363-6500
Angelo Mazzei, *CEO*
Geofffrey Whynot, *President*
Mary Mazzei, *Bd of Directors*
Celia Cobar, *Vice Pres*
▲ **EMP:** 24

SALES: 8MM
SALES (corp-wide): 8MM **Privately Held**
SIC: 3589 Water treatment equipment, industrial
PA: Mazzei Injector Corporation
    500 Rooster Dr
    Bakersfield CA 93307
    661 363-6500

(P-15540)
MCC CONTROLS LLC
Also Called: Primex
859 Cotting Ct Ste G, Vacaville
(95688-9354)
P.O. Box 1708, Detroit Lakes MN (56502-1708)
PHONE.................................218 847-1317
David Thomas, *President*
Taunia Suckert, *Corp Secy*
Todd Rammell, *Project Mgr*
Pete Santos, *Purch Agent*
Jeremy Bolin, *Manager*
EMP: 27
SALES (est): 2.9MM **Privately Held**
SIC: 3589 Sewage & water treatment equipment

(P-15541)
MD MANUFACTURING INC
34970 Mcmurtrey Ave, Bakersfield
(93308-9578)
PHONE.................................661 283-7550
Raymond Stewart, *President*
▲ **EMP:** 19
SQ FT: 34,000
SALES (est): 5.1MM **Privately Held**
SIC: 3589 Vacuum cleaners & sweepers, electric: industrial

(P-15542)
MEDIA BLAST & ABRASIVE INC
591 Apollo St, Brea (92821-3127)
PHONE.................................714 257-0484
Ronald Storer, *President*
EMP: 19
SALES (est): 3.7MM **Privately Held**
WEB: www.mediablast.com
SIC: 3589 3822 Sandblasting equipment; high pressure cleaning equipment; auto controls regulating residntl & coml environmt & applncs

(P-15543)
MICRODYN-NADIR US INC (DH)
Also Called: Trisep Corporation
93 S La Patera Ln, Goleta (93117-3246)
PHONE.................................805 964-8003
Peter Knappe, *President*
Kevin Edberg, *CFO*
Holly Wallis, *Planning*
Alfredo Rodriguez, *IT/INT Sup*
Jeffrey Flowers, *Design Engr*
◆ **EMP:** 90
SQ FT: 40,000
SALES: 23MM
SALES (corp-wide): 4.5B **Privately Held**
WEB: www.trisep.com
SIC: 3589 Water treatment equipment, industrial
HQ: Microdyn - Nadir Gmbh
    Kasteler Str. 45
    Wiesbaden 65203
    611 962-6001

(P-15544)
MONTAGUE COMPANY
1830 Stearman Ave, Hayward
(94545-1018)
P.O. Box 4954 (94540-4954)
PHONE.................................510 785-8822
Thomas M Whalen, *President*
Robert M Whalen, *Chairman*
George A Malloch, *Admin Sec*
◆ **EMP:** 105 **EST:** 1857
SQ FT: 100,000
SALES (est): 31.4MM **Privately Held**
WEB: www.montague-inc.com
SIC: 3589 Cooking equipment, commercial; commercial cooking & foodwarming equipment

(P-15545)
MYTEE PRODUCTS INC
13655 Stowe Dr, Poway (92064-6873)
PHONE.................................858 679-1191
John La Barbera, *President*

Gina La Barbera, *Corp Secy*
Paul La Barbera, *Vice Pres*
Kenny Lafoon, *Executive*
Melanie Alexander, *Department Mgr*
◆ **EMP:** 43
SQ FT: 45,000
SALES (est): 8.9MM **Privately Held**
WEB: www.mytee.com
SIC: 3589 Commercial cleaning equipment

(P-15546)
N/S CORPORATION (PA)
Also Called: NS Wash Systems
235 W Florence Ave, Inglewood
(90301-1293)
PHONE.................................310 412-7074
G Thomas Ennis Sr, *CEO*
Francis Penggardjaja, *Exec VP*
Lumen Ong, *Controller*
◆ **EMP:** 87
SQ FT: 80,000
SALES: 20MM **Privately Held**
WEB: www.nswash.com
SIC: 3589 Car washing machinery

(P-15547)
NALCO WTR PRTRTMENT SLTONS LLC
704 Richfield Rd, Placentia (92870-6760)
PHONE.................................714 792-0708
EMP: 28
SALES (corp-wide): 14.6B **Publicly Held**
SIC: 3589 Water treatment equipment, industrial
HQ: Nalco Water Pretreatment Solutions, Llc
    1601 W Diehl Rd
    Naperville IL 60563
    708 754-2550

(P-15548)
NEF TECH INC
Also Called: Ampac USA
5255 State St, Montclair (91763-6236)
PHONE.................................909 548-4900
Sammy Farag, *CEO*
Nevine Nakhla, *President*
Nevine Lewis, *CFO*
John Gunn, *Office Admin*
▼ **EMP:** 17
SQ FT: 10,000
SALES (est): 3.2MM **Privately Held**
SIC: 3589 Water treatment equipment, industrial

(P-15549)
NEW WAVE INDUSTRIES LTD (PA)
Also Called: Pur-Clean Pressure Car Wash
3315 Orange Grove Ave, North Highlands
(95660-5807)
PHONE.................................800 882-8854
Gary Hirsh, *CEO*
Nicolle Hearne, *Project Mgr*
Teresa Borchard, *Technical Staff*
Greg Oliver, *Engineer*
Dave Sharma, *Controller*
EMP: 18
SQ FT: 24,000
SALES (est): 3MM **Privately Held**
SIC: 3589 Car washing machinery

(P-15550)
NIECO CORPORATION
7950 Cameron Dr, Windsor (95492-8594)
PHONE.................................707 838-3226
Edward D Baker Sr, *President*
Edward Baker Jr, *Vice Pres*
Matthew Baker, *Vice Pres*
Patrick Baker, *Vice Pres*
Thomas Baker, *Vice Pres*
◆ **EMP:** 70
SQ FT: 80,000
SALES (est): 17.9MM
SALES (corp-wide): 2.7B **Publicly Held**
WEB: www.nieco.com
SIC: 3589 Commercial cooking & foodwarming equipment
PA: The Middleby Corporation
    1400 Toastmaster Dr
    Elgin IL 60120
    847 741-3300

(P-15551)
NIMBUS WATER SYSTEMS
42445 Avenida Alvarado, Temecula
(92590-3461)
P.O. Box 1478 (92593-1478)
PHONE.................................951 984-2800
Anthony Alexander Capone, *President*
Patricia Renee Capone, *CFO*
David See, *General Mgr*
EMP: 15
SQ FT: 25,000
SALES (est): 4.1MM
SALES (corp-wide): 546.7MM **Privately Held**
SIC: 3589 Water purification equipment, household type; water treatment equipment, industrial
HQ: Kinetico Incorporated
    10845 Kinsman Rd
    Newbury OH 44065
    440 564-9111

(P-15552)
OASIS STRUCTURES & WATER WORKS
273 Anker Ln, McKinleyville (95519-9710)
P.O. Box 2460 (95519-2460)
PHONE.................................707 839-1683
Timothy T White, *President*
Rene White, *Treasurer*
Nancy Custis, *Admin Sec*
EMP: 15
SALES (est): 724.7K **Privately Held**
SIC: 3589 Water filters & softeners, household type; water treatment equipment, industrial

(P-15553)
ORIGINCLEAR INC (PA)
525 S Hewitt St, Los Angeles (90013-2217)
PHONE.................................323 939-6645
T Riggs Eckelberry, *Ch of Bd*
Tom Marchesello, *COO*
Jean-Louis Kindler, *Ch Credit Ofcr*
EMP: 22 **EST:** 2007
SALES: 4.6MM **Publicly Held**
SIC: 3589 2869 Water treatment equipment, industrial; fuels

(P-15554)
OSMOSIS TECHNOLOGY INC
Also Called: Osmotik
6900 Hermosa Cir, Buena Park
(90620-1151)
PHONE.................................714 670-9303
Mike Joulakian, *President*
Sonia Joulakian, *Vice Pres*
EMP: 21
SQ FT: 13,000
SALES (est): 4.7MM **Privately Held**
WEB: www.osmotik.com
SIC: 3589 Water filters & softeners, household type

(P-15555)
OZOTECH INC (PA)
2401 E Oberlin Rd, Yreka (96097-9577)
PHONE.................................530 842-4189
Stephen Christiansen, *President*
▲ **EMP:** 20
SQ FT: 6,000
SALES (est): 3.7MM **Privately Held**
WEB: www.ozotech.com
SIC: 3589 Water purification equipment, household type; water treatment equipment, industrial

(P-15556)
PENTAIR FLOW TECHNOLOGIES LLC
Also Called: Pentair Water Group
2445 S Gearhart Ave, Fresno
(93725-1300)
PHONE.................................559 266-0516
Matt Miller, *Manager*
EMP: 128
SALES (corp-wide): 17.4B **Publicly Held**
WEB: www.aurorapump.com
SIC: 3589 Water purification equipment, household type
HQ: Pentair Flow Technologies, Llc
    1101 Myers Pkwy
    Ashland OH 44805
    419 289-1144

(P-15557)
PENTAIR WATER POOL AND SPA INC
Also Called: Pentair Aquatic Systems
13950 Mountain Ave, Chino (91710-9018)
PHONE.................................909 287-7800
Raul Umali, *Branch Mgr*
EMP: 45
SALES (corp-wide): 17.4B **Publicly Held**
WEB: www.pentairpool.com
SIC: 3589 Swimming pool filter & water conditioning systems
HQ: Pentair Water Pool And Spa, Inc.
    1620 Hawkins Ave
    Sanford NC 27330
    919 566-8000

(P-15558)
PENTAIR WATER POOL AND SPA INC
Also Called: Pentair Pool Products
10951 W Los Angeles Ave, Moorpark
(93021-9744)
P.O. Box 8085 (93020-8085)
PHONE.................................805 553-5003
Diane Larkin, *Manager*
Liz Mata, *Manager*
EMP: 45
SALES (corp-wide): 17.4B **Publicly Held**
WEB: www.pentairpool.com
SIC: 3589 3561 3569 3648 Swimming pool filter & water conditioning systems; pumps, domestic: water or sump; heaters, swimming pool: electric; underwater lighting fixtures; sporting & athletic goods; swimming pool & hot tub service & maintenance
HQ: Pentair Water Pool And Spa, Inc.
    1620 Hawkins Ave
    Sanford NC 27330
    919 566-8000

(P-15559)
PORIFERA INC
1575 Alvarado St, San Leandro
(94577-2640)
PHONE.................................510 695-2775
Olgica Bakajin, *CEO*
Jeff Jensen, *Chairman*
Jeffrey Mendelssohn, *Vice Pres*
Alexsander Noy, *Security Dir*
Charlie Benton, *Engineer*
EMP: 13
SQ FT: 5,000
SALES (est): 966.3K **Privately Held**
SIC: 3589 Water treatment equipment, industrial

(P-15560)
POWER KNOT LLC
2290 Ringwood Ave Ste A, San Jose
(95131-1718)
PHONE.................................408 480-2758
Iain Milnes, *President*
Agile Johns, *Engineer*
Lei Shan,
▲ **EMP:** 18
SQ FT: 1,600
SALES (est): 3.2MM **Privately Held**
SIC: 3589 Garbage disposers & compactors, commercial

(P-15561)
PRODUCT SOLUTIONS INC
1182 N Knollwood Cir, Anaheim
(92801-1307)
PHONE.................................714 545-9757
Robert Kreaton, *CEO*
Judith Keaton, *Admin Sec*
▲ **EMP:** 50
SQ FT: 25,000
SALES (est): 9.8MM **Privately Held**
WEB: www.productsolutions.net
SIC: 3589 3631 Commercial cooking & foodwarming equipment; household cooking equipment

(P-15562)
PRONTO PRODUCTS CO (PA)
9850 Siempre Viva Rd, San Diego
(92154-7247)
PHONE.................................619 661-6995
Carlos Matos, *CEO*
William E Parrot, *President*
Martha J Wagner, *Vice Pres*

Barbara Parrot, *Admin Sec*
EMP: 43
SALES (est): 10.5MM **Privately Held**
SIC: 3589 3496 Commercial cooking &
foodwarming equipment; miscellaneous
fabricated wire products

(P-15563)
PURE WATER CENTERS INC
Also Called: Absolute Aquasystems
8860 Corbin Ave Ste 382, Northridge
(91324-3309)
PHONE..................................818 316-1250
Raymundo Abad, *President*
EMP: 11
SALES (est): 1MM **Privately Held**
SIC: 3589 Water purification equipment,
household type

(P-15564)
PURI TECH INC
Also Called: Everfilt
3167 Progress Cir, Mira Loma
(91752-1112)
PHONE..................................951 360-8380
Barbara J Andrew, *President*
EMP: 25
SQ FT: 10,600
SALES (est): 5.4MM **Privately Held**
WEB: www.everfilt.com
SIC: 3589 5074 Water treatment equip-
ment, industrial; water purification equip-
ment

(P-15565)
PURONICS INCORPORATED (PA)
5775 Las Positas Rd, Livermore
(94551-7819)
PHONE..................................925 456-7000
Scott A Batiste, *President*
Mark Cosmez, *CFO*
EMP: 38
SALES (est): 19.5MM **Privately Held**
SIC: 3589 Swimming pool filter & water
conditioning systems

(P-15566)
QMP INC
25070 Avenue Tibbitts, Valencia
(91355-3447)
PHONE..................................661 294-6860
Freddy Vidal, *President*
Irma Vidal, *Vice Pres*
▲ **EMP:** 45
SQ FT: 40,000
SALES (est): 13MM **Privately Held**
WEB: www.qmpusa.com
SIC: 3589 Sewage & water treatment
equipment; water purification equipment,
household type; water treatment equip-
ment, industrial

(P-15567)
RANKIN-DELUX INC (PA)
3245 Corridor Dr, Eastvale (91752-1030)
PHONE..................................951 685-0081
L Vasan, *President*
William A Rankin, *Shareholder*
▲ **EMP:** 15 **EST:** 1965
SQ FT: 25,000
SALES (est): 2.4MM **Privately Held**
SIC: 3589 Cooking equipment, commercial

(P-15568)
RAPID RAMEN INC
9381 E Stockton Blvd # 230, Elk Grove
(95624-5070)
PHONE..................................916 479-7003
Christopher Alan Johnson, *CEO*
▲ **EMP:** 10 **EST:** 2010
SALES (est): 313.1K **Privately Held**
SIC: 3589 Commercial cooking & food-
warming equipment

(P-15569)
REMINGTON INC
28165 Avenue Crocker, Valencia
(91355-3440)
P.O. Box 800850, Santa Clarita (91380-
0850)
PHONE..................................661 257-9400
Bruce Burrows, *President*
Matt Houston, *Vice Pres*
▲ **EMP:** 21

SALES (est): 3.7MM **Privately Held**
SIC: 3589 Water purification equipment,
household type

(P-15570)
RENOVARE INTERNATIONAL INC
849 Balra Dr, El Cerrito (94530-3001)
PHONE..................................510 748-9993
George Kniazewycz, *President*
Charles Lemon, *Vice Pres*
EMP: 10
SALES (est): 1.5MM **Privately Held**
WEB: www.renovare.com
SIC: 3589 Water treatment equipment, in-
dustrial

(P-15571)
ROBERT YICK COMPANY INC
261 Bay Shore Blvd, San Francisco
(94124-1386)
PHONE..................................415 282-9707
Joseph Yick, *President*
Shew Yick, *Vice Pres*
Joe Yick, *Project Mgr*
EMP: 25
SQ FT: 10,000
SALES (est): 4.5MM **Privately Held**
SIC: 3589 3444 Cooking equipment, com-
mercial; sheet metalwork

(P-15572)
RYKO SOLUTIONS INC
3939 W Capitol Ave Ste D, West Sacra-
mento (95691-2105)
PHONE..................................916 372-8815
EMP: 21
SALES (corp-wide): 2.3B **Privately Held**
SIC: 3589 5087
HQ: Ryko Solutions, Inc.
1500 Se 37th St
Grimes IA 50111
515 986-3700

(P-15573)
S & S INSTALLATIONS INC
Also Called: Pacific Stainless
294 W Olive St, Colton (92324-1757)
PHONE..................................909 370-1730
Tom Skocilich, *President*
Ron Greg, *Vice Pres*
Robert Skocilich, *Vice Pres*
EMP: 23
SQ FT: 12,000
SALES (est): 3.8MM **Privately Held**
SIC: 3589 3556 3469 Food warming
equipment, commercial; food products
machinery; metal stampings

(P-15574)
SANTA MONICA CITY OF
Also Called: City of Santa Monica Wtr Trtmn
1228 S Bundy Dr, Los Angeles
(90025-1102)
PHONE..................................310 826-6712
Myriam Cardenas, *Branch Mgr*
Russ Maloney, *Production*
Heinz Davila, *Supervisor*
EMP: 12
SQ FT: 2,500 **Privately Held**
WEB: www.santamonicapd.org
SIC: 3589 Sewage & water treatment
equipment
PA: City Of Santa Monica
1685 Main St
Santa Monica CA 90401
310 458-8411

(P-15575)
SEACO TECHNOLOGIES INC
280 El Cerrito Dr, Bakersfield (93305-1328)
PHONE..................................661 326-1522
Bob Beck, *Branch Mgr*
EMP: 12
SALES (corp-wide): 15.1MM **Privately Held**
SIC: 3589 Water treatment equipment, in-
dustrial
PA: Seaco Technologies, Inc.
3220 Patton Way
Bakersfield CA
661 323-5115

(P-15576)
SEWER RODDING EQUIPMENT CO (PA)
Also Called: Flexible Video Systems
3217 Carter Ave, Marina Del Rey
(90292-5554)
PHONE..................................310 301-9009
Patrick Crane, *CEO*
EMP: 25
SQ FT: 24,000
SALES (est): 17.6MM **Privately Held**
SIC: 3589 Sewer cleaning equipment,
power

(P-15577)
SHEPARD BROS INC (PA)
503 S Cypress St, La Habra (90631-6126)
PHONE..................................562 697-1366
Ronald Shepard, *CEO*
Duane Shepard, *President*
Jon Wynkoop, *CFO*
Don Miller, *Vice Pres*
Manuel Solis, *Vice Pres*
▲ **EMP:** 120 **EST:** 1976
SQ FT: 57,830
SALES (est): 44MM **Privately Held**
SIC: 3589 5169 Sewage & water treat-
ment equipment; chemicals & allied prod-
ucts

(P-15578)
SJ ELECTRO SYSTEMS INC
Also Called: Primex
859 Cotting Ct Ste G, Vacaville
(95688-9354)
PHONE..................................707 449-0341
Adam Vesely, *Branch Mgr*
EMP: 26
SALES (corp-wide): 87.3MM **Privately Held**
SIC: 3589 Water treatment equipment, in-
dustrial
PA: S.J. Electro Systems, Inc.
22650 County Highway 6
Detroit Lakes MN 56501
218 847-1317

(P-15579)
SNOWPURE LLC
Also Called: Snowpure Water Technologies
130 Calle Iglesia Ste A, San Clemente
(92672-7535)
P.O. Box 73368 (92673-0113)
PHONE..................................949 240-2188
Michael Snow, *Mng Member*
Donald Mettler, *Engineer*
Ronald Ohare, *Engineer*
▲ **EMP:** 30
SALES: 5MM **Privately Held**
SIC: 3589 5074 Water purification equip-
ment, household type; water purification
equipment

(P-15580)
SPECIALTY CAR WASH SYSTEM
146 Mercury Cir, Pomona (91768-3210)
PHONE..................................909 869-6300
Mike Martorano, *Owner*
EMP: 15
SALES (est): 2.2MM **Privately Held**
SIC: 3589 Car washing machinery

(P-15581)
SPECTRA WATERMAKERS INC (HQ)
2220 S Mcdowell Blvd Ext, Petaluma
(94954-5659)
PHONE..................................415 526-2780
William Edinger, *President*
◆ **EMP:** 12
SQ FT: 8,400
SALES (est): 2.5MM
SALES (corp-wide): 3.5MM **Privately Held**
WEB: www.spectrawatermakers.com
SIC: 3589 Water treatment equipment, in-
dustrial
PA: Katadyn North America, Inc.
2495 Xenium Ln N
Minneapolis MN 55441
763 746-3500

(P-15582)
SPENUZZA INC (PA)
Also Called: Imperial Mfg Co
1128 Sherborn St, Corona (92879-2089)
PHONE..................................951 281-1830
Peter Spenuzza, *CEO*
Jennifer Mullen, *Executive*
Matt Wise, *General Mgr*
Ed Blahut, *Controller*
Miguel Betancourt, *Plant Mgr*
◆ **EMP:** 120
SQ FT: 100,000
SALES (est): 32.7MM **Privately Held**
WEB: www.imperialrange.com
SIC: 3589 3556 Cooking equipment, com-
mercial; food products machinery

(P-15583)
SPENUZZA INC
Also Called: Imperial Mfg Co
913 Oak Ave, Duarte (91010-1951)
PHONE..................................626 358-8063
Peter Spenuzza Jr, *President*
EMP: 40
SALES (corp-wide): 32.7MM **Privately Held**
WEB: www.imperialrange.com
SIC: 3589 Cooking equipment, commercial
PA: Spenuzza, Inc.
1128 Sherborn St
Corona CA 92879
951 281-1830

(P-15584)
SPOTLESS WATER SYSTEMS LLC
Also Called: Cr Spotless
372 Coogan Way, El Cajon (92020-1902)
PHONE..................................858 530-9993
Chuck Dewent, *Mng Member*
Rochelle Asbell, *General Mgr*
John Fernandez, *General Mgr*
▲ **EMP:** 12
SQ FT: 20,000
SALES: 1MM **Privately Held**
SIC: 3589 Water filters & softeners, house-
hold type

(P-15585)
STANTEC CONSULTING SVCS INC
1245 Fiddyment Rd, Lincoln (95648-9504)
P.O. Box 1050 (95648-1050)
PHONE..................................916 434-5062
Sarah McKelroy, *Branch Mgr*
Lori Van Dermark, *Marketing Staff*
EMP: 12
SALES (corp-wide): 3.2B **Privately Held**
WEB: www.ecologicengineering.com
SIC: 3589 Water treatment equipment, in-
dustrial
HQ: Stantec Consulting Services Inc.
475 5th Ave Fl 12
New York NY 10017
212 352-5160

(P-15586)
STERNO GROUP COMPANIES LLC (HQ)
Also Called: Sterno Candle Lamp
1880 Compton Ave Ste 101, Corona
(92881-2780)
PHONE..................................951 682-9600
Don Hinshaw, *CEO*
John Clark, *President*
Mike Pacharis, *Vice Pres*
Stacey Burgess, *Controller*
Robert Lanier, *Human Res Dir*
◆ **EMP:** 50
SQ FT: 110,000
SALES (est): 141.7MM **Publicly Held**
WEB: Www.candlelamp.com
SIC: 3589 3634 2899 Food warming
equipment, commercial; chafing dishes,
electric; chemical preparations

(P-15587)
STERNO GROUP LLC (DH)
1880 Compton Ave Ste 101, Corona
(92881-2780)
PHONE..................................800 669-6699
John Clark, *Mng Member*
▼ **EMP:** 32

▲ = Import ▼=Export
◆ =Import/Export

SALES (est): 57.2MM **Publicly Held**
WEB: www.sterno.com
SIC: 3589 Commercial cooking & food-warming equipment
HQ: The Sterno Group Companies Llc
1880 Compton Ave Ste 101
Corona CA 92881
951 682-9600

(P-15588)
SUEZ WTS SERVICES USA INC
5900 Silver Creek Vly Rd, San Jose
(95138-1083)
PHONE..................................408 360-5900
Thomas Hereda, *Branch Mgr*
EMP: 130
SALES (corp-wide): 94.7MM **Privately Held**
SIC: 3589 Water treatment equipment, industrial
HQ: Suez Wts Services Usa, Inc.
4545 Patent Rd
Norfolk VA 23502
757 855-9000

(P-15589)
SUEZ WTS SERVICES USA INC
7777 Industry Ave, Pico Rivera
(90660-4303)
PHONE..................................562 942-2200
Michael Dimick, *Branch Mgr*
EMP: 60
SQ FT: 32,091
SALES (corp-wide): 94.7MM **Privately Held**
WEB: www.ecolochem.com
SIC: 3589 Water treatment equipment, industrial
HQ: Suez Wts Services Usa, Inc.
4545 Patent Rd
Norfolk VA 23502
757 855-9000

(P-15590)
SUEZ WTS SERVICES USA INC
11689 Pacific Ave, Fontana (92337-8225)
PHONE..................................951 681-5555
Dennis Holley, *Manager*
EMP: 19
SALES (corp-wide): 94.7MM **Privately Held**
WEB: www.ecolochem.com
SIC: 3589 Water treatment equipment, industrial
HQ: Suez Wts Services Usa, Inc.
4545 Patent Rd
Norfolk VA 23502
757 855-9000

(P-15591)
THOUSANDS OAKS HAND WASH
Also Called: Auto Scrubber
2725 E Thousand Oaks Blvd, Thousand Oaks (91362-3257)
P.O. Box 7692, Westlake Village (91359-7692)
PHONE..................................805 379-2732
Kim Shirazi, *Owner*
EMP: 11
SALES (est): 853.6K **Privately Held**
SIC: 3589 7542 Car washing machinery; carwashes

(P-15592)
TIMBUCKTOO MANUFACTURING INC
Also Called: T M I
1633 W 134th St, Gardena (90249-2013)
PHONE..................................310 323-1134
Juen Lee, *CEO*
Kyu Lee, *President*
Kevin Lee, *Prdtn Mgr*
▲ EMP: 43
SQ FT: 50,000
SALES (est): 8.5MM **Privately Held**
SIC: 3589 Car washing machinery

(P-15593)
TOPPER MANUFACTURING CORP
23880 Madison St, Torrance (90505-6009)
PHONE..................................310 375-5000
Timothy A Beall, *CEO*
EMP: 15 EST: 2015

SQ FT: 11,000
SALES (est): 4MM **Privately Held**
SIC: 3589 Water filters & softeners, household type; water purification equipment, household type

(P-15594)
TORAY MEMBRANE USA INC
Also Called: C S M
13400 Danielson St, Poway (92064-8830)
PHONE..................................714 678-8832
Kenneth Yoon, *Branch Mgr*
EMP: 15 **Privately Held**
SIC: 3589 Water treatment equipment, industrial
HQ: Toray Membrane Usa, Inc.
13435 Danielson St
Poway CA 92064
-

(P-15595)
TST WATER LLC
Also Called: Watersentinel
42188 Rio Nedo Ste B, Temecula
(92590-3717)
PHONE..................................951 541-9517
Michael T Baird,
Mounir Ibrahim, *CFO*
Will Mott, *Info Tech Mgr*
Richard Loquet, *Design Engr*
Randy Parmley, *Design Engr*
▲ EMP: 19
SALES (est): 8.5MM **Privately Held**
WEB: www.tstwater.com
SIC: 3589 Water filters & softeners, household type

(P-15596)
UNIVERSAL FILTRATION INC
914 Westminster Ave, Alhambra
(91803-1229)
P.O. Box 400, Hamilton MT (59840-0400)
PHONE..................................626 308-1832
Brian Green, *President*
Ruth Green, *Corp Secy*
Clark R Green, *Vice Pres*
EMP: 16
SQ FT: 13,500
SALES (est): 2MM **Privately Held**
WEB: www.universalfiltration.com
SIC: 3589 3999 Swimming pool filter & water conditioning systems; hot tub & spa covers

(P-15597)
VANDERLANS & SONS INC (PA)
Also Called: Lansas Products
1320 S Sacramento St, Lodi (95240-5705)
P.O. Box 758 (95241-0758)
PHONE..................................209 334-4115
Gerald Vanderlans, *President*
Nick Bettencourt, *Corp Secy*
Victor Schuh, *Corp Secy*
April Hayles, *Bookkeeper*
Scott Sanden, *Foreman/Supr*
▲ EMP: 49
SQ FT: 30,000
SALES (est): 6.7MM **Privately Held**
WEB: www.lansas.com
SIC: 3589 Sewer cleaning equipment, power

(P-15598)
WATER ONE INDUSTRIES INC
2913 Pattern St Unit D, Brea (92821)
PHONE..................................707 747-4300
Mher Torossian, *Branch Mgr*
EMP: 10
SQ FT: 2,042 **Privately Held**
SIC: 3589 Water treatment equipment, industrial
PA: Water One Industries, Inc.
5410 Gateway Plaza Dr
Benicia CA 94510

(P-15599)
WATER ONE INDUSTRIES INC (PA)
5410 Gateway Plaza Dr, Benicia
(94510-2122)
PHONE..................................707 747-4300
Hans-Erik Fuchs, *CEO*
Erin Steiger, *Corp Secy*
Tim Russell, *Vice Pres*
EMP: 25

SQ FT: 3,500
SALES (est): 5.2MM **Privately Held**
SIC: 3589 Water treatment equipment, industrial

(P-15600)
WATER PLANET ENGINEERING LLC
8915 S La Cienega Blvd C, Inglewood
(90301-7423)
PHONE..................................424 331-7700
Eric Hoek, *CEO*
Tony Wachinski, *President*
Tom Flynn, *Vice Pres*
Jonathan Nguyen, *Mfg Staff*
EMP: 15
SQ FT: 6,000
SALES (est): 3.7MM **Privately Held**
SIC: 3589 Water treatment equipment, industrial

(P-15601)
WATERGURU INC
2 Embarcadero Ctr Fl 8, San Francisco
(94111-3833)
PHONE..................................415 269-5480
Tadmor Shalon, *President*
EMP: 10
SALES (est): 583.8K **Privately Held**
SIC: 3589 Swimming pool filter & water conditioning systems

(P-15602)
WATERHEALTH INTERNATIONAL INC
9601 Irvine Center Dr, Irvine (92618-4652)
PHONE..................................949 716-5790
Sanjay Bhatnagar, *CEO*
Jacqueline Lundquist, *Vice Pres*
EMP: 125 EST: 1995
SQ FT: 2,000
SALES (est): 10.8MM **Privately Held**
WEB: www.waterhealth.com
SIC: 3589 Water treatment equipment, industrial

(P-15603)
WATERMAN VALVE LLC (HQ)
25500 Road 204, Exeter (93221-9655)
P.O. Box 458 (93221-0458)
PHONE..................................559 562-4000
Marcus Shiveley, *President*
▲ EMP: 126
SQ FT: 175,000
SALES (est): 32MM
SALES (corp-wide): 1.2B **Privately Held**
WEB: www.watermanusa.com
SIC: 3589 Water treatment equipment, industrial
PA: Mcwane, Inc.
2900 Highway 280 S # 300
Birmingham AL 35223
205 414-3100

(P-15604)
WESFAC INC (HQ)
Also Called: Wespac
9300 Hall Rd, Downey (90241-5309)
PHONE..................................562 861-2160
Don Hyatt, *President*
Julie Hyatt, *Corp Secy*
EMP: 100 EST: 1982
SQ FT: 55,000
SALES (est): 7.9MM
SALES (corp-wide): 11.1MM **Privately Held**
WEB: www.omniteaminc.com
SIC: 3589 3431 Commercial cooking & foodwarming equipment; metal sanitary ware
PA: Omniment Industries, Inc
9300 Hall Rd
Downey CA 90241
562 923-9660

(P-15605)
WHITTIER FILTRATION INC (DH)
120 S State College Blvd, Brea
(92821-5834)
PHONE..................................714 986-5300
Jim Brown, *President*
John M Santelli, *Corp Secy*
Kenneth Severing, *Business Dir*
Sara Mendez, *Admin Asst*
◆ EMP: 24
SQ FT: 80,000

SALES (est): 6.3MM
SALES (corp-wide): 600.9MM **Privately Held**
SIC: 3589 Water treatment equipment, industrial

(P-15606)
WILBUR CURTIS CO INC
6913 W Acco St, Montebello (90640-5403)
PHONE..................................323 837-2300
EMP: 275 EST: 1946
SQ FT: 170,000
SALES: 75MM **Privately Held**
SIC: 3589

(P-15607)
YARDNEY WATER MGT SYSTEMS INC (PA)
Also Called: Yardney Water MGT Systems
6666 Box Springs Blvd, Riverside
(92507-0736)
PHONE..................................951 656-6716
Kenneth Phillips, *President*
Chris Phillips, *Vice Pres*
Tony Barrios, *Purchasing*
Mona Howell, *Marketing Staff*
Joe Barrette, *Sales Staff*
▲ EMP: 40
SQ FT: 55,000
SALES (est): 7.3MM **Privately Held**
WEB: www.yardneyfilters.com
SIC: 3589 Water treatment equipment, industrial

(P-15608)
YUBA CY WSTE WTR TRTMNT FCILTY
302 Burns Dr, Yuba City (95991-7205)
PHONE..................................530 822-7698
John Buckland, *Mayor*
EMP: 24
SALES (est): 2.8MM **Privately Held**
SIC: 3589 Water treatment equipment, industrial

(P-15609)
ZODIAC POOL SOLUTIONS LLC (DH)
2882 Whiptail Loop # 100, Carlsbad
(92010-6758)
PHONE..................................760 599-9600
Francois Mirallie, *President*
EMP: 300
SALES (est): 34.7MM
SALES (corp-wide): 2.4B **Publicly Held**
SIC: 3589 Swimming pool filter & water conditioning systems
HQ: Zodiac Pool Systems Llc
2882 Whiptail Loop # 100
Carlsbad CA 92010
760 599-9600

(P-15610)
ZODIAC POOL SYSTEMS LLC (DH)
Also Called: Jandy Pool Products
2882 Whiptail Loop # 100, Carlsbad
(92010-6758)
PHONE..................................760 599-9600
Bruce Brooks, *CEO*
Mike Allanc, *CFO*
Xavier Brunelle, *Treasurer*
Ruben Galvan, *Vice Pres*
Sarah Linton, *Executive Asst*
◆ EMP: 250
SALES (est): 597.3MM
SALES (corp-wide): 2.4B **Publicly Held**
WEB: www.jandy.com
SIC: 3589 3999 Swimming pool filter & water conditioning systems; hot tub & spa covers; atomizers; toiletry
HQ: Zodiac Pool Solutions
Parc Des Chenes
Bron 69500
800 842-340

PRODUCTS & SVCS

3592 Carburetors, Pistons, Rings & Valves

(P-15611)
B & Y MACHINE CO
1060 5th St, Calimesa (92320-1512)
P.O. Box 1208, Redlands (92373-0401)
PHONE...................................909 795-8588
John L Baker, *Manager*
EMP: 12
SQ FT: 10,000
SALES (est): 860K **Privately Held**
SIC: 3592 Valves

(P-15612)
CP-CARRILLO INC
17401 Armstrong Ave, Irvine (92614-5723)
PHONE...................................949 567-9000
Barry Calvert, *Mng Member*
EMP: 30
SALES (corp-wide): 1.7B **Privately Held**
SIC: 3592 3714 Pistons & piston rings; connecting rods, motor vehicle engine
HQ: Cp-Carrillo, Inc.
1902 Mcgaw Ave
Irvine CA 92614

(P-15613)
CP-CARRILLO INC (DH)
1902 Mcgaw Ave, Irvine (92614-0910)
PHONE...................................949 567-9000
Barry Calvert, *CEO*
Harry Glieder, *CFO*
Anita Davis-Smith, *Administration*
David Corcoran, *Info Tech Mgr*
Nathan Cser, *Engineer*
▲ EMP: 120
SQ FT: 31,840
SALES: 28.8MM
SALES (corp-wide): 1.7B **Privately Held**
SIC: 3592 3714 Pistons & piston rings; connecting rods, motor vehicle engine

(P-15614)
NOEL BURT
Also Called: Recarbco
880 Howe Rd Ste F, Martinez (94553-3485)
PHONE...................................925 439-7030
Noel Burt, *Owner*
EMP: 42
SQ FT: 20,000
SALES (est): 3.2MM **Privately Held**
WEB: www.recarbco.com
SIC: 3592 3714 Carburetors; motor vehicle parts & accessories

(P-15615)
PACIFIC PISTON RING CO INC
3620 Eastham Dr, Culver City (90232-2411)
P.O. Box 927 (90232-0927)
PHONE...................................310 836-3322
Forest Shannon, *President*
Christina Davis, *Treasurer*
Michael Shannon, *Vice Pres*
EMP: 90
SQ FT: 35,000
SALES (est): 18.5MM **Privately Held**
SIC: 3592 Pistons & piston rings

(P-15616)
PROBE RACING COMPONENTS INC
Also Called: Kwikparts.com
5022 Onyx St, Torrance (90503-2742)
PHONE...................................310 784-2977
Larry M O'Neal, *CEO*
▲ EMP: 28
SQ FT: 25,000
SALES (est): 5.5MM **Privately Held**
WEB: www.promustang.com
SIC: 3592 3463 Pistons & piston rings; engine or turbine forgings, nonferrous

(P-15617)
ROSS RACING PISTONS
625 S Douglas St, El Segundo (90245-4812)
PHONE...................................310 536-0100
Ken Roble, *President*
Joy Roble, *Corp Secy*
J B Mills, *Vice Pres*

Chris Petrini, *Creative Dir*
Ivet Lopez, *Admin Asst*
EMP: 55
SQ FT: 25,000
SALES: 4.3MM **Privately Held**
WEB: www.rosspistons.com
SIC: 3592 Pistons & piston rings

(P-15618)
RTR INDUSTRIES LLC
Also Called: Grant Piston Rings
1360 N Jefferson St, Anaheim (92807-1614)
PHONE...................................714 996-0050
Romy Laxamana,
Ramon Diaz,
Thom Nguyen,
Craig Marder, *Manager*
▲ EMP: 45
SQ FT: 44,000
SALES (est): 7.5MM **Privately Held**
SIC: 3592 Pistons & piston rings

(P-15619)
TOR C A M INDUSTRIES INC
Also Called: Venolia Pistons
2160 E Cherry Indus Cir, Long Beach (90805-4412)
PHONE...................................562 531-8463
Frank Pisino, *President*
EMP: 31
SQ FT: 10,000
SALES (est): 4.1MM **Privately Held**
WEB: www.venolia.com
SIC: 3592 3354 Pistons & piston rings; aluminum rod & bar

3593 Fluid Power Cylinders & Actuators

(P-15620)
C & H MACHINE INC
Also Called: Support Equipment
943 S Andrsen Dr Escndido Escondido, Escondido (92029)
PHONE...................................760 746-6459
Lyle J Anderson, *Exec VP*
Charles Gohlich, *Admin Sec*
Joe Viramontes, *Engineer*
EMP: 70 EST: 1964
SQ FT: 13,000
SALES (est): 16.8MM **Privately Held**
WEB: www.c-hmachine.com
SIC: 3593 3599 Fluid power cylinders & actuators; machine shop, jobbing & repair; electrical discharge machining (EDM)

(P-15621)
CAL-WEST MACHINING INC
1734 W Sequoia Ave, Orange (92868-1016)
PHONE...................................714 637-4161
Larry Lewis Sr, *President*
Marleen Lewis, *Treasurer*
EMP: 10 EST: 1981
SQ FT: 11,000
SALES (est): 2.6MM **Privately Held**
WEB: www.calwestmachine.com
SIC: 3593 3599 Fluid power actuators, hydraulic or pneumatic; machine shop, jobbing & repair

(P-15622)
GENERAL DYNMICS OTS NCVLLE INC
511 Grove St, Healdsburg (95448-4747)
PHONE...................................707 473-9200
Richard Schroeder, *General Mgr*
Timothy Finks, *Engineer*
EMP: 60 EST: 1999
SQ FT: 28,000
SALES (est): 12.4MM
SALES (corp-wide): 36.1B **Publicly Held**
WEB: www.ver.gd-ots.com
SIC: 3593 Fluid power cylinders & actuators
HQ: General Dynamics Ordnance And Tactical Systems, Inc.
11399 16th Ct N Ste 200
Saint Petersburg FL 33716
727 578-8100

(P-15623)
GENERAL GRINDING & MFG CO LLC
15100 Valley View Ave, La Mirada (90638-5226)
PHONE...................................562 921-7033
SE Heung Kim,
Rich Kim,
Silas Pak,
EMP: 25
SQ FT: 25,000
SALES: 3MM **Privately Held**
WEB: www.generalgrinding.com
SIC: 3593 3599 3471 Fluid power cylinders, hydraulic or pneumatic; grinding castings for the trade; plating & polishing

(P-15624)
HYDRAULIC PNEUMATIC INC
Also Called: Hpi Cylinders
13766 Milroy Pl, Santa Fe Springs (90670-5131)
PHONE...................................562 926-1122
James Whitney, *President*
EMP: 18
SQ FT: 18,000
SALES: 2.2MM **Privately Held**
WEB: www.hydraulic-pneumatic.com
SIC: 3593 3599 Fluid power cylinders, hydraulic or pneumatic; machine shop, jobbing & repair

(P-15625)
RTC ARSPACE - CHTSWRTH DIV INC (PA)
20409 Prairie St, Chatsworth (91311-6029)
PHONE...................................818 341-3344
James B Hart, *CEO*
BJ Schramm, *President*
Bill Hart, *Vice Pres*
Elizabeth Hart, *Vice Pres*
Robert McSweeney, *Engineer*
◆ EMP: 130
SQ FT: 42,000
SALES (est): 34.4MM **Privately Held**
SIC: 3593 3594 3599 Fluid power cylinders & actuators; fluid power pumps & motors; machine shop, jobbing & repair

3594 Fluid Power Pumps & Motors

(P-15626)
BERNELL HYDRAULICS INC (PA)
8810 Etiwanda Ave, Rancho Cucamonga (91739-9662)
P.O. Box 417 (91739-0417)
PHONE...................................909 899-1751
Terrance B Jones Sr, *Ch of Bd*
Rhonda A Garness, *President*
John S Clemons, *Vice Pres*
Carlos Aguirre, *Engineer*
EMP: 28
SQ FT: 6,000
SALES (est): 10MM **Privately Held**
WEB: www.bernellhydraulics.com
SIC: 3594 5084 3621 3593 Pumps, hydraulic power transfer; hydraulic systems equipment & supplies; motors & generators; fluid power cylinders & actuators; pumps & pumping equipment; machine tools, metal forming type

(P-15627)
CRISSAIR INC
28909 Avenue Williams, Valencia (91355-4183)
PHONE...................................661 367-3300
Linda Bradley, *President*
Mark Hughes, *Vice Pres*
Jack Mossman, *Executive*
Eric Grupp, *Business Dir*
Vivian Gonzales, *Administration*
EMP: 185
SQ FT: 40,000
SALES (est): 53.1MM
SALES (corp-wide): 771.5MM **Publicly Held**
WEB: www.crissair.com
SIC: 3594 3492 Motors, pneumatic; fluid power valves & hose fittings

PA: Esco Technologies Inc.
9900 Clayton Rd Ste A
Saint Louis MO 63124
314 213-7200

(P-15628)
DOW HYDRAULIC SYSTEMS INC
2895 Metropolitan Pl, Pomona (91767-1853)
PHONE...................................909 596-6602
Richard Dow, *Principal*
Ray Carlos, *Supervisor*
EMP: 10
SALES (est): 1.6MM
SALES (corp-wide): 12.9MM **Privately Held**
SIC: 3594 Fluid power pumps & motors
PA: Dow Hydraulic Systems, Inc.
1835 Wright Ave
La Verne CA 91750
909 596-6602

(P-15629)
EDDY PUMP CORPORATION (PA)
15405 Olde Highway 80, El Cajon (92021-2409)
PHONE...................................619 258-7020
Harry P Weinrib, *President*
Peter Weinrib, *CFO*
James J Hamill, *Treasurer*
Dan Wahlgren, *Engineer*
Kurtis Waddell, *Manager*
EMP: 13
SQ FT: 5,000
SALES (est): 4MM **Privately Held**
WEB: www.eddypump.com
SIC: 3594 8731 Pumps, hydraulic power transfer; engineering laboratory, except testing

(P-15630)
KECO INC
Also Called: Pump-A-Head
3475 Kurtz St, San Diego (92110-4430)
P.O. Box 80308 (92138-0308)
PHONE...................................619 546-9533
Anne Kenton Bleier, *President*
Andrew Bleier, *Vice Pres*
▼ EMP: 10
SQ FT: 2,000
SALES (est): 2.6MM **Privately Held**
WEB: www.pumphead.com
SIC: 3594 5084 Fluid power pumps; industrial machinery & equipment

(P-15631)
OSTOICH DIESEL SERVICE
Also Called: Diesel Injection Service
1690 Ashley Way, Colton (92324-4000)
P.O. Box 11955, San Bernardino (92423-1955)
PHONE...................................909 885-0590
Mark A Ostoich, *President*
Florence M Ostoich, *Treasurer*
Mark Ostoich, *Vice Pres*
EMP: 19
SQ FT: 5,000
SALES (est): 1.9MM **Privately Held**
SIC: 3594 Fluid power pumps & motors

(P-15632)
PARKER-HANNIFIN CORPORATION
Also Called: Parker Service Center
5650 Stewart Ave, Fremont (94538-3174)
PHONE...................................408 592-6480
Celia Osorio, *Manager*
EMP: 126
SALES (corp-wide): 14.3B **Publicly Held**
WEB: www.parker.com
SIC: 3594 Fluid power pumps
PA: Parker-Hannifin Corporation
6035 Parkland Blvd
Cleveland OH 44124
216 896-3000

(P-15633)
PARKER-HANNIFIN CORPORATION
Composite Sealing Systems Div
7664 Panasonic Way, San Diego (92154-8206)
PHONE...................................619 661-7000

▲ = Import ▼=Export
◆ =Import/Export

Jim Rando, *Manager*
Ramon Reyes, *Treasurer*
Laurie Phelts, *Program Mgr*
Frank Solis, *General Mgr*
Terry Ennis, *Administration*
EMP: 130
SALES (corp-wide): 14.3B **Publicly Held**
WEB: www.parker.com
SIC: 3594 Fluid power pumps & motors
PA: Parker-Hannifin Corporation
6035 Parkland Blvd
Cleveland OH 44124
216 896-3000

(P-15634)
PARKER-HANNIFIN CORPORATION
Also Called: Cylinder Division
221 Helicopter Cir, Corona (92880-2532)
PHONE...................................951 280-3800
Donald P Szmania, *Branch Mgr*
Joi Martin, *Administration*
Kim Santos, *Sales Staff*
Mary Zimmerman, *Sales Staff*
John Beam, *Manager*
EMP: 40
SALES (corp-wide): 14.3B **Publicly Held**
WEB: www.parker.com
SIC: 3594 3728 3593 Fluid power pumps & motors; aircraft parts & equipment; fluid power cylinders & actuators
PA: Parker-Hannifin Corporation
6035 Parkland Blvd
Cleveland OH 44124
216 896-3000

(P-15635)
PARKER-HANNIFIN CORPORATION
16666 Von Karman Ave, Irvine (92606-4997)
PHONE...................................949 833-3000
Fax: 949 851-3341
EMP: 123
SALES (corp-wide): 13B **Publicly Held**
SIC: 3594
PA: Parker-Hannifin Corporation
6035 Parkland Blvd
Cleveland OH 44124
216 896-3000

(P-15636)
PARKER-HANNIFIN CORPORATION
3007 Bunsen Ave Ste K, Ventura (93003-7633)
PHONE...................................805 658-2984
Russell Lanham, *Branch Mgr*
EMP: 12
SALES (corp-wide): 14.3B **Publicly Held**
SIC: 3594 Fluid power pumps & motors
PA: Parker-Hannifin Corporation
6035 Parkland Blvd
Cleveland OH 44124
216 896-3000

(P-15637)
PARKER-HANNIFIN CORPORATION
Also Called: Parker Medical Systems
7664 Panasonic Way, San Diego (92154-8206)
PHONE...................................714 632-6512
Steve Herman, *Branch Mgr*
Leeanne McInerny, *Executive Asst*
EMP: 126
SALES (corp-wide): 14.3B **Publicly Held**
SIC: 3594 Fluid power pumps
PA: Parker-Hannifin Corporation
6035 Parkland Blvd
Cleveland OH 44124
216 896-3000

(P-15638)
WESTERN HYDROSTATICS INC (PA)
1956 Keats Dr, Riverside (92501-1747)
PHONE...................................951 784-2133
John Starke Scott, *President*
Steve Moser, *COO*
Barnett Totten, *Treasurer*
Patrick Maluso, *Vice Pres*
Tandy W Scott, *Vice Pres*
▲ **EMP:** 30

SALES (est): 4.5MM **Privately Held**
WEB: www.weshyd.com
SIC: 3594 7699 5084 Hydrostatic drives (transmissions); hydraulic equipment repair; hydraulic systems equipment & supplies

---

3596 Scales & Balances, Exc Laboratory

(P-15639)
AMERICAN SCALE CO INC
4338 E Washington Blvd, Commerce (90023-4410)
P.O. Box 158, San Dimas (91773-0158)
PHONE...................................323 269-0305
David William Eccles III, *CEO*
EMP: 12 **EST:** 1946
SQ FT: 4,150
SALES (est): 2.2MM **Privately Held**
WEB: www.americanscaleco.com
SIC: 3596 5045 Counting scales; computers, peripherals & software

(P-15640)
BIOMICROLAB INC
2500 Dean Lesher Dr Ste A, Concord (94520-1273)
PHONE...................................925 689-1200
David B Miller, *President*
William Hess, *Vice Pres*
Brian Lechman, *Electrical Engi*
Alex Drynkin, *Engineer*
Peter Miller, *VP Opers*
EMP: 25
SALES (est): 2MM **Privately Held**
WEB: www.biomicrolab.com
SIC: 3596 Weighing machines & apparatus

(P-15641)
JONEL ENGINEERING
500 E Walnut Ave, Fullerton (92832-2540)
P.O. Box 798 (92836-0798)
PHONE...................................714 879-2360
John Lawson, *CEO*
Mike Lawson, *President*
Leon Winter, *Vice Pres*
Henry Brown, *Technician*
Christopher Haas, *Engineer*
▼ **EMP:** 20
SQ FT: 8,000
SALES (est): 3.3MM **Privately Held**
SIC: 3596 5045 Weighing machines & apparatus; computers

(P-15642)
SCALE SERVICES INC
3553a N Perris Blvd Ste 8, Perris (92571-3149)
PHONE...................................909 266-0896
Corey Stacy, *CEO*
EMP: 11
SQ FT: 1,300
SALES (est): 680.1K **Privately Held**
SIC: 3596 Counting scales; industrial scales; truck (motor vehicle) scales

---

3599 Machinery & Eqpt, Indl & Commercial, NEC

(P-15643)
2M MACHINE CORPORATION
13171 Rosecrans Ave, Santa Fe Springs (90670-4931)
PHONE...................................562 404-4225
Michael Manspeaker, *Manager*
▲ **EMP:** 13
SQ FT: 8,650
SALES (est): 1.6MM **Privately Held**
WEB: www.2mmachining.com
SIC: 3599 Machine shop, jobbing & repair

(P-15644)
3B MACHINING CO INC
2292 Trade Zone Blvd 1a, San Jose (95131-1801)
PHONE...................................408 719-9237
Bryan Bui, *President*
EMP: 10
SQ FT: 4,281
SALES (est): 1.5MM **Privately Held**
SIC: 3599 Machine shop, jobbing & repair

(P-15645)
3D MACHINE CO INC
4790 E Wesley Dr, Anaheim (92807-1941)
PHONE...................................714 777-8985
Maria Falcusan, *President*
Constantine Falcusan, *Vice Pres*
EMP: 30
SQ FT: 3,300
SALES (est): 5.9MM **Privately Held**
WEB: www.3dmachineco.com
SIC: 3599 Machine shop, jobbing & repair

(P-15646)
4-D ENGINEERING INC
1635 W 144th St, Gardena (90247-2302)
PHONE...................................310 532-2384
Ernie Thury, *President*
EMP: 22 **EST:** 1976
SQ FT: 5,000
SALES (est): 2.3MM **Privately Held**
SIC: 3599 Machine shop, jobbing & repair

(P-15647)
478826 LIMITED
Also Called: Zi Machine Manufacturing
5050 Hillsdale Cir, El Dorado Hills (95762-5706)
PHONE...................................916 933-5280
Steve Zeldag, *CEO*
EMP: 21
SQ FT: 26,000
SALES (est): 3.1MM **Privately Held**
SIC: 3599 Machine shop, jobbing & repair

(P-15648)
5TH AXIS INC
7140 Engineer Rd, San Diego (92111-1422)
PHONE...................................858 505-0432
Michelle Grangetto, *President*
Steve Grangetto, *COO*
Christopher Taylor, *Vice Pres*
▲ **EMP:** 61
SQ FT: 21,000
SALES (est): 6.8MM **Privately Held**
SIC: 3599 Machine shop, jobbing & repair

(P-15649)
A & A MACHINE & DEV CO INC
16625 Gramercy Pl, Gardena (90247-5201)
PHONE...................................310 532-7706
Arlene Hymovitz, *President*
Eric Hymovitz, *Vice Pres*
EMP: 18
SQ FT: 12,000
SALES (est): 3.6MM **Privately Held**
WEB: www.aamach.com
SIC: 3599 Machine shop, jobbing & repair

(P-15650)
A & B AEROSPACE INC
612 S Ayon Ave, Azusa (91702-5122)
PHONE...................................626 334-2976
Kenneth Smith, *President*
Malcolm Smith, *Vice Pres*
Jack Badeau, *General Mgr*
Alayne Mulree, *Sales Staff*
Joseph Nokes, *Manager*
EMP: 35
SQ FT: 23,000
SALES (est): 6.7MM **Privately Held**
SIC: 3599 Machine shop, jobbing & repair

(P-15651)
A & D PRECISION MACHINING INC
4155 Business Center Dr, Fremont (94538-6355)
PHONE...................................510 657-6781
David A Dreifort, *CEO*
Nicole Costanzo, *Info Tech Mgr*
Anson Nguyen, *Engineer*
Nick Le, *Mfg Mgr*
Caprice Dreifort, *Marketing Mgr*
EMP: 45
SQ FT: 28,000
SALES (est): 14.9MM **Privately Held**
WEB: www.adprecision.com
SIC: 3599 Machine shop, jobbing & repair

(P-15652)
A & D PRECISION MFG INC
4751 E Hunter Ave, Anaheim (92807-1940)
PHONE...................................714 779-2714

Dan Wiegel, *President*
Anthony Brown, *Vice Pres*
Tony Brown, *Vice Pres*
Allan Johnson, *QC Mgr*
EMP: 21
SQ FT: 9,000
SALES (est): 2.1MM **Privately Held**
WEB: www.adprecisionmfg.com
SIC: 3599 3728 Machine shop, jobbing & repair; aircraft parts & equipment

(P-15653)
A & H ENGINEERING & MFG INC
Also Called: A & H Tool Engineering
17109 Edwards Rd, Cerritos (90703-2423)
PHONE...................................562 623-9717
Asher Sharoni, *President*
Tova Sharoni, *CFO*
EMP: 27
SQ FT: 15,000
SALES (est): 1.6MM **Privately Held**
SIC: 3599 Grinding castings for the trade

(P-15654)
A & J MACHINING INC
16305 Vineyard Blvd Ste B, Morgan Hill (95037-7132)
PHONE...................................903 566-0304
John Zekanoski, *Vice Pres*
John Boehme, *President*
Maryann Penwacesek, *Corp Secy*
EMP: 10
SALES (est): 1MM **Privately Held**
SIC: 3599 Machine shop, jobbing & repair

(P-15655)
A & M ENGINEERING INC
15854 Salvatierra St, Irwindale (91706-6603)
PHONE...................................626 813-2020
Boris Beljak Sr, *President*
Anita Beljak, *Corp Secy*
Boris Beljak Jr, *Vice Pres*
Roy Beljak, *Vice Pres*
Mark Neiman, *Vice Pres*
EMP: 80 **EST:** 1973
SQ FT: 25,000
SALES (est): 14.1MM **Privately Held**
WEB: www.amengineeringinc.com
SIC: 3599 3812 3537 Machine shop, jobbing & repair; search & navigation equipment; industrial trucks & tractors

(P-15656)
A & R ENGINEERING CO INC
1053 E Bedmar St, Carson (90746-3601)
PHONE...................................310 603-9060
Murat Sehidoglu, *President*
Massimo Fuso, *Opers Mgr*
PHI Pham, *Prdtn Mgr*
EMP: 44
SQ FT: 23,334
SALES (est): 10.5MM **Privately Held**
WEB: www.arengr.com
SIC: 3599 Machine shop, jobbing & repair

(P-15657)
A & V ENGINEERING INC
1155 W Mahalo Pl, Compton (90220-5444)
PHONE...................................310 637-9906
Vic Kuyumjian, *President*
Vartuhi Kuyumjian, *Vice Pres*
EMP: 12
SQ FT: 8,000
SALES (est): 2.5MM **Privately Held**
WEB: www.avengineering.com
SIC: 3599 Machine shop, jobbing & repair

(P-15658)
A A A ENGINEERING & MFG CO
2118 Huntington Dr, San Marino (91108-2024)
PHONE...................................626 447-5029
Lynn Akins, *Owner*
EMP: 37
SQ FT: 500
SALES (est): 2.2MM **Privately Held**
SIC: 3599 Machine shop, jobbing & repair

(P-15659)
A C MANUFACTURING INC
3023 Mount Whitney Rd, Escondido (92029-1800)
PHONE...................................760 745-3717
Arley G Chugon, *President*
Billy Daniel, *Admin Sec*

EMP: 10
SQ FT: 12,000
SALES: 600K **Privately Held**
SIC: 3599 Machine shop, jobbing & repair

(P-15660)
A F M ENGINEERING INC
1313 E Borchard Ave, Santa Ana
(92705-4412)
PHONE.....................714 547-0194
Charles S Irwin, *President*
Jeffery Batchman, *Vice Pres*
EMP: 10 EST: 1980
SQ FT: 10,000
SALES: 1MM **Privately Held**
WEB: www.afmeng.com
SIC: 3599 3089 Machine shop, jobbing &
repair; plastic processing

(P-15661)
A H MACHINE INC
214 N Cedar Ave, Inglewood (90301-1009)
PHONE.....................310 672-0016
M P Desai, *President*
Sam Patel, *Vice Pres*
EMP: 12
SQ FT: 6,500
SALES: 2.5MM **Privately Held**
SIC: 3599 Machine shop, jobbing & repair

(P-15662)
A N TOOL & DIE INC
518 S Fair Oaks Ave, Pasadena
(91105-2690)
PHONE.....................626 795-3238
Dorothy Nettleton, *President*
John Nettleton, *Vice Pres*
Shawna Nettleton, *Office Mgr*
Leigha Nettleton, *Human Res Mgr*
EMP: 14
SQ FT: 6,000
SALES: (est) 2.3MM **Privately Held**
SIC: 3599 Machine shop, jobbing & repair

(P-15663)
A&A ENGINEERING INC
158 Santa Felicia Dr, Goleta (93117-2804)
PHONE.....................805 685-4882
Hoa Truong, *President*
EMP: 10
SQ FT: 4,000
SALES: (est) 1.2MM **Privately Held**
WEB: www.aaeng.com
SIC: 3599 Machine shop, jobbing & repair

(P-15664)
A&G MACHINE SHOP INC
1352 Burton Ave Ste B, Salinas
(93901-4417)
P.O. Box 6190 (93912-6190)
PHONE.....................831 759-2261
Anuar Molina, *President*
Edna Molina, *Vice Pres*
EMP: 16
SQ FT: 5,500
SALES: (est): 1.7MM **Privately Held**
SIC: 3599 Machine shop, jobbing & repair

(P-15665)
A&T PRECISION MACHINING
330 Piercy Rd, San Jose (95138-1401)
PHONE.....................408 363-1198
James Le, *Partner*
An Le, *Partner*
Hieu Le, *Partner*
EMP: 12
SALES: (est) 2.2MM **Privately Held**
SIC: 3599 Machine shop, jobbing & repair;
machine & other job shop work

(P-15666)
A&W PRECISION MACHINING INC
17907 S Figueroa St Ste C, Gardena
(90248-4256)
PHONE.....................310 527-7242
Walter Galich, *President*
Adelfo Varela, *Vice Pres*
EMP: 15
SQ FT: 3,700
SALES: (est): 1.1MM **Privately Held**
SIC: 3599 Machine shop, jobbing & repair

(P-15667)
A-1 JAYS MACHINING INC (PA)
2228 Oakland Rd, San Jose (95131-1414)
PHONE.....................408 262-1845
James K Machathil, *CEO*
EMP: 79
SQ FT: 10,000
SALES: (est): 16.9MM **Privately Held**
WEB: www.a1jays.com
SIC: 3599 Machine shop, jobbing & repair

(P-15668)
A-1 MACHINE MANUFACTURING INC (PA)
490 Gianni St, Santa Clara (95054-2413)
PHONE.....................408 727-0880
Yong Kil, *President*
Yong Su Pak, *Vice Pres*
▲ EMP: 131
SQ FT: 250,000
SALES: (est): 49.9MM **Privately Held**
WEB: www.a-1machine.com
SIC: 3599 Machine shop, jobbing & repair

(P-15669)
A-Z MFG INC
Also Called: AZ Manufacturing
3101 W Segerstrom Ave, Santa Ana
(92704-5811)
PHONE.....................714 444-4446
Ann Lukas, *Principal*
Gary Lukas, *Admin Sec*
EMP: 40
SQ FT: 16,096
SALES: 6.5MM **Privately Held**
WEB: www.azmfginc.com
SIC: 3599 Machine shop, jobbing & repair

(P-15670)
AAERO SWISS
22347 La Palma Ave # 105, Yorba Linda
(92887-3826)
PHONE.....................714 692-0558
Brandy Jones, *President*
Randy Jones, *Principal*
EMP: 10
SALES: (est): 1.1MM **Privately Held**
SIC: 3599 Machine shop, jobbing & repair

(P-15671)
ABLE WIRE EDM INC
440 Atlas St Ste A, Brea (92821-3136)
PHONE.....................714 255-1967
John Marquardt, *President*
Brooke Snow, *Vice Pres*
Kenny Snow, *Vice Pres*
Barbara Marquardt, *Admin Sec*
Chris Marks, *Manager*
EMP: 15
SQ FT: 5,500
SALES: 1MM **Privately Held**
SIC: 3599 Machine shop, jobbing & repair;
electrical discharge machining (EDM)

(P-15672)
ABN INDUSTRIAL CO INC (PA)
5940 Dale St, Buena Park (90621-2150)
PHONE.....................714 521-9211
Jim C K Hsieh, *President*
▲ EMP: 12
SQ FT: 10,000
SALES: 750K **Privately Held**
SIC: 3599 Machine shop, jobbing & repair

(P-15673)
ABSOLUTE MACHINE
5020 Mountain Lakes Blvd, Redding
(96003-1457)
PHONE.....................530 242-6840
Alfred Madena, *President*
EMP: 20
SALES: (est): 3.6MM **Privately Held**
SIC: 3599 Machine shop, jobbing & repair

(P-15674)
ACC PRECISION INC
321 Hearst Dr, Oxnard (93030-5158)
PHONE.....................805 278-9801
Arturo Alfaro, *President*
EMP: 15
SQ FT: 6,000
SALES: 1.2MM **Privately Held**
WEB: www.accprecision.com
SIC: 3599 Machine shop, jobbing & repair

(P-15675)
ACCU MACHINE INC
440 Aldo Ave, Santa Clara (95054-2301)
PHONE.....................408 855-8835
Tommy Dao, *Technician*
EMP: 29
SALES: (est) 5.3MM **Privately Held**
SIC: 3599 Machine shop, jobbing & repair

(P-15676)
ACCU-TECH LASER PROCESSING INC
550 S Pacific St Ste A100, San Marcos
(92078-4058)
PHONE.....................760 744-6692
Michael C Gericke, *President*
Michael Gericke, *CFO*
Roger Underwood, *CFO*
Troy Dowler, *Engineer*
Steven Slater, *Engineer*
EMP: 14 EST: 2006
SQ FT: 6,500
SALES: (est): 2.2MM **Privately Held**
SIC: 3599 Machine shop, jobbing & repair

(P-15677)
ACCUFAB INC
1326 E Francis St, Ontario (91761-5714)
PHONE.....................909 930-1751
Donna Mihovetz, *President*
EMP: 10
SQ FT: 9,000
SALES: (est): 1.1MM **Privately Held**
SIC: 3599 Machine shop, jobbing & repair

(P-15678)
ACCURATE PRFMCE MACHINING INC
2255 S Grand Ave, Santa Ana
(92705-5206)
PHONE.....................714 434-7811
Robert Keith Fischer, *CEO*
Karen Fischer, *Treasurer*
Larry Taylor, *Vice Pres*
EMP: 21 EST: 1996
SQ FT: 3,200
SALES: (est): 4.6MM **Privately Held**
SIC: 3599 Machine shop, jobbing & repair

(P-15679)
ACCURATE TECHNOLOGY MFG INC
930 Thompson Pl, Sunnyvale
(94085-4517)
PHONE.....................408 733-4344
Ivo Dukanovic, *CEO*
John Dukanovic, *Owner*
EMP: 60
SQ FT: 40,000
SALES: (est): 9.8MM **Privately Held**
SIC: 3599 Machine shop, jobbing & repair

(P-15680)
ACE INDUSTRIES INC
738 Design Ct Ste 302, Chula Vista
(91911-6161)
P.O. Box 210931 (91921-0931)
PHONE.....................619 482-2700
Bobby Yoo, *President*
Joy Yoo, *CFO*
▲ EMP: 20
SQ FT: 15,000
SALES: (est): 3.8MM **Privately Held**
WEB: www.aceindustries.com
SIC: 3599 Machine shop, jobbing & repair

(P-15681)
ACE MACHINE SHOP INC
11200 Wright Rd, Lynwood (90262-3124)
PHONE.....................310 608-2277
Pedro Gallinucci, *President*
Lucia Gallinucci, *Vice Pres*
Viran Perera, *Project Engr*
Jeff Ducas, *Purchasing*
EMP: 70 EST: 1956
SQ FT: 35,000
SALES: (est): 13.3MM **Privately Held**
SIC: 3599 Machine shop, jobbing & repair

(P-15682)
ACKLEY METAL PRODUCTS INC
Also Called: Waco Products
1311 E Saint Gertrude Pl B, Santa Ana
(92705-5216)
PHONE.....................714 979-7431
Paul Ackley, *President*
Alan Ackley, *Vice Pres*
EMP: 12
SQ FT: 3,200
SALES: (est): 2.3MM **Privately Held**
WEB: www.ackleymetal.com
SIC: 3599 Machine shop, jobbing & repair

(P-15683)
ACM MACHINING INC
Also Called: Alfred's Machining
240 State Highway 16 # 18, Plymouth
(95669-9701)
PHONE.....................916 804-9489
Carlos Balbacas, *Owner*
EMP: 32
SALES (corp-wide): 16.2MM **Privately Held**
SIC: 3599 3494 Machine shop, jobbing &
repair; valves & pipe fittings
PA: Acm Machining, Inc.
11390 Gold Dredge Way
Rancho Cordova CA 95742
916 852-8600

(P-15684)
ACM MACHINING INC (PA)
11390 Gold Dredge Way, Rancho Cordova
(95742-6867)
PHONE.....................916 852-8600
Alfred Balbach, *President*
Carlos Balbachas, *Vice Pres*
Pete Reynen, *General Mgr*
Mariano Ispas, *Engineer*
Leo Martins, *Production*
▲ EMP: 41
SQ FT: 29,000
SALES: 16.2MM **Privately Held**
SIC: 3599 Machine shop, jobbing & repair

(P-15685)
ACRA ENTERPRISES INC
5760 Thornwood Dr, Goleta (93117-3802)
PHONE.....................805 964-4757
Jack Novak, *President*
Pam Kane, *Vice Pres*
EMP: 10
SQ FT: 4,000
SALES: (est): 870K **Privately Held**
WEB: www.acraenterprises.com
SIC: 3599 Machine shop, jobbing & repair

(P-15686)
ACRO-SPEC GRINDING CO INC
4134 Indus Way, Riverside (92503-4847)
PHONE.....................951 736-1199
Haskell Boss, *President*
Clifford Boss, *Vice Pres*
Michelle Austin, *Admin Sec*
EMP: 14
SQ FT: 7,000
SALES: 1.8MM **Privately Held**
SIC: 3599 Machine shop, jobbing & repair

(P-15687)
ACROSCOPE LLC
3501 Thomas Rd Ste 7, Santa Clara
(95054-2037)
PHONE.....................408 727-6896
Gordon Erb, *Owner*
Michael Hadley, *General Mgr*
EMP: 12
SALES: (est): 1.7MM **Privately Held**
WEB: www.acroscope.com
SIC: 3599 Machine shop, jobbing & repair

(P-15688)
ACU SPEC INC
Also Called: Afi
990 Richard Ave Ste 103, Santa Clara
(95050-2828)
PHONE.....................408 748-8600
Fred Budde III, *President*
Amy Budde, *CFO*
EMP: 13
SQ FT: 9,900
SALES: (est): 133.1K **Privately Held**
WEB: www.anchorsemi.com
SIC: 3599 Machine shop, jobbing & repair

(P-15689)
ACUNA DIONISIO ABLE
Also Called: A & L Engineering
12629 Prairie Ave, Hawthorne
(90250-4611)
PHONE...............................310 978-4741
Dionisio Abel Acuna, *Owner*
EMP: 15
SQ FT: 3,700
SALES: 300K **Privately Held**
SIC: 3599 8711 5049 Machine shop, jobbing & repair; industrial engineers; engineers' equipment & supplies

(P-15690)
ADC ENTERPRISES INC
633 W Katella Ave Ste T, Orange
(92867-4621)
PHONE...............................714 538-3102
Virginia Devois, *Owner*
EMP: 17
SALES (est): 1.1MM **Privately Held**
SIC: 3599 Machine shop, jobbing & repair

(P-15691)
ADEM LLC
Also Called: Advanced Design Engrg & Mfg
1040 Di Giulio Ave # 160, Santa Clara
(95050-2847)
PHONE...............................408 727-8955
Boris Kesil, *Principal*
Jacob Obolsky,
Valery Sokolsky,
EMP: 30
SQ FT: 11,000
SALES (est): 5.3MM **Privately Held**
WEB: www.ademllc.com
SIC: 3599 8711 Machine shop, jobbing & repair; engineering services

(P-15692)
ADVANCED CERAMIC TECHNOLOGY
803 W Angus Ave, Orange (92868-1307)
PHONE...............................714 538-2524
Eric Andrew Roberts, *President*
William Roberts, *Vice Pres*
Kelly Roberts, *Program Mgr*
Jwalant Parikh, *QC Mgr*
EMP: 16
SQ FT: 9,900
SALES (est): 2.1MM **Privately Held**
WEB: www.advancedceramictech.com
SIC: 3599 Machine shop, jobbing & repair

(P-15693)
ADVANCED COMPONENTS MFG
Also Called: A C M
1415 N Carolan Ave, Burlingame
(94010-2403)
PHONE...............................650 344-6272
Craig Corey, *President*
Jack Corey, *Treasurer*
Gloria Corey, *Admin Sec*
EMP: 20
SQ FT: 6,500
SALES (est): 3.3MM **Privately Held**
SIC: 3599 3444 Machine shop, jobbing & repair; sheet metalwork

(P-15694)
ADVANCED ENGINEERING & EDM INC
13007 Kirkham Way Ste A, Poway
(92064-7152)
PHONE...............................858 679-6800
Norm Turoff, *CEO*
Lindy Bauer, *Controller*
EMP: 17
SALES (est): 1.6MM **Privately Held**
SIC: 3599 Machine shop, jobbing & repair

(P-15695)
ADVANCED ENGINERING AND EDM
13007 Kirkham Way Ste A, Poway
(92064-7152)
PHONE...............................858 679-6800
William J Bauer, *Managing Prtnr*
Norm Turoff, *Managing Prtnr*
Lindsey Bauer, *General Mgr*
EMP: 20 EST: 2011
SALES (est): 3.2MM **Privately Held**
SIC: 3599 Machine shop, jobbing & repair

(P-15696)
ADVANCED INTL TECH LLC
9909 Hibert St Ste A, San Diego
(92131-1069)
PHONE...............................858 566-2945
Margaret Yount, *President*
EMP: 10
SQ FT: 5,000
SALES (est): 907.5K **Privately Held**
WEB: www.aitechnology-usa.com
SIC: 3599 Machine shop, jobbing & repair

(P-15697)
ADVANCED LASER CUTTING INC
Also Called: Advanced Laser & Wtr Jet Cutng
820 Comstock St, Santa Clara
(95054-3404)
PHONE...............................408 486-0700
Lester Gragg, *President*
Rick Linthicum, *Principal*
EMP: 13
SQ FT: 6,800
SALES (est): 2.3MM **Privately Held**
WEB: www.adv-laser.com
SIC: 3599 Machine shop, jobbing & repair

(P-15698)
ADVANCED MCHNING SOLUTIONS INC
3523 Main St Ste 606, Chula Vista
(91911-0803)
PHONE...............................619 671-3055
Pamela Yuhm, *President*
Charles Wuennemann, *Manager*
EMP: 35
SALES (est): 4.8MM **Privately Held**
WEB: www.amsinc2005.com
SIC: 3599 Machine shop, jobbing & repair

(P-15699)
ADVANCED MCHNING TCHNIQUES INC
16205 Vineyard Blvd, Morgan Hill
(95037-7124)
PHONE...............................408 778-4500
Frank C Dutra, *President*
Susan Dutra, *Vice Pres*
Marla Abeyta, *Office Mgr*
EMP: 49
SQ FT: 24,000
SALES: 8MM **Privately Held**
WEB: www.advancedmachining.com
SIC: 3599 Machine shop, jobbing & repair

(P-15700)
ADVANCED PRCSION MACHINING INC
1649 Monrovia Ave, Costa Mesa
(92627-4404)
PHONE...............................949 650-6113
Sean McCaig, *CEO*
Russell Congelliere, *CFO*
Yasumi McCaig, *Admin Sec*
EMP: 12
SQ FT: 2,500
SALES (est): 1.3MM **Privately Held**
WEB: www.advanced-precision.com
SIC: 3599 Machine shop, jobbing & repair

(P-15701)
ADVANCED TECHNOLOGY MACHINING
28210 Avenue Crocker # 301, Valencia
(91355-3475)
PHONE...............................661 257-2313
Herbert Joe Howton, *CEO*
Vickie Howton, *President*
Joe Howton, *Vice Pres*
EMP: 15
SQ FT: 4,160
SALES (est): 3MM **Privately Held**
SIC: 3599 Machine shop, jobbing & repair

(P-15702)
AERO CHIP INC
13563 Freeway Dr, Santa Fe Springs
(90670-5633)
PHONE...............................562 404-6300
Solomon M Gavrila, *CEO*
EMP: 50
SQ FT: 17,000

SALES (est): 12.6MM **Privately Held**
WEB: www.aerochip.com
SIC: 3599 Machine shop, jobbing & repair

(P-15703)
AERO ENGINEERING INC
1020 E Elm Ave, Fullerton (92831-5022)
PHONE...............................714 879-6200
Brent Borden, *President*
Danielle Ketcham, *Engineer*
EMP: 16
SQ FT: 5,500
SALES (est): 2.4MM **Privately Held**
WEB: www.aero-e.com
SIC: 3599 Machine shop, jobbing & repair

(P-15704)
AERO INDUSTRIES LLC
139 Industrial Way, Buellton (93427)
P.O. Box 198 (93427-0198)
PHONE...............................805 688-6734
Dave Watkins, *Manager*
Francis Williams, *Site Mgr*
EMP: 30
SALES (est): 4.4MM
SALES (corp-wide): 80.4MM **Privately Held**
SIC: 3599 Machine shop, jobbing & repair
PA: Gavial Holdings, Inc.
1435 W Mccoy Ln
Santa Maria CA 93455
805 614-0060

(P-15705)
AERO MECHANISM PRECISION INC
21700 Marilla St, Chatsworth (91311-4125)
PHONE...............................818 886-1855
Palminder Sehmbey, *President*
EMP: 34 EST: 1996
SQ FT: 8,000
SALES (est): 5.3MM **Privately Held**
WEB: www.aeromechanism.com
SIC: 3599 Machine shop, jobbing & repair

(P-15706)
AERO-K INC
10764 Lower Azusa Rd, El Monte
(91731-1306)
PHONE...............................626 350-5125
Robert Krusic, *President*
Jeffrey Hines, *Info Tech Mgr*
EMP: 45
SQ FT: 14,000
SALES (est): 9.1MM **Privately Held**
WEB: www.aero-k.com
SIC: 3599 Machine shop, jobbing & repair

(P-15707)
AERO-MECHANICAL ENGRG INC
5945 Engineer Dr, Huntington Beach
(92649-1129)
PHONE...............................714 891-2423
Anders Ahlstrom, *Ch of Bd*
John Ahlstrom, *President*
EMP: 16 EST: 1974
SQ FT: 4,150
SALES: 1.5MM **Privately Held**
WEB: www.aero-mechanical.com
SIC: 3599 Machine shop, jobbing & repair

(P-15708)
AERODYNAMIC ENGINEERING INC
15495 Graham St, Huntington Beach
(92649-1205)
PHONE...............................714 891-2651
Bob Waddell, *CEO*
Alfred Mayer, *President*
Bob Waddell, *CEO*
Ewald Eisel, *Principal*
Brian Beckner, *Manager*
▲ EMP: 40
SQ FT: 12,000
SALES (est): 8.5MM **Privately Held**
WEB: www.aerodynamic.net
SIC: 3599 3769 Machine shop, jobbing & repair; guided missile & space vehicle parts & auxiliary equipment

(P-15709)
AERODYNE PRCSION MACHINING INC
5471 Argosy Ave, Huntington Beach
(92649-1038)
PHONE...............................714 891-1311
Raymond Krispel, *President*
Veronica Schultz, *CFO*
Otto Schulz, *Vice Pres*
Jason Krispel, *Executive*
Mike Trollman, *Opers Mgr*
▲ EMP: 25
SQ FT: 20,000
SALES (est): 7.7MM **Privately Held**
WEB: www.aerodyneprecision.com
SIC: 3599 Machine shop, jobbing & repair

(P-15710)
AEROLIANT MANUFACTURING INC
Also Called: Fordon Grind Industries
1613 Lockness Pl, Torrance (90501-5119)
PHONE...............................310 257-1903
Patricia A Wiacek, *President*
Greg Wiacek, *Vice Pres*
EMP: 20 EST: 2009
SQ FT: 7,200
SALES: 2.5MM **Privately Held**
SIC: 3599 Machine shop, jobbing & repair

(P-15711)
AEROSTAR ENGINEERING & MFG INC
25514 Frampton Ave, Harbor City
(90710-2907)
PHONE...............................310 326-5098
Min Lee, *President*
Connie Lee, *Admin Sec*
EMP: 11
SQ FT: 4,680
SALES (est): 1.7MM **Privately Held**
SIC: 3599 Machine shop, jobbing & repair

(P-15712)
AF MACHINE & TOOL CO INC
950 W Hyde Park Blvd D, Inglewood
(90302-3335)
PHONE...............................310 674-1919
Malka Fogel, *President*
Aaron Fogel, *Vice Pres*
Eric Fogel, *Vice Pres*
EMP: 10
SQ FT: 5,500
SALES: 1.8MM **Privately Held**
WEB: www.afmach.com
SIC: 3599 Machine shop, jobbing & repair

(P-15713)
AGA PRECISION SYSTEMS INC
122 E Dyer Rd, Santa Ana (92707-3732)
PHONE...............................714 540-3163
Ralph E Wilson, *President*
Wesley Wilson, *CFO*
EMP: 16
SQ FT: 14,100
SALES: 2.8MM **Privately Held**
WEB: www.agaprecision.com
SIC: 3599 Machine shop, jobbing & repair

(P-15714)
AIR CRAFTORS ENGINEERING INC
4040 Cheyenne Ct, Chino (91710-5457)
PHONE...............................909 900-0635
Tim Boucher, *President*
John Boucher, *Vice Pres*
EMP: 14
SQ FT: 6,000
SALES (est): 1.1MM **Privately Held**
SIC: 3599 Machine shop, jobbing & repair

(P-15715)
AIRPOINT PRECISION INC
6221 Enterprise Dr Ste D, Diamond Springs
(95619-9469)
PHONE...............................530 622-0510
Will Fanning, *President*
Clem Fanning, *President*
Jason Hanks, *CFO*
EMP: 13
SQ FT: 7,200
SALES (est): 2.3MM **Privately Held**
WEB: www.airpointinc.com
SIC: 3599 Machine shop, jobbing & repair

PRODUCTS & SVCS

(P-15716)
ALDO FRAGALE
Also Called: Turner Precision
17813 S Main St Ste 111, Gardena
(90248-3542)
PHONE..................310 324-0050
Aldo Fragale, *President*
EMP: 12
SQ FT: 2,500
SALES: 1MM **Privately Held**
SIC: 3599 Machine shop, jobbing & repair

(P-15717)
ALFREDO HERNANDEZ
Also Called: A & H Wire EDM
474 W Arrow Hwy Ste K, San Dimas
(91773-2919)
PHONE..................909 971-9320
Alfredo Hernandez, *Owner*
EMP: 10
SQ FT: 4,000
SALES (est): 1.5MM **Privately Held**
SIC: 3599 Machine shop, jobbing & repair

(P-15718)
ALL DIAMETER GRINDING INC
725 N Main St, Orange (92868-1105)
PHONE..................714 744-1200
Marvin W Goodwin, *President*
Barbara Goodwin, *Treasurer*
Jeff Goodwin, *Vice Pres*
EMP: 22
SQ FT: 9,500
SALES: 11MM **Privately Held**
WEB: www.alldiametergrinding.com
SIC: 3599 Machine shop, jobbing & repair

(P-15719)
ALL STAR PRECISION
8739 Lion St, Rancho Cucamonga
(91730-4428)
PHONE..................909 944-8373
Scott Jackson, *Owner*
Ron Jackson, *Partner*
EMP: 23
SALES (est): 366K **Privately Held**
WEB: www.allstarprecision.com
SIC: 3599 Machine shop, jobbing & repair

(P-15720)
ALL TIME MACHINE INC
2050 Del Rio Way, Ontario (91761-8037)
PHONE..................909 673-1899
Ronald J Gagnon, *President*
Allison Gagnon, *President*
EMP: 12
SQ FT: 13,000
SALES: 5.4MM **Privately Held**
WEB: www.alltimemachine.com
SIC: 3599 Machine shop, jobbing & repair

(P-15721)
ALL-TECH MACHINE & ENGRG INC
2700 Prune Ave, Fremont (94539-6780)
PHONE..................510 353-2000
Richard M Gale, *CEO*
Boydine Michaels, *Vice Pres*
Janice Moan, *Admin Sec*
EMP: 49
SALES (est): 7.9MM **Privately Held**
WEB: www.alltechinc.com
SIC: 3599 Machine shop, jobbing & repair

(P-15722)
ALLIED DISC GRINDING
2478 Maggio Cir Ste A, Lodi (95240-8815)
PHONE..................209 339-0333
Harry L Campbell, *President*
Kay Campbell, *Vice Pres*
EMP: 11 EST: 1974
SQ FT: 9,000
SALES: 1MM **Privately Held**
WEB: www.softcom.com
SIC: 3599 Grinding castings for the trade

(P-15723)
ALLOY MACHINING AND HONING INC
2808 Supply Ave, Commerce (90040-2706)
PHONE..................323 726-8248
Paul Muscet, *President*
Nada Muscet, *Admin Sec*
EMP: 12
SQ FT: 12,000

SALES (est): 1.6MM **Privately Held**
SIC: 3599 Machine shop, jobbing & repair

(P-15724)
ALLOY MACHINING SERVICES INC
2808 Supply Ave, Commerce (90040-2706)
PHONE..................323 725-2545
Paul Muscet, *President*
Christina Constantino, *Vice Pres*
EMP: 15
SALES (est): 2.1MM **Privately Held**
SIC: 3599 Machine shop, jobbing & repair

(P-15725)
ALPHA AVIATION COMPONENTS INC (PA)
16772 Schoenborn St, North Hills
(91343-6108)
PHONE..................818 894-8801
Lidia Gorko, *President*
William Tudor, *Vice Pres*
EMP: 36
SQ FT: 18,000
SALES: 3.8MM **Privately Held**
WEB: www.gorkoind.com
SIC: 3599 3451 3728 Machine shop, job-
bing & repair; screw machine products;
aircraft parts & equipment

(P-15726)
ALPHA AVIATION COMPONENTS INC
Cal-Swiss Mfg
16774 Schoenborn St, North Hills
(91343-6108)
PHONE..................818 894-8468
Lidia Gorko, *President*
EMP: 15
SALES (corp-wide): 3.8MM **Privately Held**
WEB: www.gorkoind.com
SIC: 3599 Machine shop, jobbing & repair
PA: Alpha Aviation Components, Inc.
16772 Schoenborn St
North Hills CA 91343
818 894-8801

(P-15727)
ALPHA GRINDING INC
12402 Benedict Ave, Downey
(90242-3112)
PHONE..................562 803-1509
Yanick Herrouin, *President*
Kay Marcy, *Corp Secy*
Marc Herrouin, *Vice Pres*
▲ EMP: 13 EST: 1964
SQ FT: 9,000
SALES (est): 1.6MM **Privately Held**
WEB: www.alphagrinding.com
SIC: 3599 Machine shop, jobbing & repair

(P-15728)
ALPHA MACHINE COMPANY INC
933 Chittenden Ln Ste A, Capitola
(95010-3600)
PHONE..................831 462-7400
Pemo Saraliev, *President*
Chris Jenschke, *Partner*
EMP: 18
SQ FT: 12,000
SALES (est): 5.1MM **Privately Held**
WEB: www.alphamco.com
SIC: 3599 Machine shop, jobbing & repair

(P-15729)
ALTA DESIGN AND MANUFACTURING
885 Auzerais Ave, San Jose (95126-3760)
PHONE..................408 450-5394
Steven E Hernandez, *President*
Paula Hernandez, *Vice Pres*
Griselda Rojas, *Office Mgr*
EMP: 13
SALES (est): 1.5MM **Privately Held**
SIC: 3599 Machine shop, jobbing & repair

(P-15730)
ALTAMONT MANUFACTURING INC
241 Rickenbacker Cir, Livermore
(94551-7216)
PHONE..................925 371-5401
Robert Stivers, *President*
Richard Stivers, *Vice Pres*

EMP: 18
SALES: 3MM **Privately Held**
SIC: 3599 Machine shop, jobbing & repair

(P-15731)
ALTEST CORPORATION
898 Faulstich Ct, San Jose (95112-1361)
PHONE..................408 436-9900
Savann Seng, *CEO*
Brian Sen, *President*
Amy Tung, *Vice Pres*
EMP: 29
SQ FT: 30,000
SALES (est): 6.5MM **Privately Held**
WEB: www.altestcorp.com
SIC: 3599 3672 Machine shop, jobbing &
repair; printed circuit boards

(P-15732)
ALTS TOOL & MACHINE INC (PA)
10926 Woodside Ave N, Santee
(92071-3272)
P.O. Box 712485 (92072-2485)
PHONE..................619 562-6653
Dean Alt, *President*
Kathleen Alt, *Treasurer*
EMP: 55
SQ FT: 27,000
SALES (est): 10.3MM **Privately Held**
WEB: www.altstool.com
SIC: 3599 Machine shop, jobbing & repair

(P-15733)
ALVARADO MICRO PRECISION INC
Also Called: Boring Thrading Bars Unlimited
2389 La Mirada Dr Ste 9, Vista
(92081-7863)
PHONE..................760 598-0186
Jorge E Alvarado, *President*
EMP: 10 EST: 1997
SQ FT: 5,978
SALES (est): 1.7MM **Privately Held**
WEB: www.alvaradomicro.com
SIC: 3599 Machine & other job shop work

(P-15734)
ALVELLAN INC
Also Called: East Bay Machine and Shtmtl
1030 Shary Ct, Concord (94518-2409)
P.O. Box 1206 (94522-1206)
PHONE..................925 689-2421
Sean M McLellan, *CEO*
Tim Alvey, *CFO*
EMP: 28
SQ FT: 30,000
SALES (est): 3.3MM **Privately Held**
WEB: www.eastbaymachine.com
SIC: 3599 5083 Machine shop, jobbing &
repair; lawn & garden machinery & equip-
ment

(P-15735)
AM-PAR MANUFACTURING CO INC
959 Von Geldern Way, Yuba City
(95991-4215)
PHONE..................530 671-1800
Karen Coker, *President*
Judith A Klamerus, *Vice Pres*
Karen A Coker, *Admin Sec*
EMP: 10 EST: 1962
SQ FT: 13,000
SALES: 761K **Privately Held**
SIC: 3599 Machine shop, jobbing & repair

(P-15736)
AM-TEK ENGINEERING INC
1180 E Francis St Ste C, Ontario
(91761-4802)
PHONE..................909 673-1633
Boone Bounyaseng, *CEO*
Lauren Waters, *Opers Mgr*
EMP: 18 EST: 1998
SQ FT: 10,000
SALES (est): 3MM **Privately Held**
SIC: 3599 Machine shop, jobbing & repair

(P-15737)
AMERICAN CNC INC
12430 Montague St Ste 207, Pacoima
(91331-2149)
PHONE..................818 890-3400
Patrick Talverdi Freidani, *CEO*

EMP: 10
SALES (est): 961.8K **Privately Held**
SIC: 3599 Machine shop, jobbing & repair

(P-15738)
AMERICAN DEBURRING INC
Also Called: A Fab
20742 Linear Ln, Lake Forest
(92630-7804)
PHONE..................949 457-9790
Robert L Campbell, *President*
Theresa Cook, *Admin Sec*
EMP: 25
SQ FT: 11,000
SALES: 3MM **Privately Held**
WEB: www.afabcnc.com
SIC: 3599 Machine shop, jobbing & repair

(P-15739)
AMERICAN MFG NETWRK INC
Also Called: Amanet
7001 Eton Ave, Canoga Park (91303-2112)
PHONE..................818 786-1113
Robert Barbour, *Chairman*
Sandip Desai, *President*
Natalia Garzo, *Accounting Mgr*
Maria Garcia, *Purch Mgr*
EMP: 14
SQ FT: 4,000
SALES (est): 2.4MM **Privately Held**
WEB: www.amanet.com
SIC: 3599 3469 Machine shop, jobbing &
repair; metal stampings

(P-15740)
AMERICAN PRCISION GRINDING MCH
456 Gerona Ave, San Gabriel
(91775-2938)
PHONE..................626 357-6610
Fax: 626 358-4365
EMP: 13
SQ FT: 3,500
SALES: 1.5MM **Privately Held**
SIC: 3599

(P-15741)
AMH INTERNATIONAL INC
1270 Avenida Acaso Ste J, Camarillo
(93012-8747)
PHONE..................805 388-2082
Sam Grimaldo, *Principal*
EMP: 10
SALES (est): 1.2MM **Privately Held**
SIC: 3599 Machine shop, jobbing & repair

(P-15742)
ANGULAR MACHINING INC
2040 Hartog Dr, San Jose (95131-2214)
PHONE..................408 954-8326
Kiet Nguyen, *President*
Tina Tran, *Manager*
EMP: 24 EST: 2001
SALES (est): 4.5MM **Privately Held**
WEB: www.angularmachining.com
SIC: 3599 Machine shop, jobbing & repair

(P-15743)
APPLIED PROCESS EQUIPMENT
2620 Bay Rd, Redwood City (94063-3501)
PHONE..................650 365-6895
Michael T Hertert, *Partner*
Chris Dale, *Partner*
EMP: 11
SQ FT: 5,000
SALES: 790K **Privately Held**
SIC: 3599 Machine shop, jobbing & repair

(P-15744)
ARAM PRECISION TOOL DIE INC
9758 Cozycroft Ave, Chatsworth
(91311-4417)
P.O. Box 3696 (91313-3696)
PHONE..................818 998-1000
AVI Amichai, *President*
Rona Amichai, *Corp Secy*
EMP: 13
SQ FT: 12,000
SALES (est): 1MM **Privately Held**
WEB: www.aramprecision.com
SIC: 3599 3451 Machine shop, jobbing &
repair; screw machine products

▲ = Import ▼=Export
◆ =Import/Export

(P-15745)
ARANDA TOOLING INC
13950 Yorba Ave, Chino (91710-5520)
PHONE....................................714 379-6565
Pedro Aranda, *President*
Martha Aranda, *Corp Secy*
Eric Nelson, *Engineer*
Sandra Galvan, *Human Res Mgr*
Michael Dean, *Purchasing*
▲ EMP: 70
SQ FT: 60,000
SALES (est): 35.1MM **Privately Held**
WEB: www.arandatooling.com
SIC: 3599 3469 3544 3465 Machine
shop, jobbing & repair; metal stampings;
special dies, tools, jigs & fixtures; automotive stampings

(P-15746)
AREMAC ASSOCIATES INC
2004 S Myrtle Ave, Monrovia (91016-4837)
PHONE....................................626 303-8795
Scott Sher, *CEO*
Mariela Vinas, *Vice Pres*
EMP: 35
SQ FT: 12,500
SALES (est): 5.2MM **Privately Held**
SIC: 3599 3444 Machine shop, jobbing &
repair; sheet metalwork

(P-15747)
ARMS PRECISION INC
169 Radio Rd, Corona (92879-1724)
PHONE....................................951 273-1800
Dale O Banion, *President*
Robin O Banion, *CFO*
Stephanie Clark, *Office Mgr*
EMP: 10
SQ FT: 3,900
SALES (est): 323.8K **Privately Held**
SIC: 3599 Machine shop, jobbing & repair

(P-15748)
ARMSTRONG TECHNOLOGY INC
12780 Earhart Ave, Auburn (95602-9027)
PHONE....................................530 888-6262
Arthur Armstrong, *Branch Mgr*
Julie Armstrong, *Vice Pres*
Brandy Haring, *Office Mgr*
Jim Burkhart, *Plant Mgr*
EMP: 45
SALES (corp-wide): 20MM **Privately Held**
WEB: www.armstrong-tech.com
SIC: 3599 Machine shop, jobbing & repair
PA: Armstrong Technology, Inc.
1121 Elko Dr
Sunnyvale CA 94089
408 734-4434

(P-15749)
ARNOLD-GONSALVES ENGRG INC
5731 Chino Ave, Chino (91710-5226)
PHONE....................................909 465-1579
Manuel Gonsalves, *President*
Mike Arnold, *Vice Pres*
EMP: 35
SQ FT: 10,000
SALES (est): 6MM **Privately Held**
SIC: 3599 3444 Machine shop, jobbing &
repair; sheet metal specialties, not
stamped

(P-15750)
ARROW ENGINEERING
4946 Azusa Canyon Rd, Irwindale
(91706-1940)
PHONE....................................626 960-2806
John Beaman, *President*
Jim Ballantyne, *Vice Pres*
Mark J Silk, *Agent*
Mark Silk, *Agent*
EMP: 36
SQ FT: 18,000
SALES (est): 7.7MM **Privately Held**
SIC: 3599 Machine shop, jobbing & repair

(P-15751)
ARROW SCREW PRODUCTS INC
941 W Mccoy Ln, Santa Maria
(93455-1109)
PHONE....................................805 928-2269

Robert Vine, *CEO*
Tim Vine, *Vice Pres*
Hoang Vine, *Admin Sec*
EMP: 33
SQ FT: 10,000
SALES (est): 5.9MM **Privately Held**
WEB: www.arrowscrew.com
SIC: 3599 3541 Machine shop, jobbing &
repair; machine tools, metal cutting type

(P-15752)
ASIGMA CORPORATION
2930 San Luis Rey Rd, Oceanside
(92058-1220)
PHONE....................................760 966-3103
C Dale Chudomelka, *President*
Darryl Chudomelka, *Vice Pres*
Doug Chudomelka, *Vice Pres*
▲ EMP: 16
SQ FT: 6,500
SALES (est): 2.4MM **Privately Held**
WEB: www.asigmacorp.com
SIC: 3599 Custom machinery; machine
shop, jobbing & repair

(P-15753)
ASTRO MACHINE CO INC
3734 W 139th St, Hawthorne (90250-7597)
PHONE....................................310 679-8291
William Skintauy, *President*
Ann Vellonakis, *Treasurer*
James Vellonakis, *Vice Pres*
Stasi Vellonakis, *Admin Sec*
Allen Boothe, *Mfg Mgr*
EMP: 14 EST: 1965
SQ FT: 5,000
SALES (est): 2.7MM **Privately Held**
SIC: 3599 Machine shop, jobbing & repair

(P-15754)
AUGER INDUSTRIES INC
390 E Crowther Ave, Placentia
(92870-6419)
PHONE....................................714 577-9350
John Auger, *President*
Francoise Auger, *Shareholder*
Toni Auger, *Manager*
EMP: 17 EST: 1969
SQ FT: 12,000
SALES (est): 3.3MM **Privately Held**
WEB: www.augerind.com
SIC: 3599 Machine shop, jobbing & repair

(P-15755)
AUTOMATION WEST INC
Also Called: Cameron Metal Cutting
1605 E Saint Gertrude Pl, Santa Ana
(92705-5311)
PHONE....................................714 556-7381
George Danenhauer, *President*
David Roberts, *Vice Pres*
Linda Bingham, *Admin Sec*
Dave Roberts, *Sales Staff*
▲ EMP: 15
SQ FT: 7,200
SALES (est): 1.5MM **Privately Held**
WEB: www.automationwest.se
SIC: 3599 7389 Machine shop, jobbing &
repair; metal cutting services

(P-15756)
AVATAR MACHINE LLC
18100 Mount Washington St, Fountain Valley (92708-6121)
PHONE....................................949 817-7728
Liem Do,
Frank Nguyen,
Denny Nguyen, *Mng Member*
EMP: 23
SALES (est): 2.1MM **Privately Held**
SIC: 3599 5049 Machine shop, jobbing &
repair; precision tools

(P-15757)
AVION TL MFG MACHINING CTR INC
29035 The Old Rd, Valencia (91355-1083)
PHONE....................................661 257-2915
Patrick Beaudoin, *President*
Alison Horne, *Manager*
EMP: 13
SQ FT: 6,000
SALES (est): 2.5MM **Privately Held**
SIC: 3599 Machine shop, jobbing & repair

(P-15758)
AXXIS CORPORATION
1535 Nandina Ave, Perris (92571-7010)
PHONE....................................951 436-9921
Brandy Tidball, *President*
Jo Olchawa, *Treasurer*
Susan Tidball, *Vice Pres*
Jonathan Fuerte, *Human Resources*
EMP: 35
SALES (est): 6.5MM **Privately Held**
SIC: 3599 Machine shop, jobbing & repair

(P-15759)
AZTEC MACHINE CO INC
3156 Fitzgerald Rd Ste A, Rancho Cordova
(95742-6889)
PHONE....................................916 638-4894
Alfredo Alvarez, *President*
EMP: 12
SQ FT: 7,200
SALES (est): 2.1MM **Privately Held**
SIC: 3599 Machine shop, jobbing & repair

(P-15760)
AZURE MICRODYNAMICS INC
19652 Descartes, Foothill Ranch
(92610-2600)
PHONE....................................949 699-3344
Stan Sulek, *President*
Zyta Sulek, *Shareholder*
Oliver Sulek, *Vice Pres*
Chris Nagel, *Supervisor*
EMP: 68 EST: 1997
SALES (est): 1.3MM **Privately Held**
WEB: www.azuremicrodynamics.com
SIC: 3599 3544 Machine shop, jobbing &
repair; special dies, tools, jigs & fixtures

(P-15761)
B & B MANUFACTURING CO (PA)
27940 Beale Ct, Santa Clarita
(91355-1210)
PHONE....................................661 257-2161
Kenneth Gentry, *CEO*
Fred Duncan, *President*
Jeff Lage, *Vice Pres*
Will Tiefuhr, *Vice Pres*
Kyla Kelly, *Program Mgr*
▲ EMP: 200 EST: 1961
SQ FT: 180,000
SALES (est): 50.6MM **Privately Held**
WEB: www.bbmfg.com
SIC: 3599 Machine shop, jobbing & repair

(P-15762)
B & B PIPE AND TOOL CO (PA)
3035 Walnut Ave, Long Beach
(90807-5221)
PHONE....................................562 424-0704
Craig Braly, *President*
Stephanie Braly, *Corp Secy*
▲ EMP: 23 EST: 1951
SQ FT: 2,000
SALES (est): 8.7MM **Privately Held**
WEB: www.pipesales.com
SIC: 3599 Machine shop, jobbing & repair

(P-15763)
B & B PIPE AND TOOL CO
2301 Parker Ln, Bakersfield (93308-6006)
PHONE....................................661 323-8208
Joe Keller, *General Mgr*
EMP: 12
SALES (corp-wide): 8.7MM **Privately Held**
WEB: www.pipesales.com
SIC: 3599 Machine shop, jobbing & repair
PA: B & B Pipe And Tool Co.
3035 Walnut Ave
Long Beach CA 90807
562 424-0704

(P-15764)
B & G PRECISION INC
45450 Industrial Pl Ste 9, Fremont
(94538-6474)
PHONE....................................510 438-9785
Daniel Datta, *CEO*
EMP: 19
SQ FT: 3,600
SALES (est): 3.5MM **Privately Held**
SIC: 3599 Machine shop, jobbing & repair;
machine & other job shop work

(P-15765)
B & H TECHNICAL CERAMICS INC
390 Industrial Rd, San Carlos
(94070-6285)
PHONE....................................650 637-1171
Gunther Horn, *President*
Gary Horn, *Treasurer*
Helmot Koehler, *Vice Pres*
▲ EMP: 12
SQ FT: 12,000
SALES (est): 2MM **Privately Held**
SIC: 3599 Machine shop, jobbing & repair

(P-15766)
B & M MACHINE INC
8439 Cherry Ave, Fontana (92335-3027)
PHONE....................................909 355-0998
William Fay, *President*
Robynne Fay, *Treasurer*
Kevin Bing, *Vice Pres*
Manny Jorge, *Foreman/Supr*
EMP: 11
SQ FT: 7,000
SALES (est): 1.5MM **Privately Held**
WEB: www.bmmachine.com
SIC: 3599 7699 Machine shop, jobbing &
repair; hydraulic equipment repair

(P-15767)
B & W PRECISION INC
1260 Pioneer St Ste A, Brea (92821-3725)
P.O. Box 674, Yucca Valley (92286-0674)
PHONE....................................714 447-0971
EMP: 19 EST: 1964
SQ FT: 25,000
SALES (est): 2.5MM **Privately Held**
WEB: www.bwprecision.com
SIC: 3599

(P-15768)
B P I CORP
Also Called: Banbury Precision
1208 Norman Ave Ste B, Santa Clara
(95054-2068)
PHONE....................................408 988-7888
Gordon Banbury Jr, *President*
EMP: 15
SQ FT: 6,000
SALES (est): 1.4MM **Privately Held**
SIC: 3599 Machine shop, jobbing & repair

(P-15769)
B S K T INC
Also Called: S & S Precision Sheetmetal
8447 Canoga Ave, Canoga Park
(91304-2607)
PHONE....................................818 349-1566
Steve Kim, *President*
EMP: 20 EST: 1997
SQ FT: 12,000
SALES (est): 2.8MM **Privately Held**
WEB: www.snsprecision.com
SIC: 3599 Machine shop, jobbing & repair

(P-15770)
B&Z MANUFACTURING COMPANY INC
1478 Seareel Ln, San Jose (95131-1567)
PHONE....................................408 943-1117
Dennis Kimball, *President*
Thomas Simpson, *Corp Secy*
EMP: 42 EST: 1960
SQ FT: 18,000
SALES (est): 8.1MM **Privately Held**
WEB: www.bzmfg.com
SIC: 3599 Machine shop, jobbing & repair

(P-15771)
B/E AEROSPACE INC
7155 Fenwick Ln, Westminster
(92683-5218)
PHONE....................................714 896-9001
Amin Khoury, *Chairman*
Darnell Walker, *Vice Pres*
EMP: 100
SALES (corp-wide): 66.5B **Publicly Held**
SIC: 3599 3728 Machine shop, jobbing &
repair; aircraft parts & equipment
HQ: B/E Aerospace, Inc.
1400 Corporate Center Way
Wellington FL 33414
561 791-5000

PRODUCTS & SVCS

(P-15772)
BABBITT BEARING CO INC
Also Called: B B C
1170 N 5th St, San Jose (95112-4483)
PHONE..................................408 298-1101
Stanley Sinn, *President*
Jerry Mann, *Vice Pres*
EMP: 25
SQ FT: 16,000
SALES (est): 4.3MM **Privately Held**
WEB: www.bbcmachine.com
SIC: 3599 Machine shop, jobbing & repair

(P-15773)
BAKERSFIELD MACHINE COMPANY
Also Called: BMC Industries
5605 N Chester Ave Ext, Bakersfield (93308)
P.O. Box 122 (93302-0122)
PHONE..................................661 709-1992
John L Meyer, *President*
Alfred T Meyer Jr, *Vice Pres*
Christopher Reno, *Principal*
Ruch Robert, *Network Mgr*
Pat Lewis, *Controller*
▲ EMP: 55
SQ FT: 8,276
SALES (est): 12.6MM **Privately Held**
WEB: www.bmcindustries.com
SIC: 3599 Machine shop, jobbing & repair

(P-15774)
BARRANGO (PA)
Also Called: American Rotoform
391 Forbes Blvd, South San Francisco (94080-2014)
PHONE..................................650 737-9206
William Barrango, *President*
John Barrango, *Vice Pres*
Bill Barrango, *Manager*
◆ EMP: 10 EST: 1911
SQ FT: 100,000
SALES: 3.3MM **Privately Held**
WEB: www.barrango.com
SIC: 3599 3299 3089 Carousels (merry-go-rounds); architectural sculptures: gypsum, clay, papier mache, etc.; plastic processing

(P-15775)
BAUMANN ENGINEERING INC
212 S Cambridge Ave, Claremont (91711-4843)
PHONE..................................909 621-4181
Fred Baumann, *President*
Isolde Doll, *Admin Sec*
EMP: 85 EST: 1961
SQ FT: 18,057
SALES (est): 12.3MM **Privately Held**
WEB: www.baumannengineering.com
SIC: 3599 Machine shop, jobbing & repair

(P-15776)
BAY AREA MCH & MAR REPR INC
1305 S 51st St, Richmond (94804-4627)
PHONE..................................510 815-2339
EMP: 11
SALES (est): 1.1MM **Privately Held**
SIC: 3599 Machine shop, jobbing & repair

(P-15777)
BAY PRECISION MACHINING INC
Also Called: Emkay Mfg.
815 Sweeney Ave Ste D, Redwood City (94063-3029)
PHONE..................................650 365-3010
Anne Feher, *President*
George Koncz, *Vice Pres*
EMP: 25
SQ FT: 7,500
SALES (est): 3.9MM **Privately Held**
WEB: www.emkaymfg.com
SIC: 3599 Machine shop, jobbing & repair

(P-15778)
BAY TECH MANUFACTURING INC
23334 Bernhardt St, Hayward (94545-1678)
PHONE..................................510 783-0660
Mike Niklewski, *President*
Zbigniew Niklewski, *President*

Vicki Niklewski, *CFO*
EMP: 12
SQ FT: 9,700
SALES (est): 2.1MM **Privately Held**
WEB: www.baytechmfg.com
SIC: 3599 Machine shop, jobbing & repair

(P-15779)
BAYLESS ENGINEERING INC
Also Called: Bayless Engineering & Mfg
26100 Ave Hall Valencia, Valencia (91355)
P.O. Box 914 (91380-9014)
PHONE..................................661 257-3373
Earl Bayless, *President*
Rod Smith, *Vice Pres*
EMP: 235
SQ FT: 127,000
SALES (est): 34.6MM **Privately Held**
WEB: www.baylessengineering.com
SIC: 3599 3444 Machine shop, jobbing & repair; sheet metalwork

(P-15780)
BCI INC
Also Called: Upton Engineering & Mfg Co
1822 Belcroft Ave, South El Monte (91733-3703)
PHONE..................................626 579-4234
Adam Bondra, *President*
June Bondra, *Vice Pres*
EMP: 15
SQ FT: 6,500
SALES (est): 2.3MM **Privately Held**
SIC: 3599 5084 Machine shop, jobbing & repair; welding machinery & equipment

(P-15781)
BEDARD MACHINE INC
141 Viking Ave, Brea (92821-3817)
PHONE..................................714 990-4846
Dennis Bedard, *President*
Sue Bedard, *CFO*
Jaymie Marklevits, *Mfg Staff*
EMP: 13
SQ FT: 7,200
SALES (est): 2.1MM **Privately Held**
WEB: www.bedardmachineinc.com
SIC: 3599 Machine shop, jobbing & repair

(P-15782)
BEGOVIC INDUSTRIES INC
Also Called: B & H Engineering Company
1725 Old County Rd, San Carlos (94070-5206)
PHONE..................................650 594-2861
Bakir Begovic, *CEO*
Kenan Begovic, *President*
Hamida Begovic, *Vice Pres*
Martin Villegas, *QC Mgr*
Majid Suljic, *Mfg Staff*
EMP: 20
SALES (est): 5.2MM **Privately Held**
SIC: 3599 3444 Machine shop, jobbing & repair; sheet metalwork

(P-15783)
BEL-AIR MACHINING CO
151 E Columbine Ave, Santa Ana (92707-4401)
PHONE..................................714 953-6616
Moon H Choi, *Owner*
EMP: 15
SQ FT: 5,000
SALES (est): 2.5MM **Privately Held**
WEB: www.belairmachine.com
SIC: 3599 Machine shop, jobbing & repair

(P-15784)
BELLOWS MFG & RES INC
13596 Vaughn St, San Fernando (91340-3029)
PHONE..................................818 838-1333
Arteom Art Bulgadarian, *CEO*
David Galloway, *Engineer*
EMP: 13
SQ FT: 28,000
SALES: 1.6MM **Privately Held**
SIC: 3599 Bellows, industrial: metal

(P-15785)
BENDER CCP INC
Also Called: Bender US
2150 E 37th St Vernon, Vernon (90058)
P.O. Box 847, Benicia (94510-0847)
PHONE..................................707 745-9970
Michael A Potter, *President*

Randall Potter, *Vice Pres*
▲ EMP: 75
SALES (est): 13.3MM **Privately Held**
SIC: 3599 Custom machinery

(P-15786)
BENDICK PRECISION INC
56 La Porte St, Arcadia (91006-2827)
PHONE..................................626 445-0217
Christie Joseph, *President*
Benny Joseph, *Corp Secy*
Reyes Rosales, *Production*
EMP: 12 EST: 1975
SQ FT: 5,000
SALES (est): 1.8MM **Privately Held**
SIC: 3599 3061 Machine shop, jobbing & repair; medical & surgical rubber tubing (extruded & lathe-cut)

(P-15787)
BEONCA MACHINE INC
1680 Curtiss Ct, La Verne (91750-5848)
PHONE..................................909 392-9991
Johann Bock, *President*
Danny Bock, *President*
Dennis Bock, *Vice Pres*
EMP: 17
SQ FT: 7,000
SALES (est): 2.9MM **Privately Held**
WEB: www.beoncamachine.com
SIC: 3599 Machine shop, jobbing & repair

(P-15788)
BERNS BROS INC
Also Called: De Berns Company
1250 W 17th St, Long Beach (90813-1310)
PHONE..................................562 437-0471
Steven Berns, *President*
Sue Porter, *Vice Pres*
▲ EMP: 17
SQ FT: 20,000
SALES: 2.4MM **Privately Held**
WEB: www.thebernsco.com
SIC: 3599 Machine & other job shop work

(P-15789)
BETTER-WAY & LOVELL GRINDING
Also Called: Better Way Grinding
8333 Chetle Ave, Santa Fe Springs (90670-2201)
PHONE..................................562 693-8722
Edward W Lovell, *President*
Pat Lovell, *Treasurer*
EMP: 12
SQ FT: 33,000
SALES (est): 2MM **Privately Held**
WEB: www.betterwaygrinding.com
SIC: 3599 Grinding castings for the trade

(P-15790)
BETTERLINE PRODUCTS INC
1101 E Elm Ave, Fullerton (92831-5003)
PHONE..................................760 535-5030
Byron Berkes, *President*
Bill W Berkes, *Ch of Bd*
Harriett Berkes, *Treasurer*
EMP: 23
SQ FT: 2,000
SALES (est): 2MM **Privately Held**
WEB: www.betterlineproducts.com
SIC: 3599 3949 3544 3469 Machine shop, jobbing & repair; sporting & athletic goods; special dies, tools, jigs & fixtures; metal stampings

(P-15791)
BISON ENGINEERING COMPANY
15535 Texaco Ave, Paramount (90723-3921)
PHONE..................................562 408-1525
Lothar Maertens, *President*
Neil Thompson, *Vice Pres*
EMP: 13
SQ FT: 40,000
SALES (est): 3MM **Privately Held**
SIC: 3599 3728 Machine shop, jobbing & repair; aircraft parts & equipment

(P-15792)
BLACK DIAMOND MANUFACTURING CO
755 Bliss Ave, Pittsburg (94565)
PHONE..................................925 439-9160
EMP: 10

SALES (est): 1.3MM
SALES (corp-wide): 15.7MM **Privately Held**
SIC: 3599
PA: Bishop-Wisecarver Corporation
2104 Martin Way
Pittsburg CA 94565
925 439-8272

(P-15793)
BLAGA PRECISION INC
11650 Seaboard Cir, Stanton (90680-3426)
PHONE..................................714 891-9509
Gavril Blaga, *President*
▲ EMP: 15
SQ FT: 3,600
SALES (est): 3MM **Privately Held**
SIC: 3599 Machine shop, jobbing & repair

(P-15794)
BMW PRECISION MACHINING INC
2379 Industry St, Oceanside (92054-4803)
PHONE..................................760 439-6813
Richard Blakely, *President*
EMP: 25 EST: 1981
SQ FT: 17,400
SALES (est): 4.2MM **Privately Held**
WEB: www.bmwprecision.com
SIC: 3599 Machine shop, jobbing & repair

(P-15795)
BOB LEWIS MACHINE COMPANY INC
1324 W 135th St, Gardena (90247-1909)
PHONE..................................310 538-9406
Jeff Lewis, *President*
Helen Lewis, *Treasurer*
Joe Pinela, *Vice Pres*
Jose Angel Pinela, *Vice Pres*
Albert Young, *Admin Sec*
EMP: 12
SQ FT: 10,000
SALES (est): 1.1MM **Privately Held**
WEB: www.boblewismachine.com
SIC: 3599 Machine shop, jobbing & repair

(P-15796)
BOCK MACHINE COMPANY INC
2141 S Parco Ave, Ontario (91761-5769)
PHONE..................................909 947-7250
Jacob Bock, *President*
Jack Bock, *Vice Pres*
Roy Bock, *Vice Pres*
Wilma Bock, *Admin Sec*
EMP: 15
SQ FT: 10,000
SALES (est): 1.7MM **Privately Held**
WEB: www.bockmachine.com
SIC: 3599 Machine shop, jobbing & repair

(P-15797)
BRADFORD CANNING STAHL INC
Also Called: Piranha Propeller
250 Scottsville Blvd, Jackson (95642-2671)
PHONE..................................209 257-1535
Brad Stahl, *President*
Laura Griffiths, *Representative*
▼ EMP: 10
SQ FT: 4,000
SALES (est): 1.4MM **Privately Held**
WEB: www.piranhapropellers.com
SIC: 3599 5551 Propellers, ship & boat: machined; boat dealers

(P-15798)
BROOKSHIRE TOOL & MFG CO INC
10654 Garfield Ave, South Gate (90280-7334)
PHONE..................................562 861-2567
Chrisman Chiang, *President*
▲ EMP: 10
SQ FT: 10,000
SALES (est): 1.4MM **Privately Held**
SIC: 3599 3544 3469 Machine shop, jobbing & repair; special dies, tools, jigs & fixtures; metal stampings

(P-15799)
BRUDER INDUSTRY
3920 Sandstone Dr, El Dorado Hills (95762-9652)
PHONE..................................916 939-6888

▲ = Import ▼=Export
◆ =Import/Export

Rex Kamphfner, *General Mgr*
EMP: 87
SQ FT: 35,000
SALES (est): 7.5MM
SALES (corp-wide): 39.6MM **Privately Held**
WEB: www.aero-metals.com
SIC: 3599 Machine shop, jobbing & repair
PA: Aerometals, Inc.
3920 Sandstone Dr
El Dorado Hills CA 95762
916 939-6888

(P-15800)
BTI AEROSPACE & ELECTRONICS
Also Called: B T I Areospace & Electronics
13546 Vintage Pl, Chino (91710-5243)
PHONE......................909 465-1569
Gary Rindfleisch, *President*
▲ **EMP:** 25
SQ FT: 25,000
SALES (est): 3.3MM **Privately Held**
SIC: 3599 3444 3769 Machine shop, jobbing & repair; sheet metalwork; guided missile & space vehicle parts & auxiliary equipment

(P-15801)
BUENA PARK TOOL & ENGINEERING
7661 Windfield Dr, Huntington Beach (92647-7100)
PHONE......................714 843-6215
Leo Gomez, *CEO*
Teresa Gomez, *President*
Leo Gomez Jr, *Vice Pres*
EMP: 11
SQ FT: 11,000
SALES (est): 399.3K **Privately Held**
WEB: www.buenaparktool.com
SIC: 3599 7692 3544 Machine shop, jobbing & repair; welding repair; special dies, tools, jigs & fixtures

(P-15802)
BULLSEYE LEAK DETECTION INC
4015 Seaport Blvd, West Sacramento (95691-3416)
P.O. Box 73114, Davis (95617-3114)
PHONE......................916 760-8944
Daniel Spatz, *President*
EMP: 12
SALES: 500K **Privately Held**
SIC: 3599 1623 Water leak detectors; pipe laying construction

(P-15803)
BUNDY MANUFACTURING INC
Also Called: B M I
507 S Douglas St, El Segundo (90245-4810)
PHONE......................323 772-3273
James Bundy, *President*
EMP: 25
SQ FT: 10,000
SALES (est): 4.1MM **Privately Held**
SIC: 3599 Machine shop, jobbing & repair

(P-15804)
BURNET MACHINING INC
330 S Kellogg Ave Ste N, Goleta (93117-3814)
PHONE......................805 964-6321
Michael Schock, *President*
Laurie Schock, *CFO*
EMP: 10
SQ FT: 1,800
SALES (est): 1.3MM **Privately Held**
SIC: 3599 Machine shop, jobbing & repair

(P-15805)
BURTREE INC
13513 Sherman Way, Van Nuys (91405-2899)
PHONE......................818 786-4276
Cyrus Massoudi, *President*
Farah Massoudi, *Vice Pres*
Shawn Massoudi, *Mfg Staff*
EMP: 28 **EST:** 1955
SQ FT: 13,500

SALES (est): 3.7MM **Privately Held**
WEB: www.burtree.com
SIC: 3599 7699 Machine shop, jobbing & repair; professional instrument repair services

(P-15806)
C & C DIE ENGRAVING
12510 Mccann Dr, Santa Fe Springs (90670-3337)
PHONE......................562 944-3399
Salvador J Chavez, *Owner*
EMP: 18
SQ FT: 10,000
SALES (est): 2.8MM **Privately Held**
WEB: www.cncdieengraving.com
SIC: 3599 Machine shop, jobbing & repair

(P-15807)
C & D PRECISION COMPONENTS
Also Called: Trimatic
969 S Raymond Ave, Pasadena (91105-3241)
PHONE......................626 799-7109
Coleen Ganguin, *President*
Daniel A Ganguin, *Corp Secy*
EMP: 17
SQ FT: 4,000
SALES (est): 1.1MM **Privately Held**
SIC: 3599 Machine shop, jobbing & repair

(P-15808)
C & D PRESCISION MACHINING INC
2031 Concourse Dr, San Jose (95131-1727)
PHONE......................408 383-1888
Dong Nguyen, *President*
EMP: 20
SQ FT: 10,000
SALES (est): 1.9MM **Privately Held**
SIC: 3599 Machine shop, jobbing & repair

(P-15809)
C B MACHINE PRODUCTS INC
13735 Iroquois Pl, Chino (91710-5559)
PHONE......................909 517-1828
Carl Brod, *President*
Cecilia Brod, *Vice Pres*
EMP: 13
SQ FT: 7,000
SALES (est): 1.9MM **Privately Held**
SIC: 3599 Machine shop, jobbing & repair

(P-15810)
C J PRECISION INDUSTRIES INC
2817 Cherry Ave, Signal Hill (90755-1908)
PHONE......................562 426-3708
Mike Vedder, *President*
Michael Vedder, *Vice Pres*
Thomas Vedder, *Vice Pres*
Cynthia Vedder, *Admin Sec*
EMP: 15
SQ FT: 10,000
SALES (est): 2.2MM **Privately Held**
SIC: 3599 Machine shop, jobbing & repair

(P-15811)
C K TOOL COMPANY INC
1033 Wright Ave, Mountain View (94043-4535)
PHONE......................650 968-0261
Louis Ammatuna, *President*
Sherry Ammatuna, *CFO*
Tammy Kummerehl, *Vice Pres*
EMP: 14
SQ FT: 5,352
SALES (est): 1.5MM **Privately Held**
WEB: www.cktool.com
SIC: 3599 Machine shop, jobbing & repair

(P-15812)
C L HANN INDUSTRIES INC
1020 Timothy Dr, San Jose (95133-1042)
PHONE......................408 293-4800
Colin Edison Hann, *President*
Erich Von Shofstall, *COO*
Georgette Hann, *Office Mgr*
Jack Freitas, *Manager*
Cheyne Hann, *Manager*
EMP: 18
SQ FT: 30,000

SALES (est): 3.9MM **Privately Held**
WEB: www.clhann.com
SIC: 3599 Machine shop, jobbing & repair; machine & other job shop work

(P-15813)
C M MACHINE INC
560 S Grand Ave, San Jacinto (92582-3832)
PHONE......................951 654-6019
Carmel Tomoni, *President*
Michael Tomoni, *General Mgr*
EMP: 15
SQ FT: 6,000
SALES: 910K **Privately Held**
SIC: 3599 Machine shop, jobbing & repair

(P-15814)
C N C MACHINING INC
510 S Fairview Ave, Goleta (93117-3617)
PHONE......................805 681-8855
Gary Brous, *President*
Greg Brous, *Vice Pres*
Shirley Brous, *Admin Sec*
EMP: 12
SQ FT: 2,000
SALES (est): 360.7K **Privately Held**
SIC: 3599 Machine shop, jobbing & repair

(P-15815)
CAD WORKS INC
16366 E Valley Blvd, La Puente (91744-5546)
PHONE......................626 336-5491
David Paquini, *President*
Cecilia Chavez, *CFO*
Avrahan Garcia, *Vice Pres*
Abraham Garcia, *Mktg Dir*
EMP: 20
SQ FT: 10,000
SALES: 100K **Privately Held**
WEB: www.cadworks.us
SIC: 3599 Machine shop, jobbing & repair

(P-15816)
CAE AUTOMATION AND TEST LLC
44368 Warm Springs Blvd, Fremont (94538)
PHONE......................408 204-0006
Brady Quach, *Mng Member*
James Pak, *Mng Member*
EMP: 10
SQ FT: 28,000
SALES: 2MM **Privately Held**
SIC: 3599 Custom machinery

(P-15817)
CAL PRECISION INC
1680 Commerce St, Corona (92880-1731)
PHONE......................951 273-9901
Donna Loper, *President*
Charles Loper, *Vice Pres*
Jacob Foley, *Supervisor*
EMP: 14
SQ FT: 13,140
SALES (est): 3.6MM **Privately Held**
WEB: www.calprecision.com
SIC: 3599 Machine shop, jobbing & repair

(P-15818)
CALIFORNIA BROACH COMPANY
4815 Telegraph Rd, Los Angeles (90022-3720)
PHONE......................323 260-4812
Fax: 323 263-0337
EMP: 12
SQ FT: 15,000
SALES (est): 1MM **Privately Held**
SIC: 3599 3545

(P-15819)
CALIFORNIA JIG GRINDING CO
861 N Holly Glen Dr, Long Beach (90815-4722)
PHONE......................323 723-4017
Deryl R Craig, *President*
EMP: 16
SQ FT: 10,000
SALES (est): 1.9MM **Privately Held**
WEB: www.edmexcellence.com
SIC: 3599 Grinding castings for the trade

(P-15820)
CALMAX TECHNOLOGY INC (PA)
526 Laurelwood Rd, Santa Clara (95054-2418)
PHONE......................408 748-8660
Boguslaw J Marcinkowski, *CEO*
Gary Hintz, *General Mgr*
Katherine Marcinkowski, *Office Admin*
Mark Masterson, *Info Tech Mgr*
Matt Hintz, *Project Mgr*
EMP: 50
SQ FT: 78,822
SALES (est): 25.9MM **Privately Held**
WEB: www.calmaxtechnology.com
SIC: 3599 Machine shop, jobbing & repair

(P-15821)
CAMPBELL GRINDING INC
1003 E Vine St, Lodi (95240-3127)
PHONE......................209 339-8838
Dan Fritz, *President*
EMP: 12
SQ FT: 17,000
SALES (est): 1.7MM **Privately Held**
WEB: www.campbellgrinding.com
SIC: 3599 Machine shop, jobbing & repair

(P-15822)
CANADY MANUFACTURING CO INC
500 5th St, San Fernando (91340-2299)
PHONE......................818 365-9181
Brian Koehn, *President*
Rodney Hull, *Owner*
Rod Hull, *General Mgr*
Lyndi Munchhof, *Office Mgr*
Steve Hull, *Technology*
EMP: 13 **EST:** 1943
SQ FT: 5,000
SALES (est): 2.2MM **Privately Held**
SIC: 3599 Machine shop, jobbing & repair

(P-15823)
CAPSTAN PERMAFLOW
16110 S Figueroa St, Gardena (90248-2617)
PHONE......................310 366-5999
Robert Scow, *President*
Mark Paullin, *Admin Sec*
EMP: 10
SQ FT: 8,000
SALES: 1.2MM
SALES (corp-wide): 83MM **Privately Held**
WEB: www.capstanatlantic.com
SIC: 3599 Machine shop, jobbing & repair
PA: Capstan California, Inc.
16100 S Figueroa St
Gardena CA 90248
310 366-5999

(P-15824)
CARDIC MACHINE PRODUCTS INC
17000 Keegan Ave, Carson (90746-1309)
PHONE......................310 884-3400
Joseph Trumpio, *CEO*
Calvin Crockett, *Vice Pres*
Annette Jaurequi, *Office Mgr*
EMP: 15 **EST:** 1951
SQ FT: 10,900
SALES: 7MM **Privately Held**
WEB: www.cardicmachine.com
SIC: 3599 Machine shop, jobbing & repair

(P-15825)
CARLSON & BEAULOYE AIR PWR INC
2143 Newton Ave, San Diego (92113-2296)
P.O. Box 13622 (92170-3622)
PHONE......................619 232-5719
Ronald Beauloye Jr, *President*
Eugenia B Coleman, *Treasurer*
Henry J Beauloye Jr, *Vice Pres*
EMP: 10 **EST:** 1974
SQ FT: 13,000
SALES (est): 1.6MM **Privately Held**
WEB: www.carlsonassoc.com
SIC: 3599 Machine shop, jobbing & repair

PRODUCTS & SVCS

(P-15826)
CARLSON & BEAULOYE MACH SP INC
2141 Newton Ave, San Diego (92113-2210)
P.O. Box 13622 (92170-3622)
PHONE................................619 232-5719
Ronald Beauloye, *President*
Eugena Coleman, *Treasurer*
Alfred Beauloye, *Vice Pres*
Valerie Beauloye, *Admin Sec*
EMP: 10
SQ FT: 10,000
SALES: 1MM **Privately Held**
SIC: 3599 Machine shop, jobbing & repair

(P-15827)
CARTER PUMP & MACHINE INC
635 G St, Wasco (93280-2023)
PHONE................................661 393-8620
Chet Grooman, *President*
EMP: 18
SQ FT: 6,000
SALES (est): 2.4MM **Privately Held**
SIC: 3599 7699 Machine shop, jobbing & repair; pumps & pumping equipment repair

(P-15828)
CASON ENGINEERING INC
4952 Windplay Dr Ste D, El Dorado Hills (95762-9338)
PHONE................................916 939-9311
Bradford Cason, *President*
Michelle Cason, *Executive*
EMP: 34
SQ FT: 27,500
SALES (est): 4.3MM **Privately Held**
WEB: www.casoneng.com
SIC: 3599 Machine shop, jobbing & repair

(P-15829)
CAVALLO & CAVALLO INC
Also Called: Production Engineering & Mch
14955 Hilton Dr, Fontana (92336-2082)
PHONE................................909 428-6994
Thomas H Kearns, *President*
EMP: 16
SQ FT: 16,400
SALES (est): 2.8MM **Privately Held**
WEB: www.cavallo-inc.com
SIC: 3599 Machine shop, jobbing & repair

(P-15830)
CAVANAUGH MACHINE WORKS INC
1540 Santa Fe Ave, Long Beach (90813-1239)
PHONE................................562 437-1126
John Wells, *President*
Michael Wells, *Corp Secy*
Lisa Moore, *Manager*
Tim Wells, *Supervisor*
EMP: 40
SQ FT: 19,000
SALES (est): 7.2MM **Privately Held**
WEB: www.cavmachine.com
SIC: 3599 3731 3441 Machine shop, jobbing & repair; shipbuilding & repairing; fabricated structural metal

(P-15831)
CELESTICA PRCSION MCHINING LTD
40725 Encyclopedia Cir, Fremont (94538-2451)
PHONE................................510 252-2100
EMP: 40
SALES (corp-wide): 3.1MM **Privately Held**
SIC: 3599 Machine shop, jobbing & repair
PA: Celestica Precision Machining Ltd.
49235 Milmont Dr
Fremont CA 94538
510 742-0500

(P-15832)
CENCAL CNC INC
2491 Simpson St, Kingsburg (93631-9501)
PHONE................................559 897-8706
Abe Wiebe, *President*
Ann Wiebe, *Vice Pres*
EMP: 25
SQ FT: 5,000

SALES (est): 232.5K **Privately Held**
SIC: 3599 Electrical discharge machining (EDM)

(P-15833)
CENTERPOINT MFG CO INC
2625 N San Fernando Blvd, Burbank (91504-3220)
PHONE................................818 842-2147
John C Rotunno, *President*
Carmen Rotunno, *Vice Pres*
Ricardo Servellon, *Prdtn Mgr*
Tai Thi, *Foreman/Supr*
Tony Rotunno, *Manager*
EMP: 40 EST: 1966
SQ FT: 12,000
SALES (est): 7MM **Privately Held**
SIC: 3599 Machine shop, jobbing & repair

(P-15834)
CENTURY PARTS INC
913 W 223rd St, Torrance (90502-2246)
PHONE................................310 328-0281
Lynn Hale, *CEO*
EMP: 11
SQ FT: 12,500
SALES (est): 1.8MM **Privately Held**
SIC: 3599 Machine shop, jobbing & repair

(P-15835)
CENTURY PRECISION ENGRG INC
2141 W 139th St, Gardena (90249-2451)
PHONE................................310 538-0015
Myron Yoo, *President*
Joe Kwon, *Executive*
Bruce Lee, *Admin Sec*
Sonny Shin, *Engineer*
Jean Yoo, *Opers Mgr*
EMP: 25
SQ FT: 20,000
SALES (est): 5.4MM **Privately Held**
SIC: 3599 Machine shop, jobbing & repair

(P-15836)
CENTURY PRECISION MACHINE INC
Also Called: Century Industries
1130 W Grove Ave, Orange (92865-4131)
PHONE................................714 637-3691
Donald R Bibona, *President*
Vera Bibona, *Corp Secy*
David Bibona, *Vice Pres*
EMP: 10
SQ FT: 7,800
SALES (est): 890K **Privately Held**
SIC: 3599 Machine shop, jobbing & repair

(P-15837)
CERAMIC TECH INC
46211 Research Ave, Fremont (94539-6113)
PHONE................................510 252-8500
Kanu Gandhi, *President*
Vivek Gandhi, *Treasurer*
EMP: 28
SQ FT: 30,000
SALES (est): 5.2MM **Privately Held**
WEB: www.ceramictechinc.com
SIC: 3599 3264 Machine & other job shop work; porcelain electrical supplies

(P-15838)
CHANNEL ISL OPTO MECH
1595 Walter St Ste 1, Ventura (93003-5613)
PHONE................................805 644-2153
Alan Cornelius, *President*
Roger Ransom, *Treasurer*
Mark Pennington, *Vice Pres*
Carri Jacobs, *Office Mgr*
EMP: 11
SQ FT: 5,000
SALES (est): 1MM **Privately Held**
SIC: 3599 3827 Machine shop, jobbing & repair; optical elements & assemblies, except ophthalmic

(P-15839)
CHAPMAN ENGINEERING CORP
2321 Cape Cod Way, Santa Ana (92703-3514)
PHONE................................714 542-1942
Mary M Chapman, *CEO*
Ernest D Chapman, *Admin Sec*
Adam Diethrich, *Opers Mgr*

EMP: 40
SQ FT: 25,000
SALES (est): 6.4MM **Privately Held**
WEB: www.chapmanengineering.com
SIC: 3599 3469 Machine shop, jobbing & repair; metal stampings

(P-15840)
CHAVEZ WELDING & MACHINING
1115 Campbell Ave 1a, San Jose (95126-1004)
PHONE................................408 247-4658
Ramon Chavez, *Owner*
EMP: 22
SALES (est): 1.5MM **Privately Held**
SIC: 3599 Machine & other job shop work

(P-15841)
CHE PRECISION INC
2640 Lavery Ct Ste C, Newbury Park (91320-1528)
PHONE................................805 499-8885
Claude Holguin, *President*
Charlie Holguin, *Vice Pres*
Ed Doyle, *General Mgr*
▲ EMP: 15
SQ FT: 7,500
SALES (est): 3.1MM **Privately Held**
WEB: www.cheprecision.com
SIC: 3599 Machine shop, jobbing & repair

(P-15842)
CHECK YOURSELF INC
Also Called: Check Yourself Machining
5785 Thornwood Dr, Goleta (93117-3801)
PHONE................................805 967-6190
Candice Wiesblott, *President*
Lorne Wiesblott, *CFO*
Justin Wiesblott, *Vice Pres*
EMP: 10
SQ FT: 2,300
SALES (est): 850K **Privately Held**
WEB: www.chkyourself.com
SIC: 3599 Custom machinery

(P-15843)
CHEEK MACHINE CORP
1312 S Allec St, Anaheim (92805-6303)
PHONE................................714 279-9486
Tatiana Cheek, *President*
Christopher Cheek, *Vice Pres*
Thuan Vu, *Prgrmr*
Van Vu, *Prgrmr*
Hilario Herrera, *Prdtn Mgr*
EMP: 21
SQ FT: 5,000
SALES (est): 3.5MM **Privately Held**
WEB: www.cheekmachine.com
SIC: 3599 Machine shop, jobbing & repair

(P-15844)
CHIPCO MANUFACTURING CO INC
623 Bridge St, Yuba City (95991-3817)
PHONE................................530 751-8150
Paul J Azzopardi, *President*
Lea Ann Roberts, *Office Mgr*
EMP: 14 EST: 1964
SQ FT: 22,000
SALES (est): 2.8MM **Privately Held**
SIC: 3599 Machine shop, jobbing & repair

(P-15845)
CHIPMASTERS MANUFACTURING INC (PA)
798 N Coney Ave, Azusa (91702-2239)
P.O. Box 697 (91702-0697)
PHONE................................626 804-8178
Richard Jacobsen, *President*
EMP: 16
SQ FT: 15,400
SALES: 5MM **Privately Held**
SIC: 3599 Machine shop, jobbing & repair

(P-15846)
CISCO MFG INC
3185 De La Cruz Blvd, Santa Clara (95054-2405)
PHONE................................510 584-9626
Francisco Nanez, *President*
EMP: 20
SQ FT: 500
SALES: 3.5MM **Privately Held**
SIC: 3599 Machine shop, jobbing & repair

(P-15847)
CLASSIC WIRE CUT COMPANY INC
28210 Constellation Rd, Valencia (91355-5000)
PHONE................................661 257-0558
Brett Bannerman, *Principal*
▲ EMP: 150
SQ FT: 80,000
SALES (est): 33.2MM **Privately Held**
WEB: www.classicwirecut.com
SIC: 3599 3841 Electrical discharge machining (EDM); surgical instruments & apparatus

(P-15848)
CLINT PRECISION MFG INC
7665 Formula Pl Ste A, San Diego (92121-3429)
PHONE................................858 271-4041
Michael Clint, *President*
Sharon Clint, *Treasurer*
Michael Gompper, *Vice Pres*
Rick Mills, *Prgrmr*
EMP: 14
SQ FT: 11,000
SALES (est): 2.7MM **Privately Held**
WEB: www.clintprecision.com
SIC: 3599 Machine shop, jobbing & repair

(P-15849)
CMI PRECISION MACHINING LLC
527 Fee Ana St, Placentia (92870-6702)
PHONE................................714 528-3000
EMP: 11
SALES (est): 1.7MM **Privately Held**
SIC: 3599

(P-15850)
CMI PRECISION MACHINING LLC
Also Called: CMI Precision Machining
527 Fee Ana St, Placentia (92870-6702)
PHONE................................714 528-3000
Charles Cheek, *Principal*
EMP: 10
SALES (est): 1.4MM **Privately Held**
WEB: www.cmiprecision.com
SIC: 3599 Machine shop, jobbing & repair

(P-15851)
CMS ENGINEERING INC
Also Called: Commercial Military Supply
5702 Engineer Dr, Huntington Beach (92649-1126)
PHONE................................714 899-6900
Timothy David Campbell, *CEO*
Tim Campbell, *CFO*
EMP: 12
SQ FT: 20,000
SALES (est): 2.8MM **Privately Held**
SIC: 3599 Machine shop, jobbing & repair

(P-15852)
CNC INDUSTRIES INC
10635 Monte Vista Ave, Montclair (91763-4720)
PHONE................................909 445-0300
Bob Evans, *President*
Stephanie Evans, *Treasurer*
Steve Dodds, *General Mgr*
EMP: 13 EST: 1980
SQ FT: 33,000
SALES (est): 2MM **Privately Held**
SIC: 3599 Machine shop, jobbing & repair

(P-15853)
CNC MACHINING SERVICE INC
1130 E Acequia Ave, Visalia (93292-6557)
PHONE................................559 732-5599
Greg Montgomery, *President*
EMP: 12
SQ FT: 8,000
SALES (est): 1.5MM **Privately Held**
SIC: 3599 Machine shop, jobbing & repair

(P-15854)
CNI MFG INC
Also Called: Computer-Nozzles
15627 Arrow Hwy, Irwindale (91706-2004)
PHONE................................626 962-6646
Toby Argandona, *President*
David Argandona, *Vice Pres*
Yolanda Pullen, *Admin Sec*

▲ = Import ▼=Export
◆ =Import/Export

EMP: 20
SQ FT: 32,200
SALES (est): 4MM **Privately Held**
WEB: www.cni-mfg.com
SIC: 3599 3443 Custom machinery; fabricated plate work (boiler shop)

(P-15855)
COAST COMPOSITES LLC
7 Burroughs, Irvine (92618-2804)
PHONE..................................949 455-0665
Brendan Buckel, *Manager*
EMP: 10
SALES (corp-wide): 386.8MM **Privately Held**
SIC: 3599 Machine shop, jobbing & repair
HQ: Coast Composites, Llc
   5 Burroughs
   Irvine CA 92618
   949 455-0665

(P-15856)
COAST COMPOSITES LLC (DH)
Also Called: Aip Aerospace Holdings
5 Burroughs, Irvine (92618-2804)
PHONE..................................949 455-0665
Paul Walsh, *President*
Alison Mathieu, *Vice Pres*
Tim Shumate, *Business Dir*
Calvin Le, *Program Mgr*
Graham Mitchell, *Program Mgr*
◆ EMP: 93
SQ FT: 60,000
SALES (est): 58.4MM
SALES (corp-wide): 386.8MM **Privately Held**
WEB: www.coastcomposites.com
SIC: 3599 Machine shop, jobbing & repair
HQ: Ascent Aerospace, Llc
   16445 23 Mile Rd
   Macomb MI 48042
   586 726-0500

(P-15857)
CODY CYLINDER SERVICES
1393 Dodson Way Ste A, Riverside
(92507-2073)
P.O. Box 56099 (92517-0999)
PHONE..................................951 786-3650
Art Pastoor, *President*
Jolene Cody Patoor, *Vice Pres*
EMP: 21
SALES: 3.5MM **Privately Held**
SIC: 3599 7379 Machine shop, jobbing & repair; tape recertification service

(P-15858)
COLLEEN & HERB ENTERPRISES INC
Also Called: C & H Enterprises
46939 Bayside Pkwy, Fremont
(94538-6527)
PHONE..................................510 226-6083
Herbert Schmidt, *CEO*
Colleen Schmidt, *President*
Jake Schmidt, *COO*
Ron Pervorse, *Prgrmr*
Steve Heredia, *Technology*
EMP: 115
SQ FT: 50,000
SALES (est): 16.1MM **Privately Held**
WEB: www.candhenterprises.com
SIC: 3599 7692 Machine shop, jobbing & repair; welding repair

(P-15859)
COMPLETE METAL DESIGN
154 S Valencia Ave, Glendora
(91741-3262)
PHONE..................................626 335-3636
Robert Lane, *CEO*
Crystal Lane, *Admin Sec*
EMP: 12
SALES (est): 1.3MM **Privately Held**
SIC: 3599 Machine shop, jobbing & repair

(P-15860)
COMPUTER ASSSTED MFG TECH CORP
Also Called: CAM-Tech
8710 Research Dr, Irvine (92618-4222)
PHONE..................................949 263-8911
Lance Young, *President*
David Magnuson, *Treasurer*
Greg Scott, *Vice Pres*
Susan Mc Kenzie, *Financial Exec*

EMP: 75
SQ FT: 50,000
SALES (est): 13MM **Privately Held**
WEB: www.camtechcorp.com
SIC: 3599 Machine shop, jobbing & repair

(P-15861)
COMPUTER INTGRTED MCHINING INC
10940 Wheatlands Ave, Santee
(92071-2857)
PHONE..................................619 596-9246
Michael J Brown, *President*
Terri Brock, *Opers Mgr*
EMP: 21
SQ FT: 20,000
SALES (est): 4.5MM **Privately Held**
WEB: www.cimsd.com
SIC: 3599 Machine shop, jobbing & repair

(P-15862)
CONNELLY MACHINE WORKS
420 N Terminal St, Santa Ana
(92701-4999)
PHONE..................................714 558-6855
Ray Connelly, *President*
Scott Connelly, *Vice Pres*
EMP: 22
SQ FT: 17,000
SALES (est): 4.4MM **Privately Held**
WEB: www.connellymachine.com
SIC: 3599 3492 Machine shop, jobbing & repair; fluid power valves & hose fittings

(P-15863)
CONNOR MANUFACTURING SVCS INC (PA)
1710 S Amphlett Blvd # 318, San Mateo
(94402-2706)
PHONE..................................650 591-2026
Robert Sloss, *Ch of Bd*
Maxine Harmatta, *CFO*
Dennis Kwiecinski, *Exec VP*
James Burns, *Technician*
Luke Orlando, *Engineer*
▲ EMP: 100 EST: 1912
SQ FT: 3,000
SALES (est): 68.1MM **Privately Held**
WEB: www.connorms.com
SIC: 3599 Machine shop, jobbing & repair

(P-15864)
CONSOLDTED HNGE MNFCTURED PDTS
Also Called: Champ Co
1150b Dell Ave, Campbell (95008-6640)
PHONE..................................408 379-6550
Karl L Herbst, *President*
Ursula Gueldner, *Treasurer*
Alfred Riesenhuber, *Vice Pres*
Rod Mourad, *General Mgr*
Laurie Guerra, *Production*
EMP: 17
SQ FT: 23,000
SALES (est): 2.6MM **Privately Held**
WEB: www.champcompany.com
SIC: 3599 Machine shop, jobbing & repair

(P-15865)
COUGHRAN MECHANICAL SERVICES
3053 Liberty Island Rd, Rio Vista
(94571-1018)
P.O. Box 158 (94571-0158)
PHONE..................................707 374-2100
Kirk Coughran, *President*
Karla Graham, *CFO*
EMP: 19
SQ FT: 2,400
SALES (est): 3.3MM **Privately Held**
SIC: 3599 Machine shop, jobbing & repair

(P-15866)
COZZA INC
9941 Prospect Ave, Santee (92071-4318)
PHONE..................................619 749-5663
Frank Charles Cozza, *President*
Gerry Tailor, *Vice Pres*
EMP: 13
SQ FT: 10,000
SALES (est): 2.1MM **Privately Held**
SIC: 3599 Machine & other job shop work

(P-15867)
CPK MANUFACTURING INC
2188 Del Franco St Ste 70, San Jose
(95131-1583)
PHONE..................................408 971-4019
Khamsy Syluangkhot, *President*
Paul Wendall, *Vice Pres*
EMP: 16
SALES (est): 2.7MM **Privately Held**
WEB: www.cpkmfg.com
SIC: 3599 Machine shop, jobbing & repair; machine & other job shop work

(P-15868)
CRAMER ENGINEERING INC
302 Elizabeth Ln, Corona (92880-2504)
PHONE..................................562 903-5556
David Cramer, *President*
Barbara Cramer, *Treasurer*
EMP: 20
SALES: 1.3MM **Privately Held**
WEB: www.cramerengineering.com
SIC: 3599 Machine shop, jobbing & repair

(P-15869)
CREATIVE METAL PRODUCTS CORP
6284 San Ignacio Ave D, San Jose
(95119-1366)
PHONE..................................408 281-0797
Kenneth Hutchinson, *President*
Shirley Hutchinson, *Corp Secy*
▲ EMP: 12
SQ FT: 4,606
SALES (est): 1.7MM **Privately Held**
WEB: www.creativemetalproducts.com
SIC: 3599 3544 Machine shop, jobbing & repair; special dies, tools, jigs & fixtures

(P-15870)
CRESCO MANUFACTURING INC
Also Called: Crescomfg.com
1614 N Orangethorpe Way, Anaheim
(92801-1227)
PHONE..................................714 525-2326
Jon Spielman, *President*
Alberta Spielman, *Vice Pres*
EMP: 40
SQ FT: 14,000
SALES (est): 4.9MM **Privately Held**
SIC: 3599 Machine shop, jobbing & repair

(P-15871)
CRUSH MASTER GRINDING CORP
755 Penarth Ave, Walnut (91789-3028)
PHONE..................................909 595-2249
Sherman Durousseau, *President*
Jeanne Durousseau, *Admin Sec*
Donna Gilliam, *Mfg Staff*
EMP: 35 EST: 1976
SQ FT: 11,800
SALES (est): 5.3MM **Privately Held**
WEB: www.crushmastergrinding.com
SIC: 3599 Machine shop, jobbing & repair

(P-15872)
CURLIN HEALTHCARE PRODUCTS INC
15751 Graham St, Huntington Beach
(92649-1630)
PHONE..................................714 893-2200
Ahmad Momeni, *President*
▲ EMP: 55
SQ FT: 21,000
SALES (est): 6.3MM **Privately Held**
SIC: 3599 3841 Machine shop, jobbing & repair; machine & other job shop work; surgical & medical instruments

(P-15873)
CUSTOM MICRO MACHINING INC
707 Brown Rd, Fremont (94539-7014)
PHONE..................................510 651-9434
Tao Chou, *President*
Victor Nguyen, *Vice Pres*
Christina Le, *General Mgr*
Kim Nguyen, *Planning Mgr*
EMP: 26
SQ FT: 8,000
SALES (est): 4.5MM **Privately Held**
WEB: www.cmmusa.com
SIC: 3599 Machine shop, jobbing & repair

(P-15874)
D & F STANDLER INC
195 Lewis Rd Ste 39, San Jose
(95111-2192)
PHONE..................................408 226-8188
Dennis Styczynski, *President*
Alain Styczynski, *Vice Pres*
EMP: 12
SQ FT: 11,000
SALES (est): 1.7MM **Privately Held**
SIC: 3599 Machine shop, jobbing & repair

(P-15875)
D & T MACHINING INC
3360 Victor Ct, Santa Clara (95054-2316)
PHONE..................................408 486-6035
Tom Nguyen, *President*
Thao Tran, *Manager*
EMP: 15
SQ FT: 1,800
SALES (est): 2.1MM **Privately Held**
WEB: www.dtmachining.com
SIC: 3599 Machine shop, jobbing & repair

(P-15876)
D MILLS GRNDING MACHINING INC
6131 Quail Valley Ct, Riverside
(92507-0763)
PHONE..................................951 697-6847
Anthony Puccio, *President*
Joe Puccio, *COO*
Gilles Madelmont, *CFO*
EMP: 30 EST: 1973
SQ FT: 14,000
SALES: 4.7MM
SALES (corp-wide): 14.7MM **Privately Held**
SIC: 3599 Grinding castings for the trade; machine shop, jobbing & repair
PA: Manufacturing Solutions, Inc.
   1738 N Neville St
   Orange CA 92865
   714 453-0100

(P-15877)
DAN R HUNT INC
Also Called: Hunt Enterprises
2030 S Susan St, Santa Ana (92704-4415)
PHONE..................................714 850-9383
Dan R Hunt, *President*
Phil Hunt, *Vice Pres*
Mandy Johnson, *Office Mgr*
EMP: 11
SQ FT: 6,000
SALES (est): 1.9MM **Privately Held**
WEB: www.huntenterprises.com
SIC: 3599 Machine shop, jobbing & repair

(P-15878)
DANWORTH MANUFACTURING CO
30991 Huntwood Ave # 401, Hayward
(94544-7047)
PHONE..................................510 487-8290
Maria Barath, *Co-Owner*
Daniel Barath, *Co-Owner*
EMP: 10
SQ FT: 2,400
SALES (est): 1.1MM **Privately Held**
SIC: 3599 3451 3452 Machine shop, jobbing & repair; screw machine products; bolts, nuts, rivets & washers

(P-15879)
DARCY AK CORPORATION
Also Called: AK Darcy
1760 Monrovia Ave Ste A22, Costa Mesa
(92627-4433)
PHONE..................................949 650-5566
Darrell Gilbert, *CEO*
EMP: 15
SQ FT: 9,000
SALES: 16MM **Privately Held**
SIC: 3599 5085 Machine shop, jobbing & repair; valves & fittings

(P-15880)
DARKO PRECISION INC
470 Gianni St, Santa Clara (95054-2413)
PHONE..................................408 988-6133
Dardo Simunic, *President*
Vesna Simunic, *Vice Pres*
EMP: 78
SQ FT: 35,000

(PA)=Parent Co (HQ)=Headquarters (DH)=Div Headquarters
✿ = New Business established in last 2 years
   2020 California
   Manufacturers Register
   645

SALES (est): 20.7MM **Privately Held**
WEB: www.dp-inc.com
SIC: 3599 Machine shop, jobbing & repair

(P-15881)
DARMARK CORPORATION
13225 Gregg St, Poway (92064-7120)
PHONE..................................858 679-3970
Darwin Mark Zavadil, *President*
Martin T Drake, *Vice Pres*
Lori Zavadil, *Admin Sec*
Johanna Cornellier, *Administration*
Jillian Buttler, *Technician*
EMP: 90
SQ FT: 28,000
SALES (est): 19.4MM **Privately Held**
WEB: www.darmark.com
SIC: 3599 Machine shop, jobbing & repair

(P-15882)
DAVID A NEAL INC
9825 Bell Ranch Dr, Santa Fe Springs
(90670-2953)
PHONE..................................562 941-5626
David A Neal, *President*
Debra Neal, *Admin Sec*
▲ EMP: 10
SQ FT: 12,800
SALES (est): 1.3MM **Privately Held**
WEB: www.davidoneal.com
SIC: 3599 Machine shop, jobbing & repair

(P-15883)
DAVIS GEAR & MACHINE CO
13625 S Normandie Ave, Gardena
(90249-2607)
PHONE..................................310 337-9881
Phil Davis, *Owner*
EMP: 10
SQ FT: 12,000
SALES (est): 747.6K **Privately Held**
SIC: 3599 Machine shop, jobbing & repair

(P-15884)
DELAFIELD CORPORATION (PA)
Also Called: Delafield Fluid Technology
1520 Flower Ave, Duarte (91010-2925)
PHONE..................................626 303-0740
Nik Ray, *President*
Henry Custodia, *CFO*
Jim Martin, *Vice Pres*
Hoa Le, *Info Tech Mgr*
John Schiefelbein, *Engineer*
◆ EMP: 120
SQ FT: 90,000
SALES (est): 47MM **Privately Held**
WEB: www.dftcorp.com
SIC: 3599 5085 3498 3492 Hose, flexible
metallic; valves, pistons & fittings; tube
fabricating (contract bending & shaping);
fluid power valves & hose fittings; plumbing
fixture fittings & trim; rubber & plastics
hose & beltings

(P-15885)
DELONG MANUFACTURING CO INC
967 Parker Ct, Santa Clara (95050-2808)
PHONE..................................408 727-3348
David De Long, *CEO*
William A De Long Jr, *CFO*
EMP: 16 EST: 1966
SQ FT: 8,400
SALES: 1.8MM **Privately Held**
SIC: 3599 Machine shop, jobbing & repair

(P-15886)
DELTA HI-TECH
9600 De Soto Ave, Chatsworth
(91311-5012)
PHONE..................................818 407-4000
Joe Ostrowsky, *CEO*
Chava Ostrowsky, *CFO*
Ilan Ostrowsky, *Exec VP*
Juan Casarrubias, *Vice Pres*
Gregory Elkhunovich, *Vice Pres*
▲ EMP: 130
SQ FT: 40,000
SALES (est): 31.5MM **Privately Held**
WEB: www.deltahitech.com
SIC: 3599 Machine shop, jobbing & repair

(P-15887)
DELTA MANUFACTURING INC
Also Called: Delta Engineering and Mfg
6260 Prescott Ct, Chino (91710-7111)
PHONE..................................909 590-4563
Ricardo Aguilar, *Owner*
EMP: 25
SQ FT: 1,500
SALES (est): 1.2MM **Privately Held**
WEB: www.deltamanufacturing.com
SIC: 3599 Machine shop, jobbing & repair

(P-15888)
DELTA MATRIX INC
Also Called: Delta Machine
2180 Oakland Rd, San Jose (95131-1571)
PHONE..................................408 955-9140
Tad Slowikowski, *President*
Yolanda Slowikowski, *Admin Sec*
EMP: 38
SQ FT: 9,000
SALES (est): 6.6MM **Privately Held**
WEB: www.deltamachine.com
SIC: 3599 Machine shop, jobbing & repair

(P-15889)
DESCO MANUFACTURING COMPANY (PA)
23031 Arroyo Vis Ste A, Rcho STA Marg
(92688-2605)
PHONE..................................949 858-7400
Ralph L Fabian, *President*
William Cobble, *Vice Pres*
Ruth Sistrunk, *Executive*
Tom Sistrunk, *Info Tech Mgr*
Sheri Waters, *Receptionist*
▲ EMP: 16
SALES (est): 5.2MM **Privately Held**
WEB: www.descomfg.com
SIC: 3599 Custom machinery

(P-15890)
DESERT SKY MACHINING INC
Also Called: Progressive Concepts Machining
1236 Quarry Ln Ste 104, Pleasanton
(94566-4730)
PHONE..................................925 426-0400
Chris Studzinski, *President*
Jane M Studzinski, *Vice Pres*
EMP: 25
SQ FT: 10,000
SALES (est): 3.6MM **Privately Held**
WEB: www.proconmach.com
SIC: 3599 Machine shop, jobbing & repair

(P-15891)
DETENTION DEVICE SYSTEMS
Also Called: DDS
25545 Seaboard Ln, Hayward
(94545-3209)
PHONE..................................510 783-0771
Steven R Allington, *President*
Tom Heath, *Vice Pres*
Ron Blair, *Opers Staff*
EMP: 45
SQ FT: 20,000
SALES (est): 7.6MM **Privately Held**
WEB: www.detentiondevicesystems.com
SIC: 3599 3429 Machine shop, jobbing &
repair; locks or lock sets

(P-15892)
DGA MACHINE SHOP INC
Also Called: D G A Mch Sp Blnchard Grinding
5825 Ordway St, Riverside (92504-1132)
PHONE..................................951 354-2113
Tony Diguglielmo, *President*
Angela Di Guglielmo, *Executive*
Angelo Diguglielmo, *Admin Sec*
Barbara Goodell, *Admin Sec*
EMP: 15
SALES (est): 2.9MM **Privately Held**
WEB: www.dgamachineshop.com
SIC: 3599 Machine shop, jobbing & repair

(P-15893)
DIABLO PRECISION INC
500 Park Center Dr Ste 8, Hollister
(95023-2539)
PHONE..................................831 634-0136
Conor Kelly, *CEO*
Bill Fixsen, *Vice Pres*
EMP: 11
SALES (est): 2.5MM **Privately Held**
WEB: www.diabloprecision.com
SIC: 3599 Machine shop, jobbing & repair

(P-15894)
DIAL PRECISION INC
17235 Darwin Ave, Hesperia (92345-5178)
P.O. Box 402259 (92340-2259)
PHONE..................................760 947-3557
Darryl L Tarullo, *Ch of Bd*
Bill Wolleson, *Prdtn Mgr*
Tom Jordon, *Accounts Mgr*
EMP: 95 EST: 1958
SQ FT: 15,000
SALES (est): 16.1MM **Privately Held**
WEB: www.dialprecision.com
SIC: 3599 3545 Machine shop, jobbing &
repair; machine tool accessories

(P-15895)
DIAMOND TOOL AND DIE INC
Also Called: Lab Clear
508 29th Ave, Oakland (94601-2198)
PHONE..................................510 534-7050
Darrell G Holt, *President*
Dan Welter, *Vice Pres*
Naya Pillazar, *Office Mgr*
Daniel Walter, *Admin Sec*
Larry Regas, *Prdtn Mgr*
▲ EMP: 32 EST: 1967
SQ FT: 22,000
SALES (est): 6.7MM **Privately Held**
WEB: www.dtdjobshop.com
SIC: 3599 Machine shop, jobbing & repair

(P-15896)
DIE & TOOL PRODUCTS CO INC
1842 Sabre St, Hayward (94545-1024)
PHONE..................................415 822-2888
Victor Tschirky, *President*
Mariette Tschirky, *Corp Secy*
EMP: 16
SALES (est): 2.7MM **Privately Held**
WEB: www.dieandtool.com
SIC: 3599 Machine shop, jobbing & repair

(P-15897)
DIECRAFT CORPORATION
5590 Naples Canal, Long Beach
(90803-4018)
PHONE..................................323 728-2601
Ronald W Lamb, *President*
Donald R Lamb, *Corp Secy*
EMP: 30 EST: 1941
SQ FT: 46,000
SALES (est): 3.2MM **Privately Held**
SIC: 3599 3312 3544 3469 Machine
shop, jobbing & repair; tool & die steel &
alloys; special dies, tools, jigs & fixtures;
metal stampings

(P-15898)
DILIGENT SOLUTIONS INC
Also Called: Absolute EDM
3240 Grey Hawk Ct, Carlsbad
(92010-6651)
P.O. Box 985, Murrieta (92564-0985)
PHONE..................................760 814-8960
Stephen A Bowles, *President*
EMP: 20
SALES (est): 3.4MM **Privately Held**
SIC: 3599 Machine shop, jobbing & repair

(P-15899)
DILLON PRECISION INCORPORATED
3816 Maplewood Ln, Placerville
(95667-7927)
PHONE..................................530 672-6794
EMP: 34
SQ FT: 13,700
SALES (est): 4.5MM **Privately Held**
WEB: www.dillonprec.net
SIC: 3599 Machine shop, jobbing & repair

(P-15900)
DIVERSIFIED MFG CAL INC
Also Called: Dmoc
2555 Progress St, Vista (92081-8423)
PHONE..................................760 599-9280
Thane D Rivers, *President*
Jerri Rivers, *Vice Pres*
▲ EMP: 10
SQ FT: 10,000
SALES (est): 1.5MM **Privately Held**
WEB: www.dmoc.us
SIC: 3599 Machine shop, jobbing & repair

(P-15901)
DKW PRECISION MACHINING INC
17731 Ideal Pkwy, Manteca (95336-8991)
PHONE..................................209 824-7899
Kurt Franklin, *President*
Brian Kott, *General Mgr*
EMP: 20
SQ FT: 10,000
SALES: 1.4MM **Privately Held**
SIC: 3599 Machine shop, jobbing & repair

(P-15902)
DOERKSEN PRECISION PRODUCTS
2725 Chanticleer Ave # 7, Santa Cruz
(95065-1885)
PHONE..................................831 476-1843
Robert Doerksen Jr, *President*
Dan Doerksen, *President*
EMP: 11
SQ FT: 4,500
SALES (est): 1.5MM **Privately Held**
WEB: www.doerksenppi.com
SIC: 3599 Machine shop, jobbing & repair

(P-15903)
DOLSTRA AUTOMATIC PRODUCTS
14441 Edwards St, Westminster
(92683-3607)
PHONE..................................714 894-2062
John Dolstra, *President*
Susan Dolstra, *Admin Sec*
EMP: 11
SQ FT: 3,400
SALES: 700K **Privately Held**
SIC: 3599 Machine shop, jobbing & repair

(P-15904)
DONAL MACHINE INC
591 N Mcdowell Blvd, Petaluma
(94954-2340)
P.O. Box 750637 (94975-0637)
PHONE..................................707 763-6625
John Chris Bergstedt, *President*
Donna Bergstedt, *COO*
Robert Bergstedt, *Vice Pres*
Tom Dollard, *General Mgr*
EMP: 31
SQ FT: 30,000
SALES (est): 6.2MM **Privately Held**
WEB: www.donalmachine.com
SIC: 3599 3444 3548 Machine shop, jobbing & repair; sheet metalwork; welding &
cutting apparatus & accessories

(P-15905)
DOUBLE PRECISION MFG
2273 Calle De Luna, Santa Clara
(95054-1002)
PHONE..................................408 727-7726
Michael D Corbo, *Owner*
EMP: 20
SQ FT: 8,000
SALES (est): 1.9MM **Privately Held**
WEB: www.doubleprecision.net
SIC: 3599 Machine shop, jobbing & repair

(P-15906)
DOW HYDRAULIC SYSTEMS INC (PA)
1835 Wright Ave, La Verne (91750-5817)
PHONE..................................909 596-6602
Richard P Dow, *President*
Bryan Dow, *Vice Pres*
Ryan K Dow, *Vice Pres*
Ryan Dow, *Vice Pres*
Keith Dow, *Principal*
EMP: 60
SQ FT: 11,000
SALES (est): 12.9MM **Privately Held**
WEB: www.dowprecision.com
SIC: 3599 3594 Machine shop, jobbing &
repair; fluid power pumps & motors

(P-15907)
DPM INC
Also Called: Datum Precision Machining
19641 Hirsch Ct, Anderson (96007-4941)
PHONE..................................530 378-3420
William E Holstein, *President*
Laurie Holstein, *CFO*
EMP: 14
SQ FT: 6,000

SALES (est): 1.3MM **Privately Held**
SIC: 3599 Machine shop, jobbing & repair

(P-15908)
DU-ALL SAFETY LLC
45950 Hotchkiss St, Fremont (94539-7078)
PHONE..................................510 651-8289
Terry McCarthy,
Steve Pierre, *General Mgr*
Mike Connelly, *Director*
Sean Halpin, *Manager*
EMP: 10
SALES (est): 1.4MM **Privately Held**
WEB: www.du-all.com
SIC: 3599 8742 Machine shop, jobbing & repair; industrial & labor consulting services

(P-15909)
DUNSTAN ENTERPRISES INC
Also Called: Green's Metal Cutoff
11821 Slauson Ave, Santa Fe Springs (90670-2219)
PHONE..................................562 630-6292
Renee Dunstan, *President*
EMP: 16
SALES (est): 2.9MM **Privately Held**
SIC: 3599 Machine shop, jobbing & repair

(P-15910)
DUPLAN INDUSTRIES
Also Called: Gilbert Machine & Mfg
1265 Stone Dr, San Marcos (92078-4059)
PHONE..................................760 744-4047
Nancy Duplan, *President*
Carlton Duplan, *Corp Secy*
EMP: 20
SQ FT: 15,000
SALES (est): 3MM **Privately Held**
WEB: www.gilbertmachine.com
SIC: 3599 Machine shop, jobbing & repair

(P-15911)
DYELL MACHINE (PA)
160 S Linden Ave, Rialto (92376-6204)
P.O. Box 974 (92377-0974)
PHONE..................................909 350-4101
Tom Bradley, *Partner*
Edith Dyell, *Partner*
Donna Larson, *Manager*
EMP: 30 EST: 1968
SQ FT: 20,000
SALES (est): 5.6MM **Privately Held**
WEB: www.dyellmachine.com
SIC: 3599 5084 7699 Machine shop, jobbing & repair; hydraulic systems equipment & supplies; hydraulic equipment repair

(P-15912)
DYELL MACHINE
Also Called: Dyell Machine & Hydraulic Shop
17499 Alder St, Hesperia (92345-5063)
PHONE..................................760 244-3333
Mike Coleman, *Manager*
EMP: 10
SQ FT: 10,000
SALES (est): 1.8MM
SALES (corp-wide): 5.6MM **Privately Held**
WEB: www.dyellmachine.com
SIC: 3599 5084 7699 Machine shop, jobbing & repair; hydraulic systems equipment & supplies; hydraulic equipment repair
PA: Dyell Machine
  160 S Linden Ave
  Rialto CA 92376
  909 350-4101

(P-15913)
DYLERN INCORPORATED
14444 Greenwood Cir, Nevada City (95959-9690)
PHONE..................................530 470-8785
EMP: 20
SQ FT: 9,000
SALES (est): 1.7MM **Privately Held**
SIC: 3599

(P-15914)
DYNAMIC ENTERPRISES INC
Also Called: D E I
10015 Greenleaf Ave, Santa Fe Springs (90670-3493)
PHONE..................................562 944-0271

Mildred Sudduth, *President*
Deanna Mansfield, *Corp Secy*
Alan Sudduth, *Vice Pres*
◆ EMP: 21
SQ FT: 50,000
SALES (est): 4.7MM **Privately Held**
WEB: www.dynamic-ent.com
SIC: 3599 Machine shop, jobbing & repair

(P-15915)
DYNAMIC MACHINE INC
3470 Randolph St, Huntington Park (90255-3259)
PHONE..................................323 585-0710
Brian Stevens, *President*
Mark Stevens, *Vice Pres*
EMP: 12
SQ FT: 15,000
SALES (est): 1.7MM **Privately Held**
SIC: 3599 Machine shop, jobbing & repair

(P-15916)
E & S PRECISION MACHINE INC
4631 Enterprise Way, Modesto (95356-8715)
PHONE..................................209 545-6161
Jim Elzner, *President*
Donita Elzner, *CFO*
Steve Hegedus, *Prdtn Mgr*
EMP: 18
SQ FT: 5,000
SALES (est): 3.2MM **Privately Held**
WEB: www.esprecision.com
SIC: 3599 Machine shop, jobbing & repair

(P-15917)
E D M SACRAMENTO INC
Also Called: Sac EDM & Waterjet
11341 Sunrise Park Dr, Rancho Cordova (95742-6532)
PHONE..................................916 851-9285
Daniel Folk, *CEO*
Jeffrey Foster,
EMP: 24
SQ FT: 20,000
SALES: 2.5MM **Privately Held**
WEB: www.sacedm.com
SIC: 3599 Machine shop, jobbing & repair

(P-15918)
E S M PLASTICS INC
13575 Yorba Ave, Chino (91710-5057)
P.O. Box 808 (91708-0808)
PHONE..................................909 591-7658
Earl D Silva, *CEO*
Cheryl Silva, *Admin Sec*
EMP: 15
SQ FT: 7,400
SALES (est): 2.3MM **Privately Held**
SIC: 3599 3089 Custom machinery; injection molding of plastics

(P-15919)
EASTWOOD MACHINE LLC
9346 Abraham Way, Santee (92071-2861)
PHONE..................................619 873-3660
Joseph Odneal,
Sara Odneal,
EMP: 11
SQ FT: 11,000
SALES (est): 1.3MM **Privately Held**
SIC: 3599 Machine shop, jobbing & repair

(P-15920)
EDCO DIE INC
2199 W Arrow Rte, Upland (91786-7610)
PHONE..................................909 985-4417
Dennis Ortis, *President*
Joyce Ortis, *Corp Secy*
EMP: 15 EST: 1966
SQ FT: 23,000
SALES (est): 1.4MM **Privately Held**
SIC: 3599 Machine shop, jobbing & repair

(P-15921)
EH SUDA INC (PA)
Also Called: Fabtron
615 Industrial Rd, San Carlos (94070-3301)
PHONE..................................650 622-9700
Edwin H Suda, *CEO*
EMP: 15
SQ FT: 45,000
SALES (est): 3.2MM **Privately Held**
WEB: www.fabtron-usa.com
SIC: 3599 Machine shop, jobbing & repair

(P-15922)
EH SUDA INC
Also Called: Fabtron
210 Texas Ave, Lewiston (96052)
P.O. Box 171 (96052-0171)
PHONE..................................530 778-9830
Mark Suda, *Branch Mgr*
Tasha Suda, *Finance Mgr*
EMP: 25
SALES (est): 1.4MM
SALES (corp-wide): 3.2MM **Privately Held**
WEB: www.fabtron-usa.com
SIC: 3599 Machine shop, jobbing & repair
PA: E.H. Suda, Inc.
  615 Industrial Rd
  San Carlos CA 94070
  650 622-9700

(P-15923)
EJAYS MACHINE CO INC
1108 E Valencia Dr, Fullerton (92831-4627)
PHONE..................................714 879-0558
Denise Eastin, *President*
Schuyler Eastin, *Treasurer*
EMP: 20
SALES (est): 3.7MM **Privately Held**
SIC: 3599 Machine shop, jobbing & repair

(P-15924)
EL CAMINO MACHINE & WLDG LLC (PA)
296 El Camino Real S, Salinas (93901-4511)
PHONE..................................831 758-8309
Gordon Zook,
Yvette Gnesa,
Jane Zook,
EMP: 26
SQ FT: 4,800
SALES: 4MM **Privately Held**
SIC: 3599 7692 Machine shop, jobbing & repair; welding repair

(P-15925)
ELITE METAL FABRICATION INC
2299 Ringwood Ave Ste C1, San Jose (95131-1732)
PHONE..................................408 433-9926
Mario Flores, *Manager*
EMP: 21
SALES (est): 2.5MM **Privately Held**
WEB: www.eelitemetal.com
SIC: 3599 Machine & other job shop work

(P-15926)
ELLINGSON INC
119 W Santa Fe Ave, Fullerton (92832-1831)
PHONE..................................714 773-1923
Thomas Ellingson, *President*
T C Ellingson, *CEO*
Nancy Ellingson, *Treasurer*
Steven C Ellingson, *Admin Sec*
EMP: 12
SQ FT: 7,500
SALES (est): 1.6MM **Privately Held**
WEB: www.ellingson-inc.com
SIC: 3599 Machine shop, jobbing & repair; machine & other job shop work

(P-15927)
ELLIOTT MANUFACTURING COMPANY
2664 S Cherry Ave, Fresno (93706-5494)
P.O. Box 11277 (93772-1277)
PHONE..................................559 233-6235
Terry Aluisi, *CEO*
Thomas E Cole, *Ch of Bd*
Richard E Cole, *Vice Pres*
Richard Cole, *Vice Pres*
Richard Allbritton, *Electrical Engi*
▼ EMP: 15 EST: 1929
SALES (est): 4.4MM **Privately Held**
WEB: www.elliott-mfg.com
SIC: 3599 3556 3565 7692 Machine shop, jobbing & repair; food products machinery; packaging machinery; welding repair; sheet metalwork

(P-15928)
ELY CO INC
3046 Kashiwa St, Torrance (90505-4083)
PHONE..................................310 539-5831
Walter Senff, *CEO*

Bill Senff, *Vice Pres*
Judith Senff, *Vice Pres*
Kurt Senff, *Admin Sec*
Sue Sulzbach, *Manager*
EMP: 36
SQ FT: 11,500
SALES (est): 6.7MM **Privately Held**
WEB: www.elyco.com
SIC: 3599 Machine shop, jobbing & repair

(P-15929)
EMBERTON MACHINE & TOOL INC
1215 Pioneer Way Ste A, El Cajon (92020-1665)
PHONE..................................619 401-1870
Phyllis Oatman, *CEO*
Randy Emberton, *President*
EMP: 10
SQ FT: 10,000
SALES: 1.8MM **Privately Held**
WEB: www.embertonsmachine.com
SIC: 3599 Machine shop, jobbing & repair

(P-15930)
EME TECHNOLOGIES INC
3485 Victor St, Santa Clara (95054-2319)
PHONE..................................408 720-8817
Walter Nguyen, *President*
Lien Nguyen, *Manager*
▲ EMP: 40
SQ FT: 20,000
SALES (est): 6.4MM **Privately Held**
WEB: www.emetec.com
SIC: 3599 Machine shop, jobbing & repair

(P-15931)
ENERGY LINK INDUS SVCS INC
11439 S Enos Ln, Bakersfield (93311-9452)
P.O. Box 10716 (93389-0716)
PHONE..................................661 765-4444
James R Miller III, *CEO*
Matt Knight, *Shareholder*
West Moore, *Shareholder*
Ray Miller, *President*
Gary Winters, *District Mgr*
EMP: 34
SALES (est): 5.9MM **Privately Held**
SIC: 3599 7699 Bellows, industrial: metal; compressor repair

(P-15932)
ENERGY STEEL CORPORATION
Also Called: O'Brien Iron Works
2043 Arnold Indus Way, Concord (94520-5342)
PHONE..................................925 685-5300
Diane Monaghan, *President*
Kevin Monaghan, *Officer*
EMP: 10
SQ FT: 12,000
SALES (est): 2MM **Privately Held**
SIC: 3599 Machine shop, jobbing & repair

(P-15933)
ENGINEERED PRODUCTS BY LEE LTD
Also Called: Precision Engineered Products
10444 Mcvine Ave, Sunland (91040-3102)
PHONE..................................818 352-3322
Wallace K Lee, *President*
Christine Lee, *Office Mgr*
EMP: 12 EST: 1967
SQ FT: 7,000
SALES (est): 1.3MM **Privately Held**
SIC: 3599 Machine shop, jobbing & repair

(P-15934)
ENGINEERING DESIGN INDS INC
Also Called: E D I
9649 Rush St, South El Monte (91733-1732)
PHONE..................................626 443-7741
Loc Tran, *President*
Denise Lee, *Treasurer*
EMP: 12
SQ FT: 5,000
SALES: 1.8MM **Privately Held**
WEB: www.go2edi.com
SIC: 3599 Machine shop, jobbing & repair

(P-15935)
ERB INVESTMENT COMPANY LLC
Also Called: 360 Manufacturing Solutions
3501 Thomas Rd Ste 7, Santa Clara
(95054-2037)
PHONE..................................408 727-6908
Dick Brown, *General Mgr*
EMP: 10
SALES: 950K **Privately Held**
SIC: 3599 Industrial machinery

(P-15936)
ET BALANCING INC
12823 Athens Way, Los Angeles
(90061-1146)
PHONE..................................310 538-9738
Michael Park, *President*
Jim Napora, *Corp Secy*
EMP: 10
SQ FT: 30,000
SALES (est): 1.5MM **Privately Held**
SIC: 3599 Machine shop, jobbing & repair

(P-15937)
EURO MACHINE INC
9627 Owensmouth Ave Ste 1, Chatsworth
(91311-4842)
PHONE..................................818 998-5198
Juergen Schoellkopf, *President*
Gregory Calvano, *Vice Pres*
Mane Schoellkopf, *Admin Sec*
▲ EMP: 10
SQ FT: 6,300
SALES (est): 1.7MM **Privately Held**
SIC: 3599 Machine shop, jobbing & repair

(P-15938)
EVDEN ENTERPRISES INC
2000 Wellmar Dr, Ukiah (95482-3168)
PHONE..................................707 462-0375
Dennis Mc Grath, *President*
EMP: 15 EST: 1978
SQ FT: 8,000
SALES (est): 2.6MM **Privately Held**
WEB: www.evden.com
SIC: 3599 Machine shop, jobbing & repair

(P-15939)
EXACTA-TECHNOLOGY INC
378 Wright Brothers Ave, Livermore
(94551-9489)
PHONE..................................925 443-6200
Paul Speroni, *President*
Michelle Speroni, *Vice Pres*
EMP: 14 EST: 1961
SQ FT: 16,000
SALES (est): 2.3MM **Privately Held**
WEB: www.exacta-tech.com
SIC: 3599 3826 Machine shop, jobbing & repair; liquid testing apparatus

(P-15940)
EXCEL CNC MACHINING INC
Also Called: Excel Machining
3185 De La Cruz Blvd, Santa Clara
(95054-2405)
PHONE..................................408 970-9460
Krzysztof Wisinski, *President*
EMP: 48
SALES (est): 9.2MM **Privately Held**
SIC: 3599 Machine shop, jobbing & repair

(P-15941)
EXCEL MANUFACTURING INC
20409 Prairie St, Chatsworth (91311-6029)
PHONE..................................661 257-1900
Susan Halliday, *President*
EMP: 45
SQ FT: 14,000
SALES (est): 6.8MM
SALES (corp-wide): 34.4MM **Privately Held**
SIC: 3599 Machine & other job shop work
PA: Rtc Aerospace - Chatsworth Division, Inc.
20409 Prairie St
Chatsworth CA 91311
818 341-3344

(P-15942)
EXCELSIOR MACHINE INC
2964 Phillip Ave, Clovis (93612-3934)
PHONE..................................559 291-7710
Raymond Roush, *CEO*

Heins Kart Pedersen, *Principal*
EMP: 13
SALES (est): 1.5MM **Privately Held**
SIC: 3599 Industrial machinery

(P-15943)
EXPEDITE PRECISION WORKS INC
931 Berryessa Rd, San Jose (95133-1002)
PHONE..................................408 437-1893
Orlando Teixeira, *President*
EMP: 45
SQ FT: 5,500
SALES (est): 7.4MM **Privately Held**
WEB: www.expediteprecision.com
SIC: 3599 3089 Machine shop, jobbing & repair; plastic hardware & building products

(P-15944)
EXPOL INC
2122 Ronald St, Santa Clara (95050-2820)
PHONE..................................408 567-9020
Josef Plata, *President*
Edward Amaro, *VP Opers*
EMP: 10
SQ FT: 6,000
SALES (est): 1MM **Privately Held**
WEB: www.expol.net
SIC: 3599 Machine shop, jobbing & repair

(P-15945)
EXTREME PRECISION INC
1717 Little Orchard St B, San Jose
(95125-1049)
PHONE..................................408 275-8365
Matthew Ellis, *President*
Rosa Pace, *General Mgr*
EMP: 15
SQ FT: 7,500
SALES (est): 2.1MM **Privately Held**
WEB: www.extremeprecision.com
SIC: 3599 Machine shop, jobbing & repair; machine & other job shop work

(P-15946)
EXTREME PRECISION LLC
23266 Arroyo Vis, Rcho STA Marg
(92688-2610)
PHONE..................................949 459-1062
Eric Burgers,
Carrie Burgers,
EMP: 15
SALES (est): 2.2MM **Privately Held**
SIC: 3599 7539 Machine shop, jobbing & repair; machine shop, automotive

(P-15947)
EXTRUDE HONE DEBURRING SERVICE
Also Called: Extrude Hone Abrsve Flw McHng
8800 Somerset Blvd, Paramount
(90723-4659)
PHONE..................................562 531-2976
William Melendez, *President*
EMP: 18
SQ FT: 11,000
SALES (est): 1.6MM **Privately Held**
SIC: 3599 5084 Machine shop, jobbing & repair; machine tools & accessories; machinists' precision measuring tools

(P-15948)
F E W INC
Also Called: Western Fabrication & Eqp
420 30th St, Bakersfield (93301-2514)
PHONE..................................661 323-8319
Donald Bookout, *President*
Brent E Bookout, *Vice Pres*
EMP: 10
SQ FT: 21,000
SALES (est): 880K **Privately Held**
SIC: 3599 3549 3444 Machine shop, jobbing & repair; metalworking machinery; sheet metalwork

(P-15949)
FABRI-CORP
25850 Vinedo Ln, Los Altos Hills
(94022-4435)
P.O. Box 1019, Los Altos (94023-1019)
PHONE..................................650 941-2076
Ron E Essary, *Owner*
EMP: 20
SQ FT: 4,000

SALES (est): 1.4MM **Privately Held**
SIC: 3599 3542 Custom machinery; sheet metalworking machines

(P-15950)
FABTRON
615 Industrial Rd, San Carlos
(94070-3301)
PHONE..................................650 622-9700
Edward Suda, *Principal*
EMP: 13
SALES (est): 2.3MM **Privately Held**
SIC: 3599 Machine shop, jobbing & repair

(P-15951)
FANTASY MANUFACTURING INC
7716 Bell Rd, Windsor (95492-8518)
PHONE..................................707 838-7686
Michael G Seeber, *President*
Cheryl Seeber, *Vice Pres*
EMP: 10
SQ FT: 12,000
SALES (est): 1.1MM **Privately Held**
SIC: 3599 Machine shop, jobbing & repair

(P-15952)
FARRELL BROTHERS HOLDING CORP
Also Called: Swiss Machine Products
1137 N Armando St, Anaheim
(92806-2609)
PHONE..................................714 630-3417
Doug Farrell, *President*
Myra Farrell, *Treasurer*
Kevan Farrell, *Vice Pres*
Ruby Farrell, *Admin Sec*
Ian Farrell, *Opers Mgr*
EMP: 16 EST: 1966
SQ FT: 10,000
SALES (est): 2.5MM **Privately Held**
SIC: 3599 Machine shop, jobbing & repair

(P-15953)
FAST TURN MACHINING INC
3087 Lawrence Expy, Santa Clara
(95051-0713)
PHONE..................................408 720-6888
Tom Khuu, *President*
EMP: 10
SALES (est): 1MM **Privately Held**
WEB: www.fastturninc.com
SIC: 3599 Machine shop, jobbing & repair

(P-15954)
FERAL PRODUCTIONS LLC
1935 N Macarthur Dr, Tracy (95376-2833)
PHONE..................................510 791-5392
Robert Potts,
Lynn Potts,
EMP: 28
SQ FT: 10,400
SALES: 4MM **Privately Held**
SIC: 3599 Machine shop, jobbing & repair

(P-15955)
FIBREFORM ELECTRONICS INC
Also Called: Fibreform Precision Machining
5341 Argosy Ave, Huntington Beach
(92649-1036)
PHONE..................................714 898-9641
Zachary Fischer, *Ch of Bd*
Frank Mauro, *COO*
Todd Crow, *CFO*
Joshua Ziegelhoefer, *Engineer*
Bunmee Duong, *Purchasing*
EMP: 30
SQ FT: 30,000
SALES (est): 6.2MM **Privately Held**
SIC: 3599 Machine shop, jobbing & repair

(P-15956)
FIERRITO METAL STAMPING
12358 San Fernando Rd, Sylmar
(91342-5020)
PHONE..................................818 362-6136
Henry Avila, *President*
Rosie Avila, *Manager*
EMP: 30
SALES (est): 2.6MM **Privately Held**
SIC: 3599 3469 Machine shop, jobbing & repair; metal stampings

(P-15957)
FIERRITOS INC
12358 San Fernando Rd, Sylmar
(91342-5020)
PHONE..................................818 362-6136
Henry Avila, *President*
EMP: 25
SALES (est): 2.3MM **Privately Held**
WEB: www.fierritos.com
SIC: 3599 Machine shop, jobbing & repair

(P-15958)
FINART INC (PA)
201 W Dyer Rd Ste C, Santa Ana
(92707-3426)
PHONE..................................714 957-1757
Tadeusz Kasperowicz, *President*
▲ EMP: 10
SQ FT: 10,000
SALES: 600K **Privately Held**
WEB: www.finart.com
SIC: 3599 Machine shop, jobbing & repair

(P-15959)
FINNTECH INC
1930 W 169th St, Gardena (90247-5254)
PHONE..................................310 323-0790
Renny Laitio, *President*
Peter Laitio, *Chairman*
Leila Johnson, *Treasurer*
Kari Laitio, *Vice Pres*
EMP: 13 EST: 1978
SQ FT: 2,500
SALES (est): 800K **Privately Held**
WEB: www.finntech.com
SIC: 3599 Machine shop, jobbing & repair

(P-15960)
FIVE CORNER CONSERVATION INC
13654 Victory Blvd # 327, Van Nuys
(91401-1738)
PHONE..................................818 792-1805
Michael Ball, *President*
EMP: 10
SALES (est): 719.9K **Privately Held**
SIC: 3599 Water leak detectors

(P-15961)
FLATHERS PRECISION INC
1311 E Saint Gertrude Pl D, Santa Ana
(92705-5216)
PHONE..................................714 966-8505
Jerry Flathers, *President*
Linda Flathers, *Vice Pres*
EMP: 21
SALES (est): 3.4MM **Privately Held**
WEB: www.flathersprecision.com
SIC: 3599 Machine shop, jobbing & repair

(P-15962)
FLEXAUST COMPANY INC (HQ)
1200 Prospect St Ste 325, La Jolla
(92037-3660)
P.O. Box 4275, Warsaw IN (46581-4275)
PHONE..................................619 232-8429
Richard Meyer, *President*
Mike Harvey, *Vice Pres*
Sean O'Brien, *Regional Mgr*
Chris Sharpe, *Regional Mgr*
Virginia Kugler, *Office Mgr*
EMP: 22
SALES (est): 51.9MM
SALES (corp-wide): 222MM **Privately Held**
SIC: 3599 Hose, flexible metallic

(P-15963)
FM INDUSTRIES INC
331 E Warren Ave, Fremont (94539-7966)
PHONE..................................510 673-0192
Hidenori Nanto, *Ch of Bd*
EMP: 105 **Privately Held**
SIC: 3599 Machine shop, jobbing & repair
HQ: Fm Industries, Inc.
221 E Warren Ave
Fremont CA 94539
510 668-1900

(P-15964)
FM INDUSTRIES INC (DH)
221 E Warren Ave, Fremont (94539-7916)
PHONE..................................510 668-1900
Hidenori Nanto, *Chairman*
David S Miller, *CEO*

▲ = Import ▼=Export
◆ =Import/Export

Brian West, *Program Mgr*
Gary Lok, *Technology*
Marvin Weisberg, *Technology*
EMP: 110
SQ FT: 56,000
SALES (est): 41.7MM **Privately Held**
WEB: www.fmindustries.com
SIC: 3599 3544 3999 Machine shop, job-
  bing & repair; special dies, tools, jigs &
  fixtures; atomizers, toiletry
HQ: Ngk North America, Inc.
  1105 N Market St Ste 1300
  Wilmington DE 19801
  302 654-1344

(P-15965)
FMW MACHINE SHOP
519 Claire St, Hayward (94541-6411)
PHONE.........................650 363-1313
Humberto Fabris, *General Ptnr*
Annette Fabris, *Partner*
Maria Fabris, *Partner*
EMP: 18
SALES: 2MM **Privately Held**
WEB: www.fmwmachineshop.com
SIC: 3599 Machine shop, jobbing & repair

(P-15966)
FONTAL CONTROLS INC
12725 Encinitas Ave, Sylmar (91342-3517)
PHONE.........................818 833-1127
Oscar Fontal, *President*
Gladys Fontal, *Treasurer*
Fernando Fontal, *Vice Pres*
Cristian Fontal, *Admin Sec*
EMP: 16
SQ FT: 14,200
SALES: 2.7MM **Privately Held**
WEB: www.fontalcontrols.com
SIC: 3599 Machine shop, jobbing & repair

(P-15967)
**FOREMOST PRECISION PDTS
INC**
Also Called: Diamond Precision Products
1940 Petra Ln Ste A, Placentia
  (92870-6750)
PHONE.........................714 961-0165
Paul Lavoie, *President*
EMP: 10
SQ FT: 5,000
SALES (est): 1.3MM **Privately Held**
SIC: 3599 Machine shop, jobbing & repair

(P-15968)
FORM GRIND CORPORATION
Also Called: Form Products
30062 Aventura, Rcho STA Marg
  (92688-2010)
PHONE.........................949 858-7000
Ernest Treichler, *CEO*
Gary Treichler, *Treasurer*
Joan Treichler, *Admin Sec*
Laurence Erickson, *Mfg Mgr*
Ron Bora, *Marketing Staff*
EMP: 50 **EST:** 1963
SQ FT: 30,000
SALES (est): 9.2MM **Privately Held**
WEB: www.formgrind.com
SIC: 3599 5084 Machine shop, jobbing &
  repair; industrial machinery & equipment

(P-15969)
FORTNER ENG & MFG INC
918 Thompson Ave, Glendale
  (91201-2079)
PHONE.........................818 240-7740
David W Fortner, *President*
Jimmie Fortner, *Vice Pres*
Robert S Fortner, *General Mgr*
Mike Malone, *Info Tech Mgr*
Jon Benoit, *Engineer*
EMP: 53 **EST:** 1952
SQ FT: 24,000
SALES (est): 10.5MM
SALES (corp-wide): 441.5MM **Privately
Held**
WEB: www.fortnereng.com
SIC: 3599 Machine shop, jobbing & repair
PA: Wencor Group, Llc
  416 Dividend Dr
  Peachtree City GA 30269
  678 490-0140

(P-15970)
FOURWARD MACHINE INC
Also Called: Program Precision Co
5111 Santa Fe St Ste J&I, San Diego
  (92109-1614)
PHONE.........................858 272-0601
Gary Ward, *President*
EMP: 10
SQ FT: 3,600
SALES: 750K **Privately Held**
SIC: 3599 Machine shop, jobbing & repair

(P-15971)
**FOWLERS MACHINE WORKS
INC**
300 S Riverside Dr, Modesto (95354-4007)
PHONE.........................209 522-5146
Andrew Fowler, *President*
Amanda Fowler, *Corp Secy*
EMP: 11 **EST:** 1969
SQ FT: 5,000
SALES (est): 825K **Privately Held**
WEB: www.fowlersmachine.com
SIC: 3599 Machine shop, jobbing & repair

(P-15972)
FOX HILLS MACHINING INC
7431 Belva Dr Ste 102, Huntington Beach
  (92647-6261)
PHONE.........................714 899-2211
Chris Machnicki, *President*
EMP: 10
SALES: 650K **Privately Held**
SIC: 3599 Machine shop, jobbing & repair

(P-15973)
FRANK RUSSELL INC
341 Pacific Ave, Shafter (93263-2046)
PHONE.........................661 324-5575
Andrew Russell, *President*
Cody Russell, *Parts Mgr*
EMP: 17
SQ FT: 13,000
SALES (est): 3.2MM **Privately Held**
SIC: 3599 5251 Machine shop, jobbing &
  repair; hardware

(P-15974)
**FRANKLINS INDS SAN DIEGO
INC**
12135 Dearborn Pl, Poway (92064-7111)
PHONE.........................858 486-9399
Kelly Franklin, *President*
Kim Craig, *Manager*
EMP: 44 **EST:** 1980
SQ FT: 20,000
SALES (est): 8.8MM **Privately Held**
WEB: www.franklin-ind.com
SIC: 3599 Machine shop, jobbing & repair

(P-15975)
FRED MATTER INC
Also Called: Alloy Metal Products
7801 Las Positas Rd, Livermore
  (94551-8206)
PHONE.........................925 371-1234
Fred Matter, *President*
EMP: 21 **EST:** 1977
SQ FT: 30,000
SALES: 5MM **Privately Held**
WEB: www.alloymp.com
SIC: 3599 Machine shop, jobbing & repair

(P-15976)
**FRONTIER ENGRG & MFG TECH
INC**
Also Called: Frontier Technologies
800 W 16th St, Long Beach (90813-1413)
PHONE.........................562 606-2655
John Tsai, *CEO*
Steve Hoekstra, *President*
James File, *Manager*
▲ **EMP:** 46
SQ FT: 30,000
SALES: 12MM **Privately Held**
WEB: www.frontierfittings.com
SIC: 3599 8711 Machine shop, jobbing &
  repair; engineering services

(P-15977)
FUNTASTIC FACTORY INC
Also Called: Einflatables
19703 Meadows Cir, Cerritos (90703-7734)
PHONE.........................562 777-1140
Ajay H Patel, *CEO*

Ross Andrizzi, *President*
EMP: 36 **EST:** 1994
SQ FT: 20,000
SALES (est): 4.1MM **Privately Held**
WEB: www.einflatables.com
SIC: 3599 Carnival machines & equipment,
  amusement park

(P-15978)
FUTURE TECH METALS INC
719 Palmyrita Ave, Riverside (92507-1811)
PHONE.........................951 781-4801
Tim Gearhardt, *Owner*
Art Medina, *Co-Owner*
EMP: 20
SALES (est): 3.5MM **Privately Held**
SIC: 3599 Machine shop, jobbing & repair

(P-15979)
G & H PRECISION INC
11950 Vose St, North Hollywood
  (91605-5749)
P.O. Box 16123 (91615-6123)
PHONE.........................818 982-3873
George Hallajian, *President*
Sevan Hallajian, *Vice Pres*
EMP: 14
SQ FT: 12,000
SALES: 3MM **Privately Held**
SIC: 3599 Machine shop, jobbing & repair

(P-15980)
**G & S PROCESS EQUIPMENT
INC**
Also Called: G & S Enterprises
1700 N Broadway Ave, Stockton
  (95205-3049)
PHONE.........................209 466-3630
▲ **EMP:** 10
SQ FT: 20,000
SALES (est): 1.6MM **Privately Held**
SIC: 3599 Machine shop, jobbing & repair

(P-15981)
G P MANUFACTURING INC
Also Called: Protype
541 W Briardale Ave, Orange
  (92865-4207)
PHONE.........................714 974-0288
Greg Gilbert, *President*
Lewis Pearmain, *Vice Pres*
EMP: 16
SQ FT: 13,500
SALES (est): 2.5MM **Privately Held**
SIC: 3599 3444 Machine shop, jobbing &
  repair; sheet metalwork

(P-15982)
G V INDUSTRIES INC
1346 Cleveland Ave, National City
  (91950-4207)
PHONE.........................619 474-3013
Gregory J Verdon, *President*
Joseph Verdon, *Vice Pres*
Linda Verdon, *Vice Pres*
EMP: 38
SQ FT: 14,000
SALES (est): 6.9MM **Privately Held**
SIC: 3599 Machine shop, jobbing & repair

(P-15983)
GABILAN WELDING INC
1091 San Felipe Rd, Hollister
  (95023-2813)
P.O. Box 370 (95024-0370)
PHONE.........................831 637-3360
Fax: 831 637-8853
EMP: 12 **EST:** 1951
SQ FT: 20,000
SALES (est): 1.2MM **Privately Held**
SIC: 3599

(P-15984)
**GALVIN PRECISION MACHINING
INC**
404 Yolanda Ave, Santa Rosa
  (95404-6323)
PHONE.........................707 526-5359
Jim Galvin, *President*
Jennet Simanta, *Manager*
Greg Wetterman, *Supervisor*
EMP: 13
SQ FT: 7,500
SALES (est): 2.8MM **Privately Held**
WEB: www.galvinprecisionmachining.com
SIC: 3599 Machine shop, jobbing & repair

(P-15985)
GARABEDIAN BROS INC (PA)
Also Called: Valley Welding & Machine Works
2543 S Orange Ave, Fresno (93725-1329)
P.O. Box 2455 (93745-2455)
PHONE.........................559 268-5014
Michael J Garabedian, *CEO*
Joanne Garabedian, *Corp Secy*
▼ **EMP:** 30
SQ FT: 45,000
SALES (est): 5.3MM **Privately Held**
WEB: www.vwmworks.com
SIC: 3599 3523 Machine shop, jobbing &
  repair; driers (farm): grain, hay & seed

(P-15986)
GARRETT PRECISION INC
25082 La Suen Rd, Laguna Hills
  (92653-5102)
PHONE.........................949 855-9710
Justin S Osborn, *CEO*
Dean Garrett, *President*
Lynn Garrett, *Vice Pres*
EMP: 19 **EST:** 1978
SQ FT: 6,500
SALES (est): 5.1MM **Privately Held**
SIC: 3599 Machine shop, jobbing & repair

(P-15987)
GATEWAY PRECISION INC
2300 Calle De Luna, Santa Clara
  (95054-1003)
PHONE.........................408 855-8849
Huy Nguyen, *President*
EMP: 15
SQ FT: 10,283
SALES (est): 3.4MM **Privately Held**
WEB: www.gatewayprecision.com
SIC: 3599 Machine shop, jobbing & repair

(P-15988)
GBF ENTERPRISES INC
2709 Halladay St, Santa Ana (92705-5618)
PHONE.........................714 979-7131
Cheryl Nowak, *President*
Hart Candi, *Consultant*
EMP: 25
SQ FT: 17,000
SALES (est): 4.4MM **Privately Held**
WEB: www.gbfenterprises.com
SIC: 3599 Machine shop, jobbing & repair

(P-15989)
GEIGER MANUFACTURING INC
1110 E Scotts Ave, Stockton (95205-6148)
P.O. Box 1449 (95201-1449)
PHONE.........................209 464-7746
Roger Haack, *President*
Dennis D Geiger, *Treasurer*
EMP: 16 **EST:** 1904
SQ FT: 27,250
SALES (est): 2.7MM **Privately Held**
SIC: 3599 Custom machinery; machine
  shop, jobbing & repair

(P-15990)
GENERAL GRINDING INC
Also Called: Stailess Polishing Co.
801 51st Ave, Oakland (94601-5694)
PHONE.........................510 261-5557
Michael Bardon, *President*
Daniel Bardon, *Corp Secy*
Jonathan Bardon, *Manager*
EMP: 34 **EST:** 1944
SQ FT: 22,500
SALES: 3.5MM **Privately Held**
SIC: 3599 Machine shop, jobbing & repair

(P-15991)
GENERAL INDUSTRIAL REPAIR
7417 E Slauson Ave, Commerce
  (90040-3307)
PHONE.........................323 278-0873
Henry Biazus, *President*
Richard Biazus, *CEO*
Robert Biazus, *Sales Staff*
EMP: 25
SQ FT: 75,000
SALES (est): 4.7MM **Privately Held**
WEB: www.girepair.us
SIC: 3599 Machine shop, jobbing & repair

(P-15992)
GENERAL PRODUCTION SERVICES
670 Arroyo St, San Fernando (91340-2220)
PHONE..................818 365-4211
Maria Hall, *President*
Darin Jeffries, *Officer*
Loren S Hall, *Vice Pres*
EMP: 11
SQ FT: 3,500
SALES (est): 1.5MM **Privately Held**
SIC: 3599 Machine shop, jobbing & repair

(P-15993)
GENESIS MCH & FABRICATION INC
4321 Turcon Ave, Bakersfield (93308-5263)
PHONE..................661 324-4366
Darko Skracic, *President*
William Osborne, *Vice Pres*
▲ EMP: 10
SQ FT: 4,500
SALES (est): 2.5MM **Privately Held**
SIC: 3599 Machine shop, jobbing & repair

(P-15994)
GENTEC MANUFACTURING INC
2241 Ringwood Ave, San Jose (95131-1737)
PHONE..................408 432-6220
Mark Diaz, *President*
EMP: 15
SQ FT: 5,700
SALES (est): 2.9MM **Privately Held**
WEB: www.gentecmanufacturing.com
SIC: 3599 Machine shop, jobbing & repair

(P-15995)
GEORGE FISCHER INC (HQ)
3401 Aero Jet Ave, El Monte (91731-2801)
PHONE..................626 571-2770
Chris Blumer, *CEO*
Daniel Vaterlaus, *Vice Pres*
Rudy Mangual, *Engineer*
Cathy Miller, *Accountant*
Sandi Deets, *Human Res Mgr*
◆ EMP: 37 EST: 1954
SALES (est): 187.3MM
SALES (corp-wide): 4.6B **Privately Held**
SIC: 3599 5074 3829 3559 Electrical discharge machining (EDM); pipes & fittings, plastic; testing equipment: abrasion, shearing strength, etc.; foundry machinery & equipment
PA: Georg Fischer Ag
Amsler-Laffon-Strasse 9
Schaffhausen SH 8200
526 311-111

(P-15996)
GERMAN MACHINED PRODUCTS INC
Also Called: German Machine Products
1415 W 178th St, Gardena (90248-3201)
PHONE..................310 532-4480
Jonathan Minter, *CEO*
Jonathan James Minter, *CEO*
Jacob Minter, *General Mgr*
EMP: 32 EST: 1972
SQ FT: 12,000
SALES (est): 7.9MM **Privately Held**
SIC: 3599 Machine shop, jobbing & repair

(P-15997)
GLENGARRY MANUFACTURING INC
1535 Marlborough Ave, Riverside (92507-2029)
PHONE..................951 248-1111
EMP: 10 EST: 2010
SQ FT: 5,000
SALES (est): 1.5MM **Privately Held**
SIC: 3599

(P-15998)
GOEPPNER INDUSTRIES INC
22924 Lockness Ave, Torrance (90501-5117)
PHONE..................310 784-2800
Joanne Goeppner, *President*
EMP: 12
SQ FT: 12,000

SALES (est): 1.7MM **Privately Held**
SIC: 3599 Machine shop, jobbing & repair

(P-15999)
GOLDEN WEST MACHINE INC
9930 Jordan Cir, Santa Fe Springs (90670-3305)
PHONE..................562 903-1111
Dan Goodman, *Principal*
Al Schlunegger, *Vice Pres*
Shane Downs, *Manager*
EMP: 35
SQ FT: 25,000
SALES: 5.4MM **Privately Held**
WEB: www.goldenwestmachine.com
SIC: 3599 7699 Machine shop, jobbing & repair; industrial machinery & equipment repair

(P-16000)
GOOSE MANUFACTURING INC
1853 Little Orchard St, San Jose (95125-1034)
PHONE..................408 747-0940
Donald Goossens, *President*
Rosemary Goossens, *Info Tech Mgr*
EMP: 10
SALES (est): 1.4MM **Privately Held**
WEB: www.goosemfg.com
SIC: 3599 Machine shop, jobbing & repair

(P-16001)
GP MACHINING INC
94 Commerce Dr, Buellton (93427-9500)
P.O. Box 2006 (93427-2006)
PHONE..................805 686-0852
Julian Guerra, *President*
Robert Place, *Vice Pres*
EMP: 34
SQ FT: 4,500
SALES (est): 7.1MM **Privately Held**
WEB: www.gpmachining.com
SIC: 3599 Machine shop, jobbing & repair

(P-16002)
GRACE MACHINE CO INC
4540 Cecilia St, Cudahy (90201-5812)
PHONE..................323 771-6215
Guillermo Castellanos Sr, *President*
Ivon Rodriguez, *Treasurer*
Guillermo Castellanos Jr, *Vice Pres*
Grace Castellanos, *Admin Sec*
EMP: 20
SALES: 950K **Privately Held**
SIC: 3599 Machine shop, jobbing & repair

(P-16003)
GRAMBERG MACHINE INC
500 Spectrum Cir, Oxnard (93030-8988)
PHONE..................805 278-4500
Carl Gramberg, *President*
EMP: 10
SQ FT: 5,000
SALES (est): 1.5MM **Privately Held**
SIC: 3599 Machine shop, jobbing & repair

(P-16004)
GRICO PRECISION INC
Also Called: Swiss House
128 S Valencia Ave Ste A, Glendora (91741-3271)
PHONE..................626 963-0368
Tom Grisham, *President*
Robert E Dill, *Vice Pres*
EMP: 12
SALES: 850K **Privately Held**
SIC: 3599 Machine shop, jobbing & repair

(P-16005)
GRIND FOOD COMPANY INC
Also Called: Goleta Coffee Company
177 S Turnpike Rd, Goleta (93111-2208)
PHONE..................805 964-8344
Anne Breytsbrika, *President*
EMP: 10
SALES (est): 670K **Privately Held**
SIC: 3599 Grinding castings for the trade

(P-16006)
GSP PRECISION INC
650 Town Center Dr # 950, Costa Mesa (92626-7021)
PHONE..................818 845-2212
George Gottardi, *President*
Walter D Prezioso, *CEO*
Pablo Prezioso, *Admin Sec*

EMP: 22
SQ FT: 6,000
SALES (est): 2.6MM **Privately Held**
WEB: www.gsp-precision.com
SIC: 3599

(P-16007)
GTR ENTERPRISES INCORPORATED
6352 Corte Del Abeto E, Carlsbad (92011-1408)
PHONE..................760 931-1192
Kenneth Gray, *CEO*
Martin Randant, *President*
Mike Tedesco, *President*
John Richard, *CFO*
Moe Dehghan, *Office Mgr*
EMP: 40
SQ FT: 4,000
SALES (est): 6.3MM **Privately Held**
SIC: 3599 5531 Machine shop, jobbing & repair; truck equipment & parts

(P-16008)
GUNDRILL TECH INC
10030 Greenleaf Ave, Santa Fe Springs (90670-3414)
PHONE..................562 946-9355
Joe Bati, *President*
Yolande Bati, *Vice Pres*
EMP: 22
SALES (est): 1.5MM **Privately Held**
SIC: 3599 Machine shop, jobbing & repair

(P-16009)
GUPTILL GEAR CORPORATION
874 S Rose Pl, Anaheim (92805-5337)
PHONE..................714 956-2170
Ron Guptill, *President*
EMP: 10
SQ FT: 4,000
SALES (est): 1.6MM **Privately Held**
WEB: www.guptillgear.com
SIC: 3599 Machine shop, jobbing & repair

(P-16010)
GYT SAN DIEGO INC
2253 Roll Paseo Dil Amer, San Diego (92154)
PHONE..................619 661-2568
Marco Orozco, *General Mgr*
EMP: 13
SALES (est): 1.6MM **Privately Held**
SIC: 3599 Machine shop, jobbing & repair

(P-16011)
H & M FOUR-SLIDE INC
25779 Jefferson Ave, Murrieta (92562-6903)
PHONE..................951 461-8244
Hans Klahr, *President*
EMP: 14 EST: 1978
SQ FT: 11,600
SALES (est): 1.3MM **Privately Held**
SIC: 3599 Machine shop, jobbing & repair

(P-16012)
H FAM ENGINEERING INC
2131 S Hellman Ave Ste F, Ontario (91761-8004)
PHONE..................909 930-5678
Joe Herrera, *President*
Raul Herrera, *Vice Pres*
EMP: 16
SQ FT: 7,000
SALES (est): 1MM **Privately Held**
SIC: 3599 Machine shop, jobbing & repair

(P-16013)
H Q MACHINE TECH INC
6900 8th St, Buena Park (90620-1036)
PHONE..................714 956-3388
Jason Cho, *CEO*
EMP: 23
SALES (est): 3.7MM **Privately Held**
WEB: www.hqmachine.com
SIC: 3599 Machine & other job shop work

(P-16014)
HAIG PRECISION MFG CORP
3616 Snell Ave, San Jose (95136-1305)
PHONE..................408 378-4920
Daniel S Sarkisian, *CEO*
Paul Sarkisian, *Vice Pres*
Jack Edwards, *Executive*
Aaron Valenta, *Info Tech Mgr*

John Tower, *Design Engr*
▲ EMP: 60
SQ FT: 26,000
SALES (est): 12.9MM **Privately Held**
WEB: www.haig-mfg.com
SIC: 3599 7692 Machine shop, jobbing & repair; welding repair

(P-16015)
HAMMOND ENTERPRISES INC
549 Garcia Ave Ste C, Pittsburg (94565-7402)
PHONE..................925 432-3537
Alan B Hammond, *CEO*
▲ EMP: 20
SQ FT: 12,500
SALES (est): 4MM **Privately Held**
SIC: 3599 Machine shop, jobbing & repair

(P-16016)
HANSEN HAULERS INC
Also Called: Hansen Machine Works
1628 N C St 1630, Sacramento (95811-0613)
PHONE..................916 443-7755
Jodean Mc Millan, *President*
Duke Mc Millan, *Vice Pres*
Scott Mc Millan, *Admin Sec*
EMP: 10
SQ FT: 9,000
SALES: 1.2MM **Privately Held**
SIC: 3599 3715 Machine shop, jobbing & repair; truck trailers

(P-16017)
HASALA ENGINEERING INC
125 W 155th St, Gardena (90248-2203)
PHONE..................310 538-4268
George Hasala, *President*
Emily Hasala, *Vice Pres*
EMP: 12
SQ FT: 5,000
SALES: 800K **Privately Held**
SIC: 3599 Machine shop, jobbing & repair

(P-16018)
HEIGHTEN AMERICA INC
Also Called: Heighten Manfacturing
1144 Post Rd, Oakdale (95361-9384)
PHONE..................209 845-0455
Linda Smeck, *President*
Jerrold W Smeck, *Treasurer*
EMP: 21
SQ FT: 8,000
SALES (est): 3.9MM **Privately Held**
WEB: www.heightenamericainc.com
SIC: 3599 Machine shop, jobbing & repair

(P-16019)
HELFER ENTERPRISES
Also Called: Helfer Tool Co
3030 Oak St, Santa Ana (92707-4236)
PHONE..................714 557-2733
Bennie L Helfer, *President*
EMP: 36 EST: 1973
SQ FT: 12,000
SALES (est): 5.2MM **Privately Held**
WEB: www.helfertool.com
SIC: 3599 5084 3545 3544 Machine shop, jobbing & repair; industrial machinery & equipment; machine tool accessories; special dies, tools, jigs & fixtures

(P-16020)
HERITAGE CARBIDE INC
901 S Via Rodeo, Placentia (92870-6777)
PHONE..................714 524-0222
Neal Depriest, *CEO*
Diana Depriest, *CFO*
Thomas Gill, *CTO*
EMP: 10
SALES (est): 2MM **Privately Held**
WEB: www.heritagecarbide.com
SIC: 3599 Machine shop, jobbing & repair; machine & other job shop work

(P-16021)
HI-TECH LABELS INCORPORATED (PA)
Also Called: Hi-Tech Products
8530 Roland St, Buena Park (90621-3124)
PHONE..................714 670-2150
Jeffrey T Ruch, *CEO*
Sandra Duckett, *CFO*
Damian Craig, *Vice Pres*
Jerry Oswald, *Engineer*

▲ = Import ▼=Export
◆ =Import/Export

Sandy Ruch, *Human Res Mgr*
▲ **EMP:** 34
SQ FT: 24,000
SALES (est): 7.3MM **Privately Held**
WEB: www.hi-tech-products.com
SIC: 3599 Machine shop, jobbing & repair

(P-16022)
HI-TECH PRCISION MACHINING INC
Also Called: Htpmi Contract Manufacturing
1901 Las Plumas Ave # 50, San Jose
(95133-1700)
PHONE..............................408 251-1269
Hiep Tran, *President*
Peter Lonero, *Vice Pres*
EMP: 12
SQ FT: 15,000
SALES (est): 1.8MM **Privately Held**
SIC: 3599 3334 3354 Machine shop, jobbing & repair; primary aluminum; aluminum extruded products

(P-16023)
HI-TECH WELDING & FORMING INC
1327 Fayette St, El Cajon (92020-1512)
P.O. Box 1357 (92022-1357)
PHONE..............................619 562-5929
Aubrey Burer, *CEO*
John C Monsees, *President*
Amy Fitzgerald, *Admin Sec*
EMP: 35
SQ FT: 77,000
SALES (est): 5.1MM **Privately Held**
WEB: www.hi-techwelding.com
SIC: 3599 7692 3365 Machine shop, jobbing & repair; welding repair; aerospace castings, aluminum

(P-16024)
HI-TEMP FORMING CO INC
315 Arden Ave Ste 28, Glendale
(91203-1150)
PHONE..............................714 529-6556
Marvin Rosenberg, *President*
Jay Rosenberg, *Treasurer*
Doris Rosenberg, *Vice Pres*
EMP: 65 **EST:** 1959
SQ FT: 36,000
SALES (est): 9.8MM **Privately Held**
SIC: 3599 3812 3769 Machine shop, jobbing & repair; search & navigation equipment; guided missile & space vehicle parts & auxiliary equipment

(P-16025)
HIEP NGUYEN CORPORATION
Also Called: Silicon Valley Precision Mch
1641 Rogers Ave, San Jose (95112-1126)
PHONE..............................408 451-9042
Hen Tran, *President*
Hua Tran, *Vice Pres*
Buu Thai, *Admin Sec*
EMP: 22
SQ FT: 6,400
SALES (est): 3MM **Privately Held**
SIC: 3599 Machine shop, jobbing & repair

(P-16026)
HIGH PRECISION GRINDING
1130 Pioneer Way, El Cajon (92020-1925)
PHONE..............................619 440-0303
Keith Brawner, *President*
Ken Gerhart, *Vice Pres*
Shanda Brawner, *Admin Sec*
EMP: 32
SQ FT: 20,000
SALES (est): 4.6MM **Privately Held**
SIC: 3599 Machine shop, jobbing & repair

(P-16027)
HIGH SPEED CNC
3324 Victor Ct, Santa Clara (95054-2316)
PHONE..............................408 492-0331
Joe Munich, *President*
Deanna Schmelebeck, *CFO*
EMP: 14
SQ FT: 12,000
SALES (est): 2.5MM **Privately Held**
WEB: www.highspeedcnc.com
SIC: 3599 Machine shop, jobbing & repair

(P-16028)
HIGH TECH ETCH (PA)
Also Called: High Tech Etch Research & Dev
17469 Lemon St, Hesperia (92345-5151)
PHONE..............................760 244-8916
Eric Harris, *President*
Will Ashford, *Vice Pres*
EMP: 15
SQ FT: 10,000
SALES (est): 528K **Privately Held**
SIC: 3599 Chemical milling job shop

(P-16029)
HIGHTOWER METAL PRODUCTS
2090 N Glassell St, Orange (92865-3306)
P.O. Box 5586 (92863-5586)
PHONE..............................714 637-7000
Kurt Koch, *President*
Mark Koch, *Vice Pres*
EMP: 66
SQ FT: 20,000
SALES (est): 14.7MM **Privately Held**
SIC: 3599 Machine shop, jobbing & repair

(P-16030)
HILL MARINE PRODUCTS LLC
Also Called: Signature Propellers
2683 Halladay St, Santa Ana (92705-5617)
PHONE..............................714 855-2986
Chad Hill, *Mng Member*
Ron Hill, *Partner*
▲ **EMP:** 14 **EST:** 2011
SALES (est): 972K **Privately Held**
SIC: 3599 7699 Propellers, ship & boat: machined; marine propeller repair

(P-16031)
HMCOMPANY
4464 Mcgrath St Ste 111, Ventura
(93003-7764)
PHONE..............................805 650-2651
Mark Woellert, *Owner*
EMP: 18
SQ FT: 3,500
SALES (est): 1MM **Privately Held**
WEB: www.hmcompany.net
SIC: 3599 Machine shop, jobbing & repair

(P-16032)
HOEFNER CORPORATION
9722 Rush St, South El Monte
(91733-1777)
PHONE..............................626 443-3258
Gerald Hoefner, *President*
Karen Hoefner, *Admin Sec*
EMP: 20
SQ FT: 14,800
SALES (est): 4MM **Privately Held**
WEB: www.hoefnercorp.com
SIC: 3599 3429 Machine shop, jobbing & repair; manufactured hardware (general)

(P-16033)
HOLLAND & HERRING MFG INC
Also Called: H & H MANUFACTURING
661 E Monterey Ave, Pomona
(91767-5607)
PHONE..............................909 469-4700
Jerry C Holland, *President*
Anne M Herring, *Shareholder*
Bruce N Herring, *Shareholder*
Mark B Herring, *Shareholder*
Steven R Herring, *Shareholder*
EMP: 34
SQ FT: 15,000
SALES (est): 2.7MM **Privately Held**
SIC: 3599 3471 Machine shop, jobbing & repair; cleaning, polishing & finishing

(P-16034)
HORIZON ENGINEERING INC
13200 Kirkham Way Ste 109, Poway
(92064-7126)
PHONE..............................858 679-0785
Michael Castle, *President*
Dennis Baros, *Vice Pres*
EMP: 10
SQ FT: 4,103
SALES (est): 800K **Privately Held**
WEB: www.horizon-eng.com
SIC: 3599 Machine shop, jobbing & repair

(P-16035)
HORVATH PRECISION MACHINING
Also Called: H P M
930 Thompson Pl, Sunnyvale
(94085-4517)
PHONE..............................510 683-0810
Fax: 510 683-0815
EMP: 12
SQ FT: 5,000
SALES (est): 1.2MM **Privately Held**
WEB: www.hpmquality.com
SIC: 3599

(P-16036)
HTE ACQUISITION LLC
Also Called: Hi-Tech Engineering
4610 Calle Quetzal, Camarillo
(93012-8558)
PHONE..............................805 987-5449
Shaffiq Rahim, *President*
EMP: 18
SQ FT: 15,000
SALES (est): 102.8K **Privately Held**
SIC: 3599 Machine & other job shop work

(P-16037)
HUNG TUNG
Also Called: Quality Tech Machining
3672 Bassett St, Santa Clara (95054-2001)
PHONE..............................408 496-1818
Tung Hung, *Owner*
EMP: 10
SQ FT: 1,000
SALES (est): 650K **Privately Held**
WEB: www.qualitytechmachining.com
SIC: 3599 Machine shop, jobbing & repair

(P-16038)
HYTRON MFG CO INC
15582 Chemical Ln, Huntington Beach
(92649-1505)
PHONE..............................714 903-6701
James C Rehling, *President*
Cheryll Rehling, *Corp Secy*
Robert Rehling, *Vice Pres*
Deborah Strickland, *Vice Pres*
EMP: 50
SQ FT: 13,370
SALES (est): 8.7MM **Privately Held**
WEB: www.hytronmanufacturing.com
SIC: 3599 Machine shop, jobbing & repair

(P-16039)
IMG COMPANIES LLC
225 Mountain Vista Pkwy, Livermore
(94551-8210)
PHONE..............................925 273-1100
Kam Pasha, *CEO*
Kiran Mukkamala, *CFO*
Mahesh Kumar, *Vice Pres*
▲ **EMP:** 135
SALES (est): 20MM **Privately Held**
SIC: 3599 Machine shop, jobbing & repair

(P-16040)
IMT PRECISION INC
31902 Hayman St, Hayward (94544-7925)
PHONE..............................510 324-8926
Timoteo Ilario, *President*
Jeff Nordloff, *Business Mgr*
Bekki Nguyen, *Accountant*
Peter Kunze, *QC Mgr*
Zack Lemley, *Production*
EMP: 50
SQ FT: 50,000
SALES (est): 6.5MM **Privately Held**
WEB: www.imtp.com
SIC: 3599 Machine shop, jobbing & repair

(P-16041)
INDUSTRIAL DESIGN FABRICATION
802 S San Joaquin St B, Stockton
(95206-1461)
P.O. Box 268 (95201-0268)
PHONE..............................209 937-9128
Laurie Cornell, *President*
Jerry Hicks, *Vice Pres*
▼ **EMP:** 13
SQ FT: 13,200
SALES (est): 2.8MM **Privately Held**
SIC: 3599 3589 Custom machinery; commercial cleaning equipment

(P-16042)
INDUSTRIAL POWER PRODUCTS
Also Called: Kubota Authorized Dealer
355 E Park Ave, Chico (95928-7125)
PHONE..............................530 893-0584
Tim Adkins, *President*
Robert Berger, *Vice Pres*
Shannon Palo, *General Mgr*
EMP: 30
SQ FT: 7,541
SALES (est): 2.8MM **Privately Held**
SIC: 3599 5084 5085 Machine shop, jobbing & repair; engines, gasoline; industrial supplies

(P-16043)
INFINITE ENGINEERING INC
13682 Newhope St, Garden Grove
(92843-3712)
PHONE..............................714 534-4688
Simon Ho, *President*
Kelly Ho, *Vice Pres*
EMP: 12
SALES (est): 605.7K **Privately Held**
WEB: www.infinite-eng.com
SIC: 3599 Machine shop, jobbing & repair

(P-16044)
INFINITY PRECISION INC
Also Called: Design Engineering
6919 Eton Ave, Canoga Park (91303-2110)
PHONE..............................818 447-3008
Evelina Martirosova, *President*
EMP: 10
SQ FT: 6,000
SALES (est): 1.1MM **Privately Held**
SIC: 3599 3441 Machine & other job shop work; fabricated structural metal

(P-16045)
INFINITY SYSTEMS INC
22715 La Palma Ave, Yorba Linda
(92887-4772)
PHONE..............................714 692-1722
Zoltan Karpati, *President*
Tony Karpati, *Corp Secy*
Mark Robbins, *General Mgr*
EMP: 10
SQ FT: 6,300
SALES (est): 2.1MM **Privately Held**
WEB: www.infinitysystemsinc.com
SIC: 3599 Machine shop, jobbing & repair

(P-16046)
INNO TECH MANUFACTURING INC
10109 Carroll Canyon Rd, San Diego
(92131-1109)
PHONE..............................858 565-4556
Marek Prochazka, *President*
Gail Prochazka, *CFO*
Michael Jenny, *Opers Staff*
▲ **EMP:** 19
SALES (est): 3.7MM **Privately Held**
WEB: www.innotechmachining.com
SIC: 3599 Machine shop, jobbing & repair

(P-16047)
INNOVATIVE MACHINING INC
845 Yosemite Way, Milpitas (95035-6329)
PHONE..............................408 262-2270
Thang Vo, *President*
Bich Nguyen, *Vice Pres*
EMP: 25
SQ FT: 3,000
SALES (est): 3.7MM **Privately Held**
SIC: 3599 Machine shop, jobbing & repair

(P-16048)
INNOVATIVE MANUFACTURING INC
Also Called: Innovative Mounts
1366 N Hundley St, Anaheim (92806-1301)
PHONE..............................714 524-5246
Tim Hastings, *CEO*
Greg Hastings, *CFO*
EMP: 15
SQ FT: 5,000
SALES (est): 3.1MM **Privately Held**
WEB: www.innovativemounts.com
SIC: 3599 Machine shop, jobbing & repair

PRODUCTS & SVCS

(P-16049)
INSERTS & KITS INC
1521 W Alton Ave, Santa Ana
(92704-7219)
PHONE................714 708-2888
Reinaldo J Ayala, *President*
EMP: 10
SALES (est): 1.7MM **Privately Held**
SIC: 3599 Machine shop, jobbing & repair

(P-16050)
INTEGRATED MFG TECH INC
Also Called: IMT
1477 N Milpitas Blvd, Milpitas
(95035-3160)
PHONE................510 366-8793
Andy Luong, *President*
Whyemun Chan, *Treasurer*
Sally Luong, *Vice Pres*
EMP: 27
SALES: 10MM **Privately Held**
SIC: 3599 3471 3498 7692 Machine
shop, jobbing & repair; polishing, metals
or formed products; fabricated pipe & fit-
tings; welding repair

(P-16051)
INTER CITY MANUFACTURING INC
507 Redwood Ave, Seaside (93955-3029)
PHONE................831 899-3636
Douglas A Learned, *President*
Karen Learned, *Executive*
EMP: 24
SQ FT: 12,000
SALES (est): 3.3MM **Privately Held**
SIC: 3599 Machine shop, jobbing & repair

(P-16052)
INTERCITY CENTERLESS GRINDING
11546 Coley River Cir, Fountain Valley
(92708-4219)
PHONE................714 546-5644
Mike Bell, *Owner*
Ellen Marie Gutierrez, *President*
Michael Gutierrez, *Vice Pres*
EMP: 10
SQ FT: 7,800
SALES (est): 1.1MM **Privately Held**
SIC: 3599 Machine shop, jobbing & repair

(P-16053)
INTERNATIONAL PRECISION INC
Also Called: I P
9526 Vassar Ave, Chatsworth
(91311-4168)
P.O. Box 4839 (91313-4839)
PHONE................818 882-3933
Renee M Brendel-Konrad, *CEO*
Juan Passarelli, *Mfg Mgr*
Alan Beauregard, *Sales Staff*
◆ EMP: 22
SQ FT: 12,000
SALES (est): 4.9MM **Privately Held**
WEB: www.intlprecision.com
SIC: 3599 3728 Machine shop, jobbing &
repair; aircraft parts & equipment

(P-16054)
INVERSE SOLUTIONS INC
3922 Valley Ave Ste A, Pleasanton
(94566-4873)
PHONE................925 931-9500
David Jordan, *Principal*
Ronda Jordan, *Admin Sec*
EMP: 24
SQ FT: 12,500
SALES (est): 4.4MM **Privately Held**
SIC: 3599 Machine shop, jobbing & repair

(P-16055)
IRONCLAD TOOL AND MACHINE INC
120 Old Yard Dr, Bakersfield (93307-4295)
P.O. Box 42707 (93384-2707)
PHONE................661 833-9990
Joseph Williams, *President*
EMP: 10 EST: 2016
SALES (est): 548K **Privately Held**
SIC: 3599 7692 1389 Machine & other
job shop work; machine shop, jobbing &
repair; welding repair; mud service, oil
field drilling

(P-16056)
ISI DETENTION CONTG GROUP INC
Also Called: Argyle Precision
577 N Batavia St, Orange (92868-1218)
PHONE................714 288-1770
Zach Greene, *President*
Joe Chavez, *Vice Pres*
▲ EMP: 90
SQ FT: 25,000
SALES (est): 16.7MM **Privately Held**
WEB: www.petersondetention.com
SIC: 3599 3444 Machine & other job shop
work; sheet metal specialties, not
stamped

(P-16057)
J & F MACHINE INC
6401 Global Dr, Cypress (90630-5227)
PHONE................714 527-3499
Micheline Varnum, *President*
Richard Varnum, *Vice Pres*
EMP: 22
SQ FT: 8,500
SALES (est): 4.5MM **Privately Held**
SIC: 3599 Machine shop, jobbing & repair

(P-16058)
J & R MACHINE WORKS
45420 60th St W, Lancaster (93536-8322)
PHONE................661 945-8826
Jesse Alvarado, *Partner*
Rudy Alvarado, *Partner*
EMP: 20
SQ FT: 3,500
SALES (est): 3.4MM **Privately Held**
SIC: 3599 Machine shop, jobbing & repair

(P-16059)
J & R MACHINING INC
164 Martinvale Ln, San Jose (95119-1355)
PHONE................408 365-7314
Ashur Peera, *President*
Anna Peera, *Vice Pres*
EMP: 11
SQ FT: 5,000
SALES (est): 1.4MM **Privately Held**
SIC: 3599 Machine shop, jobbing & repair

(P-16060)
J & S INC
229 E Gardena Blvd, Gardena
(90248-2800)
PHONE................310 719-7144
Joseph Brown, *President*
Sheryl Zamora, *CEO*
Margaret Brown, *Corp Secy*
EMP: 33
SQ FT: 6,141
SALES (est): 4.4MM **Privately Held**
SIC: 3599 Machine shop, jobbing & repair

(P-16061)
J & S MACHINE
Also Called: J and S Machine
8112 Freestone Ave, Santa Fe Springs
(90670-2114)
PHONE................562 945-6419
EMP: 30
SQ FT: 7,200
SALES: 1.5MM **Privately Held**
SIC: 3599

(P-16062)
J A-CO MACHINE WORKS LLC
Also Called: Jaco Machine Works
4 Carbonero Way, Scotts Valley
(95066-4200)
PHONE................877 429-8175
Andy Smith, *Mng Member*
Jeffrey A Smith, *Managing Prtnr*
EMP: 20
SQ FT: 9,000
SALES (est): 3.5MM **Privately Held**
WEB: www.jacoworks.com
SIC: 3599 Machine shop, jobbing & repair

(P-16063)
J B TOOL INC
350 E Orngthrp Ave Ste 6, Placentia
(92870-6504)
PHONE................714 993-7173
Robert Barna, *President*
EMP: 11
SQ FT: 12,000

SALES: 800K **Privately Held**
WEB: www.jbtoolinc.com
SIC: 3599 Machine shop, jobbing & repair

(P-16064)
J D INDUSTRIES
1636 E Edinger Ave Ste P, Santa Ana
(92705-5020)
PHONE................714 542-5517
Fax: 714 542-3430
EMP: 10
SQ FT: 4,000
SALES (est): 650K **Privately Held**
SIC: 3599

(P-16065)
J E S DISC GRINDING INC
2824 Metropolitan Pl, Pomona
(91767-1854)
PHONE................909 596-3823
John Schmidt, *President*
Ray Schmidt, *Vice Pres*
EMP: 13
SQ FT: 12,000
SALES (est): 1.4MM **Privately Held**
SIC: 3599 Machine shop, jobbing & repair

(P-16066)
J FLYING MACHINE INC
701 S Andreasen Dr Ste C, Escondido
(92029-1950)
PHONE................760 504-0323
Jay Hegemann, *Owner*
EMP: 15
SALES (est): 1.7MM **Privately Held**
SIC: 3599 Machine shop, jobbing & repair

(P-16067)
J&E PRECISION MACHINING INC
2814 Aiello Dr Ste A, San Jose
(95111-2197)
PHONE................408 281-1195
Eva M Sousa, *President*
Jorge Sousa, *Vice Pres*
EMP: 12
SQ FT: 6,000
SALES (est): 1.3MM **Privately Held**
WEB: www.jandeprecision.com
SIC: 3599 Machine shop, jobbing & repair

(P-16068)
J&J PRODUCTS
835 Capitolio Way Ste 4, San Luis Obispo
(93401-7127)
PHONE................805 544-4288
Earl Jeffries, *Owner*
EMP: 12
SQ FT: 3,000
SALES (est): 875.2K **Privately Held**
WEB: www.j-j-products.com
SIC: 3599 7692 Machine shop, jobbing &
repair; welding repair

(P-16069)
J3 ASSOCIATES INC
2751 Aiello Dr, San Jose (95111-2156)
PHONE................408 281-4412
John Vasapollo, *President*
James Catron, *Vice Pres*
EMP: 10
SQ FT: 10,000
SALES (est): 1.6MM **Privately Held**
WEB: www.j3associates.com
SIC: 3599 Machine shop, jobbing & repair

(P-16070)
JACK C DREES GRINDING CO INC
11815 Vose St B, North Hollywood
(91605-5748)
PHONE................818 764-8301
Jack C Drees, *President*
Dann Drees, *Vice Pres*
EMP: 20 EST: 1957
SQ FT: 12,000
SALES: 2MM **Privately Held**
SIC: 3599 7389 Grinding castings for the
trade; grinding, precision: commercial or
industrial

(P-16071)
JACK WEST CNC INC
3451 Main St Ste 111, Chula Vista
(91911-5894)
PHONE................619 421-1695
Jack West, *President*
Jenny West, *Vice Pres*
▲ EMP: 10
SALES (est): 1.8MM **Privately Held**
SIC: 3599 Machine shop, jobbing & repair

(P-16072)
JACO ENGINEERING
879 S East St, Anaheim (92805-5391)
PHONE................714 991-1680
H J Meagher, *President*
Barbara Meagher, *Vice Pres*
Frank Cabadas, *Buyer*
EMP: 35
SQ FT: 10,000
SALES (est): 7MM **Privately Held**
WEB: www.jacoengineering.com
SIC: 3599 Machine shop, jobbing & repair

(P-16073)
JAFFA PRECISION ENGRG INC
12117 Madera Way, Riverside
(92503-4849)
PHONE................951 278-8797
Raida Sayegh, *President*
Chris S Sayegh, *COO*
Joe Janini, *Accounting Mgr*
Mark Sayegh, *Manager*
EMP: 15
SQ FT: 12,500
SALES: 2.1MM **Privately Held**
SIC: 3599 Machine shop, jobbing & repair

(P-16074)
JAMES JACKSON
Also Called: J J Engineering
11021 Via El Mercado, Los Alamitos
(90720-2811)
PHONE................562 493-1402
James Jackson, *Owner*
EMP: 10
SQ FT: 7,050
SALES (est): 1.1MM **Privately Held**
SIC: 3599 Machine shop, jobbing & repair

(P-16075)
JAMES L CRAFT INC
Also Called: Genenco
1101 33rd St, Bakersfield (93301-2121)
PHONE................661 323-8251
James L Craft, *President*
EMP: 25
SALES (est): 1.8MM **Privately Held**
SIC: 3599 Machine shop, jobbing & repair

(P-16076)
JAMES STOUT
Also Called: Stg Machine
481 Gianni St, Santa Clara (95054-2414)
PHONE................408 988-8582
Jim Stout, *Owner*
EMP: 30
SQ FT: 15,000
SALES (est): 3.9MM **Privately Held**
SIC: 3599 Machine shop, jobbing & repair

(P-16077)
JARVIS MANUFACTURING INC
195 Lewis Rd Ste 36, San Jose
(95111-2192)
PHONE................408 226-2600
Tony Grewal, *CEO*
EMP: 17
SQ FT: 6,000
SALES (est): 2.9MM **Privately Held**
WEB: www.jarvismfg.com
SIC: 3599 Machine shop, jobbing & repair

(P-16078)
JCPM INC
Also Called: J C Precision
8576 Red Oak St, Rancho Cucamonga
(91730-4822)
PHONE................909 484-9040
Carlos Cajas, *President*
EMP: 14
SQ FT: 5,200
SALES (est): 2.9MM **Privately Held**
WEB: www.jcpm-inc.com
SIC: 3599 Machine shop, jobbing & repair

▲ = Import ▼=Export
◆ =Import/Export

(P-16079)
JENSON MECHANICAL INC
Also Called: J M I
32420 Central Ave, Union City
(94587-2007)
PHONE..................................510 429-8078
Greg Jenson, *President*
EMP: 20 EST: 1976
SQ FT: 30,000
SALES (est): 4.5MM **Privately Held**
SIC: 3599 7699 Custom machinery; industrial machinery & equipment repair

(P-16080)
JERAMES INDUSTRIES INC
Also Called: Jerames Tool & Mfg
460 Cypress Ln Ste F, El Cajon
(92020-1647)
PHONE..................................619 334-2204
Matthew Fromm, *President*
Harry Railton, *Shareholder*
Gary Sanchez, *General Mgr*
EMP: 20
SQ FT: 10,600
SALES (est): 4.2MM **Privately Held**
WEB: www.jerames.com
SIC: 3599 Machine shop, jobbing & repair

(P-16081)
JERRY CARROLL MACHINERY INC
Also Called: Electrocut-Pacific
993 E San Carlos Ave, San Carlos
(94070-2528)
PHONE..................................650 591-3302
Fax: 650 591-2149
EMP: 12
SQ FT: 10,000
SALES (est): 1.3MM **Privately Held**
SIC: 3599

(P-16082)
JESSEE BROTHERS MACHINE SP INC
Also Called: J B Precision
1640 Dell Ave, Campbell (95008-6901)
PHONE..................................408 866-1755
Chett Jessee, *President*
Marcia Balfour, *Sales Mgr*
EMP: 16
SQ FT: 12,500
SALES (est): 1.8MM **Privately Held**
WEB: www.jesseebrothersinc.com
SIC: 3599 Machine shop, jobbing & repair

(P-16083)
JESSOP INDUSTRIES
4645 Industrial St Ste 2c, Simi Valley
(93063-3466)
PHONE..................................805 581-6976
EMP: 11
SALES: 200K **Privately Held**
SIC: 3599

(P-16084)
JIMACHINE COMPANY INC
9720 Distribution Ave, San Diego
(92121-2310)
PHONE..................................858 695-1787
Ila Ree Piel, *President*
James Piel, *Vice Pres*
Mark Jay Piel, *Vice Pres*
Wendy Anne Piel, *Vice Pres*
Ken Gross, *VP Opers*
▲ EMP: 20
SQ FT: 15,400
SALES (est): 3.6MM **Privately Held**
WEB: www.jimachine.com
SIC: 3599 3812 Machine shop, jobbing & repair; search & navigation equipment

(P-16085)
JL HALEY ENTERPRISES INC
3510 Luyung Dr, Rancho Cordova
(95742-6872)
PHONE..................................916 631-6375
James L Haley, *CEO*
◆ EMP: 140
SQ FT: 67,000
SALES (est): 20.7MM
SALES (corp-wide): 131MM **Privately Held**
SIC: 3599 3312 7692 Machine shop, jobbing & repair; blast furnaces & steel mills; welding repair

PA: Vander-Bend Manufacturing, Inc.
2701 Orchard Pkwy
San Jose CA 95134
408 245-5150

(P-16086)
JMG MACHINE INC
17037 Industry Pl, La Mirada (90638-5819)
PHONE..................................714 522-6221
Juan Manuel Guillen, *CEO*
Ben Sanchez, *Manager*
EMP: 20
SQ FT: 10,000
SALES (est): 3.7MM **Privately Held**
WEB: www.jobshoppowersites.com
SIC: 3599 Machine shop, jobbing & repair

(P-16087)
JMT INC
14926 Bloomfield Ave, Norwalk
(90650-6065)
PHONE..................................562 404-2014
Juan Barajas, *President*
Juan C Barajas, *General Mgr*
◆ EMP: 12
SQ FT: 6,000
SALES (est): 2.3MM **Privately Held**
SIC: 3599 Machine shop, jobbing & repair

(P-16088)
JNC MACHINING
1834 Stone Ave, San Jose (95125-1306)
PHONE..................................408 920-2520
Jesus Castillon, *Owner*
EMP: 10
SALES: 700K **Privately Held**
SIC: 3599 Machine shop, jobbing & repair

(P-16089)
JNS INDUSTRIES INC
2320 S Vineyard Ave, Ontario
(91761-7767)
PHONE..................................909 923-8334
Janet Sheikh, *President*
Pamela Oates Sanders, *Manager*
EMP: 15
SQ FT: 5,000
SALES (est): 2.2MM **Privately Held**
WEB: www.jnsindustries.com
SIC: 3599 Machine shop, jobbing & repair

(P-16090)
JOHNSON MANUFACTURING INC
15201 Connector Ln, Huntington Beach
(92649-1117)
PHONE..................................714 903-0393
Colleen Johnson, *CEO*
Allan Johnson, *Vice Pres*
Sylvia Culling, *Office Mgr*
EMP: 35
SQ FT: 13,000
SALES: 5.6MM **Privately Held**
WEB: www.johnsonmfginc.com
SIC: 3599 Machine shop, jobbing & repair

(P-16091)
JOHNSON PRECISION PRODUCTS INC
1308 E Wakeham Ave, Santa Ana
(92705-4145)
PHONE..................................714 824-6971
Paul Cronin, *President*
EMP: 19 EST: 1961
SQ FT: 4,000
SALES (est): 3.7MM **Privately Held**
SIC: 3599 Machine shop, jobbing & repair

(P-16092)
JOLLY JUMPS INC
600 Via Alondra, Camarillo (93012-8733)
PHONE..................................805 484-0026
Ted Schwochow, *President*
Don Arndorfer, *Corp Secy*
EMP: 45
SQ FT: 26,000
SALES (est): 4.9MM **Privately Held**
SIC: 3599 7999 Carnival machines & equipment, amusement park; exhibition & carnival operation services

(P-16093)
JOT ENGINEERING INC
8385 Canoga Ave, Canoga Park
(91304-2605)
PHONE..................................818 727-7572
Balwinder Riat, *President*
EMP: 12
SQ FT: 2,000
SALES (est): 1.4MM **Privately Held**
SIC: 3599 Amusement park equipment

(P-16094)
JR MACHINE COMPANY INC
13245 Florence Ave, Santa Fe Springs
(90670-4509)
PHONE..................................562 903-9477
Gilbert Reyes, *President*
EMP: 29
SQ FT: 12,000
SALES (est): 2.8MM **Privately Held**
SIC: 3599 Machine shop, jobbing & repair

(P-16095)
JRD PRECISION MACHINING INC
1158 Campbell Ave, San Jose
(95126-1063)
PHONE..................................408 246-9327
Rene Diaz, *President*
EMP: 10
SALES (est): 790K **Privately Held**
SIC: 3599 Machine shop, jobbing & repair

(P-16096)
JUELL MACHINE COINC
150 Pacific St, Pomona (91768-3214)
PHONE..................................909 594-8164
Michael Starr, *President*
Ronald Starr, *Vice Pres*
Sharon Starr, *Vice Pres*
Steve Harms, *QC Mgr*
EMP: 12
SQ FT: 12,000
SALES (est): 2.2MM **Privately Held**
WEB: www.juellmachine.com
SIC: 3599 Machine shop, jobbing & repair

(P-16097)
JWP MANUFACTURING LLC
3500 De La Cruz Blvd, Santa Clara
(95054-2111)
PHONE..................................408 970-0641
Jerzy W Prokop, *Mng Member*
Peter Prokop, *Engineer*
Chris Heider, *Mfg Mgr*
Andy Eden, *Sales Staff*
Suzanna Prokop,
EMP: 25
SQ FT: 12,000
SALES (est): 4.9MM **Privately Held**
WEB: www.jwpmfg.com
SIC: 3599 Machine shop, jobbing & repair

(P-16098)
K & L PRECISION GRINDING CO
9309 Atlantic Ave, South Gate
(90280-3522)
PHONE..................................323 564-5151
Kadri Hakaj, *President*
Kadilja Hakaj, *Vice Pres*
EMP: 12
SQ FT: 6,000
SALES (est): 1.5MM **Privately Held**
SIC: 3599 Machine shop, jobbing & repair

(P-16099)
K A TOOL & TECHNOLOGY INC
1700 Sango Ct, Milpitas (95035-6838)
P.O. Box 612677, San Jose (95161-2677)
PHONE..................................408 957-9600
Henry Chung, *President*
▲ EMP: 30
SQ FT: 9,600
SALES (est): 3MM **Privately Held**
SIC: 3599 Machine shop, jobbing & repair

(P-16100)
K-P ENGINEERING CORP
2126 S Lyon St Ste A, Santa Ana
(92705-5328)
PHONE..................................714 545-7045
Kemal Pepic, *CEO*
EMP: 18
SQ FT: 7,000
SALES (est): 3.9MM **Privately Held**
SIC: 3599 8711 Machine shop, jobbing & repair; professional engineer

(P-16101)
K-TECH MACHINE INC
1377 Armorlite Dr, San Marcos
(92069-1341)
PHONE..................................800 274-9424
Kenneth Russell, *President*
Stuart John Russell, *CFO*
EMP: 134
SQ FT: 16,000
SALES (est): 32.8MM **Privately Held**
WEB: www.k-techmachine.com
SIC: 3599 3444 Machine shop, jobbing & repair; sheet metalwork

(P-16102)
KACEE COMPANY
Also Called: Kacee Discount Abrasives
3570 Hiawatha, North Highlands (95660)
PHONE..................................916 348-3204
Kenneth Cramer, *Owner*
Elizabeth Cramer, *Owner*
EMP: 10
SALES: 600K **Privately Held**
WEB: www.kacee.com
SIC: 3599 5084 5085 Machine shop, jobbing & repair; industrial machinery & equipment; abrasives

(P-16103)
KADAN CONSULTANTS INCORPORATED
5662 Research Dr, Huntington Beach
(92649-1615)
PHONE..................................562 988-1165
Rhoda Sjoberg, *CEO*
Ian Powell, *Engineer*
EMP: 15
SQ FT: 17,000
SALES: 1.6MM **Privately Held**
WEB: www.kadaninc.net
SIC: 3599 3728 3544 8711 Machine shop, jobbing & repair; aircraft parts & equipment; special dies, tools, jigs & fixtures; engineering services

(P-16104)
KAL MACHINING INC
18450 Sutter Blvd, Morgan Hill
(95037-2819)
PHONE..................................408 782-8989
Qing Ye, *President*
David Long, *Vice Pres*
James Swartzbaugh, *QC Mgr*
▲ EMP: 13
SQ FT: 10,000
SALES (est): 2.2MM **Privately Held**
WEB: www.kalmachining.com
SIC: 3599 Machine shop, jobbing & repair

(P-16105)
KALMAN MANUFACTURING INC
780 Jarvis Dr Ste 150, Morgan Hill
(95037-2886)
PHONE..................................408 776-7664
Alan D Kalman, *President*
Freia Kalman, *Vice Pres*
EMP: 43
SQ FT: 35,000
SALES: 5MM **Privately Held**
SIC: 3599 Machine shop, jobbing & repair

(P-16106)
KAP MANUFACTURING INC
327 W Allen Ave, San Dimas (91773-1441)
PHONE..................................909 599-2525
Michael D'Amato, *CFO*
Kathleen D Amato, *President*
Michael D Amato, *CEO*
Ann McConnell, *COO*
Bryan D'Amato, *Vice Pres*
EMP: 27
SQ FT: 6,000
SALES (est): 5.3MM **Privately Held**
WEB: www.kapmfg.com
SIC: 3599 Machine shop, jobbing & repair

(P-16107)
KARAPET ENGINEERING INC
Also Called: Best Engineering
11455 Vanowen St, North Hollywood
(91605-6219)
PHONE..................................818 255-0838
Arthur Alajajyan, *President*
Arthur Alajajyan, *President*
EMP: 12
SQ FT: 8,700

SALES (est): 2MM **Privately Held**
SIC: **3599** Machine shop, jobbing & repair

(P-16108)
KATCH PRECISION MACHINING INC
3953 W 139th St, Hawthorne (90250-7404)
PHONE..................................310 676-4989
George Lopez, *Owner*
Rossie Dominguez, *Executive Asst*
EMP: 10
SQ FT: 5,088
SALES (est): 928.5K **Privately Held**
WEB: www.katchdesign.com
SIC: **3599** Machine shop, jobbing & repair

(P-16109)
KAY & JAMES INC
Also Called: J&S Machine Works
14062 Balboa Blvd, Sylmar (91342-1005)
PHONE..................................818 998-0357
Kye Sook So, *CEO*
Jung M So, *Vice Pres*
Grace So, *Manager*
EMP: 75
SQ FT: 25,000
SALES (est): 14.8MM **Privately Held**
WEB: www.jandsmachineworks.com
SIC: **3599** Machine shop, jobbing & repair

(P-16110)
KEITHCO MANUFACTURING INC
15031 Parkway Loop Ste C, Tustin
(92780-6527)
PHONE..................................714 258-8933
Bernard Steel, *President*
EMP: 10 EST: 1978
SQ FT: 10,100
SALES (est): 1.4MM **Privately Held**
WEB: www.keithco-mfg.com
SIC: **3599** Machine shop, jobbing & repair

(P-16111)
KELLER ENGINEERING
136 W 157th St, Gardena (90248-2226)
PHONE..................................310 532-0554
Fax: 310 532-1086
EMP: 12
SQ FT: 12,000
SALES (est): 640K **Privately Held**
WEB: www.kellerengineering.com
SIC: **3599**

(P-16112)
KELLER ENGINEERING INC
3203 Kashiwa St, Torrance (90505-4020)
PHONE..................................310 326-6291
Kathy Keller, *President*
Claudia Keller Abate, *Treasurer*
Maya Keller Navarra, *Admin Sec*
EMP: 28
SQ FT: 20,000
SALES (est): 3.5MM **Privately Held**
WEB: www.kellereng.com
SIC: **3599** Machine shop, jobbing & repair

(P-16113)
KELLY & THOME
228 San Lorenzo St, Pomona
(91766-2336)
PHONE..................................909 623-2559
Warren C Kelly, *President*
Martha Lehr, *Office Mgr*
Sherry Caudill, *Admin Sec*
EMP: 20 EST: 1961
SQ FT: 6,000
SALES (est): 2.7MM **Privately Held**
WEB: www.kandt.com
SIC: **3599** Machine shop, jobbing & repair

(P-16114)
KEYSTONE ENGINEERING COMPANY (HQ)
4401 E Donald Douglas Dr, Long Beach
(90808-1732)
PHONE..................................562 497-3200
Ian Ballinger, *CEO*
Lili Zhou, *CFO*
◆ EMP: 37
SQ FT: 60,000
SALES (est): 8.8MM **Privately Held**
WEB: www.hamilton-standard.com
SIC: **3599** Air intake filters, internal combustion engine, except auto

PA: Ke Company Acquisition Corp.
4401 E Donald Douglas Dr
Long Beach CA 90808
562 497-3200

(P-16115)
KHUUS INC
Also Called: Kamet
1778 Mccarthy Blvd, Milpitas (95035-7421)
PHONE..................................408 522-8000
Peter Khuu, *President*
Donald Cheng, *General Mgr*
John Gitonga, *Sales Executive*
▲ EMP: 60
SQ FT: 25,000
SALES (est): 14.4MM **Privately Held**
WEB: www.kamet.com
SIC: **3599** Machine shop, jobbing & repair

(P-16116)
KILGORE MACHINE COMPANY INC
2312 S Susan St, Santa Ana (92704-4421)
PHONE..................................714 540-3659
Bryant Kilgore, *President*
Karen Sullivan, *CFO*
Doree Kilgore, *Vice Pres*
Lisa Damico, *Principal*
Linda McKenzie, *Principal*
EMP: 22 EST: 1968
SQ FT: 8,000
SALES (est): 2.1MM **Privately Held**
WEB: www.kilgoremachinecompany.com
SIC: **3599** Machine shop, jobbing & repair

(P-16117)
KIMBERLY MACHINE INC
12822 Joy St, Garden Grove (92840-6350)
PHONE..................................714 539-0151
Tam Huynh, *CEO*
Joseph Nguyen, *President*
Matias Vergara, *Project Mgr*
Valencia Ngo, *Accountant*
EMP: 24
SQ FT: 10,300
SALES (est): 4MM **Privately Held**
SIC: **3599** Machine shop, jobbing & repair

(P-16118)
KIMZEY WELDING WORKS INC
164 Kentucky Ave, Woodland
(95695-2743)
PHONE..................................530 662-9331
John W Kimzey, *President*
Edith Kimzey, *Corp Secy*
EMP: 13
SQ FT: 14,400
SALES (est): 2.1MM **Privately Held**
WEB: www.kimzeymetalproducts.com
SIC: **3599** **7692** **5251** **3842** Custom machinery; welding repair; hardware; surgical appliances & supplies; surgical & medical instruments

(P-16119)
KITCH ENGINEERING INC
12320 Montague St, Pacoima
(91331-2213)
PHONE..................................818 897-7133
Steven Kitching, *President*
Kerri Kitching, *Vice Pres*
Terry Kitching, *Vice Pres*
EMP: 30
SQ FT: 6,000
SALES (est): 5.3MM **Privately Held**
WEB: www.kitchengineering.com
SIC: **3599** **3751** Machine shop, jobbing & repair; motorcycles, bicycles & parts

(P-16120)
KLEIN INDUSTRIES INC
Also Called: Production Specialties
2380 Jerrold Ave, San Francisco
(94124-1013)
PHONE..................................415 695-9117
Lloyd Klein, *President*
EMP: 13
SQ FT: 16,000
SALES (est): 1.4MM **Privately Held**
WEB: www.kleinindustries.com
SIC: **3599** Machine shop, jobbing & repair

(P-16121)
KLN PRECISION MACHINING CORP
40725 Encyclopedia Cir, Fremont
(94538-2451)
PHONE..................................510 770-5001
Kiet Nguyen, *President*
Rinado Garofani, *Vice Pres*
EMP: 100
SQ FT: 80,000
SALES (est): 10.3MM **Privately Held**
WEB: www.klncorp.com
SIC: **3599** Machine shop, jobbing & repair

(P-16122)
KNT INC
Also Called: Knt Manufacturing
39760 Eureka Dr, Newark (94560-4808)
PHONE..................................510 651-7163
Keith Ngo, *CEO*
EMP: 150
SQ FT: 50,000
SALES (est): 29.6MM **Privately Held**
WEB: www.knt.com
SIC: **3599** Machine shop, jobbing & repair

(P-16123)
KODIAK PRECISION INC (PA)
444 S 1st St, Richmond (94804-2107)
PHONE..................................510 234-4165
Paul Bacchi, *President*
Neil Divers, *Vice Pres*
Dave Harris, *Vice Pres*
EMP: 18 EST: 1976
SQ FT: 10,000
SALES (est): 3MM **Privately Held**
WEB: www.kodiakprecision.com
SIC: **3599** Machine shop, jobbing & repair

(P-16124)
KRAMARZ ENTERPRISES
1065 Delmas Ave, San Jose (95125-1635)
PHONE..................................408 293-1187
Mike Kramarz, *Owner*
EMP: 10
SQ FT: 1,000
SALES (est): 641.6K **Privately Held**
SIC: **3599** Machine shop, jobbing & repair

(P-16125)
KRISALIS INC
Also Called: Marler Precision
3366 Golden Gate Ct, San Andreas
(95249-9625)
PHONE..................................209 286-1637
Charlie Timmy, *Manager*
EMP: 10
SALES (corp-wide): 2MM **Privately Held**
WEB: www.krisalis.com
SIC: **3599** Custom machinery
PA: Krisalis, Inc.
28216 Industrial Blvd
Hayward CA 94545
510 786-0858

(P-16126)
KRISALIS INC (PA)
Also Called: Krisalis Precision Machining
28216 Industrial Blvd, Hayward
(94545-4432)
PHONE..................................510 786-0858
William L Kannenberg, *CEO*
EMP: 10
SQ FT: 10,000
SALES: 2MM **Privately Held**
WEB: www.krisalis.com
SIC: **3599** Custom machinery

(P-16127)
KSD INC
161 W Lincoln St, Banning (92220-4976)
PHONE..................................951 849-7669
Robert S Anderson, *President*
EMP: 10 EST: 1967
SQ FT: 20,000
SALES (est): 3MM **Privately Held**
WEB: www.ksdinc.net
SIC: **3599** Machine shop, jobbing & repair

(P-16128)
KT ENGINEERING CORPORATION
2016 E Vista Bella Way, Rancho
Dominguez (90220-6109)
PHONE..................................310 537-3818

John Tajirian, *CEO*
Janice Chavez, *Engineer*
EMP: 16
SQ FT: 3,500
SALES (est): 4.8MM **Privately Held**
WEB: www.ktengineering.com
SIC: **3599** **8711** Machine shop, jobbing & repair; aviation &/or aeronautical engineering

(P-16129)
L & M MACHINING CENTER INC
1497 Poinsettia Ave # 156, Vista
(92081-8542)
PHONE..................................760 437-3810
Mike Slavinski, *President*
EMP: 14
SQ FT: 5,400
SALES: 500K **Privately Held**
WEB: www.landmmachining.com
SIC: **3599** Machine shop, jobbing & repair

(P-16130)
L & T PRECISION ENGRG INC
2395 Qume Dr, San Jose (95131-1813)
PHONE..................................408 441-1890
Luc Tran, *President*
My Truong, *General Mgr*
EMP: 40
SALES (est): 8.9MM **Privately Held**
WEB: www.lt-engineering.com
SIC: **3599** **8711** Machine shop, jobbing & repair; consulting engineer

(P-16131)
L J R GRINDING CORP
Also Called: Ljr Blanchard Grinding
445 W 164th St, Gardena (90248-2726)
PHONE..................................310 532-7232
James Garon, *President*
Robert Margolis Jr, *Vice Pres*
EMP: 13
SQ FT: 4,000
SALES (est): 1.9MM **Privately Held**
WEB: www.ljrgrinding.com
SIC: **3599** Machine shop, jobbing & repair

(P-16132)
LA GAUGE CO INC
7440 San Fernando Rd, Sun Valley
(91352-4398)
PHONE..................................818 767-7193
Harbans Bawa, *President*
Ajay Bawa, *Vice Pres*
Juan Calle, *Info Tech Mgr*
EMP: 74
SQ FT: 26,682
SALES (est): 31.8MM **Privately Held**
WEB: www.lagauge.com
SIC: **3599** Machine shop, jobbing & repair

(P-16133)
LANDMARK MFG INC
Also Called: Landmark Motor Cycle ACC
4112 Avenida De La Plata, Oceanside
(92056-6099)
PHONE..................................760 941-6626
Tom Allen, *President*
Pat Allen, *Admin Sec*
EMP: 23
SQ FT: 17,000
SALES (est): 4.3MM **Privately Held**
WEB: www.landmarkmfg.com
SIC: **3599** **3751** Machine shop, jobbing & repair; motorcycle accessories

(P-16134)
LANGE PRECISION INC
1106 E Elm Ave, Fullerton (92831-5024)
PHONE..................................714 870-5420
Gregory R Lange, *President*
Lisa Lange, *CFO*
EMP: 18
SQ FT: 35,000
SALES: 3.8MM **Privately Held**
WEB: www.lantma.org
SIC: **3599** Machine shop, jobbing & repair

(P-16135)
LANGILLS GENERAL MACHINE INC
7850 14th Ave, Sacramento (95826-4302)
PHONE..................................916 452-0167
James Langill Sr, *President*
EMP: 35
SQ FT: 10,000

▲ = Import ▼=Export
◆ =Import/Export

SALES (est): 6.2MM **Privately Held**
WEB: www.langills.com
SIC: **3599** Machine shop, jobbing & repair

(P-16136)
LANSAIR CORPORATION
25228 Anza Dr, Santa Clarita (91355-3496)
PHONE..............................661 294-9503
John Voshell, *President*
Eleanor Voshell, *Vice Pres*
EMP: 14
SQ FT: 15,000
SALES (est): 2.2MM **Privately Held**
SIC: **3599** Machine shop, jobbing & repair

(P-16137)
LARKIN PRECISION MACHINING
Also Called: Precision Cnc Mil & Turning
175 El Pueblo Rd Ste 10, Scotts Valley
(95066-4260)
PHONE..............................831 438-2700
Robert Larkin, *President*
Rob Larkin, *CEO*
Jon Larkin, *CFO*
Jonathon Larkin, *CFO*
Seth Larkin, *Admin Sec*
EMP: 35
SQ FT: 20,000
SALES (est): 6.4MM **Privately Held**
WEB: www.lpmachining.com
SIC: **3599** Amusement park equipment;
machine shop, jobbing & repair

(P-16138)
LASER INDUSTRIES INC
1351 Manhattan Ave, Fullerton
(92831-5216)
PHONE..............................714 532-3271
Robert Karim, *President*
Joseph Butterly, *Corp Secy*
John Krickl, *Vice Pres*
Gary Nadau, *Vice Pres*
EMP: 65
SQ FT: 17,500
SALES (est): 18MM **Privately Held**
WEB: www.laserindustries.com
SIC: **3599** Machine shop, jobbing & repair

(P-16139)
LASERTRON INC
909 Summit Way, Laguna Beach
(92651-3438)
PHONE..............................954 846-8600
Gary Geller, *President*
▲ EMP: 26 EST: 1979
SQ FT: 18,750
SALES (est): 4.3MM **Privately Held**
SIC: **3599** 3769 3444 3429 Machine
shop, jobbing & repair; guided missile &
space vehicle parts & auxiliary equipment; sheet metalwork; manufactured
hardware (general); porcelain electrical
supplies

(P-16140)
LASZLO J LAK
Also Called: L J L Engineering Co
3621 W Moore Ave, Santa Ana
(92704-6834)
PHONE..............................714 850-0141
Laszlo J Lak, *Owner*
Rosa Vaca, *Admin Asst*
EMP: 10
SQ FT: 17,000
SALES (est): 1.2MM **Privately Held**
SIC: **3599** Machine shop, jobbing & repair

(P-16141)
LAURELWOOD INDUSTRIES INC
Also Called: Automation Gt
1939 Palomar Oaks Way B, Carlsbad
(92011-1311)
PHONE..............................760 705-1649
Simon Grant, *President*
EMP: 20
SALES: 3MM **Privately Held**
SIC: **3599** 8734 3545 Custom machinery;
product testing laboratory, safety or per-
formance; precision measuring tools

(P-16142)
LE HUNG TUAN
Also Called: Vinaco Engineering Company
20952 Itasca St, Chatsworth (91311-4915)
PHONE..............................818 700-1008
Hung Le, *Owner*

EMP: 10
SALES: 600K **Privately Held**
SIC: **3599** Machine shop, jobbing & repair

(P-16143)
LEES PRECISION TOOLING
16751 Parkside Ave, Cerritos (90703-1840)
PHONE..............................562 926-1302
Jimmy Yoon, *Owner*
EMP: 19
SQ FT: 10,000
SALES: 3MM **Privately Held**
SIC: **3599** Machine shop, jobbing & repair

(P-16144)
LENZ PRECISION TECHNOLOGY INC
Also Called: Lenz Technology
355 Pioneer Way Ste A, Mountain View
(94041-1542)
PHONE..............................650 966-1784
Eric Lenz, *President*
Valerie Lenz, *Corp Secy*
Shannon Lenz, *Finance Mgr*
EMP: 23
SQ FT: 18,000
SALES (est): 3.7MM **Privately Held**
SIC: **3599** Machine shop, jobbing & repair

(P-16145)
LF INDUSTRIES INC
6352 Corte Del Abeto G, Carlsbad
(92011-1408)
PHONE..............................760 438-5711
Lucenda Oline, *President*
Julian Harton, *Opers Mgr*
EMP: 10
SALES (est): 466.5K **Privately Held**
SIC: **3599** Machine shop, jobbing & repair

(P-16146)
LIBERTY INDUSTRIES
10754 Lower Azusa Rd, El Monte
(91731-1391)
PHONE..............................626 575-3206
William Carter, *President*
EMP: 15 EST: 1966
SQ FT: 9,000
SALES (est): 2MM **Privately Held**
SIC: **3599** Machine shop, jobbing & repair;
machine & other job shop work

(P-16147)
LLOYD E HENNESSEY JR
Also Called: Machinist Cooperative
7200 Alexander St, Gilroy (95020-6907)
PHONE..............................408 842-8437
Lloyd E Hennessey Jr, *Owner*
Bill Horst, *Engineer*
EMP: 45 EST: 1979
SALES (est): 4.2MM **Privately Held**
WEB: www.machinistcoop.com
SIC: **3599** Machine shop, jobbing & repair

(P-16148)
LMM ENTERPRISES
Also Called: Freeway Machine & Welding Shop
1348 E Sunview Dr, Orange (92865-1739)
PHONE..............................714 543-8044
Leslie M Maude, *President*
Bill Barrett, *Principal*
Ronald Cardiel, *Principal*
EMP: 10 EST: 1951
SQ FT: 7,440
SALES (est): 1.3MM **Privately Held**
SIC: **3599** Machine shop, jobbing & repair

(P-16149)
LOGAN SMITH MACHINE CO
4190 Citrus Ave, Rocklin (95677-4000)
PHONE..............................916 632-2692
Logan Smith, *President*
Tim Smith, *Vice Pres*
EMP: 10
SQ FT: 1,200
SALES (est): 1.5MM **Privately Held**
SIC: **3599** Custom machinery; machine
shop, jobbing & repair

(P-16150)
LONG BAR GRINDING INC
13121 Arctic Cir, Santa Fe Springs
(90670-5571)
P.O. Box 3128 (90670-0128)
PHONE..............................562 921-1983

Joseph Kudron, *President*
Kade Kudron, *Finance Mgr*
EMP: 15
SQ FT: 25,000
SALES (est): 2MM **Privately Held**
SIC: **3599** Machine shop, jobbing & repair

(P-16151)
LONG MACHINE INC
27450 Colt Ct, Temecula (92590-3673)
PHONE..............................951 296-0194
Larry Long, *President*
Vicki Long, *Vice Pres*
EMP: 21
SQ FT: 15,000
SALES (est): 3.8MM **Privately Held**
WEB: www.longmachine.com
SIC: **3599** Machine shop, jobbing & repair

(P-16152)
LOWERS WLDG & FABRICATION INC
Also Called: Lowers Industrial Supply
10847 Painter Ave, Santa Fe Springs
(90670-4526)
P.O. Box 2985 (90670-0985)
PHONE..............................562 946-4521
Dawn Davis, *President*
Nora Lowers, *Vice Pres*
Sheri Lowers, *Sales Mgr*
EMP: 13
SQ FT: 4,669
SALES (est): 4.1MM **Privately Held**
WEB: www.lowerswelding.com
SIC: **3599** 7692 5085 5719 Machine
shop, jobbing & repair; welding repair; in-
dustrial supplies; metalware

(P-16153)
LURAN INC
24927 Avenue Tibbitts K, Valencia
(91355-1268)
PHONE..............................661 257-6303
Terry Decker, *President*
EMP: 18
SQ FT: 20,000
SALES (est): 2.7MM **Privately Held**
WEB: www.luraninc.com
SIC: **3599** Machine shop, jobbing & repair

(P-16154)
LUSK QUALITY MACHINE PRODUCTS
39457 15th St E, Palmdale (93550-3445)
P.O. Box 901030 (93590-1030)
PHONE..............................661 272-0630
Randall J Lusk, *CEO*
Lloyd Lusk, *President*
EMP: 27
SQ FT: 25,000
SALES (est): 5.2MM **Privately Held**
SIC: **3599** 3451 Machine shop, jobbing &
repair; screw machine products

(P-16155)
LYNCO GRINDING COMPANY INC
5950 Clara St, Bell (90201-4798)
P.O. Box 2127 (90202-2127)
PHONE..............................562 927-2631
Wayne Hogarth, *President*
Mary E Hogarth, *Vice Pres*
Jeri Hogarth, *Info Tech Mgr*
EMP: 10
SQ FT: 16,500
SALES (est): 1.7MM **Privately Held**
SIC: **3599** Machine shop, jobbing & repair

(P-16156)
LYRU ENGINEERING INC
965 San Leandro Blvd, San Leandro
(94577-1532)
PHONE..............................510 357-5951
Jeff Snyder, *President*
Greg A Snyder, *Admin Sec*
EMP: 15
SQ FT: 12,500
SALES (est): 1.4MM **Privately Held**
SIC: **3599** Machine shop, jobbing & repair

(P-16157)
M & L PRECISION MACHINING INC (PA)
18665 Madrone Pkwy, Morgan Hill
(95037-2868)
PHONE..............................408 436-3955
Mark Laisure, *President*
Harold Laisure, *Vice Pres*
Karen Laisure, *Vice Pres*
Ross Laisure, *Vice Pres*
▲ EMP: 20
SQ FT: 10,000
SALES (est): 7.2MM **Privately Held**
SIC: **3599** 3451 3444 Machine shop, job-
bing & repair; screw machine products;
sheet metalwork

(P-16158)
M & W ENGINEERING INC
3880 Dividend Dr Ste 100, Shingle Springs
(95682-7229)
PHONE..............................530 676-7185
Frank E Marsh, *President*
Kim Waters, *Treasurer*
EMP: 20
SQ FT: 10,800
SALES (est): 4.2MM **Privately Held**
SIC: **3599** Machine shop, jobbing & repair

(P-16159)
M & W MACHINE CORPORATION
Also Called: Capitol Machine Co
1642 E Edinger Ave Ste A, Santa Ana
(92705-5002)
PHONE..............................714 541-2652
George Nys, *President*
Sandra Nys, *Treasurer*
Jason Nys, *Admin Sec*
EMP: 15
SQ FT: 6,000
SALES (est): 2.5MM **Privately Held**
WEB: www.capitolmachineco.com
SIC: **3599** Machine shop, jobbing & repair

(P-16160)
M E HODGE INC
Also Called: Preco Manufacturing Co
14598 Central Ave, Chino (91710-9508)
PHONE..............................909 393-0675
Martin Munguia, *President*
Magdalene Ortega, *Shareholder*
Maggie Urrutia, *General Mgr*
EMP: 12 EST: 1957
SQ FT: 1,800
SALES (est): 1.2MM **Privately Held**
SIC: **3599** Machine shop, jobbing & repair

(P-16161)
M G DEANZA ACQUISITION INC
Also Called: Deanza Tool & Manufacturing
4010 Garner Rd, Riverside (92501-1006)
PHONE..............................951 683-3080
Mike Greenawalt, *President*
EMP: 10
SQ FT: 9,300
SALES (est): 1.3MM **Privately Held**
SIC: **3599** Machine shop, jobbing & repair

(P-16162)
MACHINE ARTS INCORPORATED
2105 S Hathaway St, Santa Ana
(92705-5238)
PHONE..............................805 965-5344
Fax: 805 564-7889
EMP: 12
SQ FT: 4,000
SALES (est): 1.2MM **Privately Held**
WEB: www.machinearts.com
SIC: **3599**

(P-16163)
MACHINE CRAFT OF SAN DIEGO
9822 Waples St, San Diego (92121-2921)
PHONE..............................858 642-0509
Chinta M Sawh, *President*
Deo Sawh, *Vice Pres*
Indra Starr, *Admin Sec*
EMP: 35
SQ FT: 4,500
SALES (est): 4.5MM **Privately Held**
WEB: www.bingoandmore.com
SIC: **3599** 3812 Machine shop, jobbing &
repair; search & navigation equipment

PRODUCTS & SVCS

(P-16164)
MACHINE EXPRNCE & DESIGN INC
Also Called: Med
2964 Phillip Ave, Clovis (93612-3934)
PHONE......................559 291-7710
David Bobbitt, *President*
Debbie Bobbitt, *Vice Pres*
EMP: 21
SQ FT: 7,100
SALES (est): 3MM **Privately Held**
SIC: 3599 Machine shop, jobbing & repair

(P-16165)
MACHINE PRECISION COMPONENTS
14014 Dinard Ave, Santa Fe Springs (90670-4923)
PHONE......................562 404-0500
Mauro Michel, *CEO*
EMP: 18
SALES (est): 2.6MM **Privately Held**
SIC: 3599 Machine shop, jobbing & repair

(P-16166)
MACHINING SPECIALIST CORP
7125 Fenwick Ln Ste O, Westminster (92683-5239)
PHONE......................714 847-1214
EMP: 20
SQ FT: 8,500
SALES (est): 197.2K **Privately Held**
SIC: 3599

(P-16167)
MADSEN PRODUCTS INCORPORATED
Also Called: Huntington Beach Machining
15321 Connector Ln, Huntington Beach (92649-1119)
PHONE......................714 894-1816
Robert Madsen, *President*
Linda Adkison, *Vice Pres*
Erik Madsen, *Vice Pres*
EMP: 16
SQ FT: 11,345
SALES (est): 3.7MM **Privately Held**
WEB: www.madsenproductions.com
SIC: 3599 5961 Machine shop, jobbing & repair; mail order house

(P-16168)
MAGNA TOOL INC
5594 Market Pl, Cypress (90630-4710)
PHONE......................714 826-2500
Bob Melton, *President*
Cindy Melton, *CFO*
Robert Aguirre, *Opers Mgr*
EMP: 20
SQ FT: 8,500
SALES (est): 3.3MM **Privately Held**
WEB: www.magnatoolinc.com
SIC: 3599 Machine shop, jobbing & repair

(P-16169)
MANTI-MACHINE CO INC
11782 Western Ave Ste 15, Stanton (90680-3466)
PHONE......................714 902-1465
William G Vlieland, *President*
Dawn Harlow, *CFO*
BJ Vlieland, *Corp Secy*
EMP: 12
SQ FT: 3,400
SALES (est): 910.9K **Privately Held**
SIC: 3599 Machine shop, jobbing & repair

(P-16170)
MAR ENGINEERING COMPANY
7350 Greenbush Ave, North Hollywood (91605-4003)
PHONE......................818 765-4805
Monte Markowitz, *CEO*
Samuel Markowitz, *President*
Barbara Markowitz, *Corp Secy*
EMP: 27
SQ FT: 12,000
SALES: 3.2MM **Privately Held**
WEB: www.marengineering.com
SIC: 3599 Machine shop, jobbing & repair

(P-16171)
MARATHON MACHINE INC
7588 Trade St, San Diego (92121-2412)
PHONE......................858 578-8670

Donald R Adcock, *President*
EMP: 11 EST: 1967
SQ FT: 5,000
SALES: 1MM **Privately Held**
SIC: 3599 8711 Machine shop, jobbing & repair; engineering services

(P-16172)
MARLIN MACHINE PRODUCTS
4071 Brewster Way, Riverside (92501-1060)
PHONE......................951 275-0050
Juan Tellez, *Partner*
Candido Tellez, *Partner*
EMP: 10
SQ FT: 5,000
SALES (est): 820K **Privately Held**
SIC: 3599 Machine shop, jobbing & repair

(P-16173)
MARONEY COMPANY
9016 Winnetka Ave, Northridge (91324-3235)
PHONE......................818 882-2722
John C Maroney Sr, *President*
Francine L Maroney, *Senior VP*
EMP: 17
SQ FT: 12,500
SALES (est): 2.9MM **Privately Held**
WEB: www.maroneycompany.com
SIC: 3599 Machine shop, jobbing & repair

(P-16174)
MARTIN-CHANDLER INC
122 E Alondra Blvd, Gardena (90248-2883)
PHONE......................323 321-5119
Paul Fihn, *CEO*
Hans Haag, *Treasurer*
EMP: 11 EST: 1951
SQ FT: 5,000
SALES (est): 1.1MM **Privately Held**
SIC: 3599 Machine shop, jobbing & repair

(P-16175)
MARTINEK MANUFACTURING
42650 Osgood Rd, Fremont (94539-5603)
PHONE......................510 438-0357
Mark Martinek, *Partner*
Charles Martinek, *Partner*
Mardell Martinek, *Partner*
EMP: 25
SQ FT: 40,000
SALES (est): 2.4MM **Privately Held**
WEB: www.martinek.com
SIC: 3599 Machine shop, jobbing & repair

(P-16176)
MARTINEZ AND TUREK INC
Also Called: Martinez & Turek
300 S Cedar Ave, Rialto (92376-9100)
PHONE......................909 820-6800
Larry Tribe, *President*
Donald A Turek, *CFO*
Thomas J Martinez, *Vice Pres*
John Romero, *Vice Pres*
Tony Elizondo, *Engineer*
EMP: 120 EST: 1980
SQ FT: 139,000
SALES (est): 32.1MM **Privately Held**
WEB: www.martinezandturek.com
SIC: 3599 Machine shop, jobbing & repair

(P-16177)
MARX DIGITAL MFG INC (PA)
Also Called: Marx Digital Cnc Machine Shop
3551 Victor St, Santa Clara (95054-2321)
PHONE......................408 748-1783
Marek Smiech, *President*
Krzysztof Juszczynski, *Treasurer*
Shane Johnson, *General Mgr*
EMP: 30
SALES (est): 9.4MM **Privately Held**
SIC: 3599 3639 3829 Machine shop, jobbing & repair; sewing machines & attachments, domestic; drafting instruments & machines: t-square, template, etc.

(P-16178)
MASTER PRECISION MACHINING
2199 Ronald St, Santa Clara (95050-2883)
PHONE......................408 727-0185
Richard Rossi, *President*
Robert Paolinetti, *Corp Secy*
William Regnani, *Vice Pres*

Mary Chavez, *Finance Mgr*
EMP: 30
SQ FT: 10,000
SALES (est): 4.8MM **Privately Held**
WEB: www.master-precision.com
SIC: 3599 Machine shop, jobbing & repair

(P-16179)
MAUL MFG INC (PA)
3041 S Shannon St, Santa Ana (92704-6320)
PHONE......................714 641-0727
Tony Johnson, *President*
Lori Deorio, *Admin Sec*
EMP: 28
SQ FT: 10,080
SALES (est): 4.3MM **Privately Held**
SIC: 3599 3491 3492 Machine shop, jobbing & repair; solenoid valves; control valves, aircraft: hydraulic & pneumatic

(P-16180)
MAX PRECISION MACHINE INC
2467 Autumnvale Dr, San Jose (95131-1802)
PHONE......................408 956-8986
Kevin Nguyen, *President*
Alvin Nguyen, *Treasurer*
Donovan Son, *Vice Pres*
Cuong Nguyen, *Admin Sec*
EMP: 10
SALES (est): 628.5K **Privately Held**
SIC: 3599 Machine shop, jobbing & repair

(P-16181)
MC CAIN & MC CAIN INC
Also Called: B&G Machine Shop
3801 Gilmore Ave, Bakersfield (93308-6211)
PHONE......................661 322-7764
Jim McCain, *President*
Gary McCain, *Vice Pres*
Yvonne Jennings, *Office Mgr*
EMP: 15 EST: 1951
SQ FT: 10,000
SALES (est): 2.4MM **Privately Held**
WEB: www.hobble-clamp.com
SIC: 3599 Machine shop, jobbing & repair

(P-16182)
MCAERO LLC
Also Called: McCullough Aero Company
12711 Imperial Hwy, Santa Fe Springs (90670-4711)
PHONE......................310 787-9911
Peter Lake, *CEO*
EMP: 10
SALES (est): 1.4MM **Privately Held**
SIC: 3599 3429 Machine shop, jobbing & repair; manufactured hardware (general)

(P-16183)
MCCOPPIN ENTERPRISES
Also Called: Accurate Manufacturing Company
6641 San Fernando Rd, Glendale (91201-1702)
PHONE......................818 240-4840
Richard J Mc Coppin, *President*
Carol Park, *Shareholder*
John Gagliardi, *Vice Pres*
Robert R Gagliardi, *Vice Pres*
EMP: 22
SQ FT: 25,000
SALES: 3MM **Privately Held**
WEB: www.acc-mfg.com
SIC: 3599 3544 3441 Machine shop, jobbing & repair; dies & die holders for metal cutting, forming, die casting; industrial molds; fabricated structural metal

(P-16184)
MCKENZIE MACHINING INC
481 Perry Ct, Santa Clara (95054-2624)
PHONE......................408 748-8885
Scott McKenzie, *Owner*
EMP: 14
SQ FT: 10,400
SALES (est): 2.6MM **Privately Held**
SIC: 3599 Machine shop, jobbing & repair

(P-16185)
MD ENGINEERING INC
1550 Consumer Cir, Corona (92880-1725)
PHONE......................951 736-5390
Mike Morgan, *President*

Ryan Cortes, *Vice Pres*
Mike McPeak, *Technician*
Danny Vu, *QC Mgr*
EMP: 37
SQ FT: 16,000
SALES (est): 3.9MM **Privately Held**
SIC: 3599 Machine shop, jobbing & repair

(P-16186)
MECHANICAL AND MCH REPR SVCS
10584 Silicon Ave, Montclair (91763-4617)
PHONE......................909 625-8705
Jose Farsaci, *President*
Hector Pinasco, *Vice Pres*
EMP: 10
SQ FT: 15,000
SALES: 2MM **Privately Held**
WEB: www.mechandmachinerepair.com
SIC: 3599 Machine shop, jobbing & repair

(P-16187)
MECHANIZED ENTERPRISES INC
1140 N Kraemer Blvd Ste M, Anaheim (92806-1919)
PHONE......................714 630-5512
George Hansel, *President*
Don Plum, *Mktg Dir*
EMP: 13
SQ FT: 12,000
SALES (est): 2.1MM **Privately Held**
WEB: www.mechanizedenterprises.com
SIC: 3599 Machine shop, jobbing & repair

(P-16188)
MECOPTRON INC
3115 Osgood Ct, Fremont (94539-5652)
PHONE......................510 226-9966
Andy Law, *President*
Christine Law, *Human Res Mgr*
EMP: 45
SQ FT: 12,000
SALES (est): 5.8MM **Privately Held**
WEB: www.mecoptron.com
SIC: 3599 3444 Machine shop, jobbing & repair; sheet metalwork

(P-16189)
MECPRO INC
980 George St, Santa Clara (95054-2705)
PHONE......................408 727-9757
Son Ho, *President*
Kelly Ho, *Vice Pres*
Colin Wintrup, *Vice Pres*
EMP: 26
SQ FT: 15,000
SALES (est): 5.1MM **Privately Held**
WEB: www.mecpro.com
SIC: 3599 Machine shop, jobbing & repair

(P-16190)
MEDLIN AND SON ENGINEERING SVC
Also Called: Medlin & Sons
12484 Whittier Blvd, Whittier (90602-1017)
PHONE......................562 464-5889
George W Medlin II, *CEO*
Susan Medlin, *Admin Sec*
EMP: 45 EST: 1959
SQ FT: 26,000
SALES: 3MM **Privately Held**
SIC: 3599 Machine shop, jobbing & repair

(P-16191)
MEERKAT INC
434 S Yucca Ave, Rialto (92376-6300)
PHONE......................909 877-0093
Ronald J Vangrouw, *President*
Dave Vangrouw, *Treasurer*
Cindy Vangrouw, *Admin Sec*
EMP: 14
SQ FT: 11,000
SALES (est): 2.1MM **Privately Held**
SIC: 3599 Machine shop, jobbing & repair

(P-16192)
MEGA PRECISION O RINGS INC
23206 Normandie Ave Ste 5, Torrance (90502-2614)
PHONE......................310 530-1166
Gerardo Sandoval, *President*
EMP: 14
SQ FT: 4,500

▲ = Import ▼=Export
◆ =Import/Export

SALES (est): 1.7MM **Privately Held**
WEB: www.megaprecisiono-rings.com
SIC: **3599** 3089 Machine shop, jobbing &
repair; plastic processing

(P-16193)
MELFRED BORZALL INC
12115 Shoemaker Ave, Santa Fe Springs
(90670-4719)
PHONE..................................562 946-7524
Fax: 562 946-2014
EMP: 12
SQ FT: 7,800
SALES (est): 920K **Privately Held**
WEB: www.melfredborzall.com
SIC: **3599**

(P-16194)
MELKES MACHINE INC
9928 Hayward Way, South El Monte
(91733-3114)
PHONE..................................626 448-5062
Isabelle Melkesian, *President*
Brent Melkesian, *Vice Pres*
Paul Novacek, *Sales Staff*
EMP: 50
SQ FT: 24,000
SALES (est): 6.3MM **Privately Held**
WEB: www.melkes.com
SIC: **3599** Machine shop, jobbing & repair

(P-16195)
MENCHES TOOL & DIE INC
30995 San Benito St, Hayward
(94544-7936)
PHONE..................................650 592-2328
John Menches Jr, *CEO*
Rosa Menches, *Admin Sec*
Joe Brider, *Sales Mgr*
Darla Stevenson, *Sales Staff*
Uwe Brinkmann, *Manager*
EMP: 20
SQ FT: 22,400
SALES (est): 3.3MM **Privately Held**
WEB: www.menches.com
SIC: **3599** Machine shop, jobbing & repair

(P-16196)
MERCURY ENGINEERING CORP
5630 Imperial Hwy, South Gate
(90280-7420)
PHONE..................................562 861-7816
David Barker, *President*
EMP: 13 EST: 1949
SQ FT: 10,000
SALES (est): 1.8MM **Privately Held**
SIC: **3599** Machine shop, jobbing & repair

(P-16197)
METALORE INC
750 S Douglas St, El Segundo
(90245-4901)
PHONE..................................310 643-0360
Kenneth Hill, *President*
Dennis Reed, *Mfg Mgr*
▲ EMP: 30
SALES (est): 5.1MM **Privately Held**
WEB: www.metalore.com
SIC: **3599** Machine shop, jobbing & repair

(P-16198)
MEZIERE ENTERPRISES INC
220 S Hale Ave Ste A, Escondido
(92029-1719)
PHONE..................................800 208-1755
Michael Meziere, *President*
Don Meziere, *Vice Pres*
Marie Meziere, *Office Mgr*
Dave Meziere, *Admin Sec*
Joel Meziere, *Admin Asst*
▲ EMP: 30
SQ FT: 15,000
SALES (est): 6.8MM **Privately Held**
WEB: www.meziere.com
SIC: **3599** Machine shop, jobbing & repair

(P-16199)
MICRON MACHINE COMPANY
12530 Stowe Dr, Poway (92064-6804)
PHONE..................................858 486-5900
Mark Conley, *CEO*
Donna Conley, *Vice Pres*
Robert Ramos, *QC Mgr*
EMP: 22
SQ FT: 16,000

SALES (est): 4.3MM **Privately Held**
SIC: **3599** 8731 3462 3369 Machine
shop, jobbing & repair; commercial physical research; iron & steel forgings; nonferrous foundries

(P-16200)
MID VALLEY MFG INC
2039 W Superior Ave, Caruthers
(93609-9531)
P.O. Box 295 (93609-0295)
PHONE..................................559 864-9441
Robert Smith, *President*
Rex Tyler, *Vice Pres*
EMP: 15
SQ FT: 7,200
SALES (est): 1.2MM **Privately Held**
WEB: www.midvalleymanufacturing.com
SIC: **3599** Machine shop, jobbing & repair

(P-16201)
MIKE KENNEY TOOL INC
Also Called: Mkt Innovations
2900 Saturn St Ste A, Brea (92821-1702)
PHONE..................................714 577-9262
Mike Kenney, *President*
Julie Kenney, *Admin Sec*
▲ EMP: 37
SALES (est): 6.2MM **Privately Held**
WEB: www.cooljet.com
SIC: **3599** Machine shop, jobbing & repair

(P-16202)
MIKES MICRO PARTS INC
1901 Potrero Ave, South El Monte
(91733-3024)
PHONE..................................626 443-0675
Robert Oganesian, *CEO*
Mike Oganesian, *President*
Henry Oganesian, *Vice Pres*
Araxi Oganesian, *Admin Sec*
EMP: 35 EST: 1964
SQ FT: 10,000
SALES (est): 5MM **Privately Held**
SIC: **3599** Machine shop, jobbing & repair

(P-16203)
MILCO WIRE EDM INC
Also Called: Milco Waterjet
15221 Connector Ln, Huntington Beach
(92649-1117)
PHONE..................................714 373-0098
Steven R Miller, *President*
John Fuhr, *QC Mgr*
Chadd Miller, *Manager*
EMP: 17
SQ FT: 14,000
SALES: 2.2MM **Privately Held**
WEB: www.milcowireedm.com
SIC: **3599** 3541 Electrical discharge ma-
chining (EDM); machine tools, metal cut-
ting type

(P-16204)
MILITARY AIRCRAFT PARTS
11265 Sunrise Gold Cir G, Rancho Cordova
(95742-6560)
PHONE..................................916 635-8010
Robert E Marin, *President*
Robert Marin, *President*
EMP: 22
SALES (corp-wide): 5.4MM **Privately
Held**
SIC: **3599** Air intake filters, internal com-
bustion engine, except auto
PA: Military Aircraft Parts
116 Oxburough Dr
Folsom CA 95630
916 635-8010

(P-16205)
MILITARY AIRCRAFT PARTS (PA)
116 Oxburough Dr, Folsom (95630-3293)
PHONE..................................916 635-8010
Robert E Marin, *President*
EMP: 28
SALES (est): 5.4MM **Privately Held**
SIC: **3599** Machine shop, jobbing & repair

(P-16206)
MILLER MACHINE INC
4055 Calle Platino # 200, Oceanside
(92056-5861)
PHONE..................................814 723-5700
Fax: 760 723-4202
EMP: 25 EST: 1981

SQ FT: 11,000
SALES (est): 4MM **Privately Held**
WEB: www.millermachine.net
SIC: **3599**

(P-16207)
MILLER MACHINE WORKS LLC
Also Called: Miller Cnc
1905 Broadway, San Diego (92102-1824)
PHONE..................................619 501-9866
Todd Cuffaro, *CEO*
Dave Miller, *President*
Gregory Hansen, *CFO*
EMP: 17
SQ FT: 7,500
SALES (est): 3.6MM **Privately Held**
WEB: www.millermachineworks.net
SIC: **3599** Machine shop, jobbing & repair

(P-16208)
MILLIPART INC (PA)
412 W Carter Dr, Glendora (91740-5998)
PHONE..................................626 963-4101
Scot Jamison, *President*
EMP: 18 EST: 1954
SQ FT: 4,000
SALES (est): 4.1MM **Privately Held**
WEB: www.millipart.com
SIC: **3599** Machine shop, jobbing & repair

(P-16209)
MILLWORX PRCSION MACHINING INC
506 Malloy Ct, Corona (92880-2045)
PHONE..................................951 371-2683
Stacy Wilson, *President*
Terry Windust, *Vice Pres*
Carson Miller, *General Mgr*
Sharon M Daniel, *Administration*
EMP: 22
SQ FT: 3,500
SALES (est): 5.4MM **Privately Held**
WEB: www.millworxprecision.com
SIC: **3599** Machine shop, jobbing & repair

(P-16210)
MILO MACHINING INC
Also Called: Milo Engineering
2675 Skypark Dr Ste 304, Torrance
(90505-5330)
PHONE..................................310 530-0925
Herman Hofer, *President*
Raymond Hofer, *Vice Pres*
EMP: 10
SQ FT: 5,000
SALES (est): 1.7MM **Privately Held**
WEB: www.miloeng.com
SIC: **3599** Machine shop, jobbing & repair

(P-16211)
MINI-FLEX CORPORATION
2472 Eastman Ave Ste 29, Ventura
(93003-5774)
PHONE..................................805 644-1474
Paul Jorgensen, *President*
◆ EMP: 13
SQ FT: 8,500
SALES (est): 2.1MM **Privately Held**
WEB: www.mini-flex.com
SIC: **3599** Bellows, industrial: metal

(P-16212)
MINIATURE PRECISION INC
4488 Mountain Lakes Blvd, Redding
(96003-1445)
PHONE..................................530 244-4131
Don Anderson, *President*
Diana Anderson, *Vice Pres*
Mike Twoney, *QC Mgr*
EMP: 13
SQ FT: 8,000
SALES (est): 1.1MM **Privately Held**
WEB: www.mpcomponents.com
SIC: **3599** Machine shop, jobbing & repair

(P-16213)
MISSION TOOL AND MFG CO INC
3440 Arden Rd, Hayward (94545-3906)
PHONE..................................510 782-8383
Gary W Smith, *President*
Carol Smith, *Vice Pres*
Sheri Albright, *General Mgr*
Tom Gazsi, *Project Mgr*
Robert Diaz, *Technology*
▲ EMP: 40 EST: 1968

SQ FT: 28,000
SALES (est): 9.1MM **Privately Held**
WEB: www.missiontool.com
SIC: **3599** 3465 3469 3544 Machine &
other job shop work; automotive stampings; metal stampings; special dies, tools,
jigs & fixtures

(P-16214)
MITCHELL-DUCKETT CORPORATION
Also Called: M & M Machine & Tool
10074 Streeter Rd Ste B, Auburn
(95602-8559)
PHONE..................................530 268-2112
Chris Duckett, *President*
Ralph Kendrick, *Treasurer*
Janis Duckett, *Vice Pres*
Jacqueline Traynor, *General Mgr*
EMP: 10
SQ FT: 4,800
SALES (est): 1.5MM **Privately Held**
SIC: **3599** Machine shop, jobbing & repair

(P-16215)
MITCO INDUSTRIES INC (PA)
2235 S Vista Ave, Bloomington
(92316-2921)
PHONE..................................909 877-0800
Larry Mitchell, *President*
Sammy Mitchell, *Corp Secy*
EMP: 34
SQ FT: 11,000
SALES (est): 4.9MM **Privately Held**
WEB: www.mitcoind.com
SIC: **3599** 3533 Machine shop, jobbing &
repair; drilling tools for gas, oil or water
wells

(P-16216)
MKT INNOVATIONS
Also Called: Cooljet Systems
2900 Saturn St Ste A, Brea (92821-1702)
PHONE..................................714 524-7668
Mike Kenney, *CEO*
Kathy Jackson, *CFO*
▲ EMP: 68
SALES (est): 11MM **Privately Held**
WEB: www.mkti.com
SIC: **3599** 3523 Machine shop, jobbing &
repair; farm machinery & equipment

(P-16217)
MODERN ENGINE INC
701 Sonora Ave, Glendale (91201-2431)
PHONE..................................818 409-9494
Vachagan Aslanian, *President*
Armond Aslanian, *Treasurer*
Razmik Aslanian, *Vice Pres*
Nora Aslanian, *Admin Sec*
▲ EMP: 43
SQ FT: 26,000
SALES (est): 6.5MM **Privately Held**
WEB: www.modernengine.com
SIC: **3599** 7539 Machine shop, jobbing &
repair; machine shop, automotive

(P-16218)
MODERN MANUFACTURING INC
4110 E La Palma Ave, Anaheim
(92807-1814)
PHONE..................................714 254-0156
▲ EMP: 26 EST: 2002
SQ FT: 20,000
SALES (est): 2.5MM **Privately Held**
WEB: www.modernmfginc.com
SIC: **3599**

(P-16219)
MOLD VISION INC
18351 Pasadena St, Lake Elsinore
(92530-2766)
PHONE..................................951 245-8020
Greg Yocum, *President*
Charles Premananthan, *Vice Pres*
EMP: 17
SALES (est): 2.1MM **Privately Held**
WEB: www.moldvision.net
SIC: **3599** Machine shop, jobbing & repair

(P-16220)
MOMENI ENGINEERING LLC
15662 Commerce Ln, Huntington Beach
(92649-1604)
PHONE..................................714 897-9301
Ahmad Momeni, *Mng Member*

EMP: 28
SQ FT: 14,000
SALES: 4.7MM **Privately Held**
SIC: 3599 3841 Machine shop, jobbing & repair; surgical & medical instruments

(P-16221)
MONO ENGINEERING CORP
20977 Knapp St, Chatsworth (91311-5926)
PHONE..................................818 772-4998
Siamak Morini, *CEO*
Joe Hernandez, *Executive*
Roujebeh Azarahishin, *Controller*
Siegfried Treichel, *Prdtn Mgr*
EMP: 50
SQ FT: 40,000
SALES: 4.5MM **Privately Held**
WEB: www.monoengineering.com
SIC: 3599 3444 8711 Machine shop, jobbing & repair; sheet metalwork; industrial engineers

(P-16222)
MONSON MACHINE INC
1802 Pomona Rd, Corona (92880-1777)
PHONE..................................951 736-6615
Kathy Monson, *President*
EMP: 18
SQ FT: 12,500
SALES: 1.8MM **Privately Held**
WEB: www.monsonmachine.com
SIC: 3599 Machine shop, jobbing & repair

(P-16223)
MONTCLAIR MACHINE SHOP INC
5621 State St, Montclair (91763-6241)
P.O. Box 2009 (91763-0509)
PHONE..................................909 986-2664
Wayne Freeberg, *President*
Thomas Freeberg, *Vice Pres*
David Peterson, *General Mgr*
EMP: 11
SQ FT: 10,000
SALES (est): 948.6K
SALES (corp-wide): 4.5MM **Privately Held**
SIC: 3599 Machine shop, jobbing & repair
PA: Montclair Bronze Inc.,
    5621 State St
    Montclair CA 91763
    909 986-2664

(P-16224)
MONTEREY MACHINE PRODUCTS
1504 W Industrial Park St, Covina (91722-3413)
PHONE..................................626 967-2242
David Griffits, *Owner*
Dave Griffith, *Partner*
EMP: 14 EST: 1953
SQ FT: 2,400
SALES (est): 2MM **Privately Held**
WEB: www.montereymachine.com
SIC: 3599 Machine shop, jobbing & repair

(P-16225)
MOONEY INDUSTRIES
8744 Remmet Ave, Canoga Park (91304-1588)
PHONE..................................818 998-0199
Alan Mooney, *CFO*
Brian Mooney, *President*
Joyce Mooney, *Vice Pres*
Al Mooney, *Train & Dev Mgr*
EMP: 15 EST: 1962
SQ FT: 9,000
SALES: 1.5MM **Privately Held**
SIC: 3599 Machine shop, jobbing & repair

(P-16226)
MORGAN HILL PRECISION INC
15500 Concord Cir Ste 100, Morgan Hill (95037-7109)
PHONE..................................408 778-7895
Michelle Rasmussen, *CEO*
George King, *President*
Janet King, *Vice Pres*
EMP: 12
SQ FT: 7,336
SALES: 1.7MM **Privately Held**
WEB: www.morganhillprecision.com
SIC: 3599 Machine shop, jobbing & repair

(P-16227)
MORGAN PRODUCTS INC
28103 Avenue Stanford, Santa Clarita (91355-1106)
PHONE..................................661 257-3022
Morris E Morgan, *President*
Mary O Morgan, *CFO*
William A Morgan, *Vice Pres*
▲ EMP: 18 EST: 1966
SQ FT: 3,250
SALES: 2MM **Privately Held**
WEB: www.morganproducts.com
SIC: 3599 3561 Machine shop, jobbing & repair; pumps & pumping equipment

(P-16228)
MOTEK INDUSTRIES
14434 Joanbridge St, Baldwin Park (91706-1746)
PHONE..................................626 960-6005
Julio Enriquez, *Owner*
EMP: 13
SQ FT: 5,000
SALES (est): 1.4MM **Privately Held**
SIC: 3599 Machine shop, jobbing & repair

(P-16229)
MOTIV DESIGN GROUP INC
430 Perrymont Ave, San Jose (95125-1444)
PHONE..................................408 441-0611
Lino R Covarrubias, *CEO*
Carlos Barrientos, *Vice Pres*
EMP: 16
SQ FT: 2,400
SALES (est): 4.7MM **Privately Held**
SIC: 3599 Custom machinery; machine & other job shop work

(P-16230)
MP TOOL INC
28110 Avenue Stanford E, Valencia (91355-1161)
PHONE..................................661 294-7711
Ed Pimentel, *President*
Dave Miller, *Vice Pres*
Sandy Pimentel, *Office Mgr*
EMP: 12
SQ FT: 26,000
SALES: 1.7MM **Privately Held**
SIC: 3599 7699 Grinding castings for the trade; industrial tool grinding

(P-16231)
MR GEARS INC
428 Stanford Ave, Redwood City (94063-3423)
PHONE..................................650 364-7793
Jack Hybl, *President*
EMP: 11
SQ FT: 4,100
SALES (est): 640K **Privately Held**
WEB: www.mrgears.com
SIC: 3599 3751 3462 3714 Machine shop, jobbing & repair; gears, motorcycle & bicycle; gears, forged steel; gears, motor vehicle

(P-16232)
MTM INDUSTRIAL INC
3230 Production Ave Ste B, Oceanside (92058-1305)
PHONE..................................760 967-1346
Mark Meddock, *President*
EMP: 14
SQ FT: 7,000
SALES (est): 2.9MM **Privately Held**
WEB: www.oilguard.com
SIC: 3599 Machine shop, jobbing & repair

(P-16233)
MUFICH ENGINEERING INC
341 W Blueridge Ave, Orange (92865-4201)
PHONE..................................714 283-0599
Mike Mufich, *President*
EMP: 20
SQ FT: 2,000
SALES (est): 2MM **Privately Held**
SIC: 3599 3444 Machine shop, jobbing & repair; sheet metalwork

(P-16234)
MUTH MACHINE WORKS (HQ)
8042 Katella Ave, Stanton (90680-3207)
PHONE..................................714 527-2239

Richard Muth, *President*
Peter G Muth, *Treasurer*
Lynn Muth, *Vice Pres*
Dwayne Gleason, *VP Opers*
▲ EMP: 20
SQ FT: 2,000
SALES (est): 6.8MM
SALES (corp-wide): 33.4MM **Privately Held**
WEB: www.orco.com
SIC: 3599 Machine shop, jobbing & repair
PA: Orco Block & Hardscape
    11100 Beach Blvd
    Stanton CA 90680
    714 527-2239

(P-16235)
MY MACHINE INC
5140 Commerce Dr, Baldwin Park (91706-1450)
PHONE..................................626 214-9223
Jamie Scott Young, *CEO*
Pedro Ignico Martinez, *Vice Pres*
EMP: 15
SALES (est): 3.2MM **Privately Held**
SIC: 3599 Machine shop, jobbing & repair

(P-16236)
N C INDUSTRIES
42147 Roick Dr, Temecula (92590-3695)
PHONE..................................951 296-9603
Richard Waltz, *Owner*
EMP: 10
SALES (est): 660K **Privately Held**
WEB: www.ncindustries.com
SIC: 3599 5112 Machine shop, jobbing & repair; stationery & office supplies

(P-16237)
NC DYNAMICS LLC
3401 E 69th St, Long Beach (90805-1872)
PHONE..................................562 634-7392
Phillip Friedman, *Principal*
EMP: 150
SALES (est): 8MM
SALES (corp-wide): 118.6MM **Privately Held**
SIC: 3599 Machine shop, jobbing & repair
PA: Harlow Aerostructures Llc
    1501 S Mclean Blvd
    Wichita KS 67213
    316 265-5268

(P-16238)
NC ENGINEERING INC
13439 S Budlong Ave, Gardena (90247-1995)
PHONE..................................310 532-4810
Patrick Mason, *President*
Gerald Fazis, *Vice Pres*
▲ EMP: 11
SQ FT: 8,000
SALES (est): 1.8MM **Privately Held**
SIC: 3599 Machine shop, jobbing & repair

(P-16239)
NELGO INDUSTRIES INC
Also Called: Nelgo Manufacturing
3265 Production Ave Ste A, Oceanside (92058-1361)
PHONE..................................760 433-6434
Peter Edward Goethel, *CEO*
EMP: 32 EST: 1966
SQ FT: 5,000
SALES (est): 7.1MM **Privately Held**
WEB: www.nelgo.com
SIC: 3599 Machine shop, jobbing & repair

(P-16240)
NELSON ENGINEERING LLC
11600 Monarch St, Garden Grove (92841-1817)
PHONE..................................714 893-7999
Ed McKenna,
▲ EMP: 48
SQ FT: 17,600
SALES (est): 6MM **Privately Held**
WEB: www.nel-eng.com
SIC: 3599 Machine shop, jobbing & repair

(P-16241)
NELSON THREAD GRINDING INC
8205 Lankershim Blvd, North Hollywood (91605-1614)
PHONE..................................818 768-2578

Raymond Nelson, *President*
Phyllis Nelson, *CEO*
Brian Nelson, *Manager*
▲ EMP: 10
SQ FT: 5,000
SALES (est): 1.4MM **Privately Held**
WEB: www.nelsonthread.com
SIC: 3599 Machine shop, jobbing & repair

(P-16242)
NEW WORLD MACHINING INC
2799 Aiello Dr, San Jose (95111-2156)
PHONE..................................408 227-3810
Marvin Elsten, *President*
Dianne Elsten, *Vice Pres*
Norma Gonzalez, *Purchasing*
EMP: 25 EST: 1973
SQ FT: 30,000
SALES (est): 3.9MM **Privately Held**
WEB: www.newworldmachining.com
SIC: 3599 5084 Machine shop, jobbing & repair; industrial machinery & equipment

(P-16243)
NEXT INTENT INC
865 Via Esteban, San Luis Obispo (93401-7178)
PHONE..................................805 781-6755
Rodney Babcock, *CEO*
Catherine B Babcock, *CFO*
EMP: 30
SQ FT: 8,500
SALES (est): 6.7MM **Privately Held**
WEB: www.nextintent.com
SIC: 3599 Machine shop, jobbing & repair

(P-16244)
NICHOLS MANUFACTURING INC
913 Hanson Ct, Milpitas (95035-3166)
PHONE..................................408 945-0911
Lettie Nichols, *President*
John Nichols, *Vice Pres*
Chris Napolitano, *Prgrmr*
Kevin Mar, *Senior Engr*
EMP: 14
SQ FT: 11,000
SALES (est): 2.6MM **Privately Held**
WEB: www.nicholsmfg.com
SIC: 3599 Machine shop, jobbing & repair

(P-16245)
NICKSONS MACHINE SHOP INC
914 W Betteravia Rd, Santa Maria (93455-1194)
P.O. Box 5200 (93456-5200)
PHONE..................................805 925-2525
Dennis William Leal, *CEO*
Barbara Leal, *Corp Secy*
Gary Winters, *Vice Pres*
EMP: 24
SQ FT: 23,800
SALES (est): 4MM **Privately Held**
WEB: www.nicksons.com
SIC: 3599 Machine shop, jobbing & repair

(P-16246)
NIEDWICK CORPORATION
Also Called: Niedwick Machine Co
967 N Eckhoff St, Orange (92867-5432)
P.O. Box 63851, Irvine (92602-6132)
PHONE..................................714 771-9999
Theodore R Niedwick, *President*
EMP: 45
SQ FT: 8,200
SALES (est): 7.5MM **Privately Held**
WEB: www.niedwickmachine.com
SIC: 3599 Machine shop, jobbing & repair

(P-16247)
NM MACHINING INC
175 Lewis Rd Ste 25, San Jose (95111-2175)
PHONE..................................408 972-8978
Mike Tran, *President*
Sylvia MAI, *Manager*
EMP: 27
SQ FT: 8,272
SALES (est): 5.1MM **Privately Held**
WEB: www.nmmachining.com
SIC: 3599 Machine shop, jobbing & repair

(P-16248)
NOROTOS INC
201 E Alton Ave, Santa Ana (92707-4416)
PHONE..................................714 662-3113

▲ = Import ▼=Export
◆ =Import/Export

Ronald Soto, *President*
John Soto, *Vice Pres*
Linda Soto, *Human Res Mgr*
Rob Prendergast, *Mfg Staff*
▲ **EMP:** 116
SQ FT: 12,000
SALES (est): 16.2MM **Privately Held**
WEB: www.norotos.com
SIC: 3599 3842 Machine shop, jobbing & repair; surgical appliances & supplies

(P-16249)
NOTRON MANUFACTURING INC
801 Milford St, Glendale (91203-1520)
PHONE..............................818 247-7739
Theone Notron, *President*
James Notron, *Treasurer*
David Notron Jr, *Vice Pres*
David Norton, *Office Mgr*
▲ **EMP:** 15
SQ FT: 13,000
SALES (est): 1.8MM **Privately Held**
SIC: 3599 5084 Machine & other job shop work; pneumatic tools & equipment

(P-16250)
NQ ENGINEERING INC
1852 W 11th St Pmb 532, Tracy (95376-3736)
PHONE..............................209 836-3255
Noel C Quigg, *President*
Loretta Quigg, *Admin Sec*
EMP: 10
SQ FT: 4,000
SALES (est): 900K **Privately Held**
WEB: www.inrich.com
SIC: 3599 Machine shop, jobbing & repair

(P-16251)
NSD INDUSTRIES INC
5027 Gayhurst Ave, Baldwin Park (91706-1813)
PHONE..............................626 813-2001
Ed Siapno, *President*
Chona Siapno, *Vice Pres*
EMP: 14
SQ FT: 2,496
SALES (est): 1.6MM **Privately Held**
SIC: 3599 Machine shop, jobbing & repair

(P-16252)
NTL PRECISION MACHINING INC
1355 Vander Way, San Jose (95112-2809)
PHONE..............................408 298-6650
Henry Ngo, *CEO*
Thao Ngo, *Admin Sec*
EMP: 15
SQ FT: 7,500
SALES (est): 2.5MM **Privately Held**
WEB: www.ntlprecision.com
SIC: 3599 Machine shop, jobbing & repair

(P-16253)
NU ENGINEERING
12121 Bartlett St, Garden Grove (92845-1525)
PHONE..............................714 894-1206
Robert Kozlowski, *Owner*
EMP: 26
SQ FT: 4,500
SALES (est): 1.3MM **Privately Held**
SIC: 3599 8742 Machine shop, jobbing & repair; automation & robotics consultant

(P-16254)
O-S INC
Also Called: All Weld Mch & Fabrication Co
541 W Capitol Expy Ste 10, San Jose (95136-3962)
PHONE..............................408 946-5890
Kim Green, *President*
Ann Owen, *Corp Secy*
John Heywood, *Plant Mgr*
EMP: 13
SQ FT: 12,000
SALES (est): 2.4MM **Privately Held**
WEB: www.allweld.com
SIC: 3599 7692 3444 Machine shop, jobbing & repair; welding repair; sheet metal specialties, not stamped

(P-16255)
ODONNELL MANUFACTURING INC
14811 Via Defrancesco Ave, Riverside (92508-9005)
P.O. Box 6245, Norco (92860-8041)
PHONE..............................562 944-9671
Steve O'Donnell, *President*
▲ **EMP:** 12
SQ FT: 10,000
SALES (est): 1.5MM **Privately Held**
WEB: www.odonnellracing.com
SIC: 3599 Machine shop, jobbing & repair

(P-16256)
OFFERMAN INDUSTRIES
43154 Via Dos Picos Ste F, Temecula (92590-3478)
P.O. Box 2000 (92593-2000)
PHONE..............................951 676-5016
Fax: 951 676-5031
EMP: 10
SQ FT: 2,000
SALES (est): 1.4MM **Privately Held**
SIC: 3599 3769

(P-16257)
OMEGA INTERCONNECT INC
1207 Brooks St, Ontario (91762-3609)
PHONE..............................909 986-1933
Eric Vasquez, *President*
EMP: 10
SALES (est): 1.2MM **Privately Held**
SIC: 3599 Machine shop, jobbing & repair

(P-16258)
OMEGA PRECISION
13040 Telegraph Rd, Santa Fe Springs (90670-4078)
PHONE..............................562 946-2491
Richard Venegas, *CEO*
Joseph M Venegas, *President*
Steve Venegas, *COO*
Richard M Venegas, *Corp Secy*
Chris Klosowski, *Human Resources*
EMP: 25 **EST:** 1965
SQ FT: 16,332
SALES (est): 4.8MM **Privately Held**
WEB: www.omegaprecision.com
SIC: 3599 Machine shop, jobbing & repair

(P-16259)
OMEGA PRECISION MACHINE
Also Called: Opmp
320 W Larch Rd Ste 15, Tracy (95304-1646)
PHONE..............................209 833-6502
Mark Orner, *President*
EMP: 12
SQ FT: 5,000
SALES (est): 2.1MM **Privately Held**
WEB: www.omegaprecisionmachine.com
SIC: 3599 Machine shop, jobbing & repair

(P-16260)
OMICRON ENGINEERING INC
1513 Plaza Del Amo, Torrance (90501-4935)
PHONE..............................310 328-4017
Alfons Ribitsch, *President*
Louis Ribitsch, *Vice Pres*
Aloisia Ribitsch, *Agent*
EMP: 10 **EST:** 1970
SQ FT: 12,500
SALES (est): 1.7MM **Privately Held**
WEB: www.omicron-eng.com
SIC: 3599 Machine shop, jobbing & repair

(P-16261)
OMNITEC PRECISION MFG INC
435 Queens Ln, San Jose (95112-4309)
PHONE..............................408 437-9056
Eric Thomas Kawano, *President*
EMP: 15
SQ FT: 22,000
SALES (est): 3MM **Privately Held**
SIC: 3599 Machine shop, jobbing & repair

(P-16262)
OPTEL-MATIC INC
11221 Thienes Ave, El Monte (91733-3777)
PHONE..............................626 444-2671
Max Buettiker, *President*
Justina Buettiker, *Vice Pres*

Elizabeth Buettiker, *Admin Sec*
EMP: 13 **EST:** 1966
SQ FT: 10,000
SALES: 900K **Privately Held**
WEB: www.optelmatic.com
SIC: 3599 Machine shop, jobbing & repair

(P-16263)
ORANGE COUNTY SCREW PRODUCTS
2993 E La Palma Ave, Anaheim (92806-2620)
PHONE..............................714 630-7433
Robert Andri, *President*
EMP: 20
SQ FT: 8,000
SALES (est): 2.5MM **Privately Held**
SIC: 3599 3451 Machine shop, jobbing & repair; screw machine products

(P-16264)
OT PRECISION INC
1450 Seareel Ln, San Jose (95131-1580)
PHONE..............................408 435-8818
Tam Dang, *President*
Minh Ly, *Manager*
EMP: 25
SQ FT: 2,000
SALES (est): 4MM **Privately Held**
WEB: www.otprecision.com
SIC: 3599 Machine shop, jobbing & repair

(P-16265)
OVERBECK MACHINE
2620 Mission St, Santa Cruz (95060-5703)
PHONE..............................831 425-5912
Wayne Overbeck, *Owner*
Wayne O Overbeck, *COO*
EMP: 20
SQ FT: 2,700
SALES (est): 1.9MM **Privately Held**
WEB: www.overbeckmachine.com
SIC: 3599 Machine shop, jobbing & repair

(P-16266)
OWENS DESIGN INCORPORATED
47427 Fremont Blvd, Fremont (94538-6504)
PHONE..............................510 659-1800
John Apgar, *President*
Doug Putnam-Pite, *Director*
EMP: 45
SQ FT: 30,000
SALES (est): 13.8MM **Privately Held**
SIC: 3599 Custom machinery

(P-16267)
P & F MACHINE INC
301 S Broadway, Turlock (95380-5414)
PHONE..............................209 667-2515
Wayne D Rickey, *President*
EMP: 10
SQ FT: 2,000
SALES (est): 1.6MM **Privately Held**
WEB: www.pfmetals.com
SIC: 3599 Machine shop, jobbing & repair

(P-16268)
P J MACHINING CO INC
17056 Hercules St Ste 101, Hesperia (92345-7608)
PHONE..............................760 948-2722
EMP: 11
SQ FT: 5,000
SALES (est): 1.7MM **Privately Held**
SIC: 3599

(P-16269)
P M S D INC (PA)
Also Called: Danco Machine
950 George St, Santa Clara (95054-2705)
PHONE..............................408 988-5235
Timothy Rohr, *CEO*
Denise Bachur, *Admin Mgr*
Marcel Miceal, *Info Tech Mgr*
Dennis Aymar, *Opers Staff*
Rod Dincoff, *Manager*
EMP: 57
SQ FT: 20,000
SALES: 14MM **Privately Held**
WEB: www.dancomachine.com
SIC: 3599 Machine shop, jobbing & repair

(P-16270)
P M S D INC
Also Called: K-Fab
3411 Leonard Ct, Santa Clara (95054-2053)
PHONE..............................408 727-5322
Bruce Alger, *General Mgr*
Hudson Wheldon, *Materials Mgr*
Tam Hoang, *Prdtn Mgr*
Neil Starr, *QC Mgr*
EMP: 40
SALES (corp-wide): 14MM **Privately Held**
SIC: 3599 Machine shop, jobbing & repair
PA: P M S D Inc
950 George St
Santa Clara CA 95054
408 988-5235

(P-16271)
PACIFIC AEROSPACE MACHINE INC
3002 S Rosewood Ave, Santa Ana (92707-3822)
PHONE..............................714 534-1444
Paul Nguyen, *CEO*
Kirk Nguyen, *CFO*
EMP: 40
SQ FT: 50,000
SALES: 7MM **Privately Held**
WEB: www.pacificmachine.net
SIC: 3599 Machine shop, jobbing & repair

(P-16272)
PACIFIC BROACH & ENGRG ASSOC
1513 N Kraemer Blvd, Anaheim (92806-1407)
PHONE..............................714 632-5678
Steven R Yetzke, *President*
Michael Yetzke, *Vice Pres*
Elaine Montgomery, *Admin Sec*
▲ **EMP:** 19
SQ FT: 18,000
SALES (est): 2.8MM **Privately Held**
SIC: 3599 Machine shop, jobbing & repair

(P-16273)
PACIFIC CNC MACHINE CO
2702 Gateway Rd, Carlsbad (92009-1730)
PHONE..............................760 431-7558
John McClain, *Owner*
EMP: 12
SQ FT: 2,500
SALES (est): 907.5K **Privately Held**
SIC: 3599 Machine shop, jobbing & repair

(P-16274)
PACIFIC MFG INC SAN DIEGO
1520 Corporate Center Dr, San Diego (92154-6634)
PHONE..............................619 423-0316
Raymundo Montalvo, *President*
Maria A Montalvo, *Vice Pres*
Richard Valenzuela, *Manager*
EMP: 20
SQ FT: 9,500
SALES (est): 3.5MM **Privately Held**
SIC: 3599 Machine shop, jobbing & repair

(P-16275)
PACIFIC WSTN AROSTRUCTURES INC
27771 Avenue Hopkins, Valencia (91355-1223)
PHONE..............................661 607-0100
Steve Cormier, *CEO*
EMP: 12 **EST:** 2015
SALES (est): 580K **Privately Held**
SIC: 3599 Machine shop, jobbing & repair

(P-16276)
PACON MFG INC
4777 Bennett Dr Ste H, Livermore (94551-4860)
PHONE..............................925 961-0445
Steven McClure, *CEO*
EMP: 20 **EST:** 2013
SALES (est): 3.5MM **Privately Held**
SIC: 3599 Machine shop, jobbing & repair

PRODUCTS & SVCS

(P-16277)
PAMCO MACHINE WORKS INC
9359 Feron Blvd, Rancho Cucamonga
(91730-4516)
PHONE....................909 941-7260
James Fredrick Wilkinson, *CEO*
Diane Wilkinson, *Admin Sec*
EMP: 20 **EST:** 1956
SQ FT: 17,000
SALES: 5MM **Privately Held**
WEB: www.pamcomachine.com
SIC: 3599 3462 Machine shop, jobbing & repair; iron & steel forgings

(P-16278)
PAPADATOS ENTERPRISES INC
Also Called: Dp Products
2015 Stone Ave, San Jose (95125-1447)
PHONE....................408 299-0190
Danny Papadatos, *President*
Robert Cobb, *Vice Pres*
EMP: 10
SQ FT: 3,500
SALES: 650K **Privately Held**
WEB: www.dpprod.com
SIC: 3599 3089 Machine shop, jobbing & repair; plastic processing

(P-16279)
PARAGON MACHINE WORKS INC
253 S 25th St, Richmond (94804-2856)
PHONE....................510 232-3223
Mark Norstad, *Owner*
EMP: 60
SQ FT: 55,000
SALES (est): 6.9MM **Privately Held**
WEB: www.paragonmachineworks.com
SIC: 3599 Machine shop, jobbing & repair

(P-16280)
PARAGON SWISS INC
545 Aldo Ave Ste 1, Santa Clara
(95054-2206)
PHONE....................408 748-1617
Kevin Beatty, *President*
David R Beatty, *Vice Pres*
Joanne Beatty, *Admin Sec*
Christopher Kay, *Prdtn Mgr*
EMP: 30
SQ FT: 10,200
SALES (est): 5.1MM **Privately Held**
WEB: www.paragonswiss.com
SIC: 3599 3451 Machine shop, jobbing & repair; screw machine products

(P-16281)
PARAMETRIC MANUFACTURING INC
3465 Edward Ave, Santa Clara
(95054-2131)
PHONE....................408 654-9845
Jon Drury, *President*
EMP: 16
SQ FT: 7,500
SALES: 2MM **Privately Held**
SIC: 3599 Machine shop, jobbing & repair

(P-16282)
PARAMOUNT GRINDING SERVICE
7311 Madison St Ste C, Paramount
(90723-4038)
P.O. Box 893 (90723-0893)
PHONE....................562 630-6940
John F Jaramillo, *President*
Lisa Jaramillo, *Vice Pres*
EMP: 12
SQ FT: 3,000
SALES: 740K **Privately Held**
SIC: 3599 Grinding castings for the trade

(P-16283)
PARAMOUNT MACHINE CO INC
10824 Edison Ct, Rancho Cucamonga
(91730-3868)
PHONE....................909 484-3600
Gregory A Harsen, *President*
Gail Harsen, *Vice Pres*
Maree Guest, *Office Mgr*
Sally Miller, *Manager*
EMP: 36
SQ FT: 12,000

SALES (est): 6.2MM **Privately Held**
WEB: www.paramountmachine.com
SIC: 3599 Machine shop, jobbing & repair

(P-16284)
PARK ENGINEERING AND MFG CO
Also Called: Pem
6430 Roland St, Buena Park (90621-3122)
P.O. Box 2275 (90621-0775)
PHONE....................714 521-4660
Joanna Tenney, *CEO*
Jeff Tenney, *President*
EMP: 30 **EST:** 1959
SQ FT: 6,000
SALES (est): 5MM **Privately Held**
WEB: www.park-engineering.com
SIC: 3599 Machine shop, jobbing & repair

(P-16285)
PARKER-HANNIFIN CORPORATION
Also Called: X Cell Tool & Manufacturing Co
13850 Van Ness Ave, Gardena
(90249-2476)
PHONE....................310 308-0389
Art Siler, *Manager*
EMP: 80
SALES (corp-wide): 14.3B **Publicly Held**
WEB: www.parker.com
SIC: 3599 3769 Machine shop, jobbing & repair; guided missile & space vehicle parts & auxiliary equipment
PA: Parker-Hannifin Corporation
6035 Parkland Blvd
Cleveland OH 44124
216 896-3000

(P-16286)
PAULCO PRECISION INC
Also Called: Precision Resources
13916 Cordary Ave, Hawthorne
(90250-7916)
PHONE....................310 679-4900
Paul Ruby, *President*
EMP: 16
SQ FT: 15,000
SALES (est): 2.4MM **Privately Held**
SIC: 3599 Machine shop, jobbing & repair

(P-16287)
PAULI SYSTEMS INC
1820 Walters Ct, Fairfield (94533-2759)
PHONE....................707 429-2434
Robert Pauli, *CEO*
Josef Spridgen, *Sales Staff*
Daniel Myers, *Director*
EMP: 22
SQ FT: 13,500
SALES: 3MM **Privately Held**
WEB: www.paulisystems.com
SIC: 3599 Custom machinery

(P-16288)
PCS MACHINING SERVICE INC
Also Called: Pcs Company
784 Edale Dr, Sunnyvale (94087-2316)
PHONE....................408 735-9974
Paul V Camenzind, *President*
Barbara Camenzind, *Treasurer*
▲ **EMP:** 12
SQ FT: 6,300
SALES: 1MM **Privately Held**
SIC: 3599 Machine shop, jobbing & repair

(P-16289)
PDQ ENGINEERING INC
1199 Avenida Acaso Ste F, Camarillo
(93012-8739)
PHONE....................805 482-1334
Shannon Clark, *President*
Elmer Clark, *Vice Pres*
Scott Jenkins, *Manager*
EMP: 28
SQ FT: 10,000
SALES: 3.3MM **Privately Held**
WEB: www.pdqeng.com
SIC: 3599 Machine shop, jobbing & repair

(P-16290)
PEDAVENA MOULD AND DIE CO INC
Also Called: PMD INC.
12464 Mccann Dr, Santa Fe Springs
(90670-3335)
PHONE....................310 327-2814
Steve Scardenzan, *President*
Paul Weisbrich, *Admin Sec*
▲ **EMP:** 28
SQ FT: 12,000
SALES (est): 5MM **Privately Held**
WEB: www.pmd-inc.net
SIC: 3599 Machine & other job shop work

(P-16291)
PENDARVIS MANUFACTURING INC
1808 N American St, Anaheim
(92801-1001)
PHONE....................714 992-0950
Robert D Pendarvis, *CEO*
Brian Pendarvis, *General Mgr*
EMP: 25
SQ FT: 8,000
SALES (est): 5.5MM **Privately Held**
WEB: www.pendarvismanufacturing.com
SIC: 3599 Machine shop, jobbing & repair

(P-16292)
PEREZ MACHINE INC
1501 W 134th St, Gardena (90249-2215)
PHONE....................310 217-9090
Mario Perez, *President*
Marcia Perez, *Vice Pres*
EMP: 10
SQ FT: 10,000
SALES (est): 1.7MM **Privately Held**
SIC: 3599 Machine shop, jobbing & repair

(P-16293)
PERFECTION MACHINE AND TL WORK
Also Called: Perfection Machine & Tl Works
1568 E 22nd St, Los Angeles (90011-1389)
PHONE....................213 749-5095
Steve Hix, *President*
Bryan Hix, *Engineer*
▲ **EMP:** 50
SQ FT: 93,000
SALES (est): 7.5MM **Privately Held**
WEB: www.pmtw.com
SIC: 3599 3469 3544 Machine shop, jobbing & repair; stamping metal for the trade; special dies, tools, jigs & fixtures

(P-16294)
PERFORMANCE CNC INC
3210 Production Ave Ste A, Oceanside
(92058-1306)
PHONE....................760 722-1129
Michael Stark, *CEO*
EMP: 10
SQ FT: 1,600
SALES (est): 783.7K **Privately Held**
WEB: www.performancecnc.com
SIC: 3599 Machine shop, jobbing & repair

(P-16295)
PERFORMANCE MACHINE TECH INC
25141 Avenue Stanford, Valencia
(91355-1227)
PHONE....................661 294-8617
Dennis Moran, *President*
Carolyn Moran, *Corp Secy*
EMP: 33
SQ FT: 10,000
SALES (est): 5.3MM **Privately Held**
SIC: 3599 Machine shop, jobbing & repair

(P-16296)
PERFORMEX MACHINING INC
963 Terminal Way, San Carlos
(94070-3224)
PHONE....................650 595-2228
Joseph Iffla, *Owner*
EMP: 20
SQ FT: 5,600
SALES (est): 3.9MM **Privately Held**
WEB: www.performexmachining.com
SIC: 3599 Machine shop, jobbing & repair

(P-16297)
PETERSEN PRECISION ENGRG LLC
611 Broadway St, Redwood City
(94063-3102)
PHONE....................650 365-4373
Fred Petersen, *Mng Member*
Sunil Chandar, *Engineer*
Brian Malenfant, *Engineer*
Milton Philip Olson,
EMP: 120
SQ FT: 55,000
SALES (est): 19.1MM **Privately Held**
SIC: 3599 Machine shop, jobbing & repair

(P-16298)
PISOR INDUSTRIES INC
7201 32nd St, North Highlands
(95660-2500)
PHONE....................916 944-2851
Tony Free, *President*
Joy Pisor, *Corp Secy*
EMP: 20
SQ FT: 4,500
SALES (est): 3MM **Privately Held**
SIC: 3599 3498 3446 Machine shop, jobbing & repair; fabricated pipe & fittings; architectural metalwork

(P-16299)
PLANETARY MACHINE AND ENGRG
976 S Andreasen Dr Ste A, Escondido
(92029-1949)
PHONE....................760 489-5571
William Heath, *President*
Layne Oaks, *Vice Pres*
EMP: 11
SQ FT: 6,000
SALES (est): 2MM **Privately Held**
SIC: 3599 Machine shop, jobbing & repair

(P-16300)
PLASMA COATING CORPORATION
13309 S Western Ave, Gardena
(90249-1925)
PHONE....................310 532-1951
James M Emery, *President*
Willard A Emery, *Vice Pres*
EMP: 22
SQ FT: 25,000
SALES (est): 4.2MM
SALES (corp-wide): 225.3B **Publicly Held**
WEB: www.plasmacoatingcorp.com
SIC: 3599 Machine shop, jobbing & repair
HQ: Southwest United Industries, Inc.
422 S Saint Louis Ave
Tulsa OK 74120
918 587-4161

(P-16301)
PLAYA TOOL & MARINE INC
1746 E Borchard Ave, Santa Ana
(92705-4695)
PHONE....................714 972-2722
Kirk Schroeder, *President*
EMP: 10
SQ FT: 8,400
SALES (est): 990K **Privately Held**
SIC: 3599 Machine shop, jobbing & repair

(P-16302)
PLEASANTON TOOL & MFG INC
1181 Quarry Ln Ste 450, Pleasanton
(94566-8460)
PHONE....................925 426-0500
Chester Thomas, *President*
Rich Thomas, *President*
Shirley Thomas, *CFO*
Ray Forbes, *General Mgr*
Linda Malcolm, *Manager*
EMP: 25
SQ FT: 18,000
SALES (est): 4MM **Privately Held**
WEB: www.pleasantontool.com
SIC: 3599 Machine shop, jobbing & repair

(P-16303)
PNM COMPANY
2547 N Business Park Ave, Fresno
(93727-8637)
PHONE....................559 291-1986
Dave Counts, *Partner*

▲ = Import ▼=Export
◆ =Import/Export

Precision Numeric Machine, *Partner*
Mark Winters, *Partner*
Mario Persicone, *Director*
Bev Caldwell, *Manager*
▲ EMP: 48
SQ FT: 5,500
SALES (est): 8.6MM **Privately Held**
WEB: www.pnmcnc.com
SIC: 3599 Machine shop, jobbing & repair

(P-16304)
POL-TECH PRECISION INC
Also Called: Pol Tech Precision Co
4447 Enterprise St, Fremont (94538-6306)
PHONE....................................510 656-6832
Mark Nowicki, *President*
EMP: 10
SQ FT: 900
SALES (est): 169.3K **Privately Held**
WEB: www.pol-tech.com
SIC: 3599 Machine shop, jobbing & repair

(P-16305)
POLYTEC PRODUCTS CORPORATION
1190 Obrien Dr, Menlo Park (94025-1411)
PHONE....................................650 322-7555
John Parissenti, *President*
Tony Hertado, *Principal*
Peggy Blevins, *Director*
EMP: 45
SQ FT: 12,000
SALES (est): 8MM **Privately Held**
WEB: www.polytecproducts.com
SIC: 3599 Machine shop, jobbing & repair

(P-16306)
POWERS BROS MACHINE INC
8100 Slauson Ave, Montebello
(90640-6622)
PHONE....................................323 728-2010
Mitchell Power, *President*
Charles Powers, *Treasurer*
Dee Kesler, *Office Mgr*
EMP: 12
SQ FT: 21,300
SALES (est): 2.1MM **Privately Held**
SIC: 3599 Machine shop, jobbing & repair

(P-16307)
PPM PRODUCTS INC
1538 Gladding Ct, Milpitas (95035-6814)
PHONE....................................408 946-4710
Yasuhiro Hayashi, *President*
Kathy Sato, *Executive Asst*
Clifford Hayashi, *Info Tech Dir*
EMP: 13
SQ FT: 3,000
SALES (est): 2.2MM **Privately Held**
WEB: www.ppmproducts.com
SIC: 3599 Machine shop, jobbing & repair

(P-16308)
PRECISION ARCFT MACHINING INC
Also Called: Pamco
10640 Elkwood St, Sun Valley
(91352-4631)
PHONE....................................818 768-5900
Donald A Pisano, *President*
Kimberly Pisano, *CFO*
Joyce Pisano, *Treasurer*
Jim Asseltyne, *Sales Mgr*
Jim Thompson, *Sales Staff*
▲ EMP: 50
SQ FT: 6,500
SALES (est): 9MM **Privately Held**
SIC: 3599 3678 Machine shop, jobbing & repair; electronic connectors

(P-16309)
PRECISION IDENTITY CORPORATION
804 Camden Ave, Campbell (95008-4119)
PHONE....................................408 374-2346
Karl Kamber, *President*
Pierre Kamber, *Vice Pres*
Roland Kamber, *Vice Pres*
Jennifer Birch, *Bookkeeper*
EMP: 24
SQ FT: 12,000
SALES (est): 3.5MM **Privately Held**
WEB: www.precisionidentity.com
SIC: 3599 3451 Machine shop, jobbing & repair; screw machine products

(P-16310)
PRECISION WATERJET INC
880 W Crowther Ave, Placentia
(92870-6348)
PHONE....................................888 538-9287
Shane Strowski, *President*
Mark Tierheimer, *Sales Associate*
Michelle Hotta, *Sales Staff*
EMP: 39
SALES: 7.8MM **Privately Held**
SIC: 3599 Machine shop, jobbing & repair

(P-16311)
PREFERRED MFG SVCS INC (PA)
Also Called: Snowline Engineering
4261 Business Dr, Cameron Park
(95682-7217)
PHONE....................................530 677-2675
Calvin Reynolds, *President*
Lee Block, *Exec VP*
Tim Bartosh, *Engineer*
Vern Holzer, *QC Mgr*
Danette Hart, *Manager*
EMP: 85
SQ FT: 34,000
SALES (est): 13MM **Privately Held**
WEB: www.snowlineengineering.com
SIC: 3599 Machine shop, jobbing & repair

(P-16312)
PREMAC INC
Also Called: Precision Machining
625 Thompson Ave, Glendale
(91201-2032)
PHONE....................................818 241-8370
Michael Warme, *CEO*
Victoria Warme, *CFO*
Rainer H Warme, *Principal*
EMP: 14
SQ FT: 6,000
SALES (est): 2.8MM **Privately Held**
SIC: 3599 Machine shop, jobbing & repair

(P-16313)
PRO FAB TECH LLC
970 W Foothill Blvd, Azusa (91702-2842)
PHONE....................................626 804-7200
James M Probst, *President*
Sandy Probst, *Manager*
EMP: 10
SQ FT: 20,000
SALES (est): 1.9MM **Privately Held**
SIC: 3599 Machine shop, jobbing & repair

(P-16314)
PRODUCTION LAPPING COMPANY
124 E Chestnut Ave, Monrovia
(91016-3432)
PHONE....................................626 359-0611
Hans Herzig, *President*
Steve Herzig, *President*
Vangie Lozada, *Office Mgr*
Trudy Herzig, *Admin Sec*
George Avelar, *Supervisor*
EMP: 20 EST: 1959
SQ FT: 4,500
SALES (est): 3MM **Privately Held**
SIC: 3599 Machine shop, jobbing & repair

(P-16315)
PROFESSIONAL BEARING SVC INC
3831 Catalina St Ste K, Los Alamitos
(90720-5447)
PHONE....................................562 596-5023
Christopher Mandryk, *CEO*
Martina Mandryk, *CFO*
EMP: 24 EST: 1978
SQ FT: 10,840
SALES (est): 2.4MM **Privately Held**
SIC: 3599 Machine shop, jobbing & repair

(P-16316)
PRONTO DRILLING INC (PA)
9501 Santa Fe Springs Rd, Santa Fe
Springs (90670-2624)
PHONE....................................562 777-0900
Miguel A Montanez, *President*
Orlando M Montanez, *Purch Mgr*
EMP: 24 EST: 1976
SALES (est): 3.8MM **Privately Held**
SIC: 3599 Machine shop, jobbing & repair

(P-16317)
PROTO SPACE ENGINEERING INC
2214 Loma Ave, South El Monte
(91733-2518)
PHONE....................................626 442-8273
Linda Dabbs, *CEO*
Michael Dabbs, *President*
EMP: 30 EST: 1965
SQ FT: 24,000
SALES (est): 5.5MM **Privately Held**
WEB: www.psengr.com
SIC: 3599 Machine shop, jobbing & repair

(P-16318)
PROTOQUICK INC
3412 Investment Blvd, Hayward
(94545-3811)
PHONE....................................510 264-0101
Carl Anderson, *President*
John Harrigan, *Vice Pres*
Ken Stall, *Vice Pres*
EMP: 10 EST: 2009
SQ FT: 7,000
SALES (est): 1.7MM **Privately Held**
SIC: 3599 Machine shop, jobbing & repair

(P-16319)
PTEC SOLUTIONS INC
48633 Warm Springs Blvd, Fremont
(94539-7782)
PHONE....................................510 358-3578
Peter Pham, *President*
Chris Arigna, *QC Mgr*
▲ EMP: 67
SQ FT: 25,000
SALES (est): 9MM **Privately Held**
WEB: www.pthsolutions.com
SIC: 3599 8711 3357 Machine shop, jobbing & repair; engineering services; fiber optic cable (insulated)

(P-16320)
PTR MANUFACTURING INC
Also Called: Ptr Sheet Metal & Fabrication
33390 Transit Ave, Union City
(94587-2014)
PHONE....................................510 477-9654
SAI La, *President*
Phong La, *General Mgr*
EMP: 40
SQ FT: 45,000
SALES (est): 6.6MM **Privately Held**
SIC: 3599 3444 Machine shop, jobbing & repair; sheet metalwork

(P-16321)
PVA TEPLA AMERICA INC (HQ)
Also Called: Plasma Division
251 Corporate Terrace St, Corona
(92879-6000)
PHONE....................................951 371-2500
Bill Marsh, *President*
Walt Royolson, *Executive*
EMP: 20
SQ FT: 15,000
SALES: 9MM
SALES (corp-wide): 110.8MM **Privately Held**
WEB: www.plasmapen.com
SIC: 3599 Custom machinery
PA: Pva Tepla Ag
Im Westpark 10-12
Wettenberg 35435
641 686-900

(P-16322)
PYRAMID PRECISION MACHINE INC
6721 Cobra Way, San Diego (92121-4110)
PHONE....................................858 642-0713
Robert Taylor, *President*
Walter Gieffels, *COO*
Arnie Amaya, *Prgrmr*
Juan Flores, *Engineer*
Cecylia Romeo, *Purchasing*
EMP: 100
SQ FT: 23,800
SALES (est): 27.9MM **Privately Held**
WEB: www.pyramidprecision.com
SIC: 3599 Machine shop, jobbing & repair

(P-16323)
Q3-CNC INC
9091 Kenamar Dr, San Diego
(92121-2421)
PHONE....................................858 790-0002
David Trainor, *President*
Christopher Campbell, *Treasurer*
Teresa Mayor, *Office Mgr*
Luis Ramos, *Admin Sec*
EMP: 13
SQ FT: 10,000
SALES (est): 2MM **Privately Held**
WEB: www.q3cnc.com
SIC: 3599 Machine shop, jobbing & repair

(P-16324)
QUALITASK INCORPORATED
2840 E Gretta Ln, Anaheim (92806-2512)
PHONE....................................714 237-0900
Som Suntharaphat, *President*
Eduvigis Suntharaphat, *Principal*
Deb Beds, *Admin Sec*
EMP: 17
SQ FT: 13,100
SALES (est): 3.1MM **Privately Held**
WEB: www.qualitask.net
SIC: 3599 Machine shop, jobbing & repair

(P-16325)
QUALITY CONTROLLED MFG INC
9429 Abraham Way, Santee (92071-2854)
PHONE....................................619 443-3997
William Grande, *President*
Jane Currie, *Treasurer*
James Hiebing, *Vice Pres*
Jeff Grande, *Mfg Staff*
Doug Grande, *Director*
EMP: 70
SQ FT: 25,000
SALES (est): 8.8MM **Privately Held**
SIC: 3599 Machine shop, jobbing & repair

(P-16326)
QUALITY EDM INC
8025 E Crystal Dr, Anaheim (92807-2523)
PHONE....................................714 283-9220
Michael Gervais, *President*
EMP: 10
SQ FT: 8,000
SALES: 2.2MM **Privately Held**
SIC: 3599 Machine shop, jobbing & repair

(P-16327)
QUALITY MACHINE ENGRG INC
2559 Grosse Ave, Santa Rosa
(95404-2608)
PHONE....................................707 528-1900
Rudy Hirschnitz, *President*
Shawn Barnett, *Vice Pres*
John F Wright, *Vice Pres*
EMP: 40
SQ FT: 13,500
SALES (est): 6MM **Privately Held**
WEB: www.qme1.com
SIC: 3599 Machine shop, jobbing & repair

(P-16328)
QUALITY MACHINE SHOP INC
1676 N Ventura Ave, Ventura (93001-1576)
PHONE....................................805 653-7944
David V Gudino, *President*
EMP: 10
SQ FT: 4,800
SALES: 250K **Privately Held**
SIC: 3599 Machine shop, jobbing & repair

(P-16329)
QUALONTIME CORPORATION
19 Senisa, Irvine (92612-2112)
PHONE....................................714 523-4751
Douglas J Siemer, *President*
EMP: 16
SQ FT: 7,500
SALES (est): 1.6MM **Privately Held**
SIC: 3599 Machine shop, jobbing & repair

(P-16330)
QUANTECH MACHINING INC
25647 Rye Canyon Rd, Valencia
(91355-1110)
PHONE....................................661 775-3990
Riad Hussein, *President*
Josie Muniz, *Office Mgr*
Jocelane Fanol, *Contract Mgr*

PRODUCTS & SVCS

Raul R Serrato, *Purch Mgr*
Jamaal Hussein, *QC Mgr*
EMP: 45
SALES: 8MM **Privately Held**
SIC: 3599 Machine shop, jobbing & repair

(P-16331)
R & B PLASTICS INC
227 E Meats Ave, Orange (92865-3311)
PHONE....................714 229-8419
Richard T Young, *President*
Nancy Young, *Vice Pres*
EMP: 14
SQ FT: 10,000
SALES (est): 3.1MM **Privately Held**
SIC: 3599 Machine shop, jobbing & repair

(P-16332)
R & L ENTERPRISES INC
Also Called: RAND MACHINE WORKS
1955 S Mary St, Fresno (93721-3309)
PHONE....................559 233-1608
Robert Rand, *President*
Linda Rand, *Vice Pres*
Kristin Henson, *Executive*
Terri Groth, *Office Mgr*
Leon Malding, *Plant Mgr*
EMP: 26
SQ FT: 27,000
SALES: 3MM **Privately Held**
WEB: www.randmachineworks.com
SIC: 3599 7692 Machine shop, jobbing & repair; welding repair

(P-16333)
R C IP INC
Also Called: R C Industries
1476 N Hundley St, Anaheim (92806-1322)
PHONE....................714 630-1239
Robert Champlin, *CEO*
EMP: 16
SQ FT: 4,400
SALES (est): 3.4MM **Privately Held**
WEB: www.rcip.com
SIC: 3599 Machine shop, jobbing & repair

(P-16334)
R L BENNETT ENGINEERING INC
Also Called: CMI
26945 Cabot Rd Ste 112, Laguna Hills (92653-7009)
PHONE....................949 367-0700
Richard Bennett, *President*
Jeff Bennett, *CFO*
EMP: 10
SQ FT: 3,000
SALES: 550K **Privately Held**
WEB: www.rlbennettengineering.com
SIC: 3599 Machine shop, jobbing & repair

(P-16335)
R M BAKER MACHINE & TOOL INC
815 W Front St, Covina (91722-3613)
PHONE....................562 697-4007
Richard Baker, *President*
Faith Baker, *Admin Sec*
EMP: 16
SQ FT: 6,700
SALES (est): 2.7MM **Privately Held**
SIC: 3599 Machine shop, jobbing & repair

(P-16336)
R STEPHENSON & D CRAM MFG INC
Also Called: R & D Mfg Services
800 Faulstich Ct, San Jose (95112-1361)
PHONE....................408 452-0882
Rick Stephenson, *President*
EMP: 30 **EST:** 1976
SQ FT: 14,000
SALES (est): 5.1MM **Privately Held**
SIC: 3599 3369 3324 Machine shop, jobbing & repair; nonferrous foundries; steel investment foundries

(P-16337)
RA INDUSTRIES LLC
2230 S Anne St, Santa Ana (92704-4411)
PHONE....................714 557-2322
Robert J Follman, *President*
Brian Goodman, *COO*
Carole A Follman,
Robin Follman-Otta,

Thomas Hyland,
◆ **EMP:** 30 **EST:** 1969
SQ FT: 30,000
SALES: 6.4MM **Privately Held**
WEB: www.ra-industries.com
SIC: 3599 3593 Machine shop, jobbing & repair; fluid power cylinders & actuators

(P-16338)
RA-WHITE INC
2736 W Industry Rd, Delano (93215-9565)
PHONE....................661 725-1840
Debbie Bushnell, *President*
Carl Bushnell, *Vice Pres*
EMP: 10 **EST:** 1951
SQ FT: 20,000
SALES: 1MM **Privately Held**
WEB: www.rawhite.com
SIC: 3599 Machine & other job shop work

(P-16339)
RALC INC
Also Called: Cnc Manufacturing
42158 Sarah Way, Temecula (92590-3401)
PHONE....................951 693-0098
Lydia Cruz, *President*
Refugio Cruz, *Vice Pres*
Rich Cruz, *General Mgr*
EMP: 12 **EST:** 1996
SQ FT: 6,800
SALES (est): 1.6MM **Privately Held**
SIC: 3599 Machine shop, jobbing & repair

(P-16340)
RALPH E AMES MACHINE WORKS
2301 Dominguez Way, Torrance (90501-6200)
PHONE....................310 328-8523
Mike Ames, *President*
Ron Ames, *Vice Pres*
EMP: 45 **EST:** 1942
SQ FT: 11,000
SALES (est): 8.8MM **Privately Held**
WEB: www.amesmachine.com
SIC: 3599 Machine shop, jobbing & repair

(P-16341)
RAPID PRECISION MFG INC
1516 Montague Expy, San Jose (95131-1408)
PHONE....................408 617-0771
Paul Yi, *CEO*
EMP: 35
SQ FT: 11,000
SALES (est): 6.1MM **Privately Held**
SIC: 3599 Machine shop, jobbing & repair

(P-16342)
RAPID PRODUCT SOLUTIONS INC
2240 Celsius Ave Ste D, Oxnard (93030-8015)
PHONE....................805 485-7234
Max Gerdts, *President*
Richard Fitch, *President*
Douglas Wallis, *President*
Shawn Tester, *Sales Staff*
▲ **EMP:** 30
SQ FT: 10,000
SALES (est): 5.5MM **Privately Held**
WEB: www.rapid-products.com
SIC: 3599 Machine shop, jobbing & repair

(P-16343)
RB MACHINING INC
39360 3rd St E Ste B203, Palmdale (93550-3256)
PHONE....................661 274-4611
Barbara Mc Millan, *CEO*
Robert McMillan, *Owner*
John Wiget, *Engineer*
EMP: 10
SALES (est): 1.3MM **Privately Held**
SIC: 3599 Machine shop, jobbing & repair

(P-16344)
RDC MACHINE INC
384 Laurelwood Rd, Santa Clara (95054-2311)
PHONE....................408 970-0721
Randolph D Cuilla, *President*
Janene Cuilla, *Treasurer*
Mark Cuilla, *Vice Pres*
EMP: 41
SQ FT: 30,000

SALES (est): 7.5MM **Privately Held**
SIC: 3599 Machine shop, jobbing & repair

(P-16345)
RDL MACHINE INC
Also Called: Hall Machine
7775 Arjons Dr, San Diego (92126-4366)
PHONE....................858 693-3975
Richard G Hall, *President*
Debbie Hall, *Corp Secy*
Dave Lopez, *Sales Executive*
EMP: 30
SQ FT: 12,200
SALES: 2.7MM **Privately Held**
WEB: www.hallmachinesd.com
SIC: 3599 Machine shop, jobbing & repair

(P-16346)
RE BILT METALIZING CO
Also Called: Rebuilt Metalizing Chrome Pltg
2229 E 38th St, Vernon (90058-1628)
P.O. Box 58808, Los Angeles (90058-0808)
PHONE....................323 277-8200
Dave Dehota, *Owner*
EMP: 14
SQ FT: 18,000
SALES (est): 1.4MM **Privately Held**
SIC: 3599 Machine shop, jobbing & repair

(P-16347)
RED LINE ENGINEERING INC
4616 Weed Patch Ct, Greenwood (95635-9507)
P.O. Box 399 (95635-0399)
PHONE....................530 333-2134
Matt Johnson, *CEO*
Michaela Johnson, *Vice Pres*
EMP: 14
SQ FT: 15,000
SALES (est): 1MM **Privately Held**
WEB: www.randyjohnson.com
SIC: 3599 Machine shop, jobbing & repair

(P-16348)
REGAL MACHINE & ENGRG INC
5200 E 60th St, Maywood (90270-3557)
PHONE....................323 773-7462
Val Darie, *President*
EMP: 27
SQ FT: 20,500
SALES (est): 5MM **Privately Held**
WEB: www.regalmachine.com
SIC: 3599 3769 Machine shop, jobbing & repair; guided missile & space vehicle parts & auxiliary equipment

(P-16349)
REID PRODUCTS INC
21430 Waalew Rd, Apple Valley (92307-1026)
P.O. Box 1507 (92307-0028)
PHONE....................760 240-1355
Kevin Reid, *President*
Cliff R Carter, *Treasurer*
Shelby Reid, *Vice Pres*
Steve Childs, *General Mgr*
Lisa Grinser, *Admin Sec*
EMP: 48
SQ FT: 15,000
SALES (est): 8.9MM **Privately Held**
SIC: 3599 Machine shop, jobbing & repair

(P-16350)
REISNER ENTERPRISES INC
Also Called: Westcorp Engineering
1403 W Linden St, Riverside (92507-6804)
PHONE....................951 786-9478
Tom Reisner, *President*
EMP: 12
SQ FT: 9,000
SALES (est): 1.3MM **Privately Held**
SIC: 3599 Machine shop, jobbing & repair

(P-16351)
RELIANCE MACHINE PRODUCTS INC
4265 Solar Way, Fremont (94538-6389)
PHONE....................510 438-6760
Kelly L Hill, *President*
EMP: 45
SQ FT: 12,000
SALES (est): 7.1MM **Privately Held**
SIC: 3599 Machine shop, jobbing & repair

(P-16352)
REMCO MCH & FABRICATION INC
1966 S Date Ave, Bloomington (92316-2442)
PHONE....................909 877-3530
Jacque Lewis Russell, *CEO*
Jerry Gilson, *Vice Pres*
▲ **EMP:** 19 **EST:** 1979
SALES (est): 3.9MM **Privately Held**
SIC: 3599 3441 Machine shop, jobbing & repair; fabricated structural metal

(P-16353)
RENAISSANCE PRECISION MFG INC
Also Called: R P M
2551 Stanwell Dr Concord, Concord (94520-4818)
PHONE....................925 691-5997
Wade Carbone, *CEO*
Bill Burmeister, *President*
Kelly Burmeister, *Corp Secy*
EMP: 10
SQ FT: 10,000
SALES (est): 1.8MM **Privately Held**
SIC: 3599 Machine shop, jobbing & repair

(P-16354)
RESEARCH METAL INDUSTRIES INC
1970 W 139th St, Gardena (90249-2408)
PHONE....................310 352-3200
Harish Brahmbhatt, *President*
Kamla Brahmbhatt, *Vice Pres*
Leigh Thompson, *General Mgr*
Diana Guhin, *Office Mgr*
Steve Oldakowski, *Technology*
◆ **EMP:** 35
SQ FT: 24,000
SALES (est): 9.1MM **Privately Held**
WEB: www.researchmetal.com
SIC: 3599 3469 Electrical discharge machining (EDM); spinning metal for the trade

(P-16355)
RICAURTE PRECISION INC
1550 E Mcfadden Ave, Santa Ana (92705-4308)
PHONE....................714 667-0632
Luis Ricaurte, *CEO*
Marina Ricaurte, *President*
EMP: 22
SQ FT: 72,000
SALES (est): 4.1MM **Privately Held**
SIC: 3599 Machine shop, jobbing & repair

(P-16356)
RICHARDS MACHINING CO INC
2161 Del Franco St, San Jose (95131-1570)
PHONE....................408 526-9219
Gustavo Chavez, *President*
Odin Chavez, *Vice Pres*
Yamir Chavez, *Admin Sec*
EMP: 16
SQ FT: 6,500
SALES: 1.2MM **Privately Held**
SIC: 3599 Machine shop, jobbing & repair

(P-16357)
RICMAN MFG INC
2273 American Ave Ste 1, Hayward (94545-1813)
PHONE....................510 670-1785
Richard Mann, *President*
EMP: 20
SQ FT: 5,000
SALES (est): 3.7MM **Privately Held**
SIC: 3599 Machine shop, jobbing & repair

(P-16358)
RIGGINS ENGINEERING INC
13932 Saticoy St, Van Nuys (91402-6587)
PHONE....................818 782-7010
Joe Grossnickle, *President*
Michael Riggins, *Vice Pres*
Casey Evans, *Office Mgr*
Nana Grossnickle, *Admin Sec*
Jackson Yeung, *Engineer*
EMP: 40 **EST:** 1967
SQ FT: 18,000

▲ = Import ▼=Export
◆ =Import/Export

SALES (est): 6.4MM **Privately Held**
WEB: www.rigginseng.com
SIC: **3599** Machine shop, jobbing & repair

(P-16359)
RINCON ENGINEERING CORPORATION
6325 Carpinteria Ave, Carpinteria (93013-2901)
P.O. Box 87 (93014-0087)
PHONE..................................805 684-0935
Alberto Hugo, *CEO*
Roger Hugo, *President*
Richard Hugo, *Vice Pres*
Colleen Hugo CPA, *General Mgr*
Ed Preston, *Plant Mgr*
EMP: 43
SQ FT: 12,000
SALES (est): 9MM **Privately Held**
WEB: www.rinconeng.com
SIC: **3599** 3444 3441 Machine shop, jobbing & repair; sheet metalwork; fabricated structural metal

(P-16360)
RIVERSIDE MACHINE WORKS INC
6301 Baldwin Ave, Riverside (92509-6014)
PHONE..................................951 685-7416
Kerry Townsend, *President*
EMP: 14
SQ FT: 7,500
SALES (est): 1.9MM **Privately Held**
SIC: **3599** 7692 3444 Machine shop, jobbing & repair; welding repair; sheet metalwork

(P-16361)
RJ MACHINE INC
7985 Dunbrook Rd Ste E, San Diego (92126-6307)
PHONE..................................858 547-9482
Reed Jackson, *President*
Sandra Jackson, *CFO*
Jonathan Jackson, *Prdtn Mgr*
EMP: 10
SQ FT: 7,000
SALES (est): 1.7MM **Privately Held**
WEB: www.rjmachine.net
SIC: **3599** Machine shop, jobbing & repair

(P-16362)
RMC ENGINEERING CO INC (PA)
255 Mayock Rd, Gilroy (95020-7032)
P.O. Box 575 (95021-0575)
PHONE..................................408 842-2525
Betty Mc Kenzie, *President*
Shawna Mc Kenzie, *Corp Secy*
Kevin Mc Kenzie, *Vice Pres*
Scott Mc Kenzie, *Vice Pres*
▲ EMP: 30
SQ FT: 14,000
SALES (est): 7.5MM **Privately Held**
SIC: **3599** 7692 7538 3715 Machine shop, jobbing & repair; automotive welding; general automotive repair shops; truck trailers

(P-16363)
ROBERT H OLIVA INC
Also Called: Romakk Engineering
19863 Nordhoff St, Northridge (91324-3331)
PHONE..................................818 700-1035
Robert Oliva, *President*
Kim Oliva, *Vice Pres*
EMP: 25
SQ FT: 4,000
SALES (est): 4.2MM **Privately Held**
SIC: **3599** Machine shop, jobbing & repair

(P-16364)
ROBERT W WIESMANTEL
Also Called: Cebe Co
15345 Allen St, Paramount (90723-4011)
P.O. Box 620 (90723-0620)
PHONE..................................562 634-0442
Robert W Wiesmantel, *Owner*
EMP: 14
SQ FT: 24,000
SALES (est): 1.2MM **Privately Held**
SIC: **3599** Machine shop, jobbing & repair

(P-16365)
ROBERTS PRECISION ENGRG INC
Also Called: Robert's Engineering
1345 S Allec St, Anaheim (92805-6304)
PHONE..................................714 635-4485
Robert Flores II, *President*
EMP: 25
SQ FT: 23,000
SALES (est): 5.8MM **Privately Held**
SIC: **3599** Machine shop, jobbing & repair

(P-16366)
ROBSON TECHNOLOGIES INC
Also Called: R T I
135 E Main Ave Ste 130, Morgan Hill (95037-7522)
PHONE..................................408 779-8008
William W Robson, *President*
Ryan Block, *Vice Pres*
Lori Robson, *Vice Pres*
EMP: 27
SQ FT: 3,000
SALES (est): 5.9MM **Privately Held**
WEB: www.geminiwriter.com
SIC: **3599** 3823 Machine shop, jobbing & repair; computer interface equipment for industrial process control

(P-16367)
ROC-AIRE CORP
2198 Pomona Blvd, Pomona (91768-3332)
PHONE..................................909 784-3385
Thomas L Collins, *CEO*
Jason Collins, *Treasurer*
EMP: 22
SQ FT: 52,000
SALES (est): 4.5MM **Privately Held**
WEB: www.rocaire.com
SIC: **3599** Machine shop, jobbing & repair

(P-16368)
ROMI INDUSTRIES INC
Also Called: Romi Machine Shop
25443 Rye Canyon Rd, Valencia (91355-1206)
PHONE..................................661 294-1142
Jay Patel, *President*
EMP: 10
SQ FT: 6,000
SALES (est): 1.2MM **Privately Held**
SIC: **3599** Machine shop, jobbing & repair

(P-16369)
RON GROSE RACING INC
488 E Kettleman Ln, Lodi (95240-5945)
PHONE..................................209 368-2571
Joey Grose, *President*
EMP: 10
SQ FT: 8,600
SALES (est): 860K **Privately Held**
WEB: www.rgracing.com
SIC: **3599** 5531 7539 Machine shop, jobbing & repair; speed shops, including race car supplies; machine shop, automotive

(P-16370)
RON WITHERSPOON INC
13525 Blackie Rd, Castroville (95012-3211)
PHONE..................................831 633-3568
Les Oglesby, *Manager*
Ken Nelson, *Facilities Mgr*
EMP: 85
SALES (corp-wide): 18.7MM **Privately Held**
SIC: **3599** Machine shop, jobbing & repair
PA: Ron Witherspoon Inc.
    1551 Dell Ave
    Campbell CA 95008
    408 370-6620

(P-16371)
RONLO ENGINEERING LTD
955 Flynn Rd, Camarillo (93012-8704)
PHONE..................................805 388-3227
Ronnie Lowe, *CEO*
Rick Slaney, *President*
Tracy Slaney, *Treasurer*
Karen Mc Master, *Vice Pres*
EMP: 30
SQ FT: 23,650
SALES (est): 5.3MM **Privately Held**
WEB: www.ronlo.com
SIC: **3599** Machine shop, jobbing & repair

(P-16372)
ROOKE MANUFACTURING CO
3360 W Harvard St, Santa Ana (92704-3920)
PHONE..................................714 540-6943
Deward Rooke, *Owner*
EMP: 10 EST: 1977
SQ FT: 5,000
SALES (est): 600K **Privately Held**
SIC: **3599** Machine shop, jobbing & repair

(P-16373)
ROTHLISBERGER MFG A CAL CORP
Also Called: R M I
14718 Arminta St, Van Nuys (91402-5904)
PHONE..................................818 786-9462
Jerry Rothlisberger, *President*
Korena Rothlisberger, *Admin Sec*
EMP: 16
SQ FT: 8,000
SALES (est): 2.2MM **Privately Held**
WEB: www.mag-hytec.com
SIC: **3599** Machine shop, jobbing & repair

(P-16374)
ROY & VAL TOOL GRINDING INC
10131 Canoga Ave, Chatsworth (91311-3006)
PHONE..................................818 341-2434
Val Goelz, *President*
Jim Tweety, *Vice Pres*
Mark Goelz, *Admin Sec*
EMP: 11
SQ FT: 4,800
SALES (est): 500K **Privately Held**
SIC: **3599** 7389 Machine shop, jobbing & repair; grinding, precision: commercial or industrial

(P-16375)
ROZAK ENGINEERING INC
556 S State College Blvd, Fullerton (92831-5114)
PHONE..................................714 446-8855
Solomon Kilaghbian, *President*
EMP: 11
SQ FT: 1,920
SALES (est): 1.1MM **Privately Held**
SIC: **3599** Machine shop, jobbing & repair

(P-16376)
RPM GRINDING CO INC
Also Called: R P M Centerless Grinding
1755 Commerce St, Norco (92860-2934)
PHONE..................................951 273-0602
Rudy Miller, *Owner*
EMP: 13
SQ FT: 10,500
SALES (est): 1.7MM **Privately Held**
WEB: www.rudymiller.com
SIC: **3599** Machine shop, jobbing & repair

(P-16377)
RS MACHINING CO INC
9726 Cozycroft Ave, Chatsworth (91311-4401)
PHONE..................................818 718-0097
Crystal C Crawford, *CEO*
Amado J Edghill, *CFO*
EMP: 10
SQ FT: 4,500
SALES (est): 1.3MM **Privately Held**
SIC: **3599** Machine shop, jobbing & repair

(P-16378)
S & H MACHINE INC (PA)
900 N Lake St, Burbank (91502-1622)
PHONE..................................818 846-9847
Fisher, *Principal*
Kenneth Fisher, *Vice Pres*
Pamela Fisher, *Vice Pres*
Cindy Martinez, *Purch Agent*
Art Martinez, *Mfg Mgr*
EMP: 13
SQ FT: 17,107
SALES (est): 7.6MM **Privately Held**
WEB: www.shmachine.com
SIC: **3599** Machine shop, jobbing & repair

(P-16379)
S & S NUMERICAL CONTROL INC
19841 Nordhoff St, Northridge (91324-3331)
PHONE..................................818 341-4141
John Satterfield, *President*
Roberta J Satterfield, *Admin Sec*
Celeste Zabala, *Opers Mgr*
EMP: 20
SQ FT: 9,000
SALES (est): 3.1MM **Privately Held**
WEB: www.ssnumerical.com
SIC: **3599** Machine shop, jobbing & repair

(P-16380)
S & S PRECISION MFG INC
2509 S Broadway, Santa Ana (92707-3411)
PHONE..................................714 754-6664
David Mosier, *President*
EMP: 45
SQ FT: 10,000
SALES (est): 9MM **Privately Held**
SIC: **3599** Machine shop, jobbing & repair

(P-16381)
S F ENTERPRISES INCORPORATED
707 Warrington Ave, Redwood City (94063-3525)
PHONE..................................650 455-3223
Ben Schloss, *President*
EMP: 12
SQ FT: 4,000
SALES: 2MM **Privately Held**
SIC: **3599** Air intake filters, internal combustion engine, except auto

(P-16382)
S R MACHINING-PROPERTIES LLC
640 Parkridge Ave, Norco (92860-3124)
PHONE..................................951 520-9486
Lawrence Kaford, *President*
Larry Novak, *Vice Pres*
▲ EMP: 134
SQ FT: 28,000
SALES (est): 30.2MM **Privately Held**
WEB: www.srmachining.com
SIC: **3599** 3089 Machine shop, jobbing & repair; injection molding of plastics

(P-16383)
SAM MACHINING INC
Also Called: A D Machine
1140 N Kraemer Blvd Ste M, Anaheim (92806-1919)
PHONE..................................714 632-7035
Promila Dutt, *President*
Navgiwan Dutt, *Vice Pres*
EMP: 10
SALES: 1.2MM **Privately Held**
SIC: **3599** Machine shop, jobbing & repair

(P-16384)
SAMAX PRECISION INC
926 W Evelyn Ave, Sunnyvale (94086-5957)
PHONE..................................408 245-9555
Vicki Murray, *President*
Jodi McCash, *Admin Sec*
Scott McClung, *QC Dir*
EMP: 36 EST: 1963
SQ FT: 10,000
SALES (est): 7.8MM **Privately Held**
WEB: www.samaxinc.com
SIC: **3599** Custom machinery

(P-16385)
SANTA FE MACHINE WORKS INC
14578 Rancho Vista Dr, Fontana (92335-4277)
PHONE..................................909 350-6877
Dennis Kelly, *President*
Scott Kelly, *CFO*
Todd Kelly, *Treasurer*
Patricia Kelly, *Vice Pres*
Gilbert Robinson, *Vice Pres*
EMP: 24
SQ FT: 30,000
SALES (est): 4.8MM **Privately Held**
WEB: www.santafemachine-phoenix.com
SIC: **3599** Machine shop, jobbing & repair

(P-16386)
SARR INDUSTRIES INC
8975 Fullbright Ave, Chatsworth
(91311-6124)
PHONE..................................818 998-7735
Richard L Joice Jr, *President*
Angela Suszka, *Corp Secy*
Sharon Mills-Roche, *Accountant*
EMP: 14
SQ FT: 5,500
SALES (est): 2.4MM **Privately Held**
SIC: 3599 Machine shop, jobbing & repair

(P-16387)
SCHNEIDERS MANUFACTURING INC
11122 Penrose St, Sun Valley
(91352-2724)
PHONE..................................818 771-0082
Nick Schneider, *President*
Trudy Schneider, *Corp Secy*
Tom Schneider, *Vice Pres*
Christina Kephart, *Production*
EMP: 30 EST: 1967
SQ FT: 18,000
SALES (est): 5.1MM **Privately Held**
SIC: 3599 Machine shop, jobbing & repair

(P-16388)
SCHROEDER TOOL & DIE CORP
25448 Cumberland Ln, Calabasas
(91302-3156)
PHONE..................................818 786-9360
Steve Schroeder, *President*
Patricia Schroeder-Deckard, *Shareholder*
EMP: 40
SQ FT: 45,000
SALES (est): 3.7MM **Privately Held**
SIC: 3599 3545 3544 Machine shop, jobbing & repair; machine tool accessories; special dies, tools, jigs & fixtures

(P-16389)
SCOTT CRAFT CO (PA)
4601 Cecilia St, Cudahy (90201-5813)
P.O. Box 430, Bell (90201-0430)
PHONE..................................323 560-3949
Merry An Cejka, *Owner*
Robert Cejka, *Sales Staff*
EMP: 15 EST: 1966
SQ FT: 12,000
SALES (est): 3MM **Privately Held**
WEB: www.scottcraft.com
SIC: 3599 3544 Custom machinery; machine shop, jobbing & repair; special dies, tools, jigs & fixtures

(P-16390)
SCOTT CRAFT CO
Also Called: Scott Craft Co & STC
5 Stallion Rd, Rancho Palos Verdes
(90275-5257)
PHONE..................................323 560-3949
Merry An Cejka, *Branch Mgr*
EMP: 10
SALES (corp-wide): 3MM **Privately Held**
WEB: www.scottcraft.com
SIC: 3599 Custom machinery
PA: Scott Craft Co
    4601 Cecilia St
    Cudahy CA 90201
    323 560-3949

(P-16391)
SCREWMATIC INC
925 W 1st St, Azusa (91702-4222)
P.O. Box 518 (91702-0518)
PHONE..................................626 334-7831
Louis E Zimmerli, *CEO*
Alice Zimmerli, *Vice Pres*
Jeff Clow, *Admin Sec*
Oscar Carpio, *Finance Mgr*
Wayne Dobloer, *Prdtn Mgr*
EMP: 65
SQ FT: 40,000
SALES (est): 10.2MM **Privately Held**
WEB: www.screwmaticinc.com
SIC: 3599 Machine shop, jobbing & repair

(P-16392)
SDI LLC
21 Morgan Ste 150, Irvine (92618-2086)
PHONE..................................949 351-1866
Jon Korbonski, *President*
EMP: 20

SALES (est): 1.2MM **Privately Held**
SIC: 3599 Custom machinery

(P-16393)
SENGA ENGINEERING INC
1525 E Warner Ave, Santa Ana
(92705-5419)
PHONE..................................714 549-8011
Roy Jones, *President*
Elvia Rodriguez, *Human Res Mgr*
Kim Truitt, *Buyer*
EMP: 48
SQ FT: 25,000
SALES (est): 8.4MM **Privately Held**
WEB: www.senga-eng.com
SIC: 3599 Machine shop, jobbing & repair

(P-16394)
SENIOR AEROSPACE JET PDTS CORP
9150 Balboa Ave, San Diego (92123-1512)
PHONE..................................858 278-8400
Willis Fletcher, *Branch Mgr*
EMP: 10
SALES (corp-wide): 1.3B **Privately Held**
SIC: 3599 Machine shop, jobbing & repair
HQ: Senior Aerospace Jet Products Corp.
    9106 Balboa Ave
    San Diego CA 92123
    858 278-8400

(P-16395)
SENIOR OPERATIONS LLC
Also Called: Senior Flexonics
9106 Balboa Ave, San Diego (92123-1512)
PHONE..................................858 278-8400
James Young, *Vice Pres*
EMP: 258
SALES (corp-wide): 1.3B **Privately Held**
SIC: 3599 Bellows, industrial: metal; hose, flexible metallic; tubing, flexible metallic
HQ: Senior Operations Llc
    300 E Devon Ave
    Bartlett IL 60103
    630 372-3500

(P-16396)
SENIOR OPERATIONS LLC
Also Called: Capo Industries Division
790 Greenfield Dr, El Cajon (92021-3101)
PHONE..................................909 627-2723
Jim Watkins, *Branch Mgr*
EMP: 70
SALES (corp-wide): 1.3B **Privately Held**
SIC: 3599 Hose, flexible metallic; tubing, flexible metallic; bellows, industrial: metal
HQ: Senior Operations Llc
    300 E Devon Ave
    Bartlett IL 60103
    630 372-3500

(P-16397)
SENIOR OPERATIONS LLC
Also Called: Jet Products
9106 Balboa Ave, San Diego (92123-1512)
PHONE..................................858 278-8400
Damon Evans, *Branch Mgr*
Daniel Fee, *Engineer*
EMP: 160
SALES (corp-wide): 1.3B **Privately Held**
SIC: 3599 Hose, flexible metallic; tubing, flexible metallic; bellows, industrial: metal
HQ: Senior Operations Llc
    300 E Devon Ave
    Bartlett IL 60103
    630 372-3500

(P-16398)
SERRANO INDUSTRIES INC
9922 Tabor Pl, Santa Fe Springs
(90670-3300)
PHONE..................................562 777-8180
Hoberto Serrano Jr, *President*
Bobby Serrano, *Vice Pres*
Maria Serrano, *Vice Pres*
Daniel Mota, *General Mgr*
Cristal Serrano, *Purchasing*
EMP: 34
SQ FT: 30,000
SALES (est): 8.1MM **Privately Held**
WEB: www.serrano-ind.com
SIC: 3599 Machine shop, jobbing & repair

(P-16399)
SHARKEY TECHNOLOGY GROUP INC
Also Called: C and T Machining
39450 3rd St E Ste 154, Palmdale
(93550-3253)
PHONE..................................661 267-2118
John P Sharkey, *Treasurer*
Judy Sharkey, *President*
EMP: 10
SQ FT: 5,000
SALES (est): 1.2MM **Privately Held**
SIC: 3599 Machine shop, jobbing & repair

(P-16400)
SHARP DIMENSION INC
4240 Business Center Dr, Fremont
(94538-6356)
PHONE..................................510 656-8938
Scott Vo, *President*
EMP: 21
SQ FT: 12,000
SALES (est): 4.4MM **Privately Held**
WEB: www.sharpdimension.com
SIC: 3599 Machine shop, jobbing & repair

(P-16401)
SHEFFIELD MANUFACTURING INC
13849 Magnolia Ave, Chino (91710-7028)
PHONE..................................818 767-4948
Dave Hilton, *CEO*
EMP: 40 EST: 2013
SALES (est): 6.8MM **Privately Held**
SIC: 3599 3444 Machine shop, jobbing & repair; sheet metalwork

(P-16402)
SHERMAN CORPORATION
10803 Los Jardines E, Fountain Valley
(92708-3936)
PHONE..................................310 671-2117
EMP: 27
SQ FT: 14,000
SALES (est): 3.8MM **Privately Held**
SIC: 3599

(P-16403)
SHORT RUN SWISS INC
714 E Edna Pl, Covina (91723-1408)
PHONE..................................626 974-9373
Paul Ellis, *President*
Bud Ellis, *Vice Pres*
EMP: 10 EST: 1968
SQ FT: 4,650
SALES (est): 800K **Privately Held**
WEB: www.shortrunswiss.com
SIC: 3599 Machine shop, jobbing & repair

(P-16404)
SIERRA PACIFIC MACHINING INC
530 Parrott St, San Jose (95112-4120)
PHONE..................................408 924-0281
Richard Wagner, *President*
Steven Young, *Vice Pres*
EMP: 18
SALES (est): 2.7MM **Privately Held**
SIC: 3599 Machine shop, jobbing & repair

(P-16405)
SILICON VALLEY ELITE MFG
460 Aldo Ave, Santa Clara (95054-2301)
PHONE..................................408 654-9534
Kim Oanh Ngo, *CEO*
EMP: 10 EST: 2012
SALES (est): 1.1MM **Privately Held**
SIC: 3599 Machine shop, jobbing & repair

(P-16406)
SIX SIGMA PRECISION INC
7706 Bell Rd Ste C, Windsor (95492-8546)
PHONE..................................707 836-0869
Dan E McCrady, *CEO*
Patrick A McCrady, *CFO*
EMP: 10
SQ FT: 4,000
SALES (est): 1.8MM **Privately Held**
SIC: 3599 Machine shop, jobbing & repair

(P-16407)
SMI CA INC
Also Called: Saeilo Manufacturing Inds
14340 Iseli Rd, Santa Fe Springs
(90670-5204)
PHONE..................................562 926-9407
Katsuhiko Tsukamoto, *CEO*
David Tsukamoto, *President*
Erik Kawakami, *Corp Secy*
EMP: 26
SQ FT: 10,000
SALES (est): 4MM
SALES (corp-wide): 30MM **Privately Held**
WEB: www.saeilo-smi.com
SIC: 3599 Machine & other job shop work
PA: Saeilo Enterprises Inc
    105 Kahr Ave
    Greeley PA 18425
    845 735-6500

(P-16408)
SMITH BROTHERS MANUFACTURING
5304 Banks St, San Diego (92110-4008)
PHONE..................................619 296-3171
Larry D Smith, *President*
Karen Amberg, *Treasurer*
Billie L Mc Farland, *Vice Pres*
EMP: 18 EST: 1945
SQ FT: 5,700
SALES (est): 2.8MM **Privately Held**
WEB: www.smithbrosmfg.com
SIC: 3599 3548 Machine shop, jobbing & repair; electrodes, electric welding

(P-16409)
SOLO ENTERPRISE CORP
Also Called: Solo Golf
220 N California Ave, City of Industry
(91744-4323)
PHONE..................................626 961-3591
Richard F Mugica, *CEO*
Edward Mugica, *Vice Pres*
Cheryl Haskett, *Accountant*
Edward A Mugica, *VP Mfg*
EMP: 50
SQ FT: 20,000
SALES (est): 7.4MM **Privately Held**
SIC: 3599 3812 Machine shop, jobbing & repair; search & navigation equipment

(P-16410)
SOUTH ALLIANCE INDUSTRIAL MCH
2423 Troy Ave, South El Monte
(91733-1431)
PHONE..................................626 442-3744
Miguel Hidalgo, *President*
EMP: 10
SQ FT: 9,000
SALES: 1MM **Privately Held**
SIC: 3599 Machine shop, jobbing & repair

(P-16411)
SOUTH BAY SOLUTIONS INC (PA)
Also Called: SBS
37399 Centralmont Pl, Fremont
(94536-6549)
PHONE..................................650 843-1800
Adam Drewniany, *CEO*
Valerie Guseva, *Vice Pres*
EMP: 30
SQ FT: 20,000
SALES (est): 16.6MM **Privately Held**
WEB: www.southbaysolutions.com
SIC: 3599 Machine shop, jobbing & repair

(P-16412)
SOUTHERN CAL TCHNICAL ARTS INC
370 E Crowther Ave, Placentia
(92870-6419)
PHONE..................................714 524-2626
John H Robson IV, *President*
Matt Robson, *COO*
Kristi A Robson, *CFO*
Christine Robson, *Corp Secy*
Paul Kiralla, *Admin Asst*
EMP: 48
SQ FT: 9,400

SALES (est): 8.9MM **Privately Held**
WEB: www.technicalarts.com
SIC: **3599** 3827 Machine shop, jobbing &
repair; optical instruments & lenses

(P-16413)
SPACETRON METAL BILLOWS CORP
15303 Ventura Blvd # 900, Sherman Oaks
(91403-3110)
PHONE..................................818 633-1075
Naborina Martinez, *President*
Lawrence Miller, *CFO*
Rick Montoya, *Senior VP*
EMP: 15
SQ FT: 12,000
SALES (est): 1.1MM **Privately Held**
SIC: **3599** Bellows, industrial: metal

(P-16414)
SPARTAN MANUFACTURING CO
7081 Patterson Dr, Garden Grove
(92841-1435)
PHONE..................................714 894-1955
R J Horton, *President*
Terry Danielson, *Vice Pres*
EMP: 26 EST: 1957
SQ FT: 16,000
SALES (est): 5.4MM **Privately Held**
WEB: www.spartanmfg.com
SIC: **3599** Machine shop, jobbing & repair

(P-16415)
SPEC ENGINEERING CO INC
13754 Saticoy St, Van Nuys (91402-6518)
PHONE..................................818 780-3045
Gregory Viksman, *President*
Anna Viksman, *Vice Pres*
EMP: 25
SQ FT: 5,200
SALES: 3.5MM **Privately Held**
SIC: **3599** 3412 Machine shop, jobbing &
repair; metal barrels, drums & pails

(P-16416)
SPECIALTY SURFACE GRINDING
345 W 131st St, Los Angeles (90061-1103)
PHONE..................................310 538-4352
Piero Casadio, *President*
Jone Casadio, *Corp Secy*
Paul Casadio, *General Mgr*
EMP: 15
SQ FT: 11,000
SALES: 700K **Privately Held**
SIC: **3599** Grinding castings for the trade;
machine shop, jobbing & repair

(P-16417)
SPENCO MACHINE & MANUFACTURING
27556 Commerce Center Dr, Temecula
(92590-2518)
PHONE..................................951 699-5566
Robert L Spencer, *Owner*
EMP: 14
SQ FT: 11,000
SALES (est): 1.9MM **Privately Held**
WEB: www.spencomachine.com
SIC: **3599** Machine shop, jobbing & repair

(P-16418)
SPIN TEK MACHINING INC
540 Parrott St Ste A, San Jose
(95112-4124)
PHONE..................................408 298-8223
Trung Nguyen, *Principal*
EMP: 15
SALES (est): 1.9MM **Privately Held**
SIC: **3599** Machine shop, jobbing & repair

(P-16419)
SQUAGLIA MANUFACTURING (PA)
275 Polaris Ave, Mountain View
(94043-4588)
PHONE..................................650 965-9644
Pat Pellizzari, *President*
Ken Pellizzari, *Vice Pres*
EMP: 22 EST: 1962
SQ FT: 10,000
SALES (est): 4.2MM **Privately Held**
WEB: www.squaglia.com
SIC: **3599** Machine shop, jobbing & repair

(P-16420)
SRCO INC
2305 Merced Ave, El Monte (91733-2624)
PHONE..................................626 350-8321
John Barkune, *President*
Van Roush, *Vice Pres*
EMP: 10 EST: 1975
SQ FT: 6,200
SALES: 1.7MM **Privately Held**
SIC: **3599** Machine shop, jobbing & repair

(P-16421)
STAR PRODUCTS
312 Brokaw Rd, Santa Clara (95050-4336)
PHONE..................................408 727-8421
Jody Kidambi,
EMP: 35
SALES: 950K **Privately Held**
SIC: **3599** Machine shop, jobbing & repair

(P-16422)
STAR TOOL & ENGINEERING CO INC
49235 Milmont Dr, Fremont (94538-7349)
PHONE..................................510 742-0500
Darren Myers, *CEO*
Angelo Grestoni, *President*
John S Winter, *Vice Pres*
EMP: 48
SQ FT: 40,000
SALES (est): 4.2MM **Privately Held**
WEB: www.startoolusa.com
SIC: **3599** 3566 3469 3544 Gears, power
transmission, except automotive; machine
shop, jobbing & repair; stamping metal for
the trade; special dies & tools

(P-16423)
STEVEN VARRATI
Also Called: Acme Machine Products
5237 American Ave, Modesto
(95356-9022)
PHONE..................................209 545-0107
Steven Varrati, *Owner*
EMP: 10 EST: 1957
SQ FT: 10,000
SALES (est): 747.6K **Privately Held**
SIC: **3599** Machine shop, jobbing & repair

(P-16424)
STIGTEC MANUFACTURING LLC
1125 Linda Vista Dr # 110, San Marcos
(92078-3819)
PHONE..................................760 744-7239
Ed Stiglic,
Teresa Stiglic, *Co-Owner*
Shaylee Welch, *General Mgr*
Donna Hein, *Manager*
EMP: 19
SQ FT: 10,000
SALES (est): 2.2MM **Privately Held**
WEB: www.stigtec.com
SIC: **3599** Machine shop, jobbing & repair

(P-16425)
STINES MACHINE INC
2481 Coral St, Vista (92081-8431)
PHONE..................................760 599-9955
Edward L Huston, *President*
Tri Tran, *Vice Pres*
EMP: 35
SQ FT: 15,000
SALES (est): 6.4MM **Privately Held**
WEB: www.stinesmachine.com
SIC: **3599** Machine shop, jobbing & repair

(P-16426)
SUMMIT MACHINE LLC
2880 E Philadelphia St, Ontario
(91761-8523)
PHONE..................................909 923-2744
▼ EMP: 120
SQ FT: 103,000
SALES: 20MM
SALES (corp-wide): 225.3B **Publicly Held**
WEB: www.summitmachining.com
SIC: **3599** 3728 Machine shop, jobbing &
repair; aircraft parts & equipment
HQ: Precision Castparts Corp.
4650 Sw Mcdam Ave Ste 300
Portland OR 97239
503 946-4800

(P-16427)
SUN PRECISION MACHINING INC
1651 Market St Ste A, Corona
(92880-1710)
PHONE..................................951 817-0056
Eric Zembower, *President*
EMP: 17
SALES (est): 2.6MM **Privately Held**
SIC: **3599** Machine shop, jobbing & repair

(P-16428)
SUNLAND TOOL INC
1819 N Case St, Orange (92865-4234)
PHONE..................................714 974-6500
Douglas P Brown, *President*
EMP: 10 EST: 1967
SQ FT: 10,000
SALES: 760K **Privately Held**
SIC: **3599** Machine shop, jobbing & repair

(P-16429)
SUNVAIR INC (HQ)
29145 The Old Rd, Valencia (91355-1015)
PHONE..................................661 294-3777
Robert Dann, *President*
Dale Roberts, *COO*
Melba Waschak, *Corp Secy*
Edward Waschak, *Vice Pres*
Cindy Guzman, *Admin Asst*
EMP: 65
SQ FT: 26,000
SALES (est): 19.3MM
SALES (corp-wide): 30MM **Privately Held**
WEB: www.sunvair.com
SIC: **3599** 7699 Machine shop, jobbing &
repair; aircraft & heavy equipment repair
services
PA: Sunvair Aerospace Group, Inc.
29145 The Old Rd
Valencia CA 91355
661 294-3777

(P-16430)
SUPREME MACHINE PRODUCTS INC
302 Sequoia Ave, Ontario (91761-1543)
PHONE..................................909 974-0349
Harold Hal Peterson, *President*
Isac Gomez, *Vice Pres*
Lyn Kaplan, *Manager*
EMP: 18
SQ FT: 7,800
SALES: 4.9MM **Privately Held**
SIC: **3599** Machine shop, jobbing & repair

(P-16431)
SURFACE MANUFACTURING INC
2025 Airpark Ct Ste 10, Auburn
(95602-9069)
PHONE..................................530 885-0700
Lee Baker, *President*
Richard Peattie, *CFO*
Jane Peattie, *Corp Secy*
EMP: 16
SQ FT: 10,000
SALES (est): 2.4MM **Privately Held**
WEB: www.surfacemfg.com
SIC: **3599** 3577 Machine shop, jobbing &
repair; computer peripheral equipment

(P-16432)
SUST MANUFACTURING COMPANY
2380 Wilcox Rd, Stockton (95215-2318)
PHONE..................................209 931-9571
Peter Sust, *President*
EMP: 10
SQ FT: 5,000
SALES (est): 1.2MM **Privately Held**
SIC: **3599** Machine shop, jobbing & repair

(P-16433)
SUTTER P DAHLGLEN ENTPS INC
Also Called: Metalfab
1650 Grant St, Santa Clara (95050-3981)
PHONE..................................408 727-4640
Linda Terestra, *President*
Jack Paravagna, *President*
EMP: 16
SQ FT: 16,000

SALES (est): 2.8MM **Privately Held**
SIC: **3599** 1611 Machine & other job shop
work; grading

(P-16434)
SWISS SCREW PRODUCTS INC
339 Mathew St, Santa Clara (95050-3113)
PHONE..................................408 748-8400
Sung H Hwang, *President*
Young S Hwang, *Vice Pres*
EMP: 25
SQ FT: 12,750
SALES (est): 4.2MM **Privately Held**
WEB: www.swissscrew.com
SIC: **3599** 3541 3451 Machine shop, job-
bing & repair; machine tools, metal cutting
type; screw machine products

(P-16435)
SWISS WIRE EDM
3505 Cadillac Ave Ste J1, Costa Mesa
(92626-1432)
PHONE..................................714 540-2903
Malcolm Schneer, *President*
Nola Schneer, *Vice Pres*
EMP: 15
SQ FT: 10,000
SALES (est): 2.9MM **Privately Held**
WEB: www.swedm.com
SIC: **3599** Machine shop, jobbing & repair

(P-16436)
T & M MACHINING INC
331 Irving Dr, Oxnard (93030-5172)
PHONE..................................805 983-6716
Mario Mangone, *President*
Kay Mangone, *Controller*
EMP: 20
SALES (est): 2.5MM **Privately Held**
SIC: **3599** 3544 Machine shop, jobbing &
repair; special dies, tools, jigs & fixtures

(P-16437)
T C QUALITY MACHINING INC
12155 Magnolia Ave 10d, Riverside
(92503-4905)
PHONE..................................951 509-4633
Dale Caldwell, *President*
Michael Taylor, *CEO*
Theresa A Taylor, *Principal*
Ronda A Caldwell, *Admin Sec*
EMP: 12 EST: 1997
SQ FT: 6,500
SALES (est): 1.9MM **Privately Held**
SIC: **3599** Machine shop, jobbing & repair

(P-16438)
T E B INC
8754 Lion St, Rancho Cucamonga
(91730-4427)
PHONE..................................909 941-8100
Michael Harding, *President*
EMP: 15 EST: 1961
SQ FT: 8,500
SALES (est): 2MM **Privately Held**
SIC: **3599** Machine shop, jobbing & repair

(P-16439)
T T E PRODUCTS INC
1701 Fortune Dr Ste N, San Jose
(95131-1702)
PHONE..................................408 955-0100
Sherman K Chu, *President*
EMP: 10
SQ FT: 2,500
SALES (est): 1.3MM **Privately Held**
SIC: **3599** Machine shop, jobbing & repair

(P-16440)
T&T PRECISION MACHINING
9812 Atlantic Ave, South Gate
(90280-5219)
PHONE..................................323 583-0064
German Torres, *Principal*
EMP: 11
SALES (est): 1.2MM **Privately Held**
SIC: **3599** Machine shop, jobbing & repair

(P-16441)
T/Q SYSTEMS INC
25131 Arctic Ocean Dr, Lake Forest
(92630-8852)
PHONE..................................949 455-0478
Victor Buytkus, *President*
Scott Moebius, *Vice Pres*
EMP: 42

PRODUCTS & SVCS

SALES: 7.1MM **Privately Held**
WEB: www.tqsystems.net
SIC: **3599** Machine shop, jobbing & repair

(P-16442)
TALOS CORPORATION
Also Called: Paramount Tool & Machine Co
512 2nd Ave, Redwood City (94063-3848)
PHONE..................................650 364-7364
Gerald G Popplewell, *President*
Adelina Popplewell, *Treasurer*
EMP: 20
SQ FT: 20,000
SALES: 1.5MM **Privately Held**
WEB: www.talosinstruments.com
SIC: **3599** Machine shop, jobbing & repair

(P-16443)
TAPEMATION MACHINING INC (PA)
13 Janis Way, Scotts Valley (95066-3537)
PHONE..................................831 438-3069
Ericka Stevens, *President*
Josolyn Bradshaw, *Vice Pres*
EMP: 12 EST: 1961
SALES (est): 3.6MM **Privately Held**
WEB: www.tapemation.com
SIC: **3599** Machine shop, jobbing & repair

(P-16444)
TAPEMATION MACHINING INC
15 Janis Way, Scotts Valley (95066-3537)
PHONE..................................831 438-3069
EMP: 14
SALES (corp-wide): 3.6MM **Privately Held**
SIC: **3599** Machine shop, jobbing & repair
PA: Tapemation Machining Inc.
    13 Janis Way
    Scotts Valley CA 95066
    831 438-3069

(P-16445)
TCT ADVANCED MACHINING INC
2454 Fender Ave Ste C, Fullerton (92831-4320)
PHONE..................................714 871-9371
James Chang, *President*
EMP: 14
SQ FT: 2,400
SALES (est): 878.4K **Privately Held**
SIC: **3599** Machine shop, jobbing & repair

(P-16446)
TECFAR MANUFACTURING INC
8525 Telfair Ave, Sun Valley (91352-3928)
PHONE..................................818 767-0677
Joe Simpson, *President*
Charles Ahn, *CEO*
Rick Shirinian, *COO*
Joe Richardson, *Prdtn Mgr*
Michael Caputo, *QC Mgr*
EMP: 17
SQ FT: 8,500
SALES: 900K **Privately Held**
WEB: www.tecfar.com
SIC: **3599** Machine shop, jobbing & repair

(P-16447)
TECH-STAR INDUSTRIES INC
1171 Sonora Ct, Sunnyvale (94086-5384)
PHONE..................................650 369-7214
James Stephens, *President*
Lolo Stephens, *CFO*
Mike Walker, *General Mgr*
▲ EMP: 12
SQ FT: 9,000
SALES (est): 2.1MM **Privately Held**
WEB: www.techstarindustries.com
SIC: **3599** Machine shop, jobbing & repair

(P-16448)
TECHNICAL TROUBLE SHOOTING INC
27822 Fremont Ct B, Valencia (91355-1130)
PHONE..................................661 257-1202
Sergey Levkov, *President*
EMP: 20
SQ FT: 15,000
SALES (est): 3.1MM **Privately Held**
SIC: **3599** Bellows, industrial: metal; propellers, ship & boat: machined

(P-16449)
TECNO INDUSTRIAL ENGINEERING
13528 Pumice St, Norwalk (90650-5249)
PHONE..................................562 623-4517
Juan Giner, *President*
Enrique Viano, *Vice Pres*
EMP: 45
SQ FT: 17,000
SALES: 2.2MM **Privately Held**
WEB: www.tecnoest.net
SIC: **3599** **3728** Machine shop, jobbing & repair; aircraft parts & equipment

(P-16450)
TEMECULA PRECISON FABRICATION
Also Called: Temecula Precision Mfg
42201 Sarah Way, Temecula (92590-3463)
PHONE..................................951 699-4066
Steve Leckband, *President*
Teri Leckband, *Vice Pres*
EMP: 13
SALES (est): 2.8MM **Privately Held**
SIC: **3599** Machine shop, jobbing & repair

(P-16451)
TEMPCO ENGINEERING INC
8866 Laurel Canyon Blvd A, Sun Valley (91352-2998)
PHONE..................................818 767-2326
David Shushereba, *Principal*
EMP: 102 EST: 1966
SQ FT: 26,000
SALES (est): 11MM **Privately Held**
WEB: www.lmiaerospace.com
SIC: **3599** Machine shop, jobbing & repair
HQ: Lmi Aerospace, Inc.
    411 Fountain Lakes Blvd
    Saint Charles MO 63301
    636 946-6525

(P-16452)
TER INC
Also Called: T E R
306 Mathew St, Santa Clara (95050-3104)
PHONE..................................408 986-9920
Edward Cech III, *President*
Daryl Gillum, *COO*
Tom Cech, *Vice Pres*
EMP: 30
SQ FT: 12,000
SALES (est): 4.2MM **Privately Held**
SIC: **3599** **3444** Machine shop, jobbing & repair; sheet metalwork

(P-16453)
TER PRECISION MACHINING INC
306 Mathew St, Santa Clara (95050-3104)
PHONE..................................408 986-9920
Thomas Cech, *President*
Edward Cech III, *Principal*
Randall Cech, *Principal*
Scott Jacobs, *General Mgr*
EMP: 25
SQ FT: 12,000
SALES (est): 4.2MM **Privately Held**
SIC: **3599** Machine shop, jobbing & repair

(P-16454)
TETRAD SERVICES INC
960 Diamond Ave, Red Bluff (96080-4358)
P.O. Box 8099 (96080-8099)
PHONE..................................530 527-5889
Roger Meyer, *CEO*
EMP: 12
SQ FT: 20,000
SALES (est): 2.4MM **Privately Held**
WEB: www.tetradservice.com
SIC: **3599** Machine shop, jobbing & repair

(P-16455)
THIESSEN PRODUCTS INC
Also Called: Jim's Machining
555 Dawson Dr Ste A, Camarillo (93012-5085)
PHONE..................................805 482-6913
Jim Thiessen, *President*
Jay R Thiessen, *Corp Secy*
Debra Thiessen, *Vice Pres*
Paul Platts, *Executive*
Denise Hughes, *Sales Mgr*
EMP: 130
SQ FT: 44,000

SALES (est): 26.1MM **Privately Held**
WEB: www.jimsusa.com
SIC: **3599** Machine shop, jobbing & repair

(P-16456)
THOMAS CNC MACHINING
23650 Via Del Rio, Yorba Linda (92887-2714)
PHONE..................................714 692-9373
Kim Rose, *Owner*
EMP: 10
SQ FT: 11,000
SALES (est): 1MM **Privately Held**
SIC: **3599** Machine shop, jobbing & repair

(P-16457)
THUNDERBOLT MANUFACTURING INC
641 S State College Blvd, Fullerton (92831-5115)
PHONE..................................714 632-0397
Minh Son To, *President*
EMP: 26
SQ FT: 5,800
SALES: 3MM **Privately Held**
SIC: **3599** Machine shop, jobbing & repair

(P-16458)
TIM GUZZY SERVICES INC
5136 Calmview Ave, Baldwin Park (91706-1803)
P.O. Box 1457 (91706-7457)
PHONE..................................626 813-0626
Tim Guzzy, *President*
Mariana Guzzy, *Vice Pres*
EMP: 11
SQ FT: 5,500
SALES (est): 1.9MM **Privately Held**
SIC: **3599** Machine shop, jobbing & repair

(P-16459)
TMX ENGINEERING AND MFG CORP
2141 S Standard Ave, Santa Ana (92707-3034)
PHONE..................................714 641-5884
Souhil Toubia, *CEO*
Gus Toubia, *President*
Mauricio Escarcega, *Principal*
Steve Korn, *Principal*
Ali Ossaily, *General Mgr*
EMP: 75
SQ FT: 23,000
SALES (est): 16.5MM **Privately Held**
WEB: www.tmxengineering.com
SIC: **3599** **3728** **3544** Machine shop, jobbing & repair; aircraft parts & equipment; special dies, tools, jigs & fixtures

(P-16460)
TOMI ENGINEERING INC
414 E Alton Ave, Santa Ana (92707-4242)
PHONE..................................714 556-1474
Michael F Falbo, *CEO*
Anthony Falbo, *President*
Julia McElroy, *Human Res Mgr*
EMP: 52 EST: 1975
SQ FT: 15,000
SALES (est): 9.7MM **Privately Held**
WEB: www.tomiengineering.com
SIC: **3599** Machine shop, jobbing & repair

(P-16461)
TORRANCE PRECISION MACHINING
Also Called: Torrance Manufacturing
9530 Owensmouth Ave Ste 8, Chatsworth (91311-8026)
PHONE..................................818 709-7838
Fred Torrance, *President*
Lajauna Torrance, *CFO*
Scott Brossard, *General Mgr*
EMP: 13
SQ FT: 8,000
SALES (est): 1.9MM **Privately Held**
WEB: www.torranceprecision.com
SIC: **3599** Machine shop, jobbing & repair

(P-16462)
TOWER INDUSTRIES INC
Also Called: Allied Mechanical Products
1720 S Bon View Ave, Ontario (91761-4411)
PHONE..................................909 947-2723
Mark Slater, *Manager*

EMP: 110
SQ FT: 60,794
SALES (corp-wide): 30.8MM **Privately Held**
SIC: **3599** Machine shop, jobbing & repair
PA: Tower Industries, Inc.
    1518 N Endeavor Ln Ste C
    Anaheim CA 92801
    -

(P-16463)
TRACET MANUFACTURING INC
40 Kirby Ave, Morgan Hill (95037-9391)
PHONE..................................408 779-8846
Tim Westmoreland, *President*
William Lattin, *Vice Pres*
EMP: 10
SQ FT: 5,000
SALES (est): 1.4MM **Privately Held**
WEB: www.tracet.com
SIC: **3599** Machine shop, jobbing & repair

(P-16464)
TREPANNING SPCIALTY A CAL CORP
Also Called: Trepanning Specialties
16201 Illinois Ave, Paramount (90723-4903)
PHONE..................................562 408-0044
Donald B Laughlin, *President*
Patricia Laughlin, *Vice Pres*
▲ EMP: 23
SQ FT: 7,000
SALES: 2.1MM **Privately Held**
WEB: www.trepanningspec.com
SIC: **3599** Machine shop, jobbing & repair

(P-16465)
TRI STATE MANUFACTURING INC
27212 Burbank, El Toro (92610-2504)
PHONE..................................949 855-9121
Bill Smith, *President*
Deanna Smith, *Corp Secy*
EMP: 10
SQ FT: 5,000
SALES (est): 1.5MM **Privately Held**
SIC: **3599** Machine shop, jobbing & repair

(P-16466)
TRI-C MACHINE CORPORATION (PA)
Also Called: Tri C Machine Shop
520 Harbor Blvd, West Sacramento (95691-2227)
PHONE..................................916 371-8090
Lilburn C Lamar Jr, *Principal*
L Lamar, *CFO*
Marion Lamar, *Vice Pres*
EMP: 10 EST: 1970
SQ FT: 12,000
SALES (est): 4.2MM **Privately Held**
SIC: **3599** **3552** **7389** Machine shop, jobbing & repair; fabric forming machinery & equipment; design services

(P-16467)
TRIAD BELLOWS DESIGN & MFG INC
2897 E La Cresta Ave, Anaheim (92806-1817)
PHONE..................................714 204-4444
Michael G Moore, *President*
EMP: 26
SALES (est): 1.6MM **Privately Held**
SIC: **3599** Bellows, industrial: metal

(P-16468)
TRIANGLE TOOL & DIE CORP
13189 Flores St, Santa Fe Springs (90670-4041)
PHONE..................................562 944-2117
Michael J Beyer, *Principal*
Barbara Beyer, *Vice Pres*
EMP: 15
SQ FT: 14,000
SALES (est): 2.2MM **Privately Held**
SIC: **3599** **3542** Electrical discharge machining (EDM); die casting & extruding machines

(P-16469)
TRIDECS CORPORATION
3513 Arden Rd, Hayward (94545-3907)
PHONE..................................510 785-2620

▲ = Import ▼=Export
◆ =Import/Export

Frank Schenkhuizen Sr, *Ch of Bd*
Frank Schenkhuizen Jr, *President*
Emma J Schenkhuizen, *Admin Sec*
Alpha Diallo, *Opers Spvr*
John Homa, *QC Mgr*
EMP: 25
SQ FT: 15,000
SALES: 3MM **Privately Held**
WEB: www.tridecs.com
SIC: 3599 Machine shop, jobbing & repair

(P-16470)
TRONSON MANUFACTURING INC
3421 Yale Way, Fremont (94538-6171)
PHONE..............................408 533-0369
Michael Lieu, *President*
▲ **EMP:** 20 **EST:** 1998
SQ FT: 11,040
SALES (est): 2.6MM **Privately Held**
SIC: 3599 Machine shop, jobbing & repair

(P-16471)
TRU MACHINING
45979 Warm Springs Blvd, Fremont
(94539-6765)
PHONE..............................510 573-3408
Quocthuy Truong, *President*
Diep Nguyen, *Director*
EMP: 15 **EST:** 2013
SALES (est): 135K **Privately Held**
SIC: 3599 3569 Machine shop, jobbing &
repair; liquid automation machinery &
equipment

(P-16472)
TRUE POSITION TECHNOLOGIES LLC
24900 Avenue Stanford, Valencia
(91355-1272)
PHONE..............................661 294-0030
Allen Sumian, *President*
EMP: 82
SQ FT: 25,000
SALES (est): 18.2MM
SALES (corp-wide): 260.7MM **Privately
Held**
WEB: www.truepositiontech.com
SIC: 3599 Machine shop, jobbing & repair
PA: Hbd Industries Inc
    5200 Upper Metro
    Dublin OH 43017
    614 526-7000

(P-16473)
TRUE PRECISION MACHINING INC
175 Indstrial Way Bellton Buellton, Buellton
(93427)
PHONE..............................805 964-4545
Todd Ackert, *President*
EMP: 22
SQ FT: 17,000
SALES (est): 3MM **Privately Held**
WEB: www.trueprecision.net
SIC: 3599 Machine shop, jobbing & repair

(P-16474)
TRUPART MANUFACTURING INC
Also Called: Trupart Mfg
4450 Dupont Ct Ste A, Ventura
(93003-7790)
PHONE..............................805 644-4107
Shane Prukop, *President*
EMP: 10
SALES (est): 2.1MM **Privately Held**
SIC: 3599 Machine shop, jobbing & repair

(P-16475)
TSC PRECISION MACHINING INC
1311 E Saint Gertrude Pl A, Santa Ana
(92705-5216)
PHONE..............................714 542-3182
Steve Salazar, *President*
EMP: 10
SQ FT: 6,298
SALES (est): 1.7MM **Privately Held**
SIC: 3599 3452 8711 Machine shop, job-
bing & repair; bolts, nuts, rivets & wash-
ers; screws, metal; mechanical
engineering

(P-16476)
TSCHIDA ENGINEERING
1812 Yajome St, NAPA (94559-1306)
PHONE..............................707 224-4482
Bruce Tschida, *President*
EMP: 10
SQ FT: 3,600
SALES (est): 1.7MM **Privately Held**
WEB: www.tschidaeng.com
SIC: 3599 Machine shop, jobbing & repair

(P-16477)
TTN MACHINING INC
9105 Olive Dr, Spring Valley (91977-2304)
PHONE..............................619 303-4573
Hung Troung, *President*
Phuc Truong, *VP Opers*
EMP: 16
SALES (est): 2.5MM **Privately Held**
WEB: www.ttnmachining.com
SIC: 3599 Machine shop, jobbing & repair

(P-16478)
TURNKEY TECHNOLOGIES INC
Also Called: Accuvac Technology Division
4650 E 2nd St Ste C, Benicia
(94510-1038)
P.O. Box 205 (94510-0205)
PHONE..............................707 745-9520
Satish Chohan, *President*
EMP: 21 **EST:** 1969
SQ FT: 24,000
SALES (est): 2MM **Privately Held**
WEB: www.accuvac.com
SIC: 3599 Machine shop, jobbing & repair

(P-16479)
TURRET LATHE SPECIALISTS INC
875 S Rose Pl, Anaheim (92805-5337)
PHONE..............................714 520-0058
Robert McBride, *President*
EMP: 18
SQ FT: 6,000
SALES (est): 2.9MM **Privately Held**
SIC: 3599 Machine shop, jobbing & repair

(P-16480)
TWO BEARS METAL PRODUCTS
723 N Meyler St, San Pedro (90731-1428)
PHONE..............................310 326-2533
Jeffrey Allen, *Owner*
EMP: 20
SALES (est): 1.5MM **Privately Held**
SIC: 3599 Machine shop, jobbing & repair

(P-16481)
UNITECH TOOL & MACHINE INC
3025 Stender Way, Santa Clara
(95054-3216)
PHONE..............................408 566-0333
Ramin Lak, *CEO*
▲ **EMP:** 20
SALES (est): 3.2MM **Privately Held**
SIC: 3599 Machine shop, jobbing & repair

(P-16482)
UNITED DRILLING CO
11807 Slauson Ave, Santa Fe Springs
(90670-2219)
PHONE..............................562 945-8833
Peter Arjona, *Owner*
Tony Flota, *Finance Mgr*
EMP: 24
SQ FT: 6,500
SALES (est): 2MM **Privately Held**
SIC: 3599 Machine shop, jobbing & repair

(P-16483)
UNITED PRO FAB MFG INC
Also Called: Pro Fab Manufacturing
45300 Industrial Pl Ste 5, Fremont
(94538-6453)
PHONE..............................510 651-5570
Rajesh Gupta, *President*
Seema Gupta, *Vice Pres*
▲ **EMP:** 10
SQ FT: 5,000
SALES (est): 1.7MM **Privately Held**
WEB: www.pfmfg.com
SIC: 3599 Machine shop, jobbing & repair

(P-16484)
UNITED WESTERN INDUSTRIES INC
3515 N Hazel Ave, Fresno (93722-4913)
P.O. Box 13099 (93794-3099)
PHONE..............................559 226-7236
L G Simmons, *President*
EMP: 49 **EST:** 1971
SQ FT: 15,000
SALES (est): 9.2MM **Privately Held**
SIC: 3599 3469 3544 Custom machinery;
machine shop, jobbing & repair; metal
stampings; die sets for metal stamping
(presses)

(P-16485)
UNIVERSAL PLANT SERVICES CAL (HQ)
20545a Belshaw Ave, Carson
(90746-3505)
PHONE..............................310 618-1600
Bradley Jones, *CEO*
Stewart Jones, *President*
Reagan Busbee, *COO*
Shawn Enarson, *Vice Pres*
EMP: 16
SALES (est): 9.7MM
SALES (corp-wide): 164.8MM **Privately
Held**
SIC: 3599 Custom machinery
PA: Jones Industrial Holdings, Inc.
    806 Seaco Ct
    Deer Park TX 77536
    281 479-6000

(P-16486)
V & S ENGINEERING COMPANY LTD
5766 Research Dr, Huntington Beach
(92649-1617)
PHONE..............................714 898-7869
Dino Dukovic, *President*
Dino Dokovic, *President*
EMP: 15
SQ FT: 10,000
SALES (est): 2.5MM **Privately Held**
SIC: 3599 Machine shop, jobbing & repair

(P-16487)
V-TECH MANUFACTURING INC
Also Called: V Tech
1140 W Evelyn Ave, Sunnyvale
(94086-5742)
PHONE..............................408 730-9200
Robert Gluchowski, *President*
Jamie Sandidge, *Office Mgr*
EMP: 15
SQ FT: 2,000
SALES (est): 2.1MM **Privately Held**
WEB: www.vtechmanufacturing.com
SIC: 3599 Machine shop, jobbing & repair

(P-16488)
VAL-AERO INDUSTRIES INC
25319 Rye Canyon Rd, Valencia
(91355-1205)
PHONE..............................661 295-8645
Ralph O Smith Jr, *President*
EMP: 12
SQ FT: 4,800
SALES (est): 1.4MM **Privately Held**
SIC: 3599 Machine shop, jobbing & repair

(P-16489)
VALLEY PERFORATING LLC
3201 Gulf St, Bakersfield (93308-4905)
PHONE..............................661 324-4964
Mike Dover, *President*
Dorothy Reynolds, *Vice Pres*
Alice Lomas, *Admin Sec*
Nicole McKenzie, *Human Res Mgr*
EMP: 65
SQ FT: 10,440
SALES (est): 10.7MM **Privately Held**
WEB: www.valleyperf.com
SIC: 3599 Machine shop, jobbing & repair

(P-16490)
VALLEY PRECISION INC
536 Hi Tech Pkwy, Oakdale (95361-9371)
PHONE..............................209 847-1758
Donald R Faubion, *President*
Michael P Faubion, *Admin Sec*
EMP: 11 **EST:** 1977
SQ FT: 5,000

SALES (est): 4.3MM **Privately Held**
SIC: 3599 3545 3544 Machine shop, jobbing & repair; machine tool accessories;
special dies, tools, jigs & fixtures

(P-16491)
VALLEY TOOL & MFG CO INC
2507 Tully Rd, Hughson (95326-9824)
P.O. Box 220 (95326-0220)
PHONE..............................209 883-4093
Fred G Brenda, *CEO*
Carol Finn, *Treasurer*
Vaughn Brenda, *Vice Pres*
Daniel C Finn, *Vice Pres*
Richard Kohl, *Vice Pres*
▲ **EMP:** 40
SQ FT: 50,000
SALES (est): 9.8MM **Privately Held**
WEB: www.valleytoolmfg.com
SIC: 3599 Machine shop, jobbing & repair

(P-16492)
VALLEY TOOL AND MACHINE CO INC
111 Explorer St, Pomona (91768-3278)
PHONE..............................909 595-2205
Chuck Rogers, *CEO*
Jim Rogers, *President*
Nancy Larson, *Corp Secy*
EMP: 32 **EST:** 1982
SQ FT: 34,000
SALES (est): 5.8MM **Privately Held**
WEB: www.valleytool-inc.com
SIC: 3599 7692 3544 Machine shop, job-
bing & repair; welding repair; special dies,
tools, jigs & fixtures

(P-16493)
VALVEX ENTERPRISES INC
Also Called: DC Valve Mfg & Precision Mchs
885 Jarvis Dr, Morgan Hill (95037-2858)
PHONE..............................408 928-2510
Cuu Banh, *CEO*
EMP: 43
SQ FT: 3,200
SALES (est): 8.3MM **Privately Held**
WEB: www.dcvalvemfg.com
SIC: 3599 Machine shop, jobbing & repair

(P-16494)
VANDER-BEND MANUFACTURING INC
Also Called: J.L. Haley
3510 Luyung Dr, Rancho Cordova
(95742-6872)
PHONE..............................916 631-6375
Steve Butts, *Branch Mgr*
EMP: 140
SALES (corp-wide): 131MM **Privately
Held**
SIC: 3599 3312 7692 Machine shop, job-
bing & repair; blast furnaces & steel mills;
welding repair
PA: Vander-Bend Manufacturing, Inc.
    2701 Orchard Pkwy
    San Jose CA 95134
    408 245-5150

(P-16495)
VANDERHULST ASSOCIATES INC
3300 Victor Ct, Santa Clara (95054-2316)
PHONE..............................408 727-1313
Hank Vanderhulst, *CEO*
Sandy Thompson, *Vice Pres*
Corrie Vanderhulst, *Admin Sec*
Chad Weaver, *Prgrmr*
EMP: 30 **EST:** 1975
SQ FT: 11,000
SALES: 3.5MM **Privately Held**
WEB: www.vanderhulst.com
SIC: 3599 Machine shop, jobbing & repair

(P-16496)
VANS MANUFACTURING INC
330 E Easy St Ste C, Simi Valley
(93065-7526)
PHONE..............................805 522-6267
Louis Tignac, *President*
EMP: 19
SQ FT: 8,500
SALES (est): 2.4MM **Privately Held**
SIC: 3599 Custom machinery

(P-16497)
VEECO PROCESS EQUIPMENT INC
Slider Process Division
112 Robin Hill Rd, Goleta (93117-3107)
PHONE..................................805 967-2700
Ed Wagner, *Manager*
Joshua Kaiman, *Manager*
EMP: 70
SALES (corp-wide): 542MM **Publicly Held**
SIC: 3599 3545 3544 3291 Machine shop, jobbing & repair; machine tool accessories; special dies, tools, jigs & fixtures; abrasive products
HQ: Veeco Process Equipment Inc.
   1 Terminal Dr
   Plainview NY 11803

(P-16498)
VELLIOS MACHINE SHOP INC
Also Called: Vellios Automotive Machine Sp
4625 29th Mnhattan Bch Bl, Lawndale (90260)
PHONE..................................310 643-8540
Harry Vellios, *President*
Carolyn Vellios, *Corp Secy*
Mark Vellios, *Vice Pres*
EMP: 12
SQ FT: 6,500
SALES (est): 1.6MM **Privately Held**
SIC: 3599 3714 5013 Machine shop, jobbing & repair; rebuilding engines & transmissions, factory basis; automotive supplies & parts

(P-16499)
VENTURA HYDRULIC MCH WORKS INC
1555 Callens Rd, Ventura (93003-5606)
PHONE..................................805 656-1760
Fred H Malzacher, *President*
Elaine Z Malzacher, *Vice Pres*
EMP: 20
SQ FT: 15,700
SALES (est): 4.2MM **Privately Held**
WEB: www.venturahydraulics.com
SIC: 3599 Machine shop, jobbing & repair

(P-16500)
VESCIO THREADING CO
Also Called: Vescio Manufacturing Intl
14002 Anson Ave, Santa Fe Springs (90670-5202)
PHONE..................................562 802-1868
Gregory Vescio, *CEO*
Robert Vescio, *President*
Greg Vescio, *CEO*
Bob Vescio, *CFO*
Verna Vescio, *Treasurer*
EMP: 73
SQ FT: 13,000
SALES (est): 15.3MM **Privately Held**
WEB: www.vesciothreading.com
SIC: 3599 Machine shop, jobbing & repair

(P-16501)
VI-TEC MANUFACTURING INC
288 Boeing Ct, Livermore (94551-9258)
PHONE..................................925 447-8200
James Vice, *President*
Linda Vice, *CFO*
EMP: 10
SQ FT: 12,000
SALES (est): 1.4MM **Privately Held**
WEB: www.vi-tec.com
SIC: 3599 Machine shop, jobbing & repair

(P-16502)
VIANH COMPANY INC
13841 A Better Way 10c, Garden Grove (92843-3930)
PHONE..................................714 590-9808
Tam Nguyen, *President*
Vianh Nguyen, *CFO*
Jimmy Nguyen, *CTO*
EMP: 25
SQ FT: 8,000
SALES: 300K **Privately Held**
WEB: www.vianhcompany.com
SIC: 3599 Machine shop, jobbing & repair

(P-16503)
VISGER PRECISION INC
1815 Russell Ave, Santa Clara (95054-2035)
PHONE..................................408 988-0184
Terrance M Visger, *President*
Terry Visger, *Manager*
EMP: 18
SQ FT: 10,000
SALES (est): 2.8MM **Privately Held**
WEB: www.visger.com
SIC: 3599 Machine shop, jobbing & repair

(P-16504)
VMG ENGINEERING INC
1046 Griswold Ave, San Fernando (91340-1455)
P.O. Box 507 (91341-0507)
PHONE..................................818 837-6320
Vicente Corona, *President*
Maribel Corona, *Corp Secy*
Marie Corona, *Vice Pres*
EMP: 10
SQ FT: 8,000
SALES (est): 1.7MM **Privately Held**
WEB: www.vmgengineering.com
SIC: 3599 3429 Machine shop, jobbing & repair; manufactured hardware (general)

(P-16505)
VULTURES ROW AVIATION LLC
Also Called: Vra Manufacturing
3152 Cameron Park Dr, Cameron Park (95682-7623)
PHONE..................................530 676-9245
Charles Wahl, *Owner*
Carol Wahl,
EMP: 11 EST: 2010
SQ FT: 15,000
SALES (est): 1.4MM **Privately Held**
SIC: 3599 3724 3728 Machine & other job shop work; aircraft engines & engine parts; ailerons, aircraft

(P-16506)
W MACHINE WORKS INC
13814 Del Sur St, San Fernando (91340-3440)
PHONE..................................818 890-8049
Marzel Neckien, *President*
Randy Neckien, *Vice Pres*
Michael Gonzaga, *Production*
JP Walz, *VP Sales*
Anna Martirosyan, *Accounts Mgr*
EMP: 45
SQ FT: 25,000
SALES (est): 9MM **Privately Held**
WEB: www.wmachineworksinc.com
SIC: 3599 Machine shop, jobbing & repair

(P-16507)
WACKER DEVELOPMENT INC
36 Hollywood Ave, Los Gatos (95030-6235)
PHONE..................................408 356-0208
Roland Wacker, *President*
Doris Wacker, *Treasurer*
EMP: 10 EST: 1960
SQ FT: 16,000
SALES (est): 750K **Privately Held**
SIC: 3599 Machine shop, jobbing & repair

(P-16508)
WAHLCO INC
15 Marconi Ste B, Irvine (92618-2779)
PHONE..................................714 979-7300
Alonso Munoz, *CEO*
Robert R Wahier, *CEO*
Dennis Nickel, *CFO*
Barry J Southam, *Exec VP*
Barry Southam, *Exec VP*
◆ EMP: 106
SQ FT: 54,000
SALES (est): 36.7MM **Privately Held**
WEB: www.wahlco.com
SIC: 3599 Custom machinery

(P-16509)
WALLACE E MILLER INC
Also Called: Micro-TEC
9155 Alabama Ave Ste B, Chatsworth (91311-5867)
PHONE..................................818 998-0444
Gary Case, *President*
Roxanne Case, *Vice Pres*
EMP: 19

SQ FT: 8,000
SALES: 1.4MM **Privately Held**
WEB: www.microtecmfg.com
SIC: 3599 Machine shop, jobbing & repair

(P-16510)
WARD ENTERPRISES
10332 Trumbull St, California City (93505-1550)
P.O. Box 803231, Santa Clarita (91380-3231)
PHONE..................................661 251-4890
EMP: 15
SQ FT: 16,000
SALES: 1.1MM **Privately Held**
SIC: 3599

(P-16511)
WARMELIN PRECISION PDTS LLC
12705 Daphne Ave, Hawthorne (90250-3311)
PHONE..................................323 777-5003
Doug Horton, *President*
Avner Applbaum, *CFO*
Ron Bohannon, *Vice Pres*
Sherri Henkel, *Senior Buyer*
Quintero Daniel, *Mfg Mgr*
EMP: 65
SQ FT: 50,000
SALES (est): 10MM
SALES (corp-wide): 22.7MM **Privately Held**
SIC: 3599 Machine shop, jobbing & repair
PA: Aerostar Aerospace Manufacturing, Llc
   2688 E Rose Garden Ln
   Phoenix AZ 85050
   602 861-1145

(P-16512)
WATSONS PROFILING CORP
1460 S Balboa Ave, Ontario (91761-7609)
PHONE..................................909 923-5500
James Watson, *President*
EMP: 13
SALES (est): 3MM **Privately Held**
SIC: 3599 Machine shop, jobbing & repair

(P-16513)
WATTS MACHINING INC
2339 Calle Del Mundo, Santa Clara (95054-1008)
PHONE..................................408 654-9300
Doug Watts, *President*
Serkadis Negussie, *Buyer*
Bob Hazle, *Prdtn Mgr*
Travis Erk, *Production*
EMP: 30
SQ FT: 17,000
SALES (est): 3.7MM **Privately Held**
WEB: www.wattsmachining.com
SIC: 3599 Machine shop, jobbing & repair

(P-16514)
WEBB-STOTLER ENGINEERING
1701 Commerce St, Corona (92880-1734)
PHONE..................................951 735-2040
David Stotler, *Owner*
EMP: 10
SQ FT: 5,700
SALES (est): 740K **Privately Held**
SIC: 3599 Machine shop, jobbing & repair

(P-16515)
WELDMAC MANUFACTURING COMPANY
1451 N Johnson Ave, El Cajon (92020-1615)
PHONE..................................619 440-2300
Marshall J Rugg, *President*
Barbara Bloomfield, *Corp Secy*
Robert L Rugg, *Vice Pres*
EMP: 122
SQ FT: 100,000
SALES: 29.6MM **Privately Held**
WEB: www.weldmac.com
SIC: 3599 3444 7692 Machine shop, jobbing & repair; sheet metalwork; brazing

(P-16516)
WES MANUFACTURING INC
3241 Keller St, Santa Clara (95054-2646)
PHONE..................................408 727-0750
Garn Nelson, *CEO*
Carl Michaels, *Vice Pres*
Dennis Whightman, *Vice Pres*

EMP: 20
SALES (est): 4MM **Privately Held**
SIC: 3599 8711 Machine shop, jobbing & repair; consulting engineer

(P-16517)
WEST COAST FORM GRINDING
Also Called: Precision Corepins
2548 S Fairview St, Santa Ana (92704-5335)
PHONE..................................714 540-5621
Adrian Calderon, *President*
Danny Deu Tran, *Treasurer*
Henry Busane, *Admin Sec*
EMP: 10
SQ FT: 3,000
SALES (est): 869.4K **Privately Held**
SIC: 3599 Grinding castings for the trade; machine shop, jobbing & repair

(P-16518)
WEST COAST MACHINING INC
14560 Marquardt Ave, Santa Fe Springs (90670-5121)
PHONE..................................562 229-1087
Sonia Duran, *CEO*
Carolina Beas, *CFO*
EMP: 15
SQ FT: 18,000
SALES (est): 3.3MM **Privately Held**
WEB: www.westcoastmachining.com
SIC: 3599 Machine shop, jobbing & repair

(P-16519)
WESTCOAST GRINDING CORPORATION
Also Called: Accurate Double Disc Grinding
10517 San Fernando Rd, Pacoima (91331-2624)
PHONE..................................818 890-1841
William C Birch, *President*
EMP: 15
SQ FT: 6,000
SALES: 1MM **Privately Held**
SIC: 3599 Machine shop, jobbing & repair

(P-16520)
WESTCOAST PRECISION INC
2091 Fortune Dr, San Jose (95131-1824)
PHONE..................................408 943-9998
Sang A Nhin, *President*
Helen Nhin, *Principal*
EMP: 45
SALES (est): 8.2MM **Privately Held**
SIC: 3599 3559 Machine shop, jobbing & repair; semiconductor manufacturing machinery

(P-16521)
WESTERN CNC INC
1001 Park Center Dr, Vista (92081-8340)
PHONE..................................760 597-7000
Danny Ashcraft, *President*
April Ashcraft Ramirez, *Vice Pres*
Carolyn Ashcraft, *Admin Sec*
Tommy Asaro, *Engineer*
Wences De La Mora, *Engineer*
EMP: 100
SQ FT: 57,000
SALES (est): 20.2MM **Privately Held**
WEB: www.westerncnc.com
SIC: 3599 Machine shop, jobbing & repair

(P-16522)
WESTERN GRINDING SERVICE INC
2375 De La Cruz Blvd, Santa Clara (95050-2920)
PHONE..................................650 591-2635
David P Wilson, *Ch of Bd*
Ethan C Wilson, *President*
Rob Brindle, *VP Mfg*
EMP: 30 EST: 1953
SQ FT: 28,000
SALES (est): 5.8MM **Privately Held**
WEB: www.westerngrinding.com
SIC: 3599 Machine shop, jobbing & repair

(P-16523)
WESTERN PRECISION AERO LLC
11600 Monarch St, Garden Grove (92841-1817)
PHONE..................................714 893-7999
Ed McKenna, *Mng Member*

▲ = Import ▼=Export
◆ =Import/Export

Norma Davis, *CFO*
EMP: 37
SQ FT: 16,000
SALES (est): 6.7MM
SALES (corp-wide): 702.5MM **Publicly Held**
SIC: 3599 Machine shop, jobbing & repair
PA: Rbc Bearings Incorporated
102 Willenbrock Rd
Oxford CT 06478
203 267-7001

(P-16524)
WESTERN WIDGETS CNC INC
915 Commercial St, San Jose (95112-1440)
PHONE..............................408 436-1230
Laszlo Molnar, *President*
Tony Fricano, *CEO*
EMP: 10
SQ FT: 7,000
SALES (est): 1.5MM **Privately Held**
SIC: 3599 Machine shop, jobbing & repair

(P-16525)
WHITTEN MACHINE SHOP
4770 S K St, Tulare (93274-7149)
PHONE..............................559 686-3428
John Whitten, *President*
Larry Whitten, *Shareholder*
Steve Whitten, *Shareholder*
Geraldine Whitten, *Corp Secy*
Ron Whitten, *Vice Pres*
EMP: 13
SALES (est): 1.4MM **Privately Held**
WEB: www.whittenmachine.com
SIC: 3599 Machine shop, jobbing & repair

(P-16526)
WILCOX MACHINE CO
7180 Scout Ave, Bell Gardens (90201-3202)
P.O. Box 2159, Bell (90202-2159)
PHONE..............................562 927-5353
George Schofhauser, *President*
Jill Wigney, *Corp Secy*
Kurt Anderegg, *Vice Pres*
Tom Anderegg, *Vice Pres*
Karen Mathis, *Persnl Dir*
◆ **EMP:** 60 **EST:** 1955
SALES (est): 12.1MM **Privately Held**
WEB: www.wilcoxmachine.com
SIC: 3599 Machine shop, jobbing & repair; custom machinery

(P-16527)
WILKINSON MFG INC
332 Piercy Rd, San Jose (95138-1401)
PHONE..............................408 988-3588
Douglas M Greene, *President*
EMP: 13
SQ FT: 4,400
SALES (est): 2.3MM **Privately Held**
WEB: www.wilkinsonmfg.com
SIC: 3599 Machine shop, jobbing & repair

(P-16528)
WILLIS MACHINE INC
200 Kinetic Dr, Oxnard (93030-7920)
PHONE..............................805 604-4500
Harlan Willis, *President*
EMP: 10
SQ FT: 20,000
SALES (est): 3.9MM **Privately Held**
WEB: www.willismachine.com
SIC: 3599 Machine shop, jobbing & repair

(P-16529)
WILMINGTON MACHINE INC
Also Called: Wilmington Ironworks
432 W C St, Wilmington (90744-5714)
PHONE..............................310 518-3213
Walter C Richards III, *President*
Elva Richards, *Treasurer*
J W Richards, *Admin Sec*
EMP: 14
SQ FT: 13,000
SALES (est): 2.4MM **Privately Held**
WEB: www.wilmingtonironworks.com
SIC: 3599 Machine shop, jobbing & repair

(P-16530)
WILSHIRE PRECISION PDTS INC
7353 Hinds Ave, North Hollywood (91605-3704)
PHONE..............................818 765-4571

Thomas G Lewis, *President*
Dana Lewis, *Corp Secy*
Shoshona Lewis, *Corp Secy*
Wendy Lewis, *Vice Pres*
Dana Ullerich, *Controller*
EMP: 31 **EST:** 1951
SQ FT: 10,000
SALES (est): 5.7MM **Privately Held**
WEB: www.wilshireprecision.com
SIC: 3599 3621 Machine shop, jobbing & repair; motors, electric; electric motor & generator auxillary parts

(P-16531)
WIRE CUT COMPANY INC
6750 Caballero Blvd, Buena Park (90620-1134)
PHONE..............................714 994-1170
Milton M Thomas, *CEO*
Tina Thomas, *Treasurer*
EMP: 30
SQ FT: 20,000
SALES (est): 5.2MM **Privately Held**
WEB: www.wirecut-co.com
SIC: 3599 Machine shop, jobbing & repair

(P-16532)
WMC PRECISION MACHINING
1234 E Ash Ave Ste A, Fullerton (92831-5013)
PHONE..............................714 773-0059
Richard Mourey, *President*
Leigh Thompson, *General Mgr*
EMP: 15
SQ FT: 10,000
SALES (est): 2.7MM **Privately Held**
SIC: 3599 Machine shop, jobbing & repair

(P-16533)
WOLFS PRECISION WORKS INC
3549 Haven Ave Ste F, Menlo Park (94025-1070)
PHONE..............................650 364-1341
Wolfgang Pohl, *President*
Karen Pohl, *Corp Secy*
EMP: 15
SQ FT: 5,000
SALES (est): 2.2MM **Privately Held**
WEB: www.wpw-inc.com
SIC: 3599 Machine shop, jobbing & repair

(P-16534)
WOODRUFF CORPORATION
109 Calle Mayor, Redondo Beach (90277-6509)
PHONE..............................310 378-1611
Ronald D Woodruff, *President*
Dan Watts, *Vice Pres*
EMP: 32
SQ FT: 16,000
SALES (est): 3.5MM **Privately Held**
SIC: 3599 Machine shop, jobbing & repair

(P-16535)
YOUNG MACHINE INC
Also Called: California Machine Specialties
12282 Colony Ave, Chino (91710-2095)
PHONE..............................909 464-0405
Anand Jagani, *President*
Gilbert Fresquez, *Consultant*
EMP: 19
SQ FT: 11,000
SALES (est): 3.6MM **Privately Held**
SIC: 3599 Machine shop, jobbing & repair

(P-16536)
YUHAS TOOLING & MACHINING
Also Called: Slawomira Sobczyk
1031 Pecten Ct, Milpitas (95035-6804)
PHONE..............................408 934-9196
Slava Sobczyk, *CEO*
EMP: 15
SQ FT: 6,000
SALES: 1MM **Privately Held**
WEB: www.yuhasmachining.com
SIC: 3599 Machine shop, jobbing & repair

(P-16537)
ZET-TEK PRECISION MACHINING (PA)
Also Called: Zet-Tek Machining
22951 La Palma Ave, Yorba Linda (92887-6701)
PHONE..............................714 777-8770
Daniel Zettler, *CEO*
Sandra Rubino, *Vice Pres*

EMP: 15
SQ FT: 25,000
SALES (est): 3.8MM **Privately Held**
WEB: www.zet-tek.com
SIC: 3599 3444 Machine shop, jobbing & repair; sheet metalwork

---

3612 Power, Distribution & Specialty Transformers

(P-16538)
ABB ENTERPRISE SOFTWARE INC
1321 Harbor Bay Pkwy # 101, Alameda (94502-6582)
PHONE..............................510 987-7111
Beth Reid, *Branch Mgr*
EMP: 76
SALES (corp-wide): 36.4B **Privately Held**
WEB: www.elsterelectricity.com
SIC: 3612 Transformers, except electric
HQ: Abb Inc.
305 Gregson Dr
Cary NC 27511
-

(P-16539)
ABBOTT TECHNOLOGIES INC
8203 Vineland Ave, Sun Valley (91352-3956)
PHONE..............................818 504-0644
Kerima Marie Batte, *CEO*
Yasmin Morales, *Admin Asst*
Jacob Shalgian, *Electrical Engi*
Albert Rieker, *Opers Mgr*
John Batte, *Sales Associate*
EMP: 50
SQ FT: 12,000
SALES (est): 9.9MM **Privately Held**
WEB: www.abbott-tech.com
SIC: 3612 3559 3677 Transformers, except electric; electronic component making machinery; transformers power supply, electronic type

(P-16540)
ALECTRO INC
Also Called: Protech Systems
6770 Central Ave Ste B, Riverside (92504-1443)
PHONE..............................909 590-9521
Tim Stevens, *CEO*
Gail A Stephens, *President*
Remy Hernandez, *Purchasing*
EMP: 15 **EST:** 1978
SQ FT: 18,000
SALES (est): 2.1MM **Privately Held**
WEB: www.protechsystems.com
SIC: 3612 1731 Transformers, except; safety & security specialization

(P-16541)
ALGONQUIN POWER SANGER LLC
1125 Muscat Ave, Sanger (93657-4000)
P.O. Box 397 (93657-0397)
PHONE..............................559 875-0800
Ian Robertson, *Mng Member*
EMP: 22
SQ FT: 16,225
SALES (est): 5MM
SALES (corp-wide): 1.6B **Privately Held**
SIC: 3612 Power transformers, electric
PA: Algonquin Power & Utilities Corp
354 Davis Rd
Oakville ON L6J 2
905 465-4500

(P-16542)
CALIFORNIA PAK INTL INC
1700 S Wilmington Ave, Compton (90220-5116)
PHONE..............................310 223-2500
Edward Kwon, *President*
Byung Yull Kwon, *CEO*
Barry Casper, *Vice Pres*
Charles Kim, *Vice Pres*
Judy Kwon, *Finance Mgr*
▲ **EMP:** 20
SQ FT: 15,000

SALES (est): 3.9MM **Privately Held**
WEB: www.calpaks.com
SIC: 3612 Distribution transformers, electric

(P-16543)
CALIFORNIA ST UNI CHANNEL ISLA
45 Rincon Dr Unit 104a, Camarillo (93012-8423)
PHONE..............................805 437-2670
Erik Blaine, *Exec Dir*
EMP: 25
SQ FT: 5,000
SALES (est): 2.7MM **Privately Held**
SIC: 3612 Power & distribution transformers

(P-16544)
CGR/THOMPSON INDUSTRIES INC
7155 Fenwick Ln, Westminster (92683-5218)
PHONE..............................714 678-4200
Michael B Baughan, *CEO*
Vince Corti, *General Mgr*
Kevin Rowan, *Sales Staff*
EMP: 70
SQ FT: 10,000
SALES (est): 11.2MM
SALES (corp-wide): 66.5B **Publicly Held**
SIC: 3612 Machine tool transformers
HQ: B/E Aerospace, Inc.
1400 Corporate Center Way
Wellington FL 33414
561 791-5000

(P-16545)
CPI ADVANCED INC
Also Called: Enaba-Kbw USA
14708 Central Ave, Chino (91710-9502)
PHONE..............................909 597-5533
Charles Pyong Cha, *President*
Yarnee Arias, *Manager*
▲ **EMP:** 120
SQ FT: 2,500
SALES (est): 14.4MM **Privately Held**
WEB: www.cpipower.com
SIC: 3612 Fluorescent lighting transformers

(P-16546)
DATATRONICS ROMOLAND INC
28151 Us Highway 74, Menifee (92585-8916)
P.O. Box 1579 (92585-1579)
PHONE..............................951 928-7700
Paul Y Siu, *CEO*
Randy Eller, *Chief Mktg Ofcr*
Nancy Johnston, *Administration*
Brock Baker, *Engineer*
Melissa Mobley, *Engineer*
▲ **EMP:** 75
SQ FT: 38,800
SALES: 12.2MM **Privately Held**
WEB: www.datatronicsromoland.com
SIC: 3612 3677 Transformers, except electric; inductors, electronic

(P-16547)
DOW-ELCO INC
1313 W Olympic Blvd, Montebello (90640-5010)
P.O. Box 669 (90640-0669)
PHONE..............................323 723-1288
Linda Su, *President*
Cecile SE Kay, *Vice Pres*
Grace Park, *Admin Sec*
Ronald Cheung, *Director*
Annie Su, *Director*
EMP: 25
SQ FT: 8,100
SALES (est): 4.9MM **Privately Held**
SIC: 3612 3829 3061 Vibrators, interrupter; measuring & controlling devices; mechanical rubber goods

(P-16548)
ENERGY CNVRSION APPLCTIONS INC
Also Called: Eca
582 Explorer St, Brea (92821-3108)
PHONE..............................714 256-2166
Akbal Grewal, *CEO*
Robert De Luca, *Manager*

EMP: 17
SQ FT: 10,000
SALES (est): 3.9MM **Privately Held**
WEB: www.eca-mfg.com
SIC: 3612 8748 Transformers, except electric; telecommunications consultant

(P-16549)
FALCON ELECTRIC INC
5116 Azusa Canyon Rd, Baldwin Park (91706-1846)
PHONE..................................626 962-7770
Arthur Seredian, *CEO*
▲ EMP: 13
SALES (est): 3.1MM **Privately Held**
SIC: 3612 Transformers, except electric

(P-16550)
FENIX INTERNATIONAL INC
30 Cleveland St, San Francisco (94103-4014)
PHONE..................................415 754-9222
Brian Warshawsky, *CEO*
Ivan Topalov, *CFO*
Junior Zerebela Kwebiiha, *Ch Credit Ofcr*
Luke Hodgkinson, *Engineer*
Ian Wogan, *Engineer*
EMP: 350
SALES (est): 5.2MM
SALES (corp-wide): 31.8B **Privately Held**
SIC: 3612 Transformers, except electric
PA: Engie
1 Place Samuel De Champlain
Courbevoie
144 220-000

(P-16551)
FORTRON/SOURCE CORPORATION (PA)
23181 Antonio Pkwy, Rcho STA Marg (92688-2652)
PHONE..................................949 766-9240
Jackson Wang, *President*
Charlie Shih, *Vice Pres*
Jeff Tseng, *Vice Pres*
Monica Mao, *Executive*
Ed Lee, *Purch Mgr*
▲ EMP: 24
SQ FT: 10,000
SALES (est): 2.4MM **Privately Held**
SIC: 3612 3679 3577 Transformers, except electric; power supplies, all types: static; computer peripheral equipment

(P-16552)
FULHAM CO INC
12705 S Van Ness Ave, Hawthorne (90250-3322)
PHONE..................................323 779-2980
Antony Corrie, *President*
James Cooke, *CFO*
Deborah Knuckles, *CFO*
Mike Hu, *Vice Pres*
Harry Libby, *Vice Pres*
▲ EMP: 40
SQ FT: 48,000
SALES (est): 6.3MM **Privately Held**
WEB: www.fulham.com
SIC: 3612 Ballasts for lighting fixtures
HQ: Fulham Company Gmbh
Torstr. 138
Berlin

(P-16553)
GRAND GENERAL ACCESSORIES LLC
1965 E Vista Bella Way, Rancho Dominguez (90220-6106)
PHONE..................................310 631-2589
Shu-Hui Lin Huang, *CEO*
Kevin Huang, *Manager*
Tina Ward, *Manager*
Susie Velasco, *Accounts Mgr*
▲ EMP: 39
SALES (est): 8.9MM **Privately Held**
SIC: 3612 5531 3713 Transformers, except electric; truck equipment & parts; truck & bus bodies

(P-16554)
HAMMOND POWER SOLUTIONS INC
17715 S Susana Rd, Compton (90221-5409)
PHONE..................................310 537-4690
Raymundo Regalado, *Manager*
Ray Regalado, *General Mgr*
EMP: 25
SALES (corp-wide): 238.1MM **Privately Held**
WEB: www.hammondpowersolutions.com
SIC: 3612 Power transformers, electric
HQ: Hammond Power Solutions, Inc.
1100 Lake St
Baraboo WI 53913
608 356-3921

(P-16555)
HIS COMPANY INC
Also Called: Hisco
2215 Pseo De Las Amrcas S, San Diego (92154-7908)
PHONE..................................858 513-7748
William Bland, *Manager*
Richard French, *Branch Mgr*
EMP: 30
SALES (corp-wide): 263.1MM **Privately Held**
WEB: www.hiscoinc.com
SIC: 3612 5063 Distribution transformers, electric; electronic wire & cable; insulators, electrical
PA: His Company, Inc.
6650 Concord Park Dr
Houston TX 77040
713 934-1600

(P-16556)
HOME PORTAL LLC
Also Called: Future Home
3351 La Cienega Pl, Los Angeles (90016-3116)
PHONE..................................310 559-6100
Murray S Kunis, *President*
Glenn Hahn, *Manager*
EMP: 10
SQ FT: 5,000
SALES: 2.5MM **Privately Held**
WEB: www.futurehome.net
SIC: 3612 Voltage regulators, transmission & distribution

(P-16557)
HYBRINETICS INC
Also Called: Voltage Valet Division
225 Sutton Pl, Santa Rosa (95407-8123)
P.O. Box 14399 (95402-6399)
PHONE..................................707 585-0333
Richard Rosa, *President*
▲ EMP: 95 EST: 1965
SQ FT: 15,000
SALES (est): 11.2MM **Privately Held**
WEB: www.voltagevalet.com
SIC: 3612 5064 3621 3634 Voltage regulating transformers, electric power; electric household appliances; irons; motors & generators; irons, electric: household

(P-16558)
INTERCOM ENERGY INC
1330 Orange Ave 300-30, Coronado (92118-2949)
PHONE..................................619 863-9644
Ernesto Pallares, *CEO*
EMP: 13
SALES (est): 1.2MM **Privately Held**
SIC: 3612 Transformers, except electric

(P-16559)
JUSTIN INC
2663 Lee Ave, El Monte (91733-1411)
PHONE..................................626 444-4516
Frank Justin Jr, *President*
Jeffrey Ross Justin, *CEO*
Jeff Justin, *Vice Pres*
EMP: 50
SQ FT: 4,000
SALES (est): 10.2MM **Privately Held**
WEB: www.justininc.com
SIC: 3612 Specialty transformers

(P-16560)
LORAN INC
Also Called: Nightscaping Outdoor Lighting
1705 E Colton Ave, Redlands (92374-4971)
PHONE..................................405 340-0660
Lavesta Locklin, *President*
▲ EMP: 42
SQ FT: 100,000
SALES (est): 6MM **Privately Held**
WEB: www.loraninc.com
SIC: 3612 3645 Transformers, except electric; garden, patio, walkway & yard lighting fixtures: electric

(P-16561)
MAGCOMP INC
982 N Batavia St, Orange (92867-5502)
PHONE..................................714 532-3584
Thang Nguyen, *Partner*
Huong Vu, *Partner*
John Nguyen, *Prdtn Mgr*
EMP: 10
SALES (est): 1.3MM **Privately Held**
WEB: www.magcomp.com
SIC: 3612 Specialty transformers

(P-16562)
MGM TRANSFORMER CO
5701 Smithway St, Commerce (90040-1583)
PHONE..................................323 726-0888
Patrick Gogerchin, *President*
David Walker, *Officer*
Luis Otero, *Vice Pres*
Shekhar Patwardhan, *Materials Mgr*
Fafar Aliabadi, *Sales Engr*
◆ EMP: 70
SQ FT: 40,000
SALES (est): 34.8MM **Privately Held**
WEB: www.mgm-transformer.com
SIC: 3612 Transformers, except electric

(P-16563)
MPS INDUSTRIES INCORPORATED (PA)
19210 S Vermont Ave # 405, Gardena (90248-4431)
PHONE..................................310 325-1043
Chiging Jean Wang, *President*
▲ EMP: 25
SQ FT: 25,000
SALES (est): 6.5MM **Privately Held**
SIC: 3612 3499 Power transformers, electric; magnets, permanent: metallic

(P-16564)
NRG ENERGY SERVICES LLC
100302 Yates Well Rd, Nipton (92364)
PHONE..................................702 815-2023
Dick Dusmely, *Manager*
EMP: 60 **Publicly Held**
SIC: 3612 Machine tool transformers
HQ: Nrg Energy Services Llc
990 Peiffers Ln
Harrisburg PA 17109

(P-16565)
ON-LINE POWER INCORPORATED (PA)
Also Called: Power Services
14000 S Broadway, Los Angeles (90061-1018)
PHONE..................................323 721-5017
Abbie Gougerchian, *President*
Brad Goodman, *General Mgr*
Vivian Meza, *Administration*
▲ EMP: 46
SQ FT: 36,000
SALES (est): 18.5MM **Privately Held**
WEB: www.onlinepower.com
SIC: 3612 3621 3613 3677 Transformers, except electric; motors & generators; regulators, power; electronic coils, transformers & other inductors

(P-16566)
PACIFIC TRANSFORMER CORP
5399 E Hunter Ave, Anaheim (92807-2054)
PHONE..................................714 779-0450
Patrick A Thomas, *CEO*
Jim Richardson, *CFO*
Jackie Wood, *Executive*
Ray Artsdalen, *General Mgr*

Emmanuel Izaguirre, *Engineer*
▲ EMP: 205
SQ FT: 37,000
SALES: 16.9MM **Privately Held**
WEB: www.pactran.com
SIC: 3612 Power transformers, electric

(P-16567)
PIONEER CUSTOM ELEC PDTS CORP
10640 Springdale Ave, Santa Fe Springs (90670-3843)
PHONE..................................562 944-0626
Geo Murickan, *President*
EMP: 68 EST: 2013
SALES (est): 18MM **Publicly Held**
SIC: 3612 Electronic meter transformers
PA: Pioneer Power Solutions, Inc.
400 Kelby St Ste 12
Fort Lee NJ 07024

(P-16568)
POWER PARAGON INC (DH)
Also Called: Power Systems Group
901 E Ball Rd, Anaheim (92805-5916)
PHONE..................................714 956-9200
David R Riley, *President*
Bruce Moore, *President*
Michael R Allen, *Vice Pres*
Michael Benthale, *Vice Pres*
Klaus Kahrs, *Vice Pres*
▼ EMP: 585
SQ FT: 120,000
SALES (est): 158MM
SALES (corp-wide): 6.8B **Publicly Held**
WEB: www.powerparagon.com
SIC: 3612 3613 3621 3643 Transformers, except electric; switchgear & switchboard apparatus; motors & generators; current-carrying wiring devices
HQ: L3 Technologies, Inc.
600 3rd Ave Fl 34
New York NY 10016
212 697-1111

(P-16569)
POWER PARAGON INC
Also Called: Power Magnetics
711 W Knox St, Gardena (90248-4410)
PHONE..................................310 523-4443
J J Garcia, *Manager*
EMP: 16
SALES (corp-wide): 6.8B **Publicly Held**
WEB: www.powerparagon.com
SIC: 3612 Transformers, except electric
HQ: Power Paragon, Inc.
901 E Ball Rd
Anaheim CA 92805
714 956-9200

(P-16570)
POWERTRONIX CORPORATION
1120 Chess Dr, Foster City (94404-1103)
PHONE..................................650 345-6800
Carl A Svensson, *CEO*
Mike Bradley, *Vice Pres*
John Scott, *Vice Pres*
Anita Svensson, *Admin Sec*
Michael Fortaleza, *Engineer*
▲ EMP: 25
SQ FT: 1,800
SALES (est): 5.9MM **Privately Held**
WEB: www.powertronix.com
SIC: 3612 Power & distribution transformers

(P-16571)
PULSE ELECTRONICS INC (DH)
15255 Innovation Dr # 100, San Diego (92128-3410)
PHONE..................................858 674-8100
Mark Twaalfhoven, *CEO*
Renuka Ayer, *CFO*
Mike Bond, *Senior VP*
John R D Dickson, *Senior VP*
John Houston, *Senior VP*
▲ EMP: 270
SQ FT: 49,750
SALES (est): 457.2MM
SALES (corp-wide): 652.7MM **Privately Held**
WEB: www.pulseeng.com
SIC: 3612 3674 3677 Specialty transformers; modules, solid state; filtration devices, electronic

HQ: Pulse Electronics Corporation
15255 Innovation Dr # 100
San Diego CA 92128
858 674-8100

(P-16572)
QUALITY TRANSFORMER & ELEC
Also Called: Quality Transformer & Elec Co
963 Ames Ave, Milpitas (95035-6326)
PHONE....................................408 935-0231
Carl Clift, *CEO*
Frank W Hendershot, *President*
Adam Clouse, *General Mgr*
Dwight Ennis, *Info Tech Mgr*
Lukasz Skowronski, *Engineer*
EMP: 40 EST: 1964
SQ FT: 32,500
SALES (est): 12.3MM **Privately Held**
WEB: www.qte.com
SIC: 3612 Transformers, except electric

(P-16573)
RING LLC (HQ)
1523 26th St, Santa Monica (90404-3507)
PHONE....................................800 656-1918
Jamie Siminoff, *CEO*
Rob Harris, *Vice Pres*
Matthew Lehman, *Vice Pres*
Emma Hsiao, *Office Admin*
Gilbert Monterrosa, *IT/INT Sup*
▲ EMP: 300
SQ FT: 40,000
SALES (est): 165MM **Publicly Held**
SIC: 3612 5065 Doorbell transformers, electric; security control equipment & systems

(P-16574)
RWNM INC
1240 Simpson Way, Escondido (92029-1406)
PHONE....................................760 489-1245
Randy Allen Weisser, *President*
Nate Mullen, *Vice Pres*
Brian Collins, *District Mgr*
Steve Lauritsen, *Regl Sales Mgr*
▲ EMP: 55
SQ FT: 2,200
SALES (est): 9.1MM **Privately Held**
WEB: www.uniquelighting.com
SIC: 3612 Transformers, except electric

(P-16575)
SEMPRA GLOBAL (HQ)
488 8th Ave, San Diego (92101-7123)
PHONE....................................619 696-2000
Debra L Reed, *CEO*
Francisco Andalon, *Prgrmr*
Chris Ward, *Project Mgr*
Craig Sheridan, *Facilities Mgr*
EMP: 65
SALES (est): 43.6MM
SALES (corp-wide): 11.6B **Publicly Held**
SIC: 3612 Transformers, except electric
PA: Sempra Energy
488 8th Ave
San Diego CA 92101
619 696-2000

(P-16576)
SOMA MAGNETICS CORPORATION
585 S State College Blvd, Fullerton (92831-5113)
PHONE....................................714 447-0782
Harry Sidhu, *President*
Soma Sidhu, *Vice Pres*
EMP: 20
SQ FT: 10,000
SALES (est): 1.1MM **Privately Held**
WEB: www.somamagnetics.com
SIC: 3612 3677 3496 5999 Transformers, except electric; inductors, electronic; cable, uninsulated wire: made from purchased wire; electronic parts & equipment; transformers, electric

(P-16577)
STARLINEOEM INC
3183 Airway Ave Ste 112f, Costa Mesa (92626-4629)
PHONE....................................949 342-8889
Rosario Pozzi, *President*
EMP: 12

SALES (est): 1.7MM **Privately Held**
SIC: 3612 3613 Distribution transformers, electric; panelboards & distribution boards, electric

(P-16578)
STEWARD TERRA INC
4323 Palm Ave, La Mesa (91941-6528)
PHONE....................................619 713-0028
Christopher D'Avignon, *CEO*
Jim Ribicic, *VP Finance*
EMP: 25
SALES (est): 1.6MM **Privately Held**
SIC: 3612 Transformers, except electric

(P-16579)
STREAMLINE AVIONICS INC
17672 Armstrong Ave, Irvine (92614-5728)
PHONE....................................949 861-8151
Daniel Frahm, *President*
Diane Adams, *General Mgr*
Wally Sandberg, *Engineer*
EMP: 22
SALES (est): 3.8MM **Privately Held**
SIC: 3612 Transformers, except electric

(P-16580)
UTOPIA LIGHTING
2329 E Pacifica Pl, Compton (90220-6210)
PHONE....................................310 327-7711
▲ EMP: 14
SALES (est): 2.4MM **Privately Held**
SIC: 3612

(P-16581)
ZETTLER MAGNETICS INC
75 Columbia, Aliso Viejo (92656-5386)
PHONE....................................949 831-5000
Gunther Rueb, *CEO*
▲ EMP: 50
SQ FT: 80,000
SALES (est): 5.8MM **Privately Held**
WEB: www.buytransformers.com
SIC: 3612 Transformers, except electric
PA: Zettler Components, Inc.
75 Columbia
Orange CA 92868

3613 Switchgear & Switchboard Apparatus

(P-16582)
3M COMPANY
8357 Canoga Ave, Canoga Park (91304-2605)
PHONE....................................818 882-0606
Clint Hinze, *Branch Mgr*
Cheli Bertaud, *Technology*
Kavneet Pujji, *Marketing Staff*
EMP: 10
SALES (corp-wide): 32.7B **Publicly Held**
SIC: 3613 Switchgear & switchboard apparatus
PA: 3m Company
3m Center
Saint Paul MN 55144
651 733-1110

(P-16583)
ABD EL & LARSON HOLDINGS LLC (PA)
Also Called: Industrial Electric Mfg
48205 Warm Springs Blvd, Fremont (94539-7654)
PHONE....................................510 656-1600
Ed Rossi, *President*
Cindy Goodsell, *CFO*
Bruce Baumann, *Exec VP*
Frank Cavezza, *Exec VP*
Guy Anderson, *Vice Pres*
▲ EMP: 25
SALES (est): 40.5MM **Privately Held**
SIC: 3613 Switchboards & parts, power; switchboard apparatus, except instruments; control panels, electric; switchgear & switchgear accessories

(P-16584)
AEM (HOLDINGS) INC
6610 Cobra Way, San Diego (92121-4107)
PHONE....................................858 481-0210
Daniel H Chang, *Ch of Bd*
Xiang Ming LI, *Senior VP*

Caili Chang, *Vice Pres*
▲ EMP: 77
SQ FT: 45,000
SALES (est): 20.2MM **Privately Held**
WEB: www.aem-usa.com
SIC: 3613 3677 7699 Fuses & fuse equipment; inductors, electronic; metal re-shaping & replating services

(P-16585)
AGE INCORPORATED
14831 Spring Ave, Santa Fe Springs (90670-5109)
PHONE....................................562 483-7300
Vasken Imasdounian, *President*
Annie Imasdounian, *Corp Secy*
Daniel Imasdounian, *Vice Pres*
▲ EMP: 35 EST: 1975
SALES (est): 4.2MM **Privately Held**
SIC: 3613 3625 Control panels, electric; electric controls & control accessories, industrial

(P-16586)
BRILLIANT HOME TECHNOLOGY INC
155 Bovet Rd Ste 500, San Mateo (94402-3157)
PHONE....................................650 539-5320
Aaron Emigh, *CEO*
Brian Cardanha, *Vice Pres*
Steven Stanek, *CTO*
EMP: 11 EST: 2016
SALES: 500K **Privately Held**
SIC: 3613 Switchgear & switchboard apparatus

(P-16587)
BUFFALO DISTRIBUTION INC
30750 San Clemente St, Hayward (94544-7131)
PHONE....................................510 324-3800
Earl I Ramer Jr, *CEO*
▲ EMP: 40
SALES (est): 3.5MM **Privately Held**
SIC: 3613 Distribution cutouts

(P-16588)
CALHOUN & POXON COMPANY INC
5330 Alhambra Ave, Los Angeles (90032-3485)
PHONE....................................323 225-2328
Garrett Calhoun, *President*
Lois Calhoun, *Vice Pres*
EMP: 15
SQ FT: 22,000
SALES (est): 1.7MM **Privately Held**
WEB: www.calhounandpoxon.com
SIC: 3613 Control panels, electric

(P-16589)
CHRONTROL CORPORATION (PA)
Also Called: Chron Trol
6611 Jackson Dr, San Diego (92119-3333)
P.O. Box 19537 (92159-0537)
PHONE....................................619 282-8686
James Durham, *CEO*
EMP: 10
SQ FT: 4,461
SALES (est): 950.8K **Privately Held**
WEB: www.chrontrol.com
SIC: 3613 3625 Time switches, electrical switchgear apparatus; relays & industrial controls

(P-16590)
COBEL TECHNOLOGIES INC
822 N Grand Ave, Covina (91724-2418)
PHONE....................................626 332-2100
Mike Warner, *President*
EMP: 20
SQ FT: 5,600
SALES (est): 1.4MM **Privately Held**
WEB: www.cobeltech.com
SIC: 3613 3625 Control panels, electric; relays & industrial controls

(P-16591)
CROWN TECHNICAL SYSTEMS
13470 Philadelphia Ave, Fontana (92337-7700)
PHONE....................................951 332-4170
Naim Siddiqui, *President*

Khawar Siddiqui, *Vice Pres*
Jake Tibbetts, *Project Mgr*
Nabil Samara, *Electrical Engi*
Richard Coronado, *Engineer*
▲ EMP: 210
SQ FT: 92,000
SALES (est): 42MM **Privately Held**
SIC: 3613 Control panels, electric

(P-16592)
CUSTOM CONTROL SENSORS LLC (PA)
Also Called: Custom Aviation Supply
21111 Plummer St, Chatsworth (91311-4905)
P.O. Box 2516 (91313-2516)
PHONE....................................818 341-4610
Henry P Acuff, *President*
Thomas Pilgrim, *CFO*
Tom Pilgrim, *CFO*
Joann D Acuff, *Corp Secy*
Linda Ruiz, *Executive Asst*
EMP: 153
SALES (est): 31.4MM **Privately Held**
WEB: www.ccsdualsnap.com
SIC: 3613 3643 3625 Switches, electric power except snap, push button, etc.; current-carrying wiring devices; relays & industrial controls

(P-16593)
DAZ INC
Also Called: Duramar Interior Surfaces
2500 White Rd Ste B, Irvine (92614-6276)
PHONE....................................949 724-8800
Farhad Abdollahi, *President*
Nikkisa Abdollahi, *Exec Dir*
EMP: 15
SQ FT: 60,000
SALES: 10MM **Privately Held**
SIC: 3613 Panelboards & distribution boards, electric

(P-16594)
DIGITAL LOGGERS INC
2695 Walsh Ave, Santa Clara (95051-0920)
PHONE....................................408 330-5599
▲ EMP: 34 EST: 2009
SQ FT: 21,000
SALES (est): 2.8MM **Privately Held**
SIC: 3613 3679

(P-16595)
DOBLE ENGINEERING COMPANY
Also Called: Vanguard Instruments
1520 S Hellman Ave, Ontario (91761-7634)
PHONE....................................909 923-9390
Hai Nguyen, *Director*
EMP: 10
SALES (corp-wide): 771.5MM **Publicly Held**
SIC: 3613 3825 Power circuit breakers; electrical energy measuring equipment
HQ: Doble Engineering Company
85 Walnut St
Watertown MA 02472
617 926-4900

(P-16596)
DVTECH SOLUTION CORP
Also Called: Dvxtreme
13937 Magnolia Ave, Chino (91710-7033)
PHONE....................................909 308-0358
Daniel Wang, *CEO*
EMP: 10
SALES: 100K **Privately Held**
SIC: 3613 Switchboard apparatus, except instruments; control panels, electric; distribution boards, electric

(P-16597)
ELECTRO SWITCH CORP
Also Called: Digitran
10410 Trademark St, Rancho Cucamonga (91730-5826)
PHONE....................................909 581-0855
Robert M Pineau, *President*
Daniel Walls, *Program Mgr*
George Nguyen, *Engineer*
Edgar Mancenido, *Purch Mgr*
Amparo Concha, *Sales Staff*
EMP: 140

SALES (corp-wide): 88.3MM **Privately Held**
WEB: www.electroswitch.com
SIC: **3613** 3625 Switches, electric power except snap, push button, etc.; control panels, electric; industrial controls: push button, selector switches, pilot
HQ: Electro Switch Corp.
775 Pleasant St Ste 1
Weymouth MA 02189
781 335-1195

(P-16598)
ELECTRO-MECH COMPONENTS INC (PA)
1826 Floradale Ave, South El Monte (91733-3689)
PHONE.....................................626 442-7180
Walter Trumbull Jr, *President*
Terry Trumbull, *Vice Pres*
Carlos Melchor, *Engineer*
Livier Ramirez, *Buyer*
EMP: 10 EST: 1963
SQ FT: 7,500
SALES (est): 1.3MM **Privately Held**
WEB: www.electromechcomp.com
SIC: **3613** Switchgear & switchboard apparatus

(P-16599)
ELECTRONIC STAMPING CORP
Also Called: Esc
19920 S Alameda St, Compton (90221-6210)
PHONE.....................................310 639-2120
Hang Up Moon, *President*
Madhu RAO, *CEO*
▲ EMP: 24
SQ FT: 42,000
SALES (est): 4MM **Privately Held**
WEB: www.electronic-stamping.com
SIC: **3613** 3678 3469 Bus bar structures; electronic connectors; metal stampings

(P-16600)
HYDRA-ELECTRIC COMPANY (PA)
3151 N Kenwood St, Burbank (91505-1052)
PHONE.....................................818 843-6211
David E Schmidt, *CEO*
Sylvia Avina, *President*
Anne Keeley, *Administration*
Tim Wright, *Project Mgr*
Jonathan Dye, *Project Engr*
EMP: 178
SQ FT: 90,000
SALES (est): 18.5MM **Privately Held**
SIC: **3613** Switches, electric power except snap, push button, etc.

(P-16601)
KREGO CORPORATION
Also Called: Panel Shop, The
12971 Arroyo St, San Fernando (91340-1548)
PHONE.....................................818 837-1494
Walter Krego, *President*
Cynthia Krego, *Corp Secy*
Manny Nunes, *Engineer*
EMP: 10
SQ FT: 8,232
SALES (est): 2.5MM **Privately Held**
SIC: **3613** Panelboards & distribution boards, electric

(P-16602)
KT INDUSTRIES INC
3203 Fletcher Dr, Los Angeles (90065-2919)
PHONE.....................................323 255-7143
Leonor Vaca, *President*
Frank Vaca, *Admin Sec*
EMP: 12
SQ FT: 3,500
SALES (est): 2.3MM **Privately Held**
WEB: www.ktiengineering.com
SIC: **3613** Switchgear & switchgear accessories; control panels, electric

(P-16603)
MARWELL CORPORATION
1094 Wabash Ave, Mentone (92359)
P.O. Box 139 (92359-0139)
PHONE.....................................909 794-4192
Larry R Blackwell, *President*

Kelle A Blackwell, *Corp Secy*
Robert Ashford, *Manager*
Karrie Matcham, *Supervisor*
EMP: 18
SQ FT: 3,500
SALES (est): 3.6MM **Privately Held**
WEB: www.marwellcorp.com
SIC: **3613** Panel & distribution boards & other related apparatus

(P-16604)
NEW IEM LLC
Also Called: Industrial Electric Mfg
48205 Warm Springs Blvd, Fremont (94539-7654)
PHONE.....................................510 656-1600
Edward Herman, *CEO*
John Hulme, *CFO*
Andy Pardue, *Vice Pres*
Vickie Kakolewska, *Admin Asst*
Keith Rhodes, *Prgrmr*
▲ EMP: 100
SQ FT: 131,000
SALES (est): 40.5MM **Privately Held**
SIC: **3613** Switchboards & parts, power; switchboard apparatus, except instruments; control panels, electric; switchgear & switchgear accessories
PA: Abd El & Larson Holdings, Llc
48205 Warm Springs Blvd
Fremont CA 94539
510 656-1600

(P-16605)
PANEL SHOP INC
Also Called: Electrical Systems
2800 Palisades Dr, Corona (92880-9427)
PHONE.....................................951 739-7000
Michael Hellmers, *President*
Carol Crawford, *President*
David Hellmers, *President*
EMP: 30
SQ FT: 36,000
SALES (est): 4.1MM **Privately Held**
WEB: www.eslsys.com
SIC: **3613** 3625 Control panels, electric; relays & industrial controls

(P-16606)
PHAOSTRON INSTR ELECTRONIC CO
Also Called: Phaostron Instr Electronic Co
717 N Coney Ave, Azusa (91702-2205)
PHONE.....................................626 969-6801
Paul R Mc Guirk, *President*
Jackie Cangialosi, *CFO*
Andrew McGuirk, *Vice Pres*
Jacqueline Cangialosi, *Admin Sec*
Steve Light, *Engineer*
EMP: 80
SQ FT: 50,000
SALES (est): 12.4MM **Privately Held**
SIC: **3613** Metering panels, electric; bus bar structures
PA: Westbase Inc
717 N Coney Ave
Azusa CA 91702

(P-16607)
POWER AIRE INC
8055 E Crystal Dr, Anaheim (92807-2523)
PHONE.....................................800 526-7661
Harry Ellis Sr, *President*
Jean Blasko, *Treasurer*
Harry Ellis Jr, *Vice Pres*
Michael Ellis, *Vice Pres*
EMP: 20
SQ FT: 3,800
SALES (est): 1.6MM **Privately Held**
WEB: www.poweraire.com
SIC: **3613** 5084 Panel & distribution boards & other related apparatus; industrial machinery & equipment

(P-16608)
POWERTYE MANUFACTURING
1640 E Miraloma Ave, Placentia (92870-6622)
P.O. Box 17904, Anaheim (92817-7904)
PHONE.....................................714 993-7400
▲ EMP: 10
SALES (est): 1.3MM **Privately Held**
SIC: **3613** 5571

(P-16609)
R & J WLDG MET FABRICATION INC
2182 Maple Privado, Ontario (91761-7602)
PHONE.....................................909 930-2900
Jose Fregoso, *CEO*
EMP: 11
SALES (est): 2.3MM **Privately Held**
SIC: **3613** 3444 Generator control & metering panels; sheet metalwork

(P-16610)
RELECTRIC INC
2390 Zanker Rd, San Jose (95131-1115)
PHONE.....................................408 467-2222
Anthony Robinson, *President*
Kelly Pihera, *Purch Agent*
Dan Arnold, *Director*
Bill Davis, *Accounts Exec*
▲ EMP: 30
SQ FT: 35,000
SALES (est): 9.9MM **Privately Held**
WEB: www.allbreakers.com
SIC: **3613** 3625 5063 8734 Switchgear & switchboard apparatus; relays & industrial controls; electrical apparatus & equipment; testing laboratories

(P-16611)
ROMAC SUPPLY CO INC
7400 Bandini Blvd, Commerce (90040-3339)
PHONE.....................................323 721-5810
David B Rosenfield, *President*
Victoria Rosenfield, *Treasurer*
Lisa R Podolsky, *Vice Pres*
Phillip Rosenfield, *Vice Pres*
Edith Rosenfield, *Admin Sec*
EMP: 60
SQ FT: 105,000
SALES (est): 22.2MM **Privately Held**
WEB: www.romacsupply.com
SIC: **3613** 3621 3612 5063 Switchgear & switchgear accessories; motors & generators; transformers, except electric; motors, electric

(P-16612)
SCHNEIDER ELECTRIC USA INC
10805 Thornmint Rd # 140, San Diego (92127-2429)
PHONE.....................................858 385-5040
Rusty King, *Manager*
EMP: 136
SALES (corp-wide): 177.9K **Privately Held**
WEB: www.squared.com
SIC: **3613** Switchgear & switchboard apparatus
HQ: Schneider Electric Usa, Inc.
201 Wshington St Ste 2700
Boston MA 02108
978 975-9600

(P-16613)
SCHULTZ CONTROLS INC
565 Draft Horse Pl, Norco (92860-4145)
PHONE.....................................714 693-2900
Rick Schultz, *President*
Kathy Schultz, *Corp Secy*
EMP: 10
SQ FT: 3,000
SALES (est): 1.7MM **Privately Held**
WEB: www.schultzcontrols.com
SIC: **3613** Control panels, electric

(P-16614)
SIEMENS INDUSTRY INC
10855 Business Center Dr, Cypress (90630-5252)
PHONE.....................................714 252-3100
Donald House, *Principal*
EMP: 92
SALES (corp-wide): 95B **Privately Held**
WEB: www.sea.siemens.com
SIC: **3613** Switchboard apparatus, except instruments
HQ: Siemens Industry, Inc.
1000 Deerfield Pkwy
Buffalo Grove IL 60089
847 215-1000

(P-16615)
SILICON VLY WORLD TRADE CORP
Also Called: American Skynet Electronics
1474 Gladding Ct, Milpitas (95035-6831)
PHONE.....................................408 945-6355
Ching-Hung Liang, *President*
▲ EMP: 17
SQ FT: 10,000
SALES (est): 1.5MM **Privately Held**
WEB: www.skynetusa.com
SIC: **3613** 7379 Power switching equipment; computer related maintenance services
PA: Skynet Electronic Co., Ltd.
4f, No. 76,78,80, Chenggong Rd., Sec. 1
Taipei City TAP 11570
-

(P-16616)
SOLARBOS (HQ)
310 Stealth Ct, Livermore (94551-9303)
PHONE.....................................925 456-7744
William Lawrence Vietas, *CEO*
Letisia Ruano, *Accountant*
EMP: 53
SQ FT: 20,000
SALES (est): 21.1MM
SALES (corp-wide): 1B **Publicly Held**
SIC: **3613** Switchgear & switchboard apparatus
PA: Gibraltar Industries, Inc.
3556 Lake Shore Rd # 100
Buffalo NY 14219
716 826-6500

(P-16617)
STACO SYSTEMS INC (HQ)
Also Called: Staco Switch
7 Morgan, Irvine (92618-2005)
PHONE.....................................949 297-8700
Patrick Hutchins, *President*
Andy Bain, *Vice Pres*
Jeff Bowen, *Vice Pres*
Tom Lanni, *Vice Pres*
Brett Meinsen, *Vice Pres*
◆ EMP: 69
SQ FT: 35,000
SALES (est): 12.3MM
SALES (corp-wide): 44.2MM **Privately Held**
WEB: www.stacoswitch.com
SIC: **3613** Switches, electric power except snap, push button, etc.; panelboards & distribution boards, electric
PA: Components Corporation Of America
5950 Berkshire Ln # 1500
Dallas TX 75225
214 969-0166

(P-16618)
TE CONNECTIVITY CORPORATION
Te Circuit Protection
308 Constitution Dr, Menlo Park (94025-1111)
PHONE.....................................650 361-3333
John McGraw,
EMP: 400
SALES (corp-wide): 13.9B **Privately Held**
WEB: www.raychem.com
SIC: **3613** Switchgear & switchboard apparatus
HQ: Te Connectivity Corporation
1050 Westlakes Dr
Berwyn PA 19312
610 893-9800

(P-16619)
TRAYER ENGINEERING CORPORATION
1569 Alvarado St, San Leandro (94577-2640)
PHONE.....................................415 285-7770
John Trayer, *President*
Neil Morris, *COO*
Kirit Patel, *COO*
Julie Elliott, *General Mgr*
David Trayer, *Electrical Engi*
▼ EMP: 84
SQ FT: 21,000

▲ = Import ▼=Export
◆ =Import/Export

SALES (est): 35.8MM **Privately Held**
WEB: www.trayer.com
SIC: **3613** Switchgear & switchgear accessories

(P-16620)
VERTIV CORPORATION
6960 Koll Center Pkwy # 300, Pleasanton
(94566-3160)
PHONE...................................925 734-8660
Tony Thomas, *Manager*
EMP: 268
SALES (corp-wide): 2.9B **Privately Held**
SIC: **3613** Regulators, power
HQ: Vertiv Corporation
    1050 Dearborn Dr
    Columbus OH 43085
    614 888-0246

(P-16621)
VERTIV CORPORATION
325 Weakley St 4, Calexico (92231-9659)
P.O. Box 2887 (92232-2887)
PHONE...................................760 768-7522
Steve Benton, *Branch Mgr*
EMP: 10
SALES (corp-wide): 2.9B **Privately Held**
SIC: **3613** 3585 7629 3625 Regulators, power; air conditioning equipment, complete; electronic equipment repair; relays & industrial controls; computer peripheral equipment; blowers & fans
HQ: Vertiv Corporation
    1050 Dearborn Dr
    Columbus OH 43085
    614 888-0246

(P-16622)
WABENJAMIN ELECTRIC CO
1615 Staunton Ave, Los Angeles
(90021-3118)
PHONE...................................213 749-7731
D E Benjamin, *President*
Mauricio Mena, *CIO*
Julie Gomez, *Accountant*
Jack Clark, *Marketing Staff*
EMP: 50
SALES (est): 11.7MM **Privately Held**
WEB: www.benjaminelectric.com
SIC: **3613** Panelboards & distribution boards, electric; switchgear & switchgear accessories

(P-16623)
WEST COAST SWITCHGEAR (HQ)
13837 Bettencourt St, Cerritos
(90703-1009)
PHONE...................................562 802-3441
Alfred P Cisternelli, *CEO*
▲ EMP: 93
SQ FT: 20,000
SALES: 20MM
SALES (corp-wide): 76.6MM **Privately Held**
WEB: www.westcoastswitchgear.com
SIC: **3613** 5063 Power circuit breakers; switchgear
PA: Resa Power, Llc
    8300 Cypress Pkwy Ste 225
    Houston TX 77070
    832 900-8340

(P-16624)
WESTBASE INC (PA)
717 N Coney Ave, Azusa (91702-2205)
PHONE...................................626 969-6801
Paul R McGuirk, *President*
EMP: 10
SQ FT: 50,000
SALES (est): 13.8MM **Privately Held**
SIC: **3613** Metering panels, electric

3621 Motors & Generators

(P-16625)
ABB MOTORS AND MECHANICAL INC
Also Called: Golden Gate Baldor
21056 Forbes Ave, Hayward (94545-1116)
PHONE...................................510 785-9900
Deryl Rippy, *Manager*
EMP: 10

SALES (corp-wide): 36.4B **Privately Held**
WEB: www.baldor.com
SIC: **3621** Motors, electric
HQ: Abb Motors And Mechanical Inc.
    5711 Rs Boreham Jr St
    Fort Smith AR 72901
    479 646-4711

(P-16626)
AC PROPULSION
446 Borrego Ct, San Dimas (91773-2937)
PHONE...................................909 592-5399
EMP: 20
SALES (est): 903.7K **Privately Held**
SIC: **3621** Motors & generators

(P-16627)
ACTON INC
2400 Lincoln Ave Ste 238, Altadena
(91001-5436)
PHONE...................................323 250-0685
Janelle Wang, *CEO*
▲ EMP: 10
SALES: 120K **Privately Held**
SIC: **3621** 7519 Generators for gas-electric or oil-electric vehicles; recreational vehicle rental

(P-16628)
ADVANCED POWER & CONTROLS LLC
605 E Alton Ave Ste A, Santa Ana
(92705-5647)
PHONE...................................714 540-9010
David Tavares, *Mng Member*
Gary Rasmussen,
▲ EMP: 12
SQ FT: 3,600
SALES (est): 2.4MM **Privately Held**
WEB: www.advancedpowercontrols.com
SIC: **3621** 3625 7629 Motor generator sets; motor controls, electric; generator repair

(P-16629)
AIH LLC (DH)
Also Called: Astec International Holding
5810 Van Allen Way, Carlsbad
(92008-7300)
PHONE...................................760 930-4600
Jay Geldmacher, *CEO*
Tom Rosenast, *CFO*
EMP: 22
SALES (est): 1.2B
SALES (corp-wide): 718.8MM **Publicly Held**
SIC: **3621** 3679 3629 Power generators; power supplies, all types: static; power conversion units, a.c. to d.c.: static-electric
HQ: Artesyn Embedded Technologies, Inc.
    2900 S Diablo Way B100
    Tempe AZ 85282
    646 617-0186

(P-16630)
AMERICAN SD POWER INC
14181 Fern Ave, Chino (91710-9013)
PHONE...................................909 947-0673
Xin Wang, *President*
▲ EMP: 10
SALES (est): 1.8MM **Privately Held**
SIC: **3621** Generator sets: gasoline, diesel or dual-fuel

(P-16631)
AMETEK INC
Aerospace Gst
17032 Armstrong Ave, Irvine (92614-5716)
PHONE...................................949 642-2400
Dave McGinley, *Vice Pres*
Brian Denien, *Program Mgr*
Mitra Mosallaie, *Analyst*
Mike Proulx, *Purch Agent*
Karen Dellaria, *Sales Staff*
EMP: 68
SALES (corp-wide): 4.8B **Publicly Held**
SIC: **3621** 3823 Motors & generators; industrial instrmnts msrmnt display/control process variable
PA: Ametek, Inc.
    1100 Cassatt Rd
    Berwyn PA 19312
    610 647-2121

(P-16632)
BARTA-SCHOENEWALD INC (PA)
Also Called: Advanced Motion Controls
3805 Calle Tecate, Camarillo (93012-5068)
PHONE...................................805 389-1935
Sandor Barta, *President*
Daniel Schoenewald, *Exec VP*
▲ EMP: 120
SQ FT: 86,000
SALES (est): 27.5MM **Privately Held**
WEB: www.a-m-c.com
SIC: **3621** 3699 Servomotors, electric; electric motor & generator parts; electrical equipment & supplies

(P-16633)
BOSCH ENRGY STOR SOLUTIONS LLC
Also Called: Robert Bosch Stiftung GMBH
4005 Miranda Ave Ste 200, Palo Alto
(94304-1232)
PHONE...................................650 320-2933
EMP: 11
SALES (est): 1.1MM
SALES (corp-wide): 261.7MM **Privately Held**
SIC: **3621**
PA: R O B E R T B O S C H S T I F T U N G Gesellschaft Mit Beschrankter Haftung
    Heidehofstr. 31
    Stuttgart 70184
    711 460-840

(P-16634)
CALNETIX TECHNOLOGIES LLC
16323 Shoemaker Ave, Cerritos
(90703-2244)
PHONE...................................562 293-1660
Vatche Artinian, *Chairman*
Herman Artinian, *CEO*
Ian Hart, *CFO*
Pana Shenoy, *Vice Pres*
Andrea Matiauda, *Admin Sec*
EMP: 82
SALES: 22MM **Privately Held**
SIC: **3621** Motors & generators
PA: Calnetix, LLC.
    16323 Shoemaker Ave
    Cerritos CA 90703
    562 293-1660

(P-16635)
CLO SYSTEMS LLC
15312 Valley Blvd, City of Industry
(91746-3324)
P.O. Box 360752, Los Angeles (90036-1251)
PHONE...................................626 939-4226
▲ EMP: 10
SQ FT: 6,000
SALES (est): 2.1MM **Privately Held**
WEB: www.closystems.com
SIC: **3621**

(P-16636)
COLE INSTRUMENT CORP
2650 S Croddy Way, Santa Ana
(92704-5238)
P.O. Box 25063 (92799-5063)
PHONE...................................714 556-3100
Ric Garcia, *President*
Manuel Garcia, *Exec VP*
Roshan Sarode, *Design Engr*
Ed Brigham, *Safety Mgr*
Ruchi Raval, *Sales Staff*
EMP: 70
SQ FT: 16,000
SALES (est): 13.9MM **Privately Held**
WEB: www.cole-switches.com
SIC: **3621** 3679 Motors & generators; electronic switches

(P-16637)
CONCENTRIC COMPONENTS INC
913 5th St, Modesto (95351-2809)
PHONE...................................209 529-4840
Phillip Nachatelo, *President*
EMP: 10

SALES (est): 1.2MM **Privately Held**
SIC: **3621** 7537 5531 Torque motors, electric; automotive transmission repair shops; automobile & truck equipment & parts

(P-16638)
DIRECT DRIVE SYSTEMS INC
621 Burning Tree Rd, Fullerton
(92833-1448)
PHONE...................................714 872-5500
James Pribble, *CEO*
Michael Slater, *COO*
Robert Clark, *CFO*
EMP: 57
SALES (est): 11.3MM
SALES (corp-wide): 12.6B **Privately Held**
WEB: www.directdrivesystems.net
SIC: **3621** Electric motor & generator parts
HQ: Fmc Technologies, Inc.
    11740 Katy Fwy Enrgy Twr
    Houston TX 77079
    281 591-4000

(P-16639)
ECO-GEN DISTRIBUTORS INC
340 Goddard, Irvine (92618-4601)
PHONE...................................760 712-7460
Bruce Kaylor, *President*
Robert Zannasdale, *CEO*
Garrtt Adams, *COO*
Stacey Zannasdale, *Vice Pres*
EMP: 12
SALES (est): 2.8MM **Privately Held**
SIC: **3621** Motors & generators

(P-16640)
ECO-GEN ENERGY INC
7247 Hayvenhurst Ave A6, Van Nuys
(91406-2871)
PHONE...................................818 756-4700
Raoul Hamilton, *President*
Julia A Otey, *Treasurer*
▲ EMP: 11
SALES (est): 1.7MM **Privately Held**
SIC: **3621** Motors & generators

(P-16641)
ELITE GENERATORS INC
9007 De Soto Ave, Canoga Park
(91304-1968)
PHONE...................................818 718-0200
Jeffrey Peter Giedt, *CEO*
Lupean Campos, *CFO*
EMP: 11
SQ FT: 1,500
SALES (est): 1.4MM **Privately Held**
SIC: **3621** 7629 Power generators; generator repair

(P-16642)
ENER-CORE INC (PA)
30100 Town Center Dr, Laguna Niguel
(92677-2064)
PHONE...................................949 732-4400
Domonic J Carney, *Interim Pres*
Douglas A Hamrin, *VP Engrg*
EMP: 10
SALES (est): 10.1MM
SALES (corp-wide): 9.1MM **Publicly Held**
SIC: **3621** Power generators

(P-16643)
ES WEST COAST LLC
Also Called: Energy Systems
7100 Longe St Ste 300, Stockton
(95206-3962)
PHONE...................................209 870-1900
Don Richter, *President*
EMP: 45
SALES (est): 5.5MM
SALES (corp-wide): 68.1MM **Privately Held**
SIC: **3621** Electric motor & generator auxiliary parts
HQ: The Shane Group Llc
    215 W Mechanic St
    Hillsdale MI 49242
    517 439-4316

(P-16644)
EURUS ENERGY AMERICA CORP (DH)
9255 Towne Centre Dr # 840, San Diego
(92121-3041)
PHONE...................................858 638-7115

P R O D U C T S & S V C S

Mark E Anderson, *President*
Sergio Moya, *President*
Cathy Syme, *President*
Tony Dorazio, *Vice Pres*
Nick Henriksen, *Vice Pres*
EMP: 16
SQ FT: 3,000
SALES (est): 15MM **Privately Held**
WEB: www.eurusenergy.com
SIC: 3621 Windmills, electric generating

(P-16645)
FARASIS ENERGY USA INC
21363 Cabot Blvd, Hayward (94545-1650)
PHONE.................................510 732-6600
Yu Wang, *CEO*
EMP: 67
SALES (est): 2MM **Privately Held**
SIC: 3621 Generators for storage battery chargers

(P-16646)
FLAMESTOWER INC
127 Kissling St, San Francisco (94103-3726)
PHONE.................................415 699-8650
Andrew Gordon Byrnes, *CEO*
Andrew Byrnes, *General Mgr*
EMP: 55
SQ FT: 2,000
SALES (est): 6.5MM **Privately Held**
SIC: 3621 Generators & sets, electric

(P-16647)
FREEWIRE TECHNOLOGIES INC
1933 Davis St Ste 301a, San Leandro (94577-1259)
PHONE.................................415 779-5515
Arcady Sosinov, *CEO*
Martin Lynch, *COO*
Yesica Rodriguez, *Office Mgr*
Richard Steele, *Engineer*
Ivan Cooper, *Director*
EMP: 50
SALES (est): 1.5MM **Privately Held**
SIC: 3621 3714 7389 Storage battery chargers, motor & engine generator type; motor vehicle electrical equipment;

(P-16648)
GLENTEK INC
208 Standard St, El Segundo (90245-3818)
PHONE.................................310 322-3026
Richard C Vasak, *CEO*
Heidi Lara, *CFO*
Helen Sysel, *CFO*
Helen M Vasak, *Corp Secy*
Bill Vasak, *Information Mgr*
◆ **EMP:** 71
SQ FT: 105,000
SALES (est): 6MM **Privately Held**
WEB: www.glentek.com
SIC: 3621 Motors & generators

(P-16649)
GLOBE MOTORS INC
1507 Gladding Ct, Milpitas (95035-6813)
PHONE.................................408 935-8989
Surinder Singh, *General Mgr*
EMP: 175
SALES (corp-wide): 310.6MM **Publicly Held**
SIC: 3621 Motors, electric
HQ: Globe Motors, Inc.
2275 Stanley Ave
Dayton OH 45404
334 983-3542

(P-16650)
GO GREEN MOBILE POWER LLC
171 Pier Ave Ste 105, Santa Monica (90405-5311)
PHONE.................................877 800-4467
James P Caulfield, *Mng Member*
James Montoya, *Exec VP*
EMP: 10
SALES (est): 3MM **Privately Held**
SIC: 3621 3648 Power generators; lighting equipment

(P-16651)
GOHZ INC
23555 Golden Springs Dr K1, Diamond Bar (91765-2176)
PHONE.................................800 603-1219
Zhuge Fusheng, *President*
Sameh Gouda, *Manager*
EMP: 30
SQ FT: 1,200
SALES: 5.1MM **Privately Held**
SIC: 3621 Frequency converters (electric generators)

(P-16652)
HARMONIC DESIGN INC
13367 Krkrham Way Ste 110, Poway (92064)
PHONE.................................858 391-9085
Michel Pouvreau, *CEO*
▲ **EMP:** 32
SALES (est): 5.6MM **Privately Held**
SIC: 3621 Motors & generators

(P-16653)
HEEGER INC
Also Called: Lmb Heeger
6446 Flotilla St, Commerce (90040-1712)
PHONE.................................323 728-5108
Robert Heeger, *President*
Christine Avila, *Vice Pres*
EMP: 19 EST: 1946
SQ FT: 16,000
SALES (est): 1.5MM **Privately Held**
SIC: 3621 3469 3444 Motors & generators; metal stampings; sheet metalwork

(P-16654)
HI PERFORMANCE ELECTRIC VEHICL
620 S Magnolia Ave Ste B, Ontario (91762-4030)
PHONE.................................909 923-1973
Brian Guy Seymour, *CEO*
Toni Seymour, *Corp Secy*
Bill Ritchie, *Sales Staff*
▲ **EMP:** 15
SQ FT: 9,000
SALES (est): 3.4MM **Privately Held**
WEB: www.hiperformancegolfcars.com
SIC: 3621 Motors, electric

(P-16655)
HITACHI AUTOMOTIVE SYSTEMS
Also Called: Los Angeles Plant
6200 Gateway Dr, Cypress (90630-4842)
PHONE.................................310 212-0200
Fred Pakshir, *Branch Mgr*
Charles Withey, *Senior Mgr*
Jun Kawano, *Director*
EMP: 100 **Privately Held**
SIC: 3621 3714 Electric motor & generator parts; motor vehicle parts & accessories
HQ: Hitachi Automotive Systems Americas, Inc.
955 Warwick Rd
Harrodsburg KY 40330
859 734-9451

(P-16656)
IMAGE MICRO SPARE PARTS INC
6301 Chalet Dr, Commerce (90040-3705)
PHONE.................................562 776-9808
Hassan Mohrekesh, *President*
Brian Buhro, *Vice Pres*
Levy Antal, *VP Bus Dvlpt*
Igor Murashov, *Administration*
EMP: 11
SQ FT: 17,000
SALES (est): 260K **Privately Held**
SIC: 3621 Generating apparatus & parts, electrical

(P-16657)
INTEGRATED MAGNETICS INC
11250 Playa Ct, Culver City (90230-6127)
PHONE.................................310 391-7213
Anil Nanji, *President*
EMP: 40
SQ FT: 120,000

SALES (est): 7.1MM
SALES (corp-wide): 47.2MM **Privately Held**
SIC: 3621 3679 3764 Rotors, for motors; servomotors, electric; cores, magnetic; rocket motors, guided missiles
PA: Integrated Technologies Group, Inc.
11250 Playa Ct
Culver City CA 90230
310 391-7213

(P-16658)
KOLLMORGEN CORPORATION
33 S La Patera Ln, Santa Barbara (93117-3214)
PHONE.................................805 696-1236
David Cline, *Engineer*
EMP: 383
SALES (corp-wide): 1.1B **Publicly Held**
SIC: 3621 Servomotors, electric
HQ: Kollmorgen Corporation
203a W Rock Rd
Radford VA 24141
540 639-9045

(P-16659)
LEOCH BATTERY CORPORATION (PA)
19751 Descartes Unit A, Foothill Ranch (92610-2620)
PHONE.................................949 588-5853
Hui Peng, *President*
Gil Franke, *Engineer*
Crystal He, *Sales Mgr*
Kelly Liu, *Sales Mgr*
John McGovern, *Sales Staff*
▲ **EMP:** 39
SALES (est): 34MM **Privately Held**
SIC: 3621 Storage battery chargers, motor & engine generator type

(P-16660)
LIN ENGINEERING INC
16245 Vineyard Blvd, Morgan Hill (95037-7123)
PHONE.................................408 919-0200
Ted T Lin, *President*
Rouyu Loughry, *CFO*
Cynthia Lin, *Treasurer*
Ryan Lin, *Vice Pres*
Timmy Nguyen, *Design Engr*
▲ **EMP:** 125
SQ FT: 16,000
SALES: 26.6MM
SALES (corp-wide): 259.6MM **Privately Held**
WEB: www.linengineering.com
SIC: 3621 Motors, electric
HQ: Moons' International Trading (Shanghai) Co., Ltd.
Caohejing Hi-Tech Zone
Shanghai 20023

(P-16661)
MAGICALL INC
4550 Calle Alto, Camarillo (93012-8509)
P.O. Box 3730 (93011-3730)
PHONE.................................805 484-4300
Joel Wacknov, *CEO*
Dan Qin, *VP Engrg*
Vicki Clifford, *Purch Mgr*
Matt Cullinane, *VP Sales*
▲ **EMP:** 33
SALES (est): 6.7MM **Privately Held**
SIC: 3621 3612 3677 3679 Motors & generators; power transformers, electric; electronic coils, transformers & other inductors; static power supply converters for electronic applications

(P-16662)
MC CULLY MAC M CORPORATION
Also Called: Mac M McCully Co
12012 Hertz Ave, Moorpark (93021-7130)
PHONE.................................805 529-0661
Guy Mc Cully, *President*
Martha L McCully, *Corp Secy*
Ernest Krier, *Manager*
EMP: 35
SQ FT: 8,000
SALES (est): 5.6MM **Privately Held**
SIC: 3621 Motors, electric

(P-16663)
MOTOR TECHNOLOGY INC
2301 Wardlow Cir, Corona (92880-2801)
PHONE.................................951 270-6200
Robert Buchwalder, *President*
Phyllis Buchwalder, *Corp Secy*
George Teets, *Manager*
EMP: 37
SQ FT: 12,600
SALES (est): 5.1MM
SALES (corp-wide): 1.1B **Publicly Held**
WEB: www.motortech.com
SIC: 3621 Motors, electric
PA: Circor International, Inc.
30 Corporate Dr Ste 200
Burlington MA 01803
781 270-1200

(P-16664)
MOTRAN INDUSTRIES INC
3037 Golf Course Dr Ste 4, Ventura (93003-7608)
PHONE.................................661 257-4995
Charles Willard, *President*
▲ **EMP:** 10
SQ FT: 8,200
SALES: 1.7MM **Privately Held**
WEB: www.motran.com
SIC: 3621 Electric motor & generator parts

(P-16665)
NATURENER USA LLC (HQ)
435 Pacific Ave Fl 4, San Francisco (94133-4611)
PHONE.................................415 217-5500
Jose M S Seara,
Scott Hooper, *Vice Pres*
Marc Denarie, *CIO*
Antonio Utrillas, *Engineer*
Yi Shen, *Analyst*
EMP: 40
SALES (est): 12.8MM
SALES (corp-wide): 863.1K **Privately Held**
SIC: 3621 Windmills, electric generating
PA: Grupo Naturener, Sa
Calle Nulez De Balboa, 120 - 7
Madrid 28006
915 625-410

(P-16666)
NOODOE INC
Also Called: Rhema Net Corp
829 S Lemon Ave Ste A-11c, Walnut (91789-2901)
PHONE.................................909 468-1118
Jennifer Chang, *CEO*
Grace Lee, *Administration*
Steve Kuo, *VP Mktg*
EMP: 10
SALES: 1MM **Privately Held**
SIC: 3621 Generators for gas-electric or oil-electric vehicles
PA: Noodoe Corporation
15f, No. 19-13, Sanchong Rd.,
Taipei City TAP 11501

(P-16667)
NOVATORQUE INC
281 Greenoaks Dr, Atherton (94027-2114)
PHONE.................................510 933-2700
Emily Liggett, *CEO*
Tim McNally, *CFO*
Kim Baker, *Vice Pres*
Scott Johnson, *Vice Pres*
Joe Weber, *Vice Pres*
▲ **EMP:** 40
SQ FT: 27,000
SALES (est): 9MM **Privately Held**
WEB: www.novatorque.com
SIC: 3621 Motors & generators

(P-16668)
POWER EFFICIENCY CORPORATION
5744 Pcf Ctr Blvd Ste 311, San Diego (92121)
PHONE.................................858 750-3875
Steven Z Strasser, *CEO*
Thomas A Mills Jr, *Vice Pres*
Brian C Chan, *Admin Sec*
▲ **EMP:** 13
SALES (est): 1.7MM **Privately Held**
WEB: www.powerefficiency.com
SIC: 3621 Motors & generators

▲ = Import ▼=Export
◆ =Import/Export

(P-16669)
R K LARRABEE COMPANY INC
Also Called: Construction Electrical Pdts
7800 Las Positas Rd, Livermore
(94551-8240)
PHONE..................925 828-9420
Robert Larrabee, *President*
Colin Christian, *Vice Pres*
Nancy Larrabee, *Vice Pres*
Christine Jeffery, *Credit Mgr*
Scott Larrabee, *Mfg Dir*
▲ EMP: 65
SALES (est): 15.8MM **Privately Held**
WEB: www.cepnow.com
SIC: 3621 3699 3648 3646 Power generators; electrical equipment & supplies; lighting equipment; commercial indusl & institutional electric lighting fixtures; non-current-carrying wiring services; nonferrous wiredrawing & insulating

(P-16670)
RESMED MOTOR TECHNOLOGIES INC
9540 De Soto Ave, Chatsworth
(91311-5010)
PHONE..................818 428-6400
David B Sears, *CEO*
Michael Fliss, *President*
Maureen Foster, *Data Proc Staff*
Aleksandr Nagorny, *Engineer*
Kathy Reed, *Manager*
▲ EMP: 170
SQ FT: 35,000
SALES (est): 34.6MM **Publicly Held**
WEB: www.resmed.com
SIC: 3621 3714 3841 Coils, for electric motors or generators; collector rings, for electric motors or generators; propane conversion equipment, motor vehicle; surgical & medical instruments
PA: Resmed Inc.
9001 Spectrum Center Blvd
San Diego CA 92123

(P-16671)
REULAND ELECTRIC CO (PA)
17969 Railroad St, City of Industry
(91748-1192)
P.O. Box 1464, La Puente (91749)
PHONE..................626 964-6411
Noel C Reuland, *President*
William Kramer III, *CFO*
Howard Lees, *Vice Pres*
Dick Blumer, *Info Tech Dir*
Scott Chalfin, *Engineer*
▲ EMP: 130 EST: 1937
SQ FT: 100,000
SALES (est): 42.4MM **Privately Held**
WEB: www.reuland.com
SIC: 3621 3566 3363 3625 Motors, electric; drives, high speed industrial, except hydrostatic; aluminum die-castings; electric controls & control accessories, industrial; fluid power motors

(P-16672)
ROCKETSTAR ROBOTICS INC
177 Estaban Dr, Camarillo (93010-1611)
PHONE..................805 529-7769
EMP: 10
SALES (est): 640K **Privately Held**
WEB: www.rocketstarrobotics.com
SIC: 3621

(P-16673)
SKURKA AEROSPACE INC (DH)
4600 Calle Bolero, Camarillo (93012-8575)
P.O. Box 2869 (93011-2869)
PHONE..................216 706-2939
Victoria Alonzo, *Administration*
Loren Hesz, *Technology*
Taylor Kane, *Electrical Engi*
Robert Hurwich, *Engineer*
Chuck McGregor, *Engineer*
EMP: 140 EST: 1950
SQ FT: 70,000
SALES (est): 45.7MM
SALES (corp-wide): 3.8B **Publicly Held**
WEB: www.skurka-aero.com
SIC: 3621 3679 Motors, electric; transducers, electrical

(P-16674)
SOFTWARE MOTOR COMPANY
1295 Forgewood Ave, Sunnyvale
(94089-2216)
PHONE..................408 601-7781
Mark Johnston, *CEO*
Mike Petouhoff, *Vice Pres*
Spencer Worley, *Vice Pres*
Paul Ternes, *Research*
Earl Zuchelli, *Manager*
EMP: 10
SALES (est): 2.6MM **Privately Held**
SIC: 3621 7389 Motors, electric; design services

(P-16675)
SOUTH AMRCN IMGING SLTIONS INC
2360 Eastman Ave Ste 110, Oxnard
(93030-7287)
PHONE..................805 824-4036
Rogelio Zavala, *CEO*
EMP: 10
SALES (est): 636.8K **Privately Held**
SIC: 3621 Electric motor & generator parts

(P-16676)
THINGAP LLC
4035 Via Pescador, Camarillo
(93012-5050)
PHONE..................805 477-9741
Sarah Gallagher, *President*
Len Wedman, *President*
Jannelle Taylor, *Office Mgr*
Travis Kenney, *Prdtn Mgr*
Aaron Budgor,
EMP: 20
SALES (est): 2.5MM **Privately Held**
SIC: 3621 Coils, for electric motors or generators

(P-16677)
THINGAP HOLDINGS LLC
Also Called: Thingap.com
4035 Via Pescador, Camarillo
(93012-5050)
PHONE..................805 477-9741
Sarah Gallagher, *CEO*
Evan Frank, *Director*
▲ EMP: 10
SQ FT: 6,826
SALES (est): 1.7MM **Privately Held**
WEB: www.thingap.com
SIC: 3621 Motors, electric

(P-16678)
VALLEY POWER SERVICES INC
425 S Hacienda Blvd, City of Industry
(91745-1123)
PHONE..................909 969-9345
Clark Lee, *President*
▲ EMP: 20
SQ FT: 17,802
SALES (est): 3.9MM **Privately Held**
SIC: 3621 Motor housings

3624 Carbon & Graphite Prdts

(P-16679)
ADVANCE CARBON PRODUCTS INC
2036 National Ave, Hayward (94545-1712)
PHONE..................510 293-5930
Ronald D Crader, *President*
James Michael Crader, *Vice Pres*
Geoff Carbon, *Engineer*
Sharlene Crader, *Purch Agent*
EMP: 40
SQ FT: 20,000
SALES (est): 7.2MM **Privately Held**
WEB: www.advancecarbon.com
SIC: 3624 3678 3643 3568 Brush blocks, carbon or molded graphite; electronic connectors; current-carrying wiring devices; power transmission equipment; gaskets, packing & sealing devices; industrial inorganic chemicals

(P-16680)
ALLIANCE SPACESYSTEMS LLC
4398 Corporate Center Dr, Los Alamitos
(90720-2537)
PHONE..................714 226-1400
Rick Byrens, *President*
Greg Golanoski, *Director*
EMP: 155
SQ FT: 101,000
SALES: 25MM
SALES (corp-wide): 118.2MM **Privately Held**
SIC: 3624 Carbon & graphite products
PA: Solaero Technologies Corp.
10420 Res Rd Se Bldg 1
Albuquerque NM 87123
505 332-5000

(P-16681)
AMERICAN ACTIVATED CARBON CORP
7310 Deering Ave, Canoga Park
(91303-1503)
PHONE..................310 491-2842
Anthony Pathirana, *CEO*
Tony Pathirana, *Marketing Staff*
▲ EMP: 10
SALES (est): 1.8MM **Privately Held**
SIC: 3624 Fibers, carbon & graphite

(P-16682)
BAKERCORP
Also Called: Baker Filtration
5500 Rawlings Ave, South Gate
(90280-7412)
PHONE..................562 904-3680
Chris Ritchie, *Branch Mgr*
EMP: 15
SALES (corp-wide): 8B **Publicly Held**
SIC: 3624 Carbon & graphite products
HQ: Bakercorp
100 Stamford Pl Ste 700
Stamford CT 06902
562 430-6262

(P-16683)
CARBON SOLUTIONS INC
5094 Victoria Hill Dr, Riverside
(92506-1450)
PHONE..................909 234-2738
Robert Haddon, *President*
Irina Kalinina, *Research*
EMP: 12 EST: 1999
SALES (est): 990K **Privately Held**
WEB: www.carbonsolution.com
SIC: 3624 Carbon & graphite products

(P-16684)
CDG TECHNOLOGY LLC
779 Twin View Blvd, Redding (96003-2008)
PHONE..................530 243-4451
Manny Ornellas,
EMP: 15
SALES: 1MM **Privately Held**
SIC: 3624 Fibers, carbon & graphite

(P-16685)
FRONTERA SOLUTIONS INC
1913 E 17th St Ste 210, Santa Ana
(92705-8627)
PHONE..................714 368-1631
Earl B Johnson, *President*
John Drake, *CFO*
Ben Rawski, *Vice Pres*
EMP: 100
SALES: 450K **Privately Held**
WEB: www.mtidebaja.com
SIC: 3624 3231 Fibers, carbon & graphite; insulating glass: made from purchased glass

(P-16686)
KBR INC
Also Called: Electro-Tech Machining Div
2000 W Gaylord St, Long Beach
(90813-1032)
P.O. Box 92610, Rochester NY (14692-0610)
PHONE..................562 436-9281
Ryan McMahon, *President*
▲ EMP: 32
SQ FT: 39,000
SALES (est): 6.7MM **Privately Held**
SIC: 3624 Carbon & graphite products

(P-16687)
MIKUNI COLOR USA INC
855 Riverside Pkwy Ste 80, West Sacramento (95605-1504)
PHONE..................916 572-0704
Hiroyoshi Tojima, *President*
EMP: 12
SALES (est): 4.1MM **Privately Held**
SIC: 3624 Carbon specialties for electrical use

(P-16688)
MITSUBISHI CHEMICAL CRBN FBR (DH)
5900 88th St, Sacramento (95828-1109)
PHONE..................916 386-1733
Susumu Sasaki, *CEO*
Donald Carter, *CFO*
Masayoshi Ozeki, *Vice Pres*
Takeshi Sasaki, *Vice Pres*
Denise Di Fabbio, *Admin Asst*
▲ EMP: 125
SQ FT: 60,000
SALES (est): 50.6MM **Privately Held**
WEB: www.grafil.com
SIC: 3624 Fibers, carbon & graphite

(P-16689)
QUATRO COMPOSITES LLC
13250 Gregg St Ste A1, Poway
(92064-7164)
PHONE..................712 707-9200
Karash Quepin, *Manager*
EMP: 35
SALES (corp-wide): 168.2MM **Privately Held**
SIC: 3624 Carbon & graphite products
HQ: Quatro Composites, L.L.C.
403 14th St Se
Orange City IA 51041
712 707-9200

(P-16690)
SIGMATEX HIGH TECH FABRICS INC (HQ)
6001 Egret Ct, Benicia (94510-1205)
PHONE..................707 751-0573
Scott Tolson, *President*
Jonah Jimemez, *President*
Crystal Shipp, *Admin Asst*
Mary Ann Reyes, *Controller*
Pamela Butala, *Human Resources*
▲ EMP: 52
SQ FT: 10,000
SALES: 28MM
SALES (corp-wide): 78.5MM **Privately Held**
WEB: www.sigmatex.com
SIC: 3624 Carbon & graphite products
PA: Sigmatex (Uk) Limited
1 Manor Farm Road
Runcorn WA7 1
192 857-0050

(P-16691)
SPACESYSTEMS HOLDINGS LLC
4398 Corporate Center Dr, Los Alamitos
(90720-2537)
PHONE..................714 226-1400
Terence Lyons, *CEO*
Rick Byrens, *President*
Jeffrey David Lassiter, *CFO*
EMP: 144 EST: 2012
SQ FT: 101,000
SALES: 30MM **Privately Held**
SIC: 3624 Carbon & graphite products

3625 Relays & Indl Controls

(P-16692)
A P SEEDORFF & COMPANY INC
Also Called: Seedorff Acme
1338 N Knollwood Cir, Anaheim
(92801-1311)
PHONE..................714 252-5330
Kurt Simon, *President*
Helmut Simon, *Treasurer*
Ernie Gasteiger, *Prdtn Mgr*
EMP: 15
SQ FT: 10,000

PRODUCTS & SVCS

SALES (est): 4.4MM **Privately Held**
WEB: www.acmewelders.com
SIC: 3625 Resistance welder controls

(P-16693)
ABSOLUTE GRAPHIC TECH USA INC
Also Called: Agt
235 Jason Ct, Corona (92879-6199)
PHONE..............................909 597-1133
Steven J Barberi, *President*
John O'Neill, *COO*
Karina Stoltz, *CFO*
Constance Rogers, *General Counsel*
Lou Barberi, *Manager*
EMP: 49
SQ FT: 25,800
SALES (est): 10MM **Privately Held**
SIC: 3625 3577 Industrial electrical relays & switches; printers & plotters

(P-16694)
AIRSPACE SYSTEMS INC
1933 Davis St Ste 229, San Leandro (94577-1257)
PHONE..............................310 704-7155
Jasminder Banga, *CEO*
Guy Bar-Nahum, *Vice Pres*
Rob Coneybeer, *Director*
Steve Schimmel, *Director*
EMP: 30
SALES (est): 421K **Privately Held**
SIC: 3625 Control equipment, electric

(P-16695)
AISIN ELECTRONICS INC
199 Frank West Cir, Stockton (95206-4002)
PHONE..............................209 983-4988
Yasuhito Mori, *President*
Yuji Tomisawa, *Admin Sec*
Timothy Willis, *Engineer*
EMP: 230
SQ FT: 22,000
SALES (est): 63.6MM **Privately Held**
WEB: www.aisin-electronics.com
SIC: 3625 3714 Control circuit relays, industrial; relays, electric power; relays, for electronic use; switches, electronic applications; motor vehicle parts & accessories
HQ: Aisin Holdings Of America, Inc.
1665 E 4th Street Rd
Seymour IN 47274
812 524-8144

(P-16696)
AMERICAN RELAYS INC
15537 Blackburn Ave, Norwalk (90650-6846)
PHONE..............................562 926-2837
Hyo Lee, *President*
Richard Lenning, *Vice Pres*
EMP: 40
SQ FT: 12,000
SALES (est): 6.3MM **Privately Held**
WEB: www.americanrelays.com
SIC: 3625 Relays, for electronic use

(P-16697)
AMES FIRE WATERWORKS
1485 Tanforan Ave, Woodland (95776-6108)
PHONE..............................530 666-2493
Nancy West, *CEO*
Steve Loya, *Prdtn Mgr*
▲ EMP: 88
SQ FT: 10,000
SALES (est): 18.2MM
SALES (corp-wide): 1.5B **Publicly Held**
WEB: www.amesfirewater.com
SIC: 3625 3494 Relays & industrial controls; valves & pipe fittings
PA: Watts Water Technologies, Inc.
815 Chestnut St
North Andover MA 01845
978 688-1811

(P-16698)
ANAHEIM AUTOMATION INC
4985 E Landon Dr, Anaheim (92807-1972)
PHONE..............................714 992-6990
Faithe Reimbold, *Vice Pres*
Nannette Israel, *CFO*
John Witt, *Vice Pres*
Alan Harmon, *General Mgr*

Joann Witt, *Admin Sec*
◆ EMP: 47
SQ FT: 9,000
SALES (est): 9.7MM **Privately Held**
WEB: www.anaheimautomation.com
SIC: 3625 3545 3566 Control equipment, electric; machine tool accessories; speed changers, drives & gears

(P-16699)
APPLIED CONTROL ELECTRONICS
5480 Merchant Cir, Placerville (95667-8250)
PHONE..............................530 626-5181
Terry Burke, *President*
Natalie Burke, *CFO*
Edd Todd, *Prdtn Mgr*
EMP: 12
SQ FT: 10,000
SALES (est): 1.1MM **Privately Held**
SIC: 3625 8711 Motor controls & accessories; electrical or electronic engineering; consulting engineer

(P-16700)
AQUADYNE COMPUTER CORPORATION
9434 Chesapeake Dr # 1204, San Diego (92123-1390)
PHONE..............................858 495-1040
Dean McDaniel, *President*
EMP: 16
SQ FT: 2,100
SALES (est): 2MM **Privately Held**
WEB: www.aquadyne.com
SIC: 3625 Control equipment, electric

(P-16701)
ASCOR INC (HQ)
4650 Norris Canyon Rd, San Ramon (94583-1320)
PHONE..............................925 328-4650
Jeffrey Lum, *President*
John Regazzi, *CEO*
EMP: 12
SQ FT: 19,000
SALES: 3.8MM
SALES (corp-wide): 11.1MM **Publicly Held**
WEB: www.ascor.com
SIC: 3625 Switches, electronic applications
PA: Giga-Tronics Incorporated
5990 Gleason Dr
Dublin CA 94568
925 328-4650

(P-16702)
BALBOA WATER GROUP LLC (PA)
Also Called: Controlmyspa
3030 Airway Ave Ste B, Costa Mesa (92626-6036)
PHONE..............................714 384-0384
David J Cline, *President*
◆ EMP: 120 EST: 2007
SALES (est): 90.1MM **Privately Held**
WEB: www.balboainstruments.com
SIC: 3625 3599 Electric controls & control accessories, industrial; machine shop, jobbing & repair

(P-16703)
BASIC MICROCOM INC
38595 Rancho Christina Rd, Temecula (92592-8025)
PHONE..............................951 708-1268
Lisa M Kubin, *Administration*
Lisa Kubin, *President*
EMP: 10 EST: 2011
SALES (est): 1.3MM **Privately Held**
SIC: 3625 Control equipment, electric

(P-16704)
CALIFORNIA ECONOMIZER
Also Called: Zonex Systems
5622 Engineer Dr, Huntington Beach (92649-1124)
PHONE..............................714 898-9963
Jeff Osheroff, *President*
▲ EMP: 50
SQ FT: 16,000

SALES (est): 9MM **Privately Held**
WEB: www.hvaccomfort.com
SIC: 3625 3822 Control equipment, electric; auto controls regulating residntl & coml environmt & applncs

(P-16705)
CALIFORNIA MOTOR CONTROLS INCO
3070 Bay Vista Ct, Benicia (94510-1235)
PHONE..............................707 746-6255
Tom Duling, *President*
Susan Duling, *Vice Pres*
Kristi Duling, *Office Mgr*
Dave Troxell, *Project Mgr*
Calvin Domantay, *Engineer*
EMP: 13
SQ FT: 8,000
SALES (est): 4.3MM **Privately Held**
SIC: 3625 Motor controls, electric

(P-16706)
COMSTAR INDUSTRIES INC
Also Called: Industrial Graphic
22465 La Palma Ave, Yorba Linda (92887-3803)
PHONE..............................714 556-1400
David Goff, *President*
EMP: 30
SALES (est): 4.3MM **Privately Held**
WEB: www.comstarindustries.com
SIC: 3625 3674 3643 3613 Relays & industrial controls; semiconductors & related devices; current-carrying wiring devices; switchgear & switchboard apparatus; screen printing

(P-16707)
CONTROL SWITCHES INC (PA)
2425 Mira Mar Ave, Long Beach (90815-1757)
PHONE..............................562 498-7331
Susana Moore, *Principal*
Donald J Armstrong, *President*
Susan Moore, *CFO*
Doug Uyemura, *Engineer*
EMP: 15
SALES (est): 10.4MM **Privately Held**
SIC: 3625 5063 Industrial electrical relays & switches; electrical apparatus & equipment

(P-16708)
CONTROL SWITCHES INTL INC
2425 Mira Mar Ave, Long Beach (90815-1757)
P.O. Box 92349 (90809-2349)
PHONE..............................562 498-7331
Margerate Turner, *Exec VP*
Susan Moore, *CFO*
Susan A Moore, *CFO*
Judith Steward, *Vice Pres*
Peggy Turner, *Vice Pres*
EMP: 25
SQ FT: 10,000
SALES (est): 3.4MM
SALES (corp-wide): 10.4MM **Privately Held**
WEB: www.controlswitches.com
SIC: 3625 Switches, electronic applications
PA: Control Switches, Inc.
2425 Mira Mar Ave
Long Beach CA 90815
562 498-7331

(P-16709)
CRYDOM INC (DH)
2320 Paseo Delas Amer 2, San Diego (92154)
PHONE..............................619 210-1590
Martha Sullivan, *President*
Oscar Fernandez, *CFO*
Jeffrey Cote, *Director*
▲ EMP: 266
SQ FT: 20,000
SALES (est): 119.2MM
SALES (corp-wide): 3.5B **Privately Held**
WEB: www.crydom.com
SIC: 3625 5065 3674 3643 Control equipment, electric; electronic parts & equipment; semiconductors & related devices; current-carrying wiring devices
HQ: Sensata Technologies, Inc.
529 Pleasant St
Attleboro MA 02703
508 236-3800

(P-16710)
CTI-CONTROLTECH INC
22 Beta Ct, San Ramon (94583-1202)
PHONE..............................925 208-4250
George P Constas, *President*
Eric Nilsson, *Technician*
Watson Bob, *Sales Mgr*
EMP: 15
SQ FT: 5,000
SALES (est): 4.4MM **Privately Held**
WEB: www.cticontroltech.com
SIC: 3625 5084 Relays & industrial controls; controlling instruments & accessories

(P-16711)
CYNERGY3 COMPONENTS CORP (PA)
2475 Pseo De Las Americas, San Diego (92154-7255)
PHONE..............................858 715-7200
John Royan, *CEO*
Wilfred Corrigan, *Ch of Bd*
Wayne Carlyle, *COO*
Bob Fenton, *Exec VP*
Robert T Borawski, *Admin Sec*
▲ EMP: 10
SQ FT: 12,000
SALES (est): 50.3MM **Privately Held**
WEB: www.ampsabundant.com
SIC: 3625 Relays & industrial controls

(P-16712)
DOW-KEY MICROWAVE CORPORATION
4822 Mcgrath St, Ventura (93003-7718)
PHONE..............................805 650-0260
David Wightman, *President*
EMP: 150
SQ FT: 26,000
SALES (est): 32MM
SALES (corp-wide): 6.9B **Publicly Held**
WEB: www.dowkey.com
SIC: 3625 3678 3643 3613 Switches, electronic applications; electronic connectors; current-carrying wiring devices; switchgear & switchboard apparatus
PA: Dover Corporation
3005 Highland Pkwy # 200
Downers Grove IL 60515
630 541-1540

(P-16713)
EAGLE ACCESS CONTROL SYSTEMS
12953 Foothill Blvd, Sylmar (91342-4929)
PHONE..............................818 837-7900
Yossi Afriat, *CEO*
Oren Afriat, *CFO*
AVI Afriat, *Vice Pres*
Carolina Hilton, *Sales Staff*
◆ EMP: 22 EST: 1996
SQ FT: 13,000
SALES (est): 5MM **Privately Held**
WEB: www.eagleoperators.com
SIC: 3625 Control equipment, electric

(P-16714)
EATON CORPORATION
200 New Stine Rd, Bakersfield (93309-2651)
PHONE..............................661 396-2557
David Madrid, *Branch Mgr*
EMP: 218 **Privately Held**
SIC: 3625 Motor controls & accessories
HQ: Eaton Corporation
1000 Eaton Blvd
Cleveland OH 44122
440 523-5000

(P-16715)
EMBEDDED SYSTEMS INC
Also Called: Esi Motion
2250a Union Pl, Simi Valley (93065-1660)
PHONE..............................805 624-6030
Earnie Beem, *President*
Sheila D'Angelo, *Vice Pres*
EMP: 40
SALES (est): 530.9K **Privately Held**
WEB: www.esimotion.com
SIC: 3625 Motor starters & controllers, electric

▲ = Import ▼=Export
◆ =Import/Export

(P-16716)
FIRE & SAFETY ELECTRONICS INC
Also Called: Phase Research
3160 Pullman St, Costa Mesa
(92626-3315)
PHONE.................................714 850-1320
John M Ludutsky, *President*
Thomas M Mitchell, *Chairman*
▼ EMP: 25
SQ FT: 5,400
SALES (est): 3.5MM **Privately Held**
WEB: www.phaseresearch.com
SIC: 3625 3873 Timing devices, electronic; watches, clocks, watchcases & parts

(P-16717)
GENERAL DYNAMICS MISSION
General Dynamics Global
7603 Saint Andrews Ave H, San Diego
(92154-8216)
PHONE.................................619 671-5400
Bud Jenkins, *Executive*
Larry Brown, *Design Engr*
Derrick Thomas, *Technology*
EMP: 72
SALES (corp-wide): 36.1B **Publicly Held**
WEB: www.axsys.com
SIC: 3625 3824 3825 3621 Relays & industrial controls; fluid meters & counting devices; instruments to measure electricity; motors & generators
HQ: General Dynamics Mission Systems, Inc.
12450 Fair Lakes Cir # 200
Fairfax VA 22033
703 263-2800

(P-16718)
GENERAL DYNMICS MTION CTRL LLC
7603 Saint Andrews Ave H, San Diego
(92154-8216)
PHONE.................................619 671-5400
Firat Gezen, *Mng Member*
Del Dameron, *Mng Member*
EMP: 12
SALES (est): 805.8K
SALES (corp-wide): 36.1B **Publicly Held**
SIC: 3625 Motor control centers
HQ: General Dynamics Ots (Niceville), Inc.
115 Hart St
Niceville FL 32578
850 897-9700

(P-16719)
GNA INDUSTRIES INC
Also Called: Alex Tronix
4761 W Jacquelyn Ave, Fresno
(93722-6438)
PHONE.................................559 276-0953
George Alexanian, *President*
Dominic Shows, *CFO*
Charles Alexanian, *Manager*
EMP: 29 EST: 1976
SQ FT: 5,000
SALES (est): 4.8MM **Privately Held**
WEB: www.alex-tronix.com
SIC: 3625 Timing devices, electronic; motor starters & controllers, electric

(P-16720)
H2W TECHNOLOGIES INC
26380 Ferry Ct, Santa Clarita
(91350-2998)
PHONE.................................661 291-1620
Fred Wilson, *CEO*
Mark Wilson, *President*
Alexander Hinds, *Exec VP*
EMP: 16 EST: 2000
SQ FT: 12,000
SALES (est): 5.2MM **Privately Held**
WEB: www.h2wtech.com
SIC: 3625 Relays & industrial controls

(P-16721)
I/O CONTROLS CORPORATION (PA)
1357 W Foothill Blvd, Azusa (91702-2853)
PHONE.................................626 812-5353
Jeffrey Ying, *President*
Renee Hsiaspin Ying, *Vice Pres*
Kody Wu, *Project Leader*
Michael Kuang, *VP Engrg*

Scott Shellman, *Technical Staff*
▲ EMP: 65
SALES (est): 13MM **Privately Held**
WEB: www.iocontrols.com
SIC: 3625 Control equipment, electric; control equipment for buses or trucks, electric

(P-16722)
ITS GROUP INC
Also Called: Its
266 Viking Ave, Brea (92821-3821)
PHONE.................................714 256-4100
Art Yee, *President*
EMP: 10
SQ FT: 2,400
SALES (est): 2.1MM **Privately Held**
SIC: 3625 Solenoid switches (industrial controls)

(P-16723)
ITT CORPORATION
I T T Cannon
56 Technology Dr, Irvine (92618-2301)
PHONE.................................714 557-4700
Mike Kuchenbrod, *Branch Mgr*
Mimi Ohara, *General Mgr*
Russ Gross, *Project Engr*
John Gruppetta, *Engineer*
Steve Nguyen, *Engineer*
EMP: 500
SQ FT: 100,000
SALES (corp-wide): 2.7B **Publicly Held**
WEB: www.ittind.com
SIC: 3625 Control equipment, electric
HQ: Itt Llc
1133 Westchester Ave N-100
White Plains NY 10604
914 641-2000

(P-16724)
ITT LLC
ITT Goulds Pumps
3951 Capitol Ave, City of Industry
(90601-1734)
P.O. Box 1254, La Puente (91749)
PHONE.................................562 908-4144
Shashank Patel, *General Mgr*
Marco Garcia, *Electrical Engi*
EMP: 75
SQ FT: 85,000
SALES (corp-wide): 2.7B **Publicly Held**
WEB: www.ittind.com
SIC: 3625 Control equipment, electric
HQ: Itt Llc
1133 Westchester Ave N-100
White Plains NY 10604
914 641-2000

(P-16725)
ITT LLC
1400 S Shamrock Ave, Monrovia
(91016-4267)
PHONE.................................626 305-6100
EMP: 15
SALES (corp-wide): 2.7B **Publicly Held**
SIC: 3625 Control equipment, electric
HQ: Itt Llc
1133 Westchester Ave N-100
White Plains NY 10604
914 641-2000

(P-16726)
KAPSCH TRAFFICCOM USA INC
4256 Hacienda Dr Ste 100, Pleasanton
(94588-8595)
PHONE.................................925 225-1600
David Dimlich, *President*
William Hargreaves, *Technician*
Micah Mowery, *Technician*
Tom Kramek, *Director*
Timothy McGuire, *Supervisor*
EMP: 18
SALES (corp-wide): 1.4B **Privately Held**
SIC: 3625 Industrial electrical relays & switches
HQ: Kapsch Trafficcom Usa, Inc.
8201 Greensboro Dr # 1002
Mc Lean VA 22102
703 885-1976

(P-16727)
KENSINGTON LABORATORIES LLC (PA)
6200 Village Pkwy, Dublin (94568-3004)
PHONE.................................510 324-0126

Raj Kaul, *Mng Member*
EMP: 17
SQ FT: 72,000
SALES (est): 6.7MM **Privately Held**
WEB: www.kenlabs.com
SIC: 3625 3825 3674 Positioning controls, electric; measuring instruments & meters, electric; semiconductors & related devices

(P-16728)
LEACH INTERNATIONAL CORP
Also Called: Reach International
6900 Orangethorpe Ave, Buena Park
(90620-1390)
PHONE.................................714 739-0770
Mark Chek, *President*
EMP: 386
SALES (corp-wide): 3.8B **Publicly Held**
SIC: 3625 3679 3674 Relays, electric power; relays, for electronic use; electronic switches; semiconductors & related devices
HQ: Leach International Corporation
6900 Orangethorpe Ave
Buena Park CA 90620
714 736-7537

(P-16729)
LEFTON TECHNOLOGIES INC
1140 Brooklawn Dr, Los Angeles
(90077-3509)
PHONE.................................818 986-1728
Norman Lefton, *CEO*
EMP: 30
SQ FT: 100,000
SALES: 5MM **Privately Held**
SIC: 3625 Motor control centers

(P-16730)
LIGHT GUARD SYSTEMS INC
2292 Airport Blvd, Santa Rosa
(95403-1003)
PHONE.................................707 542-4547
Michael A Harrison, *President*
▼ EMP: 11
SQ FT: 2,500
SALES (est): 1.9MM **Privately Held**
WEB: www.lightguardsystems.com
SIC: 3625 Relays & industrial controls

(P-16731)
LOCIX INC
901 Sneath Ln 210, San Bruno
(94066-2400)
PHONE.................................650 231-2180
Vikram Pavate, *CEO*
Elad Alon, *Principal*
Vivek Subramanian, *Principal*
EMP: 10
SALES (est): 753.6K **Privately Held**
SIC: 3625 5084 8731 Control equipment, electric; controlling instruments & accessories; electronic research

(P-16732)
MICROSEMI CORP-POWER MGT GROUP
11861 Western Ave, Garden Grove
(92841-2119)
PHONE.................................714 994-6500
James J Peterson, *President*
John W Hohener, *CFO*
Rob Warren, *Vice Pres*
David Goren, *Asst Sec*
EMP: 250 EST: 1977
SQ FT: 135,000
SALES (est): 30.1MM **Privately Held**
SIC: 3625 3677 3679 3613 Relays, for electronic use; electronic transformers; liquid crystal displays (LCD); switchgear & switchboard apparatus; transformers, except electric; computer peripheral equipment
PA: Microsemi Corp.-Power Management Group Holding
11861 Western Ave
Garden Grove CA 92841
714 994-6500

(P-16733)
MOOG INC
Also Called: Moog Jon Street Warehouse
1218 W Jon St, Torrance (90502-1208)
PHONE.................................310 533-1178
Alberto Bilalon, *Manager*

Barry Schmitt, *General Mgr*
John P Yu, *Engineer*
EMP: 500
SALES (corp-wide): 2.9B **Publicly Held**
SIC: 3625 8711 3812 Relays & industrial controls; aviation &/or aeronautical engineering; aircraft/aerospace flight instruments & guidance systems
PA: Moog Inc.
400 Jamison Rd
Elma NY 14059
716 805-2604

(P-16734)
MWSAUSSE & CO INC (PA)
Also Called: Vibrex
28744 Witherspoon Pkwy, Valencia
(91355-5425)
PHONE.................................661 257-3311
Torbjorn Helland, *President*
Paul Azevedo, *Vice Pres*
Gregory Hall, *Vice Pres*
Dan Robinson, *Vice Pres*
▲ EMP: 59
SQ FT: 12,000
SALES (est): 10.4MM **Privately Held**
WEB: www.mwsausse.com
SIC: 3625 Control equipment, electric

(P-16735)
NEXTINPUT INC (PA)
980 Linda Vista Ave, Mountain View
(94043-1903)
PHONE.................................408 770-9293
Ali Foughi, *CEO*
Philip Thach, *Vice Pres*
EMP: 18
SALES: 5MM **Privately Held**
SIC: 3625 Switches, electronic applications

(P-16736)
PARKER-HANNIFIN CORPORATION
Compumotor
5500 Business Park Dr, Rohnert Park
(94928-7904)
PHONE.................................707 584-7558
Kenneth Sweet, *Branch Mgr*
Mark Calahan, *Engineer*
Mark Gary, *Senior Buyer*
Laura McMullen, *Buyer*
Nathan Barrows, *Manager*
EMP: 200
SQ FT: 32,000
SALES (corp-wide): 14.3B **Publicly Held**
WEB: www.parker.com
SIC: 3625 3823 Motor controls, electric; industrial instrmnts msrmnt display/control process variable
PA: Parker-Hannifin Corporation
6035 Parkland Blvd
Cleveland OH 44124
216 896-3000

(P-16737)
PEAK SERVO CORPORATION
Also Called: Peak Servo Corp / Eltrol
5931 Sea Lion Pl Ste 108, Carlsbad
(92010-6622)
PHONE.................................760 438-4986
David Olstad, *President*
EMP: 10
SQ FT: 2,000
SALES (est): 1.1MM **Privately Held**
WEB: www.peakservo.com
SIC: 3625 Motor controls, electric

(P-16738)
PECO CONTROLS CORPORATION
Also Called: Peco Inspx
1616 Culpepper Ave Ste A, Modesto
(95351-1220)
PHONE.................................209 576-3345
Dan Kemnitz, *Manager*
EMP: 14
SALES (corp-wide): 7.3MM **Privately Held**
WEB: www.pecocontrols.com
SIC: 3625 Relays & industrial controls
PA: Peco Inspx
1050 Commercial St
San Carlos CA 94070
209 576-3345

PRODUCTS & SVCS

(P-16739)
PIVOTAL SYSTEMS CORPORATION
48389 Fremont Blvd # 100, Fremont (94538-6559)
PHONE...............................510 770-9125
John Hoffman, *CEO*
EMP: 20
SQ FT: 1,000
SALES (est): 4.8MM **Privately Held**
WEB: www.pivotalsys.com
SIC: 3625 Control equipment, electric

(P-16740)
PULVER LABORATORIES INC
Also Called: Electromagnetics Division
320 N Santa Cruz Ave, Los Gatos (95030-7243)
PHONE...............................408 399-7000
Lee J Pulver, *President*
EMP: 12
SALES (est): 970K **Privately Held**
WEB: www.pulverlabs.com
SIC: 3625 8742 8734 Brakes, electro-magnetic; marketing consulting services; product testing laboratories

(P-16741)
QULSAR INC (PA)
90 Great Oaks Blvd # 204, San Jose (95119-1314)
PHONE...............................408 715-1098
Rajen Datta, *CEO*
Ola Andersson, *COO*
Rajendra Datta, *Marketing Staff*
David Spencer, *Marketing Staff*
EMP: 11 EST: 2014
SALES (est): 1.1MM **Privately Held**
SIC: 3625 Relays & industrial controls

(P-16742)
RCD ENGINEERING INC
17100 Salmon Mine Rd, Nevada City (95959-9350)
P.O. Box 119, North San Juan (95960-0119)
PHONE...............................530 292-3133
Steve Leach, *CEO*
Pat Leach, *Admin Sec*
EMP: 22
SQ FT: 12,000
SALES (est): 4MM **Privately Held**
WEB: www.rcdengineering.com
SIC: 3625 3714 Motor controls & accessories; motor starters & controllers, electric; motor vehicle parts & accessories

(P-16743)
RF-LAMBDA USA LLC
10509 Vista Sorrento Pkwy # 120, San Diego (92121-2743)
PHONE...............................972 767-5998
Jon Abalos, *Mfg Staff*
EMP: 10
SALES (corp-wide): 5.3MM **Privately Held**
SIC: 3625 Switches, electronic applications
PA: Rf-Lambda Usa, Llc
4300 Marsh Ridge Rd # 110
Carrollton TX 75010
972 767-5998

(P-16744)
RIGHT HAND MANUFACTURING INC
180 Otay Lakes Rd Ste 205, Bonita (91902-2444)
PHONE...............................619 819-5056
Pedro Zaragoza, *CEO*
Luis Resendiz, *QC Mgr*
▲ EMP: 150
SALES: 7MM **Privately Held**
WEB: www.rightandsynergy.com
SIC: 3625 Control circuit devices, magnet & solid state

(P-16745)
ROCKWELL AUTOMATION INC
2125 E Katella Ave # 250, Anaheim (92806-6024)
PHONE...............................714 938-9000
Brian Holte, *Branch Mgr*
EMP: 67 **Publicly Held**
SIC: 3625 Electric controls & control accessories, industrial

PA: Rockwell Automation, Inc.
1201 S 2nd St
Milwaukee WI 53204
-

(P-16746)
ROCKWELL AUTOMATION INC
5836 Corporate Ave, Cypress (90630-4742)
PHONE...............................714 828-1800
Rick Johnston, *Branch Mgr*
EMP: 40 **Publicly Held**
SIC: 3625 Relays & industrial controls
PA: Rockwell Automation, Inc.
1201 S 2nd St
Milwaukee WI 53204
-

(P-16747)
ROCKWELL AUTOMATION INC
111 N Market St Ste 200, San Jose (95113-1116)
PHONE...............................408 443-5425
EMP: 67 **Publicly Held**
SIC: 3625
PA: Rockwell Automation, Inc.
1201 S 2nd St
Milwaukee WI 53204
-

(P-16748)
ROCKWELL AUTOMATION INC
3000 Executive Pkwy # 210, San Ramon (94583-2300)
PHONE...............................925 242-5700
Mary P Farrell, *Branch Mgr*
EMP: 35 **Publicly Held**
SIC: 3625 Electric controls & control accessories, industrial
PA: Rockwell Automation, Inc.
1201 S 2nd St
Milwaukee WI 53204
-

(P-16749)
ROTORK CONTROLS INC
419 1st St, Petaluma (94952-4226)
PHONE...............................707 769-4880
Howard Williams, *Branch Mgr*
EMP: 12
SALES (corp-wide): 893.6MM **Privately Held**
SIC: 3625 Actuators, industrial
HQ: Rotork Controls Inc.
675 Mile Crossing Blvd
Rochester NY 14624
585 247-2304

(P-16750)
S & C ELECTRIC COMPANY
1135 Atlantic Ave Ste 100, Alameda (94501-1174)
PHONE...............................510 864-9300
Witold Bik, *Vice Pres*
Leo Soroka, *Engineer*
Manuel Mendez, *Sales Staff*
EMP: 50
SALES (corp-wide): 553.9MM **Privately Held**
SIC: 3625 3823 3822 Relays & industrial controls; industrial instrmnts msrmnt display/control process variable; auto controls regulating residntl & coml environmt & applncs
PA: S & C Electric Company
6601 N Ridge Blvd
Chicago IL 60626
773 338-1000

(P-16751)
S R C DEVICES INCCUSTOMER (PA)
6295 Ferris Sq Ste D, San Diego (92121-3248)
PHONE...............................866 772-8668
Richard W Carlyle, *President*
Mark McCabe, *Senior VP*
EMP: 10
SQ FT: 2,000
SALES (est): 16.1MM **Privately Held**
SIC: 3625 3643 5065 Switches, electronic applications; current-carrying wiring devices; electronic parts & equipment

(P-16752)
SCHMARTBOARD INC
37423 Fremont Blvd, Fremont (94536-3704)
PHONE...............................510 744-9900
Andrew Yaung, *President*
Neal Greenberg, *Principal*
EMP: 10
SALES (est): 1.4MM **Privately Held**
WEB: www.schmartboard.com
SIC: 3625 Switches, electronic applications

(P-16753)
SENSATA TECHNOLOGIES INC
Also Called: Gigavac, LLC
6382 Rose Ln, Carpinteria (93013-2922)
PHONE...............................805 684-8401
Rick Danchuk, *President*
Scott Hickman, *Vice Pres*
Jim Lanum, *Vice Pres*
Bernard Bush, *Engineer*
Dan Sullivan, *Senior Engr*
▲ EMP: 15
SALES (est): 7.2MM
SALES (corp-wide): 3.5B **Privately Held**
WEB: www.gigavac.com
SIC: 3625 Relays, electric power
PA: Sensata Technologies Holding Plc
Interface House
Swindon WILTS SN4 8

(P-16754)
SILICON MICROSTRUCTURES INC
1701 Mccarthy Blvd, Milpitas (95035-7416)
PHONE...............................408 473-9700
Frank D Guidone, *President*
▲ EMP: 76
SQ FT: 34,000
SALES (est): 16.9MM
SALES (corp-wide): 13.9B **Privately Held**
WEB: www.si-micro.com
SIC: 3625 3823 Relays & industrial controls; industrial instrmnts msrmnt display/control process variable
HQ: Measurement Specialties, Inc.
1000 Lucas Way
Hampton VA 23666
757 766-1500

(P-16755)
SILVERON INDUSTRIES INC
182 S Brent Cir, City of Industry (91789-3050)
PHONE...............................909 598-4533
Steve Lee, *President*
Sam Kwon, *Purchasing*
Brad Yi, *Purchasing*
Eddy Kim, *Sales Staff*
Daniel Baek, *Manager*
▲ EMP: 16
SQ FT: 24,000
SALES (est): 5.2MM **Privately Held**
WEB: www.silveronusa.com
SIC: 3625 5065 Industrial controls: push button, selector switches, pilot; electronic parts

(P-16756)
SKJONBERG CONTROLS INC
1363 Donlon St Ste 6, Ventura (93003-8387)
PHONE...............................805 650-0877
Knut Skjonberg, *President*
Monica Skjonberg, *Corp Secy*
EMP: 12
SQ FT: 3,600
SALES (est): 2.9MM **Privately Held**
WEB: www.skjonberg.com
SIC: 3625 Motor controls, electric

(P-16757)
SOUNDCOAT COMPANY INC
16901 Armstrong Ave, Irvine (92606-4914)
PHONE...............................631 242-2200
Clay Simpson, *Branch Mgr*
Ernie Murrieta, *Purch Agent*
EMP: 30
SALES (corp-wide): 305.9MM **Privately Held**
WEB: www.soundcoat.com
SIC: 3625 3086 3296 Noise control equipment; plastics foam products; mineral wool

HQ: The Soundcoat Company Inc
1 Burt Dr
Deer Park NY 11729
631 242-2200

(P-16758)
SURFACE TECHNOLOGIES CORP
3170 Commercial St, San Diego (92113-1427)
PHONE...............................619 564-8320
Bernard Meartz, *Manager*
EMP: 35
SQ FT: 29,617
SALES (corp-wide): 42.6MM **Privately Held**
WEB: www.surfacetechcorp.net
SIC: 3625 Marine & navy auxiliary controls
PA: Surface Technologies Corporation
2440 Mayport Rd Ste 7
Jacksonville FL 32233
904 241-1501

(P-16759)
SYSTEM TECHNICAL SUPPORT CORP
960 Knox St Bldg B, Torrance (90502-1086)
PHONE...............................310 845-9400
Eric Leskly, *President*
▲ EMP: 20
SQ FT: 10,000
SALES (est): 6MM **Privately Held**
WEB: www.stscorp.net
SIC: 3625 Relays & industrial controls

(P-16760)
SYSTEMS MACHINES AUTOMATIO (PA)
Also Called: Smac
5807 Van Allen Way, Carlsbad (92008-7309)
PHONE...............................760 929-7575
Ed Neff, *CEO*
Robert Berry, *CFO*
Karl Stocks, *Engineer*
Gerald Fernandez, *Controller*
Donovan Hastie, *Recruiter*
◆ EMP: 165
SQ FT: 102,000
SALES (est): 50.3MM **Privately Held**
WEB: www.smac-mca.com
SIC: 3625 2822 3549 Actuators, industrial; synthetic rubber; assembly machines, including robotic

(P-16761)
TE CONNECTIVITY CORPORATION
Also Called: Kilovac
550 Linden Ave, Carpinteria (93013-2038)
PHONE...............................805 684-4560
Mike Moschitto, *Branch Mgr*
Joy Glatfelter-Jone, *Technical Staff*
Danny Uehara, *Regl Sales Mgr*
EMP: 110
SALES (corp-wide): 13.9B **Privately Held**
WEB: www.raychem.com
SIC: 3625 Relays, for electronic use
HQ: Te Connectivity Corporation
1050 Westlakes Dr
Berwyn PA 19312
610 893-9800

(P-16762)
TEAL ELECTRONICS CORPORATION (PA)
10350 Sorrento Valley Rd, San Diego (92121-1642)
PHONE...............................858 558-9000
Glen Kassan, *Ch of Bd*
Donald Klein, *CEO*
David Nuzzo, *Treasurer*
William Bickel, *Vice Pres*
Gary Jasinski, *Vice Pres*
◆ EMP: 79
SQ FT: 36,059
SALES (est): 30MM **Privately Held**
WEB: www.teal.com
SIC: 3625 2631 3612 Noise control equipment; transformer board; transformers, except electric

▲ = Import ▼=Export
◆ =Import/Export

(P-16763)
UNIVERSAL CTRL SOLUTIONS CORP
Also Called: Dnf Controls
19770 Bahama St, Northridge
(91324-3303)
PHONE...................................818 898-3380
Daniel Fogel, *CEO*
▲ EMP: 15
SALES (est): 2.9MM
SALES (corp-wide): 16.9MM **Privately Held**
WEB: www.dnfcontrols.com
SIC: 3625 Control equipment, electric
HQ: Tsl Professional Products Ltd.
Unit 1-2
Marlow BUCKS
162 856-4610

(P-16764)
VAREDAN TECHNOLOGIES LLC
3860 Del Amo Blvd Ste 401, Torrance
(90503-7704)
PHONE...................................310 542-2320
John Vasak,
Craig Hammond, *CFO*
EMP: 11
SQ FT: 1,350
SALES: 2MM **Privately Held**
SIC: 3625 Control equipment, electric

(P-16765)
VARIOUS TECHNOLOGIES INC
2720 Aiello Dr Ste C, San Jose
(95111-2186)
PHONE...................................408 972-4460
Kurt Sebben, *President*
EMP: 40
SQ FT: 8,300
SALES (est): 5MM **Privately Held**
WEB: www.vari-tech.com
SIC: 3625 Solenoid switches (industrial controls); electric controls & control accessories, industrial

(P-16766)
VISHAY TECHNO COMPONENTS LLC
Also Called: Vishay Spectro
4051 Greystone Dr, Ontario (91761-3100)
PHONE...................................909 923-3313
Felix Zandman PHD, *President*
Robert A Freece, *Vice Pres*
William J Spiers, *Admin Sec*
▲ EMP: 100
SQ FT: 30,000
SALES (est): 9.6MM
SALES (corp-wide): 3B **Publicly Held**
SIC: 3625 Resistors & resistor units
HQ: Dale Vishay Electronics Llc
1122 23rd St
Columbus NE 68601
605 665-9301

(P-16767)
WARTSILA DYNMC POSITIONING INC (DH)
12131 Community Rd Ste A, Poway
(92064-8893)
PHONE...................................858 679-5500
Anthony Gardiner, *President*
Mika Verronen, *Treasurer*
Aaron Bresmahan, *Vice Pres*
Martha Vasquez, *Finance Dir*
◆ EMP: 38
SQ FT: 50,000
SALES: 12MM
SALES (corp-wide): 5.9B **Privately Held**
SIC: 3625 3699 Marine & navy auxiliary controls; underwater sound equipment
HQ: Wartsila Holding, Inc.
11710 N Gessner Rd Ste A
Houston TX 77064
281 233-6200

(P-16768)
WEMS INC
Vacuum Atmospheres Co
4652 W Rosecrans Ave, Hawthorne
(90250-6841)
P.O. Box 528 (90251-0528)
PHONE...................................310 644-0255
Terry Sweem, *Branch Mgr*
Gary Fleming, *Information Mgr*
EMP: 50

SALES (corp-wide): 17.6MM **Privately Held**
WEB: www.wems.com
SIC: 3625 Relays & industrial controls
PA: Wems Inc.
4650 W Rosecrans Ave
Hawthorne CA 90250
310 644-0251

(P-16769)
WOODWARD HRT INC (HQ)
25200 Rye Canyon Rd, Santa Clarita
(91355-1204)
PHONE...................................661 294-6000
Thomas A Gendron, *CEO*
Martin V Glass, *President*
Abdul Bigirumwami, *Vice Pres*
Lisa Tanner, *Vice Pres*
Austin Smith, *Network Enginr*
▲ EMP: 650 EST: 1954
SQ FT: 200,000
SALES (est): 214.8MM
SALES (corp-wide): 2.3B **Publicly Held**
SIC: 3625 3492 Actuators, industrial; electrohydraulic servo valves, metal
PA: Woodward, Inc.
1081 Woodward Way
Fort Collins CO 80524
970 482-5811

(P-16770)
WOODWARD HRT INC
25200 Rye Canyon Rd, Santa Clarita
(91355-1204)
PHONE...................................661 702-5552
Ronald Delet, *Manager*
Leslie Olston, *Engineer*
Stephen Tranovich, *Engineer*
Melissa Aguilar-Robles, *Consultant*
EMP: 70
SALES (corp-wide): 2.3B **Publicly Held**
SIC: 3625 3492 Actuators, industrial; electrohydraulic servo valves, metal
HQ: Woodward Hrt, Inc.
25200 Rye Canyon Rd
Santa Clarita CA 91355
661 294-6000

(P-16771)
ZBE INC
1035 Cindy Ln, Carpinteria (93013-2905)
PHONE...................................805 576-1600
Zac Bogart, *President*
Rod Martinez, *Engineer*
Tom Coniglio, *Manager*
▲ EMP: 45
SQ FT: 7,500
SALES (est): 7.5MM **Privately Held**
WEB: www.zbe.com
SIC: 3625 3861 3577 Electric controls & control accessories, industrial; photographic equipment & supplies; computer peripheral equipment

(P-16772)
ZMP AQUISITION CORPORATION
Also Called: Adams Rite Aerospace
4141 N Palm St, Fullerton (92835-1025)
PHONE...................................714 278-6500
Charles Collins, *President*
EMP: 200
SQ FT: 100,000
SALES (est): 17.9MM **Privately Held**
WEB: www.adamsriteaerospace.com
SIC: 3625 3743 3728 3429 Electric controls & control accessories, industrial; marine & navy auxiliary controls; railroad locomotives & parts, electric or nonelectric; aircraft parts & equipment; aircraft hardware; marine hardware

┌─────────────────────────┐
│ **3629 Electrical Indl** │
│ **Apparatus, NEC** │
└─────────────────────────┘

(P-16773)
ADVANCED CHARGING TECH INC
Also Called: A C T
16855 Knott Ave, La Mirada (90638-6014)
PHONE...................................877 228-5922
Robert J Istwan, *President*
Anthony Capalino, *Admin Sec*
Lara Lemley, *Media Spec*

Cynthia Partida, *Manager*
▲ EMP: 21
SALES: 14MM **Privately Held**
SIC: 3629 3691 Battery chargers, rectifying or nonrotating; alkaline cell storage batteries

(P-16774)
ALTERGY SYSTEMS
140 Blue Ravine Rd, Folsom (95630-4703)
PHONE...................................916 458-8590
Eric S Mettler, *President*
Nate Cammack, *CFO*
Jeremy Wolfe, *CFO*
Stapor Bernard, *Vice Pres*
James Oros, *Vice Pres*
▼ EMP: 29
SQ FT: 37,000
SALES (est): 7.7MM **Privately Held**
WEB: www.altergysystems.com
SIC: 3629 Electrochemical generators (fuel cells)

(P-16775)
AMERICAN BATTERY CHARGING LLC
15272 Newsboy Cir, Huntington Beach
(92649-1202)
PHONE...................................401 231-5227
Ronald J Stutzbach, *President*
Joan Stutzbach, *Admin Sec*
▼ EMP: 20
SQ FT: 20,000
SALES (est): 3.5MM **Privately Held**
WEB: www.abc-chargers.com
SIC: 3629 Battery chargers, rectifying or nonrotating

(P-16776)
APOLLO MANUFACTURING SERVICES
10360 Sorrento Valley Rd A, San Diego
(92121-1600)
PHONE...................................858 271-8009
Jenny Truong, *President*
EMP: 15
SQ FT: 5,000
SALES (est): 1.5MM **Privately Held**
SIC: 3629 8742 Battery chargers, rectifying or nonrotating; manufacturing management consultant

(P-16777)
ARECONT VISION COSTAR LLC
400 N Brand Blvd Ste 860, Glendale
(91203-9709)
PHONE...................................818 937-0700
Raul Calderon, *President*
Edmond Deravanessian, *CFO*
Troy Fairchild, *Vice Pres*
EMP: 100
SALES (est): 3.4MM
SALES (corp-wide): 19.6MM **Publicly Held**
SIC: 3629 Electronic generation equipment
PA: Costar Technologies, Inc.
101 Wrangler Dr Ste 201
Coppell TX 75019
469 635-6800

(P-16778)
AVEOX INC
2265 Ward Ave Ste A, Simi Valley
(93065-1864)
PHONE...................................805 915-0200
David Palombo, *President*
Tony Dematteis, *Engineer*
Robin Loboda, *VP Human Res*
▲ EMP: 35
SQ FT: 22,000
SALES (est): 7.7MM **Privately Held**
WEB: www.aveox.com
SIC: 3629 Electronic generation equipment

(P-16779)
BLUE SKY ENERGY INC
2598 Fortune Way Ste K, Vista
(92081-8442)
PHONE...................................760 597-1642
Alex Mevay, *President*
Jared Craft, *Officer*
Alexan Mardigian, *Engineer*
▲ EMP: 10
SQ FT: 2,500

SALES: 2.1MM **Privately Held**
WEB: www.blueskyenergyinc.com
SIC: 3629 Battery chargers, rectifying or nonrotating

(P-16780)
CAPAX TECHNOLOGIES INC
24842 Avenue Tibbitts, Valencia
(91355-3404)
PHONE...................................661 257-7666
Jagdish Patel, *President*
Nina Patel, *Corp Secy*
Jagdish C Patel, *Engineer*
Kira Patel, *VP Mktg*
EMP: 28
SQ FT: 17,000
SALES (est): 4.7MM **Privately Held**
WEB: www.capaxtechnologies.com
SIC: 3629 3675 Capacitors, fixed or variable; electronic capacitors

(P-16781)
CHARGEPOINT INC (PA)
254 E Hacienda Ave, Campbell
(95008-6617)
PHONE...................................408 841-4500
Pasquale Romano, *President*
Rex Jackson, *CFO*
Colleen Jansen, *Chief Mktg Ofcr*
Bill Loewenthal, *Senior VP*
Eric Sidle, *Senior VP*
◆ EMP: 277
SQ FT: 120,000
SALES (est): 119.3MM **Privately Held**
SIC: 3629 Battery chargers, rectifying or nonrotating

(P-16782)
CHARGETEK INC
409 Calle San Pablo # 104, Camarillo
(93012-8565)
PHONE...................................805 444-7792
Louis C Josephs, *President*
Terri Shackelford, *Sales Staff*
▲ EMP: 20
SALES (est): 3MM **Privately Held**
WEB: www.chargetek.com
SIC: 3629 3679 3677 Battery chargers, rectifying or nonrotating; static power supply converters for electronic applications; transformers power supply, electronic type

(P-16783)
COOPER BUSSMANN LLC
5735 W Las Positas Blvd # 100, Pleasanton
(94588-4002)
PHONE...................................925 924-8500
Hundi Kamath, *Manager*
EMP: 14 **Privately Held**
WEB: www.bussmann.com
SIC: 3629 5065 Capacitors & condensers; capacitors, electronic
HQ: Cooper Bussmann, Llc
114 Old State Rd
Ellisville MO 63021
636 527-1324

(P-16784)
CURRENT WAYS INC
10221 Buena Vista Ave, Santee
(92071-4484)
PHONE...................................619 596-3984
James Gevarges, *President*
Forest Tracko, *CFO*
Craig Miller, *Admin Sec*
EMP: 15
SQ FT: 26,000
SALES (est): 2MM **Privately Held**
WEB: www.CurrentWays.com
SIC: 3629 Battery chargers, rectifying or nonrotating

(P-16785)
ENGINEERED MAGNETICS INC
Also Called: Aap Division
10524 S La Cienega Blvd, Inglewood
(90304-1116)
PHONE...................................310 649-9000
Josh Shachar, *Ch of Bd*
Kathy Tran, *President*
Tony Truong, *Project Mgr*
Isabella Yi Sha Li, *Director*
Maya Vu, *Director*
EMP: 26
SQ FT: 57,000

SALES (est): 7.4MM **Privately Held**
SIC: 3629 3812 3369 Power conversion units, a.c. to d.c.: static-electric; missile guidance systems & equipment; aerospace castings, nonferrous: except aluminum

(P-16786)
EPC POWER CORP
13250 Gregg St Ste A2, Poway (92064-7164)
PHONE..................................858 748-5590
Devin Dilley, *CEO*
Allan Abela, *COO*
Bill Graham, *CFO*
William Granham, *CFO*
John Bryan, *Vice Pres*
▼ EMP: 42
SQ FT: 10,000
SALES (est): 2.1MM **Privately Held**
WEB: www.epcpower.com
SIC: 3629 Battery chargers, rectifying or nonrotating; inverters, nonrotating: electrical

(P-16787)
HI-Z TECHNOLOGY INC
Also Called: Ethernal Electric Company
7606 Miramar Rd Ste 7400, San Diego (92126-4210)
PHONE..................................858 695-6660
Jill Elsner, *CEO*
Dan Krommenhoek, *President*
Alexander Kushch, *Vice Pres*
Kavon Kazemzadeh, *Engineer*
◆ EMP: 20
SQ FT: 6,800
SALES (est): 4.4MM **Privately Held**
WEB: www.hi-z.com
SIC: 3629 Thermo-electric generators

(P-16788)
IAMPLUS LLC
809 N Cahuenga Blvd, Los Angeles (90038-3703)
PHONE..................................323 210-3852
Phil Molyneux, *President*
Rosemary Peschken, *CFO*
Will Adams, *Founder*
Chandrasekar Rathakrishnan, *Director*
EMP: 56 EST: 2012
SQ FT: 3,900
SALES: 4.8MM
SALES (corp-wide): 19.5MM **Privately Held**
SIC: 3629 Electronic generation equipment
PA: I.Am.Plus Electronics, Inc.
809 N Cahuenga Blvd
Los Angeles CA 90038
323 210-3852

(P-16789)
INTELLIGENT TECHNOLOGIES LLC
Also Called: Itech
9454 Waples St, San Diego (92121-2919)
PHONE..................................858 458-1500
Rod Bolton, *President*
Frank Cooper, *Exec VP*
Andrew Buchanan, *Technology*
▲ EMP: 125
SQ FT: 17,846
SALES (est): 33.6MM
SALES (corp-wide): 90.9MM **Privately Held**
WEB: www.itecheng.com
SIC: 3629 3356 Battery chargers, rectifying or nonrotating; battery metal
PA: Universal Power Group, Inc.
488 S Royal Ln
Coppell TX 75019
469 892-1122

(P-16790)
ISC ENGINEERING LLC
4351 Schaefer Ave, Chino (91710-5451)
PHONE..................................909 596-3315
Steve Burk, *Mng Member*
Steven H Burk, *Mng Member*
▲ EMP: 70 EST: 1999
SQ FT: 15,000
SALES (est): 14MM **Privately Held**
WEB: www.iscengineering.com
SIC: 3629 Electronic generation equipment

(P-16791)
LUMATRONIX MFG INC
1141 Ringwood Ct Ste 150, San Jose (95131-1759)
PHONE..................................408 435-7820
Paul E Shin, *President*
▲ EMP: 15
SQ FT: 7,000
SALES (est): 3.2MM **Privately Held**
SIC: 3629 Capacitors, a.c., for motors or fluorescent lamp ballasts

(P-16792)
MULTIMETRIXS LLC
1025 Solano Ave, Albany (94706-1617)
PHONE..................................510 527-6769
Boris Kesil,
EMP: 15
SALES (est): 1.3MM **Privately Held**
SIC: 3629 Electronic generation equipment

(P-16793)
PINNACLE WORLDWIDE INC
315 S Las Palmas Ave, Los Angeles (90020-4813)
PHONE..................................909 628-2200
Vishal Uttamchandani, *CEO*
EMP: 15
SALES (est): 1.5MM **Privately Held**
SIC: 3629 Electronic generation equipment

(P-16794)
PRO POWER PRODUCTS INC
Also Called: Battery Hut
913 S Victory Blvd, Burbank (91502-2430)
PHONE..................................818 558-6222
Bernard A Tessmar, *President*
James L Tessmar, *Vice Pres*
EMP: 10
SQ FT: 2,000
SALES (est): 1MM **Privately Held**
SIC: 3629 3691 7699 5531 Electronic generation equipment; storage batteries; battery service & repair; batteries, automotive & truck; batteries, dry cell

(P-16795)
Q C M INC
Also Called: Veris Manufacturing
285 Gemini Ave, Brea (92821-3704)
PHONE..................................714 414-1173
Jay Cadler, *CEO*
Bill McIlvene, *General Mgr*
Sandra Martinez, *Engineer*
Mark Vasquez, *Accountant*
Breanna Rorer, *Buyer*
▲ EMP: 45
SALES (est): 18.9MM **Privately Held**
WEB: www.verismfg.com
SIC: 3629 Electronic generation equipment

(P-16796)
ROI DEVELOPMENT CORP
15272 Newsboy Cir, Huntington Beach (92649-1202)
PHONE..................................714 751-0488
James Kaplan, *CTO*
EMP: 24
SALES (corp-wide): 13MM **Privately Held**
SIC: 3629 Battery chargers, rectifying or nonrotating
PA: Roi Development Corp.
2911 W Garry Ave
Santa Ana CA 92704
714 751-0488

(P-16797)
SCOTT ENGINEERING INC
5051 Edison Ave, Chino (91710-5716)
PHONE..................................909 594-9637
Luis Ernesto Lujan, *CEO*
Paul Sapien, *Senior Buyer*
Siahna Barba, *Buyer*
Todd Hoover, *Opers Staff*
Matt Nipper, *Director*
▲ EMP: 50 EST: 1967
SQ FT: 102,660
SALES (est): 21.9MM **Privately Held**
SIC: 3629 3613 Electronic generation equipment; switchgear & switchboard apparatus

(P-16798)
SIMCO-ION TECHNOLOGY GROUP (PA)
1601 Harbor Bay Pkwy # 150, Alameda (94502-3028)
PHONE..................................510 217-0600
Craig Hindman, *CEO*
Ronald Weigner, *President*
Michael Sheperia, *Managing Dir*
Berry Brown, *General Mgr*
▲ EMP: 110
SQ FT: 55,000
SALES (est): 10.9MM **Privately Held**
WEB: www.mksinst.com
SIC: 3629 Static elimination equipment, industrial

(P-16799)
SKYWORKS SOLUTIONS
1767 Carr Rd Ste 105, Calexico (92231-9506)
PHONE..................................301 874-6408
David J Aldrich, *President*
Paul Vincet, *Vice Pres*
▲ EMP: 18
SALES (est): 2.9MM **Privately Held**
SIC: 3629 Capacitors & condensers

(P-16800)
SOLAREDGE TECHNOLOGIES INC (PA)
47505 Seabridge Dr, Fremont (94538-6546)
PHONE..................................510 498-3200
Zvi Lando, *CEO*
Uri Bechor, *COO*
Ronen Faier, *CFO*
Nadav Zafrir, *Co-COB*
Lior Handelsman, *Vice Pres*
◆ EMP: 106 EST: 2006
SALES (est): 113.7MM **Privately Held**
SIC: 3629 Power conversion units, a.c. to d.c.: static-electric

(P-16801)
SOUTH BAY SOLUTIONS TEXAS LLC
37399 Centralmont Pl, Fremont (94536-6549)
PHONE..................................936 494-0180
Theresa Brooks, *Vice Pres*
Parveen Johal, *QC Mgr*
▲ EMP: 35
SALES (est): 4.6MM **Privately Held**
SIC: 3629 Electronic generation equipment

(P-16802)
SPARQTRON CORPORATION
5079 Brandin Ct, Fremont (94538-3140)
PHONE..................................510 657-7198
Shu Hung Kung, *CEO*
Mitchell Kung, *President*
Stephanie Nelson, *CFO*
Johnny Chen, *Vice Pres*
Alana Shi, *Program Mgr*
▲ EMP: 100 EST: 1998
SQ FT: 70,000
SALES (est): 33.6MM **Privately Held**
SIC: 3629 3672 Static elimination equipment, industrial; printed circuit boards

(P-16803)
STRATA TECHNOLOGIES
1800 Irvine Blvd Ste 205, Tustin (92780)
PHONE..................................714 368-9785
Jack Mazarone, *President*
EMP: 45 EST: 1997
SALES (est): 4.8MM **Privately Held**
WEB: www.strata-tech.net
SIC: 3629 Electronic generation equipment

(P-16804)
TOMAHAWK POWER LLC
501 W Broadway Ste 2020, San Diego (92101-3548)
PHONE..................................866 577-4476
Lawrence S Nora, *President*
▲ EMP: 12
SALES (est): 1MM **Privately Held**
SIC: 3629 Electronic generation equipment

(P-16805)
YUTAKA ELECTRIC INTL INC
Also Called: Falcon Electric
5116 Azusa Canyon Rd, Baldwin Park (91706-1846)
PHONE..................................626 962-7770
Arthur Seredian, *President*
Jitsuo Mase, *Vice Pres*
▲ EMP: 11
SQ FT: 10,000
SALES (est): 1.6MM **Privately Held**
SIC: 3629 3612 Power conversion units, a.c. to d.c.: static-electric; power & distribution transformers

(P-16806)
ZPOWER LLC
4765 Calle Quetzal, Camarillo (93012-8546)
PHONE..................................805 445-7789
Ross E Dueber, *President*
Herbert V Weigel II, *COO*
Dennis Dugan, *CFO*
Dennis J Dugan, *Vice Pres*
Barry A Freeman, *Vice Pres*
EMP: 210
SALES (est): 28.4MM **Privately Held**
WEB: www.zincmatrix.com
SIC: 3629 Battery chargers, rectifying or nonrotating

3631 Household Cooking Eqpt

(P-16807)
CONAIR CORPORATION
Also Called: Allegro
9350 Rayo Ave, South Gate (90280-3613)
PHONE..................................323 724-0101
Pjbrice, *Branch Mgr*
Teresa Dionsio, *Info Tech Dir*
Kazusa Nishii, *Marketing Staff*
EMP: 80
SALES (corp-wide): 2B **Privately Held**
SIC: 3631 3639 3999 3634 Household cooking equipment; major kitchen appliances, except refrigerators & stoves; barber & beauty shop equipment; hair dryers, electric
PA: Conair Corporation
1 Cummings Point Rd
Stamford CT 06902
203 351-9000

(P-16808)
DACOR
14425 Clark Ave, City of Industry (91745-1235)
PHONE..................................626 799-1000
EMP: 55 **Privately Held**
SIC: 3631 Convection ovens, including portable: household
HQ: Dacor
14425 Clark Ave
City Of Industry CA 91745
626 799-1000

(P-16809)
DACOR
Also Called: Dacor Purchasing Industry
14425 Clark Ave, City of Industry (91745-1235)
PHONE..................................626 799-1000
EMP: 12 **Privately Held**
SIC: 3631 Convection ovens, including portable: household
HQ: Dacor
14425 Clark Ave
City Of Industry CA 91745
626 799-1000

(P-16810)
DURO CORPORATION
Also Called: Nexrange Industries
17018 Evergreen Pl, City of Industry (91745-1819)
PHONE..................................626 839-6541
Saban Chang, *President*
Grace Cho,
▲ EMP: 15
SQ FT: 10,000
SALES (est): 22MM **Privately Held**
SIC: 3631 Gas ranges, domestic

(P-16811)
FILTHY GRILL INC
70 N Dewey Ave, Newbury Park
(91320-4359)
PHONE.............................818 282-2017
Thomas Hudgins, *Principal*
EMP: 15
SALES (est): 2.3MM **Privately Held**
SIC: 3631 Barbecues, grills & braziers
(outdoor cooking)

(P-16812)
JADE RANGE LLC
Also Called: Jade Products
2650 Orbiter St, Brea (92821-6265)
PHONE.............................714 961-2400
Timothy J Fitzgerald, *CFO*
Martin M Lindsay, *Treasurer*
Deanna Cook, *Administration*
Anindita Mazumder, *Engineer*
Jad Sidani, *Accountant*
▲ EMP: 120
SALES (est): 23.4MM
SALES (corp-wide): 2.7B **Publicly Held**
WEB: www.jaderange.com
SIC: 3631 3589 Household cooking equipment; commercial cooking & foodwarming
equipment
PA: The Middleby Corporation
1400 Toastmaster Dr
Elgin IL 60120
847 741-3300

(P-16813)
LYNX GRILLS INC (HQ)
7300 Flores St, Downey (90242-4010)
PHONE.............................323 722-4324
James Buch, *CEO*
Kirk Cleveland, *President*
Scott Grugel, *Vice Pres*
Patricia Rodriguez, *Technical Staff*
Tim French, *Engineer*
◆ EMP: 17
SALES (est): 6MM
SALES (corp-wide): 2.7B **Publicly Held**
SIC: 3631 Barbecues, grills & braziers
(outdoor cooking)
PA: The Middleby Corporation
1400 Toastmaster Dr
Elgin IL 60120
847 741-3300

(P-16814)
MAGMA PRODUCTS INC
3940 Pixie Ave, Lakewood (90712-4136)
PHONE.............................562 627-0500
Jerry Mashburn, *President*
James Mashburn, *Vice Pres*
Sheila Comeau, *Financial Exec*
Greg Schicora, *VP Opers*
Tom Dougherty, *Manager*
◆ EMP: 70
SQ FT: 22,000
SALES (est): 10.4MM **Privately Held**
WEB: www.magmaproducts.com
SIC: 3631 3634 Barbecues, grills & braziers (outdoor cooking); griddles or grills,
electric: household

(P-16815)
PACIFIC COAST MFG INC
5270 Edison Ave, Chino (91710-5719)
PHONE.............................909 627-7040
Bruce Doran, *President*
James Poremba, *Vice Pres*
▲ EMP: 72
SQ FT: 40,000
SALES (est): 15MM **Privately Held**
SIC: 3631 Barbecues, grills & braziers
(outdoor cooking)

(P-16816)
ROYAL RANGE CALIFORNIA INC
Also Called: Royal Industries
3245 Corridor Dr, Eastvale (91752-1030)
PHONE.............................951 360-1600
L Vasan, *CEO*
Patricia Woods, *Vice Pres*
▼ EMP: 65
SQ FT: 52,000
SALES (est): 13.9MM **Privately Held**
WEB: www.royalranges.com
SIC: 3631 Household cooking equipment

(P-16817)
SUPERIOR EQUIPMENT SOLUTIONS
1085 Bixby Dr, Hacienda Heights
(91745-1704)
PHONE.............................323 722-7900
Jeffrey Bernstein, *CEO*
Stephan Bernstein, *Principal*
Neil Silcock, *Engineer*
▲ EMP: 60
SQ FT: 45,000
SALES: 750MM **Privately Held**
WEB: www.bestgrille.com
SIC: 3631 5046 Household cooking equipment; restaurant equipment & supplies

(P-16818)
TELEDYNE WIRELESS INC
Also Called: Teledyne Microwave
3236 Scott Blvd, Santa Clara (95054-3011)
PHONE.............................408 986-5060
EMP: 110
SALES (corp-wide): 2.3B **Publicly Held**
SIC: 3631
HQ: Teledyne Wireless, Llc
1274 Terra Bella Ave
Mountain View CA 94043
650 691-9800

(P-16819)
TWIN EAGLES INC
13259 166th St, Cerritos (90703-2203)
PHONE.............................562 802-3488
Dante L Cantal, *CEO*
Epifania Cantal, *Vice Pres*
Eric Pitones, *Purchasing*
▲ EMP: 85
SQ FT: 45,000
SALES (est): 31.3MM **Privately Held**
WEB: www.twineaglesinc.com
SIC: 3631 Barbecues, grills & braziers
(outdoor cooking)

3632 Household Refrigerators & Freezers

(P-16820)
LARRY SCHLUSSLER
Also Called: Sun Frost
824 L St Ste 7, Arcata (95521-5766)
P.O. Box 1101 (95518-1101)
PHONE.............................707 822-9095
Larry Schussler, *Owner*
▼ EMP: 16
SQ FT: 6,000
SALES (est): 1.6MM **Privately Held**
WEB: www.sunfrost.com
SIC: 3632 Household refrigerators & freezers

(P-16821)
PANASONIC APPLIANCES REF
Also Called: Paprsa
2001 Sanyo Ave, San Diego (92154-6212)
PHONE.............................619 661-1134
Shusaku Nagae, *CEO*
Kazuya Jinno, *President*
Hiroyuki Maotani, *Treasurer*
Shigeki Muneyasu, *Treasurer*
◆ EMP: 64
SALES (est): 60.6MM **Privately Held**
WEB: www.sanyousa.com
SIC: 3632 3821 3585 Household refrigerators & freezers; freezers, laboratory;
cabinets, show & display, refrigerated
HQ: Panasonic Corporation Of North America
2 Riverfront Plz Ste 200
Newark NJ 07102
201 348-7000

(P-16822)
REFRIGERATOR MANUFACTERS INC (PA)
Also Called: Econocold Refrigerators
17018 Edwards Rd, Cerritos (90703-2422)
PHONE.............................562 926-2006
Lawrence E Jaffe, *President*
Paula Donohoo, *President*
Russell E Anthony, *Exec VP*
Leo R Lewis, *Exec VP*
EMP: 24
SQ FT: 40,000

SALES (est): 4.9MM **Privately Held**
WEB: www.rmi-econocold.com
SIC: 3632 3585 Household refrigerators &
freezers; refrigeration & heating equipment

(P-16823)
RITEMP REFRIGERATION INC
9155 Archibald Ave # 503, Rancho Cucamonga (91730-5255)
PHONE.............................909 941-0444
Jesse A Saldamando, *President*
Angelina Saldamando, *Treasurer*
EMP: 10 EST: 2002
SQ FT: 7,000
SALES: 188K **Privately Held**
SIC: 3632 1711 Refrigerator cabinets,
household: metal & wood; refrigeration
contractor

3634 Electric Household Appliances

(P-16824)
AG GLOBAL PRODUCTS LLC
Also Called: Fhi Brands
15301 Blackburn Ave, Norwalk
(90650-6842)
PHONE.............................323 334-2900
Shauky Gulamani, *President*
Jayson Dodo, *CFO*
Nicolas Bobroff, *Senior VP*
Daniel Bobroff, *Mng Member*
▲ EMP: 35
SALES (est): 6.8MM **Privately Held**
SIC: 3634 3999 Hair curlers, electric; hair
& hair-based products

(P-16825)
BODY CARE RESORT INC
22125 S Vermont Ave, Torrance
(90502-2132)
PHONE.............................310 328-8888
David Hsiung, *President*
EMP: 10
SALES (est): 132.2K **Privately Held**
WEB: www.bodycareonline.com
SIC: 3634 Massage machines, electric, except for beauty/barber shops

(P-16826)
BRAVA HOME INC
312 Chestnut St, Redwood City
(94063-2222)
PHONE.............................408 675-2569
John Pleasants, *CEO*
Shih Yu Cheng, *COO*
Dan Yue,
Mark Janoff, *Admin Sec*
EMP: 26
SALES (est): 220.6K **Privately Held**
SIC: 3634 Ovens, portable: household

(P-16827)
ESMART MASSAGE INC
339 N Berry St, Brea (92821-3140)
PHONE.............................657 341-0360
Demitry Pevzner, *Vice Pres*
EMP: 15
SALES (est): 1.4MM **Privately Held**
SIC: 3634 Massage machines, electric, except for beauty/barber shops

(P-16828)
FOLDIMATE INC
879 White Pine Ct, Oak Park (91377-4769)
PHONE.............................805 876-4418
Gal Rozov, *CEO*
Ori Kaplan, *COO*
EMP: 22 EST: 2012
SALES (est): 1MM **Privately Held**
SIC: 3634 Personal electrical appliances

(P-16829)
INSEAT SOLUTIONS LLC
1871 Wright Ave, La Verne (91750-5817)
PHONE.............................562 447-1780
Arthur Liu,
Dickson Liu,
▲ EMP: 22
SALES (est): 4MM **Privately Held**
WEB: www.relaxor.com
SIC: 3634 Massage machines, electric, except for beauty/barber shops

(P-16830)
J & J ACTION INC
3210 S Standard Ave, Santa Ana
(92705-5630)
PHONE.............................877 327-5268
Przemyslaw Maslowiec, *President*
EMP: 10 EST: 2012
SQ FT: 30,000
SALES: 2.5MM **Privately Held**
SIC: 3634 Toothbrushes, electric

(P-16831)
KATADYN DESALINATION LLC
Also Called: Spectra Watermakers
2220 S Mcdowell Blvd Ext, Petaluma
(94954-5659)
PHONE.............................415 526-2780
Shawn Hostetter, *Mng Member*
Chris Voxland,
EMP: 20
SQ FT: 8,400
SALES: 4MM **Privately Held**
SIC: 3634 3732 Water pulsating devices,
electric; yachts, building & repairing

(P-16832)
KIZURE PRODUCT CO INC
Also Called: Kizure Hair Products & Irons
1950 N Central Ave, Compton
(90222-3102)
P.O. Box 2556, Gardena (90247-0120)
PHONE.............................310 604-0058
Jerry White, *President*
Lucky White, *Exec VP*
EMP: 33
SQ FT: 40,000
SALES: 2.3MM **Privately Held**
SIC: 3634 2844 Hair dryers, electric;
shampoos, rinses, conditioners: hair

(P-16833)
LUMA COMFORT LLC
6600 Katella Ave, Cypress (90630-5104)
PHONE.............................855 963-9247
Luke Peters, *President*
Mariella Peters, *Admin Sec*
▲ EMP: 50
SQ FT: 30,000
SALES (est): 3.6MM **Privately Held**
SIC: 3634 Electric housewares & fans

(P-16834)
MILA USA INC
11 Laurel Ave, Belvedere Tiburon
(94920-2305)
PHONE.............................415 734-8540
Grant Prigge, *CEO*
EMP: 20
SALES (est): 746.9K **Privately Held**
SIC: 3634 7389 Air purifiers, portable;

(P-16835)
MIST & COOL LLC
707 E Hueneme Rd, Oxnard (93033-8654)
PHONE.............................805 986-4125
Mike Davis, *Mng Member*
Barry Hanish, *Mng Member*
▲ EMP: 18
SQ FT: 9,500
SALES (est): 2.3MM **Privately Held**
SIC: 3634 Water pulsating devices, electric

(P-16836)
OLISO INC
1200 Harbour Way S 215, Richmond
(94804-3636)
PHONE.............................415 864-7600
Ehsan Alipour, *CEO*
Ankit Pandey, *Executive*
Janice Wong, *Administration*
Jonathan Seclow, *Technology*
▲ EMP: 16
SQ FT: 7,000
SALES (est): 3.4MM **Privately Held**
WEB: www.oliso.com
SIC: 3634 Personal electrical appliances

(P-16837)
OMEGA 2000 GROUP CORP
160 S Carmalita St, Hemet (92543-4230)
PHONE.............................951 775-5815
George E Sararu, *President*
Burlacu Lilioara, *CFO*
William Hull, *Director*
▲ EMP: 95
SQ FT: 5,200

PRODUCTS & SVCS

SALES: 12.4MM **Privately Held**
WEB: www.omega2000group.com
SIC: 3634 Heating units, for electric appliances

(P-16838)
PACIFIC ACCENT INCORPORATED
623 S Doubleday Ave, Ontario (91761-1520)
PHONE............................909 563-1600
Sophia Juang, *CEO*
▲ **EMP:** 14 **EST:** 2010
SQ FT: 600
SALES: 4MM **Privately Held**
SIC: 3634 Housewares, excluding cooking appliances & utensils

(P-16839)
QYK BRANDS LLC
Also Called: Qyksonic
9 Macarthur Pl, Santa Ana (92707-6738)
PHONE............................949 312-7119
Rakesh Tammabattula,
Yijun Fan, *Marketing Mgr*
Preston Ketchum, *Marketing Staff*
Frank Mueller, *Manager*
EMP: 35
SQ FT: 2,000
SALES: 350K **Privately Held**
SIC: 3634 Massage machines, electric, except for beauty/barber shops

(P-16840)
REPOSE CORP
16826 Edwards Rd, Cerritos (90703-2418)
PHONE............................562 921-9299
Johnny Lee, *Principal*
Jon Austin, *Sales Mgr*
EMP: 10
SALES (est): 861.9K **Privately Held**
SIC: 3634 Massage machines, electric, except for beauty/barber shops

(P-16841)
TOUCH COFFEE & BEVERAGES LLC
15312 Valley Blvd, City of Industry (91746-3324)
P.O. Box 360752, Los Angeles (90036-1251)
PHONE............................626 968-0300
Samuel Kim, *Mng Member*
▲ **EMP:** 14
SALES (est): 2.2MM **Privately Held**
SIC: 3634 5149 Coffee makers, electric: household; coffee & tea

(P-16842)
VAPORBROTHERS INC
2908 Oregon Ct Ste I9, Torrance (90503-2651)
PHONE............................310 618-1188
Bertram Balch, *President*
Michelle Gilpin, *Office Mgr*
Naomi Hinzo, *Sales Staff*
EMP: 12
SALES (est): 2.1MM **Privately Held**
WEB: www.vaporbrothers.com
SIC: 3634 Electric housewares & fans

3635 Household Vacuum Cleaners

(P-16843)
BETTER CLEANING SYSTEMS INC
Also Called: Kleenrite
1122 Maple St, Madera (93637-5368)
P.O. Box 359 (93639-0359)
PHONE............................559 673-5700
William Hachtmann, *CEO*
Bill Hachtmann, *President*
Pat Hibben, *Controller*
Christine Farinelli, *Purch Mgr*
Laura Wheeler, *Sales Staff*
◆ **EMP:** 37
SQ FT: 27,620
SALES (est): 4.5MM **Privately Held**
SIC: 3635 Carpet shampooer

(P-16844)
MINI VAC INC
634 E Colorado St, Glendale (91205-1710)
P.O. Box 10850 (91209-3850)
PHONE............................818 244-6777
Eric Miglins, *CEO*
▲ **EMP:** 12
SALES (est): 774.9K **Privately Held**
WEB: www.mini-vac.com
SIC: 3635 5064 Household vacuum cleaners; vacuum cleaners

(P-16845)
TECHKO KOBOT INC
Also Called: Techko Maid
11 Marconi Ste A, Irvine (92618-2786)
PHONE............................949 380-7300
Joseph Ko, *President*
▲ **EMP:** 12
SQ FT: 4,500
SALES: 2.5MM **Privately Held**
SIC: 3635 5065 Household vacuum cleaners; security control equipment & systems

(P-16846)
UNOVO LLC
Also Called: Oliso
1200 Hrbour Way S Ste 215, Richmond (94804)
PHONE............................415 864-7600
Ehsan Alipour, *Mng Member*
EMP: 10 **EST:** 2015
SQ FT: 1,400
SALES: 2.3MM **Privately Held**
SIC: 3635 3634 Household vacuum cleaners; irons, electric: household

---
3639 Household Appliances, NEC

(P-16847)
BRENTWOOD APPLIANCES INC
3088 E 46th St, Vernon (90058-2422)
PHONE............................323 266-4600
Poorad B Panahi, *President*
Maurice Araghi, *Vice Pres*
John Yadgari, *Vice Pres*
◆ **EMP:** 13
SQ FT: 65,000
SALES (est): 2.4MM **Privately Held**
SIC: 3639 Major kitchen appliances, except refrigerators & stoves

(P-16848)
BSH HOME APPLIANCES CORP (DH)
1901 Main St Ste 600, Irvine (92614-0521)
PHONE............................949 440-7100
Michael Traub, *President*
Christofer Von Nagel, *President*
Vivian Lira, *Administration*
Sylvia Mejia, *Administration*
Christoph Cochius, *Info Tech Mgr*
◆ **EMP:** 220
SQ FT: 52,000
SALES (est): 535MM
SALES (corp-wide): 294.8MM **Privately Held**
WEB: www.bsh-group.us
SIC: 3639 Major kitchen appliances, except refrigerators & stoves
HQ: Bsh Hausgerate Gmbh
Carl-Wery-Str. 34
Munchen 81739
894 590-01

(P-16849)
CNP INDUSTRIES INC
351 Thor Pl, Brea (92821-4133)
PHONE............................714 482-2320
Harold R Piszczek, *CEO*
Steven L Kirkley, *President*
▲ **EMP:** 12
SQ FT: 10,000
SALES (est): 2.7MM **Privately Held**
WEB: www.windcrestcnp.com
SIC: 3639 Major kitchen appliances, except refrigerators & stoves

(P-16850)
FISHER & PAYKEL APPLIANCES INC (DH)
695 Town Center Dr # 180, Costa Mesa (92626-1902)
PHONE............................949 790-8900
Peter Lockwell, *President*
Matt McConnell, *Vice Pres*
Mindy Herrera, *Administration*
Tina Ngo, *Credit Staff*
Sofia Reyes, *Credit Staff*
◆ **EMP:** 190
SQ FT: 26,000
SALES (est): 50.4MM
SALES (corp-wide): 7.8K **Privately Held**
WEB: www.fisherandpaykelappliances.com
SIC: 3639 3631 5064 Dishwashing machines, household; household cooking equipment; electric household appliances; refrigeration equipment & supplies
HQ: Fisher & Paykel Appliances Usa Holdings Inc.
695 Town Center Dr # 180
Costa Mesa CA 92626
888 936-7872

(P-16851)
HESTAN COMMERCIAL CORPORATION
3375 E La Palma Ave, Anaheim (92806-2815)
PHONE............................714 869-2380
Stanley Kin Sui Cheng, *President*
Eric Deng, *President*
Chris Moy, *Vice Pres*
Alex Santana, *Vice Pres*
Hans Wenzel, *Design Engr*
▲ **EMP:** 125 **EST:** 2013
SQ FT: 70,000
SALES: 8.4MM **Privately Held**
SIC: 3639 Major kitchen appliances, except refrigerators & stoves
HQ: Meyer Corporation, U.S.
1 Meyer Plz
Vallejo CA 94590
707 551-2800

(P-16852)
NRC USA INC
3700 Wilshire Blvd # 300, Los Angeles (90010-2919)
PHONE............................213 325-2780
Jibaek Heo, *President*
Kweon Lee, *Vice Pres*
▲ **EMP:** 14
SALES: 3.5MM **Privately Held**
SIC: 3639 Major kitchen appliances, except refrigerators & stoves
PA: Nr Communication
648-1 Yeoksam-Dong, Kangnam-Gu
Seoul

(P-16853)
SHARKNINJA OPERATING LLC
16300 Fern Ave, Chino (91708-9003)
PHONE............................909 325-4412
Daniel Rios, *Manager*
EMP: 11 **Privately Held**
SIC: 3639 Major kitchen appliances, except refrigerators & stoves
HQ: Sharkninja Operating Llc
89 A St Ste 100
Needham MA 02494
617 243-0235

(P-16854)
THERMA-TEK RANGE CORP
9121 Atlanta Ave Ste 331, Huntington Beach (92646-6309)
PHONE............................570 455-9491
EMP: 25
SQ FT: 30,000
SALES (est): 3.1MM **Privately Held**
SIC: 3639

(P-16855)
TLM INTERNATIONAL INC
Also Called: Dr Heater USA
860 Mahler Rd, Burlingame (94010-1604)
PHONE............................650 952-2257
Mr Vincent MA, *President*
James Tan, *Owner*
EMP: 12

SALES: 500K **Privately Held**
SIC: 3639 2519 3634 Hot water heaters, household; household furniture, except wood or metal: upholstered; massage machines, electric, except for beauty/barber shops

---
3641 Electric Lamps

(P-16856)
APPLIED PHOTON TECHNOLOGY INC
3346 Arden Rd, Hayward (94545-3923)
PHONE............................510 780-9500
Leonard Goldfine, *President*
Rafael Olano, *Vice Pres*
Rodney Romero, *Vice Pres*
Barry Smith, *Vice Pres*
▲ **EMP:** 29
SQ FT: 12,850
SALES (est): 4.6MM **Privately Held**
WEB: www.appliedphoton.com
SIC: 3641 Ultraviolet lamps

(P-16857)
BHK INC
760 E Sunkist St, Ontario (91761-1861)
PHONE............................909 983-2973
Steve Boland, *President*
Walter Chapman, *Engineer*
Suzie Garcia, *Sales Staff*
▲ **EMP:** 24
SALES: 4.4MM **Privately Held**
SIC: 3641 Health lamps, infrared or ultraviolet

(P-16858)
DA GLOBAL ENERGY INC
548 Market St Ste 32810, San Francisco (94104-5401)
PHONE............................408 916-6303
Donald James Ashley, *CEO*
EMP: 13
SALES (est): 1.1MM **Privately Held**
SIC: 3641 5063 7389 Electric light bulbs, complete; lamps, fluorescent, electric; light bulbs & related supplies;

(P-16859)
DASOL INC
Also Called: Coronet Lighting
16210 S Avalon Blvd, Gardena (90248-2908)
P.O. Box 2065 (90247-0010)
PHONE............................310 327-6700
Sol Smith, *Ch of Bd*
David Smith, *President*
Mark Smith, *Vice Pres*
▲ **EMP:** 225 **EST:** 1944
SQ FT: 120,000
SALES (est): 37.3MM **Privately Held**
WEB: www.coronetlighting.com
SIC: 3641 Electric lamps & parts for generalized applications

(P-16860)
DURALED LTG TECHNOLGIES CORP
15285 Alton Pkwy Ste 200, Irvine (92618-2372)
PHONE............................949 753-0162
Allen Fann, *President*
EMP: 16 **EST:** 2000
SQ FT: 10,000
SALES (est): 1.5MM **Privately Held**
WEB: www.duraled.com
SIC: 3641 3674 Electric lamps; semiconductors & related devices

(P-16861)
ESTAR LIMITED
15216 Daphne Ave, Gardena (90249-4122)
PHONE............................310 989-6265
Rick McCoy, *President*
EMP: 50
SALES (est): 5.2MM **Privately Held**
SIC: 3641 5047 Electric lamps; hospital equipment & supplies; dental equipment & supplies; industrial safety devices: first aid kits & masks

▲ = Import ▼=Export
◆ =Import/Export

(P-16862)
FANLIGHT CORPORATION INC
Also Called: Plusrite
3992 Mission Blvd, Montclair (91763-6035)
PHONE...............................909 868-6538
Song Qian, *CEO*
EMP: 14
SALES (corp-wide): 10.8MM **Privately Held**
SIC: 3641 Electric lamps & parts for generalized applications; electric lamp (bulb) parts; electric light bulbs, complete; glow lamp bulbs
PA: Fanlight Corporation, Inc.
    2000 S Grove Ave Bldg B
    Ontario CA 91761
    909 930-6868

(P-16863)
FANLIGHT CORPORATION INC (PA)
Also Called: Plusrite and Ledirect
2000 S Grove Ave Bldg B, Ontario (91761-4800)
PHONE...............................909 930-6868
Song Qian, *CEO*
Koji Sasaki, *President*
Cecilia Liem, *Treasurer*
Winsome Lo, *Graphic Designe*
◆ **EMP:** 21
SQ FT: 32,000
SALES (est): 10.8MM **Privately Held**
WEB: www.fanlightinc.com
SIC: 3641 Electric lamps & parts for generalized applications; electric lamp (bulb) parts; electric light bulbs, complete; glow lamp bulbs

(P-16864)
HOLLYWOOD LAMP & SHADE CO
Also Called: Kimberly Lighting
2928 Leonis Blvd, Vernon (90058-2916)
PHONE...............................323 585-3999
Fred Nadal, *President*
EMP: 15
SALES (est): 2.1MM **Privately Held**
WEB: www.hollywoodshades.com
SIC: 3641 3648 3645 Lamps, fluorescent, electric; lamps, incandescent filament, electric; lighting equipment; lamp shades, metal

(P-16865)
IRTRONIX INC
Also Called: Euri Lighting
20900 Normandie Ave B, Torrance (90502-1602)
PHONE...............................310 787-1100
Danny Joon OH, *CEO*
Suk J OH, *CFO*
Claudia Funk, *Executive*
Albert Burgos, *Sales Mgr*
▲ **EMP: 12 EST:** 2000
SQ FT: 23,000
SALES (est): 6.3MM **Privately Held**
WEB: www.irtronix.com
SIC: 3641 5065 Electric lamps & parts for generalized applications; semiconductor devices

(P-16866)
LITEPANELS INC
20600 Plummer St, Chatsworth (91311-5111)
PHONE...............................818 752-7009
Rudy Pohlert, *President*
Tim Latham, *Project Mgr*
Richard Rosen, *Research*
Victor Chen, *Engineer*
Helen Craig, *Human Res Dir*
▲ **EMP:** 11
SALES (est): 1.1MM
SALES (corp-wide): 495MM **Privately Held**
WEB: www.litepanels.com
SIC: 3641 Electric lamps
HQ: Vitec Group Holdings Limited
    Bridge House
    Richmond
    208 332-4600

(P-16867)
NIA ENERGY LLC
23679 Calabasas Rd, Calabasas (91302-1502)
PHONE...............................818 422-8000
Linying Du,
Angelina Leo, *Mng Member*
EMP: 10 EST: 2012
SQ FT: 10,000
SALES: 20MM **Privately Held**
SIC: 3641 Electric lamp (bulb) parts

(P-16868)
OSRAM SYLVANIA INC
13350 Gregg St Ste 101, Poway (92064-7137)
PHONE...............................858 748-5077
Dennis Cohen, *Branch Mgr*
EMP: 377
SALES (corp-wide): 4.7B **Privately Held**
SIC: 3641 Electric lamps
HQ: Osram Sylvania Inc
    200 Ballardvale St # 305
    Wilmington MA 01887
    978 570-3000

(P-16869)
TIVOLI LLC
15602 Mosher Ave, Tustin (92780-6427)
PHONE...............................714 957-6101
Marie Paris, *CEO*
Susan Larson, *CEO*
Nigel Coppins, *Financial Exec*
Barbara Cobos, *Credit Mgr*
Eric Kramer, *Mng Member*
◆ **EMP:** 50
SALES (est): 13.7MM **Privately Held**
SIC: 3641 3646 Tubes, electric light; ceiling systems, luminous

(P-16870)
TOPSTAR INTERNATIONAL INC
13668 Valley Blvd Unit D2, City of Industry (91746-2572)
PHONE...............................909 595-8807
Sheng Wang, *CEO*
▲ **EMP:** 10
SQ FT: 20,000
SALES (est): 1.7MM **Privately Held**
SIC: 3641 Electric light bulbs, complete

3643 Current-Carrying Wiring Devices

(P-16871)
1891 ALTON A CALIFORNIA CO
1891 Alton Pkwy Ste A, Irvine (92606-4985)
PHONE...............................949 261-6402
Elias Khamis, *Owner*
EMP: 15
SALES (est): 1MM **Privately Held**
SIC: 3643 Power line cable

(P-16872)
ABRAMS ELECTRONICS INC
Also Called: Thor Electronics of California
420 W Market St, Salinas (93901-1422)
PHONE...............................831 758-6400
Stephen Abrams, *President*
Jeff Abrams, *Vice Pres*
Carol Villagran, *Accounting Mgr*
EMP: 42
SQ FT: 28,000
SALES (est): 8MM **Privately Held**
SIC: 3643 3496 Connectors & terminals for electrical devices; cable, uninsulated wire: made from purchased wire

(P-16873)
AEI MANUFACTURING INC
Also Called: Air Electro
9452 De Soto Ave, Chatsworth (91311-4910)
P.O. Box 2231 (91313-2231)
PHONE...............................818 407-5400
Steven Strull, *President*
EMP: 10
SALES (est): 1.1MM **Privately Held**
WEB: www.aeimanufacturing.com
SIC: 3643 Current-carrying wiring devices

(P-16874)
AERO-ELECTRIC CONNECTOR INC (PA)
2280 W 208th St, Torrance (90501-1452)
PHONE...............................310 618-3737
Walter Neubauer, *Chairman*
Walter Neubauer Jr, *CEO*
Rolando Hernandez, *Manager*
EMP: 71
SQ FT: 65,000
SALES (est): 62.8MM **Privately Held**
WEB: www.aero-electric.com
SIC: 3643 3678 Connectors & terminals for electrical devices; electronic connectors

(P-16875)
ALLAN KIDD
Also Called: AK Industries
3115 E Las Hermanas St, Compton (90221-5512)
PHONE...............................310 762-1600
Allan Kidd, *Owner*
Loni Miller, *Marketing Mgr*
EMP: 20
SQ FT: 17,000
SALES: 2MM **Privately Held**
WEB: www.ak-ind.com
SIC: 3643 Electric connectors

(P-16876)
AMPHENOL DC ELECTRONICS INC
1870 Little Orchard St, San Jose (95125-1041)
P.O. Box 28463 (95159-8463)
PHONE...............................408 947-4500
David Cianciulli Sr, *CEO*
David Cianciulli Jr, *President*
Adrienne Bugayong, *Program Mgr*
Bang Tran, *Technical Staff*
Rio Ebbah, *Engineer*
EMP: 300
SQ FT: 33,000
SALES (est): 58.2MM
SALES (corp-wide): 8.2B **Publicly Held**
WEB: www.dcelectronics.com
SIC: 3643 Current-carrying wiring devices
PA: Amphenol Corporation
    358 Hall Ave
    Wallingford CT 06492
    203 265-8900

(P-16877)
AUTOSPLICE INC (PA)
10431 Wtridge Cir Ste 110, San Diego (92121)
PHONE...............................858 535-0077
Santosh RAO, *CEO*
Kevin Barry, *COO*
Jeffrey Cartwright, *CFO*
John Donaldson, *Administration*
Brendan Lydon, *Info Tech Dir*
▲ **EMP: 200 EST:** 1954
SQ FT: 20,000
SALES (est): 151.2MM **Privately Held**
SIC: 3643 Electric connectors

(P-16878)
BIZLINK TECHNOLOGY INC (HQ)
47211 Bayside Pkwy, Fremont (94538-6517)
PHONE...............................510 252-0786
Annie Kuo, *President*
David McKee, *CEO*
Ted Hsiao, *Vice Pres*
Roger Liang, *Vice Pres*
Anders Peterson, *Vice Pres*
▲ **EMP: 80 EST:** 1996
SQ FT: 62,000
SALES (est): 32.8MM **Privately Held**
WEB: www.bizlinktech.com
SIC: 3643 Current-carrying wiring devices

(P-16879)
CABLE CONNECTION INC
Also Called: Lorom West
1035 Mission Ct, Fremont (94539-8203)
PHONE...............................510 249-9000
Greg Gaches, *President*
Nikki Del Campo, *Administration*
Diane Sowerbrower, *Human Res Mgr*
Al Franco, *Buyer*
Steve Winklepleck, *Mfg Mgr*

▲ **EMP:** 100
SQ FT: 55,000
SALES (est): 26.6MM **Privately Held**
WEB: www.cable-connection.com
SIC: 3643 Current-carrying wiring devices

(P-16880)
CABLETEK INC
525 Finney Ct, Gardena (90248-2037)
P.O. Box 39 (90248-0039)
PHONE...............................310 523-5000
Rosa G Lockwood, *President*
Rosa M Garcia, *General Mgr*
▲ **EMP:** 10
SALES (est): 1.4MM **Privately Held**
SIC: 3643 Current-carrying wiring devices

(P-16881)
CALPICO INC
1387 San Mateo Ave, South San Francisco (94080-6511)
PHONE...............................650 588-2241
Carey Wilson, *President*
Edna Wilson, *Treasurer*
▲ **EMP:** 23
SQ FT: 20,000
SALES (est): 3.9MM **Privately Held**
WEB: www.calpicoinc.com
SIC: 3643 3317 3089 3498 Current-carrying wiring devices; steel pipe & tubes; plastic hardware & building products; fabricated pipe & fittings; gaskets, packing & sealing devices

(P-16882)
CARR MANUFACTURING COMPANY INC
19675 Descartes, Foothill Ranch (92610-2609)
PHONE...............................949 215-7952
Michelle R Carraway, *CEO*
▲ **EMP:** 11
SQ FT: 5,000
SALES (est): 2.4MM **Privately Held**
WEB: www.carrmfg.com
SIC: 3643 3672 3679 Power line cable; printed circuit boards; harness assemblies for electronic use: wire or cable

(P-16883)
CELESTICA LLC
280 Campillo St Ste G, Calexico (92231-3200)
PHONE...............................760 357-4880
Michael Garmon,
EMP: 400
SALES (est): 260K **Privately Held**
SIC: 3643 Current-carrying wiring devices

(P-16884)
COAST AIR SUPPLY CO INC
26501 Summit Cir, Santa Clarita (91350-3049)
PHONE...............................310 472-5612
Fred W Sutherland, *CEO*
EMP: 12
SQ FT: 15,000
SALES (est): 2.2MM **Privately Held**
WEB: www.coastair.com
SIC: 3643 Current-carrying wiring devices

(P-16885)
CONNECTEC COMPANY INC (PA)
1701 Reynolds Ave, Irvine (92614-5711)
PHONE...............................949 252-1077
Rassool Kavezade, *CEO*
Lora Taleb, *CFO*
Mike Taleb, *Treasurer*
▲ **EMP:** 90
SQ FT: 12,000
SALES (est): 14MM **Privately Held**
WEB: www.connectecco.com
SIC: 3643 3678 Electric connectors; electronic connectors

(P-16886)
CONNECTEC COMPANY INC
3901 S Main St, Santa Ana (92707-5711)
PHONE...............................949 252-1077
Lora Taleb, *Branch Mgr*
EMP: 10

(PA)=Parent Co (HQ)=Headquarters (DH)=Div Headquarters
✪ = New Business established in last 2 years

2020 California
Manufacturers Register

683

PRODUCTS & SVCS

SALES (est): 533.7K
SALES (corp-wide): 14MM **Privately Held**
SIC: **3643** 3678 Electric connectors; electronic connectors
PA: Connectec Company, Inc.
1701 Reynolds Ave
Irvine CA 92614
949 252-1077

(P-16887)
CONNECTION ENTERPRISES INC
4130 Flat Rock Dr Ste 140, Riverside (92505-5864)
PHONE..................................951 688-8133
Marabell Lucioto, *Principal*
EMP: 10
SALES (est): 1MM **Privately Held**
SIC: **3643** 3679 Current-carrying wiring devices; electronic circuits; electronic loads & power supplies

(P-16888)
COOPER INTERCONNECT INC (DH)
750 W Ventura Blvd, Camarillo (93010-8382)
PHONE..................................805 484-0543
Revathi Advaithi, *President*
Tamra Kluczynski, *Info Tech Mgr*
John White, *Engineer*
EMP: 77 EST: 1945
SQ FT: 113,000
SALES (est): 23.6MM **Privately Held**
WEB: www.ghtech.com
SIC: **3643** 3678 Electric connectors; electronic connectors
HQ: Eaton Corporation
1000 Eaton Blvd
Cleveland OH 44122
440 523-5000

(P-16889)
CTC GLOBAL CORPORATION (PA)
2026 Mcgaw Ave, Irvine (92614-0911)
PHONE..................................949 428-8500
J D Sitton, *CEO*
John Mansfield, *President*
Anne McDowell, *President*
Gabriel Tashjian, *COO*
Dean Hagen, *CFO*
▲ EMP: 129
SALES (est): 62.6MM **Privately Held**
SIC: **3643** Power line cable

(P-16890)
DATA SOLDER INC
2915 Kilson Dr, Santa Ana (92707-3716)
PHONE..................................714 429-9866
Irma Gomez, *President*
Guillermo Gomez, *Vice Pres*
EMP: 14 EST: 1997
SQ FT: 4,000
SALES (est): 1.7MM **Privately Held**
WEB: www.solddata.com
SIC: **3643** Solderless connectors (electric wiring devices)

(P-16891)
DC ELECTRONICS INC
1870 Little Orchard St, San Jose (95125-1041)
P.O. Box 67126, Scotts Valley (95067-7126)
PHONE..................................408 947-4531
Dave Cianciulli, *President*
Ruben Macias Jr, *COO*
Eric Hynes, *CFO*
Steve Gulesserian, *Vice Pres*
Alice Cheung, *Director*
EMP: 18
SALES (est): 5.7MM **Privately Held**
SIC: **3643** Current-carrying wiring devices

(P-16892)
DDH ENTERPRISE INC (PA)
2220 Oak Ridge Way, Vista (92081-8341)
PHONE..................................760 599-0171
David Du, *CEO*
Danny Du, *President*
Monika Friend, *Office Mgr*
Mike Schold, *MIS Dir*
Arceli Laguna, *Engineer*

▲ EMP: 160
SQ FT: 42,000
SALES: 30.5MM **Privately Held**
WEB: www.ddhent.com
SIC: **3643** 3644 3699 Current-carrying wiring devices; noncurrent-carrying wiring services; electrical equipment & supplies

(P-16893)
DIGGIMAC INC DBA LTG ELEMENT
16885 W Bernardo Dr # 380, San Diego (92127-1618)
PHONE..................................858 322-6000
Madeleine Kent, *CEO*
EMP: 10
SALES: 8MM **Privately Held**
SIC: **3643** 8748 Lightning protection equipment; lighting consultant

(P-16894)
DMC POWER INC (PA)
623 E Artesia Blvd, Carson (90746-1201)
PHONE..................................310 323-1616
Tony Ward, *CEO*
Eben Kane, *CFO*
Ed Cox, *Vice Pres*
Michael Yazdanpanah, *Vice Pres*
Jenny Huo, *Planning*
▲ EMP: 77
SQ FT: 40,000
SALES (est): 25.5MM **Privately Held**
SIC: **3643** Current-carrying wiring devices

(P-16895)
EARTHWISE PACKAGING INC
12 Goddard, Irvine (92618-4600)
PHONE..................................714 602-2169
Kenneth Loritz, *President*
EMP: 13
SALES (est): 394K **Privately Held**
SIC: **3643** Caps & plugs, electric: attachment

(P-16896)
ELECTRO ADAPTER INC
Also Called: Plating
20640 Nordhoff St, Chatsworth (91311-6189)
P.O. Box 2560 (91313-2560)
PHONE..................................818 998-1198
Ray Fish, *President*
Terrill Fish, *Admin Sec*
Sam Clarke, *Info Tech Mgr*
Ken Ivers, *Info Tech Mgr*
Gary Fish, *Engineer*
EMP: 67
SQ FT: 54,000
SALES (est): 12.1MM
SALES (corp-wide): 15.5MM **Privately Held**
WEB: www.electroadapter.com
SIC: **3643** Electric connectors
PA: Intritec
20640 Nordhoff St
Chatsworth CA 91311
818 998-1198

(P-16897)
EMP CONNECTORS INC
548 Amapola Ave, Torrance (90501-1472)
PHONE..................................310 533-6799
EMP: 20
SQ FT: 39,000
SALES (est): 3.8MM **Privately Held**
WEB: www.empconnectors.com
SIC: **3643** 3678 3612

(P-16898)
ESL POWER SYSTEMS INC
2800 Palisades Dr, Corona (92880-9427)
PHONE..................................800 922-4188
Michael Hellmers, *President*
David Hellmers, *Vice Pres*
◆ EMP: 55
SQ FT: 36,000
SALES (est): 15.5MM **Privately Held**
WEB: www.eslpwr.com
SIC: **3643** Outlets, electric: convenience

(P-16899)
FOXLINK INTERNATIONAL INC (HQ)
3010 Saturn St Ste 200, Brea (92821-6220)
PHONE..................................714 256-1777
Ching Fan Pu, *CEO*
James Lee, *President*
▲ EMP: 44
SALES (est): 12.8MM **Privately Held**
WEB: www.foxlink.com
SIC: **3643** 3678 3679 3691 Current-carrying wiring devices; electronic connectors; electronic circuits; storage batteries; household audio & video equipment; computer peripheral equipment

(P-16900)
G D M ELECTRONIC ASSEMBLY INC
Also Called: Gdm Electronic & Medical
2070 Ringwood Ave, San Jose (95131-1745)
PHONE..................................408 945-4100
Grant Murphy, *Partner*
Susie Perches, *Partner*
Diego Martinez, *Controller*
Shawn Hines, *Marketing Staff*
EMP: 77
SQ FT: 24,000
SALES (est): 18MM **Privately Held**
WEB: www.gdm1.com
SIC: **3643** 3565 Current-carrying wiring devices; packaging machinery

(P-16901)
GOLD TECHNOLOGIES INC
Also Called: Goldtec USA
1648 Mabury Rd Ste A, San Jose (95133-1097)
PHONE..................................408 321-9568
Patricia Tran, *President*
EMP: 25 EST: 1998
SQ FT: 12,000
SALES (est): 3.8MM **Privately Held**
WEB: www.goldtec.com
SIC: **3643** Electric connectors

(P-16902)
HI REL CONNECTORS INC
Also Called: Hirel Connectors
760 Wharton Dr, Claremont (91711-4800)
PHONE..................................909 626-1820
Fred Baumann, *CEO*
Frederick Bb Baumann, *CEO*
George Argiriadis, *Engineer*
Isaac Medrano, *Engineer*
David Neitzke, *Engineer*
EMP: 300
SQ FT: 25,000
SALES (est): 60.8MM **Privately Held**
WEB: www.hirelco.net
SIC: **3643** 3678 Connectors & terminals for electrical devices; electronic connectors

(P-16903)
HUBBELL INCORPORATED
Also Called: Hubbel Wiring Device Kellems
1392 Sarah Pl Ste A, Ontario (91761-1433)
PHONE..................................909 390-8002
Les Green, *Manager*
Hawkins Kelly, *Engineer*
EMP: 30
SALES (corp-wide): 4.4B **Publicly Held**
WEB: www.hubbell.com
SIC: **3643** Current-carrying wiring devices
PA: Hubbell Incorporated
40 Waterview Dr
Shelton CT 06484
475 882-4000

(P-16904)
HUBBELL INCORPORATED
1829 Thunderbolt Dr, Porterville (93257-9300)
PHONE..................................559 783-0470
Mona Satterfield, *Branch Mgr*
EMP: 40
SALES (corp-wide): 4.4B **Publicly Held**
WEB: www.hubbell.com
SIC: **3643** Current-carrying wiring devices

PA: Hubbell Incorporated
40 Waterview Dr
Shelton CT 06484
475 882-4000

(P-16905)
IMPULSE ENTERPRISE
Also Called: Teledyne Impulse
9855 Carroll Canyon Rd, San Diego (92131-1103)
PHONE..................................858 565-7050
▲ EMP: 20
SALES (est): 3.6MM **Privately Held**
SIC: **3643** Connectors & terminals for electrical devices

(P-16906)
IMPULSE ENTERPRISE
Also Called: Teledyne Impulse
8254 Ronson Rd, San Diego (92111-2015)
PHONE..................................858 565-7050
Francis G Faber, *President*
Lois Faber, *CFO*
Raymond Hom, *Vice Pres*
Heather Butler, *Admin Sec*
▲ EMP: 55
SQ FT: 20,000
SALES (est): 9.5MM **Privately Held**
SIC: **3643** Connectors & terminals for electrical devices

(P-16907)
INTERCONNECT SOLUTIONS GR
5855 Green Valley Cir # 2, Culver City (90230-6946)
PHONE..................................323 691-5485
David Gregory Moore, *Principal*
EMP: 13
SALES (est): 1.6MM **Privately Held**
SIC: **3643** Electric connectors

(P-16908)
ITT LLC
ITT BIW Connector Systems
500 Tesconi Cir, Santa Rosa (95401-4665)
PHONE..................................707 523-2300
Robert Roeser, *Branch Mgr*
Eckhard Konkel, *Vice Pres*
Volodymyr Skrypka, *Project Engr*
Rob Condron, *Engineer*
Pedro Andrade, *Warehouse Mgr*
EMP: 109
SQ FT: 35,000
SALES (corp-wide): 2.7B **Publicly Held**
SIC: **3643** Connectors & terminals for electrical devices
HQ: Itt Llc
1133 Westchester Ave N-100
White Plains NY 10604
914 641-2000

(P-16909)
JOY SIGNAL TECHNOLOGY LLC
1020 Marauder St Ste A, Chico (95973-9028)
PHONE..................................530 891-3551
John Joy, *Mng Member*
EMP: 50
SQ FT: 21,000
SALES (est): 10.6MM **Privately Held**
SIC: **3643** Power line cable

(P-16910)
KCB PRECISION
Also Called: K C B
29009 Avenue Penn, Valencia (91355-5426)
PHONE..................................661 295-5695
Kenny Bayer, *Principal*
Chris Bayer, *Principal*
EMP: 10
SQ FT: 5,000
SALES (est): 950K **Privately Held**
WEB: www.kcbprecision.com
SIC: **3643** Contacts, electrical; power outlets & sockets

(P-16911)
LEVITON MANUFACTURING CO INC
3760 Kilroy Airport Way # 660, Long Beach (90806-6832)
PHONE..................................631 812-6041
Joann Parks, *Manager*
EMP: 25

▲ = Import ▼=Export
◆ =Import/Export

SALES (corp-wide): 1.4B **Privately Held**
SIC: 3643 Plugs, electric
PA: Leviton Manufacturing Co., Inc.
201 N Service Rd
Melville NY 11747
631 812-6000

(P-16912)
LEVITON MANUFACTURING CO INC
6020 Progressive Ave # 500, San Diego (92154-6638)
PHONE................................619 205-8600
John Nelson, *Principal*
EMP: 319
SALES (corp-wide): 1.4B **Privately Held**
SIC: 3643 Current-carrying wiring devices
PA: Leviton Manufacturing Co., Inc.
201 N Service Rd
Melville NY 11747
631 812-6000

(P-16913)
LIGHTNING DVERSION SYSTEMS LLC
16572 Burke Ln, Huntington Beach (92647-4538)
PHONE................................714 841-1080
Dave Wilmot, *President*
EMP: 14
SQ FT: 6,284
SALES (est): 2.9MM
SALES (corp-wide): 629.3MM **Publicly Held**
WEB: www.lightningdiversion.com
SIC: 3643 3812 Lightning protection equipment; antennas, radar or communications
HQ: Ls Holdings Company, Llc
16572 Burke Ln
Huntington Beach CA 92647
714 841-1080

(P-16914)
LUCIDPORT TECHNOLOGY INC
19287 San Marcos Rd, Saratoga (95070-5677)
PHONE................................408 720-8800
WEI T Liu, *CEO*
EMP: 11
SALES (est): 1.3MM **Privately Held**
SIC: 3643 Bus bars (electrical conductors)

(P-16915)
LYNCOLE GRUNDING SOLUTIONS LLC
Also Called: Lyncole Xit Grounding
3547 Voyager St Ste 204, Torrance (90503-1673)
PHONE................................310 214-4000
Elizabeth B Robertson,
Helen Knapp,
EMP: 25
SQ FT: 10,000
SALES (est): 5.4MM **Privately Held**
WEB: www.lyncole.com
SIC: 3643 8711 Current-carrying wiring devices; consulting engineer

(P-16916)
MERCOTAC INC
6195 Corte Del Cedro # 100, Carlsbad (92011-1549)
PHONE................................760 431-7723
Timothy Leslie, *President*
Dave Brunet, *Treasurer*
Chris Rechlin, *Admin Sec*
▼ EMP: 17
SQ FT: 12,000
SALES (est): 3.9MM **Privately Held**
WEB: www.mercotac.com
SIC: 3643 Connectors & terminals for electrical devices

(P-16917)
MICRO PLASTICS INC
20821 Dearborn St, Chatsworth (91311-5916)
P.O. Box 189, San Marcos (92079-0189)
PHONE................................818 882-0244
Lynda Eurton, *President*
Anacleto Gonzalez, *Vice Pres*
Agripina Eurton, *Admin Sec*
EMP: 20 EST: 1956
SQ FT: 11,000

SALES: 2MM **Privately Held**
WEB: www.microplastics.net
SIC: 3643 3089 Connectors & terminals for electrical devices; molding primary plastic

(P-16918)
NEWVAC LLC (HQ)
9330 De Soto Ave, Chatsworth (91311-4926)
PHONE................................310 525-1205
Ted Anderson, *CEO*
Mike Davidson, *CFO*
Garrett Hoffman, *Vice Pres*
Heather Wynne, *Controller*
EMP: 140
SQ FT: 44,000
SALES (est): 6.8MM
SALES (corp-wide): 49MM **Privately Held**
SIC: 3643 Current-carrying wiring devices
PA: Adi American Distributors, Llc
2 Emery Ave Ste 1
Randolph NJ 07869
973 328-1181

(P-16919)
PASS & SEYMOUR INC
9415 Kruse Rd, Pico Rivera (90660-1430)
PHONE................................562 505-4072
EMP: 534
SALES (corp-wide): 21.2MM **Privately Held**
SIC: 3643 Current-carrying wiring devices
HQ: Pass & Seymour, Inc.
50 Boyd Ave
Syracuse NY 13209
315 468-6211

(P-16920)
PLT ENTERPRISES INC
Also Called: So-Cal Value Added
809 Calle Plano, Camarillo (93012-8516)
PHONE................................805 389-5335
Pamela L Tunis, *President*
Marco Day, *Vice Pres*
Peter L Tunis, *Vice Pres*
EMP: 75
SQ FT: 41,000
SALES (est): 13.2MM **Privately Held**
WEB: www.so-calvalueadded.com
SIC: 3643 3679 Current-carrying wiring devices; harness assemblies for electronic use: wire or cable

(P-16921)
PRECISION STAMPINGS INC (PA)
Also Called: P S I
500 Egan Ave, Beaumont (92223-2132)
PHONE................................951 845-1174
Herman Viets, *Ch of Bd*
Peter Gailing, *Shareholder*
Frauke Roth, *Shareholder*
Keith Roth, *Shareholder*
Herta Viets, *Shareholder*
EMP: 39
SQ FT: 25,000
SALES (est): 12.8MM **Privately Held**
WEB: www.precisionstampingsinc.com
SIC: 3643 5084 7539 Contacts, electrical; tool & die makers' equipment; machine shop, automotive

(P-16922)
Q-LITE USA LLC
3691 Lenawee Ave, Los Angeles (90016-4310)
PHONE................................310 736-2977
Halston Mikail, *Mng Member*
EMP: 220 EST: 2013
SQ FT: 80,000
SALES: 27MM **Privately Held**
SIC: 3643 Lightning arrestors & coils

(P-16923)
SIMPLY AUTOMATED INC
6108 Avd Encinas Ste B, Carlsbad (92011-1044)
PHONE................................760 431-2100
▲ EMP: 11
SQ FT: 7,300
SALES (est): 1.8MM **Privately Held**
WEB: www.simply-automated.com
SIC: 3643

(P-16924)
SOURIAU USA INC (DH)
1750 Commerce Way, Paso Robles (93446-3620)
PHONE................................805 238-2840
Rob Hanes, *President*
◆ EMP: 46
SQ FT: 55,000
SALES: 35MM
SALES (corp-wide): 3.8B **Publicly Held**
SIC: 3643 Bus bars (electrical conductors)
HQ: Souriau
9 Rue De La Porte De Buc
Versailles 78000
130 847-799

(P-16925)
SPIRE MANUFACTURING INC
49016 Milmont Dr, Fremont (94538-7301)
PHONE................................510 226-1070
Christine Bui, *CEO*
Achilleas Vezirir, *President*
Hai Dau, *VP Engrg*
Christopher Devera, *Manager*
▲ EMP: 20
SALES (est): 3.3MM **Privately Held**
SIC: 3643 3674 Power outlets & sockets; lamp sockets & receptacles (electric wiring devices); integrated circuits, semiconductor networks, etc.

(P-16926)
SULLINS ELECTRONICS CORP (PA)
Also Called: Sullins Connector Solutions
801 E Mission Rd B, San Marcos (92069-3002)
PHONE................................760 744-0125
Kayvan Sullins, *CEO*
▲ EMP: 44
SQ FT: 33,000
SALES (est): 9.9MM **Privately Held**
WEB: www.edgecards.com
SIC: 3643 3678 Connectors & terminals for electrical devices; electronic connectors

(P-16927)
SUPERIOR GROUNDING SYSTEMS
Also Called: S G S
16021 Arrow Hwy Ste A, Baldwin Park (91706-2062)
P.O. Box 2171, Irwindale (91706-1112)
PHONE................................626 814-1981
Steve Phan, *General Ptnr*
EMP: 50
SQ FT: 15,000
SALES (est): 6.1MM **Privately Held**
WEB: www.sgscorp.com
SIC: 3643 Connectors & terminals for electrical devices

(P-16928)
T MCGEE ELECTRIC INC
12375 Mills Ave Ste 2, Chino (91710-2082)
PHONE................................909 591-6461
Trent McGee, *President*
EMP: 10
SQ FT: 15,000
SALES (est): 1.7MM **Privately Held**
SIC: 3643 Solderless connectors (electric wiring devices); ground clamps (electric wiring devices)

(P-16929)
TE CONNECTIVITY CORPORATION
301 Constitution Dr, Menlo Park (94025-1110)
PHONE................................650 361-3333
Thomas Lynch, *President*
EMP: 800
SALES (corp-wide): 13.9B **Privately Held**
SIC: 3643 Connectors & terminals for electrical devices
HQ: Te Connectivity Corporation
1050 Westlakes Dr
Berwyn PA 19312
610 893-9800

(P-16930)
TE CONNECTIVITY CORPORATION
Also Called: Raychem Product Division
501 Oakside Ave Side, Redwood City (94063-3800)
PHONE................................650 361-2495
Janae De Guzman, *Admin Asst*
EMP: 14
SALES (corp-wide): 13.9B **Privately Held**
SIC: 3643 Connectors & terminals for electrical devices
HQ: Te Connectivity Corporation
1050 Westlakes Dr
Berwyn PA 19312
610 893-9800

(P-16931)
TE CONNECTIVITY CORPORATION
Also Called: Elcon Power Conectr Pdts Group
307 Constitution Dr, Menlo Park (94025-1110)
PHONE................................650 361-3306
Don Wood, *Branch Mgr*
EMP: 20
SALES (corp-wide): 13.9B **Privately Held**
WEB: www.raychem.com
SIC: 3643 Current-carrying wiring devices
HQ: Te Connectivity Corporation
1050 Westlakes Dr
Berwyn PA 19312
610 893-9800

(P-16932)
TE CONNECTIVITY CORPORATION
Also Called: Raychem Wire Division
501 Oakside Ave Side, Redwood City (94063-3800)
PHONE................................650 361-2495
Don Reed, *Director*
EMP: 400
SALES (corp-wide): 13.9B **Privately Held**
WEB: www.raychem.com
SIC: 3643 Connectors & terminals for electrical devices
HQ: Te Connectivity Corporation
1050 Westlakes Dr
Berwyn PA 19312
610 893-9800

(P-16933)
TECHNICAL RESOURCE INDUSTRIES (PA)
Also Called: T R I
12854 Daisy Ct, Yucaipa (92399-2026)
PHONE................................909 446-1109
Reinhard Thalmayer, *President*
EMP: 25
SQ FT: 5,000
SALES: 3MM **Privately Held**
SIC: 3643 Electric connectors

(P-16934)
TELEDYNE INSTRUMENTS INC
Also Called: Teledyne Impulse
9855 Carroll Canyon Rd, San Diego (92131-1103)
PHONE................................858 565-7050
Raymond Hom, *Manager*
Heather Butler, *General Mgr*
Michael Solorzano, *QC Mgr*
Joseph Bester, *Regl Sales Mgr*
Nicholas Lucero, *Regl Sales Mgr*
EMP: 67
SALES (corp-wide): 2.9B **Publicly Held**
WEB: www.teledyne.com
SIC: 3643 Connectors & terminals for electrical devices
HQ: Teledyne Instruments, Inc.
1049 Camino Dos Rios
Thousand Oaks CA 91360
805 373-4545

(P-16935)
TOBAR INDUSTRIES
912 Olinder Ct, San Jose (95122-2619)
PHONE................................408 494-3530
Elias Antoun, *CEO*
Farid Ghantous, *COO*
William Delaney, *CFO*
Jeffrey Reitman, *Office Mgr*
Brian Eugeni, *Sales Mgr*
EMP: 95

SQ FT: 58,516
SALES (est): 11.3MM **Privately Held**
WEB: www.tobar-ind.com
SIC: 3643 3444 Current-carrying wiring devices; sheet metalwork

(P-16936)
TRI-STAR ELECTRONICS INTL INC (HQ)
Also Called: Carlisle Interconnect
2201 Rosecrans Ave, El Segundo (90245-4910)
PHONE....................310 536-0444
John Berlin, *President*
Amelia Murillo, *Vice Pres*
Ben Damon, *Info Tech Dir*
Ken Raihala, *Engineer*
Henry Le, *Business Mgr*
◆ EMP: 270 EST: 1975
SQ FT: 80,000
SALES (est): 96MM
SALES (corp-wide): 4.4B **Publicly Held**
WEB: www.tri-starelectronics.com
SIC: 3643 Connectors, electric cord
PA: Carlisle Companies Incorporated
16430 N Scottsdale Rd # 400
Scottsdale AZ 85254
480 781-5000

(P-16937)
TRS INTERNATIONAL MFG INC
27152 Burbank, Foothill Ranch (92610-2503)
PHONE....................949 855-0673
Kevin Yin, *President*
Y P Ting, *Shareholder*
Ling Yin, *Treasurer*
▲ EMP: 10
SQ FT: 7,500
SALES (est): 2.2MM **Privately Held**
WEB: www.trsintl.com
SIC: 3643 Power line cable

(P-16938)
WASCO SALES & MARKETING INC
2245 A St, Santa Maria (93455-1008)
PHONE....................805 739-2747
Ronald Way, *President*
Brenda Way, *Shareholder*
Dave Way, *Shareholder*
Kari Way, *Exec VP*
Dana Way, *Admin Sec*
◆ EMP: 20
SQ FT: 9,000
SALES (est): 3.1MM **Privately Held**
WEB: www.wascoinc.com
SIC: 3643 Electric switches

(P-16939)
WATT STOPPER INC (DH)
Also Called: Watt Stopper Le Grand
2700 Zanker Rd Ste 168, San Jose (95134-2140)
PHONE....................408 988-5331
Tom Lowery, *CEO*
Bill Horton, *Vice Pres*
Aaron Lee, *Admin Sec*
Ting Chu, *Technician*
Britton Dickey, *Project Mgr*
▲ EMP: 30
SQ FT: 16,000
SALES (est): 52.4MM
SALES (corp-wide): 21.2MM **Privately Held**
WEB: www.wattstopper.com
SIC: 3643 3646 3645 Current-carrying wiring devices; commercial indusl & institutional electric lighting fixtures; residential lighting fixtures
HQ: Legrand Holding, Inc.
60 Woodlawn St
West Hartford CT 06110
860 233-6251

(P-16940)
WATT STOPPER INC
Engineering Division
2234 Rutherford Rd, Carlsbad (92008-8814)
PHONE....................760 804-9701
Bella Kolek, *Manager*
EMP: 11

SALES (corp-wide): 21.2MM **Privately Held**
WEB: www.wattstopper.com
SIC: 3643 Current-carrying wiring devices
HQ: The Watt Stopper Inc
2700 Zanker Rd Ste 168
San Jose CA 95134
408 988-5331

3644 Noncurrent-Carrying Wiring Devices

(P-16941)
CHASE CORPORATION
132 E Colorado Blvd, Pasadena (91105-1919)
PHONE....................626 395-7706
Paul Schwab, *Branch Mgr*
EMP: 11
SALES (corp-wide): 281.3MM **Publicly Held**
SIC: 3644 Noncurrent-carrying wiring services
PA: Chase Corporation
295 University Ave
Westwood MA 02090
781 332-0700

(P-16942)
CHASE CORPORATION
20001 Brookhurst St, Huntington Beach (92646-4922)
PHONE....................714 964-6268
EMP: 11
SALES (corp-wide): 281.3MM **Publicly Held**
SIC: 3644 Noncurrent-carrying wiring services
PA: Chase Corporation
295 University Ave
Westwood MA 02090
781 332-0700

(P-16943)
COOPER INTERCONNECT INC
Burton Electrical Engineering
750 W Ventura Blvd, Camarillo (93010-8382)
PHONE....................805 553-9632
Richard Busch, *Branch Mgr*
Terry Storms, *Info Tech Mgr*
EMP: 40 **Privately Held**
WEB: www.vikcon.com
SIC: 3644 3643 3728 3699 Outlet boxes (electric wiring devices); current-carrying wiring devices; aircraft parts & equipment; electrical equipment & supplies; electronic connectors
HQ: Cooper Interconnect, Inc.
750 W Ventura Blvd
Camarillo CA 93010
805 484-0543

(P-16944)
CREFTCON INDUSTRIES INC
Also Called: Regal Mfg Co
900 Ajax Ave, City of Industry (91748-1128)
PHONE....................203 377-5944
Leonard W Freibott, *President*
Win Freibott, *Corp Secy*
Mary M Butler, *Vice Pres*
Kathy Freibott, *Vice Pres*
Michael E Freibott, *Vice Pres*
EMP: 160
SQ FT: 85,000
SALES (est): 16.5MM **Privately Held**
WEB: www.regalfittings.com
SIC: 3644 3432 Electric conduits & fittings; plumbers' brass goods: drain cocks, faucets, spigots, etc.

(P-16945)
CWI TRADING
714 Elaine Dr, Stockton (95207-4803)
PHONE....................209 981-7023
Richard Chu, *Principal*
EMP: 10
SALES: 500K **Privately Held**
SIC: 3644 Noncurrent-carrying wiring services

(P-16946)
DRIVEN RACEWAY AND FAMILY ENTE
4601 Redwood Dr, Rohnert Park (94928-7941)
PHONE....................707 585-3748
Rodney Towery, *Principal*
EMP: 17 EST: 2009
SALES (est): 2.6MM **Privately Held**
SIC: 3644 Raceways

(P-16947)
ENOVA ENGINEERING LLC (PA)
Also Called: Garlord Manufacturing Company
1088 Mt Clair Dr, Ceres (95307)
P.O. Box 547 (95307-0547)
PHONE....................209 538-3313
Howard Logsdon,
Keith Mello,
EMP: 16
SQ FT: 30,000
SALES (est): 2.9MM **Privately Held**
SIC: 3644 3469 Fuse boxes, electric; metal stampings

(P-16948)
FRASE ENTERPRISES
Also Called: Kortick Manufacturer Co
2261 Carion Ct, Pittsburg (94565-4029)
PHONE....................510 856-3600
Robert C Frase, *CEO*
Robert Spigel, *President*
Jorge Yuikeng, *Technology*
Julius Malone, *Opers Mgr*
▲ EMP: 26 EST: 1891
SQ FT: 90,000
SALES (est): 6.9MM **Privately Held**
WEB: www.kortick.com
SIC: 3644 3462 Insulators & insulation materials, electrical; pole line hardware forgings, ferrous

(P-16949)
GUND COMPANY INC
4701 E Airport Dr, Ontario (91761-7817)
PHONE....................909 890-9300
Ricardo Beinar, *Manager*
EMP: 15
SALES (corp-wide): 70MM **Privately Held**
WEB: www.thegundcompany.com
SIC: 3644 Insulators & insulation materials, electrical
PA: The Gund Company Inc
2121 Walton Rd
Saint Louis MO 63114
314 423-5200

(P-16950)
INDUSTRIAL INSULATIONS INC (PA)
10509 Business Dr Ste A, Fontana (92337-8249)
PHONE....................909 574-7433
Barbara Malone, *CEO*
Terry M Grill, *President*
Eduardo Gomez, *CFO*
Barbara Rhoads, *Purch Mgr*
John Dodson, *Sales Executive*
▲ EMP: 38
SQ FT: 53,000
SALES (est): 10.2MM **Privately Held**
SIC: 3644 Electric conduits & fittings

(P-16951)
MB2 RACEWAY CLOVIS INC (PA)
1200 Shaw Ave, Clovis (93612-3929)
PHONE....................559 298-7223
Eric Arima, *Principal*
EMP: 10
SALES (est): 1MM **Privately Held**
SIC: 3644 Raceways

(P-16952)
ONE TIME UTILITY SALES INC
Also Called: One Time Utilities Sales
501 N Garfield St, Santa Ana (92701-4756)
PHONE....................714 953-5700
Brian Elliott, *President*
Joe Castro, *General Mgr*
EMP: 20 EST: 2011

SALES (est): 2.3MM **Privately Held**
SIC: 3644 5051 5063 5087 Electric conduits & fittings; cable, wire; rods, wire (not insulated); electrical fittings & construction materials; cable conduit; concrete burial vaults & boxes

(P-16953)
PRECISION FIBERGLASS PRODUCTS
3105 Kashiwa St, Torrance (90505-4089)
PHONE....................310 539-7470
Robby D Ross, *President*
Lucille Ross, *Vice Pres*
Randal A Ross, *Vice Pres*
EMP: 25
SQ FT: 13,300
SALES (est): 4.2MM **Privately Held**
SIC: 3644 Insulators & insulation materials, electrical

(P-16954)
SAF-T-CO SUPPLY
Also Called: All American Pipe Bending
1300 E Normandy Pl, Santa Ana (92705-4138)
PHONE....................714 547-9975
Patricia McDonald, *President*
Paul McDonald, *Corp Secy*
Robyn Dague, *Vice Pres*
EMP: 50
SQ FT: 24,000
SALES (est): 15.2MM **Privately Held**
WEB: www.saftco.com
SIC: 3644 5032 5251 5074 Noncurrent-carrying wiring services; brick, stone & related material; hardware; pipes & fittings, plastic; electrical apparatus & equipment

(P-16955)
TODAY PVC BENDING INC
501 N Garfield St, Santa Ana (92701-4756)
PHONE....................714 953-5707
Joe Castro, *President*
Juan Martinez, *Principal*
Marcellino Rios, *Principal*
EMP: 14
SALES (est): 2.1MM **Privately Held**
SIC: 3644 Electric conduits & fittings

(P-16956)
WESTERN TUBE & CONDUIT CORP (HQ)
2001 E Dominguez St, Long Beach (90810-1088)
PHONE....................310 537-6300
Barry Zekelman, *CEO*
Andy Hardesty, *Regional Mgr*
Kathy Bowden, *Prgrmr*
Kevin Carroll, *Engineer*
Jackie McField, *Credit Mgr*
▲ EMP: 216 EST: 2004
SQ FT: 420,000
SALES (est): 200MM **Privately Held**
WEB: www.westerntube.com
SIC: 3644 3446 3317 Electric conduits & fittings; fences or posts, ornamental iron or steel; tubing, mechanical or hypodermic sizes: cold drawn stainless

(P-16957)
WIRE GUARD SYSTEMS INC
2050 E Slauson Ave, Huntington Park (90255-2799)
PHONE....................323 588-2166
Frank Spitzer, *President*
Ann Spitzer, *Vice Pres*
EMP: 10
SALES (est): 1.6MM **Privately Held**
SIC: 3644 Junction boxes, electric

3645 Residential Lighting Fixtures

(P-16958)
ALGER-TRITON INC
Also Called: Alger International
5600 W Jefferson Blvd, Los Angeles (90016-3131)
PHONE....................310 229-9500
Mishel Michael, *Principal*
◆ EMP: 28

▲ = Import ▼=Export
◆ =Import/Export

SALES (est): 5.9MM **Privately Held**
WEB: www.algerco.com
SIC: 3645 Residential lighting fixtures

(P-16959)
AMERICAN NAIL PLATE LTG INC
Also Called: Anp Lighting
9044 Del Mar Ave, Montclair (91763-1627)
PHONE................................909 982-1807
Harry Foster, *CEO*
Ron Foster, *Treasurer*
Joan Foster, *Vice Pres*
Bob Foster, *Admin Sec*
Armin Ahrari, *Manager*
▲ EMP: 70
SQ FT: 13,000
SALES (est): 13.2MM **Privately Held**
SIC: 3645 3646 Residential lighting fixtures; commercial indusl & institutional electric lighting fixtures

(P-16960)
ANTHONY CALIFORNIA INC (PA)
14485 Monte Vista Ave, Chino (91710-5728)
PHONE................................909 627-0351
Kuei-Lan Yeh, *CEO*
Cindy Chang, *Treasurer*
Darien Chung, *Sales Mgr*
◆ EMP: 30
SALES (est): 3.2MM **Privately Held**
SIC: 3645 5063 5023 Residential lighting fixtures; lighting fixtures; lamps: floor, boudoir, desk

(P-16961)
APEX DIGITAL INC
4401 Eucalyptus Ave # 110, Chino (91710-9707)
PHONE................................909 366-2028
David Ji, *CEO*
Alice Hsu, *COO*
Ancle Hsu, *COO*
Scott Popovich, *Exec VP*
Shannon Tang, *Human Res Mgr*
▲ EMP: 18
SQ FT: 14,000
SALES (est): 4.4MM **Privately Held**
WEB: www.apexdigitalinc.com
SIC: 3645 Residential lighting fixtures

(P-16962)
ART MANUFACTURERS INC
623 Young St, Santa Ana (92705-5633)
PHONE................................714 540-9125
Rafio Franco, *President*
EMP: 30
SQ FT: 11,000
SALES (est): 2.1MM **Privately Held**
SIC: 3645 3648 Residential lighting fixtures; lighting equipment

(P-16963)
ARTIVA USA INC
12866 Ann St Ste 1, Santa Fe Springs (90670-3064)
PHONE................................562 298-8968
Jane Wang, *Manager*
EMP: 50 **Privately Held**
SIC: 3645 5063 Residential lighting fixtures; lighting fixtures
PA: Artiva Usa Inc.
13901 Magnolia Ave
Chino CA 91710

(P-16964)
ARTIVA USA INC (PA)
13901 Magnolia Ave, Chino (91710-7030)
PHONE................................909 628-1388
PO Y Webb, *President*
▲ EMP: 35
SQ FT: 20,000
SALES: 12MM **Privately Held**
SIC: 3645 5063 Residential lighting fixtures; lighting fixtures

(P-16965)
B-K LIGHTING INC
40429 Brickyard Dr, Madera (93636-9515)
PHONE................................559 438-5800
Douglas W Hagen, *President*
Nathan Sloan, *President*
Mark Hansston, *Design Engr*
Craig Reed, *Technical Staff*

Leilani Talty, *Controller*
▲ EMP: 90
SQ FT: 70,000
SALES (est): 20.2MM **Privately Held**
WEB: www.bklighting.com
SIC: 3645 3646 5063 Residential lighting fixtures; commercial indusl & institutional electric lighting fixtures; electrical apparatus & equipment

(P-16966)
BASE LITE CORPORATION
Also Called: Baselite
12260 Eastend Ave, Chino (91710-2008)
PHONE................................909 444-2776
Moaaa A Teixeira, *CEO*
Nick Jones, *Sales Executive*
EMP: 38
SQ FT: 10,000
SALES (est): 10.2MM **Privately Held**
WEB: www.baselite.com
SIC: 3645 3646 Residential lighting fixtures; commercial indusl & institutional electric lighting fixtures

(P-16967)
BRUCE EICHER INC (PA)
8755 Melrose Ave, Los Angeles (90069-5014)
PHONE................................310 657-4630
Hugh Duff Rubertson, *President*
Evan James Buchannan, *Vice Pres*
EMP: 15
SQ FT: 7,500
SALES (est): 2.2MM **Privately Held**
SIC: 3645 3646 Residential lighting fixtures; commercial indusl & institutional electric lighting fixtures

(P-16968)
CRAFTSMAN LIGHTING
14266 Valley Blvd Ste A, La Puente (91746-2927)
PHONE................................626 330-8512
Gilbert Orosco, *Owner*
Onelio Orozco, *General Mgr*
EMP: 11
SQ FT: 5,000
SALES: 500K **Privately Held**
WEB: www.craftsmanoutdoorlighting.com
SIC: 3645 Residential lighting fixtures

(P-16969)
FEIT ELECTRIC COMPANY INC (PA)
4901 Gregg Rd, Pico Rivera (90660-2108)
PHONE................................562 463-2852
Aaron Feit, *CEO*
Toby Feit, *CFO*
◆ EMP: 160 EST: 1978
SQ FT: 300,000
SALES (est): 50.2MM **Privately Held**
WEB: www.feit.com
SIC: 3645 3641 5023 3646 Residential lighting fixtures; electric light bulbs, complete; lamps, fluorescent, electric; home furnishings; commercial indusl & institutional electric lighting fixtures; pressed & blown glass

(P-16970)
GENERATION ALPHA INC (PA)
853 Sandhill Ave, Carson (90746-1210)
PHONE................................888 998-8881
Alan Lien, *CEO*
Alvin Hao, *President*
Tiffany Davis, *COO*
EMP: 15
SQ FT: 19,060
SALES: 3.3MM **Publicly Held**
SIC: 3645 Garden, patio, walkway & yard lighting fixtures: electric

(P-16971)
GLOBALUX LIGHTING LLC
14750 Nelson Ave Unit B, City of Industry (91744-4320)
PHONE................................909 591-7506
Esmail K Parekh, *Mng Member*
Nausheen Tabani,
Esamail K Parekh, *Mng Member*
▲ EMP: 16

SALES (est): 3.3MM **Privately Held**
SIC: 3645 3646 5063 Residential lighting fixtures; commercial indusl & institutional electric lighting fixtures; lighting fittings & accessories

(P-16972)
HIVE LIGHTING INC
525 S Hewitt St, Los Angeles (90013-2217)
PHONE................................310 773-4362
Robert Bruce Rutherford, *President*
Trent Lorenz, *Technician*
Jamie Patterson, *Mktg Dir*
Mitch Gross, *Consultant*
EMP: 12
SALES (est): 962K **Privately Held**
SIC: 3645 Residential lighting fixtures

(P-16973)
KABUSHIKI KISHA HIGUCHI SHOKAI
Also Called: Higuchi Inc., USA
2281 W 205th St Ste 107, Torrance (90501-1450)
PHONE................................310 212-7234
Mikio Morinaga, *Principal*
Kabushiki Shokai, *Principal*
Carmine Sapienza, *Administration*
▲ EMP: 11
SALES (est): 1.5MM **Privately Held**
SIC: 3645 Residential lighting fixtures

(P-16974)
KONCEPT TECHNOLOGIES INC
429 E Huntington Dr, Monrovia (91016-3632)
PHONE................................323 261-8999
Kenneth Ng, *President*
William Lam, *Opers Spvr*
Gerardo Tovar, *Sales Staff*
▲ EMP: 10
SQ FT: 14,000
SALES (est): 8.6MM **Privately Held**
WEB: koncept.com
SIC: 3645 3646 Residential lighting fixtures; commercial indusl & institutional electric lighting fixtures

(P-16975)
LIGHTCRAFT OTDOOR ENVIRONMENTS
Also Called: Lightclub USA
9811 Owensmouth Ave Ste 1, Chatsworth (91311-3800)
PHONE................................818 349-2663
Bruce Dennis, *President*
Rachel Ciavarello, *Cust Svc Dir*
◆ EMP: 16
SQ FT: 5,000
SALES (est): 3.5MM **Privately Held**
SIC: 3645 5063 Garden, patio, walkway & yard lighting fixtures: electric; lighting fittings & accessories

(P-16976)
LIGHTS OF AMERICA INC (PA)
611 Reyes Dr, Walnut (91789-3098)
PHONE................................909 594-7883
Usman Vakil, *CEO*
Farooq Vakil, *Exec VP*
Elizabeth Gardner, *Managing Dir*
Kamran Mirza, *General Mgr*
Joan Munoz, *Human Res Dir*
▲ EMP: 500
SQ FT: 210,000
SALES (est): 229.8MM **Privately Held**
WEB: www.lightsofamerica.com
SIC: 3645 3646 3641 Fluorescent lighting fixtures, residential; fluorescent lighting fixtures, commercial; electric lamps

(P-16977)
LIGHTWAVE PDL INC
1246 E Lexington Ave, Pomona (91766-5561)
PHONE................................909 548-3677
Paul Loh, *President*
Peter Lau, *CFO*
▲ EMP: 10
SQ FT: 7,500
SALES (est): 1.7MM **Privately Held**
WEB: www.lwlight.com
SIC: 3645 Fluorescent lighting fixtures, residential

SALES (est): 3.3MM **Privately Held**
SIC: 3645 3646 5063 Residential lighting fixtures; commercial indusl & institutional electric lighting fixtures; lighting fittings & accessories

(P-16978)
LUNA SCIENCES CORPORATION
18218 Mcdurmott E Ste A, Irvine (92614-4746)
PHONE................................949 225-0000
▲ EMP: 13 EST: 2010
SALES (est): 1.8MM **Privately Held**
SIC: 3645 Residential lighting fixtures

(P-16979)
MAXIM LIGHTING INTL INC (PA)
253 Vineland Ave, City of Industry (91746-2319)
PHONE................................626 956-4200
Jacob Sperling, *CEO*
Michael S Andrews, *CFO*
Mike Andrews, *CFO*
Zvi Sperling, *Corp Secy*
Jessica Tseng, *Admin Asst*
▲ EMP: 250
SQ FT: 26,000
SALES (est): 75MM **Privately Held**
SIC: 3645 Residential lighting fixtures

(P-16980)
MAXIM LIGHTING INTL INC
247 Vineland Ave, City of Industry (91746-2319)
PHONE................................626 956-4200
EMP: 51
SALES (corp-wide): 75MM **Privately Held**
SIC: 3645 Residential lighting fixtures
PA: Maxim Lighting International, Inc.
253 Vineland Ave
City Of Industry CA 91746
626 956-4200

(P-16981)
NIC PROTECTION INC
7135 Foothill Blvd, Tujunga (91042-2716)
PHONE................................818 249-2539
Vahik Arzoomanian, *President*
EMP: 12
SALES (est): 1.5MM **Privately Held**
SIC: 3645 1521 Residential lighting fixtures; repairing fire damage, single-family houses

(P-16982)
NL&A COLLECTIONS INC
Also Called: Nova
6323 Maywood Ave, Huntington Park (90255-4531)
P.O. Box 661820, Los Angeles (90066-8820)
PHONE................................323 277-6266
Daniel Edelist, *President*
Minal Chaudhary, *Vice Pres*
◆ EMP: 40
SQ FT: 48,675
SALES (est): 8.3MM **Privately Held**
WEB: www.novalamps.com
SIC: 3645 5023 Boudoir lamps; lamps: floor, boudoir, desk

(P-16983)
ORIGINALS 22 INC
13889 Pipeline Ave, Chino (91710-5418)
PHONE................................909 993-5050
Andrew Braden, *Principal*
EMP: 10
SALES (est): 1.2MM **Privately Held**
SIC: 3645 Light shades, metal

(P-16984)
ORION CHANDELIER INC
2202 S Wright St, Santa Ana (92705-5316)
PHONE................................714 668-9668
Paul Depersis, *President*
Kirk Fisher, *Assistant VP*
◆ EMP: 17
SQ FT: 3,000
SALES (est): 3MM **Privately Held**
WEB: www.orionchandelier.com
SIC: 3645 Chandeliers, residential

(P-16985)
PATIO PARADISE INC
444 Athol St, San Bernardino (92401-1907)
PHONE................................626 715-4869
Peng Sun, *CEO*
EMP: 10
SALES (est): 419K **Privately Held**
SIC: 3645 Garden, patio, walkway & yard lighting fixtures: electric

(P-16986)
PHILIPS NORTH AMERICA LLC
11201 Iberia St Ste A, Jurupa Valley
(91752-3280)
PHONE....................909 574-1800
Kenneth Parivar, *Branch Mgr*
EMP: 20
SALES (corp-wide): 20.8B **Privately Held**
WEB: www.lightguard.com
SIC: 3645 3648 3646 Residential lighting
fixtures; garden, patio, walkway & yard
lighting fixtures: electric; fluorescent lighting fixtures, residential; outdoor lighting
equipment; decorative area lighting fixtures; underwater lighting fixtures; ceiling
systems, luminous
HQ: Philips North America Llc
3000 Minuteman Rd Ms1203
Andover MA 01810
978 659-3000

(P-16987)
PHOENIX DAY CO INC
3431 Regatta Blvd, Richmond
(94804-4594)
PHONE....................415 822-4414
Tony Brenta, *President*
▲ EMP: 15
SQ FT: 8,000
SALES (est): 2.4MM **Privately Held**
WEB: www.phoenixday.com
SIC: 3645 3646 3446 Residential lighting
fixtures; commercial indusl & institutional
electric lighting fixtures; ornamental met-
alwork

(P-16988)
**RICHARD RAY CUSTOM
DESIGNS**
11350 Alethea Dr, Sunland (91040-2206)
PHONE....................323 937-5685
Richard Ray, *President*
EMP: 17
SQ FT: 4,500
SALES (est): 1.9MM **Privately Held**
WEB: www.richardraycustomdesigns.com
SIC: 3645 Residential lighting fixtures

(P-16989)
S&H INTERNATIONAL INC
1240 Palmetto St, Los Angeles
(90013-2227)
PHONE....................213 626-7112
Loan L Tran, *President*
▲ EMP: 12 EST: 2006
SALES (est): 1.5MM **Privately Held**
SIC: 3645 Residential lighting fixtures

(P-16990)
SEASCAPE LAMPS INC
125a Lee Rd, Watsonville (95076-9422)
PHONE....................831 728-5699
Michael Shenk, *President*
▲ EMP: 17
SQ FT: 16,000
SALES (est): 3.1MM **Privately Held**
WEB: www.seascapelamps.com
SIC: 3645 Boudoir lamps; lamp & light
shades

(P-16991)
SILVER MOON LIGHTING INC
12225 World Trade Dr F, San Diego
(92128-3768)
P.O. Box 501104 (92150-1104)
PHONE....................858 613-3600
Kyle R Finley, *CEO*
EMP: 15 EST: 2005
SALES (est): 2.3MM **Privately Held**
SIC: 3645 Garden, patio, walkway & yard
lighting fixtures: electric

(P-16992)
SPADIA INC
Also Called: Vortex Enterprise
10440 Pioneer Blvd Ste 1, Santa Fe
Springs (90670-8234)
PHONE....................562 206-2505
Jihoon Park, *President*
▲ EMP: 10 EST: 2012
SALES (est): 1MM **Privately Held**
SIC: 3645 3646 5719 3634 Desk lamps;
desk lamps, commercial; lighting, lamps &
accessories; air purifiers, portable; light-
ing fixtures

(P-16993)
TECHTRON PRODUCTS INC
2694 W Winton Ave, Hayward
(94545-1108)
PHONE....................510 293-3500
William Swen, *President*
Shiow Shya Swen, *Vice Pres*
EMP: 43
SQ FT: 50,500
SALES (est): 8.7MM **Privately Held**
WEB: www.techtronproducts.com
SIC: 3645 5063 Residential lighting fix-
tures; lighting fixtures, residential

(P-16994)
TROY-CSL LIGHTING INC
14508 Nelson Ave, City of Industry
(91744-3514)
P.O. Box 514310, Los Angeles (90051-
4310)
PHONE....................626 336-4511
David Littman, *CEO*
Steve Nadell, *President*
Anne Wilcox, *CFO*
Ian Wilcox, *Admin Sec*
▲ EMP: 80
SALES (est): 26.2MM **Privately Held**
WEB: www.troycsl.com
SIC: 3645 3646 Wall lamps; ornamental
lighting fixtures, commercial

(P-16995)
TYLERCO INC
17831 Sky Park Cir Ste A, Irvine
(92614-6105)
PHONE....................949 769-3991
Richard D Ashoff, *President*
◆ EMP: 45
SQ FT: 5,500
SALES (est): 5.2MM **Privately Held**
SIC: 3645 Residential lighting fixtures

(P-16996)
USPAR ENTERPRISES INC
2037 S Vineyard Ave, Ontario
(91761-8066)
PHONE....................909 591-7506
Khalid Parekh, *President*
Esmail K Parekh, *CEO*
Irfan Parekh, *Vice Pres*
▲ EMP: 25
SQ FT: 50,000
SALES (est): 4.8MM **Privately Held**
WEB: www.uspar.com
SIC: 3645 3646 3641 5063 Fluorescent
lighting fixtures, residential; fluorescent
lighting fixtures, commercial; electric
lamps; lighting fixtures

(P-16997)
VIDESSENCE LLC (PA)
10768 Lower Azusa Rd, El Monte
(91731-1306)
PHONE....................626 579-0943
Toni Swarens, *President*
Gregg Maines, *MIS Staff*
Gary Thomas, *Regl Sales Mgr*
Lee Hedberg, *Manager*
Amanda McGinnis, *Manager*
▲ EMP: 25 EST: 1951
SQ FT: 35,000
SALES (est): 4.4MM **Privately Held**
WEB: www.elplighting.com
SIC: 3645 3648 Residential lighting fix-
tures; stage lighting equipment

(P-16998)
VODE LIGHTING LLC
21684 8th St E Ste 700, Sonoma
(95476-2818)
PHONE....................707 996-9898
Thomas Warton, *President*
George Mieling, *COO*
Tracy Irving, *Admin Sec*
G Padilla-Nuno, *Technician*
Lily Fischer, *Project Mgr*
▲ EMP: 19
SALES (est): 7.4MM **Privately Held**
WEB: www.vode.com
SIC: 3645 3646 Residential lighting fix-
tures; commercial indusl & institutional
electric lighting fixtures

(P-16999)
**WANGS ALLIANCE
CORPORATION**
Also Called: Wac Lighting
1750 S Archibald Ave, Ontario
(91761-1239)
PHONE....................909 230-9401
Nina Chou, *Principal*
EMP: 20
SALES (corp-wide): 44.6MM **Privately
Held**
SIC: 3645 Residential lighting fixtures
PA: Wangs Alliance Corporation
44 Harbor Park Dr
Port Washington NY 11050
516 515-5000

(P-17000)
WASHOE EQUIPMENT INC
Also Called: Sunoptics Prismatic Skylights
6201 27th St, Sacramento (95822-3712)
PHONE....................916 395-4700
Jim Blomberg, *President*
Jerry Blomberg, *Treasurer*
Thomas Blomberg, *Vice Pres*
Grant Grabble, *VP Sales*
▼ EMP: 34
SQ FT: 16,000
SALES (est): 11.1MM
SALES (corp-wide): 3.6B **Publicly Held**
SIC: 3645 3646 5031 Residential lighting
fixtures; commercial indusl & institutional
electric lighting fixtures; skylights, all ma-
terials
PA: Acuity Brands, Inc.
1170 Peachtree St Ne # 23
Atlanta GA 30309
404 853-1400

(P-17001)
XICATO INC (PA)
101 Daggett Dr, San Jose (95134-2110)
PHONE....................408 829-4758
Menko Deroos, *CEO*
Mark Pugh, *President*
John Yriberri, *President*
Steve Workman, *CFO*
Joanna Brace, *Exec VP*
▲ EMP: 39
SALES (est): 7.4MM **Privately Held**
SIC: 3645 Garden, patio, walkway & yard
lighting fixtures: electric

(P-17002)
YAWITZ INC
Also Called: Evergreen Lighting
1379 Ridgeway St, Pomona (91768-2701)
PHONE....................909 865-5599
John Klena, *CEO*
Victor Rosen, *Treasurer*
George Cole III, *Vice Pres*
Mayte Arias, *Office Mgr*
Robert Allen, *Natl Sales Mgr*
▲ EMP: 42
SQ FT: 23,000
SALES (est): 10.4MM **Privately Held**
WEB: www.evergreenlighting.com
SIC: 3645 3646 Fluorescent lighting fix-
tures, residential; fluorescent lighting fix-
tures, commercial

**3646 Commercial, Indl &
Institutional Lighting
Fixtures**

(P-17003)
1LE CALIFORNIA INC
3224 Mchenry Ave Ste F, Modesto
(95350-1400)
PHONE....................209 846-7541
EMP: 40
SALES (est): 5MM **Privately Held**
SIC: 3646 3645

(P-17004)
515 W SEVENTH LLC
Also Called: Candella Lighting Company
430 S Pecan St, Los Angeles
(90033-4212)
PHONE....................323 278-8116
Luis A Flores Avalos, *Principal*
Renee Toomey, *CFO*

EMP: 11
SALES (est): 1.1MM **Privately Held**
SIC: 3646 3645 Ornamental lighting fixtures, commercial; residential lighting fixtures

(P-17005)
A V POLES AND LIGHTING INC
43827 Division St, Lancaster (93535-4061)
P.O. Box 9054 (93539-9054)
PHONE....................661 945-2731
Luis Romero, *CEO*
Roberta Wood, *President*
▼ EMP: 20
SQ FT: 12,000
SALES (est): 1.5MM **Privately Held**
SIC: 3646 Commercial indusl & institu-
tional electric lighting fixtures

(P-17006)
ACCLAIM LIGHTING LLC
6122 S Eastern Ave, Commerce
(90040-3402)
PHONE....................323 213-4626
Charles J Davies, *Principal*
Jennie Picard, *Administration*
Jodie Moore, *Project Mgr*
Blaine Engle, *Natl Sales Mgr*
▲ EMP: 11
SALES (est): 1.6MM **Privately Held**
SIC: 3646 3679 5063 Commercial indusl
& institutional electric lighting fixtures;
electronic loads & power supplies; wire &
cable

(P-17007)
ACUITY BRANDS LIGHTING INC
Peerless Lighting
55 Harrison St 200, Oakland (94607-3790)
PHONE....................510 845-2760
Thor Scordelis, *Manager*
Mike Lu, *Director*
EMP: 40
SALES (corp-wide): 3.6B **Publicly Held**
SIC: 3646 Fluorescent lighting fixtures,
commercial
HQ: Acuity Brands Lighting, Inc.
1 Acuity Way
Conyers GA 30012

(P-17008)
**ADVANCED LIGHTING
CONCEPTS INC**
Also Called: Environmental Lights
11235 W Bernardo Ct # 102, San Diego
(92127-1628)
PHONE....................888 880-1880
Gregory D Thorson, *CEO*
Jamison Day, *CFO*
Anne M Thorson, *Vice Pres*
Dusty Harkleroad, *Technology*
Chris Dawson, *Engineer*
◆ EMP: 50
SQ FT: 30,000
SALES (est): 10.8MM **Privately Held**
WEB: www.environmentallights.com
SIC: 3646 Commercial indusl & institu-
tional electric lighting fixtures

(P-17009)
ALPHABET LIGHTING
15774 Gateway Cir, Tustin (92780-6469)
PHONE....................714 259-0990
Alex Ladjevardi,
Vahid Ladjevardi,
Helmuth Unger,
▲ EMP: 11
SQ FT: 3,000
SALES (est): 1.5MM **Privately Held**
SIC: 3646 Commercial indusl & institu-
tional electric lighting fixtures

(P-17010)
ALUMAFAB
Also Called: Showcase Components
14335 Iseli Rd, Santa Fe Springs
(90670-5203)
PHONE....................562 630-6440
Robert Lockwood, *President*
Art Lockwood, *Vice Pres*
EMP: 12 EST: 1978
SQ FT: 12,000

▲ = Import ▼=Export
◆ =Import/Export

SALES (est): 1.9MM **Privately Held**
WEB: www.showcasecomponents.com
SIC: 3646 Commercial indusl & institutional electric lighting fixtures

(P-17011)
AMERICA ASIAN TRADE ASSN PROM
4633 Old Ironside Ste 308, Santa Rosa (95404)
PHONE.................................408 588-0008
Jeff Barrera, *Sales Mgr*
EMP: 99
SALES (est): 4.2MM **Privately Held**
SIC: 3646 Commercial indusl & institutional electric lighting fixtures

(P-17012)
ARTE DE MEXICO INC
5506 Riverton Ave, North Hollywood (91601)
PHONE.................................818 753-4510
David Staffers, *Manager*
EMP: 30
SALES (corp-wide): 22.5MM **Privately Held**
WEB: www.artedemexico.com
SIC: 3646 3446 Commercial indusl & institutional electric lighting fixtures; architectural metalwork
PA: Arte De Mexico, Inc.
   1000 Chestnut St
   Burbank CA 91506
   818 753-4559

(P-17013)
AXP TECHNOLOGY INC
41041 Trimboli Way # 1761, Fremont (94538-8001)
PHONE.................................510 683-1180
Justin Wang, *President*
EMP: 10
SALES (est): 600K **Privately Held**
SIC: 3646 Commercial indusl & institutional electric lighting fixtures

(P-17014)
B-EFFICIENT INC
11545 W Bernardo Ct # 209, San Diego (92127-1631)
PHONE.................................209 663-9199
Tom Comery, *President*
EMP: 20 EST: 2012
SQ FT: 3,000
SALES (est): 2.4MM **Privately Held**
SIC: 3646 5063 Commercial indusl & institutional electric lighting fixtures; lighting fixtures, commercial & industrial

(P-17015)
BORDEN LIGHTING
2355 Verna Ct, San Leandro (94577-4205)
PHONE.................................510 357-0171
Randy Borden, *Principal*
James Borden, *CEO*
Barry Gould, *Site Mgr*
EMP: 24 EST: 1962
SALES (est): 5.6MM **Privately Held**
WEB: www.bordenlighting.com
SIC: 3646 3645 Fluorescent lighting fixtures, commercial; ornamental lighting fixtures, commercial; fluorescent lighting fixtures, residential

(P-17016)
BOYD LIGHTING FIXTURE CO (PA)
30 Liberty Ship Way # 3150, Sausalito (94965-1757)
PHONE.................................415 778-4300
John S Sweet Jr, *President*
Udell Blackham, *CFO*
Dave Votava, *Engineer*
Jane Culligan, *Credit Mgr*
Alice Whalen, *Opers Staff*
▲ EMP: 20
SQ FT: 13,000
SALES (est): 12.9MM **Privately Held**
WEB: www.boydlighting.com
SIC: 3646 3645 Commercial indusl & institutional electric lighting fixtures; residential lighting fixtures

(P-17017)
C W COLE & COMPANY INC
Also Called: Cole Lighting
2560 Rosemead Blvd, South El Monte (91733-1593)
PHONE.................................626 443-2473
Russell W Cole, *Ch of Bd*
Stephen W Cole, *President*
Donald Cole, *Vice Pres*
Melissa Kelemen, *Administration*
Gary Summers, *Design Engr*
EMP: 41
SQ FT: 25,000
SALES (est): 10.4MM **Privately Held**
WEB: www.colelighting.com
SIC: 3646 Commercial indusl & institutional electric lighting fixtures

(P-17018)
CAL BEST CEILINGS INC
979 Seaboard Ct, Upland (91786-4572)
PHONE.................................909 946-1565
Karen Doi Parker, *President*
Jennifer Doi, *Vice Pres*
EMP: 10
SQ FT: 12,500
SALES: 960K **Privately Held**
SIC: 3646 3446 1742 Ceiling systems, luminous; acoustical suspension systems, metal; acoustical & ceiling work

(P-17019)
CANDELLA LIGHTING CO INC
430 S Pecan St, Los Angeles (90033-4212)
PHONE.................................323 798-1091
Eva Axelsson, *President*
Lillemor Greenhut, *Admin Sec*
▲ EMP: 10
SQ FT: 30,000
SALES: 174K **Privately Held**
WEB: www.candella.com
SIC: 3646 3645 2514 3648 Commercial indusl & institutional electric lighting fixtures; residential lighting fixtures; metal household furniture; lighting equipment

(P-17020)
CONTRACT ILLUMINATION
Also Called: Old California Lantern Company
975 N Enterprise St, Orange (92867-5448)
PHONE.................................714 771-5223
Tom Richard, *President*
Leslie Richard, *Corp Secy*
EMP: 20
SQ FT: 6,000
SALES (est): 4.4MM **Privately Held**
WEB: www.oldcalifornia.com
SIC: 3646 Commercial indusl & institutional electric lighting fixtures

(P-17021)
COOL LUMENS INC
1334 Brommer St Ste B6, Santa Cruz (95062-2955)
PHONE.................................831 471-8084
Thomas D McClellan, *President*
EMP: 12
SQ FT: 3,500
SALES (est): 1.9MM **Privately Held**
SIC: 3646 Commercial indusl & institutional electric lighting fixtures

(P-17022)
CRYSTAL LIGHTING CORP
13182 Flores St, Santa Fe Springs (90670-4023)
PHONE.................................562 944-0223
Manolo Naranjo, *CEO*
Fabian Naranjo, *Treasurer*
Robert Naranjo, *Vice Pres*
◆ EMP: 14
SQ FT: 10,000
SALES (est): 4.1MM **Privately Held**
WEB: www.crystallighting.us
SIC: 3646 3645 Ornamental lighting fixtures, commercial; residential lighting fixtures

(P-17023)
DECO ENTERPRISES INC
Also Called: Deco Lighting
2917 Vail Ave, Commerce (90040-2615)
PHONE.................................323 726-2575
Saman Sinai, *CEO*
Benjamin Pouladian, *President*

Ben Peterson, *Vice Pres*
Sheree Nelson, *Executive Asst*
Christopher Louie, *Engineer*
▲ EMP: 60
SQ FT: 100,000
SALES (est): 47.4MM **Privately Held**
SIC: 3646 Commercial indusl & institutional electric lighting fixtures

(P-17024)
DEXIN INTERNATIONAL INC (PA)
677 Arrow Grand Cir, Covina (91722-2146)
PHONE.................................626 859-7475
Simon LI, *President*
May Lee, *Vice Pres*
▲ EMP: 200
SQ FT: 2,500
SALES (est): 16.8MM **Privately Held**
WEB: www.dexinintl.com
SIC: 3646 5063 5199 Commercial indusl & institutional electric lighting fixtures; lighting fixtures; bags, baskets & cases

(P-17025)
ECO WORLD USA LLC
9950 Baldwin Pl, El Monte (91731-2204)
PHONE.................................626 433-1333
Shen Yen,
EMP: 12
SALES (est): 1.2MM **Privately Held**
SIC: 3646 Commercial indusl & institutional electric lighting fixtures

(P-17026)
ELATION LIGHTING INC
Also Called: Elation Professional
6122 S Eastern Ave, Commerce (90040-3402)
PHONE.................................323 582-3322
Toby Velazquez, *President*
John Dunn, *Natl Sales Mgr*
Gary Fallon, *Regl Sales Mgr*
Chuck Green, *Sales Mgr*
Scott Kinnebrew, *Sales Staff*
▲ EMP: 60
SQ FT: 50,000
SALES: 15MM **Privately Held**
SIC: 3646 Commercial indusl & institutional electric lighting fixtures

(P-17027)
ENERTRON TECHNOLOGIES INC
3030 Enterprise Ct Ste D, Vista (92081-8358)
PHONE.................................800 537-7649
Ronald Curley, *President*
EMP: 50
SQ FT: 80,000
SALES (est): 8.9MM **Privately Held**
SIC: 3646 3645 Fluorescent lighting fixtures, commercial; fluorescent lighting fixtures, residential

(P-17028)
ENLIGHTED INC (PA)
930 Benecia Ave, Sunnyvale (94085-2804)
PHONE.................................650 964-1094
Joe Costello, *Ch of Bd*
▲ EMP: 39
SALES (est): 22.5MM **Privately Held**
SIC: 3646 Commercial indusl & institutional electric lighting fixtures

(P-17029)
ENVEL DESIGN CORPORATION
3579 Old Conejo Rd, Newbury Park (91320-2122)
PHONE.................................805 376-8111
Quinn B Mayer, *President*
Pamela K Mayer, *Exec VP*
Pam Mayer, *Vice Pres*
Shawn Mayer, *Vice Pres*
EMP: 10
SALES (est): 1.8MM **Privately Held**
WEB: www.enveldesign.com
SIC: 3646 Ceiling systems, luminous

(P-17030)
ENVIRONMENTAL LTG FOR ARCH INC
Also Called: E L A Custom Architectural Div
17891 Arenth Ave, City of Industry (91748-1129)
PHONE.................................626 965-0821
Elsie U Dahlin, *CEO*
Scott Jones, *President*
Ken Annette, *Purch Mgr*
▲ EMP: 42
SQ FT: 50,000
SALES: 8MM **Privately Held**
WEB: www.ela-lighting.com
SIC: 3646 Commercial indusl & institutional electric lighting fixtures

(P-17031)
EPTRONICS INC
19210 S Vermont Ave # 300, Gardena (90248-4426)
PHONE.................................310 536-0700
Chris Chen, *President*
Quincie Lane, *Office Admin*
Jerry Gao, *IT/INT Sup*
Tom O'Neil, *Engineer*
Steve Turner, *VP Sales*
EMP: 18
SALES (est): 3MM **Privately Held**
SIC: 3646 Commercial indusl & institutional electric lighting fixtures

(P-17032)
EXIT LIGHT CO INC
Also Called: Light Fixture Industries
3170 Scott St, Vista (92081-8318)
PHONE.................................877 352-3948
Jeannette L Carrico, *President*
Paul Carrico, *CFO*
◆ EMP: 15
SQ FT: 11,000
SALES (est): 3.2MM **Privately Held**
WEB: www.exitlightco.com
SIC: 3646 5063 3993 Commercial indusl & institutional electric lighting fixtures; signaling equipment, electrical; electric signs

(P-17033)
EXIT SIGN WAREHOUSE INC
16123 Cohasset St, Van Nuys (91406-2908)
PHONE.................................888 953-3948
Josh Roman, *CEO*
John Scalco, *President*
EMP: 12
SALES: 1MM **Privately Held**
SIC: 3646 Commercial indusl & institutional electric lighting fixtures

(P-17034)
FARLIGHT LLC
460 W 5th St, San Pedro (90731-2616)
PHONE.................................310 830-0181
Robert Wolfenden, *General Mgr*
Western Land and Investment LL,
Burger Robert, *Associate*
▲ EMP: 10
SQ FT: 5,000
SALES (est): 2MM **Privately Held**
WEB: www.farlight.com
SIC: 3646 Commercial indusl & institutional electric lighting fixtures

(P-17035)
FINELITE INC (PA)
30500 Whipple Rd, Union City (94587-1530)
PHONE.................................510 441-1100
Jerome Mix, *CEO*
Mark Benguerel, *COO*
Margaret Fenton, *CFO*
Walter B Clark, *Chairman*
Attila Bardos, *Officer*
◆ EMP: 135
SQ FT: 140,132
SALES (est): 32.3MM **Privately Held**
WEB: www.finelite.com
SIC: 3646 Commercial indusl & institutional electric lighting fixtures

(P-17036)
FLUORESCENT SUPPLY CO INC
Also Called: Fsc Lighting
9120 Center Ave, Rancho Cucamonga (91730-5310)
PHONE.................................909 948-8878

Edward Yawitz, *CEO*
John Watkins, *President*
Chad Treadwell, *Senior VP*
Josh Bond, *Vice Pres*
Guy Esposito, *Vice Pres*
▲ **EMP:** 40
SQ FT: 80,000
SALES (est): 20MM **Privately Held**
WEB: www.fsclighting.com
SIC: 3646 3645 Commercial indusl & institutional electric lighting fixtures; residential lighting fixtures

(P-17037)
FOCUS INDUSTRIES INC
Also Called: Focus Landscape
25301 Commercentre Dr, Lake Forest (92630-8808)
PHONE..................................949 830-1350
Stan Shibata, *President*
Luis Mejia, *CFO*
June Shibata, *Vice Pres*
Vance Kozik, *Software Engr*
Linda Lindgren, *Human Res Mgr*
▲ **EMP:** 100
SQ FT: 40,000
SALES (est): 24.9MM **Privately Held**
WEB: www.focusindustries.com
SIC: 3646 5063 Commercial indusl & institutional electric lighting fixtures; electrical apparatus & equipment

(P-17038)
GARA INC
Also Called: First Source Lighting
1730 Industrial Dr, Auburn (95603-9587)
PHONE..................................530 887-1110
Robert Glenn Gara, *CEO*
James Gara, *Chief Mktg Ofcr*
▲ **EMP:** 16
SQ FT: 10,000
SALES (est): 4.1MM **Privately Held**
WEB: www.1stsourcelight.com
SIC: 3646 Fluorescent lighting fixtures, commercial

(P-17039)
GENERAL ELECTRIC COMPANY
11600 Philadelphia Ave, Mira Loma (91752-1135)
PHONE..................................951 360-2400
Fax: 951 360-3235
EMP: 50
SALES (corp-wide): 122B **Publicly Held**
SIC: 3646
PA: General Electric Company
41 Farnsworth St
Boston MA 02210
617 443-3000

(P-17040)
HALLMARK LIGHTING LLC
9631 De Soto Ave, Chatsworth (91311-5013)
PHONE..................................818 885-5010
Christopher Larocca, *CEO*
Robert Godlewski, *President*
Julie Winfield, *Officer*
Dan Harrison, *Info Tech Dir*
Isaac Clark, *Design Engr*
◆ **EMP:** 80
SQ FT: 56,320
SALES (est): 16.2MM **Privately Held**
WEB: www.hallmarklighting.com
SIC: 3646 3645 3641 Commercial indusl & institutional electric lighting fixtures; wall lamps; electric lamps

(P-17041)
HAMILTON TECHNOLOGY CORP
14900 S Figueroa St, Gardena (90248-1715)
PHONE..................................310 217-1191
Mark Rambod, *President*
▲ **EMP:** 13
SQ FT: 2,000
SALES (est): 2MM **Privately Held**
SIC: 3646 Commercial indusl & institutional electric lighting fixtures

(P-17042)
HARVATEK INTERNATIONAL CORP
3350 Scott Blvd Ste 4101, Santa Clara (95054-3120)
PHONE..................................408 844-9698

Jitfu Lim, *CEO*
Putt Choon Yong, *President*
EMP: 10
SALES (est): 1.4MM **Privately Held**
SIC: 3646 Commercial indusl & institutional electric lighting fixtures

(P-17043)
HI-LITE MANUFACTURING CO INC
13450 Monte Vista Ave, Chino (91710-5149)
PHONE..................................909 465-1999
Dorothy A Ohai, *President*
Lava Bobbermin, *Human Resources*
Maria Flynn, *Manager*
Jeffrey Ohai, *Manager*
▲ **EMP:** 90 EST: 1959
SQ FT: 157,000
SALES (est): 18.7MM **Privately Held**
SIC: 3646 3645 Commercial indusl & institutional electric lighting fixtures; residential lighting fixtures

(P-17044)
HUBBELL LIGHTING INC
Precision-Paragon
17760 Rowland St, Rowland Heights (91748-1119)
PHONE..................................714 386-5550
Joe Martin, *General Mgr*
EMP: 70
SALES (corp-wide): 4.4B **Publicly Held**
SIC: 3646 Commercial indusl & institutional electric lighting fixtures
HQ: Hubbell Lighting, Inc.
701 Millennium Blvd
Greenville SC 29607
-

(P-17045)
INTENSE LIGHTING LLC
3340 E La Palma Ave, Anaheim (92806-2814)
PHONE..................................714 630-9877
Kenny Eidsvold, *President*
Kenneth Eidsvold, *President*
Angelica Jurado, *Administration*
Steve Snow, *Technical Staff*
Warren Woody, *Engineer*
◆ **EMP:** 80 EST: 2001
SQ FT: 153,000
SALES (est): 30.1MM
SALES (corp-wide): 1.4B **Privately Held**
WEB: www.intenselighting.com
SIC: 3646 3645 Commercial indusl & institutional electric lighting fixtures; residential lighting fixtures
PA: Leviton Manufacturing Co., Inc.
201 N Service Rd
Melville NY 11747
631 812-6000

(P-17046)
JISHAN USA INC
Also Called: Kerilígthing
15257 Don Julian Rd, City of Industry (91745-1002)
PHONE..................................408 609-3286
Weiping Wang, *CEO*
EMP: 10
SQ FT: 15,000
SALES (est): 736.2K **Privately Held**
SIC: 3646 Commercial indusl & institutional electric lighting fixtures

(P-17047)
KONTECH USA LLC
18045 Rowland St, City of Industry (91748-1205)
PHONE..................................626 622-1325
Miguel Martinez, *Branch Mgr*
EMP: 10
SALES (corp-wide): 2.5MM **Privately Held**
SIC: 3646 3663 Commercial indusl & institutional electric lighting fixtures; television monitors
PA: Kontech Usa Llc
600 W Owens Ave
Las Vegas NV 89106
626 321-8741

(P-17048)
LA SPEC INDUSTRIES INC
Also Called: Laspec Lighting
2315 E 52nd St, Vernon (90058-3499)
PHONE..................................323 588-8746
Jacob Melamed, *Principal*
J Melamed, *President*
▲ **EMP:** 15
SQ FT: 30,000
SALES: 3MM **Privately Held**
WEB: www.laspec.com
SIC: 3646 3648 Commercial indusl & institutional electric lighting fixtures; decorative area lighting fixtures

(P-17049)
LAMPS PLUS INC
Also Called: Pacific Coast Lighting
4723 Telephone Rd, Ventura (93003-5242)
PHONE..................................805 642-9007
David Hillard, *Manager*
EMP: 13
SALES (corp-wide): 329MM **Privately Held**
WEB: www.lampsplus.com
SIC: 3646 5719 5064 Commercial indusl & institutional electric lighting fixtures; lamps & lamp shades; fans; household: electric
PA: Lamps Plus, Inc.
20250 Plummer St
Chatsworth CA 91311
818 886-5267

(P-17050)
LEXSTAR INC (PA)
Also Called: Lites On West Soho
4959 Kalamis Way, Oceanside (92056-7411)
PHONE..................................845 947-1415
Uri Redlich, *President*
Kyle Anderson, *General Mgr*
▲ **EMP:** 30
SQ FT: 15,000
SALES (est): 2.9MM **Privately Held**
WEB: www.lexstar.com
SIC: 3646 Commercial indusl & institutional electric lighting fixtures

(P-17051)
LF ILLUMINATION LLC
9200 Deering Ave, Chatsworth (91311-5803)
PHONE..................................818 885-1335
Jack Zukerman, *CEO*
Loren Kessel, *President*
Eileen S Cheng, *CFO*
Terri Roberts, *Vice Pres*
▲ **EMP:** 51 EST: 2013
SALES (est): 11.3MM **Privately Held**
SIC: 3646 3645 5719 Commercial indusl & institutional electric lighting fixtures; residential lighting fixtures; lighting fixtures; lighting, lamps & accessories

(P-17052)
LIGHTWAY INDUSTRIES INC
28435 Industry Dr, Valencia (91355-4107)
PHONE..................................661 257-0286
Jeffrey Bargman, *President*
Gary N Patten, *Vice Pres*
Delia Cerpa, *Purchasing*
EMP: 28 EST: 1980
SQ FT: 22,300
SALES: 5.5MM **Privately Held**
WEB: www.lightwayind.com
SIC: 3646 3645 Commercial indusl & institutional electric lighting fixtures; residential lighting fixtures

(P-17053)
LOS ANGELES LTG MFG CO INC
Also Called: L A Lighting
10141 Olney St, El Monte (91731-2311)
PHONE..................................626 454-8300
William D Shapiro, *President*
Mieko Shapiro, *Treasurer*
◆ **EMP:** 55
SQ FT: 50,000
SALES (est): 15.3MM **Privately Held**
WEB: www.lalighting.com
SIC: 3646 Commercial indusl & institutional electric lighting fixtures

(P-17054)
LUMASCAPE USA INC
1300 Industrial Rd Ste 19, San Carlos (94070-4130)
PHONE..................................650 595-5862
Michael Agustin, *President*
Jordan Agustin, *Manager*
▲ **EMP:** 10
SQ FT: 7,000
SALES (est): 2.8MM **Privately Held**
WEB: www.lumascape.com
SIC: 3646 Commercial indusl & institutional electric lighting fixtures
PA: Lumascape Pty Ltd
18 Brandl St
Eight Mile Plains QLD 4113

(P-17055)
LUMIGROW INC
6550 Vallejo St Ste 200, Emeryville (94608-2166)
PHONE..................................800 514-0487
Jay Albere II, *CEO*
Kevin Wells, *President*
EMP: 28
SALES (est): 10.2MM **Privately Held**
WEB: www.lumigrow.com
SIC: 3646 Ornamental lighting fixtures, commercial

(P-17056)
LUMINATION LIGHTING & TECH INC
1515 240th St, Harbor City (90710-1308)
PHONE..................................855 283-1100
EMP: 150
SALES (est): 4.9MM **Privately Held**
SIC: 3646

(P-17057)
LUMINUS INC (HQ)
Also Called: Lightera
1145 Sonora Ct, Sunnyvale (94086-5384)
PHONE..................................408 708-7000
Decai Sun, *CEO*
Mark Pugh, *Exec VP*
Tom Jory, *Vice Pres*
Mike Kennedy, *Vice Pres*
Chao Guo, *Web Dvlpr*
EMP: 120
SALES (est): 24.1MM
SALES (corp-wide): 1.2B **Privately Held**
SIC: 3646 Fluorescent lighting fixtures, commercial
PA: Sanan Optoelectronics Co., Ltd.
No.1721-1725, Luling Road, Siming District
Xiamen
592 593-7130

(P-17058)
LUXBRIGHT INC
685 Cochran St Ste 200, Simi Valley (93065-1921)
PHONE..................................323 871-4120
Ramin Rostami, *CEO*
▲ **EMP:** 15 EST: 2013
SALES (est): 2.1MM **Privately Held**
SIC: 3646 3674 Commercial indusl & institutional electric lighting fixtures; light emitting diodes

(P-17059)
MAXLITE INC
1148 N Ocean Cir, Anaheim (92806-1939)
PHONE..................................714 678-5000
EMP: 65 **Privately Held**
SIC: 3646 Commercial indusl & institutional electric lighting fixtures
PA: Maxlite, Inc.
12 York Ave
West Caldwell NJ 07006
-

(P-17060)
NOELS LIGHTING INC
9335 Stephens St Unit I, Pico Rivera (90660-2160)
PHONE..................................562 908-6181
Humberto Arguelles, *President*
EMP: 30
SQ FT: 15,000

▲ = Import ▼=Export
◆ =Import/Export

SALES (est): 4.9MM **Privately Held**
SIC: 3646 3648 Commercial indusl & institutional electric lighting fixtures; lighting equipment

(P-17061)
OPTIC ARTS INC
716 Monterey Pass Rd, Monterey Park (91754-3607)
PHONE....................213 250-6069
Jason Mullen, *CEO*
Mason Barker, *Exec VP*
Christy Lee, *General Mgr*
Dorian L Hicklin, *Admin Sec*
Mary Gacho, *Project Mgr*
EMP: 47 **EST:** 2011
SQ FT: 15,750
SALES (est): 9.4MM
SALES (corp-wide): 19.5MM **Privately Held**
SIC: 3646 3645 3648 Commercial indusl & institutional electric lighting fixtures; residential lighting fixtures; decorative area lighting fixtures
PA: Luminii Corp
7777 N Merrimac Ave
Niles IL 60714
224 333-6033

(P-17062)
PACIFIC LTG & STANDARDS CO
2815 Los Flores Blvd, Lynwood (90262-2416)
PHONE....................310 603-9344
Frank Munoz, *President*
Enrique Garcia, *Vice Pres*
▲ **EMP:** 34
SQ FT: 17,000
SALES (est): 8.2MM **Privately Held**
WEB: www.pacificlighting.com
SIC: 3646 Commercial indusl & institutional electric lighting fixtures

(P-17063)
PACLIGHTS LLC (PA)
15830 El Prado Rd Ste F, Chino (91708-9127)
P.O. Box 928, Chino Hills (91709-0031)
PHONE....................888 983-2165
Tommy Zhen, *CEO*
Fiona Zhao, *President*
Rick Acevedo, *Sales Dir*
Tyler Segovia, *Sales Dir*
Janine Pothier, *Accounts Mgr*
▲ **EMP:** 20
SQ FT: 20,000
SALES (est): 2.4MM **Privately Held**
SIC: 3646 Commercial indusl & institutional electric lighting fixtures

(P-17064)
PATRIOT LIGHTING INC
Also Called: U.S. Patriot Lite
2305 S Main St, Los Angeles (90007-2725)
PHONE....................213 741-9757
Young E Lee, *President*
▲ **EMP:** 10
SALES (est): 910K **Privately Held**
WEB: www.patriotltg.com
SIC: 3646 5063 Commercial indusl & institutional electric lighting fixtures; lighting fixtures

(P-17065)
PRECISION FLUORESCENT WEST INC (DH)
Also Called: Precision Energy Efficient Ltg
23281 La Palma Ave, Yorba Linda (92887-4768)
PHONE....................352 692-5900
Raymond Pustinger, *President*
Dan Rodriguez, *Vice Pres*
▲ **EMP:** 67
SQ FT: 31,000
SALES (est): 14.6MM
SALES (corp-wide): 4.4B **Publicly Held**
WEB: www.precisionfluorescent.com
SIC: 3646 Commercial indusl & institutional electric lighting fixtures

(P-17066)
PRUDENTIAL LIGHTING CORP (PA)
Also Called: P L M
1774 E 21st St, Los Angeles (90058-1082)
P.O. Box 58736 (90058-0736)
PHONE....................213 477-1694
Stanely J Ellis, *CEO*
Jeffrey Ellis, *President*
Jolie Ellis, *Corp Secy*
Elliot Ellis, *Vice Pres*
▲ **EMP:** 120 **EST:** 1955
SQ FT: 112,000
SALES (est): 27.4MM **Privately Held**
WEB: www.prulite.com
SIC: 3646 Fluorescent lighting fixtures, commercial

(P-17067)
R W SWARENS ASSOCIATES INC
Also Called: Engineered Lighting Products
10768 Lower Azusa Rd, El Monte (91731-1306)
PHONE....................626 579-0943
Toni Swarens, *CEO*
Lauri Maines, *President*
Jerry Caron, *Purch Agent*
John Linell, *Regl Sales Mgr*
Pete Morales-Elp, *Regl Sales Mgr*
▲ **EMP:** 45 **EST:** 1984
SALES (est): 7.1MM **Privately Held**
SIC: 3646 Commercial indusl & institutional electric lighting fixtures

(P-17068)
SAPPHIRE CHANDELIER LLC
505 Porter Way, Placentia (92870-6454)
PHONE....................714 630-3660
Hector Garibay, *Mng Member*
Hayley Hustedt,
▲ **EMP:** 13
SQ FT: 10,000
SALES (est): 3.2MM **Privately Held**
SIC: 3646 Commercial indusl & institutional electric lighting fixtures

(P-17069)
SCIENTIFIC COMPONENTS SYSTEMS
1514 N Susan St Ste C, Santa Ana (92703-1435)
PHONE....................714 554-3960
Juan L Flores, *President*
Juan Flores, *President*
Elizabeth Flores, *Admin Sec*
EMP: 10 **EST:** 1983
SQ FT: 5,000
SALES (est): 726K **Privately Held**
WEB: www.scsix18.com
SIC: 3646 5063 Commercial indusl & institutional electric lighting fixtures; lighting fixtures

(P-17070)
SCOTT LAMP COMPANY INC
Also Called: Scott Architectural
355 Watt Dr, Fairfield (94534-4207)
PHONE....................707 864-2066
Dennis J Scott, *CEO*
Dennis Scott, *CEO*
Paul R Scott, *Vice Pres*
Eileen Emerson, *Office Mgr*
Eileen K Scott-Emerson, *Admin Sec*
▲ **EMP:** 90
SQ FT: 71,000
SALES (est): 18MM **Privately Held**
WEB: www.scottlamp.com
SIC: 3646 3645 Ceiling systems, luminous; chandeliers, commercial; desk lamps, commercial; ornamental lighting fixtures, commercial; residential lighting fixtures

(P-17071)
SPOTLITE POWER CORPORATION
9937 Jefferson Blvd # 110, Culver City (90232-3528)
PHONE....................310 838-2367
Halston Mikail, *President*
▲ **EMP:** 30

SALES (est): 1.8MM
SALES (corp-wide): 24.7MM **Privately Held**
SIC: 3646 Commercial indusl & institutional electric lighting fixtures
PA: Spotlite America Corporation
9937 Jefferson Blvd # 110
Culver City CA 90232
310 829-0200

(P-17072)
STACK LABS INC
Also Called: Stack Lighting
10052 Pasadena Ave Ste A, Cupertino (95014-5956)
PHONE....................503 453-5172
Neil Joseph, *CEO*
Jack McFarland, *CFO*
Pedraam Behroozi, *Technical Staff*
EMP: 20
SQ FT: 5,000
SALES: 7.5MM **Privately Held**
SIC: 3646 Commercial indusl & institutional electric lighting fixtures

(P-17073)
SUN & SUN INDUSTRIES INC
2101 S Yale St, Santa Ana (92704-4424)
PHONE....................714 210-5141
Lynda Sun-Frederick, *CEO*
Duncan Frederick, *President*
Ken Flockblower, *Vice Pres*
EMP: 100
SQ FT: 11,000
SALES (est): 18.3MM
SALES (corp-wide): 4.2MM **Privately Held**
WEB: www.sunindustriesinc.com
SIC: 3646 Fluorescent lighting fixtures, commercial
PA: Eco-Shift Power Corp
125 Mcgovern Dr Unit 10
Cambridge ON N3H 4

(P-17074)
SUN VALLEY LTG STANDARDS INC
Also Called: US Architectural Lighting
660 W Avenue O, Palmdale (93551-3610)
PHONE....................661 233-2000
Joseph Straus, *President*
Judith Straus, *Vice Pres*
EMP: 260
SQ FT: 30,000
SALES (est): 25MM
SALES (corp-wide): 67.6MM **Privately Held**
WEB: www.usaltg.com
SIC: 3646 3648 Ornamental lighting fixtures, commercial; electrical apparatus & equipment; lighting equipment
PA: U.S. Pole Company, Inc.
660 W Avenue O
Palmdale CA 93551
800 877-6537

(P-17075)
T-1 LIGHTING INC
9929 Pioneer Blvd, Santa Fe Springs (90670-3219)
PHONE....................626 234-2328
Artur Saakyan, *CEO*
An Bao Vu, *COO*
Pang Chun Zhang, *CFO*
EMP: 16
SQ FT: 19,660
SALES: 10MM **Privately Held**
SIC: 3646 Commercial indusl & institutional electric lighting fixtures

(P-17076)
TANKO STREETLIGHTING INC
Also Called: Tanko Streetlighting Services
220 Bay Shore Blvd, San Francisco (94124-1323)
PHONE....................415 254-7579
Jason Tanko, *President*
Clare Bressani, *Vice Pres*
Jaclyn Blackwell, *Project Mgr*
Joe Bollinger, *Engineer*
Chris Pettengill, *Opers Mgr*
▲ **EMP:** 31
SQ FT: 5,000

SALES (est): 5.5MM **Privately Held**
SIC: 3646 Commercial indusl & institutional electric lighting fixtures

(P-17077)
TEMPO LIGHTING INC
Also Called: Tempo Industries
1961 Mcgaw Ave, Irvine (92614-0909)
PHONE....................949 442-1601
Dennis Pearson, *CEO*
Mike Bremser, *Vice Pres*
Jason Luck, *Technician*
Shaun Toms, *Design Engr*
Jignesh Bhagat, *Engineer*
▲ **EMP:** 31 **EST:** 1986
SQ FT: 27,000
SALES (est): 9.9MM **Privately Held**
WEB: www.tempoindustries.com
SIC: 3646 Commercial indusl & institutional electric lighting fixtures

(P-17078)
TRITON CHANDELIER INC
1301 Dove St Ste 900, Newport Beach (92660-2473)
PHONE....................714 957-9600
Richard Cooley, *President*
▲ **EMP:** 43
SQ FT: 10,000
SALES (est): 5.4MM **Privately Held**
WEB: www.tritonchandelier.com
SIC: 3646 Chandeliers, commercial

(P-17079)
TUJAYAR ENTERPRISES INC
Also Called: Tube Lighting Products
1346 Pioneer Way, El Cajon (92020-1626)
PHONE....................619 442-0577
Rick Tempkin, *President*
Donna Rogers, *General Mgr*
Jake Valenzuela, *Prdtn Mgr*
Pete Olson, *Natl Sales Mgr*
▲ **EMP:** 21
SQ FT: 9,000
SALES (est): 3.9MM **Privately Held**
WEB: www.tubelightingproducts.com
SIC: 3646 3645 Commercial indusl & institutional electric lighting fixtures; residential lighting fixtures

(P-17080)
UNIVERSAL METAL SPINNING INC
2543 W Winton Ave Ste 5j, Hayward (94545-1153)
PHONE....................510 782-0980
Stewart Blunck, *President*
Maria Blunck, *Treasurer*
Rudolf Blunck, *Vice Pres*
EMP: 11
SALES (est): 1.2MM **Privately Held**
WEB: www.universalmetalspinning.com
SIC: 3646 Commercial indusl & institutional electric lighting fixtures

(P-17081)
USHIO AMERICA INC
14 Mason, Irvine (92618-2705)
PHONE....................714 236-8600
Holger Claus, *Vice Pres*
Almeemo Ahmad, *Engineer*
EMP: 30 **Privately Held**
SIC: 3646 Fluorescent lighting fixtures, commercial
HQ: Ushio America, Inc.
5440 Cerritos Ave
Cypress CA 90630
714 236-8600

(P-17082)
VISION ENGRG MET STAMPING INC
114 Grand Cypress Ave, Palmdale (93551-3617)
PHONE....................661 575-0933
Joseph Avila, *CEO*
EMP: 100
SQ FT: 72,000
SALES (est): 9.6MM **Privately Held**
SIC: 3646 Ceiling systems, luminous

(P-17083)
VISIONAIRE LIGHTING LLC
19645 S Rancho Way, Rancho Dominguez (90220-6028)
PHONE....................310 512-6480

Fred Kayne, *CEO*
Cheryl Moorman, *CFO*
Calvin Wong, *Managing Dir*
John Dabevsky, *Info Tech Mgr*
Hugo Mendoza, *Tech/Comp Coord*
◆ **EMP:** 650
SQ FT: 36,000
SALES (est): 66.5MM **Privately Held**
WEB: www.visionairelighting.com
SIC: 3646 Commercial indusl & institutional electric lighting fixtures

(P-17084)
WESTERN ILLUMINATED PLAS INC
14451 Edwards St, Westminster
(92683-3607)
PHONE....................714 895-3067
Cornelius Crompvoets, *President*
Irene Crompvoets, *Treasurer*
Charles Crompvoets, *Vice Pres*
Sandra Crompvoets-Katanjian, *Admin Sec*
EMP: 18
SQ FT: 8,800
SALES (est): 3.4MM **Privately Held**
WEB: www.westernplastics.com
SIC: 3646 1761 Ceiling systems, luminous; ceilings, metal: erection & repair

(P-17085)
WESTERN LIGHTING INDS INC
Also Called: Orgatech Omegalux
205 W Blueridge Ave, Orange
(92865-4226)
PHONE....................626 969-6820
Lawrence St Ives, *CEO*
Victor Ortiz, *Opers Staff*
Asha Narayan, *Accounts Mgr*
▲ **EMP:** 22
SQ FT: 16,000
SALES (est): 4.1MM **Privately Held**
WEB: www.orgatechomegalux.com
SIC: 3646 Commercial indusl & institutional electric lighting fixtures

(P-17086)
YANKON INDUSTRIES INC
Also Called: Energetic Lighting
13445 12th St, Chino (91710-5206)
PHONE....................909 591-2345
WEI Chen, *CEO*
David Liu, *CEO*
Kristen Tai, *CFO*
▲ **EMP:** 25 **EST:** 2009
SQ FT: 100,627
SALES (est): 5.2MM **Privately Held**
SIC: 3646 Commercial indusl & institutional electric lighting fixtures

---

3647 Vehicular Lighting Eqpt

(P-17087)
AMP PLUS INC
Also Called: Elco Lighting
2042 E Vernon Ave, Vernon (90058-1613)
PHONE....................323 231-2600
Steve Cohen, *President*
▲ **EMP:** 55
SQ FT: 100,000
SALES (est): 9.1MM **Privately Held**
SIC: 3647 5063 3645 Vehicular lighting equipment; electrical apparatus & equipment; residential lighting fixtures

(P-17088)
DELTA TECH INDUSTRIES LLC
1901 S Vineyard Ave, Ontario
(91761-7747)
PHONE....................909 673-1900
Bogdan G Durian, *Mng Member*
James Jimenez, *Executive*
▲ **EMP:** 14
SQ FT: 12,000
SALES (est): 2.1MM **Privately Held**
WEB: www.deltalights.com
SIC: 3647 Automotive lighting fixtures

(P-17089)
ELDEMA PRODUCTS
10145 Via De La Amistad # 5, San Diego
(92154-5217)
PHONE....................619 661-5113
Chuy Valles, *Owner*

Maria Valles, *Co-Owner*
EMP: 10
SALES (est): 560K **Privately Held**
SIC: 3647 3825 Parking lights, automotive; indicating instruments, electric

(P-17090)
JKL COMPONENTS CORPORATION
13343 Paxton St, Pacoima (91331-2340)
PHONE....................818 896-0019
Joseph Velas, *President*
Mark Hori, *Vice Pres*
Kent Koerting, *Principal*
Percy Andres, *Info Tech Mgr*
Larry Rushefsky, *Engineer*
EMP: 32 **EST:** 1974
SQ FT: 7,000
SALES (est): 6MM **Privately Held**
WEB: www.jkllamps.com
SIC: 3647 3827 3699 Automotive lighting fixtures; optical instruments & lenses; electrical equipment & supplies

(P-17091)
K C HILITES INC
13637 Cimarron Ave, Gardena
(90249-2461)
P.O. Box 155, Williams AZ (86046-0155)
PHONE....................928 635-2607
Michael Dehaas, *President*
Andy Wang, *Managing Prtnr*
Rosanna Marmolejo, *Graphic Designe*
Michele Dehaas, *Marketing Staff*
Ron Pryczynski, *Marketing Staff*
◆ **EMP:** 36 **EST:** 1970
SQ FT: 25,000
SALES (est): 8.5MM **Privately Held**
WEB: www.kchilites.com
SIC: 3647 Vehicular lighting equipment

(P-17092)
SIERRA DESIGN MFG INC (PA)
Also Called: Dry Launch Light Co
1113 Greenville Rd, Livermore
(94550-9714)
PHONE....................925 443-3140
Dennis Moore, *President*
Cindy Moore, *Vice Pres*
▲ **EMP:** 40
SQ FT: 15,000
SALES (est): 3.1MM **Privately Held**
WEB: www.dry-launch.com
SIC: 3647 Taillights, motor vehicle

(P-17093)
SODERBERG MANUFACTURING CO INC
20821 Currier Rd, Walnut (91789-3018)
PHONE....................909 595-1291
B W Soderberg, *CEO*
Kathy Kirkeby, *Corp Secy*
Kari Levario, *Vice Pres*
Rick Soderberg, *Vice Pres*
Sam Tapia, *Project Engr*
EMP: 85
SALES (est): 16.5MM **Privately Held**
WEB: www.soderberg-mfg.com
SIC: 3647 3812 Aircraft lighting fixtures; search & navigation equipment

(P-17094)
STREET GLOW INC
2710 E El Presidio St, Carson
(90810-1117)
PHONE....................310 631-1881
EMP: 60 **Privately Held**
SIC: 3647
PA: Street Glow Inc
160 Gregg St Ste 7
Lodi NJ
973 709-9000

(P-17095)
SUNBEAM TRAILER PRODUCTS INC
5312 Production Dr, Huntington Beach
(92649-1523)
PHONE....................714 373-5000
EMP: 20 **EST:** 1939
SQ FT: 11,000
SALES (est): 1.7MM **Privately Held**
SIC: 3647

3648 Lighting Eqpt, NEC

(P-17096)
A&R LIGHTING CO
7644 Emil Ave, Bell (90201-4940)
PHONE....................562 927-8617
Rosemary Picon, *Owner*
EMP: 12
SALES (est): 1.3MM **Privately Held**
WEB: www.arlighting.com
SIC: 3648 3999 Lighting equipment; advertising display products

(P-17097)
AL KRAMP SPECIALTIES
Also Called: J K Lighting Systems
1707 El Pinal Dr, Stockton (95205-2553)
P.O. Box 8867 (95208-0867)
PHONE....................209 464-7539
Al Kramp, *Owner*
Sharon Lundquist, *Controller*
EMP: 25
SQ FT: 67,000
SALES (est): 3.6MM **Privately Held**
WEB: www.jk-lighting.com
SIC: 3648 5063 3699 Lighting equipment; lighting fixtures; electrical equipment & supplies

(P-17098)
ALL ACCESS STGING PRDCTONS INC (PA)
1320 Storm Pkwy, Torrance (90501-5041)
PHONE....................310 784-2464
Clive Forrester, *CEO*
Erik Eastland, *President*
Robert Achlimbari, *Vice Pres*
James Casalino, *General Mgr*
Richard Lucas, *Administration*
▲ **EMP:** 71
SQ FT: 42,000
SALES (est): 14.5MM **Privately Held**
SIC: 3648 Stage lighting equipment

(P-17099)
ALL ENERGY INC
3401 Adams Ave A28, San Diego
(92116-2490)
PHONE....................619 988-7030
Kenneth Ramcharan, *President*
EMP: 15
SALES (est): 1.2MM **Privately Held**
SIC: 3648 Area & sports luminaries

(P-17100)
AMERICAN GRIP INC
8468 Kewen Ave, Sun Valley (91352-3118)
PHONE....................818 768-8922
Lance Snoke, *President*
EMP: 25
SQ FT: 15,000
SALES (est): 3MM **Privately Held**
WEB: www.americangrip.com
SIC: 3648 3861 Stage lighting equipment; stands, camera & projector

(P-17101)
AMERICAN POWER SOLUTIONS INC
14355 Industry Cir, La Mirada
(90638-5810)
PHONE....................714 626-0300
Bansik Yoon, *CEO*
Thomas Hyun, *Sales Staff*
Wayne Kim, *Sales Staff*
Peter Yoon, *Manager*
▲ **EMP:** 20
SALES (est): 10.4MM **Privately Held**
WEB: www.americanpowersolutions.com
SIC: 3648 Lighting equipment

(P-17102)
AMERILLUM LLC
Also Called: Alumen-8
3728 Maritime Way, Oceanside
(92056-2702)
PHONE....................760 727-7675
Ronald S Lancial, *Mng Member*
Spike Atkinson, *Partner*
Peter Clarke, *Finance*
Serge Lambert,
Guy St Pierre,
▲ **EMP:** 54
SQ FT: 27,000

SALES (est): 15.9MM **Privately Held**
WEB: www.amerillum.com
SIC: 3648 Lighting equipment

(P-17103)
ARCHITECTURAL CATHODE LIGHTING
Also Called: Archigraphics
12123 Pantheon St, Norwalk (90650-1822)
PHONE....................323 581-8800
Eric Zimmerman, *President*
Leo Silva, *Manager*
EMP: 12
SQ FT: 8,000
SALES (est): 2MM **Privately Held**
WEB: www.archigraphics.com
SIC: 3648 3641 Decorative area lighting fixtures; electric lamps

(P-17104)
BEGA/US INC
1000 Bega Way, Carpinteria (93013-2902)
PHONE....................805 684-0533
Don Kinderdick, *CEO*
Mark Reed, *Vice Pres*
Scott Sorensen, *Vice Pres*
Kenneth Neppach, *Regional Mgr*
Scott Knouse, *Administration*
▲ **EMP:** 100
SQ FT: 60,000
SALES (est): 34MM **Privately Held**
WEB: www.bega-us.com
SIC: 3648 3646 Outdoor lighting equipment; commercial indusl & institutional electric lighting fixtures

(P-17105)
BIRCHWOOD LIGHTING INC
3340 E La Palma Ave, Anaheim
(92806-2814)
PHONE....................714 550-7118
Darrin Weedon, *President*
Linda Allen, *Admin Sec*
EMP: 25
SQ FT: 1,900
SALES (est): 5.8MM
SALES (corp-wide): 1.4B **Privately Held**
WEB: www.birchwoodlighting.com
SIC: 3648 3646 3645 Decorative area lighting fixtures; commercial indusl & institutional electric lighting fixtures; residential lighting fixtures
PA: Leviton Manufacturing Co., Inc.
201 N Service Rd
Melville NY 11747
631 812-6000

(P-17106)
BLISS HOLDINGS LLC
745 S Vinewood St, Escondido
(92029-1928)
PHONE....................626 506-8696
Allan Lee,
▲ **EMP:** 50
SALES (est): 1MM **Privately Held**
SIC: 3648 Lighting equipment

(P-17107)
BLISSLIGHTS LLC
100 E San Marcos Blvd # 308, San Marcos
(92069-2989)
PHONE....................888 868-4603
Ravi Bhagavatula,
Brent Hunter, *Finance Dir*
EMP: 20
SQ FT: 4,573
SALES (est): 1.2MM **Privately Held**
SIC: 3648 Lighting equipment

(P-17108)
C W ENTERPRISES INC
2111 Iowa Ave Ste D, Riverside
(92507-7414)
PHONE....................951 786-9999
William Noyes, *CEO*
Charlotte Noyes, *CFO*
EMP: 10
SALES: 1.6MM **Privately Held**
SIC: 3648 Lighting equipment

(P-17109)
CALCO SUPPLY INC
1460 Yosemite Ave, San Francisco
(94124-3322)
PHONE....................415 760-7793
John Lowe, *CEO*

2020 California
Manufacturers Register

▲ = Import ▼=Export
◆ =Import/Export

Mike Kwong, *Admin Sec*
EMP: 20
SALES (est): 2.1MM **Privately Held**
SIC: 3648 Lighting equipment

(P-17110)
CINEMILLS CORPORATION (PA)
2021 N Lincoln St, Burbank (91504-3334)
PHONE..............................818 843-4560
Marcos M Demattos, *CEO*
Carlos Demattos, *President*
▲ **EMP:** 10 **EST:** 1976
SQ FT: 5,000
SALES (est): 1.9MM **Privately Held**
WEB: www.cinemills.com
SIC: 3648 7359 3646 Lighting equipment;
sound & lighting equipment rental; com-
mercial indusl & institutional electric light-
ing fixtures

(P-17111)
CLARUS LIGHTING LLC
Also Called: Casella
10183 Croydon Way Ste C, Sacramento
(95827-2103)
PHONE..............................916 363-2888
Chuck Bird,
▲ **EMP:** 11
SQ FT: 5,000
SALES (est): 1.5MM **Privately Held**
WEB: www.claruslighting.com
SIC: 3648 Lighting equipment

(P-17112)
CLEAR BLUE ENERGY CORP
Also Called: Cbec
17150 Via Del Ca, San Diego (92127)
PHONE..............................858 451-1549
Paul Santina, *CEO*
Jim Kelly, *President*
EMP: 80
SALES (est): 4MM **Privately Held**
SIC: 3648 1731 Lighting equipment; light-
ing contractor

(P-17113)
COOPER LIGHTING LLC
3350 Enterprise Dr, Bloomington
(92316-3538)
PHONE..............................909 605-6615
John Seiler, *Manager*
Maurice Townsend, *Opers Staff*
EMP: 35 **Privately Held**
WEB: www.corelite.com
SIC: 3648 Lighting equipment
HQ: Cooper Lighting, Llc
1121 Highway 74 S
Peachtree City GA 30269
770 486-4800

(P-17114)
CYRON INC
21029 Itasca St Ste C, Chatsworth
(91311-8510)
PHONE..............................818 772-1900
Al Javadi, *President*
Jim Adair, *Sales Staff*
▲ **EMP:** 10
SQ FT: 5,700
SALES (est): 1.4MM **Privately Held**
WEB: www.cyron.com
SIC: 3648 Lighting equipment

(P-17115)
DABMAR LIGHTING INC (PA)
320 Graves Ave, Oxnard (93030-5184)
PHONE..............................805 604-9090
Dan Davidson, *President*
Bilha Davidson, *Vice Pres*
◆ **EMP:** 23 **EST:** 1990
SALES (est): 4.5MM **Privately Held**
WEB: www.dabmar.com
SIC: 3648 Lighting equipment

(P-17116)
DANA CREATH DESIGNS LTD
3030 Kilson Dr, Santa Ana (92707-4203)
PHONE..............................714 662-0111
Dana E Creath, *Partner*
James K Creath, *Partner*
Raylene R Creath, *Partner*
EMP: 30

SALES (est): 4.2MM **Privately Held**
WEB: www.danacreathdesigns.com
SIC: 3648 3646 3645 Lighting equipment;
commercial indusl & institutional electric
lighting fixtures; residential lighting fixtures

(P-17117)
DELRAY LIGHTING INC
7545 N Lockheed Dr, Burbank
(91505-1045)
PHONE..............................818 767-3793
Steven Feig, *CEO*
▲ **EMP:** 28
SQ FT: 20,000
SALES (est): 7.1MM **Privately Held**
WEB: www.delraylighting.com
SIC: 3648 Lighting equipment

(P-17118)
EEMA INDUSTRIES INC
Also Called: Liton Lighting
5461 W Jefferson Blvd, Los Angeles
(90016-3715)
PHONE..............................323 904-0200
Amir Esmail Zadeh, *President*
Tony Phan, *Marketing Staff*
Noel Madrid, *Manager*
◆ **EMP:** 40
SQ FT: 40,000
SALES (est): 8.1MM **Privately Held**
WEB: www.eema.net
SIC: 3648 5063 Lighting equipment; elec-
trical apparatus & equipment

(P-17119)
ELECTRONIC THEATRE CONTRLS INC
Also Called: Etc
1120 Scott Rd, Burbank (91504-4237)
PHONE..............................323 461-0216
Randy Pybas, *Regional Mgr*
Mike Kiktavi, *Design Engr*
David Drake, *Engineer*
Dave Liu, *Engineer*
Stanley Wong, *Engineer*
EMP: 18
SALES (corp-wide): 321.3MM **Privately Held**
WEB: www.etcasia.com
SIC: 3648 5049 Lighting equipment; the-
atrical equipment & supplies
PA: Electronic Theatre Controls, Inc.
3031 Pleasant View Rd
Middleton WI 53562
608 831-4116

(P-17120)
ELEMENTAL LED LLC (PA)
1195 Park Ave Ste 211, Emeryville
(94608-3655)
PHONE..............................877 564-5051
Randy Holleschau, *Mng Member*
Craig Anderson, *Vice Pres*
Gurpreet Khangura, *Vice Pres*
April Mitchell, *Vice Pres*
Jim Puchbauer, *Vice Pres*
EMP: 39
SQ FT: 32,000
SALES (est): 24.1MM **Privately Held**
SIC: 3648 Lighting equipment

(P-17121)
ELITE LIGHTING
5424 E Slauson Ave, Commerce
(90040-2919)
PHONE..............................323 888-1973
Babak Rashididoust, *CEO*
Rudy Godinez, *Sales Staff*
Hovik Hambarsoomian, *Warehouse Mgr*
Hamid Rashidi, *Manager*
◆ **EMP:** 200
SQ FT: 25,000
SALES (est): 63.2MM **Privately Held**
SIC: 3648 3646 3645 Lighting equipment;
commercial indusl & institutional electric
lighting fixtures; boudoir lamps

(P-17122)
EMAZING LIGHTS LLC
240 S Loara St, Anaheim (92802-1020)
PHONE..............................626 628-6482
Brian Lim, *Principal*
Joel Ruiz, *Store Mgr*
Randolth Yuson, *Technical Staff*
Matthew Marchione, *Director*

▲ **EMP:** 13
SALES (est): 2.6MM **Privately Held**
SIC: 3648 3229 Spotlights; bulbs for elec-
tric lights

(P-17123)
ENERGY MANAGEMENT GROUP INC (PA)
Also Called: Lighting Company, The
1621 Browning, Irvine (92606-4828)
PHONE..............................949 296-0764
Steve Espinosa, *President*
EMP: 13
SQ FT: 16,000
SALES (est): 2.6MM **Privately Held**
SIC: 3648 Lighting fixtures, except electric:
residential

(P-17124)
EXCELITAS TECHNOLOGIES CORP
44370 Christy St, Fremont (94538-3180)
PHONE..............................510 979-6500
John Lucero, *Branch Mgr*
Nam Dao, *Project Engr*
Terry Gilchrist, *Engineer*
Chuck Laughlin, *Engineer*
Naresh Rthy, *Engineer*
EMP: 87
SALES (corp-wide): 1.2B **Privately Held**
SIC: 3648 3845 Lighting equipment; elec-
tromedical apparatus
HQ: Excelitas Technologies Corp.
200 West St
Waltham MA 02451

(P-17125)
FNTECH
18107 Mount Washington St, Fountain Val-
ley (92708-6120)
PHONE..............................714 429-1686
EMP: 15
SALES (est): 2.5MM **Privately Held**
SIC: 3648 Stage lighting equipment

(P-17126)
FNTECH
3000 W Segerstrom Ave, Santa Ana
(92704-6526)
PHONE..............................714 429-7833
Jeremy Muir, *CEO*
EMP: 11
SALES (est): 487.3K **Privately Held**
SIC: 3648 Lighting equipment

(P-17127)
FOXFURY LLC
Also Called: Foxfury Lighting Solution
3528 Seagate Way Ste 100, Oceanside
(92056-6040)
PHONE..............................760 945-4231
Mario A Cugini,
▲ **EMP:** 24
SALES (est): 4.7MM **Privately Held**
WEB: www.foxfury.com
SIC: 3648 Lighting equipment

(P-17128)
FREELAND EXCEED INC
1820 E Locust St, Ontario (91761-7737)
PHONE..............................626 695-8031
Yeung Fan Lam, *CEO*
Zhiwei Xu, *CFO*
Xin Miao Yang, *Admin Sec*
EMP: 27
SALES (est): 959.2K **Privately Held**
SIC: 3648 Outdoor lighting equipment

(P-17129)
GALLAGHER RENTAL INC
15701 Heron Ave, La Mirada (90638-5206)
PHONE..............................714 690-1559
Joseph Gallagher, *CEO*
Megan Gallagher, *Manager*
EMP: 30 **EST:** 2012
SALES (est): 4.7MM **Privately Held**
SIC: 3648 Stage lighting equipment

(P-17130)
GREENSHINE NEW ENERGY LLC
23661 Birtcher Dr, Lake Forest
(92630-1770)
PHONE..............................949 609-9636

Alex Chen, *Sales Mgr*
Scott Douglas, *General Mgr*
Kevin Laurent, *Project Mgr*
◆ **EMP:** 100
SQ FT: 200
SALES: 1MM **Privately Held**
SIC: 3648 Lighting equipment

(P-17131)
H K LIGHTING GROUP INC
3529 Old Conejo Rd # 118, Newbury Park
(91320-6152)
PHONE..............................805 480-4881
Hiroshi Kira, *President*
Shirley Zien, *CFO*
William Steinbrink, *Sales Staff*
◆ **EMP:** 12
SALES (est): 2.3MM **Privately Held**
SIC: 3648 Decorative area lighting fixtures

(P-17132)
HANSON BRASS INC
Also Called: Hanson Heat Lamps
7530 San Fernando Rd, Sun Valley
(91352-4344)
PHONE..............................818 767-3501
Tom Hanson Jr, *President*
James Hanson, *Vice Pres*
EMP: 10
SQ FT: 6,000
SALES: 1.8MM **Privately Held**
WEB: www.hansonbrass.com
SIC: 3648 Infrared lamp fixtures

(P-17133)
HYDROFARM LLC (PA)
2249 S Mcdowell Blvd Ext, Petaluma
(94954-5661)
PHONE..............................707 765-9990
Peter Wardenburg, *Mng Member*
Tri Meter, *Products*
Doktor Doom, *Master*
Hanna Instruments, *Master*
Jeffrey Peterson,
◆ **EMP:** 38
SALES (est): 12.8MM **Privately Held**
WEB: www.hydrofarm.com
SIC: 3648 3999 Lighting equipment; hy-
droponic equipment

(P-17134)
ILOS CORP
Also Called: Meteor Lighting
1300 John Reed Ct Ste B, City of Industry
(91745-2422)
PHONE..............................213 255-2060
Ming Hsin Lu, *President*
▲ **EMP:** 10
SALES (est): 740.8K **Privately Held**
SIC: 3648 Lighting equipment

(P-17135)
IN PRO CAR WEAR INC
Also Called: I P C W
6363 Corsair St, Commerce (90040-2503)
PHONE..............................323 724-0568
Ken Liao, *Vice Pres*
Danny Serny, *Sales Executive*
▲ **EMP:** 11
SALES (est): 1.2MM **Privately Held**
WEB: www.inprocarwear.com
SIC: 3648 Lighting equipment

(P-17136)
INNOVALIGHT INC
965 W Maude Ave, Sunnyvale
(94085-2802)
PHONE..............................408 419-4400
Thomas Linn, *CEO*
Michael Johnson, *CFO*
Conrad Burke, *Principal*
▲ **EMP:** 40
SALES (est): 6.7MM
SALES (corp-wide): 30.6B **Publicly Held**
WEB: www.innovalight.com
SIC: 3648 Lighting equipment
HQ: E. I. Du Pont De Nemours And Com-
pany
974 Centre Rd Bldg 735
Wilmington DE 19805
302 485-3000

(PA)=Parent Co (HQ)=Headquarters (DH)=Div Headquarters
✪ = New Business established in last 2 years
2020 California
Manufacturers Register

PRODUCTS & SVCS

(P-17137)
JIMWAY INC
Also Called: Altair Lighting
20101 S Santa Fe Ave, Compton
(90221-5917)
PHONE..................................310 886-3718
Hsing-Min Keng, *CEO*
Irene Wang, *Admin Sec*
Singh Chang, *Info Tech Mgr*
Joseph Yale, *Graphic Designe*
Edmond Daniels, *Manager*
▲ EMP: 100
SQ FT: 200,000
SALES (est): 20.3MM **Privately Held**
SIC: 3648 3221 5063 Lighting equipment;
　glass containers; electrical apparatus &
　equipment

(P-17138)
KUSTOM LIGHTING PRODUCTS INC
2107 Chico Ave, South El Monte
(91733-1606)
PHONE..................................626 443-0166
Paul Lestz, *President*
Augustine Haro, *Shareholder*
Brett Browning, *Vice Pres*
▲ EMP: 50 EST: 1998
SQ FT: 11,500
SALES (est): 6.7MM **Privately Held**
SIC: 3648 Lighting equipment

(P-17139)
LIGHT & MOTION INDUSTRIES
711 Neeson Rd, Marina (93933-5104)
PHONE..................................831 645-1525
Daniel T Emerson, *President*
Tom Brady, *VP Mktg*
Daniel Delehanty, *VP Sales*
Adriane Fells, *Manager*
▲ EMP: 55
SALES (est): 11.6MM **Privately Held**
WEB: www.lightandmotion.com
SIC: 3648 Underwater lighting fixtures

(P-17140)
LIGHTING CONTROL & DESIGN INC
Also Called: LCD&d
9144 Deering Ave, Chatsworth
(91311-5801)
PHONE..................................323 226-0000
EMP: 26
SQ FT: 10,000
SALES (est): 4.1MM
SALES (corp-wide): 3.6B **Publicly Held**
WEB: www.lcdtest.com
SIC: 3648 3643 5719 Lighting equipment;
　current-carrying wiring devices; lighting
　fixtures
PA: Acuity Brands, Inc.
　1170 Peachtree St Ne # 23
　Atlanta GA 30309
　404 853-1400

(P-17141)
LUMENTON INC
Also Called: Lumenton Lighting
5461 W Jefferson Blvd, Los Angeles
(90016-3715)
PHONE..................................323 904-0202
A J Esmailzadeh, *President*
▲ EMP: 26
SQ FT: 100,000
SALES (est): 4.3MM **Privately Held**
SIC: 3648 Outdoor lighting equipment

(P-17142)
LUMENYTE INTERNATIONAL CORP
535 4th St, San Fernando (91340-2521)
PHONE..................................949 279-8687
Peter D Costigan, *President*
Steven Strickler, *Principal*
▲ EMP: 10
SQ FT: 5,000
SALES (est): 2.2MM **Privately Held**
WEB: www.lumenyte.com
SIC: 3648 8748 Lighting equipment; light-
　ing consultant

(P-17143)
LUMINUS DEVICES INC
1145 Sonora Ct, Sunnyvale (94086-5384)
PHONE..................................978 528-8000
Decai Sun, *CEO*
Kevin Shih, *CFO*
Mark Pugh, *Exec VP*
Ting LI, *Vice Pres*
Pamela Matos, *Admin Asst*
▲ EMP: 48
SALES (est): 17.5MM
SALES (corp-wide): 1.2B **Privately Held**
WEB: www.luminusdevices.com
SIC: 3648 Lighting equipment
HQ: Luminus, Inc.
　1145 Sonora Ct
　Sunnyvale CA 94086
　408 708-7000

(P-17144)
MAG INSTRUMENT INC (PA)
2001 S Hellman Ave, Ontario (91761-8019)
P.O. Box 50600 (91761-1083)
PHONE..................................909 947-1006
Anthony Maglica, *CEO*
Brent Flaharty, *Officer*
Malissa Peace, *Officer*
David Hefner, *Vice Pres*
John Maglica, *Vice Pres*
▲ EMP: 277 EST: 1955
SQ FT: 1,000,000
SALES (est): 175.8MM **Privately Held**
WEB: www.maglite.com
SIC: 3648 Flashlights

(P-17145)
MNC BLISS ENTERPRISES INC
1715 Fulton Ave, Sacramento
(95825-2415)
PHONE..................................916 483-1167
Marshall Bliss, *CEO*
Cassie Bliss, *CFO*
EMP: 13
SQ FT: 10,000
SALES: 4MM **Privately Held**
SIC: 3648 Outdoor lighting equipment

(P-17146)
MW MCWONG INTERNATIONAL INC
Also Called: Pacific Lighting & Electrical
1921 Arena Blvd, Sacramento
(95834-3770)
PHONE..................................916 371-8080
Margaret Y Wong, *CEO*
Emily MEI, *CFO*
Blane Goettle, *Vice Pres*
Stephen Zhou, *Vice Pres*
Christina Dyson, *Administration*
▲ EMP: 32
SQ FT: 47,430
SALES (est): 15MM **Privately Held**
SIC: 3648 Lighting fixtures, except electric:
　residential

(P-17147)
NATIONAL BRIGHT LIGHTING INC
1480 Adelia Ave, South El Monte
(91733-3003)
PHONE..................................909 818-9188
Helen Lin, *President*
EMP: 22
SALES (est): 3MM **Privately Held**
SIC: 3648 3646 Street lighting fixtures; air-
　port lighting fixtures: runway approach,
　taxi or ramp; commercial indusl & institu-
　tional electric lighting fixtures

(P-17148)
NEW BEDFORD PANORAMEX CORP
Also Called: Nbp
1480 N Claremont Blvd, Claremont
(91711-3538)
PHONE..................................909 982-9806
Steven Robert Ozuna, *President*
Bryce Nielsen, *Admin Sec*
Kenneth Gauthier, *Materials Mgr*
Kenneth Harter, *Mfg Mgr*
Michael Nielsen, *QC Mgr*
EMP: 35
SQ FT: 65,000
SALES (est): 9.3MM **Privately Held**
WEB: www.nbpcorp.com
SIC: 3648 Airport lighting fixtures: runway
　approach, taxi or ramp

(P-17149)
NITERIDER TECHNICAL LIGHTING &
12255 Crosthwaite Cir A, Poway
(92064-8825)
PHONE..................................858 268-9316
Thomas Edward Carroll, *CEO*
Mark Schultz, *COO*
▲ EMP: 35
SALES (est): 6.3MM **Privately Held**
WEB: www.niterideroffroad.com
SIC: 3648 3646 Lighting equipment; com-
　mercial indusl & institutional electric light-
　ing fixtures

(P-17150)
ONESOLUTION LIGHT AND CONTROL
Also Called: Nsi Architectural
225 S Loara St, Anaheim (92802-1019)
PHONE..................................714 490-5540
John C Ortiz, *President*
EMP: 20
SQ FT: 14,000
SALES (est): 3.2MM **Privately Held**
WEB: www.nsi-inc.com
SIC: 3648 Lighting equipment

(P-17151)
PACIFIC COAST LIGHTING INC (PA)
Also Called: Pacific Coast Lighting Group
20238 Plummer St, Chatsworth
(91311-5365)
PHONE..................................818 886-9751
Dennis K Swanson, *CEO*
Dick Idol, *Partner*
Adrienne Quarto, *President*
Clark Linstone, *CEO*
Richard Spicer, *Treasurer*
◆ EMP: 300
SQ FT: 100,000
SALES (est): 55.2MM **Privately Held**
WEB: www.pacificcoastlighting.com
SIC: 3648 3641 5719 Lighting equipment;
　electric lamps; lighting fixtures

(P-17152)
PAN-A-LITE PRODUCTS INC
1601 Ritchey St, Santa Ana (92705-5123)
PHONE..................................714 258-7111
Nina Rahe, *President*
EMP: 15
SQ FT: 3,200
SALES (est): 1.9MM **Privately Held**
SIC: 3648 Lighting equipment

(P-17153)
PANELIGHT COMPONENTS GROUP LLC
1601 Ritchey St, Santa Ana (92705-5123)
PHONE..................................714 258-7111
Nina Rahe, *Mng Member*
Richard Rahe,
EMP: 15 EST: 2000
SALES (est): 2.6MM **Privately Held**
WEB: www.panelightcomponents.com
SIC: 3648 Lighting equipment

(P-17154)
PELICAN PRODUCTS INC (PA)
23215 Early Ave, Torrance (90505-4002)
PHONE..................................310 326-4700
Lyndon J Faulkner, *CEO*
Peter Pace, *Ch of Bd*
Phil Gyori, *President*
Dave Williams, *President*
John Padian, *COO*
◆ EMP: 277
SQ FT: 150,000
SALES (est): 208.2MM **Privately Held**
WEB: www.pelican.com
SIC: 3648 3161 3089 Flashlights; lug-
　gage; plastic containers, except foam

(P-17155)
POWERLUX CORPORATION
1260 Liberty Way Ste E, Vista
(92081-8320)
PHONE..................................760 727-2360
Kenneth Lau, *President*
Theodora Lau, *Vice Pres*
Donald Maund, *Director*
EMP: 13
SQ FT: 6,000
SALES (est): 2.2MM **Privately Held**
WEB: www.powerlux.com
SIC: 3648 Lighting equipment

(P-17156)
PRIMUS LIGHTING INC
3570 Lexington Ave, El Monte
(91731-2608)
PHONE..................................626 442-4600
Jaime Calderon, *President*
EMP: 13
SQ FT: 5,300
SALES (est): 1.9MM **Privately Held**
WEB: www.primuslighting.com
SIC: 3648 Outdoor lighting equipment

(P-17157)
Q TECHNOLOGY INC
336 Lindbergh Ave, Livermore
(94551-9511)
PHONE..................................925 373-3456
Samuel S Lee, *President*
▲ EMP: 30
SQ FT: 10,000
SALES: 10MM **Privately Held**
WEB: www.qtechnology.net
SIC: 3648 Lighting equipment

(P-17158)
REMOTE OCEAN SYSTEMS INC (PA)
Also Called: R O S
5618 Copley Dr, San Diego (92111-7902)
PHONE..................................858 565-8500
Robert Acks, *CEO*
Christine Acks, *Admin Sec*
EMP: 34
SQ FT: 27,000
SALES (est): 5.5MM **Privately Held**
WEB: www.rosys.com
SIC: 3648 3861 3812 3643 Underwater
　lighting fixtures; photographic equipment
　& supplies; search & navigation equip-
　ment; current-carrying wiring devices; ve-
　hicular lighting equipment

(P-17159)
RICHEE LIGHTING INC
1600 W Washington Blvd, Los Angeles
(90007-1115)
PHONE..................................213 814-1638
James Lee, *Administration*
Angela Yi, *Admin Sec*
EMP: 10
SALES (est): 956.6K **Privately Held**
SIC: 3648 Public lighting fixtures

(P-17160)
S T E U INC
Also Called: Vista Landscape Lighting
1625 Surveyor Ave, Simi Valley
(93063-3387)
PHONE..................................805 527-0987
Dan Cunado, *President*
Phil Kerchner, *Business Dir*
Bryan Tanger, *Administration*
Ankur Vyas, *Design Engr*
Lorenzo Garcia, *Technical Staff*
▲ EMP: 30
SALES (est): 11.9MM **Privately Held**
WEB: www.vistapro.com
SIC: 3648 Decorative area lighting fixtures

(P-17161)
SHIMADA ENTERPRISES INC
Also Called: Celestial Lighting
14009 Dinard Ave, Santa Fe Springs
(90670-4922)
PHONE..................................562 802-8811
Tak Shimada, *President*
Mick Shimada, *Vice Pres*
Alex Gaxiola, *Sales Mgr*
▲ EMP: 30
SQ FT: 11,000
SALES (est): 5.6MM **Privately Held**
WEB: www.celestiallighting.com
SIC: 3648 Decorative area lighting fixtures

(P-17162)
SPIN SHADES CORPORATION
3115 Breaker Dr, Ventura (93003-1009)
PHONE..................................805 650-4849
Wendy Gayner, *President*
▲ EMP: 20

▲ = Import ▼=Export
◆ =Import/Export

SALES (est): 3MM **Privately Held**
WEB: www.spinshades.com
SIC: 3648 Lighting equipment

(P-17163)
STERIL-AIRE INC
2840 N Lima St, Burbank (91504-2506)
PHONE...........................818 565-1128
Robert Scheir, *President*
Bob Culbert, *Engineer*
Jose Barba, *Purchasing*
Tim Jones, *Plant Mgr*
Daryl Frahn, *Marketing Mgr*
◆ EMP: 23
SQ FT: 15,000
SALES (est): 5.5MM **Privately Held**
WEB: www.steril-aire-usa.com
SIC: 3648 Ultraviolet lamp fixtures

(P-17164)
SUN POWER SOURCE (PA)
1650 Palma Dr, Ventura (93003-5749)
PHONE...........................805 644-2520
Sean Frye, *President*
Tammy Frye, *Vice Pres*
EMP: 15
SQ FT: 1,850
SALES (est): 2.4MM **Privately Held**
SIC: 3648 7299 Sun tanning equipment,
incl. tanning beds; tanning salon

(P-17165)
SUREFIRE LLC
18300 Mount Baldy Cir, Fountain Valley
(92708-6122)
PHONE...........................714 545-9444
Joel Smith, *Manager*
Matt Richardson, *Engineer*
William Wells, *Engineer*
EMP: 25 **Privately Held**
SIC: 3648 Lighting equipment

(P-17166)
TEC LIGHTING INC
115 Arovista Cir, Brea (92821-3830)
PHONE...........................714 529-5068
Kamal S Hodhodc, *CEO*
David Hodhod, *President*
Paul Hebert, *COO*
Alex Platt, *Technician*
Moses Nuno, *Engineer*
◆ EMP: 15
SALES: 7.5MM **Privately Held**
WEB: www.teclighting.com
SIC: 3648 Lighting equipment

(P-17167)
TEKA ILLUMINATION INC
40429 Brickyard Dr, Madera (93636-9515)
PHONE...........................559 438-5800
Douglas W Hagen, *President*
Daniel Cravins, *Technical Staff*
EMP: 15
SQ FT: 3,000
SALES (est): 2.8MM **Privately Held**
WEB: www.tekaillumination.com
SIC: 3648 Lighting equipment

(P-17168)
THE SLOAN COMPANY INC (PA)
Also Called: Sloanled
5725 Olivas Park Dr, Ventura (93003-7697)
PHONE...........................805 676-3200
Tom Beyer, *President*
Angela Davanzo, *CFO*
Angela Delonzo, *CFO*
Kevin Stoll, *Vice Pres*
Allen Kim, *Executive*
◆ EMP: 120
SQ FT: 25,545
SALES (est): 55MM **Privately Held**
WEB: www.sloanled.com
SIC: 3648 Lighting equipment

(P-17169)
THIN-LITE CORPORATION
530 Constitution Ave, Camarillo
(93012-8595)
PHONE...........................805 987-5021
Alan Griffin, *President*
Lilian Cross Szymanek, *Co-President*
▲ EMP: 47 EST: 1970
SQ FT: 27,000

SALES (est): 7MM **Privately Held**
WEB: www.thinlite.com
SIC: 3648 3612 3646 Lighting equipment;
transformers, except electric; fluorescent
lighting fixtures, commercial

(P-17170)
TIVOLI INDUSTRIES INC
1550 E Saint Gertrude Pl, Santa Ana
(92705-5310)
PHONE...........................714 957-6101
Peter Jang, *CEO*
▲ EMP: 50
SALES: 1MM **Privately Held**
SIC: 3648 Lighting equipment

(P-17171)
TOTAL STRUCTURES INC
1696 Walter St, Ventura (93003-5619)
PHONE...........................805 676-3322
Martijn Kuijper, *President*
Danielle Magdaleno, *Office Admin*
Miguel Guillen, *Sales Executive*
Douglas Debusschere, *Sales Mgr*
◆ EMP: 32
SQ FT: 24,000
SALES (est): 14.6MM **Privately Held**
WEB: www.newwavetruss.com
SIC: 3648 3441 Lighting equipment; fabri-
cated structural metal

(P-17172)
TRULY GREEN SOLUTIONS LLC
9601 Variel Ave, Chatsworth (91311-4914)
PHONE...........................818 206-4404
Rubina Jadwet, *CEO*
Jennifer Cataffo, *Admin Asst*
Marolyn Merrell, *Regl Sales Mgr*
Blake Murphy, *Sales Staff*
Johana Romero, *Cust Mgr*
▲ EMP: 25 EST: 2010
SALES (est): 6MM **Privately Held**
SIC: 3648 Lighting equipment

(P-17173)
US POLE COMPANY INC (PA)
Also Called: U S Architectural Lighting
660 W Avenue O, Palmdale (93551-3610)
PHONE...........................800 877-6537
Joseph Straus, *President*
Gabby Castro, *Purch Agent*
Roger Rosales, *Production*
Ward Fulcher, *Sales Staff*
Javier Garcia, *Manager*
◆ EMP: 140
SQ FT: 112,000
SALES (est): 75.1MM
SALES (corp-wide): 67.6MM **Privately
Held**
WEB: www.usaltg.com
SIC: 3648 Outdoor lighting equipment

(P-17174)
V2 LIGHTING GROUP INC
276 E Gish Rd, San Jose (95112-4706)
PHONE...........................707 383-4600
Chris Varrin, *CEO*
Michelle Varrin, *Admin Sec*
Bradley Becker, *Sales Staff*
▲ EMP: 12 EST: 2010
SQ FT: 1,200
SALES (est): 2.9MM **Privately Held**
SIC: 3648 Lighting equipment

(P-17175)
VARIANT TECHNOLOGY INC
635 Hampton Rd, Arcadia (91006-2102)
PHONE...........................626 278-4343
Kamran Sarmadi, *President*
Maryam Mosallaie, *CFO*
EMP: 10
SALES: 2MM **Privately Held**
SIC: 3648 Lighting equipment

(P-17176)
VIDESSENCE LLC
10768 Lower Azusa Rd, El Monte
(91731-1306)
PHONE...........................626 579-0943
Toni Warrens, *Owner*
EMP: 20
SALES (corp-wide): 4.4MM **Privately
Held**
WEB: www.elplighting.com
SIC: 3648 Stage lighting equipment

PA: Videssence Llc
10768 Lower Azusa Rd
El Monte CA 91731
626 579-0943

(P-17177)
XENONICS HOLDINGS INC
3186 Lionshead Ave # 100, Carlsbad
(92010-4700)
PHONE...........................760 477-8900
Alan P Magerman, *Ch of Bd*
Jeffrey P Kennedy, *President*
Richard S Kay, *CFO*
EMP: 10
SQ FT: 13,200
SALES: 830K **Privately Held**
WEB: www.xenonics.com
SIC: 3648 Infrared lamp fixtures

**3651 Household Audio &
Video Eqpt**

(P-17178)
360 SYSTEMS
3281 Grande Vista Dr, Newbury Park
(91320-1193)
PHONE...........................818 991-0360
Robert Easton, *President*
Daren Francom, *Controller*
John Hall, *Sales Dir*
Brad Cox, *Cust Mgr*
EMP: 12
SQ FT: 17,000
SALES (est): 2.5MM **Privately Held**
WEB: www.360systems.com
SIC: 3651 Audio electronic systems

(P-17179)
ABCRON CORPORATION
3002 Dow Ave Ste 408, Tustin
(92780-7236)
PHONE...........................714 730-9988
Sopa Ker, *Office Mgr*
Mike Chen, *President*
▲ EMP: 12
SQ FT: 2,100
SALES: 9MM **Privately Held**
WEB: www.abcron.com
SIC: 3651 Household audio & video equip-
ment

(P-17180)
ABSOLUTE USA INC
Also Called: Absolute Pro Music
1800 E Washington Blvd, Los Angeles
(90021-3127)
PHONE...........................213 744-0044
Mohammad K Razipour, *President*
Junior Perez, *Sales Executive*
Juan Barragan, *Sales Dir*
Jesse Rosales, *Sales Staff*
◆ EMP: 47
SQ FT: 35,000
SALES (est): 12.2MM **Privately Held**
WEB: www.absoluteusa.com
SIC: 3651 Audio electronic systems

(P-17181)
ACTI CORPORATION INC
Also Called: California Acti
3 Jenner Ste 160, Irvine (92618-3834)
PHONE...........................949 753-0352
Juber Chu, *President*
Kelvin Wong, *CFO*
Dennis Eversole, *Regl Sales Mgr*
Frank Fang, *Sales Dir*
Joe Hudak, *Sales Staff*
EMP: 20
SALES (est): 3.7MM **Privately Held**
SIC: 3651 3663 3699 Household audio &
video equipment; cameras, television; se-
curity devices
PA: Acti Corporation
7f, No. 1, Alley 20, Lane 407, Tiding
Blvd., Sec. 2
Taipei City TAP 11493

(P-17182)
ACTIVEON INC (PA)
10905 Technology Pl, San Diego
(92127-1811)
PHONE...........................858 798-3300
John Lee, *CEO*

Jonathan Zupnik, *Vice Pres*
▲ EMP: 17
SALES (est): 3.5MM **Privately Held**
SIC: 3651 Household audio & video equip-
ment

(P-17183)
AEA RIBBON MICS
1029 N Allen Ave, Pasadena (91104-3202)
PHONE...........................626 798-9128
Wes Dooley, *Owner*
EMP: 12
SALES (est): 760.7K **Privately Held**
SIC: 3651 Microphones

(P-17184)
AFTER HOURS
7310 Adams St Ste F, Paramount
(90723-4043)
PHONE...........................562 925-5737
Raul Uc, *Owner*
EMP: 16
SALES (est): 1.6MM **Privately Held**
SIC: 3651 Video camera-audio recorders,
household use

(P-17185)
AL SHELLCO LLC (HQ)
9330 Scranton Rd Ste 600, San Diego
(92121-7706)
PHONE...........................570 296-6444
Mark Lucas, *Mng Member*
George Stelling, *President*
Ross Gatlin, *CEO*
Richard P Horner, *CFO*
Edward Anchel,
▲ EMP: 160
SQ FT: 120,000
SALES (est): 84.1MM
SALES (corp-wide): 863.9MM **Privately
Held**
WEB: www.alteclansing.com
SIC: 3651 3577 Radio receiving sets;
computer peripheral equipment
PA: Prophet Equity Lp
1460 Main St Ste 200
Southlake TX 76092
817 898-1500

(P-17186)
ALPHA ALARM & AUDIO INC
1400 Belden Ct, Dixon (95620-4823)
P.O. Box 911 (95620-0911)
PHONE...........................707 452-8334
Loren Dougherty, *CEO*
EMP: 14
SALES (est): 2.3MM **Privately Held**
SIC: 3651 Household audio & video equip-
ment

(P-17187)
ALURATEK INC
15241 Barranca Pkwy, Irvine (92618-2201)
PHONE...........................949 468-2046
John Wolikow, *CEO*
Akash Patel, *CFO*
Dave Song, *Vice Pres*
Andrew Wang, *Vice Pres*
Victor Wang, *Principal*
▲ EMP: 25
SQ FT: 5,000
SALES (est): 4.9MM **Privately Held**
SIC: 3651 5045 Home entertainment
equipment, electronic; audio electronic
systems; computers, peripherals & soft-
ware

(P-17188)
**ANACOM GENERAL
CORPORATION**
Also Called: Anacom Medtek
1240 S Claudina St, Anaheim
(92805-6232)
PHONE...........................714 774-8484
Daniel S Haines, *President*
William K Haines, *Chairman*
Joe Kuciera, *General Mgr*
Don Boulla, *Info Tech Mgr*
Shannon Williams, *Purch Agent*
▲ EMP: 48
SQ FT: 20,000
SALES (est): 10.9MM **Privately Held**
WEB: www.anacom-medtek.com
SIC: 3651 3577 Speaker monitors; com-
puter peripheral equipment

(P-17189)
ANCHOR AUDIO INC
5931 Darwin Ct, Carlsbad (92008-7302)
PHONE................................760 827-7100
Janet Jacobs, CEO
David Jacobs, President
Dwight Garbe, CFO
Manuel Tapia, Electrical Engi
◆ EMP: 58
SQ FT: 31,200
SALES (est): 13.6MM Privately Held
WEB: www.anchoraudio.com
SIC: 3651 Public address systems

(P-17190)
APOGEE ELECTRONICS CORPORATION
1715 Berkeley St, Santa Monica
(90404-4104)
PHONE................................310 584-9394
Betty A Bennett, CEO
Henry Lam, CFO
Hatem Nassar, Administration
▲ EMP: 35
SQ FT: 5,000
SALES (est): 7.8MM Privately Held
WEB: www.apogeedigital.com
SIC: 3651 3621 8748 Audio electronic
systems; motors & generators; communi-
cations consulting

(P-17191)
AQUATIC AV INC
282 Kinney Dr, San Jose (95112-4433)
PHONE................................408 559-1668
Robert Fils, CEO
Janet Goldstein, Treasurer
Erin Williams, General Mgr
Raylene Neves,
▲ EMP: 12 EST: 2005
SQ FT: 3,000
SALES (est): 2MM Privately Held
SIC: 3651 Audio electronic systems

(P-17192)
ARLO TECHNOLOGIES INC (PA)
3030 Orchard Pkwy, San Jose
(95134-2028)
PHONE................................408 890-3900
Matthew McRae, CEO
Ralph E Faison, Ch of Bd
Christine M Gorjanc, CFO
Patrick J Collins III, Senior VP
Brian Busse, Admin Sec
EMP: 77
SQ FT: 77,800
SALES: 464.9MM Publicly Held
SIC: 3651 7372 Household audio & video
equipment; video camera-audio
recorders, household use; application
computer software

(P-17193)
AUDEZE LLC (PA)
3410 S Susan St, Santa Ana (92704-6936)
PHONE................................714 581-8010
Alexander Rosson, CEO
Sankar Thiagasamudram, President
Mark Harper, Chief Mktg Ofcr
Mark Cohen, Vice Pres
Paul Blumhorst, Buyer
▲ EMP: 15 EST: 2012
SALES (est): 3MM Privately Held
SIC: 3651 Audio electronic systems

(P-17194)
AUDIO DYNAMIX INC
2770 S Harbor Blvd Ste D, Santa Ana
(92704-5828)
PHONE................................714 549-5100
Teresa Schmidt, President
Denise Denicola, Sls & Mktg Exec
EMP: 10
SQ FT: 3,645
SALES (est): 1.6MM Privately Held
WEB: www.audiodynamix.com
SIC: 3651 5065 Audio electronic systems;
electronic parts & equipment

(P-17195)
AUDIO FX LLC
Also Called: Audio Fx Home Theater
1415 Howe Ave, Sacramento (95825-3203)
PHONE................................916 929-2100
Chris Malone,
William Chrisman,

EMP: 11
SQ FT: 4,000
SALES (est): 1.4MM Privately Held
WEB: www.audiofx.net
SIC: 3651 5735 Household audio equip-
ment; records, audio discs & tapes

(P-17196)
AUDIONICS SYSTEM INC
21541 Nordhoff St Ste C, Chatsworth
(91311-6983)
PHONE................................818 345-9599
Khalid Jaffer, President
Sameera Khalid, Admin Sec
▲ EMP: 14
SQ FT: 6,000
SALES (est): 4.5MM Privately Held
SIC: 3651 Household audio & video equip-
ment

(P-17197)
AUERNHEIMER LABS INC
Also Called: ALC
4561 E Florence Ave, Fresno (93725-1197)
PHONE................................559 442-1048
Clarence Auernheimer, President
Dwayne Auernheimer, Corp Secy
Warren Auernheimer, Vice Pres
EMP: 11
SQ FT: 40,000
SALES (est): 1.1MM Privately Held
SIC: 3651 5169 Household audio & video
equipment; chemicals & allied products

(P-17198)
AV NOW INC
225 Technology Cir, Scotts Valley
(95066-3525)
PHONE................................831 425-2500
Robert Dehart, President
Max Duimstra, General Mgr
Ken Lyon, Opers Mgr
▲ EMP: 20
SQ FT: 2,000
SALES (est): 4.6MM Privately Held
WEB: www.avnow.com
SIC: 3651 7929 Audio electronic systems;
disc jockey service

(P-17199)
AXESS PRODUCTS CORP
9409 Owensmouth Ave, Chatsworth
(91311-6904)
PHONE................................818 785-4000
David Bakhaj, President
Danny Aghaee, COO
Kevin Hedvat, CFO
Sion Nabati,
Hector Guardado, Accounts Exec
EMP: 10
SQ FT: 20,000
SALES (est): 14MM Privately Held
SIC: 3651 Home entertainment equipment,
electronic

(P-17200)
BALTIC LTVIAN UNVRSAL ELEC LLC
Also Called: Blue Microphone
5706 Corsa Ave Ste 102, Westlake Village
(91362-4057)
PHONE................................818 879-5200
John Maier, CEO
Bart E Thielen, CFO
Thomas Andersen, Vice Pres
Henrik Brusgaard, Vice Pres
Bailey Beechler, Administration
▲ EMP: 35
SQ FT: 6,300
SALES (est): 8.2MM
SALES (corp-wide): 2.7B Privately Held
SIC: 3651 5731 Microphones; consumer
electronic equipment
PA: Logitech International S.A.
Les Chatagnis
Apples VD
218 635-511

(P-17201)
BEATS ELECTRONICS LLC (HQ)
Also Called: Beats By Dre
8600 Hayden Pl, Culver City (90232-2902)
PHONE................................424 326-4679
Timothy Cook, CEO
▲ EMP: 92

SALES (est): 135MM
SALES (corp-wide): 260.1B Publicly
Held
SIC: 3651 3679 Speaker systems; head-
phones, radio
PA: Apple Inc.
1 Apple Park Way
Cupertino CA 95014
408 996-1010

(P-17202)
BEGA SUPPLY INC
Also Called: Bega Video Supplies
1613 W 134th St Ste 3, Gardena
(90249-2036)
PHONE................................310 719-1252
Hae Won Kim, President
Charlie Kim, Vice Pres
Sung J Kim, Admin Sec
EMP: 11
SQ FT: 5,000
SALES (est): 1.2MM Privately Held
SIC: 3651 5099 2759 Video cassette
recorders/players & accessories; video
cassettes, accessories & supplies; labels
& seals: printing

(P-17203)
BELKIN INC
12045 Waterfront Dr, Playa Vista
(90094-2999)
PHONE................................800 223-5546
Chester J Pipkin, President
George Platisa, CFO
Ryan Kim, Vice Pres
Vj Nalwad, Vice Pres
Jenny Ng, Vice Pres
▲ EMP: 145
SALES (est): 47.2MM Privately Held
SIC: 3651 Electronic kits for home assem-
bly: radio, TV, phonograph

(P-17204)
BETA BOX INC
12021 Wilshire Blvd, Los Angeles
(90025-1206)
PHONE................................323 383-9820
Guy Fleming, Principal
EMP: 15
SALES (est): 1MM Privately Held
SIC: 3651 Home entertainment equipment,
electronic

(P-17205)
BIG 5 ELECTRONICS INC
Also Called: Big Five Electronics
13452 Alondra Blvd, Cerritos (90703-2315)
PHONE................................562 941-4669
Amina Bawaney, CEO
Latif Bawaney, President
Rizwan Bawaney, CFO
Carlos Ibarra, Sales Mgr
Anibal Sanchez, Sales Mgr
▲ EMP: 22
SQ FT: 4,500
SALES (est): 6.3MM Privately Held
WEB: www.big5electronics.net
SIC: 3651 5099 5065 Audio electronic
systems; video & audio equipment; elec-
tronic parts & equipment

(P-17206)
BLUE MICROPHONES LLC
5706 Corsa Ave Ste 102, Westlake Village
(91362-4057)
PHONE................................818 879-5200
Fax: 818 879-7258
EMP: 17 EST: 2008
SALES (est): 2.4MM Privately Held
SIC: 3651

(P-17207)
BOGNER AMPLIFICATION
11411 Vanowen St, North Hollywood
(91605-6219)
PHONE................................818 765-8929
Jorg Dorschner, Partner
Gregory Bayeles, Partner
Reinhold Bogner, Partner
EMP: 10
SQ FT: 5,000
SALES (est): 1.2MM Privately Held
WEB: www.bogneramplification.com
SIC: 3651 5099 Amplifiers: radio, public
address or musical instrument; musical
instruments

(P-17208)
BOOM MOVEMENT LLC
1 Viper Way Ste 3, Vista (92081-7811)
PHONE................................410 358-3600
Jim Minark, Principal
EMP: 100
SALES (est): 7MM Privately Held
SIC: 3651 Household audio equipment

(P-17209)
BRISTOL SOUNDS ELECTRONICS
Also Called: Bristol Sounds Elec Whse
2604 S Bristol St, Santa Ana (92704-5727)
PHONE................................714 549-5923
Mike Khan, Owner
▲ EMP: 14
SALES (est): 1.4MM Privately Held
SIC: 3651 5731 Sound reproducing equip-
ment; sound equipment, automotive

(P-17210)
BRITE LITE ENTERPRISES
11661 San Vicente Blvd, Los Angeles
(90049-5103)
PHONE................................310 363-7120
Arash Shamoeil, President
Ray Oribello, Senior VP
▲ EMP: 12
SALES (est): 20.2MM Privately Held
SIC: 3651 Household audio equipment

(P-17211)
CEENEE INC
683 River Oaks Pkwy, San Jose
(95134-1907)
PHONE................................408 890-5018
Kim Tran, President
Kiwi Dang, Sales Mgr
EMP: 27
SQ FT: 15,000
SALES (est): 1.7MM Privately Held
SIC: 3651 Home entertainment equipment,
electronic

(P-17212)
CLARKE PB & ASSOCIATES INC
Also Called: Pacific Accesory
2500 E Francis St, Ontario (91761-7730)
PHONE................................714 835-3022
Bob Clarke, President
▲ EMP: 25
SQ FT: 10,000
SALES (est): 3MM Privately Held
SIC: 3651 Audio electronic systems

(P-17213)
COHUHD COSTAR LLC
7330 Trade St, San Diego (92121-2456)
PHONE................................858 391-1800
Doug Means, President
James Arbuckle, Vice Pres
Phil Cutler, Vice Pres
Kris Amundson, Administration
Neil Alan, Sr Software Eng
EMP: 70
SQ FT: 26,304
SALES: 5MM
SALES (corp-wide): 19.6MM Publicly
Held
SIC: 3651 Video camera-audio recorders,
household use
PA: Costar Technologies, Inc.
101 Wrangler Dr Ste 201
Coppell TX 75019
469 635-6800

(P-17214)
COUNTRYMAN ASSOCIATES INC
195 Constitution Dr, Menlo Park
(94025-1106)
PHONE................................650 364-9988
Carl Countryman, President
William Meckfessel, CFO
Carolyn Countryman, Treasurer
Andy Davies, Engineer
▲ EMP: 17
SQ FT: 4,000
SALES (est): 2.7MM Privately Held
SIC: 3651 5065 Audio electronic systems;
electronic parts & equipment

▲ = Import ▼=Export
◆ =Import/Export

(P-17215)
COVAN SYSTEMS INC
Also Called: Covan Alarm Company
569 Leisure St, Livermore (94551-5148)
P.O. Box 4237, Manteca (95337-0004)
PHONE.................................510 226-9886
David Coon, *President*
Leilani Coon, *Vice Pres*
Timothy Coon, *Admin Sec*
EMP: 12
SQ FT: 1,500
SALES (est): 1.6MM **Privately Held**
WEB: www.covansystems.com
SIC: 3651 1731 Home entertainment
equipment, electronic; fire detection &
burglar alarm systems specialization

(P-17216)
DANA INNOVATIONS
Also Called: Sonance
991 Calle Amanecer, San Clemente
(92673-6212)
PHONE.................................949 492-7777
ARI Supran, *CEO*
Scott Struthers, *President*
Mike Simmons, *CFO*
Geoffrey L Spencer, *Corp Secy*
Rob Roland, *Exec VP*
▲ **EMP:** 59 **EST:** 1981
SQ FT: 42,320
SALES (est): 15.4MM **Privately Held**
WEB: www.sonance.com
SIC: 3651 5731 7629 Speaker systems;
radio, television & electronic stores; elec-
trical repair shops

(P-17217)
**DAVENPORT INTERNATIONAL
CORP**
7230 Coldwater Canyon Ave, North Holly-
wood (91605-4203)
P.O. Box 16539 (91615-6539)
PHONE.................................818 765-6400
Daniel Mamane, *President*
▲ **EMP:** 50
SQ FT: 50,000
SALES (est): 6.3MM **Privately Held**
SIC: 3651 7819 7812 7334 Household
audio & video equipment; reproduction
services, motion picture production; mo-
tion picture & video production; photo-
copying & duplicating services

(P-17218)
**DIGITAL PERIPH SOLUTIONS
INC**
Also Called: Q-See
160 S Old Springs Rd, Anaheim
(92808-1260)
PHONE.................................714 998-3440
Priti Sharma, *President*
Rajeev Sharma, *CFO*
Terry McConnell, *Controller*
▲ **EMP:** 40
SQ FT: 30,000
SALES (est): 21.2MM **Privately Held**
WEB: www.q-see.com
SIC: 3651 7382 Video camera-audio
recorders, household use; confinement
surveillance systems maintenance &
monitoring

(P-17219)
**DIGITAL VIDEO SYSTEMS INC
(PA)**
357 Castro St Ste 5, Mountain View
(94041-1258)
PHONE.................................650 938-8815
Mali Kuo, *Ch of Bd*
Shaun Kang, *President*
Dean Clarke Seniff, *CFO*
Delle V Vedove, *Marketing Mgr*
EMP: 40
SQ FT: 2,130
SALES (est): 14.8MM **Privately Held**
WEB: www.dvsystems.com
SIC: 3651 Household video equipment

(P-17220)
DOLBY LABORATORIES INC
Also Called: Doremi Labs
1020 Chestnut St, Burbank (91506-1623)
PHONE.................................818 562-1101
Andy Sherman, *Exec VP*
Doug Darrow, *Vice Pres*

Todd Pendleton, *Vice Pres*
Linda Rogers, *Vice Pres*
EMP: 40
SALES (corp-wide): 1.1B **Publicly Held**
SIC: 3651 Audio electronic systems
PA: Dolby Laboratories, Inc.
1275 Market St
San Francisco CA 94103
415 558-0200

(P-17221)
**DOLBY LABORATORIES INC
(PA)**
1275 Market St, San Francisco
(94103-1410)
PHONE.................................415 558-0200
Kevin Yeaman, *President*
Peter Gotcher, *Ch of Bd*
Lewis Chew, *CFO*
Todd Pendleton, *Chief Mktg Ofcr*
Andy Sherman, *Exec VP*
▲ **EMP:** 277
SALES (est): 1.1B **Publicly Held**
WEB: www.dolby.com
SIC: 3651 7819 Audio electronic systems;
laboratory service, motion picture

(P-17222)
DTS LLC
5220 Las Virgenes Rd, Calabasas
(91302-1064)
PHONE.................................818 436-1000
Jon Kirchner,
EMP: 100
SALES (est): 7.6MM
SALES (corp-wide): 406.1MM **Publicly
Held**
SIC: 3651 3845 Audio electronic systems;
audiological equipment, electromedical
HQ: Dts, Inc.
5220 Las Virgenes Rd
Calabasas CA 91302

(P-17223)
DWI ENTERPRISES
11081 Winners Cir Ste 100, Los Alamitos
(90720-2894)
PHONE.................................714 842-2236
Fred Delgleize, *President*
Amanda Delgleize, *CFO*
Dave Dain, *Vice Pres*
Dan Delgleize, *Vice Pres*
Mike Delgleize, *Vice Pres*
◆ **EMP:** 25 **EST:** 1980
SQ FT: 9,500
SALES (est): 1.9MM **Privately Held**
WEB: www.dwienterprises.com
SIC: 3651 3669 Audio electronic systems;
visual communication systems

(P-17224)
E VIRTUAL CORPORATION
Also Called: Product Virtual Gt
192 22nd St Apt D, Costa Mesa
(92627-6726)
PHONE.................................949 515-3670
Paul Stary, *President*
James McGlynn, *Partner*
John Coute, *Vice Pres*
EMP: 10
SALES: 1MM **Privately Held**
SIC: 3651 Home entertainment equipment,
electronic

(P-17225)
**ECOLINK INTELLIGENT TECH
INC**
2055 Corte Del Nogal, Carlsbad
(92011-1412)
PHONE.................................855 432-6546
Michael Lamb, *CEO*
EMP: 18
SALES (est): 2.8MM
SALES (corp-wide): 680.2MM **Publicly
Held**
SIC: 3651 Video triggers (remote control
TV devices)
PA: Universal Electronics Inc.
15147 N Scottsdale Rd
Scottsdale AZ 85254
480 530-3000

(P-17226)
EI CORP
13355 Grass Valley Ave A, Grass Valley
(95945-9521)
PHONE.................................530 274-1240
Michael Castorino, *Principal*
Syed Zaidi, *CFO*
Michael Ahmadi, *Exec VP*
EMP: 25
SQ FT: 27,000
SALES (est): 4.8MM **Privately Held**
WEB: www.eigen.com
SIC: 3651 3845 3841 Recording ma-
chines, except dictation & telephone an-
swering; electromedical equipment;
surgical & medical instruments

(P-17227)
**ELECTRONIC AUTO SYSTEMS
INC**
9855 Joe Vargas Way, South El Monte
(91733-3107)
PHONE.................................626 280-3855
Chang Ye Tong, *President*
Virginia Young, *Treasurer*
Eduardo Lo, *Exec VP*
Julio Young, *Vice Pres*
◆ **EMP:** 15
SQ FT: 9,000
SALES (est): 2MM **Privately Held**
SIC: 3651 Speaker systems

(P-17228)
ETI SOUND SYSTEMS INC
Also Called: Eti B Si Professional
3383 E Gage Ave, Huntington Park
(90255-5530)
PHONE.................................323 835-6660
Eli El-Kiss, *President*
AVI El-Kiss, *Vice Pres*
▲ **EMP:** 45
SQ FT: 73,000
SALES (est): 8.3MM **Privately Held**
WEB: www.b-52pro.com
SIC: 3651 Speaker monitors

(P-17229)
**EUREKA RECORD WORKS INC
(PA)**
Also Called: Works, The
210 C St, Eureka (95501-0339)
PHONE.................................707 442-8121
Larry Glass, *President*
EMP: 10
SQ FT: 1,200
SALES (est): 1MM **Privately Held**
SIC: 3651 Compact disk players; video
camera-audio recorders, household use;
video cassette recorders/players & acces-
sories

(P-17230)
FRESNO DISTRIBUTING CO
Also Called: Fresno D"
2055 E Mckinley Ave, Fresno (93703-2997)
P.O. Box 6078 (93703-6078)
PHONE.................................559 442-8800
Stephen Ronald Cloud, *CEO*
Mary Iness, *Corp Secy*
Ryan Cloud, *Vice Pres*
Steve Cloud Jr, *Vice Pres*
EMP: 33
SALES (est): 13.1MM **Privately Held**
WEB: www.fresnodistributing.com
SIC: 3651 3494 Home entertainment
equipment, electronic; plumbing & heating
valves

(P-17231)
**GALLIEN TECHNOLOGY INC
(PA)**
Also Called: Galliien Krueger
2234 Industrial Dr, Stockton (95206-4937)
PHONE.................................209 234-7300
Robert Gallien, *President*
Christine Simpson, *Sales Staff*
Veronica Almada,
Ricardo Almada, *Manager*
Enrique Hernandez, *Manager*
▲ **EMP:** 59
SQ FT: 21,000
SALES (est): 9.8MM **Privately Held**
WEB: www.gallien-krueger.com
SIC: 3651 Amplifiers: radio, public address
or musical instrument

(P-17232)
GILDERFLUKE & COMPANY INC
205 S Flower St, Burbank (91502-2102)
PHONE.................................818 840-9484
Douglas Mobley, *President*
Carolyn Rowley, *CFO*
Mariel Deaver, *Office Mgr*
Richard Smith, *Technician*
Sofia Vilner, *Accountant*
EMP: 10
SQ FT: 6,599
SALES (est): 1.8MM **Privately Held**
WEB: www.gilderfluke.com
SIC: 3651 7819 7999 Audio electronic
systems; sound reproducing equipment;
sound (effects & music production), mo-
tion picture; visual effects production;
tourist attractions, amusement park con-
cessions & rides

(P-17233)
GOTO CALIFORNIA INC (HQ)
Also Called: GCI
6120 Bus Ctr Ct Ste F200, San Diego
(92154)
PHONE.................................619 691-8722
Saburo Goto, *CEO*
▲ **EMP:** 200
SALES (est): 22MM **Privately Held**
WEB: www.goto-california.com
SIC: 3651 Speaker systems

(P-17234)
GUY G VERALRUD
Also Called: Vertek
10141 Evening Star Dr # 1, Grass Valley
(95945-9060)
P.O. Box 1437, Cedar Ridge (95924-1437)
PHONE.................................530 477-7323
Guy G Veralrud, *Owner*
Lee Comstock, *Manager*
EMP: 16
SQ FT: 20,000
SALES (est): 490K **Privately Held**
WEB: www.vertek.com
SIC: 3651 Household audio & video equip-
ment

(P-17235)
H&F TECHNOLOGIES INC
Also Called: Audio 2000's
650 Flinn Ave Unit 4, Moorpark
(93021-2004)
PHONE.................................805 523-2759
Haw-Renn Chen, *President*
Faye Chen, *Vice Pres*
▲ **EMP:** 10
SQ FT: 2,000
SALES (est): 2MM **Privately Held**
WEB: www.audio2000s.com
SIC: 3651 5099 Audio electronic systems;
video & audio equipment

(P-17236)
H&N BROTHERS CO LTD
Also Called: Cadence Acoustics
918 Canada Ct, City of Industry
(91748-1136)
PHONE.................................626 465-3383
Larry Nai-Ning Chen, *CEO*
Hernando Mares, *Director*
◆ **EMP:** 10
SQ FT: 4,000
SALES (est): 2.2MM **Privately Held**
SIC: 3651 5999 Audio electronic systems;
audio-visual equipment & supplies

(P-17237)
HARMAN PROFESSIONAL INC
24950 Grove View Rd, Moreno Valley
(92551-9552)
PHONE.................................951 242-2927
Clara Diaz, *Sales Staff*
EMP: 405 **Privately Held**
SIC: 3651 Household audio equipment
HQ: Harman Professional, Inc.
8500 Balboa Blvd
Northridge CA 91329
818 893-8411

PRODUCTS & SVCS

(P-17238)
HARMAN PROFESSIONAL INC (DH)
8500 Balboa Blvd, Northridge (91329-0003)
P.O. Box 2200 (91328-2200)
PHONE...................................818 893-8411
Mohit Parasher, *President*
Buzz Goodwin, *Exec VP*
Diane Ettinger, *Vice Pres*
Mark Gander, *Vice Pres*
Jeffory Grenke, *Vice Pres*
◆ EMP: 300
SALES (est): 156.8MM **Privately Held**
SIC: 3651 Audio electronic systems
HQ: Harman International Industries Incorporated
400 Atlantic St Ste 15
Stamford CT 06901
203 328-3500

(P-17239)
HDKARAOKE LLC
2400 Lincoln Ave, Altadena (91001-5436)
PHONE...................................626 296-6200
Meng Guo,
Wayne Sheng, *Manager*
▲ EMP: 12
SALES (est): 500K **Privately Held**
SIC: 3651 Home entertainment equipment, electronic

(P-17240)
HENRYS ADIO VSUAL SLUTIONS INC
Also Called: Audio Images
1582 Parkway Loop Ste F, Tustin (92780-6505)
PHONE...................................714 258-7238
Mark Ontiveros, *CEO*
Chris Kokesch, *Prgrmr*
Nathan Hesson, *Technical Staff*
EMP: 30
SQ FT: 5,400
SALES (est): 6.4MM **Privately Held**
SIC: 3651 Household audio & video equipment

(P-17241)
HILL PRODUCTS INC
19160 Arminta St, Reseda (91335-1105)
PHONE...................................818 877-9256
Jerry Hill, *President*
Kim Hill, *Corp Secy*
EMP: 10
SQ FT: 1,500
SALES (est): 666.9K **Privately Held**
SIC: 3651 Video camera-audio recorders, household use

(P-17242)
HILLO AMERICA INC
10727 7th St Ste A, Rancho Cucamonga (91730-5464)
PHONE...................................626 570-8899
Jeff Chang, *CEO*
Chengjia Wang, *President*
▲ EMP: 12
SALES: 5MM **Privately Held**
SIC: 3651 Household audio equipment

(P-17243)
HITACHI HOME ELEC AMER INC (DH)
2420 Fenton St 200, Chula Vista (91914-3516)
PHONE...................................619 591-5200
Kenji Nakamura, *CEO*
Tomomi ITOH, *President*
Tsuneo Yuki, *Treasurer*
Gary Bennett, *Exec VP*
Tatsou Hagiwara, *Exec VP*
◆ EMP: 170
SQ FT: 260,000
SALES (est): 50.2MM **Privately Held**
WEB: www.hitachiserviceusa.com
SIC: 3651 Television receiving sets; tape recorders: cassette, cartridge or reel: household use; video cassette recorders/players & accessories
HQ: Hitachi America Ltd
50 Prospect Ave
Tarrytown NY 10591
914 332-5800

(P-17244)
HPV TECHNOLOGIES INC
301 E Alton Ave, Santa Ana (92707-4418)
PHONE...................................949 476-7000
Vahan Simidian, *President*
Phillip Hamilton, *Vice Pres*
▲ EMP: 20
SQ FT: 6,250
SALES: 2MM **Privately Held**
WEB: www.hpvtech.com
SIC: 3651 Speaker systems

(P-17245)
IMATTE INC
20945 Plummer St, Chatsworth (91311-4902)
P.O. Box 1831, Simi Valley (93062-1831)
PHONE...................................818 993-8007
Paul E Vlahos, *President*
Joesph Parker, *COO*
Jay Dunn, *Manager*
EMP: 10
SALES (est): 1.4MM **Privately Held**
WEB: www.imatte.com
SIC: 3651 Audio electronic systems; video camera-audio recorders, household use

(P-17246)
ISOLATION NETWORK INC (PA)
Also Called: Ingrooves
55 Francisco St Ste 350, San Francisco (94133-2112)
PHONE...................................415 489-7000
Jay Boberg, *Ch of Bd*
Adam Hiles, *President*
Bob Roback, *CEO*
Vincent Freda, *COO*
Clifton Wong, *CFO*
EMP: 28
SQ FT: 5,000
SALES (est): 5.6MM **Privately Held**
SIC: 3651 7929 Music distribution apparatus; musical entertainers

(P-17247)
JEFF BURGESS & ASSOCIATES INC (PA)
Also Called: JB&a Distribution
1050 Northgate Dr Ste 200, San Rafael (94903-2562)
PHONE...................................415 256-2800
Jeff Burgess, *CEO*
Gregory Burgess, *President*
Nicholas Smith, *Info Tech Dir*
Jeff Briggs, *Regl Sales Mgr*
Jenny Burr, *Regl Sales Mgr*
EMP: 45
SQ FT: 10,000
SALES (est): 17.4MM **Privately Held**
WEB: www.jbanda.com
SIC: 3651 Household audio equipment

(P-17248)
JODEL ENTERPRISES
340 Gateway Dr Apt 105, Pacifica (94044-1155)
PHONE...................................650 343-4510
Josh Jodel, *Owner*
EMP: 10
SALES (est): 663.3K **Privately Held**
SIC: 3651 Audio electronic systems

(P-17249)
KAZMERE ENTERTAINMENT
400 N La Brea Ave Ste 500, Inglewood (90302-5145)
PHONE...................................323 448-9009
Shameka Peters, *Owner*
EMP: 10
SALES (est): 528.5K **Privately Held**
WEB: www.kazmereentertainment.com
SIC: 3651 Household audio & video equipment

(P-17250)
KEYFAX NEWMEDIA INC
911 Center St Ste A, Santa Cruz (95060-3831)
P.O. Box 1151, Aptos (95001-1151)
PHONE...................................831 477-1205
Julian K C Colbeck, *President*
Rachel Dean, *Opers Mgr*
EMP: 15
SALES (est): 2MM **Privately Held**
WEB: www.keyfaxnewmedia.com
SIC: 3651 Music distribution apparatus

(P-17251)
KSC INDUSTRIES INC
9771 Clairemont Mesa Blvd E, San Diego (92124-1300)
PHONE...................................619 671-0110
Jeffrey W King Jr, *President*
Bill McCarty, *President*
Malcolm Hollombe, *Vice Pres*
William McCarty, *Vice Pres*
Lisa Michaud, *Vice Pres*
▲ EMP: 25
SQ FT: 10,000
SALES (est): 4.9MM **Privately Held**
WEB: www.kscind.com
SIC: 3651 Speaker systems

(P-17252)
LRAD CORPORATION (PA)
Also Called: Genasys Inc.
16262 W Bernardo Dr, San Diego (92127-1879)
PHONE...................................858 676-1112
Richard S Danforth, *CEO*
John G Coburn, *Ch of Bd*
Dennis D Klahn, *CFO*
Simon Finburgh, *Engineer*
◆ EMP: 50
SQ FT: 31,360
SALES (est): 26.3MM **Publicly Held**
WEB: www.lradx.com
SIC: 3651 Sound reproducing equipment; speaker systems; loudspeakers, electrodynamic or magnetic

(P-17253)
LYNX STUDIO TECHNOLOGY INC
190 Mccormick Ave, Costa Mesa (92626-3307)
PHONE...................................714 545-4700
Robert J Bauman, *President*
David A Hoatson, *CFO*
Phil Moon, *Vice Pres*
EMP: 11
SQ FT: 6,400
SALES (est): 2.3MM **Privately Held**
WEB: www.lynxstudio.com
SIC: 3651 Audio electronic systems

(P-17254)
M KLEMME TECHNOLOGY CORP
Also Called: K-Tek
1384 Poinsettia Ave Ste F, Vista (92081-8505)
PHONE...................................760 727-0593
Brenda L Parker, *President*
Tino Liberatore, *Sales Staff*
▲ EMP: 12
SALES: 2.5MM **Privately Held**
SIC: 3651 Audio electronic systems

(P-17255)
MAGICO LLC
3170 Corporate Pl, Hayward (94545-3916)
PHONE...................................510 649-9700
Alon Wolf, *CEO*
Pete Maher, *CFO*
Peter Maher, *CFO*
Tuan Trinh, *CFO*
Peter Mackay, *Vice Pres*
◆ EMP: 26 EST: 1996
SQ FT: 12,000
SALES: 6.2MM **Privately Held**
WEB: www.magico.net
SIC: 3651 Speaker systems

(P-17256)
MANLEY LABORATORIES INC
13880 Magnolia Ave, Chino (91710-7027)
PHONE...................................909 627-4256
Eveanna Manley-Collins, *CEO*
Gamaliel Ibarra, *COO*
▲ EMP: 40
SQ FT: 11,000
SALES (est): 8.2MM **Privately Held**
WEB: www.manleylabs.com
SIC: 3651 3312 3663 Audio electronic systems; tool & die steel; radio & TV communications equipment

(P-17257)
MATRIX STREAM TECHNOLOGIES INC
1840 Gateway Dr Ste 200, San Mateo (94404-4029)
PHONE...................................650 292-4982
Jack Chung, *President*
Robert Liu, *Manager*
EMP: 12
SALES (est): 1.1MM **Privately Held**
WEB: www.matrixstream.com
SIC: 3651 Household audio equipment

(P-17258)
MEDIAPOINTE INC
3952 Camino Ranchero, Camarillo (93012-5066)
PHONE...................................805 480-3700
Stephen Villoria, *CEO*
EMP: 11 EST: 2011
SALES (est): 1.9MM **Privately Held**
SIC: 3651 Audio electronic systems

(P-17259)
MESA/BOOGIE LIMITED (PA)
1317 Ross St, Petaluma (94954-1124)
PHONE...................................707 765-1805
Randall Smith, *President*
Tom Waugh, *Engineer*
Jo Leach, *Controller*
Shawn Farbman, *Sales Mgr*
Bill Kelly, *Supervisor*
▲ EMP: 100 EST: 1975
SQ FT: 47,000
SALES (est): 16.4MM **Privately Held**
WEB: www.mesaboogie.com
SIC: 3651 5736 Amplifiers: radio, public address or musical instrument; musical instrument stores

(P-17260)
MEYER SOUND LABORATORIES INC (PA)
Also Called: Meyer Sound Labs
2832 San Pablo Ave, Berkeley (94702-2258)
PHONE...................................510 486-1166
John D Meyer, *President*
Brad Friedman, *CFO*
John McMahon, *Senior VP*
Helen Meyer, *Admin Sec*
Dawn Liao, *Accounting Mgr*
◆ EMP: 140 EST: 1979
SQ FT: 15,800
SALES (est): 30.1MM **Privately Held**
WEB: www.msli.com
SIC: 3651 Loudspeakers, electrodynamic or magnetic

(P-17261)
MICRONAS USA INC
560 S Winchester Blvd, San Jose (95128-2560)
PHONE...................................408 625-1200
James Mannos, *President*
Rainer Hoffmann, *President*
Frank Brooks, *CFO*
EMP: 115
SQ FT: 39,000
SALES (est): 11.3MM **Privately Held**
WEB: www.micronas.com
SIC: 3651 Household audio & video equipment

(P-17262)
MIDAS TECHNOLOGY INC
Also Called: Phoenix Audio Technologies
2552 White Rd Ste A, Irvine (92614-6272)
PHONE...................................818 937-4774
Jacob Marash, *CEO*
Joseph Marash, *Ch of Bd*
Jonathan Boaz, *Vice Pres*
Baruch Berdugo, *CTO*
Zachary Flanagan, *Manager*
▲ EMP: 24
SALES (est): 4.2MM **Privately Held**
SIC: 3651 Speaker systems

(P-17263)
MOKI INTERNATIONAL (USA) INC
21700 Oxnard St Ste 850, Woodland Hills (91367-7566)
PHONE...................................205 208-0179
Michael Smit, *CEO*

▲ = Import ▼=Export
◆ =Import/Export

EMP: 20
SALES (est): 1.1MM **Privately Held**
SIC: 3651 3678 Audio electronic systems;
  electronic connectors

(P-17264)
NADY SYSTEMS INC
3341 Vincent Rd, Pleasant Hill
(94523-4354)
PHONE..................................510 652-2411
John Nady, *President*
Joy Ferrer, *Manager*
▲ EMP: 30
SALES (est): 5.9MM **Privately Held**
WEB: www.nady.com
SIC: 3651 3669 Audio electronic systems;
  intercommunication systems, electric

(P-17265)
NCA LABORATORIES INC
Also Called: The Clearwater Company
11305 Sunrise Gold Cir D, Rancho Cordova
(95742-7213)
P.O. Box 428, Folsom (95763-0428)
PHONE..................................916 852-7029
Glenn A Stasky, *President*
▲ EMP: 17
SALES (est): 2.8MM **Privately Held**
WEB: www.clearwateraudio.com
SIC: 3651 Audio electronic systems

(P-17266)
NO STATIC PRO AUDIO INC
2070 Floyd St, Burbank (91504-3408)
PHONE..................................818 729-8554
Eugene Gordon, *President*
Adam Beck-Slaten, *Vice Pres*
Brian Peairs, *Engineer*
Dare Gaskin, *Director*
EMP: 11 EST: 1985
SALES (est): 4.1MM **Privately Held**
WEB: www.nsav.com
SIC: 3651 Audio electronic systems

(P-17267)
O W I INC
Also Called: Movits
17141 Kingsview Ave, Carson
(90746-1207)
PHONE..................................310 515-1900
Ned Morioka, *CEO*
Craig Morioka, *President*
Kristin Martinez, *Treasurer*
Joseph Martinez, *Vice Pres*
June Morioka, *Admin Sec*
▲ EMP: 13
SQ FT: 17,000
SALES (est): 3MM **Privately Held**
WEB: www.owi-inc.com
SIC: 3651 5064 3944 5099 Speaker sys-
  tems; high fidelity equipment; electronic
  toys; robots, service or novelty

(P-17268)
PARASOUND PRODUCTS INC
2250 Mckinnon Ave, San Francisco
(94124-1327)
PHONE..................................415 397-7100
Richard Schram, *President*
Jean Schram PHD, *Vice Pres*
▲ EMP: 13
SQ FT: 2,500
SALES (est): 2.2MM **Privately Held**
WEB: www.parasound.com
SIC: 3651 Audio electronic systems

(P-17269)
PASS LABORATORIES INC
13395 New Arprt Rd Ste G, Auburn
(95602)
P.O. Box 219, Foresthill (95631-0219)
PHONE..................................530 878-5350
Desmond Harrinton, *President*
Desmond Harrington, *President*
▲ EMP: 15
SQ FT: 4,000
SALES (est): 3MM **Privately Held**
SIC: 3651 Amplifiers: radio, public address
  or musical instrument

(P-17270)
PETCUBE INC (PA)
555 De Haro St Ste 280a, San Francisco
(94107-2363)
PHONE..................................424 302-6107
Iaroslav Azhniuk, *CEO*

Alexander Neskin, *CFO*
Christopher Madeiras, *Officer*
Andrii Kulbaba, *Admin Sec*
EMP: 27 EST: 2013
SALES: 8.1MM **Privately Held**
SIC: 3651 Video camera-audio recorders,
  household use

(P-17271)
PHORUS LLC
16255 Ventura Blvd # 310, Encino
(91436-2327)
PHONE..................................310 995-2521
Jon Kirchner,
Melvin Flanigan,
Sharon Graves,
Brian Towne,
▲ EMP: 14
SALES (est): 1.3MM **Privately Held**
SIC: 3651 Audio electronic systems

(P-17272)
PIONEER SPEAKERS INC (DH)
2050 W 190th St Ste 100, Torrance
(90504-6229)
PHONE..................................310 952-2000
Hiroyuki Mineta, *CEO*
Kazuo Goto, *CFO*
Makoto Takano, *Principal*
Nobuhiko Yamaguchi, *Principal*
▲ EMP: 50
SQ FT: 2,500
SALES (est): 74.3MM
SALES (corp-wide): 242.1K **Privately
Held**
WEB: www.piomsystems.com
SIC: 3651 Speaker systems

(P-17273)
PLUOT COMMUNICATIONS INC
1925 48th Ave, San Francisco
(94116-1050)
PHONE..................................202 258-9223
Kwindla Hultman Kramer, *CEO*
EMP: 10 EST: 2015
SALES: 100K **Privately Held**
SIC: 3651 7371 Household video equip-
  ment; computer software development &
  applications

(P-17274)
POLK AUDIO LLC
1 Viper Way Ste 3, Vista (92081-7811)
PHONE..................................888 267-5495
Peter Kriz, *Manager*
EMP: 50 **Privately Held**
SIC: 3651 Audio electronic systems
HQ: Polk Audio, Llc
  11500 Cronridge Dr # 110
  Owings Mills MD 21117
  410 358-3600

(P-17275)
QSC LLC (PA)
1675 Macarthur Blvd, Costa Mesa
(92626-1468)
PHONE..................................714 754-6175
Joe Pham, *President*
Jatan Shah, *COO*
Aravind Yarlagadda, *Exec VP*
Barry Ferrell, *Senior VP*
Eric Andersen, *Vice Pres*
◆ EMP: 277 EST: 1979
SQ FT: 180,000
SALES (est): 96.1MM **Privately Held**
WEB: www.qscaudio.com
SIC: 3651 Audio electronic systems

(P-17276)
RENKUS-HEINZ INC
19201 Cook St, Foothill Ranch
(92610-3501)
PHONE..................................949 588-9997
Harro Heinz, *President*
Roscoe L Anthony III, *CEO*
Erika Heinz, *Admin Sec*
Gregg Lewis, *Technician*
Kk Tan, *Engineer*
▲ EMP: 80
SQ FT: 48,500
SALES (est): 20.3MM **Privately Held**
WEB: www.renkus-heinz.com
SIC: 3651 Audio electronic systems

(P-17277)
**ROCK-OLA MANUFACTURING
CORP**
Also Called: Antique Apparatus Company
2335 W 208th St, Torrance (90501-1443)
PHONE..................................310 328-1306
Glenn S Streeter, *President*
▲ EMP: 80
SQ FT: 60,000
SALES (est): 13.8MM **Privately Held**
SIC: 3651 Coin-operated phonographs,
  juke boxes; speaker systems

(P-17278)
RODE MICROPHONES LLC
2745 Raymond Ave, Signal Hill
(90755-2129)
P.O. Box 91028, Long Beach (90809-1028)
PHONE..................................310 328-7456
Mark Ludmer, *CEO*
Peter Freedmon, *President*
Brian Swbaringen, *District Mgr*
▲ EMP: 140
SALES (est): 18.8MM **Privately Held**
WEB: www.rodemicrophones.com
SIC: 3651 Microphones
HQ: Freedman Electronics Pty Ltd
  107 Carnarvon St
  Silverwater NSW 2128

(P-17279)
S2E INC
Also Called: Mee Audio
817 Lawson St, City of Industry
(91748-1104)
PHONE..................................626 965-1008
Martie Shieh, *President*
Jerry Shieh, *Vice Pres*
Jones Mike, *Mktg Dir*
▲ EMP: 15
SQ FT: 7,000
SALES (est): 2.9MM **Privately Held**
SIC: 3651 Household audio & video equip-
  ment

(P-17280)
SARGAM INTERNATIONAL INC
Also Called: Agent 18
719 Huntley Dr, West Hollywood
(90069-5043)
PHONE..................................310 855-9694
Sargam Patel, *President*
▲ EMP: 11
SALES (est): 1.8MM **Privately Held**
SIC: 3651 Audio electronic systems

(P-17281)
SCOSCHE INDUSTRIES INC
1550 Pacific Ave, Oxnard (93033-2451)
P.O. Box 2901 (93034-2901)
PHONE..................................805 486-4450
Roger Alves, *CEO*
Steven R Klinger, *CFO*
Steven Klinger, *CFO*
Kasidy Alves, *Exec VP*
Vincent Alves, *Exec VP*
▲ EMP: 150
SQ FT: 83,000
SALES: 150MM **Privately Held**
WEB: www.scosche.com
SIC: 3651 Audio electronic systems

(P-17282)
SIGMATRONIX INC
2109 S Susan St, Santa Ana (92704-4416)
PHONE..................................714 436-1618
Michael Dang, *President*
EMP: 15
SQ FT: 5,600
SALES: 1MM **Privately Held**
WEB: www.sigmatronix.com
SIC: 3651 Electronic kits for home assem-
  bly: radio, TV, phonograph

(P-17283)
SONOS INC (PA)
614 Chapala St, Santa Barbara
(93101-3312)
PHONE..................................805 965-3001
Patrick Spence, *President*
Kristen Dailey, *Partner*
Michelangelo Volpi, *Ch of Bd*
David Perri, *COO*
Brittany Bagley, *CFO*
◆ EMP: 91

SQ FT: 33,280
SALES: 1.1B **Publicly Held**
WEB: www.sonos.com
SIC: 3651 Household audio & video equip-
  ment

(P-17284)
SONY ELECTRONICS INC (DH)
16535 Via Esprillo Bldg 1, San Diego
(92127-1738)
PHONE..................................858 942-2400
Phil Molyneux, *President*
Hideki Komiyama, *Ch of Bd*
Charles Gregory, *President*
Neal Manowitz, *President*
Rintaro Miyoshi, *CFO*
◆ EMP: 1000 EST: 1960
SALES (est): 3.5B **Privately Held**
WEB: news.sel.sony.com/en
SIC: 3651 5064 3695 3671 Household
  audio & video equipment; television receiving sets; radio receiving sets; tape
  recorders: cassette, cartridge or reel:
  household use; electrical appliances, television & radio; television sets; radios;
  video cassette recorders & accessories;
  video recording tape, blank; audio range
  tape, blank; television tubes; computer
  tape drives & components; semiconductors & related devices
HQ: Sony Corporation Of America
  25 Madison Ave Fl 27
  New York NY 10010
  212 833-8000

(P-17285)
SONY ELECTRONICS INC
Also Called: Sony Style
16530 Via Esprillo, San Diego
(92127-1708)
PHONE..................................858 942-2400
Bill Lunger, *Principal*
Bao Gore, *Info Tech Mgr*
Luxi Choi, *Technical Staff*
Kirk Steinhauff, *Engineer*
Brad Stephenson, *Engineer*
EMP: 159 **Privately Held**
SIC: 3651 Household audio & video equip-
  ment
HQ: Sony Electronics Inc.
  16535 Via Esprillo Bldg 1
  San Diego CA 92127
  858 942-2400

(P-17286)
**SOUND STORM LABORATORY
LLC**
3451 Lunar Ct, Oxnard (93030-8976)
PHONE..................................805 983-8008
Nasrin Rouhani,
Cameron Arbani,
▲ EMP: 50
SQ FT: 72,000
SALES (est): 4.8MM **Privately Held**
SIC: 3651 5731 Audio electronic systems;
  radio, television & electronic stores

(P-17287)
SOUNDVIEW APPLICATIONS INC
2390 Lindbergh St Ste 101, Auburn
(95602-9529)
PHONE..................................530 888-7593
Robert Lazor, *President*
EMP: 10
SALES (est): 850K **Privately Held**
WEB: www.svatech.com
SIC: 3651 Microphones

(P-17288)
**TECHNICOLOR THOMSON
GROUP**
Also Called: Thompson Multimedia
3233 Mission Oaks Blvd, Camarillo
(93012-5097)
PHONE..................................805 445-7652
Marjorie Martinez, *Human Resources*
EMP: 2000
SALES (corp-wide): 62.9MM **Privately
Held**
WEB: www.technicolor.com
SIC: 3651 3652 Household video equip-
  ment; pre-recorded records & tapes
HQ: Technicolor Thomson Group, Inc
  2233 N Ontario St Ste 300
  Burbank CA 91504
  818 260-3600

PRODUCTS & SVCS

(P-17289)
TECHNICOLOR USA INC
Also Called: Technicolor Connected USA
4049 Industrial Pkwy Dr, Lebec
(93243-9719)
PHONE.............................661 496-1309
EMP: 143
SALES (corp-wide): 62.9MM **Privately Held**
SIC: 3651 Household audio & video equipment
HQ: Technicolor Usa, Inc.
101 W 103rd St
Indianapolis IN 46290
317 587-4287

(P-17290)
TECHNICOLOR USA INC
1507 Railroad St, Glendale (91204-2774)
PHONE.............................818 500-9090
EMP: 143
SALES (corp-wide): 82MM **Privately Held**
SIC: 3651
HQ: Technicolor Usa, Inc.
4 Research Way
Princeton NJ 46290
317 587-3000

(P-17291)
TECHNICOLOR USA INC
Also Called: Technicolor Content Services
440 W Los Feliz Rd, Glendale
(91204-2776)
PHONE.............................818 260-3651
EMP: 143
SALES (corp-wide): 115.5MM **Privately Held**
SIC: 3651 3861 3661
HQ: Technicolor Usa, Inc.
101 W 103rd St
Indianapolis IN 46290
317 587-3000

(P-17292)
TELEVIC US CORP
4620 Northgate Blvd # 120, Sacramento
(95834-1124)
PHONE.............................916 920-0900
Danneels Lieven, CEO
Thomas Verstraeten, President
EMP: 11
SQ FT: 6,029
SALES: 1.7MM
SALES (corp-wide): 41.8MM **Privately Held**
SIC: 3651 Audio electronic systems
PA: Televic Rail
Leo Bekaertlaan 1
Izegem 8870
513 030-45

(P-17293)
THETA DIGITAL CORPORATION
1749 Chapin Rd, Montebello (90640-6609)
PHONE.............................818 572-4300
Neil Sinclair, President
▲ EMP: 21
SQ FT: 12,000
SALES (est): 3.3MM **Privately Held**
WEB: www.thetadigital.com
SIC: 3651 5731 Audio electronic systems;
radio, television & electronic stores

(P-17294)
**TOSHIBA AMERICA
ELECTRONIC (DH)**
5231 California Ave, Irvine (92617-3073)
PHONE.............................949 462-7700
Hideya Yamaguchi, CEO
Hitoshi Otsuka, President
Ichiro Hirata, Exec VP
Farhad Mafie, Vice Pres
Richard Tobias, Vice Pres
◆ EMP: 300
SQ FT: 100,000
SALES (est): 3B **Privately Held**
SIC: 3651 3631 3674 3679 Television receiving sets; video cassette recorders/players & accessories; microwave ovens, including portable: household; semiconductors & related devices; electronic circuits; electronic parts & equipment; video cassette recorders & accessories; high fidelity equipment

HQ: Toshiba America Inc
1251 Ave Of Ameri
New York NY 10020
212 596-0600

(P-17295)
**TR THEATER RESEARCH INC
(PA)**
Also Called: Dogg Digital
11150 Hope St, Cypress (90630-5236)
PHONE.............................714 894-5888
Glenn Smith, President
▲ EMP: 12
SQ FT: 15,000
SALES: 10.5MM **Privately Held**
WEB: www.dcssound.com
SIC: 3651 5099 Speaker systems; video & audio equipment

(P-17296)
ULTIMATE GAME CHAIR INC
5089 Lone Tree Way, Antioch
(94531-8016)
PHONE.............................925 756-6944
Jamie Duran, CEO
Richard Florez, CEO
▲ EMP: 25
SQ FT: 3,000
SALES: 12MM **Privately Held**
WEB: www.ultimategamechair.com
SIC: 3651 Home entertainment equipment, electronic

(P-17297)
ULTIMATE SOUND INC
1200 S Diamond Bar Blvd # 200, Diamond
Bar (91765-2298)
PHONE.............................909 861-6200
Robert Chiu, President
Cindy Chiu, Vice Pres
▼ EMP: 300
SQ FT: 20,000
SALES (est): 10.3MM **Privately Held**
WEB: www.ultimate-sound.com
SIC: 3651 5731 Loudspeakers, electrodynamic or magnetic; amplifiers: radio, public address or musical instrument; radio, television & electronic stores

(P-17298)
UME VOICE INC
Also Called: Theboom Headsets
1435 Technology Ln Ste B4, Petaluma
(94954-7615)
PHONE.............................707 939-8607
Adithya Padala, President
Jane Neve, Sales Staff
▲ EMP: 13
SQ FT: 2,000
SALES (est): 2.1MM **Privately Held**
WEB: www.umevoice.com
SIC: 3651 Microphones

(P-17299)
VANDERSTEEN AUDIO INC
116 W 4th St, Hanford (93230-5021)
PHONE.............................559 582-0324
Richard J Vandersteen, President
Eneke Vandersteen, Principal
▲ EMP: 21 EST: 1977
SQ FT: 20,000
SALES: 2MM **Privately Held**
SIC: 3651 5731 Speaker systems; radio, television & electronic stores

(P-17300)
**VANTAGE POINT PRODUCTS
CORP (PA)**
Also Called: Vpt Direct
9115 Dice Rd Ste 18, Santa Fe Springs
(90670-2538)
P.O. Box 2485 (90670-0485)
PHONE.............................562 946-1718
Donald R Burns, CEO
Mick Mulcahey, President
Glenn Hamilton, Design Engr
Prabir Chaudhury, Technical Staff
Jing Gayoba, QC Mgr
▲ EMP: 60
SQ FT: 62,000
SALES (est): 10.3MM **Privately Held**
WEB: www.vanptc.com
SIC: 3651 Audio electronic systems

(P-17301)
VELODYNE ACOUSTICS INC
345 Digital Dr, Morgan Hill (95037-2878)
PHONE.............................408 465-2800
David Hall, CEO
Joseph B Culkin, Shareholder
Vincent C Hall, Shareholder
Bruce Hall, President
Michael Jellen, President
▲ EMP: 70
SQ FT: 48,000
SALES (est): 28.8MM **Privately Held**
WEB: www.velodyne.com
SIC: 3651 5731 Speaker systems; radio, television & electronic stores

(P-17302)
VIBES AUDIO LLC
Also Called: Vibes Modular
36 Argonaut Ste 140, Aliso Viejo
(92656-1467)
PHONE.............................866 866-8484
Shane Wilder,
Charles Wilder,
EMP: 12 EST: 2016
SQ FT: 40,068
SALES (est): 649.3K **Privately Held**
SIC: 3651 Audio electronic systems

(P-17303)
VIZIO INC (PA)
39 Tesla, Irvine (92618-4603)
PHONE.............................855 833-3221
William Wang, CEO
Ken Lowe, President
Franky Lo, Vice Pres
Mark Nelson, Vice Pres
Jessica Lin, Executive Asst
◆ EMP: 154
SQ FT: 27,300
SALES (est): 91.8MM **Privately Held**
SIC: 3651 Television receiving sets; compact disk players

(P-17304)
VTL AMPLIFIERS INC
4774 Murietta St Ste 10, Chino
(91710-5155)
PHONE.............................909 627-5944
Luke Manley, President
▲ EMP: 24
SQ FT: 6,000
SALES (est): 3.6MM **Privately Held**
SIC: 3651 Audio electronic systems

(P-17305)
WINNOV INC
3945 Freedom Cir Ste 560, Santa Clara
(95054-1269)
PHONE.............................888 315-9460
Olivier Garbe, CEO
EMP: 16
SALES (est): 3.2MM **Privately Held**
WEB: www.winnov.com
SIC: 3651 Household audio & video equipment

(P-17306)
WIRELESS TECHNOLOGY INC
Also Called: Wti
2064 Eastman Ave Ste 113, Ventura
(93003-7787)
PHONE.............................805 339-9696
Phil Fancher, CEO
Arlene Fancher, CFO
Eric Myers, Executive
David Scales, CIO
Dale Roche, Engineer
EMP: 30
SQ FT: 7,000
SALES: 10.7MM **Privately Held**
SIC: 3651 Household audio & video equipment

(P-17307)
WYRED 4 SOUND LLC
4235 Traffic Way, Atascadero (93422-3002)
PHONE.............................805 466-9973
Ej Sarmento, Mng Member
Clint Hartman,
▲ EMP: 11
SALES (est): 1.9MM **Privately Held**
SIC: 3651 Audio electronic systems

(P-17308)
ZAOLLA
6650 Caballero Blvd, Buena Park
(90620-1132)
PHONE.............................714 736-9270
Sho Sato, Owner
EMP: 30
SALES (est): 2.5MM **Privately Held**
WEB: www.zaolla.com
SIC: 3651 Audio electronic systems

(P-17309)
ZED AUDIO CORPORATION
2624 Lavery Ct Ste 203, Newbury Park
(91320-1500)
PHONE.............................805 499-5559
Stephen Mantz, President
Joyce Mantz, Corp Secy
▲ EMP: 10
SALES (est): 1.4MM **Privately Held**
WEB: www.zedaudiocorp.com
SIC: 3651 Audio electronic systems

**3652 Phonograph Records
& Magnetic Tape**

(P-17310)
AUDIO PARTNERS PUBLISHING
131 E Placer St, Auburn (95603-5241)
PHONE.............................530 888-7803
Linda D Olsen, President
Grady Hesters, CEO
EMP: 10
SQ FT: 6,000
SALES (est): 1MM **Privately Held**
WEB: www.audiopartners.com
SIC: 3652 Pre-recorded records & tapes

(P-17311)
C M H RECORDS INC
Also Called: Dwell Records
2898 Rowena Ave Ste 201, Los Angeles
(90039-2096)
P.O. Box 39439 (90039-0439)
PHONE.............................323 663-8098
David Haerle, President
EMP: 20
SQ FT: 3,303
SALES (est): 2.7MM **Privately Held**
WEB: www.cmhrecords.com
SIC: 3652 7929 Phonograph records, prerecorded; entertainers & entertainment groups

(P-17312)
**CAV DISTRIBUTING
CORPORATION**
Also Called: California Audio Video Distrg
389 Oyster Point Blvd # 6, South San Francisco (94080-1951)
PHONE.............................650 588-2228
Stanford Martin, President
Jay Douglas, Vice Pres
Alex Alexzander, Director
◆ EMP: 13
SALES (est): 2.7MM **Privately Held**
WEB: www.cavd.com
SIC: 3652 5099 Compact laser discs, prerecorded; video & audio equipment

(P-17313)
**CORD INTRNATIONAL/HANA
OLA REC**
1874 Terrace Dr, Ventura (93001-2351)
P.O. Box 152 (93002-0152)
PHONE.............................805 648-7881
Michael Cord, Owner
EMP: 12
SQ FT: 6,000
SALES: 2MM **Privately Held**
WEB: www.cordinternational.com
SIC: 3652 Pre-recorded records & tapes

(P-17314)
DICARLO CONCRETE INC
8657 Pecan Ave Ste 100, Rancho Cucamonga (91739-9465)
PHONE.............................909 261-4294
Mario Dicarlo, President
EMP: 12
SQ FT: 10,000

SALES (est): 3.6MM **Privately Held**
SIC: 3652 Master records or tapes, preparation of

(P-17315)
DISC REPLICATOR INC
21137 Commerce Point Dr, Walnut
(91789-3054)
PHONE..................909 385-0118
Jingtao Xie, *CEO*
Amelyn Binagy, *Manager*
EMP: 15
SALES (est): 1.8MM **Privately Held**
SIC: 3652 Compact laser discs, prerecorded

(P-17316)
DISCOPYLABS (PA)
Also Called: Dcl
48641 Milmont Dr, Fremont (94538-7354)
PHONE..................510 651-5100
Norman Tu, *CEO*
David Tu, *President*
Antonia Tu, *Corp Secy*
Swapna Doddapaneni, *Software Dev*
Vikhar Baquer, *Human Resources*
▲ EMP: 50
SQ FT: 300,000
SALES (est): 28.7MM **Privately Held**
WEB: www.dclcorp.com
SIC: 3652 4225 7379 7389 Pre-recorded records & tapes; general warehousing & storage; ; ; materials mgmt. (purchasing, handling, inventory) consultant

(P-17317)
DISCOPYLABS
4455 E Philadelphia St, Ontario
(91761-2329)
PHONE..................909 390-3800
Larry Shaker, *Director*
Mannix De Leon, *General Mgr*
Stephanie Moya, *Accounts Mgr*
EMP: 81
SALES (corp-wide): 28.7MM **Privately Held**
WEB: www.dclcorp.com
SIC: 3652 4225 7379 7389 Pre-recorded records & tapes; general warehousing & storage; ; ; materials mgmt. (purchasing, handling, inventory) consultant
PA: Discopylabs
48641 Milmont Dr
Fremont CA 94538
510 651-5100

(P-17318)
ENAS MEDIA INC
1316 Michillinda Ave, Arcadia
(91006-1921)
PHONE..................626 962-1115
Nagapet Keshishian, *President*
Avetis Keshishian, *Vice Pres*
Serop Keshishian, *Vice Pres*
Nick Keshian, *Mfg Staff*
EMP: 34
SALES (est): 5.1MM **Privately Held**
SIC: 3652 Phonograph records, prerecorded

(P-17319)
ERIKA RECORDS INC
6300 Caballero Blvd, Buena Park
(90620-1126)
PHONE..................714 228-5420
Liz Dunster, *President*
Erzsebet Dunster, *CEO*
▲ EMP: 20
SALES (est): 3.9MM **Privately Held**
WEB: www.erikarecords.com
SIC: 3652 5735 Phonograph records, prerecorded; compact laser discs, prerecorded; records

(P-17320)
EXTREME GROUP HOLDINGS LLC
Also Called: Extreme Production Music
1531 14th St, Santa Monica (90404-3302)
PHONE..................310 899-3200
Emanuel Russell, *Branch Mgr*
EMP: 20 **Privately Held**
WEB: www.extrememusic.com
SIC: 3652 Pre-recorded records & tapes

HQ: Extreme Group Holdings Llc
25 Madison Ave Fl 19
New York NY 10010

(P-17321)
FANTASY INC
Also Called: Contemporary Records
2600 10th St Ste 100, Berkeley
(94710-2512)
PHONE..................510 486-2038
Saul Zaentz, *Ch of Bd*
Ralph Kaffel, *President*
Frank Noonan, *Treasurer*
Albert M Bendich, *Admin Sec*
Jesse Nichols, *Engineer*
EMP: 100
SQ FT: 40,000
SALES (est): 10.7MM **Privately Held**
SIC: 3652 2741 7389 Pre-recorded records & tapes; music book & sheet music publishing; recording studio, non-commercial records

(P-17322)
FAT WRECK CHORDS INC
2196 Palou Ave, San Francisco
(94124-1503)
PHONE..................415 284-1790
Michael Burkett, *President*
▲ EMP: 14
SALES (est): 1.3MM **Privately Held**
SIC: 3652 Master records or tapes, preparation of

(P-17323)
GC INTERNATIONAL INC (PA)
Also Called: Alj
4671 Calle Carga, Camarillo (93012-8560)
PHONE..................805 389-4631
Richard R Carlson, *President*
F Willard Griffith, *CEO*
Terry Carlson, *Vice Pres*
Mark R Griffith, *Vice Pres*
Marilyn Good, *Controller*
▼ EMP: 43
SQ FT: 45,000
SALES: 7MM **Publicly Held**
WEB: www.aljcast.com
SIC: 3652 3365 3695 3369 Phonograph record blanks; aluminum & aluminum-based alloy castings; magnetic & optical recording media; nonferrous foundries; mechanical rubber goods

(P-17324)
GC INTERNATIONAL INC
Also Called: Al Johnson Company
4671 Calle Carga, Camarillo (93012-8560)
PHONE..................805 389-4631
Mark Griffith, *Principal*
Ricardo Garcia, *Opers Mgr*
EMP: 43
SALES (corp-wide): 7MM **Publicly Held**
SIC: 3652 3369 Phonograph record blanks; lead, zinc & white metal
PA: Gc International, Inc.
4671 Calle Carga
Camarillo CA 93012
805 389-4631

(P-17325)
GOSPEL RECORDINGS INC
41823 Enterprise Cir N, Temecula
(92590-5681)
PHONE..................951 719-1650
Colin Stott, *Exec Dir*
Mac Timm, *President*
Ralph Loper, *CFO*
Bill Cornthwaite, *Vice Pres*
Dale Rickards, *Exec Dir*
EMP: 35 EST: 1943
SQ FT: 20,000
SALES: 1.4MM **Privately Held**
WEB: www.grnusa.net
SIC: 3652 Pre-recorded records & tapes

(P-17326)
GRAND MOTIF RECORDS
Also Called: Monopoly Music
8304 Enramada Ave, Whittier
(90605-1207)
PHONE..................562 698-8538
David Esterson, *Owner*
EMP: 11

SALES (est): 955.3K **Privately Held**
SIC: 3652 Pre-recorded records & tapes

(P-17327)
HOLLYWOOD RECORDS INC
500 S Buena Vista St, Burbank
(91521-0002)
PHONE..................818 560-5670
Abbey Konowitch, *General Mgr*
EMP: 50
SALES (est): 6.1MM
SALES (corp-wide): 90.2B **Publicly Held**
SIC: 3652 Pre-recorded records & tapes
HQ: Walt Disney Company
500 S Buena Vista St
Burbank CA 91521
818 560-1000

(P-17328)
INSIGHT MANAGEMENT CORPORATION (PA)
1130 E Clark Ave, Santa Maria
(93455-5178)
PHONE..................866 787-3588
Kevin Jasper, *CEO*
EMP: 50
SALES (est): 3.2MM **Privately Held**
SIC: 3652 Pre-recorded records & tapes

(P-17329)
INTERNATIONAL DISC MFR INC
Also Called: IDM
4906 W 1st St, Santa Ana (92703-3110)
PHONE..................714 210-1780
Thoai Tang, *President*
Tri Tang, *Vice Pres*
EMP: 25
SQ FT: 50,000
SALES (est): 3.6MM **Privately Held**
WEB: www.idmdvd.com
SIC: 3652 Compact laser discs, prerecorded

(P-17330)
ISOMEDIA LLC
41380 Christy St, Fremont (94538-3115)
PHONE..................510 668-1656
Howard Xu,
Scott Krouskup, *Sales Staff*
Bob Beck, *Manager*
▲ EMP: 25
SQ FT: 15,000
SALES: 2.2MM **Privately Held**
WEB: www.isoptix.com
SIC: 3652 Compact laser discs, prerecorded

(P-17331)
MASTERING LAB INC
911 Bryant Pl, Ojai (93023-3321)
PHONE..................805 640-2900
EMP: 10
SQ FT: 2,000
SALES (est): 850K **Privately Held**
WEB: www.masteringlab.com
SIC: 3652

(P-17332)
NUTRITION RESOURCE CONNECTION
Also Called: Exxel Media
254 May Ct, Cardiff By The Sea
(92007-2411)
PHONE..................760 803-8234
Carol Venditti, *President*
EMP: 10
SALES (est): 960K **Privately Held**
SIC: 3652 Pre-recorded records & tapes

(P-17333)
PIRATES PRESS INC
1260 Powell St, Emeryville (94608-2641)
PHONE..................415 738-2268
Eric Mueller, *President*
Ian Clark, *Merchandising*
Damon Beebe, *Sales Staff*
EMP: 17
SALES: 10MM **Privately Held**
SIC: 3652 7384 Phonograph record blanks; film developing & printing

(P-17334)
PRECISE MEDIA SERVICES INC
Also Called: Precise-Full Service Media
888 Vintage Ave, Ontario (91764-5392)
PHONE..................909 481-3305
Choy Tim Lee, *CEO*
Robert Miller, *President*
▲ EMP: 25
SQ FT: 112,000
SALES (est): 5.4MM **Privately Held**
SIC: 3652 7819 Pre-recorded records & tapes; video tape or disk reproduction

(P-17335)
RAINBO RECORD MFG CORP (PA)
Also Called: Rainbo Records & Cassettes
8960 Eton Ave, Canoga Park (91304-1621)
PHONE..................818 280-1100
Jack Brown, *Principal*
Kandra Anderson, *Accounts Mgr*
▲ EMP: 150
SQ FT: 50,000
SALES (est): 45.7MM **Privately Held**
WEB: www.rainborecords.com
SIC: 3652 5099 Compact laser discs, pre-recorded; compact discs

(P-17336)
RECORD TECHNOLOGY INC
486 Dawson Dr Ste 4s, Camarillo
(93012-8049)
PHONE..................805 484-2747
Don Mac Innis, *President*
Melodie Innis, *Vice Pres*
Melodie Mac Innis, *Vice Pres*
Sharon Waldron, *Admin Asst*
Rick Hoshamoto, *Plant Mgr*
▲ EMP: 28 EST: 1972
SQ FT: 30,000
SALES (est): 5.2MM **Privately Held**
WEB: www.recordtech.com
SIC: 3652 Master records or tapes, preparation of; phonograph record blanks; compact laser discs, prerecorded

(P-17337)
SONY ELECTRONICS INC
Also Called: Sony Network Studios Division
5510 Morehouse Dr Ste 100, San Diego
(92121-3721)
PHONE..................858 824-6960
Komei Kataoka, *Director*
James Wong, *Supervisor*
EMP: 20 **Privately Held**
SIC: 3652 Pre-recorded records & tapes
HQ: Sony Electronics Inc.
16535 Via Esprillo Bldg 1
San Diego CA 92127
858 942-2400

(P-17338)
UNIQUE MEDIA INC
2991 Corvin Dr, Santa Clara (95051-0705)
PHONE..................408 733-9999
Champion Chen, *President*
▲ EMP: 10
SQ FT: 2,000
SALES (est): 1.6MM **Privately Held**
WEB: www.unimediainc.com
SIC: 3652 Pre-recorded records & tapes

(P-17339)
WARNER MUSIC GROUP CORP
3300 Warner Blvd, Burbank (91505-4632)
PHONE..................818 846-9090
Todd Moscowitz, *Branch Mgr*
Rubino Talia, *Manager*
EMP: 13 **Privately Held**
SIC: 3652 Pre-recorded records & tapes
HQ: Warner Music Group Corp.
1633 Broadway Fl 11
New York NY 10019
212 275-2000

(P-17340)
WARNER MUSIC INC
3400 W Riverside Dr # 900, Burbank
(91505-4669)
PHONE..................818 953-2600
David Archambault, *Technology*
James Theodoulou, *Manager*
EMP: 60 **Privately Held**
SIC: 3652 Pre-recorded records & tapes

P R O D U C T S & S V C S

HQ: Warner Music Inc.
1633 Broadway Fl 11
New York NY 10019
-

3661 Telephone & Telegraph Apparatus

(P-17341)
ADAPS PHOTONICS INC
97 E Brokaw Rd, San Jose (95112-1031)
PHONE...................................650 521-6390
EMP: 12
SALES (corp-wide): 1MM Privately Held
SIC: 3661 Fiber optics communications equipment
PA: Adaps Photonics Inc
252 Corral Ave
Sunnyvale CA 94086
650 521-3925

(P-17342)
AEI COMMUNICATIONS CORP
1001 Broadway Ste 2d, Millbrae (94030-1977)
PHONE...................................650 552-9416
Mario Jauryegui, CEO
Mario Jauregui, CTO
Peter Chen, Engineer
Abel Soria, Manager
▲ EMP: 20
SALES (est): 2.5MM Privately Held
SIC: 3661 Telephones & telephone apparatus

(P-17343)
ALCATEL-LUCENT USA INC
30971a San Benito St, Hayward (94544-7936)
PHONE...................................510 475-5000
EMP: 25
SALES (corp-wide): 27.3B Privately Held
SIC: 3661
HQ: Nokia Of America Corporation
600 Mountain Ave Ste 700
New Providence NJ 07974

(P-17344)
ALCATEL-LUCENT USA INC
26801 Agoura Rd, Calabasas (91301-5122)
PHONE...................................818 880-3500
Menandro Canelo, Executive
Arun Dhakne, Software Engr
Rishi Bhaskar, Research
Pierre Chaume, Sales Dir
EMP: 23
SALES (corp-wide): 25.8B Privately Held
WEB: www.rfsworld.com
SIC: 3661 Telephone & telegraph apparatus
HQ: Nokia Of America Corporation
600 Mountain Ave Ste 700
New Providence NJ 07974

(P-17345)
ALSTON TASCOM INC
5171 Edison Ave Ste C, Chino (91710-5758)
PHONE...................................909 517-3660
Wayne Scaggs, President
Maxine Sage, Accountant
Joanne Scaggs, Marketing Mgr
EMP: 20
SQ FT: 7,500
SALES (est): 3.2MM Privately Held
WEB: www.alstontascom.com
SIC: 3661 Telephones & telephone apparatus

(P-17346)
ALTIGEN COMMUNICATIONS INC
670 N Mccarthy Blvd, Milpitas (95035-5119)
PHONE...................................408 597-9000
Jeremiah J Fleming, President
Philip M McDermott, CFO
Simon Chouldjian, Vice Pres
Mike Plumer, Vice Pres
Shirley Sun, Vice Pres
▲ EMP: 115

SQ FT: 27,576
SALES (est): 20.2MM Privately Held
SIC: 3661 1731 Telephone & telegraph apparatus; communications specialization

(P-17347)
ANDA NETWORKS INC (PA)
1100 La Avenida St Ste A, Mountain View (94043-1453)
PHONE...................................408 519-4900
Charles R Kenmore, President
Wufu Chen, Ch of Bd
Tracy Tang, Principal
EMP: 18
SQ FT: 102,291
SALES (est): 8.4MM Privately Held
WEB: www.andanetworks.com
SIC: 3661 Telephone & telegraph apparatus

(P-17348)
AYANTRA INC
47873 Fremont Blvd, Fremont (94538-6506)
PHONE...................................510 623-7526
Ashok Teckchandani, President
Harbans Rattia, Vice Pres
Dornadula Kailasnath, VP Engrg
Albert Calpito, Technical Staff
▲ EMP: 15
SQ FT: 2,300
SALES (est): 2.6MM Privately Held
WEB: www.ayantra.com
SIC: 3661 Telephone & telegraph apparatus

(P-17349)
BALAJI TRADING INC
Also Called: City of Industry
4850 Eucalyptus Ave, Chino (91710-9255)
PHONE...................................909 444-7999
Mukesh Batta, CEO
Batta Rohit, Senior Mgr
▲ EMP: 91
SALES (est): 14MM Privately Held
SIC: 3661 Headsets, telephone; telephone cords, jacks, adapters, etc.

(P-17350)
BLACK POINT PRODUCTS INC
2700 Rydin Rd Ste G, Richmond (94804-5800)
P.O. Box 70074 (94807-0074)
PHONE...................................510 232-7723
Thomas Tognetti, President
Karin M Ashford, Vice Pres
▲ EMP: 30
SALES (est): 3.6MM Privately Held
WEB: www.blkpoint.com
SIC: 3661 3651 Telephones & telephone apparatus; video cassette recorders/players & accessories

(P-17351)
CALIENT TECHNOLOGIES INC (PA)
25 Castilian Dr, Goleta (93117-3026)
PHONE...................................805 562-5500
Atiq Raza, CEO
Saiyed Atiq Raza, CEO
Jag Setlur, COO
Kevin Welsh, Senior VP
Erik Leonard, Vice Pres
▲ EMP: 30 EST: 1999
SQ FT: 150,000
SALES (est): 46.4MM Privately Held
WEB: www.calient.net
SIC: 3661 Fiber optics communications equipment

(P-17352)
CALMAR OPTCOM INC
Also Called: Calmar Laser
951 Commercial St, Palo Alto (94303-4908)
PHONE...................................408 733-7800
Anthony Lin, President
Sha Tong, Director
EMP: 20
SQ FT: 7,000
SALES (est): 3.5MM Privately Held
WEB: www.calmaropt.com
SIC: 3661 3699 Fiber optics communications equipment; pulse amplifiers; laser systems & equipment

(P-17353)
CELLSCOPE INC
5537 Claremont Ave Apt 1, Oakland (94618-1151)
PHONE...................................510 282-0674
Erik Scott Douglas, CEO
Phil Henson, Engineer
EMP: 11
SALES (est): 1.3MM Privately Held
SIC: 3661 Telephones & telephone apparatus

(P-17354)
CHANNELL COMMERCIAL CORP (PA)
33380 Ziders Rd, Temecula (92591)
P.O. Box 9022 (92589-9022)
PHONE...................................951 719-2600
William H Channell Jr, CEO
Jacqueline M Channell, Ch of Bd
Guy E Marge, President
Michael Perica, Treasurer
Ray Pawley, Vice Pres
◆ EMP: 100
SQ FT: 210,000
SALES (est): 68.6MM Privately Held
WEB: www.channellcomm.com
SIC: 3661 3663 3088 3083 Telephone & telegraph apparatus; television broadcasting & communications equipment; plastics plumbing fixtures; laminated plastics plate & sheet; thermoplastic laminates: rods, tubes, plates & sheet

(P-17355)
COADNA PHOTONICS INC (HQ)
1012 Stewart Dr, Sunnyvale (94085-3914)
PHONE...................................408 736-1100
Jim Yuan, CEO
Fang Wang, COO
Irene Yum, CFO
Jack Kelly, Vice Pres
▲ EMP: 60
SQ FT: 12,000
SALES (est): 9.4MM
SALES (corp-wide): 1.3B Publicly Held
SIC: 3661 Fiber optics communications equipment
PA: Ii-Vi Incorporated
375 Saxonburg Blvd
Saxonburg PA 16056
724 352-4455

(P-17356)
COASTAL CONNECTIONS
2085 Sperry Ave Ste B, Ventura (93003-7452)
PHONE...................................805 644-5051
Andy Devine, President
Nancy Devine, Treasurer
Marisol Diaz, Project Mgr
Duane Smeckert, Director
◆ EMP: 34
SQ FT: 9,000
SALES (est): 3.9MM Privately Held
SIC: 3661 Fiber optics communications equipment

(P-17357)
DANTEL INC
4210 N Brawley Ave 108, Fresno (93722-3979)
PHONE...................................559 292-1111
Alan J Brown, Chairman
Alan G Hutcheson, CEO
Frank Martinez, Vice Pres
Paul Wright, CTO
Ifty Husain, Research
EMP: 23
SALES (est): 5MM Privately Held
WEB: www.dantel.com
SIC: 3661 Telephones & telephone apparatus

(P-17358)
DARE TECHNOLOGIES INC (HQ)
674 Via De La Valle # 100, Solana Beach (92075-3407)
PHONE...................................714 634-5900
Xinyue Huang, CEO
Xinkang Chen, Chairman
Liyao LI, Senior VP
EMP: 13

SALES (est): 928.8K
SALES (corp-wide): 66.4MM Privately Held
WEB: www.usdare.com
SIC: 3661 5021 5023 5085 Fiber optics communications equipment; household furniture; office furniture; floor coverings; bearings, bushings, wheels & gears; packaging materials; computers, peripherals & software
PA: Shanghai Dareglobal Technologies Co., Ltd.
Block B, Floor 1, No.1555, Kongjiang Rd.
Shanghai 20009
216 563-5566

(P-17359)
DASAN ZHONE SOLUTIONS INC (HQ)
Also Called: DZS
7195 Oakport St, Oakland (94621-1947)
PHONE...................................510 777-7000
IL Yung Kim, President
Min Woo Nam, Ch of Bd
Philip Yim, COO
Seonggyun Kim, Bd of Directors
Anthony Contos, Vice Pres
◆ EMP: 167 EST: 1997
SALES: 282.3MM Publicly Held
WEB: www.tellium.com
SIC: 3661 4813 Fiber optics communications equipment;

(P-17360)
DIALOGIC INC
2890 Zanker Rd Ste 107, San Jose (95134-2118)
PHONE...................................800 755-4444
Jim Alpaugh, Planning
Jamie Colwill, Software Engr
Huw Carpenter, Engineer
EMP: 82
SALES (corp-wide): 449.4K Privately Held
SIC: 3661 3577 7371 Telephone & telegraph apparatus; data conversion equipment, media-to-media: computer; computer software development & applications
HQ: Dialogic Inc.
4 Gatehall Dr Ste 9
Parsippany NJ 07054
973 967-6000

(P-17361)
DITECH NETWORKS INC (HQ)
3099 N 1st St, San Jose (95134-2006)
PHONE...................................408 883-3636
Thomas L Beaudoin, President
Paul A Ricci, CEO
William Tamblyn, Vice Pres
EMP: 29
SQ FT: 20,100
SALES (est): 7.7MM Publicly Held
WEB: www.ditechcom.com
SIC: 3661 Telephones & telephone apparatus

(P-17362)
DYNAMETRIC INC
1715 Business Center Dr, Duarte (91010-2860)
PHONE...................................626 358-2559
Alan Morse, CEO
EMP: 10 EST: 1958
SQ FT: 8,500
SALES: 1MM Privately Held
WEB: www.dynametric.com
SIC: 3661 Telephones & telephone apparatus

(P-17363)
EARLY BIRD ALERT INC
70 Mitchell Blvd Ste 106, San Rafael (94903-2019)
PHONE...................................415 479-7902
Andrew Kluger, CEO
MI Kosasa, Treasurer
Gen Ronald Blank, Vice Pres
Michael Pecht PHD, Vice Pres
Patrick Souter, Admin Sec
EMP: 11
SALES (est): 1.4MM Privately Held
SIC: 3661 Telephone & telegraph apparatus

▲ = Import ▼=Export
◆ =Import/Export

(P-17364)
ENABLENCE USA COMPONENTS INC
2933 Bayview Dr, Fremont (94538-6520)
PHONE.....................................510 226-8900
Evan Chen, *CEO*
Andy Spector, *Surgery Dir*
Jacob Sun, *Principal*
Peter Sung, *Finance Dir*
Fang Wang, *Sales Staff*
EMP: 98
SQ FT: 26,000
SALES (est): 17.1MM
SALES (corp-wide): 3.3MM **Privately Held**
WEB: www.andevices.com
SIC: **3661** Fiber optics communications equipment
PA: Enablence Technologies Inc
390 March Rd Suite 119
Kanata ON K2K 0
613 656-2850

(P-17365)
ENGAGE COMMUNICATION INC (PA)
9565 Soquel Dr Ste 201, Aptos (95003-4155)
PHONE.....................................831 688-1021
Mark Doyle, *President*
Edmund Doyle, *Ch of Bd*
Skip Norton, *VP Bus Dvlpt*
Chris Copus, *Administration*
Shaun Tomaszewski, *Sr Software Eng*
EMP: 24
SQ FT: 3,000
SALES (est): 3.8MM **Privately Held**
WEB: www.engageinc.com
SIC: **3661** Modems

(P-17366)
EPIC TECHNOLOGIES LLC (HQ)
Also Called: Natel Engineering
9340 Owensmouth Ave, Chatsworth (91311-6915)
PHONE.....................................701 426-2192
Bhawnesh Mathur, *Mng Member*
Robert T Howard,
Jochen Lipp,
John J Sammut,
Marcus Wedner,
▲ EMP: 200
SQ FT: 52,000
SALES (est): 656.1MM
SALES (corp-wide): 1.1B **Privately Held**
SIC: **3661** 3577 3679 Telephone & telegraph apparatus; computer peripheral equipment; electronic circuits
PA: Natel Engineering Company, Llc
9340 Owensmouth Ave
Chatsworth CA 91311
818 495-8617

(P-17367)
EXTREME NETWORKS INC (PA)
6480 Via Del Oro, San Jose (95119-1208)
PHONE.....................................408 579-2800
Edward B Meyercord, *President*
Robert Gault, *Risk Mgmt Dir*
Julian Critchlow, *General Mgr*
◆ EMP: 400
SQ FT: 185,000
SALES: 995.7MM **Publicly Held**
WEB: www.extremenetworks.com
SIC: **3661** 7373 7372 Telephone & telegraph apparatus; computer integrated systems design; systems integration services; prepackaged software

(P-17368)
FERMINICS OPTO-TECHNOLOGY CORP
4555 Runway St, Simi Valley (93063-3586)
PHONE.....................................805 582-0155
Ock-KY Kim, *President*
Larry Perillo, *Corp Secy*
Lawrence Perillo, *Vice Pres*
EMP: 12
SQ FT: 23,000
SALES: 3MM **Privately Held**
WEB: www.fermionics.com
SIC: **3661** Telegraph & related apparatus

(P-17369)
FIBER SYSTEMS INC
380 Encinal St Ste 150, Santa Cruz (95060-2183)
PHONE.....................................831 430-0700
Mitchell K Hutchison, *President*
▲ EMP: 21
SQ FT: 3,000
SALES (est): 3.1MM **Privately Held**
WEB: www.fibersys.com
SIC: **3661** Fiber optics communications equipment

(P-17370)
FIBERSENSE & SIGNALS INC
4423 Fortran Ct Ste 111, San Jose (95134-2323)
PHONE.....................................408 941-1900
Joan Davies, *President*
EMP: 15
SALES (est): 1.5MM **Privately Held**
WEB: www.fibersensefirst.com
SIC: **3661** Fiber optics communications equipment

(P-17371)
FINISAR CORPORATION (HQ)
1389 Moffett Park Dr, Sunnyvale (94089-1134)
PHONE.....................................408 548-1000
▲ EMP: 24
SQ FT: 92,000
SALES: 1.2B
SALES (corp-wide): 1.3B **Publicly Held**
WEB: www.finisar.com
SIC: **3661** 3663 Fiber optics communications equipment; antennas, transmitting & communications; receiver-transmitter units (transceiver)
PA: Ii-Vi Incorporated
375 Saxonburg Blvd
Saxonburg PA 16056
724 352-4455

(P-17372)
FONEGEAR LLC
14726 Ramona Ave Ste 208, Chino (91710-5730)
PHONE.....................................909 627-7999
Hong Lip Yow,
▲ EMP: 15
SALES (est): 3.5MM **Privately Held**
WEB: www.fonegear.com
SIC: **3661** Carrier equipment, telephone or telegraph

(P-17373)
FRANKLIN WIRELESS CORP
9707 Waples St Ste 150, San Diego (92121-2954)
PHONE.....................................858 623-0000
Oc Kim, *President*
Gary Nelson, *Ch of Bd*
Yun J Lee, *COO*
Anna Jung, *Executive*
Chris Baldwin, *Program Mgr*
▲ EMP: 76 EST: 1982
SQ FT: 12,775
SALES: 36.4MM **Privately Held**
WEB: www.franklin-wireless.com
SIC: **3661** Modems

(P-17374)
GENERAL PHOTONICS CORP
14351 Pipeline Ave, Chino (91710-5642)
PHONE.....................................909 590-5473
Steve Yao, *President*
▲ EMP: 50
SQ FT: 20,000
SALES (est): 3.1MM
SALES (corp-wide): 42.9MM **Publicly Held**
WEB: www.generalphotonics.com
SIC: **3661** Fiber optics communications equipment
HQ: Luna Technologies, Inc.
301 1st St Sw Ste 200
Roanoke VA 24011
540 769-8400

(P-17375)
GRASS VALLEY USA LLC (HQ)
125 Crown Point Ct, Grass Valley (95945-9515)
P.O. Box 599000, Nevada City (95959-7900)
PHONE.....................................800 547-8949
Marco Lopez, *President*
Amit Eshet, *Vice Pres*
Steve Stubelt, *Vice Pres*
Jared Timmins, *Vice Pres*
Kc Najarian, *Executive*
▲ EMP: 300
SALES (est): 214.9MM
SALES (corp-wide): 2.5B **Publicly Held**
SIC: **3661** 3999 3651 3663 Telephone sets, all types except cellular radio; ; television receiving sets; radio & TV communications equipment
PA: Belden Inc.
1 N Brentwood Blvd Fl 15
Saint Louis MO 63105
314 854-8000

(P-17376)
GREENBERG TELEPRMPT
868 N Main St, Orange (92868-1108)
PHONE.....................................714 633-1111
EMP: 16
SALES (corp-wide): 286.2K **Privately Held**
SIC: **3661** Telephone dialing devices, automatic
PA: Greenberg Teleprmpt
1431 Truman St
San Fernando CA 91340
818 838-4437

(P-17377)
GT SAPPHIRE SYSTEMS GROUP LLC
1911 Airport Blvd, Santa Rosa (95403-1001)
PHONE.....................................707 571-1911
Raja Bal, *CFO*
Dan Squiller, *COO*
David W Keck, *Exec VP*
Dr PS Raghavan, *CTO*
Thomas Gutierrez,
EMP: 24
SALES (est): 314.5K **Privately Held**
SIC: **3661** 3845 Telephone dialing devices, automatic; telephone sets, all types except cellular radio; electromedical equipment; electromedical apparatus
PA: Gt Advanced Technologies Inc.
5 Wentworth Dr Ste 1
Hudson NH 03051

(P-17378)
HOTRONIC INC
1875 Winchester Blvd # 100, Campbell (95008-1168)
PHONE.....................................408 378-3883
Andy Ho, *President*
EMP: 25
SQ FT: 841
SALES (est): 4.4MM **Privately Held**
WEB: www.hotronic.com
SIC: **3661** Carrier equipment, telephone or telegraph

(P-17379)
INFINERA CORPORATION (PA)
140 Caspian Ct, Sunnyvale (94089-1000)
PHONE.....................................408 572-5200
Thomas J Fallon, *CEO*
Kambiz Y Hooshmand, *Ch of Bd*
David W Heard, *COO*
Nancy Erba, *CFO*
▼ EMP: 450
SQ FT: 321,000
SALES: 943.3MM **Publicly Held**
SIC: **3661** 7372 Fiber optics communications equipment; prepackaged software

(P-17380)
INSIEME NETWORKS LLC
210 W Tasman Dr Bldg F, San Jose (95134-1714)
PHONE.....................................408 424-1227
Luca Cafiero, *Principal*
Phuong Than, *Office Mgr*
EMP: 13 EST: 2012

SALES (est): 1.7MM
SALES (corp-wide): 51.9B **Publicly Held**
SIC: **3661** Telephone & telegraph apparatus
PA: Cisco Systems, Inc.
170 W Tasman Dr
San Jose CA 95134
408 526-4000

(P-17381)
INTERNTNAL CNNCTORS CABLE CORP
Also Called: I C C
2100 E Valencia Dr Ste D, Fullerton (92831-4811)
PHONE.....................................888 275-4422
Mike Lin, *President*
Eugene Chyun Tsai, *Shareholder*
Chuck Dodson, *Opers Staff*
▲ EMP: 110
SQ FT: 38,720
SALES (est): 20.5MM **Privately Held**
WEB: www.cat6.com
SIC: **3661** 5065 Telephone & telegraph apparatus; telephone & telegraphic equipment; communication equipment

(P-17382)
INTERNTNAL VIRTUAL PDT MGT INC
Also Called: I V P
8957 De Soto Ave, Canoga Park (91304-5901)
PHONE.....................................818 812-9500
Sergey Tishkin, *CEO*
EMP: 11
SQ FT: 1,200
SALES (est): 2.2MM
SALES (corp-wide): 123.2MM **Privately Held**
SIC: **3661** 2813 Autotransformers for telephone switchboards; oxygen, compressed or liquefied
HQ: Ivp Group Germany Gmbh
Gewerbestr. 3
Buchenbach 79256
766 190-160

(P-17383)
K S TELECOM INC
2350 Humphrey Rd, Penryn (95663-9500)
P.O. Box 330 (95663-0330)
PHONE.....................................916 652-4735
Kent Vander Linden, *President*
Suzan Vander Linden, *CFO*
Eric V Linden, *General Mgr*
Ian V Linden, *General Mgr*
Tammy Kirby, *Office Mgr*
EMP: 10 EST: 1995
SALES: 1MM **Privately Held**
WEB: www.kstelecom.com
SIC: **3661** Fiber optics communications equipment

(P-17384)
LG-ERICSSON USA INC
20 Mason, Irvine (92618-2706)
PHONE.....................................877 828-2673
Seok B Mun, *President*
Pierre Kerbage, *Vice Pres*
Jack Weaver, *Admin Sec*
Bernd Hesse, *Director*
◆ EMP: 47
SQ FT: 22,000
SALES (est): 5.4MM
SALES (corp-wide): 23.4B **Privately Held**
WEB: www.lgericssonus.com
SIC: **3661** 5065 Telephone sets, all types except cellular radio; modems, computer
HQ: Ericsson-Lg Co., Ltd.
382 Gangnam-Daero, Gangnam-Gu
Seoul 06232

(P-17385)
LYNX PHTNIC NTWORKS A DEL CORP
6303 Owensmouth Ave Fl 10, Woodland Hills (91367-2262)
PHONE.....................................818 878-7500
EMP: 13 EST: 1998
SQ FT: 30,000
SALES (est): 1.7MM **Privately Held**
WEB: www.lynxpn.com
SIC: **3661**

(P-17386)
METROPHONES UNLIMITED INC
15675 La Jolla Ct, Morgan Hill
(95037-5679)
PHONE..................................650 630-5400
Gregg James, *CEO*
EMP: 28
SALES (est): 3.4MM **Privately Held**
SIC: 3661 Telephone sets, all types except
cellular radio

(P-17387)
MYNTAHL CORPORATION
Also Called: East Electronics
48273 Lakeview Blvd, Fremont
(94538-6519)
PHONE..................................510 413-0002
Tingyi Xu, *CEO*
▲ EMP: 30
SQ FT: 7,000
SALES (est): 6MM **Privately Held**
WEB: www.myntahl.com
SIC: 3661 Communication headgear, tele-
phone

(P-17388)
NANOMETER TECHNOLOGIES INC
2985 Theatre Dr Ste 3, Paso Robles
(93446-4500)
PHONE..................................805 226-7332
Mike Buzzetti, *President*
Mike Mowrey, *Vice Pres*
Terri Bonnema, *Admin Sec*
▲ EMP: 10
SQ FT: 10,000
SALES (est): 1.2MM **Privately Held**
WEB: www.nanometer.com
SIC: 3661 3679 3827 Fiber optics com-
munications equipment; attenuators; opti-
cal instruments & lenses

(P-17389)
NETGEAR INC (PA)
350 E Plumeria Dr, San Jose (95134-1911)
PHONE..................................408 907-8000
Patrick C S Lo, *Ch of Bd*
Ralph Faison, *Bd of Directors*
Andrew W Kim, *Senior VP*
Tamesa T Rogers, *Senior VP*
Michael A Werdann, *Senior VP*
◆ EMP: 130
SQ FT: 142,700
SALES: 1B **Publicly Held**
WEB: www.netgear.com
SIC: 3661 3577 Modems; carrier equip-
ment, telephone or telegraph; computer
peripheral equipment

(P-17390)
NOKIA OF AMERICA CORPORATION
Also Called: Alcatel-Lucent USA
5390 Hellyer Ave, San Jose (95138-1003)
PHONE..................................408 363-5906
EMP: 13
SALES (corp-wide): 27.3B **Privately Held**
SIC: 3661
HQ: Nokia Of America Corporation
600 Mountain Ave Ste 700
New Providence NJ 07974

(P-17391)
NOKIA SLUTIONS NETWORKS US LLC
701 E Middlefield Rd, Mountain View
(94043-4079)
PHONE..................................650 623-2767
Thomas Biggs, *Branch Mgr*
EMP: 16
SALES (corp-wide): 25.8B **Privately Held**
SIC: 3661 Telephone & telegraph appara-
tus
HQ: Nokia Solutions And Networks Us Llc
6000 Connection Dr
Irving TX 75039

(P-17392)
OCCAM NETWORKS INC (HQ)
6868 Cortona Dr, Santa Barbara
(93117-1360)
PHONE..................................805 692-2900
Carl Russo, *CEO*

Michael Ashby, *Exec VP*
EMP: 23 EST: 1996
SQ FT: 51,000
SALES (est): 11.5MM
SALES (corp-wide): 441.3MM **Publicly
Held**
WEB: www.acceleratednetworks.com
SIC: 3661 Carrier equipment, telephone or
telegraph
PA: Calix, Inc.
2777 Orchard Pkwy
San Jose CA 95134
408 514-3000

(P-17393)
OCLARO (NORTH AMERICA) INC (DH)
252 Charcot Ave, San Jose (95131)
PHONE..................................408 383-1400
Jerry Turin, *CEO*
Pete Mangan, *CEO*
Paul Jiang, *Senior VP*
Kate Rundle, *Admin Sec*
EMP: 433 EST: 2000
SQ FT: 54,000
SALES (est): 38MM
SALES (corp-wide): 1.5B **Publicly Held**
WEB: www.avanex.com
SIC: 3661 Fiber optics communications
equipment
HQ: Oclaro, Inc.
400 N Mccarthy Blvd
Milpitas CA 95035
408 383-1400

(P-17394)
OCLARO SUBSYSTEMS INC
400 N Mccarthy Blvd, Milpitas
(95035-5112)
PHONE..................................408 383-1400
Jerry Turin, *CEO*
Bob Barron, *Partner*
Shri Dodani, *President*
Bruce D Horn, *CFO*
John Ralston, *Vice Pres*
▲ EMP: 200 EST: 2008
SALES (est): 36.2MM
SALES (corp-wide): 1.5B **Publicly Held**
WEB: www.stratalight.com
SIC: 3661 Fiber optics communications
equipment
HQ: Oclaro Fiber Optics, Inc.
400 N Mccarthy Blvd
Milpitas CA 95035
408 383-1400

(P-17395)
OCLARO TECHNOLOGY INC (DH)
400 N Mccarthy Blvd, Milpitas
(95035-5112)
PHONE..................................408 383-1400
Greg Dougherty, *CEO*
Jim Haynes, *President*
Terry Unter, *COO*
Pete Mangan, *CFO*
Adam Carter, *Officer*
EMP: 74
SALES (est): 55.9MM
SALES (corp-wide): 1.5B **Publicly Held**
WEB: www.bookham.com
SIC: 3661 Fiber optics communications
equipment
HQ: Oclaro, Inc.
400 N Mccarthy Blvd
Milpitas CA 95035
408 383-1400

(P-17396)
OPTICAL ZONU CORPORATION
7510 Hazeltine Ave, Van Nuys
(91405-1419)
PHONE..................................818 780-9701
Meir Bartur, *President*
Frazad Ghadooshay, *Vice Pres*
Hoang Bui, *Engineer*
John Rice, *Engineer*
Hanoch Eldar, *VP Opers*
▲ EMP: 18
SALES (est): 4.2MM **Privately Held**
WEB: www.zonu.com
SIC: 3661 Fiber optics communications
equipment

(P-17397)
OPTOPLEX CORPORATION (PA)
48500 Kato Rd, Fremont (94538-7338)
PHONE..................................510 490-9930
James C Sha, *President*
Dar-Yuan Song, *Exec VP*
Vincent Chien, *Vice Pres*
Emily Wang, *Office Mgr*
Yung-Chieh Hsieh, *CTO*
EMP: 69 EST: 2000
SQ FT: 16,000
SALES (est): 44.5MM **Privately Held**
WEB: www.optoplex.com
SIC: 3661 7361 3827 Fiber optics com-
munications equipment; employment
agencies; optical instruments & lenses

(P-17398)
PLANTRONICS INC (PA)
345 Encinal St, Santa Cruz (95060-2146)
PHONE..................................831 426-5858
Joe Burton, *President*
Robert Hagerty, *Ch of Bd*
Charles Boynton, *CFO*
Pamela Strayer, *CFO*
Marv Tseu, *Vice Ch Bd*
▲ EMP: 277
SQ FT: 183,653
SALES: 1.6B **Publicly Held**
WEB: www.plantronics.com
SIC: 3661 3679 Telephones & telephone
apparatus; headsets, telephone; tele-
phone sets, all types except cellular radio;
headphones, radio

(P-17399)
PLANTRONICS INC
Also Called: Plantronics BV
1470 Expo Way Ste 130, San Diego
(92154)
PHONE..................................831 458-7089
Jesus Barrera, *Branch Mgr*
Kevin Blank, *Credit Staff*
Elvira Oregel, *Buyer*
EMP: 16
SALES (corp-wide): 1.6B **Publicly Held**
SIC: 3661 Telephone & telegraph appara-
tus
PA: Plantronics, Inc.
345 Encinal St
Santa Cruz CA 95060
831 426-5858

(P-17400)
PLANTRONICS INC
Also Called: Plantronics BV
345 Encinal St, Santa Cruz (95060-2146)
P.O. Box 635 (95061-0635)
PHONE..................................831 426-5858
Robert Cecil, *President*
EMP: 34
SALES (corp-wide): 1.6B **Publicly Held**
SIC: 3661 Telephone & telegraph appara-
tus
PA: Plantronics, Inc.
345 Encinal St
Santa Cruz CA 95060
831 426-5858

(P-17401)
POLYCOM INC
25212 S Schulte Rd, Tracy (95377-9703)
PHONE..................................209 830-5083
Wendy Wam, *Branch Mgr*
EMP: 38
SALES (corp-wide): 1.6B **Publicly Held**
WEB: www.polycom.com
SIC: 3661 Telephones & telephone appara-
tus
HQ: Polycom, Inc.
345 Encinal St
Santa Cruz CA 95060
831 426-5858

(P-17402)
POLYCOM INC
3553 N 1st St, San Jose (95134-1803)
PHONE..................................408 526-9000
Michael Kourey, *Branch Mgr*
Valerie Hardy, *Executive*
Jennifer Valencia, *Executive Asst*
Randy Clinton, *Sr Software Eng*
Wendi Byres, *Project Mgr*
EMP: 38

SALES (corp-wide): 1.6B **Publicly Held**
WEB: www.polycom.com
SIC: 3661 Telephones & telephone appara-
tus
HQ: Polycom, Inc.
345 Encinal St
Santa Cruz CA 95060
831 426-5858

(P-17403)
POLYCOM INC (HQ)
345 Encinal St, Santa Cruz (95060-2132)
PHONE..................................831 426-5858
Joe Burton, *President*
Julie Azzarello, *Partner*
Marco Landi, *President*
Chuck Boynton, *CFO*
Amy Barzdukas, *Chief Mktg Ofcr*
▲ EMP: 277
SALES (est): 800.7MM
SALES (corp-wide): 1.6B **Publicly Held**
WEB: www.polycom.com
SIC: 3661 Telephones & telephone
apparatus; headphones, radio
PA: Plantronics, Inc.
345 Encinal St
Santa Cruz CA 95060
831 426-5858

(P-17404)
QUAKE GLOBAL INC (PA)
4711 Vewridge Ave Ste 150, San Diego
(92123)
PHONE..................................858 277-7290
George Lingenbrink, *Chairman*
Polina Braunstein, *President*
William Ater, *CFO*
Michael Geffroy, *Vice Pres*
James Miller, *Vice Pres*
▲ EMP: 77
SQ FT: 8,700
SALES (est): 17.6MM **Privately Held**
WEB: www.quakeglobal.com
SIC: 3661 Modems

(P-17405)
QUINTRON SYSTEMS INC (PA)
2105 S Blosser Rd, Santa Maria
(93458-7300)
PHONE..................................805 928-4343
James E Mc Glothlin, *CEO*
David Wilhite, *President*
Sharon Lewis, *CFO*
Elton L Hammers, *Treasurer*
Juan Gonzalez, *Project Mgr*
EMP: 70
SQ FT: 20,000
SALES (est): 15.1MM **Privately Held**
WEB: www.quintron.com
SIC: 3661 1731 Telephone & telegraph
apparatus; telephone & telephone equip-
ment installation

(P-17406)
RADICOM RESEARCH INC (PA)
671 E Brokaw Rd, San Jose (95112-1005)
PHONE..................................408 383-9006
Ming Hsieh, *President*
▲ EMP: 10
SQ FT: 5,000
SALES (est): 1.6MM **Privately Held**
WEB: www.radi.com
SIC: 3661 8732 Modems; research serv-
ices, except laboratory

(P-17407)
RAYMAR INFORMATION TECH INC (PA)
Also Called: Computer Exchange, The
7325 Roseville Rd, Sacramento
(95842-1600)
PHONE..................................916 783-1951
Donald L Breidenbach, *CEO*
Corinna Gross, *Technology*
EMP: 14
SALES (est): 6.3MM **Privately Held**
WEB: www.raymarinc.com
SIC: 3661 5045 Telephone & telegraph
apparatus; computers

(P-17408)
RAYSPAN CORPORATION
1493 Poinsettia Ave # 139, Vista
(92081-8544)
PHONE..................................858 259-9596
EMP: 13

▲ = Import ▼=Export
◆ =Import/Export

SALES (est): 1.6MM **Privately Held**
SIC: **3661**

(P-17409)
RLH INDUSTRIES INC (PA)
936 N Main St, Orange (92867-5403)
PHONE..................................714 532-1672
James B Harris, *CEO*
Thomas Vo, *Vice Pres*
Tim Harris, *General Mgr*
Carol E Harris, *Admin Sec*
Randall Mears, *VP Engrg*
▲ EMP: 40
SQ FT: 16,000
SALES: 8MM **Privately Held**
WEB: www.fiberopticlink.com
SIC: **3661** 5065 5999 Telephone & telegraph apparatus; communication equipment; telephone equipment & systems

(P-17410)
SIEMENS HLTHCARE DGNOSTICS INC
Also Called: Siemens Medical Systems
725 Potter St, Berkeley (94710-2722)
P.O. Box 2466 (94702-0466)
PHONE..................................510 982-4000
Jan Turczyn, *Principal*
Maria Silveira, *Mfg Staff*
EMP: 13
SALES (corp-wide): 95B **Privately Held**
WEB: www.dpcweb.com
SIC: **3661** Telephones & telephone apparatus
HQ: Siemens Healthcare Diagnostics Inc.
511 Benedict Ave
Tarrytown NY 10591
914 631-8000

(P-17411)
SOLONICS INC (PA)
31082 San Antonio St, Hayward (94544-7904)
PHONE..................................650 589-9798
Eddy Lee, *President*
▲ EMP: 10
SQ FT: 15,000
SALES (est): 1MM **Privately Held**
WEB: www.solonics.com
SIC: **3661** Telephone & telegraph apparatus

(P-17412)
SONANT CORPORATION
6215 Ferris Sq Ste 220, San Diego (92121-3251)
PHONE..................................858 623-8180
Charles W Smith, *President*
James B Reeg, *CFO*
Jack A Buell Jr, *Vice Pres*
Murray S Judy, *Vice Pres*
EMP: 15
SQ FT: 7,000
SALES (est): 2.1MM **Privately Held**
WEB: www.sonant.com
SIC: **3661** Computer software development & applications; systems software development services

(P-17413)
SORRENTO NETWORKS CORPORATION (DH)
7195 Oakport St, Oakland (94621-1947)
PHONE..................................510 577-1400
Phillip W Arneson, *President*
Joe R Armstrong, *CFO*
Richard L Jacobson, *Senior VP*
EMP: 18
SQ FT: 36,000
SALES (est): 10.2MM **Publicly Held**
WEB: www.sorrentonet.com
SIC: **3661** Telephones & telephone apparatus; switching equipment, telephone; multiplex equipment, telephone & telegraph; fiber optics communications equipment
HQ: Dasan Zhone Solutions, Inc.
7195 Oakport St
Oakland CA 94621
510 777-7000

(P-17414)
SPECTRASWITCH INC
445 Tesconi Cir, Santa Rosa (95401-4619)
PHONE..................................707 568-7000
Nick Lawrence, *President*
EMP: 41

SALES (est): 2.5MM **Privately Held**
WEB: www.spectraswitch.com
SIC: **3661** Fiber optics communications equipment; switching equipment, telephone

(P-17415)
SPROUTLING INC
8 California St Ste 300, San Francisco (94111-4822)
PHONE..................................415 323-3270
Christopher Sinclair, *CEO*
EMP: 10
SQ FT: 335,000
SALES (est): 1.7MM
SALES (corp-wide): 4.5B **Publicly Held**
SIC: **3661** Switching equipment, telephone
PA: Mattel, Inc.
333 Continental Blvd
El Segundo CA 90245
310 252-2000

(P-17416)
SWEDCOM CORPORATION
851 Burlway Rd Ste 300, Burlingame (94010-1712)
PHONE..................................650 348-1190
Sven E Kjaersgaard, *President*
Kersin Kjaersgaard, *Vice Pres*
Lola Cornell, *Office Mgr*
Dan Leonetti, *Purchasing*
▲ EMP: 16
SQ FT: 2,400
SALES (est): 1.7MM **Privately Held**
SIC: **3661** 5063 Multiplex equipment, telephone & telegraph; antennas, receiving, satellite dishes

(P-17417)
SYMMETRICOM INC
3870 N 1st St, San Jose (95134-1702)
PHONE..................................408 433-0910
EMP: 20
SALES (est): 3.6MM **Privately Held**
SIC: **3661** Telephone & telegraph apparatus

(P-17418)
SYSTEM STUDIES INCORPORATED (PA)
21340 E Cliff Dr, Santa Cruz (95062-4800)
PHONE..................................831 475-5777
Robert A Simpkins, *President*
Diane Bordoni, *CFO*
William D Simpkins, *Vice Pres*
Sheryll Hiatt, *Sales Mgr*
EMP: 42
SQ FT: 11,000
SALES (est): 9MM **Privately Held**
WEB: www.airtalk.com
SIC: **3661** Telephone & telegraph apparatus

(P-17419)
SYSTEM STUDIES INCORPORATED
2900 Research Park Dr, Soquel (95073-2000)
PHONE..................................831 475-5777
Gary Cramer, *Branch Mgr*
EMP: 38
SALES (corp-wide): 9MM **Privately Held**
SIC: **3661** Telephone & telegraph apparatus
PA: System Studies Incorporated
21340 E Cliff Dr
Santa Cruz CA 95062
831 475-5777

(P-17420)
TATUNG TELECOM CORPORATION
2660 Marine Way, Mountain View (94043-1124)
P.O. Box 2012, Menlo Park (94026-2012)
PHONE..................................650 961-2288
Douglas Lau, *President*
T S Lin, *Ch of Bd*
Grace Lau, *CFO*
Sue J Lau, *Admin Sec*
EMP: 100
SQ FT: 10,000
SALES (est): 8MM **Privately Held**
SIC: **3661** Telephone & telegraph apparatus

PA: Tatung Co.
22, Zhongshan N. Rd., Sec. 3,
Taipei City TAP 10435
-

(P-17421)
THALES TRANSPORT & SEC INC (HQ)
51 Discovery, Irvine (92618-3119)
PHONE..................................949 790-2500
John Brohm, *President*
Jean Pierre Forestier, *Vice Pres*
▲ EMP: 23
SALES (est): 4MM
SALES (corp-wide): 262.1MM **Privately Held**
WEB: www.alcatelusa.com
SIC: **3661** Telephone & telegraph apparatus
PA: Thales
Tour Carpe Diem Esplanade Nord
Courbevoie 92400
157 778-000

(P-17422)
TITAN PHOTONICS INC
1241 Quarry Ln Ste 140, Pleasanton (94566-8462)
PHONE..................................510 687-0488
Eric Liu, *President*
Charlie Chen, *Treasurer*
▲ EMP: 25
SQ FT: 2,000
SALES (est): 6MM **Privately Held**
WEB: www.titanphotonics.com
SIC: **3661** Telephone & telegraph apparatus

(P-17423)
U-BLOX SAN DIEGO INC
12626 High Bluff Dr, San Diego (92130-2070)
PHONE..................................858 847-9611
David W Carey, *President*
Brian N Richardson, *President*
EMP: 17
SALES (est): 2.4MM
SALES (corp-wide): 395.7MM **Privately Held**
SIC: **3661** 3571 5045 Modems; personal computers (microcomputers); computers, peripherals & software
HQ: U-Blox Ag
Zurcherstrasse 68
Thalwil ZH 8800
447 227-444

(P-17424)
UNITED OPTRONICS INC
1323 Great Mall Dr, Milpitas (95035-8013)
PHONE..................................408 503-8900
J J Pang, *Ch of Bd*
EMP: 10
SQ FT: 50,000
SALES (est): 1MM **Privately Held**
WEB: www.unitedoptronics.com
SIC: **3661** Fiber optics communications equipment

(P-17425)
UTSTARCOM INC (HQ)
1732 N 1st St Ste 200, San Jose (95112-4518)
PHONE..................................510 749-1503
William Wong, *CEO*
Leon Hong, *COO*
Jin Jiang, *CFO*
Tianruo Pu, *CFO*
Evelyn Trant, *CFO*
▲ EMP: 102
SALES (est): 99.2MM **Privately Held**
WEB: www.utstar.com
SIC: **3661** 3663 Message concentrators; mobile communication equipment

(P-17426)
VELLO SYSTEMS INC
1530 Obrien Dr, Menlo Park (94025-1454)
PHONE..................................650 324-7688
Karl May, *CEO*
Armineh Baghoomian, *CFO*
EMP: 85

SALES (est): 13.5MM **Privately Held**
SIC: **3661** 5999 5065 7622 Telephone station equipment & parts, wire; communication equipment; communication equipment; communication equipment repair

(P-17427)
VESTA SOLUTIONS INC (DH)
42555 Rio Nedo, Temecula (92590-3726)
P.O. Box 9007 (92589-9007)
PHONE..................................951 719-2100
Gino Bonanotte, *CEO*
John Molloy, *President*
Uygar Gazioglu, *Treasurer*
Andrew Sinclair, *Senior VP*
Daniel Pekofske, *Vice Pres*
▲ EMP: 272
SQ FT: 100,000
SALES (est): 97.8MM
SALES (corp-wide): 7.3B **Publicly Held**
WEB: www.peinc.com
SIC: **3661** Telephone station equipment & parts, wire
HQ: Plant Holdings, Inc.
42555 Rio Nedo
Temecula CA 92590
951 719-2100

(P-17428)
VIAVI SOLUTIONS INC
3601 Calle Tecate, Camarillo (93012-5056)
PHONE..................................805 465-1875
EMP: 75
SALES (corp-wide): 811.4MM **Publicly Held**
SIC: **3661**
PA: Viavi Solutions Inc.
6001 America Center Dr # 6
San Jose CA 95002
408 404-3600

(P-17429)
VSR NETWORK TECHNOLOGIES LLC
11760 Atwood Rd Ste 8, Auburn (95603-9075)
PHONE..................................530 889-1500
Mark Cederloff, *Mng Member*
Rhonda Cederloff,
EMP: 21
SQ FT: 2,000
SALES (est): 2.1MM **Privately Held**
WEB: www.vsrusa.com
SIC: **3661** Telephones & telephone apparatus

(P-17430)
WEST COAST VENTURE CAPITAL LLC (PA)
10050 Bandley Dr, Cupertino (95014-2102)
PHONE..................................408 725-0700
Carl Berg, *President*
EMP: 700
SALES (est): 52MM **Privately Held**
SIC: **3661** Telephone & telegraph apparatus

(P-17431)
Y B S ENTERPRISES INC
Also Called: Electro-Comm
3116 W Vanowen St, Burbank (91505-1237)
PHONE..................................818 848-7790
Y B Song, *President*
Grace Song, *Admin Sec*
Yung Kim, *VP Opers*
EMP: 13
SQ FT: 30,000
SALES (est): 6.5MM **Privately Held**
SIC: **3661** Communication headgear, telephone

(PA)=Parent Co (HQ)=Headquarters (DH)=Div Headquarters
✪ = New Business established in last 2 years

3663 Radio & T V Communications, Systs & Eqpt, Broadcast/Studio

(P-17432)
24/7 STUDIO EQUIPMENT INC
Also Called: Hertz Entertainment Services
3111 N Kenwood St, Burbank
(91505-1041)
PHONE..................................818 840-8247
Lance Sorenson, *President*
Gary Mielke, *Vice Pres*
EMP: 92
SALES (est): 23MM
SALES (corp-wide): 9.5B **Publicly Held**
WEB: www.247studioequipment.com
SIC: 3663 Studio equipment, radio & television broadcasting
PA: Hertz Global Holdings, Inc.
8501 Williams Rd Fl 3
Estero FL 33928
239 301-7000

(P-17433)
2J ANTENNAS USA
7420 Carroll Rd Ste D, San Diego
(92121-2304)
PHONE..................................858 866-1072
Ruben Cuadras, *Engineer*
EMP: 12
SALES (est): 1.4MM **Privately Held**
SIC: 3663 Radio & TV communications equipment

(P-17434)
2XWIRELESS INC
1065 Marauder St, Chico (95973-9039)
PHONE..................................877 581-8002
James Higgins, *CEO*
EMP: 60 EST: 2013
SALES (est): 4.9MM **Privately Held**
SIC: 3663 Television antennas (transmitting) & ground equipment

(P-17435)
ABEKAS INC
1233 Midas Way, Sunnyvale (94085-4021)
PHONE..................................650 470-0900
Junaid Sheikh, *President*
Anna Higgins, *Software Engr*
Phil Bennett, *Engineer*
Mayli Jew, *Mfg Mgr*
EMP: 12
SQ FT: 5,700
SALES (est): 2.7MM
SALES (corp-wide): 198MM **Privately Held**
WEB: www.abekas.com
SIC: 3663 Television broadcasting & communications equipment
HQ: Ross Europe B.V.
Strawinskylaan 411
Amsterdam
205 752-727

(P-17436)
ACROAMATICS INC
7230 Hollister Ave, Goleta (93117-2807)
PHONE..................................805 967-9909
Geoffrey Johnson, *President*
Patricia Johnson, *CFO*
Robert Danford, *Vice Pres*
John Foondle, *Vice Pres*
Howard Chang, *Engineer*
EMP: 24
SALES (est): 4.6MM **Privately Held**
WEB: www.acroamatics.com
SIC: 3663 Telemetering equipment, electronic

(P-17437)
ADAPTIVE DIGITAL SYSTEMS INC
20322 Sw Acacia St # 200, Newport Beach
(92660-1504)
PHONE..................................949 955-3116
Attila W Mathe, *President*
Ralph Boehringer, *Vice Pres*
Susan Cameron, *Admin Sec*
Anna Cameron, *Administration*
Anna Gnegy, *Prdtn Mgr*
▲ EMP: 27
SQ FT: 6,500
SALES: 9.5MM **Privately Held**
WEB: www.adaptivedigitalsystems.com
SIC: 3663 Marine radio communications equipment

(P-17438)
ADVANCED ENTERPRISES LLC
Also Called: Advanced Dealer Services
48511 Warm Springs Blvd # 202, Fremont
(94539-7746)
PHONE..................................408 923-5000
James Landes, *Principal*
EMP: 11 EST: 1998
SQ FT: 1,600
SALES (est): 1.1MM **Privately Held**
WEB: www.adsmobile.net
SIC: 3663 Mobile communication equipment

(P-17439)
AETHERCOMM INC
3205 Lionshead Ave, Carlsbad
(92010-4710)
PHONE..................................760 208-6002
William Todd Thornton, *CEO*
Todd Thornton, *President*
Richard Martinez, *CFO*
Terri Thornton, *Vice Pres*
David Burgess, *CTO*
EMP: 125
SQ FT: 46,000
SALES (est): 38.2MM **Privately Held**
WEB: www.aethercomm.com
SIC: 3663 Radio & TV communications equipment

(P-17440)
AGUDA WILSON RAMOS
Also Called: Filipino Channel
5409 Asbury Way, Stockton (95219-7163)
PHONE..................................209 942-2446
Wilson Aguda, *Owner*
EMP: 13
SALES: 100K **Privately Held**
SIC: 3663 Satellites, communications

(P-17441)
AIR-TRAK
15090 Avenue Of Science # 103, San
Diego (92128-3412)
PHONE..................................858 677-9950
Greg White, *President*
Dennis Clark, *Chairman*
Marc Bernard, *Vice Pres*
Steve Porter, *Vice Pres*
EMP: 17
SQ FT: 5,600
SALES: 5MM **Privately Held**
WEB: www.air-trak.com
SIC: 3663

(P-17442)
AIRGAIN INC (PA)
3611 Valley Centre Dr # 150, San Diego
(92130-3331)
PHONE..................................760 579-0200
James K Sims, *Ch of Bd*
Jacob Suen, *President*
Anil Doradla, *CFO*
Kevin Thill, *Senior VP*
EMP: 118
SQ FT: 10,300
SALES: 60.6MM **Publicly Held**
WEB: www.airgain.com
SIC: 3663 5731 Antennas, transmitting & communications; antennas, satellite dish

(P-17443)
AJA VIDEO SYSTEMS INC (PA)
180 Litton Dr, Grass Valley (95945-5076)
P.O. Box 1033 (95945-1033)
PHONE..................................530 274-2048
John O ABT, *Principal*
Darlene ABT, *CFO*
Robert Stacy, *General Mgr*
Dustin Graham, *Software Dev*
Chris Anderson, *Software Engr*
▲ EMP: 30
SQ FT: 9,800
SALES (est): 7.5MM **Privately Held**
WEB: www.aja.com
SIC: 3663 Television broadcasting & communications equipment

(P-17444)
ALDETEC INC
3560 Business Dr Ste 100, Sacramento
(95820-2161)
PHONE..................................916 453-3382
Jeff Russ, *President*
Teresa Robertson, *Office Mgr*
Richard Silvers, *Engineer*
David Dwssem, *Purch Mgr*
John McCarthy, *Director*
EMP: 45
SQ FT: 16,038
SALES (est): 4.4MM **Privately Held**
WEB: www.aldetec.com
SIC: 3663 Amplifiers, RF power & IF

(P-17445)
ALE USA INC
26801 Agoura Rd, Calabasas
(91301-5122)
PHONE..................................818 878-4816
Stanley Stopka, *Principal*
Michel Emelianoff, *CEO*
Stan Stopka, *Vice Pres*
Alan Pullen, *Engineer*
Brendan Flaherty, *Sales Staff*
EMP: 550
SQ FT: 50,000
SALES: 130MM
SALES (corp-wide): 9.9MM **Privately Held**
SIC: 3663 3613 Mobile communication equipment; switchgear & switchboard apparatus
HQ: China Huaxin Post And Telecom Technologies Co.,Ltd.
Building 4(West Building), Chang An Xing Rong Center, No.1 Court
Beijing 10003
105 852-8866

(P-17446)
ALIEN TECHNOLOGY LLC (PA)
845 Embedded Way, San Jose
(95138-1085)
PHONE..................................408 782-3900
Weijie Yun, *CEO*
Patrick Ervin, *President*
Glenn Gengel, *President*
John Payne, *COO*
Robert K Eulau, *CFO*
▲ EMP: 50
SQ FT: 81,000
SALES (est): 28.6MM **Privately Held**
WEB: www.alientechnology.com
SIC: 3663 Radio broadcasting & communications equipment; transmitting apparatus, radio or television

(P-17447)
ALTINEX INC
500 S Jefferson St, Placentia (92870-6617)
PHONE..................................714 990-0877
Jack Gershfeld, *President*
Sergey Alayev, *Project Engr*
▲ EMP: 50
SALES (est): 16.9MM **Privately Held**
SIC: 3663 3577 3651 5099 Radio & TV communications equipment; computer peripheral equipment; household audio & video equipment; video & audio equipment

(P-17448)
AMINO TECHNOLOGIES (US) LLC (HQ)
20823 Stevens Creek Blvd, Cupertino
(95014-2108)
PHONE..................................408 861-1400
Steve D McKay, *Bd of Directors*
Brian Garrett, *Partner*
Gary Spicer, *Controller*
Sandra Wong, *QC Mgr*
Dan Carufel, *Sales Staff*
◆ EMP: 60
SALES (est): 8.2MM **Privately Held**
SIC: 3663 5064 Television broadcasting & communications equipment; electrical appliances, television & radio; television sets

(P-17449)
AMPLIFIER TECHNOLOGIES INC
1749 Chapin Rd, Montebello (90640-6609)
PHONE..................................323 278-0001
Morris Kessler, *President*
▲ EMP: 25
SQ FT: 84,000
SALES (est): 4.9MM **Privately Held**
WEB: www.ati-amp.com
SIC: 3663 Television broadcasting & communications equipment
PA: Macey Investment Corp
1749 Chapin Rd
Montebello CA 90640
323 278-0001

(P-17450)
ANACOM INC
1961 Concourse Dr, San Jose
(95131-1708)
PHONE..................................408 519-2062
James Tom, *CEO*
May Tom, *President*
Christopher Nguyen, *CFO*
Ram Chandran, *Vice Pres*
Dan Miller, *Sr Software Eng*
▲ EMP: 40
SQ FT: 5,000
SALES (est): 8MM **Privately Held**
WEB: www.anacominc.com
SIC: 3663 Receiver-transmitter units (transceiver)

(P-17451)
ANRITSU COMPANY (DH)
490 Jarvis Dr, Morgan Hill (95037-2834)
P.O. Box 39000, San Francisco (94139-0001)
PHONE..................................800 267-4878
Hirokazu Hashimoto, *CEO*
Lisa Aragon, *President*
Donn Mulder, *President*
Neil Tomlinson, *COO*
Toshihiko Takahashi, *Senior VP*
▲ EMP: 485
SQ FT: 242,000
SALES (est): 185.1MM **Privately Held**
WEB: www.us.anritsu.com
SIC: 3663 3825 5065 Radio & TV communications equipment; test equipment for electronic & electric measurement; electronic parts & equipment
HQ: Anritsu U.S. Holding, Inc.
490 Jarvis Dr
Morgan Hill CA 95037
408 778-2000

(P-17452)
ANTCOM CORPORATION
367 Van Ness Way Ste 602, Torrance
(90501-6246)
PHONE..................................310 782-1076
Michael Ritter, *CEO*
Sean Huynh, *Vice Pres*
Doug Reid, *General Mgr*
Tran Phil, *Engineer*
Kathleen Fasenfest, *Chief Engr*
EMP: 45 EST: 1997
SQ FT: 15,000
SALES (est): 11.4MM **Privately Held**
WEB: www.antcom.com
SIC: 3663 Antennas, transmitting & communications

(P-17453)
ANTYPAS & ASSOCIATES INC
749 Thorsen Ct, Los Altos (94024-6630)
PHONE..................................650 961-4311
EMP: 12
SQ FT: 20,000
SALES (est): 1.1MM **Privately Held**
WEB: www.crystacomm.com
SIC: 3663 3661

(P-17454)
APHEX SYSTEMS LTD
3500 N San Fernando Blvd, Burbank
(91505-1000)
PHONE..................................818 767-2929
Marvin Caesar, *President*
Robbie Jo Dungey, *Manager*
EMP: 27

2020 California
Manufacturers Register

▲ = Import ▼=Export
◆ =Import/Export

SALES (est): 3.9MM **Privately Held**
WEB: www.aphex.com
SIC: **3663** Radio & TV communications
equipment

(P-17455)
APPLE INC (PA)
1 Apple Park Way, Cupertino (95014-0642)
PHONE..................................408 996-1010
Timothy D Cook, *CEO*
Arthur D Levinson, *Ch of Bd*
Jeff Williams, *COO*
◆ EMP: 2000
SALES: 260.1B **Publicly Held**
WEB: www.apple.com
SIC: **3663** 3571 3575 3577 Mobile com-
munication equipment; personal comput-
ers (microcomputers); computer
terminals, monitors & components; print-
ers, computer; sound reproducing equip-
ment; operating systems computer
software; application computer software

(P-17456)
APPLICA INC
11651 Vanowen St, North Hollywood
(91605-6128)
PHONE..................................818 565-0011
Albert Cohen, *President*
Shlomo Barash, *Treasurer*
James Viray, *General Mgr*
EMP: 20
SALES (est): 3.1MM **Privately Held**
SIC: **3663** Radio & TV communications
equipment

(P-17457)
AQUILA SPACE INC
Nasa Ames Research Park, Moffett Field
(94035)
PHONE..................................650 224-8559
Chris Biddy, *President*
EMP: 13
SALES (est): 1.4MM **Privately Held**
SIC: **3663** Space satellite communications
equipment

(P-17458)
ARDAX SYSTEMS INC
1669 Industrial Rd, San Carlos
(94070-4112)
PHONE..................................650 591-2656
Fax: 650 591-8249
EMP: 10
SQ FT: 5,800
SALES (est): 960K **Privately Held**
WEB: www.ardax.com
SIC: **3663**

(P-17459)
ARUBA NETWORKS INC
392 Acoma Way, Fremont (94539-7508)
PHONE..................................408 227-4500
EMP: 29
SALES (corp-wide): 50.1B **Publicly Held**
SIC: **3663**
HQ: Aruba Networks, Inc.
3333 Scott Blvd
Santa Clara CA 95054
408 227-4500

(P-17460)
ARUBA NETWORKS INC
390 W Caribbean Dr, Sunnyvale
(94089-1010)
PHONE..................................408 227-4500
Vinay Agarwala, *Engineer*
Jim Bergkamp, *Finance*
Kathy Winters, *Human Resources*
Tiago Garjaka, *Opers Staff*
EMP: 10
SALES (corp-wide): 30.8B **Publicly Held**
SIC: **3663** 3577 7371 Mobile communica-
tion equipment; data conversion equip-
ment; media-to-media: computer; graphic
displays, except graphic terminals; com-
puter software development
HQ: Aruba Networks, Inc.
3333 Scott Blvd
Santa Clara CA 95054
408 227-4500

(P-17461)
ASTRA COMMUNICATIONS INC
1101 Chestnut St, Burbank (91506-1624)
P.O. Box 391 (91503-0391)
PHONE..................................818 859-7305
EMP: 12
SQ FT: 11,000
SALES (est): 1.7MM **Privately Held**
WEB: www.astracomm.com
SIC: **3663**

(P-17462)
**ATX NETWORKS (SAN DIEGO)
CORP (DH)**
8880 Rehco Rd, San Diego (92121-3265)
PHONE..................................858 546-5050
Charlie Vogp, *President*
Carlos Shteremberg, *COO*
Ian A Lerner, *Officer*
Jose Rivero, *Vice Pres*
Jessica Finkler, *Office Mgr*
◆ EMP: 70
SQ FT: 7,000
SALES (est): 26.3MM
SALES (corp-wide): 132.8MM **Privately
Held**
WEB: www.picomacom.com
SIC: **3663** 5065 3678 Radio & TV com-
munications equipment; electronic parts &
equipment; electronic connectors
HQ: Atx Networks Corp
501 Clements Rd W Suite 1
Ajax ON L1S 7
905 428-6068

(P-17463)
AVIAT NETWORKS INC (PA)
860 N Mccarthy Blvd # 20, Milpitas
(95035-5110)
PHONE..................................408 941-7100
Stan Gallagher, *CEO*
John Mutch, *Ch of Bd*
Eric Chang, *Senior VP*
Shaun McFall, *Senior VP*
▲ EMP: 106
SQ FT: 19,000
SALES: 243.8MM **Publicly Held**
WEB: www.harrisstratex.com
SIC: **3663** Radio broadcasting & communi-
cations equipment

(P-17464)
AVIAT US INC (HQ)
860 N Mccarthy Blvd # 200, Milpitas
(95035-5117)
PHONE..................................408 941-7100
John Mutch, *Ch of Bd*
Ralph Marimon, *CFO*
Shaun McFall, *Chief Mktg Ofcr*
Meena L Elliott, *Senior VP*
John J Madigan, *Vice Pres*
▼ EMP: 450
SQ FT: 60,000
SALES (est): 121.7MM **Publicly Held**
SIC: **3663** 3661 Radio broadcasting &
communications equipment; transmitter-
receivers, radio; mobile communication
equipment; fiber optics communications
equipment

(P-17465)
AVID SYSTEMS INC (HQ)
280 Bernardo Ave, Mountain View
(94043-5238)
PHONE..................................650 526-1600
Ken A Sexton, *CEO*
Patti S Hart, *Ch of Bd*
Georg Blinn, *President*
Ajay Chopra, *President*
Arthur D Chadwick, *CFO*
EMP: 225
SQ FT: 106,000
SALES (est): 81MM
SALES (corp-wide): 413.2MM **Publicly
Held**
WEB: www.ipinnacle.com
SIC: **3663** 3577 Radio & TV communica-
tions equipment; computer peripheral
equipment
PA: Avid Technology, Inc.
75 Network Dr
Burlington MA 01803
978 640-6789

(P-17466)
AVX ANTENNA INC (DH)
5501 Oberlin Dr Ste 100, San Diego
(92121-1718)
PHONE..................................858 550-3820
Laurent Desclos, *President*
Vahid Manian, *COO*
Rick Johnson, *CFO*
Sung-Ki Jung, *Officer*
Trent Bartow, *Marketing Staff*
▲ EMP: 23
SALES (est): 5.8MM **Publicly Held**
WEB: www.ethertronics.com
SIC: **3663** Antennas, transmitting & com-
munications
HQ: Avx Corporation
1 Avx Blvd
Fountain Inn SC 29644
864 967-2150

(P-17467)
**AXXCELERA BRDBAND
WIRELESS INC (DH)**
82 Coromar Dr, Santa Barbara
(93117-3024)
PHONE..................................805 968-9621
Jamal Hamdani, *CEO*
Bruce Tarr, *CFO*
Tony Masters, *Senior VP*
Philip Rushton, *Senior VP*
▲ EMP: 19
SQ FT: 56,000
SALES (est): 1.7MM
SALES (corp-wide): 42MM **Privately
Held**
WEB: www.axxcelera.com
SIC: **3663** Radio & TV communications
equipment
HQ: Moseley Associates, Inc.
82 Coromar Dr
Goleta CA 93117
805 968-9621

(P-17468)
BIG SHINE LOS ANGELES INC
27211 Branbury Ct, Valencia (91354-2112)
PHONE..................................818 346-0770
Jae Ho Lee, *President*
EMP: 10
SALES (est): 1.1MM **Privately Held**
SIC: **3663** Telemetering equipment, elec-
tronic

(P-17469)
BLITZZ TECHNOLOGY INC
53 Parker, Irvine (92618-1605)
PHONE..................................949 380-7709
▲ EMP: 25
SQ FT: 10,000
SALES: 4MM **Privately Held**
SIC: **3663** 5065

(P-17470)
**BLUE DANUBE SYSTEMS INC
(PA)**
3131 Jay St Ste 201, Santa Clara
(95054-3340)
PHONE..................................650 316-5010
Mark Pinto, *CEO*
Mihai Banu, *Vice Pres*
James Emerick, *Engineer*
Akansha Sharma, *Human Resources*
Justin Walsh, *Opers Staff*
EMP: 15
SALES (est): 3.7MM **Privately Held**
SIC: **3663** Radio broadcasting & communi-
cations equipment

(P-17471)
BOEING COMPANY
900 N Pacific Coast Hwy, El Segundo
(90245-2710)
P.O. Box 92919, Los Angeles (90009-2919)
PHONE..................................310 662-9000
EMP: 25
SALES (corp-wide): 101.1B **Publicly
Held**
SIC: **3663** Satellites, communications;
space satellite communications equip-
ment
PA: The Boeing Company
100 N Riverside Plz
Chicago IL 60606
312 544-2000

(P-17472)
BOEING COMPANY
2201 Seal Beach Blvd, Seal Beach
(90740-5603)
PHONE..................................714 372-5361
Gary Black, *Officer*
EMP: 1000
SALES (corp-wide): 101.1B **Publicly
Held**
SIC: **3663** 3812 Satellites, communica-
tions; search & navigation equipment
PA: The Boeing Company
100 N Riverside Plz
Chicago IL 60606
312 544-2000

(P-17473)
**BOEING SATELLITE SYSTEMS
INC (HQ)**
900 N Pacific Coast Hwy, El Segundo
(90245-2710)
P.O. Box 92919, Los Angeles (90009-2919)
PHONE..................................310 791-7450
Craig R Cooning, *President*
Dave Ryan, *Vice Pres*
Charles Toups, *Vice Pres*
Bertha Calderon, *Admin Asst*
John Ziavras, *Design Engr*
▲ EMP: 25
SALES (est): 1.1B
SALES (corp-wide): 101.1B **Publicly
Held**
SIC: **3663** Satellites, communications;
space satellite communications equip-
ment
PA: The Boeing Company
100 N Riverside Plz
Chicago IL 60606
312 544-2000

(P-17474)
**BROADCAST MICROWAVE
SERVICES (PA)**
Also Called: B M S
12305 Crosthwaite Cir, Poway
(92064-6817)
PHONE..................................858 391-3050
Graham Bunney, *CEO*
Sharon Desuacido, *Vice Pres*
Jeff Jones, *Admin Sec*
Randy Angelito, *Software Engr*
Chris Blazie, *Software Engr*
EMP: 109
SQ FT: 37,000
SALES (est): 30.4MM **Privately Held**
WEB: www.bms-inc.com
SIC: **3663** Microwave communication
equipment

(P-17475)
CABLE AML INC (PA)
2271 W 205th St Ste 101, Torrance
(90501-1449)
PHONE..................................310 222-5599
Francisco Bernues, *President*
Eddie Nakamura, *CFO*
Norman Woods, *Admin Sec*
▼ EMP: 14
SQ FT: 15,000
SALES: 2.5MM **Privately Held**
SIC: **3663** 8711 Radio & TV communica-
tions equipment; consulting engineer

(P-17476)
CALAMP CORP (PA)
15635 Alton Pkwy Ste 250, Irvine
(92618-7328)
PHONE..................................949 600-5600
Michael Burdiek, *President*
A J Moyer, *Ch of Bd*
Kurtis Binder, *CFO*
Garo Sarkissian, *Senior VP*
Paul Washicko, *Senior VP*
◆ EMP: 226
SQ FT: 16,000
SALES: 363.8MM **Publicly Held**
SIC: **3663** Microwave communication
equipment

(P-17477)
CALAMP CORP
2231 Rutherford Rd # 110, Carlsbad
(92008-8811)
PHONE..................................760 438-9010
Frank Perna Jr, *Chairman*

PRODUCTS & SVCS

EMP: 10 EST: 2012
SALES (est): 1.2MM
SALES (corp-wide): 363.8MM **Publicly Held**
SIC: 3663 Radio & TV communications equipment
PA: Calamp Corp.
15635 Alton Pkwy Ste 250
Irvine CA 92618
949 600-5600

(P-17478)
CALIX INC (PA)
2777 Orchard Pkwy, San Jose (95134-2008)
PHONE.....................408 514-3000
Carl Russo, *President*
Don Listwin, *Ch of Bd*
Cory Sindelar, *CFO*
Michael Weening, *Exec VP*
Gregory Billings, *Senior VP*
◆ EMP: 277
SQ FT: 82,100
SALES: 441.3MM **Publicly Held**
WEB: www.calix-networks.com
SIC: 3663 4899 4813 Radio & TV communications equipment; data communication services; communication signal enhancement network system; telephone communication, except radio

(P-17479)
CANAM TECHNOLOGY INC
5318 E 2nd St Ste 700, Long Beach (90803-5324)
PHONE.....................562 856-0178
Michael Martinez, *President*
▲ EMP: 10
SQ FT: 2,200
SALES (est): 2.3MM **Privately Held**
WEB: www.canamtechnology.com
SIC: 3663 8711 Antennas, transmitting & communications; consulting engineer

(P-17480)
CANARY COMMUNICATIONS INC
6040 Hellyer Ave Ste 150, San Jose (95138-1041)
PHONE.....................408 365-0609
Vinh Tran, *President*
Roland Yamaguchi, *Vice Pres*
Charles McKee, *Executive*
▲ EMP: 15
SALES (est): 2.2MM **Privately Held**
WEB: www.canarycom.com
SIC: 3663 Receiver-transmitter units (transceiver)

(P-17481)
CARLSON WIRELESS TECH INC
3134 Jacobs Ave Ste C, Eureka (95501-0960)
PHONE.....................707 443-0100
James R Carlson, *CEO*
Mindy Hiley, *Opers Staff*
EMP: 15
SQ FT: 6,000
SALES (est): 3.1MM **Privately Held**
WEB: www.carlsonwireless.com
SIC: 3663 Airborne radio communications equipment; receivers, radio communications; transmitter-receivers, radio

(P-17482)
CARRIERCOMM INC
82 Coromar Dr, Goleta (93117-3024)
PHONE.....................805 968-9621
Jamal N Hamdani, *President*
Bruce Tarr, *CFO*
EMP: 50
SQ FT: 18,000
SALES (est): 6.9MM
SALES (corp-wide): 42MM **Privately Held**
WEB: www.carriercom.com
SIC: 3663 Radio & TV communications equipment
PA: Axxcss Wireless Solutions Inc
82 Coromar Dr
Goleta CA 93117
805 968-9621

(P-17483)
CELLCO PARTNERSHIP
Also Called: Verizon
3770 W Mcfadden Ave Ste H, Santa Ana (92704-1395)
PHONE.....................714 775-0600
Roberto Espinosa, *Manager*
EMP: 20
SALES (corp-wide): 130.8B **Publicly Held**
SIC: 3663 5999 3661 Mobile communication equipment; telephone equipment & systems; telephone & telegraph apparatus
HQ: Cellco Partnership
1 Verizon Way
Basking Ridge NJ 07920

(P-17484)
CELLPHONE-MATE INC
Also Called: Surecall
48346 Milmont Dr, Fremont (94538-7324)
PHONE.....................510 770-0469
Hongtao Zhan, *President*
Frankie Smith, *Vice Pres*
Beverley Tate, *Accounting Mgr*
Bethany Mangold, *Marketing Mgr*
Roman Vizvary, *Marketing Staff*
▲ EMP: 52
SQ FT: 22,800
SALES: 7MM **Privately Held**
SIC: 3663 Amplifiers, RF power & IF; antennas, transmitting & communications; cable television equipment

(P-17485)
CENTRON INDUSTRIES INC
441 W Victoria St, Gardena (90248-3528)
PHONE.....................310 324-6443
Yong W Kim, *CEO*
Erin Roche, *Vice Pres*
Hye S Kim, *Admin Sec*
Mandeep Kaur, *Accountant*
Jim Perretti, *Supervisor*
▲ EMP: 37
SQ FT: 10,000
SALES (est): 9.6MM **Privately Held**
WEB: www.centronind.com
SIC: 3663 Radio & TV communications equipment

(P-17486)
CLEAR-COM LLC
Also Called: Clear-Com Communications
1301 Marina Vil Pkwy 10, Alameda (94501)
PHONE.....................510 337-6600
Mitzi Dominguez, *CEO*
Bob Boster, *President*
Harry Miyahira, *Chairman*
Chris Willis, *Vice Pres*
Ana Alas-Young, *Executive*
▲ EMP: 801
SQ FT: 23,700
SALES (est): 73.3MM
SALES (corp-wide): 509.9MM **Privately Held**
WEB: www.clearcom.com
SIC: 3663 Radio & TV communications equipment
PA: H. M. Electronics, Inc.
2848 Whiptail Loop
Carlsbad CA 92010
858 535-6000

(P-17487)
COASTLINE HIGH PRFMCE COATINGS
7181 Orangewood Ave, Garden Grove (92841-1409)
PHONE.....................714 372-3263
Phil Viljoen, *President*
EMP: 15
SALES (est): 2MM **Privately Held**
SIC: 3663 Satellites, communications

(P-17488)
COBHAM TRIVEC-AVANT INC
Also Called: Trivec-Avant Corporation
17831 Jamestown Ln, Huntington Beach (92647-7136)
PHONE.....................714 841-4976
Jill Kale, *CEO*
Mike Berberet, *Vice Pres*
David Macy, *Vice Pres*
▲ EMP: 45

SQ FT: 15,000
SALES (est): 9.8MM
SALES (corp-wide): 2.3B **Privately Held**
WEB: www.trivec.com
SIC: 3663 Antennas, transmitting & communications
HQ: Cobham Aes Holdings Inc.
2121 Crystal Dr Ste 625
Arlington VA 22202

(P-17489)
COLUMBIA COMMUNICATIONS INC
22480 Parrotts Ferry Rd, Columbia (95310-9731)
PHONE.....................203 533-0252
Wallace Ratzlaff, *President*
Carolyn Ratzlaff, *Vice Pres*
Heidi Perlewitz, *Admin Sec*
EMP: 10
SQ FT: 3,000
SALES: 1MM **Privately Held**
WEB: www.columbia-comm.com
SIC: 3663 Radio broadcasting & communications equipment

(P-17490)
COMMSYSTEMS LLC
12225 World Trade Dr I, San Diego (92128-3767)
PHONE.....................858 824-0056
Karl Kapusta, *President*
Preston Vorlicek,
Liane Schreffler, *Manager*
EMP: 10 EST: 1996
SQ FT: 1,500
SALES: 899.3K **Privately Held**
WEB: www.comm-systems.com
SIC: 3663 Satellites, communications

(P-17491)
COMMUNICATIONS & PWR INDS LLC
Also Called: CPI
811 Hansen Way, Palo Alto (94304-1031)
PHONE.....................650 846-3729
Robert Sickett, *Manager*
Andy Tafler, *President*
Michael Wong, *Technician*
Rasheda Begum, *Engineer*
Mark Tom, *Engineer*
EMP: 1500
SQ FT: 25,000
SALES (corp-wide): 399.2MM **Privately Held**
WEB: www.cpii.com
SIC: 3663 Radio & TV communications equipment
HQ: Communications & Power Industries Llc
607 Hansen Way
Palo Alto CA 94304

(P-17492)
COMMUNICATIONS & PWR INDS LLC
CPI
6385 San Ignacio Ave, San Jose (95119-1206)
P.O. Box 51110, Palo Alto (94303-0687)
PHONE.....................650 846-2900
EMP: 130
SALES (corp-wide): 399.2MM **Privately Held**
SIC: 3663 Radio & TV communications equipment
HQ: Communications & Power Industries Llc
607 Hansen Way
Palo Alto CA 94304

(P-17493)
COMTECH XICOM TECHNOLOGY INC (HQ)
3550 Bassett St, Santa Clara (95054-2704)
PHONE.....................408 213-3000
Fred Kornberg, *CEO*
EMP: 141
SQ FT: 40,000

SALES (est): 49.2MM
SALES (corp-wide): 671.8MM **Publicly Held**
WEB: www.xicomtech.com
SIC: 3663 3679 Amplifiers, RF power & IF; power supplies, all types: static
PA: Comtech Telecommunications Corp.
68 S Service Rd Ste 230
Melville NY 11747
631 962-7000

(P-17494)
CONNECT SYSTEMS INC
1802 Eastman Ave Ste 116, Ventura (93003-5759)
PHONE.....................805 642-7184
▲ EMP: 22
SQ FT: 10,000
SALES (est): 3.5MM **Privately Held**
WEB: www.connectsystems.com
SIC: 3663

(P-17495)
CPI MALIBU DIVISION
3760 Calle Tecate Ste A, Camarillo (93012-5060)
PHONE.....................805 383-1829
Joel Littman, *CFO*
Elizabeth McKenzie, *QA Dir*
Eunice Szejn, *Info Tech Mgr*
Scott Hanchar, *Project Engr*
Sunil Tambat, *Engineer*
EMP: 80 EST: 1975
SQ FT: 32,500
SALES (est): 15.3MM
SALES (corp-wide): 399.2MM **Privately Held**
WEB: www.maliburesearch.com
SIC: 3663 Antennas, transmitting & communications
HQ: Communications & Power Industries Llc
607 Hansen Way
Palo Alto CA 94304

(P-17496)
CREDENCE ID LLC
5801 Christie Ave Ste 500, Emeryville (94608-1938)
PHONE.....................888 243-5452
Bruce D Hanson, *CEO*
Yash Shah, *Vice Pres*
Rob Garrigan, *VP Sales*
Machiel Vander Harst, *VP Sales*
EMP: 32
SALES (est): 4.2MM **Privately Held**
SIC: 3663 Mobile communication equipment

(P-17497)
CRL SYSTEMS INC
Also Called: Orban
14798 Wicks Blvd, San Leandro (94577-6718)
PHONE.....................510 351-3500
Derek Pilkington, *President*
C J Brentlinger, *President*
Robert McMartin, *CFO*
EMP: 65 EST: 1969
SQ FT: 75,000
SALES (est): 8.3MM
SALES (corp-wide): 10.6MM **Publicly Held**
WEB: www.orban.com
SIC: 3663 Radio & TV communications equipment
PA: Circuit Research Labs, Inc.
7970 S Kyrene Rd
Tempe AZ 85284
480 403-8300

(P-17498)
CTT INC (PA)
5870 Hellyer Ave Ste 70, San Jose (95138-1004)
PHONE.....................408 541-0596
David Tai, *President*
Thanh Thai, *Vice Pres*
John Campbell, *Admin Sec*
Ken Pickard, *Technical Staff*
Darre Brokeshoulder, *Engineer*
▼ EMP: 81
SQ FT: 45,000

SALES (est): 8.2MM **Privately Held**
WEB: www.cttinc.com
SIC: 3663 Microwave communication equipment; amplifiers, RF power & IF

(P-17499)
D X COMMUNICATIONS INC
Also Called: Tpl Communications
8160 Van Nuys Blvd, Panorama City (91402-4806)
PHONE....................323 256-3000
Richard H Myers, *CEO*
John Ehret, *President*
Richard Myers, *CEO*
EMP: 28
SALES (est): 9.3MM **Privately Held**
WEB: www.tplcom.com
SIC: 3663 Satellites, communications

(P-17500)
DATRON WRLD COMMUNICATIONS INC (PA)
3055 Enterprise Ct, Vista (92081-8347)
PHONE....................760 597-1500
Art Barter, *President*
John C Goehring, *CFO*
Jimmy Diaz, *Bd of Directors*
Christopher Barter, *Program Mgr*
Lisa Courtemanche, *Executive Asst*
▲ **EMP:** 122 **EST:** 1971
SQ FT: 62,100
SALES (est): 55.9MM **Privately Held**
WEB: www.dtwc.com
SIC: 3663 Receiver-transmitter units (transceiver)

(P-17501)
DIGI GROUP LLC
Also Called: Thor Fiber
2421 W 205th St Ste D204, Torrance (90501-6263)
PHONE....................800 521-8467
Slawomir Sochur, *Principal*
EMP: 10 **EST:** 1997
SALES (est): 881.1K **Privately Held**
SIC: 3663 Television broadcasting & communications equipment

(P-17502)
DIGITAL PROTOTYPE SYSTEMS INC
Also Called: Dps Telecom
4955 E Yale Ave, Fresno (93727-1523)
PHONE....................559 454-1600
Robert A Berry, *CEO*
Marshall Denhartog, *President*
Ron Stover, *Vice Pres*
Samantha Johnson, *Executive Asst*
Richard Howell, *Software Engr*
EMP: 46
SQ FT: 50,000
SALES (est): 11.2MM **Privately Held**
WEB: www.dpstele.com
SIC: 3663 Telemetering equipment, electronic

(P-17503)
DJH ENTERPRISES
Also Called: Channel Vision Technology
234 Fischer Ave, Costa Mesa (92626-4515)
PHONE....................714 424-6500
Darrel Eugene Hauk, *President*
▲ **EMP:** 35
SALES (est): 5.7MM **Privately Held**
WEB: www.channelvision.com
SIC: 3663 Radio & TV communications equipment

(P-17504)
DOLBY LABORATORIES INC
432 Lakeside Dr, Sunnyvale (94085-4703)
PHONE....................408 730-5543
Carlo Basile, *President*
EMP: 14
SALES (corp-wide): 1.1B **Publicly Held**
SIC: 3663 Radio & TV communications equipment
PA: Dolby Laboratories, Inc.
1275 Market St
San Francisco CA 94103
415 558-0200

(P-17505)
DOLBY LABORATORIES INC
Also Called: Dolby Labs
175 S Hill Dr, Brisbane (94005-1203)
PHONE....................415 715-2500
Jeff Griffith, *Vice Pres*
Cory Iwatsu, *Buyer*
EMP: 76
SALES (corp-wide): 1.1B **Publicly Held**
WEB: www.dolby.com
SIC: 3663 3651 Radio broadcasting & communications equipment; household audio & video equipment
PA: Dolby Laboratories, Inc.
1275 Market St
San Francisco CA 94103
415 558-0200

(P-17506)
DSS-CCTV INC
1280 Activity Dr Ste A, Vista (92081-8508)
PHONE....................609 850-9498
Jiang Cheng, *President*
▲ **EMP:** 10
SALES: 6MM **Privately Held**
SIC: 3663 5065 Television closed circuit equipment; closed circuit television

(P-17507)
DYNAMIC SCIENCES INTL INC
9400 Lurline Ave Unit B, Chatsworth (91311-6022)
PHONE....................818 226-6262
Eli Shiri, *President*
Robert Cook, *Vice Pres*
Oren Shiri, *VP Sales*
James Zheng, *Sales Mgr*
Sylvia Shuter, *Director*
EMP: 35
SQ FT: 20,000
SALES (est): 5.7MM **Privately Held**
WEB: www.dynamicsciences.com
SIC: 3663 Radio receiver networks

(P-17508)
E-BAND COMMUNICATIONS LLC
17034 Camino San Bernardo, San Diego (92127-5708)
PHONE....................858 408-0660
Sam Smookler, *CEO*
Russ Kinsch, *CFO*
Saul Umbrasas, *Senior VP*
Mark Tomlinson, *Technician*
Joey England, *Technical Staff*
EMP: 30
SALES (est): 5.9MM
SALES (corp-wide): 42MM **Privately Held**
WEB: www.ebandcom.com
SIC: 3663 Carrier equipment, radio communications; microwave communication equipment
PA: Axxcss Wireless Solutions Inc
82 Coromar Dr
Goleta CA 93117
805 968-9621

(P-17509)
ECTRON CORPORATION
8159 Engineer Rd, San Diego (92111-1980)
PHONE....................858 278-0600
Karl E Cunningham, *CEO*
Gautam Kavipurapu, *Officer*
Carol C Cunningham, *Admin Sec*
Roger Elswood, *Supervisor*
EMP: 35
SQ FT: 9,500
SALES (est): 6.3MM **Privately Held**
WEB: www.ectron.com
SIC: 3663 3829 3577 3823 Amplifiers, RF power & IF; measuring & controlling devices; data conversion equipment, media-to-media: computer; industrial instrmnts msrmnt display/control process variable

(P-17510)
EKA TECHNOLOGIES INC
Also Called: EKA Designs
2985 E Hillcrest Dr # 203, Westlake Village (91362-3192)
PHONE....................805 379-8668
Arun Madhav, *President*
▲ **EMP:** 20

SQ FT: 800
SALES: 268K **Privately Held**
SIC: 3663 7336 Cameras, television; art design services

(P-17511)
EMPOWER RF SYSTEMS INC (PA)
316 W Florence Ave, Inglewood (90301-1104)
PHONE....................310 412-8100
Barry Phelps, *Ch of Bd*
Jon Jacocks, *President*
Larisa Spanisic, *CFO*
Larisa Stanisic, *CFO*
Efraim Bainvoll, *Founder*
EMP: 90
SQ FT: 30,000
SALES: 20MM **Privately Held**
WEB: www.empowerrf.com
SIC: 3663 Amplifiers, RF power & IF

(P-17512)
ENERGOUS CORPORATION
3590 N 1st St Ste 210, San Jose (95134-1812)
PHONE....................408 963-0200
Stephen R Rizzone, *President*
Robert J Griffin, *Ch of Bd*
Cesar Johnston, *COO*
Brian Sereda, *CFO*
Neeraj Sahejpal, *Senior VP*
EMP: 68
SALES: 514.8K **Privately Held**
SIC: 3663 3674 Radio broadcasting & communications equipment; antennas, transmitting & communications; semiconductors & related devices

(P-17513)
ERICSSON INC
1055 La Avenida St, Mountain View (94043-1421)
PHONE....................972 583-0000
Flicka Enloe, *Branch Mgr*
EMP: 29
SALES (corp-wide): 23.4B **Privately Held**
SIC: 3663 Radio & TV communications equipment
HQ: Ericsson Inc.
6300 Legacy Dr
Plano TX 75024
972 583-0000

(P-17514)
ERICSSON INC
250 Holger Way, San Jose (95134-1300)
PHONE....................408 970-2000
EMP: 24
SALES (corp-wide): 30.8B **Publicly Held**
SIC: 3663
HQ: Ericsson Inc.
6300 Legacy Dr
Plano TX 75024
972 583-0000

(P-17515)
ESCAPE COMMUNICATIONS INC
2790 Skypark Dr Ste 203, Torrance (90505-5345)
PHONE....................310 997-1300
Micheal Stewart, *President*
Gregory Caso PHD, *Exec VP*
James Nadeau, *Admin Sec*
EMP: 17
SQ FT: 5,300
SALES (est): 2.3MM **Privately Held**
WEB: www.escapecom.com
SIC: 3663 8711 8731 Microwave communication equipment; engineering services; commercial physical research

(P-17516)
ETM—ELECTROMATIC INC (PA)
35451 Dumbarton Ct, Newark (94560-1100)
PHONE....................510 797-1100
Thomas M Hayse, *CEO*
Ramesh Garg, *Vice Pres*
Jesse Iverson, *Vice Pres*
Kayte Mariani, *Vice Pres*
Richard Marquez, *Vice Pres*
◆ **EMP:** 100
SQ FT: 56,000

SALES (est): 23.4MM **Privately Held**
WEB: www.etm-inc.com
SIC: 3663 3825 Microwave communication equipment; amplifiers, RF power & IF; test equipment for electronic & electric measurement

(P-17517)
EUPHONIX INC (HQ)
280 Bernardo Ave, Mountain View (94043-5238)
PHONE....................650 526-1600
Jeffrey A Chew, *CEO*
Paul L Hammel, *Senior VP*
▲ **EMP:** 95
SQ FT: 40,000
SALES (est): 8.4MM
SALES (corp-wide): 413.2MM **Publicly Held**
WEB: www.euphonix.com
SIC: 3663 Studio equipment, radio & television broadcasting
PA: Avid Technology, Inc.
75 Network Dr
Burlington MA 01803
978 640-6789

(P-17518)
EVISSAP INC
800 Charcot Ave, San Jose (95131-2211)
PHONE....................408 432-7393
Hong Yin Wang, *Branch Mgr*
EMP: 25
SALES (corp-wide): 6.4MM **Privately Held**
SIC: 3663 Radio & TV communications equipment
PA: Evissap Inc.
812 Charcot Ave
San Jose CA 95131
408 943-8266

(P-17519)
FEI-ZYFER INC (HQ)
7321 Lincoln Way, Garden Grove (92841-1428)
PHONE....................714 933-4000
Steve Strang, *President*
David Williamson, *Vice Pres*
Dydan Nguyen, *Administration*
Steve Baillargeon, *Engineer*
Edward Moran, *Engineer*
EMP: 41
SQ FT: 50,000
SALES (est): 56.1MM
SALES (corp-wide): 49.5MM **Publicly Held**
WEB: www.fei-zyfer.com
SIC: 3663 Television broadcasting & communications equipment; encryption devices
PA: Frequency Electronics, Inc.
55 Charles Lindbergh Blvd # 2
Uniondale NY 11553
516 794-4500

(P-17520)
FLEET MANAGEMENT SOLUTIONS INC
7391 Lincoln Way, Garden Grove (92841-1428)
PHONE....................800 500-6009
Tony Eales, *CEO*
Sheila Henley Roth, *CFO*
EMP: 26
SALES (est): 2.5MM
SALES (corp-wide): 6.4B **Publicly Held**
WEB: www.fmsgps.com
SIC: 3663 4899 Radio & TV communications equipment; satellite earth stations
HQ: Teletrac Navman (Uk) Ltd
K1 Business Park, Timbold Drive
Milton Keynes BUCKS MK7 6
123 475-9000

(P-17521)
FLO TV INCORPORATED
5775 Morehouse Dr, San Diego (92121-1714)
PHONE....................858 651-1645
Gilbert P John, *Principal*
EMP: 15

SALES (est): 2.2MM
SALES (corp-wide): 24.2B **Publicly Held**
WEB: www.mediaflousa.com
SIC: 3663 Transmitting apparatus, radio or television
PA: Qualcomm Incorporated
5775 Morehouse Dr
San Diego CA 92121
858 587-1121

(P-17522)
FM SYSTEMS INC
3877 S Main St, Santa Ana (92707-5710)
PHONE................................714 979-0537
Donald Mc Clatchie, *CFO*
Frank Mc Clatchie, *President*
EMP: 10
SQ FT: 3,300
SALES: 300K **Privately Held**
WEB: www.fmsystems-inc.com
SIC: 3663 Radio broadcasting & communications equipment

(P-17523)
GENERAL DYNMICS STCOM TECH INC
2205 Fortune Dr, San Jose (95131-1806)
PHONE................................408 955-1900
Steve Michaud, *Branch Mgr*
Christopher Marzilli, *President*
Jennifer Young, *Human Res Mgr*
Will Nickerson, *Director*
EMP: 70
SALES (corp-wide): 36.1B **Publicly Held**
WEB: www.tripointglobal.com
SIC: 3663 Radio & TV communications equipment
HQ: General Dynamics Satcom Technologies, Inc.
1700 Cable Dr Ne
Conover NC 28613
704 462-7330

(P-17524)
GENERAL DYNMICS STCOM TECH INC
3111 Fujita St, Torrance (90505-4006)
PHONE................................310 539-6704
Sandra Seto, *Branch Mgr*
Manfred Stupnik, *Agent*
EMP: 67
SALES (corp-wide): 36.1B **Publicly Held**
WEB: www.tripointglobal.com
SIC: 3663 Antennas, transmitting & communications
HQ: General Dynamics Satcom Technologies, Inc.
1700 Cable Dr Ne
Conover NC 28613
704 462-7330

(P-17525)
GPS LOGIC LLC
1327 Calle Avanzado, San Clemente (92673-6351)
P.O. Box 999, San Juan Capistrano (92693-0999)
PHONE................................949 812-6942
Ronald Cedillos, *CEO*
Nicole Pete, *Office Mgr*
EMP: 12 **EST:** 2010
SALES (est): 1.5MM **Privately Held**
SIC: 3663 Space satellite communications equipment

(P-17526)
GRASS VALLEY INC
125 Crown Point Ct, Grass Valley (95945-9515)
P.O. Box 599000, Nevada City (95959-7900)
PHONE................................530 478-3000
Marc Valentine, *President*
Katy Hanna, *Opers Mgr*
Janet Spangler, *Production*
Wayne Schrand, *Manager*
▲ **EMP:** 750
SALES (est): 128.8MM
SALES (corp-wide): 127.3MM **Privately Held**
WEB: www.grassvalley.com
SIC: 3663 Radio & TV communications equipment

PA: Grass Valley Canada
3499 Rue Douglas-B.-Floreani
Saint-Laurent QC H4S 2
514 333-1772

(P-17527)
GRASS VALLEY INC (HQ)
Also Called: Miranda
125 Crown Point Ct, Grass Valley (95945-9515)
P.O. Box 1658, Nevada City (95959-1658)
PHONE................................530 265-1000
Strath Goodship, *CEO*
Luc St-Georges, *COO*
Kevin Joyce, *Chief Mktg Ofcr*
Chuck Meyer, *Officer*
Sydney Lovely, *Vice Pres*
EMP: 97
SQ FT: 42,000
SALES (est): 19.2MM
SALES (corp-wide): 127.3MM **Privately Held**
WEB: www.nvision1.com
SIC: 3663 Radio & TV communications equipment
PA: Grass Valley Canada
3499 Rue Douglas-B.-Floreani
Saint-Laurent QC H4S 2
514 333-1772

(P-17528)
GROUND CONTROL SYSTEMS INC
3100 El Camino Real, Atascadero (93422-2544)
P.O. Box 4459, San Luis Obispo (93403-4459)
PHONE................................805 783-4600
Jeff Staples, *CEO*
Kurt Wright, *COO*
Branden Jenkins, *CFO*
Kirk Williams, *Business Mgr*
Joe Garrison, *Prdtn Mgr*
EMP: 17
SQ FT: 20,200
SALES (est): 3.9MM
SALES (corp-wide): 9.6MM **Privately Held**
WEB: www.groundcontrol.com
SIC: 3663 Satellites, communications
HQ: Wireless Innovation Limited
Unit D2
Gloucester GLOS GL2 8

(P-17529)
GRYPHON MOBILE ELECTRONICS LLC
159 W Orangethorpe Ave A, Placentia (92870-6901)
PHONE................................626 810-7770
Nelson Yen, *CEO*
Carol Ko, *CFO*
Julio Hernandez, *Vice Pres*
Mark Elkins, *Mng Member*
▲ **EMP:** 15
SALES (est): 354.3K **Privately Held**
SIC: 3663 Mobile communication equipment

(P-17530)
GTX CORP
117 W 9th St Ste 1214, Los Angeles (90015-1524)
PHONE................................213 489-3019
Patrick E Bertagna, *Ch of Bd*
Alex McKean, *CFO*
Andrew Duncan, *Treasurer*
Louis Rosenbaum, *Vice Pres*
EMP: 10
SQ FT: 1,230
SALES: 687K **Privately Held**
SIC: 3663 ; light communications equipment

(P-17531)
HARMONIC INC (PA)
4300 N 1st St, San Jose (95134-1258)
PHONE................................408 542-2500
Patrick J Harshman, *President*
Nimrod Ben-Natan, *Senior VP*
Neven Haltmayer, *Senior VP*
Eric Louvet, *Senior VP*
◆ **EMP:** 277
SQ FT: 143,000

SALES: 403.5MM **Publicly Held**
WEB: www.harmonicinc.com
SIC: 3663 3823 Television broadcasting & communications equipment; industrial instrmnts msrmnt display/control process variable

(P-17532)
HARMONIC INC
641 Baltic Way, Sunnyvale (94089-1140)
PHONE................................408 542-2500
Anthony Ley, *President*
Ian Graham, *Vice Pres*
Baruch Levi, *Research*
Doron Cohen, *Technical Staff*
Ajay Anandteertha, *Engineer*
EMP: 18
SALES (corp-wide): 403.5MM **Publicly Held**
SIC: 3663 Television broadcasting & communications equipment
PA: Harmonic Inc.
4300 N 1st St
San Jose CA 95134
408 542-2500

(P-17533)
HAWAII PACIFIC TELEPORT LP
1145 Beasley Way, Sonoma (95476-7466)
PHONE................................707 938-7057
Christopher Guthrie, *Managing Prtnr*
EMP: 10
SQ FT: 200
SALES: 1MM **Privately Held**
SIC: 3663 8999 Satellites, communications; communication services

(P-17534)
HBC SOLUTIONS HOLDINGS LLC
10877 Wilshire Blvd Fl 18, Los Angeles (90024-4373)
PHONE................................321 727-9100
Daniel Abrams, *Mng Member*
EMP: 1002 **EST:** 2013
SALES (est): 54.9MM **Privately Held**
SIC: 3663 Radio broadcasting & communications equipment; television broadcasting & communications equipment

(P-17535)
HEROTEK INC
155 Baytech Dr, San Jose (95134-2303)
PHONE................................408 941-8399
Cheng W Lai, *President*
John Gilman, *Engng Exec*
James Wong, *Engineer*
Ted Wadholm, *Sales Mgr*
Susan Hartman, *Sales Staff*
EMP: 46
SQ FT: 9,600
SALES (est): 8.3MM **Privately Held**
WEB: www.herotek.com
SIC: 3663 3812 Microwave communication equipment; search & navigation equipment

(P-17536)
HILLSIDE CAPITAL INC
6222 Fallbrook Ave, Woodland Hills (91367-1601)
PHONE................................650 367-2011
Becky Tran, *President*
EMP: 115
SALES (est): 7.5MM **Privately Held**
SIC: 3663 Radio & TV communications equipment

(P-17537)
HONEYWELL INTERNATIONAL INC
325 Maple Ave, Torrance (90503-2602)
P.O. Box 2033 (90510)
PHONE................................310 618-2140
Salim Idris, *Director*
Patty Smith, *Manager*
EMP: 74
SALES (corp-wide): 41.8B **Publicly Held**
WEB: www.honeywell.com
SIC: 3663 Radio & TV communications equipment
PA: Honeywell International Inc.
300 S Tryon St
Charlotte NC 28202
973 455-2000

(P-17538)
HUGHES NETWORK SYSTEMS LLC
Also Called: H N S
9605 Scranton Rd Ste 500, San Diego (92121-1770)
PHONE................................858 455-9550
Douglas H Austin, *President*
Janet Williamson, *Vice Pres*
Ramam Sheshabhattar, *Program Mgr*
Sarah Xie, *Technical Staff*
Becerril Aicsa, *Engineer*
EMP: 50 **Publicly Held**
WEB: www.hnseu.com
SIC: 3663 Satellites, communications
HQ: Hughes Network Systems, Llc
11717 Exploration Ln
Germantown MD 20876
301 428-5500

(P-17539)
IGO INC (PA)
6001 Oak Cyn, Irvine (92618-5200)
PHONE................................888 205-0093
Terry R Gibson, *President*
Jack L Howard, *Ch of Bd*
Leonard J McGill, *Vice Pres*
◆ **EMP:** 10
SALES (est): 53.5MM **Privately Held**
WEB: www.mobilityelectronics.com
SIC: 3663 Mobile communication equipment

(P-17540)
IMAGINE COMMUNICATIONS CORP
1493 Poinsettia Ave # 143, Vista (92081-8544)
PHONE................................760 936-4000
Jack Williams, *Branch Mgr*
EMP: 11
SALES (corp-wide): 3.8B **Privately Held**
SIC: 3663 Radio broadcasting & communications equipment; television broadcasting & communications equipment
HQ: Imagine Communications Corp.
3001 Dallas Pkwy Ste 300
Frisco TX 75034
469 803-4900

(P-17541)
IMPAC TECHNOLOGIES INC
3050 Red Hill Ave, Costa Mesa (92626-4524)
PHONE................................714 427-2000
Louis Parker, *President*
EMP: 89
SQ FT: 24,000
SALES (est): 8.2MM **Privately Held**
SIC: 3663 Radio & TV communications equipment

(P-17542)
INGENU INC (PA)
10301 Meanley Dr, San Diego (92131-3011)
P.O. Box 22628 (92192-2628)
PHONE................................858 201-6000
John Horn, *CEO*
Tom Gregor, *President*
Dan Halvorson, *CFO*
Jason Wilson, *Senior VP*
Josh Builta, *Vice Pres*
EMP: 50
SALES (est): 12.4MM **Privately Held**
SIC: 3663 Radio & TV communications equipment

(P-17543)
INTERSTATE ELECTRONICS CORP
604 E Vermont Ave, Anaheim (92805-5607)
PHONE................................714 758-3395
Thomas Jackson, *Branch Mgr*
EMP: 50
SALES (corp-wide): 6.8B **Publicly Held**
WEB: www.iechome.com
SIC: 3663 3621 Telemetering equipment, electronic; motors & generators
HQ: Interstate Electronics Corporation
602 E Vermont Ave
Anaheim CA 92805
714 758-0500

▲ = Import ▼=Export
◆ =Import/Export

(P-17544)
IPITEK GROUP INC
2330 Faraday Ave, Carlsbad (92008-7243)
P.O. Box 130878 (92013-0878)
PHONE.................................760 438-8362
Michael Salour, *Ch of Bd*
EMP: 150
SALES (est): 15.5MM **Privately Held**
SIC: 3663 Television broadcasting & communications equipment

(P-17545)
J M MILLS COMMUNICATIONS INC (HQ)
4686 Mission Gorge Pl, San Diego
(92120-4133)
PHONE.................................613 321-2100
John Mills, *President*
Lisa Mills, *Vice Pres*
Michael Olivarez, *Technician*
EMP: 21
SQ FT: 9,000
SALES (est): 2.2MM
SALES (corp-wide): 8.2MM **Privately Held**
WEB: www.millscom.com
SIC: 3663 Radio & TV communications equipment

(P-17546)
JAMPRO ANTENNAS INC
6340 Sky Creek Dr, Sacramento
(95828-1025)
PHONE.................................916 383-1177
Alex Perchevitch, *President*
Doug McCabe, *COO*
Ken Mueller, *CFO*
Cyndi Sanderson, *Vice Pres*
◆ EMP: 60
SQ FT: 12,000
SALES (est): 13.8MM **Privately Held**
WEB: www.jampro.com
SIC: 3663 Antennas, transmitting & communications; television antennas (transmitting) & ground equipment

(P-17547)
JANTEQ CORP (PA)
9975 Toledo Way Ste 150, Irvine
(92618-1827)
PHONE.................................949 215-2603
John A Porter, *President*
Andrew Fox, *Director*
Nigel Pedersen, *Director*
EMP: 24
SQ FT: 33,000
SALES: 29.3MM **Privately Held**
SIC: 3663 Radio & TV communications equipment

(P-17548)
JUST CELLULAR INC
9327 Deering Ave, Chatsworth
(91311-5858)
PHONE.................................818 701-3039
James Eric Kirkland, *President*
▲ EMP: 35
SQ FT: 6,700
SALES (est): 7.3MM **Privately Held**
SIC: 3663 Cellular radio telephone; mobile communication equipment

(P-17549)
JW WIRELESS
846 E Valley Blvd Ste A, San Gabriel
(91776-4602)
PHONE.................................626 532-2511
Leo Lee, *Owner*
Ben Her, *Partner*
EMP: 10
SALES (est): 1.3MM **Privately Held**
SIC: 3663 Cellular radio telephone

(P-17550)
K TECH TELECOMMUNICATIONS INC
9555 Owensmouth Ave Ste 2, Chatsworth
(91311-8083)
PHONE.................................818 773-0333
Steve Kuh, *President*
EMP: 10
SALES (est): 1.8MM **Privately Held**
SIC: 3663 Radio & television switching equipment

(P-17551)
KATEEVA INC
7015 Gateway Blvd, Newark (94560-1011)
PHONE.................................510 953-7600
Alain Harrus, *CEO*
Conor Madigan, *President*
Eli Vronsky,
May Su, *Officer*
Tom Wu, *Exec VP*
▲ EMP: 300
SQ FT: 11,000
SALES (est): 19.6MM **Privately Held**
SIC: 3663 Cable television equipment

(P-17552)
KATZ MILLENNIUM SLS & MKTG INC
Also Called: Clear Channel Radio Sales
5700 Wilshire Blvd # 100, Los Angeles
(90036-3659)
PHONE.................................323 966-5066
Nathan Brown, *Manager*
EMP: 100 **Publicly Held**
WEB: www.millenniumtvsales.com
SIC: 3663 Radio receiver networks
HQ: Katz Millennium Sales & Marketing Inc.
125 W 55th St Frnt 3
New York NY 10019

(P-17553)
KIRSEN TECHNOLOGIES INC
2041 Bancroft Way Ste 201, Berkeley
(94704-1443)
PHONE.................................510 540-5383
EMP: 10
SALES (est): 1.4MM **Privately Held**
WEB: www.kirsentech.com
SIC: 3663

(P-17554)
KMIC TECHNOLOGY INC
2095 Ringwood Ave Ste 10, San Jose
(95131-1786)
PHONE.................................408 240-3600
David Kim, *President*
Paul Truong, *Design Engr*
Jinho Park, *Opers Mgr*
EMP: 28
SQ FT: 15,800
SALES (est): 5.2MM **Privately Held**
SIC: 3663 Receivers, radio communications

(P-17555)
KRATOS DEF & SEC SOLUTIONS INC (PA)
10680 Treena St Ste 600, San Diego
(92131-2440)
PHONE.................................858 812-7300
Eric M Demarco, *President*
Scot Jarvis, *Bd of Directors*
Benjamin Goodwin, *Senior VP*
George Baker, *Vice Pres*
Maria Cervantes De Burgreen, *Vice Pres*
EMP: 300
SALES: 618MM **Publicly Held**
WEB: www.kratosdefense.com/
SIC: 3663 3761 7382 8711 Microwave communication equipment; satellites, communications; guided missiles & space vehicles; security systems services; engineering services; facilities support services

(P-17556)
KWORLD (USA) COMPUTER INC
499 Nibus Ste D, Brea (92821-3211)
PHONE.................................626 581-0867
Chung-Chieh Wang, *President*
▲ EMP: 12
SQ FT: 4,600
SALES (est): 2.8MM **Privately Held**
WEB: www.kworldcomputer.com
SIC: 3663 Cable television equipment
PA: Kworld Computer Co., Ltd.
6f, 113, Chien 2nd Rd.,
New Taipei City TAP 23585

(P-17557)
L-3 COMMUNICATIONS CORPORATION
Telemetry & Rf Products
9020 Balboa Ave, San Diego (92123-1510)
PHONE.................................858 694-7500
Fax: 619 670-0127
EMP: 16
SALES (corp-wide): 10.4B **Publicly Held**
SIC: 3663
HQ: L-3 Communications Corporation
600 3rd Ave
New York NY 10016
212 697-1111

(P-17558)
L3 APPLIED TECHNOLOGIES INC (DH)
Also Called: L-3 Applied Technologies, Inc.
10180 Barnes Canyon Rd, San Diego
(92121-2724)
PHONE.................................858 404-7824
Michael T Strainese, *CEO*
Robert A Huffman, *President*
Patricia Hernandez, *General Mgr*
Cliff Moore, *Admin Asst*
▼ EMP: 94
SALES (est): 16.1MM
SALES (corp-wide): 6.8B **Publicly Held**
SIC: 3663 3669 3769 Telemetering equipment, electronic; receiver-transmitter units (transceiver); amplifiers, RF power & IF; signaling apparatus, electric; intercommunication systems, electric; guided missile & space vehicle parts & auxiliary equipment
HQ: L3 Technologies, Inc.
600 3rd Ave Fl 34
New York NY 10016
212 697-1111

(P-17559)
L3 APPLIED TECHNOLOGIES INC
10180 Barnes Canyon Rd, San Diego
(92121-2724)
PHONE.................................858 404-7824
Janet Luna, *Controller*
EMP: 102
SALES (corp-wide): 6.8B **Publicly Held**
SIC: 3663 3669 3769 Telemetering equipment, electronic; receiver-transmitter units (transceiver); amplifiers, RF power & IF; signaling apparatus, electric; intercommunication systems, electric; guided missile & space vehicle parts & auxiliary equipment
HQ: L3 Applied Technologies, Inc.
10180 Barnes Canyon Rd
San Diego CA 92121
858 404-7824

(P-17560)
L3 TECHNOLOGIES INC
Also Called: L-3 Telemetry & Rf Products
9020 Balboa Ave, San Diego (92123-1510)
PHONE.................................858 279-0411
Burt Smith, *Branch Mgr*
Ron Waltman, *Director*
Damon Handley, *Manager*
EMP: 358
SALES (corp-wide): 6.8B **Publicly Held**
SIC: 3663 3669 3812 3679 Telemetering equipment, electronic; receiver-transmitter units (transceiver); amplifiers, RF power & IF; signaling apparatus, electric; intercommunication systems, electric; search & navigation equipment; aircraft control systems, electronic; microwave components; guided missile & space vehicle parts & auxiliary equipment
HQ: L3 Technologies, Inc.
600 3rd Ave Fl 34
New York NY 10016
212 697-1111

(P-17561)
L3 TECHNOLOGIES INC
Electron Devices
3100 Lomita Blvd, Torrance (90505-5104)
PHONE.................................650 591-8411
James D Benham, *President*
EMP: 398

(P-17562)
L3 TECHNOLOGIES INC
602 E Vermont Ave, Anaheim
(92805-5607)
PHONE.................................714 758-4222
Robert Vanwechel, *Branch Mgr*
Prima Pamplona, *Analyst*
EMP: 220
SALES (corp-wide): 6.8B **Publicly Held**
SIC: 3663 Telemetering equipment, electronic
HQ: L3 Technologies, Inc.
600 3rd Ave Fl 34
New York NY 10016
212 697-1111

(P-17563)
L3 TECHNOLOGIES INC
Narda Microwave West
107 Woodmere Rd, Folsom (95630-4706)
PHONE.................................916 351-4556
Michael Claggett, *Division Pres*
EMP: 165
SALES (corp-wide): 6.8B **Publicly Held**
SIC: 3663 Telemetering equipment, electronic
HQ: L3 Technologies, Inc.
600 3rd Ave Fl 34
New York NY 10016
212 697-1111

(P-17564)
L3 TECHNOLOGIES INC
L3 Rccs
10180 Barnes Canyon Rd, San Diego
(92121-2724)
PHONE.................................858 552-9716
Jonathan Roy, *CFO*
David Duggan, *CEO*
EMP: 100
SALES (corp-wide): 6.8B **Publicly Held**
SIC: 3663 Telemetering equipment, electronic
HQ: L3 Technologies, Inc.
600 3rd Ave Fl 34
New York NY 10016
212 697-1111

(P-17565)
L3 TECHNOLOGIES INC
Datron Advanced Tech Div
200 W Los Angeles Ave, Simi Valley
(93065-1650)
PHONE.................................805 584-1717
John Digioia, *Branch Mgr*
EMP: 100
SALES (corp-wide): 6.8B **Publicly Held**
SIC: 3663 Satellites, communications
HQ: L3 Technologies, Inc.
600 3rd Ave Fl 34
New York NY 10016
212 697-1111

(P-17566)
L3 TECHNOLOGIES INC
Also Called: Communction Systms-Wst/Lnkabit
9890 Towne Centre Dr # 100, San Diego
(92121-1983)
PHONE.................................858 552-9500
Andrew Ivers, *Branch Mgr*
Ralph Williams, *President*
EMP: 325
SALES (corp-wide): 6.8B **Publicly Held**
SIC: 3663 Space satellite communications equipment
HQ: L3 Technologies, Inc.
600 3rd Ave Fl 34
New York NY 10016
212 697-1111

(P-17567)
L3 TECHNOLOGIES INC
Also Called: Randtron Antenna Systems
130 Constitution Dr, Menlo Park
(94025-1141)
PHONE.................................650 326-9500
Robert Friedman, *Branch Mgr*

PRODUCTS & SVCS

Kevin McCullough, *President*
David Butler, *Vice Pres*
Dennis Kanzawa, *MIS Mgr*
Barbara Maynard, *Buyer*
EMP: 160
SALES (corp-wide): 6.8B **Publicly Held**
SIC: 3663 Telemetering equipment, electronic; antennas, transmitting & communications
HQ: L3 Technologies, Inc.
600 3rd Ave Fl 34
New York NY 10016
212 697-1111

(P-17568)
L3 TECHNOLOGIES INC
15825 Roxford St, Sylmar (91342-3537)
PHONE..................818 367-0111
EMP: 208
SALES (corp-wide): 6.8B **Publicly Held**
SIC: 3663 Radio & TV communications equipment
HQ: L3 Technologies, Inc.
600 3rd Ave Fl 34
New York NY 10016
212 697-1111

(P-17569)
L3 TECHNOLOGIES INC
Also Called: L-3 Communication
2700 Merced St, San Leandro (94577-5602)
PHONE..................858 499-0284
Jim Clemmons, *Branch Mgr*
EMP: 208
SALES (corp-wide): 6.8B **Publicly Held**
SIC: 3663 Telemetering equipment, electronic; receiver-transmitter units (transceiver); amplifiers, RF power & IF
HQ: L3 Technologies, Inc.
600 3rd Ave Fl 34
New York NY 10016
212 697-1111

(P-17570)
LEGEND SILICON CORP
22 Stirling Way, Hayward (94542-7945)
PHONE..................408 735-9888
Zhengyu Zhang, *President*
Hong Dong, *Vice Chairman*
Lin Yang, *Chairman*
EMP: 50
SQ FT: 8,000
SALES (est): 5.8MM **Privately Held**
WEB: www.legendsilicon.com
SIC: 3663 8733 Antennas, transmitting & communications; research institute

(P-17571)
LENNTEK CORPORATION
Also Called: Sonix
1610 Lockness Pl, Torrance (90501-5119)
PHONE..................310 534-2738
Danny Tsai, *Principal*
Steven Reymond, *Sales Staff*
▲ **EMP:** 50
SQ FT: 15,000
SALES: 20MM **Privately Held**
SIC: 3663 Mobile communication equipment

(P-17572)
LGC WIRELESS INC
541 E Trimble Rd, San Jose (95131-1224)
PHONE..................408 952-2400
Ian Sugarbroad, *President*
John Niedermaier, *CFO*
Michael Frausing, *Senior VP*
Dermot Conlon, *Vice Pres*
▲ **EMP:** 227
SQ FT: 30,000
SALES (est): 21.7MM **Publicly Held**
WEB: www.lgcwireless.com
SIC: 3663 Carrier equipment, radio communications
HQ: Commscope Connectivity Solutions Llc
1100 Commscope Pl Se
Hickory NC 28602
828 324-2200

(P-17573)
LOCKHEED MARTIN CORPORATION
3130 Zanker Rd, San Jose (95134-1965)
P.O. Box 3504, Sunnyvale (94088-3504)
PHONE..................408 473-3000

Magda Clyne, *Manager*
Steve Billmire, *Software Engr*
Carlos Bettencourt, *Engineer*
Kristy Dalrymple, *Engineer*
Mark Ptak, *Engineer*
EMP: 1665 **Publicly Held**
WEB: www.lockheedmartin.com
SIC: 3663 7373 8711 Satellites, communications; computer integrated systems design; engineering services
PA: Lockheed Martin Corporation
6801 Rockledge Dr
Bethesda MD 20817

(P-17574)
LOCKHEED MARTIN CORPORATION
Bldg 8310, Lompoc (93437)
PHONE..................805 606-4860
John Goodwin, *Administration*
EMP: 300 **Publicly Held**
WEB: www.lockheedmartin.com
SIC: 3663 3761 Satellites, communications; space vehicles, complete; guided missiles, complete; ballistic missiles, complete; guided missiles & space vehicles, research & development
PA: Lockheed Martin Corporation
6801 Rockledge Dr
Bethesda MD 20817

(P-17575)
LOMA SCIENTIFIC INTERNATIONAL
3115 Kashiwa St, Torrance (90505-4010)
PHONE..................310 539-8655
J Patrick Loughboro, *President*
EMP: 20
SQ FT: 16,000
SALES (est): 3.1MM **Privately Held**
WEB: www.lomasci.com
SIC: 3663 Transmitting apparatus, radio or television

(P-17576)
LORIMAR GROUP INC
Also Called: Lorimar Communications
1488 Pioneer Way Ste 14, El Cajon (92020-1633)
PHONE..................619 954-9300
George M Johnson, *CEO*
Sue Cole, *CFO*
Lori Johnson, *Technology*
EMP: 13
SQ FT: 2,400
SALES (est): 2.6MM **Privately Held**
SIC: 3663 7622 Radio & TV communications equipment; radio repair & installation

(P-17577)
LPN WIRELESS INC
4170 Redwood Hwy, San Rafael (94903-2618)
PHONE..................707 781-9210
EMP: 12
SQ FT: 2,500
SALES (est): 1.1MM **Privately Held**
SIC: 3663

(P-17578)
M G WATANABE INC
Also Called: West Coast Microwave
17031 Roseton Ave, Artesia (90701-2642)
PHONE..................562 402-8989
Mike Watanabe, *President*
EMP: 13
SQ FT: 1,500
SALES (est): 1.8MM **Privately Held**
SIC: 3663 Microwave communication equipment

(P-17579)
MACOM TECHNOLOGY SOLUTIONS INC
Also Called: Commercial Electronics Pho
4000 Macarthur Blvd # 101, Newport Beach (92660-2546)
PHONE..................310 320-6160
Gary Lopes, *Principal*
Gary Shah, *Vice Pres*
Sean Felstead, *Deputy Dir*
EMP: 16 **Publicly Held**
WEB: www.macom.com

SIC: 3663 2752 3674 Radio & TV communications equipment; catalogs, lithographed; semiconductors & related devices
HQ: Macom Technology Solutions Inc.
100 Chelmsford St
Lowell MA 01851

(P-17580)
MATCHLESS LLC
8423 Wilshire Blvd, Beverly Hills (90211)
PHONE..................310 473-5100
Geoff Emery, *Manager*
EMP: 23
SALES (est): 2MM **Privately Held**
SIC: 3663 Amplifiers, RF power & IF

(P-17581)
MCV TECHNOLOGIES INC
Also Called: McV Microwave
6349 Nancy Ridge Dr, San Diego (92121-6203)
PHONE..................858 450-0468
Edward Liang, *President*
Marian Liang, *President*
▲ **EMP:** 15
SQ FT: 5,000
SALES: 3MM **Privately Held**
WEB: www.mcvtech.com
SIC: 3663 3679 3629 Microwave communication equipment; microwave components; power conversion units, a.c. to d.c.: static-electric

(P-17582)
MDA CMMUNICATIONS HOLDINGS LLC
3825 Fabian Way, Palo Alto (94303-4604)
PHONE..................650 852-4000
Anil Wirasekara,
William McCombe,
EMP: 2800 EST: 2015
SALES (est): 133MM
SALES (corp-wide): 2.1B **Publicly Held**
SIC: 3663 Satellites, communications
PA: Maxar Technologies Inc.
1300 W 120th Ave
Westminster CO 80234
303 684-2207

(P-17583)
MERCURY NETWORKS LLC
1800 Wyatt Dr Ste 2, Santa Clara (95054-1527)
PHONE..................408 859-1345
Matt Cox, *Principal*
▲ **EMP:** 16 EST: 2014
SQ FT: 3,000
SALES: 1.4MM **Privately Held**
SIC: 3663 Light communications equipment

(P-17584)
METRIC SYSTEMS CORPORATION
2091 Las Palmas Dr Ste D, Carlsbad (92011-1551)
PHONE..................760 560-0348
William M Brown, *President*
Lori Daub, *Executive Asst*
Peter Brown, *Admin Sec*
EMP: 10
SALES (est): 1.9MM **Privately Held**
WEB: www.metricsystems.com
SIC: 3663 Mobile communication equipment

(P-17585)
MICRO-MODE PRODUCTS INC
1870 John Towers Ave, El Cajon (92020-1193)
PHONE..................619 449-3844
Vincent De Marco, *President*
Michael Cuban, *CEO*
Ruby Marco, *Treasurer*
Dick Robinson, *Vice Pres*
Emily Clagett, *Department Mgr*
EMP: 110 **EST:** 1971
SALES (est): 24.3MM **Privately Held**
WEB: www.micromode.com
SIC: 3663 3678 7389 Microwave communication equipment; electronic connectors;

(P-17586)
MICROVOICE CORPORATION
Also Called: Microvoice Systems
345 Willis Ave, Camarillo (93010-8558)
PHONE..................805 389-2922
EMP: 50
SQ FT: 10,000
SALES (est): 4.1MM **Privately Held**
WEB: www.microvoice.com
SIC: 3663

(P-17587)
MICROWAVE DYNAMICS
16541 Scientific, Irvine (92618-4356)
PHONE..................949 679-7788
Shoja Peter Adel, *CEO*
Brian Adel, *Admin Sec*
EMP: 18
SQ FT: 10,000
SALES (est): 3.8MM **Privately Held**
WEB: www.microwave-dynamics.com
SIC: 3663 5065 Microwave communication equipment; electronic parts & equipment

(P-17588)
MISSION MICROWAVE TECH LLC
9924 Norwalk Blvd, Santa Fe Springs (90670-3322)
PHONE..................951 893-4925
Francis Auricchio, *President*
Michael Delisio, *CTO*
Tami Dias, *Sales Staff*
EMP: 23 EST: 2014
SALES: 210K **Privately Held**
SIC: 3663 Satellites, communications

(P-17589)
MOBILE TONE INC
5430 Westhaven St, Los Angeles (90016-3314)
PHONE..................323 939-6928
Michael Towner, *President*
EMP: 12
SALES (est): 1.1MM **Privately Held**
SIC: 3663 Mobile communication equipment

(P-17590)
MODULAR COMMUNICATIONS SYSTEMS
Also Called: Moducom
373 N Western Ave Ste 15, Los Angeles (90004-2616)
PHONE..................818 764-1333
Robert A Moesch, *President*
Bernard Brandt, *Vice Pres*
Peter Hong, *Vice Pres*
Robert Moesch, *Principal*
Steve Simpkins, *Managing Dir*
EMP: 21
SQ FT: 10,000
SALES (est): 4MM **Privately Held**
WEB: www.moducom.com
SIC: 3663 Radio & TV communications equipment

(P-17591)
MOPHIE INC (HQ)
15495 Sand Canyon Ave # 4, Irvine (92618-3152)
PHONE..................888 866-7443
Daniel Huang, *CEO*
▲ **EMP:** 37
SALES (est): 17.6MM **Publicly Held**
SIC: 3663 Mobile communication equipment

(P-17592)
MOSELEY ASSOCIATES INC (HQ)
82 Coromar Dr, Goleta (93117-3024)
PHONE..................805 968-9621
Jamal N Hamdani, *President*
Bruce Tarr, *CFO*
Rodney Bryant, *Director*
▲ **EMP:** 109
SQ FT: 56,000
SALES (est): 58.7MM
SALES (corp-wide): 42MM **Privately Held**
WEB: www.moseleysb.com
SIC: 3663 Radio & TV communications equipment

▲ = Import ▼=Export
◆ =Import/Export

PA: Axxcss Wireless Solutions Inc
82 Coromar Dr
Goleta CA 93117
805 968-9621

(P-17593)
MOTOROLA MOBILITY LLC
1633 Bayshore Hwy, Burlingame
(94010-1544)
PHONE..................................206 383-7785
David Zhao, *Branch Mgr*
EMP: 58 **Privately Held**
SIC: **3663** Radio & TV communications
equipment
HQ: Motorola Mobility Llc
222 Mdse Mart Plz # 1800
Chicago IL 60654

(P-17594)
MOTOROLA MOBILITY LLC
809 Eleventh Ave Bldg 4, Sunnyvale
(94089-4731)
PHONE..................................847 576-5000
EMP: 58 **Privately Held**
WEB: www.motorola.com
SIC: **3663** Radio & TV communications
equipment
HQ: Motorola Mobility Llc
222 Mdse Mart Plz # 1800
Chicago IL 60654
-

(P-17595)
MOTOROLA SOLUTIONS INC
1101 Marina Village Pkwy # 200, Alameda
(94501-6472)
PHONE..................................510 217-7400
EMP: 142
SALES (corp-wide): 6.3B **Publicly Held**
SIC: **3663** 5046 3674 3571
PA: Motorola Solutions, Inc.
500 W Monroe St Ste 4400
Chicago IL 60661
847 576-5000

(P-17596)
MOTOROLA SOLUTIONS INC
725 S Figueroa St # 1855, Los Angeles
(90017-5458)
PHONE..................................213 362-6706
Jim Hardimon, *General Mgr*
EMP: 40
SALES (corp-wide): 7.3B **Publicly Held**
SIC: **3663** Transmitter-receivers, radio
PA: Motorola Solutions, Inc.
500 W Monroe St Ste 4400
Chicago IL 60661
847 576-5000

(P-17597)
MOTOROLA SOLUTIONS INC
6101 W Century Blvd, Los Angeles
(90045-5310)
PHONE..................................954 723-4730
EMP: 142
SALES (corp-wide): 5.7B **Publicly Held**
SIC: **3663**
PA: Motorola Solutions, Inc.
1303 E Algonquin Rd
Schaumburg IL 60661
847 576-5000

(P-17598)
MOTOROLA SOLUTIONS INC
805 E Middlefield Rd, Mountain View
(94043-4025)
PHONE..................................650 318-3200
Maulik Desai, *Manager*
EMP: 60
SALES (corp-wide): 7.3B **Publicly Held**
WEB: www.motorola.com
SIC: **3663** Radio & TV communications
equipment
PA: Motorola Solutions, Inc.
500 W Monroe St Ste 4400
Chicago IL 60661
847 576-5000

(P-17599)
MTI LABORATORY INC
Also Called: Mtil
201 Continental Blvd # 300, El Segundo
(90245-4500)
PHONE..................................310 955-3700
Davis Kent, *President*

Alister Hsu, *CFO*
Pam Montellano, *Vice Pres*
▼ EMP: 26
SQ FT: 12,000
SALES: 6.7MM **Privately Held**
SIC: **3663** Microwave communication
equipment; mobile communication equip-
ment; radio broadcasting & communica-
tions equipment
PA: Microelectronics Technology, Inc.
1, Innovation 2nd Rd., Science-Based
Industrial Park,
Hsinchu City 30076

(P-17600)
NAVCOM TECHNOLOGY INC
(HQ)
20780 Madrona Ave, Torrance
(90503-3777)
PHONE..................................310 381-2000
Tony Thelen, *CEO*
Craig Fawcept, *President*
Michael Linzy, *COO*
Alisobhani Jalal, *Principal*
EMP: 49
SQ FT: 55,000
SALES (est): 9.6MM
SALES (corp-wide): 37.3B **Publicly Held**
WEB: www.navcomtech.com
SIC: **3663** 8748 Satellites, communica-
tions; communications consulting
PA: Deere & Company
1 John Deere Pl
Moline IL 61265
309 765-8000

(P-17601)
NERDIST CHANNEL LLC
Also Called: Nerdist Industries
2525 N Naomi St, Burbank (91504-3236)
PHONE..................................818 333-2705
Peter Levin,
EMP: 30
SALES (est): 2.9MM **Privately Held**
SIC: **3663** Digital encoders

(P-17602)
NEVION USA INC
400 W Ventura Blvd # 155, Camarillo
(93010-9137)
PHONE..................................805 247-8575
Geir Bryn-Jensen, *CEO*
Petter Kvaal Djupvik, *COO*
Nils Fredriksen, *CFO*
Hans Hasselbach, *Officer*
John Glass, *Exec VP*
EMP: 61
SQ FT: 12,000
SALES (est): 12.4MM **Privately Held**
WEB: www.nevion.com
SIC: **3663** 3669 3661 Radio & TV com-
munications equipment; emergency
alarms; telephones & telephone appara-
tus
HQ: Network Electronics Holdings, Inc.
1600 Emerson Ave
Oxnard CA 93033

(P-17603)
NEXTEC MICROWAVE & RF INC
3010 Scott Blvd, Santa Clara (95054-3323)
PHONE..................................408 727-1189
Dongwook Lee, *President*
EMP: 10
SALES (est): 2.4MM **Privately Held**
WEB: www.nextec-rf.com
SIC: **3663** Radio & TV communications
equipment

(P-17604)
NEXTIVITY INC (PA)
16550 W Bernardo Dr # 550, San Diego
(92127-1889)
PHONE..................................858 485-9442
Werner Sievers, *CEO*
Tom Cooper, *President*
Alan Benson, *Bd of Directors*
Thomas Cooper, *Vice Pres*
George Lamb, *Vice Pres*
▲ EMP: 69
SALES (est): 13.9MM **Privately Held**
SIC: **3663** Airborne radio communications
equipment

(P-17605)
NORDEN MILLIMETER INC
5441 Merchant Cir Ste C, Placerville
(95667-8643)
PHONE..................................530 642-9123
JC Rosenberg, *Chairman*
Duncan Smith, *President*
Kary Robertson, *Treasurer*
Pete Mastin, *CTO*
Ross Ecker, *Senior Engr*
EMP: 22
SQ FT: 10,000
SALES (est): 4.4MM **Privately Held**
WEB: www.nordengroup.com
SIC: **3663** Amplifiers, RF power & IF

(P-17606)
**NORTHROP GRUMMAN
SYSTEMS CORP**
Space Systems Division
1 Space Park Blvd, Redondo Beach
(90278-1071)
PHONE..................................310 812-5149
James Hthwy, *Program Mgr*
Ronald Tom, *Branch Mgr*
Ellen Gerber, *Administration*
Dennis Long, *Info Tech Dir*
Scott Ninegar, *Info Tech Dir*
EMP: 101 **Publicly Held**
WEB: www.trw.com
SIC: **3663** 3674 3679 3761 Airborne
radio communications equipment; satel-
lites, communications; semiconductors &
related devices; antennas, satellite:
household use; guided missiles & space
vehicles; guided missile & space vehicle
propulsion unit parts; navigational systems & instruments
HQ: Northrop Grumman Systems Corporation
2980 Fairview Park Dr
Falls Church VA 22042
703 280-2900

(P-17607)
**NVIDIA US INVESTMENT
COMPANY**
2701 San Tomas Expy, Santa Clara
(95050-2519)
PHONE..................................408 615-2500
Jen-Hsun Huang, *President*
EMP: 850 EST: 2000
SALES (est): 44.8MM **Publicly Held**
WEB: www.nvidia.com
SIC: **3663** Radio & TV communications
equipment
PA: Nvidia Corporation
2788 San Tomas Expy
Santa Clara CA 95051

(P-17608)
OMNEON INC (HQ)
4300 N 1st St, San Jose (95134-1258)
PHONE..................................408 585-5000
Suresh Vasudevan, *President*
Darwin Kuan, *President*
Laura Perrone, *CFO*
Ron Howe, *Senior VP*
Denis R Maynard, *Senior VP*
▲ EMP: 117
SQ FT: 68,000
SALES (est): 9.8MM
SALES (corp-wide): 403.5MM **Publicly
Held**
SIC: **3663** 7375 Television broadcasting &
communications equipment; information
retrieval services
PA: Harmonic Inc.
4300 N 1st St
San Jose CA 95134
408 542-2500

(P-17609)
OPHIR RF INC
5300 Beethoven St Fl 3, Los Angeles
(90066-7068)
PHONE..................................310 306-5556
Ilan Israely, *President*
Albert Barrios, *Vice Pres*
Mary Ellen Smith, *Materials Mgr*
EMP: 42
SQ FT: 11,800
SALES: 6.9MM **Privately Held**
WEB: www.ophirrf.com
SIC: **3663** Amplifiers, RF power & IF

(P-17610)
OPTIM MICROWAVE INC
4020 Adolfo Rd, Camarillo (93012-6793)
PHONE..................................805 482-7093
Jack Peterson, *President*
Cynthia Espino, *Shareholder*
John Mahon, *Vice Pres*
William Faust, *Admin Sec*
Tom Bohner, *Prdtn Mgr*
EMP: 23
SQ FT: 15,000
SALES (est): 3.7MM **Privately Held**
WEB: www.optim-microwave.com
SIC: **3663** Antennas, transmitting & com-
munications

(P-17611)
OPTODYNE INCORPORATION
1180 W Mahalo Pl, Rancho Dominguez
(90220-5443)
PHONE..................................310 635-7481
Charles Wang, *CEO*
Lily Wang, *CFO*
Lichen Wang, *Vice Pres*
▲ EMP: 25
SQ FT: 7,500
SALES (est): 4.6MM **Privately Held**
WEB: www.optodyne.com
SIC: **3663** 3829 3827 Light communica-
tions equipment; measuring & controlling
devices; optical instruments & lenses

(P-17612)
OTI ENGINEERING CONS INC
24926 State Highway 108, MI Wuk Village
(95346-9714)
PHONE..................................209 586-1022
Thomas A Olson, *CEO*
Janice Sue Olson, *Vice Pres*
EMP: 30
SQ FT: 2,600
SALES (est): 4.2MM
SALES (corp-wide): 135.1MM **Privately
Held**
WEB: www.olson-technology.com
SIC: **3663** Cable television equipment
HQ: Antronix Of California, Inc.
24926 State Highway 108
Mi Wuk Village CA 95346
800 545-1022

(P-17613)
OVATION R&G LLC (PA)
2850 Ocean Park Blvd # 225, Santa Monica
(90405-2955)
PHONE..................................310 430-7575
Charles D D Segars,
Phil Gilligan, *CFO*
Liz Janneman, *Exec VP*
Brad Samuels, *Exec VP*
EMP: 42
SALES (est): 12.1MM **Privately Held**
SIC: **3663** Satellites, communications; tele-
vision broadcasting & communications
equipment

(P-17614)
**P C I MANUFACTURING
DIVISION**
Also Called: Pagecorp Industries
2103 N Ross St, Santa Ana (92706-2507)
PHONE..................................714 543-3496
Sue Edwards, *President*
Jamie Edwards, *Admin Sec*
▲ EMP: 10
SQ FT: 3,500
SALES: 1.2MM **Privately Held**
WEB: www.pagecorp.com
SIC: **3663** 3823 5065 Pagers (one-way);
programmers, process type; paging & sig-
naling equipment

(P-17615)
P H MACHINING INC
1099 N 5th St, San Jose (95112-4414)
PHONE..................................408 627-4222
Mike Hanover, *President*
Jagdish Patel, *Vice Pres*
EMP: 11
SQ FT: 4,000
SALES: 3MM **Privately Held**
WEB: www.euro-inter-pharma.com
SIC: **3663** Microwave communication
equipment

PRODUCTS & SVCS

(P-17616)
PACE AMERICAS INC
887 N Douglas St 200, El Segundo
(90245-2801)
PHONE..................................310 606-8300
Bill Ryan, *Vice Pres*
▲ EMP: 27 EST: 2007
SALES (est): 2MM Privately Held
SIC: 3663 Cable television equipment

(P-17617)
PACIFIC WAVE SYSTEMS INC
2525 W 190th St, Torrance (90504-6002)
PHONE..................................714 893-0152
Carl Esposito, *CEO*
John J Tus, *CFO*
Victor Jay Miller, *Admin Sec*
Robert B Topolski, *Director*
EMP: 68
SALES (est): 10.4MM Privately Held
WEB: www.pacificwavesystems.com
SIC: 3663 Satellites, communications

(P-17618)
PACIFITEK SYSTEMS INC
344 Coogan Way, El Cajon (92020-1902)
PHONE..................................619 401-1968
EMP: 10
SQ FT: 3,300
SALES (est): 1.1MM Privately Held
SIC: 3663

(P-17619)
PALM INC (HQ)
950 W Maude Ave, Sunnyvale
(94085-2801)
PHONE..................................408 617-7000
Jonathan J Rubinstein, *President*
▲ EMP: 400
SQ FT: 347,144
SALES (est): 171.3MM
SALES (corp-wide): 9.3MM Privately
Held
WEB: www.palm.com
SIC: 3663 Mobile communication equip-
ment

(P-17620)
PEARPOINT INC
39740 Garand Ln Ste B, Palm Desert
(92211-7176)
PHONE..................................760 343-7350
Paul Tistai, *CEO*
Vince Monteleone, *CFO*
EMP: 33
SQ FT: 15,000
SALES (est): 4.4MM
SALES (corp-wide): 2B Publicly Held
WEB: www.pearpoint.com
SIC: 3663 3829 5065 Television closed
circuit equipment; measuring & controlling
devices; closed circuit television
HQ: Radiodetection Limited
Western Drive
Bristol BS14

(P-17621)
**PENINSULA ENGRG SOLUTIONS
INC**
288 Love Ln, Danville (94526-2447)
P.O. Box 1095 (94526-1095)
PHONE..................................925 837-2243
Frank Martens, *President*
John Saefke, *VP Sales*
EMP: 10
SQ FT: 1,200
SALES: 1.6MM Privately Held
WEB: www.peninsulaengineering.com
SIC: 3663 Microwave communication
equipment

(P-17622)
PHONESUIT INC
1431 7th St Ste 201, Santa Monica
(90401-2638)
PHONE..................................310 774-0282
Sumeet Gupta, *CEO*
EMP: 25
SQ FT: 4,000
SALES: 10MM Privately Held
SIC: 3663 Mobile communication equip-

(P-17623)
PINNACLE SYSTEMS INC
280 Bernardo Ave, Mountain View
(94043-5238)
PHONE..................................650 237-1900
EMP: 12
SALES (est): 1.1MM Privately Held
SIC: 3663 Radio & TV communications
equipment

(P-17624)
**PIONEER AUTOMOTIVE TECH
INC**
8701 Siempre Viva Rd, San Diego
(92154-6294)
PHONE..................................937 746-6600
Jenna Heaston, *Branch Mgr*
EMP: 10
SALES (corp-wide): 242.1K Privately
Held
SIC: 3663 Cable television equipment
HQ: Pioneer Automotive Technologies, Inc.
100 S Pioneer Blvd
Springboro OH 45066

(P-17625)
**POSITRON ACCESS SOLUTIONS
INC**
1640 2nd St Ste 207, Norco (92860-2983)
PHONE..................................951 272-9100
Reginald Weiser, *CEO*
Pierre Trudeau, *President*
Claude Samson, *CFO*
Alan W Pritchard, *Senior VP*
Bob Williams, *Engineer*
EMP: 10
SALES (est): 1.4MM
SALES (corp-wide): 54.8MM Privately
Held
SIC: 3663 4899 Mobile communication
equipment; data communication services
HQ: Positron Access Solutions Corporation
5101 Rue Buchan Bureau 220
Montreal QC H4P 2
514 345-2220

(P-17626)
PRECISION CONTACTS INC
990 Suncast Ln, El Dorado Hills
(95762-9626)
PHONE..................................916 939-4147
Mat Wroblewski, *President*
Mathew Wroblewski, *President*
Nancy Wroblewski, *Corp Secy*
Dean Wroblewski, *Vice Pres*
Steven Wroblewski, *Vice Pres*
EMP: 37
SQ FT: 24,000
SALES (est): 5.3MM Privately Held
WEB: www.precisioncontacts.com
SIC: 3663 3829 Radio & TV communica-
tions equipment; measuring & controlling
devices

(P-17627)
PRISM SKYLABS INC
799 Market St Fl 8, San Francisco
(94103-2044)
PHONE..................................415 243-0834
Stephen Russell, *CEO*
Bob Cutting, *Vice Pres*
Constantin Kisly, *Engineer*
Andrew Potseluieff, *Controller*
Whit Moses, *Marketing Staff*
EMP: 14
SALES (est): 2.1MM Privately Held
SIC: 3663 Space satellite communications
equipment

(P-17628)
PROMPTER PEOPLE INC
Also Called: Flolight
126 Dillon Ave, Campbell (95008-3002)
PHONE..................................408 353-6000
Mark R Ditmanson, *CEO*
▲ EMP: 12
SALES: 5MM Privately Held
SIC: 3663 3651 Telemetering equipment,
electronic; household video equipment

(P-17629)
PROSHOT INVESTORS LLC
Also Called: Proshot Golf
18007 Sky Park Cir Ste F, Irvine
(92614-6515)
PHONE..................................949 586-9500
David Kuhn, *President*
▲ EMP: 15
SALES (est): 1.1MM
SALES (corp-wide): 1.8MM Privately
Held
SIC: 3663
PA: Izon Network, Inc.
2600 N Central Ave # 1700
Phoenix AZ 85004
480 626-2423

(P-17630)
PUREWAVE NETWORKS INC
3951 Burton Dr, Santa Clara (95054-1583)
P.O. Box 970, Pleasanton (94566-0970)
PHONE..................................650 528-5200
Don Meiners, *CEO*
Chris Sommers, *President*
Mike Seifert, *CFO*
Peter Carson, *Senior VP*
Reza Golshan, *Vice Pres*
▲ EMP: 35
SALES (est): 6.7MM Privately Held
WEB: www.purewavenetworks.com
SIC: 3663 Light communications equip-
ment

(P-17631)
**QUALCOMM INCORPORATED
(PA)**
5775 Morehouse Dr, San Diego
(92121-1714)
PHONE..................................858 587-1121
Steve Mollenkopf, *CEO*
Mark McLaughlin, *Ch of Bd*
Cristiano R Amon, *President*
Alexander H Rogers, *President*
Akash Palkhiwala, *CFO*
EMP: 277
SALES: 24.2B Publicly Held
WEB: www.qualcomm.com
SIC: 3663 3674 7372 6794 Mobile com-
munication equipment; semiconductors &
related devices; integrated circuits, semi-
conductor networks, etc.; hybrid inte-
grated circuits; business oriented
computer software; patent buying, licens-
ing, leasing

(P-17632)
QUALCOMM INCORPORATED
3165 Kifer Rd, Santa Clara (95051-0804)
PHONE..................................858 587-1121
Stephen Zee, *Branch Mgr*
Jeff Freebairn, *Vice Pres*
Nayeem Islam, *Vice Pres*
Je W Kim, *Vice Pres*
Vinay Ravuri, *Vice Pres*
EMP: 13
SALES (corp-wide): 24.2B Publicly Held
WEB: www.qualcomm.com
SIC: 3663 Radio & TV communications
equipment
PA: Qualcomm Incorporated
5775 Morehouse Dr
San Diego CA 92121
858 587-1121

(P-17633)
QUALCOMM INCORPORATED
5525 Morehouse Dr, San Diego
(92121-1710)
PHONE..................................858 587-1121
Derek May, *Vice Pres*
Julia Chernova, *Human Resources*
Shelley Tancil, *Buyer*
EMP: 100
SALES (corp-wide): 24.2B Publicly Held
SIC: 3663 Space satellite communications
equipment
PA: Qualcomm Incorporated
5775 Morehouse Dr
San Diego CA 92121
858 587-1121

(P-17634)
QULSAR USA INC
90 Great Oaks Blvd # 204, San Jose
(95119-1314)
PHONE..................................408 715-1098

Rajendra Datta, *CEO*
Ola Andersson, *COO*
James Werner, *CFO*
EMP: 12
SQ FT: 1,400
SALES (est): 785.7K Privately Held
SIC: 3663 3661 3625 Mobile communica-
tion equipment; carrier equipment, tele-
phone or telegraph; timing devices,
electronic

(P-17635)
**RADIAN AUDIO ENGINEERING
INC**
600 N Batavia St, Orange (92868-1221)
PHONE..................................714 288-8900
Richard Kontrimas, *CEO*
Raimonda Kontrimas, *Admin Sec*
▲ EMP: 26
SQ FT: 17,000
SALES (est): 4.9MM Privately Held
WEB: www.radianaudio.com
SIC: 3663 5731 3651 Radio broadcasting
& communications equipment; radio, tele-
vision & electronic stores; household
audio & video equipment

(P-17636)
**RADIO FREQUENCY SYSTEMS
INC**
Also Called: Radio Frqency Systems Ferro-
com
6276 San Ignacio Ave E, San Jose
(95119-1363)
PHONE..................................408 281-6100
Tam Nguyen, *Branch Mgr*
Dalila Samatua, *Production*
EMP: 12
SALES (corp-wide): 25.8B Privately Held
WEB: www.rfsworld.com
SIC: 3663 Radio & TV communications
equipment
HQ: Radio Frequency Systems, Inc.
200 Pond View Dr
Meriden CT 06450
203 630-3311

(P-17637)
RADITEK INC (PA)
1702 Meridian Ave Ste L, San Jose
(95125-5586)
PHONE..................................408 266-7404
Malcolm R Lee, *President*
Peter Corbett, *COO*
Hima Thakkar, *Sales Staff*
▲ EMP: 79
SALES: 5.5MM Privately Held
WEB: www.raditek.com
SIC: 3663 Microwave communication
equipment

(P-17638)
RADITEK INC
44253 Old Warm Sprng Blvd, Fremont
(94538-6168)
PHONE..................................408 266-7404
Peter Corbett, *COO*
EMP: 15
SALES (est): 765.1K Privately Held
SIC: 3663 Microwave communication
equipment
PA: Raditek Inc.
1702 Meridian Ave Ste L
San Jose CA 95125

(P-17639)
RAMONA RESEARCH INC
13741 Danielson St Ste J, Poway
(92064-6895)
PHONE..................................858 679-0717
Todd Jones, *General Mgr*
Carlos Macau, *Treasurer*
EMP: 19
SALES (est): 990.6K Publicly Held
SIC: 3663 Microwave communication
equipment
PA: Heico Corporation
3000 Taft St
Hollywood FL 33021

(P-17640)
RAVEON TECHNOLOGIES CORP
2320 Cousteau Ct, Vista (92081-8363)
PHONE..................................760 444-5995

▲ = Import ▼=Export
◆ =Import/Export

John Richard Sonnenberg, *President*
Sam Sonnenberg, *Info Tech Mgr*
Eunice Hanson, *Accountant*
Medina Andrew, *Production*
Curt Buck, *Sales Mgr*
EMP: 37
SQ FT: 7,300
SALES (est): 7.4MM **Privately Held**
WEB: www.raveontech.com
SIC: 3663 Airborne radio communications

(P-17641)
RAYTHEON APPLIED SIGNAL (HQ)
460 W California Ave, Sunnyvale (94086-5148)
P.O. Box 660425, Dallas TX (75266-0425)
PHONE..................................408 749-1888
John R Treichler, *CEO*
Mark M Andersson, *COO*
James E Doyle, *CFO*
R Fred Roscher, *Exec VP*
Roger W Anderson, *Vice Pres*
EMP: 168
SQ FT: 266,077
SALES (est): 27B **Publicly Held**
SIC: 3663 Radio & TV communications equipment
PA: Raytheon Company
870 Winter St
Waltham MA 02451
781 522-3000

(P-17642)
RECOMAX SOFTWARE INC
706 La Para Ave, Palo Alto (94306-3157)
PHONE..................................408 592-0851
Vladimir Kardonskiy, *President*
EMP: 11
SALES (est): 1.1MM **Privately Held**
SIC: 3663

(P-17643)
REMEC BROADBAND WIRE
17034 Camino San Bernardo, San Diego (92127-5708)
PHONE..................................858 312-6900
Jamal Hamdani, *CEO*
Bruce Tarr, *CFO*
EMP: 180
SALES (est): 9MM
SALES (corp-wide): 42MM **Privately Held**
SIC: 3663 Mobile communication equipment
PA: Axxcss Wireless Solutions Inc
82 Coromar Dr
Goleta CA 93117
805 968-9621

(P-17644)
REMEC BROADBAND WIRELESS LLC (PA)
17034 Camino San Bernardo, San Diego (92127-5708)
PHONE..................................858 312-6900
David K Newman, *Mng Member*
Mark McMillen, *Sr Software Eng*
Vanmeurs Michiel, *Info Tech Mgr*
Michiel Van Meurs, *Info Tech Mgr*
Dan Bryson, *Engineer*
EMP: 102
SALES (est): 17.6MM **Privately Held**
SIC: 3663 Radio & TV communications equipment

(P-17645)
ROSELM INDUSTRIES INC
2510 Seaman Ave, South El Monte (91733-1928)
PHONE..................................626 442-6840
Conrad Arguijo, *President*
EMP: 20 **EST:** 1965
SQ FT: 13,000
SALES (est): 3.2MM **Privately Held**
WEB: www.socaltech.com
SIC: 3663 Radio & TV communications equipment

(P-17646)
ROTATING PRCSION MCHANISMS INC
Also Called: RPM
8750 Shirley Ave, Northridge (91324-3409)
PHONE..................................818 349-9774
Kathy Flynn-Nikolai, *CEO*
Jerome Smith, *Shareholder*
Daniel P Flynn, *President*
Kathleen Nikolai, *Vice Pres*
Tyler Banta, *Engineer*
EMP: 46
SQ FT: 40,000
SALES (est): 12.5MM **Privately Held**
WEB: www.rpm-psi.com
SIC: 3663 Radio & TV communications equipment

(P-17647)
RUCKUS WIRELESS INC
Also Called: General Instrument
2450 Walsh Ave, Santa Clara (95051-1303)
PHONE..................................408 235-5500
EMP: 39
SALES (corp-wide): 6.7B **Privately Held**
WEB: www.motorola.com
SIC: 3663 Radio & TV communications equipment
HQ: Ruckus Wireless, Inc.
350 W Java Dr
Sunnyvale CA 94089
650 265-4200

(P-17648)
RUDEX BROADCASTING LTD CORP
12272 Sarazen Pl, Granada Hills (91344-2635)
PHONE..................................213 494-3377
John Cooper, *CEO*
EMP: 12
SALES (est): 1.2MM **Privately Held**
SIC: 3663 Radio broadcasting & communications equipment

(P-17649)
RURISOND INC
2725 Ohio Ave, Redwood City (94061-3237)
PHONE..................................650 395-7136
Robert Stevenson, *CEO*
EMP: 10
SALES (est): 503K **Privately Held**
SIC: 3663 Carrier equipment, radio communications

(P-17650)
SATELLITE 2000 SYSTEMS
741 Lakefield Rd Ste I, Westlake Village (91361-2677)
P.O. Box 4453, Thousand Oaks (91359-1453)
PHONE..................................818 991-9794
Fred Joubert, *CEO*
EMP: 10
SQ FT: 7,500
SALES (est): 2.3MM **Privately Held**
SIC: 3663 Radio & TV communications equipment

(P-17651)
SAVI TECHNOLOGY HOLDINGS INC (PA)
615 Tasman Dr, Sunnyvale (94089-1707)
PHONE..................................650 316-4950
Vikram Verma, *President*
George De Urioste, *CFO*
William Clark, *Vice Pres*
David Sutton, *Program Mgr*
David Kranzler, *Engineer*
▲ **EMP:** 43
SQ FT: 35,000
SALES (est): 23.9MM **Privately Held**
SIC: 3663 3999 Radio & TV communications equipment; identification tags, except paper

(P-17652)
SEASPACE CORPORATION
13000 Gregg St Ste A, Poway (92064-7151)
PHONE..................................858 746-1100
Erik Park, *CEO*
Daniel Lee, *Vice Pres*

Jihong Park, *Admin Sec*
Anthony Burunoff, *Project Engr*
Daniel Waltman, *Senior Engr*
EMP: 25
SQ FT: 24,000
SALES (est): 6.1MM **Privately Held**
WEB: www.seaspace.com
SIC: 3663 3829 Satellites, communications; measuring & controlling devices

(P-17653)
SECURE COMM SYSTEMS INC (HQ)
Also Called: Secure Technology
1740 E Wilshire Ave, Santa Ana (92705-4615)
PHONE..................................714 547-1174
Allen B Ronk, *CEO*
Andrew Lewes, *CFO*
Kim Diulio, *Officer*
Mike Boice, *Vice Pres*
Keith Heinzig, *Vice Pres*
▲ **EMP:** 185
SQ FT: 38,000
SALES (est): 107.4MM
SALES (corp-wide): 2.5B **Publicly Held**
WEB: www.securecomm.com
SIC: 3663 3829 3577 3571 Encryption devices; vibration meters, analyzers & calibrators; computer peripheral equipment; electronic computers
PA: Benchmark Electronics, Inc.
56 S Rockford Dr
Tempe AZ 85281
623 300-7000

(P-17654)
SECURE COMM SYSTEMS INC
1740 E Wilshire Ave, Santa Ana (92705-4615)
PHONE..................................714 547-1174
Allen Ronk, *Branch Mgr*
EMP: 15
SALES (corp-wide): 2.5B **Publicly Held**
WEB: www.securecomm.com
SIC: 3663 3829 Encryption devices; vibration meters, analyzers & calibrators
HQ: Secure Communication Systems, Inc.
1740 E Wilshire Ave
Santa Ana CA 92705
714 547-1174

(P-17655)
SEKAI ELECTRONICS INC (PA)
38 Waterworks Way, Irvine (92618-3107)
PHONE..................................949 783-5740
Roland Soohoo, *CEO*
Mattias Nilsson,
Douglas Cebik, *Director*
Francis Pang, *Director*
EMP: 30
SQ FT: 7,000
SALES (est): 5.3MM **Privately Held**
WEB: www.sekai-electronics.com
SIC: 3663 5065 Radio & TV communications equipment; video equipment, electronic

(P-17656)
SHELDONS HOBBY SHOP
2135 Oakland Rd, San Jose (95131-1578)
P.O. Box 611147 (95161-1147)
PHONE..................................408 943-0220
Ronald Sheldon, *Owner*
EMP: 19
SQ FT: 21,000
SALES (est): 1.7MM **Privately Held**
WEB: www.sheldonshobbies.com
SIC: 3663 5945 Radio & TV communications equipment; hobbies

(P-17657)
SIERRA AUTOMATED SYS/ENG CORP
2821 Burton Ave, Burbank (91504-3224)
PHONE..................................818 840-6749
Edward O Fritz, *President*
Al Salci, *Vice Pres*
Giovanni Morales, *General Mgr*
Norm Avery, *Engineer*
Kevin Nose, *Engineer*
EMP: 20
SALES (est): 3.9MM **Privately Held**
SIC: 3663 Radio broadcasting & communications equipment

(P-17658)
SIERRA NEVADA CORPORATION
39465 Paseo Padre Pkwy # 2900, Fremont (94538-5350)
PHONE..................................510 446-8400
Fatih Ozmen, *CEO*
Eren Ozmen, *President*
EMP: 30
SALES (corp-wide): 1.9B **Privately Held**
WEB: www.sncorp.com
SIC: 3663 4812 Radio & TV communications equipment; radio telephone communication
PA: Sierra Nevada Corporation
444 Salomon Cir
Sparks NV 89434
775 331-0222

(P-17659)
SILKE COMMUNICATIONS INC
1050 Riverside Pkwy # 110, West Sacramento (95605-1519)
PHONE..................................916 245-6555
James D Silke, *President*
Carol Silke, *Corp Secy*
EMP: 11
SQ FT: 2,800
SALES (est): 2.7MM **Privately Held**
WEB: www.silkecom.com
SIC: 3663 Radio & TV communications equipment

(P-17660)
SILVUS TECHNOLOGIES INC (PA)
10990 Wilshire Blvd # 1500, Los Angeles (90024-3913)
PHONE..................................310 479-3333
Babak Daneshrad, *Chairman*
Phillip Duncan, *COO*
Jimi Henderson, *Vice Pres*
Weijun Zhu, *Vice Pres*
Amanda Kahenasa, *Office Admin*
EMP: 30
SQ FT: 7,200
SALES (est): 6.4MM **Privately Held**
SIC: 3663 8731 Radio & TV communications equipment; commercial physical research

(P-17661)
SITUNE CORPORATION
2216 Ringwood Ave, San Jose (95131-1714)
PHONE..................................408 324-1711
Vahid Toosi, *President*
EMP: 10
SQ FT: 3,000
SALES (est): 550K **Privately Held**
SIC: 3663 Television closed circuit equipment

(P-17662)
SMARTRUNK SYSTEMS INC
867 Bowsprit Rd, Chula Vista (91914-4529)
PHONE..................................619 426-3781
EMP: 25
SQ FT: 11,300
SALES (est): 2.6MM **Privately Held**
WEB: www.smartrunk.com
SIC: 3663

(P-17663)
SOCKET MOBILE INC
39700 Eureka Dr, Newark (94560-4808)
PHONE..................................510 933-3000
Kevin J Mills, *President*
Charlie Bass, *Ch of Bd*
Lynn Zhao, *CFO*
▲ **EMP:** 56
SQ FT: 37,100
SALES: 16.4MM **Privately Held**
WEB: www.socketcom.com
SIC: 3663 Mobile communication equipment

(P-17664)
SOLECTEK CORPORATION
8375 Cmino Santa Fe Ste A, San Diego (92121)
PHONE..................................858 450-1220
Seung Joon Lee, *CEO*
Eric Lee, *President*
Helena Adams, *COO*
Robert Milliken, *CFO*

Dan Sparks, *Vice Pres*
▲ **EMP:** 20
SQ FT: 10,000
SALES (est): 4.1MM **Privately Held**
WEB: www.solectek.com
SIC: 3663 Television broadcasting & communications equipment

(P-17665)
SONY MOBILE COMMUNICATIONS USA
2207 Bridgepoint Pkwy, San Mateo (94404)
PHONE................................866 766-9374
Kunihiko Shiomi, *CEO*
Hideki Komiyama, *President*
Francisco Lazardi, *CFO*
Paul Hamnett, *Vice Pres*
Ron Louks, *Vice Pres*
▲ **EMP:** 170
SQ FT: 10,000
SALES (est): 107.6MM **Privately Held**
WEB: www.ericsson.se
SIC: 3663 5999 Mobile communication equipment; mobile telephones & equipment

(P-17666)
SPACE MICRO INC
15378 Ave Of Science # 200, San Diego (92128-3451)
PHONE................................858 332-0700
David J Strobel, *CEO*
David R Czajkowski, *President*
David Czajkowski, *COO*
Patricia Ellison, *Vice Pres*
Michael Jacox, *Vice Pres*
EMP: 100
SALES: 18.6MM **Privately Held**
WEB: www.spacemicro.com
SIC: 3663 Space satellite communications equipment

(P-17667)
SPACE SYSTEMS/LORAL LLC
5130 Rbert J Mathews Pkwy, El Dorado Hills (95762-5703)
PHONE................................916 605-5448
Bob White, *Plant Mgr*
Larry Wray, *Vice Pres*
EMP: 20
SALES (corp-wide): 2.1B **Publicly Held**
SIC: 3663 Space satellite communications equipment
HQ: Space Systems/Loral, Llc
3825 Fabian Way
Palo Alto CA 94303
650 852-7320

(P-17668)
SPERRY WEST INC
5575 Magnatron Blvd Ste J, San Diego (92111-1309)
PHONE................................858 551-2000
Allie Levine, *President*
Diana Morrow, *Office Mgr*
▲ **EMP:** 12
SALES (est): 2.3MM **Privately Held**
WEB: www.sperrywest.com
SIC: 3663 Television closed circuit equipment

(P-17669)
SPOSATO JOHN
Also Called: Silicon Valley Launch
257 Vera Ave, Redwood City (94061-1702)
PHONE................................408 215-8727
John Sposato, *Owner*
EMP: 10
SALES (est): 677.6K **Privately Held**
SIC: 3663 3761 3812 3825 Radio receiver networks; guided missiles & space vehicles, research & development; antennas, radar or communications; oscillators, audio & radio frequency (instrument types); energy research;

(P-17670)
STARIX TECHNOLOGY INC
9120 Irvine Center Dr # 200, Irvine (92618-4682)
PHONE................................949 387-8120
Ran-Hong Yan, *CEO*
Nancy Chiang, *General Mgr*
Inanc Inan, *Technical Mgr*
Andrei Miclea, *Software Engr*

EMP: 20
SALES: 950K **Privately Held**
SIC: 3663 Radio & TV communications equipment

(P-17671)
STM NETWORKS INC
Also Called: Stm Wireless
2 Faraday, Irvine (92618-2737)
PHONE................................949 273-6800
Emil Youssefzadeh, *CEO*
Faramarz Yousefzaheh, *Ch of Bd*
Albert Yousefzaheh, *Treasurer*
Umar Javed, *Senior VP*
Richard Forberg, *Vice Pres*
▲ **EMP:** 27
SQ FT: 22,000
SALES (est): 4.6MM **Privately Held**
WEB: www.stmnetworks.com
SIC: 3663 Satellites, communications

(P-17672)
STONECROP TECHNOLOGIES LLC
103 H St Ste B, Petaluma (94952-5125)
PHONE................................781 659-0007
Michael Grow, *Vice Pres*
Jeff Baum, *VP Bus Dvlpt*
Michelle Cloyd, *Engineer*
Roya Platsis, *Director*
Jimmy Williamson, *Manager*
EMP: 29
SALES (corp-wide): 1.5MM **Privately Held**
SIC: 3663 Microwave communication equipment
PA: Stonecrop Technologies, Llc
80 Washington St Ste M50
Norwell MA 02061
781 829-9919

(P-17673)
SUNAR RF MOTION INC
6780 Sierra Ct Ste R, Dublin (94568-2600)
PHONE................................925 833-9936
Jason Fong, *General Mgr*
Donald R Shepherd, *Shareholder*
EMP: 10
SALES: 1MM **Privately Held**
SIC: 3663 Amplifiers, RF power & IF

(P-17674)
SUNBRITETV LLC
2630 Townsgate Rd Ste F, Westlake Village (91361-2780)
PHONE................................805 214-7250
Cameron Hill, *CEO*
Jonathan Johnson, *Manager*
▲ **EMP:** 50
SALES (est): 13.8MM **Privately Held**
SIC: 3663 Transmitting apparatus, radio or television
HQ: Sunbrite Holding Corporation
2001 Anchor Ct
Thousand Oaks CA 91320
805 214-7250

(P-17675)
SWIFT NAVIGATION INC (PA)
650 Townsend St Ste 410, San Francisco (94103-6246)
PHONE................................415 484-9026
Timothy Harris, *CEO*
Michael Horne, *Exec VP*
Stefan Witanis, *Engineer*
Andrew Shannon, *Opers Mgr*
EMP: 42
SQ FT: 15,000
SALES (est): 9MM **Privately Held**
SIC: 3663 Radio & TV communications equipment

(P-17676)
TACHYON NETWORKS INCORPORATED
9339 Carroll Park Dr # 150, San Diego (92121-3278)
PHONE................................858 882-8100
Peter A Carides, *CEO*
Laurence A Hinz, *CFO*
EMP: 52
SQ FT: 18,000
SALES (est): 7.6MM **Privately Held**
WEB: www.tachyon.net
SIC: 3663 Antennas, transmitting & communications

(P-17677)
TANGOME INC (PA)
615 National Ave, Sunnyvale (94085)
PHONE................................650 375-2620
Eric Setton, *CEO*
Uri Raz, *Ch of Bd*
Gary Chevsky, *Vice Pres*
Gregory Dorso, *Vice Pres*
Uli Galoz, *Vice Pres*
▲ **EMP:** 40
SALES (est): 13.1MM **Privately Held**
SIC: 3663 Mobile communication equipment

(P-17678)
TARANA WIRELESS INC (PA)
590 Alder Dr, Milpitas (95035-7443)
PHONE................................408 365-8483
Sergiu Nedeski, *President*
Kranti Kiluru, *President*
Harry May, *Vice Pres*
Rabin K Patra, *Vice Pres*
Kamaraj Karuppiah, *Exec Dir*
EMP: 15
SALES: 2MM **Privately Held**
SIC: 3663 Radio & TV communications equipment

(P-17679)
TATUNG COMPANY AMERICA INC (HQ)
2850 E El Presidio St, Long Beach (90810-1119)
PHONE................................310 637-2105
Huei-Jihn Jih, *President*
Danny Huang, *CFO*
Mike Lee, *Vice Pres*
Alvin Ramali, *Info Tech Mgr*
Vivien Ho, *Project Mgr*
▲ **EMP:** 98
SQ FT: 95,000
SALES (est): 25.3MM **Privately Held**
WEB: www.tatungusa.com
SIC: 3663 3575 3944 3651 Television closed circuit equipment; computer terminals, monitors & components; video game machines, except coin-operated; television receiving sets; video cassette recorders/players & accessories; refrigerators, mechanical & absorption: household; microwave ovens (cooking equipment), commercial

(P-17680)
TCI INTERNATIONAL INC (HQ)
3541 Gateway Blvd, Fremont (94538-6585)
PHONE................................510 687-6100
Slobodan Tkalcevic, *Vice Pres*
Stephen Stein, *Vice Pres*
Roy Woolsey, *Vice Pres*
▲ **EMP:** 103
SQ FT: 60,000
SALES (est): 30.3MM
SALES (corp-wide): 1.5B **Publicly Held**
WEB: www.tcibr.com
SIC: 3663 3812 3661 Radio broadcasting & communications equipment; antennas, transmitting & communications; antennas, radar or communications; modems
PA: Spx Corporation
13320a Balntyn Corp Pl
Charlotte NC 28277
980 474-3700

(P-17681)
TCOMT INC
111 N Market St Ste 670, San Jose (95113-1112)
PHONE................................408 351-3340
Clifford Rhee, *President*
Michael Luther, *Chairman*
Vito Picicci, *Vice Pres*
EMP: 89
SALES: 90MM **Privately Held**
WEB: www.tcomt.net
SIC: 3663 Mobile communication equipment

(P-17682)
TECHNICOLOR USA INC
400 Providence Mine Rd, Nevada City (95959-2953)
PHONE................................530 478-3000
Jeff Rosica, *Senior VP*
EMP: 513

SALES (corp-wide): 62.9MM **Privately Held**
SIC: 3663 Radio & TV communications equipment
HQ: Technicolor Usa, Inc.
101 W 103rd St
Indianapolis IN 46290
317 587-4287

(P-17683)
TELECOMMUNICATIONS ENGRG ASSOC
1160 Industrial Rd Ste 15, San Carlos (94070-4128)
PHONE................................650 590-1801
Daryl Jones, *President*
EMP: 13
SQ FT: 5,500
SALES (est): 1.9MM **Privately Held**
WEB: www.tcomeng.com
SIC: 3663 7622 Radio & TV communications equipment; communication equipment repair

(P-17684)
TELEDESIGN SYSTEMS
1729 S Main St, Milpitas (95035-6756)
PHONE................................408 941-1808
Mark Hubbard, *CEO*
Bruce Delevaux, *Vice Pres*
Oscar Nevarez, *Production*
Hazel Wolfe, *Manager*
EMP: 10
SQ FT: 5,000
SALES (est): 1.8MM **Privately Held**
WEB: www.teledesignsystems.com
SIC: 3663 Radio & TV communications equipment

(P-17685)
TELEMTRY CMMNCTONS SYSTEMS INC
Also Called: TCS
10020 Remmet Ave, Chatsworth (91311-3854)
PHONE................................818 718-6248
Sarin Michel Roy, *President*
Mihail Mateescu, *Vice Pres*
EMP: 24
SQ FT: 14,500
SALES: 7MM **Privately Held**
WEB: www.telcoms.com
SIC: 3663 Antennas, transmitting & communications

(P-17686)
TELEWAVE INC
660 Giguere Ct, San Jose (95133-1742)
PHONE................................408 929-4400
Roberta Boward, *President*
Allen Collins, *COO*
Larry Davis, *Vice Pres*
Jeff Cornehl, *Engineer*
Caroline Tooma, *Accounting Mgr*
◆ **EMP:** 46
SQ FT: 30,000
SALES: 9MM **Privately Held**
SIC: 3663 Radio broadcasting & communications equipment

(P-17687)
TERABIT RADIOS INC
1551 Mccarthy Blvd # 210, Milpitas (95035-7442)
PHONE................................408 431-6032
Srinivas Sivaprakasam, *President*
Carpenter Bruce, *Vice Pres*
EMP: 14 EST: 2014
SALES (est): 2.2MM **Privately Held**
SIC: 3663 Radio broadcasting & communications equipment

(P-17688)
TERRALINK COMMUNICATIONS INC
5145 Golden Foothill Pkwy, El Dorado Hills (95762-9640)
PHONE................................916 439-4367
Casey Janssen, *President*
Gary Fann, *Project Mgr*
EMP: 10
SQ FT: 3,525

▲ = Import ▼ =Export
◆ =Import/Export

SALES: 6.7MM **Privately Held**
WEB: www.terralinkcommunications.com
SIC: **3663** Antennas, transmitting & communications

(P-17689)
TERRASAT COMMUNICATIONS INC
315 Digital Dr, Morgan Hill (95037-2878)
PHONE..................................408 782-5911
Jit Patel, *President*
Rod Benson, *Vice Pres*
Jose Hecht, *Vice Pres*
Carl Hurst, *Vice Pres*
Ernesto Vargas, *Design Engr*
▲ EMP: 47
SALES (est): 15MM **Privately Held**
WEB: www.terrasatinc.com
SIC: **3663** Satellites, communications

(P-17690)
THAWTE INC
Also Called: Thawte Consulting USA
487 E Middlefield Rd, Mountain View (94043-4047)
PHONE..................................650 426-7400
Mark Shuttleworth, *President*
EMP: 20 EST: 1995
SQ FT: 5,000
SALES (est): 1.7MM
SALES (corp-wide): 4.7B **Publicly Held**
WEB: www.thawte.com
SIC: **3663** 7371 Digital encoders; custom computer programming services
PA: Nortonlifelock Inc.
60 E Rio Salado Pkwy # 1
Tempe AZ 85281
650 527-8000

(P-17691)
THOMSON REUTERS CORPORATION
Also Called: Reuters Television La
633 W 5th St Ste 2300, Los Angeles (90071-2049)
PHONE..................................877 518-2761
Kevin Regan, *Principal*
EMP: 15
SALES (corp-wide): 10.6B **Publicly Held**
SIC: **3663** Satellites, communications
HQ: Thomson Reuters Corporation
3 Times Sq
New York NY 10036
646 223-4000

(P-17692)
TIM HOOVER ENTERPRISES
8532 Yarrow Ln, Riverside (92508-2926)
PHONE..................................951 237-9210
Tim Hoover, *Owner*
EMP: 60
SALES (est): 3.5MM **Privately Held**
SIC: **3663** Space satellite communications equipment

(P-17693)
TINI AEROSPACE INC
2505 Kerner Blvd, San Rafael (94901-5571)
PHONE..................................415 524-2124
Michael Bokaie, *President*
Vicki Lasky, *Treasurer*
David Bokaie, *Vice Pres*
Trudy Sachs, *Vice Pres*
Evelyn Cabrera, *Office Mgr*
▼ EMP: 30 EST: 1996
SQ FT: 5,400
SALES (est): 6.7MM **Privately Held**
WEB: www.tiniaerospace.com
SIC: **3663** Space satellite communications equipment

(P-17694)
TRACKONOMY SYSTEMS INC
2350 Mission College Blvd # 490, Santa Clara (95054-1532)
PHONE..................................833 872-2566
Erik Volkerink, *CEO*
Steve Roeser, *Admin Sec*
Ajay Khoche, *CTO*
Jake Medwell, *Director*
EMP: 13
SALES (est): 1.5MM **Privately Held**
SIC: **3663** Radio & TV communications equipment

(P-17695)
TRICOM RESEARCH INC
17791 Sky Park Cir Ste J, Irvine (92614-6150)
PHONE..................................949 250-6024
Paula Wright, *President*
John W Wright, *CFO*
Richard Taras, *Engineer*
Scott Snyder, *Director*
EMP: 64
SALES (est): 9.4MM **Privately Held**
SIC: **3663** Radio & TV communications equipment

(P-17696)
TRIQUINT WJ INC
3099 Orchard Dr, San Jose (95134-2005)
PHONE..................................408 577-6200
W Dexter Paine III, *Ch of Bd*
Bruce W Diamond, *President*
Ralph G Quinsey, *CEO*
R Gregory Miller, *CFO*
Haresh P Patel, *Senior VP*
EMP: 92
SQ FT: 124,000
SALES (est): 12.7MM
SALES (corp-wide): 3B **Publicly Held**
WEB: www.triquint.com
SIC: **3663** 3674 Radio broadcasting & communications equipment; semiconductors & related devices
HQ: Qorvo Us, Inc.
2300 Ne Brookwood Pkwy
Hillsboro OR 97124
336 664-1233

(P-17697)
ULTIMATTE CORPORATION
5828 Calvin Ave, Tarzana (91356-1111)
PHONE..................................818 993-8007
Lynne Sauve, *President*
Petro Vlahos, *Shareholder*
Paul Vlahos, *Treasurer*
Nina Michalko, *Admin Sec*
▲ EMP: 26
SALES (est): 4.3MM **Privately Held**
SIC: **3663** 3651 7371 Television broadcasting & communications equipment; household audio & video equipment; computer software development & applications
PA: Blackmagic Design Pty Ltd
11 Gateway Ct
Port Melbourne VIC 3207

(P-17698)
USGLOBALSAT INC
14740 Yorba Ct, Chino (91710-9210)
PHONE..................................909 597-8525
Shirley Cheng, *President*
▲ EMP: 10
SQ FT: 62,000
SALES (est): 3.2MM **Privately Held**
WEB: www.usglobalsat.com
SIC: **3663** Radio & TV communications equipment

(P-17699)
VERIFONE INC
1400 W Stanford Ranch Rd, Rocklin (95765-3750)
PHONE..................................808 623-2911
Frank Brown, *Branch Mgr*
Richard Char, *Senior VP*
Andrew McIntosh, *Opers Staff*
Suman Kothari, *Manager*
EMP: 160
SALES (corp-wide): 183MM **Privately Held**
SIC: **3663** Radio & TV communications equipment
HQ: Verifone, Inc.
88 W Plumeria Dr
San Jose CA 95134
408 232-7800

(P-17700)
VIASAT INC (PA)
6155 El Camino Real, Carlsbad (92009-1602)
PHONE..................................760 476-2200
Mark D Dankberg, *Ch of Bd*
Richard Baldridge, *President*
Ken Peterman, *President*
David Ryan, *President*

Shawn Duffy, *CFO*
▲ EMP: 277
SQ FT: 695,000
SALES: 2B **Publicly Held**
WEB: www.viasat.com
SIC: **3663** Space satellite communications equipment; receiver-transmitter units (transceiver); mobile communication equipment; antennas, transmitting & communications

(P-17701)
VIGOR SYSTEMS INC
4660 La Jolla Village Dr # 500, San Diego (92122-4605)
PHONE..................................866 748-4467
Magnus Sorlander, *CEO*
Shayna Smith, *COO*
Ian Loyo, *Info Tech Mgr*
▲ EMP: 35
SALES (est): 4.5MM **Privately Held**
WEB: www.vigorsys.com
SIC: **3663** Studio equipment, radio & television broadcasting

(P-17702)
VISTA POINT TECHNOLOGIES INC
847 Gibraltar Dr, Milpitas (95035-6332)
PHONE..................................408 576-7000
Walter Sheram, *Principal*
EMP: 51
SALES (est): 251.2K
SALES (corp-wide): 406.1MM **Publicly Held**
SIC: **3663** Cellular radio telephone
HQ: Digitaloptics Corporation
3025 Orchard Packway
San Jose CA 95101

(P-17703)
WATER ASSOCIATES LLC
Also Called: Redtrac
34929 Flyover Ct, Bakersfield (93308-9725)
PHONE..................................661 281-6077
Jeff Young, *Managing Prtnr*
Michael McAllister, *Business Mgr*
Bob Simonian, *Sales Mgr*
Michael Young,
EMP: 20
SQ FT: 7,000
SALES (est): 4MM **Privately Held**
SIC: **3663** 3523 Radio & TV communications equipment; irrigation equipment, self-propelled

(P-17704)
WBWALTON ENTERPRISES INC
4185 Hallmark Pkwy, San Bernardino (92407-1832)
P.O. Box 9010 (92427-0010)
PHONE..................................951 683-0930
William B Walton Jr, *President*
Jane Walton, *Corp Secy*
Ray Powers, *Sales Staff*
EMP: 26
SQ FT: 30,000
SALES (est): 5.7MM **Privately Held**
WEB: www.de-ice.com
SIC: **3663** 1731 Satellites, communications; electrical work

(P-17705)
WEST-COM NRSE CALL SYSTEMS INC (PA)
Also Called: Wc
2200 Cordelia Rd, Fairfield (94534-1912)
PHONE..................................707 428-5900
C Larry Peters, *CEO*
Dania Atanassova-Een, *CFO*
Colleen Ryan, *Managing Dir*
David Daum, *Regional Mgr*
Denise Peters, *Admin Sec*
EMP: 44
SQ FT: 15,000
SALES (est): 6.9MM **Privately Held**
WEB: www.westcall.com
SIC: **3663** Radio broadcasting & communications equipment

(P-17706)
WI2WI INC (PA)
1879 Lundy Ave Ste 218, San Jose (95131-1881)
PHONE..................................408 416-4200
Zachariah J Mathews, *President*
Barry Arneson, *Vice Pres*
EMP: 31
SALES (est): 9.2MM **Privately Held**
SIC: **3663** Radio & TV communications equipment

(P-17707)
WILMANCO
5350 Kazuko Ct, Moorpark (93021-1790)
PHONE..................................805 523-2390
Harold B Williams, *Owner*
Harold Williams Jr, *Co-Owner*
Marie Williams, *Co-Owner*
Marci Padgett, *Graphic Designe*
EMP: 16
SQ FT: 11,000
SALES (est): 1.9MM **Privately Held**
WEB: www.wilmanco.com
SIC: **3663** Microwave communication equipment

(P-17708)
WOHLER TECHNOLOGIES INC
1280 San Luis Obispo St, Hayward (94544-7916)
PHONE..................................510 870-0810
Michael Kelly, *President*
John Palmer, *Chairman*
Jerry Kocher, *Vice Pres*
Aaron Aiken, *Admin Sec*
Hitone Nakamura, *Administration*
▲ EMP: 25
SALES (est): 8.2MM **Privately Held**
WEB: www.wohler.com
SIC: **3663** Radio & TV communications equipment

(P-17709)
WV COMMUNICATIONS INC
1125 Bus Ctr Cir Ste A, Newbury Park (91320)
PHONE..................................805 376-1820
Uri Yulzari, *President*
Jim Tranovich, *Vice Pres*
Ron Bosi, *Admin Sec*
Gerri Yulzari, *QC Mgr*
Don Berryman, *Sales Staff*
▲ EMP: 40
SQ FT: 18,000
SALES (est): 10MM **Privately Held**
WEB: www.wv-comm.com
SIC: **3663** Microwave communication equipment

(P-17710)
XCOM WIRELESS INC
2700 Rose Ave Ste E, Signal Hill (90755-1929)
PHONE..................................562 981-0077
Dan Hyman, *President*
Peter Bogdanoff, *Shareholder*
Ardesta LLC, *Shareholder*
Mark Hyman, *Corp Secy*
Lance Harrison, *Technician*
EMP: 12
SQ FT: 3,500
SALES (est): 1.3MM **Privately Held**
WEB: www.xcomwireless.net
SIC: **3663** Mobile communication equipment

(P-17711)
YAESU USA INC
6125 Phyllis Dr, Cypress (90630-5242)
PHONE..................................714 827-7600
Jun Hasegawa, *CEO*
Dennis Motschenbacher, *Exec VP*
Gary Doshay, *Credit Mgr*
Nori Romero, *Sales Staff*
▲ EMP: 40
SALES (est): 10MM **Privately Held**
SIC: **3663** Radio & TV communications equipment

(P-17712)
ZYPCOM INC
29400 Kohoutek Way # 170, Union City (94587-1212)
PHONE..................................510 324-2501
Karl Zorzi, *President*

Heidi Zorzi, *Manager*
▲ EMP: 11
SQ FT: 7,200
SALES (est): 2.7MM **Privately Held**
SIC: 3669 3661 Multiplex equipment; modems

3669 Communications Eqpt, NEC

(P-17713)
ALSTOM SIGNALING OPERATION LLC
7337 Central Ave, Riverside (92504-1440)
PHONE..........................951 343-9699
Jeff Utterbach, *Manager*
EMP: 192
SALES (corp-wide): 1.4B **Privately Held**
WEB: www.proyard.com
SIC: 3669 Railroad signaling devices, electric
PA: Alstom Signaling Operation, Llc
2712 S Dillingham Rd
Grain Valley MO 64029
816 650-3112

(P-17714)
ATI SOLUTIONS INC (PA)
Also Called: Ucview
18425 Napa St, Northridge (91325-3619)
PHONE..........................818 772-7900
Guy Avital, *CEO*
Leah Avital, *Vice Pres*
Eileen Dela Cruz, *Accountant*
EMP: 15
SALES (est): 2.8MM **Privately Held**
WEB: www.atisol.com
SIC: 3669 Visual communication systems

(P-17715)
BDFCO INC
Also Called: Damac
1926 Kauai Dr, Costa Mesa (92626-3542)
PHONE..........................714 228-2900
Frank J Kubat Jr, *CEO*
Robert Mc Clory, *Shareholder*
John Sapone, *CFO*
Daniel L Davis, *Admin Sec*
▲ EMP: 80
SQ FT: 120,000
SALES (est): 14.3MM **Privately Held**
WEB: www.damac.com
SIC: 3669 Intercommunication systems, electric

(P-17716)
BITMAX LLC (PA)
6255 W Sunset Blvd # 1515, Los Angeles (90028-7416)
PHONE..........................323 978-7878
Nancy Bennett, *Mng Member*
Jim Riley, *Officer*
Marjorie Bach, *Exec VP*
Tom Jones, *Managing Dir*
Kathyren Dugenia, *Project Mgr*
EMP: 22
SQ FT: 7,500
SALES (est): 2.3MM **Privately Held**
WEB: www.bitmax.net
SIC: 3669 7929 Visual communication systems; entertainment service

(P-17717)
BLUE SKY REMEDIATION SVCS INC
Also Called: United Traffic Services & Sup
14000 Valley Blvd, La Puente (91746-2801)
PHONE..........................626 961-5736
Dora Pina, *President*
EMP: 14 EST: 1994
SQ FT: 15,000
SALES (est): 2.5MM **Privately Held**
SIC: 3669 Pedestrian traffic control equipment; traffic signals, electric

(P-17718)
BLUE SQUIRREL INC
8295 Aero Pl, San Diego (92123-2031)
PHONE..........................858 268-0717
Steve Deal, *CEO*
Jack Hetzel, *CFO*
Larry Cleary, *Vice Pres*
Philip Joosten, *Vice Pres*

Bill Kepner, *Vice Pres*
▲ EMP: 80
SQ FT: 20,000
SALES (est): 13MM **Privately Held**
WEB: www.indyme.com
SIC: 3669 3663 Burglar alarm apparatus, electric; airborne radio communications equipment

(P-17719)
CAL SIGNAL CORP
384 Beach Rd, Burlingame (94010-2004)
PHONE..........................650 343-6100
Tom Mori, *Vice Pres*
EMP: 11
SALES (est): 2.2MM **Privately Held**
SIC: 3669 Traffic signals, electric

(P-17720)
CANOGA PERKINS CORPORATION (HQ)
20600 Prairie St, Chatsworth (91311-6008)
PHONE..........................818 718-6300
Alfred Tim Champion, *President*
Anhtuan Trinh, *IT/INT Sup*
Muhammed Suhail, *Engineer*
Cynthia Lewis, *Finance*
Mercedes Agta Soa, *Human Resources*
◆ EMP: 100 EST: 1965
SQ FT: 64,000
SALES (est): 24.2MM
SALES (corp-wide): 1B **Privately Held**
WEB: www.canoga.com
SIC: 3669 Intercommunication systems, electric
PA: Rowan Technologies, Inc.
10 Indel Ave
Rancocas NJ 08073
609 267-9000

(P-17721)
COMPUTER SERVICE COMPANY
Also Called: Steiny & Company
210 N Delilah St, Corona (92879-1883)
PHONE..........................951 738-1444
Justin Cataldo, *Manager*
Gayle Kappelman, *Admin Sec*
EMP: 30
SALES (corp-wide): 2.5MM **Privately Held**
WEB: www.computerservicecompany.com
SIC: 3669 7629 Traffic signals, electric; electrical repair shops
PA: Computer Service Company
855 N Todd Ave
Azusa CA 91702
951 738-1444

(P-17722)
CONTINENTAL SECURITY INDS
19425b Soledad Canyon Rd # 126, Canyon Country (91351-2632)
PHONE..........................661 251-8800
Gregory Basse, *President*
EMP: 15
SALES (est): 1.7MM **Privately Held**
SIC: 3669 Fire alarm apparatus, electric

(P-17723)
D-TECH OPTOELECTRONICS INC (DH)
18062 Rowland St, City of Industry (91748-1205)
PHONE..........................626 956-1100
An Baoxin, *President*
EMP: 20
SALES: 20MM **Privately Held**
SIC: 3669 Intercommunication systems, electric
HQ: Global Communication Semiconductors, Llc
23155 Kashiwa Ct
Torrance CA 90505
310 530-7274

(P-17724)
DEI HEADQUARTERS INC
Also Called: Sound United
3002 Wintergreen Dr, Carlsbad (92008-6883)
PHONE..........................760 598-6200
James E Minarik, *President*
Kevin P Duffy, *President*
Blair Tripodi, *President*
Veysel P Goker, *CFO*
Josh Talge, *Chief Mktg Ofcr*

▲ EMP: 385
SALES (est): 38MM **Privately Held**
WEB: www.directed.com
SIC: 3669 Burglar alarm apparatus, electric
HQ: Dei Holdings, Inc.
1 Viper Way Ste 3
Vista CA 92081
760 598-6200

(P-17725)
DEI HOLDINGS INC (HQ)
1 Viper Way Ste 3, Vista (92081-7811)
PHONE..........................760 598-6200
Kevin P Duffy, *CEO*
Robert J Struble, *CEO*
Veysel Goker, *CFO*
Pete Harper, *CFO*
Dan Brockman, *Treasurer*
◆ EMP: 102
SQ FT: 198,000
SALES (est): 201MM **Privately Held**
WEB: www.directed.com
SIC: 3669 3651 Burglar alarm apparatus, electric; amplifiers: radio, public address or musical instrument

(P-17726)
DULCE SYSTEMS INC
26893 Bouquet Canyon Rd L, Santa Clarita (91350-2374)
PHONE..........................818 435-6007
Carmen Palacios, *President*
▲ EMP: 10
SALES (est): 1.4MM **Privately Held**
WEB: www.dulcesystems.com
SIC: 3669 3572 Sirens, electric: vehicle, marine, industrial & air raid; signaling apparatus, electric; visual communication systems; computer storage devices; tape storage units, computer; computer auxiliary storage units

(P-17727)
ECONOLITE CONTROL PRODUCTS INC (PA)
1250 N Tustin Ave, Anaheim (92807-1617)
P.O. Box 6150 (92816-0150)
PHONE..........................714 630-3700
Michael C Doyle, *CEO*
David St Amant, *President*
Douglas Wiersig, *Vice Pres*
Peter Sweatman, *Principal*
Tanya Feaster, *Admin Asst*
▼ EMP: 160
SQ FT: 95,000
SALES (est): 73MM **Privately Held**
WEB: www.econolite.com
SIC: 3669 Traffic signals, electric

(P-17728)
EXCELLENCE OPTO INC
20047 Tipico St, Chatsworth (91311-3443)
PHONE..........................818 674-1921
Fanny Huang, *President*
Kuo Hsin Huang, *President*
Tyson Tien, *Director*
EMP: 10
SQ FT: 7,000
SALES (est): 781.5K **Privately Held**
SIC: 3669 Traffic signals, electric

(P-17729)
FTC - FORWARD THREAT CONTROL
234 Jason Way, Mountain View (94043-4866)
PHONE..........................650 906-7917
Frank Zajac, *Principal*
EMP: 14
SALES (est): 1.7MM **Privately Held**
WEB: www.threatcon.info
SIC: 3669 Communications equipment

(P-17730)
GENERAL DYNAMICS MISSION
2688 Orchard Pkwy, San Jose (95134-2020)
PHONE..........................408 908-7300
Christopher Brady, *President*
Terry McLachlan, *Info Tech Dir*
Tuan Tran, *Electrical Engi*
Thomas Hanna, *Engineer*
Norman Nakahara, *Engineer*
EMP: 449

SALES (corp-wide): 36.1B **Publicly Held**
SIC: 3669 3812 Transportation signaling devices; search & navigation equipment
HQ: General Dynamics Mission Systems, Inc.
12450 Fair Lakes Cir # 200
Fairfax VA 22033
703 263-2800

(P-17731)
GENERAL DYNMICS MSSION SYSTEMS
112 S Lakeview Canyon Rd, Westlake Village (91362-3925)
PHONE..........................805 497-5042
Tom Melatis, *Branch Mgr*
Christopher Marzilli, *President*
Mike Starzyk, *General Mgr*
EMP: 209
SALES (corp-wide): 36.1B **Publicly Held**
SIC: 3669 3812 7373 8711 Intercommunication systems, electric; search & navigation equipment; computer integrated systems design; engineering services
HQ: General Dynamics Mission Systems, Inc.
12450 Fair Lakes Cir # 200
Fairfax VA 22033
703 263-2800

(P-17732)
GENERAL MONITORS INC (DH)
26776 Simpatica Cir, Lake Forest (92630-8128)
PHONE..........................949 581-4464
Nish Vartanian, *Vice Pres*
Richard Lamishaw, *CFO*
◆ EMP: 110
SQ FT: 60,000
SALES (est): 63.1MM
SALES (corp-wide): 1.3B **Publicly Held**
WEB: www.generalmonitors.com
SIC: 3669 1799 3812 Fire detection systems, electric; gas leakage detection; infrared object detection equipment
HQ: Mine Safety Appliances Company, Llc
1000 Cranberry Woods Dr
Cranberry Township PA 16066
724 776-8600

(P-17733)
HIGHBALL SIGNAL INC
6767 Di Carlo Pl, Rancho Cucamonga (91739-9155)
PHONE..........................909 341-5367
Lupita Mejia, *President*
Miguel Mejia Jr, *Vice Pres*
EMP: 12
SALES (est): 2.3MM **Privately Held**
SIC: 3669 Railroad signaling devices, electric

(P-17734)
ISMART ALARM INC
120 San Lucar Ct, Sunnyvale (94086-5213)
PHONE..........................408 245-2551
Qingwei Meng, *President*
Justin CHI, *Manager*
Jake Fox, *Manager*
Jerry Yu, *Manager*
▲ EMP: 20
SALES (est): 1.2MM **Privately Held**
SIC: 3669 5063 7382 Burglar alarm apparatus, electric; burglar alarm systems; security systems services

(P-17735)
JOHNSON CONTROLS
3568 Ruffin Rd, San Diego (92123-2597)
PHONE..........................858 633-9100
Bob Jamieson, *Branch Mgr*
Erin McAdam, *Human Res Mgr*
Wes Reynolds, *Sales Staff*
EMP: 150 **Privately Held**
WEB: www.simplexgrinnell.com
SIC: 3669 1731 1711 3873 Emergency alarms; fire detection & burglar alarm systems specialization; fire sprinkler system installation; watches, clocks, watchcases & parts; surgical appliances & supplies
HQ: Johnson Controls Fire Protection Lp
6600 Congress Ave
Boca Raton FL 33487
561 988-7200

(P-17736)
JOHNSON CONTROLS
6952 Preston Ave Ste A, Livermore
(94551-9545)
PHONE.....................925 273-0100
Michael Fisher, *Branch Mgr*
Brian Spears, *Sales Staff*
EMP: 185 **Privately Held**
WEB: www.simplexgrinnell.com
SIC: 3669 1731 1711 Emergency alarms;
fire detection & burglar alarm systems
specialization; fire sprinkler system instal-
lation
HQ: Johnson Controls Fire Protection Lp
6600 Congress Ave
Boca Raton FL 33487
561 988-7200

(P-17737)
JOHNSON CONTROLS
13504 Skypark Industrial, Chico
(95973-8859)
PHONE.....................530 893-0110
Christine Gilbert, *Branch Mgr*
EMP: 15 **Privately Held**
WEB: www.simplexgrinnell.com
SIC: 3669 3569 Fire alarm apparatus,
electric; fire detection systems, electric;
firefighting apparatus
HQ: Johnson Controls Fire Protection Lp
6600 Congress Ave
Boca Raton FL 33487
561 988-7200

(P-17738)
JOHNSON CONTROLS
4650 Beloit Dr, Sacramento (95838-2426)
PHONE.....................916 283-0300
Ron Ricketts, *General Mgr*
Joey Turner, *Controller*
Randy Low, *Sales Staff*
Justin Bradshaw, *Supervisor*
EMP: 85 **Privately Held**
WEB: www.simplexgrinnell.com
SIC: 3669 Emergency alarms
HQ: Johnson Controls Fire Protection Lp
6600 Congress Ave
Boca Raton FL 33487
561 988-7200

(P-17739)
JTB SUPPLY COMPANY INC
1030 N Batavia St Ste A, Orange
(92867-5541)
PHONE.....................714 639-9558
Jeff York, *President*
Mindy Myers, *Administration*
Matt Pieper, *Regl Sales Mgr*
EMP: 13
SQ FT: 10,000
SALES (est): 3.9MM **Privately Held**
WEB: www.jtbsupplyco.com
SIC: 3669 Traffic signals, electric

(P-17740)
KENDRA GROUP INC
Also Called: Bell Enterprise
2394 Saratoga Way, San Bernardino
(92407-1861)
PHONE.....................909 473-7206
Ed Campana, *CFO*
Debbie Campana, *President*
Brian Linton, *Office Mgr*
Brandon Bell, *Opers Staff*
Sue Ingalls, *VP Mktg*
▼ **EMP:** 11
SALES (est): 5MM **Privately Held**
SIC: 3669 4953 Intercommunication sys-
tems, electric; recycling, waste materials

(P-17741)
L3 TECHNOLOGIES INC
Also Called: Photonics Division
5957 Landau Ct, Carlsbad (92008-8803)
PHONE.....................760 431-6800
Tim Call, *Vice Pres*
EMP: 150
SALES (corp-wide): 6.8B **Publicly Held**
SIC: 3669 Intercommunication systems,
electric
HQ: L3 Technologies, Inc.
600 3rd Ave Fl 34
New York NY 10016
212 697-1111

(P-17742)
LIFELINE SYSTEMS COMPANY
450 E Romie Ln, Salinas (93901-4029)
PHONE.....................831 755-0788
Lynn Brooks, *Director*
EMP: 150
SALES (corp-wide): 20.8B **Privately Held**
SIC: 3669 Emergency alarms
HQ: Lifeline Systems Company
111 Lawrence St
Framingham MA 01702
508 988-1000

(P-17743)
LUMENS AUDIO VISUAL INC
127 27th St Apt A, Newport Beach
(92663-3461)
PHONE.....................970 988-6268
Thomas Vanden Berge, *President*
Don Berge, *Vice Pres*
Robert Cannon, *Regl Sales Mgr*
EMP: 15
SALES (est): 1.2MM **Privately Held**
SIC: 3669 Communications equipment

(P-17744)
LUMENTUM HOLDINGS INC (PA)
400 N Mccarthy Blvd, Milpitas
(95035-5112)
PHONE.....................408 546-5483
Alan S Lowe, *President*
EMP: 168
SQ FT: 126,000
SALES: 1.5B **Publicly Held**
SIC: 3669 3674 3826 Emergency alarms;
semiconductors & related devices; optical
isolators; analytical instruments; laser sci-
entific & engineering instruments

(P-17745)
**LUMENTUM OPERATIONS LLC
(HQ)**
400 N Mccarthy Blvd, Milpitas
(95035-5112)
PHONE.....................408 546-5483
Alan Lowe, *CEO*
Aaron Tachibana, *CFO*
Craig Cocchi, *Senior VP*
Sharon Parker, *Senior VP*
Vince Retort, *Senior VP*
▲ **EMP:** 217
SALES (est): 11.2MM
SALES (corp-wide): 1.5B **Publicly Held**
SIC: 3669 8748 3999 Emergency alarms;
telecommunications consultant; atomiz-
ers, toiletry
PA: Lumentum Holdings Inc.
400 N Mccarthy Blvd
Milpitas CA 95035
408 546-5483

(P-17746)
MERU NETWORKS INC (HQ)
894 Ross Dr, Sunnyvale (94089-1403)
PHONE.....................408 215-5300
Ken Xie, *CEO*
Michael Xie, *President*
Andrew Del Matto, *CFO*
Tom Palomaki, *Vice Pres*
Kishore Reddy, *Vice Pres*
▲ **EMP:** 75
SQ FT: 44,000
SALES (est): 81MM
SALES (corp-wide): 1.8B **Publicly Held**
WEB: www.merunetworks.com
SIC: 3669 Intercommunication systems,
electric
PA: Fortinet, Inc.
899 Kifer Rd
Sunnyvale CA 94086
408 235-7700

(P-17747)
MOBILE WIRELESS TECH LLC
125 W Cerritos Ave, Anaheim
(92805-6547)
PHONE.....................714 239-1535
Charles Jones, *CEO*
Harold Sabbagh, *Vice Pres*
Richard Succa, *Vice Pres*
EMP: 15 **EST:** 1994
SQ FT: 5,000

SALES (est): 1MM **Privately Held**
WEB: www.gomobilewireless.com
SIC: 3669 Transportation signaling devices; intercommunication systems, electric

(P-17748)
**MYERS & SONS HI-WAY SAFETY
INC**
520 W Grand Ave, Escondido
(92025-2502)
P.O. Box 1030, Chino (91708-1030)
PHONE.....................909 591-1781
Rod Lowry, *Manager*
EMP: 30
SALES (corp-wide): 47.8MM **Privately
Held**
WEB: www.hiwaysafety.com
SIC: 3669 3499 Transportation signaling
devices; barricades, metal
PA: Myers & Son's Hi-Way Safety Inc.
13310 5th St
Chino CA 91710
909 591-1781

(P-17749)
**MYERS & SONS HI-WAY SAFETY
INC (PA)**
13310 5th St, Chino (91710-5125)
P.O. Box 1030 (91708-1030)
PHONE.....................909 591-1781
Michael Rodgers, *CEO*
Brandon Myer, *Exec VP*
Jensen Carson, *Manager*
▲ **EMP:** 120
SQ FT: 36,400
SALES (est): 47.8MM **Privately Held**
WEB: www.hiwaysafety.com
SIC: 3669 Pedestrian traffic control equip-
ment

(P-17750)
NIGHT OPTICS USA INC
605 Oro Dam Blvd E, Oroville
(95965-5718)
PHONE.....................714 899-4475
Ilya Reyngold, *CEO*
Rimma Epelbaum, *CFO*
Israel Reyngold, *Vice Pres*
◆ **EMP:** 13
SQ FT: 4,600
SALES (est): 1.9MM
SALES (corp-wide): 2B **Publicly Held**
WEB: www.nightopticsusa.com
SIC: 3669 3827 Visual communication
systems; optical instruments & apparatus
PA: Vista Outdoor Inc.
1 Vista Way
Anoka MN 55303
801 447-3000

(P-17751)
OPTEX INCORPORATED
18730 S Wilmington Ave # 100, Compton
(90220-5924)
PHONE.....................800 966-7839
Makoto Kokobo, *CEO*
Tohru Kobayashi, *Ch of Bd*
James Quick, *President*
Michael La Chere, *CFO*
Clint Choate, *Vice Pres*
▲ **EMP:** 17
SQ FT: 35,000
SALES (est): 3.2MM **Privately Held**
WEB: www.optexamerica.com
SIC: 3669 Emergency alarms
PA: Optex Group Company, Limited
5-8-12, Ogoto
Otsu SGA 520-0

(P-17752)
PALOMAR PRODUCTS INC
23042 Arroyo Vis, Rcho STA Marg
(92688-2604)
PHONE.....................949 858-8836
Kevin Moschetti, *CEO*
Val Policky, *President*
Fred Ekstein, *Vice Pres*
Nick Moore, *Info Tech Mgr*
EMP: 79 **EST:** 1997
SQ FT: 35,000

SALES (est): 17.1MM
SALES (corp-wide): 3.8B **Publicly Held**
WEB: www.palpro.com
SIC: 3669 Intercommunication systems,
electric
HQ: Esterline Technologies Corp
500 108th Ave Ne Ste 1500
Bellevue WA 98004
425 453-9400

(P-17753)
PROTO SERVICES INC
Also Called: PSI
1991 Concourse Dr, San Jose
(95131-1708)
PHONE.....................408 321-8688
Nicky Wu, *CEO*
Norman Lee, *Vice Pres*
EMP: 40
SQ FT: 25,000
SALES: 4MM **Privately Held**
WEB: www.protoservices.com
SIC: 3669 Visual communication systems

(P-17754)
**PROXIM WIRELESS
CORPORATION (PA)**
2114 Ringwood Ave, San Jose
(95131-1715)
PHONE.....................408 383-7600
Greg Marzullo, *President*
Steve Button, *CFO*
David Porte, *Senior VP*
David L Renauld, *Vice Pres*
David Sumi, *Vice Pres*
▲ **EMP:** 55
SQ FT: 42,500
SALES (est): 34.1MM **Publicly Held**
SIC: 3669 Signaling apparatus, electric

(P-17755)
Q I S INC
28005 Oregon Pl, Quail Valley
(92587-9045)
P.O. Box 1220, Garden Grove (92842-
1220)
PHONE.....................951 244-0500
Dennis Daigle, *President*
Shelly Daigle, *Admin Sec*
EMP: 10
SQ FT: 2,000
SALES (est): 1.3MM **Privately Held**
SIC: 3669 Intercommunication systems,
electric

(P-17756)
**QUALCOMM MEMS
TECHNOLOGIES INC**
5775 Morehouse Dr, San Diego
(92121-1714)
PHONE.....................858 587-1121
Greg Heinzinger, *Senior VP*
Derek Aberle, *Exec VP*
Adrian Ong, *VP Bus Dvlpt*
Junchen Du, *Engineer*
Jenny Gong, *Engineer*
EMP: 31
SQ FT: 9,000
SALES (est): 17.9MM
SALES (corp-wide): 24.2B **Publicly Held**
WEB: www.iridigm.com
SIC: 3669 Visual communication systems
PA: Qualcomm Incorporated
5775 Morehouse Dr
San Diego CA 92121
858 587-1121

(P-17757)
RAYTHEON APPLIED SIGNAL
160 N Rverview Dr Ste 300, Anaheim
(92808)
PHONE.....................714 917-0255
John McGrory, *Branch Mgr*
Oliver Curtis, *Fellow*
Coronado Martha, *Fellow*
EMP: 10
SALES (corp-wide): 27B **Publicly Held**
SIC: 3669 Signaling apparatus, electric
HQ: Raytheon Applied Signal Technology,
Inc.
460 W California Ave
Sunnyvale CA 94086
408 749-1888

(P-17758)
RSG/AAMES SECURITY INC
3300 E 59th St, Long Beach (90805-4504)
PHONE..................................562 529-5100
Louis J Finkle, *President*
Danielle Roberts, *Shareholder*
Michelle Reuven, *Office Mgr*
Helen Moyer, *Sales Executive*
▲ EMP: 20
SQ FT: 17,000
SALES (est): 3.2MM **Privately Held**
WEB: www.rsgsecurity.com
SIC: 3669 Fire alarm apparatus, electric

(P-17759)
SAFARILAND LLC (DH)
3120 E Mission Blvd, Ontario (91761-2900)
PHONE..................................925 219-1097
Scott O'Brien, *CEO*
Scott Detillo, *Vice Pres*
Bill Moles, *Vice Pres*
Phyllis Bonser, *Executive Asst*
Leanne McKenzie, *Executive Asst*
EMP: 22
SQ FT: 2,000
SALES (est): 2.6MM
SALES (corp-wide): 1B **Privately Held**
WEB: www.tacticalcommand.com
SIC: 3669 Intercommunication systems, electric
HQ: Safariland, Llc
13386 International Pkwy
Jacksonville FL 32218
904 741-5400

(P-17760)
SENSYS NETWORKS INC (HQ)
Also Called: Senetrics International
1608 4th St Ste 200, Berkeley
(94710-1749)
PHONE..................................510 548-4620
Amine Haoui, *President*
Brian Fuller, *President*
Robert Kavaler, *Senior VP*
Hamed Benouar, *Vice Pres*
Floyd Williams, *Vice Pres*
▲ EMP: 76
SALES (est): 14.8MM
SALES (corp-wide): 21.7MM **Privately Held**
SIC: 3669 Transportation signaling devices
PA: Tagmaster Ab
Kronborgsgrand 11
Kista 164 4
863 219-50

(P-17761)
SIEMENS RAIL AUTOMATION CORP
9568 Archibald Ave, Rancho Cucamonga
(91730-5744)
PHONE..................................909 532-5405
Jay Aslam, *Opers Mgr*
Richard V Peel, *Mfg Staff*
EMP: 250
SALES (corp-wide): 95B **Privately Held**
SIC: 3669 Railroad signaling devices, electric
HQ: Siemens Rail Automation Corporation
2400 Nelson Miller Pkwy
Louisville KY 40223
800 626-2710

(P-17762)
SIERRA TRAFFIC SERVICE INC
225 W Loop Dr, Camarillo (93010-2038)
P.O. Box 222, Somis (93066-0222)
PHONE..................................805 388-2474
Terry Quinones, *President*
EMP: 12
SALES (est): 1.9MM **Privately Held**
SIC: 3669 Pedestrian traffic control equipment

(P-17763)
SIGTRONICS CORPORATION
178 E Arrow Hwy, San Dimas
(91773-3336)
PHONE..................................909 305-9399
Mark Kelley, *President*
Tim Theis, *Vice Pres*
Frank M Sigona, *Principal*
Jane Sigona, *Principal*
Steve Daw, *Info Tech Mgr*
EMP: 20
SQ FT: 12,000

SALES (est): 4.1MM **Privately Held**
WEB: www.sigtronics.com
SIC: 3669 Intercommunication systems, electric

(P-17764)
STATEWIDE SAFETY AND SIGNS I
522 Lindon Ln, Nipomo (93444-9222)
PHONE..................................714 468-1919
Greg Grosch, *CEO*
Don Nicholas, *President*
Chris Burns, *CFO*
Tony Wood, *Buyer*
EMP: 300
SALES (est): 69.2MM **Privately Held**
SIC: 3669 Pedestrian traffic control equipment

(P-17765)
SYSTECH CORPORATION
10908 Technology Pl, San Diego
(92127-1874)
PHONE..................................858 674-6500
D Mark Fowler, *President*
Zenon Barelka, *COO*
Don Armerding, *Vice Pres*
Jon Goby, *Vice Pres*
Cheri Houchin, *Vice Pres*
▲ EMP: 35 EST: 1980
SQ FT: 25,000
SALES (est): 6.9MM **Privately Held**
WEB: www.systech.com
SIC: 3669 7371 3661 3577 Intercommunication systems, electric; custom computer programming services; telephone & telegraph apparatus; computer peripheral equipment

(P-17766)
TACTICAL COMMUNICATIONS CORP
473 Post St, Camarillo (93010-8553)
PHONE..................................805 987-4100
Gregory Peacock, *Ch of Bd*
E Carey Walter, *CEO*
Carey Walters, *Info Tech Mgr*
Doug Fuller, *Manager*
EMP: 25
SQ FT: 11,000
SALES (est): 4.1MM **Privately Held**
SIC: 3669 Intercommunication systems, electric

(P-17767)
TC COMMUNICATIONS INC
17881 Cartwright Rd, Irvine (92614-6216)
PHONE..................................949 852-1972
Kai Liang, *President*
Daphne Wang, *CFO*
Matt McMillin, *Graphic Designe*
Chin Tang, *Senior Buyer*
Kevin Chang, *Prdtn Mgr*
◆ EMP: 42
SQ FT: 54,000
SALES (est): 7.2MM **Privately Held**
WEB: www.tccomm.com
SIC: 3669 Visual communication systems

(P-17768)
TEAM ECONOLITE
Also Called: Aegis Its
4120 Business Center Dr, Fremont
(94538-6354)
PHONE..................................408 577-1733
John Cane, *General Mgr*
EMP: 10
SALES (est): 1.2MM **Privately Held**
WEB: www.teameconolite.com
SIC: 3669 Traffic signals, electric

(P-17769)
TRAFFIX DEVICES INC (PA)
160 Avenida La Pata, San Clemente
(92673-6304)
PHONE..................................949 361-5663
Jack H Kulp, *President*
Maurice Havens, *General Mgr*
Albert Idowu, *General Mgr*
Roger Peck, *Office Mgr*
Andrew Maxwell, *Web Dvlpr*
◆ EMP: 15
SQ FT: 10,000
SALES (est): 13MM **Privately Held**
WEB: www.traffixdevices.com
SIC: 3669 Transportation signaling devices

(P-17770)
UNICOM ELECTRIC INC
565 Brea Canyon Rd Ste A, Walnut
(91789-3004)
PHONE..................................626 964-7873
Jeffrey Lo, *President*
Christopher Lin, *Engineer*
Raul Zeledon, *Sales Staff*
▲ EMP: 32
SQ FT: 25,000
SALES (est): 1.5MM **Privately Held**
WEB: www.unicomlink.com
SIC: 3669 3678 3577 Intercommunication systems, electric; electronic connectors; computer peripheral equipment

(P-17771)
VERSACALL TECHNOLOGIES INC
7047 Carroll Rd, San Diego (92121-3273)
PHONE..................................858 677-6766
Robert A Giese, *President*
EMP: 11 EST: 2000
SQ FT: 5,000
SALES (est): 2.6MM **Privately Held**
WEB: www.versacall.com
SIC: 3669 Visual communication systems

(P-17772)
VOCERA COMMUNICATIONS INC (PA)
525 Race St Ste 150, San Jose
(95126-3497)
PHONE..................................408 882-5100
Brent D Lang, *Ch of Bd*
Justin R Spencer, *CFO*
M Bridget Duffy, *Chief Mktg Ofcr*
Sue Dooley, *Officer*
Paul T Johnson, *Exec VP*
▲ EMP: 174
SQ FT: 70,000
SALES: 179.6MM **Publicly Held**
WEB: www.vocera.com
SIC: 3669 Intercommunication systems, electric

(P-17773)
WESTEK ELECTRONICS INC
185 Westridge Dr, Watsonville
(95076-4167)
PHONE..................................831 740-6300
Kevin Larkin, *CEO*
Michael Hushaw, *COO*
Amy Eades, *Principal*
Susie Freitas, *Principal*
Javier Ramirez, *Principal*
▲ EMP: 40
SQ FT: 1,220
SALES (est): 8.1MM **Privately Held**
WEB: www.westekelectronics.com
SIC: 3669 Intercommunication systems, electric

(P-17774)
WESTERN PACIFIC SIGNAL LLC
15890 Foothill Blvd, San Leandro
(94578-2101)
PHONE..................................510 276-6400
Heidi Shupp, *President*
Donald R Shupp, *Vice Pres*
Pedro Lopez, *Technical Staff*
Aron McEvoy, *Manager*
EMP: 15
SQ FT: 6,500
SALES (est): 3.2MM **Privately Held**
WEB: www.wpsignal.com
SIC: 3669 Traffic signals, electric

3671 Radio & T V Receiving Electron Tubes

(P-17775)
ACCURATE SOLUTIONS INC
2273 Wales Dr, Cardiff By The Sea
(92007-1509)
PHONE..................................760 753-6524
Tod Kilgore, *President*
Steven Freeman, *Corp Secy*
Eric Pinson, *Vice Pres*
EMP: 10
SQ FT: 2,400

SALES (est): 714.2K **Privately Held**
SIC: 3671 Electronic tube parts, except glass blanks

(P-17776)
AQUA BACKFLOW AND CHLORINATION
1060 Northgate St Ste C, Riverside
(92507-2172)
P.O. Box 396, Walnut (91788-0396)
PHONE..................................909 598-7251
Shirley Rogers, *President*
Duane Rogers, *Treasurer*
Chris Spaulding, *Principal*
Nicole Spaulding, *Director*
EMP: 10
SQ FT: 1,200
SALES (est): 2.1MM **Privately Held**
SIC: 3671 7699 Electron tubes, industrial; industrial equipment services

(P-17777)
COMMUNICATIONS & PWR INDS LLC
CPI
811 Hansen Way, Palo Alto (94304-1031)
PHONE..................................650 846-3494
Michael Cheng, *Branch Mgr*
Gemma Guzman, *Admin Asst*
Melissa Moran, *Administration*
Joe Rapuano, *Engineer*
Richard Dobbs, *Senior Engr*
EMP: 150
SQ FT: 25,000
SALES (corp-wide): 399.2MM **Privately Held**
WEB: www.cpii.com
SIC: 3671 Electron tubes
HQ: Communications & Power Industries Llc
607 Hansen Way
Palo Alto CA 94304

(P-17778)
COMMUNICATIONS & PWR INDS LLC (HQ)
Also Called: CPI
607 Hansen Way, Palo Alto (94304-1015)
PHONE..................................650 846-2900
Robert A Fickett, *President*
Don C Coleman, *Vice Pres*
Andrew Tafler, *Principal*
Keith Rhinehart, *Admin Sec*
Renee Butler, *Administration*
◆ EMP: 720
SQ FT: 429,000
SALES (est): 401.5MM
SALES (corp-wide): 399.2MM **Privately Held**
WEB: www.cpii.com
SIC: 3671 3679 3699 3663 Vacuum tubes; microwave components; power supplies, all types: static; electrical equipment & supplies; radio & TV communications equipment
PA: Cpi International, Inc.
811 Hansen Way
Palo Alto CA 94304
650 846-2801

(P-17779)
COMMUNICATIONS & PWR INDS LLC
Also Called: Microwave Power Products Div
811 Hansen Way, Palo Alto (94304-1031)
PHONE..................................650 846-2900
Jennifer Trainor, *Vice Pres*
Andy Moyer, *Programmer Anys*
Justin Thomaszvic, *Electrical Engi*
Steve Cauffman, *Senior Engr*
Thomas Cox, *Contract Mgr*
EMP: 130
SALES (corp-wide): 399.2MM **Privately Held**
SIC: 3671 Vacuum tubes
HQ: Communications & Power Industries Llc
607 Hansen Way
Palo Alto CA 94304

▲ = Import ▼=Export
◆ =Import/Export

(P-17780)
CPI INTERNATIONAL INC (PA)
811 Hansen Way, Palo Alto (94304-1031)
PHONE................................650 846-2801
Robert A Fickett, *CEO*
Robert J Kemp, *CFO*
Jim Bell, *Vice Pres*
John Overstreet, *Vice Pres*
Andrew E Tafler, *Vice Pres*
EMP: 10
SQ FT: 418,300
SALES (est): 399.2MM **Privately Held**
WEB: www.cpiinternational.net
SIC: 3671 3679 3699 3825 Traveling
wave tubes; vacuum tubes; microwave
components; power supplies, all types:
static; electrical equipment & supplies;
radio frequency measuring equipment

(P-17781)
DCX-CHOL ENTERPRISES INC (PA)
Also Called: Smi, Scb
12831 S Figueroa St, Los Angeles
(90061-1157)
PHONE..................................310 516-1692
Neal Castleman, *President*
Brian Gamberg, *Vice Pres*
Garret Hoffman, *Vice Pres*
Travis Cooper, *Natl Sales Mgr*
▲ **EMP:** 80
SQ FT: 50,000
SALES (est): 120.5MM **Privately Held**
SIC: 3671 Electron tubes

(P-17782)
DCX-CHOL ENTERPRISES INC
Teletronic Div Dcx-Chol Entp
12831 S Figueroa St, Los Angeles
(90061-1157)
PHONE..................................310 516-1692
Neil Levy, *Director*
EMP: 80
SALES (corp-wide): 120.5MM **Privately Held**
SIC: 3671 3679 Electron tubes; harness
assemblies for electronic use: wire or
cable
PA: Dcx-Chol Enterprises, Inc.
12831 S Figueroa St
Los Angeles CA 90061
310 516-1692

(P-17783)
DCX-CHOL ENTERPRISES INC
Also Called: Masterite Division
12831 S Figueroa St, Los Angeles
(90061-1157)
PHONE..................................310 516-1692
Brian Gamberg, *Branch Mgr*
EMP: 16
SALES (corp-wide): 120.5MM **Privately Held**
SIC: 3671 3365 Electron tubes; aerospace
castings, aluminum
PA: Dcx-Chol Enterprises, Inc.
12831 S Figueroa St
Los Angeles CA 90061
310 516-1692

(P-17784)
DCX-CHOL ENTERPRISES INC
12831 S Figueroa St, Los Angeles
(90061-1157)
PHONE..................................310 525-1205
Neil Castleman, *President*
EMP: 46
SALES (corp-wide): 120.5MM **Privately Held**
SIC: 3671 3365 Electron tubes; aerospace
castings, aluminum
PA: Dcx-Chol Enterprises, Inc.
12831 S Figueroa St
Los Angeles CA 90061
310 516-1692

(P-17785)
ECOATM LLC (HQ)
10121 Barnes Canyon Rd, San Diego
(92121-2725)
PHONE................................858 999-3200
David Maquera,
Larry Heminger, *Vice Pres*
Yuri Pitko, *Vice Pres*
Brian Lawson, *Technician*
Jim Snook, *Engineer*

EMP: 250
SALES (est): 382.5MM **Publicly Held**
SIC: 3671 Electron tubes

(P-17786)
HEATWAVE LABS INC
195 Aviation Way Ste 100, Watsonville
(95076-2059)
PHONE................................831 722-9081
Kim Gunther, *President*
Marc Curtis, *Sales Mgr*
EMP: 18
SQ FT: 10,000
SALES (est): 3.1MM **Privately Held**
WEB: www.cathode.com
SIC: 3671 Electron tubes

(P-17787)
L3 ELECTRON DEVICES INC (DH)
3100 Lomita Blvd, Torrance (90505-5104)
P.O. Box 2999 (90509-2999)
PHONE..................................310 517-6000
Michael Strianese, *CEO*
Jose Chavez, *Engineer*
▲ **EMP:** 508
SALES (est): 109.8MM
SALES (corp-wide): 6.8B **Publicly Held**
SIC: 3671 3764 Traveling wave tubes;
guided missile & space vehicle propulsion
unit parts
HQ: L3 Technologies, Inc.
600 3rd Ave Fl 34
New York NY 10016
212 697-1111

(P-17788)
LEEMAH CORPORATION (PA)
155 S Hill Dr, Brisbane (94005-1203)
PHONE..................................415 394-1288
Efrem Mah, *CEO*
Bing Hong Mah, *President*
Warren Gee, *CFO*
Dick Wong, *Vice Pres*
Brenda Ly, *Technology*
▲ **EMP:** 150
SQ FT: 60,000
SALES (est): 101MM **Privately Held**
WEB: www.leemah.com
SIC: 3671 3672 3669 3663 Electron
tubes; printed circuit boards; intercommu-
nication systems, electric; radio & TV
communications equipment; computer pe-
ripheral equipment

(P-17789)
NEWVAC LLC
Also Called: Newvac Division
9330 Desoto Ave, Chatsworth (91311)
PHONE..................................310 990-0401
Garrett Hoffman, *Branch Mgr*
EMP: 114
SALES (corp-wide): 49MM **Privately Held**
SIC: 3671 3678 3679 Electron tubes;
electronic connectors; harness assem-
blies for electronic use: wire or cable
HQ: Newvac, Llc
9330 De Soto Ave
Chatsworth CA 91311
310 525-1205

(P-17790)
NEWVAC LLC
Also Called: ADI American Def Interconnect
9330 De Soto Ave, Chatsworth
(91311-4926)
PHONE..................................310 990-0401
EMP: 14
SALES (corp-wide): 49MM **Privately Held**
SIC: 3671 3672 3429 Electron tubes;
printed circuit boards; manufactured hard-
ware (general)
HQ: Newvac, Llc
9330 De Soto Ave
Chatsworth CA 91311
310 525-1205

(P-17791)
NEWVAC LLC
New-Vac Division
9330 Desoto Ave, Chatsworth (91311)
PHONE..................................310 516-1692
Garrett Hoffman, *Branch Mgr*
Shirley Harshman, *Manager*

EMP: 80
SALES (corp-wide): 49MM **Privately Held**
SIC: 3671 3678 3679 3643 Electron
tubes; electronic connectors; harness assemblies for electronic use: wire or cable;
current-carrying wiring devices; noncurrent-carrying wiring services
HQ: Newvac, Llc
9330 De Soto Ave
Chatsworth CA 91311
310 525-1205

(P-17792)
PENTA FINANCIAL INC
Also Called: Penta Laboratories
2359 Knoll Dr, Ventura (93003-5875)
PHONE..................................818 882-3872
Steve Sanett, *CEO*
▲ **EMP:** 24
SQ FT: 28,000
SALES (est): 4.4MM **Privately Held**
WEB: www.pentalabs.com
SIC: 3671 3589 Electron tubes; mi-
crowave ovens (cooking equipment),
commercial

(P-17793)
PENTA LABORATORIES LLC
7868 Deering Ave, Canoga Park
(91304-5005)
PHONE..................................818 882-3872
Susan E Sanett,
Wayne Coturri, *President*
Neil Towey, *Vice Pres*
Peter Russell, *Chief Engr*
Jonathan Erazo, *Finance*
▲ **EMP:** 15
SALES (est): 4MM **Privately Held**
SIC: 3671 5065 Electron tubes; electronic
tubes: receiving & transmitting or indus-
trial

(P-17794)
THERMO KEVEX X-RAY INC
320 El Pueblo Rd, Scotts Valley
(95066-4219)
PHONE..................................831 438-5940
Marijn Dekkers, *President*
Donna Gaulard, *Project Mgr*
EMP: 34
SQ FT: 16,800
SALES (est): 5.6MM
SALES (corp-wide): 24.3B **Publicly Held**
WEB: www.thermo.com
SIC: 3671 3679 3844 Transmittal, indus-
trial & special purpose electron tubes;
power supplies, all types: static; X-ray ap-
paratus & tubes
PA: Thermo Fisher Scientific Inc.
168 3rd Ave
Waltham MA 02451
781 622-1000

(P-17795)
VACUUM TUBE LOGIC OF AMERICA
4774 Murietta St Ste 10, Chino
(91710-5155)
P.O. Box 2604, Sunnyvale (94087-0604)
PHONE..................................909 627-5944
Luke Manley, *President*
EMP: 15
SALES (est): 1.5MM **Privately Held**
SIC: 3671 Electron tubes

(P-17796)
VARIAN MEDICAL SYSTEMS INC
Also Called: Varian Thin Film Systems
3175 Hanover St, Palo Alto (94304-1130)
P.O. Box 10032 (94303-0896)
PHONE..................................650 493-4000
Boris Lipkin, *General Mgr*
EMP: 15

SALES (corp-wide): 2.6B **Publicly Held**
SIC: 3671 3663 3699 3563 Electron
tubes, special purpose; transmitting apparatus, radio or television; amplifiers, RF
power & IF; electrical equipment & supplies; linear accelerators; air & gas compressors; vacuum pumps, except
laboratory; industrial instrmnts msrmnt
display/control process variable; chromatographs, industrial process type; analytical instruments; spectrometers;
photometers
PA: Varian Medical Systems, Inc.
3100 Hansen Way
Palo Alto CA 94304
650 493-4000

3672 Printed Circuit Boards

(P-17797)
A & M ELECTRONICS INC
25018 Avenue Kearny, Valencia
(91355-1253)
PHONE..................................661 257-3680
Ron Simpson, *President*
Tiffiny Simpson, *Vice Pres*
Dan Simpson, *Manager*
EMP: 30
SQ FT: 12,000
SALES (est): 7MM **Privately Held**
WEB: www.aandmelectronics.com
SIC: 3672 Circuit boards, television & radio
printed

(P-17798)
A AND C ELECTRONICS
18153 Napa St, Northridge (91325-3377)
PHONE..................................818 886-8900
Frank Sampo, *President*
Louis Pacent III, *Treasurer*
EMP: 10
SQ FT: 6,000
SALES (est): 4.2MM **Privately Held**
WEB: www.acelectronics.com
SIC: 3672 Circuit boards, television & radio
printed

(P-17799)
ABC ASSEMBLY INC
43006 Osgood Rd, Fremont (94539-5629)
PHONE..................................408 293-3560
Tim Suleymanov, *CEO*
Mike Suleymanov, *Chairman*
Carlos Navarro, *Executive*
Tofik Kasumov, *Purch Mgr*
Lora Suleymanova, *Prdtn Mgr*
EMP: 12
SQ FT: 9,000
SALES (est): 2.9MM **Privately Held**
WEB: www.abcassembly.com
SIC: 3672 Printed circuit boards

(P-17800)
ABSOLUTE TURNKEY SERVICES INC
555 Aldo Ave, Santa Clara (95054-2205)
PHONE..................................408 850-7530
Jeffrey Bullis, *CEO*
Michelle Gaynor, *Vice Pres*
Dorothy Litle, *Purch Mgr*
EMP: 40
SQ FT: 17,000
SALES (est): 8.7MM **Privately Held**
WEB: www.absoluteturnkey.com
SIC: 3672 Printed circuit boards

(P-17801)
ACCU-SEMBLY INC
1835 Huntington Dr, Duarte (91010-2635)
PHONE..................................626 357-3447
John Hykes, *CEO*
Jan Shimmin, *Shareholder*
John Shimmin, *Shareholder*
Marilyn Hykes, *Admin Dir*
Joseph Santana, *Program Mgr*
▲ **EMP:** 95
SQ FT: 15,000
SALES (est): 29.3MM **Privately Held**
WEB: www.accu-sembly.com
SIC: 3672 Printed circuit boards

(P-17802)
ACCURATE CIRCUIT ENGRG INC
Also Called: Ace
3019 Kilson Dr, Santa Ana (92707-4202)
PHONE..............................714 546-2162
Charles Lowe, CEO
James Hofer, General Mgr
Charels Lowe, Info Tech Mgr
Tim Waddell, Engineer
Michael Ciccoianni, Controller
▲ EMP: 70
SQ FT: 15,000
SALES: 7.2MM Privately Held
WEB: www.ace-pcb.com
SIC: 3672 Printed circuit boards

(P-17803)
ACCURATE ENGINEERING INC
8710 Telfair Ave, Sun Valley (91352-2530)
PHONE..............................818 768-3919
Rush Patel, President
Ramesh Jasani, Shareholder
Gautam Jasani, CFO
Suresh Jasani, Treasurer
Hiten Golakiea, Vice Pres
EMP: 25
SQ FT: 15,000
SALES (est): 4.7MM
SALES (corp-wide): 10.2MM Privately
Held
WEB: www.accueng.com
SIC: 3672 Printed circuit boards
PA: Austin Engineering Company Limited
Village Patla, Taluka Bhesan
Junagadh GJ 36203
287 325-2223

(P-17804)
**ACTION ELECTRONIC
ASSEMBLY INC**
Also Called: Prowave Manufacturing
2872 S Santa Fe Ave, San Marcos
(92069-6046)
PHONE..............................760 510-0003
Salim Khalfan, President
Deborah A Walker, Treasurer
EMP: 25
SQ FT: 4,000
SALES: 2.7MM Privately Held
WEB: www.prowavemfg.com
SIC: 3672 Printed circuit boards

(P-17805)
ADDISON TECHNOLOGY INC
Also Called: Addison Engineering
150 Nortech Pkwy, San Jose (95134-2305)
PHONE..............................408 749-1000
Gibson Cobb, President
Jim Landis, Vice Pres
Mark Ridgeway, Vice Pres
Jeff Besterman, Accounts Mgr
Charles Lyons, Accounts Mgr
▲ EMP: 45
SQ FT: 40,000
SALES (est): 4.7MM Privately Held
WEB: www.addisonengineering.com
SIC: 3672 5065 Printed circuit boards;
semiconductor devices

(P-17806)
ADURA LED SOLUTIONS LLC
511 Princeland Ct, Corona (92879-1383)
PHONE..............................714 660-2944
Kris Vasoya,
▲ EMP: 10
SALES (est): 1.5MM Privately Held
SIC: 3672 5719 Printed circuit boards;
lighting fixtures

(P-17807)
**ADVANCE ELECTRONIC
SERVICE**
44141 Fremont Blvd, Fremont
(94538-6044)
PHONE..............................510 490-1065
Patrick Chan, President
EMP: 20
SALES (est): 500K Privately Held
SIC: 3672 Circuit boards, television & radio
printed

(P-17808)
ADVANCED CIRCUITS INC
Also Called: Coastal Circuit
1602 Tacoma Way, Redwood City
(94063-1109)
PHONE..............................415 602-6834
Ralph Richart Jr, President
EMP: 56 Publicly Held
SIC: 3672 Circuit boards, television & radio
printed
HQ: Advanced Circuits, Inc.
21101 E 32nd Pkwy
Aurora CO 80011
303 576-6610

(P-17809)
ALL QUALITY & SERVICES INC
Also Called: Aqs
47817 Fremont Blvd, Fremont
(94538-6506)
PHONE..............................510 249-5800
So Jin Lee, President
John Park, Chief Mktg Ofcr
Kang Samuel, Vice Pres
Raymond Luk, Business Dir
Hans Krasnow, MIS Dir
▲ EMP: 120
SALES (est): 38.2MM Privately Held
WEB: www.aqs-inc.com
SIC: 3672 3651 Printed circuit boards;
electronic kits for home assembly: radio,
TV, phonograph

(P-17810)
ALLIED ELECTRONIC SERVICES
1342 E Borchard Ave, Santa Ana
(92705-4413)
PHONE..............................714 245-2500
Dave Vadodaria, President
Bharati Vadodaria, CFO
EMP: 15
SQ FT: 6,000
SALES (est): 2.1MM Privately Held
SIC: 3672 Printed circuit boards

(P-17811)
ALMATRON ELECTRONICS INC
644 Young St, Santa Ana (92705-5633)
PHONE..............................714 557-6000
Margarito Alvarez, President
Margarita Alvarez, Owner
Sergio Rivera, Purch Agent
EMP: 30
SQ FT: 11,500
SALES (est): 4.8MM Privately Held
WEB: www.almatron.com
SIC: 3672 Circuit boards, television & radio
printed

(P-17812)
ALPHA EMS CORPORATION
44193 S Grimmer Blvd, Fremont
(94538-6350)
PHONE..............................510 498-8788
Eric Chang, President
Tom Lin, Vice Pres
Shu Lin Chen, General Mgr
Micol Hung, Engineer
Benjamin Lai, Engineer
EMP: 150
SQ FT: 50,000
SALES: 18.6MM Privately Held
SIC: 3672 Printed circuit boards

(P-17813)
ALTA MANUFACTURING INC
47650 Westinghouse Dr, Fremont
(94539-7473)
PHONE..............................510 668-1870
Anne Lee, CEO
EMP: 30
SQ FT: 24,000
SALES: 8MM Privately Held
WEB: www.altamfg.com
SIC: 3672 Printed circuit boards

(P-17814)
ALTAFLEX
336 Martin Ave, Santa Clara (95050-3112)
PHONE..............................408 727-6614
Paul Morben, President
Robert Jung, General Mgr
EMP: 70 EST: 2000
SQ FT: 20,200
SALES: 13MM
SALES (corp-wide): 1.1B Publicly Held
WEB: www.altaflex.com
SIC: 3672 Printed circuit boards
HQ: Osi Electronics, Inc.
12533 Chadron Ave
Hawthorne CA 90250
310 978-0516

(P-17815)
AMBAY CIRCUITS INC
Also Called: Delta Dvh Circuits
16117 Leadwell St, Van Nuys
(91406-3417)
PHONE..............................818 786-8241
Kana Khunti, President
EMP: 12 EST: 1973
SQ FT: 5,500
SALES (est): 1.9MM Privately Held
SIC: 3672 Circuit boards, television & radio
printed

(P-17816)
**AMERICAN BOARD ASSEMBLY
INC**
5456 Endeavour Ct, Moorpark
(93021-1705)
PHONE..............................805 523-0274
Cindy Murray, CEO
Gene Difabritis, President
▲ EMP: 140
SQ FT: 11,000
SALES (est): 40.9MM Privately Held
WEB: www.americanboard.com
SIC: 3672 Printed circuit boards

(P-17817)
**AMERICAN CIRCUIT TECH INC
(PA)**
5330 E Hunter Ave, Anaheim (92807-2053)
PHONE..............................714 777-2480
Ravi Kheni, President
Labith Lavadia, Vice Pres
Labheu Zalavadia, Vice Pres
Kanu Patel, Executive
Ankur Kheni, General Mgr
EMP: 40 EST: 1975
SQ FT: 22,000
SALES (est): 6.3MM Privately Held
WEB: www.act-cw.com
SIC: 3672 Circuit boards, television & radio
printed

(P-17818)
AMPRO SYSTEMS INC
1000 Page Ave, Fremont (94538-7340)
PHONE..............................510 624-9000
Elliot Wang, President
▲ EMP: 45 EST: 1997
SQ FT: 21,000
SALES (est): 7.5MM Privately Held
WEB: www.amprosystems.com
SIC: 3672 Printed circuit boards

(P-17819)
**AMTECH MICROELECTRONICS
INC**
485 Cochrane Cir, Morgan Hill
(95037-2831)
PHONE..............................408 612-8888
Walter Chavez, President
EMP: 42
SQ FT: 14,500
SALES (est): 6.8MM Privately Held
WEB: www.amtechmicro.com
SIC: 3672 Printed circuit boards

(P-17820)
ANC TECHNOLOGY LLC
Also Called: Shanghai Anc Electronic Tech
10195 Stockton Rd, Moorpark
(93021-9755)
PHONE..............................805 530-3958
Dennis Noble, Principal
▲ EMP: 100
SQ FT: 60,000
SALES (est): 10MM Privately Held
WEB: www.anctech.com
SIC: 3672 5083 Printed circuit boards; irri-
gation equipment

(P-17821)
APCT INC (PA)
Also Called: (FORMER: ADVANCED
PRINTED CIRCUIT TECHNOLOGY)
3495 De La Cruz Blvd, Santa Clara
(95054-2110)
PHONE..............................408 727-6442
Steve Robinson, CEO
Greg Elder, CFO
Bruce McMaster, Exec VP
Eric Schmidt, Exec VP
Randy Peterson, Program Mgr
▲ EMP: 79
SQ FT: 30,000
SALES (est): 26.7MM Privately Held
WEB: www.apctcircuits.com
SIC: 3672 Circuit boards, television & radio
printed

(P-17822)
APT ELECTRONICS INC
241 N Crescent Way, Anaheim
(92801-6704)
PHONE..............................714 687-6760
Tae Myoung Kim, CEO
EMP: 112
SQ FT: 20,000
SALES (est): 21.3MM Privately Held
WEB: www.aptelectronics.com
SIC: 3672 Printed circuit boards

(P-17823)
ARDENT SYSTEMS INC
2040 Ringwood Ave, San Jose
(95131-1728)
PHONE..............................408 526-0100
Thomas Han, President
Young C Kang, Admin Sec
Tom Han, Opers Mgr
EMP: 24
SQ FT: 8,000
SALES (est): 3.9MM Privately Held
SIC: 3672 Printed circuit boards

(P-17824)
ARNOLD ELECTRONICS INC
1907 Nancita Cir, Placentia (92870-6737)
PHONE..............................714 646-8343
Sam Z Bhayani, President
Tushar Patel, Vice Pres
Charlene Newmyer, Manager
▲ EMP: 12
SQ FT: 2,500
SALES (est): 5.8MM Privately Held
WEB: www.arnoldelectronics.com
SIC: 3672 Circuit boards, television & radio
printed

(P-17825)
ASROCK AMERICA INC
13848 Magnolia Ave, Chino (91710-7027)
PHONE..............................909 590-8308
James Teng, President
▲ EMP: 20
SALES (est): 2.8MM Privately Held
SIC: 3672 Printed circuit boards
HQ: Firstplace International Limited
C/O: Offshore Incorporations Limited
Road Town

(P-17826)
**ASSEMBLY TECHNOLOGIES CO
LLC**
Also Called: Atc
2921 W Central Ave Ste B, Santa Ana
(92704-5336)
PHONE..............................714 979-4400
David Mathisen,
Esther Mathisen, Partner
Rick Mathisen, General Mgr
EMP: 11
SQ FT: 2,000
SALES (est): 1.1MM Privately Held
SIC: 3672 Printed circuit boards

(P-17827)
ASTEELFLASH USA CORP (HQ)
4211 Starboard Dr, Fremont (94538-6427)
PHONE..............................510 440-2840
Gilles Benhamou, President
Craig Young, President
Claude Savard, CFO
Pierre Laboisse, Exec VP
Vince Pradia, Exec VP
▲ EMP: 211 EST: 2011

SALES (est): 134.5MM
SALES (corp-wide): 7MM **Privately Held**
SIC: 3672 3679 Printed circuit boards; electronic circuits
PA: Asteelflash Group
    6 Rue Vincent Van Gogh
    Neuilly Plaisance 93360
    149 445-300

(P-17828)
ASTRONIC
2 Orion, Aliso Viejo (92656-4200)
PHONE...................................949 454-1180
Sang H Choi, *CEO*
Kristine Cynn, *COO*
OK Kay Choi, *Corp Secy*
Dolly Carreon, *Executive*
Dolores Carreon, *Controller*
▲ **EMP:** 143 **EST:** 1976
SQ FT: 41,000
SALES (est): 38.4MM **Privately Held**
SIC: 3672 1742 Printed circuit boards; acoustical & insulation work

(P-17829)
AURUM ASSEMBLY PLUS INC
8829 Production Ave, San Diego (92121-2220)
PHONE...................................858 578-8710
Karl Northwang, *President*
Karl E Nothwang, *CFO*
Robert Mosley, *Vice Pres*
Robert Nothwang, *Vice Pres*
Bobby Northwang, *General Mgr*
EMP: 20
SQ FT: 7,000
SALES (est): 3.7MM **Privately Held**
WEB: www.aurumassembly.com
SIC: 3672 2298 Circuit boards, television & radio printed; wire rope centers

(P-17830)
AVANTEC MANUFACTURING INC
1811 N Case St, Orange (92865-4234)
PHONE...................................714 532-6197
Alan E McNeeney, *CEO*
▲ **EMP:** 20
SALES (est): 5.7MM **Privately Held**
WEB: www.avantecusa.com
SIC: 3672 Printed circuit boards

(P-17831)
BAY AREA CIRCUITS INC
44358 Old Warm Sprng Blvd, Fremont (94538-6148)
PHONE...................................510 933-9000
Barbara Nobriga, *President*
Brian Paper, *COO*
Cassandra Mubayed, *Office Mgr*
James Vansant, *Info Tech Mgr*
James Vant, *Engineer*
▲ **EMP:** 48
SQ FT: 7,500
SALES (est): 8.6MM **Privately Held**
WEB: www.bacircuits.com
SIC: 3672 Circuit boards, television & radio printed

(P-17832)
BAY AREA EMS SOLUTIONS LLC
Also Called: Baems
147 Walker Ranch Pkwy, Patterson (95363-8811)
PHONE...................................408 753-3651
EMP: 11 **EST:** 2011
SQ FT: 12,000
SALES (est): 1.4MM **Privately Held**
SIC: 3672

(P-17833)
BAY ELCTRNIC SPPORT TRNICS INC
Also Called: Bestronics
2090 Fortune Dr, San Jose (95131-1823)
PHONE...................................408 432-3222
Nat Mani, *CEO*
Ron Menigoz, *Vice Pres*
Connie Andrade, *Program Mgr*
Sohee Jung, *Program Mgr*
Dana Song, *Program Mgr*
▲ **EMP:** 155
SQ FT: 150,000

SALES (est): 71.5MM **Privately Held**
WEB: www.bestronicsinc.com
SIC: 3672 Circuit boards, television & radio printed
PA: Bestronics Holdings, Inc.
    2090 Fortune Dr
    San Jose CA 95131
    408 385-7777

(P-17834)
BENCHMARK ELEC MFG SLTIONS INC (HQ)
5550 Hellyer Ave, San Jose (95138-1005)
PHONE...................................805 222-1303
Jayne Desorcie, *Administration*
Bruce McCreary, *Bd of Directors*
Jeffrey Lalmond, *Engineer*
Vinette Hailey, *Analyst*
Carmen Shahrokhfar, *Buyer*
▲ **EMP:** 100 **EST:** 1986
SQ FT: 80,000
SALES (est): 118.3MM
SALES (corp-wide): 2.5B **Publicly Held**
WEB: www.smtek.com
SIC: 3672 Printed circuit boards
PA: Benchmark Electronics, Inc.
    56 S Rockford Dr
    Tempe AZ 85281
    623 300-7000

(P-17835)
BENCHMARK ELEC PHOENIX INC
1659 Gailes Blvd, San Diego (92154-8230)
PHONE...................................619 397-2402
Roberto Perez, *Branch Mgr*
EMP: 300
SALES (corp-wide): 2.5B **Publicly Held**
SIC: 3672 3577 Printed circuit boards; computer peripheral equipment
HQ: Benchmark Electronics Phoenix, Inc.
    56 S Rockford Dr
    Tempe AZ 85281
    623 300-7000

(P-17836)
BENCHMARK ELECTRONICS INC
42701 Christy St, Fremont (94538-3146)
PHONE...................................510 360-2800
Robert Pruett, *Vice Pres*
EMP: 100
SALES (corp-wide): 2.5B **Publicly Held**
SIC: 3672 Printed circuit boards
PA: Benchmark Electronics, Inc.
    56 S Rockford Dr
    Tempe AZ 85281
    623 300-7000

(P-17837)
BENCHMARK ELECTRONICS INC
2301 Arnold Ind Way Ste G, Concord (94520-5379)
PHONE...................................925 363-1151
Steve Tate, *Branch Mgr*
EMP: 257
SALES (corp-wide): 2.5B **Publicly Held**
SIC: 3672 Printed circuit boards
PA: Benchmark Electronics, Inc.
    56 S Rockford Dr
    Tempe AZ 85281
    623 300-7000

(P-17838)
BINH-NHAN D NGO
Also Called: Prototype Solutions
1751 Fortune Dr Ste F, San Jose (95131-1705)
PHONE...................................408 641-1721
Binh-Nhan Ngo, *Owner*
EMP: 10
SALES (est): 757.3K **Privately Held**
SIC: 3672 Printed circuit boards

(P-17839)
CAL-COMP USA (SAN DIEGO) INC
1940 Camino Vida Roble, Carlsbad (92008-6516)
PHONE...................................858 587-6900
Peter Pan, *President*
Marlena Aragon, *Program Mgr*
Richard Lucas, *Controller*
Nia Inthilath, *Senior Buyer*

John Wolfe, *Senior Buyer*
EMP: 215
SQ FT: 65,000
SALES (est): 63.7MM **Privately Held**
WEB: www.smstech.com
SIC: 3672 Circuit boards, television & radio printed

(P-17840)
CALIFORNIA INTEGRATION COORDIN
6048 Enterprise Dr, Diamond Springs (95619-9394)
PHONE...................................530 626-6168
Cherie Myers, *President*
Kim Ishmael, *Office Mgr*
Ray Presgrave, *Admin Sec*
Debby Verry, *Manager*
EMP: 14
SALES (est): 5MM **Privately Held**
WEB: www.cic-inc.com
SIC: 3672 Circuit boards, television & radio printed

(P-17841)
CALPAK USA INC
2110 Artesia Blvd B202, Redondo Beach (90278-3073)
PHONE...................................310 937-7335
Danish Qureshi, *President*
▲ **EMP:** 20
SALES: 5MM **Privately Held**
WEB: www.calpak-usa.com
SIC: 3672 3679 8742 4813 Printed circuit boards; commutators, electronic; management consulting services; telephone communication, except radio

(P-17842)
CAPELLA MICROSYSTEMS INC
2201 Laurelwood Rd, Santa Clara (95054-1516)
PHONE...................................408 988-8000
Cheng-Chung Shih, *CEO*
EMP: 22
SQ FT: 6,600
SALES (est): 2MM
SALES (corp-wide): 3B **Publicly Held**
WEB: www.capellamicro.com
SIC: 3672 3674 Circuit boards, television & radio printed; semiconductors & related devices
HQ: Vishay Capella Microsystems (Taiwan) Limited
    6f, 43, Fuxing Rd.,
    New Taipei City TAP 23150

(P-17843)
CELESTICA AEROSPACE TECH CORP
Also Called: Celestica-Aerospace
895 S Rockefeller Ave, Ontario (91761-8145)
PHONE...................................512 310-7540
Jeffrey Bain, *President*
Thomas Lovelock, *President*
Leslie K Sladek, *Admin Sec*
Barry Trejo, *Technology*
▲ **EMP:** 200
SQ FT: 55,000
SALES (est): 47MM
SALES (corp-wide): 23.7B **Privately Held**
WEB: www.celestica.com
SIC: 3672 Printed circuit boards
HQ: Celestica Inc
    844 Don Mills Rd
    Toronto ON M3C 1
    416 448-5800

(P-17844)
CENTURY TECHNOLOGY INC
3020 26th Ave, San Francisco (94132-1546)
PHONE...................................650 583-8908
Henry Han Ho, *President*
Kayle Hoad, *Vice Pres*
▲ **EMP:** 15 **EST:** 1993
SALES: 2MM **Privately Held**
WEB: www.century-technology.com
SIC: 3672 Printed circuit boards

(P-17845)
CHINA CIRCUIT TECH CORP N AMER
Also Called: C C T C North America
11 Thomas Owens Way, Monterey (93940-5816)
PHONE...................................831 646-2194
Doug Humble, *President*
▲ **EMP:** 10
SALES (est): 25.9MM
SALES (corp-wide): 711.7MM **Privately Held**
WEB: www.cctcna.com
SIC: 3672 Printed circuit boards
HQ: China Circuit Technology(Shantou) Corporation
    North Section Of Dongxia Road
    Shantou 51504
    754 881-9228

(P-17846)
CHOOSE MANUFACTURING CO LLC
1638 E Edinger Ave Ste A, Santa Ana (92705-5022)
PHONE...................................714 327-1698
Herbert Chiu, *Mng Member*
Tim Lynch, *Purch Agent*
Doreen Swaze, *QC Dir*
▲ **EMP:** 20 **EST:** 2000
SALES: 3MM **Privately Held**
WEB: www.choosemfg.com
SIC: 3672 Printed circuit boards

(P-17847)
CIRCUIT CONNECTIONS
Also Called: Innovative Circuits Engrg
2310 Lundy Ave, San Jose (95131-1827)
PHONE...................................408 955-9505
Narendra Narayan, *President*
Steven Poe, *Engineer*
EMP: 30
SALES (est): 3.8MM **Privately Held**
WEB: www.circuitconnections.com
SIC: 3672 Circuit boards, television & radio printed

(P-17848)
CIRCUIT EXPRESS INC
67 W Easy St Ste 129, Simi Valley (93065-6204)
PHONE...................................805 581-2172
Himmat Desai, *CEO*
Vinny Kathrota, *Admin Sec*
EMP: 12
SQ FT: 5,000
SALES: 1.2MM **Privately Held**
WEB: www.circuitexpressinc.com
SIC: 3672 Circuit boards, television & radio printed

(P-17849)
CIRCUIT SERVICES LLC
Also Called: Career Tech Circuit Services
9134 Independence Ave, Chatsworth (91311-5902)
PHONE...................................818 701-5391
Theodore Brudzinski, *CEO*
Anahit Stepanian, *Purch Mgr*
Tim Blackburn, *Marketing Mgr*
Artin Minas, *Marketing Mgr*
Armen Hayrapetian,
EMP: 43
SALES (est): 11.3MM **Privately Held**
WEB: www.careertech-usa.com
SIC: 3672 Printed circuit boards

(P-17850)
CIRCUIT SPECTRUM INC
988 Morse St, San Jose (95126-1414)
PHONE...................................408 946-8484
Zaven Tashjian, *President*
EMP: 10
SQ FT: 75,000
SALES (est): 1.6MM **Privately Held**
WEB: www.circuitspectrum.com
SIC: 3672 Printed circuit boards

(P-17851)
CIREXX CORPORATION
791 Nuttman St, Santa Clara (95054-2623)
PHONE...................................408 988-3980
Phillip Menges, *President*
Al Wasserzug, *Business Mgr*
EMP: 49

SQ FT: 22,000
SALES (est): 9.3MM **Privately Held**
WEB: www.cirexx.com
SIC: **3672** 8711 Printed circuit boards; engineering services

(P-17852)
CIREXX INTERNATIONAL INC (PA)
791 Nuttman St, Santa Clara (95054-2623)
PHONE..............................408 988-3980
Philip Menges, *President*
Kurt H Menges, *Vice Pres*
Erica Padilla,
EMP: 115
SALES (est): 33.3MM **Privately Held**
WEB: www.cirexxintl.com
SIC: **3672** Circuit boards, television & radio printed

(P-17853)
CMS CIRCUIT SOLUTIONS INC
41549 Cherry St, Murrieta (92562-9193)
P.O. Box 1031 (92564-1031)
PHONE..............................951 698-4452
Clark M Steddom, *President*
Wendy Nieves, *Office Mgr*
EMP: 20
SALES (est): 931.7K **Privately Held**
SIC: **3672** Circuit boards, television & radio printed

(P-17854)
COAST TO COAST CIRCUITS INC (PA)
Also Called: Speedy Circuits
5331 Mcfadden Ave, Huntington Beach (92649-1204)
PHONE..............................714 891-9441
Walter Stender, *CEO*
Ronald Scott Lawhead, *CFO*
Mike Schlehr, *CFO*
Albert Martinez, *Vice Pres*
Paul Chiary, *Controller*
◆ EMP: 41
SQ FT: 40,000
SALES (est): 13.8MM **Privately Held**
WEB: www.speedycircuits.com
SIC: **3672** Circuit boards, television & radio printed

(P-17855)
CONCEPT DEVELOPMENT LLC
Also Called: CDI
1881 Langley Ave, Irvine (92614-5623)
PHONE..............................949 623-8000
James M Reardon, *President*
Young Ha, *Engineer*
Dennis Yunker, *Mfg Staff*
EMP: 20 EST: 1972
SQ FT: 12,880
SALES (est): 4.5MM
SALES (corp-wide): 37MM **Publicly Held**
WEB: www.cdvinc.com
SIC: **3672** 8711 Printed circuit boards; consulting engineer
PA: One Stop Systems, Inc.
2235 Entp St Ste 110
Escondido CA 92029
760 745-9883

(P-17856)
CREATION TECH CALEXICO INC (HQ)
Also Called: Aisling Industries
1778 Zinetta Rd Ste A, Calexico (92231-9511)
P.O. Box 1833, El Centro (92244-1833)
PHONE..............................760 336-8543
Bhawnesh Mathur, *CEO*
Michael J Logue, *President*
Sergio Quiroz, *Vice Pres*
▲ EMP: 205
SQ FT: 10,000
SALES (est): 39.4MM
SALES (corp-wide): 792.1MM **Privately Held**
WEB: www.aislinginc.com
SIC: **3672** 3679 Printed circuit boards; electronic circuits
PA: Creation Technologies Inc
8999 Fraserton Crt
Burnaby BC V5J 5
604 430-4336

(P-17857)
CREATION TECH SANTA CLARA INC
2801 Northwestern Pkwy, Santa Clara (95051-0903)
PHONE..............................408 235-7500
Arthur Tymos, *CEO*
Dennis Kottke, *Ch of Bd*
Simon Ip, *Vice Pres*
Kurt Pagnini, *Vice Pres*
▲ EMP: 275
SQ FT: 32,000
SALES (est): 50.3MM
SALES (corp-wide): 792.1MM **Privately Held**
WEB: www.pro-works.com
SIC: **3672** Printed circuit boards
PA: Creation Technologies Inc
8999 Fraserton Crt
Burnaby BC V5J 5
604 430-4336

(P-17858)
CROWN CIRCUITS INC
6070 Avenida Encinas, Carlsbad (92011-1001)
PHONE..............................949 922-0144
Kamran A Saffari, *CEO*
Nilofar Saffari, *Ch of Bd*
Bert Arucnn, *President*
EMP: 70
SQ FT: 20,000
SALES (est): 5.9MM **Privately Held**
SIC: **3672** Printed circuit boards

(P-17859)
CTS CORPORATION
2271 Ringwood Ave, San Jose (95131-1717)
PHONE..............................408 955-9001
Richard Dinh, *Manager*
EMP: 125
SALES (corp-wide): 470.4MM **Publicly Held**
WEB: www.ctscorp.com
SIC: **3672** Printed circuit boards
PA: Cts Corporation
4925 Indiana Ave
Lisle IL 60532
630 577-8800

(P-17860)
DALLAS ELECTRONICS INC
2151 Delaware Ave Ste A, Santa Cruz (95060-5788)
P.O. Box 2489 (95063-2489)
PHONE..............................831 457-3610
Geneva Matta, *President*
Dallas Matta, *Vice Pres*
▲ EMP: 50
SQ FT: 16,000
SALES (est): 9.5MM **Privately Held**
WEB: www.dallaselectronics.com
SIC: **3672** 3674 Printed circuit boards; semiconductors & related devices

(P-17861)
DE LEON ENTPS ELEC SPCLIST INC
11934 Allegheny St, Sun Valley (91352-1833)
PHONE..............................818 252-6690
Miguel De Leon, *President*
▲ EMP: 24
SQ FT: 11,000
SALES (est): 4.5MM **Privately Held**
SIC: **3672** Printed circuit boards

(P-17862)
DELTA D V H CIRCUITS INC
16117 Leadwell St, Van Nuys (91406-3417)
PHONE..............................818 786-8241
Kana Khunai, *Owner*
EMP: 20
SQ FT: 10,000
SALES (est): 2.4MM **Privately Held**
WEB: www.deltacircuittech.com
SIC: **3672** Printed circuit boards

(P-17863)
DIAMOND MULTIMEDIA SYSTEMS
2880 Junction Ave, San Jose (95134-1922)
PHONE..............................408 868-9613

William J Schroeder, *Ch of Bd*
Franz Fichtner, *President*
James M Walker, *CFO*
C Scott Holt, *Senior VP*
Hyung Hwe Huh, *Senior VP*
EMP: 290
SQ FT: 80,000
SALES (est): 608.5MM **Privately Held**
SIC: **3672** 3577 3661 Printed circuit boards; computer peripheral equipment; modems

(P-17864)
DIGICOM ELECTRONICS INC
7799 Pardee Ln, Oakland (94621-1425)
PHONE..............................510 639-7003
Mohammed R Ohady, *CEO*
MO Ohady, *General Mgr*
Norma Criglar, *Controller*
Arthur Fung, *Manager*
EMP: 27
SALES (est): 7.8MM **Privately Held**
WEB: www.de-crypt.com
SIC: **3672** Printed circuit boards

(P-17865)
DYNASTY ELECTRONIC COMPANY LLC
Also Called: Dec
1790 E Mcfadden Ave, Santa Ana (92705-4638)
PHONE..............................714 550-1197
Fredrick Rodenhuis, *Mng Member*
Mark Clark,
EMP: 65
SQ FT: 10,000
SALES (est): 8.2MM **Privately Held**
SIC: **3672** Printed circuit boards

(P-17866)
ELECTRO SURFACE TECH INC
Also Called: E S T
2281 Las Palmas Dr 101, Carlsbad (92011-1527)
PHONE..............................760 431-8306
Hiroo Kirpalani, *President*
EMP: 61
SQ FT: 31,500
SALES (est): 9MM **Privately Held**
WEB: www.est.com
SIC: **3672** Circuit boards, television & radio printed

(P-17867)
ELECTROMAX INC
1960 Concourse Dr, San Jose (95131-1719)
PHONE..............................408 428-9474
Aaron Wong, *President*
Ken Wong, *Vice Pres*
▲ EMP: 50
SQ FT: 30,000
SALES (est): 11MM **Privately Held**
WEB: www.electromaxinc.com
SIC: **3672** Printed circuit boards

(P-17868)
ELECTRONIC SURFC MOUNTED INDS
Also Called: Esmi
6731 Cobra Way, San Diego (92121-4110)
PHONE..............................858 455-1710
Henry Kim, *President*
Lynn Kim, *Vice Pres*
▼ EMP: 40
SQ FT: 25,000
SALES: 4MM **Privately Held**
WEB: www.esmiinc.com
SIC: **3672** Printed circuit boards

(P-17869)
EMD SPECIALTY MATERIALS LLC
Also Called: Arlon EMD
9433 Hyssop Dr, Rancho Cucamonga (91730-6107)
PHONE..............................909 987-9533
Matt Young,
Brad Foster, *Vice Pres*
EMP: 10
SALES: 347.8K **Privately Held**
SIC: **3672** Circuit boards, television & radio printed

(P-17870)
EMSOLUTIONS INC
2152 Zanker Rd, San Jose (95131-2113)
PHONE..............................510 668-1118
Jun Huo, *President*
EMP: 10
SQ FT: 5,000
SALES (est): 1.8MM **Privately Held**
SIC: **3672** Printed circuit boards

(P-17871)
EXCELLO CIRCUITS INC
1924 Nancita Cir, Placentia (92870-6737)
PHONE..............................714 993-0560
Sam Bhayani, *President*
Tushar Patel, *Vice Pres*
Rax Ribadia, *Vice Pres*
EMP: 30
SQ FT: 11,000
SALES (est): 5.1MM **Privately Held**
WEB: www.excello.com
SIC: **3672** Circuit boards, television & radio printed

(P-17872)
EXPERT ASSEMBLY SERVICES INC
14312 Chambers Rd Ste B, Tustin (92780-6967)
PHONE..............................714 258-8880
Jack Quinn, *CEO*
EMP: 30
SALES (est): 6.2MM **Privately Held**
WEB: www.expertassembly.com
SIC: **3672** Printed circuit boards

(P-17873)
FABRICATED COMPONENTS CORP
Also Called: Summit Interconnect Orange
130 W Bristol Ln, Orange (92865-2640)
PHONE..............................714 974-8590
Shane Whiteside, *President*
▼ EMP: 140 EST: 1979
SQ FT: 40,000
SALES (est): 24MM **Privately Held**
WEB: www.mei4pcbs.com
SIC: **3672** Printed circuit boards

(P-17874)
FINE ELECTRONIC ASSEMBLY INC
4887 Mercury St, San Diego (92111-2104)
PHONE..............................858 573-0887
Rick Bajaria, *President*
David Nason, *Principal*
EMP: 20
SQ FT: 10,000
SALES: 1.5MM **Privately Held**
WEB: www.fineelectronic.com
SIC: **3672** 3699 Printed circuit boards; electrical equipment & supplies

(P-17875)
FINE PTCH ELCTRNIC ASSMBLY LLC
5106 Azusa Canyon Rd, Irwindale (91706-1846)
PHONE..............................626 337-2800
Ashish Sheladiya, *General Mgr*
Mayur Savalia,
EMP: 20
SQ FT: 15,000
SALES: 2.5MM **Privately Held**
WEB: www.finepitchassembly.com
SIC: **3672** Printed circuit boards

(P-17876)
FINELINE CIRCUITS & TECHNOLOGY
594 Apollo St Ste A, Brea (92821-3134)
PHONE..............................714 529-2942
Rick Bajaria, *President*
Ken Pansuria, *Vice Pres*
Vinny Kathrotia, *Admin Sec*
Sharon Long, *Accounting Mgr*
EMP: 30
SQ FT: 20,000
SALES (est): 4.5MM **Privately Held**
WEB: www.finelinecircuits.com
SIC: **3672** Circuit boards, television & radio printed

▲ = Import ▼=Export
◆ =Import/Export

(P-17877)
FIRST CIRCUIT INC
Also Called: Precision Circuits San Diego
7701 Garboso Pl, Carlsbad (92009-8325)
PHONE..................................760 560-0530
Tom Smiley, *President*
Christine Smiley, *Admin Sec*
EMP: 12
SALES: 1MM **Privately Held**
WEB: www.precisionpcbs.com
SIC: 3672 Printed circuit boards

(P-17878)
FLEXTRONICS AMERICA LLC (DH)
6201 America Center Dr, San Jose
(95002-2563)
PHONE..................................408 576-7000
David Bennett, *Mng Member*
Chris Collier,
▲ **EMP:** 230 **EST:** 2008
SALES (est): 797.8MM
SALES (corp-wide): 26.2B **Privately Held**
SIC: 3672 Printed circuit boards

(P-17879)
FLEXTRONICS INTERNATIONAL USA
260 S Milpitas Blvd # 15, Milpitas
(95035-5420)
PHONE..................................408 576-7000
Matt Bryan, *Branch Mgr*
Marcel Davis, *Administration*
Boonheng Lim, *Info Tech Mgr*
Giamberto Scaccia, *Engineer*
Khai Vu, *Engineer*
EMP: 650
SALES (corp-wide): 26.2B **Privately Held**
SIC: 3672 3679 Printed circuit boards;
power supplies, all types: static; harness
assemblies for electronic use: wire or
cable
HQ: Flextronics International Usa, Inc.
6201 America Center Dr
San Jose CA 95002
-

(P-17880)
FLEXTRONICS INTL USA INC
1177 Gibraltar Dr Bldg 9, Milpitas
(95035-6337)
PHONE..................................408 678-3268
EMP: 11
SALES (corp-wide): 26.2B **Privately Held**
SIC: 3672 Printed circuit boards
HQ: Flextronics International Usa, Inc.
6201 America Center Dr
San Jose CA 95002

(P-17881)
FLEXTRONICS INTL USA INC
925 Lightpost Way, Morgan Hill
(95037-2869)
PHONE..................................408 577-2262
EMP: 298
SALES (corp-wide): 26.2B **Privately Held**
SIC: 3672 Printed circuit boards
HQ: Flextronics International Usa, Inc.
6201 America Center Dr
San Jose CA 95002

(P-17882)
FLEXTRONICS INTL USA INC
847 Gibraltar Dr, Milpitas (95035-6332)
PHONE..................................408 576-7000
Amanda LI, *Bd of Directors*
Tom Linton, *Officer*
Subodh Gupta, *Vice Pres*
Kevin Hart, *Vice Pres*
Phuong Huynh, *Vice Pres*
EMP: 2000
SALES (corp-wide): 26.2B **Privately Held**
SIC: 3672 Printed circuit boards
HQ: Flextronics International Usa, Inc.
6201 America Center Dr
San Jose CA 95002

(P-17883)
FOXLINK WORLD CIRCUIT TECH
925 W Lambert Rd Ste C, Brea
(92821-2943)
PHONE..................................714 256-0877

EMP: 20
SQ FT: 6,000
SALES (est): 1.6MM **Privately Held**
SIC: 3672

(P-17884)
FTG CIRCUITS INC (DH)
20750 Marilla St, Chatsworth (91311-4407)
PHONE..................................818 407-4024
Brad Bourne, *CEO*
Michael Labrador, *President*
Joe Ricci, *CFO*
Ed Hanna, *Director*
▼ **EMP:** 100
SQ FT: 38,000
SALES (est): 31.1MM
SALES (corp-wide): 84.2MM **Privately Held**
SIC: 3672 3644 Printed circuit boards; ter-
minal boards
HQ: Firan Technology Group (Usa) Corpo-
ration
20750 Marilla St
Chatsworth CA 91311
818 407-4024

(P-17885)
GAVIAL ENGINEERING & MFG INC (HQ)
1435 W Mccoy Ln, Santa Maria
(93455-1002)
PHONE..................................805 614-0060
Don Connors, *President*
Stanley D Connors, *CEO*
Ken Hicks, *Vice Pres*
Ramona Castano, *Division Mgr*
Cathy Castor, *Office Mgr*
EMP: 45 **EST:** 2012
SQ FT: 25,000
SALES (est): 6.8MM
SALES (corp-wide): 80.4MM **Privately Held**
SIC: 3672 3679 Printed circuit boards;
electronic circuits
PA: Gavial Holdings, Inc.
1435 W Mccoy Ln
Santa Maria CA 93455
805 614-0060

(P-17886)
GEERIRAJ INC
Also Called: Mer-Mar Electronics
7042 Santa Fe Ave E A1, Hesperia
(92345-5711)
PHONE..................................760 244-6149
Kanjibhai Ghadia, *President*
Suresh Patel, *Vice Pres*
EMP: 28 **EST:** 1974
SQ FT: 22,000
SALES: 450K **Privately Held**
WEB: www.mermarinc.com
SIC: 3672 Printed circuit boards

(P-17887)
GEMINI CONSULTANTS INC
Also Called: Twin Industries
2303 Camino Ramon Ste 106, San Ramon
(94583-1389)
PHONE..................................925 866-8946
David M Wisser, *President*
▲ **EMP:** 10
SALES: 650K **Privately Held**
SIC: 3672 3825 Printed circuit boards; in-
struments to measure electricity

(P-17888)
GENERAL ELEC ASSEMBLY INC
1525 Atteberry Ln, San Jose (95131-1412)
PHONE..................................408 980-8819
Eric Chang, *President*
Matthew McClendon, *Program Mgr*
Donna Field, *QC Mgr*
EMP: 45
SQ FT: 16,000
SALES (est): 10.3MM **Privately Held**
WEB: www.geamfg.com
SIC: 3672 Wiring boards

(P-17889)
GENERATION CIRCUITS LLC
Also Called: RB Design
621 S Andreasen Dr Ste B, Escondido
(92029-1904)
PHONE..................................760 743-7459
David E Maudlin, *CEO*
Max P Henzi, *Ch of Bd*

Thomas F Beales, *President*
EMP: 20
SQ FT: 7,000
SALES: 2MM **Privately Held**
WEB: www.rbdpcb.com
SIC: 3672 Circuit boards, television & radio
printed

(P-17890)
GOLDEN WEST TECHNOLOGY
1180 E Valencia Dr, Fullerton (92831-4627)
PHONE..................................714 738-3775
Dan P Rieth, *President*
Mike Kutzle, *Purch Dir*
EMP: 60 **EST:** 1974
SQ FT: 30,000
SALES (est): 12.7MM **Privately Held**
SIC: 3672 Printed circuit boards

(P-17891)
GORILLA CIRCUITS (PA)
1445 Oakland Rd, San Jose (95112-1203)
PHONE..................................408 294-9897
Fermin Aviles, *Managing Prtnr*
Hershel Petty, *President*
Jaime Gutierrez, *Vice Pres*
Mario Borjon, *Finance*
Al Castaneda, *Accounts Mgr*
▲ **EMP:** 166
SQ FT: 60,000
SALES: 36.2MM **Privately Held**
WEB: www.gorillacircuits.com
SIC: 3672 Circuit boards, television & radio
printed

(P-17892)
GRAPHIC RESEARCH INC
9334 Mason Ave, Chatsworth
(91311-5295)
PHONE..................................818 886-7340
Govind R Vaghashia, *President*
Pete Vaghashia, *Vice Pres*
▲ **EMP:** 50
SQ FT: 42,000
SALES (est): 9.7MM **Privately Held**
WEB: www.graphicresearch.com
SIC: 3672 Printed circuit boards

(P-17893)
GREEN CIRCUITS INC
1130 Ringwood Ct, San Jose (95131-1726)
PHONE..................................408 526-1700
Joseph O'Neil, *CEO*
Ted Park, *COO*
Michael Nguyen, *Vice Pres*
Collin Vo, *Program Mgr*
Dung Huynh, *Technology*
▲ **EMP:** 187
SQ FT: 15,000
SALES (est): 31.5MM **Privately Held**
SIC: 3672 Printed circuit boards

(P-17894)
HI-TECH ELECTRONIC MFG CORP
Also Called: Hitem
7420 Carroll Rd, San Diego (92121-2304)
PHONE..................................858 657-0908
Vinh Lam, *President*
Tran Vu, *Vice Pres*
Yoshi Otani, *Program Mgr*
Thai Nguyen, *Marketing Staff*
▲ **EMP:** 80
SQ FT: 20,000
SALES (est): 29.4MM **Privately Held**
WEB: www.hitem.com
SIC: 3672 Circuit boards, television & radio
printed

(P-17895)
HUGHES CIRCUITS INC (PA)
Also Called: Hci
546 S Pacific St, San Marcos
(92078-4070)
PHONE..................................760 744-0300
Barbara Hughes, *CEO*
Jerry Hughes, *President*
Michelle Glatts, *Vice Pres*
Joe Hughes, *Vice Pres*
Steve Hughes, *Vice Pres*
EMP: 45 **EST:** 1999
SQ FT: 50,000
SALES (est): 32.7MM **Privately Held**
WEB: www.hughescircuits.com
SIC: 3672 Circuit boards, television & radio
printed

(P-17896)
HUGHES CIRCUITS INC
Also Called: Pcb Fabrication Facility
540 S Pacific St, San Marcos
(92078-4050)
PHONE..................................760 744-0300
Barbara Hughes, *Branch Mgr*
EMP: 115
SALES (corp-wide): 32.7MM **Privately
Held**
SIC: 3672 Circuit boards, television & radio
printed
PA: Hughes Circuits, Inc.
546 S Pacific St
San Marcos CA 92078
760 744-0300

(P-17897)
HYTEK R&D INC (PA)
Also Called: R & D Tech
2044 Corporate Ct, Milpitas (95035)
PHONE..................................408 761-5271
Richard Hernandez, *President*
EMP: 22
SALES (est): 2.3MM **Privately Held**
SIC: 3672 5063 Printed circuit boards;
electrical supplies

(P-17898)
IMPACT PROJECT MANAGEMENT INC
2872 S Santa Fe Ave, San Marcos
(92069-6046)
PHONE..................................760 747-6616
Randy Scott Walker, *President*
Debbie Walker, *Vice Pres*
▲ **EMP:** 27
SALES (est): 5.2MM **Privately Held**
WEB: www.impactprojects.com
SIC: 3672 Printed circuit boards

(P-17899)
INDTEC CORPORATION
3348 Paul Davis Dr # 109, Marina
(93933-2258)
P.O. Box 1998, Seaside (93955-1998)
PHONE..................................831 582-9388
Dung Van Trinh, *President*
Lily Pham, *Admin Sec*
Lani Visesio, *Accounts Mgr*
EMP: 20
SQ FT: 5,000
SALES (est): 3.4MM **Privately Held**
WEB: www.indtec.net
SIC: 3672 Circuit boards, television & radio
printed

(P-17900)
INFINITI SOLUTIONS USA INC (PA)
Also Called: Adaptive Electronics
3910 N 1st St, San Jose (95134-1501)
PHONE..................................408 923-7300
Inderjit Singh, *President*
Kumar Patel, *President*
Pin Patel, *Vice Pres*
Dhaval Patel, *Executive*
EMP: 76 **EST:** 1975
SQ FT: 70,000
SALES (est): 20.8MM **Privately Held**
WEB: www.adaptivecircuits.com
SIC: 3672 3825 8711 Printed circuit
boards; test equipment for electronic &
electrical circuits; engineering services

(P-17901)
INNERSTEP BSE (PA)
4742 Scotts Valley Dr, Scotts Valley
(95066-4231)
PHONE..................................831 461-5600
Don Landry, *CEO*
Jim Kingman, *President*
James Kingman, *CEO*
Karen Bish, *Program Mgr*
▲ **EMP:** 54
SQ FT: 25,000
SALES (est): 15.9MM **Privately Held**
WEB: www.innerstep.com
SIC: 3672 3679 Printed circuit boards;
power supplies, all types: static

(P-17902)
IPC CAL FLEX INC
13337 South St 307, Cerritos (90703-7308)
PHONE..................................714 952-0373

Scott Kohno, *President*
EMP: 40
SQ FT: 25,000
SALES (est): 5.4MM **Privately Held**
WEB: www.calflex.com
SIC: 3672 Printed circuit boards

(P-17903)
IRVINE ELECTRONICS INC
1601 Alton Pkwy Ste A, Irvine
(92606-4843)
PHONE....................................949 250-0315
Jane Zerounian, *President*
Vahan Zerounian, *CFO*
Onnig Zerounian, *Vice Pres*
Jime Kim, *Project Mgr*
Toni Wilkerson, *QC Mgr*
EMP: 100
SQ FT: 48,000
SALES (est): 14.1MM **Privately Held**
WEB: www.irvine-electronics.com
SIC: 3672 Circuit boards, television & radio
printed

(P-17904)
ISU PETASYS CORP
12930 Bradley Ave, Sylmar (91342-3829)
PHONE....................................818 833-5800
Yong Kyoun Kim, *President*
Arleen Masangkay, *CFO*
John Stephens, *VP Bus Dvlpt*
Dave Hwang, *CIO*
John Lyday, *Purch Mgr*
▲ EMP: 95
SQ FT: 50,000
SALES (est): 17.8MM **Privately Held**
WEB: www.isupetasys.com
SIC: 3672 Printed circuit boards
PA: Isu Chemical Co., Ltd.
84 Sapyeong-Daero, Seocho-Gu
Seoul 06575

(P-17905)
JABIL CIRCUIT INC
1925 Lundy Ave, San Jose (95131-1847)
PHONE....................................408 361-3200
Thomas Costkel, *Manager*
EMP: 100
SALES (corp-wide): 25.2B **Publicly Held**
SIC: 3672 Printed circuit boards
PA: Jabil Inc.
10560 Dr Mrtn Lther King
Saint Petersburg FL 33716
727 577-9749

(P-17906)
JABIL INC
Also Called: Jabil Chad Automation
1565 S Sinclair St, Anaheim (92806-5934)
PHONE....................................714 938-0080
Babak Naderi, *Director*
EMP: 50
SALES (corp-wide): 25.2B **Publicly Held**
SIC: 3672 Printed circuit boards
PA: Jabil Inc.
10560 Dr Mrtn Lther King
Saint Petersburg FL 33716
727 577-9749

(P-17907)
JABIL INC
30 Great Oaks Blvd, San Jose
(95119-1309)
PHONE....................................408 361-3200
EMP: 500
SALES (corp-wide): 25.2B **Publicly Held**
WEB: www.jabil.com
SIC: 3672 Printed circuit boards
PA: Jabil Inc.
10560 Dr Mrtn Lther King
Saint Petersburg FL 33716
727 577-9749

(P-17908)
JATON CORPORATION
47677 Lakeview Blvd, Fremont
(94538-6544)
PHONE....................................510 933-8888
Vicky Hong, *President*
J S Chiang, *CEO*
Jenny Hao, *Persnl Dir*
Aurora Wao, *Human Res Mgr*
▲ EMP: 255
SQ FT: 85,000

SALES (est): 28.5MM **Privately Held**
WEB: www.jaton.com
SIC: 3672 3674 3661 3577 Printed circuit
boards; modules, solid state; modems;
computer peripheral equipment

(P-17909)
JMP ELECTRONICS INC
2685 Dow Ave Ste A1, Tustin (92780-7241)
PHONE....................................714 730-2086
Joseph Manea, *President*
Martha Manea, *Senior VP*
Petru Pantis, *Vice Pres*
Dorel Bila, *Manager*
▲ EMP: 18
SQ FT: 12,500
SALES (est): 4.1MM **Privately Held**
WEB: www.jmpelectronics.com
SIC: 3672 Printed circuit boards

(P-17910)
KCA ELECTRONICS INC
Also Called: Summit Interconnect - Anaheim
223 N Crescent Way, Anaheim
(92801-6704)
PHONE....................................714 239-2433
Shane Whiteside, *President*
▲ EMP: 180
SQ FT: 60,000
SALES (est): 35.3MM **Privately Held**
WEB: www.kcamerica.com
SIC: 3672 Circuit boards, television & radio
printed
HQ: Equity Hci Management L P
1730 Pennsylvania Ave Nw
Washington DC

(P-17911)
KL ELECTRONICS INC
3083 S Harbor Blvd, Santa Ana
(92704-6448)
PHONE....................................714 751-5611
Khanh Ton, *President*
Michael Ton, *CEO*
Luon Ton, *Corp Secy*
Charlie Tran, *Mfg Staff*
EMP: 20
SQ FT: 4,000
SALES (est): 3.3MM **Privately Held**
WEB: www.klelectronics.com
SIC: 3672 Printed circuit boards

(P-17912)
LAMINATING COMPANY OF AMERICA
Also Called: Lcoa
20322 Windrow Dr Ste 100, Lake Forest
(92630-8150)
PHONE....................................949 587-3300
Tim Redfern, *President*
Brad Biddol, *CFO*
▲ EMP: 50
SALES (est): 8.4MM **Privately Held**
WEB: www.tristarlaminates.com
SIC: 3672 Printed circuit boards

(P-17913)
LARITECH INC
5898 Condor Dr, Moorpark (93021-2603)
PHONE....................................805 529-5000
Bill Larrick, *President*
William C Larrick, *CEO*
Joel Butler, *COO*
Scott Ishii, *CFO*
Terry Gonzales, *Treasurer*
EMP: 120 EST: 2001
SQ FT: 13,000
SALES: 10MM **Privately Held**
WEB: www.laritech.com
SIC: 3672 Printed circuit boards

(P-17914)
LIFETIME MEMORY PRODUCTS INC
2505 Da Vinci Ste A, Irvine (92614-0170)
P.O. Box 1207, Laguna Beach (92652-
1207)
PHONE....................................949 794-9000
Paul Columbus, *CEO*
Cameron Hum, *President*
◆ EMP: 40
SQ FT: 16,000

SALES (est): 7.6MM **Privately Held**
WEB: www.lifetimememory.com
SIC: 3672 5045 3674 Printed circuit
boards; computers, peripherals & software; semiconductors & related devices

(P-17915)
LOGI GRAPHICS INCORPORATED
17592 Metzler Ln, Huntington Beach
(92647-6241)
PHONE....................................714 841-3686
Greg Otterbach, *President*
Terri Otterbach, *Admin Sec*
EMP: 17
SQ FT: 12,000
SALES (est): 1.3MM **Privately Held**
SIC: 3672 Printed circuit boards

(P-17916)
LUMISTAR INC (DH)
2270 Camino Vida Roble L, Carlsbad
(92011-1503)
PHONE....................................760 431-2181
Eric Demarco, *President*
Deanna Lund, *CEO*
Laura Siegal, *Treasurer*
Michael Fink, *Vice Pres*
Bryan Graber, *Principal*
EMP: 13
SQ FT: 6,000
SALES (est): 1.7MM **Publicly Held**
WEB: www.lumi-star.com
SIC: 3672 Printed circuit boards
HQ: Kratos Rt Logic, Inc.
12515 Academy Ridge Vw
Colorado Springs CO 80921
719 598-2801

(P-17917)
MARCEL ELECTRONICS INC
240 W Bristol Ln, Orange (92865-2645)
PHONE....................................714 974-8590
EMP: 15
SALES (est): 2.2MM **Privately Held**
SIC: 3672 Printed circuit boards

(P-17918)
MARCEL ELECTRONICS INC
130 W Bristol Ln, Orange (92865-2637)
PHONE....................................714 974-8590
EMP: 14
SALES (est): 2MM **Privately Held**
SIC: 3672 Printed circuit boards

(P-17919)
MATRIX USA INC
2730 S Main St, Santa Ana (92707-3435)
PHONE....................................714 825-0404
Kieran Healy, *President*
Rick Lovelady, *Technical Mgr*
George Potocska, *Controller*
▲ EMP: 25 EST: 2005
SALES (est): 5.1MM **Privately Held**
SIC: 3672 Printed circuit boards
HQ: Matrix Electronics Limited
1124 Mid-Way Blvd
Mississauga ON L5T 2
905 670-8400

(P-17920)
MAXTROL CORPORATION
1701 E Edinger Ave Ste B6, Santa Ana
(92705-5010)
PHONE....................................714 245-0506
Uri Ranon, *President*
Leo Pardo, *Vice Pres*
EMP: 40
SQ FT: 5,000
SALES (est): 3.6MM **Privately Held**
WEB: www.maxtrol.com
SIC: 3672 Printed circuit boards

(P-17921)
MEGA PLUS PCB INCORPORATED
1479 E Warner Ave, Santa Ana
(92705-5434)
PHONE....................................714 550-0265
Nadim S Kazempoor, *CEO*
Noorya Kazempoor, *Vice Pres*
EMP: 15
SALES: 500K **Privately Held**
SIC: 3672 Printed circuit boards

(P-17922)
MERCURY SYSTEMS INC
1000 Avenida Acaso, Camarillo
(93012-8712)
PHONE....................................805 388-1345
Stephen Bouchard, *CEO*
EMP: 110
SALES (corp-wide): 654.7MM **Publicly
Held**
SIC: 3672 Printed circuit boards
PA: Mercury Systems, Inc.
50 Minuteman Rd
Andover MA 01810
978 256-1300

(P-17923)
MERCURY SYSTEMS INC
85 Nicholson Ln, San Jose (95134-1366)
PHONE....................................669 226-5800
Charles Leader, *CEO*
EMP: 10
SQ FT: 3,990
SALES (corp-wide): 654.7MM **Publicly
Held**
WEB: www.amlj.com
SIC: 3672 Printed circuit boards
PA: Mercury Systems, Inc.
50 Minuteman Rd
Andover MA 01810
978 256-1300

(P-17924)
MERITRONICS INC (PA)
500 Yosemite Dr Ste 108, Milpitas
(95035-5467)
PHONE....................................408 969-0888
Cherng Dior Wu, *President*
▲ EMP: 43
SQ FT: 34,000
SALES (est): 16.6MM **Privately Held**
WEB: www.meritronics.com
SIC: 3672 Printed circuit boards

(P-17925)
MERITRONICS MATERIALS INC
500 Yosemite Dr Ste 112, Milpitas
(95035-5467)
PHONE....................................408 390-5642
Richard Maldonado, *President*
EMP: 18
SALES (est): 2.2MM **Privately Held**
SIC: 3672 3679 Printed circuit boards;
electronic circuits

(P-17926)
MI TECHNOLOGIES INC
Also Called: Discount Merchant.com
2215 Pseo De Las Americas, San Diego
(92154-7908)
PHONE....................................619 710-2637
Amir Tafreshi, *CEO*
John Celms, *CFO*
Ali Irani-Tehrani, *Principal*
Sostenes Ibarra, *Business Mgr*
Juan Diaz, *Controller*
▲ EMP: 130
SQ FT: 8,000
SALES: 21.6MM **Privately Held**
WEB: www.mitechnologies.net
SIC: 3672 3469 3089 Printed circuit
boards; metal stampings; injection mold-
ing of plastics

(P-17927)
MODULUS INC
518 Sycamore Dr, Milpitas (95035-7412)
PHONE....................................408 457-3712
Mir Imran, *CEO*
Marvin Ackerman, *Shareholder*
Syed Zaidi, *Vice Pres*
▲ EMP: 10
SQ FT: 85,040
SALES (est): 2.5MM **Privately Held**
WEB: www.modulusinc.com
SIC: 3672 Printed circuit boards

(P-17928)
**MULTI-FINELINE ELECTRONIX
INC (HQ)**
Also Called: Mflex
101 Academy Ste 250, Irvine (92617-3035)
PHONE....................................949 453-6800
Reza Meshgin, *President*
Tom Kampfer, *CFO*
Christine Besnard, *Exec VP*
Thomas Lee, *Exec VP*

▲ = Import ▼=Export
◆ =Import/Export

Choong-Pew Lee, *Vice Pres*
EMP: 583
SQ FT: 20,171
SALES (est): 551.9MM
SALES (corp-wide): 2.8B **Privately Held**
WEB: www.mflex.com
SIC: 3672 Printed circuit boards
PA: Suzhou Dongshan Precision Manufacturing Co., Ltd.
No.8, Shiheshan Road, Dongshan Industrial Park, Wuzhong District
Suzhou 21510
512 663-0620

(P-17929)
MULTILAYER PROTOTYPES INC
Also Called: Mpi
2513 Teller Rd, Newbury Park
(91320-2220)
PHONE..................................805 498-9390
Steve Ferris, *President*
Dara Garza, *Corp Secy*
EMP: 19
SQ FT: 11,000
SALES (est): 3.1MM **Privately Held**
WEB: www.mpi-pcb.com
SIC: 3672 Circuit boards, television & radio printed

(P-17930)
MULTIMEK INC
357 Reed St, Santa Clara (95050-3107)
PHONE..................................408 653-1300
Doug McCown, *President*
Doug Mc Cown, *VP Human Res*
Kevin McCown, *Materials Mgr*
EMP: 20
SQ FT: 8,000
SALES (est): 3.2MM **Privately Held**
WEB: www.multimek.com
SIC: 3672 Printed circuit boards

(P-17931)
N D E INC
Also Called: New Dimension Electronics
3301 Keller St, Santa Clara (95054-2601)
PHONE..................................408 727-3955
Richard Le, *CEO*
EMP: 30
SQ FT: 6,000
SALES (est): 4MM **Privately Held**
SIC: 3672 3679 Printed circuit boards; harness assemblies for electronic use: wire or cable

(P-17932)
NAPROTEK INC
90 Rose Orchard Way, San Jose
(95134-1356)
PHONE..................................408 830-5000
Najat Badriyeh, *CEO*
Liz Davidson, *Vice Pres*
Minh Doan, *Engineer*
Larry Morrissey, *VP Opers*
Arlis Greco, *QC Mgr*
EMP: 60
SQ FT: 24,000
SALES: 19.6MM **Privately Held**
WEB: www.naprotek.com
SIC: 3672 Circuit boards, television & radio printed

(P-17933)
NASO INDUSTRIES CORPORATION
Also Called: Naso Technologies
3007 Bunsen Ave Ste Q, Ventura
(93003-7634)
PHONE..................................805 650-1231
Jahansooz Saleh, *CEO*
Bill Thorpe, *President*
Soraya Saleh, *CEO*
Bryan Howe, *Vice Pres*
Namdar Saleh, *Vice Pres*
EMP: 40
SQ FT: 20,000
SALES (est): 15MM **Privately Held**
WEB: www.naso.com
SIC: 3672 3599 Printed circuit boards; machine shop, jobbing & repair

(P-17934)
NATEL ENGINEERING COMPANY INC
Also Called: Powercube
9340 Owensmouth Ave, Chatsworth
(91311-6915)
PHONE..................................818 734-6552
Sudesh Arora, *Branch Mgr*
EMP: 20
SALES (corp-wide): 1.1B **Privately Held**
WEB: www.natelengr.com
SIC: 3672 Printed circuit boards
PA: Natel Engineering Company, Llc
9340 Owensmouth Ave
Chatsworth CA 91311
818 495-8617

(P-17935)
NATEL ENGINEERING COMPANY INC
2243 Lundy Ave, San Jose (95131-1822)
PHONE..................................408 228-5462
EMP: 130
SALES (corp-wide): 1.1B **Privately Held**
SIC: 3672 Printed circuit boards
PA: Natel Engineering Company, Llc
9340 Owensmouth Ave
Chatsworth CA 91311
818 495-8617

(P-17936)
NATEL ENGINEERING COMPANY INC
2066 Aldergrove Ave, Escondido
(92029-1901)
PHONE..................................760 737-6777
Keith Butler, *Branch Mgr*
EMP: 130
SALES (corp-wide): 1.1B **Privately Held**
SIC: 3672 Printed circuit boards
PA: Natel Engineering Company, Llc
9340 Owensmouth Ave
Chatsworth CA 91311
818 495-8617

(P-17937)
NETWORK PCB INC
1914 Otoole Way, San Jose (95131-2237)
PHONE..................................408 943-8760
EMP: 30
SALES (est): 4.6MM **Privately Held**
WEB: www.networkpcb.com
SIC: 3672 Circuit boards, television & radio printed

(P-17938)
NEW BRUNSWICK INDUSTRIES INC
1850 Gillespie Way, El Cajon (92020-1094)
PHONE..................................619 448-4900
Jim Krehbiel, *President*
Sue Harnack, *Vice Pres*
Sue Krehbiel, *Vice Pres*
David Carrilho, *Prgrmr*
EMP: 30
SALES (est): 7MM **Privately Held**
WEB: www.nbiinc.com
SIC: 3672 Circuit boards, television & radio printed

(P-17939)
NEXLOGIC TECHNOLOGIES INC
2085 Zanker Rd, San Jose (95131-2107)
PHONE..................................408 436-8150
Zulki Khan, *President*
Tariq Nisar, *Program Mgr*
Sanam Shaikh, *Sr Software Eng*
Johnny Hasan, *Engineer*
Yaseen Haroon, *Controller*
▲ **EMP:** 76
SALES (est): 16.1MM **Privately Held**
WEB: www.nxtcommercial.com
SIC: 3672 Printed circuit boards

(P-17940)
NORTHWEST CIRCUITS CORP
8660 Avenida Costa Blanca, San Diego
(92154-6232)
PHONE..................................619 661-1701
Toribio Lobato, *President*
▲ **EMP:** 65
SQ FT: 12,000
SALES (est): 19.1MM **Privately Held**
WEB: www.northwestcircuitscorp.com
SIC: 3672 Printed circuit boards

(P-17941)
NOVA DRILLING SERVICES INC
1500 Buckeye Dr, Milpitas (95035-7418)
PHONE..................................408 732-6682
Mike McKibbin, *President*
Michael Doherty, *Vice Pres*
Stephanie Bell, *Admin Sec*
Kathleen McKibbin, *Admin Sec*
EMP: 32
SQ FT: 15,000
SALES (est): 4.1MM **Privately Held**
WEB: www.novadrill-fab.com
SIC: 3672 3083 Printed circuit boards; laminated plastics plate & sheet

(P-17942)
NPI SERVICES INC
1580 Corporate Dr Ste 124, Costa Mesa
(92626-1460)
PHONE..................................714 850-0550
Judith Greenspon, *President*
EMP: 11
SQ FT: 5,880
SALES (est): 2.8MM **Privately Held**
WEB: www.npiservices.com
SIC: 3672 Printed circuit boards

(P-17943)
ONCORE MANUFACTURING LLC
6600 Stevenson Blvd, Fremont
(94538-2471)
PHONE..................................510 516-5488
James Liow, *Branch Mgr*
EMP: 99
SALES (corp-wide): 1.1B **Privately Held**
SIC: 3672 8711 Printed circuit boards; electrical or electronic engineering
HQ: Oncore Manufacturing Llc
9340 Owensmouth Ave
Chatsworth CA 91311
-

(P-17944)
ONCORE MANUFACTURING LLC
Also Called: Oncore Velocity
237 Via Vera Cruz, San Marcos
(92078-2617)
PHONE..................................760 737-6777
Arnulfo Villa, *Principal*
EMP: 130
SALES (corp-wide): 1.1B **Privately Held**
SIC: 3672 Printed circuit boards
HQ: Oncore Manufacturing Llc
9340 Owensmouth Ave
Chatsworth CA 91311

(P-17945)
ONCORE MANUFACTURING SVCS INC
Also Called: Neo Tech Natel Epic Oncore
9340 Owensmouth Ave, Chatsworth
(91311-6915)
PHONE..................................510 360-2222
Sudesh Arora, *CEO*
Walt Hussey, *COO*
Sajjad Malik, *Exec VP*
David Brakenwagen, *Senior VP*
Magdy Henry, *Vice Pres*
▲ **EMP:** 230
SALES (est): 116.4MM
SALES (corp-wide): 1.1B **Privately Held**
WEB: www.victron.com
SIC: 3672 Printed circuit boards
PA: Natel Engineering Company, Llc
9340 Owensmouth Ave
Chatsworth CA 91311
818 495-8617

(P-17946)
ORCA SYSTEMS INC
3990 Old Town Ave, San Diego
(92110-2930)
PHONE..................................858 679-9295
Guruswami Sridharan, *President*
Kartik Sridharan, *Vice Pres*
Rajanish Telang, *IT/INT Sup*
EMP: 35
SALES (est): 6.4MM **Privately Held**
WEB: www.orcasystems.com
SIC: 3672 Circuit boards, television & radio printed

(P-17947)
ORION MANUFACTURING INC
5550 Hellyer Ave, San Jose (95138-1005)
PHONE..................................408 955-9001
Matthew L Davis, *President*
EMP: 125
SALES (est): 1.4MM **Privately Held**
SIC: 3672 Printed circuit boards

(P-17948)
OSI ELECTRONICS INC (HQ)
12533 Chadron Ave, Hawthorne
(90250-4807)
PHONE..................................310 978-0516
Paul Morben, *President*
Bruce Macdonald, *President*
Alex Colquhoun, *COO*
Lou Campana, *Vice Pres*
Al Wascher, *Manager*
▲ **EMP:** 148
SQ FT: 60,000
SALES (est): 30.8MM
SALES (corp-wide): 1.1B **Publicly Held**
WEB: www.osielectronics.com
SIC: 3672 Printed circuit boards
PA: Osi Systems, Inc.
12525 Chadron Ave
Hawthorne CA 90250
310 978-0516

(P-17949)
PACTRON
3000 Patrick Henry Dr, Santa Clara
(95054-1814)
PHONE..................................408 329-5500
Sriram Iyer, *CEO*
Lokesh Verma, *COO*
Ravi Iyer, *Executive*
Martin Barajas, *Engineer*
Vikram RAO, *Engineer*
EMP: 99
SQ FT: 35,000
SALES (est): 33.2MM **Privately Held**
WEB: www.pactroninc.com
SIC: 3672 Printed circuit boards

(P-17950)
PALPILOT INTERNATIONAL CORP
15991 Red Hill Ave # 102, Tustin
(92780-7320)
PHONE..................................714 460-0718
Bruce Lee, *Branch Mgr*
Win Cheng, *President*
Sarah Beach, *Sales Staff*
EMP: 33 **Privately Held**
SIC: 3672 Printed circuit boards
PA: Palpilot International Corporation
500 Yosemite Dr
Milpitas CA 95035

(P-17951)
PALPILOT INTERNATIONAL CORP (PA)
500 Yosemite Dr, Milpitas (95035-5467)
PHONE..................................408 855-8866
Eddy C Niu, *President*
Alex Shih, *Officer*
Jerry Barnes, *Vice Pres*
Yichien Hwang, *Vice Pres*
Bruce Lee, *Vice Pres*
▲ **EMP:** 40
SQ FT: 7,000
SALES (est): 66MM **Privately Held**
SIC: 3672 3089 Printed circuit boards; injection molding of plastics

(P-17952)
PARAMIT CORPORATION (PA)
Also Called: Lathrop Engineering
18735 Madrone Pkwy, Morgan Hill
(95037-2876)
PHONE..................................408 782-5600
Balbir Rataul, *President*
Balbir S Rataul, *President*
Bruce Richardson, *President*
Faiyaz Syed, *COO*
Tom La Rose, *CFO*
▲ **EMP:** 287 **EST:** 1990
SQ FT: 150,000
SALES (est): 135MM **Privately Held**
WEB: www.paramit.com
SIC: 3672 Printed circuit boards

(P-17953)
PARK ELECTROCHEMICAL CORP
1100 E Kimberly Ave, Anaheim (92801-1101)
PHONE.....................714 459-4400
George Frantz, *Branch Mgr*
EMP: 40
SALES (corp-wide): 51.1MM **Publicly Held**
WEB: www.parkelectro.com
SIC: 3672 Printed circuit boards
PA: Park Aerospace Corp.
  48 S Service Rd
  Melville NY 11747
  631 465-3600

(P-17954)
PARPRO TECHNOLOGIES INC
Also Called: P T I
2700 S Fairview St, Santa Ana (92704-5947)
PHONE.....................714 545-8886
Thomas Sparrvik, *CEO*
Keith Knight, *President*
Ngathuong Le, *COO*
Eduardo Serrano, *CFO*
Ken Haney, *Vice Pres*
EMP: 190
SALES: 34.2MM **Privately Held**
SIC: 3672 Printed circuit boards
PA: Parpro Corporation
  No. 67-1, Dongyuan Rd., Zhongli Industrial Park
  Taoyuan City TAY
  -

(P-17955)
PDM SOLUTIONS INC
Also Called: Protech Design & Manufacturing
8451 Miralani Dr Ste J, San Diego (92126-4388)
PHONE.....................858 348-1000
James O'Shea, *President*
Michelle Kim, *Vice Pres*
EMP: 20
SQ FT: 5,700
SALES (est): 4.6MM **Privately Held**
SIC: 3672 Printed circuit boards

(P-17956)
PHOTO FABRICATORS INC
7648 Burnet Ave, Van Nuys (91405-1043)
PHONE.....................818 781-1010
Steve L Brooks, *President*
John R Brooks, *Chairman*
Susan Brooks, *Corp Secy*
▲ EMP: 75
SQ FT: 14,000
SALES (est): 11.2MM **Privately Held**
WEB: www.photofabricators.com
SIC: 3672 Circuit boards, television & radio printed

(P-17957)
PIONEER CIRCUITS INC
3000 S Shannon St, Santa Ana (92704-6387)
PHONE.....................714 641-3132
Robert Lee, *Principal*
James Y Lee, *President*
Moises Reynoso, *Engineer*
EMP: 260
SQ FT: 50,000
SALES: 37.8MM **Privately Held**
WEB: www.pioneercircuits.com
SIC: 3672 Circuit boards, television & radio printed

(P-17958)
PLEXUS CORP
431 Kato Ter, Fremont (94539-8333)
P.O. Box 156, Neenah WI (54957-0156)
PHONE.....................510 668-9000
Fax: 510 668-9090
EMP: 120
SALES (corp-wide): 2.6B **Publicly Held**
SIC: 3672
PA: Plexus Corp.
  1 Plexus Way
  Neenah WI 54956
  920 969-6000

(P-17959)
POWER CIRCUITS INC
2630 S Harbor Blvd, Santa Ana (92704-5829)
PHONE.....................714 327-3000
Kenton K Alder, *President*
EMP: 350
SALES (est): 53.9MM
SALES (corp-wide): 2.8B **Publicly Held**
WEB: www.ttmtek.com
SIC: 3672 Printed circuit boards
PA: Ttm Technologies, Inc.
  200 Sandpointe Ave # 400
  Santa Ana CA 92707
  714 327-3000

(P-17960)
PRECISION CIRCUITS WEST INC
3310 W Harvard St, Santa Ana (92704-3920)
PHONE.....................714 435-9670
Chatur Patel, *President*
Sam Akbari, *Executive*
Prabhudas Patel, *Admin Sec*
Kelly Akbari, *Controller*
John Sunu, *Opers Staff*
EMP: 15
SQ FT: 12,000
SALES (est): 1.2MM **Privately Held**
WEB: www.pcwesti.com
SIC: 3672 Circuit boards, television & radio printed

(P-17961)
PRECISION DESIGN INC
Also Called: Pdi
1160 Industrial Rd Ste 16, San Carlos (94070-4128)
PHONE.....................650 508-8041
Alexandra Sgolombis, *President*
EMP: 25
SQ FT: 5,030
SALES (est): 3.4MM **Privately Held**
SIC: 3672 7373 Printed circuit boards; computer integrated systems design

(P-17962)
PRINTED CIRCUIT SOLUTIONS INC
2040 S Yale St, Santa Ana (92704-3923)
PHONE.....................714 825-1090
Jose Lara, *CEO*
Ofelia Lara, *COO*
Joe Lara, *VP Bus Dvlpt*
EMP: 10 EST: 2012
SALES (est): 1.1MM **Privately Held**
SIC: 3672 Printed circuit boards

(P-17963)
PRINTED CIRCUIT TECHNOLOGY
Also Called: Pct
44081 Old Warm Sprng Blvd, Fremont (94538-6158)
PHONE.....................510 659-1866
Scott Lew, *President*
EMP: 80
SQ FT: 13,000
SALES (est): 9.1MM **Privately Held**
WEB: www.pctnet.com
SIC: 3672 Printed circuit boards

(P-17964)
QOSTRONICS INC
2044 Corporate Ct, San Jose (95131-1753)
PHONE.....................408 719-1286
Shawn Do, *Principal*
MAI Tran, *Admin Sec*
EMP: 33
SQ FT: 5,500
SALES: 4MM **Privately Held**
WEB: www.qostronics.com
SIC: 3672 3845 Circuit boards, television & radio printed; electromedical equipment

(P-17965)
QUAL-PRO CORPORATION (HQ)
18510 S Figueroa St, Gardena (90248-4519)
PHONE.....................310 329-7535
Brian Jeffrey Shane, *CEO*
Richard Fitzgerald, *COO*
Kirk Waldron, *Exec VP*
Bob Miller, *Vice Pres*

David Soden, *Vice Pres*
EMP: 200
SQ FT: 55,000
SALES (est): 68.5MM
SALES (corp-wide): 166.2MM **Privately Held**
WEB: www.qual-pro.com
SIC: 3672 Circuit boards, television & radio printed
PA: Sfo Technologies Private Limited
  Plot No. 2, Cochin Special Economic Zone,
  Kochi KL 68203
  484 661-4300

(P-17966)
QUALITEK INC (HQ)
1116 Elko Dr, Sunnyvale (94089-2207)
PHONE.....................408 734-8686
Louise Crisham, *CEO*
▲ EMP: 75
SQ FT: 20,000
SALES (est): 8.8MM
SALES (corp-wide): 53.1MM **Privately Held**
SIC: 3672 Printed circuit boards
PA: Westak, Inc
  1116 Elko Dr
  Sunnyvale CA 94089
  408 734-8686

(P-17967)
QUALITEK INC
Also Called: Westak
1272 Forgewood Ave, Sunnyvale (94089-2215)
PHONE.....................408 752-8422
Ray Giancola, *Manager*
EMP: 90
SALES (corp-wide): 53.1MM **Privately Held**
SIC: 3672 Printed circuit boards
HQ: Qualitek Inc
  1116 Elko Dr
  Sunnyvale CA 94089
  408 734-8686

(P-17968)
QUALITY CIRCUIT ASSEMBLY INC
Also Called: Q C A
1709 Junction Ct Ste 380, San Jose (95112-1044)
PHONE.....................408 441-1001
Jeff Moss, *President*
Dwight Hargrave, *Vice Pres*
Nancy L Moss, *Sales Executive*
EMP: 65
SQ FT: 30,000
SALES (est): 20.6MM **Privately Held**
WEB: www.qcamfg.com
SIC: 3672 Circuit boards, television & radio printed

(P-17969)
QUALITY SYSTEMS INTGRATED CORP
6740 Top Gun St, San Diego (92121-4114)
PHONE.....................858 587-9797
Kiem T Le, *CEO*
Thui Trong, *Shareholder*
Cecile Le, *CFO*
John Le, *Executive*
Hai Bach, *Principal*
▲ EMP: 275
SQ FT: 50,000
SALES (est): 82.3MM **Privately Held**
WEB: www.qsic.com
SIC: 3672 Printed circuit boards

(P-17970)
QUALTECH CIRCUITS INC
1101 Comstock St, Santa Clara (95054-3407)
PHONE.....................408 727-4125
Jim Khosh, *President*
EMP: 12
SQ FT: 25,000
SALES (est): 1.8MM **Privately Held**
SIC: 3672 Circuit boards, television & radio printed

(P-17971)
R F CIRCUITS AND ASSEMBLY INC
3533 Old Conejo Rd # 107, Newbury Park (91320-6163)
PHONE.....................805 499-7788
Pankaj Patell, *President*
EMP: 12
SALES: 500K **Privately Held**
WEB: www.rfassembly.com
SIC: 3672 Printed circuit boards

(P-17972)
R&D ALTANOVA INC
6389 San Ignacio Ave, San Jose (95119-1206)
PHONE.....................408 225-7011
James Russell, *CEO*
Ken Pawloski, *CFO*
Luz Rubio, *Sales Staff*
EMP: 38
SQ FT: 15,000
SALES (est): 7.1MM
SALES (corp-wide): 36.8MM **Privately Held**
WEB: www.altanova1.com
SIC: 3672 7389 Printed circuit boards; design services
PA: R & D Circuits Inc
  3601 S Clinton Ave
  South Plainfield NJ 07080
  732 549-4554

(P-17973)
RACAAR CIRCUIT INDUSTRIES INC
9225 Alabama Ave Ste F, Chatsworth (91311-5843)
PHONE.....................818 998-7566
Stephen Serup, *President*
Julie Serup, *Corp Secy*
EMP: 40
SQ FT: 4,000
SALES (est): 1.5MM **Privately Held**
SIC: 3672 3433 Printed circuit boards; heating equipment, except electric

(P-17974)
RASTERGRAF INC (PA)
7145 Marlborough Ter, Berkeley (94705-1736)
PHONE.....................510 849-4801
Victor R Gold Jr, *President*
EMP: 14
SALES (est): 2.4MM **Privately Held**
WEB: www.rastergraf.com
SIC: 3672 Printed circuit boards

(P-17975)
REALTIME TECHNOLOGIES INC
1230 Mtn View Alviso Rd, Sunnyvale (94089-2286)
PHONE.....................408 745-6434
Patrick White, *President*
Sheila White, *Shareholder*
EMP: 15
SQ FT: 4,000
SALES (est): 1.4MM **Privately Held**
SIC: 3672 Printed circuit boards

(P-17976)
RIGIFLEX TECHNOLOGY INC
1166 N Grove St, Anaheim (92806-2109)
PHONE.....................714 688-1500
Dhiru Sorathia, *President*
EMP: 25
SQ FT: 15,000
SALES (est): 4.4MM **Privately Held**
SIC: 3672 Printed circuit boards

(P-17977)
ROCKET EMS INC
2950 Patrick Henry Dr, Santa Clara (95054-1813)
PHONE.....................408 727-3700
Craig Arcuri, *CEO*
Michael Kottke, *President*
EMP: 140
SQ FT: 40,000
SALES (est): 62.2MM **Privately Held**
SIC: 3672 Printed circuit boards

(P-17978)
ROGER INDUSTRY
11552 Knott St Ste 5, Garden Grove
(92841-1833)
PHONE..............................714 896-0765
Shann-Mou Lee, *President*
Jiin-Sheue Lee, *Vice Pres*
▲ EMP: 16
SQ FT: 10,000
SALES (est): 1.3MM **Privately Held**
WEB: www.rogerindustry.com
SIC: 3672 3479 Printed circuit boards;
coating of metals with plastic or resins

(P-17979)
ROYAL CIRCUIT SOLUTIONS INC (PA)
21 Hamilton Ct, Hollister (95023-2535)
PHONE..............................831 636-7789
Milan Shah, *President*
Mary Nydegger, *Accountant*
Amber Marini, *Regl Sales Mgr*
Johnny Dearmas, *Sales Staff*
Tara Jewell, *Director*
▲ EMP: 33
SQ FT: 15,000
SALES (est): 5.5MM **Privately Held**
SIC: 3672 Circuit boards, television & radio printed

(P-17980)
ROYAL FLEX CIRCUITS INC
15505 Cornet St, Santa Fe Springs
(90670-5511)
PHONE..............................562 404-0626
Milan Shah, *CEO*
EMP: 27 EST: 2013
SALES (est): 4.7MM
SALES (corp-wide): 5.5MM **Privately Held**
SIC: 3672 Wiring boards
PA: Royal Circuit Solutions, Inc.
21 Hamilton Ct
Hollister CA 95023
831 636-7789

(P-17981)
RUSH PCB INC
2149 Otoole Ave Ste 20, San Jose
(95131-1341)
PHONE..............................408 469-6013
Neelkanta R Dantu, *Principal*
Roy Akber, *Administration*
EMP: 10 EST: 2007
SALES (est): 10MM **Privately Held**
SIC: 3672 7389 Printed circuit boards;

(P-17982)
SAEHAN ELECTRONICS AMERICA INC (PA)
7880 Airway Rd Ste B5g, San Diego
(92154-8308)
PHONE..............................858 496-1500
Bongsu Jeong, *CEO*
John Kim, *President*
Maria Bravo, *Human Res Mgr*
▲ EMP: 13
SALES (est): 8MM **Privately Held**
WEB: www.saehanusa.com
SIC: 3672 Printed circuit boards

(P-17983)
SAN DIEGO PCB DESIGN LLC
9909 Mira Mesa Blvd # 250, San Diego
(92131-1056)
PHONE..............................858 271-5722
P Michael Stoehr, *Mng Member*
EMP: 18
SALES (est): 718K **Privately Held**
SIC: 3672 Circuit boards, television & radio printed

(P-17984)
SAN FRANCISCO CIRCUITS INC
1660 S Amphlett Blvd # 200, San Mateo
(94402-2525)
PHONE..............................650 655-7202
Alex Danovich, *President*
Sam Danovich, *Vice Pres*
Andrew Gonzales, *Vice Pres*
Victor Bilandzic, *General Mgr*
Robert Boten, *QA Dir*
EMP: 12
SQ FT: 1,000

SALES (est): 2.7MM **Privately Held**
SIC: 3672 7379 Circuit boards, television
& radio printed; computer related consulting services

(P-17985)
SANMINA CORPORATION
425 El Camino Real Bldg A, Santa Clara
(95050-4366)
PHONE..............................408 244-0266
Ed Carignan, *Manager*
EMP: 1200 **Publicly Held**
SIC: 3672 Printed circuit boards
PA: Sanmina Corporation
2700 N 1st St
San Jose CA 95134

(P-17986)
SANMINA CORPORATION
San Jose Plant 1337
2700 N 1st St, San Jose (95134-2015)
PHONE..............................408 964-3500
Thomas Mosier, *President*
Alejandro Avila, *Vice Pres*
Daniel Liddle, *Vice Pres*
Bob Moffat, *Vice Pres*
Erik Swennumson, *Vice Pres*
EMP: 20 **Publicly Held**
WEB: www.sanmina.com
SIC: 3672 Printed circuit boards
PA: Sanmina Corporation
2700 N 1st St
San Jose CA 95134

(P-17987)
SANMINA CORPORATION
2701 Zanker Rd, San Jose (95134-2112)
PHONE..............................408 964-3500
Paul Hopwood, *Branch Mgr*
Gene Delaney, *Bd of Directors*
Carl Boklund, *Vice Pres*
Joseph Mello, *Vice Pres*
Tracy Trahan, *Engineer*
EMP: 20
SQ FT: 77,712 **Publicly Held**
WEB: www.sanmina.com
SIC: 3672 Printed circuit boards
PA: Sanmina Corporation
2700 N 1st St
San Jose CA 95134

(P-17988)
SANMINA CORPORATION
2050 Bering Dr, San Jose (95131-2009)
PHONE..............................408 964-6400
Eileen Card, *Branch Mgr*
Jure Sola, *CEO*
Brenda Lugo, *Vice Pres*
John Ghinazzi, *Business Dir*
Jessica Clark, *Engineer*
EMP: 375 **Publicly Held**
WEB: www.sanmina.com
SIC: 3672 Printed circuit boards
PA: Sanmina Corporation
2700 N 1st St
San Jose CA 95134

(P-17989)
SANMINA CORPORATION
Also Called: Sanmina-Sci
2036 Bering Dr, San Jose (95131-2009)
PHONE..............................408 964-3500
Norman Evans, *Branch Mgr*
Ed Attanasio, *President*
Dennis Young, *President*
Patrick Macdonald, *Vice Pres*
Khalid Ruhullah, *Vice Pres*
EMP: 300 **Publicly Held**
SIC: 3672 Printed circuit boards
PA: Sanmina Corporation
2700 N 1st St
San Jose CA 95134

(P-17990)
SANMINA CORPORATION
60 E Plumeria Dr B2db, San Jose
(95134-2102)
PHONE..............................408 557-7210
Randy Furr, *President*
Helen Ng, *Vice Pres*
Chris K Sadeghian, *Vice Pres*

Shannon Wesley, *Administration*
Michelle N Dang, *VP Finance*
EMP: 300 **Publicly Held**
WEB: www.sanmina.com
SIC: 3672 3643 Printed circuit boards;
current-carrying wiring devices
PA: Sanmina Corporation
2700 N 1st St
San Jose CA 95134

(P-17991)
SANMINA CORPORATION
42735 Christy St, Fremont (94538-3146)
PHONE..............................510 897-2000
Tony Princiotta, *Branch Mgr*
Mohammed Israr, *Vice Pres*
Ante Kutlesa, *Program Mgr*
Maria Madrigal, *Administration*
Eduardo Davalos, *IT/INT Sup*
EMP: 500
SQ FT: 155,000 **Publicly Held**
WEB: www.sanmina.com
SIC: 3672 Printed circuit boards
PA: Sanmina Corporation
2700 N 1st St
San Jose CA 95134

(P-17992)
SANMINA CORPORATION
60 E Plumeria Dr, San Jose (95134-2102)
PHONE..............................408 964-3000
Kishan Patel, *Manager*
Jackie Ward, *Bd of Directors*
EMP: 56 **Publicly Held**
WEB: www.sanmina.com
SIC: 3672 3679 Circuit boards, television
& radio printed; harness assemblies for
electronic use: wire or cable
PA: Sanmina Corporation
2700 N 1st St
San Jose CA 95134

(P-17993)
SANMINA CORPORATION
2945 Airway Ave, Costa Mesa
(92626-6007)
PHONE..............................714 371-2800
Dox Scream, *Manager*
Ellen Mattox, *Prgrmr*
George Trinite, *Engineer*
Thu Nguyen, *Director*
EMP: 100
SQ FT: 60,580 **Publicly Held**
WEB: www.sanmina.com
SIC: 3672 Printed circuit boards
PA: Sanmina Corporation
2700 N 1st St
San Jose CA 95134

(P-17994)
SANMINA CORPORATION (PA)
2700 N 1st St, San Jose (95134-2015)
P.O. Box 7, Huntsville AL (35804-0007)
PHONE..............................408 964-3500
Hartmut Liebel, *CEO*
Dennis Young, *Exec VP*
Brent Billinger, *Senior VP*
▲ EMP: 318
SALES: 8.2B **Publicly Held**
WEB: www.sanmina.com
SIC: 3672 3674 Printed circuit boards;
semiconductors & related devices; light
emitting diodes

(P-17995)
SANMINA CORPORATION
Viking Modular Solutions
2950 Red Hill Ave, Costa Mesa
(92626-5935)
PHONE..............................714 913-2200
Hamid Shokrgovar, *President*
Rick Hazell, *Vice Pres*
Chip Bellisime, *Business Dir*
Miguel Bynes, *Program Mgr*
Tayeba Salhi, *Program Mgr*
EMP: 110 **Publicly Held**
WEB: www.sanmina.com
SIC: 3672 Printed circuit boards
PA: Sanmina Corporation
2700 N 1st St
San Jose CA 95134

(P-17996)
SELECT CIRCUITS
3700 W Segerstrom Ave, Santa Ana
(92704-6410)
PHONE..............................714 825-1090
Esther Lara, *Partner*
Jose Lara, *Partner*
Ofelia Lara, *Partner*
EMP: 10
SALES (est): 703.8K **Privately Held**
WEB: www.selectcircuits.com
SIC: 3672 Printed circuit boards

(P-17997)
SEMI-KINETICS INC
20191 Windrow Dr Ste A, Lake Forest
(92630-8161)
PHONE..............................949 830-7364
Gary H Gonzalez, *CEO*
Michael Perdue, *General Mgr*
Justine Leedom, *Admin Asst*
Kevin Loomans, *Buyer*
Chuck Mountain, *Manager*
▲ EMP: 95
SALES (est): 9.9MM
SALES (corp-wide): 57.7MM **Privately Held**
WEB: www.semi-kinetics.com
SIC: 3672 Circuit boards, television & radio printed
PA: Gonzalez Production Systems, Inc.
1670 Highwood E
Pontiac MI 48340
248 548-6010

(P-17998)
SIERRA CIRCUITS INC
Also Called: Sierra Proto Express
1108 W Evelyn Ave, Sunnyvale
(94086-5745)
PHONE..............................408 735-7137
Kenneth Bahl, *CEO*
Steve Arobio, *Vice Pres*
S Bala Bahl, *Vice Pres*
Nilesh Parate, *General Mgr*
Edgar Gel, *Info Tech Dir*
▲ EMP: 105 EST: 1978
SQ FT: 22,000
SALES (est): 58MM **Privately Held**
WEB: www.protoexpress.com
SIC: 3672 Printed circuit boards

(P-17999)
SIGMA CIRCUIT TECHNOLOGY LLC
4624 Calle Mar De Armonia, San Diego
(92130-2689)
PHONE..............................858 523-0146
Daniel Duong,
EMP: 99
SALES (est): 800K **Privately Held**
SIC: 3672 Printed circuit boards

(P-18000)
SIGMATRON INTERNATIONAL INC
30000 Eigenbrodt Way, Union City
(94587-1226)
PHONE..............................510 477-5000
Raj Upadhyaya, *Vice Pres*
Bo Trygg, *Engineer*
EMP: 185 **Publicly Held**
WEB: www.sigmatronintl.com
SIC: 3672 Printed circuit boards
PA: Sigmatron International, Inc.
2201 Landmeier Rd
Elk Grove Village IL 60007

(P-18001)
SLP LIMITED LLC
Also Called: Www.slp-Formx.com
2031 E Cerritos Ave Ste H, Anaheim
(92806-5705)
PHONE..............................714 517-1955
Bruce Stuart, *Manager*
▲ EMP: 10
SQ FT: 5,000
SALES: 500K **Privately Held**
WEB: www.form-x.com
SIC: 3672 Circuit boards, television & radio printed

PRODUCTS & SVCS

(P-18002)
SMART ELEC & ASSEMBLY INC
2000 W Corporate Way, Anaheim
(92801-5373)
PHONE...............................714 772-2651
Robert Swelgin, *President*
Shou-Lee Wang, *CEO*
Dave Wopschall, *CFO*
Patrick Huang, *Officer*
Getaneh Bekele, *Vice Pres*
▲ **EMP:** 120
SQ FT: 34,500
SALES: 100.2MM
SALES (corp-wide): 2.5B **Publicly Held**
WEB: www.smartelec.com
SIC: 3672 Circuit boards, television & radio
printed
HQ: Secure Communication Systems, Inc.
1740 E Wilshire Ave
Santa Ana CA 92705
714 547-1174

(P-18003)
SMTC CORPORATION
431 Kato Ter, Fremont (94539-8333)
PHONE...............................510 737-0700
John Caldwell, *CEO*
Joe Bustos, *Vice Pres*
▲ **EMP:** 100 **EST:** 1994
SALES (est): 22.1MM
SALES (corp-wide): 216.1MM **Privately
Held**
SIC: 3672 Printed circuit boards
PA: Smtc Corporation
7050 Woodbine Ave Suite 300
Markham ON L3R 4
905 479-1810

(P-18004)
**SMTC MANUFACTURING CORP
CAL**
431 Kato Ter, Fremont (94539-8333)
PHONE...............................408 934-7100
Larry Silber, *CEO*
John Caldwell, *President*
Claude Germain, *President*
Alex Walker, *President*
Jane Todd, *CFO*
▲ **EMP:** 1875
SALES (est): 175MM
SALES (corp-wide): 216.1MM **Privately
Held**
SIC: 3672 Printed circuit boards
HQ: Smtc Manufacturing Corporation Of
Canada
7050 Woodbine Ave Suite 300
Markham ON L3R 4
905 479-1810

(P-18005)
SNA ELECTRONICS INC
3249 Laurelview Ct, Fremont (94538-6535)
PHONE...............................510 656-3903
Sung W Shin, *CEO*
CHI Shin, *CFO*
EMP: 44
SQ FT: 40,800
SALES: 5MM **Privately Held**
WEB: www.sna-electronic.com/
SIC: 3672 Printed circuit boards

(P-18006)
SOLDERMASK INC
17905 Metzler Ln, Huntington Beach
(92647-6258)
PHONE...............................714 842-1987
Frank S Kurisu, *President*
Son Pham, *General Mgr*
▲ **EMP:** 15
SQ FT: 10,000
SALES (est): 2.4MM **Privately Held**
SIC: 3672 3577 Printed circuit boards;
printers & plotters

(P-18007)
SOMACIS INC
13500 Danielson St, Poway (92064-6874)
PHONE...............................858 513-2200
Giovanni Tridenti, *CEO*
Armando Osuna, *Administration*
Sean Cowan, *Opers Dir*
Michael Gleason, *Regl Sales Mgr*
Clay Christoffersen, *Sales Mgr*
▲ **EMP:** 120
SQ FT: 76,000

SALES (est): 19.3MM
SALES (corp-wide): 83.5K **Privately Held**
SIC: 3672 Circuit boards, television & radio
printed
HQ: So.Ma.Ci.S. Spa
Via Jesina 17
Castelfidardo AN 60022
071 721-531

(P-18008)
**SONIC MANUFACTURING TECH
INC**
47951 Westinghouse Dr, Fremont
(94539-7483)
PHONE...............................510 580-8500
Kenneth Raab, *President*
Robert Pereyda, *Vice Pres*
Henry Woo, *Vice Pres*
▲ **EMP:** 300
SQ FT: 80,000
SALES (est): 111.9MM **Privately Held**
WEB: www.sonicmfg.com
SIC: 3672 Printed circuit boards

(P-18009)
SOUTH COAST CIRCUITS INC
3506 W Lake Center Dr A, Santa Ana
(92704-6985)
PHONE...............................714 966-2108
Charles R Benson, *CEO*
Dan Benson, *Vice Pres*
Daniel Alderete, *Purch Agent*
Patrick Bacon, *Mfg Staff*
Brad Harline, *Director*
▲ **EMP:** 68
SQ FT: 30,000
SALES: 9MM **Privately Held**
WEB: www.sccircuits.com
SIC: 3672 Circuit boards, television & radio
printed

(P-18010)
**SPECIALIZED COATING
SERVICES**
42680 Christy St, Fremont (94538-3135)
PHONE...............................510 226-8700
Richard Ramirez, *President*
Kim Atkins, *Vice Pres*
EMP: 62
SALES (est): 1.8MM **Privately Held**
WEB: www.speccoat.com
SIC: 3672 Circuit boards, television & radio
printed

(P-18011)
SPECTRUM ASSEMBLY INC
Also Called: Spectrum Electronics
6300 Yarrow Dr Ste 100, Carlsbad
(92011-1542)
PHONE...............................760 930-4000
Ronald Tupp, *President*
Michael Baldwin, *Vice Pres*
Mike Baldwin, *Vice Pres*
Jordan Topp, *Info Tech Mgr*
Stephen Wong, *Purchasing*
EMP: 85
SQ FT: 20,000
SALES (est): 25.8MM **Privately Held**
WEB: www.saicorp.com
SIC: 3672 Printed circuit boards

(P-18012)
**STREAMLINE ELECTRONICS
MFG INC**
Also Called: S E M
4285 Technology Dr, Fremont
(94538-6339)
PHONE...............................408 263-3600
Shahab Jafri, *President*
EMP: 50 **EST:** 1975
SQ FT: 26,000
SALES (est): 506.4K **Privately Held**
WEB: www.sem-inc.com
SIC: 3672 8711 2542 Printed circuit
boards; engineering services; partitions &
fixtures, except wood

(P-18013)
SUBA TECHNOLOGY INC
46501 Landing Pkwy, Fremont
(94538-6421)
PHONE...............................408 434-6500
Rolando M Suba, *CEO*
Alex Obice, *COO*
Winston Punzalan, *Executive*

EMP: 25
SQ FT: 35,000
SALES (est): 4.2MM **Privately Held**
WEB: www.subatech.com
SIC: 3672 Printed circuit boards

(P-18014)
SUMITRONICS USA INC
9335 Airway Rd Ste 203c, San Diego
(92154-7930)
PHONE...............................619 661-0450
Yukio Nagata, *President*
Ryuji Sumi, *CFO*
◆ **EMP:** 30
SQ FT: 800
SALES (est): 10MM **Privately Held**
SIC: 3672 Printed circuit boards
HQ: Sumitronics Corporation
1-2-2, Hitotsubashi
Chiyoda-Ku TKY 100-0

(P-18015)
**SUMMIT INTERCONNECT INC
(PA)**
220 N Crescent Way Ste B, Anaheim
(92801-6706)
PHONE...............................714 239-2433
Shane Whiteside, *President*
Clay Swain, *Vice Pres*
EMP: 150
SALES (est): 35.3MM **Privately Held**
SIC: 3672 Printed circuit boards

(P-18016)
SUMMIT INTERCONNECT INC
Also Called: Santa Clara Facility
1401 Martin Ave, Santa Clara
(95050-2614)
PHONE...............................408 727-1418
Shane Whiteside, *Branch Mgr*
EMP: 240
SALES (corp-wide): 35.3MM **Privately
Held**
SIC: 3672 Printed circuit boards
PA: Summit Interconnect, Inc.
220 N Crescent Way Ste B
Anaheim CA 92801
714 239-2433

(P-18017)
SUNNYTECH
2243 Ringwood Ave, San Jose
(95131-1737)
PHONE...............................408 943-8100
Siu Fong Chow, *President*
Virgil Chen, *Vice Pres*
▲ **EMP:** 18
SQ FT: 5,500
SALES (est): 3.5MM **Privately Held**
SIC: 3672 Printed circuit boards

(P-18018)
SYMPROTEK CO
950 Yosemite Dr, Milpitas (95035-5452)
PHONE...............................408 956-0700
Eric Chon, *President*
Maria Madriaga, *IT Specialist*
▲ **EMP:** 35
SQ FT: 36,000
SALES (est): 7.1MM **Privately Held**
WEB: www.symprotek.com
SIC: 3672 Printed circuit boards

(P-18019)
TC COSMOTRONIC INC
4663 E Guasti Rd Ste A, Ontario
(91761-8196)
PHONE...............................949 660-0740
James R Savage, *CEO*
Tracyconrad Enriquez, *CFO*
EMP: 100
SALES (est): 16.3MM **Privately Held**
SIC: 3672 Printed circuit boards

(P-18020)
TECHNOTRONIX INC
1381 N Hundley St, Anaheim (92806-1301)
PHONE...............................714 630-9200
Jayshree Kapuria, *CEO*
Chris Paris, *Sales Engr*
Ken Ghadia, *Manager*
EMP: 20
SALES (est): 2.3MM **Privately Held**
SIC: 3672 Printed circuit boards

(P-18021)
TECHSERVE INDUSTRIES INC
6032 E West View Dr, Orange
(92869-4357)
PHONE...............................714 505-2755
Al Aryamane, *President*
▲ **EMP:** 40
SQ FT: 4,500
SALES (est): 6.7MM **Privately Held**
SIC: 3672 Printed circuit boards

(P-18022)
TELIRITE TECHNICAL SVCS INC
2857 Lakeview Ct, Fremont (94538-6534)
PHONE...............................510 440-3888
Patrick Chan, *CEO*
Kue Chau Loh, *CFO*
Henry Gong, *Vice Pres*
Melissa Chow, *Accountant*
▲ **EMP:** 22
SQ FT: 12,000
SALES (est): 6.4MM **Privately Held**
WEB: www.telirite.com
SIC: 3672 Printed circuit boards

(P-18023)
TEMPO AUTOMATION INC
2460 Alameda St, San Francisco
(94103-4806)
PHONE...............................415 320-1261
Jeffrey McAlvay, *CEO*
Jesse Koenig, *COO*
Mike Borozdin, *Vice Pres*
Brady Bruce, *Vice Pres*
Anton Frolov, *Sr Software Eng*
EMP: 35
SQ FT: 2,000
SALES (est): 1.8MM **Privately Held**
SIC: 3672 Printed circuit boards

(P-18024)
TRANSLINE TECHNOLOGY INC
1106 S Technology Cir, Anaheim
(92805-6329)
PHONE...............................714 533-8300
Kishor Patel, *President*
Larry Padmani, *Vice Pres*
▲ **EMP:** 33 **EST:** 1996
SQ FT: 20,000
SALES: 1.9MM **Privately Held**
WEB: www.translinetech.com
SIC: 3672 Printed circuit boards

(P-18025)
TRANTRONICS INC
1822 Langley Ave, Irvine (92614-5624)
PHONE...............................949 553-1234
Tom Tran, *President*
Thien Luc, *Prgrmr*
EMP: 32
SALES (est): 7MM **Privately Held**
WEB: www.trantronics.com
SIC: 3672 3599 Printed circuit boards;
machine & other job shop work

(P-18026)
TRI-PHASE INC
Also Called: Valley Services Electronics
6190 San Ignacio Ave, San Jose
(95119-1378)
PHONE...............................408 284-7700
Andy Pecota, *CEO*
Beth Kendrick, *President*
Jeff Trambley, *Exec VP*
Steven Buchholz, *Engineer*
Leslie Hanson, *Engineer*
EMP: 160
SQ FT: 52,000
SALES (est): 36.7MM **Privately Held**
WEB: www.boinglures.com
SIC: 3672 Printed circuit boards

(P-18027)
TRI-STAR LAMINATES INC
Also Called: Laminating Company of America
20322 Windrow Dr Ste 100, Lake Forest
(92630-8150)
PHONE...............................949 587-3200
Patrick Redfern, *President*
Rob Wassem, *President*
Rachel Moreno, *Sales Staff*
EMP: 45
SQ FT: 50,000
SALES (est): 8MM **Privately Held**
WEB: www.lcoa.com
SIC: 3672 Printed circuit boards

(P-18028)
TTM PRINTED CIRCUIT GROUP INC
407 Mathew St, Santa Clara (95050-3105)
PHONE................................408 486-3100
Jeff Gonsman, *Manager*
Ho Raymond, *Engineer*
LI Feng, *Manager*
Chen Chris, *Assistant*
EMP: 250
SALES (corp-wide): 2.8B **Publicly Held**
SIC: 3672 Printed circuit boards
HQ: Ttm Printed Circuit Group, Inc.
   2630 S Harbor Blvd
   Santa Ana CA 92704

(P-18029)
TTM PRINTED CIRCUIT GROUP INC (HQ)
2630 S Harbor Blvd, Santa Ana
(92704-5829)
PHONE................................714 327-3000
Thomas T Edman, *President*
Steve Richards, *CFO*
▲ EMP: 52
SALES (est): 147.2MM
SALES (corp-wide): 2.8B **Publicly Held**
WEB: www.ttmtechnologies.com
SIC: 3672 Printed circuit boards
PA: Ttm Technologies, Inc.
   200 Sandpointe Ave # 400
   Santa Ana CA 92707
   714 327-3000

(P-18030)
TTM TECHNOLOGIES INC
407 Mathew St, Santa Clara (95050-3105)
PHONE................................408 486-3100
EMP: 260
SALES (corp-wide): 2.8B **Publicly Held**
SIC: 3672 Printed circuit boards
PA: Ttm Technologies, Inc.
   200 Sandpointe Ave # 400
   Santa Ana CA 92707
   714 327-3000

(P-18031)
TTM TECHNOLOGIES INC (PA)
200 Sandpointe Ave # 400, Santa Ana
(92707-5747)
PHONE................................714 327-3000
Thomas T Edman, *President*
Daniel J Weber, *Senior VP*
Todd Amy, *Vice Pres*
David Moore, *General Mgr*
Christopher Carrillo, *Engineer*
EMP: 500 EST: 1978
SQ FT: 11,775
SALES: 2.8B **Publicly Held**
WEB: www.ttmtechnologies.com
SIC: 3672 Printed circuit boards

(P-18032)
TTM TECHNOLOGIES INC
3140 E Coronado St, Anaheim
(92806-1914)
PHONE................................714 688-7200
Dave Rosato, *Engineer*
EMP: 290
SALES (corp-wide): 2.8B **Publicly Held**
WEB: www.ddiglobal.com
SIC: 3672 Printed circuit boards
PA: Ttm Technologies, Inc.
   200 Sandpointe Ave # 400
   Santa Ana CA 92707
   714 327-3000

(P-18033)
TTM TECHNOLOGIES INC
5037 Ruffner St, San Diego (92111-1107)
PHONE................................858 874-2701
Mark Micale, *Manager*
EMP: 100
SALES (corp-wide): 2.8B **Publicly Held**
WEB: www.ttmtechnologies.com
SIC: 3672 Printed circuit boards
PA: Ttm Technologies, Inc.
   200 Sandpointe Ave # 400
   Santa Ana CA 92707
   714 327-3000

(P-18034)
TTM TECHNOLOGIES INC
2630 S Harbor Blvd, Santa Ana
(92704-5829)
PHONE................................714 327-3000
Joe Ruane, *Vice Pres*
EMP: 330
SALES (corp-wide): 2.8B **Publicly Held**
WEB: www.ttmtechnologies.com
SIC: 3672 Printed circuit boards
PA: Ttm Technologies, Inc.
   200 Sandpointe Ave # 400
   Santa Ana CA 92707
   714 327-3000

(P-18035)
TTM TECHNOLOGIES INC
355 Turtle Creek Ct, San Jose
(95125-1316)
PHONE................................408 280-0422
Arnold Amaral, *Branch Mgr*
Joanna Zhao, *Program Mgr*
EMP: 118
SALES (corp-wide): 2.8B **Publicly Held**
SIC: 3672 Printed circuit boards
PA: Ttm Technologies, Inc.
   200 Sandpointe Ave # 400
   Santa Ana CA 92707
   714 327-3000

(P-18036)
TTM TECHNOLOGIES N AMER LLC
355 Turtle Creek Ct, San Jose
(95125-1316)
PHONE................................408 719-4000
EMP: 118
SALES (corp-wide): 2.8B **Publicly Held**
WEB: www.ddiglobal.com
SIC: 3672 Printed circuit boards
HQ: Ttm Technologies North America, Llc
   520 Maryville Centre Dr
   Saint Louis MO 63141
   314 719-1845

(P-18037)
TWIN INDUSTRIES INC
2303 Camino Ramon Ste 106, San Ramon
(94583-1389)
PHONE................................925 866-8946
Joe O'Neil, *General Mgr*
Adom Moutafian, *President*
▲ EMP: 85
SQ FT: 26,000
SALES (est): 8.1MM **Privately Held**
SIC: 3672 Printed circuit boards

(P-18038)
UNITED SUPERTEK INC
Also Called: U S I
14930 Vintner Ct, Saratoga (95070-9712)
PHONE................................408 922-0730
Samson Zarnegar, *President*
EMP: 35
SQ FT: 25,000
SALES (est): 4.6MM **Privately Held**
SIC: 3672 Printed circuit boards

(P-18039)
URI TECH INC
1340 Norman Ave, Santa Clara
(95054-2056)
PHONE................................408 456-0115
Sea Heon Kim, *President*
EMP: 13
SQ FT: 20,000
SALES: 1.2MM **Privately Held**
WEB: www.uritech.net
SIC: 3672 Printed circuit boards

(P-18040)
VALLEY CIRCUITS
Also Called: Valley Syncom Circuits
24940 Avenue Tibbitts, Valencia
(91355-3426)
PHONE................................661 294-0077
Christine Janes, *President*
Drew Janes, *Vice Pres*
EMP: 12
SALES: 3.2MM **Privately Held**
WEB: www.valleycircuits.com
SIC: 3672 Circuit boards, television & radio printed

(P-18041)
VECTOR ELECTRONICS & TECH INC
11115 Vanowen St, North Hollywood
(91605-6371)
PHONE................................818 985-8208
Rakesh Bajaria, *CEO*
Ken Pansuriah, *Vice Pres*
Jerry Rodriguez, *Vice Pres*
Viny Kathrotia, *Admin Sec*
▲ EMP: 25 EST: 2001
SALES (est): 4.8MM **Privately Held**
WEB: www.vectorelect.com
SIC: 3672 Printed circuit boards

(P-18042)
VECTOR FABRICATION INC (PA)
1629 Watson Ct, Milpitas (95035-6806)
PHONE................................408 942-9800
Quang Luong, *President*
Issac Stringer, *Vice Pres*
▲ EMP: 20
SQ FT: 18,000
SALES (est): 4.3MM **Privately Held**
WEB: www.vectorfab.com
SIC: 3672 Printed circuit boards

(P-18043)
VEECO ELECTRO FAB INC
1176 N Osprey Cir, Anaheim (92807-1709)
PHONE................................714 630-8020
Jagjit Singh, *President*
Joginda Singh, *Vice Pres*
EMP: 21
SQ FT: 10,000
SALES (est): 2.5MM **Privately Held**
SIC: 3672 7629 Printed circuit boards; circuit board repair

(P-18044)
VENTURE ELECTRONICS INTL INC
6701 Mowry Ave, Newark (94560-4927)
PHONE................................510 744-3720
C T Wong, *President*
EMP: 19
SALES (est): 2.6MM
SALES (corp-wide): 2.5B **Privately Held**
WEB: www.venture.com.sg
SIC: 3672 Printed circuit boards
PA: Venture Corporation Limited
   5006 Ang Mo Kio Avenue 5
   Singapore 56987
   648 217-55

(P-18045)
VINATRONIC INC
15571 Industry Ln, Huntington Beach
(92649-1534)
PHONE................................714 845-3480
Lan Nguyen, *CEO*
Kem Strano, *President*
EMP: 30
SQ FT: 13,000
SALES (est): 4.3MM **Privately Held**
WEB: www.vinatronic.com
SIC: 3672 Printed circuit boards

(P-18046)
VITRON ELECTRONIC SERVICES INC
Also Called: Vitron Electronics Mfg & Svcs
5400 Hellyer Ave, San Jose (95138-1019)
PHONE................................408 251-1600
Huan Cong Tran, *CEO*
Hien Duong, *Purchasing*
▲ EMP: 60
SQ FT: 3,500
SALES: 15MM **Privately Held**
WEB: www.vitronmfg.com
SIC: 3672 Printed circuit boards

(P-18047)
VYCOM AMERICA INC
39252 Winchester Rd 107-3, Murrieta
(92563-3509)
PHONE................................800 235-9195
Roberto Simeon, *CEO*
Sonny Dawoodjee, *Principal*
Tammy Ginsburg, *Principal*
EMP: 35 EST: 2013
SALES (est): 1.3MM **Privately Held**
SIC: 3672 Circuit boards, television & radio printed

(P-18048)
WE IMAGINE INC
9371 Canoga Ave, Chatsworth
(91311-5879)
P.O. Box 5696 (91313-5696)
PHONE................................818 709-0064
Barry Henley, *President*
Diana Reiter, *COO*
Claudia Henley, *Corp Secy*
EMP: 53 EST: 1974
SQ FT: 65,000
SALES (est): 8.7MM **Privately Held**
WEB: www.weimagineinc.com
SIC: 3672 Printed circuit boards

(P-18049)
WESTAK INC (PA)
Also Called: A2
1116 Elko Dr, Sunnyvale (94089-2207)
PHONE................................408 734-8686
Louise Crisham, *CEO*
Lou George, *COO*
Dicie Hinaga, *CFO*
Curtis Okumura, *Vice Pres*
Lisa Kennedy, *Office Mgr*
EMP: 100 EST: 1972
SQ FT: 20,000
SALES (est): 53.1MM **Privately Held**
WEB: www.westak.com
SIC: 3672 Circuit boards, television & radio printed

(P-18050)
WESTAK INTERNATIONAL SALES INC (HQ)
1116 Elko Dr, Sunnyvale (94089-2207)
PHONE................................408 734-8686
Louise Crisham, *President*
▲ EMP: 130
SQ FT: 20,000
SALES (est): 14.7MM
SALES (corp-wide): 53.1MM **Privately Held**
SIC: 3672 Printed circuit boards
PA: Westak, Inc
   1116 Elko Dr
   Sunnyvale CA 94089
   408 734-8686

(P-18051)
WHIZZ SYSTEMS INC
3240 Scott Blvd, Santa Clara (95054-3011)
PHONE................................408 207-0400
Munawar Karimjee, *CEO*
Muhammad Irfan, *President*
Yome Salinas, *Administration*
Asif Hassan, *Design Engr*
▲ EMP: 50 EST: 1999
SQ FT: 35,000
SALES (est): 28.8MM **Privately Held**
WEB: www.whizzsystems.com
SIC: 3672 Printed circuit boards

(P-18052)
WINONICS INC
Also Called: Bench 2 Bench Technologies
1257 S State College Blvd, Fullerton
(92831-5336)
PHONE................................714 626-3755
Tom Sciulli, *General Mgr*
Robert Froehlich, *Admin Mgr*
Octavio Ruelas, *Prdtn Mgr*
Xavier Pacheco, *Manager*
EMP: 120
SALES (corp-wide): 42MM **Privately Held**
WEB: www.winonics.com
SIC: 3672 Printed circuit boards
HQ: Winonics Inc.
   660 N Puente St
   Brea CA
   714 256-8700

(P-18053)
XILINX INC (PA)
2100 All Programable, San Jose
(95124-4355)
PHONE................................408 559-7778
Victor Peng, *President*
Mark David Wadlington, *Senior VP*
EMP: 988
SQ FT: 588,000

P R O D U C T S & S V C S

SALES: 3B **Publicly Held**
WEB: www.xilinx.com
SIC: 3672 3674 7372 Printed circuit boards; microcircuits, integrated (semiconductor); application computer software

(P-18054)
YAMAMOTO MANUFACTURING USA INC (HQ)
2025 Gateway Pl Ste 450, San Jose (95110-1146)
PHONE..................................408 387-5250
Takashi Toshishige, *President*
Carl Olin, *Director*
EMP: 12
SALES (est): 898.6K **Privately Held**
WEB: www.yusa.com
SIC: 3672 8711 Printed circuit boards; engineering services

(P-18055)
YUN INDUSTRIAL CO LTD
Also Called: Y I C
161 Selandia Ln, Carson (90746-1412)
PHONE..................................310 715-1898
Ilun Yun, *President*
Stephen Yun, *Vice Pres*
William Yun, *Admin Sec*
◆ EMP: 40
SQ FT: 16,000
SALES (est): 7.4MM **Privately Held**
WEB: www.yic-assm.com
SIC: 3672 Printed circuit boards

(P-18056)
ZOLLNER ELECTRONICS INC
575 Cottonwood Dr, Milpitas (95035-7402)
PHONE..................................408 434-5400
Stephan Weiss, *COO*
Michael Diep, *Program Mgr*
Nessa Hunt, *Admin Sec*
Cesar Quiason, *Technical Staff*
Bill Carlton, *Engineer*
▲ EMP: 29
SALES (est): 21.4MM
SALES (corp-wide): 1.7B **Privately Held**
SIC: 3672 Printed circuit boards
PA: Zollner Elektronik Ag
　　Manfred-Zollner-Str. 1
　　Zandt 93499
　　994 420-10

(P-18057)
ZYREL INC
15322 Lkeshore Dr Ste 301, Clearlake (95422)
P.O. Box 54157, San Jose (95154-0157)
PHONE..................................707 995-2551
▲ EMP: 11
SQ FT: 1,100
SALES (est): 1.9MM **Privately Held**
WEB: www.zyrel.com
SIC: 3672

(P-18058)
ZYTEK CORP
Also Called: Zytek Ems
1755 Mccarthy Blvd, Milpitas (95035-7416)
PHONE..................................408 520-4287
Rabia Khan, *President*
EMP: 40
SQ FT: 21,000
SALES (est): 8.3MM **Privately Held**
SIC: 3672 Printed circuit boards

3674 Semiconductors

(P-18059)
ACCELERATED MEMORY PROD INC
Also Called: AMP
1317 E Edinger Ave, Santa Ana (92705-4416)
PHONE..................................714 460-9800
Richard McCauley, *President*
Cathleen McCauley, *Vice Pres*
◆ EMP: 49
SQ FT: 10,000
SALES (est): 11.7MM **Privately Held**
WEB: www.ampinc.biz
SIC: 3674 Memories, solid state

(P-18060)
ACHRONIX SEMICONDUCTOR CORP
2903 Bunker Hill Ln # 200, Santa Clara (95054-1148)
PHONE..................................408 889-4100
Robert Blake, *President*
John Holt, *Ch of Bd*
Howard Brodsky, *CFO*
Kamal Chaudhary, *Vice Pres*
Virantha Ekanayake, *Vice Pres*
EMP: 75
SQ FT: 25,000
SALES (est): 16.3MM **Privately Held**
SIC: 3674 Integrated circuits, semiconductor networks, etc.

(P-18061)
ADESTO TECHNOLOGIES CORP (PA)
3600 Peterson Way, Santa Clara (95054-2808)
PHONE..................................408 400-0578
Narbeh Derhacobian, *President*
Nelson Chan, *Ch of Bd*
Ron Shelton, *CFO*
David Aaron, *Vice Pres*
Seyed Attaran, *Vice Pres*
◆ EMP: 71
SQ FT: 34,000
SALES: 83.4MM **Publicly Held**
SIC: 3674 Semiconductors & related devices

(P-18062)
ADEX ELECTRONICS INC
3 Watson, Irvine (92618-2716)
PHONE..................................949 597-1772
Casey Huang, *President*
Cheryl Roberts, *Treasurer*
▲ EMP: 15
SQ FT: 10,330
SALES (est): 1.4MM **Privately Held**
WEB: www.adexelec.com
SIC: 3674 8711 Semiconductors & related devices; engineering services

(P-18063)
ADVANCED ANALOGIC TECH INC
2740 Zanker Rd, San Jose (95134-2128)
PHONE..................................408 330-1400
Richard K Williams, *President*
David J Aldrich, *CEO*
Parviz Ghaffaripour, *COO*
Ashok Chandran, *CFO*
Bijan Mohandes, *Exec VP*
EMP: 47 EST: 1962
SQ FT: 42,174
SALES (est): 10.5MM
SALES (corp-wide): 3.3B **Publicly Held**
SIC: 3674 Integrated circuits, semiconductor networks, etc.
PA: Skyworks Solutions, Inc.
　　20 Sylvan Rd
　　Woburn MA 01801
　　781 376-3000

(P-18064)
ADVANCED COMPONENT LABS INC
Also Called: A C L
990 Richard Ave Ste 118, Santa Clara (95050-2828)
PHONE..................................408 327-0200
Michael J Oswald, *CEO*
Deborah Herting, *Vice Pres*
Nerissa De Ramos, *Sales Mgr*
EMP: 20
SQ FT: 20,000
SALES (est): 3.6MM **Privately Held**
WEB: www.aclusa.com
SIC: 3674 Semiconductor circuit networks

(P-18065)
ADVANCED LINEAR DEVICES INC
415 Tasman Dr, Sunnyvale (94089-1706)
PHONE..................................408 747-1155
Robert L Chao, *President*
EMP: 25
SQ FT: 12,000

SALES (est): 2.8MM **Privately Held**
WEB: www.aldinc.com
SIC: 3674 8711 Integrated circuits, semiconductor networks, etc.; engineering services

(P-18066)
ADVANCED MICRO DEVICES INC (PA)
2485 Augustine Dr, Santa Clara (95054-3002)
PHONE..................................408 749-4000
Lisa T Su, *President*
John E Caldwell, *Ch of Bd*
Devinder Kumar, *CFO*
Ahmed Al Idrissi, *Bd of Directors*
Robert Gama, *Officer*
EMP: 277
SALES: 6.4B **Publicly Held**
WEB: www.amd.com
SIC: 3674 Integrated circuits, semiconductor networks, etc.; microprocessors; memories, solid state; microcircuits, integrated (semiconductor)

(P-18067)
ADVANCED SEMICONDUCTOR INC (PA)
Also Called: A S I
7525 Ethel Ave Ste I, North Hollywood (91605-1912)
PHONE..................................818 982-1200
Fred Golob, *CEO*
Don Wolf, *Executive*
Maria Arias, *Purch Mgr*
▲ EMP: 58
SQ FT: 9,000
SALES (est): 8.8MM **Privately Held**
WEB: www.advancedsemiconductor.com
SIC: 3674 Integrated circuits, semiconductor networks, etc.

(P-18068)
ADVANCED THERMAL SCIENCES
3355 E La Palma Ave, Anaheim (92806-2815)
PHONE..................................714 688-4200
Bruce Thayer, *President*
Masashi Iwao, *Vice Pres*
Erin Carey, *Administration*
James Yoo, *Electrical Engi*
▲ EMP: 15
SALES (est): 2.3MM
SALES (corp-wide): 66.5B **Publicly Held**
SIC: 3674 Semiconductors & related devices
HQ: B/E Aerospace, Inc.
　　1400 Corporate Center Way
　　Wellington FL 33414
　　561 791-5000

(P-18069)
ADVANTEST AMERICA INC (HQ)
3061 Zanker Rd, San Jose (95134-2127)
PHONE..................................408 456-3600
Douglas Lefever, *CEO*
Keith Hardwick, *CFO*
Tony Loi, *Manager*
▲ EMP: 90
SALES (est): 71.3MM **Privately Held**
SIC: 3674 Semiconductors & related devices

(P-18070)
ADVANTEST TEST SOLUTIONS INC
4 Goodyear, Irvine (92618-2002)
PHONE..................................949 523-6900
Debbora Ahlgren, *Principal*
EMP: 29
SALES (est): 99K **Privately Held**
SIC: 3674 Semiconductors & related devices
HQ: Advantest America, Inc.
　　3061 Zanker Rd
　　San Jose CA 95134
　　408 456-3600

(P-18071)
ADVIN SYSTEMS INC
11693 Vineyard Spring Ct, Cupertino (95014-5135)
PHONE..................................408 243-7000
Wing F Hui, *President*

Ken Spink, *Controller*
Carl Buck, *VP Mktg*
EMP: 10
SQ FT: 2,680
SALES (est): 970K **Privately Held**
WEB: www.advin.com
SIC: 3674 Integrated circuits, semiconductor networks, etc.

(P-18072)
AGILE TECHNOLOGIES INC
2 Orion, Aliso Viejo (92656-4200)
PHONE..................................949 454-8030
Martin Munzer, *CEO*
David A Krohn, *President*
Rick Brooks, *Vice Pres*
Toni Sweeney, *Buyer*
EMP: 19
SQ FT: 40,000
SALES (est): 4.7MM **Privately Held**
WEB: www.agiletech.org
SIC: 3674 Photoelectric magnetic devices

(P-18073)
AIXTRON INC
1700 Wyatt Dr Ste 15, Santa Clara (95054-1526)
PHONE..................................669 228-3759
Martin Goetzeler, *CEO*
Randy Singh, *CFO*
Bill Bentinck, *Vice Pres*
Brian Lu, *Vice Pres*
Michael Patten, *Information Mgr*
▲ EMP: 156
SQ FT: 100,500
SALES: 196.4K
SALES (corp-wide): 307.7MM **Privately Held**
WEB: www.genus.com
SIC: 3674 Semiconductors & related devices
PA: Aixtron Se
　　Dornkaulstr. 2
　　Herzogenrath 52134
　　240 790-300

(P-18074)
AJILE SYSTEMS INC (PA)
920 Saratoga Ave Ste 104, San Jose (95129-3408)
PHONE..................................408 557-0829
George Hwang, *President*
Danh Lengoc, *Vice Pres*
EMP: 20
SQ FT: 3,000
SALES (est): 1.2MM **Privately Held**
WEB: www.ajile.com
SIC: 3674 Semiconductors & related devices

(P-18075)
AKM SEMICONDUCTOR INC
Also Called: A K M
1731 Tech Dr Ste 500, San Jose (95110)
PHONE..................................408 436-8580
S Kido, *President*
Makoto Konosu, *CEO*
Lyle Knudsen, *Vice Pres*
Masahiko Fukasawa, *Engineer*
▲ EMP: 22
SQ FT: 5,402
SALES (est): 4MM **Privately Held**
WEB: www.akm.com
SIC: 3674 Semiconductors & related devices
PA: Asahi Kasei Microdevices Corporation
　　1-1-2, Yurakucho
　　Chiyoda-Ku TKY 100-0

(P-18076)
AL FRESCO CONCEPTS INC
Also Called: Fresco Solar
16875 Joleen Way Unit 170, Morgan Hill (95037-4604)
PHONE..................................408 497-1579
Sean Kenny, *CEO*
EMP: 15
SALES (est): 2MM **Privately Held**
SIC: 3674 Solar cells

(P-18077)
ALCATEL-LUCENT USA INC
701 E Middlefield Rd, Mountain View (94043-4079)
PHONE..................................408 878-6500

▲ = Import ▼=Export
◆ =Import/Export

Oscar Rodriguez, *Manager*
SRI Reddy, *Vice Pres*
Mike McKeon, *Business Dir*
Sanjiv Doshi, *Sr Software Eng*
Raman Krishnaprasad, *Technical Staff*
EMP: 421
SALES (corp-wide): 25.8B **Privately Held**
WEB: www.lucent.com
SIC: 3674 Integrated circuits, semiconductor networks, etc.
HQ: Nokia Of America Corporation
600 Mountain Ave Ste 700
New Providence NJ 07974

(P-18078)
ALION ENERGY INC
2200 Central St D, Richmond
(94801-1213)
PHONE....................510 965-0868
Mark Kingsley, *President*
Jesse Atkinson, *Vice Pres*
Linda Ramos, *Office Mgr*
Craig Wildman, *Engineer*
Mark Olsen, *Controller*
▲ **EMP:** 51
SALES (est): 11MM **Privately Held**
SIC: 3674 Solar cells

(P-18079)
ALL SENSORS CORPORATION
16035 Vineyard Blvd, Morgan Hill
(95037-5480)
PHONE....................408 776-9434
Dennis Dauenhauer, *President*
Gary Arnold, *Vice Pres*
Markus Schwan, *General Mgr*
Delly Paiva, *Admin Asst*
Tim Shotter, *Planning*
◆ **EMP:** 38
SQ FT: 20,000
SALES (est): 9.1MM
SALES (corp-wide): 8.2B **Publicly Held**
WEB: www.allsensors.com
SIC: 3674 Infrared sensors, solid state
PA: Amphenol Corporation
358 Hall Ave
Wallingford CT 06492
203 265-8900

(P-18080)
ALLIANCE MEMORY INC
511 Taylor Way, San Carlos (94070-6201)
PHONE....................650 610-6800
David A Bagby, *President*
Kim Bagby, *CFO*
▲ **EMP:** 15
SQ FT: 3,000
SALES (est): 2MM **Privately Held**
WEB: www.alliancememory.com
SIC: 3674 Semiconductors & related devices

(P-18081)
ALLTEQ INDUSTRIES INC
215 Rustic Pl, San Ramon (94582-5618)
PHONE....................925 833-7666
Phil Davies, *President*
Tony Draga, *Vice Pres*
William Miller, *Vice Pres*
EMP: 14
SQ FT: 11,000
SALES (est): 1.3MM **Privately Held**
WEB: www.allteq.com
SIC: 3674 3825 Semiconductors & related devices; integrated circuit testers

(P-18082)
ALLVIA INC
657 N Pastoria Ave, Sunnyvale
(94085-2917)
PHONE....................408 720-3333
Sergey Savastiouk, *CEO*
EMP: 20
SQ FT: 17,900
SALES (est): 4.1MM **Privately Held**
WEB: www.trusi.com
SIC: 3674 Integrated circuits, semiconductor networks, etc.

(P-18083)
ALPHA AND OMEGA SEMICDTR INC (HQ)
475 Oakmead Pkwy, Sunnyvale
(94085-4709)
PHONE....................408 789-0008

Mike F Chang, *CEO*
Mary Dotz, *CFO*
Rachel Xun, *Treasurer*
Jenkon Chen, *Bd of Directors*
King Owyang PHD, *Bd of Directors*
▲ **EMP:** 120
SQ FT: 50,000
SALES (est): 31.4MM **Privately Held**
WEB: www.aos.com
SIC: 3674 Semiconductors & related devices

(P-18084)
ALTA DEVICES INC
545 Oakmead Pkwy, Sunnyvale
(94085-4023)
PHONE....................408 988-8600
Jian Ding, *CEO*
Mallorie Burak, *CFO*
Harry Atwater, *Bd of Directors*
Eli Yablonovitch, *Bd of Directors*
Thomas Giap, *Surgery Dir*
EMP: 250
SQ FT: 115,000
SALES (est): 3MM
SALES (corp-wide): 782.7MM **Privately Held**
SIC: 3674 Semiconductors & related devices
PA: Jinjiang Hydroelectric Power Group Co., Ltd.
No.0-A, Anli Road, Chaoyang Dist.
Beijing 10010
108 391-4567

(P-18085)
ALTASENS INC (HQ)
2201 E Dominguez St, Long Beach
(90810-1009)
PHONE....................818 338-9400
Kensuke Kawai, *CEO*
Clint Elsemore, *CFO*
Giuseppe Rossi, *Vice Pres*
John Von Colln, *Program Mgr*
Lester Kozlowski, *CTO*
▲ **EMP:** 48
SQ FT: 15,000
SALES (est): 6.2MM **Privately Held**
WEB: www.altasens.com
SIC: 3674 Semiconductors & related devices

(P-18086)
ALTERA CORPORATION (HQ)
101 Innovation Dr, San Jose (95134-1941)
PHONE....................408 544-7000
John P Daane, *Ch of Bd*
Ronald J Pasek, *CFO*
Greg Holste, *Treasurer*
Danny Biran, *Senior VP*
William Y Hata, *Senior VP*
▲ **EMP:** 277
SQ FT: 505,000
SALES: 1.9B
SALES (corp-wide): 70.8B **Publicly Held**
WEB: www.altera.com
SIC: 3674 7371 Semiconductors & related devices; computer software development & applications
PA: Intel Corporation
2200 Mission College Blvd
Santa Clara CA 95054
408 765-8080

(P-18087)
ALTIERRE CORPORATION
1980 Concourse Dr, San Jose
(95131-1719)
PHONE....................408 435-7343
Tony Alvarez, *CEO*
Anurag Goel, *COO*
Shan Kumar, *CFO*
Ken Cioffi, *Vice Pres*
Dave Wetle, *Vice Pres*
▲ **EMP:** 50
SQ FT: 85,367
SALES (est): 16.7MM **Privately Held**
WEB: www.altierre.com
SIC: 3674 Integrated circuits, semiconductor networks, etc.

(P-18088)
AMBARELLA INC
3101 Jay St, Santa Clara (95054-3329)
PHONE....................408 734-8888
Feng-Ming Wang, *Ch of Bd*

Kevin C Eichler, *CFO*
Christopher Paisley, *Bd of Directors*
Andrew Verhalen, *Bd of Directors*
Didier Legall, *Exec VP*
EMP: 750
SQ FT: 50,000
SALES: 227.7MM **Privately Held**
SIC: 3674 Semiconductors & related devices

(P-18089)
AMD INTERNATIONAL SLS SVC LTD (HQ)
1 Amd Pl, Sunnyvale (94085-3905)
P.O. Box 3453 (94088-3453)
PHONE....................408 749-4000
Lisa Su, *President*
Bob Rivet, *CFO*
Chekib Akrout, *Senior VP*
John Byrne, *Senior VP*
Darrell L Ford, *Senior VP*
◆ **EMP:** 26
SALES (est): 25.4MM
SALES (corp-wide): 6.4B **Publicly Held**
SIC: 3674 Semiconductors & related devices
PA: Advanced Micro Devices, Inc.
2485 Augustine Dr
Santa Clara CA 95054
408 749-4000

(P-18090)
AMD VENTURES LLC
1 Amd Pl, Sunnyvale (94085-3905)
P.O. Box 3453 (94088-3453)
PHONE....................408 749-4000
Rory Read, *Principal*
EMP: 115
SALES (est): 11.4MM **Privately Held**
SIC: 3674 Semiconductors & related devices

(P-18091)
AMERICA TECHCODE SEMICDTR INC
10456 San Fernando Ave, Cupertino
(95014-2867)
PHONE....................408 910-2028
Fong Lok-Cheung, *President*
EMP: 20 **EST:** 2010
SALES (est): 1.2MM **Privately Held**
SIC: 3674 Semiconductors & related devices

(P-18092)
AMERICAN ARIUM INC
17791 Fitch, Irvine (92614-6019)
PHONE....................949 623-7090
Larry Traylor, *President*
Diane George, *CFO*
Diane Dirks, *Corp Secy*
Jassy Mukherjee, *Finance*
EMP: 36
SQ FT: 32,330
SALES: 6MM **Privately Held**
WEB: www.arium.com
SIC: 3674 3577 Microprocessors; computer logic modules; computer peripheral equipment

(P-18093)
AMERICAN SOLAR ADVANTAGE INC
7056 Archibald St 102-432, Corona
(92880-8713)
PHONE....................951 496-1075
Bobby D Harris, *President*
EMP: 20
SALES: 800K **Privately Held**
SIC: 3674 1731 Solar cells; electrical work

(P-18094)
AMEST CORPORATION
30394 Esperanza, Rcho STA Marg
(92688-2118)
PHONE....................949 766-9692
John P Iest, *President*
Linda Iest, *Admin Sec*
Cung Le, *Technician*
Todd Montgomery, *Senior Engr*
EMP: 10 **EST:** 1975
SQ FT: 5,400
SALES (est): 1.8MM **Privately Held**
WEB: www.amestcorp.com
SIC: 3674 Microprocessors

(P-18095)
AMKOR TECHNOLOGY INC
5465 Morehouse Dr Ste 210, San Diego
(92121-4764)
PHONE....................858 320-6280
Susan Kim, *Bd of Directors*
John Osborne, *Bd of Directors*
Rebecca Craft, *Vice Pres*
Bob Filipski, *Vice Pres*
Tracy Keller, *Payroll Mgr*
EMP: 84
SALES (corp-wide): 4.3B **Publicly Held**
SIC: 3674 Semiconductors & related devices
PA: Amkor Technology, Inc.
2045 E Innovation Cir
Tempe AZ 85284
480 821-5000

(P-18096)
AMKOR TECHNOLOGY INC
3 Corporate Park Ste 230, Irvine
(92606-5161)
PHONE....................949 724-9370
Davren Mc Millan, *Manager*
EMP: 25
SALES (corp-wide): 4.3B **Publicly Held**
WEB: www.amkor.com
SIC: 3674 Semiconductors & related devices
PA: Amkor Technology, Inc.
2045 E Innovation Cir
Tempe AZ 85284
480 821-5000

(P-18097)
AMLOGIC INC
2518 Mission College Blvd, Santa Clara
(95054-1239)
PHONE....................408 850-9688
John Zhong, *President*
Yeeping Zhong, *Vice Pres*
Rose Kung, *Office Mgr*
Mike Yip, *VP Engrg*
Kedar Roy, *Technology*
EMP: 20
SALES (est): 4.1MM **Privately Held**
SIC: 3674 Integrated circuits, semiconductor networks, etc.

(P-18098)
ANALOG BITS
945 Stewart Dr, Sunnyvale (94085-3861)
PHONE....................650 279-9323
Alan Rogers, *Owner*
Jessica Huang, *Engineer*
Liting Huang, *Engineer*
Will Wong, *Mktg Dir*
EMP: 30
SALES (est): 3.8MM **Privately Held**
WEB: www.analogbits.com
SIC: 3674 Semiconductors & related devices

(P-18099)
ANALOG DEVICES INC
1530 Buckeye Dr, Milpitas (95035-7418)
PHONE....................408 727-9222
Jerry Fishman, *Sales/Mktg Mgr*
Richard Cheung, *Engineer*
Mark Lewis, *Engineer*
Derek Maravilla, *Engineer*
Harry WEI, *Engineer*
EMP: 300
SALES (corp-wide): 6.2B **Publicly Held**
WEB: www.analog.com
SIC: 3674 Integrated circuits, semiconductor networks, etc.
PA: Analog Devices, Inc.
1 Technology Way
Norwood MA 02062
781 329-4700

(P-18100)
ANALOG DEVICES INC
940 S Coast Dr Ste 230, Costa Mesa
(92626-7802)
PHONE....................714 641-9391
Jay Feldman, *Manager*
EMP: 20
SALES (corp-wide): 6.2B **Publicly Held**
WEB: www.analog.com
SIC: 3674 Integrated circuits, semiconductor networks, etc.

P
R
O
D
U
C
T
S

&

S
V
C
S

PA: Analog Devices, Inc.
1 Technology Way
Norwood MA 02062
781 329-4700

(P-18101)
ANALOGIX SEMICONDUCTOR INC
Also Called: Pacific Analogix Semiconductor
3211 Scott Blvd Ste 100, Santa Clara
(95054-3009)
PHONE.....................408 988-8848
Kewei Yang, *Ch of Bd*
Bill Eichen, *President*
Patrick LI, *President*
Mike Seifert, *CFO*
Hing Chu, *Vice Pres*
▲ EMP: 24
SALES (est): 7.7MM **Privately Held**
WEB: www.analogixsemi.com
SIC: 3674 Integrated circuits, semiconductor networks, etc.

(P-18102)
ANOKIWAVE INC (PA)
11236 El Camino Real # 100, San Diego
(92130-2617)
PHONE.....................858 792-9910
Nitin Jain, *Ch of Bd*
Robert S Donahue, *CEO*
Carl Frank, *COO*
William Boecke, *CFO*
Deborah Dendy, *Vice Pres*
EMP: 37
SQ FT: 5,766
SALES (est): 8.6MM **Privately Held**
WEB: www.anokiwave.com
SIC: 3674 Semiconductors & related devices

(P-18103)
APIC CORPORATION
5800 Uplander Way, Culver City
(90230-6608)
PHONE.....................310 642-7975
James Chan, *Officer*
Birendra Dutt, *President*
Todd Shays, *COO*
Denise Lortie, *Vice Pres*
Anguel Nikolov, *Vice Pres*
EMP: 58
SQ FT: 14,416
SALES (est): 11.2MM **Privately Held**
WEB: www.apichip.com
SIC: 3674 Semiconductors & related devices

(P-18104)
APLUS FLASH TECHNOLOGY INC
780 Montague Expy Ste 103, San Jose
(95131-1315)
PHONE.....................408 382-1100
Peter W Lee, *President*
EMP: 15 EST: 1998
SQ FT: 7,000
SALES (est): 1.9MM **Privately Held**
WEB: www.aplusflash.com
SIC: 3674 Monolithic integrated circuits (solid state)

(P-18105)
APPLIED CERAMICS INC (PA)
48630 Milmont Dr, Fremont (94538-7353)
PHONE.....................510 249-9700
Matt Darko Sertic, *CEO*
Melina Deong, *Sales Engr*
Alan Omerovic, *Sales Staff*
Genner Escalante, *Director*
Brandon Talaich, *Manager*
▲ EMP: 14
SQ FT: 57,000
SALES (est): 16.9MM **Privately Held**
WEB: www.aceramic.com
SIC: 3674 3264 Semiconductors & related devices; porcelain electrical supplies

(P-18106)
APPLIED FILMS CORPORATION
3050 Bowers Ave, Santa Clara
(95054-3201)
PHONE.....................408 727-5555
Thomas T Edman, *President*
Richard P Beck, *Ch of Bd*
Lawrence D Firestone, *CFO*
Joachim Nell, *Exec VP*

James P Scholhamer, *Senior VP*
▲ EMP: 28
SQ FT: 87,000
SALES (est): 2.7MM
SALES (corp-wide): 17.2B **Publicly Held**
SIC: 3674 Semiconductors & related devices
PA: Applied Materials, Inc.
3050 Bowers Ave
Santa Clara CA 95054
408 727-5555

(P-18107)
APPLIED MATERIALS INC
3320 Scott Blvd, Santa Clara (95054-3101)
PHONE.....................408 727-5555
Mary Ryan, *Branch Mgr*
Murali Narasimhan, *General Mgr*
Wen Chang, *Systems Dir*
Sean Herbert, *Software Engr*
Thuc Tran, *Technician*
EMP: 50
SALES (corp-wide): 17.2B **Publicly Held**
SIC: 3674 Semiconductors & related devices
PA: Applied Materials, Inc.
3050 Bowers Ave
Santa Clara CA 95054
408 727-5555

(P-18108)
APPLIED MATERIALS INC
4675 Macarthur Ct, Newport Beach
(92660-1875)
PHONE.....................949 244-1600
EMP: 46
SALES (corp-wide): 17.2B **Publicly Held**
SIC: 3674 Semiconductors & related devices
PA: Applied Materials, Inc.
3050 Bowers Ave
Santa Clara CA 95054
408 727-5555

(P-18109)
APPLIED MATERIALS INC
1285 Walsh Ave, Santa Clara
(95050-2662)
PHONE.....................406 752-2107
Gary Dickerson, *President*
Abbas Rastegar, *Technology*
Tugrul Samir PHD, *Engineer*
EMP: 48
SALES (corp-wide): 17.2B **Publicly Held**
SIC: 3674 Semiconductors & related devices
PA: Applied Materials, Inc.
3050 Bowers Ave
Santa Clara CA 95054
408 727-5555

(P-18110)
APPLIED MATERIALS INC
380 Fairview Way, Milpitas (95035-3062)
PHONE.....................408 727-5555
Stacey Brown, *Principal*
EMP: 48
SALES (corp-wide): 17.2B **Publicly Held**
SIC: 3674 Semiconductors & related devices
PA: Applied Materials, Inc.
3050 Bowers Ave
Santa Clara CA 95054
408 727-5555

(P-18111)
APPLIED MATERIALS INC
3340 Scott Blvd, Santa Clara (95054-3101)
PHONE.....................408 727-5555
Gary E Dickerson, *Branch Mgr*
Bob Bettencourt, *General Mgr*
David Waterfall, *Comp Spec*
Larry Elizaga, *Engineer*
Ron Williams, *Engineer*
EMP: 56
SALES (corp-wide): 17.2B **Publicly Held**
SIC: 3674 Semiconductors & related devices
PA: Applied Materials, Inc.
3050 Bowers Ave
Santa Clara CA 95054
408 727-5555

(P-18112)
APPLIED MATERIALS INC
3101 Scott Blvd, Santa Clara (95054-3318)
PHONE.....................512 272-3692
Bill McClintock, *Vice Pres*
Melinda Loveday, *Executive Asst*
Hemkar Manish, *Info Tech Dir*
Thuc Tran, *Technician*
Jin Kim, *Technical Staff*
EMP: 12
SALES (corp-wide): 17.2B **Publicly Held**
SIC: 3674 Semiconductors & related devices
PA: Applied Materials, Inc.
3050 Bowers Ave
Santa Clara CA 95054
408 727-5555

(P-18113)
APPLIED MATERIALS INC
3535 Garrett Dr Bldg 100, Santa Clara
(95054-2811)
P.O. Box 58039 (95052-8039)
PHONE.....................408 727-5555
Darren Mattingly, *Manager*
Jamini Samantaray, *Software Engr*
Eashpreet Bajwa, *Network Enginr*
Satish Baskaran, *IT/INT Sup*
Valery Preygerzon, *IT/INT Sup*
EMP: 48
SALES (corp-wide): 17.2B **Publicly Held**
SIC: 3674 Semiconductors & related devices
PA: Applied Materials, Inc.
3050 Bowers Ave
Santa Clara CA 95054
408 727-5555

(P-18114)
APPLIED MATERIALS INC
44050 Fremont Blvd, Fremont
(94538-6042)
PHONE.....................510 687-8018
Dianne Dougherty, *Manager*
EMP: 48
SALES (corp-wide): 17.2B **Publicly Held**
WEB: www.appliedmaterials.com
SIC: 3674 Semiconductors & related devices
PA: Applied Materials, Inc.
3050 Bowers Ave
Santa Clara CA 95054
408 727-5555

(P-18115)
APPLIED MATERIALS INC
2821 Scott Blvd Bldg 17, Santa Clara
(95050-2549)
P.O. Box 58039 (95052-8039)
PHONE.....................408 727-5555
Johnny Singh, *Principal*
Sharon Timoner, *Managing Dir*
Donn Turner, *General Mgr*
Yvonne Tai, *Info Tech Mgr*
Yoke W Mun, *Technology*
EMP: 100
SALES (corp-wide): 17.2B **Publicly Held**
WEB: www.appliedmaterials.com
SIC: 3674 Semiconductors & related devices
PA: Applied Materials, Inc.
3050 Bowers Ave
Santa Clara CA 95054
408 727-5555

(P-18116)
APPLIED MICRO CIRCUITS CORP (HQ)
4555 Great America Pkwy # 601, Santa
Clara (95054-1243)
PHONE.....................408 542-8600
Paramesh Gopi, *President*
Martin S McDermut, *CFO*
L William Caraccio,
Bruce Roberts, *Engineer*
▲ EMP: 179
SQ FT: 55,000
SALES: 159.2MM **Publicly Held**
WEB: www.amcc.com
SIC: 3674 Microcircuits, integrated (semiconductor)

(P-18117)
APPLIED MICRO CIRCUITS CORP
Also Called: Amcc Sales
4555 Great America Pkwy # 601, Santa
Clara (95054-1243)
PHONE.....................408 542-8600
Kambiz Hooshmand, *Manager*
EMP: 27 **Publicly Held**
WEB: www.amcc.com
SIC: 3674 Microcircuits, integrated (semiconductor)
HQ: Applied Micro Circuits Corp
4555 Great America Pkwy # 601
Santa Clara CA 95054
408 542-8600

(P-18118)
APPLIED WIRELESS INC
1250 Avenida Acaso Ste F, Camarillo
(93012-8729)
PHONE.....................805 383-9600
David Nichols, *President*
▲ EMP: 14
SQ FT: 8,000
SALES (est): 2.5MM **Privately Held**
WEB: www.appliedwireless.com
SIC: 3674 Semiconductors & related devices

(P-18119)
APTA GROUP INC (PA)
Also Called: Advanced Packaging Tech Amer
7580 Britannia Ct, San Diego
(92154-7424)
PHONE.....................619 710-8170
Per Tonnesen, *President*
EMP: 21
SQ FT: 25,000
SALES (est): 2.3MM **Privately Held**
WEB: www.aptagroup.com
SIC: 3674 Hybrid integrated circuits; modules, solid state

(P-18120)
AQUANTIA CORP (HQ)
91 E Tasman Dr Ste 100, San Jose
(95134-1620)
PHONE.....................408 228-8300
Matt Murphy, *President*
EMP: 89
SQ FT: 66,943
SALES: 120.7MM **Privately Held**
WEB: www.aquantia.com
SIC: 3674 Semiconductors & related devices

(P-18121)
ARDICA TECHNOLOGIES INC
2325 3rd St Ste 424, San Francisco
(94107-4305)
PHONE.....................415 568-9270
Jeff Scheinrock, *CEO*
Daniel Braithwaite, *President*
Dick Martin, *President*
Jim Retzlaff, *CFO*
Brandon Buzarde, *Vice Pres*
EMP: 12
SQ FT: 5,000
SALES: 50K **Privately Held**
WEB: www.ardica.com
SIC: 3674 Fuel cells, solid state

(P-18122)
ARM INC (DH)
150 Rose Orchard Way, San Jose
(95134-1358)
PHONE.....................408 576-1500
Simon Segars, *CEO*
EMP: 270
SQ FT: 54,489
SALES (est): 205.5MM **Privately Held**
SIC: 3674 Integrated circuits, semiconductor networks, etc.

(P-18123)
ARM INC
5375 Mira Sorrento Pl # 540, San Diego
(92121-3809)
PHONE.....................858 453-1900
Todd Vierra, *Branch Mgr*
Stuart Siu, *Manager*
EMP: 127 **Privately Held**
SIC: 3674 Integrated circuits, semiconductor networks, etc.

▲ = Import ▼=Export
◆ =Import/Export

HQ: Arm, Inc.
150 Rose Orchard Way
San Jose CA 95134

(P-18124)
ARRIVE TECHNOLOGIES INC (PA)
3693 Westchester Dr, Roseville
(95747-6353)
PHONE..................................888 864-6959
Peter W Keeler, *Ch of Bd*
Murat Uraz, *President*
EMP: 15 **EST:** 2001
SALES: 11K **Privately Held**
SIC: 3674 Integrated circuits, semiconductor networks, etc.

(P-18125)
ART MICROELECTRONICS CORP
5917 Oak Ave Ste 201, Temple City
(91780-2028)
PHONE..................................626 447-7503
Richard King, *President*
▲ **EMP:** 15
SQ FT: 800
SALES (est): 1.4MM **Privately Held**
WEB: www.alpha-sci.com
SIC: 3674 5065 Semiconductors & related devices; semiconductor devices

(P-18126)
ARTERIS INC
595 Millich Dr Ste 200, Campbell
(95008-0550)
PHONE..................................408 470-7300
Charles K Janac, *President*
Stephane Mehat, *CFO*
Bhavin Vaidya, *IT/INT Sup*
Farnaz Alim, *Technical Staff*
EMP: 40
SQ FT: 6,287
SALES: 10.4MM **Privately Held**
SIC: 3674 Semiconductors & related devices

(P-18127)
ARTERIS HOLDINGS INC
591 W Hamilton Ave # 250, Campbell
(95008-0559)
PHONE..................................408 470-7300
Charles K Janac, *President*
Stephane Mehat, *CFO*
Ty Garibay, *CTO*
Boon Chuan, *Engineer*
Jennifer Samaripa, *Accountant*
EMP: 45
SQ FT: 4,500
SALES (est): 5.8MM **Privately Held**
WEB: www.arteris.com
SIC: 3674 Semiconductors & related devices

(P-18128)
ASC GROUP INC
12243 Branford St, Sun Valley
(91352-1010)
PHONE..................................818 896-1101
Chuck Rogers, *President*
Esther Kirk, *Director*
EMP: 250
SQ FT: 80,000
SALES (est): 13MM
SALES (corp-wide): 2.5B **Privately Held**
WEB: www.ascgroup.com
SIC: 3674 Semiconductors & related devices
HQ: Pmc, Inc.
12243 Branford St
Sun Valley CA 91352
818 896-1101

(P-18129)
ASI SEMICONDUCTOR INC
Also Called: A S I
7525 Ethel Ave, North Hollywood
(91605-1912)
PHONE..................................818 982-1200
Steve Golob, *Principal*
Mike Lincoln, *COO*
Fred Golob, *Principal*
EMP: 25
SQ FT: 15,000

SALES (est): 4.3MM **Privately Held**
SIC: 3674 Semiconductors & related devices

(P-18130)
ASIC ADVANTAGE INC
3850 N 1st St, San Jose (95134-1702)
PHONE..................................408 541-8686
EMP: 52
SQ FT: 20,077
SALES (est): 6.7MM **Privately Held**
WEB: www.asicadvantage.com
SIC: 3674

(P-18131)
ATOMERA INCORPORATED
750 University Ave # 280, Los Gatos
(95032-7698)
PHONE..................................408 442-5248
Scott Bibaud, *President*
John Gerber, *Ch of Bd*
Francis Laurencio, *CFO*
Erwin Trautmann, *Exec VP*
Robert Mears, *CTO*
EMP: 17 **EST:** 2001
SQ FT: 3,396
SALES: 246K **Privately Held**
SIC: 3674 Semiconductors & related devices

(P-18132)
AUDIENCE INC (HQ)
331 Fairchild Dr, Mountain View
(94043-2200)
PHONE..................................650 254-2800
Jeffrey Niew, *President*
Paul Dickinson, *President*
Christian Scherp, *President*
Gordon Walker, *President*
David Wightman, *President*
EMP: 57
SQ FT: 87,565
SALES: 74.3MM
SALES (corp-wide): 826.9MM **Publicly Held**
SIC: 3674 Microprocessors
PA: Knowles Corporation
1151 Maplewood Dr
Itasca IL 60143
630 250-5100

(P-18133)
AUXIN SOLAR INC
6835 Via Del Oro, San Jose (95119-1315)
PHONE..................................408 225-4380
Sherry Tai, *CEO*
Mamum Rashid, *Vice Pres*
▲ **EMP:** 45
SQ FT: 100,000
SALES (est): 5.6MM **Privately Held**
SIC: 3674 Solar cells; modules, solid state

(P-18134)
AVAGO TECHNOLOGIES US INC
1730 Fox Dr, San Jose (95131-2311)
PHONE..................................408 433-4068
Hock E Tan, *Branch Mgr*
Dennis Tan, *Engineer*
EMP: 11
SALES (corp-wide): 20.8B **Publicly Held**
SIC: 3674 Semiconductors & related devices
HQ: Avago Technologies U.S. Inc.
1320 Ridder Park Dr
San Jose CA 95131
800 433-8778

(P-18135)
AVAGO TECHNOLOGIES US INC (HQ)
1320 Ridder Park Dr, San Jose
(95131-2313)
P.O. Box 3643, Santa Clara (95055-3643)
PHONE..................................800 433-8778
Hock E Tan, *President*
Bryan Ingram, *Senior VP*
Tze Siong Chong, *Vice Pres*
Mitchell Fields, *Vice Pres*
Philip Gadd, *Vice Pres*
▲ **EMP:** 400
SALES (est): 1.2B
SALES (corp-wide): 20.8B **Publicly Held**
WEB: www.avagotech.com
SIC: 3674 Semiconductor diodes & rectifiers

PA: Broadcom Inc.
1320 Ridder Park Dr
San Jose CA 95131
408 433-8000

(P-18136)
AVALANCHE TECHNOLOGY INC
3450 W Warren Ave, Fremont
(94538-6425)
PHONE..................................510 438-0148
Petro Estakhri, *President*
Yiming Huai, *Vice Pres*
Simon Nguyen, *Vice Pres*
Michael Ofstedahl, *Vice Pres*
Suzanne Marzouk, *Admin Asst*
EMP: 25
SALES (est): 4.4MM **Privately Held**
SIC: 3674 Magnetic bubble memory device

(P-18137)
AVID IDNTIFICATION SYSTEMS INC (PA)
3185 Hamner Ave, Norco (92860-1937)
PHONE..................................951 371-7505
Hannis L Stoddard, *CEO*
Trade Show, *Vice Pres*
Peter Troesch, *Vice Pres*
Mary Metzner, *Administration*
Neil King, *Info Tech Mgr*
▲ **EMP:** 100
SQ FT: 30,000
SALES (est): 14.3MM **Privately Held**
WEB: www.avidplc.com
SIC: 3674 5999 Semiconductors & related devices; pets & pet supplies

(P-18138)
AVOGY INC
677 River Oaks Pkwy, San Jose
(95134-1907)
PHONE..................................408 684-5200
Dinesh Ramanathan, *CEO*
Pierre Lamond, *Ch of Bd*
Isik Kizilyalli, *CEO*
Jeff Shealy, *Vice Pres*
Eve Cohen, *Finance Dir*
EMP: 20
SALES (est): 6.3MM **Privately Held**
SIC: 3674 Semiconductor diodes & rectifiers

(P-18139)
AXIS GROUP INC
1220 Whipple Rd, Union City (94587-2026)
P.O. Box 1192 (94587-1192)
PHONE..................................510 487-7393
Kofi A Tawiah, *President*
EMP: 17
SQ FT: 15,000
SALES (est): 1.5MM **Privately Held**
WEB: www.theaxisgroup.com
SIC: 3674 Semiconductors & related devices

(P-18140)
AXT INC
Also Called: American Etal Technology
4311 Solar Way, Fremont (94538-6389)
PHONE..................................510 683-5900
Maureen Wang, *Manager*
Bob Ochrym, *VP Bus Dvlpt*
EMP: 23
SALES (corp-wide): 102.4MM **Publicly Held**
SIC: 3674 Integrated circuits, semiconductor networks, etc.
PA: Axt, Inc.
4281 Technology Dr
Fremont CA 94538
510 438-4700

(P-18141)
AXT INC (PA)
4281 Technology Dr, Fremont
(94538-6339)
PHONE..................................510 438-4700
Morris S Young, *CEO*
Jesse Chen, *Ch of Bd*
Gary L Fischer, *CFO*
David Chang, *Bd of Directors*
Gary Fischer, *Officer*
▲ **EMP:** 25
SQ FT: 19,467

SALES: 102.4MM **Publicly Held**
WEB: www.axt.com
SIC: 3674 Semiconductors & related devices; integrated circuits, semiconductor networks, etc.; diodes, solid state (germanium, silicon, etc.)

(P-18142)
AZIMUTH INDUSTRIAL CO INC
Also Called: Azimuth Semiconductor Assembly
30593 Un Cy Blvd Ste 110, Union City
(94587)
PHONE..................................510 441-6000
David Lee, *President*
Sandra Lee, *Officer*
Sunny Tseng, *Accountant*
▲ **EMP:** 20
SQ FT: 16,000
SALES (est): 3.5MM **Privately Held**
SIC: 3674 Semiconductors & related devices

(P-18143)
BAE SYSTEMS IMGING SLTIONS INC
1841 Zanker Rd Ste 50, San Jose
(95112-4223)
PHONE..................................408 433-2500
Terry Crimmins, *President*
Victoria Madamba, *Project Mgr*
George Wang, *Engineer*
Bonnie Trifilo, *Director*
Colin Earle, *Manager*
EMP: 120
SQ FT: 60,000
SALES (est): 34.4MM
SALES (corp-wide): 21.6B **Privately Held**
WEB: www.fairchildimaging.com
SIC: 3674 Semiconductors & related devices; computer peripheral equipment
HQ: Bae Systems Information And Electronic Systems Integration Inc.
65 Spit Brook Rd
Nashua NH 03060
603 885-4321

(P-18144)
BAR MANUFACTURING INC
3921 Sandstone Dr Ste 1, El Dorado Hills
(95762-9343)
P.O. Box 4664 (95762-0022)
PHONE..................................916 939-0551
S S Wong, *Ch of Bd*
▲ **EMP:** 68
SALES: 14MM
SALES (corp-wide): 458.3MM **Privately Held**
WEB: www.barmfg.us
SIC: 3674 Semiconductor circuit networks
HQ: Compart Engineering, Inc.
1730 E Philadelphia St
Ontario CA 91761
909 947-6688

(P-18145)
BAYWA RE SOLAR PROJECTS LLC
Also Called: Baywa R.E.renewable Energy
17901 Von Karman Ave # 1050, Irvine
(92614-6297)
PHONE..................................949 398-3915
Jam Attari, *CEO*
David Sanders, *COO*
Gaby Grullon, *Office Mgr*
Tommy Nelson, *Project Mgr*
Gilbert Quintana, *Sales Mgr*
▲ **EMP:** 40 **EST:** 2014
SALES (est): 8.9MM
SALES (corp-wide): 19B **Privately Held**
SIC: 3674 Solar cells
HQ: Baywa R.E. Renewable Energy Gmbh
Arabellastr. 4
Munchen 81925
893 839-320

(P-18146)
BERKELEY DESIGN AUTOMATION INC
46871 Bayside Pkwy, Fremont
(94538-6572)
PHONE..................................408 496-6600
Ravi Subramanian PH D, *President*
Paul Estrada, *COO*
Kelly Perey, *Vice Pres*
Nafees Qureshy, *Vice Pres*

EMP: 25
SQ FT: 25,000
SALES (est): 3MM
SALES (corp-wide): 95B **Privately Held**
WEB: www.berkeley-da.com
SIC: 3674 Integrated circuits, semiconductor networks, etc.
HQ: Mentor Graphics Corporation
8005 Sw Boeckman Rd
Wilsonville OR 97070
503 685-7000

(P-18147)
BIPOLARICS INC
45920 Sentinel Pl, Fremont (94539-6942)
PHONE...........................408 372-7574
Dr Charles Leung, *President*
Colin Levy, *Treasurer*
Jessica Leung, *Controller*
EMP: 50
SALES (est): 7MM **Privately Held**
WEB: www.bipolarics.com
SIC: 3674 3677 Integrated circuits, semiconductor networks, etc.; electronic coils, transformers & other inductors

(P-18148)
BLACK HILLS NANOSYSTEMS CORP
1941 Jackson St 9, Oakland (94612-4600)
PHONE...........................605 341-3641
EMP: 10
SQ FT: 4,000
SALES (est): 790K **Privately Held**
WEB: www.blackhillsnano.com
SIC: 3674

(P-18149)
BLOOM ENERGY CORPORATION (PA)
4353 N 1st St, San Jose (95134-1259)
PHONE...........................408 543-1500
K R Sridhar, *Ch of Bd*
Susan Brennan, *COO*
Randy Furr, *CFO*
Matt Ross, *Chief Mktg Ofcr*
Glen Griffiths, *Exec VP*
▲ EMP: 300
SQ FT: 181,000
SALES: 742MM **Publicly Held**
WEB: www.bloomenergy.com
SIC: 3674 Fuel cells, solid state

(P-18150)
BRIDGELUX INC
46430 Fremont Blvd, Fremont (94538-6469)
PHONE...........................925 583-8400
Tim Lester, *CEO*
David Plumer, *Chief Mktg Ofcr*
David Connors, *Vice Pres*
Brian Cumpston, *Vice Pres*
Long Yang, *Vice Pres*
▲ EMP: 90
SALES (est): 20.5MM **Privately Held**
WEB: www.bridgelux.com
SIC: 3674 Light emitting diodes

(P-18151)
BROADCOM CORPORATION
250 Innovation Dr, San Jose (95134-3390)
PHONE...........................408 922-7000
Carol Barrett, *Branch Mgr*
Ming Lei, *Principal*
Bob McMahon, *Software Engr*
Duong Phan, *Technician*
Rahul Durve, *Design Engr*
EMP: 39
SALES (corp-wide): 20.8B **Publicly Held**
SIC: 3674 Integrated circuits, semiconductor networks, etc.
HQ: Broadcom Corporation
1320 Ridder Park Dr
San Jose CA 95131

(P-18152)
BROADCOM CORPORATION (HQ)
1320 Ridder Park Dr, San Jose (95131-2313)
P.O. Box 57013, Irvine (92619-7013)
PHONE...........................408 433-8000
Hock Tan, *CEO*
Jeff Chung, *Principal*

Charlie Kawwas, *Security Dir*
Michael Kreplik, *Program Mgr*
Henry Samueli, *CTO*
▲ EMP: 277
SALES (est): 3.3B
SALES (corp-wide): 20.8B **Publicly Held**
WEB: www.broadcom.com
SIC: 3674 Integrated circuits, semiconductor networks, etc.
PA: Broadcom Inc.
1320 Ridder Park Dr
San Jose CA 95131
408 433-8000

(P-18153)
BROADCOM CORPORATION
16340 W Bernardo Dr A, San Diego (92127-1802)
PHONE...........................858 385-8800
Bell Philip Andrew, *Branch Mgr*
Marcos Camargo, *Design Engr*
Bruce Kent, *Technical Staff*
WEI Chen, *Engineer*
Kevin Chou, *Engineer*
EMP: 860
SALES (corp-wide): 20.8B **Publicly Held**
WEB: www.broadcom.com
SIC: 3674 Integrated circuits, semiconductor networks, etc.
HQ: Broadcom Corporation
1320 Ridder Park Dr
San Jose CA 95131
-

(P-18154)
BROADCOM INC (PA)
1320 Ridder Park Dr, San Jose (95131-2313)
PHONE...........................408 433-8000
Hock E Tan, *President*
Henry Samueli, *Ch of Bd*
Thomas H Krause Jr, *CFO*
Boon Ooi, *Treasurer*
Mark D Brazeal,
EMP: 17
SALES: 20.8B **Publicly Held**
SIC: 3674 Semiconductor diodes & rectifiers

(P-18155)
BROADLIGHT INC
2901 Tasman Dr Ste 218, Santa Clara (95054-1138)
PHONE...........................408 982-4210
Raanan Gewirtzman, *CEO*
Dror Heldenberg, *CFO*
Didi Ivancovsky, *Vice Pres*
Eli Weitz, *CTO*
EMP: 11
SALES (est): 2.6MM
SALES (corp-wide): 20.8B **Publicly Held**
WEB: www.broadlight.com
SIC: 3674 Semiconductors & related devices
HQ: Broadcom Corporation
1320 Ridder Park Dr
San Jose CA 95131

(P-18156)
CAMTEK USA INC
48389 Fremont Blvd # 112, Fremont (94538-6558)
PHONE...........................510 624-9905
Cathy Hamilton, *Principal*
Amy Zhong, *Treasurer*
Tommy Weiss, *Vice Pres*
EMP: 28
SQ FT: 10,000
SALES (est): 4.8MM
SALES (corp-wide): 26.6MM **Privately Held**
WEB: www.camtekusa.com
SIC: 3674 Integrated circuits, semiconductor networks, etc.
PA: Camtek Ltd
Ramat Gavriel Ind Zone Migdal Ha'emek
Migdal Haemek
460 481-00

(P-18157)
CANADIAN SOLAR (USA) INC
3000 Oak Rd Ste 400, Walnut Creek (94597-2051)
PHONE...........................925 807-7499

Shawn Qu, *CEO*
Robert Patterson, *President*
Guangchun Zhang, *COO*
Michael G Potter, *CFO*
Yan Zhuang, *Senior VP*
◆ EMP: 10
SQ FT: 2,000
SALES (est): 5.5MM
SALES (corp-wide): 3.7B **Privately Held**
SIC: 3674 Solar cells
PA: Canadian Solar Inc
545 Speedvale Ave W
Guelph ON N1K 1
519 837-1881

(P-18158)
CAVIUM LLC (HQ)
Also Called: Cavium, Inc.
5488 Marvell Ln, Santa Clara (95054-3606)
P.O. Box 67151, Scotts Valley (95067-7151)
PHONE...........................408 222-2500
Jean Hu, *President*
Sanjay Mehrotra, *Bd of Directors*
Guy Hutchison, *Assoc VP*
Raghib Hussain, *Exec VP*
Brent Carlson, *Vice Pres*
EMP: 265
SALES: 984MM **Privately Held**
WEB: www.cavium.com
SIC: 3674 Semiconductors & related devices

(P-18159)
CAVIUM NETWORKS INTL INC (DH)
2315 N 1st St, San Jose (95131-1010)
PHONE...........................650 625-7000
Syed Ali, *CEO*
Rakesh Bindlish, *General Mgr*
Raj Singh, *General Mgr*
Iqbal Rana, *IT/INT Sup*
Len Cabeceiras, *Tech Recruiter*
EMP: 12
SALES (est): 8MM **Privately Held**
WEB: www.cavium.com
SIC: 3674 Semiconductor diodes & rectifiers

(P-18160)
CELESTICA LLC
5325 Hellyer Ave, San Jose (95138-1013)
PHONE...........................408 574-6000
Joel Bustos, *General Mgr*
Shlomo Bibas, *Vice Pres*
Arnold Villanueva, *Engineer*
Tom Wappes, *Engineer*
EMP: 250
SALES (corp-wide): 23.7B **Privately Held**
SIC: 3674 Semiconductors & related devices
HQ: Celestica Llc
11 Continental Blvd # 103
Merrimack NH 03054

(P-18161)
CHRONTEL INC (PA)
2210 Otoole Ave Ste 100, San Jose (95131-1300)
PHONE...........................408 383-9328
Bruce Wooley, *Ch of Bd*
David C SOO, *President*
James Lin, *CFO*
Demonder Chan, *Officer*
Teh Lee, *Office Mgr*
EMP: 150
SQ FT: 40,000
SALES (est): 30.2MM **Privately Held**
WEB: www.chrontel.com
SIC: 3674 8711 Integrated circuits, semiconductor networks, etc.; engineering services

(P-18162)
CIRRUS LOGIC INC
45630 Northport Loop E, Fremont (94538-6477)
PHONE...........................510 226-1204
Halappa Ravindra, *Branch Mgr*
David D French, *President*
EMP: 100
SQ FT: 57,952

SALES (corp-wide): 1.1B **Publicly Held**
WEB: www.cirrus.com
SIC: 3674 7371 Integrated circuits, semiconductor networks, etc.; custom computer programming services
PA: Cirrus Logic, Inc.
800 W 6th St
Austin TX 78701
512 851-4000

(P-18163)
CISC SEMICONDUCTOR CORP
800 W El Camino Real, Mountain View (94040-2567)
PHONE...........................847 553-4204
Markus Pistauer, *President*
Debangana Mukherjee, *Director*
EMP: 10
SALES (est): 779.8K **Privately Held**
SIC: 3674 Integrated circuits, semiconductor networks, etc.

(P-18164)
CLARIPHY COMMUNICATIONS INC (HQ)
7585 Irvine Center Dr # 100, Irvine (92618-2985)
PHONE...........................949 861-3074
Nariman Yousefi, *President*
William J Ruehle, *CFO*
Brandon Ferguson, *Office Admin*
Norman L Swenson, *CTO*
EMP: 91
SALES (est): 35.9MM
SALES (corp-wide): 294.4MM **Publicly Held**
WEB: www.clariphy.com
SIC: 3674 Integrated circuits, semiconductor networks, etc.
PA: Inphi Corporation
2953 Bunker Hill Ln # 300
Santa Clara CA 95054
408 217-7300

(P-18165)
CM MANUFACTURING INC (HQ)
6321 San Ignacio Ave, San Jose (95119-1202)
PHONE...........................408 284-7200
Chet Farris, *CEO*
Vineet Dharmadhikari, *COO*
Bob Beisner, *Vice Pres*
Howard Lee, *Vice Pres*
Isabelle Roch-Jeune, *Regl Sales Mgr*
▲ EMP: 128
SALES (est): 68.3MM **Privately Held**
WEB: www.stion.com
SIC: 3674 Semiconductors & related devices

(P-18166)
CMOS SENSOR INC
20045 Stevens Creek Blvd 1a, Cupertino (95014-2355)
PHONE...........................408 366-2898
Bill Wang, *President*
Michael Chern, *Vice Pres*
Simon Lin, *Engineer*
Shirley Cheng, *Finance Mgr*
EMP: 10
SALES: 2.2MM **Privately Held**
SIC: 3674 Semiconductors & related devices

(P-18167)
CNEX LABS INC
2880 Stevens Creek Blvd # 300, San Jose (95128-4608)
PHONE...........................408 695-1045
Alan Armstrong, *CEO*
Joe Defranco, *Vice Pres*
Ronnie Huang, *Vice Pres*
Bernie Sardinha, *VP Opers*
Ted Lam, *Director*
EMP: 50 EST: 2013
SALES: 10MM **Privately Held**
SIC: 3674 Semiconductors & related devices

(P-18168)
COLLECTION DEVELOPMENT
Also Called: Collection Led
710 Nogales St, City of Industry (91748-1306)
PHONE...........................909 595-8588
▲ EMP: 12

▲ = Import ▼=Export
◆ =Import/Export

SALES: 950K **Privately Held**
SIC: 3674

(P-18169)
COMMNEXUS SAN DIEGO
4225 Executive Sq # 1110, La Jolla
(92037-9122)
PHONE...................................888 926-3987
Rory Moore, *Principal*
EMP: 17 EST: 2010
SALES: 1.2MM **Privately Held**
SIC: 3674 Semiconductor circuit networks

(P-18170)
COMPONENT RE-ENGINEERING INC
Also Called: C. R. C
3508 Bassett St, Santa Clara (95054-2704)
PHONE...................................408 562-4000
Brent Elliot, *President*
Frank Balma, *COO*
EMP: 12
SALES (est): 4.7MM **Privately Held**
SIC: 3674 Integrated circuits, semiconductor networks, etc.

(P-18171)
COMPUGRAPHICS USA INC (HQ)
43455 Osgood Rd, Fremont (94539-5609)
PHONE...................................510 249-2600
Lawrence Amon, *President*
Joe Lister, *Database Admin*
Laurie Sullivan, *Manager*
Cathy Widner, *Manager*
Narciso Cruz, *Supervisor*
EMP: 56
SQ FT: 25,000
SALES (est): 11MM
SALES (corp-wide): 1.4B **Privately Held**
SIC: 3674 Integrated circuits, semiconductor networks, etc.
PA: Vectra Co.
120 S Central Ave Ste 200
Saint Louis MO 63105
314 797-8600

(P-18172)
CONCEPT SYSTEMS MFG INC
2047 Zanker Rd, San Jose (95131-2107)
PHONE...................................408 855-8595
Richard Diehl, *President*
Christie Shannon, *CFO*
Perry Hough, *Engineer*
▲ EMP: 15
SALES (est): 3.8MM **Privately Held**
SIC: 3674 Semiconductors & related devices

(P-18173)
CONDOR RELIABILITY SERVICES
2175 De La Cruz Blvd # 8, Santa Clara
(95050-3036)
PHONE...................................408 486-9600
Punam Patel, *President*
EMP: 120 EST: 1980
SQ FT: 5,000
SALES (est): 11.3MM **Privately Held**
SIC: 3674 8999 8734 8731 Semiconductors & related devices; weather information services; testing laboratories; commercial physical research

(P-18174)
CONEXANT HOLDINGS INC
4000 Macarthur Blvd, Newport Beach
(92660-2558)
PHONE...................................415 983-2706
David Dominik, *CEO*
Carl Mills, *CFO*
Saleel Awsare, *Vice Pres*
Nic Rossi, *Vice Pres*
John Knoll, *Admin Sec*
EMP: 600
SALES (est): 30.2MM **Privately Held**
SIC: 3674 5065 Semiconductors & related devices; semiconductor devices

(P-18175)
CONEXANT SYSTEMS LLC (HQ)
1901 Main St Ste 300, Irvine (92614-0512)
PHONE...................................949 483-4600
Jan Johannessen, *CEO*
EMP: 45
SQ FT: 140,000

SALES (est): 50.4MM
SALES (corp-wide): 1.6B **Publicly Held**
SIC: 3674 5065 Semiconductors & related devices; semiconductor devices
PA: Synaptics Incorporated
1251 Mckay Dr
San Jose CA 95131
408 904-1100

(P-18176)
CONEXANT SYSTEMS WORLDWIDE INC
4000 Macarthur Blvd, Newport Beach
(92660-2558)
PHONE...................................949 483-4600
Sailesh Chittipeddi, *President*
Gerard Carrillo, *Controller*
EMP: 86
SALES (est): 14.4MM **Privately Held**
SIC: 3674 Semiconductors & related devices

(P-18177)
CONTECH SOLUTIONS INCORPORATED
631 Montague St, San Leandro
(94577-4323)
PHONE...................................510 357-7900
Afshin Nouri, *President*
Mehran Jafarcadeh, *Vice Pres*
Jafarzaden Mehran, *Director*
EMP: 21
SQ FT: 4,000
SALES: 2.6MM **Privately Held**
WEB: www.contechsolutions.com
SIC: 3674 Semiconductors & related devices

(P-18178)
CONVERGENT MOBILE INC
870 Knight St, Sonoma (95476-7258)
P.O. Box 269 (95476-0269)
PHONE...................................707 343-1200
Mickey Breen, *CEO*
Tom Conery, *CEO*
EMP: 13 EST: 2007
SALES (est): 1.3MM **Privately Held**
SIC: 3674 Semiconductors & related devices

(P-18179)
COOPER MICROELECTRONICS INC
Also Called: CMI
1671 Reynolds Ave, Irvine (92614-5709)
PHONE...................................949 553-8352
Kenneth B Cooper III, *President*
Lily Cooper, *Vice Pres*
▲ EMP: 37
SQ FT: 10,000
SALES (est): 5.9MM **Privately Held**
WEB: www.coopermicro.com
SIC: 3674 7371 Semiconductors & related devices; custom computer programming services

(P-18180)
CORPORATECOUCH
Also Called: Corp Couch
260 Vicente St, San Francisco
(94127-1331)
PHONE...................................415 312-6078
Farzaneh Amini, *CEO*
Fatemh Amini, *Admin Sec*
EMP: 25 EST: 2011
SALES (est): 2MM **Privately Held**
SIC: 3674 Integrated circuits, semiconductor networks, etc.

(P-18181)
CORSAIR MEMORY INC
47100 Bayside Pkwy, Fremont
(94538-6563)
PHONE...................................510 657-8747
Andrew J Paul, *President*
Ronald Van Veen, *Vice Pres*
Don Lieberman, *CTO*
▲ EMP: 150
SQ FT: 44,000
SALES (est): 41.5MM **Privately Held**
WEB: www.corsairmicro.com
SIC: 3674 7373 8731 Memories, solid state; computer integrated systems design; computer (hardware) development

PA: Corsair Components, Inc.
47100 Bayside Pkwy
Fremont CA 94538

(P-18182)
CORTINA SYSTEMS INC (HQ)
2953 Bunker Hill Ln # 300, Santa Clara
(95054-1131)
PHONE...................................408 481-2300
Amir Nayyerhabibi, *President*
Bruce Margtson, *CFO*
EMP: 120
SQ FT: 41,645
SALES (est): 46.7MM
SALES (corp-wide): 294.4MM **Publicly Held**
WEB: www.cortina-systems.com
SIC: 3674 Integrated circuits, semiconductor networks, etc.
PA: Inphi Corporation
2953 Bunker Hill Ln # 300
Santa Clara CA 95054
408 217-7300

(P-18183)
COSEMI TECHNOLOGIES INC (PA)
1370 Reynolds Ave Ste 100, Irvine
(92614-5504)
PHONE...................................949 623-9816
Wenbin Jiang, *CTO*
EMP: 15
SQ FT: 3,000
SALES (est): 3.9MM **Privately Held**
WEB: www.cosemi.com
SIC: 3674 Light sensitive devices

(P-18184)
COVE20 LLC
Also Called: Kbc Networks USA
15 Brookline, Aliso Viejo (92656-1461)
PHONE...................................949 297-4930
Steve Kuntz, *President*
▲ EMP: 11
SALES (est): 1.3MM **Privately Held**
SIC: 3674 3663 Integrated circuits, semiconductor networks, etc.; radio & TV communications equipment

(P-18185)
CREATIVE INTGRATED SYSTEMS INC
Also Called: CIS
1700 E Garry Ave Ste 112, Santa Ana
(92705-5828)
PHONE...................................949 261-6577
Jim Komarek, *President*
Shiro Fujioka, *Vice Pres*
EMP: 25
SQ FT: 4,500
SALES: 1MM **Privately Held**
WEB: www.cisdesign.com
SIC: 3674 7371 3672 3661 Microcircuits, integrated (semiconductor); custom computer programming services; printed circuit boards; telephone & telegraph apparatus; electrical or electronic engineering; computer integrated systems design

(P-18186)
CROSSBAR INC
3200 Patrick Henry Dr # 110, Santa Clara
(95054-1865)
PHONE...................................408 884-0281
George Minassian, *CEO*
Mike Holland, *Vice Pres*
WEI Lu, *Vice Pres*
Peter Deutschman, *Surgery Dir*
Ashish Pancholy, *General Mgr*
EMP: 20
SALES (est): 3.6MM **Privately Held**
SIC: 3674 Semiconductors & related devices

(P-18187)
CSDR INTERNATIONAL INC
7701 Woodley Ave, Van Nuys
(91406-1732)
PHONE...................................844 330-0664
Randall H Roth, *President*
EMP: 10
SQ FT: 1,000
SALES (est): 27.3K **Privately Held**
SIC: 3674 Solar cells

(P-18188)
CYPRESS SEMICONDUCTOR CORP
195 Champion Ct Bldg 2, San Jose
(95134-1709)
PHONE...................................408 943-2600
Emmanuel Hernandez, *Principal*
EMP: 13
SQ FT: 60,370
SALES (corp-wide): 2.4B **Publicly Held**
WEB: www.cypress.com
SIC: 3674 Integrated circuits, semiconductor networks, etc.
PA: Cypress Semiconductor Corporation
198 Champion Ct
San Jose CA 95134
408 943-2600

(P-18189)
CYPRESS SEMICONDUCTOR CORP (PA)
198 Champion Ct, San Jose (95134-1709)
PHONE...................................408 943-2600
Hassane El-Khoury, *President*
Thad Trent, *CFO*
Christopher Cook, *Chief Mktg Ofcr*
Michael Balow, *Exec VP*
Sabbas Daniel, *Exec VP*
◆ EMP: 1149
SQ FT: 171,370
SALES: 2.4B **Publicly Held**
WEB: www.cypress.com
SIC: 3674 Semiconductors & related devices; integrated circuits, semiconductor networks, etc.; random access memory (RAM); read-only memory (ROM)

(P-18190)
CYPRESS SEMICONDUCTOR INTL INC (PA)
4001 N 1st St, San Jose (95134-1503)
PHONE...................................408 943-2600
Neil Weiss, *Vice Pres*
Kazu Yamada, *Vice Pres*
Anil Kumar, *Engineer*
Toan Ong, *Engineer*
Jennifer Sirrine, *Engineer*
EMP: 26
SALES (est): 13.4MM **Privately Held**
SIC: 3674 Semiconductors & related devices

(P-18191)
D-TEK MANUFACTURING
3245 Woodward Ave, Santa Clara
(95054-2626)
PHONE...................................408 588-1574
Dung Nguyen, *President*
Thanh L Dang, *Vice Pres*
EMP: 20 EST: 2010
SQ FT: 5,000
SALES (est): 5.7MM **Privately Held**
SIC: 3674 Semiconductors & related devices

(P-18192)
DATA CIRCLE INC
3333 Michelson Dr Ste 735, Irvine
(92612-7679)
PHONE...................................949 260-6569
Steve Oren, *CEO*
EMP: 13
SQ FT: 12,000
SALES (est): 1.2MM **Privately Held**
WEB: www.datacircle.com
SIC: 3674 Integrated circuits, semiconductor networks, etc.

(P-18193)
DAYLIGHT SOLUTIONS INC (DH)
Also Called: Drs Daylight Solutions
16465 Via Esprillo # 100, San Diego
(92127-1701)
PHONE...................................858 432-7500
Timothy Day, *CEO*
Paul Larson, *President*
Michelle Molina, *Office Mgr*
Enrique Lopez, *Research*
Jose Urbina, *Buyer*
EMP: 166
SALES (est): 60.2MM
SALES (corp-wide): 9.2B **Privately Held**
WEB: www.daylightsolutions.net
SIC: 3674 5084 Molecular devices, solid state; instruments & control equipment

P
R
O
D
U
C
T
S

&

S
V
C
S

HQ: Leonardo Drs, Inc.
2345 Crystal Dr Ste 1000
Arlington VA 22202
703 416-8000

(P-18194)
DAYSTAR TECHNOLOGIES INC
1010 S Milpitas Blvd, Milpitas
(95035-6307)
PHONE..........................408 582-7100
Tina Carrillo, *Branch Mgr*
EMP: 60
SALES (corp-wide): 10.4MM **Publicly Held**
WEB: www.daystartech.com
SIC: 3674 Solar cells
PA: Daystar Technologies Inc.
3556 Alvarado Niles Rd S
Union City CA 94587
408 582-7100

(P-18195)
DIALOG SEMICONDUCTOR INC (DH)
2560 Mission College Blvd # 110, Santa Clara (95054-1217)
P.O. Box 2369, Clifton NJ (07015-2369)
PHONE..........................408 845-8500
Jalal Bagherli, *CEO*
Karim Arabi, *Vice Pres*
Andrew Austin, *Vice Pres*
Jim Caravella, *Vice Pres*
Christophe Chene, *Vice Pres*
EMP: 28
SALES (est): 23MM
SALES (corp-wide): 1.4B **Privately Held**
SIC: 3674 Semiconductors & related devices
HQ: Dialog Semiconductor Gmbh
Neue Str. 95
Kirchheim Unter Teck 73230
702 180-50

(P-18196)
DNP AMERICA LLC
2099 Gateway Pl Ste 490, San Jose (95110-1087)
PHONE..........................408 616-1200
Yasuhiro Yamamura, *Principal*
EMP: 12 **Privately Held**
SIC: 3674 5084 Semiconductors & related devices; industrial machinery & equipment
HQ: Dnp America, Llc
335 Madison Ave Fl 3
New York NY 10017
212 503-1060

(P-18197)
DONGBU ELECTRONICS CO
Also Called: Dongbu Hi-Tech
2953 Bunker Hill Ln # 206, Santa Clara (95054-1131)
PHONE..........................408 330-0330
B J Yoon, *Manager*
EMP: 13 **Privately Held**
SIC: 3674 Wafers (semiconductor devices)

(P-18198)
DPA LABS INC
Also Called: Dpa Components International
2251 Ward Ave, Simi Valley (93065-7556)
PHONE..........................805 581-9200
Douglas Young, *President*
Phil Young, *Vice Pres*
Philip Young, *Vice Pres*
Steve Green, *Executive*
Hector Aponte, *Technician*
EMP: 50
SQ FT: 38,000
SALES (est): 11.1MM **Privately Held**
WEB: www.dpaci.com
SIC: 3674 8734 Semiconductors & related devices; testing laboratories

(P-18199)
DRS ADVANCED ISR LLC
10600 Valley View St, Cypress (90630-4833)
PHONE..........................714 220-3800
Jim Womble, *Branch Mgr*
Gary Roberts, *General Mgr*
Cathie Meister, *Info Tech Mgr*
EMP: 200

SALES (corp-wide): 9.2B **Privately Held**
SIC: 3674 8731 Infrared sensors, solid state; commercial physical research
HQ: Drs Icas, Llc
2601 Mission Point Blvd
Beavercreek OH 45431
-

(P-18200)
DRS NTWORK IMAGING SYSTEMS LLC
Also Called: Drs Snsors Trgting Systems Inc
10600 Valley View St, Cypress (90630-4833)
PHONE..........................714 220-3800
Shawn Black,
Timothy Harrison, *President*
Kevin Balsley, *Webmaster*
EMP: 100 EST: 2009
SALES: 34.4MM
SALES (corp-wide): 9.2B **Privately Held**
SIC: 3674 8731 Infrared sensors, solid state; commercial physical research
HQ: Leonardo Drs, Inc.
2345 Crystal Dr Ste 1000
Arlington VA 22202
703 416-8000

(P-18201)
DSP GROUP INC (PA)
2055 Gateway Pl Ste 480, San Jose (95110-1019)
PHONE..........................408 986-4300
Ofer Elyakim, *CEO*
Dror Levy, *CFO*
Naama Luquer, *Vice Pres*
Eric Stauffer, *Vice Pres*
Wayne Sun, *Business Dir*
EMP: 71
SQ FT: 1,723
SALES: 117.4MM **Publicly Held**
WEB: www.dspg.com
SIC: 3674 7371 Integrated circuits, semiconductor networks, etc.; computer software development

(P-18202)
DYNAMIC ENGINEERING
150 Dubois St Ste C, Santa Cruz (95060-2114)
PHONE..........................831 457-8891
Keith V Leisses, *CEO*
Vicki C Leisses, *Vice Pres*
▼ EMP: 12
SQ FT: 4,000
SALES (est): 3MM **Privately Held**
SIC: 3674 8711 5734 Integrated circuits, semiconductor networks, etc.; engineering services; computer peripheral equipment

(P-18203)
DYNAMIC INTGRTED SOLUTIONS LLC
1710 Fortune Dr, San Jose (95131-1744)
PHONE..........................408 727-3400
EMP: 13 **Privately Held**
SIC: 3674 Semiconductors & related devices
PA: Dynamic Integrated Solutions Llc
3964 Rivermark Plz # 104
Santa Clara CA 95054

(P-18204)
DYNAMIC INTGRTED SOLUTIONS LLC (PA)
3964 Rivermark Plz # 104, Santa Clara (95054-4155)
PHONE..........................408 727-3400
David Diep,
EMP: 32
SALES (est): 8.6MM **Privately Held**
SIC: 3674 Semiconductors & related devices

(P-18205)
E/G ELECTRO-GRAPH INC
Also Called: Electrograph
1491 Poinsettia Ave # 138, Vista (92081-8541)
PHONE..........................760 438-9090
Mike Reilly, *President*
Mary Poniktera, *CFO*
EMP: 60

SQ FT: 24,500
SALES (est): 11.4MM
SALES (corp-wide): 242.1K **Privately Held**
WEB: www.egraph.com
SIC: 3674 Semiconductor diodes & rectifiers
HQ: Plansee Se
Metallwerk Plansee-StraBe 71
Reutte 6600
567 260-00

(P-18206)
EASIC CORPORATION
3940 Freedom Cir 100, Santa Clara (95054-1204)
PHONE..........................408 855-9200
Ronnie Vasishta, *President*
Kaushik Banerjee, *President*
Patrick Little, *President*
Richard Heye, *COO*
Larry Borras, *CFO*
EMP: 30
SQ FT: 12,195
SALES (est): 8.2MM **Privately Held**
SIC: 3674 Semiconductors & related devices

(P-18207)
EDGE COMPUTE INC
5201 Great America Pkwy, Santa Clara (95054-1122)
PHONE..........................408 209-0368
Vinay Ravuri, *CEO*
EMP: 10
SALES (est): 398.2K **Privately Held**
SIC: 3674 Semiconductors & related devices

(P-18208)
EDISON OPTO USA CORPORATION
1809 Excise Ave Ste 201, Ontario (91761-8558)
PHONE..........................909 284-9710
Wen-Jui Cheng, *CEO*
Adrian Cheng, *Executive*
▲ EMP: 12
SALES (est): 1.2MM **Privately Held**
SIC: 3674 Light emitting diodes

(P-18209)
EG SYSTEMS LLC (PA)
Also Called: Electroglas
6200 Village Pkwy, Dublin (94568-3004)
PHONE..........................510 324-0126
Raj Kaul, *Mng Member*
▲ EMP: 24
SALES (est): 30.4MM **Privately Held**
SIC: 3674 Semiconductors & related devices

(P-18210)
ELEKTRON TECHNOLOGY CORP (HQ)
11849 Telegraph Rd, Santa Fe Springs (90670-3716)
PHONE..........................760 343-3650
John Wilson, *President*
Charlie Fixa, *Vice Pres*
Paul Thatcher, *Project Engr*
Chris Moodie, *Engineer*
Scott Jensen, *Service Dir*
◆ EMP: 10 EST: 1966
SALES (est): 1.7MM
SALES (corp-wide): 42.3MM **Privately Held**
WEB: www.arcolectric.com
SIC: 3674 3613 3648 3641 Semiconductors & related devices; switches, electric power except snap, push button, etc.; lighting equipment; electric lamps
PA: Checkit Plc
Broers Building
Cambridge CAMBS CB3 0
122 337-1000

(P-18211)
ELEMENTCXI
25 E Trimble Rd, San Jose (95131-1108)
PHONE..........................408 935-8090
EMP: 20
SALES (est): 2.4MM **Privately Held**
WEB: www.elementcxi.com
SIC: 3674

(P-18212)
EMCORE CORPORATION
8674 Thornton Ave, Newark (94560-3330)
PHONE..........................510 896-2139
EMP: 13
SALES (corp-wide): 174.7MM **Publicly Held**
SIC: 3674
PA: Emcore Corporation
2015 Chestnut St
Alhambra CA 91803
626 293-3400

(P-18213)
EMCORE CORPORATION (PA)
2015 Chestnut St, Alhambra (91803-1542)
PHONE..........................626 293-3400
Jeffrey Rittichier, *CEO*
Gerald J Fine, *Ch of Bd*
Jikun Kim, *CFO*
Albert Lu, *Senior VP*
David Wojciechowski, *VP Sales*
▲ EMP: 230
SQ FT: 75,000
SALES: 85.6MM **Publicly Held**
WEB: www.emcore.com
SIC: 3674 3559 Integrated circuits, semiconductor networks, etc.; metal oxide silicon (MOS) devices; wafers (semiconductor devices); semiconductor manufacturing machinery

(P-18214)
EMCORE CORPORATION
Emcore-Ortel Division
2015 Chestnut St, Alhambra (91803-1542)
PHONE..........................626 293-3400
Hone Hu, *Vice Pres*
EMP: 175
SALES (corp-wide): 85.6MM **Publicly Held**
WEB: www.emcore.com
SIC: 3674 Semiconductors & related devices
PA: Emcore Corporation
2015 Chestnut St
Alhambra CA 91803
626 293-3400

(P-18215)
EMISENSE TECHNOLOGIES LLC (DH)
Also Called: Emisense CA
999 Corporate Dr Ste 100, Ladera Ranch (92694-2149)
PHONE..........................949 502-8440
Patrick Thompson, *CEO*
Mary Brooks, *Admin Asst*
Joe Fitzpatrick, *Engineer*
EMP: 11
SALES (est): 783.8K
SALES (corp-wide): 407.6MM **Privately Held**
SIC: 3674 Radiation sensors
HQ: Coorstek Sensors, Llc
2453 Riverside Pkwy
Grand Junction CO 81505
303 271-7000

(P-18216)
ENCOMPASS DIST SVCS LLC
Also Called: EDS
3502 Mars Way Ste 161, Tracy (95377-8002)
PHONE..........................925 249-0988
Bob Swor, *President*
▲ EMP: 12
SQ FT: 3,500
SALES (est): 1.8MM **Privately Held**
SIC: 3674 Silicon wafers, chemically doped

(P-18217)
ENDURA TECHNOLOGIES LLC
7310 Miramar Rd Fl 5, San Diego (92126-4222)
P.O. Box 928769 (92192-8769)
PHONE..........................858 412-2135
Massih Tayebi, *CEO*
EMP: 13
SQ FT: 55,000
SALES (est): 1MM **Privately Held**
SIC: 3674 Microcircuits, integrated (semiconductor)

▲ = Import ▼=Export
◆ =Import/Export

(P-18218)
ENGINEERED OUTSOURCE SOLUTIONS
557 E California Ave, Sunnyvale (94086-5147)
PHONE..............................408 617-2800
Lance Nelson, *CEO*
Scott Mobley, *President*
EMP: 23
SQ FT: 44,000
SALES (est): 5.7MM **Privately Held**
WEB: www.engrsolutions.com
SIC: 3674 Computer logic modules

(P-18219)
ENPHASE ENERGY INC (PA)
47281 Bayside Pkwy, Fremont (94363-6517)
PHONE..............................707 774-7000
Badrinarayanan, *CEO*
Jeff McNeil, *COO*
Eric Branderiz, *CFO*
Humberto Garcia, *CFO*
David Ranhoff, *Ch Credit Ofcr*
▲ **EMP:** 230
SQ FT: 100,000
SALES: 316.1MM **Publicly Held**
WEB: www.enphaseenergy.com
SIC: 3674 Semiconductors & related devices

(P-18220)
ENSPHERE SOLUTIONS INC
2870 Briarwood Dr, San Jose (95125-5020)
PHONE..............................408 598-2441
Hessam Mohajeri, *President*
Emad Afifi, *Vice Pres*
EMP: 14
SALES (est): 2.1MM **Privately Held**
SIC: 3674 Semiconductors & related devices

(P-18221)
ENTROPIC COMMUNICATIONS LLC (HQ)
5966 La Place Ct Ste 100, Carlsbad (92008-8830)
PHONE..............................858 768-3600
Kishore Seendripu, *President*
Andrew Chartrand, *President*
Ted Tewksbury, *President*
Adam Spice, *Treasurer*
William R Bradford, *Senior VP*
▲ **EMP:** 50
SQ FT: 90,000
SALES (est): 35.5MM
SALES (corp-wide): 385MM **Publicly Held**
WEB: www.entropic.com
SIC: 3674 Semiconductor circuit networks; prepackaged software
PA: Maxlinear, Inc.
    5966 La Place Ct Ste 100
    Carlsbad CA 92008
    760 692-0711

(P-18222)
ENVIRON-CLEAN TECHNOLOGY INC
Also Called: Environ Clean Technology
1710 Ringwood Ave, San Jose (95131-1711)
PHONE..............................408 487-1770
Christopher Tracey, *Manager*
EMP: 16
SALES (corp-wide): 215.9MM **Privately Held**
SIC: 3674 Semiconductors & related devices
HQ: Environ-Clean Technology Inc
    3844 E University Dr # 2
    Phoenix AZ 85034
    602 438-9131

(P-18223)
EOPLLY USA INC
1670 S Amphlett Blvd # 140, San Mateo (94402-2533)
PHONE..............................650 225-9400
EMP: 10 **EST:** 2012
SALES (est): 1.2MM **Privately Held**
SIC: 3674

(P-18224)
EPSON ELECTRONICS AMERICA INC (DH)
214 Devcon Dr, San Jose (95112-4210)
PHONE..............................408 922-0200
Koji Abe, *President*
Craig Hodowski, *Admin Sec*
Stevi Sterns, *Marketing Staff*
▲ **EMP:** 32
SQ FT: 28,000
SALES (est): 12.3MM **Privately Held**
SIC: 3674 5065 8731 Semiconductors & related devices; electronic parts & equipment; commercial physical research

(P-18225)
ESILICON CORPORATION (PA)
2130 Gold St Ste 100, Alviso (95002-3700)
PHONE..............................408 635-6300
Seth Neiman, *Ch of Bd*
Jens Andersen, *President*
Jack Harding, *President*
Hugh Durdan, *COO*
Dennis Hollenbeck, *COO*
EMP: 125
SALES (est): 57.8MM **Privately Held**
WEB: www.esilicon.com
SIC: 3674 Integrated circuits, semiconductor networks, etc.; hybrid integrated circuits

(P-18226)
ESS TECHNOLOGY INC (HQ)
237 S Hillview Dr, Milpitas (95035-5417)
PHONE..............................408 643-8818
Robert L Blair, *President*
Robert Plachno, *President*
John A Marsh, *CFO*
Dan Christman, *Chief Mktg Ofcr*
Peter Frith, *Officer*
▲ **EMP:** 135
SQ FT: 35,000
SALES (est): 31MM
SALES (corp-wide): 14.4MM **Privately Held**
WEB: www.esstech.com
SIC: 3674 Microcircuits, integrated (semiconductor); semiconductor circuit networks
PA: Imperium Partners Group, Llc
    509 Madison Ave
    New York NY 10022
    212 433-1360

(P-18227)
ESSEX ELECTRONICS INC
1130 Mark Ave, Carpinteria (93013-2918)
PHONE..............................805 684-7601
Stewart Frisch, *Ch of Bd*
Garrett Kaufman, *President*
Fred Zimmermann, *President*
Jesse Moore, *CEO*
Dean Benjamin, *Vice Pres*
▲ **EMP:** 23
SQ FT: 7,000
SALES (est): 4.5MM **Privately Held**
WEB: www.keyless.com
SIC: 3674 Semiconductors & related devices

(P-18228)
ETD PRECISION CERAMICS CORP
580 Charcot Ave, San Jose (95131-2201)
PHONE..............................408 577-0405
Thanh Duong, *President*
EMP: 10
SQ FT: 7,000
SALES (est): 1.8MM **Privately Held**
SIC: 3674 Semiconductors & related devices

(P-18229)
EVERGREEN AVIONICS INC (PA)
Also Called: Evergreen Systems Intl
880 Calle Plano Ste J, Camarillo (93012-8573)
PHONE..............................805 445-6492
Robert Hulle, *President*
Linda Magallanes, *Vice Pres*
EMP: 12
SQ FT: 6,500

SALES (est): 1.5MM **Privately Held**
WEB: www.trackballs.com
SIC: 3674 Semiconductors & related devices

(P-18230)
EXAR CORPORATION (HQ)
1060 Rincon Cir, San Jose (95131-1325)
PHONE..............................669 265-6100
Ryan A Benton, *CEO*
Keith Tainsky, *CFO*
Ronald W Guire, *Exec VP*
Sherry Lin,
Jessica Wu, *Admin Sec*
EMP: 163 **EST:** 1971
SQ FT: 151,000
SALES: 149.3MM
SALES (corp-wide): 385MM **Publicly Held**
WEB: www.exar.com
SIC: 3674 Integrated circuits, semiconductor networks, etc.; metal oxide silicon (MOS) devices; microcircuits, integrated (semiconductor)
PA: Maxlinear, Inc.
    5966 La Place Ct Ste 100
    Carlsbad CA 92008
    760 692-0711

(P-18231)
EXAR CORPORATION
S I P E X
48760 Kato Rd, Fremont (94538-7312)
PHONE..............................408 927-9975
Jim Donegan, *Branch Mgr*
Thomas Werner, *COO*
Ray Wallin, *CFO*
Thomas Hollman, *Division VP*
David Matteucci, *Division VP*
EMP: 280
SALES (corp-wide): 385MM **Publicly Held**
WEB: www.sipex.com
SIC: 3674 Semiconductors & related devices
HQ: Exar Corporation
    1060 Rincon Cir
    San Jose CA 95131
    669 265-6100

(P-18232)
EXCLARA INC
4701 Patrick Henry Dr # 1701, Santa Clara (95054-1819)
PHONE..............................408 329-9319
Shrichand Dodani, *President*
Stephanie Leung, *CFO*
▲ **EMP:** 20 **EST:** 2006
SALES (est): 2.1MM **Privately Held**
SIC: 3674 3677 Semiconductors & related devices; transformers power supply, electronic type

(P-18233)
FAIRCHILD SEMICDTR INTL INC (HQ)
1272 Borregas Ave, Sunnyvale (94089-1310)
PHONE..............................408 822-2000
Keith D Jackson, *President*
William A Schromm, *COO*
Bernard Gutmann, *CFO*
George H Cave, *Exec VP*
William M Hall, *Exec VP*
EMP: 27
SALES: 1.3B
SALES (corp-wide): 5.8B **Publicly Held**
WEB: www.fairchildsemi.com
SIC: 3674 Semiconductors & related devices
PA: On Semiconductor Corporation
    5005 E Mcdowell Rd
    Phoenix AZ 85008
    602 244-6600

(P-18234)
FALKOR PARTNERS LLC
Also Called: Semicoa
333 Mccormick Ave, Costa Mesa (92626-3422)
PHONE..............................714 721-8772
Allen Ronk, *CEO*
John Park, *Principal*
EMP: 62
SQ FT: 24,000

SALES (est): 5.5MM **Privately Held**
SIC: 3674 Semiconductors & related devices

(P-18235)
FINISAR CORPORATION
41762 Christy St, Fremont (94538-5106)
PHONE..............................408 548-1000
Fariba Daneh, *Manager*
Anthony Pham, *Technician*
Ziv Lipkin, *Design Engr*
Tim Moran, *Design Engr*
Yuehao Peng, *Engineer*
EMP: 12
SALES (corp-wide): 1.3B **Publicly Held**
SIC: 3674 Semiconductors & related devices
HQ: Finisar Corporation
    1389 Moffett Park Dr
    Sunnyvale CA 94089
    408 548-1000

(P-18236)
FIRST SOLAR INC
Also Called: First Solar Electric
135 Main St Fl 6, San Francisco (94105-8113)
PHONE..............................415 935-2500
EMP: 15
SALES (corp-wide): 2.2B **Publicly Held**
SIC: 3674 3433 Solar cells; heating equipment, except electric
PA: First Solar, Inc.
    350 W Washington St # 600
    Tempe AZ 85281
    602 414-9300

(P-18237)
FLEXTRONICS SEMICONDUCTOR (DH)
2241 Lundy Ave Bldg 2, San Jose (95131-1822)
PHONE..............................408 576-7000
Ash Bhardwaj, *President*
Vikas Desai, *Vice Pres*
Duncan Robertson, *Vice Pres*
Angela Wright, *Vice Pres*
Scott Jarvis, *Administration*
EMP: 40
SQ FT: 54,000
SALES (est): 9.8MM
SALES (corp-wide): 26.2B **Privately Held**
SIC: 3674 8711 Semiconductors & related devices; engineering services

(P-18238)
FOCUS ENHANCEMENTS INC (DH)
Also Called: Focus Enhncments Systems Group
931 Benecia Ave, Sunnyvale (94085-2805)
PHONE..............................650 230-2400
Brett A Moyer, *President*
Gary Williams, *CFO*
▲ **EMP:** 27
SQ FT: 27,500
SALES (est): 5.7MM **Privately Held**
WEB: www.focusinfo.com
SIC: 3674 3861 Semiconductors & related devices; wafers (semiconductor devices); editing equipment, motion picture; viewers, splicers, etc.
HQ: Vitec Multimedia, Inc.
    2200 Century Pkwy Ne # 900
    Atlanta GA 30345
    404 320-0110

(P-18239)
FORMFACTOR INC
7545 Longard Rd, Livermore (94551)
PHONE..............................925 290-4000
Tom St Dennis, *CEO*
EMP: 13 **Publicly Held**
SIC: 3674 Semiconductors & related devices
PA: Formfactor, Inc.
    7005 Southfront Rd
    Livermore CA 94551

(P-18240)
FORMFACTOR INC (PA)
7005 Southfront Rd, Livermore (94551-8201)
PHONE..............................925 290-4000
Michael D Slessor, *CEO*

PRODUCTS & SVCS

Todd Swart, *Surgery Dir*
Warren Ng, *Technician*
Susumu Kaneko, *Design Engr*
Nicholas Jansen, *Engineer*
▲ EMP: 200
SQ FT: 168,636
SALES: 529.6MM **Publicly Held**
WEB: www.formfactor.com
SIC: **3674** Thermoelectric devices, solid
state

(P-18241)
FORTEMEDIA INC (PA)
4051 Burton Dr, Santa Clara (95054-1585)
PHONE...............................408 716-8028
Paul Huang, *CEO*
Wilson or, *Vice Pres*
Elaine Yeh, *Finance*
▼ EMP: 25
SQ FT: 9,000
SALES (est): 10.3MM **Privately Held**
WEB: www.fortemedia.com
SIC: **3674** Semiconductors & related devices

(P-18242)
FOVEON INC
2249 Zanker Rd, San Jose (95131-1120)
PHONE...............................408 855-6800
Carver A Mead, *Ch of Bd*
Jim Lau, *President*
Rudy Guttosch, *Vice Pres*
Ivana Lukacova, *Office Mgr*
Tony Velazquez, *Engineer*
EMP: 50 EST: 1997
SALES (est): 7.4MM **Privately Held**
WEB: www.foveon.com
SIC: **3674** 7221 Light sensitive devices,
solid state; photographic studios, portrait

(P-18243)
FOXSEMICON INTEGRATED TECH INC
96 Bonaventura Dr, San Jose (95134-2124)
PHONE...............................408 383-9880
Jackson C Hwang, *CEO*
Jennifer Wang, *Purchasing*
Jeff Chang, *Director*
Charles Tao, *Manager*
▲ EMP: 13
SQ FT: 3,000
SALES (est): 4.3MM **Privately Held**
SIC: **3674** Semiconductors & related devices
PA: Hon Hai Precision Industry Co., Ltd.
66, Zhongshan Rd.,
New Taipei City TAP 23680

(P-18244)
FRONTIER SEMICONDUCTOR (PA)
Also Called: Fsm
165 Topaz St, Milpitas (95035-5430)
PHONE...............................408 432-8338
Yuen F Lim, *CEO*
Aruna Aiyer, *CIO*
Louis Lau, *Sales Mgr*
EMP: 35
SQ FT: 40,000
SALES (est): 3.6MM **Privately Held**
WEB: www.frontiersemi.com
SIC: **3674** Integrated circuits, semiconductor networks, etc.

(P-18245)
FULCRUM MICROSYSTEMS INC
26660 Agoura Rd, Calabasas (91302-1954)
PHONE...............................818 871-8100
Robert R Nunn, *CEO*
Mike Zeile, *President*
Dale Bartos, *CFO*
Harry Liu, *Sr Software Eng*
Uri Cummings, *CTO*
EMP: 58 EST: 1999
SQ FT: 17,077
SALES (est): 6MM
SALES (corp-wide): 70.8B **Publicly Held**
WEB: www.fulcrummicro.com
SIC: **3674** Semiconductors & related devices

PA: Intel Corporation
2200 Mission College Blvd
Santa Clara CA 95054
408 765-8080

(P-18246)
GAZE INC
1 Market Spear Twr, San Francisco (94105)
PHONE...............................415 374-9193
Tero Heinonen, *CEO*
EMP: 10
SALES (est): 398.2K **Privately Held**
SIC: **3674** 7371 Radiation sensors; computer software development

(P-18247)
GENOA CORPORATION
41762 Christy St, Fremont (94538-5106)
PHONE...............................510 979-3000
Fariba Danesh, *CEO*
August Capital LLC, *Shareholder*
Jeff Walker, *Shareholder*
Jim Witham, *Senior VP*
Tim Gallgher, *VP Opers*
EMP: 45 EST: 1998
SQ FT: 44,000
SALES (est): 3.9MM **Privately Held**
SIC: **3674** Semiconductors & related devices

(P-18248)
GEO SEMICONDUCTOR INC (PA)
101 Metro Dr Ste 620, San Jose (95110-1342)
PHONE...............................408 638-0400
Paul Russo, *CEO*
John Casey, *President*
Simon Westbrook, *CFO*
Ronald Allard, *Vice Pres*
Michael Hopton, *Vice Pres*
EMP: 24
SALES (est): 8.5MM **Privately Held**
SIC: **3674** Semiconductors & related devices

(P-18249)
GIGAMAT TECHNOLOGIES INC
47269 Fremont Blvd, Fremont (94538-6502)
PHONE...............................510 770-8008
Edmond Abrahamians, *CEO*
EMP: 17
SQ FT: 7,000
SALES (est): 3.2MM **Privately Held**
SIC: **3674** Semiconductors & related devices

(P-18250)
GIGPEAK INC (DH)
6024 Silver Creek Vly Rd, San Jose (95138-1011)
PHONE...............................408 546-3316
Gregory L Waters, *President*
Brian C White, *CFO*
Matthew D Brandalise, *Admin Sec*
EMP: 132
SQ FT: 32,805
SALES (est): 58.7MM **Privately Held**
WEB: www.iterrac.com
SIC: **3674** Integrated circuits, semiconductor networks, etc.; hybrid integrated circuits
HQ: Integrated Device Technology, Inc.
6024 Silver Creek Vly Rd
San Jose CA 95138
408 284-8200

(P-18251)
GLO-USA INC
Also Called: G L O
1225 Bordeaux Dr, Sunnyvale (94089-1203)
PHONE...............................408 598-4400
Fariba Danesh, *CEO*
Christian Wittmann, *President*
James McCanna, *CFO*
Monier Nessim, *VP Opers*
Henry Chiu, *VP Sales*
EMP: 55
SALES (est): 14.2MM **Privately Held**
WEB: www.glo.se
SIC: **3674** Light emitting diodes

(P-18252)
GLOBAL COMM SEMICONDUCTORS LLC (HQ)
Also Called: G C S
23155 Kashiwa Ct, Torrance (90505-4026)
PHONE...............................310 530-7274
Bau-Hsing Ann, *President*
Ta-Lun Huang, *Chairman*
Darren Huang, *Bd of Directors*
Dave Wang, *Exec VP*
Sam Wang, *Vice Pres*
EMP: 20
SQ FT: 38,000
SALES (est): 20MM **Privately Held**
WEB: www.gcsincorp.com
SIC: **3674** Semiconductors & related devices

(P-18253)
GLOBAL POWER TECH GROUP INC
20692 Prism Pl, Lake Forest (92630-7803)
PHONE...............................949 273-4373
Sung Joon Kim, *President*
Josta Hogervorst, *Office Mgr*
Brian Patterson, *Electrical Engi*
EMP: 16
SALES: 450K **Privately Held**
SIC: **3674** 7389 Semiconductors & related devices;

(P-18254)
GOLD COAST SOLAR LLC
Also Called: Colored Solar
1975 Hillgate Way Apt G, Simi Valley (93065-2977)
PHONE...............................310 351-7229
Michael Mrozek, *CEO*
Paul Meyer, *CFO*
Paul Wise, *Officer*
EMP: 42
SQ FT: 10,000
SALES: 4MM **Privately Held**
SIC: **3674** 7373 3861 Solar cells; modules, solid state; systems integration services; photographic equipment & supplies

(P-18255)
GREENLIANT SYSTEMS INC
3970 Freedom Cir Ste 100, Santa Clara (95054-1298)
PHONE...............................408 217-7400
EMP: 105 EST: 2010
SALES: 14.4MM **Privately Held**
SIC: **3674** 5065 Semiconductors & related devices; electronic parts & equipment

(P-18256)
GRINDING & DICING SERVICES INC
Also Called: Gdsi
925 Berryessa Rd, San Jose (95133-1002)
PHONE...............................408 451-2000
Joe D Collins, *CEO*
Laila H Collins, *Vice Pres*
Saira Haq, *Vice Pres*
Mira Kalika, *Accountant*
Laila Haq, *Sales Mgr*
▲ EMP: 24
SQ FT: 14,500
SALES (est): 3.9MM **Privately Held**
SIC: **3674** 2672 Semiconductors & related devices; adhesive papers, labels or tapes: from purchased material

(P-18257)
GSI TECHNOLOGY INC
2360 Owen St, Santa Clara (95054-3210)
PHONE...............................408 980-8388
Shu Lee-Lean, *Branch Mgr*
EMP: 78 **Publicly Held**
SIC: **3674** Semiconductors & related devices
PA: Gsi Technology, Inc.
1213 Elko Dr
Sunnyvale CA 94089

(P-18258)
GSI TECHNOLOGY INC (PA)
1213 Elko Dr, Sunnyvale (94089-2211)
PHONE...............................408 331-8800
Lee-Lean Shu, *Ch of Bd*
Douglas M Schirle, *CFO*
Didier Lasserre, *Vice Pres*

Bor-Tay Wu, *Vice Pres*
Ping Wu, *Vice Pres*
EMP: 58
SQ FT: 44,277
SALES: 51.4MM **Publicly Held**
WEB: www.gsitechnology.com
SIC: **3674** 3572 Integrated circuits, semiconductor networks, etc.; computer storage devices

(P-18259)
GT ADVANCED TECHNOLOGIES INC
1911 Airport Blvd, Santa Rosa (95403-1001)
PHONE...............................707 571-1911
EMP: 24 **Privately Held**
SIC: **3674** Photovoltaic devices, solid state
PA: Gt Advanced Technologies Inc.
5 Wentworth Dr Ste 1
Hudson NH 03051

(P-18260)
GULSHAN INTERNATIONAL CORP
Also Called: Invax Technologies
1355 Geneva Dr, Sunnyvale (94089-1121)
PHONE...............................408 745-6090
Abid Khan, *President*
Susy Khan, *Office Mgr*
Brandon Shalin, *Engineer*
EMP: 14 EST: 1980
SALES (est): 2.4MM **Privately Held**
WEB: www.invax.com
SIC: **3674** Modules, solid state

(P-18261)
GYRFALCON TECHNOLOGY INC
1900 Mccarthy Blvd # 208, Milpitas (95035-7414)
PHONE...............................408 944-9219
Frank Lyn, *President*
EMP: 50
SALES (est): 579.8K **Privately Held**
SIC: **3674** Semiconductors & related devices

(P-18262)
H-SQUARE CORPORATION
Also Called: H2 Co
3100 Patrick Henry Dr, Santa Clara (95054-1850)
PHONE...............................408 732-1240
Bud Barclay, *President*
Larry Dean, *Shareholder*
▲ EMP: 42 EST: 1975
SQ FT: 20,000
SALES (est): 8MM **Privately Held**
WEB: www.h-square.com
SIC: **3674** Semiconductor circuit networks; solid state electronic devices; stud bases or mounts for semiconductor devices

(P-18263)
HALCYON MICROELECTRONICS INC
5467 2nd St, Irwindale (91706-2072)
PHONE...............................626 814-4688
Patricia Martin, *CEO*
Dennis Martin, *President*
EMP: 16
SQ FT: 9,100
SALES (est): 1.7MM **Privately Held**
WEB: www.halcyonmicro.com
SIC: **3674** Microcircuits, integrated (semiconductor)

(P-18264)
HANA MICROELECTRONICS INC
3100 De La Cruz Blvd # 204, Santa Clara (95054-2438)
PHONE...............................408 452-7474
Sanjay Mitra, *President*
EMP: 13
SQ FT: 2,500
SALES (est): 1.3MM **Privately Held**
WEB: www.hanaus.com
SIC: **3674** Semiconductors & related devices
HQ: Hana Semiconductor (Bkk) Company Limited
65/98 Soi Vibhavadi Rangsit 64 Yeak 2
Lak Si

(P-18265)
HANERGY HOLDING (AMERICA) LLC (HQ)
1350 Bayshore Hwy, Burlingame (94010-1823)
PHONE...................................650 288-3722
Yi Wu, *CEO*
EMP: 17
SALES (est): 40.4MM
SALES (corp-wide): 782.7MM **Privately Held**
SIC: 3674 6719 Solar cells; investment holding companies, except banks
PA: Jinjiang Hydroelectric Power Group Co., Ltd.
No.0-A, Anli Road, Chaoyang Dist.
Beijing 10010
108 391-4567

(P-18266)
HANWHA Q CELLS AMERICA INC
400 Spectrum Center Dr # 1400, Irvine (92618-5021)
PHONE...................................949 748-5996
Koo Yung Lee, *CEO*
EMP: 11
SALES (est): 212.3K **Privately Held**
SIC: 3674 Solar cells

(P-18267)
HAYWARD QUARTZ TECHNOLOGY
Also Called: Hayward Quartz Machining Co
1700 Corporate Way, Fremont (94539-6107)
PHONE...................................510 657-9605
Nhe Thi Le, *CEO*
Ha Vinh Ly, *President*
Ken Jacoby, *Project Mgr*
Dean Gehrman, *Sales Mgr*
Jimmy Phan, *Facilities Mgr*
▲ **EMP:** 250
SQ FT: 250,000
SALES (est): 62.4MM **Privately Held**
WEB: www.haywardquartz.com
SIC: 3674 Semiconductor circuit networks

(P-18268)
HELITEK COMPANY LTD
4033 Clipper Ct, Fremont (94538-6540)
PHONE...................................510 933-7688
Ping-Hai Chiao, *President*
Art Tao, *Project Mgr*
Nancy Lin, *Purchasing*
▲ **EMP:** 15
SQ FT: 30,000
SALES (est): 2.7MM **Privately Held**
SIC: 3674 Semiconductors & related devices
PA: Wafer Works Corporation
100, Longyuan 1st Rd.,
Taoyuan City TAY 32542

(P-18269)
HERMES-MICROVISION INC
1762 Automation Pkwy, San Jose (95131-1873)
PHONE...................................408 597-8600
Jack Jau, *CEO*
Chung Shih Pan, *President*
Charles Yang, *Electrical Engi*
Vincent Chang, *Engineer*
Bill Chiang, *Engineer*
▲ **EMP:** 25
SQ FT: 80,000
SALES (est): 10.8MM
SALES (corp-wide): 12.5B **Privately Held**
WEB: www.hermesmicrovision.com
SIC: 3674 Integrated circuits, semiconductor networks, etc.
HQ: Hermes Microvision Incorporated B.V.
De Run 6501
Veldhoven

(P-18270)
HI RELBLITY MCRELECTRONICS INC
1804 Mccarthy Blvd, Milpitas (95035-7410)
PHONE...................................408 764-5500
Zafar Malik, *President*
Alex Barrios, *Vice Pres*
Larry Jorstad, *CTO*

Fatemeh Kiaei, *Finance Mgr*
Catherine Tijo, *Finance Mgr*
EMP: 32
SALES (est): 4.9MM
SALES (corp-wide): 83.4MM **Privately Held**
SIC: 3674 7389 Semiconductors & related devices; inspection & testing services
HQ: Silicon Turnkey Solutions, Inc.
1804 Mccarthy Blvd
Milpitas CA 95035
408 904-0200

(P-18271)
HI/FN INC (DH)
48720 Kato Rd, Fremont (94538-7312)
PHONE...................................408 778-2944
Albert E Sisto, *Ch of Bd*
William R Walker, *CFO*
Russell S Dietz, *Vice Pres*
John Matze, *Vice Pres*
Dr Jiebing Wang, *Vice Pres*
EMP: 13
SQ FT: 20,000
SALES (est): 6.2MM
SALES (corp-wide): 385MM **Publicly Held**
WEB: www.hifn.com
SIC: 3674 7372 Semiconductors & related devices; prepackaged software
HQ: Exar Corporation
1060 Rincon Cir
San Jose CA 95131
669 265-6100

(P-18272)
HONEYWELL INTERNATIONAL INC
1804 Mccarthy Blvd, Milpitas (95035-7410)
PHONE...................................408 954-1100
Chris Cartsonas, *Branch Mgr*
EMP: 250
SALES (corp-wide): 41.8B **Publicly Held**
WEB: www.honeywell.com
SIC: 3674 Strain gages, solid state
PA: Honeywell International Inc.
300 S Tryon St
Charlotte NC 28202
973 455-2000

(P-18273)
HOTECH CORPORATION
9320 Santa Anita Ave # 100, Rancho Cucamonga (91730-6147)
PHONE...................................909 987-8828
David Ho, *President*
Hai CHI Yang, *Manager*
▲ **EMP:** 20
SQ FT: 3,000
SALES (est): 1.8MM **Privately Held**
WEB: www.hotechusa.com
SIC: 3674 Semiconductors & related devices

(P-18274)
I2A TECHNOLOGIES INC
3399 W Warren Ave, Fremont (94538-6424)
PHONE...................................510 770-0322
Victor Batinovich, *President*
Ann Batinovich, *Ch of Bd*
▲ **EMP:** 40
SQ FT: 35,000
SALES (est): 15.3MM **Privately Held**
SIC: 3674 8711 Semiconductors & related devices; engineering services

(P-18275)
IC SENSORS INC
45738 Northport Loop W, Fremont (94538-6476)
PHONE...................................510 498-1570
Frank Guibone, *President*
Victor Chatigny, *General Mgr*
EMP: 100
SQ FT: 34,000
SALES (est): 7.9MM
SALES (corp-wide): 13.9B **Privately Held**
SIC: 3674 8711 3625 Semiconductors & related devices; engineering services; switches, electronic applications
HQ: Measurement Specialties, Inc.
1000 Lucas Way
Hampton VA 23666
757 766-1500

(P-18276)
ICHIA USA INC
509 Telegraph Canyon Rd, Chula Vista (91910-6436)
PHONE...................................619 482-2222
Simon Goh, *General Mgr*
◆ **EMP:** 200
SQ FT: 3,000
SALES (est): 20.3MM **Privately Held**
WEB: www.ichia.com
SIC: 3674 Semiconductors & related devices
PA: Ichia Technologies, Inc.
268, Huaya 2nd Rd.,
Taoyuan City TAY 33383

(P-18277)
ICHOR SYSTEMS INC (HQ)
3185 Laurelview Ct, Fremont (94538-6535)
PHONE...................................510 897-5200
Thomas M Rohrs, *CEO*
▲ **EMP:** 20
SALES (est): 371.3MM
SALES (corp-wide): 823.6MM **Publicly Held**
SIC: 3674 Semiconductors & related devices
PA: Ichor Holdings, Ltd.
3185 Laurelview Ct
Fremont CA 94538
510 897-5200

(P-18278)
IKANOS COMMUNICATIONS INC (DH)
5775 Morehouse Dr, San Diego (92121-1714)
PHONE...................................858 587-1121
Rahul Patel, *President*
Sanjay Mehta, *CFO*
Meilin Tye, *Manager*
▲ **EMP:** 155
SQ FT: 73,500
SALES: 48.3MM
SALES (corp-wide): 24.2B **Publicly Held**
WEB: www.ikanos.com
SIC: 3674 Semiconductors & related devices
HQ: Qualcomm Atheros, Inc.
1700 Technology Dr
San Jose CA 95110
408 773-5200

(P-18279)
ILLINOIS TOOL WORKS INC
Also Called: ITW-Opto Diode
1260 Calle Suerte, Camarillo (93012-8053)
PHONE...................................805 499-0335
Russ Dahl, *General Mgr*
EMP: 40
SALES (corp-wide): 14.7B **Publicly Held**
SIC: 3674 Semiconductors & related devices
PA: Illinois Tool Works Inc.
155 Harlem Ave
Glenview IL 60025
847 724-7500

(P-18280)
ILLINOIS TOOL WORKS INC
ITW Rippey
5000 Hillsdale Cir, El Dorado Hills (95762-5706)
PHONE...................................916 939-4332
Brent Best, *Manager*
EMP: 69
SALES (corp-wide): 14.7B **Publicly Held**
SIC: 3674 Semiconductors & related devices
PA: Illinois Tool Works Inc.
155 Harlem Ave
Glenview IL 60025
847 724-7500

(P-18281)
IMAGERLABS INC
1995 S Myrtle Ave, Monrovia (91016-4854)
PHONE...................................949 310-9560
Eugene Atlas, *CEO*
Sarit Neter, *Vice Pres*
Mark Wadsworth, *CTO*
◆ **EMP:** 10
SQ FT: 4,500

SALES: 750K **Privately Held**
SIC: 3674 Infrared sensors, solid state; radiation sensors; ultra-violet sensors, solid state

(P-18282)
INFINEON TECH AMERICAS CORP (HQ)
Also Called: I R
101 N Pacific Coast Hwy, El Segundo (90245-4318)
PHONE...................................310 726-8000
Oleg Khaykin, *CEO*
Ilan Daskal, *CFO*
Alain Charles, *Vice Pres*
Pat Schreffler, *Vice Pres*
Abhijit Pathak, *Executive*
▲ **EMP:** 900 **EST:** 1979
SALES (est): 1.1B
SALES (corp-wide): 8.7B **Privately Held**
WEB: www.irf.com
SIC: 3674 Integrated circuits, semiconductor networks, etc.
PA: Infineon Technologies Ag
Am Campeon 1-15
Neubiberg 85579
892 340-

(P-18283)
INFINEON TECH AMERICAS CORP
Crydom Controls
233 Kansas St, El Segundo (90245-4316)
PHONE...................................310 726-8000
Derek Lidow, *Manager*
Elisa Sanchez, *Controller*
EMP: 1200
SALES (corp-wide): 8.7B **Privately Held**
SIC: 3674 Semiconductor circuit networks; rectifiers, solid state
HQ: Infineon Technologies Americas Corp.
101 N Pacific Coast Hwy
El Segundo CA 90245
310 726-8000

(P-18284)
INFINEON TECH AMERICAS CORP
640 N Mccarthy Blvd, Milpitas (95035-5113)
PHONE...................................866 951-9519
Robert Lefort, *President*
Sandra Garcia, *Technician*
Michelle Andersen, *Manager*
Shawn Ferrell, *Manager*
EMP: 1200
SALES (corp-wide): 8.7B **Privately Held**
SIC: 3674 Semiconductors & related devices
HQ: Infineon Technologies Americas Corp.
101 N Pacific Coast Hwy
El Segundo CA 90245
310 726-8000

(P-18285)
INFINEON TECH AMERICAS CORP
1521 E Grand Ave, El Segundo (90245-4339)
P.O. Box 2788, Rancho Cucamonga (91729-2788)
PHONE...................................310 252-7116
Fred Farris, *Vice Pres*
John Lambert, *Program Mgr*
Dana Wilhelm, *Design Engr*
EMP: 133
SALES (corp-wide): 8.7B **Privately Held**
SIC: 3674 Semiconductors & related devices
HQ: Infineon Technologies Americas Corp.
101 N Pacific Coast Hwy
El Segundo CA 90245
310 726-8000

(P-18286)
INFINEON TECH N AMER CORP (DH)
640 N Mccarthy Blvd, Milpitas (95035-5113)
PHONE...................................408 503-2642
Robert Lefort, *President*
Andrew Prillwitz, *CFO*
David Ho, *Vice Pres*
Alexander Peschke, *Vice Pres*
Cynthia Tan, *Executive*

PRODUCTS & SVCS

▲ EMP: 500
SQ FT: 400,000
SALES (est): 719MM
SALES (corp-wide): 8.7B Privately Held
WEB: www.infineon-ncs.com
SIC: 3674 Semiconductors & related devices
HQ: Infineon Technologies Us Holdco Inc.
   640 N Mccarthy Blvd
   Milpitas CA 95035
   866 951-9519

(P-18287)
INFINEON TECH US HOLDCO INC (HQ)
Also Called: Infineon Technologies AG
640 N Mccarthy Blvd, Milpitas
(95035-5113)
PHONE...................866 951-9519
David Lewis, CEO
Stefan Marquardt, Partner
Andrew Prillwitz, CFO
Michael Pinczolits, Treasurer
Gernot Langguth, Sr Corp Ofcr
EMP: 75
SQ FT: 62,874
SALES (est): 739.1MM
SALES (corp-wide): 8.7B Privately Held
SIC: 3674 Integrated circuits, semiconductor networks, etc.
PA: Infineon Technologies Ag
   Am Campeon 1-15
   Neubiberg 85579
   892 340-

(P-18288)
INFINERA CORPORATION
1338 Bordeaux Dr, Sunnyvale
(94089-1005)
PHONE...................408 572-5200
Debby Schuster, Branch Mgr
Mohit Misra, Director
EMP: 20
SALES (corp-wide): 943.3MM Publicly Held
SIC: 3674 Light sensitive devices
PA: Infinera Corporation
   140 Caspian Ct
   Sunnyvale CA 94089
   408 572-5200

(P-18289)
INFORMATION STORAGE DVCS INC
2727 N 1st St, San Jose (95134-2029)
PHONE...................408 943-6666
David L Angel, CEO
Jock Ochiltree, President
Felix J Rosengarten, CFO
James Brennan Jr, Vice Pres
Michael Geilhufe, Vice Pres
▲ EMP: 165
SQ FT: 60,000
SALES (est): 10.7MM Privately Held
WEB: www.isd.com
SIC: 3674 Semiconductors & related devices
PA: Winbond Electronics Corp.
   8, Keya 1st Rd.,
   Taichung City 42881

(P-18290)
INITIO CORPORATION
2050 Ringwood Ave Ste A, San Jose
(95131-1783)
PHONE...................408 943-3189
Jui liang, President
▲ EMP: 26
SQ FT: 14,000
SALES (est): 4.6MM Privately Held
SIC: 3674 7371 3577 Semiconductors & related devices; custom computer programming services; computer peripheral equipment
PA: Initio Semiconductor Corporation
   8f, 192, Jui Kuang Rd.,
   Taipei City TAP 11491

(P-18291)
INNODISK USA CORPORATION
42996 Osgood Rd, Fremont (94539-5627)
PHONE...................510 770-9421
Victor Le, President
▲ EMP: 30

SALES (est): 3.4MM Privately Held
SIC: 3674 Random access memory (RAM)
PA: Innodisk Corporation
   5f, No. 237, Datong Rd., Sec. 1,
   New Taipei City 22161

(P-18292)
INNOPHASE INC
6815 Flanders Dr Ste 150, San Diego
(92121-3925)
PHONE...................619 541-8280
Yang Xu, CEO
Thomas Lee, Vice Pres
EMP: 100 EST: 2011
SALES (est): 10.5MM Privately Held
SIC: 3674 Semiconductors & related devices

(P-18293)
INNOVATIVE MICRO TECH INC
Also Called: IMT Analytical
75 Robin Hill Rd, Goleta (93117-3108)
PHONE...................805 681-2807
Craig H Ensley, President
Peter Altavilla, CFO
Jim McGibbon, CFO
Eric Sigler, Senior VP
Richard Brossart, Vice Pres
EMP: 115
SQ FT: 130,000
SALES (est): 22MM Privately Held
WEB: www.imtmems.com
SIC: 3674 Semiconductors & related devices

(P-18294)
INOLUX CORPORATION (PA)
3350 Scott Blvd Ste 4102, Santa Clara
(95054-3120)
PHONE...................408 844-8734
Holton Lee, President
EMP: 12 EST: 2012
SALES (est): 1.7MM Privately Held
SIC: 3674 Light emitting diodes

(P-18295)
INPHENIX INC
250 N Mines Rd, Livermore (94551-2238)
PHONE...................925 606-8809
David Eu, President
Gene Covell, Vice Pres
Tao Huang, Engineer
Beverly Rogers, Human Res Mgr
Steve Vitkovsky, Sales Mgr
EMP: 25
SALES (est): 5.9MM Privately Held
WEB: www.inphenix.com
SIC: 3674 Semiconductors & related devices

(P-18296)
INPHI CORPORATION (PA)
2953 Bunker Hill Ln # 300, Santa Clara
(95054-1131)
PHONE...................408 217-7300
Ford Tamer, President
Diosdado P Banatao, Ch of Bd
John Edmunds, CFO
Eric Hayes, Senior VP
Charles Roach, Senior VP
EMP: 229 EST: 2000
SQ FT: 57,914
SALES: 294.4MM Publicly Held
WEB: www.inphi-corp.com
SIC: 3674 Integrated circuits, semiconductor networks, etc.

(P-18297)
INPHI INTERNATIONAL PTE LTD
112 S Lakeview Canyon Rd, Westlake Village (91362-3925)
PHONE...................805 719-2300
Ford Tamer, President
John Edmunds, CFO
EMP: 21
SALES (est): 922.2K Privately Held
SIC: 3674 Semiconductors & related devices

(P-18298)
INSILIXA INC
1000 Hamlin Ct, Sunnyvale (94089-1400)
PHONE...................408 809-3000
Arjang Hassibi, CEO
Nader Gamini, COO

Michael Taylor, Engineer
Kshama Jirage, Consultant
EMP: 12
SQ FT: 1,500
SALES: 2.6MM Privately Held
SIC: 3674 Semiconductors & related devices

(P-18299)
INTEGRA TECH SILICON VLY LLC (DH)
1635 Mccarthy Blvd, Milpitas (95035-7415)
PHONE...................408 618-8700
Matt Bergeron, CEO
Janice Pinson, Program Mgr
Jonny Corrao, Engineer
Chip Greely, Engineer
Angie Smead, Senior Buyer
EMP: 109
SQ FT: 48,000
SALES (est): 22.4MM Privately Held
WEB: www.corwil.com
SIC: 3674 3825 Semiconductors & related devices; semiconductor test equipment
HQ: Integra Technologies Llc
   3450 N Rock Rd Ste 100
   Wichita KS 67226
   316 630-6800

(P-18300)
INTEGRA TECHNOLOGIES INC
321 Coral Cir, El Segundo (90245-4620)
PHONE...................310 606-0855
Paul Aken, President
Jeff Burger, Vice Pres
WEI Cheng, Engineer
Christine Carter, Accounting Mgr
Michael Silva, Buyer
EMP: 50 EST: 1997
SQ FT: 15,000
SALES (est): 17.5MM Privately Held
WEB: www.integratech.com
SIC: 3674 Modules, solid state; transistors

(P-18301)
INTEGRA TECHNOLOGIES LLC
Also Called: Viko Test Labs
2006 Martin Ave, Santa Clara
(95050-2700)
PHONE...................408 923-7300
Ed Nunes, Principal
George Liu, Vice Pres
Swee Khim, CTO
Jerry Kirby, VP Sales
Jinesh Desai, Manager
EMP: 100 Privately Held
WEB: www.adaptivecircuits.com
SIC: 3674 Semiconductors & related devices
HQ: Integra Technologies Silicon Valley Llc
   1635 Mccarthy Blvd
   Milpitas CA 95035

(P-18302)
INTEGRATED DEVICE TECH INC (HQ)
Also Called: I D T
6024 Silver Creek Vly Rd, San Jose
(95138-1011)
P.O. Box 67071, Scotts Valley (95067-7071)
PHONE...................408 284-8200
Gregory L Waters, President
Brian C White, CFO
Kenneth Kannappan, Bd of Directors
Matthew D Brandalise,
Anja Hamilton,
▲ EMP: 277
SQ FT: 263,000
SALES: 842.7MM Privately Held
WEB: www.idt.com
SIC: 3674 Integrated circuits, semiconductor networks, etc.

(P-18303)
INTEGRATED DEVICE TECH INC
Purchase Office
6024 Silver Creek Vly, San Jose
(95138-1011)
PHONE...................408 284-1433
Regi John, Vice Pres
Bob Valderrama, Purchasing
EMP: 291 Privately Held
WEB: www.idt.com

SIC: 3674 Semiconductors & related devices
HQ: Integrated Device Technology, Inc.
   6024 Silver Creek Vly Rd
   San Jose CA 95138
   408 284-8200

(P-18304)
INTEGRTED SILICON SOLUTION INC (PA)
1623 Buckeye Dr, Milpitas (95035-7423)
PHONE...................408 969-6600
Jimmy Lee, CEO
Scott Howarth, President
Allen Chang, Vice Pres
John Cobb, Vice Pres
Shou-Kong Fan, Vice Pres
▲ EMP: 57
SQ FT: 55,612
SALES (est): 215.8MM Privately Held
WEB: www.issi.com
SIC: 3674 Semiconductors & related devices

(P-18305)
INTEL CORPORATION
1200 Creekside Dr, Folsom (95630-3431)
PHONE...................916 943-6809
Milind Konnur, Program Mgr
Jim Sutorka, Info Tech Dir
Thomas Lyda, Design Engr
Georgna Gonzalez-Hall, Technology
Pradeep Golconda, Engineer
EMP: 58
SALES (corp-wide): 70.8B Publicly Held
SIC: 3674 Microprocessors
PA: Intel Corporation
   2200 Mission College Blvd
   Santa Clara CA 95054
   408 765-8080

(P-18306)
INTEL CORPORATION
530 Technology Dr Ste 100, Irvine
(92618-1350)
PHONE...................408 765-8080
Van Truong, Design Engr
Elvyn Donawerth, Engineer
EMP: 10
SALES (corp-wide): 70.8B Publicly Held
SIC: 3674 Microprocessors
PA: Intel Corporation
   2200 Mission College Blvd
   Santa Clara CA 95054
   408 765-8080

(P-18307)
INTEL CORPORATION
44235 Nobel Dr, Fremont (94538-3178)
PHONE...................510 651-9841
Mike Ricci, General Mgr
EMP: 35
SALES (corp-wide): 70.8B Publicly Held
WEB: www.intel.com
SIC: 3674 Microprocessors
PA: Intel Corporation
   2200 Mission College Blvd
   Santa Clara CA 95054
   408 765-8080

(P-18308)
INTEL CORPORATION
1900 Prairie City Rd, Folsom (95630-9599)
PHONE...................916 356-8080
Conrad Wiederhold, Manager
Suzanne Listar, President
Gregorio Martinez, President
Dan Lecam, Vice Pres
Alan Bumgarner, Program Mgr
EMP: 57
SALES (corp-wide): 70.8B Publicly Held
WEB: www.intel.com
SIC: 3674 3572 3577 Microprocessors; computer storage devices; computer peripheral equipment
PA: Intel Corporation
   2200 Mission College Blvd
   Santa Clara CA 95054
   408 765-8080

(P-18309)
INTEL FEDERAL LLC
2200 Mission College Blvd, Santa Clara
(95054-1549)
PHONE...................302 644-3756
David Patterson,

Ron Dickel, *Vice Pres*
Ravi Jacob, *Vice Pres*
Steve Lund, *Vice Pres*
EMP: 20
SALES (est): 2MM
SALES (corp-wide): 70.8B **Publicly Held**
SIC: 3674 Semiconductors & related devices
PA: Intel Corporation
2200 Mission College Blvd
Santa Clara CA 95054
408 765-8080

(P-18310)
INTEL INTERNATIONAL LIMITED (HQ)
2200 Mission College Blvd, Santa Clara (95054-1549)
PHONE...........................408 765-8080
Lee Johnny, *Principal*
EMP: 15
SALES (est): 3.1MM
SALES (corp-wide): 70.8B **Publicly Held**
SIC: 3674 3571 Memories, solid state; computers, digital, analog or hybrid
PA: Intel Corporation
2200 Mission College Blvd
Santa Clara CA 95054
408 765-8080

(P-18311)
INTEL NETWORK SYSTEMS INC
3600 Juliette Ln, Santa Clara (95054-1540)
PHONE...........................408 765-8080
Brian Dharmanto, *Software Engr*
Alfred Kohanteb, *Software Engr*
Jantz Tran, *Software Engr*
Sunil Hegde, *IT/INT Sup*
Muhammad Kazmi, *Design Engr*
EMP: 27
SALES (corp-wide): 70.8B **Publicly Held**
SIC: 3674 Semiconductors & related devices
HQ: Intel Network Systems Inc
77 Reed Rd
Hudson MA 01749
978 553-4000

(P-18312)
INTEL PUERTO RICO INC
2200 Mission College Blvd, Santa Clara (95054-1549)
PHONE...........................408 765-8080
Craig Barrett, *President*
Patrick Terranova,
EMP: 50
SALES (est): 4.5MM
SALES (corp-wide): 70.8B **Publicly Held**
WEB: www.intel.com
SIC: 3674 3571 Memories, solid state; microprocessors; computers, digital, analog or hybrid
PA: Intel Corporation
2200 Mission College Blvd
Santa Clara CA 95054
408 765-8080

(P-18313)
INTERCONNECT SYSTEMS INC (DH)
Also Called: I S I
741 Flynn Rd, Camarillo (93012-8056)
PHONE...........................805 482-2870
William P Miller, *President*
Louis Buldain, *Vice Pres*
Glen Griswold, *Vice Pres*
▲ **EMP:** 90
SQ FT: 48,000
SALES (est): 50.9MM
SALES (corp-wide): 40.6B **Privately Held**
WEB: www.isipkg.com
SIC: 3674 Computer logic modules
HQ: Molex, Llc
2222 Wellington Ct
Lisle IL 60532
630 969-4550

(P-18314)
INTERMOLECULAR INC (HQ)
3011 N 1st St, San Jose (95134-2004)
PHONE...........................408 582-5700
Chris Kramer, *President*
C Richard Neely, *CFO*
Bill Roeschlein, *CFO*
Scot A Griffin, *Exec VP*
Judy Ajifu, *Vice Pres*

EMP: 106
SQ FT: 146,000
SALES: 33.6MM
SALES (corp-wide): 16.9B **Privately Held**
WEB: www.intermolecular.com
SIC: 3674 Integrated circuits, semiconductor networks, etc.
PA: Merck Kg Auf Aktien
Frankfurter Str. 250
Darmstadt 64293
615 172-0

(P-18315)
INTERNATIONAL RECTIFIER CORP (PA)
17885 Von Karman Ave # 100, Irvine (92614-5256)
PHONE...........................949 453-1008
Fax: 949 453-8748
EMP: 23
SQ FT: 6,000
SALES (est): 3.9MM **Privately Held**
SIC: 3674 3672

(P-18316)
INTEST CORPORATION
47777 Warm Springs Blvd, Fremont (94539-7470)
PHONE...........................408 678-9123
Dale Christman, *Manager*
Deborah Cook, *Controller*
Rick Baze, *Manager*
EMP: 45
SALES (corp-wide): 78.5MM **Publicly Held**
WEB: www.intest.com
SIC: 3674 Semiconductors & related devices
PA: Intest Corporation
804 E Gate Dr Ste 200
Mount Laurel NJ 08054
856 505-8800

(P-18317)
INTEST SILICON VALLEY CORP
47777 Warm Springs Blvd, Fremont (94539-7470)
PHONE...........................408 678-9123
Dale Christman, *General Mgr*
Hugh Tregan Jr, *CFO*
Leonard Torres, *Manager*
EMP: 45
SALES (est): 6.1MM
SALES (corp-wide): 78.5MM **Publicly Held**
SIC: 3674 Semiconductors & related devices
PA: Intest Corporation
804 E Gate Dr Ste 200
Mount Laurel NJ 08054
856 505-8800

(P-18318)
INVECAS INC
3385 Scott Blvd, Santa Clara (95054-3115)
PHONE...........................408 758-5636
Dasaradha Gude, *CEO*
Prasad Chalasani, *President*
Khanh Le, *President*
Ian Williams, *Vice Pres*
Arvind Shenoy, *Surgery Dir*
EMP: 25
SQ FT: 8,536
SALES: 68MM **Privately Held**
SIC: 3674 Semiconductors & related devices

(P-18319)
INVENLUX CORPORATION
168 Mason Way Ste B5, City of Industry (91746-2339)
PHONE...........................626 277-4163
Chunhui Yan, *President*
EMP: 29
SQ FT: 18,000
SALES (est): 4.2MM **Privately Held**
SIC: 3674 Light emitting diodes

(P-18320)
INVENSAS CORPORATION
3025 Orchard Pkwy, San Jose (95134-2017)
PHONE...........................408 324-5100
Craig Mitchell, *President*
Javier Delacruz, *President*
Kazumi Allen, *Vice Pres*

Benny Fuentes, *Technician*
Hong Shen, *Engineer*
EMP: 27
SALES (est): 5.9MM
SALES (corp-wide): 406.1MM **Publicly Held**
SIC: 3674 Integrated circuits, semiconductor networks, etc.
HQ: Tessera Technologies, Inc.
3025 Orchard Pkwy
San Jose CA 95134
408 321-6000

(P-18321)
IOG PRODUCTS LLC
Also Called: Impact-O-Graph Devices
9737 Lurline Ave, Chatsworth (91311-4404)
PHONE...........................818 350-5070
Mark Newgreen,
Ron Ginther, *Executive*
Darryl Termine, *VP Sales*
Brandon Collier, *Sales Staff*
Kristen Payton, *Cust Mgr*
EMP: 15
SALES (est): 2.2MM **Privately Held**
SIC: 3674 3669 Radiation sensors; visual communication systems

(P-18322)
IQ-ANALOG CORPORATION
12348 High Bluff Dr # 110, San Diego (92130-3545)
PHONE...........................858 200-0388
Michael S Kappes, *President*
Ken Pettit, *Vice Pres*
Mikko Waltari, *Vice Pres*
Randy Wayland, *Vice Pres*
Nitin Nidhi, *Engineer*
EMP: 25
SALES (est): 3.4MM **Privately Held**
SIC: 3674 Semiconductors & related devices

(P-18323)
IRVINE SENSORS CORPORATION
3000 Airway Ave Ste A1, Costa Mesa (92626-6033)
PHONE...........................714 444-8700
John C Carson, *President*
Anthony Mastrangelo, *Vice Pres*
James Justice, *Admin Sec*
EMP: 43 **EST:** 2013
SALES (est): 4.4MM **Privately Held**
SIC: 3674 8731 Semiconductors & related devices; electronic research

(P-18324)
IWATT INC (DH)
Also Called: Dialog Semiconductor
675 Campbell Tech Pkwy # 150, Campbell (95008-5053)
PHONE...........................408 374-4200
Ronald P Edgerton, *CEO*
James V McCanna, *CFO*
Alex Sinar, *Vice Pres*
Kaj Den Daas, *Principal*
Brian McDonald, *Principal*
▲ **EMP:** 45
SQ FT: 26,000
SALES: 50MM
SALES (corp-wide): 1.4B **Privately Held**
WEB: www.iwatt.com
SIC: 3674 Semiconductors & related devices
HQ: Dialog Semiconductor Gmbh
Neue Str. 95
Kirchheim Unter Teck 73230
702 180-50

(P-18325)
IXYS LLC (HQ)
1590 Buckeye Dr, Milpitas (95035-7418)
PHONE...........................408 457-9000
Nathan Zommer, *CEO*
Neil Lejeune, *Vice Pres*
Vladimir Tsukanov, *Research*
Gonzalo Martinez, *Engineer*
Chad Kolowrat, *Sales Staff*
EMP: 85
SQ FT: 51,000

SALES: 322.1MM
SALES (corp-wide): 1.7B **Publicly Held**
WEB: www.ixys.com
SIC: 3674 Integrated circuits, semiconductor networks, etc.
PA: Littelfuse, Inc.
8755 W Higgins Rd Ste 500
Chicago IL 60631
773 628-1000

(P-18326)
IXYS INTGRTD CRCTS DIV AV INC
145 Columbia, Aliso Viejo (92656-1413)
PHONE...........................949 831-4622
Nathan Zommer, *Ch of Bd*
Uzi Sasson, *CFO*
Bret Howe, *Design Engr*
EMP: 26
SQ FT: 28,000
SALES (est): 4MM
SALES (corp-wide): 1.7B **Publicly Held**
WEB: www.ixys.com
SIC: 3674 7389 Microcircuits, integrated (semiconductor); design services
HQ: Ixys, Llc
1590 Buckeye Dr
Milpitas CA 95035
408 457-9000

(P-18327)
IXYS LONG BEACH INC (DH)
2500 Mira Mar Ave, Long Beach (90815-1758)
PHONE...........................562 296-6584
Nathan Zommer, *CEO*
Arnold Agbayani, *CFO*
▲ **EMP:** 25
SQ FT: 20,000
SALES (est): 4MM
SALES (corp-wide): 1.7B **Publicly Held**
SIC: 3674 5065 Semiconductors & related devices; electronic parts & equipment
HQ: Ixys, Llc
1590 Buckeye Dr
Milpitas CA 95035
408 457-9000

(P-18328)
JA SOLAR USA INC
2570 N 1st St Ste 360, San Jose (95131-1029)
PHONE...........................408 586-0000
Jian Xie, *CEO*
Anthea Chung, *CFO*
Ming Yang, *Vice Pres*
▲ **EMP:** 10
SQ FT: 6,527
SALES (est): 4.4MM
SALES (corp-wide): 1.2MM **Privately Held**
SIC: 3674 Solar cells
HQ: Hefei Ja Solar Technology Co., Ltd.
No.999, Changning Avenue, High-Tech Zone
Hefei 23000
551 671-9099

(P-18329)
JAZZ SEMICONDUCTOR INC (DH)
Also Called: Towerjazz
4321 Jamboree Rd, Newport Beach (92660-3007)
PHONE...........................949 435-8000
Amir Elstein, *Ch of Bd*
Itzhak Edrei, *President*
Rafi Mor, *COO*
Oren Shirazi, *CFO*
Andy Chan, *Vice Pres*
▲ **EMP:** 700
SQ FT: 300,000
SALES (est): 221.4MM
SALES (corp-wide): 352MM **Privately Held**
WEB: www.jazzsemi.com
SIC: 3674 Wafers (semiconductor devices)

(P-18330)
JINKOSOLAR (US) INC
595 Market St Ste 2200, San Francisco (94105-2834)
PHONE...........................415 402-0502
Duan Yang Chen, *Accounts Mgr*
John McLaughlin, *Director*
◆ **EMP:** 13

SALES (est): 16.3MM
SALES (corp-wide): 14.7MM **Privately Held**
SIC: **3674** Semiconductors & related devices
PA: Jinkosolar (U.S.) Holding Inc.
595 Market St Ste 2200
San Francisco CA 94105
415 402-0502

(P-18331)
K LIVE
Also Called: Bulb Star
300 W Valley Blvd 33, Alhambra (91803-3338)
PHONE....................626 289-2885
Ken Lively, *CEO*
▲ **EMP:** 10
SALES (est): 2MM **Privately Held**
WEB: www.bulbstar.com
SIC: **3674** Light emitting diodes

(P-18332)
KEYSSA INC (PA)
655 Campbell Technology P, Campbell (95008-5064)
PHONE....................408 637-2300
Tony Fadell, *CEO*
Gordon Almquist, *Vice Pres*
Nick Antonopoulos, *Vice Pres*
Satish Ganesan, *Vice Pres*
Srikanth Gondi, *Vice Pres*
EMP: 37
SALES (est): 9.5MM **Privately Held**
SIC: **3674** 3577 Semiconductors & related devices; computer peripheral equipment

(P-18333)
KISCO CONFORMAL COATING LLC (PA)
6292 San Ignacio Ave C, San Jose (95119-1385)
PHONE....................408 224-6533
Yoshiya Wasa, *Mng Member*
Takatoshi Masuda, *Mng Member*
▲ **EMP:** 10
SALES (est): 1.3MM **Privately Held**
SIC: **3674** Light emitting diodes

(P-18334)
KLA-TENCOR ASIA-PAC DIST CORP
1 Technology Dr, Milpitas (95035-7916)
PHONE....................408 875-4144
Mark Nordstrom, *Principal*
Dan Wack, *Surgery Dir*
▲ **EMP:** 29
SALES (est): 3.7MM
SALES (corp-wide): 4.5B **Publicly Held**
WEB: www.tencor.com
SIC: **3674** Semiconductors & related devices
PA: Kla Corporation
1 Technology Dr
Milpitas CA 95035
408 875-3000

(P-18335)
KOPIN CORPORATION
501 Tevis Trl, Hollister (95023-9367)
PHONE....................831 636-5556
Jeff Jacobson, *Manager*
EMP: 45
SALES (corp-wide): 24.4MM **Publicly Held**
WEB: www.kopin.com
SIC: **3674** Semiconductors & related devices
PA: Kopin Corporation
125 North Dr
Westborough MA 01581
508 870-5959

(P-18336)
KSM CORP
1959 Concourse Dr, San Jose (95131-1708)
PHONE....................408 514-2400
Jooswan Kim, *CEO*
Harvinder P Singh, *President*
EMP: 500
SQ FT: 18,000
SALES: 100MM **Privately Held**
SIC: **3674** Semiconductors & related devices

PA: Ksm Component Co., Ltd.
90 Wolha-Ro 589beon-Gil, Haseong-Myeon
Gimpo 10011

(P-18337)
KYOCERA INTERNATIONAL INC (HQ)
8611 Balboa Ave, San Diego (92123-1580)
PHONE....................858 492-1456
Robert Whisler, *President*
William Edwards, *Vice Pres*
George Woodworth, *Vice Pres*
Eric Klein, *Admin Sec*
Patrick Wood, *Design Engr*
◆ **EMP:** 150
SQ FT: 16,000
SALES (est): 67.2MM **Publicly Held**
SIC: **3674** 5023 5731 Semiconductors & related devices; kitchen tools & utensils; radio, television & electronic stores

(P-18338)
L & M ELECTRONICS
541 Taylor Way Ste 10, San Carlos (94070-6254)
PHONE....................650 341-1608
Ed Luzzi, *President*
EMP: 15
SQ FT: 1,800
SALES: 300K **Privately Held**
SIC: **3674** 8731 Solid state electronic devices; commercial physical research

(P-18339)
LAM RESEARCH CORPORATION
3590 N 1st St Ste 200, San Jose (95134-1808)
PHONE....................408 434-6109
John Newman, *Principal*
Daniel Phan, *Technician*
Kenneth Finnegan, *Engineer*
Wenchi Liu, *Engineer*
Denis Syomin, *Engineer*
EMP: 45
SALES (corp-wide): 9.6B **Publicly Held**
WEB: www.lamrc.com
SIC: **3674** Semiconductors & related devices
PA: Lam Research Corporation
4650 Cushing Pkwy
Fremont CA 94538
510 572-0200

(P-18340)
LAM RESEARCH CORPORATION (PA)
4650 Cushing Pkwy, Fremont (94538-6401)
PHONE....................510 572-0200
Timothy M Archer, *President*
Stephen G Newberry, *Ch of Bd*
Douglas R Bettinger, *CFO*
Sarah A O'Dowd,
Richard A Gottscho, *Exec VP*
EMP: 100
SALES: 9.6B **Publicly Held**
WEB: www.lamrc.com
SIC: **3674** Wafers (semiconductor devices)

(P-18341)
LAM RESEARCH CORPORATION
1 Portola Ave, Livermore (94551-7647)
PHONE....................510 572-8400
Marcus Musselman, *Engineer*
Rich Witherspoon, *Business Mgr*
Kristopher Poor, *Manager*
EMP: 25
SALES (corp-wide): 9.6B **Publicly Held**
SIC: **3674** Semiconductors & related devices
PA: Lam Research Corporation
4650 Cushing Pkwy
Fremont CA 94538
510 572-0200

(P-18342)
LAM RESEARCH CORPORATION
4400 Cushing Pkwy, Fremont (94538-6429)
PHONE....................510 572-0200
Robin Mancuso Grady, *Branch Mgr*
Kim Jisoo, *Technical Staff*
Helen Zhu, *Engineer*
Lisa Agnelli, *Director*

EMP: 86
SALES (corp-wide): 9.6B **Publicly Held**
WEB: www.lamrc.com
SIC: **3674** Semiconductors & related devices
PA: Lam Research Corporation
4650 Cushing Pkwy
Fremont CA 94538
510 572-0200

(P-18343)
LASER OPERATIONS LLC
Also Called: Qpc Laser
15632 Roxford St, Sylmar (91342-1265)
PHONE....................818 986-0000
Morris Lichtenstein, *CEO*
Mikhail Leibov, *President*
Robert Lammert, *Vice Pres*
Kulya Ponek, *General Mgr*
Jeffrey Ungar, *CTO*
EMP: 27
SQ FT: 40,320
SALES (est): 6.2MM **Privately Held**
SIC: **3674** Semiconductors & related devices

(P-18344)
LATTICE SEMICONDUCTOR CORP
2115 Onel Dr, San Jose (95131-2032)
PHONE....................408 826-6000
Al Chan, *Manager*
Srinivas Perisetty, *Engineer*
EMP: 300
SALES (corp-wide): 398.8MM **Publicly Held**
WEB: www.latticesemi.com
SIC: **3674** Integrated circuits, semiconductor networks, etc.
PA: Lattice Semiconductor Corp
5555 Ne Moore Ct
Hillsboro OR 97124
503 268-8000

(P-18345)
LED ONE CORPORATION (PA)
12437 Bellegrave Ave, Eastvale (91752-1014)
PHONE....................510 770-1189
Jonathan Chu, *CEO*
Shen Jen WA Ng, *Admin Sec*
Susan Miller, *Marketing Mgr*
Ivan Chu, *Sales Mgr*
John Burns, *Accounts Mgr*
▲ **EMP:** 10
SQ FT: 17,000
SALES (est): 3.6MM **Privately Held**
SIC: **3674** Light emitting diodes

(P-18346)
LEDCONN CORP
301 Thor Pl, Brea (92821-4133)
PHONE....................714 256-2111
Tsanyu Wang, *President*
Wan Ting Huang, *CFO*
Michael McDonald, *Vice Pres*
Lien-Chung Lin, *Design Engr*
Desiree Ortiz, *Project Mgr*
▲ **EMP:** 15
SQ FT: 2,000
SALES (est): 4MM **Privately Held**
SIC: **3674** Light emitting diodes

(P-18347)
LEDENGIN INC (PA)
651 River Oaks Pkwy, San Jose (95134-1907)
PHONE....................408 922-7200
▲ **EMP:** 35
SQ FT: 15,037
SALES (est): 8.8MM **Privately Held**
WEB: www.ledengin.com
SIC: **3674** Light emitting diodes

(P-18348)
LEDTRONICS INC
23105 Kashiwa Ct, Torrance (90505-4026)
PHONE....................310 534-1505
Pervaiz Lodhie, *President*
Almas Lodhie, *Vice Pres*
Eugene Enriquez, *Engineer*
Joannes Hsuean, *QC Mgr*
Mazvar Rizvi, *Manager*
▲ **EMP:** 130
SQ FT: 60,000

SALES: 13.8MM **Privately Held**
WEB: www.led.net
SIC: **3674** 3825 3641 Light emitting diodes; instruments to measure electricity; electric lamps

(P-18349)
LEVEL 5 NETWORKS INC
840 W California Ave, Sunnyvale (94086-4828)
PHONE....................408 245-9300
Ashfaq Munshi, *CEO*
Steve Pope, *CTO*
EMP: 50
SQ FT: 12,759
SALES (est): 5MM **Privately Held**
SIC: **3674** Semiconductor diodes & rectifiers

(P-18350)
LINEAR INTEGRATED SYSTEMS INC
4042 Clipper Ct, Fremont (94538-6540)
PHONE....................510 490-9160
Cindy Cook Johnson, *CEO*
Tim McCune, *President*
Timothy McCune, *President*
Michael Ansberry, *Vice Pres*
Peter Tang, *Sales Staff*
EMP: 17
SQ FT: 5,000
SALES (est): 2.8MM **Privately Held**
SIC: **3674** Integrated circuits, semiconductor networks, etc.

(P-18351)
LINEAR TECHNOLOGY CORPORATION
Also Called: Linear Express
720 Sycamore Dr, Milpitas (95035-7406)
PHONE....................408 428-2050
Quang Ndyem, *Branch Mgr*
Todd Reimund, *Chief Mktg Ofcr*
Leo Chan, *Engineer*
Fernando Ferreira, *Production*
David S Lee, *Director*
EMP: 14
SALES (corp-wide): 6.2B **Publicly Held**
SIC: **3674** Integrated circuits, semiconductor networks, etc.
HQ: Linear Technology Llc
1630 Mccarthy Blvd
Milpitas CA 95035
408 432-1900

(P-18352)
LINEAR TECHNOLOGY CORPORATION
1530 Buckeye Dr, Milpitas (95035-7418)
PHONE....................408 434-6237
EMP: 54
SALES (corp-wide): 6.2B **Publicly Held**
SIC: **3674** Integrated circuits, semiconductor networks, etc.
HQ: Linear Technology Llc
1630 Mccarthy Blvd
Milpitas CA 95035
408 432-1900

(P-18353)
LINEAR TECHNOLOGY LLC (HQ)
1630 Mccarthy Blvd, Milpitas (95035-7417)
PHONE....................408 432-1900
Lothar Maier, *CEO*
Vicki A Hembree, *President*
Alexander R McCann, *COO*
Donald P Zerio, *CFO*
Robert C Dobkin, *Vice Pres*
▲ **EMP:** 900
SQ FT: 430,000
SALES: 1.4B
SALES (corp-wide): 6.2B **Publicly Held**
WEB: www.linear.com
SIC: **3674** Integrated circuits, semiconductor networks, etc.
PA: Analog Devices, Inc.
1 Technology Way
Norwood MA 02062
781 329-4700

(P-18354)
LINEAR TECHNOLOGY LLC
911 Olive St, Santa Barbara (93101-1406)
PHONE....................805 965-6400
Robert Swanson, *CEO*

▲ = Import ▼=Export
◆ =Import/Export

EMP: 54
SALES (corp-wide): 6.2B **Publicly Held**
SIC: 3674 Integrated circuits, semiconductor networks, etc.
HQ: Linear Technology Llc
1630 Mccarthy Blvd
Milpitas CA 95035
408 432-1900

(P-18355)
LINEAR TECHNOLOGY LLC
5465 Morehouse Dr Ste 155, San Diego (92121-4713)
PHONE...................................408 432-1900
Ralf Butz, *Manager*
Kirk Albrektsen, *Engineer*
EMP: 54
SALES (corp-wide): 6.2B **Publicly Held**
SIC: 3674 Integrated circuits, semiconductor networks, etc.
HQ: Linear Technology Llc
1630 Mccarthy Blvd
Milpitas CA 95035
408 432-1900

(P-18356)
LION SEMICONDUCTOR INC
332 Townsend St, San Francisco (94107-1607)
PHONE...................................415 462-4933
Wonyoung Kim, *CEO*
John Crossley, *Vice Pres*
Hanhphuc Le, *Engineer*
Thomas LI, *Engineer*
Hans Meyvaert, *Engineer*
EMP: 13 EST: 2012
SALES (est): 146.2K **Privately Held**
SIC: 3674 Microcircuits, integrated (semiconductor)

(P-18357)
LOCKWOOD INDUSTRIES LLC
Also Called: Fralock
28525 Industry Dr, Valencia (91355-5424)
PHONE...................................661 702-6999
Marcelo Norona, *CEO*
Bobbi Booher, *CFO*
David Leon, *Executive*
Mayra Arroyo, *Technician*
Kc Calderon, *Project Mgr*
EMP: 200 EST: 1966
SQ FT: 62,500
SALES (est): 84.8MM **Privately Held**
WEB: www.fralock.com
SIC: 3674 3842 3089 2891 Semiconductors & related devices; prosthetic appliances; plastic containers, except foam; sealants; laminated plastics plate & sheet

(P-18358)
LONGI SOLAR TECHNOLOGY US INC
2603 Camino Ramon Ste 423, San Ramon (94583-9128)
PHONE...................................925 380-6084
Baoshen Zhong, *CEO*
Lixing Zhang, *CFO*
Archimedes Flores, *Admin Sec*
EMP: 13
SALES (est): 635.7K
SALES (corp-wide): 3.1B **Privately Held**
SIC: 3674 Solar cells
HQ: Longi Solar Technologie Gmbh
Sebastian-Kneipp-Str. 41
Frankfurt Am Main 60439
695 050-6425

(P-18359)
LSI CORPORATION (DH)
Also Called: Broadcom
1320 Ridder Park Dr, San Jose (95131-2313)
PHONE...................................408 433-8000
Abhijit Talwalkar, *President*
Abhijit Y Talwalkar, *President*
D Jeffrey Richardson, *COO*
Bryon Look, *CFO*
Jean F Rankin, *Exec VP*
▲ EMP: 2400
SQ FT: 240,000
SALES (est): 2.5B
SALES (corp-wide): 20.8B **Publicly Held**
WEB: www.lsi.com
SIC: 3674 Microcircuits, integrated (semiconductor)

HQ: Avago Technologies Wireless (U.S.A.) Manufacturing Llc
4380 Ziegler Rd
Fort Collins CO 80525
970 288-2575

(P-18360)
LSI CORPORATION
9745 Prospect Ave, Santee (92071-6209)
PHONE...................................619 312-0903
EMP: 49
SALES (corp-wide): 4.2B **Privately Held**
SIC: 3674
HQ: Lsi Corporation
1320 Ridder Park Dr
San Jose CA 95131
408 433-8000

(P-18361)
LSI CORPORATION
Also Called: LSI Logic
2 Park Plz Ste 440, Irvine (92614-2535)
PHONE...................................800 372-2447
Al Di Cicco, *Branch Mgr*
EMP: 20
SALES (corp-wide): 20.8B **Publicly Held**
SIC: 3674 Semiconductors & related devices
HQ: Lsi Corporation
1320 Ridder Park Dr
San Jose CA 95131
408 433-8000

(P-18362)
LSI CORPORATION
1310 Ridder Park Dr, San Jose (95131-2313)
PHONE...................................408 436-8379
Kay Framan, *Branch Mgr*
Trinh Tran, *Director*
EMP: 16
SALES (corp-wide): 20.8B **Publicly Held**
SIC: 3674 Semiconductors & related devices
HQ: Lsi Corporation
1320 Ridder Park Dr
San Jose CA 95131
408 433-8000

(P-18363)
LUMIO INC
6355 Topanga Canyon Blvd # 335, Woodland Hills (91367-2102)
PHONE...................................586 861-2408
Freddy Raitan, *CEO*
Mario Neves, *Senior VP*
Dan Gunders, *Vice Pres*
EMP: 12
SALES (est): 2.3MM **Privately Held**
SIC: 3674 Radiation sensors

(P-18364)
LUXTERA LLC
Also Called: Luxtera, Inc.
2320 Camino Vida Roble # 100, Carlsbad (92011-1562)
PHONE...................................760 448-3520
Greg Young, *President*
Joseph Balardeta, *Vice Pres*
Rocky Leblanc, *Engineer*
Karen Warrington, *Accountant*
EMP: 105
SALES (est): 4MM
SALES (corp-wide): 51.9B **Publicly Held**
WEB: www.luxtera.com
SIC: 3674 Semiconductors & related devices
PA: Cisco Systems, Inc.
170 W Tasman Dr
San Jose CA 95134
408 526-4000

(P-18365)
M-PULSE MICROWAVE INC
576 Charcot Ave, San Jose (95131-2201)
PHONE...................................408 432-1480
Billy Long, *President*
Wendell Sanders, *Shareholder*
EMP: 25
SQ FT: 24,000
SALES (est): 3.5MM **Privately Held**
WEB: www.mpulsemw.com
SIC: 3674 Integrated circuits, semiconductor networks, etc.

(P-18366)
MACKENZIE LABORATORIES INC
1163 Nicole Ct, Glendora (91740-5387)
P.O. Box 1416 (91740-1416)
PHONE...................................909 394-9007
Nagy Khattar, *President*
Joe Coussa, *Vice Pres*
Robert Satchell, *Research*
Jorge Ocana, *Engineer*
Chantel Najera, *Personnel*
▲ EMP: 25 EST: 1952
SQ FT: 20,000
SALES (est): 4.4MM **Privately Held**
WEB: www.macklabs.com
SIC: 3674 3663 Semiconductors & related devices; radio & TV communications equipment

(P-18367)
MACQUARIE ELECTRONICS INC
2153 Otoole Ave Ste 20, San Jose (95131-1331)
PHONE...................................408 965-3860
John Doricko, *Vice Pres*
Ben Lu, *Vice Pres*
▲ EMP: 12
SALES (est): 1.7MM **Privately Held**
SIC: 3674 Semiconductors & related devices

(P-18368)
MAGNUM SEMICONDUCTOR INC
6024 Silver Creek Vly Rd, San Jose (95138-1011)
PHONE...................................408 934-3700
Gopal Solanki, *President*
▲ EMP: 233
SALES (est): 32.7MM **Privately Held**
WEB: www.magnumsemi.com
SIC: 3674 Integrated circuits, semiconductor networks, etc.
HQ: Gigpeak, Inc.
6024 Silver Creek Vly Rd
San Jose CA 95138
408 546-3316

(P-18369)
MAGTEK INC
20725 Annalee Ave, Carson (90746-3572)
PHONE...................................562 631-8602
James Niu, *Engineer*
Jose Bonilla, *Admin Sec*
EMP: 13
SALES (corp-wide): 63.4MM **Privately Held**
SIC: 3674 Semiconductors & related devices
PA: Magtek, Inc.
1710 Apollo Ct
Seal Beach CA 90740
562 546-6400

(P-18370)
MARTEQ PROCESS SOLUTIONS INC
1721 S Grand Ave, Santa Ana (92705-4808)
PHONE...................................714 495-4275
Danny L Richter, *President*
Charles Edwards, *Surgery Dir*
Kevin Jacobs, *VP Finance*
▼ EMP: 10
SQ FT: 7,000
SALES (est): 1.1MM **Privately Held**
WEB: www.marteqpro.com
SIC: 3674 Semiconductors & related devices

(P-18371)
MARVELL SEMICONDUCTOR INC
15485 Sand Canyon Ave, Irvine (92618-3154)
PHONE...................................949 614-7700
Robert E Romney, *Principal*
EMP: 12 **Privately Held**
SIC: 3674 Semiconductors & related devices
HQ: Marvell Semiconductor, Inc.
5488 Marvell Ln
Santa Clara CA 95054

(P-18372)
MARVELL SEMICONDUCTOR INC (HQ)
5488 Marvell Ln, Santa Clara (95054-3606)
PHONE...................................408 222-2500
Matt Murphy, *CEO*
Allan Brown, *Bd of Directors*
Juergen Gromer, *Bd of Directors*
Neil Kim, *Exec VP*
Nafea Bishara, *Vice Pres*
◆ EMP: 900
SALES (est): 663.2MM **Privately Held**
WEB: www.marvel.com
SIC: 3674 Semiconductors & related devices

(P-18373)
MASIMO SEMICONDUCTOR INC
52 Discovery, Irvine (92618-3105)
PHONE...................................603 595-8900
Mark P De Raad, *President*
Gerry Hammarth, *Treasurer*
Hugh Ferguson, *Accounts Mgr*
EMP: 20
SALES (est): 2.4MM **Publicly Held**
SIC: 3674 Light emitting diodes
PA: Masimo Corporation
52 Discovery
Irvine CA 92618

(P-18374)
MATTSON TECHNOLOGY INC (HQ)
47131 Bayside Pkwy, Fremont (94538-6517)
PHONE...................................510 657-5900
Fusen Chen, *President*
J Michael Dodson, *COO*
Subhash Deshmukh, *Officer*
Michael Z Shi, *Officer*
Suzette Sanchez, *Executive Asst*
▲ EMP: 224
SQ FT: 101,000
SALES: 251.4MM
SALES (corp-wide): 3.5MM **Privately Held**
SIC: 3674 Semiconductors & related devices
PA: Beijing E-Town International Investment & Development Co., Ltd.
Building 61, Bda International Business Avenue, No.2, Jingyuan (
Beijing 10017
108 716-2565

(P-18375)
MAXIM INTEGRATED PRODUCTS INC (PA)
160 Rio Robles, San Jose (95134-1813)
PHONE...................................408 601-1000
Tunc Doluca, *President*
EMP: 956
SQ FT: 435,000
SALES: 2.3B **Publicly Held**
WEB: www.maxim-ic.com
SIC: 3674 Semiconductors & related devices; microcircuits, integrated (semiconductor)

(P-18376)
MAXIM-DALLAS DIRECT INC
120 San Gabriel Dr, Sunnyvale (94086-5125)
PHONE...................................800 659-5909
Tunc Doluca, *President*
EMP: 14
SALES (est): 1.2MM **Privately Held**
SIC: 3674 Semiconductors & related devices

(P-18377)
MAXLINEAR INC (PA)
5966 La Place Ct Ste 100, Carlsbad (92008-8830)
PHONE...................................760 692-0711
Kishore Seendripu, *Ch of Bd*
Kimihiko Imura, *Vice Pres*
Michael J Lachance, *Vice Pres*
Raja Pullela, *Vice Pres*
Madhukar Reddy, *Vice Pres*
▲ EMP: 45
SQ FT: 68,000

PRODUCTS & SVCS

SALES: 385MM **Publicly Held**
WEB: www.maxlinear.com
SIC: **3674** Semiconductors & related devices

(P-18378)
MDC VACUUM PRODUCTS LLC (PA)
30962 Santana St, Hayward (94544-7058)
P.O. Box 398436, San Francisco (94139-8436)
PHONE.................................510 265-3500
David L Dutton, *CEO*
Tim Lima, *CFO*
Timothy Lima, *CFO*
Rob Holoboff, *General Mgr*
Neil Spector, *Engineer*
▲ EMP: 100 EST: 1976
SQ FT: 45,000
SALES: 41MM **Privately Held**
WEB: www.mdcvacuum.com
SIC: **3674** 3491 Wafers (semiconductor devices); pressure valves & regulators, industrial

(P-18379)
MEGACHIPS TECHNOLOGY AMER CORP (HQ)
Also Called: Kawasaki Micro Elec Amer
2755 Orchard Pkwy, San Jose (95134-2008)
PHONE.................................408 570-0555
Koichi Akeyama, *CEO*
Shujiro Matsusaka, *CFO*
Koji Takano, *CFO*
Tommy Aizawa, *Vice Pres*
Amir Sheikholeslami, *Vice Pres*
▲ EMP: 40
SQ FT: 16,000
SALES (est): 13.4MM **Publicly Held**
WEB: www.klsi.com
SIC: **3674** Integrated circuits, semiconductor networks, etc.

(P-18380)
MEIVAC INCORPORATED
5830 Hellyer Ave, San Jose (95138-1004)
PHONE.................................408 362-1000
Richard Meidinger, *CEO*
David Meidinger, *President*
EMP: 30
SQ FT: 27,000
SALES (est): 8.9MM **Privately Held**
WEB: www.meivac.com
SIC: **3674** Semiconductors & related devices

(P-18381)
MELLANOX TECHNOLOGIES INC
Also Called: Accounts Payable
350 Oakmead Pkwy Ste 100, Sunnyvale (94085-5423)
P.O. Box 67143, Scotts Valley (95067-7143)
PHONE.................................408 970-3400
Eyal Waldman, *CEO*
Hong Liang, *Engineer*
Peter Zhou, *Engineer*
Bhavin Bijlani, *Senior Engr*
Pegah Seddighian, *Senior Engr*
EMP: 31
SALES (corp-wide): 293.8MM **Privately Held**
SIC: **3674** Semiconductors & related devices
HQ: Mellanox Technologies, Inc.
350 Oakmead Pkwy
Sunnyvale CA 94085
408 970-3400

(P-18382)
MELLANOX TECHNOLOGIES INC (HQ)
350 Oakmead Pkwy, Sunnyvale (94085-5400)
PHONE.................................408 970-3400
Eyal Waldman, *Ch of Bd*
Chris Shea, *President*
Alon Webman, *President*
Shai Cohen, *COO*
Michael Gray, *CFO*
EMP: 260
SQ FT: 39,000

SALES: 1B
SALES (corp-wide): 293.8MM **Privately Held**
SIC: **3674** Integrated circuits, semiconductor networks, etc.
PA: Mellanox Technologies, Ltd.
26 Hakidma
Upper Yokneam
747 237-200

(P-18383)
MENLO MICROSYSTEMS INC
49 Discovery Ste 150, Irvine (92618-6710)
PHONE.................................949 771-0277
Russ Garcia, *CEO*
EMP: 23
SALES (est): 3MM **Privately Held**
SIC: **3674** Semiconductors & related devices

(P-18384)
MERLIN SOLAR TECHNOLOGIES INC
5891 Rue Ferrari, San Jose (95138-1857)
PHONE.................................650 740-1160
Arthur Tan, *CEO*
Olaf Gresens, *President*
Venkatesan Murali, *Founder*
Becky Neto, *Office Mgr*
Dong Xu, *Senior Engr*
EMP: 40
SQ FT: 26,773
SALES (est): 1.8MM
SALES (corp-wide): 2MM **Privately Held**
SIC: **3674** Solar cells
PA: Aci Solar Holdings Na Inc
303 Twin Dolphin Dr # 600
Redwood City CA 94065
650 227-3271

(P-18385)
MIASOLE
2590 Walsh Ave, Santa Clara (95051-1315)
PHONE.................................408 919-5700
Jeff Zhou, *CEO*
Merle McClendon, *CFO*
Atiye Bayman, *CTO*
▲ EMP: 315
SALES (est): 55.1MM **Privately Held**
WEB: www.miasole.com
SIC: **3674** Solar cells

(P-18386)
MIASOLE HI-TECH CORP (DH)
2590 Walsh Ave, Santa Clara (95051-1315)
PHONE.................................408 919-5700
Jie Zhang, *CEO*
Lyndsey Zhang, *CFO*
Jason Corneille, *Vice Pres*
Dartt Wagner, *Executive*
Niem Nguyen, *Administration*
EMP: 250
SQ FT: 111,585
SALES (est): 40.4MM
SALES (corp-wide): 782.7MM **Privately Held**
SIC: **3674** 5074 Solar cells; heating equipment & panels, solar
HQ: Hanergy Holding (America) Llc
1350 Bayshore Hwy
Burlingame CA 94010
650 288-3722

(P-18387)
MICREL LLC
2180 Fortune Dr, San Jose (95131-1815)
PHONE.................................408 944-0800
Raymond Zinn, *CEO*
Lisa Jones, *Administration*
Tien Pham, *Engineer*
Jenny Sun, *Engineer*
Lia N Punches, *Pub Rel Mgr*
EMP: 728
SALES (corp-wide): 5.3B **Publicly Held**
SIC: **3674** Integrated circuits, semiconductor networks, etc.
HQ: Micrel, Llc
2355 W Chandler Blvd
Chandler AZ 85224
480 792-7200

(P-18388)
MICREL LLC
Also Called: Micrel Semiconductor
1849 Fortune Dr, San Jose (95131-1724)
PHONE.................................408 944-0800
Mark Lunsford, *Branch Mgr*
John Holman, *Prgrmr*
Karen Jakabcin, *Technical Staff*
John Kirby, *Technical Staff*
EMP: 250
SALES (corp-wide): 5.3B **Publicly Held**
WEB: www.micrel.com
SIC: **3674** Semiconductors & related devices
HQ: Micrel, Llc
2355 W Chandler Blvd
Chandler AZ 85224
480 792-7200

(P-18389)
MICREL LLC
1931 Fortune Dr, San Jose (95131-1724)
PHONE.................................408 944-0800
Jung-Chen Lin, *Branch Mgr*
Satoshi Ibuki, *Design Engr*
EMP: 250
SALES (corp-wide): 5.3B **Publicly Held**
WEB: www.micrel.com
SIC: **3674** Semiconductors & related devices
HQ: Micrel, Llc
2355 W Chandler Blvd
Chandler AZ 85224
480 792-7200

(P-18390)
MICRO ANALOG INC
1861 Puddingstone Dr, La Verne (91750-5825)
PHONE.................................909 392-8277
Hung T Nguyen, *CEO*
Khanh Van Nguyen, *CFO*
KV Nguyen, *Vice Pres*
Tuan Nguyen, *Executive*
Tuan Tran, *Engineer*
▲ EMP: 160
SQ FT: 27,000
SALES (est): 48.5MM **Privately Held**
SIC: **3674** Semiconductors & related devices

(P-18391)
MICRO GAGE INC
9537 Telstar Ave Ste 131, El Monte (91731-2912)
PHONE.................................626 443-1741
Bruce Talmo, *President*
Martin Chinn, *Vice Pres*
EMP: 35 EST: 1972
SQ FT: 9,000
SALES (est): 5.4MM **Privately Held**
SIC: **3674** Semiconductors & related devices

(P-18392)
MICRO SEMICDTR RESEARCHES LLC
805 Aldo Ave Ste 101, Santa Clara (95054-2200)
PHONE.................................408 492-1369
Seiji Yamashita, *Branch Mgr*
EMP: 25
SALES (corp-wide): 1.7MM **Privately Held**
SIC: **3674** 8748 Semiconductors & related devices; test development & evaluation service
PA: Micro Semiconductor Researches, Llc
310 W 52nd St Apt 12b
New York NY 10019
646 863-6070

(P-18393)
MICROCHIP TECHNOLOGY INC
450 Holger Way, San Jose (95134-1368)
PHONE.................................408 735-9110
Greg Winner, *CEO*
Thuan Vu, *Design Engr*
Michael Huynh, *Engineer*
Jin-Ho Kim, *Engineer*
Kevin McAdams, *Engineer*
EMP: 166
SALES (corp-wide): 5.3B **Publicly Held**
SIC: **3674** Integrated circuits, semiconductor networks, etc.

PA: Microchip Technology Inc
2355 W Chandler Blvd
Chandler AZ 85224
480 792-7200

(P-18394)
MICROFLEX TECHNOLOGIES LLC
430 W Collins Ave, Orange (92867-5508)
PHONE.................................714 937-1507
Micheal Doyle, *Mng Member*
EMP: 11
SALES (est): 2.3MM **Privately Held**
WEB: www.microflexseals.com
SIC: **3674** Semiconductors & related devices

(P-18395)
MICRON TECHNOLOGY INC
570 Alder Dr Bldg 2, Milpitas (95035-7443)
PHONE.................................408 855-4000
Dana Krelle, *Vice Pres*
Leagong Chen, *Engineer*
Lichieh Chien, *Engineer*
Dan Nguyen, *Engineer*
Jihye Shin, *Engineer*
EMP: 48
SALES (corp-wide): 23.4B **Publicly Held**
WEB: www.micron.com
SIC: **3674** Random access memory (RAM)
PA: Micron Technology, Inc.
8000 S Federal Way
Boise ID 83716
208 368-4000

(P-18396)
MICRON TECHNOLOGY INC
2235 Iron Point Rd, Folsom (95630-8765)
PHONE.................................916 458-3003
Glen Hawk, *Branch Mgr*
Jose Suez, *IT/INT Sup*
Rick Baer, *Engineer*
Dustin Carter, *Engineer*
Jiajia Guo, *Engineer*
EMP: 512
SALES (corp-wide): 23.4B **Publicly Held**
SIC: **3674** Integrated circuits, semiconductor networks, etc.
PA: Micron Technology, Inc.
8000 S Federal Way
Boise ID 83716
208 368-4000

(P-18397)
MICROPLEX INC
1070 Ortega Way, Placentia (92870-7124)
PHONE.................................714 630-8220
Clay Kucenas, *President*
Catherine A Kucenas, *Executive*
EMP: 15
SQ FT: 10,500
SALES: 2MM **Privately Held**
WEB: www.microplexinc.com
SIC: **3674** Semiconductors & related devices

(P-18398)
MICROSEMI COMMUNICATIONS INC
11861 Western Ave, Garden Grove (92841-2119)
PHONE.................................805 388-3700
Martin S McDermut, *Principal*
EMP: 30
SALES (corp-wide): 5.3B **Publicly Held**
WEB: www.cicada-semi.com
SIC: **3674** Semiconductors & related devices
HQ: Microsemi Communications, Inc.
4721 Calle Carga
Camarillo CA 93012
805 388-3700

(P-18399)
MICROSEMI COMMUNICATIONS INC (DH)
Also Called: Catawba County Schools
4721 Calle Carga, Camarillo (93012-8541)
PHONE.................................805 388-3700
Christopher R Gardner, *President*
Martin S McDermut, *CFO*
Jacob Nielsen, *CIO*
EMP: 105
SQ FT: 111,000

SALES (est): 84.3MM
SALES (corp-wide): 5.3B **Publicly Held**
WEB: www.vitesse.com
SIC: 3674 Semiconductors & related devices
HQ: Microsemi Corporation
1 Enterprise
Aliso Viejo CA 92656
949 380-6100

(P-18400)
MICROSEMI CORP - PWR PRDTS GRP
3000 Oakmead Village Dr, Santa Clara (95051-0819)
PHONE..................408 986-8031
Cindy Matts, *Vice Pres*
EMP: 15
SALES (corp-wide): 5.3B **Publicly Held**
WEB: www.advancedpower.com
SIC: 3674 Transistors
HQ: Microsemi Corp. - Power Products Group
405 Sw Columbia St
Bend OR 97702
541 382-8028

(P-18401)
MICROSEMI CORP- RF INTEGRATED (DH)
Also Called: Microsemi Rfis
105 Lake Forest Way, Folsom (95630-4708)
PHONE..................916 850-8640
James J Peterson, *President*
Ralph Brandi, *COO*
John W Hohener, *CFO*
David H Hall, *Vice Pres*
▲ **EMP:** 115
SALES (est): 8.7MM
SALES (corp-wide): 5.3B **Publicly Held**
SIC: 3674 Semiconductors & related devices
HQ: Microsemi Corporation
1 Enterprise
Aliso Viejo CA 92656
949 380-6100

(P-18402)
MICROSEMI CORP-ANALOG
3850 N 1st St, San Jose (95134-1702)
PHONE..................408 643-6000
Shafy Eltoukhy, *General Mgr*
EMP: 35
SALES (corp-wide): 5.3B **Publicly Held**
SIC: 3674 Semiconductors & related devices
HQ: Microsemi Corp. - Analog Mixed Signal Group
11861 Western Ave
Garden Grove CA 92841

(P-18403)
MICROSEMI CORP-ANALOG (DH)
Also Called: Linfinity Microelectronics
11861 Western Ave, Garden Grove (92841-2119)
PHONE..................714 898-8121
James Peterson, *CEO*
Paul Pickle, *COO*
John Hohener, *CFO*
Russ Garcia, *Exec VP*
Steve Litchfield, *Security Dir*
EMP: 74
SALES (est): 157.6MM
SALES (corp-wide): 5.3B **Publicly Held**
SIC: 3674 Semiconductor circuit networks
HQ: Microsemi Corporation
1 Enterprise
Aliso Viejo CA 92656
949 380-6100

(P-18404)
MICROSEMI CORPORATION
Also Called: Microsemi Corp - Santa Ana
11861 Western Ave, Garden Grove (92841-2119)
PHONE..................714 898-7112
Lane Jorgensen, *Manager*
Todd Wiviott, *Plant Mgr*
EMP: 350
SQ FT: 93,000

SALES (corp-wide): 5.3B **Publicly Held**
SIC: 3674 Semiconductors & related devices
HQ: Microsemi Corporation
1 Enterprise
Aliso Viejo CA 92656
949 380-6100

(P-18405)
MICROSEMI CORPORATION (HQ)
1 Enterprise, Aliso Viejo (92656-2606)
PHONE..................949 380-6100
James J Peterson, *CEO*
Paul H Pickle, *President*
John W Hohener, *CFO*
Thomas Anderson, *Bd of Directors*
Bill Healey, *Bd of Directors*
EMP: 50
SALES: 1.8B
SALES (corp-wide): 5.3B **Publicly Held**
SIC: 3674 Integrated circuits, semiconductor networks, etc.; rectifiers, solid state; Zener diodes; diodes, solid state (germanium, silicon, etc.)
PA: Microchip Technology Inc
2355 W Chandler Blvd
Chandler AZ 85224
480 792-7200

(P-18406)
MICROSEMI CORPORATION
3843 Brickway Blvd # 100, Santa Rosa (95403-9060)
PHONE..................707 568-5900
Amanda Lando, *President*
EMP: 121
SALES (corp-wide): 5.3B **Publicly Held**
SIC: 3674 Semiconductors & related devices
HQ: Microsemi Corporation
1 Enterprise
Aliso Viejo CA 92656
949 380-6100

(P-18407)
MICROSEMI CORPORATION
3850 N 1st St, San Jose (95134-1702)
PHONE..................408 643-6000
Jim Peterson, *CEO*
Jih-Jong Wang, *Engineer*
Stephen Yu, *Senior Mgr*
Madhu Raman, *Manager*
Solomon Wolday, *Manager*
EMP: 10
SALES (corp-wide): 5.3B **Publicly Held**
SIC: 3674 Semiconductors & related devices
HQ: Microsemi Corporation
1 Enterprise
Aliso Viejo CA 92656
949 380-6100

(P-18408)
MICROSEMI CORPORATION
3870 N 1st St, San Jose (95134-1702)
PHONE..................650 318-4200
Pierre Irisso, *Branch Mgr*
EMP: 52
SALES (corp-wide): 5.3B **Publicly Held**
SIC: 3674 Semiconductors & related devices
HQ: Microsemi Corporation
1 Enterprise
Aliso Viejo CA 92656
949 380-6100

(P-18409)
MICROSEMI FREQUENCY TIME CORP
3750 Westwind Blvd, Santa Rosa (95403-9072)
PHONE..................707 528-1230
John Dutil, *Manager*
EMP: 100
SALES (corp-wide): 5.3B **Publicly Held**
WEB: www.symmetricom.com
SIC: 3674 Semiconductors & related devices
HQ: Microsemi Frequency And Time Corporation
3870 N 1st St
San Jose CA 95134

(P-18410)
MICROSEMI FREQUENCY TIME CORP
802 Calle Plano, Camarillo (93012-8557)
PHONE..................805 465-1700
EMP: 30
SALES (corp-wide): 5.3B **Publicly Held**
WEB: www.symmetricom.com
SIC: 3674 Semiconductors & related devices
HQ: Microsemi Frequency And Time Corporation
3870 N 1st St
San Jose CA 95134

(P-18411)
MICROSEMI FREQUENCY TIME CORP
2300 Orchard Pkwy, San Jose (95131-1017)
P.O. Box 39000, San Francisco (94139-0001)
PHONE..................408 433-0910
EMP: 12
SALES (corp-wide): 5.3B **Publicly Held**
SIC: 3674 Semiconductors & related devices
HQ: Microsemi Frequency And Time Corporation
3870 N 1st St
San Jose CA 95134

(P-18412)
MICROSEMI SOC CORP (DH)
3870 N 1st St, San Jose (95134-1702)
PHONE..................408 643-6000
James J Peterson, *CEO*
John W Hohener, *CFO*
Esmat Z Hamdy, *Senior VP*
Fares N Mubarak, *Senior VP*
David L Van De Hey, *Vice Pres*
▲ **EMP:** 96
SQ FT: 158,000
SALES (est): 162.4MM
SALES (corp-wide): 5.3B **Publicly Held**
WEB: www.actel.com
SIC: 3674 7371 Microcircuits, integrated (semiconductor); computer software development
HQ: Microsemi Corporation
1 Enterprise
Aliso Viejo CA 92656
949 380-6100

(P-18413)
MICROSEMI SOC CORP
2051 Stierlin Ct, Mountain View (94043-4655)
PHONE..................650 318-4200
Mary Segura, *Manager*
EMP: 31
SALES (corp-wide): 5.3B **Publicly Held**
SIC: 3674 Microcircuits, integrated (semiconductor)
HQ: Microsemi Soc Corp.
3870 N 1st St
San Jose CA 95134
408 643-6000

(P-18414)
MICROSEMI STOR SOLUTIONS INC (DH)
1380 Bordeaux Dr, Sunnyvale (94089-1005)
PHONE..................408 239-8000
Paul Pickle, *President*
Adhir Mattu, *President*
John W Hohener, *CFO*
EMP: 82
SQ FT: 85,000
SALES (est): 277.6MM
SALES (corp-wide): 5.3B **Publicly Held**
SIC: 3674 Modules, solid state
HQ: Microsemi Corporation
1 Enterprise
Aliso Viejo CA 92656
949 380-6100

(P-18415)
MICROSEMI STOR SOLUTIONS INC
101 Creekside Ridge Ct # 100, Roseville (95678-3595)
PHONE..................916 788-3300
Jim Dabney, *CEO*
EMP: 13
SALES (corp-wide): 5.3B **Publicly Held**
SIC: 3674 Semiconductors & related devices
HQ: Microsemi Storage Solutions, Inc.
1380 Bordeaux Dr
Sunnyvale CA 94089
408 239-8000

(P-18416)
MINDSPEED TECHNOLOGIES LLC (HQ)
Also Called: Mindspeed Technologies, Inc.
4000 Macarthur Blvd, Newport Beach (92660-2558)
PHONE..................949 579-3000
Raouf Y Halim, *CEO*
Stephen N Ananias, *CFO*
Abdelnaser M Adas, *Senior VP*
Najabat H Bajwa, *Senior VP*
Gerald J Hamilton, *Senior VP*
EMP: 68 **EST:** 2002
SQ FT: 97,000
SALES (est): 61MM **Publicly Held**
WEB: www.mindspeed.com
SIC: 3674 Semiconductors & related devices

(P-18417)
MINUS K TECHNOLOGY INC
460 Hindry Ave Ste C, Inglewood (90301-2044)
PHONE..................310 348-9656
David L Platus, *President*
Nancee Schwartz, *Admin Sec*
Jason AIN, *Production*
EMP: 110
SQ FT: 2,500
SALES (est): 13.8MM **Privately Held**
WEB: www.minusk.com
SIC: 3674 Optical isolators

(P-18418)
MIPS TECH INC (HQ)
300 Orchard Cy Dr Ste 170, Campbell (95008)
PHONE..................408 530-5000
Sandeep Vij, *President*
Krishna Raghavan, *COO*
William Slater, *CFO*
Brad Holtzinger, *Vice Pres*
Gideon Intrater, *VP Mktg*
▲ **EMP:** 80
SALES (est): 24MM
SALES (corp-wide): 32.6MM **Privately Held**
WEB: www.mips.com
SIC: 3674 Microprocessors
PA: Wave Computing, Inc.
300 Orchard Cy Dr Ste 170
Campbell CA 95008
408 412-8645

(P-18419)
MOBIVEIL INC
890 Hillview Ct Ste 250, Milpitas (95035-4574)
PHONE..................408 791-2977
Ravikumar R Thummarukudy, *CEO*
Dale Olstinske, *Vice Pres*
Amit Saxena, *Vice Pres*
D Srinivasan, *Principal*
Nisha Dalal, *Finance Mgr*
EMP: 13 **EST:** 2011
SALES (est): 1.9MM **Privately Held**
SIC: 3674 Semiconductors & related devices

(P-18420)
MONTAGE TECHNOLOGY INC
101 Metro Dr Ste 500, San Jose (95110-1342)
PHONE..................408 982-2788
Howard Yang, *Principal*
Lee Khem, *Sales Staff*
EMP: 16

PRODUCTS & SVCS

SALES (est): 2.9MM **Privately Held**
SIC: **3674** Semiconductors & related devices

(P-18421)
MOSYS INC
2309 Bering Dr, San Jose (95131-1125)
PHONE..............................408 418-7500
Thomas Riordan, *COO*
James W Sullivan, *CFO*
Michael Miller, *CTO*
John Monson, *VP Mktg*
EMP: 68
SQ FT: 47,000
SALES: 16.6MM **Privately Held**
WEB: www.mosysinc.com
SIC: **3674** Integrated circuits, semiconductor networks, etc.

(P-18422)
MOTOROLA SOLUTIONS INC
9665 Chesapeake Dr # 220, San Diego (92123-1367)
PHONE..............................858 541-2163
Amanda Hornik, *Manager*
EMP: 17
SALES (corp-wide): 7.3B **Publicly Held**
WEB: www.motorola.com
SIC: **3674** Semiconductors & related devices
PA: Motorola Solutions, Inc.
500 W Monroe St Ste 4400
Chicago IL 60661
847 576-5000

(P-18423)
MPS INTERNATIONAL LTD
79 Great Oaks Blvd, San Jose (95119-1311)
PHONE..............................408 826-0600
Michael R Hsing, *CEO*
▼ EMP: 1000 EST: 1997
SQ FT: 100,000
SALES (est): 388.6MM **Publicly Held**
SIC: **3674** Semiconductors & related devices
PA: Monolithic Power Systems, Inc.
4040 Lake Wash Blvd Ne
Kirkland WA 98033

(P-18424)
NANOSILICON INC
2461 Autumnvale Dr, San Jose (95131-1802)
PHONE..............................408 263-7341
Lincoln Bejan, *President*
Jackie Bejan, *CFO*
John Ayala, *Vice Pres*
EMP: 22
SQ FT: 30,000
SALES: 3.5MM **Privately Held**
SIC: **3674** Semiconductors & related devices

(P-18425)
NANOSYS INC
233 S Hillview Dr, Milpitas (95035-5417)
PHONE..............................408 240-6700
Jason Hartlove, *CEO*
Martin Devenney, *COO*
Noland Granberry, *Exec VP*
John Hanlow, *Senior VP*
Ophelia Skiver, *Executive Asst*
EMP: 113
SQ FT: 32,000
SALES (est): 36.5MM **Privately Held**
WEB: www.nanosysinc.com
SIC: **3674** Semiconductors & related devices

(P-18426)
NATEL ENGINEERING COMPANY LLC (PA)
Also Called: Neotech
9340 Owensmouth Ave, Chatsworth (91311-6915)
PHONE..............................818 495-8617
Sudesh K Arora,
James Howe, *Vice Pres*
Asdrubal Macias, *Vice Pres*
Anthony Lautieri, *Business Dir*
Mark Hiett, *Info Tech Mgr*
▲ EMP: 210
SQ FT: 200,000

SALES (est): 1.1B **Privately Held**
WEB: www.natelengr.com
SIC: **3674** **3679** Semiconductors & related devices; antennas, receiving

(P-18427)
NATIONAL SEMICONDUCTOR CORP (HQ)
2900 Semiconductor Dr, Santa Clara (95051-0695)
PHONE..............................408 721-5000
Ellen L Barker, *CEO*
Lewis Chew, *CFO*
Todd M Duchene, *Senior VP*
Edward J Sweeney, *Senior VP*
Jamie E Samath, *Vice Pres*
▲ EMP: 1700 EST: 1959
SALES (est): 421.6MM
SALES (corp-wide): 15.7B **Publicly Held**
WEB: www.national.com
SIC: **3674** Microprocessors
PA: Texas Instruments Incorporated
12500 Ti Blvd
Dallas TX 75243
214 479-3773

(P-18428)
NDSP DELAWARE INC
Also Called: Ndsp Crp
224 Airport Pkwy Ste 400, San Jose (95110-1095)
PHONE..............................408 626-1640
Ven L Lee, *President*
Leonard Liu, *Chairman*
Hongmin Zhang, *CTO*
EMP: 51
SQ FT: 9,285
SALES (est): 2.6MM
SALES (corp-wide): 76.5MM **Publicly Held**
WEB: www.pixelworks.com
SIC: **3674** Integrated circuits, semiconductor networks, etc.
PA: Pixelworks, Inc.
226 Airport Pkwy Ste 595
San Jose CA 95110
408 200-9200

(P-18429)
NEOCONIX INC
4020 Moorpark Ave Ste 108, San Jose (95117-1845)
PHONE..............................408 530-9393
Asuri Raghavan, *President*
Jim Witham, *CEO*
Dirk Brown, *Exec VP*
Phil Damberg, *Vice Pres*
Dinesh Kalakkad, *Vice Pres*
EMP: 40
SQ FT: 5,000
SALES (est): 6.3MM **Privately Held**
SIC: **3674** Semiconductors & related devices

(P-18430)
NEOPHOTONICS CORPORATION
40931 Encyclopedia Cir, Fremont (94538-2436)
PHONE..............................408 232-9200
Larry Martin, *Engineer*
EMP: 10 **Publicly Held**
SIC: **3674** Semiconductors & related devices
PA: Neophotonics Corporation
2911 Zanker Rd
San Jose CA 95134

(P-18431)
NEOPHOTONICS CORPORATION (PA)
2911 Zanker Rd, San Jose (95134-2125)
PHONE..............................408 232-9200
Timothy S Jenks, *Ch of Bd*
CHI Yue Cheung, *COO*
Elizabeth EBY, *CFO*
Wupen Yuen,
Yang Chiah Yee, *Senior VP*
EMP: 291
SQ FT: 103,314
SALES: 322.5MM **Publicly Held**
WEB: www.neophotonics.com
SIC: **3674** Semiconductors & related devices

(P-18432)
NETHRA IMAGING INC (PA)
2855 Bowers Ave, Santa Clara (95051-0917)
PHONE..............................408 257-5880
Ramesh Singh, *President*
EMP: 13
SALES (est): 3.6MM **Privately Held**
WEB: www.nethra-imaging.com
SIC: **3674** Semiconductors & related devices

(P-18433)
NETLIST INC (PA)
175 Technology Dr Ste 150, Irvine (92618-2479)
PHONE..............................949 435-0025
Chun K Hong, *Ch of Bd*
Gail Sasaki, *CFO*
Jun Cho, *Bd of Directors*
Soon Choi, *Bd of Directors*
Vahid Ordoubadian, *Vice Pres*
EMP: 82
SQ FT: 8,200
SALES: 33.5MM **Publicly Held**
WEB: www.netlistinc.com
SIC: **3674** Random access memory (RAM)

(P-18434)
NEWPORT FAB LLC
Also Called: Jazz Semiconductor
4321 Jamboree Rd, Newport Beach (92660-3007)
PHONE..............................949 435-8000
Susanna Bennette,
Gary Petzer, *Director*
EMP: 99
SALES (est): 1,000K
SALES (corp-wide): 352MM **Privately Held**
SIC: **3674** Wafers (semiconductor devices)
HQ: Jazz Semiconductor, Inc.
4321 Jamboree Rd
Newport Beach CA 92660
949 435-8000

(P-18435)
NEXGEN POWER SYSTEMS INC
2010 El Camino Real, Santa Clara (95050-4051)
PHONE..............................408 230-7698
Dinesh Ramanathan, *President*
Narayanan Karu, *CFO*
EMP: 30 EST: 2017
SQ FT: 3,400
SALES (est): 111.7K **Privately Held**
SIC: **3674** Semiconductor circuit networks

(P-18436)
NGCODEC INC
440 N Wolfe Rd Ste 2187, Sunnyvale (94085-3869)
PHONE..............................408 766-4382
Oliver Gunasekara, *CEO*
Alberto Duenas, *Chairman*
EMP: 20 EST: 2012
SALES (est): 892.3K **Privately Held**
SIC: **3674** Semiconductors & related devices

(P-18437)
NVIDIA CORPORATION (PA)
2788 San Tomas Expy, Santa Clara (95051-0952)
PHONE..............................408 486-2000
Jen-Hsun Huang, *President*
Colette M Kress, *CFO*
Ajay K Puri, *Exec VP*
Debora Shoquist, *Exec VP*
Timothy S Teter, *Exec VP*
◆ EMP: 458
SALES: 11.7B **Publicly Held**
WEB: www.nvidia.com
SIC: **3674** Semiconductors & related devices

(P-18438)
NVIDIA CORPORATION
2001 Walsh Ave, Santa Clara (95050-2522)
PHONE..............................408 566-5364
Marvin D Burkett, *President*
Michael Griffith, *Info Tech Dir*
Subhash Gutti, *Software Engr*
Vishwanath Kadam, *Software Engr*
Tezaswi Raja, *Design Engr*

EMP: 17 **Publicly Held**
SIC: **3674** Semiconductors & related devices
PA: Nvidia Corporation
2788 San Tomas Expy
Santa Clara CA 95051

(P-18439)
NVIDIA DEVELOPMENT INC
2701 San Tomas Expy, Santa Clara (95050-2519)
PHONE..............................408 486-2000
EMP: 27
SALES (est): 5.8MM **Publicly Held**
SIC: **3674** Semiconductors & related devices
PA: Nvidia Corporation
2788 San Tomas Expy
Santa Clara CA 95051

(P-18440)
NXEDGE SAN CARLOS LLC
1000 Commercial St, San Carlos (94070-4024)
PHONE..............................650 422-2269
EMP: 10
SALES (est): 1.7MM **Privately Held**
SIC: **3674** Semiconductors & related devices

(P-18441)
NXP USA INC
2680 Zanker Rd Ste 200, San Jose (95134-2144)
PHONE..............................408 518-5500
Rob Shane, *Branch Mgr*
Ruediger Stroh, *Exec VP*
Bogdan Costinescu, *Engineer*
Maryann Little, *Buyer*
Kwame Adwere, *Counsel*
EMP: 75
SALES (corp-wide): 9.4B **Privately Held**
SIC: **3674** Semiconductors & related devices
HQ: Nxp Usa, Inc.
6501 W William Cannon Dr
Austin TX 78735
512 933-8214

(P-18442)
NXP USA INC
411 E Plumeria Dr, San Jose (95134-1924)
PHONE..............................408 518-5500
Fari Assaderaghi, *Senior VP*
Maria Hough, *Manager*
EMP: 500
SALES (corp-wide): 9.4B **Privately Held**
SIC: **3674** Integrated circuits, semiconductor networks, etc.
HQ: Nxp Usa, Inc.
6501 W William Cannon Dr
Austin TX 78735
512 933-8214

(P-18443)
NXP USA INC
Also Called: Philips Semiconductors
690 E Arques Ave, Sunnyvale (94085-3829)
PHONE..............................408 991-2700
Susie Ostrega, *Manager*
EMP: 39
SALES (corp-wide): 9.4B **Privately Held**
WEB: www.philipslogic.com
SIC: **3674** Integrated circuits, semiconductor networks, etc.
HQ: Nxp Usa, Inc.
6501 W William Cannon Dr
Austin TX 78735
512 933-8214

(P-18444)
NXP USA INC
440 N Wolfe Rd, Sunnyvale (94085-3869)
PHONE..............................408 991-2000
Scott McGregor, *President*
EMP: 39
SALES (corp-wide): 9.4B **Privately Held**
WEB: www.philipslogic.com
SIC: **3674** Integrated circuits, semiconductor networks, etc.

HQ: Nxp Usa, Inc.
6501 W William Cannon Dr
Austin TX 78735
512 933-8214

(P-18445)
NXP USA INC
9 Cushing Ste 100, Irvine (92618-4225)
PHONE..................................949 399-4000
Roger Schalk, *Branch Mgr*
EMP: 16
SALES (corp-wide): 9.4B **Privately Held**
WEB: www.freescale.com
SIC: 3674 Integrated circuits, semiconductor networks, etc.
HQ: Nxp Usa, Inc.
6501 W William Cannon Dr
Austin TX 78735
512 933-8214

(P-18446)
OCLARO INC (HQ)
400 N Mccarthy Blvd, Milpitas
(95035-5112)
PHONE..................................408 383-1400
Greg Dougherty, *CEO*
Craig Cocchi, *COO*
Pete Mangan, *CFO*
Adam Carter, *Ch Credit Ofcr*
Lisa Paul, *Exec VP*
EMP: 89
SALES: 543.1MM
SALES (corp-wide): 1.5B **Publicly Held**
SIC: 3674 3826 3827 Light emitting diodes; laser scientific & engineering instruments; optical instruments & apparatus
PA: Lumentum Holdings Inc.
400 N Mccarthy Blvd
Milpitas CA 95035
408 546-5483

(P-18447)
OCLARO FIBER OPTICS INC (DH)
400 N Mccarthy Blvd, Milpitas
(95035-5112)
PHONE..................................408 383-1400
Harry L Bosco, *President*
Robert J Nobile, *CFO*
Atsushi Horiuchi, *Senior VP*
Justin J O'Neill, *Senior VP*
Pinaki Mohapatra, *Controller*
EMP: 37 EST: 2000
SALES (est): 42.8MM
SALES (corp-wide): 1.5B **Publicly Held**
WEB: www.opnext.com
SIC: 3674 Photoconductive cells; photoelectric cells, solid state (electronic eye)
HQ: Oclaro, Inc.
400 N Mccarthy Blvd
Milpitas CA 95035
408 383-1400

(P-18448)
OEPIC SEMICONDUCTORS INC
1231 Bordeaux Dr, Sunnyvale
(94089-1203)
PHONE..................................408 747-0388
Yi-Ching Pao, *President*
EMP: 35 EST: 2000
SQ FT: 18,000
SALES (est): 7.7MM **Privately Held**
SIC: 3674 Semiconductors & related devices

(P-18449)
OMNISIL
5401 Everglades St, Ventura (93003-6523)
PHONE..................................805 644-2514
David Clark, *President*
Karin Clark, *Corp Secy*
Dennis Strang, *Vice Pres*
▲ EMP: 21
SQ FT: 9,800
SALES (est): 4.5MM **Privately Held**
WEB: www.omnisil.com
SIC: 3674 Silicon wafers, chemically doped

(P-18450)
OMNIVISION TECHNOLOGIES INC (PA)
4275 Burton Dr, Santa Clara (95054-1512)
PHONE..................................408 567-3000
Shaw Hong, *CEO*

Henry Yang, *COO*
Anson Chan, *CFO*
Tina Sze, *Executive Asst*
Howard Rhodes, *CTO*
▲ EMP: 129
SQ FT: 207,000
SALES (est): 1.1B **Privately Held**
WEB: www.ovt.com
SIC: 3674 Semiconductors & related devices

(P-18451)
OMTEK INC
3722 Calle Cita, Santa Barbara
(93105-2411)
PHONE..................................805 687-9629
EMP: 23
SQ FT: 15,000
SALES (est): 1.3MM **Privately Held**
SIC: 3674

(P-18452)
ON SEMICONDUCTOR CONNECTIVITY (HQ)
1704 Automation Pkwy, San Jose
(95131-1873)
PHONE..................................669 209-5500
Keith D Jackson, *President*
Lionel Bonnot, *Senior VP*
EMP: 61
SQ FT: 84,000
SALES: 220.4MM
SALES (corp-wide): 5.8B **Publicly Held**
SIC: 3674 Semiconductors & related devices
PA: On Semiconductor Corporation
5005 E Mcdowell Rd
Phoenix AZ 85008
602 244-6600

(P-18453)
ONESUN LLC
27 Gate 5 Rd, Sausalito (94965-1401)
PHONE..................................415 230-4277
Paul Hawken,
Eitan Zeira, *CTO*
EMP: 10
SALES (est): 1.3MM **Privately Held**
SIC: 3674 Semiconductors & related devices

(P-18454)
ONSPEC TECHNOLOGY PARTNERS INC
Also Called: Bi Cmos Foundry
975 Comstock St, Santa Clara
(95054-3407)
PHONE..................................408 654-7627
Peter Liljegren, *Vice Pres*
EMP: 20
SALES (est): 3MM **Privately Held**
SIC: 3674 Wafers (semiconductor devices)

(P-18455)
ONTERA INC
2161 Delaware Ave Ste B, Santa Cruz
(95060-5790)
PHONE..................................831 222-2193
Murielle Thinard McLane, *CEO*
Raparti Swayambhu, *Vice Pres*
William Dunbar, *Principal*
Trevor Morin, *Principal*
Rose Carman, *Executive Asst*
EMP: 107
SQ FT: 12,000
SALES (est): 903.8K **Privately Held**
SIC: 3674 3826 Semiconductors & related devices; analytical instruments

(P-18456)
OPTASENSE INC
3350 Scott Blvd Bldg 1, Santa Clara
(95054-3107)
PHONE..................................408 970-3500
Lew Stolpner, *Vice Pres*
EMP: 11 **Privately Held**
SIC: 3674 Semiconductors & related devices
HQ: Optasense, Inc.
12709 Haynes Rd
Houston TX 77066
713 493-0348

(P-18457)
OPTOELECTRONIX INC (PA)
111 W Saint John St # 588, San Jose
(95113-1105)
PHONE..................................408 437-9488
Chuck Berghoff, *President*
Tom Thayer, *COO*
Dato Yap Peng Hooi, *Vice Pres*
Robert Kow, *Vice Pres*
Jim Schenck, *Sales Staff*
EMP: 18 EST: 2008
SALES (est): 2.5MM **Privately Held**
SIC: 3674 Light emitting diodes

(P-18458)
ORBOTECH LT SOLAR LLC
Also Called: Olt Solar
5970 Optical Ct, San Jose (95138-1400)
PHONE..................................408 414-3777
Georg Bremer, *Mng Member*
Bobby Hulter, *Electrical Engi*
Kam Law,
Matt Toshima,
EMP: 20
SALES: 3.8MM
SALES (corp-wide): 4.5B **Publicly Held**
SIC: 3674 Integrated circuits, semiconductor networks, etc.
PA: Kla Corporation
1 Technology Dr
Milpitas CA 95035
408 875-3000

(P-18459)
ORTEL A DIVISION EMCORE CO (HQ)
2015 Chestnut St, Alhambra (91803-1542)
PHONE..................................626 293-3400
Mary E Ortel, *President*
EMP: 15
SALES (est): 1MM
SALES (corp-wide): 85.6MM **Publicly Held**
WEB: www.forceinc.com
SIC: 3674 3559 Integrated circuits, semiconductor networks, etc.; semiconductor manufacturing machinery
PA: Emcore Corporation
2015 Chestnut St
Alhambra CA 91803
626 293-3400

(P-18460)
OSE USA INC (HQ)
1737 N 1st St Ste 350, San Jose
(95112-4523)
PHONE..................................408 452-9080
Edmond Tseng, *President*
Adonai Mack, *Analyst*
EMP: 12
SALES: 4.5MM **Privately Held**
WEB: www.ose.com.tw
SIC: 3674 Integrated circuits, semiconductor networks, etc.

(P-18461)
OSI OPTOELECTRONICS INC
Also Called: Advanced Photonix
1240 Avenida Acaso, Camarillo
(93012-8754)
PHONE..................................805 987-0146
Jean-Pierre Maufras, *General Mgr*
EMP: 50
SALES (corp-wide): 1.1B **Publicly Held**
SIC: 3674 Semiconductors & related devices
HQ: Osi Optoelectronics, Inc.
12525 Chadron Ave
Hawthorne CA 90250
310 978-0516

(P-18462)
OSI SYSTEMS INC (PA)
12525 Chadron Ave, Hawthorne
(90250-4807)
PHONE..................................310 978-0516
Deepak Chopra, *Ch of Bd*
Robert Kephart, *COO*
Alan Edrick, *CFO*
Rick Merritt, *Officer*
Ajay Mehra, *Exec VP*
EMP: 325
SQ FT: 88,000

SALES: 1.1B **Publicly Held**
WEB: www.osi-systems.com
SIC: 3674 3845 Integrated circuits, semiconductor networks, etc.; photoconductive cells; photoelectric cells, solid state (electronic eye); electromedical equipment; ultrasonic scanning devices, medical

(P-18463)
OSRAM SYLVANIA INC
Also Called: Led Engine
651 River Oaks Pkwy, San Jose
(95134-1907)
PHONE..................................408 922-7200
EMP: 40
SALES (corp-wide): 4.7B **Privately Held**
SIC: 3674 Light emitting diodes
HQ: Osram Sylvania Inc
200 Ballardvale St # 305
Wilmington MA 01887
978 570-3000

(P-18464)
PAC TECH USA PACKG TECH INC
328 Martin Ave, Santa Clara (95050-3112)
PHONE..................................408 588-1925
Heinrich Ldeke, *CEO*
Thorsten Teutsch, *President*
Lucyany Everett, *Admin Asst*
Bernd Otto, *Engineer*
Axel Scheffler, *Engineer*
EMP: 14 EST: 2001
SALES: 12.7MM **Privately Held**
SIC: 3674 Wafers (semiconductor devices)
HQ: Pac Tech - Packaging Technologies Gmbh
Am Schlangenhorst 7-9
Nauen 14641
332 144-9510

(P-18465)
PANTRONIX CORPORATION
2710 Lakeview Ct, Fremont (94538-6534)
PHONE..................................510 656-5898
Stanley Wang, *President*
Bret Buckler, *President*
Franny Wang, *Corp Secy*
Dave Toledo, *Data Proc Staff*
Susan Bristow, *Human Res Mgr*
▲ EMP: 250
SQ FT: 82,000
SALES (est): 37.7MM **Privately Held**
WEB: www.pantronix.com
SIC: 3674 8734 Integrated circuits, semiconductor networks, etc.; testing laboratories

(P-18466)
PATRIOT MEMORY LLC (PA)
47027 Benicia St, Fremont (94538-7331)
PHONE..................................510 979-1021
Paul Jones, *Mng Member*
Jim Jones, *Accounting Dir*
Doug Diggs,
▲ EMP: 125
SALES (est): 22.7MM **Privately Held**
WEB: www.patriotmem.com
SIC: 3674 5045 Semiconductors & related devices; computers

(P-18467)
PAYTON TECHNOLOGY CORPORATION
17665 Newhope St Ste B, Fountain Valley
(92708-8209)
PHONE..................................714 885-8000
John Tu, *President*
David Sun, *Admin Sec*
John Leitgeb, *CIO*
Tim Westland, *Marketing Mgr*
Cenk Akkurt, *Marketing Staff*
▲ EMP: 161
SALES (est): 15.8MM **Privately Held**
SIC: 3674 Semiconductors & related devices

(P-18468)
PERFECTVIPS INC (PA)
2099 Gateway Pl Ste 240, San Jose
(95110-1017)
PHONE..................................408 912-2316
Prasana Kumari, *Principal*
Abira Das, *Human Resources*
EMP: 10

PRODUCTS & SVCS

SALES (est): 1.5MM **Privately Held**
SIC: 3674 Semiconductors & related devices

(P-18469)
PIEZO-METRICS INC (PA)
Also Called: Micron Instruments
4509 Runway St, Simi Valley (93063-3479)
PHONE...................................805 522-4676
Herbert Chelner, *President*
Sharon Chelner, *Vice Pres*
Geoff Dunsterville, *General Mgr*
EMP: 35
SQ FT: 9,000
SALES (est): 6.6MM **Privately Held**
WEB: www.microninstruments.com
SIC: 3674 3829 Strain gages, solid state; pressure transducers

(P-18470)
PIXELWORKS INC (PA)
226 Airport Pkwy Ste 595, San Jose
(95110-3704)
PHONE...................................408 200-9200
Todd A Debonis, *President*
Elias Nader, *CFO*
Daniel Heneghan, *Bd of Directors*
Peter Carson, *Vice Pres*
Perry Chappell, *Vice Pres*
EMP: 49
SQ FT: 19,000
SALES: 76.5MM **Publicly Held**
WEB: www.pixelworks.com
SIC: 3674 7372 Semiconductors & related devices; prepackaged software; utility computer software

(P-18471)
PMC-SIERRA US INC
1380 Bordeaux Dr, Sunnyvale
(94089-1005)
PHONE...................................408 239-8000
Steve Geiser, *CEO*
EMP: 10
SALES (est): 1.4MM
SALES (corp-wide): 5.3B **Publicly Held**
SIC: 3674 Microprocessors
HQ: Microsemi Storage Solutions, Inc.
1380 Bordeaux Dr
Sunnyvale CA 94089
408 239-8000

(P-18472)
PNY TECHNOLOGIES INC
2099 Gateway Pl Ste 220, San Jose
(95110-1017)
PHONE...................................408 392-4100
Clint Rosenthal, *Director*
Jenna Battistini, *Sales Staff*
EMP: 20
SALES (corp-wide): 128.1MM **Privately Held**
SIC: 3674 5045 Memories, solid state; computers, peripherals & software
PA: Pny Technologies, Inc.
100 Jefferson Rd
Parsippany NJ 07054
973 515-9700

(P-18473)
POINT NINE TECHNOLOGIES INC (PA)
2697 Lavery Ct Ste 8, Newbury Park
(91320-1585)
PHONE...................................805 375-6600
Fred Quigg, *Ch of Bd*
Dixie Quigg, *President*
Laura Vega, *CFO*
Fred Roth, *Manager*
EMP: 15
SQ FT: 7,000
SALES: 7MM **Privately Held**
WEB: www.rfmosfet.com
SIC: 3674 Transistors

(P-18474)
POLISHING CORPORATION AMERICA
Also Called: PCA
442 Martin Ave, Santa Clara (95050-2911)
PHONE...................................888 892-3377
Stuart Becker, *CEO*
▲ EMP: 26
SQ FT: 10,000

SALES (est): 2.1MM **Privately Held**
WEB: www.pcasilicon.com
SIC: 3674 Silicon wafers, chemically doped

(P-18475)
POLYFET RF DEVICES INC
1110 Avenida Acaso, Camarillo
(93012-8725)
PHONE...................................805 484-9582
S K Leong, *President*
EMP: 25
SQ FT: 7,500
SALES (est): 4.5MM **Privately Held**
WEB: www.polyfet.com
SIC: 3674 Transistors

(P-18476)
POLYSTAK INC
1159 Sonora Ct 109, Sunnyvale
(94086-5384)
PHONE...................................408 441-1400
Kyung Suk Kang, *President*
Christina Kim, *Administration*
EMP: 18 EST: 1999
SQ FT: 4,300
SALES (est): 2.1MM **Privately Held**
WEB: www.polystak.com
SIC: 3674 Modules, solid state

(P-18477)
POWER INTEGRATIONS INC (PA)
5245 Hellyer Ave, San Jose (95138-1002)
PHONE...................................408 414-9200
Balu Balakrishnan, *President*
Radu Barsan, *Vice Pres*
David Matthews, *Vice Pres*
Raja Petrakian, *Vice Pres*
Ben Sutherland, *Vice Pres*
EMP: 221
SALES: 415.9MM **Publicly Held**
WEB: www.powerint.com
SIC: 3674 Integrated circuits, semiconductor networks, etc.

(P-18478)
POWER INTEGRATIONS INTERNATION
5245 Hellyer Ave, San Jose (95138-1002)
PHONE...................................408 414-8528
Balu Balakrishnan, *President*
Wolfgang Ademmer, *Vice Pres*
Joe Schiffer, *Director*
EMP: 392
SALES (est): 15.7MM
SALES (corp-wide): 415.9MM **Publicly Held**
SIC: 3674 Integrated circuits, semiconductor networks, etc.
PA: Power Integrations, Inc.
5245 Hellyer Ave
San Jose CA 95138
408 414-9200

(P-18479)
PRIME SOLUTIONS INC
4261 Business Center Dr, Fremont
(94538-6357)
PHONE...................................510 490-2255
Harry H Moroyan, *President*
Vera Moroyan, *Admin Sec*
EMP: 17
SQ FT: 1,200
SALES (est): 2.4MM **Privately Held**
WEB: www.primesol.com
SIC: 3674 Integrated circuits, semiconductor networks, etc.

(P-18480)
PRINTEC HT ELECTRONICS LLC
501 Sally Pl, Fullerton (92831-5014)
PHONE...................................714 484-7597
Nancy Cheng,
Greg Morton, *Manager*
▲ EMP: 50
SQ FT: 12,000
SALES: 10MM **Privately Held**
SIC: 3674 3629 Modules, solid state; electronic generation equipment
PA: Printec H. T. Electronics Corp.
No. 38, Liyan St.,
New Taipei City TAP 23557

(P-18481)
PROCESS SPECIALTIES INC
1660 W Linne Rd Ste A, Tracy
(95377-8025)
PHONE...................................209 832-1344
Edward Morris, *President*
Mark Hinkle, *Vice Pres*
Manny D Arroz, *Admin Sec*
Garry Jenkins, *Engineer*
Pam Yao, *Accountant*
EMP: 27
SQ FT: 35,910
SALES: 10.3MM **Privately Held**
WEB: www.processspecialties.com
SIC: 3674 Wafers (semiconductor devices)

(P-18482)
PROMEX INDUSTRIES INCORPORATED
Also Called: Quik-Pak
10987 Via Frontera, San Diego
(92127-1703)
PHONE...................................858 674-4676
Steve Swendrowski, *General Mgr*
EMP: 28
SALES (corp-wide): 20.7MM **Privately Held**
SIC: 3674 Integrated circuits, semiconductor networks, etc.
PA: Promex Industries, Incorporated
3075 Oakmead Village Dr
Santa Clara CA 95051
408 496-0222

(P-18483)
PROMEX INDUSTRIES INCORPORATED (PA)
3075 Oakmead Village Dr, Santa Clara
(95051-0811)
PHONE...................................408 496-0222
Richard F Otte, *CEO*
Chris Pugh, *Vice Pres*
Dr Edward Binkley, *Principal*
▲ EMP: 65 EST: 1999
SQ FT: 30,000
SALES (est): 20.7MM **Privately Held**
SIC: 3674 Modules, solid state; hybrid integrated circuits; integrated circuits, semiconductor networks, etc.

(P-18484)
PROTONEX LLC
2331 Circadian Way, Santa Rosa
(95407-5437)
PHONE...................................707 566-2260
Eric Walters,
Becky OH,
EMP: 18
SALES (est): 797.1K **Privately Held**
SIC: 3674 Radiation sensors

(P-18485)
PSEMI CORPORATION (DH)
9369 Carroll Park Dr, San Diego
(92121-3264)
PHONE...................................858 731-9400
Sumit Tomar, *CEO*
Go Maruyama, *Senior VP*
Rajappan Balagopal, *Vice Pres*
Takaki Murata, *Vice Pres*
Anil Tata, *Vice Pres*
▲ EMP: 70
SQ FT: 96,384
SALES (est): 127.4MM **Privately Held**
WEB: www.psemi.com
SIC: 3674 Silicon wafers, chemically doped
HQ: Murata Electronics North America, Inc.
2200 Lake Park Dr Se
Smyrna GA 30080
770 436-1300

(P-18486)
PSIBER DATA SYSTEMS INC
7075 Mission Gorge Rd K, San Diego
(92120-2454)
PHONE...................................619 287-9970
Darrell J Johnson, *President*
Cameron Fedeli, *Mfg Mgr*
▲ EMP: 10
SQ FT: 3,000
SALES (est): 1.6MM **Privately Held**
SIC: 3674 Semiconductors & related devices

(P-18487)
PYRAMID SEMICONDUCTOR CORP
1249 Reamwood Ave, Sunnyvale
(94089-2226)
PHONE...................................408 542-9430
Joe Rothstein, *President*
Douglas Beaubien, *Vice Pres*
Dr Jagtar Sandhu, *Vice Pres*
EMP: 11
SQ FT: 8,400
SALES (est): 2.1MM **Privately Held**
WEB: www.pyramidsemiconductor.com
SIC: 3674 Integrated circuits, semiconductor networks, etc.

(P-18488)
QLOGIC LLC (DH)
15485 Sand Canyon Ave, Irvine
(92618-3154)
PHONE...................................949 389-6000
Syed Ali,
Connie Williams, *IT Executive*
Joseph Carnuccio, *Software Engr*
Nasir Moinuddin, *Software Engr*
Pat Tansey, *Software Engr*
▲ EMP: 138
SQ FT: 161,000
SALES (est): 371.7MM **Privately Held**
WEB: www.qlogic.com
SIC: 3674 Integrated circuits, semiconductor networks, etc.

(P-18489)
QMAT INC
Also Called: Quenta Material
2424 Walsh Ave, Santa Clara
(95051-1303)
P.O. Box 110644, Campbell (95011-0644)
PHONE...................................498 228-5858
Francois Henley, *Principal*
Kristine Ryan, *Admin Sec*
EMP: 25
SALES (est): 4.6MM **Privately Held**
SIC: 3674 Wafers (semiconductor devices)

(P-18490)
QORVO US INC
3099 Orchard Dr, San Jose (95134-2005)
PHONE...................................408 493-4304
Timothy R Richardson, *Manager*
Michael Zybura, *Senior Mgr*
Cheng-Hui Lin, *Manager*
EMP: 43
SALES (corp-wide): 3B **Publicly Held**
WEB: www.rfmd.com
SIC: 3674 Integrated circuits, semiconductor networks, etc.
HQ: Qorvo Us, Inc.
2300 Ne Brookwood Pkwy
Hillsboro OR 97124
336 664-1233

(P-18491)
QPC LASERS INC
15632 Roxford St, Sylmar (91342-1265)
PHONE...................................818 986-0000
Hao Zhao, *CEO*
EMP: 13
SALES (est): 516.3K **Privately Held**
SIC: 3674 Semiconductors & related devices

(P-18492)
QUALCOMM ATHEROS INC (HQ)
1700 Technology Dr, San Jose
(95110-1383)
PHONE...................................408 773-5200
Steve Mollenkopf, *CEO*
Lilia Munoz, *Executive*
Gary Szilagyi, *General Mgr*
Thu Nguyen, *Software Engr*
MAI Hoang, *Technician*
▲ EMP: 600
SALES (est): 225MM
SALES (corp-wide): 24.2B **Publicly Held**
WEB: www.airvia.com
SIC: 3674 4899 Integrated circuits, semiconductor networks, etc.; communication signal enhancement network system
PA: Qualcomm Incorporated
5775 Morehouse Dr
San Diego CA 92121
858 587-1121

(P-18493)
QUALCOMM DATACENTER TECH INC (HQ)
5775 Morehouse Dr, San Diego (92121-1714)
PHONE..............................858 567-1121
Dileep Bhandarkar, *Vice Pres*
Anand Chandrasekher, *General Mgr*
EMP: 17
SALES (est): 36.1K
SALES (corp-wide): 24.2B **Publicly Held**
SIC: 3674 Integrated circuits, semiconductor networks, etc.
PA: Qualcomm Incorporated
5775 Morehouse Dr
San Diego CA 92121
858 587-1121

(P-18494)
QUALCOMM INCORPORATED
2016 Palomar Airport Rd # 100, Carlsbad (92011-4400)
PHONE..............................858 651-8481
David Lieber, *Principal*
Jonathan David, *Engineer*
Nathan Frost, *Engineer*
Congyi Liu, *Engineer*
Dingyi LI, *Engineer*
EMP: 350
SALES (corp-wide): 24.2B **Publicly Held**
SIC: 3674 Integrated circuits, semiconductor networks, etc.
PA: Qualcomm Incorporated
5775 Morehouse Dr
San Diego CA 92121
858 587-1121

(P-18495)
QUALCOMM INCORPORATED
3135 Kifer Rd, Santa Clara (95051-0804)
PHONE..............................408 216-6797
Vincent Jones, *Branch Mgr*
Thach Tran, *Design Engr*
EMP: 350
SALES (corp-wide): 24.2B **Publicly Held**
SIC: 3674 Integrated circuits, semiconductor networks, etc.
PA: Qualcomm Incorporated
5775 Morehouse Dr
San Diego CA 92121
858 587-1121

(P-18496)
QUALCOMM INCORPORATED
5751 Pacific Center Blvd, San Diego (92121-4252)
PHONE..............................858 909-0316
Margaret L Johnson, *Branch Mgr*
EMP: 350
SALES (corp-wide): 24.2B **Publicly Held**
WEB: www.qualcomm.com
SIC: 3674 Integrated circuits, semiconductor networks, etc.
PA: Qualcomm Incorporated
5775 Morehouse Dr
San Diego CA 92121
858 587-1121

(P-18497)
QUALCOMM INCORPORATED
9393 Waples St Ste 150, San Diego (92121-3931)
PHONE..............................858 587-1121
Richard Archer, *Network Enginr*
EMP: 350
SALES (corp-wide): 24.2B **Publicly Held**
WEB: www.qualcomm.com
SIC: 3674 7372 Integrated circuits, semiconductor networks, etc.; prepackaged software
PA: Qualcomm Incorporated
5775 Morehouse Dr
San Diego CA 92121
858 587-1121

(P-18498)
QUALCOMM INCORPORATED
10160 Pacific Mesa Blvd # 100, San Diego (92121-4390)
PHONE..............................858 587-1121
EMP: 350
SALES (corp-wide): 24.2B **Publicly Held**
SIC: 3674 7372 6794 Integrated circuits, semiconductor networks, etc.; business oriented computer software; patent buying, licensing, leasing

PA: Qualcomm Incorporated
5775 Morehouse Dr
San Diego CA 92121
858 587-1121

(P-18499)
QUALCOMM LIMITED PARTNER INC
5775 Morehouse Dr, San Diego (92121-1714)
PHONE..............................858 587-1121
Anthony Thornley, *President*
Richard Sulpivil, *President*
EMP: 25
SALES (est): 1.6MM
SALES (corp-wide): 24.2B **Publicly Held**
SIC: 3674 Semiconductors & related devices
PA: Qualcomm Incorporated
5775 Morehouse Dr
San Diego CA 92121
858 587-1121

(P-18500)
QUALCOMM TECHNOLOGIES INC (HQ)
5775 Morehouse Dr, San Diego (92121-1714)
PHONE..............................858 587-1121
Steve Mollenkopf, *CEO*
Cristiano Amon, *President*
Dileep Bhandarkar, *Vice Pres*
Thomas Nindl, *Business Dir*
Lori Chantrachuck, *Executive Asst*
▲ **EMP:** 199
SALES (est): 2.7B
SALES (corp-wide): 24.2B **Publicly Held**
SIC: 3674 7372 6794 Integrated circuits, semiconductor networks, etc.; business oriented computer software; patent buying, licensing, leasing
PA: Qualcomm Incorporated
5775 Morehouse Dr
San Diego CA 92121
858 587-1121

(P-18501)
QUANTUM 3D HEADQUARTERS
6330 San Ignacio Ave, San Jose (95119-1209)
PHONE..............................408 361-9999
Gordon Campbell, *Principal*
▲ **EMP:** 11
SALES (est): 691.1K **Privately Held**
SIC: 3674 Semiconductors & related devices

(P-18502)
QUANTUM SOLAR INC
6 Endeavor Dr, Corte Madera (94925-2024)
PHONE..............................415 924-8140
Tom Faust, *CEO*
EMP: 10
SALES (est): 800.3K **Privately Held**
SIC: 3674 Semiconductors & related devices

(P-18503)
QUANTUMSCAPE CORPORATION
1730 Technology Dr, San Jose (95110-1331)
PHONE..............................408 452-2000
Jagdeep Singh, *President*
Tim Holme, *Officer*
Howard Lukens, *Officer*
Mike McCarthy, *Officer*
Ann Truong, *Controller*
EMP: 121
SALES (est): 576.7K **Privately Held**
SIC: 3674 Semiconductors & related devices

(P-18504)
QUELLAN INC
Also Called: Intersil Quellan
1001 Murphy Ranch Rd, Milpitas (95035-7912)
PHONE..............................408 546-3487
Tony Stelliga, *CEO*
Donald Macleod, *Ch of Bd*
James Diller, *CEO*
Guy Anthony, *CFO*
Joy Laskar, *CTO*

EMP: 27
SALES (est): 1.4MM **Privately Held**
SIC: 3674 Semiconductors & related devices
HQ: Renesas Electronics America Inc.
1001 Murphy Ranch Rd
Milpitas CA 95035
408 432-8888

(P-18505)
QUICKLOGIC CORPORATION (PA)
2220 Lundy Ave, San Jose (95131-1816)
PHONE..............................408 990-4000
Brian C Faith, *President*
Suping Cheung, *CFO*
Timothy Saxe, *Senior VP*
Rajiv Jain, *Vice Pres*
EMP: 72
SQ FT: 24,164
SALES: 12.6MM **Publicly Held**
WEB: www.quicklogic.com
SIC: 3674 3823 Integrated circuits, semiconductor networks, etc.; programmers, process type

(P-18506)
QUORUM SYSTEMS INC
5960 Cornerstone Ct W # 200, San Diego (92121-3780)
PHONE..............................858 546-0895
Bernard Xavier PHD, *President*
EMP: 10
SALES (est): 1.2MM **Privately Held**
WEB: www.quorumsystems.com
SIC: 3674 Semiconductors & related devices

(P-18507)
R2 SEMICONDUCTOR INC
1196 Borregas Ave Ste 201, Sunnyvale (94089-1340)
PHONE..............................408 745-7400
David Fisher, *President*
Frank Sasselli, *Vice Pres*
Larry Burns, *Principal*
Andrew Hartland, *Principal*
Ravi Ramachandran, *Principal*
EMP: 20
SALES (est): 3.4MM **Privately Held**
SIC: 3674 Integrated circuits, semiconductor networks, etc.

(P-18508)
RAMBUS INC (PA)
1050 Entp Way Ste 700, Sunnyvale (94089)
PHONE..............................408 462-8000
Luc Seraphin, *President*
Boris Vinarsky, *Administration*
Jahnavi Addaguduri, *Sr Software Eng*
Kurt Starkey, *Research*
Srikanth Kandhuri, *Technology*
◆ **EMP:** 272
SALES: 231.2MM **Publicly Held**
WEB: www.rambus.com
SIC: 3674 6794 Integrated circuits, semiconductor networks, etc.; patent owners & lessors

(P-18509)
RAMBUS INC
Lighting Technology Division
1050 Enterprise Way # 700, Sunnyvale (94089-1417)
PHONE..............................408 462-8000
Jeff Parker, *Senior VP*
EMP: 12
SALES (corp-wide): 231.2MM **Publicly Held**
SIC: 3674 Semiconductors & related devices
PA: Rambus Inc.
1050 Entp Way Ste 700
Sunnyvale CA 94089
408 462-8000

(P-18510)
REACTION TECHNOLOGY INC (PA)
3400 Bassett St, Santa Clara (95054-2703)
PHONE..............................408 970-9601
Uzi Sasson, *CEO*
James Jacobson, *President*
David Sallous, *Vice Pres*
Janice Baker, *Office Mgr*

EMP: 21
SQ FT: 10,800
SALES (est): 3.6MM **Privately Held**
WEB: www.reactiontechnology.com
SIC: 3674 Integrated circuits, semiconductor networks, etc.

(P-18511)
REDPINE SIGNALS INC (PA)
2107 N 1st St Ste 540, San Jose (95131-2028)
PHONE..............................408 748-3385
Venkat Mattela, *CEO*
Kalpana Atluri, *President*
David Casey, *Vice Pres*
Ram Gutta, *Vice Pres*
Narasimha Anumolu, *Software Engr*
EMP: 27
SALES (est): 19MM **Privately Held**
SIC: 3674 Integrated circuits, semiconductor networks, etc.

(P-18512)
REFLEX PHOTONICS INC
1250 Oakmead Pkwy, Sunnyvale (94085-4027)
PHONE..............................408 501-8886
EMP: 30
SALES (est): 1.8MM **Privately Held**
WEB: www.reflexphotonics.com
SIC: 3674

(P-18513)
RELIANCE COMPUTER CORP
2451 Mission College Blvd, Santa Clara (95054-1214)
PHONE..............................408 492-1915
▲ **EMP:** 115
SALES (est): 6MM
SALES (corp-wide): 4.2B **Publicly Held**
SIC: 3674 3672
HQ: Broadcom Corporation
5300 California Ave
Irvine CA 95131
949 926-5000

(P-18514)
RENESAS ELECTRONICS AMER INC
205 Llagas Rd, Morgan Hill (95037-3079)
PHONE..............................408 546-3434
Kevin Ellis, *Principal*
EMP: 600 **Privately Held**
SIC: 3674 Semiconductors & related devices
HQ: Renesas Electronics America Inc.
1001 Murphy Ranch Rd
Milpitas CA 95035
408 432-8888

(P-18515)
RENESAS ELECTRONICS AMER INC
Also Called: Intersil Design Center
10865 Rancho Bernardo Rd, San Diego (92127-2113)
PHONE..............................858 451-7240
Steve Trunkett, *Branch Mgr*
EMP: 600 **Privately Held**
SIC: 3674 Semiconductors & related devices
HQ: Renesas Electronics America Inc.
1001 Murphy Ranch Rd
Milpitas CA 95035
408 432-8888

(P-18516)
RESONANT INC (PA)
175 Cremona Dr Ste 200, Goleta (93117-3197)
PHONE..............................805 308-9803
George B Holmes, *CEO*
John E Major, *Ch of Bd*
Martin S McDermut, *CFO*
Michael Fox, *Bd of Directors*
Neal Fenzi, *Exec VP*
EMP: 53
SALES: 524K **Publicly Held**
SIC: 3674 Semiconductors & related devices

(P-18517)
RF DIGITAL CORPORATION
1601 Pcf Cast Hwy Ste 290, Hermosa Beach (90254)
PHONE..............................949 610-0008

PRODUCTS & SVCS

Armen Kazanchian, *President*
Rod Landers, *COO*
EMP: 105
SQ FT: 5,000
SALES (est): 17.9MM
SALES (corp-wide): 1.6B **Privately Held**
SIC: 3674 Modules, solid state
HQ: Heptagon Usa, Inc.
　　465 N Whisman Rd Ste 200
　　Mountain View CA 94043
　　650 336-7990

(P-18518)
RKD ENGINEERING CORP INC
316 S Navarra Dr, Scotts Valley
(95066-3622)
PHONE.................................831 430-9464
Kirk Martin, *President*
Daniel Kaschala, *Vice Pres*
EMP: 10
SALES (est): 908.9K **Privately Held**
SIC: 3674 Semiconductor circuit networks

(P-18519)
ROCKLEY PHOTONICS INC (HQ)
234 E Colo Blvd Ste 600, Pasadena
(91101)
PHONE.................................626 304-9960
Andrew George Rickman, *CEO*
Grant Bristow, *Info Tech Mgr*
Caroline Lai, *Engineer*
Melissa Valdez, *Human Res Mgr*
Esthepany Aragon, *Manager*
EMP: 87
SALES (est): 30.8MM
SALES (corp-wide): 19.4MM **Privately Held**
SIC: 3674 Semiconductors & related devices

(P-18520)
ROCKLEY PHOTONICS INC
333 W San Carlos St, San Jose
(95110-2726)
PHONE.................................408 579-9210
Andrew George Rickman, *Branch Mgr*
EMP: 15
SALES (corp-wide): 19.4MM **Privately Held**
SIC: 3674 Semiconductors & related devices
HQ: Rockley Photonics, Inc.
　　234 E Colo Blvd Ste 600
　　Pasadena CA 91101
　　626 304-9960

(P-18521)
RTG INC
4030 Spencer St Ste 108, Torrance
(90503-2463)
P.O. Box 3986 (90510-3986)
PHONE.................................310 534-3016
Kurt Rasmussen, *President*
Mojca Rasmussen, *Corp Secy*
EMP: 10
SQ FT: 5,000
SALES (est): 1.3MM **Privately Held**
WEB: www.rtg.com
SIC: 3674 8731 Integrated circuits, semiconductor networks, etc.; electronic research

(P-18522)
S-ENERGY AMERICA INC (HQ)
18022 Cowan Ste 260, Irvine (92614-1600)
PHONE.................................949 281-7897
David Kim, *President*
EMP: 13
SALES (est): 3MM **Privately Held**
SIC: 3674 Solar cells

(P-18523)
S3 GRAPHICS INC
940 Mission Ct, Fremont (94539-8202)
PHONE.................................510 687-4900
Wenchih Chen, *President*
Roger Niu, *Vice Pres*
Michael Shiuan, *Vice Pres*
Joyce Cheng, *Engineer*
Fan Lu, *Engineer*
EMP: 129
SALES (est): 14.8MM **Privately Held**
WEB: www.s3graphics.com
SIC: 3674 Semiconductors & related devices

PA: S3 Graphics Co., Ltd
　　C/O: Card Corporate Services Ltd
　　George Town GR CAYMAN
　　-

(P-18524)
SAAZ MICRO INC
94 W Cochran St Ste A, Simi Valley
(93065-0948)
PHONE.................................805 405-0700
Atul Joshi, *CEO*
EMP: 10
SALES (est): 512.7K **Privately Held**
SIC: 3674 Semiconductors & related devices

(P-18525)
SAC-TEC LABS INC (PA)
24301 Wilmington Ave, Carson
(90745-6139)
PHONE.................................310 375-5295
Robert Kunesh, *President*
Marylin Hafermalz, *Shareholder*
Bruce Kaufman, *Executive*
Charles Spencer, *Engineer*
Kelley Owen, *Train & Dev Mgr*
EMP: 28
SQ FT: 10,000
SALES (est): 3.5MM **Privately Held**
SIC: 3674 Semiconductors & related devices

(P-18526)
SAMIL POWER US LTD
3478 Buskirk Ave Ste 1000, Pleasant Hill
(94523-4378)
PHONE.................................925 930-3924
Peter Peiju Cui, *CEO*
▲ **EMP:** 600
SQ FT: 2,000
SALES (est): 22.2MM
SALES (corp-wide): 81.6K **Privately Held**
SIC: 3674 Solar cells
PA: Wuxi Samil Power Co., Ltd.
　　No.52, Huigu Venture Park, Zhenghe
　　Boulevard, Huishan District
　　Wuxi 21417
　　510 835-9313

(P-18527)
SANTIER INC
10103 Carroll Canyon Rd, San Diego
(92131-1109)
PHONE.................................858 271-1993
Kevin Cotner, *CEO*
Warren Bartholomew, *CFO*
▼ **EMP:** 64
SQ FT: 23,000
SALES (est): 10MM
SALES (corp-wide): 17.3MM **Privately Held**
SIC: 3674 Semiconductors & related devices
HQ: Egide (Usa), Llc
　　4 Washington St
　　Cambridge MD 21613
　　410 901-6100

(P-18528)
SCALABLE SYSTEMS RES LABS INC
2680 N 1st St Ste 200, San Jose
(95134-2039)
PHONE.................................650 322-6507
Axel K Kloth, *President*
EMP: 28
SALES: 3MM **Privately Held**
SIC: 3674 7371 7373 8731 Semiconductors & related devices; computer software development; computer integrated systems design; electronic research

(P-18529)
SCINTERA NETWORKS INC
160 Rio Robles, San Jose (95134-1813)
PHONE.................................408 636-2600
Davin Lee, *CEO*
Scott M Gibson, *CFO*
Steffen Hahn, *Vice Pres*
Bob Koupal, *Vice Pres*
Rajeev Krishnamoorthy, *Vice Pres*
EMP: 30
SQ FT: 20,000

SALES (est): 5.5MM **Privately Held**
WEB: www.scintera.com
SIC: 3674 Semiconductors & related devices

(P-18530)
SEMI AUTOMATION & TECH INC
Also Called: Noel Technologies
1510 Dell Ave Ste C, Campbell
(95008-6917)
PHONE.................................408 374-9549
Kristin Boyce, *President*
Brenda Hill, *Vice Pres*
▲ **EMP:** 42
SQ FT: 7,500
SALES (est): 7.5MM **Privately Held**
WEB: www.noeltech.com
SIC: 3674 Semiconductors & related devices

(P-18531)
SEMICNDCTOR CMPONENTS INDS LLC
2975 Stender Way, Santa Clara
(95054-3214)
PHONE.................................408 542-1000
Gelu Voicu, *Manager*
EMP: 250
SALES (corp-wide): 5.8B **Publicly Held**
SIC: 3674 Semiconductors & related devices
HQ: Semiconductor Components Industries, Llc
　　5005 E Mcdowell Rd
　　Phoenix AZ 85008
　　800 282-9855

(P-18532)
SEMICOA CORPORATION
333 Mccormick Ave, Costa Mesa
(92626-3479)
PHONE.................................714 979-1900
Thomas E Epley, *CEO*
Ramesh Ramchandani, *President*
Perry Denning, *COO*
Gary B Joyce, *CFO*
▲ **EMP:** 60
SALES (est): 13MM **Privately Held**
SIC: 3674 Semiconductors & related devices

(P-18533)
SEMICONDUCTOR COMPONENTS INC
Also Called: SCI
1353 E Edinger Ave, Santa Ana
(92705-4430)
PHONE.................................714 547-6059
Archie L Brainard, *President*
EMP: 20 **EST:** 1959
SQ FT: 2,500
SALES (est): 2.4MM **Privately Held**
WEB: www.semiconductorcomponents.com
SIC: 3674 Semiconductor circuit networks

(P-18534)
SEMICONDUCTOR LOGISTICS CORP
14409 Iseli Rd, Santa Fe Springs
(90670-5205)
PHONE.................................562 921-0399
Clarine Reed, *Manager*
EMP: 11
SALES (est): 785.8K **Privately Held**
WEB: www.slc-semiconductors.com
SIC: 3674 Semiconductors & related devices

(P-18535)
SEMICONDUCTOR PROCESS EQP CORP
Also Called: Spec
27963 Franklin Pkwy, Valencia
(91355-4110)
PHONE.................................661 257-0934
Arnold J Gustin, *CEO*
Robin Douglas, *President*
Kevin McGillivray, *Vice Pres*
◆ **EMP:** 35
SQ FT: 139,000
SALES (est): 9.8MM **Privately Held**
WEB: www.team-spec.com
SIC: 3674 Semiconductors & related devices

(P-18536)
SEMICONIX CORP (PA)
2968 Scott Blvd, Santa Clara (95054-3322)
PHONE.................................408 986-8026
Serban Porumbescu, *President*
Mihaela Porumbescu, *CFO*
Crick Waters, *Senior VP*
Thuan Lai, *Vice Pres*
EMP: 12
SALES: 2.5MM **Privately Held**
WEB: www.semiconix.com
SIC: 3674 Semiconductors & related devices

(P-18537)
SEMINET INC
150 Great Oaks Blvd, San Jose
(95119-1347)
PHONE.................................408 754-8537
Humayun Kabir, *Principal*
Greg Krikorian, *Principal*
EMP: 10
SALES (est): 1.2MM **Privately Held**
WEB: www.seminet.com
SIC: 3674 Semiconductors & related devices

(P-18538)
SEMTECH CORPORATION (PA)
200 Flynn Rd, Camarillo (93012-8790)
PHONE.................................805 498-2111
Mohan R Maheswaran, *President*
Rockell N Hankin, *Ch of Bd*
Emeka N Chukwu, *CFO*
James P Burra, *Vice Ch Bd*
Charles B Ammann, *Exec VP*
▲ **EMP:** 180 **EST:** 1960
SQ FT: 88,000
SALES: 627.2MM **Publicly Held**
WEB: www.semtech.com
SIC: 3674 Semiconductors & related devices

(P-18539)
SEMTECH SAN DIEGO CORPORATION
10021 Willow Creek Rd, San Diego
(92131-1657)
PHONE.................................858 695-1808
Mark Drucker, *President*
Nancy Ricks, *Office Mgr*
Sylvia Rodriguez, *Administration*
Robert Grambo, *Technical Staff*
Alan Burchfield, *Marketing Mgr*
EMP: 46
SQ FT: 25,000
SALES (est): 4.5MM
SALES (corp-wide): 627.2MM **Publicly Held**
WEB: www.semtech.com
SIC: 3674 Integrated circuits, semiconductor networks, etc.
PA: Semtech Corporation
　　200 Flynn Rd
　　Camarillo CA 93012
　　805 498-2111

(P-18540)
SENSONETICS INC
11164 Young River Ave, Fountain Valley
(92708-4109)
PHONE.................................714 799-1616
Gary Sahagen, *CEO*
Laurie Childress, *Business Mgr*
◆ **EMP:** 17 **EST:** 1998
SQ FT: 8,000
SALES (est): 3.6MM **Privately Held**
WEB: www.sensonetics.com
SIC: 3674 Semiconductors & related devices

(P-18541)
SENSORONIX INC
16181 Scientific, Irvine (92618-4325)
PHONE.................................949 528-0906
Sid M Gomman, *President*
Gina Blair, *Admin Asst*
Jeff Kolodziejski, *Technician*
Stephen Rasmussen, *Project Mgr*
Arqam Chowdhry, *Engineer*
EMP: 12
SALES (est): 1.7MM **Privately Held**
WEB: www.sensoronix.com
SIC: 3674 Infrared sensors, solid state

▲ = Import ▼=Export
◆ =Import/Export

(P-18542)
SII SEMICONDUCTOR USA CORP
21221 S Wstn Ave Ste 250, Torrance (90501)
PHONE..................................310 517-7771
James Schlumpberger, *Vice Pres*
EMP: 11
SALES (est): 577.7K **Privately Held**
SIC: 3674 Semiconductors & related devices

(P-18543)
SILICON ELECTRONICS (PA)
1148 Sonora Ct, Sunnyvale (94086-5308)
P.O. Box 2297 (94087-0297)
PHONE..................................408 738-8236
Miten Marfatia, *President*
EMP: 35
SQ FT: 3,070
SALES (est): 198.3K **Privately Held**
SIC: 3674 7379 Semiconductors & related devices; computer related consulting services

(P-18544)
SILICON IMAGE INC (HQ)
2115 Onel Dr, San Jose (95131-2032)
PHONE..................................408 616-4000
Joe Bedewi, *CFO*
Kurt Thielen, *President*
Byron Milstead, *Vice Pres*
David L Rutledge, *CTO*
Victor Da Costa, *Engng Exec*
▲ EMP: 57
SQ FT: 128,154
SALES (est): 69.4MM
SALES (corp-wide): 398.8MM **Publicly Held**
WEB: www.siimage.com
SIC: 3674 7371 Semiconductors & related devices; computer software development & applications; computer software systems analysis & design, custom
PA: Lattice Semiconductor Corp
5555 Ne Moore Ct
Hillsboro OR 97124
503 268-8000

(P-18545)
SILICON LABS INTEGRATION INC (HQ)
Also Called: Silicon Laboratories
2708 Orchard Pkwy 30, San Jose (95134-1968)
PHONE..................................408 702-1400
Jean Luc Nauleau, *President*
Pierre Lamond, *Chairman*
Eric Radza, *Engineer*
Vivek Mohan, *Senior Mgr*
EMP: 17
SALES (est): 3.5MM **Publicly Held**
WEB: www.integration.com
SIC: 3674 Semiconductors & related devices

(P-18546)
SILICON LIGHT MACHINES CORP (DH)
820 Kifer Rd, Sunnyvale (94086-5200)
PHONE..................................408 240-4700
Lars Eng, *CEO*
Ken Fukui, *Senior VP*
EMP: 11
SQ FT: 18,000
SALES (est): 2.3MM **Privately Held**
WEB: www.siliconlight.com
SIC: 3674 Semiconductors & related devices
HQ: Screen North America Holdings, Inc.
5110 Tollview Dr
Rolling Meadows IL 60008
847 870-7400

(P-18547)
SILICON MOTION INC
690 N Mccarthy Blvd # 200, Milpitas (95035-5134)
PHONE..................................408 501-5300
Wallace Kou, *President*
Richard Chang, *Vice Pres*
Bernadette Aguilon, *Admin Asst*
Robert Abutan, *Software Engr*
Sara Hsu, *Project Mgr*
EMP: 60

SQ FT: 12,000
SALES (est): 9.6MM **Privately Held**
WEB: www.siliconmotion.com
SIC: 3674 Integrated circuits, semiconductor networks, etc.
PA: Silicon Motion, Inc.
8f-1, 36, Tai Yuan St.,
Chupei City HSI 30265

(P-18548)
SILICON SPECIALISTS INC
2487 Industrial Pkwy W, Hayward (94545-5007)
PHONE..................................510 732-9796
Wayne Cheung, *President*
Kimberly Nguyen, *Vice Pres*
EMP: 10
SQ FT: 8,000
SALES (est): 1MM **Privately Held**
SIC: 3674 Wafers (semiconductor devices)

(P-18549)
SILICON STANDARD CORP
Also Called: SSC
4701 Patrick Henry Dr # 16, Santa Clara (95054-1863)
PHONE..................................408 234-6964
EMP: 20
SALES (est): 2.2MM **Privately Held**
WEB: www.siliconstandard.com
SIC: 3674

(P-18550)
SILICON TURNKEY SOLUTIONS INC (HQ)
1804 Mccarthy Blvd, Milpitas (95035-7410)
PHONE..................................408 904-0200
Richard Kingdon, *President*
Michael Rooney, *CFO*
Jerry Chang, *General Mgr*
Larry Jorstad, *CTO*
Wasim Khan, *Engineer*
EMP: 17
SQ FT: 35,000
SALES (est): 16.3MM
SALES (corp-wide): 83.4MM **Privately Held**
WEB: www.siliconturnkey.com
SIC: 3674 5065 Microcircuits, integrated (semiconductor); semiconductor devices
PA: Micross Components, Inc.
7725 N Orange Blossom Trl
Orlando FL 32810
407 298-7100

(P-18551)
SILICON VLY MCRELECTRONICS INC
2985 Kifer Rd, Santa Clara (95051-0802)
PHONE..................................408 844-7100
Patrick Callinan, *President*
Van Pham, *Accounting Mgr*
Sean D'Angelo, *Sales Mgr*
Brian Miller, *Manager*
Shirley Sun, *Manager*
◆ EMP: 30
SQ FT: 30,000
SALES: 28MM **Privately Held**
WEB: www.svmi.com
SIC: 3674 Silicon wafers, chemically doped

(P-18552)
SILICONCORE TECHNOLOGY INC
890 Hillview Ct Ste 120, Milpitas (95035-4573)
PHONE..................................408 946-8185
Eric LI, *President*
Sonny Tang, *President*
Robert Young, *President*
Heng Liu, *Officer*
Nicos Syrimis, *Senior VP*
▲ EMP: 23
SQ FT: 6,000
SALES (est): 24.3MM **Privately Held**
WEB: www.silicon-core.com
SIC: 3674 Integrated circuits, semiconductor networks, etc.

(P-18553)
SILICONIX INCORPORATED (HQ)
2585 Junction Ave, San Jose (95134-1923)
PHONE..................................408 988-8000

Serge Jaunay, *CEO*
King Owyang, *President*
Nick Bacile, *COO*
▲ EMP: 610
SQ FT: 220,100
SALES (est): 322.9MM
SALES (corp-wide): 3B **Publicly Held**
SIC: 3674 Transistors
PA: Vishay Intertechnology, Inc.
63 Lancaster Ave
Malvern PA 19355
610 644-1300

(P-18554)
SILICONIX SEMICONDUCTOR INC
2201 Laurelwood Rd, Santa Clara (95054-1593)
PHONE..................................408 988-8000
EMP: 121
SALES (est): 4.2MM
SALES (corp-wide): 3B **Publicly Held**
SIC: 3674 Semiconductors & related devices
HQ: Siliconix Incorporated
2585 Junction Ave
San Jose CA 95134
408 988-8000

(P-18555)
SILVER PEAK SYSTEMS INC (PA)
2860 De La Cruz Blvd # 100, Santa Clara (95050-2635)
PHONE..................................408 935-1800
David Hughes, *CEO*
Eric Yeaman, *CFO*
Rick Valentine, *Ch Credit Ofcr*
John Vincenzo, *Chief Mktg Ofcr*
Kathleen Swift, *Senior VP*
EMP: 120
SQ FT: 29,000
SALES (est): 33.8MM **Privately Held**
WEB: www.silver-peak.com
SIC: 3674 Integrated circuits, semiconductor networks, etc.

(P-18556)
SIPEX CORPORATION (DH)
48720 Kato Rd, Fremont (94538-7312)
PHONE..................................510 668-7000
Ralph Schmitt, *CEO*
Clyde R Wallin, *CFO*
Lee Cleveland, *Senior VP*
Khem Chhabra, *Engineer*
Patong Yang, *Engineer*
EMP: 126
SQ FT: 95,700
SALES (est): 11.9MM
SALES (corp-wide): 385MM **Publicly Held**
WEB: www.sipex.com
SIC: 3674 Integrated circuits, semiconductor networks, etc.; monolithic integrated circuits (solid state)
HQ: Exar Corporation
1060 Rincon Cir
San Jose CA 95131
669 265-6100

(P-18557)
SIRF TECHNOLOGY HOLDINGS INC (DH)
1060 Rincon Cir, San Jose (95131-1325)
PHONE..................................408 523-6500
Diosdado B Banatao, *Ch of Bd*
Diosdado P Banatao, *Ch of Bd*
Dennis Bencala, *CFO*
Geoffrey Ribar, *CFO*
Kanwar Chadha, *Vice Pres*
EMP: 75
SQ FT: 48,000
SALES (est): 30.9MM
SALES (corp-wide): 24.2B **Publicly Held**
WEB: www.sirf.com
SIC: 3674 3663 Semiconductors & related devices;
HQ: Csr Limited
Churchill House
Cambridge CAMBS CB4 0
122 369-2000

(P-18558)
SITEK PROCESS SOLUTIONS
233 Technology Way Ste 3, Rocklin (95765-1208)
PHONE..................................916 797-9000
James Mullany, *President*
Terri Mullany, *Vice Pres*
Danielle Johnson, *Mktg Coord*
▲ EMP: 13
SQ FT: 8,000
SALES (est): 2.5MM **Privately Held**
WEB: www.sitekprocess.com
SIC: 3674 Semiconductors & related devices

(P-18559)
SITIME CORPORATION (HQ)
5451 Patrick Henry Dr, Santa Clara (95054-1167)
PHONE..................................408 328-4400
Rajesh Vashist, *CEO*
Mark Lunsford, *President*
Craig Garber, *CFO*
Piyush Sevalia, *Exec VP*
David Hsieh, *Vice Pres*
EMP: 135
SQ FT: 32,000
SALES: 85.2MM **Publicly Held**
WEB: www.sitime.com
SIC: 3674 Semiconductors & related devices

(P-18560)
SJT TECH INDUSTRIES INC
1400 Coleman Ave Ste E28, Santa Clara (95050-4358)
PHONE..................................408 980-9547
Jake Rhee, *Principal*
EMP: 10
SALES (est): 1MM **Privately Held**
SIC: 3674 Semiconductors & related devices

(P-18561)
SK HYNIX MEMORY SOLUTIONS INC
3103 N 1st St, San Jose (95134-1934)
PHONE..................................408 514-3500
Tony Yoon, *CEO*
Sang SOO Son, *CFO*
Chee Hoe Chu, *Vice Pres*
Jon Haswell, *Vice Pres*
Khaled Labib, *Vice Pres*
EMP: 24
SALES (est): 34.9MM **Privately Held**
SIC: 3674 Semiconductors & related devices
PA: Sk Hynix Inc.
2091 Gyeongchung-Daero, Bubal-Eup
Icheon 17336

(P-18562)
SKYWORKS SOLUTIONS INC
2427 W Hillcrest Dr, Newbury Park (91320-2202)
PHONE..................................805 480-4400
Michael Gooch, *Manager*
Terry Pope, *COO*
Ernesto Ambrocio, *Engineer*
Maxwell Thomas, *Engineer*
Brian Chaughnessy, *Safety Mgr*
EMP: 56
SALES (corp-wide): 3.3B **Publicly Held**
WEB: www.alphaind.com
SIC: 3674 Semiconductors & related devices
PA: Skyworks Solutions, Inc.
20 Sylvan Rd
Woburn MA 01801
781 376-3000

(P-18563)
SKYWORKS SOLUTIONS INC
730 Lawrence Dr, Newbury Park (91320-2207)
PHONE..................................805 480-4227
Xiao-Ping LI, *Engineer*
EMP: 56
SALES (corp-wide): 3.3B **Publicly Held**
SIC: 3674 Semiconductors & related devices
PA: Skyworks Solutions, Inc.
20 Sylvan Rd
Woburn MA 01801
781 376-3000

PRODUCTS & SVCS

(P-18564)
SMART GLOBAL HOLDINGS INC (PA)
39870 Eureka Dr, Newark (94560-4809)
PHONE.....................510 623-1231
Ajay Shah, *Ch of Bd*
Bruce Goldberg,
Jack Pacheco, *Officer*
Tom Coull, *Senior VP*
Kiwan Kim, *Senior VP*
EMP: 25 EST: 1988
SQ FT: 79,480
SALES: 1.2B **Publicly Held**
SIC: 3674 Semiconductors & related devices

(P-18565)
SMART MODULAR TECH DE INC (HQ)
45800 Northport Loop W, Fremont (94538-6413)
PHONE.....................510 623-1231
Jack Pacheco, *CEO*
Frank Perezalonso, *Vice Pres*
Lee C CBA, *Credit Staff*
Alex Zaldivar, *Manager*
EMP: 175
SALES (est): 166.5MM
SALES (corp-wide): 1.2B **Publicly Held**
SIC: 3674 Semiconductors & related devices
PA: Smart Global Holdings, Inc.
39870 Eureka Dr
Newark CA 94560
510 623-1231

(P-18566)
SMART MODULAR TECHNOLOGIES INC (HQ)
39870 Eureka Dr, Newark (94560-4809)
PHONE.....................510 623-1231
Ajay Shah, *President*
Bruce Goldberg, *Vice Pres*
Kiwan Kim, *Vice Pres*
Jack Pacheco, *Vice Pres*
Mike Rubino, *Vice Pres*
▲ EMP: 103
SALES (est): 1.8MM
SALES (corp-wide): 1.2B **Publicly Held**
WEB: www.smartm.com
SIC: 3674 Semiconductors & related devices
PA: Smart Global Holdings, Inc.
39870 Eureka Dr
Newark CA 94560
510 623-1231

(P-18567)
SMT ELECTRONICS MFG INC
2630 S Shannon St, Santa Ana (92704-5230)
PHONE.....................714 751-8894
Henry T Tran, *CEO*
EMP: 35
SQ FT: 12,104
SALES (est): 4.6MM **Privately Held**
WEB: www.smtelectronics.com
SIC: 3674 3672 Integrated circuits, semiconductor networks, etc.; printed circuit boards

(P-18568)
SOLAICX
600 Clipper Dr, Belmont (94002-4119)
PHONE.....................408 988-5000
David Ranhoff, *President*
Guy Anthony, *CFO*
John T Sedgwick, *Founder*
Peter Bostock PHD, *Vice Pres*
Peter Schwartz, *Vice Pres*
▲ EMP: 83
SQ FT: 36,000
SALES (est): 8.9MM
SALES (corp-wide): 2.4B **Privately Held**
WEB: www.solaicx.com
SIC: 3674 Silicon wafers, chemically doped
PA: Sunedison, Inc.
13736 Riverport Dr
Maryland Heights MO 63043

(P-18569)
SOLARTECH POWER INC
901 E Cedar St, Ontario (91761-5572)
PHONE.....................909 673-0178
Sherry Fu, *President*
Rachel Seadschlag, *Sales Staff*
EMP: 10 EST: 2005
SALES (est): 1.4MM **Privately Held**
SIC: 3674 Solar cells

(P-18570)
SOLID STATE DEVICES INC
Also Called: Ssdi
14701 Firestone Blvd, La Mirada (90638-5918)
PHONE.....................562 404-4474
Arnold N Applebaum, *President*
David Franz, *CFO*
Mike Faucher, *Officer*
Eli Dexter, *Engineer*
David Guy, *Engineer*
▲ EMP: 110
SQ FT: 32,000
SALES (est): 21.9MM **Privately Held**
WEB: www.ssdi-power.com
SIC: 3674 Diodes, solid state (germanium, silicon, etc.)

(P-18571)
SONIC TECHNOLOGY PRODUCTS INC
108 Boulder St, Nevada City (95959-2610)
P.O. Box 539, Grass Valley (95945-0539)
PHONE.....................530 272-4607
Melanie Sullivan, *CEO*
Justin Reinholz, *President*
Jo Alsing, *COO*
Craig Ashcraft, *Vice Pres*
▲ EMP: 29
SQ FT: 2,000
SALES (est): 7.6MM **Privately Held**
SIC: 3674 3651 Semiconductors & related devices; household audio & video equipment

(P-18572)
SORAA INC (PA)
6500 Kaiser Dr Ste 110, Fremont (94555-3662)
PHONE.....................510 456-2200
Jeffery Parker, *Ch of Bd*
Kieran Drain, *COO*
Neal Woods, *Senior VP*
Nahid Afshar, *Vice Pres*
Todd Antes, *Vice Pres*
▲ EMP: 90
SQ FT: 50,000
SALES (est): 27.7MM **Privately Held**
SIC: 3674 3641 Semiconductors & related devices; electric lamps; electric lamp (bulb) parts

(P-18573)
SPANSION INC (HQ)
198 Champion Ct, San Jose (95134-1709)
P.O. Box 3453, Sunnyvale (94088-3453)
PHONE.....................408 962-2500
John H Kispert, *President*
Gary Wang, *President*
Randy W Furr, *CFO*
Glenda Dorchak, *Exec VP*
Robin J Jigour, *Senior VP*
▲ EMP: 10
SALES (est): 915.4MM
SALES (corp-wide): 2.4B **Publicly Held**
WEB: www.spansion.com
SIC: 3674 Integrated circuits, semiconductor networks, etc.
PA: Cypress Semiconductor Corporation
198 Champion Ct
San Jose CA 95134
408 943-2600

(P-18574)
SPANSION LLC (HQ)
198 Champion Ct, San Jose (95134-1709)
P.O. Box 3453, Sunnyvale (94088-3453)
PHONE.....................512 691-8500
Tom Moon, *Opers Staff*
Thad Trent, *President*
Eugene Spevakov, *Treasurer*
Tom EBY, *Exec VP*
Eric Price, *IT/INT Sup*
▲ EMP: 89

SALES (est): 88.5MM
SALES (corp-wide): 2.4B **Publicly Held**
SIC: 3674 Semiconductors & related devices
PA: Cypress Semiconductor Corporation
198 Champion Ct
San Jose CA 95134
408 943-2600

(P-18575)
SPATIAL PHOTONICS INC
930 Hamlin Ct, Sunnyvale (94089-1401)
PHONE.....................408 940-8800
Wald Siskens, *President*
Shaoher Pan, *CTO*
EMP: 40
SALES (est): 5.3MM **Privately Held**
SIC: 3674 Semiconductors & related devices

(P-18576)
SPECTROLAB INC
12500 Gladstone Ave, Sylmar (91342-5373)
P.O. Box 9209 (91392-9209)
PHONE.....................818 365-4611
David Lillington, *President*
Paul Ballew, *CFO*
Nasser Karam, *Vice Pres*
Jeff Peacock, *Vice Pres*
Edward Ringo, *Vice Pres*
EMP: 400
SQ FT: 50,000
SALES (est): 89.8MM
SALES (corp-wide): 101.1B **Publicly Held**
WEB: www.spectrolab.com
SIC: 3674 3679 Solar cells; power supplies, all types: static
HQ: Boeing Satellite Systems, Inc.
900 N Pacific Coast Hwy
El Segundo CA 90245

(P-18577)
SPIN MEMORY INC
45500 Northport Loop W, Fremont (94538-6498)
PHONE.....................510 933-8200
Tom Sparkman, *President*
Antoine Bruyns, *CFO*
Mustafa Pinarbasi, *Senior VP*
Les Crudele, *Vice Pres*
Amitay Levi, *Vice Pres*
▲ EMP: 50
SALES (est): 52MM **Privately Held**
SIC: 3674 Random access memory (RAM)

(P-18578)
SPT MICROTECHNOLOGIES
1755 Junction Ave, San Jose (95112-1029)
PHONE.....................408 571-1400
EMP: 10
SALES (est): 1.3MM **Privately Held**
SIC: 3674 Semiconductors & related devices

(P-18579)
STATS CHIPPAC INC (DH)
46429 Landing Pkwy, Fremont (94538-6496)
PHONE.....................510 979-8000
Tan Lay Koon, *President*
Wan Choong Hoe, *Exec VP*
Han Byung Joon, *Exec VP*
John Lau Tai Chong, *Senior VP*
Janet Taylor, *Senior VP*
▲ EMP: 50
SQ FT: 190,000
SALES (est): 12.5MM **Privately Held**
WEB: www.statschippac.com
SIC: 3674 Integrated circuits, semiconductor networks, etc.
HQ: Stats Chippac Pte. Ltd.
5 Yishun Street 23
Singapore 76844
695 771-12

(P-18580)
STATS CHIPPAC TEST SVCS INC
Also Called: Fastramp
9710 Scranton Rd Ste 360, San Diego (92121-1711)
PHONE.....................858 228-4084
Louis Benton, *Manager*
Srinivas RAO, *Technician*

Paul Isaac, *Consultant*
EMP: 25 **Privately Held**
SIC: 3674 Semiconductors & related devices
HQ: Stats Chippac Test Services, Inc.
46429 Landing Pkwy
Fremont CA 94538

(P-18581)
STATS CHIPPAC TEST SVCS INC (DH)
Also Called: Fastramp
46429 Landing Pkwy, Fremont (94538-6496)
PHONE.....................510 979-8000
Tan Lay Koon, *President*
David Goldberg, *Admin Sec*
EMP: 15
SALES (est): 3.4MM **Privately Held**
SIC: 3674 Semiconductors & related devices
HQ: Stats Chippac Pte. Ltd.
5 Yishun Street 23
Singapore 76844
695 771-12

(P-18582)
STMICROELECTRONICS INC
85 Enterprise Ste 300, Aliso Viejo (92656-2614)
PHONE.....................949 347-0717
EMP: 34
SALES (corp-wide): 7.4B **Privately Held**
SIC: 3674
HQ: Stmicroelectronics, Inc
750 Canyon Dr Ste 300
Coppell TX 75019
972 466-6000

(P-18583)
STRATAMET INC
46009 Hotchkiss St, Fremont (94539-7081)
PHONE.....................510 651-7176
▲ EMP: 25
SQ FT: 13,000
SALES (est): 2.2MM **Privately Held**
WEB: www.stratamet.com
SIC: 3674 3671 3699 3264 Semiconductors & related devices; electron tubes; electrical equipment & supplies; porcelain electrical supplies

(P-18584)
STRATEDGE CORPORATION
Also Called: Strat Edge
9424 Abraham Way Ste A, Santee (92071-5640)
PHONE.....................866 424-4962
Tim Going, *President*
Josie Santos, *CFO*
Casey Krawiec, *Vice Pres*
EMP: 40
SALES (est): 8MM **Privately Held**
WEB: www.stratedge.com
SIC: 3674 Semiconductors & related devices

(P-18585)
STRETCH INC
48720 Kato Rd, Fremont (94538-7312)
PHONE.....................408 543-2700
Craig Lytle, *President*
Thomas Daniel, *Vice Pres*
Wayne P Heideman, *Vice Pres*
Daniel Wark, *Vice Pres*
Elena Gonzalez, *Executive Asst*
EMP: 65
SALES (est): 6.7MM
SALES (corp-wide): 385MM **Publicly Held**
WEB: www.stretchinc.com
SIC: 3674 Integrated circuits, semiconductor networks, etc.
HQ: Exar Corporation
1060 Rincon Cir
San Jose CA 95131
669 265-6100

(P-18586)
SUBSTANCE ABUSE PROGRAM
1370 S State St Ste A, Hemet (92543)
PHONE.....................951 791-3350
Mark Thuve, *Business Mgr*
EMP: 30

▲ = Import ▼=Export
◆ =Import/Export

SALES (est): 1.4MM **Privately Held**
SIC: 3674 Semiconductors & related devices

(P-18587)
SUMCO PHOENIX CORPORATION
2099 Gateway Pl Ste 400, San Jose (95110-1017)
PHONE..................408 352-3880
EMP: 67 **Privately Held**
SIC: 3674 Silicon wafers, chemically doped
HQ: Sumco Phoenix Corporation
19801 N Tatum Blvd
Phoenix AZ 85050
480 473-6000

(P-18588)
SUMMIT WIRELESS TECH INC
6840 Via Del Oro Ste 280, San Jose (95119-1380)
PHONE..................408 627-4716
Brett Moyer, *Ch of Bd*
Gary Williams, *CFO*
James Cheng, *Vice Pres*
EMP: 49
SQ FT: 1,500
SALES: 1.3MM **Privately Held**
SIC: 3674 Semiconductors & related devices

(P-18589)
SUNCORE INC
3200 El Camino Real # 100, Irvine (92602-1378)
PHONE..................949 450-0054
Steven Brimmer, *President*
Donald A Nevins, *Treasurer*
Jennifer Mansoor, *Executive Asst*
Richard Sanett, *Director*
▲ **EMP:** 20
SQ FT: 5,000
SALES (est): 2.4MM **Privately Held**
SIC: 3674 5063 5065 Solar cells; batteries; electronic parts & equipment

(P-18590)
SUNLINE ENERGY INC
7546 Trade St, San Diego (92121-2412)
PHONE..................858 997-2408
Matthew Margolin, *CEO*
Tony Hubanks, *Manager*
Demian Martinez, *Manager*
Gerry Ebert, *Consultant*
EMP: 48
SQ FT: 5,000
SALES (est): 483.1K **Privately Held**
SIC: 3674 3829 Solar cells; solarimeters

(P-18591)
SUNPOWER CORPORATION (DH)
51 Rio Robles, San Jose (95134-1858)
PHONE..................408 240-5500
Thomas H Werner, *Ch of Bd*
Erin Nelson, *Exec VP*
Douglas J Richards, *Exec VP*
Vichheka Heang, *Vice Pres*
John Kauffmann, *Vice Pres*
▲ **EMP:** 600
SQ FT: 129,000
SALES: 1.7B
SALES (corp-wide): 8.4B **Publicly Held**
WEB: www.sunpowercorp.com
SIC: 3674 3679 Solar cells; photoelectric cells, solid state (electronic eye); power supplies, all types: static
HQ: Total Solar Intl
La Defense
Courbevoie 92400
147 444-546

(P-18592)
SUNPREME INC
4701 Patrick Henry Dr # 25, Santa Clara (95054-1863)
PHONE..................408 419-9281
Ashok K Sinha, *CEO*
Mike Wanebo, *President*
Ratson Morad, *COO*
Surinder S Bedi, *Exec VP*
Homi Fateni, *Senior VP*
◆ **EMP:** 30 **EST:** 2009
SALES (est): 8.4MM **Privately Held**
SIC: 3674 Solar cells

(P-18593)
SUNSIL INC (PA)
3174 Danville Blvd Ste 1, Alamo (94507-1919)
P.O. Box 220 (94507-0220)
PHONE..................925 648-7779
Seth Alavi, *President*
Frank Muscolino, *Sales Staff*
Terry Snowden, *Sales Staff*
▲ **EMP:** 10 **EST:** 1999
SALES: 8.1MM **Privately Held**
WEB: www.sunsil.com
SIC: 3674 Semiconductors & related devices

(P-18594)
SUNSYSTEM TECHNOLOGY LLC
Also Called: Next Phase Solar
2802 10th St, Berkeley (94710-2711)
PHONE..................510 984-2027
Adam Burstein, *Branch Mgr*
EMP: 375
SALES (corp-wide): 41.6MM **Privately Held**
SIC: 3674 Photovoltaic devices, solid state
PA: Sunsystem Technology Llc
2731 Citrus Rd Ste D
Rancho Cordova CA 95742
916 671-3351

(P-18595)
SUNWORKS INC (PA)
1030 Winding Creek Rd # 100, Roseville (95678-7046)
PHONE..................916 409-6900
Charles Cargile, *CEO*
Joshua Schechter, *Ch of Bd*
Paul McDonnel, *CFO*
EMP: 84
SALES: 70.9MM **Publicly Held**
WEB: www.machinetalker.com
SIC: 3674 Integrated circuits, semiconductor networks, etc.

(P-18596)
SUPERTEX INC (HQ)
1235 Bordeaux Dr, Sunnyvale (94089-1203)
PHONE..................408 222-8888
Henry C Pao PH D, *President*
Benedict C K Choy, *Senior VP*
John Billingsley, *Engineer*
Dean Converse, *Engineer*
Linda Lam, *Director*
▲ **EMP:** 62
SQ FT: 42,000
SALES: 51.2MM
SALES (corp-wide): 5.3B **Publicly Held**
SIC: 3674 Integrated circuits, semiconductor networks, etc.; light emitting diodes; semiconductor circuit networks; monolithic integrated circuits (solid state)
PA: Microchip Technology Inc
2355 W Chandler Blvd
Chandler AZ 85224
480 792-7200

(P-18597)
SURFACE ART ENGINEERING INC
81 Bonaventura Dr, San Jose (95134-2105)
PHONE..................408 433-4700
Jennifer Lee, *CEO*
Richard Kundert, *President*
Kay Park, *Exec Dir*
Angela Choi, *Program Mgr*
▲ **EMP:** 50
SQ FT: 24,000
SALES (est): 12.3MM **Privately Held**
WEB: www.surface-art.com
SIC: 3674 Computer logic modules

(P-18598)
SYMMETRY ELECTRONICS LLC (DH)
Also Called: Semiconductorstore.com
222 N Pacific Coast Hwy, El Segundo (90245-5648)
PHONE..................310 536-6190
Joe Caravana, *Co-Founder*
Scott Wing, *President*
Gil Zaharoni, *Co-Founder*
▲ **EMP:** 35
SQ FT: 15,000

SALES (est): 9.9MM
SALES (corp-wide): 225.3B **Publicly Held**
WEB: www.semiconductorstore.com
SIC: 3674 Semiconductors & related devices
HQ: Tti, Inc.
2441 Northeast Pkwy
Fort Worth TX 76106
817 740-9000

(P-18599)
SYNTIANT CORP
7555 Irvine Center Dr, Irvine (92618-2930)
PHONE..................948 774-4887
Kurt Busch, *CEO*
EMP: 11
SALES (est): 1.2MM **Privately Held**
SIC: 3674 Semiconductors & related devices

(P-18600)
T-RAM SEMICONDUCTOR INC
2109 Landings Dr, Mountain View (94043-0839)
PHONE..................408 597-3670
Dado Banatao, *Ch of Bd*
Sam R Nakib, *President*
Scott Robins, *Vice Pres*
EMP: 21 **EST:** 2000
SQ FT: 28,000
SALES (est): 2.8MM **Privately Held**
WEB: www.t-ram.com
SIC: 3674 Semiconductors & related devices

(P-18601)
TAHOE RF SEMICONDUCTOR INC
12834 Earhart Ave, Auburn (95602-9027)
PHONE..................530 823-9786
Irshad A Rasheed, *CEO*
Brian Kabaker, *CFO*
Christopher Saint, *Vice Pres*
EMP: 15
SQ FT: 6,000
SALES (est): 2.6MM **Privately Held**
WEB: www.tahoerf.com
SIC: 3674 8711 Semiconductors & related devices; engineering services

(P-18602)
TAKEX AMERICA INC
151 San Zeno Way, Sunnyvale (94086-5307)
PHONE..................877 371-2727
Yuji Egawa, *President*
▲ **EMP:** 23
SALES (est): 3.4MM **Privately Held**
SIC: 3674 Infrared sensors, solid state

(P-18603)
TECH-SEMI INC
2355 Paragon Dr Ste A, San Jose (95131-1334)
PHONE..................408 451-9588
Jintu Wang, *Administration*
◆ **EMP:** 10
SALES (est): 1MM **Privately Held**
SIC: 3674 Semiconductors & related devices

(P-18604)
TECHNOPROBE AMERICA INC
2526 Qume Dr Ste 27, San Jose (95131-1870)
PHONE..................408 573-9911
Stefano Felici, *President*
Aberash Tefera, *Human Resources*
Sithon Im, *Mfg Staff*
Hugh Obyrne, *Sales Mgr*
Steve Radford, *Sales Staff*
EMP: 25
SQ FT: 800
SALES: 450K **Privately Held**
SIC: 3674 Semiconductors & related devices

(P-18605)
TECK ADVANCED MATERIALS INC (DH)
Also Called: Cominco Advanced Material
13670 Danielson St Ste H, Poway (92064-6890)
PHONE..................858 391-2935
Donald R Lindsay, *CEO*

Norman B Keevil, *Ch of Bd*
Mike Martin, *President*
▲ **EMP:** 17
SALES: 3.1MM
SALES (corp-wide): 9.5B **Privately Held**
SIC: 3674 Semiconductors & related devices
HQ: Teck American Incorporated
501 N Riverpoint Blvd # 300
Spokane WA 99202
509 747-6111

(P-18606)
TELA INNOVATIONS INC
475 Alberto Way Ste 120, Los Gatos (95032-5480)
PHONE..................408 558-6300
Scott Becker, *CEO*
Carney Becker, *President*
Peter Calverley, *CFO*
Liz Stewart, *Vice Pres*
EMP: 45
SALES (est): 5.2MM **Privately Held**
SIC: 3674 Integrated circuits, semiconductor networks, etc.

(P-18607)
TELEDYNE DEFENSE ELEC LLC
Also Called: Teledyne E2v Hirel Electronics
765 Sycamore Dr, Milpitas (95035-7465)
PHONE..................408 737-0992
EMP: 105
SALES (corp-wide): 2.9B **Publicly Held**
SIC: 3674 Semiconductors & related devices
HQ: Teledyne Defense Electronics, Llc
1274 Terra Bella Ave
Mountain View CA 94043
650 691-9800

(P-18608)
TELEDYNE E2V, INC.
Also Called: Teledyne Hirel Electronics
765 Sycamore Dr, Milpitas (95035-7465)
PHONE..................408 737-0992
EMP: 44
SALES (est): 20.4MM
SALES (corp-wide): 2.9B **Publicly Held**
WEB: www.e2v.com/aero
SIC: 3674 Semiconductors & related devices
HQ: E2v Holdings Inc.
660 White Plains Rd # 525
Tarrytown NY 10591
415 987-2211

(P-18609)
TELEDYNE INSTRUMENTS INC
9855 Carroll Canyon Rd, San Diego (92131-1103)
PHONE..................858 842-3127
Mark Page, *Manager*
EMP: 20
SALES (corp-wide): 2.9B **Publicly Held**
WEB: www.teledynesolutions.com
SIC: 3674 3678 3613 3423 Semiconductors & related devices; electronic connectors; switchgear & switchboard apparatus; hand & edge tools
HQ: Teledyne Instruments, Inc.
1049 Camino Dos Rios
Thousand Oaks CA 91360
805 373-4545

(P-18610)
TELEDYNE TECHNOLOGIES INC
Also Called: Teledyne Cougar
290 Santa Ana Ct, Sunnyvale (94085-4512)
PHONE..................408 773-8814
Sheila Pugatch, *Branch Mgr*
EMP: 305
SALES (corp-wide): 2.9B **Publicly Held**
WEB: www.teledyne.com
SIC: 3674 Semiconductors & related devices
PA: Teledyne Technologies Inc
1049 Camino Dos Rios
Thousand Oaks CA 91360
805 373-4545

(P-18611)
TELEGENT SYSTEMS USA INC
10180 Telesis Ct Ste 500, San Diego (92121-2787)
PHONE..................408 523-2800

Ford Tamer, *CEO*
Weijie Yun, *Ch of Bd*
Samuel Sheng, *CTO*
EMP: 25
SQ FT: 6,437
SALES (est): 2.2MM
SALES (corp-wide): 220.2K **Privately Held**
WEB: www.telegentsystems.com
SIC: 3674 Microcircuits, integrated (semi-conductor)
HQ: Spreadtrum Communications (Shanghai) Co., Ltd.
　　Building 1, Exhibition Center, No.2288,
　　Zuchongzhi Road, China (
　　Shanghai 20120
　　212 036-0600

(P-18612)
TENSORCOM INC
3530 John Hopkins Ct, San Diego
(92121-1121)
PHONE..................760 496-3264
Patrick Soon-Shiong, *CEO*
Felix Madrigal, *General Mgr*
Gt Tanisawa, *Business Anlyst*
Melissa Cota, *Technology*
Bethany Steidl, *Technology*
◆ **EMP:** 32
SQ FT: 5,000
SALES (est): 1.3MM **Privately Held**
SIC: 3674 Microcircuits, integrated (semi-conductor)

(P-18613)
TERIDIAN SEMICONDUCTOR CORP (DH)
6440 Oak Cyn Ste 100, Irvine
(92618-5208)
PHONE..................714 508-8800
Mark Casper, *CEO*
John Silk, *Vice Pres*
Pete Todd, *Vice Pres*
David Gruetter, *CTO*
EMP: 90
SALES (est): 5.5MM
SALES (corp-wide): 2.3B **Publicly Held**
WEB: www.teridian.com
SIC: 3674 Semiconductors & related devices

(P-18614)
TESSERA INC (DH)
3025 Orchard Pkwy, San Jose
(95134-2017)
PHONE..................408 321-6000
Richard Chernicoff, *President*
Simon McElrea, *President*
Tudor Brown, *Bd of Directors*
Christopher Seams, *Bd of Directors*
Alan Massengale, *Vice Pres*
EMP: 12
SQ FT: 51,000
SALES (est): 10.2MM
SALES (corp-wide): 406.1MM **Publicly Held**
WEB: www.tessera.com
SIC: 3674 8999 Integrated circuits, semiconductor networks, etc.; inventor
HQ: Tessera Technologies, Inc.
　　3025 Orchard Pkwy
　　San Jose CA 95134
　　408 321-6000

(P-18615)
TESSERA INTELLECTUAL PRPTS INC
3025 Orchard Pkwy, San Jose
(95134-2017)
PHONE..................408 321-6000
Tom Lacey, *Principal*
EMP: 68 **EST:** 2012
SALES (est): 383.3K
SALES (corp-wide): 406.1MM **Publicly Held**
SIC: 3674 Integrated circuits, semiconductor networks, etc.
HQ: Tessera, Inc.
　　3025 Orchard Pkwy
　　San Jose CA 95134

(P-18616)
TESSERA INTLLCTUAL PRPRTY CORP
3025 Orchard Pkwy, San Jose
(95134-2017)
PHONE..................408 321-6000
Tom Lacey, *CEO*
Murali Dharan, *President*
Robert A Young PHD, *President*
Robert Andersen, *CFO*
EMP: 40 **EST:** 2011
SALES (est): 4.4MM
SALES (corp-wide): 406.1MM **Publicly Held**
SIC: 3674 Microcircuits, integrated (semiconductor)
HQ: Tessera Technologies, Inc.
　　3025 Orchard Pkwy
　　San Jose CA 95134
　　408 321-6000

(P-18617)
TESSERA TECHNOLOGIES INC (HQ)
3025 Orchard Pkwy, San Jose
(95134-2017)
PHONE..................408 321-6000
Tom Lacey, *CEO*
Jon E Kirchner, *President*
Robert Andersen, *CFO*
Peter Van Deventer, *Chief Mktg Ofcr*
Kevin Doohan, *Officer*
▲ **EMP:** 37
SALES: 273.3MM
SALES (corp-wide): 406.1MM **Publicly Held**
WEB: www.tessera.com
SIC: 3674 6794 Integrated circuits, semiconductor networks, etc.; memories, solid state; patent buying, licensing, leasing
PA: Xperi Corporation
　　3025 Orchard Pkwy
　　San Jose CA 95134
　　408 321-6000

(P-18618)
TEXAS INSTRUMENTS INCORPORATED
165 Gibraltar Ct, Sunnyvale (94089-1301)
PHONE..................408 541-9900
Al Wagner, *Manager*
Bjoy Santos, *Technology*
Dipa RAO, *Engineer*
Neel Seshan, *Marketing Mgr*
Kenny Grant, *Regl Sales Mgr*
EMP: 27
SALES (corp-wide): 15.7B **Publicly Held**
WEB: www.ti.com
SIC: 3674 Microprocessors
PA: Texas Instruments Incorporated
　　12500 Ti Blvd
　　Dallas TX 75243
　　214 479-3773

(P-18619)
TEXAS INSTRUMENTS INCORPORATED
2900 Semiconductor Dr, Santa Clara
(95051-0606)
PHONE..................669 721-5000
Ming Hwang, *Engineer*
Darryl Jeong, *Engineer*
Demetrius Lim, *Engineer*
Trung Nguyen, *Marketing Staff*
Andrew Devlin, *Facilities Mgr*
EMP: 24
SALES (corp-wide): 15.7B **Publicly Held**
SIC: 3674 3613 3822 3578 Microprocessors; microcircuits, integrated (semiconductor); computer logic modules; memories, solid state; power circuit breakers; thermostats & other environmental sensors; calculators & adding machines
PA: Texas Instruments Incorporated
　　12500 Ti Blvd
　　Dallas TX 75243
　　214 479-3773

(P-18620)
TEXAS INSTRUMENTS INCORPORATED
14351 Myford Rd, Tustin (92780-7074)
PHONE..................714 731-7110
EMP: 190

SALES (corp-wide): 12.2B **Publicly Held**
SIC: 3674
PA: Texas Instruments Incorporated
　　12500 Ti Blvd
　　Dallas TX 75243
　　214 479-3773

(P-18621)
THINCI INC (PA)
4659 Gldn Fthl Pkwy # 201, El Dorado Hills
(95762-9766)
PHONE..................916 235-8466
Dinakar C Munagala, *CEO*
EMP: 10
SALES (est): 0 **Privately Held**
SIC: 3674 Semiconductors & related devices

(P-18622)
TOUCHDOWN TECHNOLOGIES INC
5188 Commerce Dr, Baldwin Park
(91706-1450)
PHONE..................626 472-6732
Haruo Matsuno, *President*
Patrick Flynn, *President*
Raffi Garabedian, *Vice Pres*
Brian Flowers, *Admin Sec*
▼ **EMP:** 103
SQ FT: 30,000
SALES (est): 17.2MM **Privately Held**
SIC: 3674 Semiconductor diodes & rectifiers

(P-18623)
TOWER SEMICONDUCTOR USA INC
2570 N 1st St Ste 480, San Jose
(95131-1018)
PHONE..................408 770-1320
Doron Simon, *President*
Marco Racanelli, *Vice Pres*
David Lipsett, *Sales Dir*
Greg Hunsinger, *Marketing Staff*
Oren Shirazi, *Director*
EMP: 15
SQ FT: 4,100
SALES (est): 2.9MM
SALES (corp-wide): 352MM **Privately Held**
SIC: 3674 Semiconductors & related devices
PA: Tower Semiconductor Ltd
　　20 Shaul Amor Blvd
　　Migdal Haemek 23530
　　465 066-11

(P-18624)
TROPIAN INC
20813 Stevens Creek Blvd, Cupertino
(95014-2185)
PHONE..................408 865-1300
Tim Unger, *President*
Earl Mc Cune, *CTO*
▲ **EMP:** 60
SQ FT: 26,000
SALES (est): 4.4MM **Privately Held**
SIC: 3674 Semiconductors & related devices

(P-18625)
TSI SEMICONDUCTORS AMERICA LLC (PA)
Also Called: Telefunken Semiconductors Amer
7501 Foothills Blvd, Roseville
(95747-6504)
PHONE..................916 786-3900
Bruce Gray, *CEO*
Michael Gontar, *Ch of Bd*
John Doricko, *President*
Roger Lee, *COO*
Randy Ruegg, *CFO*
▲ **EMP:** 139
SALES (est): 39.3MM **Privately Held**
SIC: 3674 Semiconductors & related devices

(P-18626)
TSMC TECHNOLOGY INC
2585 Junction Ave, San Jose (95134-1923)
PHONE..................408 382-8052
Lora Ho, *President*
Dick Thurston, *President*
Wendell Huang, *Treasurer*

EMP: 57
SALES (est): 10.3MM **Privately Held**
SIC: 3674 Semiconductor circuit networks
HQ: Tsmc Partners Ltd.
　　C/O: Portcullis Trusnet (Bvi) Limited
　　Road Town
　　-

(P-18627)
TWILIGHT TECHNOLOGY INC (PA)
325 N Shepard St, Anaheim (92806-2832)
P.O. Box 1149, Placentia (92871-1149)
PHONE..................714 257-2257
Randy Greene, *President*
James Donaghy, *Vice Pres*
Gale Greene, *Admin Sec*
Scott Teson, *Sales Mgr*
Kathy Gibson, *Manager*
EMP: 20 **EST:** 1997
SQ FT: 12,000
SALES (est): 3MM **Privately Held**
WEB: www.forcetechnologies.co.uk
SIC: 3674 Integrated circuits, semiconductor networks, etc.

(P-18628)
TWIN CREEKS TECHNOLOGIES INC (PA)
3930 N 1st St Ste 10, San Jose
(95134-1501)
P.O. Box 1476, Los Gatos (95031-1476)
PHONE..................408 368-3733
Srinivasan Sivaram, *President*
EMP: 14
SALES (est): 2.6MM **Privately Held**
WEB: www.twincreekstechnologies.com
SIC: 3674 Semiconductors & related devices

(P-18629)
UBICOM INC
195 Baypointe Pkwy, San Jose
(95134-1697)
PHONE..................408 433-3330
Gangesh Ganesan, *CEO*
Douglas C Spreng, *Ch of Bd*
Alain Martinez, *CFO*
Josiane Valverde, *Vice Pres*
Linda Fu, *Accountant*
EMP: 75
SQ FT: 15,000
SALES (est): 6.6MM **Privately Held**
WEB: www.ubicom.com
SIC: 3674 Integrated circuits, semiconductor networks, etc.

(P-18630)
UHV SPUTTERING INC
275 Digital Dr, Morgan Hill (95037-2878)
PHONE..................408 779-2826
Rick Wooden, *President*
Linda Wooden, *CFO*
Mila Clement, *Sales Staff*
EMP: 19
SQ FT: 10,000
SALES (est): 3.8MM **Privately Held**
SIC: 3674 3471 Thin film circuits; electroplating & plating

(P-18631)
ULTRASIL LLC
3527 Breakwater Ave, Hayward
(94545-3610)
PHONE..................510 266-3700
Nghia Nguyen, *CEO*
Len Anderson, *Vice Pres*
EMP: 20
SALES (est): 712.7K **Privately Held**
SIC: 3674 Silicon wafers, chemically doped

(P-18632)
UMC GROUP(USA)
488 De Guigne Dr, Sunnyvale
(94085-3903)
PHONE..................408 523-7800
Robert Tsao, *Chairman*
Ing-Dar Liu, *Vice Chairman*
Peter Chang, *President*
Fu Tai Liou, *President*
Jason S Wang, *CEO*
▲ **EMP:** 75 **EST:** 1997
SQ FT: 40,000

▲ = Import ▼=Export
◆ =Import/Export

SALES (est): 14.4MM **Privately Held**
WEB: www.hope-umc.com
SIC: 3674 5065 Wafers (semiconductor devices); electronic parts & equipment
PA: United Microelectronics Corp.
3, Li Hsin 2nd Rd., Science-Based Industrial Park,
Hsinchu City 30077

(P-18633)
UNIREX CORP
Also Called: Unirex Technology
2288 E 27th St, Vernon (90058-1131)
PHONE..................................323 589-4000
Bijan Neman, *President*
Behzad Neman, *Admin Sec*
Vener Venerc, *Bookkeeper*
Farzad Neman, *VP Human Res*
Herlinda F Garcia, *Sales Staff*
▲ EMP: 13
SQ FT: 33,000
SALES (est): 2.5MM **Privately Held**
WEB: www.unirex.net
SIC: 3674 3572 Magnetic bubble memory device; computer storage devices

(P-18634)
UNISEM (SUNNVALE) INC (PA)
2241 Calle De Luna, Santa Clara (95054-1002)
PHONE..................................408 734-3222
Marita Erickson, *President*
James K Cook, *CFO*
EMP: 14
SQ FT: 5,798
SALES (est): 3.5MM **Privately Held**
SIC: 3674 Integrated circuits, semiconductor networks, etc.

(P-18635)
US SENSOR CORP
1832 W Collins Ave, Orange (92867-5425)
PHONE..................................714 639-1000
Roger W Dankert, *CEO*
Dan Dankert, *President*
EMP: 100
SQ FT: 30,000
SALES (est): 20.9MM
SALES (corp-wide): 1.7B **Publicly Held**
WEB: www.ussensor.com
SIC: 3674 3676 Semiconductors & related devices; thermistors, except temperature sensors
PA: Littelfuse, Inc.
8755 W Higgins Rd Ste 500
Chicago IL 60631
773 628-1000

(P-18636)
V-SILICON INC
47467 Fremont Blvd, Fremont (94538-6504)
PHONE..................................510 897-0168
Thinh Tran, *CEO*
EMP: 10
SALES (est): 398.2K **Privately Held**
SIC: 3674 Semiconductors & related devices

(P-18637)
VEECO INSTRUMENTS INC
Also Called: Veeco C V C
3100 Laurelview Ct, Santa Clara (95054)
PHONE..................................510 657-8523
EMP: 28
SALES (corp-wide): 392.8MM **Publicly Held**
SIC: 3674 5065
PA: Veeco Instruments Inc.
Terminal Dr
Plainview NY 11803
516 677-0200

(P-18638)
VENTURA TECHNOLOGY GROUP
855 E Easy St Ste 104, Simi Valley (93065-1825)
PHONE..................................805 581-0800
Douglas E Lafountaine, *President*
EMP: 47
SQ FT: 7,400
SALES (est): 12.5MM **Privately Held**
WEB: www.venturatech.com
SIC: 3674 Random access memory (RAM)

(P-18639)
VERISILICON INC (HQ)
2150 Gold St Ste 200, San Jose (95002-3702)
P.O. Box 1090 (95108-1090)
PHONE..................................408 844-8560
Wayne WEI Ming Dai, *President*
Robert Brown, *CFO*
Jonser Chan, *Vice Pres*
Davud Jarmon, *Vice Pres*
Ichiro Nakamura, *Vice Pres*
▲ EMP: 17
SQ FT: 55,000
SALES (est): 6.8MM **Privately Held**
WEB: www.verisilicon.com
SIC: 3674 Semiconductors & related devices

(P-18640)
VESTA TECHNOLOGY INC
3973 Soutirage Ln, San Jose (95135-1735)
PHONE..................................408 519-5800
Karl W Markert, *CEO*
Sang-In Lee, *Vice Pres*
EMP: 10
SALES (est): 930K **Privately Held**
SIC: 3674 Semiconductors & related devices

(P-18641)
VIA TELECOM INC
3390 Carmel Mountain Rd # 100, San Diego (92121-1053)
PHONE..................................858 350-5560
Ker Zhang, *CEO*
Chenwei Yan, *COO*
Mark Davis, *Vice Pres*
Howen Chen, *Director*
▲ EMP: 107
SALES (est): 14.3MM
SALES (corp-wide): 275.8K **Privately Held**
WEB: www.viatelecom.com
SIC: 3674 Semiconductors & related devices
PA: Jingrui Science And Technology (Beijing) Limited Company
Weisheng Building, Building 7, No.1 Courtyard , Qinghua Park, Zh
Beijing
105 985-3386

(P-18642)
VIAVI SOLUTIONS INC
80 Rose Orchard Way, San Jose (95134-1356)
PHONE..................................408 577-1478
Sergei Pacht, *Branch Mgr*
Oliver Kevin, *VP Mngmt*
Baker Dave, *Accounts Mgr*
EMP: 129
SALES (corp-wide): 1.1B **Publicly Held**
SIC: 3674 Optical isolators
PA: Viavi Solutions Inc.
6001 America Center Dr # 6
San Jose CA 95002
408 404-3600

(P-18643)
VIOLIN MMORY FDRAL SYSTEMS INC
4555 Great America Pkwy, Santa Clara (95054-1243)
PHONE..................................650 396-1500
John Kapitula, *President*
EMP: 10
SQ FT: 1,000
SALES (est): 753.8K
SALES (corp-wide): 50.8MM **Privately Held**
SIC: 3674 7389 Semiconductors & related devices;
PA: Violin Memory, Inc.
4555 Great America Pkwy # 150
Santa Clara CA 95054
650 396-1500

(P-18644)
VIRAGE LOGIC CORPORATION (HQ)
700 E Middlefield Rd, Mountain View (94043-4024)
PHONE..................................650 584-5000
Alexander Shubat, *President*
Brian Sereda, *CFO*

Jian Y Pan, *Vice Pres*
David Sowards, *Vice Pres*
Andreas Kuehlmann, *General Mgr*
EMP: 354
SQ FT: 61,500
SALES (est): 43.7MM
SALES (corp-wide): 3.1B **Publicly Held**
WEB: www.viragelogic.com
SIC: 3674 Integrated circuits, semiconductor networks, etc.
PA: Synopsys, Inc.
690 E Middlefield Rd
Mountain View CA 94043
650 584-5000

(P-18645)
VISHAY THIN FILM LLC
Also Called: Vishay Spectoral Electronics
4051 Greystone Dr, Ontario (91761-3100)
PHONE..................................909 923-3313
Robert Leon, *Mng Member*
Sheila Rigg, *Principal*
EMP: 70
SALES (est): 950K **Privately Held**
SIC: 3674 Thin film circuits

(P-18646)
VISHAY TRANSDUCERS LTD
2930 Inland Empire Blvd # 100, Ontario (91764-4802)
PHONE..................................626 363-7500
Dubi Zandman, *CEO*
Philx Zanman, *General Ptnr*
▲ EMP: 50
SALES (est): 6MM
SALES (corp-wide): 299.7MM **Publicly Held**
SIC: 3674 Semiconductors & related devices
PA: Vishay Precision Group, Inc.
3 Great Valley Pkwy # 150
Malvern PA 19355
484 321-5300

(P-18647)
VISIONARY ELECTRONICS INC
141 Parker Ave, San Francisco (94118-2607)
PHONE..................................415 751-8811
Brad Mc Millan, *President*
Roger Peterson, *Shareholder*
Jeff Fearn, *Treasurer*
EMP: 73 EST: 1974
SALES (est): 8.6MM **Privately Held**
WEB: www.viselect.com
SIC: 3674 3679 Microprocessors; recording & playback heads, magnetic

(P-18648)
VITESSE MANUFACTURING & DEV
Also Called: Vitesse Semiconductor
11861 Western Ave, Garden Grove (92841-2119)
PHONE..................................805 388-3700
Chris Gardner, *President*
EMP: 200
SALES (est): 25.1MM
SALES (corp-wide): 5.3B **Publicly Held**
WEB: www.vitesse.com
SIC: 3674 Microcircuits, integrated (semiconductor)
HQ: Microsemi Communications, Inc.
4721 Calle Carga
Camarillo CA 93012
805 388-3700

(P-18649)
VOLTAGE MULTIPLIERS INC (PA)
Also Called: V M I
8711 W Roosevelt Ave, Visalia (93291-9458)
PHONE..................................559 651-1402
Dennis J Kemp, *President*
John Yakura, *Corp Secy*
Kenneth Hage, *Vice Pres*
Robbie Hodgkins, *Engineer*
Brian Loehner, *Engineer*
EMP: 176
SQ FT: 24,000
SALES (est): 23.2MM **Privately Held**
WEB: www.voltagemultipliers.com
SIC: 3674 Diodes, solid state (germanium, silicon, etc.)

(P-18650)
VOLTERRA SEMICONDUCTOR LLC (HQ)
Also Called: Volterra Semiconductor Corp
160 Rio Robles, San Jose (95134-1813)
PHONE..................................408 601-1000
Mark Casper, *President*
Christopher Paisley, *Ch of Bd*
Craig Teuscher, *COO*
Mike Burns, *CFO*
William Numann, *Senior VP*
EMP: 32 EST: 1996
SQ FT: 73,000
SALES (est): 12.2MM
SALES (corp-wide): 2.3B **Publicly Held**
WEB: www.volterra.com
SIC: 3674 3612 Semiconductors & related devices; voltage regulators, transmission & distribution
PA: Maxim Integrated Products, Inc.
160 Rio Robles
San Jose CA 95134
408 601-1000

(P-18651)
W G HOLT INC
Also Called: Holt Integrated Circuits
23351 Madero, Mission Viejo (92691-2730)
PHONE..................................949 859-8800
David Mead, *CEO*
Jerry Donaldson, *Chief Mktg Ofcr*
William Holt, *Executive*
Chris Zenter, *Info Tech Dir*
James Yu, *Info Tech Mgr*
EMP: 65
SQ FT: 17,000
SALES (est): 12.7MM **Privately Held**
WEB: www.holtic.com
SIC: 3674 Integrated circuits, semiconductor networks, etc.

(P-18652)
W2 OPTRONICS INC
39523 Pardee Ct, Fremont (94538-1250)
PHONE..................................510 220-2796
Xinshi Xu, *Branch Mgr*
Dana Wu, *President*
EMP: 11
SALES (corp-wide): 1.6MM **Privately Held**
SIC: 3674 Microprocessors
PA: W2 Optronics Inc.
5500 Stewart Ave
Fremont CA 94538
510 207-8320

(P-18653)
WAFER PROCESS SYSTEMS INC
3641 Charter Park Dr, San Jose (95136-1312)
PHONE..................................408 445-3010
Douglas H Caldwell, *CEO*
Christopher J Schmitz, *Vice Pres*
EMP: 15
SALES (est): 3.4MM **Privately Held**
WEB: www.waferprocess.com
SIC: 3674 Semiconductors & related devices

(P-18654)
WAFERNET INC
2142 Paragon Dr, San Jose (95131-1305)
PHONE..................................408 437-9747
Lori L Vann, *President*
Brian Schmidt, *COO*
Dave Mewes, *Vice Pres*
Jon Mewes, *Vice Pres*
Marie Maraschin, *CIO*
▲ EMP: 17
SALES (est): 4.2MM **Privately Held**
WEB: www.wafernet.com
SIC: 3674 Semiconductors & related devices

(P-18655)
WAVEXING INC
3200 Scott Blvd, Santa Clara (95054-3007)
PHONE..................................408 896-1982
EMP: 10
SALES: 500K **Privately Held**
SIC: 3674

(P-18656)
WELDEX CORPORATION (PA)
6751 Katella Ave, Cypress (90630-5105)
PHONE..............................714 761-2100
G W Goddard, *CEO*
William Jung, *President*
Tyler Pierce, *Sales Staff*
Nicole Donovan, *Accounts Mgr*
June Hwang, *Accounts Mgr*
▲ **EMP:** 32
SQ FT: 15,000
SALES (est): 23.4MM **Privately Held**
WEB: www.weldex.com
SIC: 3674 3663 Light emitting diodes; television closed circuit equipment

(P-18657)
WINSLOW AUTOMATION INC
Also Called: Six Sigma
905 Montague Expy, Milpitas (95035-6817)
PHONE..............................408 262-9004
Russell Winslow, *CEO*
Daryl Sawtelle, *CFO*
Scott Pon, *Info Tech Mgr*
Amy Phan, *Controller*
Tisha Wolf, *Opers Mgr*
EMP: 58
SQ FT: 24,784
SALES (est): 12.4MM **Privately Held**
WEB: www.solderquik.com
SIC: 3674 Semiconductors & related devices

(P-18658)
WINWAY USA INC
1800 Wyatt Dr Ste 2, Santa Clara (95054-1527)
PHONE..............................203 775-9311
Mark Wang, *CEO*
Stephen A Evans, *President*
Robert Bollo, *CFO*
EMP: 45
SQ FT: 5,000
SALES: 10MM **Privately Held**
SIC: 3674 Semiconductors & related devices
PA: Winway Technology Co., Ltd.
68, Chuangyi S. Rd.,
Kaohsiung City 81156

(P-18659)
WORLDWIDE ENERGY & MFG USA INC (PA)
1675 Rollins Rd Ste F, Burlingame (94010-2320)
PHONE..............................650 692-7788
John Ballard, *Ch of Bd*
Tiffany Margaret Shum, *Director*
▲ **EMP:** 23
SQ FT: 9,680
SALES (est): 28MM **Privately Held**
WEB: www.wwmusa.com
SIC: 3674 Semiconductors & related devices

(P-18660)
XEL USA INC
Also Called: XEL Group
21 Argonaut Ste B, Aliso Viejo (92656-4150)
PHONE..............................949 425-8686
Paul Kuszka, *CEO*
Wendy Luttrell, *Info Tech Mgr*
EMP: 25
SALES (est): 4.6MM **Privately Held**
SIC: 3674 Magnetic bubble memory device

(P-18661)
XILINX INC
42063 Benbow Dr, Fremont (94539-5002)
PHONE..............................510 770-9449
David Liu, *Principal*
Luis Bielich, *Engineer*
Joe Luka, *Sales Staff*
EMP: 62
SALES (corp-wide): 3B **Publicly Held**
SIC: 3674 Microcircuits, integrated (semiconductor)
PA: Xilinx, Inc.
2100 All Programable
San Jose CA 95124
408 559-7778

(P-18662)
XILINX INC
2050 All Programable # 4, San Jose (95124-4355)
PHONE..............................408 879-6563
Kung Demi, *Manager*
EMP: 10
SALES (corp-wide): 3B **Publicly Held**
WEB: www.xilinx.com
SIC: 3674 Microcircuits, integrated (semiconductor)
PA: Xilinx, Inc.
2100 All Programable
San Jose CA 95124
408 559-7778

(P-18663)
XILINX DEVELOPMENT CORPORATION (HQ)
2100 All Programable, San Jose (95124-4355)
P.O. Box 240010 (95154-2410)
PHONE..............................408 559-7778
Jon A Olson, *CEO*
EMP: 13
SALES (est): 964.8K
SALES (corp-wide): 3B **Publicly Held**
SIC: 3674 Semiconductors & related devices
PA: Xilinx, Inc.
2100 All Programable
San Jose CA 95124
408 559-7778

(P-18664)
XPERI CORPORATION (PA)
3025 Orchard Pkwy, San Jose (95134-2017)
PHONE..............................408 321-6000
Jon Kirchner, *CEO*
Richard S Hill, *Ch of Bd*
Robert Andersen, *CFO*
George Riedel, *Bd of Directors*
Geir Skaaden, *Officer*
EMP: 69
SALES: 406.1MM **Publicly Held**
SIC: 3674 7379 7819 8742 Semiconductors & related devices; data processing consultant; ; consultants, motion picture; management information systems consultant

(P-18665)
YADAV TECHNOLOGY INC
48371 Fremont Blvd # 101, Fremont (94538-6554)
PHONE..............................510 438-0148
Petro Estakhri, *CEO*
Rani Ranjan, *Principal*
EMP: 11
SALES (est): 947.3K **Privately Held**
SIC: 3674 Semiconductors & related devices

(P-18666)
YIELD ENGINEERING SYSTEMS INC
203 Lawrence Dr Ste A, Livermore (94551-5152)
PHONE..............................925 373-8353
Ken Macwilliams, *CEO*
Dan Dunkly, *President*
Fred Garcy, *CFO*
William A Moffat, *Founder*
Lori Cantrell, *Exec VP*
EMP: 36
SQ FT: 20,000
SALES (est): 7MM **Privately Held**
WEB: www.yieldengineering.com
SIC: 3674 Semiconductors & related devices

(P-18667)
YIELD ENHANCEMENT SERVICES INC
Also Called: Yes-Tek
364 Sunpark Ct, San Jose (95136-2145)
PHONE..............................408 410-5825
Rick Torres, *President*
Efren Q Ebreo, *CFO*
EMP: 10
SQ FT: 7,000
SALES (est): 904.8K **Privately Held**
SIC: 3674 Semiconductors & related devices

(P-18668)
ZENVERGE INC
2680 Zanker Rd Ste 200, San Jose (95134-2144)
PHONE..............................408 350-5052
Amir Mobini, *CEO*
Tony Masterson, *COO*
Vincent A McCord, *CFO*
Raghu RAO, *Vice Pres*
EMP: 70
SALES (est): 13.4MM **Privately Held**
SIC: 3674 Semiconductors & related devices

(P-18669)
ZEP SOLAR LLC (DH)
161 Mitchell Blvd Ste 104, San Rafael (94903-2085)
PHONE..............................415 479-6900
Michael John Miskovsky, *CEO*
Peter David, *CFO*
Christina Manansala, *Vice Pres*
Jack West, *CTO*
▲ **EMP:** 28
SQ FT: 8,200
SALES (est): 11MM
SALES (corp-wide): 21.4B **Publicly Held**
SIC: 3674 Photovoltaic devices, solid state

(P-18670)
ZEST LABS INC (HQ)
2349 Bering Dr, San Jose (95131-1125)
PHONE..............................408 200-6500
Peter Mehring, *CEO*
Scott Durgin, *CTO*
EMP: 33
SQ FT: 8,000
SALES (est): 1.5MM **Publicly Held**
WEB: www.intelleflex.com
SIC: 3674 Semiconductors & related devices

(P-18671)
ZF MICRO SOLUTIONS INC
1000 Elwell Ct Ste 134, Palo Alto (94303-4306)
PHONE..............................650 846-6500
David L Feldman, *President*
David Feldman, *President*
Jerry Masterson, *CFO*
EMP: 11
SQ FT: 3,500
SALES (est): 1.2MM **Privately Held**
SIC: 3674 7371 Computer logic modules; custom computer programming services

(P-18672)
ZILOG INC (DH)
1590 Buckeye Dr, Milpitas (95035-7418)
PHONE..............................408 513-1500
Darin G Billerbeck, *President*
Mike Speckman, *President*
Perry J Grace, *CFO*
Steve Darrough, *Vice Pres*
Dan Eaton, *Vice Pres*
EMP: 30
SQ FT: 42,000
SALES (est): 19.5MM
SALES (corp-wide): 1.7B **Publicly Held**
WEB: www.zilog.com
SIC: 3674 Microcircuits, integrated (semiconductor)
HQ: Ixys, Llc
1590 Buckeye Dr
Milpitas CA 95035
408 457-9000

(P-18673)
ZORAN CORPORATION (DH)
1060 Rincon Cir, San Jose (95131-1325)
PHONE..............................972 673-1600
Daniel Willard Gardiner, *CEO*
Mustafa Ozgen, *President*
Karl Schneider, *CFO*
Isaac Shenberg PHD, *Senior VP*
Robert Kirk, *Vice Pres*
◆ **EMP:** 45
SQ FT: 89,000
SALES (est): 101.6MM
SALES (corp-wide): 24.2B **Publicly Held**
WEB: www.zoran.com
SIC: 3674 Integrated circuits, semiconductor networks, etc.

HQ: Csr Limited
Churchill House
Cambridge CAMBS CB4 0
122 369-2000

(P-18674)
ZT PLUS
1321 Mountain View Cir, Azusa (91702-1649)
PHONE..............................626 208-3440
Sandy Grouf, *Principal*
▲ **EMP:** 12
SALES (est): 839.5K **Privately Held**
SIC: 3674 Thermoelectric devices, solid state

3675 Electronic Capacitors

(P-18675)
AMERICAN CAPACITOR CORPORATION
5367 3rd St, Irwindale (91706-2085)
PHONE..............................626 814-4444
Joseph Latourelle, *President*
EMP: 25 **EST:** 1979
SQ FT: 14,200
SALES (est): 3.1MM **Privately Held**
WEB: www.americancapacitor.com
SIC: 3675 5065 Electronic capacitors; electronic parts & equipment

(P-18676)
BESTRONICS HOLDINGS INC (PA)
2090 Fortune Dr, San Jose (95131-1823)
PHONE..............................408 385-7777
Nat Mani, *CEO*
Steve Yetso, *Vice Pres*
Ron Menigoz, *CTO*
Ben Calub, *VP Mfg*
Shane OH, *Manager*
EMP: 42
SQ FT: 73,000
SALES (est): 71.5MM **Privately Held**
SIC: 3675 Electronic capacitors

(P-18677)
CSI TECHNOLOGIES INC
2540 Fortune Way, Vista (92081-8441)
PHONE..............................760 682-2222
Gary W Greiser, *President*
Perry Sheth, *Shareholder*
Narendra C Soni, *Shareholder*
▲ **EMP:** 18
SQ FT: 18,000
SALES (est): 3.3MM **Privately Held**
SIC: 3675 Electronic capacitors

(P-18678)
I M B ELECTRONIC PRODUCTS
1800 E Via Burton, Anaheim (92806-1213)
PHONE..............................714 523-2110
Steve Binnix, *President*
EMP: 55
SQ FT: 18,000
SALES (est): 3.6MM
SALES (corp-wide): 116.4MM **Publicly Held**
WEB: www.selas.com
SIC: 3675 Electronic capacitors
PA: Intricon Corporation
1260 Red Fox Rd
Arden Hills MN 55112
651 636-9770

(P-18679)
INCA ONE CORPORATION
1632 1/2 W 134th St, Gardena (90249-2014)
PHONE..............................310 808-0001
Adriana Roberts, *President*
Tupac Roberts, *Vice Pres*
Roger Fortier,
▲ **EMP:** 35 **EST:** 1971
SALES (est): 6.6MM **Privately Held**
WEB: www.inca-tvlifts.com
SIC: 3675 Electronic capacitors

(P-18680)
JENNINGS TECHNOLOGY CO LLC (DH)
970 Mclaughlin Ave, San Jose (95122-2611)
PHONE..............................408 292-4025

▲ = Import ▼=Export
◆ =Import/Export

W David Smith,
Kurt Gallo, *Vice Pres*
Jamie Horton, *Vice Pres*
Jeff Hilderbrand, *Regl Sales Mgr*
▲ **EMP:** 70
SALES (est): 12MM
SALES (corp-wide): 36.4B **Privately Held**
WEB: www.jenningstech.com
SIC: 3675 3679 3625 Electronic capacitors; electronic circuits; relays, for electronic use
HQ: Abb Installation Products Inc.
860 Ridge Lake Blvd
Memphis TN 38120
901 252-5000

(P-18681)
JOHANSON DIELECTRICS INC (HQ)
4001 Calle Tecate, Camarillo (93012-5087)
PHONE..................................805 389-1166
N Eric Johanson, *CEO*
Justin Greene, *CFO*
Tian Tan, *Engineer*
▲ **EMP:** 132
SALES (est): 26.4MM **Privately Held**
WEB: www.johansondielectrics.com
SIC: 3675 Electronic capacitors

(P-18682)
JOHANSON TECHNOLOGY INC
4001 Calle Tecate, Camarillo (93012-5087)
PHONE..................................805 389-1166
John Petrinec, *CEO*
D Ick Crawford, *Plant Mgr*
▲ **EMP:** 159
SQ FT: 30,000
SALES (est): 21MM **Privately Held**
WEB: www.johansontechnology.com
SIC: 3675 5065 3674 Electronic capacitors; electronic parts & equipment; semiconductors & related devices
PA: Johanson Ventures, Inc.
4001 Calle Tecate
Sylmar CA 93012

(P-18683)
NEMCO ELECTRONICS CORP
40 Roan Pl, Woodside (94062-4249)
PHONE..................................650 571-1234
Eugene J Porto, *Chairman*
John Nolan, *President*
James Rapoport, *Exec VP*
Ann Nolan, *Admin Sec*
EMP: 150
SQ FT: 10,000
SALES (est): 23MM **Privately Held**
WEB: www.nemcocaps.com
SIC: 3675 Electronic capacitors

(P-18684)
PACIFIC CAPACITOR CO
288 Digital Dr, Morgan Hill (95037-2877)
PHONE..................................408 778-6670
Steven Francis, *President*
Harold Francis, *President*
EMP: 12 **EST:** 1967
SQ FT: 10,000
SALES (est): 1.5MM **Privately Held**
SIC: 3675 Electronic capacitors

(P-18685)
TRIGON COMPONENTS INC
935 Mariner St, Brea (92821-3827)
PHONE..................................714 990-1367
Yeankai Chorng, *CEO*
Maria Chorng, *Office Mgr*
▲ **EMP:** 18
SALES (est): 2.9MM **Privately Held**
WEB: www.trigoncomp.com
SIC: 3675 5065 Condensers, electronic; electronic parts & equipment

(P-18686)
VIRGIL WALKER INC
Also Called: Auton Motorized Systems
29102 Hancock Pkwy, Valencia (91355-1066)
PHONE..................................661 294-9142
Fax: 310 295-5639
◆ **EMP:** 32
SQ FT: 15,000
SALES (est): 4.6MM **Privately Held**
WEB: www.auton.com
SIC: 3675

(P-18687)
WRIGHT CAPACITORS INC
Also Called: WCI
2610 Oak St, Santa Ana (92707-3720)
PHONE..................................714 546-2490
Casey Crandall, *President*
Pendra Lafee, *CFO*
Bev Woods, *Bookkeeper*
▲ **EMP:** 15 **EST:** 1977
SQ FT: 6,500
SALES (est): 2.6MM **Privately Held**
WEB: www.wrightcap.com
SIC: 3675 Electronic capacitors

(P-18688)
ZF ARRAY TECHNOLOGY INC
2302 Trade Zone Blvd, San Jose (95131-1819)
PHONE..................................408 433-9920
Robert Zinn, *CEO*
Richard Freiberger, *COO*
Jim Viviani, *Vice Pres*
▲ **EMP:** 55
SQ FT: 33,000
SALES (est): 4.3MM
SALES (corp-wide): 216.1MM **Privately Held**
WEB: www.zfarray.com
SIC: 3675 Electronic capacitors
PA: Smtc Corporation
7050 Woodbine Ave Suite 300
Markham ON L3R 4
905 479-1810

3676 Electronic Resistors

(P-18689)
CALIFORNIA MICRO DEVICES CORP (HQ)
3001 Stender Way, Santa Clara (95054-3216)
PHONE..................................408 542-1051
Robert V Dickinson, *President*
John Jorgensen, *President*
Kevin J Berry, *CFO*
Kyle D Baker, *Vice Pres*
Daniel Hauck, *Vice Pres*
▲ **EMP:** 21 **EST:** 1980
SQ FT: 26,800
SALES (est): 7.8MM
SALES (corp-wide): 5.8B **Publicly Held**
WEB: www.calmicro.com
SIC: 3676 3675 3672 3674 Electronic resistors; electronic capacitors; printed circuit boards; microcircuits, integrated (semiconductor)
PA: On Semiconductor Corporation
5005 E Mcdowell Rd
Phoenix AZ 85008
602 244-6600

(P-18690)
MICRO-OHM CORPORATION
1088 Hamilton Rd, Duarte (91010-2742)
PHONE..................................626 357-5377
Byron Ritchey, *CEO*
Charles Schwab, *President*
Barbette Bowers, *Corp Secy*
Mark Craven, *Vice Pres*
▲ **EMP:** 26 **EST:** 1961
SQ FT: 10,000
SALES (est): 3.4MM **Privately Held**
WEB: www.micro-ohm.com
SIC: 3676 Electronic resistors

(P-18691)
RIEDON INC (PA)
300 Cypress Ave, Alhambra (91801-3001)
PHONE..................................626 284-9901
Michael A Zoeller, *President*
Duane Ebbert, *Vice Pres*
Greg Wood, *Vice Pres*
Phil Ebbert, *CIO*
Becky Hinojosa, *Technology*
▲ **EMP:** 150
SQ FT: 12,000
SALES (est): 20.2MM **Privately Held**
WEB: www.riedon.com
SIC: 3676 Electronic resistors

(P-18692)
VISHAY THIN FILM LLC
Also Called: Vishay Spectrol
4051 Greystone Dr, Ontario (91761-3100)
PHONE..................................909 923-3313
▲ **EMP:** 50
SALES (est): 6.4MM **Privately Held**
SIC: 3676 3861 3577 Electronic resistors; photographic equipment & supplies; computer peripheral equipment

(P-18693)
YAGEO AMERICA CORPORATION
2550 N 1st St Ste 480, San Jose (95131-1038)
PHONE..................................408 240-6200
CHI Wen Chang, *President*
Dean Rambo, *Regl Sales Mgr*
Lisa Ramirez, *Sales Associate*
Ana Pinto, *Cust Mgr*
▲ **EMP:** 20
SALES (est): 2.5MM **Privately Held**
SIC: 3676 Electronic resistors
PA: Yageo Corporation
3f, 233-1, 233-2, Baoqiao Rd.,
New Taipei City TAP 23145

3677 Electronic Coils & Transformers

(P-18694)
ADTEC TECHNOLOGY INC
48625 Warm Springs Blvd, Fremont (94539-7782)
PHONE..................................510 226-5766
Shuitsu Fujii, *President*
Jor Amster, *President*
Nobuyuki Horita, *Exec Dir*
Junko Szymanski, *Admin Sec*
EMP: 13
SQ FT: 6,703
SALES (est): 6.2MM **Privately Held**
WEB: www.adtecusa.com
SIC: 3677 Electronic coils, transformers & other inductors
PA: Adtec Plasma Technology Co.,Ltd.
5-6-10, Hikinocho
Fukuyama HIR 721-0

(P-18695)
ADVANCED CHIP MAGNETICS INC
4225 Spencer St, Torrance (90503-2421)
PHONE..................................310 370-8188
Denise Nguyen, *CEO*
Steven Nguyen, *Admin Sec*
EMP: 10
SQ FT: 10,000
SALES (est): 1.3MM **Privately Held**
SIC: 3677 Electronic coils, transformers & other inductors

(P-18696)
AEM ELECTRONICS (USA) INC
6610 Cobra Way, San Diego (92121-4107)
PHONE..................................858 481-0210
Daniel H Chang, *CEO*
Cai L Chang, *CFO*
EMP: 32
SALES (est): 9MM **Privately Held**
SIC: 3677 3613 8742 3559 Inductors, electronic; fuses, electric; planning consultant; electronic component making machinery; metal powders, pastes & flakes; chemical preparations

(P-18697)
AHN ENTERPRISES LLC
Also Called: Santronics
1240 Birchwood Dr Ste 2, Sunnyvale (94089-2205)
PHONE..................................408 734-1878
Raymond Ahn,
Joanna Abes,
Garrick Ahn,
Grant Ahn,
Jeewon Ahn,
▲ **EMP:** 19
SQ FT: 5,000

SALES (est): 1.4MM **Privately Held**
WEB: www.santronics-usa.com
SIC: 3677 Electronic transformers

(P-18698)
ALLIED COMPONENTS INTL
19671 Descartes, Foothill Ranch (92610-2609)
PHONE..................................949 356-1780
Neal McDonald, *President*
Ruben Ramirez, *CFO*
▲ **EMP:** 25
SQ FT: 9,000
SALES (est): 5.4MM **Privately Held**
WEB: www.alliedcomponents.com
SIC: 3677 Electronic coils, transformers & other inductors

(P-18699)
AMI/COAST MAGNETICS INC
5333 W Washington Blvd, Los Angeles (90016-1191)
PHONE..................................323 936-6188
Satya Dosaj, *CEO*
Phillis Dosaj, *Shareholder*
Dev Dosaj, *President*
Austin Dosaj, *Administration*
EMP: 49 **EST:** 1965
SQ FT: 25,000
SALES (est): 8.5MM **Privately Held**
WEB: www.coastmagnetics.com
SIC: 3677 3549 Electronic transformers; coil winding machines for springs

(P-18700)
ARAS POWER TECHNOLOGIES (PA)
371 Fairview Way, Milpitas (95035-3024)
PHONE..................................408 935-8877
Fariborz RAD, *President*
▲ **EMP:** 15
SQ FT: 5,000
SALES (est): 1.8MM **Privately Held**
WEB: www.arastech.com
SIC: 3677 3679 Transformers power supply, electronic type; static power supply converters for electronic applications

(P-18701)
ASTRON CORPORATION
9 Autry, Irvine (92618-2768)
PHONE..................................949 458-7277
Loren Pochirowski, *President*
William Pochirowski, *Officer*
▲ **EMP:** 40
SQ FT: 18,000
SALES (est): 7.9MM **Privately Held**
WEB: www.astroncorp.com
SIC: 3677 3679 Transformers power supply, electronic type; electronic circuits

(P-18702)
BECKER SPECIALTY CORPORATION
15310 Arrow Blvd, Fontana (92335-3249)
PHONE..................................909 356-1095
Jack McGrew, *Branch Mgr*
EMP: 12
SALES (corp-wide): 882MM **Privately Held**
WEB: www.beckers-bic.com
SIC: 3677 Electronic coils, transformers & other inductors
HQ: Becker Specialty Corporation
2526 Delta Ln
Elk Grove Village IL 60007

(P-18703)
BEL POWER SOLUTIONS INC
Also Called: Power One
2390 Walsh Ave, Santa Clara (95051-1301)
PHONE..................................866 513-2839
Dennis Ackerman, *President*
Colin Dunn, *Vice Pres*
Steve Dawson, *Director*
▲ **EMP:** 2000
SALES (est): 9.7MM
SALES (corp-wide): 548.1MM **Publicly Held**
SIC: 3677 Electronic coils, transformers & other inductors

PA: Bel Fuse Inc.
206 Van Vorst St
Jersey City NJ 07302
201 432-0463

(P-18704)
BOURNS INC (PA)
1200 Columbia Ave, Riverside
(92507-2129)
PHONE..................................951 781-5500
Gordon L Bourns, *CEO*
Erik Meijer, *President*
James Heiken, *CFO*
Gregg Gibbons, *Exec VP*
Kelly Vogt, *Senior VP*
◆ **EMP:** 171
SQ FT: 205,000
SALES (est): 550MM **Privately Held**
WEB: www.bourns.com
SIC: 3677 3676 3661 3639 Electronic
transformers; electronic resistors; tele-
phone & telegraph apparatus; major
kitchen appliances, except refrigerators &
stoves; electronic circuits; connectors &
terminals for electrical devices

(P-18705)
CAL COIL MAGNETICS INC
2523 Seaman Ave, El Monte (91733-1927)
PHONE..................................626 455-0011
Scott Alvarado, *President*
Lisa Alvarado, *Admin Sec*
▲ **EMP:** 30 **EST:** 1954
SQ FT: 7,000
SALES (est): 4.2MM **Privately Held**
WEB: www.calcoilmagnetics.com
SIC: 3677 3612 Transformers power sup-
ply, electronic type; coil windings, elec-
tronic; transformers, except electric

(P-18706)
**COAST/DVNCED CHIP
MGNETICS INC**
Also Called: Coast/A C M
4225 Spencer St, Torrance (90503-2421)
PHONE..................................310 370-8188
Benjamin Nguyen, *CEO*
Allen Adams, *President*
Ben Nguyen, *CEO*
Karlis Lossing, *Info Tech Mgr*
Jessica Ortiz, *Agent*
EMP: 19
SQ FT: 3,000
SALES (est): 4.5MM **Privately Held**
WEB: www.coastacm.com
SIC: 3677 Electronic coils, transformers &
other inductors

(P-18707)
COIL WINDING SPECIALIST INC
Also Called: Cws
353 W Grove Ave, Orange (92865-3205)
PHONE..................................714 279-9010
James Lau, *President*
Benny Ortiz, *Opers Mgr*
Kian Chow, *VP Sales*
▲ **EMP:** 15
SQ FT: 1,000
SALES (est): 4.9MM **Privately Held**
SIC: 3677 Inductors, electronic

(P-18708)
COMPONETICS INC
2492 Turquoise Cir, Newbury Park
(91320-1209)
PHONE..................................805 498-0939
Oscar Maldonado, *President*
EMP: 11
SQ FT: 6,275
SALES (est): 2.1MM **Privately Held**
WEB: www.componeticsinc.com
SIC: 3677 Coil windings, electronic

(P-18709)
CORONA MAGNETICS INC
Also Called: C M I
201 Corporate Terrace St, Corona
(92879-6000)
P.O. Box 1355 (92878-1355)
PHONE..................................951 735-7558
Jay Paasch, *CEO*
Heike Paasch, *COO*
Cory Villa, *COO*
Ubaldo Jimenez, *Engineer*
Susan Paasch, *Financial Exec*
EMP: 120 **EST:** 1968

SQ FT: 17,000
SALES (est): 21.6MM **Privately Held**
WEB: www.corona-magnetics.com
SIC: 3677 3679 Transformers power sup-
ply, electronic type; electronic circuits

(P-18710)
CUSTOM COILS INC
4000 Industrial Way, Benicia (94510-1242)
PHONE..................................707 752-8633
Tom Quinn, *President*
John Quinn, *CEO*
Brian Quinn, *Vice Pres*
EMP: 15
SQ FT: 7,200
SALES (est): 3.4MM **Privately Held**
WEB: www.ccoils.com
SIC: 3677 Electronic coils, transformers &
other inductors

(P-18711)
CYPRESS MAGNETICS INC
8753 Industrial Ln, Rancho Cucamonga
(91730-4527)
PHONE..................................909 987-3570
Suresh Mahajan, *President*
EMP: 10
SALES (est): 438K **Privately Held**
SIC: 3677 Electronic coils, transformers &
other inductors

(P-18712)
DSPM INC
Also Called: Digital Signal Power Mfg
1921 S Quaker Ridge Pl, Ontario
(91761-8041)
PHONE..................................714 970-2304
Milton Hanson, *President*
Kenneth Carter, *Technician*
Carey Neill, *Controller*
▲ **EMP:** 20
SQ FT: 30,000
SALES (est): 6MM **Privately Held**
WEB: www.dspm.com
SIC: 3677 Transformers power supply,
electronic type

(P-18713)
DUCOMMUN INCORPORATED
Dbp Microwave Div
1321 Mountain View Cir, Azusa
(91702-1649)
P.O. Box 1062, Rancho Santa Fe (92067-
1062)
PHONE..................................626 812-9666
EMP: 35
SALES (corp-wide): 550.6MM **Publicly
Held**
SIC: 3677 3674 3625 3613
PA: Ducommun Incorporated
200 Sandpointe Ave # 700
Santa Ana CA 92707
657 335-3665

(P-18714)
**FILTER CONCEPTS
INCORPORATED**
22895 Eastpark Dr, Yorba Linda
(92887-4653)
PHONE..................................714 545-7003
Peter Murphy, *President*
Lester Edelberg, *President*
EMP: 38
SQ FT: 15,000
SALES (est): 5.1MM **Privately Held**
WEB: www.audiopower.com
SIC: 3677 Filtration devices, electronic
PA: Astrodyne Corporation
36 Newburgh Rd
Hackettstown NJ 07840

(P-18715)
**FILTRATION DEVELOPMENT CO
LLC**
Also Called: Fdc Aerofilter
3920 Sandstone Dr, El Dorado Hills
(95762-9652)
PHONE..................................415 884-0555
Andrew Rowen, *Bd of Directors*
Sharon Stark, *Sales Staff*
EMP: 19 **EST:** 1998
SQ FT: 3,000
SALES (est): 10MM **Privately Held**
WEB: www.fdcaerofilter.com
SIC: 3677 Filtration devices, electronic

(P-18716)
FRONTIER ELECTRONICS CORP
667 Cochran St, Simi Valley (93065-1939)
PHONE..................................805 522-9998
Jeannie Gu, *President*
Winston Gu, *Vice Pres*
Jean Pope, *Controller*
▲ **EMP:** 18
SQ FT: 15,246
SALES (est): 5MM **Privately Held**
WEB: www.frontierusa.com
SIC: 3677 3674 Inductors, electronic;
transformers power supply, electronic
type; semiconductors & related devices

(P-18717)
**FROST MAGNETICS
INCORPORATED**
49643 Hartwell Rd, Oakhurst (93644-8522)
PHONE..................................559 642-2536
Michael E Frost, *President*
Anita Frost, *Vice Pres*
▲ **EMP:** 30 **EST:** 1964
SQ FT: 16,200
SALES (est): 6.4MM **Privately Held**
WEB: www.frostmagnetics.com
SIC: 3677 Electronic transformers

(P-18718)
FSP GROUP USA CORP
14284 Albers Way, Chino (91710-6940)
PHONE..................................909 606-0960
Joseph Huang, *President*
John Chen, *Accounts Exec*
▲ **EMP:** 10
SALES (est): 1.9MM **Privately Held**
SIC: 3677 Transformers power supply,
electronic type
PA: Fsp Technology Inc.
22, Jianguo E. Rd.,
Taoyuan City TAY 33068

(P-18719)
H B R INDUSTRIES INC
2261 Fortune Dr Ste B, San Jose
(95131-1861)
PHONE..................................408 988-0800
Henk Ryssemus, *Owner*
Teresa Ryssemus, *Admin Sec*
▲ **EMP:** 10 **EST:** 1979
SQ FT: 5,000
SALES (est): 1.7MM **Privately Held**
SIC: 3677 3679 3555 5065 Electronic
transformers; cores, magnetic; printing
trades machinery; electronic parts &
equipment

(P-18720)
INDUCTOR SUPPLY INC
Also Called: ISI
11542 Knott St Ste 3, Garden Grove
(92841-1826)
PHONE..................................714 894-9050
Diana Klimek, *President*
▲ **EMP:** 10 **EST:** 1979
SQ FT: 5,000
SALES (est): 1.7MM **Privately Held**
WEB: www.inductorsupply.com
SIC: 3677 Electronic coils, transformers &
other inductors

(P-18721)
INTELLIPOWER INC
1746 N Saint Thomas Cir, Orange
(92865-4247)
PHONE..................................714 921-1580
G W Bill Shipman, *CEO*
Dana Helmes, *CFO*
Dan Johnson, *CFO*
Michael Bautista, *Vice Pres*
Edward Legault, *Business Mgr*
EMP: 100
SQ FT: 22,000
SALES (est): 21.3MM **Privately Held**
SIC: 3677 Transformers power supply,
electronic type

(P-18722)
**JAMES L HALL CO
INCORPORATED**
Also Called: Jetronics Company
218 Roberts Ave, Santa Rosa
(95401-6146)
P.O. Box U (95402-0280)
PHONE..................................707 544-2436
Stephen Vallarino, *Mng Member*
EMP: 55
SALES (est): 9.7MM
SALES (corp-wide): 8.2MM **Privately
Held**
SIC: 3677 3679 Electronic coils, trans-
formers & other inductors; electronic cir-
cuits
PA: James L. Hall Co., Incorporated
360 Tesconi Cir Ste B
Santa Rosa CA 95401
707 547-0775

(P-18723)
MAGNETIC COILS INC
150 San Hedrin Cir, Willits (95490-8753)
PHONE..................................707 459-5994
Don Setzco, *Manager*
EMP: 35
SALES (corp-wide): 5.2MM **Privately
Held**
WEB: www.mcitransformer.com
SIC: 3677 Electronic coils, transformers &
other inductors
PA: Magnetic Coils Inc.
411 Manhattan Ave
West Babylon NY
631 587-0510

(P-18724)
**MAGNOTEK MANUFACTURING
INC**
6510 Box Springs Blvd, Riverside
(92507-0740)
PHONE..................................951 653-8461
Donald K Furness, *CEO*
▲ **EMP:** 80
SQ FT: 500
SALES (est): 9.6MM **Privately Held**
SIC: 3677 Electronic transformers

(P-18725)
**MAGTECH & POWER
CONVERSION INC**
Also Called: Speciality Labs
1146 E Ash Ave, Fullerton (92831-5018)
PHONE..................................714 451-0106
Viet Pho, *President*
Linh Pho, *Vice Pres*
Hien Pham, *General Mgr*
Tien Tran, *Engineer*
EMP: 40
SQ FT: 9,000
SALES (est): 1MM **Privately Held**
WEB: www.magtechpower.com
SIC: 3677 Electronic transformers

(P-18726)
MERCURY MAGNETICS INC
Also Called: Gulf Enterprises
10050 Remmet Ave, Chatsworth
(91311-3854)
PHONE..................................818 998-7791
Sergio Hamernik, *President*
Susan Hamernik, *Vice Pres*
▲ **EMP:** 20
SQ FT: 21,000
SALES (est): 5.1MM **Privately Held**
WEB: www.mercurymagnetics.com
SIC: 3677 Electronic transformers

(P-18727)
MIL-SPEC MAGNETICS INC
169 Pacific St, Pomona (91768-3215)
PHONE..................................909 598-8116
Shelton Gunewardena, *CEO*
Tony Gunewardena, *President*
Andrew Gunewardena, *Principal*
Nathan Schanfein, *Project Engr*
EMP: 30
SQ FT: 6,000
SALES: 2.8MM **Privately Held**
SIC: 3677 3675 Electronic transformers;
inductors, electronic; electronic capacitors

(P-18728)
NATIONAL CERTIFIED FABRICATORS
Also Called: Griswold Water Systems
1525 E 6th St, Corona (92879-1716)
PHONE..................................951 278-8992
David E Griswold, *President*
Markus Reichert, *Manager*
EMP: 10
SQ FT: 21,000
SALES (est): 1.8MM **Privately Held**
WEB: www.griswoldfiltration.com
SIC: 3677 3585 Filtration devices, electronic; parts for heating, cooling & refrigerating equipment

(P-18729)
PARKER-HANNIFIN CORPORATION
Also Called: Water Purification
19610 S Rancho Way, Rancho Dominguez (90220-6039)
PHONE..................................310 608-5600
Jaime Garcia, *Principal*
EMP: 150
SALES (corp-wide): 14.3B **Publicly Held**
SIC: 3677 Filtration devices, electronic
PA: Parker-Hannifin Corporation
6035 Parkland Blvd
Cleveland OH 44124
216 896-3000

(P-18730)
PAYNE MAGNETICS INC
854 W Front St, Covina (91722-3614)
PHONE..................................626 332-6207
George Payne, *Chairman*
Jon S Payne, *President*
▲ **EMP:** 100
SQ FT: 6,600
SALES (est): 15.1MM **Privately Held**
WEB: www.payne-magnetics.com
SIC: 3677 3699 Electronic transformers; inductors, electronic; electrical equipment & supplies

(P-18731)
PCA ELECTRONICS INC
16799 Schoenborn St, North Hills (91343-6194)
PHONE..................................818 892-0761
Morris Weinberg, *President*
Benjamin Weinberg, *Vice Pres*
Ira Goldstein, *Technology*
Bruce Luisi, *Sales Mgr*
Toni Essman, *Manager*
EMP: 44
SQ FT: 30,000
SALES (est): 7.7MM **Privately Held**
WEB: www.pcainc.com
SIC: 3677 Electronic transformers

(P-18732)
PEARSON ELECTRONICS INC
4009 Transport St, Palo Alto (94303-4914)
PHONE..................................650 494-6444
Paul A Pearson, *President*
Patricia Pearson, *Vice Pres*
Cathy Breton, *Sales Staff*
Sherry Morfin, *Manager*
EMP: 18
SQ FT: 14,400
SALES: 3MM **Privately Held**
WEB: www.pearsonelectronics.com
SIC: 3677 Electronic transformers

(P-18733)
POWER DISTRIBUTION INC
4011 W Carriage Dr, Santa Ana (92704-6301)
PHONE..................................714 513-1500
David Hensley, *President*
Keith Waterman, *Sales Mgr*
Helen Chun, *Manager*
EMP: 10 **Privately Held**
SIC: 3677 3612 3613 Electronic coils, transformers & other inductors; transformers, except electric; switchgear & switchboard apparatus
HQ: Power Distribution, Inc.
4200 Oakleys Ln
Richmond VA 23223
804 737-9880

(P-18734)
PREMIER MAGNETICS INC
20381 Barents Sea Cir, Lake Forest (92630-8807)
PHONE..................................949 452-0511
James Earley, *President*
▲ **EMP:** 30
SALES (est): 5.8MM **Privately Held**
WEB: www.premiermag.com
SIC: 3677 3612 Electronic coils, transformers & other inductors; specialty transformers

(P-18735)
PUROFLUX CORPORATION
2121 Union Pl, Simi Valley (93065-1661)
PHONE..................................805 579-0216
Henry Nmi Greenberg, *President*
Santos Lopez, *Purchasing*
▼ **EMP:** 17
SQ FT: 25,000
SALES (est): 3.7MM **Privately Held**
SIC: 3677 3613 Filtration devices, electronic; control panels, electric

(P-18736)
R & M COILS
27547 Terrytown Rd, Sun City (92586-3217)
PHONE..................................951 672-9855
Rudolph Hesse, *Owner*
EMP: 12
SALES: 260K **Privately Held**
SIC: 3677 Electronic coils, transformers & other inductors

(P-18737)
R H BARDEN INC
Also Called: Lodestone Pacific
4769 E Wesley Dr, Anaheim (92807-1941)
PHONE..................................714 970-0900
Richard H Barden III, *President*
Susan Barden, *Mktg Coord*
▲ **EMP:** 15
SQ FT: 12,000
SALES (est): 2.8MM **Privately Held**
WEB: www.lodestonepacific.com
SIC: 3677 Electronic coils, transformers & other inductors

(P-18738)
RAYCO ELECTRONIC MFG INC
1220 W 130th St, Gardena (90247-1502)
PHONE..................................310 329-2660
Mahendra P Patel, *CEO*
Steve Mardani, *Vice Pres*
Mayan Patel, *Vice Pres*
EMP: 50 **EST:** 1941
SQ FT: 20,000
SALES (est): 11.9MM **Privately Held**
WEB: www.raycoelectronics.com
SIC: 3677 3612 3621 Electronic transformers; filtration devices, electronic; transformers, except electric; motors & generators

(P-18739)
ROBERT M HADLEY COMPANY INC
4054 Transport St, Ventura (93003-8323)
PHONE..................................805 658-7286
James A Hadley, *CEO*
Jim Hadley, *President*
Christopher Waian, *Vice Pres*
Chris Waian, *General Mgr*
Mary Hadley Waian, *Admin Sec*
EMP: 90
SQ FT: 28,000
SALES: 4.7MM **Privately Held**
WEB: www.rmhco.com
SIC: 3677 Transformers power supply, electronic type

(P-18740)
RODON PRODUCTS INC
15481 Electronic Ln Ste A, Huntington Beach (92649-1355)
PHONE..................................714 898-3528
Robert W Bertels Jr, *President*
Sandra Bertels, *Vice Pres*
Steve Freeman, *Vice Pres*
EMP: 25

SALES (est): 3.4MM **Privately Held**
WEB: www.rodonproducts.com
SIC: 3677 3679 Electronic coils, transformers & other inductors; electronic circuits

(P-18741)
SCOTTS VALLEY MAGNETICS INC
300 El Pueblo Rd Ste 107, Scotts Valley (95066-4238)
P.O. Box 66575 (95067-6575)
PHONE..................................831 438-3600
Norma Humphries, *President*
Karina Humphries, *Treasurer*
Jerry Humphries, *Vice Pres*
John F Humphries, *Admin Sec*
Donna Humphries, *Purch Agent*
▲ **EMP:** 24
SQ FT: 15,000
SALES (est): 4.5MM **Privately Held**
WEB: www.svmagnetics.com
SIC: 3677 3679 3829 Filtration devices, electronic; electronic transformers; inductors, electronic; transformers power supply, electronic type; power supplies, all types: static; measuring & controlling devices

(P-18742)
SI MANUFACTURING INC
1440 S Allec St, Anaheim (92805-6305)
PHONE..................................714 956-7110
James R Reed, *President*
Ata Shafizadeh, *Vice Pres*
▲ **EMP:** 50
SALES (est): 9.5MM **Privately Held**
WEB: www.simfg.com
SIC: 3677 3612 3679 3613 Electronic coils, transformers & other inductors; transformers, except electric; electronic loads & power supplies; switchgear & switchboard apparatus; engineering services

(P-18743)
SMART WIRES INC (PA)
Also Called: S W G
3292 Whipple Rd, Union City (94587-1217)
PHONE..................................415 800-5555
Gregg Rotenberg, *President*
Deniz Gundogdu, *Mfg Staff*
EMP: 86
SALES (est): 5.9MM **Privately Held**
SIC: 3677 Electronic coils, transformers & other inductors

(P-18744)
SONOMA PHOTONICS INC
1750 Northpoint Pkwy C, Santa Rosa (95407-7597)
PHONE..................................707 568-1202
Mark A Caylor, *President*
Wesley G Bush, *President*
Karen Wallen, *General Mgr*
Craig Witt, *Design Engr*
Annie Lee, *Controller*
EMP: 50 **EST:** 2000
SQ FT: 30,000
SALES (est): 8.8MM **Publicly Held**
WEB: www.sonomaphotonics.com
SIC: 3677 3827 Filtration devices, electronic; optical instruments & lenses
HQ: Northrop Grumman Systems Corporation
2980 Fairview Park Dr
Falls Church VA 22042
703 280-2900

(P-18745)
STANGENES INDUSTRIES INC (PA)
1052 E Meadow Cir, Palo Alto (94303-4271)
PHONE..................................650 855-9926
Magne Stangenes, *CEO*
Kari Stangenes, *CFO*
Lill Runge, *Vice Pres*
Christopher Rivers, *Technician*
Chris Yeckel, *Electrical Engi*
▲ **EMP:** 113 **EST:** 1974
SQ FT: 15,500
SALES (est): 19.3MM **Privately Held**
WEB: www.stangenes.com
SIC: 3677 Electronic transformers

(P-18746)
SYNDER INC (PA)
Also Called: Synder Filtration
4941 Allison Pkwy, Vacaville (95688-8795)
PHONE..................................707 451-6060
Edward Yeh, *CEO*
Joseph Y Wang, *President*
Y C Jao PHD, *Vice Pres*
▲ **EMP:** 33
SQ FT: 26,000
SALES (est): 8.1MM **Privately Held**
WEB: www.synderfiltration.com
SIC: 3677 8748 8742 Filtration devices, electronic; systems analysis or design; industry specialist consultants

(P-18747)
TUR-BO JET PRODUCTS CO INC
5025 Earle Ave, Rosemead (91770-1197)
PHONE..................................626 285-1294
Richard Bloom, *President*
Richard L Bloom, *Vice Pres*
Viviana Gomez, *Project Mgr*
Michael Bloom, *Engineer*
Tom Hagan, *Chief Engr*
▲ **EMP:** 95 **EST:** 1945
SQ FT: 27,000
SALES (est): 20.9MM **Privately Held**
WEB: www.turbojetproducts.com
SIC: 3677 Coil windings, electronic

(P-18748)
WJLP COMPANY INC
Also Called: West Coast Magnetics
4848 Frontier Way Ste 100, Stockton (95215-9649)
P.O. Box 31330 (95213-1330)
PHONE..................................800 628-1123
Weyman Lundquist, *President*
Luz Jimenez, *Admin Sec*
Vivien Yang, *Engineer*
Toni Jimenez, *Purch Mgr*
Lisa Reyes, *Prdtn Mgr*
▲ **EMP:** 100
SQ FT: 8,000
SALES: 5MM **Privately Held**
WEB: www.wcmagnetics.com
SIC: 3677 3357 Electronic transformers; inductors, electronic; coaxial cable, nonferrous

---

3678 Electronic Connectors

(P-18749)
ADVANCED GLOBAL TECH GROUP
8015 E Treeview Ct, Anaheim (92808-1553)
PHONE..................................714 281-8020
▲ **EMP:** 21
SALES: 2.5MM **Privately Held**
SIC: 3678 3652 4813 0191

(P-18750)
ALPHA PRODUCTS INC
351 Irving Dr, Oxnard (93030-5173)
PHONE..................................805 981-8666
Tony Gulrajani, *President*
Elaine Schaeffer, *General Mgr*
▲ **EMP:** 27
SQ FT: 12,000
SALES (est): 4.9MM **Privately Held**
SIC: 3678 5065 Electronic connectors; electronic parts & equipment

(P-18751)
AMPHENOL CORPORATION
Amphenol Rf
5069 Maureen Ln Ste B, Moorpark (93021-7149)
PHONE..................................805 378-6464
Mike Comer, *Manager*
EMP: 11
SALES (corp-wide): 8.2B **Publicly Held**
SIC: 3678 Electronic connectors
PA: Amphenol Corporation
358 Hall Ave
Wallingford CT 06492
203 265-8900

(P-18752)
BRANTNER AND ASSOCIATES INC (DH)
Also Called: Te Connectivity MOG
1700 Gillespie Way, El Cajon (92020-1874)
PHONE......................................619 562-7070
Patrick G Simar, *President*
Denton Seilhan, *Exec VP*
▲ EMP: 142
SQ FT: 35,000
SALES (est): 35.2MM
SALES (corp-wide): 13.9B **Privately Held**
SIC: 3678 3643 Electronic connectors;
　current-carrying wiring devices
HQ: Brantner Holding Llc
　501 Oakside Ave
　Redwood City CA 94063
　650 361-5292

(P-18753)
CHINA LOCO SZHOU PRECISE INDUS
4125 Business Center Dr, Fremont
(94538-6355)
PHONE......................................510 429-3700
Alex Wang, *Branch Mgr*
May Benass, *CFO*
EMP: 20
SALES (corp-wide): 24MM **Privately Held**
WEB: www.leoco.net
SIC: 3678 Electronic connectors
PA: Leoco (Suzhou) Precise Industrial Co.,
　Ltd.
　No.300, Liuxu Rd., Economic And
　Technological Development Zone,
　Wujiang 21520
　512 634-5546

(P-18754)
CIRCUIT ASSEMBLY CORP (PA)
3 Vanderbilt Ste A, Irvine (92618-2777)
PHONE......................................949 855-7887
Andrew Lang, *President*
Terri Lang, *Vice Pres*
Vicky Vasquez, *QC Mgr*
Paulette Cox, *Sales Associate*
Charles Luevano, *Sales Staff*
▲ EMP: 30 EST: 1969
SQ FT: 62,000
SALES (est): 4.1MM **Privately Held**
WEB: www.circuitassembly.com
SIC: 3678 Electronic connectors

(P-18755)
COMPONENT EQUIPMENT COINC
Also Called: Ceco
3050 Camino Del Sol, Oxnard
(93030-7275)
PHONE......................................805 988-8004
Bill Rigby, *President*
Thomas Conway, *Vice Pres*
Sheila Richmond, *Human Res Dir*
EMP: 75
SQ FT: 32,000
SALES (est): 10.4MM **Privately Held**
WEB: www.ceco-inc.com
SIC: 3678 Electronic connectors

(P-18756)
CONESYS INC (PA)
2280 W 208th St, Torrance (90501-1452)
PHONE......................................310 618-3737
Walter Neubauer Jr, *CEO*
John Vinke, *CFO*
Andrew Dawson, *Vice Pres*
Andres Murillo, *General Mgr*
Darren Magana, *Graphic Designe*
EMP: 78
SQ FT: 95,000
SALES (est): 27.9MM **Privately Held**
WEB: www.conesys.com
SIC: 3678 Electronic connectors

(P-18757)
CONESYS INC
548 Amapola Ave, Torrance (90501-1472)
PHONE......................................310 212-0065
Teresa Lynn De Foreest, *Administration*
Karim Louanchi, *General Mgr*
Mark Edwards, *CIO*
Laurent Gonin, *Technology*
Odin Becerra, *Engineer*
EMP: 12

SALES (est): 1.9MM
SALES (corp-wide): 27.9MM **Privately Held**
SIC: 3678 Electronic connectors
PA: Conesys, Inc.
　2280 W 208th St
　Torrance CA 90501
　310 618-3737

(P-18758)
CONNECTOR KINGS CORPORATION
Also Called: Connectorkings.com
2110 Mcallister St, Riverside (92503-6704)
P.O. Box 1507, Kodak TN (37764-7507)
PHONE......................................951 710-1180
William B Furlong, *President*
Ralph Davis, *Manager*
EMP: 12
SALES (est): 2MM **Privately Held**
SIC: 3678 Electronic connectors

(P-18759)
COOPER CROUSE-HINDS LLC
Also Called: General Connector
750 W Ventura Blvd, Camarillo
(93010-8382)
PHONE......................................805 484-0543
Alexander M Cutler, *CEO*
Robert Sierra, *Principal*
EMP: 135 **Privately Held**
SIC: 3678 3663 3451 Electronic connec-
　tors; radio & TV communications equip-
　ment; screw machine products
HQ: Cooper Crouse-Hinds, Llc
　1201 Wolf St
　Syracuse NY 13208
　315 477-7000

(P-18760)
COOPER INTERCONNECT INC
750 W Ventura Blvd, Camarillo
(93010-8382)
PHONE......................................805 553-9632
EMP: 100 **Privately Held**
SIC: 3678 3643 Electronic connectors;
　current-carrying wiring devices
HQ: Cooper Interconnect, Inc.
　750 W Ventura Blvd
　Camarillo CA 93010
　805 484-0543

(P-18761)
CORSAIR ELEC CONNECTORS INC
17100 Murphy Ave, Irvine (92614-5916)
PHONE......................................949 833-0273
Amir Saket, *President*
Margot Rodelli, *Administration*
Brian Pace, *Engrg Dir*
Steve Simmons, *Controller*
Francisco Mendez, *Director*
EMP: 140
SQ FT: 34,554
SALES (est): 20.6MM **Privately Held**
SIC: 3678 Electronic connectors

(P-18762)
CRISTEK INTERCONNECTS INC (PA)
5395 E Hunter Ave, Anaheim (92807-2054)
PHONE......................................714 696-5200
Cristi Cristich, *President*
Julie Barker, *CFO*
John B Pollock, *Vice Pres*
Rebecca Lopez, *Sales Staff*
EMP: 135
SALES (est): 26.7MM **Privately Held**
WEB: www.cristek.com
SIC: 3678 Electronic connectors

(P-18763)
CS MANFACTURING INDUS SVCS INC (PA)
619 Paulin Ave Ste 105, Calexico
(92231-2671)
P.O. Box 2914 (92232-2914)
PHONE......................................760 890-7746
Cesar Samaniego Silva, *President*
EMP: 15
SQ FT: 1,000
SALES (est): 1.5MM **Privately Held**
SIC: 3678 Electronic connectors

(P-18764)
DETORONICS CORP
13071 Rosecrans Ave, Santa Fe Springs
(90670-4930)
PHONE......................................626 579-7130
Kenneth S Clark, *CEO*
Marcia Baroda, *CFO*
Jamie Saltos, *General Mgr*
Nancy Chavez, *Sales Mgr*
EMP: 37
SQ FT: 20,000
SALES (est): 7.5MM **Privately Held**
WEB: www.detoronics.com
SIC: 3678 Electronic connectors

(P-18765)
DS CYPRESS MAGNETICS INC
8753 Industrial Ln, Rancho Cucamonga
(91730-4527)
PHONE......................................909 987-3570
Suresh S Mahajan, *President*
Dan Reimders, *Vice Pres*
▲ EMP: 10 EST: 2005
SALES (est): 1.5MM **Privately Held**
SIC: 3678 8742 Electronic connectors;
　management consulting services

(P-18766)
DUEL SYSTEMS INC
2025 Galeway Pl Ste 235, San Jose
(95110)
PHONE......................................408 453-9500
Don Duda, *President*
▲ EMP: 25
SQ FT: 34,000
SALES (est): 3.4MM
SALES (corp-wide): 1B **Publicly Held**
WEB: www.methode.com
SIC: 3678 Electronic connectors
PA: Methode Electronics, Inc
　8750 W Bryn Mawr Ave # 1000
　Chicago IL 60631
　708 867-6777

(P-18767)
EVENSPHERE INCORPORATION
1249 S Diamond Bar Blvd, Diamond Bar
(91765-4122)
PHONE......................................909 247-3030
Jeng H Yuh, *President*
Joanne Lu, *Office Mgr*
EMP: 50
SALES (est): 3.8MM **Privately Held**
SIC: 3678 3229 3357 Electronic connec-
　tors; fiber optics strands; fiber optic cable
　(insulated)

(P-18768)
FEI EFA INC (DH)
Also Called: Dcg Systems
3400 W Warren Ave, Fremont
(94538-6425)
PHONE......................................510 897-6800
Israel Niv, *CEO*
Ronen Benzion, *President*
Bob Conners, *CFO*
Tameyasu Anayama, *Vice Pres*
Vincent Hong, *Info Tech Mgr*
EMP: 95
SQ FT: 45,000
SALES (est): 68.7MM
SALES (corp-wide): 24.3B **Publicly Held**
SIC: 3678 Electronic connectors
HQ: Fei Company
　5350 Ne Dawson Creek Dr
　Hillsboro OR 97124
　503 726-7500

(P-18769)
FLEXIBLE MANUFACTURING LLC
Also Called: F M I
1719 S Grand Ave, Santa Ana
(92705-4808)
PHONE......................................714 259-7996
Frank Meza, *President*
Tom Rendina, *CFO*
Ross Silberfarb, *Vice Pres*
Bart Pacetti, *Program Mgr*
Carlos Cortes,
▲ EMP: 100
SQ FT: 15,000
SALES (est): 20.8MM **Privately Held**
WEB: www.flexiblemanufacturing.com
SIC: 3678 Electronic connectors

(P-18770)
GLEN-MAC SWISS CO
12848 Weber Way, Hawthorne
(90250-5537)
PHONE......................................310 978-4555
Torkom Postajian, *President*
Armen Postajian, *Corp Secy*
▲ EMP: 15
SQ FT: 12,676
SALES: 1.2MM **Privately Held**
SIC: 3678 3429 3451 3599 Electronic
　connectors; manufactured hardware (gen-
　eral); screw machine products; machine
　shop, jobbing & repair

(P-18771)
HCC INDUSTRIES INC (HQ)
4232 Temple City Blvd, Rosemead
(91770-1552)
PHONE......................................626 443-8933
Richard Ferraid, *President*
EMP: 15
SQ FT: 36,000
SALES: 148.6MM
SALES (corp-wide): 4.8B **Publicly Held**
WEB: www.hccmachining.com
SIC: 3678 Electronic connectors
PA: Ametek, Inc.
　1100 Cassatt Rd
　Berwyn PA 19312
　610 647-2121

(P-18772)
HIGH CONNECTION DENSITY INC
820 Kifer Rd Ste A, Sunnyvale
(94086-5200)
PHONE......................................408 743-9700
Tsuyoshi Taira, *President*
Charlie Stevenson, *COO*
EMP: 25
SALES (est): 2.7MM **Privately Held**
WEB: www.hcdcorp.com
SIC: 3678 8734 Electronic connectors;
　testing laboratories

(P-18773)
I O INTERCONNECT LTD (PA)
Also Called: I/O Interconnect
1202 E Wakeham Ave, Santa Ana
(92705-4145)
PHONE......................................714 564-1111
Gary Kung, *CEO*
Roland Balusek, *Vice Pres*
▲ EMP: 50
SQ FT: 38,000
SALES (est): 222MM **Privately Held**
WEB: www.iointerconnect.com
SIC: 3678 3679 Electronic connectors;
　harness assemblies for electronic use:
　wire or cable

(P-18774)
ICONN INC
Also Called: Iconn Technologies
8909 Irvine Center Dr, Irvine (92618-4249)
PHONE......................................949 297-8448
Rob Tondreault, *President*
Turker Hidirlar, *COO*
▲ EMP: 39
SQ FT: 9,920
SALES (est): 6.1MM **Privately Held**
SIC: 3678 3643 5063 3613 Electronic
　connectors; connectors & terminals for
　electrical devices; connectors, electric
　cord; lugs & connectors, electrical; power
　connectors, electric; booster (jump-start)
　cables, automotive

(P-18775)
INFINITE ELECTRONICS INTL INC (DH)
17792 Fitch, Irvine (92614-6020)
PHONE......................................949 261-1920
Penny Cotner, *CEO*
Jim Dauw, *COO*
Scott Rosner, *CFO*
David Quinn, *Exec VP*
Eugene Halona, *Administration*
▲ EMP: 240
SQ FT: 40,000

▲ = Import ▼=Export
◆ =Import/Export

SALES (est): 300MM **Privately Held**
WEB: www.pasternack.com
SIC: **3678** 3357 3651 3643 Electronic connectors; coaxial cable, nonferrous; household audio & video equipment; current-carrying wiring devices
HQ: Infinite Electronics, Inc.
17792 Fitch
Irvine CA 92614
949 261-1920

(P-18776)
J-T E C H
548 Amapola Ave, Torrance (90501-1472)
PHONE..................................310 533-6700
Walter Naubauer Jr, *Principal*
EMP: 136
SALES (est): 5.9MM **Privately Held**
SIC: **3678** Electronic connectors

(P-18777)
JOSLYN SUNBANK COMPANY LLC
1740 Commerce Way, Paso Robles (93446-3620)
PHONE..................................805 238-2840
Angel Cruz, *Principal*
Nayan Patel, *Program Mgr*
Preston Cole, *Maintence Staff*
Eric Lardiere,
Marlo Oliver,
EMP: 500
SQ FT: 80,000
SALES (est): 113.5MM
SALES (corp-wide): 3.8B **Publicly Held**
WEB: www.sunbankcorp.com
SIC: **3678** 3643 5065 Electronic connectors; connectors & terminals for electrical devices; connectors, electronic
HQ: Esterline Technologies Corp
500 108th Ave Ne Ste 1500
Bellevue WA 98004
425 453-9400

(P-18778)
L & M MACHINING CORPORATION
550 S Melrose St, Placentia (92870-6327)
PHONE..................................714 414-0923
Mike MAI, *President*
EMP: 55
SQ FT: 31,000
SALES: 3MM **Privately Held**
WEB: www.lmcnc.com
SIC: **3678** Electronic connectors

(P-18779)
MIN-E-CON LLC
17312 Eastman, Irvine (92614-5522)
PHONE..................................949 250-0087
Wendell Jacob, *Mng Member*
John M Brown,
Wendell P Jacob,
William Charette, *Manager*
▼ EMP: 60 EST: 1974
SALES (est): 9.5MM **Privately Held**
WEB: www.min-e-con.com
SIC: **3678** Electronic connectors

(P-18780)
MOLEX LLC
Also Called: Custom Goods Warehouse
12200 Arrow Rte, Rancho Cucamonga (91739-9610)
PHONE..................................909 803-1362
John Franco, *Branch Mgr*
EMP: 26
SALES (corp-wide): 40.6B **Privately Held**
SIC: **3678** 3643 3357 3679 Electronic connectors; connectors & terminals for electrical devices; communication wire; electronic circuits
HQ: Molex, Llc
2222 Wellington Ct
Lisle IL 60532
630 969-4550

(P-18781)
NEA ELECTRONICS INC
14370 White Sage Rd, Moorpark (93021-8720)
PHONE..................................805 292-4010
Steven Perkins, *President*
EMP: 24
SQ FT: 20,000
SALES (est): 5.8MM **Privately Held**
WEB: www.neaelectronics.com
SIC: **3678** 3629 3592 Electronic connectors; battery chargers, rectifying or nonrotating; valves

(P-18782)
NOVA MOBILE SYSTEMS INC
2888 Loker Ave E Ste 311, Carlsbad (92010-6686)
PHONE..................................800 734-9885
George Ecker, *President*
EMP: 10
SALES (est): 1.4MM **Privately Held**
SIC: **3678** Electronic connectors

(P-18783)
ONANON INC
720 S Milpitas Blvd, Milpitas (95035-5449)
PHONE..................................408 262-8990
Dennis Joel Johnson, *CEO*
Thomas R Sahakian, *CFO*
Suzanne Figueroa, *Office Mgr*
Brian Fang, *Engineer*
Katie Hoose, *Engineer*
EMP: 49
SQ FT: 25,000
SALES (est): 10.4MM **Privately Held**
WEB: www.onanon.com
SIC: **3678** 3089 Electronic connectors; laminating of plastic

(P-18784)
P W WIRING SYSTEMS LLC
Also Called: Pw Wiring Systems
9415 Kruse Rd, Pico Rivera (90660-1430)
PHONE..................................562 463-9055
Steven Koundouriotis,
EMP: 36
SALES (est): 5.2MM **Privately Held**
WEB: www.pwwiringsystems.com
SIC: **3678** Electronic connectors

(P-18785)
R KERN ENGINEERING & MFG CORP
13912 Mountain Ave, Chino (91710-9018)
PHONE..................................909 664-2440
Richard Kern, *CEO*
Roland A Kern, *Ch of Bd*
Helga Kern, *Treasurer*
Jose Nunez, *Vice Pres*
Jay Nunez, *IT/INT Sup*
▲ EMP: 54 EST: 1966
SQ FT: 34,000
SALES (est): 15.3MM **Privately Held**
WEB: www.kerneng.com
SIC: **3678** 3599 Electronic connectors; machine shop, jobbing & repair

(P-18786)
RAYCON TECHNOLOGY INC (PA)
5252 Mcfadden Ave, Huntington Beach (92649-1237)
PHONE..................................714 799-4100
Raymond Smith, *President*
▲ EMP: 10
SQ FT: 20,000
SALES (est): 1.5MM **Privately Held**
WEB: www.raycontech.com
SIC: **3678** Electronic connectors

(P-18787)
RF INDUSTRIES LTD (PA)
7610 Miramar Rd Ste 6000, San Diego (92126-4238)
PHONE..................................858 549-6340
Robert D Dawson, *President*
Mark Turfler, *CFO*
Howard Hill, *Bd of Directors*
Jesse Fuller, *Sales Staff*
Mona Sabaot, *Manager*
EMP: 86
SQ FT: 21,908
SALES: 50.2MM **Publicly Held**
WEB: www.rfindustries.com
SIC: **3678** 3643 3663 Electronic connectors; electric connectors; connectors & terminals for electrical devices; transmitter-receivers, radio

(P-18788)
TE CONNECTIVITY
5733 W Whittier Ave, Hemet (92545-9030)
PHONE..................................951 765-2200

EMP: 16 EST: 2013
SALES (est): 4.8MM **Privately Held**
SIC: **3678** Electronic connectors

(P-18789)
TE CONNECTIVITY CORPORATION
6900 Paseo Padre Pkwy, Fremont (94555-3641)
PHONE..................................650 361-3333
Christine Brown, *Branch Mgr*
Rosalyn Thomas, *Manager*
EMP: 31
SALES (corp-wide): 13.9B **Privately Held**
WEB: www.raychem.com
SIC: **3678** Electronic connectors
HQ: Te Connectivity Corporation
1050 Westlakes Dr
Berwyn PA 19312
610 893-9800

(P-18790)
TE CONNECTIVITY CORPORATION
300 Constitution Dr, Menlo Park (94025-1140)
PHONE..................................650 361-3333
Jeff Harrison, *Branch Mgr*
EMP: 350
SALES (corp-wide): 13.9B **Privately Held**
WEB: www.raychem.com
SIC: **3678** Electronic connectors
HQ: Te Connectivity Corporation
1050 Westlakes Dr
Berwyn PA 19312
610 893-9800

(P-18791)
TE CONNECTIVITY CORPORATION
Also Called: Deutsch Industrial Products
700 S Hathaway St, Banning (92220-5904)
PHONE..................................951 929-3323
Teri Elrod, *Manager*
EMP: 476
SALES (corp-wide): 13.9B **Privately Held**
WEB: www.deutschecd.com
SIC: **3678** 3643 Electronic connectors; current-carrying wiring devices
HQ: Te Connectivity Corporation
1050 Westlakes Dr
Berwyn PA 19312
610 893-9800

(P-18792)
TE CONNECTIVITY CORPORATION
5733 W Whittier Ave, Hemet (92545-9030)
PHONE..................................951 765-2250
EMP: 98
SALES (corp-wide): 13.9B **Privately Held**
WEB: www.deutschecd.com
SIC: **3678** Electronic connectors
HQ: Te Connectivity Corporation
1050 Westlakes Dr
Berwyn PA 19312
610 893-9800

(P-18793)
TE CONNECTIVITY CORPORATION
Defense Aerospace Operations
3390 Alex Rd, Oceanside (92058-1319)
PHONE..................................760 757-7500
Richard Niemi, *Branch Mgr*
EMP: 501
SALES (corp-wide): 13.9B **Privately Held**
WEB: www.deutschecd.com
SIC: **3678** Electronic connectors
HQ: Te Connectivity Corporation
1050 Westlakes Dr
Berwyn PA 19312
610 893-9800

(P-18794)
TE CONNECTIVITY CORPORATION
1455 Adams Dr, Menlo Park (94025-1438)
PHONE..................................650 361-3302
Dwayne Goodwin, *Manager*
EMP: 150
SALES (corp-wide): 13.9B **Privately Held**
WEB: www.raychem.com
SIC: **3678** Electronic connectors

HQ: Te Connectivity Corporation
1050 Westlakes Dr
Berwyn PA 19312
610 893-9800

(P-18795)
TE CONNECTIVITY CORPORATION
Also Called: Wireless Systems Segment
5300 Hellyer Ave, San Jose (95138-1003)
PHONE..................................408 624-3000
Robert Tavares, *Vice Pres*
EMP: 307
SALES (corp-wide): 13.9B **Privately Held**
WEB: www.raychem.com
SIC: **3678** Electronic connectors
HQ: Te Connectivity Corporation
1050 Westlakes Dr
Berwyn PA 19312
610 893-9800

(P-18796)
TE CONNECTIVITY CORPORATION
Also Called: Tyco Electronics
9543 Henrich Dr Ste 7, San Diego (92154)
PHONE..................................619 454-5176
Enrique Aristi, *Office Mgr*
EMP: 20
SALES (corp-wide): 13.9B **Privately Held**
SIC: **3678** 3643 Electronic connectors; current-carrying wiring devices; connectors & terminals for electrical devices
HQ: Te Connectivity Corporation
1050 Westlakes Dr
Berwyn PA 19312
610 893-9800

(P-18797)
TE CONNECTIVITY CORPORATION
6900 Paseo Padre Pkwy, Fremont (94555-3641)
PHONE..................................650 361-3615
Thomas J Lynch, *CEO*
EMP: 600
SALES (corp-wide): 13.9B **Privately Held**
SIC: **3678** Electronic connectors
HQ: Te Connectivity Corporation
1050 Westlakes Dr
Berwyn PA 19312
610 893-9800

(P-18798)
TE CONNECTIVITY CORPORATION
Defense Aerospace Operations
5733 W Whittier Ave, Hemet (92545-9030)
PHONE..................................951 765-2200
Richard Niemi, *Director*
EMP: 297
SALES (corp-wide): 13.9B **Privately Held**
WEB: www.deutschecd.com
SIC: **3678** 3643 3577 Electronic connectors; current-carrying wiring devices; computer peripheral equipment
HQ: Te Connectivity Corporation
1050 Westlakes Dr
Berwyn PA 19312
610 893-9800

(P-18799)
TEKTEST INC
Also Called: E-Z-Hook Test Products Div
225 N 2nd Ave, Arcadia (91006-3286)
P.O. Box 660729 (91066-0729)
PHONE..................................626 446-6175
Phelps M Wood, *President*
Beverly Wood, *Vice Pres*
EMP: 20 EST: 1970
SQ FT: 24,000
SALES: 2.7MM **Privately Held**
WEB: www.e-z-hook.com
SIC: **3678** Electronic connectors

(P-18800)
TIMCO/CAL RF INC
3910 Royal Ave Ste A, Simi Valley (93063-3270)
PHONE..................................805 582-1777
James V Clarizio Jr, *President*
EMP: 20
SQ FT: 13,000
SALES (est): 2.5MM **Privately Held**
SIC: **3678** Electronic connectors

(P-18801)
ULTI-MATE CONNECTOR INC
1872 N Case St, Orange (92865-4233)
PHONE...............................714 637-7099
Bruce I Billington, *CEO*
Thierry Pombart, *Vice Pres*
Truong Trinh, *Human Res Mgr*
Isabel Mendoza, *Purchasing*
Frank Malczyk, *Sales Staff*
▲ EMP: 45
SQ FT: 11,000
SALES: 8MM Privately Held
WEB: www.umi-c.com
SIC: 3678 Electronic connectors

(P-18802)
UNIT INDUSTRIES INC (PA)
3122 Maple St, Santa Ana (92707-4408)
PHONE...............................714 871-4161
Anthony Codet, *President*
J W Abouchar, *CEO*
Lizabeth Mulligan Codet, *Admin Sec*
EMP: 35
SQ FT: 16,000
SALES (est): 8.9MM Privately Held
WEB: www.unitindustries.com
SIC: 3678 Electronic connectors

3679 Electronic Components, NEC

(P-18803)
2 S 2 INC
Also Called: Display Integration Tech
1357 Rocky Point Dr, Oceanside
(92056-5864)
PHONE...............................760 599-9225
Benjamin G Chapman, *President*
Robert Hover, *Sales Mgr*
EMP: 10 Privately Held
SIC: 3679 Liquid crystal displays (LCD)
PA: 2 S 2, Inc.
    1702 A St Ste C
    Sparks NV 89431
    -

(P-18804)
3Y POWER TECHNOLOGY INC
80 Bunsen, Irvine (92618-4210)
PHONE...............................949 450-0152
Yuan Yu, *President*
▲ EMP: 17
SQ FT: 13,800
SALES (est): 3.1MM Privately Held
WEB: www.3ypower.com
SIC: 3679 Power supplies, all types: static;
electronic circuits

(P-18805)
A R ELECTRONICS INC
Also Called: Audiolink
31290 Plantation Dr, Thousand Palms
(92276-6604)
PHONE...............................760 343-1200
Larry N Rich, *President*
Larry Rich, *President*
Cheryl Rich, *Admin Sec*
EMP: 25
SQ FT: 10,000
SALES (est): 3.6MM Privately Held
SIC: 3679 5065 Electronic circuits; elec-
tronic parts & equipment

(P-18806)
ACCRATRONICS SEALS CORPORATION
Also Called: A T S
2211 Kenmere Ave, Burbank (91504-3493)
PHONE...............................818 843-1500
William Fisch, *CEO*
Corby Jones, *President*
Delbert Jones, *Vice Pres*
Troy Jones, *Vice Pres*
Deken Jones, *Admin Sec*
EMP: 72
SQ FT: 10,000
SALES (est): 6.6MM Privately Held
WEB: www.accratronics.com
SIC: 3679 Hermetic seals for electronic
equipment

(P-18807)
ACCU-GLASS PRODUCTS INC
25047 Anza Dr, Valencia (91355-3414)
PHONE...............................818 365-4215
Charles Miltenberger, *President*
Jamie Faulconer, *COO*
EMP: 10
SQ FT: 4,000
SALES (est): 1.9MM Privately Held
WEB: www.accuglassproducts.com
SIC: 3679 Electronic circuits

(P-18808)
ADCO PRODUCTS INC
23091 Mill Creek Dr, Laguna Hills
(92653-1258)
PHONE...............................937 339-6267
George Adkins, *President*
Randy Adkins, *Vice Pres*
EMP: 60
SQ FT: 12,500
SALES (est): 10.1MM Privately Held
SIC: 3679 2499 Electronic circuits; har-
ness assemblies for electronic use: wire
or cable; surveyors' stakes, wood

(P-18809)
ADVANCED ASSEMBLIES INC
990 Richard Ave Ste 109, Santa Clara
(95050-2828)
PHONE...............................408 988-1016
Kim N Tran, *President*
EMP: 12
SQ FT: 7,450
SALES (est): 974.3K Privately Held
WEB: www.advancedassemblies.net
SIC: 3679 Electronic circuits

(P-18810)
ADVANCED MICROWAVE INC
333 Moffett Park Dr, Sunnyvale
(94089-1208)
PHONE...............................408 739-4214
Mike Ghandehari, *President*
Susan Ghandehari, *Corp Secy*
EMP: 12
SQ FT: 5,000
SALES (est): 1.3MM Privately Held
WEB: www.advmic.com
SIC: 3679 Microwave components

(P-18811)
AEI ELECTECH CORP
Also Called: Sunpower USA
33485 Western Ave, Union City
(94587-3201)
PHONE...............................510 489-5088
David Shu, *President*
▲ EMP: 15
SALES (est): 2.1MM Privately Held
WEB: www.sunpower-usa.com
SIC: 3679 Power supplies, all types: static

(P-18812)
AHEAD MAGNETICS INC
Also Called: Aheadtek
6410 Via Del Oro, San Jose (95119-1208)
PHONE...............................408 226-9800
Tim Higgins, *Principal*
Ed Soldani, *CFO*
Patrick Johnston, *Vice Pres*
Yolanda Verdugo, *Executive*
Leslie Ungos, *Administration*
▲ EMP: 78
SQ FT: 32,000
SALES (est): 13.3MM Privately Held
WEB: www.aheadtek.com
SIC: 3679 Recording & playback heads,
magnetic
PA: Huritga International Holding (S) Pte.
    Ltd.
    10 Anson Road
    Singapore
    -

(P-18813)
ALYN INDUSTRIES INC
Also Called: Electronic Source Company
16028 Arminta St, Van Nuys (91406-1808)
PHONE...............................818 988-7696
Scott J Alyn, *CEO*
Marty McGinnis, *Engineer*
Lukas Sanchez, *Engineer*
Nina Ning, *Program Dir*
Bobby Ferdosi, *Director*
▼ EMP: 100

SALES (est): 18.5MM Privately Held
SIC: 3679 Electronic circuits

(P-18814)
AMERICAN AUDIO COMPONENT INC
Also Called: AAC
20 Fairbanks Ste 198, Irvine (92618-1673)
PHONE...............................909 596-3788
David Plekenpol, *CEO*
Richard Monk, *CFO*
Willie Maglonso, *Manager*
▲ EMP: 26
SALES: 3MM Privately Held
WEB: www.american-audio.com
SIC: 3679 Transducers, electrical
HQ: Aac Acoustic Technologies (Shenzhen)
    Co., Ltd.
    (Office), 6/F, Block A, Nanjing Univer-
    sity Technology Research B
    Shenzhen 51805

(P-18815)
AMERICAN INDUS SYSTEMS INC
Also Called: A I S
1768 Mcgaw Ave, Irvine (92614-5732)
PHONE...............................888 485-6688
Nelson Tsay, *CEO*
Joe Fijak, *COO*
Tony Gu, *Accounting Mgr*
▲ EMP: 30
SQ FT: 25,000
SALES (est): 5.9MM Privately Held
WEB: www.aispro.com
SIC: 3679 Liquid crystal displays (LCD)
PA: Ennoconn Corporation
    3-6f, 10, Jiankang Rd.,
    New Taipei City TAP 23586

(P-18816)
AMSCO US INC
15341 Texaco Ave, Paramount
(90723-3946)
PHONE...............................562 630-0333
Mike Yazdi, *President*
Victor Yazdi, *Vice Pres*
Karina Vega, *Purch Dir*
Tarane Yazdi, *VP Opers*
Liset Morando, *Accounts Mgr*
EMP: 110
SALES (est): 20.6MM Privately Held
WEB: www.amscous.com
SIC: 3679 Harness assemblies for elec-
tronic use: wire or cable

(P-18817)
APEM INC
Also Called: Ch Products
970 Park Center Dr, Vista (92081-8301)
PHONE...............................760 598-2518
Peter Brouilette, *President*
Bryan Murphy, *Regl Sales Mgr*
EMP: 81 Privately Held
SIC: 3679 3577 Electronic switches; com-
puter peripheral equipment
HQ: Apem, Inc.
    63 Neck Rd
    Haverhill MA 01835

(P-18818)
APPLIED THIN-FILM PRODUCTS (PA)
Also Called: Atp
3620 Yale Way, Fremont (94538-6182)
PHONE...............................510 661-4287
David J Adams, *CEO*
Ryan Nguyen, *COO*
Steven Cheung, *Bd of Directors*
Franco Pietroforte, *Vice Pres*
Russell Alm, *VP Business*
EMP: 112
SQ FT: 18,000
SALES: 25MM Privately Held
WEB: www.thinfilm.com
SIC: 3679 Microwave components

(P-18819)
APPLIED THIN-FILM PRODUCTS
3439 Edison Way, Fremont (94538-6179)
PHONE...............................510 661-4287
David Adams, *Branch Mgr*
EMP: 16 Privately Held
SIC: 3679 Microwave components

PA: Applied Thin-Film Products
    3620 Yale Way
    Fremont CA 94538
    -

(P-18820)
ARTECH INDUSTRIES INC
1966 Keats Dr, Riverside (92501-1747)
PHONE...............................951 276-3331
Mansukh R Bera, *President*
Girish Bera, *CFO*
Madan Bera, *Vice Pres*
▲ EMP: 36
SQ FT: 24,500
SALES (est): 5.4MM Privately Held
WEB: www.artech-loadcell.com
SIC: 3679 Loads, electronic

(P-18821)
ASEA POWER SYSTEMS
15272 Newsboy Cir, Huntington Beach
(92649-1202)
PHONE...............................714 896-9695
Mark A Woodward, *President*
Russ Engle, *Exec VP*
Thomas Short, *Prdtn Mgr*
◆ EMP: 30
SQ FT: 6,100
SALES (est): 5.8MM Privately Held
WEB: www.aseapower.com
SIC: 3679 Static power supply converters
for electronic applications

(P-18822)
ASTRO SEAL INC
827 Palmyrita Ave Ste B, Riverside
(92507-1820)
PHONE...............................951 787-6670
Michael Hammer, *President*
Karen Upfold, *Opers Staff*
Roger Hammer, *Director*
▲ EMP: 34 EST: 1964
SQ FT: 42,000
SALES (est): 6.4MM Privately Held
WEB: www.astroseal.com
SIC: 3679 3678 Hermetic seals for elec-
tronic equipment; electronic connectors

(P-18823)
ATLAS MAGNETICS INC
1121 N Kraemer Pl, Anaheim (92806-1923)
PHONE...............................714 632-9718
Maurice Brear, *CEO*
Perry Preece, *VP Opers*
EMP: 15
SALES (est): 2.2MM Privately Held
SIC: 3679 3592 Solenoids for electronic
applications; valves, aircraft

(P-18824)
AVI
431 Janemar Rd, Fallbrook (92028-2631)
PHONE...............................760 451-9379
EMP: 17
SQ FT: 8,000
SALES (est): 1.7MM Privately Held
SIC: 3679

(P-18825)
AVR GLOBAL TECHNOLOGIES INC (PA)
500 La Terraza Blvd, Escondido
(92025-3875)
P.O. Box 3814, Dana Point (92629-8814)
PHONE...............................949 391-1180
Andy Bowman, *President*
Val Pontes, *Treasurer*
EMP: 10 EST: 2016
SALES (est): 11.2MM Privately Held
SIC: 3679 3714 5065 5063 Harness assemblies for electronic use: wire or cable;
automotive wiring harness sets; electronic
parts & equipment; electronic parts; connectors, electronic; wire & cable; control &
signal wire & cable, including coaxial;
electronic wire & cable

(P-18826)
AZ DISPLAYS INC
75 Columbia, Aliso Viejo (92656-5386)
PHONE...............................949 831-5000
Reiner Moegling, *President*
▲ EMP: 50
SALES (est): 7.5MM Privately Held
WEB: www.azettler.com
SIC: 3679 Liquid crystal displays (LCD)

HQ: American Zettler Inc.
75 Columbia
Aliso Viejo CA 92656
949 831-5000

(P-18827)
B & G ELECTRONIC ASSEMBLY INC
10350 Regis Ct, Rancho Cucamonga (91730-3055)
PHONE...............................909 608-2077
Robert M Odell, *CEO*
Lillian Odell, *Vice Pres*
Liz Odell, *Vice Pres*
EMP: 18
SQ FT: 8,900
SALES (est): 3.4MM **Privately Held**
WEB: www.bgelectronic.com
SIC: 3679 Harness assemblies for electronic use: wire or cable

(P-18828)
B T E DELTEC INC
Also Called: Powerware
2727 Kurtz St, San Diego (92110-3109)
PHONE...............................619 291-4211
Dan Jackson, *President*
Chris Peavey, *VP Finance*
EMP: 250
SQ FT: 80,000
SALES (est): 9.3MM **Privately Held**
SIC: 3679 Electronic circuits; power supplies, all types: static
HQ: Eaton Corporation
1000 Eaton Blvd
Cleveland OH 44122
440 523-5000

(P-18829)
BANH AN BINH
1965 Stonewood Ln, San Jose (95132-1354)
PHONE...............................408 935-8950
EMP: 20
SALES (est): 1.9MM **Privately Held**
SIC: 3679

(P-18830)
BARTOLINI GUITARS
Also Called: Bartolini Pickups
2133 Research Dr Ste 16, Livermore (94550-3854)
PHONE...............................386 517-6823
William Bartolini, *Partner*
EMP: 16
SALES (est): 1.5MM **Privately Held**
WEB: www.bartolini.net
SIC: 3679 Recording & playback apparatus, including phonograph

(P-18831)
BASIC ELECTRONICS INC
11371 Monarch St, Garden Grove (92841-1406)
PHONE...............................714 530-2400
Nancy Balzano, *President*
Al Balzano, *Vice Pres*
Aurora Medina, *Info Tech Dir*
EMP: 30
SQ FT: 20,000
SALES (est): 4.9MM **Privately Held**
WEB: www.basicinc.com
SIC: 3679 3672 3613 Electronic circuits; power supplies, all types: static; printed circuit boards; switchgear & switchboard apparatus

(P-18832)
BEATS ELECTRONICS LLC (PA)
Also Called: Beats By Dr. Dre
8600 Hayden Pl, Culver City (90232-2902)
PHONE...............................424 268-3055
EMP: 13 EST: 2010
SALES (est): 6.1MM **Privately Held**
SIC: 3679 3651

(P-18833)
BEI NORTH AMERICA LLC (DH)
1461 Lawrence Dr, Thousand Oaks (91320-1303)
PHONE...............................805 716-0642
Martha Sullivan, *President*
Jeffrey Cote, *Vice Pres*
Alison Roelke, *Vice Pres*
EMP: 12

SALES: 54MM
SALES (corp-wide): 3.5B **Privately Held**
SIC: 3679 Electronic circuits
HQ: Custom Sensors & Technologies, Inc.
1461 Lawrence Dr
Thousand Oaks CA 91320
805 716-0322

(P-18834)
BEMA ELECTRONIC MFG INC
4545 Cushing Pkwy, Fremont (94538-6466)
PHONE...............................510 490-7770
Helen Kwong, *President*
Suju Kwong, *CFO*
Charles Evans, *Program Mgr*
Nancy Lo, *Program Mgr*
Luis Medina, *Program Mgr*
▲ EMP: 79
SQ FT: 26,205
SALES (est): 23.4MM **Privately Held**
WEB: www.bemaelectronics.com
SIC: 3679 Electronic circuits

(P-18835)
BENCHMARK ELEC MFG SOL MOORPK
200 Science Dr, Moorpark (93021-2003)
PHONE...............................805 532-2800
Bill Lehr, *Director*
EMP: 523
SALES (est): 66.1MM
SALES (corp-wide): 2.5B **Publicly Held**
WEB: www.smtek.com
SIC: 3679 Electronic circuits
HQ: Benchmark Electronics Manufacturing Solutions Inc.
5550 Hellyer Ave
San Jose CA 95138
805 222-1303

(P-18836)
BENTEK CORPORATION
Also Called: Bentek Solar
1991 Senter Rd, San Jose (95112-2631)
PHONE...............................408 954-9600
Mitchell Schoch, *President*
Lou Marzano, *President*
Mel Pagdanganan, *Info Tech Mgr*
Alan Duong, *Technology*
Jamie Aimonetti, *Human Res Dir*
▲ EMP: 100
SALES (est): 39.8MM **Privately Held**
SIC: 3679 Electronic circuits

(P-18837)
BERKELEY SCIENTIFIC
21 Westminster Ave, Kensington (94708-1036)
PHONE...............................510 525-1945
Lee Donaghey, *President*
EMP: 10
SQ FT: 2,000
SALES (est): 656.5K **Privately Held**
WEB: www.berkeleyscientific.com
SIC: 3679 8999 Electronic circuits; inventor

(P-18838)
BI TECHNOLOGIES CORPORATION
413 Rood Rd Ste 7, Calexico (92231-9765)
PHONE...............................714 447-2402
EMP: 21
SALES (corp-wide): 551.6MM **Privately Held**
WEB: www.bitechnologies.com
HQ: Bi Technologies Corporation
120 S State College Blvd
Brea CA 92821
714 447-2300

(P-18839)
BI-SEARCH INTERNATIONAL INC
17550 Gillette Ave, Irvine (92614-5610)
PHONE...............................714 258-4500
Kevin Y Kim, *President*
Yong Su Kim, *CFO*
◆ EMP: 50
SQ FT: 45,000
SALES (est): 21.2MM **Privately Held**
WEB: www.bisearch.com
SIC: 3679 Liquid crystal displays (LCD)

(P-18840)
BIVAR INC
4 Thomas, Irvine (92618-2593)
PHONE...............................949 951-8808
Thomas Silber, *CEO*
Kurt Baron, *Design Engr*
Jay Enciso, *Plant Mgr*
▲ EMP: 40
SQ FT: 26,040
SALES (est): 7.8MM **Privately Held**
WEB: www.bivar.com
SIC: 3679 Electronic circuits

(P-18841)
BRANDT ELECTRONICS INC
1971 Tarob Ct, Milpitas (95035-6825)
PHONE...............................408 240-0014
Phillip D Duvall, *CEO*
Steve Hall, *Vice Pres*
Rogelio Jose, *Engineer*
EMP: 40
SQ FT: 12,000
SALES (est): 7.3MM **Privately Held**
WEB: www.brandtelectronics.com
SIC: 3679 Power supplies, all types: static

(P-18842)
BREE ENGINEERING CORP
1275 Stone Dr Ste A, San Marcos (92078-4097)
PHONE...............................760 510-4950
Dan Bree, *President*
Jackie Bree, *CFO*
Daniel Czagany, *Sales Staff*
Bree Dan, *Agent*
EMP: 30
SQ FT: 7,600
SALES: 2MM **Privately Held**
WEB: www.breeeng.com
SIC: 3679 Electronic circuits

(P-18843)
C & A TRANSDUCERS INC
14329 Commerce Dr, Garden Grove (92843-4949)
PHONE...............................714 554-9188
Daniel Toledo, *President*
EMP: 25
SQ FT: 6,000
SALES: 2.5MM **Privately Held**
WEB: www.ca-transducers.com
SIC: 3679 3677 3674 Transducers, electrical; electronic coils, transformers & other inductors; semiconductors & related devices

(P-18844)
C & S ASSEMBLY INC
1150 N Armando St, Anaheim (92806-2609)
PHONE...............................866 779-8939
Sandra A Foley, *President*
Chris Foley, *Vice Pres*
Christopher Foley, *Vice Pres*
EMP: 15
SQ FT: 12,000
SALES (est): 2.4MM **Privately Held**
WEB: www.cnsassembly.com
SIC: 3679 5063 Harness assemblies for electronic use: wire or cable; electronic wire & cable

(P-18845)
C D INTERNATIONAL TECH INC
695 Pinnacle Pl, Livermore (94550-9705)
PHONE...............................408 986-0725
Zhong Cao, *President*
▲ EMP: 15
SQ FT: 10,000
SALES (est): 2.4MM **Privately Held**
WEB: www.cdint.com
SIC: 3679 Transducers, electrical

(P-18846)
CABLE HARNESS SYSTEMS INC
7462 Talbert Ave, Huntington Beach (92648-1239)
PHONE...............................714 841-9650
Mike Fuchs, *President*
Mark Fuchs, *Purchasing*
Shelly Martin, *Manager*
Cherene Prenger, *Manager*
EMP: 30

SALES (est): 5MM **Privately Held**
WEB: www.cableharness.com
SIC: 3679 Harness assemblies for electronic use: wire or cable

(P-18847)
CAC INC
20322 Windrow Dr Ste 100, Lake Forest (92630-8150)
PHONE...............................949 587-3328
Patrick Redfern, *President*
▲ EMP: 12
SALES (est): 1.6MM **Privately Held**
WEB: www.cacproducts.com
SIC: 3679 Electronic circuits

(P-18848)
CAL SOUTHERN BRAIDING INC
Also Called: Scb Division
7450 Scout Ave, Bell Gardens (90201-4932)
PHONE...............................562 927-5531
Neal Castleman, *President*
EMP: 60
SQ FT: 38,000
SALES: 10.9MM
SALES (corp-wide): 120.5MM **Privately Held**
WEB: www.socalbraid.com
SIC: 3679 Harness assemblies for electronic use: wire or cable
PA: Dcx-Chol Enterprises, Inc.
12831 S Figueroa St
Los Angeles CA 90061
310 516-1692

(P-18849)
CALEX MFG CO INC
2401 Stanwell Dr Frnt, Concord (94520-4872)
PHONE...............................925 687-4411
Paul S Cuff, *CEO*
Robert Zorovic, *Buyer*
Goble Loren, *Mfg Mgr*
Kathy Waldron, *Mfg Staff*
Jillda Hahn, *Sales Staff*
▲ EMP: 45
SALES (est): 11.9MM **Privately Held**
WEB: www.calex.com
SIC: 3679 Static power supply converters for electronic applications; power supplies, all types: static

(P-18850)
CARDIGAN ROAD PRODUCTIONS
1999 Ave Of The Sts 110, Los Angeles (90067)
PHONE...............................310 289-1442
Marc Friedland, *President*
EMP: 38 EST: 2001
SALES (est): 2.1MM **Privately Held**
SIC: 3679 Electronic circuits

(P-18851)
CARROS AMERICAS INC
Also Called: Innovista Sensors
2945 Townsgate Rd Ste 200, Westlake Village (91361-5866)
PHONE...............................805 267-7176
Eric Pilaud, *President*
Ben Watt, *CFO*
EMP: 29
SALES (est): 18.7MM **Privately Held**
SIC: 3679 3577 Electronic circuits; encoders, computer peripheral equipment

(P-18852)
CARROS SENSORS SYSTEMS CO LLC
Also Called: Systron Donner Inertial
355 Lennon Ln, Walnut Creek (94598-2475)
PHONE...............................925 979-4400
Mark Collins, *Design Engr*
Victor Dragotti, *Design Engr*
David Hoyh, *Sales Dir*
Mark Chamberlain, *Sales Staff*
Harry Angus, *Manager*
EMP: 125
SALES (corp-wide): 3.5B **Privately Held**
SIC: 3679 Electronic circuits

PRODUCTS & SVCS

HQ: Carros Sensors & Systems Company,
   Llc
   1461 Lawrence Dr
   Thousand Oaks CA 91320

(P-18853)
**CARROS SENSORS SYSTEMS
CO LLC (DH)**
Also Called: BEI Industrial Encoders
1461 Lawrence Dr, Thousand Oaks
(91320-1303)
PHONE..............................805 968-0782
Eric Pilaud, *CEO*
Jean-Yves Mouttet, *Treasurer*
Victor Copeland, *Admin Sec*
Jean-Yves Vo, *CTO*
Yasmina Belkahla, *Sales Staff*
▲ EMP: 125
SALES (est): 100.9MM
SALES (corp-wide): 3.5B **Privately Held**
SIC: 3679 Electronic circuits
HQ: Sensata Technologies, Inc.
   529 Pleasant St
   Attleboro MA 02703
   508 236-3800

(P-18854)
CCM ASSEMBLY & MFG INC
2275 Michael Faraday Dr # 6, San Diego
(92154-7927)
PHONE..............................760 560-1310
Erika Marcela Murillo, *CEO*
Sergio Murillo, *President*
John Savage, *Vice Pres*
Esthela Mena, *Purchasing*
▲ EMP: 50 EST: 1997
SQ FT: 10,000
SALES (est): 9MM **Privately Held**
WEB: www.ccmassembly.com
SIC: 3679 3441 Harness assemblies for
   electronic use: wire or cable; fabricated
   structural metal

(P-18855)
**CELESCO TRANSDUCER
PRODUCTS**
20630 Plummer St, Chatsworth
(91311-5111)
PHONE..............................818 701-2701
Hernan Cortez, *Principal*
▲ EMP: 13
SALES (est): 1.8MM **Privately Held**
SIC: 3679 1541 Transducers, electrical;
   industrial buildings & warehouses

(P-18856)
CELESTICA LLC
Also Called: D&H Manufacturing
49235 Milmont Dr, Fremont (94538-7349)
PHONE..............................510 770-5100
Mark Morris, *Branch Mgr*
EMP: 200
SALES (corp-wide): 23.7B **Privately Held**
SIC: 3679 Electronic circuits
HQ: Celestica Llc
   11 Continental Blvd # 103
   Merrimack NH 03054

(P-18857)
CELLTRON INC
19860 Plummer St, Chatsworth
(91311-5652)
P.O. Box 98, Galena KS (66739-0098)
PHONE..............................620 783-1333
Stacey Williams, *CFO*
EMP: 10
SALES (est): 398.2K **Privately Held**
SIC: 3679 Harness assemblies for elec-
   tronic use: wire or cable

(P-18858)
**CENTERLINE MANUFACTURING
INC**
Also Called: Centerline Engineering
1234 E Ash Ave Ste D, Fullerton
(92831-5013)
PHONE..............................714 525-9890
David Khoe, *President*
Jack Antes, *Ch of Bd*
Randolph Scott, *President*
▲ EMP: 10
SQ FT: 6,000

SALES: 50K **Privately Held**
WEB: www.centerline-engineering.com
SIC: 3679 Harness assemblies for elec-
   tronic use: wire or cable

(P-18859)
CERNEX INC
1710 Zanker Rd Ste 103, San Jose
(95112-4219)
PHONE..............................408 541-9226
Chanh Huynh, *President*
▲ EMP: 25
SQ FT: 5,200
SALES (est): 5.5MM **Privately Held**
WEB: www.cernex.com
SIC: 3679 Microwave components

(P-18860)
CIAO WIRELESS INC
4000 Via Pescador, Camarillo
(93012-5044)
PHONE..............................805 389-3224
Glen Wasylewski, *President*
Glen Wasyleuski, *VP Sales*
Etzon Garcia, *Sales Staff*
Justin Harrison, *Manager*
Felipe Roque, *Assistant*
▼ EMP: 55
SQ FT: 42,000
SALES (est): 12MM **Privately Held**
WEB: www.ciaowireless.com
SIC: 3679 3699 Microwave components;
   pulse amplifiers

(P-18861)
CICON ENGINEERING INC
8345 Canoga Ave, Canoga Park
(91304-2605)
PHONE..............................818 909-6060
Eric Lopez, *Manager*
EMP: 20
SALES (est): 990.1K
SALES (corp-wide): 27.5MM **Privately
Held**
SIC: 3679 Harness assemblies for elec-
   tronic use: wire or cable
PA: Cicon Engineering, Inc.
   6633 Odessa Ave
   Van Nuys CA 91406
   818 909-6060

(P-18862)
CICON ENGINEERING INC
21421 Schoenborn St, Canoga Park
(91304-2630)
PHONE..............................818 882-6508
Richard McKee, *Manager*
EMP: 10
SALES (est): 619.8K
SALES (corp-wide): 27.5MM **Privately
Held**
WEB: www.cicon.com
SIC: 3679 Harness assemblies for elec-
   tronic use: wire or cable
PA: Cicon Engineering, Inc.
   6633 Odessa Ave
   Van Nuys CA 91406
   818 909-6060

(P-18863)
CICON ENGINEERING INC (PA)
6633 Odessa Ave, Van Nuys (91406-5746)
PHONE..............................818 909-6060
Ali Kolahi, *President*
Farah Kolahi, *Shareholder*
Hamid Kolahi, *Shareholder*
Peter Boskovich, *COO*
Brian Rash, *CFO*
EMP: 102
SQ FT: 50,000
SALES (est): 27.5MM **Privately Held**
WEB: www.cicon.com
SIC: 3679 Harness assemblies for elec-
   tronic use: wire or cable

(P-18864)
CICON ENGINEERING INC
9300 Mason Ave, Chatsworth
(91311-5201)
PHONE..............................818 909-6060
Ali Kolahi, *Branch Mgr*
EMP: 49
SALES (corp-wide): 27.5MM **Privately
Held**
SIC: 3679 Harness assemblies for elec-
   tronic use: wire or cable

PA: Cicon Engineering, Inc.
   6633 Odessa Ave
   Van Nuys CA 91406
   818 909-6060

(P-18865)
CINEMAG INC
4487 Ish Dr, Simi Valley (93063-7665)
PHONE..............................818 993-4644
David Garen, *President*
Thomas Reichenbach, *President*
EMP: 12
SALES (est): 1.6MM **Privately Held**
SIC: 3679 Antennas, receiving

(P-18866)
CIRCUIT AUTOMATION INC
5292 System Dr, Huntington Beach
(92649-1527)
PHONE..............................714 763-4180
Thomas Meeker, *President*
Yuki Kojima, *President*
Sherlene Meeker, *CFO*
Masayuki Kojima, *Vice Pres*
◆ EMP: 18
SQ FT: 15,000
SALES: 2MM **Privately Held**
WEB: www.circuitautomation.com
SIC: 3679 Electronic circuits

(P-18867)
**CKS SOLUTION
INCORPORATED**
556 Vanguard Way Ste C, Brea
(92821-3929)
PHONE..............................714 292-6307
Patrick Park, *Manager*
EMP: 25
SALES (corp-wide): 6.3MM **Privately
Held**
SIC: 3679 Liquid crystal displays (LCD)
PA: Cks Solution Incorporated
   4293 Muhlhauser Rd
   Fairfield OH 45014
   513 947-1277

(P-18868)
CLARY CORPORATION
150 E Huntington Dr, Monrovia
(91016-3415)
PHONE..............................626 359-4486
John G Clary, *Ch of Bd*
Donald G Ash, *Treasurer*
Jerry Satterfield, *Technician*
Wahid Nawabi, *Director*
Leo Tran, *Manager*
EMP: 40
SQ FT: 26,000
SALES (est): 7.8MM **Privately Held**
WEB: www.clary.com
SIC: 3679 3612 Electronic loads & power
   supplies; power supplies, all types: static;
   transformers, except electric

(P-18869)
**COASTAL COMPONENT INDS
INC**
Also Called: C C I
133 E Bristol Ln, Orange (92865-2749)
PHONE..............................714 685-6677
Ronna Coe, *Chairman*
Mark Coe, *President*
Donald B Coe, *CEO*
Donald Coe, *CEO*
Diana Romero, *Vice Pres*
EMP: 20
SQ FT: 6,027
SALES (est): 3.9MM **Privately Held**
WEB: www.ccicoastal.com
SIC: 3679 5065 3643 3678 Electronic cir-
   cuits; electronic parts & equipment; elec-
   tric connectors; electronic connectors;
   relays & industrial controls; manufactured
   hardware (general)

(P-18870)
COHERENT ASIA INC
5100 Patrick Henry Dr, Santa Clara
(95054-1112)
PHONE..............................408 764-4000
John R Ambroseo, *President*
John Ambroseo, *President*
Helene Simonet, *Exec VP*
EMP: 98

PA: Cicon Engineering, Inc.
   6633 Odessa Ave
   Van Nuys CA 91406
   818 909-6060

(P-18865) *(already above — see left)*

SALES (est): 12.3MM
SALES (corp-wide): 1.9B **Publicly Held**
SIC: 3679 3827 Electronic crystals; optical
   instruments & lenses
PA: Coherent, Inc.
   5100 Patrick Henry Dr
   Santa Clara CA 95054
   408 764-4000

(P-18871)
COLLARIS LLC
Also Called: Collaris Defense
685 Jarvis Dr Ste C, Morgan Hill
(95037-2813)
PHONE..............................510 825-9995
Yasser Khan, *Principal*
Ajmal Khan, *Principal*
EMP: 56
SALES (est): 179.3K **Privately Held**
SIC: 3679 3812 Rheostats, for electronic
   end products; search & navigation equip-
   ment

(P-18872)
**COMMUNICATIONS & PWR INDS
LLC**
CPI
6385 San Ignacio Ave, San Jose
(95119-1206)
PHONE..............................650 846-2900
Gordon Ballantyne, *Branch Mgr*
EMP: 130
SALES (corp-wide): 399.2MM **Privately
Held**
SIC: 3679 3699 3671 3663 Microwave
   components; electrical equipment & sup-
   plies; vacuum tubes; radio & TV commu-
   nications equipment
HQ: Communications & Power Industries
   Llc
   607 Hansen Way
   Palo Alto CA 94304

(P-18873)
**COMPASS COMPONENTS INC
(PA)**
Also Called: Compass Manufacturing Service
48133 Warm Springs Blvd, Fremont
(94539-7498)
PHONE..............................510 656-4700
Jack Maxwell, *CEO*
Bob Duplantier, *President*
Irene Madrid, *Associate Dir*
Arthur Morrison, *IT/INT Sup*
Minh Nguyen, *IT/INT Sup*
EMP: 110 EST: 1979
SQ FT: 36,000
SALES: 51.9MM **Privately Held**
WEB: www.ccicms.com
SIC: 3679 5065 Harness assemblies for
   electronic use: wire or cable; electronic
   parts

(P-18874)
COMPSERV INC
42 Golf Rd, Pleasanton (94566-9752)
PHONE..............................415 331-4571
Michael J Maslana, *President*
Christopher Alessio, *Vice Pres*
Robert Boguski, *Vice Pres*
EMP: 19
SQ FT: 9,000
SALES (est): 1.8MM **Privately Held**
WEB: www.compserv-inc.com
SIC: 3679 Electronic circuits

(P-18875)
**CPI INTERNATIONAL HOLDING
CORP**
811 Hansen Way, Palo Alto (94304-1031)
PHONE..............................650 846-2900
O Joe Caldarelli, *CEO*
Robert A Fickett, *President*
John R Beighley, *Vice Pres*
John Overstreet, *Vice Pres*
Andrew E Tafler, *Vice Pres*
EMP: 18
SALES: 494.6MM **Privately Held**
SIC: 3679 Electronic circuits
PA: Cpi International Holding Llc
   811 Hansen Way
   Palo Alto CA 94304

(P-18876)
CRANE CO
Also Called: Crane Valves Services Division
3948 Teal Ct, Benicia (94510-1202)
PHONE..................................707 748-7166
Evan Russell, *Manager*
EMP: 11
SALES (corp-wide): 3.3B **Publicly Held**
WEB: www.stellarinteractivesolutions.com
SIC: 3679 Oscillators
PA: Crane Co.
100 1st Stamford Pl # 300
Stamford CT 06902
203 363-7300

(P-18877)
CRUCIAL POWER PRODUCTS
14000 S Broadway, Los Angeles
(90061-1018)
PHONE..................................323 721-5017
Abbie Gougerchian, *Principal*
Alan Stone, *Vice Pres*
EMP: 12
SALES (est): 1.1MM **Privately Held**
WEB: www.crucialpower.com
SIC: 3679 Electronic circuits

(P-18878)
CRYSTAL CAL LAB INC
3981 E Miraloma Ave, Anaheim
(92806-6201)
PHONE..................................714 991-1580
EMP: 26
SQ FT: 7,600
SALES (est): 3MM **Privately Held**
SIC: 3679 3825

(P-18879)
CSR TECHNOLOGY INC (DH)
1060 Rincon Cir, San Jose (95131-1325)
PHONE..................................408 523-6500
Brett Gladden, *CEO*
Ron Mackintosh, *Chairman*
Chris Ladas, *Exec VP*
Igor Chirashnya, *Vice Pres*
Dennis Bencala, *Director*
▲ EMP: 120
SALES (est): 53.6MM
SALES (corp-wide): 24.2B **Publicly Held**
SIC: 3679 3812 3674 Electronic circuits;
search & navigation equipment; semiconductors & related devices
HQ: Qualcomm Technologies International,
Ltd.
Unit 2 The Legacy Building
Belfast BT3 9
289 046-3140

(P-18880)
CURTIS TECHNOLOGY INC
11391 Sorrento Valley Rd, San Diego
(92121-1303)
PHONE..................................858 453-5797
Alex Jvirblis, *President*
Daksha Dave, *Corp Secy*
EMP: 15 EST: 1959
SQ FT: 18,000
SALES (est): 2.3MM **Privately Held**
WEB: www.curtistechnology.com
SIC: 3679 8711 3229 Electronic circuits;
consulting engineer; pressed & blown
glass

(P-18881)
**CUSTOM MICROWAVE
COMPONENTS**
44249 Old Warm Sprng Blvd, Fremont
(94538-6168)
PHONE..................................510 651-3434
Gregory Mau, *President*
EMP: 10
SQ FT: 12,000
SALES (est): 1.5MM **Privately Held**
WEB: www.customwave.com
SIC: 3679 Microwave components

(P-18882)
**CUSTOM SENSORS & TECH INC
(HQ)**
Also Called: C S T
1461 Lawrence Dr, Thousand Oaks
(91320-1303)
PHONE..................................805 716-0322
Martha Sullivan, *CEO*
Remi Chazalmartin, *General Mgr*

Greg Smyers, *Sr Software Eng*
Carolyn Kolb, *Human Res Dir*
Jeffrey Cote, *Director*
▲ EMP: 83
SALES (est): 668.5MM
SALES (corp-wide): 3.5B **Privately Held**
WEB: www.cst.schneider-electric.com
SIC: 3679 Electronic circuits

(P-18883)
DAWN VME PRODUCTS
47915 Westinghouse Dr, Fremont
(94539-7483)
PHONE..................................510 657-4444
Barry W Burnsides, *CEO*
Cheryl A Burnsides, *Vice Pres*
Tim Collins, *Program Mgr*
Robert Holguin, *Engineer*
Sharnjit Sekhon, *QC Mgr*
▲ EMP: 45
SQ FT: 20,000
SALES (est): 9.7MM **Privately Held**
WEB: www.dawnvme.com
SIC: 3679 Electronic circuits

(P-18884)
DCX-CHOL ENTERPRISES INC
Also Called: Scb Division of Dcx-Chol
7450 Scout Ave, Bell (90201-4932)
PHONE..................................562 927-5531
Ben Dose, *Branch Mgr*
EMP: 60
SALES (corp-wide): 120.5MM **Privately
Held**
SIC: 3679 Harness assemblies for electronic use: wire or cable
PA: Dcx-Chol Enterprises, Inc.
12831 S Figueroa St
Los Angeles CA 90061
310 516-1692

(P-18885)
**DE ANZA MANUFACTURING
SVCS INC**
1271 Reamwood Ave, Sunnyvale
(94089-2275)
PHONE..................................408 734-2020
Art Takahara, *President*
Michael Takahara, *Vice Pres*
Kristine Walker, *Admin Asst*
Dale Walker, *Engineer*
Sarah Walker, *Marketing Staff*
▼ EMP: 60
SQ FT: 24,000
SALES (est): 11.3MM **Privately Held**
WEB: www.deanzamfg.com
SIC: 3679 3643 Harness assemblies for
electronic use: wire or cable; current-carrying wiring devices

(P-18886)
**DELTA GROUP ELECTRONICS
INC**
10180 Scripps Ranch Blvd, San Diego
(92131-1234)
PHONE..................................858 569-1681
Bill West, *Manager*
John Pollock, *Manager*
EMP: 55
SALES (corp-wide): 149.2MM **Privately
Held**
WEB: www.deltagroupinc.com
SIC: 3679 3577 3672 Electronic circuits;
computer peripheral equipment; printed
circuit boards
PA: Delta Group Electronics, Inc.
4521a Osuna Rd Ne
Albuquerque NM 87109
505 883-7674

(P-18887)
DICON FIBEROPTICS INC (PA)
1689 Regatta Blvd Bldg W1, Richmond
(94804-7438)
PHONE..................................510 620-5000
Ho-Shang Lee, *President*
Dr Gilles Corcos, *Ch of Bd*
Robert Schleicher, *Vice Pres*
Hoffman Cheung, *QA Dir*
Wuucheng Huang, *Info Tech Mgr*
▲ EMP: 119
SQ FT: 202,000
SALES (est): 81.1MM **Privately Held**
WEB: www.diconfiber.com
SIC: 3679 3827 Electronic switches; optical instruments & lenses

(P-18888)
**DIGITAL POWER CORPORATION
(HQ)**
48430 Lakeview Blvd, Fremont
(94538-6532)
PHONE..................................510 657-2635
Amos Kohn, *President*
Milton C Ault III, *Ch of Bd*
William B Horne, *CFO*
Moti Rosenberg, *Bd of Directors*
Olga Chupric, *Controller*
▲ EMP: 26 EST: 1969
SQ FT: 12,396
SALES: 27.1MM **Publicly Held**
WEB: www.digipwr.com
SIC: 3679 Electronic switches
PA: Dpw Holdings, Inc.
201 Shipyard Way Ste E
Newport Beach CA 92663
949 444-5464

(P-18889)
DIGITAL VIEW INC
18440 Tech Dr Ste 130, Morgan Hill
(95037)
PHONE..................................408 782-7773
James Robert Henry, *CEO*
Neil Wood, *VP Engrg*
Renato Ceja, *Technical Staff*
Rob Warren, *Engineer*
Dawn Kersey, *Business Mgr*
◆ EMP: 10
SQ FT: 6,000
SALES (est): 2.1MM
SALES (corp-wide): 6.5MM **Privately
Held**
WEB: www.digitalview.com
SIC: 3679 7313 Liquid crystal displays
(LCD); electronic media advertising representatives
HQ: Digital View Limited
Rm 705-708 7/F Texwood Plz
Kwun Tong KLN

(P-18890)
**DIVERSFIED TCHNCAL
SYSTEMS INC (PA)**
1720 Apollo Ct, Seal Beach (90740-5617)
PHONE..................................562 493-0158
Stephen D Pruitt, *CEO*
Steve Pruitt, *President*
Kirsten Larsen, *CFO*
George M Beckage, *Vice Pres*
Tim Kippen, *Vice Pres*
▲ EMP: 29
SQ FT: 55,000
SALES (est): 15MM **Privately Held**
WEB: www.dtsweb.com
SIC: 3679 3825 Electronic circuits; analog-digital converters, electronic instrumentation type

(P-18891)
DJ GREY COMPANY INC
455 Allan Ct, Healdsburg (95448-4802)
PHONE..................................707 431-2779
Marla J Grey, *President*
Michele Perry, *Vice Pres*
EMP: 15
SQ FT: 4,500
SALES (est): 2.3MM **Privately Held**
WEB: www.djgreycompany.com
SIC: 3679 Electronic circuits

(P-18892)
**DREAMCTCHERS
EMPWERMENT NETWRK**
2201 Tuolumne St, Vallejo (94589-2524)
PHONE..................................707 558-1775
George Lytal, *Ch of Bd*
EMP: 25
SALES (est): 368.5K **Privately Held**
SIC: 3679 Voice controls

(P-18893)
DYNALLOY INC
1562 Reynolds Ave, Irvine (92614-5612)
PHONE..................................714 436-1206
Wayne Brown, *CEO*
Jess Brown, *Vice Pres*
EMP: 20
SQ FT: 8,000

SALES (est): 4.8MM **Privately Held**
WEB: www.dynalloy.com
SIC: 3679 3357 5065 Electronic circuits;
nonferrous wiredrawing & insulating; electronic parts

(P-18894)
DYTRAN INSTRUMENTS INC
21592 Marilla St, Chatsworth (91311-4137)
PHONE..................................818 700-7818
Nicholas D Change II, *President*
Michael Change, *Vice Pres*
Anne Hackney, *Vice Pres*
Vanessa Villasenor, *Administration*
Roy Alaman, *Info Tech Dir*
EMP: 160
SQ FT: 8,000
SALES (est): 35.9MM **Privately Held**
WEB: www.dytran.com
SIC: 3679 3829 Transducers, electrical;
measuring & controlling devices

(P-18895)
ECLIPSE MICROWAVE INC
2095 Ringwood Ave Ste 60, San Jose
(95131-1786)
PHONE..................................408 526-1100
Jeffrey P Rapadas, *President*
EMP: 14
SALES (est): 2MM **Privately Held**
WEB: www.eclipsemicrowave.com
SIC: 3679 Microwave components

(P-18896)
ELCON INC
1009 Timothy Dr, San Jose (95133-1043)
PHONE..................................408 292-7800
Anthony J Barraco, *CEO*
Timothy Dyer, *Vice Pres*
Steve Loveless, *Principal*
Trinh Tran,
Jesus Perez, *Supervisor*
EMP: 50
SQ FT: 31,000
SALES (est): 8.4MM **Privately Held**
WEB: www.elcon-inc.com
SIC: 3679 Commutators, electronic

(P-18897)
ELECTRO SWITCH CORP
Also Called: Arga Controls A Unit
10410 Trademark St, Rancho Cucamonga
(91730-5826)
PHONE..................................909 581-0855
Kathy Brown, *Branch Mgr*
EMP: 15
SALES (corp-wide): 90.3MM **Privately
Held**
SIC: 3679 Transducers, electrical
HQ: Electro Switch Corp.
775 Pleasant St Ste 1
Weymouth MA 02189
781 335-1195

(P-18898)
**ELECTRO-SUPPORT SYSTEMS
CORP**
Also Called: IMS-Ess
27449 Colt Ct, Temecula (92590-3674)
P.O. Box 50067, Irvine (92619-0067)
PHONE..................................951 676-2751
Richard Olson, *President*
Mark Bridgeford, *Admin Sec*
EMP: 20
SQ FT: 12,500
SALES (est): 3.3MM **Privately Held**
WEB: www.ims-ess.com
SIC: 3679 3845 3728 Electronic circuits;
electromedical equipment; military aircraft
equipment & armament

(P-18899)
**ELECTRO-TECH PRODUCTS
INC**
2001 E Gladstone St Ste A, Glendora
(91740-5381)
PHONE..................................909 592-1434
Ramzi Bader, *President*
▲ EMP: 30
SQ FT: 11,000
SALES (est): 6.1MM **Privately Held**
WEB: www.etp-inc.com
SIC: 3679 Electronic circuits; power supplies, all types: static

PRODUCTS & SVCS

(P-18900)
ELECTROCUBE INC (PA)
Also Called: Southern Electronics
3366 Pomona Blvd, Pomona (91768-3234)
PHONE..................................909 595-1821
Langdon Clay Parrill, *President*
Don Duquette, *Vice Pres*
Donald Duquette, *Vice Pres*
Scott Wieland, *Principal*
William Jaacks, *Senior Engr*
◆ EMP: 62
SQ FT: 27,000
SALES (est): 9.2MM Privately Held
WEB: www.electrocube.com
SIC: 3679 3675 Electronic circuits; electronic capacitors

(P-18901)
ELMECH INC
195 San Pedro Ave Ste E15, Morgan Hill
(95037-5140)
P.O. Box 2606 (95038-2606)
PHONE..................................408 782-2990
Paul Balog, *President*
Mathew Schreyer, *Supervisor*
EMP: 12
SQ FT: 4,400
SALES (est): 2.5MM Privately Held
WEB: www.elmechinc.com
SIC: 3679 Harness assemblies for electronic use: wire or cable

(P-18902)
EMAC ASSEMBLY CORP
21615 Parthenia St, Canoga Park
(91304-1517)
PHONE..................................818 882-2999
Lupe Garcia, *President*
EMP: 15
SALES (est): 1.6MM Privately Held
SIC: 3679 3469 Electronic circuits; stamping metal for the trade

(P-18903)
EMBER ACQUISITION SUB INC (HQ)
2015 Chestnut St, Alhambra (91803-1542)
PHONE..................................626 293-3400
Jeffrey Rittichier, *CEO*
EMP: 117
SALES (est): 7.3MM
SALES (corp-wide): 85.6MM Publicly Held
SIC: 3679 3829 Electronic circuits; accelerometers
PA: Emcore Corporation
2015 Chestnut St
Alhambra CA 91803
626 293-3400

(P-18904)
EMI SOLUTIONS INC
13805 Alton Pkwy Ste B, Irvine
(92618-1690)
PHONE..................................949 206-9960
Julie Ydens, *Ch of Bd*
Bob Ydens, *President*
Robert Zarrow, *Business Dir*
▼ EMP: 18
SQ FT: 6,500
SALES (est): 1.7MM Privately Held
WEB: www.4emi.com
SIC: 3679 Electronic circuits

(P-18905)
EMLINQ LLC
Also Called: Electronic Mfg Leaders & Qulty
2125 N Madera Rd Ste C, Simi Valley
(93065-7711)
PHONE..................................805 409-4807
Tamara Bitticks, *Mng Member*
Michael Peter, *Vice Pres*
Linda Hana, *Program Mgr*
Mallory Simonoff, *Program Mgr*
Andrew Homiak, *Engineer*
▲ EMP: 58
SALES (est): 21.2MM Privately Held
SIC: 3679 Electronic circuits

(P-18906)
ENFORA INC
9645 Scranton Rd Ste 205, San Diego
(92121-1764)
PHONE..................................972 234-1689
Mark Weinzierl, *President*
Kenneth Leddon, *Senior VP*

Catherine F Ratcliffe, *Senior VP*
Slim S Souissi, *Senior VP*
▲ EMP: 100
SQ FT: 27,000
SALES (est): 13.7MM
SALES (corp-wide): 202.4MM Publicly Held
SIC: 3679 Commutators, electronic
HQ: Novatel Wireless, Inc.
9605 Scranton Rd Ste 300
San Diego CA 92121
858 812-3400

(P-18907)
ESP CORP
1175 W Victoria St, Compton (90220-5813)
PHONE..................................310 639-2535
Bayasouk Ounthaung, *President*
EMP: 20
SALES (est): 1.8MM Privately Held
SIC: 3679 Electronic components

(P-18908)
EXPRESS MANUFACTURING INC (PA)
3519 W Warner Ave, Santa Ana
(92704-5214)
PHONE..................................714 979-2228
Chauk Pan Chin, *President*
Catherine Lee Chin, *Treasurer*
C M Chin, *Vice Pres*
Stana Marko, *Vice Pres*
Owen James, *Program Mgr*
▲ EMP: 211
SQ FT: 96,000
SALES (est): 158.6MM Privately Held
WEB: www.eminc.com
SIC: 3679 3672 Electronic circuits; printed circuit boards

(P-18909)
FABRI-TECH COMPONENTS INC
49038 Milmont Dr, Fremont (94538-7301)
PHONE..................................510 249-2000
Terry Anest, *President*
Teo Seow Phong, *CEO*
Allison Bates, *Manager*
EMP: 15
SQ FT: 7,000
SALES (est): 3.8MM
SALES (corp-wide): 19.3MM Privately Held
WEB: www.fabritech.net
SIC: 3679 Electronic circuits
PA: Fabri-Tech Components (S) Pte Ltd
3 Tuas Basin Link
Singapore 63875
686 282-22

(P-18910)
FABRICAST INC (PA)
2517 Seaman Ave, South El Monte
(91733-1927)
P.O. Box 3176 (91733-0176)
PHONE..................................626 443-3247
H Phelps Wood III, *President*
Phelps Wood, *CIO*
EMP: 25 EST: 1960
SQ FT: 6,250
SALES (est): 2.4MM Privately Held
WEB: www.fabricast.com
SIC: 3679 3621 Electronic circuits; motors & generators

(P-18911)
FASTRAK MANUFACTURING SVCS INC
1275 Alma Ct, San Jose (95112-5943)
PHONE..................................408 298-6414
Phillip Guzman, *CEO*
Michelle Hilty, *President*
EMP: 20
SALES (est): 3.7MM Privately Held
SIC: 3679 8711 Harness assemblies for electronic use: wire or cable; electronic circuits; electrical or electronic engineering

(P-18912)
FEASIBLE INC
1175 Park Ave, Emeryville (94608-3631)
PHONE..................................310 702-5803
Andrew Hsieh, *Partner*
Daniel Steingart, *Partner*
Barry Van Tassell, *Partner*
EMP: 10

SALES (est): 258.5K Privately Held
SIC: 3679 3823 3826 3829 Electronic circuits; industrial process measurement equipment; analytical instruments; stress, strain & flaw detecting/measuring equipment

(P-18913)
FEDERAL CUSTOM CABLE LLC
1891 Alton Pkwy Ste A, Irvine
(92606-4985)
PHONE..................................949 851-3114
Juliette Khamis,
Jabra Khamis, *Admin Asst*
Violet Kamis, *Human Res Mgr*
Jan Deckert, *Purch Agent*
Abe Kamis, *Safety Mgr*
EMP: 50
SALES (est): 9.8MM Privately Held
WEB: www.fccable.com
SIC: 3679 Electronic circuits

(P-18914)
FEMA ELECTRONICS CORPORATION
22 Corporate Park, Irvine (92606-3112)
PHONE..................................714 825-0140
Bob Cheng, *CEO*
Chinyun Cheng, *Treasurer*
George Cheng, *Vice Pres*
▲ EMP: 30
SQ FT: 3,000
SALES (est): 5.5MM Privately Held
WEB: www.femacorp.com
SIC: 3679 Electronic crystals

(P-18915)
FERRARI INTRCNNECT SLTIONS INC
4385 E Lowell St Ste A, Ontario
(91761-2228)
PHONE..................................951 684-8034
David Ferrari, *President*
EMP: 10
SQ FT: 2,700
SALES (est): 760.3K Privately Held
SIC: 3679 Electronic circuits

(P-18916)
FLEX INTERCONNECT TECH INC
1603 Watson Ct, Milpitas (95035-6806)
PHONE..................................408 956-8204
Chetan Shah, *CEO*
Dean Matsuo, *Corp Secy*
Nitin Desai, *Engineer*
Yaqub Obaidi, *Engineer*
Victoria Ramires, *QC Mgr*
EMP: 41
SQ FT: 15,000
SALES (est): 9.6MM Privately Held
WEB: www.fit4flex.com
SIC: 3679 Electronic circuits

(P-18917)
FLEXTRONICS CORPORATION (DH)
6201 America Center Dr, Alviso
(95002-2563)
PHONE..................................803 936-5200
Marc A Onetto, *President*
Adeline Tan, *Bd of Directors*
Paul Baldassari, *Officer*
Mindy Dodson, *Vice Pres*
Scott Graybeal, *Vice Pres*
▲ EMP: 277
SQ FT: 350,000
SALES (est): 185.3MM
SALES (corp-wide): 26.2B Privately Held
SIC: 3679 3577 3571 Electronic circuits; computer peripheral equipment; electronic computers

(P-18918)
FREQUENCY MANAGEMENT INTL (PA)
15302 Bolsa Chica St, Huntington Beach
(92649-1245)
PHONE..................................714 373-8100
Kouros Sariri, *President*
Kevin Panizza, *Mktg Dir*
Gary Slacum, *Sales Staff*
EMP: 13
SQ FT: 16,000

SALES (est): 2.6MM Privately Held
WEB: www.frequencymanagement.com
SIC: 3679 Antennas, receiving

(P-18919)
FUELBOX INC
201 W Montecito St, Santa Barbara
(93101-3824)
PHONE..................................919 949-9179
Robert Herr, *CEO*
Ryan Heinberg, *CFO*
EMP: 11
SQ FT: 900
SALES: 450K Privately Held
SIC: 3679 Antennas, receiving

(P-18920)
GAR ENTERPRISES
Also Called: K.G.S.electronics Inc.
1396 W 9th St, Upland (91786-5724)
PHONE..................................909 985-4575
Alex Morales, *Manager*
EMP: 20
SALES (est): 874K
SALES (corp-wide): 34.4MM Privately Held
WEB: www.kgselectronics.com
SIC: 3679 3621 3577 Electronic loads & power supplies; motors & generators; computer peripheral equipment
PA: Gar Enterprises
418 E Live Oak Ave
Arcadia CA 91006
626 574-1175

(P-18921)
GAVIAL HOLDINGS INC (PA)
Also Called: Gavial Engineering & Mfg
1435 W Mccoy Ln, Santa Maria
(93455-1002)
PHONE..................................805 614-0060
Morgan Maxwell Connor, *CEO*
Dennis Levinski, *Engineer*
EMP: 15
SQ FT: 24,500
SALES (est): 80.4MM Privately Held
WEB: www.gavial.com
SIC: 3679 4911 6799 Electronic circuits; electric services; investors

(P-18922)
GAVIAL HOLDINGS INC
Also Called: Arrow Industries
139 Industrial Way, Buellton (93427-9592)
P.O. Box 198 (93427-0198)
PHONE..................................805 688-6734
Dave Watkins, *Branch Mgr*
EMP: 33
SALES (corp-wide): 80.4MM Privately Held
WEB: www.gavial.com
SIC: 3679 3545 Electronic circuits; machine tool accessories
PA: Gavial Holdings, Inc.
1435 W Mccoy Ln
Santa Maria CA 93455
805 614-0060

(P-18923)
GAVIAL ITC LLC
869 Ward Dr, Santa Barbara (93111-2920)
PHONE..................................805 614-0060
Morgan Connor, *President*
EMP: 99
SQ FT: 30,000
SALES (est): 2.7MM Privately Held
SIC: 3679 Transducers, electrical

(P-18924)
GES US (NEW ENGLAND) INC
1051 S East St, Anaheim (92805-5749)
PHONE..................................978 459-4434
Riachard Pelletier, *General Mgr*
EMP: 150
SQ FT: 70,000
SALES (est): 12.7MM
SALES (corp-wide): 2.5B Privately Held
WEB: www.ges-us.com
SIC: 3679 3672 Electronic circuits; printed circuit boards
HQ: Ges Investment Pte. Ltd.
28 Marsiling Lane
Singapore 73915
673 298-98

(P-18925)
GM ASSOCIATES INC
Also Called: G M Quartz
9824 Kitty Ln, Oakland (94603-1070)
PHONE...................................510 430-0806
Melvyn Nutter, *President*
Deborah Camp, *Vice Pres*
Terri Hartman, *Vice Pres*
Mark Lowe, *Technical Staff*
Bill Fesmire, *Mfg Mgr*
▲ EMP: 58
SQ FT: 8,000
SALES (est): 9.7MM **Privately Held**
WEB: www.gmassoc.com
SIC: 3679 3229 Quartz crystals, for electronic application; scientific glassware

(P-18926)
GOOCH & HOUSEGO PALO ALTO LLC (HQ)
Also Called: Crystal Technology
44247 Nobel Dr, Fremont (94538-3178)
PHONE...................................650 856-7911
Jon Fowler, *President*
Mark Batzdorf, *CFO*
▲ EMP: 65
SQ FT: 25,000
SALES (est): 10.7MM
SALES (corp-wide): 159.2MM **Privately Held**
WEB: www.crystaltechnology.com
SIC: 3679 Electronic crystals
PA: Gooch & Housego Plc
Dowlish Ford
Ilminster TA19
146 025-6440

(P-18927)
GROWTHSTOCK INC
2921 Daimler St, Santa Ana (92705-5810)
PHONE...................................949 660-9473
John T Sandberg, *Ch of Bd*
Michele Sandberg, *Vice Pres*
EMP: 200
SALES: 15MM **Privately Held**
WEB: www.sandberg.com
SIC: 3679 3825 8711 5999 Electronic circuits; test equipment for electronic & electrical circuits; consulting engineer; telephone equipment & systems

(P-18928)
GTRAN INC (PA)
829 Flynn Rd, Camarillo (93012-8702)
PHONE...................................805 445-4500
Ray Yu, *President*
Deepak Mehrotra, *CEO*
Douglas Holmes, *Vice Pres*
▲ EMP: 46
SQ FT: 226,000
SALES (est): 2.5MM **Privately Held**
WEB: www.gtran.com
SIC: 3679 Electronic circuits

(P-18929)
HARBOR ELECTRONICS INC (PA)
3021 Kenneth St, Santa Clara (95054-3416)
PHONE...................................408 988-6544
Michael Brannan, *President*
Paul Diehl, *Vice Pres*
EMP: 190
SQ FT: 50,000
SALES (est): 45MM **Privately Held**
WEB: www.harbor-electronics.com
SIC: 3679 3672 Harness assemblies for electronic use: wire or cable; printed circuit boards

(P-18930)
HARPER & TWO INC (PA)
2937 Cherry Ave, Signal Hill (90755-1910)
PHONE...................................562 424-3030
Dan Kilstofte, *President*
Jim Quilty, *Admin Sec*
EMP: 18
SALES (est): 2.7MM **Privately Held**
WEB: www.harperandtwo.com
SIC: 3679 Electronic circuits

(P-18931)
HART ELECTRONIC ASSEMBLY INC
21726 Lassen St, Chatsworth (91311-3623)
PHONE...................................818 709-2761
Lanell Allen, *Owner*
EMP: 100
SQ FT: 10,000
SALES (est): 12.5MM **Privately Held**
WEB: www.hartelectronic.com
SIC: 3679 3672 3441 Electronic circuits; printed circuit boards; fabricated structural metal

(P-18932)
HARWIL PRECISION PRODUCTS
541 Kinetic Dr, Oxnard (93030-7923)
PHONE...................................805 988-6800
Geoffrey Strand, *President*
Teresa Bowmar, *Treasurer*
Bruce Bowmar, *Vice Pres*
Cynthia Strand, *Admin Sec*
Ellis Anderson, *Sales Executive*
EMP: 30
SQ FT: 33,000
SALES (est): 5.9MM **Privately Held**
WEB: www.harwil.com
SIC: 3679 3625 3823 Electronic circuits; flow actuated electrical switches; industrial instrmnts msrmnt display/control process variable

(P-18933)
HELIOVOLT CORPORATION
3945 Freedom Cir Ste 560, Santa Clara (95054-1269)
PHONE...................................512 767-6079
Dong S Kim, *President*
Billy J Stanbery, *President*
John Prater, *Vice Pres*
Steve Darnell, *Principal*
Louay Eldada, *CTO*
▲ EMP: 98
SALES (est): 13.6MM **Privately Held**
WEB: www.heliovolt.com
SIC: 3679 Power supplies, all types: static

(P-18934)
HERLEY INDUSTRIES INC
4820 Estgate Mall Ste 200, San Diego (92121)
PHONE...................................858 812-7300
Brad Shear, *Manager*
EMP: 65
SALES (corp-wide): 984.8MM **Privately Held**
SIC: 3679 Microwave components
HQ: Herley Industries, Inc.
3061 Industry Dr
Lancaster PA 17603
717 397-2777

(P-18935)
HERMETIC SEAL CORPORATION (DH)
Also Called: Ametek HCC
4232 Temple City Blvd, Rosemead (91770-1592)
PHONE...................................626 443-8931
Andrew Goldfarb, *President*
Pedro Almanza, *IT/INT Sup*
George McCormack, *Sales Mgr*
Rene Ayala, *Warehouse Mgr*
EMP: 200
SQ FT: 36,000
SALES (est): 76.6MM
SALES (corp-wide): 4.8B **Publicly Held**
SIC: 3679 3469 Hermetic seals for electronic equipment; metal stampings
HQ: Hcc Industries Inc.
4232 Temple City Blvd
Rosemead CA 91770
626 443-8933

(P-18936)
HILLTRON CORPORATION
2528 Qume Dr Ste 4, San Jose (95131-1836)
PHONE...................................408 597-4424
Tanya Ahmed, *President*
EMP: 13
SALES (est): 1.8MM **Privately Held**
SIC: 3679 Electronic circuits

(P-18937)
HTI TURNKEY MANUFACTURING SVCS
2200 Zanker Rd Ste A, San Jose (95131-1111)
PHONE...................................408 955-0807
MAI Linh Tran, *CEO*
Thanah MAI Tran, *Admin Sec*
Vic Tinio, *Consultant*
EMP: 25
SQ FT: 10,000
SALES (est): 2MM **Privately Held**
WEB: www.hti9001.com
SIC: 3679 Harness assemblies for electronic use: wire or cable

(P-18938)
HUNTER TECHNOLOGY CORPORATION (DH)
1940 Milmont Dr, Milpitas (95035-2578)
PHONE...................................408 957-1300
Joseph F O'Neil, *President*
Mark Evans, *COO*
▲ EMP: 135 EST: 1987
SQ FT: 62,500
SALES (est): 45.7MM
SALES (corp-wide): 374.9MM **Privately Held**
WEB: www.hunterpcb.com
SIC: 3679 Microwave components
HQ: Sparton Corporation
425 N Martingale Rd
Schaumburg IL 60173
847 762-5800

(P-18939)
HWA IN AMERICA INC (PA)
Also Called: ORANGE PACK SOLUTION
1541 Santiago Ridge Way, San Diego (92154-7704)
PHONE...................................619 567-4539
Sun Duk Kim, *President*
Ji Lee, *Principal*
▲ EMP: 14 EST: 1997
SALES (est): 4.2MM **Privately Held**
SIC: 3679 5199 Static power supply converters for electronic applications; packaging materials

(P-18940)
I J RESEARCH INC
2919 Tech Ctr, Santa Ana (92705-5657)
PHONE...................................714 546-8522
Rick Yoon, *President*
Kevin Danh, *COO*
Sandy Yoon, *CFO*
Carla Guzman, *Manager*
◆ EMP: 35
SQ FT: 12,500
SALES (est): 6.1MM **Privately Held**
WEB: www.ijresearch.com
SIC: 3679 Hermetic seals for electronic equipment

(P-18941)
I SOURCE TECHNICAL SVCS INC
575 Rancho Cir, Irvine (92618)
PHONE...................................949 453-1500
Irene Horvath, *Branch Mgr*
EMP: 10 **Privately Held**
SIC: 3679 Electronic circuits
PA: I Source Technical Services, Inc.
5 Rancho Cir
Lake Forest CA 92630

(P-18942)
I SOURCE TECHNICAL SVCS INC (PA)
5 Rancho Cir, Lake Forest (92630-8324)
PHONE...................................949 453-1500
Irene Horvath, *President*
Mik Horvath, *Vice Pres*
David Tuza, *General Mgr*
EMP: 17
SALES (est): 1.7MM **Privately Held**
WEB: www.i-source.com
SIC: 3679 Electronic circuits

(P-18943)
IMERGY POWER SYSTEMS INC
3945 Freedom Cir Ste 560, Santa Clara (95054-1269)
PHONE...................................510 668-1485

William D Watkins, *CEO*
Kelly Truman, *President*
Jack Jenkins-Stark, *CFO*
Viraj Patel, *CFO*
Gilles Champagne, *Vice Pres*
▲ EMP: 40
SQ FT: 35,000
SALES (est): 9MM **Privately Held**
WEB: www.deeyaenergy.com
SIC: 3679 Electronic loads & power supplies

(P-18944)
IMPACT LLC
22521 Avenida Empresa # 107, Rcho STA Marg (92688-2041)
PHONE...................................714 546-6000
Phil Laney,
Tim Scanlon, *VP Sales*
EMP: 28
SALES (est): 3.3MM **Privately Held**
WEB: www.impactllc.com
SIC: 3679 3829 Electronic circuits; measuring & controlling devices

(P-18945)
INFINITE ELECTRONICS INC (HQ)
17792 Fitch, Irvine (92614-6020)
PHONE...................................949 261-1920
Penny Cotner, *President*
Krishnan Iyer, *Vice Pres*
EMP: 40
SQ FT: 40,000
SALES: 300MM **Privately Held**
SIC: 3679 Electronic circuits

(P-18946)
INSTRUMENT DESIGN ENG ASSOC I
Also Called: Idea
2923 Saturn St Ste F, Brea (92821-6260)
PHONE...................................714 525-3302
Sabrina Lu, *President*
EMP: 20
SALES (est): 2.7MM **Privately Held**
WEB: www.ledidea.com
SIC: 3679 3674 Electronic circuits; semiconductors & related devices

(P-18947)
INTEGRATED MICROWAVE CORP
Also Called: Imcsd
11353 Sorrento Valley Rd, San Diego (92121-1303)
PHONE...................................858 259-2600
Mary Ellen Clark, *CEO*
Allen Hobbs, *Vice Pres*
Wayne Mandak, *Vice Pres*
Steven Porter, *Vice Pres*
Kathy Hoof, *Executive*
◆ EMP: 85 EST: 1982
SQ FT: 24,142
SALES (est): 17.6MM **Privately Held**
WEB: www.imcsd.com
SIC: 3679 Microwave components

(P-18948)
INTEGRITY TECHNOLOGY CORP
2505 Technology Dr, Hayward (94545-4869)
PHONE...................................270 812-8867
J P Young, *President*
Paul Wagner, *Engineer*
Susan Whichard, *VP Sales*
J Garcia, *Manager*
EMP: 40
SQ FT: 4,000
SALES: 2.5MM **Privately Held**
WEB: www.integritytechnology.net
SIC: 3679 3677 Electronic circuits; electronic coils, transformers & other inductors

(P-18949)
INTERCTIVE DSPLAY SLUTIONS INC
490 Wald, Irvine (92618-4638)
PHONE...................................949 727-9493
Brian Chung, *President*
Paul Kitzerow, *Senior VP*
Son Park, *Vice Pres*
Danny Lee, *Opers Staff*
▲ EMP: 12

(PA)=Parent Co (HQ)=Headquarters (DH)=Div Headquarters
✿ = New Business established in last 2 years

2020 California
Manufacturers Register

769

P R O D U C T S & S V C S

SALES: 8.8MM **Privately Held**
WEB: www.pvdisplay.com
SIC: 3679 Liquid crystal displays (LCD)

(P-18950)
INTERFACE MASTERS TECH INC
150 E Brokaw Rd, San Jose (95112-4203)
PHONE................................408 441-9341
Benjamin Askarinam, *CEO*
Sima Askarinam, *President*
Jennifer Hang, *Program Mgr*
Modest Kravchuk, *Sr Software Eng*
Bill Kish, *CTO*
EMP: 50
SQ FT: 3,000
SALES (est): 13.8MM **Privately Held**
SIC: 3679 Electronic switches

(P-18951)
INTERLOG CORPORATION
Also Called: Interlog Construction
1295 N Knollwood Cir, Anaheim
(92801-1310)
PHONE................................714 529-7808
Justin H Kwon, *CEO*
Nathanael Kim, *Info Tech Mgr*
Jonathan Lee, *Purch Mgr*
Sunny Yim, *Manager*
▲ **EMP:** 20
SALES (est): 8MM **Privately Held**
SIC: 3679 Electronic circuits

(P-18952)
INTERNATIONAL ELECTRONIC DESIG (PA)
Also Called: Ied Group
2630 S Shannon St, Santa Ana
(92704-5230)
PHONE................................714 662-1018
Eben Benade, *CEO*
Eben Denade, *President*
▲ **EMP:** 10
SQ FT: 16,000
SALES: 4MM **Privately Held**
SIC: 3679 Electronic circuits

(P-18953)
IQD FREQUENCY PRODUCTS INC
777 E Tahqtz Cyn Way # 200, Palm Springs
(92262-6784)
PHONE................................760 318-2824
Neil Floodgate, *President*
EMP: 43
SALES (est): 277K
SALES (corp-wide): 13.6MM **Privately Held**
SIC: 3679 Microwave components
HQ: Iqd Frequency Products Limited
Station Road
Crewkerne
146 027-0200

(P-18954)
ISOLINK INC
880 Yosemite Way, Milpitas (95035-6360)
PHONE................................408 946-1968
David Aldrich, *CEO*
Jorge Rosario, *Treasurer*
Bill Cantarini, *Engrg Dir*
▲ **EMP:** 32
SQ FT: 16,600
SALES (est): 5.5MM
SALES (corp-wide): 3.3B **Publicly Held**
WEB: www.isolink.com
SIC: 3679 3827 Electronic circuits; optical
instruments & lenses
PA: Skyworks Solutions, Inc.
20 Sylvan Rd
Woburn MA 01801
781 376-3000

(P-18955)
J & L DIGITAL PRECISION INC
551 Taylor Way Ste 15, San Carlos
(94070-6252)
PHONE................................650 592-0170
John L Obertelli, *President*
Loretta Obertelli, *Corp Secy*
Gail Firpo, *Vice Pres*
Louis Firpo, *Vice Pres*
EMP: 11
SALES (est): 2MM **Privately Held**
WEB: www.jldigital.com
SIC: 3679 Electronic circuits

(P-18956)
J L COOPER ELECTRONICS INC
Also Called: Jlcooper
142 Arena St, El Segundo (90245-3901)
PHONE................................310 322-9990
James Loren Cooper, *President*
Mark Van Kirk, *Director*
▲ **EMP:** 25
SALES (est): 4.1MM **Privately Held**
WEB: www.jlcooper.com
SIC: 3679 Recording & playback apparatus, including phonograph

(P-18957)
J R V PRODUCTS INC
1314 N Harbor Blvd # 302, Santa Ana
(92703-1300)
P.O. Box 5645, Orange (92863-5645)
PHONE................................714 259-9772
Curt Shoup, *President*
John Beckingham, *President*
▲ **EMP:** 13
SQ FT: 6,000
SALES (est): 990K **Privately Held**
WEB: www.jrvproductsinc.com
SIC: 3679 Electronic switches; electronic
circuits; electronic loads & power supplies

(P-18958)
J&M MANUFACTURING INC
430 Aaron St, Cotati (94931-3016)
P.O. Box 2435, Rohnert Park (94927-2435)
PHONE................................707 795-8223
James O Judd Jr, *Owner*
Paul L Matthias, *CFO*
▲ **EMP:** 34
SQ FT: 25,000
SALES (est): 7.1MM **Privately Held**
WEB: www.jmmfg.com
SIC: 3679 3444 Electronic circuits; metal
housings, enclosures, casings & other
containers

(P-18959)
JAMES L HALL CO INCORPORATED (PA)
360 Tesconi Cir Ste B, Santa Rosa
(95401-4677)
P.O. Box 309 (95402-0309)
PHONE................................707 547-0775
Steve Vallarino, *President*
Morey Serpa, *CFO*
Linda Beyce, *Corp Secy*
EMP: 55 **EST:** 1919
SQ FT: 1,400
SALES (est): 8.2MM **Privately Held**
WEB: www.jetronics.com
SIC: 3679 Electronic circuits

(P-18960)
JASPER ELECTRONICS
1580 N Kellogg Dr, Anaheim (92807-1902)
PHONE................................714 917-0749
Robert Nishimoto, *CEO*
Hiroshi Tango, *Chairman*
Chandra Mehta, *Vice Pres*
Shailesh Patel, *Design Engr*
Bill Galey, *Project Mgr*
▲ **EMP:** 30
SQ FT: 17,000
SALES (est): 6.2MM **Privately Held**
WEB: www.jasperelectronics.com
SIC: 3679 Electronic loads & power supplies; power supplies, all types: static

(P-18961)
JAVAD EMS INC
900 Rock Ave, San Jose (95131-1615)
PHONE................................408 770-1700
Javad Ashjaee, *President*
Gary Walker, *Vice Pres*
Linda Bezoni, *Principal*
Pam Walke, *Principal*
▲ **EMP:** 95
SALES (est): 20MM **Privately Held**
SIC: 3679 Electronic circuits

(P-18962)
JAXX MANUFACTURING INC
Also Called: Craig Kackert Design Tech
1912 Angus Ave, Simi Valley (93063-3494)
PHONE................................805 526-4979
Greg Liu, *President*
Robert Barr, *Program Mgr*
Veronica Liu, *General Mgr*
Dan Smith, *CIO*

EMP: 45
SALES (est): 8.4MM **Privately Held**
SIC: 3679 Electronic circuits

(P-18963)
JAYCO INTERFACE TECHNOLOGY INC
1351 Pico St, Corona (92881-3373)
PHONE................................951 738-2000
Hemant Mistry, *President*
Shaila RAO, *Treasurer*
EMP: 40
SQ FT: 23,000
SALES (est): 7.6MM **Privately Held**
WEB: www.jaycopanels.com
SIC: 3679 5065 Electronic circuits; electronic parts & equipment

(P-18964)
JAYCO MMI INC
1351 Pico St, Corona (92881-3373)
PHONE................................951 738-2000
Shaila Mistry, *President*
Hemant Mistry, *Vice Pres*
EMP: 42 **EST:** 1992
SQ FT: 24,000
SALES (est): 5.3MM **Privately Held**
SIC: 3679 5065 3577 2759 Electronic circuits; electronic parts & equipment; computer peripheral equipment; commercial
printing; engineering services

(P-18965)
JDI DISPLAY AMERICA INC (PA)
1740 Tech Dr Ste 460, San Jose (95110)
PHONE................................408 501-3720
Atsuhiko Tokinosu, *President*
Shuichi Odsuka, *CEO*
Koichiro Taniyama, *CFO*
Michael Du, *Vice Pres*
Robert Bogdanoff, *District Mgr*
EMP: 19
SALES (est): 3.2MM **Privately Held**
SIC: 3679 7374 Liquid crystal displays
(LCD); computer processing services

(P-18966)
JDS TECHNOLOGIES
12200 Thatcher Ct, Poway (92064-6876)
PHONE................................858 486-8787
Jeff Stein, *Owner*
EMP: 14
SQ FT: 7,000
SALES (est): 1MM **Privately Held**
SIC: 3679 Electronic circuits

(P-18967)
JIC INDUSTRIAL CO INC
978 Hanson Ct, Milpitas (95035-3165)
PHONE................................408 935-9880
Frank Yen, *President*
▲ **EMP:** 15
SALES (est): 1.7MM **Privately Held**
WEB: www.jicusa.com
SIC: 3679 3678 3357 Electronic circuits;
electronic connectors; nonferrous wire-drawing & insulating

(P-18968)
JOLO INDUSTRIES INC
10432 Brightwood Dr, Santa Ana
(92705-1591)
PHONE................................714 554-6840
James S Giampiccolo, *President*
Theresa Giampiccolo, *Corp Secy*
Chip Giampiccolo, *Vice Pres*
EMP: 20 **EST:** 1968
SQ FT: 8,000
SALES (est): 1.8MM **Privately Held**
SIC: 3679 3678 Electronic circuits; electronic connectors

(P-18969)
JOMAR MACHINING INC
180 Constitution Dr Ste 8, Menlo Park
(94025-1137)
PHONE................................650 324-2143
Joe Bencsik, *President*
Margaret Bencsik, *Corp Secy*
EMP: 14
SQ FT: 3,600
SALES (est): 1.5MM **Privately Held**
SIC: 3679 Antennas, receiving; antennas,
satellite: household use; cores, magnetic;
cryogenic cooling devices for infrared detectors, masers

(P-18970)
K S EQUIPMENT INC
17 Hangar Way, Watsonville (95076-2454)
PHONE................................831 722-7173
Jeff Kidwell, *President*
Margaret Kidwell, *Corp Secy*
▲ **EMP:** 10
SQ FT: 13,000
SALES (est): 1.5MM **Privately Held**
WEB: www.ksequipment.com
SIC: 3679 Switches, stepping

(P-18971)
KAMA INTERCONNECT INC
8030 Remmet Ave Ste 3, Canoga Park
(91304-6411)
PHONE................................818 713-9810
Amir Behzadi, *President*
Abbas Ghasemi, *Corp Secy*
Ali Kolahi, *Vice Pres*
Ruberto Domanis, *Manager*
EMP: 10
SQ FT: 5,000
SALES (est): 1.6MM **Privately Held**
SIC: 3679 Electronic circuits; harness assemblies for electronic use: wire or cable

(P-18972)
KATOLEC DEVELOPMENT INC
6120 Business Center Ct, San Diego
(92154)
PHONE................................619 710-0075
Eisuke Kato, *President*
▲ **EMP:** 20
SALES (est): 6.8MM **Privately Held**
SIC: 3679 Electronic circuits
PA: Katolec Corporation
2-8-7, Edagawa
Koto-Ku TKY 135-0

(P-18973)
KAVLICO CORPORATION (DH)
1461 Lawrence Dr, Thousand Oaks
(91320-1303)
PHONE................................805 523-2000
Martha Sullivan, *President*
Nicolas Cortes, *Engineer*
Magdalena Manlulu, *Production*
Jeffrey Cote, *Director*
▲ **EMP:** 1390
SQ FT: 284,000
SALES (est): 479.9MM
SALES (corp-wide): 3.5B **Privately Held**
SIC: 3679 3829 3823 Transducers, electrical; measuring & controlling devices; industrial instrmnts msrmnt display/control
process variable
HQ: Custom Sensors & Technologies, Inc.
1461 Lawrence Dr
Thousand Oaks CA 91320
805 716-0322

(P-18974)
KAVLICO CORPORATION
2475 Pseo De Las Americas, San Diego
(92154-7255)
PHONE................................805 523-2000
EMP: 30
SALES (corp-wide): 3.5B **Privately Held**
SIC: 3679 3829 Transducers, electrical;
measuring & controlling devices
HQ: Kavlico Corporation
1461 Lawrence Dr
Thousand Oaks CA 91320
805 523-2000

(P-18975)
KELYTECH CORPORATION
1482 Gladding Ct, Milpitas (95035-6831)
PHONE................................408 935-0888
K C Wong, *President*
Stanley Chiu, *Vice Pres*
Kevin Wong, *Office Mgr*
Irene Wong, *Admin Sec*
EMP: 40
SQ FT: 8,500
SALES (est): 2MM **Privately Held**
WEB: www.kelytech.com
SIC: 3679 Electronic circuits

(P-18976)
KENJITSU USA CORP
9830 Siempre Viva Rd # 14, San Diego
(92154-7236)
PHONE................................619 734-5862

▲ = Import ▼=Export
◆ =Import/Export

Tien-Chen Tsou, *President*
▲ EMP: 15
SQ FT: 2,000
SALES: 800K **Privately Held**
SIC: 3679 2899 3674 Electronic loads &
power supplies; power supplies, all types:
static; static power supply converters for
electronic applications; battery acid; light
emitting diodes

(P-18977)
KG TECHNOLOGIES INC
6028 State Farm Dr, Rohnert Park
(94928-2133)
P.O. Box 7089, Cotati (94931-7089)
PHONE....................................888 513-1874
Philipp Gruner, *President*
Thomas Gruner, *Treasurer*
Lorene Rivera, *Sales Staff*
Aaron Buchholz, *Manager*
Satia Healey, *Accounts Mgr*
▲ EMP: 12
SQ FT: 5,600
SALES (est): 2.6MM
SALES (corp-wide): 991MM **Privately
Held**
WEB: www.kgtechnologies.net
SIC: 3679 Electronic circuits
HQ: Clodi L.L.C.
429 E Cotati Ave
Cotati CA 94931
707 664-5006

(P-18978)
KMW USA INC (HQ)
Also Called: KMW Communications
1818 E Orangethorpe Ave, Fullerton
(92831-5324)
PHONE....................................714 515-1100
Duk Y Kim, *President*
Burton Calloway, *Vice Pres*
Yeong Kim, *Vice Pres*
▲ EMP: 27
SQ FT: 4,500
SALES (est): 5.7MM **Privately Held**
WEB: www.kmwinc.com
SIC: 3679 5063 Electronic circuits; electri-
cal apparatus & equipment; control & sig-
nal wire & cable, including coaxial

(P-18979)
KRITECH CORPORATION (PA)
333 W 131st St, Los Angeles (90061-1103)
PHONE....................................310 538-9940
Louis Riberio, *President*
EMP: 15
SQ FT: 6,000
SALES (est): 1.3MM **Privately Held**
SIC: 3679 3053 Electronic circuits; gas-
kets, packing & sealing devices

(P-18980)
KRYTAR INC
1288 Anvilwood Ave, Sunnyvale (94089)
PHONE....................................408 734-5999
Nancy Russell, *Ch of Bd*
Douglas Hagan, *President*
Amy Renwald, *Admin Asst*
Michael Romero, *Engineer*
Hilda Clayton, *Purchasing*
EMP: 20
SALES (est): 3.8MM **Privately Held**
WEB: www.krytar.com
SIC: 3679 Microwave components; elec-
tronic circuits

(P-18981)
L P GLASSBLOWING INC
2322 Calle Del Mundo, Santa Clara
(95054-1007)
PHONE....................................408 988-7561
Leopold Pivk, *President*
Hilda Pivk, *Vice Pres*
EMP: 30
SQ FT: 6,700
SALES (est): 4.5MM **Privately Held**
WEB: www.lpglassblowing.com
SIC: 3679 3229 Quartz crystals, for elec-
tronic application; pressed & blown glass

(P-18982)
LABWORKS INC
2950 Airway Ave Ste A16, Costa Mesa
(92626-6019)
PHONE....................................714 549-1981
Gary Curtis Butts, *CEO*

Nick Lus, *Vice Pres*
EMP: 10
SQ FT: 5,000
SALES (est): 1.5MM **Privately Held**
WEB: www.labworks-inc.com
SIC: 3679 3812 Electronic circuits; search
& navigation equipment

(P-18983)
LANDMARK LCDS INC
12453 Blue Meadow Ct, Saratoga
(95070-3820)
PHONE....................................408 386-4257
Richard Kim, *President*
EMP: 10 EST: 2015
SALES (est): 512.7K **Privately Held**
SIC: 3679 Liquid crystal displays (LCD)

(P-18984)
LANDMARK TECHNOLOGY INC
1660 Mckee Rd, San Jose (95116-1263)
PHONE....................................408 435-8890
Sun Lu, *President*
Jean Lu, *CFO*
Fanny Yip, *Admin Asst*
▲ EMP: 22
SQ FT: 13,000
SALES (est): 3MM **Privately Held**
WEB: www.landmarktek.com
SIC: 3679 3674 Liquid crystal displays
(LCD); semiconductors & related devices

(P-18985)
LE VU
4234 54th St, McClellan (95652-2100)
PHONE....................................916 231-1594
Fred Frasier, *Chief*
EMP: 50
SALES (est): 3.2MM **Privately Held**
SIC: 3679 Electronic components

(P-18986)
**LEACH INTERNATIONAL CORP
(DH)**
6900 Orangethorpe Ave, Buena Park
(90620-1390)
P.O. Box 5032 (90622-5032)
PHONE....................................714 736-7537
Richard Brad Lawrence, *CEO*
Mark Thek, *President*
John Danley, *COO*
Alain Durand, *Vice Pres*
Grace Quintero, *Exec Dir*
EMP: 500 EST: 1919
SALES (est): 207.4MM
SALES (corp-wide): 3.8B **Publicly Held**
SIC: 3679 Electronic circuits
HQ: Esterline Technologies Corp
500 108th Ave Ne Ste 1500
Bellevue WA 98004
425 453-9400

(P-18987)
LG INNOTEK USA INC (HQ)
2540 N 1st St Ste 400, San Jose
(95131-1016)
PHONE....................................408 955-0364
Sung IL Yang, *President*
Harry Kang, *Marketing Mgr*
▲ EMP: 19
SQ FT: 71,168
SALES (est): 18MM **Privately Held**
SIC: 3679 Antennas, receiving

(P-18988)
**LHV POWER CORPORATION
(PA)**
10221 Buena Vista Ave A, Santee
(92071-4484)
PHONE....................................619 258-7700
James Gevarges, *President*
Ladge Leitner, *Technology*
▲ EMP: 25
SQ FT: 20,000
SALES (est): 3.5MM **Privately Held**
WEB: www.hitekpower.com
SIC: 3679 Power supplies, all types: static

(P-18989)
**LIBRA CABLE TECHNOLOGIES
INC**
Monterey Business Park 27, Torrance
(90503)
PHONE....................................310 618-8182
Palle Gravesen Jensen, *CEO*

Anne Sletto, *Sales Staff*
EMP: 12
SALES (est): 1.7MM
SALES (corp-wide): 7.5MM **Privately
Held**
SIC: 3679 Harness assemblies for elec-
tronic use: wire or cable
PA: Electronic House Uab
Dariaus Ir Gireno G. 149
Vilnius LT-02
523 067-51

(P-18990)
LIEDER DEVELOPMENT INC
1839 S Lake Pl, Ontario (91761-5789)
PHONE....................................909 947-7722
Kimball Chase, *CEO*
Paul Caraway, *President*
Beth Thomas, *Office Mgr*
EMP: 15
SQ FT: 7,200
SALES (est): 2.4MM **Privately Held**
WEB: www.liederdev.com
SIC: 3679 Microwave components

(P-18991)
LIGHTCROSS INC
2630 Corporate Pl, Monterey Park
(91754-7645)
PHONE....................................626 236-4500
Robert Barron, *President*
Daniel Kim, *Corp Secy*
Tom Smith, *Vice Pres*
EMP: 34 EST: 2000
SQ FT: 23,000
SALES (est): 3.2MM **Privately Held**
WEB: www.lightcross.com
SIC: 3679 Electronic circuits

(P-18992)
LIGHTECH FIBEROPTIC INC
1987 Adams Ave, San Leandro
(94577-1005)
PHONE....................................510 567-8700
Tracy Scott, *COO*
Jimmy Ko, *President*
EMP: 40
SQ FT: 11,000
SALES (est): 4.8MM **Privately Held**
WEB: www.lightech.net
SIC: 3679 3229 Electronic switches;
pressed & blown glass

(P-18993)
LITHIUMSTART INC
865 Hinckley Rd, Burlingame (94010-1502)
PHONE....................................800 520-8864
James Voss, *Principal*
Manavendra Sial, *Principal*
Edward Yocum, *Principal*
▲ EMP: 20
SQ FT: 20,000
SALES (est): 3.7MM **Privately Held**
SIC: 3679 Electronic loads & power sup-
plies
PA: Eaglepicher Technologies, Llc
C & Porter St
Joplin MO 64801

(P-18994)
**LOGITECH STREAMING MEDIA
INC**
7600 Gateway Blvd, Newark (94560-1159)
PHONE....................................510 795-8500
Bracken Darrell, *CEO*
Jeff Eisenman, *Sr Ntwrk Engine*
Dean Blackketter, *CTO*
Vishnu Vadla, *Info Tech Dir*
Michael Chen, *Software Engr*
▲ EMP: 24
SQ FT: 18,000
SALES (est): 2.5MM
SALES (corp-wide): 2.7B **Privately Held**
WEB: www.slimdevices.com
SIC: 3679 Electronic circuits
PA: Logitech International S.A.
Les Chatagnis
Apples VD
218 635-511

(P-18995)
LOTW LIGHT OF WORLD
1301 Maulhardt Ave, Oxnard (93030-7963)
PHONE....................................805 278-4806
Andrew Romero, *Owner*

Francisco Romero, *Production*
EMP: 10
SQ FT: 6,000
SALES (est): 981.7K **Privately Held**
SIC: 3679 Electronic circuits

(P-18996)
LUCERO CABLES INC
193 Stauffer Blvd, San Jose (95125-1042)
PHONE....................................408 536-0340
Madeline Eliasnia, *CEO*
Surendra Gupta, *President*
Art Eliasnia, *Chairman*
Iraj Pessian, *Treasurer*
Serjik Avanes, *Vice Pres*
▲ EMP: 110 EST: 1978
SQ FT: 50,000
SALES (est): 17.6MM **Privately Held**
WEB: www.luceromfg.com
SIC: 3679 3571 Harness assemblies for
electronic use: wire or cable; electronic
computers

(P-18997)
LUCIX CORPORATION (HQ)
800 Avenida Acaso Ste E, Camarillo
(93012-8758)
PHONE....................................805 987-6645
Mark Shahriary, *President*
Cheryl Johnson, *CFO*
D Ick Fanucchi, *Vice Pres*
▲ EMP: 83
SQ FT: 48,000
SALES (est): 31.5MM **Publicly Held**
WEB: www.lucix.com
SIC: 3679 8731 Microwave components;
commercial physical research

(P-18998)
M R F TECHNIQUES INC
Also Called: Rf Techniques
2245b Fortune Dr Ste B, San Jose
(95131-1806)
PHONE....................................408 433-1941
Sara Mathew, *President*
Moni Mathew, *Admin Sec*
EMP: 11
SQ FT: 3,000
SALES (est): 1.3MM **Privately Held**
WEB: www.rftechniques.com
SIC: 3679 3676 3674 3672 Electronic cir-
cuits; electronic resistors; integrated cir-
cuits, semiconductor networks, etc.;
semiconductor circuit networks; thin film
circuits; printed circuit boards

(P-18999)
M WAVE DESIGN CORPORATION
94 W Cochran St Ste B, Simi Valley
(93065-0948)
PHONE....................................805 499-8825
Ken Boswell, *CEO*
Bonnie Murray, *Admin Sec*
EMP: 10
SQ FT: 6,600
SALES (est): 1.5MM **Privately Held**
SIC: 3679 5065 Microwave components;
electronic parts & equipment

(P-19000)
M2 ANTENNA SYSTEMS INC
Also Called: Msquared
4402 N Selland Ave, Fresno (93722-4191)
PHONE....................................559 221-2271
Myrna Staal, *President*
Mike Staal, *Vice Pres*
EMP: 15
SQ FT: 10,000
SALES (est): 3MM **Privately Held**
WEB: www.m2inc.com
SIC: 3679 5999 3625 Antennas, receiv-
ing; mobile telephones & equipment; posi-
tioning controls, electric

(P-19001)
**MAGNETIC CIRCUIT ELEMENTS
INC**
Also Called: M C E
1540 Moffett St, Salinas (93905-3351)
PHONE....................................831 757-8752
John S Conklin, *CEO*
Lisa Battaglia, *Admin Sec*
Mark Pepple, *Design Engr*
EMP: 49
SQ FT: 11,000

SALES (est): 7.8MM **Privately Held**
WEB: www.mcemagnetics.com
SIC: 3679 3677 Electronic circuits; electronic coils, transformers & other inductors

(P-19002)
MAGNETIC DESIGN LABS INC
1636 E Edinger Ave Ste H, Santa Ana (92705-5020)
PHONE....................714 558-3355
ABI Kazem, *Principal*
Judith Kazem, *President*
Judith A Kazem, *CEO*
Kamran Kazem, *Vice Pres*
EMP: 15
SQ FT: 6,000
SALES (est): 1.3MM **Privately Held**
WEB: www.magneticdesign.com
SIC: 3679 5065 Power supplies, all types: static; electronic parts & equipment

(P-19003)
MAGNETIC SENSORS CORP
1365 N Mccan St, Anaheim (92806-1316)
PHONE....................714 630-8380
Charles Boudakian, *President*
Don Payne, *Vice Pres*
Mario Gregory, *Electrical Engi*
Grace Bagwell, *Finance Dir*
Pauline Garcia, *Marketing Staff*
EMP: 43
SQ FT: 15,000
SALES (est): 9.2MM **Privately Held**
WEB: www.magsensors.com
SIC: 3679 3677 Transducers, electrical; coil windings, electronic

(P-19004)
MAGNITUDE ELECTRONICS LLC
926 Bransten Rd, San Carlos (94070-4029)
PHONE....................650 551-1850
Hal White, *Mng Member*
Gilles Grosgurin,
▲ **EMP:** 12
SQ FT: 2,500
SALES (est): 5MM **Privately Held**
WEB: www.magnitude-electronics.com
SIC: 3679 Electronic circuits

(P-19005)
MANUTRONICS INC
736 S Hillview Dr, Milpitas (95035-5455)
PHONE....................408 262-6579
Cuong Tran, *CEO*
EMP: 14 **EST:** 2013
SALES (est): 2.3MM **Privately Held**
SIC: 3679 Electronic circuits

(P-19006)
MARKI MICROWAVE INC
215 Vineyard Ct, Morgan Hill (95037-7121)
PHONE....................408 778-4200
Ferenc A Marki, *President*
Christine Marki, *CFO*
Justin Boyle, *Technical Staff*
Lance Bassett, *Controller*
EMP: 45
SQ FT: 9,800
SALES (est): 10.8MM **Privately Held**
WEB: www.markimicrowave.com
SIC: 3679 Microwave components

(P-19007)
MASK TECHNOLOGY INC
2601 Oak St, Santa Ana (92707-3720)
PHONE....................714 557-3383
Andrew Holzmann, *President*
Joanne Deblis, *Director*
EMP: 25
SQ FT: 9,800
SALES (est): 3.1MM **Privately Held**
WEB: www.masktek.com
SIC: 3679 Electronic circuits

(P-19008)
MAURY MICROWAVE INC
2900 Inland Empire Blvd, Ontario (91764-4804)
PHONE....................909 987-4715
Gregory M Maury, *CEO*
Marc A Maury, *President*
Ted Lewis, *Vice Pres*
Jane Cary, *General Mgr*

Monica Amos, *Admin Asst*
▲ **EMP:** 115
SQ FT: 6,000
SALES (est): 39.2MM **Privately Held**
WEB: www.maurymw.com
SIC: 3679 Microwave components

(P-19009)
MC ELECTRONICS LLC
1891 Airway Dr, Hollister (95023-9099)
PHONE....................831 637-1651
Jan Kreminski,
Christy Trevino, *Program Mgr*
Lou Murfillo, *Engrg Dir*
Crystal Herrera, *Accounting Mgr*
Rick Dresser, *Purchasing*
EMP: 399
SQ FT: 6,000
SALES (est): 90MM
SALES (corp-wide): 372.1MM **Privately Held**
WEB: www.mcelectronics.com
SIC: 3679 Harness assemblies for electronic use: wire or cable
PA: Volex Plc
Holbrook House
Richmond TW10
203 370-8830

(P-19010)
MEAN WELL USA INC
44030 Fremont Blvd, Fremont (94538-6042)
PHONE....................510 683-8886
Shiao Ta Tung, *CEO*
David Tung, *President*
Mike Shien, *MIS Staff*
Benny Cheung, *Engineer*
Kai LI, *Engineer*
▲ **EMP:** 19
SQ FT: 13,500
SALES (est): 4.4MM **Privately Held**
WEB: www.meanwellusa.com
SIC: 3679 Static power supply converters for electronic applications
PA: Mean Well Enterprises Co., Ltd.
No. 28, Wu Chuan 3rd Rd.,
New Taipei City TAP 24891

(P-19011)
MEMBRANE SWITCH AND PANEL INC
3198 Arprt Loop Dr Ste K, Costa Mesa (92626)
PHONE....................714 957-6905
John B Corzine, *President*
EMP: 16
SQ FT: 5,000
SALES (est): 2.1MM **Privately Held**
WEB: www.membraneusa.com
SIC: 3679 Antennas, receiving

(P-19012)
MERCURY UNITED ELECTRONICS INC
Also Called: Global Electronics Intl
9804 Cres Ctr Dr Ste 603, Rancho Cucamonga (91730-5782)
PHONE....................909 466-0427
Chih-Hsun Yen, *CEO*
Jason Yen, *President*
Jean Hsi, *Corp Secy*
Jyh Yaw Yen, *Vice Pres*
EMP: 25
SQ FT: 8,460
SALES (est): 3MM **Privately Held**
SIC: 3679 5065 Quartz crystals, for electronic application; paging & signaling equipment

(P-19013)
MICRO CHIPS OF AMERICA INC
5302 Comercio Ln Apt 1, Woodland Hills (91364-2049)
PHONE....................818 577-9543
Sara Baires, *President*
Steve Levy, *CEO*
David Levy, *Treasurer*
Erets Levy, *Vice Pres*
EMP: 25
SQ FT: 3,000
SALES (est): 2MM **Privately Held**
SIC: 3679 3674 Electronic circuits; semiconductors & related devices

(P-19014)
MICRO LAMBDA WIRELESS INC
46515 Landing Pkwy, Fremont (94538-6421)
PHONE....................510 770-9221
John Nguyen, *President*
Alexander Chenakin, *Vice Pres*
David Suddarth, *Vice Pres*
Myra Verret, *Administration*
Susan Sun, *Info Tech Mgr*
EMP: 39
SQ FT: 19,000
SALES (est): 8MM **Privately Held**
WEB: www.microlambdawireless.com
SIC: 3679 5065 3663 Microwave components; electronic parts & equipment; radio & TV communications equipment

(P-19015)
MICROFABRICA INC
7911 Haskell Ave, Van Nuys (91406-1909)
PHONE....................888 964-2763
Eric Miller, *Principal*
Uri Frodis, *Senior VP*
Richard Chen, *Vice Pres*
Greg Schmitz, *Vice Pres*
Arun Veeramani, *Design Engr*
EMP: 50
SQ FT: 39,000
SALES (est): 12.4MM **Privately Held**
WEB: www.microfabrica.com
SIC: 3679 Electronic circuits

(P-19016)
MICROMETALS INC (PA)
5615 E La Palma Ave, Anaheim (92807-2109)
PHONE....................714 970-9400
Richard H Barden, *CEO*
Chris Oliver, *Admin Mgr*
Pedro Lopez, *QA Dir*
Steve Collier, *Info Tech Dir*
Dale Nicol, *Engineer*
▲ **EMP:** 90 **EST:** 1951
SQ FT: 50,000
SALES (est): 34MM **Privately Held**
WEB: www.micrometals.com
SIC: 3679 Cores, magnetic

(P-19017)
MICROMETALS/TEXAS INC
5615 E La Palma Ave, Anaheim (92807-2109)
PHONE....................325 677-8753
Richard H Barden, *President*
Angie Moore, *Human Res Dir*
◆ **EMP:** 250
SQ FT: 20,000
SALES (est): 32MM
SALES (corp-wide): 34MM **Privately Held**
WEB: www.micrometals.com
SIC: 3679 Cores, magnetic
PA: Micrometals, Inc.
5615 E La Palma Ave
Anaheim CA 92807
714 970-9400

(P-19018)
MICROSEMI SEMICONDUCTOR US INC
3843 Brickway Blvd # 100, Santa Rosa (95403-9059)
PHONE....................707 568-5900
Julio Perdomo, *CEO*
Hiroshi Kondoh, *COO*
Jerome C Nathan, *CFO*
Jeff Meyer, *CTO*
▼ **EMP:** 72
SQ FT: 26,000
SALES (est): 9.5MM
SALES (corp-wide): 5.3B **Publicly Held**
WEB: www.centellax.com
SIC: 3679 Microwave components
HQ: Cnt Acquisition Corp.
1 Enterprise
Aliso Viejo CA 92656
949 380-6100

(P-19019)
MICROWAVE TECHNOLOGY INC (DH)
4268 Solar Way, Fremont (94538-6335)
PHONE....................510 651-6700
Nathan Zommer, *CEO*

Cynthia Tran, *Chief Mktg Ofcr*
Jerry Lee, *Officer*
Shawn Smith, *Engineer*
Ted Tu, *Engineer*
EMP: 45
SQ FT: 30,800
SALES (est): 7MM
SALES (corp-wide): 1.7B **Publicly Held**
WEB: www.mwtinc.com
SIC: 3679 3663 Commutators, electronic; amplifiers, RF power & IF
HQ: Ixys, Llc
1590 Buckeye Dr
Milpitas CA 95035
408 457-9000

(P-19020)
MINATRONIC INC
1139 13th St, Paso Robles (93446-2644)
PHONE....................805 239-8864
Max Clinger, *President*
David Kudija, *Executive*
EMP: 19
SALES (est): 2MM **Privately Held**
SIC: 3679 5065 Electronic circuits; electronic parts & equipment

(P-19021)
MITSUBISHI ELECTRIC VISUAL
Also Called: Mevsa
10833 Valley View St # 300, Cypress (90630-5046)
PHONE....................800 553-7278
Tadashi Hiraoka, *CEO*
Kenichiro Yamanishi, *Chairman*
Perry Pappous, *Admin Sec*
▲ **EMP:** 150
SALES (est): 56.8MM **Privately Held**
SIC: 3679 Liquid crystal displays (LCD)
PA: Mitsubishi Electric Corporation
2-7-3, Marunouchi
Chiyoda-Ku TKY 100-0

(P-19022)
MULTIMEDIA LED INC (PA)
4225 Prado Rd Ste 108, Corona (92880-7443)
PHONE....................951 280-7500
Steven Craig, *CEO*
Alex Birner, *President*
Rick Vanrensselaer, *Engineer*
Ernest Lai, *Controller*
▲ **EMP:** 14
SALES (est): 1.6MM **Privately Held**
SIC: 3679 Electronic circuits

(P-19023)
MUSTARD SEED TECHNOLOGIES INC
Also Called: P K C
3000 W Warner Ave, Santa Ana (92704-5311)
PHONE....................714 556-7007
Bruce T McCleave Sr, *President*
Roger Litz, *CFO*
James R Seiler Jr, *Admin Sec*
Jorge Andrade, *Engineer*
Joel Longoria, *Natl Sales Mgr*
▲ **EMP:** 134
SQ FT: 26,000
SALES (est): 41MM **Privately Held**
WEB: www.4pkc.com
SIC: 3679 5065 Harness assemblies for electronic use: wire or cable; electronic parts & equipment

(P-19024)
MUZIK INC (PA)
9220 W Sunset Blvd # 112, West Hollywood (90069-3501)
PHONE....................973 615-1223
Jason Hardi, *CEO*
Marc Greenspoon, *President*
Joakim Ostarson, *COO*
Greenspoon Marc, *Vice Pres*
EMP: 34
SQ FT: 4,140
SALES (est): 1.4MM **Privately Held**
SIC: 3679 Headphones, radio

(P-19025)
NEW VISION DISPLAY INC (DH)
1430 Blue Oaks Blvd # 100, Roseville (95747-5156)
PHONE....................916 786-8111

▲ = Import ▼=Export
◆ =Import/Export

Jeff Olyniec, *CEO*
Owen Chen, *Ch of Bd*
Alan M Lefko, *CFO*
Jack Powers, *Engineer*
◆ **EMP:** 28
SQ FT: 2,000
SALES: 300MM
SALES (corp-wide): 297.1MM **Privately Held**
SIC: 3679 Liquid crystal displays (LCD)

(P-19026)
NEWAYS INC
28202 Cabot Rd Ste 100, Laguna Niguel (92677-1247)
PHONE.................................949 264-1542
EMP: 38
SALES (est): 1.9MM **Privately Held**
SIC: 3679

(P-19027)
NEWVAC LLC
American Def Interconnect Div
9330 De Soto Ave, Chatsworth (91311-4926)
PHONE.................................310 525-1205
Garrett Hoffman, *Vice Pres*
George Fry, *Manager*
EMP: 26
SALES (corp-wide): 49MM **Privately Held**
SIC: 3679 Harness assemblies for electronic use: wire or cable
HQ: Newvac, Llc
9330 De Soto Ave
Chatsworth CA 91311
310 525-1205

(P-19028)
NEXYN CORPORATION
1287 Forgewood Ave, Sunnyvale (94089-2216)
PHONE.................................408 962-0895
Joyce Benton, *CEO*
Ll Benton, *Ch of Bd*
Robert Benton, *President*
Jim Chen, *CFO*
EMP: 10
SQ FT: 5,000
SALES (est): 1.5MM **Privately Held**
WEB: www.nexyn.com
SIC: 3679 Oscillators

(P-19029)
NORTRA CABLES INC
570 Gibraltar Dr, Milpitas (95035-6315)
PHONE.................................408 942-1106
Jim Love, *President*
Lyn Hickey, *Shareholder*
Andy O'Brien, *Programmer Anys*
Pat Wilder, *QC Mgr*
Gabriel Venegas, *Facilities Mgr*
EMP: 60
SQ FT: 14,000
SALES (est): 14.8MM **Privately Held**
WEB: www.nortra-cables.com
SIC: 3679 Harness assemblies for electronic use: wire or cable

(P-19030)
NOVANTA CORPORATION
4575 Cushing Pkwy, Fremont (94538-6466)
PHONE.................................510 770-1417
EMP: 20 **Publicly Held**
SIC: 3679 3825 8711 Liquid crystal displays (LCD); digital test equipment, electronic & electrical circuits; engineering services
HQ: Novanta Corporation
125 Middlesex Tpke
Bedford MA 01730
781 266-5700

(P-19031)
NOVANTA CORPORATION
Also Called: Reach Technology
5750 Hellyer Ave, San Jose (95138-1000)
PHONE.................................408 754-4176
Kariem Khadr, *Branch Mgr*
Cindy Tofa, *Purchasing*
Dan Neumann, *Opers Staff*
Sarah Harrington, *Marketing Staff*
Janis Marshall, *Sales Staff*
EMP: 20 **Publicly Held**
SIC: 3679 Liquid crystal displays (LCD)

HQ: Novanta Corporation
125 Middlesex Tpke
Bedford MA 01730
781 266-5700

(P-19032)
NRC MANUFACTURING INC
47690 Westinghouse Dr, Fremont (94539-7473)
PHONE.................................510 438-9400
Rata Chea, *President*
David Hang, *CFO*
EMP: 18
SQ FT: 16,000
SALES: 3MM **Privately Held**
SIC: 3679 Electronic circuits

(P-19033)
O M JONES INC
Also Called: Micro-Tronics
18897 Microtronics Way, Sonora (95370-9288)
P.O. Box 4375 (95370-1375)
PHONE.................................209 532-1008
Lawrence Jones, *President*
Olga Jones, *CFO*
Kevin Jones, *Vice Pres*
Mark Knowles, *Vice Pres*
Gina Prock, *Vice Pres*
EMP: 23 **EST:** 1978
SQ FT: 7,300
SALES (est): 2.4MM **Privately Held**
WEB: www.micro-tronics.net
SIC: 3679 Microwave components

(P-19034)
OASIS MATERIALS COMPANY LP
12131 Community Rd Ste D, Poway (92064-8893)
PHONE.................................858 486-8846
Frank Polese, *President*
Christopher Bateman, *Partner*
Stephen Nootens, *Partner*
Ryan Dutcher, *Graphic Designe*
Shane Lenihan, *Engineer*
EMP: 35
SQ FT: 22,000
SALES (est): 7.9MM **Privately Held**
SIC: 3679 Electronic circuits; hermetic seals for electronic equipment

(P-19035)
OBERON CO
7216 Via Colina, San Jose (95139-1130)
PHONE.................................408 227-3730
Inez Termerson, *President*
Ian Temerson, *Manager*
EMP: 85
SALES (est): 5.2MM **Privately Held**
WEB: www.oberon.net
SIC: 3679 Electronic circuits

(P-19036)
OCG INC
17952 Lyons Cir, Huntington Beach (92647-7167)
PHONE.................................714 375-4024
Jocelyn Lucas-Skarzenski, *President*
▲ **EMP:** 75
SALES (est): 10.5MM **Privately Held**
WEB: www.ocgconnect.com
SIC: 3679 Harness assemblies for electronic use: wire or cable

(P-19037)
OMEGA LEADS INC
Also Called: Wire Harness & Cable Assembly
1509 Colorado Ave, Santa Monica (90404-3316)
PHONE.................................310 394-6786
Jeff Sweet Sr, *President*
Carole Faxon, *Technology*
Cynthia Gonzalez, *Technology*
EMP: 20
SQ FT: 7,200
SALES (est): 4.3MM **Privately Held**
WEB: www.omegaleads.com
SIC: 3679 Harness assemblies for electronic use: wire or cable

(P-19038)
OMNI CONNECTION INTL INC
126 Via Trevizio, Corona (92879-1772)
PHONE.................................951 898-6232
Henry Cheng, *President*

Phyllis Ting, *Vice Pres*
▲ **EMP:** 410
SQ FT: 65,000
SALES (est): 77.7MM **Privately Held**
WEB: www.omni-conn.com
SIC: 3679 Harness assemblies for electronic use: wire or cable

(P-19039)
OMNIYIG INC
3350 Scott Blvd Bldg 66, Santa Clara (95054-3174)
PHONE.................................408 988-0843
William Capogeannis, *Ch of Bd*
Cathleen Capogeannis, *Treasurer*
Maria Rosales, *Office Mgr*
Michaela Nieblas, *Assistant*
EMP: 26
SQ FT: 12,000
SALES (est): 4.4MM **Privately Held**
WEB: www.omniyig.com
SIC: 3679 Microwave components

(P-19040)
ONSHORE TECHNOLOGIES INC
2771 Plaza Dl Amo 802-8, Torrance (90503)
PHONE.................................310 533-4888
Max Van Orden, *President*
EMP: 25
SALES (est): 5.9MM **Privately Held**
SIC: 3679 Harness assemblies for electronic use: wire or cable

(P-19041)
OPTIMUM DESIGN ASSOCIATES INC (PA)
1075 Serpentine Ln Ste A, Pleasanton (94566-4809)
PHONE.................................925 401-2004
Nick A Barbin, *CEO*
Roger Hileman, *CFO*
Everett Frank, *General Mgr*
Clinton Gann, *Engineer*
Nick Barbin, *Director*
◆ **EMP:** 68
SQ FT: 22,000
SALES: 20MM **Privately Held**
WEB: www.optimumdesign.com
SIC: 3679 3577 8711 Electronic circuits; computer peripheral equipment; engineering services

(P-19042)
OPTO 22
43044 Business Park Dr, Temecula (92590-3614)
PHONE.................................951 695-3000
Mark Engman, *President*
Kathleen Roe, *Corp Secy*
Benson Hougland, *Vice Pres*
Bob Sheffres, *Vice Pres*
Jonathan Fischer, *Software Dev*
◆ **EMP:** 200 **EST:** 1974
SQ FT: 135,000
SALES (est): 54.8MM **Privately Held**
WEB: www.opto22.com
SIC: 3679 3823 3625 Electronic switches; industrial instrmnts msrmnt display/control process variable; relays & industrial controls

(P-19043)
ORMET CIRCUITS INC
6555 Nncy Rdge Dr Ste 200, San Diego (92121)
PHONE.................................858 831-0010
Till Langner, *CEO*
◆ **EMP:** 22
SQ FT: 18,000
SALES (est): 1.6MM
SALES (corp-wide): 16.9B **Privately Held**
SIC: 3679 Electronic circuits
HQ: Emd Performance Materials Corp.
1200 Intrepid Ave Ste 3
Philadelphia PA 19112
888 367-3275

(P-19044)
OXFORD INSTRUMENTS X-RAY TECH
Also Called: X-Ray Technology Group
360 El Pueblo Rd, Scotts Valley (95066-4228)
PHONE.................................831 439-9729
Bernard Scanlan, *CEO*

Bryant Grigsby, *Engrg Dir*
Randy Nolan, *Engineer*
Viveka Barnes, *Controller*
▲ **EMP:** 69
SQ FT: 6,600
SALES (est): 14.9MM
SALES (corp-wide): 429.1MM **Privately Held**
WEB: www.oxfordxtg.com
SIC: 3679 3844 Power supplies, all types: static; X-ray apparatus & tubes
HQ: Oxford Instruments Holdings, Inc.
600 Milik St
Carteret NJ 07008
732 541-1300

(P-19045)
PACMAG INC
Also Called: Pacific Magnetics
87 Georgina St, Chula Vista (91910-6121)
PHONE.................................619 872-0343
Mary Hill, *President*
Francisco Perez, *Engineer*
▲ **EMP:** 17
SALES (est): 2.8MM **Privately Held**
SIC: 3679 Electronic circuits

(P-19046)
PARTSEARCH TECHNOLOGIES INC (DH)
Also Called: Andrews Electronics
27460 Avenue Scott D, Valencia (91355-3472)
PHONE.................................800 289-0300
Hubert Joly, *CEO*
EMP: 23
SQ FT: 10,000
SALES (est): 5.9MM
SALES (corp-wide): 42.8B **Publicly Held**
WEB: www.partsearch.com
SIC: 3679 Commutators, electronic

(P-19047)
PCH INTERNATIONAL USA INC
Also Called: Pch Lime Lab
135 Mississippi St Fl 1, San Francisco (94107-2536)
PHONE.................................415 643-5463
William Casey, *CEO*
Sean Peters, *VP Bus Dvlpt*
Matt Crichton, *Business Dir*
Diane Sullivan, *Business Dir*
Dan Klempay, *Comms Mgr*
EMP: 36
SALES (est): 25.9MM **Privately Held**
SIC: 3679 Antennas, receiving

(P-19048)
PENUMBRA BRANDS INC
1010 S Coast Highway 101, Encinitas (92024-5002)
PHONE.................................385 336-6120
Gentry Jensen, *CEO*
Anne McKnight, *VP Mktg*
EMP: 16
SALES (est): 3.1MM **Privately Held**
SIC: 3679 Antennas, receiving

(P-19049)
PLANAR MONOLITHICS INDS INC
4921 Robert J Mathews, El Dorado Hills (95762-5772)
PHONE.................................916 542-1401
Ashok Gorwara, *President*
EMP: 40
SQ FT: 40,000 **Privately Held**
SIC: 3679 3677 Attenuators; electronic circuits; electronic switches; oscillators; filtration devices, electronic
PA: Planar Monolithics Industries, Inc.
7311 Grove Rd Ste F
Frederick MD 21704

(P-19050)
PPST INC (PA)
17692 Fitch, Irvine (92614-6022)
PHONE.................................800 421-1921
Kevin J Voelcker, *President*
▲ **EMP:** 35
SALES (est): 17.5MM **Privately Held**
SIC: 3679 Power supplies, all types: static

PRODUCTS & SVCS

(P-19051)
PRECISION ENGINEERING INDS
Also Called: Precision Engineering Industry
11627 Cantara St, North Hollywood
(91605-1604)
PHONE...............................818 767-8590
Greg Kellzi, *President*
▲ EMP: 15
SQ FT: 23,975
SALES (est): 1.8MM **Privately Held**
SIC: 3679 5063 Electronic circuits; burglar
alarm systems

(P-19052)
PRECISION HERMETIC TECH INC
1940 W Park Ave, Redlands (92373-8042)
PHONE...............................909 381-6011
Daniel B Schachtel, *President*
Sari Schachtel, *CFO*
Richard Martin, *Engineer*
Jim Padilla, *Senior Engr*
Tony Mejia, *Plant Mgr*
EMP: 77
SQ FT: 25,000
SALES (est): 13.5MM **Privately Held**
WEB: www.pht.net
SIC: 3679 Hermetic seals for electronic
equipment

(P-19053)
PRED TECHNOLOGIES USA INC
7855 Fay Ave Ste 310, La Jolla
(92037-4280)
PHONE...............................858 999-2114
Charles Speidel, *CEO*
EMP: 70 EST: 2016
SALES (est): 162.8K **Privately Held**
SIC: 3679 Headphones, radio

(P-19054)
PSC CIRCUITS INC
5160 Rivergrade Rd, Baldwin Park
(91706-1406)
PHONE...............................626 373-1728
Pashih Oliver Su, *President*
▲ EMP: 30 EST: 2000
SALES (est): 2.8MM **Privately Held**
WEB: www.psccircuits.com
SIC: 3679 Electronic circuits

(P-19055)
PULSE ELECTRONICS CORPORATION (HQ)
15255 Innovation Dr # 100, San Diego
(92128-3410)
PHONE...............................858 674-8100
Mark C J Twaalfhoven, *CEO*
Kimerbly Gillette, *Executive*
Alan Wong, *Technology*
James Butler, *Finance*
Bruce Elliott, *Sales Mgr*
▲ EMP: 65 EST: 1947
SQ FT: 50,000
SALES (est): 457.3MM
SALES (corp-wide): 652.7MM **Privately
Held**
WEB: www.pulseelectronics.com
SIC: 3679 3612 3663 Electronic circuits;
transformers, except electric; antennas,
transmitting & communications
PA: Ocm Pe Holdings, L.P.
333 S Grand Ave Fl 28
Los Angeles CA 90071
213 830-6213

(P-19056)
Q MICROWAVE INC
1591 Pioneer Way, El Cajon (92020-1637)
PHONE...............................619 258-7322
Eric Maat, *CEO*
Craig Higginson, *President*
Craig Shauan, *Vice Pres*
Leah Diehl, *Purch Agent*
Tom Lake, *QC Mgr*
EMP: 84
SQ FT: 18,000
SALES (est): 12MM **Privately Held**
WEB: www.qmicrowave.com
SIC: 3679 5065 Microwave components;
electronic parts & equipment

(P-19057)
Q TECH CORPORATION
10150 Jefferson Blvd, Culver City
(90232-3502)
PHONE...............................310 836-7900
Sally Phillips, *President*
Rosa Menendez, *Vice Pres*
Richard Taylor, *Executive*
Minh Dao, *Program Mgr*
Basheer Remtulla, *Program Mgr*
EMP: 200
SQ FT: 21,000
SALES (est): 48.7MM **Privately Held**
WEB: www.q-tech.com
SIC: 3679 Oscillators

(P-19058)
Q-FLEX INC
1301 E Hunter Ave, Santa Ana
(92705-4133)
PHONE...............................714 664-0101
Nayna Uka, *President*
Nalini Celio, *Corp Secy*
Pete Uka, *Vice Pres*
▲ EMP: 22 EST: 1988
SQ FT: 7,200
SALES (est): 3.7MM **Privately Held**
SIC: 3679 Electronic circuits

(P-19059)
QORVO CALIFORNIA INC
Also Called: Qorvo US
950 Lawrence Dr, Newbury Park
(91320-1522)
PHONE...............................805 480-5050
Charles J Abronson, *Ch of Bd*
Mark Lampenfeld, *President*
Paul O Daughenbaugh, *CEO*
Ralph G Quinsey, *Chairman*
Susan Liles, *Treasurer*
EMP: 49
SQ FT: 11,000
SALES (est): 9.7MM
SALES (corp-wide): 3B **Publicly Held**
WEB: www.capwireless.com
SIC: 3679 Electronic circuits
HQ: Qorvo Us, Inc.
2300 Ne Brookwood Pkwy
Hillsboro OR 97124
336 664-1233

(P-19060)
QORVO US INC
950 Lawrence Dr, Newbury Park
(91320-1522)
PHONE...............................805 480-5099
Paul Daughenbaugh, *Branch Mgr*
EMP: 49
SALES (corp-wide): 3B **Publicly Held**
SIC: 3679 Electronic circuits
HQ: Qorvo Us, Inc.
2300 Ne Brookwood Pkwy
Hillsboro OR 97124
336 664-1233

(P-19061)
QUALITY QUARTZ ENGINEERING INC (PA)
8484 Central Ave, Newark (94560-3430)
PHONE...............................510 791-1013
Scott Moseley, *CEO*
Kevin Cordia, *Vice Pres*
Mezhgan Karim, *Office Mgr*
Melissa Richards, *Accounts Mgr*
▲ EMP: 24
SQ FT: 20,000
SALES (est): 11.7MM **Privately Held**
WEB: www.qqe.com
SIC: 3679 Quartz crystals, for electronic
application

(P-19062)
QUANTUM DIGITAL TECHNOLOGY INC
1525 W Alton Ave, Santa Ana
(92704-7219)
PHONE...............................310 325-4949
Kaveh Ayria, *CEO*
EMP: 15
SQ FT: 3,000
SALES (est): 2.5MM **Privately Held**
WEB: www.quantumdigitaltechnology.com
SIC: 3679 Electronic crystals

(P-19063)
RADARSONICS INC
1190 N Grove St, Anaheim (92806-2109)
PHONE...............................714 630-7288
Deborah Rhea, *President*
▲ EMP: 15
SQ FT: 12,000
SALES (est): 2.3MM **Privately Held**
SIC: 3679 5099 Transducers, electrical;
firearms & ammunition, except sporting

(P-19064)
RANTEC MICROWAVE SYSTEMS INC
Microwave Specialty Company
2066 Wineridge Pl, Escondido
(92029-1930)
PHONE...............................760 744-1544
Ben Walpole, *President*
Brenda Grohe, *Info Tech Mgr*
Myrna Baker, *Purchasing*
Eric Robyn, *Prdtn Mgr*
EMP: 27
SALES (corp-wide): 13.9MM **Privately
Held**
SIC: 3679 Antennas, receiving; microwave
components
PA: Rantec Microwave Systems, Inc.
31186 La Baya Dr
Westlake Village CA 91362
818 223-5000

(P-19065)
REEDEX INC
15526 Commerce Ln, Huntington Beach
(92649-1602)
PHONE...............................714 894-0311
Dan Reed, *President*
Ted Reed, *Vice Pres*
Stephanie Reed, *Office Mgr*
▲ EMP: 49
SALES (est): 9.4MM **Privately Held**
WEB: www.reedex.com
SIC: 3679 Harness assemblies for elec-
tronic use: wire or cable

(P-19066)
REGAL ELECTRONICS INC (PA)
2029 Otoole Ave, San Jose (95131-1301)
P.O. Box 60008, Sunnyvale (94088-0008)
PHONE...............................408 988-2288
Tony Lee, *President*
Madeleine Lee, *CEO*
Dr William Kunz, *Exec VP*
▲ EMP: 23
SQ FT: 26,000
SALES (est): 2.3MM **Privately Held**
WEB: www.regalusa.com
SIC: 3679 3678 3612 Electronic circuits;
electronic connectors; transformers, ex-
cept electric

(P-19067)
RELCOMM INC
4868 Highway 4 Ste G, Angels Camp
(95222)
P.O. Box 640 (95222-0640)
PHONE...............................209 736-0421
Robert Henkel, *Ch of Bd*
Carolyn A Henkel, *Admin Sec*
EMP: 12
SQ FT: 8,000
SALES (est): 1.8MM **Privately Held**
SIC: 3679 Commutators, electronic

(P-19068)
RENESAS ELECTRONICS AMER INC (HQ)
1001 Murphy Ranch Rd, Milpitas
(95035-7912)
PHONE...............................408 432-8888
Necip Sayiner, *President*
Richard Crowley, *CFO*
Sandra Gallego, *CFO*
Ryan Roderick, *Exec VP*
Mark Downing, *Vice Pres*
▲ EMP: 277
SQ FT: 126,000
SALES (est): 439.1MM **Privately Held**
SIC: 3679 3674 Electronic circuits; inte-
grated circuits, semiconductor networks,
etc.

(P-19069)
RJA INDUSTRIES INC
Also Called: Automation Electronics
9640 Topanga Canyon Pl J, Chatsworth
(91311-0880)
PHONE...............................818 998-5124
Robert Aiani, *President*
Lynn Aiani, *Corp Secy*
Chris Aiani, *Vice Pres*
Sandra Acnason, *Controller*
EMP: 20 EST: 1974
SQ FT: 10,000
SALES (est): 4MM **Privately Held**
SIC: 3679 Harness assemblies for elec-
tronic use: wire or cable; electronic cir-
cuits

(P-19070)
ROCKER SOLENOID COMPANY
Also Called: Rocker Industries
1500 240th St, Harbor City (90710-1309)
PHONE...............................310 534-5660
Francis E Goodyear, *CEO*
Raymond Hatashita, *Chairman*
Milton A Mather, *Vice Pres*
Alexia Perry, *Info Tech Mgr*
Milt Mather, *Chief Engr*
▼ EMP: 70 EST: 1954
SQ FT: 23,000
SALES (est): 18.1MM **Privately Held**
WEB: www.rockerindustries.com
SIC: 3679 Solenoids for electronic applica-
tions

(P-19071)
ROGAR MANUFACTURING INC
Also Called: Ro Gar Mfg
866 E Ross Ave, El Centro (92243-9652)
PHONE...............................760 335-3700
Pat Lewis, *Principal*
EMP: 126
SALES (corp-wide): 17.6MM **Privately
Held**
SIC: 3679 Electronic circuits
PA: Rogar Manufacturing Incorporated
1520 Montague Expy
San Jose CA 95131
408 894-9800

(P-19072)
ROTECH ENGINEERING INC
1020 S Melrose St Ste A, Placentia
(92870-7169)
PHONE...............................714 632-0532
Ralph Ono, *President*
EMP: 20
SQ FT: 10,000
SALES (est): 5.6MM **Privately Held**
WEB: www.rotech-busbar.com
SIC: 3679 Electronic circuits

(P-19073)
RTIE HOLDINGS LLC
1800 E Via Burton, Anaheim (92806-1213)
PHONE...............................714 765-8200
Mark Schelbert,
Jonathan Smith,
EMP: 80
SALES (est): 7.2MM **Privately Held**
SIC: 3679 Electronic circuits

(P-19074)
S AND C PRECISION INC
5045 Calmview Ave, Baldwin Park
(91706-1802)
PHONE...............................626 338-7149
Jose Sanchez, *President*
EMP: 12
SQ FT: 3,000
SALES: 1,000K **Privately Held**
SIC: 3679 3721 3599 Microwave compo-
nents; aircraft; machine shop, jobbing &
repair

(P-19075)
SAFE ENVIRONMENT ENGINEERING
28320 Constellation Rd, Valencia
(91355-5078)
PHONE...............................661 295-5500
David Lamensdorf, *Managing Prtnr*
Sue Springer, *VP Mktg*
EMP: 10
SQ FT: 3,000

▲ = Import ▼=Export
◆ =Import/Export

SALES (est): 1.8MM **Privately Held**
WEB: www.safeenv.com
SIC: 3679 7629 5084 Electronic circuits; electrical repair shops; safety equipment

(P-19076)
SAS MANUFACTURING INC
405 N Smith Ave, Corona (92880-6905)
PHONE.................................951 734-1808
Theo F Smit Jr, *CEO*
Sharon Smit, *Vice Pres*
Harry Welsh, *Purchasing*
Jereme Painter, *Mfg Mgr*
EMP: 45
SQ FT: 24,000
SALES (est): 8.5MM **Privately Held**
WEB: www.sasmanufacturing.com
SIC: 3679 Harness assemblies for electronic use: wire or cable

(P-19077)
SCEPTRE INC
Also Called: E-Scepter
16800 Gale Ave, City of Industry (91745-1804)
PHONE.................................626 369-3698
Stephen Liu, *CEO*
Kieu Dao, *Marketing Mgr*
▲ **EMP:** 50
SALES (est): 12.7MM **Privately Held**
WEB: www.sceptre.com
SIC: 3679 Liquid crystal displays (LCD)

(P-19078)
SCHNEIDER ELECTRIC IT USA
Also Called: APC By Scheineder Electric
1660 Scenic Ave, Costa Mesa (92626-1410)
PHONE.................................714 513-7313
Alex Aguilar, *Branch Mgr*
Donthi Ravikumar, *Vice Pres*
Mike Habibi, *Technology*
Paul Marchand, *Technical Staff*
Michael Weiss, *Sales Mgr*
EMP: 450
SALES (corp-wide): 177.9K **Privately Held**
SIC: 3679 Power supplies, all types: static
HQ: Schneider Electric It Usa, Inc.
132 Fairgrounds Rd
West Kingston RI 02892

(P-19079)
SEASONIC ELECTRONICS INC
301 Aerojet Ave, Azusa (91702)
PHONE.................................626 969-9966
Hsiu-Cheng Chang, *CEO*
Vincent Chang, *Principal*
Sabine Delbauve, *Sales Mgr*
Simon Wu, *Sales Mgr*
Warren Chen, *Marketing Staff*
▲ **EMP:** 14
SALES (est): 2.2MM **Privately Held**
WEB: www.seasonic.com
SIC: 3679 Electronic loads & power supplies

(P-19080)
SECURITY PEOPLE INC
Also Called: Digilock
9 Willowbrook Ct, Petaluma (94954-6507)
PHONE.................................707 766-6000
Asil Gokcebay, *CEO*
Bill Gordon, *President*
Elisabeth Boaz, *Executive Asst*
Shu Sun, *Accounting Mgr*
Julie Advocate, *Sales Mgr*
◆ **EMP:** 30
SALES (est): 11.9MM **Privately Held**
WEB: www.digilock.com
SIC: 3679 Electronic circuits

(P-19081)
SIGNATURE TECH GROUP INC
Also Called: A & A Electronic Assembly
11960 Borden Ave, San Fernando (91340-1808)
PHONE.................................818 890-7611
Victor Castro, *Owner*
EMP: 20
SQ FT: 10,000
SALES (est): 2.4MM **Privately Held**
SIC: 3679 3672 Electronic circuits; printed circuit boards

(P-19082)
SINKPAD LLC
511 Princeland Ct, Corona (92879-1383)
PHONE.................................714 660-2944
Kris K Vasoya, *President*
Tushar Patel, *Exec VP*
Deannae Childress, *Technology*
Abdul Aslami, *Sales Staff*
Sam Bhayani,
EMP: 10
SQ FT: 11,500
SALES: 3.2MM **Privately Held**
SIC: 3679 Antennas, receiving

(P-19083)
SMART WIRELESS COMPUTING INC (HQ)
39870 Eureka Dr, Newark (94560-4809)
PHONE.................................510 683-9999
Jagat R Acharya, *President*
Yohana Komensen, *Office Admin*
Akhil Xavier, *Software Engr*
Nicole Ellis, *Human Res Mgr*
EMP: 10 **EST:** 2007
SALES (est): 2.1MM
SALES (corp-wide): 1.2B **Publicly Held**
SIC: 3679 Electronic circuits
PA: Smart Global Holdings, Inc.
39870 Eureka Dr
Newark CA 94560
510 623-1231

(P-19084)
SMITHS INTERCONNECT INC
Also Called: Channel Microwave
375 Conejo Ridge Ave, Thousand Oaks (91361-4928)
PHONE.................................805 267-0100
Ken Boswell, *Manager*
Serge Taylor, *President*
Harold Aikins, *Manager*
David Raymond, *Manager*
EMP: 14
SALES (corp-wide): 4.2B **Privately Held**
SIC: 3679 Microwave components
HQ: Smiths Interconnect, Inc.
4726 Eisenhower Blvd
Tampa FL 33634
813 901-7200

(P-19085)
SMITHS INTRCNNECT AMERICAS INC
1550 Scenic Ave Ste 150, Costa Mesa (92626-1465)
PHONE.................................714 371-1100
Dom Matos, *President*
Sandra Mariscal, *Project Mgr*
Ashley Bender, *Accounting Mgr*
EMP: 300
SALES (corp-wide): 4.2B **Privately Held**
SIC: 3679 Microwave components
HQ: Smiths Interconnect Americas, Inc.
5101 Richland Ave
Kansas City KS 66106
913 342-5544

(P-19086)
SMT MFG INCORPORATAED
970 S Loyola Dr, Anaheim (92807-5111)
PHONE.................................714 738-9999
Abid Ali Mirza, *CEO*
EMP: 20
SALES (est): 2.3MM **Privately Held**
WEB: www.smtmfg.com
SIC: 3679 Electronic circuits

(P-19087)
SO-CAL VALUE ADDED LLC
809 Calle Plano, Camarillo (93012-8516)
PHONE.................................805 389-5335
Marco Muniz Day, *Vice Pres*
EMP: 35
SQ FT: 40,000
SALES: 4MM **Privately Held**
SIC: 3679 3643 Harness assemblies for electronic use: wire or cable; current-carrying wiring devices

(P-19088)
SORA POWER INC (PA)
1141 Olympic Dr, Corona (92881-3391)
PHONE.................................951 479-9880
Ramesh Patel, *CEO*
Remy Lacroix, *Vice Pres*

Jim Virden, *QC Mgr*
▲ **EMP:** 10 **EST:** 1956
SALES: 5MM **Privately Held**
WEB: www.sorapower.com
SIC: 3679 Electronic circuits

(P-19089)
SOUTH BAY CIRCUITS INC
210 Hillsdale Ave, San Jose (95136-1392)
PHONE.................................408 978-8992
EMP: 164
SALES (corp-wide): 70.7MM **Privately Held**
SIC: 3679
PA: South Bay Circuits, Inc.
99 N Mckemy Ave
Chandler AZ 85226
480 940-3125

(P-19090)
SPARTON IRVINE LLC
Also Called: Electronic Manufacturing Tech
2802 Kelvin Ave Ste 100, Irvine (92614-5897)
PHONE.................................949 855-6625
Michael Wayne Leedom,
Anne Kaiser, *Human Res Dir*
Leah Dupre,
EMP: 75
SQ FT: 30,000
SALES (est): 30.4MM
SALES (corp-wide): 374.9MM **Privately Held**
WEB: www.emtllc.com
SIC: 3679 Harness assemblies for electronic use: wire or cable
HQ: Sparton Emt, Llc
425 N Martingale Rd Ste 2
Schaumburg IL 60173
800 772-7866

(P-19091)
STANDARD CRYSTAL CORP
17626 Barber Ave, Artesia (90701-3832)
PHONE.................................626 443-2121
James Zhang, *President*
EMP: 10
SQ FT: 12,300
SALES (est): 1.3MM **Privately Held**
WEB: www.standardcrystalcorp.com
SIC: 3679 5065 Oscillators; electronic crystals; electronic parts & equipment

(P-19092)
STARLED INC
2059 E Del Amo Blvd, Rancho Dominguez (90220-6131)
PHONE.................................310 603-0403
Andres Alvarez, *President*
David Cheselske, *Treasurer*
Dennis Nishio, *Engineer*
EMP: 18
SQ FT: 4,500
SALES (est): 2.7MM **Privately Held**
WEB: www.starled.com
SIC: 3679 Electronic circuits

(P-19093)
STATEK CORPORATION (HQ)
512 N Main St, Orange (92868-1182)
PHONE.................................714 639-7810
Brian McCarthy, *President*
Shih Chuang, *COO*
Michael Dastmalchian, *Co-President*
Charolette Koren, *Vice Pres*
Leslie Rock, *Executive*
▲ **EMP:** 57
SQ FT: 71,000
SALES (est): 28.3MM
SALES (corp-wide): 75.1MM **Privately Held**
WEB: www.statek.com
SIC: 3679 Electronic circuits; quartz crystals, for electronic application; oscillators
PA: Technicorp International Ii, Inc.
512 N Main St
Orange CA 92868
714 639-7810

(P-19094)
STEWART AUDIO (HQ)
100 W El Camino Real # 72, Mountain View (94040-2649)
PHONE.................................209 588-8111
Richard Otte, *President*
Tom Kritzer, *VP Engrg*

Phil Martin, *Engineer*
Yvonne Esquet, *Human Res Dir*
Neil Conley, *Manager*
▲ **EMP:** 15
SQ FT: 3,000
SALES (est): 7.5MM
SALES (corp-wide): 20.7MM **Privately Held**
WEB: www.stewartaudio.com
SIC: 3679 8711 3651 Recording & playback apparatus, including phonograph; designing: ship, boat, machine & product; household audio & video equipment
PA: Promex Industries, Incorporated
3075 Oakmead Village Dr
Santa Clara CA 95051
408 496-0222

(P-19095)
STRIKE TECHNOLOGY INC
Also Called: Wilorco
24311 Wilmington Ave, Carson (90745-6139)
PHONE.................................562 437-3428
Robert Kunesh, *Ch of Bd*
John Cardall, *Sales Staff*
Manouk Ohanes Yan, *Director*
EMP: 25 **EST:** 2001
SQ FT: 9,800
SALES (est): 5.1MM **Privately Held**
WEB: www.striketechnology.com
SIC: 3679 Static power supply converters for electronic applications

(P-19096)
SUNTSU ELECTRONICS INC
Also Called: Nemco
142 Technology Dr Ste 150, Irvine (92618-2429)
PHONE.................................949 783-7300
Casey Conlan, *President*
Shireen Balou, *Administration*
James Braithwaite, *Technical Staff*
Akiko Harada, *Finance Dir*
Kenneth Butte, *Manager*
▲ **EMP:** 35
SQ FT: 14,000
SALES (est): 7.7MM **Privately Held**
WEB: www.suntsuinc.com
SIC: 3679 5065 Electronic circuits; recording & playback apparatus, including phonograph; electronic parts & equipment

(P-19097)
SUPPORT SYSTEMS INTL CORP
Also Called: Fiber Optic Cable Shop
136 S 2nd St Dept B, Richmond (94804-2110)
PHONE.................................510 234-9090
Ben G Parsons, *President*
Richard St John, *Vice Pres*
▼ **EMP:** 65
SQ FT: 15,000
SALES (est): 7.3MM **Privately Held**
WEB: www.support-systems-intl.com
SIC: 3679 Harness assemblies for electronic use: wire or cable

(P-19098)
SURE POWER INC
Also Called: Martek Power
1111 Knox St, Torrance (90502-1034)
PHONE.................................310 542-8561
Maricela Sanchez, *Branch Mgr*
Rene San Pedro, *MIS Mgr*
Bob Duarte, *Natl Sales Mgr*
EMP: 45 **Privately Held**
WEB: www.martekpower.com
SIC: 3679 Power supplies, all types: static
HQ: Sure Power, Inc.
10955 Sw Avery St
Tualatin OR 97062
503 692-5360

(P-19099)
SYSTRON DONNER INERTIAL INC
2700 Systron Dr, Concord (94518-1399)
PHONE.................................925 979-4400
Dave Peace, *CEO*
EMP: 117
SALES (est): 7.3MM
SALES (corp-wide): 85.6MM **Publicly Held**
SIC: 3679 3829 Electronic circuits; accelerometers

HQ: Aerospace Newco Holdings, Inc.
2700 Systron Dr
Concord CA 94518
925 979-4400

(P-19100)
TANGO SYSTEMS INC
1980 Concourse Dr, San Jose
(95131-1719)
PHONE..................408 526-2330
Ravi Mullapudi, *CEO*
Fang Lin, *Engineer*
EMP: 52
SQ FT: 15,000
SALES (est): 14MM **Privately Held**
SIC: 3679 3641 Attenuators; lamps, vapor

(P-19101)
TE CONNECTIVITY LTD
Also Called: Te Circuit Protection
6900 Paseo Padre Pkwy, Fremont
(94555-3641)
PHONE..................650 361-4923
Thomas J Lynch, *CEO*
Terrence Curtin, *President*
Joe Donahue, *COO*
Mario Calastri, *CFO*
John Jenkins, *Exec VP*
EMP: 43
SALES (est): 9MM
SALES (corp-wide): 1.7B **Publicly Held**
SIC: 3679 Electronic circuits
PA: Littelfuse, Inc.
8755 W Higgins Rd Ste 500
Chicago IL 60631
773 628-1000

(P-19102)
TECH ELECTRONIC SYSTEMS INC
404 S Euclid Ave, Ontario (91762-4309)
PHONE..................909 986-4395
Robert B Contreras, *CEO*
EMP: 15
SQ FT: 14,000
SALES (est): 2.8MM **Privately Held**
WEB: www.techelectronicsys.com
SIC: 3679 3499 Liquid crystal displays (LCD); locks, safe & vault: metal

(P-19103)
TEK ENTERPRISES INC
7730 Airport Bus Pkwy, Van Nuys (91406)
PHONE..................818 785-5971
Tek T Tjia, *President*
Amy Tjia, *COO*
Anthony Fredrick, *Vice Pres*
EMP: 31
SALES (est): 2.7MM **Privately Held**
SIC: 3679 3621 Harness assemblies for electronic use: wire or cable; coils, for electric motors or generators

(P-19104)
TELEDYNE DEFENSE ELEC LLC
Teledyne Relays
12525 Daphne Ave, Hawthorne
(90250-3308)
PHONE..................323 777-0077
Hamid Emami, *Manager*
Thomas Clark, *Design Engr*
Kien Trinh, *Research*
Jack Shropshire, *Engineer*
Billy Wong, *Engineer*
EMP: 107
SQ FT: 86,000
SALES (corp-wide): 2.9B **Publicly Held**
WEB: www.teledyne.com
SIC: 3679 Microwave components
HQ: Teledyne Defense Electronics, Llc
1274 Terra Bella Ave
Mountain View CA 94043
650 691-9800

(P-19105)
TELEDYNE DEFENSE ELEC LLC
Also Called: Teledyne Reynolds
1001 Knox St, Torrance (90502-1030)
PHONE..................310 823-5491
Jim McCosky, *Manager*
Al Andry, *General Mgr*
Danielle Shafran, *Office Admin*
Cesar Aldana, *Project Engr*
Henri Cadena, *Purchasing*
EMP: 14
SQ FT: 4,500

SALES (corp-wide): 2.9B **Publicly Held**
WEB: www.teledynereynolds.com
SIC: 3679 Microwave components
HQ: Teledyne Defense Electronics, Llc
1274 Terra Bella Ave
Mountain View CA 94043
650 691-9800

(P-19106)
TELEDYNE DEFENSE ELEC LLC
Also Called: Teledyne Reynolds
1001 Knox St, Torrance (90502-1030)
PHONE..................310 823-5491
Mark Kotilinek, *Branch Mgr*
James E Bailey, *Surgery Dir*
EMP: 160
SALES (corp-wide): 2.9B **Publicly Held**
SIC: 3679 Microwave components
HQ: Teledyne Defense Electronics, Llc
1274 Terra Bella Ave
Mountain View CA 94043
650 691-9800

(P-19107)
TELEDYNE DEFENSE ELEC LLC
Also Called: Teledyne Microwave Solutions
11361 Sunrise Park Dr, Rancho Cordova
(95742-6587)
PHONE..................916 638-3344
Bob Dipple, *Branch Mgr*
David A Zavadil, *Vice Pres*
John Tennant, *Program Mgr*
Russell Shaller, *General Mgr*
Jerry Pennello, *Planning*
EMP: 200
SALES (corp-wide): 2.9B **Publicly Held**
SIC: 3679 3672 3663 3651 Microwave components; printed circuit boards; radio & TV communications equipment; household audio & video equipment; traveling wave tubes
HQ: Teledyne Defense Electronics, Llc
1274 Terra Bella Ave
Mountain View CA 94043
650 691-9800

(P-19108)
TELEDYNE DEFENSE ELEC LLC (HQ)
Also Called: Teledyne Microwave Solutions
1274 Terra Bella Ave, Mountain View
(94043-1820)
PHONE..................650 691-9800
Richard Pailonis, *CEO*
Ralph Fullerton, *Engineer*
Kiet Pham, *Engineer*
Lee Koolpe, *Opers Mgr*
Susan L Main,
▲ EMP: 25
SALES: 104MM
SALES (corp-wide): 2.9B **Publicly Held**
SIC: 3679 Microwave components
PA: Teledyne Technologies Inc
1049 Camino Dos Rios
Thousand Oaks CA 91360
805 373-4545

(P-19109)
TELEDYNE TECHNOLOGIES INC
Also Called: Teledyne Controls
501 Continental Blvd, El Segundo
(90245-5036)
P.O. Box 1026 (90245-1026)
PHONE..................310 765-3600
Masood Hassan, *Vice Pres*
Joe Allen, *President*
Marshall Dormire, *Vice Pres*
Martin Leiderman, *Executive*
Shervin Malmir, *Program Mgr*
EMP: 300
SALES (corp-wide): 2.9B **Publicly Held**
WEB: www.teledyne.com
SIC: 3679 8731 3812 3519 Electronic circuits; commercial physical research; search & navigation equipment; internal combustion engines
PA: Teledyne Technologies Inc
1049 Camino Dos Rios
Thousand Oaks CA 91360
805 373-4545

(P-19110)
TELEDYNE TECHNOLOGIES INC
3350 Moore St, Los Angeles (90066-1704)
P.O. Box 25964 (90025-0964)
PHONE..................310 820-4616

Kim Rosol, *Branch Mgr*
Jody Glasser, *President*
EMP: 300
SALES (corp-wide): 2.9B **Publicly Held**
SIC: 3679 Electronic circuits
PA: Teledyne Technologies Inc
1049 Camino Dos Rios
Thousand Oaks CA 91360
805 373-4545

(P-19111)
TELEDYNE TECHNOLOGIES INC (PA)
1049 Camino Dos Rios, Thousand Oaks
(91360-2362)
PHONE..................805 373-4545
Robert Mehrabian, *Ch of Bd*
George C Bobb III, *President*
Janice L Hess, *President*
Aldo Pichelli, *President*
Michael Read, *President*
EMP: 250
SALES: 2.9B **Publicly Held**
WEB: www.teledyne.com
SIC: 3679 3761 3519 3724 Electronic circuits; guided missiles & space vehicles; internal combustion engines; gasoline engines; engines, diesel & semi-diesel or dual-fuel; aircraft engines & engine parts; research & development on aircraft engines & parts; aircraft control systems, electronic; navigational systems & instruments; semiconductors & related devices

(P-19112)
TELEDYNE TECHNOLOGIES INC
12964 Panama St, Los Angeles (90066)
PHONE..................310 822-8229
Bruce Gecks, *Manager*
Matthew Bakker, *President*
Sam Calvillo, *President*
Jody Glasser, *President*
Melisa Santos, *Technology*
EMP: 360
SALES (corp-wide): 2.9B **Publicly Held**
WEB: www.teledyne.com
SIC: 3679 Electronic circuits
PA: Teledyne Technologies Inc
1049 Camino Dos Rios
Thousand Oaks CA 91360
805 373-4545

(P-19113)
TELEDYNE WIRELESS LLC
Also Called: Teledyne Microwave Solutions
1274 Terra Bella Ave, Mountain View
(94043-1820)
PHONE..................650 691-9800
Daniel Cheadle Sr, *Branch Mgr*
EMP: 107
SALES (corp-wide): 2.9B **Publicly Held**
SIC: 3679 Microwave components
HQ: Teledyne Defense Electronics, Llc
1274 Terra Bella Ave
Mountain View CA 94043
650 691-9800

(P-19114)
TELEDYNE WIRELESS LLC
11361 Sunrise Park Dr, Rancho Cordova
(95742-6587)
PHONE..................916 638-3344
EMP: 111
SALES (corp-wide): 2.3B **Publicly Held**
SIC: 3679
HQ: Teledyne Wireless, Llc
1274 Terra Bella Ave
Mountain View CA 94043
650 691-9800

(P-19115)
TERADYNE INC
30701 Agoura Rd, Agoura Hills
(91301-5928)
PHONE..................818 991-2900
Greg Beecher, *Manager*
Kevin Giebel, *Vice Pres*
Lori Dunn, *Executive*
Joel Justin, *Info Tech Mgr*
Nguyen Fabre, *Project Mgr*
EMP: 290
SALES (corp-wide): 2.1B **Publicly Held**
WEB: www.teradyne.com
SIC: 3679 Electronic circuits

PA: Teradyne, Inc.
600 Riverpark Dr
North Reading MA 01864
978 370-2700

(P-19116)
THERMAL ELECTRONICS INC
403 W Minthorn St, Lake Elsinore
(92530-2801)
PHONE..................951 674-3555
David Zackerson, *CEO*
Gerald Barnes, *Shareholder*
James Mikesell, *President*
Butch Noll, *President*
David McCullagh, *CFO*
EMP: 15 EST: 1977
SQ FT: 10,000
SALES (est): 4.3MM **Privately Held**
WEB: www.thermalelectronics.com
SIC: 3679 Electronic circuits

(P-19117)
THIN FILM ELECTRONICS INC
Also Called: NFC Innovation Center
2581 Junction Ave, San Jose (95134-1923)
PHONE..................408 503-7300
Peter Fischer, *CEO*
EMP: 70 EST: 2011
SQ FT: 61,000
SALES: 18.6MM **Privately Held**
SIC: 3679 Electronic circuits
PA: Thin Film Electronics Asa
House Of Business Fridtjof Nansens
Plass 4
Oslo 0160

(P-19118)
THOMPSON MAGNETICS INC
Also Called: Auto Doctor
42255 Baldaray Cir Ste C, Temecula
(92590-3632)
P.O. Box 2019 (92593-2019)
PHONE..................951 676-0243
Howard M Thompson Sr, *Ch of Bd*
Betty J Thompson, *Corp Secy*
David Thompson, *Vice Pres*
Howard M Thompson Jr, *Vice Pres*
EMP: 14 EST: 1969
SQ FT: 16,000
SALES: 2.7MM **Privately Held**
SIC: 3679 7538 Cores, magnetic; general automotive repair shops

(P-19119)
TNP INSTRUMENTS INC
119 Star Of India Ln, Carson (90746-1415)
PHONE..................310 532-2222
Vu Tran, *President*
EMP: 14
SQ FT: 5,000
SALES: 1.4MM **Privately Held**
WEB: www.tnpinstruments.com
SIC: 3679 5065 Liquid crystal displays (LCD); electronic parts & equipment

(P-19120)
TOWERJAZZ TEXAS INC (DH)
4321 Jamboree Rd, Newport Beach
(92660-3007)
PHONE..................949 435-8000
Russell Ellwanger, *CEO*
Dani Ashkenazi, *Vice Pres*
Dalit Dahan, *Vice Pres*
Fra Drumm, *Vice Pres*
Ori Galzur, *Vice Pres*
EMP: 69 EST: 2015
SALES (est): 20MM
SALES (corp-wide): 352MM **Privately Held**
SIC: 3679 Electronic circuits

(P-19121)
TR MANUFACTURING LLC (HQ)
33210 Central Ave, Union City
(94587-2010)
PHONE..................510 657-3850
Dom Tran, *CEO*
Jack Cho, *COO*
Asprer Steve, *Program Mgr*
Hilary Wurr, *Program Mgr*
Armando Manlutac, *Engineer*
▲ EMP: 250
SQ FT: 52,000

▲ = Import ▼=Export
◆ =Import/Export

SALES (est): 97.2MM
SALES (corp-wide): 11.2B **Publicly Held**
WEB: www.trmfginc.com
SIC: 3679 Electronic circuits
PA: Corning Incorporated
    1 Riverfront Plz
    Corning NY 14831
    607 974-9000

(P-19122)
TRANSDUCER TECHNIQUES LLC
42480 Rio Nedo, Temecula (92590-3734)
PHONE..................................951 719-3965
Randy A Baker, *Mng Member*
Gary Mann, *Systems Mgr*
EMP: 37
SQ FT: 27,000
SALES (est): 8.8MM **Privately Held**
WEB: www.ttloadcells.com
SIC: 3679 Electronic circuits

(P-19123)
TRANSKO ELECTRONICS INC
3981 E Miraloma Ave, Anaheim (92806-6201)
PHONE..................................714 528-8000
Ae Duk Chun, *CEO*
Jimmy Tim, *Opers Mgr*
▲ EMP: 12
SQ FT: 7,000
SALES (est): 2.2MM **Privately Held**
WEB: www.transko.com
SIC: 3679 Electronic loads & power supplies; oscillators; electronic crystals

(P-19124)
TRI TEK ELECTRONICS INC
25358 Avenue Stanford, Valencia (91355-1214)
PHONE..................................661 295-0020
James Gillson, *President*
Josie Gillson, *CFO*
Anthony Lopez, *Principal*
Joe Fattrusso, *Purch Mgr*
Dan Huffman, *QC Mgr*
EMP: 40
SQ FT: 22,000
SALES (est): 8.1MM **Privately Held**
WEB: www.tri-tekelectronics.com
SIC: 3679 Harness assemblies for electronic use: wire or cable; electronic circuits

(P-19125)
TRI-MAG INC
1601 Clancy Ct, Visalia (93291-9253)
Rural Route 4079 (93278)
PHONE..................................559 651-2222
Jia Ming LI, *Ch of Bd*
Donna Vongpanya,
▲ EMP: 27
SQ FT: 27,000
SALES (est): 3.8MM **Privately Held**
WEB: www.tri-mag.com
SIC: 3679 3677 Electronic switches; filtration devices, electronic

(P-19126)
TRUE CIRCUITS INC
4300 El Camino Real # 200, Los Altos (94022-1090)
PHONE..................................650 949-3400
Stephen Maneatis, *CEO*
Don Draper, *VP Engrg*
EMP: 10
SALES (est): 1.5MM **Privately Held**
WEB: www.truecircuits.com
SIC: 3679 8711 Electronic circuits; engineering services

(P-19127)
TRUE VISION DISPLAYS INC
16402 Berwyn Rd, Cerritos (90703-2440)
PHONE..................................562 407-0630
Steven H Yu, *CEO*
▲ EMP: 12
SQ FT: 30,460
SALES (est): 2MM **Privately Held**
SIC: 3679 Liquid crystal displays (LCD)

(P-19128)
TURTLE BEACH CORPORATION (PA)
11011 Via Frontera Ste A, San Diego (92127-1752)
PHONE..................................914 345-2255
Juergen Stark, *President*
Sara Kell, *Executive Asst*
Ron Gonzalez, *Technical Staff*
Javier Roman, *Technical Staff*
John Bolton, *Engineer*
▲ EMP: 39
SQ FT: 30,000
SALES: 287.4MM **Publicly Held**
SIC: 3679 Parametric amplifiers

(P-19129)
TXC TECHNOLOGY INC (HQ)
451 W Lambert Rd Ste 201, Brea (92821-3920)
PHONE..................................714 990-5510
Peter Wan Shing Lin, *President*
Lou Lee, *CEO*
EMP: 12
SQ FT: 1,900
SALES (est): 1.2MM **Privately Held**
SIC: 3679 Electronic circuits

(P-19130)
U S CIRCUIT INC
2071 Wineridge Pl, Escondido (92029-1931)
PHONE..................................760 489-1413
Michael Fariba, *President*
Mukesh Patel, *Vice Pres*
T J Sojitra, *Vice Pres*
Rupal Sojitra, *General Mgr*
Connie Wolff, *Human Resources*
EMP: 80
SQ FT: 40,000
SALES: 14.4MM **Privately Held**
WEB: www.uscircuit.com
SIC: 3679 3672 Electronic circuits; printed circuit boards

(P-19131)
UNIQUIFY INC
2030 Fortune Dr Ste 200, San Jose (95131-1835)
PHONE..................................408 235-8810
Josh Lee, *CEO*
Jung Ho Lee, *President*
Sam Kim, *COO*
Robert Sheffield, *CFO*
Robert Smith, *Senior VP*
EMP: 50
SALES (est): 9.2MM **Privately Held**
SIC: 3679 Electronic circuits

(P-19132)
US ETA INC
Also Called: Eta USA
16170 Vineyard Blvd # 180, Morgan Hill (95037-5498)
PHONE..................................408 778-2793
Hiroshi Kitagawa, *CEO*
Amir Safakish, *President*
Sousan Manteghi, *General Mgr*
Keon Safakish, *Opers Mgr*
◆ EMP: 12
SQ FT: 8,000
SALES: 3MM **Privately Held**
WEB: www.eta-usa.com
SIC: 3679 5063 Electronic switches; transformers & transmission equipment

(P-19133)
VANDER-BEND MANUFACTURING INC (PA)
2701 Orchard Pkwy, San Jose (95134-2008)
PHONE..................................408 245-5150
Greg Biggs, *President*
Jason Bortoli, *Program Mgr*
Jill De Dios, *Admin Sec*
Abhinawa Ghimire, *Technology*
Holly Bugaj, *Human Res Dir*
▲ EMP: 277
SQ FT: 207,000
SALES (est): 131MM **Privately Held**
WEB: www.vander-bend.com
SIC: 3679 3444 3549 Harness assemblies for electronic use: wire or cable; sheet metalwork; metalworking machinery

(P-19134)
VAS ENGINEERING INC
4750 Viewridge Ave, San Diego (92123-1640)
PHONE..................................858 569-1601
Rohak Vora, *CEO*
T J Sojitra, *Shareholder*
Greg Atzmiller, *Treasurer*
Jim Strum, *Engineer*
John Greenwood, *QC Mgr*
▲ EMP: 50
SQ FT: 19,200
SALES (est): 14.3MM **Privately Held**
WEB: www.vasengineering.com
SIC: 3679 3823 Electronic circuits; harness assemblies for electronic use: wire or cable; temperature measurement instruments, industrial

(P-19135)
VASTCIRCUITS & MFG LLC
2226 Goodyear Ave Unit B, Ventura (93003-7746)
PHONE..................................805 421-4299
Erica Gonzalez-Preciado, *President*
EMP: 10
SALES (est): 398.2K **Privately Held**
SIC: 3679 Electronic circuits

(P-19136)
VERTEX LCD INC
600 S Jefferson St Ste K, Placentia (92870-6634)
P.O. Box 206 (92871-0206)
PHONE..................................714 223-7111
Gene Huh, *President*
Andy Tseng, *CFO*
Brian Yi, *Electrical Engi*
EMP: 35
SQ FT: 5,000
SALES (est): 6.2MM **Privately Held**
SIC: 3679 Liquid crystal displays (LCD)

(P-19137)
VERTIV JV HOLDINGS LLC (PA)
360 N Crescent Dr, Beverly Hills (90210-4874)
PHONE..................................310 712-1195
EMP: 33
SALES (est): 2.9B **Privately Held**
SIC: 3679 3585 6719 Power supplies, all types: static; air conditioning units, complete: domestic or industrial; investment holding companies, except banks

(P-19138)
VICTOR WIETESKI
Also Called: Vic Company
9427 Santa Fe Springs Rd, Santa Fe Springs (90670-2622)
PHONE..................................562 946-9715
Wieteski Victor, *Owner*
Victor Wieteski, *Owner*
EMP: 15
SALES (est): 680.3K **Privately Held**
SIC: 3679 Electronic circuits

(P-19139)
VOICE ASSIST INC
Also Called: (A DEVELOPMENT STAGE COMPANY)
15 Enterprise Ste 350, Aliso Viejo (92656-2655)
PHONE..................................949 655-1611
Michael Metcalf, *Ch of Bd*
EMP: 16
SALES: 564.6K **Privately Held**
SIC: 3679 Voice controls

(P-19140)
WAIN INDUSTRIES
5688 Via Bonita, Newbury Park (91320-6818)
PHONE..................................805 581-5900
Michael Wainess, *President*
Ellen Wainess, *Corp Secy*
EMP: 14
SALES: 1MM **Privately Held**
WEB: www.wainindustries.com
SIC: 3679 Harness assemblies for electronic use: wire or cable

(P-19141)
WAVESTREAM CORPORATION (HQ)
545 W Terrace Dr, San Dimas (91773-2915)
PHONE..................................909 599-9080
Robert Huffman, *CEO*
Nimrod Itach, *CFO*
Francis Auricchio, *Exec VP*
Larry Cooke, *Program Mgr*
Bruce Morris, *Program Mgr*
EMP: 103
SQ FT: 33,000
SALES (est): 27.5MM
SALES (corp-wide): 71.9MM **Privately Held**
WEB: www.wavestream.com
SIC: 3679 8731 Microwave components; commercial physical research
PA: Gilat Satellite Networks Ltd.
    21 Yegia Kapaim
    Petah Tikva 49130
    392 520-00

(P-19142)
WELLEX CORPORATION (PA)
551 Brown Rd, Fremont (94539-7003)
PHONE..................................510 743-1818
Tzu Tai Tsai, *CEO*
Richard Fitzgerald, *President*
Jackson Wang, *Chairman*
Evelyn Chu, *Executive*
Wesley Chen, *MIS Mgr*
▲ EMP: 108
SQ FT: 88,516
SALES (est): 38.9MM **Privately Held**
WEB: www.wellex.com
SIC: 3679 3672 Harness assemblies for electronic use: wire or cable; printed circuit boards

(P-19143)
WIRELESS INNOVATION INC
Also Called: Hte
1024 Iron Point Rd, Folsom (95630-8013)
PHONE..................................916 357-6700
Ken Arnold, *President*
Henry Brown III, *Vice Pres*
Elizabeth Leblanc, *Office Mgr*
Liz Leblanc, *IT/INT Sup*
Chuck Sams, *Prdtn Mgr*
EMP: 12
SQ FT: 10,000
SALES (est): 960.8K **Privately Held**
SIC: 3679 8711 3577 3571 Electronic circuits; engineering services; computer peripheral equipment; electronic computers

(P-19144)
WRIGHT TECHNOLOGIES INC
1352 Blue Oaks Blvd # 140, Roseville (95678-7028)
PHONE..................................916 773-4424
Chuck Allen, *CEO*
Barbara Allen, *CFO*
EMP: 10
SALES: 1MM **Privately Held**
SIC: 3679 3825 8711 Microwave components; radio frequency measuring equipment; electrical or electronic engineering

(P-19145)
WYVERN TECHNOLOGIES INC
1205 E Warner Ave, Santa Ana (92705-5431)
PHONE..................................714 966-0710
James J Weber, *President*
Debbie Hansen, *Office Mgr*
Carole Gordon, *Controller*
EMP: 30
SQ FT: 10,000
SALES: 3.7MM **Privately Held**
WEB: www.wyverncorp.com
SIC: 3679 Microwave components

(P-19146)
XCEIVE CORPORATION
3900 Freedom Cir Ste 200, Santa Clara (95054-1222)
PHONE..................................408 486-5610
Jean-Louis Bories, *President*
Alain-Serge Porret, *President*
Meryl Rains, *CFO*
Peter Cohn, *Admin Sec*
EMP: 45
SQ FT: 3,500

PRODUCTS & SVCS

SALES (est): 6.4MM **Privately Held**
WEB: www.xceive.com
SIC: 3679 Electronic circuits

(P-19147)
Z-COMMUNICATIONS INC
6779 Mesa Ridge Rd # 150, San Diego
(92121-2932)
PHONE.................................858 621-2700
Zdravko Divjak, *President*
EMP: 15
SALES (corp-wide): 2.8MM **Privately
Held**
SIC: 3679 Oscillators
PA: Z-Communications, Inc.
    16481 Prospect Ln
    Broomfield CO 80023
    858 621-2700

(P-19148)
Z-TRONIX INC
Also Called: Manufacturer
6327 Alondra Blvd, Paramount
(90723-3750)
PHONE.................................562 808-0800
Kamran Jahangard-Mahboob, *CEO*
Roy R Jahangard, *President*
▲ EMP: 20
SQ FT: 18,000
SALES (est): 5.8MM **Privately Held**
WEB: www.z-tronix.com
SIC: 3679 5063 5065 Harness assem-
blies for electronic use: wire or cable; wire
& cable; connectors, electronic

(P-19149)
ZENTEC GROUP
26190 Entp Way Ste 200, Lake Forest
(92630)
PHONE.................................949 586-3609
Giles Denning, *President*
Mary Gentile, *CFO*
EMP: 10
SALES (est): 940K **Privately Held**
WEB: www.pectelusa.com
SIC: 3679 Harness assemblies for elec-
tronic use: wire or cable

3691 Storage Batteries

(P-19150)
AA PORTABLE POWER
CORPORATION
825 S 19th St, Richmond (94804-3808)
PHONE.................................510 525-2328
Xiao Ping Jiang, *President*
Reiko Aso, *Admin Sec*
▲ EMP: 35
SQ FT: 15,000
SALES (est): 6.1MM **Privately Held**
WEB: www.aaportablepower.com
SIC: 3691 Storage batteries

(P-19151)
ADARA POWER INC
15466 Los Gatos Blvd # 109351, Los Gatos
(95032-2542)
PHONE.................................844 223-2969
Neil Maguire, *CEO*
Greg Maguire, *Vice Pres*
◆ EMP: 11
SQ FT: 5,000
SALES (est): 320K **Privately Held**
SIC: 3691 Storage batteries

(P-19152)
BATTERY TECHNOLOGY INC
(PA)
Also Called: B T I
16651 E Johnson Dr, City of Industry
(91745-2413)
PHONE.................................626 336-6878
Christopher Chu, *President*
Andy Tong, *Vice Pres*
Mike Tobin, *Sales Mgr*
▲ EMP: 62
SQ FT: 20,000
SALES (est): 7.5MM **Privately Held**
WEB: www.batterytech.com
SIC: 3691 Storage batteries

(P-19153)
CABAN SYSTEMS INC
858 Stanton Rd, Burlingame (94010-1404)
PHONE.................................650 270-0113
Alexandra Rasch, *CEO*
EMP: 10
SALES (est): 2MM **Privately Held**
SIC: 3691 Storage batteries

(P-19154)
CALEB TECHNOLOGY
CORPORATION
2905 Lomita Blvd, Torrance (90505-5106)
PHONE.................................310 257-4780
Thomas S Lin, *President*
Lily W Lin, *Treasurer*
EMP: 20
SQ FT: 14,000
SALES (est): 279.9K **Privately Held**
WEB: www.caleb-battery.com
SIC: 3691 Batteries, rechargeable

(P-19155)
COMPONENT CONCEPTS LLC
1732 Ord Way, Oceanside (92056-1501)
PHONE.................................760 722-9559
Chuck Eshom, *CEO*
Dan Perry, *Accounts Exec*
▲ EMP: 14
SALES (est): 3.3MM **Privately Held**
WEB: www.componentconcepts.com
SIC: 3691 Batteries, rechargeable

(P-19156)
CONTOUR ENERGY SYSTEMS
INC
Also Called: Cfx Battery
1300 W Optical Dr Ste 100, Irwindale
(91702-3284)
PHONE.................................626 610-0660
Louis E Lupo, *President*
Lc Chiu, *COO*
Liew-Chuang Chiu, *COO*
Lee Sailor, *CFO*
Joe Carcone, *Vice Pres*
▲ EMP: 34 EST: 2008
SALES (est): 3.5MM **Privately Held**
SIC: 3691 3692 Storage batteries; primary
batteries, dry & wet

(P-19157)
EAST PENN MANUFACTURING
CO
3701 Parkway Pl Ste B, West Sacramento
(95691-5044)
PHONE.................................916 374-9965
EMP: 14
SALES (corp-wide): 2.8B **Privately Held**
SIC: 3691 Storage batteries
PA: East Penn Manufacturing Co.
    102 Deka Rd
    Lyon Station PA 19536
    610 682-6361

(P-19158)
ENERGY SALES LLC (PA)
2030 Ringwood Ave, San Jose
(95131-1728)
PHONE.................................503 690-9000
Kathryn Wilke, *President*
Jean-Pierre Gueguen, *COO*
Valerie Franco, *Vice Pres*
▲ EMP: 13 EST: 1972
SQ FT: 8,100
SALES (est): 4.3MM **Privately Held**
WEB: www.energy-sales.com
SIC: 3691 5063 5065 Storage batteries;
batteries; electronic parts & equipment

(P-19159)
ENERSYS
30069 Ahern Ave, Union City (94587-1234)
PHONE.................................510 887-8080
Tom Larkin, *Branch Mgr*
EMP: 15
SALES (corp-wide): 2.8B **Publicly Held**
SIC: 3691 Lead acid batteries (storage bat-
teries)
PA: Enersys
    2366 Bernville Rd
    Reading PA 19605
    610 208-1991

(P-19160)
ENERSYS
5580 Edison Ave, Chino (91710-6936)
PHONE.................................909 464-8251
Ken Hill, *Branch Mgr*
EMP: 88
SALES (corp-wide): 2.8B **Publicly Held**
SIC: 3691 Lead acid batteries (storage bat-
teries)
PA: Enersys
    2366 Bernville Rd
    Reading PA 19605
    610 208-1991

(P-19161)
ENERVAULT CORPORATION
1100 La Avenida St Ste A, Mountain View
(94043-1453)
PHONE.................................408 636-7519
Ron Mosso, *CEO*
Denis Giorno, *Ch of Bd*
Thomas E Colson, *COO*
Thomas Jahn, *CFO*
Craig Horne, *Officer*
▲ EMP: 14
SALES (est): 3MM **Privately Held**
SIC: 3691 Storage batteries

(P-19162)
ENEVATE CORPORATION
101 Theory Ste 200, Irvine (92617-3089)
PHONE.................................949 243-0399
Robert A Rango, *President*
John B Kennedy, *CFO*
Sameer V RAO, *CFO*
Heidi Houghton, *Officer*
Jarvis Tou, *Exec VP*
▲ EMP: 43
SQ FT: 17,000
SALES (est): 9.8MM **Privately Held**
SIC: 3691 Storage batteries

(P-19163)
EREPLACEMENTS LLC
16885 W Bernardo Dr # 370, San Diego
(92127-1618)
PHONE.................................714 361-2652
Thomas M Peck, *Branch Mgr*
EMP: 30 **Privately Held**
SIC: 3691 Storage batteries
PA: Ereplacements, Llc
    600 E Dallas Rd Ste 200
    Grapevine TX 76051

(P-19164)
EXIDE TECHNOLOGIES
345 Cessna Cir Ste 101, Corona
(92880-2519)
PHONE.................................951 520-0677
Adam Sicre, *Manager*
EMP: 25
SALES (corp-wide): 2.3B **Privately Held**
WEB: www.exideworld.com
SIC: 3691 3629 Storage batteries; battery
chargers, rectifying or nonrotating
PA: Exide Technologies
    13000 Deerfield Pkwy # 200
    Milton GA 30004
    678 566-9000

(P-19165)
FIRST LITHIUM LLC
17244 S Main St, Carson (90749)
PHONE.................................310 489-6266
Dazhe Wong, *Mng Member*
EMP: 10
SALES (est): 308.9K **Privately Held**
SIC: 3691 Storage batteries

(P-19166)
FLUX POWER HOLDINGS INC
(PA)
2685 S Melrose Dr, Vista (92081-8783)
PHONE.................................877 505-3589
Ronald F Dutt, *President*
Christopher L Anthony, *Ch of Bd*
Jonathan A Berry, *COO*
Charles A Scheiwe, *CFO*
Theresa Weaver, *Asst Controller*
▲ EMP: 53
SQ FT: 22,054
SALES: 9.3MM **Publicly Held**
SIC: 3691 5063 Storage batteries; batter-
ies, rechargeable; storage batteries, in-
dustrial

(P-19167)
FRONT EDGE TECHNOLOGY
INC
13455 Brooks Dr Ste A, Baldwin Park
(91706-2254)
PHONE.................................626 856-8979
Simon Nieh, *President*
Roger Lin, *CFO*
James Liang, *Vice Pres*
EMP: 26
SQ FT: 18,000
SALES (est): 3.1MM **Privately Held**
WEB: www.frontedgetechnology.com
SIC: 3691 Batteries, rechargeable

(P-19168)
INDUSTRIAL BATTERY ENGRG
INC
Also Called: I B E
9121 De Garmo Ave, Sun Valley
(91352-2697)
PHONE.................................818 767-7067
Birger Holmquist, *CEO*
Michael Sloan, *President*
Javier Sanchez, *Corp Secy*
Ralph Holanov, *Vice Pres*
Derek Sloan, *Vice Pres*
EMP: 30
SQ FT: 20,000
SALES (est): 5.9MM **Privately Held**
WEB: www.ibe-inc.com
SIC: 3691 3629 Storage batteries; elec-
tronic generation equipment

(P-19169)
INEVIT INC
541 Jefferson Ave Ste 100, Redwood City
(94063-1700)
PHONE.................................650 298-6001
Michael Miskovsky, *CEO*
Mark White, *Admin Sec*
EMP: 74
SALES (est): 121.1K
SALES (corp-wide): 1.6MM **Privately
Held**
SIC: 3691 Storage batteries
HQ: Sf Motors, Inc.
    3303 Scott Blvd
    Santa Clara CA 95054
    408 617-7878

(P-19170)
M B S INC
Also Called: Accu Rack
18514 Yorba Linda Blvd, Yorba Linda
(92886-4179)
PHONE.................................714 693-9952
Roy Benavidez, *Director*
EMP: 13
SALES (corp-wide): 1.7MM **Privately
Held**
SIC: 3691 Storage batteries
PA: M B S Inc
    1961 E Miraloma Ave Ste D
    Placentia CA 92870
    714 693-9952

(P-19171)
POWERSTORM HOLDINGS INC
Also Called: Powerstorm Ess
31244 Palos Verdes Dr W # 245, Rancho
Palos Verdes (90275-5370)
PHONE.................................424 327-2991
Michel J Freni, *Ch of Bd*
Shailesh Upreti, *Vice Pres*
EMP: 12
SQ FT: 2,000
SALES: 128.9K **Privately Held**
SIC: 3691 4911 5063 Storage batteries; ;
; storage batteries, industrial

(P-19172)
SILA NANOTECHNOLOGIES INC
2450 Mariner Square Loop, Alameda
(94501-1010)
PHONE.................................408 475-7452
Gene Berdichevsky, *CEO*
Justin Yen, *Engineer*
EMP: 27
SQ FT: 87,531
SALES (est): 8.7MM **Privately Held**
SIC: 3691 Storage batteries

▲ = Import ▼=Export
◆ =Import/Export

(P-19173)
SIMPLIPHI POWER INC
3100 Camino Del Sol, Oxnard
(93030-7257)
PHONE................................805 640-6700
Catherine Von Burg, *CEO*
Edwin F Moore, *President*
Bill Sechrest, *CFO*
Stuart Lennox, *CTO*
Dan Sauer, *Manager*
▲ EMP: 12
SQ FT: 5,300
SALES: 2.9MM **Privately Held**
SIC: 3691 Storage batteries

(P-19174)
TELEDYNE TECHNOLOGIES INC
Also Called: Teledyne Battery Products
840 W Brockton Ave, Redlands
(92374-2902)
P.O. Box 7950 (92375-1150)
PHONE................................909 793-3131
Greg Donahey, *Branch Mgr*
Christine Delmar, *Vice Pres*
Jim Ellison, *Engineer*
Janak Rajpara, *Engineer*
Joe Barnhill, *Business Mgr*
EMP: 58
SALES (corp-wide): 2.9B **Publicly Held**
WEB: www.teledyne.com
SIC: 3691 3692 Storage batteries; primary
batteries, dry & wet
PA: Teledyne Technologies Inc
1049 Camino Dos Rios
Thousand Oaks CA 91360
805 373-4545

(P-19175)
TENERGY CORPORATION
Also Called: All-Battery.com
436 Kato Ter, Fremont (94539-8332)
PHONE................................510 687-0388
Xiangbing LI, *CEO*
Ling Ch Liang, *Admin Sec*
Lydia Del Real, *Accounts Mgr*
▲ EMP: 90
SALES (est): 18.7MM **Privately Held**
SIC: 3691 5063 Alkaline cell storage bat-
teries; batteries

(P-19176)
VYCON INC
16323 Shoemaker Ave # 600, Cerritos
(90703-2244)
PHONE................................562 282-5500
Vatche Artinian, *CEO*
Frank Delattre, *President*
Ken Demirjian, *COO*
Patrick T McMullen, *CTO*
▲ EMP: 52
SQ FT: 38,000
SALES (est): 9.9MM
SALES (corp-wide): 22MM **Privately
Held**
SIC: 3691 Storage batteries
PA: Calnetix, Inc.
16323 Shoemaker Ave
Cerritos CA 90703
562 293-1660

(P-19177)
ZEROBASE ENERGY LLC
Also Called: Zero Base
46609 Fremont Blvd, Fremont
(94538-6410)
PHONE................................888 530-9376
Steve Hogge, *President*
Roger Rose, *Vice Pres*
Wayne Labrie, *Production*
Mark Lucas, *Sales Staff*
EMP: 22
SALES: 5.5MM **Privately Held**
SIC: 3691 3699 4911 Storage batteries;
generators, ultrasonic;

3692 Primary Batteries: Dry & Wet

(P-19178)
B & B BATTERY (USA) INC (PA)
6415 Randolph St, Commerce
(90040-3511)
PHONE................................323 278-1900
Jack Liu, *President*

George Liu, *Vice Pres*
▲ EMP: 20
SQ FT: 20,000
SALES (est): 15.3MM **Privately Held**
WEB: www.bb-battery.com
SIC: 3692 Primary batteries, dry & wet

(P-19179)
CONCORDE BATTERY CORP (PA)
2009 W San Bernardino Rd, West Covina
(91790-1006)
PHONE................................626 813-1234
Donald W Godber, *President*
Glenn Hollett, *Vice Pres*
Coral Ferguson, *General Mgr*
Greg Gomez, *Info Tech Mgr*
Anthony Tapia, *Info Tech Mgr*
▲ EMP: 27
SQ FT: 36,000
SALES (est): 23.3MM **Privately Held**
WEB: www.concordebattery.com
SIC: 3692 Dry cell batteries, single or mul-
tiple cell

(P-19180)
PRIMUS POWER CORPORATION
3967 Trust Way, Hayward (94545-3723)
PHONE................................510 342-7600
Thomas Stepien, *CEO*
Jorg Heinemann, *Officer*
Brian Dillard, *VP Bus Dvlpt*
Richard Winter, *CTO*
Andrew Bookholt, *Engineer*
EMP: 50
SALES (est): 14.9MM **Privately Held**
SIC: 3692 Primary batteries, dry & wet

(P-19181)
QUALLION LLC
12744 San Fernando Rd # 100, Sylmar
(91342-3854)
PHONE................................818 833-2000
Alfred E Mann,
Jackie York, *CFO*
▲ EMP: 155
SALES (est): 40.1MM
SALES (corp-wide): 2.8B **Publicly Held**
WEB: www.quallion.com
SIC: 3692 Primary batteries, dry & wet
PA: Enersys
2366 Bernville Rd
Reading PA 19605
610 208-1991

(P-19182)
SOLID STATE BATTERY INC
7825 Industry Ave, Pico Rivera
(90660-4305)
PHONE................................310 753-6769
Lloyd Goldwater, *Principal*
EMP: 11
SALES (est): 1.2MM **Privately Held**
SIC: 3692 5063 Dry cell batteries, single
or multiple cell; batteries

(P-19183)
TROJAN BATTERY COMPANY LLC (HQ)
10375 Slusher Dr, Santa Fe Springs
(90670-3748)
PHONE................................562 236-3000
Armand Lauzon, *President*
Edward Dunlap, *CFO*
David Godber, *Exec VP*
Phil Taylor, *Senior VP*
Phil McGreevy, *Vice Pres*
◆ EMP: 365 EST: 1925
SQ FT: 160,000
SALES (est): 189.2MM
SALES (corp-wide): 670MM **Privately
Held**
WEB: www.trojan-battery.com
SIC: 3692 3691 Primary batteries, dry &
wet; lead acid batteries (storage batteries)
PA: C&D Technologies, Inc.
1400 Union Meeting Rd # 110
Blue Bell PA 19422
215 619-2700

3694 Electrical Eqpt For Internal Combustion Engines

(P-19184)
ALTERNATORS STARTERS ETC
Also Called: Auto Lectrics
1360 White Oaks Rd Ste H, Campbell
(95008-6749)
PHONE................................408 559-3540
Muhammed Osman, *President*
EMP: 12
SQ FT: 2,500
SALES (est): 1.9MM **Privately Held**
WEB: www.autolectrics.com
SIC: 3694 Automotive electrical equipment

(P-19185)
AST POWER LLC
54 Coral Reef, Newport Coast
(92657-1904)
PHONE................................949 226-2275
Ali Navid, *Mng Member*
◆ EMP: 20
SQ FT: 2,500
SALES (est): 1.7MM **Privately Held**
SIC: 3694 2834 3841 2086 Engine electrical equipment; pharmaceutical preparations; surgical & medical instruments;
mineral water, carbonated: packaged in
cans, bottles, etc.; computer software development & applications

(P-19186)
BARRETT ENGINEERING INC
Also Called: Racemate Alternators
1725 Burton St, San Diego (92111-7001)
PHONE................................858 256-9194
John Barrett, *President*
Kay Barrett, *Treasurer*
EMP: 15
SQ FT: 4,000
SALES: 300K **Privately Held**
WEB: www.racemate.com
SIC: 3694 5531 Alternators, automotive;
speed shops, including race car supplies

(P-19187)
BATTERY-BIZ INC
Also Called: Ebatts.com
1380 Flynn Rd, Camarillo (93012-8016)
PHONE................................805 437-7777
Ophir Marish, *CEO*
Yossi Jakubovits, *Admin Sec*
▲ EMP: 63
SQ FT: 60,000
SALES (est): 14.3MM **Privately Held**
WEB: www.batterybiz.net
SIC: 3694 Battery charging generators, au-
tomobile & aircraft

(P-19188)
BYD ENERGY LLC
1800 S Figueroa St, Los Angeles
(90015-3422)
PHONE................................661 949-2918
EMP: 30
SALES (est): 693.2K
SALES (corp-wide): 2.4MM **Privately
Held**
SIC: 3694 Engine electrical equipment
HQ: Byd Motors Llc
1800 S Figueroa St
Los Angeles CA 90015

(P-19189)
DSM&T CO INC
10609 Business Dr, Fontana (92337-8212)
PHONE................................909 357-7960
Sergio Corona, *CEO*
David Serrano, *Administration*
Jesus Granados, *Research*
Carolyn Richards, *Buyer*
Alicia Rebolledo, *VP Opers*
▲ EMP: 170 EST: 1982
SQ FT: 41,000

SALES (est): 45.9MM **Privately Held**
WEB: www.dsmt.com
SIC: 3694 3357 3634 3643 Harness
wiring sets, internal combustion engines;
nonferrous wiredrawing & insulating;
heating pads, electric; connectors, electric
cord

(P-19190)
ELECTRICAL REBUILDERS SLS INC (PA)
Also Called: Vapex-Genex-Precision
1559 W 134th St, Gardena (90249-2215)
PHONE................................323 249-7545
Mike Klapper, *President*
Mary Ann Klapper, *Corp Secy*
David Klapper, *Vice Pres*
▲ EMP: 75
SQ FT: 90,000
SALES (est): 7.2MM **Privately Held**
SIC: 3694 3592 3714 Distributors, motor
vehicle engine; carburetors; motor vehicle
brake systems & parts

(P-19191)
ENGINE ELECTRONICS INC
Also Called: Compu-Fire
12155 Pangborn Ave, Downey
(90241-5624)
P.O. Box 189, La Verne (91750-0189)
PHONE................................562 803-1700
Lewis Hemphill, *President*
EMP: 10
SQ FT: 17,000
SALES: 2.6MM **Privately Held**
WEB: www.compufire.com
SIC: 3694 Engine electrical equipment

(P-19192)
INTERNATIONAL RES DEV CORP NEV (PA)
Also Called: IRD
5212 Chelsea St, La Jolla (92037-7910)
PHONE................................858 488-9900
Robert E Kane, *President*
Anthony Renda, *Vice Pres*
▲ EMP: 15
SALES (est): 1.5MM **Privately Held**
SIC: 3694 Automotive electrical equipment

(P-19193)
JAPAN ENGINE INC
2131 Williams St, San Leandro
(94577-3224)
PHONE................................510 532-7878
Yu Feng Lin, *CEO*
Michael Yi, *Principal*
▲ EMP: 20
SALES (est): 3.9MM **Privately Held**
SIC: 3694 Engine electrical equipment

(P-19194)
JET PERFORMANCE PRODUCTS INC
Also Called: Jet Transmission
17491 Apex Cir, Huntington Beach
(92647-5728)
PHONE................................714 848-5500
Bryant Seller, *President*
Dan Nicholas, *Mktg Dir*
EMP: 25
SQ FT: 8,500
SALES (est): 4.1MM **Privately Held**
WEB: www.jetchip.com
SIC: 3694 3714 Automotive electrical
equipment; motor vehicle parts & acces-
sories

(P-19195)
MAXWELL TECHNOLOGIES INC (HQ)
3888 Calle Fortunada, San Diego
(92123-1825)
PHONE................................858 503-3300
Franz Fink, *President*
David Lyle, *CFO*
Thibault Kassir, *Vice Pres*
Emily Lough, *Vice Pres*
Everett Wiggins, *Vice Pres*
▲ EMP: 277
SQ FT: 30,500

SALES: 90.4MM
SALES (corp-wide): 21.4B **Publicly Held**
WEB: www.maxwell.com
SIC: 3694 3629 Engine electrical equipment; capacitors & condensers; capacitors, a.c., for motors or fluorescent lamp ballasts; capacitors, fixed or variable; power conversion units, a.c. to d.c.: static-electric
PA: Tesla, Inc.
3500 Deer Creek Rd
Palo Alto CA 94304
650 681-5000

(P-19196)
MYOTEK INDUSTRIES INCORPORATED (PA)
1278 Glenneyre St Ste 431, Laguna Beach (92651-3103)
PHONE..............................949 502-3776
Robert Harrington, *President*
▲ **EMP:** 90
SQ FT: 1,800
SALES (est): 14.3MM **Privately Held**
SIC: 3694 5013 Automotive electrical equipment; automotive servicing equipment

(P-19197)
NGK SPARK PLUGS (USA) INC
68 Fairbanks, Irvine (92618-1602)
P.O. Box 30745, Los Angeles (90030-0745)
PHONE..............................949 580-2639
Mark Pratt, *Branch Mgr*
EMP: 25 **Privately Held**
SIC: 3694 Ignition apparatus & distributors
HQ: Ngk Spark Plugs (U.S.A.), Inc.
46929 Magellan
Wixom MI 48393
248 926-6900

(P-19198)
ORIGINAL DISTRIBUTOR EXCHANGE
2538 E 52nd St, Huntington Park (90255-2501)
PHONE..............................323 583-8707
Jose Luis Veloz, *Owner*
EMP: 12 **EST:** 1975
SQ FT: 3,000
SALES (est): 1.1MM **Privately Held**
SIC: 3694 3621 Automotive electrical equipment; generators, automotive & aircraft; distributors, motor vehicle engine; starters, for motors

(P-19199)
PARTS OUT INC (PA)
Also Called: Ats International
1875 Century Park E # 2200, Los Angeles (90067-2337)
PHONE..............................626 560-1540
Siong Tan, *President*
▲ **EMP:** 15 **EST:** 2001
SQ FT: 100,000
SALES: 6MM **Privately Held**
SIC: 3694 Distributors, motor vehicle engine

(P-19200)
PERTRONIX INC
Also Called: Patriot Products
15601 Cypress Ave Unit B, Irwindale (91706-2120)
PHONE..............................909 599-5955
Jack Porter, *Manager*
Bill Hoge, *Accounts Mgr*
EMP: 40
SALES (corp-wide): 13.8MM **Privately Held**
WEB: www.pertronix.com
SIC: 3694 5013 Ignition apparatus, internal combustion engines; automotive supplies & parts
PA: Pertronix, Inc.
440 E Arrow Hwy
San Dimas CA 91773
909 599-5955

(P-19201)
PRECO AIRCRAFT MOTORS INC
1133 Mission St, South Pasadena (91030-3211)
P.O. Box 189 (91031-0189)
PHONE..............................626 799-3549
Peter Kingston Jr, *President*

Peter Kingston Sr, *Chairman*
Linda D Kingston, *Vice Pres*
EMP: 29
SQ FT: 10,000
SALES (est): 3.3MM **Privately Held**
SIC: 3694 Motors, starting: automotive & aircraft

(P-19202)
TELEMETRIA TELEPHONY TECH INC
2635 N 1st St Ste 205, San Jose (95134-2032)
PHONE..............................408 428-0101
Allen Nejah, *President*
Mike Wallach, *CFO*
EMP: 10
SALES (est): 1.1MM **Privately Held**
SIC: 3694 Engine electrical equipment

(P-19203)
TRADEMARK CONSTRUCTION CO INC (PA)
Also Called: Jmw Truss and Components
15916 Bernardo Center Dr, San Diego (92127-1828)
PHONE..............................760 489-5647
Richard D Wilson, *President*
Nancy Wilson, *Corp Secy*
John Cao, *Vice Pres*
EMP: 100
SQ FT: 12,000
SALES (est): 20.9MM **Privately Held**
WEB: www.jmwtruss.com
SIC: 3694 Engine electrical equipment

(P-19204)
URIMAN INC (HQ)
650 N Puente St, Brea (92821-2880)
PHONE..............................714 257-2080
Kyeong Ho Lee, *CEO*
Kyung Hoon Park, *COO*
Young Hak Yun, *CFO*
Jason Kim, *Sales Mgr*
◆ **EMP:** 122
SQ FT: 42,144
SALES (est): 26.2MM **Privately Held**
WEB: www.uriman.com
SIC: 3694 3625 3714 Alternators, automotive; starter, electric motor; power steering equipment, motor vehicle

(P-19205)
VANTAGE VEHICLE INTL INC
Also Called: Vantage Vehicle Group
1740 N Delilah St, Corona (92879-1893)
PHONE..............................951 735-1200
Michael Pak, *President*
▲ **EMP:** 30
SQ FT: 50,000
SALES (est): 5.6MM **Privately Held**
WEB: www.vantagevehicle.com
SIC: 3694 Distributors, motor vehicle engine

(P-19206)
WAN LI INDUSTRIAL DEV INC
1967 W Holt Ave, Pomona (91768-3352)
PHONE..............................909 594-1818
Yanlin Zhang, *President*
▲ **EMP:** 10 **EST:** 1992
SALES (est): 1.8MM **Privately Held**
SIC: 3694 Alternators, automotive

(P-19207)
WELLS MFG USA INC
9698 Telstar Ave Ste 312, El Monte (91731-3010)
PHONE..............................626 575-2886
Jackson You, *President*
▲ **EMP:** 10
SQ FT: 4,000
SALES (est): 1.4MM **Privately Held**
SIC: 3694 Engine electrical equipment
PA: Hong Kong Wells Limited
Rm 3-4 10/F Hermes Coml Ctr
Tsim Sha Tsui KLN

3695 Recording Media

(P-19208)
3DCD
3233 Mission Oaks Blvd, Camarillo (93012-5138)
PHONE..............................805 383-3837
John Town, *Principal*
Tim Belcher, *VP Opers*
EMP: 17
SALES: 950K **Privately Held**
SIC: 3695 Magnetic & optical recording media

(P-19209)
ALPHALOGIX INC
5811 Mcfadden Ave, Huntington Beach (92649-1323)
PHONE..............................714 901-1456
Robert D McCandless, *CEO*
EMP: 52
SALES (est): 5.1MM **Privately Held**
SIC: 3695 Computer software tape & disks: blank, rigid & floppy

(P-19210)
BERKLEY INTEGRATED AUDIO SOFTW
Also Called: B I A S
121 H St, Petaluma (94952-5125)
PHONE..............................707 782-1866
Steve Berkley, *President*
Christine Anuszkiewicz, *CFO*
Christine Berkley, *Vice Pres*
EMP: 20
SALES (est): 2.2MM **Privately Held**
WEB: www.bias-inc.com
SIC: 3695 Computer software tape & disks: blank, rigid & floppy

(P-19211)
CAMSOFT CORPORATION
32295 Mission Trl Ste 8, Lake Elsinore (92530-2305)
PHONE..............................951 674-8100
Gary J Corey, *President*
Diane Corey, *Vice Pres*
EMP: 20
SQ FT: 3,000
SALES (est): 1.5MM **Privately Held**
WEB: www.camsoftcorp.com
SIC: 3695 Computer software tape & disks: blank, rigid & floppy

(P-19212)
CD VIDEO MANUFACTURING INC
Also Called: C D Video
12650 Westminster Ave, Santa Ana (92706-2139)
PHONE..............................714 265-0770
Minh T Nguyen, *President*
Charles Schredder, *Vice Pres*
Dave Nickelson, *Office Mgr*
Joe Brunatti, *Sales Staff*
▲ **EMP:** 60
SQ FT: 11,000
SALES (est): 24MM **Privately Held**
WEB: www.cdvideomfg.com
SIC: 3695 3652 7819 Video recording tape, blank; compact laser discs, prerecorded; services allied to motion pictures

(P-19213)
CVC AUDIO & VIDEO SUPPLY INC
3845 S Main St, Santa Ana (92707-5710)
PHONE..............................714 526-5725
Frank Childs, *President*
Roger Childs, *Treasurer*
Carling H Childs, *Vice Pres*
EMP: 12
SALES (est): 2.1MM **Privately Held**
WEB: www.cvcaudiovideo.com
SIC: 3695 Audio range tape, blank; video recording tape, blank

(P-19214)
ECLIPSE DATA TECHNOLOGIES INC
5139 Johnson Dr, Pleasanton (94588-3343)
PHONE..............................925 224-8880

Kevin McDonnell, *President*
Siew Chuah, *Research*
Johnathan Dacquisto, *Engineer*
Bob Edmonds, *VP Sales*
▲ **EMP:** 10
SQ FT: 1,500
SALES (est): 1.5MM **Privately Held**
WEB: www.eclipsedata.com
SIC: 3695 7371 Computer software tape & disks: blank, rigid & floppy; custom computer programming services

(P-19215)
ELECTRONIC ARTS REDWOOD INC (HQ)
Also Called: Ea Sports
209 Redwood Shores Pkwy, Redwood City (94065-1175)
PHONE..............................650 628-1500
Larry Probst, *CEO*
Stuart Lang, *Vice Pres*
Yeray Romera, *Marketing Staff*
William Payne, *Director*
Scott Mackay, *Manager*
EMP: 69
SALES: 2.9MM
SALES (corp-wide): 4.9B **Publicly Held**
SIC: 3695 Video recording tape, blank
PA: Electronic Arts Inc.
209 Redwood Shores Pkwy
Redwood City CA 94065
650 628-1500

(P-19216)
ELM SYSTEM INC
11622 El Carmino Real 1, San Diego (92130)
PHONE..............................408 694-2750
Ingyeom Kim, *CEO*
EMP: 18
SALES (est): 4MM **Privately Held**
SIC: 3695 Computer software tape & disks: blank, rigid & floppy

(P-19217)
ERISS
1124 Glen Ellen Pl 201, San Marcos (92078-1029)
PHONE..............................858 722-2177
Barbara Nyegaard, *Principal*
EMP: 10
SQ FT: 12,000
SALES (est): 1.4MM **Privately Held**
WEB: www.eriss.com
SIC: 3695 Computer software tape & disks: blank, rigid & floppy

(P-19218)
FARSTONE TECHNOLOGY INC
184 Technology Dr Ste 205, Irvine (92618-2435)
PHONE..............................949 336-4321
Thomas Lin, *President*
Mary Chuang, *Exec VP*
Tom Fedro, *Exec VP*
EMP: 110
SALES (est): 3.1MM
SALES (corp-wide): 208.7MM **Privately Held**
WEB: www.farstone.com
SIC: 3695 Computer software tape & disks: blank, rigid & floppy
PA: Solartech Energy Corp.
16, Guangfu N. Rd.,
Hukou Hsiang HSI 30351
352 768-88

(P-19219)
HOFFMAN MAGNETICS INC
19528 Ventura Blvd, Tarzana (91356-2917)
PHONE..............................818 717-5095
EMP: 20
SALES (est): 1.7MM **Privately Held**
SIC: 3695

(P-19220)
INTERMAG INC
1650 Santa Ana Ave, Sacramento (95838-1752)
PHONE..............................916 568-6744
T C Lin, *President*
CM Chen, *CFO*
EMP: 222
SQ FT: 117,288

SALES (est): 18MM Privately Held
SIC: 3695 Computer software tape & disks: blank, rigid & floppy

(P-19221)
JULY SYSTEMS INC (PA)
533 Airport Blvd Ste 395, Burlingame (94010-2012)
PHONE..................................650 685-2460
BJ Arun, *CEO*
Rajash Reddy, *President*
Ashook Narasimhan, *Principal*
Deann Swanson, *Consultant*
EMP: 18
SALES (est): 7.7MM Privately Held
WEB: www.julysystems.com
SIC: 3695 Computer software tape & disks: blank, rigid & floppy

(P-19222)
KEYIN INC
Also Called: Acca Recording Products
511 S Harbor Blvd Ste C, La Habra (90631-9376)
P.O. Box 90533, City of Industry (91715-0533)
PHONE..................................562 690-3888
Fax: 562 690-8788
▲ EMP: 12
SQ FT: 12,000
SALES (est): 1.9MM Privately Held
SIC: 3695

(P-19223)
MICROTECH SYSTEMS INC
5619 Scotts Valley Dr # 160, Scotts Valley (95066-3474)
PHONE..................................650 596-1900
Corwin Nichols, *CEO*
Sara Kumar, *COO*
Michael Fallavollita, *Vice Pres*
Lance Danbe, *Executive*
Russell Mendola, *Executive*
EMP: 15
SALES (est): 3.2MM Privately Held
WEB: www.rotech.com
SIC: 3695 Optical disks & tape, blank

(P-19224)
MONTEREY DESIGN SYSTEMS INC
2171 Landings Dr, Mountain View (94043-0837)
PHONE..................................408 747-7370
Jacques Benkoski, *President*
Aidan Cullen, *CFO*
James Koford, *Chairman*
John Larbie, *IT/INT Sup*
▲ EMP: 128 EST: 1996
SALES (est): 12.1MM Privately Held
SIC: 3695 5045 3675 Computer software tape & disks: blank, rigid & floppy; computer software; electronic capacitors

(P-19225)
MOTA GROUP INC (PA)
Also Called: Unorth
60 S Market St Ste 1100, San Jose (95113-2366)
PHONE..................................408 370-1248
Michael Faro, *CEO*
Jeffrey L Garon, *CFO*
Lily Q Ju, *Admin Sec*
◆ EMP: 25
SALES (est): 3.8MM Privately Held
SIC: 3695 Computer software tape & disks: blank, rigid & floppy

(P-19226)
MSE MEDIA SOLUTIONS INC
Also Called: M S E Media Solutions
5533 E Slauson Ave, Commerce (90040-2920)
PHONE..................................323 721-1656
Fernando Antonio Ruballos, *CEO*
▲ EMP: 24
SALES (est): 2.9MM Privately Held
WEB: www.msemedia.com
SIC: 3695 Video recording tape, blank

(P-19227)
NEURAL ID LLC
203 Redwood Shr Pkwy # 250, Redwood City (94065-6103)
PHONE..................................650 394-8800
EMP: 11

SQ FT: 2,500
SALES (est): 1.5MM Privately Held
SIC: 3695

(P-19228)
NORDSON CALIFORNIA INC
Also Called: Nordson Asymtek
2747 Loker Ave W, Carlsbad (92010-6601)
PHONE..................................760 918-8490
Michael F Hilton, *CEO*
Gregory A Thaxton, *Senior VP*
Robert E Veillette, *Vice Pres*
Joy Ladner, *Executive Asst*
Devin Morrow, *Software Engr*
◆ EMP: 94
SALES (est): 53.8MM
SALES (corp-wide): 2.2B Publicly Held
SIC: 3695 3561 Computer software tape & disks: blank, rigid & floppy; pump jacks & other pumping equipment
PA: Nordson Corporation
    28601 Clemens Rd
    Westlake OH 44145
    440 892-1580

(P-19229)
PARALLOCITY INC
440 N Wolfe Rd, Sunnyvale (94085-3869)
PHONE..................................408 524-1530
Shekhar Ambe, *President*
David Cowan, *VP Sales*
EMP: 25 EST: 2007
SALES (est): 1.8MM Privately Held
SIC: 3695 Computer software tape & disks: blank, rigid & floppy

(P-19230)
QUARTIC WEST TECHNOLOGIES
425 W 235th St, Carson (90745-5116)
PHONE..................................909 202-7038
Manny Mendoza, *Partner*
EMP: 12
SALES (est): 100K Privately Held
SIC: 3695 Instrumentation type tape, blank

(P-19231)
RECOMMIND INC (HQ)
550 Kearny St Ste 700, San Francisco (94108-2589)
PHONE..................................415 394-7899
Steve King, *CEO*
Bernard Huger, *CFO*
Ewaryst Missiuro, *Vice Pres*
Eric S Cissp, *Regional Mgr*
Nick Ball, *Sr Software Eng*
EMP: 100
SQ FT: 15,000
SALES (est): 50.1MM
SALES (corp-wide): 2.8B Privately Held
WEB: www.recommind.com
SIC: 3695 Computer software tape & disks: blank, rigid & floppy
PA: Open Text Corporation
    275 Frank Tompa Dr
    Waterloo ON N2L 0
    519 888-7111

(P-19232)
REEL PICTURE PRODUCTIONS LLC
5330 Eastgate Mall, San Diego (92121-2804)
PHONE..................................858 587-0301
Michael Ishayik, *Mng Member*
David Smiljkovich, *CFO*
Rodney Schroder, *Plant Engr*
▲ EMP: 75
SQ FT: 45,000
SALES (est): 17.3MM Privately Held
SIC: 3695 Optical disks & tape, blank

(P-19233)
SCENEWISE INC
Also Called: Comchoice
2201 Park Pl Ste 100, El Segundo (90245-5167)
PHONE..................................310 466-7692
Bob D Hively, *Ch of Bd*
Duncan Wain, *President*
Leslie Hively, *Corp Secy*
EMP: 70
SQ FT: 19,000
SALES (est): 6.6MM Privately Held
SIC: 3695 0971 Magnetic tape; game services

(P-19234)
SONY DADC US INC
4499 Glencoe Ave, Marina Del Rey (90292-6357)
PHONE..................................310 760-8500
Geoff Cambel, *Branch Mgr*
EMP: 30 Privately Held
SIC: 3695 Audio range tape, blank
HQ: Sony Dadc Us Inc.
    1800 N Fruitridge Ave
    Terre Haute IN 47804
    812 462-8100

(P-19235)
SUSTAIN TECHNOLOGIES INC (PA)
915 E 1st St, Los Angeles (90012-4050)
PHONE..................................213 229-5300
Jerry Salzman, *President*
Chris Forslund, *Technical Staff*
EMP: 10
SALES: 3MM Privately Held
SIC: 3695 Computer software tape & disks: blank, rigid & floppy

(P-19236)
TARGET TECHNOLOGY COMPANY LLC
564 Wald, Irvine (92618-4637)
PHONE..................................949 788-0909
Han H Nee,
Valerie Genrelly, *Asst Controller*
Stephene Nguyen, *Accountant*
Kazuo Furuyama, *Sales Staff*
EMP: 50 EST: 1998
SALES (est): 8.3MM Privately Held
WEB: www.targettechnology.com
SIC: 3695 Magnetic & optical recording media

(P-19237)
TECHNICOLOR DISC SERVICES CORP (HQ)
3233 Mission Oaks Blvd, Camarillo (93012-5097)
PHONE..................................805 445-1122
Mary Fialkowski, *President*
Orlando F Raimondo, *Sr Exec VP*
O F Raimondo, *Executive*
▲ EMP: 200
SQ FT: 62,000
SALES (est): 27.8MM
SALES (corp-wide): 62.9MM Privately Held
SIC: 3695 7361 Computer software tape & disks: blank, rigid & floppy; audio range tape, blank; video recording tape, blank; employment agencies

(P-19238)
THINKWAVE INC
7959 Covert Ln, Sebastopol (95472-2757)
P.O. Box 2418 (95473-2418)
PHONE..................................707 824-6200
Jim Kiriakis, *CEO*
EMP: 15
SALES (est): 1.5MM Privately Held
WEB: www.thinkwave.com
SIC: 3695 7371 Computer software tape & disks: blank, rigid & floppy; custom computer programming services

(P-19239)
UNITED AUDIO VIDEO GROUP INC
6855 Vineland Ave, North Hollywood (91605-6410)
PHONE..................................818 980-6700
Miriam Newman, *President*
Lauri Newman, *Corp Secy*
Steven Newman, *Vice Pres*
Larry Schwartz, *General Mgr*
Karol Wagner-Loy, *Accounts Mgr*
▲ EMP: 25
SQ FT: 11,500
SALES (est): 3.9MM Privately Held
WEB: www.unitedavg.com
SIC: 3695 5065 Audio range tape, blank; video recording tape, blank; tapes, audio & video recording

(P-19240)
VIDA CORPORATION
17807 Maclaren St Ste A, City of Industry (91744-5700)
PHONE..................................626 839-4912
Eva Chang Hsu, *President*
Tony Hsu, *Vice Pres*
EMP: 30
SQ FT: 40,000
SALES (est): 314.8K Privately Held
SIC: 3695 5099 Magnetic tape; video recording tape, blank; video cassettes, accessories & supplies

(P-19241)
WD MEDIA LLC
1710 Automation Pkwy, San Jose (95131-1873)
PHONE..................................408 576-2000
Timothy D Harris, *CEO*
Kathleen A Bayless, *CFO*
Mr Jan Schwartz, *Treasurer*
Richard A Kashnow, *Bd of Directors*
Peter S Norris, *Exec VP*
▲ EMP: 426
SQ FT: 188,000
SALES (est): 73.3MM
SALES (corp-wide): 16.5B Publicly Held
WEB: www.komag.com
SIC: 3695 Magnetic & optical recording media
PA: Western Digital Corporation
    5601 Great Oaks Pkwy
    San Jose CA 95119
    408 717-6000

(P-19242)
WEBALO INC
1990 S Bundy Dr Ste 540, Los Angeles (90025-5244)
PHONE..................................310 828-7335
Peter Price, *CEO*
Ashish Agarwal, *Vice Pres*
Will Trogdon, *Vice Pres*
Michael Berlin, *Office Mgr*
Seth Bruder, *CTO*
EMP: 12
SALES (est): 1.7MM Privately Held
SIC: 3695 Computer software tape & disks: blank, rigid & floppy

(P-19243)
WEFEA INC
4695 Chabot Dr Ste 200, Pleasanton (94588-2756)
PHONE..................................925 218-1839
Jay K Patel, *President*
EMP: 25
SQ FT: 900
SALES: 10MM Privately Held
SIC: 3695 Computer software tape & disks: blank, rigid & floppy

---

3699 Electrical Machinery, Eqpt & Splys, NEC

(P-19244)
3D ROBOTICS INC (PA)
Also Called: Diy Drones
1608 4th St Ste 410, Berkeley (94710-1749)
PHONE..................................415 599-1404
Chris Anderson, *CEO*
Jordi Munoz, *President*
Andy Jensen, *COO*
John Cherbini, *Vice Pres*
Kimberly Saunders, *Vice Pres*
▲ EMP: 70 EST: 2009
SALES (est): 11.7MM Privately Held
SIC: 3699 Electrical equipment & supplies

(P-19245)
A T PARKER INC (PA)
Also Called: Solar Electronics Company
10866 Chandler Blvd, North Hollywood (91601-2945)
PHONE..................................818 755-1700
Tom A Parker, *President*
Jo Ann Dennis, *Vice Pres*
Sue Parker, *Asst Sec*
▼ EMP: 22
SQ FT: 7,500

PRODUCTS & SVCS

SALES (est): 3.1MM **Privately Held**
WEB: www.parker-inc.com
SIC: **3699** Electrical equipment & supplies

(P-19246)
AAMP OF AMERICA
2500 E Francis St, Ontario (91761-7730)
PHONE..................................805 338-6800
Dennis Hill, *Owner*
▲ EMP: 11
SALES (est): 2.1MM **Privately Held**
SIC: **3699** Electrical equipment & supplies

(P-19247)
ACCSYS TECHNOLOGY INC
1177 Quarry Ln, Pleasanton (94566-4787)
PHONE..................................925 462-6949
Hirofumi Hiro Seki, *CEO*
Takao Kuboniwa, *President*
Keenan Moore, *Engineer*
David Ryan, *Engineer*
Kazuko Omoto, *Accounting Mgr*
▲ EMP: 26
SQ FT: 15,400
SALES (est): 7.3MM **Privately Held**
WEB: www.linacs.com
SIC: **3699** 8731 3663 Linear accelerators;
commercial physical research; amplifiers,
RF power & IF
PA: Hitachi, Ltd.
1-6-6, Marunouchi
Chiyoda-Ku TKY 100-0

(P-19248)
ADVANCED MANUFACTURING TECH
3140a E Coronado St, Anaheim
(92806-1914)
PHONE..................................714 238-1488
Tom Lee, *Director*
Craig M Riedel, *CFO*
Wayne Wilson, *General Mgr*
EMP: 120
SQ FT: 54,000
SALES (est): 11.4MM
SALES (corp-wide): 2.8B **Privately Held**
WEB: www.mflex.com
SIC: **3699** Electrical equipment & supplies
HQ: Multi-Fineline Electronix, Inc.
101 Academy Ste 250
Irvine CA 92617
949 453-6800

(P-19249)
ADVANCED RTRCRAFT TRINING SVCS
Also Called: Arts
938 W Evelyn Ave Unit B, Sunnyvale
(94086-5957)
PHONE..................................650 967-6300
Jerry Sun, *President*
Charles Lee, *CFO*
EMP: 20
SALES (est): 1.3MM **Privately Held**
SIC: **3699** Flight simulators (training aids),
electronic

(P-19250)
AGENTS WEST INC
Also Called: Electrical Products Rep
6 Hughes Ste 210, Irvine (92618-2063)
PHONE..................................949 614-0293
Aldo Pellicciotti, *President*
Hank Marino, *COO*
Clyde Collins, *Treasurer*
Stephen Benshoof, *Vice Pres*
Robert Rathburn, *Admin Sec*
EMP: 23
SQ FT: 30,000
SALES (est): 3MM **Privately Held**
SIC: **3699** 5063 Electrical equipment &
supplies; electrical apparatus & equip-
ment; electrical supplies

(P-19251)
AITECH DEFENSE SYSTEMS INC
19756 Prairie St, Chatsworth (91311-6531)
PHONE..................................818 700-2000
Moshe Tal, *CEO*
Erez Konfino, *CFO*
Heuy Tran, *Design Engr*
AVI Lahat, *Engineer*
Luwana Alvarado, *Human Res Mgr*
◆ EMP: 48
SQ FT: 22,000

SALES: 15.7MM **Privately Held**
WEB: www.rugged.com
SIC: **3699** Electrical equipment & supplies
PA: Aitech Rugged Group, Inc.
19756 Prairie St
Chatsworth CA 91311

(P-19252)
AITECH RUGGED GROUP INC (PA)
19756 Prairie St, Chatsworth (91311-6531)
PHONE..................................818 700-2000
Moshe Tal, *CEO*
Erez Konfino, *CFO*
EMP: 50
SALES: 29.9MM **Privately Held**
SIC: **3699** Electrical equipment & supplies

(P-19253)
AKT AMERICA INC (HQ)
3101 Scott Blvd Bldg 91, Santa Clara
(95054-3318)
PHONE..................................408 563-5455
In Doo Kang, *Vice Pres*
Chang Olivia, *Admin Asst*
Jun Yang, *Software Engr*
Henry Vargas, *Electrical Engi*
Balakrishnam Jampana, *Engineer*
▲ EMP: 400
SQ FT: 200,000
SALES: 8B
SALES (corp-wide): 17.2B **Publicly Held**
WEB: www.appliedmaterials.com
SIC: **3699** Electrical equipment & supplies
PA: Applied Materials, Inc.
3050 Bowers Ave
Santa Clara CA 95054
408 727-5555

(P-19254)
ALPHA LASER
302 Elizabeth Ln, Corona (92880-2504)
PHONE..................................951 582-0285
Kaan Cakmak, *President*
Sule Cakmak, *Office Mgr*
EMP: 13
SALES (est): 1.1MM **Privately Held**
SIC: **3699** Laser welding, drilling & cutting
equipment

(P-19255)
ALTA PROPERTIES INC
Also Called: Sonatech Division
879 Ward Dr, Santa Barbara (93111-2920)
PHONE..................................805 683-1431
Karen Vaughn, *Administration*
EMP: 475
SALES (corp-wide): 197.5MM **Privately Held**
WEB: www.sonatech.com
SIC: **3699** Electrical equipment & supplies
PA: Alta Properties, Inc.
879 Ward Dr
Santa Barbara CA 93111
805 967-0171

(P-19256)
ALTA PROPERTIES INC
Sonatech
879 Ward Dr, Santa Barbara (93111-2920)
PHONE..................................805 690-5382
Geoff Warner, *IT/INT Sup*
Chuck Randall, *Engineer*
EMP: 475
SALES (corp-wide): 197.5MM **Privately Held**
SIC: **3699** Underwater sound equipment
PA: Alta Properties, Inc.
879 Ward Dr
Santa Barbara CA 93111
805 967-0171

(P-19257)
AMREX-ZETRON INC
Also Called: Amrex Electrotherapy Equipment
7034 Jackson St, Paramount (90723-4835)
PHONE..................................310 527-6868
George Bell, *President*
Carina Bassett, *Manager*
▲ EMP: 35
SQ FT: 20,000

SALES (est): 5.7MM **Privately Held**
WEB: www.amrex-zetron.com
SIC: **3699** 3845 High-energy particle
physics equipment; electromedical equipment

(P-19258)
AOPTIX TECHNOLOGIES INC
695 Campbell Tech Pkwy # 100, Campbell
(95008-5076)
PHONE..................................408 558-3300
Michael Klayko, *CEO*
Dean Senner, *Ch of Bd*
Anthony Mazzarella, *President*
Earl C Charles, *CFO*
Chandrasekhar Pusarla, *Senior VP*
EMP: 65 EST: 2000
SQ FT: 12,000
SALES (est): 1.2MM **Privately Held**
WEB: www.aoptix.com
SIC: **3699** Laser systems & equipment

(P-19259)
AREESYS CORPORATION
4055 Clipper Ct, Fremont (94538-6540)
PHONE..................................510 979-9601
Kai-An Wang, *CEO*
Ning Zhao, *CFO*
EMP: 40
SALES (est): 5.5MM **Privately Held**
SIC: **3699** Electrical equipment & supplies

(P-19260)
ARM ELECTRONICS INC
8860 Industrial Ave # 140, Roseville
(95678-6204)
P.O. Box 1388 (95678-8388)
PHONE..................................916 787-1100
Mark Haney, *CEO*
▲ EMP: 44 EST: 2000
SQ FT: 45,000
SALES (est): 5MM **Privately Held**
WEB: www.armelectronics.com
SIC: **3699** Security control equipment &
systems

(P-19261)
ASSA ABLOY ENTRANCE SYS US INC
Also Called: Besam Entrance Solutions
9733 Kent St 100, Elk Grove (95624-8800)
PHONE..................................916 686-4116
Jim Dill, *Branch Mgr*
EMP: 18
SALES (corp-wide): 9.3B **Privately Held**
SIC: **3699** 1796 3442 Door opening &
closing devices, electrical; installing build-
ing equipment; metal doors
HQ: Assa Abloy Entrance Systems Us Inc.
1900 Airport Rd
Monroe NC 28110
704 290-5520

(P-19262)
ASSA ABLOY ENTRANCE SYSTEMS US
Also Called: Besam Entrance Solutions
1520 S Sinclair St, Anaheim (92806-5933)
PHONE..................................714 578-0526
Erik Huber, *Branch Mgr*
EMP: 53
SALES (corp-wide): 9.3B **Privately Held**
SIC: **3699** 1796 3442 Door opening &
closing devices, electrical; installing build-
ing equipment; metal doors
HQ: Assa Abloy Entrance Systems Us Inc.
1900 Airport Rd
Monroe NC 28110
704 290-5520

(P-19263)
AVIVA BIOSCIENCES CORPORATION
7700 Ronson Rd Ste 100, San Diego
(92111-1553)
PHONE..................................858 552-0888
Norrie Russell, *President*
Lei Wu PHD, *COO*
Peter Wilding, *Chairman*
Xiaobo Wang, *Surgery Dir*
Weiping Yang, *Surgery Dir*
EMP: 26 EST: 1999
SALES (est): 5.2MM **Privately Held**
WEB: www.avivabio.com
SIC: **3699** Electrical equipment & supplies

(P-19264)
AZTECH PRODUCTS INTERNATIONAL
326 10th St, Del Mar (92014-2825)
PHONE..................................858 481-8412
Chris Underhill, *President*
▲ EMP: 27
SALES: 2.5MM **Privately Held**
SIC: **3699** Electrical equipment & supplies

(P-19265)
BLISSLIGHTS INC
100 E San Marcos Blvd # 308, San Marcos
(92069-2989)
PHONE..................................888 868-4603
Alan Lee, *President*
▲ EMP: 43
SALES (est): 30.5MM **Privately Held**
SIC: **3699** Laser systems & equipment

(P-19266)
BOLIDE TECHNOLOGY GROUP INC
Also Called: Bolide International
468 S San Dimas Ave, San Dimas
(91773-4045)
PHONE..................................909 305-8889
David Liu, *President*
Angela Wang, *Office Mgr*
Mike Lugo, *Engineer*
Fiona Du, *Accountant*
Camilo Avila, *Sales Mgr*
◆ EMP: 70
SQ FT: 16,000
SALES (est): 11.6MM **Privately Held**
WEB: www.bolideco.com
SIC: **3699** Security devices

(P-19267)
BYRUM TECHNOLOGIES INC
550 S Pacific St Ste 100, San Marcos
(92078-4058)
PHONE..................................760 744-6692
James E Byrum, *President*
Kathleen J Byrum, *Admin Sec*
EMP: 28
SQ FT: 12,000
SALES (est): 2.8MM **Privately Held**
SIC: **3699** 7692 Laser welding, drilling &
cutting equipment; welding repair

(P-19268)
C C T LASER SERVICES INC
25421 S Schulte Rd, Tracy (95377-9709)
PHONE..................................209 833-1110
Roger Underwood, *President*
EMP: 10
SQ FT: 10,000
SALES (est): 1.4MM **Privately Held**
WEB: www.cctlaser.com
SIC: **3699** Laser welding, drilling & cutting
equipment

(P-19269)
CAL STAR SYSTEMS GROUP INC
Also Called: Quikstor
6613 Valjean Ave, Van Nuys (91406-5817)
PHONE..................................818 922-2000
Dennis Levitt, *President*
April Lee, *Technical Staff*
Shaina Cossairt, *Sales Staff*
▲ EMP: 22
SALES (est): 3.4MM **Privately Held**
WEB: www.quikstor.com
SIC: **3699** 7371 Security devices; com-
puter software development

(P-19270)
CARTTRONICS LLC
8 Studebaker, Irvine (92618-2012)
PHONE..................................888 696-2278
John R French,
Donald Testa, *Vice Pres*
▲ EMP: 31 EST: 1997
SQ FT: 14,000
SALES (est): 5.2MM
SALES (corp-wide): 17.1MM **Privately Held**
WEB: www.carttronics.com
SIC: **3699** 7382 5065 Security devices;
security systems services; security control
equipment & systems

PA: Gatekeeper Systems, Inc.
90 Icon
Foothill Ranch CA 92610
949 268-1414

(P-19271)
CED ANAHEIM 018
Also Called: California Electric Supply
1304 S Allec St, Anaheim (92805-6303)
PHONE.................................714 956-5156
Steve Richardson, *Manager*
Tom A Catullo, *Manager*
EMP: 14
SALES (est): 2.5MM **Privately Held**
SIC: 3699 5063 Electrical equipment &
supplies; electrical apparatus & equip-
ment

(P-19272)
CENTRAL TECH INC
2271 Ringwood Ave, San Jose
(95131-1717)
PHONE.................................408 955-0919
EMP: 13
SALES (est): 2.7MM **Privately Held**
SIC: 3699 Electronic training devices

(P-19273)
CLEAN AMERICA INC
Also Called: EDM Performance Accessories
1400 Pioneer St, Brea (92821-3720)
PHONE.................................562 694-5990
Jim E Swartzbaugh, *President*
Tom Adams, *Vice Pres*
Dave Liukkonen, *Sales Mgr*
Jeff Daneke, *Sales Staff*
Reese Remy, *Sales Staff*
▲ EMP: 15
SQ FT: 14,000
SALES (est): 3.7MM **Privately Held**
WEB: www.cleanup-america.com
SIC: 3699 Electrical equipment & supplies

(P-19274)
CLEAR PATH TECHNOLOGIES INC
561 W Rincon St, Corona (92880-2019)
P.O. Box 1996 (92878-1996)
PHONE.................................951 278-3520
William Nitze, *President*
Roger Spillmann, *CEO*
EMP: 10
SALES (est): 1.4MM **Privately Held**
SIC: 3699 Fire control or bombing equip-
ment, electronic

(P-19275)
CODA ENERGY HOLDINGS LLC
111 N Artsakh St Ste 300, Glendale
(91206-4097)
PHONE.................................626 775-3900
Paul Detering, *CEO*
Peter Nortman, *COO*
John Bryan, *Vice Pres*
Davnette Librando,
Edward Solar,
▲ EMP: 43
SALES (est): 8.3MM **Privately Held**
SIC: 3699 Household electrical equipment

(P-19276)
COHERENT INC
Also Called: Coherent Auburn Group, The
5100 Patrick Henry Dr, Santa Clara
(95054-1112)
PHONE.................................408 764-4000
Robin Henderson, *General Mgr*
EMP: 700
SALES (corp-wide): 1.7B **Publicly Held**
SIC: 3699 3827 3674 Laser systems &
equipment; optical instruments & lenses;
semiconductors & related devices
PA: Coherent, Inc.
5100 Patrick Henry Dr
Santa Clara CA 95054
408 764-4000

(P-19277)
COMPULOCKS BRANDS INC
9115 Dice Rd Ste 18, Santa Fe Springs
(90670-2538)
PHONE.................................562 201-2913
Martin Noble, *President*
EMP: 19

SALES (est): 3MM **Privately Held**
SIC: 3699 5065 7382 Security devices;
security control equipment & systems; security systems services

(P-19278)
CONSTRUCTION INNOVATIONS LLC
Also Called: Ci
10630 Mather Blvd Ste 200, Mather
(95655-4125)
PHONE.................................855 725-9555
Larry A Devore, *President*
James B Littlejohn, *CFO*
Kevin Austin, *Director*
Rob Stubben, *Director*
John Lathouwers, *Manager*
EMP: 150
SQ FT: 17,000
SALES: 160MM **Privately Held**
SIC: 3699 Electrical equipment &
supplies; consulting engineer
PA: Bdg Innovations, Llc
6001 Outfall Cir
Sacramento CA 95828
855 725-9555

(P-19279)
CONTROLLED ENTRANCES INC
27525 Valley Center Rd A, Valley Center
(92082-6556)
PHONE.................................760 749-1212
Bruce Clark, *President*
Shaun Clark, *Manager*
EMP: 15
SQ FT: 6,000
SALES (est): 2.2MM **Privately Held**
WEB: www.controlledentrancesinc.com
SIC: 3699 1799 5211 Security devices;
fence construction; fencing

(P-19280)
CONVERGINT TECHNOLOGIES LLC
1667 N Batavia St, Orange (92867-3508)
PHONE.................................714 546-2780
Mike Mathis, *Branch Mgr*
EMP: 20
SALES (corp-wide): 13.4MM **Privately Held**
WEB: www.convergint.com
SIC: 3699 Security devices
HQ: Convergint Technologies Llc
1 Commerce Dr
Schaumburg IL 60173
847 620-5000

(P-19281)
COZZIA USA LLC
861 S Oak Park Rd, Covina (91724-3624)
PHONE.................................626 667-2272
Mark Holmes, *COO*
Jimmy Lo, *CFO*
▲ EMP: 20
SQ FT: 5,500
SALES: 21MM
SALES (corp-wide): 784.6MM **Privately Held**
SIC: 3699 Electrical equipment & supplies
PA: Xiamen Comfort Science&Technology
Group Co., Ltd.
No.31, Anling 2nd Road, Huli High-
Tech Park
Xiamen 36100
592 379-5700

(P-19282)
CUBIC DEFENSE APPLICATIONS INC
CMS Secure Comms
9333 Balboa Ave, San Diego (92123-1515)
PHONE.................................858 505-2870
Jerry Madigan, *Vice Pres*
EMP: 200
SALES (corp-wide): 1.2B **Publicly Held**
SIC: 3699 7382 Security devices; security
systems services
HQ: Cubic Defense Applications, Inc.
9333 Balboa Ave
San Diego CA 92123
858 277-6780

(P-19283)
CUBIC DEFENSE APPLICATIONS INC (HQ)
9333 Balboa Ave, San Diego (92123-1515)
P.O. Box 85587 (92186-5587)
PHONE.................................858 277-6780
William J Toti, *CEO*
John D Thomas, *CFO*
Janice Hamby, *Bd of Directors*
James R Edwards, *Senior VP*
Mark A Harrison, *Senior VP*
◆ EMP: 589
SQ FT: 130,000
SALES (est): 1.6B
SALES (corp-wide): 1.2B **Publicly Held**
SIC: 3699 3663 3812 Flight simulators
(training aids), electronic; radio & TV
communications equipment; aircraft/aero-
space flight instruments & guidance sys-
tems; navigational systems &
instruments; defense systems & equip-
ment; search & detection systems & in-
struments
PA: Cubic Corporation
9333 Balboa Ave
San Diego CA 92123
858 277-6780

(P-19284)
CXC SIMULATIONS LLC
3160 W El Segundo Blvd, Hawthorne
(90250-4842)
PHONE.................................888 918-2010
Chris Considine,
Christopher X Considine,
Jochen Repolust,
EMP: 11 EST: 2007
SALES (est): 1.3MM **Privately Held**
SIC: 3699 Flight simulators (training aids),
electronic

(P-19285)
CYBER SWITCHING INC
2050 Ringwood Ave Frnt, San Jose
(95131-1783)
PHONE.................................408 595-3670
Charles H Reynolds, *President*
Shelly Paiva, *CFO*
Richard Yeadon, *Vice Pres*
EMP: 25
SQ FT: 25,000
SALES (est): 4.5MM **Privately Held**
WEB: www.cyberswitching.com
SIC: 3699 Electrical equipment & supplies

(P-19286)
CYMER LLC (HQ)
Also Called: Asml USA
17075 Thornmint Ct, San Diego
(92127-2413)
PHONE.................................858 385-7300
Joost Stienen, *CEO*
Robert P Akins, *Senior VP*
Richard L Sandstrom, *Senior VP*
Marshall Benham, *Vice Pres*
Geert Beullens, *Vice Pres*
▲ EMP: 555
SALES: 606.7MM
SALES (corp-wide): 12.5B **Privately Held**
SIC: 3699 3827 Laser systems & equip-
ment; lens mounts
PA: Asml Holding N.V.
De Run 6501
Veldhoven 5504
402 683-000

(P-19287)
D & D SECURITY RESOURCES INC (PA)
Also Called: D&D Security Enterprises
200 Mason Cir Ste C, Concord
(94520-1249)
PHONE.................................800 453-4195
Dean Smith, *President*
Tanya Pickett, *Purch Mgr*
Jeff Rogers, *Sales Staff*
Randy Clarke, *Accounts Mgr*
▲ EMP: 15
SQ FT: 4,500
SALES: 8.5MM **Privately Held**
WEB: www.ddsecurity.com
SIC: 3699 5712 Security devices; office
furniture

(P-19288)
DATA STORM INC
Also Called: Mytek America
2001 Manistee Dr, La Canada Flintridge
(91011-1209)
PHONE.................................818 352-4994
Byung Woo Min, *President*
Chunghee Min, *Admin Sec*
▲ EMP: 13
SQ FT: 8,000
SALES (est): 1.9MM **Privately Held**
WEB: www.mytekalarms.com
SIC: 3699 5999 Security control equip-
ment & systems; alarm signal systems

(P-19289)
DELTA TURNSTILES LLC
Also Called: Delta Turnstile Controls
1011 Detroit Ave, Concord (94518-2410)
P.O. Box 3664, Santa Clara (95055-3664)
PHONE.................................925 969-1498
Thomas Howell, *Mng Member*
Vanessa Howell, *Project Mgr*
EMP: 10
SALES (est): 1.3MM **Privately Held**
WEB: www.deltaturnstile.com
SIC: 3699 Security devices

(P-19290)
DESIGNER SOUND SEC SYSTEMS
13547 Ventura Blvd # 338, Sherman Oaks
(91423-3825)
PHONE.................................818 981-9249
Anthony Stampfer, *President*
EMP: 12
SALES (est): 1.7MM **Privately Held**
SIC: 3699 7382 1731 Security control
equipment & systems; security systems
services; safety & security specialization

(P-19291)
DISTRIBUTION ELECTRNICS VLUED
Also Called: Deva
2651 Dow Ave, Tustin (92780-7207)
PHONE.................................714 368-1717
Rodger Dale Baker, *CEO*
Ken Plock, *COO*
Gary Bata, *Opers Mgr*
Michael Woods, *Opers Staff*
Maureen Supple, *Sales Staff*
◆ EMP: 23 EST: 1974
SQ FT: 13,800
SALES (est): 5.6MM **Privately Held**
SIC: 3699 5065 Electrical equipment &
supplies; electronic parts & equipment
HQ: Deva, Inc.
450 W 15th St Ste 501
New York NY 10011
212 223-2466

(P-19292)
DIY CO
3360 20th St, San Francisco (94110-2655)
PHONE.................................844 564-6349
Zach Klein, *CEO*
Ashley Qian, *Software Engr*
EMP: 16
SALES (est): 1.6MM **Privately Held**
SIC: 3699 Teaching machines & aids, elec-
tronic
HQ: Littlebits Electronics Inc.
601 W 26th St Rm M274
New York NY 10001

(P-19293)
DOORKING INC (PA)
120 S Glasgow Ave, Inglewood
(90301-1502)
PHONE.................................310 645-0023
Thomas Richmond, *President*
Pat Kochie, *Vice Pres*
Susan Richmond, *Admin Sec*
Mario Sanchez, *Info Tech Mgr*
Kevin Lee, *Design Engr*
◆ EMP: 185 EST: 1948
SQ FT: 16,000
SALES: 55MM **Privately Held**
WEB: www.dkaccess.com
SIC: 3699 5065 3829 Security control
equipment & systems; security control
equipment & systems; measuring & con-
trolling devices

(P-19294)
DPSS LASERS INC
2525 Walsh Ave, Santa Clara
(95051-1316)
PHONE..................................408 988-4300
Alex Laymon, *President*
Thomas Hogan, *CEO*
Timothy Houtz, *Technician*
Malinna Tian, *Accounting Mgr*
EMP: 30
SQ FT: 25,000
SALES (est): 6MM **Privately Held**
WEB: www.dpss-lasers.com
SIC: 3699 Laser systems & equipment

(P-19295)
DUNAN SENSING LLC
1953 Concourse Dr, San Jose
(95131-1708)
PHONE..................................408 613-1015
Tom Nguyen, *Principal*
Annie Tran, *Manager*
◆ EMP: 36
SQ FT: 15,000
SALES: 1.8MM **Privately Held**
SIC: 3699 Laser welding, drilling & cutting
equipment

(P-19296)
DUTEK INCORPORATED
2228 Oak Ridge Way, Vista (92081-8341)
PHONE..................................760 566-8888
David Du, *CEO*
Bill Marsh, *Vice Pres*
Dee Trabert, *Financial Exec*
Greg Skodacek, *QC Mgr*
Ivan Auffret, *Opers Staff*
EMP: 50
SQ FT: 4,500
SALES (est): 9.8MM
SALES (corp-wide): 30.5MM **Privately
Held**
SIC: 3699 3629 3643 Electrical equip-
ment & supplies; electronic generation
equipment; current-carrying wiring de-
vices
PA: Ddh Enterprise, Inc.
2220 Oak Ridge Way
Vista CA 92081
760 599-0171

(P-19297)
DYNAMIC FABRICATION INC
2615 S Hickory St, Santa Ana
(92707-3713)
PHONE..................................714 662-2440
Andrew Crook, *President*
Olga Garcia Crook, *Corp Secy*
EMP: 15
SQ FT: 22,000
SALES (est): 3.9MM **Privately Held**
WEB: www.dynamicfab.com
SIC: 3699 3728 3764 3761 Laser weld-
ing, drilling & cutting equipment; aircraft
parts & equipment; engines & engine
parts, guided missile; guided missiles &
space vehicles

(P-19298)
E E SYSTEMS GROUP INC
12346 Valley Blvd Unit A, El Monte
(91732-3682)
PHONE..................................626 452-8988
Randall Wang, *President*
▲ EMP: 12
SALES (est): 1.2MM **Privately Held**
SIC: 3699 Security devices

(P-19299)
E-FUEL CORPORATION
15466 Los Gatos Blvd 37, Los Gatos
(95032-2542)
PHONE..................................408 267-2667
EMP: 32
SALES (est): 3MM **Privately Held**
SIC: 3699

(P-19300)
EASTERNCCTV (USA) LLC
Also Called: Ens Security
525 Parriott Pl W, Hacienda Heights
(91745-1033)
PHONE..................................626 961-8810
Xianjie Xiong, *Mng Member*
Ramon Rincon, *Sales Staff*
EMP: 74

SALES (corp-wide): 12.9MM **Privately
Held**
SIC: 3699 Security devices
PA: Easterncctv (Usa), Llc
50 Commercial St
Plainview NY 11803
516 870-3779

(P-19301)
EATON CORPORATION
Also Called: Cutler-Hammer
11120 Philadelphia Ave, Jurupa Valley
(91752-1168)
PHONE..................................951 685-5788
Rich Kilar, *Manager*
EMP: 16 **Privately Held**
WEB: www.eaton.com
SIC: 3699 Electrical equipment & supplies
HQ: Eaton Corporation
1000 Eaton Blvd
Cleveland OH 44122
440 523-5000

(P-19302)
ELECTRIC GATE STORE INC
(PA)
421 Park Ave, San Fernando (91340-2525)
PHONE..................................818 504-2300
Jorge Nunez, *President*
Karla Nunez, *Vice Pres*
▲ EMP: 150
SQ FT: 4,725
SALES (est): 18.9MM **Privately Held**
WEB: www.gatestore.com
SIC: 3699 Security devices

(P-19303)
ELECTRIC GATE STORE INC
15342 Chatsworth St, Mission Hills
(91345-2041)
PHONE..................................818 361-6872
Jorge Nunez, *Branch Mgr*
EMP: 150
SALES (corp-wide): 18.9MM **Privately
Held**
SIC: 3699 Security devices
PA: Electric Gate Store, Inc.
421 Park Ave
San Fernando CA 91340
818 504-2300

(P-19304)
**ELECTRONIC INTERFACE CO
INC**
Also Called: Applied Engineering
6341 San Ignacio Ave # 10, San Jose
(95119-1202)
PHONE..................................408 286-2134
Jack Yao, *President*
Katherine Nguyen, *Controller*
John Villadsen, *Opers Staff*
Brian McMorris, *Sales Staff*
Eric Miller, *Supervisor*
EMP: 75
SALES (est): 17.3MM **Privately Held**
SIC: 3699 7694 Electrical equipment &
supplies; armature rewinding shops

(P-19305)
ENVIA SYSTEMS INC
7979 Gateway Blvd Ste 101, Newark
(94560-1157)
P.O. Box 14142, Fremont (94539-1342)
PHONE..................................510 509-1367
Sujeet Kumar, *President*
▲ EMP: 50 EST: 2007
SALES (est): 9.2MM **Privately Held**
SIC: 3699 Electrical equipment & supplies

(P-19306)
EOPLEX INC
1321 Ridder Park Dr 10, San Jose
(95131-2306)
PHONE..................................408 638-5100
Arthur L Chait, *CEO*
EMP: 13
SALES (est): 1.6MM **Privately Held**
SIC: 3699 Electrical equipment & supplies

(P-19307)
EOPLEX TECHNOLOGIES INC
2940 N 1st St, San Jose (95134-2021)
PHONE..................................408 638-5100
Arthur Chait, *President*
Charles Taylor, *Founder*
Philip E Rogren, *VP Mktg*

Sean Foote, *Director*
Michio Fujimura, *Director*
▲ EMP: 15
SALES (est): 3MM **Privately Held**
WEB: www.eoplex.com
SIC: 3699 Electrical equipment & supplies

(P-19308)
ETON CORPORATION
1015 Corporation Way, Palo Alto
(94303-4305)
PHONE..................................650 903-3866
Esmail Amid-Hozour, *President*
John Smith, *Senior VP*
Esmail Hozour, *Executive*
Skip Orvis, *Engineer*
Winston Wang, *Engineer*
▲ EMP: 45
SQ FT: 10,400
SALES (est): 11.9MM **Privately Held**
WEB: www.etoncorp.com
SIC: 3699 Electrical equipment & supplies

(P-19309)
FAAC
357 S Acacia Ave Unit 357 # 357, Fullerton
(92831-4748)
PHONE..................................800 221-8278
Andrea Marcellan, *Branch Mgr*
EMP: 10
SALES (corp-wide): 3.7MM **Privately
Held**
SIC: 3699 Door opening & closing devices,
electrical
PA: Faac
3160 Murrell Rd
Rockledge FL 32955

(P-19310)
**FEITIAN TECHNOLOGIES US
INC**
4677 Old Ironsides Dr # 312, Santa Clara
(95054-1857)
PHONE..................................408 352-5553
Yu Huang, *CEO*
EMP: 10
SALES (est): 795.1K **Privately Held**
SIC: 3699 Security devices

(P-19311)
**FLYTHISSIM TECHNOLOGIES
INC**
3534 Empleo St Ste B, San Luis Obispo
(93401-7333)
PHONE..................................844 746-2846
Roland Nissim, *Director*
Carl Suttle, *Director*
EMP: 10
SALES (est): 714.1K **Privately Held**
SIC: 3699 Flight simulators (training aids),
electronic

(P-19312)
FORMAX TECHNOLOGIES INC
Also Called: Fti
305 S Soderquist Rd, Turlock
(95380-5130)
PHONE..................................209 668-1001
Ryan Lindsay, *President*
T Ryan Lindsay, *President*
Timothy D Lindsay, *CEO*
Melody Wright, *Cust Svc Dir*
▲ EMP: 35
SQ FT: 66,000
SALES (est): 5.4MM **Privately Held**
SIC: 3699 Electrical equipment & supplies

(P-19313)
FREEDOM PHOTONICS LLC
41 Aero Camino, Santa Barbara
(93117-3104)
PHONE..................................805 967-4900
Milan Mashanovitch,
Misty Cuellar, *Office Admin*
Brian Ehrsam, *Engineer*
Henry Garrett, *Senior Engr*
Miranda Tang, *Finance*
EMP: 33
SQ FT: 14,500
SALES (est): 7.5MM **Privately Held**
WEB: www.freedomphotonics.com
SIC: 3699 3827 3674 Laser systems &
equipment; optical test & inspection
equipment; light sensitive devices

(P-19314)
FULLER MANUFACTURING INC
130 Ridge Rd, Sutter Creek (95685)
P.O. Box 999 (95685-0999)
PHONE..................................209 267-5071
Christopher Fuller, *President*
Shirley Fuller, *Corp Secy*
EMP: 15
SQ FT: 5,000
SALES: 1.4MM **Privately Held**
SIC: 3699 3694 3679 Electrical equip-
ment & supplies; automotive electrical
equipment; electronic circuits

(P-19315)
FUTURE FIBRE TECH US INC
(HQ)
800 W El Cam, Mountain View (94040)
PHONE..................................650 903-2222
Eric Reynolds, *Vice Pres*
Leigh Davis, *CFO*
EMP: 14
SALES (est): 4MM **Privately Held**
SIC: 3699 Security control equipment &
systems

(P-19316)
GATEKEEPER SYSTEMS INC
(PA)
90 Icon, Foothill Ranch (92610-3000)
PHONE..................................949 268-1414
Michael Lawler, *CEO*
Stephen Hannah, *President*
Erik Paulson, *President*
Ashley Morgan, *Officer*
R J Brandes, *Vice Pres*
◆ EMP: 35
SQ FT: 15,000
SALES (est): 17.1MM **Privately Held**
WEB: www.gatekeepersystems.com
SIC: 3699 Security devices

(P-19317)
GEFEN LLC
1800 S Mcdowell Blvd Ext, Petaluma
(94954-6962)
PHONE..................................818 772-9100
Hagai Gefen, *CEO*
Tony Dowzall, *President*
Jill Gefen, *Vice Pres*
Aaron Hernandez, *Director*
Robert Lemer, *Director*
▲ EMP: 42
SQ FT: 8,000
SALES: 44MM
SALES (corp-wide): 11B **Privately Held**
WEB: www.gefen.com
SIC: 3699 High-energy particle physics
equipment
HQ: Nortek Security & Control Llc
5919 Sea Otter Pl Ste 100
Carlsbad CA 92010
760 438-7000

(P-19318)
GEMFIRE CORPORATION
2570 N 1st St Ste 440, San Jose
(95131-1018)
PHONE..................................408 519-6015
Rick Tompane, *CEO*
Carl Yordan, *CFO*
William Bischel, *Vice Pres*
EMP: 85
SQ FT: 50,000
SALES (est): 11.2MM **Privately Held**
SIC: 3699 8731 Laser systems & equip-
ment; commercial physical research

(P-19319)
**GLOBAL CUSTOM SECURITY
INC**
755 Lakefield Rd Ste B, Westlake Village
(91361-2646)
PHONE..................................818 889-6900
Delaney Broussard, *President*
Carla Broussard, *Corp Secy*
Marty Howard, *Vice Pres*
Rupert Talbot, *General Mgr*
Erin Seamans, *Sales Staff*
EMP: 12
SQ FT: 2,400
SALES (est): 2.4MM **Privately Held**
WEB: www.globalcustom.com
SIC: 3699 1731 Security devices; electri-
cal work

(P-19320)

GORES RADIO HOLDINGS LLC
10877 Wilshire Blvd # 1805, Los Angeles (90024-4341)
PHONE..................................310 209-3010
Alex Gores, *President*
EMP: 1501
SALES (est): 58MM
SALES (corp-wide): 3.8B **Privately Held**
SIC: 3699 7382 Security devices; security systems services
PA: The Gores Group Llc
9800 Wilshire Blvd
Beverly Hills CA 90212
310 209-3010

(P-19321)

HESS PRECISION LASER INC
4747 Stratos Way Ste D, Modesto (95356-8893)
P.O. Box 747, Denair (95316-0747)
PHONE..................................209 575-1634
Randall R Hess, *President*
Belinda M Hess, *CFO*
Weston Hess, *Opers Mgr*
EMP: 10
SQ FT: 7,200
SALES (est): 2.1MM **Privately Held**
WEB: www.hessprecisionlaser.com
SIC: 3699 Laser systems & equipment

(P-19322)

IJK & CO INC
Also Called: Bayshore Lights
225 Industrial St, San Francisco (94124-1928)
PHONE..................................415 826-8899
Michael Tseng, *CEO*
EMP: 50
SALES: 20MM **Privately Held**
SIC: 3699 5063 Electrical equipment & supplies; electrical supplies; plumbing, heating, air-conditioning contractors; lighting maintenance service

(P-19323)

IMPEVA LABS INC (PA)
2570 W El Cam, Mountain View (94040)
PHONE..................................650 559-0103
Bradley H Feldman, *President*
Gregory L Tanner, *Treasurer*
Randall L Shepard, *Senior VP*
Thomas A Echols, *Vice Pres*
William L Hoese, *Vice Pres*
EMP: 13
SQ FT: 3,400
SALES (est): 3.1MM **Privately Held**
WEB: www.impeva.com
SIC: 3699 Security devices

(P-19324)

INNOVATIVETEK INC
1271 W 9th St, Upland (91786-5706)
PHONE..................................909 981-3401
Sandy Samudrala, *President*
Theresa Romero, *Exec VP*
Paul Trinh, *Vice Pres*
Terri Romero, *CIO*
Ashley McBride, *Clerk*
EMP: 23
SALES: 3MM **Privately Held**
SIC: 3699 Electronic training devices

(P-19325)

INTEGRITY SECURITY SVCS LLC
30 W Sola St, Santa Barbara (93101-2508)
PHONE..................................805 965-6044
Jeffrey R Hazarian, *President*
Alan Meyer, *Vice Pres*
Cameron Durham, *Software Engr*
Jason Isaacs, *General Counsel*
EMP: 14
SALES (est): 2.2MM
SALES (corp-wide): 23.4MM **Privately Held**
WEB: www.valicore.com
SIC: 3699 7371 Security control equipment & systems; custom computer programming services; computer software systems analysis & design, custom; computer software development
HQ: Green Hills Software Llc
30 W Sola St
Santa Barbara CA 93101
805 965-6044

(P-19326)

INTELLIGENCE SUPPORT GROUP LTD
Also Called: I S G
7100 Monache Mtn, Inyokern (93527)
PHONE..................................800 504-3341
Richard Disabatino, *CEO*
William Alden, *President*
Richard Di Sabatino, *Manager*
EMP: 20
SQ FT: 20,000
SALES (est): 2.4MM **Privately Held**
WEB: www.isghq.com
SIC: 3699 Security control equipment & systems

(P-19327)

INTERGEN INC
1145 Tasman Dr, Sunnyvale (94089-2228)
PHONE..................................408 245-2737
Kris Madeyski, *President*
John Horn, *Admin Sec*
EMP: 11
SQ FT: 7,000
SALES (est): 1.3MM **Privately Held**
SIC: 3699 7371 Laser systems & equipment; computer software development & applications

(P-19328)

IONETIX CORPORATION (PA)
101 The Embarcadero # 210, San Francisco (94105-1222)
PHONE..................................415 944-1440
Kevin Cameron, *CEO*
David Eve, *Vice Pres*
Carrie Busch, *VP Finance*
Joe Lambert, *Controller*
Skip Turek, *Purchasing*
EMP: 35
SALES (est): 4.7MM **Privately Held**
SIC: 3699 Cyclotrons

(P-19329)

IRONWOOD ELECTRIC INC
1239 N Tustin Ave, Anaheim (92807-1603)
PHONE..................................714 630-2350
Raymond Chafe, *Principal*
Joe Moreno, *Project Mgr*
Anders Howmann, *Technology*
Ray Chafe, *Sales Staff*
Joey Hanson, *Superintendent*
EMP: 28 EST: 2011
SALES (est): 6.6MM **Privately Held**
SIC: 3699 1731 Electrical equipment & supplies; electrical work

(P-19330)

IWERKS ENTERTAINMENT INC
Also Called: Simex-Iwerks
27509 Avenue Hopkins, Santa Clarita (91355-3910)
PHONE..................................661 678-1800
Gary Matus, *CEO*
Donald Stults, *COO*
Jeff Dahl, *CFO*
Mark Cornell, *Senior VP*
Mairead McKeron, *Mktg Coord*
EMP: 75
SQ FT: 23,000
SALES (est): 1.5MM
SALES (corp-wide): 17.7MM **Privately Held**
WEB: www.iwerks.com
SIC: 3699 7819 Electrical equipment & supplies; developing & printing of commercial motion picture film
PA: Simex Inc
600-210 King St E
Toronto ON M5A 1
416 597-1585

(P-19331)

JACK J ENGEL MANUFACTURING INC
Also Called: Creative Automation
11641 Pendleton St, Sun Valley (91352-2502)
PHONE..................................818 767-6220
Jack Engel, *President*
Jack J Engel, *President*
Ilene Rosen, *CFO*
Ilene Engel, *Corp Secy*
James Crawford, *Mktg Dir*
EMP: 34

(P-19332)

JANTEK ELECTRONICS INC
4820 Arden Dr, Temple City (91780-4001)
PHONE..................................626 350-4198
Danny Jan, *President*
Joe Jan, *Exec VP*
Zon Jan, *Project Leader*
Shirley Jan, *Controller*
◆ EMP: 15
SQ FT: 5,700
SALES (est): 1.5MM **Privately Held**
WEB: www.jantek.com
SIC: 3699 8748 5063 Security control equipment & systems; communications consulting; electric alarms & signaling equipment

(P-19333)

JBB INC
Also Called: Precision Waterjet
880 W Crowther Ave, Placentia (92870-6348)
PHONE..................................888 538-9287
Jack Budd, *President*
EMP: 25
SQ FT: 17,000
SALES (est): 5.1MM **Privately Held**
WEB: www.h20jet.com
SIC: 3699 Laser welding, drilling & cutting equipment

(P-19334)

JDSU PHOTONIC POWER (HQ)
1768 Automation Pkwy, San Jose (95131-1873)
PHONE..................................408 546-5000
Kevin Kennedy, *Owner*
▲ EMP: 10
SALES (est): 2MM
SALES (corp-wide): 1.1B **Publicly Held**
SIC: 3699 Laser systems & equipment
PA: Viavi Solutions Inc.
6001 America Center Dr # 6
San Jose CA 95002
408 404-3600

(P-19335)

JEICO SECURITY INC
Also Called: Camtron US
1525 N Endeavor Ln Ste Q, Anaheim (92801-1156)
EMP: 10
SQ FT: 3,000
SALES (est): 83.7K **Privately Held**
SIC: 3699

(P-19336)

JELUZ ELECTRIC LTD LLC
Also Called: Fbs Floor Box Systems
25060 Hancock Ave, Murrieta (92562-5930)
PHONE..................................800 216-8307
Cecilia Quenardelle,
Jorge Luis Muttoni Jr,
EMP: 20
SQ FT: 10,000
SALES: 2MM **Privately Held**
SIC: 3699 Pulse amplifiers

(P-19337)

KANEX
3 Pointe Dr Ste 300, Brea (92821-7624)
PHONE..................................714 332-1681
Kelvin Yan, *CEO*
▲ EMP: 25
SQ FT: 20,000
SALES (est): 7.5MM **Privately Held**
WEB: www.apogeeinc.net
SIC: 3699 5065 Electrical equipment & supplies; electronic parts & equipment

(P-19338)

KELLY PNEUMATICS INC
711 W 17th St Ste F8, Costa Mesa (92627-4346)
PHONE..................................800 704-7552
Ed Kelly, *President*
John McDaniel, *Mfg Staff*
▲ EMP: 15
SQ FT: 1,350

SALES (est): 2.3MM **Privately Held**
WEB: www.kpiwebsite.com
SIC: 3699 Electrical equipment & supplies

(P-19339)

KERI SYSTEMS INC (PA)
302 Enzo Dr Ste 190, San Jose (95138-1801)
PHONE..................................408 435-8400
Ted Geiszler, *President*
Ken Geiszler, *President*
Elisabeth Morton, *Admin Sec*
Steve Henderson, *Technical Mgr*
Vince Deiuliis, *Marketing Mgr*
▲ EMP: 53
SQ FT: 20,000
SALES (est): 10.2MM **Privately Held**
WEB: www.entraguard.com
SIC: 3699 3829 Security control equipment & systems; measuring & controlling devices

(P-19340)

KINETIC ELECTRIC CORPORATION
944 Industrial Blvd 946, Chula Vista (91911-1608)
PHONE..................................619 654-1157
Camilo Sanchez Fernandez, *President*
Luz Fernandez, *CFO*
EMP: 50
SALES (est): 3.3MM **Privately Held**
SIC: 3699 Electrical equipment & supplies

(P-19341)

KNIGHTSCOPE INC
1070 Terra Bella Ave, Mountain View (94043-1830)
PHONE..................................650 924-1025
William Santana LI, *CEO*
Jack Schenk, *President*
Marina Hardof, *CFO*
EMP: 10
SALES (est): 579.2K **Privately Held**
SIC: 3699 Security devices

(P-19342)

KULICKE SFFA WEDGE BONDING INC
Also Called: Kulicke & Soffa Industries
1821 E Dyer Rd Ste 200, Santa Ana (92705-5700)
PHONE..................................949 660-0440
Scott Kulicke, *President*
Tom Naves, *Information Mgr*
Orlando Valentin, *Research*
Dang Tran, *Electrical Engi*
Chong Chen, *Engineer*
▲ EMP: 200
SALES (est): 36.6MM
SALES (corp-wide): 809MM **Publicly Held**
WEB: www.kns.com
SIC: 3699 Electrical equipment & supplies
PA: Kulicke And Soffa Industries, Inc.
1005 Virginia Dr
Fort Washington PA 19034
215 784-6000

(P-19343)

L T SEROGE INC
Also Called: Laser Tech
7400 Jurupa Ave, Riverside (92504-1030)
PHONE..................................951 354-7141
Anthony Di Guglielmo, *CEO*
Chuck Markley, *Manager*
EMP: 15
SQ FT: 50,000
SALES: 3.6MM **Privately Held**
WEB: www.lasertech911.com
SIC: 3699 Laser welding, drilling & cutting equipment

(P-19344)

LASEROD TECHNOLOGIES LLC
20312 Gramercy Pl, Torrance (90501-1511)
PHONE..................................310 328-5869
Charles T Moffitt, *Mng Member*
David V Adams Jr, *Mng Member*
▼ EMP: 20
SQ FT: 8,000
SALES (est): 3.7MM **Privately Held**
SIC: 3699 Laser systems & equipment; laser welding, drilling & cutting equipment

(P-19345)
LGPHILIPS LCD AMER FIN CORP
150 E Brokaw Rd, San Jose (95112-4203)
PHONE.....................................408 350-7600
Kyoung Park, *Principal*
Jeong James, *CFO*
▲ EMP: 26
SALES (est): 3.3MM **Privately Held**
SIC: 3699 3651 3634 Electrical equipment & supplies; household audio & video equipment; electric housewares & fans

(P-19346)
LIFELINE SEC & AUTOMTN INC
2081 Arena Blvd Ste 260, Sacramento
(95834-2309)
PHONE.....................................916 285-9078
Gordon Johnson, *President*
EMP: 76
SALES (est): 2MM **Privately Held**
SIC: 3699 Security devices
PA: Ghs Interactive Security Llc
     21031 Warner Center Ln D
     Woodland Hills CA 91367

(P-19347)
LINTELLE ENGINEERING INC
380 El Pueblo Rd Ste 105, Scotts Valley
(95066-4212)
PHONE.....................................831 439-8400
Levon Billuts, *President*
Clara Diane, *Shareholder*
William L Turne, *Shareholder*
EMP: 30
SQ FT: 32,000
SALES (est): 5MM
SALES (corp-wide): 85.8MM **Privately Held**
WEB: www.lintelle.com/corp-profile.html
SIC: 3699 Electrical equipment & supplies
PA: Creo Capital Partners Llc
     6455 S Yosemite St # 140
     Greenwood Village CO 80111
     720 398-6500

(P-19348)
LORENZ INC
Also Called: Karel Manufacturing
1749 Stergios Rd, Calexico (92231-9657)
PHONE.....................................760 427-1815
Zaven Arakelian, *President*
▲ EMP: 400
SQ FT: 73,000
SALES (est): 85.2MM **Privately Held**
SIC: 3699 Electrical equipment & supplies

(P-19349)
LOW VOLTAGE ARCHITECTURE INC
11715 San Vicente Blvd, Los Angeles
(90049-6628)
P.O. Box 1182, Malibu (90265-1182)
PHONE.....................................310 573-7588
Matthew Denos, *President*
EMP: 22
SALES: 5MM **Privately Held**
SIC: 3699 8712 Security control equipment & systems; architectural services

(P-19350)
LT SECURITY INC
Also Called: L T S
18738 San Jose Ave, City of Industry
(91748-1323)
PHONE.....................................626 435-2838
Tzu Ping Ho, *CEO*
Grant Long, *President*
Carlo Yu, *Vice Pres*
Bobby Chang, *General Mgr*
Patrick Yang, *Webmaster*
▲ EMP: 36
SALES (est): 8.5MM **Privately Held**
SIC: 3699 Security devices

(P-19351)
MAAS-ROWE CARILLONS INC
2255 Meyers Ave, Escondido (92029-1007)
P.O. Box 462366 (92046-2366)
PHONE.....................................760 743-1311
Paul H Rowe, *President*
Elaine Rowe, *Vice Pres*
▲ EMP: 25 EST: 1958
SQ FT: 10,500

SALES (est): 4.2MM **Privately Held**
SIC: 3699 Bells, electric

(P-19352)
MACON INDUSTRIES INC
Also Called: Lightwave Laser
3186 Coffey Ln, Santa Rosa (95403-2555)
PHONE.....................................707 566-2116
Jhon Macon, *President*
Laura Larsen, *Graphic Designe*
Malcolm Lapera, *Prdtn Mgr*
Rick Pepper, *Production*
EMP: 10
SQ FT: 5,000
SALES (est): 1.3MM **Privately Held**
WEB: www.lightwavelaser.com
SIC: 3699 Laser welding, drilling & cutting equipment

(P-19353)
MARTRONIC ENGINEERING INC (PA)
874 Patriot Dr Unit D, Moorpark
(93021-3605)
PHONE.....................................805 583-0808
Richard Marsh, *President*
Ellen Marsh, *Corp Secy*
Matt Marsh, *Purchasing*
EMP: 11 EST: 1975
SQ FT: 6,700
SALES: 1.7MM **Privately Held**
WEB: www.meilaser.com
SIC: 3699 Laser systems & equipment

(P-19354)
MEDIA KING INC
140 W Valley Blvd 201a, San Gabriel
(91776-3760)
PHONE.....................................626 288-4558
▲ EMP: 22
SALES (est): 2.5MM **Privately Held**
SIC: 3699

(P-19355)
MEGGITT SAFETY SYSTEMS INC (HQ)
Also Called: Meggitt Control Systems
1785 Voyager Ave, Simi Valley
(93063-3363)
PHONE.....................................805 584-4100
Dennis Hutton, *President*
Dolores Watai, *Vice Pres*
Aimee Birkner, *General Mgr*
Mila Calderon, *Administration*
Sheila Welch, *Administration*
▲ EMP: 210
SQ FT: 180,000
SALES (est): 124.2MM
SALES (corp-wide): 2.6B **Privately Held**
WEB: www.meggittsafety.com
SIC: 3699 3724 3728 Betatrons; exhaust systems, aircraft; engine heaters, aircraft; aircraft parts & equipment
PA: Meggitt Plc
     Atlantic House, Aviation Park West
     Christchurch BH23
     120 259-7597

(P-19356)
MERCURY SECURITY PRODUCTS LLC
2355 Mira Mar Ave, Long Beach
(90815-1755)
PHONE.....................................562 986-9105
Joseph Grillo, *CEO*
Michael Serafin, *President*
Hing Hung, *Exec VP*
▲ EMP: 19
SQ FT: 12,000
SALES (est): 4.4MM
SALES (corp-wide): 9.3B **Privately Held**
WEB: www.mercury-security.com
SIC: 3699 8742 Security control equipment & systems; industry specialist consultants
HQ: Hid Global Corporation
     611 Center Ridge Dr
     Austin TX 78753
     800 237-7769

(P-19357)
MICROLUX INC
1065 Asbury St, San Jose (95126-1855)
P.O. Box 4095, Santa Clara (95056-4095)
PHONE.....................................408 435-1700
Edic Sliva, *President*
EMP: 12
SQ FT: 20,000
SALES (est): 1.7MM **Privately Held**
WEB: www.microlux.com
SIC: 3699 Laser welding, drilling & cutting equipment

(P-19358)
MOBIUS PHOTONICS INC
110 Pioneer Way Ste A, Mountain View
(94041-1519)
PHONE.....................................408 496-1084
Robert L Mortensen, *CEO*
Robert L Byer, *Ch of Bd*
Kiyomi Monro, *CEO*
Mark Byer, *COO*
Manuel Leonardo, *CTO*
EMP: 10
SQ FT: 500
SALES (est): 1.1MM
SALES (corp-wide): 1.4B **Publicly Held**
WEB: www.mobiusphotonics.com
SIC: 3699 Laser systems & equipment
PA: Ipg Photonics Corporation
     50 Old Webster Rd
     Oxford MA 01540
     508 373-1100

(P-19359)
MOTICONT
6901 Woodley Ave, Van Nuys
(91406-4844)
PHONE.....................................818 785-1800
Joseph Hank, *Partner*
Aaron Eghbal, *Partner*
EMP: 22
SALES: 3.4MM **Privately Held**
SIC: 3699 Linear accelerators; electron linear accelerators

(P-19360)
MULTI POWER PRODUCTS INC
47931 Westinghouse Dr, Fremont
(94539-7483)
PHONE.....................................415 883-6300
Paul Chait, *President*
EMP: 13
SALES (corp-wide): 2.4MM **Privately Held**
WEB: www.power-products.com
SIC: 3699 Electrical equipment & supplies
PA: Multi Power Products, Inc.
     2901 Tasman Dr Ste 111
     Santa Clara CA
     415 354-5688

(P-19361)
MYE TECHNOLOGIES INC
28460 Westinghouse Pl, Valencia
(91355-0929)
PHONE.....................................661 964-0217
Anthony Garcia, *President*
Virg Kasputis, *General Mgr*
Lin Hazen, *Director*
Val Levey, *Manager*
▲ EMP: 45
SQ FT: 5,000
SALES (est): 8.6MM **Privately Held**
WEB: www.myeclubtv.com
SIC: 3699 Electric sound equipment

(P-19362)
NANOTRONICS IMAGING INC
Also Called: Nanotronics Automation
777 Flynn Rd, Hollister (95023-9558)
PHONE.....................................831 630-0700
Randy Griffith, *Branch Mgr*
EMP: 15
SALES (corp-wide): 2.9MM **Privately Held**
SIC: 3699 Electronic training devices
PA: Nanotronics Imaging, Inc.
     2251 Front St Ste 109-111
     Cuyahoga Falls OH 44221
     330 926-9809

(P-19363)
NETWORK CHEMISTRY INC
1804 Embarcadero Rd # 201, Palo Alto
(94303-3341)
PHONE.....................................650 858-3120
Lou Ryan, *Ch of Bd*
Robert Mirkovich, *CEO*
EMP: 14
SQ FT: 2,700
SALES (est): 1.8MM **Privately Held**
WEB: www.networkchemistry.com
SIC: 3699 Security devices

(P-19364)
NETWORKED ENERGY SERVICES CORP (HQ)
Also Called: Grid Modernization Division
5215 Hellyer Ave Ste 150, San Jose
(95138-1089)
PHONE.....................................408 622-9900
Michael Anderson, *CEO*
Will Mathieson, *CFO*
Damian Inglin, *VP Bus Dvlpt*
Fremont Bainbridge, *Sr Software Eng*
Carlos Cuturrufo, *Engineer*
▲ EMP: 31
SALES (est): 8.2MM
SALES (corp-wide): 1.1B **Privately Held**
SIC: 3699 Grids, electric
PA: S&T Ag
     Industriezeile 35
     Linz 4021
     732 766-40

(P-19365)
NEW WAVE RESEARCH INCORPORATED (DH)
48660 Kato Rd, Fremont (94538-7339)
PHONE.....................................510 249-1550
Pei Hsien Fang, *Chairman*
Rick Wong, *CFO*
▲ EMP: 110
SQ FT: 65,000
SALES (est): 7.9MM
SALES (corp-wide): 2B **Publicly Held**
WEB: www.new-wave.com
SIC: 3699 3674 Laser systems & equipment; semiconductors & related devices
HQ: Electro Scientific Industries, Inc.
     13900 Nw Science Park Dr
     Portland OR 97229
     503 641-4141

(P-19366)
NEWAGE PAVILIONS LLC
9360 Penfield Ave, Chatsworth
(91311-6550)
PHONE.....................................818 701-9600
Ron Hay, *President*
▲ EMP: 12
SQ FT: 29,000
SALES (est): 1.2MM **Privately Held**
SIC: 3699 Electrical equipment & supplies

(P-19367)
NEWPORT CORPORATION
Also Called: Spectra-Physics Laser Div
3635 Peterson Way, Santa Clara
(95054-2809)
P.O. Box 7013, Mountain View (94039)
PHONE.....................................408 980-4300
Peggy Bradley, *Planning*
Jeri Loman, *Engineer*
Curt Rettig, *Engineer*
Rimas Viselga, *Engineer*
Ly Le, *Accountant*
EMP: 800
SALES (corp-wide): 2B **Publicly Held**
SIC: 3699 5049 Laser systems & equipment; scientific instruments
HQ: Newport Corporation
     1791 Deere Ave
     Irvine CA 92606
     949 863-3144

(P-19368)
NM LASER PRODUCTS INC
337 Piercy Rd, San Jose (95138-1403)
PHONE.....................................408 227-8299
David Woodruff, *President*
EMP: 10
SQ FT: 3,000
SALES (est): 1.2MM **Privately Held**
SIC: 3699 Laser systems & equipment

▲ = Import ▼=Export
◆ =Import/Export

(P-19369)
NORTEK SECURITY & CONTROL LLC
12471 Riverside Dr, Eastvale (91752-1007)
PHONE....................................760 438-7000
John West, *Principal*
EMP: 10
SALES (corp-wide): 11B **Privately Held**
SIC: 3699 Security control equipment & systems
HQ: Nortek Security & Control Llc
    5919 Sea Otter Pl Ste 100
    Carlsbad CA 92010
    760 438-7000

(P-19370)
NUPHOTON TECHNOLOGIES INC
41610 Corning Pl, Murrieta (92562-7023)
PHONE....................................951 696-8366
Ramadas Pillai, *CEO*
Dan Vera, *COO*
Vish Govindan, *CFO*
Norm Nelson, *Vice Pres*
Sindu Pillai, *Vice Pres*
EMP: 16
SQ FT: 12,000
SALES (est): 5MM **Privately Held**
WEB: www.nuphoton.com
SIC: 3699 Laser systems & equipment

(P-19371)
O & S CALIFORNIA INC
Also Called: Osca-Arcosa
9731 Siempre Viva Rd E, San Diego (92154-7200)
PHONE....................................619 661-1800
Kazuo Murata, *President*
Jos Luis Furlong, *Vice Pres*
Ramon Leyva, *MIS Mgr*
Faustino Gomez, *Technology*
Satoshi Imamasa, *Accounting Mgr*
▲ EMP: 400
SQ FT: 4,676
SALES (est): 164.7MM **Privately Held**
WEB: www.osca-arcosa.com
SIC: 3699 Electrical equipment & supplies
PA: Onamba Co., Ltd.
    3-1-27, Fukaekita, Higashinari-Ku
    Osaka OSK 537-0

(P-19372)
OBSERVABLES INC
117 N Milpas St, Santa Barbara (93103-3345)
PHONE....................................805 272-9255
Abraham Schryer, *President*
Doug Weinstein, *Manager*
EMP: 12
SALES (est): 536.6K **Privately Held**
SIC: 3699 Security control equipment & systems

(P-19373)
OSI SUBSIDIARY INC
12525 Chadron Ave, Hawthorne (90250-4807)
PHONE....................................310 978-0516
Deepak Chopra, *CEO*
Ajay Mehra, *President*
Alan Edrick, *CFO*
EMP: 400
SALES (est): 70.5MM
SALES (corp-wide): 1.1B **Publicly Held**
WEB: www.osioptoelectronics.com
SIC: 3699 Laser systems & equipment
PA: Osi Systems, Inc.
    12525 Chadron Ave
    Hawthorne CA 90250
    310 978-0516

(P-19374)
PACIFIC CONTROLS INC
Also Called: Pacific Controls E D M
4949 Newcastle Ave, Encino (91316-4210)
PHONE....................................818 345-1970
George Jariabek, *President*
Tamara G Jariabek, *Treasurer*
EMP: 19 EST: 1971
SQ FT: 5,000
SALES (est): 1.6MM **Privately Held**
WEB: www.pacificcontrols.com
SIC: 3699 Electrical equipment & supplies

(P-19375)
PEC MANUFACTURING INC
675 Sycamore Dr, Milpitas (95035-7430)
PHONE....................................408 577-1839
Eric Truong, *President*
EMP: 10
SALES (est): 2.3MM **Privately Held**
WEB: www.pecmfg.com
SIC: 3699 Extension cords

(P-19376)
PHASE-A-MATIC INC
39360 3rd St E Ste C301, Palmdale (93550-3257)
PHONE....................................661 947-8485
Colin G Johnstone, *President*
Juan Ochoa, *Technician*
Donna Johnstone, *Engineer*
Monica Varelas, *Accounting Mgr*
Mike Jones, *Controller*
▲ EMP: 12 EST: 1965
SQ FT: 10,000
SALES: 2.3MM **Privately Held**
WEB: www.phase-a-matic.com
SIC: 3699 Electrical equipment & supplies

(P-19377)
PHILATRON INTERNATIONAL (PA)
Also Called: Santa Fe Supply Company
15315 Cornet St, Santa Fe Springs (90670-5531)
PHONE....................................562 802-0452
Phillip M Ramos Jr, *CEO*
Phillip M Ramos Sr, *Exec VP*
Phillip Ramos, *Exec VP*
Isela Cid, *Executive*
Joel Jarquin, *Technician*
EMP: 140 EST: 1978
SQ FT: 100,000
SALES (est): 26.9MM **Privately Held**
WEB: www.philatron.com
SIC: 3699 3694 3357 Electrical equipment & supplies; engine electrical equipment; communication wire

(P-19378)
PINE GROVE GROUP INC
25500 State Highway 88, Pioneer (95666-9647)
PHONE....................................209 295-7733
Dan Nolting, *CEO*
EMP: 30
SQ FT: 8,000
SALES (est): 5.3MM **Privately Held**
WEB: www.pinegrovegroup.com
SIC: 3699 Electrical equipment & supplies

(P-19379)
POWER PARAGON INC
Also Called: Power Systems Group
901 E Ball Rd, Anaheim (92805-5916)
PHONE....................................714 956-9200
Harvey Cohen, *Manager*
EMP: 350
SALES (corp-wide): 6.8B **Publicly Held**
WEB: www.powerparagon.com
SIC: 3699 8721 8741 3612 Electrical equipment & supplies; accounting, auditing & bookkeeping; management services; personnel management; transformers, except electric
HQ: Power Paragon, Inc.
    901 E Ball Rd
    Anaheim CA 92805
    714 956-9200

(P-19380)
POWERFLARE CORPORATION
37 Ringwood Ave, Atherton (94027-2231)
P.O. Box 7615, Menlo Park (94026-7615)
PHONE....................................650 208-2580
Kenneth Dueker, *CEO*
Kahan Modi, *Chief*
EMP: 11
SALES (est): 1.2MM **Privately Held**
SIC: 3699 Electrical equipment & supplies

(P-19381)
PRECISION FLIGHT CONTROLS
2747 Merc Dr Ste 100, Rancho Cordova (95742)
PHONE....................................916 414-1310
Mike Altman, *President*
Bart Altman, *Vice Pres*
EMP: 13

SQ FT: 11,000
SALES (est): 3.1MM **Privately Held**
WEB: www.flypfc.com
SIC: 3699 Flight simulators (training aids), electronic

(P-19382)
PRIORITY TECH SYSTEMS INC
Also Called: Pts Security
14040 Runnymede St, Van Nuys (91405-2511)
PHONE....................................818 756-5413
Mauricio Navarro, *President*
EMP: 15
SALES (est): 1.7MM **Privately Held**
SIC: 3699 1731 Security devices; fire detection & burglar alarm systems specialization

(P-19383)
PRO SYSTEMS FABRICATORS INC (PA)
14643 Hawthorne Ave, Fontana (92335-2544)
PHONE....................................909 350-9147
Edith Sugarman, *President*
Lynn Sugarman, *Treasurer*
Trina Jackson, *Admin Sec*
▲ EMP: 15
SQ FT: 11,000
SALES (est): 1.3MM **Privately Held**
SIC: 3699 3677 3564 Electrical equipment & supplies; filtration devices, electronic; blowers & fans

(P-19384)
PRO-SPOT INTERNATIONAL INC
5932 Sea Otter Pl, Carlsbad (92010-6630)
PHONE....................................760 407-1414
Joran Olsson, *President*
Wendy Olsson, *Admin Sec*
Lorinda Teague, *Administration*
Tessie Ortega, *Project Mgr*
Fred Sather, *Electrical Engi*
▲ EMP: 17
SALES (est): 5.8MM **Privately Held**
WEB: www.prospot.com
SIC: 3699 Electrical welding equipment

(P-19385)
PROTOTYPE EXPRESS LLC
3506 W Lake Center Dr D, Santa Ana (92704-6985)
PHONE....................................714 751-3533
Bob Tavi, *Mng Member*
EMP: 15
SQ FT: 7,000
SALES (est): 2.7MM **Privately Held**
WEB: www.prototypexpress.com
SIC: 3699 Electrical equipment & supplies

(P-19386)
QED SYSTEMS INC
1330 30th St Ste C, San Diego (92154-3471)
PHONE....................................619 802-0020
Ed Vacin, *President*
EMP: 30
SALES (corp-wide): 147.1MM **Privately Held**
SIC: 3699 Electrical equipment & supplies
PA: Qed Systems, Inc.
    4646 N Witchduck Rd
    Virginia Beach VA 23455
    757 490-5000

(P-19387)
QUARTON USA INC
Also Called: Infiniter
3230 Fallow Field Dr, Diamond Bar (91765-3479)
PHONE....................................888 532-2221
Chao-CHI Huang, *President*
Cindy Lin, *Controller*
▲ EMP: 15
SALES: 2MM **Privately Held**
WEB: www.quarton.com
SIC: 3699 Laser systems & equipment

(P-19388)
R J R TECHNOLOGIES INC (PA)
7875 Edgewater Dr, Oakland (94621-2001)
PHONE....................................510 638-5901
Wil Salhuana, *President*
Tony Bregante, *CFO*
Richard J Ross, *Principal*

Diane Holcomb, *Purch Agent*
EMP: 105
SQ FT: 50,000
SALES (est): 25MM **Privately Held**
WEB: www.rjrpolymers.com
SIC: 3699 Cleaning equipment, ultrasonic, except medical & dental

(P-19389)
RACHE CORPORATION
1160 Avenida Acaso, Camarillo (93012-8719)
PHONE....................................805 389-6868
Steven Wisuri, *President*
Steve Garcia, *Project Engr*
Andy Varahamurthy, *Mktg Dir*
Ed Prado, *Manager*
EMP: 10
SQ FT: 8,500
SALES: 1MM **Privately Held**
WEB: www.rache.com
SIC: 3699 7389 Laser welding, drilling & cutting equipment; metal cutting services

(P-19390)
RACO MANUFACTURING & ENGRG CO
1400 62nd St, Emeryville (94608-2099)
PHONE....................................510 658-6713
Constance Brown, *President*
Connie Brown, *Vice Pres*
James Brown, *Vice Pres*
Sam Siggins, *CTO*
Gene Cottom, *Sales Mgr*
EMP: 14 EST: 1947
SQ FT: 5,500
SALES (est): 3.3MM **Privately Held**
WEB: www.racoman.com
SIC: 3699 3823 Electrical equipment & supplies; temperature instruments: industrial process type

(P-19391)
RAYTHEON COMPANY
6380 Hollister Ave, Goleta (93117-3114)
PHONE....................................805 967-5511
Jack Gressingh, *General Mgr*
Randy Brown, *President*
Brian Hatt, *President*
Carl Jelinex, *Principal*
Adolph Schulbach, *Principal*
EMP: 200
SQ FT: 102,570
SALES (corp-wide): 27B **Publicly Held**
SIC: 3699 3812 Countermeasure simulators, electric; search & navigation equipment
PA: Raytheon Company
    870 Winter St
    Waltham MA 02451
    781 522-3000

(P-19392)
RELDOM CORPORATION
3241 Industry Dr, Signal Hill (90755-4013)
PHONE....................................562 498-3346
Peter Modler, *CEO*
EMP: 20
SALES (est): 4.4MM **Privately Held**
WEB: www.reldom.com
SIC: 3699 Security devices

(P-19393)
RGBLASE LLC
3984 Washington Blvd # 306, Fremont (94538-4954)
PHONE....................................510 585-8449
Pan MA, *Mng Member*
EMP: 12
SALES (est): 993.2K **Privately Held**
WEB: www.rgblase.com
SIC: 3699 Laser systems & equipment

(P-19394)
RHUB COMMUNICATIONS INC
4340 Stevens Creek Blvd, San Jose (95129-1102)
PHONE....................................408 899-2830
Larry Dorie, *President*
John Mao, *CTO*
EMP: 13
SQ FT: 1,000
SALES (est): 665.5K **Privately Held**
SIC: 3699 Electrical equipment & supplies

(P-19395)
RIGOLI ENTERPRISES INC
Also Called: Rignoli Pacific
1983 Potrero Grande Dr, Monterey Park (91755-7420)
PHONE....................................626 573-0242
Arthur R Rigoli, *President*
Adam Rigoli, *Vice Pres*
EMP: 14
SALES (est): 1.3MM **Privately Held**
WEB: www.mindpik.com
SIC: 3699 Fire control or bombing equipment, electronic

(P-19396)
RKS INC (HQ)
1955 Cordell Ct Ste 104, El Cajon (92020-0901)
PHONE....................................858 571-4444
Russell Leonard Scheppmann, *CEO*
Allen Thomas, *COO*
Scott Skillman, *CFO*
Mike McMinn, *Vice Pres*
Brian Shultz, *Vice Pres*
EMP: 18
SQ FT: 7,747
SALES (est): 4.4MM
SALES (corp-wide): 36.4B **Privately Held**
WEB: www.aps-technology.com
SIC: 3699 Door opening & closing devices, electrical; security devices; security control equipment & systems
PA: Abb Ltd
Affolternstrasse 44
ZUrich ZH 8050
433 177-111

(P-19397)
ROMEO SYSTEMS INC
Also Called: Romeo Power
4380 Ayers Ave, Vernon (90058-4306)
PHONE....................................323 675-2180
Michael Patterson, *CEO*
Erik Fleming, *COO*
Lauren Webb, *CFO*
Cody Boggs, *Vice Pres*
Bryan Ovalle, *Vice Pres*
◆ EMP: 202
SQ FT: 114,000
SALES (est): 97.4K **Privately Held**
SIC: 3699 8731 High-energy particle physics equipment; energy research

(P-19398)
SACO
Also Called: S A C O Your Manufacturing Co
3525 Old Conejo Rd # 107, Newbury Park (91320-2154)
PHONE....................................805 499-7788
Samuel Bernstein, *Owner*
Phil Bernstein, *Owner*
EMP: 20
SALES: 250K **Privately Held**
SIC: 3699 3651 Electrical equipment & supplies; household audio & video equipment

(P-19399)
SEA BREEZE TECHNOLOGY INC
Also Called: Tech 22
1160 Joshua Way, Vista (92081-7836)
PHONE....................................760 727-6366
Thomas Skarvada, *President*
EMP: 17
SQ FT: 3,000
SALES (est): 2.1MM **Privately Held**
SIC: 3699 Electrical equipment & supplies

(P-19400)
SERRA LASER AND WATERJET INC
1740 N Orangethorpe Park, Anaheim (92801-1138)
PHONE....................................714 680-6211
Glenn Kline, *CEO*
EMP: 30
SALES (est): 1.6MM **Privately Held**
SIC: 3699 Laser welding, drilling & cutting equipment

(P-19401)
SIDUS SOLUTIONS LLC (PA)
7352 Trade St, San Diego (92121-2422)
P.O. Box 420698 (92142-0698)
PHONE....................................619 275-5533
Leonard Pool, *Mng Member*
EMP: 12 EST: 2000
SQ FT: 1,000
SALES: 1.5MM **Privately Held**
WEB: www.sidus-solutions.com
SIC: 3699 Security devices

(P-19402)
SIENNA CORPORATION INC
41350 Christy St, Fremont (94538-3115)
PHONE....................................510 440-0200
EMP: 21 EST: 1995
SALES (est): 3.2MM **Privately Held**
SIC: 3699

(P-19403)
SIERRA NEVADA CORPORATION
145 Parkshore Dr, Folsom (95630-4726)
PHONE....................................916 985-8799
Carolyn Cain, *Branch Mgr*
David Hanifan, *Engineer*
EMP: 30
SALES (corp-wide): 1.9B **Privately Held**
WEB: www.sncorp.com
SIC: 3699 Countermeasure simulators, electric
PA: Sierra Nevada Corporation
444 Salomon Cir
Sparks NV 89434
775 331-0222

(P-19404)
SIGMA 6 ELECTRONICS INC
7030 Alamitos Ave Ste E, San Diego (92154-4764)
P.O. Box 711094 (92171-1094)
PHONE....................................858 279-4300
Scott Housman, *President*
Samantha Herrera, *Administration*
EMP: 11
SALES (est): 3.2MM **Privately Held**
SIC: 3699 Electrical equipment & supplies

(P-19405)
SKYGUARD LLC
2945 Townsgate Rd Ste 200, Westlake Village (91361-5866)
PHONE....................................703 262-0500
EMP: 25
SALES (est): 2.5MM **Privately Held**
SIC: 3699

(P-19406)
SOLIANT ENERGY INC
1100 La Avenida St Ste A, Mountain View (94043-1453)
PHONE....................................626 396-9500
Terry Bailey, *President*
Michael Deck, *CFO*
▲ EMP: 47
SQ FT: 4,500
SALES (est): 5.7MM **Privately Held**
WEB: www.practicalinstruments.com
SIC: 3699 Electrical equipment & supplies

(P-19407)
SONNET TECHNOLOGIES INC
8 Autry, Irvine (92618-2708)
PHONE....................................949 587-3500
Robert Farnsworth, *President*
Mike Leber, *CFO*
Luis Camano, *Officer*
Brad Horn, *Vice Pres*
Glen Peden, *Vice Pres*
▲ EMP: 27
SQ FT: 17,000
SALES (est): 6.4MM **Privately Held**
WEB: www.sonnettech.com
SIC: 3699 Electrical equipment & supplies

(P-19408)
SONY BIOTECHNOLOGY INC
1730 N 1st St Fl 2, San Jose (95112-4508)
PHONE....................................800 275-5963
Allen Poirson, *President*
Narayan Prabhu, *CFO*
EMP: 65
SALES (est): 12.8MM **Privately Held**
WEB: www.i-cyt.com
SIC: 3699 7372 Laser systems & equipment; prepackaged software

HQ: Sony Corporation Of America
25 Madison Ave Fl 27
New York NY 10010
212 833-8000

(P-19409)
SORAA LASER DIODE INC (PA)
Also Called: Sld Laser
485 Pine Ave, Goleta (93117-3709)
PHONE....................................805 696-6999
Steven Denbaars, *CEO*
James Raring, *President*
Eric B Kim, *CEO*
Thomas Caulfield, *COO*
George Stringer, *Senior VP*
EMP: 40 EST: 2013
SQ FT: 3,000
SALES (est): 16.3MM **Privately Held**
SIC: 3699 Laser systems & equipment

(P-19410)
SORAA LASER DIODE INC
6500 Kaiser Dr, Fremont (94555-3661)
PHONE....................................805 696-6999
Steven Denbaars, *CEO*
EMP: 40
SALES (corp-wide): 16.3MM **Privately Held**
SIC: 3699 Laser systems & equipment
PA: Soraa Laser Diode, Inc.
485 Pine Ave
Goleta CA 93117
805 696-6999

(P-19411)
SOUNDCRAFT INC
Also Called: Secura Key
20301 Nordhoff St, Chatsworth (91311-6128)
PHONE....................................818 882-0020
Joel Smulson, *President*
Martin Casden, *Vice Pres*
Frank Tajbakhsh, *Design Engr*
Wayne Dow, *Technology*
Rene Aldaya, *Controller*
◆ EMP: 35
SQ FT: 12,000
SALES (est): 8.7MM **Privately Held**
WEB: www.securakey.com
SIC: 3699 1731 3829 Security control equipment & systems; safety & security specialization; measuring & controlling devices

(P-19412)
SPECTRA-PHYSICS INC
Also Called: Laser Division
3635 Peterson Way, Santa Clara (95054-2809)
P.O. Box 19607, Irvine (92623-9607)
PHONE....................................650 961-2550
Robert J Phillippy, *CEO*
Pete Williams, *Vice Pres*
Tim Keiper, *Software Engr*
ADI Diner, *Project Mgr*
Dirk Mortag, *Research*
▼ EMP: 800
SQ FT: 129,500
SALES (est): 104.7MM
SALES (corp-wide): 2B **Publicly Held**
WEB: www.spectraphysics.com
SIC: 3699 8731 Laser systems & equipment; commercial physical research
HQ: Newport Corporation
1791 Deere Ave
Irvine CA 92606
949 863-3144

(P-19413)
SSG ALLIANCE LLC (PA)
2550 Somersville Rd # 55, Antioch (94509-8700)
PHONE....................................925 526-6050
Mohammed J Khan,
EMP: 10 EST: 2015
SALES: 300K **Privately Held**
SIC: 3699 Security devices

(P-19414)
STERIS CORPORATION
9020 Activity Rd Ste D, San Diego (92126-4454)
PHONE....................................858 586-1166
Walt Rosebrough, *Manager*
EMP: 60 **Privately Held**
SIC: 3699 Electrical equipment & supplies

HQ: Steris Corporation
5960 Heisley Rd
Mentor OH 44060
440 354-2600

(P-19415)
STIR
2210 Lincoln Ave, Pasadena (91103)
PHONE....................................626 657-0918
Jean-Paul Labrosse, *CEO*
Warren Horton, *Engineer*
EMP: 15
SALES (est): 1.5MM **Privately Held**
SIC: 3699 Electrical equipment & supplies

(P-19416)
STRACON INC
1672 Kaiser Ave Ste 1, Irvine (92614-5700)
PHONE....................................949 851-2288
Son Pham, *President*
Lisette Nguyen, *Executive*
EMP: 17
SQ FT: 10,000
SALES (est): 4.1MM **Privately Held**
WEB: www.straconinc.com
SIC: 3699 Electrical equipment & supplies

(P-19417)
SUMMIT ELECTRIC & DATA INC
28338 Constellation Rd # 920, Valencia (91355-5098)
PHONE....................................661 775-9901
Ray Vasquez, *President*
EMP: 26 EST: 2010
SALES (est): 4.9MM **Privately Held**
SIC: 3699 1731 Electrical equipment & supplies; electrical work

(P-19418)
SUSS MCRTEC PHTNIC SYSTEMS INC
220 Klug Cir, Corona (92880-5409)
PHONE....................................951 817-3700
Courtney T Sheets, *CEO*
Debbie Brown, *CFO*
Courtney Sheets, *Bd of Directors*
Courtney T Sheets, *Principal*
Debora Blanchard, *Admin Sec*
EMP: 90
SALES (est): 20MM
SALES (corp-wide): 233.4MM **Privately Held**
WEB: www.tamsci.com
SIC: 3699 7389 Electrical equipment & supplies;
PA: SUss Microtec Se
SchleiBheimer Str. 90
Garching B. Munchen 85748
893 200-70

(P-19419)
TASCENT INC
475 Alberto Way Ste 200, Los Gatos (95032-5480)
PHONE....................................650 799-4611
Dean Senner, *CEO*
Scott Clark, *Vice Pres*
Anthony Hay, *Vice Pres*
Alastair Partington, *Vice Pres*
Joey Pritikin, *Vice Pres*
EMP: 16 EST: 2015
SALES (est): 2.7MM **Privately Held**
SIC: 3699 Security control equipment & systems

(P-19420)
TECHKO INC
27301 Calle De La Rosa, San Juan Capistrano (92675-1875)
PHONE....................................949 486-0678
Joseph Y Ko, *CEO*
Rosemary Borne, *Vice Pres*
▲ EMP: 1000
SQ FT: 18,000
SALES (est): 80MM **Privately Held**
WEB: www.techkousa.com
SIC: 3699 3589 Security devices; shredders, industrial & commercial

(P-19421)
TEKLINK SECURITY INC
Also Called: Securityman
4601 E Airport Dr, Ontario (91761-7869)
PHONE....................................909 230-6668
Sam Hsien Jung Yu, *President*
Mike Chen, *Vice Pres*

▲ = Import ▼=Export
◆ =Import/Export

▲ EMP: 50
SALES (est): 4.9MM **Privately Held**
SIC: 3699 Security control equipment & systems

(P-19422)
TELEDYNE INSTRUMENTS INC
Also Called: Teledyne Blueview
14020 Stowe Dr, Poway (92064-6846)
PHONE.................................425 492-7400
James Volz, *Branch Mgr*
EMP: 26
SALES (corp-wide): 2.9B **Publicly Held**
SIC: 3699 Electrical equipment & supplies
HQ: Teledyne Instruments, Inc.
1049 Camino Dos Rios
Thousand Oaks CA 91360
805 373-4545

(P-19423)
TRI POWER ELECTRIC INC
1211 N La Loma Cir, Anaheim
(92806-1802)
P.O. Box 5968, Huntington Beach (92615-5968)
PHONE.................................714 630-6445
Ronald Staley, *Owner*
Mike Diaz, *Purch Mgr*
EMP: 14
SALES (est): 2.5MM **Privately Held**
SIC: 3699 1731 Electrical equipment & supplies; electrical work

(P-19424)
TRIGON ELECTRONICS INC
22865 Savi Ranch Pkwy A, Yorba Linda
(92887-4626)
PHONE.................................714 633-7442
Milton L Sneller, *CEO*
Lorna R Sneller, *President*
EMP: 14
SALES (est): 3.4MM **Privately Held**
WEB: www.trigonelectronics.com
SIC: 3699 Security control equipment & systems

(P-19425)
TURNER DESIGNS HYDROCARBON INS
2027 N Gateway Blvd # 109, Fresno
(93727-1648)
PHONE.................................559 253-1414
Gary Bartman, *President*
Mark Fletcher, *Corp Secy*
EMP: 43
SALES (est): 8.5MM **Privately Held**
WEB: www.oilinwatermonitors.com
SIC: 3699 Electrical equipment & supplies

(P-19426)
ULTRA-STEREO LABS INC
Also Called: U S L
181 Bonetti Dr, San Luis Obispo
(93401-7397)
PHONE.................................805 549-0161
James A Cashin, *President*
Jack Cashin, *President*
Dave Cogley, *Sr Software Eng*
Dj Layland, *Info Tech Mgr*
Michael Aarons, *Engineer*
▲ EMP: 48
SQ FT: 15,000
SALES (est): 10.3MM
SALES (corp-wide): 96.1MM **Privately Held**
WEB: www.uslinc.com
SIC: 3699 Electric sound equipment
PA: Qsc, Llc
1675 Macarthur Blvd
Costa Mesa CA 92626
714 754-6175

(P-19427)
UNDERSEA SYSTEMS INTL INC
Also Called: Ocean Technology Systems
3133 W Harvard St, Santa Ana
(92704-3912)
PHONE.................................714 754-7848
Michael R Pelissier, *President*
Jerry Peck, *Chairman*
Dennis Martinez, *Vice Pres*
Cindy Pelissier, *Finance Mgr*
Kurt Schmid, *Sales Staff*
◆ EMP: 62
SQ FT: 18,000

SALES (est): 13.3MM **Privately Held**
WEB: www.oceantechnologysystems.com
SIC: 3699 8711 Underwater sound equipment; acoustical engineering; electrical or electronic engineering

(P-19428)
UNITED SECURITY PRODUCTS INC
Also Called: Amtek
13250 Gregg St Ste B, Poway
(92064-7164)
P.O. Box 785 (92074-0785)
PHONE.................................800 227-1592
Ted R Greene, *President*
Nieves Aquino, *Production*
▲ EMP: 32
SQ FT: 16,000
SALES (est): 6.5MM **Privately Held**
SIC: 3699 5999 Security devices; alarm signal systems; safety supplies & equipment

(P-19429)
UNIVERSAL ELECTRONICS INC
2055 Corte Del Miguel, Carlsbad (92008)
PHONE.................................760 431-8804
Michael Lamb, *Branch Mgr*
▲ EMP: 15
SALES (corp-wide): 680.2MM **Publicly Held**
SIC: 3699 Security devices
PA: Universal Electronics Inc.
15147 N Scottsdale Rd
Scottsdale AZ 85254
480 530-3000

(P-19430)
USA TOPDON LLC
18351 Colima Rd Unit 255, Rowland Heights (91748-2791)
PHONE.................................833 233-5535
Ke Lou,
EMP: 10
SALES: 350K **Privately Held**
SIC: 3699 Automotive driving simulators (training aids), electronic

(P-19431)
USA VISION SYSTEMS INC (HQ)
9301 Irvine Blvd, Irvine (92618-1669)
PHONE.................................949 583-1519
Kuang Cheng Tai, *President*
Mike Liu, *General Mgr*
Ray Lee, *Business Mgr*
Ryan Clark, *Accounts Mgr*
▲ EMP: 40
SALES (est): 14.4MM **Privately Held**
WEB: www.usavisionsys.com
SIC: 3699 Security control equipment & systems

(P-19432)
VIAVI SOLUTIONS INC
Also Called: Jsdu
2789 Northpoint Pkwy, Santa Rosa
(95407-7350)
PHONE.................................707 545-6440
Toni McWilliamns, *Principal*
Fred Van Milligen, *General Mgr*
Clifford Ferrell, *Engineer*
Mark Lyon, *Engineer*
Tj Mills, *Engineer*
EMP: 200
SALES (corp-wide): 1.1B **Publicly Held**
WEB: www.jdsuniphase.com
SIC: 3699 Laser systems & equipment
PA: Viavi Solutions Inc.
6001 America Center Dr # 6
San Jose CA 95002
408 404-3600

(P-19433)
VIAVI SOLUTIONS INC
Also Called: Jdsu
1750 Automation Pkwy, San Jose
(95131-1873)
PHONE.................................408 546-5000
Garry Ronco, *Manager*
Paul McNab, *Exec VP*
Ralph Rondione, *Senior VP*
Kevin Siebert, *Vice Pres*
Matthew Lorenzo, *Administration*
EMP: 200

SALES (corp-wide): 1.1B **Publicly Held**
WEB: www.jdsuniphase.com
SIC: 3699 Electrical equipment & supplies
PA: Viavi Solutions Inc.
6001 America Center Dr # 6
San Jose CA 95002
408 404-3600

(P-19434)
VIDEO SIMPLEX INC
5160 Mercury Pt Ste C, San Diego
(92111-1225)
PHONE.................................858 467-9762
Richard Hinckley, *President*
EMP: 15
SALES (est): 1.6MM **Privately Held**
WEB: www.videosimplex.com
SIC: 3699 Electrical equipment & supplies

(P-19435)
VIGITRON INC
7810 Trade St 100, San Diego
(92121-2445)
PHONE.................................858 484-5209
Ali Eghbal, *President*
Heller Neil, *VP Bus Dvlpt*
Jeff Wood, *General Mgr*
John Neilson, *Engineer*
Loi Thai, *Buyer*
▲ EMP: 10
SALES (est): 2.3MM **Privately Held**
WEB: www.vigitron.com
SIC: 3699 Security devices; visual communication systems

(P-19436)
VIKING ACCESS SYSTEMS LLC
631 Wald, Irvine (92618-4628)
PHONE.................................949 753-1280
Ali Tehranchi, *Mng Member*
Chris Mazzuckis, *Natl Sales Mgr*
Carolina Alvarez, *Mktg Mgr*
Gio Carrillo, *Regl Sales Mgr*
Bahar Tehranchi,
▲ EMP: 23
SALES (est): 4.6MM **Privately Held**
SIC: 3699 3625 Security control equipment & systems; relays & industrial controls; control equipment, electric

(P-19437)
VISIONARY SOLUTIONS INC
2060 Alameda Padre Serra, Santa Barbara
(93103-1713)
PHONE.................................805 845-8900
Jordan Christoff, *President*
William Bakewell, *Vice Pres*
Scott Freshman, *Vice Pres*
EMP: 11
SQ FT: 3,600
SALES (est): 4.5MM **Privately Held**
WEB: www.vsicam.com
SIC: 3699 8731 Electrical equipment & supplies; electronic research

(P-19438)
VORTRAN LASER TECHNOLOGY INC
21 Golden Land Ct Ste 200, Sacramento
(95834-2426)
PHONE.................................916 283-8208
Doug Wilner, *CEO*
Gordon Wong, *President*
James Lee, *Exec VP*
EMP: 10
SALES: 684.8K
SALES (corp-wide): 3.8MM **Privately Held**
SIC: 3699 Laser systems & equipment
PA: Vortran Medical Technology 1, Inc
21 Golden Land Ct Ste 100
Sacramento CA 95834
916 648-8460

(P-19439)
VTI INSTRUMENTS CORPORATION (HQ)
2031 Main St, Irvine (92614-6509)
PHONE.................................949 955-1894
Paul Dhillon, *CEO*
Jasdeep Dhillon, *President*
Andy Haddad, *Business Dir*
Eddie Cabezas, *Purchasing*
Lee Labo, *Mktg Dir*
▲ EMP: 40
SQ FT: 11,500

SALES (corp-wide): 1.1B **Publicly Held**
WEB: www.jdsuniphase.com
SIC: 3699 Electrical equipment & supplies
PA: Viavi Solutions Inc.
6001 America Center Dr # 6
San Jose CA 95002
408 404-3600

(P-19440)
WALLARM INC (PA)
415 Brannan St 2, San Francisco
(94107-1703)
PHONE.................................415 940-7077
Ivan Novikov, *CEO*
EMP: 17
SALES (est): 7.4MM **Privately Held**
SIC: 3699 Security control equipment & systems

(P-19441)
WEST COAST CHAIN MFG CO
Also Called: Key-Bak
4245 Pacific Privado, Ontario
(91761-1588)
P.O. Box 9088 (91762-9088)
PHONE.................................909 923-7800
Boake Paugh, *President*
Michael Winegar, *Vice Pres*
Mike Winegar, *Vice Pres*
▲ EMP: 50 EST: 1948
SQ FT: 31,000
SALES (est): 10.9MM **Privately Held**
WEB: www.keybak.com
SIC: 3699 Security devices

(P-19442)
WESTERN DNING - SCHNEIDER CAFE
3500 Never Forget Ln, Clovis
(93612-5628)
PHONE.................................559 292-1981
Hakim Eslami, *Security Dir*
Alfio Marrone, *Purchasing*
Marcel Mendes, *QC Mgr*
John K Carpenter, *Senior Mgr*
▲ EMP: 28
SALES (est): 6.6MM **Privately Held**
SIC: 3699 Electrical equipment & supplies

(P-19443)
WESTGATE MFG INC
2462 E 28th St, Vernon (90058-1402)
PHONE.................................877 805-2252
Eryeh Hadjian, *President*
AVI Hadjian, *CFO*
Andrew Gonzales, *Officer*
Isaac Hadjyan, *Vice Pres*
Mark Sakaue, *Regional*
▲ EMP: 11
SALES: 2.5MM **Privately Held**
SIC: 3699 Electrical equipment & supplies

(P-19444)
WESTPAK USA INC
1235 N Red Gum St, Anaheim
(92806-1821)
PHONE.................................714 530-6995
Steven Tyler, *President*
Linh Cao, *COO*
Julie Bui, *CFO*
▲ EMP: 10
SQ FT: 1,900
SALES (est): 1MM **Privately Held**
WEB: www.westpakusa.com
SIC: 3699 8711 Cleaning equipment, ultrasonic, except medical & dental; engineering services

(P-19445)
WG SECURITY PRODUCTS INC
591 W Hamilton Ave # 260, Campbell
(95008-0568)
PHONE.................................408 241-8000
Xiao Hui Yang, *CEO*
Graham Handyside, *Vice Pres*
Ed Wolfe, *VP Bus Dvlpt*
Tonya Williams, *Administration*
Bryan Linsky, *Natl Sales Mgr*
▲ EMP: 40
SALES (est): 8.9MM **Privately Held**
WEB: www.wgspi.com
SIC: 3699 5065 Security devices; security control equipment & systems

SALES (est): 10.4MM
SALES (corp-wide): 4.8B **Publicly Held**
WEB: www.vxitech.com
SIC: 3699 Electrical equipment & supplies
PA: Ametek, Inc.
1100 Cassatt Rd
Berwyn PA 19312
610 647-2121

(right margin, vertical) **PRODUCTS & SVCS**

(P-19446)
WHISTLE LABS INC
1355 Market St Fl 2, San Francisco
(94103-1307)
PHONE...........................623 337-3679
Benjamin Jacobs, CEO
Steven Eidelman, COO
Scott Neuberger, CFO
Heather Wajer, Chief Mktg Ofcr
Kevin Lloyd, CTO
EMP: 30
SQ FT: 3,000
SALES (est): 5.2MM
SALES (corp-wide): 37.6B Privately Held
SIC: 3699 3824 Electrical equipment &
supplies; totalizing meters, consumption
registering
HQ: Mars Petcare Us, Inc.
2013 Ovation Pkwy
Franklin TN 37067
615 807-4626

(P-19447)
XENONICS INC
3186 Lionshead Ave # 100, Carlsbad
(92010-4700)
PHONE...........................760 477-8900
Alan Magerman, Ch of Bd
Jeff Kennedy, President
Rick Kay, CFO
EMP: 10
SQ FT: 10,000
SALES (est): 2.4MM Privately Held
WEB: www.xenonics.com
SIC: 3699 High-energy particle physics
equipment

(P-19448)
XIRGO TECHNOLOGIES LLC
188 Camino Ruiz Fl 2, Camarillo
(93012-6700)
PHONE...........................805 319-4079
Roberto Piolanti, CEO
Shawn Aleman, Chief Mktg Ofcr
Nader Barakat Sr, Principal
Don Bosch Sr, Principal
Joel Young, CTO
EMP: 30
SALES (est): 7.5MM Privately Held
SIC: 3699 Electronic training devices

```
3711 Motor Vehicles & Car
            Bodies
```

(P-19449)
**AFTERMARKET PARTS
COMPANY LLC**
10293 Birtcher Dr, Jurupa Valley
(91752-1827)
PHONE...........................951 681-2751
Bill Coryell, Branch Mgr
EMP: 302
SALES (corp-wide): 2.5B Privately Held
SIC: 3711 Motor vehicles & car bodies
HQ: The Aftermarket Parts Company Llc
3229 Sawmill Pkwy
Delaware OH 43015
740 369-1056

(P-19450)
**ALAN JOHNSON PRFMCE
ENGRG INC**
Also Called: Johnson Racing
1097 Foxen Canyon Rd, Santa Maria
(93454-9146)
PHONE...........................805 922-1202
Alan P Johnson, President
▲ EMP: 24
SQ FT: 25,000
SALES (est): 3.7MM Privately Held
SIC: 3711 Motor vehicles & car bodies

(P-19451)
ALEPH GROUP INC
1900 E Alessndro Blvd # 105, Riverside
(92508-2311)
PHONE...........................951 213-4815
Jales Mello, CEO
Karina Resendiz, Bookkeeper
▼ EMP: 20 EST: 2012
SALES: 4.5MM Privately Held
SIC: 3711 Motor vehicles & car bodies

(P-19452)
AMERICAN CARRIER SYSTEMS
2285 E Date Ave, Fresno (93706-5426)
PHONE...........................559 442-1500
Philip Sweet, President
David Sweet, Admin Sec
▲ EMP: 90
SQ FT: 36,552
SALES (est): 9.9MM Privately Held
SIC: 3711 Motor vehicles & car bodies

(P-19453)
AMERICAN HX AUTO TRADE INC
Also Called: U.S. Specialty Vehicles
9455 Hyssop Dr, Rancho Cucamonga
(91730-6107)
PHONE...........................909 484-1010
Amy Lin, Mng Member
▲ EMP: 72
SALES (est): 555.1K Privately Held
SIC: 3711 Automobile bodies, passenger
car, not including engine, etc.

(P-19454)
**ARTISAN VEHICLE SYSTEMS
INC**
2385 Pleasant Valley Rd, Camarillo
(93012-8589)
PHONE...........................805 512-9955
Michael Kasaba, President
Russell Davis, COO
Joe Beck, Project Mgr
Kyle Hickey, Research
Brian Huff, Engineer
EMP: 60
SALES (est): 3MM
SALES (corp-wide): 11.1B Privately Held
SIC: 3711 Personnel carriers (motor vehi-
cles), assembly of
PA: Sandvik Ab
Hogbovagen 45
Sandviken 811 3
262 600-00

(P-19455)
ATIEVA USA INC (HQ)
Also Called: Lucid Motors
7373 Gateway Blvd, Newark (94560-1149)
PHONE...........................510 648-3553
Peter Rawlinson, CEO
Dave Haskell, Vice Pres
Derek Jenkins, Vice Pres
Bryce Brown, Principal
Rick Griffith, CIO
▲ EMP: 320 EST: 2007
SQ FT: 65,000
SALES (est): 133.1MM Privately Held
SIC: 3711 8711 Motor vehicles & car bod-
ies; engineering services

(P-19456)
AUTOANYTHING INC
Also Called: Autoanything.com
6602 Convoy Ct Ste 200, San Diego
(92111-1000)
PHONE...........................858 569-8111
Brandon Proctor, President
EMP: 132
SALES (est): 4.5MM
SALES (corp-wide): 19.1MM Privately
Held
SIC: 3711 Motor vehicles & car bodies
PA: Azaa Investments, Inc.
6602 Convoy Ct Ste 200
San Diego CA 92111
858 569-8111

(P-19457)
AZAA INVESTMENTS INC (PA)
6602 Convoy Ct Ste 200, San Diego
(92111-1000)
P.O. Box 2198, Memphis TN (38101-2198)
PHONE...........................858 569-8111
Selwyn Klein, President
William Rhodes III, President
David Klein, COO
William Giles, Treasurer
Harry Goldsmith, Admin Sec
▼ EMP: 19
SALES (est): 19.1MM Privately Held
SIC: 3711 Motor vehicles & car bodies

(P-19458)
BAATZ ENTERPRISES INC
Also Called: Tow Industries
2223 W San Bernardino Rd, West Covina
(91790-1008)
PHONE...........................323 660-4866
Mark Ormonde Baatz, CEO
John O Baatz, President
Helen Baatz, Corp Secy
Juan Calvillo, General Mgr
Jessica Tow, Admin Asst
▼ EMP: 17
SALES: 20MM Privately Held
SIC: 3711 5013 7538 Motor vehicles &
car bodies; truck parts & accessories;
truck engine repair, except industrial

(P-19459)
**BECKER AUTOMOTIVE
DESIGNS INC**
Also Called: Becker Automotive Design USA
1711 Ives Ave, Oxnard (93033-1866)
PHONE...........................805 487-5227
Howard Bernard Becker, CEO
Debra Becker, Corp Secy
◆ EMP: 39
SQ FT: 35,000
SALES (est): 7.5MM Privately Held
SIC: 3711 Cars, armored, assembly of

(P-19460)
BESPOKE COACHWORKS INC
7641 Burnet Ave, Van Nuys (91405-1006)
PHONE...........................818 571-9900
Gabi Mashal, CEO
Elie Rothstein, Vice Pres
EMP: 12
SALES (est): 2.4MM Privately Held
SIC: 3711 3713 5511 Motor vehicles &
car bodies; van bodies; vans, new & used

(P-19461)
BYTON NORTH AMERICA CORP
4201 Burton Dr, Santa Clara (95054-1512)
PHONE...........................408 966-5078
Carsten Breitfeld, CEO
Albert LI, CFO
Scott Bang, Engineer
Andrew Hussey, Director
EMP: 120 EST: 2016
SALES (est): 62.4MM
SALES (corp-wide): 111.9MM Privately
Held
SIC: 3711 Cars, electric, assembly of
PA: Nanjing Byton Electric Vehicle Co., Ltd.
Building D4, Hongfeng Science And
Technology Park, Etdz
Nanjing 21003
256 959-2000

(P-19462)
CANOO INC
19951 Mariner Ave, Torrance (90503-1672)
PHONE...........................318 849-6327
Ulrich Kranz, CEO
Rasmus Vandercolff, CFO
Richard Kim, Vice Pres
Karl-Thomas Neumann, CTO
EMP: 230
SQ FT: 90,000
SALES (est): 19.2MM Privately Held
SIC: 3711 Motor vehicles & car bodies

(P-19463)
CENTRIC PARTS INC
14528 Bonelli St, City of Industry
(91746-3022)
PHONE...........................626 961-5775
Dino Crescentini, CEO
Dan Lelchuk, President
Cynthia Clarke, Vice Pres
Cynthia Windle, Vice Pres
Bryan Germain, Info Tech Mgr
◆ EMP: 106
SALES (est): 31.2MM Privately Held
SIC: 3711 Automobile assembly, including
specialty automobiles

(P-19464)
COACHWORKS HOLDINGS INC
1863 Service Ct, Riverside (92507-2341)
PHONE...........................951 684-9585
Dale Carson, President
Terri L Carson, Admin Sec
EMP: 300

SALES (est): 30.4MM
SALES (corp-wide): 58.9MM Privately
Held
SIC: 3711 Motor buses, except trackless
trollies, assembly of
PA: D/T Carson Enterprises, Inc.
42882 Ivy St
Murrieta CA 92562
951 684-9585

(P-19465)
DEINY AUTOMOTIVE INC
13040 Bradley Ave, Sylmar (91342-3831)
PHONE...........................818 362-5865
Ken Sapper, President
Diana Deiny, Vice Pres
Frank Deiny Jr, Vice Pres
Joan Sapper, Admin Sec
▼ EMP: 19
SQ FT: 14,000
SALES (est): 2.4MM Privately Held
WEB: www.1speedway.com
SIC: 3711 Chassis, motor vehicle

(P-19466)
**DIME RESEARCH AND
DEVELOPMENT**
Also Called: Dime Racing
5542 Research Dr, Huntington Beach
(92649-1614)
PHONE...........................714 969-7879
Jonathan Kennedy, Principal
EMP: 50
SALES: 52MM Privately Held
SIC: 3711 Automobile assembly, including
specialty automobiles

(P-19467)
DIMORA ENTERPRISES
1775 E Palm Canyon Dr # 105, Palm
Springs (92264-1623)
PHONE...........................760 832-9070
Alfred Dimora, Principal
EMP: 15
SALES: 950K Privately Held
SIC: 3711 Motor vehicles & car bodies

(P-19468)
**ELDORADO NATIONAL CAL INC
(HQ)**
9670 Galena St, Riverside (92509-3089)
PHONE...........................951 727-9300
Peter Orthwein, CEO
◆ EMP: 350
SQ FT: 62,000
SALES (est): 94.7MM Publicly Held
WEB: www.enconline.com
SIC: 3711 Buses, all types, assembly of

(P-19469)
**FEDERAL SIGNAL
CORPORATION**
1108 E Raymond Way, Anaheim
(92801-1119)
PHONE...........................714 871-3336
EMP: 25
SALES (corp-wide): 707.9MM Publicly
Held
SIC: 3711
PA: Federal Signal Corporation
1415 W 22nd St Ste 1100
Oak Brook IL 60523
630 954-2000

(P-19470)
**FISKER AUTO & TECH GROUP
LLC**
3080 Airway Ave, Costa Mesa
(92626-6034)
PHONE...........................714 723-3247
EMP: 233
SALES: 300K Privately Held
SIC: 3711

(P-19471)
FLYER DEFENSE LLC
151 W 135th St, Los Angeles (90061-1645)
PHONE...........................310 674-5030
Gerald M Friedman, CEO
Sefe Emokpae, Marketing Staff
▲ EMP: 20 EST: 2000

SALES (est): 3MM
SALES (corp-wide): 223.5MM **Privately Held**
SIC: 3711 3714 Military motor vehicle assembly; motor vehicle parts & accessories
PA: Marvin Engineering Co., Inc.
261 W Beach Ave
Inglewood CA 90302
310 674-5030

(P-19472)
GLOBAL ENVIRONMENTAL PDTS INC
Also Called: Global Sweeping Solutions
5405 Industrial Pkwy, San Bernardino (92407-1803)
PHONE..................................909 713-1600
Walter Pusic, *Principal*
Chad Bormann, *Vice Pres*
Bashkim Abdulla, *Electrical Engi*
Geoff Odgers, *Engineer*
Donald Barnes, *Parts Mgr*
▲ EMP: 67
SQ FT: 104,000
SALES (est): 25.1MM **Privately Held**
SIC: 3711 Street sprinklers & sweepers (motor vehicles), assembly of

(P-19473)
GOLDEN STATE FIRE APPRATUS INC
7400 Reese Rd, Sacramento (95828-3706)
PHONE..................................916 330-1638
Ryan Wright, *President*
Marie Wright, *Admin Sec*
EMP: 16
SQ FT: 5,000
SALES: 25MM **Privately Held**
WEB: www.goldenstatefire.com
SIC: 3711 3713 Truck & tractor truck assembly; truck & bus bodies

(P-19474)
GREENKRAFT INC
2530 S Birch St, Santa Ana (92707-3444)
PHONE..................................714 545-7777
George Gemayel, *Ch of Bd*
George Patrick, *COO*
Sosi Bardakjian, *CFO*
Frank Ziegler, *Sales Staff*
EMP: 18
SQ FT: 51,942
SALES: 434.1K **Privately Held**
SIC: 3711 3519 Motor vehicles & car bodies; internal combustion engines

(P-19475)
GREENPOWER MOTOR COMPANY INC
1700 Hope Ave, Porterville (93257)
PHONE..................................604 563-4144
Fraser Atkinson, *Principal*
EMP: 13
SALES (est): 2MM
SALES (corp-wide): 4.6MM **Privately Held**
SIC: 3711 Motor vehicles & car bodies
PA: Greenpower Motor Company Inc
209 Carrall St Suite 240
Vancouver BC V6B 2
604 563-4144

(P-19476)
HACKROD INC
2220 N Ventura Ave Ste A, Ventura (93001-1363)
PHONE..................................347 331-8919
Michael McCoy, *CEO*
EMP: 10 EST: 2017
SALES: 500K **Privately Held**
SIC: 3711 7373 Automobile assembly, including specialty automobiles; computer-aided engineering (CAE) systems service

(P-19477)
HALCORE GROUP INC
Leader Industries
10941 Weaver Ave, South El Monte (91733-2752)
PHONE..................................626 575-0880
Gary Hunter, *Manager*
Garry Hunter, *Manager*
EMP: 100 **Publicly Held**
WEB: www.hortonambulance.com

SIC: 3711 Motor vehicles & car bodies
HQ: Halcore Group, Inc.
3800 Mcdowell Rd
Grove City OH 43123
614 539-8181

(P-19478)
HCHD
1175 S Grove Ave Ste 104, Ontario (91761-3470)
PHONE..................................909 923-8889
Hui Luo, *President*
EMP: 13
SALES (est): 1.4MM
SALES (corp-wide): 392.6MM **Privately Held**
SIC: 3711 Automobile assembly, including specialty automobiles
PA: Huachangda Intelligent Equipment Group Co., Ltd.
No.9, Dongyi Avenue
Shiyan 44201
719 876-7909

(P-19479)
HYBRID KINETIC MOTORS CORP
800 E Colo Blvd Ste 880, Pasadena (91101)
PHONE..................................626 683-7330
Chuantao Wang, *CEO*
Yung Yeung, *President*
Jurgelsky Kathy, *Vice Pres*
Xuejun Liu, *Vice Pres*
John Shelburne, *Vice Pres*
EMP: 10
SALES (est): 1.3MM **Privately Held**
SIC: 3711 Automobile assembly, including specialty automobiles

(P-19480)
JAPANESE TRUCK DISMANTLING
940 Alameda St, Wilmington (90744-3841)
PHONE..................................310 835-3100
Don Mahrin, *President*
▲ EMP: 15
SQ FT: 20,000
SALES: 1.2MM **Privately Held**
SIC: 3711 5015 Automobile assembly, including specialty automobiles; automotive parts & supplies, used

(P-19481)
KANDI USA INC
738 Epperson Dr, City of Industry (91748-1336)
PHONE..................................909 941-4588
Wangyuan Hu, *CEO*
Tim Pei, *General Mgr*
▲ EMP: 10
SALES (est): 1.5MM
SALES (corp-wide): 41.6MM **Privately Held**
SIC: 3711 Motor vehicles & car bodies
PA: Zhejiang Kandi Vehicles Co., Ltd.
Inside Of Kangdi Automobile City, Industrial Park
Jinhua 32101
579 822-3988

(P-19482)
KARMA AUTOMOTIVE LLC
9950 Jeronimo Rd, Irvine (92618-2014)
PHONE..................................949 722-7121
Pamela Cordova, *Executive Asst*
William Gooding, *Director*
EMP: 10
SALES (corp-wide): 2.9B **Privately Held**
SIC: 3711 Motor vehicles & car bodies
HQ: Karma Automotive Llc
9950 Jeronimo Rd
Irvine CA 92618
714 723-3247

(P-19483)
KARMA AUTOMOTIVE LLC (DH)
9950 Jeronimo Rd, Irvine (92618-2014)
PHONE..................................714 723-3247
Liang Zhou, *CEO*
John Wilson, *Officer*
Mikael Elley, *Vice Pres*
Todd George, *Vice Pres*
Devries Joost, *Vice Pres*
EMP: 277
SQ FT: 262,463

SALES (est): 110.1MM
SALES (corp-wide): 2.9B **Privately Held**
SIC: 3711 Motor vehicles & car bodies

(P-19484)
LIPPERT COMPONENTS INC
168 S Spruce Ave, Rialto (92376-9005)
PHONE..................................909 873-0061
Andrew Zanschoick, *Manager*
EMP: 70
SALES (corp-wide): 2.4B **Publicly Held**
WEB: www.lci1.com
SIC: 3711 3469 3444 3714 Chassis, motor vehicle; stamping metal for the trade; metal roofing & roof drainage equipment; motor vehicle parts & accessories; welding on site
HQ: Lippert Components, Inc.
3501 County Road 6 E
Elkhart IN 46514
574 312-7480

(P-19485)
MARS MEDICAL RIDE CORP
23702 Main St, Carson (90745-5744)
PHONE..................................310 518-1024
Ernie Soriano, *President*
Flordeliza Soriano, *Vice Pres*
EMP: 10
SQ FT: 900
SALES (est): 1MM **Privately Held**
SIC: 3711 4119 Ambulances (motor vehicles), assembly of; ambulance service

(P-19486)
MARVIN LAND SYSTEMS INC
Also Called: Marvin Group The
261 W Beach Ave, Inglewood (90302-2904)
PHONE..................................310 674-5030
Gerald M Friedman, *President*
Leon Tsimmerman, *CFO*
Mike Hershewe, *Info Tech Mgr*
▲ EMP: 44
SQ FT: 200,000
SALES (est): 13.7MM
SALES (corp-wide): 223.5MM **Privately Held**
WEB: www.marvineng.com
SIC: 3711 Military motor vehicle assembly
PA: Marvin Engineering Co., Inc.
261 W Beach Ave
Inglewood CA 90302
310 674-5030

(P-19487)
MILLENWORKS
1361 Valencia Ave, Tustin (92780-6459)
PHONE..................................714 426-5500
Ellen M Lord, *CEO*
Dean Banks, *President*
Rod Millen, *CEO*
▲ EMP: 75
SQ FT: 76,000
SALES (est): 13.1MM
SALES (corp-wide): 13.9B **Publicly Held**
WEB: www.millenworks.com
SIC: 3711 5012 7549 8731 Military motor vehicle assembly; commercial vehicles; automotive customizing services, non-factory basis; electronic research
HQ: Textron Systems Corporation
201 Lowell St
Wilmington MA 01887
978 657-5111

(P-19488)
MODA ENTERPRISES INC
Also Called: Southern California Tow Eqp
1334 N Knollwood Cir, Anaheim (92801-1311)
PHONE..................................714 484-0076
Kamy Modarres, *President*
Hector Rivas, *General Mgr*
EMP: 11
SQ FT: 9,000
SALES: 7MM **Privately Held**
WEB: www.towequipments.com
SIC: 3711 Wreckers (tow truck), assembly of

(P-19489)
MULLEN TECHNOLOGIES INC (PA)
1405 Pioneer St, Brea (92821-3721)
PHONE..................................714 613-1900

David Michery, *CEO*
Jerry Alban, *CFO*
William Johnston, *Exec VP*
Mary Winter, *Vice Pres*
Francis McMahon, *CTO*
EMP: 40
SQ FT: 24,730
SALES (est): 5.8MM **Privately Held**
SIC: 3711 5013 Motor vehicles & car bodies; motor vehicle supplies & new parts

(P-19490)
NAVISTAR INC
14651 Ventura Blvd, Sherman Oaks (91403-3617)
PHONE..................................818 907-0129
EMP: 60
SALES (corp-wide): 10.2B **Publicly Held**
SIC: 3711 Truck & tractor truck assembly
HQ: Navistar, Inc.
2701 Navistar Dr
Lisle IL 60532
331 332-5000

(P-19491)
NEWFIELD TECHNOLOGY CORP (PA)
4230 E Airport Dr Ste 105, Ontario (91761-3702)
P.O. Box 1290, Upland (91785-1290)
PHONE..................................909 931-4405
Minoru Nitta, *President*
▲ EMP: 40
SALES (est): 4.1MM **Privately Held**
SIC: 3711 Motor vehicles & car bodies

(P-19492)
NIO USA INC
Also Called: Nextev
3200 N 1st St, San Jose (95134-1936)
PHONE..................................408 518-7000
Padmasree Warrior, *CEO*
Thomas Schaeffer, *Vice Pres*
Alan Zeng, *Vice Pres*
Vivek Hajela, *Engineer*
Mutti Kocbayindiran, *Engineer*
EMP: 98 EST: 2015
SALES (est): 39.2MM **Privately Held**
SIC: 3711 Motor vehicles & car bodies
HQ: Nio Co., Ltd.
Building 20, Auto Innovation Port, No. 56, Antuo Road, Jiading D
Shanghai 20180
216 908-2000

(P-19493)
PHOENIX CARS LLC
Also Called: Phoenix Motorcars
401 S Doubleday Ave, Ontario (91761-1501)
PHONE..................................909 987-0815
Alexander Lee, *CEO*
Hamada Will, *Engineer*
Joseph Tobia, *Accountant*
Archie Kimes, *Production*
▲ EMP: 16
SQ FT: 40,000
SALES (est): 4.5MM
SALES (corp-wide): 57.1MM **Privately Held**
SIC: 3711 Cars, electric, assembly of
HQ: Al Yousuf Motors Llc
Next Noor Bank Metro Station Between 2nd, 3rd Interchange, Sheik Dubai
433 910-50

(P-19494)
PROTERRA INC (PA)
1815 Rollins Rd, Burlingame (94010-2204)
PHONE..................................864 438-0000
Ryan Popple, *President*
Amy Ard, *CFO*
Matt Horton, *Ch Credit Ofcr*
Joann Covington, *Officer*
Josh Ensign, *Officer*
▲ EMP: 110
SQ FT: 14,000
SALES (est): 36.1MM **Privately Held**
WEB: www.proterra.com
SIC: 3711 Bus & other large specialty vehicle assembly

PRODUCTS & SVCS

(PA)=Parent Co (HQ)=Headquarters (DH)=Div Headquarters
✿ = New Business established in last 2 years

(P-19495)
RACEPAK LLC
Also Called: Race Pak
30402 Esperanza, Rcho STA Marg
(92688-2144)
PHONE.....................................888 429-4709
Fax: 949 709-5556
▲ EMP: 29
SQ FT: 6,000
SALES (est): 5.5MM Privately Held
WEB: www.csisensors.com
SIC: 3711

(P-19496)
RAMON LOPEZ
Also Called: Prestige Limousine
4752 Ijams Rd, Stockton (95210-3605)
PHONE.....................................209 478-9500
Ramon R Lopez, Owner
EMP: 10
SALES: 1MM Privately Held
WEB: www.prestigelimos.com
SIC: 3711 4119 Automobile assembly, in-
cluding specialty automobiles; limousine
rental, with driver

(P-19497)
RAYTHEON COMPANY
9400 Santa Fe Springs Rd, Santa Fe
Springs (90670-2623)
PHONE.....................................310 884-1825
Lisa Nguyen, Manager
EMP: 200
SALES (corp-wide): 27B Publicly Held
SIC: 3711 8711 Motor vehicles & car bod-
ies; engineering services
PA: Raytheon Company
870 Winter St
Waltham MA 02451
781 522-3000

(P-19498)
RIPON VOLUNTEER FIREMANS
ASSN
142 S Stockton Ave, Ripon (95366-2759)
PHONE.....................................209 599-4209
Dennis Ditters, Chief
EMP: 18
SALES: 27K Privately Held
SIC: 3711 Ambulances (motor vehicles),
assembly of; fire department vehicles
(motor vehicles), assembly of

(P-19499)
SABA MOTORS INC
521 Charcot Ave Ste 165, San Jose
(95131-1152)
PHONE.....................................408 219-8675
Simon Saba, President
Chris Arcus, Director
EMP: 10 EST: 2009
SALES (est): 753.3K Privately Held
SIC: 3711 Motor vehicles & car bodies

(P-19500)
SALEEN INCORPORATED (PA)
2735 Wardlow Rd, Corona (92882-2869)
PHONE.....................................714 400-2121
Paul Wilbur, President
Stephen Saleen, CEO
Brian Walsh, Senior VP
Michael Simmons, Sales Staff
EMP: 500
SALES (est): 73.7MM Privately Held
SIC: 3711 Automobile assembly, including
specialty automobiles; motor trucks, ex-
cept off-highway, assembly of

(P-19501)
SF MOTORS INC (DH)
3303 Scott Blvd, Santa Clara (95054-3102)
PHONE.....................................408 617-7878
Michael Deng, CEO
Martin Eberhard, Officer
Mike Miskovsky, Officer
Shen Chen, Info Tech Mgr
EMP: 250
SQ FT: 18,000
SALES (est): 2.8MM
SALES (corp-wide): 1.6MM Privately
Held
SIC: 3711 Cars, electric, assembly of

HQ: Chongqing Jinkang New Energy Auto-
mobile Co., Ltd.
No.229, Fusheng Avenue, Jiangbei
District
Chongqing 40003
238 909-5666

(P-19502)
SHELBY CARROLL INTL INC
(PA)
19021 S Figueroa St, Gardena
(90248-4510)
PHONE.....................................310 538-2914
Carroll Shelby, Principal
Schechner Gary, VP Mktg
Mike Lambert, Relations
EMP: 28
SALES (est): 9.3MM Privately Held
SIC: 3711 Motor vehicles & car bodies

(P-19503)
TCI ENGINEERING INC
Also Called: Total Cost Involved
1416 Brooks St, Ontario (91762-3613)
PHONE.....................................909 984-1773
Edward Moss, President
Sherlly Prakarsa, CFO
Ruben Perez, Purchasing
EMP: 54
SQ FT: 25,000
SALES (est): 12.4MM Privately Held
WEB: www.totalcostinvolved.com
SIC: 3711 5531 3714 Chassis, motor ve-
hicle; automotive & home supply stores;
motor vehicle parts & accessories

(P-19504)
TESLA INC
Also Called: Tesla Motors Inc.
18260 S Harlan Rd, Lathrop (95330-8757)
PHONE.....................................209 647-7037
Robyn Denholm, Ch of Bd
EMP: 18
SALES (corp-wide): 21.4B Publicly Held
SIC: 3711 Motor vehicles & car bodies
PA: Tesla, Inc.
3500 Deer Creek Rd
Palo Alto CA 94304
650 681-5000

(P-19505)
TESLA INC
38503 Cherry St Ste I, Newark
(94560-4717)
PHONE.....................................510 896-6400
EMP: 663
SALES (corp-wide): 21.4B Publicly Held
SIC: 3711 Motor vehicles & car bodies
PA: Tesla, Inc.
3500 Deer Creek Rd
Palo Alto CA 94304
650 681-5000

(P-19506)
TESLA INC
Also Called: Tesla Solar
1055 Page Ave, Fremont (94538-7341)
PHONE.....................................707 373-4035
EMP: 21
SALES (corp-wide): 21.4B Publicly Held
SIC: 3711 Motor vehicles & car bodies
PA: Tesla, Inc.
3500 Deer Creek Rd
Palo Alto CA 94304
650 681-5000

(P-19507)
TESLA INC (PA)
3500 Deer Creek Rd, Palo Alto
(94304-1317)
PHONE.....................................650 681-5000
Elon Musk, CEO
Robyn Denholm, Ch of Bd
Zach Kirkhorn, CFO
Zachary Kirkhorn, CFO
Vaibhav Taneja,
▲ EMP: 225
SQ FT: 350,000
SALES: 21.4B Publicly Held
WEB: www.teslamotors.com
SIC: 3711 3714 3674 Automobile assem-
bly, including specialty automobiles; cars,
electric, assembly of; motor vehicle parts
& accessories; solar cells

(P-19508)
TIFFANY COACHWORKS INC
420 N Mckinley St 111-465, Corona
(92879-8099)
PHONE.....................................951 657-2680
William Auden, CEO
James Powel, CEO
◆ EMP: 115
SQ FT: 57,000
SALES (est): 10.1MM Privately Held
SIC: 3711 Motor vehicles & car bodies

(P-19509)
UNDERCAR EXPRESS INC
57 N Altadena Dr, Pasadena (91107-3331)
PHONE.....................................626 683-2787
Shahe Kalaydjian, CEO
Ruben Dekhbachyan, Vice Pres
EMP: 10 EST: 1995
SALES (est): 1.4MM Privately Held
SIC: 3711 Automobile assembly, including
specialty automobiles
PA: Undercar Plus Inc.
4100 Goodwin Ave
Los Angeles CA 90039

(P-19510)
VALLEY MOTOR CENTER INC
Also Called: Star Racecars
10639 Glenoaks Blvd, Pacoima
(91331-1613)
PHONE.....................................818 686-3350
▲ EMP: 10
SQ FT: 30,000
SALES (est): 1.4MM Privately Held
WEB: www.valleymotorcenter.com
SIC: 3711

(P-19511)
WARLOCK INDUSTRIES
Also Called: Tiffany Coach Builders
23129 Cajalco Rd Ste A, Perris
(92570-7298)
PHONE.....................................951 657-2680
Carter J Read, CEO
Mike Sears, Finance Mgr
David Perry, Controller
▼ EMP: 46 EST: 2009
SQ FT: 118,600
SALES (est): 7.9MM Privately Held
SIC: 3711 Motor vehicles & car bodies

(P-19512)
WEST COAST UNLIMITED
Also Called: West Coast Airlines
11161 Pierce St, Riverside (92505-2713)
PHONE.....................................951 352-1234
H J Manning, Manager
L K Manning, President
EMP: 11
SQ FT: 6,000
SALES (est): 1MM Privately Held
SIC: 3711 7699 Fire department vehicles
(motor vehicles), assembly of; fire control
(military) equipment repair

(P-19513)
WIDE OPEN INDUSTRIES LLC
21088 Bake Pkwy Ste 100, Lake Forest
(92630-2165)
PHONE.....................................949 635-2292
Christian Hammarskjold, Mng Member
EMP: 20
SALES: 950K Privately Held
SIC: 3711 3714 5012 Motor vehicles &
car bodies; motor vehicle parts & acces-
sories; automobiles & other motor vehi-
cles

(P-19514)
ZOOX INC (PA)
Also Called: Zoox Labs
1149 Chess Dr, Foster City (94404-1102)
PHONE.....................................650 733-9669
Carl Bass, Chairman
Jesse Levinson, CTO
Michael Batty, Controller
Rebekah Baratho, Recruiter
Bruce Baumgartner, Director
EMP: 222
SALES (est): 161.5MM Privately Held
SIC: 3711 Automobile assembly, including
specialty automobiles

3713 Truck & Bus Bodies

(P-19515)
ACCESS MFG INC
Also Called: Tradesman Trucktops
1805 Railroad Ave, Winters (95694-2011)
P.O. Box 519 (95694-0519)
PHONE.....................................530 795-0720
John Neil, CEO
Maria Rodriguez, Office Mgr
EMP: 11
SQ FT: 20,000
SALES (est): 1.8MM Privately Held
WEB: www.accessmfg.com
SIC: 3713 Truck tops

(P-19516)
AMERICAN CUSTOM COACH
INC
1255 W Colton Ave, Redlands
(92374-2861)
PHONE.....................................909 796-4747
Jales Mello, President
EMP: 14
SQ FT: 10,000
SALES (est): 2.3MM Privately Held
WEB: www.americancc.com
SIC: 3713 Specialty motor vehicle bodies

(P-19517)
AMERICAN TRCK TRLR BDY CO
INC (PA)
100 W Valpico Rd Ste D, Tracy
(95376-8198)
PHONE.....................................209 836-8985
Clint Garner, President
Michael A Garner, President
Toni Ageno, CFO
Adam Garner, Corp Secy
Dallas Dodson, Vice Pres
EMP: 42
SQ FT: 40,000
SALES (est): 8.6MM Privately Held
WEB: www.attbcinc.com
SIC: 3713 Truck bodies (motor vehicles)

(P-19518)
ARMENCO CATRG TRCK MFG
CO INC
11819 Vose St, North Hollywood
(91605-5748)
PHONE.....................................818 768-0400
Gerhayr Djahani, President
Yres Mardros, Vice Pres
EMP: 12
SQ FT: 6,000
SALES: 1.7MM Privately Held
WEB: www.cateringtruck.com
SIC: 3713 Truck bodies (motor vehicles)

(P-19519)
ARROW TRUCK BODIES &
EQUIPMENT
1639 S Campus Ave, Ontario (91761-4364)
PHONE.....................................909 947-3991
Raymond A Glaze, President
Keith Wysocki, President
Richard Rubio, Corp Secy
EMP: 27
SQ FT: 33,980
SALES: 2.5MM Privately Held
WEB: www.arrowtruckbodies.com
SIC: 3713 Truck bodies (motor vehicles)

(P-19520)
ARROW TRUCK SALES
INCORPORATED
10175 Cherry Ave, Fontana (92335-5217)
PHONE.....................................909 829-2365
Corey Garland, Manager
Bruce Brancato, Director
EMP: 11
SALES (corp-wide): 43.4B Privately Held
WEB: www.arrowtruckatlanta.com
SIC: 3713 Truck bodies & parts
HQ: Arrow Truck Sales Incorporated
3200 Manchester Trfy L-70
Kansas City MO 64129
816 923-5000

▲ = Import ▼=Export
◆ =Import/Export

(P-19521)
BETTS COMPANY
2867 S Maple Ave, Fresno (93725-2217)
PHONE....................................559 498-8624
Carlos Holdin, *Branch Mgr*
EMP: 46
SQ FT: 56,672
SALES (corp-wide): 77.4MM **Privately Held**
WEB: www.bettspring.com
SIC: 3713 3495 3452 3493 Truck & bus bodies; wire springs; bolts, nuts, rivets & washers; automobile springs
PA: Betts Company
2843 S Maple Ave
Fresno CA 93725
559 498-3304

(P-19522)
CALIFORNIA SUPERTRUCKS INC
14385 Veterans Way, Moreno Valley (92553-9059)
PHONE....................................951 656-2903
Chris Robinson, *President*
Tim Clark, *Vice Pres*
Bradley Myers, *Vice Pres*
EMP: 27 **EST:** 1996
SQ FT: 20,000
SALES (est): 4.6MM **Privately Held**
WEB: www.californiasupertrucks.com
SIC: 3713 3011 5014 5013 Truck bodies & parts; inner tubes, all types; pneumatic tires, all types; truck tires & tubes; truck parts & accessories

(P-19523)
COMPLETE TRUCK BODY REPAIR INC
1217 N Alameda St Compton, Compton (90222)
PHONE....................................323 445-2675
Rodrigo Robles, *President*
EMP: 10
SQ FT: 10,225
SALES: 25MM **Privately Held**
SIC: 3713 Truck bodies & parts

(P-19524)
COOKS TRUCK BODY MFG INC
9600 Del Rd, Roseville (95747-9108)
PHONE....................................916 784-3220
Jerry Cook Jr, *President*
Brian Diamond, *Corp Secy*
Cindy Diamond, *Vice Pres*
EMP: 13
SQ FT: 11,400
SALES (est): 2.3MM **Privately Held**
WEB: www.cookstruckbody.com
SIC: 3713 Truck bodies (motor vehicles)

(P-19525)
DADEE MANUFACTURING LLC
911 N Poinsettia St, Santa Ana (92701-3827)
PHONE....................................602 276-4390
Paul Campbell,
EMP: 22 **EST:** 2007
SALES (est): 5.7MM **Privately Held**
SIC: 3713 Garbage, refuse truck bodies

(P-19526)
DELTA STAG MANUFACTURING
Also Called: Delta-Stag Truck Body
1818 E Rosslynn Ave, Fullerton (92831-5140)
PHONE....................................562 904-6444
George Cashman Sr, *President*
EMP: 60
SQ FT: 100,000
SALES (est): 9.8MM **Privately Held**
WEB: www.deltastag.com
SIC: 3713 7549 Truck bodies (motor vehicles); specialty motor vehicle bodies; automotive maintenance services

(P-19527)
DENBESTE MANUFACTURING INC
810 Den Beste Ct Ste 107, Windsor (95492-6843)
PHONE....................................707 838-1407
Lori Denbeste, *President*
EMP: 11

SALES (est): 1.7MM **Privately Held**
SIC: 3713 Tank truck bodies

(P-19528)
DIAMOND TRUCK BODY MFG INC
1908 E Fremont St, Stockton (95205-4523)
PHONE....................................209 943-1655
Tony Teresi, *President*
Frances Teresi, *Treasurer*
EMP: 14 **EST:** 1978
SQ FT: 11,250
SALES (est): 2.7MM **Privately Held**
WEB: www.diamondtruckbody.com
SIC: 3713 Truck bodies (motor vehicles)

(P-19529)
DOUGLASS TRUCK BODIES INC
231 21st St, Bakersfield (93301-4138)
PHONE....................................661 327-0258
Rick Douglass, *President*
Jean Raley, *Corp Secy*
Deborah Douglass, *Vice Pres*
Michael Ledford, *Vice Pres*
Rey Mesa, *Mfg Staff*
EMP: 24
SQ FT: 5,000
SALES (est): 5.8MM **Privately Held**
WEB: www.douglasstruckbodies.com
SIC: 3713 Truck bodies (motor vehicles)

(P-19530)
DYNAFLEX PRODUCTS (PA)
Also Called: EXHAUST TECH
6466 Gayhart St, Commerce (90040-2506)
PHONE....................................323 724-1555
Robert L McGovern, *President*
Gil Contreras, *Vice Pres*
Christopher Salisbury, *Engineer*
Rich Schevis, *Engineer*
Peter Jensen, *Maint Spvr*
EMP: 75
SQ FT: 64,000
SALES: 19.9MM **Privately Held**
WEB: www.dynaflexproducts.com
SIC: 3713 3498 3714 Truck & bus bodies; fabricated pipe & fittings; exhaust systems & parts, motor vehicle

(P-19531)
EBUS INC
9250 Washburn Rd, Downey (90242-2909)
PHONE....................................562 904-3474
Anders B Eklov, *Ch of Bd*
Chris Mejia, *Engineer*
Lou Ellen Pruden, *Controller*
Lou Pruden, *Controller*
EMP: 45
SALES (est): 6MM **Privately Held**
WEB: www.ebus.com
SIC: 3713 Bus bodies (motor vehicles)

(P-19532)
ERF ENTERPRISES INC
Also Called: Colton Truck Terminal Garage
863 E Valley Blvd, Colton (92324-3125)
PHONE....................................909 825-4080
Ed Doltar, *President*
Rich Doltar, *Principal*
Fran Fields, *Principal*
EMP: 18
SALES (est): 720.2K **Privately Held**
SIC: 3713 Truck bodies (motor vehicles)

(P-19533)
FLEMING METAL FABRICATORS
2810 Tanager Ave, Commerce (90040-2716)
PHONE....................................323 723-8203
Wade M Fleming, *President*
Marc Fleming, *Vice Pres*
Mark Miles, *Engineer*
EMP: 30
SQ FT: 36,000
SALES (est): 6.4MM **Privately Held**
WEB: www.flemingmetal.com
SIC: 3713 3441 3714 3577 Truck bodies & parts; fabricated structural metal; motor vehicle parts & accessories; computer peripheral equipment; electronic computers

(P-19534)
GAYLORDS INC (PA)
13538 Excelsior Dr, Santa Fe Springs (90670-5616)
PHONE....................................562 529-7543

William G Lunney IL, *President*
Jose Escudero, *Purchasing*
EMP: 12
SQ FT: 4,800
SALES (est): 8.9MM **Privately Held**
SIC: 3713 Truck tops

(P-19535)
GENERAL TRUCK BODY INC
1130 S Vail Ave, Montebello (90640-6021)
PHONE....................................323 276-1933
Kam C Law, *President*
Peter Lee, *Treasurer*
Dana Pearce, *General Mgr*
Miles Olsen, *Manager*
◆ **EMP:** 99
SQ FT: 43,000
SALES (est): 15.3MM **Privately Held**
SIC: 3713 Truck bodies (motor vehicles)

(P-19536)
GILLIG LLC
451 Discovery Dr, Livermore (94551-9534)
PHONE....................................510 785-1500
Derek Maunus, *President*
Joe Policarpio, *Vice Pres*
Greg Vismara, *Vice Pres*
Bob Birdwell, *Exec Dir*
Deirdre Fenelon, *Administration*
▲ **EMP:** 277
SQ FT: 150,000
SALES (est): 207.6MM
SALES (corp-wide): 1.5B **Privately Held**
WEB: www.gillig.com
SIC: 3713 Truck & bus bodies
PA: Henry Crown And Company
222 N La Salle St # 2000
Chicago IL 60601
312 236-6300

(P-19537)
HARBOR TRUCK BODIES INC
Also Called: Harbor Truck Body
255 Voyager Ave, Brea (92821-6223)
PHONE....................................714 996-0411
Ken Lindt, *President*
John Houng, *Engineer*
Randy Dickerson, *Human Res Dir*
Alex Ledezma, *Purchasing*
Brian Divine, *Opers Staff*
EMP: 79
SQ FT: 50,000
SALES (est): 22.3MM **Privately Held**
WEB: www.harbortruck.com
SIC: 3713 7532 Truck bodies (motor vehicles); body shop, automotive

(P-19538)
HARDWARE IMPORTS INC
Also Called: Western Hardware Company
161 Commerce Way, Walnut (91789-2719)
PHONE....................................909 595-6201
Gayle Pacheco, *President*
Robert Pacheco, *CFO*
▲ **EMP:** 15
SQ FT: 6,000
SALES (est): 2.8MM **Privately Held**
SIC: 3713 3429 Truck & bus bodies; furniture hardware

(P-19539)
JJS TRUCK EQUIPMENT LLC
Also Called: D & H Trucking Equipment
9685 Via Excelencia # 200, San Diego (92126-7500)
PHONE....................................858 566-1155
James Coffman,
James Aland,
EMP: 25
SQ FT: 45,000
SALES (est): 442.3K **Privately Held**
SIC: 3713 7538 5013 Truck bodies (motor vehicles); truck engine repair, except industrial; truck parts & accessories

(P-19540)
LEE BROTHERS TRUCK BODY INC
18915 Roselle Ave, Torrance (90504-5618)
PHONE....................................310 532-7980
Richard Lee, *President*
Ron Lee, *Vice Pres*
EMP: 10
SQ FT: 1,800

SALES: 1.5MM **Privately Held**
WEB: www.leebrostruck.com
SIC: 3713 7532 5531 Truck bodies & parts; body shop, trucks; truck equipment & parts

(P-19541)
LIMOS BY TIFFANY INC
Also Called: Tiffany Coachworks
23129 Cajalco Rd, Perris (92570-7298)
P.O. Box 46 (92572-0046)
PHONE....................................951 657-2680
William Auden, *President*
Carter Read, *Corp Secy*
EMP: 35
SQ FT: 56,000
SALES (est): 6.5MM **Privately Held**
SIC: 3713 Specialty motor vehicle bodies

(P-19542)
MCLELLAN EQUIPMENT INC (PA)
251 Shaw Rd, South San Francisco (94080-6605)
PHONE....................................650 873-8100
Molly Mausser, *CEO*
Kristi Parres, *Corp Secy*
Scott McLellan, *Vice Pres*
Annette De Maria, *Executive Asst*
▲ **EMP:** 80 **EST:** 1965
SQ FT: 12,000
SALES (est): 9.8MM **Privately Held**
SIC: 3713 3532 7532 3312 Truck bodies (motor vehicles); truck beds; mining machinery; tops (canvas or plastic), installation or repair: automotive; blast furnaces & steel mills

(P-19543)
MCLELLAN EQUIPMENT INC
13221 Crown Ave, Hanford (93230-9508)
PHONE....................................559 582-8100
Scott McLellan, *Vice Pres*
Russ Huffman, *Prdtn Mgr*
EMP: 70
SALES (est): 10.9MM
SALES (corp-wide): 9.8MM **Privately Held**
SIC: 3713 3532 7532 3312 Truck bodies (motor vehicles); truck beds; mining machinery; tops (canvas or plastic), installation or repair: automotive; blast furnaces & steel mills
PA: Mclellan Equipment, Inc.
251 Shaw Rd
South San Francisco CA 94080
650 873-8100

(P-19544)
MCLELLAN INDUSTRIES INC
13221 Crown Ave, Hanford (93230-9508)
PHONE....................................650 873-8100
Victor Resendez, *Manager*
Shawn Quinn, *General Mgr*
Ranae Agurrie, *Sales Mgr*
Megan Ogle, *Sales Staff*
EMP: 80
SALES (corp-wide): 23.2MM **Privately Held**
WEB: www.mclellanindustries.com
SIC: 3713 Truck bodies (motor vehicles)
PA: Mclellan Industries, Inc.
251 Shaw Rd
South San Francisco CA 94080
650 873-8100

(P-19545)
MCNEILUS TRUCK AND MFG INC
401 N Pepper Ave, Colton (92324-1817)
P.O. Box 1588 (92324-0849)
PHONE....................................909 370-2100
Liza Langley, *Branch Mgr*
EMP: 33
SALES (corp-wide): 7.7B **Publicly Held**
WEB: www.mcneiluscompanies.com
SIC: 3713 5511 3711 3531 Cement mixer bodies; pickups, new & used; truck & tractor truck assembly; construction machinery
HQ: Mcneilus Truck And Manufacturing, Inc.
524 E Highway St
Dodge Center MN 55927
507 374-6321

(P-19546)
METRO TRUCK BODY INCORPORATED
1201 W Jon St, Torrance (90502-1288)
PHONE..................................310 532-5570
Vincent Rigali, *CEO*
Vincint X Rigali, *President*
Philip W Rigali, *CEO*
Sid Halushka, *Corp Secy*
Virginia Rigali, *Vice Pres*
▲ **EMP:** 47 **EST:** 1968
SQ FT: 20,000
SALES (est): 8.3MM **Privately Held**
WEB: www.metrotruckbody.com
SIC: 3713 7532 5012 5531 Truck bodies (motor vehicles); body shop, automotive; truck bodies; truck equipment & parts

(P-19547)
NOR-CAL VANS INC
1300 Nord Ave, Chico (95926-4235)
PHONE..................................530 892-0150
Todd Lapant, *CEO*
Laura Lapant, *CFO*
Amanda Perez, *Mktg Dir*
Matt McTavish, *Asst Mgr*
EMP: 15
SALES (est): 3.9MM **Privately Held**
SIC: 3713 Van bodies

(P-19548)
NORCAL WASTE EQUIPMENT CO
299 Park St, San Leandro (94577-1501)
PHONE..................................510 568-8336
Otto C Ganter, *President*
EMP: 20
SQ FT: 10,000
SALES (est): 3.4MM **Privately Held**
SIC: 3713 Truck bodies (motor vehicles)

(P-19549)
PACIFIC TRUCK EQUIPMENT INC
11655 Washington Blvd, Whittier (90606-2424)
PHONE..................................562 464-9674
Julie Hargrave, *CEO*
John Hargrave, *President*
EMP: 73
SALES (est): 18.4MM **Privately Held**
WEB: www.pacifictruckequipment.com
SIC: 3713 Truck bodies (motor vehicles)

(P-19550)
PACIFIC TRUCK TANK INC
7029 Florin Perkins Rd A, Sacramento (95828-2656)
PHONE..................................916 379-9280
Kirby Fleming, *President*
Jerry Jones, *Vice Pres*
EMP: 20
SQ FT: 22,000
SALES (est): 4.3MM **Privately Held**
WEB: www.pacifictrucktank.com
SIC: 3713 Truck beds

(P-19551)
PHENIX ENTERPRISES INC (PA)
Also Called: Phenix Truck Bodies and Eqp
1785 Mount Vernon Ave, Pomona (91768-3330)
PHONE..................................909 469-0411
Benjamin Albertini, *Chairman*
Norma E Albertini, *President*
Rick Albertini, *CEO*
Paul Albertini, *Corp Secy*
Todd Davis, *General Mgr*
EMP: 40
SQ FT: 100,000
SALES (est): 7.6MM **Privately Held**
WEB: www.phenixent.com
SIC: 3713 3711 Truck bodies (motor vehicles); motor vehicles & car bodies

(P-19552)
RYANGMW INC
13861 Dry Creek Rd, Auburn (95602-8482)
PHONE..................................530 305-2499
Ryan Gangemi, *Principal*
EMP: 13 **EST:** 2008
SALES (est): 1.3MM **Privately Held**
SIC: 3713 Automobile wrecker truck bodies

(P-19553)
SAF-T-CAB INC (PA)
3241 S Parkway Dr, Fresno (93725-2319)
P.O. Box 2587 (93745-2587)
PHONE..................................559 268-5541
Fred Mattern, *President*
Dan Lockie, *Corp Secy*
Eric Valdivia, *Chief Engr*
▲ **EMP:** 54
SQ FT: 12,000
SALES (est): 9.7MM **Privately Held**
WEB: www.saftcab.com
SIC: 3713 3532 Truck cabs for motor vehicles; truck beds; mining machinery

(P-19554)
SKAUG TRUCK BODY WORKS
1404 1st St, San Fernando (91340-2795)
PHONE..................................818 365-9123
George L Skaug, *President*
William Reeves, *Vice Pres*
EMP: 18
SQ FT: 3,200
SALES (est): 3.2MM **Privately Held**
SIC: 3713 Truck bodies (motor vehicles)

(P-19555)
SOUTHERN CAL TRCK BDIES SLS IN
1131 E 2nd St, Pomona (91766-2115)
PHONE..................................909 469-1132
Miguel Sanchez, *President*
Silvia Sanchez, *Admin Sec*
EMP: 15
SQ FT: 6,035
SALES (est): 2.3MM **Privately Held**
SIC: 3713 5531 Truck bodies & parts; automotive parts

(P-19556)
SOUTHLAND MIXER SERVICE
12231 Hibiscus Rd, Adelanto (92301-1702)
PHONE..................................760 246-6080
Esteban Castilleja, *Owner*
Pedro Chavez, *Principal*
EMP: 11
SQ FT: 15,220
SALES (est): 1.7MM **Privately Held**
SIC: 3713 Truck bodies & parts

(P-19557)
SPARTAN TRUCK COMPANY INC
12266 Branford St, Sun Valley (91352-1009)
PHONE..................................818 899-1111
Myan Spaccarelli, *President*
Dan Spaccarelli, *Sales Mgr*
EMP: 35
SQ FT: 25,000
SALES (est): 7.3MM **Privately Held**
SIC: 3713 7532 3537 Garbage, refuse truck bodies; top & body repair & paint shops; industrial trucks & tractors

(P-19558)
SPECIALTY EQUIPMENT CO
1921 E Pomona St, Santa Ana (92705-5119)
PHONE..................................714 258-1622
Richard Page, *President*
EMP: 25
SALES (est): 4.9MM **Privately Held**
SIC: 3713 3711 Truck bodies & parts; motor vehicles & car bodies

(P-19559)
SUPREME CORPORATION
Also Called: Supreme Truck Body
22135 Alessandro Blvd, Moreno Valley (92553-8215)
PHONE..................................951 656-6101
Mike Oium, *General Mgr*
Cynthia Consorte, *Purch Agent*
Jon Buchholz, *Plant Mgr*
EMP: 115
SALES (corp-wide): 2.2B **Publicly Held**
SIC: 3713 Truck bodies (motor vehicles)
HQ: Supreme Corporation
2581 Kercher Rd
Goshen IN 46528
574 642-4888

(P-19560)
VAHE ENTERPRISES INC
Also Called: Aa Leasing
750 E Slauson Ave, Los Angeles (90011-5236)
PHONE..................................323 235-6657
Vahe Karapetian, *CEO*
Clarence Stokes, *Asst Controller*
▲ **EMP:** 90
SQ FT: 60,000
SALES (est): 17.5MM **Privately Held**
WEB: www.aacatertruck.com
SIC: 3713 7513 Truck bodies (motor vehicles); truck leasing, without drivers

---

3714 Motor Vehicle Parts & Access

(P-19561)
6F RESOLUTION INC
5100 W Goldleaf Cir, Los Angeles (90056-1658)
PHONE..................................209 467-0490
Pete Warinne, *Manager*
EMP: 80
SALES (corp-wide): 12.3MM **Privately Held**
SIC: 3714 Motor vehicle parts & accessories
PA: 6f Resolution, Inc.
5100 W Goldleaf Cir # 215
Los Angeles CA 90056
323 292-6644

(P-19562)
A TERRYCABLE CALIFORNIA CORP
17376 Eucalyptus St, Hesperia (92345-5118)
PHONE..................................760 244-9351
Terry P Davis, *President*
EMP: 21
SQ FT: 10,000
SALES (est): 1.5MM **Privately Held**
WEB: www.terrycable.com
SIC: 3714 Motor vehicle parts & accessories

(P-19563)
ACME HEADLINING CO
Also Called: Acme Auto Headlining
550 W 16th St, Long Beach (90813-1510)
P.O. Box 847 (90801-0847)
PHONE..................................562 432-0281
Bob Westmoreland, *Vice Pres*
Don Young, *Director*
▲ **EMP:** 75
SQ FT: 18,000
SALES: 7.2MM **Privately Held**
SIC: 3714 Tops, motor vehicle

(P-19564)
ACSCO PRODUCTS INC
313 N Lake St, Burbank (91502-1816)
PHONE..................................818 953-2240
Thomas W Mc Intyre, *President*
Yolanda Piroli, *Info Tech Mgr*
Luigi Cervantes, *Engineer*
EMP: 20 **EST:** 1963
SQ FT: 4,000
SALES (est): 4.4MM **Privately Held**
WEB: www.acsco.net
SIC: 3714 Motor vehicle parts & accessories

(P-19565)
ADOMANI INC
4740 Green River Rd, Corona (92880-9185)
PHONE..................................951 407-9860
James L Reynolds, *Ch of Bd*
Richard A Eckert, *COO*
Michael K Menerey, *CFO*
Kevin G Kanning, *Vice Pres*
Robert E Williams, *Vice Pres*
EMP: 11
SALES: 5MM **Privately Held**
SIC: 3714 Motor vehicle parts & accessories

(P-19566)
ADVANCE ADAPTERS INC
4320 Aerotech Center Way, Paso Robles (93446-8529)
P.O. Box 247 (93447-0247)
PHONE..................................805 238-7000
Mike Partridge, *President*
John Partridge, *Vice Pres*
Charles Althausen, *Engineer*
Kevin Dill, *Engineer*
Mario Darg, *Purchasing*
▲ **EMP:** 44
SQ FT: 44,000
SALES (est): 10.1MM **Privately Held**
WEB: www.advanceadapters.com
SIC: 3714 Transmission housings or parts, motor vehicle

(P-19567)
ADVANCED CLUTCH TECHNOLOGY INC
206 E Avenue K4, Lancaster (93535-4685)
PHONE..................................661 940-7555
Tracy Nunez, *CEO*
Dirk Starksen, *President*
Daniel Starksen, *Officer*
Chris Bernal, *Exec VP*
Danette Starksen, *Admin Sec*
▲ **EMP:** 30
SQ FT: 18,000
SALES (est): 6.9MM **Privately Held**
WEB: www.advancedclutch.com
SIC: 3714 Clutches, motor vehicle

(P-19568)
ADVANCED ENGINE MANAGEMENT INC (PA)
Also Called: A E M
2205 W 126th St Ste A, Hawthorne (90250-3367)
PHONE..................................310 484-2322
Gregory David Neuwirth, *President*
Wilson Tam, *CFO*
Peter Neuwirth, *Chairman*
Andrew Zheng, *Bd of Directors*
Cynthia Isom, *General Mgr*
▲ **EMP:** 115
SQ FT: 78,000
SALES (est): 39.1MM **Privately Held**
SIC: 3714 Motor vehicle engines & parts

(P-19569)
ADVANCED FLOW ENGINEERING INC (PA)
Also Called: Afe Power
252 Granite St, Corona (92879-1283)
PHONE..................................951 493-7155
Shahriar Nick Niakan, *President*
David Howey, *CFO*
Chris Barron, *Vice Pres*
Eric Griffith, *Vice Pres*
Stuart Miyagishima, *Vice Pres*
▲ **EMP:** 90
SQ FT: 60,000
SALES (est): 20.5MM **Privately Held**
WEB: www.afefilters.com
SIC: 3714 Motor vehicle engines & parts

(P-19570)
ADVANTI RACING USA LLC (DH)
10721 Business Dr Ste 1, Fontana (92337-8252)
PHONE..................................951 272-5930
Raymond Chan, *Principal*
EMP: 20
SALES (est): 2.5MM
SALES (corp-wide): 326.3MM **Privately Held**
SIC: 3714 Wheel rims, motor vehicle
HQ: Yhi Corporation (Singapore) Pte Ltd
2 Pandan Road
Singapore 60925
626 421-55

(P-19571)
AEC GROUP INC
Also Called: Advantage Engrg & Chemistry
3600 W Carriage Dr, Santa Ana (92704-6416)
PHONE..................................714 444-1395
Mike Lau, *President*
Erik Waelput, *Vice Pres*
EMP: 15
SQ FT: 12,000

▲ = Import ▼=Export
◆ =Import/Export

SALES (est): 3.5MM **Privately Held**
WEB: www.aecgroup.net
SIC: 3714 Lubrication systems & parts, motor vehicle

(P-19572)
AEP-CALIFORNIA LLC
10729 Wheatlands Ave C, Santee (92071-2887)
PHONE.....................619 596-1925
Melvin Sheldon, *Principal*
EMP: 12
SALES (est): 2.1MM **Privately Held**
SIC: 3714 Sanders, motor vehicle safety

(P-19573)
AGILITY FUEL SYSTEMS LLC (DH)
1815 Carnegie Ave, Santa Ana (92705-5527)
PHONE.....................949 236-5520
Kathleen Ligocki, *CEO*
Ron Eickeleman, *President*
William Nowicke, *COO*
Tom Russell, *CFO*
Scott Lucero, *Vice Pres*
▲ **EMP:** 161
SALES (est): 107.4MM
SALES (corp-wide): 282.1MM **Privately Held**
SIC: 3714 Fuel systems & parts, motor vehicle
HQ: Agility Fuel Solutions Llc
3335 Susan St Ste 100
Costa Mesa CA 92626
949 236-5520

(P-19574)
AIR FLOW RESEARCH HEADS INC
28611 Industry Dr, Valencia (91355-5413)
PHONE.....................661 257-8124
Rick Sperling, *President*
Beverly Sperling, *Vice Pres*
Chris Sperling, *Technician*
Chris Paul, *Plant Mgr*
Jess Ulloa, *Prdtn Mgr*
▲ **EMP:** 40
SQ FT: 14,000
SALES (est): 9.2MM **Privately Held**
WEB: www.airflowresearch.com
SIC: 3714 Cylinder heads, motor vehicle

(P-19575)
ALL SALES MANUFACTURING INC
Also Called: AMI
5121 Hillsdale Cir, El Dorado Hills (95762-5708)
PHONE.....................916 933-0236
Steve Dringenberg, *President*
Joanne Dringenberg, *Vice Pres*
Dringenberg Heath, *Vice Pres*
▲ **EMP:** 50 **EST:** 1994
SQ FT: 1,200
SALES (est): 3.8MM **Privately Held**
WEB: www.allsalesmfg.com
SIC: 3714 Motor vehicle parts & accessories

(P-19576)
AMCOR INDUSTRIES INC
Also Called: Gorilla Automotive Products
2011 E 49th St, Vernon (90058-2801)
PHONE.....................323 585-2852
Peter J Schermer, *President*
◆ **EMP:** 25
SQ FT: 30,000
SALES (est): 4.7MM **Privately Held**
SIC: 3714 3429 Motor vehicle wheels & parts; manufactured hardware (general)
PA: Wheel Pros, Llc
5347 S Valentia Way # 200
Greenwood Village CO 80111

(P-19577)
AMERICAN CYLINDER HEAD INC
499 Lesser St, Oakland (94601-4916)
PHONE.....................510 261-1590
Arvid Elbeck, *Principal*
Einer Elbeck, *Corp Secy*
EMP: 10

SALES (est): 2.4MM **Privately Held**
SIC: 3714 Motor vehicle parts & accessories

(P-19578)
AMERICAN CYLNDR HD RPR/EXCG
499 Lesser St, Oakland (94601-4916)
PHONE.....................510 536-1764
Arvid E Elbeck, *President*
Einer Elbeck, *Vice Pres*
EMP: 14
SQ FT: 17,000
SALES (est): 1.9MM **Privately Held**
SIC: 3714 Cylinder heads, motor vehicle

(P-19579)
AMERICAN FABRICATION CORP (PA)
Also Called: American Best Car Parts
2891 E Via Martens, Anaheim (92806-1751)
PHONE.....................714 632-1709
Greg Knox, *President*
Jodee Jensen Smith, *Vice Pres*
▲ **EMP:** 175
SALES (est): 25.1MM **Privately Held**
WEB: www.teamxenon.com
SIC: 3714 Motor vehicle parts & accessories

(P-19580)
AMERICAN INTERNATIONAL RACING
1132 W Kirkwall Rd, Azusa (91702-5128)
PHONE.....................626 969-7733
Harold Hannemann, *President*
John Brewer, *Manager*
▲ **EMP:** 12
SALES (est): 1MM **Privately Held**
WEB: www.americaninternationalracing.com
SIC: 3714 Motor vehicle parts & accessories

(P-19581)
AMERICAN RIM SUPPLY INC
1955 Kellogg Ave, Carlsbad (92008-6582)
PHONE.....................760 431-3666
Robert D Ward, *President*
Aj Ward, *Prdtn Mgr*
▼ **EMP:** 40
SQ FT: 20,000
SALES (est): 10.1MM **Privately Held**
SIC: 3714 Wheel rims, motor vehicle

(P-19582)
ANGELUS PLATING WORKS
1713 W 134th St, Gardena (90249-2083)
PHONE.....................310 516-1883
Gerald Bozajian, *President*
EMP: 10
SQ FT: 10,000
SALES (est): 1.5MM **Privately Held**
WEB: www.angelusplating.com
SIC: 3714 3471 Exhaust systems & parts, motor vehicle; plating & polishing

(P-19583)
APEX PRECISION TECH INC
23622 Calabasas Rd # 323, Calabasas (91302-1594)
PHONE.....................317 821-1000
Robert Oswald, *Ch of Bd*
Jerry Jackson, *President*
Bryson Ocker, *President*
EMP: 45
SQ FT: 40,000
SALES (est): 11.7MM **Privately Held**
WEB: www.apexprecision.com
SIC: 3714 3586 3498 3462 Motor vehicle parts & accessories; measuring & dispensing pumps; fabricated pipe & fittings; iron & steel forgings

(P-19584)
APTIV SERVICES 3 (US) LLC (HQ)
30 Corporate Park Ste 303, Irvine (92606-5133)
P.O. Box 439018, San Diego (92143-9018)
PHONE.....................949 458-3100
Kevin Clark, *Ch of Bd*
Amy Milhorne, *Research*
Kristine Bello, *Opers Staff*

Laurie Prew, *Manager*
Kate Simmons, *Manager*
▲ **EMP:** 12
SALES (est): 88.5MM
SALES (corp-wide): 16.6B **Privately Held**
SIC: 3714 Motor vehicle parts & accessories
PA: Aptiv Plc
Queensway House Hilgrove Street
Jersey JE1 1
163 422-4000

(P-19585)
ARIAS INDUSTRIES INC
Also Called: Arias Pistons
275 Roswell Ave, Long Beach (90803-1538)
PHONE.....................310 532-9737
Nicholas Arias Jr, *President*
Carmen Arias, *Vice Pres*
EMP: 20
SQ FT: 20,000
SALES (est): 3.3MM **Privately Held**
WEB: www.ariaspistons.com
SIC: 3714 Motor vehicle engines & parts

(P-19586)
AUTOMOCO LLC
Also Called: B & M Racing & Prfmce Pdts
9142 Independence Ave, Chatsworth (91311-5902)
PHONE.....................707 544-4761
Brian Applegate, *President*
EMP: 80
SALES (est): 6.3MM **Privately Held**
SIC: 3714 Transmission housings or parts, motor vehicle

(P-19587)
AUTOMOTIVE EXCH & SUP OF CAL (PA)
Also Called: AES
4354 Twain Ave Ste G, San Diego (92120-3419)
PHONE.....................619 282-3207
John Matheson, *CEO*
Mark James Matheson, *President*
EMP: 25
SQ FT: 6,000
SALES: 1.5MM **Privately Held**
SIC: 3714 Motor vehicle engines & parts

(P-19588)
AZUSA ENGINEERING INC
1542 W Industrial Park St, Covina (91722-3487)
P.O. Box 2909 (91722-8909)
PHONE.....................626 966-4071
James M Patronite, *CEO*
Tom Patronite, *President*
Janice M Patronite, *Admin Sec*
David Stillwell, *Supervisor*
▲ **EMP:** 17
SQ FT: 17,000
SALES (est): 3MM **Privately Held**
WEB: www.azusaeng.com
SIC: 3714 Transmission housings or parts, motor vehicle

(P-19589)
B & I FENDER TRIMS INC
1401 Air Wing Rd, San Diego (92154-7705)
PHONE.....................718 326-4323
Albert Sasson, *President*
Yzhak Faigenblat, *Vice Pres*
Dylan Mc Cue, *Manager*
▲ **EMP:** 90
SQ FT: 80,000
SALES (est): 11.9MM **Privately Held**
SIC: 3714 Motor vehicle body components & frame; motor vehicle wheels & parts

(P-19590)
BAB STEERING HYDRAULICS (PA)
Also Called: Bab Hydraulics
14554 Whittram Ave, Fontana (92335-3108)
PHONE.....................208 573-4502
William Carlson, *President*
▲ **EMP:** 20
SQ FT: 15,000

SALES (est): 4.9MM **Privately Held**
WEB: www.babsteering.com
SIC: 3714 3713 5084 Hydraulic fluid power pumps for auto steering mechanism; truck & bus bodies; hydraulic systems equipment & supplies

(P-19591)
BEKO RADIATOR CORES INC
2322 Bates Ave Ste A, Concord (94520-8565)
PHONE.....................925 671-2975
John Bekakis, *President*
Bernice Bekakis, *Treasurer*
Maria Bekakis, *Admin Sec*
EMP: 20
SQ FT: 8,000
SALES (est): 2.7MM **Privately Held**
WEB: www.bekoradiator.com
SIC: 3714 Radiators & radiator shells & cores, motor vehicle

(P-19592)
BESTOP BAJA LLC
Also Called: Baja Designs
185 Bosstick Blvd, San Marcos (92069-5932)
PHONE.....................760 560-2252
Deanne Moore, *CEO*
Pauline Salazar, *Admin Asst*
Chris Johnson, *Engineer*
Trent Kirby, *Mktg Dir*
Diego Land, *Sales Staff*
▲ **EMP:** 24
SQ FT: 14,000
SALES: 5MM
SALES (corp-wide): 123.4MM **Privately Held**
WEB: www.bajadesigns.com
SIC: 3714 5013 5571 Motor vehicle electrical equipment; motorcycle parts; motorcycle parts & accessories
PA: Bestop, Inc.
333 Centennial Pkwy Ste B
Louisville CO 80027
800 845-3567

(P-19593)
BIG GUN INC
Also Called: Big Gun Exhaust
190 Business Center Dr B, Corona (92880-1713)
PHONE.....................714 970-0423
Larry Riggs, *President*
▲ **EMP:** 10
SALES (est): 1.2MM **Privately Held**
SIC: 3714 Exhaust systems & parts, motor vehicle

(P-19594)
BLOWER DRIVE SERVICE CO
Also Called: BDS
1280 W Lambert Rd Ste B, Brea (92821-2820)
PHONE.....................562 693-4302
Craig Railsback, *Partner*
Lance Railsback, *Partner*
Lance E Railsback, *Vice Pres*
EMP: 20 **EST:** 1969
SQ FT: 11,000
SALES (est): 3.2MM **Privately Held**
WEB: www.blowerdriveservice.com
SIC: 3714 Motor vehicle engines & parts

(P-19595)
BLUETONE MUFFLER MFG CO
9366 Klingerman St, South El Monte (91733-2545)
PHONE.....................626 442-1073
Yuki Mashiro, *Owner*
Yuki Yamashiro, *President*
Aurelia Yamashiro, *Admin Sec*
EMP: 20 **EST:** 1964
SALES (est): 1.8MM **Privately Held**
SIC: 3714 Mufflers (exhaust), motor vehicle

(P-19596)
BNP ENTERPRISES LLC
22902 Roebuck St, Lake Forest (92630-2952)
PHONE.....................949 770-5438
William Paulson,
EMP: 10

(PA)=Parent Co (HQ)=Headquarters (DH)=Div Headquarters
✪ = New Business established in last 2 years

SALES: 100K Privately Held
SIC: 3714 Motor vehicle parts & accessories

(P-19597)
BSST LLC
5462 Irwindale Ave Ste A, Irwindale
(91706-2074)
PHONE...................................626 593-4500
Lon Bell,
Sandy Grouf, *CFO*
▲ EMP: 17
SQ FT: 12,000
SALES: 5MM
SALES (corp-wide): 1B Publicly Held
WEB: www.bsst.com
SIC: 3714 Heaters, motor vehicle; air conditioner parts, motor vehicle; cleaners, air, motor vehicle
PA: Gentherm Incorporated
21680 Haggerty Rd Ste 101
Northville MI 48167
248 504-0500

(P-19598)
BULLS-EYE MARKETING INC
Also Called: GTC Manufacturing
6610 Goodyear Rd, Benicia (94510-1250)
P.O. Box 5466, Walnut Creek (94596-1466)
PHONE...................................707 745-5278
EMP: 10
SALES (est): 619.7K Privately Held
SIC: 3714 3566 Clutches, motor vehicle; torque converters, except automotive

(P-19599)
BUNKER CORP (PA)
Also Called: Energy Suspension
1131 Via Callejon, San Clemente
(92673-6230)
PHONE...................................949 361-3935
Donald Bunker, *CEO*
Heather Mills, *HR Admin*
Mark Kranz, *Purchasing*
Bill Wainscott, *Plant Supt*
Sean Crary, *Sales Mgr*
▼ EMP: 100
SQ FT: 78,000
SALES (est): 20.2MM Privately Held
WEB: www.energysuspension.com
SIC: 3714 Motor vehicle body components & frame

(P-19600)
BURNS STAINLESS LLC
1041 W 18th St Ste B104, Costa Mesa
(92627-4583)
PHONE...................................949 631-5120
Jack Burns,
Rick Popovits,
EMP: 10
SQ FT: 6,200
SALES (est): 118.4K Privately Held
WEB: www.burnsstainless.com
SIC: 3714 Exhaust systems & parts, motor vehicle

(P-19601)
BUS SERVICES CORPORATION
Also Called: Trams International
6801 Suva St, Bell Gardens (90201-1937)
PHONE...................................562 231-1770
Don Duffy, *President*
Linda Duffy, *Corp Secy*
Newton Montano, *Vice Pres*
▼ EMP: 35
SQ FT: 70,000
SALES (est): 7.7MM Privately Held
SIC: 3714 Motor vehicle body components & frame

(P-19602)
BYD MOTORS LLC (HQ)
1800 S Figueroa St, Los Angeles
(90015-3422)
PHONE...................................213 748-3980
Stella LI, *CEO*
Ke LI, *President*
Michael Auftin, *Vice Pres*
Sandra Itkoff, *Vice Pres*
Fred Ni, *Vice Pres*
▲ EMP: 39

SALES (est): 2.5MM
SALES (corp-wide): 2.4MM Privately Held
SIC: 3714 Motor vehicle electrical equipment
PA: Byd Us Holding Inc.
1800 S Figueroa St
Los Angeles CA 90015
213 748-3980

(P-19603)
C F MANUFACTURING
11867 Sheldon St, Sun Valley
(91352-1508)
PHONE...................................818 504-9899
Angela Fluke, *President*
EMP: 10
SALES (est): 1.5MM Privately Held
SIC: 3714 Wheels, motor vehicle

(P-19604)
C R LAURENCE CO INC (HQ)
Also Called: Crl
2503 E Vernon Ave, Vernon (90058-1826)
PHONE...................................323 588-1281
Fred Altamirano, *Vice Pres*
Will Armstrong, *Branch Mgr*
Debbie Zanelli, *Credit Mgr*
Lamar Harris, *Analyst*
Srilekha Kottapalli, *Analyst*
◆ EMP: 380
SQ FT: 170,000
SALES: 423.1MM
SALES (corp-wide): 30.6B Privately Held
WEB: www.crlaurence.com
SIC: 3714 5072 5039 Sun roofs, motor vehicle; hand tools; glass construction materials
PA: Crh Public Limited Company
Stonemasons Way
Dublin D16 K
140 410-00

(P-19605)
CALIFORNIA MINI TRUCK INC
Also Called: Full-Traction Suspension
12539 Jomani Dr, Bakersfield
(93312-3456)
PHONE...................................661 398-9585
Steven D Kramer, *President*
Randall Kramer, *Vice Pres*
EMP: 10
SALES (est): 1.1MM Privately Held
WEB: www.full-traction.com
SIC: 3714 Motor vehicle parts & accessories

(P-19606)
CALMINI PRODUCTS INC
6951 Mcdivitt Dr, Bakersfield (93313-2020)
PHONE...................................661 398-9500
Randy Kramer, *President*
Steven D Kramer, *Vice Pres*
David Kampa, *Info Tech Dir*
▲ EMP: 10
SQ FT: 12,000
SALES (est): 1.8MM Privately Held
WEB: www.calmini.com
SIC: 3714 5961 Motor vehicle engines & parts; automotive supplies & equipment, mail order

(P-19607)
CAR SOUND EXHAUST SYSTEM INC
Magnaflow Performance Exhaust
22961 Arroyo Vis, Rcho STA Marg
(92688-2603)
PHONE...................................949 858-5900
Cody Spakes, *Technology*
Thomas Hopkins, *Engineer*
Marc Mendez, *Director*
EMP: 51
SALES (corp-wide): 101.4MM Privately Held
SIC: 3714 Mufflers (exhaust), motor vehicle
PA: Car Sound Exhaust System, Inc.
1901 Corporate Ctr
Oceanside CA 92056
949 858-5900

(P-19608)
CAR SOUND EXHAUST SYSTEM INC (PA)
Also Called: Magnaflow
1901 Corporate Ctr, Oceanside
(92056-5831)
PHONE...................................949 858-5900
Jerry Paolone, *CEO*
Dan Paolone, *President*
Stephen Kasprisin, *CFO*
Lindsay Monge, *Officer*
Andrew Blocksidge, *Vice Pres*
◆ EMP: 20
SQ FT: 45,000
SALES (est): 101.4MM Privately Held
SIC: 3714 Exhaust systems & parts, motor vehicle

(P-19609)
CAR SOUND EXHAUST SYSTEM INC
Also Called: Magnaslow
30142 Ave De Las Bndras, Rcho STA Marg
(92688-2116)
PHONE...................................949 858-5900
Don Billings, *Manager*
Nick Paolone, *VP Opers*
EMP: 84
SALES (corp-wide): 104.4MM Privately Held
SIC: 3714 Exhaust systems & parts, motor vehicle
PA: Car Sound Exhaust System, Inc.
1901 Corporate Ctr
Oceanside CA 92056
949 858-5900

(P-19610)
CAR SOUND EXHAUST SYSTEM INC
23201 Antonio Pkwy, Rcho STA Marg
(92688-2653)
PHONE...................................949 858-5900
James Mayor, *Engineer*
EMP: 20
SALES (corp-wide): 101.4MM Privately Held
SIC: 3714 Exhaust systems & parts, motor vehicle
PA: Car Sound Exhaust System, Inc.
1901 Corporate Ctr
Oceanside CA 92056
949 858-5900

(P-19611)
CARLSTAR GROUP LLC
10730 Production Ave, Fontana
(92337-8008)
PHONE...................................909 829-1703
EMP: 16
SALES (corp-wide): 1.4B Privately Held
SIC: 3714 Motor vehicle parts & accessories
PA: The Carlstar Group Llc
725 Cool Springs Blvd
Franklin TN 37067
615 503-0220

(P-19612)
CENERGY SOLUTIONS INC
40967 Albrae St, Fremont (94538-2486)
PHONE...................................510 474-7593
Gary Fanger, *President*
Michael Maxey, *Admin Sec*
Greg Fanger, *Director*
Laura Skinner, *Manager*
EMP: 10 EST: 2012
SQ FT: 2,945
SALES: 300K Privately Held
SIC: 3714 Propane conversion equipment, motor vehicle

(P-19613)
CENTER LINE WHEEL CORPORATION
Also Called: Center Line Performance Wheels
23 Corporate Plaza Dr # 150, Newport Beach (92660-7908)
PHONE...................................562 921-9637
Ray Lipper, *President*
▲ EMP: 100 EST: 1963
SALES (est): 15.1MM Privately Held
WEB: www.centerlinewheels.com
SIC: 3714 Wheels, motor vehicle

(P-19614)
CHAMPION LABORATORIES INC
740 Palmyrita Ave Ste A, Riverside
(92507-1826)
PHONE...................................951 275-0715
Genaro Iniguez, *Branch Mgr*
EMP: 11
SALES (corp-wide): 553.7MM Privately Held
SIC: 3714 Filters: oil, fuel & air, motor vehicle
HQ: Champion Laboratories, Inc.
200 S 4th St
Albion IL 62806
618 445-6011

(P-19615)
CIRCLE RACING WHEELS INC (PA)
14955 Don Julian Rd, City of Industry
(91746-3112)
PHONE...................................800 959-2100
Michael Stallings, *President*
Bob Strickland, *CFO*
Sherrie Stallings, *Corp Secy*
EMP: 15
SQ FT: 45,000
SALES (est): 1.9MM Privately Held
WEB: www.wheelvintiques.com
SIC: 3714 5013 Wheel rims, motor vehicle; wheels, motor vehicle

(P-19616)
COATES INCORPORATED
Also Called: Les Schwab
73816 S Delleker Rd, Portola
(96122-6401)
PHONE...................................530 832-1533
Stoages Bill, *President*
EMP: 13
SALES (corp-wide): 1MM Privately Held
SIC: 3714 7534 Motor vehicle brake systems & parts; tire retreading & repair shops
PA: Coates Incorporated
73816 S Delleker Rd
Portola CA 96122
530 832-1533

(P-19617)
COBRA ENGINEERING INC
23801 La Palma Ave, Yorba Linda
(92887-5540)
PHONE...................................714 692-8180
Timothy D McCool, *Principal*
Tim Mc Cool, *President*
Linda Mc Cool, *Admin Sec*
Ken Boyko, *Technical Staff*
▲ EMP: 70
SQ FT: 33,000
SALES (est): 14.2MM Privately Held
SIC: 3714 Exhaust systems & parts, motor vehicle

(P-19618)
CODA AUTOMOTIVE INC
12101 W Olympic Blvd, Los Angeles
(90064-1017)
PHONE...................................310 820-3611
Phil Murtaugh, *CEO*
EMP: 48 Privately Held
SIC: 3714 Motor vehicle parts & accessories
PA: Coda Automotive Inc
2340 S Fairfax Ave
Los Angeles CA 90016

(P-19619)
CODA AUTOMOTIVE INC
1441 Camino Del Rio S, San Diego
(92108-3521)
PHONE...................................619 291-2040
EMP: 64 Privately Held
SIC: 3714 Motor vehicle parts & accessories
PA: Coda Automotive Inc
2340 S Fairfax Ave
Los Angeles CA 90016

(P-19620)
CODA AUTOMOTIVE INC
14 Auto Center Dr, Irvine (92618-2802)
PHONE...................................949 830-7000
EMP: 57 Privately Held
SIC: 3714 Motor vehicle parts & accessories
PA: Coda Automotive Inc
2340 S Fairfax Ave
Los Angeles CA 90016
-

(P-19621)
CONTINNTAL ADVNCED LDAR SLTONS
6307 Crpinteria Ave Ste A, Santa Barbara (93103)
PHONE...................................805 318-2072
Arnaud Lagandre, CEO
Kevin P Collins, Officer
Bert Franks, Officer
George R Jurch, Officer
Rick Ledsinger, Officer
EMP: 13 EST: 2015
SALES (est): 907.1K
SALES (corp-wide): 50.8B Privately Held
SIC: 3714 Motor vehicle brake systems & parts
HQ: Continental Automotive Systems, Inc.
1 Continental Dr
Auburn Hills MI 48326
248 393-5300

(P-19622)
COUNTERPART AUTOMOTIVE INC
420 W Brenna Ln, Orange (92867-5637)
PHONE...................................714 771-1732
Walter T Froemke, President
Eric Froemke, CFO
Eric G Froemke, CFO
Daniel Bowers, Vice Pres
▲ EMP: 10
SQ FT: 8,000
SALES (est): 1.5MM Privately Held
SIC: 3714 Motor vehicle parts & accessories

(P-19623)
CRAIG MANUFACTURING COMPANY (PA)
8129 Slauson Ave, Montebello (90640-6621)
PHONE...................................323 726-7355
Craig Taslitt, President
Julie Taslitt Gross, Vice Pres
EMP: 60 EST: 1976
SQ FT: 16,000
SALES (est): 5.9MM Privately Held
WEB: www.craigmanufacturing.com
SIC: 3714 Radiators & radiator shells & cores, motor vehicle

(P-19624)
CROWER ENGRG & SLS CO INC
Also Called: Crower Cams
6180 Business Center Ct, San Diego (92154-5604)
PHONE...................................619 690-7810
Doug Evans, President
H Bruce Crower, CEO
Loren Harris, Vice Pres
▲ EMP: 150
SQ FT: 40,000
SALES (est): 31MM Privately Held
WEB: www.crower.com
SIC: 3714 Camshafts, motor vehicle

(P-19625)
CUMMINS ELECTRIFIED POWER NA (HQ)
1181 Cadillac Ct, Milpitas (95035-3055)
PHONE...................................408 624-1231
Joerg Ferchau, CEO
Andrew Frank, CTO
Dana Morton, Human Resources
Kristal Ferchau, Marketing Staff
Laurie A Miller, Counsel
EMP: 11
SALES (est): 3.5MM
SALES (corp-wide): 23.7B Publicly Held
SIC: 3714 Motor vehicle electrical equipment

PA: Cummins Inc.
500 Jackson St
Columbus IN 47201
812 377-5000

(P-19626)
CURRIE ENTERPRISES
382 N Smith Ave, Corona (92880-6971)
PHONE...................................714 528-6957
Raymond Currie, President
Charles Currie, Vice Pres
John Currie, Admin Sec
Lorraine Currie, Manager
◆ EMP: 50
SQ FT: 13,000
SALES (est): 11.2MM Privately Held
WEB: www.new9inch.com
SIC: 3714 3599 Differentials & parts, motor vehicle; gears, motor vehicle; machine shop, jobbing & repair

(P-19627)
CUSTOM WHEELS AND ACC INC
41710 Reagan Way, Murrieta (92562-6934)
PHONE...................................714 827-5200
Connie Buck, President
Chris Buck, Opers Mgr
Dan Mon, Manager
◆ EMP: 10
SQ FT: 18,000
SALES (est): 4.5MM Privately Held
WEB: www.cwausa.com
SIC: 3714 Motor vehicle wheels & parts

(P-19628)
CYLINDER HEAD EXCHANGE INC
12677 San Fernando Rd, Sylmar (91342-3727)
PHONE...................................818 364-2371
Dennis Woolsey, President
Wayne Heinis, Sales Executive
EMP: 12
SQ FT: 8,000
SALES (est): 2MM Privately Held
SIC: 3714 Cylinder heads, motor vehicle

(P-19629)
D & S CUSTOM PLATING INC
11552 Anabel Ave, Garden Grove (92843-3707)
PHONE...................................714 537-5411
Fax: 714 537-5413
EMP: 13
SQ FT: 1,500
SALES (est): 1.3MM Privately Held
SIC: 3714

(P-19630)
DAA DRAEXLMAIER AUTO AMER LLC
801 Challenger St, Livermore (94551-9536)
PHONE...................................864 485-1000
Andrew Bailey, Branch Mgr
EMP: 100
SALES (corp-wide): 177.9K Privately Held
SIC: 3714 Motor vehicle parts & accessories
HQ: Daa Draexlmaier Automotive Of America Llc
1751 E Main St
Duncan SC 29334
-

(P-19631)
DANCHUK MANUFACTURING INC
3201 S Standard Ave, Santa Ana (92705-5640)
PHONE...................................714 540-4363
Arthur Danchuk, President
Daniel Danchuk, CEO
Bobbie Black, Sales Staff
Mike Martin, Director
▲ EMP: 71
SQ FT: 33,000
SALES (est): 13.6MM Privately Held
WEB: www.danchuk.com
SIC: 3714 3465 Motor vehicle parts & accessories; automotive stampings

(P-19632)
DEE ENGINEERING INC (PA)
3100 Airway Ave Ste 106, Costa Mesa (92626-4604)
PHONE...................................714 979-4990
Edward C Fulton, President
Gary T Fulton, Vice Pres
▲ EMP: 35
SALES (est): 7.9MM Privately Held
WEB: www.deeeng.com
SIC: 3714 Motor vehicle parts & accessories

(P-19633)
DEE ENGINEERING INC
1893 S Lake Pl, Ontario (91761-8331)
PHONE...................................909 947-5616
Gary Fulton, Vice Pres
EMP: 23
SQ FT: 25,000
SALES (corp-wide): 7.9MM Privately Held
WEB: www.deeeng.com
SIC: 3714 Mufflers (exhaust), motor vehicle
PA: Dee Engineering, Inc.
3100 Airway Ave Ste 106
Costa Mesa CA 92626
714 979-4990

(P-19634)
DEL WEST ENGINEERING INC (PA)
Also Called: Del West USA
28128 Livingston Ave, Valencia (91355-4115)
PHONE...................................661 295-5700
Al Sommer, Chairman
Mark Sommer, President
Rosemarie Chegwin, Vice Pres
Guido Keijzers, Vice Pres
Guido Keyzers, VP Engrg
EMP: 135
SQ FT: 50,000
SALES (est): 22.6MM Privately Held
WEB: www.delwestusa.com
SIC: 3714 Motor vehicle parts & accessories

(P-19635)
DELPHI CONNECTION SYSTEMS LLC
8662 Siempre Viva Rd, San Diego (92154-6211)
PHONE...................................949 458-3155
EMP: 15 Privately Held
SIC: 3714
HQ: Delphi Connection Systems, Llc
30 Corporate Park Ste 303
Irvine CA 92606

(P-19636)
DENSO INTERNATIONAL AMER INC
Also Called: Dwam
2251 Rutherford Rd 100, Carlsbad (92008-8815)
PHONE...................................760 597-7400
Loraine Graves, Principal
EMP: 13 Privately Held
SIC: 3714 Motor vehicle parts & accessories
HQ: Denso International America, Inc.
24777 Denso Dr
Southfield MI 48033
248 350-7500

(P-19637)
DENSO PDTS & SVCS AMERICAS INC
41673 Corning Pl, Murrieta (92562-7023)
PHONE...................................951 698-3379
Yoshihiko Yamada, President
Robert Navarro, Prgrmr
Keiko Asada, Enginr/R&D Asst
William Coffelt, Senior Buyer
Jackie J Brundage, Sales Staff
EMP: 150 Privately Held
SIC: 3714 Motor vehicle parts & accessories

HQ: Denso Products And Services Americas, Inc.
3900 Via Oro Ave
Long Beach CA 90810
310 834-6352

(P-19638)
DONALDSON COMPANY INC
26235 Technology Dr, Valencia (91355-1147)
PHONE...................................661 295-0800
Paul Akian, President
EMP: 99
SALES (corp-wide): 2.8B Publicly Held
WEB: www.donaldson.com
SIC: 3714 Mufflers (exhaust), motor vehicle
PA: Donaldson Company, Inc.
1400 W 94th St
Minneapolis MN 55431
952 887-3131

(P-19639)
DONOVAN ENGINEERING CORP
Also Called: Donovan Aluminum Racing Engine
2305 Border Ave, Torrance (90501-3614)
PHONE...................................310 320-3772
Kathleen Donovan, President
Norman Woodruff, Vice Pres
EMP: 12
SQ FT: 15,000
SALES (est): 1.7MM Privately Held
WEB: www.donovanengineering.com
SIC: 3714 Motor vehicle engines & parts

(P-19640)
DOUGLAS TECHNOLOGIES GROUP INC (PA)
Also Called: Douglas Wheel
1340 N Melrose Dr, Vista (92083-2916)
PHONE...................................760 758-5560
Johnny Leach, President
▲ EMP: 40
SQ FT: 60,000
SALES (est): 10.6MM Privately Held
WEB: www.douglaswheel.com
SIC: 3714 Wheel rims, motor vehicle

(P-19641)
DUKES RESEARCH AND MFG INC
9060 Winnetka Ave, Northridge (91324-3293)
PHONE...................................818 998-9811
Patricia Huffman, President
EMP: 40
SALES (est): 3.2MM Privately Held
SIC: 3714 Fuel pumps, motor vehicle

(P-19642)
DYNATRAC PRODUCTS CO INC
7392 Count Cir, Huntington Beach (92647-4551)
PHONE...................................714 596-4461
Jim McGean, President
Robert Brewer, Technical Staff
EMP: 15
SQ FT: 1,600
SALES (est): 4MM Privately Held
WEB: www.dynatrac.com
SIC: 3714 5013 5531 Motor vehicle transmissions, drive assemblies & parts; motor vehicle supplies & new parts; truck equipment & parts

(P-19643)
EAGLE ENTERPRISES INC
Also Called: Webers Auto Parts
604 W Whittier Blvd, Montebello (90640-5236)
P.O. Box 1579 (90640-7579)
PHONE...................................323 721-4741
Steve Weber, Owner
EMP: 23
SQ FT: 1,824
SALES (corp-wide): 36.1B Publicly Held
SIC: 3714 5531 Automotive wiring harness sets; automotive parts
HQ: Eagle Enterprises, Inc.
604 W Whittier Blvd
Montebello CA 90640
323 721-4741

(PA)=Parent Co (HQ)=Headquarters (DH)=Div Headquarters
✪ = New Business established in last 2 years

(P-19644)
EDELBROCK HOLDINGS INC
2301 Dominguez Way, Torrance
(90501-6200)
PHONE..............................310 781-2290
Jeff Paige, *Manager*
EMP: 117 **Privately Held**
SIC: 3714 Motor vehicle parts & accessories
PA: Edelbrock Holdings, Inc.
2700 California St
Torrance CA 90503

(P-19645)
EDELBROCK HOLDINGS INC
1380 S Buena Vista St, San Jacinto
(92583-4665)
PHONE..............................951 654-6677
EMP: 204 **Privately Held**
SIC: 3714 Motor vehicle parts & accessories
PA: Edelbrock Holdings, Inc.
2700 California St
Torrance CA 90503

(P-19646)
EFI TECHNOLOGY INC
2741 Plaza Del Amo # 211, Torrance
(90503-7319)
PHONE..............................310 793-2505
Graham Western, *President*
EMP: 20
SALES (est): 2MM **Privately Held**
WEB: www.efitechnology.com
SIC: 3714 8748 8731 Fuel systems & parts, motor vehicle; communications consulting; electronic research

(P-19647)
EGR INCORPORATED (DH)
4000 Greystone Dr, Ontario (91761-3101)
PHONE..............................909 923-7075
John Whitten, *President*
▲ **EMP: 110**
SQ FT: 70,000
SALES (est): 21.8MM **Privately Held**
WEB: www.egrinc.com
SIC: 3714 Motor vehicle parts & accessories

(P-19648)
ENDERLE FUEL INJECTION
1830 Voyager Ave, Simi Valley
(93063-3348)
PHONE..............................805 526-3838
Kent H Enderle, *President*
Joan C Enderle, *Corp Secy*
Jim Rehfeld, *Vice Pres*
EMP: 20 EST: 1966
SQ FT: 18,000
SALES (est): 4.2MM **Privately Held**
SIC: 3714 Fuel systems & parts, motor vehicle

(P-19649)
ENGINE WORLD LLC
1487 67th St, Emeryville (94608-1015)
PHONE..............................510 653-4444
Parviz Jabbari,
Said Saffari,
◆ **EMP: 25**
SQ FT: 60,000
SALES (est): 5.1MM **Privately Held**
SIC: 3714 Rebuilding engines & transmissions, factory basis

(P-19650)
ESSLINGER ENGINEERING INC
5946 Freedom Dr, Chino (91710-7014)
PHONE..............................909 539-0544
Dwaine E Esslinger, *President*
Dan Esslinger, *Vice Pres*
Elizabeth Esslinger, *Admin Sec*
▲ **EMP: 20**
SQ FT: 4,000
SALES (est): 4.3MM **Privately Held**
WEB: www.esslingeracing.com
SIC: 3714 Motor vehicle engines & parts

(P-19651)
EVANS WALKER ENTERPRISES
Also Called: Evans, Walker Racing
2304 Fleetwood Dr, Riverside
(92509-2409)
P.O. Box 2469 (92516-2469)
PHONE..............................951 784-7223
Walker Evans, *President*
Phyllis Evans, *Corp Secy*
Randall Anderson, *Vice Pres*
Phillis Evans, *Executive*
Don Barker, *Manager*
▲ **EMP: 20 EST:** 1978
SQ FT: 20,000
SALES (est): 11.5MM **Privately Held**
WEB: www.walkerevansracing.com
SIC: 3714 Motor vehicle parts & accessories

(P-19652)
EXHAUST GAS TECHNOLOGIES INC
15642 Dupont Ave Ste B, Chino
(91710-7615)
PHONE..............................909 548-8100
Dennis Lawler, *President*
Maria Lawler, *Vice Pres*
EMP: 12
SQ FT: 5,000
SALES (est): 1.9MM **Privately Held**
WEB: www.exhaustgas.com
SIC: 3714 3829 Exhaust systems & parts, motor vehicle; thermocouples

(P-19653)
FABCO HOLDINGS INC
151 Lawrence Dr, Livermore (94551-5126)
PHONE..............................925 454-9500
Gerard Giucidi, *CEO*
Allen Sunderland, *President*
David Doden, *Vice Pres*
Michael Chapman, *Controller*
▲ **EMP: 2635**
SALES (est): 228.8MM **Privately Held**
SIC: 3714 Axles, motor vehicle

(P-19654)
FACTORY REPRODUCTIONS
13353 Benson Ave, Chino (91710-5246)
PHONE..............................909 590-5252
Suzy Nelson, *Chief Mktg Ofcr*
Mike Deberry, *Manager*
▲ **EMP: 10**
SQ FT: 18,000
SALES (est): 1.5MM **Privately Held**
WEB: www.factoryreproductions.com
SIC: 3714 Wheels, motor vehicle

(P-19655)
FAT PERFORMANCE INC
1558 N Case St, Orange (92867-3635)
PHONE..............................714 637-2889
Ronald Fleming, *President*
J Greg Aronson, *Vice Pres*
EMP: 10 EST: 1975
SQ FT: 6,600
SALES (est): 1.3MM **Privately Held**
WEB: www.fatperformance.com
SIC: 3714 5961 7538 Motor vehicle engines & parts; automotive supplies & equipment, mail order; general automotive repair shops

(P-19656)
FLOWMASTER INC
1500 Overland Ct, West Sacramento
(95691-3490)
PHONE..............................916 371-2345
Bill Rider, *Branch Mgr*
EMP: 150
SALES (corp-wide): 113.2MM **Privately Held**
SIC: 3714 Mufflers (exhaust), motor vehicle
HQ: Flowmaster, Inc.
100 Stony Point Rd # 125
Santa Rosa CA 95401
707 544-4761

(P-19657)
FLOWMASTER INC (HQ)
100 Stony Point Rd # 125, Santa Rosa
(95401-4131)
PHONE..............................707 544-4761
Brian Appelgate, *President*
Ross Mignoli, *Treasurer*

Thomas J Caracciolo, *Admin Sec*
▲ **EMP: 50**
SQ FT: 160,000
SALES (est): 23.3MM
SALES (corp-wide): 113.2MM **Privately Held**
SIC: 3714 Mufflers (exhaust), motor vehicle
PA: Driven Performance Brands, Inc.
100 Stony Point Rd # 125
Santa Rosa CA 95401
707 544-4761

(P-19658)
FOOTE AXLE & FORGE LLC
3954 Whiteside St, Los Angeles
(90063-1615)
PHONE..............................323 268-4151
Michael F Denton Sr, *Mng Member*
Merrie N Denton,
Scott Lutz, *Director*
▲ **EMP: 32**
SQ FT: 66,000
SALES: 3MM **Privately Held**
WEB: www.footeaxle.com
SIC: 3714 Differentials & parts, motor vehicle

(P-19659)
FORGIATO INC
11915 Wicks St, Sun Valley (91352-1908)
PHONE..............................818 771-9779
Nisan G Celik, *CEO*
▲ **EMP: 62**
SQ FT: 60,000
SALES (est): 13.5MM **Privately Held**
WEB: www.forgiato.com
SIC: 3714 Motor vehicle wheels & parts

(P-19660)
FOX FACTORY HOLDING CORP
Also Called: Fox Racing Shox
750 Vernon Way, El Cajon (92020-1979)
PHONE..............................619 768-1800
EMP: 11
SALES (corp-wide): 619.2MM **Publicly Held**
SIC: 3714 Motor vehicle parts & accessories
PA: Fox Factory Holding Corp.
915 Disc Dr
Scotts Valley CA 95066
831 274-6500

(P-19661)
FOX FACTORY INC (HQ)
Also Called: Fox Racing Shox
130 Hangar Way, Watsonville
(95076-2406)
PHONE..............................831 274-6500
Larry L Enterline, *CEO*
Robert C Fox Jr, *President*
Mario Galasso, *President*
Robert Fox, *Bd of Directors*
Bonnie Chesser, *Technician*
◆ **EMP: 143 EST:** 1978
SQ FT: 86,000
SALES (est): 70.7MM
SALES (corp-wide): 619.2MM **Publicly Held**
WEB: www.foxracingshox.com
SIC: 3714 Shock absorbers, motor vehicle
PA: Fox Factory Holding Corp.
915 Disc Dr
Scotts Valley CA 95066
831 274-6500

(P-19662)
FRIEDL CORPORATION
Also Called: Axles Now
1291 N Patt St, Anaheim (92801-2550)
P.O. Box 3233, Orange (92857-0233)
PHONE..............................714 443-0122
Daniel Friedl, *CEO*
EMP: 15 EST: 2014
SQ FT: 5,000
SALES: 1.2MM **Privately Held**
SIC: 3714 Axles, motor vehicle

(P-19663)
FTG INC (PA)
Also Called: Filtration Technology Group
12750 Center Court Dr S # 280, Cerritos
(90703-8593)
PHONE..............................562 865-9200
Pino Pathak, *President*

▲ **EMP: 20**
SQ FT: 1,500
SALES: 4MM **Privately Held**
WEB: www.ftginc.com
SIC: 3714 5085 3069 3053 Filters: oil, fuel & air, motor vehicle; industrial supplies; bushings, rubber; castings, rubber; grommets, rubber; packing, rubber

(P-19664)
FUEL INJECTION CORPORATION
2246 N Macarthur Dr, Tracy (95376-2823)
PHONE..............................925 371-6551
Robert B White, *President*
Bob White, *CFO*
Janet White, *Treasurer*
Kathy White, *Admin Sec*
▲ **EMP: 15**
SQ FT: 10,000
SALES: 2MM **Privately Held**
WEB: www.fuelinjectioncorp.com
SIC: 3714 Motor vehicle parts & accessories

(P-19665)
FUEL INJECTION ENGINEERING CO
Also Called: Hilborn Fuel Injection Company
22892 Glenwood Dr, Aliso Viejo
(92656-1520)
PHONE..............................949 360-0909
Duane Hilborn, *President*
Edrias Snipes, *Vice Pres*
EMP: 12 EST: 1948
SALES (est): 1.7MM **Privately Held**
SIC: 3714 Motor vehicle parts & accessories

(P-19666)
GAHH LLC (HQ)
11128 Gault St, North Hollywood
(91605-6305)
PHONE..............................800 722-2292
Rodney Wells, *CEO*
Bryan Auney, *President*
Jack Dekirmendjian, *Vice Pres*
Jean Hilado, *Accountant*
Brian Aune, *Controller*
▲ **EMP: 10**
SQ FT: 7,000
SALES (est): 1.9MM
SALES (corp-wide): 807.5K **Privately Held**
WEB: www.gahhinc.com
SIC: 3714 7532 Motor vehicle parts & accessories; upholstery & trim shop, automotive
PA: Topdown, Inc.
633 Chestnut St Ste 1640
Chattanooga TN 37450
423 755-0888

(P-19667)
GARY SCHROEDER ENTERPRISES
158 W Verdugo Ave, Burbank
(91502-2132)
PHONE..............................818 565-1133
Gary Schroeder, *CEO*
EMP: 10
SALES (est): 1MM **Privately Held**
SIC: 3714 Motor vehicle parts & accessories

(P-19668)
GEAR VENDORS INC
1717 N Magnolia Ave, El Cajon
(92020-1243)
PHONE..............................619 562-0060
Ken R Johnson, *CEO*
Rick Johnson, *President*
Jordan Eiler, *Technical Staff*
Randy Palmer, *Sales Associate*
Jan Storck, *Sales Associate*
▲ **EMP: 35 EST:** 1981
SQ FT: 35,000
SALES (est): 6.3MM **Privately Held**
WEB: www.gearvendors.com
SIC: 3714 Transmissions, motor vehicle

▲ = Import ▼=Export
◆ =Import/Export

(P-19669)
GENTHERM INCORPORATED
5462 Irwindale Ave Ste A, Irwindale
(91706-2074)
PHONE..................................626 593-4500
EMP: 10
SALES (corp-wide): 1B **Publicly Held**
SIC: 3714 Motor vehicle parts & accessories
PA: Gentherm Incorporated
   21680 Haggerty Rd Ste 101
   Northlle MI 48167
   248 504-0500

(P-19670)
GERHARDT GEAR CO INC
133 E Santa Anita Ave, Burbank
(91502-1926)
PHONE..................................818 842-6700
Ronald J Gerhardt, *CEO*
Mitch Gerhardt, *President*
Kurht Gerhardt, *Vice Pres*
John Kim, *General Mgr*
EMP: 46
SQ FT: 30,000
SALES: 8.8MM **Privately Held**
WEB: www.gerhardtgear.com
SIC: 3714 3728 3769 3462 Gears, motor vehicle; gears, aircraft power transmission; guided missile & space vehicle parts & auxiliary equipment; iron & steel forgings

(P-19671)
GERMANEX IMPORTS INC
19015 Parthenia St, Northridge
(91324-3727)
PHONE..................................818 700-0441
Agop Tarpinian, *President*
EMP: 12 **EST:** 1987
SALES (est): 1.8MM **Privately Held**
SIC: 3714 Tops, motor vehicle

(P-19672)
GIBSON PERFORMANCE CORPORATION
Also Called: Gibson Exhaust Systems
1270 Webb Cir, Corona (92879-5760)
PHONE..................................951 372-1220
Ronald Gibson, *President*
Victor Lopez, *Owner*
▲ **EMP:** 75
SQ FT: 50,000
SALES (est): 15.7MM **Privately Held**
WEB: www.gibsonperformance.com
SIC: 3714 5013 Exhaust systems & parts, motor vehicle; motor vehicle supplies & new parts

(P-19673)
GLORIOUS EMPIRE LLC
Also Called: Tge Distribution
2460 S Santa Fe Ave Ste B, Vista
(92084-8002)
PHONE..................................760 598-5000
Andrew David Broussard, *Mng Member*
▲ **EMP:** 10 **EST:** 2011
SQ FT: 7,500
SALES (est): 1.7MM **Privately Held**
SIC: 3714 Acceleration equipment, motor vehicle

(P-19674)
GRANATELLI MOTOR SPORTS INC
1000 Yarnell Pl, Oxnard (93033-2454)
PHONE..................................805 486-6644
Joseph R Granatelli, *CEO*
Jassper Esteban, *Info Tech Mgr*
▲ **EMP:** 31
SQ FT: 49,000
SALES (est): 5.4MM **Privately Held**
WEB: www.granatellimotorsports.com
SIC: 3714 Fuel systems & parts, motor vehicle

(P-19675)
GROVER PRODUCTS CO (PA)
3424 E Olympic Blvd, Los Angeles
(90023-3000)
P.O. Box 23966 (90023-0966)
PHONE..................................323 263-9981
John Adam Roesch Jr, *CEO*
William Marting, *VP Sales*
▲ **EMP:** 40

SQ FT: 60,000
SALES (est): 12.2MM **Privately Held**
WEB: www.airhorns.com
SIC: 3714 3494 5999 Motor vehicle brake systems & parts; valves & pipe fittings; plumbing & heating supplies

(P-19676)
GROVER PRODUCTS CO
3424 E Olympic Blvd, Los Angeles
(90023-3000)
PHONE..................................323 263-9981
EMP: 95
SALES (corp-wide): 12.2MM **Privately Held**
WEB: www.airhorns.com
SIC: 3714 Motor vehicle parts & accessories
PA: Grover Products Co.
   3424 E Olympic Blvd
   Los Angeles CA 90023
   323 263-9981

(P-19677)
HALDEX BRAKE PRODUCTS CORP
291 Kettering Dr, Ontario (91761-8132)
PHONE..................................909 974-1200
EMP: 14
SALES (corp-wide): 528.7MM **Privately Held**
SIC: 3714 Motor vehicle parts & accessories
HQ: Haldex Brake Products Corporation
   10930 N Pomona Ave
   Kansas City MO 64153
   816 891-2470

(P-19678)
HANNEMANN FIBERGLASS INC
1132 W Kirkwall Rd, Azusa (91702-5128)
PHONE..................................626 969-7317
Harold H Hannemann, *President*
EMP: 12
SQ FT: 9,000
SALES (est): 2.1MM **Privately Held**
WEB: www.hannemannfiberglass.com
SIC: 3714 Motor vehicle parts & accessories

(P-19679)
HEDMAN MANUFACTURING (PA)
Also Called: Hedman Hedders
12438 Putnam St, Whittier (90602-1002)
PHONE..................................562 204-1031
Robert Bandergriff, *President*
Ron Funfar, *Vice Pres*
Lee Robinson, *Natl Sales Mgr*
Phillip Wigginton, *Sales Staff*
▲ **EMP:** 45 **EST:** 1978
SALES (est): 13.2MM **Privately Held**
WEB: www.hedman.com
SIC: 3714 Exhaust systems & parts, motor vehicle

(P-19680)
HELLWIG PRODUCTS COMPANY INC
16237 Avenue 296, Visalia (93292-9675)
PHONE..................................559 734-7451
Donald Hellwig, *Ch of Bd*
Mark Hellwig, *President*
▲ **EMP:** 30
SQ FT: 37,000
SALES (est): 10.6MM **Privately Held**
WEB: www.hellwigproducts.com
SIC: 3714 3493 3499 Motor vehicle parts & accessories; automobile springs; stabilizing bars (cargo), metal

(P-19681)
HILBORN MANUFACTURING CORP
Also Called: Fuel Injection Engineering
22892 Glenwood Dr, Aliso Viejo
(92656-1520)
PHONE..................................949 360-0909
Stuart Hilborn, *Director*
Duane Hilborn, *President*
Kathy Hilborn, *Treasurer*
Virgina Hilborn, *Corp Secy*
Edris Snipes, *Vice Pres*
EMP: 13 **EST:** 1954
SQ FT: 17,000

SALES (est): 1.7MM **Privately Held**
WEB: www.hilborninjection.com
SIC: 3714 Fuel systems & parts, motor vehicle

(P-19682)
HONEYWELL INTERNATIONAL INC
510 W Aten Rd, Imperial (92251-9718)
PHONE..................................760 355-3420
Mike Billasenor, *Manager*
EMP: 24
SALES (corp-wide): 41.8B **Publicly Held**
WEB: www.honeywell.com
SIC: 3714 Motor vehicle parts & accessories
PA: Honeywell International Inc.
   300 S Tryon St
   Charlotte NC 28202
   973 455-2000

(P-19683)
HORSTMAN MANUFACTURING CO INC
1970 Peacock Blvd, Oceanside
(92056-3538)
PHONE..................................760 598-2100
Allen Bourgeois, *President*
Gary Gebhart, *COO*
▲ **EMP:** 30 **EST:** 1963
SALES (est): 3.5MM **Privately Held**
WEB: www.horstmanclutches.com
SIC: 3714 3944 Motor vehicle engines & parts; games, toys & children's vehicles

(P-19684)
HOWCO INC
Also Called: C N C
1221 W Morena Blvd, San Diego
(92110-3837)
PHONE..................................619 275-1663
Charles H Neal, *President*
Delores Neal, *Vice Pres*
EMP: 16
SQ FT: 5,000
SALES (est): 2.5MM **Privately Held**
SIC: 3714 Motor vehicle brake systems & parts

(P-19685)
HT MULTINATIONAL INC
Also Called: Unisun Multinational
12851 Reservoir St Apt A, Chino
(91710-2908)
PHONE..................................626 964-2686
Chunli Zhao, *CEO*
▲ **EMP:** 21
SALES (est): 8.7MM **Privately Held**
SIC: 3714 3429 5072 Motor vehicle brake systems & parts; filters: oil, fuel & air, motor vehicle; manufactured hardware (general); hardware
HQ: Sinatex, S.A. De C.V.
   Industriales No. 1188 Pte.
   Cajeme SON. 85210

(P-19686)
IDDEA CALIFORNIA LLC
Also Called: Go Rhino
589 Apollo St, Brea (92821-3127)
PHONE..................................714 257-7389
Manuel Alvarez, *Mng Member*
Peter Taylor, *General Mgr*
Ron Storer,
Ann Eonyea, *Manager*
▲ **EMP:** 14
SQ FT: 50,000
SALES (est): 3.6MM **Privately Held**
WEB: www.gorhino.com
SIC: 3714 Motor vehicle parts & accessories

(P-19687)
IDRIVE INC
249 N Turnpike Rd, Santa Barbara
(93111-1928)
PHONE..................................805 308-6094
Sean O'Neil, *President*
Curt Andrews, *Vice Pres*
Lucian Dragomir, *Principal*
Kelli O'Neil, *Mktg Dir*
EMP: 17
SQ FT: 1,500

SALES (est): 3.3MM **Privately Held**
SIC: 3714 Motor vehicle parts & accessories

(P-19688)
IMPCO TECHNOLOGIES INC (HQ)
3030 S Susan St, Santa Ana (92704-6435)
PHONE..................................714 656-1200
Massimo Fracchia, *General Mgr*
Ro Blackwood, *Vice Pres*
Peter Chase, *Principal*
Vahagn Israelyan, *Electrical Engi*
Daniel Breslow, *Engineer*
◆ **EMP:** 160 **EST:** 1958
SQ FT: 108,000
SALES (est): 123.8MM
SALES (corp-wide): 270.2MM **Privately Held**
WEB: www.impcotechnologies.com
SIC: 3714 3592 7363 Fuel systems & parts, motor vehicle; carburetors; engineering help service
PA: Westport Fuel Systems Inc
   1750 75th Ave W Suite 101
   Vancouver BC
   604 718-2000

(P-19689)
INDIAN HEAD INDUSTRIES INC
Also Called: MGM Brakes
1184 S Cloverdale Blvd, Cloverdale
(95425-4412)
P.O. Box 249 (95425-0249)
PHONE..................................707 894-3333
Bob Stutsman, *Manager*
EMP: 75
SALES (corp-wide): 64.3MM **Privately Held**
WEB: www.indianheadindustries.com
SIC: 3714 Motor vehicle brake systems & parts
PA: Indian Head Industries, Inc.
   6200 Hars Tech Blvd
   Charlotte NC 28269
   704 547-7411

(P-19690)
INLAND EMPIRE DRIVE LINE SVC (PA)
4035 E Guasti Rd Ste 301, Ontario
(91761-1532)
PHONE..................................909 390-3030
Gregory Frick, *President*
Carolyn Frick, *Corp Secy*
Jeff Gilroy, *Vice Pres*
EMP: 16
SQ FT: 7,500
SALES (est): 2MM **Privately Held**
WEB: www.iedls.com
SIC: 3714 7539 Drive shafts, motor vehicle; automotive repair shops; powertrain components repair services

(P-19691)
INNOVA ELECTRONICS CORPORATION
Also Called: Equipment & Tool Institute
17352 Von Karman Ave, Irvine
(92614-6204)
PHONE..................................714 241-6800
Ieon C Chenn, *President*
Phuong Pham, *Engineer*
Jonathan Kim, *Sales Staff*
EMP: 29
SQ FT: 12,000
SALES (est): 14.5MM **Privately Held**
WEB: www.iequus.com
SIC: 3714 Motor vehicle electrical equipment

(P-19692)
INTERNATIONAL MERCANTILE
6102 Avenida Encinas, Carlsbad
(92011-1005)
PHONE..................................760 438-2205
Terry Morehouse, *Owner*
▲ **EMP:** 10
SQ FT: 4,000
SALES (est): 835.7K **Privately Held**
WEB: www.im356-911.com
SIC: 3714 Motor vehicle parts & accessories

(P-19693)
J C S VOLKS MACHINE
Also Called: Jcs
15626 Cypress Ave, Irwindale
(91706-2119)
PHONE...................626 338-6003
Jeff Jarosz, *Partner*
Jorge Contreras, *Partner*
Brad Jarosz, *Partner*
Dave Jarosz, *Partner*
EMP: 19
SQ FT: 7,000
SALES: 700K **Privately Held**
WEB: www.jcsvwparts.com
SIC: 3714 Rebuilding engines & transmissions, factory basis

(P-19694)
JASPER ENGINE EXCHANGE INC
1477 E Cedar St Ste D, Ontario
(91761-8330)
PHONE...................800 827-7455
Roger Brenner, *Manager*
EMP: 14
SALES (corp-wide): 521.6MM **Privately Held**
SIC: 3714 4225 Rebuilding engines & transmissions, factory basis; fuel systems & parts, motor vehicle; gears, motor vehicle; general warehousing & storage
PA: Jasper Engine Exchange, Inc.
815 Wernsing Rd
Jasper IN 47546
812 482-1041

(P-19695)
JOHN BOYD ENTERPRISES INC
Also Called: JB Radiator Specialties
8441 Specialty Cir, Sacramento
(95828-2523)
PHONE...................916 504-3622
Phillip King, *Branch Mgr*
EMP: 105
SALES (corp-wide): 57.7MM **Privately Held**
SIC: 3714 Motor vehicle parts & accessories
PA: John Boyd Enterprises, Inc.
8401 Specialty Cir
Sacramento CA 95828
916 381-4790

(P-19696)
JOHN BOYD ENTERPRISES INC (PA)
Also Called: J B Enterprises
8401 Specialty Cir, Sacramento
(95828-2523)
P.O. Box 292460 (95829-2460)
PHONE...................916 381-4790
Donna Boyd, *Treasurer*
Barney Gonzales, *Manager*
▲ **EMP:** 123
SQ FT: 14,000
SALES (est): 57.7MM **Privately Held**
SIC: 3714 3433 Radiators & radiator shells & cores, motor vehicle; heating equipment, except electric

(P-19697)
JOHNSON CONTROLS INC
6383 Las Positas Rd, Livermore
(94551-5103)
PHONE...................925 447-9200
Carol Skelly, *Branch Mgr*
EMP: 345 **Privately Held**
SIC: 3714 Motor vehicle body components & frame
HQ: Johnson Controls, Inc.
5757 N Green Bay Ave
Milwaukee WI 53209
414 524-1200

(P-19698)
KAMM INDUSTRIES INC
Also Called: Prp Seats
43352 Business Park Dr, Temecula
(92590-3665)
PHONE...................800 317-6253
Aaron Wedeking, *CEO*
Mike Doherty, *Co-Owner*
▲ **EMP:** 43

SALES: 6.4MM **Privately Held**
SIC: 3714 Motor vehicle parts & accessories

(P-19699)
KARBZ INC
Also Called: SSC Racing
77806 Flora Rd Ste E, Palm Desert
(92211-4108)
PHONE...................760 567-9953
Joe Ramos, *President*
Jim Boltz, *Vice Pres*
▲ **EMP:** 15 **EST:** 1994
SQ FT: 40,000
SALES (est): 1.1MM **Privately Held**
WEB: www.sscracing.com
SIC: 3714 Motor vehicle parts & accessories

(P-19700)
KENNEDY ENGINEERED PRODUCTS
38830 17th St E, Palmdale (93550-3915)
PHONE...................661 272-1147
Hobert Kennedy, *Owner*
▲ **EMP:** 14
SQ FT: 5,900
SALES: 2MM **Privately Held**
WEB: www.kennedyeng.com
SIC: 3714 Motor vehicle parts & accessories

(P-19701)
KF FIBERGLASS INC (PA)
8247 Phlox St, Downey (90241-4841)
PHONE...................562 869-1536
Ron Belk, *President*
David Ruiz, *Vice Pres*
EMP: 25
SQ FT: 35,000
SALES (est): 3.8MM **Privately Held**
SIC: 3714 Motor vehicle parts & accessories

(P-19702)
KING SHOCK TECHNOLOGY INC
12472 Edison Way, Garden Grove
(92841-2821)
PHONE...................714 530-8701
Brett King, *President*
Lance King, *President*
Ross King, *CFO*
Sharon King, *Vice Pres*
Ricky Koutzoukis, *Engineer*
◆ **EMP:** 99
SQ FT: 18,000
SALES (est): 16.2MM **Privately Held**
WEB: www.kingshocks.com
SIC: 3714 Motor vehicle body components & frame

(P-19703)
KW AUTOMOTIVE NORTH AMER INC
300 W Pontiac Way, Clovis (93612-5606)
PHONE...................800 445-3767
Klaus M Wohlfarth, *President*
Darrell Edwards, *General Mgr*
Freddie Breine, *Opers Staff*
▲ **EMP:** 40
SQ FT: 115,000
SALES (est): 9MM
SALES (corp-wide): 53.1MM **Privately Held**
SIC: 3714 Motor vehicle parts & accessories
PA: Kw Automotive Gmbh
Aspachweg 14
Fichtenberg 74427
797 196-300

(P-19704)
LIQUID ROBOTICS INC (HQ)
1329 Moffett Park Dr, Sunnyvale
(94089-1134)
PHONE...................408 636-4200
Gary Gysin, *President*
Graham Hine, *Partner*
Caryn Nightengale, *CFO*
Daniel J Middleton, *Exec VP*
Mark Bindon, *Vice Pres*
▲ **EMP:** 100
SQ FT: 5,000

SALES (est): 16.3MM
SALES (corp-wide): 101.1B **Publicly Held**
WEB: www.liquidr.com
SIC: 3714 Hydraulic fluid power pumps for auto steering mechanism
PA: The Boeing Company
100 N Riverside Plz
Chicago IL 60606
312 544-2000

(P-19705)
LLOYD DESIGN CORPORATION
Also Called: Lloyd Mats
19731 Nordhoff St, Northridge
(91324-3330)
PHONE...................818 768-6001
Lloyd S Levine, *CEO*
Brendan Dooley, *President*
Mary Freeman, *Human Res Dir*
▲ **EMP:** 55
SALES (est): 7.6MM **Privately Held**
WEB: www.lloydmats.com
SIC: 3714 Motor vehicle parts & accessories

(P-19706)
LOS ANGELES SLEEVE CO INC
Also Called: L.A. Sleeve
12051 Rivera Rd, Santa Fe Springs
(90670-2211)
PHONE...................562 945-7578
Nick G Metchkoff, *President*
Sarah Metchkoff, *Shareholder*
James G Metchkoff, *Corp Secy*
David Metchkoff, *Vice Pres*
Tim Efseaff, *Engineer*
▲ **EMP:** 29
SQ FT: 33,000
SALES (est): 5.6MM **Privately Held**
WEB: www.lasleeve.com
SIC: 3714 Exhaust systems & parts, motor vehicle

(P-19707)
LSI PRODUCTS INC
12885 Wildflower Ln, Riverside
(92503-9772)
PHONE...................951 343-9270
Alex Danze, *CEO*
▲ **EMP:** 70
SALES (est): 14.1MM **Privately Held**
SIC: 3714 Motor vehicle parts & accessories

(P-19708)
LUND MOTION PRODUCTS INC
Also Called: AMP Research
15651 Mosher Ave, Tustin (92780-6426)
PHONE...................949 221-0023
Mitch Fogle, *President*
John Houng, *CTO*
Eric Bajza, *Engineer*
EMP: 35 **Privately Held**
SIC: 3714 Motor vehicle parts & accessories
HQ: Lund Motion Products, Inc.
4325 Hamilton Mill Rd
Buford GA 30518
678 804-3767

(P-19709)
M C O INC
13925 Benson Ave, Chino (91710-7024)
PHONE...................909 627-3574
Leon O Martin, *President*
Vicki Martin, *Corp Secy*
EMP: 15
SQ FT: 10,000
SALES (est): 2.2MM **Privately Held**
SIC: 3714 Frames, motor vehicle

(P-19710)
M E D INC
14001 Marquardt Ave, Santa Fe Springs
(90670-5088)
PHONE...................562 921-0464
Steven Moore, *CEO*
Susan Lowe, *CFO*
EMP: 70 **EST:** 1974
SQ FT: 40,000
SALES (est): 16MM **Privately Held**
WEB: www.dmeexpansionjoints.com
SIC: 3714 3429 Exhaust systems & parts, motor vehicle; clamps, couplings, nozzles & other metal hose fittings

(P-19711)
MAGNUSON PRODUCTS LLC
Also Called: Magnuson Superchargers
1990 Knoll Dr Ste A, Ventura (93003-7309)
PHONE...................805 642-8833
Kim Pendergast, *CEO*
Tim Krauskopf, *President*
Jeff Wright, *Executive*
Kerry Tresback, *Info Tech Mgr*
Owen Peterson, *Project Mgr*
EMP: 49
SQ FT: 45,600
SALES (est): 20.9MM **Privately Held**
WEB: www.magnusonproducts.com
SIC: 3714 Motor vehicle parts & accessories

(P-19712)
MAIER RACING ENTERPRISES INC
22215 Meekland Ave, Hayward
(94541-3855)
PHONE...................510 581-7600
William G Maier, *President*
Shirley J Maier, *Treasurer*
Margaret H Maier, *Vice Pres*
EMP: 11
SQ FT: 14,200
SALES (est): 1.5MM **Privately Held**
WEB: www.maierracing.com
SIC: 3714 5531 Motor vehicle parts & accessories; automotive & home supply stores

(P-19713)
MANUFACTURING & PROD SVCS CORP
Also Called: M P S
2222 Enterprise St, Escondido
(92029-2015)
PHONE...................760 796-4300
Michael McGowen, *President*
EMP: 10
SQ FT: 5,400
SALES (est): 1.5MM **Privately Held**
SIC: 3714 Motor vehicle parts & accessories

(P-19714)
MARGUS AUTOMOTIVE ELC EXCH
165 E Jefferson Blvd, Los Angeles
(90011-2330)
PHONE...................323 232-5281
Donald Lopez, *President*
Carolyn Lopez, *CFO*
EMP: 61
SQ FT: 28,570
SALES (est): 6.2MM **Privately Held**
SIC: 3714 3694 3621 3568 Motor vehicle parts & accessories; motor generator sets, automotive; motors, starting: automotive & aircraft; motors & generators; power transmission equipment

(P-19715)
MAXON INDUSTRIES INC
11921 Slauson Ave, Santa Fe Springs
(90670-2221)
P.O. Box 3434, Los Angeles (90078-3434)
PHONE...................562 464-0099
Murray Lugash, *President*
Larry Lugash, *Exec VP*
Brenda Leung, *Vice Pres*
Howard Smith, *Vice Pres*
Jeffrey Urquhart, *Info Tech Mgr*
EMP: 75 **EST:** 1957
SQ FT: 250,000
SALES (est): 13.5MM **Privately Held**
SIC: 3714 Motor vehicle parts & accessories

(P-19716)
MCLEOD RACING LLC
1570 Lakeview Loop, Anaheim
(92807-1819)
PHONE...................714 630-2764
Paul Lee, *President*
Mark Restivo, *Officer*
Lana Chrisman, *Vice Pres*
EMP: 10
SQ FT: 17,500
SALES (est): 2.1MM **Privately Held**
SIC: 3714 Clutches, motor vehicle

▲ = Import ▼=Export
◆ =Import/Export

(P-19717)
MERITOR SPECIALTY PRODUCTS LLC (HQ)
151 Lawrence Dr, Livermore (94551-5126)
PHONE....................248 435-1000
Carl D Anderson II,
Michael Chapman, *Controller*
Steve Montano, *Senior Buyer*
Brett L Ellander,
▲ EMP: 19
SQ FT: 85,000
SALES (est): 304.2MM **Publicly Held**
WEB: www.fabcoautomotive.com
SIC: 3714 Axles, motor vehicle; gears, motor vehicle; transmission housings or parts, motor vehicle; transmissions, motor vehicle

(P-19718)
METRA ELECTRONICS CORPORATION
Also Called: Antenna Works
3201 E 59th St, Long Beach (90805-4501)
PHONE....................562 470-6601
Steve Hertel, *Manager*
EMP: 15
SALES (corp-wide): 164.1MM **Privately Held**
WEB: www.metraonline.com
SIC: 3714 Motor vehicle body components & frame
PA: Metra Electronics Corporation
460 Walker St
Holly Hill FL 32117
386 257-1186

(P-19719)
MGM BRAKES
1184 S Cloverdale Blvd, Cloverdale (95425-4412)
P.O. Box 249 (95425-0249)
PHONE....................707 894-3333
Ron Parker, *Owner*
◆ EMP: 65 EST: 2015
SALES (est): 284.4K **Privately Held**
SIC: 3714 3625 Air brakes, motor vehicle; brakes, electromagnetic

(P-19720)
MID-WEST FABRICATING CO
Also Called: West Bent Bolt Division
8623 Dice Rd, Santa Fe Springs (90670-2511)
PHONE....................562 698-9615
Steve Petersen, *Manager*
Stephen Petersen, *Vice Pres*
EMP: 40
SQ FT: 40,000
SALES (corp-wide): 25.5MM **Privately Held**
WEB: www.midwestfab.com
SIC: 3714 3452 3316 3312 Tie rods, motor vehicle; bolts, nuts, rivets & washers; cold finishing of steel shapes; wire products, steel or iron
PA: Mid-West Fabricating Co.
313 N Johns St
Amanda OH 43102
740 969-4411

(P-19721)
MILODON INCORPORATED
2250 Agate Ct, Simi Valley (93065-1842)
PHONE....................805 577-5950
Steve Morrison, *President*
▲ EMP: 40 EST: 1957
SQ FT: 32,000
SALES (est): 7.4MM **Privately Held**
WEB: www.milodon.net
SIC: 3714 Motor vehicle engines & parts

(P-19722)
MOBIS PARTS AMERICA LLC
10550 Talbert Ave 4, Fountain Valley (92708-6031)
PHONE....................949 450-0014
H S Lee,
EMP: 270 **Privately Held**
SIC: 3714 Motor vehicle body components & frame
HQ: Mobis Parts America, Llc
10550 Talbert Ave Fl 4
Fountain Valley CA 92708
786 515-1101

(P-19723)
MORENO INDUSTRIES INC
Also Called: Intro Designs
1225 N Knollwood Cir, Anaheim (92801-1310)
PHONE....................714 229-9696
Jose L Moreno, *President*
Victor Moreno, *Vice Pres*
▲ EMP: 10
SQ FT: 1,400
SALES (est): 1.8MM **Privately Held**
WEB: www.introwheels.com
SIC: 3714 Wheels, motor vehicle

(P-19724)
MOTORCAR PARTS OF AMERICA INC (PA)
Also Called: MPA
2929 California St, Torrance (90503-3914)
PHONE....................310 212-7910
Selwyn Joffe, *Ch of Bd*
David Lee, *CFO*
Philip Gay, *Bd of Directors*
Doug Schooner, *Senior VP*
Steve Kratz, *Vice Pres*
◆ EMP: 833
SQ FT: 231,000
SALES (est): 472.8MM **Publicly Held**
WEB: www.motorcarparts.com
SIC: 3714 3694 3625 5013 Motor vehicle parts & accessories; alternators, automotive; starter, electric motor; motor vehicle supplies & new parts

(P-19725)
MUSCLE ROAD INC
Also Called: Classic Soft Trim Central Cal
28838 Ave 15 One Half, Madera (93638)
P.O. Box 1013 (93639-1013)
PHONE....................559 499-6888
Dennis Patterson, *President*
EMP: 10
SQ FT: 15,000
SALES (est): 1.4MM **Privately Held**
SIC: 3714 Automotive wiring harness sets

(P-19726)
MYGRANT GLASS COMPANY INC
10220 Camino Santa Fe, San Diego (92121-3105)
PHONE....................858 455-8022
Tom Andia, *President*
EMP: 20
SQ FT: 32,185
SALES (corp-wide): 191.1MM **Privately Held**
SIC: 3714 5013 Motor vehicle parts & accessories; motor vehicle supplies & new parts
PA: Mygrant Glass Company, Inc.
3271 Arden Rd
Hayward CA 94545
510 785-4360

(P-19727)
NEW CENTURY INDUSTRIES INC
7231 Rosecrans Ave, Paramount (90723-2501)
P.O. Box 1845 (90723-1845)
PHONE....................562 634-9551
Michael Mason, *CEO*
EMP: 50
SQ FT: 32,000
SALES (est): 9.3MM **Privately Held**
SIC: 3714 3465 3469 Wheels, motor vehicle; automotive stampings; stamping metal for the trade

(P-19728)
NICE RACK TOWER ACCESSORIES
Also Called: Billet Industries
8850 Muraoka Dr, Gilroy (95020-3684)
PHONE....................408 846-1919
Horacio Longoria, *President*
EMP: 10
SALES (est): 268.6K **Privately Held**
SIC: 3714 3334 Motor vehicle parts & accessories; primary aluminum

(P-19729)
NOLOGY ENGINEERING INC
1333 Keystone Way, Vista (92081-8311)
PHONE....................760 591-0888
Werner Funk, *President*
Jan Quigley, *CFO*
EMP: 14
SQ FT: 11,000
SALES (est): 1.1MM **Privately Held**
WEB: www.nology.com
SIC: 3714 Motor vehicle parts & accessories

(P-19730)
OCTILLION POWER SYSTEMS INC
721 Sandoval Way, Hayward (94544-7112)
PHONE....................510 397-5952
Peng Zhou, *CEO*
Paul Beach, *President*
Josh Bender, *Engineer*
▲ EMP: 14 EST: 2010
SALES (est): 1.9MM **Privately Held**
SIC: 3714 Transmissions, motor vehicle

(P-19731)
OFFENHAUSER SALES CORP
5300 Alhambra Ave, Los Angeles (90032-3405)
P.O. Box 32219 (90032-0219)
PHONE....................323 225-1307
Fred C Offenhauser Jr, *President*
EMP: 13
SQ FT: 15,000
SALES (est): 2.1MM **Privately Held**
SIC: 3714 Motor vehicle parts & accessories

(P-19732)
ONKI CORP
294 Hegenberger Rd, Oakland (94621-1436)
PHONE....................510 567-8875
Daren On, *President*
▲ EMP: 10
SALES (est): 830K **Privately Held**
WEB: www.onkicorp.com
SIC: 3714 5013 Motor vehicle parts & accessories; truck parts & accessories

(P-19733)
ORGAN-O-SIL FIBER CO INC
Also Called: Organosil Fiber Co
17616 Gothard St Ste B, Huntington Beach (92647-6215)
P.O. Box 86 (92648-0086)
PHONE....................714 847-8310
Ruby Riggs, *President*
Margaret Riggs, *President*
EMP: 27
SQ FT: 3,000
SALES (est): 2MM **Privately Held**
SIC: 3714 Mufflers (exhaust), motor vehicle

(P-19734)
P & S SALES INC
20943 Cabot Blvd, Hayward (94545-1155)
PHONE....................510 732-2628
Robert Phillips, *President*
Diane Phillips, *Treasurer*
Dave Phillips, *Vice Pres*
David Phillips, *Vice Pres*
Edwin Morrison, *Manager*
EMP: 12
SQ FT: 40,000
SALES (est): 3.5MM **Privately Held**
SIC: 3714 5013 Motor vehicle parts & accessories; automotive supplies

(P-19735)
PANA-PACIFIC CORPORATION (HQ)
838 N Laverne Ave, Fresno (93727-6868)
PHONE....................559 457-4700
Kristina Reed, *President*
Harrison Brix, *COO*
▲ EMP: 150 EST: 2004
SALES (est): 13.9MM
SALES (corp-wide): 144.1MM **Privately Held**
WEB: www.brixcom.com
SIC: 3714 Motor vehicle parts & accessories

PA: The Brix Group Inc
838 N Laverne Ave
Fresno CA 93727
559 457-4700

(P-19736)
PARTS EXPEDITING AND DIST CO
Also Called: Pedco
10805 Artesia Blvd # 112, Cerritos (90703-2699)
PHONE....................562 944-3199
Virgil Cooley, *President*
Rachel Cooley, *Vice Pres*
EMP: 40 EST: 1975
SQ FT: 32,000
SALES (est): 5.5MM **Privately Held**
WEB: www.pedco.net
SIC: 3714 3519 Rebuilding engines & transmissions, factory basis; internal combustion engines

(P-19737)
POWER BRAKE EXCHANGE INC
6853 Suva St, Bell (90201-1937)
PHONE....................562 806-6661
Charles Pitts, *President*
Pamela Pitts, *CFO*
EMP: 15
SALES (corp-wide): 4.2MM **Privately Held**
WEB: www.power-brake-exchange.com
SIC: 3714 Motor vehicle brake systems & parts
PA: Power Brake Exchange, Inc.
45 Affonso Dr
Carson City NV 89706
408 292-1305

(P-19738)
POWER PROS RACG EXHUST SYSTEMS
Also Called: Power Pros Exhaust Systems
817 S Lakeview Ave Ste J, Placentia (92870-6718)
PHONE....................714 777-3278
Don Kistler, *President*
Thomas Kistler, *CEO*
EMP: 12
SQ FT: 7,000
SALES: 1.2MM **Privately Held**
WEB: www.thepowerpros.com
SIC: 3714 5013 Exhaust systems & parts, motor vehicle; motorcycle parts

(P-19739)
PRECISION DIE CUTTING INC
Also Called: Precision Film & Tape
150 Doolittle Dr, San Leandro (94577-1014)
PHONE....................510 636-9654
Glenn Yamagata, *CEO*
Arthur N Aronsen, *President*
Joan Yamagata, *CEO*
EMP: 33
SQ FT: 25,000
SALES (est): 3.9MM
SALES (corp-wide): 3.7MM **Privately Held**
SIC: 3714 2675 Motor vehicle parts & accessories; die-cut paper & board
PA: Aronsen & Company
150 Doolittle Dr
San Leandro CA
510 636-9654

(P-19740)
PRIME WHEEL CORPORATION
23920 Vermont Ave, Harbor City (90710-1602)
PHONE....................310 326-5080
Eddie Chen, *Manager*
Ramon Limon, *Opers Spvr*
EMP: 500
SQ FT: 200,000
SALES (corp-wide): 331.7MM **Privately Held**
WEB: www.primewheel.com
SIC: 3714 3471 5013 Motor vehicle wheels & parts; plating & polishing; automotive supplies & parts
PA: Prime Wheel Corporation
17705 S Main St
Gardena CA 90248
310 516-9126

P
R
O
D
U
C
T
S

&

S
V
C
S

(P-19741)
PRIME WHEEL CORPORATION
250 W Apra St, Compton (90220-5521)
PHONE..............................310 516-9126
Lynn Biscocho, *Branch Mgr*
EMP: 20
SALES (corp-wide): 331.7MM **Privately Held**
SIC: 3714 Motor vehicle parts & accessories
PA: Prime Wheel Corporation
17705 S Main St
Gardena CA 90248
310 516-9126

(P-19742)
PRIME WHEEL CORPORATION
Also Called: Prime Wheel of Figueroa
17680 S Figueroa St, Gardena (90248)
PHONE..............................310 819-4123
Peter Liang, *Branch Mgr*
EMP: 25
SALES (corp-wide): 331.7MM **Privately Held**
SIC: 3714 Wheels, motor vehicle
PA: Prime Wheel Corporation
17705 S Main St
Gardena CA 90248
310 516-9126

(P-19743)
PRIME WHEEL CORPORATION (PA)
17705 S Main St, Gardena (90248-3516)
PHONE..............................310 516-9126
Henry Chen, *CEO*
Webb Carter, *Vice Chairman*
Philip Chen, *President*
Mitchell M Tung, *President*
Phillip Chen, *Vice Pres*
◆ **EMP:** 600
SQ FT: 320,000
SALES (est): 331.7MM **Privately Held**
WEB: www.primewheel.com
SIC: 3714 Wheels, motor vehicle

(P-19744)
PROGRESS GROUP
1600 E Miraloma Ave, Placentia (92870-6622)
PHONE..............................714 630-9017
Jeff Cheechov, *President*
Michelle Broyles, *Info Tech Dir*
▲ **EMP:** 14 **EST:** 2009
SALES (est): 2.9MM **Privately Held**
SIC: 3714 Motor vehicle parts & accessories

(P-19745)
PROGRESSIVE HOUSING INC
Also Called: Happy Daze Rv's
5605 Southfront Rd, Livermore (94551-9513)
PHONE..............................916 920-8255
EMP: 15
SALES (corp-wide): 19.4MM **Privately Held**
SIC: 3714 Motor vehicle parts & accessories
PA: Progressive Housing Inc
1199 El Camino Ave
Sacramento CA 95815
916 920-8255

(P-19746)
PURE FORGE
13011 Kirkham Way, Poway (92064-7112)
PHONE..............................760 201-0951
Nathan K Meckel, *President*
EMP: 11 **EST:** 2011
SALES (est): 867.9K **Privately Held**
SIC: 3714 Motor vehicle parts & accessories

(P-19747)
QF LIQUIDATION INC
25242 Arctic Ocean Dr, Lake Forest (92630-8821)
PHONE..............................949 399-4500
Brian Olson, *CFO*
EMP: 35 **Privately Held**
SIC: 3714 8731 Fuel systems & parts, motor vehicle; commercial physical research

PA: Qf Liquidation, Inc.
25242 Arctic Ocean Dr
Lake Forest CA 92630
-

(P-19748)
QF LIQUIDATION INC (PA)
Also Called: Quantum Technologies
25242 Arctic Ocean Dr, Lake Forest (92630-8821)
PHONE..............................949 930-3400
W Brian Olson, *President*
Bradley J Timon, *CFO*
Mark Arold, *Vice Pres*
Kenneth R Lombardo, *Vice Pres*
David M Mazaika, *Exec Dir*
◆ **EMP:** 172
SQ FT: 156,000
SALES (est): 37.5MM **Privately Held**
SIC: 3714 3764 8711 Motor vehicle parts & accessories; guided missile & space vehicle propulsion unit parts; engineering services

(P-19749)
R F P & WELDING
310 E Easy St Ste E, Simi Valley (93065-7531)
P.O. Box 940370 (93094-0370)
PHONE..............................805 526-3425
Randy Miller, *Owner*
EMP: 10
SQ FT: 1,500
SALES (est): 1.1MM **Privately Held**
WEB: www.rfpwelding.com
SIC: 3714 7692 Exhaust systems & parts, motor vehicle; welding repair

(P-19750)
R3 PERFORMANCE PRODUCTS INC
531 Old Woman Springs Rd, Yucca Valley (92284-1613)
PHONE..............................760 364-3001
Roger Ketelslger, *CEO*
Robert Istwan, *CFO*
EMP: 15
SALES (est): 2.4MM **Privately Held**
SIC: 3714 Shock absorbers, motor vehicle

(P-19751)
RACE TECHNOLOGIES LLC
17422 Murphy Ave, Irvine (92614-5922)
PHONE..............................714 438-1118
Jaime Trimble,
Chris Villasenor, *Manager*
▲ **EMP:** 14
SALES (est): 3MM **Privately Held**
WEB: www.racetechnologies.com
SIC: 3714 5013 Motor vehicle brake systems & parts; automotive brakes

(P-19752)
RACEPAK LLC
30402 Esperanza, Rcho STA Marg (92688-2144)
PHONE..............................949 709-5555
Tom Tomlinson, *President*
Jeff Greene, *Vice Pres*
Brian Woodard, *Creative Dir*
Donny Cummins, *VP Opers*
EMP: 28
SALES: 8.9MM
SALES (corp-wide): 133MM **Privately Held**
SIC: 3714 Motor vehicle parts & accessories
PA: Holley Performance Products Inc.
1801 Russellville Rd
Bowling Green KY 42101
270 782-2900

(P-19753)
RADFLO SUSPENSION TECHNOLOGY
11233 Condor Ave, Fountain Valley (92708-6105)
PHONE..............................714 965-7828
Glenn Classen, *CEO*
▲ **EMP:** 11
SQ FT: 5,000
SALES (est): 1.6MM **Privately Held**
WEB: www.radflo.com
SIC: 3714 Shock absorbers, motor vehicle

(P-19754)
RAM OFF ROAD ACCESSORIES INC
3901 Medford St, Los Angeles (90063-1608)
PHONE..............................323 266-3850
Chris Foterek, *President*
William Longo, *Vice Pres*
EMP: 30
SQ FT: 103,000
SALES (est): 4.8MM **Privately Held**
SIC: 3714 Motor vehicle body components & frame

(P-19755)
RB RACING
1234 W 134th St, Gardena (90247-1903)
PHONE..............................310 515-5720
Lynn Hilkemeyer Behn, *Owner*
EMP: 15
SQ FT: 2,500
SALES (est): 1.7MM **Privately Held**
WEB: www.rbracing-rsr.com
SIC: 3714 Motor vehicle parts & accessories

(P-19756)
RICARDO DEFENSE INC (DH)
175 Cremona Dr Ste 140, Goleta (93117-3197)
PHONE..............................805 882-1884
Chester Gryzcan, *President*
Brian Smith, *Vice Pres*
Rick Wyrembelski, *Vice Pres*
Harvey Lin, *Software Engr*
Jay Lobb, *Project Mgr*
EMP: 49
SALES: 17.5MM
SALES (corp-wide): 509.5MM **Privately Held**
WEB: www.control-pt.com
SIC: 3714 8711 Motor vehicle brake systems & parts; consulting engineer

(P-19757)
RICH PRODUCTS
1041 Broadway Ave, San Pablo (94806-2260)
PHONE..............................510 234-7547
Donald Rich, *Partner*
Mary Rich, *Partner*
Maribeth Wasmund, *Manager*
EMP: 10
SQ FT: 3,000
SALES (est): 1.2MM **Privately Held**
WEB: www.richproductsco.com
SIC: 3714 Exhaust systems & parts, motor vehicle

(P-19758)
RK SPORT INC
26900 Jefferson Ave, Murrieta (92562-9112)
PHONE..............................951 894-7883
Mike Lozano, *President*
Robert Smith, *President*
Julie Lozano, *Vice Pres*
EMP: 20
SQ FT: 15,000
SALES: 2MM **Privately Held**
WEB: www.rksport.com
SIC: 3714 5531 5013 Motor vehicle parts & accessories; automotive parts; automotive supplies & parts

(P-19759)
RLV TUNED EXHAUST PRODUCTS
2351 Thompson Way Bldg A, Santa Maria (93455-1041)
PHONE..............................805 925-5461
Rodney L Verlengiere, *President*
Arthur R Verlengiere, *Treasurer*
▲ **EMP:** 23 **EST:** 1978
SQ FT: 5,000
SALES (est): 4.5MM **Privately Held**
SIC: 3714 Exhaust systems & parts, motor vehicle

(P-19760)
ROADSTER WHEELS INC
14955 Don Julian Rd, City of Industry (91746-3112)
PHONE..............................626 333-3007
Yvette Marchisset, *Vice Pres*

EMP: 14
SQ FT: 52,000
SALES (est): 1.1MM **Privately Held**
SIC: 3714 Wheels, motor vehicle

(P-19761)
RUFFSTUFF INC
3237 Rippey Rd Ste 200, Loomis (95650-7661)
PHONE..............................916 600-1945
Daniel Fredrickson, *CEO*
Mallory Kittredge, *CFO*
Louis Staley, *Sales Mgr*
Zack Fredrickson, *Manager*
EMP: 11
SALES (est): 2MM **Privately Held**
SIC: 3714 Motor vehicle parts & accessories

(P-19762)
S&B FILTERS INC
15461 Slover Ave Ste A, Fontana (92337-1306)
PHONE..............................909 947-0015
Berry Carter, *President*
▲ **EMP:** 58
SALES (est): 11.4MM **Privately Held**
WEB: www.sbfilters.com
SIC: 3714 3564 Filters: oil, fuel & air, motor vehicle; filters, air: furnaces, air conditioning equipment, etc.

(P-19763)
SANKO ELECTRONICS AMERICA INC (HQ)
20700 Denker Ave Ste A, Torrance (90501-6415)
PHONE..............................310 618-1677
Hironori Saigusa, *CEO*
Akio Saigusa, *President*
Toshiaki Yamashita, *President*
▲ **EMP:** 19
SQ FT: 35,000
SALES (est): 3.9MM **Privately Held**
SIC: 3714 Motor vehicle parts & accessories

(P-19764)
SEDENQUIST-FRASER ENTPS INC
Also Called: Leisure Components
16730 Gridley Rd, Cerritos (90703-1730)
PHONE..............................562 924-5763
Jitu Patel, *President*
EMP: 20 **EST:** 1974
SQ FT: 22,000
SALES (est): 3.1MM **Privately Held**
WEB: www.sftech.com
SIC: 3714 3089 3544 Motor vehicle parts & accessories; plastic processing; special dies, tools, jigs & fixtures

(P-19765)
SHARK WHEEL INC
22600 Lambert St Ste 704, Lake Forest (92630-1619)
PHONE..............................818 216-8001
David Patrick,
EMP: 14 **EST:** 2014
SALES (est): 2.2MM **Privately Held**
SIC: 3714 Motor vehicle parts & accessories

(P-19766)
SHRIN CORPORATION
Also Called: Cover King
900 E Arlee Pl, Anaheim (92805-5645)
P.O. Box 9860 (92812-7860)
PHONE..............................714 850-0303
Narendra K Gupta, *President*
Robby Gupta, *Vice Pres*
Ramin Edalat, *Engineer*
Bansari Shah, *Accounting Mgr*
Anita Gupta, *Director*
◆ **EMP:** 150
SQ FT: 90,000
SALES (est): 34.1MM **Privately Held**
WEB: www.coverking.com
SIC: 3714 5013 Motor vehicle parts & accessories; automotive supplies & parts

(P-19767)
SIMWON AMERICA CORP
400 Darcy Pkwy, Lathrop (95330-9796)
PHONE..............................925 276-3412
Yong Joon Bae, *CEO*

▲ = Import ▼=Export
◆ =Import/Export

EMP: 15
SALES (est): 6.7MM **Privately Held**
SIC: 3714 Acceleration equipment, motor vehicle

(P-19768)
SINISTER MFG COMPANY INC
Also Called: Mkm Customs
2025 Opportunity Dr Ste 7, Roseville (95678-3010)
PHONE...................................916 772-9253
Brian P George, *President*
Mike Mitchell, *CFO*
Robert McCrickard, *General Mgr*
Rosa Gutierrez, *Manager*
▲ EMP: 45
SQ FT: 11,000
SALES: 20MM **Privately Held**
SIC: 3714 Motor vehicle parts & accessories

(P-19769)
SLAM SPECIALTIES LLC (PA)
5845 E Terrace Ave, Fresno (93727-1398)
PHONE...................................559 348-9038
Harry Solakian, *Mng Member*
Nick Solakian,
Sheryl Solakian,
▼ EMP: 16
SQ FT: 10,000
SALES (est): 2.3MM **Privately Held**
WEB: www.slamspecialties.com
SIC: 3714 Motor vehicle engines & parts

(P-19770)
SOUTHLAND CLUTCH INC
Also Called: Clutches New or Rebuilt
101 E 18th St, National City (91950-4529)
PHONE...................................619 477-2105
Dan Levine, *President*
Colleen Llanos, *Office Mgr*
EMP: 11
SQ FT: 8,000
SALES: 2MM **Privately Held**
WEB: www.southlandclutch.com
SIC: 3714 Clutches, motor vehicle

(P-19771)
SPECIAL DEVICES INCORPORATED
Also Called: Sdi
2655 1st St Ste 300, Simi Valley (93065-1580)
PHONE...................................805 387-1000
Yasuhiro Sakaki, *CEO*
Mike Mendonca, *COO*
Harry Rector, *CFO*
Nicholas J Bruge, *Ch Credit Ofcr*
Richard Richins, *Planning*
▲ EMP: 600
SQ FT: 170,000
SALES (est): 1.1MM **Privately Held**
WEB: www.specialdevices.com
SIC: 3714 Motor vehicle parts & accessories
PA: Daicel Corporation
3-1, Ofukacho, Kita-Ku
Osaka OSK 530-0
-

(P-19772)
SPECIALTY PRODUCTS DESIGN INC
11252 Sunco Dr, Rancho Cordova (95742-6515)
PHONE...................................916 635-8108
Chris Hill, *President*
Carol Hill, *Corp Secy*
EMP: 11 EST: 1970
SQ FT: 22,000
SALES (est): 2.2MM **Privately Held**
WEB: www.spdexhaust.com
SIC: 3714 Exhaust systems & parts, motor vehicle

(P-19773)
SPECTRUM ACCESSORY DISTRS
9770 Carroll Centre Rd, San Diego (92126-6504)
PHONE...................................858 653-6470
C Dwight Anderson, *President*
EMP: 115

SALES (est): 8.5MM **Privately Held**
SIC: 3714 5013 Motor vehicle body components & frame; motor vehicle supplies & new parts

(P-19774)
SUNNY AMERICA & GLOBAL AUTOTEC
2681 Dow Ave Ste A, Tustin (92780-7244)
PHONE...................................714 544-0400
Alex Han, *Owner*
▲ EMP: 65
SALES (est): 5.7MM **Privately Held**
SIC: 3714 Motor vehicle engines & parts

(P-19775)
SUPERIOR INDS INTL HLDINGS LLC (HQ)
7800 Woodley Ave, Van Nuys (91406-1722)
PHONE...................................818 781-4973
Steven J Borick, *Ch of Bd*
Emory Brown, *Vice Pres*
Paul Icinkoff, *Admin Asst*
Dustin Schumm, *Administration*
Cotterell Melanie, *Business Mgr*
▲ EMP: 29
SALES (est): 1.8MM
SALES (corp-wide): 1.5B **Publicly Held**
SIC: 3714 Motor vehicle wheels & parts
PA: Superior Industries International, Inc.
26600 Telg Rd Ste 400
Southfield MI 48033
248 352-7300

(P-19776)
TABC INC (DH)
6375 N Paramount Blvd, Long Beach (90805-3301)
PHONE...................................562 984-3305
Michael Bafan, *CEO*
Yoshiaki Nishino, *Treasurer*
◆ EMP: 117
SQ FT: 8,820
SALES (est): 133.4MM **Privately Held**
SIC: 3714 3713 3469 Motor vehicle parts & accessories; truck beds; metal stampings

(P-19777)
TAP MANUFACTURING LLC
Also Called: Pro Comp
2360 Boswell Rd, Chula Vista (91914-3510)
PHONE...................................619 216-1444
Darren M Salvin, *Principal*
Josh Weber, *Project Mgr*
▲ EMP: 18
SALES (est): 4.1MM **Privately Held**
SIC: 3714 Motor vehicle parts & accessories

(P-19778)
TASKER METAL PRODUCTS INC
1823 S Hope St, Los Angeles (90015-4197)
P.O. Box 15368 (90015-0368)
PHONE...................................213 765-5400
Eugene L Golling, *President*
Rudi Verstegen, *Vice Pres*
Rudy Verstegen, *Vice Pres*
▲ EMP: 15
SQ FT: 12,000
SALES (est): 550K **Privately Held**
WEB: www.taskermetalproducts.com
SIC: 3714 Motor vehicle body components & frame; hoods, motor vehicle

(P-19779)
TEECO PRODUCTS INC
Paca
7471 Reese Rd, Sacramento (95828-3721)
PHONE...................................916 688-3535
Tom Valvered, *Manager*
EMP: 30
SALES (est): 3.8MM
SALES (corp-wide): 19.4MM **Privately Held**
WEB: www.teecoproducts.com
SIC: 3714 5084 3443 Propane conversion equipment, motor vehicle; propane conversion equipment; fabricated plate work (boiler shop)

PA: Teeco Products Inc.
16881 Armstrong Ave
Irvine CA 92606
949 261-6295

(P-19780)
TENNECO AUTOMOTIVE OPER CO INC
6925 Atlantic Ave, Long Beach (90805-1415)
PHONE...................................562 630-0700
Danny Walker, *Manager*
EMP: 65
SALES (corp-wide): 11.7B **Publicly Held**
WEB: www.tenneco-automotive.com
SIC: 3714 3713 Motor vehicle parts & accessories; truck & bus bodies
HQ: Tenneco Automotive Operating Company, Inc.
500 N Field Dr
Lake Forest IL 60045
847 482-5000

(P-19781)
TESLA INC
3203 Jack Northrop Ave, Hawthorne (90250-4424)
PHONE...................................310 219-4652
Anne Lemperle, *Manager*
EMP: 13
SALES (corp-wide): 21.4B **Publicly Held**
SIC: 3714 3711 Motor vehicle parts & accessories; cars, electric, assembly of
PA: Tesla, Inc.
3500 Deer Creek Rd
Palo Alto CA 94304
650 681-5000

(P-19782)
THERMAL SOLUTIONS MFG INC
Also Called: THERMAL SOLUTIONS MANUFACTURING
1390 S Tippecanoe Ave B, San Bernardino (92408-2998)
PHONE...................................909 796-0754
Maureen Baker, *Branch Mgr*
Glenn Hollis, *CFO*
EMP: 34
SALES (corp-wide): 30.1MM **Privately Held**
WEB: www.mytinytiger.com
SIC: 3714 Radiators & radiator shells & cores, motor vehicle
PA: Thermal Solutions Manufacturing, Inc.
15 Century Blvd Ste 102
Nashville TN 37214
800 359-9186

(P-19783)
THYSSENKRUPP BILSTEIN AMER INC
14102 Stowe Dr, Poway (92064-7147)
PHONE...................................858 386-5900
Doug Robertson, *Vice Pres*
Brian Giczkowski, *Technology*
Alireza Mohammadi, *Sr Project Mgr*
EMP: 42
SALES (corp-wide): 39.8B **Publicly Held**
SIC: 3714 5013 Motor vehicle parts & accessories; motor vehicle supplies & new parts
HQ: Thyssenkrupp Bilstein Of America, Inc.
8685 Bilstein Blvd
Hamilton OH 45015
513 881-7600

(P-19784)
TILTON ENGINEERING INC
25 Easy St, Buellton (93427-9566)
P.O. Box 1787 (93427-1787)
PHONE...................................805 688-2353
Jason Wahl, *President*
Todd Cooper, *Vice Pres*
Casey Lund, *Chief Engr*
Jon Conway, *Purch Agent*
▲ EMP: 50 EST: 1972
SQ FT: 15,000
SALES (est): 10.8MM **Privately Held**
WEB: www.tiltonracing.com
SIC: 3714 Motor vehicle parts & accessories

(P-19785)
TOYO AUTOMOTIVE PARTS USA INC
5665 Plaza Dr Ste 200, Cypress (90630-5066)
PHONE...................................714 229-6125
Iori Suzuki, *President*
Motook Unihira, *Principal*
Ron Craddock, *Credit Staff*
Robert McDonald, *Train & Dev Mgr*
Marc Sanzenbacher, *Senior Mgr*
◆ EMP: 60
SALES (est): 21.8MM **Privately Held**
WEB: www.toyo-rubber.co.jp
SIC: 3714 Motor vehicle body components & frame
PA: Toyo Tire Corporation
2-2-13, Fujinoki
Itami HYO 664-0

(P-19786)
TRANSGO
Also Called: Transco
2621 Merced Ave, El Monte (91733-1905)
PHONE...................................626 443-7456
Gilbert W Younger, *Principal*
David Hardin, *General Mgr*
Sema Reyes, *Admin Sec*
Jim Mobley, *Technician*
EMP: 25
SQ FT: 4,560
SALES (est): 4.2MM **Privately Held**
SIC: 3714 Motor vehicle parts & accessories

(P-19787)
TRANSPORTATION POWER INC
Also Called: Transpower
2415 Auto Park Way, Escondido (92029-1222)
PHONE...................................858 248-4255
Michael C Simon, *President*
Paul Scott, *Vice Pres*
James Burns, *Chief*
EMP: 45
SALES (est): 10.1MM **Privately Held**
WEB: www.transpowerusa.com
SIC: 3714 Motor vehicle parts & accessories

(P-19788)
TRISTAR GLOBAL INC
Also Called: Pinnacle
526 Coralridge Pl, La Puente (91746-3000)
PHONE...................................626 363-6978
Benjamin Chau, *President*
▼ EMP: 10
SALES (est): 1.4MM **Privately Held**
WEB: www.tristarglobal.com
SIC: 3714 Motor vehicle parts & accessories

(P-19789)
TUBE TECHNOLOGIES INC
Also Called: TTI Performance Exhaust
1555 Consumer Cir, Corona (92880-1726)
PHONE...................................951 371-4878
Sam Davis, *President*
Trini Respico, *Corp Secy*
Tom Nakawatase, *Vice Pres*
Raul Rodriguez, *Vice Pres*
▲ EMP: 30
SQ FT: 18,400
SALES (est): 4.7MM **Privately Held**
WEB: www.ttiexhaust.com
SIC: 3714 3498 Exhaust systems & parts, motor vehicle; tube fabricating (contract bending & shaping)

(P-19790)
TURBONETICS HOLDINGS INC
14399 Princeton Ave, Moorpark (93021-1481)
PHONE...................................805 581-0333
Brad Lewis, *Vice Pres*
Ron Reeves, *Partner*
Greg Papp, *Finance Dir*
Danny Lapinid, *Senior Buyer*
Tyler Tanaka, *Marketing Mgr*
▲ EMP: 49
SQ FT: 50,000
SALES (est): 9.3MM
SALES (corp-wide): 4.3B **Publicly Held**
SIC: 3714 Motor vehicle parts & accessories

PRODUCTS & SVCS

PA: Westinghouse Air Brake Technologies
Corporation
30 Isabella St
Pittsburgh PA 15212
412 825-1000

(P-19791)
U S WHEEL CORPORATION
Also Called: US Wheel
15702 Producer Ln, Huntington Beach
(92649-1303)
PHONE......................714 892-0021
Eliot Mason, *President*
Larry Van Es, *Manager*
◆ **EMP:** 15
SQ FT: 135,000
SALES (est): 14.6MM **Privately Held**
WEB: www.uswheel.com
SIC: 3714 5013 Wheels, motor vehicle;
wheels, motor vehicle

(P-19792)
UFO DESIGNS
Also Called: S F Technology
16730 Gridley Rd, Cerritos (90703-1730)
PHONE......................562 924-5763
Jitu Patel, *President*
EMP: 22
SALES (corp-wide): 3.8MM **Privately
Held**
WEB: www.ufodesign.com
SIC: 3714 3089 Motor vehicle parts & ac-
cessories; plastic processing
PA: U.F.O. Designs
5812 Machine Dr
Huntington Beach CA 92649
714 892-4420

(P-19793)
UNI FILTER INC
1468 Manhattan Ave, Fullerton
(92831-5222)
PHONE......................714 535-6933
Lanny R Mitchell, *President*
Kenneth E Mitchell, *Shareholder*
Robert A Nichols, *Shareholder*
Kathi Perry, *Treasurer*
Tom Gross, *Vice Pres*
EMP: 60 **EST:** 1971
SQ FT: 26,000
SALES: 3MM **Privately Held**
WEB: www.unifilter.com
SIC: 3714 Filters: oil, fuel & air, motor vehi-
cle

(P-19794)
UNITED RESEARCH & MFG
Also Called: U R M
2630 Progress St, Vista (92081-8412)
PHONE......................760 727-4320
Danny Horrell, *President*
▲ **EMP:** 10
SQ FT: 15,000
SALES (est): 730K **Privately Held**
SIC: 3714 3599 Motor vehicle brake sys-
tems & parts; machine shop, jobbing & re-
pair

(P-19795)
US HYBRID CORPORATION (PA)
445 Maple Ave, Torrance (90503-3807)
PHONE......................310 212-1200
Abas Goodarzi, *CEO*
Don C Kang, *President*
Daniel Orlowski, *Program Mgr*
Christophe Salgues, *Engineer*
Paul Nguyen, *Mfg Spvr*
▲ **EMP:** 42
SQ FT: 18,000
SALES (est): 7.1MM **Privately Held**
WEB: www.ushybrid.com
SIC: 3714 Motor vehicle engines & parts

(P-19796)
US MOTOR WORKS LLC (PA)
14722 Anson Ave, Santa Fe Springs
(90670-5306)
PHONE......................562 404-0488
Gil Benjaman,
Doron Goren, *Executive*
Avram Ben-Yehuda,
◆ **EMP:** 104
SQ FT: 37,000
SALES (est): 20.8MM **Privately Held**
WEB: www.usmotorworks.com
SIC: 3714 Water pump, motor vehicle

(P-19797)
**US RADIATOR CORPORATION
(PA)**
4423 District Blvd, Vernon (90058-3111)
PHONE......................323 826-0965
Donald Armstrong, *President*
William Zimmerman, *Treasurer*
Tim Armstrong, *Vice Pres*
▲ **EMP:** 30
SQ FT: 35,000
SALES (est): 4.5MM **Privately Held**
WEB: www.usradiator.com
SIC: 3714 Radiators & radiator shells &
cores, motor vehicle

(P-19798)
**VIGILANT MARINE SYSTEMS
LLC**
2045 S Baker Ave, Ontario (91761-8027)
PHONE......................909 597-9508
Craig Mason,
▲ **EMP:** 11 **EST:** 2002
SALES (est): 1.6MM **Privately Held**
SIC: 3714 Filters: oil, fuel & air, motor vehi-
cle

(P-19799)
VINTIQUE INC
1828 W Sequoia Ave, Orange
(92868-1018)
PHONE......................714 634-1932
Chad Looney, *President*
Judy Looney, *Treasurer*
Denise Looney, *Vice Pres*
▲ **EMP:** 23
SQ FT: 17,000
SALES (est): 4MM **Privately Held**
WEB: www.vintique.com
SIC: 3714 Motor vehicle parts & acces-
sories

(P-19800)
VOYOMOTIVE LLC
2443 Fillmore St Ste 157, San Francisco
(94115-1814)
PHONE......................888 321-4633
Peter Yorke, *Bd of Directors*
Harald Ekman, *CFO*
EMP: 12
SALES (est): 1.1MM **Privately Held**
SIC: 3714 5045 Motor vehicle parts & ac-
cessories; computer software

(P-19801)
WAH HUNG GROUP INC (PA)
1000 E Garvey Ave, Monterey Park
(91755-3031)
PHONE......................626 571-8700
Man Kwong Ng, *CEO*
EMP: 28
SALES (est): 8.4MM **Privately Held**
SIC: 3714 Wheel rims, motor vehicle

(P-19802)
WAH HUNG GROUP INC
283 E Garvey Ave, Monterey Park
(91755-1811)
PHONE......................626 571-8700
EMP: 26
SALES (corp-wide): 8.4MM **Privately
Held**
SIC: 3714 Wheel rims, motor vehicle
PA: Wah Hung Group, Inc.
1000 E Garvey Ave
Monterey Park CA 91755
626 571-8700

(P-19803)
WALKER PRODUCTS (PA)
14291 Commerce Dr, Garden Grove
(92843-4944)
PHONE......................714 554-5151
Michael Gerard Weaver, *President*
Grant Kitching, *Vice Pres*
Timothy A Weaver, *Admin Sec*
Jeff Weaver, *Info Tech Dir*
Ronda Bowen, *Finance Dir*
▲ **EMP:** 25
SQ FT: 125,000
SALES (est): 50MM **Privately Held**
WEB: www.walkerproducts.com
SIC: 3714 Motor vehicle parts & acces-
sories

(P-19804)
WEB CAM INC
Also Called: Web Cam
1815 Massachusetts Ave, Riverside
(92507-2616)
PHONE......................951 369-5144
Laurie Dunlap, *Vice Pres*
EMP: 13
SQ FT: 6,000
SALES (est): 2.3MM **Privately Held**
WEB: www.webcaminc.net
SIC: 3714 Camshafts, motor vehicle

(P-19805)
WILWOOD ENGINEERING
4700 Calle Bolero, Camarillo (93012-8561)
PHONE......................805 388-1188
William H Wood, *President*
Douglas Burke, *Vice Pres*
Larry Wolff, *General Mgr*
Dave Brzozowski, *Software Dev*
Jill Domke, *IT/INT Sup*
▲ **EMP:** 120 **EST:** 1977
SALES (est): 29.1MM **Privately Held**
WEB: www.wilwood.com
SIC: 3714 Motor vehicle parts & acces-
sories

(P-19806)
**WINDSHIELD PROS
INCORPORATED**
4501 E Airport Dr, Ontario (91761-7877)
PHONE......................951 272-2867
Michael Fox, *Principal*
EMP: 27
SALES (est): 2.1MM **Privately Held**
WEB: www.windshieldpros.com
SIC: 3714 Windshield frames, motor vehi-
cle

(P-19807)
**WORKS PERFORMANCE
PRODUCTS INC**
21045 Osborne St, Canoga Park
(91304-1744)
PHONE......................818 701-1010
Gilles Vaillancourt, *President*
Douglas Yerkes, *Vice Pres*
EMP: 43
SQ FT: 14,700
SALES (est): 9MM **Privately Held**
WEB: www.worksperformance.com
SIC: 3714 Shock absorbers, motor vehicle

(P-19808)
WRIGHTSPEED INC
650 W Tower Ave, Alameda (94501-5047)
PHONE......................866 960-9482
Ian Wright, *CEO*
Mark Schmitz, *CFO*
Ian Welch, *Director*
▲ **EMP:** 39
SQ FT: 108,000
SALES (est): 14.2MM **Privately Held**
SIC: 3714 Differentials & parts, motor vehi-
cle

(P-19809)
WSW CORP (PA)
Also Called: Waag
16000 Strathern St, Van Nuys
(91406-1316)
PHONE......................818 989-5008
Gary Waagenaar, *CEO*
Mike Calka, *President*
Jennifer Waagenaar, *Vice Pres*
▲ **EMP:** 45
SQ FT: 55,000
SALES (est): 1.2MM **Privately Held**
WEB: www.waag.com
SIC: 3714 5712 Motor vehicle parts & ac-
cessories; beds & accessories; bedding &
bedsprings

(P-19810)
YINLUN TDI LLC
Also Called: Thermal Dynamics
760 S Milliken Ave Ste A, Ontario
(91761-7894)
PHONE......................800 266-5645
EMP: 11
SALES (corp-wide): 723MM **Privately
Held**
SIC: 3714 Motor vehicle parts & acces-
sories

HQ: Yinlun Tdi, Llc
4850 E Airport Dr
Ontario CA 91761
909 390-3944

(P-19811)
YINLUN TDI LLC (HQ)
Also Called: Thermal Dynamics
4850 E Airport Dr, Ontario (91761-7818)
PHONE......................909 390-3944
Thomas Thielen, *Mng Member*
George Gray, *Senior Buyer*
Virgil Darga, *Manager*
EMP: 80
SQ FT: 85,000
SALES (est): 29.5MM
SALES (corp-wide): 723MM **Privately
Held**
SIC: 3714 Motor vehicle engines & parts
PA: Zhejiang Yinlun Machinery Co., Ltd.
No.8, East Shifeng Road, Fuxi Street
Tiantai County 31720
576 839-3839

3715 Truck Trailers

(P-19812)
ACE TRAILER CO
Also Called: American Carrier Equipment
2285 E Date Ave, Fresno (93706-5477)
PHONE......................559 442-1500
Phillip Sweet, *President*
David Sweet, *Treasurer*
Darlene Reece, *Purch Agent*
EMP: 40
SALES: 6.9MM **Privately Held**
SIC: 3715 Truck trailers

(P-19813)
ANDERSEN INDUSTRIES INC
17079 Muskrat Ave, Adelanto
(92301-2259)
PHONE......................760 246-8766
Steven Andersen, *CEO*
Neil Andersen, *Vice Pres*
Wayne Andersen, *Vice Pres*
Judy McCalmon, *Admin Asst*
Dave Andersen, *Mfg Dir*
EMP: 25
SQ FT: 110,000
SALES (est): 7.2MM **Privately Held**
WEB: www.andersenmp.com
SIC: 3715 3441 3444 Truck trailers; fabri-
cated structural metal; hoppers, sheet
metal

(P-19814)
BLACKSERIES CAMPERS INC
19501 E Walnut Dr S, City of Industry
(91748-2318)
PHONE......................626 579-1069
Hongwei Qiu, *CEO*
Yichun Chen, *Admin Sec*
EMP: 20
SALES: 1MM **Privately Held**
SIC: 3715 Trailers or vans for transporting
horses

(P-19815)
**CALIFORNIA CART BUILDER
LLC**
29375 Hunco Way, Lake Elsinore
(92530-2756)
PHONE......................951 245-1114
Elma M Eaton, *Mng Member*
Rodney Eaton,
EMP: 10
SALES (est): 1.8MM **Privately Held**
SIC: 3715 Trailer bodies

(P-19816)
**CIMC INTERMODAL EQUIPMENT
LLC (DH)**
10530 Sessler St, South Gate
(90280-7252)
PHONE......................562 904-8600
Frank Sonzela, *CEO*
Chris Ratliff, *Vice Pres*
Missy Pinksaw, *Executive*
Ed Gill, *Exec Dir*
Sean Lambright, *Info Tech Dir*
▲ **EMP:** 70

▲ = Import ▼=Export
◆ =Import/Export

SALES (est): 56MM **Privately Held**
SIC: 3715 7539 Truck trailer chassis; trailer repair
HQ: China International Marine Containers (Group) Co., Ltd.
8/F, Cimc R&D Center, No.2 Gangwan Avenue, Shekou Industrial Zon
Shenzhen 51806
755 268-0263

(P-19817)
CONCEPT VEHICLE TECHNOLOGIES
Also Called: Concept Transporters
2695 S Cherry Ave Ste 120, Fresno (93706-5488)
PHONE...................................559 233-1313
Bruce Canepa, *President*
Jeff Gardner, *Vice Pres*
EMP: 12
SALES (est): 1.5MM **Privately Held**
SIC: 3715 7539 3711 Truck trailers; trailer repair; motor trucks, except off-highway, assembly of

(P-19818)
COZAD TRAILER SALES LLC
4907 E Waterloo Rd, Stockton (95215-2096)
PHONE...................................209 931-3000
Tom G Pistacchio,
Steve Clark, *Partner*
Randy Askins, *Purch Agent*
Delores Pistacchio,
▲ EMP: 92 EST: 1953
SQ FT: 78,000
SALES (est): 28.2MM **Privately Held**
WEB: www.cozadtrailers.com
SIC: 3715 7539 Trailer bodies; trailer repair

(P-19819)
DEXTER AXLE COMPANY
Also Called: Unique Functional Products
135 Sunshine Ln, San Marcos (92069-1733)
PHONE...................................760 744-1610
Steve Moore, *Director*
Damian Sullivan, *Sales Mgr*
Jackie Lipford, *Sales Staff*
EMP: 125
SALES (corp-wide): 324.9MM **Privately Held**
SIC: 3715 3714 Trailer bodies; motor vehicle parts & accessories
HQ: Dexter Axle Company
2900 Industrial Pkwy
Elkhart IN 46516

(P-19820)
ERMM CORPORATION
Also Called: J & L Tank Co
5415 Martin Luther King, Lynwood (90262-3961)
PHONE...................................310 635-0524
Norma Ritterbush, *President*
Michael Ritterbush, *Vice Pres*
EMP: 23 EST: 1968
SQ FT: 450,000
SALES (est): 4.2MM **Privately Held**
SIC: 3715 3795 5561 7538 Truck trailers; tanks & tank components; recreational vehicle dealers; general automotive repair shops; motor vehicle parts & accessories

(P-19821)
FIVE STAR TRAILERS INC
221 M St, Fresno (93721-3007)
PHONE...................................559 498-0337
Ricardo Vargas, *President*
Norma Saldana, *Admin Sec*
EMP: 11
SALES (est): 1.7MM **Privately Held**
SIC: 3715 Bus trailers, tractor type

(P-19822)
GLENN ENGINEERING INC
9850 3rd St, Delhi (95315-9624)
PHONE...................................209 667-4555
Thomas Glenn, *President*
Mary Glenn, *Treasurer*
EMP: 10
SQ FT: 7,000
SALES (est): 1.5MM **Privately Held**
SIC: 3715 Truck trailers

(P-19823)
HARLEY MURRAY INC
Also Called: Murray Trailers
1754 E Mariposa Rd, Stockton (95205)
PHONE...................................209 466-0266
Douglas G Murray, *President*
EMP: 54
SQ FT: 41,000
SALES: 4.5MM **Privately Held**
WEB: www.murraytrailer.com
SIC: 3715 7539 Semitrailers for truck tractors; trailer repair

(P-19824)
IRON WORKS ENTERPRISES INC
801 S 7th St, Modesto (95351-3903)
PHONE...................................209 572-7450
EMP: 20
SALES (est): 1.8MM **Privately Held**
SIC: 3715

(P-19825)
JACOBSEN TRAILER INC
1128 E South Ave, Fowler (93625-9798)
PHONE...................................559 834-5971
Eugene Jacobsen, *President*
Joetta Jacobsen, *Corp Secy*
EMP: 23
SQ FT: 9,400
SALES (est): 4.4MM **Privately Held**
WEB: www.jacobsentrailers.com
SIC: 3715 5013 7519 5084 Truck trailers; trailer parts & accessories; trailer rental; trailers, industrial

(P-19826)
MCQUAIDE BROTHERS CORPORATION
Also Called: F E Trailers
11919 Woodside Ave, Lakeside (92040-2913)
PHONE...................................619 444-9932
John McQuaide, *President*
Alan McQuaide, *Vice Pres*
EMP: 10
SQ FT: 13,000
SALES (est): 1.2MM **Privately Held**
WEB: www.fetrailers.com
SIC: 3715 7539 5599 Truck trailers; trailer repair; utility trailers

(P-19827)
OWEN TRAILERS INC
9020 Jurupa Rd, Riverside (92509-3106)
PHONE...................................951 361-4557
Loren Owen Jr, *President*
Angela P Owen, *Corp Secy*
Jeff Owen, *General Mgr*
EMP: 25 EST: 1946
SQ FT: 34,000
SALES: 3MM **Privately Held**
WEB: www.owentrailers.com
SIC: 3715 Truck trailers

(P-19828)
PERFORMANCE TRAILERS INC
2901 Falcon Dr, Madera (93637-9287)
PHONE...................................559 673-6300
Kevin D Gerhardt Sr, *President*
Kevin Gerhardt, *President*
EMP: 25
SQ FT: 24,000
SALES: 1.5MM **Privately Held**
WEB: www.perftrlrs.com
SIC: 3715 Trailer bodies

(P-19829)
PERFORMANCE TRUCK AND TRLR LLC
2429 Peck Rd, Whittier (90601-1605)
PHONE...................................909 605-0323
Bryan Kobus, *CFO*
EMP: 12
SALES (est): 1.5MM **Privately Held**
SIC: 3715 Truck trailers

(P-19830)
R A PHILLIPS INDUSTRIES INC
Phillips Coml Vhcl Pdts Div
12070 Burke St, Santa Fe Springs (90670-2676)
PHONE...................................562 781-2100
Bob Phillips, *President*
Patti Peterson, *Vice Pres*

EMP: 300
SALES (corp-wide): 88.7MM **Privately Held**
SIC: 3715 3713 Truck trailers; truck & bus bodies
PA: R. A. Phillips Industries, Inc.
12012 Burke St
Santa Fe Springs CA 90670
562 781-2121

(P-19831)
R V GAMBLER
6966 Saxon Rd Spc 14, Adelanto (92301-9513)
PHONE...................................928 927-5966
Russel Peralta, *Owner*
EMP: 16
SALES (est): 1.3MM **Privately Held**
SIC: 3715 Truck trailers

(P-19832)
SUNWAY MECHANICAL & ELEC TECH
1650 S Grove Ave Ste A, Ontario (91761-4018)
PHONE...................................909 673-7959
Zili Xu, *President*
WEI Liu, *CFO*
Yan Guo, *Admin Sec*
EMP: 16
SALES (est): 1.3MM **Privately Held**
SIC: 3715 Truck trailers

(P-19833)
TRU-TRAILERS INC
Also Called: Tru-Trailers Manufacturing
4444 E Lincoln Ave, Fresno (93725-9709)
PHONE...................................559 251-7591
Judy A True, *Vice Pres*
Tom M True, *President*
Terry True, *Admin Sec*
EMP: 13
SQ FT: 4,000
SALES (est): 3.3MM **Privately Held**
SIC: 3715 7699 5013 Trailers or vans for transporting horses; trailer bodies; tractor repair; trailer parts & accessories

(P-19834)
TUFF BOY HOLDING INC
Also Called: Tuff Boy Trailers
5151 Almondwood Rd, Manteca (95337-8868)
PHONE...................................209 239-1361
Martin Harris, *President*
John Cambra, *Vice Pres*
EMP: 44
SQ FT: 1,500
SALES (est): 5.1MM **Privately Held**
SIC: 3715 Semitrailers for truck tractors

(P-19835)
UNITED STATES LOGISTICS GROUP
Also Called: US Logistics
2700 Rose Ave Ste A, Signal Hill (90755-1929)
P.O. Box 10129, Glendale (91209-3129)
PHONE...................................562 989-9555
Khachatur Khudikyan, *CEO*
Chester Whisenant, *Manager*
EMP: 32
SALES (est): 5.7MM **Privately Held**
SIC: 3715 Truck trailers

(P-19836)
UNLIMITED TRCK TRLR MAINT INC
825 S Maple Ave Ste D, Montebello (90640-5400)
PHONE...................................323 727-2500
Yoan Leon, *President*
EMP: 25
SALES (est): 3.1MM **Privately Held**
SIC: 3715 Truck trailers

(P-19837)
UTILITY TRAILER MFG CO
Tautliner Division
17295 Railroad St Ste A, City of Industry (91748-1043)
PHONE...................................909 594-6026
Linda Baker, *Manager*
EMP: 315

SALES (corp-wide): 1.2B **Privately Held**
WEB: www.utm.com
SIC: 3715 5199 Truck trailers; tarpaulins
PA: Utility Trailer Manufacturing Company
17295 Railroad St Ste A
City Of Industry CA 91748
626 964-7319

(P-19838)
UTILITY TRAILER MFG CO
Also Called: Utility Trlr Sls Southern Cal
15567 Valley Blvd, Fontana (92335-6351)
PHONE...................................909 428-8300
Thayne Stanger, *Branch Mgr*
EMP: 45
SALES (corp-wide): 1.2B **Privately Held**
SIC: 3715 Semitrailers for truck tractors
PA: Utility Trailer Manufacturing Company
17295 Railroad St Ste A
City Of Industry CA 91748
626 964-7319

(P-19839)
VINTAGE TRANSPORT INC
161 Fair Ln, Placerville (95667-3929)
PHONE...................................530 622-3046
Lisa Nadeau, *President*
James Nadeau, *Vice Pres*
EMP: 11
SALES (est): 1.3MM **Privately Held**
WEB: www.vintagetransport.com
SIC: 3715 Demountable cargo containers

3716 Motor Homes

(P-19840)
B & B RV INC
Also Called: B&B Rv Center
3750 Auto Mall Dr, Anderson (96007-4929)
PHONE...................................530 365-7043
Marcu Lemoni, *CEO*
Brent Moody, *COO*
Melvin Flanagan, *CFO*
Karin Bell, *Admin Sec*
EMP: 20
SALES (est): 3.7MM
SALES (corp-wide): 4.7B **Publicly Held**
SIC: 3716 Recreational van conversion (self-propelled), factory basis
PA: Camping World Holdings, Inc.
250 Parkway Dr Ste 270
Lincolnshire IL 60069
847 808-3000

(P-19841)
CT COACHWORKS LLC
9700 Indiana Ave, Riverside (92503-5563)
PHONE...................................951 343-8787
Steven Thomas, *Principal*
Susan Thomas,
▲ EMP: 11
SALES (est): 2.4MM **Privately Held**
SIC: 3716 Recreational van conversion (self-propelled), factory basis

(P-19842)
FLEETWOOD MOTOR HOMES-CALIFINC (DH)
Also Called: Fleetwood Homes
3125 Myers St, Riverside (92503-5527)
P.O. Box 7638 (92513-7638)
PHONE...................................951 354-3000
Edward B Caudill, *CEO*
Elden L Smith, *President*
Boyd R Plowman, *CFO*
Lyle N Larkin, *Treasurer*
Christopher J Braun, *Senior VP*
▲ EMP: 37
SQ FT: 262,900
SALES (est): 91.2MM
SALES (corp-wide): 2.6B **Privately Held**
SIC: 3716 Motor homes
HQ: Fleetwood Enterprises, Inc.
1351 Pomona Rd Ste 230
Corona CA 92882
951 354-3000

(P-19843)
REXHALL INDUSTRIES INC
26857 Tannahill Ave, Canyon Country (91387-3969)
PHONE...................................661 726-5470
William Jonathan Rex, *Ch of Bd*
James C Rex, *Vice Pres*

Cheryl Rex, *Admin Sec*
▲ **EMP:** 46
SQ FT: 120,000
SALES (est): 7.5MM **Privately Held**
WEB: www.rexhall.com
SIC: 3716 Motor homes

(P-19844)
UNIVERSAL SPECIALTY VEHICLES
7879 Pine Crest Dr, Riverside (92506-5401)
PHONE..............................951 943-7747
Andrew Hall, *President*
Mary Hall, *Vice Pres*
EMP: 16
SQ FT: 14,000
SALES (est): 3.2MM **Privately Held**
WEB: www.usv1.com
SIC: 3716 Motor homes

3721 Aircraft

(P-19845)
ADVANCED TACTICS INC
3339 Airport Dr, Torrance (90505-6152)
PHONE..............................310 701-3659
Don Shaw, *President*
Lori K Tang, *Marketing Staff*
EMP: 12
SALES (est): 1.7MM **Privately Held**
SIC: 3721 Aircraft

(P-19846)
AERCAP US GLOBAL AVIATION LLC (HQ)
Also Called: Aercap Los Angeles
10250 Constellation Blvd, Los Angeles (90067-6200)
PHONE..............................310 788-1999
Sean Sullivan,
Keith Helming, *CFO*
Khalid Akhrif, *Vice Pres*
Dan Donahue, *Vice Pres*
Julie Harris, *Technology*
EMP: 23
SALES (est): 257.7MM
SALES (corp-wide): 52.7MM **Privately Held**
SIC: 3721 4581 6159 Aircraft; airport leasing, if operating airport; equipment & vehicle finance leasing companies
PA: Aercap Holdings N.V.
   Onbekend Nederlands Adres

   353 163-6065

(P-19847)
AERO CORPORATION
3061 Quail Run Rd, Los Alamitos (90720-2901)
PHONE..............................562 598-2281
J Strom, *President*
EMP: 20 **EST:** 2010
SALES (est): 1.3MM **Privately Held**
SIC: 3721 Aircraft

(P-19848)
AEROSYSNG INC
Also Called: Aerosystems Engineering
1112 W Barkley Ave, Orange (92868-1213)
PHONE..............................714 633-1901
Minna Chae, *Partner*
EMP: 10
SALES: 1.2MM **Privately Held**
SIC: 3721 Aircraft

(P-19849)
AEROVIRONMENT INC
1610 S Magnolia Ave, Monrovia (91016-4547)
PHONE..............................626 357-9983
Diaz Carmen, *Executive Asst*
Baker Gene, *Sales Mgr*
EMP: 58
SALES (corp-wide): 314.2MM **Publicly Held**
SIC: 3721 Aircraft
PA: Aerovironment, Inc.
   900 Innovators Way
   Simi Valley CA 93065
   805 581-2187

(P-19850)
AEROVIRONMENT INC (PA)
900 Innovators Way, Simi Valley (93065-2072)
P.O. Box 5031, Monrovia (91017-7131)
PHONE..............................805 581-2187
Wahid Nawabi, *President*
Brian Shackley, *CFO*
Stephen Page, *Bd of Directors*
Melissa Brown, *Vice Pres*
Brett Hush, *Vice Pres*
▲ **EMP:** 60
SQ FT: 85,000
SALES (est): 314.2MM **Publicly Held**
WEB: www.avinc.com
SIC: 3721 Gliders (aircraft)

(P-19851)
AEROVIRONMENT INC
1725 Peck Rd, Monrovia (91016)
PHONE..............................626 357-9983
Tim Conver, *Ch of Bd*
EMP: 11
SALES (corp-wide): 314.2MM **Publicly Held**
SIC: 3721 8711 Aircraft; engineering services
PA: Aerovironment, Inc.
   900 Innovators Way
   Simi Valley CA 93065
   805 581-2187

(P-19852)
AEROVIRONMENT INC
222 E Huntington Dr # 118, Monrovia (91016-8014)
PHONE..............................626 357-9983
Eric Sornborger, *Program Mgr*
Chuck Strawbridge, *Program Mgr*
Keith Kolb, *Software Engr*
Jeff Roper, *Engineer*
Kelly Ramirez, *Senior Engr*
EMP: 29
SALES (corp-wide): 314.2MM **Publicly Held**
SIC: 3721 Aircraft
PA: Aerovironment, Inc.
   900 Innovators Way
   Simi Valley CA 93065
   805 581-2187

(P-19853)
AEROVIRONMENT INC
2290 Agate Ct, Simi Valley (93065-1935)
PHONE..............................626 357-9983
David Villa, *Manager*
EMP: 10
SALES (corp-wide): 314.2MM **Publicly Held**
SIC: 3721 1541 Aircraft; industrial buildings & warehouses
PA: Aerovironment, Inc.
   900 Innovators Way
   Simi Valley CA 93065
   805 581-2187

(P-19854)
AEROVIRONMENT INC
825 S Myrtle Ave, Monrovia (91016-3424)
PHONE..............................626 357-9983
Stewart Hindle, *Manager*
Richard Childress, *Info Tech Dir*
Ronald Norton, *Engineer*
EMP: 20
SALES (corp-wide): 314.2MM **Publicly Held**
WEB: www.avinc.com
SIC: 3721 Aircraft
PA: Aerovironment, Inc.
   900 Innovators Way
   Simi Valley CA 93065
   805 581-2187

(P-19855)
AMERICAN SCENCE TECH AS T CORP (PA)
50 California St Fl 21, San Francisco (94111-4624)
P.O. Box 9148, Laguna Beach (92652-7142)
PHONE..............................415 251-2800
James Johnson, *President*
Jake Soujah, *President*
EMP: 135

SALES: 348MM **Privately Held**
SIC: 3721 3724 3761 3764 Aircraft; aircraft engines & engine parts; guided missiles & space vehicles; guided missile & space vehicle propulsion unit parts; guided missile & space vehicle parts & auxiliary equipment

(P-19856)
AMERICAN SCENCE TECH AS T CORP
2372 Morse Ave Ste 571, Irvine (92614-6234)
PHONE..............................310 773-1978
Kinda Assouad, *Branch Mgr*
EMP: 85
SALES (corp-wide): 348MM **Privately Held**
SIC: 3721 3724 3761 3764 Aircraft; aircraft engines & engine parts; guided missiles & space vehicles; guided missile & space vehicle propulsion unit parts; guided missile & space vehicle parts & auxiliary equipment
PA: American Science & Technology (As&T) Corporation
   50 California St Fl 21
   San Francisco CA 94111
   415 251-2800

(P-19857)
APM MANUFACTURING (HQ)
Also Called: Anaheim Precision Shtmtl Mfg
1738 N Neville St, Orange (92865-4214)
PHONE..............................714 453-0100
Anthony Puccio, *CEO*
Joe Puccio, *COO*
Gilles Madelmont, *CFO*
EMP: 116
SQ FT: 57,000
SALES: 9.5MM
SALES (corp-wide): 14.7MM **Privately Held**
WEB: www.anaheimprecision.com
SIC: 3721 3444 3728 3479 Motorized aircraft; culverts, flumes & pipes; aircraft body & wing assemblies & parts; aircraft landing assemblies & brakes; aircraft assemblies, subassemblies & parts; etching & engraving; machine & other job shop work
PA: Manufacturing Solutions, Inc.
   1738 N Neville St
   Orange CA 92865
   714 453-0100

(P-19858)
ASTRAEUS AEROSPACE LLC
16255 Ventura Blvd # 625, Encino (91436-2302)
PHONE..............................310 907-9205
David Wagreich, *CEO*
Sariah Dorbin,
EMP: 12
SALES (est): 487.7K **Privately Held**
SIC: 3721 Research & development on aircraft by the manufacturer

(P-19859)
BOEING COMPANY
Lemoore Nval Base Hnger 1, Lemoore (93245)
P.O. Box 1160 (93245-1160)
PHONE..............................559 998-8260
George Baldwin, *Manager*
EMP: 50
SALES (corp-wide): 101.1B **Publicly Held**
SIC: 3721 Aircraft
PA: The Boeing Company
   100 N Riverside Plz
   Chicago IL 60606
   312 544-2000

(P-19860)
BOEING COMPANY
22308 Harbor Ridge Ln, Torrance (90502-2451)
PHONE..............................310 662-7286
EMP: 1005
SALES (corp-wide): 101.1B **Publicly Held**
SIC: 3721 Airplanes, fixed or rotary wing; helicopters; research & development on aircraft by the manufacturer

PA: The Boeing Company
   100 N Riverside Plz
   Chicago IL 60606
   312 544-2000

(P-19861)
BOEING COMPANY
2201 Seal Beach Blvd, Seal Beach (90740-5603)
PHONE..............................562 797-5831
James Albaugh, *Branch Mgr*
EMP: 1000
SALES (corp-wide): 101.1B **Publicly Held**
SIC: 3721 Aircraft
PA: The Boeing Company
   100 N Riverside Plz
   Chicago IL 60606
   312 544-2000

(P-19862)
BOEING COMPANY
5463 Plumeria Ln, Cypress (90630-7912)
PHONE..............................714 952-1509
EMP: 895
SALES (corp-wide): 101.1B **Publicly Held**
SIC: 3721 Airplanes, fixed or rotary wing
PA: The Boeing Company
   100 N Riverside Plz
   Chicago IL 60606
   312 544-2000

(P-19863)
BOEING COMPANY
24172 Via Madrugada, Mission Viejo (92692-1907)
PHONE..............................949 452-0259
EMP: 895
SALES (corp-wide): 101.1B **Publicly Held**
SIC: 3721 Airplanes, fixed or rotary wing
PA: The Boeing Company
   100 N Riverside Plz
   Chicago IL 60606
   312 544-2000

(P-19864)
BOEING COMPANY
122 E Jones Rd Bldg 151, Edwards (93524-8202)
PHONE..............................661 810-4686
Kenneth R Westman, *CEO*
EMP: 1005
SALES (corp-wide): 101.1B **Publicly Held**
SIC: 3721 Airplanes, fixed or rotary wing; helicopters; research & development on aircraft by the manufacturer
PA: The Boeing Company
   100 N Riverside Plz
   Chicago IL 60606
   312 544-2000

(P-19865)
BOEING COMPANY
3521 E Spring St, Long Beach (90806-2431)
PHONE..............................714 317-1070
Cesar Quintanilla, *Engineer*
Agustin Romo, *Internal Med*
EMP: 996
SALES (corp-wide): 101.1B **Publicly Held**
SIC: 3721 Airplanes, fixed or rotary wing
PA: The Boeing Company
   100 N Riverside Plz
   Chicago IL 60606
   312 544-2000

(P-19866)
BOEING COMPANY
2400 E Wardlow Rd, Long Beach (90807-5310)
PHONE..............................562 593-6668
EMP: 996
SALES (corp-wide): 101.1B **Publicly Held**
SIC: 3721 Airplanes, fixed or rotary wing
PA: The Boeing Company
   100 N Riverside Plz
   Chicago IL 60606
   312 544-2000

▲ = Import ▼=Export
◆ =Import/Export

(P-19867)
BOEING COMPANY
12203 Hillwood Dr, Whittier (90604-3109)
PHONE..................................562 944-6583
EMP: 895
SALES (corp-wide): 101.1B **Publicly
Held**
SIC: 3721 Airplanes, fixed or rotary wing
PA: The Boeing Company
100 N Riverside Plz
Chicago IL 60606
312 544-2000

(P-19868)
BOEING COMPANY
3460 Cherry Ave Bldg 56, Long Beach
(90807-4912)
PHONE..................................562 425-3613
EMP: 996
SALES (corp-wide): 101.1B **Publicly
Held**
SIC: 3721 Airplanes, fixed or rotary wing
PA: The Boeing Company
100 N Riverside Plz
Chicago IL 60606
312 544-2000

(P-19869)
BOEING COMPANY
18310 Readiness St, Victorville
(92394-7911)
PHONE..................................760 246-0273
Ray Rich, *Manager*
EMP: 996
SALES (corp-wide): 101.1B **Publicly
Held**
SIC: 3721 Airplanes, fixed or rotary wing
PA: The Boeing Company
100 N Riverside Plz
Chicago IL 60606
312 544-2000

(P-19870)
BOEING COMPANY
15400 Graham St Ste 101, Huntington
Beach (92649-1257)
PHONE..................................714 934-9801
Ray Murillo, *Branch Mgr*
EMP: 996
SALES (corp-wide): 101.1B **Publicly
Held**
SIC: 3721 Airplanes, fixed or rotary wing
PA: The Boeing Company
100 N Riverside Plz
Chicago IL 60606
312 544-2000

(P-19871)
BOEING COMPANY
222 N Pacific Coast Hwy # 2050, El Se-
gundo (90245-5660)
PHONE..................................310 426-4100
Barry Waldman, *Manager*
EMP: 100
SALES (corp-wide): 101.1B **Publicly
Held**
SIC: 3721 Airplanes, fixed or rotary wing
PA: The Boeing Company
100 N Riverside Plz
Chicago IL 60606
312 544-2000

(P-19872)
BOEING COMPANY
5301 Bolsa Ave, Huntington Beach
(92647-2048)
PHONE..................................714 896-3311
Jim Albaugh, *Branch Mgr*
EMP: 996
SALES (corp-wide): 101.1B **Publicly
Held**
SIC: 3721 3761 Airplanes, fixed or rotary
wing; guided missiles & space vehicles
PA: The Boeing Company
100 N Riverside Plz
Chicago IL 60606
312 544-2000

(P-19873)
BOEING COMPANY
4000 N Lakewood Blvd, Long Beach
(90808-1700)
PHONE..................................562 496-1000
Nan Bouchard, *Vice Pres*
Troy Ball, *Partner*
Keith Bruno, *Program Mgr*

Kambiz Moghaddam, *Program Mgr*
Sandra Cossio, *Executive Asst*
EMP: 2000
SALES (corp-wide): 101.1B **Publicly
Held**
SIC: 3721 Airplanes, fixed or rotary wing
PA: The Boeing Company
100 N Riverside Plz
Chicago IL 60606
312 544-2000

(P-19874)
BOEING COMPANY
5301 Bolsa Ave, Huntington Beach
(92647-2048)
PHONE..................................714 896-1301
Dave Bullock, *CFO*
EMP: 559
SALES (corp-wide): 101.1B **Publicly
Held**
SIC: 3721 Aircraft
PA: The Boeing Company
100 N Riverside Plz
Chicago IL 60606
312 544-2000

(P-19875)
BOEING COMPANY
4000 N Lakewood Blvd, Long Beach
(90808-1700)
P.O. Box 200 (90801-0200)
PHONE..................................562 593-5511
Linda Van Reeden, *Manager*
Carola Najera, *Office Admin*
Wael Elaref, *Project Mgr*
Kimberly De La Torre, *Technical Staff*
Craig Anderson, *Engineer*
EMP: 1400
SALES (corp-wide): 101.1B **Publicly
Held**
SIC: 3721 Airplanes, fixed or rotary wing
PA: The Boeing Company
100 N Riverside Plz
Chicago IL 60606
312 544-2000

(P-19876)
BOEING COMPANY
14441 Astronautics Ln, Huntington Beach
(92647-2080)
PHONE..................................714 896-1670
EMP: 996
SALES (corp-wide): 101.1B **Publicly
Held**
SIC: 3721 Airplanes, fixed or rotary wing
PA: The Boeing Company
100 N Riverside Plz
Chicago IL 60606
312 544-2000

(P-19877)
BOEING COMPANY
451 1st St, Travis Afb (94535-2186)
P.O. Box 1415 (94535-0415)
PHONE..................................707 437-8574
Steve Andrews, *Branch Mgr*
EMP: 996
SALES (corp-wide): 101.1B **Publicly
Held**
SIC: 3721 Airplanes, fixed or rotary wing
PA: The Boeing Company
100 N Riverside Plz
Chicago IL 60606
312 544-2000

(P-19878)
BOEING COMPANY
5301 Bolsa Ave, Huntington Beach
(92647-2048)
PHONE..................................714 896-1839
John Vaswani, *Vice Pres*
EMP: 3500
SALES (corp-wide): 101.1B **Publicly
Held**
SIC: 3721 Aircraft
PA: The Boeing Company
100 N Riverside Plz
Chicago IL 60606
312 544-2000

(P-19879)
BOEING COMPANY
5222 Rancho Rd, Huntington Beach
(92647-2052)
PHONE..................................714 896-3311
Paula Hutt, *Branch Mgr*

EMP: 30
SALES (corp-wide): 101.1B **Publicly
Held**
SIC: 3721 Aircraft
PA: The Boeing Company
100 N Riverside Plz
Chicago IL 60606
312 544-2000

(P-19880)
BOEING COMPANY
1700 E Imperial Ave, El Segundo
(90245-2646)
PHONE..................................310 416-9319
Joe Buford, *Principal*
Joe N Buford, *Principal*
EMP: 996
SALES (corp-wide): 101.1B **Publicly
Held**
SIC: 3721 Airplanes, fixed or rotary wing
PA: The Boeing Company
100 N Riverside Plz
Chicago IL 60606
312 544-2000

(P-19881)
BOEING COMPANY
8900 De Soto Ave, Canoga Park
(91304-1967)
PHONE..................................818 428-1154
Archi Burds, *Principal*
EMP: 1005
SALES (corp-wide): 101.1B **Publicly
Held**
SIC: 3721 Airplanes, fixed or rotary wing
PA: The Boeing Company
100 N Riverside Plz
Chicago IL 60606
312 544-2000

(P-19882)
BOEING COMPANY
5250 Tanker Way, March ARB
(92518-1748)
PHONE..................................951 571-0122
EMP: 996
SALES (corp-wide): 101.1B **Publicly
Held**
SIC: 3721 Airplanes, fixed or rotary wing
PA: The Boeing Company
100 N Riverside Plz
Chicago IL 60606
312 544-2000

(P-19883)
BOEING INTELLECTUAL
3501 Bolsa Ave, Huntington Beach (92647)
PHONE..................................562 797-2020
Gary Black, *Officer*
Chia-WEI Chow, *Vice Pres*
Lacey Jones, *Vice Pres*
Russell Kuchynka, *Vice Pres*
Wayne Howe, *Program Mgr*
EMP: 28
SALES (est): 3.2MM
SALES (corp-wide): 101.1B **Publicly
Held**
SIC: 3721 Airplanes, fixed or rotary wing;
helicopters; research & development on
aircraft by the manufacturer
PA: The Boeing Company
100 N Riverside Plz
Chicago IL 60606
312 544-2000

(P-19884)
**BOEING SATELLITE SYSTEMS
INC**
2300 E Imperial Hwy, El Segundo
(90245-2813)
P.O. Box 92919, Los Angeles (90009-2919)
PHONE..................................310 568-2735
Steve Tsukamoto, *Manager*
Pamela Campadonia, *Purch Mgr*
Diane Safarik, *Buyer*
Jesse Arroyo, *Manager*
Irina Dubovitsky, *Manager*
EMP: 10
SALES (corp-wide): 101.1B **Publicly
Held**
SIC: 3721 Aircraft
HQ: Boeing Satellite Systems, Inc.
900 N Pacific Coast Hwy
El Segundo CA 90245

(P-19885)
**BOEING SATELLITE SYSTEMS
INC**
1950 E Imperial Hwy, El Segundo
(90245-2701)
PHONE..................................310 364-6444
Patrick Bailleul, *Manager*
Michael Bohman, *Design Engr*
Mike Trujillo, *Engineer*
Paul Ajari, *Senior Engr*
Dorica Stroe, *Accountant*
EMP: 22
SQ FT: 36,220
SALES (corp-wide): 101.1B **Publicly
Held**
SIC: 3721 Aircraft
HQ: Boeing Satellite Systems, Inc.
900 N Pacific Coast Hwy
El Segundo CA 90245

(P-19886)
CALIFORNIA BLIMPS
738 W 17th St Ste D, Costa Mesa
(92627-4340)
PHONE..................................949 650-1183
Paul Pacelli, *Owner*
EMP: 10
SQ FT: 1,900
SALES (est): 1MM **Privately Held**
WEB: www.californiablimps.com
SIC: 3721 Blimps

(P-19887)
CHIPTON-ROSS INC
420 Culver Blvd, Playa Del Rey
(90293-7706)
PHONE..................................310 414-7800
Judith Hinkley, *President*
Morgan Amic, *Administration*
Carla Bernal, *Administration*
Tama Nathanson, *Administration*
Chris Guldimann, *CIO*
EMP: 100
SQ FT: 6,000
SALES: 9MM **Privately Held**
SIC: 3721 3731 8731 7363 Motorized
aircraft; military ships, building & repair-
ing; commercial physical research; tem-
porary help service; engineering services

(P-19888)
**CLEAN WAVE MANAGEMENT
INC**
Also Called: Impact Bearing
1291 Puerta Del Sol, San Clemente
(92673-6310)
PHONE..................................949 488-2922
Fax: 949 488-2923
▲ EMP: 15
SALES (est): 2.1MM **Privately Held**
WEB: www.aircraftbearing.com
SIC: 3721

(P-19889)
CNS AVIATION INC
1240 N Simon Cir, Anaheim (92806-1814)
PHONE..................................714 901-7072
Scott David Dantuono, *President*
EMP: 10
SALES (est): 2.1MM **Privately Held**
SIC: 3721 Aircraft

(P-19890)
**COMAC AMERICA
CORPORATION**
4350 Von Karman Ave # 400, Newport
Beach (92660-2007)
PHONE..................................760 616-9614
WEI Ye, *CEO*
EMP: 15
SALES (est): 1.4MM
SALES (corp-wide): 855.9MM **Privately
Held**
SIC: 3721 Aircraft
PA: Commercial Aircraft Corporation Of
China, Ltd.
China Commercial Aircraft Mansion,
No. 1919 Shibo Avenue, Pudong
Shanghai 20012
212 088-8888

(P-19891)
DAYTON SUPERIOR
CORPORATION
10780 Mulberry Ave, Fontana
(92337-7062)
PHONE............................909 957-7271
EMP: 30
SALES (corp-wide): 43B Publicly Held
SIC: 3721 Aircraft
HQ: Dayton Superior Corporation
1125 Byers Rd
Miamisburg OH 45342
937 866-0711

(P-19892)
ES3 PRIME LOGISTICS GROUP
INC (PA)
550 W C St Ste 1630, San Diego
(92101-3569)
PHONE............................619 338-0380
Teri Sgammato, Ch of Bd
Doug Wiser, COO
Chuck Dahms, CFO
Brett Bailey, CIO
Clint Forrest, CTO
EMP: 16
SALES (est): 3.1MM Privately Held
SIC: 3721 8711 Aircraft; engineering services

(P-19893)
EXPERIMENTAL AIRCRAFT
ASSN
7026 Lasaine Ave, Van Nuys (91406-3544)
PHONE............................818 705-2744
Charles Ducat, President
EMP: 12
SALES (est): 871.5K Privately Held
SIC: 3721 Aircraft

(P-19894)
GDAS-LINCOLN INC
Also Called: Gulfstream California
1501 Aviation Blvd, Lincoln (95648-9388)
PHONE............................916 645-8961
David Pearman, General Mgr
EMP: 53
SALES (est): 7.9MM Privately Held
SIC: 3721 Aircraft

(P-19895)
GENERAL ATOMIC AERON
14040 Danielson St, Poway (92064-6857)
PHONE............................858 455-4560
EMP: 15 Privately Held
SIC: 3721 Aircraft
HQ: General Atomics Aeronautical Systems, Inc.
14200 Kirkham Way
Poway CA 92064
-

(P-19896)
GENERAL ATOMIC AERON
13330 Evening Creek Dr N, San Diego
(92128-4110)
PHONE............................858 964-6700
Neal Blue, President
Saleha Saidani, Design Engr
Roland Hogue, Opers Staff
EMP: 500 Privately Held
SIC: 3721 Aircraft
HQ: General Atomics Aeronautical Systems, Inc.
14200 Kirkham Way
Poway CA 92064
-

(P-19897)
GENERAL ATOMIC AERON
9779 Yucca Rd, Adelanto (92301-2265)
PHONE............................760 246-3660
Jim Machin, Manager
EMP: 135 Privately Held
WEB: www.ga-asi.com
SIC: 3721 Aircraft
HQ: General Atomics Aeronautical Systems, Inc.
14200 Kirkham Way
Poway CA 92064

(P-19898)
GENERAL ATOMIC AERON
3550 General Atomics Ct, San Diego
(92121-1122)
PHONE............................858 455-2810
Brian Hornby, Administration
Bruce Trumbo, Info Tech Mgr
Susie Khuu, Technical Staff
Electrical Rodriguez, Engineer
Marcel Danko, VP Finance
EMP: 500 Privately Held
SIC: 3721 Aircraft
HQ: General Atomics Aeronautical Systems, Inc.
14200 Kirkham Way
Poway CA 92064

(P-19899)
GENERAL ATOMIC AERON
Mission Systems
16761 Via Del Campo Ct, San Diego
(92127-1713)
PHONE............................858 455-4309
Cyndra Flanagen, Director
Michael Neale, President
Ross Malmberg, Program Mgr
Charles Wright, Program Mgr
Andrew Hausner, Admin Asst
EMP: 500 Privately Held
WEB: www.ga-asi.com
SIC: 3721 Aircraft
HQ: General Atomics Aeronautical Systems, Inc.
14200 Kirkham Way
Poway CA 92064
-

(P-19900)
GENERAL ATOMIC AERON
73 El Mirage Airport Rd B, Adelanto
(92301-9540)
PHONE............................760 388-8208
Gary Bener, Branch Mgr
EMP: 200
SQ FT: 34,425 Privately Held
WEB: www.generalatomics.com
SIC: 3721 Aircraft
HQ: General Atomics Aeronautical Systems, Inc.
14200 Kirkham Way
Poway CA 92064
-

(P-19901)
GENERAL ATOMIC AERON (DH)
Also Called: US Gov GA Aeronautical Uav
14200 Kirkham Way, Poway (92064-7103)
PHONE............................858 312-2810
Neal Blue, President
Tony Navarra, Treasurer
Brad Clark, Vice Pres
Stacy Jakuttis, Vice Pres
Stephen Bell, Program Mgr
◆ EMP: 500
SQ FT: 900,000
SALES (est): 1.6B Privately Held
WEB: www.ga-asi.com
SIC: 3721 Aircraft

(P-19902)
GENERAL ATOMIC AERON
14115 Stowe Dr, Poway (92064-7145)
PHONE............................858 312-2543
Deborah Mettas, Contractor
EMP: 500 Privately Held
SIC: 3721 Aircraft
HQ: General Atomics Aeronautical Systems, Inc.
14200 Kirkham Way
Poway CA 92064
-

(P-19903)
GENERAL ELECTRIC COMPANY
18000 Phantom St, Victorville
(92394-7913)
PHONE............................760 530-5200
John Hardell, Principal
Dave Kiehl, Engineer
Noah Demerly, Maintence Staff
EMP: 50
SALES (corp-wide): 121.6B Publicly Held
SIC: 3721 Aircraft

PA: General Electric Company
41 Farnsworth St
Boston MA 02210
617 443-3000

(P-19904)
GULF STREAMS
4150 E Donald Douglas Dr, Long Beach
(90808-1725)
PHONE............................562 420-1818
Mike Kambourian, Owner
Thomas Anderson, General Mgr
Andrew Miller, Network Analyst
Mike Anderson, Buyer
Jim Curby, Safety Mgr
▲ EMP: 19
SALES (est): 3.5MM Privately Held
SIC: 3721 Aircraft

(P-19905)
GULFSTREAM AEROSPACE
CORP GA
9818 Mina Ave, Whittier (90605-3035)
PHONE............................562 907-9300
EMP: 1189
SALES (corp-wide): 36.1B Publicly Held
SIC: 3721 Airplanes, fixed or rotary wing
HQ: Gulfstream Aerospace Corporation (Georgia)
500 Gulfstream Rd
Savannah GA 31408
912 965-3000

(P-19906)
IMPOSSIBLE AEROSPACE CORP
2222 Ronald St, Santa Clara (95050-2846)
PHONE............................707 293-9367
Albert Spencer Gore, CEO
EMP: 15
SALES (est): 2.6MM Privately Held
SIC: 3721 Aircraft

(P-19907)
JETEFFECT INC (PA)
3250 Airflite Way Fl 3, Long Beach
(90807-5312)
PHONE............................562 989-8800
Bryan Comstock, President
Walt Wakefield, Exec VP
Kari Chandler, Office Mgr
John Padrick, Sales Dir
Chris Warners, Sales Dir
EMP: 10 EST: 2001
SALES (est): 1.4MM Privately Held
WEB: www.jeteffect.com
SIC: 3721 Aircraft

(P-19908)
JVR SHEETMETAL
FABRICATION INC
Also Called: Talsco
7101 Patterson Dr, Garden Grove
(92841-1415)
PHONE............................714 841-2464
Jose Castaneda, CEO
EMP: 33
SQ FT: 1,000
SALES: 3.8MM Privately Held
SIC: 3721 Aircraft

(P-19909)
KAY AND ASSOCIATES INC
300 Reeves Blvd, Lemoore (93246-7400)
PHONE............................559 410-0917
Gregory Kay, President
Dianna Chinn Heinz, CFO
EMP: 40
SALES (est): 1.8MM Privately Held
SIC: 3721 Aircraft

(P-19910)
KOREA AEROSPACE
INDUSTRIES LTD
16700 Valley View Ave # 205, La Mirada
(90638-5852)
PHONE............................714 868-8560
Jy Moon, Branch Mgr
EMP: 11 Privately Held
WEB: www.samsungamerica.com
SIC: 3721 Aircraft
PA: Korea Aerospace Industries. Ltd
78 Gongdan 1-Ro, Sanam-Myeon
Sacheon 52529

(P-19911)
LOCKHEED MARTIN (HQ)
1111 Lockheed Martin Way, Sunnyvale
(94089-1212)
PHONE............................408 834-9741
Dave Turkington, Principal
EMP: 33
SALES (est): 8.5MM Publicly Held
SIC: 3721 Aircraft

(P-19912)
LOCKHEED MARTIN
CORPORATION
2655 S Macarthur Dr, Tracy (95376-8188)
PHONE............................408 756-3008
EMP: 430
SALES (corp-wide): 45.3B Publicly Held
SIC: 3721
PA: Lockheed Martin Corporation
6801 Rockledge Dr
Bethesda MD 20817
301 897-6000

(P-19913)
LOCKHEED MARTIN
CORPORATION
1374 Holland Ct, San Jose (95118-3423)
PHONE............................408 742-5219
EMP: 430
SALES (corp-wide): 47.1B Publicly Held
SIC: 3721
PA: Lockheed Martin Corporation
6801 Rockledge Dr
Bethesda MD 20817
301 897-6000

(P-19914)
LOCKHEED MARTIN
CORPORATION
1330 30th St Ste A, San Diego
(92154-3471)
PHONE............................619 298-8453
EMP: 435
SALES (corp-wide): 46.1B Publicly Held
SIC: 3721
PA: Lockheed Martin Corporation
6801 Rockledge Dr
Bethesda MD 20817
301 897-6000

(P-19915)
MISSION RESEARCH
CORPORATION (DH)
Also Called: Atk Mission Research
6750 Navigator Way # 200, Goleta
(93117-3657)
PHONE............................805 690-2447
Kevin Vogel, Principal
Jeff Vosburgh, Vice Pres
Patrick Figge, Senior Mgr
EMP: 10
SQ FT: 40,000
SALES (est): 15.8MM Publicly Held
WEB: www.mrcla.com
SIC: 3721 Research & development on aircraft by the manufacturer
HQ: Northrop Grumman Innovation Systems, Inc.
45101 Warp Dr
Dulles VA 20166
703 406-5000

(P-19916)
MOLLER INTERNATIONAL INC
1855 N 1st St Unit C, Dixon (95620-9758)
PHONE............................530 756-5086
Paul S Moller, President
Jim Toreson, Chairman
Faulkner White, Corp Secy
EMP: 12
SQ FT: 13,000
SALES: 500K Privately Held
SIC: 3721 3724 Aircraft; aircraft engines & engine parts; research & development on aircraft engines & parts

(P-19917)
NORTHROP GRUMMAN
SYSTEMS CORP
Also Called: Electronic Systems Co Esco
401 E Hendy Ave, Sunnyvale (94086-5100)
P.O. Box 3499 (94088-3499)
PHONE............................408 735-2241
William Pitts, Branch Mgr

▲ = Import ▼=Export
◆ =Import/Export

Rudy Quejado, *General Mgr*
Hanif Subedar, *Engrg Dir*
William Ho, *Technical Staff*
Rick Leon, *Project Engr*
EMP: 305 **Publicly Held**
WEB: www.sperry.ngc.com
SIC: 3721 Motorized aircraft; research &
development on aircraft by the manufac-
turer
HQ: Northrop Grumman Systems Corpora-
tion
2980 Fairview Park Dr
Falls Church VA 22042
703 280-2900

(P-19918)
**NORTHROP GRUMMAN
SYSTEMS CORP**
Also Called: Air Combat Systems
3520 E Avenue M, Palmdale (93550-7401)
PHONE..............................661 272-7000
David G Hogarth, *Manager*
Alex Welsh, *Bd of Directors*
Patricia Helke, *Administration*
Yvonne Ramirez, *Technical Staff*
William Ekstrand, *Engineer*
EMP: 300 **Publicly Held**
WEB: www.sperry.ngc.com
SIC: 3721 3812 3761 Aircraft; search &
navigation equipment; guided missiles &
space vehicles
HQ: Northrop Grumman Systems Corpora-
tion
2980 Fairview Park Dr
Falls Church VA 22042
703 280-2900

(P-19919)
**NORTHROP GRUMMAN
SYSTEMS CORP**
1 Hornet Way, El Segundo (90245-2804)
PHONE..............................310 332-1000
Kevin Witherell, *Principal*
EMP: 200 **Publicly Held**
WEB: www.sperry.ngc.com
SIC: 3721 Aircraft
HQ: Northrop Grumman Systems Corpora-
tion
2980 Fairview Park Dr
Falls Church VA 22042
703 280-2900

(P-19920)
**NORTHROP GRUMMAN
SYSTEMS CORP**
Also Called: Northrop Grumman Mar Systems
401 E Hendy Ave Ms33-3, Sunnyvale
(94086-5100)
P.O. Box 3499 (94088-3499)
PHONE..............................408 735-3011
J Hupton, *Branch Mgr*
Gary Murray, *Software Engr*
David Fursh, *Engineer*
Nandor Horvath, *Engineer*
John Hultin, *Engineer*
EMP: 1000 **Publicly Held**
WEB: www.sperry.ngc.com
SIC: 3721 3519 3511 Aircraft; internal
combustion engines; turbines & turbine
generator sets
HQ: Northrop Grumman Systems Corpora-
tion
2980 Fairview Park Dr
Falls Church VA 22042
703 280-2900

(P-19921)
**NORTHROP GRUMMAN
SYSTEMS CORP**
Also Called: Aerospace Systems
1 Space Park Blvd, Redondo Beach
(90278-1071)
PHONE..............................310 812-1089
Gary Ervin, *Branch Mgr*
Dora Cabrera, *Administration*
Theodore Lau, *Planning*
Philip Hutson, *Software Engr*
Thomas Le, *Software Engr*
EMP: 305 **Publicly Held**

SIC: 3721 3761 3728 3812 Airplanes,
fixed or rotary wing; research & development on aircraft by the manufacturer;
guided missiles, complete; guided missiles & space vehicles, research & development; fuselage assembly, aircraft; wing
assemblies & parts, aircraft; research &
dev by manuf., aircraft parts & auxiliary
equip; inertial guidance systems; gyroscopes; warfare counter-measure equipment; search & detection systems &
instruments; test equipment for electronic
& electrical circuits; aircraft servicing & repairing
HQ: Northrop Grumman Systems Corporation
2980 Fairview Park Dr
Falls Church VA 22042
703 280-2900

(P-19922)
**NORTHROP GRUMMAN
SYSTEMS CORP**
1 Space Park Blvd D, Redondo Beach
(90278-1071)
PHONE..............................310 812-4321
Bruce Gaines, *Principal*
Michelle Costley, *Admin Sec*
Susan Christie, *Admin Asst*
Edison Bautista, *Administration*
Walter Freeman, *Info Tech Mgr*
EMP: 305 **Publicly Held**
SIC: 3721 3761 3728 Airplanes, fixed or
rotary wing; research & development on
aircraft by the manufacturer; guided missiles, complete; guided missiles & space
vehicles, research & development; fuselage assembly, aircraft; wing assemblies
& parts, aircraft; research & dev by
manuf., aircraft parts & auxiliary equip
HQ: Northrop Grumman Systems Corporation
2980 Fairview Park Dr
Falls Church VA 22042
703 280-2900

(P-19923)
POSITEX INC
2569 Mccabe Way Ste 210, Irvine
(92614-5220)
PHONE..............................307 201-0601
Mark Azzarito, *Principal*
EMP: 11 **EST:** 2016
SALES (est): 453.6K **Privately Held**
SIC: 3721 Aircraft

(P-19924)
**PRECISION AEROFORM
CORPORATION**
12619 Hoover St, Garden Grove
(92841-4170)
PHONE..............................714 725-6611
Lynn Nguyen, *CEO*
Thanh Quang, *CFO*
Loan Hong, *General Mgr*
EMP: 12
SALES: 500K **Privately Held**
SIC: 3721 Airships

(P-19925)
QUALITY TECH MFG INC
170 W Mindanao St, Bloomington
(92316-2946)
PHONE..............................909 465-9565
Rudolph A Gutierrez, *President*
Camilio Gutierrez, *Vice Pres*
Danielle Alacron, *Administration*
Chris Gutierrez, *Engineer*
EMP: 37
SQ FT: 18,000
SALES (est): 6.3MM **Privately Held**
WEB: www.qualitytechmfg.com
SIC: 3721 Aircraft

(P-19926)
**QUICKSILVER AERONAUTICS
LLC**
40084 Villa Venecia, Temecula
(92591-1667)
PHONE..............................951 506-0061
Guillermo F Escutia Nunez,
Daniel Perez Munoz,
EMP: 10
SALES (est): 1.5MM **Privately Held**
WEB: www.quicksilveraircraft.com
SIC: 3721 Aircraft

(P-19927)
ROBERT GROVE
Also Called: Grove Aircraft Co
1860 Joe Crosson Dr, El Cajon
(92020-1227)
PHONE..............................619 562-1268
Robert Grove, *Owner*
▲ **EMP:** 12
SALES (est): 650K **Privately Held**
WEB: www.groveaircraft.com
SIC: 3721 8748 Aircraft; test development
& evaluation service

(P-19928)
**ROBINSON HELICOPTER CO
INC**
2901 Airport Dr, Torrance (90505-6115)
PHONE..............................310 539-0508
Kurt L Robinson, *CEO*
Frank Robinson, *President*
Tim Goetz, *CFO*
Daniel Huesca, *Technical Staff*
P Wayne Walden, *VP Mfg*
◆ **EMP:** 970 **EST:** 1973
SQ FT: 260,000
SALES (est): 222.6MM **Privately Held**
WEB: www.robinsonheli.com
SIC: 3721 Helicopters

(P-19929)
**SAN-JOAQUIN HELICOPTERS
INC**
Also Called: S J Helicopter Service
1408 S Lexington St, Delano (93215-9783)
PHONE..............................661 725-6603
Jim Josephson, *Branch Mgr*
EMP: 10
SALES (corp-wide): 39.2MM **Privately
Held**
WEB: www.sjhelicopters.com
SIC: 3721 Helicopters
PA: San-Joaquin Helicopters Inc.
1408 S Lexington St
Delano CA 93215
661 725-1898

(P-19930)
SCALED COMPOSITES LLC
1624 Flight Line, Mojave (93501-1663)
PHONE..............................661 824-4541
Kevin Mickey, *President*
Mark Taylor, *CFO*
Cory Bird, *Vice Pres*
Ben Diachun, *Vice Pres*
Jason Kelley, *Vice Pres*
EMP: 500
SQ FT: 160,000
SALES (est): 228.1MM **Publicly Held**
WEB: www.scaled.com
SIC: 3721 3999 8711 Aircraft; models, ex-
cept toy; aviation &/or aeronautical engi-
neering
HQ: Northrop Grumman Systems Corpora-
tion
2980 Fairview Park Dr
Falls Church VA 22042
703 280-2900

(P-19931)
**SOARING AMERICA
CORPORATION**
Also Called: Mooney International
8354 Kimball Ave F360, Chino
(91708-9267)
P.O. Box 2937, Chino Hills (91709-0098)
PHONE..............................909 270-2628
Cheng-Yuan Jerry Chen, *CEO*
Albert LI, *CFO*
EMP: 45
SALES (est): 9.7MM **Privately Held**
SIC: 3721 3728 Research & development
on aircraft by the manufacturer; motorized
aircraft; research & dev by manuf., aircraft
parts & auxiliary equip

(P-19932)
SPORT KITES INC
Also Called: Wills Wing
500 W Blueridge Ave, Orange
(92865-4206)
PHONE..............................714 998-6359
Steven Pearson, *President*
Michael Meier, *Vice Pres*
Linda Meier, *Admin Sec*
▲ **EMP:** 18 **EST:** 1973

SQ FT: 16,000
SALES: 3.5MM **Privately Held**
SIC: 3721 Hang gliders

(P-19933)
TDL AERO ENTERPRISES
44 Macready Dr, Merced (95341-6405)
P.O. Box 249, Hilmar (95324-0249)
PHONE..............................209 722-7300
Tom Lopez, *President*
EMP: 19
SALES (est): 2.2MM **Privately Held**
SIC: 3721 5088 7389 Airplanes, fixed or
rotary wing; transportation equipment &
supplies;

(P-19934)
TELEXCA INC
13463 Nomwaket Rd, Apple Valley
(92308-6591)
PHONE..............................760 247-4277
Roberto Brand, *President*
Elba Brand, *Vice Pres*
Victor Brand, *Engineer*
EMP: 16
SALES (est): 2.8MM **Privately Held**
SIC: 3721 Aircraft

(P-19935)
TRI MODELS INC
5191 Oceanus Dr, Huntington Beach
(92649-1026)
PHONE..............................714 896-0823
Prince A Herzog Sr, *CEO*
Jeff Herzog, *President*
Sharmon Herzog, *Administration*
Wayne Herzog, *Project Leader*
Frederick Herzog, *Sales Executive*
▲ **EMP:** 58
SALES: 17.4MM **Privately Held**
SIC: 3721 Airplanes, fixed or rotary wing

(P-19936)
**UNMANNED INNOVATION INC
(PA)**
Also Called: Airware
2625 Franklin St Apt 301, San Francisco
(94123-4522)
PHONE..............................877 714-4828
Yvonne Wassenaar, *CEO*
David Milanes, *President*
Kartik Ghorakavi, *Technical Staff*
Rob Poulsen, *Engineer*
Kate Englander, *Accountant*
EMP: 53
SALES (est): 11.9MM **Privately Held**
SIC: 3721 Aircraft

(P-19937)
**WEST E CMNTY ACCESS
NETWRK INC**
Also Called: We Can Foundation
646 W 60th St, Los Angeles (90044-6331)
PHONE..............................323 967-0520
Michael McLaughlin, *Exec Dir*
EMP: 100
SALES (est): 774K **Privately Held**
SIC: 3721 Research & development on air-
craft by the manufacturer

(P-19938)
WORLDWIDE AEROS CORP
1734 Aeros Way, Montebello (90640-6504)
PHONE..............................818 344-3999
Igor Pasternak, *President*
Carrie Cass, *CFO*
Aric Hirami, *Info Tech Mgr*
▲ **EMP:** 82
SALES (est): 16.9MM **Privately Held**
WEB: www.aerosml.com
SIC: 3721 8711 Airships; aviation &/or
aeronautical engineering

(P-19939)
ZODIAC AEROSPACE
11340 Jersey Blvd, Rancho Cucamonga
(91730-4919)
PHONE..............................909 652-9700
Robert Tom, *COO*
Margarita Vazquez, *Program Mgr*
Chris Breceda, *Planning*
Rozairo Miralles, *Design Engr*
Jim Seaton, *Project Mgr*
EMP: 13
SALES (est): 1MM **Privately Held**
SIC: 3721 Aircraft

P R O D U C T S & S V C S

3724 Aircraft Engines & Engine Parts

(P-19940)
3-D PRECISION MACHINE INC
42132 Remington Ave, Temecula
(92590-2547)
PHONE...............................951 296-5449
Linda Luoma, *President*
Roy Luoma, *Founder*
EMP: 25
SQ FT: 14,000
SALES: 3.5MM **Privately Held**
SIC: 3724 Research & development on aircraft engines & parts

(P-19941)
A F B SYSTEMS INC
Also Called: Sierra Tech
20400 Prairie St Unit B, Chatsworth
(91311-8129)
PHONE...............................818 775-0151
Frank Carbone, *Principal*
Norberto A Cusiuato, *President*
Jose A Nicosis, *Admin Sec*
EMP: 10
SQ FT: 20,719
SALES (est): 720K **Privately Held**
SIC: 3724 Aircraft engines & engine parts

(P-19942)
AC&A ENTERPRISES LLC (HQ)
25671 Commercentre Dr, Lake Forest
(92630-8801)
PHONE...............................949 716-3511
Justin Uchida, *CEO*
Justin Schultz,
Steve Smith, *Director*
▲ EMP: 87
SALES (est): 36.6MM
SALES (corp-wide): 30.3MM **Privately Held**
SIC: 3724 3511 Aircraft engines & engine parts; turbines & turbine generator sets
PA: Ac&A Enterprises Holdings, Llc
25692 Atlantic Ocean Dr
Lake Forest CA 92630
949 716-3511

(P-19943)
ACCURATE GRINDING AND MFG CORP
807 E Parkridge Ave, Corona (92879-6609)
PHONE...............................951 479-0909
Douglas Nilsen, *CEO*
Hans J Nilsen, *President*
David Nilsen, *Admin Sec*
Anthony Fall, *QC Mgr*
▲ EMP: 35
SQ FT: 15,000
SALES (est): 8.9MM **Privately Held**
WEB: www.accurategrindingmfg.com
SIC: 3724 3812 Aircraft engines & engine parts; search & navigation equipment

(P-19944)
ADVANCED GROUND SYSTEMS (HQ)
Also Called: Agse
10805 Painter Ave, Santa Fe Springs
(90670-4502)
PHONE...............................562 906-9300
Diane Henderson, *CEO*
Frank Judge, *COO*
David Chetwood, *CFO*
Tony Romero, *General Mgr*
Joel Morey, *CIO*
▲ EMP: 40
SALES (est): 14MM
SALES (corp-wide): 23.6MM **Privately Held**
WEB: www.westmont.com
SIC: 3724 Aircraft engines & engine parts
PA: Westmont Industries
10805 Painter Ave Uppr
Santa Fe Springs CA 90670
562 944-6137

(P-19945)
AERO TURBINE INC
6800 Lindbergh St, Stockton (95206-3934)
PHONE...............................209 983-1112

Douglas R Clayton, *President*
C W Dinsley, *Treasurer*
David Mattson, *Exec VP*
▲ EMP: 60
SQ FT: 51,000
SALES (est): 14.8MM **Privately Held**
WEB: www.aeroturbine.aero
SIC: 3724 Aircraft engines & engine parts

(P-19946)
APPROVED TURBO COMPONENTS
1545 E Acequia Ave, Visalia (93292-6652)
PHONE...............................559 627-3600
Michael Rogers, *President*
▲ EMP: 10 EST: 1998
SALES (est): 1.1MM **Privately Held**
SIC: 3724 Turbo-superchargers, aircraft

(P-19947)
DTI HOLDINGS INC
213 Technology Dr, Irvine (92618-2437)
PHONE...............................949 485-1725
Lisa Nguyen, *Vice Pres*
EMP: 10
SALES (est): 1.5MM **Privately Held**
SIC: 3724 Research & development on aircraft engines & parts

(P-19948)
DUCOMMUN AEROSTRUCTURES INC (HQ)
268 E Gardena Blvd, Gardena
(90248-2814)
PHONE...............................310 380-5390
Anthony J Reardon, *CEO*
George Coe, *Branch Mgr*
◆ EMP: 450
SQ FT: 300,000
SALES (est): 314.6MM
SALES (corp-wide): 629.3MM **Publicly Held**
SIC: 3724 3812 3728 Aircraft engines & engine parts; search & navigation equipment; aircraft parts & equipment
PA: Ducommun Incorporated
200 Sandpointe Ave # 700
Santa Ana CA 92707
657 335-3665

(P-19949)
DUCOMMUN AEROSTRUCTURES INC
1885 N Batavia St, Orange (92865-4105)
PHONE...............................714 637-4401
Kent T Christensen, *Branch Mgr*
EMP: 18
SALES (corp-wide): 629.3MM **Publicly Held**
SIC: 3724 3812 3728 Aircraft engines & engine parts; search & navigation equipment; aircraft parts & equipment
HQ: Ducommun Aerostructures, Inc.
268 E Gardena Blvd
Gardena CA 90248
310 380-5390

(P-19950)
DUCOMMUN AEROSTRUCTURES INC
23301 Wilmington Ave, Carson
(90745-6209)
PHONE...............................310 513-7200
Eugene Conese Jr, *Director*
EMP: 39
SALES (corp-wide): 629.3MM **Publicly Held**
SIC: 3724 Aircraft engines & engine parts
HQ: Ducommun Aerostructures, Inc.
268 E Gardena Blvd
Gardena CA 90248
310 380-5390

(P-19951)
ENCORE INTERNATIONAL
5511 Skylab Rd, Huntington Beach
(92647-2068)
PHONE...............................949 559-0930
Tom McFarland, *CEO*
Jude Dozor, *COO*
Mike Melancon, *CFO*
Antonio Perez, *Admin Sec*
▲ EMP: 250 EST: 2015
SQ FT: 80,000

SALES: 9.3MM **Privately Held**
SIC: 3724 Aircraft engines & engine parts

(P-19952)
GKN AEROSPACE CHEM-TRONICS INC
1148 Bert Acosta St, El Cajon
(92020-1101)
P.O. Box 1604 (92022-1604)
PHONE...............................619 258-5012
Mike Worthen, *Branch Mgr*
EMP: 19
SALES (corp-wide): 11B **Privately Held**
SIC: 3724 Aircraft engines & engine parts
HQ: Gkn Aerospace Chem-Tronics Inc.
1150 W Bradley Ave
El Cajon CA 92020
619 448-2320

(P-19953)
GKN AEROSPACE CHEM-TRONICS INC (DH)
1150 W Bradley Ave, El Cajon
(92020-1504)
P.O. Box 1604 (92022-1604)
PHONE...............................619 448-2320
Marcus J Bryson, *CEO*
Michael A Beck, *President*
Les Emanuel, *CFO*
Stacey Clapp, *Vice Pres*
Elizabeth Alford, *General Mgr*
▲ EMP: 648 EST: 1953
SQ FT: 400,000
SALES (est): 216.2MM
SALES (corp-wide): 11B **Privately Held**
WEB: www.chem-tronics.com
SIC: 3724 7699 Aircraft engines & engine parts; aircraft & heavy equipment repair services
HQ: Gkn Limited
Po Box 4128
Redditch WORCS
152 751-7715

(P-19954)
HONEYWELL INTERNATIONAL INC
22 Centerpointe Dr # 100, La Palma
(90623-2566)
PHONE...............................714 562-3000
Phil O'Leary, *Manager*
Neveen Farag, *Program Mgr*
EMP: 200
SALES (corp-wide): 41.8B **Publicly Held**
WEB: www.honeywell.com
SIC: 3724 Aircraft engines & engine parts
PA: Honeywell International Inc.
300 S Tryon St
Charlotte NC 28202
973 455-2000

(P-19955)
HONEYWELL INTERNATIONAL INC
6452 Morion Cir, Huntington Beach
(92647-6532)
PHONE...............................310 512-4237
EMP: 556
SALES (corp-wide): 41.8B **Publicly Held**
WEB: www.honeywell.com
SIC: 3724 Aircraft engines & engine parts
PA: Honeywell International Inc.
300 S Tryon St
Charlotte NC 28202
973 455-2000

(P-19956)
HONEYWELL INTERNATIONAL INC
2525 W 190th St, Torrance (90504-6002)
PHONE...............................310 323-9500
Ken Defusco, *Branch Mgr*
Kevin Haf, *Engineer*
EMP: 1000
SALES (corp-wide): 41.8B **Publicly Held**
WEB: www.honeywell.com
SIC: 3724 Aircraft engines & engine parts
PA: Honeywell International Inc.
300 S Tryon St
Charlotte NC 28202
973 455-2000

(P-19957)
HONEYWELL INTERNATIONAL INC
3105 Prince Valiant Ln, Modesto
(95350-1414)
PHONE...............................951 500-6086
EMP: 694
SALES (corp-wide): 41.8B **Publicly Held**
SIC: 3724 Aircraft engines & engine parts
PA: Honeywell International Inc.
300 S Tryon St
Charlotte NC 28202
973 455-2000

(P-19958)
HONEYWELL INTERNATIONAL INC
27831 Abadejo, Mission Viejo
(92692-2521)
PHONE...............................949 425-3992
EMP: 694
SALES (corp-wide): 41.8B **Publicly Held**
SIC: 3724 Aircraft engines & engine parts
PA: Honeywell International Inc.
300 S Tryon St
Charlotte NC 28202
973 455-2000

(P-19959)
HONEYWELL INTERNATIONAL INC
25 S Stockton St Ste C, Lodi (95240-2978)
PHONE...............................209 323-8520
EMP: 673
SALES (corp-wide): 41.8B **Publicly Held**
SIC: 3724 Aircraft engines & engine parts
PA: Honeywell International Inc.
300 S Tryon St
Charlotte NC 28202
973 455-2000

(P-19960)
HONEYWELL INTERNATIONAL INC
2100 Geer Rd Ste C, Turlock (95382-2452)
PHONE...............................209 480-6733
EMP: 673
SALES (corp-wide): 41.8B **Publicly Held**
SIC: 3724 Aircraft engines & engine parts
PA: Honeywell International Inc.
300 S Tryon St
Charlotte NC 28202
973 455-2000

(P-19961)
HONEYWELL INTERNATIONAL INC
22775 Savi Ranch Pkwy D, Yorba Linda
(92887-4622)
PHONE...............................714 337-6864
EMP: 673
SALES (corp-wide): 41.8B **Publicly Held**
SIC: 3724 Aircraft engines & engine parts
PA: Honeywell International Inc.
300 S Tryon St
Charlotte NC 28202
973 455-2000

(P-19962)
HONEYWELL INTERNATIONAL INC
6201 W Imperial Hwy, Los Angeles
(90045-6306)
PHONE...............................310 410-9605
Harvey Ticlo, *Manager*
Patricia Giovacchini, *Admin Asst*
Matt Kaszynski, *Technical Staff*
EMP: 300
SQ FT: 145,000
SALES (corp-wide): 41.8B **Publicly Held**
WEB: www.honeywell.com
SIC: 3724 Research & development on aircraft engines & parts
PA: Honeywell International Inc.
300 S Tryon St
Charlotte NC 28202
973 455-2000

(P-19963)
HONEYWELL INTERNATIONAL INC
6 Center Pt Ste 300, La Palma (90623)
PHONE...............................714 562-3016
John Gruss, *General Mgr*

2020 California
Manufacturers Register

▲ = Import ▼=Export
◆ =Import/Export

EMP: 75
SALES (corp-wide): 41.8B Publicly Held
WEB: www.honeywell.com
SIC: 3724 Aircraft engines & engine parts
PA: Honeywell International Inc.
   300 S Tryon St
   Charlotte NC 28202
   973 455-2000

(P-19964)
HONEYWELL INTERNATIONAL INC
233 Paulin Ave 8500, Calexico (92231-2615)
PHONE.................................760 312-5300
William Bouscher, *Principal*
EMP: 657
SALES (corp-wide): 41.8B Publicly Held
WEB: www.honeywell.com
SIC: 3724 Aircraft engines & engine parts
PA: Honeywell International Inc.
   300 S Tryon St
   Charlotte NC 28202
   973 455-2000

(P-19965)
INFINITY AEROSPACE INC (PA)
9060 Winnetka Ave, Northridge (91324-3235)
PHONE.................................818 998-9811
Chet Huffman, *CEO*
R Lloyd Huffman, *Ch of Bd*
Steve Lonngren, *President*
Elaine Marino, *Human Res Mgr*
Elias Garcia, *Senior Buyer*
EMP: 67
SQ FT: 30,000
SALES (est): 10.9MM Privately Held
WEB: www.dukesinc.com
SIC: 3724 Pumps, aircraft engine

(P-19966)
INTERNATIONAL WIND INC (PA)
137 N Joy St, Corona (92879-1321)
PHONE.................................562 240-3963
Cory Arendt, *President*
EMP: 49
SALES: 7MM Privately Held
SIC: 3724 8711 8742 Turbines, aircraft type; engineering services; aviation &/or aeronautical engineering; consulting engineer; management consulting services; maintenance management consultant

(P-19967)
JAMES HUNKINS
Also Called: Hunkins Enterprises
601 Lairport St, El Segundo (90245-5005)
PHONE.................................310 640-8243
James Hunkins, *Owner*
EMP: 14
SALES (est): 979.3K Privately Held
WEB: www.jdh-stech.com
SIC: 3724 Aircraft engines & engine parts

(P-19968)
JET/BRELLA INC
6849 Hayvenhurst Ave, Van Nuys (91406-4718)
PHONE.................................818 786-5480
William Onasch, *President*
EMP: 30
SQ FT: 18,000
SALES: 500K Privately Held
WEB: www.jetbrella.com
SIC: 3724 3728 5088 Aircraft engines & engine parts; aircraft parts & equipment; aircraft & parts

(P-19969)
KINGS CRATING INC (PA)
Also Called: Reyes Machining
1364 Pioneer Way, El Cajon (92020-1626)
PHONE.................................619 590-1664
Manuel Reyes, *President*
Sheila Reyes, *CFO*
Lynn Mason, *Admin Sec*
EMP: 20
SQ FT: 25,000
SALES (est): 3.2MM Privately Held
SIC: 3724 Aircraft engines & engine parts

(P-19970)
LOGISTICAL SUPPORT LLC
Also Called: RTC Aerospace
20409 Prairie St, Chatsworth (91311-6029)
PHONE.................................818 341-3344
Jerry Hill,
EMP: 125
SQ FT: 14,600
SALES (est): 11MM Privately Held
WEB: www.logisticalsupport.com
SIC: 3724 Aircraft engines & engine parts

(P-19971)
MAPE ENGINEERING INC
Also Called: America Manufacturing
9840 6th St, Rancho Cucamonga (91730-5714)
PHONE.................................626 338-7964
Manny Perales, *CEO*
Iraida Andrade, *President*
EMP: 10
SALES: 350K Privately Held
SIC: 3724 Research & development on aircraft engines & parts

(P-19972)
MARTON PRECISION MFG LLC
1365 S Acacia Ave, Fullerton (92831-5315)
PHONE.................................714 808-6523
Daniel J Marton, *President*
Mary Marton, *CFO*
EMP: 47
SQ FT: 20,000
SALES: 7.5MM Privately Held
WEB: www.martoninc.com
SIC: 3724 3599 3827 Aircraft engines & engine parts; machine & other job shop work; optical instruments & apparatus

(P-19973)
PACIFIC AERODYNAMIC INC
889 N Main St, Orange (92868-1107)
PHONE.................................714 450-9140
George Kassaseya, *President*
EMP: 12
SALES: 1.5MM Privately Held
SIC: 3724 Aircraft engines & engine parts

(P-19974)
PARAGON PRECISION INC
25620 Rye Canyon Rd Ste A, Valencia (91355-1139)
PHONE.................................661 257-1380
Allan Smith, *President*
Mike Keithley, *CFO*
EMP: 35
SQ FT: 14,000
SALES: 3.2MM Privately Held
WEB: www.paragon-precision.com
SIC: 3724 Aircraft engines & engine parts

(P-19975)
PARKER-HANNIFIN CORPORATION
Fluid Systems Division
16666 Von Karman Ave, Irvine (92606-4997)
PHONE.................................949 833-3000
Matthew Stafford, *Manager*
WEI Chiu, *Software Engr*
Paul Sandner, *Network Analyst*
Brian Ault, *Research*
Dennis Dinh, *Engineer*
EMP: 400
SALES (corp-wide): 14.3B Publicly Held
WEB: www.parker.com
SIC: 3724 3728 Aircraft engines & engine parts; aircraft parts & equipment
PA: Parker-Hannifin Corporation
   6035 Parkland Blvd
   Cleveland OH 44124
   216 896-3000

(P-19976)
QUALITY AEROSTRUCTURES COMPANY
10291 Trademark St Ste A, Rancho Cucamonga (91730-5847)
PHONE.................................909 987-4888
Fred Quinones, *President*
Michael Cabral, *Senior VP*
Rosa Rios, *Controller*
EMP: 15
SQ FT: 15,000

SALES (est): 1.2MM Privately Held
SIC: 3724 Aircraft engines & engine parts

(P-19977)
SAFRAN PWR UNITS SAN DIEGO LLC
4255 Ruffin Rd Ste 100, San Diego (92123-1247)
PHONE.................................858 223-2228
Rick Elgin, *Vice Pres*
EMP: 70 EST: 2015
SQ FT: 22,000
SALES (est): 6.8MM
SALES (corp-wide): 833.4MM Privately Held
SIC: 3724 Research & development on aircraft engines & parts
HQ: Safran Power Units
   8 Chemin Du Pont De Rupe
   Toulouse 31200
   561 701-651

(P-19978)
SALVADOR RAMIREZ
Also Called: S & R Cnc Machining
25334 Avenue Stanford B, Valencia (91355-1214)
PHONE.................................661 702-1813
Salvador Ramirez, *Owner*
EMP: 19
SQ FT: 2,700
SALES (est): 2.9MM Privately Held
WEB: www.srcncmachining.com
SIC: 3724 3714 3599 Aircraft engines & engine parts; motor vehicle parts & accessories; machine & other job shop work

(P-19979)
SENIOR AEROSPACE JET PDTS CORP (HQ)
9106 Balboa Ave, San Diego (92123-1512)
PHONE.................................858 278-8400
Willis H Fletcher, *Ch of Bd*
Ronald R Blair, *President*
John Shepherd, *COO*
Steven Konold, *Admin Sec*
Francoise Pierquin, *Administration*
EMP: 142 EST: 1965
SQ FT: 125,000
SALES (est): 47.1MM
SALES (corp-wide): 1.3B Privately Held
WEB: www.jetproducts.com
SIC: 3724 3462 3444 Aircraft engines & engine parts; iron & steel forgings; sheet metalwork

(P-19980)
SIERRA AEROSPACE LLC
2263 Ward Ave, Simi Valley (93065-1863)
PHONE.................................805 526-8669
EMP: 16
SQ FT: 7,500
SALES (est): 2.6MM Privately Held
SIC: 3724

(P-19981)
TELEDYNE RISI INC
Also Called: Teledyne Elctronic Safety Pdts
19735 Dearborn St, Chatsworth (91311-6510)
PHONE.................................818 718-6640
Mike Summer, *Branch Mgr*
EMP: 12
SALES (corp-wide): 2.9B Publicly Held
WEB: www.teledyne.com
SIC: 3724 Aircraft engines & engine parts
HQ: Teledyne Risi, Inc.
   32727 W Corral Hollow Rd
   Tracy CA 95376
   925 456-9700

(P-19982)
THERMAL STRUCTURES INC (DH)
2362 Railroad St, Corona (92880-5421)
PHONE.................................951 736-9911
Vaughn Barnes, *President*
Jerry Brantley, *Info Tech Mgr*
Joe Riley, *Project Mgr*
Nick Todd, *Technology*
Javier Garcia, *Engineer*
EMP: 270
SQ FT: 175,000

SALES (est): 94.1MM Publicly Held
WEB: www.thermalstructures.com
SIC: 3724 Aircraft engines & engine parts
HQ: Heico Aerospace Holdings Corp.
   3000 Taft St
   Hollywood FL 33021
   954 987-4000

(P-19983)
THOMPSON AEROSPACE INC (PA)
8687 Research Dr Ste 250, Irvine (92618-4290)
PHONE.................................949 264-1600
Mark Thompson, *President*
Heiko Wiedmann, *CFO*
Trevor Coolidge, *Vice Pres*
Fred Esch, *Vice Pres*
Craig Jones, *VP Bus Dvlpt*
EMP: 10
SALES (est): 1.2MM Privately Held
SIC: 3724 3728 Aircraft engines & engine parts; aircraft parts & equipment

(P-19984)
THRUN MFG INC
31947 Corydon St Ste 170, Lake Elsinore (92530-8531)
PHONE.................................949 677-2461
Christine N Thrun, *President*
Scott Gordon, *Vice Pres*
EMP: 23
SQ FT: 25,000
SALES: 21MM Privately Held
WEB: www.thrun.com
SIC: 3724 3769 Aircraft engines & engine parts; guided missile & space vehicle parts & auxiliary equipment

(P-19985)
TMJ PRODUCTS INC
515 S Palm Ave Ste 6, Alhambra (91803-1430)
PHONE.................................626 576-4063
Jones Tsui, *President*
S L Tsui, *Vice Pres*
▲ EMP: 14
SQ FT: 1,600
SALES (est): 2.1MM Privately Held
SIC: 3724 Aircraft engines & engine parts

(P-19986)
TURBINE COMPONENTS INC
Also Called: T C I
8985 Crestmar Pt, San Diego (92121-3222)
PHONE.................................858 678-8568
Raffee Esmailians, *President*
Tom Hughes, *Vice Pres*
EMP: 48
SQ FT: 55,000
SALES: 5MM
SALES (corp-wide): 702.5MM Publicly Held
WEB: www.turbinecomponents.com
SIC: 3724 Turbines, aircraft type
PA: Rbc Bearings Incorporated
   102 Willenbrock Rd
   Oxford CT 06478
   203 267-7001

(P-19987)
UNITED TECHNOLOGIES CORP
Also Called: Chemical Systems Div
600 Metcalf Rd, San Jose (95138-9601)
PHONE.................................408 779-9121
Greg Fatobic, *Branch Mgr*
EMP: 660
SALES (corp-wide): 66.5B Publicly Held
WEB: www.utc.com
SIC: 3724 3769 3489 Rocket motors, aircraft; guided missile & space vehicle parts & auxiliary equipment; ordnance & accessories
PA: United Technologies Corporation
   10 Farm Springs Rd
   Farmington CT 06032
   860 728-7000

(P-19988)
UNITED TECHNOLOGIES CORP
Also Called: Space Propulsions Div
600 Metcalf Rd, San Jose (95138-9601)
P.O. Box 109600, West Palm Beach FL (33410-9600)
PHONE.................................408 779-9121

PRODUCTS & SVCS

Mark Mounsey, *Manager*
EMP: 750
SALES (corp-wide): 66.5B **Publicly Held**
WEB: www.utc.com
SIC: 3724 3585 3534 3721 Aircraft engines & engine parts; refrigeration & heating equipment; elevators & moving stairways; aircraft; surgical appliances & supplies; motor vehicle parts & accessories
PA: United Technologies Corporation
10 Farm Springs Rd
Farmington CT 06032
860 728-7000

(P-19989)
UNITED TECHNOLOGIES CORP
4384 Enterprise Pl, Fremont (94538-6365)
PHONE.....................510 438-1300
Richard Haswell, *Branch Mgr*
EMP: 255
SALES (corp-wide): 66.5B **Publicly Held**
SIC: 3724 Aircraft engines & engine parts
PA: United Technologies Corporation
10 Farm Springs Rd
Farmington CT 06032
860 728-7000

(P-19990)
VIP MANUFACTURING & ENGRG
Also Called: VIP Mfg & Engr
1084 Martin Ave, Santa Clara (95050-2609)
PHONE.....................408 727-6545
L A Vargo Jr, *President*
Emma Vargo, *CFO*
EMP: 14
SQ FT: 10,500
SALES (est): 1.7MM **Privately Held**
WEB: www.vip10.com
SIC: 3724 3451 3599 Aircraft engines & engine parts; screw machine products; machine shop, jobbing & repair

(P-19991)
WKF (FRIEDMAN ENTERPRISES INC (PA)
Also Called: Eff Aero
2334 Stagecoach Rd Ste B, Stockton (95215-7939)
PHONE.....................925 673-9100
Wayne Friedman, *President*
EMP: 19
SALES (est): 1.3MM **Privately Held**
SIC: 3724 Aircraft engines & engine parts

(P-19992)
ZURICH ENGINEERING INC
Also Called: Vf Engineering USA
1365 N Dynamics St Ste E, Anaheim (92806-1904)
PHONE.....................714 528-0066
Nikhil Saran, *President*
▲ **EMP:** 10
SQ FT: 4,000
SALES (est): 1.4MM **Privately Held**
SIC: 3724 Turbo-superchargers, aircraft

3728 Aircraft Parts & Eqpt, NEC

(P-19993)
A & A AEROSPACE INC
1442 Hayes Ave, Long Beach (90813-1124)
PHONE.....................562 901-6803
Arnie Puentes, *President*
EMP: 17
SALES (corp-wide): 5MM **Privately Held**
SIC: 3728 Aircraft parts & equipment
PA: A & A Aerospace, Inc.
13649 Pumice St
Santa Fe Springs CA 90670
562 901-6803

(P-19994)
A & A AEROSPACE INC
1987 W 16th St, Long Beach (90813-1136)
PHONE.....................562 901-6803
Arnie Puentes, *President*
EMP: 12
SALES (corp-wide): 5MM **Privately Held**
SIC: 3728 Aircraft parts & equipment

PA: A & A Aerospace, Inc.
13649 Pumice St
Santa Fe Springs CA 90670
562 901-6803

(P-19995)
A-INFO INC
60 Tesla, Irvine (92618-4603)
PHONE.....................949 346-7326
Linda Williams, *Asst Mgr*
EMP: 35
SALES (est): 1.3MM **Privately Held**
SIC: 3728 3812 5049 Aircraft parts & equipment; antennas, radar or communications; analytical instruments; scientific instruments; scientific recording equipment

(P-19996)
AAA AIR SUPPORT
13723 Harvard Pl, Gardena (90249-2527)
PHONE.....................310 538-1377
Matthew D Kerster, *President*
Joan Robinson- Berry, *Vice Pres*
Kent Fisher, *Vice Pres*
Jack House, *Vice Pres*
Matthew Kerster, *Vice Pres*
EMP: 12
SQ FT: 15,000
SALES: 3.6MM **Privately Held**
SIC: 3728 5088 Aircraft parts & equipment; aircraft & space vehicle supplies & parts

(P-19997)
ABL AERO INC
Also Called: Able Aerospace Adhesives
25032 Anza Dr, Valencia (91355-3917)
PHONE.....................661 257-2500
Alicia Hed-Ram, *President*
Lata Wadhwani, *Office Mgr*
Kiran Singh, *Purch Agent*
Desai Sujay, *Sales Mgr*
EMP: 20
SQ FT: 10,000
SALES (est): 4.8MM **Privately Held**
WEB: www.ablaero.com
SIC: 3728 Aircraft parts & equipment

(P-19998)
ACE AIR MANUFACTURING
1430 W 135th St, Gardena (90249-2218)
PHONE.....................310 323-7246
Roger Brandt, *President*
EMP: 17 **EST:** 1957
SQ FT: 12,000
SALES: 2MM **Privately Held**
SIC: 3728 Aircraft parts & equipment

(P-19999)
ACE AVIATION SERVICE INC
3239 Roymar Rd Ste B, Oceanside (92058-1342)
PHONE.....................760 721-2804
Donald Nicolai, *President*
EMP: 12
SQ FT: 2,000
SALES (est): 1.3MM **Privately Held**
SIC: 3728 3714 Aircraft assemblies, sub-assemblies & parts; motor vehicle parts & accessories

(P-20000)
ACE CLEARWATER ENTERPRISES INC (PA)
19815 Magellan Dr, Torrance (90502-1107)
PHONE.....................310 323-2140
James D Dodson, *President*
Kellie Johnson, *CEO*
Agustin Gonzalez, *Officer*
William Schauerman, *Program Mgr*
Cesar Tello, *Administration*
EMP: 100 **EST:** 1961
SALES (est): 42.8MM **Privately Held**
WEB: www.aceclearwater.com
SIC: 3728 3544 7692 3812 Aircraft parts & equipment; special dies, tools, jigs & fixtures; welding repair; search & navigation equipment; sheet metalwork

(P-20001)
ACROMIL LLC (HQ)
18421 Railroad St, City of Industry (91748-1233)
PHONE.....................626 964-2522
John T Cave II,

PA: A & A Aerospace, Inc.
13649 Pumice St
Santa Fe Springs CA 90670
562 901-6803

David Patterson, *Vice Pres*
Jon Konheim,
Gerald A Niznick,
EMP: 204 **EST:** 2015
SQ FT: 96,000
SALES (est): 12.7MM
SALES (corp-wide): 23.6MM **Privately Held**
SIC: 3728 Aircraft body & wing assemblies & parts
PA: Acromil Corporation
18421 Railroad St
City Of Industry CA 91748
626 964-2522

(P-20002)
ACROMIL LLC
1168 Sherborn St, Corona (92879-2089)
PHONE.....................951 808-9929
David Nguyen, *President*
EMP: 60
SALES (corp-wide): 23.6MM **Privately Held**
SIC: 3728 Aircraft body & wing assemblies & parts
HQ: Acromil, Llc
18421 Railroad St
City Of Industry CA 91748
626 964-2522

(P-20003)
ACROMIL CORPORATION (PA)
18421 Railroad St, City of Industry (91748-1281)
PHONE.....................626 964-2522
Gerald A Niznick, *President*
John Stock, *President*
Jon Konheim, *COO*
Jeanne Aguilera, *CFO*
◆ **EMP:** 105
SQ FT: 100,000
SALES (est): 23.6MM **Privately Held**
WEB: www.acromil.com
SIC: 3728 Aircraft body & wing assemblies & parts

(P-20004)
ACUFAST AIRCRAFT PRODUCTS INC
12445 Gladstone Ave, Sylmar (91342-5321)
PHONE.....................818 365-7077
Art Dovlatian, *President*
Jaime Salazar, *Vice Pres*
EMP: 40
SALES: 6MM **Privately Held**
SIC: 3728 Aircraft parts & equipment

(P-20005)
ADAMS RITE AEROSPACE INC (DH)
4141 N Palm St, Fullerton (92835-1025)
PHONE.....................714 278-6500
John Schaefer, *President*
Aleem Shaikh, *Business Dir*
Ivonne Saldana, *Admin Asst*
Faustino Gutierrez, *Administration*
Rhoneil Ramos, *Technical Staff*
EMP: 149
SQ FT: 100,000
SALES (est): 65.3MM
SALES (corp-wide): 3.8B **Publicly Held**
WEB: www.ar-aero.com
SIC: 3728 Aircraft parts & equipment

(P-20006)
ADAPTIVE AEROSPACE CORPORATION
20304 W Valley Blvd Ste H, Tehachapi (93561-8697)
PHONE.....................661 822-2850
Bill McCune, *CEO*
Sean Dineen, *Design Engr*
Brian Foster, *Engineer*
Duana Pera, *Controller*
EMP: 15
SQ FT: 4,000
SALES: 3MM **Privately Held**
WEB: www.adaptaero.com
SIC: 3728 Aircraft parts & equipment

(P-20007)
ADVANCED MTLS JOINING CORP (PA)
Also Called: Advanced Technology Co
2858 E Walnut St, Pasadena (91107-3755)
PHONE.....................626 449-2696
Jean L De Silvestri, *President*
Mohammed Islam, *President*
Gilbert Figueroa, *Facilities Mgr*
EMP: 41
SQ FT: 23,000
SALES (est): 7.8MM **Privately Held**
WEB: www.at-co.com
SIC: 3728 3724 Aircraft parts & equipment; aircraft engines & engine parts

(P-20008)
AEG INDUSTRIES INC
1219 Briggs Ave, Santa Rosa (95401-4761)
PHONE.....................707 575-0697
Peggy McIlnay Moe, *President*
Peg McIlnay-Moe, *President*
William Pottorff, *President*
Dennis McIlnay Moe, *Vice Pres*
EMP: 20
SQ FT: 6,500
SALES: 3MM **Privately Held**
WEB: www.aegindustries.com
SIC: 3728 Aircraft parts & equipment

(P-20009)
AERO DYNAMIC MACHINING INC
11841 Monarch St, Garden Grove (92841-2110)
PHONE.....................714 379-1073
David Nguyen, *President*
Wendy Nguyen, *CFO*
Kevin Tran, *Vice Pres*
John Fairris, *Technical Staff*
Rick Zulawski, *QC Mgr*
▲ **EMP:** 60 **EST:** 1998
SALES (est): 20.5MM **Privately Held**
WEB: www.aerodynamicinc.com
SIC: 3728 Aircraft parts & equipment

(P-20010)
AERO ENGINEERING & MFG CO CAL
28217 Avenue Crocker, Valencia (91355-1249)
PHONE.....................661 295-0875
Dennis L Junker, *CEO*
Lance R Junker, *President*
Richard Jucksch, *Vice Pres*
Rick Jucksch, *General Mgr*
Bob Singley, *Info Tech Mgr*
▼ **EMP:** 49
SQ FT: 21,000
SALES (est): 14MM **Privately Held**
WEB: www.aeroeng.com
SIC: 3728 5088 Aircraft assemblies, sub-assemblies & parts; aircraft & parts

(P-20011)
AERO PACIFIC CORPORATION (PA)
Also Called: Merco Manufacturing Co
588 Porter Way, Placentia (92870-6453)
PHONE.....................714 961-9200
Mark Heasley, *President*
Bridget Hopkins, *Vice Pres*
Sharon Mosher, *Program Mgr*
EMP: 80
SQ FT: 60,000
SALES: 15MM **Privately Held**
WEB: www.mercomfg.com
SIC: 3728 Aircraft parts & equipment

(P-20012)
AERO PACIFIC CORPORATION
Aero Pacific Mfg
7100 Belgrave Ave, Garden Grove (92841-2809)
PHONE.....................714 961-9200
Mark Heasley, *Branch Mgr*
EMP: 50
SALES (corp-wide): 15MM **Privately Held**
SIC: 3728 Aircraft parts & equipment
PA: Aero Pacific Corporation
588 Porter Way
Placentia CA 92870
714 961-9200

(P-20013)
AERO PRECISION INDUSTRIES LLC (PA)
201 Lindbergh Ave, Livermore (94551-7667)
PHONE..................925 455-9900
Darryl Mayhorn, *CEO*
Angel Flores, *Vice Pres*
Carol Knepper, *Admin Asst*
Tami Farro, *Administration*
Tammy Ficarra, *Administration*
▼ **EMP:** 128
SQ FT: 45,000
SALES: 150MM **Privately Held**
WEB: www.apiinc.net
SIC: 3728 Aircraft parts & equipment

(P-20014)
AERO SENSE INC
26074 Avenue Hall Ste 18, Valencia (91355-3445)
PHONE..................661 257-1608
Sohail Tabrizi, *President*
Ro Missaghian, *CFO*
Amin Mozaffarian, *Program Mgr*
▲ **EMP:** 15
SALES (est): 3MM **Privately Held**
SIC: 3728 Aircraft parts & equipment

(P-20015)
AERO-CRAFT HYDRAULICS INC
392 N Smith Ave, Corona (92880-6971)
PHONE..................951 736-4690
Rod Guzman Sr, *President*
Suzane Treneer, *Ch of Bd*
Brad Davidson, *CFO*
Carol Thoe, *Engineer*
Sharon Sanna, *Controller*
EMP: 43
SQ FT: 16,500
SALES (est): 9.3MM **Privately Held**
WEB: www.aero-craft.com
SIC: 3728 5084 7699 Aircraft body & wing assemblies & parts; hydraulic systems equipment & supplies; aircraft & heavy equipment repair services

(P-20016)
AEROJET ROCKETDYNE INC (HQ)
2001 Aerojet Rd, Rancho Cordova (95742-6418)
P.O. Box 13222, Sacramento (95813-3222)
PHONE..................916 355-4000
Warren M Boley Jr, *CEO*
Kathleen E Redd, *CFO*
John Joy, *Treasurer*
Steve Warren, *Ch Credit Ofcr*
Jose Ruiz Jr, *Officer*
▲ **EMP:** 1400
SALES (est): 867.2MM
SALES (corp-wide): 1.9B **Publicly Held**
SIC: 3728 3764 3769 3761 Aircraft body & wing assemblies & parts; propulsion units for guided missiles & space vehicles; guided missile & space vehicle parts & auxiliary equipment; guided missiles & space vehicles
PA: Aerojet Rocketdyne Holdings, Inc.
222 N Pacific Coast Hwy # 50
El Segundo CA 90245
310 252-8100

(P-20017)
AEROJET ROCKETDYNE INC
Also Called: Rocket Shop
1180 Iron Point Rd # 350, Folsom (95630-8321)
PHONE..................916 355-4000
Craig Halterman, *Vice Pres*
Warren Yasuhara, *Vice Pres*
Gene Goldman, *Exec Dir*
Michael Gagne, *Project Engr*
David Knoll, *Electrical Engi*
EMP: 14
SALES (corp-wide): 1.9B **Publicly Held**
SIC: 3728 Aircraft body & wing assemblies & parts
HQ: Aerojet Rocketdyne, Inc.
2001 Aerojet Rd
Rancho Cordova CA 95742
916 355-4000

(P-20018)
AEROMETALS INC (PA)
3920 Sandstone Dr, El Dorado Hills (95762-9652)
PHONE..................916 939-6888
Lorie Symon, *President*
Lori Symon, *Chief Mktg Ofcr*
Tony Bohm, *Program Mgr*
David Postema, *General Mgr*
Teresa Rathstone, *Administration*
◆ **EMP:** 76
SQ FT: 150,000
SALES: 39.6MM **Privately Held**
SIC: 3728 Aircraft parts & equipment

(P-20019)
AEROSHEAR AVIATION SVCS INC (PA)
7701 Woodley Ave 200, Van Nuys (91406-1732)
PHONE..................818 779-1650
Lonnie Paschal, *CEO*
Christine Paschal, *CFO*
Ryan Hogan,
EMP: 32
SQ FT: 42,000
SALES (est): 4.3MM **Privately Held**
WEB: www.aeroshearaviation.com
SIC: 3728 3599 1799 Aircraft parts & equipment; machine shop, jobbing & repair; welding on site

(P-20020)
AEROSPACE COMPOSITE PRODUCTS (PA)
Also Called: Acp Composites
78 Lindbergh Ave, Livermore (94551-9503)
PHONE..................925 443-5900
George William Sparr, *President*
Barbara Sparr, *Admin Sec*
Michele Flores, *Data Proc Staff*
Connie Austin, *Human Res Mgr*
EMP: 20
SALES (est): 7.8MM **Privately Held**
WEB: www.acp-composites.com
SIC: 3728 5961 3624 Aircraft assemblies, subassemblies & parts; mail order house; carbon & graphite products

(P-20021)
AEROSPACE DYNAMICS INTL INC
Also Called: ADI
25540 Rye Canyon Rd, Valencia (91355-1169)
PHONE..................661 257-3535
Joseph I Snowden, *CEO*
▲ **EMP:** 450
SQ FT: 250,000
SALES (est): 180.5MM
SALES (corp-wide): 225.3B **Publicly Held**
WEB: www.adi-aero.com
SIC: 3728 Aircraft parts & equipment
HQ: Precision Castparts Corp.
4650 Sw Mcdam Ave Ste 300
Portland OR 97239
503 946-4800

(P-20022)
AEROSPACE ENGINEERING CORP
2632 Saturn St, Brea (92821-6701)
PHONE..................714 996-8178
Trevor Burdge, *President*
EMP: 70
SALES: 9.1MM **Privately Held**
SIC: 3728 3541 Aircraft parts & equipment; numerically controlled metal cutting machine tools

(P-20023)
AEROSPACE PARTS HOLDINGS INC
Also Called: Cadence Aerospace
3150 E Miraloma Ave, Anaheim (92806-1906)
PHONE..................949 877-3630
Ron Case, *CEO*
Mike Coburn, *COO*
Don Devore, *CFO*
EMP: 1175
SALES: 301MM **Privately Held**
SIC: 3728 Aircraft parts & equipment

(P-20024)
AHF-DUCOMMUN INCORPORATED (HQ)
Also Called: Ducommun Arostructures-Gardena
268 E Gardena Blvd, Gardena (90248-2814)
PHONE..................310 380-5390
Joseph C Berenato, *Principal*
◆ **EMP:** 250
SQ FT: 105,000
SALES (est): 314.6MM
SALES (corp-wide): 629.3MM **Publicly Held**
SIC: 3728 3812 3769 3469 Aircraft body & wing assemblies & parts; search & navigation equipment; guided missile & space vehicle parts & auxiliary equipment; metal stampings
PA: Ducommun Incorporated
200 Sandpointe Ave # 700
Santa Ana CA 92707
657 335-3665

(P-20025)
AIRBORNE TECHNOLOGIES INC
999 Avenida Acaso, Camarillo (93012-8700)
P.O. Box 2210 (93011-2210)
PHONE..................805 389-3700
EMP: 67
SQ FT: 40,000
SALES: 15.1MM **Privately Held**
SIC: 3728 5088 7699 3812 Aircraft parts & equipment; aircraft equipment & supplies; aircraft & heavy equipment repair services; search & navigation equipment

(P-20026)
AIRCRAFT HINGE INC
28338 Constellation Rd # 970, Santa Clarita (91355-5801)
PHONE..................661 257-3434
Doug Silva, *President*
Robbie Johnson, *President*
Brianne Dautel, *Office Mgr*
Terrina Arroyo, *Finance Dir*
Jose Nunez, *Foreman/Supr*
▲ **EMP:** 20
SQ FT: 11,000
SALES (est): 5.5MM **Privately Held**
WEB: www.aircrafthinge.com
SIC: 3728 Aircraft parts & equipment

(P-20027)
AIRPARTS EXPRESS INC
3420 W Macarthur Blvd G, Santa Ana (92704-6853)
PHONE..................714 308-2764
Mike Sweney, *CEO*
Thomas J Murphy, *President*
Shaun Murphy, *CFO*
Hardy Blackman, *Vice Pres*
Jeff Parker, *Admin Sec*
▲ **EMP:** 54
SQ FT: 2,000
SALES (est): 5.7MM **Privately Held**
WEB: www.airpartsexpress.net
SIC: 3728 Aircraft parts & equipment

(P-20028)
AIRTECH INTERNATIONAL INC (PA)
Also Called: Airtech Advanced Mtls Group
5700 Skylab Rd, Huntington Beach (92647-2055)
PHONE..................714 899-8100
Jeff Dahlgren, *President*
Bryan Driskill, *General Mgr*
William R Dahlgren, *Info Tech Mgr*
Chhien Chauv, *Engineer*
Jeffrey Dahlgren, *Engineer*
◆ **EMP:** 130
SQ FT: 150,000
SALES (est): 59.4MM **Privately Held**
WEB: www.airtechintl.com
SIC: 3728 3081 5088 2673 Aircraft parts & equipment; unsupported plastics film & sheet; aeronautical equipment & supplies; bags: plastic, laminated & coated; coated & laminated paper; packaging paper & plastics film, coated & laminated

(P-20029)
ALATUS AEROSYSTEMS (PA)
Also Called: F.K.a Trmph Strctrs-Los Angles
17055 Gale Ave, City of Industry (91745-1808)
PHONE..................610 251-1000
Scott Holland, *CEO*
Mark Peterman, *COO*
Richard Yang, *CFO*
Rich Oak, *Exec VP*
Mariano Velarde, *Exec VP*
◆ **EMP:** 184
SQ FT: 350,000
SALES (est): 85.8MM **Privately Held**
WEB: www.triumphgroup.com
SIC: 3728 3489 Aircraft parts & equipment; wing assemblies & parts, aircraft; alighting (landing gear) assemblies, aircraft; artillery or artillery parts, over 30 mm.

(P-20030)
ALATUS AEROSYSTEMS
9301 Mason Ave, Chatsworth (91311-5202)
PHONE..................626 498-7376
Richard Oak, *Manager*
Hector Zaldivar, *Maint Spvr*
Alice Calzada, *Director*
Greg Rogozinski, *Manager*
EMP: 80
SALES (corp-wide): 85.8MM **Privately Held**
WEB: www.triumphgroup.com
SIC: 3728 3489 Aircraft parts & equipment; wing assemblies & parts, aircraft; alighting (landing gear) assemblies, aircraft; artillery or artillery parts, over 30 mm.
PA: Alatus Aerosystems
17055 Gale Ave
City Of Industry CA 91745
610 251-1000

(P-20031)
ALIGN AEROSPACE LLC (DH)
9401 De Soto Ave, Chatsworth (91311-4920)
PHONE..................818 727-7800
Ian Cohen,
Leticia Guillermo, *Finance Spvr*
Sandra Sanchez, *Purch Agent*
Olivier Lafrance, *Manager*
EMP: 220
SQ FT: 73,000
SALES (est): 118.3MM
SALES (corp-wide): 43.3B **Privately Held**
SIC: 3728 Aircraft parts & equipment

(P-20032)
AMG TORRANCE LLC (DH)
Also Called: Metric Precision
5401 Business Dr, Huntington Beach (92649-1225)
PHONE..................310 515-2584
Omar Khan, *CEO*
Victor Bonus, *Controller*
Angelique Flores, *Controller*
EMP: 69
SQ FT: 37,800
SALES (est): 15.9MM **Privately Held**
SIC: 3728 Ailerons
HQ: Aerospace Manufacturing Group Inc
5401 Business Dr
Huntington Beach CA 92649
714 894-9802

(P-20033)
AMRO FABRICATING CORPORATION
17101 Heacock St, Moreno Valley (92551-9560)
PHONE..................951 842-6140
EMP: 49
SALES (corp-wide): 53.6MM **Privately Held**
SIC: 3728
PA: Amro Fabricating Corporation
1430 Adelia Ave
South El Monte CA 91733
626 579-2200

PRODUCTS & SVCS

(P-20034)
AMRO FABRICATING CORPORATION (PA)
1430 Adelia Ave, South El Monte (91733-3003)
PHONE...............................626 579-2200
John Hammond, *President*
Michael Riley, *CEO*
Steve M Riley, *Vice Pres*
Joe Bianchi, *Program Mgr*
Maria Robles, *Admin Asst*
EMP: 250
SQ FT: 150,000
SALES (est): 73.8MM **Privately Held**
WEB: www.amrofab.com
SIC: 3728 3769 3544 5088 Aircraft parts & equipment; guided missile & space vehicle parts & auxiliary equipment; special dies, tools, jigs & fixtures; aircraft & space vehicle supplies & parts; guided missiles & space vehicles

(P-20035)
AMRON MANUFACTURING INC
Also Called: Amron Urethane Products
635 Gregory Cir, Corona (92881-3596)
PHONE...............................714 278-9204
Daniel Horvath, *President*
Irene Munoz, *Office Mgr*
Norma Horvath, *Admin Sec*
EMP: 12
SQ FT: 15,000
SALES: 1.1MM **Privately Held**
SIC: 3728 Aircraft parts & equipment

(P-20036)
ANMAR PRECISION COMPONENTS
7424 Greenbush Ave, North Hollywood (91605-4005)
PHONE...............................818 764-0901
Bruno Mudy, *President*
Teresa Mudy, *Corp Secy*
Anthony Mudy, *Vice Pres*
EMP: 18
SQ FT: 10,000
SALES (est): 1.6MM **Privately Held**
SIC: 3728 Aircraft parts & equipment

(P-20037)
APPLIED AROSPC STRUCTURES CORP (PA)
Also Called: Aasc
3437 S Airport Way, Stockton (95206-3853)
P.O. Box 6189 (95206-0189)
PHONE...............................209 982-0160
John E Rule, *President*
Rhonda Ward, *Corp Secy*
Burton Weil, *Admin Sec*
Mike Merit, *Info Tech Dir*
Gary Van Waters, *Business Mgr*
▲ EMP: 230
SQ FT: 100,000
SALES (est): 44.7MM **Privately Held**
WEB: www.aascworld.com
SIC: 3728 Aircraft parts & equipment

(P-20038)
APPLIED CMPSITE STRUCTURES INC (HQ)
1195 Columbia St, Brea (92821-2922)
PHONE...............................714 990-6300
David Horner, *CEO*
Jorge Garcia, *CFO*
Bobby Breaux, *Vice Pres*
Kelly Tingen, *Vice Pres*
Teri Morales, *Executive*
EMP: 120 EST: 1975
SQ FT: 100,000
SALES (est): 55.7MM
SALES (corp-wide): 30.3MM **Privately Held**
WEB: www.bradleyspareparts.com
SIC: 3728 Aircraft parts & equipment
PA: Ac&A Enterprises Holdings, Llc
25692 Atlantic Ocean Dr
Lake Forest CA 92630
949 716-3511

(P-20039)
APPROVED AERONAUTICS LLC
1240 Graphite Dr, Corona (92881-3308)
PHONE...............................951 200-3730
David A Janes,

EMP: 10
SQ FT: 3,000
SALES (est): 2.1MM **Privately Held**
WEB: www.approvedaeronautics.com
SIC: 3728 Aircraft parts & equipment

(P-20040)
ARDEN ENGINEERING INC (DH)
3130 E Miraloma Ave, Anaheim (92806-1906)
PHONE...............................949 877-3642
Thomas Hutton, *CEO*
Michael J Stow, *President*
John R Meisenbach Sr, *CEO*
Michael Stow, *Vice Pres*
Mark Metsker, *Manager*
▲ EMP: 21
SQ FT: 25,000
SALES (est): 33MM
SALES (corp-wide): 192.6MM **Privately Held**
WEB: www.arden-engr.com
SIC: 3728 Aircraft body assemblies & parts
HQ: Arden Engineering Holdings, Inc.
1878 N Main St
Orange CA
714 998-6410

(P-20041)
ARDEN ENGINEERING INC
1878 N Main St, Orange (92865-4117)
Rural Route 3130, Anaheim (92806)
PHONE...............................714 998-6410
Thorin Southworth, *Director*
EMP: 20
SALES (corp-wide): 192.6MM **Privately Held**
SIC: 3728 Aircraft body assemblies & parts
HQ: Arden Engineering, Inc.
3130 E Miraloma Ave
Anaheim CA 92806
949 877-3642

(P-20042)
ARMORSTRUXX LLC
850 Thurman St, Lodi (95240-8228)
PHONE...............................209 365-9400
Aaron Starkovich, *CEO*
Benvinda Chaves, *Purch Mgr*
Hugo Castrejon, *Opers Dir*
EMP: 24
SQ FT: 100,000
SALES: 20MM **Privately Held**
WEB: www.armorstruxx.com
SIC: 3728 3795 3711 Military aircraft equipment & armament; tanks & tank components; motor vehicles & car bodies

(P-20043)
ARROWHEAD PRODUCTS CORPORATION
4411 Katella Ave, Los Alamitos (90720-3599)
PHONE...............................714 828-7770
Andrew Whelan, *President*
Bill Gardner, *Vice Pres*
Dominic Ruiz, *Vice Pres*
Bob Sweet, *Executive*
Erick Reinhold, *Exec Dir*
▲ EMP: 640
SQ FT: 250,000
SALES (est): 184.8MM
SALES (corp-wide): 508.4MM **Privately Held**
WEB: www.arrowheadproducts.net
SIC: 3728 Aircraft parts & equipment
HQ: Industrial Manufacturing Company Llc
8223 Brecksville Rd Ste 1
Brecksville OH 44141
440 838-4700

(P-20044)
ASTOR MANUFACTURING
779 Anita St Ste B, Chula Vista (91911-3937)
PHONE...............................661 645-5585
Erick Muschenheim, *President*
EMP: 25
SQ FT: 3,500
SALES: 1.2MM **Privately Held**
SIC: 3728 Aircraft body assemblies & parts

(P-20045)
ASTRO-TEK INDUSTRIES LLC
1198 N Kraemer Blvd, Anaheim (92806-1916)
PHONE...............................714 238-0022
Terry Smith, *Vice Pres*
Jack Wright II, *Manager*
EMP: 80
SQ FT: 50,000
SALES (est): 21.3MM **Privately Held**
WEB: www.astro-tek.com
SIC: 3728 3599 3548 3449 Aircraft parts & equipment; electrical discharge machining (EDM); welding apparatus; miscellaneous metalwork

(P-20046)
ASTURIES MANUFACTURING CO INC
310 Cessna Cir, Corona (92880-2509)
PHONE...............................951 270-1766
Manuel Perez, *President*
Luis Perez, *Vice Pres*
EMP: 25
SQ FT: 50,850
SALES (est): 6.1MM **Privately Held**
SIC: 3728 3559 Aircraft parts & equipment; semiconductor manufacturing machinery

(P-20047)
AVCORP CMPSITE FABRICATION INC
1600 W 135th St, Gardena (90249-2506)
P.O. Box 1007 (90249-0007)
PHONE...............................310 970-5658
Marcus Maria Van Rooij, *President*
Andy Koeck, *General Mgr*
Hardeep Sidhu, *Info Tech Mgr*
Eric Sorenson, *VP Engrg*
Brendan Connelly, *Engineer*
EMP: 400 EST: 2015
SQ FT: 350,000
SALES: 75MM
SALES (corp-wide): 129.4MM **Privately Held**
SIC: 3728 Aircraft parts & equipment
PA: Avcorp Industries Inc
10025 River Way
Delta BC V4G 1
604 582-1137

(P-20048)
AVCORP CMPSTES FABRICATION INC
1551 W 139th St, Gardena (90249-2603)
PHONE...............................310 527-0700
EMP: 12
SALES (est): 2.1MM **Privately Held**
SIC: 3728 Aircraft parts & equipment

(P-20049)
AVIATOR SYSTEMS INC
37440 Calle De Lobo, Murrieta (92562-7109)
PHONE...............................949 677-2461
Scott Gordon, *President*
EMP: 10 EST: 2014
SALES (est): 624.7K **Privately Held**
SIC: 3728 Aircraft parts & equipment

(P-20050)
AVIBANK MFG INC (DH)
11500 Sherman Way, North Hollywood (91605-5827)
P.O. Box 9909 (91609-1909)
PHONE...............................818 392-2100
Dan Welter, *President*
John Duran, *Vice Pres*
▲ EMP: 115 EST: 1945
SALES (est): 92.7MM
SALES (corp-wide): 225.3B **Publicly Held**
SIC: 3728 Aircraft parts & equipment
HQ: Sps Technologies, Llc
301 Highland Ave
Jenkintown PA 19046
215 572-3000

(P-20051)
B & E MANUFACTURING CO INC
12151 Monarch St, Garden Grove (92841-2927)
PHONE...............................714 898-2269
Larry Solinger, *President*

Ann Lee Solinger, *Corp Secy*
Randy Solinger, *Vice Pres*
Rachel Sollinger, *Production*
Rob Force, *Manager*
EMP: 45
SQ FT: 26,000
SALES (est): 11MM **Privately Held**
WEB: www.bandmfg.com
SIC: 3728 Aircraft parts & equipment

(P-20052)
B/E AEROSPACE INC
Also Called: Teklam Corporation
350 W Rincon St, Corona (92880-2004)
PHONE...............................951 278-4563
Gordon McKauley, *Branch Mgr*
EMP: 100
SALES (corp-wide): 66.5B **Publicly Held**
SIC: 3728 Aircraft parts & equipment
HQ: B/E Aerospace, Inc.
1400 Corporate Center Way
Wellington FL 33414
561 791-5000

(P-20053)
B/E AEROSPACE INC
7155 Fenwick Ln, Westminster (92683-5218)
PHONE...............................714 896-9001
Jim Melrose, *Manager*
EMP: 250
SALES (corp-wide): 66.5B **Publicly Held**
WEB: www.beaerospace.com
SIC: 3728 3647 Aircraft parts & equipment; aircraft lighting fixtures
HQ: B/E Aerospace, Inc.
1400 Corporate Center Way
Wellington FL 33414
561 791-5000

(P-20054)
B/E AEROSPACE INC
Collins Aerospace
3355 E La Palma Ave, Anaheim (92806-2815)
PHONE...............................714 688-4200
Bruce Thayer, *General Mgr*
Kevin Lehnert, *Executive*
Masashi Iwao, *General Mgr*
Peggy Packard, *Administration*
Ken Cowans, *Research*
EMP: 300
SALES (corp-wide): 66.5B **Publicly Held**
WEB: www.beaerospace.com
SIC: 3728 3585 Aircraft parts & equipment; refrigeration & heating equipment
HQ: B/E Aerospace, Inc.
1400 Corporate Center Way
Wellington FL 33414
561 791-5000

(P-20055)
BAILEY INDUSTRIES INC
25256 Terreno Dr, Mission Viejo (92691-5528)
PHONE...............................949 461-0807
Nonny Bailey, *President*
EMP: 12
SALES (est): 1.1MM **Privately Held**
WEB: www.baileyindustries.com
SIC: 3728 4783 2679 5088 Aircraft parts & equipment; packing & crating; labels, paper: made from purchased material; aircraft equipment & supplies

(P-20056)
BANDY MANUFACTURING LLC
3420 N San Fernando Blvd, Burbank (91504-2532)
P.O. Box 7716 (91510-7716)
PHONE...............................818 846-9020
Tom Fulton, *President*
Kevin L Cummings, *CEO*
Tom Hoffa, *Design Engr*
Henry Moore, *Facilities Mgr*
EMP: 93 EST: 1952
SQ FT: 60,000
SALES (est): 22.5MM **Privately Held**
SIC: 3728 Aircraft parts & equipment

(P-20057)
BERANEK INC
2340 W 205th St, Torrance (90501-1436)
PHONE...............................310 328-9094
George Beranek, *CEO*
Douglas Beranek, *President*

Hector D Beranek, *Exec VP*
Vilma N Beranek, *Admin Sec*
Eric Beranek, *Opers Mgr*
EMP: 22
SQ FT: 20,000
SALES: 8.8MM **Privately Held**
WEB: www.beranekinc.com
SIC: 3728 Aircraft parts & equipment

(P-20058)
BISH INC
2820 Via Orange Way Ste G, Spring Valley
(91978-1742)
PHONE...............................619 660-6220
William L Cary, *President*
Shane Nonthavet, *Vice Pres*
Allison Sauer,
EMP: 23
SQ FT: 16,000
SALES: 6MM **Privately Held**
SIC: 3728 Aircraft parts & equipment

(P-20059)
BRICE MANUFACTURING CO INC
Also Called: Haeco Americas Cabin Solutions
10262 Norris Ave, Pacoima (91331-2217)
PHONE...............................818 896-2938
Richard Kendall, *CEO*
Mark Peterman, *President*
Lee Fox, *CFO*
▲ **EMP:** 25
SQ FT: 60,000
SALES (est): 11.9MM **Privately Held**
WEB: www.bricemfg.com
SIC: 3728 7641 Aircraft parts & equipment; furniture repair & maintenance
HQ: Haeco Americas, Llc
623 Radar Rd
Greensboro NC 27410
336 668-4410

(P-20060)
C & H HYDRAULICS INC
Also Called: Acme Divac Industries
1585 Monrovia Ave, Newport Beach
(92663-2806)
PHONE...............................949 646-6230
James F Andreae Jr, *CEO*
Cindy Bender, *Purchasing*
EMP: 17
SQ FT: 8,000
SALES (est): 2.9MM **Privately Held**
SIC: 3728 8734 3769 3812 Aircraft parts & equipment; testing laboratories; guided missile & space vehicle parts & auxiliary equipment; search & navigation equipment; current-carrying wiring devices; hydraulic equipment repair

(P-20061)
CAD MANUFACTURING INC
7320 Adams St, Paramount (90723-4008)
PHONE...............................562 408-1113
John Mburu, *President*
Harry Samat, *Vice Pres*
EMP: 10
SQ FT: 8,000
SALES (est): 1.5MM **Privately Held**
WEB: www.cadmanufacturing.com
SIC: 3728 3544 Aircraft parts & equipment; special dies, tools, jigs & fixtures

(P-20062)
CADENCE AEROSPACE LLC (PA)
3150 E Miraloma Ave, Anaheim
(92806-1906)
PHONE...............................949 877-3630
Ron Case, *Mng Member*
Lanny Shirk, *President*
Joyce Pae, *CFO*
Robert J Saia, *Senior VP*
Richard Brighenti, *Vice Pres*
EMP: 47 **EST:** 2010
SQ FT: 5,000
SALES (est): 192.6MM **Privately Held**
SIC: 3728 Aircraft body assemblies & parts

(P-20063)
CAL TECH PRECISION INC
1830 N Lemon St, Anaheim (92801-1000)
PHONE...............................714 992-4130
Guy W Haarlammert, *President*
▲ **EMP:** 99

SALES (est): 11.1MM **Privately Held**
WEB: www.caltechprecision.com
SIC: 3728 Aircraft parts & equipment

(P-20064)
CALIFORNIA COMPOSITES MGT INC
1935 E Occidental St, Santa Ana
(92705-5115)
PHONE...............................714 258-0405
Fred Good, *Ch of Bd*
EMP: 25
SQ FT: 30,000
SALES (est): 4.2MM **Privately Held**
WEB: www.ccdicomposites.com
SIC: 3728 3812 3624 Aircraft parts & equipment; search & navigation equipment; carbon & graphite products

(P-20065)
CANYON COMPOSITES INCORPORATED
1548 N Gemini Pl, Anaheim (92801-1152)
PHONE...............................714 991-8181
BJ Rutkoski, *President*
Eric Collins, *Treasurer*
Robert Gray, *Vice Pres*
Blake Vanier, *Technology*
Van H Pat, *Senior Engr*
EMP: 40
SQ FT: 31,500
SALES (est): 11.3MM **Privately Held**
WEB: www.canyoncomposites.com
SIC: 3728 8711 Aircraft parts & equipment; engineering services

(P-20066)
CANYON ENGINEERING PDTS INC
28909 Avenue Williams, Valencia
(91355-4183)
PHONE...............................661 294-0084
Todd Strickland, *President*
Paul Knerr, *Vice Pres*
EMP: 88
SQ FT: 70,000
SALES (est): 11.6MM
SALES (corp-wide): 771.5MM **Publicly Held**
WEB: www.canyonengineering.com
SIC: 3728 Aircraft assemblies, subassemblies & parts
PA: Esco Technologies Inc.
9900 Clayton Rd Ste A
Saint Louis MO 63124
314 213-7200

(P-20067)
CARBON BY DESIGN LLC
1491 Poinsettia Ave # 136, Vista
(92081-8541)
PHONE...............................760 643-1300
Dominick Consalvi,
John Schauer, *Partner*
Mitchell Pearl, *Engineer*
EMP: 75
SQ FT: 65,000
SALES: 4.7MM **Publicly Held**
WEB: www.carbonbydesign.com
SIC: 3728 3761 Airframe assemblies, except for guided missiles; guided missiles & space vehicles; guided missiles & space vehicles, research & development
HQ: Flight Support Group Inc
161 Turnberry Cir
New Smyrna FL 32168
954 987-4000

(P-20068)
CARDONA MANUFACTURING CORP
1869 N Victory Pl, Burbank (91504-3476)
PHONE...............................818 841-8358
Louis Cardona, *President*
Jo Ann Cardona, *Corp Secy*
Joe Martinez, *Info Tech Mgr*
Cathy Martinez, *Purchasing*
EMP: 26
SQ FT: 10,000
SALES (est): 3.9MM **Privately Held**
WEB: www.cardonamfg.com
SIC: 3728 3812 Aircraft parts & equipment; search & navigation equipment

(P-20069)
CAVOTEC DABICO US INC
5665 Corporate Ave, Cypress
(90630-4727)
PHONE...............................714 947-0005
Gary Matthews, *President*
Christian Bernadotte, *Admin Sec*
Chris Clayton, *Accountant*
Dorothy Chen, *Controller*
Lejo Joseph, *Manager*
▲ **EMP:** 36
SALES (est): 9.4MM **Privately Held**
SIC: 3728 Aircraft parts & equipment

(P-20070)
CHOL ENTERPRISES INC
12831 S Figueroa St, Los Angeles
(90061-1157)
PHONE...............................310 516-1328
Neal Castleman, *President*
Brian Gamberg, *Vice Pres*
EMP: 26
SQ FT: 25,000
SALES (est): 3.1MM **Privately Held**
SIC: 3728 3769 3678 3357 Aircraft assemblies, subassemblies & parts; guided missile & space vehicle parts & auxiliary equipment; electronic connectors; nonferrous wiredrawing & insulating

(P-20071)
CIRCOR AEROSPACE INC
2301 Wardlow Cir, Corona (92880-2801)
PHONE...............................951 270-6200
Christopher R Celtruda, *General Mgr*
Bill Asmus, *Principal*
▲ **EMP:** 315
SQ FT: 80,000
SALES: 44.2MM
SALES (corp-wide): 1.1B **Publicly Held**
WEB: www.circor.com
SIC: 3728 3625 Alighting (landing gear) assemblies, aircraft; actuators, industrial
PA: Circor International, Inc.
30 Corporate Dr Ste 200
Burlington MA 01803
781 270-1200

(P-20072)
COATING SPECIALTIES INC
Also Called: Aero Products Co.
815 E Rosecrans Ave, Los Angeles
(90059-3510)
PHONE...............................310 639-6900
Martha Taylor, *Admin Sec*
EMP: 14
SQ FT: 31,000
SALES: 3MM **Privately Held**
WEB: www.aeroproductsco.com
SIC: 3728 3812 Aircraft assemblies, subassemblies & parts; search & navigation equipment

(P-20073)
COI CERAMICS INC
Also Called: Coic
7130 Miramar Rd Ste 100b, San Diego
(92121-2340)
PHONE...............................858 621-5700
David A Shanahan, *CEO*
Steve Atmur, *Director*
Andy Szweda, *Director*
EMP: 41
SQ FT: 3,000
SALES (est): 12.9MM **Publicly Held**
WEB: www.coi-world.com
SIC: 3728 Aircraft parts & equipment
HQ: Northrop Grumman Innovation Systems, Inc.
45101 Warp Dr
Dulles VA 20166
703 406-5000

(P-20074)
COMPOSITES HORIZONS LLC (HQ)
1629 W Industrial Park St, Covina
(91722-3418)
PHONE...............................626 331-0861
Jeff Hynes, *President*
Renee Fahmy, *Vice Pres*
Tom Schulz, *Administration*
Rod Wolfe, *Facilities Mgr*
▲ **EMP:** 140
SQ FT: 25,000

SALES (est): 26.4MM
SALES (corp-wide): 386.8MM **Privately Held**
WEB: www.chi-covina.com
SIC: 3728 3844 2821 Aircraft parts & equipment; X-ray apparatus & tubes; nuclear irradiation equipment; plastics materials & resins
PA: Ascent Aerospace Holdings Llc
16445 23 Mile Rd
Macomb MI 48042
212 916-8142

(P-20075)
COMPUCRAFT INDUSTRIES INC
Also Called: Cii
8787 Olive Ln, Santee (92071-4137)
P.O. Box 712529 (92072-2529)
PHONE...............................619 448-0787
Maurice Brear, *President*
Margarita Brear, *CFO*
EMP: 50
SQ FT: 85,000
SALES: 6MM **Privately Held**
WEB: www.ccind.com
SIC: 3728 Aircraft assemblies, subassemblies & parts

(P-20076)
CONDOR PACIFIC INDS CAL INC
905 Rancho Conejo Blvd, Newbury Park
(91320-1716)
PHONE...............................818 889-2150
Sidney Meltzner, *President*
Cher Gibson, *Program Mgr*
Charles Shuman, *Financial Exec*
EMP: 20
SALES: 3MM **Privately Held**
SIC: 3728 Aircraft parts & equipment

(P-20077)
CORONADO MANUFACTURING INC
8991 Glenoaks Blvd, Sun Valley
(91352-2038)
PHONE...............................818 768-5010
Allen F Gowing, *President*
Phillip Belmonte, *Vice Pres*
Scott Wilke, *Managing Dir*
Mylinn Dasalla, *Mktg Dir*
▼ **EMP:** 50
SQ FT: 19,000
SALES (est): 9MM **Privately Held**
WEB: www.coronadomfg.com
SIC: 3728 5084 Military aircraft equipment & armament; aircraft assemblies, subassemblies & parts; industrial machine parts

(P-20078)
CUSTOM AIRCRAFT INTERIORS INC
3701 Industry Ave, Lakewood
(90712-4113)
PHONE...............................562 426-5098
William Erwin, *CEO*
Kurt Erwin, *Vice Pres*
Linda Seale, *General Mgr*
EMP: 10
SQ FT: 11,000
SALES (est): 1.8MM **Privately Held**
SIC: 3728 Aircraft parts & equipment

(P-20079)
CYNTHIA GARCIA
Also Called: Aero Space Composites
11782 Western Ave Ste 7, Stanton
(90680-3458)
PHONE...............................714 897-4654
Cynthia Garcia, *Owner*
EMP: 10
SQ FT: 6,000
SALES: 800K **Privately Held**
SIC: 3728 3812 8711 Aircraft parts & equipment; search & navigation equipment; aviation &/or aeronautical engineering

(P-20080)
D & D GEAR INCORPORATED
Also Called: Absolute Technologies
4890 E La Palma Ave, Anaheim
(92807-1911)
PHONE...............................714 692-6570
Bill Beverage, *President*
Don Beverage, *Vice Pres*

Kim Helms, *Executive*
Jason Praditbatuga, *Engineer*
Scott Reid, *Engineer*
▲ **EMP:** 210
SQ FT: 82,500
SALES (est): 59.8MM **Privately Held**
WEB: www.absolutetechnologies.com
SIC: 3728 Aircraft parts & equipment

(P-20081)
D & S INDUSTRIES INC
4515 E Eisenhower Cir, Anaheim
(92807-1852)
PHONE..................................714 779-8074
David Pierce Jr, *President*
Lisa Wilson, *Manager*
EMP: 13
SQ FT: 8,000
SALES (est): 3MM **Privately Held**
SIC: 3728 Aircraft parts & equipment

(P-20082)
DANIEL VOSCLOO JR
Also Called: Danvo Machining Company
2107 S Hathaway St, Santa Ana
(92705-5238)
PHONE..................................714 751-1401
Daniel Vosloo Jr, *Owner*
Jeffrey Hudson, *QC Mgr*
EMP: 10 **EST:** 1977
SQ FT: 400
SALES (est): 1.2MM **Privately Held**
WEB: www.danvomachiningcompany.com
SIC: 3728 Aircraft body assemblies & parts

(P-20083)
DASCO ENGINEERING CORP
24747 Crenshaw Blvd, Torrance
(90505-5308)
PHONE..................................310 326-2277
Ward Olson, *President*
John Karle, *Vice Pres*
Glen Olson, *Vice Pres*
◆ **EMP:** 105 **EST:** 1964
SQ FT: 50,000
SALES (est): 22.9MM **Privately Held**
WEB: www.dascoeng.com
SIC: 3728 Aircraft body & wing assemblies
& parts

(P-20084)
DATUM PRECISION INC
345 Crown Point Cir # 800, Grass Valley
(95945-9526)
PHONE..................................530 272-8415
John T Jans III, *President*
EMP: 10
SQ FT: 3,000
SALES (est): 1.4MM **Privately Held**
SIC: 3728 3599 Aircraft assemblies, sub-
assemblies & parts; machine shop, job-
bing & repair

(P-20085)
DIAGNOSTIC SOLUTIONS INTL
LLC
2580 E Philadelphia St C, Ontario
(91761-8093)
PHONE..................................909 930-3600
Brian Hatcher, *General Mgr*
Neil Seamon, *Technical Staff*
Elena Buckley,
EMP: 16
SQ FT: 5,000
SALES (est): 3.2MM **Privately Held**
SIC: 3728 Aircraft parts & equipment

(P-20086)
DJI SERVICE LLC
17301 Edwards Rd, Cerritos (90703-2427)
PHONE..................................818 235-0788
Hao Shen,
EMP: 15
SALES (est): 4.9MM **Privately Held**
SIC: 3728 Aircraft parts & equipment

(P-20087)
DMEA MSC
5584 Patrol Rd Bldg 1069, McClellan
(95652-2200)
PHONE..................................916 568-4087
Tamara Sullivan, *Principal*
EMP: 22
SALES (est): 3.2MM **Privately Held**
SIC: 3728 Military aircraft equipment & ar-
mament

(P-20088)
DOWNEY MANUFACTURING INC
11421 Downey Ave, Downey (90241-4934)
PHONE..................................562 862-3311
Bill Read, *President*
EMP: 10
SQ FT: 15,000
SALES: 750K **Privately Held**
WEB: www.downeymfg.com
SIC: 3728 7699 Alighting (landing gear)
assemblies, aircraft; aircraft flight instru-
ment repair

(P-20089)
DPI LABS INC
1350 Arrow Hwy, La Verne (91750-5218)
PHONE..................................909 392-5777
Vicki Brown, *CEO*
Al Snow, *CFO*
Pam Archibald, *Vice Pres*
Greg Desmet, *Vice Pres*
Alfonso Loera, *Technician*
EMP: 35
SALES (est): 8MM **Privately Held**
WEB: www.dpilabs.com
SIC: 3728 Aircraft parts & equipment

(P-20090)
DRETLOH AIRCRAFT SUPPLY
INC (PA)
2830 E La Cresta Ave, Anaheim
(92806-1816)
PHONE..................................714 632-6982
Eugene Holte, *President*
Freda Holte, *Corp Secy*
Randy Holte, *Vice Pres*
Carol Snyder, *Manager*
▲ **EMP:** 15
SQ FT: 10,000
SALES (est): 2.3MM **Privately Held**
SIC: 3728 5199 Aircraft parts & equip-
ment; foam rubber

(P-20091)
DUCOMMUN
AEROSTRUCTURES INC
801 Royal Oaks Dr, Monrovia
(91016-3630)
PHONE..................................626 358-3211
Maurice Harris, *General Mgr*
EMP: 30
SALES (corp-wide): 629.3MM **Publicly
Held**
SIC: 3728 Aircraft parts & equipment
HQ: Ducommun Aerostructures, Inc.
268 E Gardena Blvd
Gardena CA 90248
310 380-5390

(P-20092)
DUCOMMUN
AEROSTRUCTURES INC
4001 El Mirage Rd, Adelanto (92301-9489)
PHONE..................................760 246-4191
Art McFarlan, *Manager*
EMP: 34
SQ FT: 1,152
SALES (corp-wide): 629.3MM **Publicly
Held**
SIC: 3728 Aircraft parts & equipment
HQ: Ducommun Aerostructures, Inc.
268 E Gardena Blvd
Gardena CA 90248
310 380-5390

(P-20093)
DUCOMMUN INCORPORATED
(PA)
200 Sandpointe Ave # 700, Santa Ana
(92707-5759)
PHONE..................................657 335-3665
Stephen G Oswald, *President*
Christopher D Wampler, *CFO*
Rosalie F Rogers, *Officer*
Jerry L Redondo, *Senior VP*
▲ **EMP:** 146 **EST:** 1849
SALES: 629.3MM **Publicly Held**
SIC: 3728 3679 Aircraft body & wing as-
semblies & parts; microwave components

(P-20094)
DUCOMMUN LABARGE TECH
INC (HQ)
Also Called: American Electronics
23301 Wilmington Ave, Carson
(90745-6209)
PHONE..................................310 513-7200
Stephen G Oswald, *CEO*
Douglas L Groves, *CFO*
Amy M Paul, *Admin Sec*
Steven Moorman, *Mfg Staff*
Ross Bilodeau, *Manager*
▲ **EMP:** 180 **EST:** 1958
SQ FT: 117,000
SALES (est): 61.7MM
SALES (corp-wide): 629.3MM **Publicly
Held**
WEB: www.ductech.com
SIC: 3728 3769 5065 3812 Aircraft parts
& equipment; guided missile & space ve-
hicle parts & auxiliary equipment; elec-
tronic parts & equipment; search &
navigation equipment; current-carrying
wiring devices; relays & industrial controls
PA: Ducommun Incorporated
200 Sandpointe Ave # 700
Santa Ana CA 92707
657 335-3665

(P-20095)
DYNAMATION RESEARCH INC
2301 Pontius Ave, Los Angeles
(90064-1809)
PHONE..................................909 864-2310
Gal Lipkin, *President*
EMP: 15
SQ FT: 5,500
SALES (est): 3MM **Privately Held**
SIC: 3728 3812 Aircraft parts & equip-
ment; search & navigation equipment

(P-20096)
EATON INDUSTRIAL
CORPORATION
Also Called: Ground Fueling
9650 Jeronimo Rd, Irvine (92618-2024)
PHONE..................................949 425-9700
Keith Mayer, *Branch Mgr*
Debby Reynolds, *General Mgr*
EMP: 300 **Privately Held**
SIC: 3728 3594 3561 3492 Aircraft parts
& equipment; fluid power pumps & mo-
tors; pumps & pumping equipment; fluid
power valves & hose fittings
HQ: Eaton Industrial Corporation
23555 Euclid Ave
Cleveland OH 44117
216 523-4205

(P-20097)
ENCORE INTERIORS INC (HQ)
Also Called: Lift By Encore
5511 Skylab Rd Ste 101, Huntington Beach
(92647-2071)
PHONE..................................949 559-0930
Thomas McFarland, *President*
Kevin Tran, *IT/INT Sup*
Kashif Ahmed, *Project Engr*
Wade Delaney, *Project Engr*
Heath White, *Engineer*
▲ **EMP:** 130
SQ FT: 42,000
SALES (est): 61MM
SALES (corp-wide): 101.1B **Publicly
Held**
WEB: www.compositesunlimited.com
SIC: 3728 1799 Aircraft parts & equip-
ment; renovation of aircraft interiors
PA: The Boeing Company
100 N Riverside Plz
Chicago IL 60606
312 544-2000

(P-20098)
ENCORE INTERIORS INC
5511 Skylab Rd Ste 101, Huntington Beach
(92647-2071)
PHONE..................................562 344-1700
Karl Jonson, *Vice Pres*
EMP: 200
SALES (corp-wide): 101.1B **Publicly
Held**
SIC: 3728 Aircraft parts & equipment

HQ: Encore Interiors, Inc.
5511 Skylab Rd Ste 101
Huntington Beach CA 92647
949 559-0930

(P-20099)
ENCORE SEATS INC
Also Called: Lift By Encore
5511 Skylab Rd, Huntington Beach
(92647-2068)
PHONE..................................949 559-0930
Thomas McFarland, *CEO*
Mike Melancon, *CFO*
Aram Krikorian, *Vice Pres*
EMP: 46 **EST:** 2015
SQ FT: 80,000
SALES (est): 8.5MM **Privately Held**
SIC: 3728 Aircraft assemblies, subassem-
blies & parts; seat ejector devices, aircraft

(P-20100)
ENGINEERING JK AEROSPACE
& DEF
23231 La Palma Ave, Yorba Linda
(92887-4768)
PHONE..................................714 414-6722
Jonathan Crisan, *President*
EMP: 15 **EST:** 2017
SALES (est): 587.5K **Privately Held**
SIC: 3728 Aircraft parts & equipment

(P-20101)
F & L TOOLS CORPORATION
Also Called: F & L Tls Precision Machining
245 Jason Ct, Corona (92879-6199)
PHONE..................................951 279-1555
Tracey Pratt, *President*
Larry Pratt, *President*
Daryl Pratt, *General Mgr*
Shawn Wolfe, *Sales Staff*
EMP: 18
SQ FT: 8,100
SALES (est): 3.9MM **Privately Held**
WEB: www.fltcorp.com
SIC: 3728 Aircraft parts & equipment

(P-20102)
FARRAR GRINDING COMPANY
347 E Beach Ave, Inglewood (90302-3191)
PHONE..................................323 678-4879
Clarke Farrar, *President*
Darryl Farrar, *Administration*
EMP: 14 **EST:** 1957
SQ FT: 6,000
SALES: 1.2MM **Privately Held**
WEB: www.farrar-grinding.com
SIC: 3728 3599 Aircraft parts & equip-
ment; machine shop, jobbing & repair

(P-20103)
FEDERAL AVIATION ADM
Also Called: Flight Standards District Off
2250 E Imperial Hwy # 140, El Segundo
(90245-3543)
PHONE..................................310 640-9640
Richard Falcon, *Manager*
EMP: 40 **Publicly Held**
WEB: www.faa.gov
SIC: 3728 Airplane brake expanders; air-
craft armament, except guns
HQ: Federal Aviation Administration
800 Independence Ave Sw
Washington DC 20591
-

(P-20104)
FLARE GROUP
Also Called: Aviation Equipment Processing
1571 Macarthur Blvd, Costa Mesa
(92626-1407)
PHONE..................................714 850-2080
Dennis Heider, *President*
Steve Osorio, *Vice Pres*
Daryl Silva, *Principal*
Eric Trainor, *Principal*
Jim Vinyard, *Principal*
EMP: 25
SALES (est): 6.1MM **Privately Held**
SIC: 3728 Aircraft parts & equipment; air-
craft body assemblies & parts

(P-20105)
FLEXCO INC
6855 Suva St, Bell Gardens (90201-1999)
PHONE..................................562 927-2525
Erik Moller, *President*

EMP: 36
SQ FT: 14,000
SALES: 3MM **Privately Held**
WEB: www.flexcoinc.com
SIC: 3728 3496 Aircraft parts & equipment; miscellaneous fabricated wire products

(P-20106)
FLIGHT ENVIRONMENTS INC
570 Linne Rd Ste 100, Paso Robles
(93446-9460)
P.O. Box 3169 (93447-3169)
PHONE.................................805 226-2912
Eamon F Halpin, *CEO*
Viviana Gutierrez, *Executive Asst*
Sergio Flores, *Prdtn Mgr*
EMP: 25
SQ FT: 11,000
SALES (est): 3.1MM **Privately Held**
WEB: www.flightenvironments.com
SIC: 3728 Aircraft parts & equipment

(P-20107)
FMH AEROSPACE CORP
Also Called: F M H
17072 Daimler St, Irvine (92614-5548)
PHONE.................................714 751-1000
Rick Busch, *CEO*
Valerie Gorman, *CFO*
David Difranco, *Admin Sec*
▲ **EMP:** 100
SQ FT: 15,000
SALES (est): 28.2MM
SALES (corp-wide): 4.8B **Publicly Held**
WEB: www.flexiblemetalhose.com
SIC: 3728 Aircraft parts & equipment
PA: Ametek, Inc.
    1100 Cassatt Rd
    Berwyn PA 19312
    610 647-2121

(P-20108)
FORMING SPECIALTIES INC
1309 W Walnut Pkwy, Compton
(90220-5030)
PHONE.................................310 639-1122
Darrell E Madole, *President*
Kevin Herbert, *Vice Pres*
EMP: 33
SQ FT: 40,000
SALES (est): 4.9MM **Privately Held**
WEB: www.formingspecialties.com
SIC: 3728 3444 Aircraft parts & equipment; sheet metalwork

(P-20109)
FORREST MACHINING INC
Also Called: Forrestmachining.com
27756 Avenue Mentry, Valencia
(91355-3453)
PHONE.................................661 257-0231
Joanne Butler, *CEO*
Joe Velazquez, *Executive*
Andrew Kim, *Program Mgr*
Tony Montoya, *Program Mgr*
Steve Wooten, *General Mgr*
▲ **EMP:** 200 **EST:** 1977
SALES: 47.9MM **Privately Held**
WEB: www.forrestmachining.com
SIC: 3728 Aircraft parts & equipment

(P-20110)
FRAZIER AVIATION INC
445 N Fox St, San Fernando (91340-2501)
PHONE.................................818 898-1998
Robert L Frazier, *CEO*
Robert Frazier III, *President*
Marcia Cooper, *Vice Pres*
Charles E Ricard, *Vice Pres*
Tamara Druschen, *Administration*
EMP: 42 **EST:** 1956
SQ FT: 44,000
SALES (est): 9.9MM **Privately Held**
WEB: www.frazieraviation.com
SIC: 3728 5088 Aircraft body assemblies & parts; transportation equipment & supplies

(P-20111)
GALI CORPORATION
Also Called: Dynamation Research
2301 Pontius Ave, Los Angeles
(90064-1809)
PHONE.................................310 477-1224
Gal Lipkin, *CEO*

EMP: 14
SALES (est): 2.2MM **Privately Held**
WEB: www.dynamation.com
SIC: 3728 3812 Aircraft parts & equipment; aircraft control instruments

(P-20112)
GE AVIATION SYSTEMS LLC
Also Called: Mechancal Systm-Rial Refueling
23695 Via Del Rio, Yorba Linda
(92887-2715)
PHONE.................................714 692-0200
Mary Normand, *Controller*
EMP: 250
SALES (corp-wide): 121.6B **Publicly Held**
SIC: 3728 Aircraft assemblies, subassemblies & parts
HQ: Ge Aviation Systems Llc
    1 Neumann Way
    Cincinnati OH 45215
    937 898-9600

(P-20113)
GEAR MANUFACTURING INC
Also Called: G M I
3701 E Miraloma Ave, Anaheim
(92806-2123)
PHONE.................................714 792-2895
Gary M Smith, *CEO*
Aaron Smith, *Info Tech Mgr*
Bob Bennett, *Mfg Mgr*
Dave Mackley, *QC Mgr*
George Abbascia, *Sales Staff*
EMP: 50
SQ FT: 26,500
SALES (est): 11.7MM **Privately Held**
WEB: www.gearmfg.com
SIC: 3728 3714 3566 3568 Gears, aircraft power transmission; bearings, motor vehicle; speed changers, drives & gears; power transmission equipment; motorcycles, bicycles & parts

(P-20114)
GFMI AEROSPACE & DEFENSE INC
17375 Mount Herrmann St, Fountain Valley
(92708-4103)
PHONE.................................714 361-4444
EMP: 30 **EST:** 2011
SALES (est): 2.6MM **Privately Held**
WEB: www.gfmiaero.com
SIC: 3728 8711

(P-20115)
GLEDHILL/LYONS INC
Also Called: Accurate Technology
1521 N Placentia Ave, Anaheim
(92806-1236)
PHONE.................................714 502-0274
David M Lyons, *President*
EMP: 43
SQ FT: 31,200
SALES (est): 13.5MM **Privately Held**
WEB: www.accuratetechnology.net
SIC: 3728 Aircraft parts & equipment

(P-20116)
GLOBAL AEROSPACE TECH CORP
25109 Rye Canyon Loop, Valencia
(91355-5004)
PHONE.................................818 407-5600
Steve Cormier, *CEO*
EMP: 22
SQ FT: 40,000
SALES (est): 5.2MM **Privately Held**
WEB: www.globalatcorp.com
SIC: 3728 Aircraft parts & equipment

(P-20117)
GLOBAL AEROSTRUCTURES
10291 Trademark St Ste C, Rancho Cucamonga (91730-5847)
PHONE.................................909 987-4888
EMP: 15
SALES: 2MM **Privately Held**
SIC: 3728

(P-20118)
GME MFG INC
10641 Pullman Ct, Rancho Cucamonga
(91730-4847)
PHONE.................................909 989-4478
Leo Garcia, *President*

Olivia Gutierrez, *Admin Sec*
EMP: 10
SQ FT: 8,000
SALES (est): 2MM **Privately Held**
SIC: 3728 Accumulators, aircraft propeller

(P-20119)
GOODRICH CORPORATION
Goodrich Super Temp Division
11120 Norwalk Blvd, Santa Fe Springs
(90670-3830)
PHONE.................................562 906-7372
Michael Grundelsky, *Manager*
Jerry T Toms, *Design Engr*
EMP: 10
SALES (corp-wide): 66.5B **Publicly Held**
WEB: www.goodrich.com
SIC: 3728 Aircraft parts & equipment
HQ: Goodrich Corporation
    2730 W Tyvola Rd 4
    Charlotte NC 28217
    704 423-7000

(P-20120)
GOODRICH CORPORATION
Also Called: Goodrich Aerostructures
850 Lagoon Dr, Chula Vista (91910-2001)
PHONE.................................619 691-4111
David Gitlin, *President*
Jared Hippe, *Vice Pres*
Susan Segal, *Vice Pres*
Beth Garrison, *Administration*
Olivier Vanoli, *Administration*
▲ **EMP:** 84
SALES (est): 32MM **Privately Held**
SIC: 3728 Aircraft parts & equipment

(P-20121)
GOODRICH CORPORATION
2727 E Imperial Hwy, Brea (92821-6713)
PHONE.................................714 984-1461
Rob Gibbs, *General Mgr*
Lydia Kirk, *General Mgr*
Tedd Wong, *Engineer*
Mike Fox, *Manager*
EMP: 140
SALES (corp-wide): 66.5B **Publicly Held**
WEB: www.bfgoodrich.com
SIC: 3728 Aircraft parts & equipment
HQ: Goodrich Corporation
    2730 W Tyvola Rd 4
    Charlotte NC 28217
    704 423-7000

(P-20122)
GOODRICH CORPORATION
Goodrich Wheel and Brake Svcs
9920 Freeman Ave, Santa Fe Springs
(90670-3421)
PHONE.................................562 944-4441
Hosrow Bordbar, *Manager*
Mark Posada, *Purch Dir*
EMP: 55
SALES (corp-wide): 66.5B **Publicly Held**
WEB: www.bfgoodrich.com
SIC: 3728 Aircraft parts & equipment
HQ: Goodrich Corporation
    2730 W Tyvola Rd 4
    Charlotte NC 28217
    704 423-7000

(P-20123)
GST INDUSTRIES INC
9060 Winnetka Ave, Northridge
(91324-3235)
PHONE.................................818 350-1900
EMP: 24
SQ FT: 9,700
SALES (est): 2.3MM
SALES (corp-wide): 8.4MM **Privately Held**
WEB: www.gstindustries.net
SIC: 3728
PA: Infinity Aerospace, Inc.
    9060 Winnetka Ave
    Northridge CA 91324
    818 998-9811

(P-20124)
HAGER MFG INC
14610 Industry Cir, La Mirada
(90638-5815)
PHONE.................................714 522-8870
Donald L Bowley, *President*
Patricia Bowley, *CFO*
EMP: 25 **EST:** 1969

SQ FT: 10,800
SALES (est): 3.8MM **Privately Held**
SIC: 3728 3599 Aircraft assemblies, subassemblies & parts; machine shop, jobbing & repair

(P-20125)
HELICOPTER TECH CO LTD PARTNR
12902 S Broadway, Los Angeles
(90061-1118)
PHONE.................................310 523-2750
Frank Palminteri, *President*
Gary Burdorf, *Executive*
Bob Bouchard, *General Mgr*
Robert Bouchard, *General Mgr*
James Fackler, *VP Opers*
◆ **EMP:** 24
SQ FT: 197,000
SALES (est): 5.8MM **Privately Held**
SIC: 3728 3721 Aircraft parts & equipment; helicopters

(P-20126)
HILLER AIRCRAFT CORPORATION
925 M St, Firebaugh (93622-2234)
P.O. Box 246 (93622-0246)
PHONE.................................559 659-5959
Steven Palm, *General Mgr*
EMP: 30
SQ FT: 100,000
SALES (est): 4.9MM **Privately Held**
SIC: 3728 Aircraft parts & equipment

(P-20127)
HQ MACHINE TECH LLC
6900 8th St, Buena Park (90620-1036)
PHONE.................................714 956-3388
Robert Groner, *President*
EMP: 35 **EST:** 2017
SALES (est): 1.9MM **Privately Held**
SIC: 3728 Aircraft parts & equipment

(P-20128)
HUGO ENGINEERING CO INC
837 Van Ness Ave, Torrance (90501-2230)
PHONE.................................310 320-0288
Loreto Gonzalez, *President*
Angie Gonzalez, *Vice Pres*
EMP: 10
SQ FT: 5,500
SALES (est): 1.9MM **Privately Held**
SIC: 3728 Aircraft parts & equipment

(P-20129)
HUTCHINSON AROSPC & INDUST INC
Also Called: ARS
4510 W Vanowen St, Burbank
(91505-1135)
PHONE.................................818 843-1000
Shano Cristilli, *Branch Mgr*
Gigi Tran, *General Mgr*
Alana Dunne, *Project Engr*
Roberto Sarjeant, *Engineer*
Ron Yeager, *Human Res Mgr*
EMP: 165
SALES (corp-wide): 8.4B **Publicly Held**
SIC: 3728 Aircraft parts & equipment
HQ: Hutchinson Aerospace & Industry, Inc.
    82 South St
    Hopkinton MA 01748
    508 417-7000

(P-20130)
HYDRAULICS INTERNATIONAL INC (PA)
9201 Independence Ave, Chatsworth
(91311-5905)
PHONE.................................818 998-1231
Nicky Ghaemmaghami, *CEO*
Shah Banifazl, *CFO*
Linda Ghaemmaghami, *Vice Pres*
Jeffrey Riley, *Vice Pres*
Shane Faulkwell, *Engineer*
◆ **EMP:** 277 **EST:** 1976
SQ FT: 78,000
SALES: 105.6MM **Privately Held**
WEB: www.hiifsu.com
SIC: 3728 Aircraft parts & equipment

(P-20131)
HYDRAULICS INTERNATIONAL INC
9000 Mason Ave, Chatsworth (91311-6178)
PHONE.................818 998-1236
Chuck Sherman, *Branch Mgr*
EMP: 62
SALES (corp-wide): 105.6MM **Privately Held**
WEB: www.hiifsu.com
SIC: 3728 Aircraft parts & equipment
PA: Hydraulics International, Inc.
9201 Independence Ave
Chatsworth CA 91311
818 998-1231

(P-20132)
HYDRO-AIRE INC (DH)
3000 Winona Ave, Burbank (91504-2540)
PHONE.................818 526-2600
Brendan J Curran, *CEO*
Tazewell Rowe, *Treasurer*
Ermine Adzhemyan, *Administration*
Travis Bevelaqua, *IT/INT Sup*
Sean Santos, *Engineer*
▲ EMP: 43
SQ FT: 173,000
SALES (est): 123.1MM
SALES (corp-wide): 3.3B **Publicly Held**
WEB: www.craneco.com
SIC: 3728 Aircraft parts & equipment

(P-20133)
HYDROFORM USA INCORPORATED
2848 E 208th St, Carson (90810-1101)
PHONE.................310 632-6353
Chester K Jablonski, *CEO*
George Curiel, *COO*
Ulrich Gottschling, *CFO*
Mauricio Salazar, *CFO*
Steven Hsu, *Info Tech Dir*
▼ EMP: 154
SQ FT: 95,000
SALES: 35MM **Privately Held**
WEB: www.hydroformusa.com
SIC: 3728 Aircraft parts & equipment

(P-20134)
ICON AIRCRAFT INC (PA)
2141 Icon Way, Vacaville (95688-8766)
PHONE.................707 564-4000
Kirk Hawkins, *CEO*
Thomas Wieners, *COO*
David Crook, *CFO*
Olivier Bellin, *Vice Pres*
Rich Bridge, *Vice Pres*
EMP: 81
SALES (est): 28.3MM **Privately Held**
SIC: 3728 Aircraft parts & equipment

(P-20135)
IKHANA GROUP INC
Also Called: Ikhana Aircraft Services
37260 Sky Canyon Dr # 20, Murrieta (92563-2680)
PHONE.................951 600-0009
John A Zublin, *President*
Marcos M Carvalhal, *CFO*
Stanley R Fisher, *Exec VP*
Marilyn Meyer, *Executive Asst*
Rick Broulik, *Design Engr*
▲ EMP: 120 EST: 2007
SALES (est): 21MM **Privately Held**
SIC: 3728 Flaps, aircraft wing

(P-20136)
IMPRESA AEROSPACE LLC (PA)
344 W 157th St, Gardena (90248-2135)
PHONE.................310 354-1200
Scott Smith, *CEO*
David Hirsch, *Vice Pres*
Jose Banuelos, *General Mgr*
Gustavo Alcala, *Engineer*
Federico Cisneros, *Engineer*
EMP: 16 EST: 1987
SQ FT: 26,000
SALES (est): 48MM **Privately Held**
WEB: www.ventureaircraft.com
SIC: 3728 3444 Aircraft parts & equipment; sheet metalwork

(P-20137)
IMPRESA AEROSPACE LLC
344 W 157th St, Gardena (90248-2135)
PHONE.................843 553-2021
Charles Vangraan, *Manager*
Scott Smith, *CEO*
EMP: 16
SALES (corp-wide): 48MM **Privately Held**
SIC: 3728 3444 Aircraft parts & equipment; sheet metalwork
PA: Impresa Aerospace, Llc
344 W 157th St
Gardena CA 90248
310 354-1200

(P-20138)
INFLIGHT WARNING SYSTEMS INC
Also Called: Iws Predictive Technologies
3910 Prospect Ave Unit P, Yorba Linda (92886-1746)
PHONE.................714 993-9394
Joseph Barclay, *President*
Dirk Fichtner, *President*
Jeff Bulkin, *CFO*
George Orff, *Admin Sec*
EMP: 19
SQ FT: 6,000
SALES (est): 1.6MM **Privately Held**
WEB: www.iws-llc.com
SIC: 3728 Aircraft assemblies, subassemblies & parts

(P-20139)
INTEGRAL AEROSPACE LLC
2040 E Dyer Rd, Santa Ana (92705-5710)
PHONE.................949 250-3123
John Alves, *President*
John Kutler, *Ch of Bd*
Terence Lyons, *CEO*
Jeff Lassiter, *CFO*
Bryan McLean, *Vice Pres*
EMP: 150
SQ FT: 275,000
SALES (est): 481.6K **Privately Held**
SIC: 3728 Aircraft propellers & associated equipment

(P-20140)
INTERTRADE AVIATION CORP
5722 Buckingham Dr, Huntington Beach (92649-1130)
PHONE.................714 895-3335
Ted Newfield, *President*
Bill Stuckert, *QC Mgr*
▲ EMP: 45 EST: 1980
SQ FT: 65,000
SALES (est): 6.6MM **Privately Held**
SIC: 3728 5088 Aircraft assemblies, subassemblies & parts; transportation equipment & supplies

(P-20141)
IRWIN AVIATION INC
Also Called: Aero Performance
225 Airport Cir, Corona (92880-2527)
PHONE.................951 372-9555
James Irwin, *CEO*
Nanci Irwin, *Vice Pres*
EMP: 30
SALES (est): 6.2MM **Privately Held**
SIC: 3728 Aircraft parts & equipment

(P-20142)
ITT AEROSPACE CONTROLS LLC
ITT Aerospace Controls Unit S
28150 Industry Dr, Valencia (91355-4101)
PHONE.................661 295-4000
Robert Briggs, *Manager*
Farrokh Batliwala, *President*
Mark Wu, *Project Engr*
Mostafa Donyanavard, *Engineer*
Peter Marlow, *Engineer*
EMP: 300
SALES (corp-wide): 2.7B **Publicly Held**
WEB: www.ittind.com
SIC: 3728 Aircraft parts & equipment
HQ: Itt Aerospace Controls Llc
28150 Industry Dr
Valencia CA 91355
315 568-7258

(P-20143)
ITT AEROSPACE CONTROLS LLC
28150 Industry Dr, Valencia (91355-4101)
PHONE.................661 295-4000
Jim Dauw, *President*
Art E Lewis, *Manager*
EMP: 27
SALES (corp-wide): 2.7B **Publicly Held**
SIC: 3728 Aircraft parts & equipment
HQ: Itt Aerospace Controls Llc
28150 Industry Dr
Valencia CA 91355
315 568-7258

(P-20144)
IVOPROP CORPORATION
15903 Lakewood Blvd # 103, Bellflower (90706-4300)
PHONE.................562 602-1451
Ivo Zdarskty, *President*
EMP: 12
SALES (est): 1.4MM **Privately Held**
WEB: www.ivoprop.com
SIC: 3728 Aircraft propellers & associated equipment

(P-20145)
JET AIR FBO LLC
681 Kenney St, El Cajon (92020-1278)
PHONE.................619 448-5991
Dan Gayet,
Liz Nunery, *Manager*
Wafaa Stele, *Manager*
EMP: 30
SQ FT: 250,000
SALES (est): 2.2MM **Privately Held**
SIC: 3728 Refueling equipment for use in flight, airplane

(P-20146)
JETSTREAM TRADING CO
1005 E Las Tunas Dr U356, San Gabriel (91776-1614)
PHONE.................818 921-7158
Jimmy Xiao Zhu, *CEO*
Jie Zhu, *President*
EMP: 10
SQ FT: 500
SALES (est): 1.1MM **Privately Held**
SIC: 3728 Aircraft parts & equipment

(P-20147)
JOHNSON CALDRAUL INC
Also Called: Cal-Draulics
220 N Delilah St Ste 101, Corona (92879-1883)
PHONE.................951 340-1067
Douglas Johnson, *President*
Kenneth W Johnson, *Vice Pres*
EMP: 30
SQ FT: 12,000
SALES: 3MM **Privately Held**
WEB: www.caldraulics.com
SIC: 3728 3593 Aircraft parts & equipment; fluid power cylinders & actuators

(P-20148)
K & E INC
Also Called: Micro Space Products
3906 W 139th St, Hawthorne (90250-7497)
PHONE.................310 675-3309
Cathy Riegler, *CEO*
Rudi Riegler, *President*
Rina Marquez, *Controller*
◆ EMP: 12
SQ FT: 10,000
SALES: 1MM **Privately Held**
SIC: 3728 Aircraft parts & equipment

(P-20149)
KLUNE INDUSTRIES INC (DH)
7323 Coldwater Canyon Ave, North Hollywood (91605-4206)
PHONE.................818 503-8100
Joseph I Snowden, *CEO*
Kenneth Ward, *CFO*
Juan Tovar, *Human Res Mgr*
Brad Jackson, *Purchasing*
Pamela Mayes, *Purch Agent*
▲ EMP: 358
SQ FT: 125,000
SALES (est): 131.1MM
SALES (corp-wide): 225.3B **Publicly Held**
SIC: 3728 Aircraft parts & equipment

(P-20150)
KOITO AVIATION LLC
25011 Avenue Stanford D, Valencia (91355-4771)
PHONE.................661 257-2878
Robet Ayvazian,
Chitoshi Fujii,
▲ EMP: 10
SALES (est): 1MM **Privately Held**
SIC: 3728 Aircraft parts & equipment

(P-20151)
KS ENGINEERING INC
14948 Shoemaker Ave, Santa Fe Springs (90670-5552)
PHONE.................562 483-7788
Clifford Yu, *President*
Mindy Ketchum, *Finance Mgr*
Amber Hermrack, *Client Mgr*
Kap Yu, *Manager*
EMP: 10
SQ FT: 14,000
SALES (est): 1.5MM **Privately Held**
SIC: 3728 Aircraft body & wing assemblies & parts

(P-20152)
LAMART CALIFORNIA INC
7560 Bristow Ct Ste C, San Diego (92154-7428)
PHONE.................510 489-8100
EMP: 11 EST: 2017
SALES (est): 1.8MM **Privately Held**
SIC: 3728 Aircraft parts & equipment

(P-20153)
LAMSCO WEST INC
Also Called: Shimtech US
29101 The Old Rd, Santa Clarita (91355-1014)
PHONE.................661 295-8620
Steve Griffith, *President*
Rick Casillas, *COO*
Scott Wilkinson, *CFO*
EMP: 99
SQ FT: 31,280
SALES (est): 42.8MM
SALES (corp-wide): 113.5MM **Privately Held**
WEB: www.lamscowest.com
SIC: 3728 Aircraft parts & equipment
HQ: Shimtech Industries U.S., Inc.
29101 The Old Rd
Valencia CA 91355
661 295-8620

(P-20154)
LANIC ENGINEERING INC (PA)
Also Called: LANIC AEROSPACE
12144 6th St, Rancho Cucamonga (91730-6111)
PHONE.................877 763-0411
S Robert Leaming, *CEO*
Shaun Arnold, *President*
Rick Villanueva, *Buyer*
EMP: 36
SQ FT: 30,000
SALES: 2.5MM **Privately Held**
WEB: www.lanicengineering.com
SIC: 3728 3721 Aircraft parts & equipment; aircraft

(P-20155)
LAVI SYSTEMS INC
13731 Saticoy St, Van Nuys (91402-6517)
PHONE.................818 373-5400
Leonard Gross, *Chairman*
Ray Lavi, *President*
Bernard Shapiro, *Vice Pres*
Leonard Shapiro, *Admin Sec*
EMP: 18
SQ FT: 11,500
SALES (est): 3.5MM
SALES (corp-wide): 72.3MM **Privately Held**
WEB: www.lavisystems.com
SIC: 3728 Aircraft parts & equipment
PA: Shapco Inc.
1666 20th St Ste 100
Santa Monica CA 90404
310 264-1666

▲ = Import ▼=Export
◆ =Import/Export

(P-20156)
LEE AEROSPACE PRODUCTS INC
90 W Easy St Ste 5, Simi Valley (93065-6206)
PHONE..............................805 527-1811
Darrell Lee, *President*
Estelle Lee, *Treasurer*
EMP: 10
SQ FT: 25,000
SALES (est): 1.3MM **Privately Held**
WEB: www.leeaerospace-ca.com
SIC: 3728 Aircraft parts & equipment

(P-20157)
LLAMAS PLASTICS INC
12970 Bradley Ave, Sylmar (91342-3851)
PHONE..............................818 362-0371
Ricardo M Llamas, *CEO*
Oswald Llamas, *President*
Jeff Mabry, *Corp Secy*
Richard Llamas, *Prdtn Mgr*
EMP: 105
SQ FT: 37,000
SALES (est): 30.7MM **Privately Held**
WEB: www.llamasplastics.com
SIC: 3728 3089 3083 Aircraft parts & equipment; plastic containers, except foam; laminated plastics plate & sheet

(P-20158)
LMI AEROSPACE INC
1351 Specialty Dr, Vista (92081-8521)
PHONE..............................760 597-7066
EMP: 170 **Privately Held**
SIC: 3728 Aircraft parts & equipment
HQ: Lmi Aerospace, Inc.
411 Fountain Lakes Blvd
Saint Charles MO 63301
636 946-6525

(P-20159)
LMI AEROSPACE INC
1377 Specialty Dr, Vista (92081-8521)
PHONE..............................760 599-4477
Ed Campbell, *General Mgr*
EMP: 132 **Privately Held**
SIC: 3728 Aircraft parts & equipment
HQ: Lmi Aerospace, Inc.
411 Fountain Lakes Blvd
Saint Charles MO 63301
636 946-6525

(P-20160)
LPJ AEROSPACE LLC
741 E 223rd St, Carson (90745-4111)
PHONE..............................310 834-5700
Louie Labadie,
EMP: 15
SALES (est): 1.5MM **Privately Held**
SIC: 3728 Aircraft parts & equipment

(P-20161)
LUXFER INC (DH)
Also Called: Luxfer Gas Cylinder
3016 Kansas Ave Bldg 1, Riverside (92507-3445)
PHONE..............................951 684-5110
John Rhodes, *President*
Anthony Barnes, *President*
Micheal Edwards, *Vice Pres*
Richard Lintin, *Info Tech Mgr*
◆ **EMP:** 70
SQ FT: 120,000
SALES (est): 127.7MM
SALES (corp-wide): 487.9MM **Privately Held**
WEB: www.luxfer-ecare.com
SIC: 3728 3354 Aircraft parts & equipment; shapes, extruded aluminum

(P-20162)
MACHINETEK LLC
1985 Palomar Oaks Way, Carlsbad (92011-1307)
PHONE..............................760 438-6644
Kevin S Darroch,
Donald Firm, *COO*
Hanns O Lindberg,
EMP: 18
SQ FT: 21,000
SALES (est): 2.5MM **Privately Held**
WEB: www.machinetek.com
SIC: 3728 Aircraft assemblies, subassemblies & parts

(P-20163)
MACHINEWORKS MANUFACTURING
20540 Superior St Ste D, Chatsworth (91311-4445)
PHONE..............................818 527-1327
Lenci Diaz, *COO*
EMP: 10
SALES (est): 1.1MM **Privately Held**
SIC: 3728 3599 Aircraft parts & equipment; custom machinery

(P-20164)
MANEY AIRCRAFT INC
1305 S Wanamaker Ave, Ontario (91761-2237)
PHONE..............................909 390-2500
Martin T Bright, *CEO*
David A Ederer, *Shareholder*
Michael Neely, *Shareholder*
Melinda Gerard, *General Mgr*
EMP: 30
SQ FT: 14,700
SALES (est): 7.1MM **Privately Held**
WEB: www.maneyaircraft.com
SIC: 3728 5088 3829 3812 Aircraft assemblies, subassemblies & parts; aircraft & parts; aircraft & motor vehicle measurement equipment; search & navigation equipment; guided missile & space vehicle parts & auxiliary equipment; aircraft, self-propelled

(P-20165)
MARINO ENTERPRISES INC
Also Called: Gear Technology
10671 Civic Center Dr, Rancho Cucamonga (91730-3804)
PHONE..............................909 476-0343
Thomas Marino, *President*
Paul Marino, *Technician*
Ronald Poat, *Engineer*
Sharon Nevius, *Human Res Mgr*
William Esterline, *Senior Buyer*
EMP: 35
SQ FT: 16,320
SALES (est): 7.2MM **Privately Held**
SIC: 3728 3769 Gears, aircraft power transmission; guided missile & space vehicle parts & auxiliary equipment

(P-20166)
MARVIN ENGINEERING CO INC (PA)
Also Called: Marvin Group, The
261 W Beach Ave, Inglewood (90302-2904)
PHONE..............................310 674-5030
Gerald M Friedman, *CEO*
Howard Gussman, *President*
Wade Morse, *COO*
Leon Tsimmerman, *CFO*
Carrie Ignacia, *Vice Pres*
▲ **EMP:** 580
SQ FT: 300,000
SALES (est): 223.5MM **Privately Held**
WEB: www.marvineng.com
SIC: 3728 Aircraft parts & equipment

(P-20167)
MASON ELECTRIC CO
13955 Balboa Blvd, Sylmar (91342-1084)
PHONE..............................818 361-3366
Steven Brune, *Vice Pres*
Arturo Goche, *Project Engr*
Hamed Bashizadeh, *Engineer*
Rick Dinger, *Engineer*
Ray Francisco, *Engineer*
EMP: 350
SQ FT: 105,000
SALES (est): 60.6MM
SALES (corp-wide): 3.8B **Publicly Held**
WEB: www.mason-electric.com
SIC: 3728 Aircraft parts & equipment
HQ: Esterline Technologies Corp
500 108th Ave Ne Ste 1500
Bellevue WA 98004
425 453-9400

(P-20168)
MASTER RESEARCH & MFG INC
13528 Pumice St, Norwalk (90650-5249)
PHONE..............................562 483-8789
Enrique Viano, *Vice Pres*
EMP: 52 **EST:** 1977

SQ FT: 31,200
SALES (est): 15.1MM **Privately Held**
WEB: www.master-research.com
SIC: 3728 Aircraft body assemblies & parts

(P-20169)
MATTERNET INC (PA)
161 E Evelyn Ave, Mountain View (94041-1510)
PHONE..............................650 260-2727
Andreas Ratopoulos, *CEO*
EMP: 28
SALES (est): 5.3MM **Privately Held**
SIC: 3728 Target drones

(P-20170)
MAVERICK AEROSPACE INC
3718 Capitol Ave, City of Industry (90601-1731)
PHONE..............................714 578-1700
David Feltch, *CEO*
George Ono, *President*
Nigel Young, *Vice Pres*
EMP: 16
SQ FT: 12,000
SALES (est): 3MM **Privately Held**
WEB: www.kjackaero.com
SIC: 3728 Aircraft assemblies, subassemblies & parts

(P-20171)
MAVERICK AEROSPACE LLC
3718 Capitol Ave, City of Industry (90601-1731)
PHONE..............................714 578-1700
Steve Crisanti, *CEO*
Val Darie, *Exec VP*
George Ono, *Vice Pres*
EMP: 44
SQ FT: 40,000
SALES (est): 781.9K **Privately Held**
SIC: 3728 3544 3761 3441 Aircraft parts & equipment; special dies, tools, jigs & fixtures; guided missiles & space vehicles; fabricated structural metal; guided missile & space vehicle parts & auxiliary equipment; machine shop, jobbing & repair

(P-20172)
MEGGITT
1785 Voyager Ave Ste 100, Simi Valley (93063-3365)
PHONE..............................877 666-0712
Greg Brostek, *CFO*
Doug Webb, *CFO*
Phyllis Pearce, *Senior VP*
Steve Fackler, *Vice Pres*
Robin Johnson, *Vice Pres*
EMP: 112
SALES (est): 15.1MM **Privately Held**
SIC: 3728 Aircraft parts & equipment

(P-20173)
MEGGITT (SAN DIEGO) INC (DH)
Also Called: Meggitt Polymers & Composites
6650 Top Gun St, San Diego (92121-4112)
PHONE..............................858 824-8976
Michael Louderback, *General Mgr*
Richard Ramirez, *Treasurer*
Tom Little, *Senior VP*
Eric Lardiere, *Vice Pres*
Sherri Stack, *General Mgr*
EMP: 120
SQ FT: 120,000
SALES (est): 40.9MM
SALES (corp-wide): 2.6B **Privately Held**
SIC: 3728 Roto-blades for helicopters
HQ: Meggitt-Usa, Inc.
1955 Surveyor Ave
Simi Valley CA 93063
805 526-5700

(P-20174)
MEGGITT DEFENSE SYSTEMS INC
9801 Muirlands Blvd, Irvine (92618-2521)
PHONE..............................949 465-7700
Roger Brum, *President*
Greg Brostek, *CFO*
Jeffrey Grunewald, *Engineer*
Bob Bettwy, *VP Finance*
Denice Brown, *Human Res Mgr*
EMP: 353 **EST:** 1998
SQ FT: 153,000

SALES (est): 92.9MM
SALES (corp-wide): 2.6B **Privately Held**
WEB: www.wd.com
SIC: 3728 Military aircraft equipment & armament
PA: Meggitt Plc
Atlantic House, Aviation Park West
Christchurch BH23
120 259-7597

(P-20175)
MEGGITT SAFETY SYSTEMS INC
Also Called: Htl Manufacturing Div
1785 Voyager Ave, Simi Valley (93063-3363)
PHONE..............................805 584-4100
Dennis Hutton, *President*
Steve Kahm, *Vice Pres*
Alison G Obe, *Exec Dir*
Bruce Bringhurst, *MIS Dir*
Alan Randle, *Engineer*
EMP: 52
SALES (corp-wide): 2.6B **Privately Held**
WEB: www.pacsci.com
SIC: 3728 Aircraft parts & equipment
HQ: Meggitt Safety Systems, Inc.
1785 Voyager Ave
Simi Valley CA 93063
805 584-4100

(P-20176)
MEGGITT-USA INC (HQ)
Also Called: Meggitt Polymers & Composites
1955 Surveyor Ave, Simi Valley (93063-3369)
PHONE..............................805 526-5700
Eric Lardiere, *President*
Peter Stammers, *President*
Robert W Soukup, *Treasurer*
Barney Rosenberg, *Vice Pres*
Kevin Wright, *Vice Pres*
▲ **EMP:** 223
SQ FT: 3,000
SALES (est): 391MM
SALES (corp-wide): 2.6B **Privately Held**
SIC: 3728 3829 3679 Aircraft parts & equipment; vibration meters, analyzers & calibrators; electronic switches
PA: Meggitt Plc
Atlantic House, Aviation Park West
Christchurch BH23
120 259-7597

(P-20177)
MGB INDUSTRIES INC
679 Anita St Ste B, Chula Vista (91911-4662)
PHONE..............................619 247-9284
EMP: 16
SALES (est): 200K **Privately Held**
SIC: 3728 5949

(P-20178)
MIKELSON MACHINE SHOP INC
2546 Merced Ave, South El Monte (91733-1924)
PHONE..............................626 448-3920
James Michaelson, *President*
James M Mikelson, *President*
▼ **EMP:** 23 **EST:** 1967
SQ FT: 14,000
SALES (est): 5.4MM **Privately Held**
SIC: 3728 Aircraft parts & equipment

(P-20179)
MILCOMM INC
10291 Trademark St Ste C, Rancho Cucamonga (91730-5847)
PHONE..............................626 523-8305
Candy Benevides, *CEO*
Michael Cabral, *President*
EMP: 13
SQ FT: 13,603
SALES: 900K **Privately Held**
SIC: 3728 Aircraft assemblies, subassemblies & parts

(P-20180)
MISSION CRTICAL COMPOSITES LLC
15400 Graham St Ste 102, Huntington Beach (92649-1257)
PHONE..............................714 831-2100
Robert Hartman, *Mng Member*
Julie Hagen, *Controller*

P R O D U C T S & S V C S

EMP: 22 EST: 2012
SALES: 3.4MM **Privately Held**
SIC: 3728 3721 3724 3761 Aircraft assemblies, subassemblies & parts; aircraft; aircraft engines & engine parts; guided missiles & space vehicles; guided missile & space vehicle propulsion unit parts; airframe assemblies, guided missiles

(P-20181)
MONAERO ENGINEERING INC
17011 Industry Pl, La Mirada (90638-5819)
PHONE..............................714 994-5463
Harish Bhutani, *President*
Stephen Russo, *Design Engr*
Gloria Contreras, *Purch Mgr*
Jerry Claustor, *QC Mgr*
Monisha Cohen, *Sls & Mktg Exec*
▲ EMP: 10
SQ FT: 8,750
SALES (est): 1.7MM **Privately Held**
WEB: www.monaero.com
SIC: 3728 Aircraft parts & equipment

(P-20182)
MONOGRAM SYSTEMS
Also Called: Zodiac Aerospace
1500 Glenn Curtiss St, Carson
(90746-4012)
PHONE..............................801 400-7944
Perrie Weiner, *Manager*
Dawn Garrett, *Program Mgr*
Oscar Lopez, *Design Engr*
Joel Montiel, *Project Engr*
Edita Salcepuedes, *Engineer*
EMP: 18
SALES (est): 3.4MM **Privately Held**
SIC: 3728 Aircraft parts & equipment

(P-20183)
**MULGREW ARCFT
COMPONENTS INC**
1810 S Shamrock Ave, Monrovia
(91016-4251)
PHONE..............................626 256-1375
Mike Houshiar, *CEO*
Adrian Velasquez, *Engineer*
EMP: 58
SQ FT: 45,000
SALES: 8.2MM **Privately Held**
WEB: www.mulgrewaircraft.com
SIC: 3728 Aircraft assemblies, subassemblies & parts

(P-20184)
N2 DEVELOPMENT INC
Also Called: N2 Aero
1819 Dana St Ste A, Glendale
(91201-2007)
PHONE..............................323 210-3251
Gregory Nelson, *President*
Olen Nelson, *Vice Pres*
EMP: 15
SQ FT: 4,000
SALES (est): 600K **Privately Held**
SIC: 3728 Aircraft parts & equipment

(P-20185)
NASCO AIRCRAFT BRAKE INC
Also Called: Meggitt Arcft Braking Systems
13300 Estrella Ave, Gardena (90248-1519)
PHONE..............................310 532-4430
Daniel Aron, *CEO*
Phil Friedman, *Corp Secy*
Sara Kruse, *Vice Pres*
Terry Jones, *Business Dir*
Leah Garcia, *General Mgr*
EMP: 100
SQ FT: 25,000
SALES (est): 20.8MM
SALES (corp-wide): 2.6B **Privately Held**
WEB: www.nascoaircraft.com
SIC: 3728 Brakes, aircraft
HQ: Meggitt Aircraft Braking Systems Corporation
1204 Massillon Rd
Akron OH 44306
330 796-4400

(P-20186)
NC DYNAMICS INCORPORATED
Also Called: Ncdi
6925 Downey Ave, Long Beach
(90805-1823)
PHONE..............................562 634-7392
Kevin Minter, *CEO*

Randall L Bazz, *President*
Vince Braun, *President*
Steve Woodhouse, *Officer*
Chris Thompson, *Vice Pres*
▲ EMP: 151
SALES (est): 49.6MM
SALES (corp-wide): 118.6MM **Privately Held**
WEB: www.ncdynamics.com
SIC: 3728 Aircraft parts & equipment
PA: Harlow Aerostructures Llc
1501 S Mclean Blvd
Wichita KS 67213
316 265-5268

(P-20187)
NEILL AIRCRAFT CO
1260 W 15th St, Long Beach (90813-1390)
PHONE..............................562 432-7981
Judith L Carpenter, *President*
Gonzalo Rivas, *General Mgr*
Jesus Vejar, *Design Engr*
Kim Mageo, *Human Resources*
Allison Reyes, *Buyer*
EMP: 275 EST: 1956
SQ FT: 150,000
SALES (est): 57.4MM **Privately Held**
WEB: www.neillaircraft.com
SIC: 3728 Aircraft body & wing assemblies & parts

(P-20188)
OMNIA INC
2831 N San Fernando Blvd, Burbank
(91504-2521)
PHONE..............................818 843-1620
William Marcy, *Principal*
EMP: 11
SALES (est): 1.6MM **Privately Held**
SIC: 3728 Aircraft assemblies, subassemblies & parts

(P-20189)
ORCON AEROSPACE
2600 Central Ave Ste E, Union City
(94587-3187)
P.O. Box 2936, Douglas GA (31534-2936)
PHONE..............................510 489-8100
Hollis Bascom, *President*
Dennis Murray, *Vice Pres*
EMP: 150
SQ FT: 200,000
SALES (est): 13MM **Privately Held**
WEB: www.orcon.com
SIC: 3728 Aircraft parts & equipment

(P-20190)
**OTTO INSTRUMENT SERVICE
INC (PA)**
1441 Valencia Pl, Ontario (91761-7639)
PHONE..............................909 930-5800
William R Otto Jr, *President*
Elizabeth Otto, *Corp Secy*
Ben Rosenthal, *Exec VP*
Richard Delman, *Vice Pres*
Lynnae Otto, *Vice Pres*
EMP: 45
SQ FT: 36,800
SALES: 29.5MM **Privately Held**
SIC: 3728 5088 7699 Aircraft parts & equipment; aircraft equipment & supplies; aircraft flight instrument repair

(P-20191)
**PACIFIC AERO COMPONENTS
INC (PA)**
Also Called: Aero Component Engineering
28887 Industry Dr, Valencia (91355-5419)
PHONE..............................818 841-9258
David Bill, *President*
Carmody Tom, *Marketing Staff*
EMP: 10
SQ FT: 4,000
SALES (est): 869.2K **Privately Held**
WEB: www.aerocomponent.com
SIC: 3728 3492 Aircraft assemblies, subassemblies & parts; hose & tube fittings & assemblies, hydraulic/pneumatic

(P-20192)
PACIFIC AIR INDUSTRIES INC
9650 De Soto Ave, Chatsworth
(91311-5012)
PHONE..............................310 829-4345
Paul H Ridley-Tree, *CEO*
Fred Gaunt, *President*

Sally Van Arnam, *Vice Pres*
Ron Munzlinger, *Purch Dir*
Tom Nolet, *VP Mktg*
▲ EMP: 45
SQ FT: 45,000
SALES (est): 5.6MM **Privately Held**
WEB: www.pac-air.com
SIC: 3728 Aircraft parts & equipment

(P-20193)
PACIFIC SKY SUPPLY INC
8230 San Fernando Rd, Sun Valley
(91352-3218)
PHONE..............................818 768-3700
Emilio B Perez, *CEO*
Emilio Perez, *President*
Valorie Stromer, *Executive*
Cathy Wise, *Executive*
Kelly Anderson, *Admin Sec*
EMP: 59
SQ FT: 27,000
SALES (est): 15.8MM **Privately Held**
WEB: www.pacsky.com
SIC: 3728 3724 5088 Aircraft parts & equipment; aircraft engines & engine parts; transportation equipment & supplies

(P-20194)
PARAMOUNT PANELS INC
Also Called: California Plasteck
1531 E Cedar St, Ontario (91761-5762)
PHONE..............................909 947-5168
John Thorne, *Vice Pres*
Arthur Thorne, *President*
EMP: 30
SALES (est): 1.3MM
SALES (corp-wide): 6.8MM **Privately Held**
SIC: 3728 Aircraft body & wing assemblies & parts
PA: Paramount Panels, Inc.
1531 E Cedar St
Ontario CA 91761
909 947-8008

(P-20195)
**PARKER-HANNIFIN
CORPORATION**
Also Called: Fluid Systems Division
16666 Von Karman Ave, Irvine
(92606-4997)
PHONE..............................216 896-2663
Greg Crowe, *General Mgr*
Robert Wells, *Engineer*
EMP: 100
SALES (corp-wide): 14.3B **Publicly Held**
WEB: www.parker.com
SIC: 3728 3724 Aircraft parts & equipment; aircraft engines & engine parts
PA: Parker-Hannifin Corporation
6035 Parkland Blvd
Cleveland OH 44124
216 896-3000

(P-20196)
**PARKER-HANNIFIN
CORPORATION**
Also Called: Parker Aerospace
1666 Don Carmen, Irvine (92618)
PHONE..............................949 833-3000
Robert Bond, *Branch Mgr*
Peter Seth, *Vice Pres*
James Beverly, *Executive*
Scott Bierman, *Program Mgr*
Bashir Ali, *Administration*
EMP: 93
SQ FT: 180,000
SALES (corp-wide): 14.3B **Publicly Held**
SIC: 3728 Aircraft assemblies, subassemblies & parts
PA: Parker-Hannifin Corporation
6035 Parkland Blvd
Cleveland OH 44124
216 896-3000

(P-20197)
**PARKER-HANNIFIN
CORPORATION**
Control Systems Division
14300 Alton Pkwy, Irvine (92618-1898)
PHONE..............................949 833-3000
Carl Moffitt, *General Mgr*
EMP: 700

SALES (corp-wide): 14.3B **Publicly Held**
WEB: www.parker.com
SIC: 3728 Aircraft body & wing assemblies & parts
PA: Parker-Hannifin Corporation
6035 Parkland Blvd
Cleveland OH 44124
216 896-3000

(P-20198)
**PARKER-HANNIFIN
CORPORATION**
Also Called: Stratoflex Product Division
3800 Calle Tecate, Camarillo (93012-5070)
PHONE..............................805 484-8533
William Cartmill, *Opers Mgr*
Philip Berg, *Engineer*
Ricardo Garcia, *Engineer*
EMP: 150
SALES (corp-wide): 14.3B **Publicly Held**
WEB: www.parker.com
SIC: 3728 3769 3568 Aircraft parts & equipment; guided missile & space vehicle parts & auxiliary equipment; power transmission equipment
PA: Parker-Hannifin Corporation
6035 Parkland Blvd
Cleveland OH 44124
216 896-3000

(P-20199)
PCA AEROSPACE INC (PA)
17800 Gothard St, Huntington Beach
(92647-6217)
PHONE..............................714 841-1750
Brian Murray, *CEO*
Gregory Ruffalo, *COO*
▲ EMP: 71 EST: 1963
SQ FT: 58,000
SALES (est): 19MM **Privately Held**
WEB: www.pcaaerospace.com
SIC: 3728 3599 Aircraft parts & equipment; machine shop, jobbing & repair

(P-20200)
PERFORMANCE PLASTICS INC
7919 Saint Andrews Ave, San Diego
(92154-8224)
PHONE..............................619 482-5031
Lance Brean, *President*
Michael Kerr, *Finance*
EMP: 99
SQ FT: 50,000
SALES (est): 28.6MM
SALES (corp-wide): 113.5MM **Privately Held**
SIC: 3728 Aircraft parts & equipment
HQ: Shimtech Industries U.S., Inc.
29101 The Old Rd
Valencia CA 91355
661 295-8620

(P-20201)
**PIEDRAS MACHINE
CORPORATION**
15154 Downey Ave Ste B, Paramount
(90723-4595)
PHONE..............................562 602-1500
Salvador Piedra, *President*
Ruben Piedra, *CFO*
Monica Piedra, *Executive Asst*
EMP: 19
SALES: 1.2MM **Privately Held**
SIC: 3728 Aircraft parts & equipment

(P-20202)
PMC INC (HQ)
12243 Branford St, Sun Valley
(91352-1010)
PHONE..............................818 896-1101
Christopher Lette, *President*
EMP: 36 EST: 1962
SALES (est): 542.7MM
SALES (corp-wide): 2.5B **Privately Held**
WEB: www.pmcwichita.com
SIC: 3728 3724 Bodies, aircraft; engine mount parts, aircraft
PA: Pmc Global, Inc.
12243 Branford St
Sun Valley CA 91352
818 896-1101

(P-20203)
PRECISE AERO PRODUCTS INC
4120 Indus Way, Riverside (92503-4847)
PHONE..............................951 340-4554

▲ = Import ▼=Export
◆ =Import/Export

Bud Andrews, *President*
Catherine Andrews, *Admin Sec*
EMP: 10
SQ FT: 5,414
SALES: 850K **Privately Held**
WEB: www.preciseaero.com
SIC: 3728 3599 Aircraft parts & equipment; machine shop, jobbing & repair

(P-20204)
PRECISION AEROSPACE CORP
11155 Jersey Blvd Ste A, Rancho Cucamonga (91730-5148)
PHONE.................................909 945-9604
Jim Hudson, *President*
EMP: 70
SQ FT: 50,000
SALES (est): 15.1MM **Privately Held**
WEB: www.pac.cc
SIC: 3728 Aircraft assemblies, subassemblies & parts

(P-20205)
PROGRAMMED COMPOSITES INC
250 Klug Cir, Corona (92880-5409)
PHONE.................................951 520-7300
Fax: 951 520-7300
EMP: 250
SALES: 20MM
SALES (corp-wide): 3.1B **Publicly Held**
SIC: 3728 3769
PA: Orbital Atk, Inc.
45101 Warp Dr
Dulles VA 20166
703 406-5000

(P-20206)
PTI TECHNOLOGIES INC (DH)
501 Del Norte Blvd, Oxnard (93030-7983)
PHONE.................................805 604-3700
Rowland Ellis, *President*
Beth Kozlowski, *Vice Pres*
Jim Martin, *Vice Pres*
Eric R Schram, *Vice Pres*
Sharon Cordray, *Executive*
▲ **EMP:** 212
SQ FT: 225,000
SALES (est): 30.2MM
SALES (corp-wide): 771.5MM **Publicly Held**
WEB: www.ptitechnologies.com
SIC: 3728 Aircraft parts & equipment
HQ: Esco Technologies Holding Llc
9900 Clayton Rd Ste A
Saint Louis MO 63124
314 213-7200

(P-20207)
Q1 TEST INC
1100 S Grove Ave Ste B2, Ontario (91761-4574)
PHONE.................................909 390-9718
Allen Riley, *CEO*
Jason Riley, *President*
EMP: 21
SQ FT: 10,500
SALES (est): 2.5MM **Privately Held**
SIC: 3728 Turret test fixtures, aircraft

(P-20208)
QUALITY FORMING LLC
Also Called: Qfi Prv Aerospace
22906 Frampton Ave, Torrance (90501-5035)
PHONE.................................310 539-2855
Mark Severns, *President*
Brian Valparaiso, *Opers Mgr*
▲ **EMP:** 100
SALES (est): 22.2MM
SALES (corp-wide): 192.6MM **Privately Held**
WEB: www.qfinc.com
SIC: 3728 Aircraft assemblies, subassemblies & parts
HQ: Qpi Holdings, Inc.
22906 Frampton Ave
Torrance CA 90501
310 539-2855

(P-20209)
RADIUS AROSPC - SAN DIEGO INC
203 N Johnson Ave, El Cajon (92020-3111)
PHONE.................................619 440-2504
Richard C III, *CEO*

Mark Gobin, *President*
EMP: 160
SALES (est): 34.8MM
SALES (corp-wide): 263.8MM **Privately Held**
WEB: www.triumphgrp.com
SIC: 3728 Aircraft body & wing assemblies & parts
PA: Arlington Capital Partners, L.P.
5425 Wisconsin Ave # 200
Chevy Chase MD 20815
202 337-7500

(P-20210)
RAM AEROSPACE INC
581 Tamarack Ave, Brea (92821-3206)
PHONE.................................714 853-1703
Rajen Rathod, *CEO*
Ravin Rathod, *President*
EMP: 10
SQ FT: 8,000
SALES (est): 1.2MM **Privately Held**
WEB: www.rjproductsllc.com
SIC: 3728 3599 3769 Aircraft parts & equipment; machine shop, jobbing & repair; guided missile & space vehicle parts & auxiliary equipment

(P-20211)
ROGERS HOLDING COMPANY INC
Also Called: V & M Precision Grinding Co.
1130 Columbia St, Brea (92821-2921)
PHONE.................................714 257-4850
Aldo Devile, *Principal*
Maynard Hallman, *Partner*
Tom Rogers, *Vice Pres*
William Fickling 1111, *Program Mgr*
Valerie Miller, *Manager*
EMP: 30 **EST:** 1946
SQ FT: 65,000
SALES: 5MM **Privately Held**
WEB: www.vm-machining.com
SIC: 3728 Alighting (landing gear) assemblies, aircraft

(P-20212)
ROHR INC (HQ)
Also Called: Collins Aerospace
850 Lagoon Dr, Chula Vista (91910-2001)
PHONE.................................619 691-4111
Greg Peters, *President*
Curtis Reusser, *President*
Laurence A Chapman, *CFO*
Brian Broderick, *Vice Pres*
Robert A Gustafson, *Vice Pres*
▲ **EMP:** 2100
SQ FT: 2,770,000
SALES (est): 934.1MM
SALES (corp-wide): 66.5B **Publicly Held**
SIC: 3728 Nacelles, aircraft
PA: United Technologies Corporation
10 Farm Springs Rd
Farmington CT 06032
860 728-7000

(P-20213)
RSA ENGINEERED PRODUCTS LLC
110 W Cochran St Ste A, Simi Valley (93065-6228)
PHONE.................................805 584-4150
Ray Scarcello, *President*
Leslie Fernandes, *President*
Scott Leeds, *CFO*
John Yi, *Program Mgr*
Cindy Estrada, *Administration*
◆ **EMP:** 90
SQ FT: 43,000
SALES: 27.8MM **Privately Held**
SIC: 3728 Aircraft parts & equipment

(P-20214)
SAFRAN CABIN GALLEYS US INC
Also Called: Zodiac Electrical Inserts USA
14505 Astronautics Ln, Huntington Beach (92647-2067)
PHONE.................................714 861-7300
EMP: 50
SALES (corp-wide): 833.4MM **Privately Held**
SIC: 3728 Aircraft parts & equipment

HQ: Safran Cabin Galleys Us, Inc.
17311 Nichols Ln
Huntington Beach CA 92647
714 861-7300

(P-20215)
SAFRAN CABIN GALLEYS US INC (HQ)
17311 Nichols Ln, Huntington Beach (92647-5721)
PHONE.................................714 861-7300
Matthew Stafford, *CEO*
Vincent Kozar, *CFO*
Frank Delos Santos, *Controller*
◆ **EMP:** 717
SQ FT: 90,000
SALES (est): 277.6MM
SALES (corp-wide): 833.4MM **Privately Held**
WEB: www.driessenusa.com
SIC: 3728 Aircraft parts & equipment
PA: Safran
2 Bd Du General Martial Valin
Paris 15e Arrondissement 75015
140 608-080

(P-20216)
SAFRAN CABIN INC
Also Called: 4 Flight
8595 Milliken Ave Ste 101, Rancho Cucamonga (91730-4942)
PHONE.................................909 652-9700
Tom McFarland, *CEO*
Leticia Zamora, *Human Res Mgr*
EMP: 200
SALES (corp-wide): 833.4MM **Privately Held**
SIC: 3728 Aircraft parts & equipment
HQ: Safran Cabin Inc.
5701 Bolsa Ave
Huntington Beach CA 92647
714 934-0000

(P-20217)
SAFRAN CABIN INC
12472 Industry St, Garden Grove (92841-2819)
PHONE.................................714 901-2672
Mike Boyd, *Branch Mgr*
EMP: 250
SALES (corp-wide): 833.4MM **Privately Held**
SIC: 3728 Aircraft parts & equipment
HQ: Safran Cabin Inc.
5701 Bolsa Ave
Huntington Beach CA 92647
714 934-0000

(P-20218)
SAFRAN CABIN INC (HQ)
5701 Bolsa Ave, Huntington Beach (92647-2063)
PHONE.................................714 934-0000
Christophe Bernardini, *CEO*
Norman Jordan, *CEO*
Jeff Henry, *CFO*
Scott Savian, *Exec VP*
Julee Nishimi, *Creative Dir*
▲ **EMP:** 500
SQ FT: 150,000
SALES (est): 1.1B
SALES (corp-wide): 833.4MM **Privately Held**
WEB: www.zodiac.com
SIC: 3728 Aircraft assemblies, subassemblies & parts
PA: Safran
2 Bd Du General Martial Valin
Paris 15e Arrondissement 75015
140 608-080

(P-20219)
SAFRAN CABIN INC
2850 Skyway Dr, Santa Maria (93455-1410)
PHONE.................................805 922-3013
Jude F Dozor, *Branch Mgr*
EMP: 19
SALES (corp-wide): 833.4MM **Privately Held**
SIC: 3728 Aircraft parts & equipment
HQ: Safran Cabin Inc.
5701 Bolsa Ave
Huntington Beach CA 92647
714 934-0000

(P-20220)
SAFRAN CABIN INC
11240 Warland Dr, Cypress (90630-5035)
PHONE.................................562 344-4780
Gary Reese, *Branch Mgr*
EMP: 248
SALES (corp-wide): 833.4MM **Privately Held**
SIC: 3728 Aircraft assemblies, subassemblies & parts
HQ: Safran Cabin Inc.
5701 Bolsa Ave
Huntington Beach CA 92647
714 934-0000

(P-20221)
SAFRAN CABIN INC
Also Called: C & D Aerospace
7330 Lincoln Way, Garden Grove (92841-1427)
PHONE.................................714 891-1906
Alec Azarian, *Branch Mgr*
EMP: 330
SALES (corp-wide): 833.4MM **Privately Held**
SIC: 3728 3443 Aircraft assemblies, subassemblies & parts; fabricated plate work (boiler shop)
HQ: Safran Cabin Inc.
5701 Bolsa Ave
Huntington Beach CA 92647
714 934-0000

(P-20222)
SAFRAN CABIN INC
Also Called: C&D Aerodesign
6754 Calle De Linea # 111, San Diego (92154-8021)
PHONE.................................619 671-0430
Jose Martinez, *Manager*
EMP: 223
SALES (corp-wide): 833.4MM **Privately Held**
SIC: 3728 Aircraft parts & equipment
HQ: Safran Cabin Inc.
5701 Bolsa Ave
Huntington Beach CA 92647
714 934-0000

(P-20223)
SAFRAN CABIN INC
1945 S Grove Ave, Ontario (91761-5616)
PHONE.................................909 947-2725
Danny Martin, *Branch Mgr*
EMP: 300
SALES (corp-wide): 833.4MM **Privately Held**
SIC: 3728 Aircraft assemblies, subassemblies & parts
HQ: Safran Cabin Inc.
5701 Bolsa Ave
Huntington Beach CA 92647
714 934-0000

(P-20224)
SAFRAN CABIN MATERIALS LLC
1945 S Grove Ave, Ontario (91761-5616)
PHONE.................................909 947-4115
Lek Makpaiboon, *President*
EMP: 17
SALES (est): 2.4MM
SALES (corp-wide): 833.4MM **Privately Held**
SIC: 3728 Aircraft parts & equipment
PA: Safran
2 Bd Du General Martial Valin
Paris 15e Arrondissement 75015
140 608-080

(P-20225)
SAFRAN SEATS SANTA MARIA LLC
Also Called: Zodiac Seat Shells U.S. LLC
2641 Airpark Dr, Santa Maria (93455-1415)
PHONE.................................805 922-5995
Klaus Koester, *Principal*
Manolito Corpuz, *Design Engr*
▲ **EMP:** 650
SALES (est): 184.9MM
SALES (corp-wide): 833.4MM **Privately Held**
SIC: 3728 Aircraft parts & equipment

PRODUCTS & SVCS

HQ: Safran Seats Usa Llc
2000 Weber Dr
Gainesville TX 76240
940 668-4825

(P-20226)
SANDERS COMPOSITES INC (DH)
Also Called: Sanders Composites Industries
3701 E Conant St, Long Beach
(90808-1783)
PHONE....................................562 354-2800
Larry O'Toole, *CEO*
Larry O Toole, *CEO*
EMP: 39
SQ FT: 44,400
SALES (est): 7.7MM
SALES (corp-wide): 53.9MM **Privately Held**
WEB: www.sanderscomposites.com
SIC: 3728 Aircraft assemblies, subassemblies & parts
HQ: Integrated Polymer Solutions, Inc.
3701 E Conant St
Long Beach CA 90808
562 354-2920

(P-20227)
SANTA MONICA PROPELLER SVC INC
3135 Dnald Douglas Loop S, Santa Monica
(90405-3210)
PHONE....................................310 390-6233
Leonid Polyakov, *CEO*
▲ **EMP:** 15
SQ FT: 11,000
SALES (est): 2.1MM **Privately Held**
WEB: www.santamonicapropeller.com
SIC: 3728 5088 Aircraft propellers & associated equipment; aircraft assemblies, subassemblies & parts; aircraft & parts

(P-20228)
SANTOS PRECISION INC
2220 S Anne St, Santa Ana (92704-4411)
PHONE....................................714 957-0299
Francisco Santos, *President*
Evelyn Santos, *Corp Secy*
Richard Santos, *Vice Pres*
EMP: 34 **EST:** 1979
SQ FT: 14,800
SALES (est): 7.6MM **Privately Held**
WEB: www.santosprecision.com
SIC: 3728 Aircraft parts & equipment

(P-20229)
SEAMAN PRODUCTS OF CALIFORNIA
12329 Gladstone Ave, Sylmar
(91342-5319)
PHONE....................................818 361-2012
Carol Haisten, *President*
EMP: 17
SQ FT: 13,000
SALES: 2.3MM **Privately Held**
SIC: 3728 Aircraft assemblies, subassemblies & parts

(P-20230)
SEHANSON INC
2121 E Via Burton, Anaheim (92806-1220)
PHONE....................................714 778-1900
Stanley E Hanson, *President*
Chris Jones, *CFO*
Christopher J Jones, *CFO*
Judy Trumbull, *Executive*
Dan Chicarella, *Marketing Staff*
EMP: 40
SQ FT: 18,000
SALES (est): 6.9MM **Privately Held**
WEB: www.acraaerospace.com
SIC: 3728 3429 Aircraft parts & equipment; manufactured hardware (general)

(P-20231)
SENIOR OPERATIONS LLC
Senior Aerospace SSP
2980 N San Fernando Blvd, Burbank
(91504-2522)
PHONE....................................818 260-2900
Launie Flemning, *Manager*
Mark Flohr, *Vice Pres*
Krist Khodjasaryan, *Vice Pres*
Halston Howard, *Program Mgr*
Anisa Marino, *Admin Asst*

EMP: 380
SALES (corp-wide): 1.3B **Privately Held**
SIC: 3728 3599 Aircraft parts & equipment; bellows, industrial: metal
HQ: Senior Operations Llc
300 E Devon Ave
Bartlett IL 60103
630 372-3500

(P-20232)
SHIM-IT CORPORATION
1691 California Ave, Corona (92881-3375)
PHONE....................................562 467-8600
Jeff Johnson, *President*
Diane Hesson, *Vice Pres*
Heidi Stout, *General Mgr*
EMP: 13 **EST:** 1961
SQ FT: 8,500
SALES (est): 1.3MM **Privately Held**
SIC: 3728 3542 Aircraft parts & equipment; machine tools, metal forming type

(P-20233)
SHIMTECH INDUSTRIES US INC (DH)
29101 The Old Rd, Valencia (91355-1014)
PHONE....................................661 295-8620
Scott Wilkinson, *CFO*
EMP: 99
SQ FT: 75,000
SALES (est): 94MM
SALES (corp-wide): 113.5MM **Privately Held**
SIC: 3728 Aircraft parts & equipment
HQ: Shimtech Industries Limited
7a/B Millington Road
Hayes MIDDX UB3 4
208 571-0055

(P-20234)
SKYLOCK INDUSTRIES
1290 W Optical Dr, Azusa (91702-3249)
PHONE....................................626 334-2391
Jeff Creoiserat, *Ch of Bd*
Jim Pease, *President*
Candy Perez, *Office Mgr*
Arthur Martinez, *Opers Mgr*
Iris Ascunce, *Sales Staff*
EMP: 70
SQ FT: 14,000
SALES (est): 17.9MM **Privately Held**
WEB: www.skylock.com
SIC: 3728 Aircraft parts & equipment

(P-20235)
SOUTHWEST MACHINE & PLASTIC CO
Also Called: Southwest Plastics Co
620 W Foothill Blvd, Glendora
(91741-2403)
PHONE....................................626 963-6919
W Thomas Jorgensen, *President*
Alfred D Jorgensen, *Vice Pres*
▲ **EMP:** 30 **EST:** 1937
SALES (est): 4.5MM **Privately Held**
SIC: 3728 3089 3544 Aircraft parts & equipment; injection molding of plastics; special dies, tools, jigs & fixtures

(P-20236)
SPACE-LOK INC
13306 Halldale Ave, Gardena
(90249-2204)
P.O. Box 2919 (90247-1119)
PHONE....................................310 527-6150
Scott F Wade, *President*
Jeffrey Wade, *CFO*
EMP: 138 **EST:** 1962
SALES (est): 12.3MM
SALES (corp-wide): 165.3MM **Privately Held**
WEB: www.space-lok.com
SIC: 3728 3542 3812 3452 Aircraft assemblies, subassemblies & parts; machine tools, metal forming type; search & navigation equipment; bolts, nuts, rivets & washers
HQ: Novaria Fastening Systems, Llc
6300 Ridglea Pl Ste 800
Fort Worth TX 76116
817 381-3810

(P-20237)
STEECON INC
5362 Indl Dr, Huntington Beach (92649)
PHONE....................................714 895-5313

Charles Steel, *CEO*
Chris Steel, *CEO*
Anita Kelleher, *Executive*
Linda Steel, *Project Mgr*
Jared Dominguez, *Engineer*
EMP: 11
SQ FT: 12,000
SALES (est): 3MM **Privately Held**
WEB: www.steecon.com
SIC: 3728 Aircraft body assemblies & parts

(P-20238)
STOCKTON PROPELLER INC
2478 Wilcox Rd, Stockton (95215-2319)
PHONE....................................209 982-4000
Robert C Hake, *President*
Diane Sullivan, *Accountant*
EMP: 10
SQ FT: 8,000
SALES (est): 1.2MM **Privately Held**
WEB: www.stocktonpropeller.com
SIC: 3728 Aircraft propellers & associated equipment

(P-20239)
STRATOFLIGHT (DH)
Also Called: Western Methods
25540 Rye Canyon Rd, Valencia
(91355-1109)
PHONE....................................949 622-0700
Joseph I Snowden, *CEO*
▲ **EMP:** 81
SALES (est): 29MM
SALES (corp-wide): 225.3B **Publicly Held**
WEB: www.stratoflightcorp.com
SIC: 3728 Aircraft parts & equipment
HQ: Precision Castparts Corp.
4650 Sw Mcdam Ave Ste 300
Portland OR 97239
503 946-4800

(P-20240)
SUNGEAR INC
8535 Arjons Dr Ste G, San Diego
(92126-4360)
PHONE....................................858 549-3166
Don Brown, *President*
Randall Palinski, *Vice Pres*
EMP: 42
SQ FT: 16,000
SALES (est): 8.5MM
SALES (corp-wide): 59.4MM **Privately Held**
WEB: www.sungearinc.com
SIC: 3728 Gears, aircraft power transmission
PA: H-D Advanced Manufacturing Company
2200 Georgetown Dr # 300
Sewickley PA 15143
724 759-2850

(P-20241)
SUNVAIR OVERHAUL INC
Also Called: A H Plating
29145 The Old Rd, Valencia (91355-1015)
PHONE....................................661 257-6123
John Waschak, *CEO*
Robert Waschak, *Officer*
Timothy Waschak, *Officer*
EMP: 45
SQ FT: 35,000
SALES (est): 5.5MM **Privately Held**
SIC: 3728 5088 Alighting (landing gear) assemblies, aircraft; aircraft & parts

(P-20242)
SYMBOLIC DISPLAYS INC
1917 E Saint Andrew Pl, Santa Ana
(92705-5143)
PHONE....................................714 258-2811
Candy Suits, *CEO*
▼ **EMP:** 76 **EST:** 1964
SQ FT: 15,860
SALES: 11.9MM **Privately Held**
WEB: www.symbolicdisplays.com
SIC: 3728 3812 3577 Aircraft parts & equipment; search & navigation equipment; computer peripheral equipment

(P-20243)
T M W ENGINEERING INC
14810 S San Pedro St, Gardena
(90248-2000)
PHONE....................................310 768-8211

Bernard Welsch, *President*
EMP: 10
SQ FT: 5,552
SALES (est): 800K **Privately Held**
WEB: www.tmwengineering.com
SIC: 3728 8711 3599 Aircraft parts & equipment; industrial engineers; machine shop, jobbing & repair

(P-20244)
TCA PRECISION PRODUCTS LLC
Also Called: V&M Prcsion Machining Grinding
1130 Columbia St, Brea (92821-2921)
PHONE....................................714 257-4850
Gregory Felix,
Alyce Schreiber,
EMP: 14
SALES (est): 671.1K **Privately Held**
SIC: 3728 Aircraft parts & equipment

(P-20245)
TDG AEROSPACE INC
2180 Chablis Ct Ste 106, Escondido
(92029-2076)
PHONE....................................760 466-1040
Virginia Richard, *Ch of Bd*
Gerry Bench, *President*
Fred Bond, *CFO*
Mike Baggett, *QC Mgr*
EMP: 18 **EST:** 1991
SALES (est): 3.6MM **Privately Held**
WEB: www.tdgaerospace.com
SIC: 3728 Aircraft parts & equipment

(P-20246)
TDK MACHINING
10772 Capital Ave Ste 7n, Garden Grove
(92843-4969)
PHONE....................................714 554-4166
Kenney Nguyen, *President*
EMP: 10
SALES (est): 1.7MM **Privately Held**
SIC: 3728 Aircraft parts & equipment

(P-20247)
THALES AVIONICS INC
48 Discovery, Irvine (92618-3151)
PHONE....................................949 381-3033
Dominique Giannoni, *Owner*
EMP: 16
SALES (corp-wide): 262.1MM **Privately Held**
SIC: 3728 Aircraft parts & equipment
HQ: Thales Avionics, Inc.
140 Centennial Ave
Piscataway NJ 08854
732 242-6300

(P-20248)
THALES AVIONICS INC
Also Called: Inflight Entrmt & Connectivity
51 Discovery, Irvine (92618-3119)
PHONE....................................949 790-2500
Brad Foreman, *Manager*
EMP: 225
SALES (corp-wide): 262.1MM **Privately Held**
SIC: 3728 3663 Aircraft parts & equipment; radio & TV communications equipment
HQ: Thales Avionics, Inc.
140 Centennial Ave
Piscataway NJ 08854
732 242-6300

(P-20249)
THOMPSON INDUSTRIES LTD
Also Called: Thompson ADB Industries
7155 Fenwick Ln, Westminster
(92683-5218)
PHONE....................................310 679-9193
Werner Lieberherr, *CEO*
EMP: 22
SQ FT: 52,000
SALES (est): 7.2MM
SALES (corp-wide): 66.5B **Publicly Held**
WEB: www.thompsonindustriesltd.com
SIC: 3728 Aircraft parts & equipment
HQ: B/E Aerospace, Inc.
1400 Corporate Center Way
Wellington FL 33414
561 791-5000

▲ = Import ▼=Export
♦ =Import/Export

(P-20250)
TMC AEROSPACE INC
2865 Pullman St, Santa Ana (92705-5713)
PHONE.................................949 250-4999
Scott Holland, *President*
Bob Yari, *President*
William Gresher, *CFO*
EMP: 40
SALES (est): 323.1K **Privately Held**
SIC: 3728 Aircraft parts & equipment

(P-20251)
TOPNOTCH QUALITY WORKS INC
12455 Branford St Ste 8, Pacoima (91331-3461)
PHONE.................................818 897-7679
Eric Wong, *President*
Veerayakit Patcsaranaparat, *President*
EMP: 10
SALES: 800K **Privately Held**
SIC: 3728 Aircraft parts & equipment

(P-20252)
TRANSDIGM INC
Also Called: Adel Wiggins Group
5000 Triggs St, Commerce (90022-4833)
P.O. Box 14088, Newark NJ (07198-0088)
PHONE.................................323 269-9181
Brady Fitzpatrick, *Branch Mgr*
Ida Crowl, *Administration*
Gloria Gutierrez, *Administration*
Katrina Ureno, *Administration*
Kin Ong, *Info Tech Mgr*
EMP: 50
SALES (corp-wide): 3.8B **Publicly Held**
WEB: www.electromotion.com
SIC: 3728 Aircraft parts & equipment
HQ: Transdigm, Inc.
      4223 Monticello Blvd
      Cleveland OH 44121

(P-20253)
TRANSDIGM INC
Adel Wggins Grp-Commercial Div
5000 Triggs St, Commerce (90022-4833)
P.O. Box 22228, Los Angeles (90022-0228)
PHONE.................................323 269-9181
Cindy Terakawa, *Branch Mgr*
EMP: 163
SALES (corp-wide): 3.8B **Publicly Held**
WEB: www.electromotion.com
SIC: 3728 3365 Aircraft parts & equipment; aerospace castings, aluminum
HQ: Transdigm, Inc.
      4223 Monticello Blvd
      Cleveland OH 44121

(P-20254)
TRANSDIGM INC
Adel Wggins Grup- Military Div
5000 Triggs St, Commerce (90022-4833)
P.O. Box 22228, Los Angeles (90022-0228)
PHONE.................................323 269-9181
Brady Fitzpatrick, *Branch Mgr*
EMP: 163
SALES (corp-wide): 3.8B **Publicly Held**
WEB: www.electromotion.com
SIC: 3728 3365 Aircraft parts & equipment; aerospace castings, aluminum
HQ: Transdigm, Inc.
      4223 Monticello Blvd
      Cleveland OH 44121

(P-20255)
TRI-FITTING MFG COMPANY
10414 Rush St, South El Monte (91733-3344)
PHONE.................................626 442-2000
Ralph Bernal, *President*
EMP: 15 **EST:** 1977
SQ FT: 13,000
SALES (est): 2.6MM **Privately Held**
SIC: 3728 3494 3492 Aircraft assemblies, subassemblies & parts; valves & pipe fittings; fluid power valves & hose fittings

(P-20256)
TRI-TECH PRECISION INC
1863 N Case St, Orange (92865-4234)
PHONE.................................714 970-1363
Ernie Husted, *President*
EMP: 17

SALES (est): 2.7MM **Privately Held**
SIC: 3728 3544 Aircraft parts & equipment; special dies, tools, jigs & fixtures

(P-20257)
TRIO MANUFACTURING INC
601 Lairport St, El Segundo (90245-5005)
PHONE.................................310 640-6123
Michael Hunkins, *President*
Brian Hunkins, *Vice Pres*
Tony Cisneros, *Engineer*
▲ **EMP:** 60
SALES (est): 18.8MM **Privately Held**
WEB: www.triomanufacturing.com
SIC: 3728 3829 3812 3663 Aircraft parts & equipment; measuring & controlling devices; search & navigation equipment; radio & TV communications equipment

(P-20258)
TRIUMPH ACTUATION SYSTMS-VALEN
28150 Harrison Pkwy, Valencia (91355-4109)
PHONE.................................661 295-1015
Daniel J Crowley, *President*
Jim McCabe, *CFO*
Lance Turner, *Senior VP*
John B Wright II, *Senior VP*
Gary Tenison, *Vice Pres*
EMP: 250
SALES (est): 68.9MM **Publicly Held**
WEB: www.efs-calif.com
SIC: 3728 Aircraft parts & equipment
PA: Triumph Group, Inc.
      899 Cassatt Rd Ste 210
      Berwyn PA 19312

(P-20259)
TRIUMPH AEROSTRUCTURES LLC
Also Called: Triumph Arstrctres - Vght Coml
3901 Jack Northrop Ave, Hawthorne (90250-4442)
PHONE.................................310 322-1000
Marty Jones, *Branch Mgr*
EMP: 680 **Publicly Held**
WEB: www.voughtaircraft.com
SIC: 3728 Aircraft parts & equipment
HQ: Triumph Aerostructures, Llc
      300 Austin Blvd
      Red Oak TX 75154

(P-20260)
TRIUMPH EQUIPMENT INC
13434 S Ontario Ave, Ontario (91761-7956)
PHONE.................................909 947-5983
Brigitte A De Laura, *President*
EMP: 35
SQ FT: 2,700
SALES (est): 2.3MM **Privately Held**
SIC: 3728 Aircraft parts & equipment

(P-20261)
TRIUMPH GROUP INC
2401 Portico Blvd, Calexico (92231-9604)
PHONE.................................760 768-1700
Manuel Estrada, *Branch Mgr*
▲ **EMP:** 13 **Publicly Held**
SIC: 3728 Aircraft parts & equipment
PA: Triumph Group, Inc.
      899 Cassatt Rd Ste 210
      Berwyn PA 19312

(P-20262)
TRIUMPH INSULATION SYSTEMS LLC
Also Called: Triumph Group
1754 Carr Rd Ste 103, Calexico (92231-9509)
PHONE.................................949 250-4999
Scott Holland, *Vice Pres*
Jeffry L McRao, *CFO*
R Jamed Cudd, *Vice Pres*
Robin Derogatis, *Vice Pres*
John B Wright II, *Vice Pres*
▲ **EMP:** 900
SALES (est): 192.9MM **Publicly Held**
SIC: 3728 Aircraft parts & equipment

HQ: Triumph Aerospace Systems Group, Inc.
      899 Cassatt Rd Ste 210
      Berwyn PA 19312

(P-20263)
TRIYAR CAPITAL CALIFORNIA LLC (PA)
10850 Wilshire Blvd, Los Angeles (90024-4305)
PHONE.................................310 441-5654
Steven Yari, *Mng Member*
Bob Yari, *Mng Member*
EMP: 10
SALES (est): 1.2MM **Privately Held**
SIC: 3728 6719 Aircraft parts & equipment; investment holding companies, except banks

(P-20264)
UNITED STATES DEPT OF NAVY
Also Called: Naval Maint Training Group
672 13th St Ste 1, Port Hueneme (93042-5011)
PHONE.................................805 989-5402
Dave Atkins, *Branch Mgr*
EMP: 30 **Publicly Held**
SIC: 3728 9711 Aircraft training equipment; Navy
HQ: United States Department Of The Navy
      1200 Navy Pentagon
      Washington DC 20350

(P-20265)
UNITED TECHNOLOGIES CORP
Also Called: UTC Aerospace Systems
11120 Norwalk Blvd, Santa Fe Springs (90670-3830)
PHONE.................................562 944-6244
Louis R Chenevert, *CEO*
EMP: 18
SALES (est): 2.7MM **Privately Held**
SIC: 3728 3312 Brakes, aircraft; wheels

(P-20266)
VANTAGE ASSOCIATES INC
Also Called: Vantage Master Machine Company
900 Civic Center Dr, National City (91950-1013)
PHONE.................................619 477-6940
Paul Roy, *Branch Mgr*
EMP: 40
SALES (corp-wide): 63.6MM **Privately Held**
SIC: 3728 Aircraft assemblies, subassemblies & parts
PA: Vantage Associates Inc.
      900 Civic Center Dr
      National City CA 91950
      619 477-6940

(P-20267)
VENTURA AEROSPACE INC
31355 Agoura Rd, Westlake Village (91361-4610)
PHONE.................................818 540-3130
Mark L Snow, *CEO*
Michael Snow, *Vice Pres*
EMP: 16
SQ FT: 2,000
SALES (est): 4.1MM **Privately Held**
WEB: www.venturaaerospace.com
SIC: 3728 Aircraft parts & equipment

(P-20268)
WESANCO INC
14870 Desman Rd, La Mirada (90638-5746)
PHONE.................................714 739-4989
Andrew D Shyer, *President*
▲ **EMP:** 30
SQ FT: 30,000
SALES: 12MM
SALES (corp-wide): 1.2MM **Privately Held**
WEB: www.wesanco.com
SIC: 3728 Oleo struts, aircraft
HQ: Zsi-Foster, Inc.
      45065 Michigan Ave
      Canton MI 48188

(P-20269)
WESTERN METHODS MACHINERY CORP
2344 Pullman St, Santa Ana (92705-5507)
PHONE.................................949 252-6600
Mark Heasley, *President*
EMP: 120 **EST:** 1977
SALES (est): 15MM **Privately Held**
WEB: www.compassaerospace.com
SIC: 3728 3769 Aircraft parts & equipment; guided missile & space vehicle parts & auxiliary equipment

(P-20270)
WHITTAKER CORPORATION
1955 Surveyor Ave Fl 2, Simi Valley (93063-3369)
PHONE.................................805 526-5700
Erick Lardiere, *President*
▲ **EMP:** 40
SQ FT: 276,000
SALES (est): 12.4MM
SALES (corp-wide): 2.6B **Privately Held**
WEB: www.whittakercorporation.com
SIC: 3728 3669 7373 Aircraft parts & equipment; fire detection systems, electric; smoke detectors; systems integration services
PA: Meggitt Plc
      Atlantic House, Aviation Park West
      Christchurch BH23
      120 259-7597

(P-20271)
WOODWARD HRT INC
Also Called: Woodward Duarte
1700 Business Center Dr, Duarte (91010-2859)
PHONE.................................626 359-9211
Don Grimes, *Manager*
Lisa Wolsey, *Partner*
Doug Salter, *Business Dir*
Rose Brookins, *Info Tech Dir*
David Farness, *Technician*
EMP: 250
SALES (corp-wide): 2.3B **Publicly Held**
SIC: 3728 5084 Aircraft parts & equipment; hydraulic systems equipment & supplies
HQ: Woodward Hrt, Inc.
      25200 Rye Canyon Rd
      Santa Clarita CA 91355
      661 294-6000

(P-20272)
YEAGER MANUFACTURING CORP (PA)
Also Called: Cummins Aerospace
2320 E Orangethorpe Ave, Anaheim (92806-1223)
PHONE.................................714 879-2800
William B Cummins, *CEO*
Sean Cummins, *President*
Nieves Medina, *Train & Dev Mgr*
EMP: 30
SQ FT: 35,000
SALES (est): 6.2MM **Privately Held**
WEB: www.cumminsaerospace.com
SIC: 3728 3812 3519 Aircraft parts & equipment; search & navigation equipment; internal combustion engines

(P-20273)
ZENITH MANUFACTURING INC
Also Called: Zipco
3087 12th St, Riverside (92507-4904)
PHONE.................................818 767-2106
James Phoung, *President*
EMP: 25
SQ FT: 47,000
SALES: 3MM **Privately Held**
SIC: 3728 Aircraft parts & equipment

(P-20274)
ZODIAC WTR WASTE AERO SYSTEMS
Also Called: Monogram Systems
1500 Glenn Curtiss St, Carson (90746-4012)
PHONE.................................310 884-7000
David Conrad, *Vice Pres*
Edward Gloss, *Engineer*
Thelma Stewart, *Engineer*
EMP: 45 **EST:** 1958

PRODUCTS & SVCS

SALES (est): 12.1MM
SALES (corp-wide): 833.4MM **Privately Held**
SIC: **3728** Aircraft parts & equipment
PA: Safran
2 Bd Du General Martial Valin
Paris 15e Arrondissement 75015
140 608-080

(P-20275)
ZODIAK SERVICES AMERICA
6734 Valjean Ave, Van Nuys (91406-5818)
PHONE..................................310 884-7200
Lou Pedonne, *President*
EMP: 56
SQ FT: 10,000
SALES (est): 5.6MM
SALES (corp-wide): 833.4MM **Privately Held**
WEB: www.aircruisers.com
SIC: **3728** 5088 Oxygen systems, aircraft; transportation equipment & supplies
HQ: Air Cruisers Company, Llc
1747 State Route 34
Wall Township NJ 07727
732 681-3527

3731 Shipbuilding & Repairing

(P-20276)
ALLIANCE TECHNICAL SVCS INC
1785 Utah Ave, Lompoc (93437-6020)
PHONE..................................805 606-3020
EMP: 12
SQ FT: 5,734
SALES (corp-wide): 10.2MM **Privately Held**
SIC: **3731**
PA: Alliance Technical Services, Inc.
400 W 24th St
Norfolk VA 23510
757 628-9500

(P-20277)
APR ENGINEERING INC
Also Called: Oceanwide Repairs
1812 W 9th St, Long Beach (90813-2614)
P.O. Box 9100 (90810-0100)
PHONE..................................562 983-3800
Roy Herington, *President*
Trina Young, *Treasurer*
Nicholas Berry, *Purchasing*
▲ EMP: 33
SALES (est): 6.8MM **Privately Held**
WEB: www.oceanwiderepair.com
SIC: **3731** Shipbuilding & repairing

(P-20278)
BAE SYSTEMS SAN DIEGO
2205 Belt St, San Diego (92113-3634)
P.O. Box 13308 (92170-3308)
PHONE..................................619 238-1000
Erwin Bieber, *President*
James M Blue, *Vice Pres*
Alice M Eldridge, *Vice Pres*
Karen Odermatt, *Executive Asst*
Sara Madrid, *Administration*
◆ EMP: 1278 EST: 1976
SALES (est): 228.8MM
SALES (corp-wide): 21.6B **Privately Held**
WEB: www.baesystems-sandiego-shiprepair.com
SIC: **3731** Shipbuilding & repairing; barges, building & repairing; lighters, marine: building & repairing; ferryboats, building & repairing
HQ: Bae Systems Ship Repair Inc.
750 W Berkley Ave
Norfolk VA 23523
757 494-4000

(P-20279)
BAY CITY MARINE INC
1625 Cleveland Ave, National City (91950-4212)
PHONE..................................619 477-3991
Fred Hays, *Manager*
EMP: 25

SALES (corp-wide): 4.8MM **Privately Held**
WEB: www.baycitymarine.com
SIC: **3731** Military ships, building & repairing
PA: Bay City Marine, Inc.
1625 Cleveland Ave
National City CA 91950
619 477-3991

(P-20280)
BAY SHIP & YACHT CO (PA)
2900 Main St Ste 2100, Alameda (94501-7739)
PHONE..................................510 337-9122
William Elliott, *CEO*
Bill Elliott, *President*
Vicki Elliott, *Treasurer*
Alan Cameron, *Vice Pres*
William Shamis, *Executive*
▲ EMP: 210
SQ FT: 20,000
SALES (est): 85.1MM **Privately Held**
WEB: www.bay-ship.com
SIC: **3731** 3732 Commercial cargo ships, building & repairing; combat vessels, building & repairing; barges, building & repairing; yachts, building & repairing

(P-20281)
CAL LLC BREAKWATER INTL
327 Lecouvreur Ave, Wilmington (90744-6033)
PHONE..................................310 518-1718
Robert Schuchardt, *Vice Pres*
EMP: 14
SQ FT: 6,500
SALES (est): 2.6MM **Privately Held**
SIC: **3731** 5087 Shipbuilding & repairing; firefighting equipment

(P-20282)
COASTAL DECKING INC
2050 Wilson Ave Ste A, National City (91950-6500)
PHONE..................................619 477-0567
Frank Safely, *President*
EMP: 24
SQ FT: 3,000
SALES (est): 2.6MM **Privately Held**
SIC: **3731** Shipbuilding & repairing

(P-20283)
COASTAL MARINE MAINT CO LLC (PA)
Also Called: Cmmc
250 W Wardlow Rd, Long Beach (90807-4429)
PHONE..................................562 432-8066
Joe Gregorio,
Gary Beale,
Erick Garcia,
▲ EMP: 13
SQ FT: 6,626
SALES (est): 949K **Privately Held**
SIC: **3731** Cargo vessels, building & repairing

(P-20284)
COLONNAS SHIPYARD WEST LLC
105 S 31st St, San Diego (92113-1403)
PHONE..................................619 557-8373
Robert Boyd, *Principal*
EMP: 30
SALES (est): 2.9MM **Privately Held**
SIC: **3731** Shipbuilding & repairing

(P-20285)
CONTINENTAL MARITIME INDS INC
1995 Bay Front St, San Diego (92113-2122)
PHONE..................................619 234-8851
David H Mc Queary, *President*
Lee E Wilson, *Vice Pres*
Davis Ann, *Human Res Mgr*
Maryanne Davis, *Human Res Mgr*
EMP: 429
SQ FT: 90,000
SALES (est): 87.6MM **Publicly Held**
SIC: **3731** Shipbuilding & repairing

PA: Huntington Ingalls Industries, Inc.
4101 Washington Ave
Newport News VA 23607
-

(P-20286)
CRAFT LABOR & SUPPORT SVCS LLC
1545 Tidelands Ave Ste C, National City (91950-4240)
PHONE..................................619 336-9977
Michael Greene, *Branch Mgr*
Jackie Vazquez, *Manager*
EMP: 100
SALES (corp-wide): 10.3MM **Privately Held**
SIC: **3731** Shipbuilding & repairing
PA: Craft Labor And Support Services, Llc
7636 230th St Sw Apt B
Edmonds WA 98026
206 304-4543

(P-20287)
GENERAL DYNAMICS CORPORATION
General Dynamics Nassco
2798 Harbor Dr, San Diego (92113-3650)
PHONE..................................619 544-3400
Steven Strobel, *Vice Pres*
Michael Askew, *President*
Christopher Barnes, *President*
Bill Hale, *Vice Pres*
Valerie Fusco, *Admin Asst*
EMP: 42
SALES (corp-wide): 36.1B **Publicly Held**
SIC: **3731** Shipbuilding & repairing
PA: General Dynamics Corporation
11011 Sunset Hills Rd
Reston VA 20190
703 876-3000

(P-20288)
HII SAN DIEGO SHIPYARD INC
1995 Bay Front St, San Diego (92113-2122)
PHONE..................................619 234-8851
Christopher Joseph Miner, *CEO*
Ronald Sugar, *President*
Carl Vancio, *Chief Mktg Ofcr*
Bryan Herring, *Vice Pres*
Mike Chandler, *Administration*
EMP: 325
SQ FT: 90,000
SALES (est): 66.4MM **Publicly Held**
WEB: www.cmsd.net
SIC: **3731** Military ships, building & repairing
PA: Huntington Ingalls Industries, Inc.
4101 Washington Ave
Newport News VA 23607

(P-20289)
INTEGRATED MARINE SERVICES INC
Also Called: IMS
2320 Main St, Chula Vista (91911-4610)
PHONE..................................619 429-0300
Larry Samano, *President*
EMP: 55
SALES: 11MM **Privately Held**
SIC: **3731** Shipbuilding & repairing

(P-20290)
LARSON AL BOAT SHOP
1046 S Seaside Ave, San Pedro (90731-7334)
PHONE..................................310 514-4100
Jack Wall, *CEO*
George Wall, *Vice Pres*
Gloria Wall, *Vice Pres*
Kelly Wall, *Asst Controller*
Linda Shiffer, *Manager*
▲ EMP: 70
SQ FT: 65,000
SALES (est): 17MM **Privately Held**
WEB: www.larsonboat.com
SIC: **3731** 4493 Military ships, building & repairing; commercial cargo ships, building & repairing; marinas

(P-20291)
MARE ISLAND DRY DOCK LLC
1180 Nimitz Ave, Vallejo (94592-1053)
PHONE..................................707 652-7356

Stephen Dileo, *Mng Member*
Harry Nicholsen, *CFO*
William Dunbar, *Vice Pres*
Dale Lacey, *Vice Pres*
Paul Gates, *Program Mgr*
EMP: 60 EST: 2012
SALES (est): 32.4MM **Privately Held**
SIC: **3731** Shipbuilding & repairing

(P-20292)
MAXON CRS LLC
5400 W Rosecrans Ave # 105, Hawthorne (90250-6682)
PHONE..................................424 236-4660
Isaac Zaharoni, *President*
Tom Carmody,
Letty Mercado,
EMP: 21
SQ FT: 9,411
SALES (est): 855.5K **Privately Held**
SIC: **3731** Shipbuilding & repairing

(P-20293)
MILLER MARINE
2275 Manya St, San Diego (92154-4713)
PHONE..................................619 791-1500
Pauline Senter, *CEO*
Edward Senter, *President*
Miller Marine, *Admin Sec*
Gonzalez Miguel, *Purch Mgr*
EMP: 45
SQ FT: 13,500
SALES (est): 10.7MM **Privately Held**
WEB: www.millermarine.us
SIC: **3731** 7389 Shipbuilding & repairing; grinding, precision: commercial or industrial; metal slitting & shearing

(P-20294)
MORRISON MAR & INTERMODAL INC
753 Tunbridge Rd Ste A150, Danville (94526-4319)
PHONE..................................925 362-4599
Scott Morrison, *President*
Dave Burns, *General Mgr*
Laura Forslund, *Opers Mgr*
▲ EMP: 25
SQ FT: 1,500
SALES (est): 1MM **Privately Held**
WEB: www.morrisonmarine.com
SIC: **3731** 4789 Cargo vessels, building & repairing; cargo loading & unloading services

(P-20295)
NATIONAL STL & SHIPBUILDING CO (HQ)
Also Called: Nassco
2798 Harbor Dr, San Diego (92113-3650)
P.O. Box 85278 (92186-5278)
PHONE..................................619 544-3400
Frederick J Harris, *President*
Michael Toner, *Ch of Bd*
D H Fogg, *Treasurer*
John Keane, *Bd of Directors*
Phebe Novakoviz, *Exec VP*
◆ EMP: 277
SQ FT: 100,000
SALES (est): 474.2MM
SALES (corp-wide): 36.1B **Publicly Held**
WEB: www.nassco.com
SIC: **3731** Military ships, building & repairing; commercial cargo ships, building & repairing
PA: General Dynamics Corporation
11011 Sunset Hills Rd
Reston VA 20190
703 876-3000

(P-20296)
NAVIGATIONAL SERVICES INC
34 E 17th St Ste C, National City (91950-4501)
P.O. Box 2444 (91951-2444)
PHONE..................................619 477-1564
Frank Soto Sr, *President*
Don Fritz, *CFO*
Lupita Lopez, *Manager*
EMP: 12 EST: 1998
SQ FT: 3,800
SALES (est): 1.9MM **Privately Held**
SIC: **3731** Commercial passenger ships, building & repairing

▲ = Import ▼=Export
◆ =Import/Export

(P-20297)
OC FLEET SERVICE INC
8270 Monroe Ave, Stanton (90680-2612)
PHONE.....................................714 460-8069
Russell Loud, *President*
Evell Stanley, *Vice Pres*
EMP: 15
SQ FT: 150,000
SALES: 2MM **Privately Held**
SIC: 3731 Shipbuilding & repairing

(P-20298)
PACIFIC SHIP REPR FBRCTION INC (PA)
1625 Rigel St, San Diego (92113-3887)
P.O. Box 13428 (92170-3428)
PHONE.....................................619 232-3200
David J Moore, *CEO*
David Moore, *CFO*
David Bain, *Vice Pres*
Marvin Cannegieter, *Program Mgr*
Christopher Stein, *Planning Mgr*
EMP: 287
SQ FT: 136,000
SALES: 45.1MM **Privately Held**
WEB: www.pacship.com
SIC: 3731 3444 Combat vessels, building & repairing; sheet metalwork

(P-20299)
PACORD INC
Also Called: L-3 Pacord
240 W 30th St, National City (91950-7204)
PHONE.....................................619 336-2200
Russell J Pearce, *Branch Mgr*
EMP: 50
SALES (corp-wide): 6.8B **Publicly Held**
SIC: 3731 1731 Shipbuilding & repairing; electrical work
HQ: Pacord Inc
    3835 E Princess Anne Rd
    Norfolk VA 23502
    757 855-8037

(P-20300)
PAIGE SITTA & ASSOCIATES INC (PA)
Also Called: Paige Floor Cvg Specialists
2050 Wilson Ave Ste B, National City (91950-6500)
PHONE.....................................619 233-5912
Scott Nicholson, *President*
Peter Sitta, *Vice Pres*
Debbie Kelley, *Controller*
EMP: 35
SQ FT: 9,000
SALES (est): 4.7MM **Privately Held**
WEB: www.paigefc.com
SIC: 3731 1752 Shipbuilding & repairing; floor laying & floor work

(P-20301)
PATRIOT MRITIME COMPLIANCE LLC
1320 Willow Pass Rd # 485, Concord (94520-7940)
PHONE.....................................925 296-2000
Richard Naccara, *Mng Member*
Judy Collins,
Timothy Gill,
Jordan Truchan,
EMP: 13
SALES (est): 1.4MM **Privately Held**
SIC: 3731 Shipbuilding & repairing

(P-20302)
PYR PRESERVATION SERVICES
2393 Newton Ave Ste B, San Diego (92113-3666)
PHONE.....................................619 338-8395
Daniel R Cummins, *CEO*
EMP: 30
SQ FT: 12,500
SALES (est): 1.1MM **Privately Held**
SIC: 3731 3589 3479 2851 Commercial cargo ships, building & repairing; sandblasting equipment; etching & engraving; epoxy coatings

(P-20303)
ROBERT E BLAKE INC
Also Called: General Engrg & Mch Works
135 Clara St, San Francisco (94107-1120)
PHONE.....................................415 391-2255
Peter J Blake, *President*

Robert Blake, *President*
EMP: 15 EST: 1967
SQ FT: 11,000
SALES (est): 1.5MM **Privately Held**
SIC: 3731 3599 3519 3444 Shipbuilding & repairing; machine shop, jobbing & repair; engines, diesel & semi-diesel or dual-fuel; sheet metalwork

(P-20304)
SEA TEK SPARS & RIGGING INC
508 E E St Ste B, Wilmington (90744-6059)
PHONE.....................................310 549-1800
Maria Almazan, *President*
EMP: 11
SALES (est): 1.2MM **Privately Held**
SIC: 3731 Marine rigging

(P-20305)
SOUTHERN CALIFORNIA INSULATION
Also Called: SCI
2050 Wilson Ave Ste C, National City (91950-6500)
PHONE.....................................619 477-1303
Mitch Spenst, *President*
EMP: 20
SALES (est): 2.2MM **Privately Held**
SIC: 3731 1742 Shipbuilding & repairing; plastering, drywall & insulation

(P-20306)
TECNICO CORPORATION
1670 Brandywine Ave Ste D, Chula Vista (91911-6071)
PHONE.....................................619 426-7385
Jerald Steen, *Manager*
EMP: 45 **Privately Held**
SIC: 3731 Shipbuilding & repairing
HQ: Tecnico Corporation
    831 Industrial Ave
    Chesapeake VA 23324
    757 545-4013

(P-20307)
WALASHEK INDUSTRIAL & MAR INC
2826 Eighth St, Berkeley (94710-2707)
PHONE.....................................206 624-2880
Frank Walashek, *Manager*
EMP: 11
SALES (corp-wide): 29.3MM **Privately Held**
WEB: www.walashek.com
SIC: 3731 Shipbuilding & repairing
HQ: Walashek Industrial & Marine, Inc.
    3411 Amherst St
    Norfolk VA 23513
    -

(P-20308)
WALASHEK INDUSTRIAL & MAR INC
1428 Mckinley Ave, National City (91950-4217)
PHONE.....................................619 498-1711
Frank Walashek, *Manager*
EMP: 43
SALES (corp-wide): 29.3MM **Privately Held**
WEB: www.walashek.com
SIC: 3731 Shipbuilding & repairing
HQ: Walashek Industrial & Marine, Inc.
    3411 Amherst St
    Norfolk VA 23513

(P-20309)
WALKER DESIGN INC
Also Called: Walker Engineering Enterprises
9255 San Fernando Rd, Sun Valley (91352-1416)
PHONE.....................................818 252-7788
Robert A Walker Jr, *CEO*
Shari Goodgame, *Corp Secy*
Michael Delillo, *Vice Pres*
Leo Larue, *Technical Staff*
Emilio Gomez, *QC Mgr*
▲ EMP: 33
SQ FT: 29,800
SALES (est): 7.4MM **Privately Held**
WEB: www.walkerairsep.com
SIC: 3731 Lighters, marine: building & repairing

3732 Boat Building & Repairing

(P-20310)
ADEPT PROCESS SERVICES INC
Also Called: APS Marine
1505 Cleveland Ave, National City (91950-4210)
P.O. Box 2130, Imperial Beach (91933-2130)
PHONE.....................................619 434-3194
Gary Southerland, *President*
David Carlisle, *Program Mgr*
Carolyn R Southerland, *Manager*
EMP: 34
SQ FT: 30,000
SALES: 4.2MM **Privately Held**
WEB: www.adeptworks.net
SIC: 3732 4493 7699 Boat building & repairing; boat yards, storage & incidental repair; boat repair

(P-20311)
AIR & GAS TECH INC
3191 Commercial St, San Diego (92113-1426)
PHONE.....................................619 557-8373
Anthony Greenwell, *President*
Keith Mallder, *Sales Mgr*
EMP: 25
SQ FT: 18,000
SALES (est): 5.9MM **Privately Held**
WEB: www.cemcorp.net
SIC: 3732 Boat building & repairing

(P-20312)
ANACAPA MARINE SERVICES (PA)
Also Called: Anacapa Boatyard
151 Shipyard Way Ste 5, Newport Beach (92663-4460)
PHONE.....................................805 985-1818
Richard Fairchild, *President*
Jj Marine Acquisition, *Principal*
EMP: 17 EST: 1973
SQ FT: 8,000
SALES (est): 3.4MM **Privately Held**
WEB: www.amsboatyard.com
SIC: 3732 5088 Boat building & repairing; marine supplies

(P-20313)
BALBOA BOAT YARD INC
2414 Newport Blvd, Newport Beach (92663-3704)
PHONE.....................................949 673-6834
Arthur Lewis, *President*
EMP: 10
SQ FT: 1,700
SALES (est): 1.1MM **Privately Held**
SIC: 3732 Boat building & repairing

(P-20314)
BASIN MARINE INC
Also Called: Basin Marine Shipyard
829 Harbor Island Dr A, Newport Beach (92660-7235)
PHONE.....................................949 673-0360
Paul Smith, *President*
Augie Gonzaleez, *Clerk*
▲ EMP: 18 EST: 1956
SQ FT: 44,000
SALES (est): 4.7MM **Privately Held**
SIC: 3732 5551 Boat building & repairing; marine supplies

(P-20315)
BAY MARINE BOATWORKS INC
310 W Cutting Blvd, Richmond (94804-2018)
PHONE.....................................510 237-0140
Erik Mattson, *President*
Brenda Tostenson, *Office Mgr*
Kim Desenberg, *Project Mgr*
Octavia Taylor, *Purchasing*
Rolfe Brittain, *Opers Mgr*
▲ EMP: 36
SQ FT: 500

SALES (est): 6.9MM
SALES (corp-wide): 85.1MM **Privately Held**
WEB: www.bay-ship.com
SIC: 3732 Boat building & repairing
PA: Bay Ship & Yacht Co.
    2900 Main St Ste 2100
    Alameda CA 94501
    510 337-9122

(P-20316)
BOATWORKS
2251 Townsgate Rd, Westlake Village (91361-2404)
PHONE.....................................805 374-9455
Alex Toller, *Owner*
EMP: 10
SALES (est): 815.9K **Privately Held**
SIC: 3732 Boat building & repairing

(P-20317)
CATALINA YACHTS INC (PA)
Also Called: Morgan Marine
21200 Victory Blvd, Woodland Hills (91367-2582)
PHONE.....................................818 884-7700
Frank W Butler, *President*
Sharon Day, *Corp Secy*
◆ EMP: 200
SQ FT: 200,000
SALES (est): 52.2MM **Privately Held**
WEB: www.catalinayachts.com
SIC: 3732 5551 Sailboats, building & repairing; boat dealers

(P-20318)
COBRA PERFORMANCE BOATS INC
5109 Holt Blvd, Montclair (91763-4820)
PHONE.....................................909 482-0047
Jeff Bohn, *President*
EMP: 10
SQ FT: 18,000
SALES (est): 1.3MM **Privately Held**
SIC: 3732 5551 7699 Boat building & repairing; boat dealers; boat repair

(P-20319)
CRYSTALINER CORP
1626 Placentia Ave, Costa Mesa (92627-4385)
PHONE.....................................949 548-0292
Jerry Norek, *President*
Jack L Norek Jr, *Treasurer*
Dorothy La Rose, *Admin Sec*
EMP: 20
SQ FT: 9,000
SALES (est): 2.5MM **Privately Held**
SIC: 3732 5551 5088 Boat building & repairing; marine supplies; marine supplies

(P-20320)
DAVIS BOATS
2601 Engine Ave, Paso Robles (93446)
PHONE.....................................805 227-1170
Harold Davis, *President*
Ardith Davis, *Corp Secy*
Larry Davis, *Vice Pres*
EMP: 10
SQ FT: 4,000
SALES (est): 1.3MM **Privately Held**
WEB: www.davisboats.com
SIC: 3732 5551 Motorboats, inboard or outboard: building & repairing; motor boat dealers

(P-20321)
DEEP OCEAN ENGINEERING INC
2403 Qume Dr, San Jose (95131-1821)
PHONE.....................................408 436-1102
Fang Li, *CEO*
EMP: 15
SALES (est): 3MM **Privately Held**
SIC: 3732 Boat building & repairing

(P-20322)
DR RADON BOATBUILDING INC (PA)
67 Depot Rd, Goleta (93117-3430)
PHONE.....................................805 692-2170
Donald Rae Radon, *CEO*
Linda Radon, *Treasurer*
EMP: 13
SQ FT: 20,000

PRODUCTS & SVCS

SALES (est): 1.4MM **Privately Held**
WEB: www.radonboats.com
SIC: 3732 Fishing boats: lobster, crab, oyster, etc.: small

(P-20323)
DRISCOLL INC
Also Called: Driscoll Boat Works
2500 Shelter Island Dr, San Diego
(92106-3114)
PHONE..............................619 226-2500
Thomas Driscoll, *President*
John Gerald Driscoll, *Ch of Bd*
Mary-Carol Driscoll, *Corp Secy*
Joseph E Driscoll, *Vice Pres*
▲ EMP: 50 EST: 1947
SQ FT: 2,400
SALES (est): 9.8MM **Privately Held**
WEB: www.driscollinc.com
SIC: 3732 Yachts, building & repairing

(P-20324)
DRISCOLL MISSION BAY LLC
1500 Quivira Way Ste 2, San Diego
(92109-8300)
PHONE..............................619 223-5191
Mary Carol Driscoll,
▲ EMP: 13
SQ FT: 1,000
SALES (est): 2.4MM **Privately Held**
WEB: www.driscoll-boats.com
SIC: 3732 Boat building & repairing

(P-20325)
DUFFIELD MARINE INC
Also Called: Duffy Electric Boat Company
16732 Pacific Coast, Sunset Beach
(90742)
PHONE..............................949 650-4633
Heather Gorrie, *Manager*
EMP: 10
SALES (corp-wide): 10MM **Privately Held**
WEB: www.duffyboats.com
SIC: 3732 Boat building & repairing
PA: Duffield Marine Inc.
670 W 17th St Ste E7
Costa Mesa CA 92627
760 246-1211

(P-20326)
DUFFIELD MARINE INC (PA)
Also Called: Duffield Electric Boat Company
670 W 17th St Ste E7, Costa Mesa
(92627-3664)
PHONE..............................760 246-1211
Marshall Duffield, *President*
Raul Sanchez, *Manager*
EMP: 25
SALES (est): 10.9MM **Privately Held**
WEB: www.duffyboats.com
SIC: 3732 Boat building & repairing

(P-20327)
DUFFIELD MARINE INC
Also Called: Duffy Electric Boat
2001 W Coast Hwy, Newport Beach
(92663-4713)
PHONE..............................949 645-6812
Karl Tahti, *Manager*
EMP: 25
SALES (corp-wide): 10.9MM **Privately Held**
WEB: www.duffyboats.com
SIC: 3732 Boat building & repairing
PA: Duffield Marine Inc.
670 W 17th St Ste E7
Costa Mesa CA 92627
760 246-1211

(P-20328)
EPIC BOATS LLC (PA)
2755 Dos Aarons Way Ste A, Vista
(92081-8359)
PHONE..............................760 542-6060
Chris Anthony,
Karen Callow,
EMP: 14
SQ FT: 30,000
SALES (est): 2.3MM **Privately Held**
WEB: www.epicboats.com
SIC: 3732 Boats, fiberglass: building & repairing

(P-20329)
FANTASEA ENTERPRISES INC
Also Called: Pacific Avalon Yacht Charters
2901 W Coast Hwy Ste 160, Newport
Beach (92663-4030)
PHONE..............................949 673-8545
John Gueola, *President*
Roy King, *President*
EMP: 10 EST: 1994
SQ FT: 3,000
SALES (est): 1.7MM **Privately Held**
WEB: www.pacificavalon.com
SIC: 3732 Yachts, building & repairing

(P-20330)
FASHION BLACKSMITH INC
121 Starfish Way, Crescent City
(95531-4447)
PHONE..............................707 464-9219
Dale Long, *President*
EMP: 10
SQ FT: 9,000
SALES (est): 980K **Privately Held**
SIC: 3732 Boat building & repairing

(P-20331)
FINELINE INDUSTRIES INC (PA)
Also Called: Centurion
2047 Grogan Ave, Merced (95341-6440)
PHONE..............................209 384-0255
Richard D Lee, *President*
Clark Bird, *CFO*
Pamela Lee, *Treasurer*
Jeffrey Polan, *Vice Pres*
Rick Lee, *Engineer*
▼ EMP: 121
SQ FT: 38,000
SALES (est): 36.8MM **Privately Held**
WEB: www.centurionboats.com
SIC: 3732 Boats, fiberglass: building & repairing

(P-20332)
GAMBOL INDUSTRIES INC
1825 W Pier D St, Long Beach
(90802-1033)
PHONE..............................562 901-2470
Robert A Stein, *President*
John Bridwell, *Vice Pres*
▲ EMP: 45
SALES (est): 8.9MM **Privately Held**
WEB: www.gambolindustries.com
SIC: 3732 7699 4493 Yachts, building & repairing; boat repair; boat yards, storage & incidental repair

(P-20333)
GLOBAL MARINE GROUP INC
Also Called: Inmar Marine Group
6020 Progressive Ave # 800, San Diego
(92154-6633)
PHONE..............................800 729-1665
Joshua Palmer, *CEO*
EMP: 15
SALES (est): 587.5K **Privately Held**
SIC: 3732 Boat building & repairing

(P-20334)
GREGOR INC
Also Called: Gregor Boat Co
3565 N Hazel Ave, Fresno (93722-4913)
PHONE..............................559 441-7703
Wilton W Gregory, *President*
Dusan Milicevic, *Vice Pres*
EMP: 10 EST: 1964
SQ FT: 70,000
SALES (est): 825K **Privately Held**
WEB: www.gregorboats.com
SIC: 3732 5551 Fishing boats: lobster, crab, oyster, etc.: small; boat dealers

(P-20335)
HALLETT BOATS
180 S Irwindale Ave, Azusa (91702-3211)
PHONE..............................626 969-8844
Nick Barron, *President*
Shirley Barron, *Corp Secy*
EMP: 25
SQ FT: 21,000
SALES (est): 3.9MM **Privately Held**
WEB: www.hallettboats.com
SIC: 3732 5091 Motorboats, inboard or outboard: building & repairing; boats, canoes, watercrafts & equipment

(P-20336)
HENDERSON SERVICES INC
Also Called: Valco Boats
6722 N Stonebridge Dr, Fresno
(93711-1194)
PHONE..............................559 435-8874
Donald L Henderson, *President*
Linda Henderson, *Treasurer*
EMP: 25
SQ FT: 22,000
SALES (est): 2MM **Privately Held**
SIC: 3732 Motorboats, inboard or outboard: building & repairing

(P-20337)
HOBIE CAT COMPANY
4925 Oceanside Blvd, Oceanside
(92056-3099)
PHONE..............................760 758-9100
Richard Rogers, *CEO*
Doug Skidmore, *President*
Bill Baldwin, *CFO*
Denis Mackessy, *Info Tech Mgr*
Bill Van Vooren, *Info Tech Mgr*
◆ EMP: 150 EST: 1995
SQ FT: 60,000
SALES (est): 34.8MM **Privately Held**
WEB: www.hobiecat.com
SIC: 3732 Sailboats, building & repairing

(P-20338)
INDEL ENGINEERING INC
Also Called: Marina Shipyard
6400 E Marina Dr, Long Beach
(90803-4618)
PHONE..............................562 594-0995
D E Bud Tretter, *President*
D E Tretter, *President*
Kurt Tretter, *Corp Secy*
Jerry Tretter, *Vice Pres*
EMP: 35
SQ FT: 3,000
SALES (est): 6.6MM **Privately Held**
WEB: www.marinashipyard.com
SIC: 3732 Houseboats, building & repairing; motorboats, inboard or outboard: building & repairing

(P-20339)
INNESPACE PRODUCTIONS
20172 Charlanne Dr, Redding
(96002-9222)
PHONE..............................530 241-2800
Robert Innes, *President*
Dan Tazza, *Vice Pres*
▼ EMP: 12 EST: 2010
SALES (est): 1.7MM **Privately Held**
SIC: 3732 Boat building & repairing

(P-20340)
INTERNATIONAL INBOARD MAR INC
2556 W 16th St, Merced (95348-4355)
PHONE..............................209 384-2566
Roger Cruser, *President*
Robert Jessen, *Vice Pres*
EMP: 32
SQ FT: 6,000
SALES (est): 5.1MM **Privately Held**
WEB: www.calabriaboats.com
SIC: 3732 Motorboats, inboard or outboard: building & repairing

(P-20341)
JAMES BETTS ENTERPRISES INC
100 Sierra Terrace Rd, Tahoe City (96145)
P.O. Box 991, Friday Harbor WA (98250-0991)
PHONE..............................530 581-1331
James Betts, *President*
Janis Betts, *Treasurer*
EMP: 20
SQ FT: 22,000
SALES (est): 2.5MM **Privately Held**
SIC: 3732 Yachts, building & repairing

(P-20342)
KAYE SANDY ENTERPRISES INC
Also Called: Porta-Bote International
1074 Independence Ave, Mountain View
(94043-1602)
PHONE..............................650 961-5334
Alex R Kaye, *President*
Frances Kaye, *Corp Secy*

▼ EMP: 35
SQ FT: 4,000
SALES (est): 6.1MM **Privately Held**
WEB: www.porta-bote.com
SIC: 3732 5551 Boat building & repairing; boat dealers

(P-20343)
LAVEY CRAFT PRFMCE BOATS INC
175 Vander St, Corona (92880-6972)
PHONE..............................951 273-9690
Jeff A Camire, *CEO*
Jeff Camire, *CEO*
Nathalie Sampson, *Senior VP*
Chris Camire, *Admin Sec*
EMP: 13
SQ FT: 4,500
SALES (est): 1.4MM **Privately Held**
WEB: www.laveycraft.com
SIC: 3732 Boats, fiberglass: building & repairing

(P-20344)
LEAR BAYLOR INC
7215 Garden Grove Blvd C, Garden Grove
(92841-4221)
PHONE..............................714 799-9396
Shanda Lear-Baylor, *President*
EMP: 25
SALES (est): 3MM **Privately Held**
WEB: www.learbaylor.com
SIC: 3732 Boats, fiberglass: building & repairing

(P-20345)
MACGREGOR YACHT CORPORATION
1631 Placentia Ave, Costa Mesa
(92627-4311)
PHONE..............................310 621-2206
Roger Mac Gregor, *President*
Mary Lou Mac Gregor, *Corp Secy*
EMP: 74 EST: 1963
SQ FT: 10,000
SALES (est): 9.5MM **Privately Held**
SIC: 3732 5551 Sailboats, building & repairing; boat dealers

(P-20346)
MARINE GROUP BOAT WORKS LLC
997 G St, Chula Vista (91910-3414)
PHONE..............................619 427-6767
Herb Engel, *Mng Member*
Arthur E Engel, *Chairman*
Karen Ramos, *Department Mgr*
Brooks Detchon, *Project Mgr*
Cliff Mayo, *Project Mgr*
▲ EMP: 115
SALES (est): 42.2MM **Privately Held**
WEB: www.marinegroupbw.com
SIC: 3732 Boat building & repairing

(P-20347)
MARINE TECH
1500 Quivira Way Ste 1, San Diego
(92109-8300)
PHONE..............................619 225-0448
Ezobrio Netto, *Owner*
Carla Kralagodri, *Principal*
EMP: 16
SALES (est): 989.7K **Privately Held**
SIC: 3732 Boat building & repairing

(P-20348)
MARITIME SOLUTIONS LLC
1616 Newton Ave, San Diego
(92113-1013)
PHONE..............................619 234-2676
Kim M Zeledon,
EMP: 30 EST: 1999
SQ FT: 4,000
SALES (est): 5.6MM **Privately Held**
SIC: 3732 3731 8711 Boat building & repairing; shipbuilding & repairing; engineering services

(P-20349)
MAURER MARINE INC
873 W 17th St, Costa Mesa (92627-4308)
PHONE..............................949 645-7673
Craig Maurer, *President*
Jay S Maurer, *Vice Pres*
EMP: 18

SALES (est): 4MM **Privately Held**
WEB: www.maurermarine.com
SIC: 3732 7389 Yachts, building & repairing; yacht brokers

(P-20350)
MB SPORTS INC
280 Airpark Rd, Atwater (95301-9535)
PHONE..................................209 357-4153
Myung Bo Hong, *CEO*
▲ **EMP:** 40
SQ FT: 16,000
SALES (est): 9.8MM **Privately Held**
WEB: www.mbsports.net
SIC: 3732 5551 5091 Motorboats, inboard or outboard: building & repairing; boat dealers; boats, canoes, watercrafts & equipment

(P-20351)
MOOSE BOATS INC
1175 Nimitz Ave Ste 115, Vallejo (94592-1003)
PHONE..................................707 778-9828
Christian Lind, *CEO*
Aaron Lind, *Treasurer*
EMP: 16
SQ FT: 20,000
SALES (est): 3.4MM **Privately Held**
WEB: www.mooseboats.com
SIC: 3732 Boat building & repairing

(P-20352)
NAVIGATOR YACHTS AND PDTS INC
364 Malbert St, Perris (92570-8336)
PHONE..................................951 657-2117
Xia Wang, *CEO*
Jule Marshall, *Principal*
Cheryl Bond, *Director*
EMP: 150
SQ FT: 30,000
SALES (est): 16.1MM **Privately Held**
SIC: 3732 Yachts, building & repairing

(P-20353)
OCEAN PROTECTA INCORPORATED
10743 Progress Way, Cypress (90630-4714)
PHONE..................................714 891-2628
Edgar Chong Tan, *CEO*
Myron Reyes, *President*
EMP: 50
SALES (est): 5.8MM **Privately Held**
SIC: 3732 Boat building & repairing

(P-20354)
OCEANSIDE MARINE CENTER INC (PA)
1550 Harbor Dr N, Oceanside (92054-1031)
PHONE..................................760 722-1833
John Tyrell, *President*
Myrtle Tyrell, *Vice Pres*
EMP: 10 **EST:** 1964
SQ FT: 5,000
SALES (est): 1MM **Privately Held**
SIC: 3732 Boat building & repairing

(P-20355)
PACIFIC YACHT TOWERS
165 Balboa St Ste C10, San Marcos (92069-1347)
PHONE..................................760 744-4831
Tom Newton, *President*
EMP: 10
SQ FT: 5,000
SALES (est): 1.3MM **Privately Held**
WEB: www.pacificyachttowers.com
SIC: 3732 5091 Motorized boat, building & repairing; boat accessories & parts

(P-20356)
R & D RACING PRODUCTS USA INC
12983 Los Nietos Rd, Santa Fe Springs (90670-3011)
PHONE..................................562 906-1190
Glenn Dickinson, *President*
Bill Chapin, *Vice Pres*
▲ **EMP:** 15
SQ FT: 5,000

SALES (est): 2.3MM **Privately Held**
WEB: www.rd-performance.com
SIC: 3732 Boat building & repairing

(P-20357)
SHELTER ISLAND YACHTWAYS LTD
Also Called: Shelter Island Boatyard
2330 Shelter Island Dr # 1, San Diego (92106-3126)
PHONE..................................619 222-0481
William Roberts, *General Ptnr*
Lori Kimmelmann, *Controller*
▲ **EMP:** 30 **EST:** 1953
SQ FT: 20,000
SALES (est): 5.4MM **Privately Held**
SIC: 3732 6512 Boat building & repairing; lessors of piers, docks, associated buildings & facilities

(P-20358)
STONE BOAT YARD INC
2517 Blanding Ave, Alameda (94501-1599)
PHONE..................................510 523-3030
David Olson, *President*
EMP: 15
SQ FT: 47,250
SALES (est): 1.7MM **Privately Held**
SIC: 3732 3731 Boats, fiberglass: building & repairing; shipbuilding & repairing

(P-20359)
TBYCI LLC
Also Called: Boatyard-Channel Islands, The
3615 Victoria Ave, Oxnard (93035-4360)
PHONE..................................805 985-6800
Gregory Schem,
Craig Campbell, *General Mgr*
EMP: 16 **EST:** 2013
SQ FT: 7,500
SALES (est): 682K **Privately Held**
SIC: 3732 3731 Motorized boat, building & repairing; motorboats, inboard or outboard: building & repairing; sailboats, building & repairing; patrol boats, building & repairing; crew boats, building & repairing

(P-20360)
VENTURA HARBOR BOATYARD INC
1415 Spinnaker Dr, Ventura (93001-4339)
PHONE..................................805 654-1433
Robert Bartosh, *President*
Dale Morris, *CFO*
Kim Morris, *Vice Pres*
Stephen James, *Admin Sec*
EMP: 35
SQ FT: 2,000
SALES: 4.8MM **Privately Held**
SIC: 3732 4493 Boat building & repairing; boat yards, storage & incidental repair

(P-20361)
VINTAGE AERO ENGINES
1582 Goodrick Dr Ste 8a, Tehachapi (93561-1672)
PHONE..................................661 822-4107
Michael Nixon, *Owner*
EMP: 16
SALES (est): 1.4MM **Privately Held**
SIC: 3732 Tenders (small motor craft), building & repairing

(P-20362)
WESTERLY MARINE INC
3535 W Garry Ave, Santa Ana (92704-6422)
PHONE..................................714 966-8550
Lynn Bowser, *President*
Steven Lee, *Vice Pres*
▲ **EMP:** 26
SQ FT: 18,000
SALES (est): 6.1MM **Privately Held**
WEB: www.westerly-marine.com
SIC: 3732 Boat building & repairing

(P-20363)
WHEELS MAGAZINE INC
1409 Centinela Ave, Inglewood (90302-1141)
P.O. Box 2617, Gardena (90247-0617)
PHONE..................................310 402-9013
Terry Taylor, *Principal*
EMP: 50

SALES (est): 1.9MM **Privately Held**
SIC: 3732 Non-motorized boat, building & repairing

(P-20364)
WILLARD MARINE INC
1250 N Grove St, Anaheim (92806-2130)
PHONE..................................714 630-4018
George L Angle, *Chairman*
Ulrich Gottschling, *President*
Jojo Nery, *President*
Gabriella M Carrera, *CFO*
Dave Gutierrez, *Vice Pres*
▲ **EMP:** 55
SQ FT: 45,000
SALES (est): 17.2MM **Privately Held**
WEB: www.willardmarine.com
SIC: 3732 Boats, fiberglass: building & repairing

(P-20365)
WINDWARD YACHT & REPAIR INC
Also Called: Windward Yacht Center
13645 Fiji Way, Venice (90292-6986)
PHONE..................................310 823-4581
Jacob Wood, *President*
Arlen Wood, *Vice Pres*
Simon Landt, *Manager*
Chris Waid, *Manager*
▲ **EMP:** 14
SQ FT: 5,000
SALES (est): 1.9MM **Privately Held**
SIC: 3732 Boat building & repairing

3743 Railroad Eqpt

(P-20366)
AQ TRANSPORTATION
326 Boyd St Ste C, Los Angeles (90013-1550)
PHONE..................................626 143-4552
Najam Javed, *CEO*
EMP: 10
SALES (est): 561K **Privately Held**
SIC: 3743 Freight cars & equipment

(P-20367)
BOMBARDIER TRANSPORTATION
1555 N San Fernando Rd, Los Angeles (90065-1261)
PHONE..................................323 224-3461
Robert Young, *Manager*
EMP: 100
SALES (corp-wide): 16.2B **Privately Held**
SIC: 3743 Railroad equipment
HQ: Bombardier Transportation (Holdings) Usa Inc.
1251 Waterfront Pl
Pittsburgh PA 15222
412 655-5700

(P-20368)
CABLE CAR CLASSICS INC
3239 Rio Lindo Ave, Healdsburg (95448-9495)
PHONE..................................707 433-6810
Matthew Etchell, *President*
Robert Etchell Sr, *Admin Sec*
Michelle Buchignani, *Purchasing*
▲ **EMP:** 10
SQ FT: 10,000
SALES (est): 940K **Privately Held**
WEB: www.cablecarclassics.com
SIC: 3743 Interurban cars & car equipment; streetcars & car equipment

(P-20369)
EAGLE SYSTEMS INC
1601 Atlas Rd, Richmond (94806-1101)
PHONE..................................510 231-2686
EMP: 10 **Privately Held**
SIC: 3743 Railway motor cars
HQ: Eagle Systems, Inc.
230 Grant Rd Ste A1
East Wenatchee WA 98802
509 884-7575

(P-20370)
HITACHI RAIL USA INC (PA)
101 The Embarcadero # 210, San Francisco (94105-1222)
PHONE..................................415 397-7010

Giancarlo Fantappie, *President*
▲ **EMP:** 14
SQ FT: 5,000
SALES (est): 28.3MM **Privately Held**
SIC: 3743 Train cars & equipment, freight or passenger

(P-20371)
KINKISHARYO INTERNATIONAL LLC (HQ)
1960 E Grand Ave Ste 1210, El Segundo (90245-5061)
PHONE..................................424 276-1803
Akiyoshi Oba, *President*
Hiroshi Okamoto, *CFO*
Masaya Wakuda, *Vice Pres*
▲ **EMP:** 19 **EST:** 1999
SQ FT: 6,000
SALES (est): 30.9MM **Privately Held**
WEB: www.kinkisharyo-usa.com
SIC: 3743 3321 Train cars & equipment, freight or passenger; railroad car wheels & brake shoes, cast iron

(P-20372)
KNORR BRAKE COMPANY LLC
29471 Kohoutek Way, Union City (94587-1237)
PHONE..................................510 475-0770
Paul Akins, *Branch Mgr*
Raymond LI, *Mfg Staff*
EMP: 10
SALES (corp-wide): 711.6K **Privately Held**
WEB: www.knorrbrakecorp.com
SIC: 3743 Railroad equipment
HQ: Knorr Brake Company Llc
1 Arthur Peck Dr
Westminster MD 21157
410 875-0900

(P-20373)
LEVAC SPECIALTIES INC
2305 Cemo Cir, Gold River (95670-4424)
PHONE..................................916 362-3795
Leo Levac, *Owner*
EMP: 14 **EST:** 1999
SQ FT: 6,000
SALES (est): 2.4MM **Privately Held**
SIC: 3743 Rapid transit cars & equipment

(P-20374)
MBF TRANSPORTATION LLC
13610 Imperial Hwy Ste 6, Santa Fe Springs (90670-4875)
PHONE..................................562 282-0540
Michael Marchica,
EMP: 10 **EST:** 2014
SALES (est): 886.3K **Privately Held**
SIC: 3743 Freight cars & equipment

(P-20375)
PACIFIC GREEN TRUCKING INC
512 E C St, Wilmington (90744-6618)
PHONE..................................310 830-4528
Adrian Zarate, *CEO*
EMP: 11 **EST:** 2009
SALES (est): 1.3MM **Privately Held**
SIC: 3743 Freight cars & equipment

(P-20376)
PARAGON PRODUCTS LLC (PA)
4475 Golden Foothill Pkwy, El Dorado Hills (95762-9638)
PHONE..................................916 941-9717
Ted Keefer, *President*
Renee Lajou, *CFO*
Paul Davies,
◆ **EMP:** 40
SQ FT: 12,000
SALES (est): 13.2MM **Privately Held**
WEB: www.paragonproducts.net
SIC: 3743 Railroad locomotives & parts, electric or nonelectric; locomotives & parts

(P-20377)
ULTIMATE RAIL EQUIPMENT INC
30914 San Antonio St, Hayward (94544-7110)
PHONE..................................510 324-5000
Geoffrey Nelson, *CEO*
◆ **EMP:** 10
SALES (est): 1.5MM **Privately Held**
SIC: 3743 Railroad equipment

(P-20378)
UNION TANK CAR COMPANY
175 W Jackson Blvd, Bakersfield (93311)
PHONE 312 431-3111
Bill Constantino, *Director*
EMP: 153
SALES (corp-wide): 225.3B **Publicly Held**
SIC: 3743 Train cars & equipment, freight or passenger
HQ: Union Tank Car Company
175 W Jackson Blvd # 2100
Chicago IL 60604
312 431-3111

(P-20379)
WOOJIN IS AMERICA INC
5108 Azusa Canyon Rd, Irwindale (91706-1846)
PHONE 626 386-0101
Sharon Peck, *President*
Rich Lee, *Administration*
▲ **EMP:** 10
SALES (est): 1.8MM **Privately Held**
SIC: 3743 4789 Railroad equipment; railroad maintenance & repair services
HQ: Woojin Industrial Systems Co., Ltd.
95 Sari-Ro, Sari-Myeon
Goesan 28046
824 382-0414

3751 Motorcycles, Bicycles & Parts

(P-20380)
ALL AMERICAN RACERS INC
Also Called: Dan Gurneys All Amercn Racers
2334 S Broadway, Santa Ana (92707-3250)
P.O. Box 2186 (92707-0186)
PHONE 714 557-2116
Daniel S Gurney, *CEO*
Justin B Gurney, *CEO*
Kathy Weida, *Vice Pres*
Ellen La Bond, *Accountant*
Jimmy Gurney, *VP Sales*
EMP: 162 **EST:** 1962
SQ FT: 25,000
SALES: 36.2MM **Privately Held**
WEB: www.allamericanracers.com
SIC: 3751 Motorcycles & related parts

(P-20381)
AMERICAN PERFORMANCE ENGI
7347 W Rosamond Blvd, Rosamond (93560-7284)
PHONE 661 256-7309
Jay Eshbach, *Owner*
EMP: 11
SALES (est): 1.6MM **Privately Held**
SIC: 3751 5013 Motorcycles & related parts; motorcycle parts

(P-20382)
B & E ENTERPRISES
1380 N Mccan St, Anaheim (92806-1316)
PHONE 714 630-3731
Michael Banister, *President*
Edward Miller, *Vice Pres*
EMP: 13
SQ FT: 9,100
SALES (est): 2.3MM **Privately Held**
WEB: www.tubebender.com
SIC: 3751 3714 3599 Frames, motorcycle & bicycle; motor vehicle parts & accessories; machine shop, jobbing & repair

(P-20383)
BARNETT TOOL & ENGINEERING
Also Called: Barnett Performance Products
2238 Palma Dr, Ventura (93003-8068)
PHONE 805 642-9435
Michael Taylor, *President*
Colleen Taylor, *CFO*
EMP: 60
SQ FT: 43,000
SALES (est): 12.2MM **Privately Held**
SIC: 3751 Motorcycle accessories; motorcycles & related parts

(P-20384)
BELT DRIVES LTD
Also Called: B D L
505 W Lambert Rd, Brea (92821-3909)
PHONE 714 693-1313
Steve R Yetzke, *CEO*
Kathy Yetzke, *Shareholder*
EMP: 21
SQ FT: 30,000
SALES (est): 5.3MM **Privately Held**
WEB: www.beltdrives.com
SIC: 3751 Motorcycles & related parts

(P-20385)
BILLS PIPES INC
226 N Maple St, Corona (92880-6913)
PHONE 951 371-1329
William Cervera, *President*
EMP: 15
SQ FT: 4,500
SALES (est): 2.1MM **Privately Held**
WEB: www.billspipes.com
SIC: 3751 Motorcycle accessories; motorcycles & related parts

(P-20386)
BROOKSHIRE INNOVATIONS LLC
502 Giuseppe Ct Ste 7, Roseville (95678-6306)
PHONE 916 786-7601
Kelly Nippear,
▲ **EMP:** 35
SQ FT: 60,000
SALES: 3.7MM **Privately Held**
SIC: 3751 Motorcycle accessories

(P-20387)
BUCHANANS SPOKE & RIM
805 W 8th St, Azusa (91702-2247)
PHONE 626 969-4655
Robert Buchanan, *CEO*
Kenny Buchanan, *Vice Pres*
▲ **EMP:** 21
SQ FT: 21,000
SALES (est): 2.9MM **Privately Held**
WEB: www.buchananspokes.com
SIC: 3751 Motorcycles & related parts

(P-20388)
CAL MOTO
2490 Old Middlefield Way, Mountain View (94043-2317)
PHONE 650 966-1183
Kari W Prager, *President*
Anya Meissner, *Office Mgr*
Ian Clements, *Manager*
▲ **EMP:** 18
SALES (est): 7.2MM **Privately Held**
SIC: 3751 Bicycles & related parts

(P-20389)
CEE BAILEYS AIRCRAFT PLAS INC
6900 W Acco St, Montebello (90640-5435)
P.O. Box 1028 (90640-1028)
PHONE 323 721-4900
Jeff Johnston, *CEO*
Bryan Elliot, *Controller*
EMP: 24
SQ FT: 5,000
SALES: 3MM **Privately Held**
SIC: 3751 3728 3089 Motorcycle accessories; aircraft parts & equipment; windows, plastic

(P-20390)
CORBIN PACIFIC INC
11445 Commercial Pkwy, Castroville (95012-3201)
PHONE 408 633-2500
EMP: 35
SALES (corp-wide): 11.9MM **Privately Held**
SIC: 3751 Saddles & seat posts, motorcycle & bicycle
PA: Corbin Pacific, Inc.
2360 Technology Pkwy
Hollister CA 95023
831 634-1100

(P-20391)
CORBIN PACIFIC INC (PA)
2360 Technology Pkwy, Hollister (95023-2512)
PHONE 831 634-1100
Michael W Hanagan, *CEO*
Beverly Hanagan, *Admin Sec*
▲ **EMP:** 64
SQ FT: 80,000
SALES (est): 11.9MM **Privately Held**
SIC: 3751 Saddles & seat posts, motorcycle & bicycle

(P-20392)
CRITERION COMPOSITES INC
14349 Commerce Dr, Garden Grove (92843-4949)
PHONE 714 554-2717
Don Guichard, *President*
EMP: 13 **EST:** 2008
SALES (est): 1.8MM **Privately Held**
SIC: 3751 3624 Bicycles & related parts; carbon & graphite products

(P-20393)
CULT CVLT
1555 E Saint Gertrude Pl, Santa Ana (92705-5309)
PHONE 714 435-2858
Robert Morales, *Principal*
▲ **EMP:** 12
SALES (est): 1.7MM **Privately Held**
SIC: 3751 Motorcycles, bicycles & parts

(P-20394)
CUSTOM CHROME MANUFACTURING
15750 Vineyard Blvd # 100, Morgan Hill (95037-7119)
PHONE 408 825-5000
Dan Cook, *Principal*
Bill Prescott, *VP Admin*
Jeremy Yearton, *Sales Mgr*
Sharon Dela Cruz, *Marketing Staff*
Bill McClure, *Manager*
◆ **EMP:** 206
SALES (est): 35.3MM **Privately Held**
WEB: www.customchrome.com
SIC: 3751 Motorcycle accessories; frames, motorcycle & bicycle
HQ: Dae-Il Usa, Inc.
112 Robert Young Blvd
Murray KY 42071
-

(P-20395)
CYCLE SHACK INC
816 Murchison Dr, Millbrae (94030-3026)
PHONE 650 583-7014
Homer H Dyer, *President*
Buzz Dyer, *President*
Grove Hoover II, *Vice Pres*
Steve Reedy, *Admin Sec*
EMP: 59
SQ FT: 35,000
SALES (est): 9.9MM **Privately Held**
WEB: www.cycle-shack.com
SIC: 3751 Motorcycles & related parts; motorcycle accessories

(P-20396)
D & D MOTORCYCLE SERVICE INC
10401 Alameda St, Lynwood (90262-1758)
PHONE 323 567-9480
Ken Harold, *President*
EMP: 25
SQ FT: 17,000
SALES (est): 2.8MM **Privately Held**
WEB: www.danddservicesinc.com
SIC: 3751 Motorcycles & related parts

(P-20397)
DAYTEC CENTER LLC
Also Called: Jpm Finishing Company
17469 Lemon St, Hesperia (92345-5151)
P.O. Box 401328 (92340-1328)
PHONE 760 995-3515
Phil Day,
▲ **EMP:** 24
SQ FT: 40,000
SALES (est): 3.7MM **Privately Held**
SIC: 3751 3479 Frames, motorcycle & bicycle; coating of metals with plastic or resins

(P-20398)
EDELBROCK LLC (HQ)
2700 California St, Torrance (90503-3907)
PHONE 310 781-2222
Don Barry, *President*
Wayne Murray, *President*
John Colaianne, *CEO*
Steve Zitkus, *CFO*
Frank Lonigro, *General Mgr*
▲ **EMP:** 300
SQ FT: 290,000
SALES (est): 117.1MM **Privately Held**
WEB: www.edelbrock.com
SIC: 3751 3714 Motorcycle accessories; manifolds, motor vehicle

(P-20399)
ELECTRIC BIKE COMPANY LLC
519 Superior Ave, Newport Beach (92663-3630)
PHONE 949 264-4080
Sean Lupton-Smith, *Mng Member*
Kim King, *Office Mgr*
Cristina Salvador, *Assistant*
EMP: 10
SALES: 1MM **Privately Held**
SIC: 3751 Motorcycles, bicycles & parts

(P-20400)
ENDURANCE PTC
8 Madrona St, Mill Valley (94941-1812)
PHONE 415 445-9155
Andrea Kennedy, *CEO*
Tim Fleming, *Manager*
EMP: 10
SALES (est): 1.3MM **Privately Held**
SIC: 3751 Motorcycles & related parts; motorcycle accessories; brakes, friction clutch & other; bicycle

(P-20401)
FMF RACING
Also Called: Flying Machine Factory
18033 S Santa Fe Ave, Compton (90221-5514)
PHONE 310 631-4363
Don Emler, *CEO*
Raul Mandujano, *COO*
Eric Van Tichelin, *Managing Dir*
Richard King, *MIS Dir*
Erik Mattson, *Design Engr*
▲ **EMP:** 150
SALES (est): 25.5MM **Privately Held**
WEB: www.fmfracing.com
SIC: 3751 5571 Motorcycle accessories; motorcycle parts & accessories

(P-20402)
FOX FACTORY HOLDING CORP (PA)
915 Disc Dr, Scotts Valley (95066-4543)
PHONE 831 274-6500
Larry L Enterline, *CEO*
Dudley Mendenhall, *Ch of Bd*
Elizabeth Fetter, *Bd of Directors*
Ted Waitman, *Bd of Directors*
Zvi Glasman, *Officer*
EMP: 44
SALES: 619.2MM **Publicly Held**
SIC: 3751 Motorcycles, bicycles & parts

(P-20403)
FOX FACTORY INC (HQ)
Also Called: Fox Racing Shox
915 Disc Dr, Scotts Valley (95066-4543)
PHONE 831 274-6500
Larry Enterline, *CEO*
Bob Fox, *President*
Dale A Silvia, *Officer*
Mario Galasso, *Exec VP*
John Blocher, *Vice Pres*
EMP: 103
SALES (est): 35.6MM **Publicly Held**
SIC: 3751 Bicycles & related parts

(P-20404)
GLOBAL MOTORSPORT PARTS INC
155 E Main Ave Ste 150, Morgan Hill (95037-7521)
PHONE 408 778-0500
Joseph F Keenan, *Ch of Bd*
Seth Murdock, *CFO*
Leland Katsuda, *Controller*
◆ **EMP:** 102

SQ FT: 13,000
SALES (est): 8.1MM **Privately Held**
SIC: 3751 5013 Motorcycle accessories;
motorcycle parts
HQ: Dae-Il Usa, Inc.
112 Robert Young Blvd
Murray KY 42071
-

(P-20405)
GPR STABILIZER LLC
8715 Dead Stick Rd, San Diego
(92154-7710)
PHONE....................................619 661-0101
Randy Norman,
EMP: 10
SALES (est): 1.4MM **Privately Held**
SIC: 3751 Motorcycles & related parts

(P-20406)
HEADWINDS
Also Called: Tradewinds
221 W Maple Ave, Monrovia (91016-3329)
PHONE....................................626 359-8044
Joel Felty, *Owner*
Julie Felty, *Co-Owner*
EMP: 13
SQ FT: 10,000
SALES (est): 1.5MM **Privately Held**
WEB: www.headwinds.com
SIC: 3751 3599 Motorcycle accessories;
machine shop, jobbing & repair

(P-20407)
HIGH END SEATING SOLUTIONS LLC
1919 E Occidental St, Santa Ana
(92705-5115)
PHONE....................................714 259-0177
Lars Roulund, *CEO*
EMP: 35 EST: 1998
SQ FT: 23,000
SALES (est): 5.1MM **Privately Held**
WEB: www.highendseats.com
SIC: 3751 Saddles & seat posts, motorcycle & bicycle

(P-20408)
IMS PRODUCTS INC
6240 Box Springs Blvd E, Riverside
(92507-0748)
PHONE....................................951 653-7720
C H Wheat, *President*
Chris Hardin, *General Mgr*
EMP: 16 EST: 1976
SQ FT: 10,000
SALES (est): 2.3MM **Privately Held**
WEB: www.imsproducts.com
SIC: 3751 5571 Motorcycles & related
parts; motorcycle accessories; motorcycle
dealers

(P-20409)
INBOARD TECHNOLOGY INC
1347 Pacific Ave Ste 201, Santa Cruz
(95060-3940)
PHONE....................................844 846-2627
Ryan Evans, *CEO*
Timothy Miller, *COO*
Tim Miller, *Officer*
EMP: 10
SALES (est): 324.9K **Privately Held**
SIC: 3751 Motor scooters & parts

(P-20410)
K & N ENGINEERING INC (PA)
1455 Citrus St, Riverside (92507-1603)
P.O. Box 1329 (92502-1329)
PHONE....................................951 826-4000
Richard Bisson, *CEO*
Jesse Spungin, *Chief Mktg Ofcr*
Patrick Jacobs, *Technician*
Richard Smith, *Business Mgr*
Tom Fumoto, *Analyst*
◆ EMP: 565
SQ FT: 270,000
SALES (est): 124.3MM **Privately Held**
WEB: www.kandn.org
SIC: 3751 3599 3714 Handle bars, motorcycle & bicycle; air intake filters, internal
combustion engine, except auto; filters:
oil, fuel & air, motor vehicle

(P-20411)
KDF INC
Also Called: Pro-Cision Machining
15875 Concord Cir, Morgan Hill
(95037-5448)
PHONE....................................408 779-3731
Ken Fredenburg, *President*
Bonnie Lambert, *QC Mgr*
EMP: 30
SQ FT: 20,000
SALES (est): 3MM **Privately Held**
SIC: 3751 3599 Bicycles & related parts;
machine & other job shop work; electrical
discharge machining (EDM)

(P-20412)
KIBBLWHITE PRECISION MACHINING
580 Crespi Dr Ste H, Pacifica
(94044-3426)
PHONE....................................650 359-4704
Will Kibblewhite, *President*
Maria Kibblewhite, *Purchasing*
▲ EMP: 23
SQ FT: 3,000
SALES (est): 4.1MM **Privately Held**
WEB: www.blackdiamondvalves.com
SIC: 3751 3599 Motorcycles & related
parts; machine shop, jobbing & repair

(P-20413)
KRAFT TECH INC
661 Arroyo St, San Fernando
(91340-2219)
PHONE....................................818 837-3520
Javier Mendoza, *President*
▲ EMP: 13 EST: 1990
SQ FT: 40,000
SALES (est): 3MM **Privately Held**
WEB: www.krafttech.com
SIC: 3751 Motorcycle accessories

(P-20414)
LEPERA ENTERPRISES INC
8207 Lankershim Blvd, North Hollywood
(91605-1614)
PHONE....................................818 767-5110
Robert Lepera, *President*
Robert Le Pera, *President*
Christine Le Pera, *Admin Sec*
Christine Lepera, *Admin Sec*
EMP: 26
SQ FT: 7,000
SALES (est): 2.8MM **Privately Held**
WEB: www.lepera.com
SIC: 3751 Saddles & seat posts, motorcycle & bicycle

(P-20415)
LOADED BOARDS INC
10575 Virginia Ave, Culver City
(90232-3520)
PHONE....................................310 839-1800
Don Tashman, *CEO*
Maria Alarcon, *Accounting Mgr*
Brian Dolen, *Mktg Dir*
Dan Briggs, *Sales Mgr*
Danny Carper, *Director*
▲ EMP: 17
SQ FT: 5,500
SALES (est): 3.8MM **Privately Held**
WEB: www.loadedboards.com
SIC: 3751 Bicycles & related parts; frames,
motorcycle & bicycle

(P-20416)
MAHINDRA TRACTOR ASSEMBLY INC (DH)
Also Called: Mahindra Genze
48016 Fremont Blvd, Fremont
(94538-6500)
PHONE....................................650 779-5180
Vish Palekar, *CEO*
Deven Kataria, *COO*
Sangeeta Laud, *Treasurer*
Shabbir Boxwala, *Administration*
Siddhesh Ozarkar, *Manager*
▲ EMP: 30
SALES (est): 11.7MM
SALES (corp-wide): 7.4B **Privately Held**
SIC: 3751 Motor scooters & parts

(P-20417)
MAIER MANUFACTURING INC
416 Crown Point Cir Ste 1, Grass Valley
(95945-9558)
PHONE....................................530 272-9036
Charles A Maier, *President*
George Maier, *Vice Pres*
Mark Maier, *Vice Pres*
▲ EMP: 45
SQ FT: 79,000
SALES (est): 6.7MM **Privately Held**
WEB: www.maier-mfg.com
SIC: 3751 3082 Motorcycle accessories;
unsupported plastics profile shapes

(P-20418)
MARKLAND INDUSTRIES INC (PA)
1111 E Mcfadden Ave, Santa Ana
(92705-4103)
PHONE....................................714 245-2850
Donald R Markland, *President*
▲ EMP: 74 EST: 1978
SQ FT: 100,000
SALES (est): 32.2MM **Privately Held**
WEB: www.marklandindustries.com
SIC: 3751 Motorcycle accessories

(P-20419)
MEGACYCLE ENGINEERING INC
Also Called: Megacycle Cams
90 Mitchell Blvd, San Rafael (94903-2039)
PHONE....................................415 472-3195
James H Dour, *President*
Barbara Dour, *Treasurer*
Lisa Dour, *Office Mgr*
EMP: 14
SQ FT: 7,500
SALES (est): 2MM **Privately Held**
WEB: www.megacyclecams.com
SIC: 3751 3714 5013 Motorcycles & related parts; camshafts, motor vehicle; automotive supplies & parts; motorcycle parts

(P-20420)
MOVEMENT PRODUCTS INC
22365 El Toro Rd Ste 295, Lake Forest
(92630-5053)
PHONE....................................949 206-0000
James K Miansian, *President*
EMP: 10 EST: 2012
SALES: 250K **Privately Held**
SIC: 3751 5013 Motorcycles, bicycles &
parts; automotive supplies & parts

(P-20421)
MPLUS MOTORS CORP
15375 Barranca Pkwy Ste K, Irvine
(92618-2217)
PHONE....................................510 259-8435
Yiling Guo, *Administration*
▲ EMP: 13
SALES (est): 1.7MM
SALES (corp-wide): 6.3MM **Privately Held**
SIC: 3751 Motorcycles, bicycles & parts
HQ: Jiangsu Sinski Sonik Motor Technology
Co. Ltd.
Rm 201,Hongyuan Rd,Hongshan
Town.
Wuxi 21400
-

(P-20422)
PRO CIRCUIT PRODUCTS INC
2388 Railroad St, Corona (92880-5410)
PHONE....................................951 734-3320
Randy Fleisher, *Manager*
EMP: 15
SALES (corp-wide): 8.9MM **Privately Held**
WEB: www.procircuit.com
SIC: 3751 Motorcycles & related parts
PA: Pro Circuit Products, Inc.
2771 Wardlow Rd
Corona CA 92882
951 738-8050

(P-20423)
REDLANDS CCI INC
721 Nevada St Ste 308, Redlands
(92373-8053)
P.O. Box 365 (92373-0121)
PHONE....................................909 307-6500
Michael E Lyon, *President*

Michael Lyon, *President*
Robert Lyon, *Vice Pres*
EMP: 25
SALES (est): 3.7MM **Privately Held**
SIC: 3751 5091 Bicycles & related parts;
bicycle equipment & supplies

(P-20424)
RITCHEY DESIGN INC (PA)
236 N Santa Cruz Ave # 238, Los Gatos
(95030-7262)
PHONE....................................650 368-4018
Thomas W Ritchey, *President*
Maris Adamovics, *Manager*
Eric Breedy, *Manager*
▲ EMP: 17
SQ FT: 10,000
SALES (est): 1.3MM **Privately Held**
WEB: www.ritcheylogic.com
SIC: 3751 Bicycles & related parts

(P-20425)
SPINERGY INC
1914 Palomar Oaks Way # 100, Carlsbad
(92008-6515)
PHONE....................................760 496-2121
Martin Connolly, *President*
Rene Leyva, *Director*
▲ EMP: 80
SQ FT: 63,000
SALES (est): 14.7MM **Privately Held**
WEB: www.spinergy.com
SIC: 3751 3949 7389 Bicycles & related
parts; exercise equipment; design services

(P-20426)
SPYKE INC
12155 Pangborn Ave, Downey
(90241-5624)
PHONE....................................562 803-1700
Steve Campbell, *President*
▲ EMP: 23 EST: 1996
SQ FT: 15,000
SALES (est): 4.1MM **Privately Held**
WEB: www.spyke1.com
SIC: 3751 Motorcycles, bicycles & parts

(P-20427)
SUPER73 INC
16591 Noyes Ave, Irvine (92606-5102)
PHONE....................................949 313-6340
Legrand Crewse, *CEO*
▼ EMP: 29
SALES (est): 1.8MM **Privately Held**
SIC: 3751 5012 Motorcycles, bicycles &
parts; motorcycles

(P-20428)
T3 MOTION INC
425 Klug Cir, Corona (92880-5406)
PHONE....................................951 737-7300
Lucy LI, *CEO*
William Tsumpes, *COO*
EMP: 25
SALES (est): 899.4K **Privately Held**
SIC: 3751 Motorcycles, bicycles & parts

(P-20429)
TOLEMAR INC
Also Called: Tolemar Manufacturing
5221 Oceanus Dr, Huntington Beach
(92649-1028)
PHONE....................................714 362-8166
Steve Ramelot, *CEO*
▲ EMP: 45
SQ FT: 25,000
SALES (est): 8MM **Privately Held**
WEB: www.tolemar.com
SIC: 3751 Motorcycles & related parts; motorcycle accessories

(P-20430)
TOOMEY RACING USA
5050 Wing Way, Paso Robles
(93446-9528)
PHONE....................................805 239-8870
Stuart Toomey, *Owner*
▼ EMP: 10
SQ FT: 5,000
SALES (est): 440K **Privately Held**
WEB: www.toomey.com
SIC: 3751 5012 5571 Motorcycles & related parts; motorcycles; motorcycle parts & accessories

PRODUCTS & SVCS

(P-20431)
TORCANO INDUSTRIES INC
20381 Lk Frest Dr Ste B10, Lake Forest (92630)
PHONE...............................855 359-3339
John Denson, *CEO*
EMP: 40 EST: 2013
SALES (est): 3MM **Privately Held**
SIC: 3751 Bicycles & related parts

(P-20432)
TRICO SPORTS INC
13541 Desmond St, Pacoima (91331-2301)
PHONE...............................818 899-7705
Paul Yates, *President*
George R Yates, *Vice Pres*
▲ EMP: 90
SQ FT: 60,000
SALES (est): 9.5MM **Privately Held**
SIC: 3751 Bicycles & related parts; saddles & seat posts, motorcycle & bicycle

(P-20433)
TRY ALL 3 SPORTS
Also Called: Tri All
931 Calle Negocio Ste O, San Clemente (92673-6224)
P.O. Box 73833 (92673-0128)
PHONE...............................949 492-2255
Bill Langford, *Owner*
Eric Tothan, *Manager*
EMP: 12
SALES: 500K **Privately Held**
WEB: www.triall3sports.com
SIC: 3751 5091 Bicycles & related parts; bicycle equipment & supplies

(P-20434)
TWO BROTHERS RACING INC
167 Via Trevizio, Corona (92879-1773)
PHONE...............................714 550-6070
Craig A Erion, *President*
Mark Jacobs, *Sales Mgr*
Greg Miranda, *Sales Staff*
James Saechao, *Sales Staff*
◆ EMP: 18
SALES (est): 3.9MM **Privately Held**
SIC: 3751 5013 Motorcycles & related parts; motorcycle parts

(P-20435)
V&H PERFORMANCE LLC
Also Called: Vance & Hines
13861 Rosecrans Ave, Santa Fe Springs (90670-5207)
PHONE...............................562 921-7461
Andrew Graves, *CEO*
Byron Hines, *Shareholder*
Mike Kennedy, *President*
Terry Vance, *Vice Pres*
Steve Derksen, *Info Tech Dir*
▼ EMP: 65
SQ FT: 12,000
SALES (est): 26.6MM **Privately Held**
WEB: www.maggroup.com
SIC: 3751 5013 Motorcycles, bicycles & parts; motorcycle parts
HQ: Motorsport Aftermarket Group, Inc.
651 Canyon Dr Ste 100
Coppell TX 75019
469 283-7777

(P-20436)
WESTERN MFG & DISTRG LLC
Also Called: I.V. League Medical
835 Flynn Rd, Camarillo (93012-8702)
P.O. Box 7192, Rancho Santa Fe (92067-7192)
PHONE...............................805 988-1010
Bill Nichols,
Ryan Nichols, *Safety Mgr*
Donnell Nichols,
EMP: 40
SQ FT: 25,000
SALES (est): 6.5MM **Privately Held**
WEB: www.mcenterprisesusa.com
SIC: 3751 3841 3599 Motorcycles & related parts; motorcycle accessories; surgical & medical instruments; machine shop, jobbing & repair

(P-20437)
WILDERNESS TRAIL BIKES INC (PA)
475 Miller Ave, Mill Valley (94941-2941)
PHONE...............................415 389-5040
Patrick Seidler, *President*
Charlie Cunningham, *Vice Pres*
Stephen M Potts, *Vice Pres*
Mark J Slate, *Vice Pres*
Susan Weaber, *Principal*
▲ EMP: 15
SQ FT: 2,000
SALES (est): 1.7MM **Privately Held**
SIC: 3751 5941 Bicycles & related parts; bicycle & bicycle parts

(P-20438)
WORKS CONNECTION
4130 Product Dr, Cameron Park (95682-8459)
PHONE...............................530 642-9488
Eric Phipps, *Owner*
▲ EMP: 11
SQ FT: 2,800
SALES (est): 1.7MM **Privately Held**
WEB: www.worksconnection.com
SIC: 3751 Motorcycles & related parts

(P-20439)
YUKON TRAIL INC
1175 Woodlawn St, Ontario (91761-4559)
PHONE...............................909 218-5286
Michael Du, *CEO*
Jun Wu Liu, *President*
▲ EMP: 12 EST: 2010
SALES (est): 1.5MM **Privately Held**
SIC: 3751 Motorcycles, bicycles & parts

(P-20440)
ZERO GRAVITY CORPORATION
Also Called: Zero Gravity Group
912 Pancho Rd Ste A, Camarillo (93012-8597)
PHONE...............................805 388-8803
Glenn Cook, *President*
◆ EMP: 35
SQ FT: 2,800
SALES (est): 5.7MM **Privately Held**
WEB: www.zerogravity-racing.com
SIC: 3751 Motorcycle accessories

(P-20441)
ZING RACING PRODUCTS
27430 Bostik Ct Ste 101, Temecula (92590-5511)
PHONE...............................760 219-4700
Bob Zingg, *Partner*
Dr Calvin Spoolstra, *Partner*
EMP: 10 EST: 1997
SQ FT: 8,000
SALES (est): 1.2MM **Privately Held**
WEB: www.zingracing.com
SIC: 3751 Motorcycles, bicycles & parts

```
3761 Guided Missiles &
Space Vehicles
```

(P-20442)
ARCTURUS UAV INC
1035 N Mcdowell Blvd, Petaluma (94954-1173)
PHONE...............................707 206-9372
D'Milo Hallerberg,
Hallerberg Chase, *Manager*
EMP: 10
SQ FT: 80,000
SALES (est): 2MM **Privately Held**
SIC: 3761 3728 Guided missiles & space vehicles; military aircraft equipment & armament

(P-20443)
BOEING COMPANY
5301 Bolsa Ave, Huntington Beach (92647-2048)
PHONE...............................714 896-3311
James McNerney, *Branch Mgr*
R Gale Schluter, *Vice Pres*
Will Trafton, *Vice Pres*
EMP: 368
SQ FT: 2,200,000

SALES (corp-wide): 101.1B **Publicly Held**
SIC: 3761 3769 Guided missiles & space vehicles; guided missile & space vehicle parts & auxiliary equipment
PA: The Boeing Company
100 N Riverside Plz
Chicago IL 60606
312 544-2000

(P-20444)
CENIC NTWRK OPERATIONS WEBSITE
5757 Plaza Dr Ste 205, Cypress (90630-5048)
PHONE...............................714 220-3494
Bill Clebsch, *Principal*
Tammy Sopo, *Admin Asst*
Christine Goodheart, *Consultant*
EMP: 11 EST: 2010
SALES (est): 1.2MM **Privately Held**
SIC: 3761 Guided missiles & space vehicles, research & development

(P-20445)
CLIFFDALE LLC
20409 Prairie St, Chatsworth (91311-6029)
PHONE...............................818 885-0300
William Hart,
EMP: 16
SQ FT: 24,000
SALES (est): 2MM **Privately Held**
SIC: 3761 Guided missiles & space vehicles

(P-20446)
FENIX SPACE INC
294 S Leland, San Bernardino (92408)
PHONE...............................909 382-5677
Jason Lee, *President*
EMP: 10
SALES (est): 360.4K **Privately Held**
SIC: 3761 4522 Guided missiles & space vehicles; air cargo carriers, nonscheduled

(P-20447)
JACOBS TECHNOLOGY INC
8 Draco Dr Bldg 8350, Edwards (93524-7200)
PHONE...............................661 275-6100
Frank Costanza, *Manager*
Bonnadeene Trimble, *Assistant*
EMP: 20
SALES (corp-wide): 10B **Publicly Held**
SIC: 3761 Rockets, space & military, complete
HQ: Jacobs Technology Inc.
600 William Northern Blvd
Tullahoma TN 37388
931 455-6400

(P-20448)
LOCKHEED MARTIN CORPORATION
16020 Empire Grade, Santa Cruz (95060-9628)
PHONE...............................831 425-6000
Joane Meguior, *Manager*
Bill Rose, *Engineer*
David Barauna, *Controller*
EMP: 85 **Publicly Held**
WEB: www.lockheedmartin.com
SIC: 3761 8734 8731 Guided missiles & space vehicles, research & development; space vehicles, complete; testing laboratories; commercial physical research
PA: Lockheed Martin Corporation
6801 Rockledge Dr
Bethesda MD 20817

(P-20449)
LOCKHEED MARTIN CORPORATION
Lockheed Martin Metrology Svcs
1111 Lockheed Martin Way, Sunnyvale (94089-1212)
PHONE...............................408 756-5751
Terri Garcia, *Exec Dir*
Neil Etling, *Program Mgr*
Stu Lowenthal, *Program Mgr*
James Daniel, *Administration*
Greg Yenner, *Sr Software Eng*
EMP: 64 **Publicly Held**

SIC: 3761 Space vehicles, complete; guided missiles, complete; ballistic missiles, complete; guided missiles & space vehicles, research & development
PA: Lockheed Martin Corporation
6801 Rockledge Dr
Bethesda MD 20817

(P-20450)
LOCKHEED MARTIN CORPORATION
160 E Tasman Dr, San Jose (95134-1619)
P.O. Box 3504, Sunnyvale (94088-3504)
PHONE...............................408 747-2626
John Limdquist, *Manager*
EMP: 400 **Publicly Held**
WEB: www.lockheedmartin.com
SIC: 3761 3663 Guided missiles & space vehicles; radio & TV communications equipment
PA: Lockheed Martin Corporation
6801 Rockledge Dr
Bethesda MD 20817

(P-20451)
LOCKHEED MARTIN CORPORATION
1111 Lockheed Martin Way, Sunnyvale (94089-1212)
P.O. Box 3504 (94088-3504)
PHONE...............................408 742-4321
Christin Kulinski, *CEO*
Vinh Nguyen, *Program Mgr*
Rodrick Harkness, *Electrical Engi*
Kevin Chiu, *Engineer*
John Gibb, *Engineer*
EMP: 584 **Publicly Held**
WEB: www.lockheedmartin.com
SIC: 3761 3663 Radio & TV communications equipment; ballistic missiles, complete
PA: Lockheed Martin Corporation
6801 Rockledge Dr
Bethesda MD 20817

(P-20452)
MASTEN SPACE SYSTEMS INC
1570 Sabovich St 25, Mojave (93501-1681)
PHONE...............................661 824-3423
Joel Scotkin, *CEO*
Shawn Mahoney, *COO*
David Masten, *CTO*
Sean Mahoney, *Info Tech Mgr*
Chris Hofmann, *Technician*
EMP: 14
SQ FT: 6,000
SALES (est): 3.3MM **Privately Held**
WEB: www.masten-space.com
SIC: 3761 Guided missiles & space vehicles

(P-20453)
ORBITAL SCIENCES CORPORATION
Talo Rd Bldg 1555, Lompoc (93437)
PHONE...............................805 734-5400
Eric Denbrook, *Manager*
EMP: 100 **Publicly Held**
WEB: www.orbital.com
SIC: 3761 Space vehicles, complete
HQ: Orbital Sciences Corporation
45101 Warp Dr
Dulles VA 20166
703 406-5000

(P-20454)
PARABILIS SPACE TECH INC
1195 Linda Vista Dr Ste F, San Marcos (92078-3824)
PHONE...............................855 727-2245
David J Streich, *CEO*
Richard Slansky, *Exec VP*
Christopher Grainger, *Vice Pres*
Frank Macklin, *Chief Engr*
David Brynes, *VP Finance*
EMP: 10 EST: 2014
SQ FT: 3,242
SALES (est): 890.3K **Privately Held**
SIC: 3761 Guided missiles & space vehicles, research & development

(P-20455)
SPACE EXPLORATION TECH CORP (PA)
Also Called: Spacex
1 Rocket Rd, Hawthorne (90250-6844)
PHONE..................................310 363-6000
Elon R Musk, *CEO*
Gwynne Shotwell, *President*
Bret Johnsen, *CFO*
Mark Juncosa, *Vice Pres*
Hans Koenigsmann, *Vice Pres*
◆ **EMP:** 1215
SQ FT: 964,000
SALES (est): 1.1B **Privately Held**
WEB: www.spacex.com
SIC: 3761 Rockets, space & military, complete

(P-20456)
STELLAR EXPLORATION INC
835 Airport Dr, San Luis Obispo (93401-8370)
PHONE..................................805 459-1425
Tomas Svitek, *President*
Iva Svitek, *Admin Sec*
EMP: 12
SQ FT: 3,000
SALES: 1.3MM **Privately Held**
SIC: 3761 Space vehicles, complete

(P-20457)
TAYCO ENGINEERING INC
10874 Hope St, Cypress (90630-5214)
P.O. Box 6034 (90630-0034)
PHONE..................................714 952-2240
Jay Chung, *President*
Ann Taylor, *COO*
Sheri T Nikolakopulos, *CFO*
Brent Taylor, *Vice Pres*
Hamida Sadghzah, *Executive*
EMP: 130
SQ FT: 55,600
SALES: 15.8MM **Privately Held**
WEB: www.taycoeng.com
SIC: 3761 Guided missiles & space vehicles

(P-20458)
TERRAN ORBITAL CORPORATION (PA)
15330 Barranca Pkwy, Irvine (92618-2215)
PHONE..................................212 496-2300
Anthony Previte, *CEO*
Jordi Puig-Suari, *Admin Sec*
EMP: 20
SALES (est): 6.6MM **Privately Held**
SIC: 3761 3764 Space vehicles, complete; guided missiles & space vehicles, research & development; guided missile & space vehicle engines, research & devel.

(P-20459)
TSC LLC (DH)
Also Called: Spaceship Company, The
16555 Spceship Landing Wa, Mojave (93501-1534)
PHONE..................................661 824-6600
George Whitesides,
Matt Launder, *Technician*
Dan Shippey, *Technician*
Neil Jagoda, *Design Engr*
Igor Temkin, *Design Engr*
EMP: 850
SQ FT: 200,000
SALES (est): 112.7MM **Privately Held**
SIC: 3761 Rockets, space & military, complete

(P-20460)
TYVAK NN-SATELLITE SYSTEMS INC
15330 Barranca Pkwy, Irvine (92618-2215)
PHONE..................................949 753-1020
Anthony Previte, *CEO*
Marco Villa, *Treasurer*
Austin Williams, *Vice Pres*
Krystle Curnette, *Admin Sec*
Nicholas Ryhajlo, *Software Engr*
EMP: 75

SALES (est): 6.3MM
SALES (corp-wide): 6.6MM **Privately Held**
WEB: www.tyvak.com
SIC: 3761 3764 Space vehicles, complete; guided missiles & space vehicles, research & development; guided missile & space vehicle propulsion unit parts; guided missile & space vehicle engines, research & devel.
PA: Terran Orbital Corporation
15330 Barranca Pkwy
Irvine CA 92618
212 496-2300

(P-20461)
UNITED LAUNCH ALLIANCE LLC
1579 Utah Ave Bldg 7525, Vandenberg Afb (93437)
PHONE..................................303 269-5876
Deborah Settit, *Principal*
EMP: 100
SALES (corp-wide): 1.1B **Privately Held**
SIC: 3761 Guided missiles & space vehicles
PA: United Launch Alliance, L.L.C.
9501 E Panorama Cir
Centennial CO 80112
720 922-7100

(P-20462)
US ROCKETS
Munsey Rd Mile 11, Cantil (93519)
P.O. Box 1242, Claremont (91711-1242)
PHONE..................................707 267-3393
Jerry Irvine, *Owner*
EMP: 14 **EST:** 1998
SQ FT: 6,000
SALES (est): 648.3K **Privately Held**
SIC: 3761 Rockets, space & military, complete

(P-20463)
VIRGIN ORBIT LLC (PA)
4022 E Conant St, Long Beach (90808-1777)
PHONE..................................562 384-4400
Dan Hart Became, *CEO*
Dan Hart, *President*
Jon Campagna, *Vice Pres*
Pavel Roskin, *Sr Software Eng*
Scott Macklin, *Chief Engr*
EMP: 171 **EST:** 2016
SQ FT: 150,000
SALES (est): 174.2MM **Privately Held**
SIC: 3761 3764 Guided missiles & space vehicles; guided missile & space vehicle propulsion unit parts

---

3764 Guided Missile/Space Vehicle Propulsion Units & parts

(P-20464)
INTERNET SCIENCE EDUCATION PRJ
805 Chestnut St, San Francisco (94133-2245)
PHONE..................................415 806-3156
Jack Sarfatti, *President*
EMP: 10 **EST:** 1995
SALES: 172.6K **Privately Held**
SIC: 3764 3812 8731 Guided missile & space vehicle engines, research & devel.; defense systems & equipment; commercial physical research; energy research

(P-20465)
MICROCOSM INC
3111 Lomita Blvd, Torrance (90505-5108)
PHONE..................................310 219-2700
James Wertz, *President*
Alice Wertz, *Corp Secy*
Dr Robert E Conger, *Vice Pres*
EMP: 40
SQ FT: 50,000

SALES (est): 7.9MM **Privately Held**
WEB: www.smad.com
SIC: 3764 2731 3769 Guided missile & space vehicle propulsion unit parts; book publishing; guided missile & space vehicle parts & auxiliary equipment

(P-20466)
NORTHROP GRUMMAN INNOVATION
Also Called: Ca75 Atk
9617 Distribution Ave, San Diego (92121-2307)
PHONE..................................858 621-5700
David W Thompson, *President*
Dean Dubey, *Analyst*
Kelly Enriquez, *Director*
EMP: 300 **Publicly Held**
SIC: 3764 Guided missile & space vehicle propulsion unit parts
HQ: Northrop Grumman Innovation Systems, Inc.
45101 Warp Dr
Dulles VA 20166
703 406-5000

(P-20467)
NORTHROP GRUMMAN INNOVATION
250 Klug Cir, Corona (92880-5409)
PHONE..................................951 520-7300
Dave Shanahan, *Branch Mgr*
EMP: 63 **Publicly Held**
WEB: www.mrcwdc.com
SIC: 3764 Guided missile & space vehicle propulsion unit parts
HQ: Northrop Grumman Innovation Systems, Inc.
45101 Warp Dr
Dulles VA 20166
703 406-5000

(P-20468)
ORBITAL SCIENCES CORPORATION
1151 W Reeves Ave, Ridgecrest (93555-2313)
PHONE..................................818 887-8345
David Rocca, *Branch Mgr*
Leah Olufson, *Analyst*
EMP: 10 **Publicly Held**
SIC: 3764 Propulsion units for guided missiles & space vehicles
HQ: Orbital Sciences Corporation
45101 Warp Dr
Dulles VA 20166
703 406-5000

(P-20469)
THALES ALENIA SPACE NORTH AMER
20400 Stevens Creek Blvd # 245, Cupertino (95014-2217)
PHONE..................................408 973-9845
EMP: 11
SQ FT: 1,200
SALES: 2MM
SALES (corp-wide): 305.4MM **Privately Held**
SIC: 3764 3769 3761
HQ: Thales Alenia Space Italia Spa
Via Saccomuro 24
Roma RM 00131
064 151-1

(P-20470)
WASK ENGINEERING INC
3905 Dividend Dr, Cameron Park (95682-7214)
PHONE..................................530 672-2795
Wendel Burkhardt, *President*
John Crapuchettes, *Chief Engr*
EMP: 11
SQ FT: 3,500
SALES (est): 1.6MM **Privately Held**
WEB: www.waskengr.com
SIC: 3764 Engines & engine parts, guided missile

3769 Guided Missile/Space Vehicle Parts & Eqpt, NEC

(P-20471)
AEROWIND CORPORATION
1959 John Towers Ave, El Cajon (92020-1117)
PHONE..................................619 569-1960
William L Kousens, *CEO*
Tam Nguyen, *Engineer*
EMP: 15 **EST:** 1946
SQ FT: 20,000
SALES (est): 3.9MM **Privately Held**
WEB: www.aerowind.com
SIC: 3769 3469 Guided missile & space vehicle parts & aux eqpt, rsch & dev; machine parts, stamped or pressed metal

(P-20472)
AMERICAN AUTOMATED ENGRG INC
Also Called: A A E Aerospace & Coml Tech
5382 Argosy Ave, Huntington Beach (92649-1037)
PHONE..................................714 898-9951
Kenneth Christensen, *President*
EMP: 85
SQ FT: 48,000
SALES: 26MM **Privately Held**
WEB: www.aaeaerospace.com
SIC: 3769 Guided missile & space vehicle parts & auxiliary equipment

(P-20473)
CLIFFDALE MANUFACTURING LLC
Also Called: RTC Aerospace
20409 Prairie St, Chatsworth (91311-6029)
PHONE..................................818 341-3344
Jason Darley, *CEO*
Jerry Koger, *President*
EMP: 130 **EST:** 1943
SQ FT: 42,000
SALES (est): 17MM **Privately Held**
WEB: www.robertstool.net
SIC: 3769 3599 Guided missile & space vehicle parts & auxiliary equipment; machine shop, jobbing & repair

(P-20474)
DATA DEVICE CORPORATION
13000 Gregg St Ste C, Poway (92064-7151)
PHONE..................................858 503-3300
Dan Veenstra, *Branch Mgr*
Robert Hillman, *Engineer*
EMP: 35
SALES (corp-wide): 3.8B **Publicly Held**
SIC: 3769 Guided missile & space vehicle parts & aux eqpt, rsch & dev
HQ: Data Device Corporation
105 Wilbur Pl
Bohemia NY 11716
631 567-5600

(P-20475)
GOODRICH CORPORATION
Also Called: UTC Aerospace Systems
3530 Branscombe Rd, Fairfield (94533)
P.O. Box Kk (94533-0659)
PHONE..................................707 422-1880
Aaron Bennetts, *Manager*
EMP: 25
SALES (corp-wide): 66.5B **Publicly Held**
SIC: 3769 Guided missile & space vehicle parts & auxiliary equipment
HQ: Goodrich Corporation
2730 W Tyvola Rd 4
Charlotte NC 28217
704 423-7000

(P-20476)
HYDROMACH INC
20400 Prairie St, Chatsworth (91311-8129)
PHONE..................................818 341-0915
Norberto A Cusinato, *CEO*
Jose Nicosia, *Vice Pres*
Anna M Cusinato, *Admin Sec*
Hector Sampedro, *QC Mgr*
Hamid Lari, *Production*
EMP: 40

SQ FT: 23,000
SALES (est): 8.2MM **Privately Held**
SIC: 3769 3599 Guided missile & space vehicle parts & auxiliary equipment; machine shop, jobbing & repair

(P-20477)
KDL PRECISION MOLDING CORP
Also Called: Custom Silicone Technologies
11381 Bradley Ave, Pacoima (91331-2358)
PHONE..............................818 896-9899
David Wyckoff, *President*
Lee Brown, *CFO*
Ben Bensal, *Vice Pres*
EMP: 70
SQ FT: 10,000
SALES (est): 13.9MM **Privately Held**
WEB: www.kdlprecision.com
SIC: 3769 2822 3061 Guided missile & space vehicle parts & auxiliary equipment; silicone rubbers; oil & gas field machinery rubber goods (mechanical)

(P-20478)
LEDA CORPORATION
7080 Kearny Dr, Huntington Beach (92648-6254)
PHONE..............................714 841-7821
Joseph K Tung, *President*
David Tung, *Vice Pres*
Dorothy Tung, *Vice Pres*
EMP: 30
SQ FT: 15,000
SALES (est): 4.1MM **Privately Held**
WEB: www.ledacorp.net
SIC: 3769 Guided missile & space vehicle parts & aux eqpt, rsch & dev

(P-20479)
MICRO STEEL INC
7850 Alabama Ave, Canoga Park (91304-4905)
PHONE..............................818 348-8701
Lazar Hersko, *President*
Claudia Scelo, *Vice Pres*
Tova Hersko, *Admin Sec*
EMP: 25
SQ FT: 14,500
SALES: 3.7MM **Privately Held**
WEB: www.microsteel.com
SIC: 3769 Guided missile & space vehicle parts & auxiliary equipment

(P-20480)
STANFORD MU CORPORATION
Also Called: Airborne Components
20725 Annalee Ave, Carson (90746-3503)
PHONE..............................310 605-2888
Stanford Mu, *President*
Robert Friend, *Exec VP*
Lynn Price, *Vice Pres*
Edgar Maldonado, *Project Engr*
EMP: 40
SALES (est): 8MM **Privately Held**
WEB: www.stanfordmu.com
SIC: 3769 3764 7699 Guided missile & space vehicle parts & auxiliary equipment; guided missile & space vehicle propulsion unit parts; propulsion units for guided missiles & space vehicles; aircraft & heavy equipment repair services

(P-20481)
VANTAGE ASSOCIATES INC (PA)
900 Civic Center Dr, National City (91950-1013)
PHONE..............................619 477-6940
Paul Roy, *CEO*
Eric Clack, *President*
Andrea Alpinieri Glover, *CFO*
Maggie Ambrose, *Admin Asst*
EMP: 35
SQ FT: 15,000
SALES (est): 63.6MM **Privately Held**
WEB: www.vantagemmc.com
SIC: 3769 2821 3728 3083 Guided missile & space vehicle parts & auxiliary equipment; plastics materials & resins; aircraft parts & equipment; laminated plastics plate & sheet

---

3792 Travel Trailers & Campers

(P-20482)
COMPOSITE PLASTIC SYSTEMS INC
1701a River Rock Rd, Santa Maria (93454-2581)
PHONE..............................805 354-1391
Rienk Ayers, *Regional Mgr*
EMP: 17 **EST:** 2013
SALES (est): 1.3MM **Privately Held**
SIC: 3792 1623 3728 House trailers, except as permanent dwellings; transmitting tower (telecommunication) construction; research & dev by manuf., aircraft parts & auxiliary equip

(P-20483)
CUSTOM FIBREGLASS MFG CO
Also Called: Custom Hardtops
1711 Harbor Ave, Long Beach (90813-1300)
PHONE..............................562 432-5454
Hartmut W Schroeder, *President*
Joel Thiefburg, *CFO*
Robert L Edwards, *Senior VP*
Pete Lopa, *Production*
◆ **EMP:** 165 **EST:** 1966
SQ FT: 135,000
SALES: 48.5MM
SALES (corp-wide): 1.2B **Privately Held**
WEB: www.snugtop.com
SIC: 3792 Pickup covers, canopies or caps
HQ: Truck Accessories Group, Llc
28858 Ventura Dr
Elkhart IN 46517
574 522-5337

(P-20484)
FLEETWOOD TRAVEL TRLRS IND INC (DH)
3125 Myers St, Riverside (92503-5527)
P.O. Box 7638 (92513-7638)
PHONE..............................951 354-3000
Edward B Caudill, *President*
Boyd R Plowman, *CFO*
Lyle N Larkin, *Treasurer*
Christopher J Braun, *Senior VP*
Forrest D Theobald, *Senior VP*
EMP: 14 **EST:** 1971
SQ FT: 262,900
SALES (est): 9.3MM
SALES (corp-wide): 2.6B **Privately Held**
SIC: 3792 Travel trailers & campers
HQ: Fleetwood Enterprises, Inc.
1351 Pomona Rd Ste 230
Corona CA 92882
951 354-3000

(P-20485)
FOREST RIVER INC
255 S Pepper Ave, Rialto (92376-6721)
PHONE..............................909 873-3777
Ty Miller, *Owner*
EMP: 20
SALES (corp-wide): 225.3B **Publicly Held**
WEB: www.forestriverinc.com
SIC: 3792 Tent-type camping trailers
HQ: Forest River, Inc.
900 County Road 1 N
Elkhart IN 46514

(P-20486)
FOUR WHEEL CAMPERS INC
109 Pioneer Ave, Woodland (95776-6123)
PHONE..............................530 666-1442
Tom Hanagan, *President*
Sonam Chand, *Admin Asst*
Stan Kennedy, *Sales Executive*
▲ **EMP:** 25
SQ FT: 24,000
SALES (est): 5.6MM **Privately Held**
SIC: 3792 5561 Travel trailers & campers; recreational vehicle dealers

(P-20487)
GOLDEN OFFICE TRAILERS INC
18257 Grand Ave, Lake Elsinore (92530-6159)
P.O. Box 669, Wildomar (92595-0669)
PHONE..............................951 678-2177
Hal D Woods, *President*
EMP: 25
SALES (est): 4.6MM **Privately Held**
SIC: 3792 5271 Travel trailers & campers; mobile homes

(P-20488)
LIFETIME CAMPER SHELLS INC
1375 N E St, San Bernardino (92405-4506)
PHONE..............................909 885-2814
Joe Malotte, *President*
Gwen Malotte, *Corp Secy*
EMP: 20 **EST:** 1980
SQ FT: 1,000
SALES (est): 3.2MM **Privately Held**
SIC: 3792 Campers, for mounting on trucks

(P-20489)
LIN CONSULTING LLC
Also Called: Airstream of Orange County
15086 Beach Blvd, Midway City (92655-1414)
PHONE..............................714 650-8595
Margaret Bayston, *CEO*
Ira Cohen, *Principal*
Ken Kaiden, *Principal*
Dale Johnson, *Manager*
EMP: 11
SALES (est): 202.9K **Privately Held**
SIC: 3792 4725 Travel trailers & campers; tour operators

(P-20490)
MVP RV INC
40 E Verdugo Ave, Burbank (91502-1931)
PHONE..............................951 848-4288
Brad Williams, *President*
Pablo Carmona, *COO*
Roger Humeston, *CFO*
▲ **EMP:** 50
SALES (est): 6.5MM **Privately Held**
SIC: 3792 Travel trailer chassis

(P-20491)
PACIFIC COACHWORKS INC
3411 N Perris Blvd Bldg 1, Perris (92571-3100)
PHONE..............................951 686-7294
Brett Bashaw, *CEO*
Michael Rhodes, *Admin Sec*
EMP: 155
SALES (est): 48MM **Privately Held**
WEB: www.pacificcoachworks.com
SIC: 3792 Travel trailers & campers

(P-20492)
PROTO HOMES LLC
917 W 17th St, Los Angeles (90015-3317)
PHONE..............................310 271-7544
Frank Vafaee,
Garden Carpio, *Office Mgr*
EMP: 40
SQ FT: 8,000
SALES: 9MM **Privately Held**
SIC: 3792 House trailers, except as permanent dwellings

(P-20493)
SHADOW INDUSTRIES INC
Also Called: Shadow Trailers
8941 Electric St, Cypress (90630-2240)
PHONE..............................714 995-4353
Fritz Stanley Owner, *President*
EMP: 14
SQ FT: 2,804
SALES: 1,000K **Privately Held**
WEB: www.shadowtrailers.com
SIC: 3792 5599 Travel trailers & campers; utility trailers

(P-20494)
TAILGATER INC
Also Called: Versarack
881 Vertin Ave, Salinas (93901-4524)
P.O. Box 629 (93902-0629)
PHONE..............................831 424-7710
Warren P Landon, *President*
Barbara Landon, *Treasurer*
Barbara H Landon, *Corp Secy*

Dick Renard, *Vice Pres*
Robbie Hohstadt, *Office Mgr*
EMP: 15
SALES (est): 1.4MM **Privately Held**
WEB: www.tailgater.net
SIC: 3792 3713 Pickup covers, canopies or caps; truck & bus bodies

(P-20495)
TRUCK ACCESSORIES GROUP LLC
Leer West
1686 E Beamer St, Woodland (95776-6219)
PHONE..............................530 666-0176
Dave Madison, *Manager*
Danny Lamb, *Opers Mgr*
EMP: 115
SALES (corp-wide): 1.2B **Privately Held**
WEB: www.leer.com
SIC: 3792 3713 Pickup covers, canopies or caps; truck & bus bodies
HQ: Truck Accessories Group, Llc
28858 Ventura Dr
Elkhart IN 46517
574 522-5337

3795 Tanks & Tank Components

(P-20496)
BAE SYSTEMS LAND ARMAMENTS LP
6331 San Ignacio Ave, San Jose (95119-1202)
PHONE..............................408 289-0111
EMP: 60
SALES (corp-wide): 21.6B **Privately Held**
WEB: www.bradleyspareparts.com
SIC: 3795 Tanks & tank components
HQ: Bae Systems Land & Armaments L.P.
2000 15th St N Fl 11
Arlington VA 22201
703 907-8250

(P-20497)
DN TANKS INC (PA)
351 Cypress Ln, El Cajon (92020-1603)
PHONE..............................619 440-8181
Charles Crowley, *CEO*
Bill Hendrickson, *Co-CEO*
Jim Diggins, *Vice Pres*
Joe Manzi, *Vice Pres*
Christopher Young, *Regional Mgr*
▼ **EMP:** 152
SALES (est): 80MM **Privately Held**
SIC: 3795 8711 1542 Tanks & tank components; engineering services; nonresidential construction

(P-20498)
DYK INCORPORATED (HQ)
Also Called: Dyk Prestressed Tanks
351 Cypress Ln, El Cajon (92020-1603)
P.O. Box 696 (92022-0696)
PHONE..............................619 440-8181
Charles Crowley, *CEO*
Max R Dykmans, *President*
Don Paula, *CFO*
Danish Ihsan, *Officer*
David Gourley, *Exec VP*
▲ **EMP:** 25
SALES (est): 4.8MM **Privately Held**
WEB: www.dyk.com
SIC: 3795 8711 1542 Tanks & tank components; engineering services; nonresidential construction

(P-20499)
PREMIER TANK SERVICE INC
34933 Imperial St, Bakersfield (93308)
PHONE..............................661 833-2960
Lupe Lopez, *President*
EMP: 40 **EST:** 2007
SQ FT: 5,000
SALES (est): 3.5MM **Privately Held**
SIC: 3795 7699 Tanks & tank components; tank repair

▲ = Import ▼=Export
◆ =Import/Export

(P-20500)
SANTA ROSA STAIN
1400 Airport Blvd, Santa Rosa
(95403-1023)
P.O. Box 518 (95402-0518)
PHONE..............................707 544-7777
Mark Ferronato, *President*
Michele Cotta, *Corp Secy*
Rod Ferronato, *Vice Pres*
EMP: 45
SQ FT: 12,000
SALES (est): 17.2MM **Privately Held**
WEB: www.srss.com
SIC: 3795 Tanks & tank components

(P-20501)
TIGER TANKS INC
3397 Edison Hwy, Bakersfield
(93307-2234)
P.O. Box 21041 (93390-1041)
PHONE..............................661 363-8335
Toll Free:..888 -
Robert E Bimat, *Ch of Bd*
Darryck Selk, *President*
Bryan Lewis, *CFO*
Roger Burns, *Vice Pres*
Carol Bimat, *Admin Sec*
EMP: 30
SQ FT: 55,000
SALES (est): 6MM **Privately Held**
WEB: www.tigertanksinc.com
SIC: 3795 3443 Tanks & tank compo-
nents; fabricated plate work (boiler shop)

3799 Transportation Eqpt, NEC

(P-20502)
ADVANCED DISPLAY SYSTEMS INC
8614 Central Ave, Stanton (90680-2720)
PHONE..............................714 995-2200
Roger J Nichols, *President*
EMP: 11
SQ FT: 12,000
SALES (est): 1MM **Privately Held**
WEB: www.advanceddisplaysystems.com
SIC: 3799 Golf carts, powered; trailers &
trailer equipment; pushcarts & wheelbar-
rows

(P-20503)
ASSAULT INDUSTRIES INC
12691 Monarch St, Garden Grove
(92841-3918)
PHONE..............................714 799-6711
Marcelo Danze, *President*
Elliott Mungarro, *Accounts Exec*
▲ EMP: 10
SALES: 469.3K **Privately Held**
SIC: 3799 All terrain vehicles (ATV)

(P-20504)
CLR ANALYTICS INC
25 Mauchly Ste 315, Irvine (92618-2361)
PHONE..............................949 864-6696
Lianyu Chu, *President*
◆ EMP: 10
SALES (est): 758.3K **Privately Held**
SIC: 3799 Trailers & trailer equipment

(P-20505)
CLUB CAR LLC
Also Called: Engersall
1203 Hall Ave, Riverside (92509-2214)
PHONE..............................951 735-4675
Adam Burke, *Manager*
EMP: 30 **Privately Held**
WEB: www.clubcar.com
SIC: 3799 5088 Golf carts, powered; golf
carts
HQ: Club Car, Llc
4125 Washington Rd
Evans GA 30809
706 863-3000

(P-20506)
DG PERFORMANCE SPC INC
4100 E La Palma Ave, Anaheim
(92807-1814)
PHONE..............................714 961-8850
Mark W Dooley, *President*
William J Dooley, *Ch of Bd*
Joan K Dooley, *Corp Secy*

EMP: 100
SQ FT: 25,000
SALES (est): 16.4MM **Privately Held**
WEB: www.dgperf.com
SIC: 3799 3751 5012 5961 Recreational
vehicles; motorcycles & related parts;
recreation vehicles, all-terrain; fitness &
sporting goods, mail order; motor vehicle
parts & accessories; carburetors, pistons,
rings, valves

(P-20507)
DHM ENTERPRISES INC
7609 Wilbur Way, Sacramento
(95828-4927)
PHONE..............................916 688-7767
George Backovich, *President*
John Pennell, *Treasurer*
Bruce Pennell, *Vice Pres*
EMP: 25
SALES (est): 3.1MM **Privately Held**
WEB: www.dhmenterprises.com
SIC: 3799 5551 Boat trailers; boat dealers

(P-20508)
EKKO MATERIAL HDLG EQP MFG INC
1761 W Holt Ave, Pomona (91768-3315)
PHONE..............................909 212-1962
Xiaobo Liu, *CEO*
Don Hwang, *Director*
EMP: 10
SQ FT: 9,000
SALES: 500K **Privately Held**
SIC: 3799 Towing bars & systems

(P-20509)
FLEETWOOD ENTERPRISES INC (DH)
1351 Pomona Rd Ste 230, Corona
(92882-7165)
PHONE..............................951 354-3000
Nelson Potter, *President*
Christopher J Braun, *Exec VP*
Paul C Eskritt, *Exec VP*
Charley Lott, *Exec VP*
Todd L Inlander, *Senior VP*
EMP: 237 EST: 1950
SALES (est): 1.9B
SALES (corp-wide): 2.6B **Privately Held**
WEB: www.fleetwood.com
SIC: 3799 2451 5561 Recreational vehi-
cles; mobile homes; recreational vehicle
parts & accessories

(P-20510)
G & F HORSE TRAILER REPAIR
Also Called: G & F White Wedding Carriages
2175 S Willow Ave, Bloomington
(92316-2970)
PHONE..............................909 820-4600
George E Liblin, *Owner*
EMP: 15
SQ FT: 15,000
SALES (est): 750K **Privately Held**
SIC: 3799 7539 4789 Horse trailers, ex-
cept fifth-wheel type; trailer repair; horse
drawn transportation services

(P-20511)
GENESIS SUPREME RV INC
23129 Cajalco Rd, Perris (92570-7298)
PHONE..............................951 337-0254
Pablo Carmona, *CEO*
EMP: 28
SALES (est): 6.3MM **Privately Held**
SIC: 3799 Recreational vehicles

(P-20512)
HALL ASSOCIATES RACG PDTS INC
23104 Normandie Ave, Torrance
(90502-2619)
PHONE..............................310 326-4111
Ammie Armstrong, *CEO*
Kennith C Hall, *President*
EMP: 17
SQ FT: 7,000
SALES (est): 3.5MM **Privately Held**
WEB: www.hallassociatesmachine.com
SIC: 3799 8733 3699 Recreational vehi-
cles; research institute; security devices

(P-20513)
HUA RONG INTERNATIONAL CORP
Also Called: Excalibur Motorsports
14020 Cent Ave Ste 530, Chino (91710)
PHONE..............................909 591-8800
Wade W Liu, *CEO*
Jin Lee, *Vice Pres*
▲ EMP: 11
SQ FT: 10,000
SALES (est): 1.4MM **Privately Held**
WEB: www.atv4usa.com
SIC: 3799 5013 All terrain vehicles (ATV);
wheels, motor vehicle

(P-20514)
IPC INDUSTRIES INC (PA)
Also Called: Innovative Products Co
27230 Madison Ave Ste C2, Temecula
(92590-5690)
PHONE..............................951 695-2720
Michael P Highsmith, *CEO*
Doug Highsmith, *Vice Pres*
Stacy Hammond, *Office Mgr*
Stacy Highsmith, *Office Mgr*
Stacy Lindsey, *Administration*
EMP: 14
SQ FT: 11,000
SALES (est): 2.6MM **Privately Held**
SIC: 3799 Trailers & trailer equipment

(P-20515)
LIQUIDSPRING TECHNOLOGIES INC
10400 Pioneer Blvd Ste 1, Santa Fe
Springs (90670-3728)
PHONE..............................562 941-4344
Richard J Meyer, *President*
Carl Harr, *Marketing Staff*
Tony Wade, *Director*
▼ EMP: 11 EST: 1982
SQ FT: 6,000
SALES (est): 1.2MM **Privately Held**
SIC: 3799 3714 Automobile trailer chassis;
universal joints, motor vehicle

(P-20516)
NATIONAL SIGNAL INC
2440 Artesia Ave, Fullerton (92833-2543)
PHONE..............................714 441-7707
Marcos Fernandez, *President*
Lupe Mertinez, *Vice Pres*
◆ EMP: 50
SQ FT: 55,000
SALES (est): 14.2MM **Privately Held**
SIC: 3799 Trailers & trailer equipment

(P-20517)
OMF PERFORMANCE PRODUCTS
Also Called: Orchard's Metal Fabrication
8199 Mar Vista Ct, Riverside (92504-4372)
PHONE..............................951 354-8272
Tim Orchard, *Owner*
EMP: 10
SQ FT: 2,000
SALES: 1.3MM **Privately Held**
WEB: www.omfperformance.com
SIC: 3799 All terrain vehicles (ATV)

(P-20518)
PACIFIC BOAT TRAILERS INC (PA)
13643 5th St, Chino (91710-5168)
PHONE..............................909 902-0094
Roger Treichler, *President*
Vicky Treichler, *Vice Pres*
Sergio Acosta, *Sales Staff*
Karen Ash, *Agent*
EMP: 20
SQ FT: 30,000
SALES (est): 1MM **Privately Held**
WEB: www.pacifictrailers.com
SIC: 3799 Boat trailers

(P-20519)
PREMIER TRAILER MANUFACTURING
30517 Ivy Rd, Visalia (93291-9553)
P.O. Box 191 (93279-0191)
PHONE..............................559 651-2212
Gene A Cuelho Jr, *President*
Sally Cuelho, *Admin Sec*
EMP: 50

SALES (est): 14.1MM **Privately Held**
SIC: 3799 Trailers & trailer equipment

(P-20520)
S&S INVESTMENT CLUB (PA)
5340 Gateway Plaza Dr, Benicia
(94510-2123)
PHONE..............................707 747-5508
Michael Combest, *CFO*
Scott Murphy, *President*
EMP: 14
SQ FT: 10,200
SALES (est): 2.7MM **Privately Held**
WEB: www.nicksgolfcarts.com
SIC: 3799 5012 7999 5599 Golf carts,
powered; recreational vehicles, motor
homes & trailers; golf services & profes-
sionals; golf cart, powered

(P-20521)
SPORT BOAT TRAILERS INC
430 C St, Patterson (95363-2724)
P.O. Box 1686 (95363-1686)
PHONE..............................209 892-5388
Robert J Kehl, *President*
EMP: 12
SQ FT: 3,700
SALES (est): 5MM **Privately Held**
SIC: 3799 7539 Boat trailers; trailer repair

(P-20522)
STIERS RV CENTERS LLC
Also Called: American Rv
25410 The Old Rd, Santa Clarita
(91381-1704)
PHONE..............................661 254-6000
Nancy Houck, *Manager*
EMP: 14
SALES (corp-wide): 4.7B **Publicly Held**
SIC: 3799 Recreational vehicles; automo-
bile trailer chassis; carriages, horse
drawn
HQ: Stier's Rv Centers, Llc
5500 Wible Rd
Bakersfield CA 93313
661 323-8000

(P-20523)
UNIVERSAL TRAILERS INC
2750 Mulberry St, Riverside (92501-2531)
PHONE..............................951 784-0543
Nghiem Nguyen, *Principal*
Thuan Nguyen, *Principal*
EMP: 15
SQ FT: 22,000
SALES (est): 1.3MM **Privately Held**
SIC: 3799 5599 Trailers & trailer equip-
ment; utility trailers

(P-20524)
WAGONMASTERS CORPORATION
Also Called: Joe's Trailer Repair
11060 Cherry Ave, Fontana (92337-7119)
PHONE..............................909 823-6188
Joseph M Burt, *President*
EMP: 10
SQ FT: 10,200
SALES (est): 930K **Privately Held**
WEB: www.trailerrepairusa.com
SIC: 3799 Trailers & trailer equipment

(P-20525)
WHILL INC (PA)
951 Mariners Island Blvd # 300, San Mateo
(94404-1560)
PHONE..............................844 699-4455
Satoshi Sugie, *CEO*
Kenji Goho, *CFO*
Muneaki Fukuoka, *CTO*
Hiromi Katsutani, *Accountant*
EMP: 10
SALES: 1.3MM **Privately Held**
SIC: 3799 Off-road automobiles, except
recreational vehicles

PRODUCTS & SVCS

3812 Search, Detection, Navigation & Guidance Systs & Instrs

(P-20526)
3H COMMUNICATION SYSTEMS INC
4000 Barranca Pkwy # 250, Irvine (92604-4710)
PHONE.................949 529-1583
Purna Subedi, *CEO*
Michael Giarratano, *President*
Luis Wong, *Principal*
EMP: 48 **EST:** 2014
SALES (est): 6.2MM **Privately Held**
SIC: 3812 4813 4812 3663 Search & navigation equipment; voice telephone communications; radio telephone communication; radio & TV communications equipment; rockets, space & military, complete

(P-20527)
ABL SPACE SYSTEMS COMPANY
224 Oregon St, El Segundo (90245-4214)
P.O. Box 1608 (90245-6608)
PHONE.................650 996-8214
Harrison O'Hanley, *CEO*
Daniel Piemont, *CFO*
EMP: 10 **EST:** 2017
SALES: 671.9K **Privately Held**
SIC: 3812 Acceleration indicators & systems components, aerospace

(P-20528)
ACCUTURN CORPORATION
7189 Old 215 Frontage Rd, Moreno Valley (92553-7903)
PHONE.................951 656-6621
Ignatius C Araujo, *CEO*
Henri Rahmon, *Shareholder*
Mark Sayegh, *Shareholder*
Iggy Araujo, *President*
EMP: 26 **EST:** 1974
SQ FT: 15,000
SALES (est): 3.8MM **Privately Held**
WEB: www.accuturncorp.com
SIC: 3812 3089 3599 Acceleration indicators & systems components, aerospace; automotive parts, plastic; machine shop, jobbing & repair

(P-20529)
AERO CHIP INTGRTED SYSTEMS INC
13565 Freeway Dr, Santa Fe Springs (90670-5633)
PHONE.................310 329-8600
Solomon M Gavrila, *President*
Liviu Pribac, *Vice Pres*
EMP: 13
SQ FT: 50,000
SALES (est): 3.4MM **Privately Held**
WEB: www.AeroChip.com
SIC: 3812 Acceleration indicators & systems components, aerospace

(P-20530)
AEROANTENNA TECHNOLOGY INC
20732 Lassen St, Chatsworth (91311-4507)
PHONE.................818 993-3842
Yosef Klein, *President*
Joe Klein, *President*
Carmela Klein, *Admin Sec*
▲ **EMP:** 140
SALES (est): 35.6MM **Publicly Held**
WEB: www.aeroantenna.com
SIC: 3812 3663 Antennas, radar or communications; antennas, transmitting & communications
HQ: Heico Electronic Technologies Corp.
3000 Taft St
Hollywood FL 33021
954 987-6101

(P-20531)
AEROJET RCKETDYNE HOLDINGS INC (PA)
222 N Pacific Coast Hwy # 50, El Segundo (90245-5648)
P.O. Box 537012, Sacramento (95853-7012)
PHONE.................310 252-8100
Eileen Drake, *President*
Warren G Lichtenstein, *Ch of Bd*
Mark Tucker, *COO*
Paul R Lundstrom, *CFO*
Tyler Evans, *Senior VP*
EMP: 75 **EST:** 1915
SALES: 1.9B **Publicly Held**
WEB: www.gencorp.com
SIC: 3812 3764 3769 6552 Defense systems & equipment; propulsion units for guided missiles & space vehicles; guided missile & space vehicle parts & auxiliary equipment; subdividers & developers; real property lessors

(P-20532)
ALLIANT TCHSYSTEMS OPRTONS LLC
9401 Corbin Ave, Northridge (91324-2400)
PHONE.................818 887-8195
Albert Calabrese, *President*
EMP: 14 **Publicly Held**
WEB: www.mrcwdc.com
SIC: 3812 Search & navigation equipment
HQ: Alliant Techsystems Operations Llc
601 Carlson Pkwy Ste 600
Minnetonka MN 55305

(P-20533)
AMETEK AMERON LLC
4750 Littlejohn St, Baldwin Park (91706-2274)
PHONE.................626 337-4640
EMP: 35
SALES (corp-wide): 3.5B **Publicly Held**
SIC: 3812
HQ: Ametek Ameron, Llc
4750 Littlejohn St
Baldwin Park CA 91706
626 337-4640

(P-20534)
AO SKY CORPORATION
4989 Pedro Hill Rd, Pilot Hill (95664-9610)
PHONE.................415 717-9901
Craig Miller, *President*
EMP: 11
SALES (est): 1.7MM **Privately Held**
SIC: 3812 Aircraft/aerospace flight instruments & guidance systems

(P-20535)
APEX TECHNOLOGY HOLDINGS INC
Also Called: Apex Design Technology
2850 E Coronado St, Anaheim (92806-2503)
PHONE.................714 688-7188
Lance Schroeder, *President*
EMP: 120
SQ FT: 80,000
SALES (est): 19MM **Privately Held**
SIC: 3812 Acceleration indicators & systems components, aerospace

(P-20536)
AQUA-LUNG AMERICA INC (DH)
2340 Cousteau Ct, Vista (92081-8346)
PHONE.................760 597-5000
Vernon Brock, *President*
Graham Church, *CFO*
Jean-Noel Picard, *CFO*
James Hay, *Vice Pres*
Richard Vaughn, *Division Mgr*
◆ **EMP:** 135
SQ FT: 135,000
SALES (est): 61.8MM **Privately Held**
WEB: www.sea-quest.com
SIC: 3812 3949 Search & navigation equipment; sporting & athletic goods

(P-20537)
ARMTEC COUNTERMEASURES CO (DH)
85901 Avenue 53, Coachella (92236-2607)
PHONE.................760 398-0143

Paul Heidenreich, *Vice Pres*
Freeman Swank, *Vice Pres*
Miguel Ortega, *Design Engr*
Charles Jaeck, *Project Engr*
Rob Dautermann, *Engineer*
◆ **EMP:** 12
SQ FT: 100,000
SALES (est): 71.9MM
SALES (corp-wide): 3.8B **Publicly Held**
WEB: www.armtecdefense.com
SIC: 3812 Defense systems & equipment
HQ: Armtec Defense Products Co.
85901 Avenue 53
Coachella CA 92236
760 398-0143

(P-20538)
ASCENT TOOLING GROUP LLC
1395 S Lyon St, Santa Ana (92705-4608)
PHONE.................949 455-0665
Brian Williams, *CEO*
Paul Walsh, *COO*
Steve Littauer, *CFO*
Sandra Hall, *Administration*
EMP: 1108
SALES (est): 67MM
SALES (corp-wide): 386.8MM **Privately Held**
SIC: 3812 Acceleration indicators & systems components, aerospace
PA: Ascent Aerospace Holdings Llc
16445 23 Mile Rd
Macomb MI 48042
212 916-8142

(P-20539)
ASRC AEROSPACE CORP
Nasa Ames Research Ctr, Mountain View (94035)
PHONE.................650 604-5946
Ted Price, *Manager*
EMP: 50
SALES (corp-wide): 2.9B **Privately Held**
WEB: www.asrcaerospace.com
SIC: 3812 7371 7373 5088 Search & navigation equipment; custom computer programming services; computer integrated systems design; transportation equipment & supplies
HQ: Asrc Aerospace Corp
7000 Muirkirk Meadows Dr # 100
Beltsville MD 20705
301 837-5500

(P-20540)
ASTRO AEROSPACE
2601 Camino Del Sol, Oxnard (93030-7996)
PHONE.................805 684-6641
Albert F Myers, *CEO*
Richard Nelson, *President*
Daniel Hoyt, *Marketing Staff*
EMP: 110
SQ FT: 70,000
SALES (est): 41.1MM **Publicly Held**
WEB: www.trw.com
SIC: 3812 Search & navigation equipment
HQ: Northrop Grumman Systems Corporation
2980 Fairview Park Dr
Falls Church VA 22042
703 280-2900

(P-20541)
ATK SPACE SYSTEMS INC (DH)
Also Called: Space Components
6033 Bandini Blvd, Commerce (90040-2968)
PHONE.................323 722-0222
Daniel J Murphy, *CEO*
Ronald D Dittemore, *Senior VP*
James Armor, *Vice Pres*
Thomas R Wilson, *Vice Pres*
◆ **EMP:** 50
SQ FT: 104,000
SALES (est): 426.9MM **Publicly Held**
WEB: www.psi-pci.com
SIC: 3812 Search & navigation equipment
HQ: Northrop Grumman Innovation Systems, Inc.
45101 Warp Dr
Dulles VA 20166
703 406-5000

(P-20542)
ATK SPACE SYSTEMS INC
600 Pine Ave, Goleta (93117-3831)
PHONE.................805 685-2262
Blake Larson, *CEO*
EMP: 100 **Publicly Held**
WEB: www.mrcwdc.com
SIC: 3812 Search & navigation equipment
HQ: Atk Space Systems Inc.
6033 Bandini Blvd
Commerce CA 90040
323 722-0222

(P-20543)
ATK SPACE SYSTEMS INC
1960 E Grand Ave Ste 1150, El Segundo (90245-5061)
PHONE.................310 343-3799
Dale Woolheater, *Director*
EMP: 600 **Publicly Held**
SIC: 3812 Search & navigation equipment
HQ: Atk Space Systems Inc.
11310 Frederick Ave
Beltsville MD 20705
301 595-5500

(P-20544)
BAE SYSTEMS LAND ARMAMENTS LP
6331 San Ignacio Ave, San Jose (95119-1202)
P.O. Box 5300958 (95153-5398)
PHONE.................408 289-0111
Mark Pedrazzi, *Manager*
Robert Sankovich, *Vice Pres*
Ted Kimes, *Program Mgr*
Loren Van Huystee, *Program Mgr*
Raj Jacapl, *General Mgr*
EMP: 1000
SALES (corp-wide): 21.6B **Privately Held**
WEB: www.udlp.com
SIC: 3812 Search & navigation equipment
HQ: Bae Systems Land & Armaments L.P.
2000 15th St N Fl 11
Arlington VA 22201
703 907-8250

(P-20545)
BAE SYSTEMS TECH SOL SRVC INC
9650 Chesapeake Dr, San Diego (92123-1307)
PHONE.................858 278-3042
Rabie Kohan, *Software Engr*
EMP: 10
SALES (corp-wide): 21.6B **Privately Held**
SIC: 3812 Navigational systems & instruments
HQ: Bae Systems Technology Solutions & Services Inc.
520 Gaither Rd
Rockville MD 20850
703 847-5820

(P-20546)
BENMAR MARINE ELECTRONICS INC
2225 S Huron Dr, Santa Ana (92704-4941)
PHONE.................714 540-5120
Norton W Lazarus, *President*
Ronald J Klammer, *Ch of Bd*
EMP: 10
SQ FT: 3,000
SALES: 10MM **Privately Held**
SIC: 3812 Navigational systems & instruments

(P-20547)
BIOSPHERICAL INSTRUMENTS INC
5340 Riley St, San Diego (92110-2621)
PHONE.................619 686-1888
Charles Booth, *CEO*
Dr John Morrow, *President*
Randy Lind, *Engineer*
Tom Comer, *Prdtn Mgr*
EMP: 14
SQ FT: 7,000
SALES (est): 3MM **Privately Held**
WEB: www.biospherical.com
SIC: 3812 8733 3826 Light or heat emission operating apparatus; research institute; photometers

▲ = Import ▼=Export
◆ =Import/Export

(P-20548)
BOEING COMPANY
210 Reeves Blvd Bldg 210 # 210, Lemoore (93246-7200)
PHONE....................................559 998-8214
Steven Bruce, *Branch Mgr*
EMP: 20
SALES (corp-wide): 101.1B **Publicly Held**
SIC: **3812** Acceleration indicators & systems components, aerospace
PA: The Boeing Company
100 N Riverside Plz
Chicago IL 60606
312 544-2000

(P-20549)
BOEING COMPANY
3855 N Lakewood Blvd D35-0072, Long Beach (90846-0001)
PHONE....................................562 593-5511
Marcia Solomon, *Branch Mgr*
Sean Frankel, *Administration*
Sanober Khan, *Network Enginr*
Steven Chan, *Project Mgr*
Becky Kent, *Project Mgr*
EMP: 30
SALES (corp-wide): 101.1B **Publicly Held**
SIC: **3812** Search & navigation equipment
PA: The Boeing Company
100 N Riverside Plz
Chicago IL 60606
312 544-2000

(P-20550)
BOEING COMPANY
1500 E Avenue M, Palmdale (93550-1501)
PHONE....................................661 212-0024
Dan Brown, *Manager*
Kimberly Robidoux, *Engineer*
EMP: 342
SALES (corp-wide): 101.1B **Publicly Held**
SIC: **3812** Space vehicle guidance systems & equipment; missile guidance systems & equipment
PA: The Boeing Company
100 N Riverside Plz
Chicago IL 60606
312 544-2000

(P-20551)
BOEING SATELLITE SYSTEMS
2060 E Imperial Hwy Fl 1, El Segundo (90245-3507)
PHONE....................................310 364-5088
EMP: 54
SALES (corp-wide): 96.1B **Publicly Held**
SIC: **3812**
HQ: Boeing Satellite Systems International, Inc.
2260 E Imperial Hwy
El Segundo CA 90245
310 364-4000

(P-20552)
CAL-SENSORS INC (PA)
1260 Calle Suerte, Camarillo (93012-8053)
PHONE....................................707 303-3837
Craig A Hindman, *CEO*
Jane Howard, *General Mgr*
EMP: 38
SQ FT: 14,800
SALES (est): 2.7MM **Privately Held**
WEB: www.calsensors.com
SIC: **3812** 3674 Infrared object detection equipment; semiconductors & related devices

(P-20553)
COBHAM ADV ELEC SOL INC
9404 Chesapeake Dr, San Diego (92123-1303)
PHONE....................................858 560-1301
Vincent Trnka, *Branch Mgr*
John Andrews, *Business Anlyst*
Chani Moy, *Business Anlyst*
Mario Cano, *Technician*
Scott Goerke, *Technician*
EMP: 208
SALES (corp-wide): 2.3B **Privately Held**
SIC: **3812** Search & navigation equipment

HQ: Cobham Advanced Electronic Solutions Inc.
305 Richardson Rd
Lansdale PA 19446

(P-20554)
COBHAM ADV ELEC SOL INC
5300 Hellyer Ave, San Jose (95138-1003)
PHONE....................................408 624-3000
Charles Stuff, *President*
Judy Huynh, *Lab Dir*
Scott Sacks, *Program Mgr*
Kathleen Thomas, *Program Mgr*
Mary Watson, *Program Mgr*
EMP: 316
SALES (corp-wide): 2.3B **Privately Held**
SIC: **3812** 3679 Search & navigation equipment; microwave components
HQ: Cobham Advanced Electronic Solutions Inc.
305 Richardson Rd
Lansdale PA 19446

(P-20555)
CODAR OCEAN SENSORS LTD (PA)
1914 Plymouth St, Mountain View (94043-1796)
PHONE....................................408 773-8240
Donald E Barrick, *President*
Peter M Lilleboe, *Treasurer*
Belinda J Lipa, *Vice Pres*
James Isaacson, *Admin Sec*
Janice Tran, *Admin Asst*
EMP: 14
SQ FT: 2,000
SALES (est): 2MM **Privately Held**
WEB: www.codaros.com
SIC: **3812** 7629 Antennas, radar or communications; electrical repair shops

(P-20556)
COMANT INDUSTRIES INCORPORATED (DH)
577 Burning Tree Rd, Fullerton (92833-1445)
PHONE....................................714 870-2420
Walter G Stierhoff, *CEO*
Dave Holloway, *Design Engr*
Irwin Bettman, *Controller*
EMP: 30
SQ FT: 30,000
SALES (est): 4.7MM
SALES (corp-wide): 2.3B **Privately Held**
WEB: www.comant.com
SIC: **3812** Search & navigation equipment
HQ: Chelton Avionics, Inc.
6400 Wilkinson Dr
Prescott AZ 86301
928 708-1500

(P-20557)
COMPUTATIONAL SENSORS CORP
1042 Via Los Padres, Santa Barbara (93111-1345)
PHONE....................................805 962-1175
EMP: 22 EST: 1999
SQ FT: 5,500
SALES: 3MM **Privately Held**
SIC: **3812**

(P-20558)
CONNECT PHILLIPS TECH LLC (HQ)
12012 Burke St, Santa Fe Springs (90670-2676)
PHONE....................................800 423-4512
Michael William Wittenberg,
Bill Ellis, *President*
EMP: 11
SALES (est): 423.1K
SALES (corp-wide): 88.7MM **Privately Held**
SIC: **3812** Search & navigation equipment
PA: R. A. Phillips Industries, Inc.
12012 Burke St
Santa Fe Springs CA 90670
562 781-2121

(P-20559)
CONSOLIDATED AEROSPACE MFG LLC (PA)
Also Called: CAM
1425 S Acacia Ave, Fullerton (92831-5317)
PHONE....................................714 989-2797
Dave Werner, *Mng Member*
Jordan Law,
EMP: 18
SALES (est): 167.6MM **Privately Held**
SIC: **3812** Search & navigation equipment

(P-20560)
CORETEX USA INC
15110 Avenue O, San Diego (92128)
PHONE....................................877 247-8725
Selwyn Pellett, *CEO*
Steve Clark, *Director*
EMP: 24
SALES (est): 5.2MM
SALES (corp-wide): 2.2MM **Privately Held**
SIC: **3812** Acceleration indicators & systems components, aerospace
PA: Coretex Limited
Level 4, 8 Nugent Street, Grafton
Auckland 1149

(P-20561)
CPP IND
16800 Chestnut St, City of Industry (91748-1017)
PHONE....................................909 595-2252
Alan Hill, *President*
EMP: 12 EST: 2010
SALES (est): 1.4MM **Privately Held**
SIC: **3812** Acceleration indicators & systems components, aerospace

(P-20562)
CRANE AEROSPACE INC
Crane Aerospace & Electronics
3000 Winona Ave, Burbank (91504-2540)
PHONE....................................818 526-2600
Brendan Curran, *President*
Bob Tavares, *President*
Gregg Robison, *Vice Pres*
Jeff Campbell, *Program Mgr*
Michael Rohona, *Program Mgr*
EMP: 59
SALES (corp-wide): 3.3B **Publicly Held**
SIC: **3812** Defense systems & equipment
HQ: Crane Aerospace, Inc.
100 Stamford Pl
Stamford CT 06902

(P-20563)
CREATIVE ELECTRON INC
201 Trade St, San Marcos (92078-4373)
PHONE....................................760 752-1192
Guilherme Cardoso, *President*
Bill Cardoso, *President*
Glen Thomas, *Vice Pres*
Brian Wagner, *Vice Pres*
Tom Gasaway, *Software Dev*
▲ EMP: 11
SQ FT: 10,000
SALES (est): 2.9MM **Privately Held**
SIC: **3812** 3826 Detection apparatus: electronic/magnetic field, light/heat; electron paramagnetic spin type apparatus

(P-20564)
CUBIC CORPORATION (PA)
9333 Balboa Ave, San Diego (92123-1589)
PHONE....................................858 277-6780
Bradley H Feldmann, *CEO*
Brian Laroche, *COO*
Anshooman AGA, *CFO*
Rhys V Williams, *Treasurer*
Mike Barthlow, *Senior VP*
EMP: 1243
SQ FT: 500,000
SALES: 1.2B **Publicly Held**
WEB: www.cubic.com
SIC: **3812** 3699 7372 Defense systems & equipment; flight simulators (training aids), electronic; application computer software

(P-20565)
DAVIS INSTRUMENTS CORPORATION
3465 Diablo Ave, Hayward (94545-2778)
PHONE....................................510 732-9229
James S Acquistapace, *Ch of Bd*
Robert W Selig Jr, *President*
Kevin McCarthy, *COO*
Diane Padilla, *CFO*
Susan Tatum, *CFO*
◆ EMP: 100
SQ FT: 77,000
SALES (est): 25.4MM **Privately Held**
WEB: www.davisnet.com
SIC: **3812** 3429 3829 3823 Navigational systems & instruments; marine hardware; measuring & controlling devices; industrial instrmnts msrmnt display/control process variable; farm machinery & equipment

(P-20566)
DAVTRON
427 Hillcrest Way, Emerald Hills (94062-4012)
PHONE....................................650 369-1188
Betty Torresdal, *Ch of Bd*
Kevin Torresdal, *President*
Brock Torresdal, *CFO*
▼ EMP: 14
SALES (est): 2.5MM **Privately Held**
WEB: www.davtron.com
SIC: **3812** Aircraft flight instruments

(P-20567)
DECA INTERNATIONAL CORP
Also Called: Golf Buddy
10700 Norwalk Blvd, Santa Fe Springs (90670-3824)
PHONE....................................714 367-5900
Seung Wook Jung, *CEO*
Chris Bartlow, *Sales Staff*
▲ EMP: 28
SQ FT: 3,000
SALES (est): 12MM **Privately Held**
SIC: **3812** Navigational systems & instruments

(P-20568)
DECATUR ELECTRONICS INC (HQ)
15890 Bernardo Center Dr, San Diego (92127-2320)
PHONE....................................888 428-4315
Brian Brown, *CEO*
Luisa Nechodom, *Treasurer*
◆ EMP: 70
SQ FT: 10,000
SALES (est): 9.1MM **Privately Held**
WEB: www.decaturradar.com
SIC: **3812** Radar systems & equipment

(P-20569)
DECATUR ELECTRONICS INC
Also Called: Thunderworks Division
10729 Wheatlands Ave C, Santee (92071-2887)
PHONE....................................619 596-1925
Kevin Mitchell, *Manager*
EMP: 35 **Privately Held**
WEB: www.decaturradar.com
SIC: **3812** Radar systems & equipment
HQ: Decatur Electronics, Inc.
15890 Bernardo Center Dr
San Diego CA 92127
888 428-4315

(P-20570)
DG ENGINEERING CORP (PA)
Also Called: Schulz Engineering
13326 Ralston Ave, Sylmar (91342-7608)
PHONE....................................818 364-9024
Gary Gilmore, *Ch of Bd*
Aret Demiral, *President*
▲ EMP: 26
SQ FT: 7,000
SALES (est): 3.4MM **Privately Held**
WEB: www.dge-corp.com
SIC: **3812** 3845 Aircraft control systems, electronic; electromedical equipment

(P-20571)
EATON AEROSPACE LLC
E E M C O Div
2905 Winona Ave, Burbank (91504-2539)
PHONE..818 550-4200
John H Morris, *Branch Mgr*
EMP: 35 **Privately Held**
SIC: 3812 3621 Acceleration indicators &
systems components, aerospace; motors,
electric
HQ: Eaton Aerospace Llc
1000 Eaton Blvd
Cleveland OH 44122
216 523-5000

(P-20572)
EATON AEROSPACE LLC
9650 Jeronimo Rd, Irvine (92618-2024)
PHONE..949 452-9500
Lily Bridenbaker, *Manager*
EMP: 25 **Privately Held**
SIC: 3812 3365 Acceleration indicators &
systems components, aerospace; aero-
space castings, aluminum
HQ: Eaton Aerospace Llc
1000 Eaton Blvd
Cleveland OH 44122
216 523-5000

(P-20573)
ECTEC INC
Also Called: Electrnic Cmbat Test Evluation
38638 Palms Pl, Palmdale (93552-2412)
PHONE..661 451-1098
Nancy Fitzhugh, *President*
William Fitzhugh, *Vice Pres*
EMP: 11
SALES (est): 1.3MM **Privately Held**
WEB: www.ectecinc.com
SIC: 3812 8748 8731 Search & naviga-
tion equipment; communications consult-
ing; electronic research

(P-20574)
ELITE AVIATION PRODUCTS INC
1641 Reynolds Ave, Irvine (92614-5709)
PHONE..949 536-7199
EMP: 50 EST: 2013
SALES (est): 1.8MM
SALES (corp-wide): 7MM **Privately Held**
SIC: 3812
PA: Elite Aerospace Group, Inc.
15773 Gateway Cir
Tustin CA 92780
949 536-7199

(P-20575)
**ENSIGN-BICKFORD AROSPC
DEF CO**
14370 White Sage Rd, Moorpark
(93021-8720)
P.O. Box 429 (93020-0429)
PHONE..805 292-4000
Brendan Walsh, *Vice Pres*
EMP: 23
SALES (corp-wide): 196.2MM **Privately
Held**
SIC: 3812 Search & navigation equipment
HQ: Ensign-Bickford Aerospace & Defense
Co
640 Hopmeadow St
Simsbury CT 06070
860 843-2289

(P-20576)
FIBCO COMPOSITES INC
1220 Hearthside Ct, Fullerton
(92831-1070)
PHONE..714 269-1118
Anthony J Rivera, *President*
EMP: 12
SQ FT: 16,544
SALES (est): 890K **Privately Held**
SIC: 3812 3728 Radar systems & equip-
ment; aircraft body assemblies & parts

(P-20577)
**FIRAN TECH GROUP USA CORP
(HQ)**
20750 Marilla St, Chatsworth (91311-4407)
PHONE..818 407-4024
Brad Bourne, *President*
Heather Levesque,
EMP: 12

SALES (est): 52.1MM
SALES (corp-wide): 84.2MM **Privately
Held**
SIC: 3812 Aircraft control systems, elec-
tronic
PA: Firan Technology Group Corporation
250 Finchdene Sq
Scarborough ON M1X 1
416 299-4000

(P-20578)
FLIGHT METALS LLC
879 W 190th St Ste 400, Gardena
(90248-4223)
PHONE..800 838-9047
Jay Sheehan, *Principal*
EMP: 11
SALES (est): 1.3MM **Privately Held**
SIC: 3812 Aircraft/aerospace flight instru-
ments & guidance systems

(P-20579)
FLIR SYSTEMS INC
6769 Hollister Ave # 100, Goleta
(93117-5572)
PHONE..805 964-9797
James Woolaway, *CEO*
Austin Richards, *Executive Asst*
Stephanie Marasciullo, *Software Engr*
Devin Walsh, *Engineer*
Bill Williamson, *Engineer*
EMP: 40
SALES (corp-wide): 1.7B **Publicly Held**
SIC: 3812 Aircraft/aerospace flight instru-
ments & guidance systems
PA: Flir Systems, Inc.
27700 Sw Parkway Ave
Wilsonville OR 97070
503 498-3547

(P-20580)
FORT ORD WORKS INC
791 Neeson Rd, Marina (93933-5106)
PHONE..831 275-1294
Joe Johnson, *CEO*
EMP: 20
SALES (est): 896.6K **Privately Held**
SIC: 3812 Aircraft/aerospace flight instru-
ments & guidance systems

(P-20581)
GARNER PRODUCTS INC
10620 Industrial Ave # 100, Roseville
(95678-6241)
PHONE..916 784-0200
Ronald Stofan, *CEO*
Michelle M Stofan, *Admin Sec*
Jason McMillen, *Manager*
EMP: 15
SQ FT: 24,000
SALES (est): 3.2MM **Privately Held**
SIC: 3812 3663 7389 Degaussing equip-
ment; radio broadcasting & communica-
tions equipment; document & office
record destruction

(P-20582)
**GENERAL DYNMICS OTS
NCVLLE INC**
950 Iron Point Rd Ste 110, Folsom
(95630-8303)
PHONE..916 355-7700
Marshall Cousineau, *Director*
EMP: 62
SALES (est): 1.8MM **Privately Held**
SIC: 3812 3769 Search & navigation
equipment; guided missile & space vehi-
cle parts & auxiliary equipment

(P-20583)
GEODETICS INC
2649 Ariane Dr, San Diego (92117-3422)
PHONE..858 729-0872
Lydia Bock, *President*
Jeffrey Fayman, *Vice Pres*
Hondo Geodetics, *Vice Pres*
Christina Mainland, *Controller*
Megan Adams, *Sales Staff*
EMP: 30 EST: 1999
SQ FT: 2,500
SALES (est): 6.7MM **Privately Held**
WEB: www.geodetics.com
SIC: 3812 Search & navigation equipment

(P-20584)
**GLOBAL TECH INSTRUMENTS
INC**
18380 Enterprise Ln, Huntington Beach
(92648-1201)
PHONE..714 375-1811
John Frampton, *President*
EMP: 12
SALES (est): 1.5MM **Privately Held**
WEB: www.globaltechinstruments.com
SIC: 3812 Search & navigation equipment

(P-20585)
GOLDAK INC
15835 Monte St Ste 104, Sylmar
(91342-7674)
PHONE..818 240-2666
Dan Mulcahey, *President*
Jeanie Mulcahey, *CFO*
Thomas Mulcahey, *CFO*
Butch Mulcahey, *Vice Pres*
EMP: 25
SQ FT: 3,000
SALES (est): 4.5MM **Privately Held**
WEB: www.goldak.com
SIC: 3812 Detection apparatus: elec-
tronic/magnetic field, light/heat

(P-20586)
**GRAMERCY AEROSPACE MFG
LLC**
17224 Gramercy Pl, Gardena
(90247-5211)
PHONE..310 515-0576
Edward Navarro, *President*
Frank Peckham, *Vice Pres*
▼ EMP: 11
SALES: 1.5MM **Privately Held**
SIC: 3812 Acceleration indicators & sys-
tems components, aerospace

(P-20587)
HOYA CORPORATION USA
680 N Mccarthy Blvd # 120, Milpitas
(95035-5120)
PHONE..408 654-2200
Hiroshi Suzuki, *President*
Robert Gusello, *Vice Pres*
Hiromichi Okutsu, *Director*
Lynn Brown, *Manager*
EMP: 10 **Privately Held**
WEB: www.hoyaoptics.com
SIC: 3812 3211 Search & navigation
equipment; flat glass
HQ: Hoya Corporation Usa
680 N Mccarthy Blvd # 120
Milpitas CA 95035

(P-20588)
INTELLISENSE SYSTEMS INC
20600 Gramercy Pl Ste 101, Torrance
(90501-1870)
PHONE..310 320-1827
Frank Willis, *President*
EMP: 130 EST: 2017
SQ FT: 43,000
SALES (est): 26.1MM **Privately Held**
SIC: 3812 Search & navigation equipment

(P-20589)
INTEROCEAN INDUSTRIES INC
Also Called: Interocean Systems
3738 Ruffin Rd, San Diego (92123-1812)
PHONE..858 292-0808
Michael Pearlman, *CEO*
Stephen Pearlman, *Admin Sec*
Paul Pruitt, *Info Tech Mgr*
▼ EMP: 31 EST: 1945
SQ FT: 65,000
SALES (est): 7.3MM **Privately Held**
WEB: www.interoceansystems.com
SIC: 3812 3699 3826 3531 Search &
navigation equipment; underwater sound
equipment; environmental testing equip-
ment; marine related equipment; indus-
trial flow & liquid measuring instruments;
geophysical & meteorological testing
equipment

(P-20590)
INTEROCEAN SYSTEMS LLC
Also Called: Interocean Systems, Inc.
3738 Ruffin Rd, San Diego (92123-1812)
PHONE..858 565-8400

Michael D Pearlman, *President*
EMP: 35
SALES: 2.5MM
SALES (corp-wide): 112.9MM **Privately
Held**
SIC: 3812 3699 Search & navigation
equipment; underwater sound equipment
PA: Delmar Systems, Inc.
8114 Highway 90 E
Broussard LA 70518
337 365-0180

(P-20591)
INVENSENSE INC (HQ)
1745 Tech Dr Ste 200, San Jose (95110)
PHONE..408 501-2200
Amit Shah, *Ch of Bd*
Behrooz Abdi, *President*
Mark Dentinger, *CFO*
Daniel Goehl, *Vice Pres*
MO Maghsoudnia, *Vice Pres*
EMP: 122
SQ FT: 159,000
SALES (est): 418.4MM **Privately Held**
WEB: www.invensense.com
SIC: 3812 Gyroscopes

(P-20592)
JARIET TECHNOLOGIES INC
103 W Torrance Blvd, Redondo Beach
(90277-3633)
PHONE..310 698-1001
Charles Harper, *CEO*
David Clark, *Vice Pres*
Monica Gilbert, *Vice Pres*
Matthew Hoppe, *Vice Pres*
Craig Hornbuckle, *Principal*
EMP: 35
SQ FT: 20,000
SALES: 3.9MM
SALES (corp-wide): 6.8B **Publicly Held**
SIC: 3812 Search & navigation equipment
PA: L3harris Technologies, Inc.
1025 W Nasa Blvd
Melbourne FL 32919
321 727-9100

(P-20593)
JENNINGS AERONAUTICS INC
3183 Duncan Ln Ste C, San Luis Obispo
(93401-6781)
PHONE..805 544-0932
Gordon Jennings, *President*
EMP: 39
SQ FT: 19,000
SALES: 12MM **Privately Held**
SIC: 3812 7371 Electronic detection systems (aeronautical); aircraft control systems, electronic; defense systems &
equipment; computer software development & applications; computer software
development

(P-20594)
KRATOS INSTRUMENTS LLC
Also Called: Kratos Pressure Products
2201 Alton Pkwy, Irvine (92606-5033)
PHONE..949 660-0666
Lewis Wise, *Principal*
EMP: 18
SALES (est): 3.1MM **Privately Held**
SIC: 3812 Search & navigation equipment

(P-20595)
**L-3 COMMUNICATIONS
WESCAM**
428 Aviation Blvd Ste 3I, Santa Rosa
(95403-1069)
PHONE..707 568-3000
Dan Heibel, *President*
EMP: 30
SALES (est): 7MM
SALES (corp-wide): 6.8B **Publicly Held**
SIC: 3812 3861 Search & navigation
equipment; photographic equipment &
supplies
HQ: L3 Technologies, Inc.
600 3rd Ave Fl 34
New York NY 10016
212 697-1111

(P-20596)
L3 TECHNOLOGIES INC
Ocean Systems Division
15825 Roxford St, Sylmar (91342-3537)
PHONE..818 833-2500

▲ = Import ▼=Export
◆ =Import/Export

Alex Miseirvitch, *Vice Pres*
EMP: 200
SALES (corp-wide): 6.8B **Publicly Held**
SIC: 3812 Search & navigation equipment
HQ: L3 Technologies, Inc.
  600 3rd Ave Fl 34
  New York NY 10016
  212 697-1111

(P-20597)
L3HARRIS TECHNOLOGIES INC
Also Called: Harris Corporation
7821 Orion Ave, Van Nuys (91406-2029)
P.O. Box 7713 (91409-7713)
PHONE...................................818 901-2523
J Malloy, *Vice Pres*
EMP: 350
SALES (corp-wide): 6.8B **Publicly Held**
WEB: www.ittind.com
SIC: 3812 Search & navigation equipment
PA: L3harris Technologies, Inc.
  1025 W Nasa Blvd
  Melbourne FL 32919
  321 727-9100

(P-20598)
L3HARRIS TECHNOLOGIES INC
Also Called: Edo Rcnnssnce Srvllnce Sys-
tems
7821 Orion Ave, Van Nuys (91406-2029)
PHONE...................................408 201-8000
EMP: 325
SALES (corp-wide): 6.8B **Publicly Held**
SIC: 3812 Defense systems & equipment
PA: L3harris Technologies, Inc.
  1025 W Nasa Blvd
  Melbourne FL 32919
  321 727-9100

(P-20599)
L3HARRIS TECHNOLOGIES INC
Also Called: Rf Communiactions
9201 Spectrum Center Blvd, San Diego
(92123-1407)
PHONE...................................619 684-7511
Bill Bry, *Manager*
EMP: 25
SALES (corp-wide): 6.8B **Publicly Held**
SIC: 3812 Search & navigation equipment
PA: L3harris Technologies, Inc.
  1025 W Nasa Blvd
  Melbourne FL 32919
  321 727-9100

(P-20600)
LAIRD R & F PRODUCTS INC (DH)
2091 Rutherford Rd, Carlsbad
(92008-7316)
PHONE...................................760 916-9410
Scott Griffiths, *President*
▲ **EMP:** 50
SQ FT: 62,000
SALES (est): 7.9MM **Privately Held**
WEB: www.randf.com
SIC: 3812 Radar systems & equipment
HQ: Laird Technologies, Inc.
  16401 Swingley
  Chesterfield MO 63017
  636 898-6000

(P-20601)
LITE MACHINES CORPORATION
2222 Faraday Ave, Carlsbad (92008-7235)
PHONE...................................765 463-0959
Paul Arlton, *President*
David Arlton, *Vice Pres*
Donna Arlton, *Assistant VP*
EMP: 12
SALES (est): 1.8MM **Privately Held**
WEB: www.litemachines.com
SIC: 3812 3721 Aircraft control systems,
  electronic; automatic pilots, aircraft; air-
  craft; research & development on aircraft
  by the manufacturer

(P-20602)
LOCKHEED MARTIN CORPORATION
4203 Smith Grade, Santa Cruz
(95060-9705)
P.O. Box 3504 (95063-3504)
PHONE...................................831 425-6000
Dave Murphey, *Branch Mgr*
EMP: 4536 **Publicly Held**
WEB: www.lockheedmartin.com

SIC: 3812 Search & navigation equipment
PA: Lockheed Martin Corporation
  6801 Rockledge Dr
  Bethesda MD 20817
  -

(P-20603)
LOCKHEED MARTIN CORPORATION
1330 30th St Ste A, San Diego
(92154-3471)
PHONE...................................619 542-3273
Darrell Griffin, *Manager*
EMP: 12 **Publicly Held**
WEB: www.lockheedmartin.com
SIC: 3812 Search & navigation equipment
PA: Lockheed Martin Corporation
  6801 Rockledge Dr
  Bethesda MD 20817
  -

(P-20604)
LOCKHEED MARTIN CORPORATION
1523 Crom St, Manteca (95337-6507)
PHONE...................................408 756-1400
Gari Young, *Mfg Mgr*
EMP: 473 **Publicly Held**
SIC: 3812 Search & navigation equipment
PA: Lockheed Martin Corporation
  6801 Rockledge Dr
  Bethesda MD 20817
  -

(P-20605)
LOCKHEED MARTIN CORPORATION
1001 Lockheed Way, Palmdale
(93599-0001)
PHONE...................................661 572-2974
Robert J Stevens, *Branch Mgr*
Eufracio Benavides, *Project Engr*
Dorian Racey, *Supervisor*
EMP: 14 **Publicly Held**
SIC: 3812 Search & navigation equipment
PA: Lockheed Martin Corporation
  6801 Rockledge Dr
  Bethesda MD 20817
  -

(P-20606)
LOCKHEED MARTIN CORPORATION
2770 De La Cruz Blvd, Santa Clara
(95050-2624)
PHONE...................................408 734-4980
Ed Novak, *Director*
Stan Nakaso, *Project Mgr*
Carol Crose, *Director*
EMP: 1018 **Publicly Held**
WEB: www.lockheedmartin.com
SIC: 3812 Search & navigation equipment
PA: Lockheed Martin Corporation
  6801 Rockledge Dr
  Bethesda MD 20817
  -

(P-20607)
LOCKHEED MARTIN CORPORATION
4524 Chancery Ln, Dublin (94568-1314)
PHONE...................................925 756-4594
S Larson, *Principal*
EMP: 473 **Publicly Held**
SIC: 3812 Search & navigation equipment
PA: Lockheed Martin Corporation
  6801 Rockledge Dr
  Bethesda MD 20817
  -

(P-20608)
LOCKHEED MARTIN CORPORATION
1105 Remington Ct, Sunnyvale
(94087-2072)
PHONE...................................408 756-1868
Mark Ellson, *Principal*
EMP: 473 **Publicly Held**
SIC: 3812 Search & navigation equipment
PA: Lockheed Martin Corporation
  6801 Rockledge Dr
  Bethesda MD 20817
  -

(P-20609)
LOCKHEED MARTIN CORPORATION
Also Called: Buellton Advanced Materials
153 Industrial Way, Buellton (93427-9592)
PHONE...................................805 686-4069
EMP: 491 **Publicly Held**
SIC: 3812 Search & navigation equipment
PA: Lockheed Martin Corporation
  6801 Rockledge Dr
  Bethesda MD 20817
  -

(P-20610)
LOCKHEED MARTIN CORPORATION
3251 Hanover St, Palo Alto (94304-1121)
PHONE...................................650 424-2000
Aram Mica, *Vice Pres*
Marillyn Lewson, *President*
Tom Lupo, *IT/INT Sup*
Norman Strampach, *Research*
Michael Acree, *Engineer*
EMP: 625
SQ FT: 350,000 **Publicly Held**
WEB: www.lockheedmartin.com
SIC: 3812 Search & navigation equipment
PA: Lockheed Martin Corporation
  6801 Rockledge Dr
  Bethesda MD 20817
  -

(P-20611)
LOCKHEED MARTIN CORPORATION
266 Caspian Dr, Sunnyvale (94089-1014)
PHONE...................................408 781-8570
Robert Butler III, *Manager*
William G Conrad Jr, *Manager*
Mark Ellson, *Manager*
EMP: 17 **Publicly Held**
WEB: www.lockheedmartin.com
SIC: 3812 Search & navigation equipment
PA: Lockheed Martin Corporation
  6801 Rockledge Dr
  Bethesda MD 20817
  -

(P-20612)
LOCKHEED MARTIN CORPORATION
3100 Zanker Rd, San Jose (95134-1965)
PHONE...................................408 473-7498
David Turkington, *Branch Mgr*
EMP: 3000 **Publicly Held**
WEB: www.lockheedmartin.com
SIC: 3812 3761 Search & navigation
  equipment; guided missiles & space vehi-
  cles
PA: Lockheed Martin Corporation
  6801 Rockledge Dr
  Bethesda MD 20817
  -

(P-20613)
LOCKHEED MARTIN CORPORATION
3201 Airpark Dr Ste 204, Santa Maria
(93455-1833)
PHONE...................................805 614-3671
Mike Berdeguez, *Principal*
EMP: 3000 **Publicly Held**
WEB: www.lockheedmartin.com
SIC: 3812 3761 Search & navigation
  equipment; guided missiles & space vehi-
  cles
PA: Lockheed Martin Corporation
  6801 Rockledge Dr
  Bethesda MD 20817
  -

(P-20614)
LOCKHEED MARTIN CORPORATION
Also Called: Lockheed Martin Aeronautics Co
225 N Flightline Rd, Edwards
(93524-0001)
PHONE...................................661 277-0691
Brian Larson, *Manager*
EMP: 1539 **Publicly Held**
WEB: www.lockheedmartin.com
SIC: 3812 Search & navigation equipment

PA: Lockheed Martin Corporation
  6801 Rockledge Dr
  Bethesda MD 20817
  -

(P-20615)
LOCKHEED MARTIN CORPORATION
1111 Lockheed Martin Way, Sunnyvale
(94089-1212)
P.O. Box 3504 (94088-3504)
PHONE...................................408 742-6688
B H Rogers, *Branch Mgr*
Todd Mortensen, *General Mgr*
Daren Heidgerken, *Project Engr*
Bill Henninger, *Manager*
EMP: 25 **Publicly Held**
WEB: www.lockheedmartin.com
SIC: 3812 Search & navigation equipment
PA: Lockheed Martin Corporation
  6801 Rockledge Dr
  Bethesda MD 20817
  -

(P-20616)
LOCKHEED MARTIN CORPORATION
10325 Meanley Dr, San Diego
(92131-3011)
PHONE...................................858 740-5100
Mike Berdeguez, *Manager*
EMP: 250 **Publicly Held**
WEB: www.lockheedmartin.com
SIC: 3812 Search & navigation equipment
PA: Lockheed Martin Corporation
  6801 Rockledge Dr
  Bethesda MD 20817
  -

(P-20617)
LOCKHEED MARTIN CORPORATION
2895 Golf Course Dr, Ventura
(93003-7610)
PHONE...................................805 650-4600
Ben Egerton, *General Mgr*
EMP: 26 **Publicly Held**
WEB: www.lockheedmartin.com
SIC: 3812 Search & navigation equipment
PA: Lockheed Martin Corporation
  6801 Rockledge Dr
  Bethesda MD 20817
  -

(P-20618)
LOCKHEED MARTIN CORPORATION
Also Called: Lockheed Martin Aeronautics Co
1011 Lockheed Way, Palmdale
(93599-0001)
PHONE...................................661 572-7428
Rick Baker, *Vice Pres*
John Petersen, *Project Mgr*
Jeffrey Doran, *Engineer*
EMP: 4000 **Publicly Held**
WEB: www.lockheedmartin.com
SIC: 3812 Search & navigation equipment
PA: Lockheed Martin Corporation
  6801 Rockledge Dr
  Bethesda MD 20817
  -

(P-20619)
LOCKHEED MARTIN CORPORATION
Also Called: Lockheed Martin Space Sys
16020 Empire Grade, Santa Cruz
(95060-9628)
PHONE...................................831 425-6375
Byron Ravenscraft, *Manager*
EMP: 85 **Publicly Held**
WEB: www.lockheedmartin.com
SIC: 3812 Search & navigation equipment
PA: Lockheed Martin Corporation
  6801 Rockledge Dr
  Bethesda MD 20817
  -

(P-20620)
LOCKHEED MARTIN CORPORATION
Santa Barbara Focal Plane
346 Bollay Dr, Goleta (93117-5550)
PHONE...................................805 571-2346
Bryan Butler, *Manager*

Mary Mendoza, *Manager*
EMP: 100
SQ FT: 8,500 **Publicly Held**
WEB: www.lockheedmartin.com
SIC: 3812 Infrared object detection equipment
PA: Lockheed Martin Corporation
      6801 Rockledge Dr
      Bethesda MD 20817

(P-20621)
LOCKHEED MARTIN CORPORATION
1111 Lockheed Martin Way, Sunnyvale (94089-1212)
PHONE........................408 756-5836
Paul Johnson, *Manager*
EMP: 1261 **Publicly Held**
WEB: www.lockheedmartin.com
SIC: 3812 7371 Nautical instruments; custom computer programming services
PA: Lockheed Martin Corporation
      6801 Rockledge Dr
      Bethesda MD 20817

(P-20622)
LOCKHEED MARTIN CORPORATION
10325 Meanley Dr, San Diego (92131-3011)
PHONE........................858 740-5100
Jeff Zeimantz, *Manager*
Chris Andert, *Principal*
EMP: 250 **Publicly Held**
WEB: www.lockheedmartin.com
SIC: 3812 Search & navigation equipment
PA: Lockheed Martin Corporation
      6801 Rockledge Dr
      Bethesda MD 20817

(P-20623)
LOCKHEED MARTIN CORPORATION
22630 Aguadero Pl, Santa Clarita (91350-1301)
PHONE........................661 572-7363
Robert Scobie, *Manager*
EMP: 430 **Publicly Held**
SIC: 3812 Search & navigation equipment
PA: Lockheed Martin Corporation
      6801 Rockledge Dr
      Bethesda MD 20817

(P-20624)
LOCKHEED MARTIN CORPORATION
1643 Kitchener Dr, Sunnyvale (94087-4133)
PHONE........................408 756-4386
Martha Steiner, *Branch Mgr*
EMP: 430 **Publicly Held**
SIC: 3812 Search & navigation equipment
PA: Lockheed Martin Corporation
      6801 Rockledge Dr
      Bethesda MD 20817

(P-20625)
LOCKHEED MARTIN CORPORATION
1111 Lockheed Martin Way, Sunnyvale (94089-1212)
PHONE........................408 742-4321
Jim Harrington, *Manager*
Melina Snider, *Export Mgr*
EMP: 10 **Publicly Held**
WEB: www.lockheedmartin.com
SIC: 3812 Search & navigation equipment
PA: Lockheed Martin Corporation
      6801 Rockledge Dr
      Bethesda MD 20817

(P-20626)
LOCKHEED MARTIN CORPORATION
Also Called: Lockheed Martin Naval
1121 W Reeves Ave, Ridgecrest (93555-2313)
PHONE........................760 446-1700
John Polak, *Branch Mgr*

Donna Mayfield, *Manager*
EMP: 232 **Publicly Held**
SIC: 3812 Search & navigation equipment
PA: Lockheed Martin Corporation
      6801 Rockledge Dr
      Bethesda MD 20817
-

(P-20627)
LYTX INC (PA)
9785 Towne Centre Dr, San Diego (92121-1968)
PHONE........................858 430-4000
Brandon Nixon, *CEO*
Dave Riordan, *COO*
David Riordan, *COO*
Steve Lifshatz, *CFO*
Paul J Pucino, *CFO*
EMP: 300
SQ FT: 100,000
SALES (est): 121.8MM **Privately Held**
WEB: www.drivecam.com
SIC: 3812 Search & detection systems & instruments

(P-20628)
MEGGITT (ORANGE COUNTY) INC
Also Called: Meggitt Aerospace
355 N Pastoria Ave, Sunnyvale (94085-4110)
PHONE........................408 739-3533
Joseph Fragala, *Principal*
EMP: 15
SALES (corp-wide): 2.6B **Privately Held**
SIC: 3812 8731 3829 Search & navigation equipment; commercial physical research; measuring & controlling devices
HQ: Meggitt (Orange County), Inc.
      14600 Myford Rd
      Irvine CA 92606

(P-20629)
MEGGITT SAFETY SYSTEMS INC
Meggitt Control Systems
1785 Voyager Ave, Simi Valley (93063-3363)
PHONE........................805 584-4100
Jim Healy, *Director*
EMP: 200
SALES (corp-wide): 2.6B **Privately Held**
SIC: 3812 Aircraft control systems, electronic
HQ: Meggitt Safety Systems, Inc.
      1785 Voyager Ave
      Simi Valley CA 93063
      805 584-4100

(P-20630)
METROTECH CORPORATION (PA)
Also Called: Vivax-Metrotech
3251 Olcott St, Santa Clara (95054-3006)
PHONE........................408 734-3880
Christian Stolz, *CEO*
Andrew Hoare, *President*
Mark Drew, *Vice Pres*
Mark Royle, *Vice Pres*
Dee Hoare, *General Mgr*
▲ **EMP:** 78 **EST:** 1976
SQ FT: 65,000
SALES (est): 17.1MM **Privately Held**
WEB: www.metrotech.com
SIC: 3812 3599 3829 Detection apparatus: electronic/magnetic field, light/heat; water leak detectors; measuring & controlling devices

(P-20631)
MILLENNIUM SPACE SYSTEMS INC (HQ)
2265 E El Segundo Blvd, El Segundo (90245-4608)
PHONE........................310 683-5840
Stan Dubyn, *CEO*
Tiffany Guthrie, *COO*
Laura White, *CFO*
EMP: 32
SQ FT: 10,000

SALES (est): 13.3MM
SALES (corp-wide): 101.1B **Publicly Held**
WEB: www.millennium-space.com
SIC: 3812 Search & navigation equipment
PA: The Boeing Company
      100 N Riverside Plz
      Chicago IL 60606
      312 544-2000

(P-20632)
MOBILE CROSSING INC
Also Called: Everything Mobile
1230 Oakmead Pkwy Ste 304, Sunnyvale (94085-4017)
PHONE........................916 485-2773
Raymond Hou, *President*
Chris Stocker, *Vice Pres*
▲ **EMP:** 12
SQ FT: 1,500
SALES: 1.5MM **Privately Held**
SIC: 3812 Navigational systems & instruments

(P-20633)
MOOG INC
21339 Nordhoff St, Chatsworth (91311-5819)
PHONE........................818 341-5156
Ruben Nalbandian, *Sales Mgr*
Scott Phillip, *Info Tech Dir*
Phil Scott, *Technology*
Carmen Aguilar, *Engineer*
Steven Macias, *Engineer*
EMP: 150
SALES (corp-wide): 2.9B **Publicly Held**
WEB: www.moog.com
SIC: 3812 Aircraft control systems, electronic
PA: Moog Inc.
      400 Jamison Rd
      Elma NY 14059
      716 805-2604

(P-20634)
MOOG INC
7406 Hollister Ave, Goleta (93117-2583)
PHONE........................805 618-3900
Robert W Urban, *General Mgr*
Chris Leslie, *Program Mgr*
EMP: 300
SALES (corp-wide): 2.9B **Publicly Held**
SIC: 3812 3492 3625 3769 Aircraft control systems, electronic; electrohydraulic servo valves, metal; relays & industrial controls; actuators, industrial; guided missile & space vehicle parts & auxiliary equipment; airframe assemblies, guided missiles; aircraft parts & equipment; motors & generators
PA: Moog Inc.
      400 Jamison Rd
      Elma NY 14059
      716 805-2604

(P-20635)
MOOG INC
Also Called: Moog Aircraft Group
20263 S Western Ave, Torrance (90501-1310)
PHONE........................310 533-1178
Alberto Bilalon, *Manager*
Julie Mazzu, *Project Mgr*
Tom Elwell, *Technology*
Richard Delecki, *Project Engr*
Anthony Rabano, *Project Engr*
EMP: 450
SALES (corp-wide): 2.9B **Publicly Held**
WEB: www.moog.com
SIC: 3812 Search & navigation equipment
PA: Moog Inc.
      400 Jamison Rd
      Elma NY 14059
      716 805-2604

(P-20636)
MOUNTAIN LAKE LABS
Also Called: Mlabs
2675 Lands End Dr, Lakeport (95453-9605)
PHONE........................707 331-3297
Stanley Snow, *Principal*
EMP: 10 **EST:** 2015

SALES (est): 581.8K **Privately Held**
SIC: 3812 3761 3764 3769 Aircraft/aerospace flight instruments & guidance systems; guided missiles & space vehicles, research & development; guided missile & space vehicle engines, research & devel.; airframe assemblies, guided missiles; nose cones, guided missiles;

(P-20637)
MTI DE BAJA INC
42941 Madio St Ste 2, Indio (92201-1978)
PHONE........................951 654-2333
Monty Merkin, *CEO*
EMP: 28
SALES (est): 1.9MM **Privately Held**
SIC: 3812 Acceleration indicators & systems components, aerospace

(P-20638)
NAVCOM DEFENSE ELECTRONICS INC (PA)
9129 Stellar Ct, Corona (92883-4924)
PHONE........................951 268-9205
Clifford C Christ, *President*
David Eliasson, *CFO*
EMP: 52
SQ FT: 61,000
SALES (est): 9.5MM **Privately Held**
WEB: www.navcom.com
SIC: 3812 Navigational systems & instruments

(P-20639)
NEVWEST INC
1225 S Expo Way Ste 140, San Diego (92154)
PHONE........................619 420-8100
Alfredo Liburd, *President*
Virginia Burd, *Vice Pres*
EMP: 30
SALES (est): 7.1MM **Privately Held**
SIC: 3812 Warfare counter-measure equipment

(P-20640)
NORTHROP GRUMMAN CORPORATION
14099 Champlain Ct, Fontana (92336-3506)
PHONE........................626 812-2842
Eugene Kanechika, *Branch Mgr*
Minh Vu, *Design Engr*
Diane Brackett, *Buyer*
John St Rock, *Manager*
EMP: 735 **Publicly Held**
SIC: 3812 Aircraft/aerospace flight instruments & guidance systems
PA: Northrop Grumman Corporation
      2980 Fairview Park Dr
      Falls Church VA 22042

(P-20641)
NORTHROP GRUMMAN CORPORATION
9736 Trigger Pl, Chatsworth (91311-2655)
PHONE........................818 715-3264
Kevin Kern, *Branch Mgr*
EMP: 735 **Publicly Held**
SIC: 3812 Aircraft/aerospace flight instruments & guidance systems
PA: Northrop Grumman Corporation
      2980 Fairview Park Dr
      Falls Church VA 22042

(P-20642)
NORTHROP GRUMMAN CORPORATION
Northrop Grumman Aviation
1 Hornet Way, El Segundo (90245-2804)
PHONE........................310 332-1000
Ray Pollok, *Manager*
Richard G Matthews, *Vice Pres*
Keith Nobuhara, *Department Mgr*
Peggy Polite, *Administration*
David Blackburn, *Sr Ntwrk Engine*
EMP: 200 **Publicly Held**
SIC: 3812 Search & navigation equipment
PA: Northrop Grumman Corporation
      2980 Fairview Park Dr
      Falls Church VA 22042

▲ = Import ▼=Export
◆ =Import/Export

(P-20643)
NORTHROP GRUMMAN CORPORATION
18701 Caminito Pasadero, San Diego (92128-6162)
PHONE.............................858 967-1221
Dagnall Barry, *Branch Mgr*
John Paterson, *Program Mgr*
Jason Graham, *Administration*
Jorge Romo, *Network Enginr*
Michael Insalaco, *Design Engr*
EMP: 735 Publicly Held
SIC: 3812 Search & detection systems & instruments
PA: Northrop Grumman Corporation
2980 Fairview Park Dr
Falls Church VA 22042

(P-20644)
NORTHROP GRUMMAN CORPORATION
28063 Liana Ln, Valencia (91354-1483)
PHONE.............................310 332-0412
Ed Huey, *Branch Mgr*
Stacey Huey, *Analyst*
EMP: 735 Publicly Held
SIC: 3812 Search & navigation equipment
PA: Northrop Grumman Corporation
2980 Fairview Park Dr
Falls Church VA 22042

(P-20645)
NORTHROP GRUMMAN CORPORATION
17311 Santa Barbara St, Fountain Valley (92708-3321)
PHONE.............................310 332-6653
EMP: 735 Publicly Held
SIC: 3812 Aircraft/aerospace flight instruments & guidance systems
PA: Northrop Grumman Corporation
2980 Fairview Park Dr
Falls Church VA 22042

(P-20646)
NORTHROP GRUMMAN CORPORATION
18701 Wilmington Ave, Carson (90746-2819)
PHONE.............................310 764-3000
Howard Rosenthal, *Branch Mgr*
Sheila Gee, *Software Engr*
EMP: 735 Publicly Held
SIC: 3812 Search & navigation equipment
PA: Northrop Grumman Corporation
2980 Fairview Park Dr
Falls Church VA 22042

(P-20647)
NORTHROP GRUMMAN CORPORATION
10806 Willow Ct, San Diego (92127-2428)
PHONE.............................858 618-7617
Jeff Machler, *Branch Mgr*
Nhatnam Nguyen, *Engineer*
EMP: 735 Publicly Held
SIC: 3812 Aircraft/aerospace flight instruments & guidance systems
PA: Northrop Grumman Corporation
2980 Fairview Park Dr
Falls Church VA 22042

(P-20648)
NORTHROP GRUMMAN CORPORATION
4010 Sorrento Valley Blvd, San Diego (92121-1432)
PHONE.............................858 514-9259
Thomas Adam, *Principal*
Michael Schwerin, *Officer*
EMP: 735 Publicly Held
SIC: 3812 Aircraft/aerospace flight instruments & guidance systems
PA: Northrop Grumman Corporation
2980 Fairview Park Dr
Falls Church VA 22042

(P-20649)
NORTHROP GRUMMAN CORPORATION
4020 Redondo Beach Ave, Redondo Beach (90278-1109)
PHONE.............................310 812-4321
EMP: 40 Publicly Held
SIC: 3812 Search & navigation equipment
PA: Northrop Grumman Corporation
2980 Fairview Park Dr
Falls Church VA 22042

(P-20650)
NORTHROP GRUMMAN CORPORATION
21050 Burbank Blvd, Woodland Hills (91367-6602)
PHONE.............................818 715-2383
Deehan Fagan, *Manager*
Aida Ruiz, *Technology*
Daryl Sakaida, *Technical Staff*
Darrell Freiwald, *Engineer*
Michael Medina, *Engineer*
EMP: 15 Publicly Held
SIC: 3812 Search & navigation equipment
PA: Northrop Grumman Corporation
2980 Fairview Park Dr
Falls Church VA 22042

(P-20651)
NORTHROP GRUMMAN INNOVATION
9401 Corvin Ave, Woodland Hills (91367)
PHONE.............................818 887-8100
Ron Hill, *Branch Mgr*
Peter Pavia, *Director*
EMP: 500 Publicly Held
SIC: 3812 Aircraft/aerospace flight instruments & guidance systems
HQ: Northrop Grumman Innovation Systems, Inc.
45101 Warp Dr
Dulles VA 20166
703 406-5000

(P-20652)
NORTHROP GRUMMAN INNOVATION
6750 Navigator Way # 200, Goleta (93117-3657)
PHONE.............................805 961-8600
John Nisbet, *Branch Mgr*
Kimberly Langley, *Admin Asst*
Ruth Cholvibul, *Engineer*
EMP: 63 Publicly Held
WEB: www.mrcwdc.com
SIC: 3812 Search & navigation equipment
HQ: Northrop Grumman Innovation Systems, Inc.
45101 Warp Dr
Dulles VA 20166
703 406-5000

(P-20653)
NORTHROP GRUMMAN INTL TRDG INC
21240 Burbank Blvd, Woodland Hills (91367-6680)
PHONE.............................818 715-3607
Tina Davis, *Administration*
EMP: 958 EST: 2014
SALES: 24MM Publicly Held
SIC: 3812 Search & navigation equipment
HQ: Northrop Grumman International, Inc.
2980 Fairview Park Dr
Falls Church VA 22042

(P-20654)
NORTHROP GRUMMAN SYSTEMS CORP
Litton Navigation Systems Div
21240 Burbank Blvd Ms29, Woodland Hills (91367-6680)
PHONE.............................818 715-4040
Bill Allison, *Division Pres*
James McHugh, *Program Mgr*
Patricia White, *Program Mgr*
Cammy Reynoso, *Executive Asst*
Jim Kemp, *Admin Asst*
EMP: 1000 Publicly Held
WEB: www.sperry.ngc.com

(P-20655)
NORTHROP GRUMMAN SYSTEMS CORP
1 Hornet Way Dept Mt00w5, El Segundo (90245-2804)
PHONE.............................310 632-1846
Richard A Lautzenheiser, *Manager*
Kenneth L Bedingfield, *Vice Pres*
Randy Agura, *General Mgr*
EMP: 317 Publicly Held
SIC: 3812 Search & navigation equipment
HQ: Northrop Grumman Systems Corporation
2980 Fairview Park Dr
Falls Church VA 22042
703 280-2900

(P-20656)
NORTHROP GRUMMAN SYSTEMS CORP
2700 Camino Del Sol, Oxnard (93030-7967)
PHONE.............................805 278-2074
Pierre Courduroux, *Branch Mgr*
EMP: 508 Publicly Held
SIC: 3812 Aircraft/aerospace flight instruments & guidance systems
HQ: Northrop Grumman Systems Corporation
2980 Fairview Park Dr
Falls Church VA 22042
703 280-2900

(P-20657)
NORTHROP GRUMMAN SYSTEMS CORP
9112 Spectrum Center Blvd, San Diego (92123-1439)
PHONE.............................858 514-9020
EMP: 11 Publicly Held
SIC: 3812 Search & navigation equipment
HQ: Northrop Grumman Systems Corporation
2980 Fairview Park Dr
Falls Church VA 22042
703 280-2900

(P-20658)
NORTHROP GRUMMAN SYSTEMS CORP
California Microwave Systems
21200 Burbank Blvd, Woodland Hills (91367-6675)
PHONE.............................818 715-2597
Roy Medlin, *Opers Mgr*
Lisle Sherwin, *Engineer*
EMP: 50 Publicly Held
WEB: www.sperry.ngc.com
SIC: 3812 Search & navigation equipment
HQ: Northrop Grumman Systems Corporation
2980 Fairview Park Dr
Falls Church VA 22042
703 280-2900

(P-20659)
NORTHROP GRUMMAN SYSTEMS CORP
Also Called: Field Support Services
N Island Naval A Sta, Coronado (92118)
P.O. Box 181160 (92178-1160)
PHONE.............................619 437-4231
Tom Whited, *Manager*
EMP: 25 Publicly Held
WEB: www.sperry.ngc.com
SIC: 3812 Search & navigation equipment
HQ: Northrop Grumman Systems Corporation
2980 Fairview Park Dr
Falls Church VA 22042
703 280-2900

(P-20660)
NORTHROP GRUMMAN SYSTEMS CORP
2550 Honolulu Ave, Montrose (91020-1858)
PHONE.............................818 249-5252

Arthur F Brown, *Enginr/R&D Mgr*
EMP: 18 Publicly Held
WEB: www.logicon.com
SIC: 3812 Search & navigation equipment
HQ: Northrop Grumman Systems Corporation
2980 Fairview Park Dr
Falls Church VA 22042
703 280-2900

(P-20661)
NORTHROP GRUMMAN SYSTEMS CORP
17066 Goldentop Rd, San Diego (92127-2412)
PHONE.............................858 618-4349
Gerald Dufresne, *Manager*
Ed Boyce, *Program Mgr*
Daniel Ip, *Design Engr*
Chad Homan, *Engng Exec*
EMP: 2000 Publicly Held
SIC: 3812 3761 7373 3721 Search & detection systems & instruments; guided missiles, complete; computer integrated systems design; airplanes, fixed or rotary wing; aircraft servicing & repairing; ordnance & accessories
HQ: Northrop Grumman Systems Corporation
2980 Fairview Park Dr
Falls Church VA 22042
703 280-2900

(P-20662)
NORTHROP GRUMMAN SYSTEMS CORP
1100 W Hollyvale St, Azusa (91702-3305)
P.O. Box 296 (91702-0296)
PHONE.............................626 812-1000
Carl Fischer, *Manager*
Larry Tiller, *General Mgr*
James Lott, *Sr Ntwrk Engine*
Mike Pettey, *Comp Lab Dir*
Marc Lavertu, *Network Mgr*
EMP: 210 Publicly Held
WEB: www.sperry.ngc.com
SIC: 3812 Search & navigation equipment
HQ: Northrop Grumman Systems Corporation
2980 Fairview Park Dr
Falls Church VA 22042
703 280-2900

(P-20663)
NORTHROP GRUMMAN SYSTEMS CORP
Western Region
3520 E Avenue M, Palmdale (93550-7401)
PHONE.............................661 540-0446
Jim Pace, *Branch Mgr*
EMP: 305 Publicly Held
WEB: www.sperry.ngc.com
SIC: 3812 Search & navigation equipment
HQ: Northrop Grumman Systems Corporation
2980 Fairview Park Dr
Falls Church VA 22042
703 280-2900

(P-20664)
NORTHROP GRUMMAN SYSTEMS CORP
Northrop Grumman Info Systems
5441 Luce Ave, McClellan (95652-2417)
PHONE.............................916 570-4454
John Dydiw, *Manager*
Ron Garrison, *Design Engr*
EMP: 25 Publicly Held
WEB: www.trw.com
SIC: 3812 Search & navigation equipment
HQ: Northrop Grumman Systems Corporation
2980 Fairview Park Dr
Falls Church VA 22042
703 280-2900

(P-20665)
NORTHROP GRUMMAN SYSTEMS CORP
2477 Manhattan Beach Blvd, Redondo Beach (90278-1544)
PHONE.............................310 812-4321
Bruce R Gerding, *Vice Pres*
EMP: 305 Publicly Held
WEB: www.sperry.ngc.com

SIC: **3812** Search & navigation equipment
HQ: Northrop Grumman Systems Corporation
2980 Fairview Park Dr
Falls Church VA 22042
703 280-2900

(P-20666)
NORTHROP GRUMMAN SYSTEMS CORP
1111 W 3rd St, Azusa (91702-3328)
PHONE..........................626 812-1464
Michael Clayton, *Manager*
EMP: 305 **Publicly Held**
WEB: www.sperry.ngc.com
SIC: **3812** Search & navigation equipment
HQ: Northrop Grumman Systems Corporation
2980 Fairview Park Dr
Falls Church VA 22042
703 280-2900

(P-20667)
NORTHROP GRUMMAN SYSTEMS CORP
Also Called: Northrop Grumman Space
9326 Spectrum Center Blvd, San Diego (92123-1443)
PHONE..........................858 514-9000
Mike Twyman, *Branch Mgr*
EMP: 220 **Publicly Held**
WEB: www.trw.com
SIC: **3812** Search & navigation equipment
HQ: Northrop Grumman Systems Corporation
2980 Fairview Park Dr
Falls Church VA 22042
703 280-2900

(P-20668)
NORWICH AERO PRODUCTS INC (DH)
6900 Orangethorpe Ave B, Buena Park (90620-1390)
P.O. Box 109, Norwich NY (13815-0109)
PHONE..........................607 336-7636
Curtis Reusser, *CEO*
Roger Alan Ross, *President*
Robert D George, *CFO*
Christoper Ainsworth, *VP Opers*
EMP: 47
SQ FT: 56,000
SALES (est): 9.3MM
SALES (corp-wide): 3.8B **Publicly Held**
WEB: www.norwichaero.com
SIC: **3812** 3829 3823 Search & navigation equipment; measuring & controlling devices; temperature instruments: industrial process type
HQ: Esterline Technologies Corp
500 108th Ave Ne Ste 1500
Bellevue WA 98004
425 453-9400

(P-20669)
OCEAN AERO INC
10350 Sorrento Valley Rd, San Diego (92121-1642)
PHONE..........................858 945-3768
Eric Patten, *CEO*
EMP: 30
SALES (est): 330K **Privately Held**
SIC: **3812** Search & detection systems & instruments

(P-20670)
ORBITAL SCIENCES CORPORATION
Also Called: Space Systems Division
20 Ryan Ranch Rd Ste 214, Monterey (93940-6439)
PHONE..........................703 406-5000
Steven Mumma, *Director*
EMP: 99 EST: 1990
SALES (est): 6.9MM **Privately Held**
SIC: **3812** Search & navigation equipment

(P-20671)
PACIFIC DESIGN TECH INC
Also Called: PDT
6300 Lindmar Dr, Goleta (93117-3112)
PHONE..........................805 961-9110
David Zapico, *CEO*
Ed Sweeney, *District Mgr*
Mark Kukawski, *Regl Sales Mgr*

EMP: 28
SQ FT: 19,000
SALES (est): 9MM
SALES (corp-wide): 4.8B **Publicly Held**
WEB: www.pd-tech.com
SIC: **3812** Acceleration indicators & systems components, aerospace
PA: Ametek, Inc.
1100 Cassatt Rd
Berwyn PA 19312
610 647-2121

(P-20672)
PACIFIC SCIENTIFIC COMPANY (DH)
Also Called: Electro Kinetics Division
1785 Voyager Ave, Simi Valley (93063-3363)
PHONE..........................805 526-5700
James Simpkins, *Principal*
James Healey, *General Mgr*
David Penner, *Finance Dir*
◆ EMP: 23
SALES (est): 71.7MM
SALES (corp-wide): 2.6B **Privately Held**
WEB: www.pacsci.com
SIC: **3812** 3669 3621 3694 Aircraft control systems, electronic; fire detection systems; generators & sets, electric; motors, electric; servomotors, electric; alternators, automotive; water quality monitoring & control systems; control equipment, electric
HQ: Meggitt-Usa, Inc.
1955 Surveyor Ave
Simi Valley CA 93063
805 526-5700

(P-20673)
PANEL PRODUCTS INC
21818 S Wilmington Ave # 411, Long Beach (90810-1642)
PHONE..........................310 830-3331
Nabil Abdou, *CEO*
Sherine Attia, *Vice Pres*
EMP: 20
SALES: 5MM **Privately Held**
SIC: **3812** Aircraft control instruments

(P-20674)
PNEUDRAULICS INC
8575 Helms Ave, Rancho Cucamonga (91730-4591)
PHONE..........................909 980-5366
Michael Saville, *CEO*
Dain Miller, *President*
Herbert Cruz, *Technician*
Ralph Palomino, *Design Engr*
Bryan Akioka, *Project Engr*
▼ EMP: 275
SQ FT: 48,000
SALES (est): 52.4MM
SALES (corp-wide): 3.8B **Publicly Held**
WEB: www.pneudraulics.com
SIC: **3812** Acceleration indicators & systems components, aerospace
PA: Transdigm Group Incorporated
1301 E 9th St Ste 3000
Cleveland OH 44114
216 706-2960

(P-20675)
POLYNESIAN EXPLORATION INC
2210 Otoole Ave Ste 240, San Jose (95131-1300)
PHONE..........................540 808-7538
Senlin Peng, *Principal*
EMP: 12
SALES (est): 548.9K **Privately Held**
SIC: **3812** Search & navigation equipment

(P-20676)
PRENAV INC
121 Beech St, Redwood City (94063-2135)
PHONE..........................650 264-7279
Nathan Schuett, *CEO*
Nick Rossi, *President*
Marc Ausman, *COO*
Asa Hammond, *Chief Engr*
EMP: 15
SQ FT: 11,000
SALES (est): 1MM **Privately Held**
SIC: **3812** Aircraft/aerospace flight instruments & guidance systems

(P-20677)
QUANERGY SYSTEMS INC (PA)
482 Mercury Dr, Sunnyvale (94085-4706)
PHONE..........................408 245-9500
Louay Eldada, *President*
Axel Fuchs, *President*
Mike Healy, *CFO*
Enzo Signore, *Chief Mktg Ofcr*
Gary Saunders, *Officer*
EMP: 94
SALES (est): 12.6MM **Privately Held**
SIC: **3812** Infrared object detection equipment

(P-20678)
QUANTUM3D INC (PA)
1759 Mccarthy Blvd, Milpitas (95035-7416)
PHONE..........................408 600-2500
Clayton Conrad, *President*
Murat Kose, *CFO*
Tim Stewart, *Officer*
Jocelyn Walter, *Controller*
Ed Herradura, *Production*
◆ EMP: 19
SQ FT: 20,000
SALES (est): 13.3MM **Privately Held**
SIC: **3812** Aircraft control instruments

(P-20679)
RADTEC ENGINEERING INC
1780 La Costa Meadows Dr # 102, San Marcos (92078-9101)
PHONE..........................760 510-2715
Mohammad Haq, *Manager*
EMP: 12 **Privately Held**
WEB: www.radar-sales.com
SIC: **3812** 5065 Radar systems & equipment; radar detectors
PA: Radtec Engineering, Inc.
2150 W 6th Ave Ste F
Broomfield CO 80020

(P-20680)
RANTEC MICROWAVE SYSTEMS INC (PA)
31186 La Baya Dr, Westlake Village (91362-4003)
PHONE..........................818 223-5000
Carl Grindle, *CEO*
Carl E Grindle, *CEO*
Steven Chegwin, *CFO*
Steven B Chegwin, *Treasurer*
Graham R Wilson, *Admin Sec*
EMP: 55
SQ FT: 35,000
SALES (est): 13.9MM **Privately Held**
WEB: www.rantecmdm.com
SIC: **3812** Antennas, radar or communications

(P-20681)
RAYTHEON COMPANY
14471 Danes Cir, Huntington Beach (92647-2223)
PHONE..........................310 334-0430
Steve Chu,
Brian Armstrong, *Engineer*
EMP: 15
SALES (corp-wide): 27B **Publicly Held**
SIC: **3812** 8711 3663 3674 Defense systems & equipment; engineering services; radio & TV communications equipment; semiconductors & related devices
PA: Raytheon Company
870 Winter St
Waltham MA 02451
781 522-3000

(P-20682)
RAYTHEON COMPANY
1921 Mariposa St, El Segundo (90245)
PHONE..........................310 647-1000
David Wajsgras, *Branch Mgr*
BAC Tran, *Engineer*
EMP: 100
SALES (corp-wide): 27B **Publicly Held**
SIC: **3812** 4899 Sonar systems & equipment; satellite earth stations
PA: Raytheon Company
870 Winter St
Waltham MA 02451
781 522-3000

(P-20683)
RAYTHEON COMPANY
16035 E Bridger St, Covina (91722-3323)
PHONE..........................626 675-2584
EMP: 170
SALES (corp-wide): 27B **Publicly Held**
SIC: **3812** Defense systems & equipment
PA: Raytheon Company
870 Winter St
Waltham MA 02451
781 522-3000

(P-20684)
RAYTHEON COMPANY
1801 Hughes Dr, Fullerton (92833-2200)
P.O. Box 902, El Segundo (90245-0902)
PHONE..........................714 446-2584
John Coarse, *Branch Mgr*
John Panetta, *Executive*
Robert Eland, *Program Mgr*
David Heine, *Info Tech Mgr*
Daniel Sandoval, *Electrical Engi*
EMP: 15
SALES (corp-wide): 27B **Publicly Held**
SIC: **3812** Sonar systems & equipment
PA: Raytheon Company
870 Winter St
Waltham MA 02451
781 522-3000

(P-20685)
RAYTHEON COMPANY
1801 Hughes Dr, Fullerton (92833-2200)
P.O. Box 3310 (92834-3310)
PHONE..........................714 446-3513
Jeff Leiter, *Principal*
Richard Ascheri, *Sr Ntwrk Engine*
Steve Tarr, *Electrical Engi*
Benjamin Rodriguez, *Engineer*
Scott Gacki, *Finance Mgr*
EMP: 99
SALES (corp-wide): 27B **Publicly Held**
SIC: **3812** 8711 Defense systems & equipment; engineering services
PA: Raytheon Company
870 Winter St
Waltham MA 02451
781 522-3000

(P-20686)
RAYTHEON COMPANY
350 E Ridgecrest Blvd # 202, Ridgecrest (93555-3928)
PHONE..........................760 384-3295
Jim Lemon, *Manager*
EMP: 25
SALES (corp-wide): 27B **Publicly Held**
SIC: **3812** Sonar systems & equipment
PA: Raytheon Company
870 Winter St
Waltham MA 02451
781 522-3000

(P-20687)
RAYTHEON COMPANY
8650 Balboa Ave, San Diego (92123-1502)
PHONE..........................619 628-3345
Tom Harwell, *Manager*
Calvin Trinh, *Admin Sec*
Lou Grein, *Engineer*
EMP: 250
SALES (corp-wide): 27B **Publicly Held**
SIC: **3812** Sonar systems & equipment
PA: Raytheon Company
870 Winter St
Waltham MA 02451
781 522-3000

(P-20688)
RAYTHEON COMPANY
1801 Hughes Dr, Fullerton (92833-2200)
P.O. Box 3310 (92834-3310)
PHONE..........................714 732-0119
Barry Bolton, *Contract Mgr*
Kelly Allison, *Principal*
Katherine Gjevre, *Software Engr*
Richard Heske, *Senior Engr*
EMP: 132
SALES (corp-wide): 27B **Publicly Held**
SIC: **3812** 7371 Sonar systems & equipment; computer software development & applications
PA: Raytheon Company
870 Winter St
Waltham MA 02451
781 522-3000

(P-20689)
RAYTHEON COMPANY
2000 E El Segundo Blvd, El Segundo
(90245-4501)
PHONE.................................310 647-1000
John Jones, *Manager*
Joan Procopio, *Officer*
Patsy Chan, *Program Mgr*
Tim McGoldrick, *Program Mgr*
Thomas Traylor, *Planning Mgr*
EMP: 500
SALES (corp-wide): 27B **Publicly Held**
SIC: 3812 Defense systems & equipment
PA: Raytheon Company
   870 Winter St
   Waltham MA 02451
   781 522-3000

(P-20690)
RAYTHEON COMPANY
2000 Elsegundo Blvd, El Segundo (90245)
PHONE.................................310 647-8334
Pam Nullmayer, *Branch Mgr*
EMP: 400
SALES (corp-wide): 27B **Publicly Held**
SIC: 3812 Radar systems & equipment
PA: Raytheon Company
   870 Winter St
   Waltham MA 02451
   781 522-3000

(P-20691)
RAYTHEON COMPANY
Bldg 471 North End, Port Hueneme
(93043-0001)
PHONE.................................805 985-6851
Jackie Samuel, *Manager*
EMP: 16
SALES (corp-wide): 27B **Publicly Held**
SIC: 3812 Sonar systems & equipment
PA: Raytheon Company
   870 Winter St
   Waltham MA 02451
   781 522-3000

(P-20692)
RAYTHEON COMPANY
1120 S Vineyard Ave, Ontario
(91761-7753)
P.O. Box 7651, Van Nuys (91409-7651)
PHONE.................................310 338-1324
Mike Rabens, *Sales/Mktg Mgr*
Patrick Partikian, *Software Engr*
Joseph Merfalen, *Electrical Engi*
Paul Rodriguez, *Electrical Engi*
Jessica Donaldson, *Engineer*
EMP: 75
SALES (corp-wide): 27B **Publicly Held**
SIC: 3812 Sonar systems & equipment
PA: Raytheon Company
   870 Winter St
   Waltham MA 02451
   781 522-3000

(P-20693)
RAYTHEON COMPANY
2000 E El Segundo Blvd, El Segundo
(90245-4501)
PHONE.................................310 647-9438
Donna McCullough, *Branch Mgr*
EMP: 1000
SALES (corp-wide): 27B **Publicly Held**
SIC: 3812 3663 3761 3231 Defense systems & equipment; space satellite communications equipment; airborne radio communications equipment; guided missiles & space vehicles, research & development; rockets, space & military, complete; scientific & technical glassware: from purchased glass; integrated circuits, semiconductor networks, etc.; semiconductor circuit networks
PA: Raytheon Company
   870 Winter St
   Waltham MA 02451
   781 522-3000

(P-20694)
RAYTHEON COMPANY
2000 E El Segundo Blvd, El Segundo
(90245-4501)
P.O. Box 902 (90245-0902)
PHONE.................................310 647-1000
Christine Combs, *Manager*
Hon Tran, *Technology*
EMP: 500

SALES (corp-wide): 27B **Publicly Held**
SIC: 3812 Search & navigation equipment
PA: Raytheon Company
   870 Winter St
   Waltham MA 02451
   781 522-3000

(P-20695)
RAYTHEON COMPANY
2000 E El Segundo Blvd, El Segundo
(90245-4501)
PHONE.................................310 647-1000
William Swanson, *Principal*
EMP: 50
SALES (corp-wide): 27B **Publicly Held**
SIC: 3812 Radar systems & equipment
PA: Raytheon Company
   870 Winter St
   Waltham MA 02451
   781 522-3000

(P-20696)
RAYTHEON COMPANY
1901 W Malvern Ave 618, Fullerton
(92833-2177)
PHONE.................................714 446-3232
Dan Buranham, *President*
EMP: 400
SALES (corp-wide): 27B **Publicly Held**
SIC: 3812 3829 Defense systems & equipment; aircraft & motor vehicle measurement equipment
PA: Raytheon Company
   870 Winter St
   Waltham MA 02451
   781 522-3000

(P-20697)
RAYTHEON COMPANY
10606 7th St, Rancho Cucamonga
(91730-5438)
PHONE.................................909 483-4040
Raul Mendoza, *Manager*
EMP: 75
SALES (corp-wide): 27B **Publicly Held**
SIC: 3812 Sonar systems & equipment
PA: Raytheon Company
   870 Winter St
   Waltham MA 02451
   781 522-3000

(P-20698)
RAYTHEON COMPANY
2175 Park Pl, El Segundo (90245-4705)
PHONE.................................310 334-7675
Raymond T Wheeler, *Manager*
EMP: 50
SALES (corp-wide): 27B **Publicly Held**
SIC: 3812 Sonar systems & equipment
PA: Raytheon Company
   870 Winter St
   Waltham MA 02451
   781 522-3000

(P-20699)
RAYTHEON COMPANY
75 Coromar Dr, Goleta (93117-3088)
PHONE.................................805 562-4611
Mike E Allgeier, *Manager*
Stephen Black, *COO*
Stefan Baur, *Info Tech Dir*
Floyd Cordisco, *Engineer*
Frank Mesh, *Engineer*
EMP: 100
SALES (corp-wide): 27B **Publicly Held**
SIC: 3812 8731 3845 3825 Sonar systems & equipment; commercial research laboratory; electronic research; electromedical equipment; instruments to measure electricity
PA: Raytheon Company
   870 Winter St
   Waltham MA 02451
   781 522-3000

(P-20700)
RAYTHEON COMPANY
2000 E El Segundo Blvd, El Segundo
(90245-4501)
P.O. Box 902 (90245-0902)
PHONE.................................310 647-9438
Rick Yuse, *Branch Mgr*
EMP: 10000
SALES (corp-wide): 27B **Publicly Held**
SIC: 3812 Defense systems & equipment

PA: Raytheon Company
   870 Winter St
   Waltham MA 02451
   781 522-3000

(P-20701)
RAYTHEON COMPANY
8650 Balboa Ave, San Diego (92123-1502)
PHONE.................................858 571-6598
Greg Pendleton, *Senior Mgr*
EMP: 80
SALES (corp-wide): 27B **Publicly Held**
SIC: 3812 Sonar systems & equipment
PA: Raytheon Company
   870 Winter St
   Waltham MA 02451
   781 522-3000

(P-20702)
RAYTHEON COMPANY
63 Hollister St, Goleta (93117)
PHONE.................................805 967-5511
Randy Brown, *President*
John Thornburg, *General Mgr*
Karen Steinfeld, *Engineer*
Paul Gardner, *Director*
EMP: 131
SALES (corp-wide): 27B **Publicly Held**
SIC: 3812 Defense systems & equipment
PA: Raytheon Company
   870 Winter St
   Waltham MA 02451
   781 522-3000

(P-20703)
RAYTHEON DGITAL FORCE TECH LLC
6779 Mesa Ridge Rd # 150, San Diego
(92121-2996)
PHONE.................................858 546-1244
Jeanette Hughes, *Vice Pres*
Frank R Jimenez, *Vice Pres*
Taylor W Lawrence, *Vice Pres*
David C Wajsgras, *Vice Pres*
Nick Moreau, *General Mgr*
EMP: 40
SQ FT: 14,500
SALES (est): 8MM
SALES (corp-wide): 27B **Publicly Held**
WEB: www.digitalforcetech.com
SIC: 3812 8711 Defense systems & equipment; engineering services
HQ: Raytheon Bbn Technologies Corp.
   10 Moulton St
   Cambridge MA 02138
   617 873-8000

(P-20704)
REMCOR TECHNICAL INDUSTRIES
7025 Alamitos Ave, San Diego
(92154-4709)
PHONE.................................619 424-8878
Ron Mueller, *President*
Ellie Mueller, *Admin Sec*
▲ **EMP:** 25
SQ FT: 6,000
SALES (est): 2MM **Privately Held**
WEB: www.remcortech.com
SIC: 3812 Detection apparatus: electronic/magnetic field, light/heat

(P-20705)
REVEAL IMAGING TECH INC
10260 Campus Point Dr # 6133, San Diego
(92121-1522)
PHONE.................................858 826-9909
Joseph S Secker, *CEO*
Bill Aitkenhead PHD, *President*
James Buckley, *President*
Carol Raymond, *President*
David Reissfelder, *CFO*
▲ **EMP:** 65
SQ FT: 2,000
SALES (est): 7.6MM
SALES (corp-wide): 10.1B **Publicly Held**
WEB: www.revealimaging.com
SIC: 3812 7372 Search & detection systems & instruments; application computer software
HQ: Leidos, Inc.
   11951 Freedom Dr Ste 500
   Reston VA 20190
   571 526-6000

(P-20706)
ROCKWELL COLLINS INC
1733 Alton Pkwy, Irvine (92606-4901)
PHONE.................................714 929-3000
EMP: 89
SALES (corp-wide): 66.5B **Publicly Held**
WEB: www.kaiserelectronics.com
SIC: 3812 Search & navigation equipment
HQ: Rockwell Collins, Inc.
   400 Collins Rd Ne
   Cedar Rapids IA 52498
   -

(P-20707)
ROCKWELL COLLINS INC
1757 Carr Rd Ste 100e, Calexico
(92231-9781)
PHONE.................................760 768-4732
Nicolas Pineda, *Manager*
Nick Trent, *Manager*
EMP: 25
SALES (corp-wide): 66.5B **Publicly Held**
WEB: www.keo.com
SIC: 3812 Search & navigation equipment
HQ: Rockwell Collins, Inc.
   400 Collins Rd Ne
   Cedar Rapids IA 52498

(P-20708)
ROCKWELL COLLINS OPTRONICS INC
2752 Loker Ave W, Carlsbad (92010-6603)
PHONE.................................319 295-1000
Melissa Ospby, *Branch Mgr*
Charles Micka, *Engineer*
EMP: 13
SALES (corp-wide): 66.5B **Publicly Held**
WEB: www.keo.com
SIC: 3812 Search & navigation equipment
HQ: Rockwell Collins Optronics, Inc.
   400 Collins Rd Ne
   Cedar Rapids IA 52498

(P-20709)
ROGERSON AIRCRAFT CORPORATION (PA)
2201 Alton Pkwy, Irvine (92606-5033)
PHONE.................................949 660-0666
Michael J Rogerson, *President*
Gordon Neil, *President*
Jonathan C Smith, *CFO*
Michael Miller, *Vice Pres*
Milton R Pizinger, *Vice Pres*
EMP: 80 **EST:** 1975
SQ FT: 50,000
SALES (est): 37.7MM **Privately Held**
WEB: www.rogerson.com
SIC: 3812 3545 3492 3728 Aircraft flight instruments; machine tool accessories; fluid power valves & hose fittings; fuel tanks, aircraft

(P-20710)
ROGERSON KRATOS
403 S Raymond Ave, Pasadena
(91105-2609)
PHONE.................................626 449-3090
Lawrence Smith, *CEO*
Cannon Mathews, *CFO*
Michael Rogerson, *Chairman*
Milton R Pizinger, *Vice Pres*
EMP: 160
SQ FT: 28,000
SALES (est): 38MM
SALES (corp-wide): 37.7MM **Privately Held**
WEB: www.rogersonkratos.com
SIC: 3812 3825 3699 Aircraft flight instruments; instruments to measure electricity; electrical equipment & supplies
PA: Rogerson Aircraft Corporation
   2201 Alton Pkwy
   Irvine CA 92606
   949 660-0666

(P-20711)
ROZENDAL ASSOCIATES INC
9530 Pathway St Ste 101, Santee
(92071-4171)
PHONE.................................619 562-5596
Tim Rozendal, *President*
Jean Rozendal, *Vice Pres*
EMP: 10

PRODUCTS & SVCS

SQ FT: 5,500
SALES: 1MM **Privately Held**
WEB: www.rozendalassociates.com
SIC: **3812** 3663 8711 Radar systems &
equipment; antennas, transmitting & com-
munications; engineering services

(P-20712)
**SAFRAN ELEC DEF AVNICS USA
LLC**
3184 Pullman St, Costa Mesa
(92626-3319)
PHONE..................................949 642-2427
Parice Smith, *CEO*
EMP: 170
SQ FT: 56,000
SALES (corp-wide): 833.4MM **Privately
Held**
WEB: www.eaton.com
SIC: **3812** Aircraft/aerospace flight instru-
ments & guidance systems
HQ: Safran Electronics & Defense, Avionics
Usa, Llc
2802 Safran Dr
Grand Prairie TX 75052
972 314-3600

(P-20713)
SAGO SYSTEMS INC
10455 Pacific Center Ct, San Diego
(92121-4339)
PHONE..................................858 646-5300
John Lovberg, *President*
EMP: 10
SQ FT: 5,000
SALES: 1.1MM **Privately Held**
WEB: www.sagosystems.com
SIC: **3812** Search & navigation equipment

(P-20714)
SANDEL AVIONICS INC
2405 Dogwood Way, Vista (92081-8409)
PHONE..................................760 727-4900
Gerald Block, *Branch Mgr*
EMP: 169
SALES (corp-wide): 90MM **Privately
Held**
SIC: **3812** Aircraft control instruments; air-
craft flight instruments; air traffic control
systems & equipment, electronic; anten-
nas, radar or communications
PA: Sandel Avionics, Inc.
2401 Dogwood Way
Vista CA 92081
760 727-4900

(P-20715)
SANDEL AVIONICS INC (PA)
2401 Dogwood Way, Vista (92081-8409)
PHONE..................................760 727-4900
Gerald Block, *President*
Grant Miller, *CFO*
Charla Parks, *Admin Asst*
Bret Strain, *Software Engr*
John Huebner, *Electrical Engi*
EMP: 31
SQ FT: 16,000
SALES: 90MM **Privately Held**
WEB: www.sandel.com
SIC: **3812** Aircraft control instruments; air-
craft flight instruments; air traffic control
systems & equipment, electronic; anten-
nas, radar or communications

(P-20716)
SANDERS AIRCRAFT INC
Also Called: Sanders Aircraft Technologies
17149 Lambert Rd, Ione (95640-9527)
P.O. Box 1088 (95640-1088)
PHONE..................................209 274-2955
Ruth Sanders, *President*
Brian Sanders, *Vice Pres*
EMP: 10
SQ FT: 18,000
SALES: 1MM **Privately Held**
WEB: www.sandersaircraft.com
SIC: **3812** Aircraft/aerospace flight instru-
ments & guidance systems

(P-20717)
**SATCOM SOLUTIONS
CORPORATION**
31119 Via Colinas Ste 501, Westlake Vil-
lage (91362-3933)
PHONE..................................818 991-9794
Fred Joubert, *President*

Ellie Bahadori, *Office Mgr*
▼ EMP: 10
SQ FT: 7,500
SALES: 2MM **Privately Held**
SIC: **3812** 3669 Navigational systems &
instruments; intercommunication systems,
electric

(P-20718)
SCIENTIFIC-ATLANTA LLC
Scientific Atlanta
13112 Evening Creek Dr S, San Diego
(92128-4108)
PHONE..................................619 679-6000
Richard Lapointe, *Controller*
EMP: 350
SALES (corp-wide): 51.9B **Publicly Held**
WEB: www.scientific-atlanta.com
SIC: **3812** Navigational systems & instru-
ments
HQ: Scientific-Atlanta, Llc
5030 Sugarloaf Pkwy 1
Lawrenceville GA 30044
678 277-1000

(P-20719)
**SENSOR CONCEPTS
INCORPORATED**
7950 National Dr, Livermore (94550-8811)
P.O. Box 2657 (94551-2657)
PHONE..................................925 443-9001
Michael Sanders, *President*
Barbara Peter, *Officer*
John Ashton, *Vice Pres*
George Blenis, *Pharmacy Dir*
Matthew Bogdanov, *Info Tech Mgr*
EMP: 55
SALES (est): 5.2MM **Privately Held**
WEB: www.sensorconcepts.com
SIC: **3812** 8711 Radar systems & equip-
ment; engineering services

(P-20720)
SENSOR SYSTEMS INC
8929 Fullbright Ave, Chatsworth
(91311-6179)
PHONE..................................818 341-5366
Mary E Bazar, *CEO*
Si Robin, *Vice Pres*
Dennis E Bazar, *Admin Sec*
Adriana Bardon, *Buyer*
Craig Miller, *Manager*
EMP: 258
SQ FT: 60,000
SALES (est): 48.6MM **Privately Held**
WEB: www.sensorantennas.com
SIC: **3812** Aircraft flight instruments

(P-20721)
SIERRA MONOLITHICS INC
5141 California Ave # 200, Irvine
(92617-3061)
PHONE..................................949 269-4400
Emeka Chukwu, *Owner*
EMP: 11
SALES (corp-wide): 627.2MM **Publicly
Held**
SIC: **3812** Search & navigation equipment
HQ: Sierra Monolithics, Inc.
103 W Torrance Blvd
Redondo Beach CA 90277
310 698-1000

(P-20722)
SIEVA NETWORKS INC (PA)
281 Countrybrook Loop, San Ramon
(94583-4476)
PHONE..................................408 475-1953
Vijay Pillai, *President*
EMP: 10
SQ FT: 2,000
SALES (est): 1.6MM **Privately Held**
SIC: **3812** Search & navigation equipment

(P-20723)
SKYDIO INC
114 Hazel Ave, Redwood City
(94061-3112)
PHONE..................................408 203-8497
Adam P Bry, *CEO*
Abraham Bachrach, *CTO*
Peter Henry, *Software Engr*
Dan Adams, *Engineer*
Patrick Stahl, *Marketing Staff*
EMP: 18
SQ FT: 15,000

SALES (est): 961.6K **Privately Held**
SIC: **3812** Acceleration indicators & systems components, aerospace

(P-20724)
SNAPTRACS INC
5775 Morehouse Dr, San Diego
(92121-1714)
PHONE..................................858 587-1121
Scott L Neuberger, *CEO*
EMP: 14 EST: 2012
SALES (est): 2.8MM **Privately Held**
SIC: **3812** Search & navigation equipment

(P-20725)
**SONCELL NORTH AMERICA INC
(HQ)**
Also Called: AEP Cali
10729 Whelt Lands Ave C, San Diego
(92107)
PHONE..................................619 795-4600
Luisa Nechodom, *CEO*
Jessica Faustino, *Controller*
EMP: 23 EST: 2011
SALES (est): 10.6MM
SALES (corp-wide): 1.2B **Privately Held**
SIC: **3812** Radar systems & equipment
PA: Bowmer And Kirkland Limited
High Edge Court
Belper DE56
177 385-3131

(P-20726)
SPACE INFORMATION LABS LLC
Also Called: Sil
2260 Meredith Ln Ste A, Santa Maria
(93455-1117)
PHONE..................................805 925-9010
Edmund Burke, *CEO*
Denise Burke, *CFO*
EMP: 15
SALES (est): 3.1MM **Privately Held**
SIC: **3812** Search & navigation equipment

(P-20727)
SPEC TOOL COMPANY
Also Called: Alice G Fink-Painter
11805 Wakeman St, Santa Fe Springs
(90670-2130)
P.O. Box 1056, Pico Rivera (90660-1056)
PHONE..................................323 723-9533
Alice G Fink-Painter, *President*
D B Fink, *CEO*
Albert G Fink Jr, *Vice Pres*
EMP: 50 EST: 1954
SALES (est): 8.7MM **Privately Held**
SIC: **3812** Aircraft control systems, elec-
tronic

(P-20728)
**TECNOVA ADVANCED SYSTEMS
INC**
Also Called: Tecnadyne
9770 Carroll Centre Rd, San Diego
(92126-6504)
P.O. Box 676086, Rancho Santa Fe
(92067-6086)
PHONE..................................858 586-9660
Andrew Bazeley, *President*
Ute Pelzer, *CFO*
Barry Sears, *Vice Pres*
EMP: 20
SQ FT: 17,150
SALES (est): 4.1MM **Privately Held**
WEB: www.tecnadyne.com
SIC: **3812** Search & navigation equipment

(P-20729)
TELEDYNE CONTROLS LLC
501 Continental Blvd, El Segundo
(90245-5036)
P.O. Box 1026 (90245-1026)
PHONE..................................310 765-3600
Aldo Pichelli, *CEO*
Robert Mehrabian, *Ch of Bd*
Masood Hassan, *President*
Susan L Main, *CFO*
George C Bobb III, *Ch Credit Ofcr*
EMP: 616
SALES (est): 92.7MM
SALES (corp-wide): 2.9B **Publicly Held**
SIC: **3812** Search & navigation equipment
PA: Teledyne Technologies Inc
1049 Camino Dos Rios
Thousand Oaks CA 91360
805 373-4545

(P-20730)
TELEDYNE INSTRUMENTS INC
Also Called: Teledyne Rd Instruments
14020 Stowe Dr, Poway (92064-6846)
PHONE..................................858 842-2600
Dennis Klahn, *Branch Mgr*
Jeff McNicholl, *Info Tech Dir*
Boby George, *Software Engr*
Robert Abirgas, *Design Engr*
Ian Cassimatis, *Electrical Engi*
EMP: 140
SALES (corp-wide): 2.9B **Publicly Held**
SIC: **3812** 3829 Search & navigation
equipment; measuring & controlling de-
vices
HQ: Teledyne Instruments, Inc.
1049 Camino Dos Rios
Thousand Oaks CA 91360
805 373-4545

(P-20731)
TELENAV INC (PA)
4655 Great America Pkwy # 300, Santa
Clara (95054-1236)
PHONE..................................408 245-3800
H P Jin, *Ch of Bd*
Salman Dhanani, *President*
Hassan Wahla, *President*
Adeel Manzoor, *CFO*
Michael Strambi, *Treasurer*
EMP: 142
SQ FT: 55,000
SALES: 220.9MM **Publicly Held**
WEB: www.telenav.com
SIC: **3812** Navigational systems & instru-
ments

(P-20732)
**TMC ICE PROTECTION
SYSTEMS LLC**
Also Called: TMC Aero
25775 Jefferson Ave, Murrieta
(92562-6903)
PHONE..................................951 677-6934
Edward Rigney, *COO*
EMP: 20
SALES (corp-wide): 3MM **Privately Held**
SIC: **3812** 8711 Aircraft/aerospace flight
instruments & guidance systems; aviation
&/or aeronautical engineering
PA: Tmc Ice Protection Systems Llc
10850 Wilshire Blvd # 1250
Los Angeles CA 90024
760 672-0559

(P-20733)
**TOWER MECHANICAL
PRODUCTS INC**
Also Called: Allied Mechanical Products
1720 S Bon View Ave, Ontario
(91761-4411)
PHONE..................................714 947-2723
Richard B Slater, *President*
Susan J Hardy, *Corp Secy*
James W Longcrier, *Vice Pres*
EMP: 126
SQ FT: 148,000
SALES (est): 13.3MM
SALES (corp-wide): 30.8MM **Privately
Held**
SIC: **3812** Acceleration indicators & sys-
tems components, aerospace
PA: Tower Industries, Inc.
1518 N Endeavor Ln Ste C
Anaheim CA 92801

(P-20734)
TRIMBLE INC
945 Stewart Dr Ste 100, Sunnyvale
(94085-3940)
PHONE..................................408 481-8490
EMP: 11
SALES (corp-wide): 3.1B **Publicly Held**
SIC: **3812** Navigational systems & instru-
ments
PA: Trimble Inc.
935 Stewart Dr
Sunnyvale CA 94085
408 481-8000

(P-20735)
TRIMBLE INC
1720 Prairie City Rd, Folsom (95630-4043)
PHONE..................................916 294-2000

Sarah Berggren, *Sales Staff*
EMP: 40
SALES (corp-wide): 3.1B **Publicly Held**
SIC: 3812 Navigational systems & instruments
PA: Trimble Inc.
935 Stewart Dr
Sunnyvale CA 94085
408 481-8000

(P-20736)
TRIMBLE INC
510 Deguigne Dr, Sunnyvale (94085)
PHONE..................................408 481-8000
EMP: 11
SALES (corp-wide): 3.1B **Publicly Held**
WEB: www.trimble.com
SIC: 3812 3829 5049 Navigational systems & instruments; measuring & controlling devices; surveyors' instruments
PA: Trimble Inc.
935 Stewart Dr
Sunnyvale CA 94085
408 481-8000

(P-20737)
TRIMBLE MILITARY & ADVNCED SYS
510 De Guigne Dr, Sunnyvale
(94085-3920)
P.O. Box 3642 (94088-3642)
PHONE..................................408 481-8000
Ron Smith, *President*
▼ **EMP:** 55
SQ FT: 22,000
SALES (est): 4MM
SALES (corp-wide): 3.1B **Publicly Held**
WEB: www.trimble.com
SIC: 3812 3829 Search & navigation equipment; measuring & controlling devices
PA: Trimble Inc.
935 Stewart Dr
Sunnyvale CA 94085
408 481-8000

(P-20738)
TUFFER MANUFACTURING CO INC
163 E Liberty Ave, Anaheim (92801-1012)
PHONE..................................714 526-3077
Cathy Kim, *President*
Edward Yang, *COO*
Ken Kim, *Vice Pres*
Ryan Hamilton, *Project Mgr*
David Walters, *Human Res Dir*
EMP: 39 **EST:** 1977
SQ FT: 12,000
SALES (est): 6.6MM **Privately Held**
WEB: www.tuffermfg.com
SIC: 3812 3599 Search & navigation equipment; machine shop, jobbing & repair

(P-20739)
UVIFY INC
1 Market Ste 3600, San Francisco
(94105-5102)
PHONE..................................628 200-4469
Hyon Lim, *Mng Member*
EMP: 13
SALES (est): 540.7K **Privately Held**
SIC: 3812 Electronic detection systems (aeronautical)

(P-20740)
VALENCE SURFACE TECH LLC
Valence San Carlos
1000 Commercial St, San Carlos
(94070-4024)
PHONE..................................323 770-0240
John Garin, *Manager*
EMP: 50
SALES (corp-wide): 103MM **Privately Held**
SIC: 3812 Aircraft/aerospace flight instruments & guidance systems
PA: Valence Surface Technologies Llc
1790 Hughes Landing Blvd
The Woodlands TX 77380
855 370-5920

(P-20741)
VELODYNE LIDAR INC
345 Digital Dr, Morgan Hill (95037-2878)
PHONE..................................408 465-2800

Jaime Gonzalez, *Manager*
EMP: 300
SALES (corp-wide): 53.5MM **Privately Held**
SIC: 3812 5731 Altimeters, standard & sensitive; radio, television & electronic stores
PA: Velodyne Lidar, Inc.
5521 Hellyer Ave
San Jose CA 95138
408 465-2800

(P-20742)
VIASAT INC
Also Called: Enerdyne Division
1935 Cordell Ct, El Cajon (92020-0911)
PHONE..................................619 438-6000
Brandon Nixon, *President*
Ron Wangerin, *CFO*
Mike Kulinski, *Vice Pres*
Steve Gardner, *CTO*
Richard Jaramillo, *Software Engr*
EMP: 60
SQ FT: 20,000
SALES (est): 8.3MM
SALES (corp-wide): 2B **Publicly Held**
WEB: www.enerdyne.com
SIC: 3812 Search & navigation equipment
PA: Viasat, Inc.
6155 El Camino Real
Carlsbad CA 92009
760 476-2200

(P-20743)
VOTAW PRECISION TECH INC
13153 Lakeland Rd, Santa Fe Springs
(90670-4520)
P.O. Box 314, Seal Beach (90740-0314)
PHONE..................................562 944-0661
Steve Lamb, *CEO*
David Takes, *President*
Jonathan Miller, *CFO*
Steve Crisanti, *Exec VP*
Tamara Williams, *Principal*
▲ **EMP:** 10 **EST:** 1964
SQ FT: 240,000
SALES: 40MM
SALES (corp-wide): 121.3MM **Privately Held**
WEB: www.votaw.com
SIC: 3812 Acceleration indicators & systems components, aerospace; aircraft/aerospace flight instruments & guidance systems; navigational systems & instruments
PA: Burtek Holdings Inc.
50325 Patricia St
Chesterfield MI

(P-20744)
WESCAM USA INC (DH)
424 Aviation Blvd, Santa Rosa
(95403-1069)
PHONE..................................707 236-1077
Michael T Strianese, *CEO*
John Dehne, *President*
EMP: 11
SALES (est): 2MM
SALES (corp-wide): 6.8B **Publicly Held**
SIC: 3812 Search & navigation equipment
HQ: L3 Technologies, Inc.
600 3rd Ave Fl 34
New York NY 10016
212 697-1111

3821 Laboratory Apparatus & Furniture

(P-20745)
ADVANCE ENGINEERING & TECH CO
Also Called: Advance Lab Instr & Sups
717 W Temple St Ste 203, Los Angeles
(90012-2616)
PHONE..................................213 250-8338
Kimberly Hannah, *Sales Staff*
EMP: 12
SQ FT: 3,000
SALES (est): 500K **Privately Held**
SIC: 3821 Laboratory equipment: fume hoods, distillation racks, etc.

(P-20746)
BERLIN FOOD & LAB EQUIPMENT CO
43 S Linden Ave, South San Francisco
(94080-6407)
PHONE..................................650 589-4231
Michael F Ulrich, *President*
Mark Cottonaro, *COO*
Bron Cottonaro, *Vice Pres*
Jackie McClymond, *Admin Asst*
Keith Kozuch, *Project Leader*
EMP: 23 **EST:** 1947
SQ FT: 50,000
SALES (est): 5.7MM **Privately Held**
WEB: www.berlinusa.com
SIC: 3821 1799 Laboratory apparatus & furniture; home/office interiors finishing, furnishing & remodeling; food service equipment installation

(P-20747)
BICO INC
Also Called: Bico-Braun International
3116 W Valhalla Dr, Burbank (91505-1296)
P.O. Box 6339 (91510-6339)
PHONE..................................818 842-7179
Robert De Palma, *Principal*
Margaret De Palma, *Vice Pres*
EMP: 10 **EST:** 1888
SQ FT: 15,453
SALES (est): 2.6MM **Privately Held**
WEB: www.bicoinc.com
SIC: 3821 Laboratory apparatus, except heating & measuring

(P-20748)
CERA INC
14180 Live Oak Ave Ste I, Baldwin Park
(91706-1350)
P.O. Box 1608 (91706-7608)
PHONE..................................626 814-2688
Philip Dimson, *Owner*
◆ **EMP:** 21
SQ FT: 2,000
SALES (est): 4.8MM **Privately Held**
SIC: 3821 Chemical laboratory apparatus

(P-20749)
CHEMAT TECHNOLOGY INC
Also Called: Chemat Vision
9036 Winnetka Ave, Northridge
(91324-3235)
PHONE..................................818 727-9786
Haixing Zheng, *CEO*
Haixing Zhou, *Sls & Mktg Exec*
Tammy Barrett, *Manager*
Thomas Zhang, *Manager*
▲ **EMP:** 32
SQ FT: 30,000
SALES (est): 6.6MM **Privately Held**
WEB: www.chemat.com
SIC: 3821 3827 Chemical laboratory apparatus; optical test & inspection equipment

(P-20750)
CHROMACODE INC
2330 Faraday Ave Ste 100, Carlsbad
(92008-7244)
PHONE..................................442 244-4369
Alex Dickinson, *Bd of Directors*
Gregory Gosch, *CEO*
Lynne Rollins, *CFO*
EMP: 27 **EST:** 2014
SALES (est): 394.1K **Privately Held**
SIC: 3821 Clinical laboratory instruments, except medical & dental

(P-20751)
CLEATECH LLC
2106 N Glassell St, Orange (92865-3308)
PHONE..................................714 754-6668
Sam Kashanchi,
Angelica Rosales, *Representative*
EMP: 27
SALES: 3.9MM **Privately Held**
WEB: www.cleatech.com
SIC: 3821 Laboratory apparatus & furniture

(P-20752)
COUNTY OF SAN BERNARDINO
Also Called: Arrow Head Regional Med Ctr
400 N Pepper Ave, Colton (92324-1801)
PHONE..................................909 580-0015
Carolyn Leech, *Director*
Adrian Martinez, *Nursing Mgr*

Susan Peterson, *Human Res Dir*
Martha L Melendez, *Family Practiti*
Yvette Bynum, *Legal Staff*
EMP: 50 **Privately Held**
SIC: 3821 8071 Clinical laboratory instruments, except medical & dental; blood analysis laboratory
PA: County Of San Bernardino
385 N Arrowhead Ave
San Bernardino CA 92415
909 387-3841

(P-20753)
COVALENT METROLOGY SVCS INC
921 Thompson Pl, Sunnyvale
(94085-4518)
PHONE..................................408 498-4611
Craig Hunter, *CEO*
Mark Harrison, *COO*
EMP: 11
SQ FT: 3,500
SALES (est): 500K **Privately Held**
SIC: 3821 Laboratory apparatus & furniture

(P-20754)
DICKINSON CORPORATION
31 Commercial Blvd Ste G, Novato
(94949-6114)
PHONE..................................415 883-7147
Matthew Bishop, *CEO*
Jon Myers, *CEO*
Steve Tanner, *Chairman*
Abhay Thomas, *Research*
Wayne Dickinson, *Chief Engr*
EMP: 12
SQ FT: 7,400
SALES: 500K **Privately Held**
SIC: 3821 Physics laboratory apparatus

(P-20755)
DUKE SCIENTIFIC CORPORATION
46360 Fremont Blvd, Fremont
(94538-6406)
P.O. Box 50005, Palo Alto (94303-0005)
PHONE..................................650 424-1177
Stanley D Duke, *CEO*
Philip Warren, *President*
Ellen Layendecker, *Treasurer*
Heather Vail, *Admin Sec*
EMP: 26 **EST:** 1970
SQ FT: 14,000
SALES: 5MM
SALES (corp-wide): 24.3B **Publicly Held**
WEB: www.dukescientific.com
SIC: 3821 Laboratory apparatus & furniture
PA: Thermo Fisher Scientific Inc.
168 3rd Ave
Waltham MA 02451
781 622-1000

(P-20756)
ENDRESS + HAUSER INC
Also Called: Endresshouser Conducta
4123 E La Palma Ave # 200, Anaheim
(92807-1867)
PHONE..................................714 577-5600
Wolfgang Bable, *Branch Mgr*
Abdul Halim, *Controller*
Ron Loring, *Mfg Mgr*
Joe Garnica, *Manager*
EMP: 14
SALES (corp-wide): 2.8B **Privately Held**
SIC: 3821 Laboratory measuring apparatus
HQ: Endress + Hauser Inc
2350 Endress Pl
Greenwood IN 46143
317 535-7138

(P-20757)
ENDRUN TECHNOLOGIES LLC
2270 Northpoint Pkwy, Santa Rosa
(95407-7398)
PHONE..................................707 573-8633
Bruce Penrod, *Vice Pres*
Georgia Johnson, *CFO*
Michael Korreng, *Engineer*
David Lobsinger, *Marketing Staff*
Susan Coryell,
EMP: 13
SQ FT: 7,400

SALES (est): 3.8MM **Privately Held**
WEB: www.endruntechnologies.com
SIC: 3821 3825 Time interval measuring equipment, electric (lab type); frequency meters: electrical, mechanical & electronic

(P-20758)
GARDNER SYSTEMS INC
3321 S Yale St, Santa Ana (92704-6446)
PHONE................................714 668-9018
Joe Gardner, *President*
Claudia Gardner, *Treasurer*
▲ EMP: 15
SQ FT: 8,000
SALES (est): 3MM **Privately Held**
WEB: www.gardner-systems.com
SIC: 3821 Laboratory apparatus & furniture

(P-20759)
GENETRONICS INC
11494 Sorrento Valley Rd A, San Diego (92121-1318)
PHONE................................858 597-6006
James Heppell, *Chairman*
Avtar Dhillon, *President*
Peter Kies, *CFO*
Babak Nemati PH, *Vice Pres*
Douglas Murdock, *Admin Sec*
EMP: 26
SQ FT: 25,000
SALES (est): 5.8MM **Publicly Held**
WEB: www.genetronics.com
SIC: 3821 8731 3826 Laboratory apparatus, except heating & measuring; biotechnical research, commercial; analytical instruments
PA: Inovio Pharmaceuticals, Inc.
660 W Germantown Pike
Plymouth Meeting PA 19462

(P-20760)
HANSON LAB FURNITURE INC
747 Calle Plano, Camarillo (93012-8556)
PHONE................................805 498-3121
Mike Hanson, *President*
Joseph F Matta, *COO*
Joe Matta, *Vice Pres*
▲ EMP: 30
SQ FT: 40,000
SALES (est): 7.8MM **Privately Held**
WEB: www.hansonlab.com
SIC: 3821 Laboratory furniture

(P-20761)
HITACHI CHEM DIAGNOSTICS INC
630 Clyde Ct, Mountain View (94043-2239)
PHONE................................650 961-5501
Takashi Miyamoto, *CEO*
Kazuyoshi Tsunoda, *President*
Keiichi Takeda, *CFO*
Steve Schwalen, *Administration*
Elizabeth Jeung, *Research*
EMP: 190
SQ FT: 31,000
SALES (est): 35.7MM **Privately Held**
WEB: www.hcdiagnostics.com
SIC: 3821 2835 8071 Laboratory measuring apparatus; in vitro diagnostics; medical laboratories
PA: Hitachi Chemical Company, Ltd.
1-9-2, Marunouchi
Chiyoda-Ku TKY 100-0

(P-20762)
IDEX HEALTH & SCIENCE LLC (HQ)
600 Park Ct, Rohnert Park (94928-7906)
PHONE................................707 588-2000
Jeff Cannon, *President*
Abhi Khandelwal, *Vice Pres*
Christal Morris, *Vice Pres*
Dan Salliotte, *Vice Pres*
Lisa Walsh, *Vice Pres*
▲ EMP: 87
SQ FT: 70,000
SALES (est): 202.5MM
SALES (corp-wide): 2.4B **Publicly Held**
SIC: 3821 3829 3826 3823 Laboratory apparatus & furniture; measuring & controlling devices; analytical instruments; industrial instrmnts msrmnt display/control process variable; valves & pipe fittings

PA: Idex Corporation
1925 W Field Ct Ste 200
Lake Forest IL 60045
847 498-7070

(P-20763)
ISEC INCORPORATED
5735 Krny Vlla Rd Ste 105, San Diego (92123)
PHONE................................858 279-9085
Stan Nagle, *Project Mgr*
Jose Alvarez, *Master*
EMP: 248
SALES (corp-wide): 295.9MM **Privately Held**
SIC: 3821 Laboratory apparatus & furniture
PA: Isec, Incorporated
6000 Greenwood Plaza Blvd # 200
Greenwood Village CO 80111
410 381-6049

(P-20764)
LASER REFERENCE INC
151 Martinvale Ln, San Jose (95119-1454)
PHONE................................408 361-0220
Lee Robson, *President*
Christopher Middleton, *Treasurer*
Mike Middleton, *Admin Sec*
▲ EMP: 35
SQ FT: 9,500
SALES (est): 6.1MM **Privately Held**
WEB: www.proshotlaser.com
SIC: 3821 3829 3699 Laser beam alignment devices; measuring & controlling devices; electrical equipment & supplies

(P-20765)
MARVAC SCIENTIFIC MFG CO
3231 Monument Way Ste I, Concord (94518-2444)
PHONE................................925 825-4636
George Marin, *President*
Steve Marin, *Treasurer*
Douglas Marin, *Vice Pres*
EMP: 18
SQ FT: 20,000
SALES (est): 4MM **Privately Held**
WEB: www.marvacscientific.com
SIC: 3821 Vacuum pumps, laboratory

(P-20766)
MYC DIRECT INC
19977 Harrison Ave, Walnut (91789-2848)
PHONE................................909 287-9919
Michael Chen, *Owner*
▲ EMP: 10
SQ FT: 20,000
SALES (est): 1.2MM **Privately Held**
SIC: 3821 Laboratory apparatus & furniture

(P-20767)
NEWPORT CORPORATION (HQ)
1791 Deere Ave, Irvine (92606-4814)
P.O. Box 19607 (92623-9607)
PHONE................................949 863-3144
Seth Bagshaw, *President*
Derek D'Antilio, *Treasurer*
Jeff Parker, *Vice Pres*
Greg Reischlein, *Vice Pres*
Jackson Sapudar, *Lab Dir*
◆ EMP: 277 EST: 1938
SALES (est): 641MM
SALES (corp-wide): 2B **Publicly Held**
WEB: www.newport.com
SIC: 3821 3699 3827 3826 Worktables, laboratory; laser systems & equipment; optical instruments & lenses; mirrors, optical; prisms, optical; analytical optical instruments; laser scientific & engineering instruments
PA: Mks Instruments, Inc.
2 Tech Dr Ste 201
Andover MA 01810
978 645-5500

(P-20768)
NORTHRDGE TR-MDLITY IMGING INC
Also Called: Trifoil Imaging
9457 De Soto Ave, Chatsworth (91311-4920)
PHONE................................818 709-2468
Kevin Parnham, *President*
Ryan Weirich, *CFO*
EMP: 15 EST: 2013
SQ FT: 11,000

SALES (est): 3.8MM **Privately Held**
SIC: 3821 7699 Clinical laboratory instruments, except medical & dental; medical equipment repair, non-electric

(P-20769)
PARTER MEDICAL PRODUCTS INC
17015 Kingsview Ave, Carson (90746-1220)
PHONE................................310 327-4417
Hormonz Foroughi, *President*
Parviz Hassanzadeh, *Shareholder*
Veronica Andrande, *Manager*
▲ EMP: 160
SQ FT: 40,000
SALES (est): 46.9MM **Privately Held**
WEB: www.partermedical.com
SIC: 3821 Sterilizers

(P-20770)
PASADENA BIO CLLBRTIVE INCBTOR
Also Called: PASADENA BIOSCIENCE COLLOBORAT
2265 E Foothill Blvd, Pasadena (91107-3658)
PHONE................................626 507-8487
Robert Bishop, *President*
Bruce Blonstrom, *President*
EMP: 12
SALES: 689.2K **Privately Held**
SIC: 3821 Incubators, laboratory

(P-20771)
PERFORMANCE PLUS LABORATORIES
3609 Vista Mercado, Camarillo (93012-8055)
P.O. Box 2690 (93011-2690)
PHONE................................805 383-7871
Anthony J Von Teuber, *President*
Dr Tim Barber, *COO*
EMP: 112
SQ FT: 25,000
SALES (est): 1.1MM **Privately Held**
SIC: 3821 Laboratory apparatus, except heating & measuring

(P-20772)
QUALIGEN INC (PA)
2042 Corte Del Nogal A, Carlsbad (92011-1438)
PHONE................................760 918-9165
Paul A Rosinack, *CEO*
Chris Lotz, *CFO*
Christopher L Lotz, *CFO*
Michael S Poirier, *Senior VP*
Wajdi Ahad, *Vice Pres*
EMP: 45
SQ FT: 23,000
SALES (est): 8.5MM **Privately Held**
WEB: www.qualigeninc.com
SIC: 3821 3841 Laboratory apparatus & furniture; surgical & medical instruments

(P-20773)
RYSS LAB INC
29540 Kohoutek Way, Union City (94587-1221)
PHONE................................510 477-9570
Ming Lee, *CEO*
EMP: 13
SQ FT: 1,000
SALES (est): 2.3MM **Privately Held**
WEB: www.ryss.com
SIC: 3821 Chemical laboratory apparatus

(P-20774)
SEPOR INC
718 N Fries Ave, Wilmington (90744-5403)
PHONE................................310 830-6601
Tim Lee Miller, *CEO*
Drew Willis, *COO*
Bud Metcalf, *Engineer*
Allen Souary, *Controller*
Lucy Ortiz, *Manager*
◆ EMP: 11
SQ FT: 6,000
SALES (est): 2.7MM **Privately Held**
WEB: www.sepor.com
SIC: 3821 Sample preparation apparatus; laboratory heating apparatus; crushing & grinding apparatus, laboratory; furnaces, laboratory

(P-20775)
TECAN SYSTEMS INC
2450 Zanker Rd, San Jose (95131-1126)
PHONE................................408 953-3100
David Martyr, *CEO*
Rudolf Eugster, *CFO*
Martin Brusdeilins, *Exec VP*
Michael Winniman, *Regional Mgr*
Sean Leu, *Software Engr*
▲ EMP: 100 EST: 1972
SQ FT: 23,400
SALES (est): 28.2MM
SALES (corp-wide): 597.4MM **Privately Held**
WEB: www.tecansystems.com
SIC: 3821 3829 3561 3494 Laboratory apparatus, except heating & measuring; measuring & controlling devices; pumps & pumping equipment; valves & pipe fittings; unsupported plastics profile shapes; commercial physical research
HQ: Tecan U.S. Group, Inc.
9401 Globe Center Dr # 140
Morrisville NC 27560
919 361-5200

(P-20776)
THERMOGENESIS HOLDINGS INC (PA)
Also Called: Cesca Therapeutics
2711 Citrus Rd, Rancho Cordova (95742-6228)
PHONE................................916 858-5100
Xiaochun Xu, *Ch of Bd*
Jeff Cauble, *CFO*
James Xu, *Senior VP*
Paul Hoseit, *Vice Pres*
Elana McVay, *Office Mgr*
▲ EMP: 53
SQ FT: 28,000
SALES (est): 9.6MM **Publicly Held**
WEB: www.thermogenesis.com
SIC: 3821 Freezers, laboratory

(P-20777)
TLI ENTERPRISES INC (PA)
3118 Depot Rd, Hayward (94545-2708)
P.O. Box 3711 (94540-3711)
PHONE................................510 538-3304
John Trujillo, *CEO*
Shawn Trujillo, *President*
EMP: 30 EST: 1937
SQ FT: 18,000
SALES (est): 12MM **Privately Held**
WEB: www.thermionicscorp.com
SIC: 3821 3471 Vacuum pumps, laboratory; cleaning, polishing & finishing

(P-20778)
TORREY PINES SCIENTIFIC INC
2713 Loker Ave W, Carlsbad (92010-6601)
PHONE................................760 930-9400
Michael Cassiano, *CEO*
Caroline Cassiano, *President*
Anthony Cassiano, *Chairman*
▲ EMP: 10
SALES (est): 4MM **Privately Held**
WEB: www.torreypinesscientific.com
SIC: 3821 Laboratory equipment: fume hoods, distillation racks, etc.

(P-20779)
TOTAL SOURCE MANUFACTURING
Also Called: Total Source Manufacturing Co
1445 Engineer St, Vista (92081-8846)
PHONE................................760 598-2146
Stacy Camp, *President*
▲ EMP: 1800
SALES (est): 146.6MM **Privately Held**
WEB: www.tsmfg.com
SIC: 3821 Laboratory equipment: fume hoods, distillation racks, etc.

3822 Automatic Temperature Controls

(P-20780)
ACS CONTROLS CORPORATION
4704 Roseville Rd Ste 101, North Highlands (95660-5173)
PHONE................................916 640-8800
Mitch Slavensky, *President*

EMP: 13
SQ FT: 4,000
SALES: 2.2MM **Privately Held**
WEB: www.acscontrols.net
SIC: 3822 Building services monitoring controls, automatic

(P-20781)
AIR DRY CO OF AMERICA LLC
1740 Commerce Way, Paso Robles (93446-3620)
PHONE..................................805 238-2840
Jeff Watson, *President*
Patricia Harris, *Manager*
EMP: 20
SQ FT: 20,000
SALES (est): 2.8MM **Privately Held**
SIC: 3822 Auto controls regulating residntl & coml environmt & applncs

(P-20782)
AIR MONITOR CORPORATION (PA)
1050 Hopper Ave, Santa Rosa (95403-1695)
P.O. Box 6358 (95406-0358)
PHONE..................................707 544-2706
Dean De Baun, *CEO*
Sharon Hughes, *CFO*
Chris De Baun, *Admin Sec*
Paresh Dave, *Manager*
EMP: 70
SQ FT: 50,000
SALES (est): 12.5MM **Privately Held**
WEB: www.airmonitor.com
SIC: 3822 Air flow controllers, air conditioning & refrigeration

(P-20783)
AROMYX CORPORATION
319 Bernardo Ave, Mountain View (94043-5225)
PHONE..................................650 430-8100
Josh Silverman, *CEO*
Christopher Hanson, *Chairman*
Luke Schneider, *Bd of Directors*
Ed Costello, *Vice Pres*
Victor Cushman, *Vice Pres*
EMP: 14
SALES (est): 1.9MM **Privately Held**
WEB: www.pervasivebiosensors.com
SIC: 3822 Auto controls regulating residntl & coml environmt & applncs

(P-20784)
AVC SPECIALISTS INC
5146 N Commerce Ave Ste G, Moorpark (93021-7138)
PHONE..................................513 458-2600
Tom Shideler, *President*
Barbara Shideler, *Admin Sec*
▼ **EMP:** 20 **EST:** 1977
SQ FT: 5,000
SALES (est): 4MM
SALES (corp-wide): 337.3MM **Publicly Held**
WEB: www.avcspecialists.com
SIC: 3822 Electric air cleaner controls, automatic
PA: Ceco Environmental Corp.
14651 Dallas Pkwy Ste 50
Dallas TX 75254
214 357-6181

(P-20785)
C3-ILEX LLC (PA)
46609 Fremont Blvd, Fremont (94538-6410)
P.O. Box 3224, Los Altos (94024-0224)
PHONE..................................510 659-8300
Sue Schwee, *President*
John Klimaszewski, *Vice Pres*
EMP: 21
SQ FT: 15,000
SALES (est): 4.9MM **Privately Held**
WEB: www.c3ilex.com
SIC: 3822 Auto controls regulating residntl & coml environmt & applncs

(P-20786)
CATALYTIC SOLUTIONS INC (HQ)
1700 Fiske Pl, Oxnard (93033-1863)
PHONE..................................805 486-4649
David Gann, *CEO*
Charlie Karl, *CEO*

Kevin McDonnell, *CFO*
Dan McGuire, *Vice Pres*
Steven Golden, *CTO*
▲ **EMP:** 69
SQ FT: 75,000
SALES (est): 22.4MM **Privately Held**
WEB: www.catsoln.com
SIC: 3822 Auto controls regulating residntl & coml environmt & applncs

(P-20787)
CHRONOMITE LABORATORIES INC
17451 Hurley St, City of Industry (91744-5106)
P.O. Box 3527 (91744-0527)
PHONE..................................310 534-2300
Donald E Morris, *CEO*
Cathy Milostan, *Sales Staff*
▲ **EMP:** 34
SALES: 6.5MM
SALES (corp-wide): 85MM **Privately Held**
WEB: www.chronomite.com
SIC: 3822 8731 3432 Water heater controls; commercial physical research; plumbing fixture fittings & trim
PA: Acorn Engineering Company
15125 Proctor Ave
City Of Industry CA 91746
800 488-8999

(P-20788)
CLEAR SKIES SOLUTIONS INC
2345 Mirada Ct, Tracy (95377-0217)
PHONE..................................925 570-4471
Scott Vaughn, *CEO*
EMP: 12
SALES: 950K **Privately Held**
SIC: 3822 Auto controls regulating residntl & coml environmt & applncs

(P-20789)
CONTRCTOR CMPLIANCE MONITORING
2343 Donnington Way, San Diego (92139-2927)
PHONE..................................619 472-9065
Deborah Wilder, *Branch Mgr*
Jessica Finau, *Opers Mgr*
EMP: 22
SALES (corp-wide): 2.5MM **Privately Held**
SIC: 3822 5082 Building services monitoring controls, automatic; general construction machinery & equipment
PA: Contractor Compliance & Monitoring Inc
635 Mariners Island Blvd 200b
San Mateo CA 94404
650 522-4403

(P-20790)
CRGSYNERGY
21 Commercial Blvd Ste 14, Novato (94949-6109)
PHONE..................................415 497-0182
Eli Cohen, *Ch of Bd*
EMP: 20
SQ FT: 20,000
SALES (est): 1.5MM **Privately Held**
SIC: 3822 Building services monitoring controls, automatic

(P-20791)
EARTHSAVERS EROSION CTRL LLC
12972 County Road 102, Woodland (95776-9119)
P.O. Box 2083 (95776-2083)
PHONE..................................530 662-7700
Darrell Hinz, *Mng Member*
Doug Bailey,
Greg Baker,
EMP: 13 **EST:** 2009
SALES (est): 4.8MM **Privately Held**
SIC: 3822 5039 Auto controls regulating residntl & coml environmt & applncs; soil erosion control fabrics

(P-20792)
ECO GLOBAL SOLUTIONS INC
221 Gateway Rd W Ste 403, NAPA (94558-6623)
P.O. Box 4350 (94558-0567)
PHONE..................................707 254-9844
Joseph Chuang, *CEO*
Jessie Hastings, *CTO*
EMP: 10
SALES (est): 1.3MM **Privately Held**
SIC: 3822 3826 Auto controls regulating residntl & coml environmt & applncs; environmental testing equipment

(P-20793)
ELECTRASEM CORP
372 Elizabeth Ln, Corona (92880-2528)
PHONE..................................951 371-6140
Don S Edwards, *President*
▲ **EMP:** 17
SALES (est): 3MM
SALES (corp-wide): 1.3B **Publicly Held**
WEB: www.generalmonitors.com
SIC: 3822 Electric heat proportioning controls, modulating controls
HQ: General Monitors, Inc.
26776 Simpatica Cir
Lake Forest CA 92630
949 581-4464

(P-20794)
FIRST AMERICAN BUILDING SVCS
6 Commodore Dr Unit 530, Emeryville (94608-1639)
PHONE..................................415 299-7597
Justin Sina Moayed, *President*
EMP: 10 **EST:** 2017
SALES (est): 542.6K **Privately Held**
SIC: 3822 Building services monitoring controls, automatic

(P-20795)
GEM MOBILE TREATMENT SVCS INC (HQ)
2525 Cherry Ave Ste 105, Signal Hill (90755-2054)
PHONE..................................562 595-7075
Paul Anderson, *COO*
Shane Whittington, *CFO*
Pam Patterson, *Manager*
EMP: 22
SALES (est): 24.5MM **Privately Held**
SIC: 3822 1629 Vapor heating controls; waste water & sewage treatment plant construction

(P-20796)
HONEYWELL INTERNATIONAL INC
2055 Dublin Dr, San Diego (92154-8203)
PHONE..................................619 671-5612
Virgel McCormick, *Manager*
Enrique Del Villar, *Design Engr*
EMP: 110
SALES (corp-wide): 41.8B **Publicly Held**
WEB: www.honeywell.com
SIC: 3822 3494 Auto controls regulating residntl & coml environmt & applncs; valves & pipe fittings
PA: Honeywell International Inc.
300 S Tryon St
Charlotte NC 28202
973 455-2000

(P-20797)
LINK4 CORPORATION
175 E Freedom Ave, Anaheim (92801-1006)
PHONE..................................714 524-0004
Yen Pham, *President*
Fred Kaifer, *Vice Pres*
▲ **EMP:** 11
SALES (est): 2.6MM **Privately Held**
WEB: www.link4corp.com
SIC: 3822 Auto controls regulating residntl & coml environmt & applncs

(P-20798)
MICRO GROW GREENHOUSE SYSTEMS
42065 Zevo Dr Ste B1, Temecula (92590-3746)
PHONE..................................951 296-3340
Thomas Piini, *President*

Hunter Weeks, *Software Dev*
Dane Martin, *Prdtn Mgr*
▲ **EMP:** 10
SQ FT: 4,000
SALES (est): 2.3MM **Privately Held**
WEB: www.microgrow.com
SIC: 3822 Controls, combination limit & fan

(P-20799)
MOLEKULE INC (PA)
1301 Folsom St, San Francisco (94103-3818)
PHONE..................................352 871-3803
Lovely Goswami, *President*
Dilip Goswami, *CEO*
Jaya RAO, *COO*
Peter Riering-Czekalla, *Chief Mktg Ofcr*
Gaurav Agarwal, *Vice Pres*
EMP: 10
SALES (est): 2.9MM **Privately Held**
SIC: 3822 3829 Air flow controllers, air conditioning & refrigeration; measuring & controlling devices

(P-20800)
NEWMATIC ENGINEERING INC (PA)
355 Goddard Ste 250, Irvine (92618-4644)
PHONE..................................415 824-2664
Richard Yardley, *President*
Sydney Kwan, *Treasurer*
EMP: 12
SQ FT: 21,000
SALES (est): 3.1MM **Privately Held**
WEB: www.newmatic.net
SIC: 3822 Air flow controllers, air conditioning & refrigeration

(P-20801)
NVENT THERMAL LLC (DH)
899 Broadway St, Redwood City (94063-3104)
PHONE..................................650 474-7414
Brad Faulconer, *President*
Pele Myers, *Mktg Dir*
Spencer Leslie, *Director*
▲ **EMP:** 300
SQ FT: 65,000
SALES: 750MM **Privately Held**
WEB: www.tycothermal.com
SIC: 3822 1711 Auto controls regulating residntl & coml environmt & applncs; heating & air conditioning contractors
HQ: Nvent Management Company
1665 Utica Ave S Ste 700
Saint Louis Park MN 55416
763 204-7700

(P-20802)
OLS CONTROLS
15215 Old Ranch Rd, Los Gatos (95033-8329)
PHONE..................................408 353-6564
Joseph Ols, *Principal*
EMP: 10
SALES: 500K **Privately Held**
SIC: 3822 Auto controls regulating residntl & coml environmt & applncs

(P-20803)
PARAGON CONTROLS INCORPORATED
Also Called: PCI
2371 Circadian Way, Santa Rosa (95407-5439)
P.O. Box 99, Forestville (95436-0099)
PHONE..................................707 579-1424
Richard Thomas Reis, *President*
Cheryl Reis, *Treasurer*
Larry E Winterbourne, *Vice Pres*
Dennis Reis, *Admin Sec*
▲ **EMP:** 15
SQ FT: 8,200
SALES (est): 3.7MM **Privately Held**
WEB: www.paragoncontrols.com
SIC: 3822 3823 Air flow controllers, air conditioning & refrigeration; fan control, temperature responsive; pressure controllers, air-conditioning system type; primary elements for process flow measurement

---

(P-20804)
PERTRONIX INC (PA)
440 E Arrow Hwy, San Dimas
(91773-3340)
PHONE....................................909 599-5955
Thomas A Reh, *CEO*
Thomas Reh, *CFO*
Joh R Sherer, *Vice Pres*
▲ EMP: 40
SQ FT: 22,000
SALES (est): 13.8MM Privately Held
WEB: www.pertronix.com
SIC: 3822 3694 Auto controls regulating
residntl & coml environmt & applncs; igni-
tion apparatus, internal combustion en-
gines

(P-20805)
REC SOLAR COMMERCIAL CORP
3450 Broad St Ste 105, San Luis Obispo
(93401-7214)
PHONE....................................844 732-7652
Matt Walz, *CEO*
Gary Morris, *CFO*
EMP: 120 EST: 2013
SQ FT: 15,000
SALES (est): 303.1K
SALES (corp-wide): 24.5B Publicly Held
SIC: 3822 Energy cutoff controls, residen-
tial or commercial types
PA: Duke Energy Corporation
550 S Tryon St
Charlotte NC 28202
704 382-3853

(P-20806)
RED MOUNTAIN INC
Also Called: J&B Mountain Holding
17767 Mitchell N, Irvine (92614-6028)
PHONE....................................949 595-4475
Brian Slezak, *President*
Jay Murata, *CFO*
▼ EMP: 12
SALES (est): 1.9MM Privately Held
WEB: www.redmtnengr.com
SIC: 3822 Auto controls regulating residntl
& coml environmt & applncs

(P-20807)
RESIDENTIAL CTRL SYSTEMS INC
Also Called: R C S
11481 Sunrise Gold Cir # 1, Rancho Cor-
dova (95742-6545)
PHONE....................................916 635-6784
Michael Kuhlmann, *President*
Mike Hoffman, *Vice Pres*
Michael Hoffman, *CTO*
Gene Goodell, *VP Mktg*
EMP: 25
SALES (est): 2MM Privately Held
SIC: 3822 Damper operators: pneumatic,
thermostatic, electric; pneumatic relays,
air-conditioning type; energy cutoff con-
trols, residential or commercial types

(P-20808)
SALUS NORTH AMERICA INC
Also Called: Salus Enterprises of N Amer
850 Main St, Redwood City (94063-1902)
PHONE....................................888 387-2587
Shen Owyang, *President*
Janine M Kinney, *Admin Sec*
Rebecca Tiu, *Finance Dir*
EMP: 13
SALES (est): 4.1MM Privately Held
SIC: 3822 Thermostats & other environ-
mental sensors
HQ: Computime Group Limited
6/F Hong Kong Science Park Bldg 20e
Ph 3
Sha Tin NT

(P-20809)
SENSIT INC
1652 Plum Ln Ste 106, Redlands
(92374-4594)
PHONE....................................909 793-5816
Shudong Zhou, *President*
Huiling Chen, *Admin Sec*
▲ EMP: 14

SALES (est): 1.4MM Privately Held
SIC: 3822 Thermostats & other environmental sensors

(P-20810)
SENTINEL OFFENDER SERVICES LLC
16046 Amar Rd, City of Industry
(91744-2203)
PHONE....................................626 336-5150
James Barrios, *Manager*
EMP: 10
SALES (corp-wide): 71.6MM Privately
Held
WEB: www.sentrak.com
SIC: 3822 Auto controls regulating residntl
& coml environmt & applncs
PA: Sentinel Offender Services Llc
1290 N Hancock St Ste 103
Anaheim CA 92807
949 453-1550

(P-20811)
SFC COMMUNICATIONS INC
65 Post Ste 1000, Irvine (92618-5216)
PHONE....................................949 553-8566
Saundra Jacobs, *President*
EMP: 10 EST: 2010
SALES (est): 1.4MM Privately Held
SIC: 3822 Auto controls regulating residntl
& coml environmt & applncs

(P-20812)
SIEMENS INDUSTRY INC
6 Journey Ste 200, Aliso Viejo
(92656-5321)
PHONE....................................949 448-0600
Linda Wang, *Principal*
EMP: 97
SALES (corp-wide): 95B Privately Held
SIC: 3822 Air conditioning & refrigeration
controls
HQ: Siemens Industry, Inc.
1000 Deerfield Pkwy
Buffalo Grove IL 60089
847 215-1000

(P-20813)
SIEMENS INDUSTRY INC
2775 Goodrick Ave, Richmond
(94801-1109)
PHONE....................................510 237-2325
EMP: 81
SALES (corp-wide): 95B Privately Held
SIC: 3822 Air conditioning & refrigeration
controls
HQ: Siemens Industry, Inc.
1000 Deerfield Pkwy
Buffalo Grove IL 60089
847 215-1000

(P-20814)
SIEMENS INDUSTRY INC
3650 Industrial Blvd # 100, West Sacra-
mento (95691-6512)
PHONE....................................916 553-4444
Rick Glaser, *Principal*
BEI Xu, *Software Engr*
Aaldrik Metting, *Project Mgr*
Walter Bixby, *Engineer*
Sebastian Ziegler, *Finance*
EMP: 13
SALES (corp-wide): 95B Privately Held
WEB: www.sibt.com
SIC: 3822 Thermostats & other environ-
mental sensors
HQ: Siemens Industry, Inc.
1000 Deerfield Pkwy
Buffalo Grove IL 60089
847 215-1000

(P-20815)
SIEMENS INDUSTRY INC
7464 French Rd, Sacramento
(95828-4600)
PHONE....................................916 681-3000
Oliver Hauck, *Branch Mgr*
Nicola Terry, *Executive Asst*
Vasiliy Karamalak, *Electrical Engi*
Lennart Bergstrom, *Engineer*
George Long, *Engineer*
EMP: 200

SALES (corp-wide): 95B Privately Held
SIC: 3822 5063 3669 1731 Air conditioning & refrigeration controls; thermostats &
other environmental sensors; electric
alarms & signaling equipment; emergency
alarms; safety & security specialization;
security systems services; relays & industrial controls
HQ: Siemens Industry, Inc.
1000 Deerfield Pkwy
Buffalo Grove IL 60089
847 215-1000

(P-20816)
T&L AIR CONDITIONING INC
164 W Live Oak Ave, Arcadia (91007-8562)
PHONE....................................626 294-9888
Shinn Liu, *President*
EMP: 15
SQ FT: 2,928
SALES (est): 2.8MM Privately Held
SIC: 3822 Air flow controllers, air condition-
ing & refrigeration

(P-20817)
TRANSFIRST CORPORATION
900 E Blanco Rd, Salinas (93901-4419)
P.O. Box 1788 (93902-1788)
PHONE....................................831 424-2911
James Lugg, *President*
Richard Macleod, *Vice Pres*
Teresa Scattini, *Vice Pres*
Norma Johnson, *Executive Asst*
Cathy Kuehl, *Controller*
▲ EMP: 27
SALES (est): 7.8MM Privately Held
WEB: www.transfresh.com
SIC: 3822 Air conditioning & refrigeration
controls

(P-20818)
TRUE FRESH HPP LLC
6535 Caballero Blvd B, Buena Park
(90620-8106)
PHONE....................................949 629-7645
Veronica Gomez, *VP Human Res*
Patrick Jacobi, *Director*
EMP: 15 EST: 2015
SALES (est): 3.4MM Privately Held
SIC: 3822 Refrigeration controls (pressure)

(P-20819)
VERMILLIONS ENVIRONMENTAL
Also Called: Envirnmental Pdts Applications
78900 Avenue 47 Ste 106, La Quinta
(92253-2070)
PHONE....................................760 777-8035
John Vermillion, *President*
EMP: 20
SALES (est): 5.6MM Privately Held
SIC: 3822 Auto controls regulating residntl
& coml environmt & applncs

(P-20820)
VIGILENT CORPORATION (PA)
1111 Broadway Fl 3, Oakland
(94607-4139)
PHONE....................................888 305-4451
David Hudson, *CEO*
Dave Hudson, *Officer*
Andrew Gordon, *Vice Pres*
Jeff Rauenhorst, *Vice Pres*
Jonathan Lee, *Sr Software Eng*
EMP: 32
SALES (est): 4.8MM Privately Held
SIC: 3822 Auto controls regulating residntl
& coml environmt & applncs

(P-20821)
VOLTUS INC
2442 Fillmore St, San Francisco
(94115-1815)
PHONE....................................415 617-9602
Gregg Dixon, *CEO*
Matthew Plante, *President*
Stephanie Hendricks, *Vice Pres*
EMP: 45 EST: 2016
SALES (est): 386.1K Privately Held
SIC: 3822 3829 Auto controls regulating
residntl & coml environmt & applncs;
measuring & controlling devices

(P-20822)
WATER HEATER WAREHOUSE LLC
1853 W Commonwealth Ave, Fullerton
(92833-3035)
PHONE....................................714 244-8562
Christian Flores, *Mng Member*
EMP: 13 EST: 2014
SALES (est): 2.4MM Privately Held
SIC: 3822 Water heater controls

(P-20823)
X CONTROLS INC
6640 Lusk Blvd Ste A101, San Diego
(92121-2771)
PHONE....................................858 717-0004
Tom Karpecki, *President*
Boris Batiyenko, *Vice Pres*
EMP: 12
SALES (est): 1MM Privately Held
SIC: 3822 3699 1731 7382 Building serv-
ices monitoring controls, automatic; secu-
rity control equipment & systems;
computerized controls installation; secu-
rity systems services; auditing services

3823 Indl Instruments For Meas, Display & Control

(P-20824)
3D INSTRUMENTS LP (DH)
Also Called: Sierra Precision
4990 E Hunter Ave, Anaheim (92807-2057)
PHONE....................................714 399-9200
Felix Brockmeyer, *VP Opers*
Michael Gerster, *President*
Garey Cooper, *Vice Pres*
Agus Kusumadi, *Engineer*
Sheila Ivy, *Purchasing*
EMP: 41
SQ FT: 22,500
SALES (est): 13.1MM
SALES (corp-wide): 533.8MM Privately
Held
WEB: www.3dhb.com
SIC: 3823 Pressure gauges, dial & digital
HQ: Wika Holding, L P
1000 Wiegand Blvd
Lawrenceville GA 30043
770 513-8200

(P-20825)
ACCU-GAGE & THREAD GRINDING CO
40 S San Gabriel Blvd, Pasadena
(91107-3750)
PHONE....................................626 568-2932
Conrad A Vios, *President*
EMP: 10
SQ FT: 4,000
SALES: 1MM Privately Held
WEB: www.accugageandthread.com
SIC: 3823 Pressure measurement instru-
ments, industrial

(P-20826)
ACS INSTRUMENTATION VALVES INC
3065 Richmond Pkwy # 106, Richmond
(94806-5719)
PHONE....................................510 262-1880
Elizabeth Niemczyk, *CEO*
EMP: 99
SALES (est): 3.5MM Privately Held
SIC: 3823 Industrial instrmnts msrmnt dis-
play/control process variable

(P-20827)
ADS LLC
Also Called: A D S Environmental Srvs
15205 Springdale St, Huntington Beach
(92649-1156)
PHONE....................................714 379-9778
Paul Mitchell, *Manager*
EMP: 25
SALES (corp-wide): 2.4B Publicly Held
SIC: 3823 8748 Flow instruments, indus-
trial process type; environmental consult-
ant

▲ = Import ▼=Export
◆ =Import/Export

HQ: Ads Llc
    340 The Bridge St Ste 204
    Huntsville AL 35806
    256 430-3366

(P-20828)
ADVANCED ELECTROMAGNETICS INC
Also Called: Aemi
1320 Air Wing Rd Ste 101, San Diego
(92154-7707)
PHONE.....................................619 449-9492
Per Iversen, *President*
Doriana Maciel, *Admin Asst*
Monica Jaramillo, *Controller*
Eder Marengo, *Production*
◆ **EMP:** 37 **EST:** 1980
SQ FT: 16,000
SALES (est): 9.5MM
SALES (corp-wide): 16.5MM **Privately Held**
SIC: 3823 3825 Absorption analyzers: infrared, X-ray, etc.: industrial; instruments to measure electricity
HQ: Orbit/Fr, Inc.
    650 Louis Dr Ste 100
    Warminster PA 18974
    -

(P-20829)
ADVANCED PRESSURE TECHNOLOGY
Also Called: AP Tech
687 Technology Way, NAPA (94558-7512)
PHONE.....................................707 259-0102
Rene Zakhour, *President*
Kambiz Farnaam, *Vice Pres*
Barbara Cornelius, *Admin Asst*
Roman Sheykhet, *Project Engr*
Elisa McClure, *Opers Mgr*
▲ **EMP:** 95
SALES (est): 32.8MM **Privately Held**
WEB: www.aptech-online.com
SIC: 3823 Pressure gauges, dial & digital

(P-20830)
ALPHA SENSORS INC
Also Called: Alpha Technics
125 S Tremont St Ste 100, Oceanside
(92054-3028)
PHONE.....................................949 250-6578
Daniel M O'Brien, *CEO*
Lisa Marie Ryan, *President*
David Boydston, *Engineer*
Linda Lee, *Accountant*
EMP: 24
SALES (est): 5.4MM **Privately Held**
WEB: www.alphatechnics.com
SIC: 3823 Temperature measurement instruments, industrial

(P-20831)
ALPHA TECHNICS INC
125 S Tremont St Ste 100, Oceanside
(92054-3028)
PHONE.....................................949 250-6578
Lisa Marie Ryan, *President*
EMP: 200 **EST:** 2011
SQ FT: 6,000
SALES (est): 30.4MM
SALES (corp-wide): 13.9B **Privately Held**
SIC: 3823 Industrial instrmnts msrmnt display/control process variable
HQ: Te Connectivity Inc.
    601 13th St Nw Ste 850s
    Washington DC 20005
    202 471-3400

(P-20832)
AMETEK AMERON LLC (HQ)
Also Called: Mass Systems
4750 Littlejohn St, Baldwin Park
(91706-2274)
PHONE.....................................626 856-0101
Keith Marsicola, *Mng Member*
Ramy Ghebrial, *General Mgr*
Michael Mallari, *Engineer*
Maria Gomez, *Buyer*
Ken Wright, *VP Mfg*
EMP: 55
SQ FT: 2,600

SALES (est): 17.3MM
SALES (corp-wide): 4.8B **Publicly Held**
SIC: 3823 3999 3728 8711 Pressure gauges, dial & digital; fire extinguishers, portable; aircraft parts & equipment; industrial engineers; clothing, fire resistant & protective
PA: Ametek, Inc.
    1100 Cassatt Rd
    Berwyn PA 19312
    610 647-2121

(P-20833)
AMOBEE INC
10201 Wtridge Cir Ste 200, San Diego
(92121)
PHONE.....................................858 638-1515
Steven Kline, *Surgery Dir*
EMP: 13
SALES (corp-wide): 13MM **Privately Held**
SIC: 3823 Digital displays of process variables
HQ: Amobee, Inc.
    901 Marshall St 200
    Redwood City CA 94063

(P-20834)
ANALYTICAL INDUSTRIES INC
Also Called: Advanced Instruments
2855 Metropolitan Pl, Pomona
(91767-1853)
PHONE.....................................909 392-6900
Frank S Gregus, *President*
Patrick J Prindible, *Vice Pres*
Mohammad Razaq, *Vice Pres*
Paul Espiritu, *Purch Mgr*
Mark Gregus, *VP Opers*
EMP: 45
SQ FT: 15,000
SALES (est): 9.3MM **Privately Held**
WEB: www.aii1.com
SIC: 3823 On-stream gas/liquid analysis instruments, industrial

(P-20835)
APPLIED INSTRUMENT TECH INC
2121 Aviation Dr, Upland (91786-2195)
PHONE.....................................909 204-3700
Joseph Laconte, *President*
EMP: 40
SALES (est): 10.4MM
SALES (corp-wide): 177.9K **Privately Held**
SIC: 3823 Industrial instrmnts msrmnt display/control process variable
HQ: Schneider Electric Usa, Inc.
    201 Wshington St Ste 2700
    Boston MA 02108
    978 975-9600

(P-20836)
ARGA CONTROLS INC
10410 Trademark St, Rancho Cucamonga
(91730-5826)
PHONE.....................................626 799-3314
Bob Pineau, *President*
Linda Halsey, *President*
EMP: 18
SALES (est): 3.5MM **Privately Held**
WEB: www.arizonasunsales.com
SIC: 3823 3829 3625 3613 Industrial instrmnts msrmnt display/control process variable; measuring & controlling devices; relays & industrial controls; switchgear & switchboard apparatus

(P-20837)
AUTOFLOW PRODUCTS CO
15915 S San Pedro St, Gardena
(90248-2555)
PHONE.....................................310 515-2866
EMP: 15
SQ FT: 6,500
SALES (est): 1.5MM **Privately Held**
WEB: www.autoflowproducts.com
SIC: 3823 3491

(P-20838)
BAMBECK SYSTEMS INC (PA)
1921 Carnegie Ave Ste 3a, Santa Ana
(92705-5510)
PHONE.....................................949 250-3100
Robert J Bambeck, *President*

Robert Deweerd, *Vice Pres*
Melinda Yoshida, *Finance*
EMP: 19
SQ FT: 6,100
SALES (est): 3.2MM **Privately Held**
WEB: www.bambecksystems.com
SIC: 3823 Boiler controls: industrial, power & marine type

(P-20839)
BESTEST INTERNATIONAL
Also Called: Bestest Medical
181 W Orangethorpe Ave C, Placentia
(92870-6931)
PHONE.....................................714 974-8837
Pamela Bogart, *President*
John Bogart, *CFO*
EMP: 15
SQ FT: 9,200
SALES (est): 5MM **Privately Held**
SIC: 3823 3841 Industrial instrmnts msrmnt display/control process variable; surgical & medical instruments

(P-20840)
BIODOT INC (PA)
2852 Alton Pkwy, Irvine (92606-5104)
PHONE.....................................949 440-3685
Thomas C Tisone, *CEO*
Barbara McIntosh, *Vice Pres*
Trish Morley, *Office Mgr*
Annette Payer, *Office Mgr*
Steven Chang, *Sr Software Eng*
EMP: 30
SQ FT: 24,000
SALES (est): 4.6MM **Privately Held**
WEB: www.biodot.com
SIC: 3823 3826 Industrial instrmnts msrmnt display/control process variable; analytical instruments

(P-20841)
BRILLIANT INSTRUMENTS INC
1622 W Campbell Ave 107, Campbell
(95008-1535)
PHONE.....................................408 866-0426
Shalom Kattan, *CEO*
EMP: 12
SALES (est): 1.8MM **Privately Held**
SIC: 3823 Industrial process control instruments

(P-20842)
BROADLEY-JAMES-CORPORATION
19 Thomas, Irvine (92618-2704)
PHONE.....................................949 829-5555
Leighton S Broadley, *CFO*
Dan Folwell, *General Mgr*
Catherine A Broadley, *Admin Sec*
Joseph Cracchiolo, *Info Tech Dir*
Leighton Broadley, *Prgrmr*
EMP: 65
SQ FT: 24,000
SALES (est): 17.9MM **Privately Held**
WEB: www.broadleyjames.com
SIC: 3823 3822 Electrodes used in industrial process measurement; auto controls regulating residntl & coml environmt & applncs

(P-20843)
CALIFRNIA ANLYTICAL INSTRS INC
1312 W Grove Ave, Orange (92865-4136)
PHONE.....................................714 974-5560
R Pete Furton, *President*
Loren T Mathews, *Corp Secy*
Harold J Peper, *Exec VP*
Jim Mabe, *Design Engr*
Todd Harrison, *Technical Staff*
EMP: 55
SQ FT: 26,400
SALES (est): 14.6MM **Privately Held**
WEB: www.gasanalyzers.com
SIC: 3823 Industrial instrmnts msrmnt display/control process variable

(P-20844)
CAMERON TECHNOLOGIES US INC
Also Called: Cameron's Measurement Systems
4040 Capitol Ave, Whittier (90601-1735)
PHONE.....................................562 222-8440

Victor Hart, *Plant Mgr*
EMP: 100 **Publicly Held**
SIC: 3823 Industrial flow & liquid measuring instruments
HQ: Cameron Technologies Us, Inc.
    1000 Mcclaren Woods Dr
    Coraopolis PA 15108

(P-20845)
CANNALINK INC
110 W C St Ste 1300, San Diego
(92101-3978)
PHONE.....................................310 921-1955
Robert Plomgren, *CEO*
Robert Malasek, *CFO*
James Truher, *Chairman*
Ed Hart, *Vice Pres*
Robert L McCauley, *CTO*
EMP: 10 **EST:** 1997
SQ FT: 37,000
SALES (est): 1.4MM **Privately Held**
SIC: 3823 4899 4841 Computer interface equipment for industrial process control; data communication services; cable & other pay television services

(P-20846)
CARMEL INSTRUMENTS LLC
1622 W Campbell Ave, Campbell
(95008-1535)
PHONE.....................................408 866-0426
Shulamith Sofge, *General Mgr*
EMP: 10
SQ FT: 5,000
SALES (est): 591.5K **Privately Held**
SIC: 3823 Industrial process control instruments

(P-20847)
CBRITE INC
421 Pine Ave, Goleta (93117-3709)
PHONE.....................................805 722-1121
Boo Nilsson, *President*
EMP: 17
SALES (est): 4.3MM **Privately Held**
SIC: 3823 8731 Industrial instrmnts msrmnt display/control process variable; electronic research

(P-20848)
CELAMARK CORP
8 Digital Dr Ste 100, Novato (94949-5759)
P.O. Box 2333 (94948-2333)
PHONE.....................................415 883-3386
Charles Ray, *President*
▲ **EMP:** 25
SALES (est): 3.2MM **Privately Held**
WEB: www.celamark.com
SIC: 3823 2389 3822 2671 Controllers for process variables, all types; disposable garments & accessories; auto controls regulating residntl & coml environmt & applncs; packaging paper & plastics film, coated & laminated

(P-20849)
CK TECHNOLOGIES INC (PA)
Also Called: Ckt
3629 Vista Mercado, Camarillo
(93012-8055)
PHONE.....................................805 987-4801
Karl F Zimmermann, *President*
Heidi Zimmerman, *Vice Pres*
Heidi Zimmermann, *Info Tech Mgr*
Serban Lungu, *VP Engrg*
EMP: 33
SQ FT: 34,000
SALES (est): 9.6MM **Privately Held**
WEB: www.ckt.com
SIC: 3823 3825 5065 Water quality monitoring & control systems; instruments to measure electricity; electronic parts & equipment

(P-20850)
CONDOR ELECTRONICS INC
990 San Antonio Rd, Palo Alto
(94303-4917)
PHONE.....................................408 745-7141
Christian Dorward, *President*
▲ **EMP:** 30
SQ FT: 7,300

SALES: 11MM **Privately Held**
WEB: www.condorelectronics.net
SIC: **3823** 5065 Panelboard indicators, recorders & controllers: receiver; electronic parts & equipment

(P-20851)
CONTINENTAL CONTROLS CORP
7720 Kenamar Ct Ste C, San Diego (92121-2425)
PHONE.................................858 453-9880
Carlyn Ross Fisher, *CEO*
Ross Fisher, *President*
David Fisher, *Vice Pres*
Richard Fisher, *Vice Pres*
Rick Fisher, *Vice Pres*
▲ EMP: 24
SQ FT: 17,000
SALES (est): 7.5MM **Privately Held**
WEB: www.continentalcontrols.com
SIC: **3823** Industrial instrmnts msrmnt display/control process variable

(P-20852)
COUNTY OF NAPA
Also Called: Flood Ctrl Wtr Cnservation Dst
804 1st St, NAPA (94559-2623)
PHONE.................................707 259-8620
Robert Peterson, *Director*
EMP: 15 **Privately Held**
WEB: www.billkeller.com
SIC: **3823** Water quality monitoring & control systems
PA: County Of Napa
  1195 Third St Ste 310
  Napa CA 94559
  707 253-4421

(P-20853)
CRYSTAL ENGINEERING CORP
708 Fiero Ln Ste 9, San Luis Obispo (93401-7945)
P.O. Box 3033 (93403-3033)
PHONE.................................805 595-5477
David Porter, *President*
Matthew Haas, *Vice Pres*
Nielson Sean, *Marketing Mgr*
Jeff Gartner, *Sales Staff*
Jim Pronge, *Sales Staff*
▲ EMP: 38
SALES (est): 9.8MM
SALES (corp-wide): 4.8B **Publicly Held**
WEB: www.crystalengineering.net
SIC: **3823** Pressure gauges, dial & digital; industrial process measurement equipment
PA: Ametek, Inc.
  1100 Cassatt Rd
  Berwyn PA 19312
  610 647-2121

(P-20854)
CYBERWARE LABORATORY INC
12835 Corte Cordillera, Salinas (93908-8964)
PHONE.................................831 484-1064
David Addleman, *President*
Lloyd Addleman, *Treasurer*
Stephen Addleman, *Vice Pres*
Sue Addleman, *Vice Pres*
Pat Addleman, *Admin Sec*
EMP: 16
SQ FT: 12,000
SALES (est): 1.6MM **Privately Held**
WEB: www.cyberware.com
SIC: **3823** Digital displays of process variables

(P-20855)
DELPHI CONTROL SYSTEMS INC
2806 Metropolitan Pl, Pomona (91767-1854)
PHONE.................................909 593-8099
Beth A Barbonc, *President*
Scott Crail, *Vice Pres*
EMP: 15
SQ FT: 11,000
SALES: 3MM **Privately Held**
WEB: www.delphicontrolsystems.com
SIC: **3823** 3613 Industrial process control instruments; control panels, electric

(P-20856)
DESERT MICROSYSTEMS INC
3387 Chicago Ave, Riverside (92507-6815)
PHONE.................................951 682-3867
Albert Johnson, *President*
EMP: 25
SALES (est): 2.9MM **Privately Held**
WEB: www.desertmicrosys.com
SIC: **3823** 3577 3571 Computer interface equipment for industrial process control; computer peripheral equipment; electronic computers

(P-20857)
DIGITAL DYNAMICS INC
5 Victor Sq, Scotts Valley (95066-3531)
PHONE.................................831 438-4444
Jerde, *President*
William P Ledeen, *Ch of Bd*
Carolyn Jerde, *Admin Sec*
William Waggoner, *Info Tech Mgr*
Craig Nelson, *Electrical Engi*
EMP: 45
SQ FT: 18,000
SALES (est): 12.3MM **Privately Held**
WEB: www.digitaldynamics.com
SIC: **3823** Industrial instrmnts msrmnt display/control process variable

(P-20858)
DIGIVISION INC
9830 Summers Ridge Rd, San Diego (92121-3083)
PHONE.................................858 530-0100
Randy Millar, *Exec VP*
Richard Hier, *Vice Pres*
EMP: 13
SQ FT: 10,000
SALES (est): 1.4MM **Privately Held**
WEB: www.digivision.com
SIC: **3823** 8731 Digital displays of process variables; commercial physical research

(P-20859)
DONNASHI ENTERPRISES INC
43644 Parkway Esplanade W, La Quinta (92253-4097)
PHONE.................................760 200-3402
Jill Ames, *General Mgr*
EMP: 30 EST: 2011
SALES (est): 2.2MM **Privately Held**
SIC: **3823** Water quality monitoring & control systems

(P-20860)
DURO-SENSE CORP
869 Sandhill Ave, Carson (90746-1210)
PHONE.................................310 533-6877
Jay Waterman, *President*
Roger S Waterman, *Ch of Bd*
EMP: 15
SQ FT: 8,000
SALES (est): 3.5MM **Privately Held**
WEB: www.duro-sense.com
SIC: **3823** Temperature instruments: industrial process type

(P-20861)
DUSOUTH INDUSTRIES
Also Called: Dst Controls
651 Stone Rd, Benicia (94510-1141)
PHONE.................................707 745-5117
William P Southard, *President*
Read Hayward, *Vice Pres*
EMP: 30
SQ FT: 14,000
SALES (est): 10.9MM **Privately Held**
SIC: **3823** Industrial instrmnts msrmnt display/control process variable

(P-20862)
EAGLE TECH MANUFACTURING INC
841 Walker St, Watsonville (95076-4116)
PHONE.................................831 768-7467
Alfredo Madrigal, *President*
Hector Madrigal, *Vice Pres*
Bertha Guerrero, *Bookkeeper*
Jesus Navarro, *Buyer*
Enrique Hernandez, *Marketing Staff*
▲ EMP: 35
SQ FT: 5,000
SALES (est): 7.3MM **Privately Held**
WEB: www.eagletechman.com
SIC: **3823** Electrolytic conductivity instruments, industrial process

(P-20863)
EDC-BIOSYSTEMS INC (PA)
49090 Milmont Dr, Fremont (94538-7301)
PHONE.................................510 257-1500
Roger Williams, *CEO*
Greg Stephens, *President*
Chuck Reichel, *Vice Pres*
◆ EMP: 25
SQ FT: 18,600
SALES (est): 2.8MM **Privately Held**
WEB: www.edcbiosystems.com
SIC: **3823** Industrial process measurement equipment

(P-20864)
ELDRIDGE PRODUCTS INC
465 Reservation Rd, Marina (93933-3430)
PHONE.................................831 648-7777
Mark F Eldridge, *President*
Joseph Limon, *Purchasing*
Craig Schieding, *Manager*
▼ EMP: 20
SQ FT: 8,500
SALES (est): 4.9MM **Privately Held**
WEB: www.epiflow.com
SIC: **3823** 3824 Flow instruments, industrial process type; fluid meters & counting devices

(P-20865)
EMBEDDED DESIGNS INC
Also Called: K I C
16120 W Bernardo Dr Ste A, San Diego (92127-1875)
PHONE.................................858 673-6050
Casey Kazmierowicz, *Chairman*
Bjorn Dahle, *President*
Henryk J Kazmier, *CFO*
Henryk Kazmier, *CFO*
Miles Moreau, *Vice Pres*
EMP: 32
SQ FT: 9,500
SALES (est): 6.7MM **Privately Held**
WEB: www.kicthermal.com
SIC: **3823** Temperature measurement instruments, industrial

(P-20866)
EMERSON PROCESS MANAGEMENT
5466 Complex St Ste 203, San Diego (92123-1124)
PHONE.................................858 492-1069
Ron Buchholz, *Manager*
EMP: 20
SALES (corp-wide): 17.4B **Publicly Held**
WEB: www.emersonprocesspowerwater.com
SIC: **3823** Industrial instrmnts msrmnt display/control process variable
HQ: Emerson Process Management Power & Water Solutions, Inc.
  200 Beta Dr
  Pittsburgh PA 15238
  412 963-4000

(P-20867)
ESYS ENERGY CONTROL COMPANY
12881 Knott St Ste 227, Garden Grove (92841-3947)
PHONE.................................714 372-3322
Abio Russeniello, *Owner*
Tyler Adkins, *Manager*
EMP: 25
SALES (est): 1.7MM **Privately Held**
SIC: **3823** Combustion control instruments

(P-20868)
FLOWMETRICS INC
9201 Independence Ave, Chatsworth (91311-5905)
PHONE.................................818 407-3420
Hormoz Ghaemmaghami, *President*
Irfan Ahmad, *Purch Dir*
EMP: 22
SQ FT: 4,000
SALES (est): 4MM **Privately Held**
WEB: www.flowmetrics.com
SIC: **3823** Industrial flow & liquid measuring instruments

(P-20869)
FLUID COMPONENTS INTL LLC (PA)
Also Called: F C I
1755 La Costa Meadows Dr A, San Marcos (92078-5187)
PHONE.................................760 744-6950
Dan McQueen, *CEO*
Daniel M McQueen, *President*
Barbara Succetti, *CFO*
Mike Noel, *Vice Pres*
Jim Delee, *Regional Mgr*
▲ EMP: 187
SQ FT: 49,000
SALES: 41.4MM **Privately Held**
WEB: www.fluidcomponents.com
SIC: **3823** Industrial instrmnts msrmnt display/control process variable

(P-20870)
FLUID POWER CTRL SYSTEMS INC
1400 E Valencia Dr, Fullerton (92831-4733)
PHONE.................................714 525-3727
Harsoyo Lukito, *President*
EMP: 21
SALES (est): 3.4MM **Privately Held**
SIC: **3823** Fluidic devices, circuits & systems for process control

(P-20871)
FORTREND ENGINEERING CORP
2220 Otoole Ave, San Jose (95131-1326)
PHONE.................................408 734-9311
Chris Wu PHD, *CEO*
Joseph MA PHD, *Chairman*
Richard Morgan, *Vice Pres*
Harriet West, *Executive*
EMP: 41
SQ FT: 20,000
SALES (est): 8.9MM **Privately Held**
WEB: www.fortrend.com
SIC: **3823** Industrial instrmnts msrmnt display/control process variable

(P-20872)
FOX THERMAL INSTRUMENTS INC
399 Reservation Rd, Marina (93933-3229)
PHONE.................................831 384-4300
William Roller, *CEO*
Bradley Philip Lesko, *President*
Al Arreola, *Regional Mgr*
Matthew Evans, *Engineer*
Kamal Pillay, *Accountant*
▲ EMP: 20 EST: 1993
SQ FT: 8,000
SALES: 4.7MM
SALES (corp-wide): 1.4B **Privately Held**
WEB: www.foxthermalinstruments.com
SIC: **3823** Industrial instrmnts msrmnt display/control process variable
HQ: Onicon Incorporated
  11451 Belcher Rd S
  Largo FL 33773
  727 447-6140

(P-20873)
FRONTLINE ENVIRONMENTAL TEC
Also Called: Frontline Technologies
3195 Park Rd Ste C, Benicia (94510-1185)
P.O. Box 426 (94510-0426)
PHONE.................................707 745-1116
Randall L Sherwood, *President*
EMP: 15
SQ FT: 5,000
SALES (est): 3MM **Privately Held**
WEB: www.frontlineworldwide.com
SIC: **3823** 1731 Industrial instrmnts msrmnt display/control process variable; environmental system control installation

(P-20874)
FUNDAMENTAL TECH INTL INC
Also Called: F T I
2900 E 29th St, Long Beach (90806-2315)
PHONE.................................562 595-0661
Maarten Propper, *CEO*
John Jacobson, *President*
▼ EMP: 21
SQ FT: 20,000

▲ = Import ▼=Export
◆ =Import/Export

SALES (est): 3.5MM **Privately Held**
SIC: **3823** Liquid analysis instruments, industrial process type

(P-20875)
FUNKTION TECHNOLOGIES INC
2110 Artesia Blvd B202, Redondo Beach (90278-3073)
PHONE..................................310 937-7335
Danish Qureshi, *CEO*
EMP: 10
SALES (est): 577K **Privately Held**
SIC: **3823** Industrial process measurement equipment

(P-20876)
FUTEK ADVANCED SENSOR TECH INC
10 Thomas, Irvine (92618-2702)
PHONE..................................949 465-0900
Javad Mokhberi, *CEO*
Mark Chepelyuk, *Administration*
Thomas Bowles, *CIO*
Ericson Palermo, *Info Tech Dir*
Javad Von Mokhbery, *Info Tech Dir*
EMP: 140
SQ FT: 23,000
SALES: 30MM **Privately Held**
WEB: www.futek.com
SIC: **3823** 8711 Industrial instrmnts msrmnt display/control process variable; engineering services

(P-20877)
GALIL MOTION CONTROL INC
270 Technology Way, Rocklin (95765-1228)
PHONE..................................800 377-6329
Jacob Tal, *Principal*
Wayne Baron, *President*
Brian Kambe, *Vice Pres*
Kaushal Shah, *Vice Pres*
John Thompson, *Vice Pres*
EMP: 36
SQ FT: 30,000
SALES (est): 9.2MM **Privately Held**
WEB: www.galilmc.com
SIC: **3823** Industrial instrmnts msrmnt display/control process variable

(P-20878)
GATEWORKS CORPORATION
3026 S Higuera St, San Luis Obispo (93401-6606)
PHONE..................................805 781-2000
Gordon Edmonds, *President*
Doug Hollingsworth, *Vice Pres*
Ron Eisworth, *Admin Sec*
EMP: 12 EST: 1995
SQ FT: 2,100
SALES (est): 3.8MM **Privately Held**
WEB: www.gateworks.com
SIC: **3823** Computer interface equipment for industrial process control

(P-20879)
GEORG FISCHER SIGNET LLC
3401 Aero Jet Ave, El Monte (91731-2801)
PHONE..................................626 571-2770
Charlotte Hill, *Mng Member*
Thad Snowden, *Maintence Staff*
▲ EMP: 90 EST: 1953
SQ FT: 27,000
SALES (est): 20.1MM
SALES (corp-wide): 4.6B **Privately Held**
WEB: www.gfsignet.com
SIC: **3823** Industrial process control instruments
HQ: Georg Fischer Spa
Via Sondrio 1
Cernusco Sul Naviglio MI 20063
029 218-61

(P-20880)
GET ENGINEERING CORP
9350 Bond Ave, El Cajon (92021-2850)
PHONE..................................619 443-8295
L Adams, *CEO*
Guille Tuttle, *Shareholder*
Rodney Tuttle, *Shareholder*
Leslie Adams, *CEO*
David Shaw, *COO*
EMP: 20
SQ FT: 14,500

SALES (est): 5MM **Privately Held**
WEB: www.getntds.com
SIC: **3823** 7373 3812 3679 Computer interface equipment for industrial process control; computer integrated systems design; search & navigation equipment; electronic circuits

(P-20881)
GRAPHTEC AMERICA INC (DH)
17462 Armstrong Ave, Irvine (92614-5724)
PHONE..................................949 770-6010
Yasutaka Arakawa, *CEO*
Noriko Slijk, *Director*
◆ EMP: 50
SQ FT: 35,000
SALES (est): 6.7MM **Privately Held**
WEB: www.graphtecusa.com
SIC: **3823** 5064 Industrial instrmnts msrmnt display/control process variable; video cassette recorders & accessories

(P-20882)
HARDY PROCESS SOLUTIONS
9440 Carroll Park Dr # 150, San Diego (92121-5201)
PHONE..................................858 278-2900
Eric Schellenberger, *President*
Steve Hanes, *CFO*
Stan Modzel, *Business Mgr*
Lorilee Kanner, *Buyer*
Michael Hunt, *Opers Staff*
◆ EMP: 50 EST: 1980
SQ FT: 63,000
SALES (est): 13MM
SALES (corp-wide): 5.1B **Publicly Held**
WEB: www.hardyinst.com
SIC: **3823** 3829 3596 Industrial instrmnts msrmnt display/control process variable; measuring & controlling devices; scales & balances, except laboratory
HQ: Dynamic Instruments, Inc.
10737 Lexington Dr
Knoxville TN 37932
858 278-4900

(P-20883)
HEWITT INDUSTRIES LOS ANGELES
1455 Crenshaw Blvd # 290, Torrance (90501-2438)
PHONE..................................714 891-9300
John T Hewitt, *President*
▲ EMP: 45 EST: 1955
SALES (est): 7.9MM **Privately Held**
WEB: www.hewittindustries.com
SIC: **3823** 3714 3625 Pyrometers, industrial process type; temperature instruments: industrial process type; motor vehicle parts & accessories; relays & industrial controls

(P-20884)
HONEYWELL INTERNATIONAL INC
13125 Danielson St, Poway (92064-8873)
PHONE..................................858 848-3187
Scott Covey, *Branch Mgr*
EMP: 668
SALES (corp-wide): 41.8B **Publicly Held**
SIC: **3823** Industrial instrmnts msrmnt display/control process variable
PA: Honeywell International Inc.
300 S Tryon St
Charlotte NC 28202
973 455-2000

(P-20885)
I DES INC
864 Saint Francis Way, Rio Vista (94571-1250)
PHONE..................................707 374-7500
Dan Simpson, *President*
▲ EMP: 35
SALES (est): 4.7MM **Privately Held**
SIC: **3823** Hydrometers, industrial process type

(P-20886)
I T I ELECTRO-OPTIC CORP (PA)
Also Called: Ccd
11500 W Olympic Blvd, Los Angeles (90064-1524)
PHONE..................................310 445-8900
MEI Shi, *Ch of Bd*
Robert Nevins, *President*

Henry Hong, *Executive*
John Sun, *Systems Staff*
James Wang, *VP Finance*
▲ EMP: 40
SQ FT: 5,000
SALES (est): 4.8MM **Privately Held**
SIC: **3823** Infrared instruments, industrial process type

(P-20887)
I T I ELECTRO-OPTIC CORP
1500 E Olympic Blvd # 400, Los Angeles (90021-1900)
PHONE..................................310 312-4526
John Sun, *Manager*
EMP: 20
SALES (corp-wide): 4.8MM **Privately Held**
SIC: **3823** Infrared instruments, industrial process type
PA: I T I Electro-Optic Corporation
11500 W Olympic Blvd
Los Angeles CA 90064
310 445-8900

(P-20888)
INFRAREDVISION TECHNOLOGY CORP
Also Called: I T C
140 Industrial Way, Buellton (93427-9507)
PHONE..................................805 686-8848
James Giacobazzi, *President*
Kenneth Hay, *Vice Pres*
EMP: 20
SALES (est): 2.1MM
SALES (corp-wide): 718.8MM **Publicly Held**
SIC: **3823** Industrial instrmnts msrmnt display/control process variable
HQ: Lumasense Technologies Holdings, Inc.
3301 Leonard Ct
Santa Clara CA 95054
408 727-1600

(P-20889)
INNOVATIVE INTEGRATION INC
741 Flynn Rd, Camarillo (93012-8056)
PHONE..................................805 520-3300
Jim Henderson, *President*
Dan McLane, *Vice Pres*
▲ EMP: 30
SQ FT: 11,000
SALES (est): 8.9MM **Privately Held**
WEB: www.innovative-dsp.com
SIC: **3823** 3571 Industrial instrmnts msrmnt display/control process variable; electronic computers

(P-20890)
INSTRUMENT & VALVE SERVICES CO
6851 Walthall Way A, Paramount (90723-2028)
PHONE..................................562 633-0179
Larry Baumber, *Manager*
EMP: 77
SALES (corp-wide): 17.4B **Publicly Held**
WEB: www.instrum3nt.com
SIC: **3823** Industrial instrmnts msrmnt display/control process variable
HQ: Instrument & Valve Services Company
205 S Center St
Marshalltown IA 50158
-

(P-20891)
INSTRUMENT & VALVE SERVICES CO
531 Getty Ct Ste D, Benicia (94510-1180)
PHONE..................................707 745-4664
George Noland, *Manager*
EMP: 11
SALES (corp-wide): 17.4B **Publicly Held**
WEB: www.instrum3nt.com
SIC: **3823** Industrial instrmnts msrmnt display/control process variable
HQ: Instrument & Valve Services Company
205 S Center St
Marshalltown IA 50158
-

(P-20892)
JR3 INC
22 Harter Ave Ste 1, Woodland (95776-5901)
PHONE..................................530 661-3677
John E Ramming, *President*
Joe Coehlo, *Engineer*
EMP: 11
SQ FT: 7,500
SALES (est): 877.7K **Privately Held**
WEB: www.jr3.com
SIC: **3823** Industrial instrmnts msrmnt display/control process variable

(P-20893)
KASHIYAMA USA INC
41432 Christy St, Fremont (94538-5105)
PHONE..................................510 979-0070
Take Hirabayashi, *President*
Take Hiraboyashi, *President*
Jim Gentleman, *Manager*
Richard Lenhard, *Accounts Mgr*
▲ EMP: 10
SALES (est): 1.3MM **Privately Held**
WEB: www.kashiyama.com
SIC: **3823** 3826 Thermal conductivity instruments, industrial process type; electrolytic conductivity instruments

(P-20894)
KEYSIGHT TECHNOLOGIES INC (PA)
1400 Fountaingrove Pkwy, Santa Rosa (95403-1738)
P.O. Box 4026 (95402-4026)
PHONE..................................800 829-4444
Ronald S Nersesian, *Ch of Bd*
Satish Dhanasekaran, *President*
Soon Chai Gooi, *President*
Bethany Mayer, *President*
John Page, *President*
EMP: 277
SALES: 3.8B **Publicly Held**
SIC: **3823** 3829 7629 Industrial instrmnts msrmnt display/control process variable; measuring & controlling devices; electronic equipment repair

(P-20895)
KING INSTRUMENT COMPANY INC
12700 Pala Dr, Garden Grove (92841-3924)
PHONE..................................714 891-0008
Clyde F King, *President*
EMP: 50
SQ FT: 46,000
SALES (est): 12.6MM **Privately Held**
WEB: www.kinginstrumentco.com
SIC: **3823** Flow instruments, industrial process type

(P-20896)
KING NUTRONICS CORPORATION
6421 Independence Ave, Woodland Hills (91367-2608)
PHONE..................................818 887-5460
J Robert King, *President*
Leslie King, *Admin Sec*
Dan Fredrickson, *Electrical Engi*
Chris Crocker, *Purch Mgr*
Brandi Kaufman, *Prdtn Mgr*
EMP: 20
SQ FT: 21,000
SALES (est): 5.1MM **Privately Held**
WEB: www.kingnutronics.com
SIC: **3823** 3825 Pressure measurement instruments, industrial; temperature instruments: industrial process type; instruments to measure electricity

(P-20897)
KOCO MOTION US LLC
335 Cochrane Cir, Morgan Hill (95037-2831)
PHONE..................................408 612-4970
Max Wietharn, *Principal*
Karen McGeough, *Manager*
▲ EMP: 13 EST: 2011
SALES (est): 2.2MM **Privately Held**
SIC: **3823** Industrial process control instruments

PRODUCTS & SVCS

(P-20898)

L3HARRIS TECHNOLOGIES INC

Also Called: Harris Corporation
591 Camno De La Reina 5, San Diego
(92108)
PHONE..............................619 296-6900
Jim Wantrobski, *Branch Mgr*
EMP: 195
SALES (corp-wide): 6.8B **Publicly Held**
SIC: 3823 3812 Industrial instrmnts
msrmnt display/control process variable;
search & navigation equipment
PA: L3harris Technologies, Inc.
1025 W Nasa Blvd
Melbourne FL 32919
321 727-9100

(P-20899)

LAIRD TECHNOLOGIES INC

2040 Fortune Dr Ste 102, San Jose
(95131-1850)
PHONE..............................408 544-9500
Troy Hodges, *Owner*
EMP: 50 **Privately Held**
SIC: 3823 Absorption analyzers: infrared,
X-ray, etc.: industrial
HQ: Laird Technologies, Inc.
16401 Swingley
Chesterfield MO 63017
636 898-6000

(P-20900)

LOGIC BEACH INC (PA)

8363 Center Dr Ste 6f, La Mesa
(91942-2942)
PHONE..............................619 698-3300
David Parks, *President*
Martha Osterling, *Vice Pres*
EMP: 10
SQ FT: 2,000
SALES (est): 2MM **Privately Held**
WEB: www.logicbeach.com
SIC: 3823 3825 Data loggers, industrial
process type; battery testers, electrical

(P-20901)

MANNING HOLOFF CO INC

15610 Moorpark St Apt 3, Encino
(91436-1639)
PHONE..............................818 407-2500
Geraldine Holoff, *President*
Susan Holoff, *Vice Pres*
James Krasne, *Admin Sec*
Sue Holoff, *VP Finance*
EMP: 25
SALES: 2.1MM **Privately Held**
WEB: www.magna-lite.com
SIC: 3823 3648 Industrial instrmnts
msrmnt display/control process variable;
lighting equipment

(P-20902)

MARINESYNC CORPORATION

3235 Hancock St, San Diego (92110-4419)
P.O. Box 80174 (92138-0174)
PHONE..............................619 578-2953
Austin Bleier, *CEO*
EMP: 10
SALES (est): 1.5MM **Privately Held**
SIC: 3823 Telemetering instruments, indus-
trial process type

(P-20903)

MICRO LITHOGRAPHY INC

1247 Elko Dr, Sunnyvale (94089-2211)
PHONE..............................408 747-1769
Yung-Tsai Yen, *CEO*
Chris Yen, *President*
Sandy Yen, *Exec VP*
John T Liu, *General Mgr*
David Wang, *Administration*
▲ EMP: 225
SQ FT: 100,000
SALES (est): 58.1MM **Privately Held**
WEB: www.mliusa.com
SIC: 3823 3674 Industrial instrmnts
msrmnt display/control process variable;
semiconductors & related devices

(P-20904)

MICROCOOL

72216 Northshore St # 103, Thousand
Palms (92276-2325)
PHONE..............................760 322-1111
Mike Lemche, *President*
Christopher Stanley, *Vice Pres*

James Murphy, *Admin Sec*
▲ EMP: 15
SQ FT: 5,800
SALES (est): 3.4MM **Privately Held**
WEB: www.microcool.com
SIC: 3823 Humidity instruments, industrial
process type

(P-20905)

MODUTEK CORP

6387 San Ignacio Ave, San Jose
(95119-1206)
PHONE..............................408 362-2000
Douglas G Wagner, *President*
Robert Brody, *Vice Pres*
EMP: 21
SQ FT: 21,000
SALES (est): 5.4MM **Privately Held**
WEB: www.modutek.com
SIC: 3823 7373 Temperature instruments:
industrial process type; systems integra-
tion services

(P-20906)

MOUNTZ INC (PA)

Also Called: Dg Mountz Associates
1080 N 11th St, San Jose (95112-2927)
PHONE..............................408 292-2214
Brad Mountz, *President*
David Aviles, *CFO*
Lorna U Mountz, *Treasurer*
Sanjar Chakamian, *Bd of Directors*
Maria Luna, *Technology*
▲ EMP: 43
SQ FT: 30,000
SALES: 15MM **Privately Held**
SIC: 3823 5085 Industrial instrmnts
msrmnt display/control process variable;
fasteners & fastening equipment

(P-20907)

MYRON L COMPANY

2450 Impala Dr, Carlsbad (92010-7226)
PHONE..............................760 438-2021
Gary O Robinson, *President*
Jerry Adams, *Vice Pres*
Scott Macdonald, *Mfg Staff*
Buddy Taylor, *Production*
◆ EMP: 80
SQ FT: 43,000
SALES (est): 24.5MM **Privately Held**
WEB: www.myronl.com
SIC: 3823 3825 3613 Electrodes used in
industrial process measurement; instru-
ments to measure electricity; switchgear
& switchboard apparatus

(P-20908)

N A SUEZ

Also Called: West Bsin Wtr Rclamation Plant
1935 S Hughes Way, El Segundo
(90245-4729)
PHONE..............................310 414-0183
Reza Nabegh, *Manager*
Jaime Patriarca, *Buyer*
Temitayo Abegunde, *Manager*
EMP: 45
SALES (corp-wide): 94.7MM **Privately
Held**
WEB: www.unitedwaterservices.com
SIC: 3823 Water quality monitoring & con-
trol systems
HQ: Suez Water Indiana Llc
461 From Rd Ste F400
Paramus NJ 07652
201 767-9300

(P-20909)

NON-LINEAR SYSTEMS

Also Called: Nls
4561 Mission Gorge Pl F, San Diego
(92120-4113)
PHONE..............................619 521-2161
Pamela Finley, *Owner*
Jesse L Finley, *Co-Owner*
▼ EMP: 10
SQ FT: 6,000
SALES (est): 986.5K **Privately Held**
WEB: www.nonlinearsystems.com
SIC: 3823 3825 Temperature instruments:
industrial process type; test equipment for
electronic & electric measurement; cur-
rent measuring equipment; oscillographs
& oscilloscopes; volt meters

(P-20910)

NORDSON ASYMTEK INC

2475 Ash St, Vista (92081-8424)
PHONE..............................760 727-2880
Dave Padgett, *Branch Mgr*
Juan Villagomez, *Supervisor*
EMP: 15
SALES (corp-wide): 2.2B **Publicly Held**
SIC: 3823 Industrial instrmnts msrmnt dis-
play/control process variable
HQ: Nordson Asymtek, Inc.
2747 Loker Ave W
Carlsbad CA 92010
760 431-1919

(P-20911)

NORDSON ASYMTEK INC (HQ)

2747 Loker Ave W, Carlsbad (92010-6601)
PHONE..............................760 431-1919
Peter Bierhuis, *CEO*
Hector Pulido, *Vice Pres*
Payman Tayebi, *Program Mgr*
Jerry Wilder, *Branch Mgr*
Bernard McHugh, *General Mgr*
▲ EMP: 200
SQ FT: 100,000
SALES: 57.9MM
SALES (corp-wide): 2.2B **Publicly Held**
WEB: www.asymtek.com
SIC: 3823 Industrial flow & liquid measur-
ing instruments
PA: Nordson Corporation
28601 Clemens Rd
Westlake OH 44145
440 892-1580

(P-20912)

OLEUMTECH CORPORATION

19762 Pauling, Foothill Ranch
(92610-2611)
PHONE..............................949 305-9009
Paul Gregory, *CEO*
Vrej ISA, *COO*
Colin Miller, *Software Engr*
Tho Ngo, *Engineer*
Franchel Williams, *Engineer*
EMP: 57
SQ FT: 55,000
SALES: 15MM **Privately Held**
WEB: www.oleumtech.com
SIC: 3823 Industrial instrmnts msrmnt dis-
play/control process variable

(P-20913)

OMRON SCIENTIFIC TECH INC (DH)

Also Called: Optical Sensor Division
6550 Dumbarton Cir, Fremont
(94555-3605)
PHONE..............................510 608-3400
Joseph J Lazzara, *President*
James A Ashford, *Senior VP*
James A Lazzara, *Senior VP*
Man Nguyen, *Software Engr*
Marcel Pardorla, *Technician*
◆ EMP: 250 EST: 1979
SQ FT: 95,700
SALES (est): 47.3MM **Privately Held**
SIC: 3823 3827 Industrial instrmnts
msrmnt display/control process variable;
optical instruments & lenses
HQ: Omron Management Center Of Amer-
ica, Inc.
2895 Greenspoint Pkwy
Hoffman Estates IL 60169
224 520-7650

(P-20914)

PAC 21

11888 Western Ave, Stanton (90680-3438)
PHONE..............................714 891-7000
Will G Durant, *President*
George Lindsley, *Shareholder*
Will Durant, *President*
Ariel Durant, *Admin Sec*
EMP: 10
SQ FT: 9,000
SALES (est): 1.3MM **Privately Held**
WEB: www.pac21.com
SIC: 3823 Industrial process control instru-
ments

(P-20915)

PARKER-HANNIFIN CORPORATION

Veriflo Division
250 Canal Blvd, Richmond (94804-2002)
PHONE..............................510 235-9590
Pera Horne, *General Mgr*
Joe Lis, *Engineer*
Anil Raina, *Engineer*
Jeff Michael, *Senior Engr*
Judy Codling, *Manager*
EMP: 100
SALES (corp-wide): 14.3B **Publicly Held**
WEB: www.parker.com
SIC: 3823 3842 3841 3625 Industrial
process control instruments; respirators;
surgical & medical instruments; relays &
industrial controls; industrial valves
PA: Parker-Hannifin Corporation
6035 Parkland Blvd
Cleveland OH 44124
216 896-3000

(P-20916)

PATTEN SYSTEMS INC

15598 Producer Ln, Huntington Beach
(92649-1308)
PHONE..............................714 799-5656
John Capitano, *CEO*
Jason Neves, *Sales Staff*
EMP: 17
SALES (est): 3MM **Privately Held**
SIC: 3823 Analyzers, industrial process
type

(P-20917)

PENSANDO SYSTEMS INC

1730 Technology Dr, San Jose
(95110-1331)
PHONE..............................408 451-9012
Prem Chand Jain, *CEO*
John Chambers, *Chairman*
EMP: 19
SALES (est): 8.3MM **Privately Held**
SIC: 3823 Computer interface equipment
for industrial process control

(P-20918)

PHOTON INC

1671 Dell Ave Ste 208, Campbell
(95008-6900)
PHONE..............................408 226-1000
John Fleisher, *President*
Judith Fleisher, *Corp Secy*
EMP: 17
SQ FT: 10,000
SALES (est): 3.6MM **Privately Held**
SIC: 3823 8711 Industrial instrmnts
msrmnt display/control process variable;
consulting engineer

(P-20919)

PHYN LLC

1855 Del Amo Blvd, Torrance (90501-1302)
PHONE..............................310 400-4001
Ryan Kim, *CEO*
Chester J Pipkin, *President*
EMP: 10 EST: 2016
SALES (est): 1.5MM **Privately Held**
SIC: 3823 Water quality monitoring & con-
trol systems
HQ: Belkin International, Inc.
12045 Waterfront Dr
Playa Vista CA 90094
310 751-5100

(P-20920)

PRESSURE PROFILE SYSTEMS INC

5757 W Century Blvd # 600, Los Angeles
(90045-6429)
PHONE..............................310 641-8100
Denis A O'Connor, *CEO*
Jae S Son, *CEO*
Huan Tran, *COO*
Steven Sanchez, *Treasurer*
David Ables, *Admin Sec*
EMP: 17
SALES (est): 3.9MM **Privately Held**
WEB: www.pressureprofile.com
SIC: 3823 Industrial instrmnts msrmnt dis-
play/control process variable

▲ = Import ▼=Export
◆ =Import/Export

(P-20921)
PROCESS SOLUTIONS INC
Also Called: PSI
1077 Dell Ave Ste A, Campbell
(95008-6628)
PHONE.............................408 370-6540
Brent Simmons, *CEO*
Gunnar Thortarson, *Vice Pres*
Gunnar Thordarson, *Human Res Mgr*
Allison Petsche, *Sales Staff*
Gary Turner, *Director*
▲ EMP: 32
SALES (est): 11.2MM **Privately Held**
WEB: www.4psi.net
SIC: 3823 Water quality monitoring & control systems

(P-20922)
PROTEUS INDUSTRIES INC
340 Pioneer Way, Mountain View
(94041-1577)
PHONE.............................650 964-4163
Jon Heiner, *CEO*
Mark Nicewonger, *Vice Pres*
Jane Rendon, *Info Tech Mgr*
Fred Luu, *Engineer*
Rene Truong, *Engineer*
▲ EMP: 50
SQ FT: 40,000
SALES (est): 12.6MM **Privately Held**
WEB: www.proteusind.com
SIC: 3823 3829 3826 3824 Industrial instrmnts msrmnt display/control process variable; measuring & controlling devices; analytical instruments; fluid meters & counting devices; relays & industrial controls

(P-20923)
Q-MARK MANUFACTURING INC
Also Called: Quality Components Co
30051 Comercio, Rcho STA Marg
(92688-2106)
PHONE.............................949 457-1913
Mark Osterstock, *President*
EMP: 14
SQ FT: 5,120
SALES: 2.7MM **Privately Held**
WEB: www.cmms.com
SIC: 3823 3599 Industrial instrmnts msrmnt display/control process variable; machine shop, jobbing & repair

(P-20924)
QED INC
2920 Halladay St, Santa Ana (92705-5623)
PHONE.............................714 546-6010
Erik K Moller, *CEO*
Randy Heartfield, *President*
Mary C Heartfield, *Admin Sec*
Lizbeth Santibanez, *Info Tech Mgr*
Chris Barr, *Engineer*
▲ EMP: 43
SQ FT: 14,000
SALES: 5.6MM **Privately Held**
WEB: www.qedinstruments.com
SIC: 3823 3829 3812 Pressure gauges, dial & digital; accelerometers; pressure & vacuum indicators, aircraft engine; aircraft/aerospace flight instruments & guidance systems; aircraft flight instruments; aircraft control systems, electronic

(P-20925)
QUANTUM-DYNAMICS CO INC
6414 Independence Ave, Woodland Hills
(91367-2607)
PHONE.............................818 719-0142
Arnold F Liu, *President*
Frederick F Liu, *President*
Lily Liu, *Corp Secy*
Arnold Liu, *Vice Pres*
EMP: 18
SQ FT: 25,000
SALES: 1.5MM **Privately Held**
SIC: 3823 8731 Flow instruments, industrial process type; engineering laboratory, except testing

(P-20926)
R G HANSEN ASSOCIATES (PA)
5951 Encina Rd Ste 106, Goleta
(93117-6251)
P.O. Box 160 (93116-0160)
PHONE.............................805 564-3388
Ian Wood, *President*

Dan Swets, *Mfg Spvr*
EMP: 12 EST: 1972
SQ FT: 10,000
SALES (est): 1.1MM **Privately Held**
WEB: www.cryostat.com
SIC: 3823 Industrial instrmnts msrmnt display/control process variable

(P-20927)
RAIN MSTR IRRGTION SYSTEMS INC
5825 Jasmine St, Riverside (92504-1144)
P.O. Box 489 (92502-0489)
PHONE.............................805 527-4498
Jim Sieminski, *President*
John Torosiani, *Admin Sec*
EMP: 32
SQ FT: 13,000
SALES (est): 4.7MM
SALES (corp-wide): 2.6B **Publicly Held**
WEB: www.toro.com
SIC: 3823 Industrial instrmnts msrmnt display/control process variable
PA: The Toro Company
8111 Lyndale Ave S
Bloomington MN 55420
952 888-8801

(P-20928)
RENAU CORPORATION
Also Called: Renau Electronic Laboratories
9309 Deering Ave, Chatsworth
(91311-5858)
PHONE.............................818 341-1994
Karol Renau, *CEO*
Christine Renau, *Admin Sec*
Jackie Renau, *Technology*
Roman Pyrzynski, *Engineer*
Mike Ryland, *Engineer*
▲ EMP: 20
SQ FT: 10,000
SALES (est): 6.4MM **Privately Held**
WEB: www.renau.com
SIC: 3823 Controllers for process variables, all types; time cycle & program controllers, industrial process type

(P-20929)
ROHRBACK COSASCO SYSTEMS INC (DH)
11841 Smith Ave, Santa Fe Springs
(90670-3226)
PHONE.............................562 949-0123
Bryan Sanderlin, *CEO*
David Price, *IT/INT Sup*
Carl Vaughn, *Technician*
Jim Robinson, *Technology*
Long Sung, *Technology*
▼ EMP: 71
SQ FT: 37,000
SALES (est): 17.3MM
SALES (corp-wide): 1.5B **Privately Held**
WEB: www.rohrbackcosasco.com
SIC: 3823 8742 Industrial instrmnts msrmnt display/control process variable; industry specialist consultants

(P-20930)
RONAN ENGINEERING COMPANY (PA)
Also Called: Ronan Engnrng/Rnan Msrment Div
28209 Avenue Stanford, Valencia
(91355-3984)
P.O. Box 129, Castaic (91310-0129)
PHONE.............................661 702-1344
John A Hewitson, *CEO*
▼ EMP: 56
SQ FT: 50,000
SALES (est): 15.7MM **Privately Held**
WEB: www.ronanmeasure.com
SIC: 3823 3825 Industrial instrmnts msrmnt display/control process variable; measuring instruments & meters, electric

(P-20931)
SABIA INCORPORATED (PA)
10919 Technology Pl Ste A, San Diego
(92127-1882)
PHONE.............................858 217-2200
Steve Foster, *CEO*
Craig Belnap, *President*
Clinton L Lingren, *President*
James Miller, *Vice Pres*
Edward Nunn, *Vice Pres*
EMP: 27

SALES (est): 6.7MM **Privately Held**
WEB: www.sabiainc.com
SIC: 3823 Industrial instrmnts msrmnt display/control process variable

(P-20932)
SANTA BARBARA CONTROL SYSTEMS
Also Called: CHEMTROL
5375 Overpass Rd, Santa Barbara
(93111-3015)
PHONE.............................805 683-8833
Pablo Navarro, *President*
Jacques Steininger, *CEO*
Karen Blomsprand, *Office Mgr*
Karen Grigsby, *Office Mgr*
Nader Swich, *Info Tech Dir*
EMP: 19
SQ FT: 8,000
SALES: 5.6MM **Privately Held**
WEB: www.sbcontrol.com
SIC: 3823 3589 7699 Water quality monitoring & control systems; swimming pool filter & water conditioning systems; cash register repair

(P-20933)
SCHNEIDER ELC SYSTEMS USA INC
Also Called: Triconex
26561 Rancho Pkwy S, Lake Forest
(92630-8301)
PHONE.............................949 885-0700
Morgan England, *Branch Mgr*
Rose Folli, *Executive*
Paul Groner, *Engineer*
James Jordan, *Engineer*
Vivanne Matheson, *Human Resources*
EMP: 10
SALES (corp-wide): 177.9K **Privately Held**
WEB: www.foxboro.com
SIC: 3823 Controllers for process variables, all types
HQ: Schneider Electric Systems Usa, Inc.
38 Neponset Ave
Foxboro MA 02035
508 543-8750

(P-20934)
SCIENTIFIC REPAIR INC
Also Called: SRI Instruments
20720 Earl St Ste 2, Torrance
(90503-3034)
PHONE.............................310 214-5092
Hugh Goldsmith, *President*
Summer Goldsmith, *Technician*
EMP: 12
SQ FT: 5,000
SALES: 6MM **Privately Held**
WEB: www.srigc.com
SIC: 3823 Chromatographs, industrial process type

(P-20935)
SEMIFAB INC
150 Great Oaks Blvd, San Jose
(95119-1347)
PHONE.............................408 414-5928
Hauynium Kabir, *President*
Greg Krikorian, *CFO*
Gerry Reynolds, *VP Sales*
◆ EMP: 60 EST: 1978
SQ FT: 55,000
SALES (est): 10.1MM **Privately Held**
WEB: www.semifab.com
SIC: 3823 3822 Industrial instrmnts msrmnt display/control process variable; temperature instruments: industrial process type; temperature controls, automatic

(P-20936)
SENSORTECH SYSTEMS INC
Also Called: Sensor Engineering
341 Bernoulli Cir, Oxnard (93030-5164)
PHONE.............................805 981-3735
Colin Hanson, *President*
Roger Carlson, *Shareholder*
Susan Hanson, *Office Admin*
John Fordham, *Admin Sec*
Martine Hunter, *Marketing Staff*
▲ EMP: 12
SQ FT: 4,000

SALES (est): 3MM **Privately Held**
WEB: www.sensortech.com
SIC: 3823 3826 3829 Digital displays of process variables; analytical instruments; measuring & controlling devices

(P-20937)
SENSOSCIENTIFIC INC
685 Cochran St Ste 200, Simi Valley
(93065-1921)
PHONE.............................800 279-3101
Ramin Rostami, *CEO*
Mike Zarei, *Vice Pres*
Isabelle Diep, *Finance Dir*
Jennifer Davis, *Regl Sales Mgr*
Dana Deignan, *Regl Sales Mgr*
▲ EMP: 25
SQ FT: 4,000
SALES: 5MM **Privately Held**
SIC: 3823 Industrial instrmnts msrmnt display/control process variable

(P-20938)
SILENX CORPORATION
10606 Shoemaker Ave Ste A, Santa Fe Springs (90670-4071)
PHONE.............................562 941-4200
Peter Kim, *President*
Chris Kim, *Treasurer*
Annie Kim, *Accounts Mgr*
◆ EMP: 15
SQ FT: 10,000
SALES: 1MM **Privately Held**
WEB: www.silenx.com
SIC: 3823 5063 Computer interface equipment for industrial process control; lighting fixtures, commercial & industrial

(P-20939)
SJCONTROLS INC
2248 Obispo Ave Ste 203, Long Beach
(90755-4026)
PHONE.............................562 494-1400
David J Olszewski, *President*
Frederick D Hesley Jr, *Chairman*
Stephen Czaus, *Vice Pres*
Jazmin Jones, *Office Mgr*
EMP: 11
SQ FT: 8,000
SALES (est): 2.8MM **Privately Held**
WEB: www.sjcontrols.com
SIC: 3823 5084 3824 Industrial instrmnts msrmnt display/control process variable; controlling instruments & accessories; fluid meters & counting devices

(P-20940)
SOUND WAVES INSULATION INC
1406 Ritchey St Ste D, Santa Ana
(92705-4735)
PHONE.............................714 556-2110
Todd Terray, *President*
Wally Fisk, *Vice Pres*
EMP: 20
SALES: 1.5MM **Privately Held**
SIC: 3823 Thermal conductivity instruments, industrial process type

(P-20941)
SPARLING INSTRUMENTS LLC
4097 Temple City Blvd, El Monte
(91731-1046)
PHONE.............................626 444-0571
Yosufi Tyebkhan, *Mng Member*
▲ EMP: 25
SQ FT: 56,000
SALES (est): 7MM **Privately Held**
WEB: www.sparlinginstruments.com
SIC: 3823 5084 3824 Industrial instrmnts msrmnt display/control process variable; industrial machinery & equipment; fluid meters & counting devices

(P-20942)
SST TECHNOLOGIES
Also Called: Sst Vacuum Reflow Systems
9801 Everest St, Downey (90242-3113)
PHONE.............................562 803-3361
Anthony Wilson, *President*
Ralph Burroughs, *CFO*
Dan Ross, *Engineer*
Estela Torres, *Accountant*
Jorge Garcia, *Purch Mgr*
◆ EMP: 30
SQ FT: 20,000

SALES (est): 7.4MM **Privately Held**
WEB: www.edmsupply.com
SIC: 3823 Thermal conductivity instruments, industrial process type
PA: Palomar Technologies, Inc.
2728 Loker Ave W
Carlsbad CA 92010

(P-20943)
STAR-LUCK ENTERPRISE INC
11807 Harrington St, Bakersfield
(93311-9278)
PHONE.................................661 665-9999
Xiaodong Zhou, *President*
Stephen Thompson, *Senior VP*
David Johnson, *Vice Pres*
▲ EMP: 12
SQ FT: 11,800
SALES (est): 4MM **Privately Held**
SIC: 3823 Pressure measurement instruments, industrial

(P-20944)
SUPERFISH INC
2595 E Byshore Rd Ste 150, Palo Alto
(94303)
PHONE.................................650 752-6564
Shaul Gal-Oz, *President*
EMP: 18 EST: 2008
SALES (est): 3.8MM **Privately Held**
SIC: 3823 Analyzers, industrial process type

(P-20945)
TELEDYNE INSTRUMENTS INC
Also Called: Teledyne Analytical Instrs
16830 Chestnut St, City of Industry
(91748-1017)
PHONE.................................626 934-1500
Tom Compas, *Branch Mgr*
Tony Ho, *Technology*
Steve Broy, *Engineer*
Connie Favela, *Engineer*
John Medici, *Engineer*
EMP: 170
SQ FT: 70,000
SALES (corp-wide): 2.9B **Publicly Held**
SIC: 3823 Industrial instrmnts msrmnt display/control process variable
HQ: Teledyne Instruments, Inc.
1049 Camino Dos Rios
Thousand Oaks CA 91360
805 373-4545

(P-20946)
TELEDYNE INSTRUMENTS INC
Also Called: Teledyne Oceanscience
2245 Camino Vida Roble, Carlsbad
(92011-1557)
PHONE.................................760 754-2400
Dennis Klahn, *Principal*
Ed Tyburski, *President*
Shannon Searing, *General Mgr*
Brant Stewart, *Administration*
Peggy Walters, *Technical Staff*
EMP: 21
SALES (corp-wide): 2.9B **Publicly Held**
SIC: 3823 Buoyancy instruments, industrial process type
HQ: Teledyne Instruments, Inc.
1049 Camino Dos Rios
Thousand Oaks CA 91360
805 373-4545

(P-20947)
TERN DESIGN LTD
Also Called: Oceanscience
14020 Stowe Dr, Poway (92064-6846)
PHONE.................................760 754-2400
Ronald George, *President*
Ban Hoang, *Engineer*
Dennis Clark, *Buyer*
Earl Childress, *Opers Mgr*
David Marousch, *Sales Mgr*
EMP: 25
SQ FT: 4,800
SALES (est): 6.2MM **Privately Held**
WEB: www.oceanscience.com
SIC: 3823 Buoyancy instruments, industrial process type

(P-20948)
TEST ENTERPRISES INC (PA)
Also Called: Thermonics
1288 Reamwood Ave, Sunnyvale
(94089-2233)
PHONE.................................408 542-5900
James C Kufis, *CEO*
Joachim Kunkel, *General Mgr*
▲ EMP: 32
SQ FT: 22,000
SALES (est): 6MM **Privately Held**
WEB: www.thermonics.com
SIC: 3823 3825 Temperature measurement instruments, industrial; semiconductor test equipment

(P-20949)
THERMOMETRICS
CORPORATION (PA)
18714 Parthenia St, Northridge
(91324-3813)
PHONE.................................818 886-3755
Jorge Hernandez, *President*
Robert Hernandez, *Vice Pres*
Victoria Dukes, *Controller*
Cynthia Grable, *Purch Mgr*
Tom Fishwick, *Site Mgr*
EMP: 30
SQ FT: 16,897
SALES (est): 4.2MM **Privately Held**
WEB: www.thermometricscorp.com
SIC: 3823 Industrial instrmnts msrmnt display/control process variable

(P-20950)
THERMX TEMPERATURE TECH
Also Called: Thermx Southwest
7370 Opportunity Rd Ste S, San Diego
(92111-2245)
PHONE.................................858 573-0983
John Bowman, *President*
Karen Bowman, *CFO*
EMP: 11
SQ FT: 1,500
SALES (est): 2.4MM **Privately Held**
WEB: www.thermx.com
SIC: 3823 Industrial instrmnts msrmnt display/control process variable

(P-20951)
TRANSLOGIC INCORPORATED
5641 Engineer Dr, Huntington Beach
(92649-1123)
PHONE.................................714 890-0058
Donald Ross, *CEO*
Gregory Ross, *Admin Sec*
EMP: 41
SALES (est): 7.7MM **Privately Held**
WEB: www.translogicinc.com
SIC: 3823 3829 Temperature instruments: industrial process type; thermocouples, industrial process type; measuring & controlling devices

(P-20952)
U S AIR FILTRATION INC (PA)
23811 Washington Ave C110176, Murrieta
(92562-2275)
PHONE.................................951 491-7282
James H Perkins, *President*
EMP: 15
SQ FT: 3,900
SALES (est): 4.1MM **Privately Held**
WEB: www.usairfiltration.com
SIC: 3823 1796 Industrial process control instruments; pollution control equipment installation

(P-20953)
ULTRA CLEAN TECHNOLOGY
SYSTEMS (HQ)
Also Called: Uct
26462 Corporate Ave, Hayward
(94545-3914)
PHONE.................................510 576-4400
Jim Skullhammer, *CEO*
Ernest Maddock, *Bd of Directors*
Deborah Hayward, *Senior VP*
Lavi Lev, *Senior VP*
Bruce Wier, *Senior VP*
▲ EMP: 120
SQ FT: 12,000

SALES (est): 109.7MM
SALES (corp-wide): 1.1B **Publicly Held**
SIC: 3823 Industrial instrmnts msrmnt display/control process variable
PA: Ultra Clean Holdings, Inc.
26462 Corporate Ave
Hayward CA 94545
510 576-4400

(P-20954)
VALLEY CONTROLS INC
583 E Dinuba Ave, Reedley (93654-3531)
P.O. Box 1205 (93654-1205)
PHONE.................................559 638-5115
Verl A Tyler, *President*
Robin Tyler, *Corp Secy*
Doyle Anderson, *Vice Pres*
EMP: 14
SQ FT: 14,500
SALES (est): 1.4MM **Privately Held**
WEB: www.valleycontrols.com
SIC: 3823 1731 Industrial instrmnts msrmnt display/control process variable; electrical work

(P-20955)
VEEX INC
2827 Lakeview Ct, Fremont (94538-6534)
PHONE.................................510 651-0500
Cyrille Morelle, *President*
Son Nguyen, *Technician*
Timothy Badman, *Technical Staff*
Supriya Wallace, *Marketing Mgr*
Ildefonso Polo, *Marketing Staff*
EMP: 19
SQ FT: 8,000
SALES (est): 5.9MM **Privately Held**
SIC: 3823 Programmers, process type

(P-20956)
VERTIV CORPORATION
35 Parker, Irvine (92618-1605)
PHONE.................................949 457-3600
Anita Golden, *Branch Mgr*
Rj Miller, *Marketing Staff*
EMP: 50
SALES (corp-wide): 2.9B **Privately Held**
SIC: 3823 Industrial instrmnts msrmnt display/control process variable
HQ: Vertiv Corporation
1050 Dearborn Dr
Columbus OH 43085
614 888-0246

(P-20957)
WATER RESOURCES CAL DEPT
901 P St Lbby, Sacramento (95814-6424)
PHONE.................................916 651-9203
Mark Cowin, *Branch Mgr*
EMP: 99 **Privately Held**
SIC: 3823 Water quality monitoring & control systems
HQ: California Department Of Water Resources
1416 9th St
Sacramento CA 95814
916 653-9394

(P-20958)
WORLDWIDE ENVMTL PDTS INC
(PA)
Also Called: Imperials Sand Dunes
1100 Beacon St, Brea (92821-2936)
PHONE.................................714 990-2700
William Oscar Delaney, *CEO*
Dick Creagh, *CFO*
Garrett Delaney, *Chief Mktg Ofcr*
Steve N Green, *Officer*
Steven Alford, *Info Tech Mgr*
EMP: 90
SQ FT: 23,000
SALES: 18.6MM **Privately Held**
WEB: www.wep-inc.com
SIC: 3823 3694 Industrial instrmnts msrmnt display/control process variable; automotive electrical equipment

(P-20959)
XIRRUS INC
2101 Corporate Center Dr A, Thousand Oaks (91320-1419)
PHONE.................................805 262-1600
Shane Buckley, *CEO*
Steve Degennaro, *CFO*
Jillian Mansolf, *Chief Mktg Ofcr*
Sam Bass, *Vice Pres*

John Hudson, *Vice Pres*
◆ EMP: 200
SQ FT: 25,000
SALES (est): 48.3MM **Privately Held**
WEB: www.xirrus.com
SIC: 3823 Computer interface equipment for industrial process control

(P-20960)
YOUNG ENGINEERING & MFG
INC (PA)
560 W Terrace Dr, San Dimas
(91773-2914)
P.O. Box 3984 (91773-7984)
PHONE.................................909 394-3225
Winston Young, *President*
Joanne Young, *Vice Pres*
Ken Krogen, *CTO*
Adam Stubblefield, *Sales Staff*
◆ EMP: 32
SQ FT: 55,000
SALES (est): 4.5MM **Privately Held**
WEB: www.youngeng.com
SIC: 3823 5084 8711 5074 Industrial instrmnts msrmnt display/control process variable; industrial machinery & equipment; consulting engineer; water purification equipment

---
3824 Fluid Meters &
Counters

(P-20961)
BLUE-WHITE INDUSTRIES LTD
(PA)
5300 Business Dr, Huntington Beach
(92649-1224)
PHONE.................................714 893-8529
Robert E Gledhill, *President*
Cindy Henderson, *Corp Secy*
Robert E Gledhill III, *Vice Pres*
Jeanne Hendrickson, *Vice Pres*
Daniel Estrada, *General Mgr*
▲ EMP: 71 EST: 1957
SQ FT: 48,000
SALES: 20MM **Privately Held**
WEB: www.bluwhite.com
SIC: 3824 3561 3589 Water meters; industrial pumps & parts; sewage & water treatment equipment

(P-20962)
BRITELAB
6341 San Ignacio Ave, San Jose
(95119-1202)
PHONE.................................650 961-0671
Robert De Neve, *CEO*
Paul Rogan, *CFO*
Kip Smith, *Officer*
Peter Kim, *Vice Pres*
Jae Jung, *Security Dir*
▲ EMP: 65
SQ FT: 52,000
SALES (est): 29.9MM **Privately Held**
SIC: 3824 8741 8742 Mechanical & electromechanical counters & devices; management services; management consulting services

(P-20963)
COUNTY OF ALAMEDA
Also Called: Registrar of Voters Office
1225 Fallon St Ste G1, Oakland
(94612-4229)
PHONE.................................510 272-6964
Bradley Clark, *Principal*
Gerald Veras, *Manager*
EMP: 30 **Privately Held**
WEB: www.co.alameda.ca.us
SIC: 3824 9199 Registers, linear tallying; general government administration;
PA: County Of Alameda
1221 Oak St Ste 555
Oakland CA 94612
510 272-6691

(P-20964)
CURTIS INSTRUMENTS INC
Also Called: Curtis PMC
235 E Airway Blvd, Livermore
(94551-7664)
PHONE.................................925 961-1088
Steven Post, *Branch Mgr*
Steve Post, *General Mgr*

Andrea Mokros, *Administration*
Larry Piggins, *Software Engr*
Kathy Kirby, *Technology*
EMP: 70
SALES (corp-wide): 301.5MM **Privately Held**
SIC: 3824 3829 3825 3629 Speed indicators & recorders, vehicle; aircraft & motor vehicle measurement equipment; elapsed time meters, electronic; electronic generation equipment; relays & industrial controls; motors & generators
PA: Curtis Instruments, Inc.
    200 Kisco Ave
    Mount Kisco NY 10549
    914 666-2971

(P-20965)
DANAHER CORPORATION
Ketema Division
3255 W Stetson Ave, Hemet (92545-7763)
PHONE.....................951 652-6811
James Pugh, *Branch Mgr*
Steve Sheere, *Info Tech Mgr*
Mike Dyer, *Opers Staff*
EMP: 220
SALES (corp-wide): 19.8B **Publicly Held**
SIC: 3824 5084 3613 Water meters; industrial machinery & equipment; switchgear & switchboard apparatus
PA: Danaher Corporation
    2200 Penn Ave Nw Ste 800w
    Washington DC 20037
    202 828-0850

(P-20966)
DEXERIALS AMERICA CORPORATION
2001 Gateway Pl Ste 455e, San Jose (95110-1044)
PHONE.....................408 441-0846
Nelly Soudakova, *Owner*
Kentaro Matsumoto, *Sales Mgr*
Jennie Liu, *Sales Staff*
Tatsuo Nagamatsu, *Manager*
EMP: 10 **Privately Held**
SIC: 3824 Magnetic counters
HQ: Dexerials America Corporation
    215 Satellite Blvd Ne # 400
    Suwanee GA 30024
    770 945-3845

(P-20967)
EMCOR GROUP INC
2 Cromwell, Irvine (92618-1816)
PHONE.....................949 475-6020
Henry Magdaleno, *Principal*
Frank Ledda, *President*
EMP: 29
SALES (est): 12MM **Privately Held**
SIC: 3824 Fluid meters & counting devices

(P-20968)
EMITCON INC
Also Called: Airex
1175 N Van Horne Way, Anaheim (92806-2506)
PHONE.....................714 632-8595
Jack M Preston, *President*
EMP: 35
SQ FT: 45,000
SALES (est): 5.3MM **Privately Held**
SIC: 3824 Integrating & totalizing meters for gas & liquids

(P-20969)
EXELIXIS INC
Division 1
1851 Harbor Bay Pkwy, Alameda (94502-3010)
PHONE.....................650 837-7000
Michael M Morrissey, *President*
EMP: 371 **Publicly Held**
SIC: 3824 8731 Fluid meters & counting devices; commercial physical research; biological research
PA: Exelixis, Inc.
    1851 Harbor Bay Pkwy
    Alameda CA 94502

(P-20970)
INTERSCAN CORPORATION
4590 Ish Dr Ste 110, Simi Valley (93063-7682)
PHONE.....................805 823-8301

Richard Shaw, *President*
Lorienne Shaw, *Treasurer*
Michael Shaw, *Vice Pres*
Jordan Shaw, *Technical Staff*
EMP: 23
SQ FT: 10,000
SALES (est): 5.5MM **Privately Held**
WEB: www.gasdetection.com
SIC: 3824 3829 Gas meters, domestic & large capacity: industrial; measuring & controlling devices

(P-20971)
LIQUA-TECH CORPORATION
Also Called: L T C
3501 N State St, Ukiah (95482-3008)
PHONE.....................800 659-3556
Marta J Sligh, *President*
Edward L Bruce, *Director*
EMP: 14
SQ FT: 17,000
SALES (est): 3.2MM **Privately Held**
WEB: www.liqua-tech.com
SIC: 3824 Liquid meters

(P-20972)
MCCROMETER INC
3255 W Stetson Ave, Hemet (92545-7763)
PHONE.....................951 652-6811
Stephen Bell, *President*
Ian Rule, *Vice Pres*
◆ **EMP:** 230
SQ FT: 9,090
SALES (est): 64.3MM
SALES (corp-wide): 19.8B **Publicly Held**
WEB: www.mccrometer.com
SIC: 3824 Water meters
PA: Danaher Corporation
    2200 Penn Ave Nw Ste 800w
    Washington DC 20037
    202 828-0850

(P-20973)
MINDRUM PRECISION INC
Also Called: Mindrum Precision Products
10000 4th St, Rancho Cucamonga (91730-5793)
PHONE.....................909 989-1728
Diane Mindrum, *CEO*
Kurt Ponsor, *President*
Daniel Mindrum, *Corp Secy*
Dave Hamilton, *Vice Pres*
Daphne Fulayter, *Admin Asst*
EMP: 49
SQ FT: 30,000
SALES (est): 9.8MM **Privately Held**
WEB: www.mindrum.com
SIC: 3824 3827 3823 3264 Fluid meters & counting devices; optical instruments & lenses; industrial instrmnts msrmnt display/control process variable; porcelain electrical supplies; products of purchased glass

(P-20974)
PACIFIC UTILITY PRODUCTS INC
2950 E Philadelphia St, Ontario (91761-8545)
PHONE.....................909 923-1800
Diana Grootonk, *CEO*
EMP: 18 **EST:** 2013
SALES (est): 4MM **Privately Held**
SIC: 3824 Fluid meters & counting devices

(P-20975)
STEM CONSULTANTS INC
651 W Terrylynn Pl, Long Beach (90807-3121)
PHONE.....................612 987-8008
Tiroshen Fonseka, *CEO*
EMP: 10 **EST:** 2016
SALES (est): 923.4K **Privately Held**
SIC: 3824 8748 8711 7389 Mechanical & electromechanical counters & devices; systems analysis & engineering consulting services; mechanical engineering; structural engineering;

(P-20976)
THERMO GAMMA-METRICS LLC (HQ)
10010 Mesa Rim Rd, San Diego (92121-2912)
PHONE.....................858 450-9811
Ken Berger, *President*

Sandra Lambert, *Admin Sec*
▲ **EMP:** 20
SQ FT: 45,000
SALES (est): 7.5MM
SALES (corp-wide): 24.3B **Publicly Held**
WEB: www.gammametrics.com
SIC: 3824 3826 3812 3823 Controls, revolution & timing instruments; environmental testing equipment; search & detection systems & instruments; industrial instrmnts msrmnt display/control process variable
PA: Thermo Fisher Scientific Inc.
    168 3rd Ave
    Waltham MA 02451
    781 622-1000

(P-20977)
TRI-CONTINENT SCIENTIFIC INC
12740 Earhart Ave, Auburn (95602-9027)
PHONE.....................530 273-8888
Lee Carter, *CEO*
Brenton Hanlon, *President*
Sandra Zoch, *Treasurer*
Ross Waring, *Technician*
▲ **EMP:** 85
SQ FT: 34,000
SALES (est): 16MM
SALES (corp-wide): 2.6B **Publicly Held**
WEB: www.tricontinent.com
SIC: 3824 3829 3821 3561 Integrating & totalizing meters for gas & liquids; totalizing meters, consumption registering; measuring & controlling devices; laboratory apparatus & furniture; pumps & pumping equipment
HQ: Gardner Denver, Inc.
    222 E Erie St Ste 500
    Milwaukee WI 53202

(P-20978)
ZENNER PERFORMANCE METERS INC
1910 E Westward Ave, Banning (92220-6366)
P.O. Box 895 (92220-0019)
PHONE.....................951 849-8822
Ron Gallon, *CEO*
▲ **EMP:** 23
SALES (est): 5.4MM **Privately Held**
SIC: 3824 Water meters

3825 Instrs For Measuring & Testing Electricity

(P-20979)
2M MACHINING & MFG CO
8630 Santa Fe Ave, South Gate (90280-2601)
PHONE.....................323 564-9388
Kwok Lee, *President*
EMP: 15 **EST:** 1973
SQ FT: 11,000
SALES (est): 2MM **Privately Held**
SIC: 3825 Electrical power measuring equipment

(P-20980)
A H SYSTEMS INC
9710 Cozycroft Ave, Chatsworth (91311-4401)
PHONE.....................818 998-0223
Arthur C Cohen, *President*
Jodi Henderson, *Treasurer*
Michael Cohen, *Vice Pres*
Lori Weiss, *Admin Sec*
▲ **EMP:** 10
SQ FT: 5,300
SALES: 2MM **Privately Held**
WEB: www.ahsystems.com
SIC: 3825 Test equipment for electronic & electric measurement

(P-20981)
ACCEL-RF CORPORATION
4380 Viewridge Ave Ste D, San Diego (92123-1678)
PHONE.....................858 278-2074
Roland Shaw, *President*
Tucker Weaver, *CFO*
David Sanderlin, *Vice Pres*
Ellen Williams, *Principal*

Hannah Going, *General Mgr*
▲ **EMP:** 12
SALES (est): 4.2MM **Privately Held**
WEB: www.accelrf.com
SIC: 3825 Electron tube test equipment

(P-20982)
ADVANCED MICROTECHNOLOGY INC
480 Vista Way, Milpitas (95035-5406)
PHONE.....................408 945-9191
Eugene R Wertz, *President*
EMP: 15
SQ FT: 5,000
SALES (est): 2.2MM **Privately Held**
WEB: www.advancedmicrotech.com
SIC: 3825 8711 Test equipment for electronic & electrical circuits; engineering services

(P-20983)
ADVANCED SAFETY DEVICES LLC
Also Called: Asd
21430 Strathern St Unit M, Canoga Park (91304-4188)
PHONE.....................818 701-9200
Nima Parto, *General Mgr*
Mort Parto, *Sls & Mktg Exec*
▲ **EMP:** 10
SALES (est): 950K **Privately Held**
SIC: 3825 Instruments to measure electricity

(P-20984)
AEA TECHNOLOGY INC
5933 Sea Lion Pl Ste 112, Carlsbad (92010-6625)
PHONE.....................760 931-8979
George Naber, *President*
Ed Stevenson, *Vice Pres*
EMP: 10
SALES (est): 1.4MM **Privately Held**
SIC: 3825 Instruments to measure electricity

(P-20985)
AEHR TEST SYSTEMS (PA)
400 Kato Ter, Fremont (94539-8332)
PHONE.....................510 623-9400
Gayn Erickson, *President*
Rhea J Posedel, *Ch of Bd*
Kunio Sano, *President*
Kenneth B Spink, *CFO*
Mark D Allison, *Vice Pres*
▲ **EMP:** 86 **EST:** 1977
SQ FT: 51,289
SALES: 21MM **Publicly Held**
WEB: www.aehr.com
SIC: 3825 Test equipment for electronic & electrical circuits

(P-20986)
AGILENT TECH WORLD TRADE INC (HQ)
5301 Stevens Creek Blvd, Santa Clara (95051-7201)
PHONE.....................408 345-8886
Adrian Dillon, *CEO*
D Craig Norlund, *Treasurer*
Marie O Huber, *Asst Sec*
EMP: 15
SALES (est): 129.2MM
SALES (corp-wide): 4.9B **Publicly Held**
SIC: 3825 Instruments to measure electricity
PA: Agilent Technologies, Inc.
    5301 Stevens Creek Blvd
    Santa Clara CA 95051
    408 345-8886

(P-20987)
AGILENT TECHNOLOGIES INC
39201 Cherry St, Newark (94560-4967)
PHONE.....................510 794-1234
Cheol H Han, *Principal*
Doris Lee, *IT/INT Sup*
Stephan Jansen, *Engineer*
EMP: 350
SALES (corp-wide): 4.9B **Publicly Held**
WEB: www.agilent.com
SIC: 3825 Instruments to measure electricity

PRODUCTS & SVCS

PA: Agilent Technologies, Inc.
5301 Stevens Creek Blvd
Santa Clara CA 95051
408 345-8886

(P-20988)
AGILENT TECHNOLOGIES INC
91 Blue Ravine Rd, Folsom (95630-4720)
PHONE..................................916 985-7888
James T Olsen, *Branch Mgr*
EMP: 250
SALES (corp-wide): 4.9B Publicly Held
WEB: www.agilent.com
SIC: 3825 Instruments to measure electricity
PA: Agilent Technologies, Inc.
5301 Stevens Creek Blvd
Santa Clara CA 95051
408 345-8886

(P-20989)
AGILENT TECHNOLOGIES INC
1170 Mark Ave, Carpinteria (93013-2918)
PHONE..................................805 566-6655
Britt Meelby Jensen, *General Mgr*
Scott Reed, *Executive*
Jason Henry, *Administration*
Lynette Girvin, *Info Tech Dir*
Bonnie Gerstenfeld, *Project Mgr*
EMP: 17
SALES (corp-wide): 4.9B Publicly Held
SIC: 3825 Instruments to measure electricity
PA: Agilent Technologies, Inc.
5301 Stevens Creek Blvd
Santa Clara CA 95051
408 345-8886

(P-20990)
AGILENT TECHNOLOGIES INC
Agilent Santa Clara Site
5301 Stevens Creek Blvd, Santa Clara
(95051-7201)
P.O. Box 58059 (95052-8059)
PHONE..................................408 345-8886
Bill Sullivan, *CEO*
EMP: 2000
SALES (corp-wide): 4.9B Publicly Held
WEB: www.agilent.com
SIC: 3825 Instruments to measure electricity
PA: Agilent Technologies, Inc.
5301 Stevens Creek Blvd
Santa Clara CA 95051
408 345-8886

(P-20991)
AGILENT TECHNOLOGIES INC
11011 N Torrey Pines Rd, La Jolla
(92037-1007)
PHONE..................................858 373-6300
Janet King, *Principal*
Sande Hessler, *Manager*
EMP: 453
SALES (corp-wide): 4.9B Publicly Held
SIC: 3825 Instruments to measure electricity
PA: Agilent Technologies, Inc.
5301 Stevens Creek Blvd
Santa Clara CA 95051
408 345-8886

(P-20992)
AGILENT TECHNOLOGIES INC
395 Page Mill Rd, Palo Alto (94306-2065)
PHONE..................................877 424-4536
Shirley Lamkin, *Admin Asst*
Kar Tiang, *Admin Asst*
Linda Keighley, *Administration*
Amber Colandone, *Comp Spec*
Lindsay Buck, *Research*
EMP: 51
SALES (est): 5.8MM Privately Held
SIC: 3825 Instruments to measure electricity

(P-20993)
AGILENT TECHNOLOGIES INC
(PA)
5301 Stevens Creek Blvd, Santa Clara
(95051-7201)
P.O. Box 58059 (95052-8059)
PHONE..................................408 345-8886
Michael R McMullen, *President*
Henrik Ancher-Jensen, *President*
Robert W McMahon, *CFO*

Mark Doak, *Senior VP*
Dominique P Grau, *Senior VP*
▲ EMP: 277
SALES: 4.9B Publicly Held
WEB: www.agilent.com
SIC: 3825 3826 7372 Instruments to
measure electricity; analytical instruments; gas testing apparatus; instruments
measuring magnetic & electrical properties; prepackaged software

(P-20994)
AGILENT TECHNOLOGIES INC
Also Called: Agilent Labs
5301 Stevens Creek Blvd, Santa Clara
(95051-7201)
PHONE..................................408 345-8886
Gail Jacobs, *Branch Mgr*
Hewlett E Melton Jr, *Principal*
EMP: 3275
SALES (corp-wide): 4.9B Publicly Held
WEB: www.agilent.com
SIC: 3825 Instruments to measure electricity
PA: Agilent Technologies, Inc.
5301 Stevens Creek Blvd
Santa Clara CA 95051
408 345-8886

(P-20995)
AGILENT TECHNOLOGIES INC
3175 Bowers Ave, Santa Clara
(95054-3225)
P.O. Box 58059 (95052-8059)
PHONE..................................408 553-7777
Paul Sedlewicz, *Branch Mgr*
EMP: 3275
SALES (corp-wide): 4.9B Publicly Held
WEB: www.agilent.com
SIC: 3825 Instruments to measure electricity
PA: Agilent Technologies, Inc.
5301 Stevens Creek Blvd
Santa Clara CA 95051
408 345-8886

(P-20996)
AGILENT TECHNOLOGIES INC
30721 Russell Ranch Rd, Westlake Village
(91362-7382)
PHONE..................................408 345-8886
Alice Liu, *Principal*
EMP: 3275
SALES (corp-wide): 4.9B Publicly Held
WEB: www.agilent.com
SIC: 3825 Instruments to measure electricity
PA: Agilent Technologies, Inc.
5301 Stevens Creek Blvd
Santa Clara CA 95051
408 345-8886

(P-20997)
AGILENT TECHNOLOGIES INC
11011 N Torrey Pines Rd, La Jolla
(92037-1007)
PHONE..................................858 373-6300
EMP: 453
SALES (corp-wide): 4B Publicly Held
SIC: 3825
PA: Agilent Technologies, Inc.
5301 Stevens Creek Blvd
Santa Clara CA 95051
408 345-8886

(P-20998)
ALTA PROPERTIES INC
International Transducer
869 Ward Dr, Santa Barbara (93111-2920)
PHONE..................................805 683-2575
Brian Dolan, *Director*
EMP: 475
SALES (corp-wide): 197.5MM Privately Held
SIC: 3825 3812 Transducers for volts, amperes, watts, vars, frequency, etc.; search
& navigation equipment
PA: Alta Properties, Inc.
879 Ward Dr
Santa Barbara CA 93111
805 967-0171

(P-20999)
ALTA SOLUTIONS INC
12580 Stowe Dr, Poway (92064-6804)
PHONE..................................858 668-5200

Robert B Mihata, *President*
Julia K Mihata, *COO*
David S Baggest, *Vice Pres*
Dave Baggest, *Engineer*
John Polhemus, *Regl Sales Mgr*
EMP: 14
SQ FT: 12,000
SALES (est): 3.8MM Privately Held
WEB: www.altasol.com
SIC: 3825 Instruments to measure electricity

(P-21000)
**AMERICAN AMPLIFIER TECH
LLC**
7889 Lichen Dr 360, Citrus Heights
(95621-1074)
PHONE..................................530 574-3474
Steven Wild, *Mng Member*
EMP: 11 EST: 2014
SALES: 1.5MM Privately Held
SIC: 3825 5731 5065 5961 Radio set analyzers, electrical; radios, receiver type;
radio receiving & transmitting tubes;

(P-21001)
AMERICAN PROBE & TECH INC
1795 Grogan Ave, Merced (95341-6455)
PHONE..................................408 263-3356
Kenneth M Chabraya, *President*
Kim Merrill, *Vice Pres*
EMP: 11
SQ FT: 4,300
SALES: 1MM Privately Held
WEB: www.americanprobe.com
SIC: 3825 Test equipment for electronic &
electric measurement

(P-21002)
**AMETEK PROGRAMMABLE
POWER INC (HQ)**
9250 Brown Deer Rd, San Diego
(92121-2267)
PHONE..................................858 450-0085
Timothy F Croal, *CEO*
John Molinelli, *CFO*
Shawn Smith, *Vice Pres*
Dylan Mora, *Program Mgr*
Ponciano Benavides, *Technician*
▲ EMP: 219 EST: 2006
SQ FT: 110,000
SALES (est): 88.5MM
SALES (corp-wide): 4.8B Publicly Held
WEB: www.elgar.com
SIC: 3825 Instruments to measure electricity
PA: Ametek, Inc.
1100 Cassatt Rd
Berwyn PA 19312
610 647-2121

(P-21003)
ANRITSU US HOLDING INC (HQ)
Also Called: Anritsu Company
490 Jarvis Dr, Morgan Hill (95037-2834)
PHONE..................................408 778-2000
Wade Hulon, *President*
Jon Martens, *Vice Chairman*
Oneill Brian, *Principal*
Randy McNeil, *Engineer*
Andy Sailor, *Engineer*
▲ EMP: 500
SQ FT: 244,000
SALES: 323.5MM Privately Held
SIC: 3825 3663 5065 Test equipment for
electronic & electric measurement; radio
& TV communications equipment; electronic parts & equipment

(P-21004)
**APPLIED MICROSTRUCTURES
INC**
2381 Bering Dr, San Jose (95131-1125)
PHONE..................................408 907-2885
Jeffrey Chinn, *CEO*
Fred Helmrich, *Vice Pres*
EMP: 17
SQ FT: 3,500
SALES (est): 3.2MM Privately Held
SIC: 3825 Digital panel meters, electricity
measuring

(P-21005)
APRIL INSTRUMENT
1401 Fallen Leaf Ln, Los Altos
(94024-5810)
P.O. Box 62046, Sunnyvale (94088-2046)
PHONE..................................650 964-8379
Bill Chan, *Owner*
EMP: 10
SALES: 2MM Privately Held
WEB: www.aprilinstrument.com
SIC: 3825 Microwave test equipment

(P-21006)
**ARBITER SYSTEMS
INCORPORATED (PA)**
1324 Vendels Cir Ste 121, Paso Robles
(93446-3806)
PHONE..................................805 237-3831
Craig Armstrong, *President*
Bruce Roeder, *CFO*
Steve Myers, *Sales Mgr*
EMP: 30 EST: 1973
SQ FT: 15,000
SALES (est): 3.6MM Privately Held
WEB: www.arbiter.com
SIC: 3825 3829 3663 Test equipment for
electronic & electric measurement; measuring & controlling devices; radio & TV
communications equipment

(P-21007)
**ASTRONICS TEST SYSTEMS INC
(HQ)**
4 Goodyear, Irvine (92618-2002)
PHONE..................................800 722-2528
James Mulato, *President*
David Burney, *Treasurer*
Jonathan Sinskie, *Vice Pres*
◆ EMP: 130
SQ FT: 98,600
SALES (est): 99.6MM
SALES (corp-wide): 803.2MM Publicly
Held
SIC: 3825 Test equipment for electronic &
electric measurement
PA: Astronics Corporation
130 Commerce Way
East Aurora NY 14052
716 805-1599

(P-21008)
AZIMUTH ELECTRONICS INC
2605 S El Camino Real, San Clemente
(92672-3353)
PHONE..................................949 492-6481
Kenneth C Johnson, *President*
Kenneth C Johnsen, *President*
Ro Hall, *Sales Mgr*
EMP: 13
SQ FT: 3,600
SALES (est): 2.2MM Privately Held
WEB: www.azimuth-electronics.com
SIC: 3825 7389 Test equipment for electronic & electrical circuits; design, commercial & industrial

(P-21009)
**B&K PRECISION CORPORATION
(PA)**
22820 Savi Ranch Pkwy, Yorba Linda
(92887-4610)
PHONE..................................714 921-9095
Victor Tolan, *CEO*
Linda Morton, *CFO*
Jorg Hesser, *Vice Pres*
Ahmad Daouk, *Mktg Dir*
Renato Araga, *Marketing Mgr*
▲ EMP: 25
SQ FT: 17,000
SALES (est): 5.9MM Privately Held
SIC: 3825 5063 Instruments to measure
electricity; electrical apparatus & equipment

(P-21010)
**BAE SYSTEMS INFO & ELEC
SYS**
10920 Technology Pl, San Diego
(92127-1874)
PHONE..................................858 592-5000
Jordan Becker, *Vice Pres*
William Barfield, *Software Dev*
Lynne Ross, *Human Res Dir*
Angelo Hammond, *Manager*
EMP: 200

SALES (corp-wide): 21.6B **Privately Held**
SIC: 3825 7373 3812 Test equipment for electronic & electric measurement; computer integrated systems design; search & navigation equipment
HQ: Bae Systems Information And Electronic Systems Integration Inc.
65 Spit Brook Rd
Nashua NH 03060
603 885-4321

(P-21011)
BAUGHN ENGINEERING INC
2815 Metropolitan Pl, Pomona (91767-1853)
PHONE.................................909 392-0933
Daniel Baughn, *President*
Sandra Baughn, *Admin Sec*
Tracy Kiernan, *Engineer*
Mark B Baughn, *Plant Supt*
EMP: 11
SQ FT: 10,400
SALES (est): 2.3MM **Privately Held**
WEB: www.baughneng.com
SIC: 3825 8711 Test equipment for electronic & electric measurement; engineering services; aviation &/or aeronautical engineering

(P-21012)
BLUE ROCK NETWORKS LLC
1160 Battery St Ste 100, San Francisco (94111-1233)
PHONE.................................415 577-8004
Christian Beumann, *Principal*
EMP: 14
SALES (est): 1.9MM **Privately Held**
SIC: 3825 Network analyzers

(P-21013)
BOURNS INC
Bourns Sensor Controls
1200 Columbia Ave, Riverside (92507-2129)
PHONE.................................951 781-5690
James Davis, *President*
EMP: 150
SALES (corp-wide): 550MM **Privately Held**
WEB: www.bourns.com
SIC: 3825 Instruments to measure electricity
PA: Bourns, Inc.
1200 Columbia Ave
Riverside CA 92507
951 781-5500

(P-21014)
BOURNS INC
8662 Siempre Viva Rd, San Diego (92154-6211)
PHONE.................................951 781-5360
▲ EMP: 12
SALES (est): 1.5MM **Privately Held**
SIC: 3825

(P-21015)
CALOGIC LLC (PA)
237 Whitney Pl, Fremont (94539-7664)
PHONE.................................510 656-2900
Jonathan Kaye, *President*
Kathryn Kaye,
Mark Sylva, *Director*
EMP: 14
SQ FT: 10,314
SALES (est): 1.4MM **Privately Held**
WEB: www.calogic.com
SIC: 3825 Instruments to measure electricity

(P-21016)
CHROMA SYSTEMS SOLUTIONS INC (HQ)
19772 Pauling, Foothill Ranch (92610-2611)
PHONE.................................949 297-4848
Fred Sabatine, *President*
Abbas Ford, *Executive*
Philip Ngo, *Program Mgr*
Nathan Chang, *Administration*
David Kargel, *Technician*
▲ EMP: 89
SQ FT: 25,000

SALES (est): 18.7MM **Privately Held**
WEB: www.chromausa.com
SIC: 3825 Measuring instruments & meters, electric

(P-21017)
CIRCUIT CHECK INC
1764 Houret Ct, Milpitas (95035-6829)
PHONE.................................408 263-7444
Steve Herrera, *Manager*
EMP: 80 **Privately Held**
SIC: 3825 Test equipment for electronic & electric measurement
HQ: Circuit Check, Inc.
6550 Wedgwood Rd N # 120
Maple Grove MN 55311
763 694-4100

(P-21018)
COHU INC (PA)
12367 Crosthwaite Cir, Poway (92064-6817)
PHONE.................................858 848-8100
Luis A Muller, *President*
James A Donahue, *Ch of Bd*
Jeffrey D Jones, *CFO*
Steven Bilodeau, *Bd of Directors*
Andrew Caggia, *Bd of Directors*
▲ EMP: 122
SQ FT: 147,000
SALES: 451.7MM **Publicly Held**
WEB: www.cohu.com
SIC: 3825 Semiconductor test equipment

(P-21019)
COMPLIANCE PRODUCTS USA INC
Also Called: Compliance West USA
650 Gateway Center Way D, San Diego (92102-4547)
PHONE.................................619 878-9696
Jeff Lind, *President*
Raul Ruiz, *Opers Mgr*
EMP: 10
SALES (est): 1.9MM **Privately Held**
WEB: www.compwest.com
SIC: 3825 Test equipment for electronic & electric measurement; pulse (signal) generators

(P-21020)
CONCISYS INC
5452 Oberlin Dr, San Diego (92121-1715)
PHONE.................................858 292-5888
Giao Huu Nguyen, *CEO*
Vu Wing, *President*
▲ EMP: 40
SALES (est): 20.3MM **Privately Held**
SIC: 3825 Digital test equipment, electronic & electrical circuits

(P-21021)
CONNOR J INC
Also Called: Jetco
835 Meridian St, Irwindale (91010-3587)
PHONE.................................626 358-3820
Bradley G Jenkins, *President*
Deborah L Jenkins, *CFO*
▲ EMP: 10
SQ FT: 3,600
SALES (est): 2MM **Privately Held**
WEB: www.itorque.com
SIC: 3825 2951 Test equipment for electronic & electric measurement; asphalt paving mixtures & blocks

(P-21022)
DELTA DESIGN LITTLETON INC (HQ)
12367 Crosthwaite Cir, Poway (92064-6817)
PHONE.................................858 848-8100
Charles A Schwan, *Ch of Bd*
Nicholas J Cedrone, *Vice Pres*
▲ EMP: 10 EST: 1959
SQ FT: 102,000
SALES (est): 31.6MM
SALES (corp-wide): 451.7MM **Publicly Held**
SIC: 3825 Test equipment for electronic & electrical circuits
PA: Cohu, Inc.
12367 Crosthwaite Cir
Poway CA 92064
858 848-8100

(P-21023)
DYNATEST CONSULTING INC
165 S Chestnut St, Ventura (93001-2808)
PHONE.................................805 648-2230
William A Beck II, *President*
Donovan Morse, *Technician*
Reuben Williams, *Senior Engr*
Lauren Barney, *Accountant*
Richmond Ryan, *Controller*
EMP: 18
SALES (est): 2.2MM **Privately Held**
WEB: www.dynatest.com
SIC: 3825 Instruments to measure electricity

(P-21024)
ECHELON CORPORATION (HQ)
3600 Peterson Way, Santa Clara (95054-2808)
PHONE.................................408 938-5200
Ronald Sege, *President*
Andrew Maisel, *Chief Mktg Ofcr*
Alicia Jayne Moore, *Officer*
Christopher Jodoin, *Vice Pres*
Michael Milsner, *Sr Software Eng*
▲ EMP: 55
SQ FT: 32,000
SALES: 31.6MM **Publicly Held**
WEB: www.echelon.com
SIC: 3825 7371 Network analyzers; computer software systems analysis & design, custom; computer software development

(P-21025)
ECLYPSE INTERNATIONAL CORP (PA)
265 N Joy St Ste 150, Corona (92879-0600)
PHONE.................................951 371-8008
Tom Day, *Ch of Bd*
Glen Coulter, *Shareholder*
C Alan Ferguson, *CEO*
David Hieger, *Program Mgr*
Benjamin Nhan, *Programmer Anys*
EMP: 15
SQ FT: 2,000
SALES (est): 2.7MM **Privately Held**
SIC: 3825 8711 Test equipment for electronic & electrical circuits; consulting engineer

(P-21026)
EICO INC (PA)
1054 Yosemite Dr, Milpitas (95035-5410)
PHONE.................................408 945-9898
Hsun K Chou, *President*
EMP: 55
SQ FT: 18,000
SALES (est): 13.3MM **Privately Held**
WEB: www.eico.net
SIC: 3825 Instruments to measure electricity

(P-21027)
ELECRAFT INCORPORATED
125 Westridge Dr, Watsonville (95076-4167)
P.O. Box 69, Aptos (95001-0069)
PHONE.................................831 763-4211
Eric Swartz, *President*
Wayne Burdick, *Principal*
Dick Dievendorff, *Sr Software Eng*
Jones Lisa, *Info Tech Mgr*
Rene Morris, *Technician*
EMP: 35
SALES (est): 12.1MM **Privately Held**
WEB: www.elecraft.com
SIC: 3825 Oscillators, audio & radio frequency (instrument types)

(P-21028)
ELECTRIQ POWER INC
14451 Catalina St, San Leandro (94577-5515)
PHONE.................................408 393-7702
Frank Magnotti, *CEO*
Jim Lovewell, *President*
Jeffrey Besen, *Vice Pres*
Chadwick Manning, *Security Dir*
Jan Klube, *VP Engrg*
EMP: 17
SALES (est): 748.3K **Privately Held**
SIC: 3825 7371 Electrical energy measuring equipment; computer software development & applications

(P-21029)
EQUUS PRODUCTS INC
17352 Von Karman Ave, Irvine (92614-6204)
PHONE.................................714 424-6779
Ieon C Chen, *CEO*
Cynthia H Tsai, *CFO*
◆ EMP: 31
SQ FT: 36,000
SALES (est): 7.9MM **Privately Held**
SIC: 3825 3545 3714 Electrical power measuring equipment; machine tool accessories; motor vehicle parts & accessories

(P-21030)
ERP POWER LLC (PA)
893 Patriot Dr Ste E, Moorpark (93021-3357)
PHONE.................................805 517-1300
Jeffrey Frank, *CEO*
Abdul Sher-Jan, *COO*
James Kingman, *Exec VP*
Andy Williams, *Exec VP*
Laurent Jenck, *Vice Pres*
EMP: 17
SALES (est): 10.3MM **Privately Held**
SIC: 3825 Energy measuring equipment, electrical

(P-21031)
ESSAI INC (PA)
48580 Kato Rd, Fremont (94538-7338)
PHONE.................................510 580-1700
Nasser Barabi, *CEO*
Tim Abril, *Engineer*
Evan Bunce, *Engineer*
Shadaya Bridges, *Human Res Mgr*
Behrooz Sajjadi, *Plant Mgr*
EMP: 130
SALES (est): 41.4MM **Privately Held**
SIC: 3825 Semiconductor test equipment; alternator & generator testers

(P-21032)
EUGENUS INC (HQ)
677 River Oaks Pkwy, San Jose (95134-1907)
PHONE.................................669 235-8244
Pyung Yong Um, *CEO*
EMP: 78
SQ FT: 2,700
SALES (est): 10MM **Privately Held**
SIC: 3825 Semiconductor test equipment

(P-21033)
EVERETT CHARLES TECH LLC (DH)
Also Called: Factron Test Fixtures
14570 Meyer Canyon Dr # 100, Fontana (92336-4029)
PHONE.................................909 625-5551
Dave Taclli, *CEO*
David Van Loan, *President*
▲ EMP: 100 EST: 1965
SALES (est): 47.2MM
SALES (corp-wide): 451.7MM **Publicly Held**
WEB: www.ectinfo.com
SIC: 3825 3678 Test equipment for electronic & electrical circuits; electronic connectors
HQ: Xcerra Corporation
825 University Ave
Norwood MA 02062
781 461-1000

(P-21034)
EVERETT CHARLES TECH LLC
14570 Meyer Canyon Dr # 100, Fontana (92336-4029)
PHONE.................................909 625-5551
Mary Au, *Principal*
EMP: 10
SALES (corp-wide): 451.7MM **Publicly Held**
SIC: 3825 Test equipment for electronic & electrical circuits
HQ: Everett Charles Technologies, Llc
14570 Meyer Canyon Dr # 100
Fontana CA 92336
909 625-5551

(P-21035)
EXATRON INC
2842 Aiello Dr, San Jose (95111-2154)
PHONE................................408 629-7600
Robert Howell, *CEO*
Eric Hagquist, *Treasurer*
Adam Nomura, *Engineer*
Terri Nigh, *Buyer*
Gloria Matson, *Sales Staff*
EMP: 25
SQ FT: 15,500
SALES (est): 6.5MM **Privately Held**
WEB: www.exatron.com
SIC: 3825 Integrated circuit testers

(P-21036)
EXCEL PRECISION CORP USA
3350 Scott Blvd Bldg 62, Santa Clara
(95054-3125)
PHONE................................408 727-4260
John Tsai, *CEO*
Lon Allen, *Admin Sec*
EMP: 25
SQ FT: 5,500
SALES (est): 4.8MM **Privately Held**
WEB: www.excelprecision.com
SIC: 3825 3829 3827 3826 Measuring instruments & meters, electric; measuring & controlling devices; optical instruments & lenses; analytical instruments

(P-21037)
FIELDPIECE INSTRUMENTS INC
1636 W Collins Ave, Orange (92867-5421)
PHONE................................714 634-1844
Rey Harju, *President*
Jim Gregorec, *Engineer*
▲ EMP: 10
SQ FT: 4,000
SALES (est): 2.5MM **Privately Held**
WEB: www.fieldpiece.com
SIC: 3825 3829 3826 3823 Instruments for measuring electrical quantities; measuring & controlling devices; analytical instruments; industrial instrmnts msrmnt display/control process variable

(P-21038)
FISCHER CSTM
CMMUNICATIONS INC (PA)
19220 Normandie Ave B, Torrance
(90502-1011)
PHONE................................310 303-3300
Virginia Fischer, *CEO*
David Fischer, *President*
Allen Fischer, *Vice Pres*
EMP: 28
SALES (est): 7.6MM **Privately Held**
WEB: www.fischercc.com
SIC: 3825 Digital test equipment, electronic & electrical circuits; impedance measuring equipment; transducers for volts, amperes, watts, vars, frequency, etc.; transformers, portable: instrument

(P-21039)
FLUX POWER INC
2685 S Melrose Dr, Vista (92081-8783)
PHONE................................760 741-3589
Ronald F Dutt, *President*
Paul Geantil, *Engineer*
Carla Collignon, *Controller*
Gary Wellinger, *Regl Sales Mgr*
▲ EMP: 10
SALES (est): 2.5MM **Publicly Held**
SIC: 3825 Battery testers, electrical
PA: Flux Power Holdings, Inc.
2685 S Melrose Dr
Vista CA 92081

(P-21040)
FOUR DIMENSIONS INC
3140 Diablo Ave, Hayward (94545-2702)
PHONE................................510 782-1843
James T Chen, *President*
Constance Chen, *Corp Secy*
▲ EMP: 15 EST: 1978
SQ FT: 8,800
SALES (est): 3.3MM **Privately Held**
WEB: www.4dimensions.com
SIC: 3825 Semiconductor test equipment

(P-21041)
GANTNER INSTRUMENTS INC
1550 Hotel Cir N, San Diego (92108-2901)
PHONE................................858 537-2060
Robert Henley, *President*
EMP: 50 EST: 2010
SALES (est): 6.4MM
SALES (corp-wide): 4.5MM **Privately Held**
SIC: 3825 Test equipment for electronic & electric measurement
PA: Gantner Instruments Gmbh
Montafoner StraBe 4
Schruns 6780
555 677-4630

(P-21042)
GENEFORGE INC
2699 Spring St, Redwood City
(94063-3521)
PHONE................................650 219-9335
Mike Bailey, *President*
EMP: 10
SALES (est): 878.8K **Privately Held**
SIC: 3825 Frequency synthesizers

(P-21043)
GIGA-TRONICS INCORPORATED
(PA)
5990 Gleason Dr, Dublin (94568-7644)
PHONE................................925 328-4650
John R Regazzi, *CEO*
William J Thompson, *Ch of Bd*
Lutz P Henckels, *CFO*
Traci Mitchell, *Officer*
Tim Ursprung, *VP Bus Dvlpt*
EMP: 39 EST: 1980
SQ FT: 23,873
SALES: 11.1MM **Publicly Held**
WEB: www.gigatronics.com
SIC: 3825 3674 3823 Microwave test equipment; pulse (signal) generators; signal generators & averagers; sweep generators; microcircuits, integrated (semiconductor); modules, solid state; computer interface equipment for industrial process control

(P-21044)
GOLDEN ALTOS CORPORATION
402 S Hillview Dr, Milpitas (95035-5464)
PHONE................................408 956-1010
Alexander H C Chang, *CEO*
▲ EMP: 50
SQ FT: 10,000
SALES (est): 10MM
SALES (corp-wide): 13.3MM **Privately Held**
WEB: www.goldenaltos.com
SIC: 3825 3674 3672 Integrated circuit testers; semiconductors & related devices; printed circuit boards
PA: Eico, Inc.
1054 Yosemite Dr
Milpitas CA 95035
408 945-9898

(P-21045)
GOULD & BASS COMPANY INC
1431 W 2nd St, Pomona (91766-1299)
PHONE................................909 623-6793
John S Bass, *CEO*
Jim Borucki, *Vice Pres*
Don Todd, *Vice Pres*
Jeremy Basse, *Purchasing*
Ed Plachy, *Manager*
EMP: 32
SQ FT: 66,000
SALES (est): 9MM **Privately Held**
WEB: www.gould-bass.net
SIC: 3825 3535 3556 Test equipment for electronic & electric measurement; belt conveyor systems, general industrial use; packing house machinery

(P-21046)
GREENLEE TEXTRON INC
7098 Miratech Dr Ste 130, San Diego
(92121-3111)
PHONE................................858 530-3100
Robert Crick, *Principal*
EMP: 96
SALES (corp-wide): 17.4B **Publicly Held**
SIC: 3825 Battery testers, electrical

HQ: Greenlee Textron Inc.
4455 Boeing Dr
Rockford IL 61109
800 435-0786

(P-21047)
GREGORY ASSOCIATES INC
1233 Belknap Ct, Cupertino (95014-4904)
PHONE................................408 446-5725
EMP: 24
SQ FT: 21,000
SALES (est): 3.3MM **Privately Held**
SIC: 3825 8711 3674

(P-21048)
GUIDETECH INC
1300 Memorex Dr, Santa Clara
(95050-2813)
PHONE................................408 733-6555
Frank McKiney, *President*
Hans Betz, *Ch of Bd*
▲ EMP: 25
SQ FT: 50,000
SALES (est): 4.7MM **Privately Held**
WEB: www.jitter.net
SIC: 3825 Test equipment for electronic & electric measurement

(P-21049)
GUZIK TECHNICAL
ENTERPRISES
2443 Wyandotte St, Mountain View
(94043-2350)
PHONE................................650 625-8000
Nahum Guzik, *President*
▲ EMP: 51
SQ FT: 60,000
SALES (est): 16.5MM **Privately Held**
WEB: www.guzik.com
SIC: 3825 3829 3577 Test equipment for electronic & electrical circuits; measuring & controlling devices; computer peripheral equipment

(P-21050)
HEXAGON METROLOGY INC
Romer Cimcore
3536 Seagate Way, Oceanside
(92056-2672)
PHONE................................760 994-1401
Steve Ilmrud, *General Mgr*
EMP: 60
SALES (corp-wide): 4.3B **Privately Held**
SIC: 3825 Instruments to measure electricity
HQ: Hexagon Metrology, Inc.
250 Circuit Dr
North Kingstown RI 02852
401 886-2000

(P-21051)
INFORMATION SCAN TECH INC
Also Called: I S T
487 Gianni St, Santa Clara (95054-2414)
PHONE................................408 988-1908
Richard Chang, *President*
Peter Chou, *Vice Pres*
Tony Lee, *Vice Pres*
▲ EMP: 13
SQ FT: 12,000
SALES (est): 1.9MM **Privately Held**
WEB: www.infoscantech.com
SIC: 3825 Test equipment for electronic & electrical circuits

(P-21052)
INGRASYS TECHNOLOGY USA
INC
2025 Gateway Pl Ste 190, San Jose
(95110-1052)
PHONE................................863 271-8266
Taiyu Chou, *CEO*
▲ EMP: 20 EST: 2009
SALES (est): 11MM **Privately Held**
SIC: 3825 4899 Network analyzers; communication signal enhancement network system
PA: Ingrasys Technology Inc.
21f, No. 207, Fuxing Rd.
Taoyuan City TAY 33066

(P-21053)
INTELLIGENT CMPT SOLUTIONS
INC (PA)
8968 Fullbright Ave, Chatsworth
(91311-6123)
PHONE................................818 998-5805
Uzi Kohavi, *President*
Gonen Ravid, *CEO*
▲ EMP: 25
SQ FT: 21,000
SALES (est): 4.9MM **Privately Held**
SIC: 3825 3577 3572 Test equipment for electronic & electrical circuits; computer peripheral equipment; computer storage devices

(P-21054)
INTEPRO AMERICA LP (PA)
14662 Franklin Ave Ste E, Tustin
(92780-7224)
PHONE................................714 953-2686
Gary Halmbacher,
Joe Engler,
▲ EMP: 25
SALES (est): 3.6MM **Privately Held**
WEB: www.inteproate.com
SIC: 3825 Frequency meters: electrical, mechanical & electronic

(P-21055)
INTERNATIONAL TRANDUCER
CORP
Also Called: Channel Technologies Group
869 Ward Dr, Santa Barbara (93111-2920)
PHONE................................805 683-2575
R M Callahan, *Co-COB*
Kevin Ruelas, *President*
Robert F Carlson, *Co-COB*
Brian Dolan, *Director*
EMP: 160 EST: 1966
SALES (est): 50.7MM
SALES (corp-wide): 80.4MM **Privately Held**
WEB: www.itc-transducers.com
SIC: 3825 3812 Transducers for volts, amperes, watts, vars, frequency, etc.; search & navigation equipment
PA: Gavial Holdings, Inc.
1435 W Mccoy Ln
Santa Maria CA 93455
805 614-0060

(P-21056)
INTERSTATE ELECTRONICS
CORP (DH)
Also Called: L-3 Interstate Electronics
602 E Vermont Ave, Anaheim
(92805-5607)
P.O. Box 3117 (92803-3117)
PHONE................................714 758-0500
Thomas L Walsh, *President*
Carol Grogg, *Vice Pres*
Candace Lee, *Admin Sec*
EMP: 275
SQ FT: 235,700
SALES (est): 168.7MM
SALES (corp-wide): 6.8B **Publicly Held**
WEB: www.iechome.com
SIC: 3825 3812 3679 Test equipment for electronic & electric measurement; navigational systems & instruments; liquid crystal displays (LCD)
HQ: L3 Technologies, Inc.
600 3rd Ave Fl 34
New York NY 10016
212 697-1111

(P-21057)
IXIA (HQ)
26601 Agoura Rd, Calabasas
(91302-1959)
PHONE................................818 871-1800
Neil Dougherty, *President*
Jason Kary, *CFO*
Jeffrey LI, *Treasurer*
Matthew S Alexander, *Senior VP*
Stephen Williams, *Vice Pres*
EMP: 277
SQ FT: 116,000
SALES (est): 436.3MM
SALES (corp-wide): 3.8B **Publicly Held**
SIC: 3825 7371 Network analyzers; custom computer programming services

PA: Keysight Technologies, Inc.
1400 Fountaingrove Pkwy
Santa Rosa CA 95403
800 829-4444

(P-21058)
IXIA
Also Called: Ixia Communications
26701 Agoura Rd, Calabasas
(91302-1960)
PHONE..................................818 871-1800
EMP: 13
SALES (corp-wide): 3.8B Publicly Held
SIC: 3825 Network analyzers
HQ: Ixia
26601 Agoura Rd
Calabasas CA 91302
818 871-1800

(P-21059)
JEM AMERICA CORP
3000 Laurelview Ct, Fremont (94538-6575)
PHONE..................................510 683-9234
Kazumasa Okubo, Owner
Eddie Kazama, President
Phil MAI, Vice Pres
Robin Neal, Executive
Karen Wong, General Mgr
EMP: 50
SQ FT: 17,000
SALES (est): 5MM Privately Held
WEB: www.jemam.com
SIC: 3825 Test equipment for electronic &
electric measurement
PA: Japan Electronic Materials Corporation
2-5-13, Nishinagasucho
Amagasaki HYO 660-0
-

(P-21060)
**KELLY NETWORK SOLUTIONS
INC**
22650 Alcalde Rd, Cupertino (95014-3904)
PHONE..................................650 364-7201
Roland Valtierra, President
EMP: 19
SALES (est): 3.6MM Privately Held
SIC: 3825 Network analyzers

(P-21061)
KEYSIGHT TECHNOLOGIES INC
5301 Stevens Creek Blvd, Santa Clara
(95051-7201)
PHONE..................................408 553-3290
Nunes Luisa, Executive Asst
Jun LI, Project Mgr
Jia Liu, Research
EMP: 25
SALES (corp-wide): 3.8B Publicly Held
SIC: 3825 Instruments to measure electric-
ity
PA: Keysight Technologies, Inc.
1400 Fountaingrove Pkwy
Santa Rosa CA 95403
800 829-4444

(P-21062)
**KIMBALL ELECTRONICS
INDIANA**
5215 Hellyer Ave Ste 130, San Jose
(95138-1090)
PHONE..................................669 234-1110
Christopher Thyen, Vice Pres
EMP: 40
SALES (est): 2.7MM
SALES (corp-wide): 1.1B Publicly Held
SIC: 3825 Instruments to measure electric-
ity
PA: Kimball Electronics, Inc.
1205 Kimball Blvd
Jasper IN 47546
812 634-4000

(P-21063)
KLA CORPORATION
3530 Bassett St, Santa Clara (95054-2704)
PHONE..................................408 496-2055
EMP: 55
SALES (corp-wide): 4.5B Publicly Held
SIC: 3825 Instruments to measure electric-
ity
PA: Kla Corporation
1 Technology Dr
Milpitas CA 95035
408 875-3000

(P-21064)
KLA CORPORATION
850 Auburn Ct, Fremont (94538-7306)
PHONE..................................510 456-2490
Kathryn Cross, Director
EMP: 55
SALES (corp-wide): 4.5B Publicly Held
WEB: www.tencor.com
SIC: 3825 Semiconductor test equipment
PA: Kla Corporation
1 Technology Dr
Milpitas CA 95035
408 875-3000

(P-21065)
**LIQUID ROBOTICS FEDERAL
INC**
1329 Moffett Park Dr, Sunnyvale
(94089-1134)
PHONE..................................408 636-4200
Sandra McVey, Principal
Bill Vass, CEO
Steven R Springsteel, COO
Gary Gysin, Exec VP
Graham Hine, Senior VP
EMP: 11
SALES (est): 1.1MM Privately Held
SIC: 3825 Waveform measuring and/or an-
alyzing equipment

(P-21066)
LITEL INSTRUMENTS INC
10650 Scripps Ranch Blvd # 105, San
Diego (92131-2471)
PHONE..................................858 546-3788
Robert O Hunter Jr, President
EMP: 29
SALES (est): 4.5MM Privately Held
SIC: 3825 Instruments to measure electric-
ity

(P-21067)
LIVEWIRE TEST LABS INC
Also Called: Livewire Innovation
808 Calle Plano, Camarillo (93012-8557)
PHONE..................................801 293-8300
Ron Vogel, CEO
Cynthia Furse, Ch of Bd
Lucas Thomson, Electrical Engi
Brent Waddoups, Engineer
Marji Ketaily, Opers Staff
EMP: 10
SQ FT: 7,900
SALES (est): 1.6MM Privately Held
WEB: www.livewiretest.com
SIC: 3825 Test equipment for electronic &
electrical circuits; engine electrical test
equipment

(P-21068)
**LUCAS/SIGNATONE
CORPORATION (PA)**
Also Called: Lucas Labs
393 Tomkins Ct Ste J, Gilroy (95020-3632)
PHONE..................................408 848-2851
L Brent Dickson, President
Dennis Dickson, CFO
James Dickson, Technology
Marc Pinard, Sales Mgr
EMP: 30 EST: 1990
SALES (est): 4.9MM Privately Held
WEB: www.lucaslabs.com
SIC: 3825 3559 Semiconductor test equip-
ment; semiconductor manufacturing ma-
chinery

(P-21069)
LUMILEDS LLC (HQ)
370 W Trimble Rd, San Jose (95131-1008)
PHONE..................................408 964-2900
Jonathan Rich, CEO
Ilan Daskal, CFO
Cheree McAlpine, Senior VP
Ashok Agarwal, Surgery Dir
Steve Barlow, General Mgr
◆ EMP: 31
SALES (est): 148.6MM Publicly Held
WEB: www.luxeon.com
SIC: 3825 Instruments to measure electric-
ity

(P-21070)
MACHINE CONTROL TECH INC
210 Crouse Dr, Corona (92879-8093)
PHONE..................................951 808-0973

Samuel Yu, President
▲ EMP: 10
SALES (est): 1.7MM Privately Held
SIC: 3825 7389 Test equipment for elec-
tronic & electrical circuits;

(P-21071)
**MAGNEBIT HOLDING
CORPORATION (PA)**
9590 Chesapeake Dr Ste 1, San Diego
(92123-1348)
PHONE..................................858 573-0727
Catherine Jacobson, President
Peter Jacobson, Ch of Bd
EMP: 18
SALES (est): 2MM Privately Held
WEB: www.magnebit.com
SIC: 3825 3471 Instruments to measure
electricity; plating & polishing

(P-21072)
**MAGNETIC RCRDING
SOLUTIONS INC**
3080 Oakmead Village Dr, Santa Clara
(95051-0808)
PHONE..................................408 970-8266
Vladimir Pogrebinsky, President
Wayne Erickson, Exec VP
EMP: 35
SQ FT: 6,000
SALES (est): 5.1MM Privately Held
WEB: www.mrs-usa.com
SIC: 3825 Test equipment for electronic &
electrical circuits

(P-21073)
**MARVELL SEMICONDUCTOR
INC**
5450 Bayfront Plz, Santa Clara
(95054-3600)
PHONE..................................408 855-8839
EMP: 31 Privately Held
SIC: 3825
HQ: Marvell Semiconductor, Inc.
5488 Marvell Ln
Santa Clara CA 95054

(P-21074)
MARVIN TEST SOLUTIONS INC
1770 Kettering, Irvine (92614-5616)
PHONE..................................949 263-2222
Loofie Gutterman, President
Leon Tsimmerman, CFO
Gerald Friedman, Treasurer
EMP: 96
SQ FT: 31,000
SALES: 21.6MM
SALES (corp-wide): 223.5MM Privately
Held
WEB: www.geotestinc.com
SIC: 3825 Instruments to measure electric-
ity
PA: Marvin Engineering Co., Inc.
261 W Beach Ave
Inglewood CA 90302
310 674-5030

(P-21075)
**MATERIALS DEVELOPMENT
CORP (PA)**
21541 Nordhoff St Ste B, Chatsworth
(91311-6982)
PHONE..................................818 700-8290
Barton Gordon, President
Dr Robert S Harp, Corp Secy
EMP: 10
SQ FT: 6,000
SALES (est): 1.5MM Privately Held
WEB: www.mdc4cv.com
SIC: 3825 Semiconductor test equipment

(P-21076)
MAURICE LANDSTRASS
1667 Rosita Rd, Pacifica (94044-4433)
PHONE..................................650 355-5532
Maurice Landstrass, Owner
EMP: 20
SALES (est): 2MM Privately Held
SIC: 3825 Semiconductor test equipment

(P-21077)
**MEASUREMENT SPECIALTIES
INC**
Also Called: Te Connectivity
424 Crown Point Cir, Grass Valley
(95945-9089)
PHONE..................................530 273-4608
Frank Guidone, CEO
EMP: 60
SALES (corp-wide): 13.9B Privately Held
SIC: 3825 3676 Instruments to measure
electricity; electronic resistors
HQ: Measurement Specialties, Inc.
1000 Lucas Way
Hampton VA 23666
757 766-1500

(P-21078)
MEREX INC
1283 Flynn Rd, Camarillo (93012-8013)
P.O. Box 3474, Chatsworth (91313-3474)
PHONE..................................805 446-2700
Chester J Dopler, CEO
Ahmad Shams, President
Nathan Skop, Exec VP
EMP: 12 EST: 1984
SALES (est): 1.7MM Privately Held
SIC: 3825 Instruments to measure electric-
ity

(P-21079)
**MICRO-PROBE INCORPORATED
(HQ)**
Also Called: M P I
617 River Oaks Pkwy, San Jose
(95134-1907)
PHONE..................................408 457-3900
Mike Slessor, CEO
Patrick Kuhn, Vice Pres
Todd Swart, Vice Pres
Phonevixay Souriyasak, Technician
Robert Mendoza, Engineer
▲ EMP: 95
SQ FT: 43,000
SALES (est): 30.3MM Publicly Held
WEB: www.microprobe.com
SIC: 3825 Test equipment for electronic &
electrical circuits

(P-21080)
MICROSOURCE INC
5990 Gleason Dr, Dublin (94568-7644)
PHONE..................................925 328-4650
John R Regazzi, CEO
Suresh Nair, CEO
Ernie Nyiri, General Mgr
Temi Oduozor, Controller
Jim Taber, VP Sales
EMP: 55 EST: 1981
SQ FT: 24,000
SALES: 16MM
SALES (corp-wide): 11.1MM Publicly
Held
WEB: www.microsource-inc.com
SIC: 3825 Instruments to measure electric-
ity
PA: Giga-Tronics Incorporated
5990 Gleason Dr
Dublin CA 94568
925 328-4650

(P-21081)
**MITCHELL INSTRUMENTS CO
INC**
2875 Scott St Ste 101, Vista (92081-8559)
PHONE..................................760 744-2690
James Desportes, CEO
◆ EMP: 15
SALES (est): 4.3MM Privately Held
WEB: www.mitchellinstrument.net
SIC: 3825 Instruments to measure electric-
ity

(P-21082)
MRV SYSTEMS LLC
6370 Lusk Blvd Ste F100, San Diego
(92121-2754)
PHONE..................................800 645-7114
Fredric Maas, Mng Member
Michael Letchinger,
EMP: 20

SALES (est): 2.2MM **Privately Held**
WEB: www.mrvsys.com
SIC: 3825 3823 Instruments to measure electricity; temperature measurement instruments, industrial

(P-21083)
MULTITEST ELCTRNIC SYSTEMS INC (DH)
3021 Kenneth St, Santa Clara (95054-3416)
PHONE....................408 988-6544
Dave Tacelli, *President*
▲ **EMP:** 280
SQ FT: 40,000
SALES (est): 52.6MM
SALES (corp-wide): 451.7MM **Publicly Held**
WEB: www.multitest.com
SIC: 3825 3674 3624 Semiconductor test equipment; semiconductors & related devices; brushes & brush stock contacts, electric
HQ: Xcerra Corporation
825 University Ave
Norwood MA 02062
781 461-1000

(P-21084)
N H RESEARCH INCORPORATED
16601 Hale Ave, Irvine (92606-5049)
PHONE....................949 474-3900
Peter Swartz, *President*
Curtis Randall, *Engineer*
Shawn Brown, *Buyer*
Mike Nolan, *Natl Sales Mgr*
Johannes Pabbruwee, *Sales Staff*
▲ **EMP:** 75
SQ FT: 29,000
SALES (est): 17.9MM **Privately Held**
WEB: www.nhresearch.com
SIC: 3825 3829 Test equipment for electronic & electrical circuits; measuring & controlling devices

(P-21085)
NAPTECH TEST EQUIPMENT INC
9781 Pt Lkeview Rd Unit 3, Kelseyville (95451)
PHONE....................707 995-7145
Roger Briggs, *President*
◆ **EMP:** 15
SQ FT: 12,000
SALES: 2.3MM **Privately Held**
WEB: www.naptech.com
SIC: 3825 7629 Instruments to measure electricity; electrical repair shops

(P-21086)
NATIONAL INSTRUMENTS CORP
Also Called: Ni Microwave Components
4600 Patrick Henry Dr, Santa Clara (95054-1817)
PHONE....................408 610-6800
Dirk De Mol, *Branch Mgr*
EMP: 338
SALES (corp-wide): 1.3B **Publicly Held**
SIC: 3825 Instruments to measure electricity
PA: National Instruments Corporation
11500 N Mopac Expy
Austin TX 78759
512 683-0100

(P-21087)
NEARFIELD SYSTEMS INC
19730 Magellan Dr, Torrance (90502-1104)
PHONE....................310 525-7000
Greg Hindman, *President*
Dan Slater, *Vice Pres*
Bruce Williams, *Manager*
▼ **EMP:** 62
SALES (est): 18.8MM
SALES (corp-wide): 44.8MM **Privately Held**
WEB: www.nearfield.com
SIC: 3825 3829 Test equipment for electronic & electric measurement; measuring & controlling devices
PA: Nsi-Mi Technologies, Llc
1125 Satellite Blvd Nw # 100
Suwanee GA 30024
678 475-8300

(P-21088)
NEOLOGY INC (HQ)
13520 Evening Creek Dr N S, San Diego (92128-8105)
PHONE....................858 391-0260
Francisco Martinez, *CEO*
Scott Raskin, *Ch of Bd*
Charles Padgett, *CFO*
Manuel Moreno, *Vice Pres*
Doug Moran, *Director*
◆ **EMP:** 37
SQ FT: 23,050
SALES (est): 12.9MM
SALES (corp-wide): 140.8MM **Privately Held**
WEB: www.neology-rfid.com
SIC: 3825 Integrated circuit testers
PA: Smartrac N.V.
Strawinskylaan 851
Amsterdam
203 050-150

(P-21089)
NEOSEM TECHNOLOGY INC (HQ)
Also Called: Flexstar Technology, Inc
1965 Concourse Dr, San Jose (95131-1708)
PHONE....................408 643-7000
DH Yeom, *President*
Michael Bellon, *President*
Mike Rogowski, *COO*
Jin Choi, *Vice Pres*
Roger Leisy, *VP Sales*
▲ **EMP:** 20
SQ FT: 18,000
SALES (est): 14.9MM
SALES (corp-wide): 13MM **Privately Held**
WEB: www.flexstar.com
SIC: 3825 Test equipment for electronic & electrical circuits
PA: Neosem Holdings, Inc.
11001 Lakeline Blvd # 150
Austin TX 78717
512 257-5018

(P-21090)
NEXTEST SYSTEMS CORPORATION
Also Called: Nextest Systems Teradyne Co
875 Embedded Way, San Jose (95138-1030)
PHONE....................408 960-2400
Mark Jadiela, *CEO*
Tim F Moriarty, *President*
James P Moniz, *CFO*
Robin Adler, *Bd of Directors*
Paul Barics, *Vice Pres*
▲ **EMP:** 125
SQ FT: 33,200
SALES (est): 39.9MM
SALES (corp-wide): 2.1B **Publicly Held**
WEB: www.nextest.com
SIC: 3825 Instruments to measure electricity
PA: Teradyne, Inc.
600 Riverpark Dr
North Reading MA 01864
978 370-2700

(P-21091)
NIKON RESEARCH CORP AMERICA
1399 Shoreway Rd, Belmont (94002-4107)
PHONE....................800 446-4566
W Thomas Novak, *CEO*
Donis Flagello, *President*
Hamid Zarringhalam, *Exec VP*
Mitsuaki Yonekawa, *Senior VP*
Mohamad Zarringhalam, *Senior VP*
EMP: 40
SQ FT: 15,000
SALES (est): 12.2MM **Privately Held**
WEB: www.nikonrca.com
SIC: 3825 Semiconductor test equipment
HQ: Nikon Americas Inc.
1300 Walt Whitman Rd Fl 2
Melville NY 11747

(P-21092)
NOVA MEASURING INSTRUMENTS INC
3342 Gateway Blvd, Fremont (94538-6525)
PHONE....................408 200-4344
May Su, *President*
Dror David, *Officer*
EMP: 29 **EST:** 1996
SALES (est): 4.2MM
SALES (corp-wide): 67.7MM **Privately Held**
SIC: 3825 Semiconductor test equipment
PA: Nova Measuring Instruments Ltd
Rehovot
Rehovot
732 295-600

(P-21093)
NOVTEK INC
Also Called: Novtek Test Systems
7018 Mariposa St, Santee (92071-5648)
PHONE....................408 441-9934
Douglas E Eastman III, *President*
James Harper, *COO*
Ruth Eastman, *Vice Pres*
Joe Raynak, *Vice Pres*
EMP: 11
SQ FT: 13,000
SALES (est): 1.8MM **Privately Held**
WEB: www.novtek.com
SIC: 3825 8999 Integrated circuit testers; scientific consulting

(P-21094)
NOVX CORPORATION
1750 N Loop Rd Ste 100, Alameda (94502-8011)
PHONE....................408 998-5555
Steve Heymann, *President*
Lern Hollins, *Vice Pres*
Lyle Nelsen, *Vice Pres*
◆ **EMP:** 25
SQ FT: 6,000
SALES: 3MM **Privately Held**
SIC: 3825 Electrical energy measuring equipment

(P-21095)
OML INC
300 Digital Dr, Morgan Hill (95037-2896)
PHONE....................408 779-2698
Charles Oleson, *President*
Yuenie Lau, *Vice Pres*
Mitzi Chow, *General Mgr*
Jackie Lau, *Marketing Mgr*
EMP: 10
SQ FT: 2,450
SALES (est): 1.9MM **Privately Held**
WEB: www.omlinc.com
SIC: 3825 Microwave test equipment

(P-21096)
PACIFIC WESTERN SYSTEMS INC (PA)
505 E Evelyn Ave, Mountain View (94041-1613)
PHONE....................650 961-8855
Daniel A Worsham, *Ch of Bd*
Becky Worsham, *Corp Secy*
EMP: 20 **EST:** 1967
SQ FT: 40,000
SALES (est): 2.5MM **Privately Held**
WEB: www.pacificwesternsystems.com
SIC: 3825 3567 Semiconductor test equipment; industrial furnaces & ovens

(P-21097)
PERICOM SEMICONDUCTOR CORP (HQ)
1545 Barber Ln, Milpitas (95035-7409)
PHONE....................408 232-9100
Alex Chiming Hui, *President*
Kevin S Bauer, *CFO*
Angela Chen, *Senior VP*
CHi-Hung Hui, *Senior VP*
Michael Chen, *Vice Pres*
◆ **EMP:** 23
SQ FT: 85,040
SALES: 128.8MM
SALES (corp-wide): 1.2B **Publicly Held**
WEB: www.pericom.com
SIC: 3825 3674 Instruments to measure electricity; integrated circuits; semiconductor networks, etc.

PA: Diodes Incorporated
4949 Hedgcoxe Rd Ste 200
Plano TX 75024
972 987-3900

(P-21098)
PHOENIX MARINE CORPORATION (PA)
700 Larkspur Landing Cir # 175, Larkspur (94939-1715)
PHONE....................415 464-8116
David Brining, *President*
EMP: 73
SALES (est): 8.4MM **Privately Held**
SIC: 3825 3643 Synchroscopes; connectors, electric cord

(P-21099)
PHOTON DYNAMICS INC (HQ)
5970 Optical Ct, San Jose (95138-1400)
PHONE....................408 226-9900
Malcolm J Thompson PHD, *Ch of Bd*
Amichai Steimberg, *President*
Errol Moore, *CEO*
James P Moniz, *CFO*
Dr Abraham Gross, *Exec VP*
◆ **EMP:** 112
SQ FT: 128,520
SALES: 82.7MM
SALES (corp-wide): 256.3MM **Privately Held**
WEB: www.photondynamics.com
SIC: 3825 3829 Test equipment for electronic & electrical circuits; measuring & controlling devices
PA: Orbotech Ltd.
7 Hasanhedrin Blvd.
Yavne 81215
894 235-33

(P-21100)
POWER MNTRING DAGNSTC TECH LTD
Also Called: Pmdt
6840 Via Del Oro Ste 150, San Jose (95119-1373)
PHONE....................408 972-5588
Emily MA, *CEO*
Michael Nie, *Technical Staff*
Constance Chou, *Sales Staff*
Liming MA, *Manager*
EMP: 11
SALES (est): 1.8MM
SALES (corp-wide): 17.2MM **Privately Held**
SIC: 3825 Instruments to measure electricity
PA: Pdstars Electric Co., Ltd.
1-2/F, Block B, Bldg.2, No.158, Xinjunhuan Rd., Minhang Dist.
Shanghai 20111
213 429-3358

(P-21101)
POWER STANDARDS LAB INC
980 Atlantic Ave Ste 100, Alameda (94501-1098)
PHONE....................510 522-4400
Alex McEachern, *President*
Barry Tangney, *COO*
Andreas Eberhard, *Vice Pres*
Thomas Pua, *Engineer*
Christine Lancaster, *Accounting Mgr*
EMP: 32
SQ FT: 12,000
SALES (est): 8.6MM
SALES (corp-wide): 15.2MM **Privately Held**
WEB: www.powerstandards.com
SIC: 3825 8734 Power measuring equipment, electrical; testing laboratories
PA: Equipements Power Survey Ltee, Les
7880 Rte Transcanadienne
Saint-Laurent QC H4T 1
514 333-8392

(P-21102)
PROBE-RITE CORP
600 Mission St, Santa Clara (95050-6041)
P.O. Box 242 (95052-0242)
PHONE....................408 727-0100
Frank Ardezzone, *President*
EMP: 27
SQ FT: 3,000

▲ = Import ▼=Export
◆ =Import/Export

SALES (est): 1.1MM **Privately Held**
SIC: 3825 3569 3491 3535 Semiconductor test equipment; robots, assembly line: industrial & commercial; automatic regulating & control valves; robotic conveyors; hybrid integrated circuits

(P-21103)
PROGRAM DATA INCORPORATED
Also Called: Pdi
16291 Jackson Ranch Rd, Silverado (92676-9706)
PHONE.................714 649-2122
Allen Aksu, *President*
Seyyal Aksu, *Treasurer*
EMP: 17 EST: 1969
SQ FT: 25,000
SALES (est): 1.1MM **Privately Held**
WEB: www.programdata.com
SIC: 3825 3643 Test equipment for electronic & electric measurement; current-carrying wiring devices

(P-21104)
PRONK TECHNOLOGIES INC (PA)
8933 Lankershim Blvd, Sun Valley (91352-1916)
PHONE.................818 768-5600
Karl Ruiter, *President*
Christine Chee Ruiter, *Vice Pres*
Denize Machit, *Admin Sec*
▼ EMP: 12
SQ FT: 4,000
SALES (est): 1MM **Privately Held**
WEB: www.pronktech.com
SIC: 3825 Test equipment for electronic & electric measurement

(P-21105)
PULSE INSTRUMENTS
1234 Francisco St, Torrance (90502-1200)
PHONE.................310 515-5330
Sylvia Kan, *President*
David Kan, *Vice Pres*
Steven Kan, *Vice Pres*
EMP: 23 EST: 1975
SQ FT: 15,000
SALES (est): 5MM **Privately Held**
WEB: www.pulseinstruments.com
SIC: 3825 3823 3621 Instruments to measure electricity; industrial instrmnts msrmnt display/control process variable; motors & generators

(P-21106)
QUALECTRON SYSTEMS CORPORATION
321 E Brokaw Rd, San Jose (95112-4208)
PHONE.................408 986-1686
Ricky MA, *President*
▲ EMP: 10
SQ FT: 10,000
SALES (est): 1.3MM **Privately Held**
WEB: www.qualectron.com
SIC: 3825 Test equipment for electronic & electric measurement

(P-21107)
QUALITAU INCORPORATED (PA)
830 Maude Ave, Mountain View (94043-4022)
PHONE.................650 282-6226
Gadi Krieger, *CEO*
Jacob Herschmann, *President*
Nava Ben-Yehuda, *Vice Pres*
Tony Chavez, *Principal*
Peter Y Cuevas, *Principal*
EMP: 55
SQ FT: 16,000
SALES (est): 12.9MM **Privately Held**
SIC: 3825 Semiconductor test equipment

(P-21108)
QUANTUM FOCUS INSTRUMENTS CORP
2385 La Mirada Dr, Vista (92081-7863)
PHONE.................760 599-1122
Grant Albright, *President*
Victoria Albright, *Admin Sec*
▼ EMP: 13
SQ FT: 7,500

SALES (est): 3.3MM **Privately Held**
SIC: 3825 Instruments to measure electricity

(P-21109)
QXQ INC
44113 S Grimmer Blvd, Fremont (94538-6350)
PHONE.................510 252-1522
Roger Quan, *President*
Kelly Nguyen, *CFO*
Weili Aguilar, *Officer*
Jack Jenkins, *Admin Sec*
George Quan, *Opers Mgr*
▲ EMP: 33
SQ FT: 2,600
SALES (est): 7.5MM **Privately Held**
WEB: www.qxq.com
SIC: 3825 Instruments to measure electricity

(P-21110)
RADIO FREQUENCY SIMULATION
25371 Diana Cir, Mission Viejo (92691-4514)
PHONE.................714 974-7377
Richard C Damon, *President*
Diane Langius, *Administration*
EMP: 29
SALES (est): 1.7MM **Privately Held**
SIC: 3825 Radio frequency measuring equipment

(P-21111)
RADX TECHNOLOGIES INC
10650 Scripps Ranch Blvd # 100, San Diego (92131-2470)
PHONE.................619 677-1849
Cristina B Matthews, *Finance*
Ross Smith, *CEO*
Thomas Kais, *CFO*
EMP: 16
SALES (est): 2.7MM **Privately Held**
SIC: 3825 3663 7372 Instruments to measure electricity; radio & TV communications equipment; prepackaged software

(P-21112)
RIEDON INC
13065 Tom White Way Ste F, Norwalk (90650-8935)
PHONE.................562 926-2304
Greg Wood, *Branch Mgr*
EMP: 10 **Privately Held**
SIC: 3825 3679 Shunts, electrical; power supplies, all types: static
PA: Riedon, Inc.
300 Cypress Ave
Alhambra CA 91801

(P-21113)
ROD L ELECTRONICS INC (PA)
935 Sierra Vista Ave F, Mountain View (94043-1754)
P.O. Box 52158, Palo Alto (94303-0754)
PHONE.................650 322-0711
Roy Clay Sr, *Owner*
Roy Clay, *Owner*
▲ EMP: 14
SALES (est): 2.1MM **Privately Held**
SIC: 3825 Test equipment for electronic & electrical circuits

(P-21114)
ROOS INSTRUMENTS INC
Also Called: RI
2285 Martin Ave, Santa Clara (95050-2715)
PHONE.................408 748-8589
Mark D Roos, *President*
Catherine Roos, *COO*
Esther Chen, *Sr Software Eng*
Mark Brown, *Software Engr*
Matthew James, *Electrical Engi*
EMP: 21
SQ FT: 22,000
SALES (est): 5.6MM **Privately Held**
WEB: www.roos.com
SIC: 3825 Semiconductor test equipment

(P-21115)
SAGE INSTRUMENTS INC
240 Airport Blvd, Freedom (95019-2636)
PHONE.................831 761-1000

Dave McIntosh, *CEO*
Brett M Mackinnon, *President*
Ray Levasseur, *CFO*
Al Key, *Technical Staff*
Steven Glassman, *Sales Staff*
EMP: 90
SQ FT: 20,000
SALES (est): 17.5MM **Privately Held**
SIC: 3825 Test equipment for electronic & electric measurement

(P-21116)
SANGFOR TECHNOLOGIES INC
46721 Fremont Blvd, Fremont (94538-6539)
PHONE.................408 520-7898
Darwin Ceng, *CEO*
EMP: 900
SALES (est): 55.2MM **Privately Held**
SIC: 3825 Network analyzers

(P-21117)
SATELLITE TELEWORK CENTERS INC (PA)
6265 Highway 9, Felton (95018-9710)
PHONE.................831 222-2100
Barbara Sprenger, *President*
EMP: 11
SALES (est): 3.3MM **Privately Held**
SIC: 3825 7389 Network analyzers; office facilities & secretarial service rental

(P-21118)
SEAGULL SOLUTIONS INC
15105 Concord Cir Ste 100, Morgan Hill (95037-5487)
PHONE.................408 778-1127
Carol Lawless, *CFO*
Donald L Ekhoff, *CTO*
EMP: 13
SQ FT: 8,717
SALES (est): 2MM **Privately Held**
WEB: www.seagullsolutions.net
SIC: 3825 Instruments to measure electricity

(P-21119)
SENTIENT ENERGY INC (PA)
880 Mitten Rd Ste 105, Burlingame (94010-1309)
PHONE.................650 523-6680
James Keener, *CEO*
Michael Bauer, *President*
James Tracey, *Vice Pres*
Dennis Perrone, *Executive*
Nace Reader, *Software Engr*
EMP: 12
SQ FT: 15,000
SALES (est): 5.7MM **Privately Held**
SIC: 3825 Instruments to measure electricity

(P-21120)
SHB INSTRUMENTS INC
19215 Parthenia St Ste A, Northridge (91324-5168)
PHONE.................818 773-2000
Barry Megdal, *President*
▲ EMP: 10
SQ FT: 2,500
SALES (est): 2MM **Privately Held**
SIC: 3825 Test equipment for electronic & electrical circuits

(P-21121)
SIGNUM SYSTEMS CORPORATION
1211 Flynn Rd Unit 104, Camarillo (93012-6208)
PHONE.................805 383-3682
Jerry Lewandowski, *President*
Robert Chyla, *Vice Pres*
◆ EMP: 17
SQ FT: 6,000
SALES (est): 3.1MM
SALES (corp-wide): 42.7MM **Privately Held**
WEB: www.signum.com
SIC: 3825 3577 Test equipment for electronic & electrical circuits; computer peripheral equipment
PA: I.A.R. Systems Group Ab
Strandbodgatan 1
Uppsala 753 2
841 092-000

(P-21122)
SOF-TEK INTEGRATORS INC
Also Called: Op-Test
4712 Mtn Lakes Blvd # 200, Redding (96003-1479)
PHONE.................530 242-0527
Daniel C Morrow, *President*
Meredith Morrow, *CFO*
S Curt Dodds, *Vice Pres*
Morrow Annmary, *Admin Sec*
Annmary Morrow, *Admin Sec*
EMP: 16
SQ FT: 5,000
SALES (est): 800K **Privately Held**
WEB: www.op-test.com
SIC: 3825 8711 Instruments to measure electricity; engineering services

(P-21123)
SOLARIUS DEVELOPMENT INC
2390 Bering Dr, San Jose (95131-1121)
PHONE.................408 541-0151
Peter Joshua, *President*
Marco Negrete, *General Mgr*
Amy Zullo, *Office Mgr*
Abhay Paranjap, *Technical Staff*
Joshua Less, *Engineer*
EMP: 10
SQ FT: 3,600
SALES (est): 2.7MM **Privately Held**
SIC: 3825 Electrical energy measuring equipment

(P-21124)
SOTCHER MEASUREMENT INC
115 Phelan Ave Ste 10, San Jose (95112-6122)
PHONE.................408 574-0112
Marc Sotcher, *President*
Don Vuong, *Finance Mgr*
EMP: 12
SQ FT: 9,000
SALES (est): 1.5MM **Privately Held**
WEB: www.sotcher.com
SIC: 3825 Test equipment for electronic & electrical circuits

(P-21125)
SPECTRUM INSTRUMENTS INC
570 E Arrow Hwy Ste D, San Dimas (91773-3347)
PHONE.................909 971-9710
Thomas Verseput, *President*
Jeffrey Grous, *Director*
Donald REA, *Director*
EMP: 15
SALES: 830K **Privately Held**
WEB: www.spectruminstruments.com
SIC: 3825 Frequency synthesizers; time code generators

(P-21126)
SPIRENT COMMUNICATIONS INC
2708 Orchard Pkwy Ste 20, San Jose (95134-1968)
PHONE.................408 752-7100
Laura Chavez, *Manager*
EMP: 111
SALES (corp-wide): 476.9MM **Privately Held**
SIC: 3825 3829 3663 Instruments to measure electricity; measuring & controlling devices; radio & TV communications equipment
HQ: Spirent Communications Inc.
27439 Agoura Rd
Calabasas CA 91301
818 676-2300

(P-21127)
SPIRENT COMMUNICATIONS INC (HQ)
Also Called: Spirent Calabasas
27439 Agoura Rd, Calabasas (91301)
PHONE.................818 676-2300
Eric G Hutchinson, *CEO*
Bill Burns, *President*
Kumar Krishnakumar, *Surgery Dir*
David Stehlin, *General Mgr*
Michelle Bruni, *Sr Software Eng*
▲ EMP: 350

PRODUCTS & SVCS

SALES (est): 344.6MM
SALES (corp-wide): 476.9MM **Privately Held**
SIC: 3825 3829 3663 Instruments to measure electricity; measuring & controlling devices; radio & TV communications equipment
PA: Spirent Communications Plc
    Northwood Park
    Crawley W SUSSEX RH10
    129 376-7676

(P-21128)
STEM INC (PA)
100 Rollins Rd, Millbrae (94030-3115)
PHONE...................................415 937-7836
John Carrington, *CEO*
Karen Butterfield, *Officer*
John Christian, *Vice Pres*
David Erhart, *Vice Pres*
Tad Glauthier, *Vice Pres*
◆ EMP: 80
SQ FT: 20,000
SALES (est): 16.7MM **Privately Held**
SIC: 3825 Electrical power measuring equipment

(P-21129)
STRUCTURAL DIAGNOSTICS INC
Also Called: S D I
650 Via Alondra, Camarillo (93012-8733)
PHONE...................................805 987-7755
Paul R Teagle, *President*
EMP: 28
SQ FT: 30,000
SALES (est): 6MM **Privately Held**
WEB: www.sdindt.com
SIC: 3825 Instruments to measure electricity

(P-21130)
STS INSTRUMENTS INC
17711 Mitchell N, Irvine (92614-6028)
P.O. Box 1805, Ardmore OK (73402-1805)
PHONE...................................580 223-4773
Kevin Voelcker, *President*
William D Long, *Treasurer*
Barbara J Stinnett, *Admin Sec*
▲ EMP: 18
SQ FT: 20,000
SALES (est): 3MM
SALES (corp-wide): 17.5MM **Privately Held**
WEB: www.sltrco.com
SIC: 3825 Test equipment for electronic & electrical circuits
PA: Ppst, Inc.
    17692 Fitch
    Irvine CA 92614
    800 421-1921

(P-21131)
SURFACE OPTICS CORP
11555 Rancho Bernardo Rd, San Diego
(92127-1441)
PHONE...................................858 675-7404
Jonathan Dummer, *CEO*
James Jafolla, *President*
James C Jafolla, *President*
Marian Geremia, *CFO*
Marian K Geremia, *CFO*
EMP: 50
SQ FT: 18,000
SALES (est): 12.6MM **Privately Held**
WEB: www.surfaceoptics.com
SIC: 3825 8748 3829 8731 Instruments to measure electricity; business consulting; measuring & controlling devices; commercial physical research

(P-21132)
SV PROBE INC
6680 Via Del Oro, San Jose (95119-1392)
PHONE...................................480 635-4700
Kevin Kurtz, *Principal*
EMP: 100 **Privately Held**
SIC: 3825 Test equipment for electronic & electrical circuits
HQ: Sv Probe, Inc.
    7810 S Hardy Dr Ste 109
    Tempe AZ 85284

(P-21133)
SV PROBE INC
535 E Brokaw Rd, San Jose (95112-1004)
PHONE...................................408 653-2387
Trong Pham, *President*
EMP: 10 **Privately Held**
SIC: 3825 Semiconductor test equipment
HQ: Sv Probe, Inc.
    7810 S Hardy Dr Ste 109
    Tempe AZ 85284

(P-21134)
SYNTHESYS RESEARCH INC (DH)
4250 Burton Dr, Santa Clara (95054-1551)
PHONE...................................408 753-1630
Lutz Henckels, *CEO*
James Waschura, *President*
Thomas Waschura, *CTO*
EMP: 60
SQ FT: 8,000
SALES (est): 5MM
SALES (corp-wide): 6.4B **Publicly Held**
WEB: www.synthesysresearch.com
SIC: 3825 Test equipment for electronic & electric measurement
HQ: Tektronix, Inc.
    14150 Sw Karl Braun Dr
    Beaverton OR 97005
    800 833-9200

(P-21135)
TASEON INC
515 S Flower St Fl 25, Los Angeles
(90071-2228)
PHONE...................................408 240-7800
Albert Wong, *CEO*
Rachel Wang, *Technical Staff*
▲ EMP: 65
SQ FT: 21,000
SALES (est): 7.4MM **Privately Held**
SIC: 3825 Network analyzers

(P-21136)
TEKTRONIX INC
2368 Walsh Ave, Santa Clara
(95051-1323)
PHONE...................................408 496-0800
Douglas Shafer, *Branch Mgr*
EMP: 22
SALES (corp-wide): 6.4B **Publicly Held**
WEB: www.tek.com
SIC: 3825 Instruments to measure electricity
HQ: Tektronix, Inc.
    14150 Sw Karl Braun Dr
    Beaverton OR 97005
    800 833-9200

(P-21137)
TELEDYNE LECROY INC
Also Called: Lecroy Prtocol Solutions Group
765 Sycamore Dr, Milpitas (95035-7465)
PHONE...................................408 727-6600
Jason Lebeck, *Branch Mgr*
James Allen, *Technical Staff*
Amit Bakshi, *Engineer*
James Livingston, *Sales Engr*
EMP: 24
SALES (corp-wide): 2.9B **Publicly Held**
WEB: www.lecroy.com
SIC: 3825 3829 Test equipment for electronic & electrical circuits; oscillographs & oscilloscopes; measuring & controlling devices
HQ: Teledyne Lecroy, Inc.
    700 Chestnut Ridge Rd
    Chestnut Ridge NY 10977
    845 425-2000

(P-21138)
TELSOR CORPORATION
42181 Avenida Alvarado B, Temecula
(92590-3429)
PHONE...................................951 296-3066
Frank Simon, *Ch of Bd*
EMP: 10
SQ FT: 1,775
SALES (est): 800K **Privately Held**
SIC: 3825 Radio frequency measuring equipment

(P-21139)
TERADYNE INC
30801 Agoura Rd, Agoura Hills
(91301-2054)
PHONE...................................818 991-9700
Wayne Hardenberg, *Principal*
Paul Hatmaker, *Info Tech Dir*
Christopher Vosse, *Business Anlyst*
Garnik Abrahmian, *Manager*
John Grover, *Manager*
EMP: 140
SALES (corp-wide): 2.1B **Publicly Held**
SIC: 3825 Semiconductor test equipment
PA: Teradyne, Inc.
    600 Riverpark Dr
    North Reading MA 01864
    978 370-2700

(P-21140)
TERADYNE INC
Also Called: Circuit Bd Test & Insptn Sls
5251 California Ave # 100, Irvine
(92617-3075)
PHONE...................................949 453-0900
Ken Ovens, *Branch Mgr*
EMP: 55
SALES (corp-wide): 2.1B **Publicly Held**
WEB: www.teradyne.com
SIC: 3825 Semiconductor test equipment
PA: Teradyne, Inc.
    600 Riverpark Dr
    North Reading MA 01864
    978 370-2700

(P-21141)
TERADYNE INC
875 Embedded Way, San Jose
(95138-1030)
PHONE...................................408 960-2400
Ron Butler, *General Mgr*
EMP: 225
SALES (corp-wide): 2.1B **Publicly Held**
WEB: www.teradyne.com
SIC: 3825 Test equipment for electronic & electric measurement
PA: Teradyne, Inc.
    600 Riverpark Dr
    North Reading MA 01864
    978 370-2700

(P-21142)
TESEDA CORPORATION
160 Rio Robles Bldg D, San Jose
(95134-1813)
PHONE...................................650 320-8188
Jack Chen, *Branch Mgr*
EMP: 10
SALES (corp-wide): 1.9MM **Privately Held**
WEB: www.teseda.com
SIC: 3825 Test equipment for electronic & electric measurement
PA: Teseda Corporation
    6915 Sw Mcdam Ave Ste 245
    Portland OR 97219
    503 223-3315

(P-21143)
TEST CONNECTIONS INC
1146 W 9th St, Upland (91786-5728)
PHONE...................................909 981-1810
Michael A Curtis, *President*
Patrica Jones, *CFO*
Patricia Jones, *Treasurer*
EMP: 10
SQ FT: 5,000
SALES (est): 1.5MM **Privately Held**
WEB: www.tciinfo.com
SIC: 3825 3679 Test equipment for electronic & electrical circuits; electronic circuits

(P-21144)
TEST ELECTRONICS
821 Smith Rd, Watsonville (95076-9798)
PHONE...................................831 763-2000
Ed Armstrong, *Owner*
EMP: 42
SALES (est): 2.9MM **Privately Held**
WEB: www.testelectronics.com
SIC: 3825 Test equipment for electronic & electrical circuits

(P-21145)
TEST ENTERPRISES INC
Fet-Test
1288 Reamwood Ave, Sunnyvale
(94089-2233)
PHONE...................................408 778-0234
Gary Wolfe, *Principal*
EMP: 24
SQ FT: 13,777
SALES (corp-wide): 6MM **Privately Held**
WEB: www.thermonics.com
SIC: 3825 Semiconductor test equipment
PA: Test Enterprises, Inc.
    1288 Reamwood Ave
    Sunnyvale CA 94089
    408 542-5900

(P-21146)
TEST-UM INC
430 N Mccarthy Blvd, Milpitas
(95035-5112)
PHONE...................................818 464-5021
David Vellequette, *CEO*
▲ EMP: 18
SQ FT: 8,000
SALES (est): 2.7MM
SALES (corp-wide): 1.1B **Publicly Held**
WEB: www.test-um.com
SIC: 3825 Test equipment for electronic & electric measurement
PA: Viavi Solutions Inc.
    6001 America Center Dr # 6
    San Jose CA 95002
    408 404-3600

(P-21147)
TESTMETRIX INC
426 S Hillview Dr, Milpitas (95035-5464)
PHONE...................................408 730-5511
Christian Cojocneanu, *President*
Stephanie Haag, *CFO*
Mike Bulat, *Director*
EMP: 24
SQ FT: 10,000
SALES (est): 4.7MM **Privately Held**
WEB: www.testmetrix.com
SIC: 3825 3674 Test equipment for electronic & electric measurement; semiconductors & related devices

(P-21148)
TRANSLARITY INC
46575 Fremont Blvd, Fremont
(94538-6409)
PHONE...................................510 371-7900
Laura Oliphant, *CEO*
Mark Gardiner, *COO*
Michael Brannan, *Exec VP*
Nick Sporck, *Vice Pres*
Chuck Wiley,
EMP: 19
SQ FT: 20,000
SALES (est): 4.6MM **Privately Held**
WEB: www.octsci.com
SIC: 3825 Semiconductor test equipment

(P-21149)
TRENDPOINT SYSTEMS INC
283 Winfield Cir, Corona (92880-6943)
PHONE...................................925 855-0600
Lisa Mandell, *CEO*
Donna Carter, *Admin Sec*
Jonathon Trout, *CTO*
EMP: 10
SALES (est): 3.1MM **Privately Held**
WEB: www.trendpoint.com
SIC: 3825 Instruments to measure electricity

(P-21150)
TRI-NET INC
14721 Hilton Dr, Fontana (92336-4013)
PHONE...................................909 483-3555
Rosemarie V Hall, *President*
EMP: 15
SQ FT: 7,500
SALES (est): 3.3MM **Privately Held**
SIC: 3825 Test equipment for electronic & electric measurement

(P-21151)
TRT BSNESS NTWRK SOLUTIONS INC
15551 Red Hill Ave Ste A, Tustin
(92780-7325)
PHONE...................................714 380-3888

▲ = Import ▼=Export
◆ =Import/Export

Julia Swen, *President*
▲ EMP: 13
SALES (est): 1.3MM **Privately Held**
WEB: www.trtinfo.com
SIC: 3825 Network analyzers

(P-21152)
VALDOR FIBER OPTICS INC
(PA)
1838 D St, Hayward (94541-4435)
PHONE...................................510 293-1212
Las Yabut, *President*
EMP: 29
SQ FT: 12,000
SALES (est): 3.8MM **Privately Held**
SIC: 3825 Measuring instruments & meters, electric

(P-21153)
VERTOX COMPANY
11752 Garden Grove Blvd # 113, Garden Grove (92843-1423)
PHONE...................................714 530-4541
Steven L Hacker, *Owner*
▲ EMP: 12
SQ FT: 1,000
SALES (est): 838.1K **Privately Held**
WEB: www.vertox.org
SIC: 3825 Meters: electric, pocket, portable, panelboard, etc.

(P-21154)
VITREK LLC
12169 Kirkham Rd Ste C, Poway (92064-8835)
PHONE...................................858 689-2755
Kevin P Clark, *President*
Talia Stuedeman, *Buyer*
▲ EMP: 15
SQ FT: 4,000
SALES (est): 3.8MM **Privately Held**
WEB: www.vitrek.com
SIC: 3825 Test equipment for electronic & electric measurement

(P-21155)
VLSI STANDARDS INC
5 Technology Dr, Milpitas (95035-7916)
PHONE...................................408 428-1800
Ian Smith, *President*
EMP: 34
SQ FT: 17,500
SALES (est): 6.6MM
SALES (corp-wide): 4.5B **Publicly Held**
WEB: www.vlsistandards.com
SIC: 3825 Standards & calibration equipment for electrical measuring
PA: Kla Corporation
1 Technology Dr
Milpitas CA 95035
408 875-3000

(P-21156)
XANDEX INC
1360 Redwood Way Ste A, Petaluma (94954-1104)
PHONE...................................707 763-7799
Kamran Shamsavari, *President*
Nariman Manoochehri, *CEO*
▲ EMP: 93
SQ FT: 20,000
SALES (est): 20.6MM **Privately Held**
WEB: www.xandex.com
SIC: 3825 3674 Instruments to measure electricity; wafers (semiconductor devices)

┌─────────────────────────────────┐
│ **3826 Analytical Instruments** │
└─────────────────────────────────┘

(P-21157)
10X GENOMICS INC (PA)
6230 Stoneridge Mall Rd, Pleasanton (94588-3260)
PHONE...................................925 401-7300
Serge Saxonov, *CEO*
John R Stuelpnagel, *Ch of Bd*
Benjamin J Hindson, *President*
Justin J McAnear, *CFO*
Bradford J Crutchfield, *Ch Credit Ofcr*
EMP: 181
SQ FT: 200,000

SALES: 146.3MM **Publicly Held**
SIC: 3826 2836 Analytical instruments; biological products, except diagnostic

(P-21158)
AB SCIEX LLC (HQ)
1201 Radio Rd, Redwood City (94065-1217)
PHONE...................................877 740-2129
Rainer Blair, *Mng Member*
Tamara Bond, *Vice Pres*
Thomas Covey, *Vice Pres*
John Fulford, *Vice Pres*
Marian Cadiz, *Executive Asst*
EMP: 100
SALES (est): 44.3MM
SALES (corp-wide): 19.8B **Publicly Held**
SIC: 3826 Analytical instruments
PA: Danaher Corporation
2200 Penn Ave Nw Ste 800w
Washington DC 20037
202 828-0850

(P-21159)
ACCESS SYSTEMS INC
4947 Hillsdale Cir, El Dorado Hills (95762-5707)
PHONE...................................916 941-8099
Michael Herd, *President*
Barbara Ponce, *Office Mgr*
Greg Johnston, *Opers Mgr*
EMP: 11
SQ FT: 3,000
SALES (est): 2.8MM **Privately Held**
WEB: www.accesssystems.us
SIC: 3826 3699 Integrators (mathematical instruments); security control equipment & systems

(P-21160)
ACELLS CORP
Also Called: Amcells
1351 Dist Way Ste 1, Vista (92081)
PHONE...................................760 727-6666
Jenny Zhang, *President*
David Allen, *Vice Pres*
▲ EMP: 10
SQ FT: 10,000
SALES (est): 1.5MM **Privately Held**
WEB: www.amcells.com
SIC: 3826 Analytical instruments

(P-21161)
ADVANCED MICRO
INSTRUMENTS INC
Also Called: AMI
225 Paularino Ave, Costa Mesa (92626-3313)
PHONE...................................714 848-5533
Kenneth Biele, *CEO*
W William Layton, *Controller*
EMP: 23
SQ FT: 2,500
SALES (est): 5.3MM **Privately Held**
WEB: www.amio2.com
SIC: 3826 Analytical instruments

(P-21162)
AFFYMETRIX INC
3380 Central Expy, Santa Clara (95051-0704)
PHONE...................................408 731-5000
George Beers, *Branch Mgr*
EMP: 54
SALES (corp-wide): 24.3B **Publicly Held**
SIC: 3826 Analytical instruments
HQ: Affymetrix, Inc.
3380 Central Expy
Santa Clara CA 95051

(P-21163)
AFFYMETRIX INC
5893 Oberlin Dr, San Diego (92121-3773)
PHONE...................................858 642-2058
EMP: 200
SALES (corp-wide): 24.3B **Publicly Held**
SIC: 3826 Analytical instruments
HQ: Affymetrix, Inc.
3380 Central Expy
Santa Clara CA 95051

(P-21164)
AFFYMETRIX INC
3450 Central Expy, Santa Clara (95051-0703)
PHONE...................................408 731-5000
Mirasol Abriam, *Branch Mgr*
EMP: 74
SALES (corp-wide): 24.3B **Publicly Held**
WEB: www.affymetrix.com
SIC: 3826 2835 Analytical instruments; in vitro & in vivo diagnostic substances
HQ: Affymetrix, Inc.
3380 Central Expy
Santa Clara CA 95051
-

(P-21165)
AFFYMETRIX INC (HQ)
3380 Central Expy, Santa Clara (95051-0704)
PHONE...................................408 731-5000
Seth H Hoogasian, *President*
Kamalia Dam, *Exec VP*
James Bradley, *Vice Pres*
Eric Fung, *Vice Pres*
Luis Jevons, *Vice Pres*
EMP: 277
SALES (est): 262.2MM
SALES (corp-wide): 24.3B **Publicly Held**
WEB: www.affymetrix.com
SIC: 3826 Analytical instruments
PA: Thermo Fisher Scientific Inc.
168 3rd Ave
Waltham MA 02451
781 622-1000

(P-21166)
AFFYMETRIX ANATRACE
3380 Central Expy, Santa Clara (95051-0704)
P.O. Box 178 (95052-0178)
PHONE...................................408 731-5756
EMP: 14
SALES (est): 3.2MM **Privately Held**
SIC: 3826

(P-21167)
AGILONE INC (PA)
771 Vaqueros Ave, Sunnyvale (94085-3527)
PHONE...................................877 769-3047
Omer Artun, *CEO*
Mark Vashon, *Vice Pres*
Tom Kolich, *Surgery Dir*
Karen Wood, *Surgery Dir*
Michelle Viguerie, *Admin Sec*
EMP: 48 EST: 2005
SQ FT: 6,000
SALES (est): 13.5MM **Privately Held**
SIC: 3826 Analytical instruments

(P-21168)
ALZA CORPORATION
1010 Joaquin Rd, Mountain View (94043-1242)
PHONE...................................650 564-5000
Duane Frise, *Branch Mgr*
EMP: 725
SALES (corp-wide): 81.5B **Publicly Held**
WEB: www.alza.com
SIC: 3826 Analytical instruments
HQ: Alza Corporation
700 Eubanks Dr
Vacaville CA 95688
707 453-6400

(P-21169)
ALZA CORPORATION
700 Eubanks Dr, Vacaville (95688-9470)
PHONE...................................707 453-6400
David Danks, *Vice Pres*
EMP: 650
SQ FT: 23,040
SALES (corp-wide): 81.5B **Publicly Held**
WEB: www.alza.com
SIC: 3826 Analytical instruments
HQ: Alza Corporation
700 Eubanks Dr
Vacaville CA 95688
707 453-6400

(P-21170)
AMBIOS TECHNOLOGY INC (PA)
1 Technology Dr, Milpitas (95035-7916)
PHONE...................................831 427-1160
Patrick O'Hara, *President*

▲ EMP: 22
SQ FT: 5,800
SALES (est): 6.2MM **Privately Held**
WEB: www.ambiostech.com
SIC: 3826 Laser scientific & engineering instruments

(P-21171)
ANALYTCAL SCENTIFIC INSTRS
INC
Also Called: A S I
3023 Research Dr, San Pablo (94806-5206)
PHONE...................................510 669-2250
Stephen H Graham, *President*
Yasu Graham, *Vice Pres*
EMP: 30
SQ FT: 12,000
SALES (est): 8.3MM **Privately Held**
WEB: www.hplc-asi.com
SIC: 3826 3494 Analytical instruments; valves & pipe fittings

(P-21172)
ANALYTIK JENA US LLC (DH)
2066 W 11th St, Upland (91786-3509)
P.O. Box 5015 (91785-5015)
PHONE...................................909 946-3197
Monde Qhobosheane, *CEO*
Chris Griffith, *CFO*
Luis Moreno, *Accounting Mgr*
Leighton H Smith, *Mng Member*
Ulrich Krauss, *Manager*
◆ EMP: 100
SQ FT: 42,000
SALES (est): 17.4MM
SALES (corp-wide): 2.8B **Privately Held**
SIC: 3826 3641 Analytical instruments; ultraviolet lamps
HQ: Analytik Jena Ag
Konrad-Zuse-Str. 1
Jena 07745
364 177-70

(P-21173)
ANASYS INSTRUMENTS CORP
325 Chapala St, Santa Barbara (93101-3407)
PHONE...................................805 730-3310
Roshan Shetty, *President*
Kevin Kjoller, *Vice Pres*
Kristen White, *Office Mgr*
Doug Gotthard, *Engineer*
Michael Sbaraglia, *Buyer*
EMP: 15
SQ FT: 3,000
SALES (est): 2.6MM **Privately Held**
WEB: www.anasysinstruments.com
SIC: 3826 Thermal analysis instruments, laboratory type

(P-21174)
APTON BIOSYSTEMS INC
24245 Elise Ct, Los Altos Hills (94024-5117)
PHONE...................................650 284-6992
Bryan Staker, *Chief Engr*
Bart Staker, *Chief Engr*
EMP: 10
SALES (est): 713.8K **Privately Held**
SIC: 3826 Protein analyzers, laboratory type

(P-21175)
ART ROBBINS INSTRUMENTS
LLC
1293 Mountain View Alviso, Sunnyvale (94089-2241)
PHONE...................................408 734-8400
Matt Robbins, *General Mgr*
David Wright, *General Mgr*
Erik Norgren, *Design Engr*
Paul May, *Engineer*
Edward Pursifull, *Engineer*
EMP: 20
SQ FT: 6,000
SALES (est): 3.3MM **Privately Held**
WEB: www.artrobbinsinstruments.com
SIC: 3826 Analytical instruments

(P-21176)
ASA CORPORATION
3111 Sunset Blvd Ste V, Rocklin (95677-3090)
PHONE...................................530 305-3720
John Mehlhaff, *President*

EMP: 15
SALES (est): 5MM **Privately Held**
SIC: 3826 Surface area analyzers

(P-21177)
ATE MICROGRAPHICS INC
3101 Whipple Rd Ste 22, Union City
(94587-1223)
PHONE.....................510 475-5882
Edmund Monberg, *President*
Debra Rosen, *General Mgr*
EMP: 10
SQ FT: 20,000
SALES (est): 1MM **Privately Held**
WEB: www.lasermotion.com
SIC: 3826 8742 Photomicrographic apparatus; management consulting services

(P-21178)
BAUSCH HEALTH AMERICAS INC
1330 Redwood Way Ste C, Petaluma
(94954-7122)
PHONE.....................707 793-2600
EMP: 140
SALES (corp-wide): 8.3B **Privately Held**
SIC: 3826 Analytical instruments
HQ: Bausch Health Americas, Inc.
   400 Somerset Corp Blvd
   Bridgewater NJ 08807
   908 927-1400

(P-21179)
BAYSPEC INC
1101 Mckay Dr, San Jose (95131-1706)
PHONE.....................408 512-5928
William Yang, *President*
Eric Bergles, *Vice Pres*
Brad Sohnlein, *Sales Staff*
EMP: 35
SQ FT: 48,000
SALES (est): 6.6MM **Privately Held**
WEB: www.bayspec.com
SIC: 3826 Analytical instruments

(P-21180)
BECKMAN COULTER INC
15989 Cypress Ave, Chino (91708-9100)
PHONE.....................909 597-3967
EMP: 82
SALES (corp-wide): 18.3B **Publicly Held**
SIC: 3826 3821 3841
HQ: Beckman Coulter, Inc.
   250 S Kraemer Blvd
   Brea CA 92821
   714 993-5321

(P-21181)
BECKMAN COULTER INC
167 W Poplar Ave, Porterville (93257-5311)
PHONE.....................559 784-0800
Marshall Black, *Opers-Prdtn-Mfg*
Robert Baxley, *General Mgr*
Myra Aguillon, *Technician*
Bob Baxley, *Director*
EMP: 200
SQ FT: 36,000
SALES (corp-wide): 19.8B **Publicly Held**
WEB: www.beckman.com
SIC: 3826 Analytical instruments
HQ: Beckman Coulter, Inc.
   250 S Kraemer Blvd
   Brea CA 92821
   714 993-5321

(P-21182)
BECKMAN COULTER INC
2470 Faraday Ave, Carlsbad (92010-7224)
PHONE.....................760 438-9151
Claire O'Donadan, *Opers-Prdtn-Mfg*
Shaila Jain, *Finance Mgr*
EMP: 200
SALES (corp-wide): 19.8B **Publicly Held**
WEB: www.beckman.com
SIC: 3826 Analytical instruments
HQ: Beckman Coulter, Inc.
   250 S Kraemer Blvd
   Brea CA 92821
   714 993-5321

(P-21183)
BECKMAN COULTER INC
2040 Enterprise Blvd, West Sacramento
(95691-5045)
PHONE.....................916 374-3511
EMP: 77

SALES (corp-wide): 19.8B **Publicly Held**
SIC: 3826 Analytical instruments
HQ: Beckman Coulter, Inc.
   250 S Kraemer Blvd
   Brea CA 92821
   714 993-5321

(P-21184)
BEMCO INC (PA)
2255 Union Pl, Simi Valley (93065-1661)
PHONE.....................805 583-4970
Randy Jean Bruskrud, *President*
Brian Bruskrud, *Admin Sec*
EMP: 25 **EST:** 1951
SQ FT: 50,000
SALES (est): 6MM **Privately Held**
WEB: www.bemcoinc.com
SIC: 3826 Environmental testing equipment

(P-21185)
BIO-RAD LABORATORIES INC
Also Called: Finance Department
225 Linus Pauling Dr, Hercules
(94547-1816)
PHONE.....................510 741-6916
Lanette Ewing, *Branch Mgr*
Claudia Yatsko, *Executive*
Alfredo Ornelas, *Program Mgr*
Anh Lam, *Software Dev*
Serge Taran, *Software Dev*
EMP: 1500
SALES (corp-wide): 2.2B **Publicly Held**
SIC: 3826 Electrophoresis equipment
PA: Bio-Rad Laboratories, Inc.
   1000 Alfred Nobel Dr
   Hercules CA 94547
   510 724-7000

(P-21186)
BIO-RAD LABORATORIES INC
21 Technology Dr, Irvine (92618-2335)
PHONE.....................949 789-0685
EMP: 473
SALES (corp-wide): 2.2B **Publicly Held**
SIC: 3826 Analytical instruments
PA: Bio-Rad Laboratories, Inc.
   1000 Alfred Nobel Dr
   Hercules CA 94547
   510 724-7000

(P-21187)
BIO-RAD LABORATORIES INC
Bio-RAD U S S D
2000 Alfred Nobel Dr, Hercules
(94547-1804)
PHONE.....................510 741-1000
EMP: 125
SQ FT: 95,850
SALES (corp-wide): 2.2B **Publicly Held**
WEB: www.bio-rad.com
SIC: 3826 Analytical instruments
PA: Bio-Rad Laboratories, Inc.
   1000 Alfred Nobel Dr
   Hercules CA 94547
   510 724-7000

(P-21188)
BIO-RAD LABORATORIES INC
Bio-RAD Clinical Systems Div
4000 Alfred Nobel Dr, Hercules
(94547-1810)
PHONE.....................510 741-6709
EMP: 125
SQ FT: 87,750
SALES (corp-wide): 2.2B **Publicly Held**
WEB: www.bio-rad.com
SIC: 3826 Analytical instruments
PA: Bio-Rad Laboratories, Inc.
   1000 Alfred Nobel Dr
   Hercules CA 94547
   510 724-7000

(P-21189)
BIO-RAD LABORATORIES INC
2000 Alfred Nobel Dr, Hercules
(94547-1804)
PHONE.....................510 232-7000
Norman Swartz, *CEO*
Kevin Maddocks, *Opers Mgr*
Franck Villars, *Opers Mgr*
Lip Chu, *Manager*
Leeann Khoo, *Manager*
EMP: 1500

SALES (corp-wide): 19.8B **Publicly Held**
SIC: 3826 Analytical instruments
HQ: Beckman Coulter, Inc.
   250 S Kraemer Blvd
   Brea CA 92821
   714 993-5321

(P-21190)
BIO-RAD LABORATORIES INC
6000 James Watson Dr, Hercules (94547)
PHONE.....................510 741-6715
Bill Radcliff, *Manager*
EMP: 473
SALES (corp-wide): 2.2B **Publicly Held**
WEB: www.bio-rad.com
SIC: 3826 3841 3829 Analytical instruments; surgical & medical instruments; instruments to measure electricity
PA: Bio-Rad Laboratories, Inc.
   1000 Alfred Nobel Dr
   Hercules CA 94547
   510 724-7000

(P-21191)
BIO-RAD LABORATORIES INC
Also Called: Lifescience
2000 Alfred Nobel Dr, Hercules
(94547-1804)
PHONE.....................510 741-6999
Burt Zabin, *Manager*
EMP: 300
SALES (corp-wide): 2.2B **Publicly Held**
WEB: www.bio-rad.com
SIC: 3826 3841 3829 Analytical instruments; surgical & medical instruments; measuring & controlling devices
PA: Bio-Rad Laboratories, Inc.
   1000 Alfred Nobel Dr
   Hercules CA 94547
   510 724-7000

(P-21192)
BIO-RAD LABORATORIES INC
Also Called: Bio-RAD Labs
3110 Regatta Ave, Richmond (94804-6427)
PHONE.....................510 232-7000
Paul Bouchard, *Branch Mgr*
EMP: 473
SQ FT: 6,880
SALES (corp-wide): 2.2B **Publicly Held**
WEB: www.bio-rad.com
SIC: 3826 Electrophoresis equipment
PA: Bio-Rad Laboratories, Inc.
   1000 Alfred Nobel Dr
   Hercules CA 94547
   510 724-7000

(P-21193)
BIO-RAD LABORATORIES INC
5400 E 2nd St, Benicia (94510-1059)
PHONE.....................510 741-5790
Bruce Bartholomew, *Manager*
Kris Fisher, *Vice Pres*
Shannon Hall, *Vice Pres*
Christine Tsingos, *Vice Pres*
Mary Dietz, *IT/INT Sup*
EMP: 20
SALES (corp-wide): 2.2B **Publicly Held**
WEB: www.bio-rad.com
SIC: 3826 Analytical instruments
PA: Bio-Rad Laboratories, Inc.
   1000 Alfred Nobel Dr
   Hercules CA 94547
   510 724-7000

(P-21194)
BIO-RAD LABORATORIES INC
2500 Atlas Rd, Richmond (94806-1170)
PHONE.....................510 724-7000
Payal Khandelwal, *Manager*
EMP: 473
SALES (corp-wide): 2.2B **Publicly Held**
SIC: 3826 Electrophoresis equipment
PA: Bio-Rad Laboratories, Inc.
   1000 Alfred Nobel Dr
   Hercules CA 94547
   510 724-7000

(P-21195)
BIOLOG INC
21124 Cabot Blvd, Hayward (94545-1130)
PHONE.....................510 785-2564
Barry R Bochner, *President*
Edwin Fineman, *Vice Pres*
Doug Rife, *Vice Pres*

Andrew Wung, *Marketing Staff*
Joshua Martin, *Sales Staff*
EMP: 40
SQ FT: 25,000
SALES (est): 10.5MM **Privately Held**
WEB: www.biolog.com
SIC: 3826 Analytical instruments

(P-21196)
BIONANO GENOMICS INC (PA)
9540 Twne Cntre Dr Ste 10, San Diego
(92121)
PHONE.....................858 888-7600
R Erik Holmlin, *President*
Mark Borodkin, *COO*
Mike Ward, *CFO*
Warren Robinson, *Ch Credit Ofcr*
Sven Bocklandt, *Associate Dir*
EMP: 77
SQ FT: 16,521
SALES: 12MM **Publicly Held**
WEB: www.bionanogenomics.com
SIC: 3826 Analytical instruments

(P-21197)
BIOPAC SYSTEMS INC
42 Aero Camino, Goleta (93117-3105)
PHONE.....................805 685-0066
Alan Macy, *CEO*
Marc Wester, *CFO*
William McMullen, *Vice Pres*
Kevin Wasco, *Executive*
EMP: 40
SQ FT: 16,000
SALES (est): 10.6MM **Privately Held**
WEB: www.biopac.com
SIC: 3826 Analytical instruments

(P-21198)
BIORAD INC
9500 Jeronimo Rd, Irvine (92618-2017)
PHONE.....................949 598-1200
Alex Alzona, *General Mgr*
Jesse Cooper, *Administration*
Maria Al-Bayati, *Project Mgr*
Zdravko Bradic, *Research*
Raksha Inamdar, *Research*
EMP: 33
SALES (est): 4.8MM **Privately Held**
SIC: 3826 Analytical instruments

(P-21199)
BIOTAGE LLC
Also Called: Phynexus
3670 Charter Park Dr B, San Jose
(95136-1396)
PHONE.....................408 267-7214
EMP: 10
SALES (corp-wide): 101.1MM **Privately Held**
SIC: 3826 Analytical instruments
HQ: Biotage, Llc
   10430 Harris Oak Blvd C
   Charlotte NC 28269
   704 654-4900

(P-21200)
BRUKER BIOSPIN CORPORATION
Also Called: Bruker Biosciences Cad
61 Daggett Dr, San Jose (95134-2109)
PHONE.....................510 683-4300
Malcolm Bramwell, *Sales/Mktg Mgr*
EMP: 25
SALES (corp-wide): 1.9B **Publicly Held**
WEB: www.brukerbiospin.com
SIC: 3826 Analytical instruments
HQ: Bruker Biospin Corporation
   15 Fortune Dr
   Billerica MA 01821
   978 667-9580

(P-21201)
BRUKER NANO INC
112 Robin Hill Rd, Santa Barbara
(93117-3107)
PHONE.....................805 967-2700
Vladimir Fonoberov, *Software Engr*
John Vance, *IT/INT Sup*
Cole Zimmerman, *Technical Staff*
Kevin Button, *Engineer*
Shuiqing Hu, *Engineer*
EMP: 10
SALES (corp-wide): 1.9B **Publicly Held**
SIC: 3826 Analytical instruments

▲ = Import ▼=Export
◆ =Import/Export

HQ: Bruker Nano, Inc.
3400 E Britannia Dr # 150
Tucson AZ 85706
520 741-1044

(P-21202)
CENTER HEALTH SERVICES
Also Called: San Diego Lgbt Community Ctr
2313 El Cajon Blvd, San Diego
(92104-1105)
P.O. Box 3357 (92163-1357)
PHONE.....................619 692-2077
Deborah Stern-Ellis, *Director*
EMP: 10
SALES (est): 1.7MM **Privately Held**
SIC: 3826 8742 Blood testing apparatus;
hospital & health services consultant

(P-21203)
CEPHEID
904 E Caribbean Dr, Sunnyvale
(94089-1189)
PHONE.....................408 541-4191
EMP: 14
SALES (corp-wide): 18.3B **Publicly Held**
SIC: 3826
HQ: Cepheid
904 E Caribbean Dr
Sunnyvale CA 94089

(P-21204)
CEPHEID (HQ)
904 E Caribbean Dr, Sunnyvale
(94089-1189)
PHONE.....................408 541-4191
Warren Kocmond, *President*
Christopher Germak, *Vice Pres*
Paris Harris, *Vice Pres*
Robert Kwiatkowski, *Vice Pres*
Leonard Phillips, *Vice Pres*
◆ EMP: 277
SALES: 538.5MM
SALES (corp-wide): 19.8B **Publicly Held**
WEB: www.cepheid.com
SIC: 3826 3841 Analytical instruments;
surgical & medical instruments
PA: Danaher Corporation
2200 Penn Ave Nw Ste 800w
Washington DC 20037
202 828-0850

(P-21205)
CITY OF SAN DIEGO
Also Called: Public Utilites Emts
2392 Kincaid Rd, San Diego (92101-0811)
PHONE.....................619 758-2310
Steve Meyer, *Manager*
Kimberly Mathis, *Area Mgr*
Valli Clark, *Administration*
Adam Stontz, *Technician*
Francisco Bordon, *Project Engr*
EMP: 38
SQ FT: 92,782 **Privately Held**
WEB: www.eayo.com
SIC: 3826 Sewage testing apparatus
PA: City Of San Diego
202 C St
San Diego CA 92101
619 236-6330

(P-21206)
COHERENT INC (PA)
5100 Patrick Henry Dr, Santa Clara
(95054-1112)
PHONE.....................408 764-4000
John R Ambroseo, *President*
Garry W Rogerson, *Ch of Bd*
Kevin Palatnik, *CFO*
L William Krause, *Bd of Directors*
Bret M Dimarco, *Exec VP*
▲ EMP: 1082
SQ FT: 200,000
SALES: 1.9B **Publicly Held**
WEB: www.coherent.com
SIC: 3826 3845 3699 Laser scientific &
engineering instruments; laser systems &
equipment, medical; laser systems &
equipment

(P-21207)
COMBIMATRIX CORPORATION (HQ)
310 Goddard Ste 150, Irvine (92618-4617)
PHONE.....................949 753-0624
Mark McDonough, *President*

R Judd Jessup, *Ch of Bd*
Scott R Burell, *CFO*
Evan Cleaver, *Executive*
Aria Esmaeili, *Technology*
EMP: 30
SQ FT: 12,200
SALES: 12.8MM **Publicly Held**
WEB: www.combimatrix.com
SIC: 3826 8731 Analytical instruments;
biotechical research, commercial

(P-21208)
CONNECTEDYARD INC
Also Called: Phin
1841 Zanker Rd Ste 10, San Jose
(95112-4223)
PHONE.....................408 686-9466
Justin Miller, *CEO*
Mark Janes, *COO*
EMP: 25 EST: 2014
SALES (est): 3.6MM
SALES (corp-wide): 541.5MM **Privately Held**
SIC: 3826 7371 Water testing apparatus;
computer software development & applications
PA: Hayward Industries, Inc.
620 Division St
Elizabeth NJ 07201
908 351-5400

(P-21209)
CONTINUUM ELECTRO-OPTICS INC
532 Gibraltar Dr, Milpitas (95035-6315)
PHONE.....................408 727-3240
Robert Buckley, *CEO*
Larry Cramer, *President*
Frank Romero, *Treasurer*
Curt Frederickson, *Vice Pres*
◆ EMP: 75
SQ FT: 44,000
SALES (est): 21.2MM
SALES (corp-wide): 23.7MM **Privately Held**
WEB: www.continuumlasers.com
SIC: 3826 Laser scientific & engineering
instruments
PA: Amplitude Technologies
Espace Du Bois Chaland 2a4
Lisses 91090
169 112-790

(P-21210)
CORETEST SYSTEMS INC (PA)
400 Woodview Ave, Morgan Hill
(95037-2827)
PHONE.....................408 778-3771
Jared M Potter, *CEO*
Avid Lynch, *President*
EMP: 15
SQ FT: 7,000
SALES (est): 1.5MM **Privately Held**
WEB: www.coretest.com
SIC: 3826 Analytical instruments

(P-21211)
CRAIC TECHNOLOGIES INC
948 N Amelia Ave, San Dimas
(91773-1401)
PHONE.....................310 573-8180
Paul Martin, *President*
Jumi Lee, *Vice Pres*
Jonathan Burdett, *Regl Sales Mgr*
Colton Sullivan, *Manager*
EMP: 12
SQ FT: 3,500
SALES (est): 2.7MM **Privately Held**
WEB: www.microspectra.com
SIC: 3826 Analytical instruments

(P-21212)
CUPERTRONIX INC
2946 Via Torino, Santa Clara (95051-6084)
PHONE.....................408 887-5455
Larry L Shi, *CEO*
Larry Shi, *CEO*
EMP: 10 EST: 2015
SALES (est): 732K **Privately Held**
SIC: 3826 3661 Analytical optical instruments; fiber optics communications
equipment

(P-21213)
CYBORTRONICS INCORPORATED
470 Nibus, Brea (92821-3204)
PHONE.....................949 855-2814
Brian Supplee, *President*
Eric Luebben, *Vice Pres*
EMP: 12
SALES (est): 5.2MM **Privately Held**
WEB: www.cybortronics.com
SIC: 3826 3825 Environmental testing
equipment; test equipment for electronic
& electric measurement

(P-21214)
CYTEK DEVELOPMENT INC
4059 Clipper Ct, Fremont (94538-6540)
PHONE.....................510 657-0102
▲ EMP: 13
SQ FT: 3,000
SALES (est): 3.8MM **Privately Held**
SIC: 3826

(P-21215)
DATARAY INCORPORATED
1675 Market St, Redding (96001-1022)
PHONE.....................530 472-1717
Steven Garvey, *President*
Kevin Garvey, *COO*
Joy Garvey, *Corp Secy*
EMP: 10
SALES (est): 2.2MM **Privately Held**
WEB: www.dataray.com
SIC: 3826 Laser scientific & engineering
instruments

(P-21216)
DIONEX CORPORATION (HQ)
1228 Titan Way Ste 1002, Sunnyvale
(94085-4074)
P.O. Box 3603 (94088-3603)
PHONE.....................408 737-0700
Mark Casper, *President*
Craig A McCollam, *CFO*
Bruce Barton, *Exec VP*
Jasmine Gruia Gray PHD, *Vice Pres*
Bill Baker, *Regional Mgr*
EMP: 400 EST: 1986
SQ FT: 252,000
SALES (est): 290.3MM
SALES (corp-wide): 24.3B **Publicly Held**
WEB: www.dionex.com
SIC: 3826 2819 3087 3841 Chromatographic equipment, laboratory type;
chemicals, reagent grade: refined from
technical grade; custom compound purchased resins; surgical & medical instruments
PA: Thermo Fisher Scientific Inc.
168 3rd Ave
Waltham MA 02451
781 622-1000

(P-21217)
DIONEX CORPORATION
Also Called: Thermo Fisher
501 Mercury Dr, Sunnyvale (94085-4019)
P.O. Box 3603 (94088-3603)
PHONE.....................408 737-0700
Lucis Brancil, *Manager*
Jose Romero, *Buyer*
EMP: 100
SALES (corp-wide): 24.3B **Publicly Held**
WEB: www.dionex.com
SIC: 3826 Analytical instruments
HQ: Dionex Corporation
1228 Titan Way Ste 1002
Sunnyvale CA 94085
408 737-0700

(P-21218)
DRY VAC ENVIRONMENTAL INC (PA)
864 Saint Francis Way, Rio Vista
(94571-1250)
PHONE.....................707 374-7500
Dan Simpson, *President*
Greg Crocco, *Shareholder*
EMP: 25
SQ FT: 50,000
SALES (est): 2.4MM **Privately Held**
SIC: 3826 3531 Liquid testing apparatus;
construction machinery

(P-21219)
DVS SCIENCES INC
7000 Shoreline Ct Ste 100, South San
Francisco (94080-7603)
PHONE.....................408 900-7205
Joseph J Victor, *President*
Mark Tebneoer, *CFO*
Scott Tanner, *Founder*
Kevin Farrell, *Manager*
EMP: 50
SALES (est): 6.1MM
SALES (corp-wide): 112.9MM **Publicly Held**
SIC: 3826 2819 Analytical instruments;
chemicals, reagent grade: refined from
technical grade
PA: Fluidigm Corporation
7000 Shoreline Ct Ste 100
South San Francisco CA 94080
650 266-6000

(P-21220)
ELECTRON IMAGING INCORPORATED
14260 Garden Rd Ste A12, Poway
(92064-4973)
PHONE.....................858 679-1569
Ken Arnold, *Principal*
EMP: 10
SALES (est): 960K **Privately Held**
WEB: www.hte.com
SIC: 3826 Analytical instruments

(P-21221)
ELECTRONIC SENSOR TECH INC
1125 Bsneca Ctr Cir Ste B, Newbury Park
(91320)
PHONE.....................805 480-1994
William Wittmeyer, *CEO*
Kelly Dang,
EMP: 10
SQ FT: 12,700
SALES: 420K **Publicly Held**
WEB: www.estcal.com
SIC: 3826 3829 Gas chromatographic instruments; measuring & controlling devices
PA: Halfmoon Bay Capital Limited
C/O Trident Trust Company (B.V.I)
Limited
Road Town

(P-21222)
EMD MILLIPORE CORPORATION
25801 Industrial Blvd B, Hayward
(94545-2223)
PHONE.....................510 576-1367
Lawrence F Bruder, *CEO*
EMP: 180
SALES (corp-wide): 16.9B **Privately Held**
SIC: 3826 Analytical instruments
HQ: Emd Millipore Corporation
400 Summit Dr
Burlington MA 01803
781 533-6000

(P-21223)
EMD MILLIPORE CORPORATION
26578 Old Julian Hwy, Ramona
(92065-6733)
PHONE.....................760 788-9692
Haizhen Liu, *Manager*
EMP: 10
SQ FT: 9,694
SALES (corp-wide): 16.9B **Privately Held**
SIC: 3826 Analytical instruments
HQ: Emd Millipore Corporation
400 Summit Dr
Burlington MA 01803
781 533-6000

(P-21224)
EMD MILLIPORE CORPORATION
28835 Single Oak Dr, Temecula
(92590-5501)
PHONE.....................951 676-8080
Patrick Schneider, *Manager*
EMP: 180
SALES (corp-wide): 16.9B **Privately Held**
SIC: 3826 Analytical instruments

PRODUCTS & SVCS

HQ: Emd Millipore Corporation
400 Summit Dr
Burlington MA 01803
781 533-6000

(P-21225)
ENDRESS & HAUSER CONDUCTA INC
Also Called: Endresshauser Conducta
4123 E La Palma Ave, Anaheim
(92807-1867)
PHONE..............................800 835-5474
Manfred A Jagiella, *CEO*
Claude Genswein, *CFO*
Steve Ruff, *General Mgr*
Jason Huo, *Engineer*
Michael Kruger, *Engineer*
EMP: 50 EST: 1976
SQ FT: 31,000
SALES (est): 12.5MM
SALES (corp-wide): 2.8B **Privately Held**
WEB: www.conducta.endress.com
SIC: 3826 3823 Water testing apparatus;
industrial instrmnts msrmnt display/control
process variable
HQ: Endress+Hauser Conducta Gmbh+Co.
Kg
Dieselstr. 24
Gerlingen 70839
715 620-90

(P-21226)
ENTECH INSTRUMENTS INC
2207 Agate Ct, Simi Valley (93065-1839)
PHONE..............................805 527-5939
Daniel B Cardin, *CEO*
Daniel Cardin, *Vice Pres*
Jared Bossart, *Admin Sec*
Ziggy Cunanan, *Graphic Designe*
▲ EMP: 55
SQ FT: 25,000
SALES (est): 14.3MM **Privately Held**
WEB: www.entechinst.com
SIC: 3826 Environmental testing equip-
ment

(P-21227)
EUV TECH INC
2840 Howe Rd Ste A, Martinez
(94553-4035)
PHONE..............................925 229-4388
Rupert Perera, *President*
Dave Houser, *Vice Pres*
Ravisha Sellahewa, *Marketing Staff*
Derek Yegian, *Director*
EMP: 15 EST: 1996
SQ FT: 6,000
SALES (est): 3.8MM **Privately Held**
WEB: www.euvl.com
SIC: 3826 Laser scientific & engineering
instruments

(P-21228)
FIBERLITE CENTRIFUGE LLC
Also Called: Thermo Fisher Scientific
422 Aldo Ave, Santa Clara (95054-2301)
PHONE..............................408 492-1109
Al Piramoon, *Mng Member*
Tim Sgroi, *Sr Project Mgr*
Kim Vong, *Senior Mgr*
Christian Corso, *Manager*
▲ EMP: 70
SQ FT: 18,000
SALES (est): 9.4MM
SALES (corp-wide): 24.3B **Publicly Held**
WEB: www.piramoon.com
SIC: 3826 Analytical instruments
PA: Thermo Fisher Scientific Inc.
168 3rd Ave
Waltham MA 02451
781 622-1000

(P-21229)
FILMETRICS INC (PA)
10655 Roselle St Ste 200, San Diego
(92121-1557)
PHONE..............................858 573-9300
Scott Chalmers, *President*
Menno Bouman, *Technology*
Jarret Whetstone, *Technology*
Robert O'Barr, *Technical Staff*
John Coleman, *Engineer*
EMP: 20
SQ FT: 2,691

SALES (est): 4.3MM **Privately Held**
WEB: www.filmetrix.com
SIC: 3826 Analytical optical instruments

(P-21230)
FLIR EOC LLC
Also Called: Flir Elctr-Ptcal Comp Bus Unit
2223 Eastman Ave Ste B, Ventura
(93003-8050)
P.O. Box 6217 (93006-6217)
PHONE..............................805 642-4645
John Baumann, *General Mgr*
EMP: 30
SQ FT: 7,264
SALES (est): 5.8MM
SALES (corp-wide): 1.7B **Publicly Held**
WEB: www.aeriusphotonics.com
SIC: 3826 Laser scientific & engineering
instruments
PA: Flir Systems, Inc.
27700 Sw Parkway Ave
Wilsonville OR 97070
503 498-3547

(P-21231)
FLUIDIGM CORPORATION (PA)
7000 Shoreline Ct Ste 100, South San
Francisco (94080-7603)
PHONE..............................650 266-6000
Samuel D Colella, *Ch of Bd*
Vikram Jog, *CFO*
Steven C McPhail, *Ch Credit Ofcr*
William M Smith, *Exec VP*
Grace Yow, *Exec VP*
EMP: 174
SQ FT: 81,500
SALES: 112.9MM **Publicly Held**
WEB: www.fluidigm.com
SIC: 3826 8731 Analytical instruments;
biotechnical research, commercial

(P-21232)
FULL SPECTRUM GROUP LLC (PA)
Also Called: FSA
1252 Quarry Ln, Pleasanton (94566-4756)
PHONE..............................925 485-9000
Tom S Fider,
Alan Chan, *CFO*
Greg Halstead, *Regional Mgr*
Roger Reeve, *Technical Staff*
John Martin,
EMP: 10
SQ FT: 5,000
SALES (est): 8.2MM **Privately Held**
WEB: www.fullspectrum-inc.com
SIC: 3826 Analytical instruments

(P-21233)
GENETIX USA INC
120 Baytech Dr, San Jose (95134-2302)
P.O. Box 528, Richmond IL (60071-0528)
PHONE..............................408 719-6400
Mark Reid, *President*
▲ EMP: 18
SQ FT: 5,500
SALES (est): 2.9MM **Privately Held**
WEB: www.genetix.com
SIC: 3826 Analytical instruments
HQ: Launchchange Limited
19 Jessops Riverside
Sheffield

(P-21234)
HAMAX AMERICA INC (PA)
660 Baker St Ste 405s, Costa Mesa
(92626-4411)
P.O. Box 3613, Laguna Hills (92654-3613)
PHONE..............................714 641-7528
Takahira Hamada, *CEO*
▲ EMP: 10
SALES (est): 2.5MM **Privately Held**
SIC: 3826 3452 Laser scientific & engi-
neering instruments; bolts, nuts, rivets &
washers

(P-21235)
HAMILTON SUNDSTRAND CORP
Collins Aerospace
960 Overland Ct, San Dimas (91773-1742)
P.O. Box 2801, Pomona (91769-2801)
PHONE..............................909 593-5300
Bob Hertel, *Branch Mgr*
Edward Francis, *Exec Dir*
Dr Robt Hertel, *Engineer*

Pie Ngov, *Engineer*
Ronnie Bowen, *Human Res Mgr*
EMP: 240
SALES (corp-wide): 66.5B **Publicly Held**
WEB: www.hamilton-standard.com
SIC: 3826 3861 3812 Spectrometers;
cameras, still & motion picture (all types);
search & navigation equipment
HQ: Hamilton Sundstrand Corporation
1 Hamilton Rd
Windsor Locks CT 06096
860 654-6000

(P-21236)
HI-Q ENVIRONMENTAL PDTS CO INC
7386 Trade St, San Diego (92121-2422)
PHONE..............................858 549-2818
Marc A Held, *CEO*
Sherry Williams, *Office Mgr*
Nagaraj Ramakrishna, *Engineer*
▲ EMP: 12 EST: 1973
SQ FT: 5,000
SALES (est): 3MM **Privately Held**
WEB: www.hi-q.net
SIC: 3826 Analytical instruments

(P-21237)
HIGH SIERRA ELECTRONICS INC
155 Spring Hill Dr # 106, Grass Valley
(95945-5929)
PHONE..............................530 273-2080
James Logan, *CEO*
Ilse Gayl, *President*
Brian Loflin, *CFO*
EMP: 26
SQ FT: 9,100
SALES (est): 1MM **Privately Held**
SIC: 3826 8748 8731 Environmental test-
ing equipment; communications consult-
ing; electronic research

(P-21238)
HITACHI HIGH-TECHNOLOGIES
20770 Nordhoff St, Chatsworth
(91311-5900)
PHONE..............................818 280-0745
Mark Kawamura, *CEO*
Mike Takahashi, *President*
Shaul Balkan, *Senior VP*
Peter Lee, *Info Tech Mgr*
Dean Gregson, *Business Anlyst*
EMP: 17
SQ FT: 900
SALES (est): 3.9MM **Privately Held**
WEB: www.siintusa.com
SIC: 3826 Analytical instruments
PA: Hitachi High-Tech Science Corporation
1-24-14, Nishishimbashi
Minato-Ku TKY 105-0

(P-21239)
HOEFER INC
760 National Ct, Richmond (94804-2008)
PHONE..............................415 282-2307
Hugh Douglas, *COO*
Ron Miller, *Accounting Mgr*
John Kelly, *Prdtn Mgr*
▲ EMP: 30 EST: 1967
SQ FT: 30,000
SALES (est): 5.5MM **Publicly Held**
WEB: www.hoeferinc.com
SIC: 3826 Electrophoresis equipment
PA: Harvard Bioscience, Inc.
84 October Hill Rd Ste 10
Holliston MA 01746

(P-21240)
HORIBA INSTRUMENTS INC (DH)
Also Called: Horiba Automotive Test Systems
9755 Research Dr, Irvine (92618-4626)
PHONE..............................949 250-4811
Jai Hakhu, *Ch of Bd*
Pattie Jones, *Credit Staff*
▲ EMP: 195 EST: 1998
SQ FT: 80,000

SALES (est): 215.6MM **Privately Held**
WEB: www.horibalab.com
SIC: 3826 3829 3511 3825 Analytical instruments; measuring & controlling devices; turbines & turbine generator sets;
instruments to measure electricity; diagnostic equipment, medical; medical laboratory equipment; hospital equipment &
supplies; physician equipment & supplies;
industrial process measurement equipment
HQ: Horiba Americas Holding Incorporated
9755 Research Dr
Irvine CA 92618
949 250-4811

(P-21241)
HYDROLYNX SYSTEMS INC
950 Riverside Pkwy Ste 10, West Sacra-
mento (95605-1501)
PHONE..............................916 374-1800
Kimberly A Blair, *President*
David Leader, *Vice Pres*
EMP: 10 EST: 1998
SQ FT: 7,000
SALES (est): 1.9MM **Privately Held**
WEB: www.hydrolynx.com
SIC: 3826 Environmental testing equip-
ment

(P-21242)
ILLUMINA INC
9885 Towne Centre Dr, San Diego
(92121-1975)
PHONE..............................800 809-4566
William Rastetter, *Chairman*
Jay Harger, *Associate Dir*
Frank Lynch, *Associate Dir*
Stacie Young, *Associate Dir*
Karla Morrell, *Executive Asst*
EMP: 21
SALES (corp-wide): 3.3B **Publicly Held**
SIC: 3826 Analytical instruments
PA: Illumina, Inc.
5200 Illumina Way
San Diego CA 92122
858 202-4500

(P-21243)
ILLUMINA INC (PA)
5200 Illumina Way, San Diego
(92122-4616)
PHONE..............................858 202-4500
Francis A Desouza, *President*
Jay T Flatley, *Ch of Bd*
Sam A Samad, *CFO*
Aquinas Arnold, *Bd of Directors*
Aimee Hoyt, *Officer*
▲ EMP: 277
SQ FT: 1,218,000
SALES: 3.3B **Publicly Held**
WEB: www.illumina.com
SIC: 3826 3821 Analytical instruments;
clinical laboratory instruments, except
medical & dental

(P-21244)
ILLUMINA INC
200 Lincoln Centre Dr, Foster City
(94404-1122)
PHONE..............................510 670-9300
Mary Schramke, *Principal*
EMP: 22
SALES (corp-wide): 3.3B **Publicly Held**
SIC: 3826 Analytical instruments
PA: Illumina, Inc.
5200 Illumina Way
San Diego CA 92122
858 202-4500

(P-21245)
INFRARED INDUSTRIES INC
25590 Seaboard Ln, Hayward
(94545-3210)
PHONE..............................510 782-8100
Mark Russell, *President*
Martha Rykala, *CFO*
▲ EMP: 10
SQ FT: 10,000
SALES (est): 1.8MM **Privately Held**
WEB: www.infraredindustries.com
SIC: 3826 Gas analyzing equipment

▲ = Import ▼=Export
◆ =Import/Export

(P-21246)
INFRASTRUCTUREWORLD LLC
1001 Bayhill Dr Ste 200, San Bruno
(94066-5902)
PHONE..................................650 871-3950
EMP: 20
SALES (est): 1.6MM **Privately Held**
WEB: www.infrastructureworld.com
SIC: 3826

(P-21247)
INTEGENX INC (HQ)
5720 Stoneridge Dr # 300, Pleasanton
(94588-2739)
PHONE..................................925 701-3400
Robert A Schueren, *CEO*
David V Smith, *COO*
David King, *Exec VP*
▲ EMP: 69
SQ FT: 10,000
SALES (est): 13.8MM
SALES (corp-wide): 24.3B **Publicly Held**
WEB: www.microchipbiotech.com
SIC: 3826 Analytical instruments
PA: Thermo Fisher Scientific Inc.
168 3rd Ave
Waltham MA 02451
781 622-1000

(P-21248)
**INTERGLOBAL WASTE
MANAGEMENT**
820 Calle Plano, Camarillo (93012-8557)
PHONE..................................805 388-1588
Harold Katersky, *Ch of Bd*
Thomas Williams, *Shareholder*
Clay Causey, *Sales Staff*
Dwight Norris, *Sales Staff*
Tim O'Connell, *Sales Staff*
EMP: 80
SALES (est): 867.1K **Privately Held**
SIC: 3826 Analytical instruments

(P-21249)
**INTERNTIONAL THERMAL INSTR
INC**
4511 Sun Valley Rd, Del Mar (92014-4114)
P.O. Box 309 (92014-0309)
PHONE..................................858 755-4436
Norman D Greene, *General Mgr*
Derek Greene, *CEO*
EMP: 10
SQ FT: 5,000
SALES (est): 1.2MM **Privately Held**
WEB: www.iticompany.com
SIC: 3826 5084 Instruments measuring
thermal properties; instruments & control
equipment

(P-21250)
J&M ANALYTIK AG
141 California St Apt G, Arcadia
(91006-6528)
PHONE..................................626 297-2930
Biplab Bhawal, *Sales Staff*
EMP: 26
SALES (est): 2.1MM **Privately Held**
SIC: 3826 Spectroscopic & other optical
properties measuring equipment

(P-21251)
KETT
Also Called: Kett U S
9581 Featherhill Dr, Villa Park
(92861-2633)
PHONE..................................714 974-8837
John Bogart, *Managing Dir*
EMP: 12 EST: 1988
SQ FT: 10,000
SALES (est): 1.2MM **Privately Held**
WEB: www.kett.com
SIC: 3826 Analytical instruments

(P-21252)
LAB VISION CORPORATION (DH)
Also Called: Thermo Fisher Scientific
46500 Kato Rd, Fremont (94538-7310)
PHONE..................................510 979-5000
Seth H Hoogasian, *CEO*
David Bespalko, *President*
Derek Lehane, *General Mgr*
Julien Simon, *Electrical Engi*
▲ EMP: 10
SQ FT: 12,163

SALES (est): 733K
SALES (corp-wide): 24.3B **Publicly Held**
WEB: www.labvision.com
SIC: 3826 3841 5122 Analytical instru-
ments; diagnostic apparatus, medical; bi-
ologicals & allied products

(P-21253)
**LAMBDA RESEARCH OPTICS
INC**
1695 Macarthur Blvd, Costa Mesa
(92626-1440)
PHONE..................................714 327-0600
Mark W Youn, *President*
▲ EMP: 65
SQ FT: 3,500
SALES (est): 13.7MM **Privately Held**
SIC: 3826 3827 3229 Laser scientific &
engineering instruments; optical instru-
ments & lenses; pressed & blown glass

(P-21254)
**LIFE TECHNOLOGIES
CORPORATION**
500 Lincoln Centre Dr, Foster City
(94404-1158)
PHONE..................................760 603-7200
EMP: 115
SALES (corp-wide): 24.3B **Publicly Held**
SIC: 3826 Analytical instruments
HQ: Life Technologies Corporation
5781 Van Allen Way
Carlsbad CA 92008
760 603-7200

(P-21255)
MAKO INDUSTRIES SC INC
1280 N Red Gum St, Anaheim
(92806-1820)
PHONE..................................714 632-1400
John Tittelfitz, *CEO*
Gunnar Bredek, *Vice Pres*
Shane Rankin, *Sales Staff*
▲ EMP: 39 EST: 2007
SALES (est): 9.4MM **Privately Held**
WEB: www.makoindustries.com
SIC: 3826 Environmental testing equip-
ment

(P-21256)
MANTA INSTRUMENTS INC
9755 Research Dr, Irvine (92618-4626)
PHONE..................................844 633-2500
Jai Hakhu, *CEO*
Kuba Tatarkiewicz, *VP Engrg*
EMP: 13
SALES (est): 1.9MM **Privately Held**
SIC: 3826 Analytical instruments

(P-21257)
MARBIL INDUSTRIES INC
2201 N Glassell St, Orange (92865-2701)
PHONE..................................714 974-4032
Allan V Thompson, *President*
William B Thomson Jr, *Shareholder*
EMP: 20
SQ FT: 10,000
SALES (est): 1.6MM **Privately Held**
SIC: 3826 Mass spectrometers

(P-21258)
**MARINE SPILL RESPONSE
CORP**
990 W Waterfront Dr, Eureka (95501-0173)
PHONE..................................707 442-6087
EMP: 22
SALES (corp-wide): 105.4MM **Privately
Held**
SIC: 3826 Environmental testing equip-
ment
PA: Marine Spill Response Corporation
220 Spring St Ste 500
Herndon VA 20170
703 326-5600

(P-21259)
MARKES INTERNATIONAL INC
Also Called: Alms Company
2355 Gold Meadow Way # 120, Gold River
(95670-6365)
PHONE..................................513 745-0241
Elizabeth Woolfenden, *Director*
Alun Cole, *Director*
EMP: 100

SALES: 1MM
SALES (corp-wide): 222MM **Privately
Held**
SIC: 3826 Analytical instruments
HQ: Markes International Limited
Unit 3-4 Gwaun Elai, Medi Science
Campus
Pontyclun M GLAM CF72
144 323-0935

(P-21260)
MEANS ENGINEERING INC
5927 Geiger Ct, Carlsbad (92008-7305)
PHONE..................................760 931-9452
David William Means, *CEO*
Richard Howard, *Partner*
Lisa Means, *Exec VP*
Jose Figueroa, *Administration*
EMP: 70
SQ FT: 34,000
SALES (est): 17.6MM **Privately Held**
WEB: www.meanseng.com
SIC: 3826 3699 3559 Analytical instru-
ments; electrical equipment & supplies;
semiconductor manufacturing machinery

(P-21261)
**MESOTECH INTERNATIONAL
INC**
4531 Harlin Dr, Sacramento (95826-9716)
PHONE..................................916 368-2020
Michael Lydon, *President*
Johnathan Walters, *Project Engr*
Adrian Vidrio, *Electrical Engi*
EMP: 14
SALES (est): 3.3MM **Privately Held**
WEB: www.mesotech.com
SIC: 3826 Analytical instruments

(P-21262)
METAL ETCH SERVICES INC
1165 Linda Vista Dr # 106, San Marcos
(92078-3821)
PHONE..................................760 510-9476
Elias Malfavor Jr, *President*
Carlos Dugay, *Natl Sales Mgr*
EMP: 20
SALES (est): 3.5MM **Privately Held**
WEB: metaletchservices.com
SIC: 3826 3951 3479 Laser scientific &
engineering instruments; pens & mechan-
ical pencils; etching on metals

(P-21263)
METROLASER INC
22941 Mill Creek Dr, Laguna Hills
(92653-1264)
PHONE..................................949 553-0688
Cecil Hess, *Founder*
Cecil F Hess, *CEO*
James Trolinger, *Vice Pres*
Regis Morgan, *Technician*
Liang WEI, *Engineer*
EMP: 10
SQ FT: 8,157
SALES (est): 2.9MM **Privately Held**
WEB: www.metrolaserinc.com
SIC: 3826 8731 Laser scientific & engi-
neering instruments; commercial physical
research

(P-21264)
MICRO-TECH SCIENTIFIC INC
Also Called: Microtech Scientific
3059 Palm Hill Dr, Vista (92084-6555)
PHONE..................................760 597-9088
▲ EMP: 16
SQ FT: 21,100
SALES (est): 3MM **Privately Held**
WEB: www.micro-tech.us
SIC: 3826 3841

(P-21265)
MK DIGITAL DIRECT INC
Also Called: or Technology
861 Harold Pl Ste 209, Chula Vista
(91914-4555)
PHONE..................................619 661-0628
◆ EMP: 10
SQ FT: 5,600
SALES (est): 2MM **Privately Held**
SIC: 3826

(P-21266)
**MOLECULAR BIOPRODUCTS
INC (DH)**
9389 Waples St, San Diego (92121-3903)
PHONE..................................858 453-7551
Seth H Hoogasian, *CEO*
Verner Andersen, *Vice Pres*
Jodie Donina, *Vice Pres*
Clive Wingar, *Vice Pres*
Gary J Marmontello, *Admin Sec*
◆ EMP: 110
SQ FT: 45,000
SALES (est): 78.5MM
SALES (corp-wide): 24.3B **Publicly Held**
WEB: www.mbpinc.com
SIC: 3826 Analytical instruments
HQ: Fisher Scientific International Llc
81 Wyman St
Waltham MA 02451
781 622-1000

(P-21267)
**MOLECULAR BIOPRODUCTS
INC**
2200 S Mcdowell Blvd Ext, Petaluma
(94954-5659)
PHONE..................................707 762-6689
Warner Johnson, *Director*
Cathi Huntington, *Technology*
EMP: 220
SALES (corp-wide): 24.3B **Publicly Held**
WEB: www.mbpinc.com
SIC: 3826 Analytical instruments
HQ: Molecular Bioproducts, Inc.
9389 Waples St
San Diego CA 92121
858 453-7551

(P-21268)
**MOLECULAR DEVICES LLC
(HQ)**
3860 N 1st St, San Jose (95134-1702)
PHONE..................................408 747-1700
Kevin Chance, *Mng Member*
Dean Ding, *Vice Pres*
Shawn Laymon, *Vice Pres*
Susan Murphy, *Vice Pres*
Poonam Taneja, *Vice Pres*
▲ EMP: 125
SALES (est): 139.2MM
SALES (corp-wide): 19.8B **Publicly Held**
WEB: www.moleculardevices.com
SIC: 3826 3841 Analytical instruments;
surgical & medical instruments
PA: Danaher Corporation
2200 Penn Ave Nw Ste 800w
Washington DC 20037
202 828-0850

(P-21269)
MOTIONLOFT INC
550 15th Ste 29, San Francisco
(94103-5032)
PHONE..................................415 580-7671
Joyce Reitman, *CEO*
Dan Daogaru, *President*
Paul McAlpine, *Vice Pres*
Alex Hill, *Software Engr*
Kevin McCurdy, *Finance Dir*
EMP: 39
SALES (est): 8.7MM **Privately Held**
SIC: 3826 7372 Analytical instruments;
application computer software; business
oriented computer software

(P-21270)
NANOIMAGING SERVICES INC
4940 Carroll Canyon Rd # 115, San Diego
(92121-1735)
PHONE..................................888 675-8261
Clinton S Potter, *President*
Jessica Moore, *Assistant*
EMP: 14
SALES (est): 1MM **Privately Held**
SIC: 3826 Microscopes, electron & proton

(P-21271)
NANOVEA INC (PA)
6 Morgan Ste 156, Irvine (92618-1922)
PHONE..................................949 461-9292
Pierre Leroux, *President*
John Lin, *Engineer*
Patrick Valdis, *Engineer*
Craig Leising, *Manager*
EMP: 14

(PA)=Parent Co (HQ)=Headquarters (DH)=Div Headquarters
✪ = New Business established in last 2 years

SALES (est): 2.6MM **Privately Held**
SIC: 3826 Analytical instruments

(P-21272)
NEONODE INC (PA)
2880 Zanker Rd Ste 362, San Jose
(95134-2117)
PHONE..................408 496-6722
Maria Ek, *CEO*
Per Bystedt, *Ch of Bd*
Lars Lindqvist, *Treasurer*
Mats Dahlin, *Bd of Directors*
Bengt Edlund, *Vice Pres*
EMP: 60
SQ FT: 6,508
SALES: 8.5MM **Publicly Held**
SIC: 3826 Infrared analytical instruments

(P-21273)
OXFORD INSTRS ASYLUM RES INC (HQ)
6310 Hollister Ave, Santa Barbara
(93117-3115)
PHONE..................805 696-6466
Jason Cleveland, *CEO*
John Green, *President*
Roger Proksch, *President*
Richard Clark, *CFO*
Dick Clark, *Exec VP*
EMP: 55
SALES (est): 8.6MM
SALES (corp-wide): 429.1MM **Privately Held**
SIC: 3826 Analytical instruments
PA: Oxford Instruments Plc
Tubney Woods
Abingdon OXON OX13
186 539-3200

(P-21274)
PACIFIC BIOSCIENCES CAL INC (PA)
1305 Obrien Dr, Menlo Park (94025-1445)
PHONE..................650 521-8000
Michael Hunkapiller, *Ch of Bd*
Lorinda Lahiff, *Info Tech Dir*
Steve Tyson, *Software Engr*
Adam Knight, *IT/INT Sup*
Khalil Bahram, *Technician*
EMP: 241
SQ FT: 180,000
SALES: 78.6MM **Publicly Held**
WEB: www.nanofluidics.com
SIC: 3826 Analytical instruments

(P-21275)
PHENOMENEX INC (HQ)
411 Madrid Ave, Torrance (90501-1430)
PHONE..................310 212-0555
Farshad Mahjoor, *President*
Frank T McFaden, *CFO*
Robert Gramcko, *Executive*
Alex Gharagozlow, *Exec Dir*
Luke Steece, *District Mgr*
▲ **EMP:** 250
SQ FT: 100,000
SALES (est): 120.1MM
SALES (corp-wide): 19.8B **Publicly Held**
WEB: www.phenomenex.com
SIC: 3826 Analytical instruments
PA: Danaher Corporation
2200 Penn Ave Nw Ste 800w
Washington DC 20037
202 828-0850

(P-21276)
PICARRO INC (PA)
3105 Patrick Henry Dr, Santa Clara
(95054-1815)
PHONE..................408 962-3900
Alex Balkanski, *President*
Laura Perrone, *CFO*
Brenda Glaze, *Senior VP*
Jan Willem Poelmann, *Senior VP*
Eric Crosson, *Vice Pres*
EMP: 24
SQ FT: 15,250
SALES (est): 8.6MM **Privately Held**
WEB: www.picarro.com
SIC: 3826 Analytical instruments

(P-21277)
PIXON IMAGING INC
Also Called: Pixonimaging
4930 Longford St, San Diego (92117-2156)
PHONE..................858 352-0100

Chiyoko Lord, *Vice Pres*
EMP: 25
SALES: 950K **Privately Held**
SIC: 3826 Magnetic resonance imaging apparatus

(P-21278)
PROFESSIONAL IMAGING SVCS INC
Also Called: Pro Imaging
751 Main St, Chula Vista (91911-6168)
PHONE..................858 565-4217
Steven Richard Ford, *President*
Anne Ford, *Shareholder*
EMP: 10
SALES: 1.2MM **Privately Held**
WEB: www.proimagingservices.com
SIC: 3826 8742 Magnetic resonance imaging apparatus; hospital & health services consultant

(P-21279)
Q CORPORATION
4880 Adohr Ln, Camarillo (93012-8508)
PHONE..................805 383-8998
Margaret Negri, *President*
James Topp, *CEO*
Wayne Hopkins, *CFO*
Stanton Ens, *Admin Sec*
Jason Eastin, *Manager*
▲ **EMP:** 48 **EST:** 1976
SQ FT: 22,000
SALES (est): 17MM **Privately Held**
WEB: www.theqcorporation.net
SIC: 3826 Environmental testing equipment

(P-21280)
QUANTUM DESIGN INC (PA)
Also Called: Quantum Design International
10307 Pacific Center Ct, San Diego
(92121-4340)
PHONE..................858 481-4400
Greg Degeller, *President*
Martin Kugler, *COO*
David Schultz, *CFO*
Michael B Simmonds, *Vice Pres*
Doug Bird, *Technical Staff*
▲ **EMP:** 217
SQ FT: 118,000
SALES (est): 42.1MM **Privately Held**
WEB: www.qdusa.com
SIC: 3826 Laser scientific & engineering instruments

(P-21281)
QUEST DIAGNOSTICS NICHOLS INST (HQ)
33608 Ortega Hwy, San Juan Capistrano
(92675-2042)
PHONE..................949 728-4000
Catherine T Doherty, *CEO*
Nicholas Conti, *Vice Pres*
Timothy Sharpe, *Vice Pres*
Dan Haemmerle, *Exec Dir*
Michael Caulfield, *Research*
EMP: 1000
SQ FT: 240,000
SALES (est): 218.9MM
SALES (corp-wide): 7.5B **Publicly Held**
WEB: www.nicholsinstitute.com
SIC: 3826 8071 Analytical instruments; testing laboratories
PA: Quest Diagnostics Incorporated
500 Plaza Dr Ste G
Secaucus NJ 07094
973 520-2700

(P-21282)
RS TECHNICAL SERVICES INC (PA)
1327 Clegg St, Petaluma (94954-1126)
P.O. Box 750579 (94975-0579)
PHONE..................707 778-1974
Michael Sutliff, *Principal*
Kathey Sutliff, *Admin Sec*
EMP: 95
SQ FT: 15,000
SALES (est): 18.5MM **Privately Held**
WEB: www.rstechserv.com
SIC: 3826 3823 Sewage testing apparatus; industrial instrmnts msrmnt display/control process variable

(P-21283)
RTEC-INSTRUMENTS INC
1810 Oakland Rd Ste B, San Jose
(95131-2316)
PHONE..................408 456-0801
Vishal Khosla, *CEO*
Jun Xiao, *Vice Pres*
Lizhu Chen, *Marketing Staff*
EMP: 25
SQ FT: 3,000
SALES: 6.5MM **Privately Held**
SIC: 3826 Analytical instruments

(P-21284)
SAGE METERING INC
8 Harris Ct Ste D1, Monterey (93940-5716)
PHONE..................831 242-2030
Robert Steinberg, *President*
David Huey, *CFO*
Myrna Hartnett, *Office Mgr*
Robert Trescott, *VP Engrg*
Jorge Morales, *Engineer*
▲ **EMP:** 10
SQ FT: 2,400
SALES (est): 2.5MM **Privately Held**
WEB: www.sagemetering.com
SIC: 3826 Instruments measuring thermal properties

(P-21285)
SAN DIEGO INSTRUMENTS INC
9155 Brown Deer Rd Ste 8, San Diego
(92121-2260)
PHONE..................858 530-2600
Carl Lischer, *President*
Dr Richard Butcher, *Vice Pres*
Kenneth Fite, *Vice Pres*
Mark A Geyer, *Vice Pres*
James Lischer, *Purchasing*
EMP: 10
SQ FT: 5,000
SALES: 2.3MM **Privately Held**
WEB: www.sandiegoinstruments.com
SIC: 3826 Analytical instruments

(P-21286)
SCI INSTRUMENTS INC (PA)
6355 Corte Del Abeto C105, Carlsbad
(92011-1443)
PHONE..................760 634-3822
Emad S Zawaideh, *President*
EMP: 12
SQ FT: 4,000
SALES: 10MM **Privately Held**
WEB: www.sci-soft.com
SIC: 3826 Laser scientific & engineering instruments

(P-21287)
SCREENING SYSTEMS INC (PA)
36 Blackbird Ln, Aliso Viejo (92656-1765)
P.O. Box 3931, Laguna Hills (92654-3931)
PHONE..................949 855-1751
Susan L Baker, *President*
Susan Baker, *CFO*
Peter Baker, *Consultant*
EMP: 30
SQ FT: 34,000
SALES (est): 4.7MM **Privately Held**
WEB: www.scrsys.com
SIC: 3826 3829 Environmental testing equipment; measuring & controlling devices

(P-21288)
SENSOR-KINESIS CORPORATION (PA)
10604 S La Cienega Blvd, Inglewood
(90304-1115)
PHONE..................424 331-0900
Frank Adell, *CEO*
Christopher Bissell, *CFO*
EMP: 18
SQ FT: 3,750
SALES (est): 1.3MM **Privately Held**
SIC: 3826 Analytical instruments

(P-21289)
SEPRAGEN CORPORATION
1205 San Luis Obispo St, Hayward
(94544-7915)
PHONE..................510 475-0650
Vinit Saxena, *Ch of Bd*
Henry N Edmunds, *CFO*
Salah Ahmed, *Education*
EMP: 28

SQ FT: 23,000
SALES (est): 5.8MM **Privately Held**
WEB: www.sepragen.com
SIC: 3826 Liquid chromatographic instruments

(P-21290)
SHORE WESTERN MANUFACTURING
225 W Duarte Rd, Monrovia (91016-4545)
PHONE..................626 357-3251
Donald Schroeder, *President*
Alice Schroeder, *Corp Secy*
Joe Schroeder, *Vice Pres*
Matthew Schroeder, *Engineer*
Frederick Helen, *Accounting Mgr*
▲ **EMP:** 34 **EST:** 1967
SQ FT: 16,000
SALES: 5MM **Privately Held**
WEB: www.shorewestern.com
SIC: 3826 Environmental testing equipment

(P-21291)
SMITHS DETECTION LLC
1251 E Dyer Rd Ste 140, Santa Ana
(92705-5677)
PHONE..................714 258-4400
Karen Bomba, *CEO*
Chris Le, *General Mgr*
EMP: 609
SALES (corp-wide): 833.4MM **Privately Held**
SIC: 3826 3812 Magnetic resonance imaging apparatus; search & navigation equipment
HQ: Smiths Detection, Llc
7151 Gateway Blvd
Newark CA 94560
510 739-2400

(P-21292)
SPECTRASENSORS INC
11027 Arrow Rte, Rancho Cucamonga
(91730-4866)
PHONE..................909 980-4238
Jeffrey Immelt, *CFO*
EMP: 24
SALES (corp-wide): 2.8B **Privately Held**
SIC: 3826 Analytical instruments
HQ: Spectrasensors, Inc.
4333 W Sam Houston Pkwy N
Houston TX 77043
713 466-3172

(P-21293)
SPRITE INDUSTRIES INCORPORATED
Also Called: Sprite Showers
1791 Railroad St, Corona (92880-2511)
PHONE..................951 735-1015
David K Farley, *President*
Kathleen Farley, *Vice Pres*
Doris Farley, *Admin Sec*
Kathy Farley, *Human Res Mgr*
Sherry Farley, *VP Sales*
▲ **EMP:** 20 **EST:** 1974
SQ FT: 25,000
SALES (est): 3.9MM **Privately Held**
WEB: www.spritewater.com
SIC: 3826 3589 Water testing apparatus; water filters & softeners, household type

(P-21294)
STANFORD RESEARCH SYSTEMS INC
Also Called: SRS
1290 Reamwood Ave Ste D, Sunnyvale
(94089-2279)
PHONE..................408 744-9040
William R Green, *President*
John Willison, *Vice Pres*
Judi Cushing, *Info Tech Mgr*
Christopher Bochna, *Software Engr*
Ian Chan, *Design Engr*
EMP: 140
SQ FT: 20,000
SALES (est): 49.9MM **Privately Held**
WEB: www.srsys.com
SIC: 3826 Analytical instruments

▲ = Import ▼=Export
◆ =Import/Export

(P-21295)
SYAGEN TECHNOLOGY LLC
1251 E Dyer Rd Ste 140, Santa Ana
(92705-5677)
PHONE....................714 258-4400
Karen Bomba,
Quyen Tran, *Administration*
EMP: 20
SQ FT: 5,000
SALES (est): 3.9MM
SALES (corp-wide): 833.4MM **Privately Held**
WEB: www.syagen.com
SIC: 3826 Analytical instruments
HQ: Smiths Detection, Llc
7151 Gateway Blvd
Newark CA 94560
510 739-2400

(P-21296)
TALIS BIOMEDICAL CORPORATION
230 Constitution Dr, Menlo Park
(94025-1109)
PHONE....................650 433-3000
Martin Goldberg, *Branch Mgr*
EMP: 48 **Privately Held**
SIC: 3826 Analytical instruments
PA: Talis Biomedical Corporation
125 S Clark St Fl 17
Chicago IL 60603

(P-21297)
TEAM CHINA CALIFORNIA LLC
3138 Madeira Ave, Costa Mesa
(92626-2324)
PHONE....................714 424-9999
Patrick Mulcahy,
Patrick D Mulcahy,
EMP: 12
SALES: 2MM **Privately Held**
WEB: www.teamchinausa.com
SIC: 3826 8731 Environmental testing
equipment; environmental research

(P-21298)
TECHCOMP (USA) INC
Also Called: Edinburgh Instruments
3500 W Warren Ave, Fremont
(94538-6499)
PHONE....................510 683-4300
Chris O'Connor, *CEO*
James O'Connor, *Principal*
EMP: 22
SQ FT: 17,000
SALES (est): 4.5MM
SALES (corp-wide): 342.6K **Privately Held**
SIC: 3826 7371 Analytical instruments;
computer software development & applications
PA: Techcomp (Europe) Limited
Lake House
Royston HERTS

(P-21299)
TELEDYNE INSTRUMENTS INC
Teledyne Hanson Research
9810 Variel Ave, Chatsworth (91311-4316)
PHONE....................818 882-7266
Thomas Reslewic, *Branch Mgr*
EMP: 31
SALES (corp-wide): 2.9B **Publicly Held**
SIC: 3826 Analytical instruments
HQ: Teledyne Instruments, Inc.
1049 Camino Dos Rios
Thousand Oaks CA 91360
805 373-4545

(P-21300)
TELEDYNE REDLAKE MASD LLC
1049 Camino Dos Rios, Thousand Oaks
(91360-2362)
PHONE....................805 373-4545
Edwin Roks, *President*
Chris Hillman, *Electrical Engi*
Emily Tsang, *Production*
EMP: 33
SQ FT: 50,000

SALES (est): 30.6K
SALES (corp-wide): 2.9B **Publicly Held**
SIC: 3826 3861 3822 3812 Analytical instruments; photographic equipment & supplies; auto controls regulating residntl & coml environmt & applncs; search & navigation equipment
HQ: Teledyne Digital Imaging Us, Inc.
700 Technology Park Dr # 2
Billerica MA 01821
978 670-2000

(P-21301)
TERUMO AMERICAS HOLDING INC
Also Called: Cardiovascular Systems
1311 Valencia Ave, Tustin (92780-6447)
PHONE....................714 258-8001
Kevin Hoffman, *Branch Mgr*
Charlie Noel, *Vice Pres*
Gail Harris, *Sales Staff*
Shawn Miller, *Director*
EMP: 117 **Privately Held**
WEB: www.terumomedical.com
SIC: 3826 Hemoglobinometers; gas analyzing equipment
HQ: Terumo Americas Holding, Inc.
265 Davidson Ave Ste 320
Somerset NJ 08873
732 302-4900

(P-21302)
TETRA TECH EC INC
17885 Von Karman Ave # 500, Irvine
(92614-5227)
PHONE....................949 809-5000
Andrew Brack, *Branch Mgr*
EMP: 49
SALES (corp-wide): 2.9B **Publicly Held**
SIC: 3826 Environmental testing equipment
HQ: Tetra Tech Ec, Inc.
6 Century Dr Ste 3
Parsippany NJ 07054
973 630-8000

(P-21303)
THERMO FINNIGAN LLC (HQ)
355 River Oaks Pkwy, San Jose
(95134-1908)
PHONE....................408 965-6000
Anthony H Smith, *Mng Member*
Jonathan C Wilk,
▲ EMP: 500
SALES (est): 87.8MM
SALES (corp-wide): 24.3B **Publicly Held**
SIC: 3826 Analytical instruments
PA: Thermo Fisher Scientific Inc.
168 3rd Ave
Waltham MA 02451
781 622-1000

(P-21304)
THERMO FISHER SCIENTIFIC
Also Called: Thermofinnegan
355 River Oaks Pkwy, San Jose
(95134-1908)
P.O. Box 49031 (95161)
PHONE....................408 894-9835
Ian Jardin, *Branch Mgr*
Michael Antonczak, *Design Engr*
Viatcheslav Kovtoun, *Research*
Brian McLaughlin, *Engineer*
Stu Matlow, *Pub Rel Mgr*
EMP: 400
SALES (corp-wide): 24.3B **Publicly Held**
WEB: www.thermo.com
SIC: 3826 Analytical instruments
HQ: Thermo Fisher Scientific (Ashville) Llc
28 Schenck Pkwy Ste 400
Asheville NC 28803
828 658-2711

(P-21305)
THERMO FISHER SCIENTIFIC INC
15982 San Antonio Ave, Chino
(91708-7641)
PHONE....................909 393-3205
Claudia Groebner, *Branch Mgr*
Laura Uribe, *Marketing Mgr*
Jim Garn, *Director*
EMP: 307
SALES (corp-wide): 24.3B **Publicly Held**
SIC: 3826 Thermal analysis instruments,
laboratory type

PA: Thermo Fisher Scientific Inc.
168 3rd Ave
Waltham MA 02451
781 622-1000

(P-21306)
THERMO FISHER SCIENTIFIC INC
675 S Sierra Ave, Solana Beach
(92075-3200)
PHONE....................858 481-6386
Wes Woll, *Principal*
EMP: 307
SALES (corp-wide): 24.3B **Publicly Held**
SIC: 3826 Analytical instruments
PA: Thermo Fisher Scientific Inc.
168 3rd Ave
Waltham MA 02451
781 622-1000

(P-21307)
THERMO FISHER SCIENTIFIC INC
200 Oyster Point Blvd, South San Francisco (94080-1911)
PHONE....................650 876-1949
Ernest Hardy, *Branch Mgr*
EMP: 54
SALES (corp-wide): 24.3B **Publicly Held**
SIC: 3826 Analytical instruments
PA: Thermo Fisher Scientific Inc.
168 3rd Ave
Waltham MA 02451
781 622-1000

(P-21308)
THERMO FISHER SCIENTIFIC INC
3400 W Warren Ave, Fremont
(94538-6425)
PHONE....................510 979-5000
EMP: 22
SALES (corp-wide): 24.3B **Publicly Held**
SIC: 3826 Analytical instruments
PA: Thermo Fisher Scientific Inc.
168 3rd Ave
Waltham MA 02451
781 622-1000

(P-21309)
THERMO FISHER SCIENTIFIC INC
180 Oyster Point Blvd, South San Francisco (94080-1909)
PHONE....................650 246-5265
James Pire, *Administration*
Kelly LI, *Research*
Gary Lim, *Engineer*
EMP: 19
SALES (corp-wide): 24.3B **Publicly Held**
SIC: 3826 Environmental testing equipment
PA: Thermo Fisher Scientific Inc.
168 3rd Ave
Waltham MA 02451
781 622-1000

(P-21310)
THERMO FISHER SCIENTIFIC INC
Also Called: Molecular Bio Products
9389 Waples St, San Diego (92121-3903)
PHONE....................858 453-7551
Cesar Ramirez, *Branch Mgr*
EMP: 70
SALES (corp-wide): 24.3B **Publicly Held**
SIC: 3826 Analytical instruments
PA: Thermo Fisher Scientific Inc.
168 3rd Ave
Waltham MA 02451
781 622-1000

(P-21311)
THERMO FISHER SCIENTIFIC INC
7000 Shoreline Ct, South San Francisco
(94080-1945)
PHONE....................650 638-6409
EMP: 250
SALES (corp-wide): 24.3B **Publicly Held**
SIC: 3826 3845 3823 Analytical instruments; electromedical equipment; industrial instrmnts msrmnt display/control process variable

PA: Thermo Fisher Scientific Inc.
168 3rd Ave
Waltham MA 02451
781 622-1000

(P-21312)
THERMO FISHER SCIENTIFIC INC
46500 Kato Rd, Fremont (94538-7310)
PHONE....................317 490-5809
EMP: 15
SALES (corp-wide): 24.3B **Publicly Held**
SIC: 3826 Environmental testing equipment
PA: Thermo Fisher Scientific Inc.
168 3rd Ave
Waltham MA 02451
781 622-1000

(P-21313)
THERMO FISHER SCIENTIFIC INC
3380 Central Expy, Santa Clara
(95051-0704)
PHONE....................408 731-5056
Gene Tanimoto, *Branch Mgr*
Vicky Huynh, *Research*
Raul Cepeda, *Engineer*
Oscar Cuevas, *Director*
Ron O'Brien, *Director*
EMP: 29
SALES (corp-wide): 24.3B **Publicly Held**
SIC: 3826 Analytical instruments
PA: Thermo Fisher Scientific Inc.
168 3rd Ave
Waltham MA 02451
781 622-1000

(P-21314)
THERMO FISHER SCIENTIFIC INC
22801 Roscoe Blvd, West Hills
(91304-3200)
PHONE....................747 494-1413
Steve Zhang, *Branch Mgr*
Paul Aguilar, *Director*
EMP: 11
SALES (corp-wide): 24.3B **Publicly Held**
SIC: 3826 Analytical instruments
PA: Thermo Fisher Scientific Inc.
168 3rd Ave
Waltham MA 02451
781 622-1000

(P-21315)
THERMO FISHER SCIENTIFIC INC
10010 Mesa Rim Rd, San Diego
(92121-2912)
PHONE....................858 882-1286
Anand Shirur, *Branch Mgr*
Richard Leathers, *Info Tech Mgr*
Eric Strahan, *Technical Staff*
Becky Roman, *Recruiter*
Darrell Leetham, *Marketing Staff*
EMP: 14
SALES (corp-wide): 24.3B **Publicly Held**
WEB: www.thermo.com
SIC: 3826 Analytical instruments
PA: Thermo Fisher Scientific Inc.
168 3rd Ave
Waltham MA 02451
781 622-1000

(P-21316)
THERMOQUEST CORPORATION
355 River Oaks Pkwy, San Jose
(95134-1908)
P.O. Box 49031 (95161-9031)
PHONE....................408 965-6000
EMP: 1215
SALES: 431.8MM
SALES (corp-wide): 16.9B **Publicly Held**
SIC: 3826 3823
PA: Thermo Fisher Scientific Inc.
168 3rd Ave
Waltham MA 02451
781 622-1000

(P-21317)
TURNER DESIGNS INC
1995 N 1st St, San Jose (95112-4220)
PHONE....................408 749-0994
Jim Crawford, *President*
EMP: 45 **EST:** 1972

SQ FT: 20,000
SALES (est): 10.6MM Privately Held
WEB: www.turnerdesigns.com
SIC: 3826 Analytical instruments

(P-21318)
UNITED STATES THERMOELECTRIC
Also Called: Ustc
13267 Contractors Dr, Chico (95973-8851)
PHONE..................................530 345-8000
James M Kerner, *President*
▲ EMP: 30
SALES (est): 5.8MM Privately Held
WEB: www.ustechcon.com
SIC: 3826 3823 Thermal analysis instruments, laboratory type; industrial instrmnts msrmnt display/control process variable

(P-21319)
V & P SCIENTIFIC INC
9823 Pacific Heights Blvd, San Diego (92121-4704)
PHONE..................................858 455-0643
Patrick H Cleveland, *President*
Victoria Cleveland, *CFO*
Victoria L Cleveland, *Corp Secy*
John Herich, *Technical Staff*
Casey Reinholtz, *QC Dir*
▲ EMP: 11
SQ FT: 7,000
SALES (est): 2.6MM Privately Held
WEB: www.vp-scientific.com
SIC: 3826 Analytical instruments

(P-21320)
VEECO PROCESS EQUIPMENT INC
Also Called: Digital Instruments Div
112 Robin Hill Rd, Goleta (93117-3107)
PHONE..................................805 967-1400
Don Kenia, *CEO*
Brent Nelson, *Executive*
David Hibbits, *Engineer*
Sahil Pawa, *Manager*
EMP: 190
SALES (corp-wide): 542MM Publicly Held
SIC: 3826 3827 Microscopes, electron & proton; optical instruments & lenses
HQ: Veeco Process Equipment Inc.
    1 Terminal Dr
    Plainview NY 11803

(P-21321)
VIAVI SOLUTIONS INC (PA)
6001 America Center Dr # 6, San Jose (95002-2562)
PHONE..................................408 404-3600
Oleg Khaykin, *President*
Richard E Belluzzo, *Ch of Bd*
Amar Maletira, *CFO*
Paul McNab, *Chief Mktg Ofcr*
Ralph Rondinone, *Senior VP*
◆ EMP: 320
SQ FT: 37,000
SALES: 1.1B Publicly Held
WEB: www.jdsuniphase.com
SIC: 3826 3674 Analytical instruments; laser scientific & engineering instruments; optical isolators

(P-21322)
VIAVI SOLUTIONS INC
430 N Mccarthy Blvd, Milpitas (95035-5112)
PHONE..................................408 546-5000
David Fike, *Vice Pres*
Kim Quillin, *Vice Pres*
Vince Retort, *Vice Pres*
Enzo Di Luigi, *General Mgr*
Seisaku Nomura, *Info Tech Dir*
EMP: 191
SALES (corp-wide): 1.1B Publicly Held
SIC: 3826 3674 Analytical instruments; optical isolators
PA: Viavi Solutions Inc.
    6001 America Center Dr # 6
    San Jose CA 95002
    408 404-3600

(P-21323)
W R GRACE & CO-CONN
Also Called: Grace Dvson Discovery Sciences
17434 Mojave St, Hesperia (92345-7611)
PHONE..................................760 244-6107
EMP: 100
SALES (corp-wide): 1.9B Publicly Held
WEB: www.chromatography.com
SIC: 3826 Chromatographic equipment, laboratory type
HQ: W. R. Grace & Co.-Conn.
    7500 Grace Dr
    Columbia MD 21044
    410 531-4000

(P-21324)
WATERS TECHNOLOGIES CORP
18271 Mcdurmott St, Irvine (92614)
PHONE..................................949 474-4320
Bobette Frye, *Branch Mgr*
EMP: 10 Publicly Held
SIC: 3826 3829 7371 7372 Chromatographic equipment, laboratory type; spectrometers, liquid scintillation & nuclear; computer software systems analysis & design, custom; computer software development; prepackaged software
HQ: Waters Technologies Corporation,
    34 Maple St
    Milford MA 01757
    508 478-2000

(P-21325)
WYATT TECHNOLOGY CORPORATION (PA)
6330 Hollister Ave, Goleta (93117-3115)
PHONE..................................805 681-9009
Philip J Wyatt, *CEO*
Clifford D Wyatt, *President*
Geofrey K Wyatt, *President*
Carolyn Walton, *CFO*
Terry Boykin, *Accountant*
EMP: 120
SQ FT: 30,000
SALES (est): 33.6MM
SALES (corp-wide): 22.7MM Privately Held
WEB: www.mals.com
SIC: 3826 Laser scientific & engineering instruments

(P-21326)
YSI INCORPORATED
Also Called: Yellow Springs Instruments
9940 Summers Ridge Rd, San Diego (92121-2997)
PHONE..................................858 546-8327
Chris Ward, *Branch Mgr*
EMP: 50 Publicly Held
WEB: www.sontek.com
SIC: 3826 3823 3841 Water testing apparatus; industrial instrmnts msrmnt display/control process variable; temperature measurement instruments, industrial; diagnostic apparatus, medical
HQ: Ysi Incorporated
    1700 Brannum Ln 1725
    Yellow Springs OH 45387
    937 767-7241

(P-21327)
ZINSSER NA INC (DH)
19145 Parthenia St Ste C, Northridge (91324-5108)
PHONE..................................818 341-2906
Clifford Olson, *President*
EMP: 10
SQ FT: 5,000
SALES (est): 1.5MM
SALES (corp-wide): 103.7MM Privately Held
WEB: www.zinsserna.com
SIC: 3826 Mass spectroscopy instrumentation
HQ: Zinsser Analytic Gesellschaft Mit
    Beschrankter Haftung
    Schwalbacher Str. 62
    Eschborn 65760
    619 658-6930

(P-21328)
ZYGO CORPORATION
3350 Scott Blvd, Santa Clara (95054-3104)
PHONE..................................408 434-1000
Robert Plozl, *Manager*

EMP: 30
SALES (corp-wide): 4.8B Publicly Held
WEB: www.zygo.com
SIC: 3826 3829 3827 Microscopes, electron & proton; measuring & controlling devices; optical instruments & lenses
HQ: Zygo Corporation
    21 Laurel Brook Rd
    Middlefield CT 06455
    860 347-8506

3827 Optical Instruments

(P-21329)
AAREN SCIENTIFIC INC (DH)
Also Called: Carl Zeiss Meditec,
1040 S Vintage Ave Ste A, Ontario (91761-3631)
PHONE..................................909 937-1033
Hans-Joachim Miesner, *President*
Stevens Chevillotte, *Treasurer*
Eric Desjardins, *Vice Pres*
Victor Garcia, *Vice Pres*
James Thornton, *Admin Sec*
▲ EMP: 63
SQ FT: 15,000
SALES (est): 21.9MM
SALES (corp-wide): 449.3K Privately Held
SIC: 3827 3851 Optical instruments & lenses; ophthalmic goods
HQ: Carl Zeiss Meditec, Inc.
    5160 Hacienda Dr
    Dublin CA 94568
    925 557-4100

(P-21330)
ABRISA TECHNOLOGIES
200 Hallock Dr, Santa Paula (93060-9646)
P.O. Box 489 (93061-0489)
PHONE..................................805 525-4902
Blake Fennell, *CEO*
Maartin Ostendorp, *CFO*
Susan Hirst, *Vice Pres*
Dave Kwan, *Vice Pres*
Lawrence Luke, *Engineer*
EMP: 20
SALES (est): 3.2MM Privately Held
SIC: 3827 Optical instruments & lenses

(P-21331)
ADTECH PHOTONICS INC
Also Called: Adtech Optics
18007 Cortney Ct, City of Industry (91748-1203)
PHONE..................................626 956-1000
Mary Fong, *CEO*
Ed Ho, *Vice Pres*
Marvin Lee, *Administration*
Ulisses Gamboa, *Engineer*
Prita Ganatra, *Human Res Dir*
EMP: 25
SALES (est): 4.5MM Privately Held
SIC: 3827 Optical instruments & lenses

(P-21332)
ADVANCED SPECTRAL TECH INC
94 W Cochran St Ste A, Simi Valley (93065-0948)
PHONE..................................805 527-7657
Roy Brochtrup, *CFO*
Thomas Persico, *President*
Scott Persico, *Vice Pres*
Greg Kuric, *Opers Mgr*
EMP: 20
SALES (est): 625.3K Privately Held
SIC: 3827 Optical test & inspection equipment

(P-21333)
ALLUXA INC
3660 N Laughlin Rd, Santa Rosa (95403-1027)
PHONE..................................707 284-1040
Mike Scobey, *President*
Matthew Nichols, *Technician*
Jeff Johansen, *Engineer*
Joshua Howard, *Opers Mgr*
Haley Metlinger, *Marketing Staff*
EMP: 36
SALES (est): 8.1MM Privately Held
SIC: 3827 Optical instruments & lenses

(P-21334)
APOLLO INSTRUMENTS INC
55 Peters Canyon Rd, Irvine (92606-1402)
PHONE..................................949 756-3111
Alice Z Gheen, *President*
Peter Wang, *Vice Pres*
▲ EMP: 21
SALES (est): 3.5MM Privately Held
WEB: www.apolloinstruments.com
SIC: 3827 3822 Optical instruments & lenses; auto controls regulating residntl & coml environmt & applncs

(P-21335)
BLUE SKY RESEARCH INCORPORATED (PA)
510 Alder Dr, Milpitas (95035-7443)
PHONE..................................408 941-6068
Christopher Gladding, *President*
Sandip Basu, *CFO*
Joe Kulakofsky, *Vice Pres*
EMP: 49
SQ FT: 21,000
SALES (est): 9.5MM Privately Held
SIC: 3827 3674 Lenses, optical: all types except ophthalmic; semiconductors & related devices

(P-21336)
BUK OPTICS INC
Also Called: Precision Glass & Optics
3600 W Moore Ave, Santa Ana (92704-6835)
PHONE..................................714 384-9620
Daniel S Bukaty, *CEO*
Michelle Callahan, *Purchasing*
Tony Orozco, *QC Mgr*
▲ EMP: 42
SQ FT: 25,000
SALES (est): 8.5MM Privately Held
WEB: www.pgo.com
SIC: 3827 Optical instruments & apparatus

(P-21337)
CARL ZEISS INC
Humphrey Systems
5160 Hacienda Dr, Dublin (94568-7315)
P.O. Box 8111, Pleasanton (94588-8711)
PHONE..................................925 557-4100
Kieth Hunt, *Manager*
Thomas Fry, *Vice Pres*
Jeffrey Schmidt, *Vice Pres*
Markus Weber, *Vice Pres*
Miguel Gonzalez, *General Mgr*
EMP: 40
SALES (corp-wide): 449.3K Privately Held
SIC: 3827 3851 3845 3841 Optical test & inspection equipment; ophthalmic goods; electromedical equipment; surgical & medical instruments
HQ: Carl Zeiss, Inc.
    1 N Broadway Ste 401
    White Plains NY 10601
    914 747-1800

(P-21338)
CARL ZEISS MEDITEC INC (DH)
5160 Hacienda Dr, Dublin (94568-7562)
P.O. Box 100372, Pasadena (91189-0003)
PHONE..................................925 557-4100
James V Mazzo, *President*
Roberto Deger, *CFO*
Thomas Simmerer, *Officer*
Tom Fry, *Vice Pres*
Angelo Rago, *Vice Pres*
▲ EMP: 277
SALES (est): 199.5MM
SALES (corp-wide): 449.3K Privately Held
SIC: 3827 Optical instruments & apparatus
HQ: Carl Zeiss Meditec Ag
    Goschwitzer Str. 51-52
    Jena 07745
    364 122-00

(P-21339)
CARL ZEISS MEDITEC INC
5160 Hacienda Dr, Dublin (94568-7562)
PHONE..................................858 716-0661
EMP: 28
SALES (corp-wide): 449.3K Privately Held
SIC: 3827 Optical instruments & lenses

HQ: Carl Zeiss Meditec, Inc.
5160 Hacienda Dr
Dublin CA 94568
925 557-4100

(P-21340)
CASCADE OPTICAL COATING INC
1225 E Hunter Ave, Santa Ana
(92705-4131)
PHONE....................714 543-9777
Ken Romo, *Vice Pres*
Lawrence D Hundsdoerfer, *President*
Claudia J Hundsdoerfer, *Corp Secy*
Tammy Sides, *Info Tech Mgr*
EMP: 13
SQ FT: 8,500
SALES: 2.8MM **Privately Held**
WEB: www.c-optical.com
SIC: 3827 Lens coating equipment

(P-21341)
CELESTRON ACQUISITION LLC
2835 Columbia St, Torrance (90503-3877)
PHONE....................310 328-9560
Dave Anderson, *CEO*
Paul Roth, *CFO*
Sylvia Shen, *Mng Member*
▲ **EMP:** 77
SALES (est): 80MM **Privately Held**
WEB: www.celestron.com
SIC: 3827 Telescopes: elbow, panoramic, sighting, fire control, etc.
HQ: Sw Technology Corporation
2835 Columbia St
Torrance CA 90503
310 328-9560

(P-21342)
CELESTRON LLC
2835 Columbia St, Torrance (90503-3877)
PHONE....................310 328-9560
Alan Hale, *Chairman*
EMP: 50 **EST:** 2014
SALES (est): 12.2MM **Privately Held**
SIC: 3827 Telescopes: elbow, panoramic, sighting, fire control, etc.; lenses, optical: all types except ophthalmic

(P-21343)
CHEMICAL & MATERIAL TECHNOLOGY
Also Called: Cmt
229 Creekside Village Dr, Los Gatos
(95032-7351)
P.O. Box 2351 (95031-2351)
PHONE....................408 354-2656
William N Kraus, *President*
T W Ireland, *Vice Pres*
Joseph R Spaziani, *Vice Pres*
EMP: 25
SQ FT: 2,000
SALES (est): 2MM **Privately Held**
SIC: 3827 8741 3674 8742 Lenses, optical: all types except ophthalmic; management services; semiconductors & related devices; management consulting services

(P-21344)
COLLIMATED HOLES INC
460 Division St, Campbell (95008-6923)
PHONE....................408 374-5080
Richard Mead, *President*
Dan Dickerson, *Vice Pres*
EMP: 20
SQ FT: 11,600
SALES (est): 2.9MM **Privately Held**
WEB: www.collimatedholes.com
SIC: 3827 Optical instruments & apparatus; optical elements & assemblies, except ophthalmic

(P-21345)
COMCORE TECHNOLOGIES INC
Also Called: Comcore Opcital Communication
48834 Kato Rd Ste 108a, Fremont
(94538-7368)
PHONE....................510 498-8858
Yong Huang, *President*
EMP: 20
SQ FT: 22,000
SALES (est): 4MM
SALES (corp-wide): 104.3K **Privately Held**
SIC: 3827 Optical instruments & apparatus

PA: Manfredini Gennaro
Via Sant' Anna 109/B
Nocera Inferiore SA
081 927-753

(P-21346)
COSTCO WHOLESALE CORPORATION
Also Called: Price/Costco Optical Lab
1001 W 19th St Ste A, National City
(91950-5400)
PHONE....................619 336-3360
EMP: 500
SALES (corp-wide): 152.7B **Publicly Held**
SIC: 3827 Optical instruments & lenses
PA: Costco Wholesale Corporation
999 Lake Dr Ste 200
Issaquah WA 98027
425 313-8100

(P-21347)
DELTRONIC CORPORATION
Also Called: Hi-Precision Grinding
3900 W Segerstrom Ave, Santa Ana
(92704-6312)
PHONE....................714 545-5800
Robert C Larzelere, *President*
Sterling Sander, *CFO*
Diane Larzelere, *Admin Sec*
▼ **EMP:** 73
SQ FT: 40,000
SALES (est): 16.1MM **Privately Held**
WEB: www.deltronic.com
SIC: 3827 3545 Optical comparators; gauges (machine tool accessories)

(P-21348)
DIELECTRIC COATING INDUSTRIES
Also Called: DCI
30997 Huntwood Ave # 104, Hayward
(94544-7041)
PHONE....................510 487-5980
Carmen Bischer Jr, *President*
Carmen Bischer Sr, *Vice Pres*
▲ **EMP:** 10
SQ FT: 8,000
SALES (est): 1.9MM **Privately Held**
SIC: 3827 Reflectors, optical

(P-21349)
DIGILENS INC
1288 Hammerwood Ave, Sunnyvale
(94089-2232)
PHONE....................408 734-0219
Christopher Pickett, *CEO*
Ratson Morad, *COO*
Michael Angel, *CFO*
Jonathan David Waldern, *Chairman*
Gerald Buxton, *Engineer*
EMP: 40
SQ FT: 15,000
SALES (est): 4MM **Privately Held**
SIC: 3827 Optical instruments & lenses

(P-21350)
DIMAXX TECHNOLOGIES LLC
11838 Kemper Rd, Auburn (95603-9531)
P.O. Box 21810, Eugene OR (97402-0412)
PHONE....................530 888-1942
Leonard Mott,
Gary Debell,
Tony Louderback,
EMP: 16 **EST:** 2000
SALES (est): 2.7MM **Privately Held**
WEB: www.dimax.com
SIC: 3827 Optical instruments & lenses

(P-21351)
ELECTRO OPTICAL INDUSTRIES
320 Storke Rd Ste 100, Goleta
(93117-2992)
PHONE....................805 964-6701
Stephen Scopatz, *General Mgr*
Thierry Campos, *President*
Maegan Piccolo, *Admin Asst*
Derek Bond, *Manager*
EMP: 21
SALES (corp-wide): 4.9MM **Privately Held**
SIC: 3827 Optical instruments & apparatus
PA: Electro Optical Industries, Inc
50 Milk St Fl 16
Boston MA 02109
617 401-2196

(P-21352)
ENHANCED VISION SYSTEMS INC (HQ)
15301 Springdale St, Huntington Beach
(92649-1140)
PHONE....................800 440-9476
Tom Tiernan, *CEO*
Rose Mayer, *Manager*
◆ **EMP:** 59
SALES (est): 9.6MM
SALES (corp-wide): 15.2MM **Privately Held**
WEB: www.enhancedvision.com
SIC: 3827 Optical instruments & lenses
PA: Freedom Scientific Blv Group, Llc
17757 Us Highway 19 N # 560
Clearwater FL 33764
727 803-8000

(P-21353)
FLEX PRODUCTS INC
1402 Mariner Way, Santa Rosa
(95407-7370)
PHONE....................707 525-6866
Michael B Sullivan, *President*
Joseph Zils, *President*
Mary Ellen King, *IT/INT Sup*
EMP: 225
SQ FT: 70,000
SALES (est): 30.8MM
SALES (corp-wide): 1.1B **Publicly Held**
WEB: www.flexrest.com
SIC: 3827 3081 Lens coating equipment; unsupported plastics film & sheet
HQ: Optical Coating Laboratory, Llc
2789 Northpoint Pkwy
Santa Rosa CA 95407
707 545-6440

(P-21354)
FOREAL SPECTRUM INC
2370 Qume Dr Ste A, San Jose
(95131-1842)
PHONE....................408 923-1675
Anmin Zheng, *President*
Liang Zhou, *President*
Baorui Gao, *Vice Pres*
Ronggui Shen, *Vice Pres*
Dan Cifelli, *VP Sales*
▲ **EMP:** 25
SALES (est): 5MM **Privately Held**
WEB: www.forealspectrum.com
SIC: 3827 Optical instruments & lenses

(P-21355)
GMTO CORPORATION
Also Called: Giant Mgllan Tlscope Orgnztnal
465 N Halstead St Ste 250, Pasadena
(91107-3226)
PHONE....................626 204-0500
Patrick McCarthy, *President*
Dr Robert N Shelton, *President*
Alan Gordon, *CFO*
Javier Luna, *Officer*
Karla Russell, *Executive Asst*
▲ **EMP:** 70 **EST:** 2007
SQ FT: 40,000
SALES: 5.4MM **Privately Held**
WEB: www.gmto.org
SIC: 3827 Telescopes: elbow, panoramic, sighting, fire control, etc.

(P-21356)
GOOCH AND HOUSEGO CAL LLC
5390 Kazuko Ct, Moorpark (93021-1790)
PHONE....................805 529-3324
Kenneth Neczypor, *Mng Member*
Robin Whitt, *Human Res Mgr*
Ken Kistner, *QC Mgr*
Nigel Deeley, *Cust Mgr*
EMP: 80
SALES (est): 13MM
SALES (corp-wide): 159.2MM **Privately Held**
SIC: 3827 3823 Optical instruments & lenses; industrial instrmnts msrmnt display/control process variable
PA: Gooch & Housego Plc
Dowlish Ford
Ilminster TA19
146 025-6440

(P-21357)
GUIDED WAVE INC
3033 Gold Canal Dr, Rancho Cordova
(95670-6129)
PHONE....................916 638-4944
Susan Foulk, *CEO*
Don Goldman, *Vice Pres*
William Grooms, *Vice Pres*
James Low, *Info Tech Mgr*
Janell Leysath, *Marketing Staff*
EMP: 32
SQ FT: 15,000
SALES (est): 6.6MM **Privately Held**
WEB: www.guided-wave.com
SIC: 3827 Optical instruments & apparatus

(P-21358)
H SILANI & ASSOCIATES INC
Also Called: Supervision Eyewear Suppliers
210 S Robertson Blvd, Beverly Hills
(90211-2811)
PHONE....................310 623-4848
Hossein Silani, *President*
EMP: 10
SQ FT: 1,300
SALES (est): 550K **Privately Held**
SIC: 3827 5995 Optical instruments & lenses; optical goods stores; contact lenses, prescription; eyeglasses, prescription

(P-21359)
HOYA CORPORATION USA (DH)
680 N Mccarthy Blvd # 120, Milpitas
(95035-5120)
PHONE....................408 492-1069
Hiroshi Suzuki, *Principal*
▲ **EMP:** 10
SQ FT: 1,000
SALES (est): 2.6MM **Privately Held**
WEB: www.hoyaoptics.com
SIC: 3827 Optical instruments & lenses
HQ: Hoya Holdings, Inc.
680 N Mccarthy Blvd # 120
Milpitas CA 95035
408 654-2300

(P-21360)
HOYA HOLDINGS INC
Hoya Corporation USA
425 E Huntington Dr, Monrovia
(91016-3632)
PHONE....................626 739-5200
Al Benzoni, *Vice Pres*
EMP: 63 **Privately Held**
WEB: www.hoyaholdings.com
SIC: 3827 Optical instruments & lenses
HQ: Hoya Holdings, Inc.
680 N Mccarthy Blvd # 120
Milpitas CA 95035
408 654-2300

(P-21361)
I-COAT COMPANY LLC
12020 Mora Dr Ste 2, Santa Fe Springs
(90670-6082)
PHONE....................562 941-9989
Arman Bernardi, *CEO*
▲ **EMP:** 50
SQ FT: 6,000
SALES (est): 10.2MM
SALES (corp-wide): 1.4MM **Privately Held**
WEB: www.icoatcompany.com
SIC: 3827 Optical instruments & lenses
HQ: Essilor Of America, Inc.
13555 N Stemmons Fwy
Dallas TX 75234
214 496-4000

(P-21362)
IDEX HEALTH & SCIENCE LLC
2051 Palomar Airpt Rd # 200, Carlsbad
(92011-1461)
PHONE....................760 438-2131
Blake Fennell, *Branch Mgr*
Elizabeth Hernandez, *General Mgr*
Amir Marashi, *Engineer*
John Powers, *Safety Mgr*
EMP: 184
SALES (corp-wide): 2.4B **Publicly Held**
SIC: 3827 3699 Optical instruments & lenses; laser systems & equipment

HQ: Idex Health & Science Llc
600 Park Ct
Rohnert Park CA 94928
707 588-2000

(P-21363)
II-VI OPTICAL SYSTEMS INC
14192 Chambers Rd, Tustin (92780-6908)
PHONE..............................714 247-7100
Mark Maiberger, *General Mgr*
Scott Fleming, *Planning*
Kent Weed, *Engineer*
EMP: 60
SALES (corp-wide): 1.3B Publicly Held
SIC: 3827 7389 8748 Optical instruments
& apparatus; design services; business
consulting
HQ: Ii-Vi Optical Systems, Inc.
36570 Briggs Rd
Murrieta CA 92563
951 926-2994

(P-21364)
INFINITE OPTICS INC
1712 Newport Cir Ste F, Santa Ana
(92705-5118)
PHONE..............................714 557-2299
Geza Keller, *President*
Daniel Houston, *Vice Pres*
Denise Banionis, *Principal*
Steven Crawford, *Principal*
Joseph Goodhand, *Principal*
EMP: 24
SQ FT: 12,860
SALES (est): 5MM Privately Held
WEB: www.infiniteoptics.com
SIC: 3827 Lens coating & grinding equip-
ment

(P-21365)
INNEOS LLC
5700 Stoneridge Dr # 200, Pleasanton
(94588-2897)
PHONE..............................925 226-0138
Brian C Peters, *CEO*
Scott Oleary, *Vice Pres*
Stephannie Elliott, *Office Mgr*
Ihi Nzeadibe, *Design Engr*
Tony Woodward, *Design Engr*
EMP: 27
SALES (est): 8.9MM Privately Held
SIC: 3827 Optical elements & assemblies,
except ophthalmic

(P-21366)
INSCOPIX INC
2462 Embarcadero Way, Palo Alto
(94303-3313)
PHONE..............................650 600-3886
Kunal Ghosh, *President*
Valerie Vincent, *Sales Mgr*
Katrina Paraskevopoulos, *Sales Staff*
Pushkar Joshi, *Director*
Lara Cardy, *Manager*
EMP: 15
SQ FT: 6,041
SALES (est): 4.5MM Privately Held
SIC: 3827 Microscopes, except electron,
proton & corneal

(P-21367)
INTEVAC PHOTONICS INC (HQ)
3560 Bassett St, Santa Clara (95054-2704)
PHONE..............................408 986-9888
Joseph Pietras III, *President*
Timothy Justyn, *Exec VP*
EMP: 17
SALES (est): 10.5MM
SALES (corp-wide): 95.1MM Publicly
Held
SIC: 3827 Optical instruments & lenses
PA: Intevac, Inc.
3560 Bassett St
Santa Clara CA 95054
408 986-9888

(P-21368)
INTEVAC PHOTONICS INC
Also Called: Intevac Vision Systems
5909 Sea Lion Pl Ste A, Carlsbad
(92010-6634)
PHONE..............................760 476-0339
Jerome Carollo, *General Mgr*
EMP: 22

SALES (corp-wide): 95.1MM Publicly
Held
SIC: 3827 Optical instruments & lenses
HQ: Intevac Photonics, Inc.
3560 Bassett St
Santa Clara CA 95054
-

(P-21369)
IRCAMERA LLC
30 S Calle Cesar Chavez, Santa Barbara
(93103-5652)
PHONE..............................805 965-9650
Steve McHugh, *Mng Member*
Matthew Kimak, *Director*
EMP: 20
SALES (est): 4.7MM Publicly Held
SIC: 3827 3812 Optical test & inspection
equipment; infrared object detection
equipment
HQ: Santa Barbara Infrared, Inc.
30 S Calle Cesar Chavez D
Santa Barbara CA 93103
805 965-3669

(P-21370)
IT CONCEPTS LLC
1244 Quarry Ln Ste B, Pleasanton
(94566-4767)
PHONE..............................925 401-0010
Naum Pinkhasik,
Sergey Perunov, *Mfg Staff*
Alla Balashov,
Inna Boyanzhu,
▼EMP: 12
SQ FT: 9,000
SALES (est): 5.6MM Privately Held
SIC: 3827 Optical instruments & apparatus
PA: International Technology Concepts, Inc.
1244 Quarry Ln Ste B
Pleasanton CA 94566

(P-21371)
JIMS OPTICAL
Also Called: Jim & Lees Optical
5253 Jerusalem Ct Ste G, Modesto
(95356-9238)
PHONE..............................209 549-2517
Jim Lima, *Owner*
EMP: 11
SQ FT: 550
SALES (est): 1.2MM Privately Held
SIC: 3827 Optical instruments & lenses

(P-21372)
KAMA-TECH CORPORATION
3451 Main St Ste 109, Chula Vista
(91911-5894)
PHONE..............................619 421-7858
Ichiro Kamakura, *President*
▲EMP: 15
SALES (est): 5.1MM Privately Held
WEB: www.kazmisakata.com
SIC: 3827 Binoculars

(P-21373)
KLA CORPORATION (PA)
1 Technology Dr, Milpitas (95035-7916)
PHONE..............................408 875-3000
Richard P Wallace, *President*
Edward W Barnholt, *Ch of Bd*
Bren D Higgins, *CFO*
Teri A Little,
Ahmad A Khan, *Exec VP*
◆EMP: 300 EST: 1975
SQ FT: 727,302
SALES: 4.5B Publicly Held
WEB: www.tencor.com
SIC: 3827 3825 7699 7629 Optical in-
struments & lenses; optical test & inspec-
tion equipment; semiconductor test
equipment; optical instrument repair; elec-
tronic equipment repair

(P-21374)
LENS TECHNOLOGY I LLC
Also Called: LTI
45 Parker Ste 100, Irvine (92618-1658)
PHONE..............................714 690-6470
John Quinn, *President*
Sung Tark, *Vice Pres*
John W Quinn III, *General Mgr*
James J Ryan,
EMP: 16
SQ FT: 11,500

SALES (est): 4.6MM Privately Held
WEB: www.lenstech.com
SIC: 3827 5049 Lens coating equipment;
optical goods

(P-21375)
LIGHT LABS INC
725 Shasta St, Redwood City
(94063-2124)
PHONE..............................650 272-6942
Dave Grannan, *CEO*
Tom Barone, *CFO*
Bradley Lautenbach, *Senior VP*
Prashant Velagaleti, *Vice Pres*
Rajiv Laroia, *CTO*
EMP: 78
SALES (est): 24.3MM Privately Held
SIC: 3827 Optical instruments & lenses

(P-21376)
LUMENTUM OPERATIONS LLC
1750 Automation Pkwy # 400, San Jose
(95131-1873)
PHONE..............................408 546-5483
EMP: 19
SALES (corp-wide): 1.5B Publicly Held
SIC: 3827 5995 Optical instruments &
lenses; optical goods stores
HQ: Lumentum Operations Llc
400 N Mccarthy Blvd
Milpitas CA 95035
408 546-5483

(P-21377)
LUMINIT LLC (PA)
1850 W 205th St, Torrance (90501-1526)
PHONE..............................310 320-1066
Engin Arik,
Ed Kaiser, *Vice Pres*
Leo Katsenelenson, *Vice Pres*
Stanley KAO, *VP Bus Dvlpt*
Karma Burns, *Executive Asst*
▲EMP: 42
SALES (est): 13.3MM Privately Held
WEB: www.luminit.com
SIC: 3827 Optical instruments & lenses

(P-21378)
MACHINE VISION PRODUCTS
INC (PA)
3270 Corporate Vw Ste D, Vista
(92081-8570)
PHONE..............................760 438-1138
George T Ayoub, *CEO*
Olga Balakina, *Software Engr*
Fadi Nammoura, *Software Engr*
Chad Loperfido, *Engineer*
▲EMP: 73
SQ FT: 60,000
SALES (est): 15.5MM Privately Held
WEB: www.machinevisionproducts.com
SIC: 3827 7371 3229 Optical instruments
& lenses; custom computer programming
services; pressed & blown glass

(P-21379)
MARK OPTICS INC
1424 E Saint Gertrude Pl, Santa Ana
(92705-5271)
PHONE..............................714 545-6684
Julie A Houser, *President*
Judy A Chapman, *CFO*
▲EMP: 20
SALES (est): 4.1MM Privately Held
WEB: www.markoptics.com
SIC: 3827 Optical elements & assemblies,
except ophthalmic

(P-21380)
MEADE INSTRUMENTS CORP
27 Hubble, Irvine (92618-4209)
PHONE..............................949 451-1450
Wenjun Ni, *CEO*
Victor Aniceto, *President*
Dawn Kirscher, *Info Tech Mgr*
Hector Martinez, *Controller*
Lenora Hernandez, *Human Res Dir*
▲EMP: 92 EST: 1972
SQ FT: 25,000
SALES (est): 21.2MM Privately Held
WEB: www.meade.com
SIC: 3827 Telescopes: elbow, panoramic,
sighting, fire control, etc.

(P-21381)
MELLES GRIOT INC
2072 Corte Del Nogal, Carlsbad
(92011-1427)
PHONE..............................760 438-2131
Marcus Barber, *Manager*
EMP: 10
SALES (est): 236.6K Privately Held
SIC: 3827 Optical instruments & lenses

(P-21382)
METAMATERIAL TECH USA INC
5880 W Las Positas Blvd, Pleasanton
(94588-8552)
PHONE..............................650 993-9223
Boris Kobrin, *CTO*
EMP: 10
SQ FT: 5,000
SALES (est): 683.3K Privately Held
SIC: 3827 Optical instruments & lenses
PA: Metamaterial Technologies Inc
1 Research Dr
Dartmouth NS B2Y 4
902 482-5729

(P-21383)
MICRO-VU CORP CALIFORNIA
(PA)
7909 Conde Ln, Windsor (95492-9779)
PHONE..............................707 838-6272
Edward P Amormino, *President*
Virginia Amormino, *Corp Secy*
Rebecca Pozzi, *Administration*
Jordan Reese, *Administration*
Kevin Johnson, *Project Engr*
▲EMP: 80
SQ FT: 60,000
SALES (est): 17.6MM Privately Held
WEB: www.microvu.com
SIC: 3827 Optical comparators

(P-21384)
NEWPORT GLASS WORKS LTD
10564 Fern Ave, Stanton (90680-2648)
P.O. Box 127 (90680-0127)
PHONE..............................714 484-8100
Ray Larsen, *Director*
EMP: 13 EST: 1978
SQ FT: 40,000
SALES (est): 1MM
SALES (corp-wide): 2.2MM Privately
Held
SIC: 3827 Lenses, optical: all types except
ophthalmic
PA: Newport Optical Industries Ltd
10564 Fern Ave
Stanton CA 90680
714 484-8100

(P-21385)
NEWPORT OPTICAL
INDUSTRIES (PA)
Also Called: Newport Glassworks
10564 Fern Ave, Stanton (90680-2648)
P.O. Box 127 (90680-0127)
PHONE..............................714 484-8100
Ray Larsen, *President*
▲EMP: 20
SQ FT: 12,000
SALES (est): 2.2MM Privately Held
SIC: 3827 5049 Lenses, optical: all types
except ophthalmic; optical goods

(P-21386)
NORDSON YESTECH INC
2747 Loker Ave W, Carlsbad (92010-6601)
PHONE..............................949 361-2714
Don Miller, *President*
Christine Schwarzmann, *CFO*
Robert E Veillette, *Admin Sec*
EMP: 32
SQ FT: 10,000
SALES: 25MM
SALES (corp-wide): 2.2B Publicly Held
WEB: www.nordson.com
SIC: 3827 Optical test & inspection equip-
ment
PA: Nordson Corporation
28601 Clemens Rd
Westlake OH 44145
440 892-1580

▲ = Import ▼=Export
◆ =Import/Export

(P-21387)
OCLARO PHOTONICS INC (DH)
400 N Mccarthy Blvd, Milpitas
(95035-5112)
PHONE.............................408 383-1400
Ken Ibbs, *President*
▲ EMP: 100
SALES (est): 11.6MM
SALES (corp-wide): 2B **Publicly Held**
WEB: www.newfocus.com
SIC: 3827 3699 3229 Optical instruments
& lenses; electrical equipment & supplies;
pressed & blown glass
HQ: Newport Corporation
1791 Deere Ave
Irvine CA 92606
949 863-3144

(P-21388)
ONDAX INC
850 E Duarte Rd, Monrovia (91016-4275)
PHONE.............................626 357-9600
Randy Heyler, *CEO*
Christophe Moser, *President*
Ryan Park, *Sales Staff*
James Carriere, *Director*
Lawrence Ho, *Director*
EMP: 15 EST: 2000
SQ FT: 60,000
SALES (est): 3.3MM **Privately Held**
WEB: www.ondax.com
SIC: 3827 Optical instruments & apparatus

(P-21389)
ONYX OPTICS INC
6551 Sierra Ln, Dublin (94568-2798)
PHONE.............................925 833-1969
Helmuthe Meissner, *Ch of Bd*
David Meissner, *President*
Stephanie Meissner, *CEO*
EMP: 15
SQ FT: 8,500
SALES (est): 5MM **Privately Held**
WEB: www.onyxoptics.com
SIC: 3827 Optical instruments & lenses

(P-21390)
OPOTEK LLC
2233 Faraday Ave Ste E, Carlsbad
(92008-7214)
PHONE.............................760 929-0770
David Crozier, *Principal*
Renee Jones, *Principal*
Lam Nguyen, *Principal*
EMP: 10
SALES (est): 761.2K **Privately Held**
SIC: 3827 Optical instruments & lenses

(P-21391)
OPTICAL PHYSICS COMPANY
4133 Guardian St G, Simi Valley
(93063-3382)
PHONE.............................818 880-2907
Richard A Hutchin, *CEO*
Marc Jacoby, *President*
A Thomas Stanley, *Vice Pres*
EMP: 15
SQ FT: 12,000
SALES (est): 5.1MM **Privately Held**
SIC: 3827 Optical instruments & apparatus

(P-21392)
OPTISCAN LTD
48290 Vista Calico Ste A, La Quinta
(92253-8409)
PHONE.............................760 777-9595
Daniel Sherman, *President*
Howard Gurock, *Vice Pres*
EMP: 11
SQ FT: 3,000
SALES (est): 14MM **Privately Held**
WEB: www.opticscan.com
SIC: 3827 5049 Sighting & fire control
equipment, optical; periscopes; optical
test & inspection equipment; optical
goods

(P-21393)
OPTOSIGMA CORPORATION
3210 S Croddy Way, Santa Ana
(92704-6348)
PHONE.............................949 851-5881
Yosuke Kondo, *CEO*
Takayoshi Tafaka, *President*
Roger Matsunaga, *Senior VP*
Steve McNamee, *Vice Pres*

Hoganson Laury, *Admin Asst*
EMP: 25
SQ FT: 13,000
SALES (est): 4.9MM **Privately Held**
WEB: www.optosigma.com
SIC: 3827 Optical instruments & lenses
PA: Sigma Koki Co., Ltd.
1-19-9, Midori
Sumida-Ku TKY 130-0

(P-21394)
PACIFIC COAST OPTICS INC
10604 Industrial Ave # 100, Roseville
(95678-6226)
PHONE.............................916 789-0111
Shannon Rogers, *President*
▼ EMP: 20
SQ FT: 14,000
SALES (est): 732K **Privately Held**
WEB: www.pcoptics.com
SIC: 3827 Optical instruments & apparatus

(P-21395)
PACIFIC LINK CORP
Also Called: Extra Lite
15865 Chemical Ln, Huntington Beach
(92649-1510)
PHONE.............................714 897-3525
Frank Lyn, *President*
Ken Lin, *Vice Pres*
Olive Lin, *Vice Pres*
▲ EMP: 10
SQ FT: 3,500
SALES (est): 885.7K **Privately Held**
WEB: www.extralite.com
SIC: 3827 3851 Lenses, optical: all types
except ophthalmic; ophthalmic goods

(P-21396)
PACIFIC QUARTZ INC
900 Glenneyre St, Laguna Beach
(92651-2707)
PHONE.............................714 546-8133
Greg Dickson, *CEO*
E Roy Dickson, *President*
Andy Tran, *Cust Svc Dir*
EMP: 30
SALES (est): 3.5MM **Privately Held**
WEB: www.pacificquartz.com
SIC: 3827 Optical elements & assemblies,
except ophthalmic

(P-21397)
PARKS OPTICAL INC
80 W Easy St Ste 3, Simi Valley
(93065-1665)
P.O. Box 1859 (93062-1859)
PHONE.............................805 522-6722
Maurice Sweiss, *President*
▲ EMP: 28
SQ FT: 25,000
SALES (est): 4.9MM **Privately Held**
WEB: www.parksoptical.com
SIC: 3827 5999 Binoculars; telescopes:
elbow, panoramic, sighting, fire control,
etc.; telescopes

(P-21398)
PHILIPS ELEC N AMER CORP
13700 Live Oak Ave, Baldwin Park
(91706-1319)
PHONE.............................626 480-0755
EMP: 150
SALES (corp-wide): 26B **Privately Held**
SIC: 3827 3641
HQ: Philips Electronics North America Cor-
poration
3000 Minuteman Rd Ms1203
Andover MA 01810
978 687-1501

(P-21399)
PIONEER MATERIALS INC
548 Trinidad Ln, Foster City (94404-3725)
PHONE.............................650 357-7130
Leon Chiu, *President*
EMP: 20
SALES (est): 2.2MM **Privately Held**
WEB: www.pioneer-materials.com
SIC: 3827 Optical instruments & lenses

(P-21400)
**PVP ADVANCED EO SYSTEMS
INC**
14312 Franklin Ave # 100, Tustin
(92780-7011)
PHONE.............................714 508-2740
Bruce E Ferguson, *CEO*
John Le Blanc, *CFO*
Young Nguyen, *IT/INT Sup*
Dave Brandt, *Engineer*
Russell Hammett, *Engineer*
▲ EMP: 50
SQ FT: 21,000
SALES (est): 13.3MM **Privately Held**
WEB: www.pvpaeo.com
SIC: 3827 Optical instruments & apparatus

(P-21401)
**REDFERN INTEGRATED OPTICS
INC**
3350 Scott Blvd Bldg 1, Santa Clara
(95054-3107)
PHONE.............................408 970-3500
Larry Marshall, *CEO*
EMP: 20
SALES (est): 3.2MM **Privately Held**
WEB: www.rio1.com
SIC: 3827 Optical elements & assemblies,
except ophthalmic
HQ: Optasense Holdings Limited
Cody Technology Park Ively Road
Farnborough HANTS

(P-21402)
REYNARD CORPORATION
1020 Calle Sombra, San Clemente
(92673-6227)
PHONE.............................949 366-8866
Forrest Reynard, *President*
Jean Reynard, *Vice Pres*
Randy Reynard, *Vice Pres*
Jean Rogers, *Executive*
Thomas Arthur, *QC Mgr*
EMP: 32
SQ FT: 28,000
SALES (est): 10.7MM **Privately Held**
WEB: www.reynardcorp.com
SIC: 3827 Mirrors, optical; lenses, optical:
all types except ophthalmic; prisms, opti-
cal

(P-21403)
RRDS INC (PA)
12 Goodyear Ste 100, Irvine (92618-3764)
PHONE.............................949 482-6200
Troy Barnes, *CEO*
Celeste Barnes, *Accountant*
Charles Hallums, *Manager*
Brooke Davis, *Associate*
▲ EMP: 17
SALES: 210K **Privately Held**
SIC: 3827 5012 3949 5045 Optical in-
struments & lenses; automobiles & other
motor vehicles; sporting & athletic goods;
computers, peripherals & software; tanks
& tank components; motor vehicle parts &
accessories

(P-21404)
RVISION INC
2365 Paragon Dr Ste D, San Jose
(95131-1335)
PHONE.............................408 437-5777
Brian M Kelly, *President*
Ryan Wald, *President*
Robb Warwick, *Treasurer*
Daniel Spradling, *Admin Sec*
Lance Rosenzweig, *Director*
EMP: 18
SQ FT: 11,000
SALES: 4MM **Privately Held**
WEB: www.rvisionusa.com
SIC: 3827 3861 1731 5063 Optical in-
struments & lenses; cameras & related
equipment; electrical work; electrical ap-
paratus & equipment
PA: Industrial Security Alliance Partners,
Inc.
10350 Science Center Dr # 100
San Diego CA 92121
619 232-7041

(P-21405)
SCOPE CITY (PA)
2978 Topaz Ave, Simi Valley (93063-2168)
P.O. Box 1630 (93062-1630)
PHONE.............................805 522-6646
Maurice Sweiss, *CEO*
▲ EMP: 35
SQ FT: 35,000
SALES (est): 2.8MM **Privately Held**
WEB: www.scopecity.com
SIC: 3827 Optical instruments & lenses

(P-21406)
SDO COMMUNICATIONS CORP
47365 Galindo Dr, Fremont (94539-7235)
PHONE.............................408 979-0289
CHI Hao Liu, *Principal*
CHI-Sho Liu, *Treasurer*
Wuei-Fang Ko, *Director*
EMP: 52
SQ FT: 27,000
SALES (est): 5.9MM **Privately Held**
WEB: www.sdocorp.com
SIC: 3827 3229 Optical instruments & ap-
paratus; pressed & blown glass

(P-21407)
SELLERS OPTICAL INC
Also Called: Precision Optical
320 Kalmus Dr, Costa Mesa (92626-6013)
PHONE.............................949 631-6800
Alan Mixon Lambert, *Ch of Bd*
Rod Randolph, *President*
Donny Miller, *CFO*
Paul Dimeck, *Vice Pres*
Alan Lambert Jr, *Vice Pres*
EMP: 57 EST: 1981
SQ FT: 17,000
SALES (est): 8MM **Privately Held**
WEB: www.precisionoptical.com
SIC: 3827 Optical instruments & apparatus

(P-21408)
SEMPREX CORPORATION
782 Camden Ave, Campbell (95008-4102)
PHONE.............................408 379-3230
Karl Volk, *President*
Chris Cox, *Prdtn Mgr*
EMP: 13
SQ FT: 12,500
SALES (est): 2.4MM **Privately Held**
WEB: www.semprex.com
SIC: 3827 Optical instruments & lenses

(P-21409)
SHEERVISION INC (PA)
4030 Palos Verdes Dr N # 104, Rllng HLS
Est (90274-2559)
PHONE.............................310 265-8918
Suzanne Lewsadder, *CEO*
Martin Chaput, *COO*
Patrick Adams, *CFO*
Brandon Pope, *Production*
Gordon Stover, *Sales Executive*
EMP: 14 EST: 1986
SQ FT: 3,090
SALES (est): 1.2MM **Publicly Held**
WEB: www.sheervision.com
SIC: 3827 Optical instruments & lenses

(P-21410)
SIERRA PRECISION OPTICS INC
12830 Earhart Ave, Auburn (95602-9027)
PHONE.............................530 885-6979
Michael Dorich, *CEO*
Eloise Dorich, *Admin Sec*
EMP: 25
SQ FT: 15,000
SALES: 4MM **Privately Held**
WEB: www.sierraoptics.com
SIC: 3827 Optical instruments & apparatus

(P-21411)
SPECTRUM SCIENTIFIC INC
16692 Hale Ave Ste A, Irvine (92606-5052)
PHONE.............................949 260-9900
Daphnie Chakran, *President*
Kevin Suvimon, *Engineer*
EMP: 12
SALES (est): 2.8MM **Privately Held**
WEB: www.ssioptics.com
SIC: 3827 Optical instruments & lenses

PRODUCTS & SVCS

(P-21412)
STELLARVUE
11820 Kemper Rd, Auburn (95603-9500)
PHONE..................................530 823-7796
Vic Maris, *Partner*
▲ **EMP:** 10
SALES (est): 1MM **Privately Held**
WEB: www.stellarvue.com
SIC: 3827 Telescopes: elbow, panoramic, sighting, fire control, etc.

(P-21413)
SUNEX INC
3160 Lionshead Ave Ste 2, Carlsbad (92010-4705)
P.O. Box 131672 (92013-1672)
PHONE..................................760 597-2966
Alex Ning, *President*
Rob Neville, *CFO*
David Holland, *Vice Pres*
Tae Yoo, *Vice Pres*
Taylor Patterson, *Program Mgr*
EMP: 10
SALES (est): 2.8MM **Privately Held**
WEB: www.optics-online.com
SIC: 3827 Optical instruments & apparatus

(P-21414)
SVETWHEEL LLC
121 Arundel Rd, San Carlos (94070-1905)
PHONE..................................650 245-6080
Victor Faybishenko,
Vladimir Solodovnikov,
EMP: 12
SALES (est): 1.5MM **Privately Held**
SIC: 3827 Lenses, optical: all types except ophthalmic; optical alignment & display instruments

(P-21415)
TFD INCORPORATED
Also Called: Thin Film Devices
1180 N Tustin Ave, Anaheim (92807-1732)
PHONE..................................714 630-7127
Saleem Shaikh, *CEO*
Joy Shaikh, *CFO*
▲ **EMP:** 25
SQ FT: 20,000
SALES (est): 5.8MM **Privately Held**
SIC: 3827 Optical instruments & lenses

(P-21416)
TWIN COAST METROLOGY INC (PA)
333 Wshngton Blvd Ste 362, Marina Del Rey (90292)
PHONE..................................310 709-2308
Eric Stone, *President*
Jason Remillard, *Treasurer*
Amy Remillard, *Admin Sec*
EMP: 15
SQ FT: 1,200
SALES (est): 1.6MM **Privately Held**
SIC: 3827 Optical instruments & lenses

(P-21417)
V-A OPTICAL COMPANY INC
60 Red Hill Ave, San Anselmo (94960-2424)
PHONE..................................415 459-1919
Michael Valliant, *President*
EMP: 10
SQ FT: 6,000
SALES: 1MM **Privately Held**
WEB: www.vaoptical.com
SIC: 3827 Optical elements & assemblies, except ophthalmic

(P-21418)
VSP LABS INC (PA)
Also Called: Vspone
3333 Quality Dr, Rancho Cordova (95670-7985)
PHONE..................................866 569-8800
Donald E Oakley, *President*
Don Ball, *CFO*
Denise Guy, *Manager*
EMP: 39
SALES (est): 33.8MM **Privately Held**
SIC: 3827 5049 Optical instruments & lenses; optical goods

(P-21419)
WAVE PRECISION INC
5390 Kazuko Ct, Moorpark (93021-1790)
PHONE..................................805 529-3324
Kenneth L Scribner, *President*
Dennis B Hotchkiss, *Vice Pres*
EMP: 75 **EST:** 1974
SQ FT: 16,000
SALES (est): 7.1MM **Privately Held**
WEB: www.generaloptics.com
SIC: 3827 Optical instruments & apparatus

(P-21420)
WINT CORPORATION
2880 Zanker Rd Ste 203, San Jose (95134-2122)
PHONE..................................408 816-4818
Frank Wang, *President*
EMP: 200
SQ FT: 3,000
SALES (est): 14.3MM **Privately Held**
SIC: 3827 Optical instruments & lenses

(P-21421)
WINTRISS ENGINEERING CORP
9010 Kenamar Dr Ste 101, San Diego (92121-3437)
PHONE..................................858 550-7300
Andrew W Ash, *CEO*
Vic Wintriss, *President*
Chris Kiraly, *CTO*
Gareth Lewis, *Software Engr*
Jerry Rose, *Regl Sales Mgr*
▲ **EMP:** 23
SQ FT: 11,576
SALES (est): 6.3MM **Privately Held**
WEB: www.weco.com
SIC: 3827 Optical test & inspection equipment

(P-21422)
WSGLASS HOLDINGS INC
Also Called: Western States Glass
180 Main Ave, Sacramento (95838-2015)
PHONE..................................916 388-5885
Curt Colgan, *Branch Mgr*
EMP: 17 **Privately Held**
WEB: www.westernstatesglass.com
SIC: 3827 Glasses, field or opera
HQ: Wsglass Holdings, Inc.
3241 Darby Cmn
Fremont CA 94539
510 623-5000

(P-21423)
Z C & R COATING FOR OPTICS INC
1401 Abalone Ave, Torrance (90501-2889)
PHONE..................................310 381-3060
Celso Cabrera, *President*
Robert Cabrera, *General Mgr*
Abrisa Technologies, *Webmaster*
Jim Walker, *Engineer*
Fred Praudisch, *VP Opers*
EMP: 43
SQ FT: 21,781
SALES (est): 8.6MM
SALES (corp-wide): 256.5MM **Privately Held**
WEB: www.zcrcoatings.com
SIC: 3827 Lens coating equipment
HQ: Abrisa Industrial Glass, Inc.
200 Hallock Dr
Santa Paula CA 93060
805 525-4902

(P-21424)
ZYGO CORPORATION
Also Called: Zygo Optical Systems
2031 Main St, Irvine (92614-6509)
PHONE..................................714 918-7433
Eric D'Lppolito, *Manager*
EMP: 22
SALES (corp-wide): 4.8B **Publicly Held**
WEB: www.zygo.com
SIC: 3827 Optical instruments & lenses
HQ: Zygo Corporation
21 Laurel Brook Rd
Middlefield CT 06455
860 347-8506

(P-21425)
ZYGO EPO
3900 Lakeside Dr, Richmond (94806-1963)
PHONE..................................510 243-7592
EMP: 12 **EST:** 2011

SALES (est): 2.2MM **Privately Held**
SIC: 3827 Optical instruments & lenses

3829 Measuring & Controlling Devices, NEC

(P-21426)
ABAXIS INC (HQ)
3240 Whipple Rd, Union City (94587-1217)
PHONE..................................510 675-6500
Clinton H Severson, *CEO*
Ross Taylor, *CFO*
Sigrid Rose, *Exec VP*
Ilya Frumkin, *Vice Pres*
Gene Hart, *Vice Pres*
◆ **EMP:** 180
SQ FT: 158,378
SALES: 244.7MM
SALES (corp-wide): 5.8B **Publicly Held**
WEB: www.abaxis.com
SIC: 3829 2835 Medical diagnostic systems, nuclear; in vitro & in vivo diagnostic substances; veterinary diagnostic substances
PA: Zoetis Inc.
10 Sylvan Way Ste 105
Parsippany NJ 07054
973 822-7000

(P-21427)
ACLARA BIOSCIENCES INC
Also Called: A Company In Development Stage
345 Oyster Point Blvd, South San Francisco (94080-1913)
PHONE..................................800 297-2728
Thomas G Klopack, *CEO*
Thomas J Baruch, *Ch of Bd*
EMP: 62
SQ FT: 44,000
SALES (est): 7.4MM **Privately Held**
WEB: www.virologic.com
SIC: 3829 8731 3826 3821 Measuring & controlling devices; commercial physical research; analytical instruments; laboratory apparatus & furniture; chemical preparations

(P-21428)
ACO PACIFIC INC
2604 Read Ave, Belmont (94002-1520)
PHONE..................................650 595-8588
Noland Lewis, *President*
EMP: 10
SQ FT: 25,000
SALES: 870K **Privately Held**
WEB: www.acopacific.com
SIC: 3829 Measuring & controlling devices

(P-21429)
ACTSOLAR INC
2900 Semiconductor Dr, Santa Clara (95051-0606)
PHONE..................................408 721-5000
Andrew Foss, *President*
Brian Dupin, *Vice Pres*
EMP: 15
SQ FT: 3,000
SALES (est): 95.1K
SALES (corp-wide): 15.7B **Publicly Held**
WEB: www.national.com
SIC: 3829 Measuring & controlling devices
HQ: National Semiconductor Corporation
2900 Semiconductor Dr
Santa Clara CA 95051
408 721-5000

(P-21430)
ALL WEATHER INC
Also Called: AWI
1065 National Dr Ste 1, Sacramento (95834-1927)
PHONE..................................916 928-1000
Jason Hall, *President*
Steve Vansanten, *Vice Pres*
Neal Dillman, *CTO*
Bartlomiej Klusek, *Software Engr*
Rajesh Kommu, *Software Engr*
◆ **EMP:** 65
SQ FT: 50,000

SALES (est): 21.9MM **Privately Held**
WEB: www.allweather.com
SIC: 3829 8999 3674 Weather tracking equipment; weather related services; radiation sensors

(P-21431)
ALTUS POSITIONING SYSTEMS INC
20725 S Wstn Ave Ste 100, Torrance (90501)
PHONE..................................310 541-8139
Neil Vancans, *President*
Marisa Strange, *Marketing Staff*
Eric Albrecht, *Manager*
EMP: 12
SALES (est): 1.9MM **Privately Held**
WEB: www.altus-ps.com
SIC: 3829 Measuring & controlling devices

(P-21432)
ALVARADO MANUFACTURING CO INC
12660 Colony Ct, Chino (91710-2975)
PHONE..................................909 591-8431
Bret Armatas, *CEO*
▲ **EMP:** 71
SQ FT: 69,000
SALES (est): 22.3MM **Privately Held**
WEB: www.alvaradomfg.com
SIC: 3829 Turnstiles, equipped with counting mechanisms

(P-21433)
APICAL INSTRUMENTS INC
2971 Spring St, Redwood City (94063-3935)
PHONE..................................650 967-1030
Bruno Strul PHD, *CEO*
EMP: 14
SQ FT: 15,000
SALES (est): 3.7MM **Privately Held**
WEB: www.apicalinstr.com
SIC: 3829 8742 3841 Measuring & controlling devices; industry specialist consultants; surgical & medical instruments

(P-21434)
APPLIED PHYSICS SYSTEMS INC (PA)
Also Called: 2-G Enterprises
425 Clyde Ave, Mountain View (94043-2209)
PHONE..................................650 965-0500
William Goodman, *President*
Maxwell Goodman, *Vice Pres*
Robert Goodman, *Vice Pres*
Dwayne Bakaas, *General Mgr*
Christine Goodman, *Admin Sec*
EMP: 92
SALES (est): 18.5MM **Privately Held**
WEB: www.appliedphysics.com
SIC: 3829 8711 Magnetometers; consulting engineer

(P-21435)
APPLIED TECHNOLOGIES ASSOC INC (HQ)
Also Called: A T A
3025 Buena Vista Dr, Paso Robles (93446-8555)
PHONE..................................805 239-9100
William B Wade, *President*
Chris Barker, *Owner*
George Walker, *Vice Pres*
Oliver Clock, *Technology*
David Bower, *Engineer*
▲ **EMP:** 127
SALES (est): 20.8MM **Privately Held**
WEB: www.ata-sd.com
SIC: 3829 1381 Surveying instruments & accessories; drilling oil & gas wells
PA: Scientific Drilling International, Inc.
16071 Greenspoint Park
Houston TX 77060
281 443-3300

(P-21436)
AQUA MEASURE INSTRUMENT CO
Also Called: Moisture Register Products
9567 Arrow Rte Ste E, Rancho Cucamonga (91730-4550)
PHONE..................................909 941-7776
John W Lundstrom, *Principal*

▲ = Import ▼=Export
◆ =Import/Export

Dean Curd, *Principal*
Arthur B Schultz, *Principal*
▲ EMP: 13
SQ FT: 13,500
SALES (est): 3MM **Privately Held**
WEB: www.moistureregisterproducts.com
SIC: 3829 3826 Moisture density meters;
analytical instruments

(P-21437)
ASTRO HAVEN ENTERPRISES INC
555 Anton Blvd Ste 150, Costa Mesa
(92626-7036)
P.O. Box 3637, San Clemente (92674-3637)
PHONE................................949 215-3777
Priscilla Brotherston, *President*
David Brotherston, *Chief*
▼ EMP: 12
SALES (est): 573.8K **Privately Held**
SIC: 3829 Measuring & controlling devices

(P-21438)
ATMOS ENGINEERING INC
443 Dearborn Park Rd, Pescadero
(94060-9706)
P.O. Box 807 (94060-0807)
PHONE................................650 879-1674
Rodger Reinhart, *President*
EMP: 12
SALES (est): 1.7MM **Privately Held**
WEB: www.atmos.com
SIC: 3829 Temperature sensors, except in-
dustrial process & aircraft

(P-21439)
AUTOMATIC CONTROL ENGRG CORP
Also Called: Johnson Contrls Authorized Dlr
20788 Corsair Blvd, Hayward
(94545-1010)
P.O. Box 20788 (94546-8788)
PHONE................................510 293-6040
Robert Crowder, *CEO*
Stephen Crowder, *Vice Pres*
Alfred Espudo, *Project Engr*
Terry Crowder, *Opers Mgr*
Jose Espudo, *Sales Engr*
EMP: 46
SQ FT: 15,000
SALES (est): 14.5MM **Privately Held**
SIC: 3829 5084 5075 Measuring & con-
trolling devices; instruments & control
equipment; warm air heating & air condi-
tioning

(P-21440)
AXCELIS TECHNOLOGIES INC
1360 Reynolds Ave Ste 106, Irvine
(92614-5535)
PHONE................................949 477-5160
EMP: 400
SALES (corp-wide): 442.5MM **Publicly Held**
SIC: 3829 Ion chambers
PA: Axcelis Technologies, Inc.
108 Cherry Hill Dr
Beverly MA 01915
978 787-4000

(P-21441)
AXCELIS TECHNOLOGIES INC
5673 W Las Positas Blvd # 205, Pleasanton
(94588-4077)
PHONE................................510 979-1970
Ali Moghadam, *Manager*
EMP: 400
SALES (corp-wide): 442.5MM **Publicly Held**
SIC: 3829 Ion chambers
PA: Axcelis Technologies, Inc.
108 Cherry Hill Dr
Beverly MA 01915
978 787-4000

(P-21442)
BARKSDALE INC (DH)
3211 Fruitland Ave, Vernon (90058-3717)
P.O. Box 58843, Los Angeles (90058-0843)
PHONE................................323 583-6243
C Ian Dodd, *President*
Ralf Fuehr, *Vice Pres*
Doug Holland, *Vice Pres*
Tarun Shivlani, *Vice Pres*
Craig Woetzel, *Vice Pres*

▲ EMP: 152
SQ FT: 115,000
SALES (est): 25.8MM
SALES (corp-wide): 3.3B **Publicly Held**
WEB: www.barksdale.net
SIC: 3829 3491 3823 3643 Measuring &
controlling devices; industrial valves; in-
dustrial instrmnts msrmnt display/control
process variable; current-carrying wiring
devices

(P-21443)
BECHLER CAMS INC
1313 S State College Pkwy, Anaheim
(92806-5298)
PHONE................................714 774-5150
Daniel Lennert, *President*
Laura Stearman, *Corp Secy*
EMP: 16 EST: 1957
SQ FT: 11,500
SALES (est): 2.8MM **Privately Held**
WEB: www.bechlercams.com
SIC: 3829 Measuring & controlling devices

(P-21444)
BRENNER-FIEDLER & ASSOCIATES (PA)
Also Called: B F
4059 Flat Rock Dr, Riverside (92505-5859)
PHONE................................562 404-2721
James Kloman, *CEO*
Wendi Kaminski, *Train & Dev Mgr*
Mitchell Powless, *Purchasing*
Deborah Kloman, *VP Opers*
Deborah Kloman-Lichter, *VP Opers*
EMP: 39
SQ FT: 28,669
SALES (est): 15.7MM **Privately Held**
WEB: www.brenner-fiedler.com
SIC: 3829 5085 Accelerometers; pistons &
valves; valves & fittings

(P-21445)
C&C BUILDING AUTOMATION CO INC
390 Swift Ave Ste 22, South San Francisco
(94080-6221)
PHONE................................650 292-7450
Chuck Chavez, *Principal*
Lynn Meneguzzi, *Administration*
Aaron Hougton, *Technician*
Francisco Jauregui, *Design Engr*
Cliff McIntire, *Manager*
EMP: 25
SQ FT: 6,000
SALES (est): 5.6MM **Privately Held**
WEB: www.ccbac.com
SIC: 3829 Measuring & controlling devices

(P-21446)
CALIFORNIA DYNAMICS CORP (PA)
Also Called: Caldyn
5572 Alhambra Ave, Los Angeles
(90032-3195)
PHONE................................323 223-3882
Donald Benkert, *President*
Adell Benkert, *President*
Scott Sween, *Sales Staff*
▲ EMP: 25
SQ FT: 30,000
SALES (est): 3MM **Privately Held**
WEB: www.caldyn.com
SIC: 3829 Vibration meters, analyzers &
calibrators

(P-21447)
CALIFORNIA SENSOR CORPORATION
2075 Corte Del Nogal P, Carlsbad
(92011-1413)
PHONE................................760 438-0525
Ralph Miller, *CEO*
David L Byma, *President*
Richard Wilkinson, *Treasurer*
Robert Destremps, *Vice Pres*
EMP: 30
SQ FT: 6,000
SALES (est): 8.1MM **Privately Held**
WEB: www.calsense.com
SIC: 3829 5083 Measuring & controlling
devices; irrigation equipment

(P-21448)
CARGO DATA CORPORATION
1502 Eastman Ave Ste A, Ventura
(93003-8020)
P.O. Box 6553 (93006-6553)
PHONE................................805 650-5922
Bud Pohle, *President*
Roger Niebolt, *Sales Mgr*
Tammy Wylie, *Sales Mgr*
▲ EMP: 10
SALES (est): 840K **Privately Held**
SIC: 3829 Temperature sensors, except in-
dustrial process & aircraft

(P-21449)
CARTURNER INC (PA)
3444 Tripp Ct Ste B, San Diego
(92121-1000)
PHONE................................760 598-7448
Bill Schwenker, *President*
Eugene J Polley, *Accountant*
EMP: 13
SALES (est): 2.4MM **Privately Held**
SIC: 3829 3444 Turntable indicator
testers; sheet metalwork

(P-21450)
CBS SCIENTIFIC CO INC (PA)
10805 Vista Sorrento Pkwy # 100, San
Diego (92121-2701)
P.O. Box 856, Del Mar (92014-0856)
PHONE................................858 755-4959
▲ EMP: 40
SQ FT: 25,000
SALES (est): 3.6MM **Privately Held**
WEB: www.cbsscientific.com
SIC: 3829 3821

(P-21451)
CERCACOR LABORATORIES INC
40 Parker, Irvine (92618-1604)
PHONE................................949 679-6100
Joe E Kiani, *President*
Mel Chiba, *Vice Pres*
Brenda Montgomery, *Vice Pres*
Don Sanders, *Sr Software Eng*
Howard Chan, *Engineer*
EMP: 11
SALES (est): 1.7MM **Privately Held**
SIC: 3829 Pulse analyzers, nuclear moni-
toring

(P-21452)
COMET TECHNOLOGIES USA INC
Also Called: Plasma Control Technologies
2370 Bering Dr, San Jose (95131-1121)
PHONE................................408 325-8770
Paul Smith, *General Mgr*
Conor O'Mahony, *Vice Pres*
Jeff Wilkins, *Vice Pres*
Robert Jardim, *Administration*
Knut Mehr, *Engineer*
EMP: 50
SALES (corp-wide): 439MM **Privately Held**
WEB: www.cometna.com
SIC: 3829 Measuring & controlling devices
HQ: Comet Technologies Usa Inc.
100 Trap Falls Road Ext
Shelton CT 06484
203 447-3200

(P-21453)
COMPUTATIONAL SYSTEMS INC
4301 Resnik Ct, Bakersfield (93313-4852)
PHONE................................661 832-5306
Shannon Romine, *Branch Mgr*
EMP: 50
SALES (corp-wide): 17.4B **Publicly Held**
SIC: 3829 Stress, strain & flaw
detecting/measuring equipment
HQ: Computational Systems, Incorporated
8000 West Florissant Ave
Saint Louis MO 63136
314 553-2000

(P-21454)
CONNECTPV INC
13370 Kirkham Way, Poway (92064-7117)
PHONE................................858 246-6140
John Hass, *CEO*
Tom Cole, *Director*
Rick Cunningham, *Director*

Randy Rounds, *Manager*
EMP: 10 EST: 2015
SALES (est): 607.1K **Privately Held**
SIC: 3829 Solarimeters

(P-21455)
CUBIC TRNSP SYSTEMS INC (HQ)
5650 Kearny Mesa Rd, San Diego
(92111-1305)
P.O. Box 85587 (92186-5587)
PHONE................................858 268-3100
Stephen O Shewmaker, *CEO*
Walter C Zable, *Ch of Bd*
Thuston Britt, *Officer*
Steve Purcell, *Senior VP*
Raymond De Kozan, *Vice Pres*
◆ EMP: 550
SALES (est): 217.1MM
SALES (corp-wide): 1.2B **Publicly Held**
SIC: 3829 1731 Fare registers for street
cars, buses, etc.; toll booths, automatic;
telephone & telephone equipment instal-
lation
PA: Cubic Corporation
9333 Balboa Ave
San Diego CA 92123
858 277-6780

(P-21456)
CUBIC TRNSP SYSTEMS INC
1800 Sutter St Ste 900, Concord
(94520-2536)
PHONE................................925 348-9163
Derrick Benoit, *Manager*
Richard Hamai, *Database Admin*
EMP: 175
SALES (corp-wide): 1.2B **Publicly Held**
SIC: 3829 Fare registers for street cars,
buses, etc.
HQ: Cubic Transportation Systems, Inc.
5650 Kearny Mesa Rd
San Diego CA 92111
858 268-3100

(P-21457)
DAKOTA ULTRASONICS CORPORATION
1500 Green Hills Rd # 107, Scotts Valley
(95066-4945)
PHONE................................831 431-9722
Teresa Engel, *COO*
Laurie Gudhal, *CPA*
Richard Engel, *Sales Staff*
EMP: 13
SQ FT: 4,500
SALES (est): 3MM **Privately Held**
WEB: www.dakotainst.com
SIC: 3829 Gauging instruments, thickness
ultrasonic

(P-21458)
DAVIDSON OPTRONICS INC
Also Called: Doi Venture
9087 Arrow Rte Ste 180, Rancho Cuca-
monga (91730-4451)
PHONE................................626 962-5181
Eugene Dumitrascu, *Ch of Bd*
Dan State, *President*
Debra Richards, *Admin Sec*
Harvey Miller, *Sales Staff*
EMP: 22
SQ FT: 40,000
SALES (est): 3.9MM
SALES (corp-wide): 36.5MM **Privately Held**
WEB: www.davidsonoptronics.com
SIC: 3829 3827 Measuring & controlling
devices; optical instruments & apparatus
HQ: Trioptics, Inc.
9087 Arrow Rte Ste 180
Rancho Cucamonga CA 91730
626 962-5181

(P-21459)
DELTATRAK INC
1236 Doker Dr, Modesto (95351-1587)
PHONE................................209 579-5343
Allen Hui, *Manager*
EMP: 50
SQ FT: 25,468
SALES (corp-wide): 15.7MM **Privately Held**
WEB: www.deltatrak.com
SIC: 3829 Temperature sensors, except in-
dustrial process & aircraft

PRODUCTS & SVCS

PA: Deltatrak, Inc.
6140 Stoneridge Mall Rd # 180
Pleasanton CA 94588
925 249-2250

(P-21460)
DELTATRAK INC (PA)
6140 Stoneridge Mall Rd # 180, Pleasanton
(94588-3288)
P.O. Box 398 (94566-0039)
PHONE..................................925 249-2250
Frederick L Wu, *CEO*
Jeanne Solis, *Administration*
Andy Cowell, *Sr Software Eng*
Matthew Moore, *Technical Staff*
Rick Delgado, *Opers Staff*
▲ **EMP:** 25
SQ FT: 7,500
SALES (est): 15.7MM **Privately Held**
WEB: www.deltatrak.com
SIC: 3829 3823 3822 Temperature sensors, except industrial process & aircraft; industrial instrmnts msrmnt display/control process variable; auto controls regulating residntl & coml environmt & applncs

(P-21461)
DYNAMIC SOLUTIONS
631 W Rosecrans Ave # 23, Gardena
(90248-1516)
P.O. Box 7963, Northridge (91327-7963)
PHONE..................................253 273-7936
Aimmee Hagler, *Partner*
Steven Wood, *Partner*
EMP: 12
SQ FT: 10,000
SALES (est): 1.5MM **Privately Held**
WEB: www.dynsolusa.com
SIC: 3829 Vibration meters, analyzers & calibrators

(P-21462)
EAGLEMETRIC CORP
98 Discovery, Irvine (92618-3105)
PHONE..................................949 288-3363
Patrick Lee, *President*
EMP: 12 **EST:** 2010
SALES (est): 974.8K **Privately Held**
SIC: 3829 Measuring & controlling devices

(P-21463)
ECKERT ZEGLER ISOTOPE PDTS INC
1800 N Keystone St, Burbank
(91504-3417)
PHONE..................................661 309-1010
Karl Amlauer, *Branch Mgr*
EMP: 30
SALES (corp-wide): 163.4MM **Privately Held**
WEB: www.isotopeproducts.com
SIC: 3829 Nuclear radiation & testing apparatus
HQ: Eckert & Ziegler Isotope Products, Inc.
24937 Avenue Tibbitts
Valencia CA 91355
661 309-1010

(P-21464)
ECKERT ZEGLER ISOTOPE PDTS INC (HQ)
Also Called: Isotope Products Lab
24937 Avenue Tibbitts, Valencia
(91355-3427)
PHONE..................................661 309-1010
Frank Yeager, *CEO*
Joe Hathcock, *President*
Karen Haskins, *Treasurer*
Frida Tan, *Project Mgr*
Audrey Townsend, *Human Res Mgr*
EMP: 45 **EST:** 1967
SQ FT: 40,000
SALES: 44.6MM
SALES (corp-wide): 163.4MM **Privately Held**
WEB: www.isotopeproducts.com
SIC: 3829 Nuclear radiation & testing apparatus
PA: Eckert & Ziegler Strahlen- Und Medizintechnik Ag
Robert-Rossle-Str. 10
Berlin 13125
309 410-840

(P-21465)
ECKERT ZEGLER ISOTOPE PDTS INC
1800 N Keystone St, Burbank
(91504-3417)
PHONE..................................661 309-1010
EMP: 30
SALES (corp-wide): 158.2MM **Privately Held**
SIC: 3829
HQ: Eckert & Ziegler Isotope Products, Inc.
24937 Avenue Tibbitts
Valencia CA 91355
661 309-1010

(P-21466)
EMISSION METHODS INC
Also Called: Webber EMI
1307 S Wanamaker Ave, Ontario
(91761-2237)
PHONE..................................909 605-6800
Kenneth Parker, *President*
EMP: 20
SQ FT: 14,100
SALES (est): 4.4MM **Privately Held**
WEB: www.webberemi.com
SIC: 3829 3499 3599 Dynamometer instruments; aircraft & motor vehicle measurement equipment; novelties & specialties, metal; carnival machines & equipment, amusement park

(P-21467)
ET WATER SYSTEMS LLC
384 Bel Marin Keys Blvd # 145, Novato
(94949-5366)
PHONE..................................415 945-9383
Bruce J Cardinal,
Mark Coppersmith, *Managing Dir*
Kevin Heverin, *Marketing Mgr*
Leroy McGrue, *Regl Sales Mgr*
▲ **EMP:** 14
SALES (est): 1.4MM **Privately Held**
SIC: 3829 Measuring & controlling devices

(P-21468)
EXCELITAS TECHNOLOGIES CORP
1330 E Cypress St, Covina (91724-2103)
PHONE..................................626 967-6021
Patrick O'Shaunessey, *Branch Mgr*
Paul Igoe, *Admin Sec*
Chau Chan, *Engineer*
Angie Avila, *Controller*
EMP: 120
SALES (corp-wide): 1.2B **Privately Held**
SIC: 3829 3679 Thermometers & temperature sensors; electronic circuits
HQ: Excelitas Technologies Corp.
200 West St
Waltham MA 02451

(P-21469)
EXCESS TRADING INC
Also Called: Precision Designed Products
12350 Montague St Ste L, Pacoima
(91331-2201)
PHONE..................................310 212-0020
Mark L Silberberg, *President*
EMP: 25
SALES (est): 3.2MM **Privately Held**
WEB: www.excesstrading.com
SIC: 3829 Levels & tapes, surveying

(P-21470)
EXP COMPUTER
Also Called: Xeltek
1296 Kifer Rd Ste 605, Sunnyvale
(94086-5318)
PHONE..................................408 530-8080
Soonam Kim, *President*
Juok Kim, *Treasurer*
Robert Parente, *Admin Sec*
Ted Jeon, *Engineer*
▲ **EMP:** 10
SQ FT: 3,500
SALES (est): 1.7MM **Privately Held**
WEB: www.xeltek.com
SIC: 3829 5065 Measuring & controlling devices; electronic parts & equipment

(P-21471)
F & D FLORES ENTERPRISES INC
Also Called: Hardware Specialties
761 E Francis St, Ontario (91761-5514)
PHONE..................................909 975-4853
Frank Flores, *President*
Steve Saldana, *Supervisor*
▲ **EMP:** 11
SQ FT: 20,000
SALES (est): 1.4MM **Privately Held**
WEB: www.sentryturnstiles.com
SIC: 3829 5031 3446 Automatic turnstiles & related apparatus; lumber, plywood & millwork; architectural metalwork

(P-21472)
FAR WEST TECHNOLOGY INC
330 S Kellogg Ave, Goleta (93117-3814)
PHONE..................................805 964-3615
John D Rickey, *CEO*
John Handloser Jr, *Exec VP*
John Handloser, *Vice Pres*
Handloser Jr John, *Sales Mgr*
Scot Larson, *Manager*
▲ **EMP:** 17 **EST:** 1971
SQ FT: 6,100
SALES (est): 3.6MM **Privately Held**
WEB: www.fwt.com
SIC: 3829 Nuclear radiation & testing apparatus

(P-21473)
FITBIT INC (PA)
199 Fremont St Fl 14, San Francisco
(94105-2253)
PHONE..................................415 513-1000
James Park, *President*
Jessie Stehle, *Partner*
Amy McDonough, *COO*
Ronald Kisling, *CFO*
Tim Rosa, *Chief Mktg Ofcr*
EMP: 277
SQ FT: 366,000
SALES: 1.5B **Publicly Held**
SIC: 3829 Measuring & controlling devices

(P-21474)
FLOWLINE INC
Also Called: Flowline Liquid Intelligence
10500 Humbolt St, Los Alamitos
(90720-2439)
PHONE..................................562 598-3015
Stephen E Olson, *Ch of Bd*
Scott Olson, *President*
Mark Lederman, *Software Engr*
Mike Rafferty, *Engineer*
Joe Tran, *Engineer*
EMP: 25
SQ FT: 8,000
SALES (est): 4.5MM **Privately Held**
WEB: www.flowline.com
SIC: 3829 5084 Measuring & controlling devices; industrial machinery & equipment

(P-21475)
FOOTHILL INSTRUMENTS LLC
5011 Jarvis Ave, La Canada (91011-1640)
PHONE..................................818 952-5600
Glenn Houser, *Partner*
Leslie Miller, *Partner*
EMP: 10 **EST:** 1999
SALES (est): 1.1MM **Privately Held**
WEB: www.foothill-instruments.com
SIC: 3829 Measuring & controlling devices

(P-21476)
FOUR D IMAGING
808 Gilman St, Berkeley (94710-1422)
PHONE..................................510 290-3533
Glen Stevick, *President*
EMP: 12
SALES (est): 1.3MM **Privately Held**
SIC: 3829 Measuring & controlling devices

(P-21477)
FRONTLINE INSTRS & CONTRLS
Also Called: Frontline Technologies
3195 Park Rd Ste C, Benicia (94510-1185)
PHONE..................................707 747-9766
Lee Sherwood, *President*
EMP: 10
SALES: 200K **Privately Held**
SIC: 3829 Measuring & controlling devices

(P-21478)
GAMMA SCIENTIFIC INC
Also Called: Road Vista
9925 Carroll Canyon Rd, San Diego
(92131-1105)
PHONE..................................858 635-9008
Kong G Loh, *COO*
James Wray, *Technology*
Christopher Flores, *Mfg Staff*
Pete Frazier, *Regl Sales Mgr*
Susan Xanten, *Manager*
▲ **EMP:** 48
SQ FT: 20,000
SALES: 11.9MM **Privately Held**
WEB: www.gamma-sci.com
SIC: 3829 3648 3821 Measuring & controlling devices; reflectors for lighting equipment; metal; calibration tapes for physical testing machines

(P-21479)
GENERAL NUCLEONICS INC
2807 Metropolitan Pl, Pomona
(91767-1853)
PHONE..................................909 593-4985
Sam Dominey, *President*
Donald Blincow, *Vice Pres*
Teresa Estrella, *Office Mgr*
John Mahoney, *CTO*
EMP: 10
SQ FT: 14,000
SALES (est): 1.6MM **Privately Held**
WEB: www.generalnucleonics.com
SIC: 3829 Stress, strain & flaw detecting/measuring equipment; gauging instruments, thickness ultrasonic

(P-21480)
GEOMETRICS INC
2190 Fortune Dr, San Jose (95131-1815)
PHONE..................................408 428-4244
Mark Prouty, *President*
Rod Bravo, *CFO*
Ron Royal, *Vice Pres*
Ruth Beynon, *Administration*
Brenda Inthisane, *Administration*
EMP: 80
SALES: 26.6MM **Privately Held**
WEB: www.geometrics.com
SIC: 3829 Geophysical or meteorological electronic equipment
HQ: Oyo Corporation U.S.A.
245 N Carmelo Ave Ste 101
Pasadena CA 91107

(P-21481)
GUNNEBO ENTRANCE CONTROL INC (HQ)
Also Called: Omega Turnstiles
535 Getty Ct Ste F, Benicia (94510-1179)
PHONE..................................707 748-0885
John Haining, *CEO*
Susanne Larsson, *CFO*
Tomas Wngberg, *Vice Pres*
Jenifer Babbitt, *Admin Sec*
Tim Sakellariou, *Technical Mgr*
▲ **EMP:** 18
SQ FT: 20,000
SALES (est): 1.5MM
SALES (corp-wide): 677.9MM **Privately Held**
WEB: www.gunneboentrance.us
SIC: 3829 Automatic turnstiles & related apparatus
PA: Gunnebo Ab
Johan Pa Gardas Gata 7
Goteborg 412 5
102 095-000

(P-21482)
H2SCAN CORPORATION
27215 Turnberry Ln Unit A, Valencia
(91355-1068)
PHONE..................................661 775-9575
Michael Allman, *CEO*
Dennis W Reid, *President*
Kyle Hodge, *Technician*
Gid Herman, *Technical Staff*
Tim Howard, *Engineer*
EMP: 25
SQ FT: 10,000
SALES (est): 7.9MM **Privately Held**
SIC: 3829 Hydrometers, except industrial process type

▲ = Import ▼=Export
◆ =Import/Export

(P-21483)
HAMILTON SUNDSTRAND SPC SYSTMS
Also Called: Hsssi
960 Overland Ct, San Dimas (91773-1742)
PHONE..................................909 288-5300
Edward Francis, *Exec Dir*
Lawrence R McNamara, *President*
Gregory J Hayes, *CEO*
Eugene Dougherty, *Treasurer*
Clinton Gardiner, *Vice Pres*
EMP: 76
SQ FT: 134,000
SALES (est): 8.9MM
SALES (corp-wide): 66.5B **Publicly Held**
WEB: www.hsssi.com
SIC: 3829 Measuring & controlling devices
HQ: Goodrich Corporation
2730 W Tyvola Rd 4
Charlotte NC 28217
704 423-7000

(P-21484)
HIGHLAND TECHNOLOGY
650 Potrero Ave, San Francisco (94110-2117)
PHONE..................................415 551-1700
John Larkin, *President*
Denise Thiry, *Shareholder*
Hugh Callahan, *Vice Pres*
Elizabeth Larkin, *Vice Pres*
Rebecca McKee, *Admin Sec*
EMP: 20
SQ FT: 6,000
SALES (est): 4.9MM **Privately Held**
WEB: www.highlandtechnology.com
SIC: 3829 Measuring & controlling devices

(P-21485)
HILZ CABLE ASSEMBLIES INC
31889 Corydon St Ste 110, Lake Elsinore (92530-8509)
PHONE..................................951 245-0499
Darlene Hilz, *President*
▲ **EMP:** 15
SALES: 1MM **Privately Held**
SIC: 3829 Cable testing machines

(P-21486)
HORIBA INSTRUMENTS INC
430 Indio Way, Sunnyvale (94085-4202)
PHONE..................................408 730-4772
Margarita Trujillo, *Opers Mgr*
EMP: 75 **Privately Held**
SIC: 3829 Measuring & controlling devices
HQ: Horiba Instruments Incorporated
9755 Research Dr
Irvine CA 92618
949 250-4811

(P-21487)
I/O SELECT INC
9835 Carroll Centre Rd # 100, San Diego (92126-6507)
PHONE..................................858 537-2060
Rob Henley, *President*
Julie A Henley, *Exec VP*
Julie Henley, *Exec VP*
H Philip White, *Vice Pres*
EMP: 15
SQ FT: 6,100
SALES (est): 3MM **Privately Held**
SIC: 3829 Measuring & controlling devices

(P-21488)
IMDEX TECHNOLOGY USA LLC
3474 Empresa Dr Ste 150, San Luis Obispo (93401-7391)
PHONE..................................805 540-2017
George Vu,
Tim Price,
EMP: 20 **EST:** 2011
SQ FT: 3,500
SALES (est): 4.1MM **Privately Held**
SIC: 3829 8711 Surveying instruments & accessories; engineering services
PA: Imdex Ltd
216 Balcatta Rd
Balcatta WA 6021

(P-21489)
INTELLIGENT BARCODE SYSTEMS
2190 Sherwood Rd, San Marino (91108-2849)
PHONE..................................626 576-8938
Vincent Chang, *President*
Karen Lee, *Treasurer*
EMP: 10
SQ FT: 2,400
SALES (est): 1.2MM **Privately Held**
WEB: www.barcodesystems.com
SIC: 3829 Measuring & controlling devices

(P-21490)
INTERNATIONAL SENSOR TECH
3 Whatney Ste 100, Irvine (92618-2836)
PHONE..................................949 452-9000
Thomas Jack Chou, *President*
Daniel R Chuo, *CFO*
Doris Chou, *Corp Secy*
Frank Diferdinando, *Trust Officer*
Tai CAM Luu, *Admin Sec*
▲ **EMP:** 27
SQ FT: 20,000
SALES (est): 4.3MM **Privately Held**
WEB: www.intlsensor.com
SIC: 3829 Gas detectors

(P-21491)
IRROMETER COMPANY INC
Also Called: Watermark
1425 Palmyrita Ave, Riverside (92507-1600)
PHONE..................................951 682-9505
Thomas C Penning, *President*
Samuel Legget, *Treasurer*
Jeremy Sullivan, *Vice Pres*
Diganta Adhikari, *Engineer*
Brad Adams, *Sales Staff*
EMP: 18 **EST:** 1951
SQ FT: 9,000
SALES (est): 4MM **Privately Held**
WEB: www.irrometer.com
SIC: 3829 Measuring & controlling devices

(P-21492)
J L SHEPHERD AND ASSOCIATES
1010 Arroyo St, San Fernando (91340-1822)
PHONE..................................818 898-2361
Joseph L Shepherd, *President*
Dorothy Shepherd, *Treasurer*
Diana Shepherd, *Vice Pres*
Mary Shepherd, *Vice Pres*
▲ **EMP:** 27 **EST:** 1967
SQ FT: 15,000
SALES (est): 7.8MM **Privately Held**
WEB: www.jlshepherd.com
SIC: 3829 3844 Nuclear radiation & testing apparatus; irradiation equipment

(P-21493)
JOHANSON INNOVATIONS INC
2975 Hawk Hill Ln, San Luis Obispo (93405-8328)
PHONE..................................805 544-4697
Michael Belingheri, *President*
EMP: 10
SALES (est): 890K **Privately Held**
SIC: 3829 Measuring & controlling devices

(P-21494)
KALILA MEDICAL INC
1400 Dell Ave Ste C, Campbell (95008-6620)
PHONE..................................408 819-5175
Joshua Hagerman, *Surgery Dir*
EMP: 25
SQ FT: 12,536
SALES: 900K **Privately Held**
SIC: 3829 Thermometers, including digital: clinical
HQ: Terumo Americas Holding, Inc.
265 Davidson Ave Ste 320
Somerset NJ 08873
732 302-4900

(P-21495)
KAP MEDICAL
1395 Pico St, Corona (92881-3373)
PHONE..................................951 340-4360
Raj K Gowda, *President*
Enrik Tobon, *CFO*
Dave Lewis, *Vice Pres*
Dan Rosenmayer, *Vice Pres*
Maylil Gowda, *Manager*
▲ **EMP:** 35
SQ FT: 20,000
SALES (est): 13.9MM **Privately Held**
SIC: 3829 8711 Medical diagnostic systems, nuclear; consulting engineer

(P-21496)
KARL STORZ IMAGING INC (HQ)
Also Called: Optronics
1 S Los Carneros Rd, Goleta (93117-5506)
PHONE..................................805 968-5563
Miles Hartfield, *General Mgr*
Gail Lobdell, *Executive Asst*
Gail Lobdell, *Admin Sec*
Barbara Meehan, *Admin Asst*
Craig Pannett, *Info Tech Dir*
EMP: 344
SQ FT: 105,000
SALES (est): 138.5MM
SALES (corp-wide): 1.9B **Privately Held**
SIC: 3829 3841 Measuring & controlling devices; surgical & medical instruments
PA: Karl Storz Se & Co. Kg
Dr.-Karl-Storz-Str. 34
Tuttlingen 78532
746 170-80

(P-21497)
KHN SOLUTIONS INC
Also Called: Bactrack
300 Broadway Ste 26, San Francisco (94133-4529)
PHONE..................................877 334-6876
Keith Nothacker, *CEO*
Pauline Basaran, *Vice Pres*
Stacey Sachs, *Vice Pres*
Jason Farrara, *Accounts Mgr*
◆ **EMP:** 12
SQ FT: 4,000
SALES: 50MM **Privately Held**
SIC: 3829 Breathalyzers

(P-21498)
KWJ ENGINEERING INC (PA)
Also Called: Eco Sensors
8430 Central Ave Ste C, Newark (94560-3457)
PHONE..................................510 794-4296
Joseph R Stetter, *President*
Edward F Stetter, *CFO*
Edward Stetter, *Vice Pres*
Tasneem Ali, *Admin Asst*
EMP: 25
SQ FT: 10,000
SALES (est): 5.3MM **Privately Held**
WEB: www.kwjengineering.com
SIC: 3829 5084 Gas detectors; instruments & control equipment

(P-21499)
LEX PRODUCTS LLC
12701 Van Nuys Blvd Ste Q, Pacoima (91331-7296)
PHONE..................................818 768-4474
Bob Luther, *President*
Elizabeth Luther, *President*
Patrick Legler, *Sales Staff*
EMP: 14 **Privately Held**
SIC: 3829 3315 3643 3613 Measuring & controlling devices; cable, steel: insulated or armored; current-carrying wiring devices; switchboards & parts, power
PA: Lex Products Llc
15 Progress Dr
Shelton CT 06484

(P-21500)
LOIS A VALESKIE
Also Called: Municon Consultants
775 Congo St, San Francisco (94131-2809)
PHONE..................................415 641-2570
Lois A Valeskie, *Owner*
EMP: 10
SALES: 1,000K **Privately Held**
WEB: www.municon.net
SIC: 3829 8711 Vibration meters, analyzers & calibrators; consulting engineer

(P-21501)
LUFFT USA INC
1110 Eugenia Pl Ste 200, Carpinteria (93013-2081)
PHONE..................................805 335-8500
Michael Corbett, *Branch Mgr*
Ann Pattison, *CEO*
Erik Wright, *Office Mgr*
Laura Goodfellow, *Technical Staff*
Georg Heinemann, *Sales Staff*
EMP: 14
SALES (est): 2.4MM **Privately Held**
SIC: 3829 Weather tracking equipment
PA: Lufft Usa, Inc.
420 Boardwalk Dr
Youngsville NC 27596

(P-21502)
MEASUREMENT SPECIALTIES INC
9131 Oakdale Ave Ste 170, Chatsworth (91311-6502)
PHONE..................................818 701-2750
Robert Simon, *Branch Mgr*
James Bishop, *Manager*
EMP: 98
SALES (corp-wide): 13.9B **Privately Held**
SIC: 3829 Measuring & controlling devices
HQ: Measurement Specialties, Inc.
1000 Lucas Way
Hampton VA 23666
757 766-1500

(P-21503)
MECHANIZED SCIENCE SEALS INC
Also Called: Ms Bellows
5322 Mcfadden Ave, Huntington Beach (92649-1239)
PHONE..................................714 898-5602
Jon Hamren, *President*
Victoria Hamren, *Treasurer*
Robin Hamren, *Admin Sec*
Linda Welsh, *Manager*
EMP: 20 **EST:** 1964
SQ FT: 10,000
SALES (est): 4MM **Privately Held**
WEB: www.msbellows.com
SIC: 3829 Measuring & controlling devices

(P-21504)
MEGGITT (ORANGE COUNTY) INC (HQ)
Also Called: Meggitt Sensing Systems
14600 Myford Rd, Irvine (92606-1005)
PHONE..................................949 493-8181
Mel Hilderbrand, *President*
Veronica Reyes, *Treasurer*
Cheryl Tindle, *General Mgr*
Karen Goodcell, *Executive Asst*
Jim Henderson, *Sr Software Eng*
▲ **EMP:** 239
SQ FT: 125,000
SALES (est): 88MM
SALES (corp-wide): 2.6B **Privately Held**
SIC: 3829 Vibration meters, analyzers & calibrators
PA: Meggitt Plc
Atlantic House, Aviation Park West
Christchurch BH23
120 259-7597

(P-21505)
MEPS REAL-TIME INC
Also Called: Intellgard Inventory Solutions
6451 El Camino Real Ste C, Carlsbad (92009-2800)
PHONE..................................760 448-9500
Gordon Krass, *CEO*
Williams Jay, *VP Bus Dvlpt*
Melissa Knowles, *Accounting Mgr*
Valerie Fritz, *Marketing Staff*
Greg Bartels, *Sales Staff*
EMP: 50
SALES (est): 10.3MM **Privately Held**
SIC: 3829 Accelerometers

(P-21506)
METTLER-TOLEDO RAININ LLC (HQ)
7500 Edgewater Dr, Oakland (94621-3027)
PHONE..................................510 564-1600
Gerhard Keller, *General Mgr*
Olivier Filliol, *CEO*

Henri Chahine, *COO*
Shawn Vadala, *CFO*
Sam Verdickt, *General Mgr*
▲ EMP: 120
SQ FT: 55,000
SALES (est): 120.6MM
SALES (corp-wide): 2.9B **Publicly Held**
WEB: www.rainin.com
SIC: 3829 3821 Measuring & controlling
devices; pipettes, hemocytometer
PA: Mettler-Toledo International Inc.
1900 Polaris Pkwy Fl 6
Columbus OH 43240
614 438-4511

(P-21507)
MICRO-METRIC INC
1050 Commercial St, San Jose
(95112-1419)
PHONE..................................408 452-8505
Fax: 408 452-8412
EMP: 15
SQ FT: 6,500
SALES (est): 3.2MM **Privately Held**
WEB: www.micro-metric.com
SIC: 3829 7699 8734

(P-21508)
MIRION TECHNOLOGIES INC (PA)
3000 Executive Pkwy # 518, San Ramon
(94583-4355)
PHONE..................................925 543-0800
Thomas Logan, *CEO*
Anthony Rabb, *CFO*
Mike Brumbaugh, *Exec VP*
Seth Rosen, *Exec VP*
Kip Bennett, *Vice Pres*
EMP: 158
SQ FT: 10,300
SALES (est): 380.2MM **Privately Held**
WEB: www.mirion.com
SIC: 3829 Measuring & controlling devices

(P-21509)
MISTRAS GROUP INC
3551 Voyager St Ste 104, Torrance
(90503-1674)
PHONE..................................310 793-7173
Colm Walsh, *Branch Mgr*
EMP: 20 **Publicly Held**
SIC: 3829 Measuring & controlling devices
PA: Mistras Group, Inc.
195 Clarksville Rd Ste 2
Princeton Junction NJ 08550

(P-21510)
MITCHELL TEST & SAFETY INC
Also Called: Mitchell Instruments
2875 Scott St Ste 101-103, Vista
(92081-8559)
PHONE..................................760 744-2690
Sherwin Desportes, *President*
Michael Macvie, *Principal*
EMP: 12
SALES (est): 1.2MM **Privately Held**
SIC: 3829 Measuring & controlling devices

(P-21511)
NDT SYSTEMS INC
5542 Buckingham Dr Ste A, Huntington
Beach (92649-1158)
PHONE..................................714 893-2438
Grant Johnston, *CEO*
Gregory Smith, *President*
Ray Riebeling, *Executive*
Drew Courtright, *General Mgr*
Martin Leyba, *General Mgr*
EMP: 22
SALES (est): 4.9MM
SALES (corp-wide): 10B **Privately Held**
WEB: www.ndtsystems.com
SIC: 3829 Ultrasonic testing equipment
HQ: Amec Foster Wheeler Limited
4th Floor Old Change House
London EC4V
207 429-7500

(P-21512)
OMNI OPTICAL PRODUCTS INC (PA)
17282 Eastman, Irvine (92614)
PHONE..................................714 634-5700
Ken Panique, *President*
Cindy Von Hershman, *Manager*

▲ EMP: 20
SALES (est): 4.3MM **Privately Held**
WEB: www.omnisurvey.com
SIC: 3829 Surveying instruments & accessories

(P-21513)
OPTIVUS PROTON THERAPY INC
1475 Victoria Ct, San Bernardino
(92408-2831)
P.O. Box 608, Loma Linda (92354-0608)
PHONE..................................909 799-8300
Jon W Slater, *CEO*
Daryl L Anderson, *CFO*
Raymond Terry, *Administration*
EMP: 75
SQ FT: 35,000
SALES (est): 17.6MM **Privately Held**
WEB: www.optivus.com
SIC: 3829 7371 8742 3699 Nuclear radiation & testing apparatus; custom computer programming services; maintenance management consultant; electrical equipment & supplies

(P-21514)
OTSUKA AMERICA INC (HQ)
1 Embarcadero Ctr # 2020, San Francisco
(94111-3750)
PHONE..................................415 986-5300
Hiromi Yoshikawa, *Ch of Bd*
Shun Uchida, *President*
Mark Vernon, *Officer*
Marin Charles, *Vice Pres*
David Gates, *Vice Pres*
◆ EMP: 10
SALES (est): 490.1MM **Privately Held**
SIC: 3829 3499 5122 2833 Spectrometers, liquid scintillation & nuclear; magnets, permanent: metallic; pharmaceuticals; vitamins, natural or synthetic: bulk, uncompounded; wines; mineral water, carbonated: packaged in cans, bottles, etc.

(P-21515)
OUSTER INC
350 Treat Ave Ste 1, San Francisco
(94110-1948)
PHONE..................................415 949-0108
Charles Pacala, *CEO*
Mark Frichtl, *COO*
Oliver Hutaff, *CFO*
Lisa Haugh, *Vice Pres*
Myra Pasek, *General Counsel*
EMP: 85 EST: 2015
SALES (est): 383.9K **Privately Held**
SIC: 3829 Surveying instruments & accessories

(P-21516)
PACIFIC DIVERSIFIED CAPITAL CO
101 Ash St, San Diego (92101-3017)
PHONE..................................619 696-2000
Steve Baum, *Ch of Bd*
Thomas Page, *Ch of Bd*
Henry Huta, *President*
Michael Lowell, *Vice Pres*
EMP: 800
SALES (est): 49.1MM
SALES (corp-wide): 11.6B **Publicly Held**
SIC: 3829 Measuring & controlling devices
HQ: San Diego Gas & Electric Company
8326 Century Park Ct
San Diego CA 92123
619 696-2000

(P-21517)
PACIFIC INSTRUMENTS INC
4080 Pike Ln, Concord (94520-1227)
PHONE..................................925 827-9010
John Hueckel, *President*
Norm Hueckel, *Vice Pres*
Morgan Butay, *Marketing Staff*
▲ EMP: 21
SQ FT: 18,000
SALES (est): 6.4MM
SALES (corp-wide): 299.7MM **Publicly Held**
WEB: www.pacificinstruments.com
SIC: 3829 Measuring & controlling devices

HQ: Vishay Precision Israel Ltd
26 Harokmim, Entrance
Holon 58858
355 708-88

(P-21518)
PACIFIC PRECISION LABS INC
Also Called: J M A R Precision Systems
9430 Lurline Ave, Chatsworth
(91311-6003)
PHONE..................................818 700-8977
Chandu Vanjani, *President*
Ed Laiche, *Sales Staff*
▲ EMP: 25
SQ FT: 10,000
SALES (est): 4.7MM **Privately Held**
SIC: 3829 Measuring & controlling devices

(P-21519)
PAVILION INTEGRATION CORP
2528 Qume Dr Ste 1, San Jose
(95131-1836)
PHONE..................................408 453-8801
Ningyi Luo, *President*
Beningyi Luo, *President*
Jason Cao, *Vice Pres*
EMP: 11
SQ FT: 3,000
SALES (est): 617.9K **Privately Held**
SIC: 3829 Instrumentation for reactor controls, auxiliary

(P-21520)
PHOENIX AERIAL SYSTEMS INC
10131 National Blvd, Los Angeles
(90034-3804)
PHONE..................................323 577-3366
Grayson Omans, *President*
EMP: 15
SQ FT: 1,500
SALES: 500K **Privately Held**
SIC: 3829 Surveying instruments & accessories

(P-21521)
PROCESS METRIX LLC
6622 Owens Dr, Pleasanton (94588-3334)
PHONE..................................925 460-0385
Michel Bonin,
Jared Hoog, *Partner*
Aaron Stibich, *Software Engr*
Thomas L Harvill,
Donald J Holve,
EMP: 12
SQ FT: 5,100
SALES (est): 2.7MM
SALES (corp-wide): 2.3B **Privately Held**
WEB: www.processmetrix.com
SIC: 3829 Instrumentation for reactor controls, auxiliary
PA: Vesuvius Plc
165 Fleet Street
London EC4A
207 822-0000

(P-21522)
PROMEGA BSYSTEMS SUNNYVALE INC
3945 Freedom Cir Ste 200, Santa Clara
(95054-1264)
PHONE..................................408 636-2400
William A Linton, *Principal*
EMP: 35
SQ FT: 20,000
SALES (est): 6.5MM
SALES (corp-wide): 420.8MM **Privately Held**
WEB: www.turnerbiosystems.com
SIC: 3829 Measuring & controlling devices
PA: Promega Corporation
2800 Woods Hollow Rd
Fitchburg WI 53711
608 274-4330

(P-21523)
PROPRIETARY CONTROLS SYSTEMS
Also Called: P C S C
3541 Challenger St, Torrance
(90503-1641)
PHONE..................................310 303-3600
Masami Kosaka, *President*
Robert K Takahashi, *Vice Pres*
EMP: 45
SQ FT: 29,000

SALES (est): 8.2MM
SALES (corp-wide): 8.6MM **Privately Held**
WEB: www.1pcsc.com
SIC: 3829 3669 Measuring & controlling devices; burglar alarm apparatus, electric
PA: Ttik Inc
3541 Challenger St
Torrance CA 90503
310 303-3600

(P-21524)
QUALITY CONTROL SOLUTIONS INC
43339 Bus Pk Dr Ste 101, Temecula
(92590-3636)
PHONE..................................951 676-1616
Louis Todd, *President*
Denise Todd, *Admin Sec*
EMP: 25
SQ FT: 7,500
SALES (est): 4.5MM **Privately Held**
WEB: www.qc-solutions.com
SIC: 3829 5084 Measuring & controlling devices; instruments & control equipment

(P-21525)
QUANTUM GROUP INC
6827 Nancy Ridge Dr, San Diego
(92121-2233)
PHONE..................................858 566-9959
Mark K Goldstein, *President*
Ivan Nelson, *Shareholder*
Robert Banach, *Vice Pres*
▲ EMP: 100
SALES (est): 18.7MM **Privately Held**
SIC: 3829 8732 7389 Fire detector systems, non-electric; research services, except laboratory; fire protection service other than forestry or public

(P-21526)
QUINT MEASURING SYSTEMS INC
Also Called: Quint Graphics
2922 Saklan Indian Dr, Walnut Creek
(94595-3911)
PHONE..................................510 351-9405
Carol Quint, *President*
Richard Quint, *Chairman*
▲ EMP: 10
SQ FT: 5,000
SALES: 2MM **Privately Held**
WEB: www.quintmeasuring.com
SIC: 3829 3552 Measuring & controlling devices; silk screens for textile industry

(P-21527)
RADCAL PARTNERS IA CALIFORNIA
426 W Duarte Rd, Monrovia (91016-4591)
PHONE..................................626 359-4575
J Howard Marshall III, *Chairman*
Paul B Sunde, *President*
John Crawford, *Treasurer*
Timothy Harrington, *Vice Pres*
John Lumsden, *Admin Sec*
EMP: 48 EST: 1977
SQ FT: 10,000
SALES (est): 6.4MM
SALES (corp-wide): 6.7MM **Privately Held**
WEB: www.radcal.com
SIC: 3829 Nuclear radiation & testing apparatus
PA: Radcal Corporation
426 W Duarte Rd
Monrovia CA 91016
626 359-4575

(P-21528)
RADIANT DETECTOR TECH LLC
19355 Bus Center Dr Ste 8, Northridge
(91324-3576)
PHONE..................................818 709-2468
Jan S Iwanczyk, *President*
Peter Lee, *Vice Pres*
EMP: 11
SQ FT: 15,000
SALES: 190K **Privately Held**
WEB: www.radiantdetectors.com
SIC: 3829 Nuclear radiation & testing apparatus

▲ = Import ▼=Export
◆ =Import/Export

(P-21529)
RAE SYSTEMS INC (DH)
1349 Moffett Park Dr, Sunnyvale
(94089-1134)
PHONE..................................408 952-8200
Robert Chen, *President*
Christopher Toney, *COO*
Michael Hansen, *CFO*
Ming Ting Tang PHD, *Exec VP*
Thomas N Gre, *Vice Pres*
▲ EMP: 104
SQ FT: 67,000
SALES (est): 98.7MM
SALES (corp-wide): 41.8B **Publicly Held**
SIC: 3829 3812 3699 Gas detectors;
search & detection systems & instru-
ments; security control equipment & sys-
tems
HQ: Honeywell Analytics Inc.
405 Barclay Blvd
Lincolnshire IL 60069
847 955-8200

(P-21530)
RAYTHEON COMPANY
1801 Hughes Dr Dd311, Fullerton
(92833-2200)
PHONE..................................714 446-2287
John Coarse, *President*
Kelly Allison, *Principal*
EMP: 80
SALES (corp-wide): 27B **Publicly Held**
SIC: 3829 7371 3578 Toll booths, auto-
matic; custom computer programming
services; calculating & accounting equip-
ment
PA: Raytheon Company
870 Winter St
Waltham MA 02451
781 522-3000

(P-21531)
RHEOSENSE INC
2420 Camino Ramon Ste 240, San Ramon
(94583-4319)
PHONE..................................925 866-3801
Seong-Gi Baek, *CEO*
EMP: 14
SQ FT: 1,400
SALES (est): 3.5MM **Privately Held**
WEB: www.rheosense.com
SIC: 3829 Breathalyzers

(P-21532)
SANTA CLARA IMAGING
Also Called: SCI
1825 Civic Center Dr # 1, Santa Clara
(95050-7302)
PHONE..................................408 296-5555
Reza Hashemieh, *Principal*
EMP: 40
SALES (est): 4.6MM **Privately Held**
SIC: 3829 8099 Measuring & controlling
devices; blood related health services

(P-21533)
SECO MANUFACTURING
COMPANY INC
4155 Oasis Rd, Redding (96003-0859)
PHONE..................................530 225-8155
Steven W Berglund, *CEO*
Mike Dahl, *General Mgr*
▲ EMP: 120 EST: 1978
SQ FT: 73,400
SALES (est): 31.8MM
SALES (corp-wide): 3.1B **Publicly Held**
WEB: www.surveying.com
SIC: 3829 Surveying instruments & acces-
sories
PA: Trimble Inc.
935 Stewart Dr
Sunnyvale CA 94085
408 481-8000

(P-21534)
SEMCO
1495 S Gage St, San Bernardino
(92408-2835)
PHONE..................................909 799-9666
Shawn Martin, *Owner*
▲ EMP: 25
SQ FT: 5,400

SALES: 2MM **Privately Held**
SIC: 3829 3599 Physical property testing
equipment; machine shop, jobbing & repair

(P-21535)
SENSO-METRICS INC
4584 Runway St, Simi Valley (93063-3449)
PHONE..................................805 527-3640
Gary Johnson, *President*
Joan P Evans, *Corp Secy*
John Smith, *Exec VP*
EMP: 16 EST: 1972
SQ FT: 16,288
SALES: 4.5MM **Privately Held**
WEB: www.senso-metrics.com
SIC: 3829 5084 Measuring & controlling
devices; industrial machinery & equip-
ment

(P-21536)
SENTINEL HYDROSOLUTIONS
LLC
1223 Pacific Oaks Pl # 104, Escondido
(92029-2913)
PHONE..................................866 410-1134
Scott Pallais, *Chairman*
Stephanie Lafica, *Director*
EMP: 12
SQ FT: 3,500
SALES: 1.1MM **Privately Held**
SIC: 3829 Liquid leak detection equipment

(P-21537)
SENTRAN L L C (PA)
4355 E Lowell St Ste F, Ontario
(91761-2225)
PHONE..................................888 545-8988
Ken Kramer, *CEO*
Carlos Valdes, *COO*
Jorge Valdes, *Persnl Dir*
Manuel Haro, *Buyer*
Tim Petersen, *QC Mgr*
▲ EMP: 19
SQ FT: 5,000
SALES (est): 4MM **Privately Held**
WEB: www.sentranllc.com
SIC: 3829 Measuring & controlling devices

(P-21538)
SIERRA MONITOR
CORPORATION (HQ)
1991 Tarob Ct, Milpitas (95035-6840)
PHONE..................................408 262-6611
Nishan J Vartanian, *President*
▲ EMP: 56
SQ FT: 28,000
SALES: 22MM
SALES (corp-wide): 1.3B **Publicly Held**
WEB: www.sierramonitor.com
SIC: 3829 3822 Measuring & controlling
devices; auto controls regulating residntl
& coml environmt & applncs
PA: Msa Safety Incorporated
1000 Cranberry Woods Dr
Cranberry Township PA 16066
724 776-8600

(P-21539)
SIMON HARRISON
Also Called: Mri
551 5th St Ste A, San Fernando
(91340-2268)
PHONE..................................818 898-1036
Simon Harrison, *Owner*
EMP: 30
SALES (est): 1.9MM **Privately Held**
WEB: www.simonharrison.com
SIC: 3829 Torsion testing equipment

(P-21540)
SIMPA NETWORKS INC
2595 Mission St Ste 300, San Francisco
(94110-2574)
PHONE..................................415 216-3204
Michael Macharg, *Director*
EMP: 10
SALES (est): 600K **Privately Held**
SIC: 3829 Measuring & controlling devices

(P-21541)
SKF CONDITION MONITORING
INC (DH)
Also Called: SKF Aptitude Exchange
9444 Balboa Ave 150, San Diego
(92123-4377)
PHONE..................................858 496-3400
Mark McGinn, *CEO*
Kevin Haskell, *Database Admin*
Buddy Wynn, *Sales Staff*
Robert Kaufman, *Manager*
Kirk Tisdale, *Manager*
EMP: 120
SQ FT: 31,000
SALES (est): 17.9MM
SALES (corp-wide): 9.5B **Privately Held**
WEB: www.skfcm.com
SIC: 3829 Vibration meters, analyzers &
calibrators
HQ: Skf Usa Inc.
890 Forty Foot Rd
Lansdale PA 19446
267 436-6000

(P-21542)
SOBERLINK HEALTHCARE LLC
16787 Beach Blvd 211, Huntington Beach
(92647-4848)
PHONE..................................714 975-7200
Brad Keays, *CEO*
EMP: 13
SALES (est): 1.1MM **Privately Held**
SIC: 3829 Breathalyzers

(P-21543)
SOILMOISTURE EQUIPMENT
CORP
801 S Kellogg Ave, Goleta (93117-3886)
P.O. Box 30025, Santa Barbara (93130-
0025)
PHONE..................................805 964-3525
Whitney Skaling, *CEO*
Kenneth Macaulay, *CFO*
Percy E Skaling, *Principal*
Jan Skaling, *Admin Sec*
Bob Elliott,
▲ EMP: 23 EST: 1950
SQ FT: 14,000
SALES (est): 5.5MM **Privately Held**
WEB: www.soilmoisture.com
SIC: 3829 Measuring & controlling devices

(P-21544)
SOLANO DIAGNOSTICS
IMAGING
1101 B Gale Wilson Blvd # 100, Fairfield
(94533-3771)
PHONE..................................707 646-4646
Adrian Ritts, *Manager*
Laverna Hubbard, *Administration*
EMP: 15
SQ FT: 4,000
SALES (est): 2.8MM **Privately Held**
SIC: 3829 8071 8011 Medical diagnostic
systems, nuclear; medical laboratories;
radiologist

(P-21545)
SOLMETRIC CORPORATION
Also Called: Suneye
117 Morris St Ste 100, Sebastopol
(95472-3846)
PHONE..................................707 823-4600
Macdonald Willand, *President*
Robert Macdonald, *VP Finance*
▲ EMP: 26
SALES: 3.6MM
SALES (corp-wide): 757.5MM **Publicly
Held**
SIC: 3829 Solarimeters
HQ: Vivint Solar, Inc.
1800 W Ashton Blvd
Lehi UT 84043
877 404-4129

(P-21546)
SPECTRAL DYNAMICS INC (PA)
2199 Zanker Rd, San Jose (95131-2109)
PHONE..................................760 761-0440
Stewart J Slykhous, *CEO*
James D Tucker, *CFO*
▲ EMP: 20
SQ FT: 12,000

SALES (est): 8.6MM **Privately Held**
WEB: www.spectraldynamics.com
SIC: 3829 Measuring & controlling devices

(P-21547)
SPECTRAL LABS
INCORPORATED
15920 Bernardo Center Dr, San Diego
(92127-1828)
PHONE..................................858 451-0540
James H Winso, *President*
John Rolando, *Shareholder*
Eric Ackermann, *Vice Pres*
James Adams, *Project Mgr*
EMP: 20
SQ FT: 2,000
SALES (est): 400K **Privately Held**
SIC: 3829 Measuring & controlling devices

(P-21548)
SPIRACLE TECHNOLOGY LLC
10601 Calle Lee Ste 190, Los Alamitos
(90720-6788)
PHONE..................................714 418-1091
Michael Farne, *Mng Member*
▲ EMP: 10
SQ FT: 7,000
SALES (est): 1.5MM **Privately Held**
SIC: 3829 Measuring & controlling devices

(P-21549)
SYSTEMS INTEGRATED LLC
2200 N Glassell St Ste A, Orange
(92865-2771)
PHONE..................................714 998-0900
Susan Corrales-Diaz, *CEO*
John Holbrook, *Director*
EMP: 41
SQ FT: 7,000
SALES (est): 7.2MM **Privately Held**
SIC: 3829 Measuring & controlling devices

(P-21550)
SYSTEMS L C WOMACK
1615 Yeager Ave, La Verne (91750-5854)
PHONE..................................909 593-7304
Mike Rowlett, *President*
EMP: 10
SALES (corp-wide): 85.3MM **Privately
Held**
SIC: 3829 7373 3594 Aircraft & motor ve-
hicle measurement equipment; systems
integration services; pumps, hydraulic
power transfer
HQ: Womack Systems, L.C.
13835 Senlac Dr
Farmers Branch TX 75234
214 357-3871

(P-21551)
TEK84 INC
13495 Gregg St, Poway (92064-7135)
PHONE..................................858 676-5382
Steven W Smith, *Mng Member*
Barbara Hatfield,
EMP: 30
SALES (est): 825K **Privately Held**
SIC: 3829 Measuring & controlling devices

(P-21552)
TEKVISIONS INC (PA)
Also Called: Tekvisions Tuchscreen Solutions
40970 Anza Rd, Temecula (92592-9368)
PHONE..................................951 506-9709
Tom Cramer, *President*
Nicholas Christie, *Corp Secy*
Doug Bowe, *Vice Pres*
▲ EMP: 10
SQ FT: 1,880
SALES (est): 4MM **Privately Held**
WEB: www.tekvisions.com
SIC: 3829 5045 Measuring & controlling
devices; computer peripheral equipment

(P-21553)
TELATEMP CORPORATION
2910 E La Palma Ave Ste C, Anaheim
(92806-2618)
PHONE..................................714 414-0343
Daniel Stack, *President*
Evelyn Darringer, *Vice Pres*
EMP: 12
SQ FT: 3,200

SALES: 3MM **Privately Held**
WEB: www.telatemp.com
SIC: 3829 Thermometers & temperature sensors

(P-21554)
TELEDYNE DGITAL IMAGING US INC
Also Called: Teledyne RAD-Icon Imaging
765 Sycamore Dr, Milpitas (95035-7465)
PHONE..............................408 736-6000
EMP: 15
SALES (corp-wide): 2.9B **Publicly Held**
SIC: 3829 3674 Measuring & controlling devices; semiconductors & related devices
HQ: Teledyne Digital Imaging Us, Inc.
700 Technology Park Dr # 2
Billerica MA 01821
978 670-2000

(P-21555)
TELEDYNE INSTRUMENTS INC
Also Called: Teledyne API
9970 Carroll Canyon Rd A, San Diego (92131-1106)
PHONE..............................619 239-5959
Jeff Franks, *Branch Mgr*
Daryl Goodwin, *Technician*
Michael Parker, *Technology*
EMP: 100
SALES (corp-wide): 2.9B **Publicly Held**
WEB: www.teledynesolutions.com
SIC: 3829 3823 Measuring & controlling devices; industrial instrmnts msrmnt display/control process variable
HQ: Teledyne Instruments, Inc.
1049 Camino Dos Rios
Thousand Oaks CA 91360
805 373-4545

(P-21556)
TEMPTRON ENGINEERING INC
7823 Deering Ave, Canoga Park (91304-5006)
PHONE..............................818 346-4900
Edward Skei, *President*
Beverly Skei, *Treasurer*
Anna Vartanian, *Accountant*
EMP: 35 EST: 1971
SQ FT: 13,000
SALES (est): 6.9MM **Privately Held**
SIC: 3829 3769 3823 Measuring & controlling devices; guided missile & space vehicle parts & auxiliary equipment; temperature instruments: industrial process type

(P-21557)
THERM-X OF CALIFORNIA INC (PA)
3200 Investment Blvd, Hayward (94545-3807)
P.O. Box 768, Alamo (94507-0768)
PHONE..............................510 441-7566
Dan Trujillo, *CEO*
Skip Johnson, *President*
Linda Trujillo, *Corp Secy*
Otto Amezquita, *Prgrmr*
Raymund Cruz, *Engineer*
EMP: 191 EST: 1983
SQ FT: 74,300
SALES (est): 39.7MM **Privately Held**
WEB: www.therm-x.com
SIC: 3829 Measuring & controlling devices

(P-21558)
TOPCON POSITIONING SYSTEMS INC (DH)
7400 National Dr, Livermore (94550-7340)
PHONE..............................925 245-8300
Raymond O'Connor, *President*
David Mudrick, *CFO*
M Yamazaki, *Exec VP*
Mark S Bittner, *Senior VP*
Joe Brabec, *Senior VP*
◆ EMP: 122
SQ FT: 80,000
SALES (est): 108.5MM **Privately Held**
WEB: www.topconlaser.com
SIC: 3829 3625 3823 3699 Surveying instruments & accessories; relays & industrial controls; industrial instrmnts msrmnt display/control process variable; electrical equipment & supplies; surveying services; excavation work

HQ: Topcon America Corporation
111 Bauer Dr
Oakland NJ 07436
201 599-5100

(P-21559)
TRIMBLE INC (PA)
935 Stewart Dr, Sunnyvale (94085-3913)
PHONE..............................408 481-8000
Steven W Berglund, *President*
Ulf J Johansson, *Ch of Bd*
Robert G Painter, *CFO*
Michael D Bank, *Senior VP*
Ronald J Bisio, *Senior VP*
◆ EMP: 750 EST: 1978
SQ FT: 139,000
SALES: 3.1B **Publicly Held**
WEB: www.trimble.com
SIC: 3829 3812 Measuring & controlling devices; navigational systems & instruments

(P-21560)
TRUTOUCH TECHNOLOGIES INC
2020 Iowa Ave Ste 102, Riverside (92507-2417)
PHONE..............................909 703-5963
Benjamin Ver Steeg, *CEO*
Oscar Lazaro, *Partner*
David Desrochers, *CFO*
Gerald Grafe, *Admin Sec*
Ries Robinson, *Director*
EMP: 14
SQ FT: 5,000
SALES (est): 2.3MM **Privately Held**
WEB: www.trutouchtechnologies.com
SIC: 3829 Measuring & controlling devices

(P-21561)
UNITED TESTING SYSTEMS INC
1375 S Acacia Ave, Fullerton (92831-5315)
PHONE..............................714 638-2322
Carol M Watson, *President*
Paul Mumford, *Vice Pres*
Cliff Schaffer, *Vice Pres*
Thomas D Settimi, *Vice Pres*
Syed Ahmed, *Managing Dir*
▲ EMP: 52 EST: 1964
SALES: 7.9MM **Privately Held**
SIC: 3829 8734 5084 Hardness testing equipment; tensile strength testing equipment; calibration & certification; industrial machinery & equipment

(P-21562)
US NUCLEAR CORP (PA)
7051 Eton Ave, Canoga Park (91303-2112)
PHONE..............................818 296-0746
Robert Goldstein, *CEO*
Richard Landry, *COO*
Darian Andersen, *CFO*
EMP: 16
SALES (est): 1.6MM **Privately Held**
SIC: 3829 Nuclear radiation & testing apparatus

(P-21563)
VIBRATION IMPACT & PRES
Also Called: VIP Sensors
32242 Paseo Adelanto C, San Juan Capistrano (92675-3610)
PHONE..............................949 429-3558
Alex Karolys, *Owner*
EMP: 10
SALES (est): 1MM **Privately Held**
WEB: www.vipsensors.com
SIC: 3829 Measuring & controlling devices

(P-21564)
WELLBORE NAVIGATION INC (PA)
Also Called: Welnav
1240 N Jefferson St Ste M, Anaheim (92807-1632)
PHONE..............................714 259-7760
Charles Ron Adams, *President*
Sandy Adams, *Admin Sec*
EMP: 15 EST: 1981
SQ FT: 7,000
SALES (est): 2MM **Privately Held**
WEB: www.welnavinc.com
SIC: 3829 1381 7371 Surveying instruments & accessories; directional drilling oil & gas wells; computer software development

(P-21565)
XIA LLC
31057 Genstar Rd, Hayward (94544-7831)
PHONE..............................510 494-9020
William K Warburton,
Michael Sears, *Vice Pres*
Karl Meyer, *General Mgr*
Mark Daly, *Office Mgr*
Nicole Thomas, *Admin Asst*
EMP: 18
SQ FT: 8,000
SALES (est): 3.4MM **Privately Held**
WEB: www.xia.com
SIC: 3829 Measuring & controlling devices

(P-21566)
YS CONTROLS LLC
3041 S Shannon St, Santa Ana (92704-6320)
PHONE..............................714 641-0727
John Sapone, *President*
Tony Johnson, *President*
▲ EMP: 28
SQ FT: 10,080
SALES (est): 3.8MM
SALES (corp-wide): 4.3MM **Privately Held**
WEB: www.yscontrols.com
SIC: 3829 Measuring & controlling devices
PA: Maul Mfg., Inc.
3041 S Shannon St
Santa Ana CA 92704
714 641-0727

3841 Surgical & Medical Instrs & Apparatus

(P-21567)
3 GEN INC
31521 Rancho Viejo Rd # 104, San Juan Capistrano (92675-1868)
PHONE..............................949 481-6384
John Bottjer, *President*
Nizar Mullani,
Thorsten Trotzenberg,
EMP: 13
SQ FT: 3,000
SALES (est): 1.8MM **Privately Held**
WEB: www.epifluoroscope.com
SIC: 3841 Surgical & medical instruments

(P-21568)
5 I SCIENCES INC
16885 Via Del Campo Ct # 130, San Diego (92127-1744)
PHONE..............................858 943-4566
Richard M Rose MD, *CEO*
Jerome Aarestad, *Director*
EMP: 15
SALES (est): 133.1K **Privately Held**
SIC: 3841 Surgical & medical instruments

(P-21569)
AB MEDICAL TECHNOLOGIES INC
20272 Skypark Dr, Redding (96002-9250)
PHONE..............................530 605-2522
Tammy Blanton, *CEO*
Dwight Abbott, *President*
Ken Brown, *President*
EMP: 10
SQ FT: 7,000
SALES (est): 1.4MM **Privately Held**
SIC: 3841 Surgical & medical instruments

(P-21570)
ABBOTT LABORATORIES
Also Called: Abbott Diagnostics Division
4551 Great America Pkwy, Santa Clara (95054-1208)
PHONE..............................408 330-0057
Jim Janik, *Branch Mgr*
Manijeh Hosseini, *Project Mgr*
Jose Ochoa, *Project Mgr*
Karen Primero, *Project Mgr*
Ling Chen, *Research*
EMP: 450
SQ FT: 117,500
SALES (corp-wide): 30.5B **Publicly Held**
WEB: www.abbott.com
SIC: 3841 Medical instruments & equipment, blood & bone work

PA: Abbott Laboratories
100 Abbott Park Rd
Abbott Park IL 60064
224 667-6100

(P-21571)
ABBOTT LABORATORIES
Also Called: Abbott Vascular
3200 Lakeside Dr, Santa Clara (95054-2807)
P.O. Box 58167 (95052-8167)
PHONE..............................408 845-3000
Jean Reyda, *Branch Mgr*
Kathy Curtis, *Admin Sec*
Carol Parker, *Admin Asst*
Arlynne Wiley, *Project Mgr*
Jared Dodson, *Engineer*
EMP: 750
SALES (corp-wide): 30.5B **Publicly Held**
WEB: www.abbott.com
SIC: 3841 8731 Surgical & medical instruments; commercial physical research
PA: Abbott Laboratories
100 Abbott Park Rd
Abbott Park IL 60064
224 667-6100

(P-21572)
ABBOTT VASCULAR INC (HQ)
3200 Lakeside Dr, Santa Clara (95054-2807)
PHONE..............................408 845-3000
John M Capek, *President*
Charles D Foltz, *CEO*
Mark Murray, *CFO*
Chris Kinsey, *Admin Asst*
Traci Mellin, *Admin Asst*
▲ EMP: 275
SQ FT: 370,000
SALES (est): 701.6MM
SALES (corp-wide): 30.5B **Publicly Held**
WEB: www.abbottvascular.com
SIC: 3841 Surgical & medical instruments
PA: Abbott Laboratories
100 Abbott Park Rd
Abbott Park IL 60064
224 667-6100

(P-21573)
ABBOTT VASCULAR INC
42301 Zevo Dr Ste D, Temecula (92590-3731)
P.O. Box 9018 (92589-9018)
PHONE..............................951 914-2400
Rhonda Reddick, *Manager*
EMP: 31
SALES (corp-wide): 30.5B **Publicly Held**
WEB: www.abbottvascular.com
SIC: 3841 Catheters
HQ: Abbott Vascular Inc.
3200 Lakeside Dr
Santa Clara CA 95054
408 845-3000

(P-21574)
ABBOTT VASCULAR INC
30590 Cochise Cir, Murrieta (92563-2501)
P.O. Box 3020, North Chicago IL (60064-9320)
PHONE..............................408 845-3186
EMP: 200
SALES (corp-wide): 30.5B **Publicly Held**
WEB: www.abbottvascular.com
SIC: 3841 Surgical instruments & apparatus
HQ: Abbott Vascular Inc.
3200 Lakeside Dr
Santa Clara CA 95054
408 845-3000

(P-21575)
ACCESS CLOSURE INC
5452 Betsy Ross Dr, Santa Clara (95054-1101)
PHONE..............................408 610-6500
Gregory D Casciaro, *President*
Srey Soeung, *COO*
John J Buckley, *CFO*
Susan Aloyan, *Exec VP*
Stephen Mackinnon, *Vice Pres*
EMP: 344
SQ FT: 40,000

▲ = Import ▼=Export
◆ =Import/Export

SALES (est): 54.1MM
SALES (corp-wide): 145.5B **Publicly Held**
WEB: www.accessclosure.com
SIC: **3841** Surgical & medical instruments
PA: Cardinal Health, Inc.
      7000 Cardinal Pl
      Dublin OH 43017
      614 757-5000

(P-21576)
ACCESS SCIENTIFIC INC
1042 N El Camino Real, Encinitas
(92024-1322)
PHONE..............................858 354-8761
Steve Bierman, *CEO*
Bill Bold, *President*
EMP: 34
SQ FT: 2,700
SALES (est): 5.4MM **Privately Held**
SIC: **3841** Surgical & medical instruments

(P-21577)
ACCLARENT INC
31 Technology Dr Ste 200, Irvine
(92618-2302)
PHONE..............................650 687-5888
David Shepherd, *President*
John Chang, *Vice Pres*
Heather Wozniak, *Regional Mgr*
Andrew Drake, *Research*
Antoanela Gomard, *Engineer*
EMP: 400
SALES (est): 106.7MM
SALES (corp-wide): 81.5B **Publicly Held**
WEB: www.acclarent.com
SIC: **3841** Surgical & medical instruments
HQ: Ethicon Inc.
      Us Route 22
      Somerville NJ 08876
      732 524-0400

(P-21578)
ACCRIVA DGNOSTICS HOLDINGS INC (DH)
Also Called: Itc Nexus Holding Company
6260 Sequence Dr, San Diego
(92121-4358)
PHONE..............................858 404-8203
Scott Cramer, *CEO*
Greg Tibbitts, *CFO*
Tom Whalen, *Security Dir*
EMP: 350
SALES (est): 91.4MM
SALES (corp-wide): 115.1MM **Privately Held**
SIC: **3841** 2835 6719 Diagnostic apparatus, medical; blood derivative diagnostic agents; hemotology diagnostic agents; investment holding companies, except banks
HQ: Instrumentation Laboratory Company
      180 Hartwell Rd
      Bedford MA 01730
      781 861-0710

(P-21579)
ACCURAY INCORPORATED (PA)
1310 Chesapeake Ter, Sunnyvale
(94089-1100)
PHONE..............................408 716-4600
Joshua H Levine, *President*
Shigeyuki Hamamatsu, *CFO*
Suzanne Winter, *Officer*
▲ EMP: 117
SQ FT: 124,000
SALES: 418.7MM **Publicly Held**
WEB: www.accuray.com
SIC: **3841** Surgical instruments & apparatus

(P-21580)
ACCUTECH LLC
2641 La Mirada Dr, Vista (92081-8435)
PHONE..............................760 599-6555
Terrence Lee,
EMP: 30
SALES (est): 4.4MM **Privately Held**
WEB: www.cholestrak.com
SIC: **3841** Diagnostic apparatus, medical

(P-21581)
ADEPT MED INTERNATIONAL INC (PA)
665 Pleasant Valley Rd, Diamond Springs
(95619-9241)
PHONE..............................530 621-1220
Tim Quigley, *President*
Christine Quigley, *Vice Pres*
Chris Quigley, *MIS Staff*
EMP: 10
SQ FT: 6,500
SALES: 2MM **Privately Held**
WEB: www.adeptmed.com
SIC: **3841** Diagnostic apparatus, medical

(P-21582)
ADVANCED OXYGEN THERAPY INC (HQ)
3512 Seagate Way Ste 100, Oceanside
(92056-2688)
PHONE..............................760 431-4700
Mike Griffiths, *CEO*
EMP: 19
SALES (est): 3MM **Privately Held**
SIC: **3841** Diagnostic apparatus, medical
PA: Aoti, Inc.
      3512 Seagate Way Ste 100
      Oceanside CA 92056
      760 431-4700

(P-21583)
ADVANCED REFRACTIVE TECH
12518 Cavallo St, San Diego (92130-2740)
P.O. Box 910436 (92191-0436)
PHONE..............................949 940-1300
Randal Bailey, *President*
Laurence M Schreiber, *COO*
EMP: 15 EST: 1999
SQ FT: 10,000
SALES (est): 1.5MM **Privately Held**
WEB: www.advancedrefractive.com
SIC: **3841** Surgical & medical instruments

(P-21584)
ADVANCED STERILIZATION (HQ)
Also Called: A S P
33 Technology Dr, Irvine (92618-2346)
PHONE..............................800 595-0200
Bernard Zovighian, *CEO*
EMP: 45
SALES (est): 34MM
SALES (corp-wide): 6.4B **Publicly Held**
SIC: **3841** Surgical & medical instruments
PA: Fortive Corporation
      6920 Seaway Blvd
      Everett WA 98203
      425 446-5000

(P-21585)
ADVANCEDCATH TECHNOLOGIES LLC (HQ)
176 Component Dr, San Jose
(95131-1119)
PHONE..............................408 433-9505
Randall Sword, *CEO*
Lucian Bejinariu, *Vice Pres*
Tim Maes, *Vice Pres*
Monica Salathuraj, *Research*
Chris Mikkelson, *Engineer*
EMP: 32
SALES (est): 19.1MM
SALES (corp-wide): 13.9B **Privately Held**
WEB: www.advancedcath.com
SIC: **3841** Catheters
PA: Te Connectivity Ltd.
      Rheinstrasse 20
      Schaffhausen SH 8200
      526 336-677

(P-21586)
ALCON LENSX INC (DH)
15800 Alton Pkwy, Irvine (92618-3818)
PHONE..............................949 753-1393
Kevin J Buehler, *CEO*
Elaine Whitbeck,
Guy Holland, *Associate Dir*
Fei Liu, *Research*
Peter Goldbrunner, *Engineer*
EMP: 82 EST: 2006
SQ FT: 20,000
SALES (est): 22.7MM
SALES (corp-wide): 3.5B **Privately Held**
SIC: **3841** Surgical lasers

HQ: Alcon Laboratories Holding Corporation
      6201 South Fwy
      Fort Worth TX 76134
      817 293-0450

(P-21587)
ALCON VISION LLC
Also Called: Alcon Surgical
15800 Alton Pkwy, Irvine (92618-3818)
P.O. Box 19587 (92623-9587)
PHONE..............................949 753-6488
Kenneth Lickel, *Vice Pres*
Ed McGough, *Vice Pres*
Steve Ambrose, *Associate Dir*
Julie Hornung, *Admin Asst*
Jim Garwood, *Info Tech Mgr*
EMP: 600
SQ FT: 32,000
SALES (corp-wide): 3.5B **Privately Held**
WEB: www.alconlabs.com
SIC: **3841** 3851 5049 Surgical & medical instruments; ophthalmic goods; optical goods
HQ: Alcon Vision, Llc
      6201 South Fwy
      Fort Worth TX 76134
      817 293-0450

(P-21588)
ALCOTREVI INC
1133 S Central Ave 1, Glendale
(91204-2212)
PHONE..............................818 244-0400
Fredrik Der-Hacopian, *Director*
Dr Samvel Hmayakyan, *Bd of Directors*
EMP: 10
SALES (est): 680K **Privately Held**
SIC: **3841** Surgical & medical instruments

(P-21589)
ALEPH GROUP INC
Also Called: A G I
6920 Sycamore Canyon Blvd, Riverside
(92507-0781)
PHONE..............................951 213-4815
EMP: 14
SALES: 3MM **Privately Held**
SIC: **3841** 3843 8099

(P-21590)
ALL MANUFACTURERS INC
Also Called: Allied Harbor Aerospace Fas
2900 Palisades Dr, Corona (92880-9429)
PHONE..............................951 280-4200
Jon R Gerwin, *CEO*
Ron Gerwin, *President*
Jannat Robertson, *CFO*
Ron Tucker, *Manager*
EMP: 42
SQ FT: 30,000
SALES: 30MM **Privately Held**
WEB: www.allied1.com
SIC: **3841** 3694 Surgical & medical instruments; motors, starting: automotive & aircraft

(P-21591)
ALLIANCE MEDICAL PRODUCTS INC
Also Called: Siegfried Irvine
9342 9292 Jeronimo Rd, Irvine (92618)
PHONE..............................949 768-4690
Darrin Schellin, *CEO*
Brian Jones, *COO*
Dan Moore, *CFO*
Tom Lucas, *Vice Pres*
Calvin Witcher, *Info Tech Mgr*
▲ EMP: 130
SQ FT: 55,000
SALES (est): 98.7MM
SALES (corp-wide): 799.2MM **Privately Held**
SIC: **3841** 7819 Medical instruments & equipment, blood & bone work; laboratory service, motion picture
HQ: Siegfried Usa Holding , Inc.
      33 Industrial Park Rd
      Pennsville NJ 08070
      856 678-3601

(P-21592)
ALPHATEC HOLDINGS INC (PA)
5818 El Camino Real, Carlsbad
(92008-8816)
PHONE..............................760 431-9286

Terry M Rich, *CEO*
Mortimer Berkowitz III, *Ch of Bd*
Michael Plunkett, *President*
Patrick Miles, *Chairman*
Kristine M Jacques, *Chief Mktg Ofcr*
EMP: 36
SQ FT: 76,693
SALES: 91.6MM **Publicly Held**
SIC: **3841** Surgical & medical instruments

(P-21593)
ALPINE BIOMED CORP
1501 Industrial Rd, San Carlos
(94070-4111)
PHONE..............................650 802-0400
James B Hawkins, *President*
EMP: 120
SQ FT: 1,460
SALES (est): 6.4MM
SALES (corp-wide): 530.8MM **Publicly Held**
WEB: www.alpinebiomed.com
SIC: **3841** Catheters
PA: Natus Medical Incorporated
      6701 Koll Center Pkwy # 12
      Pleasanton CA 94566
      925 223-6700

(P-21594)
ALTHEA AJINOMOTO INC
Also Called: Ajinomoto Bio-Pharma Services
11040 Roselle St, San Diego (92121-1205)
PHONE..............................858 882-0123
J David Enloe Jr, *President*
Martha J Demski, *CFO*
Ej Brandreth, *Senior VP*
Chris Duffy, *Senior VP*
Bert Barbosa, *Vice Pres*
EMP: 164
SQ FT: 85,000
SALES (est): 86.2MM **Privately Held**
WEB: www.altheatech.com
SIC: **3841** 2836 Hypodermic needles & syringes; coagulation products
PA: Ajinomoto Co., Inc.
      1-15-1, Kyobashi
      Chuo-Ku TKY 104-0

(P-21595)
AMADA MIYACHI AMERICA INC
245 E El Norte St, Monrovia (91016-4828)
PHONE..............................626 303-5676
Susan Gu, *Manager*
EMP: 20 **Privately Held**
SIC: **3841** Surgical & medical instruments
HQ: Amada Miyachi America, Inc.
      1820 S Myrtle Ave
      Monrovia CA 91016

(P-21596)
AMEDICA BIOTECH INC
28301 Industrial Blvd K, Hayward
(94545-4429)
PHONE..............................510 785-5980
▲ EMP: 17
SALES (est): 1.7MM
SALES (corp-wide): 27.3B **Publicly Held**
WEB: www.amedicabiotech.com
SIC: **3841** 8731
HQ: Alere Inc.
      51 Sawyer Rd Ste 200
      Waltham MA 02453
      781 647-3900

(P-21597)
AMEDITECH INC
9940 Mesa Rim Rd, San Diego
(92121-2910)
PHONE..............................858 535-1968
Robert Joel, *Principal*
▲ EMP: 118 EST: 1999
SQ FT: 47,000
SALES (est): 22.7MM
SALES (corp-wide): 30.5B **Publicly Held**
WEB: www.ameditech.com
SIC: **3841** Medical instruments & equipment, blood & bone work
HQ: Alere Inc.
      51 Sawyer Rd Ste 200
      Waltham MA 02453
      781 647-3900

(P-21598)
AMERICAN MSTR TECH SCNTFIC INC
Also Called: American Histology Reagent Co
1330 Thurman St, Lodi (95240-3145)
P.O. Box 2539 (95241-2539)
PHONE.....................209 368-4031
Dan Eckert, *CEO*
Brandon B Jones, *President*
Kameron Teyes, *COO*
Jeff Kupp, *CFO*
▲ EMP: 126
SQ FT: 25,000
SALES (est): 5.5MM
SALES (corp-wide): 29.7MM **Privately Held**
WEB: www.americanmastertech.com
SIC: 3841 2835 Medical instruments & equipment, blood & bone work; cytology & histology diagnostic agents
PA: SImp, Llc
2090 Commerce Dr
Mckinney TX 75069
972 436-1010

(P-21599)
AMO USA INC
1700 E Saint Andrew Pl, Santa Ana (92705-4933)
PHONE.....................714 247-8200
Tom Frinzi, *President*
EMP: 200
SQ FT: 100,000
SALES: 1.1B
SALES (corp-wide): 81.5B **Publicly Held**
WEB: www.visx.com
SIC: 3841 3845 Surgical & medical instruments; laser systems & equipment, medical
HQ: Johnson & Johnson Surgical Vision, Inc.
1700 E Saint Andrew Pl
Santa Ana CA 92705
714 247-8200

(P-21600)
APAMA MEDICAL INC
745 Camden Ave Ste A, Campbell (95008-4146)
PHONE.....................408 903-4094
AMR Salahieh, *President*
John Buckley, *CFO*
Pj Iranitalab, *Development*
EMP: 15
SQ FT: 7,000
SALES (est): 3.3MM
SALES (corp-wide): 9.8B **Publicly Held**
SIC: 3841 Diagnostic apparatus, medical
PA: Boston Scientific Corporation
300 Boston Scientific Way
Marlborough MA 01752
508 683-4000

(P-21601)
APOLLO MED EXTRUSION TECH INC
3508 Seagate Way Ste 170, Oceanside (92056-2686)
PHONE.....................760 453-2944
EMP: 14
SALES (est): 2.1MM **Privately Held**
SIC: 3841 Surgical & medical instruments

(P-21602)
APPLIED CARDIAC SYSTEMS INC
1 Hughes Ste A, Irvine (92618-2021)
PHONE.....................949 855-9366
Loren A Manera, *CEO*
Tricia Meads, *CFO*
Susan Marcus, *Vice Pres*
Robert Wilks, *Admin Sec*
Sam Jaroudi, *Purch Mgr*
▲ EMP: 64 EST: 1981
SQ FT: 18,000
SALES (est): 11.8MM **Privately Held**
WEB: www.acsholter.com
SIC: 3841 Diagnostic apparatus, medical

(P-21603)
APPLIED MANUFACTURING LLC
22872 Avenida Empresa, Rcho STA Marg (92688-2650)
PHONE.....................949 713-8000

Tom Wachli, *President*
EMP: 1200
SALES (est): 30MM
SALES (corp-wide): 766.6MM **Privately Held**
SIC: 3841 Surgical & medical instruments
HQ: Applied Medical Resources Corporation
22872 Avenida Empresa
Rcho Sta Marg CA 92688
949 713-8000

(P-21604)
APPLIED MEDICAL CORPORATION (PA)
Also Called: Applied Medical Resources
22872 Avenida Empresa, Rcho STA Marg (92688-2650)
PHONE.....................949 713-8000
Said Hilal, *CEO*
Dennis Grosshans, *Vice Pres*
David Heaton, *Vice Pres*
Mary Stegwell, *Vice Pres*
Ed Judy, *District Mgr*
EMP: 150 EST: 1987
SALES (est): 766.6MM **Privately Held**
SIC: 3841 Surgical & medical instruments

(P-21605)
APPLIED MEDICAL RESOURCES CORP (HQ)
Also Called: Applied Medical Distribution
22872 Avenida Empresa, Rcho STA Marg (92688-2650)
PHONE.....................949 713-8000
Said S Hilal, *President*
Nabil Hilal, *President*
Gary Johnson, *President*
Stephen E Stanley, *President*
Michael Vaughn, *President*
▲ EMP: 277
SQ FT: 800,000
SALES: 544.3MM
SALES (corp-wide): 766.6MM **Privately Held**
WEB: www.acucise.com
SIC: 3841 Surgical & medical instruments
PA: Applied Medical Corporation
22872 Avenida Empresa
Rcho Sta Marg CA 92688
949 713-8000

(P-21606)
APPLIED SCIENCE INC (PA)
983 Golden Gate Ter, Grass Valley (95945-5938)
PHONE.....................530 273-8299
Jonathan G Morgan, *President*
Carmen Narayanan, *Office Mgr*
Robyn Perez, *Office Mgr*
Thomas Vick, *Purchasing*
Dale Richardson, *VP Sales*
◆ EMP: 17
SQ FT: 6,200
SALES (est): 1.8MM **Privately Held**
WEB: www.hemoflow.com
SIC: 3841 Surgical & medical instruments

(P-21607)
APRICOT DESIGNS INC
677 Arrow Grand Cir, Covina (91722-2146)
PHONE.....................626 966-3299
Felix Yiu, *CEO*
Xiao Duan, *Engineer*
Andrea Esparza, *Purchasing*
Jim Schools, *Mktg Dir*
Jeremy Lawton, *Sales Mgr*
▲ EMP: 38
SQ FT: 6,200
SALES (est): 8.2MM **Privately Held**
WEB: www.apricotdesign.com
SIC: 3841 Surgical & medical instruments

(P-21608)
ARDIAN INC
1380 Shorebird Way, Mountain View (94043-1338)
PHONE.....................650 417-6500
EMP: 11
SALES (est): 1.2MM **Publicly Held**
SIC: 3841
HQ: Medtronic, Inc.
710 Medtronic Pkwy
Minneapolis MN 55432
763 514-4000

(P-21609)
ARTHREX INC
460 Ward Dr Ste C, Santa Barbara (93111-2351)
PHONE.....................805 964-8104
EMP: 76
SALES (corp-wide): 400.2MM **Privately Held**
SIC: 3841 Diagnostic apparatus, medical
PA: Arthrex, Inc.
1370 Creekside Blvd
Naples FL 34108
239 643-5553

(P-21610)
ASPEN MEDICAL PRODUCTS LLC
6481 Oak Cyn, Irvine (92618-5202)
P.O. Box 22116, Pasadena (91185-0001)
PHONE.....................949 681-0200
Daniel J Williamson, *CEO*
▲ EMP: 70
SQ FT: 52,000
SALES (est): 26.2MM
SALES (corp-wide): 132MM **Privately Held**
WEB: www.aspenmp.com
SIC: 3841 Surgical & medical instruments
PA: Cogr, Inc.
140 E 45th St Fl 43
New York NY 10017
212 370-5600

(P-21611)
ASTHMATX INC
888 Ross Dr Ste 100, Sunnyvale (94089-1406)
PHONE.....................408 419-0100
Glen French, *President*
Debbie Brown, *Vice Pres*
Fearthal Hennessi, *Vice Pres*
Bill Wizeman, *Vice Pres*
Karen Passafaro, *VP Mktg*
EMP: 60
SQ FT: 22,000
SALES (est): 5.4MM
SALES (corp-wide): 9.8B **Publicly Held**
WEB: www.asthmatx.com
SIC: 3841 Surgical & medical instruments
PA: Boston Scientific Corporation
300 Boston Scientific Way
Marlborough MA 01752
508 683-4000

(P-21612)
ASTURA MEDICAL
Also Called: Hyghte Holdings
3186 Lionshead Ave # 100, Carlsbad (92010-4700)
PHONE.....................760 814-8047
Joel Gandrall, *President*
Megan Henley, *Principal*
EMP: 10
SQ FT: 4,500
SALES (est): 690.6K **Privately Held**
SIC: 3841 Surgical & medical instruments

(P-21613)
AURIS HEALTH INC (DH)
150 Shoreline Dr, Redwood City (94065-1400)
PHONE.....................650 610-0750
Frederic Moll, *CEO*
David M Styka, *CFO*
Josh Defonzo, *Officer*
Rob Rocha, *Engineer*
Joshua Wu, *Engineer*
EMP: 130 EST: 2007
SALES (est): 36.8MM
SALES (corp-wide): 81.5B **Publicly Held**
SIC: 3841 Surgical & medical instruments
HQ: Ethicon Inc.
Us Route 22
Somerville NJ 08876
732 524-0400

(P-21614)
AVAIL MEDSYSTEMS INC
380 Portage Ave, Palo Alto (94306-2244)
PHONE.....................650 772-1529
Roy Hefer, *Principal*
EMP: 20
SALES (est): 739.4K **Privately Held**
SIC: 3841 Surgical & medical instruments

(P-21615)
AVANTEC VASCULAR CORPORATION
870 Hermosa Ave, Sunnyvale (94085-4104)
PHONE.....................408 329-5400
Kiminori Toda, *CEO*
Motasim Sirhan, *President*
Jim Shy, *Vice Pres*
Nat Bowditch, *Principal*
Roger Farnholtz, *Engineer*
▲ EMP: 35
SALES: 122K **Privately Held**
WEB: www.avantecvascular.com
SIC: 3841 Medical instruments & equipment, blood & bone work

(P-21616)
AVINGER INC
400 Chesapeake Dr, Redwood City (94063-4739)
PHONE.....................650 241-7900
James G Cullen, *Ch of Bd*
Jeffrey M Soinski, *President*
Mark Weinswig, *CFO*
Donald Lucas, *Bd of Directors*
Patricia Kim, *Executive Asst*
EMP: 65
SQ FT: 44,200
SALES: 7.9MM **Privately Held**
SIC: 3841 Catheters

(P-21617)
B BRAUN MEDICAL INC
2525 Mcgaw Ave, Irvine (92614-5841)
P.O. Box 19791 (92623-9791)
PHONE.....................610 691-5400
Keith Klaes, *Manager*
Joe Garcia, *Officer*
Rose Radocha, *Admin Asst*
Nadine Nguyen, *Sr Ntwrk Engine*
Huaina LI, *Info Tech Mgr*
EMP: 1300
SALES (corp-wide): 2.6MM **Privately Held**
SIC: 3841 Catheters
HQ: B. Braun Medical Inc.
824 12th Ave
Bethlehem PA 18018
610 691-5400

(P-21618)
BAXALTA US INC
1700 Rancho Conejo Blvd, Thousand Oaks (91320-1424)
PHONE.....................805 498-8664
Paul Marshall, *Manager*
Scott Tinkel, *Business Dir*
Cristina Davis, *Project Leader*
Jesus Espinoza, *Technician*
Shawn Galastian, *Project Engr*
EMP: 500
SALES (corp-wide): 15.1B **Privately Held**
SIC: 3841 2835 2389 3842 Surgical & medical instruments; catheters; medical instruments & equipment, blood & bone work; surgical instruments & apparatus; blood derivative diagnostic agents; hospital gowns; surgical appliances & supplies; medical laboratory equipment; intravenous solutions
HQ: Baxalta Us Inc.
1200 Lakeside Dr
Bannockburn IL 60015
224 948-2000

(P-21619)
BAXTER HEALTHCARE CORPORATION
Also Called: Baxter Medication Delivery
17511 Armstrong Ave, Irvine (92614-5725)
PHONE.....................949 474-6301
Michael Mussallem, *Manager*
Charles Mooney, *Research*
James M Moralez, *Engineer*
Patti Bosalet, *Human Res Dir*
EMP: 250
SALES (corp-wide): 11.1B **Publicly Held**
SIC: 3841 Surgical & medical instruments
HQ: Baxter Healthcare Corporation
1 Baxter Pkwy
Deerfield IL 60015
224 948-2000

(P-21620)
BAXTER HEALTHCARE CORPORATION
Baxter Bentley
1402 Alton Pkwy, Irvine (92606-4838)
P.O. Box 11150, Santa Ana (92711-1150)
PHONE..............................949 250-2500
Mike Musalem, *President*
John McGrath, *Vice Pres*
Robert Reindl, *Human Res Mgr*
Joy Masline, *Manager*
EMP: 75
SQ FT: 72,000
SALES (corp-wide): 11.1B **Publicly Held**
SIC: 3841 Surgical & medical instruments
HQ: Baxter Healthcare Corporation
1 Baxter Pkwy
Deerfield IL 60015
224 948-2000

(P-21621)
BAYER CORPORATION
Pharmaceutical Division
820 Parker St, Berkeley (94710-2440)
P.O. Box 1986 (94701-1986)
PHONE.................................510 705-5000
Wolfgang Plischke, *President*
Bruce Rhodes, *Technician*
Anthony Hsieh, *Project Mgr*
Jefferson Douglas, *Research*
Nasir Hassan, *Engineer*
EMP: 500
SALES (corp-wide): 45.3B **Privately Held**
SIC: 3841 2834 Surgical & medical instruments; pharmaceutical preparations
HQ: Bayer Corporation
100 Bayer Rd Bldg 14
Pittsburgh PA 15205
412 777-2000

(P-21622)
BECKMAN COULTER INC
Beckman Coulter Diagnostics
250 S Kraemer Blvd, Brea (92821-6232)
P.O. Box 8000 (92822-8000)
PHONE.................................818 970-2161
Albert Ziegler, *Manager*
EMP: 200
SALES (corp-wide): 19.8B **Publicly Held**
WEB: www.beckman.com
SIC: 3841 3821 Surgical & medical instruments; clinical laboratory instruments, except medical & dental
HQ: Beckman Coulter, Inc.
250 S Kraemer Blvd
Brea CA 92821
714 993-5321

(P-21623)
BECTON DICKINSON AND COMPANY
10975 Torreyana Rd, San Diego (92121-1106)
PHONE.................................858 812-8800
Roger McFadden, *Branch Mgr*
EMP: 429
SALES (corp-wide): 15.9B **Publicly Held**
SIC: 3841 Hypodermic needles & syringes
PA: Becton, Dickinson And Company
1 Becton Dr
Franklin Lakes NJ 07417
201 847-6800

(P-21624)
BECTON DICKINSON AND COMPANY
Bd Biosciences
2350 Qume Dr, San Jose (95131-1812)
PHONE.................................408 432-9475
William Rhodes, *Principal*
Donna Boles, *Vice Pres*
Dinesh Gandhi, *Manager*
EMP: 332
SALES (corp-wide): 15.9B **Publicly Held**
SIC: 3841 3826 2899 2835 Surgical & medical instruments; analytical instruments; chemical preparations; in vitro & in vivo diagnostic substances
PA: Becton, Dickinson And Company
1 Becton Dr
Franklin Lakes NJ 07417
201 847-6800

(P-21625)
BECTON DICKINSON AND COMPANY
Also Called: Care Fusion Products
3750 Torrey View Ct, San Diego (92130-2622)
PHONE.................................888 876-4287
Michelle Younghouse, *Vice Pres*
Kathryn Uijtermerk, *Administration*
Nathan Dominguez, *Software Engr*
Rogina White, *Engineer*
Jeremy Woods, *Engineer*
EMP: 14
SALES (corp-wide): 15.9B **Publicly Held**
SIC: 3841 Surgical & medical instruments & equipment, blood & bone work
PA: Becton, Dickinson And Company
1 Becton Dr
Franklin Lakes NJ 07417
201 847-6800

(P-21626)
BENTEC MEDICAL OPCO LLC
1380 E Beamer St, Woodland (95776-6003)
PHONE.................................530 406-3333
JG Singh, *CEO*
Robert Nickson, *Purch Mgr*
Jason Rosecrans, *Purchasing*
EMP: 50 **EST:** 2016
SALES: 10MM **Privately Held**
SIC: 3841 Surgical & medical instruments

(P-21627)
BENTEC SCIENTIFIC LLC
1380 E Beamer St, Woodland (95776-6003)
PHONE.................................530 406-3333
Briant Benson,
EMP: 14
SQ FT: 17,000
SALES (est): 6.7MM **Privately Held**
SIC: 3841 Surgical & medical instruments

(P-21628)
BIO-MEDICAL DEVICES INC
Also Called: Maxair Systems
17171 Daimler St, Irvine (92614-5508)
PHONE.................................949 752-9642
Nick Herbert, *President*
Alan Davidner, *Shareholder*
Harry N Herbert, *CEO*
Ray Sadeghi, *General Mgr*
Areli Quezada, *Opers Staff*
▲ **EMP:** 37
SQ FT: 40,000
SALES (est): 10.2MM **Privately Held**
WEB: www.bmdi.com
SIC: 3841 2353 Surgical & medical instruments; hats, caps & millinery

(P-21629)
BIO-MEDICAL DEVICES INTL INC
17171 Daimler St, Irvine (92614-5508)
PHONE.................................800 443-3842
Nicholas Herbert, *President*
Larry Green, *Engineer*
Allan Schultz, *Director*
EMP: 11
SALES (est): 1.9MM **Privately Held**
SIC: 3841 2353 Surgical & medical instruments; hats, caps & millinery

(P-21630)
BIOCARE MEDICAL LLC
60 Berry Dr, Pacheco (94553-5601)
PHONE.................................925 603-8000
Nicolas Barthelemy, *Chairman*
Roy Yih,
Cindy Ali, *Senior Mgr*
Scott Cooper, *Accounts Exec*
▼ **EMP:** 154
SQ FT: 51,000
SALES (est): 36MM **Privately Held**
WEB: www.biocare.net
SIC: 3841 2835 5047 Diagnostic apparatus, medical; in vitro & in vivo diagnostic substances; diagnostic equipment, medical

(P-21631)
BIOCHECK INC
Also Called: Bio Check, Inc.
425 Eccles Ave, South San Francisco (94080-1902)
PHONE.................................650 573-1968

John Chen, *CEO*
EMP: 22
SQ FT: 7,000
SALES (est): 3.9MM **Privately Held**
WEB: www.biocheckinc.com
SIC: 3841 5047 Diagnostic apparatus, medical; diagnostic equipment, medical
PA: Origene Technologies, Inc.
9620 Med Ctr Dr Ste 200
Rockville MD 20850

(P-21632)
BIOFILM INC
3225 Executive Rdg, Vista (92081-8527)
PHONE.................................760 727-9030
Lisa A O'Carroll, *CEO*
Daniel Wray, *Ch of Bd*
Mike Adams, *COO*
Robert Dearmond, *Vice Pres*
Lois Wray, *Admin Sec*
EMP: 54
SQ FT: 61,000
SALES (est): 15.5MM **Privately Held**
WEB: www.biofilm.com
SIC: 3841 Surgical & medical instruments

(P-21633)
BIOGENERAL INC
9925 Mesa Rim Rd, San Diego (92121-2911)
PHONE.................................858 453-4451
Victor Wild, *President*
Carlos Alvarez, *Supervisor*
▲ **EMP:** 15
SALES (est): 3.9MM **Privately Held**
WEB: www.biogeneral.com
SIC: 3841 Surgical & medical instruments

(P-21634)
BIOGENEX LABORATORIES (PA)
49026 Milmont Dr, Fremont (94538-7301)
PHONE.................................510 824-1400
Krishan L Kalra, *CEO*
Satya Kalra, *Admin Sec*
Sunil Aggarwal, *Research*
Ajay Kumar, *Financial Analy*
Joseph Paul, *Mfg Mgr*
◆ **EMP:** 35
SQ FT: 31,000
SALES (est): 8.5MM **Privately Held**
WEB: www.biogenex.com
SIC: 3841 2835 8731 2819 Diagnostic apparatus, medical; cytology & histology diagnostic agents; commercial physical research; chemicals, reagent grade: refined from technical grade

(P-21635)
BIOINITIATIVES INC
7641 Galilee Rd Ste 110, Roseville (95678-7212)
PHONE.................................916 780-9100
Mark Sienkiewicz, *President*
Matthaus Dengler, *Vice Pres*
EMP: 36
SALES (est): 17.8MM **Privately Held**
SIC: 3841 Surgical & medical instruments

(P-21636)
BIOMERICA INC (PA)
17571 Von Karman Ave, Irvine (92614-6207)
PHONE.................................949 645-2111
Zackary Irani, *Ch of Bd*
Francis Capitanio, *President*
Janet Moore, *CFO*
Jane F Emerson, *Bd of Directors*
Patrick Garcia, *Mktg Dir*
▲ **EMP:** 39 **EST:** 1971
SQ FT: 22,000
SALES: 5.2MM **Publicly Held**
WEB: www.biomerica.com
SIC: 3841 Diagnostic apparatus, medical

(P-21637)
BIOSEAL
167 W Orangethorpe Ave, Placentia (92870-6922)
PHONE.................................714 528-4695
Bill Runion, *President*
Robert C Kopple, *Corp Secy*
Lauren Martin, *Human Resources*
Chad Carty, *Sales Staff*
Hailey Golden, *Sales Staff*
▲ **EMP:** 40

SQ FT: 8,500
SALES (est): 9MM **Privately Held**
WEB: www.biosealnet.com
SIC: 3841 5047 Surgical & medical instruments; hospital equipment & furniture

(P-21638)
BIOSIG TECHNOLOGIES INC
12424 Wilshire Blvd # 745, Los Angeles (90025-1240)
PHONE.................................310 620-9320
Kenneth L Londoner, *Ch of Bd*
Steve Chaussy, *CFO*
Seth Fischer, *Bd of Directors*
Don E Foley, *Bd of Directors*
Roy Tanaka, *Bd of Directors*
EMP: 20 **EST:** 2009
SQ FT: 4,000
SALES (est): 3.3MM **Privately Held**
SIC: 3841 Surgical & medical instruments

(P-21639)
BIT GROUP USA INC (PA)
Also Called: Bit Medtech
15870 Bernardo Center Dr, San Diego (92127-2320)
PHONE.................................858 613-1200
Marius Balger, *CEO*
Susanne Gottschalk, *CFO*
Valentin Kaiser, *Marketing Staff*
Brian Kelleher, *Mng Member*
▲ **EMP:** 70 **EST:** 1998
SQ FT: 35,000
SALES (est): 17.1MM **Privately Held**
WEB: www.bit-companies.com/bit-medtech
SIC: 3841 8711 Surgical & medical instruments; engineering services

(P-21640)
BOSTON SCIENTIFIC CORPORATION
28460 Avenue Stanford, Valencia (91355-4856)
PHONE.................................661 645-6668
Erin Fuller, *Principal*
Angela Malig, *Supervisor*
EMP: 285
SALES (corp-wide): 9.8B **Publicly Held**
SIC: 3841 Surgical & medical instruments
PA: Boston Scientific Corporation
300 Boston Scientific Way
Marlborough MA 01752
508 683-4000

(P-21641)
BOSTON SCIENTIFIC CORPORATION
Also Called: Boston Scientific - Valencia
25155 Rye Canyon Loop, Valencia (91355-5004)
PHONE.................................800 678-2575
Phill Tarves, *Manager*
Milad Girgis, *Vice Pres*
Lisa Welker-Finney, *Vice Pres*
Sandra Antoine, *Admin Asst*
Jennifer Rowland, *Admin Asst*
EMP: 45
SALES (corp-wide): 9.8B **Publicly Held**
WEB: www.bsci.com
SIC: 3841 Surgical & medical instruments
PA: Boston Scientific Corporation
300 Boston Scientific Way
Marlborough MA 01752
508 683-4000

(P-21642)
BRANAN MEDICAL CORPORATION (PA)
9940 Mesa Rim Rd, San Diego (92121-2910)
PHONE.................................949 598-7166
Cindy Horton, *CEO*
Raphael Wong, *President*
Beckie Chien, *Vice Pres*
▲ **EMP:** 30
SQ FT: 8,400
SALES (est): 4MM **Privately Held**
WEB: www.brananmedical.com
SIC: 3841 Diagnostic apparatus, medical

(P-21643)
BREG INC (HQ)
2885 Loker Ave E, Carlsbad (92010-6626)
PHONE.................................760 599-3000
Brad Lee, *President*

PRODUCTS & SVCS

Stuart M Essig, *Ch of Bd*
Aarti Gautam, *President*
Geoff Siegel, *President*
Aaron Heisler, *CFO*
▲ **EMP:** 200
SQ FT: 104,000
SALES: 24K
SALES (corp-wide): 330.2MM **Privately Held**
WEB: www.breg.com
SIC: 3841 Surgical & medical instruments
PA: Water Street Healthcare Partners Llc
　　444 W Lake St Ste 1800
　　Chicago IL 60606
　　312 506-2900

(P-21644)
BRIGHTWATER MEDICAL INC
42580 Rio Nedo, Temecula (92590-3727)
P.O. Box 1286, Murrieta (92564-1286)
PHONE....................951 290-3410
Harry Robert Smouse, *CEO*
EMP: 15 **EST:** 2014
SQ FT: 5,000
SALES (est): 550K
SALES (corp-wide): 882.7MM **Publicly Held**
SIC: 3841 Surgical & medical instruments
PA: Merit Medical Systems, Inc.
　　1600 W Merit Pkwy
　　South Jordan UT 84095
　　801 253-1600

(P-21645)
BRUIN BIOMETRICS LLC
10877 Wilshire Blvd # 1600, Los Angeles (90024-4371)
PHONE....................310 268-9494
Martin Burns, *CEO*
Michael Flesch, *CEO*
Scott Hayashi, *CFO*
Sara Barrington, *Exec VP*
Chanel Thompson, *Office Mgr*
EMP: 17
SQ FT: 3,000
SALES (est): 542.1K **Privately Held**
SIC: 3841 Diagnostic apparatus, medical

(P-21646)
CALBIOTECH INC
1935 Cordell Ct, El Cajon (92020-0911)
PHONE....................619 660-6162
Noori Barka, *President*
Ron Bonner, *Info Tech Mgr*
▼ **EMP:** 38
SQ FT: 22,500
SALES: 4MM
SALES (corp-wide): 120.7MM **Publicly Held**
WEB: www.calbiotech.com
SIC: 3841 8731 8071 Diagnostic apparatus, medical; medical research, commercial; medical laboratories
HQ: Erba Diagnostics Mannheim Gmbh
　　Mallaustr. 69-73
　　Mannheim 68219

(P-21647)
CALDERA MEDICAL INC
5171 Clareton Dr, Agoura Hills (91301-4523)
PHONE....................818 879-6555
Bryon L Merade, *Ch of Bd*
Jeff Hubauer, *COO*
David Hochman, *CFO*
Dan Keeffe, *Vice Pres*
Serena Augustine, *Engineer*
EMP: 70
SQ FT: 25,000
SALES (est): 2.6MM **Privately Held**
WEB: www.calderamedical.com
SIC: 3841 Surgical & medical instruments

(P-21648)
CAMINO NEUROCARE
5955 Pacific Center Blvd, San Diego (92121-4309)
PHONE....................858 455-1115
Tony Andrasfay, *Manager*
EMP: 100
SQ FT: 35,000
SALES (est): 9.5MM **Publicly Held**
WEB: www.integra-ls.com
SIC: 3841 Diagnostic apparatus, medical; blood pressure apparatus

PA: Integra Lifesciences Holdings Corporation
　　311 Enterprise Dr
　　Plainsboro NJ 08536

(P-21649)
CANARY MEDICAL USA LLC
2710 Loker Ave W Ste 350, Carlsbad (92010-6645)
PHONE....................760 448-5066
William Hunter, *CEO*
Constantina Darsaklis, *Administration*
Jeffrey M Gross, *CTO*
EMP: 12
SALES (est): 439K **Privately Held**
SIC: 3841 Surgical & medical instruments

(P-21650)
CAPISTRANO LABS INC
150 Calle Iglesia Ste B, San Clemente (92672-7550)
PHONE....................949 492-0390
Paul Meyers, *President*
Matt Stabley, *CFO*
Mike Martnick, *Senior Buyer*
EMP: 20
SQ FT: 8,000
SALES (est): 3.2MM **Privately Held**
WEB: www.capolabs.com
SIC: 3841 Diagnostic apparatus, medical

(P-21651)
CARDIVA MEDICAL INC
1615 Wyatt Dr, Santa Clara (95054-1587)
PHONE....................408 470-7100
John Russell, *President*
Rick Anderson, *Ch of Bd*
Glenn Foy, *President*
Malcolm Farnsworth, *CFO*
Randy Hubbell, *Officer*
EMP: 135
SALES (est): 30.7MM **Privately Held**
WEB: www.cardivamedical.com
SIC: 3841 Surgical & medical instruments

(P-21652)
CARE FUSION
10020 Pacific Mesa Blvd, San Diego (92121-4386)
PHONE....................858 617-2000
EMP: 704
SALES (est): 175.8MM **Privately Held**
SIC: 3841

(P-21653)
CAREFUSION 207 INC
1100 Bird Center Dr, Palm Springs (92262-8000)
PHONE....................760 778-7200
Edward Borkowski, *CFO*
Carol Zilm, *President*
Amarendra Duvvur, *Treasurer*
Mark Stauffer, *Officer*
Cathy Cooney, *Exec VP*
▲ **EMP:** 327
SALES (est): 31.7MM
SALES (corp-wide): 265.4MM **Privately Held**
SIC: 3841 8741 Surgical & medical instruments; nursing & personal care facility management
PA: Vyaire Holding Company
　　26125 N Riverwoods Blvd
　　Mettawa IL 60045
　　872 757-0114

(P-21654)
CAREFUSION 211 INC
22745 Savi Ranch Pkwy, Yorba Linda (92887-4668)
PHONE....................714 283-2228
David Mowry, *President*
David Stafford, *CFO*
Kevin Klemz, *Admin Sec*
EMP: 638
SALES (est): 866K
SALES (corp-wide): 265.4MM **Privately Held**
SIC: 3841 Surgical & medical instruments
HQ: Vyaire Medical, Inc.
　　26125 N Riverwoods Blvd # 1
　　Mettawa IL 60045
　　833 327-3284

(P-21655)
CAREFUSION 213 LLC (DH)
3750 Torrey View Ct, San Diego (92130-2622)
PHONE....................800 523-0502
David L Schlotterbeck, *CEO*
Dwight Windstead, *COO*
Edward Borkowski, *CFO*
◆ **EMP:** 450
SALES (est): 148.5MM
SALES (corp-wide): 15.9B **Publicly Held**
SIC: 3841 Surgical & medical instruments

(P-21656)
CAREFUSION CORPORATION
22745 Savi Ranch Pkwy, Yorba Linda (92887-4668)
PHONE....................800 231-2466
Bill Ross, *Branch Mgr*
Joshua Timmons, *Technician*
Richard Bongiovanni, *Research*
Haojun Fu, *Research*
Thomas McCollum, *Electrical Engi*
EMP: 35
SALES (corp-wide): 15.9B **Publicly Held**
SIC: 3841 Surgical & medical instruments
HQ: Carefusion Corporation
　　3750 Torrey View Ct
　　San Diego CA 92130

(P-21657)
CARL ZEISS MEDITEC PROD LLC
1040 S Vintage Ave Ste A, Ontario (91761-3631)
PHONE....................877 644-4657
Hans-Joachim Miesner, *President*
Paul Yun, *Treasurer*
James Thornton, *Admin Sec*
Min Qu, *Asst Treas*
EMP: 99
SQ FT: 67,000
SALES (est): 3.5MM
SALES (corp-wide): 449.3K **Privately Held**
SIC: 3841 Surgical & medical instruments
HQ: Carl Zeiss Meditec, Inc.
　　5160 Hacienda Dr
　　Dublin CA 94568
　　925 557-4100

(P-21658)
CARL ZEISS OPHTHALMIC SYSTEMS
5160 Hacienda Dr, Dublin (94568-7562)
PHONE....................925 557-4100
Lothar Coob, *President*
Victoria Doll, *Marketing Staff*
EMP: 230 **EST:** 2000
SALES (est): 12.4MM **Privately Held**
SIC: 3841 Medical instruments & equipment, blood & bone work

(P-21659)
CAROLINA LQUID CHMISTRIES CORP
510 W Central Ave Ste C, Brea (92821-3032)
P.O. Box 92249 (92822)
PHONE....................336 722-8910
Phil Shugart, *Branch Mgr*
Patricia Shugart, *Vice Pres*
David Dixon, *Technical Staff*
Lori Nicholson, *Technical Staff*
Bob Dupor, *Regl Sales Mgr*
EMP: 12
SALES (est): 1.5MM **Privately Held**
SIC: 3841 Surgical & medical instruments
PA: Carolina Liquid Chemistries Corporation
　　313 Gallimore Dairy Rd
　　Greensboro NC 27409

(P-21660)
CATHERA INC
627 National Ave, Mountain View (94043-2221)
PHONE....................650 388-5088
Aaron Berez, *CEO*
EMP: 15
SALES (est): 816.5K **Privately Held**
SIC: 3841 Surgical & medical instruments

(P-21661)
CEREBROTECH MEDICAL SYSTEMS (PA)
1048 Serpentine Ln # 301, Pleasanton (94566-4734)
PHONE....................925 399-5392
Carl O'Connell, *CEO*
John T Kilcoyne, *Ch of Bd*
Michell Levinson, *CEO*
EMP: 18
SALES (est): 3.3MM **Privately Held**
SIC: 3841 Diagnostic apparatus, medical

(P-21662)
CETERIX ORTHOPAEDICS INC
6500 Kaiser Dr Ste 120, Fremont (94555-3662)
PHONE....................650 241-1748
John McCutcheon, *President*
Michael Hendricksen, *COO*
Justin Saliman, *Chief Mktg Ofcr*
Patty Perla, *Human Resources*
Mark Saxton, *VP Sls/Mktg*
EMP: 28 **EST:** 2010
SALES (est): 6MM
SALES (corp-wide): 4.9B **Privately Held**
SIC: 3841 Surgical instruments & apparatus
PA: Smith & Nephew Plc
　　Building 5
　　Watford HERTS WD18
　　192 347-7100

(P-21663)
CHEN-TECH INDUSTRIES INC (DH)
Also Called: ATI Forged Products
9 Wrigley, Irvine (92618-2711)
PHONE....................949 855-6716
Richard Harshman, *CEO*
Shannon Ko, *President*
Cat Ton, *Accountant*
EMP: 38
SQ FT: 18,000
SALES (est): 13.7MM **Publicly Held**
WEB: www.aeroforge-tech.com
SIC: 3841 3769 3724 3463 Surgical & medical instruments; guided missile & space vehicle parts & auxiliary equipment; aircraft engines & engine parts; aluminum forgings
HQ: Ati Ladish Llc
　　5481 S Packard Ave
　　Cudahy WI 53110
　　414 747-2611

(P-21664)
CHROMOLOGIC LLC
1225 S Shamrock Ave, Monrovia (91016-4244)
PHONE....................626 381-9974
Naresh Menon, *Mng Member*
Tiffany Moreno, *Admin Asst*
EMP: 28
SALES (est): 4.8MM **Privately Held**
WEB: www.chromologic.com
SIC: 3841 Diagnostic apparatus, medical

(P-21665)
CIRTEC MEDICAL LLC
101b Cooper Ct, Los Gatos (95032-7604)
PHONE....................408 395-0443
Michael Forman, *Branch Mgr*
Erik Morgan, *Info Tech Dir*
Mike Mehle, *Senior Buyer*
Lisa Thorud, *Senior Buyer*
EMP: 60
SALES (corp-wide): 57.8MM **Privately Held**
WEB: www.cirtecmed.com
SIC: 3841 Surgical & medical instruments
PA: Cirtec Medical, Llc
　　99 Print Shop Rd
　　Enfield CT 55445
　　413 525-5700

(P-21666)
CLEARFLOW INC (PA)
140 Technology Dr Ste 100, Irvine (92618-2427)
PHONE....................714 916-5010
Paul Molloy, *President*
Michael Elniski, *Vice Pres*
Edward Boyle Jr, *Principal*
David Elderfield, *Managing Dir*

▲ = Import ▼=Export
◆ =Import/Export

Patty Miller, *Office Mgr*
EMP: 21
SALES: 244K **Privately Held**
SIC: 3841 3829 Surgical & medical instruments; thermometers, including digital: clinical

(P-21667)
COALIGN INNOVATIONS INC
2684 Middlefield Rd Ste A, Redwood City (94063-3479)
PHONE.........................888 714-4440
Paul Goeld, *CEO*
John Ashley, *Exec VP*
John Barrett, *Exec VP*
Joe Loy, *Vice Pres*
EMP: 20
SALES (est): 2.4MM **Privately Held**
SIC: 3841 5999 Medical instruments & equipment, blood & bone work; medical apparatus & supplies

(P-21668)
COMPANION MEDICAL INC
11011 Via Frontera Ste D, San Diego (92127-1752)
PHONE.........................858 522-0252
Sean Saint, *CEO*
Marty Holmquist, *Vice Pres*
Tiffani MAI, *Administration*
Michael Mensinger, *CTO*
EMP: 58
SALES (est): 246.5K **Privately Held**
SIC: 3841 Surgical & medical instruments

(P-21669)
COMPOSITE MANUFACTURING INC
Also Called: CMI
970 Calle Amanecer Ste D, San Clemente (92673-6250)
PHONE.........................949 361-7580
Roger Malcolm, *President*
Tim Salter, *CEO*
Louis Mahony, *CFO*
Kim Bobb, *Admin Asst*
Tawney Tucker, *Administration*
EMP: 36
SQ FT: 16,000
SALES (est): 7MM **Privately Held**
WEB: www.carbonfiber.com
SIC: 3841 3624 Operating tables; carbon & graphite products

(P-21670)
CONCENTRIC MEDICAL INC
47900 Bayside Pkwy, Fremont (94538-6515)
PHONE.........................650 938-2100
Maria Sainz, *President*
Brett Hale, *CFO*
EMP: 40
SQ FT: 22,000
SALES (est): 7.8MM
SALES (corp-wide): 13.6B **Publicly Held**
WEB: www.concentric-medical.com
SIC: 3841 Surgical & medical instruments
PA: Stryker Corporation
2825 Airview Blvd
Portage MI 49002
269 385-2600

(P-21671)
CONFLUENT MEDICAL TECH INC (PA)
47533 Westinghouse Dr, Fremont (94539-7463)
PHONE.........................510 683-2000
Dean Schauer, *CEO*
Tom Duerig, *President*
Doug Hutchison, *Officer*
Craig Bonsignore, *Vice Pres*
John Dicello, *Vice Pres*
◆ **EMP:** 300
SQ FT: 90,000
SALES (est): 182.4MM **Privately Held**
SIC: 3841 5047 Surgical & medical instruments; medical & hospital equipment

(P-21672)
COVIDIEN HOLDING INC
2101 Faraday Ave, Carlsbad (92008-7205)
PHONE.........................760 603-5020
Ed McCoy, *IT/INT Sup*
Jerome Agbayani, *Engineer*
Carlos Duran, *Analyst*

Julie Mallett, *Manager*
EMP: 21 **Privately Held**
SIC: 3841 Surgical & medical instruments
HQ: Covidien Holding Inc.
710 Medtronic Pkwy
Minneapolis MN 55432

(P-21673)
COVIDIEN HOLDING INC
Also Called: Covidien Kenmex
2475 Paseo De Las Amrcs A, San Diego (92154-7255)
PHONE.........................619 690-8500
Javira Gonzales, *Manager*
Vicente Cintora, *Engineer*
EMP: 1900 **Privately Held**
SIC: 3841 Surgical & medical instruments
HQ: Covidien Holding Inc.
710 Medtronic Pkwy
Minneapolis MN 55432

(P-21674)
COVIDIEN LP
Also Called: Vascular Therapies
9775 Toledo Way, Irvine (92618-1811)
PHONE.........................949 837-3700
Hal Hurwitz, *CFO*
Lindsay Kellner, *Buyer*
Marvin Le, *Production*
Jane Anderson, *Sales Staff*
Joel Harris, *Manager*
EMP: 500 **Privately Held**
SIC: 3841 Surgical & medical instruments
HQ: Covidien Lp
710 Medtronic Pkwy
Minneapolis MN 55432
763 514-4000

(P-21675)
CURAPHARM INC
10054 Prospect Ave Ste A, Santee (92071-4328)
PHONE.........................619 449-7388
Thomas Hnat, *CEO*
Alot Nigam, *President*
EMP: 10
SALES (est): 950.4K **Privately Held**
SIC: 3841 5047 Surgical & medical instruments; medical & hospital equipment

(P-21676)
CURE MEDICAL LLC (PA)
3471 Via Lido Ste 211, Newport Beach (92663-3929)
PHONE.........................800 570-1778
John Anderson, *CEO*
Ann E Kenowsky, *President*
Timothy Palmer, *COO*
Loren McFarland, *CFO*
▲ **EMP:** 12
SALES (est): 2.4MM **Privately Held**
SIC: 3841 Catheters

(P-21677)
DA VITA TUSTIN DIALYSIS CTR
Also Called: Devita Dialysis
2090 N Tustin Ave Ste 100, Santa Ana (92705-7869)
PHONE.........................714 835-2450
Kelly Seigler, *Administration*
EMP: 30
SALES (est): 2MM **Privately Held**
SIC: 3841 8092 Hemodialysis apparatus; kidney dialysis centers

(P-21678)
DAVID KOPF INSTRUMENTS
7324 Elmo St, Tujunga (91042-2205)
P.O. Box 636 (91043-0636)
PHONE.........................818 352-3274
Carl Koph, *CEO*
J David Kopf, *President*
Carol Kopf, *Treasurer*
Ernesto Zamudio, *Foreman/Supr*
EMP: 28
SQ FT: 13,836
SALES (est): 4.9MM **Privately Held**
WEB: www.kopfinstruments.net
SIC: 3841 Veterinarians' instruments & apparatus

(P-21679)
DEPUY SYNTHES PRODUCTS INC
130 Knowles Dr Ste E, Los Gatos (95032-1832)
PHONE.........................408 246-4300
EMP: 15
SALES (corp-wide): 81.5B **Publicly Held**
SIC: 3841 Diagnostic apparatus, medical
HQ: Depuy Synthes Products, Inc.
325 Paramount Dr
Raynham MA 02767
508 880-8100

(P-21680)
DERMANEW LLC
Also Called: Dermanew Institute
9461 Santa Monica Blvd, Beverly Hills (90210-4620)
PHONE.........................310 276-0457
Amby Longhofer, *Branch Mgr*
EMP: 10
SALES (corp-wide): 907.2K **Privately Held**
WEB: www.dermanew.com
SIC: 3841 7231 Skin grafting equipment; facial salons
PA: Dermanew, Llc
436 Smithwood Dr
Beverly Hills CA 90212
626 442-2813

(P-21681)
DESIGN CATAPULT MANUFACTURING
3609 W Macarthur Blvd # 805, Santa Ana (92704-6850)
PHONE.........................949 522-6789
Sam Iravantchi, *President*
William Wooten, *Principal*
EMP: 12 **EST:** 2018
SALES (est): 2.2MM **Privately Held**
SIC: 3841 Surgical & medical instruments

(P-21682)
DEXCOM INC (PA)
6340 Sequence Dr, San Diego (92121-4356)
PHONE.........................858 200-0200
Kevin Sayer, *Ch of Bd*
Kaare Larson, *Owner*
Quentin S Blackford, *COO*
Patrick M Murphy, *Ch Credit Ofcr*
Donald Abbey, *Exec VP*
EMP: 277
SQ FT: 470,900
SALES: 1B **Publicly Held**
WEB: www.dexcom.com
SIC: 3841 Diagnostic apparatus, medical

(P-21683)
DFINE INC (HQ)
3047 Orchard Pkwy, San Jose (95134-2024)
PHONE.........................408 321-9999
Greg Barrett, *President*
Rick Short, *CFO*
Cindee Van Vleck, *Vice Pres*
Tasha Christian, *Sales Staff*
Alex Janowski, *Sales Staff*
▲ **EMP:** 69
SQ FT: 18,000
SALES (est): 16.7MM
SALES (corp-wide): 882.7MM **Publicly Held**
SIC: 3841 Surgical & medical instruments
PA: Merit Medical Systems, Inc.
1600 W Merit Pkwy
South Jordan UT 84095
801 253-1600

(P-21684)
DIAGNOSTIXX CALIFORNIA CORP
Also Called: Immunalysis
829 Towne Center Dr, Pomona (91767-5901)
PHONE.........................909 482-0840
James R Soares PHD, *President*
Michael Vincent, *Vice Pres*
Mark Villoria, *Director*
Greg Dowdeswell, *Manager*
Guohong Wang, *Manager*
▲ **EMP:** 22
SQ FT: 11,000

SALES (est): 5.8MM **Privately Held**
WEB: www.immunalysis.com
SIC: 3841 2835 Diagnostic apparatus, medical; in vitro & in vivo diagnostic substances

(P-21685)
DIAMICS INC
6 Hamilton Landing # 200, Novato (94949-8270)
PHONE.........................415 883-0414
EMP: 12
SQ FT: 2,000
SALES (est): 97K **Privately Held**
WEB: www.diamics.com
SIC: 3841

(P-21686)
DIASOL INC (PA)
Also Called: Discount Medical Supply
1110 Arroyo St, San Fernando (91340-1824)
PHONE.........................818 838-7077
Monica Abeles, *President*
Mary Castillo, *Vice Pres*
EMP: 16
SALES (est): 10.3MM **Privately Held**
SIC: 3841 Surgical & medical instruments

(P-21687)
DIGITAL SURGERY SYSTEMS INC
315 Bollay Dr, Goleta (93117-2994)
PHONE.........................805 308-6909
Aidan Foley, *President*
Arthur Rice, *Chairman*
J Flagg Flanagan,
Kevin Foley,
Simon Raab,
EMP: 34
SQ FT: 7,800
SALES: 5MM **Privately Held**
SIC: 3841 Surgical & medical instruments

(P-21688)
DIH TECHNOLOGIES CO
8920 Activity Rd Ste A, San Diego (92126-4458)
P.O. Box 720231 (92172-0231)
PHONE.........................858 768-9816
Jason Chen, *President*
Yangning Xu, *Vice Pres*
Ian Xu, *CTO*
EMP: 10 **EST:** 2010
SQ FT: 6,000
SALES: 500K **Privately Held**
SIC: 3841 Medical instruments & equipment, blood & bone work

(P-21689)
DITEC CO
Also Called: Ditec Mfg.
1019 Mark Ave, Carpinteria (93013-2912)
PHONE.........................805 566-7800
Don L Cooper, *President*
Scott Cooper, *Vice Pres*
Deeanna Moore, *Human Res Mgr*
EMP: 13
SQ FT: 10,000
SALES (est): 1.8MM **Privately Held**
WEB: www.ditecmfg.com
SIC: 3841 3843 3545 Surgical instruments & apparatus; burs, dental; diamond cutting tools for turning, boring, burnishing, etc.

(P-21690)
DOSE MEDICAL CORPORATION
229 Avenida Fabricante, San Clemente (92672-7531)
PHONE.........................949 367-9600
Thomas W Burns, *CEO*
EMP: 15
SALES (est): 263.7K
SALES (corp-wide): 181.2MM **Publicly Held**
SIC: 3841 Eye examining instruments & apparatus
PA: Glaukos Corporation
229 Avenida Fabricante
San Clemente CA 92672
949 367-9600

(P-21691)
DUKE EMPIRICAL INC
2829 Mission St, Santa Cruz (95060-5755)
PHONE..................................831 420-1104
Robert C Laduca, *CEO*
EMP: 60
SQ FT: 9,000
SALES (est): 15.4MM **Privately Held**
WEB: www.dukeempirical.com
SIC: 3841 Diagnostic apparatus, medical

(P-21692)
DUPACO INC
4144 Avenda De La Plata, Oceanside (92056)
PHONE..................................760 758-4550
Gregory Jordan, *President*
Ken Cunningham, *CFO*
Julie Butler, *Executive*
EMP: 43
SQ FT: 30,000
SALES (est): 10.1MM **Privately Held**
WEB: www.dupacoinc.com
SIC: 3841 3845 Medical instruments &
equipment, blood & bone work; elec-
tromedical equipment

(P-21693)
EASYDIAL INC
181 Technology Dr Ste 150, Irvine (92618-2484)
PHONE..................................949 916-5851
Philippe Faurie, *CEO*
Clayton Poppe, *CTO*
Imelda Dela Torre, *Assistant*
EMP: 53
SALES (est): 10.8MM **Privately Held**
SIC: 3841 Hemodialysis apparatus

(P-21694)
ECA MEDICAL INSTRUMENTS (DH)
1107 Tourmaline Dr, Newbury Park (91320-1208)
PHONE..................................805 376-2509
John J Nino, *President*
James Schultz, *Exec VP*
Melissa Reyes, *Analyst*
Ron Zisman, *Controller*
Joe Brendle, *Director*
EMP: 22
SQ FT: 14,982
SALES (est): 5.8MM **Publicly Held**
WEB: www.ecamedical.com
SIC: 3841 Surgical & medical instruments
HQ: Acas, Llc
2 Bethesda Metro Ctr # 1200
Bethesda MD 20814
301 951-6122

(P-21695)
ECA MEDICAL INSTRUMENTS
Also Called: Electro Component Assembly
21615 Parthenia St, Canoga Park (91304-1517)
PHONE..................................818 998-7284
Yvonne Hairston, *Principal*
EMP: 20 **Publicly Held**
WEB: www.ecamedical.com
SIC: 3841 Surgical & medical instruments
HQ: Eca Medical Instruments
1107 Tourmaline Dr
Newbury Park CA 91320
805 376-2509

(P-21696)
EDWARDS LFSCIENCES CARDIAQ LLC
Also Called: Cardiaq Valve Technologies Inc
2 Jenner Ste 100, Irvine (92618-3832)
PHONE..................................949 387-2615
Robrecht Michiels, *CEO*
J Brent Ratz, *President*
Jan Champion, *Vice Pres*
Danny Baldo, *Engineer*
Julie Fan, *Analyst*
EMP: 12
SALES (est): 1.8MM
SALES (corp-wide): 3.7B **Publicly Held**
SIC: 3841 Surgical & medical instruments
PA: Edwards Lifesciences Corp
1 Edwards Way
Irvine CA 92614
949 250-2500

(P-21697)
EDWARDS LIFESCIENCES CORP
17192 Daimler St, Irvine (92614-5509)
PHONE..................................949 250-3783
EMP: 11
SALES (corp-wide): 3.7B **Publicly Held**
SIC: 3841 Surgical & medical instruments
PA: Edwards Lifesciences Corp
1 Edwards Way
Irvine CA 92614
949 250-2500

(P-21698)
EKLIN MEDICAL SYSTEMS INC
6359 Paseo Del Lago, Carlsbad (92011-1317)
PHONE..................................760 918-9626
Robert Antin, *President*
EMP: 92
SQ FT: 16,000
SALES (est): 5.7MM
SALES (corp-wide): 37.6B **Privately Held**
WEB: www.eklin.com
SIC: 3841 5047 Medical instruments &
equipment, blood & bone work; medical &
hospital equipment
HQ: Vca Inc.
12401 W Olympic Blvd
Los Angeles CA 90064
310 571-6500

(P-21699)
ELECTRONIC WAVEFORM LAB INC
5702 Bolsa Ave, Huntington Beach (92649-1128)
PHONE..................................714 843-0463
Ryan Haney, *President*
William Heaney, *President*
Kim Zink, *CFO*
Patricia Heaney, *Corp Secy*
Michael Heaney, *VP Mfg*
EMP: 25
SALES (est): 5.5MM **Privately Held**
WEB: www.h-wave.com
SIC: 3841 Anesthesia apparatus

(P-21700)
ELIXIR MEDICAL CORPORATION (PA)
920 N Mccarthy Blvd, Milpitas (95035-5128)
PHONE..................................408 636-2000
Motasim Sirhan, *CEO*
Vinayak Bhat, *Vice Pres*
Richard Castro, *Vice Pres*
Donna Collins, *Vice Pres*
Erin Mazzone, *Vice Pres*
EMP: 15
SQ FT: 15,000
SALES (est): 3.2MM **Privately Held**
SIC: 3841 Surgical & medical instruments

(P-21701)
ELLEX ISCIENCE
Also Called: Ellex Itrack
41316 Christy St, Fremont (94538-3115)
PHONE..................................510 291-1300
G Reis, *Principal*
EMP: 18
SALES (est): 3.2MM **Privately Held**
SIC: 3841 Surgical & medical instruments

(P-21702)
EMBOLX INC
530 Lakeside Dr Ste 200, Sunnyvale (94085-4063)
PHONE..................................408 990-2949
Michael Allen, *CEO*
John Layton, *Marketing Staff*
EMP: 12 EST: 2013
SALES (est): 983K **Privately Held**
SIC: 3841 Catheters

(P-21703)
ENDOLOGIX INC (PA)
2 Musick, Irvine (92618-1631)
PHONE..................................949 595-7200
John Onopchenko, *CEO*
Jeffrey S Brown, *COO*
Vaseem Mahboob, *CFO*
John D Zehren, *Ch Credit Ofcr*
Greg Morrow, *Chief Mktg Ofcr*
▲ EMP: 223

SALES: 156.4MM **Publicly Held**
WEB: www.endologix.com
SIC: 3841 Catheters

(P-21704)
ENTRA HEALTH SYSTEMS LLC
1300 N Johnson Ave # 100, El Cajon (92020-1653)
PHONE..................................877 458-2646
Richard C Strobridge, *CEO*
Bruce Ahern, *Chief Mktg Ofcr*
Larry Mahar, *CTO*
Matthew Weisensee, *VP Sales*
EMP: 25
SQ FT: 11,000
SALES: 10MM **Privately Held**
SIC: 3841 Surgical & medical instruments
HQ: Crf Inc.
4000 Chemical Rd Ste 400
Plymouth Meeting PA 19462
267 498-2300

(P-21705)
ENTROPY ENTERPRISES LLC
170 Seacliff Dr, Pismo Beach (93449-1715)
PHONE..................................805 305-1400
Kourosh Bagheri, *Principal*
EMP: 10 EST: 2013
SALES (est): 558.6K **Privately Held**
SIC: 3841 Surgical & medical instruments

(P-21706)
EPICA MEDICAL INNOVATIONS LLC
901 Calle Amanecer # 150, San Clemente (92673-4219)
PHONE..................................949 238-6323
Frank D'Amelio,
Jason Grace, *Project Mgr*
▲ EMP: 24 EST: 2012
SQ FT: 4,441
SALES: 4.5MM
SALES (corp-wide): 19.7MM **Privately Held**
SIC: 3841 5047 Surgical & medical instru-
ments; medical equipment & supplies
PA: Epica International, Inc.
901 Calle Amanecer # 150
San Clemente CA 92673
949 238-6323

(P-21707)
EPINEX DIAGNOSTICS INC
14351 Myford Rd Ste J, Tustin (92780-7038)
PHONE..................................949 660-7770
Asad R Zaidi, *President*
Jeff Byrd, *Vice Pres*
Henry J Smith, *CTO*
EMP: 30
SQ FT: 3,400
SALES (est): 5.4MM **Privately Held**
WEB: www.epinex.com
SIC: 3841 Diagnostic apparatus, medical

(P-21708)
EVOFEM INC
12400 High Bluff Dr # 600, San Diego (92130-3077)
PHONE..................................858 550-1900
Saundra Pelletier, *CEO*
Justin Jay File, *CFO*
Kelly Culwell, *Chief Mktg Ofcr*
Mary Jarosz, *Vice Pres*
Kris Larrabee, *Analyst*
▼ EMP: 12
SQ FT: 5,453
SALES (est): 4.6MM **Privately Held**
SIC: 3841 5047 8731 Surgical & medical
instruments; medical equipment & sup-
plies; biotechnical research, commercial

(P-21709)
EVOLVE MANUFACTURING TECH INC
47300 Bayside Pkwy, Fremont (94538-6516)
PHONE..................................650 968-9292
Noreen King, *President*
Dave Devine, *President*
Juliea Chu, *Purch Mgr*
Barbara Espinoza, *Purch Mgr*
Trang Tran, *Prdtn Mgr*
▲ EMP: 65
SQ FT: 45,000

SALES (est): 14.9MM **Privately Held**
WEB: www.evolvemfg.com
SIC: 3841 3674 8731 Ultrasonic medical
cleaning equipment; semiconductors &
related devices; biotechnical research,
commercial

(P-21710)
EYE CARE NETWORK OF CAL INC (PA)
345 Baker St, Costa Mesa (92626-4518)
PHONE..................................714 619-4660
Aspasia Shappet, *President*
EMP: 10 EST: 1976
SQ FT: 1,700
SALES (est): 24.6MM **Privately Held**
SIC: 3841 Eye examining instruments &
apparatus

(P-21711)
EYE MEDICAL GROUP SANTA CRUZ
515 Soquel Ave, Santa Cruz (95062-2378)
PHONE..................................831 426-2550
Laurie Marquez, *General Mgr*
EMP: 12
SALES (est): 1MM **Privately Held**
SIC: 3841 Optometers

(P-21712)
FC GLOBAL REALTY INCORPORATED
2375 Camino Vida Roble B, Carlsbad (92011-1506)
PHONE..................................760 602-3300
Jeff O'Donnel, *CEO*
Dennis M McGrath, *CFO*
Kevin Scanlon, *Exec VP*
Michele Pupach, *Director*
EMP: 25
SALES (corp-wide): 36K **Privately Held**
WEB: www.photomedex.com
SIC: 3841 Surgical lasers
PA: Fc Global Realty Incorporated
2300 Computer Rd Ste G26
Willow Grove PA 19090
215 619-3600

(P-21713)
FIRST CHOICE INTERNATIONAL
1201 W Artesia Blvd, Compton (90220-5305)
PHONE..................................310 537-1500
Mike Shah, *CEO*
Lidia Morales, *Sales Mgr*
EMP: 12
SALES: 250K **Privately Held**
SIC: 3841 Surgical & medical instruments

(P-21714)
FLUID LINE TECHNOLOGY CORP
9362 Eton Ave Ste A, Chatsworth (91311-5888)
P.O. Box 3116 (91313-3116)
PHONE..................................818 998-8848
Joseph Marcilese, *President*
Phillip Jaramilla, *Vice Pres*
▼ EMP: 25
SQ FT: 17,000
SALES (est): 4.7MM **Privately Held**
WEB: www.fluidlinetech.com
SIC: 3841 2833 Surgical & medical instru-
ments; medicinals & botanicals

(P-21715)
FLUXION BIOSCIENCES INC
1600 Harbor Bay Pkwy # 150, Alameda (94502-3011)
PHONE..................................650 241-4777
Jeff Jenson, *CEO*
Jody Beecher, *Vice Pres*
Niall Murphy, *Vice Pres*
Cristian Ionescu, *CTO*
Cristian Ionescuzanetti, *CTO*
▲ EMP: 30
SQ FT: 10,000
SALES (est): 5.4MM **Privately Held**
WEB: www.fluxionbio.com
SIC: 3841 Diagnostic apparatus, medical

▲ = Import ▼=Export
◆ =Import/Export

(P-21716)
FORSYTHE TECH WORLDWIDE
23924 Victory Blvd, Woodland Hills
(91367-1253)
PHONE..........................818 710-8694
Thomas Delahanty, President
Ingrid Vaynovsky, Manager
EMP: 10
SALES (est): 1.1MM Privately Held
WEB: www.forsythetechnologies.com
SIC: 3841 Diagnostic apparatus, medical

(P-21717)
FOUNDRY MED INNOVATIONS INC
Also Called: Toolbox Medical Innovations
1965 Kellogg Ave, Carlsbad (92008-6582)
PHONE..........................888 445-2333
John K Zeis, President
Jenn S Zeis, Vice Pres
Chris Da Costa, Engineer
Grant Ware, Marketing Staff
EMP: 17
SALES (est): 1.9MM Privately Held
SIC: 3841 Diagnostic apparatus, medical

(P-21718)
FRANS MANUFACTURING INC
126 N Vinewood St, Escondido
(92029-1332)
PHONE..........................760 741-9135
Frans Ketelaars, President
Michael Wibier, Vice Pres
EMP: 13 EST: 1980
SQ FT: 3,900
SALES (est): 2.1MM Privately Held
SIC: 3841 Surgical & medical instruments

(P-21719)
FZIOMED INC (PA)
231 Bonetti Dr, San Luis Obispo
(93401-7376)
PHONE..........................805 546-0610
John S Krelle, President
Ronald F Haynes, Ch of Bd
Sabino Loiodice, Vice Pres
Mark Miller, Senior Engr
Collette Canning, Human Resources
EMP: 40
SQ FT: 36,000
SALES (est): 8.5MM Privately Held
WEB: www.fzio.com
SIC: 3841 Surgical & medical instruments

(P-21720)
GALEN ROBOTICS INC
541 Jefferson Ave Ste 100, Redwood City
(94063-1700)
PHONE..........................408 502-5960
Bruce Lichorowic, President
Lori Munog, CFO
Feimo Shen, Vice Pres
David Sunders, CTO
EMP: 15 EST: 2016
SQ FT: 15,000
SALES (est): 528.8K Privately Held
SIC: 3841 Surgical instruments & apparatus

(P-21721)
GE VENTURES INC
2882 Sand Hill Rd Ste 240, Menlo Park
(94025-7057)
PHONE..........................650 233-3900
Sue Siegal, CEO
EMP: 30 EST: 2015
SALES (est): 3.2MM Privately Held
SIC: 3841 Surgical & medical instruments

(P-21722)
GENALYTE INC
10520 Wateridge Cir, San Diego
(92121-5782)
PHONE..........................858 956-1200
Cary Gunn, CEO
Kevin Lo, President
Todd Ritter, President
Kevin McGee, Officer
Rufus Burlingame, Vice Pres
EMP: 18
SQ FT: 4,035
SALES (est): 5MM Privately Held
WEB: www.genalyte.com
SIC: 3841 Diagnostic apparatus, medical

(P-21723)
GENMARK DIAGNOSTICS INC (PA)
5964 La Place Ct Ste 100, Carlsbad
(92008-8829)
PHONE..........................760 448-4300
Hany Massarany, President
James B McNally, Senior VP
Brian Mitchell, Senior VP
Eric Stier, Senior VP
EMP: 139
SQ FT: 53,000
SALES: 70.7MM Publicly Held
SIC: 3841 Surgical & medical instruments

(P-21724)
GLAUKOS CORPORATION (PA)
229 Avenida Fabricante, San Clemente
(92672-7531)
PHONE..........................949 367-9600
Thomas W Burns, President
William J Link, Ch of Bd
Chris M Calcaterra, COO
Joseph E Gilliam, CFO
Marc Stapley, Bd of Directors
EMP: 201
SALES: 181.2MM Publicly Held
WEB: www.glaukos.com
SIC: 3841 Eye examining instruments & apparatus

(P-21725)
GLYSENS INCORPORATED
3931 Sorrento Valley Blvd, San Diego
(92121-1402)
PHONE..........................858 638-7708
Bill Markle, CEO
Robert Engler, Officer
Timothy Routh, Vice Pres
Ott Anna, Administration
Joe Lucisano, CTO
EMP: 30
SALES (est): 360.2K Privately Held
WEB: www.glysens.com
SIC: 3841 Surgical & medical instruments

(P-21726)
GRIFFIN LABORATORIES
43379 Bus Pk Dr Ste 300, Temecula
(92590-3687)
PHONE..........................951 695-6727
Clifford J Griffin, President
Karen Griffin, Vice Pres
Eric Howell, Sales Staff
EMP: 10 EST: 1994
SQ FT: 5,000
SALES (est): 1.9MM Privately Held
WEB: www.griffinlab.com
SIC: 3841 Surgical & medical instruments

(P-21727)
GUIDANT SALES LLC
825 E Middlefield Rd, Mountain View
(94043-4025)
PHONE..........................650 965-2634
EMP: 35
SALES (corp-wide): 9.8B Publicly Held
WEB: www.guidant.com
SIC: 3841 Surgical & medical instruments
HQ: Guidant Sales Llc
4100 Hamline Ave N
Saint Paul MN 55112

(P-21728)
HAEMONETICS CORPORATION
95 Declaration Dr Ste 3, Chico
(95973-4916)
PHONE..........................530 774-2081
EMP: 317
SALES (corp-wide): 967.5MM Publicly Held
SIC: 3841 Medical instruments & equipment, blood & bone work
PA: Haemonetics Corporation
400 Wood Rd
Braintree MA 02184
781 848-7100

(P-21729)
HAEMONETICS MANUFACTURING INC (HQ)
1630 W Industrial Park St, Covina
(91722-3419)
PHONE..........................626 339-7388

Neil Ryding, CEO
◆ EMP: 33
SQ FT: 61,313
SALES (est): 26.1MM
SALES (corp-wide): 967.5MM Publicly Held
SIC: 3841 Surgical & medical instruments
PA: Haemonetics Corporation
400 Wood Rd
Braintree MA 02184
781 848-7100

(P-21730)
HANCOCK JAFFE LABORATORIES INC
70 Doppler, Irvine (92618-4306)
PHONE..........................949 261-2900
Robert A Berman, CEO
Robert Rankin, CFO
Marc H Glickman, Chief Mktg Ofcr
EMP: 10
SQ FT: 14,507
SALES: 186.5K Privately Held
SIC: 3841 Surgical & medical instruments

(P-21731)
HANSEN MEDICAL INC
Also Called: Braid Logistics
800 E Middlefield Rd, Mountain View
(94043-4030)
PHONE..........................650 404-5800
Cary Vance, President
Michael L Eagle, Ch of Bd
Cary G Vance, President
Christopher P Lowe, CFO
Robert Cathcart, Senior VP
EMP: 130
SQ FT: 63,000
SALES: 16MM
SALES (corp-wide): 81.5B Publicly Held
WEB: www.hansenmedical.com
SIC: 3841 Catheters
HQ: Auris Health, Inc.
150 Shoreline Dr
Redwood City CA 94065
650 610-0750

(P-21732)
HANTEL TECHNOLOGIES INC
3496 Breakwater Ct, Hayward
(94545-3613)
PHONE..........................510 400-1164
Mary M Pascual Gallup, CEO
David Gallup, President
Robert Brommer, Project Leader
Belita Yap, Engineer
Dennis Mello, Manager
▲ EMP: 40 EST: 1998
SQ FT: 18,000
SALES (est): 7.6MM Privately Held
WEB: www.hanteltech.com
SIC: 3841 Surgical & medical instruments

(P-21733)
HEMODIALYSIS INC
Also Called: Hunnington Dialysis Center
806 S Fair Oaks Ave, Pasadena
(91105-2601)
PHONE..........................626 792-0548
Susan Burkhart, Manager
EMP: 50
SALES (corp-wide): 10.4MM Privately Held
SIC: 3841 8011 Hemodialysis apparatus; hematologist
PA: Hemodialysis, Inc.
710 W Wilson Ave
Glendale CA 91203
818 500-8736

(P-21734)
HOWMEDICA OSTEONICS CORP
1947 W Collins Ave, Orange (92867-5426)
PHONE..........................714 557-5010
Lynn Wagnor, Branch Mgr
EMP: 27
SALES (corp-wide): 13.6B Publicly Held
SIC: 3841 Surgical & medical instruments
HQ: Howmedica Osteonics Corp.
325 Corporate Dr
Mahwah NJ 07430
201 831-5000

(P-21735)
HOYA SURGICAL OPTICS INC
15335 Fairfield Ranch Rd # 250, Chino Hills
(91709-8841)
PHONE..........................909 680-3900
Yasuro Mori, CFO
Bruno Chermette, President
EMP: 20
SALES (est): 2.6MM Privately Held
SIC: 3841 Surgical & medical instruments

(P-21736)
HYCOR BIOMEDICAL LLC
7272 Chapman Ave Ste A, Garden Grove
(92841-2103)
PHONE..........................714 933-3000
Dick Aderman, President
Eric Whitters, COO
Phil Crusco, Vice Pres
Richard Hockins, Vice Pres
Mark V Cleve, Director
▲ EMP: 120 EST: 1985
SQ FT: 76,000
SALES: 7.2MM
SALES (corp-wide): 98.7MM Privately Held
WEB: www.hycorbiomedical.com
SIC: 3841 2835 Surgical & medical instruments; in vitro & in vivo diagnostic substances
PA: Linden, Llc
111 S Wacker Dr Ste 3350
Chicago IL 60606
312 506-5657

(P-21737)
I-FLOW LLC
43 Discovery Ste 100, Irvine (92618-3773)
PHONE..........................800 448-3569
Donald Earhart, President
James J Dal Porto, COO
James R Talevich, CFO
EMP: 1100
SQ FT: 66,675
SALES (est): 96.1MM
SALES (corp-wide): 18.4B Publicly Held
WEB: www.iflo.com
SIC: 3841 Surgical instruments & apparatus
PA: Kimberly-Clark Corporation
351 Phelps Dr
Irving TX 75038
972 281-1200

(P-21738)
ICU MEDICAL INC (PA)
951 Calle Amanecer, San Clemente
(92673-6212)
PHONE..........................949 366-2183
Vivek Jain, Ch of Bd
Christian B Voigtlander, COO
Scott E Lamb, CFO
George Lopez, Bd of Directors
Alison D Burcar, Vice Pres
▲ EMP: 277
SQ FT: 39,000
SALES: 1.4B Publicly Held
SIC: 3841 3845 IV transfusion apparatus; catheters; pacemaker, cardiac

(P-21739)
ICU MEDICAL SALES INC (HQ)
951 Calle Amanecer, San Clemente
(92673-6212)
PHONE..........................949 366-2183
Vivek Jain, CEO
EMP: 10
SQ FT: 39,000
SALES (est): 2.2MM
SALES (corp-wide): 1.4B Publicly Held
SIC: 3841 IV transfusion apparatus; catheters
PA: Icu Medical, Inc.
951 Calle Amanecer
San Clemente CA 92673
949 366-2183

(P-21740)
IMMUNO CONCEPTS INC
9825 Goethe Rd Ste 350, Sacramento
(95827-3571)
PHONE..........................916 363-2649
Robert Boyes, Branch Mgr
Jack Horner, Vice Chairman
Bob Boyes, General Mgr
Natalie Zelenov, QC Mgr

EMP: 45
SALES (corp-wide): 8.8MM **Privately Held**
WEB: www.immunoconcepts.com
SIC: **3841** 2835 Diagnostic apparatus, medical; in vitro & in vivo diagnostic substances
PA: Immuno Concepts Inc
2280 Springlake Rd # 106
Dallas TX 75234
972 919-1780

(P-21741)
IMPEDIMED INC (HQ)
5900 Pasteur Ct Ste 125, Carlsbad (92008-7334)
PHONE...................760 585-2100
Richard Carreon, CEO
Steve St Amand, Technology
EMP: 20
SQ FT: 15,000
SALES (est): 4.5MM **Privately Held**
SIC: **3841** Surgical & medical instruments

(P-21742)
INARI MEDICAL INC
9 Parker Ste 100, Irvine (92618-1666)
PHONE...................949 600-8433
Bill Hoffman, CEO
Thomas M Tu, Chief Mktg Ofcr
Eben Gordon, Vice Pres
Paul Lubock, Vice Pres
Janet Byk, CPA
EMP: 22
SALES (est): 4.3MM **Privately Held**
SIC: **3841** Catheters

(P-21743)
INCELLDX INC
1541 Industrial Rd, San Carlos (94070-4111)
PHONE...................650 777-7630
Bruce Patterson, CEO
Christine Meda, Officer
Daren Abe, Office Mgr
Marion Bonneu, Technical Staff
Debra Luff, Business Mgr
EMP: 13
SQ FT: 3,500
SALES (est): 3.6MM **Privately Held**
SIC: **3841** Diagnostic apparatus, medical

(P-21744)
INOGEN INC (PA)
326 Bollay Dr, Goleta (93117-5550)
PHONE...................805 562-0500
Scott Wilkinson, President
Heath Lukatch, Ch of Bd
Alison Bauerlein, CFO
Byron Myers, Exec VP
Bart Sanford, Exec VP
◆ EMP: 208
SQ FT: 39,000
SALES: 358.1MM **Publicly Held**
WEB: www.inogen.net
SIC: **3841** 3842 7352 Surgical & medical instruments; surgical appliances & supplies; medical equipment rental

(P-21745)
INTEGER HOLDINGS CORPORATION
Also Called: Greatbatch Medical
8830 Siempre Viva Rd # 100, San Diego (92154-6278)
PHONE...................619 498-9448
Raul Mata, Branch Mgr
Dennis Diaz, VP Opers
EMP: 16
SALES (corp-wide): 1.2B **Publicly Held**
WEB: www.greatbatch.com
SIC: **3841** Surgical & medical instruments
PA: Integer Holdings Corporation
5830 Gran Pkwy Ste 1150
Plano TX 75024
214 618-5243

(P-21746)
INTEGRA LFSCNCES HOLDINGS CORP
5955 Pacific Center Blvd, San Diego (92121-4309)
PHONE...................609 529-9748
Peter Arduini, CEO
Sharon Fisher, Partner
Elizabeth Ormaza, Program Mgr

Ron Ingram, Research
Raul Davila, Engineer
EMP: 25 **Publicly Held**
SIC: **3841** 3845 Surgical & medical instruments; electromedical equipment
PA: Integra Lifesciences Holdings Corporation
311 Enterprise Dr
Plainsboro NJ 08536
-

(P-21747)
INTELLA INTERVENTIONAL SYSTEMS
Also Called: Iwi
605 W California Ave, Sunnyvale (94086-4831)
PHONE...................650 269-1375
EMP: 62
SQ FT: 14,500
SALES (est): 7.3MM **Privately Held**
WEB: www.i-i-s-i.com
SIC: **3841**

(P-21748)
INTERNATIONAL TECHNIDYNE CORP (DH)
Also Called: Accriva Diagnostics
6260 Sequence Dr, San Diego (92121-4358)
PHONE...................858 263-2300
Scott Cramer, President
Tom Whalen, COO
Greg Tibbitts, CFO
Frank Laduca, Officer
Matt Bastardi, Senior VP
EMP: 250 EST: 1969
SQ FT: 130,000
SALES (est): 78.5MM
SALES (corp-wide): 115.1MM **Privately Held**
WEB: www.itcmed.com
SIC: **3841** 3829 Diagnostic apparatus, medical; medical diagnostic systems, nuclear
HQ: Accriva Diagnostics Holdings, Inc.
6260 Sequence Dr
San Diego CA 92121
858 404-8203

(P-21749)
INTERSECT ENT INC (PA)
1555 Adams Dr, Menlo Park (94025-1439)
PHONE...................650 641-2100
Lisa D Earnhardt, President
Kieran Gallahue, Ch of Bd
Christine Kowalski, COO
Jeryl L Hilleman, CFO
Robert Binney, Vice Pres
▲ EMP: 191
SQ FT: 50,400
SALES: 108.4MM **Publicly Held**
SIC: **3841** Surgical & medical instruments

(P-21750)
INTUBRITE LLC
2460 Coral St, Vista (92081-8430)
PHONE...................760 727-1900
John Hicks, Mng Member
Leslie Tanger, Mng Member
James Tenger, Mng Member
▲ EMP: 10
SALES (est): 2MM **Privately Held**
SIC: **3841** Medical instruments & equipment, blood & bone work

(P-21751)
INTUITIVE SRGCAL OPRATIONS INC
1020 Kifer Rd, Sunnyvale (94086-5301)
PHONE...................408 523-2100
Gary S Guthart, CEO
EMP: 41 EST: 2009
SALES (est): 8.7MM **Publicly Held**
SIC: **3841** Surgical & medical instruments
PA: Intuitive Surgical, Inc.
1020 Kifer Rd
Sunnyvale CA 94086

(P-21752)
INTUITIVE SRGICAL HOLDINGS LLC (HQ)
1020 Kifer Rd, Sunnyvale (94086-5301)
PHONE...................408 523-2100

Gary S Guthart PHD, CEO
Gokul Ramaswamy, Director
▼ EMP: 10
SALES (est): 7.5MM **Publicly Held**
SIC: **3841** Surgical & medical instruments

(P-21753)
INTUITIVE SURGICAL INC
1250 Kifer Rd, Sunnyvale (94086-5304)
PHONE...................408 523-7314
John Wagner, Vice Pres
Lidia Bernardo, Executive Asst
Benjamin Velazquez, Planning
Patrick Jiang, IT/INT Sup
Richard Willia, Technical Staff
EMP: 21 **Publicly Held**
SIC: **3841** Surgical & medical instruments
PA: Intuitive Surgical, Inc.
1020 Kifer Rd
Sunnyvale CA 94086

(P-21754)
INTUITIVE SURGICAL INC
3410 Central Expy, Santa Clara (95051-0703)
PHONE...................408 523-2100
EMP: 308 **Publicly Held**
SIC: **3841** Surgical & medical instruments
PA: Intuitive Surgical, Inc.
1020 Kifer Rd
Sunnyvale CA 94086

(P-21755)
INTUITIVE SURGICAL INC (PA)
1020 Kifer Rd, Sunnyvale (94086-5301)
PHONE...................408 523-2100
Gary S Guthart, President
Marshall L Mohr, CFO
David J Rosa, Ch Credit Ofcr
Myriam J Curet, Chief Mktg Ofcr
Salvatore J Brogna, Exec VP
▲ EMP: 183
SQ FT: 927,000
SALES: 3.7B **Publicly Held**
WEB: www.intusurg.com
SIC: **3841** Surgical & medical instruments

(P-21756)
INTUITY MEDICAL INC
Also Called: Rosedale Medical
3500 W Warren Ave, Fremont (94538-6499)
PHONE...................408 530-1700
Emory Anderson, President
Emory V Anderson III, President
Robb Hesley, Vice Pres
Kelley Lipman, Vice Pres
EMP: 64
SQ FT: 18,000
SALES (est): 22.3MM **Privately Held**
SIC: **3841** Surgical & medical instruments

(P-21757)
INVENIO IMAGING INC
2310 Walsh Ave, Santa Clara (95051-1301)
PHONE...................408 753-9147
Jay Trautman, President
Jonathan Ross, CFO
Christian Freudiger, Vice Pres
◆ EMP: 10
SQ FT: 2,000
SALES (est): 1.3MM **Privately Held**
SIC: **3841** Surgical & medical instruments

(P-21758)
INVUITY INC
Also Called: Intelligent Photonics
444 De Haro St Ste 110, San Francisco (94107-2350)
PHONE...................415 665-2100
Scott Flora, CEO
James H Mackaness, CFO
Marcia Fish, Officer
Paul Davison, Vice Pres
Joseph Guido, Vice Pres
▲ EMP: 172
SQ FT: 38,135
SALES: 39.6MM
SALES (corp-wide): 13.6B **Publicly Held**
SIC: **3841** 5047 Surgical instruments & apparatus; surgical equipment & supplies

PA: Stryker Corporation
2825 Airview Blvd
Portage MI 49002
269 385-2600

(P-21759)
IOWA APPROACH INC
3715 Haven Ave Ste 110, Menlo Park (94025-1047)
PHONE...................650 422-3633
Allan Zingeler, CEO
EMP: 13
SALES (est): 2.1MM **Privately Held**
SIC: **3841** Surgical instruments & apparatus

(P-21760)
ISCIENCE INTERVENTIONAL CORP
41316 Christy St, Fremont (94538-3115)
PHONE...................650 421-2700
Michael Nash, President
Matt Franklin, CFO
Stan Conston, Vice Pres
Ernie Edwards, Vice Pres
Mark Hayward, Vice Pres
EMP: 60
SALES (est): 7.2MM **Privately Held**
WEB: www.isciencesurgical.com
SIC: **3841** Instruments, microsurgical: except electromedical

(P-21761)
ITECH MEDICAL INC
17011 Beach Blvd Ste 900, Huntington Beach (92647-5998)
PHONE...................714 841-2670
Warren G Baker, Ch of Bd
Wayne Cockburn, CFO
Karl R Wolcott, VP Sls/Mktg
EMP: 10
SALES (est): 647.6K **Privately Held**
SIC: **3841** Surgical & medical instruments

(P-21762)
IV SUPPORT SYSTEMS INC
Also Called: Siella Medical
12 Hughes Ste 105, Irvine (92618-1950)
PHONE...................888 688-6822
George Davis, Principal
EMP: 18
SALES (est): 3MM **Privately Held**
SIC: **3841** Medical instruments & equipment, blood & bone work

(P-21763)
IVERA MEDICAL LLC
Also Called: Ivera Medical Corporation
10805 Rancho Bernardo Rd # 100, San Diego (92127-5702)
PHONE...................888 861-8228
Bobby E Rogers, President
Jack Saladow, Marketing Staff
EMP: 60
SALES (est): 6.6MM
SALES (corp-wide): 32.7B **Publicly Held**
SIC: **3841** IV transfusion apparatus
PA: 3m Company
3m Center
Saint Paul MN 55144
651 733-1110

(P-21764)
J F FONG INC
Also Called: American Imex
16520 Aston, Irvine (92606-4805)
PHONE...................949 553-8885
Joan F Fong, President
Joseph Fong, Executive
▲ EMP: 15
SQ FT: 8,000
SALES (est): 3.1MM **Privately Held**
WEB: www.americanimex.com
SIC: **3841** 5047 Surgical & medical instruments; medical equipment & supplies

(P-21765)
JOHNSON & JOHNSON
Also Called: Johnson & Johnson Vision
510 Cottonwood Dr, Milpitas (95035-7403)
PHONE...................408 273-4100
Murthy Simhambhatla, Branch Mgr
John Grimaldo, Senior Buyer
Olga Chiang, Buyer
EMP: 32

SALES (corp-wide): 81.5B **Publicly Held**
SIC: **3841** Ophthalmic instruments & apparatus
HQ: Johnson & Johnson Surgical Vision, Inc.
1700 E Saint Andrew Pl
Santa Ana CA 92705
714 247-8200

(P-21766)
JOHNSON & JOHNSON
2501 Pullman St, Santa Ana (92705-5515)
PHONE..................................714 247-8200
James V Mazzo, *President*
EMP: 38
SALES (corp-wide): 81.5B **Publicly Held**
SIC: **3841** Surgical & medical instruments
HQ: Johnson & Johnson Surgical Vision, Inc.
1700 E Saint Andrew Pl
Santa Ana CA 92705
714 247-8200

(P-21767)
KARL STORZ ENDSCPY-AMERICA INC
2151 E Grand Ave Ste 100, El Segundo (90245-2838)
PHONE..................................508 248-9011
Marsha Hunter, *Branch Mgr*
David Chatenever, *Vice Pres*
Monica Botwinski, *Associate Dir*
Marc Amling, *Exec Dir*
Connie Padden, *Exec Dir*
EMP: 20
SALES (corp-wide): 1.9B **Privately Held**
WEB: www.ksela.com
SIC: **3841** Surgical & medical instruments
HQ: Karl Storz Endoscopy-America, Inc.
2151 E Grand Ave
El Segundo CA 90245
424 218-8100

(P-21768)
KARL STORZ ENDSCPY-AMERICA INC (HQ)
2151 E Grand Ave, El Segundo (90245-5017)
PHONE..................................424 218-8100
Charles Wilhelm, *CEO*
Sken Huang, *CFO*
Mark Green, *Vice Pres*
Marsha Hunter, *Branch Mgr*
Lidia Leon, *Executive Asst*
▲ EMP: 277
SQ FT: 90,000
SALES (est): 278.1MM
SALES (corp-wide): 1.9B **Privately Held**
WEB: www.ksela.com
SIC: **3841** 5047 Surgical & medical instruments; medical equipment & supplies
PA: Karl Storz Se & Co. Kg
Dr.-Karl-Storz-Str. 34
Tuttlingen 78532
746 170-80

(P-21769)
KENLOR INDUSTRIES INC
1560 E Edinger Ave Ste A1, Santa Ana (92705-4913)
PHONE..................................714 647-0770
Kamales Som PHD, *President*
Sudeep Banerjee, *Vice Pres*
EMP: 12
SQ FT: 5,000
SALES (est): 1.5MM **Privately Held**
WEB: www.kenlor.com
SIC: **3841** 2834 Surgical & medical instruments; pharmaceutical preparations

(P-21770)
KINEMATIC AUTOMATION INC
21085 Longeway Rd, Sonora (95370-8968)
P.O. Box 69, Twain Harte (95383-0069)
PHONE..................................209 532-3200
David Carlberg, *President*
Ted Meigs, *Vice Pres*
EMP: 55
SQ FT: 19,000
SALES (est): 13.2MM **Privately Held**
WEB: www.kinematic.com
SIC: **3841** 7389 Diagnostic apparatus, medical; design, commercial & industrial

(P-21771)
KONG VETERINARY PRODUCTS
Also Called: KVP
16018 Adelante St Ste C, Irwindale (91702-3236)
PHONE..................................626 633-0077
Nancy Klinkhart, *President*
Herman Klinkhart, *Vice Pres*
Roger Klinkhart, *Vice Pres*
EMP: 15 EST: 1960
SQ FT: 8,000
SALES (est): 1.4MM **Privately Held**
SIC: **3841** 3842 Surgical & medical instruments; surgical appliances & supplies

(P-21772)
KOROS USA INC
610 Flinn Ave, Moorpark (93021-2008)
PHONE..................................805 529-0825
Tibor Koros, *President*
Joanna Thompson, *Manager*
▲ EMP: 25 EST: 1974
SQ FT: 12,000
SALES (est): 4.9MM **Privately Held**
WEB: www.korosusa.com
SIC: **3841** Diagnostic apparatus, medical

(P-21773)
LEICA BIOSYSTEMS IMAGING INC
Also Called: Aperio
1360 Park Center Dr, Vista (92081-8300)
PHONE..................................760 539-1100
James F O'Reilly, *Vice Pres*
Keith B Hagen, *COO*
Jared N Schwartz, *Officer*
Greg Crandall, *Vice Pres*
Steven V Russell, *Vice Pres*
EMP: 182
SQ FT: 37,000
SALES (est): 31.7MM **Privately Held**
SIC: **3841** Surgical & medical instruments

(P-21774)
LIFE SCIENCE OUTSOURCING INC
Also Called: Medical Device Manufacturing
830 Challenger St, Brea (92821-2946)
PHONE..................................714 672-1090
Barry Kazemi, *President*
Charlie Ricci, *Vice Pres*
Mireya Lozano, *Project Mgr*
Judy Deakins, *Purchasing*
Charley Ricci, *Sales Executive*
▲ EMP: 80
SQ FT: 56,000
SALES (est): 18.3MM **Privately Held**
WEB: www.lso-inc.com
SIC: **3841** Surgical instruments & apparatus

(P-21775)
LIFEMED OF CALIFORNIA
13948 Mountain Ave, Chino (91710-9018)
P.O. Box 787 (91708-0787)
PHONE..................................800 543-3633
Thomas Hamon, *President*
Pat Brinker, *Vice Pres*
EMP: 21
SQ FT: 10,000
SALES (est): 2.4MM **Privately Held**
WEB: www.lifemedinc.com
SIC: **3841** Hemodialysis apparatus; medical instruments & equipment, blood & bone work

(P-21776)
LIFESCAN PRODUCTS LLC (HQ)
1000 Gibraltar Dr, Milpitas (95035-6312)
PHONE..................................408 719-8443
Eric Milledge, *Ch of Bd*
Louis Caro, *CFO*
Polly Ferguson, *Analyst*
Sonia Rodriguez, *Buyer*
EMP: 65
SALES (est): 52.6MM
SALES (corp-wide): 81.5B **Publicly Held**
SIC: **3841** 3845 Surgical & medical instruments; ultrasonic scanning devices, medical
PA: Johnson & Johnson
1 Johnson And Johnson Plz
New Brunswick NJ 08933
732 524-0400

(P-21777)
LIFESCIENCE PLUS INC
2520 Wyandotte St Ste A, Mountain View (94043-2381)
P.O. Box 60783, Palo Alto (94306-0783)
PHONE..................................650 565-8172
Vicky Feng, *President*
Lason Magallones, *Vice Pres*
Sally Pennington, *General Mgr*
◆ EMP: 10
SQ FT: 3,000
SALES (est): 1.3MM **Privately Held**
WEB: www.lifescienceplus.com
SIC: **3841** Surgical & medical instruments

(P-21778)
LINKS MEDICAL PRODUCTS INC (PA)
9247 Research Dr, Irvine (92618-4286)
PHONE..................................949 753-0001
Thomas L Buckley, *CEO*
Patrick Buckley, *President*
Sandy Campbell, *Office Mgr*
Joe Greco, *Sales Dir*
Spears Chris, *Sales Staff*
▲ EMP: 28
SQ FT: 8,800
SALES (est): 4.4MM **Privately Held**
WEB: www.linksmed.com
SIC: **3841** Medical instruments & equipment, blood & bone work

(P-21779)
LINVATEC CORPORATION
Also Called: Envision Medical
26 Castilian Dr Ste B, Goleta (93117-5565)
PHONE..................................805 571-8100
Bruce Smears, *Manager*
EMP: 80
SALES (corp-wide): 859.6MM **Publicly Held**
WEB: www.hallsurgical.com
SIC: **3841** 3861 Surgical & medical instruments; photographic equipment & supplies
HQ: Linvatec Corporation
11311 Concept Blvd
Largo FL 33773
727 392-6464

(P-21780)
LOMA VISTA MEDICAL INC
863a Mitten Rd Ste 100a, Burlingame (94010-1303)
PHONE..................................650 490-4747
Alex Tilson, *CEO*
Mark Scheeff, *Vice Pres*
EMP: 15
SQ FT: 4,500
SALES (est): 2.1MM
SALES (corp-wide): 15.9B **Publicly Held**
SIC: **3841** Surgical & medical instruments
PA: Becton, Dickinson And Company
1 Becton Dr
Franklin Lakes NJ 07417
201 847-6800

(P-21781)
LOMBARD MEDICAL TECH INC (PA)
6440 Oak Cyn Ste 200, Irvine (92618-5209)
PHONE..................................949 379-3750
Kurt Lemvigh, *CEO*
Simon Hubbert, *CEO*
William Kullback, *CFO*
Micheal Gioffredi, *Vice Pres*
Briana Figueroa, *Info Tech Mgr*
EMP: 20
SQ FT: 17,000
SALES (est): 13.2MM **Privately Held**
SIC: **3841** Surgical & medical instruments

(P-21782)
LUCIRA HEALTH INC
1412 62nd St, Emeryville (94608-2036)
PHONE..................................510 350-8071
Erik T Engelson, *President*
Frankie Myers, *Engineer*
EMP: 15
SALES (est): 485.3K **Privately Held**
SIC: **3841** Surgical & medical instruments

(P-21783)
LUMENIS INC (DH)
2077 Gateway Pl Ste 300, San Jose (95110-1149)
PHONE..................................408 764-3000
Tzipi Ozer Armon, *CEO*
Brad Oliver, *President*
Shlomi Cohen, *CFO*
Ido Warshavski, *Admin Sec*
Kristine Gysel, *Info Tech Mgr*
▲ EMP: 150
SQ FT: 13,500
SALES (est): 160MM **Privately Held**
SIC: **3841** Surgical & medical instruments
HQ: Lumenis Ltd.
6 Hakidma
Upper Yokneam 20692
495 990-00

(P-21784)
MAGNABIOSCIENCES LLC
6325 Lusk Blvd, San Diego (92121-3733)
PHONE..................................858 481-4400
Ron Sager,
Dave Cox,
Gerald D Daviessnager,
Greg Degeller,
Ronald E Sager,
EMP: 100
SQ FT: 2,200
SALES (est): 12.4MM
SALES (corp-wide): 42.1MM **Privately Held**
WEB: www.qdusa.com
SIC: **3841** 5047 5999 Diagnostic apparatus, medical; diagnostic equipment, medical; medical apparatus & supplies
PA: Quantum Design, Inc.
10307 Pacific Center Ct
San Diego CA 92121
858 481-4400

(P-21785)
MAGNAMOSIS INC
953 Indiana St Rm 212, San Francisco (94107-3007)
PHONE..................................707 484-8774
Michael Harrison, *President*
Michael Danty, *COO*
EMP: 10 EST: 2012
SALES (est): 456.3K **Privately Held**
SIC: **3841** Surgical & medical instruments

(P-21786)
MALLINCKRODT INC
3298 Morning Ridge Ave, Thousand Oaks (91362-1195)
PHONE..................................805 553-9303
Mark Thom, *President*
EMP: 13
SALES (est): 1MM **Privately Held**
SIC: **3841** Ultrasonic medical cleaning equipment

(P-21787)
MARLEE MANUFACTURING INC
4711 E Guasti Rd, Ontario (91761-8106)
PHONE..................................909 390-3222
Russell Wells, *President*
Shawn Cory, *President*
Patricia Wells, *Vice Pres*
EMP: 39
SQ FT: 41,000
SALES (est): 7.5MM **Privately Held**
WEB: www.marleemanufacturing.com
SIC: **3841** 3599 Surgical & medical instruments; machine shop, jobbing & repair

(P-21788)
MASIMO AMERICAS INC
52 Discovery, Irvine (92618-3105)
PHONE..................................949 297-7000
Rick Fishel, *CEO*
Ron Coverston, *Vice Pres*
Rebecca Jackvony, *Manager*
Stephen Cartwright, *Accounts Mgr*
Robert Cherrie, *Accounts Mgr*
EMP: 16
SALES (est): 2.8MM **Publicly Held**
SIC: **3841** Surgical & medical instruments
PA: Masimo Corporation
52 Discovery
Irvine CA 92618

PRODUCTS & SVCS

(P-21789)
MAST BIOSURGERY USA INC
6749 Top Gun St Ste 108, San Diego
(92121-4151)
PHONE...............................858 550-8050
Thomas Brooas, *President*
Thoms Brooas, *President*
EMP: 30
SQ FT: 10,000
SALES (est): 4.9MM **Privately Held**
WEB: www.mastbio.com
SIC: 3841 Surgical & medical instruments

(P-21790)
MATTHEY JOHNSON INC
Also Called: Shape Memory Applications
1070 Coml St Ste 110, San Jose (95112)
PHONE...............................408 727-2221
Brian Woodward, *Branch Mgr*
EMP: 50
SALES (corp-wide): 13.8B **Privately Held**
SIC: 3841 3496 3356 3357 Surgical &
medical instruments; miscellaneous fabri-
cated wire products; nonferrous rolling &
drawing; nonferrous wiredrawing & insu-
lating; steel wire & related products
HQ: Johnson Matthey Inc.
435 Devon Park Dr Ste 600
Wayne PA 19087
610 971-3000

(P-21791)
MCCASH MANUFACTURING INC
1256 Washoe Dr, San Jose (95120-4005)
PHONE...............................408 748-8991
Jason McCash, *President*
EMP: 25 EST: 1999
SQ FT: 1,200
SALES (est): 2.7MM **Privately Held**
WEB: www.mccashmfg.com
SIC: 3841 Surgical & medical instruments

(P-21792)
MED-SAFE SYSTEMS INC
10975 Torreyana Rd, San Diego
(92121-1106)
PHONE...............................855 236-2772
Joseph Taylor, *General Mgr*
◆ EMP: 200
SQ FT: 90,000
SALES (est): 11.4MM
SALES (corp-wide): 15.9B **Publicly Held**
WEB: www.becton.com
SIC: 3841 Surgical instruments & appara-
tus
PA: Becton, Dickinson And Company
1 Becton Dr
Franklin Lakes NJ 07417
201 847-6800

(P-21793)
MEDALLION THERAPEUTICS INC
25134 Rye Canyon Loop # 200, Valencia
(91355-5028)
PHONE...............................661 621-6122
Don Deyo, *CEO*
Duane Ruge, *Manager*
EMP: 23
SQ FT: 39,777
SALES (est): 389.1K
SALES (corp-wide): 507.5K **Privately
Held**
SIC: 3841 Surgical & medical instruments
PA: The Alfred E Mann Foundation For Sci-
entific Research
25134 Rye Canyon Loop
Valencia CA 91355
661 702-6700

(P-21794)
MEDEDGE INC
11965 Venice Blvd Ste 407, Los Angeles
(90066-3982)
P.O. Box 3028, Venice (90294-3028)
PHONE...............................310 745-2290
EMP: 16
SQ FT: 2,000
SALES (est): 1.2MM **Privately Held**
WEB: www.mededge-inc.com
SIC: 3841

(P-21795)
MEDEIA INC
7 W Figueroa St Ste 215, Santa Barbara
(93101-3189)
PHONE...............................800 433-4609
Slav Danev, *President*
EMP: 13
SQ FT: 1,500
SALES: 2MM **Privately Held**
SIC: 3841 Surgical instruments & appara-
tus

(P-21796)
MEDICAL AESTHETICS MENLO PARK
885 Oak Grove Ave Ste 101, Menlo Park
(94025-4400)
PHONE...............................650 336-3358
EMP: 10
SALES (est): 825K **Privately Held**
SIC: 3841 7991 Surgical lasers; spas

(P-21797)
MEDICAL DEVICE RESOURCE CORP
Also Called: M.D. Resource
5981 Graham Ct, Livermore (94550-9710)
PHONE...............................510 732-9950
Terry Meredith, *CEO*
▼ EMP: 10
SALES (est): 2.1MM
SALES (corp-wide): 8.1MM **Privately
Held**
WEB: www.mdresource.com
SIC: 3841 Surgical instruments & appara-
tus; medical instruments & equipment,
blood & bone work; suction therapy appa-
ratus
PA: Innovia Medical
815 Northwest Pkwy # 100
Saint Paul MN 55121
651 789-3939

(P-21798)
MEDICAL INSTR DEV LABS INC
Also Called: Mid Labs
557 Mccormick St, San Leandro
(94577-1107)
PHONE...............................510 357-3952
Dr Rob Peabody Sr, *CEO*
Carl Wang, *President*
Andrew Wang, *Info Tech Mgr*
Steve Heeter, *IT/INT Sup*
Jim Gaab, *Engineer*
EMP: 35
SQ FT: 17,000
SALES (est): 7.5MM **Privately Held**
WEB: www.midlabs.com
SIC: 3841 Ophthalmic instruments & appa-
ratus

(P-21799)
MEDICAL TACTILE INC
5500 W Rosecrans Ave A, Hawthorne
(90250-6643)
PHONE...............................310 641-8228
Jae Son, *Chairman*
Denis O'Connor, *CEO*
Steven Sanchez, *Admin Sec*
David Ables, *CTO*
▼ EMP: 12
SALES (est): 1.1MM **Privately Held**
SIC: 3841 Diagnostic apparatus, medical

(P-21800)
MEDICOOL INC
20460 Gramercy Pl, Torrance
(90501-1513)
PHONE...............................310 782-2200
Steve Yeager, *Principal*
Stephen Yeager, *Principal*
Liz Hernandez, *Sales Staff*
▲ EMP: 17
SQ FT: 15,000
SALES (est): 1.7MM **Privately Held**
WEB: www.medicool.com
SIC: 3841 Inhalators, surgical & medical

(P-21801)
MEDIKA THERAPEUTICS INC
Also Called: Medika Health Care
4046 Clipper Ct, Fremont (94538-6540)
PHONE...............................510 377-0898
Roy Chin, *Chairman*
EMP: 10

SALES (est): 919.7K **Privately Held**
SIC: 3841 5999 7389 Surgical & medical
instruments; medical apparatus & supplies; design services

(P-21802)
MEDINA MEDICAL INC
39684 Eureka Dr, Newark (94560-4805)
PHONE...............................650 396-7756
Erik T Engelson, *CEO*
EMP: 10
SALES (est): 1.8MM **Privately Held**
SIC: 3841 Surgical & medical instruments
HQ: Medtronic, Inc.
710 Medtronic Pkwy
Minneapolis MN 55432
763 514-4000

(P-21803)
MEDTRONIC INC
1659 Gailes Blvd, San Diego (92154-8230)
PHONE...............................949 798-3934
Araceli Rodriguez, *Branch Mgr*
Jonah Wright, *Project Mgr*
Siria Lenina Gomez, *Engineer*
Uriel Perez, *Engineer*
Sal Groppo, *Consultant*
EMP: 300 **Privately Held**
SIC: 3841 Surgical & medical instruments
HQ: Medtronic, Inc.
710 Medtronic Pkwy
Minneapolis MN 55432
763 514-4000

(P-21804)
MEDTRONIC INC
2200 Powell St, Emeryville (94608-1809)
PHONE...............................510 985-9670
Reggie Dupee, *Sales Staff*
EMP: 192 **Privately Held**
SIC: 3841 Surgical & medical instruments
HQ: Medtronic, Inc.
710 Medtronic Pkwy
Minneapolis MN 55432
763 514-4000

(P-21805)
MEDTRONIC INC
18000 Devonshire St, Northridge
(91325-1219)
PHONE...............................300 646-4633
EMP: 204 **Privately Held**
SIC: 3841 Surgical & medical instruments
HQ: Medtronic, Inc.
710 Medtronic Pkwy
Minneapolis MN 55432
763 514-4000

(P-21806)
MEDTRONIC INC
9775 Toledo Way, Irvine (92618-1811)
PHONE...............................949 837-3700
Stephen Sosnowski, *Engrg Dir*
Natasha Behrmann, *Research*
Isabella TSE, *Research*
Mike Neppl, *Technology*
Gopan Patel, *Engineer*
EMP: 27
SALES (est): 3.7MM **Privately Held**
SIC: 3841 Surgical & medical instruments

(P-21807)
MEDTRONIC INC
5345 Skyllane Blvd, Santa Rosa (95403)
PHONE...............................707 541-3144
Eric Kunz, *Branch Mgr*
EMP: 30 **Privately Held**
SIC: 3841 5047 5999 Surgical & medical
instruments; medical equipment & sup-
plies; medical apparatus & supplies
HQ: Medtronic, Inc.
710 Medtronic Pkwy
Minneapolis MN 55432
763 514-4000

(P-21808)
MEDTRONIC INC
1851 E Deere Ave, Santa Ana
(92705-5720)
PHONE...............................949 474-3943
Walter Cuevas, *Manager*
Carol Eberhardt, *Engrg Mgr*
Athar Sayeed, *Engineer*
Paul San, *Analyst*
Cecilia Lopez, *Personnel Assit*
EMP: 53

SQ FT: 47,000 **Privately Held**
WEB: www.medtronic.com
SIC: 3841 Surgical & medical instruments
HQ: Medtronic, Inc.
710 Medtronic Pkwy
Minneapolis MN 55432
763 514-4000

(P-21809)
MEDTRONIC INC
1860 Barber Ln, Milpitas (95035-7422)
PHONE...............................408 548-6618
Richard Mott, *CEO*
Jim Adzema, *Info Tech Dir*
Jason Hsieh, *Technology*
Christopher Rodahaffer, *Consultant*
EMP: 22 **Privately Held**
WEB: www.medtronic.com
SIC: 3841 Surgical & medical instruments
HQ: Medtronic, Inc.
710 Medtronic Pkwy
Minneapolis MN 55432
763 514-4000

(P-21810)
MEDTRONIC INC
11811 Landon Dr, Eastvale (91752-4002)
PHONE...............................951 332-3600
EMP: 21 **Privately Held**
SIC: 3841 Surgical & medical instruments
HQ: Medtronic, Inc.
710 Medtronic Pkwy
Minneapolis MN 55432
763 514-4000

(P-21811)
MEDTRONIC ATS MEDICAL INC
1851 E Deere Ave, Santa Ana
(92705-5720)
PHONE...............................949 380-9333
Walter Cuevas, *Branch Mgr*
EMP: 40 **Privately Held**
WEB: www.atsmedical.com
SIC: 3841 Surgical instruments & appara-
tus
HQ: Medtronic Ats Medical, Inc.
3800 Annapolis Ln N # 175
Minneapolis MN 55447
763 553-7736

(P-21812)
MEDTRONIC PS MEDICAL INC (DH)
125 Cremona Dr, Goleta (93117-5503)
PHONE...............................805 571-3769
Austin Noll, *General Mgr*
Kim Chancey, *COO*
Paul Coates, *Program Mgr*
Megan Trobridge, *Project Mgr*
Horace Johnson, *Engineer*
◆ EMP: 200
SQ FT: 82,000
SALES (est): 28.1MM **Privately Held**
SIC: 3841 Surgical & medical instruments
HQ: Medtronic, Inc.
710 Medtronic Pkwy
Minneapolis MN 55432
763 514-4000

(P-21813)
MEDTRONIC SPINE LLC
1221 Crossman Ave, Sunnyvale
(94089-1103)
PHONE...............................408 548-6500
Bill Hawkins, *President*
Karen D Talmadge, *Vice Pres*
EMP: 229 EST: 2008
SQ FT: 151,000
SALES (est): 57.6MM **Privately Held**
WEB: www.kyphon.com
SIC: 3841 Surgical & medical instruments
HQ: Medtronic, Inc.
710 Medtronic Pkwy
Minneapolis MN 55432
763 514-4000

(P-21814)
MEDWAVES INC
16760 W Bernardo Dr, San Diego
(92127-1904)
PHONE...............................858 946-0015
Theodore Ormsby, *President*
Gwo Shen, *Exec VP*
EMP: 20

▲ = Import ▼=Export
◆ =Import/Export

SALES: 2.6MM **Privately Held**
WEB: www.medwaves.com
SIC: 3841 Surgical & medical instruments

(P-21815)
MELCO ENGINEERING CORPORATION
3605 Avenida Cumbre, Calabasas
(91302-3034)
P.O. Box 8907 (91372-8907)
PHONE..................................818 591-1000
Henry B David, *President*
EMP: 10
SALES (est): 1.1MM **Privately Held**
WEB: www.melcowire.com
SIC: 3841 Surgical & medical instruments

(P-21816)
MEMRY CORPORATION
4065 Campbell Ave, Menlo Park
(94025-1006)
PHONE..................................650 463-3400
Robert Richardson, *Principal*
John Schosser, *Vice Pres*
EMP: 120
SALES (corp-wide): 60.2MM **Privately Held**
WEB: www.memry.com
SIC: 3841 Surgical & medical instruments
HQ: Memry Corporation
3 Berkshire Blvd
Bethel CT 06801
203 739-1100

(P-21817)
MERIT CABLES INCORPORATED
830 N Poinsettia St, Santa Ana
(92701-3853)
PHONE..................................714 547-3054
Ted Hendrickson, *Principal*
Ruben Mauricio, *CFO*
David Greenwald, *Vice Pres*
Rich McHugh, *Director*
▼ EMP: 25
SQ FT: 8,000
SALES (est): 4MM **Privately Held**
WEB: www.meritcables.com
SIC: 3841 Surgical & medical instruments

(P-21818)
METTLER ELECTRONICS CORP
1333 S Claudina St, Anaheim
(92805-6266)
PHONE..................................714 533-2221
Stephen C Mettler, *CEO*
Mark Mettler, *President*
Matthew Ferrari, *CFO*
Donna Mettler, *Admin Sec*
Brian Muma, *Engineer*
▲ EMP: 42 EST: 1957
SQ FT: 22,500
SALES (est): 7MM **Privately Held**
WEB: www.mettlerelec.com
SIC: 3841 Surgical & medical instruments

(P-21819)
MICRO THERAPEUTICS INC (HQ)
Also Called: Ev3 Neurovascular
9775 Toledo Way, Irvine (92618-1811)
PHONE..................................949 837-3700
Thomas C Wilder III, *President*
Thomas Berryman, *CFO*
EMP: 17
SQ FT: 43,000
SALES (est): 11.2MM **Privately Held**
SIC: 3841 Surgical & medical instruments

(P-21820)
MICROVENTION INC (DH)
Also Called: Microvention Terumo
35 Enterprise, Aliso Viejo (92656-2601)
PHONE..................................714 258-8000
Richard Cappetta, *President*
Bill Hughes, *COO*
Matt Fitz, *Senior VP*
Bruce Canter, *Vice Pres*
Thierry De Bosson, *Vice Pres*
▲ EMP: 277 EST: 1997
SQ FT: 35,000
SALES (est): 243.2MM **Privately Held**
WEB: www.microvention.com
SIC: 3841 Surgical & medical instruments

HQ: Terumo Americas Holding, Inc.
265 Davidson Ave Ste 320
Somerset NJ 08873
732 302-4900

(P-21821)
MICRUS ENDOVASCULAR LLC (HQ)
821 Fox Ln, San Jose (95131-1601)
PHONE..................................408 433-1400
P Laxminarain, *President*
Robert A Stern, *President*
John T Kilcoyne, *CEO*
Gordon T Sangster, *CFO*
Edward F Ruppel Jr, *Ch Credit Ofcr*
EMP: 139
SQ FT: 42,000
SALES (est): 32.9MM
SALES (corp-wide): 81.5B **Publicly Held**
WEB: www.micruscorp.com
SIC: 3841 Surgical instruments & apparatus
PA: Johnson & Johnson
1 Johnson And Johnson Plz
New Brunswick NJ 08933
732 524-0400

(P-21822)
MIKROSCAN TECHNOLOGIES INC
2764 Gateway Rd 100, Carlsbad
(92009-1730)
PHONE..................................760 893-8095
Robert Goerlitz, *CEO*
James Crowe, *Sr Software Eng*
Victor Casas, *CTO*
Tobias Richmond-Darbey, *Info Tech Mgr*
Cooper Nelson, *Technician*
EMP: 10
SALES: 3MM **Privately Held**
SIC: 3841 Surgical & medical instruments

(P-21823)
MINERVA SURGICAL INC
101 Saginaw Dr, Redwood City
(94063-4717)
PHONE..................................650 399-1770
David Clapper, *CEO*
▲ EMP: 14
SQ FT: 2,000
SALES (est): 3.5MM **Privately Held**
SIC: 3841 Surgical & medical instruments

(P-21824)
MINITOUCH INC
47853 Warm Springs Blvd, Fremont
(94539-7400)
PHONE..................................510 651-5000
Dinesh Mody, *President*
Sadna Kumbhani, *Vice Pres*
EMP: 11
SQ FT: 10,000
SALES (est): 655.9K **Privately Held**
SIC: 3841 Surgical & medical instruments

(P-21825)
MIZUHO ORTHOPEDIC SYSTEMS INC (HQ)
Also Called: Mizuho OSI
30031 Ahern Ave, Union City (94587-1234)
P.O. Box 1468 (94587-6468)
PHONE..................................510 429-1500
Takashi Nemoto, *CEO*
Steve Lamb, *President*
Yosup Kim, *Treasurer*
Patrick Rimroth, *General Mgr*
Veronica Yra, *Mfg Spvr*
▲ EMP: 272
SQ FT: 111,100
SALES (est): 57.5MM **Privately Held**
WEB: www.osiosi.com
SIC: 3841 Operating tables

(P-21826)
MODERN METALS INDUSTRIES INC
14000 S Broadway, Los Angeles
(90061-1018)
P.O. Box 701, El Segundo (90245-0701)
PHONE..................................800 437-6633
Lee Sherrill, *President*
Andrew Sherrill, *President*
Christopher Thomsen, *VP Bus Dvlpt*
Nick Bell, *Regl Sales Mgr*
John Goyette, *Regl Sales Mgr*

▲ EMP: 40
SQ FT: 40,000
SALES (est): 4.3MM **Privately Held**
WEB: www.mmimedcarts.com
SIC: 3841 Surgical & medical instruments

(P-21827)
MONOBIND INC (PA)
100 N Pointe Dr, Lake Forest (92630-2270)
PHONE..................................949 951-2665
Frederick Jerome, *President*
Dr Jay Singh, *Vice Pres*
Veronica Landa, *Administration*
Anthony Shatola, *QA Dir*
Tony Shatola, *QC Dir*
▲ EMP: 37 EST: 1977
SQ FT: 18,000
SALES (est): 6.4MM **Privately Held**
WEB: www.monobind.com
SIC: 3841 Diagnostic apparatus, medical

(P-21828)
MORGAN MEDESIGN INC
7700 Bell Rd Ste B, Windsor (95492-8559)
PHONE..................................707 568-2929
Jim Whitman, *CEO*
Jim Whitman, *Finance*
EMP: 11
SQ FT: 10,000
SALES: 3.6MM **Privately Held**
WEB: www.morganmedesign.com
SIC: 3841 Diagnostic apparatus, medical

(P-21829)
MPS MEDICAL INC
830 Challenger St Ste 200, Brea
(92821-2946)
PHONE..................................714 672-1090
Ryan B Kazemi, *Opers Mgr*
EMP: 27 EST: 2014
SALES (est): 2MM **Privately Held**
SIC: 3841 Surgical & medical instruments

(P-21830)
MRI INTERVENTIONS INC
5 Musick, Irvine (92618-1638)
PHONE..................................949 900-6833
Francis P Grillo, *President*
Mallory Concepcion, *Office Mgr*
Chris Kantorak, *Controller*
Mina Rodriguez, *Production*
Wendelin C Maners, *VP Sales*
EMP: 33
SQ FT: 7,400
SALES: 7.3MM **Privately Held**
SIC: 3841 Surgical & medical instruments

(P-21831)
NEOMEND INC
60 Technology Dr, Irvine (92618-2301)
PHONE..................................949 783-3300
David Renzi, *President*
Erik Reese, *President*
Ken Watson, *President*
Kevin Cousins, *CFO*
Pete Davis, *Vice Pres*
▼ EMP: 90
SQ FT: 21,000
SALES: 15.6MM
SALES (corp-wide): 15.9B **Publicly Held**
SIC: 3841 Surgical & medical instruments
HQ: C. R. Bard, Inc.
1 Becton Dr
Franklin Lakes NJ 07417
908 277-8000

(P-21832)
NEOTRACT INC (DH)
Also Called: Urolift
4155 Hopyard Rd, Pleasanton
(94588-8534)
PHONE..................................925 401-0700
David R Amerson, *President*
Doug Hughes, *CFO*
Theodore M Bender, *Vice Pres*
Lisa E Campbell, *Vice Pres*
Joseph Catanese, *Vice Pres*
EMP: 12
SALES (est): 3.9MM
SALES (corp-wide): 2.4B **Publicly Held**
SIC: 3841 8733 8011 Medical instruments
& equipment; blood & bone work; medical
research; urologist

(P-21833)
NEURAL ANALYTICS INC
2440 S Sepulveda Blvd # 115, Los Angeles
(90064-1744)
PHONE..................................818 317-4999
Leo Petrossian, *CEO*
Mark Hattendorf, *CFO*
Neil A Martin, *Chief Mktg Ofcr*
Robert Hamilton, *Vice Pres*
Dan Henchey, *Vice Pres*
EMP: 14
SQ FT: 3,000
SALES (est): 1.9MM **Privately Held**
SIC: 3841 3845 Diagnostic apparatus,
medical; ultrasonic scanning devices,
medical

(P-21834)
NEUROPTICS INC
23041 Ave D L Carlota 1, Laguna Hills
(92653)
PHONE..................................949 250-9792
Kamran Siminou, *CEO*
William Worthen, *President*
▲ EMP: 18
SALES (est): 3.6MM **Privately Held**
WEB: www.neuroptics.com
SIC: 3841 Surgical & medical instruments

(P-21835)
NEVRO CORP
411 Acacia Ave, Palo Alto (94306-2203)
PHONE..................................650 251-0005
EMP: 172 **Publicly Held**
SIC: 3841 Surgical & medical instruments
PA: Nevro Corp.
1800 Bridge Pkwy
Redwood City CA 94065

(P-21836)
NEVRO CORP (PA)
1800 Bridge Pkwy, Redwood City
(94065-1164)
PHONE..................................650 251-0005
D Keith Grossman, *Ch of Bd*
Andrew H Galligan, *CFO*
Niamh Pellegrini, *Ch Credit Ofcr*
David Caraway, *Chief Mktg Ofcr*
Jim Alecxih, *Vice Pres*
EMP: 136
SQ FT: 50,000
SALES: 387.2MM **Publicly Held**
SIC: 3841 Surgical & medical instruments

(P-21837)
NEW WORLD MEDICAL INCORPORATED
10763 Edison Ct, Rancho Cucamonga
(91730-4844)
PHONE..................................909 466-4304
A Mateen Ahmed, *President*
Rafael Chan, *Officer*
Omar Ahmed, *Vice Pres*
EMP: 17
SQ FT: 10,000
SALES: 15.9MM **Privately Held**
WEB: www.ahmedvalve.com
SIC: 3841 Ophthalmic instruments & apparatus

(P-21838)
NEWPORT MEDICAL INSTRS INC
Also Called: Covidien
1620 Sunflower Ave, Costa Mesa
(92626-1513)
PHONE..................................949 642-3910
Philippe Negre, *President*
Patti Gunter, *Info Tech Mgr*
Truc Le, *Engineer*
Karen Faber, *Manager*
Robert Gerger, *Manager*
▲ EMP: 95
SQ FT: 33,328
SALES (est): 20.8MM **Privately Held**
WEB: www.newportnmi.com
SIC: 3841 3842 3845 Surgical & medical
instruments; respirators; electromedical
equipment
HQ: Covidien Limited
20 Lower Hatch Street
Dublin 2

(P-21839)
NEXUS DX INC
6759 Mesa Ridge Rd, San Diego
(92121-4902)
PHONE...............................858 410-4600
Nam Shin, *CEO*
▼ EMP: 34
SQ FT: 39,000
SALES (est): 54.7MM
SALES (corp-wide): 96.1K **Privately Held**
SIC: 3841 Diagnostic apparatus, medical
HQ: Polaris Medinet, Llc
13571 Zinnia Hills Pl
San Diego CA 92130
858 410-4600

(P-21840)
NORDSON MED DESIGN & DEV INC
Also Called: Tdc Medical California
610 Palomar Ave, Sunnyvale (94085-2912)
PHONE...............................603 707-8753
Gary Boseck, *Branch Mgr*
Matthew Davis, *Program Mgr*
Isabel Kerschmann, *Buyer*
Ron Koronkowski, *Director*
EMP: 18
SALES (corp-wide): 2.2B **Publicly Held**
SIC: 3841 Surgical & medical instruments
HQ: Nordson Medical Design And Development, Inc.
261 Cedar Hill St Ste 1
Marlborough MA 01752
508 481-6233

(P-21841)
NORDSON MEDICAL (CA) LLC
7612 Woodwind Dr, Huntington Beach
(92647-7164)
PHONE...............................657 215-4200
David Zgonc, *Mng Member*
Donald Adams, *Technology*
Sherry Liu, *Engineer*
James Young, *Opers Staff*
John Pickett, *Director*
EMP: 51
SQ FT: 40,000
SALES (est): 21.6MM **Privately Held**
WEB: www.avalonlabs.com
SIC: 3841 Surgical & medical instruments

(P-21842)
NUMOTECH INC
9420 Reseda Blvd Ste 504, Northridge
(91324-2932)
PHONE...............................818 772-1579
Robert Felton, *President*
EMP: 100
SALES (est): 6.7MM **Privately Held**
WEB: www.numotech.com
SIC: 3841 Medical instruments & equipment, blood & bone work

(P-21843)
NUVASIVE INC (PA)
7475 Lusk Blvd, San Diego (92121-5707)
PHONE...............................858 909-1800
J Christopher Barry, *CEO*
Gregory T Lucier, *Ch of Bd*
Matthew W Link, *President*
Rajesh J Asarpota, *CFO*
Carol A Cox, *Exec VP*
▲ EMP: 75
SQ FT: 152,000
SALES: 1.1B **Publicly Held**
WEB: www.nuvasive.com
SIC: 3841 Surgical & medical instruments

(P-21844)
NUVASIVE SPCLZED ORTHPDICS INC
101 Enterprise Ste 100, Aliso Viejo
(92656-2604)
PHONE...............................949 837-3600
Edmund Roschak, *CEO*
Robert Krist, *CFO*
Jeff Rydin, *Security Dir*
Jeffrey Bacani, *Senior Buyer*
EMP: 100
SQ FT: 52,741
SALES (est): 3.6MM
SALES (corp-wide): 1.1B **Publicly Held**
SIC: 3841 Inhalation therapy equipment

PA: Nuvasive, Inc.
7475 Lusk Blvd
San Diego CA 92121
858 909-1800

(P-21845)
OBALON THERAPEUTICS INC
5421 Avd Encinas Ste F, Carlsbad
(92008-4410)
PHONE...............................760 795-6558
William J Plovanic, *President*
Kim Kamdar, *Ch of Bd*
William Plovanic, *President*
Nooshin Hussainy, *CFO*
Andrew Rasdal, *Chairman*
EMP: 113
SQ FT: 20,200
SALES: 9.1MM **Privately Held**
SIC: 3841 Surgical & medical instruments

(P-21846)
OCT MEDICAL IMAGING INC
1002 Health Sciences Rd, Irvine
(92617-3010)
PHONE...............................949 701-6656
Tirunelveli Ramalingam, *CFO*
EMP: 10
SALES (est): 1.5MM **Privately Held**
SIC: 3841 Diagnostic apparatus, medical

(P-21847)
OHADI MANAGEMENT CORPORATION
11088 Elm Ave, Rancho Cucamonga
(91730-7676)
PHONE...............................909 625-2000
Camiar Ohadi, *President*
EMP: 12 EST: 2008
SALES (est): 621.1K **Privately Held**
SIC: 3841 Diagnostic apparatus, medical

(P-21848)
ONSET MEDICAL CORPORATION
13900 Alton Pkwy Ste 120, Irvine
(92618-1621)
PHONE...............................949 716-1100
Joseph Bishop, *President*
David Richard, *CFO*
▲ EMP: 20
SALES (est): 2.6MM **Privately Held**
SIC: 3841 Surgical & medical instruments
HQ: Terumo Americas Holding, Inc.
265 Davidson Ave Ste 320
Somerset NJ 08873
732 302-4900

(P-21849)
OPTIMEDICA CORPORATION
510 Cottonwood Dr, Milpitas (95035-7403)
PHONE...............................408 850-8600
Miles White, *CEO*
Mark J Forchette, *President*
Mark A Murray, *CFO*
EMP: 140
SALES (est): 30.2MM
SALES (corp-wide): 81.5B **Publicly Held**
WEB: www.optimedica.com
SIC: 3841 Eye examining instruments & apparatus
PA: Johnson & Johnson
1 Johnson And Johnson Plz
New Brunswick NJ 08933
732 524-0400

(P-21850)
OPTISCAN BIOMEDICAL CORP
24590 Clawiter Rd, Hayward (94545-2222)
PHONE...............................510 342-5800
Cary G Vance, *President*
Peter Rule, *Ch of Bd*
Donald Webber, *COO*
Patrick Nugent, *CFO*
Jim Causey, *Vice Pres*
EMP: 50
SQ FT: 10,000
SALES (est): 10.6MM **Privately Held**
WEB: www.farir.com
SIC: 3841 Diagnostic apparatus, medical

(P-21851)
OPTOVUE INC (PA)
2800 Bayview Dr, Fremont (94538-6518)
PHONE...............................510 623-8868
Jay WEI, *CEO*
David Voris, *President*

Paul Kealey, *Senior VP*
Joe Garibaldi, *Vice Pres*
Gordon Wong, *Vice Pres*
▲ EMP: 86
SQ FT: 12,400
SALES (est): 37.1MM **Privately Held**
WEB: www.optovue.com
SIC: 3841 5048 Surgical & medical instruments; ophthalmic goods

(P-21852)
OSSEON LLC
2301 Circadian Way # 300, Santa Rosa
(95407-5461)
PHONE...............................707 636-5940
Ronald Clough, *CEO*
Spencer Hill,
EMP: 19
SQ FT: 10,000
SALES (est): 2.4MM **Privately Held**
SIC: 3841 Surgical & medical instruments

(P-21853)
P K ENGINEERING & MFG CO INC
200 E Shell Rd 2b, Ventura (93001-1261)
PHONE...............................805 628-9556
William Kilbury, *President*
Robert Kilbury, *Vice Pres*
EMP: 15
SQ FT: 8,700
SALES (est): 1.3MM **Privately Held**
SIC: 3841 Surgical instruments & apparatus; saws, surgical

(P-21854)
PACIFIC INTEGRATED MFG INC
4364 Bonita Rd Ste 454, Bonita
(91902-1421)
PHONE...............................619 921-3464
Stephen F Keane, *CEO*
Charles Peinado, *President*
EMP: 200
SALES (est): 6.6MM **Privately Held**
SIC: 3841 Diagnostic apparatus, medical

(P-21855)
PAN PROBE BIOTECH INC
7396 Trade St, San Diego (92121-2422)
PHONE...............................858 689-9936
Shujie Cui, *CEO*
Alice Yu, *Vice Pres*
▲ EMP: 18 EST: 1995
SQ FT: 5,246
SALES (est): 2.1MM **Privately Held**
WEB: www.panprobebiotech.com
SIC: 3841 Diagnostic apparatus, medical

(P-21856)
PENUMBRA INC (PA)
1 Penumbra, Alameda (94502-7676)
PHONE...............................510 748-3200
Adam Elsesser, *Ch of Bd*
EMP: 251
SQ FT: 295,000
SALES: 444.9MM **Publicly Held**
WEB: www.penumbrainc.com
SIC: 3841 Surgical & medical instruments

(P-21857)
PHARMACO-KINESIS CORPORATION
6053 W Century Blvd # 600, Los Angeles
(90045-6400)
PHONE...............................310 641-2700
Frank Adell, *Principal*
Thomas Chen, *Principal*
Peter Hirshfield, *Principal*
John Muthew, *Principal*
EMP: 26
SALES (est): 5.6MM **Privately Held**
WEB: www.pharmaco-kinesis.com
SIC: 3841 Surgical & medical instruments

(P-21858)
PHILLIPS-MEDISIZE
3545 Harbor Blvd, Costa Mesa
(92626-1406)
PHONE...............................949 477-9495
Bob Frank, *General Mgr*
Hank Mancini, *Business Mgr*
EMP: 240
SQ FT: 45,000

SALES (est): 47.2MM
SALES (corp-wide): 40.6B **Privately Held**
WEB: www.affinitymed.com
SIC: 3841 Surgical & medical instruments
HQ: Molex, Llc
2222 Wellington Ct
Lisle IL 60532
630 969-4550

(P-21859)
PNEUMRX INC
4255 Burton Dr, Santa Clara (95054-1512)
PHONE...............................650 625-4440
Erin McGurk, *CEO*
Darlene Ebeling, *Surgery Dir*
Steve Fermin, *Executive Asst*
Erik Hagen, *Controller*
Lisa Rogan, *VP Mktg*
EMP: 35
SALES (est): 7.2MM **Privately Held**
WEB: www.pneumrx.com
SIC: 3841 Surgical & medical instruments
HQ: Btg International Limited
5 Fleet Place
London EC4M

(P-21860)
POST-SRGCAL RHAB SPCALISTS LLC
12774 Florence Ave, Santa Fe Springs
(90670-3906)
PHONE...............................562 236-5600
Steven Howser, *Mng Member*
EMP: 15 EST: 2005
SALES (est): 1.8MM **Privately Held**
SIC: 3841 Surgical & medical instruments

(P-21861)
POTRERO MEDICAL INC
26142 Eden Landing Rd, Hayward
(94545-3710)
PHONE...............................888 635-7280
Joe Urban, *CEO*
Andrew Offer, *CFO*
Saheel Sutaria, *CTO*
Teresa Nguyen, *Engineer*
Jeff Matthews, *Controller*
EMP: 52
SQ FT: 15,000
SALES: 1.1MM **Privately Held**
SIC: 3841 Diagnostic apparatus, medical

(P-21862)
PRANALYTICA INC
1101 Colorado Ave, Santa Monica
(90401-3009)
PHONE...............................310 458-3345
C Kumar N Patel, *President*
Francis McGuire, *VP Finance*
EMP: 15
SQ FT: 7,350
SALES: 3MM **Privately Held**
SIC: 3841 3826 Surgical & medical instruments; laser scientific & engineering instruments

(P-21863)
PRO-DEX INC (PA)
2361 Mcgaw Ave, Irvine (92614-5831)
PHONE...............................949 769-3200
Richard L Van Kirk, *President*
Nicholas J Swenson, *Ch of Bd*
Alisha K Charlton, *CFO*
William Farrell, *Bd of Directors*
Daniel Davison, *Engineer*
EMP: 70
SQ FT: 28,180
SALES: 27.1MM **Publicly Held**
WEB: www.pro-dex.com
SIC: 3841 3843 7372 3594 Surgical & medical instruments; dental equipment; business oriented computer software; motors, pneumatic; business consulting

(P-21864)
PROMAXO INC
70 Washington St Ste 407, Oakland
(94607-3705)
PHONE...............................510 982-1202
Amit Vohra, *President*
Dinesh Kumar, *COO*
Michael Bartholomew, *Ch Credit Ofcr*
EMP: 13
SALES (est): 1.1MM **Privately Held**
SIC: 3841 Surgical & medical instruments

(P-21865)
PROSURG INC
Also Called: Ximed Medical Systems
2195 Trade Zone Blvd, San Jose
(95131-1743)
PHONE..............................408 945-4040
Ashvin H Desai, *President*
EMP: 40
SQ FT: 14,800
SALES: 4MM **Privately Held**
WEB: www.prosurg.com
SIC: 3841 3823 Surgical & medical instruments; industrial instrmnts msrmnt display/control process variable

(P-21866)
PROVASIS THERAPEUTICS INC
9177 Sky Park Ct B, San Diego
(92123-4341)
PHONE..............................858 712-2101
Terrance Bruggeman, *Ch of Bd*
John W Cardosa, *CFO*
Bruce E Bennett Jr, *Vice Pres*
Laura E Dipietro, *Vice Pres*
Gary L Loomis PHD, *Vice Pres*
EMP: 36 EST: 1995
SQ FT: 20,400
SALES (est): 2.9MM **Privately Held**
WEB: www.provasis.com
SIC: 3841 8011 Surgical instruments & apparatus; physical medicine, physician/surgeon

(P-21867)
PRYOR PRODUCTS
1819 Peacock Blvd, Oceanside
(92056-3578)
PHONE..............................760 724-8244
Jeffrey Pryor, *CEO*
Paul Pryor, *Vice Pres*
Kevin Donahue, *Engineer*
George Kemper, *VP Sales*
▲ EMP: 50
SQ FT: 29,000
SALES (est): 10.9MM **Privately Held**
WEB: www.pryorproducts.com
SIC: 3841 IV transfusion apparatus

(P-21868)
PULSAR VASCULAR INC
130 Knowles Dr Ste E, Los Gatos
(95032-1832)
PHONE..............................408 246-4300
Robert M Abrams, *President*
Chas Roue, *Vice Pres*
EMP: 15
SQ FT: 4,500
SALES (est): 2.8MM
SALES (corp-wide): 81.5B **Publicly Held**
SIC: 3841 Diagnostic apparatus, medical
HQ: Depuy Synthes Products, Inc.
325 Paramount Dr
Raynham MA 02767
508 880-8100

(P-21869)
PULSE METRIC INC
2100 Hawley Dr, Vista (92084-2615)
PHONE..............................760 842-8224
Shiu-Shin Chio, *Ch of Bd*
Jeffery Lapointe, *Design Engr*
EMP: 12
SALES (est): 1.3MM **Privately Held**
WEB: www.pulsemetric.com
SIC: 3841 Blood pressure apparatus

(P-21870)
RA MEDICAL SYSTEMS INC
2070 Las Palmas Dr, Carlsbad
(92011-1518)
PHONE..............................760 804-1648
Dean Irwin, *Ch of Bd*
Jeffrey J Kraws, *President*
Andrew Jackson, *CFO*
Thomas G Fogarty, *Ch Credit Ofcr*
Daniel Horwood, *Admin Sec*
▼ EMP: 118
SQ FT: 32,000
SALES: 6.2MM **Privately Held**
WEB: www.ramed.com
SIC: 3841 3845 Surgical lasers; laser systems & equipment, medical

(P-21871)
RADIOLOGY SUPPORT DEVICES
1904 E Dominguez St, Long Beach
(90810-1002)
PHONE..............................310 518-0527
Matthew Alderson, *CEO*
EMP: 29
SQ FT: 16,000
SALES (est): 5.5MM **Privately Held**
WEB: www.rsdphantoms.com
SIC: 3841 3844 Diagnostic apparatus, medical; X-ray apparatus & tubes

(P-21872)
REBOUND THERAPEUTICS CORP
13900 Alton Pkwy Ste 120, Irvine
(92618-1621)
PHONE..............................949 305-8111
Jeffrey Valko, *CEO*
EMP: 26 EST: 2015
SALES (est): 4.9MM **Publicly Held**
SIC: 3841 Surgical & medical instruments
PA: Integra Lifesciences Holdings Corporation
311 Enterprise Dr
Plainsboro NJ 08536

(P-21873)
RECOR MEDICAL INC (HQ)
1049 Elwell Ct, Palo Alto (94303-4308)
PHONE..............................650 542-7700
Andrew Weiss, *President*
Mano Iyer, *COO*
Matthew J Franklin, *CFO*
Toni Caruso, *Office Mgr*
Shruthi Thirumalai, *Engineer*
EMP: 11
SQ FT: 1,500
SALES (est): 2.2MM **Privately Held**
SIC: 3841 Surgical & medical instruments

(P-21874)
REPLENISH INC
73 N Vinedo Ave, Pasadena (91107-3759)
PHONE..............................626 219-7867
Sean Caffey, *Chairman*
Mark Humayun, *President*
Yu-Chong Tai, *Co-Founder*
EMP: 10
SALES (est): 1.8MM **Privately Held**
SIC: 3841 Medical instruments & equipment, blood & bone work

(P-21875)
RES MED INC
9001 Spectrum Center Blvd, San Diego
(92123-1438)
PHONE..............................858 746-2400
EMP: 35
SALES (est): 3.1MM **Privately Held**
SIC: 3841 Surgical & medical instruments

(P-21876)
RESMED INC (PA)
9001 Spectrum Center Blvd, San Diego
(92123-1438)
PHONE..............................858 836-5000
Michael J Farrell, *CEO*
Raj Sodhi, *President*
Brett Sandercock, *CFO*
David Pendarvis, *Officer*
EMP: 277
SQ FT: 230,000
SALES: 2.6B **Publicly Held**
WEB: www.resmed.com
SIC: 3841 7372 Diagnostic apparatus, medical; application computer software

(P-21877)
RESPIRATORY SUPPORT PRODUCTS
9255 Customhouse Plz N, San Diego
(92154-7636)
PHONE..............................619 710-1000
Anthony V Beran, *President*
▲ EMP: 29 EST: 1975
SQ FT: 35,000
SALES (est): 2.6MM **Privately Held**
WEB: www.rspace.com
SIC: 3841 3845 Surgical instruments & apparatus; medical instruments & equipment, blood & bone work; electromedical equipment

(P-21878)
RESTORATION ROBOTICS INC (PA)
1972 Hartog Dr, San Jose (95131-2212)
PHONE..............................408 457-1280
▲ EMP: 87
SQ FT: 23,000
SALES: 21.9MM **Privately Held**
SIC: 3841 5047 Surgical & medical instruments; electro-medical equipment

(P-21879)
REVERSE MEDICAL CORPORATION
13700 Alton Pkwy Ste 167, Irvine
(92618-1618)
PHONE..............................949 215-0660
Jeffrey Valko, *President*
Brian Strauss, *CTO*
EMP: 15
SALES (est): 2.7MM **Privately Held**
SIC: 3841 Surgical & medical instruments
HQ: Covidien Limited
20 Lower Hatch Street
Dublin 2

(P-21880)
RF SURGICAL SYSTEMS LLC
5927 Landau Ct, Carlsbad (92008-8803)
PHONE..............................855 522-7027
John Buhler, *President*
Ron Wangerin, *CFO*
William Blair, *CTO*
▲ EMP: 55
SQ FT: 24,000
SALES (est): 19.4MM **Privately Held**
WEB: www.rfsurg.com
SIC: 3841 Surgical & medical instruments
HQ: Medtronic, Inc.
710 Medtronic Pkwy
Minneapolis MN 55432
763 514-4000

(P-21881)
RH USA INC
Also Called: Lumenis
455 N Canyons Pkwy Ste B, Livermore
(94551-7682)
PHONE..............................925 245-7900
Jeannette Trujillo, *Vice Pres*
Brian Guscott, *Vice Pres*
Bob Schultz, *Engineer*
Miranda Yee, *Controller*
Gladys Copeland, *Director*
▲ EMP: 42
SQ FT: 40,000
SALES: 9.4MM
SALES (corp-wide): 97.7MM **Privately Held**
SIC: 3841 Surgical & medical instruments
PA: R.H. Technologies Ltd
5 Hatzoref
Nazareth Illit 17880
460 890-00

(P-21882)
ROBERT BOSCH LLC
Also Called: Bosch Diagnostics
2030 Alameda Padre Serra, Santa Barbara
(93103-1704)
PHONE..............................805 966-2000
Andreas Huber, *Branch Mgr*
EMP: 30
SALES (corp-wide): 294.8MM **Privately Held**
SIC: 3841 Diagnostic apparatus, medical
HQ: Robert Bosch Llc
2800 S 25th Ave
Broadview IL 60155
248 876-1000

(P-21883)
ROBERT P VON ZABERN
4121 Tigris Way, Riverside (92503-4844)
PHONE..............................951 734-7215
Robert P Von Zabern, *Owner*
EMP: 13
SQ FT: 1,500
SALES (est): 1.1MM **Privately Held**
WEB: www.vzs.net
SIC: 3841 Surgical instruments & apparatus

(P-21884)
ROXWOOD MEDICAL INC
400 Seaport Ct Ste 103, Redwood City
(94063-2799)
PHONE..............................650 779-4555
Mehrdad Farhangnia, *CEO*
John Miller, *Vice Pres*
Helen Song, *Vice Pres*
Veronica Thompson, *Senior Mgr*
Rubyrose Kozuma, *Cust Mgr*
EMP: 15
SQ FT: 3,000
SALES (est): 2.3MM **Privately Held**
SIC: 3841 Surgical & medical instruments
PA: Btg Limited
5 Fleet Place
London EC4M

(P-21885)
RUXCO ENGINEERING INC
6051 Entp Dr Ste 105, Diamond Springs
(95619)
PHONE..............................530 622-4122
Michael Ruck, *President*
Silvia Ruck, *CFO*
EMP: 13
SQ FT: 10,000
SALES (est): 1.4MM **Privately Held**
SIC: 3841 3812 Medical instruments & equipment, blood & bone work; acceleration indicators & systems components, aerospace

(P-21886)
SADRA MEDICAL INC
160 Knowles Dr, Los Gatos (95032-1828)
PHONE..............................408 370-1550
Michael F Mahoney, *President*
Ken Martin, *President*
Jon Bohane, *CFO*
Robert Chang, *Exec VP*
Dave Paul, *Vice Pres*
EMP: 20
SALES (est): 3.7MM
SALES (corp-wide): 9.8B **Publicly Held**
WEB: www.sadramedical.com
SIC: 3841 Surgical & medical instruments
PA: Boston Scientific Corporation
300 Boston Scientific Way
Marlborough MA 01752
508 683-4000

(P-21887)
SANARUS MEDICAL INCORPORATED
7068 Koll Center Pkwy # 425, Pleasanton
(94566-3158)
PHONE..............................925 460-6080
John Howe, *President*
Israel Madera, *Vice Pres*
Jeff Stevens, *Executive*
Karen Hambly, *Office Mgr*
Bryan Hanna, *Opers Staff*
EMP: 12
SQ FT: 12,000
SALES (est): 1.7MM **Privately Held**
WEB: www.sanarus.com
SIC: 3841 Surgical & medical instruments
PA: Sanarus Technologies, Inc.
1249 Quarry Ln Ste 150
Pleasanton CA 94566

(P-21888)
SANOVAS INC
2597 Kerner Blvd, San Rafael
(94901-5571)
P.O. Box 2129 (94912-2129)
PHONE..............................415 729-9391
Lawrence Gerrans, *President*
Jeff Heer, *COO*
Robert Farrell, *CFO*
Steve Budill, *Vice Pres*
Mike Humason, *Vice Pres*
EMP: 36
SALES (est): 6.8MM **Privately Held**
SIC: 3841 Surgical & medical instruments

(P-21889)
SCHOLTEN SURGICAL INSTRS INC
170 Commerce St Ste 101, Lodi
(95240-0871)
PHONE..............................209 365-1393

Arie Scholten, *President*
Jim Van Andel, *COO*
Jim V Andel, *Manager*
EMP: 15
SALES (est): 1.6MM **Privately Held**
WEB: www.bioptome.com
SIC: 3841 Surgical & medical instruments

(P-21890)
SCIGENE CORPORATION
1287 Reamwood Ave, Sunnyvale
(94089-2234)
PHONE..........................408 733-7337
James Stanchfield, *President*
Terry Gill, *Mfg Staff*
EMP: 12
SQ FT: 12,000
SALES: 2.2MM **Privately Held**
WEB: www.scigene.com
SIC: 3841 Surgical & medical instruments

(P-21891)
SCITON INC
925 Commercial St, Palo Alto
(94303-4908)
PHONE..........................650 493-9155
James Hobart, *CEO*
Shannyn Harrison, *Partner*
Ariel Weaver, *Partner*
Daniel Negus, *President*
Dan Negus, *Executive*
▼ **EMP:** 74
SQ FT: 15,000
SALES (est): 20MM **Privately Held**
WEB: www.sciton.com
SIC: 3841 Surgical lasers

(P-21892)
SEASTAR MEDICAL INC
2187 Newcastle Ave # 200, Cardiff By The
Sea (92007-1848)
PHONE..........................734 272-4772
R James Danehy, *CEO*
Mark R Morsfield, *CFO*
H David Humes, *Officer*
EMP: 13 **EST:** 2007
SALES (est): 3.8MM **Privately Held**
SIC: 3841 Surgical & medical instruments

(P-21893)
SECHRIST INDUSTRIES INC
4225 E La Palma Ave, Anaheim
(92807-1844)
PHONE..........................714 579-8400
Edward Pulwer, *CEO*
John Razzano, *CFO*
Sean Terry, *QA Dir*
Ray Tan, *Design Engr*
Fernando Cendejas, *Engineer*
▲ **EMP:** 88
SQ FT: 74,000
SALES (est): 815.2K
SALES (corp-wide): 17.4MM **Privately Held**
WEB: www.sechristind.com
SIC: 3841 Surgical & medical instruments
HQ: Wound Care Holdings, Llc
5220 Belfort Rd Ste 130
Jacksonville FL 32256
800 379-9774

(P-21894)
SECOND SIGHT MEDICAL PDTS INC (PA)
12744 San Fernando Rd, Sylmar
(91342-3853)
PHONE..........................818 833-5000
Jonathan Will McGuire, *President*
Gregg Williams, *Ch of Bd*
Patrick Ryan, *COO*
John T Blake, *CFO*
Stephen Okland, *Ch Credit Ofcr*
EMP: 112
SQ FT: 45,351
SALES: 6.9MM **Publicly Held**
WEB: www.2-sight.com
SIC: 3841 Ophthalmic instruments & apparatus

(P-21895)
SEMLER SCIENTIFIC INC
911 Bern Ct Ste 110, San Jose
(95112-1242)
PHONE..........................877 774-4211
Douglas Murphy-Chutorian, *CEO*
Herbert J Semler, *Ch of Bd*

Daniel E Conger, *CFO*
EMP: 29
SALES: 21.4MM **Privately Held**
SIC: 3841 Surgical & medical instruments

(P-21896)
SEQUENT MEDICAL INC
11 Columbia Ste A, Aliso Viejo
(92656-1427)
PHONE..........................949 830-9600
Thomas C Wilder, *President*
Kevin J Cousins, *CFO*
Andrew J Hykes, *Vice Pres*
Paul G Krell, *Vice Pres*
William R Patterson, *Vice Pres*
EMP: 65
SALES (est): 11.9MM **Privately Held**
WEB: www.sequentmedical.com
SIC: 3841 Surgical & medical instruments
HQ: Microvention, Inc.
35 Enterprise
Aliso Viejo CA 92656
714 258-8000

(P-21897)
SHEATHING TECHNOLOGIES INC
675 Jarvis Dr Ste A, Morgan Hill
(95037-2830)
PHONE..........................408 782-2720
Larry Polayes, *President*
Kipp Herman, *Personnel Assit*
▲ **EMP:** 46
SQ FT: 10,000
SALES (est): 9.4MM **Privately Held**
WEB: www.sheathes.com
SIC: 3841 Diagnostic apparatus, medical

(P-21898)
SHOCKWAVE MEDICAL INC (PA)
5403 Betsy Ross Dr, Santa Clara
(95054-1162)
PHONE..........................510 279-4262
Douglas Godshall, *President*
C Raymond Larkin Jr, *Ch of Bd*
Dan Puckett, *CFO*
Isaac Zacharias, *Ch Credit Ofcr*
Keith D Dawkins, *Chief Mktg Ofcr*
EMP: 69
SQ FT: 35,000
SALES: 12.2MM **Publicly Held**
SIC: 3841 Diagnostic apparatus, medical

(P-21899)
SILK ROAD MEDICAL INC
1213 Innsbruck Dr, Sunnyvale
(94089-1317)
PHONE..........................408 720-9002
Erica J Rogers, *President*
Lucas W Buchanan, *CFO*
Andrew S Davis, *Exec VP*
Randall Sullivan, *Exec VP*
Rhonda Barr, *Area Mgr*
EMP: 176
SQ FT: 31,000
SALES: 34.5MM **Privately Held**
SIC: 3841 Surgical & medical instruments

(P-21900)
SIMPLAY LABS LLC
1140 E Arques Ave, Sunnyvale
(94085-4602)
PHONE..........................408 616-4000
Joseph Lias,
▲ **EMP:** 31
SALES (est): 3.2MM **Privately Held**
SIC: 3841 Surgical & medical instruments

(P-21901)
SMITHS MEDICAL ASD INC
9255 Customhouse Plz N, San Diego
(92154-7636)
PHONE..........................619 710-1000
Aldo Soto, *Branch Mgr*
Sergio Ortiz, *Engineer*
EMP: 20
SALES (corp-wide): 4.2B **Privately Held**
WEB: www.smith-medical.com
SIC: 3841 Surgical & medical instruments
HQ: Smiths Medical Asd, Inc.
6000 Nathan Ln N Ste 100
Plymouth MN 55442
763 383-3000

(P-21902)
SMITHS MEDICAL ASD INC
2231 Rutherford Rd, Carlsbad
(92008-8811)
PHONE..........................760 602-4400
Donald Cornwall, *Manager*
EMP: 108
SALES (corp-wide): 4.1B **Privately Held**
SIC: 3841 IV transfusion apparatus
HQ: Smiths Medical Asd, Inc.
6000 Nathan Ln N Ste 100
Plymouth MN 55442
763 383-3000

(P-21903)
SOLTA MEDICAL INC (DH)
7031 Koll Center Pkwy # 260, Pleasanton
(94566-3134)
PHONE..........................510 786-6946
J Michael Pearson, *President*
Howard B Schiller, *Treasurer*
Robert Chai-Onn, *Admin Sec*
▲ **EMP:** 15
SQ FT: 88,000
SALES (est): 73.6MM
SALES (corp-wide): 8.3B **Privately Held**
WEB: www.thermage.com
SIC: 3841 Surgical & medical instruments
HQ: Bausch Health Americas, Inc.
400 Somerset Corp Blvd
Bridgewater NJ 08807
908 927-1400

(P-21904)
SONOMA ORTHOPEDIC PRODUCTS INC
50 W San Fernando St Fl 5, San Jose
(95113-2433)
PHONE..........................847 807-4378
Charles Nelson, *CEO*
Matt Jerome, *President*
Rick Epstein, *CEO*
Kyle Lappin, *Vice Pres*
Alex Winber, *Vice Pres*
EMP: 13
SALES (est): 2MM **Privately Held**
SIC: 3841 Surgical & medical instruments

(P-21905)
SONOMA PHARMACEUTICALS INC
1129 N Mcdowell Blvd, Petaluma
(94954-1110)
PHONE..........................707 283-0550
Amy Trombly, *CEO*
Marc Umscheid, *COO*
John Dal Poggetto, *CFO*
Robert Northey, *Vice Pres*
Bruce Thornton, *Vice Pres*
EMP: 79
SALES: 18.9MM **Privately Held**
WEB: www.oculusis.com
SIC: 3841 Surgical & medical instruments

(P-21906)
SOURCE SURGICAL INC
3130 20th St Ste 200, San Francisco
(94110-2789)
PHONE..........................415 861-7040
Craig Sparks, *President*
Todd Marinchak, *CFO*
Mattie Stone, *Sales Associate*
Casey Hales, *Education*
Sara Baker, *Manager*
EMP: 18
SQ FT: 2,300
SALES: 1.5MM **Privately Held**
WEB: www.sourcesurgical.com
SIC: 3841 Surgical instruments & apparatus

(P-21907)
SPECIALTEAM MEDICAL SVC INC
22445 La Palma Ave Ste F, Yorba Linda
(92887-3811)
PHONE..........................714 694-0348
Terry Bagwell, *President*
Erick Bickett, *CFO*
Billy Teeple, *Vice Pres*
EMP: 15
SQ FT: 7,000
SALES (est): 2.2MM **Privately Held**
WEB: www.specialteam.com
SIC: 3841 Surgical & medical instruments

(P-21908)
SPECIFIC DIAGNOSTICS INC
855 Maude Ave, Mountain View
(94043-4021)
PHONE..........................561 655-5588
Paul Rhodes, *Principal*
Karen Koski, *Officer*
Ray Martino, *Principal*
Michael Eiden, *CIO*
Richard Huang, *Director*
EMP: 20
SALES (est): 2MM **Privately Held**
SIC: 3841 Surgical & medical instruments

(P-21909)
SPECTRANETICS CORPORATION
5055 Brandin Ct, Fremont (94538-3140)
PHONE..........................510 933-7964
Gil Paet, *Principal*
EMP: 80
SALES (est): 2.1MM **Privately Held**
SIC: 3841 5047 5999 Surgical & medical
instruments; medical equipment & supplies; medical apparatus & supplies

(P-21910)
SPINALMOTION INC
201 San Antonio Cir # 115, Mountain View
(94040-1252)
PHONE..........................650 947-3472
Christine Hanni, *CFO*
EMP: 11
SALES (est): 1.4MM **Privately Held**
WEB: www.spinalmotion.com
SIC: 3841 Diagnostic apparatus, medical

(P-21911)
SPINE VIEW INC
110 Pioneer Way Ste A, Mountain View
(94041-1519)
PHONE..........................510 490-1753
Roy Chin, *CEO*
Sam Park, *COO*
EMP: 56
SALES (est): 7.3MM **Privately Held**
SIC: 3841 Surgical & medical instruments

(P-21912)
SPINEEX INC
4046 Clipper Ct, Fremont (94538-6540)
PHONE..........................510 573-1093
Roy Chin, *Ch of Bd*
Andrew Rogers, *President*
Christie Wang, *President*
George Oliva, *CFO*
Eric Blossey, *Ch Credit Ofcr*
EMP: 14 **EST:** 2017
SALES (est): 2MM **Privately Held**
SIC: 3841 5047 Surgical & medical instruments; medical equipment & supplies

(P-21913)
SPIRACUR INC (PA)
Also Called: Snap
1180 Bordeaux Dr, Sunnyvale
(94089-1209)
PHONE..........................650 364-1544
Chris Fashek, *Chairman*
Moshe Pinto, *Exec VP*
Lawrence Hu, *Vice Pres*
Linda Lamagna, *Vice Pres*
Yousuf Mazhar, *Vice Pres*
EMP: 52
SALES: 7MM **Privately Held**
SIC: 3841 Surgical & medical instruments

(P-21914)
SSCOR INC
11064 Randall St, Sun Valley (91352-2621)
PHONE..........................818 504-4054
Samuel D Say, *President*
Jonathan Kim, *Vice Pres*
Betty Say, *Admin Sec*
Gary Decosse, *Opers Staff*
Jan Say, *Marketing Staff*
▲ **EMP:** 16
SQ FT: 12,000
SALES (est): 3.5MM **Privately Held**
WEB: www.sscor.com
SIC: 3841 Suction therapy apparatus

(P-21915)
ST JUDE MEDICAL LLC
Also Called: Abbott
645 Almanor Ave, Sunnyvale (94085-2901)
PHONE............................408 738-4883
Ron Matricaria, *Principal*
Nathan Harold, *Program Mgr*
Bryan Duff, *Sr Software Eng*
Yongjian Wu, *Sr Software Eng*
Fahfu Ho, *Software Engr*
EMP: 275
SALES (corp-wide): 30.5B **Publicly Held**
WEB: www.sjm.com
SIC: 3841 Medical instruments & equip-
ment, blood & bone work
HQ: St. Jude Medical, Llc
1 Saint Jude Medical Dr
Saint Paul MN 55117
651 756-2000

(P-21916)
STRYKER CORPORATION
Also Called: Stryker Neurovascular
47900 Bayside Pkwy, Fremont
(94538-6515)
PHONE............................510 413-2500
EMP: 38
SALES (corp-wide): 13.6B **Publicly Held**
SIC: 3841 Surgical & medical instruments
PA: Stryker Corporation
2825 Airview Blvd
Portage MI 49002
269 385-2600

(P-21917)
STRYKER CORPORATION
3407 E La Palma Ave, Anaheim
(92806-2021)
PHONE............................714 764-1700
Lynn Wagnor, *Branch Mgr*
EMP: 38
SALES (corp-wide): 13.6B **Publicly Held**
SIC: 3841 Surgical & medical instruments
PA: Stryker Corporation
2825 Airview Blvd
Portage MI 49002
269 385-2600

(P-21918)
SURE INC
Also Called: Suretouch
1404 Granvia Altamira, Palos Verdes Es-
tates (90274-2131)
PHONE............................833 787-3462
Joseph Peterson, *CEO*
Henry Grause, *Treasurer*
David Ables, *Manager*
EMP: 12
SALES (est): 543.9K **Privately Held**
SIC: 3841 8011 Surgical & medical instru-
ments; offices & clinics of medical doctors

(P-21919)
SURGISTAR INC (PA)
Also Called: Sabel
2310 La Mirada Dr, Vista (92081-7862)
PHONE............................760 598-2480
Jonathan Woodward, *President*
Hema Chaudhary, *Vice Pres*
▲ EMP: 35
SQ FT: 12,000
SALES: 9MM **Privately Held**
SIC: 3841 Surgical & medical instruments

(P-21920)
SYNVASIVE TECHNOLOGY INC
4925 R J Mathews Park 1, El Dorado Hills
(95762)
PHONE............................916 939-3913
Kelly Fisher, *Principal*
EMP: 23
SALES (corp-wide): 7.9B **Publicly Held**
SIC: 3841 Surgical knife blades & handles
HQ: Synvasive Technology, Inc.
8690 Technology Way
Reno NV 89521
775 332-2726

(P-21921)
TACSENSE INC
10 N East St Ste 108, Woodland
(95776-5921)
PHONE............................530 797-0008
William Aldrich, *CEO*
Tingrui Pan, *President*
Hong Ye,

Suzanne Papamichail,
EMP: 10 EST: 2015
SQ FT: 4,000
SALES: 250K **Privately Held**
SIC: 3841 Blood pressure apparatus

(P-21922)
TACTX MEDICAL INC (DH)
Also Called: Creganna - Tactx Medical
1353 Dell Ave, Campbell (95008-6609)
PHONE............................408 364-7100
Robert Bell Hance, *CEO*
Nitin Matani, *President*
Helen Ryan, *President*
Jeff Kraus, *Vice Pres*
Doug Wilkins, *Vice Pres*
▼ EMP: 115
SQ FT: 12,000
SALES (est): 23.6MM
SALES (corp-wide): 13.9B **Privately Held**
WEB: www.tactxmed.com
SIC: 3841 Surgical stapling devices

(P-21923)
**TANDEM DIABETES CARE INC
(PA)**
11075 Roselle St, San Diego (92121-1204)
PHONE............................858 366-6900
Kim D Blickenstaff, *President*
John F Sheridan, *COO*
Leigh A Vosseller, *CFO*
Brian B Hansen, *Ch Credit Ofcr*
Howard Greene, *Bd of Directors*
EMP: 254
SQ FT: 108,000
SALES: 183.8MM **Publicly Held**
SIC: 3841 2833 Surgical & medical instru-
ments; insulin: bulk, uncompounded

(P-21924)
TEARLAB CORPORATION (PA)
150 La Terraza Blvd # 101, Escondido
(92025-3877)
PHONE............................858 455-6006
Joseph Jensen, *CEO*
Elias Vamvakas, *Ch of Bd*
Adrienne Graves, *Bd of Directors*
Paul Karpecki, *Bd of Directors*
Richard Lindstrom, *Bd of Directors*
EMP: 10
SQ FT: 14,700
SALES: 25MM **Publicly Held**
SIC: 3841 3851 Eye examining instru-
ments & apparatus; ophthalmic instru-
ments & apparatus; ophthalmic goods

(P-21925)
TECOMET INC
503 S Vincent Ave, Azusa (91702-5131)
PHONE............................626 334-1519
Ava Tenorio, *QC Mgr*
EMP: 745
SALES (corp-wide): 697.6MM **Privately
Held**
SIC: 3841 3444 Diagnostic apparatus,
medical; sheet metalwork
PA: Tecomet Inc.
115 Eames St
Wilmington MA 01887
978 642-2400

(P-21926)
TENACORE HOLDINGS INC
1525 E Edinger Ave, Santa Ana
(92705-4907)
PHONE............................714 444-4643
Peter Bonin III, *President*
Brand R Caso, *Vice Pres*
Tara Stack, *Vice Pres*
Bob Banks, *General Mgr*
David Pak, *Info Tech Dir*
▲ EMP: 100
SQ FT: 35,000
SALES: 15MM **Privately Held**
WEB: www.tenacore.com
SIC: 3841 7699 Surgical instruments &
apparatus; surgical instrument repair

(P-21927)
TENEX HEALTH INC
26902 Vista Ter, Lake Forest (92630-8123)
PHONE............................949 454-7500
William Maya, *President*
Ivan Mijatovic, *CFO*
Jagi Gill, *Officer*
Bernard Morrey, *Officer*

▲ EMP: 70
SQ FT: 15,000
SALES: 8MM **Privately Held**
SIC: 3841 Surgical & medical instruments

(P-21928)
THERANOS INC (PA)
7373 Gateway Blvd, Newark (94560-1149)
PHONE............................650 838-9292
David Taylor, *CEO*
So Han Spivey, *Controller*
EMP: 100
SALES (est): 34.8MM **Privately Held**
WEB: www.theranos.com
SIC: 3841 8748 Diagnostic apparatus,
medical; testing services

(P-21929)
THERAPEUTIC INDUSTRIES INC
72096 Dunham Way Ste E, Thousand
Palms (92276-3320)
P.O. Box 92 (92276-0092)
PHONE............................760 343-2502
Chris Lehude, *President*
Merideth Laureno, *Bd of Directors*
EMP: 15 EST: 2014
SALES (est): 1.7MM **Privately Held**
SIC: 3841 Surgical & medical instruments

(P-21930)
THERASENSE INC
1360 S Loop Rd, Alameda (94502-7000)
PHONE............................510 749-5400
W Mark Lortz, *CEO*
EMP: 11
SALES (est): 682.4K
SALES (corp-wide): 30.5B **Publicly Held**
WEB: www.abbott.com
SIC: 3841 Surgical & medical instruments
PA: Abbott Laboratories
100 Abbott Park Rd
Abbott Park IL 60064
224 667-6100

(P-21931)
TITAN MEDICAL DME INC
803 Camarillo Springs Rd A, Camarillo
(93012-9459)
P.O. Box 7746, Thousand Oaks (91359-
7746)
PHONE............................818 889-9998
Ted Nordblum, *President*
▲ EMP: 11
SQ FT: 2,800
SALES (est): 850K **Privately Held**
SIC: 3841 Muscle exercise apparatus,
ophthalmic

(P-21932)
TMJ SOLUTIONS INC
Also Called: TMJ Concepts
2233 Knoll Dr, Ventura (93003-7398)
PHONE............................805 650-3391
David Samson, *President*
William Anspach, *Shareholder*
John Perez, *Technician*
Erik Rinde, *Engineer*
Craig Rose, *Director*
EMP: 15
SQ FT: 7,280
SALES (est): 2.1MM **Privately Held**
WEB: www.tmjconcepts.com
SIC: 3841 Surgical & medical instruments

(P-21933)
TOP QUEST INC
13872 Magnolia Ave, Chino (91710-7027)
PHONE............................626 839-8618
Shaoching Sung, *CEO*
EMP: 17
SALES (est): 2.7MM **Privately Held**
SIC: 3841 7699 Surgical knife blades &
handles; knife, saw & tool sharpening &
repair

(P-21934)
**TOP SHELF MANUFACTURING
LLC**
1851 Paradise Rd Ste B, Tracy
(95304-8524)
PHONE............................209 834-8185
Mark Hirsch,
Jeff Leonard,
▲ EMP: 15

SALES (est): 3.9MM **Privately Held**
WEB: www.topshelfmfg.com
SIC: 3841 Diagnostic apparatus, medical

(P-21935)
TRANSCEND MEDICAL INC
127 Independence Dr, Menlo Park
(94025-1112)
PHONE............................650 325-2050
Fax: 650 325-2815
EMP: 10
SALES (est): 1.8MM
SALES (corp-wide): 49.1B **Privately Held**
SIC: 3841
PA: Novartis Ag
Lichtstrasse 35
Basel BS 4056
613 241-111

(P-21936)
**TRELLEBORG SEALING
SOLUTIONS (DH)**
Also Called: Issac
2761 Walnut Ave, Tustin (92780-7051)
PHONE............................714 415-0280
William Reising, *CEO*
Ron Fraleigh, *President*
Don Borje, *COO*
Tom Mazelin, *Vice Pres*
Neil Davies, *Controller*
EMP: 150
SQ FT: 1,600
SALES (est): 35.7MM
SALES (corp-wide): 3.7B **Privately Held**
SIC: 3841 Surgical & medical instruments
HQ: Trelleborg Corporation
200 Veterans Blvd Ste 3
South Haven MI 49090
269 639-9891

(P-21937)
TRIREME MEDICAL LLC
7060 Koll Center Pkwy, Pleasanton
(94566-3106)
PHONE............................925 931-1300
Eitan Konstantino, *President*
EMP: 70
SQ FT: 15,000
SALES: 10.6MM **Privately Held**
SIC: 3841 Suction therapy apparatus

(P-21938)
TRIVASCULAR INC (DH)
3910 Brickway Blvd, Santa Rosa
(95403-1070)
PHONE............................707 543-8800
Christopher G Chavez, *CEO*
Michael Chobotov, *Officer*
EMP: 40
SALES (est): 6.2MM **Publicly Held**
SIC: 3841 Surgical & medical instruments
HQ: Trivascular Technologies, Inc.
3910 Brickway Blvd
Santa Rosa CA 95403
707 543-8800

(P-21939)
**TRIVASCULAR TECHNOLOGIES
INC (HQ)**
3910 Brickway Blvd, Santa Rosa
(95403-1070)
PHONE............................707 543-8800
Christopher G Chavez, *President*
Michael R Kramer, *CFO*
Michael V Chobotov, *CTO*
Robert G Whirley, *Development*
EMP: 14
SQ FT: 110,000
SALES (est): 31.8MM **Publicly Held**
SIC: 3841 Surgical & medical instruments

(P-21940)
TRUER MEDICAL INC
1050 N Batavia St Ste C, Orange
(92867-5542)
PHONE............................714 628-9785
Timothy Truitt, *CEO*
Gerry Kritner, *Admin Sec*
EMP: 12 EST: 2008
SQ FT: 7,000
SALES (est): 562.6K **Privately Held**
SIC: 3841 Anesthesia apparatus

(P-21941)
TRUEVISION SYSTEMS INC
Also Called: Truevision 3d Surgical
315 Bollay Dr Ste 101, Goleta
(93117-2948)
PHONE.................................805 963-9700
A Burton Tripathi, CEO
Robert Reali, Vice Pres
Christin Slyngman, Administration
Charles Marson, Sr Software Eng
Charles Morison, Software Dev
▲ EMP: 43
SQ FT: 10,549
SALES (est): 4.4MM
SALES (corp-wide): 165.7MM Privately
Held
WEB: www.truevisionsys.com
SIC: 3841 Surgical & medical instruments
PA: Alcon Research, Llc
6201 South Fwy
Fort Worth TX 76134
817 551-4555

(P-21942)
U S MEDICAL INSTRUMENTS
INC (PA)
888 Prospect St Ste 100, La Jolla
(92037-8200)
P.O. Box 928439, San Diego (92192-8439)
PHONE.................................619 661-5500
Matthew Mazur, CEO
Carlos H Manjarrez, Vice Pres
George A Schapiro, Admin Sec
Eldridge Fridge, Director
William Maloney, Director
EMP: 60
SQ FT: 60,000
SALES (est): 8.7MM Privately Held
WEB: www.eusmi.com
SIC: 3841 Surgical & medical instruments

(P-21943)
UNITED ORTHOPEDIC GROUP
LLC
2885 Loker Ave E, Carlsbad (92010-6626)
PHONE.................................760 729-8585
Brad Lee, President
EMP: 12
SALES (est): 2.3MM
SALES (corp-wide): 330.2MM Privately
Held
SIC: 3841 Surgical & medical instruments
HQ: Breg, Inc.
2885 Loker Ave E
Carlsbad CA 92010
760 599-3000

(P-21944)
VACUMETRICS INC
Also Called: Vacumed
4538 Wstnghouse St Unit A, Ventura
(93003)
PHONE.................................805 644-7461
John J Hoppe, President
▲ EMP: 12
SQ FT: 6,000
SALES (est): 2.9MM Privately Held
WEB: www.vacumed.com
SIC: 3841 Surgical & medical instruments

(P-21945)
VARIAN ASSOCIATES LIMITED
3100 Hansen Way, Palo Alto (94304-1038)
PHONE.................................650 493-4000
Timothy E Guertin, President
Elisha W Finney, Vice Pres
Tai Yun Chen, Controller
EMP: 32
SALES (est): 5MM
SALES (corp-wide): 2.9B Publicly Held
SIC: 3841 3829 Diagnostic apparatus,
medical; medical diagnostic systems, nu-
clear
PA: Varian Medical Systems, Inc.
3100 Hansen Way
Palo Alto CA 94304
650 493-4000

(P-21946)
VARIAN MEDICAL SYSTEMS
INC
3120 Hansen Way, Palo Alto (94304-1030)
PHONE.................................408 321-4468
George Zdasiuk, Vice Pres
Cesar Proano, Manager

EMP: 45
SALES (corp-wide): 2.9B Publicly Held
WEB: www.varian.com
SIC: 3841 Surgical & medical instruments
PA: Varian Medical Systems, Inc.
3100 Hansen Way
Palo Alto CA 94304
650 493-4000

(P-21947)
VARIAN MEDICAL SYSTEMS
INC
660 N Mccarthy Blvd, Milpitas
(95035-5113)
PHONE.................................408 321-9400
Viki Sparks, Branch Mgr
Linda Garcia, Analyst
EMP: 200
SALES (corp-wide): 2.9B Publicly Held
WEB: www.varian.com
SIC: 3841 Surgical & medical instruments
PA: Varian Medical Systems, Inc.
3100 Hansen Way
Palo Alto CA 94304
650 493-4000

(P-21948)
VARIAN MEDICAL SYSTEMS
INC
3045 Hanover St, Palo Alto (94304-1129)
P.O. Box 10022 (94303-0922)
PHONE.................................650 493-4000
Sharon Rylander, Branch Mgr
EMP: 118
SALES (corp-wide): 2.6B Publicly Held
WEB: www.varian.com
SIC: 3841 Surgical & medical instruments
PA: Varian Medical Systems, Inc.
3100 Hansen Way
Palo Alto CA 94304
650 493-4000

(P-21949)
VASCULAR IMAGING
PROFESSIONALS (PA)
1340 N Dynamics St Ste A, Anaheim
(92806-1902)
PHONE.................................949 278-5622
Matthew Lieberman, Principal
EMP: 11
SALES (est): 4MM Privately Held
SIC: 3841 Diagnostic apparatus, medical

(P-21950)
VENTA MEDICAL INC
1971 Milmont Dr, Milpitas (95035-2577)
PHONE.................................510 429-9300
Bill Northum, General Mgr
Joseph S Coel, COO
Michael W Wimmer, CFO
EMP: 40
SALES: 7MM
SALES (corp-wide): 4.8B Publicly Held
SIC: 3841 3449 Inhalation therapy equip-
ment; curtain wall, metal
HQ: Ltc Holdings, Inc.
3021 N Delany Rd
Waukegan IL 60087
847 249-5900

(P-21951)
VENTUS MEDICAL INC
1100 La Avenida St Ste A, Mountain View
(94043-1453)
PHONE.................................408 200-5299
EMP: 25
SQ FT: 14,000
SALES (est): 6.9MM Privately Held
SIC: 3841 Surgical & medical instruments

(P-21952)
VERB SURGICAL INC
2450 Bayshore Pkwy, Mountain View
(94043-1107)
PHONE.................................408 438-3363
Kurt Azarbarzin, President
Maria Chung, Vice Pres
Dave Herrmann, Vice Pres
David Herrmann, Vice Pres
Pablo E Garcia Kilroy, Vice Pres
EMP: 60
SALES (est): 3.6MM Privately Held
SIC: 3841 Surgical & medical instruments

(P-21953)
VERRIX LLC
1330 Calle Avanzado # 200, San Clemente
(92673-6351)
PHONE.................................949 668-1234
Cameron Rouns, CEO
Tim Way, Vice Pres
Adrian Ponce,
EMP: 15
SQ FT: 10,000
SALES (est): 857.1K Privately Held
SIC: 3841 Biopsy instruments & equipment

(P-21954)
VERSATILE POWER INC
743 Camden Ave B, Campbell
(95008-4101)
PHONE.................................408 341-4600
Jerry Price, CEO
Gerald Price, President
Fred Hofmann, Technician
▲ EMP: 12
SALES (est): 1.9MM Privately Held
WEB: www.versatilepower.com
SIC: 3841 3825 Medical instruments &
equipment, blood & bone work; semicon-
ductor test equipment

(P-21955)
VERTOS MEDICAL INC
95 Enterprise Ste 325, Aliso Viejo
(92656-2612)
PHONE.................................949 349-0008
James M Corbett, CEO
Rebecca Colbert, CFO
David Lalor, Vice Pres
Stephen E Paul, VP Sales
James Hollander, Sales Staff
EMP: 62 EST: 2005
SQ FT: 25,000
SALES (est): 8.7MM Privately Held
SIC: 3841 3842 Medical instruments &
equipment, blood & bone work; surgical
appliances & supplies

(P-21956)
VESTA MEDICAL LLC
Also Called: Vestara
3750 Torrey View Ct, San Diego
(92130-2622)
PHONE.................................949 660-8648
Alan Davidner, Mng Member
Gary Brookshire, CFO
EMP: 10
SALES (est): 1.3MM
SALES (corp-wide): 15.9B Publicly Held
SIC: 3841 Medical instruments & equip-
ment, blood & bone work
HQ: Carefusion Corporation
3750 Torrey View Ct
San Diego CA 92130

(P-21957)
VIASYS RESPIRATORY CARE
INC
Also Called: Biosys Healthcare
22745 Savi Ranch Pkwy, Yorba Linda
(92887-4668)
PHONE.................................714 283-2228
William B Ross, President
EMP: 230
SQ FT: 120,000
SALES (est): 21.3MM
SALES (corp-wide): 15.9B Publicly Held
WEB: www.sensormedics.com
SIC: 3841 Diagnostic apparatus, medical
HQ: Carefusion Corporation
3750 Torrey View Ct
San Diego CA 92130

(P-21958)
VNUS MEDICAL
TECHNOLOGIES INC
5799 Fontanoso Way, San Jose
(95138-1015)
PHONE.................................408 360-7200
Brian E Farley, President
Peter Osborne, CFO
Kirti Kamdar, Senior VP
John W Kapples, Vice Pres
Mark S Saxton, Vice Pres
EMP: 208
SQ FT: 93,650

SALES (est): 24MM Privately Held
WEB: www.vnus.com
SIC: 3841 Catheters
HQ: Covidien Lp
710 Medtronic Pkwy
Minneapolis MN 55432
763 514-4000

(P-21959)
VORTRAN MEDICAL
TECHNOLOGY 1 (PA)
21 Golden Land Ct Ste 100, Sacramento
(95834-2427)
PHONE.................................916 648-8460
Gordon Wong MD, President
James Lee, Exec VP
EMP: 28
SALES (est): 3.8MM Privately Held
WEB: www.vortran.com
SIC: 3841 Inhalators, surgical & medical

(P-21960)
VOYAGE MEDICAL INC
610 Galveston Dr, Redwood City
(94063-4721)
PHONE.................................650 503-7500
Vahid Saadat, President
Allan Zingeler, President
Michael Wiley, CFO
John Allison, Vice Pres
Douglas M Bruce, Vice Pres
EMP: 35
SALES (est): 3.6MM Privately Held
SIC: 3841 Surgical & medical instruments

(P-21961)
VYAIRE MEDICAL INC
22745 Savi Ranch Pkwy, Yorba Linda
(92887-4668)
PHONE.................................714 919-3265
EMP: 22
SALES (corp-wide): 265.4MM Privately
Held
SIC: 3841 Surgical & medical instruments
HQ: Vyaire Medical, Inc.
26125 N Riverwoods Blvd # 1
Mettawa IL 60045
833 327-3284

(P-21962)
W L GORE & ASSOCIATES INC
2890 De La Cruz Blvd, Santa Clara
(95050-2619)
PHONE.................................928 864-2705
Mohan Sancheti, Branch Mgr
EMP: 184
SALES (corp-wide): 3.4B Privately Held
SIC: 3841 Surgical & medical instruments
PA: W. L. Gore & Associates, Inc.
555 Paper Mill Rd
Newark DE 19711
302 738-4880

(P-21963)
WAVE 80 BIOSCIENCES INC
1100 26th St, San Francisco (94107-3527)
PHONE.................................415 487-7976
Daniel Laser, President
EMP: 18
SALES (est): 3MM Privately Held
WEB: www.wave80.com
SIC: 3841 Diagnostic apparatus, medical

(P-21964)
WORKMAN HOLDINGS INC
Also Called: Tabco Precision
525 Industrial Way, Fallbrook (92028-2244)
PHONE.................................760 723-5283
Kyle Workman, President
Brett Taylor, Manager
EMP: 10
SALES (est): 1.5MM Privately Held
SIC: 3841 3851 Surgical & medical instru-
ments; frames & parts, eyeglass & spec-
tacle

(P-21965)
ZELTIQ AESTHETICS INC
Also Called: Coolsculpting
6723 Sierra Ct, Dublin (94568-2699)
PHONE.................................925 474-2519
Patrick Williams, Principal
EMP: 10 Privately Held
SIC: 3841 Surgical & medical instruments

▲ = Import ▼=Export
◆ =Import/Export

HQ: Zeltiq Aesthetics, Inc.
4410 Rosewood Dr
Pleasanton CA 94588
-

(P-21966)
ZELTIQ AESTHETICS INC (DH)
Also Called: Coolsculpting
4410 Rosewood Dr, Pleasanton
(94588-3050)
PHONE.....................925 474-2500
Mark J Foley, *President*
Sergio Garcia, *Senior VP*
Austin Root, *Engineer*
▲ EMP: 277
SQ FT: 71,670
SALES (est): 318.7MM **Privately Held**
WEB: www.zeltiq.com
SIC: 3841 Surgical & medical instruments
HQ: Allergan Holdco Us, Inc.
400 Interpace Pkwy Ste D
Parsippany NJ
862 261-7000

(P-21967)
ZIPLINE MEDICAL INC
747 Camden Ave Ste A, Campbell
(95008-4147)
PHONE.....................408 412-7228
John R Tighe, *President*
Amir Belson, *Founder*
Bauback Safa, *Officer*
Trish Howell, *Vice Pres*
Eric Storne, *Vice Pres*
EMP: 19
SALES (est): 3.3MM **Privately Held**
SIC: 3841 7389 Surgical & medical instruments; business services

3842 Orthopedic, Prosthetic & Surgical Appliances/Splys

(P-21968)
ACUTUS MEDICAL INC
2210 Faraday Ave Ste 100, Carlsbad
(92008-7225)
PHONE.....................858 673-1621
Randy Werneth, *CEO*
Scott Huennekens, *Ch of Bd*
John Dahldorf, *CFO*
Graydon Beatty, *CTO*
EMP: 13
SALES (est): 5.2MM **Privately Held**
SIC: 3842 Abdominal supporters, braces & trusses

(P-21969)
ADENNA LLC
2151 Michelson Dr Ste 260, Irvine
(92612-1369)
PHONE.....................909 510-6999
Thomas Friedl, *CEO*
Patrick Fitzmaurice, *CFO*
Jesilyn Duke, *Vice Pres*
Janice Adkins, *Credit Mgr*
◆ EMP: 13 EST: 1997
SQ FT: 13,000
SALES (est): 3.8MM
SALES (corp-wide): 295.9MM **Privately Held**
WEB: www.adenna.com
SIC: 3842 Surgical appliances & supplies
PA: The Tranzonic Companies
26301 Curtiss Wright Pkwy # 200
Richmond Heights OH 44143
216 535-4300

(P-21970)
ADEX MEDICAL INC
6101 Quail Valley Ct D, Riverside
(92507-0764)
P.O. Box 97, Temecula (92593-0097)
PHONE.....................951 653-9122
Michael M Ghafouri, *President*
EMP: 25 EST: 1996
SQ FT: 15,000

SALES (est): 3MM **Privately Held**
WEB: www.adexmed.com
SIC: 3842 3843 5999 5047 Surgical appliances & supplies; dental equipment & supplies; medical apparatus & supplies; medical & hospital equipment; industrial supplies

(P-21971)
ADVANCED ARM DYNAMICS (PA)
123 W Torrance Blvd # 203, Redondo Beach (90277-3614)
PHONE.....................310 372-3050
John Miguelez, *President*
Misty Carver, *Principal*
Dan Conyers, *Principal*
Carol Sorrels, *Principal*
Dan Segawa, *Technology*
EMP: 44
SALES (est): 10.7MM **Privately Held**
SIC: 3842 Prosthetic appliances

(P-21972)
ADVANCED BIONICS LLC (HQ)
Also Called: A B
12740 San Fernando Rd, Sylmar
(91342-3700)
PHONE.....................661 362-1400
Rainer Platz, *CEO*
Frank Visco, *Software Dev*
Steven Becker, *Software Engr*
Gangadhar Kurugod, *Business Anlyst*
Eugene Bravo, *IT/INT Sup*
EMP: 500
SALES (est): 73.5MM
SALES (corp-wide): 2.7B **Privately Held**
SIC: 3842 Hearing aids
PA: Sonova Holding Ag
Laubisrutistrasse 28
StAfa ZH 8712
589 283-333

(P-21973)
ADVANCED BIONICS CORPORATION (HQ)
28515 Westinghouse Pl, Valencia
(91355-4833)
PHONE.....................661 362-1400
Rainer Platz, *CEO*
Arthur Rascon, *Vice Pres*
Tom Santogrossi, *Vice Pres*
Alfred Mann, *Principal*
Johanna Bailey-Stark, *Regional Mgr*
▲ EMP: 214
SALES (est): 130MM
SALES (corp-wide): 2.7B **Privately Held**
SIC: 3842 Hearing aids
PA: Sonova Holding Ag
Laubisrutistrasse 28
StAfa ZH 8712
589 283-333

(P-21974)
ADVANCED ORTHOPAEDIC SOLUTIONS
Also Called: Aos
3203 Kashiwa St, Torrance (90505-4020)
PHONE.....................310 533-9966
Gary Sohngen, *CEO*
Barry Hubbard, *Vice Pres*
Vasso Chronis, *Regional Mgr*
Scott Epperly, *Design Engr*
Pat Quintana, *Design Engr*
EMP: 34
SALES (est): 1.2MM **Privately Held**
WEB: www.aosortho.com
SIC: 3842 Implants, surgical

(P-21975)
ADVANCED ORTHOTIC DESIGNS
9351 Narnia Dr, Riverside (92503-5634)
PHONE.....................951 710-1640
Mark Latham, *CEO*
EMP: 11
SQ FT: 1,500
SALES (est): 675.4K
SALES (corp-wide): 1.3MM **Privately Held**
WEB: www.advancedorthoticdesigns.com
SIC: 3842 Braces, orthopedic; orthopedic appliances

PA: New Day, Inc.
8026 Sitio Caucho
Carlsbad CA
-

(P-21976)
ALPHATEC HOLDINGS INC
2150 Palomar Airport Rd, Carlsbad
(92011-4406)
PHONE.....................760 431-9286
Mitsuo Asai, *Branch Mgr*
EMP: 12
SALES (corp-wide): 91.6MM **Publicly Held**
SIC: 3842 Surgical appliances & supplies
PA: Alphatec Holdings, Inc.
5818 El Camino Real
Carlsbad CA 92008
760 431-9286

(P-21977)
ALPHATEC SPINE INC (HQ)
5818 El Camino Real, Carlsbad
(92008-8816)
PHONE.....................760 494-6610
James M Corbett, *CEO*
Michael Plunkett, *COO*
M Ross Simmonds, *COO*
Jeffrey G Black, *CFO*
Michael O'Neill, *CFO*
▲ EMP: 250
SALES (est): 63.2MM
SALES (corp-wide): 91.6MM **Publicly Held**
WEB: www.alphatecspine.com
SIC: 3842 8711 5047 Surgical appliances & supplies; engineering services; medical equipment & supplies
PA: Alphatec Holdings, Inc.
5818 El Camino Real
Carlsbad CA 92008
760 431-9286

(P-21978)
AMERICAN CERAMIC TECHNOLOGY (PA)
12909 Lomas Verdes Dr, Poway
(92064-1250)
P.O. Box 461479, Escondido (92046-1479)
PHONE.....................619 992-3104
Richard Vaughn Culbertson, *CEO*
Scott McCall, *Engineer*
Sean Forehand, *Business Mgr*
Adrian Stewart, *Sales Staff*
EMP: 15 EST: 2008
SALES (est): 3.5MM **Privately Held**
SIC: 3842 3443 Radiation shielding aprons, gloves, sheeting, etc.; nuclear shielding, metal plate

(P-21979)
AMERICAN METAL ENTERPRISES INC
15855 Chemical Ln, Huntington Beach
(92649-1510)
PHONE.....................714 894-6810
Scott B Edwards, *CEO*
EMP: 10 EST: 2012
SALES (est): 414.8K **Privately Held**
SIC: 3842 Braces, elastic

(P-21980)
AMERICH CORPORATION (PA)
13212 Saticoy St, North Hollywood
(91605-3404)
PHONE.....................818 982-1711
Edward Richmond, *President*
Dino Pacifici, *Vice Pres*
Greg Richmond, *Vice Pres*
Chantal Difrancesca, *Accountant*
Lynn Hardy, *Opers Mgr*
▲ EMP: 120
SQ FT: 145,000
SALES (est): 32.5MM **Privately Held**
WEB: www.americh.com
SIC: 3842 3432 3431 3261 Whirlpool baths, hydrotherapy equipment; plumbing fixture fittings & trim; metal sanitary ware; vitreous plumbing fixtures

(P-21981)
ANSELL SNDEL MED SOLUTIONS LLC
9301 Oakdale Ave Ste 300, Chatsworth
(91311-6539)
PHONE.....................818 534-2500
Anthony B Lopez, *President*
Wendell Franke, *Associate Dir*
Stephanie Barth, *Principal*
Dan Sandel, *Consultant*
◆ EMP: 32
SQ FT: 14,600
SALES (est): 6.9MM **Privately Held**
WEB: www.sandelmedical.com
SIC: 3842 Surgical appliances & supplies
PA: Ansell Limited
L 3 678 Victoria St
Richmond VIC 3121

(P-21982)
ARS ENTERPRISES (PA)
15554 Minnesota Ave, Paramount
(90723-4119)
PHONE.....................562 946-3505
Ben Hom, *Mng Member*
Michael D Dunn, *Ch of Bd*
Glenn Caster, *President*
Carol Alvarez, *Accounting Mgr*
Marshall Geller, *Mng Member*
EMP: 14
SQ FT: 11,000
SALES (est): 2MM **Privately Held**
WEB: www.rely-ars.com
SIC: 3842 5074 Autoclaves, hospital & surgical; boilers, steam

(P-21983)
AXIOM INDUSTRIES INC
Also Called: Prime Engineering
4202 W Sierra Madre Ave, Fresno
(93722-3932)
PHONE.....................559 276-1310
Mary Wilson Boegel, *President*
Bruce Boegel, *CFO*
Mark Allen, *Vice Pres*
Rick Michael, *Natl Sales Mgr*
◆ EMP: 26
SALES (est): 4.5MM **Privately Held**
WEB: www.primeengineering.com
SIC: 3842 Technical aids for the handicapped

(P-21984)
BAUERS & COLLINS
Also Called: Community Vision
6765 Lankershim Blvd, North Hollywood
(91606-1614)
PHONE.....................818 983-1281
Robert F Collins, *Owner*
EMP: 15 EST: 1999
SALES (est): 1.6MM **Privately Held**
WEB: www.communityvisions.org
SIC: 3842 Prosthetic appliances

(P-21985)
BIO CYBERNETICS INTERNATIONAL
Also Called: Cybertech
2701 Kimball Ave, Pomona (91767-2268)
PHONE.....................909 447-7050
▲ EMP: 15
SQ FT: 10,000
SALES (est): 2MM **Privately Held**
WEB: www.cybertechmedical.com
SIC: 3842

(P-21986)
BIOM LLC
Also Called: Orthera
9655 Gran Rdge Dr Ste 200, San Diego
(92123)
PHONE.....................858 717-2995
Torc Huber, *President*
EMP: 10 EST: 2017
SALES (est): 761.1K **Privately Held**
SIC: 3842 Foot appliances, orthopedic

(P-21987)
BIOMECHANICAL ANALYSIS &
Also Called: Biomechanical Services
20509 Earlgate St, Walnut (91789-2909)
PHONE.....................714 990-5932
Greg Wolfe, *President*
Kevin Hasegawa, *Shareholder*

Brian Killeen, *Shareholder*
Dr William Sniechowski, *Shareholder*
Scott De Francisco, *Vice Pres*
EMP: 45
SQ FT: 13,000
SALES (est): 5.9MM **Privately Held**
WEB: www.biomechanical.com
SIC: 3842 5999 Orthopedic appliances;
orthopedic & prosthesis applications

(P-21988)
BIOMET SAN DIEGO LLC
1540 Rubenstein Ave, Cardiff By The Sea
(92007-2436)
PHONE..................760 942-2786
Trude Jackson, *President*
EMP: 10
SQ FT: 2,200
SALES: 4.7MM **Privately Held**
SIC: 3842 Implants, surgical

(P-21989)
BIONICSOUND INC
Also Called: Bionikear.com
390 Spar Ave Ste 104, San Jose
(95117-1643)
PHONE..................714 300-4809
Asela Jayampathy, *CEO*
EMP: 14
SQ FT: 5,000
SALES: 15MM **Privately Held**
SIC: 3842 Hearing aids

(P-21990)
**BOSTON SCIENTIFIC
CORPORATION**
150 Baytech Dr, San Jose (95134-2302)
PHONE..................408 935-3400
Tom Flemming, *Manager*
Eddie Lam, *Engineer*
Brendan Crowley, *Controller*
Shivaun Clark, *Marketing Staff*
Kenneth Gillette, *Manager*
EMP: 125
SALES (corp-wide): 9.8B **Publicly Held**
WEB: www.bsci.com
SIC: 3842 3841 Surgical appliances &
supplies; grafts, artificial: for surgery; di-
agnostic apparatus, medical
PA: Boston Scientific Corporation
300 Boston Scientific Way
Marlborough MA 01752
508 683-4000

(P-21991)
**BOSTON SCNTFIC NRMDLATION
CORP**
25129 Rye Canyon Loop, Valencia
(91355-5004)
PHONE..................661 949-4869
Jeff Greiner, *President*
EMP: 10
SALES (corp-wide): 9.8B **Publicly Held**
SIC: 3842 3841 Hearing aids; surgical in-
struments & apparatus
HQ: Boston Scientific Neuromodulation
Corporation
25155 Rye Canyon Loop
Valencia CA 91355

(P-21992)
**BOSTON SCNTFIC NRMDLATION
CORP (HQ)**
25155 Rye Canyon Loop, Valencia
(91355-5004)
PHONE..................661 949-4310
Michael F Mahoney, *CEO*
Supratim Bose, *Exec VP*
Jeffrey D Capello, *Exec VP*
Kevin Ballinger, *Senior VP*
Wendy Carruthers, *Senior VP*
▲ **EMP:** 450
SQ FT: 26,000
SALES (est): 92.7MM
SALES (corp-wide): 9.8B **Publicly Held**
SIC: 3842 3841 5047 Hearing aids; surgi-
cal & medical instruments; metabolism
apparatus; surgical instruments & appara-
tus; medical & hospital equipment; hear-
ing aids
PA: Boston Scientific Corporation
300 Boston Scientific Way
Marlborough MA 01752
508 683-4000

(P-21993)
BREATHE TECHNOLOGIES INC
15091 Bake Pkwy, Irvine (92618-2501)
PHONE..................949 988-7700
Lawrence A Mastrovich, *President*
John L Miclot, *Ch of Bd*
Paul J Lytle, *CFO*
Gary Berman, *Officer*
Rebecca Mabry, *Senior VP*
EMP: 39
SALES (est): 12.5MM
SALES (corp-wide): 2.8B **Publicly Held**
WEB: www.breathetechnologies.com
SIC: 3842 Respirators; respiratory protec-
tion equipment, personal
HQ: Hill-Rom, Inc.
1069 State Route 46 E
Batesville IN 47006
812 934-7777

(P-21994)
CASTLE HILL HOLDINGS INC
Also Called: Collier O & P
3161 Putnam Blvd, Pleasant Hill
(94523-4650)
P.O. Box 23491, Concord (94523-0491)
PHONE..................925 943-1119
Richard Todd, *President*
Leslie Wells, *CEO*
EMP: 10
SALES (est): 1.2MM **Privately Held**
SIC: 3842 Braces, orthopedic; canes, or-
thopedic; foot appliances, orthopedic

(P-21995)
CONVAID PRODUCTS INC
2830 California St, Torrance (90503-3908)
P.O. Box 4209, Pls Vrds Pnsl (90274-9571)
PHONE..................310 618-0111
Chris Braun, *CEO*
Mervyn M Watkins, *CEO*
Rachel Watkins, *Treasurer*
Justin Egli, *Engineer*
Sheryl Vargas, *Analyst*
◆ **EMP:** 89
SALES (est): 21.6MM **Privately Held**
WEB: www.convaid.com
SIC: 3842 Wheelchairs

(P-21996)
CURTISS-WRIGHT CONTROLS
Also Called: Penny & Giles Drive Technology
210 Ranger Ave, Brea (92821-6215)
PHONE..................714 982-1860
John Camp, *President*
EMP: 25
SALES (corp-wide): 2.4B **Publicly Held**
WEB: www.autronics.com
SIC: 3842 Braces, elastic
HQ: Curtiss-Wright Controls Integrated
Sensing, Inc.
28965 Avenue Penn
Valencia CA 91355

(P-21997)
DIAMOND GLOVES
1100 S Linwood Ave Ste A, Santa Ana
(92705-4345)
PHONE..................714 667-0506
John Te, *CEO*
Rachel Lai,
▲ **EMP:** 22 **EST:** 2009
SALES (est): 3.8MM **Privately Held**
SIC: 3842 Gloves, safety

(P-21998)
DJO LLC
3151 Scott St, Vista (92081-8365)
PHONE..................760 727-1280
Andi Donner, *Branch Mgr*
Rich Gildersleeve, *Vice Pres*
Jason Johnson, *Vice Pres*
Hector Marquez, *Vice Pres*
Anita Morin, *Vice Pres*
EMP: 17
SALES (corp-wide): 3.6B **Publicly Held**
SIC: 3842 Surgical appliances & supplies
HQ: Djo, Llc
10300 N Enterprise Dr
Mequon WI 53092
760 727-1283

(P-21999)
DONN & DOFF INC (PA)
Also Called: Tegerstrand Orthtics Prsthtics
2102 Civic Center Dr, Redding
(96001-2704)
PHONE..................530 241-4040
Dona Tegerstrand, *President*
Sue Mc Gaity, *Office Mgr*
Justin Tegerstrand, *Surg-Orthopdc*
EMP: 15
SQ FT: 3,000
SALES (est): 1.6MM **Privately Held**
WEB: www.donnanddoff.com
SIC: 3842 Limbs, artificial; braces, ortho-
pedic

(P-22000)
DRS OWN INC (PA)
Also Called: Good Feet
5923 Farnsworth Ct, Carlsbad
(92008-7303)
PHONE..................760 804-0751
David E Workman, *President*
Sue Austad, *CFO*
Andrea Paz, *Bookkeeper*
James Hankee, *Sales Staff*
◆ **EMP:** 35
SQ FT: 18,400
SALES (est): 5.6MM **Privately Held**
WEB: www.drsown.com
SIC: 3842 Abdominal supporters, braces &
trusses

(P-22001)
**DYNAMICS ORTHOTICS &
PROSTHETI**
Also Called: Dynamics O&P
1830 W Olympic Blvd # 123, Los Angeles
(90006-3734)
PHONE..................213 383-9212
Peter J Sean, *CEO*
Sharon Sean, *Mktg Dir*
Sharon Cho, *Manager*
EMP: 30
SQ FT: 20,662
SALES (est): 4.9MM **Privately Held**
SIC: 3842 Orthopedic appliances; limbs,
artificial

(P-22002)
EARGO INC (PA)
1600 Technology Dr Fl 6, San Jose
(95110-1382)
PHONE..................650 996-9508
Christian Gormsen, *CEO*
Adam Laponis, *CFO*
Bill Browney, *Ch Credit Ofcr*
Jurgen Pauquet, *Ch Credit Ofcr*
Daniel Shen, *Ch Credit Ofcr*
EMP: 80
SQ FT: 20,000
SALES (est): 15MM **Privately Held**
SIC: 3842 5047 7371 Hearing aids; hear-
ing aids; computer software development
& applications

(P-22003)
EARLENS CORPORATION
4045a Campbell Ave, Menlo Park
(94025-1006)
PHONE..................650 366-9000
William M Facteau, *President*
George Harter, *CFO*
Leilani Latimer, *Chief Mktg Ofcr*
Rodney Perkins, *Chief Mktg Ofcr*
Scott Durall, *Exec VP*
EMP: 14
SALES (est): 3.9MM **Privately Held**
SIC: 3842 Hearing aids

(P-22004)
EDWARDS LIFESCIENCES CORP
1402 Alton Pkwy, Irvine (92606-4838)
PHONE..................949 250-3522
Diane Nguyen, *Branch Mgr*
Takahiro Makino, *Project Mgr*
Nancy Cohen, *Manager*
EMP: 13
SALES (corp-wide): 3.7B **Publicly Held**
SIC: 3842 Surgical appliances & supplies
PA: Edwards Lifesciences Corp
1 Edwards Way
Irvine CA 92614
949 250-2500

(P-22005)
**EDWARDS LIFESCIENCES CORP
(PA)**
1 Edwards Way, Irvine (92614-5688)
PHONE..................949 250-2500
Michael A Mussallem, *Ch of Bd*
Denise E Botticelli, *Vice Pres*
Mark Konno, *Vice Pres*
Jean-Luc Lemercier, *Vice Pres*
John P McGrath, *Vice Pres*
EMP: 1600
SALES: 3.7B **Publicly Held**
WEB: www.edwards.com
SIC: 3842 Surgical appliances & supplies

(P-22006)
EDWARDS LIFESCIENCES CORP
1212 Alton Pkwy, Irvine (92606-4837)
PHONE..................949 553-0611
Rita Hernandez, *Branch Mgr*
EMP: 21
SALES (corp-wide): 3.7B **Publicly Held**
WEB: www.edwards.com
SIC: 3842 Surgical appliances & supplies
PA: Edwards Lifesciences Corp
1 Edwards Way
Irvine CA 92614
949 250-2500

(P-22007)
EKSO BIONICS HOLDINGS INC
1414 Hrbour Way S Ste 120, Richmond
(94804)
PHONE..................510 984-1761
Jack Peurach, *President*
Steven Sherman, *Ch of Bd*
John Glenn, *CFO*
Bill Shaw, *Ch Credit Ofcr*
EMP: 82
SQ FT: 45,000
SALES: 11.3MM **Privately Held**
SIC: 3842 5999 Crutches & walkers; walk-
ers; canes, orthopedic; medical apparatus
& supplies

(P-22008)
EMERGENT GROUP INC (DH)
10939 Pendleton St, Sun Valley
(91352-1522)
PHONE..................818 394-2800
Bruce J Haber, *CEO*
Louis Buther, *President*
William M McKay, *CFO*
EMP: 55
SQ FT: 13,000
SALES (est): 7.8MM
SALES (corp-wide): 242.6MM **Privately
Held**
WEB: www.primedical.net
SIC: 3842 7352 Surgical appliances &
supplies; medical equipment rental
HQ: Agiliti Health, Inc.
6625 W 78th St Ste 300
Minneapolis MN 55439
952 893-3200

(P-22009)
ENDOTEC INC
14525 Valley View Ave H, Santa Fe Springs
(90670-5237)
PHONE..................714 681-6306
Young B Shim, *CEO*
EMP: 12
SQ FT: 5,900
SALES (est): 1.9MM **Privately Held**
SIC: 3842 Orthopedic appliances
PA: Cellumed Co., Ltd.
130 Digital-Ro, Geumcheon-Gu
Seoul 08589

(P-22010)
ESP SAFETY INC
555 N 1st St, San Jose (95112-5314)
PHONE..................408 886-9746
Ivan Lukisa, *President*
Anna Trofimova, *Vice Pres*
EMP: 10
SQ FT: 8,000
SALES (est): 2.1MM **Privately Held**
WEB: www.esp-corporation.com
SIC: 3842 Personal safety equipment

▲ = Import ▼=Export
◆ =Import/Export

(P-22011)
ETHICON INC
Advanced Sterilization Pdts
33 Technology Dr, Irvine (92618-2346)
PHONE..............................949 581-5799
Charles Austin, *Branch Mgr*
EMP: 300
SALES (corp-wide): 81.5B **Publicly Held**
WEB: www.ethiconinc.com
SIC: 3842 Sutures, absorbable & non-absorbable
HQ: Ethicon Inc.
    Us Route 22
    Somerville NJ 08876
    732 524-0400

(P-22012)
FERRACO INC (HQ)
Also Called: Human Designs Pros/Ortho Lab
2933 Long Beach Blvd, Long Beach
(90806-1517)
PHONE..............................562 988-2414
Natalie Rose Cronin, *CEO*
Eric Ferraco, *President*
Brian Cronin, *CFO*
EMP: 30
SALES: 8MM
SALES (corp-wide): 1.9MM **Privately Held**
SIC: 3842 Surgical appliances & supplies
PA: Arc-V, Inc.
    1639 N Hollywood Way
    Burbank CA 91505
    732 266-1479

(P-22013)
FOOT IN MOTION INC
Also Called: Kevin Orthopedic
2239 Business Way, Riverside
(92501-2231)
PHONE..............................312 752-0990
Kevin Rosenbloom, *President*
◆ EMP: 15
SALES (est): 1.8MM **Privately Held**
SIC: 3842 Foot appliances, orthopedic

(P-22014)
FRANK STUBBS CO INC
1830 Eastman Ave, Oxnard (93030-8935)
PHONE..............................805 278-4300
Glenn Soensker, *CFO*
David Paul Pearson, *President*
Glenn Alan Slensker, *CFO*
Dan Betkhoodu, *Purch Mgr*
EMP: 49
SQ FT: 50,100
SALES (est): 6.3MM **Privately Held**
WEB: www.fstubbs.com
SIC: 3842 Supports: abdominal, ankle, arch, kneecap, etc.; personal safety equipment

(P-22015)
FREEDOM DESIGNS INC
2241 N Madera Rd, Simi Valley
(93065-1762)
PHONE..............................805 582-0077
Matthew E Monaghan, *Ch of Bd*
Kathleen P Leneghan, *CFO*
Gabriela Guerrero, *Human Res Mgr*
Rick Aimone, *Sales Staff*
◆ EMP: 120 EST: 1981
SQ FT: 40,000
SALES (est): 20.9MM
SALES (corp-wide): 972.3MM **Publicly Held**
WEB: www.freedomdesigns.com
SIC: 3842 Wheelchairs
PA: Invacare Corporation
    1 Invacare Way
    Elyria OH 44035
    440 329-6000

(P-22016)
FREEDOM INNOVATIONS LLC (HQ)
3 Morgan, Irvine (92618-1917)
PHONE..............................949 672-0032
Maynard Carkhuff,
Paul Steinert, *IT/INT Sup*
Coryn Olpin, *Marketing Staff*
Chris Wilson, *Sales Staff*
Lee Kim,
◆ EMP: 20
SQ FT: 6,800

SALES (est): 19.6MM **Privately Held**
SIC: 3842 Foot appliances, orthopedic

(P-22017)
FREUDENBERG MEDICAL LLC
5050 Rivergrade Rd, Baldwin Park
(91706-1405)
PHONE..............................626 814-9684
Coburn Pharr, *Manager*
Hamlet Haroutonian, *Project Mgr*
EMP: 149
SALES (corp-wide): 11B **Privately Held**
SIC: 3842 Prosthetic appliances
HQ: Freudenberg Medical, Llc
    1110 Mark Ave
    Carpinteria CA 93013
    805 684-3304

(P-22018)
FREUDENBERG MEDICAL LLC (DH)
Also Called: Helix Medical
1110 Mark Ave, Carpinteria (93013-2918)
PHONE..............................805 684-3304
Jorg Schneewind, *CEO*
Thomas Vassalo, *President*
Thomas Vassallo, *Exec VP*
Steve Lents, *Vice Pres*
Ward Sokoloski, *Vice Pres*
▲ EMP: 271
SQ FT: 66,000
SALES (est): 162MM
SALES (corp-wide): 11B **Privately Held**
WEB: www.helixmed.com
SIC: 3842 Prosthetic appliances

(P-22019)
GUARDIAN SURVIVAL GEAR INC
1401 S Hicks Ave, Commerce
(90023-3240)
PHONE..............................760 519-5643
Daniel Kunz, *President*
Steve Williams, *General Mgr*
▲ EMP: 15
SQ FT: 15,000
SALES: 1.5MM **Privately Held**
SIC: 3842 First aid, snake bite & burn kits

(P-22020)
HAND BIOMECHANICS LAB INC
77 Scripps Dr Ste 104, Sacramento
(95825-6209)
PHONE..............................916 923-5073
John Agee MD, *President*
Jesse Wallace, *Assistant*
EMP: 16
SQ FT: 2,600
SALES (est): 2.3MM **Privately Held**
WEB: www.handbiolab.com
SIC: 3842 Orthopedic appliances

(P-22021)
HANGER
6099 Malburg Way, Vernon (90058-3947)
PHONE..............................323 238-7738
EMP: 15 EST: 2005
SALES (est): 1.8MM **Privately Held**
SIC: 3842 Surgical appliances & supplies

(P-22022)
HANGER INC
100 Pacifica Ste 270, Irvine (92618-7447)
PHONE..............................949 408-3320
EMP: 18
SALES (corp-wide): 1B **Publicly Held**
SIC: 3842 Surgical appliances & supplies
PA: Hanger, Inc.
    10910 Domain Dr Ste 300
    Austin TX 78758
    512 777-3800

(P-22023)
HANGER PRSTHETCS & ORTHO INC
Also Called: Hanger Clinic
6300 Wilshire Blvd # 950, Los Angeles
(90048-5204)
PHONE..............................323 866-2555
Sam Liang, *Branch Mgr*
EMP: 99
SQ FT: 1,500
SALES (corp-wide): 1B **Publicly Held**
SIC: 3842 Prosthetic appliances

HQ: Hanger Prosthetics & Orthotics, Inc.
    10910 Domain Dr Ste 300
    Austin TX 78758
    512 777-3800

(P-22024)
HANGER PRSTHETCS & ORTHO INC
Also Called: Hanger Clinic
18022 Cowan Ste 285, Irvine (92614-6814)
PHONE..............................949 863-1951
EMP: 86
SALES (corp-wide): 762.8MM **Publicly Held**
SIC: 3842
HQ: Hanger Prosthetics & Orthotics, Inc.
    10910 Main Dr
    Austin TX 78758
    512 777-3800

(P-22025)
HANGER PRSTHETCS & ORTHO INC
Also Called: Nova Care Orthtics Prosthetics
15725 Pomerado Rd, Poway (92064-2068)
PHONE..............................858 487-4516
Dhruval Shah, *Branch Mgr*
EMP: 19
SALES (corp-wide): 1B **Publicly Held**
SIC: 3842 5999 Prosthetic appliances; orthopedic & prosthesis applications
HQ: Hanger Prosthetics & Orthotics, Inc.
    10910 Domain Dr Ste 300
    Austin TX 78758
    512 777-3800

(P-22026)
HANGER PRSTHETCS & ORTHO INC
4659 Las Positas Rd Ste A, Livermore
(94551-9631)
PHONE..............................925 371-5081
Regina Lnd, *Branch Mgr*
EMP: 14
SALES (corp-wide): 1B **Publicly Held**
SIC: 3842 Orthopedic appliances
HQ: Hanger Prosthetics & Orthotics, Inc.
    10910 Domain Dr Ste 300
    Austin TX 78758
    512 777-3800

(P-22027)
HONEYWELL SAFETY PDTS USA INC
7828 Waterville Rd, San Diego
(92154-8205)
PHONE..............................619 661-8383
Dave M Cote, *CEO*
EMP: 110
SALES (corp-wide): 41.8B **Publicly Held**
SIC: 3842 Ear plugs
HQ: Honeywell Safety Products Usa, Inc.
    2711 Centerville Rd
    Wilmington DE 19808
    302 636-5401

(P-22028)
IMPERATIVE CARE INC
1359 Dell Ave, Campbell (95008-6609)
PHONE..............................669 228-3814
Farhad Khosravi, *President*
Brian Armijo, *VP Opers*
EMP: 25
SQ FT: 20,000
SALES (est): 153.5K **Privately Held**
SIC: 3842 Surgical appliances & supplies

(P-22029)
IMPLANTECH ASSOCIATES INC
Also Called: Allied Bio Medical
6025 Nicolle St Ste B, Ventura
(93003-7602)
P.O. Box 392 (93002-0392)
PHONE..............................805 289-1665
William Binder, *President*
Lillie Cranfill, *Admin Mgr*
Robert Ramirez, *Graphic Designe*
EMP: 30
SQ FT: 11,000
SALES (est): 6.2MM **Privately Held**
WEB: www.implantech.com
SIC: 3842 Implants, surgical

(P-22030)
INFAB CORPORATION
1040 Avenida Acaso, Camarillo
(93012-8712)
PHONE..............................805 987-5255
Donald J Cusick, *President*
Tom Fink, *Vice Pres*
Billy Morgan, *Vice Pres*
Brian Malkin, *Natl Sales Mgr*
Justine Peterson, *VP Sales*
▲ EMP: 57
SQ FT: 40,000
SALES: 12.3MM **Privately Held**
WEB: www.infabcorp.com
SIC: 3842 Radiation shielding aprons, gloves, sheeting, etc.

(P-22031)
INHEALTH TECHNOLOGIES
1110 Mark Ave, Carpinteria (93013-2918)
PHONE..............................800 477-5969
Ed Munoz, *Principal*
Rachel McCluskey, *Human Res Mgr*
Rachel Peterson, *Human Res Mgr*
Keith Gauthier, *Mfg Mgr*
Anthony Serna, *Marketing Mgr*
EMP: 16
SALES (est): 2.2MM **Privately Held**
WEB: www.inhealth.com
SIC: 3842 Surgical appliances & supplies

(P-22032)
INLAND ARTFL LIMB & BRACE INC (PA)
680 Parkridge Ave, Norco (92860-3124)
PHONE..............................951 734-1835
Guy Savidan CP, *President*
EMP: 17
SALES (est): 2.3MM **Privately Held**
SIC: 3842 5999 Limbs, artificial; artificial limbs

(P-22033)
INTERPORE CROSS INTL INC (DH)
181 Technology Dr, Irvine (92618-2484)
PHONE..............................949 453-3200
Dan Hann, *President*
Greg Hartman, *CFO*
▲ EMP: 58
SALES (est): 17.4MM
SALES (corp-wide): 7.9B **Publicly Held**
WEB: www.interpore.com
SIC: 3842 3843 Orthopedic appliances; surgical appliances & supplies; dental equipment & supplies
HQ: Biomet, Inc.
    345 E Main St
    Warsaw IN 46580
    574 267-6639

(P-22034)
IX MEDICAL (PA)
725 W Anaheim St, Long Beach
(90813-2819)
PHONE..............................877 902-6446
Kerry Brady, *President*
EMP: 10
SQ FT: 4,000
SALES: 3.5MM **Privately Held**
SIC: 3842 Radiation shielding aprons, gloves, sheeting, etc.

(P-22035)
JACUZZI BRANDS LLC (DH)
Also Called: Jacuzzi Group Worldwide
13925 City Center Dr # 200, Chino Hills
(91709-5437)
PHONE..............................909 606-1416
Robert Rowen, *CEO*
Alex P Marini, *President*
Peter Munk, *President*
Robert I Rowan, *President*
David Broadbent, *CFO*
◆ EMP: 50
SQ FT: 15,134
SALES (est): 1.6B **Privately Held**
SIC: 3842 Whirlpool baths, hydrotherapy equipment
HQ: Jupiter Holding I Corp.
    13925 City Center Dr # 200
    Chino Hills CA 91709
    909 606-1416

(P-22036)
JOA CORPORATION (PA)
Also Called: Johnsons Orthopedic
7254 Magnolia Ave, Riverside
(92504-3829)
PHONE.............................951 785-4411
William Kearney, President
Lesli Kearney, CFO
EMP: 34
SQ FT: 6,000
SALES (est): 4.2MM Privately Held
WEB: www.johnsonsorthopedic.com
SIC: 3842 5999 8011 Braces, orthopedic;
limbs, artificial; orthopedic & prosthesis
applications; orthopedic physician

(P-22037)
JOHNSON & JOHNSON
15715 Arrow Hwy, Irwindale (91706-2006)
PHONE.............................909 839-8650
Cathy Somalis, Manager
EMP: 300
SALES (corp-wide): 81.5B Publicly Held
WEB: www.jnj.com
SIC: 3842 Dressings, surgical
PA: Johnson & Johnson
1 Johnson And Johnson Plz
New Brunswick NJ 08933
732 524-0400

(P-22038)
JOHNSON WILSHIRE INC
17343 Freedom Way, City of Industry
(91748-1001)
PHONE.............................562 777-0088
David W Pang, President
EMP: 30
SQ FT: 120,000
SALES (est): 2MM Privately Held
SIC: 3842 Personal safety equipment;
gloves, safety; linemen's safety belts

(P-22039)
**KAISE PERMA SAN FRANC
MEDIC CE**
2425 Geary Blvd, San Francisco
(94115-3358)
PHONE.............................415 833-2000
Michael Alexander, Senior VP
EMP: 23
SALES (est): 4.1MM Privately Held
SIC: 3842 Autoclaves, hospital & surgical

(P-22040)
KINAMED INC
820 Flynn Rd, Camarillo (93012-8701)
PHONE.............................805 384-2748
Clyde R Pratt, President
Vineet Sarin, President
Anthony Rose, COO
Bob Bruce, Vice Pres
Adam Nelson, Research
EMP: 26
SQ FT: 28,828
SALES (est): 520K Privately Held
WEB: www.kinamed.com
SIC: 3842 Implants, surgical
PA: Vme Acquisition Corp.
820 Flynn Rd
Camarillo CA 93012

(P-22041)
KINGSLEY MFG CO (PA)
1984 Placentia Ave, Costa Mesa
(92627-3421)
P.O. Box 5010 (92628-5010)
PHONE.............................949 645-4401
Jeffry Kingsley, President
Jane Kingsley, Treasurer
Denise Kingsley, Admin Sec
EMP: 10
SQ FT: 6,000
SALES: 1MM Privately Held
SIC: 3842 Orthopedic appliances

(P-22042)
KVP INTERNATIONAL INC
13775 Ramona Ave, Chino (91710-5405)
PHONE.............................888 411-7387
John Nelson, CEO
Ken Bowman, COO
Mary Ann Gehring, CFO
Alan McCool, Purch Mgr
Roberto Godoy, Manager
▲ EMP: 41

SALES (est): 12.5MM Privately Held
SIC: 3842 5047 Abdominal supporters,
braces & trusses; veterinarians' equipment & supplies

(P-22043)
MBK ENTERPRISES INC
Also Called: MBK Tape Solutions
9959 Canoga Ave, Chatsworth
(91311-3002)
PHONE.............................818 998-1477
Jeffrey Kaminski, President
Marcella B Kaminski, Corp Secy
Kelly Weber-Williams, Controller
Laura Kaminski, Marketing Staff
▲ EMP: 40
SQ FT: 14,000
SALES: 12.2MM Privately Held
WEB: www.mbk1.com
SIC: 3842 Adhesive tape & plasters, medicated or non-medicated

(P-22044)
MEDI KID COMPANY
448 S Palm Ave Ste A, Hemet
(92543-4819)
P.O. Box 5398 (92544-0398)
PHONE.............................951 925-8800
Melinda Siwek, CEO
EMP: 10
SALES (est): 790K Privately Held
WEB: www.medi-kid.com
SIC: 3842 Restraints, patient

(P-22045)
**MEDICAL PACKAGING
CORPORATION**
Also Called: Hygenia
941 Avenida Acaso, Camarillo
(93012-8755)
PHONE.............................805 388-2383
Frederic L Nason, President
Susan J Nason, Corp Secy
EMP: 100
SQ FT: 45,000
SALES (est): 19.4MM Privately Held
SIC: 3842 2835 Surgical appliances &
supplies; in vitro & in vivo diagnostic substances

(P-22046)
MEDLINE INDUSTRIES INC
Also Called: Medline Industires
42500 Winchester Rd, Temecula
(92590-2570)
PHONE.............................951 296-2600
Dave House, Vice Pres
Cory Dacio, Exec Dir
EMP: 11
SALES (corp-wide): 5.7B Privately Held
SIC: 3842 Surgical appliances & supplies
PA: Medline Industries, Inc.
3 Lakes Dr
Northfield IL 60093
847 949-5500

(P-22047)
MEDTRONIC INC
3576 Unocal Pl Bldg B, Santa Rosa
(95403-1774)
PHONE.............................707 541-3281
Omar Ishrak, CEO
Chris Hadland, Vice Pres
David Moeller, Vice Pres
Vipul Sheth, Vice Pres
Jason Weidman, Vice Pres
EMP: 63 Privately Held
SIC: 3842 3841 3845 Surgical appliances
& supplies; implants, surgical; surgical &
medical instruments; blood transfusion
equipment; catheters; medical instruments & equipment, blood & bone work;
pacemaker, cardiac
HQ: Medtronic, Inc.
710 Medtronic Pkwy
Minneapolis MN 55432
763 514-4000

(P-22048)
MENTOR WORLDWIDE LLC (DH)
31 Technology Dr Ste 200, Irvine
(92618-2302)
PHONE.............................800 636-8678
David Shepherd, President
Dean Freed, President
Robert Hum, President

Warren Foust, Vice Pres
Flavia Pease,
▲ EMP: 250
SALES (est): 250.9MM
SALES (corp-wide): 81.5B Publicly Held
WEB: www.mentordirect.com
SIC: 3842 3845 3841 Surgical appliances
& supplies; prosthetic appliances; implants, surgical; cosmetic restorations; ultrasonic medical equipment, except
cleaning; medical instruments & equipment, blood & bone work
HQ: Ethicon Inc.
Us Route 22
Somerville NJ 08876
732 524-0400

(P-22049)
MIRADRY INC
Also Called: Miramar Labs, Inc.
2790 Walsh Ave, Santa Clara
(95051-0963)
PHONE.............................408 940-8700
R Michael Kleine, President
Brigid A Makes, CFO
Steven W Kim, CTO
Steven M Higa, Mfg Staff
Robert Ellis, Marketing Staff
EMP: 24 EST: 2006
SALES (est): 6.6MM
SALES (corp-wide): 68.1MM Publicly
Held
SIC: 3842 Surgical appliances & supplies
PA: Sientra, Inc.
420 S Fairview Ave # 200
Santa Barbara CA 93117
805 562-3500

(P-22050)
MOLDEX-METRIC INC
10111 Jefferson Blvd, Culver City
(90232-3509)
PHONE.............................310 837-6500
Mark Magidson, CEO
Jeffrey Birkner, Vice Pres
Debra Magidson, Admin Sec
Larry Tutor, IT/INT Sup
Monica Madrid, Human Res Dir
◆ EMP: 500 EST: 1960
SQ FT: 80,000
SALES (est): 122.5MM Privately Held
WEB: www.moldex.com
SIC: 3842 Personal safety equipment; ear
plugs

(P-22051)
MULLER COMPANY
3366 N Torrey Pines Ct # 140, La Jolla
(92037-1025)
PHONE.............................858 587-9955
Stephen Muller, Branch Mgr
EMP: 11
SALES (corp-wide): 25MM Privately
Held
SIC: 3842 Hearing aids
PA: The Muller Company
18881 Von Karman Ave # 400
Irvine CA 92612
949 476-9800

(P-22052)
MY TRUE IMAGE MFG INC
Also Called: Design Veronique
999 Marina Way S, Richmond
(94804-3738)
PHONE.............................510 970-7990
Veronica C Smith, President
Michael Qi, Accounting Mgr
Macarthur Alfaro, Prdtn Mgr
▲ EMP: 80
SQ FT: 30,000
SALES (est): 12.6MM Privately Held
SIC: 3842 Surgical appliances & supplies

(P-22053)
NEUROSTRUCTURES INC
199 Technology Dr Ste 110, Irvine
(92618-2447)
PHONE.............................800 352-6103
John Stephani, CEO
Moti Altarc, Principal
EMP: 14
SALES (est): 1.8MM Privately Held
SIC: 3842 Braces, orthopedic

(P-22054)
NOBBE ORTHOPEDICS INC
3010 State St, Santa Barbara
(93105-3304)
PHONE.............................805 687-7508
Ralph W Nobbe, President
Bret Laurent, President
Erwin Nobbe, Vice Pres
Rolf Schiefel, Vice Pres
Sharadi L Nobbe,
EMP: 11
SQ FT: 2,850
SALES (est): 1.6MM Privately Held
WEB: www.nobbeorthopedics.com
SIC: 3842 2342 Cosmetic restorations;
braces, orthopedic; trusses, orthopedic &
surgical; supports: abdominal, ankle,
arch, kneecap, etc.; corsets & allied garments

(P-22055)
**NORELL PRSTHTICS
ORTHOTICS INC (PA)**
Also Called: Synergy Prosthetics
5466 Complex St Ste 207, San Diego
(92123-1124)
PHONE.............................510 770-9010
Louis Cosenza, CEO
Robert Fagnani, President
Ana Patel, IT/INT Sup
Vaibhavi Kulkarni, Sales Staff
EMP: 12
SALES (est): 1.8MM Privately Held
SIC: 3842 Limbs, artificial; braces, orthopedic

(P-22056)
NU-HOPE LABORATORIES INC
12640 Branford St, Pacoima (91331-3451)
P.O. Box 331150 (91333-1150)
PHONE.............................818 899-7711
Bradley J Galindo, CEO
Estelle Galindo, CFO
Mickey Galindo,
▲ EMP: 38
SQ FT: 25,000
SALES (est): 7.2MM Privately Held
WEB: www.nu-hope.com
SIC: 3842 Colostomy appliances

(P-22057)
NUPRODX INC
161 S Vasco Rd Ste G, Livermore
(94551-5131)
PHONE.............................925 292-0866
David Gaskell, President
EMP: 15
SALES (corp-wide): 2.4MM Privately
Held
SIC: 3842 3999 Wheelchairs; wheelchair
lifts
PA: Nuprodx, Inc.
889 Hayes St
Sonoma CA 95476
415 472-1699

(P-22058)
OCEAN HEAT INC
13610 Imperial Hwy Ste 4, Santa Fe
Springs (90670-4873)
PHONE.............................951 208-1923
Jason Johnson, CEO
EMP: 15
SQ FT: 29,000
SALES (est): 1.1MM Privately Held
SIC: 3842 Hydrotherapy equipment

(P-22059)
OMNICAL INC
557 Jessie St, San Fernando (91340-2542)
PHONE.............................818 837-7531
Ron Tinero, President
Ellen Tinero, Admin Sec
EMP: 12
SQ FT: 9,100
SALES (est): 1MM Privately Held
WEB: www.omnical.com
SIC: 3842 5047 Surgical appliances &
supplies; medical & hospital equipment

(P-22060)
ORTHO ENGINEERING INC (PA)
5759 Uplander Way, Culver City
(90230-6605)
PHONE.............................310 559-5996
George Ashkharikian, President

▲ = Import ▼=Export
◆ =Import/Export

EMP: 29
SQ FT: 4,000
SALES: 3MM Privately Held
WEB: www.orthoengineering.com
SIC: 3842 Braces, orthopedic; prosthetic appliances

(P-22061)
OSSUR AMERICAS INC (HQ)
27051 Towne Centre Dr # 100, Foothill Ranch (92610-2819)
PHONE....................949 362-3883
Mahesh Mansukhani, *CEO*
Avanindra Chaturvedi, *CFO*
Marc Larose, *Engineer*
Naomi Werner, *VP Human Res*
Nicole Carley, *Sales Staff*
▲ EMP: 277
SQ FT: 12,000
SALES (est): 121.5MM
SALES (corp-wide): 612.8MM Privately Held
SIC: 3842 Braces, orthopedic; orthopedic appliances
PA: Ossur Hf.
    Grjothalsi 5
    Reykjavik 110
    425 340-0

(P-22062)
OSSUR AMERICAS INC
19762 Pauling, Foothill Ranch (92610-2611)
PHONE....................949 382-3893
Edward Castillo, *Branch Mgr*
EMP: 13
SALES (corp-wide): 612.8MM Privately Held
SIC: 3842 Prosthetic appliances
HQ: Ossur Americas, Inc.
    27051 Towne Centre Dr # 100
    Foothill Ranch CA 92610
    949 362-3883

(P-22063)
OSSUR AMERICAS INC
Also Called: Ossur North America
27051 Towne Centre Dr # 100, Foothill Ranch (92610-2819)
P.O. Box 5194, Los Angeles (90051)
PHONE....................805 484-2600
Cathy McAnn, *Branch Mgr*
EMP: 26
SALES (corp-wide): 612.8MM Privately Held
SIC: 3842 Prosthetic appliances; limbs, artificial
HQ: Ossur Americas, Inc.
    27051 Towne Centre Dr # 100
    Foothill Ranch CA 92610
    949 362-3883

(P-22064)
PACIFIC COAST LABORATORIES
Also Called: PCL Communications
2100 Orchard Ave, San Leandro (94577-3415)
PHONE....................510 351-2770
Monte Martinez, *President*
James Kinred, *Marketing Mgr*
EMP: 15
SALES (est): 2.5MM Privately Held
WEB: www.pcl-cfa.com
SIC: 3842 Hearing aids; ear plugs; noise protectors, personal

(P-22065)
PASSY-MUIR INC
1212 Mcgaw Ave, Irvine (92614-5537)
PHONE....................949 833-8255
Joseph Agra, *Principal*
EMP: 10
SALES (corp-wide): 3.9MM Privately Held
SIC: 3842 Surgical appliances & supplies
PA: Passy-Muir, Inc.
    17992 Mitchell S Ste 200
    Irvine CA 92614
    949 833-8255

(P-22066)
PASSY-MUIR INC (PA)
17992 Mitchell S Ste 200, Irvine (92614-6813)
PHONE....................949 833-8255

Cameron Jolly, *President*
Ryan Williams, *COO*
Mary Sarris, *General Mgr*
Bert Magelo, *Info Tech Mgr*
Jose Comino Ramos, *Project Engr*
EMP: 30
SQ FT: 1,200
SALES (est): 3.9MM Privately Held
WEB: www.passy-muir.com
SIC: 3842 Orthopedic appliances

(P-22067)
PAULSON MANUFACTURING CORP (PA)
46752 Rainbow Canyon Rd, Temecula (92592-5984)
PHONE....................951 676-2451
Roy Paulson, *President*
Joyce Paulson, *Corp Secy*
Thomas V Paulson, *Vice Pres*
Jason Damore, *Engineer*
Jesus Luna, *Human Res Mgr*
▲ EMP: 100
SQ FT: 42,000
SALES: 15.3MM Privately Held
WEB: www.paulsonmfg.com
SIC: 3842 Personal safety equipment

(P-22068)
PHOENIX IMPROVING LIFE LLC
Also Called: Readysmart
148 Farley St, Mountain View (94043-4418)
PHONE....................650 248-0655
Tracy Ferea,
EMP: 15
SALES (est): 1.2MM Privately Held
SIC: 3842 Surgical appliances & supplies

(P-22069)
PHONAK LLC
47257 Fremont Blvd, Fremont (94538-6502)
PHONE....................510 743-3939
EMP: 10
SALES (corp-wide): 2.7B Privately Held
SIC: 3842 Hearing aids
HQ: Phonak, Llc
    4520 Weaver Pkwy Ste 1
    Warrenville IL 60555
    630 821-5000

(P-22070)
PONG RESEARCH CORPORATION
1010 S Coast Highway 101 # 105, Encinitas (92024-5069)
PHONE....................858 914-5299
David Pinn, *Principal*
EMP: 13 EST: 2014
SALES (est): 1.7MM Privately Held
SIC: 3842 3674 Radiation shielding aprons, gloves, sheeting, etc.; radiation sensors

(P-22071)
PROSTAT FIRST AID LLC (PA)
24922 Anza Dr Ste A, Valencia (91355-1232)
PHONE....................661 705-1256
Joseph Bratter, *Mng Member*
Karla Vasquez, *Manager*
▲ EMP: 21
SALES (est): 5.5MM Privately Held
SIC: 3842 5199 Bandages & dressings; first aid supplies

(P-22072)
PROSTAT FIRST AID LLC
1643 Puddingstone Dr, La Verne (91750-5810)
PHONE....................888 900-2920
Joseph Bratter, *Mng Member*
EMP: 24
SALES (corp-wide): 5.5MM Privately Held
SIC: 3842 Bandages & dressings
PA: Prostat First Aid, Llc
    24922 Anza Dr Ste A
    Valencia CA 91355
    661 705-1256

(P-22073)
PROSTHETIC AND ORTHOTIC GROUP (PA)
2669 Myrtle Ave Ste 101, Signal Hill (90755-2746)
PHONE....................562 595-6445
Glenn Matsushima, *President*
Sonia Marlow, *General Mgr*
Larry Wong, *Admin Sec*
Sonia Enriquez, *Opers Staff*
EMP: 12
SQ FT: 2,700
SALES (est): 1.6MM Privately Held
WEB: www.p-o-group.com
SIC: 3842 Braces, orthopedic; limbs, artificial

(P-22074)
PULSE SYSTEMS LLC
4090 Nelson Ave, Concord (94520-8513)
PHONE....................925 798-4080
Herb Bellucci,
Scott Summers, *Office Admin*
Wen Ho, *Engineer*
Bob Lamson, *Sales Staff*
Herbert J Bellucci,
EMP: 45
SQ FT: 12,600
SALES (est): 13.5MM
SALES (corp-wide): 8.4MM Publicly Held
WEB: www.pulsesystemscorp.com
SIC: 3842 3841 Surgical appliances & supplies; surgical & medical instruments
PA: United American Healthcare Corporation
    303 E Wacker Dr Ste 1040
    Chicago IL 60601
    313 393-4571

(P-22075)
RACING PLUS INC
Also Called: Parker Pumper Helmet Co
3834 Wacker Dr, Mira Loma (91752-1147)
PHONE....................951 360-5906
Harold Nicks, *President*
EMP: 11
SQ FT: 9,200
SALES (est): 1.4MM Privately Held
SIC: 3842 Helmets, space

(P-22076)
RAY-BAR ENGINEERING CORP
697 W Foothill Blvd, Azusa (91702-2346)
P.O. Box 415 (91702-0415)
PHONE....................626 969-1818
Toll Free:....................877 -
Joyce Vicky Wohler, *President*
Shirley Saldarriaga, *Admin Asst*
◆ EMP: 12
SQ FT: 15,000
SALES (est): 1.2MM Privately Held
WEB: www.raybar.net
SIC: 3842 Radiation shielding aprons, gloves, sheeting, etc.

(P-22077)
RESPIRONICS INC
14101 Rosecrans Ave Ste F, La Mirada (90638-3551)
PHONE....................562 483-6805
Jimmy Gibbs, *Manager*
EMP: 13
SALES (corp-wide): 20.8B Privately Held
WEB: www.respironics.com
SIC: 3842 7699 Surgical appliances & supplies; medical equipment repair, non-electric
HQ: Respironics, Inc.
    1001 Murry Ridge Ln
    Murrysville PA 15668
    724 387-5200

(P-22078)
REVA MEDICAL INC
5751 Copley Dr Ste B, San Diego (92111-7912)
PHONE....................858 966-3000
Jeff Anderson, *President*
C Raymond Larkin Jr, *Ch of Bd*
Leigh F Elkolli, *CFO*
EMP: 51
SQ FT: 37,000
SALES: 45K Privately Held
WEB: www.teamreva.com
SIC: 3842 Surgical appliances & supplies

(P-22079)
SAN JOAQUIN ORTHTICS & PRSTHTC
2211 N California St, Stockton (95204-5503)
PHONE....................209 932-0170
Matthew Shane Evans, *CEO*
Mike Beck, *Principal*
EMP: 11
SALES (est): 957.1K Privately Held
SIC: 3842 Orthopedic appliances

(P-22080)
SAS SAFETY CORPORATION
3031 Gardenia Ave, Long Beach (90807-5215)
PHONE....................562 427-2775
Patrick Larmon, *CEO*
James McCool, *Treasurer*
Julie Calvo, *Executive Asst*
Daniel Lett, *Admin Sec*
Delene Reifer, *QA Dir*
▲ EMP: 60
SQ FT: 90,000
SALES (est): 36MM
SALES (corp-wide): 11.6B Privately Held
WEB: www.sassafety.com
SIC: 3842 Personal safety equipment
HQ: Bunzl Usa Holdings Llc
    1 Cityplace Dr Ste 200
    Saint Louis MO 63141

(P-22081)
SEASPINE INC
Also Called: Integra Lifesciences
5770 Armada Dr, Carlsbad (92008-4608)
PHONE....................760 727-8399
Keith Valentine, *CEO*
Mike Lytle, *Vice Pres*
Sarah Stoltz, *Engineer*
Danielle Fresch, *Sales Staff*
Frank Vizesi, *Director*
EMP: 80
SQ FT: 22,000
SALES (est): 5.5MM
SALES (corp-wide): 143.4MM Publicly Held
WEB: www.seaspine.com
SIC: 3842 5999 Orthopedic appliances; orthopedic & prosthesis applications
HQ: Seaspine Orthopedics Corporation
    5770 Armada Dr
    Carlsbad CA 92008
    866 942-8698

(P-22082)
SEASPINE ORTHOPEDICS CORP (HQ)
5770 Armada Dr, Carlsbad (92008-4608)
PHONE....................866 942-8698
Keith Valentine, *CEO*
EMP: 20
SALES (est): 15.3MM
SALES (corp-wide): 143.4MM Publicly Held
SIC: 3842 5999 Orthopedic appliances; orthopedic & prosthesis applications
PA: Seaspine Holdings Corporation
    5770 Armada Dr
    Carlsbad CA 92008
    760 727-8399

(P-22083)
SECURITY PRO USA
10530 Venice Blvd Ste 200, Culver City (90232-3308)
PHONE....................310 841-5845
Al Even, *Owner*
Nelson Miranda, *Purch Mgr*
Cindy Perez, *Sales Staff*
◆ EMP: 14
SALES (est): 2.7MM Privately Held
SIC: 3842 Clothing, fire resistant & protective

(P-22084)
SHAMROCK MARKETING CO INC (HQ)
Also Called: Shamrock Manufacturing
5445 Daniels St, Chino (91710-9009)
PHONE....................909 591-8855
Hansen Jap, *CEO*
Hanson Lawrence, *President*
Angela Yiu, *Sales Mgr*

▲ **EMP:** 15 **EST:** 1997
SQ FT: 28,000
SALES (est): 2.2MM **Privately Held**
WEB: www.smcgloves.com
SIC: 3842 Gloves, safety

(P-22085)
SHAPE MEMORY MEDICAL INC
807 Aldo Ave Ste 109, Santa Clara
(95054-2254)
PHONE......................979 599-5201
Ted Ruppel, *President*
Bart Balkman, *Ch Credit Ofcr*
Scott Kraus, *VP Sales*
Carolyn Bruguera, *General Counsel*
EMP: 10 **EST:** 2009
SALES (est): 648.2K **Privately Held**
SIC: 3842 Surgical appliances & supplies

(P-22086)
SIENTRA INC (PA)
420 S Fairview Ave # 200, Santa Barbara
(93117-3654)
PHONE......................805 562-3500
Jeffrey M Nugent, *Ch of Bd*
Charles Huiner, *COO*
EMP: 129
SQ FT: 20,000
SALES: 68.1MM **Publicly Held**
SIC: 3842 Surgical appliances & supplies

(P-22087)
SIMPSON PERFORMANCE PDTS INC
Also Called: Team Simpson Racing
1407 240th St, Harbor City (90710-1306)
PHONE......................310 325-6035
Dave Nelson, *Branch Mgr*
EMP: 100 **Privately Held**
WEB: www.simpsonraceproducts.com
SIC: 3842 2326 Surgical appliances &
supplies; men's & boys' work clothing
HQ: Simpson Performance Products, Inc.
328 Fm 306
New Braunfels TX 78130
830 625-1774

(P-22088)
SMITH & NEPHEW INC
4085 Nelson Ave Ste E, Concord
(94520-1257)
PHONE......................925 681-3300
Martin Myers, *Principal*
Jeremy Hahn, *Sales Staff*
EMP: 50
SALES (corp-wide): 4.9B **Privately Held**
SIC: 3842 Surgical appliances & supplies
HQ: Smith & Nephew, Inc.
7135 Goodlett Farms Pkwy
Cordova TN 38016
901 396-2121

(P-22089)
SPECTRUM PROSTHETICS/ORTHOTICS
1844 South St, Redding (96001-1809)
PHONE......................530 243-4500
Forest Sexton, *President*
Jeff Zeller, *Admin Sec*
EMP: 11
SALES: 1.5MM **Privately Held**
SIC: 3842 Prosthetic appliances

(P-22090)
SPINAL AND ORTHOPEDIC DEVICES
5920 Noble Ave, Van Nuys (91411-3025)
PHONE......................818 908-9000
Frank McMurray, *President*
Steven McMurray, *Vice Pres*
Hal White, *General Mgr*
Cameron Ritchie, *VP Engrg*
EMP: 13
SQ FT: 1,500
SALES: 2.5MM **Privately Held**
SIC: 3842 Implants, surgical

(P-22091)
STEMRAD INC
228 Hamilton Ave Fl 3, Palo Alto
(94301-2583)
PHONE......................650 933-3377
Daniel Levitt, *CEO*
Oren Milstein, *Manager*
EMP: 12

SALES (est): 682.3K **Privately Held**
SIC: 3842 Clothing, fire resistant & protective

(P-22092)
STERIS CORPORATION
Also Called: Vts Medical Systems
324 Martin Ave, Santa Clara (95050-3102)
PHONE......................800 614-6789
Jerry Dilts, *Info Tech Mgr*
Mark Craig, *Manager*
EMP: 11 **Privately Held**
SIC: 3842 Surgical appliances & supplies
HQ: Steris Corporation
5960 Heisley Rd
Mentor OH 44060
440 354-2600

(P-22093)
STINGRAY SHIELDS CORPORATION
850 Beech St Unit 302, San Diego
(92101-2892)
PHONE......................619 325-9003
Erin Finegold, *President*
EMP: 10
SALES (est): 708.3K **Privately Held**
SIC: 3842 Radiation shielding aprons,
gloves, sheeting, etc.

(P-22094)
STJ ORTHOTIC SERVICES INC
225 Benjamin Dr Ste 103, Corona
(92879-8080)
PHONE......................951 279-5650
Michael Connor, *Manager*
EMP: 50 **Privately Held**
WEB: www.stjorthotic.com
SIC: 3842 5999 3131 Orthopedic appliances; orthopedic & prosthesis applications; footwear cut stock
PA: Stj Orthotic Services Inc
920 Wellwood Ave Ste B
Lindenhurst NY 11757

(P-22095)
STRENUMED INC
4864 Market St Ste D, Ventura
(93003-5786)
PHONE......................805 477-1000
Brenda Acosta, *CEO*
Doug Walker, *President*
▲ **EMP:** 10
SALES (est): 1.3MM **Privately Held**
WEB: www.strenumed.com
SIC: 3842 Surgical appliances & supplies

(P-22096)
SUNRISE MEDICAL (US) LLC
2842 N Business Park Ave, Fresno
(93727-1328)
PHONE......................559 292-2171
Thomas Rossnagel, *CEO*
▲ **EMP:** 99
SALES (est): 22.8MM **Privately Held**
SIC: 3842 Wheelchairs

(P-22097)
SUPER-FIT INC
1031 S Linwood Ave, Santa Ana
(92705-4323)
PHONE......................657 218-4827
Weibing Fei, *CEO*
EMP: 10
SALES (est): 439.6K **Privately Held**
SIC: 3842 2259 7218 Gloves, safety;
work gloves, knit; safety glove supply

(P-22098)
SUPERIOR SOUND TECHNOLOGY LLC
707 Vintage Ave, Suisun City (94534-7418)
PHONE......................707 863-7431
Claudia Pordes, *President*
EMP: 11
SALES (est): 1.3MM **Privately Held**
SIC: 3842 5049 5099 5999 Personal
safety equipment; ear plugs; law enforcement equipment & supplies; machine
guns; safety equipment & supplies; safety
supplies & equipment

(P-22099)
SUREFIRE LLC
17680 Newhope St Ste B, Fountain Valley
(92708-4220)
PHONE......................714 545-9444
Daniel Fischer, *Production*
EMP: 54
SALES (corp-wide): 159.3MM **Privately Held**
SIC: 3842 3484 3648 Ear plugs; guns
(firearms) or gun parts, 30 mm. & below;
flashlights
PA: Surefire, Llc
18300 Mount Baldy Cir
Fountain Valley CA 92708
714 545-9444

(P-22100)
SUREFIRE LLC
17760 Newhope St Ste A, Fountain Valley
(92708-5401)
PHONE......................714 545-9444
Daniel Fischer, *Production*
EMP: 41
SALES (corp-wide): 159.3MM **Privately Held**
SIC: 3842 3484 3648 Ear plugs; guns
(firearms) or gun parts, 30 mm. & below;
flashlights
PA: Surefire, Llc
18300 Mount Baldy Cir
Fountain Valley CA 92708
714 545-9444

(P-22101)
SUREFIRE LLC
2110 S Anne St, Santa Ana (92704-4409)
PHONE......................714 641-0483
Gustav Bonse, *Mfg Staff*
EMP: 41
SALES (corp-wide): 159.3MM **Privately Held**
SIC: 3842 3484 3648 Ear plugs; guns
(firearms) or gun parts, 30 mm. & below;
flashlights
PA: Surefire, Llc
18300 Mount Baldy Cir
Fountain Valley CA 92708
714 545-9444

(P-22102)
SUREFIRE LLC
2121 S Yale St, Santa Ana (92704-4437)
PHONE......................714 545-9444
John D Matthews, *Branch Mgr*
EMP: 49
SALES (corp-wide): 159.3MM **Privately Held**
SIC: 3842 Ear plugs
PA: Surefire, Llc
18300 Mount Baldy Cir
Fountain Valley CA 92708
714 545-9444

(P-22103)
SUREFIRE LLC
2300 S Yale St, Santa Ana (92704-5330)
PHONE......................714 641-0483
Gustav Bonse, *Manager*
EMP: 82
SALES (corp-wide): 159.3MM **Privately Held**
SIC: 3842 3484 3648 Ear plugs; guns
(firearms) or gun parts, 30 mm. & below;
flashlights
PA: Surefire, Llc
18300 Mount Baldy Cir
Fountain Valley CA 92708
714 545-9444

(P-22104)
SUREFIRE LLC (PA)
18300 Mount Baldy Cir, Fountain Valley
(92708-6122)
PHONE......................714 545-9444
John W Matthews, *President*
Sean Vo, *CFO*
Alex SOO, *Vice Pres*
Joel Smith,
Vuong Hoang, *Info Tech Dir*
◆ **EMP:** 150 **EST:** 2000
SQ FT: 45,000
SALES (est): 159.3MM **Privately Held**
SIC: 3842 3484 3648 Ear plugs; guns
(firearms) or gun parts, 30 mm. & below;
flashlights

(P-22105)
SUTURA INC
17080 Newhope St, Fountain Valley
(92708-4206)
PHONE......................714 427-0398
Anthony Nobles, *CEO*
David Kernan, *COO*
EMP: 28
SQ FT: 20,000
SALES (est): 2.6MM
SALES (corp-wide): 27.5MM **Privately Held**
WEB: www.whitebox-advisors.com
SIC: 3842 Surgical appliances & supplies;
sutures, absorbable & non-absorbable
PA: Whitebox Advisors Llc
3033 Excelsior Blvd # 300
Minneapolis MN 55416
612 253-6001

(P-22106)
SYMPHONIX DEVICES INC
1735 N 1st St, San Jose (95112-4529)
PHONE......................408 323-8218
Kirk B Davis, *President*
William Arthur, *Ch of Bd*
Terence J Griffin, *CFO*
Geoffrey R Ball, *Vice Pres*
Patrick J Rimroth, *VP Opers*
EMP: 10
SALES (est): 1.3MM **Privately Held**
SIC: 3842 Hearing aids

(P-22107)
TECHNIGLOVE INTERNATIONAL INC
3750 Pierce St, Riverside (92503-5037)
PHONE......................951 582-0890
Janine Gass, *CEO*
Darcy Maskrey, *Director*
▲ **EMP:** 10
SALES (est): 1.4MM **Privately Held**
WEB: www.techniglove.com
SIC: 3842 Gloves, safety

(P-22108)
TENDER CORPORATION
Also Called: Adventure Medical Kits
1141 Harbor Bay Pkwy # 103, Alameda
(94502-2219)
PHONE......................510 261-7414
Jonathan Greer, *Sales Staff*
EMP: 20
SALES (corp-wide): 24.4MM **Privately Held**
SIC: 3842 First aid, snake bite & burn kits
PA: Tender Corporation
944 Industrial Park Rd
Littleton NH 03561
603 444-5464

(P-22109)
THINK SURGICAL INC
47201 Lakeview Blvd, Fremont
(94538-6530)
PHONE......................510 249-2300
In K Mun, *CEO*
Hyunmo Ku, *CFO*
Paul Weiner, *CFO*
Guiwhan You, *Web Dvlpr*
Aruna Gummalla, *Software Engr*
EMP: 160 **EST:** 2007
SQ FT: 70,000
SALES (est): 34.8MM **Privately Held**
SIC: 3842 Surgical appliances & supplies

(P-22110)
THUASNE NORTH AMERICA INC (DH)
4615 Shepard St, Bakersfield
(93313-2339)
PHONE......................800 432-3466
Elizabeth Ducottet, *CEO*
EMP: 350
SALES (est): 32.4MM
SALES (corp-wide): 1.2MM **Privately Held**
SIC: 3842 Braces, orthopedic
HQ: Thuasne
118 Rue Marius Aufan
Levallois-Perret 92300
141 059-292

(P-22111)
TOTAL RESOURCES INTL INC (PA)
420 S Lemon Ave, Walnut (91789-2956)
PHONE...................................909 594-1220
George Rivera, *CEO*
Gregg Rivera, *President*
Merlyn Rivera, *Vice Pres*
▲ **EMP:** 80
SQ FT: 115,000
SALES: 12MM **Privately Held**
WEB: www.totalresourcesintl.com
SIC: 3842 First aid, snake bite & burn kits

(P-22112)
TRI QUALITY INC
Also Called: Nutec Rehab
5840 S Watt Ave Ste A, Sacramento (95829-9352)
PHONE...................................916 388-5939
Otmar H Weber, *President*
James Lindquist, *Vice Pres*
Dagmar Weber, *Admin Sec*
▲ **EMP:** 28
SQ FT: 10,000
SALES (est): 3.8MM **Privately Held**
WEB: www.triquality.com
SIC: 3842 Wheelchairs

(P-22113)
ULTIMATE EARS CONSUMER LLC
3 Jenner Ste 180, Irvine (92618-3835)
PHONE...................................949 502-8340
Mindy Harvey, *Owner*
Melinda Harvey,
Daphne X LI, *Senior Mgr*
▲ **EMP:** 24
SALES (est): 4.1MM
SALES (corp-wide): 2.7B **Privately Held**
SIC: 3842 Hearing aids
HQ: Logitech Inc.
7700 Gateway Blvd
Newark CA 94560
510 795-8500

(P-22114)
US ARMOR CORPORATION
10715 Bloomfield Ave, Santa Fe Springs (90670-3913)
PHONE...................................562 207-4240
Stephen Armellino, *President*
Victoria Rios, *Purch Mgr*
Jennifer Wright, *Purch Mgr*
▲ **EMP:** 45
SQ FT: 14,000
SALES (est): 11.3MM **Privately Held**
WEB: www.usarmor.com
SIC: 3842 2326 5999 Bulletproof vests; men's & boys' work clothing; safety supplies & equipment

(P-22115)
VCP MOBILITY INC
2842 N Business Park Ave, Fresno (93727-1328)
PHONE...................................559 292-2171
EMP: 400
SALES (corp-wide): 402.8MM **Privately Held**
SIC: 3842 Surgical appliances & supplies
HQ: Vcp Mobility, Inc.
6899 Winchester Cir # 200
Boulder CO 80301
303 218-4500

(P-22116)
VCP MOBILITY HOLDINGS INC
Also Called: Sunrise Med HM Hlth Care Group
745 Design Ct Ste 602, Chula Vista (91911-6165)
PHONE...................................619 213-6500
Steve Winston, *Manager*
EMP: 320
SALES (corp-wide): 402.8MM **Privately Held**
WEB: www.sleepcompliance.com
SIC: 3842 Wheelchairs
HQ: Vcp Mobility Holdings, Inc.
7477 Dry Creek Pkwy
Niwot CO 80503
303 218-4600

(P-22117)
VCP MOBILITY HOLDINGS INC
Also Called: Quickie Designs
2842 N Business Park Ave, Fresno (93727-1328)
PHONE...................................303 218-4500
Adtar Kooner, *Manager*
Peter Whittle, *Vice Pres*
Chris Diffey, *Administration*
Son Le, *Design Engr*
Daniel Zhou, *Design Engr*
EMP: 350
SALES (corp-wide): 402.8MM **Privately Held**
WEB: www.sleepcompliance.com
SIC: 3842 Surgical appliances & supplies
HQ: Vcp Mobility Holdings, Inc.
7477 Dry Creek Pkwy
Niwot CO 80503
303 218-4600

(P-22118)
VISALIA CTR 4 AMBLTRY MED & SV
Also Called: Visalia Cams
842 S Akers St, Visalia (93277-8309)
PHONE...................................559 740-4094
Burton Redd, *Partner*
EMP: 30
SQ FT: 5,000
SALES: 5MM **Privately Held**
SIC: 3842 Trusses, orthopedic & surgical

(P-22119)
VISION QUEST INDUSTRIES INC (PA)
Also Called: V Q Orthocare
18011 Mitchell S Ste A, Irvine (92614-6863)
PHONE...................................949 261-6382
James W Knape, *CEO*
Kevin Lunau, *COO*
Bob Blachford, *CFO*
Joe Farrell, *Engineer*
▲ **EMP:** 100
SQ FT: 35,500
SALES (est): 18.3MM **Privately Held**
WEB: www.vqorthocare.com
SIC: 3842 5999 Braces, orthopedic; medical apparatus & supplies

(P-22120)
VISION QUEST INDUSTRIES INC
Also Called: Vq Orthocare
1390 Decision St Ste A, Vista (92081-8578)
PHONE...................................760 734-1550
Kevin Lunau, *Branch Mgr*
James W Knape, *CEO*
Cynthia Castillo, *Purch Mgr*
EMP: 75
SALES (corp-wide): 18.3MM **Privately Held**
WEB: www.vqorthocare.com
SIC: 3842 5999 Braces, orthopedic; medical apparatus & supplies
PA: Vision Quest Industries Incorporated
18011 Mitchell S Ste A
Irvine CA 92614
949 261-6382

(P-22121)
VME ACQUISITION CORP (PA)
Also Called: Kinamad
820 Flynn Rd, Camarillo (93012-8701)
PHONE...................................805 384-2748
Clyde R Pratt, *President*
Lorraine Willis, *CFO*
EMP: 30
SQ FT: 14,000
SALES: 600K **Privately Held**
SIC: 3842 7342 Surgical appliances & supplies; disinfecting & pest control services

(P-22122)
WALKER CREATIONS
907 Vista Del Rio, Santa Maria (93458-8238)
PHONE...................................805 349-0755
EMP: 12
SALES (est): 879.9K **Privately Held**
SIC: 3842

(P-22123)
WEBER ORTHOPEDIC INC (PA)
Also Called: Hely & Weber Orthopedic
1185 E Main St, Santa Paula (93060-2954)
P.O. Box 832 (93061-0832)
PHONE...................................805 525-8474
Jim Weber, *President*
John P Hely, *Vice Pres*
Power Hely, *Info Tech Mgr*
Ed Marx, *Engineer*
Mark Vo, *Engineer*
▲ **EMP:** 40
SQ FT: 28,000
SALES (est): 6MM **Privately Held**
WEB: www.helyweber.net
SIC: 3842 5047 Braces, orthopedic; orthopedic equipment & supplies

(P-22124)
WEST COAST ORTHOTIC/PROSTHETIC
3215 N California St # 2, Stockton (95204-3433)
PHONE...................................209 942-4166
Dave Vera, *Principal*
EMP: 12
SALES (est): 2.2MM **Privately Held**
WEB: www.wcop.com
SIC: 3842 Braces, orthopedic

(P-22125)
WESTERN GLOVE MFG INC
10747 Norwalk Blvd, Santa Fe Springs (90670-3823)
P.O. Box 558, Paramount (90723-0558)
PHONE...................................562 903-1339
C Edward Chu, *President*
Hong Brian Choi, *Vice Pres*
EMP: 60
SALES (est): 4.8MM **Privately Held**
SIC: 3842 3151 2326 Gloves, safety; gloves, leather: work; men's & boys' work clothing

(P-22126)
WHITEHALL MANUFACTURING INC
Also Called: A Division Acom Engrg Co
15125 Proctor Ave, City of Industry (91746-3327)
P.O. Box 3527 (91744-0527)
PHONE...................................626 336-4561
Donald E Morris, *President*
Kathryn L Morris, *Corp Secy*
William D Morris, *Vice Pres*
Steve Stormes, *Vice Pres*
EMP: 750
SQ FT: 2,000
SALES (est): 18.1MM
SALES (corp-wide): 85MM **Privately Held**
WEB: www.whitehallmfg.com
SIC: 3842 Whirlpool baths, hydrotherapy equipment
PA: Acorn Engineering Company
15125 Proctor Ave
City Of Industry CA 91746
800 488-8999

(P-22127)
XR LLC
15251 Pipeline Ln, Huntington Beach (92649-1135)
PHONE...................................714 847-9292
ARI Suss,
Kelly Eberhard Allen,
Rebecca Weinberg, *Director*
▲ **EMP:** 27
SQ FT: 68,000
SALES (est): 4.4MM **Privately Held**
WEB: www.extremerestraints.com
SIC: 3842 Personal safety equipment

(P-22128)
ZIMMER INTERMED INC
1647 Yeager Ave, La Verne (91750-5854)
PHONE...................................909 392-0882
Kelly Liebhart, *President*
EMP: 50
SALES (est): 6MM **Privately Held**
SIC: 3842 Prosthetic appliances

3843 Dental Eqpt & Splys

(P-22129)
3M COMPANY
2111 Mcgaw Ave, Irvine (92614-0908)
PHONE...................................949 863-1360
David Goldinger, *Branch Mgr*
Dena Robertson, *Executive*
Kevin Foust, *Engineer*
Joel Knott, *Engineer*
David Beatty, *Manager*
EMP: 10
SQ FT: 77,656
SALES (corp-wide): 32.7B **Publicly Held**
WEB: www.mmm.com
SIC: 3843 5047 Dental equipment & supplies; dental equipment & supplies
PA: 3m Company
3m Center
Saint Paul MN 55144
651 733-1110

(P-22130)
3M UNITEK CORPORATION
2724 Peck Rd, Monrovia (91016-5097)
PHONE...................................626 445-7960
Mary Jo Abler, *CEO*
Fred Palensky, *Vice Pres*
Mike Lane, *Executive*
James Pang, *Info Tech Mgr*
Erasmo Robles, *Engineer*
▲ **EMP:** 480
SQ FT: 249,000
SALES (est): 88.9MM
SALES (corp-wide): 32.7B **Publicly Held**
WEB: www.mmm.com
SIC: 3843 Orthodontic appliances; dental hand instruments; dental laboratory equipment
PA: 3m Company
3m Center
Saint Paul MN 55144
651 733-1110

(P-22131)
ALIGN TECHNOLOGY INC (PA)
Also Called: Invisalign
2820 Orchard Pkwy, San Jose (95134-2019)
PHONE...................................408 470-1000
Joseph M Hogan, *President*
C Raymond Larkin Jr, *Ch of Bd*
John F Morici, *CFO*
Raj Pudipeddi, *Chief Mktg Ofcr*
Simon Beard, *Senior VP*
▲ **EMP:** 277
SALES: 1.9B **Publicly Held**
WEB: www.invisalign.com
SIC: 3843 Orthodontic appliances

(P-22132)
ALPHA DENTAL OF UTAH INC
12898 Towne Center Dr, Cerritos (90703-8546)
PHONE...................................562 467-7759
Anthony S Barth, *Principal*
Teresa Lanta, *Treasurer*
Shahab Haghnazari, *Systs Prg Mgr*
Michelle McBride, *Manager*
Betty Quintana, *Manager*
EMP: 21
SALES (est): 1.9MM **Privately Held**
SIC: 3843 Dental equipment & supplies

(P-22133)
AMERICAN TOOTH INDUSTRIES
1200 Stellar Dr, Oxnard (93033-2404)
PHONE...................................805 487-9868
Emilio Pozzi, *CEO*
Angela Fontenot, *President*
Bruno Pozzi, *President*
Victoria Pozzi, *Exec VP*
Roberto Trada, *Exec VP*
▲ **EMP:** 98
SQ FT: 28,000
SALES (est): 15.6MM **Privately Held**
SIC: 3843 Teeth, artificial (not made in dental laboratories)

(P-22134)
ARGEN CORPORATION
8515 Miralani Dr, San Diego (92126-4352)
PHONE...................................858 455-7900
Anton Woolf, *CEO*

Connie Wedel, *VP Human Res*
Luis Gonzalez, *Plant Mgr*
EMP: 17
SALES (est): 4.4MM **Privately Held**
SIC: 3843 Dental equipment & supplies

(P-22135)
AURIDENT INC
610 S State College Blvd, Fullerton
(92831-5138)
P.O. Box 7200 (92834-7200)
PHONE..................................714 870-1851
Howard M Hoffman, *President*
Fredelle G Hoffman, *Corp Secy*
David H Fell, *Vice Pres*
Sangdon Choi, *Technician*
My Nguyen, *Finance Mgr*
EMP: 30
SQ FT: 2,700
SALES (est): 5MM **Privately Held**
WEB: www.aurident.com
SIC: 3843 Dental alloys for amalgams

(P-22136)
BELPORT COMPANY INC (PA)
Also Called: Gingi Pak
4825 Calle Alto, Camarillo (93012-8530)
P.O. Box 240 (93011-0240)
PHONE..................................805 484-1051
Jo Pennington, *President*
Lupe Becerra, *Cust Mgr*
David Havriliak, *Manager*
EMP: 21
SQ FT: 22,000
SALES (est): 3.6MM **Privately Held**
SIC: 3843 Dental hand instruments; compounds, dental; impression material, dental

(P-22137)
BIEN AIR USA INC
8861 Research Dr Ste 100, Irvine
(92618-4255)
PHONE..................................949 477-6050
Jean Claude Maeier, *President*
Arthur Mateen, *Vice Pres*
Ashley Blanchard, *Opers Staff*
EMP: 12
SALES (est): 2.1MM
SALES (corp-wide): 71.1MM **Privately Held**
WEB: www.bienair.com
SIC: 3843 7699 5047 Dental equipment; dental instrument repair; hospital equipment & furniture
HQ: Bien-Air Dental Sa
　　Langgasse 60
　　Biel-Bienne BE 2504
　　323 446-464

(P-22138)
BIOLASE INC (PA)
4 Cromwell, Irvine (92618-1816)
PHONE..................................949 361-1200
Todd Norbe, *CEO*
Jonathan T Lord, *Ch of Bd*
John R Beaver, *CFO*
John Beaver, *Officer*
Dmitri Boutoussov, *Vice Pres*
EMP: 195
SQ FT: 57,000
SALES: 46.1MM **Publicly Held**
WEB: www.biolase.com
SIC: 3843 3841 Dental equipment & supplies; dental equipment; dental hand instruments; dental laboratory equipment; surgical lasers

(P-22139)
CONAMCO SA DE CV
3008 Palm Hill Dr, Vista (92084-6555)
PHONE..................................760 586-4356
Jane Mitchell, *Vice Pres*
Alfredo Mobarak, *Ch of Bd*
EMP: 75
SQ FT: 20,000
SALES (est): 2MM **Privately Held**
SIC: 3843 Cement, dental

(P-22140)
CYBER MEDICAL IMAGING INC
Also Called: Xdr Radiology
11300 W Olympic Blvd # 710, Los Angeles
(90064-1637)
PHONE..................................888 937-9729
Douglas Yoon, *CEO*

Joel Karafin, *COO*
Adam Chen, *Senior VP*
EMP: 25
SQ FT: 2,800
SALES: 6.1MM **Privately Held**
SIC: 3843 Dental equipment & supplies

(P-22141)
DANVILLE MATERIALS LLC
4020 E Leaverton Ct, Anaheim
(92807-1610)
PHONE..................................714 399-0334
Greg Dorsman, *Manager*
Caroline Franklin, *Admin Asst*
EMP: 20
SALES (corp-wide): 19.2MM **Privately Held**
SIC: 3843 Dental materials
HQ: Danville Materials, Llc
　　2875 Loker Ave E
　　Carlsbad CA 92010
　　760 743-7744

(P-22142)
DANVILLE MATERIALS LLC (HQ)
2875 Loker Ave E, Carlsbad (92010-6626)
PHONE..................................760 743-7744
Steve Schiess, *President*
▲ **EMP:** 36
SALES (est): 6.3MM
SALES (corp-wide): 19.2MM **Privately Held**
SIC: 3843 Dental equipment & supplies
PA: Zest Anchors, Inc.
　　2875 Loker Ave E
　　Carlsbad CA 92010
　　760 743-7744

(P-22143)
DEN-MAT HOLDINGS LLC (HQ)
1017 W Central Ave, Lompoc
(93436-2701)
P.O. Box 1729, Santa Maria (93456-1729)
PHONE..................................805 346-3700
Steven J Semmelmayer, *CEO*
Robert Cartagena, *COO*
Timothy Heher, *CFO*
Trevor Roots, *CFO*
Todd J Tiberi, *Principal*
▲ **EMP:** 10
SALES (est): 144.6MM **Privately Held**
SIC: 3843 Dental materials
PA: Cp Dental Llc
　　2727 Skyway Dr
　　Santa Maria CA 93455
　　800 433-6628

(P-22144)
DENOVO DENTAL INC
5130 Commerce Dr, Baldwin Park
(91706-1450)
P.O. Box 548 (91706-0548)
PHONE..................................626 480-0182
Richard R Parker, *President*
Joseph Parker, *Vice Pres*
Jeanette Parker, *Admin Sec*
▼ **EMP:** 20
SQ FT: 10,000
SALES (est): 5.4MM **Privately Held**
WEB: www.denovodental.com
SIC: 3843 5047 Dental equipment & supplies; dental equipment & supplies

(P-22145)
DENTIUM USA (HQ)
Also Called: Implantium
6731 Katella Ave, Cypress (90630-5105)
PHONE..................................714 226-0229
Sung Min Chung, *President*
S Ghildyal, *CEO*
Eun Kyung Son, *Vice Pres*
Martin Zamora, *CIO*
▲ **EMP:** 12
SQ FT: 5,500
SALES (est): 3MM **Privately Held**
SIC: 3843 Dental equipment

(P-22146)
DENTSPLY SIRONA INC
13553 Calimesa Blvd, Yucaipa
(92399-2303)
PHONE..................................909 795-2080
Vernon Goodwalt, *Branch Mgr*
Mark Pimentel, *Regl Sales Mgr*
EMP: 80

SALES (corp-wide): 3.9B **Publicly Held**
WEB: www.dentsply.com
SIC: 3843 5047 Dental equipment & supplies; dentists' professional supplies
PA: Dentsply Sirona Inc.
　　221 W Philadelphia St
　　York PA 17401
　　717 845-7511

(P-22147)
DENTTIO INC
116 N Maryland Ave # 125, Glendale
(91206-4291)
PHONE..................................323 254-1000
Young Han, *CEO*
EMP: 16
SALES: 2.2MM **Privately Held**
SIC: 3843 Dental equipment & supplies

(P-22148)
DEXTA CORPORATION
957 Enterprise Way, NAPA (94558-6209)
PHONE..................................707 255-2454
Mark M Rusin, *President*
Paul Rusin, *Vice Pres*
EMP: 52 **EST:** 1966
SQ FT: 19,000
SALES (est): 7.9MM **Privately Held**
WEB: www.dexta.com
SIC: 3843 Dental chairs; dental equipment

(P-22149)
DIAMODENT INC
1580 N Harmony Cir, Anaheim
(92807-2092)
PHONE..................................888 281-8850
Kazem Jeff Rassoli, *President*
EMP: 15
SALES (est): 2.6MM **Privately Held**
WEB: www.diamodent.com
SIC: 3843 Dental equipment & supplies

(P-22150)
DOCKUM RESEARCH LABORATORY
844 E Mariposa St, Altadena (91001-2421)
PHONE..................................626 794-1821
Greta Dockum, *President*
EMP: 12 **EST:** 1956
SQ FT: 5,000
SALES: 424.4K **Privately Held**
SIC: 3843 Dental equipment & supplies

(P-22151)
ECONOTEK INC (PA)
Also Called: Eti Empire Direct
2895 E Blue Star St, Anaheim
(92806-2508)
P.O. Box 6972, Orange (92863-6972)
PHONE..................................714 238-1131
Robert Wilcken, *President*
Phil Miller, *Vice Pres*
EMP: 10
SQ FT: 5,000
SALES (est): 3.4MM **Privately Held**
WEB: www.econotek.com
SIC: 3843 Plaster, dental

(P-22152)
EMDIN INTERNATIONAL CORP
15841 Business Center Dr, Irwindale
(91706-2053)
P.O. Box 660901, Arcadia (91066-0901)
PHONE..................................626 813-3740
Dinesh C Tandon, *President*
Maryann Tandon, *Vice Pres*
EMP: 10
SQ FT: 10,000
SALES: 800K **Privately Held**
WEB: www.emdin.com
SIC: 3843 Dental equipment & supplies

(P-22153)
ENDODENT INC
851 Meridian St, Duarte (91010-3588)
PHONE..................................626 359-5715
EMP: 34
SQ FT: 10,000
SALES (est): 3MM **Privately Held**
WEB: www.endodent.com
SIC: 3843

(P-22154)
ENVISTA HOLDINGS CORPORATION
200 S Kraemer Blvd Bldg E, Brea
(92821-6208)
PHONE..................................714 817-7000
Amir Aghdaei, *President*
Scott Huennekens, *Ch of Bd*
Howard H Yu, *CFO*
Curt W Bludworth, *Senior VP*
Patrik Eriksson, *Senior VP*
EMP: 12800
SALES (est): 228.8MM **Privately Held**
SIC: 3843 Dental equipment & supplies

(P-22155)
EVOLVE DENTAL TECHNOLOGIES INC
5 Vanderbilt, Irvine (92618-2011)
PHONE..................................949 713-0909
Rodger Kurthy, *CEO*
Sharon Kurthy, *President*
EMP: 14
SALES (est): 1.5MM **Privately Held**
SIC: 3843 Dental equipment & supplies

(P-22156)
G HARTZELL & SON INC
2372 Stanwell Cir, Concord (94520-4807)
P.O. Box 5988 (94524-0988)
PHONE..................................925 798-2206
Andy Hartzell, *President*
Andrew McIver, *Owner*
EMP: 30
SQ FT: 20,000
SALES (est): 3.3MM **Privately Held**
WEB: www.ghartzellandson.com
SIC: 3843 3842 Dental equipment & supplies; surgical appliances & supplies

(P-22157)
GOLDEN EMPIRE DENTAL LAB INC
929 21st St, Bakersfield (93301-4706)
PHONE..................................661 327-1888
Chuck Kim, *President*
EMP: 10
SQ FT: 2,100
SALES (est): 1.1MM **Privately Held**
WEB: www.gedentallab.com
SIC: 3843 Dental laboratory equipment

(P-22158)
HAND PIECE PARTS AND PRODUCTS
707 W Angus Ave, Orange (92868-1305)
PHONE..................................714 997-4331
Steve Bowen, *President*
Lyla Bowen, *Vice Pres*
EMP: 30
SQ FT: 18,000
SALES: 3MM **Privately Held**
WEB: www.handpieceparts.com
SIC: 3843 Dental materials

(P-22159)
HENRY J PEREZ DDS
Also Called: G & P Dntl Care Former Partnr
132 S A St Ste B, Oxnard (93030-5690)
PHONE..................................805 983-6768
Henry J Perez Jr DDS, *Owner*
Rose Kravagna, *Manager*
EMP: 10
SALES (est): 839.9K **Privately Held**
SIC: 3843 Orthodontic appliances

(P-22160)
IMPLANT DIRECT SYBRON INTL LLC (HQ)
22715 Savi Ranch Pkwy, Yorba Linda
(92887-4609)
PHONE..................................818 444-3000
Roy Chang,
Ed Buthusiem,
Henrik J Roos,
Tom Stratton,
EMP: 14 **EST:** 2010
SALES (est): 4.8MM
SALES (corp-wide): 19.8B **Publicly Held**
SIC: 3843 Dental equipment & supplies
PA: Danaher Corporation
　　2200 Penn Ave Nw Ste 800w
　　Washington DC 20037
　　202 828-0850

▲ = Import ▼=Export
◆ =Import/Export

(P-22161)
IMPLANT DIRECT SYBRON MFG LLC
3050 E Hillcrest Dr, Westlake Village (91362-3171)
PHONE...................................818 444-3300
Gerald A Niznick,
Nicole Pinion, *Technical Staff*
Barry Britzman, *Engineer*
Eduardo Bueno, *Engineer*
Oguzman Guzman, *Engineer*
EMP: 200
SQ FT: 45,622
SALES (est): 40.8MM
SALES (corp-wide): 19.8B **Publicly Held**
WEB: www.implantdirect.com
SIC: 3843 Dental equipment & supplies
PA: Danaher Corporation
2200 Penn Ave Nw Ste 800w
Washington DC 20037
202 828-0850

(P-22162)
JAZZ IMAGING LLC
800 Chartot Ave Ste 100, San Jose (95131)
PHONE...................................567 234-5299
Todd Miller, *Info Tech Mgr*
Kumar Joshi, *VP Opers*
EMP: 10 **EST:** 2014
SALES: 1MM **Privately Held**
SIC: 3843 5047 Dental equipment & supplies; dental equipment & supplies

(P-22163)
JENERIC/PENTRON INCORPORATED (HQ)
1717 W Collins Ave, Orange (92867-5422)
PHONE...................................203 265-7397
Gordon Cohen, *President*
Martin Schulman, *Exec VP*
EMP: 200 **EST:** 1977
SQ FT: 46,000
SALES (est): 10MM
SALES (corp-wide): 27.9MM **Privately Held**
WEB: www.pentron.com
SIC: 3843 Dental equipment
PA: Pentron Corporation
53 N Plains Industrial Rd
Wallingford CT
203 265-7397

(P-22164)
JMU DENTAL INC
150 E Lambert Rd, Fullerton (92835-1000)
PHONE...................................909 676-0000
Jianmin Yu, *CEO*
EMP: 10
SQ FT: 40,000
SALES (est): 414.8K **Privately Held**
SIC: 3843 Dental equipment & supplies

(P-22165)
KAINOS DENTAL TECHNOLOGIES LLC (PA)
1844 San Miguel Dr 308b, Walnut Creek (94596-8604)
PHONE...................................800 331-4834
William Gianni, *CEO*
Andrew Nam, *COO*
Michael Finke, *CTO*
EMP: 24
SQ FT: 3,000
SALES: 3.4MM **Privately Held**
SIC: 3843 3841 Dental equipment & supplies; surgical & medical instruments

(P-22166)
KERR CORPORATION (DH)
1717 W Collins Ave, Orange (92867-5422)
P.O. Box 14247 (92863-1447)
PHONE...................................714 516-7400
Damien McDonald, *CEO*
Philip Read, *President*
Steve Semmelmayer, *President*
Alexander Wallstein, *President*
Steve Dunkerken, *Treasurer*
◆ **EMP:** 218
SQ FT: 105,000

SALES (est): 347MM
SALES (corp-wide): 19.8B **Publicly Held**
WEB: www.kerrdental.com
SIC: 3843 Dental materials; dental laboratory equipment; impression material, dental; dental hand instruments

(P-22167)
KETTENBACH LP
16052 Beach Blvd Ste 221, Huntington Beach (92647-3855)
PHONE...................................877 532-2123
Daniel Parrilli, *Director*
Erik Cortes, *General Mgr*
Keith Schmitz, *Sales Mgr*
Tia Cain, *Marketing Staff*
EMP: 19
SALES (est): 2.1MM **Privately Held**
SIC: 3843 5047 Dental equipment & supplies; dental equipment & supplies

(P-22168)
KEYSTONE DENTAL INC
13645 Alton Pkwy Ste A, Irvine (92618-1693)
PHONE...................................781 328-3382
Michael Nealon, *Branch Mgr*
Rachel Morkel, *Sales Executive*
EMP: 29 **Privately Held**
SIC: 3843 Enamels, dentists'
PA: Keystone Dental, Inc.
154 Middlesex Tpke Ste 2
Burlington MA 01803

(P-22169)
LACLEDE INC
Also Called: Laclede Research Center
2103 E University Dr, Rancho Dominguez (90220-6413)
PHONE...................................310 605-4280
Michael Pellico, *President*
Stephen Pellico, *Vice Pres*
Orion Lindemann, *Technology*
▲ **EMP:** 35
SQ FT: 25,000
SALES (est): 9.6MM **Privately Held**
WEB: www.laclede.com
SIC: 3843 Dental equipment

(P-22170)
LANCER ORTHODONTICS INC (PA)
1493 Poinsettia Ave # 143, Vista (92081-8544)
PHONE...................................760 744-5585
Giorgio Beretta, *CEO*
Lisa LI, *CFO*
Janet Moore, *Admin Sec*
▲ **EMP:** 20
SQ FT: 9,240
SALES (est): 14.3MM **Privately Held**
WEB: www.lancerortho.com
SIC: 3843 5047 Orthodontic appliances; dental equipment & supplies

(P-22171)
LARES RESEARCH
295 Lockheed Ave, Chico (95973-9026)
PHONE...................................530 345-1767
Craig J Lares, *President*
Bruce Holderbein, *Electrical Engi*
Larry McCulloch, *Engineer*
Michael Peairs, *Engineer*
Juan Lopez, *Clerk*
EMP: 39 **EST:** 1956
SQ FT: 30,000
SALES (est): 9.5MM **Privately Held**
WEB: www.laresdental.com
SIC: 3843 Hand pieces & parts, dental

(P-22172)
LIGHT MOBILE INC
Also Called: Danso Dental Lab
7968 Arjons Dr Ste D, San Diego (92126-6362)
PHONE...................................858 278-1750
Mal Hoan Park, *Principal*
Daniel Park, *President*
EMP: 17 **EST:** 2008
SQ FT: 6,500
SALES (est): 1.5MM **Privately Held**
SIC: 3843 8072 Teeth, artificial (not made in dental laboratories); artificial teeth production

(P-22173)
MICROTECH LLC
17260 Newhope St, Fountain Valley (92708-4210)
PHONE...................................714 966-1645
Reed Payne, *Owner*
Tuan Nuygen,
Lance Payne,
EMP: 22
SQ FT: 1,600
SALES (est): 3.3MM **Privately Held**
SIC: 3843 Dental equipment & supplies

(P-22174)
NEIGHBORING LLC
2427 Sentinel Ln, San Marcos (92078-2138)
PHONE...................................818 271-0640
Xiaohong Liu, *President*
Sean Gelt, *Manager*
EMP: 11
SQ FT: 2,400
SALES (est): 133.1K **Privately Held**
SIC: 3843 Dental equipment & supplies

(P-22175)
NOBEL BIOCARE USA LLC
22715 Savi Ranch Pkwy, Yorba Linda (92887-4609)
PHONE...................................714 282-4800
Thomas Olsen, *President*
Anne Gonzales, *General Mgr*
Corinne Lozano, *General Mgr*
Cecelia Acker, *Administration*
Catalina Segundo, *Administration*
▲ **EMP:** 500
SQ FT: 150,000
SALES (est): 290MM
SALES (corp-wide): 19.8B **Publicly Held**
SIC: 3843 Dental equipment
HQ: Nobel Biocare Ab
Kungsgatan 15
Goteborg 411 1
318 188-00

(P-22176)
ORMCO CORPORATION (DH)
Also Called: Sybron Endo
1717 W Collins Ave, Orange (92867-5422)
PHONE...................................714 516-7400
Patrik Eriksson, *CEO*
Vicente Reynal, *President*
Jason R Davis, *Vice Pres*
Ryan Alexander, *District Mgr*
Roy Scolding, *District Mgr*
◆ **EMP:** 100
SQ FT: 104,000
SALES (est): 152.8MM
SALES (corp-wide): 19.8B **Publicly Held**
WEB: www.ormco.com
SIC: 3843 Orthodontic appliances

(P-22177)
ORTHO ORGANIZERS INC
1822 Aston Ave, Carlsbad (92008-7306)
PHONE...................................760 448-8600
David Parker, *Chairman*
Russell J Bonafede, *President*
Alison Weber, *CFO*
Ted Dreifuss, *Vice Pres*
Robert Riley, *Vice Pres*
▲ **EMP:** 226
SQ FT: 65,000
SALES (est): 33.7MM
SALES (corp-wide): 13.2B **Publicly Held**
WEB: www.orthoorganizers.com
SIC: 3843 5047 Orthodontic appliances; dental equipment & supplies
PA: Henry Schein, Inc.
135 Duryea Rd
Melville NY 11747
631 843-5500

(P-22178)
ORTHODENTAL INTERNATIONAL INC
280 Campillo St Ste J, Calexico (92231-3200)
PHONE...................................760 357-8070
Armando Lozano, *President*
▲ **EMP:** 57
SALES (est): 7.4MM
SALES (corp-wide): 3.9B **Publicly Held**
SIC: 3843 Orthodontic appliances

PA: Dentsply Sirona Inc.
221 W Philadelphia St
York PA 17401
717 845-7511

(P-22179)
PANADENT CORPORATION
580 S Rancho Ave, Colton (92324-3252)
PHONE...................................909 783-1841
Arlene Lee, *Ch of Bd*
Thomas E Lee, *President*
Brian Richardson, *Sales Associate*
Kelly Barrie, *Sales Staff*
EMP: 20
SQ FT: 1,200
SALES: 3.5MM **Privately Held**
WEB: www.panadent.com
SIC: 3843 Dental hand instruments

(P-22180)
PAR ORTHODONTIC LABORATORY
23141 La Cadena Dr Ste K, Laguna Hills (92653-1423)
P.O. Box 30010, Laguna Niguel (92607-0010)
PHONE...................................949 472-4788
Ronald N Rogowski, *President*
Patricia A Rogowski, *Treasurer*
EMP: 20
SQ FT: 3,000
SALES: 900K **Privately Held**
WEB: www.parortho.com
SIC: 3843 Orthodontic appliances

(P-22181)
PRECISION ONE MEDICAL INC
3923 Oceanic Dr Ste 200, Oceanside (92056-5866)
PHONE...................................760 945-7966
John Tyszka, *CEO*
Steve Patterson, *President*
Chip Prescott, *CFO*
Larry Alonzo, *Opers Staff*
EMP: 80
SQ FT: 10,000
SALES (est): 12.7MM **Privately Held**
SIC: 3843 Dental equipment & supplies

(P-22182)
PROMA INC
730 Kingshill Pl, Carson (90746-1219)
PHONE...................................310 327-0035
Raymond Tai, *CEO*
Harold Tai, *Ch of Bd*
▲ **EMP:** 40 **EST:** 1967
SQ FT: 37,000
SALES (est): 7MM **Privately Held**
SIC: 3843 Dental equipment & supplies

(P-22183)
PURELIFE DENTAL
201 Santa Monica Blvd # 400, Santa Monica (90401-2212)
PHONE...................................310 587-0783
April Strong, *Project Mgr*
Kirsten Brownrigg, *Marketing Staff*
EMP: 11
SALES (est): 1.9MM **Privately Held**
SIC: 3843 Dental equipment & supplies

(P-22184)
PURELINE ORALCARE INC
804 Estates Dr Ste 104, Aptos (95003-3571)
P.O. Box 1070, Capitola (95010-1070)
PHONE...................................831 662-9500
Jack Conrey, *President*
EMP: 11
SQ FT: 8,500
SALES (est): 1.5MM **Privately Held**
WEB: www.purelineoralcare.com
SIC: 3843 5047 Dental equipment; dental equipment & supplies

(P-22185)
RAY FOSTER DENTAL EQUIPMENT
5421 Commercial Dr, Huntington Beach (92649-1231)
PHONE...................................714 897-7795
John Foster, *President*
Muriel Foster, *Corp Secy*
Mark Foster, *Vice Pres*
▲ **EMP:** 15
SQ FT: 12,000

PRODUCTS & SVCS

SALES (est): 2.3MM **Privately Held**
WEB: www.fosterdental.com
SIC: **3843** Dental equipment

(P-22186)
REPLACEMENT PARTS INDS INC
Also Called: RPI
625 Cochran St, Simi Valley (93065-1939)
P.O. Box 940250 (93094-0250)
PHONE..................................818 882-8611
Ira Lapides, *President*
Albert M Lapides, *Chairman*
Sherry Lapides, *Corp Secy*
Joan Woodlock, *Vice Pres*
Phillip Grauel, *Telecomm Mgr*
◆ EMP: 25 EST: 1972
SQ FT: 15,000
SALES (est): 6.6MM **Privately Held**
WEB: www.rpiparts.com
SIC: **3843** 3841 3821 Dental equipment; surgical & medical instruments; laboratory apparatus, except heating & measuring

(P-22187)
SAESHIN AMERICA INC
216 Technology Dr Ste F, Irvine (92618-2416)
PHONE..................................949 825-6925
Richard Ryu, *General Mgr*
EMP: 23 EST: 2016
SALES (est): 3.2MM **Privately Held**
SIC: **3843** Dental equipment & supplies
PA: Saeshin Precision Co., Ltd.
52 Secheon-Ro 1-Gil, Dasa-Eup
Dalseong-Gun
Daegu 42921

(P-22188)
SANDERS ORTHODONTIC LAB INC
5653 Stoneridge Dr # 107, Pleasanton (94588-8543)
PHONE..................................925 251-0019
Tom Asai, *President*
Ida Asai, *Vice Pres*
EMP: 11
SQ FT: 1,000
SALES: 300K **Privately Held**
WEB: www.sanderslab.com
SIC: **3843** Orthodontic appliances

(P-22189)
SELANE PRODUCTS INC (PA)
Also Called: Sml Space Maintainers Labs
9129 Lurline Ave, Chatsworth (91311-5922)
P.O. Box 2101 (91313-2101)
PHONE..................................818 998-7460
Rob Veis, *CEO*
Victor Peraza, *Info Tech Mgr*
Anna McNaught, *Graphic Designe*
Wendy Kayne, *Manager*
Scott Veis, *Manager*
▲ EMP: 85
SQ FT: 12,000
SALES (est): 11.6MM **Privately Held**
WEB: www.smldent.com
SIC: **3843** 8072 Orthodontic appliances; dental laboratories

(P-22190)
SONENDO INC (PA)
26061 Merit Cir Ste 102, Laguna Hills (92653-7010)
PHONE..................................949 766-3636
Dan Miller, *Vice Pres*
Chris Rabbitt, *Principal*
Thomas Bravek, *Administration*
Roy Chen, *CTO*
Nicholas Nabavian, *Engineer*
EMP: 39
SALES (est): 5.5MM **Privately Held**
SIC: **3843** Dental equipment & supplies

(P-22191)
SWIFT HEALTH SYSTEMS INC
111 Academy Ste 150, Irvine (92617-3053)
PHONE..................................877 258-8677
Philong Pham, *CEO*
Kenneth Chang, *CFO*
Robert Lee, *Info Tech Mgr*
EMP: 35
SALES (est): 362.4K **Privately Held**
SIC: **3843** Orthodontic appliances

(P-22192)
SYBRON DENTAL SPECIALTIES INC
824 Cowan Rd, Burlingame (94010-1205)
PHONE..................................650 340-0393
EMP: 550
SALES (corp-wide): 19.8B **Publicly Held**
SIC: **3843** Dental laboratory equipment
HQ: Sybron Dental Specialties, Inc.
1717 W Collins Ave
Orange CA 92867

(P-22193)
SYBRON DENTAL SPECIALTIES INC
1332 S Lone Hill Ave, Glendora (91740-5339)
PHONE..................................909 596-0276
Andy Astadurian, *Branch Mgr*
Lars Gehlbach, *Vice Pres*
Yexenia Torres, *Planning*
Gerardo Lara, *Design Engr*
Janna Parsonage, *Project Mgr*
EMP: 550
SALES (corp-wide): 19.8B **Publicly Held**
WEB: www.sybrondentalspecialties.com
SIC: **3843** Dental equipment & supplies
HQ: Sybron Dental Specialties, Inc.
1717 W Collins Ave
Orange CA 92867

(P-22194)
SYBRON DENTAL SPECIALTIES INC (HQ)
Also Called: Analytic Endodontics
1717 W Collins Ave, Orange (92867-5422)
PHONE..................................714 516-7400
Dan Even, *CEO*
Don Schilling, *Info Tech Mgr*
Trish Tazelaar, *Info Tech Mgr*
Brendan Lee, *MIS Staff*
Muhammad Ali, *Programmer Anys*
◆ EMP: 250
SQ FT: 16,000
SALES (corp-wide): 19.8B **Publicly Held**
WEB: www.sybrondentalspecialties.com
SIC: **3843** 2834 Dental laboratory equipment; orthodontic appliances; pharmaceutical preparations
PA: Danaher Corporation
2200 Penn Ave Nw Ste 800w
Washington DC 20037
202 828-0850

(P-22195)
TALLADIUM INC (PA)
27360 Muirfield Ln, Valencia (91355-1010)
PHONE..................................661 295-0900
Eddie Harms-, *CEO*
Geoff Harms, *CFO*
Steve Brennan, *Sales Mgr*
Josephine Thomas, *Sales Staff*
Ray Gunaka, *Director*
▲ EMP: 41
SQ FT: 9,000
SALES: 12MM **Privately Held**
WEB: www.talladium.com
SIC: **3843** 3541 5047 Investment material, dental; milling machines; dental equipment & supplies

(P-22196)
TECH WEST VACUUM INC
2625 N Argyle Ave, Fresno (93727-1304)
PHONE..................................559 291-1650
John Napier, *President*
▲ EMP: 40
SQ FT: 30,000
SALES (est): 9.5MM **Privately Held**
WEB: www.tech-west.com
SIC: **3843** Dental equipment

(P-22197)
TPC ADVANCE TECHNOLOGY INC
18519 Gale Ave, City of Industry (91748-1321)
PHONE..................................626 810-4337
Chung Liang Want, *President*
Scott Beckley, *Vice Pres*
Danny Wang, *Director*
▲ EMP: 10

SALES (est): 850K **Privately Held**
WEB: www.tpcdental.com
SIC: **3843** Dental equipment & supplies

(P-22198)
TRI DENTAL INNOVATORS CORP
13902 West St, Garden Grove (92843-3915)
PHONE..................................714 554-1170
▲ EMP: 12
SALES (est): 1.1MM **Privately Held**
SIC: **3843**

(P-22199)
TRUABUTMENT INC
17742 Cowan, Irvine (92614-6012)
PHONE..................................714 956-1488
Hyungick Kim, *CEO*
Sangho Yoo, *CFO*
EMP: 59
SQ FT: 1,800
SALES: 12MM **Privately Held**
SIC: **3843** Dental equipment & supplies

(P-22200)
UNIVERSAL ORTHODONTIC LAB INC
11917 Front St, Norwalk (90650-2900)
PHONE..................................562 908-2929
Young Paul Kim, *Owner*
Sang Lee, *CTO*
Daniel Camarena, *Accountant*
Victoria Goldsmith, *Accountant*
Roman Viera, *Manager*
EMP: 30
SALES (est): 2.5MM **Privately Held**
SIC: **3843** Dental equipment

(P-22201)
US DENTAL INC
Also Called: Young Dental
13043 166th St, Cerritos (90703-2201)
PHONE..................................562 404-3500
Young Hoon Park, *CEO*
EMP: 20
SALES (est): 1.1MM **Privately Held**
SIC: **3843** Dental equipment & supplies

(P-22202)
VAN R DENTAL PRODUCTS INC
600 E Hueneme Rd, Oxnard (93033-8600)
PHONE..................................805 488-1122
Don D Porteous, *President*
Joan Porteous, *Treasurer*
Russell W Porteous Jr, *Vice Pres*
▲ EMP: 10 EST: 1953
SQ FT: 4,500
SALES (est): 1.5MM **Privately Held**
SIC: **3843** Dental equipment & supplies

(P-22203)
VIADE PRODUCTS INC
354 Dawson Dr, Camarillo (93012-8008)
PHONE..................................805 484-2114
Keith Zinser, *President*
Sandra Zinser, *Corp Secy*
John Menzie, *Vice Pres*
EMP: 20 EST: 1968
SQ FT: 8,000
SALES: 1.5MM **Privately Held**
WEB: www.viade.com
SIC: **3843** 5047 5999 Dental laboratory equipment; dental materials; dental laboratory equipment; medical apparatus & supplies

(P-22204)
VMC INTERNATIONAL LLC
Also Called: Vaniman Manufacturing
25799 Jefferson Ave, Murrieta (92562-6903)
P.O. Box 74, Fallbrook (92088-0074)
PHONE..................................760 723-1498
Don Vaniman, *General Mgr*
Kyle Galenza, *Vice Pres*
Sandra Vaniman, *Consultant*
EMP: 16
SQ FT: 7,000
SALES: 1.8MM **Privately Held**
WEB: www.vaniman.com
SIC: **3843** Dental equipment

(P-22205)
WELLS DENTAL INC
Also Called: Wells Precision Machining
5860 Flynn Creek Rd, Comptche (95427-9500)
P.O. Box 106 (95427-0106)
PHONE..................................707 937-0521
Richard B Wells, *President*
Marvin Wells, *Corp Secy*
Ginger Wells, *Exec VP*
Anita Wells, *Office Mgr*
EMP: 15
SQ FT: 15,000
SALES (est): 2.5MM **Privately Held**
WEB: www.wellsdental.com
SIC: **3843** Dental laboratory equipment

(P-22206)
WESTSIDE RESOURCES INC
Also Called: Crystal Tip
8850 Research Dr, Irvine (92618-4223)
PHONE..................................800 944-3939
Donovan Berkely, *CEO*
Derek Jenkins, *Vice Pres*
▲ EMP: 40
SQ FT: 18,000
SALES (est): 6.3MM **Privately Held**
SIC: **3843** 5047 Dental equipment & supplies; medical & hospital equipment

---

3844 X-ray Apparatus & Tubes

(P-22207)
AMERICAN MEDICAL SALES INC
218 Bronwood Ave, Los Angeles (90049-3104)
PHONE..................................310 471-8900
Daniel Giesberg, *President*
Carol Lifland, *Vice Pres*
Richard Giesberg, *Admin Sec*
EMP: 30 EST: 1955
SQ FT: 20,000
SALES (est): 4.4MM **Privately Held**
WEB: www.ams4illuminators.com
SIC: **3844** Lamps, X-ray

(P-22208)
ASHTEL STUDIOS INC
Also Called: Ashtel Dental
1610 E Philadelphia St, Ontario (91761-5759)
PHONE..................................909 434-0911
Anish Patel, *President*
Jessica Reza, *Products*
▲ EMP: 25
SQ FT: 40,000
SALES: 30.5MM **Privately Held**
WEB: www.ashteldental.com
SIC: **3844** 3991 5122 X-ray apparatus & tubes; toothbrushes, except electric; toothbrushes, except electric

(P-22209)
ASTROPHYSICS INC (PA)
21481 Ferrero, City of Industry (91789-5233)
PHONE..................................909 598-5488
Francois Zayek, *President*
John Pan, *CFO*
John Whelan, *Vice Pres*
Nick Gillett, *Program Mgr*
Elias Abdo, *Administration*
◆ EMP: 129
SQ FT: 65,376
SALES (est): 33.1MM **Privately Held**
SIC: **3844** X-ray apparatus & tubes

(P-22210)
CARL ZISS X-RAY MICROSCOPY INC
4385 Hopyard Rd Ste 100, Pleasanton (94588-2758)
PHONE..................................925 701-3600
Bobby Blair, *CEO*
Peter Jackson, *President*
Timothy Hart, *Corp Secy*
Jin Yoon, *Principal*
EMP: 66 EST: 2000

SALES (est): 19.1MM
SALES (corp-wide): 449.3K **Privately Held**
SIC: 3844 5047 X-ray apparatus & tubes;
    X-ray machines & tubes
HQ: Carl Zeiss Microscopy Gmbh
    Carl-Zeiss-Promenade 10
    Jena 07745
    364 164-0

(P-22211)
CARR CORPORATION (PA)
1547 11th St, Santa Monica (90401-2999)
PHONE...............................310 587-1113
John Carr, *President*
Paul Carr, *Exec VP*
Reese Carr, *Vice Pres*
EMP: 25 **EST:** 1946
SQ FT: 25,000
SALES (est): 6.4MM **Privately Held**
WEB: www.carrcorporation.com
SIC: 3844 3861 3842 X-ray apparatus &
    tubes; processing equipment, photo-
    graphic; surgical appliances & supplies

(P-22212)
**CURA MEDICAL
TECHNOLOGIES LLC**
1365 S Acacia Ave, Fullerton (92831-5315)
PHONE...............................949 939-4406
Tyler Bengard,
EMP: 10
SALES (est): 650K **Privately Held**
SIC: 3844 X-ray apparatus & tubes

(P-22213)
HOLOGIC INC
1240 Elko Dr, Sunnyvale (94089-2212)
PHONE...............................408 745-0975
EMP: 195
SALES (corp-wide): 3.2B **Publicly Held**
SIC: 3844 X-ray apparatus & tubes
PA: Hologic, Inc.
    250 Campus Dr
    Marlborough MA 01752
    508 263-2900

(P-22214)
IMMPORT THERAPEUTICS INC
Also Called: Antigen Discovery Inc.
1 Technology Dr Ste E309, Irvine
(92618-2343)
PHONE...............................949 679-4068
Philip Felgner, *President*
Joseph Campo, *Project Mgr*
Adam Shandling, *Research*
Andy Teng, *Research*
Angela Yee, *Controller*
EMP: 13
SALES (est): 2.3MM **Privately Held**
WEB: www.immport-inc.com
SIC: 3844 Therapeutic X-ray apparatus &
    tubes

(P-22215)
LYNCEAN TECHNOLOGIES INC
47633 Westinghouse Dr, Fremont
(94539-7474)
PHONE...............................650 320-8300
Ronald Ruth, *CEO*
Rod Loewen, *Shareholder*
Jeff Rifkin, *Vice Pres*
Benjamin Hornberger, *Director*
▲ **EMP:** 17
SALES (est): 3.2MM **Privately Held**
WEB: www.lynceantech.com
SIC: 3844 X-ray generators

(P-22216)
MATSUSADA PRECISION INC
299 Harbor Way, South San Francisco
(94080-6811)
PHONE...............................650 877-0151
Sadayoshi Matsuda, *President*
EMP: 10
SALES (est): 820.7K **Privately Held**
SIC: 3844 X-ray generators

(P-22217)
NORDSON DAGE INC
2747 Loker Ave W, Carlsbad (92010-6601)
PHONE...............................440 985-4496
John J Keane, *CEO*
Phil Vere, *CFO*
Scott Sleeman, *Area Mgr*
Robert E Veillette, *Admin Sec*

Andrea Rolf, *Planning*
▲ **EMP:** 30 **EST:** 1977
SQ FT: 6,000
SALES (est): 9.1MM
SALES (corp-wide): 2.2B **Publicly Held**
WEB: www.dageinc.com
SIC: 3844 3544 5065 3823 X-ray appa-
    ratus & tubes; special dies, tools, jigs &
    fixtures; electronic parts; industrial instrm-
    nts msrmnt display/control process vari-
    able; instruments to measure electricity;
    analytical instruments
HQ: Dage Holdings Limited
    25 Faraday Road
    Aylesbury BUCKS
    129 631-7800

(P-22218)
**NORTHERN CAL PET IMAGING
CTR**
3195 Folsom Blvd Ste 110, Sacramento
(95816-5264)
PHONE...............................916 737-3211
Ruth Tesar, *Exec Dir*
EMP: 10
SALES (est): 6.4MM **Privately Held**
WEB: www.ncpic.com
SIC: 3844 Radiographic X-ray apparatus &
    tubes

(P-22219)
NOVARAY MEDICAL INC
39655 Eureka Dr, Newark (94560-4806)
PHONE...............................510 619-9200
Marc C Whyte, *President*
EMP: 11
SALES (est): 1.2MM **Privately Held**
SIC: 3844 X-ray apparatus & tubes

(P-22220)
**RAPISCAN LABORATORIES INC
(HQ)**
3793 Spinnaker Ct, Fremont (94538-6537)
PHONE...............................408 961-9700
Shiva Kumar, *President*
Deborah Cegielski, *Vice Pres*
▲ **EMP:** 60 **EST:** 1997
SQ FT: 36,000
SALES (est): 21.1MM
SALES (corp-wide): 1.1B **Publicly Held**
WEB: www.rapiscansystems.com
SIC: 3844 X-ray apparatus & tubes
PA: Osi Systems, Inc.
    12525 Chadron Ave
    Hawthorne CA 90250
    310 978-0516

(P-22221)
RAPISCAN SYSTEMS INC (HQ)
2805 Columbia St, Torrance (90503-3804)
PHONE...............................310 978-1457
Deepak Chopra, *CEO*
Eric Luiz, *CFO*
Gordon Blythe, *Vice Pres*
Robert C Goodhouse, *Vice Pres*
Kevin Jardim, *Vice Pres*
◆ **EMP:** 181
SQ FT: 93,000
SALES (est): 152.9MM
SALES (corp-wide): 1.1B **Publicly Held**
WEB: www.rapiscan.com
SIC: 3844 X-ray apparatus & tubes
PA: Osi Systems, Inc.
    12525 Chadron Ave
    Hawthorne CA 90250
    310 978-0516

(P-22222)
**STRATEGIC MEDICAL
VENTURES LLC (PA)**
280 Newport Center Dr, Newport Beach
(92660-7526)
PHONE...............................949 355-5212
Antony Clarke, *Mng Member*
Michael McKinnon,
EMP: 20 **EST:** 2010
SALES (est): 2.6MM **Privately Held**
SIC: 3844 X-ray apparatus & tubes

(P-22223)
TRUFOCUS CORPORATION
468 Westridge Dr, Watsonville
(95076-4159)
PHONE...............................831 761-9981
George G Howard, *President*

Kevin Bedolla, *Admin Sec*
Dianne Moody, *Exec Sec*
EMP: 16
SQ FT: 12,500
SALES: 2MM **Privately Held**
WEB: www.trufocus.com
SIC: 3844 X-ray apparatus & tubes

(P-22224)
**VARIAN MEDICAL SYSTEMS
INC (PA)**
3100 Hansen Way, Palo Alto (94304-1030)
PHONE...............................650 493-4000
R Andrew Eckert, *Ch of Bd*
Kolleen T Kennedy, *President*
Chris Toth, *President*
Dow R Wilson, *President*
Gary E Bischoping Jr, *CFO*
EMP: 1710
SQ FT: 481,000
SALES: 2.9B **Publicly Held**
WEB: www.varian.com
SIC: 3844 7372 3845 Therapeutic X-ray
    apparatus & tubes; radiographic X-ray ap-
    paratus & tubes; irradiation equipment;
    prepackaged software; electromedical ap-
    paratus

(P-22225)
WILLICK ENGINEERING CO INC
12516 Lakeland Rd, Santa Fe Springs
(90670-3940)
PHONE...............................562 946-4242
Dan Guerrero, *President*
Gus Guerrero, *Mfg Mgr*
Lori Guerrero, *Manager*
◆ **EMP:** 16 **EST:** 1983
SQ FT: 10,673
SALES (est): 3.3MM **Privately Held**
WEB: www.willick.com
SIC: 3844 3612 7629 X-ray apparatus &
    tubes; specialty transformers; electrical
    equipment repair, high voltage

(P-22226)
ZIEHM INSTRUMENTARIUM
4181 Latham St, Riverside (92501-1729)
PHONE...............................407 615-8560
Wolfram Klawitter, *President*
Richard Westrick, *Treasurer*
Lars Nillson, *Vice Pres*
Stan Talaba, *Vice Pres*
Paul Holman, *Sales Staff*
EMP: 22
SQ FT: 11,000
SALES: 1.2MM **Privately Held**
SIC: 3844 X-ray apparatus & tubes

**3845 Electromedical &
Electrotherapeutic
Apparatus**

(P-22227)
ALERE CONNECT LLC
9975 Summers Ridge Rd, San Diego
(92121-2997)
PHONE...............................888 876-3327
Kent E Dicks, *CEO*
Lyle Scritsmier, *CFO*
David Teitel, *Treasurer*
Ellen Chiniars, *Admin Sec*
EMP: 22
SALES (est): 3.3MM
SALES (corp-wide): 30.5B **Publicly Held**
WEB: www.medapps.com
SIC: 3845 Electromedical equipment
PA: Abbott Laboratories
    100 Abbott Park Rd
    Abbott Park IL 60064
    224 667-6100

(P-22228)
**AVANTIS MEDICAL SYSTEMS
INC**
2367 Bering Dr, San Jose (95131-1125)
PHONE...............................408 733-1901
Matt Frushell, *President*
Anthony Ditonno, *Ch of Bd*
Scott Dodson, *President*
Larry Tannenbaum, *CFO*
Doug Gielow, *Vice Pres*
EMP: 38

SQ FT: 4,700
SALES (est): 6.1MM **Privately Held**
WEB: www.avantismedical.com
SIC: 3845 Endoscopic equipment, elec-
    tromedical

(P-22229)
**AXELGAARD MANUFACTURING
CO LTD (PA)**
520 Industrial Way, Fallbrook (92028-2244)
PHONE...............................760 723-7554
Jens Axelgaard, *CEO*
Dan Jeffery, *President*
Christian Boddaert, *COO*
Patricia Chipp, *Executive*
Rachel Horton, *Research*
▲ **EMP:** 92
SQ FT: 33,000
SALES (est): 29MM **Privately Held**
SIC: 3845 Electromedical equipment

(P-22230)
**AXELGAARD MANUFACTURING
CO LTD**
329 W Aviation Rd, Fallbrook (92028-3201)
PHONE...............................760 723-7554
Yen Axelgaard, *Manager*
Alma Gutierrez, *Administration*
Nancy Liddle, *Finance*
Janice Williams, *Controller*
Judy Phillips, *Human Res Dir*
EMP: 35
SALES (corp-wide): 29MM **Privately
Held**
SIC: 3845 Electromedical equipment
PA: Axelgaard Manufacturing Co., Ltd.
    520 Industrial Way
    Fallbrook CA 92028
    760 723-7554

(P-22231)
BARRX MEDICAL INC
Also Called: Covidien
540 Oakmead Pkwy, Sunnyvale
(94085-4022)
PHONE...............................408 328-7300
Vafa Jamali, *Vice Pres*
Richard Short, *President*
Kevin Cordell, *Vice Pres*
William Dippel, *Vice Pres*
Robert Haggerty, *Vice Pres*
EMP: 94
SQ FT: 19,000
SALES (est): 16.3MM **Privately Held**
WEB: www.barrx.com
SIC: 3845 Electromedical equipment
HQ: Covidien Limited
    20 Lower Hatch Street
    Dublin 2
    -

(P-22232)
**BIO-RAD LABORATORIES INC
(PA)**
1000 Alfred Nobel Dr, Hercules
(94547-1898)
PHONE...............................510 724-7000
Norman Schwartz, *Ch of Bd*
John Hertia, *President*
Annette Tumolo, *President*
Ilan Daskal, *CFO*
Andrew J Last, *CFO*
◆ **EMP:** 277
SALES: 2.2B **Publicly Held**
WEB: www.bio-rad.com
SIC: 3845 2835 3826 Electromedical
    equipment; in vitro & in vivo diagnostic
    substances; electrophoresis equipment

(P-22233)
BIOMED INSTRUMENTS INC
1511 Alto Ln, Fullerton (92831-2007)
PHONE...............................714 459-5716
EMP: 18
SQ FT: 3,200
SALES (est): 987.4K **Privately Held**
WEB: www.biomedinstruments.com
SIC: 3845

(P-22234)
BIONESS INC
25103 Rye Canyon Loop, Valencia
(91355-5004)
PHONE...............................661 362-4850
Todd Cushman, *President*

(PA)=Parent Co (HQ)=Headquarters (DH)=Div Headquarters
✿ = New Business established in last 2 years

Nick Hetlinger, *Technician*
Karen Lowery, *Project Mgr*
Stacey Williams, *Research*
Tim Martin, *Technology*
▲ **EMP:** 190
SQ FT: 29,000
SALES (est): 36.6MM **Privately Held**
WEB: www.bioness.com
SIC: 3845 5047 Transcutaneous electrical nerve stimulators (TENS); medical & hospital equipment

(P-22235)
BIOSENSE WEBSTER INC (HQ)
33 Technology Dr, Irvine (92618-2346)
PHONE..........................909 839-8500
Shlomi Nachman, *CEO*
David Shepherd, *President*
Mary Rex, *CFO*
Tom Turley, *Vice Pres*
Lynn Ho, *Executive*
▲ **EMP:** 150
SALES (est): 180.2MM
SALES (corp-wide): 81.5B **Publicly Held**
WEB: www.biosensewebster.com
SIC: 3845 3841 Electromedical apparatus; surgical & medical instruments
PA: Johnson & Johnson
1 Johnson And Johnson Plz
New Brunswick NJ 08933
732 524-0400

(P-22236)
CARE INNOVATIONS LLC
950 Iron Point Rd Ste 160, Folsom (95630-9304)
PHONE..........................800 450-0970
Randy Swanson, *CEO*
Bruce Pruden, *CFO*
EMP: 50
SALES (est): 7.1MM **Privately Held**
SIC: 3845 3641 Electromedical apparatus; electrotherapeutic lamp units

(P-22237)
CAREFUSION CORPORATION (HQ)
Also Called: Bd Carefusion
3750 Torrey View Ct, San Diego (92130-2622)
PHONE..........................858 617-2000
Thomas E Polen Jr, *President*
Brian Bonnell, *Vice Pres*
Jean-Michel Deckers, *Vice Pres*
Nivaldo Diaz, *Vice Pres*
Gerard Diepman, *Vice Pres*
▲ **EMP:** 277
SALES (est): 4.2B
SALES (corp-wide): 15.9B **Publicly Held**
SIC: 3845 8742 3841 Electromedical equipment; respiratory analysis equipment, electromedical; hospital & health services consultant; surgical instruments & apparatus
PA: Becton, Dickinson And Company
1 Becton Dr
Franklin Lakes NJ 07417
201 847-6800

(P-22238)
CHALGREN ENTERPRISES
Also Called: Jari Electro Supply
380 Tomkins Ct, Gilroy (95020-3631)
PHONE..........................408 847-3994
Richard Kaiser, *President*
Michael Kaiser, *Vice Pres*
Rebecca Kaiser, *Vice Pres*
EMP: 15 **EST:** 1965
SQ FT: 4,200
SALES: 2.1MM **Privately Held**
SIC: 3845 Electromedical equipment

(P-22239)
CLARIFY MEDICAL INC
10505 Sorrento Valley Rd # 450, San Diego (92121-1623)
PHONE..........................877 738-6041
George W Mahaffey, *CEO*
David Hale, *Chairman*
Sharlene Kakimoto, *Chief Mktg Ofcr*
Andre Gamelin, *Vice Pres*
EMP: 20
SALES (est): 482.2K **Privately Held**
SIC: 3845 Laser systems & equipment, medical

(P-22240)
CLI LIQUIDATING CORPORATION
47266 Benicia St, Fremont (94538-7330)
PHONE..........................510 354-0300
Fax: 510 657-4476
EMP: 81
SQ FT: 29,000
SALES (est): 11MM **Privately Held**
WEB: www.cardima.com
SIC: 3845

(P-22241)
CNC MACHINING SOLUTIONS INC
12155 Magnolia Ave 10c, Riverside (92503-4905)
PHONE..........................951 688-4267
Theresa Taylor, *CEO*
Dale Caldwell, *CFO*
Michael Taylor, *Exec VP*
Ronda Caldwell, *Admin Sec*
EMP: 10
SQ FT: 6,500
SALES: 650K **Privately Held**
SIC: 3845 Medical cleaning equipment, ultrasonic

(P-22242)
COASTLINE INTERNATIONAL
1207 Bangor St, San Diego (92106-2407)
PHONE..........................888 748-7177
Larry Angione, *President*
▲ **EMP:** 250
SQ FT: 32,000
SALES: 4.6MM **Privately Held**
WEB: www.coastlineintl.com
SIC: 3845 3841 Electromedical equipment; surgical & medical instruments

(P-22243)
CONVERSION DEVICES INC
15481 Electronic Ln Ste D, Huntington Beach (92649-1355)
PHONE..........................714 898-6551
Roland Roth, *President*
Harish Khatter, *Engrg Dir*
EMP: 25
SQ FT: 11,000
SALES (est): 3.5MM **Privately Held**
WEB: www.cdipower.com
SIC: 3845 3577 Electromedical apparatus; computer peripheral equipment

(P-22244)
COOLSYSTEMS INC (HQ)
Also Called: Game Ready
1800 Sutter St Ste 500, Concord (94520-2587)
PHONE..........................888 426-3732
John Tushar, *President*
Steven Voskuil, *CFO*
Matt Bouza, *Senior VP*
Cindy Kumar, *VP Finance*
▲ **EMP:** 104
SQ FT: 18,298
SALES: 27MM
SALES (corp-wide): 652.3MM **Publicly Held**
WEB: www.gameready.com
SIC: 3845 Laser systems & equipment, medical
PA: Avanos Medical, Inc.
5405 Windward Pkwy # 100
Alpharetta GA 30004
844 428-2667

(P-22245)
COOLTOUCH CORPORATION
Also Called: Cool Touch
9085 Foothills Blvd, Roseville (95747-7130)
PHONE..........................916 677-1975
Nina Davis, *President*
EMP: 18
SALES (est): 2.1MM **Privately Held**
WEB: www.cooltouch.com
SIC: 3845 Laser systems & equipment, medical

(P-22246)
CUTERA INC (PA)
3240 Bayshore Blvd, Brisbane (94005-1021)
PHONE..........................415 657-5500

David H Mowry, *CEO*
J Daniel Plants, *Ch of Bd*
Sandra A Gardiner, *CFO*
Larry E Laber, *Exec VP*
Peter Falzon, *Vice Pres*
EMP: 229 **EST:** 1998
SQ FT: 66,000
SALES: 162.7MM **Publicly Held**
SIC: 3845 Laser systems & equipment, medical

(P-22247)
CYTEK BIOSCIENCES INC (PA)
46107 Landing Pkwy, Fremont (94538-6407)
PHONE..........................510 657-0110
Wenbin Jiang, *CEO*
Patrik Jeanmonod, *CFO*
Steve Ziganti, *Vice Pres*
Ming Yan, *CTO*
EMP: 71 **EST:** 2014
SQ FT: 52,000
SALES (est): 3.8MM **Privately Held**
SIC: 3845 3841 Laser systems & equipment, medical; diagnostic apparatus, medical

(P-22248)
DECISION SCIENCES MED CO LLC
Also Called: Decision Medical
12345 First American Way # 100, Poway (92064-6828)
PHONE..........................858 602-1600
Stanton Sloane, *President*
George R Creel, *Managing Prtnr*
Paul Bartholomew, *CFO*
EMP: 20
SALES (est): 2.6MM **Privately Held**
SIC: 3845 3841 Electromedical equipment; surgical & medical instruments

(P-22249)
DOLPHIN MEDICAL INC (HQ)
12525 Chadron Ave, Hawthorne (90250-4807)
PHONE..........................800 448-6506
Deepak Chopra, *President*
Thomas Scharf, *Vice Pres*
▲ **EMP:** 100
SALES (est): 52.9MM
SALES (corp-wide): 1.1B **Publicly Held**
WEB: www.dolphinmedical.com
SIC: 3845 Ultrasonic medical equipment, except cleaning
PA: Osi Systems, Inc.
12525 Chadron Ave
Hawthorne CA 90250
310 978-0516

(P-22250)
EBR SYSTEMS INC (PA)
480 Oakmead Pkwy, Sunnyvale (94085-4708)
PHONE..........................408 720-1906
John McCutcheon, *President*
Stephen Oconnor, *President*
Mark Schwartz, *President*
Rick Riley, *COO*
Debra Echt, *Chief Mktg Ofcr*
EMP: 23
SQ FT: 8,500
SALES (est): 3.1MM **Privately Held**
WEB: www.ebrsystemsinc.com
SIC: 3845 Cardiographs

(P-22251)
EDWARDS LIFESCIENCES US INC
1 Edwards Way, Irvine (92614-5688)
PHONE..........................949 250-2500
Michael A Mussallem, *CEO*
Dirksen J Lehman, *Vice Pres*
Christine Z McCauley, *Vice Pres*
Stanton J Rowe, *Vice Pres*
Scott B Ullem, *Vice Pres*
EMP: 26 **EST:** 2011
SALES: 4.9MM
SALES (corp-wide): 3.7B **Publicly Held**
SIC: 3845 Patient monitoring apparatus; pacemaker, cardiac
PA: Edwards Lifesciences Corp
1 Edwards Way
Irvine CA 92614
949 250-2500

(P-22252)
EKO DEVICES INC
2600 10th St Ste 260, Berkeley (94710-2597)
PHONE..........................844 356-3384
Connor Landgraf, *CEO*
Craig Bagby, *Vice Pres*
EMP: 10
SALES (est): 1.7MM **Privately Held**
SIC: 3845 5047 3841 Electromedical equipment; medical & hospital equipment; diagnostic equipment, medical; diagnostic apparatus, medical

(P-22253)
EXAM ROOM SUPPLY LLC
2419 Hrbour Blvd Unit 126, Ventura (93001)
PHONE..........................805 298-3631
Charles Solomon, *Mng Member*
M Wash, *Mng Member*
EMP: 15
SALES (est): 1MM **Privately Held**
SIC: 3845 3841 5047 5999 Electromedical apparatus; diagnostic apparatus, medical; medical & hospital equipment; medical apparatus & supplies

(P-22254)
EXO SYSTEMS INC
333 Pali Ct, Oakland (94611-1855)
PHONE..........................510 655-5033
Sandeep Akkaraju, *President*
Janusz Bryzek, *CEO*
Yusuf Haque, *Vice Pres*
EMP: 22
SALES (est): 1.2MM **Privately Held**
SIC: 3845 Ultrasonic medical equipment, except cleaning

(P-22255)
EXPLORAMED NC7 INC
Also Called: Willow
1975 W El Camino Real, Mountain View (94040-2274)
PHONE..........................650 559-5805
Naomi Kelman, *Mng Member*
EMP: 28
SQ FT: 5,175
SALES (est): 5MM **Privately Held**
SIC: 3845 Electromedical apparatus

(P-22256)
GAMING FUND GROUP
14507 Catalina St, San Leandro (94577-5519)
PHONE..........................510 532-8881
David Chau, *President*
Lucy Trinh, *Marketing Staff*
Kaycee Tooker, *Supervisor*
EMP: 10
SALES (est): 1.3MM **Privately Held**
SIC: 3845 Pacemaker, cardiac

(P-22257)
GIVEN IMAGING LOS ANGELES LLC
5860 Uplander Way, Culver City (90230-6608)
PHONE..........................310 641-8492
Tom Parks PHD, *President*
Ron McIntyre, *CFO*
Eric Finkelman, *Vice Pres*
Jeffrey Sawyer, *Marketing Staff*
◆ **EMP:** 175
SALES (est): 25.7MM **Privately Held**
WEB: www.sierraint.com
SIC: 3845 Electromedical equipment
PA: Given Imaging Ltd.
2 Hacarmel
Upper Yokneam
490 977-77

(P-22258)
HALO NEURO INC
Also Called: Halo Neuroscience
735 Market St Fl 4, San Francisco (94103-2034)
PHONE..........................415 851-3338
Daniel Chao, *CEO*
Mark Mastalir, *Chief Mktg Ofcr*
Mark Mastlier, *Chief Mktg Ofcr*
EMP: 17
SQ FT: 8,000
SALES (est): 792.8K **Privately Held**
SIC: 3845 Electrotherapeutic apparatus

(P-22259)
HEMOSENSE INC
9975 Summers Ridge Rd, San Diego
(92121-2997)
PHONE.....................408 719-1393
James D Merselis, *President*
Gordon Sangster, *CFO*
Timothy I Still, *Exec VP*
William H Dippel, *Vice Pres*
David L Phillips, *Vice Pres*
▲ EMP: 79
SQ FT: 15,250
SALES (est): 4.8MM
SALES (corp-wide): 30.5B **Publicly Held**
WEB: www.hemosense.com
SIC: 3845 Automated blood & body fluid
  analyzers, except laboratory
HQ: Alere Inc.
  51 Sawyer Rd Ste 200
  Waltham MA 02453
  781 647-3900

(P-22260)
HOLOGIC INC
10210 Genetic Center Dr, San Diego
(92121-4362)
PHONE.....................858 410-8000
Gonzalo Martinez, *Branch Mgr*
Jorgine Ellerbrock, *Senior VP*
Jim Neal, *Vice Pres*
Steve Dickson, *Executive*
Jill Kolas, *Executive*
EMP: 36
SALES (corp-wide): 3.2B **Publicly Held**
SIC: 3845 Ultrasonic medical equipment,
  except cleaning
PA: Hologic, Inc.
  250 Campus Dr
  Marlborough MA 01752
  508 263-2900

(P-22261)
HOSPITAL SYSTEMS INC
750 Garcia Ave, Pittsburg (94565-5012)
PHONE.....................925 427-7800
Jennifer M Miller, *Ch of Bd*
David H Miller, *President*
Rebecca Miller, *President*
Laura Ortiz, *Purchasing*
Kathie Campbell, *VP Opers*
EMP: 72 EST: 1970
SQ FT: 20,000
SALES (est): 11.5MM **Privately Held**
WEB: www.hospitalsystems.com
SIC: 3845 Electromedical equipment

(P-22262)
HYGEIA II MEDICAL GROUP INC
6241 Yarrow Dr Ste A, Carlsbad
(92011-1541)
PHONE.....................714 515-7571
Mark Engler, *CEO*
Brett Nakfoor, *President*
▲ EMP: 40
SALES (est): 4.5MM **Privately Held**
SIC: 3845 Electromedical equipment

(P-22263)
HYPERBARIC TECHNOLOGIES INC
3224 Hoover Ave, National City
(91950-7224)
PHONE.....................619 336-2022
W T Gurnee, *President*
Julie Vaickus, *Controller*
EMP: 80
SQ FT: 15,000
SALES: 2.5MM **Privately Held**
WEB: www.oxyheal.com
SIC: 3845 3841 7352 3443 Electromed-
  ical equipment; medical instruments &
  equipment, blood & bone work; medical
  equipment rental; fabricated plate work
  (boiler shop)

(P-22264)
INTERSON CORP
7150 Koll Center Pkwy, Pleasanton
(94566-3164)
PHONE.....................925 462-4948
Monica Solak, *Director*
EMP: 22 EST: 2015
SALES (est): 284.7K **Privately Held**
SIC: 3845 Electromedical apparatus

(P-22265)
IOGYN INC
150 Baytech Dr, San Jose (95134-2302)
PHONE.....................408 996-2517
Csaba Truckai, *Exec Dir*
John Shadduck, *Exec Dir*
David Clapper, *Director*
Rodney Perkins, *Director*
Bruno Strul, *Director*
EMP: 13 EST: 2010
SALES (est): 2.2MM
SALES (corp-wide): 9.8B **Publicly Held**
SIC: 3845 Ultrasonic scanning devices,
  medical
PA: Boston Scientific Corporation
  300 Boston Scientific Way
  Marlborough MA 01752
  508 683-4000

(P-22266)
IRHYTHM TECHNOLOGIES INC (PA)
650 Townsend St Ste 500, San Francisco
(94103-6227)
PHONE.....................415 632-5700
Abhijit Y Talwalkar, *Ch of Bd*
EMP: 30
SQ FT: 60,873
SALES: 147.2MM **Publicly Held**
WEB: www.irhythmtech.com
SIC: 3845 3841 Electrocardiographs; di-
  agnostic apparatus, medical

(P-22267)
IRIDEX CORPORATION (PA)
1212 Terra Bella Ave, Mountain View
(94043-1824)
PHONE.....................650 940-4700
David I Bruce, *President*
EMP: 114
SQ FT: 37,166
SALES: 42.6MM **Publicly Held**
SIC: 3845 Electromedical equipment

(P-22268)
IRIS MEDICAL INSTRUMENTS INC
Also Called: Iridex
1212 Terra Bella Ave, Mountain View
(94043-1824)
PHONE.....................650 940-4700
Ted Boutacoff, *CEO*
EMP: 130
SALES (est): 7.3MM
SALES (corp-wide): 42.6MM **Publicly Held**
WEB: www.iridex.com
SIC: 3845 Laser systems & equipment,
  medical
PA: Iridex Corporation
  1212 Terra Bella Ave
  Mountain View CA 94043
  650 940-4700

(P-22269)
JOHNSON & JOHNSON (HQ)
Also Called: Johnson & Johnson Vision
1700 E Saint Andrew Pl, Santa Ana
(92705-4933)
P.O. Box 25929 (92799-5929)
PHONE.....................714 247-8200
Thomas Frinzi, *President*
Victor Chang, *President*
Cameron Rouns, *Vice Pres*
Vince Scullin, *Vice Pres*
Sharon Nagaoka, *Executive*
▲ EMP: 300
SALES (est): 1.2B
SALES (corp-wide): 81.5B **Publicly Held**
WEB: www.amo-inc.com
SIC: 3845 3841 Laser systems & equip-
  ment, medical; ophthalmic instruments &
  apparatus
PA: Johnson & Johnson
  1 Johnson And Johnson Plz
  New Brunswick NJ 08933
  732 524-0400

(P-22270)
LEAF HEALTHCARE INC
5994 W Las Positas Blvd, Pleasanton
(94588-8509)
PHONE.....................925 621-1800
Mark Weckwerth, *CEO*
Daniel Shen, *Ch Credit Ofcr*

Dana Rivinius, *Administration*
▼ EMP: 10
SQ FT: 4,400
SALES (est): 1.7MM **Privately Held**
SIC: 3845 Patient monitoring apparatus

(P-22271)
LIFETRAK INCORPORATED
8371 Central Ave Ste A, Newark
(94560-3473)
PHONE.....................510 413-9030
▲ EMP: 10
SALES: 5MM **Privately Held**
SIC: 3845
PA: Salutron Incorporated
  8371 Central Ave Ste A
  Newark CA 94560

(P-22272)
LOBUE LASER & EYE MEDICAL CTRS
40740 California Oaks Rd, Murrieta
(92562-5727)
PHONE.....................951 696-1135
EMP: 29
SALES (corp-wide): 5MM **Privately Held**
SIC: 3845 Laser systems & equipment,
  medical
PA: Lobue Laser & Eye Medical Ctrs Inc
  40700 California Oaks Rd
  Murrieta CA 92562
  951 696-1135

(P-22273)
LUMASENSE TECH HOLDINGS INC (HQ)
3301 Leonard Ct, Santa Clara
(95054-2054)
PHONE.....................408 727-1600
Steve Abely, *CEO*
Vivek Joshi, *President*
Steve Uhlir, *President*
Frederick A Ball, *Bd of Directors*
Tina M Donikowski, *Bd of Directors*
▲ EMP: 80
SQ FT: 62,000
SALES (est): 12.1MM
SALES (corp-wide): 718.8MM **Publicly Held**
WEB: www.lumasenseinc.com
SIC: 3845 3829 3825 3823 Electromed-
  ical equipment; measuring & controlling
  devices; instruments to measure electric-
  ity; temperature instruments: industrial
  process type
PA: Advanced Energy Industries, Inc.
  1625 Sharp Point Dr
  Fort Collins CO 80525
  970 221-4670

(P-22274)
MAQUET MEDICAL SYSTEMS USA LLC
120 Baytech Dr, San Jose (95134-2302)
PHONE.....................408 635-3900
Heribert Ballhaus, *CEO*
Heinz Jacqui, *Exec VP*
Reinhard Mayer, *Vice Pres*
Hilde Van Der Westhuizen, *Vice Pres*
Cathy Carder, *Accounts Mgr*
EMP: 525
SQ FT: 75,000
SALES (est): 59.9MM
SALES (corp-wide): 6.1B **Privately Held**
SIC: 3845 Ultrasonic scanning devices,
  medical
HQ: Maquet Gmbh
  Kehler Str. 31
  Rastatt 76437
  722 293-20

(P-22275)
MASIMO CORPORATION
9600 Jeronimo Rd, Irvine (92618-2024)
PHONE.....................949 297-7000
Joe Kiani, *Branch Mgr*
EMP: 50 **Publicly Held**
SIC: 3845 Electromedical equipment
PA: Masimo Corporation
  52 Discovery
  Irvine CA 92618

(P-22276)
MASIMO CORPORATION (PA)
52 Discovery, Irvine (92618-3105)
PHONE.....................949 297-7000
Joe Kiani, *Ch of Bd*
Micah Young, *CFO*
Yongsam Lee, *Exec VP*
Tom McClenahan, *Exec VP*
Michelle Hahn, *Vice Pres*
▲ EMP: 350
SQ FT: 213,400
SALES: 858.2MM **Publicly Held**
WEB: www.masimo.com
SIC: 3845 Patient monitoring apparatus;
  phonocardiographs

(P-22277)
MAUI IMAGING INC
70 Las Colinas Ln, San Jose (95119-1212)
PHONE.....................408 744-1127
David J Specht, *CEO*
EMP: 10
SALES (est): 1.3MM **Privately Held**
SIC: 3845 Electromedical equipment

(P-22278)
MC LIQUIDATION INC
Also Called: Intraop Medical Services
570 Del Rey Ave, Sunnyvale (94085-3528)
PHONE.....................408 636-1020
John Powers, *President*
J K Hullett, *CFO*
Richard A Belford, *Vice Pres*
Winfield Jones, *VP Sales*
EMP: 28
SQ FT: 14,419
SALES (est): 3.7MM **Privately Held**
SIC: 3845 Electromedical equipment

(P-22279)
MEDIVISION INC
Also Called: Medivision Optics
4883 E La Palma Ave # 503, Anaheim
(92807-1957)
PHONE.....................714 563-2772
Kevin May, *President*
EMP: 15
SQ FT: 6,000
SALES (est): 1.5MM **Privately Held**
WEB: www.medivisionusa.com
SIC: 3845 7699 5047 Endoscopic equip-
  ment, electromedical; scientific equipment
  repair service; physician equipment &
  supplies

(P-22280)
MEDTRONIC INC
125 Cremona Dr, Goleta (93117-5503)
PHONE.....................805 571-3769
EMP: 16 **Privately Held**
SIC: 3845 3842 3841 Electromedical
  equipment; implants, surgical; blood
  transfusion equipment
HQ: Medtronic, Inc.
  710 Medtronic Pkwy
  Minneapolis MN 55432
  763 514-4000

(P-22281)
MEDTRONIC MINIMED INC (DH)
18000 Devonshire St, Northridge
(91325-1219)
PHONE.....................800 646-4633
Catherine Szyman, *President*
George J Montague, *Vice Pres*
Kiem Dang, *Program Mgr*
Eric Hanson, *Program Mgr*
Cyrus Roushan, *Program Mgr*
▲ EMP: 1200
SQ FT: 250,000
SALES (est): 859.1MM **Privately Held**
WEB: www.minimed.com
SIC: 3845 Electromedical equipment
HQ: Medtronic, Inc.
  710 Medtronic Pkwy
  Minneapolis MN 55432
  763 514-4000

(P-22282)
MENTZER ELECTRONICS
858 Stanton Rd, Burlingame (94010-1404)
P.O. Box 610, Barrington IL (60011-0610)
PHONE.....................650 697-2642
Fax: 650 697-2405
EMP: 24
SQ FT: 14,000

SALES (est): 2.1MM **Privately Held**
WEB: www.mentzerelectronics.com
SIC: 3845 3672

(P-22283)
NANOSTIM INC
776 Palomar Ave, Sunnyvale (94085-2914)
PHONE......................408 530-0700
Drew Hoffmann, *CEO*
EMP: 17
SALES (est): 2.9MM
SALES (corp-wide): 30.5B **Publicly Held**
SIC: 3845 Pacemaker, cardiac
HQ: St. Jude Medical, Llc
    1 Saint Jude Medical Dr
    Saint Paul MN 55117
    651 756-2000

(P-22284)
NATUS MEDICAL
INCORPORATED
1501 Industrial Rd, San Carlos
(94070-4111)
PHONE.......................303 962-1800
James B Hawkins, *CEO*
Chris Chung, *Vice Pres*
Augusto Segredo, *Regional Mgr*
Keithia Harding, *Area Spvr*
Susan Cowan, *District Mgr*
EMP: 34
SALES (corp-wide): 530.8MM **Publicly
Held**
SIC: 3845 Electromedical equipment
PA: Natus Medical Incorporated
    6701 Koll Center Pkwy # 12
    Pleasanton CA 94566
    925 223-6700

(P-22285)
NATUS MEDICAL
INCORPORATED
5955 Pacific Center Blvd, San Diego
(92121-4309)
PHONE.......................858 260-2590
Stephen Dirocco, *Director*
EMP: 71
SALES (corp-wide): 530.8MM **Publicly
Held**
SIC: 3845 3841 Electromedical equip-
    ment; electrotherapeutic apparatus; surgi-
    cal instruments & apparatus
PA: Natus Medical Incorporated
    6701 Koll Center Pkwy # 12
    Pleasanton CA 94566
    925 223-6700

(P-22286)
NATUS MEDICAL
INCORPORATED (PA)
6701 Koll Center Pkwy # 12, Pleasanton
(94566-8061)
PHONE.......................925 223-6700
Jonathan Kennedy, *President*
Drew Davies, *CFO*
Rachun Williams, *Treasurer*
Austin F Noll III, *Ch Credit Ofcr*
Doris Engibous, *Bd of Directors*
▲ EMP: 277
SQ FT: 8,200
SALES: 530.8MM **Publicly Held**
WEB: www.natus.com
SIC: 3845 Electromedical equipment

(P-22287)
NEW SOURCE TECHNOLOGY
LLC
6678 Owens Dr Ste 105, Pleasanton
(94588-3324)
PHONE.......................925 462-6888
Gregory A Pon, *President*
Jocelyn Long, *Vice Pres*
Antonio Martinez, *Engineer*
Jenny Jiang, *Business Mgr*
Manda Tam, *Controller*
EMP: 15
SALES (est): 297.2K **Privately Held**
WEB: www.newsourcetechnology.com
SIC: 3845 Laser systems & equipment,
    medical

(P-22288)
NEW STAR LASERS INC
Also Called: Cooltouch
8331 Sierra College Blvd # 204, Roseville
(95661-9412)
PHONE.......................916 677-1900
Ilan Ben-David, *CEO*
Nina Davis, *President*
David R Hennings, *President*
EMP: 41
SQ FT: 20,000
SALES (est): 8.2MM **Privately Held**
WEB: www.newstarlasers.com
SIC: 3845 Laser systems & equipment,
    medical

(P-22289)
NIHON KOHDEN ORANGEMED
INC
15375 Barranca Pkwy C109, Irvine
(92618-2206)
PHONE.......................949 502-6448
Hong-Lin Du, *CEO*
EMP: 12
SALES: 707.1K **Privately Held**
SIC: 3845 Electromedical equipment

(P-22290)
NORCAL RESPIRATORY INC
3075 Crossroads Dr Ste A, Redding
(96003-8018)
PHONE.......................530 246-1200
Jim Rahmann, *President*
EMP: 21
SALES (est): 3.6MM **Privately Held**
SIC: 3845 Respiratory analysis equipment,
    electromedical

(P-22291)
OPOTEK INC
2233 Faraday Ave Ste E, Carlsbad
(92008-7214)
PHONE.......................760 929-0770
Eli Margalith, *President*
Larry Bay, *Vice Pres*
Renee Robinson, *Office Mgr*
Mark Little, *Sales Mgr*
EMP: 14
SQ FT: 4,000
SALES (est): 1.6MM **Privately Held**
WEB: www.opotek.com
SIC: 3845 Laser systems & equipment,
    medical

(P-22292)
OPTEK GROUP INC
23 Corporate Plaza Dr # 150, Newport
Beach (92660-7911)
PHONE.......................949 629-2558
Allan Hsieh, *President*
Perry Hsieh, *Admin Sec*
EMP: 25
SQ FT: 3,000
SALES: 3MM **Privately Held**
SIC: 3845 5084 Electromedical equip-
    ment; chemical process equipment

(P-22293)
ORATEC INTERVENTIONS INC
(DH)
3696 Haven Ave, Redwood City
(94063-4604)
PHONE.......................901 396-2121
Ron Sparks, *CEO*
Mark Frost, *Treasurer*
Jerry Goodman, *Vice Pres*
Reuben Rosales, *Vice Pres*
James Ralston, *Admin Sec*
EMP: 11
SQ FT: 37,000
SALES (est): 9.1MM
SALES (corp-wide): 4.9B **Privately Held**
WEB: www.oratec.com
SIC: 3845 8011 3841 Electromedical
    equipment; offices & clinics of medical
    doctors; surgical & medical instruments
HQ: Smith & Nephew, Inc.
    7135 Goodlett Farms Pkwy
    Cordova TN 38016
    901 396-2121

(P-22294)
PACESETTER INC
6035 Stoneridge Dr, Pleasanton
(94588-3270)
PHONE.......................925 730-4171
David Villarreal, *Branch Mgr*
Rich Bonito, *Officer*
Noushin Isadvastar, *Project Mgr*
Jesse Gage, *Research*
Steven Drake, *Engineer*
EMP: 12
SALES (corp-wide): 30.5B **Publicly Held**
SIC: 3845 Defibrillator
HQ: Pacesetter, Inc.
    15900 Valley View Ct
    Sylmar CA 91342
    -

(P-22295)
PACESETTER INC (DH)
Also Called: Ventritex
15900 Valley View Ct, Sylmar
(91342-3585)
P.O. Box 9221 (91392-9221)
PHONE.......................818 362-6822
Eric S Fain, *CEO*
Ronald A Matricaria, *President*
Ron Thompson, *Vice Pres*
Ed Ferrier, *Executive*
Jorge Amely-Velez, *Senior Engr*
▲ EMP: 725
SALES (est): 339MM
SALES (corp-wide): 30.5B **Publicly Held**
SIC: 3845 Defibrillator
HQ: St. Jude Medical, Llc
    1 Saint Jude Medical Dr
    Saint Paul MN 55117
    651 756-2000

(P-22296)
PARACOR MEDICAL INC
19200 Stevns Crk Blvd # 200, Cupertino
(95014-2530)
PHONE.......................408 207-1050
William Mavity, *President*
Pooja Joshipura, *Supervisor*
EMP: 30
SQ FT: 12,000
SALES (est): 3.7MM **Privately Held**
WEB: www.paracormedical.com
SIC: 3845 Ultrasonic scanning devices,
    medical

(P-22297)
PART HANDLING ENGRG & DEV
CORP
42175 Zevo Dr, Temecula (92590-2503)
PHONE.......................951 308-4450
Bassam A Poullath, *President*
Basil Poullath, *Vice Pres*
Brittany Poullath, *Bookkeeper*
EMP: 10
SQ FT: 8,200
SALES (est): 1.6MM **Privately Held**
SIC: 3845 3535 5084 Electromedical
    equipment; robotic conveyors; conveyor
    systems

(P-22298)
R & D NOVA INC
833 Marlborough Ave 200, Riverside
(92507-2133)
PHONE.......................951 781-7332
Scott Snyder, *President*
Martin Clajus, *General Mgr*
EMP: 15
SQ FT: 4,000
SALES (est): 2.4MM
SALES (corp-wide): 19.1MM **Privately
Held**
WEB: www.novarad.com
SIC: 3845 3812 Magnetic resonance im-
    aging device, nuclear; search & detection
    systems & instruments
PA: Kromek Group Plc
    Thomas Wright Way
    Stockton-On-Tees TS21
    174 062-6050

(P-22299)
RADLINK INC
815 N Nash St, El Segundo (90245-2824)
PHONE.......................310 643-6900
Thomas T Hacking, *Ch of Bd*
Cat Vanderlaan, *Regional Mgr*
Michelle Iafigliola, *Sales Staff*

Mehrshad Pezeshki, *Sales Staff*
Ben Purcell, *Sales Staff*
EMP: 30 EST: 1999
SQ FT: 25,000
SALES (est): 6.5MM **Privately Held**
SIC: 3845 Ultrasonic scanning devices,
    medical

(P-22300)
REAL-TIME RADIOGRAPHY INC
3825 Hopyard Rd Ste 220, Pleasanton
(94588-2786)
PHONE.......................925 416-1903
Shaul Dukeman, *President*
EMP: 24
SQ FT: 1,800
SALES (est): 1.5MM **Privately Held**
WEB: www.realtimeradiography.com
SIC: 3845 Cardiographs; pacemaker, car-
    diac

(P-22301)
REFLEXION MEDICAL INC
25841 Industrial Blvd # 275, Hayward
(94545-2991)
PHONE.......................650 239-9070
Samuel R Mazin, *President*
Todd Powell, *President*
Martyn Webster, *CFO*
Akshay Nanduri, *Admin Sec*
Jeffrey Kuan, *Electrical Engi*
EMP: 120
SALES (est): 7.2MM **Privately Held**
SIC: 3845 Electromedical equipment

(P-22302)
RESHAPE LIFESCIENCES INC
(PA)
1001 Calle Amanecer, San Clemente
(92673-6260)
PHONE.......................949 429-6680
Barton P Bandy, *President*
Dan W Gladney, *Ch of Bd*
Thomas Stankovich, *CFO*
Kevin Condrin, *Senior VP*
Donna Garceau, *Executive Asst*
EMP: 57
SQ FT: 28,388
SALES: 606.7K **Publicly Held**
WEB: www.enteromedics.com
SIC: 3845 Electromedical equipment

(P-22303)
RESONANCE TECHNOLOGY
INC
18121 Parthenia St Ste A, Northridge
(91325-3351)
PHONE.......................818 882-1997
Mokhtar Ziarati, *CEO*
Susanna Ziarati, *Shareholder*
▲ EMP: 11
SALES (est): 2.1MM **Privately Held**
WEB: www.fmri.net
SIC: 3845 Magnetic resonance imaging
    device, nuclear

(P-22304)
RFA MEDICAL SOLUTIONS
40874 Calido Pl, Fremont (94539-3633)
PHONE.......................510 583-9500
EMP: 10
SALES: 800K **Privately Held**
SIC: 3845

(P-22305)
RITA MEDICAL SYSTEMS INC
(HQ)
46421 Landing Pkwy, Fremont
(94538-6496)
PHONE.......................510 771-0400
Michael D Angel, *CFO*
Jelle W Kylstra, *Vice Pres*
Juan Soto, *Vice Pres*
Mario Martinez, *General Mgr*
Darrin Uecker, *CTO*
EMP: 77
SQ FT: 14,500
SALES (est): 13.1MM
SALES (corp-wide): 270.6MM **Publicly
Held**
SIC: 3845 3841 Electromedical equip-
    ment; surgical & medical instruments;
    catheters

PA: Angiodynamics, Inc.
14 Plaza Dr
Latham NY 12110
518 795-1400

(P-22306)
ROX MEDICAL INC (PA)
150 Calle Iglesia Ste A, San Clemente
(92672-7550)
P.O. Box 4078, Dana Point (92629-9078)
PHONE..................................949 276-8968
Mike Mackinnon, *CEO*
Keegan Harper, *Ch of Bd*
Jonathan Sackner-Bernstein, *Chief Mktg Ofcr*
Paul A Sobotka, *Officer*
Elizabeth Sheehan, *Sr Project Mgr*
EMP: 20
SQ FT: 3,500
SALES (est): 3.8MM **Privately Held**
SIC: 3845 Ultrasonic scanning devices, medical

(P-22307)
SALUTRON INCORPORATED (PA)
8371 Central Ave Ste A, Newark
(94560-3473)
PHONE..................................510 795-2876
Mike Tsai, *CEO*
Bob Gerstenberger, *Vice Pres*
Jhovendan Baroro, *Sr Software Eng*
Yong Jin Lee, *CTO*
▲ EMP: 30
SQ FT: 11,000
SALES (est): 5MM **Privately Held**
WEB: www.salutron.com
SIC: 3845 Patient monitoring apparatus

(P-22308)
SENSOR DYNAMICS INC
4568 Enterprise St, Fremont (94538-6315)
PHONE..................................510 623-1459
Wun Yann Liao, *President*
▲ EMP: 15
SQ FT: 10,000
SALES (est): 2.1MM **Privately Held**
WEB: www.sensordynamics.com
SIC: 3845 Electromedical apparatus
PA: Direction Technology Co., Ltd.
No. 88-7, Guangfu Rd., Sec. 1
New Taipei City TAP 24158

(P-22309)
SIEMENS MED SOLUTIONS USA INC
Also Called: Oncology Care Systems Group
4040 Nelson Ave, Concord (94520-1200)
PHONE..................................925 246-8200
Ajit Singh, *President*
Ross Taylor, *Managing Dir*
Daniel Lutze, *Finance Mgr*
Jens Merkel, *Finance Mgr*
Christopher Amies, *Director*
EMP: 450
SALES (corp-wide): 95B **Privately Held**
WEB: www.siemensmedical.com
SIC: 3845 3842 5047 Electromedical equipment; surgical appliances & supplies; hospital equipment & furniture
HQ: Siemens Medical Solutions Usa, Inc.
40 Liberty Blvd
Malvern PA 19355
888 826-9702

(P-22310)
SIUI AMERICA INC
780 Montague Expy Ste 608, San Jose
(95131-1320)
PHONE..................................408 432-8881
James MA, *President*
▲ EMP: 10
SALES: 3MM **Privately Held**
WEB: www.siuiamerica.com
SIC: 3845 Ultrasonic scanning devices, medical

(P-22311)
SMART CAREGIVER CORPORATION
1229 N Mcdowell Blvd, Petaluma
(94954-1112)
PHONE..................................707 781-7450
Timothy Long, *President*

Lauren Long, *Admin Sec*
Heather Hennes, *Sales Mgr*
▲ EMP: 25
SQ FT: 4,200
SALES: 10MM **Privately Held**
WEB: www.smartcaregivercorp.com
SIC: 3845 Electromedical equipment

(P-22312)
SOLTA MEDICAL INC
25901 Industrial Blvd, Hayward
(94545-2995)
PHONE..................................510 782-2286
Doug Heigo, *Branch Mgr*
Katherine Grant, *Managing Dir*
Lois Ritter, *Executive Asst*
Patrick Babcock, *Opers Staff*
Ana Cardenas, *Opers Staff*
EMP: 150
SALES (corp-wide): 8.3B **Privately Held**
SIC: 3845 Electromedical equipment
HQ: Solta Medical, Inc.
7031 Koll Center Pkwy # 260
Pleasanton CA 94566
510 786-6946

(P-22313)
SOTERA WIRELESS INC
10020 Huennekens St, San Diego
(92121-2966)
PHONE..................................858 427-4620
Tom Watlington, *CEO*
Charlie Alvarez, *President*
Younes Achkire, *COO*
Mark Spring, *CFO*
Francis Chen, *Chief Mktg Ofcr*
EMP: 104
SQ FT: 29,928
SALES (est): 24.1MM **Privately Held**
SIC: 3845 Electromedical equipment

(P-22314)
SOUND IMAGING INC
7580 Trade St Ste A, San Diego
(92121-2479)
PHONE..................................858 622-0082
Sunny Tabrizi, *CFO*
EMP: 19
SQ FT: 5,800
SALES (est): 3.3MM **Privately Held**
WEB: www.soundimaging.com
SIC: 3845 5047 5999 Laser systems & equipment, medical; medical equipment & supplies; medical apparatus & supplies

(P-22315)
SPECTRANETICS
6531 Dumbarton Cir, Fremont
(94555-3619)
PHONE..................................408 592-2111
EMP: 11
SALES (est): 1.3MM **Privately Held**
SIC: 3845 Electromedical equipment

(P-22316)
STRAND PRODUCTS INC (PA)
725 E Yanonali St, Santa Barbara
(93103-3235)
P.O. Box 4610 (93140-4610)
PHONE..................................805 568-0304
James Wilson, *President*
Wesley Prunckle, *Vice Pres*
Hamahito Hokyo, *Engineer*
John Hottinger, *Engineer*
▲ EMP: 22
SQ FT: 6,000
SALES (est): 4MM **Privately Held**
WEB: www.strandproducts.com
SIC: 3845 5063 Ultrasonic scanning devices, medical; wire & cable

(P-22317)
SYNERON INC (DH)
Also Called: Syneron Candela
3 Goodyear Ste A, Irvine (92618-2050)
PHONE..................................866 259-6661
Shimon Eckhouse, *Ch of Bd*
Fabian Tenenbaum, *CFO*
Lisa Soderquist, *Officer*
Todd Van Horn, *Officer*
Dany Berube, *Vice Pres*
EMP: 53
SALES (est): 94.1MM **Privately Held**
SIC: 3845 Laser systems & equipment, medical

HQ: Syneron Medical Ltd
Upper Yokneam
Upper Yokneam
732 442-200

(P-22318)
TAE LIFE SCIENCES LLC
1756 Cloverfield Blvd, Santa Monica
(90404-4008)
PHONE..................................310 633-5042
Dave Bush, *Mng Member*
Robert Hill, *COO*
◆ EMP: 10
SALES (est): 699.1K
SALES (corp-wide): 50.3MM **Privately Held**
SIC: 3845 2834 Laser systems & equipment, medical; pharmaceutical preparations
PA: Tae Technologies, Inc.
19631 Pauling
Foothill Ranch CA 92610
949 830-2117

(P-22319)
TENSYS MEDICAL INC
12625 High Bluff Dr # 213, San Diego
(92130-2052)
PHONE..................................858 552-1941
Stuart Gallant, *CEO*
EMP: 32
SQ FT: 25,370
SALES (est): 6.4MM **Privately Held**
WEB: www.tensysmedical.com
SIC: 3845 3841 Ultrasonic scanning devices, medical; surgical & medical instruments

(P-22320)
THORATEC LLC (HQ)
6035 Stoneridge Dr, Pleasanton
(94588-3270)
PHONE..................................925 847-8600
Donald J Zurbay,
Julie Piona, *President*
Taylor C Harris, *CFO*
David Farrar, *Vice Pres*
Lauren Hernandez, *Vice Pres*
▲ EMP: 193
SQ FT: 66,000
SALES (est): 386.8MM
SALES (corp-wide): 30.5B **Publicly Held**
WEB: www.thoratec.com
SIC: 3845 3841 Electromedical equipment; surgical & medical instruments; diagnostic apparatus, medical
PA: Abbott Laboratories
100 Abbott Park Rd
Abbott Park IL 60064
224 667-6100

(P-22321)
TOPCON MED LASER SYSTEMS INC
606 Enterprise Ct, Livermore (94550-5200)
PHONE..................................888 760-8657
Dean Scotch, *Vice Pres*
Rob Orsino, *President*
Hideharu Suzuki, *President*
Dan Van Buskirk, *Program Mgr*
Bobbie Heap, *Sales Staff*
▲ EMP: 45 EST: 2010
SALES (est): 8.4MM **Privately Held**
SIC: 3845 Laser systems & equipment, medical
HQ: Topcon America Corporation
111 Bauer Dr
Oakland NJ 07436
201 599-5100

(P-22322)
TRI-STAR TECHNOLOGIES INC
1111 E El Segundo Blvd, El Segundo
(90245-4202)
PHONE..................................310 567-9243
Alex Kerner, *President*
EMP: 13
SQ FT: 80,000
SALES: 4.4MM
SALES (corp-wide): 4.4B **Publicly Held**
WEB: www.tri-star-technologies.com
SIC: 3845 2836 3542 Laser systems & equipment, medical; plasmas; crimping machinery, metal

PA: Carlisle Companies Incorporated
16430 N Scottsdale Rd # 400
Scottsdale AZ 85254
480 781-5000

(P-22323)
TRIMEDYNE INC (PA)
530 Technology Dr Ste 275, Irvine
(92618-1349)
PHONE..................................949 951-3800
Glenn D Yeik, *President*
Marvin P Loeb, *Ch of Bd*
L Dean Crawford, *Vice Pres*
Brian T Kenney, *Vice Pres*
EMP: 43
SQ FT: 9,215
SALES (est): 7.1MM **Publicly Held**
WEB: www.trimedyne.com
SIC: 3845 7352 Laser systems & equipment, medical; medical equipment rental

(P-22324)
VAVE HEALTH INC
2350 Mission College Blvd, Santa Clara
(95054-1532)
PHONE..................................650 387-7059
Amin Nikoozadeh, *CEO*
EMP: 15
SALES (est): 1MM **Privately Held**
SIC: 3845 Ultrasonic medical equipment, except cleaning

(P-22325)
VERTIFLEX INC
2714 Loker Ave W Ste 100, Carlsbad
(92010-6640)
PHONE..................................442 325-5900
Earl Fender, *CEO*
EMP: 40 EST: 2004
SQ FT: 25,000
SALES (est): 8.4MM
SALES (corp-wide): 9.8B **Publicly Held**
SIC: 3845 Ultrasonic scanning devices, medical
PA: Boston Scientific Corporation
300 Boston Scientific Way
Marlborough MA 01752
508 683-4000

(P-22326)
VIBRYNT INC
2570 W El Camino Real # 310, Mountain View (94040-1306)
PHONE..................................650 362-6100
EMP: 30
SQ FT: 4,121
SALES (est): 3.1MM **Privately Held**
SIC: 3845

(P-22327)
VITAL CONNECT INC
224 Airport Pkwy Ste 300, San Jose
(95110-1022)
PHONE..................................408 963-4600
Nersi Nazari, *President*
Michael Dillhyon, *President*
Martin Webster, *CFO*
Bill Brodie, *Officer*
EMP: 50
SALES (est): 9.4MM **Privately Held**
SIC: 3845 Ultrasonic scanning devices, medical

(P-22328)
VIVOMETRICS INC
16030 Ventura Blvd # 470, Encino
(91436-2731)
PHONE..................................805 667-2225
Howard R Baker, *President*
EMP: 35 EST: 1999
SQ FT: 8,220
SALES (est): 3.5MM **Privately Held**
WEB: www.vivometrics.com
SIC: 3845 3842 Patient monitoring apparatus; surgical appliances & supplies

(P-22329)
VOLCANO CORPORATION (DH)
3721 Vly Cntre Dr Ste 500, San Diego
(92130)
PHONE..................................800 228-4728
R Scott Huennekens, *President*
Ronald A Matricaria, *Ch of Bd*
John T Dahldorf, *CFO*
Darin M Lippoldt, *Exec VP*
John Onopchenko, *Exec VP*

▲ **EMP:** 300
SQ FT: 92,602
SALES: 393.6MM
SALES (corp-wide): 20.8B **Privately Held**
WEB: www.volcanocorp.com
SIC: 3845 Ultrasonic medical equipment, except cleaning

(P-22330)
VOLCANO CORPORATION
Also Called: Volcano Therapeutics
2451 Merc Dr Ste 200, Rancho Cordova (95742)
PHONE....................916 281-2932
Saul Salayandia, *Manager*
EMP: 280
SALES (corp-wide): 20.8B **Privately Held**
SIC: 3845 Electromedical equipment
HQ: Volcano Corporation
3721 Vly Cntre Dr Ste 500
San Diego CA 92130
800 228-4728

(P-22331)
VOLCANO CORPORATION
1931 Old Middlefield Way, Mountain View (94043-2557)
PHONE....................650 938-5300
R Scott Huennekens, *President*
EMP: 280
SALES (corp-wide): 20.8B **Privately Held**
SIC: 3845 Electromedical equipment
HQ: Volcano Corporation
3721 Vly Cntre Dr Ste 500
San Diego CA 92130
800 228-4728

(P-22332)
VOLCANO CORPORATION
2870 Kilgore Rd, Rancho Cordova (95670-6133)
PHONE....................916 638-8008
Scott Huennekens, *CEO*
Richard Silva, *Manager*
EMP: 280
SALES (corp-wide): 20.8B **Privately Held**
WEB: www.volcanocorp.com
SIC: 3845 Ultrasonic scanning devices, medical
HQ: Volcano Corporation
3721 Vly Cntre Dr Ste 500
San Diego CA 92130
800 228-4728

(P-22333)
XINTEC CORPORATION (PA)
Also Called: Convergent Laser Technologies
1660 S Loop Rd, Alameda (94502-7091)
PHONE....................510 832-2130
Mark H K Chim, *President*
Marilyn M Chou, *Exec VP*
Michael Haskin, *Engineer*
Jenny Ha, *Purchasing*
▲ **EMP:** 20
SQ FT: 20,000
SALES (est): 3.3MM **Privately Held**
WEB: www.convergentlaser.com
SIC: 3845 Laser systems & equipment, medical

(P-22334)
ZENSE-LIFE INC
2218 Faraday Ave Ste 120, Carlsbad (92008-7234)
PHONE....................858 888-5289
Leif Bowman, *CEO*
EMP: 11 **EST:** 2018
SALES (est): 977.6K **Privately Held**
SIC: 3845 Electromedical equipment

(P-22335)
ZOLL CIRCULATION INC
2000 Ringwood Ave, San Jose (95131-1728)
PHONE....................408 541-2140
Richard A Packer, *CEO*
James Palabzolo, *President*
Rick Helkowski, *Vice Pres*
Kenneth E Ludlum, *Principal*
Jonathan A Rennert, *Principal*
▲ **EMP:** 130
SALES (est): 35.9MM **Privately Held**
WEB: www.revivant.com
SIC: 3845 3841 Electromedical equipment; surgical & medical instruments

HQ: Zoll Medical Corporation
269 Mill Rd
Chelmsford MA 01824
978 421-9655

(P-22336)
ZOLL MEDICAL CORPORATION
2000 Ringwood Ave, San Jose (95131-1728)
PHONE....................408 419-2929
Beth Barredo, *Manager*
Catherine Prophet, *Executive*
Dean Severns, *Electrical Engi*
Jeff Resnick, *Director*
EMP: 15 **Privately Held**
SIC: 3845 Defibrillator
HQ: Zoll Medical Corporation
269 Mill Rd
Chelmsford MA 01824
978 421-9655

3851 Ophthalmic Goods

(P-22337)
ABBS VISION SYSTEMS INC
Also Called: Guard-Dogs
4848 Colt St Ste 14, Ventura (93003-7732)
PHONE....................805 642-0499
Susan Lindahl, *President*
Arthur Lindahl, *Vice Pres*
▲ **EMP:** 10
SQ FT: 1,200
SALES (est): 1.4MM **Privately Held**
WEB: www.guard-dogs.com
SIC: 3851 Protective eyeware

(P-22338)
ADVANCED VISION SCIENCE INC
5743 Thornwood Dr, Goleta (93117-3801)
PHONE....................805 683-3851
Khalid Mentak, *Ch of Bd*
Karen Krebaum, *Marketing Staff*
Alan Matthews, *Research Analys*
EMP: 40 **EST:** 1976
SQ FT: 30,000
SALES (est): 9.2MM **Privately Held**
WEB: www.advancedvisionscience.com
SIC: 3851 3841 8011 Intraocular lenses; surgical & medical instruments; offices & clinics of medical doctors
PA: Santen Pharmaceutical Co., Ltd.
4-20, Ofukacho, Kita-Ku
Osaka OSK 530-0

(P-22339)
AMERON INTERNATIONAL CORP
Ameron Protective Linings
201 N Berry St, Brea (92821-3931)
P.O. Box 1629 (92822-1629)
PHONE....................714 256-7755
Micheal Carruth, *Branch Mgr*
EMP: 30
SALES (corp-wide): 8.4B **Publicly Held**
WEB: www.ameron.com
SIC: 3851 3081 Ophthalmic goods; unsupported plastics film & sheet
HQ: Ameron International Corporation
7909 Parkwood Circle Dr
Houston TX 77036
713 375-3700

(P-22340)
BARTON PERREIRA LLC (PA)
459 Wald, Irvine (92618-4639)
PHONE....................949 305-5360
William G Barton,
Carla Carpenter, *Partner*
Dwight Chiles, *Partner*
Robert Fiddler, *CIO*
Celeste Vos, *VP Sales*
▲ **EMP:** 25 **EST:** 2006
SALES (est): 4.2MM **Privately Held**
SIC: 3851 Protective eyeware

(P-22341)
BAUSCH & LOMB INCORPORATED
50 Technology Dr, Irvine (92618-2301)
PHONE....................949 788-6000
Ron Zarella, *Branch Mgr*
James Leblanc, *Info Tech Dir*

Abigail Markward, *Marketing Staff*
Edward Kennedy, *Director*
EMP: 200
SALES (corp-wide): 8.3B **Privately Held**
WEB: www.bausch.com
SIC: 3851 Ophthalmic goods
HQ: Bausch & Lomb Incorporated
400 Somerset Corp Blvd
Bridgewater NJ 08807
585 338-6000

(P-22342)
BROTHERS OPTICAL LABORATORY
870 N Eckhoff St, Orange (92868-1008)
PHONE....................714 639-9852
John Ragazzo, *President*
Joseph Ragazzo, *Corp Secy*
Peter Comoglio, *Vice Pres*
▲ **EMP:** 90 **EST:** 1973
SQ FT: 19,000
SALES (est): 12.8MM **Privately Held**
SIC: 3851 5048 Lenses, ophthalmic; ophthalmic goods

(P-22343)
CALIFORNIA COATING LAB
670 Mccormick St, San Leandro (94577-1110)
PHONE....................510 357-1800
William Lee, *Owner*
Angie Lewis-Stuber, *Admin Asst*
EMP: 20
SALES (est): 2.1MM **Privately Held**
WEB: www.californiacoatinglab.com
SIC: 3851 Lens coating, ophthalmic

(P-22344)
CARL ZEISS VISION INC (DH)
12121 Scripps Summit Dr, San Diego (92131-4608)
PHONE....................858 790-7700
Jens Boy, *President*
Joe Dunn, *Technology*
Paul Green, *Finance*
Bernadette Hiskey, *Marketing Staff*
Melissa Horne, *Sales Staff*
▲ **EMP:** 80
SQ FT: 9,000
SALES (est): 409.9MM
SALES (corp-wide): 449.3K **Privately Held**
WEB: www.zeiss.com/us
SIC: 3851 3827 Lenses, ophthalmic; lenses, optical: all types except ophthalmic
HQ: Carl Zeiss Vision International Gmbh
Turnstr. 27
Aalen 73430
736 159-10

(P-22345)
CONTEX INC
Also Called: Contex Inc Contact Lenses
4505 Van Nuys Blvd, Van Nuys (91403-2914)
PHONE....................818 788-5836
Nick Stoyan, *President*
Ann Stoyan, *Vice Pres*
Gary Stoyan, *Vice Pres*
EMP: 15
SQ FT: 5,000
SALES (est): 3.4MM **Privately Held**
WEB: www.oklens.com
SIC: 3851 8011 Contact lenses; offices & clinics of medical doctors

(P-22346)
COOPER COMPANIES INC (PA)
6140 Stoneridge Mall Rd # 590, Pleasanton (94588-3772)
PHONE....................925 460-3600
Albert G White III, *President*
A Thomas Bender, *Ch of Bd*
Allan E Rubenstein, *Vice Chairman*
Daniel G McBride, *COO*
Brian Andrews, *CFO*
EMP: 157
SQ FT: 103,990
SALES: 2.5B **Publicly Held**
WEB: www.coopercos.com
SIC: 3851 3842 Contact lenses; surgical appliances & supplies; gynecological supplies & appliances

(P-22347)
COOPERVISION INC
6150 Stoneridge Mall Rd # 370, Pleasanton (94588-3241)
PHONE....................925 251-6600
Stephen Fanning, *CEO*
Tresia O'Shea, *Director*
Jose Fabregas, *Manager*
John Herb, *Manager*
EMP: 100
SALES (corp-wide): 2.5B **Publicly Held**
SIC: 3851 Contact lenses
HQ: Coopervision, Inc.
209 High Point Dr Ste 100
Victor NY 14564

(P-22348)
DITA INC (PA)
Also Called: Dita Eyewear
1787 Pomona Rd, Corona (92880-6995)
PHONE....................949 599-2700
Sukhmeet Dhillon, *President*
Shahid Ghani, *Treasurer*
Jenn Bradley, *Vice Pres*
Dustin E Arnold, *Creative Dir*
▲ **EMP:** 33
SQ FT: 3,000
SALES (est): 5MM **Privately Held**
WEB: www.ditaeyewear.com
SIC: 3851 5995 Ophthalmic goods; optical goods stores

(P-22349)
DRAGON ALLIANCE INC
971 Calle Amanecer, San Clemente (92673-4228)
PHONE....................760 931-4900
William H Howard, *President*
Ryan Vance, *Admin Sec*
▲ **EMP:** 45
SQ FT: 3,500
SALES (est): 8MM
SALES (corp-wide): 4.4B **Privately Held**
WEB: www.dragonoptical.com
SIC: 3851 Glasses, sun or glare
HQ: Marchon Eyewear, Inc.
201 Old Country Rd Fl 3
Melville NY 11747
631 755-2020

(P-22350)
EAGLE LABS LLC
Also Called: Eagle Laboratories, LLC
10201a Trademark St Ste A, Rancho Cucamonga (91730-5849)
PHONE....................909 481-0011
Richard J De Camp, *President*
Michael Decamp, *Vice Pres*
Richard Decamp, *Vice Pres*
EMP: 65
SQ FT: 30,000
SALES (est): 6.5MM
SALES (corp-wide): 8.1MM **Privately Held**
SIC: 3851 Frames, lenses & parts, eyeglass & spectacle
PA: Innovia Medical
815 Northwest Pkwy # 100
Saint Paul MN 55121
651 789-3939

(P-22351)
ELECTRIC VISUAL EVOLUTION LLC (PA)
950 Calle Amanecer # 101, San Clemente (92673-4231)
PHONE....................949 940-9125
Eric Crane, *CEO*
Billy Benda, *Finance*
Scott Morris, *Controller*
Steve Hurst, *VP Opers*
Derek Bradley, *Opers Staff*
◆ **EMP:** 28 **EST:** 1999
SQ FT: 2,000
SALES: 5.3MM **Privately Held**
SIC: 3851 5094 5136 Glasses, sun or glare; watchcases; apparel belts, men's & boys'

(P-22352)
EMPIRE OPTICAL OF CALIFORNIA
7633 Varna Ave, North Hollywood (91605-1748)
PHONE..................................818 997-6474
Noel Diaz, *Principal*
Neil Grossman, *President*
Joanne Grossman, *Corp Secy*
Charles Thomas, *Director*
EMP: 45
SQ FT: 5,000
SALES (est): 6.2MM
SALES (corp-wide): 1.4MM **Privately Held**
SIC: 3851 Ophthalmic goods
HQ: Essilor Laboratories Of America, Inc.
13515 N Stemmons Fwy
Dallas TX 75234
972 241-4141

(P-22353)
ESSILOR LABORATORIES AMER INC
801 N Burke St, Visalia (93292-3822)
PHONE..................................800 624-6672
Real Goulet, *Principal*
Eric Dennewitz, *General Mgr*
EMP: 50
SALES (corp-wide): 1.4MM **Privately Held**
SIC: 3851 Eyeglasses, lenses & frames
HQ: Essilor Laboratories Of America, Inc.
13515 N Stemmons Fwy
Dallas TX 75234
972 241-4141

(P-22354)
ESSILOR LABORATORIES AMER INC
Also Called: Elite Optical
1450 W Walnut St, Compton (90220-5013)
PHONE..................................310 604-8668
Real Goulet, *Principal*
EMP: 50
SALES (corp-wide): 1.4MM **Privately Held**
SIC: 3851 Eyeglasses, lenses & frames
HQ: Essilor Laboratories Of America, Inc.
13515 N Stemmons Fwy
Dallas TX 75234
972 241-4141

(P-22355)
EXPRESS LENS LAB INC
17150 Newhope St Ste 305, Fountain Valley (92708-4251)
PHONE..................................714 545-1024
Brian Goldstone, *President*
EMP: 30
SQ FT: 5,000
SALES (est): 3MM **Privately Held**
SIC: 3851 8011 5049 Ophthalmic goods; offices & clinics of medical doctors; optical goods

(P-22356)
EYEBRAIN MEDICAL INC
Also Called: Neurolenses
3184 Airway Ave Ste C, Costa Mesa (92626-4619)
PHONE..................................949 339-5157
Corley Davis, *President*
Thomas J Chirillo, *Ch Credit Ofcr*
Danny Perales, *Officer*
Matt Swartz, *VP Sales*
▲ EMP: 16
SQ FT: 6,000
SALES: 392K **Privately Held**
SIC: 3851 Eyeglasses, lenses & frames

(P-22357)
EYEFLUENCE INC
1600 Amphitheatre Pkwy, Mountain View (94043-1351)
PHONE..................................408 586-8632
EMP: 29
SALES (est): 3.7MM **Privately Held**
SIC: 3851

(P-22358)
EYEONICS INC
Also Called: Bausch & Lomb Surgical Div
50 Technology Dr, Irvine (92618-2301)
PHONE..................................949 788-6000

Joseph F Gordon, *CEO*
EMP: 50
SQ FT: 5,000
SALES (est): 6.3MM
SALES (corp-wide): 8.3B **Privately Held**
SIC: 3851 Ophthalmic goods
HQ: Bausch & Lomb Incorporated
400 Somerset Corp Blvd
Bridgewater NJ 08807
585 338-6000

(P-22359)
GUNNAR OPTIKS LLC
2236 Rutherford Rd # 123, Carlsbad (92008-8836)
PHONE..................................858 769-2500
Joe Croft, *CEO*
Jennifer Michelsen, *Chief Mktg Ofcr*
Erwin Miguel, *Marketing Mgr*
Rj Snyder, *Marketing Mgr*
Annie Mighdoll, *Sales Mgr*
▲ EMP: 20
SALES (est): 10MM **Privately Held**
SIC: 3851 Contact lenses

(P-22360)
HOYA CORPORATION
Also Called: Hoya San Diego
4255 Ruffin Rd, San Diego (92123-1232)
PHONE..................................858 309-6050
Charlie Pendrell, *Principal*
EMP: 200 **Privately Held**
SIC: 3851 Ophthalmic goods
HQ: Hoya Corporation
651 E Corporate Dr
Lewisville TX 75057
972 221-4141

(P-22361)
HOYA OPTICAL INC (PA)
1400 Carpenter Ln, Modesto (95351-1102)
P.O. Box 580870 (95358-0016)
PHONE..................................209 579-7739
Fred Fink, *CEO*
Lester Thornburg, *General Mgr*
EMP: 90
SQ FT: 17,700
SALES (est): 7.6MM **Privately Held**
SIC: 3851 8011 5995 5048 Ophthalmic goods; offices & clinics of medical doctors; optical goods stores; ophthalmic goods

(P-22362)
INITIUM EYEWEAR INC
412 Olive Ave Ste 218, Huntington Beach (92648-5142)
PHONE..................................714 444-0866
Jason Kazmer, *Principal*
EMP: 11
SALES (est): 180.4K **Privately Held**
SIC: 3851 Eyeglasses, lenses & frames

(P-22363)
IRD ACQUISITIONS LLC
Also Called: Trijicon Electro Optics
12810 Earhart Ave, Auburn (95602-9027)
PHONE..................................530 210-2966
Stephen Bindon, *CEO*
EMP: 12
SQ FT: 7,500
SALES (est): 2.2MM
SALES (corp-wide): 29.9MM **Privately Held**
SIC: 3851 3949 3827 Goggles: sun, safety, industrial, underwater, etc.; target shooting equipment; telescopes: elbow, panoramic, sighting, fire control, etc.
PA: Trijicon, Inc.
49385 Shafer Ct
Wixom MI 48393
248 960-7700

(P-22364)
J G HERNANDEZ COMPANY
Also Called: Collard Rose Optical Lab
870 N Eckhoff St, Orange (92868-1008)
PHONE..................................800 242-2020
Robby J Hernandez, *President*
David Milan, *Vice Pres*
Armine Dervishian, *Manager*
EMP: 47 EST: 1948
SALES: 10MM
SALES (corp-wide): 1.4MM **Privately Held**
SIC: 3851 Lenses, ophthalmic

HQ: Essilor Laboratories Of America, Inc.
13515 N Stemmons Fwy
Dallas TX 75234
972 241-4141

(P-22365)
KATZ & KLEIN
9901 Horn Rd Ste D, Sacramento (95827-1944)
PHONE..................................916 444-2024
Corrine Hood, *President*
Candy Corcoran, *Corp Secy*
Mike Francesconi, *Vice Pres*
Magic Munson -Cs, *Manager*
EMP: 33
SQ FT: 7,500
SALES (est): 2.7MM **Privately Held**
WEB: www.katzandklein.com
SIC: 3851 5049 Ophthalmic goods; optical goods

(P-22366)
KH9100 LLC
Also Called: Lab, The
3073 N California St, Burbank (91504-2005)
PHONE..................................818 972-2580
Hye Won Kim,
Peter Wang, *Accountant*
EMP: 14
SALES (est): 2MM **Privately Held**
SIC: 3851 Ophthalmic goods

(P-22367)
LEISURE COLLECTIVE INC
Also Called: Otis Eyewear
6189 El Camino Real 101, Carlsbad (92009-1602)
PHONE..................................760 814-2840
Chat Crites, *General Mgr*
▲ EMP: 11
SALES (est): 1.8MM **Privately Held**
SIC: 3851 5099 5091 Protective eyeware; sunglasses; watersports equipment & supplies

(P-22368)
LENS C-C INC (PA)
Also Called: Con-Cise Contact Lens Co
1750 N Loop Rd Ste 150, Alameda (94502-8013)
PHONE..................................800 772-3911
Carl Moore, *President*
Lynda Baker, *Vice Pres*
Dan Davis, *Vice Pres*
EMP: 100 EST: 1949
SQ FT: 34,000
SALES (est): 7.6MM **Privately Held**
WEB: www.con-cise.com
SIC: 3851 Contact lenses

(P-22369)
LENSVECTOR INC
6203 San Ignacio Ave, San Jose (95119-1371)
PHONE..................................408 542-0300
Howard Earhart, *CEO*
Mark Gemello, *CFO*
EMP: 70
SALES (est): 11.5MM **Privately Held**
SIC: 3851 Ophthalmic goods

(P-22370)
LUXE LABORATORY
7052 Orangewood Ave Ste 8, Garden Grove (92841-1419)
PHONE..................................714 221-2330
Richard Wilhelm, *President*
EMP: 10 EST: 2012
SQ FT: 5,000
SALES (est): 1.5MM **Privately Held**
SIC: 3851 Ophthalmic goods

(P-22371)
MARCH VISION CARE INC
6701 Center Dr W Ste 790, Los Angeles (90045-1563)
PHONE..................................310 665-0975
Glen A March Jr, *President*
Shawn Shahzad, *President*
Gavin Galimi, *CFO*
Cabraini March, *Exec VP*
Ann Ritchey, *Exec VP*
EMP: 42

SALES (est): 8.3MM **Privately Held**
SIC: 3851 Frames, lenses & parts, eyeglass & spectacle
PA: March Holdings, Inc.
6701 Center Dr W Ste 790
Los Angeles CA 90045
-

(P-22372)
MEDENNIUM INC (PA)
9 Parker Ste 150, Irvine (92618-1691)
PHONE..................................949 789-9000
Jacob Feldman, *President*
James R Zullo, *CFO*
EMP: 38
SQ FT: 20,000
SALES (est): 4.6MM **Privately Held**
WEB: www.medennium.com
SIC: 3851 Intraocular lenses

(P-22373)
NITINOL DEVELOPMENT CORP
Also Called: Nitinol Devices & Components
47533 Westinghouse Dr, Fremont (94539-7463)
PHONE..................................510 683-2000
Tom Duerig, *President*
Chuck Faris, *Vice Pres*
Steve Kleshinski, *Vice Pres*
Attila Meretei, *Vice Pres*
Alan Pelton, *CTO*
EMP: 600
SQ FT: 30,000
SALES (est): 18.7MM **Privately Held**
SIC: 3851 3496 Frames & parts, eyeglass & spectacle; miscellaneous fabricated wire products

(P-22374)
NVISION LASER EYE CENTERS INC
Also Called: Meister Eye & Laser
5959 Greenback Ln Ste 310, Citrus Heights (95621-4700)
PHONE..................................916 723-7400
Ngoc Trieu, *Director*
EMP: 15
SALES (corp-wide): 11.1MM **Privately Held**
SIC: 3851 Frames & parts, eyeglass & spectacle
PA: Nvision Laser Eye Centers Inc.
3155d Sedona Ct 100
Ontario CA 91764
909 605-1975

(P-22375)
OAKLEY INC
20081 Ellipse, Foothill Ranch (92610-3001)
PHONE..................................949 672-6849
EMP: 52
SALES (corp-wide): 1.4MM **Privately Held**
SIC: 3851 Ophthalmic goods
HQ: Oakley, Inc.
1 Icon
Foothill Ranch CA 92610
949 951-0991

(P-22376)
OAKLEY SALES CORP
1 Icon, El Toro (92610-3000)
PHONE..................................949 951-0991
Link Newcomb, *President*
Derek Baker, *Vice Pres*
◆ EMP: 18
SQ FT: 400,000
SALES (est): 3.3MM
SALES (corp-wide): 1.4MM **Privately Held**
WEB: www.oakley.com
SIC: 3851 Glasses, sun or glare
HQ: Oakley, Inc.
1 Icon
Foothill Ranch CA 92610
949 951-0991

(P-22377)
OASIS MEDICAL INC (PA)
510-528 S Vermont Ave, Glendora (91741)
P.O. Box 1137 (91740-1137)
PHONE..................................909 305-5400
Norman Delgado, *Ch of Bd*
Arlene Delgado, *Treasurer*
Eduardo Carlo, *Design Engr*

PRODUCTS & SVCS

Maria Lacayo-Zuniga, *Engineer*
Richard Quach, *Engineer*
▲ EMP: 55
SQ FT: 14,000
SALES (est): 13.8MM **Privately Held**
WEB: www.oasismedical.com
SIC: 3851 5048 Ophthalmic goods; ophthalmic goods

(P-22378)
OPHTHONIX INC
900 Glenneyre St, Laguna Beach
(92651-2707)
PHONE...................................760 842-5600
Stephen J Osbaldeston, *CEO*
Jim Bergmark, *Finance Dir*
▲ EMP: 60
SQ FT: 50,000
SALES (est): 7.4MM **Privately Held**
WEB: www.ophthonix.com
SIC: 3851 Eyes, glass & plastic

(P-22379)
OPTI LITE OPTICAL
5552 W Adams Blvd, Los Angeles
(90016-2542)
PHONE...................................323 932-6828
Howard Mochayoff, *Owner*
EMP: 20
SQ FT: 5,512
SALES (est): 2.1MM **Privately Held**
SIC: 3851 Lens grinding, except prescription: ophthalmic

(P-22380)
PRESBIBIO LLC
Also Called: Presbia
36 Plateau, Aliso Viejo (92656-8026)
PHONE...................................949 502-7010
Todd Cooper, *CEO*
Neal Gonzales, *Vice Pres*
Vanessa Tasso, *Vice Pres*
Helio Gomez, *Design Engr*
Asad Jaleel, *Engineer*
EMP: 45
SALES (est): 5.5MM **Privately Held**
SIC: 3851 Frames, lenses & parts, eyeglass & spectacle
PA: Presbia Public Limited Company
120-121 Lower Baggot St
Dublin

(P-22381)
RAFI SYSTEMS INC
23453 Golden Springs Dr, Diamond Bar
(91765-2030)
PHONE...................................909 861-6574
Mohamed Rafiquzzaman, *President*
Mrs Kusum Rafiquzza, *CEO*
EMP: 95
SQ FT: 5,000
SALES (est): 8.9MM **Privately Held**
WEB: www.rafisystems.com
SIC: 3851 3843 5047 5048 Frames, lenses & parts, eyeglass & spectacle; dental equipment; dental equipment & supplies; ophthalmic goods

(P-22382)
RICHMOND OPTICAL CO
923 Berryessa Rd, San Jose (95133-1002)
PHONE...................................510 783-1420
Ronald Furr, *President*
Ken Furr, *Vice Pres*
EMP: 12
SQ FT: 1,800
SALES (est): 1.1MM **Privately Held**
SIC: 3851 5048 Ophthalmic goods; frames, ophthalmic

(P-22383)
SAFETY AMERICA INC
2766 Via Orange Way Ste D, Spring Valley
(91978-1753)
PHONE...................................619 660-6968
EMP: 12
SQ FT: 2,000
SALES (est): 1.2MM **Privately Held**
WEB: www.safetyamerica.com
SIC: 3851 7389

(P-22384)
SAM VAZIRI VANCE INC (PA)
Also Called: Sama Eyewear
10250 Santa Monica Blvd # 1867, Los Angeles (90067-6544)
PHONE...................................323 822-3955
Sheila Vance, *President*
Hossein Kazemi, *Vice Pres*
Darlene Saardphak, *Marketing Staff*
▲ EMP: 20
SALES (est): 3.7MM **Privately Held**
WEB: www.samaeyewear.net
SIC: 3851 Protective eyeware

(P-22385)
SIGNET ARMORLITE INC (DH)
5803 Newton Dr Ste A, Carlsbad
(92008-7380)
P.O. Box 3309, Carol Stream IL (60132-3309)
PHONE...................................760 744-4000
Brad Staley, *President*
Bruno Salvadori, *Ch of Bd*
Lauri Crawford, *Exec VP*
Edward P Derosa, *Exec VP*
M Kathryn Bernard, *Vice Pres*
▲ EMP: 400
SQ FT: 138,000
SALES: 76MM
SALES (corp-wide): 1.4MM **Privately Held**
WEB: www.signetarmorlite.com
SIC: 3851 Ophthalmic goods
HQ: Essilor Of America, Inc.
13555 N Stemmons Fwy
Dallas TX 75234
214 496-4000

(P-22386)
SPELLBOUND DEVELOPMENT GROUP
Also Called: Spellbound Entertainment
17192 Gillette Ave, Irvine (92614-5603)
PHONE...................................949 474-8577
Earl Votolato, *President*
Amanda Brooks, *Manager*
▲ EMP: 10
SALES (est): 1.7MM **Privately Held**
WEB: www.spellboundinc.com
SIC: 3851 7812 5099 Goggles: sun, safety, industrial, underwater, etc.; video production; safety equipment & supplies

(P-22387)
SPORTIFEYE OPTICS INC
1231 Mountain View Cir, Azusa
(91702-1601)
PHONE...................................626 521-5600
Tom Pfeiffer, *CEO*
EMP: 20
SALES (est): 1.6MM **Privately Held**
SIC: 3851 Frames, lenses & parts, eyeglass & spectacle

(P-22388)
SPORTRX INC
5070 Santa Fe St Ste C, San Diego
(92109-1610)
PHONE...................................858 571-0240
Gabby Bloch, *CEO*
Nigel Bloch, *Vice Pres*
▲ EMP: 20
SALES (est): 4.2MM **Privately Held**
WEB: www.sportrx.com
SIC: 3851 Eyeglasses, lenses & frames

(P-22389)
SPY INC (PA)
1896 Rutherford Rd, Carlsbad
(92008-7326)
PHONE...................................760 804-8420
Seth Hamot, *Ch of Bd*
Barry Buchholtz, *President*
James McGinty, *CFO*
Jim Sepanek, *Exec VP*
▲ EMP: 94
SQ FT: 32,551
SALES (est): 38.1MM **Publicly Held**
WEB: www.orangetwentyone.com
SIC: 3851 5099 Glasses, sun or glare; sunglasses

(P-22390)
STAAR SURGICAL COMPANY (PA)
1911 Walker Ave, Monrovia (91016-4846)
PHONE...................................626 303-7902
Caren Mason, *President*
Louis E Silverman, *Ch of Bd*
Deborah Andrews, *CFO*
John Moore, *Bd of Directors*
Samuel Gesten,
▲ EMP: 219 EST: 1982
SALES: 123.9MM **Publicly Held**
WEB: www.staar.com
SIC: 3851 Ophthalmic goods

(P-22391)
STAAR SURGICAL COMPANY
15102 Redhilll Ave, Tustin (92780)
PHONE...................................626 303-7902
Keith Holiday, *Branch Mgr*
EMP: 16
SALES (corp-wide): 123.9MM **Publicly Held**
SIC: 3851 Ophthalmic goods
PA: Staar Surgical Company
1911 Walker Ave
Monrovia CA 91016
626 303-7902

(P-22392)
SYNERGEYES INC (PA)
2236 Rutherford Rd # 115, Carlsbad
(92008-8836)
PHONE...................................760 476-9410
James K Kirchner, *President*
Thomas M Crews, *President*
James Gorechner, *CEO*
David Voris, *CFO*
Peg Achenbach, *Vice Pres*
▲ EMP: 68
SALES (est): 10.3MM **Privately Held**
SIC: 3851 Contact lenses

(P-22393)
TEKIA INC
17 Hammond Ste 414, Irvine (92618-1635)
PHONE...................................949 699-1300
Gene Currie, *President*
Larry Blake, *VP Engrg*
EMP: 20
SQ FT: 5,000
SALES: 2MM **Privately Held**
WEB: www.tekia.com
SIC: 3851 8742 Intraocular lenses; hospital & health services consultant

(P-22394)
VISIONARY INC
2940 E Miraloma Ave, Anaheim
(92806-1811)
PHONE...................................714 237-1900
Richard Belliveau, *President*
Cindy Belliveau, *Treasurer*
EMP: 30
SQ FT: 16,000
SALES: 2.5MM **Privately Held**
SIC: 3851 5048 Contact lenses; contact lenses

(P-22395)
WHEELER OPTICAL LAB
8200 Katella Ave Ste A, Stanton
(90680-3262)
PHONE...................................714 891-2016
Alex Aguilar, *Owner*
EMP: 10
SQ FT: 1,700
SALES (est): 862.6K **Privately Held**
SIC: 3851 Lenses, ophthalmic

(P-22396)
X WILEY INC (PA)
Also Called: Wiley X Eyewear
7800 Patterson Pass Rd, Livermore
(94550-9544)
PHONE...................................925 243-9810
Myles R Freeman Sr, *CEO*
Myles J Freeman Jr, *President*
John B Barrett, *COO*
Steve Gerlovich, *Vice Pres*
Christian G Gerlovich, *Info Tech Mgr*
▲ EMP: 75
SQ FT: 35,000

SALES (est): 18.9MM **Privately Held**
WEB: www.wileyx.com
SIC: 3851 5048 2381 2339 Frames, lenses & parts, eyeglass & spectacle; ophthalmic goods; gloves, work: woven or knit, made from purchased materials; women's & misses' athletic clothing & sportswear

(P-22397)
YOUNGER MFG CO (PA)
Also Called: Younger Optics
2925 California St, Torrance (90503-3914)
PHONE...................................310 783-1533
Joseph David Rips, *CEO*
Tom Balch, *President*
Roshan Seresinhe, *CFO*
Nancy Yamasaki, *Admin Sec*
◆ EMP: 280
SQ FT: 130,000
SALES (est): 221.8MM **Privately Held**
WEB: www.youngeroptics.com
SIC: 3851 Lenses, ophthalmic

(P-22398)
ZEROUV
16792 Burke Ln, Huntington Beach
(92647-4559)
PHONE...................................714 584-0015
Viet Tran, *Principal*
Tran Vick, *General Mgr*
EMP: 12
SALES (est): 904K **Privately Held**
SIC: 3851 Eyeglasses, lenses & frames

3861 Photographic Eqpt & Splys

(P-22399)
AB MANUFACTURING INC
115 Red River Way, San Jose
(95136-3352)
PHONE...................................408 972-5085
Dan Maurer, *President*
Anhvu Vu, *Treasurer*
Corinne Avila, *Office Mgr*
EMP: 10
SQ FT: 2,200
SALES (est): 970K **Privately Held**
WEB: www.abmfg.com
SIC: 3861 7699 Photographic equipment & supplies; photographic equipment repair

(P-22400)
AFTERMASTER INC (PA)
6671 W Sunset Blvd # 1520, Hollywood
(90028-7175)
PHONE...................................310 657-4886
Lawrence G Ryckman, *Ch of Bd*
Mirella Chavez, *CFO*
Mark Depew, *Senior VP*
Aaron Ryckman, *Senior VP*
Sheldon Yakus, *Vice Pres*
EMP: 11
SALES: 976.3K **Publicly Held**
SIC: 3861 Sound recording & reproducing equipment, motion picture

(P-22401)
ALTIA SYSTEMS INC
10020 N De Anza Blvd, Cupertino
(95014-2213)
PHONE...................................408 996-9710
Aurangzeb Khan, *CEO*
Naveed Alam, *Vice Pres*
Alex Hausman, *Executive*
Osman Ahmed, *Software Engr*
Priya Krishnan, *Marketing Mgr*
▲ EMP: 25
SALES (est): 4.4MM
SALES (corp-wide): 1.6B **Privately Held**
SIC: 3861 Cameras & related equipment
PA: Gn Store Nord A/S
Lautrupbjerg 7
Ballerup 2750
457 500-00

(P-22402)
ANSCHUTZ FILM GROUP LLC (HQ)
1888 Century Park E # 1400, Los Angeles
(90067-1718)
PHONE...................................310 887-1000

Michael Bostick, *CEO*
Marcia Wheatley, *Administration*
▲ EMP: 30
SALES (est): 2.5MM **Privately Held**
SIC: 3861 Motion picture film

(P-22403)
AVID TECHNOLOGY INC
2600 10th St Ste 100, Berkeley
(94710-2512)
PHONE...................510 486-8302
EMP: 462
SALES (corp-wide): 413.2MM **Publicly Held**
SIC: 3861 Photographic equipment & supplies
PA: Avid Technology, Inc.
75 Network Dr
Burlington MA 01803
978 640-6789

(P-22404)
AVID TECHNOLOGY INC
101 S 1st St Ste 200, Burbank
(91502-1938)
PHONE...................818 557-2520
Kristin Bedient, *Manager*
EMP: 20
SALES (corp-wide): 413.2MM **Publicly Held**
WEB: www.avid.com
SIC: 3861 Editing equipment, motion picture: viewers, splicers, etc.
PA: Avid Technology, Inc.
75 Network Dr
Burlington MA 01803
978 640-6789

(P-22405)
AVID TECHNOLOGY INC
14007 Runnymede St, Van Nuys
(91405-2510)
PHONE...................818 779-7860
EMP: 215
SALES (corp-wide): 677.9MM **Publicly Held**
SIC: 3861
PA: Avid Technology, Inc.
75 Network Dr
Burlington MA 01803
978 640-6789

(P-22406)
CDS CALIFORNIA LLC
3330 Chnga Blvd W Ste 200, Los Angeles
(90068-1354)
PHONE...................818 766-5000
Steven Balvanz, *Exec VP*
Adam Bergeron, *Administration*
Jerry Sawyer, *Technician*
Barbara Russo, *VP Sales*
Lisa Mayberry, *Manager*
EMP: 14
SALES (est): 2.1MM **Privately Held**
SIC: 3861 Photographic equipment & supplies

(P-22407)
CHRISTIE DIGITAL SYSTEMS INC (HQ)
10550 Camden Dr, Cypress (90630-4600)
PHONE...................714 236-8610
Rex Balz, *President*
Paul Estrada, *Vice Pres*
Anju Rana, *Office Mgr*
Leigh Shanks, *Administration*
Tom Clapp, *Project Mgr*
EMP: 21
SALES (est): 111.4MM **Privately Held**
SIC: 3861 6719 Projectors, still or motion picture, silent or sound; investment holding companies, except banks

(P-22408)
CINE MECHANICS INC
20610 Plummer St, Chatsworth
(91311-5111)
PHONE...................818 701-7944
Albert Beck Jr, *President*
EMP: 14
SQ FT: 11,000
SALES: 1MM **Privately Held**
SIC: 3861 Cameras & related equipment

(P-22409)
CLOVER TECHNOLOGIES GROUP LLC
315 Weakley St, Calexico (92231-9659)
PHONE...................760 357-9277
EMP: 50
SALES (corp-wide): 934MM **Privately Held**
SIC: 3861 Printing equipment, photographic
HQ: Clover Technologies Group, Llc
2700 W Higgins Rd Ste 100
Hoffman Estates IL 60169

(P-22410)
COMPUTER PROMPTING SERVICE
617 S Victory Blvd, Burbank (91502-2424)
PHONE...................818 563-3465
Bron Galleran, *President*
EMP: 12 EST: 1983
SALES: 200K **Privately Held**
WEB: www.computerprompting.com
SIC: 3861 Blueprint reproduction machines & equipment

(P-22411)
CONTINUOUS CARTRIDGE
Also Called: Acuprint.com
5973 Avenida Encinas # 140, Carlsbad
(92008-4476)
PHONE...................760 929-4808
EMP: 30
SALES (est): 1.9MM
SALES (corp-wide): 7.4MM **Privately Held**
WEB: www.ebanklink.com
SIC: 3861
PA: Acuprint, Inc.
5973 Avenida Encinas
Carlsbad CA 92008
760 929-4808

(P-22412)
CRASHCAM INDUSTRIES CORP
19627 Vision Dr, Topanga (90290-3116)
PHONE...................310 283-5379
Ed Gutentag, *President*
EMP: 10
SQ FT: 1,500
SALES (est): 1.1MM **Privately Held**
SIC: 3861 Cameras, still & motion picture (all types)

(P-22413)
DION ROSTAMIAN
Also Called: Pic Flick
1146 N Central Ave 227, Glendale
(91202-2506)
PHONE...................877 633-0293
EMP: 12 EST: 2012
SALES (est): 670K **Privately Held**
SIC: 3861

(P-22414)
DJI TECHNOLOGY INC
201 S Victory Blvd, Burbank (91502-2349)
PHONE...................818 235-0789
Jie Shen, *CEO*
EMP: 24 EST: 2015
SALES (est): 5.2MM **Privately Held**
SIC: 3861 Aerial cameras; cameras & related equipment

(P-22415)
DOREMI CINEMA LLC
1020 Chestnut St, Burbank (91506-1623)
PHONE...................818 562-1101
Camille Rizko,
Safar Ghazal,
Emil Rizko,
EMP: 45
SQ FT: 20,000
SALES: 10MM **Privately Held**
SIC: 3861 Motion picture apparatus & equipment

(P-22416)
DXG TECHNOLOGY USA INC
Also Called: Dxg USA
330 Turnbull Canyon Rd, City of Industry
(91745-1009)
PHONE...................626 820-0687
Jackson Tzu-Chiang Yu, *President*

Tien-Ta Chih, *Shareholder*
Yung-Hsi Chen, *Shareholder*
Chih WEI Shih, *General Mgr*
◆ EMP: 26
SQ FT: 28,255
SALES: 36MM **Privately Held**
SIC: 3861 Cameras & related equipment

(P-22417)
E PHOCUS INC
10455 Pacific Center Ct, San Diego
(92121-4339)
PHONE...................858 646-5462
Tzuchiang Hsieh, *President*
Tzu-Chiang Hsieh, *President*
EMP: 13
SALES (est): 1MM **Privately Held**
SIC: 3861 Photographic equipment & supplies

(P-22418)
EASTMAN KODAK COMPANY
3 Santa Elena, Rcho STA Marg
(92688-2409)
PHONE...................949 306-9034
James Saavedra, *Sales Staff*
EMP: 65
SALES (corp-wide): 1.3B **Publicly Held**
SIC: 3861 Photographic equipment & supplies
PA: Eastman Kodak Company
343 State St
Rochester NY 14650
585 724-4000

(P-22419)
ELEMENT TECHNICA LLC
4617 W Jefferson Blvd, Los Angeles
(90016-4006)
PHONE...................323 993-5329
Hector Ortega,
EMP: 12
SALES (est): 12MM **Privately Held**
WEB: www.slscine.com
SIC: 3861 Cameras & related equipment

(P-22420)
ELEPHANT FILMZ & MUSIC INC
3943 Irvine Blvd Ste 430, Irvine
(92602-2400)
PHONE...................310 925-8712
Aj Jamal, *CEO*
Abiola Lawal, *CFO*
EMP: 10
SQ FT: 800
SALES: 100K **Privately Held**
SIC: 3861 Motion picture film

(P-22421)
ESSENCE IMAGING INC
20651 Golden Springs Dr, Walnut
(91789-3866)
PHONE...................909 979-2116
Eliza Un, *CEO*
▲ EMP: 30 EST: 2006
SALES (est): 2.8MM **Privately Held**
SIC: 3861 Printing equipment, photographic

(P-22422)
FASTEC IMAGING CORPORATION
17150 Via DI Cmpo 301, San Diego
(92127)
PHONE...................858 592-2342
Stephen W Ferrell, *President*
Charles Mrdjenovich, *President*
Tony Montiel, *Vice Pres*
EMP: 25
SALES: 1,000K **Privately Held**
SIC: 3861 Cameras & related equipment

(P-22423)
GOPRO INC (PA)
3000 Clearview Way, San Mateo
(94402-3710)
PHONE...................650 332-7600
Nicholas Woodman, *Ch of Bd*
Brian McGee, *CFO*
Eve Saltman, *Vice Pres*
Todd Wagner, *Vice Pres*
Chris Clark, *Comms Dir*
◆ EMP: 495
SQ FT: 311,000

SALES: 1.1B **Publicly Held**
WEB: www.gopro.com
SIC: 3861 7372 Cameras & related equipment; prepackaged software

(P-22424)
HF GROUP INC (PA)
Also Called: Houston Fearless 76
203 W Artesia Blvd, Compton
(90220-5517)
PHONE...................310 605-0755
Myung S Lee, *Ch of Bd*
James H Lee, *President*
Virginia C Clark, *CFO*
Brendan McHugh, *Administration*
Scott McCormack, *VP Finance*
EMP: 47
SQ FT: 45,000
SALES (est): 8MM **Privately Held**
WEB: www.houstonfearless.com
SIC: 3861 Processing equipment, photographic; cameras, still & motion picture (all types); sensitized film, cloth & paper

(P-22425)
HITI DIGITAL AMERICA INC
675 Brea Canyon Rd Ste 7, Walnut
(91789-3065)
PHONE...................909 594-0099
Kuo-Hua Liang, *CEO*
Sunny LI, *Opers Mgr*
Kevin Linton, *Sales Staff*
Eva Ni, *Sales Staff*
◆ EMP: 22 EST: 2008
SALES (est): 4.4MM **Privately Held**
SIC: 3861 7384 Printing equipment, photographic; photographic services

(P-22426)
HOLLYWOOD FILM COMPANY
Also Called: Hav Holdings & Subsidiaries
9265 Borden Ave, Sun Valley (91352-2034)
PHONE...................818 683-1130
Vincent Carabello, *President*
Antonia L Carabello, *Director*
▲ EMP: 100
SQ FT: 79,000
SALES (est): 15.9MM **Privately Held**
WEB: www.hollywoodfilmco.com
SIC: 3861 7819 Editing equipment, motion picture: viewers, splicers, etc.; services allied to motion pictures

(P-22427)
HOYA HOLDINGS INC (HQ)
680 N Mccarthy Blvd # 120, Milpitas
(95035-5120)
PHONE...................408 654-2300
Hiroshi Suzuki, *CEO*
Eiichiro Ikeda, *COO*
Ryo Hirooka, *CFO*
▲ EMP: 180
SALES (est): 129.9MM **Privately Held**
WEB: www.hoyaholdings.com
SIC: 3861 3825 3827 Photographic sensitized goods; test equipment for electronic & electric measurement; optical instruments & lenses

(P-22428)
IDEAS IN MOTION
1435 Eolus Ave, Encinitas (92024-1733)
PHONE...................760 635-1181
Jake Barto, *President*
EMP: 10
SALES (est): 720K **Privately Held**
WEB: www.ideasinmotion.com
SIC: 3861 Motion picture film

(P-22429)
INDUSTRIAL SEC ALLIANC PTNRS (PA)
Also Called: Isap
10350 Science Center Dr # 100, San Diego
(92121-1129)
PHONE...................619 232-7041
Brian Kelly, *President*
Howard Landa, *Ch of Bd*
Michael Lumpkin, *CEO*
EMP: 15 EST: 1997
SALES (est): 4MM **Privately Held**
WEB: www.isapusa.com
SIC: 3861 Cameras & related equipment

PRODUCTS & SVCS

(P-22430)
INTEGRATED DESIGN TOOLS INC (PA)
Also Called: I D T
1 W Mountain St Unit 3, Pasadena (91103-3070)
P.O. Box 16488, Tallahassee FL (32317-6488)
PHONE....................850 222-5939
Luiz M Lourenco, *President*
Max Luera, *Engineer*
EMP: 11 **EST:** 1997
SALES (est): 3.7MM **Privately Held**
WEB: www.idtvision.com
SIC: 3861 5043 Cameras & related equipment; cameras & photographic equipment

(P-22431)
IQINVISION INC
27127 Calle Arroyo # 1920, San Juan Capistrano (92675-2765)
PHONE....................949 369-8100
Charles Chestnutt, *President*
Rob Ledenko, *Exec VP*
▲ **EMP:** 65 **EST:** 1998
SQ FT: 2,000
SALES (est): 10.2MM
SALES (corp-wide): 27.7MM **Privately Held**
WEB: www.iqeye.com
SIC: 3861 5946 Lens shades, camera; camera & photographic supply stores
PA: Vicon Industries, Inc.
135 Fell Ct
Hauppauge NY 11788
631 952-2288

(P-22432)
ITERIS INC (PA)
1700 Carnegie Ave Ste 100, Santa Ana (92705-5551)
PHONE....................949 270-9400
J Joseph Bergera, *President*
Andrew Schmidt, *CFO*
Andy Schmidt, *CFO*
Joseph Boissy, *Chief Mktg Ofcr*
Pete Costello, *Assoc VP*
▲ **EMP:** 146
SQ FT: 41,000
SALES: 99.1MM **Publicly Held**
WEB: www.iteris.com
SIC: 3861 8742 3699 Cameras & related equipment; driers, photographic; printing equipment, photographic; densitometers; transportation consultant; security control equipment & systems

(P-22433)
J L FISHER INC
1000 W Isabel St, Burbank (91506-1404)
PHONE....................818 846-8366
James L Fisher, *President*
Cary Clayton, *Vice Pres*
Mark Gregory, *Technician*
Jennifer Tuason, *Accounting Mgr*
Frank Kay, *Mktg Dir*
▲ **EMP:** 60
SALES (est): 10.2MM **Privately Held**
WEB: www.jlfisher.com
SIC: 3861 3663 7359 Motion picture apparatus & equipment; radio & TV communications equipment; equipment rental & leasing

(P-22434)
JONDO LTD (PA)
22700 Savi Ranch Pkwy, Yorba Linda (92887-4608)
PHONE....................714 279-2300
John Stuart DOE, *CEO*
Dave Murray, *CFO*
Maryann DOE, *Admin Sec*
Elayne Rogers, *Buyer*
EMP: 60
SQ FT: 50,000
SALES: 8MM **Privately Held**
WEB: www.harvestpro.com
SIC: 3861 Photographic equipment & supplies

(P-22435)
KALTEC ELECTRONICS INC (PA)
Also Called: Kaltec Enterprises
16220 Bloomfield Ave, Cerritos (90703-2113)
PHONE....................813 888-9555
Hee K Lee, *CEO*
Wade Thomas, *COO*
▲ **EMP:** 14
SQ FT: 13,000
SALES: 45MM **Privately Held**
WEB: www.kaltech.net
SIC: 3861 Cameras & related equipment

(P-22436)
KK AUDIO INC
12620 Raymer St, North Hollywood (91605-4307)
P.O. Box 16346 (91615-6346)
PHONE....................818 765-2921
Kurt Koesler, *President*
EMP: 12
SQ FT: 12,500
SALES (est): 1.6MM **Privately Held**
WEB: www.kkaudio.com
SIC: 3861 2517 Sound recording & reproducing equipment, motion picture; wood television & radio cabinets

(P-22437)
L-3 CMMNICATIONS SONOMA EO INC
Also Called: Wescam Sonoma Operations
428 Aviation Blvd, Santa Rosa (95403-1069)
PHONE....................707 568-3000
Andy Fordham, *General Mgr*
EMP: 200
SQ FT: 20,000
SALES (est): 38.9MM
SALES (corp-wide): 6.8B **Publicly Held**
SIC: 3861 3812 Photographic equipment & supplies; heads-up display systems (HUD), aeronautical
HQ: L3 Technologies, Inc.
600 3rd Ave Fl 34
New York NY 10016
212 697-1111

(P-22438)
LUMENS INTEGRATION INC
4116 Clipper Ct, Fremont (94538-6514)
PHONE....................510 657-8367
Andy Chang, *President*
Leeling Wang, *Officer*
▲ **EMP:** 14
SQ FT: 5,200
SALES (est): 2.6MM **Privately Held**
WEB: www.mylumens.com
SIC: 3861 5043 Projectors, still or motion picture, silent or sound; projection apparatus, motion picture & slide
PA: Lumens Digital Optics Inc.
5f-1, 20, Taiyuan St.,
Chupei City HSI 30288

(P-22439)
MATTHEWS STUDIO EQUIPMENT INC
Also Called: M S E
4520 W Valerio St, Burbank (91505-1046)
PHONE....................818 843-6715
Edward Phillips III, *President*
▲ **EMP:** 45
SALES (est): 9.7MM **Privately Held**
WEB: www.msegrip.com
SIC: 3861 Motion picture apparatus & equipment; stands, camera & projector; tripods, camera & projector

(P-22440)
ME & ME COSTUMES INC
1052 N Cahuenga Blvd, Los Angeles (90038-2636)
PHONE....................323 876-4432
Mary Ellen Fields, *President*
EMP: 10
SALES (est): 605.1K **Privately Held**
SIC: 3861 Motion picture film

(P-22441)
MODERN STUDIO EQUIPMENT INC
7414 Bellaire Ave, North Hollywood (91605-4303)
PHONE....................818 764-8574
Seno Mousally, *President*
Rina Mousally, *Vice Pres*
Rosy Valencia, *Accounts Exec*
EMP: 19
SQ FT: 22,000
SALES (est): 3.7MM **Privately Held**
SIC: 3861 Motion picture apparatus & equipment

(P-22442)
MOVING IMAGE TECHNOLOGIES LLC
17760 Newhope St Ste B, Fountain Valley (92708-5442)
PHONE....................714 751-7998
Glenn Sherman, *President*
Dan Hodgdon, *Technical Staff*
Jim Stewart, *Technical Staff*
Brandon Shaffer, *Engineer*
Thuha Nguyen, *Controller*
▲ **EMP:** 46
SQ FT: 18,000
SALES (est): 9.6MM **Privately Held**
WEB: www.movingimagetech.com
SIC: 3861 Motion picture apparatus & equipment

(P-22443)
MPO VIDEOTRONICS INC (PA)
5069 Maureen Ln, Moorpark (93021-7148)
PHONE....................805 499-8513
Larry Kaiser, *President*
Julius Barron, *Vice Pres*
Don Gaston, *Director*
EMP: 75 **EST:** 1947
SALES (est): 9.6MM **Privately Held**
WEB: www.mpo-video.com
SIC: 3861 5065 7819 3823 Motion picture apparatus & equipment; video equipment, electronic; equipment rental, motion picture; industrial instrmnts msrmnt display/control process variable; household audio & video equipment

(P-22444)
MVM PRODUCTS LLC
946 Calle Amanecer Ste E, San Clemente (92673-6221)
P.O. Box 73155 (92673-0105)
PHONE....................949 366-1470
Daniel W Loyer,
Steve L Boden,
Daniel Loyer,
EMP: 81
SQ FT: 76,000
SALES (est): 9.6MM **Privately Held**
SIC: 3861 Toners, prepared photographic (not made in chemical plants)

(P-22445)
OPTOMA TECHNOLOGY INC
47697 Westinghouse Dr # 100, Fremont (94539-7401)
PHONE....................510 897-8600
Robert Sterzing, *Principal*
Hans Wang, *Exec VP*
Gen Page, *Admin Asst*
Brad Langley, *Technical Staff*
Sindy Yip, *Controller*
▲ **EMP:** 120
SQ FT: 34,000
SALES (est): 23.5MM **Privately Held**
WEB: www.optomausa.com
SIC: 3861 Projectors, still or motion picture, silent or sound
HQ: Optoma Corporation
12f, No. 213, Beixin Rd., Sec. 3
New Taipei City TAP 23143

(P-22446)
PANAVISION INC
Also Called: Panavision Hollywood
6735 Selma Ave, Los Angeles (90028-6134)
PHONE....................323 464-3800
Lisa Harp, *Vice Pres*
Natalie Ortiz, *Marketing Staff*
EMP: 55 **Privately Held**

WEB: www.panastore.com
SIC: 3861 Photographic equipment & supplies
PA: Panavision Inc.
6101 Variel Ave
Woodland Hills CA 91367

(P-22447)
PANAVISION INTERNATIONAL LP (HQ)
6101 Variel Ave, Woodland Hills (91367-3722)
P.O. Box 4360 (91365-4360)
PHONE....................818 316-1080
Robert Beitcher, *President*
Ross Landfbuam, *CFO*
▲ **EMP:** 380
SQ FT: 150,000
SALES (est): 124.6MM **Privately Held**
WEB: www.panavision.com
SIC: 3861 Cameras & related equipment

(P-22448)
PHASESPACE INC (PA)
1937 Oak Park Blvd Ste A, Pleasant Hill (94523-4660)
PHONE....................925 945-6533
Tracy McSheery, *CEO*
Charles Luther, *CFO*
Dennis Gates, *Director*
▲ **EMP:** 14
SQ FT: 6,000
SALES (est): 3.1MM **Privately Held**
SIC: 3861 Motion picture apparatus & equipment

(P-22449)
PHOTOFLEX INC
1800 Green Hills Rd # 104, Scotts Valley (95066-4984)
PHONE....................831 786-1370
Eugene Kester, *President*
Renee Chamberlain, *Sales Staff*
▲ **EMP:** 18
SQ FT: 18,835
SALES (est): 4.9MM **Privately Held**
WEB: www.photoflex.com
SIC: 3861 5043 Photographic equipment & supplies; photographic equipment & supplies; cameras & photographic equipment

(P-22450)
PHOTRONICS INC (DH)
Also Called: Photronics California
2428 N Ontario St, Burbank (91504-3119)
PHONE....................203 740-5653
James Mac Donald Jr, *Ch of Bd*
Constantine Maristos, *CEO*
Amy Bentley, *Executive Asst*
Deborah Marshlick, *Technician*
Vicky Zhu, *Manager*
EMP: 280 **EST:** 1970
SQ FT: 30,000
SALES (est): 29.2MM
SALES (corp-wide): 535.2MM **Publicly Held**
SIC: 3861 Photographic equipment & supplies

(P-22451)
PRESTON CINEMA SYSTEMS INC
1659 11th St Ste 100, Santa Monica (90404-3739)
PHONE....................310 453-1852
Howard Preston, *President*
Paul Davi, *Administration*
Alanna Berkson, *Technical Staff*
Mirko Kovacevic, *Engineer*
Leticia De La Torre, *Sales Staff*
EMP: 11
SALES (est): 1.9MM **Privately Held**
WEB: www.prestoncinema.com
SIC: 3861 7359 Motion picture apparatus & equipment; audio-visual equipment & supply rental

(P-22452)
PRINTER CARTRIDGE USA
14276 Barrymore St, San Diego (92129-3304)
PHONE....................858 538-7630
Brad Belland, *Owner*
EMP: 10 **EST:** 2009

SALES (est): 176.9K **Privately Held**
SIC: 3861 Photographic equipment & supplies

(P-22453)
RADEX STEREO CO INC
13228 Crenshaw Blvd, Gardena
(90249-1546)
PHONE......................310 516-9015
Steven Bracker, *President*
Nina Bracker, *Vice Pres*
▲ **EMP:** 10
SQ FT: 6,500
SALES (est): 1.6MM **Privately Held**
WEB: www.radexinc.com
SIC: 3861 Photographic equipment & supplies

(P-22454)
REDCOM LLC (HQ)
Also Called: Red Digital Cinema Camera Co
34 Parker, Irvine (92618-1609)
PHONE......................949 206-7900
James H Jannard, *CEO*
Kevin Cabrera, *Officer*
Peter Coleman, *Officer*
Mike D Executive, *Vice Pres*
Steven Chen, *Administration*
▲ **EMP:** 67
SALES (est): 159.2MM **Privately Held**
SIC: 3861 Motion picture apparatus &
equipment
PA: Red Europe Limited
Pinewood Road
Iver BUCKS
175 378-5454

(P-22455)
RICOH ELECTRONICS INC (DH)
Also Called: Ricoh Development California
1100 Valencia Ave, Tustin (92780-6450)
PHONE......................714 566-2500
Jeffrey A Briwick, *President*
Yoshinori Yamashita, *CEO*
Howard Suzuki, *CFO*
Stephen Hudock, *Executive*
Braden Ruch, *Executive*
◆ **EMP:** 300
SQ FT: 146,000
SALES (est): 431.4MM **Privately Held**
WEB: www.ricohelectronicsinc.com
SIC: 3861 3695 Photocopy machines; toners, prepared photographic (not made in
chemical plants); magnetic & optical
recording media
HQ: Ricoh Usa, Inc.
300 Eagleview Blvd # 200
Exton PA 19341
610 296-8000

(P-22456)
ROSCO LABORATORIES INC
9420 Chivers Ave, Sun Valley
(91352-2654)
PHONE......................800 767-2652
Maria Szots, *Manager*
Katie-Marie O'Connor, *Technology*
Alexander Porvatov, *Accounts Mgr*
EMP: 12 **Privately Held**
SIC: 3861 Photographic equipment & supplies
HQ: Rosco Laboratories, Inc.
52 Harbor View Ave
Stamford CT 06902
203 708-8900

(P-22457)
SA HARTMAN & ASSOCIATES INC
Also Called: S A Hartman Productions
14570 Benefit St, Sherman Oaks
(91403-5508)
PHONE......................818 907-9681
Steve A Hartman, *President*
EMP: 25
SALES: 500K **Privately Held**
SIC: 3861 6211 Motion picture film; investment firm, general brokerage

(P-22458)
STEWART FILMSCREEN CORP (PA)
1161 Sepulveda Blvd, Torrance
(90502-2797)
PHONE......................310 326-1422
Grant W Stewart, *CEO*

Patrick H Stewart, *CEO*
Robert Keeler, *Vice Pres*
Donald R Stewart, *Vice Pres*
Thomas E Stewart, *Vice Pres*
◆ **EMP:** 160 **EST:** 1947
SQ FT: 43,000
SALES (est): 29.2MM **Privately Held**
SIC: 3861 Screens, projection

(P-22459)
SUNRISE IMAGING INC
1813 E Dyer Rd Ste 410, Santa Ana
(92705-5731)
PHONE......................949 252-3003
Dennis Childs, *President*
Robert Lasnik, *Vice Pres*
EMP: 10
SQ FT: 6,000
SALES (est): 1.3MM **Privately Held**
WEB: www.sunreimaging.com
SIC: 3861 Cameras, microfilm; microfilm
equipment: cameras, projectors, readers,
etc.

(P-22460)
SUSS MCRTEC PRCISION PHOTOMASK
Also Called: Image Technology
821 San Antonio Rd, Palo Alto
(94303-4618)
PHONE......................415 494-3113
Frank Averdung, *CEO*
Alex Naderi, *President*
Patricia Christiansen, *CFO*
EMP: 25
SQ FT: 10,000
SALES (est): 3.3MM
SALES (corp-wide): 233.4MM **Privately Held**
WEB: www.sussphotomask.com
SIC: 3861 Photographic equipment & supplies
HQ: Suss Microtec Inc.
220 Klug Cir
Corona CA 92880
408 940-0300

(P-22461)
SWENSON GROUP
Also Called: Swenson Group Inc Xerox
1620 S Amphlett Blvd, San Mateo (94402)
PHONE......................650 655-4990
Dean Swenson, *President*
Danielle Addis, *Office Mgr*
EMP: 15 **Privately Held**
WEB: www.theswensongroup.com
SIC: 3861 Photographic equipment & supplies
PA: The Swenson Group
207 Boeing Ct
Livermore CA 94551

(P-22462)
TECHNICAL FILM SYSTEMS INC
Also Called: T F S
4650 Calle Quetzal, Camarillo
(93012-8558)
PHONE......................805 384-9470
Manfred G Michelson, *President*
Markus Michelson, *Vice Pres*
EMP: 14
SQ FT: 1,800
SALES: 1MM **Privately Held**
WEB: www.techfilmsystems.com
SIC: 3861 Printing equipment, photographic

(P-22463)
TETRACAM INC
21601 Devonshire St # 310, Chatsworth
(91311-8423)
PHONE......................818 718-2119
George Ismael, *President*
John Edling, *Treasurer*
Steve Heinold, *Exec VP*
Dean Shen, *Vice Pres*
Gerry King, *General Mgr*
▲ **EMP:** 16
SQ FT: 4,200
SALES: 1.6MM **Privately Held**
WEB: www.tetracam.com
SIC: 3861 Microfilm equipment: cameras,
projectors, readers, etc.

(P-22464)
THERMAPRINT CORP
11 Autry Ste B, Irvine (92618-2766)
PHONE......................949 583-0800
Natalie J Hochner, *President*
Gary Larsen, *CEO*
▲ **EMP:** 25
SQ FT: 14,500
SALES (est): 3.9MM **Privately Held**
WEB: www.fiberopticdesign.com
SIC: 3861 3443 3585 2759 Graphic arts
plates, sensitized; fabricated plate work
(boiler shop); parts for heating, cooling &
refrigerating equipment; screen printing

(P-22465)
TRANSCENDENT IMAGING LLC
Also Called: Megavision
5765 Thornwood Dr, Goleta (93117-3830)
P.O. Box 60158, Santa Barbara (93160-0158)
PHONE......................805 964-1400
Ken Boydston, *Mng Member*
Lynn Watson, *Admin Sec*
EMP: 13
SQ FT: 4,000
SALES (est): 1.6MM **Privately Held**
SIC: 3861 5731 Cameras & related equipment; video cameras, recorders & accessories

(P-22466)
TRIPRISM INC
15950 Bernardo Center Dr B, San Diego
(92127-1829)
PHONE......................858 675-7552
Tim Justice, *President*
Steve Chua, *CEO*
Serge Caleca, *Admin Sec*
Audrey Lin, *Web Dvlpr*
Todd Langford, *Director*
EMP: 10
SQ FT: 3,800
SALES (est): 1.3MM **Privately Held**
WEB: www.triprism.com
SIC: 3861 Photographic equipment & supplies

(P-22467)
TWO THIRTY TWO PRODUCTINS INC
7108 Katella Ave Ste 440, Stanton
(90680-2803)
PHONE......................714 317-5317
Paul Dillon, *President*
Anna Dillon, *Exec VP*
EMP: 25
SQ FT: 6,500
SALES (est): 1.6MM **Privately Held**
SIC: 3861 Motion picture film

(P-22468)
UNIQ VISION INC
2924 Scott Blvd, Santa Clara (95054-3312)
PHONE......................408 330-0818
Chuck Woo, *President*
Minh Lam, *Vice Pres*
Rex Siu, *Vice Pres*
▲ **EMP:** 110
SALES (est): 10MM **Privately Held**
WEB: www.uniqvision.com
SIC: 3861 Cameras & related equipment

(P-22469)
UNITY SALES INTERNATIONAL INC
Also Called: Unity Digital
2950 Airway Ave Ste A12, Costa Mesa
(92626-6019)
PHONE......................714 800-1700
Timothy McCanna, *President*
EMP: 15
SQ FT: 4,000
SALES (est): 2MM **Privately Held**
WEB: www.unitydigital.com
SIC: 3861 Cameras & related equipment

(P-22470)
VELOCITY IMAGING PRODUCTS INC
8139 Center St, La Mesa (91942-2915)
PHONE......................619 433-8000
Linda Stavola, *CEO*
EMP: 15

SALES (est): 2.1MM **Privately Held**
WEB: www.velocityimagingproducts.com
SIC: 3861 Photocopy machines

(P-22471)
VICTORY STUDIO
1840 Victory Blvd, Glendale (91201-2558)
PHONE......................818 972-0737
John Ankwicz, *Principal*
John Smith, *Owner*
EMP: 10
SALES (est): 1.3MM **Privately Held**
SIC: 3861 Motion picture film

(P-22472)
VITEK INDUS VIDEO PDTS INC
28492 Constellation Rd, Valencia
(91355-5081)
PHONE......................661 294-8043
Greg Bier, *CEO*
Vic Korhonian, *CEO*
▲ **EMP:** 20 **EST:** 1998
SQ FT: 9,200
SALES (est): 4MM **Privately Held**
WEB: www.vitekcctv.com
SIC: 3861 5099 Cameras & related equipment; video & audio equipment

(P-22473)
VONNIC INC
16610 Gale Ave, City of Industry
(91745-1801)
PHONE......................626 964-2345
Kim Por Lin, *CEO*
Kitty Lam, *CFO*
▲ **EMP:** 23
SALES: 7.8MM **Privately Held**
SIC: 3861 Cameras & related equipment

(P-22474)
XEROX CORPORATION
2980 Inland Empire Blvd # 105, Ontario
(91764-6567)
PHONE......................909 605-7900
John Palmer, *Manager*
Melvin Crosby, *Analyst*
Gregory Terry, *Production*
EMP: 10
SALES (corp-wide): 405.1MM **Publicly Held**
WEB: www.xerox.com
SIC: 3861 Photographic equipment & supplies
HQ: Xerox Corporation
201 Merritt 7
Norwalk CT 06851
203 968-3000

3873 Watch & Clock Devices & Parts

(P-22475)
ACCUSPLIT (PA)
1262 Quarry Ln Ste B, Pleasanton
(94566-4733)
PHONE......................925 290-1900
W Ron Sutton, *President*
Byron Dana Lindstrom, *Exec VP*
Curtis Sutton, *Info Tech Dir*
Jan Hansen,
▲ **EMP:** 24
SALES (est): 4.2MM **Privately Held**
WEB: www.pedometer.com
SIC: 3873 3824 Watches & parts, except
crystals & jewels; controls, revolution &
timing instruments; pedometers

(P-22476)
AMG EMPLOYEE MANAGEMENT INC
Also Called: Time Masters
3235 N San Fernando Rd 1d, Los Angeles
(90065-1443)
PHONE......................323 254-7448
Tigran Galstyan, *President*
Matt Livingston, *Technical Staff*
▲ **EMP:** 17
SALES (est): 2.3MM **Privately Held**
SIC: 3873 7371 7372 3579 Timers for industrial use, clockwork mechanism only;
computer software development; business oriented computer software; time
clocks & time recording devices

(P-22477)
BLOCKS WEARABLES INC
1800 Century Park E Fl 10, Los Angeles
(90067-1513)
PHONE..............................650 307-9557
Alireza Tahmasebzadeh, *Director*
EMP: 10
SALES (est): 398.3K **Privately Held**
SIC: 3873 Watchcases

(P-22478)
CALIFORNIA CLOCK CO (PA)
Also Called: Youngs Evergreen Nursery Co
16060 Abajo Gir, Fountain Valley
(92708-1312)
P.O. Box 9901 (92728-0901)
PHONE..............................714 545-4321
Woody Young, *Owner*
EMP: 10
SALES (est): 1.4MM **Privately Held**
WEB: www.californiaclock.com
SIC: 3873 2731 5193 Clocks, assembly
of; books: publishing only; nursery stock

(P-22479)
CHASE-DURER LTD (PA)
8455 Ftn Ave Unit 515, West Hollywood
(90069)
PHONE..............................310 550-7280
Brandon Chase, *President*
Christian Nagata, *Vice Pres*
Fred Goode, *Manager*
▲ EMP: 19 EST: 1997
SALES (est): 1.2MM **Privately Held**
WEB: www.chasedurer.com
SIC: 3873 Watches, clocks, watchcases &
parts

(P-22480)
**CLUB DONATELLO OWNERS
ASSN**
501 Post St, San Francisco (94102-1228)
PHONE..............................415 474-7333
Daryl Clark, *President*
Sherwin David, *Manager*
Mandy Vergara, *Manager*
▲ EMP: 21
SALES (est): 1.9MM **Privately Held**
SIC: 3873 Timers for industrial use, clock-
work mechanism only

(P-22481)
MOD ELECTRONICS INC
Also Called: Ese
142 Sierra St, El Segundo (90245-4117)
PHONE..............................310 322-2136
William Kaiser, *President*
Brian Way, *Vice Pres*
Bill Rajaniemi, *Technical Staff*
Corey Campbell, *Chief Engr*
Fernando Vallin, *Sales Staff*
▲ EMP: 26
SQ FT: 7,500
SALES (est): 4.6MM **Privately Held**
WEB: www.ese-web.com
SIC: 3873 3663 3651 3625 Clocks, as-
sembly of; radio & TV communications
equipment; household audio & video
equipment; relays & industrial controls

(P-22482)
OLIO DEVICES INC
1100 La Avenida St Ste A, Mountain View
(94043-1453)
PHONE..............................650 918-6546
Steven Jacobs, *CEO*
EMP: 27
SALES (est): 3.2MM **Privately Held**
SIC: 3873 Watchcases

(P-22483)
PEBBLE TECHNOLOGY CORP
900 Middlefield Rd Ste 5, Redwood City
(94063-1681)
PHONE..............................888 224-5820
EMP: 44
SALES (est): 18.9MM **Privately Held**
SIC: 3873

(P-22484)
SUNBURST PRODUCTS INC
Also Called: Freestyle
1570 Corporate Dr Ste F, Costa Mesa
(92626-1428)
PHONE..............................949 722-0158

EMP: 40
SQ FT: 12,000
SALES (est): 3.3MM
SALES (corp-wide): 98.7K **Privately Held**
WEB: www.freestyleusa.com
SIC: 3873 3172 3845
HQ: Awc Liquidating Co.
1407 Broadway Rm 400
New York NY 10018
212 221-1177

(P-22485)
TAKANE USA INC (HQ)
369 Van Ness Way Ste 715, Torrance
(90501-6249)
PHONE..............................310 212-1411
Kenji Hanaoka, *President*
▲ EMP: 21
SQ FT: 47,000
SALES (est): 13.1MM **Privately Held**
SIC: 3873 Movements, watch or clock

(P-22486)
VITALE HOME DESIGNS INC
Also Called: Fancy Schmancy Art Frames
24425 Woolsey Canyon Rd # 46, Canoga
Park (91304-1131)
PHONE..............................818 888-2481
Toni Vitale, *President*
EMP: 15
SALES: 96K **Privately Held**
SIC: 3873 Watches, clocks, watchcases &
parts

**3911 Jewelry: Precious
Metal**

(P-22487)
ACE HOLDINGS INC
650 S Hill St Ste 510, Los Angeles
(90014-1753)
PHONE..............................213 972-2100
John Arzoian, *CEO*
Linda Fass, *President*
EMP: 200
SQ FT: 65,000
SALES (est): 18MM **Privately Held**
SIC: 3911 Jewelry, precious metal

(P-22488)
ADRIENNE DESIGNS LLC
Also Called: A/D Enterprises
17150 Newhope St Ste 514, Fountain Val-
ley (92708-4253)
PHONE..............................714 558-1209
Clifford E Johnston, *President*
▲ EMP: 31
SQ FT: 10,000
SALES (est): 4.7MM **Privately Held**
SIC: 3911 Jewelry, precious metal

(P-22489)
ALEX VELVET INC
3334 Eagle Rock Blvd, Los Angeles
(90065-2843)
PHONE..............................323 255-6900
Krikor Alexanian, *President*
Berj Alexanian, *CFO*
▲ EMP: 35
SQ FT: 15,000
SALES (est): 1.2MM **Privately Held**
WEB: www.alexvelvetdisplays.com
SIC: 3911 7319 5046 Jewelry mountings
& trimmings; display advertising service;
store fixtures & display equipment

(P-22490)
ALLISON-KAUFMAN CO
7640 Haskell Ave, Van Nuys (91406-2005)
PHONE..............................818 373-5100
Bart Kaufman, *President*
Jay A Kaufman, *Vice Pres*
Scott Kaufman, *Vice Pres*
Vickie Sober, *Regl Sales Mgr*
Jeffrey Liebich, *Manager*
▲ EMP: 72 EST: 1946
SQ FT: 21,000
SALES (est): 10.4MM **Privately Held**
WEB: www.allison-kaufman.com
SIC: 3911 Jewelry, precious metal

(P-22491)
ALOR INTERNATIONAL LTD
Also Called: Philippe Charriol USA
11696 Sorrento Valley Rd # 101, San Diego
(92121-1024)
PHONE..............................858 454-0011
Jack Zemer, *CEO*
Sandy Zemer, *President*
Tal Zemer, *Officer*
Ori Zemer, *Vice Pres*
▲ EMP: 45
SALES (est): 8.6MM **Privately Held**
WEB: www.charriol-usa.com
SIC: 3911 3172 3915 Vanity cases, pre-
cious metal; personal leather goods; jewel
preparing: instruments, tools, watches &
jewelry

(P-22492)
ALUMA USA INC
435 Tesconi Cir, Santa Rosa (95401-4619)
PHONE..............................707 545-9344
Doron Sharfman, *President*
▲ EMP: 22
SQ FT: 8,867
SALES: 15MM **Privately Held**
WEB: www.alumausa.net
SIC: 3911 Jewelry, precious metal

(P-22493)
AMERICAS GOLD INC
Also Called: Americas Gold - Amrcas Da-
monds
650 S Hill St Ste 224, Los Angeles
(90014-1769)
PHONE..............................213 688-4904
Rafi M Siddiqui, *President*
Samina Siddiqui, *Vice Pres*
Sami Siddiqui, *Manager*
EMP: 30
SQ FT: 4,500
SALES (est): 5.4MM **Privately Held**
WEB: www.americasgold.com
SIC: 3911 Jewelry, precious metal

(P-22494)
**AMINCO INTERNATIONAL USA
INC (PA)**
Also Called: California Premium Incentives
20571 Crescent Bay Dr, Lake Forest
(92630-8825)
PHONE..............................949 457-3261
William Wu, *President*
Ann Wu, *Treasurer*
Steve Ruiz, *Marketing Staff*
John Yarmoski, *Agent*
▲ EMP: 50 EST: 1978
SQ FT: 35,000
SALES (est): 7MM **Privately Held**
WEB: www.amincousa.com
SIC: 3911 5099 Jewelry, precious metal;
brass goods

(P-22495)
ANATOMETAL INC
165 Dubois St, Santa Cruz (95060-2108)
PHONE..............................831 454-9880
Barry Blanchard, *President*
EMP: 40
SALES (est): 6.6MM **Privately Held**
WEB: www.anatometal.com
SIC: 3911 Jewelry, precious metal

(P-22496)
AR CASTING INC
7240 Coldwater Canyon Ave B, North Holly-
wood (91605-4246)
PHONE..............................818 765-1202
Abel Rojas, *President*
EMP: 16
SALES (est): 1.3MM **Privately Held**
WEB: www.aandrcasting.com
SIC: 3911 Jewelry, precious metal

(P-22497)
ARTS ELEGANCE INC
154 W Bellevue Dr, Pasadena
(91105-2504)
PHONE..............................626 793-4794
Arutiun Mikaelian, *President*
EMP: 45
SALES (corp-wide): 8.5MM **Privately
Held**
SIC: 3911 Jewelry, precious metal

PA: Art's Elegance, Inc.
739 E Walnut St Ste 200
Pasadena CA 91101
626 405-1522

(P-22498)
ARZY COMPANY INC
Also Called: Arzy Company Fine Jewelry
650 S Hill St Ste 915, Los Angeles
(90014-1752)
PHONE..............................213 627-7344
Hossein Arzy, *President*
EMP: 10
SALES (est): 1.3MM **Privately Held**
SIC: 3911 3961 Bracelets, precious metal;
costume jewelry, ex. precious metal &
semiprecious stones

(P-22499)
ASTOURIAN JEWELRY MFG INC
635 S Hill St Ste 407, Los Angeles
(90014-1819)
PHONE..............................213 683-0436
Viken Astourian, *President*
▲ EMP: 13
SQ FT: 1,200
SALES (est): 3.5MM **Privately Held**
SIC: 3911 Jewelry, precious metal

(P-22500)
AVE JEWELRY INC
Also Called: Ave Jewelry Design Mfg
13127 Ebell St, North Hollywood
(91605-1006)
PHONE..............................213 488-0097
EMP: 15
SQ FT: 12,300
SALES (est): 1.3MM **Privately Held**
SIC: 3911

(P-22501)
BARGUEIRAS RENE INC
Also Called: R B I
621 S Victory Blvd, Burbank (91502-2424)
PHONE..............................818 500-8288
Rene Bargueiras, *President*
Sena Bargueiras, *Vice Pres*
Angie Vaca, *Controller*
EMP: 12
SQ FT: 1,300
SALES (est): 1.1MM **Privately Held**
WEB: www.rb-inc.com
SIC: 3911 5094 Jewelry apparel;
bracelets, precious metal; earrings, pre-
cious metal; rings, finger: precious metal;
jewelry & precious stones

(P-22502)
BARKEVS INC
707 S Broadway Ste 415, Los Angeles
(90014-2858)
PHONE..............................800 227-7321
Barkev Meserlian, *President*
Seta Ratevosian, *Accountant*
Marina Kurian, *Mktg Dir*
EMP: 10
SALES (est): 991.4K **Privately Held**
WEB: www.barkevs.com
SIC: 3911 5944 Jewelry, precious metal;
jewelry, precious stones & precious met-
als

(P-22503)
BASHOURA INC
539 S Glenwood Ave, Glendora
(91741-3514)
PHONE..............................626 963-7600
Jean Bashoura, *President*
Moussa Bashoura, *Treasurer*
Tony Bashoura, *Vice Pres*
Tania Bashoura, *Admin Sec*
▲ EMP: 11
SQ FT: 5,760
SALES (est): 1.2MM **Privately Held**
WEB: www.bashoura.com
SIC: 3911 Jewelry, precious metal

(P-22504)
BEZ AMBAR INC
611 Wilshire Blvd Ste 607, Los Angeles
(90017-2912)
PHONE..............................213 629-9191
Betzalael Ambar, *President*
▲ EMP: 40
SQ FT: 5,200

▲ = Import ▼ =Export
◆ =Import/Export

SALES (est): 4.1MM **Privately Held**
SIC: 3911 Jewelry, precious metal

(P-22505)
C GONSHOR FINE JEWELRY INC
640 S Hill St Ste 546a, Los Angeles
(90014-4745)
PHONE...................................213 629-1075
Chain Gonshor, *President*
Misha Kottler, *Vice Pres*
EMP: 10
SQ FT: 2,500
SALES (est): 1.2MM **Privately Held**
SIC: 3911 5094 Jewelry apparel; jewelry

(P-22506)
CHARLES LIGETI CO
611 Wilshire Blvd Ste 801, Los Angeles
(90017-2925)
PHONE...................................213 612-0831
Charles Ligeti, *Owner*
Marie Rose Cabrera, *Vice Pres*
Lulu Tupas, *Admin Sec*
Susan Burciaga, *Sales Staff*
EMP: 30 EST: 1957
SQ FT: 1,500
SALES (est): 3.1MM **Privately Held**
WEB: www.charlesligeti.com
SIC: 3911 Rings, finger: precious metal

(P-22507)
CONNERS ORO-CAL MFG CO
1720 Bird St, Oroville (95965-4806)
PHONE...................................530 533-5065
David J Conner, *President*
Susan Y Conner, *Admin Sec*
EMP: 18
SQ FT: 2,850
SALES: 9.2MM **Privately Held**
SIC: 3911 3873 5094 Jewelry, precious
metal; watches, clocks, watchcases &
parts; jewelry & precious stones; clocks,
watches & parts

(P-22508)
CPS GEM CORPORATION
Also Called: C.P.s Fine Gems Jwly Collectn
1327 S Myrtle Ave, Monrovia (91016-4150)
PHONE...................................213 627-4019
Allan Pung, *CEO*
Tina Pung, *President*
EMP: 10
SALES (est): 1.2MM **Privately Held**
WEB: www.cpsgems.com
SIC: 3911 5944 Jewelry, precious metal;
jewelry stores

(P-22509)
CUBIC ZEE JEWELRY INC
728 S Hill St Ste 900, Los Angeles
(90014-2731)
P.O. Box 811695 (90081-0012)
PHONE...................................213 614-9800
Sarkis Ulikyan, *President*
Ovakim Ulikyan, *Vice Pres*
EMP: 11 EST: 2010
SALES (est): 2.2MM **Privately Held**
SIC: 3911 Jewelry, precious metal

(P-22510)
DESIGNED BY SCORPIO INC
550 S Hill St Ste 1605, Los Angeles
(90013-2494)
PHONE...................................213 612-4440
Kirkor Yerganyan, *Partner*
Lena Yerganyan, *Partner*
EMP: 18
SQ FT: 3,000
SALES (est): 1.9MM **Privately Held**
WEB: www.designedbyscorpio.com
SIC: 3911 Jewelry mountings & trimmings

(P-22511)
DIARING INC
550 S Hill St Ste 990, Los Angeles
(90013-2466)
PHONE...................................213 489-3894
Sarju Vora, *President*
Devang Vora, *Vice Pres*
EMP: 10
SQ FT: 1,500
SALES (est): 1MM **Privately Held**
WEB: www.diaring.com
SIC: 3911 5094 5944 Jewelry, precious
metal; jewelry; jewelry, precious stones &
precious metals

(P-22512)
**DOVES JEWELRY
CORPORATION**
2860 N Naomi St, Burbank (91504-2023)
PHONE...................................818 955-8886
Egine Artinian, *President*
Helen Adji-Artinian, *Admin Sec*
EMP: 20
SQ FT: 3,000
SALES (est): 1.3MM **Privately Held**
SIC: 3911 5094 Jewelry, precious metal;
jewelry

(P-22513)
EAR CHARMS INC
Also Called: Ear Gear
1855 Laguna Canyon Rd, Laguna Beach
(92651-1121)
P.O. Box 4289 (92652-4289)
PHONE...................................949 494-4147
Sandra Callisto, *President*
Mike Callisto, *Vice Pres*
George Reynolds, *Director*
EMP: 12
SALES (est): 1.1MM **Privately Held**
WEB: www.earcuff.net
SIC: 3911 5944 Earrings, precious metal;
jewelry, precious stones & precious met-
als

(P-22514)
EJ DIAMONDS INC
631 S Olive St Ste 201, Los Angeles
(90014-3656)
PHONE...................................213 623-2329
Albert Can, *President*
EMP: 10
SALES (est): 763.8K **Privately Held**
SIC: 3911 Jewelry apparel

(P-22515)
ELBA JEWELRY INC
Also Called: Elba Company
910 N Amelia Ave, San Dimas
(91773-1401)
PHONE...................................909 394-5803
Edouard Bachoura, *President*
▼ EMP: 19
SQ FT: 10,000
SALES (est): 2.4MM **Privately Held**
WEB: www.elbainc.com
SIC: 3911 Jewelry, precious metal

(P-22516)
ELEMENTS
20314a Gramercy Pl, Torrance (90501)
PHONE...................................310 781-1384
Derrick Obatake, *Owner*
EMP: 25
SALES (est): 1.6MM **Privately Held**
SIC: 3911 Jewelry, precious metal

(P-22517)
F CONRAD FURLONG INC
Also Called: Furlong, Conrad
550 S Hill St Ste 1620, Los Angeles
(90013-2452)
PHONE...................................213 623-4191
Franklin Conrad Furlong, *President*
Irene Furlong, *Vice Pres*
EMP: 13
SQ FT: 1,600
SALES (est): 1.4MM **Privately Held**
SIC: 3911 Jewelry apparel

(P-22518)
FAITH KNIGHT INC
2340 Mountain Ave, La Crescenta
(91214-3134)
PHONE...................................213 488-1569
Faith Knight, *President*
Raul Banuelos, *Vice Pres*
EMP: 10
SALES: 200K **Privately Held**
SIC: 3911 Jewelry apparel

(P-22519)
FARSI JEWELRY MFG CO INC
631 Suth Olive St Ste 565, Los Angeles
(90014)
PHONE...................................213 624-0043
Yousef Eshaghzadeh, *President*
Masoud Eshaghzadeh, *Treasurer*
Saied Eshaghzadeh, *Admin Sec*
EMP: 13

SALES (est): 2.3MM **Privately Held**
SIC: 3911 Jewelry, precious metal

(P-22520)
GGCO INC
Also Called: Eccentric Jewelry
18380 Ventura Blvd, Tarzana (91356-4219)
PHONE...................................213 623-3636
Ghzaros Ghazarossian, *President*
EMP: 20
SQ FT: 2,400
SALES (est): 1.9MM **Privately Held**
SIC: 3911 Jewelry, precious metal

(P-22521)
GINA DESIGNS
870 Sanitarium Rd, Angwin (94576-9707)
PHONE...................................707 967-1041
EMP: 10 EST: 1991
SALES (est): 563.3K **Privately Held**
SIC: 3911

(P-22522)
GIVING KEYS INC
836 Traction Ave, Los Angeles
(90013-1816)
PHONE...................................213 935-8791
Caitlin Crosby, *CEO*
Brit Gilmore, *President*
▲ EMP: 55 EST: 2012
SQ FT: 8,000
SALES: 7.5MM **Privately Held**
SIC: 3911 Jewelry, precious metal

(P-22523)
GOLD COUTURE 22 K
6406 Kinglet Way, Carlsbad (92011-2700)
PHONE...................................760 602-0690
Himgauri Kulkarni, *Partner*
Raju Katari, *Partner*
EMP: 10
SQ FT: 2,200
SALES: 2MM **Privately Held**
SIC: 3911 5094 Jewel settings & mount-
ings, precious metal; jewelry

(P-22524)
**GOLD CRAFT JEWELRY CORP
(PA)**
Also Called: Gemma Creations
640 S Hill St Ste 650, Los Angeles
(90014-4701)
PHONE...................................213 623-8673
Vahi Urun, *President*
EMP: 14
SQ FT: 12,000
SALES (est): 2.2MM **Privately Held**
WEB: www.goldcraftco.com
SIC: 3911 Earrings, precious metal

(P-22525)
GOLD CRAFT JEWELRY CORP
Also Called: Jewelry Manufacturing
640 S Hill St Ste 650, Los Angeles
(90014-4701)
PHONE...................................213 623-8673
Nuran Urun, *Opers-Prdtn-Mfg*
EMP: 40
SALES (corp-wide): 2.2MM **Privately
Held**
WEB: www.goldcraftco.com
SIC: 3911 3599 Earrings, precious metal;
machine shop, jobbing & repair
PA: Gold Craft Jewelry Corp.
640 S Hill St Ste 650
Los Angeles CA 90014
213 623-8673

(P-22526)
HARTEN JEWELRY CO INC
8213 Villaverde Dr, Whittier (90605-1339)
PHONE...................................562 652-5006
Ofer Harten, *President*
Bessy Harten, *Vice Pres*
EMP: 20
SQ FT: 4,000
SALES (est): 1.8MM **Privately Held**
WEB: www.harten.com
SIC: 3911 5094 Jewelry apparel; jewelry

(P-22527)
HERFF JONES LLC
14321 Goose St, Eastvale (92880-0922)
PHONE...................................951 541-3938
EMP: 15

SALES (corp-wide): 1.1B **Privately Held**
SIC: 3911 Rings, finger: precious metal
HQ: Herff Jones, Llc
4501 W 62nd St
Indianapolis IN 46268
800 419-5462

(P-22528)
HOLLY YASHI INC
1300 9th St, Arcata (95521-5703)
PHONE...................................707 822-0389
Paul S Lubitz, *President*
Holly A Hosterman, *Vice Pres*
Trevor Shirk, *Research*
Danielle Demartini, *Graphic Designe*
Robin Weburg, *Accountant*
▲ EMP: 54
SQ FT: 4,800
SALES (est): 11.4MM **Privately Held**
WEB: www.hollyyashi.com
SIC: 3911 Earrings, precious metal; neck-
laces, precious metal

(P-22529)
HUMIDTECH INC
1241 Johnson Ave Ste 345, San Luis
Obispo (93401-3306)
PHONE...................................805 541-9500
Robin Marks, *President*
EMP: 10 EST: 1996
SQ FT: 6,000
SALES: 750K **Privately Held**
WEB: www.humidtech.com
SIC: 3911 Cigar & cigarette accessories

(P-22530)
ISHARYA INC
4340 Stevens Creek Blvd, San Jose
(95129-1102)
PHONE...................................415 462-6294
Radhika Tandon, *President*
EMP: 25
SQ FT: 10,000
SALES (est): 2.3MM **Privately Held**
SIC: 3911 Jewelry, precious metal

(P-22531)
JEWELRY CLUB HOUSE INC
606 S Olive St Ste 2000, Los Angeles
(90014-1656)
PHONE...................................213 362-7888
Lo Huang, *President*
Victor Han, *CEO*
John Han, *CFO*
▲ EMP: 15
SALES (est): 904.2K **Privately Held**
SIC: 3911 Jewelry, precious metal

(P-22532)
JEWELS BY ANGELO INC
9221 Rives Ave, Downey (90240-2658)
PHONE...................................562 862-6293
Angelo R Cardono, *President*
EMP: 15
SQ FT: 10,180
SALES (est): 2.1MM **Privately Held**
WEB: www.jewelsbyangelo.com
SIC: 3911 Jewelry, precious metal

(P-22533)
JOSTENS INC
Also Called: Jostens Printing & Publishing
231 S Kelsey St, Visalia (93291-7973)
P.O. Box 991 (93279-0991)
PHONE...................................559 622-5200
Bruce Mortan, *Branch Mgr*
EMP: 180
SQ FT: 10,000
SALES (corp-wide): 1.4B **Privately Held**
WEB: www.jostens.com
SIC: 3911 Rings, finger: precious metal
HQ: Jostens, Inc.
7760 France Ave S Ste 400
Minneapolis MN 55435
952 830-3300

(P-22534)
KESMOR ASSOCIATES
Also Called: American Designs
610 S Broadway Ste 717, Los Angeles
(90014-1814)
PHONE...................................213 629-2300
Joseph Keshoyan, *President*
Hasmik Keshoyan, *Vice Pres*
EMP: 20
SQ FT: 6,000

SALES (est): 2.1MM **Privately Held**
SIC: 3911 Jewelry, precious metal

(P-22535)
KITSCH LLC (PA)
307 N New Hampshire Ave, Los Angeles (90004-3408)
PHONE..............................424 240-5551
Cassandra Morales Thurswell, *CEO*
Jeremy Thurswell, *President*
Rica Romanes, *Production*
▲ EMP: 12
SQ FT: 5,000
SALES (est): 1.5MM **Privately Held**
SIC: 3911 5131 5094 Jewelry, precious metal; hair accessories; jewelry

(P-22536)
KOBI KATZ INC
Also Called: Baguette World
801 S Flower St Fl 3, Los Angeles (90017-4617)
PHONE..............................213 689-9505
Kobi Katz, *President*
Eli Sandberg, *Treasurer*
Manuel Valencia, *Accounts Exec*
EMP: 62 EST: 1981
SQ FT: 14,000
SALES (est): 9.3MM **Privately Held**
SIC: 3911 5094 Jewelry apparel; diamonds (gems)

(P-22537)
LA GEM AND JWLY DESIGN INC
Also Called: La Rocks
659 S Broadway Fl 7, Los Angeles (90014-2291)
PHONE..............................213 488-1290
Joseph W Behney, *CEO*
Ashish Arora, *CFO*
Elsa Behney, *Admin Sec*
▲ EMP: 100
SQ FT: 10,000
SALES (est): 35.2MM **Privately Held**
SIC: 3911 5094 Jewelry, precious metal; jewelry

(P-22538)
LEGACY BANDS INC
13261 Paxton St, Pacoima (91331-2357)
PHONE..............................818 890-2527
Aram Naobandain, *President*
▲ EMP: 10
SALES: 500K **Privately Held**
WEB: www.legacybands.com
SIC: 3911 Jewelry, precious metal

(P-22539)
LEONARD CRAFT CO LLC
3501 W Segerstrom Ave, Santa Ana (92704-6449)
PHONE..............................714 549-0678
Stephen D Leonard, *Mng Member*
EMP: 95
SALES (est): 10.6MM **Privately Held**
SIC: 3911 5947 Jewelry, precious metal; gift shop

(P-22540)
LINX BRACELETS INC
Also Called: Linx & More
23147 Ventura Blvd # 250, Woodland Hills (91364-1112)
PHONE..............................818 224-4050
Gina Eckstein, *CEO*
Ivette Helfend, *President*
Cheryl Bloxberg, *COO*
Alexandra Legaspi, *Cust Mgr*
EMP: 12
SQ FT: 2,400
SALES (est): 1.4MM **Privately Held**
WEB: www.linxandmore.com
SIC: 3911 5094 Jewelry, precious metal; jewelry & precious stones

(P-22541)
LIVINGSTONE JEWELRY CO INC
631 S Olive St Ste 340, Los Angeles (90014-3656)
PHONE..............................213 683-1040
Jim Shaw, *President*
EMP: 10
SQ FT: 800

SALES (est): 1.1MM **Privately Held**
WEB: www.livingstonejewelry.com
SIC: 3911 5944 Jewelry, precious metal; jewelry stores

(P-22542)
LUMINAR CREATIONS
420 N Moss St, Burbank (91502-1726)
PHONE..............................818 843-0010
Joseph Toobi, *President*
Daniel Toobi, *Corp Secy*
Jonathan Toobi, *Accounts Exec*
EMP: 30
SQ FT: 8,000
SALES (est): 3.8MM **Privately Held**
SIC: 3911 Jewelry, precious metal

(P-22543)
M & H CREATIVE DESIGN INC
550 N Hill St Ste 1030, Los Angeles (90013-1881)
PHONE..............................213 627-8881
Fax: 213 627-5999
EMP: 10
SQ FT: 1,000
SALES (est): 800K **Privately Held**
SIC: 3911

(P-22544)
MAKSE INC
Also Called: K&M Jewellery
52 E Santa Anita Ave, Burbank (91502-1962)
PHONE..............................213 622-5030
Karapet Naapatyan, *President*
EMP: 16
SQ FT: 3,500
SALES (est): 2.5MM **Privately Held**
SIC: 3911 5094 Jewelry, precious metal; jewelry

(P-22545)
MALCOLM DEMILLE INC
650 S Frontage Rd, Nipomo (93444-9148)
PHONE..............................805 929-4353
Malcolm Demille, *President*
Janet Demille, *Vice Pres*
Phil Scorsone, *Purchasing*
EMP: 15
SALES (est): 1.9MM **Privately Held**
WEB: www.mdemille.com
SIC: 3911 Jewelry mountings & trimmings

(P-22546)
MANUFACTURING USA ENTERPRISES
4220 San Fernando Rd, Glendale (91204-2520)
PHONE..............................818 409-3070
Manuel Galachyan, *President*
Naira Galachyan, *Admin Sec*
EMP: 28
SALES (est): 4.5MM **Privately Held**
SIC: 3911 Jewel settings & mountings, precious metal

(P-22547)
MASTINI DESIGNS
9454 Wilshire Blvd # 600, Beverly Hills (90212-2931)
PHONE..............................800 979-4848
Shahrad Tabibzadeh, *President*
Farokh Tabibzadeh, *Corp Secy*
Mahasti Tabibzadeh, *Vice Pres*
EMP: 10
SQ FT: 1,000
SALES (est): 1.3MM **Privately Held**
WEB: www.mastini.com
SIC: 3911 5094 Jewelry apparel; diamonds (gems); precious stones (gems)

(P-22548)
MERIDIAN JEWELRY & DESIGN INC
3814 La Cresta Ave, Oakland (94602-1727)
PHONE..............................510 428-2095
Lynn B Olander, *CEO*
Lynn Olander, *President*
Brad Olander, *CEO*
EMP: 17
SALES (est): 1.5MM **Privately Held**
SIC: 3911 Jewelry, precious metal

(P-22549)
MICHELLE ALISA DESIGNS INC
Also Called: Alisa Michelle Designs
4528 Van Noord Ave, Studio City (91604-1013)
PHONE..............................818 501-9300
Alisa M Taxe, *CEO*
EMP: 15 EST: 1998
SALES (est): 1.6MM **Privately Held**
WEB: www.alisamichelle.com
SIC: 3911 Jewelry apparel

(P-22550)
MODERN GOLD DESIGN INC
Also Called: Aaagolddesigns
650 S Hill St Ste 509, Los Angeles (90014-1753)
PHONE..............................213 614-1818
Movses Khayoyan, *President*
EMP: 20
SQ FT: 5,000
SALES (est): 2.2MM **Privately Held**
WEB: www.aaagolddesigns.com
SIC: 3911 5944 Jewelry, precious metal; jewelry stores

(P-22551)
MONTBLANC NORTH AMERICA LLC
Also Called: Montblanc Santa Clara
2855 Stevens Creek Blvd, Santa Clara (95050-6709)
PHONE..............................408 241-5188
Cindy Lawler, *Branch Mgr*
EMP: 12
SALES (corp-wide): 15.7B **Privately Held**
SIC: 3911 Mountings, gold or silver: pens, leather goods, etc.
HQ: Montblanc North America, Llc
645 5th Ave Fl 6
New York NY 10022

(P-22552)
NAREG JEWELRY INC
640 S Hill St Ste 542a, Los Angeles (90014-4704)
PHONE..............................213 683-1660
Greg Iskanian, *President*
EMP: 30
SQ FT: 5,000
SALES (est): 2.6MM **Privately Held**
SIC: 3911 Jewelry, precious metal

(P-22553)
NATIONWIDE JEWELRY MFRS INC
Also Called: B & B Jewelry Mfg
631 S Olive St Ste 790, Los Angeles (90014-3607)
PHONE..............................213 489-1215
Ben Behnam, *CEO*
Behrooz Behnam, *Vice Pres*
Parviz Behnam, *Vice Pres*
▲ EMP: 16
SQ FT: 4,000
SALES (est): 3MM **Privately Held**
SIC: 3911 5094 Jewelry, precious metal; jewelry

(P-22554)
NEW CENTURY GOLD LLC
6303 Owensmouth Ave Fl 10, Woodland Hills (91367-2262)
PHONE..............................818 936-2676
Derek Lee, *Mng Member*
EMP: 10
SALES (est): 845.4K **Privately Held**
SIC: 3911 Jewelry, precious metal

(P-22555)
NEW GOLD MANUFACTURING INC
2150 N Lincoln St, Burbank (91504-3337)
PHONE..............................818 847-1020
Mesrop Samvelian, *CEO*
▲ EMP: 60
SALES (est): 6.4MM **Privately Held**
SIC: 3911 Jewelry, precious metal

(P-22556)
OBATAKE INC
Also Called: Lucy Ann
20309 Gramercy Pl Ste A, Torrance (90501-1531)
PHONE..............................310 782-2730
Derrick Obatake, *President*
EMP: 20
SALES: 5MM **Privately Held**
WEB: www.lucyann.com
SIC: 3911 5084 Jewelry, precious metal; industrial machinery & equipment

(P-22557)
PACIFIC JEWELRY SERVICES
606 S Olive St, Los Angeles (90014-1623)
PHONE..............................213 627-3337
Richard Trujillo, *Owner*
▲ EMP: 45
SALES (est): 4.4MM **Privately Held**
SIC: 3911 Jewelry, precious metal

(P-22558)
PADILLA JEWELERS INC
6118 Venice Blvd Fl 2, Los Angeles (90034-2227)
PHONE..............................323 931-1678
Manuel Padilla Jr, *President*
EMP: 14
SALES (est): 2.5MM **Privately Held**
SIC: 3911 Jewelry, precious metal; jewelry apparel

(P-22559)
QJM CORP
606 S Olive St Ste 2170, Los Angeles (90014-1695)
PHONE..............................213 622-0264
Meenu Agarwal, *President*
Rajiv Agarwal, *Vice Pres*
EMP: 12
SALES (est): 930K **Privately Held**
WEB: www.qjmcorp.com
SIC: 3911 Jewelry, precious metal

(P-22560)
QUAD R TECH
521 W Rosecrans Ave, Gardena (90248-1514)
PHONE..............................310 851-6161
Vlademmer Reil, *President*
EMP: 150
SALES (est): 13.2MM **Privately Held**
SIC: 3911 Earrings, precious metal

(P-22561)
RANI JEWELS INC
1249 Quarry Ln Ste 100, Pleasanton (94566-8410)
PHONE..............................408 516-6807
Radha Sharma, *CEO*
EMP: 10
SALES (est): 757.8K **Privately Held**
SIC: 3911 Jewelry, precious metal

(P-22562)
RICHLINE GROUP INC
455 N Moss St, Burbank (91502-1727)
PHONE..............................818 848-5555
Bob Wagner, *Principal*
EMP: 198
SALES (corp-wide): 225.3B **Publicly Held**
WEB: www.aurafin.net
SIC: 3911 Necklaces, precious metal
HQ: Richline Group, Inc.
1385 Broadway Fl 14
New York NY 10018

(P-22563)
RICHLINE GROUP INC
Also Called: Aurafin Oroamerica
443 N Varney St, Burbank (91502-1733)
P.O. Box 7340 (91510-7340)
PHONE..............................818 848-5555
Guy Benhamou, *Branch Mgr*
EMP: 198
SALES (corp-wide): 225.3B **Publicly Held**
SIC: 3911 Necklaces, precious metal
HQ: Richline Group, Inc.
1385 Broadway Fl 14
New York NY 10018

(P-22564)
RJ JEWELRY INC
Also Called: Rubens Jewelry Mfg
650 S Hill St Ste 414, Los Angeles
(90014-1773)
PHONE.....................213 627-9936
Gevork Karapetian, *President*
Diana Karapetian, *Vice Pres*
Ruben Karapetian, *Vice Pres*
EMP: 14
SQ FT: 3,000
SALES: 923.2K **Privately Held**
SIC: 3911 5094 Jewelry, precious metal;
precious metals

(P-22565)
ROBERTO MARTINEZ INC
1050 Calle Cordillera # 103, San Clemente
(92673-6240)
PHONE.....................800 257-6462
Roberto Martinez, *CEO*
Elsa Martinez-Phillips, *President*
▲ **EMP:** 15
SQ FT: 6,000
SALES (est): 2.3MM **Privately Held**
WEB: www.rminc.ws
SIC: 3911 5094 Jewelry apparel; jewelry

(P-22566)
SAGE GODDESS INC
3830 Del Amo Blvd Ste 102, Torrance
(90503-2119)
PHONE.....................650 733-6639
Athena I Perrakis, *CEO*
David Maeizlik, *COO*
EMP: 42
SQ FT: 12,000
SALES (est): 2.4MM **Privately Held**
SIC: 3911 5944 5999 Jewelry apparel;
jewelry, precious stones & precious met-
als; perfumes & colognes

(P-22567)
SAGE MACHADO INC
133 N Gramercy Pl, Los Angeles
(90004-4013)
PHONE.....................323 931-0595
Sage Machado, *President*
EMP: 12
SQ FT: 2,600
SALES (est): 1.3MM **Privately Held**
WEB: www.sagejewelry.com
SIC: 3911 5944 5999 5621 Jewelry, pre-
cious metal; jewelry stores; perfumes &
colognes; boutiques

(P-22568)
SAKS STYLING INCORPORATED
Also Called: Charm America
641 W Harvard St, Glendale (91204-1107)
PHONE.....................818 244-0540
Sarkis Andreasian, *President*
Adrian Andreasian, *Admin Sec*
EMP: 30
SQ FT: 10,000
SALES: 5MM **Privately Held**
SIC: 3911 Jewelry, precious metal

(P-22569)
SAUSALITO CRAFTWORKS INC
Also Called: Omnirax
2342 Marinship Way, Sausalito
(94965-1463)
P.O. Box 1792 (94966-1792)
PHONE.....................415 331-4031
David Holland, *Branch Mgr*
EMP: 12
SALES (corp-wide): 1.7MM **Privately
Held**
WEB: www.sausalitocraft.com
SIC: 3911 2522 Jewelry, precious metal;
office furniture, except wood
PA: Sausalito Craftworks, Inc.
2330 Marinship Way # 160
Sausalito CA
415 332-3392

(P-22570)
**SCHNEIDERS DEISGN STUDIO
INC**
Also Called: Dave Schneider's Fine Jewelry
245 The Promenade N Fl 2, Long Beach
(90802-3179)
PHONE.....................562 437-0448
Mark Schneider, *President*
▲ **EMP:** 16 **EST:** 1946

SQ FT: 5,000
SALES (est): 2.3MM **Privately Held**
SIC: 3911 5094 Jewelry, precious metal;
jewelry

(P-22571)
SGB HOLDINGS LLC
Also Called: Secured Gold Buyers
7 Balboa Cvs, Newport Beach
(92663-3226)
PHONE.....................949 722-1149
Ryan Knott, *Mng Member*
EMP: 41 **EST:** 2008
SALES (est): 3.4MM **Privately Held**
SIC: 3911 Jewelry, precious metal

(P-22572)
SOLID 21 INCORPORATED
Also Called: 2 Awesome International
22287 Mulholland Hwy # 82, Calabasas
(91302-5157)
PHONE.....................213 688-0900
Christopher Aire, *President*
EMP: 16
SALES (est): 10MM **Privately Held**
SIC: 3911 5944 7631 Jewelry, precious
metal; jewelry, precious stones & precious
metals; watch, clock & jewelry repair

(P-22573)
STAR RING INC
Also Called: Romance Ring
4429 Summerglen Ct, Moorpark
(93021-2744)
PHONE.....................818 773-4900
Kenneth Harrison, *President*
▲ **EMP:** 60
SQ FT: 10,000
SALES (est): 14.7MM **Privately Held**
WEB: www.starringinc.com
SIC: 3911 Jewelry, precious metal

(P-22574)
STATUS COLLECTION & CO INC
8383 Wilshire Blvd # 112, Beverly Hills
(90211-2404)
PHONE.....................310 432-7788
Jeremiah Spielman, *President*
EMP: 10
SQ FT: 2,100
SALES (est): 1.2MM **Privately Held**
SIC: 3911 Jewelry, precious metal

(P-22575)
STUDIO 311 INC
466 Primero Ct Ste E, Cotati (94931-3036)
P.O. Box 179 (94931-0179)
PHONE.....................707 795-6599
Katherine Aberle, *President*
EMP: 12
SALES (est): 1.4MM **Privately Held**
SIC: 3911 Jewelry, precious metal

(P-22576)
SUNRISE JEWELRY MFG CORP
4425 Convoy St Ste 226, San Diego
(92111-3731)
PHONE.....................619 270-5624
Sol Levy, *President*
EMP: 329
SALES (est): 22.1MM **Privately Held**
SIC: 3911 Jewelry, precious metal

(P-22577)
**TARINA TARANTINO DESIGNS
LLC**
910 S Broadway Fl 6, Los Angeles
(90015-1610)
PHONE.....................213 533-8070
Alfonso Campos, *General Mgr*
Tarina Tarantino, *Creative Dir*
▲ **EMP:** 10 **EST:** 1996
SQ FT: 2,200
SALES (est): 1.9MM **Privately Held**
WEB: www.tarinatarantino.com
SIC: 3911 Jewelry, precious metal

(P-22578)
TERRYBERRY COMPANY LLC
25600 Rye Canyon Rd # 109, Santa Clarita
(91355-1166)
PHONE.....................661 257-9971
EMP: 60
SALES (corp-wide): 42.2MM **Privately
Held**
SIC: 3911 Jewelry, precious metal

PA: Terryberry Company, Llc
2033 Oak Industrial Dr Ne
Grand Rapids MI 49505
616 458-1391

(P-22579)
THREE SISTERS DESIGN INC
Also Called: Three Sisters Jewelry Design
967 S Coast Highway 101, Encinitas
(92024-4443)
PHONE.....................760 230-2813
Zoe Mohler, *CEO*
EMP: 15 **EST:** 2013
SQ FT: 1,600
SALES: 1.1MM **Privately Held**
SIC: 3911 Jewelry apparel

(P-22580)
TK AND COMPANY WATCHES
5827 W Pico Blvd, Los Angeles
(90019-3714)
PHONE.....................213 545-1971
EMP: 15
SALES (est): 656.6K **Privately Held**
SIC: 3911

(P-22581)
US GOLD TRADING INC (PA)
117 E Providencia Ave, Burbank
(91502-1922)
PHONE.....................818 558-7766
Sarkis Adamian, *CEO*
EMP: 14
SQ FT: 25,000
SALES (est): 1.1MM **Privately Held**
SIC: 3911 Jewelry, precious metal

(P-22582)
VAPE CRAFT LLC
2100 Palomar Airpt Rd # 210, Carlsbad
(92011-4402)
PHONE.....................760 295-7484
Ben Osmanson, *Mng Member*
EMP: 27
SALES (est): 845.5K **Privately Held**
SIC: 3911 Cigar & cigarette accessories

(P-22583)
VOGT WESTERN SILVER LTD
1210 Commerce Ave Ste 1, Woodland
(95776-5927)
P.O. Box 1129 (95776-1129)
PHONE.....................530 669-6840
Chester N Vogt, *President*
Casey Vogt, *Vice Pres*
Linda Baldwin, *Production*
EMP: 10 **EST:** 1970
SQ FT: 5,000
SALES (est): 1.6MM **Privately Held**
WEB: www.vogtsilversmiths.com
SIC: 3911 3199 Jewelry, precious metal;
leather belting & strapping

(P-22584)
**WESTERN IMPERIAL TRADING
INC**
Also Called: Imperial Designs
13946 Ventura Blvd, Sherman Oaks
(91423-3530)
PHONE.....................818 907-0768
Jacob Killedjian, *President*
EMP: 10 **EST:** 1975
SQ FT: 1,500
SALES (est): 1MM **Privately Held**
SIC: 3911 Jewelry, precious metal

(P-22585)
Y Y K INC
Also Called: Kim's Jewelry Manufacturer
411 W 7th St Ste 710, Los Angeles
(90014-3615)
PHONE.....................213 622-0741
Yun Bu Kim, *President*
Young Ye Kim, *Admin Sec*
▼ **EMP:** 15
SQ FT: 1,500
SALES (est): 1.6MM **Privately Held**
SIC: 3911 Jewelry, precious metal

(P-22586)
YERMA JEWELRY MFG INC
671 W Broadway, Glendale (91204-1007)
PHONE.....................818 551-0690
Hagob Yermanez, *President*
EMP: 50

SALES (est): 3.8MM **Privately Held**
SIC: 3911 Bracelets, precious metal

(P-22587)
**ZALEMARK HOLDING COMPANY
INC**
15260 Ventura Blvd # 120, Sherman Oaks
(91403-5307)
P.O. Box 280725, Northridge (91328-0725)
PHONE.....................888 682-6885
Xia Wu, *CEO*
Charels Baron, *CFO*
Caren Currier, *CFO*
Steven Zale, *Corp Secy*
EMP: 11
SQ FT: 1,000
SALES (est): 1.1MM **Privately Held**
SIC: 3911 5094 Jewelry, precious metal;
jewelry

3914 Silverware, Plated & Stainless Steel Ware

(P-22588)
CAL SIMBA INC (PA)
1680 Universe Cir, Oxnard (93033-2441)
PHONE.....................805 240-1177
Jay Schechter, *CEO*
John Stout, *Corp Secy*
Stuart Seeler, *Vice Pres*
Austin Fongemie, *Technician*
Alessia Sega, *Purchasing*
▲ **EMP:** 38
SQ FT: 18,000
SALES (est): 8.7MM **Privately Held**
SIC: 3914 2672 3452 2821 Trophies,
plated (all metals); tape (unprinted),
gummed: made from purchased materi-
als; pins; polyurethane resins; silk screen
design

(P-22589)
DYLN LIFESTYLE LLC
Also Called: Dyln Inspired
18242 Mcdurmott W Ste A, Irvine
(92614-4771)
PHONE.....................949 209-9401
Dorian Ayres,
▲ **EMP:** 15 **EST:** 2011
SALES (est): 1.9MM **Privately Held**
SIC: 3914 Stainless steel ware

(P-22590)
STEELCRAFT WEST
14575 Yorba Ave, Chino (91710-5710)
P.O. Box 981268, El Paso TX (79998-
1268)
PHONE.....................909 548-2696
Dwight White, *General Mgr*
EMP: 13
SALES (est): 1.8MM **Privately Held**
SIC: 3914 Holloware, stainless steel

(P-22591)
STREIVOR INC
Also Called: Streivor Air Systems
2150 Kitty Hawk Rd, Livermore
(94551-9522)
PHONE.....................925 960-9090
Jeffrey S Lambertson, *CEO*
EMP: 18
SQ FT: 35,250
SALES (est): 4.3MM **Privately Held**
SIC: 3914 Stainless steel ware

3915 Jewelers Findings & Lapidary Work

(P-22592)
AM CASTENADA INC
1450 University Ave Ste P, Riverside
(92507-4432)
PHONE.....................951 686-3966
EMP: 13
SALES (corp-wide): 10.9MM **Privately
Held**
SIC: 3915 Lapidary work & diamond cut-
ting & polishing
PA: Am Castenada Inc
1090 Third Ave Ste 19
Chula Vista CA 91911
619 498-1042

(P-22593)
BEAUDRY INTERNATIONAL LLC
3835 E Thousand Oaks Blvd, Westlake Village (91362-3637)
PHONE...................213 623-5025
Frank Lucero, *Mng Member*
EMP: 10
SALES (est): 1.3MM **Privately Held**
SIC: 3915 Diamond cutting & polishing

(P-22594)
CGM INC
Also Called: Cgm Findings
19611 Ventura Blvd # 211, Tarzana (91356-2907)
PHONE...................818 609-7088
Devinder Bindra, *CEO*
Imelda Provenzano, *Accounts Mgr*
▲ EMP: 25
SQ FT: 12,000
SALES (est): 3.5MM **Privately Held**
WEB: www.cgmfindings.com
SIC: 3915 5094 Jewelers' materials & lapidary work; precious metals; precious stones (gems); precious stones & metals

(P-22595)
FRESNO GEM & MINERAL SOCIETY
340 W Olive Ave, Fresno (93728-2927)
P.O. Box 9608 (93793-9608)
PHONE...................559 486-7280
Newman Gill, *President*
EMP: 12
SALES: 74.5K **Privately Held**
SIC: 3915 Lapidary work, contract or other

(P-22596)
HING WA LEE INC
19811 Colima Rd, Walnut (91789-3421)
PHONE...................909 595-3500
David Lee, *CEO*
EMP: 20
SALES (corp-wide): 4.3MM **Privately Held**
SIC: 3915 Jewelers' materials & lapidary work
PA: Hing Wa Lee, Inc.
19345 San Jose Ave
City Of Industry CA 91748
909 869-0900

(P-22597)
KIM SENG JEWELRY INC
818 N Broadway Ste 202, Los Angeles (90012-2342)
PHONE...................213 628-8566
Minh Chang, *President*
▲ EMP: 15
SQ FT: 1,400
SALES (est): 1.4MM **Privately Held**
SIC: 3915 Jewel cutting, drilling, polishing, recutting or setting

(P-22598)
NELSON JEWELLERY (USA) INC
631 S Olive St Ste 300, Los Angeles (90014-3637)
PHONE...................213 489-3323
Eddie Chung, *President*
▲ EMP: 18
SALES (est): 2.3MM **Privately Held**
SIC: 3915 Jewelers' materials & lapidary work

(P-22599)
RAMONA MINING & MANUFACTURING
Also Called: Craftstones
505 Elm St, Ramona (92065-1913)
P.O. Box 847 (92065-0847)
PHONE...................760 789-1620
Herbert Walters, *President*
Stephen Walters, *Vice Pres*
Mary Walters, *Admin Sec*
◆ EMP: 18 EST: 1953
SQ FT: 12,500
SALES (est): 2.2MM **Privately Held**
WEB: www.craftstones.com
SIC: 3915 Jewelers' materials & lapidary work

(P-22600)
ROBERT SNELL CAST SPECIALIST
110 Spring Hill Dr Ste 20, Grass Valley (95945-5928)
PHONE...................530 273-8958
Robert Snell, *Owner*
Debra Snell, *Co-Owner*
EMP: 12
SALES (est): 760K **Privately Held**
SIC: 3915 Jewelers' castings

(P-22601)
STARDUST DIAMOND CORP
Also Called: Diamonds By Design
550 S Hill St Ste 1420, Los Angeles (90013-2415)
PHONE...................213 239-9999
Gall Raiman, *President*
Albert Gad, *Shareholder*
Janet Guttmann, *CFO*
EMP: 15
SQ FT: 3,600
SALES (est): 1.7MM **Privately Held**
WEB: www.stardustdiamonds.com
SIC: 3915 5094 Jewelers' findings & materials; diamond cutting & polishing; diamonds (gems)

(P-22602)
STEINHAUSEN INC
28478 Westinghouse Pl, Valencia (91355-0929)
PHONE...................661 702-1400
▲ EMP: 12
SALES (est): 1.2MM **Privately Held**
WEB: www.steinhauseninc.com
SIC: 3915

(P-22603)
THAT CASTING PLACE INC
6229 Outlook Ave, Los Angeles (90042-3531)
PHONE...................323 258-5691
Antonio Campopiano, *President*
Isabella Campopiano, *Vice Pres*
EMP: 10
SQ FT: 3,000
SALES (est): 560K **Privately Held**
SIC: 3915 Jewelers' castings

3931 Musical Instruments

(P-22604)
AGOURA MUSIC
625 N Sycamore Ave # 313, Los Angeles (90036-2043)
PHONE...................818 991-8316
Nima Azizi, *President*
EMP: 15
SALES (est): 1.6MM **Privately Held**
WEB: www.agouramusic.com
SIC: 3931 8299 Musical instruments; musical instrument lessons

(P-22605)
ALEMBIC INC
3005 Wiljan Ct Ste A, Santa Rosa (95407-5702)
PHONE...................707 523-2611
Susan L Wickersham, *President*
Ron Wickersham, *Treasurer*
EMP: 15 EST: 1969
SQ FT: 12,472
SALES (est): 2.1MM **Privately Held**
WEB: www.alembic.com
SIC: 3931 5736 Guitars & parts, electric & nonelectric; musical instrument stores

(P-22606)
AQUARIAN ACCESSORIES CORP
Also Called: Aquarian Drumheads
1140 N Tustin Ave, Anaheim (92807-1735)
PHONE...................714 632-0230
Ronald Marquez, *President*
Dave Donahue, *Treasurer*
Ray Burns, *Vice Pres*
Rose Marquez, *Admin Sec*
Gabe Diaz, *Sales Mgr*
EMP: 20
SQ FT: 20,000
SALES (est): 3.3MM **Privately Held**
SIC: 3931 Percussion instruments & parts

(P-22607)
AUDIO IMPRESSIONS INC
6592 Oak Springs Dr, Oak Park (91377-3828)
PHONE...................818 532-7360
Christopher L Stone, *President*
Leslie Stone, *Treasurer*
EMP: 13
SALES (est): 1.1MM **Privately Held**
WEB: www.audioimpressions.com
SIC: 3931 Musical instruments, electric & electronic

(P-22608)
AXL MUSICAL INSTRUMENTS LTD
31067 San Clemente St, Hayward (94544-7813)
P.O. Box 808, Brisbane (94005-0808)
PHONE...................415 508-1398
Liu WEI Guo, *Branch Mgr*
EMP: 155 **Privately Held**
WEB: www.axlusa.com
SIC: 3931 5736 Musical instruments; musical instrument stores
PA: Shanghai Chaobo Industrial Co., Ltd.
No.2411, Xinjian No.1 Rd., Xuhang Town, Jiading Dist.
Shanghai 20180

(P-22609)
BBE SOUND INC (PA)
Also Called: G & L Musical Instruments
2548 Fender Ave Ste D, Fullerton (92831-4439)
PHONE...................714 897-6766
John C McLaren, *CEO*
John T Davey, *CFO*
David C McLaren, *Exec VP*
Paul Gagon, *Vice Pres*
Robert Ruzzito, *Vice Pres*
▲ EMP: 22
SQ FT: 10,000
SALES (est): 5.5MM **Privately Held**
SIC: 3931 3651 Guitars & parts, electric & nonelectric; amplifiers: radio, public address or musical instrument: microphones

(P-22610)
BOULDER CREEK GUITARS INC
5810 Obata Way Ste 1, Gilroy (95020-7039)
PHONE...................408 842-0222
Jeffrey Paul Strametz, *CEO*
EMP: 14 EST: 2014
SQ FT: 6,700
SALES (est): 1.9MM **Privately Held**
SIC: 3931 5099 Guitars & parts, electric & nonelectric; musical instruments

(P-22611)
DEERING BANJO COMPANY INC
3733 Kenora Dr, Spring Valley (91977-1206)
PHONE...................619 464-8252
Charles Greg Deering, *President*
Janet Deering, *Corp Secy*
Julie Luciano, *Finance*
David Bandrowski, *Marketing Staff*
▲ EMP: 40
SQ FT: 18,000
SALES (est): 6.5MM **Privately Held**
WEB: www.deeringbanjos.com
SIC: 3931 Banjos & parts

(P-22612)
DIGITAL MUSIC CORPORATION
3165 Coffey Ln, Santa Rosa (95403-2502)
PHONE...................707 545-0600
Joshua C Fiden, *President*
▲ EMP: 12
SQ FT: 2,400
SALES (est): 940K **Privately Held**
WEB: www.voodoolab.com
SIC: 3931 Musical instruments, electric & electronic

(P-22613)
DRUM WORKSHOP INC (PA)
Also Called: Dw Drum
3450 Lunar Ct, Oxnard (93030-8976)
PHONE...................805 485-6999
Christopher D Lombardi, *CEO*

Don Lombardi, *President*
John Good, *Vice Pres*
◆ EMP: 60
SQ FT: 17,000
SALES (est): 21.4MM **Privately Held**
WEB: www.dwdrums.com
SIC: 3931 Drums, parts & accessories (musical instruments)

(P-22614)
DUNCAN CARTER CORPORATION (PA)
Also Called: Seymour Duncan
5427 Hollister Ave, Santa Barbara (93111-2307)
PHONE...................805 964-9749
Seymour Duncan, *President*
Cathy Carter Duncan, *CEO*
James Keifer, *Buyer*
▲ EMP: 96 EST: 1976
SQ FT: 20,000
SALES (est): 18.1MM **Privately Held**
WEB: www.seymourduncan.com
SIC: 3931 5736 3674 3651 Guitars & parts, electric & nonelectric; musical instrument stores; semiconductors & related devices; household audio & video equipment

(P-22615)
DUNLOP MANUFACTURING INC (PA)
150 Industrial Way, Benicia (94510-1112)
P.O. Box 846 (94510-0846)
PHONE...................707 745-2722
James Andrew Dunlop, *CEO*
Julie Forristall, *CFO*
Jasmin Powell, *Vice Pres*
Joey Tosi, *Creative Dir*
Sally Balmaceda, *Info Tech Mgr*
◆ EMP: 100 EST: 1977
SQ FT: 40,000
SALES (est): 16.2MM **Privately Held**
WEB: www.jimdunlop.com
SIC: 3931 Guitars & parts, electric & nonelectric

(P-22616)
DUNLOP MANUFACTURING INC
649 Industrial Way, Benicia (94510-1163)
PHONE...................707 745-2709
Jasmin Powell, *Branch Mgr*
EMP: 45
SALES (corp-wide): 16.2MM **Privately Held**
SIC: 3931 Musical instruments
PA: Dunlop Manufacturing, Inc.
150 Industrial Way
Benicia CA 94510
707 745-2722

(P-22617)
E M G INC
675 Aviation Blvd Ste B, Santa Rosa (95403-1025)
P.O. Box 4394 (95402-4394)
PHONE...................707 525-9941
Robert A Turner, *President*
Andy Gravelle, *COO*
Gary Rush, *General Mgr*
EMP: 81
SQ FT: 10,000
SALES (est): 14.5MM **Privately Held**
WEB: www.emgpickups.com
SIC: 3931 5736 Guitars & parts, electric & nonelectric; musical instrument stores

(P-22618)
ERNIE BALL INC (PA)
4117 Earthwood Ln, San Luis Obispo (93401-7541)
PHONE...................805 544-7726
Roland S Ball, *President*
Sterling C Ball, *Vice Pres*
▲ EMP: 96
SQ FT: 50,000
SALES (est): 17.8MM **Privately Held**
WEB: www.ernieball.com
SIC: 3931 Guitars & parts, electric & nonelectric

(P-22619)
ERNIE BALL INC
53973 Polk St, Coachella (92236-3816)
PHONE...................800 543-2255
Sterling C Ball, *Manager*

EMP: 54
SALES (corp-wide): 17.8MM **Privately Held**
SIC: **3931** Guitars & parts, electric & non-electric
PA: Ernie Ball, Inc.
4117 Earthwood Ln
San Luis Obispo CA 93401
805 544-7726

(P-22620)
FENDER MUSICAL INSTRS CORP
301 Cessna Cir, Corona (92880-2521)
PHONE....................480 596-9690
Al Guzman, *Principal*
Evan Jones, *Chief Mktg Ofcr*
Eric Spitzer, *Vice Pres*
Mike Born, *Technology*
Mike Imes, *Technology*
EMP: 600
SALES (corp-wide): 711.9MM **Privately Held**
WEB: www.fender.com
SIC: **3931** Guitars & parts, electric & non-electric
PA: Fender Musical Instruments Corporation
17600 N Perimeter Dr # 100
Scottsdale AZ 85255
480 596-9690

(P-22621)
FULLTONE MUSICAL PRODUCTS INC
11018 Washington Blvd, Culver City (90232-3901)
PHONE....................310 204-0155
Michael Fuller, *President*
▲ EMP: 15
SQ FT: 3,595
SALES: 4.3MM **Privately Held**
WEB: www.fulltone.com
SIC: **3931** 5099 Musical instruments; musical instruments

(P-22622)
GIBSON BRANDS INC
Also Called: Entertainment Relations
9350 Civic Center Dr # 130, Beverly Hills (90210-3629)
PHONE....................310 300-2369
Jennifer Feeney, *Manager*
EMP: 114
SALES (corp-wide): 567.5MM **Privately Held**
WEB: www.gibson.com
SIC: **3931** Guitars & parts, electric & non-electric
PA: Gibson Brands, Inc.
309 Plus Park Blvd
Nashville TN 37217
615 871-4500

(P-22623)
GOODALL GUITARS INC
541 S Franklin St, Fort Bragg (95437-5101)
PHONE....................707 962-1620
James Goodall, *President*
Jean Goodall, *Vice Pres*
EMP: 14
SQ FT: 7,200
SALES (est): 1.5MM **Privately Held**
WEB: www.goodallguitars.com
SIC: **3931** 5099 Guitars & parts, electric & nonelectric; musical instruments

(P-22624)
GULBRANSEN INC
Also Called: Piano Exchange
2102 Hancock St, San Diego (92110-2083)
PHONE....................619 296-5760
Curtis Rex Carter Jr, *CEO*
Robert L Hill, *President*
David Starky, *Senior VP*
EMP: 10
SQ FT: 6,500
SALES (est): 660K **Privately Held**
SIC: **3931** 5099 Keyboard instruments & parts; pianos, all types: vertical, grand, spinet, player, etc.; musical instruments; pianos

(P-22625)
HARRIS ORGANS INC
Also Called: Harris' Precision Products
7047 Comstock Ave, Whittier (90602-1399)
PHONE....................562 693-3442
David C Harris, *President*
EMP: 21
SQ FT: 12,000
SALES (est): 2.5MM **Privately Held**
WEB: www.harrisorgans.com
SIC: **3931** 3599 Pipes, organ; machine shop, jobbing & repair

(P-22626)
HPF CORPORATION (PA)
Also Called: Suzuki Musical Instruments
9920 Prospect Ave Ste 102, Santee (92071-4349)
PHONE....................858 566-9710
▲ EMP: 18
SQ FT: 40,000
SALES (est): 5.3MM **Privately Held**
WEB: www.suzukicorp.com
SIC: **3931**

(P-22627)
HUPALO REPASKY PIPE ORGANS LLC
2450 Alvarado St, San Leandro (94577-4316)
PHONE....................510 483-6905
John Hupalo,
Jason Jia, *Sales Staff*
Steve Repasky,
▲ EMP: 15
SQ FT: 3,400
SALES: 239K **Privately Held**
WEB: www.hupalorepasky.com
SIC: **3931** Musical instruments

(P-22628)
KANSTUL MUSICAL INSTRS INC
Also Called: K M I
1501 E Lincoln Ave, Anaheim (92805-2220)
PHONE....................714 563-1000
Zigmant J Kanstul, *President*
EMP: 42
SQ FT: 27,000
SALES (est): 5.8MM **Privately Held**
WEB: www.kanstul.net
SIC: **3931** Brass instruments & parts

(P-22629)
LR BAGGS CORPORATION
483 N Frontage Rd, Nipomo (93444-9596)
PHONE....................805 929-3545
Lloyd R Baggs, *CEO*
Bo Lrbaggs, *General Mgr*
Caleb Elling, *Technology*
Ed Herlihy, *Technology*
Justin Rucker, *Electrical Engi*
▲ EMP: 25
SALES (est): 4.3MM **Privately Held**
SIC: **3931** 3825 3651 Guitars & parts, electric & nonelectric; transducers for volts, amperes, watts, vars, frequency, etc.; household audio & video equipment

(P-22630)
MANZANITA
Also Called: Lsl Instruments
26559 Ruether Ave, Santa Clarita (91350-2622)
PHONE....................818 785-1111
Lisa Lerman, *CEO*
Lance Lerman, *President*
EMP: 10 EST: 2010
SALES (est): 1.1MM **Privately Held**
SIC: **3931** Musical instruments

(P-22631)
PALADAR MFG INC
53973 Polk St, Coachella (92236-3816)
P.O. Box 4117, San Luis Obispo (93403-4117)
PHONE....................760 775-4222
Sterling C Ball, *President*
Roland S Ball, *Vice Pres*
▲ EMP: 52
SQ FT: 6,000
SALES (est): 8.2MM **Privately Held**
SIC: **3931** Strings, musical instrument

(P-22632)
QUILTER LABORATORIES LLC
1700 Sunflower Ave, Costa Mesa (92626-1505)
PHONE....................714 519-6114
Patrick H Quilter, *Principal*
Robert Becker, *COO*
Nicole Cheshire, *Manager*
▲ EMP: 11 EST: 2011
SALES (est): 1.6MM **Privately Held**
SIC: **3931** Guitars & parts, electric & non-electric

(P-22633)
REMO INC (PA)
28101 Industry Dr, Valencia (91355-4113)
PHONE....................661 294-5600
Remo D Belli, *President*
Yolanda Davis, *COO*
Doug Sink, *CFO*
Douglas Sink, *CFO*
AMI Belli, *Vice Pres*
◆ EMP: 300
SQ FT: 216,000
SALES (est): 47.7MM **Privately Held**
WEB: www.remo.com
SIC: **3931** Heads, drum; drums, parts & accessories (musical instruments)

(P-22634)
RICO CORPORATION (HQ)
Also Called: Rico Products
8484 San Fernando Rd, Sun Valley (91352-3227)
PHONE....................818 394-2700
James D Addario, *CEO*
▲ EMP: 45
SALES (est): 22.8MM
SALES (corp-wide): 180MM **Privately Held**
WEB: www.ricoreeds.com
SIC: **3931** 5099 Reeds for musical instruments; musical instruments
PA: D'addario & Company, Inc.
595 Smith St
Farmingdale NY 11735
631 439-3300

(P-22635)
RICO HOLDINGS INC
8484 San Fernando Rd, Sun Valley (91352-3227)
PHONE....................818 394-2700
William Carpenter, *President*
EMP: 240
SQ FT: 17,000
SALES (est): 13.3MM **Privately Held**
SIC: **3931** 5099 Reeds for musical instruments; musical instruments

(P-22636)
SANTA CRUZ GUITAR CORPORATION
151 Harvey West Blvd C, Santa Cruz (95060-2172)
PHONE....................831 425-0999
Richard Hoover, *President*
John Anderson, *CFO*
▲ EMP: 22
SQ FT: 6,800
SALES (est): 3.3MM **Privately Held**
WEB: www.santacruzguitar.com
SIC: **3931** 5736 Guitars & parts, electric & nonelectric; musical instrument stores

(P-22637)
SCHECTER GUITAR RESEARCH INC
10953 Pendleton St, Sun Valley (91352-1522)
PHONE....................818 767-1029
Michael Ciravolo, *President*
David Santiago, *CFO*
Seth Miller, *Executive*
Toshi Hayakawa, *Opers Mgr*
Todd Reich, *Opers Staff*
◆ EMP: 43
SQ FT: 11,000
SALES: 19MM **Privately Held**
WEB: www.schecterguitars.com
SIC: **3931** Musical instruments

(P-22638)
SCHOENSTEIN & CO
4001 Industrial Way, Benicia (94510-1241)
PHONE....................707 747-5858
Jack M Bethards, *President*
Louis Patterson, *Vice Pres*
Diane Delu, *Admin Sec*
EMP: 25
SQ FT: 10,000
SALES (est): 3.6MM **Privately Held**
WEB: www.schoenstein.com
SIC: **3931** 7699 Pipes, organ; organ tuning & repair

(P-22639)
SHUBB CAPOS
14471 Hwy 1, Valley Ford (94972)
P.O. Box 550 (94972-0550)
PHONE....................707 876-3001
Rick Shubb, *Partner*
Dave Coontz, *Partner*
Ruth Powers, *Executive*
▲ EMP: 22
SQ FT: 1,000
SALES (est): 2.4MM **Privately Held**
WEB: www.shubb.com
SIC: **3931** Guitars & parts, electric & non-electric

(P-22640)
SONGBIRD OCARINAS LLC
2751 E 11th St, Los Angeles (90023-3403)
PHONE....................323 269-2524
Darren Steinberg, *Mng Member*
Barbara James, *Admin Sec*
▲ EMP: 11
SQ FT: 10,000
SALES: 1MM **Privately Held**
WEB: www.songbirdocarina.com
SIC: **3931** Ocarinas

(P-22641)
THUNDER PRODUCTS INC
Also Called: Players Music Accessories
2469 Klein Rd, San Jose (95148-1800)
P.O. Box H (95151-0008)
PHONE....................408 270-7800
Tony Lalonde, *CEO*
Tony La Londe, *President*
EMP: 16
SQ FT: 6,000
SALES: 750K **Privately Held**
SIC: **3931** Musical instruments

(P-22642)
THUNDER PRODUCTS INC
Also Called: Players Music Accessories
127 Escondido Way, Portola (96122-7057)
P.O. Box 9210, Mesa AZ (85214-9210)
PHONE....................480 833-2500
Tony Lalonde, *CEO*
Jodie Lalonde, *CFO*
Monta Lalonde, *CFO*
Jodi Ann Stone, *Office Mgr*
▲ EMP: 16
SALES (est): 2.5MM **Privately Held**
SIC: **3931** Drums, parts & accessories (musical instruments)

(P-22643)
TRIPLETT HARPS
220 Suburban Rd Ste C, San Luis Obispo (93401-7526)
PHONE....................805 544-2777
Steven Triplett, *Owner*
Debbie Triplett, *General Mgr*
▼ EMP: 14
SQ FT: 7,000
SALES: 800K **Privately Held**
WEB: www.tripletharps.com
SIC: **3931** 5736 Harps & parts; musical instrument stores

(P-22644)
YAMAHA GUITAR GROUP INC (HQ)
26580 Agoura Rd, Calabasas (91302-1921)
PHONE....................818 575-3600
Joe Bentivegna, *President*
◆ EMP: 120
SQ FT: 20,000
SALES (est): 41MM **Privately Held**
WEB: www.line6.com
SIC: **3931** Musical instruments

PRODUCTS & SVCS

3942 Dolls & Stuffed Toys

(P-22645)
CUDDLY TOYS
1833 N Eastern Ave, Los Angeles
(90032-4115)
P.O. Box 41281 (90041-0281)
PHONE............................323 980-0572
Leo Ramdwar, *President*
EMP: 12
SQ FT: 30,000
SALES (est): 1MM **Privately Held**
WEB: www.cuddlytoys.com
SIC: 3942 Stuffed toys, including animals

(P-22646)
DEFINE TOYS INC
Also Called: Hugfun International
1255 Bixby Dr, City of Industry
(91745-1708)
PHONE............................626 330-8800
Ling He, *President*
Helen Wang, *Vice Pres*
▲ **EMP:** 15 **EST:** 2001
SQ FT: 15,000
SALES (est): 1.2MM **Privately Held**
SIC: 3942 Dolls & stuffed toys

(P-22647)
DREAM INTERNATIONAL USA INC
Also Called: Caltoy
7001 Village Dr Ste 280, Buena Park
(90621-2397)
PHONE............................714 521-6007
Chul Hong Min, *CEO*
Amy E Cho, *Managing Dir*
Suzette Lee, *General Mgr*
James Wang, *Admin Sec*
▲ **EMP:** 10
SALES (est): 1.4MM
SALES (corp-wide): 5.4K **Privately Held**
WEB: www.caltoy.com
SIC: 3942 5092 Stuffed toys, including animals; toys & games
PA: C&H Co., Ltd.
65 Sinbong 3-Gil
Sangju
825 453-6234

(P-22648)
KOTO INC
Also Called: Koto Bukiya
22857 Lockness Ave, Torrance
(90501-5103)
PHONE............................310 327-7359
Jeffrey Kashida, *President*
Kazuyuki Shimizu, *President*
Hiroyo Shimizu, *COO*
May Okabe, *CFO*
Aiko Shoji, *Vice Pres*
▲ **EMP:** 10
SQ FT: 5,000
SALES (est): 2MM **Privately Held**
SIC: 3942 5092 Dolls & stuffed toys; toy novelties & amusements; toys

(P-22649)
MAHAR MANUFACTURING CORP (PA)
Also Called: Fiesta Concession
2834 E 46th St, Vernon (90058-2404)
PHONE............................323 581-9988
Michael Lauber, *CEO*
◆ **EMP:** 39
SQ FT: 100,000
SALES (est): 14.1MM **Privately Held**
WEB: www.fiestatoy.com
SIC: 3942 Stuffed toys, including animals

(P-22650)
MATTEL INC (PA)
333 Continental Blvd, El Segundo
(90245-5032)
PHONE............................310 252-2000
Ynon Kreiz, *Ch of Bd*
Richard Dickson, *President*
Joseph J Euteneuer, *CFO*
Robert Normile,
Amanda J Thompson,
◆ **EMP:** 1700
SQ FT: 335,000

SALES: 4.5B **Publicly Held**
WEB: www.mattel.com
SIC: 3942 3944 Dolls & stuffed toys; dolls, except stuffed toy animals; stuffed toys, including animals; games, toys & children's vehicles

(P-22651)
ONE AT A TIME
3518 El Camino Real 195, Atascadero
(93422-2531)
PHONE............................805 461-1784
Barbara Fritch, *Partner*
Bob Fritch, *Partner*
EMP: 11
SQ FT: 2,000
SALES: 39.8K **Privately Held**
SIC: 3942 5947 Dolls & stuffed toys; gift shop

(P-22652)
PHOENIX CUSTOM PROMOTIONS
Also Called: Petite Porcelain By Barbara
2005 Casa Grande Ct, Modesto
(95355-5101)
PHONE............................209 579-1557
Abraham Angel, *President*
Barbara Angel, *Admin Sec*
▲ **EMP:** 10
SQ FT: 1,000
SALES (est): 1.2MM **Privately Held**
WEB: www.petiteporcelain.com
SIC: 3942 Dolls & stuffed toys

(P-22653)
RAYKORVAY INC
Also Called: Giant Teddy
1070 N Kraemer Pl, Anaheim
(92806-2610)
PHONE............................714 632-8680
Reza Khosravi, *CEO*
▲ **EMP:** 16
SQ FT: 10,000
SALES (est): 2.2MM **Privately Held**
SIC: 3942 5961 Stuffed toys, including animals; toys & games (including dolls & models), mail order

(P-22654)
SNAP CREATIVE MANUFACTURING
3760 Calle Tecate Ste B, Camarillo
(93012-5061)
PHONE............................818 735-3830
William Peter Howard Jr, *CEO*
▲ **EMP:** 12
SQ FT: 4,000
SALES: 20MM **Privately Held**
SIC: 3942 3069 Dolls & stuffed toys; toys, rubber

(P-22655)
UPD INC
Also Called: United Pacific Designs
4507 S Maywood Ave, Vernon
(90058-2610)
PHONE............................323 588-8811
Shahin Dardashty, *President*
Ben Hooshim, *COO*
PHI Fozo, *CFO*
Frederick Dardashti, *Vice Pres*
Fred Dardashty, *Vice Pres*
◆ **EMP:** 60
SQ FT: 140,000
SALES (est): 21.2MM **Privately Held**
SIC: 3942 5112 3944 Dolls & stuffed toys; pens &/or pencils; puzzles

3944 Games, Toys & Children's Vehicles

(P-22656)
ADOLF GOLDFARB
Also Called: Goldfarb & Associates
1434 6th St Ste 10, Santa Monica
(90401-2541)
PHONE............................310 451-1211
Adolf E Goldfarb, *Owner*
EMP: 10
SQ FT: 13,000
SALES (est): 488.7K **Privately Held**
SIC: 3944 Children's vehicles, except bicycles

(P-22657)
ANKI INC (PA)
333 S Grand Ave Ste 4100, Los Angeles
(90071-1571)
PHONE............................877 721-2654
Boris Sofman, *CEO*
Hanns Tappeiner, *President*
Anna Baird, *CFO*
Dominic Ruso, *CFO*
Mark Palatucci,
▲ **EMP:** 21
SALES (est): 10.3MM **Privately Held**
SIC: 3944 Toy trains, airplanes & automobiles

(P-22658)
ARTIFACT PUZZLES
180 Constitution Dr Ste 6, Menlo Park
(94025-1137)
PHONE............................650 283-0589
Maya Gupta, *Mng Member*
EMP: 10
SALES (est): 1MM **Privately Held**
SIC: 3944 Puzzles

(P-22659)
ASSOCIATED ELECTRICS INC
21062 Bake Pkwy Ste 100, Lake Forest
(92630-2183)
PHONE............................949 544-7500
Gary Titus, *CEO*
Chung L Lai, *President*
Clifton Lett, *Vice Pres*
▲ **EMP:** 46
SALES (est): 6.4MM **Privately Held**
WEB: www.rc10.com
SIC: 3944 Automobile & truck models, toy & hobby

(P-22660)
B DAZZLE INC
Also Called: Www.b-Dazzle.com
500 Meyer Ln, Redondo Beach
(90278-5208)
PHONE............................310 374-3000
Kathleen A Gavin, *President*
▲ **EMP:** 12
SQ FT: 5,500
SALES (est): 1.8MM **Privately Held**
WEB: www.b-dazzle.com
SIC: 3944 5092 Board games, puzzles & models, except electronic; puzzles; toys & games; puzzles; toys

(P-22661)
BANDAI AMERICA INCORPORATED (DH)
2120 Park Pl Ste 120, El Segundo
(90245-4824)
PHONE............................714 816-9751
Atsushi Takeuchi, *Principal*
Katsushi Murakami, *Ch of Bd*
Takeshi Nojima, *President*
Masayuki Matsuo, *CEO*
Brian Goldner, *COO*
▲ **EMP:** 55
SQ FT: 75,000
SALES (est): 15.2MM **Privately Held**
WEB: www.bandai.com
SIC: 3944 Games, toys & children's vehicles

(P-22662)
BEEJAY LLC
Also Called: Spinner Toys & Gifts
3450 Kurtz St Ste C, San Diego
(92110-4451)
P.O. Box 81983 (92138-1983)
PHONE............................619 220-8697
Lynda Willis, *Partner*
Jon Willis, *Vice Pres*
Richard Freeman, *Opers Staff*
Toya Davis, *Manager*
EMP: 10
SQ FT: 6,000
SALES (est): 1MM **Privately Held**
WEB: www.spinnertoys.com
SIC: 3944 5092 5199 Toy trains, airplanes & automobiles; toys & hobby goods & supplies; gifts & novelties

(P-22663)
BOTTELSEN DART CO INC
Also Called: American Dart Lines
945 W Mccoy Ln, Santa Maria
(93455-1109)
PHONE............................805 922-4519
Walter Bottelsen, *President*
Aj Norrie, *General Mgr*
Susette Bottelsen, *Admin Sec*
Terri Balderama, *Sales Staff*
▲ **EMP:** 10
SQ FT: 10,250
SALES (est): 3.5MM **Privately Held**
SIC: 3944 Darts & dart games

(P-22664)
BRAINSTORMPRODUCTS LLC
1011 S Andreasen Dr # 100, Escondido
(92029-1962)
PHONE............................760 871-1135
Randal W Joe,
Angela Burnett, *CFO*
Eric Duvauchelle, *Vice Pres*
Brian Tawa,
Scott Brady, *Director*
◆ **EMP:** 10
SQ FT: 4,000
SALES (est): 2MM **Privately Held**
SIC: 3944 Kites

(P-22665)
BROKEN TOKEN
541 N Quince St Ste 1, Escondido
(92025-2570)
PHONE............................760 294-1923
Gregory Spence, *President*
EMP: 10 **EST:** 2016
SALES (est): 1.1MM **Privately Held**
SIC: 3944 Games, toys & children's vehicles

(P-22666)
BUMBLERIDE INC
2345 Kettner Blvd Ste B, San Diego
(92101-1274)
PHONE............................619 615-0475
Matthew Reichardt, *President*
Emily Reichardt, *Vice Pres*
Sarah McKindlay-Boina, *Marketing Mgr*
Kandi Brown, *Manager*
▲ **EMP:** 10
SQ FT: 3,500
SALES (est): 1.8MM **Privately Held**
WEB: www.bumbleride.com
SIC: 3944 Strollers, baby (vehicle)

(P-22667)
CAPERON DESIGNS INC
Also Called: Beco Baby Carrier
1733 Monrovia Ave Ste N, Costa Mesa
(92627-4421)
PHONE............................714 552-3201
Gabriela Caperon, *President*
Andrew Caperon, *Vice Pres*
▲ **EMP:** 15
SQ FT: 3,000
SALES (est): 2MM **Privately Held**
SIC: 3944 Baby carriages & restraint seats

(P-22668)
CRAFTERS COMPANION
2750 E Regal Park Dr, Anaheim
(92806-2417)
PHONE............................714 630-2444
▲ **EMP:** 20 **EST:** 2012
SQ FT: 8,197
SALES (est): 1.9MM **Privately Held**
SIC: 3944

(P-22669)
CRYPTIC STUDIOS INC
980 University Ave, Los Gatos
(95032-7620)
PHONE............................408 399-1969
Jack Emmert, *CEO*
Michael C Lewis, *President*
Aaron Herkomer, *Technical Staff*
EMP: 100
SALES (est): 14.9MM
SALES (corp-wide): 260.6K **Privately Held**
WEB: www.crypticstudios.com
SIC: 3944 Video game machines, except coin-operated

▲ = Import ▼=Export
◆ =Import/Export

HQ: Perfect World Co., Ltd.
701-14, Floor 7, Building 5, No.1
Courtyard, Shangdi E. Road, Ha
Beijing 10010
105 780-5623

(P-22670)
DREAMGEAR LLC
20001 S Western Ave, Torrance
(90501-1306)
PHONE..............................310 222-5522
Yahya Ahdout, *CEO*
Olivia Arevalo, *Executive*
Moe Katouzian, *Controller*
Moris Mirzadeh, *VP Sales*
Raul Ferrero, *Sales Mgr*
◆ EMP: 49
SQ FT: 60,000
SALES (est): 10.6MM **Privately Held**
WEB: www.dreamgear.net
SIC: 3944 5023 Electronic games & toys;
electronic game machines, except coin-
operated; decorative home furnishings &
supplies

(P-22671)
DREAMPLAY TOYS LLC
11755 Wilshire Blvd # 2000, Los Angeles
(90025-1506)
PHONE..............................424 208-7010
Patrick Soon-Shiong,
EMP: 15
SALES (est): 87.6K **Publicly Held**
SIC: 3944 Electronic games & toys
PA: Jakks Pacific, Inc.
2951 28th St
Santa Monica CA 90405
-

(P-22672)
**DT MATTSON ENTERPRISES
INC**
Also Called: Proline Manufacturing
201 W Lincoln St, Banning (92220-4933)
P.O. Box 456, Beaumont (92223-0456)
PHONE..............................951 849-9781
Todd Mattson, *CEO*
Matt Wallace, *Engineer*
Cindy Cross, *Accountant*
David Hannaford, *Maint Spvr*
Tim Clark, *Manager*
▲ EMP: 40
SQ FT: 20,000
SALES (est): 6.7MM **Privately Held**
WEB: www.prolineracing.com
SIC: 3944 5521 Games, toys & children's
vehicles; trucks, tractors & trailers: used

(P-22673)
**EGGTOOTH ORIGINALS
CONSULTING**
13502 Graveyard Gulch Rd, Fort Jones
(96032-9743)
PHONE..............................530 468-5131
John West, *Owner*
Karen West, *Co-Owner*
EMP: 12
SALES (est): 852.2K **Privately Held**
SIC: 3944 Craft & hobby kits & sets

(P-22674)
ERGO BABY CARRIER INC (HQ)
617 W 7th St Fl 10, Los Angeles
(90017-3879)
PHONE..............................213 283-2090
Bill Chiasson, *CEO*
Karin A Frost, *President*
Elias Sabo, *President*
Svea Frost, *Vice Pres*
Vanessa Van Bui, *Vice Pres*
▲ EMP: 22
SALES: 67.3MM **Publicly Held**
WEB: www.ergobabycarrier.com
SIC: 3944 Baby carriages & restraint seats

(P-22675)
EXPLODING KITTENS LLC
101 S La Brea Ave A, Los Angeles
(90036-2998)
PHONE..............................310 788-8699
Elan Lee,
Jackie Yu, *Accountant*
Matthew Inman,
Carly McGinnis, *Director*
EMP: 10

SALES (est): 8.1MM **Privately Held**
SIC: 3944 7371 Board games, children's &
adults'; computer software development &
applications

(P-22676)
EXTRON CONTRACT MFG INC
Also Called: Extron Contract Packaging
496 S Abbott Ave, Milpitas (95035-5258)
PHONE..............................510 353-0177
Andy Nguyen, *President*
EMP: 125
SQ FT: 200,000
SALES (est): 12.5MM **Privately Held**
SIC: 3944 3672 Electronic games & toys;
printed circuit boards

(P-22677)
**GAMES PRODUCTION
COMPANY LLC**
Also Called: Galaxy Pest Control
21323 Pacific Coast Hwy, Malibu
(90265-5202)
PHONE..............................310 456-0099
Jamie Ottilie, *CEO*
EMP: 15 EST: 2007
SALES (est): 999.4K **Privately Held**
SIC: 3944 7371 7372 Electronic games &
toys; computer software development &
applications; home entertainment com-
puter software

(P-22678)
**HARDCORE RACING
COMPONENTS LLC**
27717 Avenue Scott, Valencia
(91355-1219)
PHONE..............................661 294-5032
Fax: 661 294-0770
EMP: 16 EST: 2000
SALES (est): 1.2MM **Privately Held**
SIC: 3944

(P-22679)
HARVEST ASIA INC
Also Called: 2 Impact Group
7888 Cherry Ave Ste G, Fontana
(92336-4273)
PHONE..............................888 800-3133
Derek Ro, *President*
Tina Kim, *Controller*
▲ EMP: 10
SQ FT: 5,000
SALES (est): 1.4MM **Privately Held**
SIC: 3944 3751 Children's vehicles, ex-
cept bicycles; motorcycles, bicycles &
parts

(P-22680)
HASBRO INC
16047 Mountain Ave, Chino (91708-9131)
PHONE..............................909 393-3248
Jeffrey Brown, *Manager*
EMP: 407
SALES (corp-wide): 4.5B **Publicly Held**
SIC: 3944 Games, toys & children's vehi-
cles
PA: Hasbro, Inc.
1027 Newport Ave
Pawtucket RI 02861
401 431-8697

(P-22681)
HORIZON HOBBY LLC
4710 E Guasti Rd Ste A, Ontario
(91761-8121)
PHONE..............................909 390-9595
Yolanda Perry, *Branch Mgr*
Dave Giglio, *Technical Staff*
Jacob Calderon, *Engineer*
Keith West, *VP Finance*
EMP: 150
SALES (corp-wide): 107.5MM **Privately
Held**
WEB: www.hangar-9.com
SIC: 3944 5092 Automobile & truck mod-
els, toy & hobby; hobby goods
PA: Horizon Hobby, Llc
2904 Research Rd
Champaign IL 61822
217 352-1913

(P-22682)
IMPERIAL TOY LLC (PA)
16641 Roscoe Pl, North Hills (91343-6104)
PHONE..............................818 536-6500

Peter Tiger, *Mng Member*
Amy Dugan, *VP Sales*
Arthur Hirsch,
Katie Fitzpatrick, *Manager*
◆ EMP: 115
SQ FT: 400,000
SALES (est): 228.3MM **Privately Held**
WEB: www.imperialtoy.com
SIC: 3944 Games, toys & children's vehi-
cles

(P-22683)
INSOMNIAC GAMES INC (PA)
2255 N Ontario St Ste 550, Burbank
(91504-3197)
PHONE..............................818 729-2400
Theodore C Price, *President*
Alex Hastings, *Vice Pres*
Brian Hastings, *Admin Sec*
EMP: 54
SALES (est): 15MM **Privately Held**
WEB: www.insomniacgames.com
SIC: 3944 Electronic games & toys

(P-22684)
**INTERACTIVE ENTERTAINMENT
INC**
Also Called: Database Dynamics
2 Enterprise Apt 7107, Aliso Viejo
(92656-8004)
PHONE..............................714 460-2343
Wayne S Schonfeld, *CEO*
Rick Odekirk, *President*
Andi Kendall, *Admin Sec*
Randy Copperman, *CIO*
Wayne Schonfeld, *VP Sales*
EMP: 17
SALES (est): 2MM **Privately Held**
WEB: www.databasedynamics.net
SIC: 3944 Electronic games & toys

(P-22685)
JADA GROUP INC
Also Called: Jada Toys
938 Hatcher Ave, City of Industry
(91748-1035)
PHONE..............................626 810-8382
William Anthony Simons, *CEO*
Manfred Duschl, *CFO*
Harvey Luong, *CFO*
Steven Sandler, *Vice Pres*
Bill Simons, *Vice Pres*
◆ EMP: 70
SQ FT: 45,000
SALES (est): 14MM
SALES (corp-wide): 37.2MM **Privately
Held**
WEB: www.jadatoys.com
SIC: 3944 Games, toys & children's vehi-
cles
PA: Simba-Dickie-Group Gmbh
Werkstr. 1
Furth 90765
911 976-501

(P-22686)
JAKKS PACIFIC INC
Also Called: Flying Colors
21749 Baker Pkwy, Walnut (91789-5234)
PHONE..............................909 594-7771
Michelle Tromp, *Branch Mgr*
EMP: 30 **Publicly Held**
SIC: 3944 5092 Games, toys & children's
vehicles; toys
PA: Jakks Pacific, Inc.
2951 28th St
Santa Monica CA 90405
-

(P-22687)
JAKKS PACIFIC INC (PA)
2951 28th St, Santa Monica (90405-2961)
PHONE..............................424 268-9444
Stephen G Berman, *President*
John J McGrath, *COO*
Joel M Bennett, *CFO*
Brent Novak, *CFO*
Anthony Mohamed, *IT/INT Sup*
EMP: 241
SALES: 567.8MM **Publicly Held**
SIC: 3944 Games, toys & children's vehi-
cles

(P-22688)
JOHN N HANSEN CO INC
740 Southpoint Blvd, Petaluma
(94954-7494)
PHONE..............................650 652-9833
Mary J Hansen, *Ch of Bd*
Lars Larsen, *President*
John Henson Jr, *COO*
Mike Krieger, *General Mgr*
◆ EMP: 13
SALES (est): 2.2MM **Privately Held**
WEB: www.johnhansenco.com
SIC: 3944 5092 Games, toys & children's
vehicles; toys & hobby goods & supplies

(P-22689)
**LEAPFROG ENTERPRISES INC
(HQ)**
6401 Hollis St Ste 100, Emeryville
(94608-1463)
PHONE..............................510 420-5000
Nick Delany, *CEO*
William To, *President*
Alec Anderson, *CFO*
Paul Bennett, *Vice Pres*
Eugene Faulkner, *Vice Pres*
▲ EMP: 357
SALES (est): 247.2MM **Privately Held**
WEB: www.leapfrog.com
SIC: 3944 Games, toys & children's vehi-
cles

(P-22690)
MAKERPLACE INC
684 Margarita Ave, Coronado
(92118-2321)
PHONE..............................619 435-1279
Steven Herrick, *President*
EMP: 15
SALES (est): 1MM **Privately Held**
SIC: 3944 Craft & hobby kits & sets

(P-22691)
MAKERSKIT LLC
Also Called: Makerskit.com
7600 Melrose Ave Ste E, Los Angeles
(90046-7451)
PHONE..............................213 973-7019
Michael Kim, *President*
John McQuade, *COO*
EMP: 20
SQ FT: 2,000
SALES (est): 2.7MM **Privately Held**
SIC: 3944 3999 5092 Craft & hobby kits &
sets; novelties, bric-a-brac & hobby kits;
arts & crafts equipment & supplies

(P-22692)
MATTEL INC
1456 E Harry Shepard Blvd, San
Bernardino (92408-0137)
PHONE..............................909 382-3780
Ron Headrick, *Manager*
Scott Butterbaugh, *Plant Mgr*
EMP: 15
SALES (corp-wide): 4.5B **Publicly Held**
WEB: www.mattel.com
SIC: 3944 Games, toys & children's vehi-
cles
PA: Mattel, Inc.
333 Continental Blvd
El Segundo CA 90245
310 252-2000

(P-22693)
**MATTEL DIRECT IMPORT INC
(HQ)**
333 Continental Blvd, El Segundo
(90245-5032)
PHONE..............................310 252-2000
Kevin Farr, *CEO*
Bryan G Stockton, *President*
Melinda Mehringer, *Vice Pres*
Lisa Steins, *Vice Pres*
Linda Gavigan, *Admin Asst*
EMP: 11
SALES (est): 4.9MM
SALES (corp-wide): 4.5B **Publicly Held**
WEB: www.mattel.com
SIC: 3944 3942 3949 Games, toys & chil-
dren's vehicles; dolls, except stuffed toy
animals; sporting & athletic goods

PRODUCTS & SVCS

PA: Mattel, Inc.
333 Continental Blvd
El Segundo CA 90245
310 252-2000

(P-22694)
MEDIUM ENTERTAINMENT INC
501 Folsom St Fl 1, San Francisco
(94105-3175)
PHONE..............................469 951-2688
Andy Yang, *President*
Raymond Lau, *CEO*
Erik Yao, *Ch Credit Ofcr*
EMP: 20
SALES (est): 3.2MM **Privately Held**
SIC: 3944 Electronic games & toys

(P-22695)
MINDJOLT
144 2nd St Fl 4, San Francisco
(94105-3721)
PHONE..............................415 543-7800
Richard Fields, *Manager*
Matthew Casertano, *Vice Pres*
Jill Schneiderman, *Senior Mgr*
EMP: 16
SALES (est): 878.8K **Privately Held**
SIC: 3944 Games, toys & children's vehicles

(P-22696)
**MOORES IDEAL PRODUCTS
LLC**
Also Called: M I P
830 W Golden Grove Way, Covina
(91722-3257)
PHONE..............................626 339-9007
Eustace Moore Jr, *Mng Member*
Alycia Moore, *Manager*
EMP: 11
SQ FT: 8,600
SALES (est): 2.2MM **Privately Held**
SIC: 3944 Automobile & truck models, toy
& hobby

(P-22697)
NEKO WORLD INC
21041 S Wstn Ave Ste 200, Torrance
(90501)
PHONE..............................301 649-1188
Mike INA, *Principal*
EMP: 40 **EST:** 2014
SQ FT: 4,000
SALES: 15MM **Privately Held**
SIC: 3944 5092 Games, toys & children's
vehicles; toys & hobby goods & supplies

(P-22698)
NEUROSMITH LLC
1000 N Studebaker Rd # 3, Long Beach
(90815-4957)
PHONE..............................562 296-1100
EMP: 23
SQ FT: 7,200
SALES (est): 2.6MM **Privately Held**
SIC: 3944

(P-22699)
**NEW YORK TOY EXCHANGE
INC**
11955 Jack Benny Dr Ste 1, Rancho Cuca-
monga (91739-9230)
PHONE..............................626 327-4547
Lucy Patterson, *CEO*
James McMullin, *President*
EMP: 12
SALES: 125K **Privately Held**
SIC: 3944 Games, toys & children's vehicles

(P-22700)
NEXTSPORT INC
106 Linden St Ste 201, Oakland
(94607-2538)
PHONE..............................510 601-8802
Edward Dua, *CEO*
Julio Deulofeu, *President*
▲ **EMP:** 14 **EST:** 2001
SQ FT: 4,000
SALES (est): 3.1MM **Privately Held**
WEB: www.nextsport.com
SIC: 3944 Games, toys & children's vehicles

(P-22701)
NINJA JUMP INC
3221 N San Fernando Rd, Los Angeles
(90065-1414)
PHONE..............................323 255-5418
Rouben Gourchounian, *President*
Jack Chaparyan, *Manager*
◆ **EMP:** 75
SQ FT: 35,000
SALES (est): 14.6MM **Privately Held**
WEB: www.ninjajump.com
SIC: 3944 Games, toys & children's vehicles

(P-22702)
NKOK INC
5354 Irwindale Ave Ste A, Irwindale
(91706-2068)
PHONE..............................626 330-1988
Shun Yun Chiu, *President*
Kohsche Koh, *Vice Pres*
Edward Gomez, *Creative Dir*
Lanny Halim, *Manager*
◆ **EMP:** 10 **EST:** 1998
SQ FT: 30,000
SALES (est): 1.8MM **Privately Held**
WEB: www.nkok.com
SIC: 3944 Games, toys & children's vehicles

(P-22703)
PACIFIC GAMING
1975 Adams Ave, San Leandro
(94577-1005)
PHONE..............................510 562-8900
Lee Fried, *Principal*
Steve Rockwell, *VP Sales*
EMP: 20
SALES (est): 2.9MM **Privately Held**
SIC: 3944 Bingo boards (games)

(P-22704)
PLAYHUT INC
18560 San Jose Ave, City of Industry
(91748-1365)
PHONE..............................909 869-8083
Yu Zheng, *CEO*
Theresa Deredin, *Manager*
▲ **EMP:** 20
SALES (est): 12.2MM **Privately Held**
SIC: 3944 Games, toys & children's vehicles
PA: Basic Fun, Inc
301 E Yamato Rd Ste 4200
Boca Raton FL 33431

(P-22705)
POCKET GEMS INC (PA)
220 Montgomery St Ste 750, San Francisco
(94104-3479)
PHONE..............................415 371-1333
Ben Liu, *CEO*
Simon Chen, *Software Engr*
Ken Domke, *Software Engr*
Yu Guan, *Software Engr*
Matthew Koontz, *Software Engr*
EMP: 84
SALES (est): 28.9MM **Privately Held**
SIC: 3944 Electronic games & toys

(P-22706)
POOLMASTER INC
770 Del Paso Rd, Sacramento
(95834-1117)
P.O. Box 340308 (95834-0308)
PHONE..............................916 567-9800
Leon H Tager, *President*
Carol Tager, *Corp Secy*
Nora Davis, *Vice Pres*
Scheri Adams, *Human Res Dir*
Will Heizer, *Safety Mgr*
◆ **EMP:** 55 **EST:** 1959
SQ FT: 100,000
SALES (est): 12.4MM **Privately Held**
WEB: www.poolmaster.net
SIC: 3944 5091 Games, toys & children's
vehicles; sporting & recreation goods

(P-22707)
PRIMARY CONCEPTS INC
1338 7th St, Berkeley (94710-1410)
P.O. Box 640, Lafayette OR (97127-0640)
PHONE..............................510 559-5545
Reid Calcott, *CEO*
Jim Whitney, *President*

▲ **EMP:** 17
SALES (est): 2.2MM **Privately Held**
WEB: www.primaryconcepts.com
SIC: 3944 Games, toys & children's vehicles

(P-22708)
RED ROBOT LABS INC
1935 Landings Dr, Mountain View
(94043-0808)
P.O. Box 61017, Palo Alto (94306-6017)
PHONE..............................650 762-8058
Mike Ouye, *CEO*
Felix Hu, *Director*
EMP: 19
SALES (est): 1.5MM **Privately Held**
SIC: 3944 Electronic game machines, ex-
cept coin-operated

(P-22709)
RED TRICYCLE INC
548 Market St, San Francisco
(94104-5401)
PHONE..............................415 729-9781
Anna Ishihara, *Executive*
Roxana Cahill, *Sales Staff*
Sandra Coulson, *Director*
Levada Gray, *Director*
Nicole Kirksey, *Director*
EMP: 29
SALES (corp-wide): 1.9MM **Privately
Held**
SIC: 3944 Tricycles
PA: Red Tricycle Inc.
40 Marina Vista Ave
Larkspur CA
-

(P-22710)
RUMBLE ENTERTAINMENT INC
Also Called: Rumble Games
2121 S El Cmino Real C1, San Mateo
(94403)
PHONE..............................650 316-8819
Greg Richardson, *CEO*
Theresa Bottenhorn, *Human Resources*
Jeremy Forson, *Director*
EMP: 45
SALES (est): 6.8MM **Privately Held**
SIC: 3944 Electronic games & toys

(P-22711)
S M L INDUSTRIES INC
10965 Hartley Rd Ste P, Santee
(92071-2893)
PHONE..............................619 258-7941
Mark R Linder, *President*
EMP: 10
SQ FT: 1,500
SALES (est): 1.2MM **Privately Held**
WEB: www.smlind.com
SIC: 3944 Craft & hobby kits & sets

(P-22712)
SHELCORE INC (PA)
Also Called: Shelcore Toys
7811 Lemona Ave, Van Nuys (91405-1139)
PHONE..............................818 883-2400
Arnold Rubin, *President*
▼ **EMP:** 13
SQ FT: 20,000
SALES (est): 61.1MM **Privately Held**
WEB: www.shelcore.com
SIC: 3944 Blocks, toy; structural toy sets

(P-22713)
SIPI COMPANY INC
34734 Williams Way, Union City
(94587-5578)
PHONE..............................650 201-1169
Vincent Tong, *Ch of Bd*
EMP: 10
SALES (est): 770K **Privately Held**
SIC: 3944 7372 Electronic games & toys;
educational computer software; home en-
tertainment computer software

(P-22714)
SKULLDUGGERY INC
5433 E La Palma Ave, Anaheim
(92807-2022)
PHONE..............................714 777-6425
Peter Koehl Sr, *CEO*
Steven Koehl, *President*
Emmy Koehl, *Mktg Dir*
▲ **EMP:** 14

SQ FT: 10,000
SALES: 2MM **Privately Held**
WEB: www.skullduggery.com
SIC: 3944 5961 Science kits: micro-
scopes, chemistry sets, etc.; mail order
house

(P-22715)
SONOMA INTERNATIONAL INC
Also Called: Dowling Magnets
462 W Napa St Fl 2, Sonoma
(95476-6556)
P.O. Box 1829 (95476-1829)
PHONE..............................707 935-0710
Niels A Chow, *President*
Rosemarie Townsend, *Buyer*
◆ **EMP:** 35
SALES (est): 4MM **Privately Held**
SIC: 3944 3499 Games, toys & children's
vehicles; magnets, permanent: metallic

(P-22716)
STREAK TECHNOLOGY INC
43575 Mission Blvd 614, Fremont
(94539-5831)
PHONE..............................408 206-2373
Robert B Stewart, *President*
Shelley Stratton, *Vice Pres*
EMP: 12
SQ FT: 10,000
SALES: 14MM **Privately Held**
WEB: www.streaktechnology.com
SIC: 3944 Video game machines, except
coin-operated

(P-22717)
SUN-MATE CORP
19730 Ventura Blvd Ste 18, Woodland Hills
(91364-6304)
PHONE..............................818 700-0572
Rami Ben-Moshe, *President*
▲ **EMP:** 18
SQ FT: 5,000
SALES (est): 2.8MM **Privately Held**
SIC: 3944 Electronic games & toys

(P-22718)
SUNS OUT INC
2915 Red Hill Ave A210c, Costa Mesa
(92626-5916)
PHONE..............................714 556-2314
Diane J Skilling, *President*
Carolyn Miller, *VP Mktg*
EMP: 10
SQ FT: 2,000
SALES (est): 673.1K **Privately Held**
WEB: www.sunsout.com
SIC: 3944 5092 Puzzles; toys & games

(P-22719)
TANGLE INC
Also Called: Tangle Creations
385 Oyster Point Blvd 8b, South San Fran-
cisco (94080-1934)
PHONE..............................650 616-7900
Richard Zawitz, *President*
Nick Zawitz, *CFO*
Nicholas Zawitz, *Treasurer*
Geoff McKee, *Vice Pres*
Anya De Marie, *Mktg Dir*
▲ **EMP:** 26
SQ FT: 5,000
SALES (est): 11.6MM **Privately Held**
WEB: www.tangletoys.com
SIC: 3944 Games, toys & children's vehicles

(P-22720)
**TELECHEM INTERNATIONAL
INC (HQ)**
927 Thompson Pl, Sunnyvale
(94085-4518)
PHONE..............................408 744-1331
Rene Schena, *Ch of Bd*
Mark Schena PHD, *President*
William L Sklar, *CFO*
Todd J Martinsky, *Senior VP*
Paul K Haje, *VP Sales*
▲ **EMP:** 47
SQ FT: 8,280
SALES (est): 1.9MM **Publicly Held**
WEB: www.arrayit.com
SIC: 3944 Science kits: microscopes,
chemistry sets, etc.

(P-22721)
TORRENCE TRADING INC
21041 S Wstn Ave Ste 200, Torrance (90501)
PHONE................................310 649-1188
EMP: 40 EST: 2014
SQ FT: 4,000
SALES (est): 2.1MM Privately Held
SIC: 3944 5092

(P-22722)
UNDERGROUND GAMES INC
2356 253rd St, Lomita (90717-2010)
P.O. Box 1214, Redondo Beach (90278-0214)
PHONE................................310 379-0100
Leroy Sawyer Jr, CEO
Adriane Sawyer, CFO
EMP: 10
SQ FT: 1,000
SALES (est): 1MM Privately Held
SIC: 3944 Board games, puzzles & models, except electronic

(P-22723)
USAOPOLY INC
5607 Palmer Way, Carlsbad (92010-7242)
PHONE................................760 431-5910
Dane Chapin, CEO
Erica Dennis, Controller
Brent Navratil, Sales Mgr
Stephanie Turl, Director
Katie Lowther, Accounts Mgr
▲ EMP: 32
SQ FT: 10,000
SALES (est): 13.4MM Privately Held
SIC: 3944 Board games, puzzles & models, except electronic

(P-22724)
VISION PLASTICS MFG INC
283 Meadowood Ln, Sonoma (95476-4545)
PHONE................................855 476-2767
Jonathan Kemmer, Director
Robert Miller, Director
Stephen Rhoads, Director
Christian Sorensen, Director
EMP: 10
SALES (est): 1.1MM Privately Held
SIC: 3944 Blocks, toy

(P-22725)
WESTAMERICA BANCORPORATION
4550 Mangels Blvd, Fairfield (94534-4083)
P.O. Box 1240, Suisun City (94585-1240)
PHONE................................707 863-6000
David Payne, Branch Mgr
Audrey King, President
Susan Myer, President
Glen Yasaki, COO
Claudia Rodriguez, Info Tech Dir
▲ EMP: 13
SALES (corp-wide): 199.8MM Publicly Held
SIC: 3944 Banks, toy
PA: Westamerica Bancorporation
1108 5th Ave
San Rafael CA 94901
707 863-6000

(P-22726)
WHAT KIDS WANT INC
19428 Londelius St, Northridge (91324-3511)
PHONE................................818 775-0375
Jordon Kort, CEO
Tony Najjar, Vice Pres
Steven Kort, Principal
Caroline Kim, Director
▲ EMP: 14 EST: 1999
SQ FT: 2,000
SALES (est): 2.6MM Privately Held
WEB: www.whatkidswant.net
SIC: 3944 Games, toys & children's vehicles

(P-22727)
WILLIAM MCCLUNG
Also Called: Red Caboose of Colorado
987 Keller Ave, Crescent City (95531-2520)
PHONE................................970 535-4601
EMP: 10
SQ FT: 5,000

SALES (est): 320K Privately Held
SIC: 3944

(P-22728)
WORLDWIDE GAMING SYSTEMS CORP
9205 Alabama Ave Ste E, Chatsworth (91311-5847)
PHONE................................818 678-9150
Peter Khai, President
Shannon Lewis, Technician
Robert Engel, Accountant
Robert Emert, Sales Staff
Roel Dulduleo, Manager
EMP: 25
SALES: 2.5MM Privately Held
SIC: 3944 Video game machines, except coin-operated

3949 Sporting & Athletic Goods, NEC

(P-22729)
800TOTAL GYM COMMERCIAL LLC
5225 Avd Encinas Ste C, Carlsbad (92008-4367)
PHONE................................858 586-6080
Jesse Campanaro, Manager
▲ EMP: 18
SALES (est): 830.8K Privately Held
SIC: 3949 Exercise equipment

(P-22730)
ABSOLUTE BOARD CO INC
4040 Calle Platino # 102, Oceanside (92056-5833)
P.O. Box 4098 (92052-4098)
PHONE................................760 295-2201
Matt Logan, CEO
▲ EMP: 23
SALES (est): 3MM Privately Held
SIC: 3949 Skateboards

(P-22731)
ACTIVA GLOBAL SPT & ENTRMT LLC
30950 Rncho Viejo Rd 125, San Juan Capistrano (92675)
PHONE................................949 265-8260
Raymond Taccolini, Mng Member
▲ EMP: 20
SQ FT: 2,700
SALES (est): 1.2MM Privately Held
SIC: 3949 Sporting & athletic goods

(P-22732)
ACUSHNET COMPANY
Also Called: Titleist
2819 Loker Ave E, Carlsbad (92010-6626)
PHONE................................760 804-6500
John Worster, Branch Mgr
Ken Larose, Vice Pres
Bob Vokey, Vice Pres
Bilal Aljanabi, Admin Asst
Jeff Meyer, Info Tech Dir
EMP: 300 Publicly Held
WEB: www.titleist.com
SIC: 3949 Shafts, golf club
HQ: Acushnet Company
333 Bridge St
Fairhaven MA 02719
508 979-2000

(P-22733)
ADVANTAGE ENGINEERING CORP
Also Called: Valley Sailboards
301 Bernoulli Cir, Oxnard (93030-5164)
PHONE................................805 216-9920
Alan K Pittman, President
EMP: 20
SALES (est): 1.9MM Privately Held
WEB: www.skirope.com
SIC: 3949 5941 2298 Water skiing equipment & supplies, except skis; sporting goods & bicycle shops; cordage & twine

(P-22734)
AFTCO MFG CO INC
Also Called: Bluewater Wear
2400 S Garnsey St, Santa Ana (92707-3335)
PHONE................................949 660-8757
Bill Shedd, President
William D Shedd, CEO
Peggie Shedd, Treasurer
Jill Shedd, General Mgr
Christie Shedd, Opers Mgr
◆ EMP: 71 EST: 1958
SQ FT: 24,000
SALES (est): 17.4MM Privately Held
WEB: www.aftco.com
SIC: 3949 2329 2339 Fishing tackle, general; men's & boys' leather, wool & down-filled outerwear; women's & misses' outerwear

(P-22735)
AIRSOFT ZONE CORPORATION (PA)
Also Called: Airsoft Megastore
138 E Longden Ave, Arcadia (91006-5242)
PHONE................................818 495-6502
Mike Chan, Owner
George Cohen, CFO
Aaron Martin, Engineer
▲ EMP: 20 EST: 2009
SALES (est): 3.4MM Privately Held
SIC: 3949 Sporting & athletic goods

(P-22736)
ALBANY SWIMMING POOL
Also Called: Albanay Aquatic Center
1311 Portland Ave, Albany (94706-1445)
PHONE................................510 559-6640
William Wong, Superintendent
Stephen Dunkle, Director
EMP: 25
SALES (est): 1MM Privately Held
SIC: 3949 Swimming pools, except plastic

(P-22737)
ALDILA INC (HQ)
1945 Kellogg Ave, Carlsbad (92008-6582)
PHONE................................858 513-1801
Peter R Mathewson, Ch of Bd
Peter H Kamin, Shareholder
Scott M Bier, CFO
John E Oldenburg, Vice Pres
Derek Hall, CIO
▲ EMP: 53
SQ FT: 125,000
SALES (est): 153.2MM Privately Held
SIC: 3949 3297 Shafts, golf club; graphite refractories: carbon bond or ceramic bond

(P-22738)
ALDILA INC
Also Called: Aldila De Poway
13450 Stowe Dr, Poway (92064-6860)
PHONE................................858 513-1801
Greg Donaldson, Manager
Sue-WEI Yeh, Controller
EMP: 200 Privately Held
SIC: 3949 3624 5091 Shafts, golf club; carbon & graphite products; golf equipment
HQ: Aldila, Inc.
1945 Kellogg Ave
Carlsbad CA 92008
858 513-1801

(P-22739)
ALDILA GOLF CORP
13450 Stowe Dr, Poway (92064-6860)
PHONE................................858 513-1801
EMP: 104 Privately Held
SIC: 3949 Shafts, golf club
HQ: Aldila Golf Corp.
1945 Kellogg Ave
Carlsbad CA 92008

(P-22740)
ALDILA GOLF CORP (DH)
1945 Kellogg Ave, Carlsbad (92008-6582)
PHONE................................858 513-1801
Peter R Mathewson, CEO
Scott Bier, CFO
Sue-WEI Yeh, Controller
▲ EMP: 78
SQ FT: 52,156

SALES (est): 15.8MM Privately Held
WEB: www.aldilagolf.com
SIC: 3949 Shafts, golf club
HQ: Aldila, Inc.
1945 Kellogg Ave
Carlsbad CA 92008
858 513-1801

(P-22741)
ALTERG INC
48368 Milmont Dr, Fremont (94538-7324)
PHONE................................510 270-5900
Sanjay Gupta, CEO
Kevin Davidge, CFO
Dev Mishra, Chief Mktg Ofcr
Gabriel Griego, Vice Pres
Clement Leung, Vice Pres
▲ EMP: 60
SQ FT: 15,247
SALES (est): 12.9MM Privately Held
WEB: www.alter-g.com
SIC: 3949 Lacrosse equipment & supplies, general

(P-22742)
AMERICAN MAPLE INC
14020 S Western Ave, Gardena (90249-3008)
PHONE................................310 515-8881
Ben Hong, President
◆ EMP: 13
SQ FT: 24,000
SALES (est): 4.4MM Privately Held
SIC: 3949 Fishing tackle, general

(P-22743)
AMERICAN PREMIER CORP
1531 S Carlos Ave, Ontario (91761-7661)
PHONE................................909 923-7070
Michael Wu, President
Ric Heat, General Mgr
▲ EMP: 48
SQ FT: 15,000
SALES (est): 2.5MM Privately Held
WEB: www.americanpremiercorp.com
SIC: 3949 Reels, fishing; rods & rod parts, fishing; fishing equipment

(P-22744)
AMERICAN UNDERWATER PRODUCTS (HQ)
Also Called: Oceanic
2002 Davis St, San Leandro (94577-1211)
PHONE................................800 435-3483
Robert R Hollis, CEO
Paul Elsinga, COO
◆ EMP: 93 EST: 1973
SQ FT: 74,000
SALES (est): 36.7MM Privately Held
WEB: www.pro-a.com
SIC: 3949 5941 Sporting & athletic goods; skin diving, scuba equipment & supplies

(P-22745)
AMERICANA SPORTS INC
422 S Vermont Ave, Glendora (91741-6256)
PHONE................................626 914-0238
Chris Wellington, President
John Yeh, Chairman
▲ EMP: 25
SALES (est): 2.1MM Privately Held
SIC: 3949 Surfboards

(P-22746)
AMRON INTERNATIONAL INC (PA)
1380 Aspen Way, Vista (92081-8349)
PHONE................................760 208-6500
Debra L Ritchie, CEO
Mike Malone, Vice Pres
Latonya Jaramillo, Buyer
Joe Esparza, Marketing Mgr
Kirby Morgan, Products
◆ EMP: 75
SQ FT: 40,000
SALES (est): 12.9MM Privately Held
WEB: www.amronintl.com
SIC: 3949 5091 Skin diving equipment, scuba type; diving equipment & supplies

(P-22747)
ANDERSON BAT COMPANY LLC
236 E Orangethorpe Ave, Placentia (92870-6442)
PHONE................................714 524-7500

▲ EMP: 53
SQ FT: 5,300
SALES (est): 538.7K **Privately Held**
WEB: www.andersonbat.com
SIC: 3949

(P-22748)
ANTHONY JONES
Also Called: Coral Reef Dive Center
14161 Beach Blvd, Westminster
(92683-4451)
PHONE..................................714 894-3483
Anthony Jones, *Owner*
▲ EMP: 15
SALES (est): 1.1MM **Privately Held**
WEB: www.coralreefusa.com
SIC: 3949 5941 5091 Water sports equipment; water sport equipment; diving equipment & supplies

(P-22749)
ARBOR SNOWBOARDS INC
102 Washington Blvd, Marina Del Rey
(90292-5126)
PHONE..................................310 577-1120
Robert Carlson, *President*
Chris Jensen, *Vice Pres*
Nate Shute, *Engineer*
Tina Goff, *Opers Mgr*
Dakota Franklin, *Merchandising*
▲ EMP: 20
SQ FT: 2,400
SALES (est): 2.4MM **Privately Held**
WEB: www.arborsports.com
SIC: 3949 Winter sports equipment

(P-22750)
ASPHALT FABRIC AND ENGRG INC
2683 Lime Ave, Signal Hill (90755-2709)
PHONE..................................562 997-4129
Bill Goldsmith, *President*
Joe Salamone, *CFO*
Doug Coulter, *Vice Pres*
EMP: 90
SQ FT: 5,000
SALES (est): 16.6MM **Privately Held**
SIC: 3949 Sporting & athletic goods

(P-22751)
ATOMIC AQUATICS INC (PA)
3585 Cadillac Ave Ste A, Costa Mesa
(92626-1495)
PHONE..................................714 375-1433
Dean Garraffa, *President*
Doug Toth, *Admin Sec*
▲ EMP: 10
SQ FT: 6,000
SALES (est): 1.4MM **Privately Held**
WEB: www.atomicaquatics.com
SIC: 3949 Water sports equipment

(P-22752)
AVET INDUSTRIES INC
9687 Topanga Canyon Pl, Chatsworth
(91311-4118)
PHONE..................................818 576-9895
Aruttyun Alajajyan, *President*
Sarkis Alajajyan, *Vice Pres*
EMP: 15
SQ FT: 19,200
SALES (est): 1.9MM **Privately Held**
WEB: www.avetreels.com
SIC: 3949 Reels, fishing

(P-22753)
AZA INDUSTRIES INC (PA)
1410 Vantage Ct, Vista (92081-8509)
PHONE..................................760 560-0440
David H Brown, *President*
Jim Passamonte, *Treasurer*
Bill Pierce, *Vice Pres*
▲ EMP: 40
SQ FT: 27,000
SALES (est): 10.5MM **Privately Held**
WEB: www.syndromedist.com
SIC: 3949 Skateboards

(P-22754)
BAHNE AND COMPANY INC
Also Called: Bahne Single Ski
585 Westlake St Ste A, Encinitas
(92024-3764)
P.O. Box 230326 (92023-0326)
PHONE..................................760 753-8847

William L Bahne, *President*
Robert Bahne, *Vice Pres*
▲ EMP: 10 EST: 1964
SQ FT: 6,000
SALES (est): 2MM **Privately Held**
WEB: www.finsunlimited.com
SIC: 3949 Water skis

(P-22755)
BASE HOCKEY LP (PA)
581 Calle Arroyo, Thousand Oaks
(91360-2506)
PHONE..................................805 405-3650
Ronald Kunisaki, *Partner*
EMP: 10
SALES (est): 2.6MM **Privately Held**
WEB: www.basehockey.com
SIC: 3949 7389 Fencing equipment (sporting goods);

(P-22756)
BBS MANUFACTURING INC
1905 Diamond St Ste A, San Marcos
(92078-5185)
PHONE..................................760 798-8011
Grant Burns, *CEO*
Angela Diaz, *Office Mgr*
Roger Orange, *Manager*
▲ EMP: 16
SQ FT: 13,000
SALES (est): 3MM **Privately Held**
SIC: 3949 Skateboards

(P-22757)
BECHHOLD & SON FLASHER & LURE
616 Keller St, Petaluma (94952-2808)
P.O. Box 967, Foresthill (95631-0967)
PHONE..................................530 367-6650
Jery Bechhold, *Partner*
Roy Bechhold, *Partner*
EMP: 10
SQ FT: 5,000
SALES (est): 1MM **Privately Held**
WEB: www.fishcatcher.com
SIC: 3949 Fishing tackle, general

(P-22758)
BECKER SURFBOARDS INC
301 Pier Ave, Hermosa Beach
(90254-3616)
PHONE..................................310 372-6554
John Leninger, *Branch Mgr*
Travis Stassart, *Manager*
EMP: 10
SALES (corp-wide): 7.3MM **Privately Held**
WEB: www.beckersurf.com
SIC: 3949 Surfboards; archery equipment, general
PA: Becker Surfboards, Inc
121 Waterworks Way # 101
Irvine CA 92618
888 673-0225

(P-22759)
BELL FOUNDRY CO (PA)
5310 Southern Ave, South Gate
(90280-3690)
P.O. Box 1070 (90280-1070)
PHONE..................................323 564-5701
Cesar Capallini, *President*
Dimitry Rabyy, *CFO*
Wanda De Wald, *Treasurer*
Edgar Cruz, *Vice Pres*
▲ EMP: 60 EST: 1924
SQ FT: 140,000
SALES (est): 7.6MM **Privately Held**
WEB: www.bfco.com
SIC: 3949 3321 Dumbbells & other weightlifting equipment; gray & ductile iron foundries

(P-22760)
BELL SPORTS INC (HQ)
Also Called: Easton Bell Sports
5550 Scotts Valley Dr, Scotts Valley
(95066-3438)
PHONE..................................469 417-6600
Dan Arment, *President*
Mark A Tripp, *Admin Sec*
◆ EMP: 75
SQ FT: 27,197

SALES (est): 181.8MM
SALES (corp-wide): 2B **Publicly Held**
WEB: www.bellsports.com
SIC: 3949 3751 Helmets, athletic; bicycles & related parts
PA: Vista Outdoor Inc.
1 Vista Way
Anoka MN 55303
801 447-3000

(P-22761)
BEYNON SPORTS SURFACES INC
4668 N Sonora Ave Ste 101, Fresno
(93722-3970)
PHONE..................................559 237-2590
John T Beynon, *Branch Mgr*
EMP: 33
SALES (est): 1.7MM
SALES (corp-wide): 17.8MM **Privately Held**
SIC: 3949 1629 Track & field athletic equipment; athletic field construction
PA: Beynon Sports Surfaces, Inc.
16 Alt Rd
Hunt Valley MD 21030
410 527-0386

(P-22762)
BILLY BEEZ USA LLC
24201 Valencia Blvd, Santa Clarita
(91355-1861)
PHONE..................................661 383-0050
EMP: 12
SALES (corp-wide): 16.7MM **Privately Held**
SIC: 3949 5137 7999 Playground equipment; women's & children's dresses, suits, skirts & blouses; amusement ride
PA: Billy Beez Usa, Llc
3 W 35th St Fl 3 # 3
New York NY 10001
646 606-2249

(P-22763)
BILLY BEEZ USA LLC
925 Blossom Hill Rd # 1397, San Jose
(95123-1230)
PHONE..................................408 300-9547
EMP: 17
SALES (corp-wide): 16.7MM **Privately Held**
SIC: 3949 5137 7999 Playground equipment; women's & children's dresses, suits, skirts & blouses; amusement ride
PA: Billy Beez Usa, Llc
3 W 35th St Fl 3 # 3
New York NY 10001
646 606-2249

(P-22764)
BLOCK ALTERNATIVES
604 W Avenue L Ste 101, Lancaster
(93534-7148)
PHONE..................................661 729-2800
Richard Bartlett, *Owner*
EMP: 11
SQ FT: 6,500
SALES (est): 817.5K **Privately Held**
WEB: www.blockalternatives.com
SIC: 3949 2262 2759 Sporting & athletic goods; screen printing: manmade fiber & silk broadwoven fabrics; screen printing

(P-22765)
BOARDS ON NORD INC
14822 Meridian Meadows Ln, Chico
(95973-9255)
PHONE..................................530 513-3922
Josh Morrow, *President*
▲ EMP: 10
SALES (est): 643.2K **Privately Held**
SIC: 3949 7389 Skateboards;

(P-22766)
BODY FLEX SPORTS INC (PA)
21717 Ferrero, Walnut (91789-5209)
PHONE..................................909 598-9876
Bob Hsiung, *President*
▲ EMP: 12
SQ FT: 10,000
SALES (est): 2.9MM **Privately Held**
WEB: www.bodyflex.com
SIC: 3949 Exercise equipment

(P-22767)
BOOSTED INC (PA)
Also Called: Boosted Boards
82 Pioneer Way Ste 200, Mountain View
(94041-1526)
PHONE..................................650 933-5151
Sanjay Dastoor, *CEO*
Ashley Wilburne, *Office Mgr*
Alberto Cayabyab, *Technician*
Jason Bluhm, *Engineer*
Oliver Riihiluoma, *Engineer*
EMP: 26
SALES (est): 6.4MM **Privately Held**
SIC: 3949 Skateboards

(P-22768)
BRAVO SPORTS
Also Called: Sector9
4370 Jutland Dr, San Diego (92117-3642)
PHONE..................................858 408-0083
Derek Oneill, *CEO*
EMP: 50
SALES (corp-wide): 26.8MM **Privately Held**
SIC: 3949 Skateboards
HQ: Bravo Sports
12801 Carmenita Rd
Santa Fe Springs CA 90670
562 484-5100

(P-22769)
BRAVO SPORTS (HQ)
12801 Carmenita Rd, Santa Fe Springs
(90670-4805)
PHONE..................................562 484-5100
Nicholas Schultz, *President*
Steven Finney, *Controller*
Meghan Sinnott, *Marketing Staff*
◆ EMP: 80
SQ FT: 100,000
SALES (est): 29.3MM
SALES (corp-wide): 26.8MM **Privately Held**
SIC: 3949 Sporting & athletic goods
PA: Transom Bravo Holdings Corp.
12801 Carmenita Rd
Santa Fe Springs CA 90670
562 484-5100

(P-22770)
BUILD AT HOME LLC
273 N Benson Ave, Upland (91786-5614)
PHONE..................................909 949-1601
Joseph Ciaglia,
EMP: 10 EST: 2015
SALES (est): 441.1K **Privately Held**
SIC: 3949 Skateboards

(P-22771)
C PREME LIMITED LLC
Also Called: C-Preme
1250 E 223rd St, Carson (90745-4266)
PHONE..................................310 355-0498
Ryan Ratner, *Mng Member*
Corey Ratner, *Mng Member*
▲ EMP: 18
SQ FT: 40,000
SALES (est): 1.8MM
SALES (corp-wide): 2B **Publicly Held**
SIC: 3949 5091 5571 5099 Skateboards; bicycles; motor scooters; luggage
PA: Vista Outdoor Inc.
1 Vista Way
Anoka MN 55303
801 447-3000

(P-22772)
CALLAWAY GOLF COMPANY
5858 Dryden Pl, Carlsbad (92008-6503)
PHONE..................................760 804-4502
Pascual Luna, *Principal*
John Cushman, *Bd of Directors*
Brian Lynch, *Exec VP*
Bramley John, *Prgrmr*
Jennifer Thomas, *Controller*
EMP: 1000
SALES (corp-wide): 1.2B **Publicly Held**
SIC: 3949 Sporting & athletic goods
PA: Callaway Golf Company
2180 Rutherford Rd
Carlsbad CA 92008
760 931-1771

(P-22773)
CALLAWAY GOLF COMPANY
44500 Indian Wells Ln, Indian Wells
(92210-8746)
PHONE................................760 345-4653
Mike Pease, *Director*
EMP: 1000
SALES (corp-wide): 1.2B **Publicly Held**
SIC: 3949 Shafts, golf club
PA: Callaway Golf Company
2180 Rutherford Rd
Carlsbad CA 92008
760 931-1771

(P-22774)
**CALLAWAY GOLF COMPANY
(PA)**
2180 Rutherford Rd, Carlsbad
(92008-7328)
PHONE................................760 931-1771
Oliver G Brewer III, *President*
Ronald S Beard, *Ch of Bd*
Brian P Lynch, *CFO*
Glenn Hickey, *Exec VP*
Mark F Leposky, *Exec VP*
◆ **EMP:** 277
SQ FT: 269,000
SALES: 1.2B **Publicly Held**
WEB: www.callawaygolf.com
SIC: 3949 2329 2339 6794 Golf equip-
ment; shafts, golf club; balls: baseball,
football, basketball, etc.; bags, golf; men's
& boys' sportswear & athletic clothing;
athletic (warmup, sweat & jogging) suits:
men's & boys'; women's & misses' ath-
letic clothing & sportswear; athletic clothing: women's, misses' & juniors'; women's
& misses' accessories; patent buying, licensing, leasing

(P-22775)
CAMELBAK ACQUISITION CORP
2000 S Mcdowell Blvd, Petaluma
(94954-6901)
PHONE................................707 792-9700
EMP: 101
SALES (est): 5.6MM
SALES (corp-wide): 2B **Publicly Held**
SIC: 3949 Camping equipment & supplies
PA: Vista Outdoor Inc.
1 Vista Way
Anoka MN 55303
801 447-3000

(P-22776)
**CAMELBAK PRODUCTS LLC
(HQ)**
2000 S Mcdowell Blvd, Petaluma
(94954-6901)
PHONE................................707 792-9700
Scott D Chaplin, *Mng Member*
Jody Brunner,
Glenn Gross,
Stephen M Nolan,
J Marty O'Donohue,
◆ **EMP:** 100
SQ FT: 50,000
SALES (est): 23.5MM
SALES (corp-wide): 2B **Publicly Held**
SIC: 3949 Camping equipment & supplies
PA: Vista Outdoor Inc.
1 Vista Way
Anoka MN 55303
801 447-3000

(P-22777)
CASA DE HERMANDAD (PA)
Also Called: WEST AREA OPPORTUNITY
CENTER
11750 W Pico Blvd, Los Angeles
(90064-1309)
PHONE................................310 477-8272
David Abelar, *President*
EMP: 30
SQ FT: 4,500
SALES: 59K **Privately Held**
SIC: 3949 Driving ranges, golf, electronic

(P-22778)
CATCH SURFBOARD CO LLC
201 Calle Pintoresco, San Clemente
(92672-7530)
PHONE................................949 218-0428
George Arzente, *President*
Chris Monroe, *Vice Pres*

Geneva Vancampen, *Opers Staff*
Joel Manalastas, *Sales Mgr*
John Schlesinger, *Director*
EMP: 12 **EST:** 2008
SALES (est): 345.1K **Privately Held**
SIC: 3949 Surfboards

(P-22779)
**CHAMPION DISCS
INCORPORATED**
Also Called: Innova Champion Discs
950 S Dupont Ave, Ontario (91761-1525)
PHONE................................800 408-8449
David B Dunipace, *President*
Charles Duvall, *Treasurer*
Harold G Duvall, *Vice Pres*
Greg Muir, *Vice Pres*
Tim Selinske, *Admin Sec*
▲ **EMP:** 11
SQ FT: 22,000
SALES (est): 2.2MM **Privately Held**
WEB: www.innovadiscs.com
SIC: 3949 Sporting & athletic goods

(P-22780)
**CHANNEL ISLANDS
SURFBOARDS INC**
1115 Mark Ave, Carpinteria (93013-2917)
PHONE................................805 745-2823
Al Merrik, *Manager*
EMP: 10
SALES (corp-wide): 188.4MM **Privately
Held**
SIC: 3949 Surfboards
HQ: Channel Islands Surfboards Inc.
36 Anacapa St
Santa Barbara CA 93101
805 966-7213

(P-22781)
**CHAPMN-WLTERS
INTRCOASTAL CORP**
Also Called: Cwic
141 Via Lampara, Rcho STA Marg
(92688-2954)
PHONE................................949 448-9940
Andrew De Camara, *Receiver*
Cindi A Walters, *President*
◆ **EMP:** 40
SQ FT: 103,000
SALES (est): 4.3MM **Privately Held**
WEB: www.cwicfluid.com
SIC: 3949 Sporting & athletic goods

(P-22782)
CITY OF SANTA FE SPRINGS
Also Called: Santafe Spg PKS&rec Lake Cntr
11641 Florence Ave, Santa Fe Springs
(90670-4353)
PHONE................................562 868-8761
Manuel Cantu, *Director*
EMP: 10 **Privately Held**
WEB: www.santafesprings.org
SIC: 3949 Track & field athletic equipment
PA: City Of Santa Fe Springs
11710 Telegraph Rd
Santa Fe Springs CA 90670
562 409-7500

(P-22783)
CLEANWORLD
2330 Gold Meadow Way, Gold River
(95670-4471)
PHONE................................916 635-7300
Michele Wong, *CEO*
Amy Tucker, *Info Tech Mgr*
Josh Rapport, *Research*
Jason Woldseth, *Engineer*
EMP: 13
SALES (est): 2MM **Privately Held**
SIC: 3949 Exercise equipment

(P-22784)
**CONDOR OUTDOOR PRODUCTS
INC (PA)**
5268 Rivergrade Rd, Baldwin Park
(91706-1336)
PHONE................................626 358-3270
Spencer Tien, *President*
Jennifer Saavedra, *Executive*
Nell Chen, *General Mgr*
Mandy Tsai, *Office Mgr*
Steve Law, *Info Tech Mgr*
◆ **EMP:** 37 **EST:** 1994
SQ FT: 11,000

SALES (est): 4.9MM **Privately Held**
WEB: www.condoroutdoor.com
SIC: 3949 Sporting & athletic goods

(P-22785)
**CONTINENTAL FIBERGLASS
INC (PA)**
17031 Muskrat Ave, Adelanto
(92301-2259)
PHONE................................760 246-6480
William Lohman, *President*
▼ **EMP:** 10
SQ FT: 25,000
SALES (est): 1.8MM **Privately Held**
SIC: 3949 Swimming pools, except plastic

(P-22786)
CRAZY INDUSTRIES
8675 Avenida Costa Norte, San Diego
(92154-6253)
PHONE................................619 270-9090
Brian Kelly, *Controller*
EMP: 40
SALES (corp-wide): 3.8MM **Privately
Held**
SIC: 3949 Sporting & athletic goods
PA: Crazy Industries
9840 Prospect Ave
Santee CA 92071
619 270-9090

(P-22787)
CYCLE HOUSE LLC
8511 Melrose Ave, West Hollywood
(90069-5114)
PHONE................................310 358-0888
Adam Gillman, *Mng Member*
Elizabeth Tabak, *Opers Staff*
Julien Crochet,
Lara Gillman,
▲ **EMP:** 35
SALES (est): 226.5K **Privately Held**
SIC: 3949 Exercising cycles

(P-22788)
D HAUPTMAN CO INC
Also Called: Fold-A-Goal
4856 W Jefferson Blvd, Los Angeles
(90016-3921)
PHONE................................323 734-2507
David Hauptman, *President*
Amy Schaub, *Treasurer*
Aaron Hauptman, *Vice Pres*
Diana Hauptman, *Admin Sec*
Merlyn Cruz, *Manager*
◆ **EMP:** 23
SQ FT: 11,000
SALES (est): 3.3MM **Privately Held**
WEB: www.fold-a-goal.com
SIC: 3949 Soccer equipment & supplies

(P-22789)
DGB LLC
Also Called: Rusty Surfboards
8495 Commerce Ave, San Diego
(92121-2608)
PHONE................................858 578-0414
Rusty Preisendorfer, *President*
EMP: 20
SALES (est): 892.1K **Privately Held**
SIC: 3949 Surfboards

(P-22790)
**DIAMOND BASEBALL COMPANY
INC**
Also Called: Diamond Sports
1880 E Saint Andrew Pl, Santa Ana
(92705-5043)
P.O. Box 55090, Irvine (92619-5090)
PHONE................................800 366-2999
Jay Hicks, *CEO*
Andrea Gordon, *President*
Robert W Ezell, *Vice Pres*
Monte Robertson, *Sales Staff*
Janet Carlton, *Cust Mgr*
◆ **EMP:** 23
SQ FT: 120,000
SALES (est): 3.8MM **Privately Held**
WEB: www.diamond-sports.com
SIC: 3949 5091 Baseball equipment &
supplies, general; athletic goods

(P-22791)
**DIVING UNLIMITED
INTERNATIONAL**
1148 Delevan Dr, San Diego (92102-2499)
PHONE................................619 236-1203
Susan Long, *CEO*
Richard Long, *President*
Dan Drake, *Engineer*
Ali Khorshidi, *Accountant*
Shahram Homayounfar, *Controller*
◆ **EMP:** 75
SQ FT: 14,500
SALES (est): 9.7MM **Privately Held**
WEB: www.dui-online.com
SIC: 3949 Skin diving equipment, scuba
type

(P-22792)
DYNA-KING INC
Also Called: Abby Precision Mfg
597 Santana Dr Ste A, Cloverdale
(95425-4250)
PHONE................................707 894-5566
Lenora Abby, *President*
Ron Abby, *Officer*
EMP: 12
SQ FT: 5,000
SALES: 800K **Privately Held**
WEB: www.dyna-king.com
SIC: 3949 5941 5091 Fishing equipment;
sporting goods & bicycle shops; sporting
& recreation goods

(P-22793)
DYNAFLEX INTERNATIONAL
Also Called: Dynabee USA
1144 N Grove St, Anaheim (92806-2109)
PHONE................................714 630-0909
▲ **EMP:** 20
SQ FT: 5,000
SALES (est): 2MM **Privately Held**
WEB: www.dynaflexpro.com
SIC: 3949

(P-22794)
EAI-JR286 INC
20100 S Vermont Ave, Torrance
(90502-1361)
PHONE................................310 297-6400
Jonathan Hirshberg, *Principal*
EMP: 12
SALES (est): 287K **Privately Held**
SIC: 3949 Baseball equipment & supplies,
general

(P-22795)
**EF COMPOSITE TECHNOLOGIES
LP**
2151 Las Palmas Dr Ste D, Carlsbad
(92011-1575)
PHONE................................800 433-6723
Ronald A Grimes, *Partner*
▲ **EMP:** 10 **EST:** 1994
SALES (est): 880.4K **Privately Held**
SIC: 3949 Sporting & athletic goods

(P-22796)
EFGP INC
Also Called: E. Force Sports
1384 Poinsettia Ave Ste E, Vista
(92081-8505)
PHONE................................760 692-3900
Ronald A Grimes, *President*
▲ **EMP:** 15
SALES (est): 1.5MM **Privately Held**
WEB: www.eforce.com
SIC: 3949 Racket sports equipment

(P-22797)
ERMICO ENTERPRISES INC
1111 17th St Ste B, San Francisco
(94107-2406)
P.O. Box 885403 (94188-5403)
PHONE................................415 822-6776
Rebekah Engel, *President*
Linda Decay, *Corp Secy*
Gwynned Vitello, *Vice Pres*
▲ **EMP:** 100
SQ FT: 19,000
SALES (est): 12.4MM **Privately Held**
SIC: 3949 3599 3365 3366 Skateboards;
machine shop, jobbing & repair; alu-
minum foundries; brass foundry

(P-22798)
EXACTACATOR INC (PA)
2237 Stagecoach Rd, Stockton
(95215-7915)
P.O. Box 8501 (95208-0501)
PHONE.....................209 464-8979
James G Nesbitt, *President*
Shelley Holcomb, *Treasurer*
John Nakashima, *Vice Pres*
Barbara Nesbitt, *Admin Sec*
David Brown, *Sales Staff*
▲ EMP: 25
SQ FT: 21,000
SALES (est): 2.4MM **Privately Held**
WEB: www.viseinserts.com
SIC: 3949 Bowling equipment & supplies;
bows, archery

(P-22799)
FAIRWAY IMPORT-EXPORT INC
Also Called: Lantic USA
2130 E Gladwick St, Rancho Dominguez
(90220-6203)
PHONE.....................310 637-6162
Guido Rietdyk, *President*
▲ EMP: 35
SQ FT: 17,000
SALES (est): 5.3MM **Privately Held**
SIC: 3949 Protective sporting equipment

(P-22800)
FINIS INC (PA)
Also Called: Finis USA
5849 W Schulte Rd Ste 104, Tracy
(95377-8135)
PHONE.....................925 454-0111
John Mix, *CEO*
Bob Bowe, *CFO*
Vicki Espiritu, *Executive*
Clarke Dolliver, *Graphic Designe*
Charbel Yamuni, *Opers Staff*
▲ EMP: 25
SALES (est): 3.5MM **Privately Held**
WEB: www.finisinc.com
SIC: 3949 Surfboards

(P-22801)
FITNESS WAREHOUSE LLC (PA)
Also Called: Hoist Fitness Systems
9990 Alesmith Ct Ste 130, San Diego
(92126-4200)
PHONE.....................858 578-7676
Jeffrey Partrick, *Partner*
Jenna Novotny, *Marketing Staff*
Lisa Shouse, *Manager*
◆ EMP: 30
SALES (est): 2.5MM **Privately Held**
SIC: 3949 Sporting & athletic goods

(P-22802)
FLOW SPORTS INC (PA)
1011 Calle Sombra Ste 220, San Clemente
(92673-4206)
PHONE.....................949 361-5260
Anthony Scaturro, *CEO*
Anthony D Scaturro, *President*
◆ EMP: 23
SALES (est): 3.5MM **Privately Held**
WEB: www.flow.com
SIC: 3949 Snow skiing equipment & sup-
plies, except skis

(P-22803)
FLYDIVE INC (PA)
3209 Midway Dr Unit 203, San Diego
(92110-4517)
PHONE.....................844 359-3483
James Plante, *CEO*
▲ EMP: 16
SQ FT: 12,000
SALES (est): 1.4MM **Privately Held**
SIC: 3949 Water sports equipment

(P-22804)
**FUJIKURA COMPOSITE
AMERICA INC**
Also Called: Fujikuria Composits
1819 Aston Ave Ste 101, Carlsbad
(92008-7338)
PHONE.....................760 598-6060
Peter Sanchez, *President*
Kenji Morita, *CFO*
▲ EMP: 20
SALES (est): 2.7MM **Privately Held**
WEB: www.fujikuragolf.com
SIC: 3949 Shafts, golf club

PA: Fujikura Composites Inc.
3-5-7, Ariake
Koto-Ku TKY 135-0
-

(P-22805)
G PUCCI & SONS INC
460 Valley Dr, Brisbane (94005-1210)
PHONE.....................415 468-0452
John Pucci, *Owner*
Stefano Pucci, *President*
Angelo Pucci, *CFO*
◆ EMP: 10
SQ FT: 50,050
SALES (est): 1.4MM **Privately Held**
WEB: www.p-line.com
SIC: 3949 Fishing tackle, general

(P-22806)
GENTRY GOLF MAINTENANCE
14893 Ball Rd, Anaheim (92806-5048)
PHONE.....................714 630-3541
Dave Graff, *Partner*
EMP: 20
SALES (est): 987.1K **Privately Held**
SIC: 3949 5941 Driving ranges, golf, elec-
tronic; golf goods & equipment

(P-22807)
GERALD GENTELLALLI
Also Called: Rancho Safari
19360 Camino Vista Rd, Ramona
(92065-6770)
P.O. Box 691 (92065-0691)
PHONE.....................760 789-2094
Gerald Gentellalli, *President*
Donald Reynolds, *Safety Dir*
Celeste Wilder, *Manager*
EMP: 15
SQ FT: 5,000
SALES: 1.3MM **Privately Held**
SIC: 3949 5961 Hunting equipment;
archery equipment, general; fishing, hunt-
ing & camping equipment & supplies: mail
order

(P-22808)
GLIMMER GEAR
4337 Alabama St, San Diego (92104-1023)
PHONE.....................619 399-9211
Kali Hussain, *Owner*
EMP: 10
SALES: 97K **Privately Held**
SIC: 3949 7389 5961 Sporting & athletic
goods; ; catalog & mail-order houses

(P-22809)
GLOBAL BILLIARD MFG CO INC
1141 Sandhill Ave, Carson (90746-1314)
PHONE.....................310 764-5000
Torben W Gramstrup, *President*
Solveig M Gramstrup, *Admin Sec*
◆ EMP: 20
SQ FT: 30,000
SALES: 1.3MM **Privately Held**
WEB: www.globalbilliard.com
SIC: 3949 Billiard & pool equipment & sup-
plies, general

(P-22810)
GOLF DESIGN INC
Also Called: Golf Design USA
10523 Humbolt St, Los Alamitos
(90720-5401)
PHONE.....................714 899-4040
John Tate, *President*
Patricia Tate, *VP Finance*
▲ EMP: 70
SQ FT: 18,000
SALES (est): 10.8MM **Privately Held**
SIC: 3949 Golf equipment

(P-22811)
GOOMBY LLC
Also Called: Goomby Skateboarding
8350 Wilshire Blvd # 200, Beverly Hills
(90211-2327)
PHONE.....................323 556-0637
John Pyle,
Dave Pyle,
◆ EMP: 13 EST: 2007
SQ FT: 2,000
SALES (est): 753.4K **Privately Held**
SIC: 3949 Skateboards

(P-22812)
GP INDUSTRIES INC
3230 Rvrsid Ave Ste 110, Paso Robles
(93446)
PHONE.....................805 227-6565
Phil Patti, *CEO*
Arthur Gutierrez, *Corp Secy*
▲ EMP: 15 EST: 1999
SALES (est): 2.6MM **Privately Held**
WEB: www.gpindinc.com
SIC: 3949 Sporting & athletic goods

(P-22813)
**GRAVITY BOARDING COMPANY
INC**
Also Called: Skateboard
2211 S Hcnda Blvd Ste 201, Hacienda
Heights (91745)
PHONE.....................760 591-4144
Michael Bream, *President*
Mary Bream, *Shareholder*
Chris Taylor, *Shareholder*
EMP: 12
SQ FT: 5,000
SALES (est): 1.3MM **Privately Held**
SIC: 3949 5941 Skateboards; skateboard-
ing equipment

(P-22814)
**GREENFIELDS OUTDOOR
FITNES INC**
2617 W Woodland Dr, Anaheim
(92801-2627)
PHONE.....................888 315-9037
Samuel Mendelsohn, *CEO*
Aviv Avivshay, *Shareholder*
◆ EMP: 15
SALES: 4MM **Privately Held**
SIC: 3949 Gymnasium equipment

(P-22815)
GSI CAPITAL PARTNERS LLC
888 Rancheros Dr Ste A, San Marcos
(92069-3044)
PHONE.....................760 745-1768
Mario F Garcia, *President*
Michael MA, *Vice Pres*
Andrew H Tarlow, *Mng Member*
▲ EMP: 13
SQ FT: 11,000
SALES (est): 1.2MM **Privately Held**
SIC: 3949 Golf equipment

(P-22816)
**HAMPTON FITNESS PRODUCTS
LTD**
1913 Portola Rd, Ventura (93003-8030)
PHONE.....................805 339-9733
Zagngang Guo, *Ch of Bd*
Shirley Jay, *CFO*
Robert Hornbuckle, *Vice Pres*
▲ EMP: 14
SQ FT: 30,000
SALES: 7MM **Privately Held**
WEB: www.hamptonfit.com
SIC: 3949 Exercise equipment

(P-22817)
HATCH OUTDOORS INC
961 Park Center Dr, Vista (92081-8312)
PHONE.....................760 734-4343
John Torok, *President*
▲ EMP: 11
SALES (est): 1.3MM **Privately Held**
SIC: 3949 Fishing equipment; bait, artifi-
cial: fishing; fishing tackle, general;
hooks, fishing

(P-22818)
HAYDENSHAPES SURFBOARDS
209 Richmond St Apt D, El Segundo
(90245-5110)
PHONE.....................310 648-8268
Hayden Cox, *Owner*
Kye Fitzgerald, *Natl Sales Mgr*
Katrina Grange, *Manager*
◆ EMP: 13
SALES (est): 1.3MM **Privately Held**
SIC: 3949 Surfboards

(P-22819)
HEART RATE INC
Also Called: Versaclimber
1411 E Wilshire Ave, Santa Ana
(92705-4422)
PHONE.....................714 850-9716
Richard D Charnitski, *President*
Redge Henn, *Vice Pres*
Dan Charnitski, *Admin Sec*
Peri Fetsch, *Controller*
Sergio Raya, *Production*
▲ EMP: 38
SQ FT: 18,000
SALES (est): 6.3MM **Privately Held**
WEB: www.heartrateinc.com
SIC: 3949 Exercise equipment

(P-22820)
HILLERICH & BRADSBY CO
Also Called: R & B Research & Development
5960 Jetton Ln, Loomis (95650-9594)
PHONE.....................916 652-4267
George Berger, *Branch Mgr*
EMP: 20
SALES (corp-wide): 96.3MM **Privately
Held**
WEB: www.slugger.com
SIC: 3949 Baseball equipment & supplies,
general; golf equipment; sticks: hockey,
lacrosse, etc.
PA: Hillerich & Bradsby Co.
800 W Main St
Louisville KY 40202
502 585-5226

(P-22821)
HILLERICH & BRADSBY CO
Also Called: H & B Sports Products Div
1800 S Archibald Ave, Ontario
(91761-7647)
PHONE.....................800 282-2287
Tom R Harris, *Branch Mgr*
EMP: 100
SALES (corp-wide): 96.3MM **Privately
Held**
WEB: www.slugger.com
SIC: 3949 3354 Baseball equipment &
supplies, general; aluminum extruded
products
PA: Hillerich & Bradsby Co.
800 W Main St
Louisville KY 40202
502 585-5226

(P-22822)
HOIST FITNESS SYSTEMS INC
11900 Community Rd, Poway
(92064-7143)
PHONE.....................858 578-7676
Jeff Partrick, *CEO*
Jody Paulsen, *Executive*
Tim Waterman, *Marketing Mgr*
Natalie Mendoza, *Sales Mgr*
Karen Kirch, *Sales Associate*
◆ EMP: 65
SQ FT: 105,000
SALES (est): 9.9MM **Privately Held**
WEB: www.hoistfitness.com
SIC: 3949 5941 Exercise equipment; exer-
cise equipment

(P-22823)
HUPA INTERNATIONAL INC
Also Called: Body Flex Sports
21717 Ferrero, Walnut (91789-5209)
PHONE.....................909 598-9876
Bob Hsiung, *President*
▲ EMP: 21
SQ FT: 30,000
SALES (est): 1.9MM **Privately Held**
WEB: www.bodychamp.com
SIC: 3949 Exercise equipment

(P-22824)
HYDRAPAK INC
6605 San Leandro St, Oakland
(94621-3317)
PHONE.....................510 632-8318
Matthew Lyon, *CEO*
Michael Massucco, *Director*
▲ EMP: 25
SALES (est): 892.3K **Privately Held**
WEB: www.hydrapak.com
SIC: 3949 Sporting & athletic goods

(P-22825)
I & I SPORTS SUPPLY COMPANY (PA)
19751 Figueroa St, Carson (90745-1004)
PHONE.................................310 715-6800
Alan Iba, *President*
▲ EMP: 20
SALES (est): 4.4MM **Privately Held**
WEB: www.ilsports.com
SIC: 3949 5091 5941 Sporting & athletic goods; sporting & recreation goods; martial arts equipment & supplies

(P-22826)
IGOLPING INC
43583 Greenhills Way, Fremont (94539-5916)
PHONE.................................866 507-4440
Doug Sumaraga, *Principal*
EMP: 10
SQ FT: 2,000
SALES (est): 680K **Privately Held**
SIC: 3949 Driving ranges, golf, electronic

(P-22827)
ILLAH SPORTS INC A CORPORATION
Also Called: Belding Golf Bag Company, The
1610 Fiske Pl, Oxnard (93033-1849)
PHONE.................................805 240-7790
Brien Patermo, *CEO*
Steve Perrin, *President*
Jackie Perrin, *Vice Pres*
▲ EMP: 50
SALES (est): 5.2MM **Privately Held**
SIC: 3949 Sporting & athletic goods

(P-22828)
INNOVATIVE EARTH PRODUCTS
232 Avenida Fabricante, San Clemente (92672-7555)
PHONE.................................888 588-5955
Steve Yates, *President*
Vicky Hastings, *Analyst*
San Clemente, *Accounts Mgr*
▲ EMP: 10
SQ FT: 4,100
SALES: 100K **Privately Held**
SIC: 3949 Camping equipment & supplies

(P-22829)
INTERNATIONAL SALES INC
Also Called: ISI
3210 Production Ave Ste B, Oceanside (92058-1306)
PHONE.................................760 722-1455
Linda Prettyman, *President*
Ed Mroz, *Vice Pres*
▲ EMP: 20
SQ FT: 11,000
SALES (est): 1.5MM **Privately Held**
SIC: 3949 2321 3751 Skateboards; men's & boys' furnishings; bicycles & related parts

(P-22830)
INTERNTNAL INDIAN TRATY CUNCIL
2940 16th St Ste 305, San Francisco (94103-3688)
PHONE.................................415 641-4482
Andrea Carmen, *Exec Dir*
Francisco Cali, *President*
Ron Lameman, *Treasurer*
Yamilka Hernandez, *Bd of Directors*
EMP: 13
SALES: 549.5K **Privately Held**
WEB: www.treatycouncil.org
SIC: 3949 Indian clubs

(P-22831)
IRON GRIP BARBELL COMPANY INC
4012 W Garry Ave, Santa Ana (92704-6300)
PHONE.................................714 850-6900
Scott Frasco, *CEO*
Michael Rojas, *President*
Irma Ramirez, *General Mgr*
Chuck Brown, *Controller*
Donna McCallum, *Sales Mgr*
▼ EMP: 85
SQ FT: 63,000

SALES (est): 18.2MM **Privately Held**
WEB: www.irongrip.com
SIC: 3949 Exercise equipment

(P-22832)
J B L ENTERPRISES INC
3219 Roymar Rd, Oceanside (92058-1311)
P.O. Box 1105, Orange (92856-0105)
PHONE.................................760 754-2727
Guy Skinner, *President*
▲ EMP: 13
SQ FT: 10,000
SALES (est): 2MM **Privately Held**
SIC: 3949 Fishing equipment; spears & spearguns, fishing

(P-22833)
J F CHRISTOPHER INC
Also Called: Bonehead Composites
3110 Indian Ave Ste D, Perris (92571-3271)
PHONE.................................951 943-1166
Chris Frisella, *President*
EMP: 15 EST: 1996
SALES (est): 1.2MM **Privately Held**
WEB: www.boneheadcomposites.com
SIC: 3949 Helmets, athletic

(P-22834)
JOHNSON OUTDOORS INC
Scuba Pro
1166 Fesler St Ste A, El Cajon (92020-1813)
PHONE.................................619 402-1023
Joe Stella, *Branch Mgr*
John Richardson, *Technician*
Jill Maucere, *Human Resources*
EMP: 45
SALES (corp-wide): 490.5MM **Publicly Held**
SIC: 3949 5091 Skin diving equipment, scuba type; diving equipment & supplies
PA: Johnson Outdoors Inc.
555 Main St
Racine WI 53403
262 631-6600

(P-22835)
KAREEM CORPORATION
Also Called: Kareem Cart Commissary & Mfg
4423 S Vermont Ave, Los Angeles (90037-2413)
PHONE.................................323 234-0724
Mona Abdul Jawwad, *President*
Magdy Mahpa, *Admin Sec*
EMP: 10
SALES (est): 1.2MM **Privately Held**
WEB: www.kareemcarts.com
SIC: 3949 Carts, caddy

(P-22836)
KAYO CORP (PA)
Also Called: Kayo Store, The
6351 Yarrow Dr Ste D, Carlsbad (92011-1545)
PHONE.................................760 918-0405
Troy Morgan, *President*
Leila Morgan, *Admin Sec*
▲ EMP: 11
SALES (est): 2.5MM **Privately Held**
WEB: www.thekayocorp.com
SIC: 3949 Skateboards

(P-22837)
KEISER CORPORATION (PA)
Also Called: Keiser Sports Health Equipment
2470 S Cherry Ave, Fresno (93706-5004)
PHONE.................................559 256-8000
Dennis L Keiser, *CEO*
Portlinn Pangburn, *CFO*
Kathy Keiser, *Treasurer*
Randy Keiser, *Vice Pres*
Gyl Keiser, *Admin Sec*
◆ EMP: 100
SQ FT: 100,000
SALES (est): 19.5MM **Privately Held**
WEB: www.keiser.com
SIC: 3949 Exercise equipment

(P-22838)
KENNY GIANNINI PUTTERS LLC
74755 N Cove Dr, Indian Wells (92210-7142)
P.O. Box 2400, Palm Desert (92261-2400)
PHONE.................................760 851-9475
EMP: 12

SALES (est): 1MM **Privately Held**
SIC: 3949

(P-22839)
L A STEEL CRAFT PRODUCTS (PA)
1975 Lincoln Ave, Pasadena (91103-1321)
P.O. Box 90365 (91109-0365)
PHONE.................................626 798-7401
Beverly Holt, *President*
John C Gaudesi, *COO*
Gene Bourgeault, *Purchasing*
Ron Coker, *Sales Staff*
▲ EMP: 23 EST: 1951
SQ FT: 200,000
SALES (est): 3.2MM **Privately Held**
WEB: www.lasteelcraft.com
SIC: 3949 Playground equipment

(P-22840)
LAB SURF COMPANY
3205 Production Ave Ste G, Oceanside (92058-1304)
PHONE.................................760 757-1975
Ivan Mendoza, *President*
EMP: 11
SALES (est): 790K **Privately Held**
SIC: 3949 Surfboards

(P-22841)
LEADMASTERS
17229 Lemon St Ste E11, Hesperia (92345-5188)
PHONE.................................760 949-6566
Jim Pearce, *Owner*
▲ EMP: 10
SQ FT: 5,800
SALES (est): 738.6K **Privately Held**
SIC: 3949 5091 Fishing tackle, general; fishing tackle

(P-22842)
LIQUID FORCE WAKEBOARDS
Also Called: Free Motion Wakeboards
1815 Aston Ave Ste 105, Carlsbad (92008-7340)
PHONE.................................760 943-8364
Tony Finn, *Owner*
◆ EMP: 50
SALES (est): 3.3MM **Privately Held**
WEB: www.liquidforce.com
SIC: 3949 Water sports equipment

(P-22843)
LOB-STER INC (PA)
Also Called: Lobster Sports
7340 Fulton Ave, North Hollywood (91605-4113)
PHONE.................................818 764-6000
Tony Potter, *President*
Melissa Bush, *Finance Mgr*
◆ EMP: 13
SQ FT: 8,000
SALES (est): 1.6MM **Privately Held**
WEB: www.lobstersports.com
SIC: 3949 Tennis equipment & supplies

(P-22844)
LOUD MOUTH INC
3840 Edna Pl Apt 1, San Diego (92116-3778)
PHONE.................................619 743-0370
Dasean Cunningham, *CEO*
Kevin Gniadek, *CFO*
EMP: 22
SALES (est): 932.9K **Privately Held**
SIC: 3949 Fencing equipment (sporting goods)

(P-22845)
LUCITE INTL PRTNR HOLDINGS INC
MRC Composite Product
5441 Avd Encinas Ste B, Carlsbad (92008-4412)
PHONE.................................760 929-0001
Hikaro Shikashi, *Vice Pres*
EMP: 38 **Privately Held**
WEB: www.ebpass.com
SIC: 3949 Golf equipment
PA: Lucite International Partnership Holdings, Inc.
1403 Foulk Rd
Wilmington DE

(P-22846)
LUCKY STRIKE ENTERTAINMENT INC (PA)
15260 Ventura Blvd # 1110, Sherman Oaks (91403-5346)
PHONE.................................818 933-3752
Steven Foster, *President*
Bryan Reis, *General Mgr*
Raj Tubati, *General Mgr*
Hector Segovia, *Information Mgr*
Melissa Ehrlich, *Human Res Mgr*
EMP: 50
SALES (est): 279.6MM **Privately Held**
SIC: 3949 5812 5813 Bowling alleys & accessories; American restaurant; bar (drinking places)

(P-22847)
MARPO KINETICS INC
1306 Stealth St, Livermore (94551-9356)
PHONE.................................925 606-6919
Marius Popescu, *President*
▲ EMP: 10
SALES (est): 1MM **Privately Held**
WEB: www.marpokinetics.com
SIC: 3949 Sporting & athletic goods

(P-22848)
MARTIN SPORTS INC (PA)
Also Called: Martin Archery
1100 Glendon Ave Ste 920, Los Angeles (90024-3513)
PHONE.................................509 529-2554
Rich Weatherford, *Principal*
Tracy Reiff, *President*
Richard Weatherford, *CEO*
Tim Larkin, *CFO*
Kevin MA, *Vice Pres*
▲ EMP: 29
SQ FT: 28,000
SALES (est): 5.4MM **Privately Held**
SIC: 3949 Sporting & athletic goods

(P-22849)
MASTER INDUSTRIES INC
1001 S Linwood Ave, Santa Ana (92705-4323)
PHONE.................................949 660-0644
Bill Norman, *President*
Steve Norman, *COO*
Helen Norman, *Corp Secy*
Steven Norman, *General Mgr*
▲ EMP: 48
SQ FT: 55,000
SALES (est): 4.4MM **Privately Held**
WEB: www.masterindustries.com
SIC: 3949 Bowling equipment & supplies

(P-22850)
MAUI TOYS
2951 28th St Ste 1000, Santa Monica (90405-2993)
PHONE.................................330 747-4333
Brian D Kessler, *President*
Cynthia Kessler, *Principal*
◆ EMP: 38
SQ FT: 17,000
SALES (est): 6.1MM **Privately Held**
SIC: 3949 3944 Exercise equipment; games, toys & children's vehicles

(P-22851)
MED-FIT SYSTEMS INC
3553 Rosa Way, Fallbrook (92028-2663)
PHONE.................................760 723-3618
Dean Sbragia, *President*
Juergen Kopf, *Vice Pres*
Alex Sbragia, *Admin Sec*
▲ EMP: 128
SQ FT: 1,500
SALES (est): 20.7MM **Privately Held**
SIC: 3949 5047 Exercise equipment; therapy equipment

(P-22852)
MEL & ASSOCIATES INC (PA)
Also Called: Freeline Design Surfboards
821 41st Ave, Santa Cruz (95062-4420)
PHONE.................................831 476-2950
John Mel, *President*
Brittney Barrios, *Buyer*
EMP: 10
SALES (est): 1.2MM **Privately Held**
WEB: www.freelinesurf.com
SIC: 3949 5941 Surfboards; surfing equipment & supplies

(P-22853)
MICHAEL HAGAN
Also Called: Racehorse Supply
17858 Laurel Dr, Fontana (92336-2835)
PHONE....................................909 213-5916
Sofia Sandoval, *Principal*
Mike Hagan, *Manager*
EMP: 22
SALES: 270K Privately Held
SIC: 3949 Sporting & athletic goods

(P-22854)
MIRAGE SPRTFSHNG & COMMRCL
1810 Kapalua Dr, Oxnard (93036-7745)
PHONE....................................805 983-0975
Joe Villareal, *CEO*
Erin Villareal, *CFO*
EMP: 12
SALES (est): 1.1MM Privately Held
SIC: 3949 Reels, fishing

(P-22855)
MISSION HOCKEY COMPANY (PA)
12 Goodyear Ste 100, Irvine (92618-3764)
PHONE....................................949 585-9390
Michael Whan, *CEO*
Christopher Lynch, *CFO*
▲ EMP: 13
SQ FT: 10,000
SALES (est): 2MM Privately Held
WEB: www.missionitech.com
SIC: 3949 Hockey equipment & supplies, general

(P-22856)
MURREY INTERNATIONAL INC
25701 Weston Dr, Laguna Niguel (92677-1482)
PHONE....................................310 532-6091
Patrick Murrey, *President*
Ron Murrey, *Corp Secy*
Rosemary Murrey, *Corp Secy*
Larry Murrey, *Vice Pres*
Ted Murrey, *Vice Pres*
▲ EMP: 25
SQ FT: 40,000
SALES (est): 3.1MM Privately Held
WEB: www.murreyintl.com
SIC: 3949 1542 Bowling alleys & accessories; custom builders, non-residential

(P-22857)
MUSCLE DYNAMICS CORPORATION
14133 Freeway Dr, Santa Fe Springs (90670-5813)
P.O. Box 3752 (90670-1752)
PHONE....................................562 926-3232
Fax: 310 323-7608
▲ EMP: 12
SQ FT: 24,000
SALES (est): 910K Privately Held
WEB: www.muscledynamics.com
SIC: 3949 5941

(P-22858)
MV EXCEL
2838 Garrison St, San Diego (92106-2720)
PHONE....................................619 223-7493
William E Poole, *Owner*
EMP: 12
SALES (est): 647.7K Privately Held
SIC: 3949 Fishing equipment

(P-22859)
NHS INC
Also Called: Santa Cruz Skateboards
104 Bronson St Ste 9, Santa Cruz (95062-3487)
P.O. Box 2718 (95063-2718)
PHONE....................................831 459-7800
Robert A Denike, *CEO*
Caylin Tardif, *CFO*
Richard H Novak, *Chairman*
Jeff Kendall, *Chief Mktg Ofcr*
Jaime Medrano, *Department Mgr*
▲ EMP: 92
SQ FT: 50,000
SALES (est): 22.3MM Privately Held
WEB: www.nhs-inc.com
SIC: 3949 2329 Skateboards; winter sports equipment; athletic (warmup, sweat & jogging) suits: men's & boys'

(P-22860)
NOR-CAL SMOKESHOP
765 Lighthouse Ave, Monterey (93940-1009)
PHONE....................................831 645-9021
Mahdi Radwan, *CEO*
EMP: 12 EST: 2010
SALES (est): 1MM Privately Held
SIC: 3949 Sporting & athletic goods

(P-22861)
NORBERTS ATHLETIC PRODUCTS
354 W Gardena Blvd, Gardena (90248-2739)
P.O. Box 1890, San Pedro (90733-1890)
PHONE....................................310 830-6672
Loren Dill, *President*
▲ EMP: 19
SQ FT: 4,000
SALES (est): 2.8MM Privately Held
WEB: www.norberts.net
SIC: 3949 Sporting & athletic goods

(P-22862)
NUTCASE INC
Also Called: Nut Case Helmets
12801 Carmenita Rd, Santa Fe Springs (90670-4805)
PHONE....................................503 243-4570
Scott Montgomery, *CEO*
Michael Morrow, *President*
Miriam L Berman, *Admin Sec*
Morgan Braaten, *Graphic Designe*
Lisa Bauso, *Marketing Staff*
▲ EMP: 14
SQ FT: 4,000
SALES (est): 9MM
SALES (corp-wide): 26.8MM Privately Held
SIC: 3949 Helmets, athletic
HQ: Bravo Sports
12801 Carmenita Rd
Santa Fe Springs CA 90670
562 484-5100

(P-22863)
PACIFIC FLYWAY DECOY ASSN
300 Marble Dr, Antioch (94509-6221)
PHONE....................................925 754-4978
Terry Avila, *President*
Donna Burcio, *Treasurer*
EMP: 11
SALES: 68.4K Privately Held
SIC: 3949 2395 Decoys, duck & other game birds; art goods for embroidering, stamped: purchased materials

(P-22864)
PARAGON TACTICAL INC
Also Called: S T I
1580 Commerce St, Corona (92880-1729)
P.O. Box 819, Brea (92822-0819)
PHONE....................................951 736-9440
Art Fransen, *CEO*
Ed Fransen, *Senior VP*
Phil Sivert, *Vice Pres*
Arthur Fransen, *Executive*
EMP: 12
SQ FT: 10,100
SALES (est): 2.3MM Privately Held
WEB: www.supertrap.com
SIC: 3949 Shooting equipment & supplies, general

(P-22865)
PRECISION SPORTS INC
Also Called: Labeda Inline Wheels & Frames
29910 Ohana Cir, Lake Elsinore (92532-2413)
PHONE....................................951 674-1665
Curt Labeda, *President*
Shelly Labeda, *Treasurer*
Sherri Labeda, *Admin Sec*
Robert Chornomud, *Sales Executive*
▲ EMP: 90
SQ FT: 9,500
SALES (est): 12.7MM Privately Held
WEB: www.labeda.com
SIC: 3949 Skates & parts, roller

(P-22866)
PROSERIES LLC
3400 Airport Ave Bldg E, Santa Monica (90405-6132)
PHONE....................................213 533-6400

Shaun Sheikh, *Mng Member*
EMP: 15
SQ FT: 2,000
SALES: 300K Privately Held
SIC: 3949 Team sports equipment

(P-22867)
RAINBOW FIN COMPANY INC
677 Beach Dr, Watsonville (95076-1904)
PHONE....................................831 728-2998
Glen Dewitt, *Principal*
Kathleen Dewitt, *Principal*
Shawd Dewitt, *Principal*
▲ EMP: 20
SQ FT: 4,000
SALES (est): 1.7MM Privately Held
WEB: www.rainbowfins.com
SIC: 3949 Windsurfing boards (sailboards) & equipment; surfboards

(P-22868)
RAP4
2345 La Mirada Dr, Vista (92081-7863)
PHONE....................................408 434-0434
Kt Tran, *President*
EMP: 20 EST: 2013
SALES (est): 1MM Privately Held
SIC: 3949 Shooting equipment & supplies, general

(P-22869)
RBG HOLDINGS CORP (PA)
7855 Haskell Ave Ste 350, Van Nuys (91406-1936)
PHONE....................................818 782-6445
Paul Harrington, *Principal*
Paul E Harrington, *Principal*
EMP: 20
SALES (est): 650.2MM Privately Held
SIC: 3949 5091 3751 Sporting & athletic goods; sporting & recreation goods; motorcycles, bicycles & parts

(P-22870)
REAL ACTION PAINTBALL INC
Also Called: MODERN COMBAT SOLUTIONS
2345 La Mirada Dr, Vista (92081-7863)
PHONE....................................408 848-2846
Nicole Nguyen, *CFO*
Kt Tran, *President*
Loc Pham, *CIO*
◆ EMP: 12
SALES: 2.5MM Privately Held
WEB: www.rap4.com
SIC: 3949 Sporting & athletic goods

(P-22871)
REVOLUTION ENTERPRISES INC
12170 Dearborn Pl, Poway (92064-7110)
PHONE....................................858 679-5785
Joseph Hadzicki, *President*
David Hadzicki, *Vice Pres*
▲ EMP: 12
SALES: 1MM Privately Held
WEB: www.revolutionenterprises.net
SIC: 3949 Sporting & athletic goods

(P-22872)
RIP CURL INC (DH)
Also Called: Rip Curl USA
3030 Airway Ave, Costa Mesa (92626-6036)
PHONE....................................714 422-3600
Kelly Gibson, *CEO*
Diem Culley, *COO*
Matt Szot, *CFO*
Kerry Joubert, *General Mgr*
Brian Kuntz, *IT/INT Sup*
◆ EMP: 60
SQ FT: 25,000
SALES (est): 39.2MM
SALES (corp-wide): 342.6MM Privately Held
WEB: www.ripcurl.com
SIC: 3949 Surfboards; shuffleboards & shuffleboard equipment

(P-22873)
ROBOWORM INC
764 Calle Plano, Camarillo (93012-8555)
PHONE....................................805 389-1636
Greg Stump, *President*
EMP: 13

SALES (est): 1MM Privately Held
WEB: www.roboworm.com
SIC: 3949 Lures, fishing: artificial

(P-22874)
ROGUE RIVER RIFLEWORKS INC
Also Called: Rogue River Super Scopes
570 Linne Rd Ste 110, Paso Robles (93446-9460)
PHONE....................................805 227-4611
Geoff Miller, *President*
Craig Boddington, *COO*
Judy Sonne, *CFO*
EMP: 10
SQ FT: 5,000
SALES: 1.5MM Privately Held
SIC: 3949 Hunting equipment

(P-22875)
ROLLER DERBY SKATE CORP
Also Called: 360,
3401 Etiwanda Ave 911c, Jurupa Valley (91752-1126)
PHONE....................................217 324-3961
Mike Maslowski, *Branch Mgr*
EMP: 10
SALES (est): 623.3K
SALES (corp-wide): 15.7MM Privately Held
WEB: www.rollerderbyskates.com
SIC: 3949 5091 Ice skates, parts & accessories; athletic goods
PA: Roller Derby Skate Corp.
311 W Edwards St
Litchfield IL 62056
217 324-3961

(P-22876)
ROSEN & ROSEN INDUSTRIES INC
Also Called: R & R Industries
204 Avenida Fabricante, San Clemente (92672-7538)
PHONE....................................949 361-9238
Richard Rosen, *President*
Daniel Rosen, *Vice Pres*
▲ EMP: 80
SQ FT: 22,500
SALES (est): 8.1MM Privately Held
WEB: www.rrind.com
SIC: 3949 7389 Sporting & athletic goods; embroidering of advertising on shirts, etc.

(P-22877)
RPSZ CONSTRUCTION LLC
1201 W 5th St Ste T340, Los Angeles (90017-1489)
PHONE....................................314 677-5831
Rick Platt, *Mng Member*
EMP: 30 EST: 2008
SQ FT: 3,500
SALES (est): 6.5MM
SALES (corp-wide): 38MM Privately Held
SIC: 3949 Trampolines & equipment
HQ: Sky Zone, Llc
1201 W 5th St Ste T340
Los Angeles CA 90017
310 734-0300

(P-22878)
RTG INVESTMENT GROUP INC
Also Called: Gym Parts Depot
149 S Barrington Ave, Los Angeles (90049-3310)
PHONE....................................310 444-5554
Roy Greenberg, *CEO*
Tania Cobb, *CFO*
EMP: 12
SALES (est): 1.2MM Privately Held
WEB: www.motususa.com
SIC: 3949 Gymnasium equipment

(P-22879)
RUSTY SURFBOARDS INC (PA)
8495 Commerce Ave, San Diego (92121-2608)
PHONE....................................858 578-0414
Angela Preidendorfer, *President*
Angela Preisendorfer, *President*
◆ EMP: 24
SALES (est): 2.9MM Privately Held
WEB: www.rustysurfboards.com
SIC: 3949 5941 Surfboards; surfing equipment & supplies

▲ = Import ▼=Export
◆ =Import/Export

(P-22880)
RUSTY SURFBOARDS INC
2170 Avenida De La Playa, La Jolla
(92037-3214)
PHONE..........................858 551-0262
Eric Graftman, *Manager*
EMP: 10
SALES (est): 770.8K
SALES (corp-wide): 2.9MM **Privately Held**
WEB: www.rustysurfboards.com
SIC: 3949 Surfboards
PA: Rusty Surfboards Inc
8495 Commerce Ave
San Diego CA 92121
858 578-0414

(P-22881)
S/R INDUSTRIES INC (HQ)
Also Called: Marksman Products
10652 Bloomfield Ave, Santa Fe Springs
(90670-3912)
PHONE..........................562 968-5800
Yu Zhisong, *President*
▲ **EMP:** 12
SQ FT: 25,000
SALES (est): 1.6MM
SALES (corp-wide): 5.4MM **Privately Held**
WEB: www.marksman.com
SIC: 3949 Sporting & athletic goods
PA: Shanghai Gongzi Machinery Manufac-
turing Co., Ltd.
No.60, Hongtu Road, Fengcheng
Town, Fengxian District
Shanghai 20140
215 717-5727

(P-22882)
SAINT NINE AMERICA INC
10700 Norwalk Blvd, Santa Fe Springs
(90670-3824)
PHONE..........................562 921-5300
Timothy Chae, *CEO*
Terry Kim, *Controller*
Max Kim, *Manager*
EMP: 40
SALES: 1.7MM **Privately Held**
SIC: 3949 Team sports equipment

(P-22883)
SAMIS SPORTS
5215 1/2 W Adams Blvd, Los Angeles
(90016-2646)
PHONE..........................323 965-8093
Alida Lopez, *Principal*
EMP: 10
SALES: 250K **Privately Held**
SIC: 3949 Sporting & athletic goods

(P-22884)
SCAPE GOAT IND
6901 Quail Pl Unit E, Carlsbad
(92009-4120)
PHONE..........................760 931-1802
EMP: 10
SALES (est): 460.9K **Privately Held**
SIC: 3949

(P-22885)
SCARLET SAINTS SOFTBALL
304 Grande Ave, Davis (95616-0212)
PHONE..........................530 613-1443
John Sleuter, *Principal*
EMP: 12
SALES: 2K **Privately Held**
SIC: 3949 8641 8661 Softball equipment
& supplies; social associations; churches,
temples & shrines

(P-22886)
SHOCK DOCTOR INC (PA)
Also Called: Shock Doctor Sports
11488 Slater Ave, Fountain Valley
(92708-5440)
PHONE..........................800 233-6956
Anthony Armand, *CEO*
Doug Pedersen, *CFO*
▲ **EMP:** 99
SALES (est): 15.9MM **Privately Held**
WEB: www.shockdoc.com
SIC: 3949 Protective sporting equipment

(P-22887)
SKATE ONE CORP
Also Called: Roller Bones
30 S La Patera Ln Ste 9, Santa Barbara
(93117-3253)
PHONE..........................805 964-1330
George Powell, *President*
Donna Calgar, *Executive*
Mike Mete, *Design Engr*
Deville Nunes, *Technology*
Leanne Turner, *Controller*
▲ **EMP:** 80
SQ FT: 67,000
SALES (est): 13MM **Privately Held**
WEB: www.skateone.com
SIC: 3949 Skateboards; skates & parts,
roller

(P-22888)
SLIVNIK MACHINING INC
1070 Linda Vista Dr Ste A, San Marcos
(92078-2653)
PHONE..........................760 744-8692
Leo Slivnik, *President*
Monica Slivnik, *CFO*
Adela Slivnik, *Vice Pres*
August Slivnik, *Vice Pres*
Christina Slivnik, *Admin Sec*
EMP: 35 **EST:** 1979
SQ FT: 22,000
SALES (est): 3.1MM **Privately Held**
WEB: www.sli-bos.com
SIC: 3949 3599 Shafts, golf club; machine
shop, jobbing & repair

(P-22889)
SMOOTH OPERATOR LLC
3388 Main St, San Diego (92113-3831)
P.O. Box 13250 (92170-3250)
PHONE..........................619 233-8177
Tod Swank, *Finance Spvr*
Tonie Morehead, *Administration*
▲ **EMP:** 20
SQ FT: 26,500
SALES (est): 1.7MM **Privately Held**
WEB: www.watsonlaminates.com
SIC: 3949 Skateboards

(P-22890)
SOCAL SKATESHOP
24002 Via Fabricante # 205, Mission Viejo
(92691-3901)
PHONE..........................949 305-5321
Mike Hirsh, *Owner*
EMP: 10
SALES (est): 944.3K **Privately Held**
SIC: 3949 Skateboards

(P-22891)
SOCCER 90
1235 Veterans Blvd, Redwood City
(94063-2608)
PHONE..........................650 599-9900
Will Clark, *Office Mgr*
EMP: 10
SALES (est): 521.7K **Privately Held**
SIC: 3949 Sporting & athletic goods

(P-22892)
SOUTH STREET INC
Also Called: Twelve Strike
2231 E Curry St, Long Beach
(90805-3209)
PHONE..........................562 984-6240
Ron W Richmond, *CEO*
Susiy Richmond, *Treasurer*
◆ **EMP:** 10 **EST:** 1997
SQ FT: 21,600
SALES (est): 1.6MM **Privately Held**
WEB: www.twelvestrike.com
SIC: 3949 Bowling equipment & supplies

(P-22893)
SPEEDPLAY INC
10151 Pacific Mesa Blvd # 107, San Diego
(92121-4329)
PHONE..........................858 453-4707
Richard Bryne, *CEO*
Sharon Worman, *President*
Rachel Barnes, *Controller*
▲ **EMP:** 25
SQ FT: 5,600
SALES (est): 2.5MM **Privately Held**
WEB: www.speedplay.com
SIC: 3949 Sporting & athletic goods

(P-22894)
SPEEDSKINS INC
Also Called: Atm Skateboards
2919 San Luis Rey Rd, Oceanside
(92058-1219)
PHONE..........................760 439-3119
John Falahee, *President*
Leah Falahee, *Vice Pres*
Ronnie Bertino, *Sales Staff*
▲ **EMP:** 16
SQ FT: 7,000
SALES (est): 1.7MM **Privately Held**
SIC: 3949 5136 Skateboards; men's &
boys' clothing

(P-22895)
SPN INVESTMENTS INC
Also Called: Einflatables
6481 Orangethorpe Ave # 12, Buena Park
(90620-1376)
PHONE..........................562 777-1140
Steven P Nero, *CEO*
Steven Nero, *CEO*
EMP: 45 **EST:** 2011
SALES (est): 5.7MM **Privately Held**
SIC: 3949 Playground equipment

(P-22896)
SPORT ROCK INTERNATIONAL INC
Also Called: Park Pets and Boulders
450 Marquita Ave, Paso Robles
(93446-5910)
P.O. Box 32, Pismo Beach (93448-0032)
PHONE..........................805 434-5474
Mike English, *President*
Kathy English, *Admin Sec*
EMP: 10
SQ FT: 13,000
SALES (est): 700K **Privately Held**
WEB: www.sportrockintl.com
SIC: 3949 Sporting & athletic goods

(P-22897)
SPORTS HOOP INC
12669 Beryl Way, Jurupa Valley
(92509-1213)
PHONE..........................626 387-6027
Kun Yuan Lin, *President*
Mie Lee, *CFO*
▲ **EMP:** 16
SALES (est): 1.5MM **Privately Held**
WEB: www.fitnessports.com
SIC: 3949 Sporting & athletic goods

(P-22898)
STA-SLIM PRODUCTS INC
600 N Pacific Ave, San Pedro
(90731-2024)
P.O. Box 1470 (90733-1470)
PHONE..........................310 514-1155
Tom Lincir, *President*
Diane Lincir, *Vice Pres*
Chet Groskreutz, *VP Sales*
EMP: 17
SQ FT: 40,000
SALES (est): 1.2MM **Privately Held**
WEB: www.ivankobarbell.com
SIC: 3949 Exercising cycles

(P-22899)
STYLE UP AMERICA INC
2600 E 8th St, Los Angeles (90023-2104)
PHONE..........................213 553-1134
Neil Miller, *President*
▲ **EMP:** 10
SQ FT: 22,000
SALES: 850K **Privately Held**
SIC: 3949 Sporting & athletic goods

(P-22900)
SUBMERSIBLE SYSTEMS INC
7413 Slater Ave, Huntington Beach
(92647-6228)
PHONE..........................714 842-6566
Anthony Buban, *President*
Christine Buban, *Corp Secy*
Christeen Buban, *Vice Pres*
Corey Brabant, *Administration*
Shannon Bermudez, *Mktg Dir*
▲ **EMP:** 15 **EST:** 1973
SQ FT: 12,000
SALES (est): 2.1MM **Privately Held**
WEB: www.submersiblesystems.com
SIC: 3949 Skin diving equipment, scuba
type

(P-22901)
SUPERIOR FOAM PRODUCTS INC
Also Called: Custom X Body Boards
394 Via El Centro, Oceanside
(92058-1237)
PHONE..........................760 722-1585
Ronald M Noric, *President*
David Cunniff, *Shareholder*
Debbie Colwell, *President*
◆ **EMP:** 10
SQ FT: 4,400
SALES (est): 1MM **Privately Held**
SIC: 3949 Surfboards

(P-22902)
SUREGRIP INTERNATIONAL CO
5519 Rawlings Ave, South Gate
(90280-7495)
PHONE..........................562 923-0724
James Ball, *Vice Pres*
Ione L Ball, *President*
▲ **EMP:** 60 **EST:** 1937
SQ FT: 30,000
SALES (est): 7.4MM **Privately Held**
WEB: www.suregrip.com
SIC: 3949 Skates & parts, roller

(P-22903)
SURF MORE PRODUCTS INC
250 Calle Pintoresco, San Clemente
(92672-7504)
PHONE..........................949 492-0753
Robert B Nealy, *President*
Sara Nealy, *Vice Pres*
Luis Benito, *Manager*
▲ **EMP:** 25
SQ FT: 5,200
SALES (est): 2.8MM **Privately Held**
WEB: www.surfmorexm.com
SIC: 3949 Surfboards

(P-22904)
SURF TO SUMMIT INC
7234 Hollister Ave, Goleta (93117-2807)
PHONE..........................805 964-1896
Eric States, *President*
Julie States, *Vice Pres*
▲ **EMP:** 18
SALES (est): 1.9MM **Privately Held**
WEB: www.surftosummit.com
SIC: 3949 Sporting & athletic goods

(P-22905)
SURFY SURFY
974 N Coast Highway 101, Encinitas
(92024-2051)
P.O. Box 230165 (92023-0165)
PHONE..........................760 452-7687
Jean Paul St Pierre, *Principal*
EMP: 12
SALES (est): 1.3MM **Privately Held**
SIC: 3949 Surfboards

(P-22906)
TAYLOR MADE GOLF COMPANY INC (HQ)
5545 Fermi Ct, Carlsbad (92008-7324)
PHONE..........................877 860-8624
Mark King, *President*
Ben Sharpe, *CEO*
Melissa Claassen, *CFO*
Bob Maggiore, *Chief Mktg Ofcr*
John Kawaja, *Exec VP*
◆ **EMP:** 495 **EST:** 1979
SALES (est): 260.4MM
SALES (corp-wide): 1.9B **Privately Held**
WEB: www.taylormade-golf.com
SIC: 3949 Shafts, golf club
PA: Kps Capital Partners, Lp
485 Lexington Ave Fl 31
New York NY 10017
212 338-5100

(P-22907)
THOUSAND LLC
915 Mateo St Ste 302, Los Angeles
(90021-1786)
PHONE..........................310 745-0110
EMP: 12 **EST:** 2016
SALES (est): 1MM **Privately Held**
SIC: 3949 Sporting & athletic goods

PRODUCTS & SVCS

(P-22908)
TONY HAWK INC
1161-A S Melrose Dr 362, Vista (92081)
PHONE.....................................760 477-2477
Steve Hawk, *Principal*
Pat Hawk, *COO*
Sandy Dusablon, *Bd of Directors*
EMP: 10
SALES: 822.8K **Privately Held**
SIC: 3949 Skateboards

(P-22909)
**TORERO SPECIALTY
PRODUCTS LLC**
Also Called: Newport Vessels
222 E Huntington Dr # 225, Monrovia
(91016-8006)
PHONE.....................................415 520-3481
Patrick Dean, *President*
Robert E Dean,
William L Shepherd IV,
▲ **EMP:** 12
SALES: 5MM **Privately Held**
SIC: 3949 3999 2392 Sporting & athletic
goods; advertising display products; boat
cushions

(P-22910)
TRIACTIVE AMERICA INC
1244 Trail View Pl, Nipomo (93444-6663)
PHONE.....................................805 595-1005
Jim Sargen, *President*
Marc Sargen, *CFO*
▲ **EMP:** 10
SQ FT: 1,600
SALES: 900K **Privately Held**
WEB: www.triactiveamerica.com
SIC: 3949 Sporting & athletic goods

(P-22911)
TRIDENT DIVING EQUIPMENT
9616 Owensmouth Ave, Chatsworth
(91311-4803)
PHONE.....................................818 998-7518
Lowell Dreyfuss, *President*
Tom Bird, *CFO*
Maria Navarro, *Office Mgr*
Barry Douglas, *Sales Staff*
◆ **EMP:** 22
SQ FT: 12,000
SALES (est): 2.7MM **Privately Held**
WEB: www.tridentdive.com
SIC: 3949 Skin diving equipment, scuba
type

(P-22912)
TRUE TEMPER SPORTS INC
9401 Waples St Ste 140, San Diego
(92121-3929)
PHONE.....................................858 404-0405
Scott Hennessy, *President*
▲ **EMP:** 24
SQ FT: 17,885
SALES (est): 3.2MM **Privately Held**
SIC: 3949 Shafts, golf club

(P-22913)
TUFFSTUFF FITNESS INTL INC
13971 Norton Ave, Chino (91710-5473)
PHONE.....................................909 629-1600
Cammie Grider, *President*
Pete Asistin, *Vice Pres*
Monida Grider, *Vice Pres*
Michael Loch, *Sales Staff*
Donald Payne, *Sales Staff*
◆ **EMP:** 180
SQ FT: 150,000
SALES (est): 24.1MM **Privately Held**
SIC: 3949 Exercise equipment

(P-22914)
TWIN PEAK INDUSTRIES INC
Also Called: Jungle Jumps
12420 Montague St Ste E, Pacoima
(91331-2140)
PHONE.....................................800 259-5906
Edmond K Keshishian, *President*
Raffi Sepanian, *Principal*
EMP: 32
SALES (est): 3.8MM **Privately Held**
WEB: www.twinpeakindustries.com
SIC: 3949 3069 Playground equipment;
air-supported rubber structures

(P-22915)
U S BOWLING CORPORATION
5480 Schaefer Ave, Chino (91710-6901)
PHONE.....................................909 548-0644
David Frewing, *President*
Dolores Frewing, *Corp Secy*
Janet Frewing, *Officer*
Daroll L Frewing, *Principal*
Donna Carmell, *Accounting Mgr*
▲ **EMP:** 15
SQ FT: 50,000
SALES (est): 2.7MM **Privately Held**
SIC: 3949 1799 Bowling alleys & acces-
sories; bowling alley installation

(P-22916)
U S DIVERS CO INC
2340 Cousteau Ct, Vista (92081-8346)
PHONE.....................................760 597-5000
Graham Church, *Corp Secy*
EMP: 126 **EST:** 1947
SALES: 40MM **Privately Held**
SIC: 3949 Water sports equipment; skin
diving equipment, scuba type
HQ: Aqua-Lung America, Inc.
2340 Cousteau Ct
Vista CA 92081
760 597-5000

(P-22917)
UNITY CLOTHING INC
Also Called: Unity Clothing Company
3788 Rockwell Ave, El Monte (91731-2384)
PHONE.....................................626 579-5588
Raymond Hwang, *President*
▲ **EMP:** 12
SQ FT: 4,000
SALES: 600K **Privately Held**
SIC: 3949 Sporting & athletic goods

(P-22918)
VF OUTDOOR LLC
Also Called: North Face, The
180 Post St, San Francisco (94108-4703)
PHONE.....................................415 433-3223
David Garcia, *Manager*
EMP: 43
SALES (corp-wide): 13.8MM **Publicly
Held**
WEB: www.thenorthface.com
SIC: 3949 Sporting & athletic goods
HQ: Vf Outdoor, Llc
2701 Harbor Bay Pkwy
Alameda CA 94502
510 618-3500

(P-22919)
VICTORIA SKIMBOARDS
2955 Laguna Canyon Rd # 1, Laguna
Beach (92651-1194)
PHONE.....................................949 494-0059
Charles Haines III, *President*
▲ **EMP:** 25
SQ FT: 4,500
SALES (est): 2.3MM **Privately Held**
WEB: www.vicskim.com
SIC: 3949 5941 Surfboards; surfing equip-
ment & supplies

(P-22920)
VISION AQUATICS INC
4542 Skidmore Ct, Moorpark (93021-2234)
PHONE.....................................818 749-2178
Peter J Gillette, *President*
Patricia Gillette, *Treasurer*
EMP: 10
SALES: 3.7MM **Privately Held**
WEB: www.visionaquatics.com
SIC: 3949 Swimming pools, plastic

(P-22921)
VISTA OUTDOOR INC
Also Called: Brg Sports
5550 Scotts Valley Dr, Scotts Valley
(95066-3438)
PHONE.....................................831 461-7500
Mark Teixeira, *Branch Mgr*
Jean Jaime, *Vice Pres*
Craig Phillips, *Sales Staff*
EMP: 73
SALES (corp-wide): 2B **Publicly Held**
SIC: 3949 Bags, rosin
PA: Vista Outdoor Inc.
1 Vista Way
Anoka MN 55303
801 447-3000

(P-22922)
WATERMANS GUILD
260 E Dyer Rd Ste L, Santa Ana
(92707-3753)
PHONE.....................................714 751-0603
Gregory Martz, *Owner*
EMP: 10
SQ FT: 3,200
SALES (est): 390K **Privately Held**
SIC: 3949 Surfboards

(P-22923)
WEST COAST TRENDS INC
Also Called: Train Reaction
17811 Jamestown Ln, Huntington Beach
(92647-7136)
PHONE.....................................714 843-9288
Jeffrey C Herold, *CEO*
Vivienne Herold, *CFO*
Jim Jamison, *Opers Staff*
Byron Slovis, *Production*
Mickey Miller, *Sales Mgr*
◆ **EMP:** 50
SQ FT: 26,000
SALES (est): 5.9MM **Privately Held**
WEB: www.clubglove.com
SIC: 3949 Golf equipment

(P-22924)
WESTERN GOLF INC
1340 N Jefferson St, Anaheim
(92807-1614)
PHONE.....................................800 448-4409
◆ **EMP:** 14
SQ FT: 15,500
SALES (est): 1.7MM **Privately Held**
WEB: www.westerngolf.com
SIC: 3949 5091

(P-22925)
WESTERN GOLF CAR MFG INC
Also Called: Western Golf Car Sales Co
69391 Dillon Rd, Desert Hot Springs
(92241-8433)
PHONE.....................................760 671-6691
Scott Stevens, *President*
Robert W Thomas, *Vice Pres*
Robert Evans, *Controller*
EMP: 55
SQ FT: 60,000
SALES (est): 35.5K **Privately Held**
SIC: 3949 3799 Sporting & athletic goods;
golf carts, powered

(P-22926)
WILLIAM GETZ CORP
539 W Walnut Ave, Orange (92868-2232)
PHONE.....................................714 516-2050
Michael Paulsen, *President*
▲ **EMP:** 27
SQ FT: 10,000
SALES (est): 2.7MM **Privately Held**
SIC: 3949 Fishing tackle, general

(P-22927)
XFIT BRANDS INC
25731 Commercentre Dr, Lake Forest
(92630-8803)
PHONE.....................................949 916-9680
J Gregory Barrow, *CEO*
Brent D Willis, *Ch of Bd*
Charles E Joiner, *President*
Robert J Miranda, *CFO*
EMP: 10 **EST:** 2003
SALES (est): 174.1K **Privately Held**
SIC: 3949 Sporting & athletic goods

(P-22928)
XS SCUBA INC (PA)
4040 W Chandler Ave, Santa Ana
(92704-5202)
PHONE.....................................714 424-0434
Daniel F Babcock, *President*
◆ **EMP:** 25
SALES (est): 3MM **Privately Held**
WEB: www.xsscuba.com
SIC: 3949 5091 Skin diving equipment,
scuba type; diving equipment & supplies

(P-22929)
YELLOW INC
Also Called: Rollin Industries
9350 Trade Pl Ste C, San Diego
(92126-6334)
PHONE.....................................858 689-4851
▲ **EMP:** 50

SALES (est): 451.7K **Privately Held**
WEB: www.pony-ex.com
SIC: 3949

(P-22930)
ZEPP LABS INC
75 E Santa Clara St # 93, San Jose
(95113-1826)
PHONE.....................................314 662-2145
Jason Fass, *CEO*
Bruce McAllister, *CFO*
Robin Han, *Senior Mgr*
▲ **EMP:** 50
SQ FT: 4,000
SALES (est): 4.7MM **Privately Held**
SIC: 3949 4832 Sporting & athletic goods;
sports

(P-22931)
ZONSON COMPANY INC
3197 Lionshead Ave, Carlsbad
(92010-4702)
PHONE.....................................760 597-0338
Jeff Yearours, *Vice Pres*
▲ **EMP:** 26
SALES (est): 2.2MM **Privately Held**
SIC: 3949 Bags, golf

3951 Pens & Mechanical Pencils

(P-22932)
**AMITY RUBBERIZED PEN
COMPANY**
612 N Commercial Ave, Covina
(91723-1309)
PHONE.....................................626 969-0863
Robert Oroumieh, *President*
▲ **EMP:** 22
SALES (est): 1.4MM **Privately Held**
SIC: 3951 Ball point pens & parts

(P-22933)
ANOTO INCORPORATED
7677 Oakport St Ste 1200, Oakland
(94621-1975)
PHONE.....................................510 777-0071
Jim Marggraff, *CEO*
EMP: 18
SALES (est): 1.6MM **Privately Held**
SIC: 3951 Pens & mechanical pencils

(P-22934)
HARTLEY COMPANY
Also Called: Hartley-Racon
1987 Placentia Ave, Costa Mesa
(92627-6265)
P.O. Box 10999 (92627-0999)
PHONE.....................................949 646-9643
Ed Kuder, *President*
Mike Quinley, *Vice Pres*
Mark Simpson, *Vice Pres*
Lance Hume, *Store Mgr*
Erik Ingersoll, *Finance Mgr*
▲ **EMP:** 22
SQ FT: 75,000
SALES (est): 3.7MM **Privately Held**
SIC: 3951 Cartridges, refill: ball point pens

(P-22935)
NATIONAL PEN CO LLC (DH)
12121 Scripps Summit Dr # 200, San Diego
(92131-4609)
P.O. Box 847203, Dallas TX (75284-7203)
PHONE.....................................866 388-9850
Peter Kelly, *CEO*
David Thompson, *Ch of Bd*
Richard N Obrigawitch, *COO*
Laurent Yung, *Vice Pres*
Christopher Coats, *Creative Dir*
◆ **EMP:** 150
SQ FT: 40,000
SALES (est): 294.5MM
SALES (corp-wide): 2.5B **Privately Held**
SIC: 3951 3993 Pens & mechanical pen-
cils; advertising novelties
HQ: Cimpress Usa Incorporated
275 Wyman St Ste 100
Waltham MA 02451
866 614-8002

▲ = Import ▼=Export
◆ =Import/Export

(P-22936)
TOLERANCE TECHNOLOGY INC
1756 Junction Ave Ste C, San Jose
(95112-1045)
PHONE...............................408 586-8811
Ke Qian, *CEO*
Shirley W Zhang, *Administration*
EMP: 10
SALES (est): 968.2K **Privately Held**
SIC: 3951 5084 Pens & mechanical pencils; industrial machinery & equipment

---

3952 Lead Pencils, Crayons & Artist's Mtrls

(P-22937)
AARDVARK CLAY & SUPPLIES INC (PA)
1400 E Pomona St, Santa Ana
(92705-4858)
PHONE...............................714 541-4157
George Johnston, *President*
K Douglas Mac Pherson, *Corp Secy*
Daniel T Carreon, *Vice Pres*
Richard Mac Pherson, *Vice Pres*
Rick Macpherson, *Vice Pres*
▲ **EMP:** 30
SQ FT: 25,000
SALES (est): 4.2MM **Privately Held**
WEB: www.aardvarkclay.com
SIC: 3952 5945 Modeling clay; arts & crafts supplies

(P-22938)
ALLIED PRESSROOM PRODUCTS INC
Also Called: Allied Litho Products
3546 Emery St, Los Angeles (90023-3908)
PHONE...............................323 266-6250
Mark Rios, *Manager*
EMP: 12
SALES (est): 2MM
SALES (corp-wide): 9.3MM **Privately Held**
SIC: 3952 5199 Lead pencils & art goods; art goods & supplies
PA: Allied Pressroom Products, Inc.
4814 Persimmon Ct
Monroe NC 28110
954 920-0909

(P-22939)
AR-CE INC
Also Called: Stretch Art
141 E 162nd St, Gardena (90248-2801)
PHONE...............................310 771-1960
Sarkis Cetinyan, *President*
Herman Artinian, *Vice Pres*
EMP: 15
SQ FT: 6,000
SALES (est): 1.1MM **Privately Held**
WEB: www.stretch-art.com
SIC: 3952 Lead pencils & art goods

(P-22940)
CONVERSION TECHNOLOGY CO INC (PA)
5360 N Commerce Ave, Moorpark
(93021-1762)
PHONE...............................805 378-0033
Jim Newkirk, *President*
Russell Greenhouse, *COO*
Terrill Newkirk, *Office Mgr*
▲ **EMP:** 50
SQ FT: 28,000
SALES (est): 7.5MM **Privately Held**
WEB: www.fluidink.com
SIC: 3952 2893 2899 Ink, drawing: black & colored; printing ink; ink or writing fluids

(P-22941)
DOSTAL STUDIO
898 Lincoln Ave, San Rafael (94901-3330)
PHONE...............................415 721-7080
Frank Dostal, *Owner*
EMP: 15
SQ FT: 4,000
SALES: 600K **Privately Held**
WEB: www.dostalstudio.com
SIC: 3952 Frames for artists' canvases

(P-22942)
J F MCCAUGHIN CO
2628 River Ave, Rosemead (91770-3302)
PHONE...............................626 573-3000
Jim Mallory, *Branch Mgr*
EMP: 30
SALES (corp-wide): 667.6MM **Privately Held**
WEB: www.argueso.com
SIC: 3952 Wax, artists'
HQ: J. F. Mccaughin Co.
2817 Mccracken St
Norton Shores MI 49441
231 759-7304

(P-22943)
MANSOOR AMARNA CORP
16923 Kinzie St, Northridge (91343-1715)
PHONE...............................818 894-8937
Henry Mansoor, *President*
EMP: 12
SALES (est): 982.6K **Privately Held**
SIC: 3952 Artists' equipment

(P-22944)
SALIS INTERNATIONAL INC
3921 Oceanic Dr Ste 802, Oceanside
(92056-5857)
PHONE...............................303 384-3588
Lawrence R Salis, *President*
▲ **EMP:** 38
SQ FT: 10,000
SALES (est): 5.2MM **Privately Held**
WEB: www.salisinternational.com
SIC: 3952 Water colors, artists'

(P-22945)
SIENA DECOR INC
1250 Philadelphia St, Pomona
(91766-5535)
PHONE...............................909 895-8585
Duc Do, *CEO*
▲ **EMP:** 10 **EST:** 2012
SQ FT: 60,000
SALES (est): 308.7K **Privately Held**
SIC: 3952 Colors, artists': water & oxide ceramic glass

(P-22946)
TARA MATERIALS INC
7615 Siempre Viva Rd, San Diego
(92154-6217)
P.O. Box 406, Cottonwood (96022-0406)
PHONE...............................619 671-1018
John I Benator, *Owner*
EMP: 20
SALES (corp-wide): 66MM **Privately Held**
WEB: www.taramaterials.com
SIC: 3952 Lead pencils & art goods
PA: Tara Materials, Inc.
322 Industrial Park Dr
Lawrenceville GA 30046
770 963-5256

(P-22947)
TREKELL & CO INC
17459 Lilac St Ste B, Hesperia
(92345-5106)
PHONE...............................800 378-3867
Brian Trekell, *President*
▲ **EMP:** 11
SALES (est): 1.2MM **Privately Held**
SIC: 3952 Brushes, air, artists'

3953 Marking Devices

(P-22948)
BRANDNEW INDUSTRIES INC
375 Pine Ave Ste 22, Santa Barbara
(93117-3725)
PHONE...............................805 964-8251
Sean David Clayton, *President*
Lisa Frey, *Partner*
Tim Sisneros, *Sales Staff*
EMP: 15 **EST:** 1991
SQ FT: 2,000
SALES (est): 1MM **Privately Held**
SIC: 3953 Irons, marking or branding

(P-22949)
GENERAL METAL ENGRAVING INC
Also Called: Kumjian Enterprises
9254 Garvey Ave, South El Monte
(91733-1020)
P.O. Box 762, San Gabriel (91778-0762)
PHONE...............................626 443-8961
Sarkis Kumjian, *President*
Val Kumjian, *Executive*
EMP: 30
SALES (est): 4.2MM **Privately Held**
WEB: www.generalmetalengraving.com
SIC: 3953 3544 Printing dies, rubber or plastic, for marking machines; special dies, tools, jigs & fixtures

(P-22950)
GREEN LAKE INVESTORS LLC
Also Called: Laser Excel
3310 Coffey Ln, Santa Rosa (95403-1917)
PHONE...............................707 577-1301
Ron Macken, *Manager*
Dan Marschall, *Director*
EMP: 25
SALES (est): 1.7MM
SALES (corp-wide): 14.5MM **Privately Held**
WEB: www.laserexcel.com
SIC: 3953 2759 3699 Stencils, painting & marking; screen printing; electrical equipment & supplies
PA: Green Lake Investors Llc
620 Cardinal Ln
Hartland WI 53029
262 369-5000

(P-22951)
HERO ARTS RUBBER STAMPS INC
1200 Hrbour Way S Ste 201, Richmond
(94804)
PHONE...............................510 232-4200
Aaron Leventhal, *CEO*
Jacqueline Leventhal, *President*
▲ **EMP:** 59 **EST:** 1974
SQ FT: 70,000
SALES (est): 6.4MM **Privately Held**
SIC: 3953 Marking devices

(P-22952)
JOY PRODUCTS CALIFORNIA INC
Also Called: Coastal Enterprises
17281 Mount Wynne Cir, Fountain Valley
(92708-4107)
PHONE...............................714 437-7250
Shayne Perkins, *President*
Susie Erickson, *Sales Staff*
▲ **EMP:** 15
SQ FT: 12,000
SALES (est): 3MM **Privately Held**
WEB: www.coastalsportswear.com
SIC: 3953 2759 Screens, textile printing; screen printing

(P-22953)
NOVA TOOL CO
Also Called: Wilbur Manufacturing
27736 Industrial Blvd, Hayward
(94545-4047)
PHONE...............................925 828-7172
Frank D Aerni, *President*
Nancy Aerni, *Vice Pres*
▲ **EMP:** 10
SQ FT: 80,000
SALES (est): 1.4MM **Privately Held**
WEB: www.novatoolco.com
SIC: 3953 Irons, marking or branding

(P-22954)
ON-LINE STAMPCO INC
Also Called: California Stamp Company
3341 Hancock St, San Diego (92110-4302)
P.O. Box 122432 (92112-2432)
PHONE...............................800 373-5614
Donna Wright, *CEO*
Neal Wright, *President*
Sean Lazar, *Vice Pres*
Gina Guerra, *Production*
EMP: 11 **EST:** 1892
SQ FT: 6,000

SALES (est): 1.7MM **Privately Held**
WEB: www.olstamp.com
SIC: 3953 2759 Embossing seals & hand stamps; engraving

(P-22955)
STENCIL MASTER INC
780 Charcot Ave, San Jose (95131-2224)
PHONE...............................408 428-9695
Sang M Yu, *President*
Grace Song, *Sls & Mktg Exec*
EMP: 17 **EST:** 1997
SQ FT: 9,000
SALES (est): 2.4MM **Privately Held**
WEB: www.stencilmaster.net
SIC: 3953 Cancelling stamps, hand: rubber or metal

(P-22956)
SVEVIA USA INC
14567 Rancho Vista Dr, Fontana
(92335-4299)
PHONE...............................909 559-4134
John Lucas, *President*
EMP: 15
SALES (est): 455.6K **Privately Held**
SIC: 3953 Stencils, painting & marking

(P-22957)
UNITED CEREBRAL PALSY ASSN SAN
Also Called: Ready Stamps
10405 Sn Dgo Mssn Rd 10, San Diego
(92108)
PHONE...............................619 282-8790
Jim Elliott, *Manager*
Barbara Cox, *Manager*
EMP: 18
SALES (corp-wide): 3.1MM **Privately Held**
WEB: www.readystamps.com
SIC: 3953 5945 Marking devices; hobby, toy & game shops
PA: United Cerebral Palsy Association Of San Diego County
8525 Gibbs Dr Ste 209
San Diego CA 92123
858 571-7803

(P-22958)
WILD SIDE WEST
1543 Truman St, San Fernando
(91340-3145)
PHONE...............................213 388-9792
Frank Gizatullin, *President*
EMP: 30
SALES (est): 1.1MM
SALES (corp-wide): 6.4MM **Privately Held**
WEB: www.thewildside.com
SIC: 3953 2752 Irons, marking or branding; commercial printing, lithographic
PA: The Wild Side West
6353 E 14 Mile Rd
Sterling Heights MI 48312
818 837-5000

3955 Carbon Paper & Inked Ribbons

(P-22959)
ACI SUPPLIES LLC
425 N Berry St, Brea (92821-3105)
PHONE...............................714 989-1821
Carlos Adeva,
Benny Adeva, *Opers Mgr*
▲ **EMP:** 29
SALES: 11MM **Privately Held**
SIC: 3955 Print cartridges for laser & other computer printers

(P-22960)
BUSHNELL RIBBON CORPORATION
300 W Brookdale Pl, Fullerton
(92832-1465)
P.O. Box 2543, Santa Fe Springs (90670-0543)
PHONE...............................562 948-1410
Jim Kinmartin, *President*
Mary Alice Milward, *Treasurer*
James C Kinmartin, *Vice Pres*
Paul C Kinmartin, *Vice Pres*
EMP: 70

SQ FT: 24,000
SALES (est): 7.8MM **Privately Held**
WEB: www.bushnellribbon.com
SIC: 3955 Ribbons, inked: typewriter, adding machine, register, etc.

(P-22961)
CALIFORNIA RIBBON CARBN CO INC
10914 Thienes Ave, South El Monte (91733-3404)
PHONE....................323 724-9100
Robert J Picou, *President*
Louis Titus, *Corp Secy*
Clara Picou, *Vice Pres*
▲ **EMP:** 100 **EST:** 1939
SQ FT: 12,000
SALES (est): 13.4MM **Privately Held**
WEB: www.californiaribbon.com
SIC: 3955 Ribbons, inked: typewriter, adding machine, register, etc.

(P-22962)
E ALKO INC
Also Called: Laser Imaging International
8201 Woodley Ave, Van Nuys (91406-1231)
PHONE....................818 587-9700
Eyal Alkoby, *President*
Beth Alkoby, *Principal*
▲ **EMP:** 190
SQ FT: 45,000
SALES (est): 17.3MM **Privately Held**
SIC: 3955 3861 Print cartridges for laser & other computer printers; photographic equipment & supplies

(P-22963)
ECMM SERVICES INC
500 S Kraemer Blvd # 100, Brea (92821-6763)
PHONE....................714 988-9388
Vincent Yang, *President*
Donald Sung, *Principal*
EMP: 250
SALES (est): 25.9MM **Privately Held**
SIC: 3955 5045 Print cartridges for laser & other computer printers; printers, computer
PA: Hon Hai Precision Industry Co., Ltd.
66, Zhongshan Rd.,
New Taipei City 23680

(P-22964)
GENERAL RIBBON CORP
Also Called: G R C
5775 E Ls Angls Ave Ste 2, Chatsworth (91311)
PHONE....................818 709-1234
Stephen R Morgan, *President*
Robert W Daggs, *Ch of Bd*
▲ **EMP:** 500
SQ FT: 110,000
SALES (est): 46.5MM **Privately Held**
WEB: www.printgrc.com
SIC: 3955 3861 Ribbons, inked: typewriter, adding machine, register, etc.; photographic equipment & supplies

(P-22965)
HYDRO FLOW FILTRATION SYS LLC
42074 Remington Ave, Temecula (92590-2551)
PHONE....................951 296-0904
Charles Lacy, *Mng Member*
Michael T Baird,
Mounir S Ibrahim,
▲ **EMP:** 15
SQ FT: 5,200
SALES: 1MM **Privately Held**
SIC: 3955 Carbon paper & inked ribbons

(P-22966)
LASER RECHARGE INC (PA)
Also Called: Encompass
9935 Horn Rd Ste A, Sacramento (95827-1954)
PHONE....................916 737-6360
Michael Mooney, *CEO*
Dave Michon, *President*
Shannon Mooney, *CFO*
EMP: 24
SQ FT: 10,000

SALES (est): 4.6MM **Privately Held**
WEB: www.laserrecharge.net
SIC: 3955 7699 5943 Print cartridges for laser & other computer printers; office equipment & accessory customizing; office forms & supplies

(P-22967)
LASER TONER & COMPUTER SUPPLY
940 Enchanted Way Ste 106, Simi Valley (93065-0907)
P.O. Box 239, Moorpark (93020-0239)
PHONE....................805 529-3300
Richard Bradbury, *President*
Jodie Bradbury, *Admin Sec*
EMP: 10
SQ FT: 8,000
SALES: 2MM **Privately Held**
SIC: 3955 7378 5943 5112 Print cartridges for laser & other computer printers; computer peripheral equipment repair & maintenance; office forms & supplies; computer & photocopying supplies

(P-22968)
LASERCARE TECHNOLOGIES INC (PA)
3375 Robertson Pl, Los Angeles (90034-3311)
PHONE....................310 202-4200
Paul Wilhelm, *President*
Ernesto Comodo, *Graphic Designe*
Marissa McFarland, *Accounts Exec*
EMP: 35
SQ FT: 12,000
SALES: 5MM **Privately Held**
WEB: www.lasercare.com
SIC: 3955 7378 5734 Print cartridges for laser & other computer printers; computer peripheral equipment repair & maintenance; printers & plotters: computers

(P-22969)
MAGNUM DATA INC
28130 Avenue Crocker # 303, Valencia (91355-3421)
PHONE....................800 869-2589
Mike Mahfouz, *CEO*
EMP: 10
SQ FT: 2,500
SALES (est): 510K **Privately Held**
SIC: 3955 Print cartridges for laser & other computer printers

(P-22970)
PACIFIC COMPUTER PRODUCTS INC
2210 S Huron Dr, Santa Ana (92704-4947)
PHONE....................714 549-7535
EMP: 25
SQ FT: 12,000
SALES (est): 1.6MM **Privately Held**
SIC: 3955 5045

(P-22971)
PLANET GREEN CARTRIDGES INC
20724 Lassen St, Chatsworth (91311-4507)
PHONE....................818 725-2596
Sean Levi, *President*
Natalya Levi, *Treasurer*
Pattie Saso, *Controller*
Tracy Whitehead, *Sales Staff*
Charlene Lajnef, *Accounts Exec*
◆ **EMP:** 84
SQ FT: 29,699
SALES (est): 13.8MM **Privately Held**
WEB: www.pginkjets.com
SIC: 3955 5093 Print cartridges for laser & other computer printers; plastics scrap

(P-22972)
RAYZIST PHOTOMASK INC (PA)
Also Called: Honor Life
955 Park Center Dr, Vista (92081-8312)
PHONE....................760 727-8561
Randy S Willis, *CEO*
James Myers, *Prdtn Mgr*
Liz Haas, *Sales Staff*
Michael H Haas, *Manager*
Jim Kemp, *Manager*
▲ **EMP:** 54
SQ FT: 28,000

SALES (est): 10.1MM **Privately Held**
WEB: www.rayzist.com
SIC: 3955 3281 3589 Stencil paper, gelatin or spirit process; cut stone & stone products; sandblasting equipment

(P-22973)
SERCOMP LLC (PA)
5401 Tech Cir Ste 200, Moorpark (93021-1713)
P.O. Box 92728, City of Industry (91715-2728)
PHONE....................805 299-0020
Mike Goodman,
Terry Mora, *Manager*
EMP: 89 **EST:** 2003
SQ FT: 67,000
SALES (est): 5.6MM **Privately Held**
WEB: www.sercomp.com
SIC: 3955 3577 Print cartridges for laser & other computer printers; computer peripheral equipment

(P-22974)
UNIVERSAL IMAGING TECH INC
4733 Torrance Blvd 997, Torrance (90503-4100)
PHONE....................310 961-2098
Shad Applegate, *President*
EMP: 16
SQ FT: 4,000
SALES: 1.6MM **Privately Held**
SIC: 3955 Print cartridges for laser & other computer printers

(P-22975)
US PRINT & TONER INC
Also Called: National Copy Cartridge
1990 Friendship Dr, El Cajon (92020-1128)
PHONE....................619 562-6995
James Meyers, *President*
▲ **EMP:** 22
SQ FT: 6,500
SALES (est): 3.4MM **Privately Held**
WEB: www.nationalcopycartridge.com
SIC: 3955 Print cartridges for laser & other computer printers

(P-22976)
VISION IMAGING SUPPLIES INC
9540 Cozycroft Ave, Chatsworth (91311-5101)
PHONE....................818 710-7200
Benard Khachi, *CEO*
Raymond Khachi, *Vice Pres*
▲ **EMP:** 50
SALES (est): 8MM **Privately Held**
WEB: www.vis-llc.com
SIC: 3955 Print cartridges for laser & other computer printers

┌─────────────────────────┐
│ **3961 Costume Jewelry &** │
│ **Novelties** │
└─────────────────────────┘

(P-22977)
A G ARTWEAR INC
Also Called: Frederic Duclos
15564 Producer Ln, Huntington Beach (92649-1308)
P.O. Box 2460 (92647-0460)
PHONE....................714 898-3636
Karen M Duclos, *President*
Frederic Duclos, *Vice Pres*
EMP: 10
SQ FT: 2,100
SALES (est): 1.3MM **Privately Held**
WEB: www.fredericduclos.com
SIC: 3961 Costume jewelry

(P-22978)
B & R ACCESSORIES INC
7508 Deering Ave Ste D, Canoga Park (91303-1436)
PHONE....................213 688-8727
Brijinder S Ahluwalia, *President*
▲ **EMP:** 10
SALES (est): 1.1MM **Privately Held**
SIC: 3961 Costume jewelry

(P-22979)
COLORON JEWELRY INC
Also Called: Coloron Jewelry Manufacturing
7242 Valjean Ave, Van Nuys (91406-3412)
PHONE....................818 565-1100

Ilan Lavian, *President*
EMP: 14 **EST:** 2000
SQ FT: 2,000
SALES (est): 2.2MM **Privately Held**
SIC: 3961 Costume jewelry

(P-22980)
DOGEARED INC
6053 Bristol Pkwy, Culver City (90230-6601)
PHONE....................310 846-4444
Marcia Maizel-Clarke, *President*
Douglas Clarke, *Treasurer*
Mimi Kim-Ison, *Vice Pres*
Chad Berryhill, *Info Tech Dir*
Francine Campos, *Human Res Mgr*
EMP: 90
SALES (est): 17.6MM **Privately Held**
WEB: www.dogearedjewelry.com
SIC: 3961 Costume jewelry

(P-22981)
EDGY SOUL
22337 Pacific Coast Hwy # 143, Malibu (90265-5030)
PHONE....................310 800-2861
Lori Roberts, *COO*
EMP: 12
SQ FT: 1,100
SALES (est): 824.6K **Privately Held**
SIC: 3961 Costume jewelry

(P-22982)
FML INC
Also Called: Dynasty Import Co
2765 16th St, San Francisco (94103-4215)
PHONE....................415 864-5084
Fred Lane, *President*
Mayling Lane, *Vice Pres*
Anyta Lane, *Opers Staff*
◆ **EMP:** 11 **EST:** 1950
SQ FT: 40,000
SALES (est): 2.2MM **Privately Held**
SIC: 3961 5094 Costume jewelry, ex. precious metal & semiprecious stones; jewelry

(P-22983)
HOORSEN BUHS LLC
2217 Main St, Santa Monica (90405-2217)
PHONE....................888 692-2997
Robert Keiths, *Mng Member*
Robert Keithns, *Mng Member*
Kether Parker, *Director*
EMP: 12
SALES (est): 138.6K **Privately Held**
SIC: 3961 Jewelry apparel, non-precious metals

(P-22984)
JAM DESIGN INC
5415 Cleon Ave, North Hollywood (91601-2834)
PHONE....................818 505-1680
Marie Van Demark, *President*
EMP: 12
SQ FT: 1,500
SALES (est): 870K **Privately Held**
SIC: 3961 Jewelry apparel, non-precious metals

(P-22985)
JMGJ GROUP INC
10120 Wexted Way, Elk Grove (95757-5501)
PHONE....................866 293-2872
Jacque Ojadidi, *CEO*
EMP: 10 **EST:** 2017
SQ FT: 3,900
SALES: 500K **Privately Held**
SIC: 3961 5944 5094 Costume jewelry, ex. precious metal & semiprecious stones; jewelry stores; jewelry

(P-22986)
KEY ITEM SALES INC
21037 Superior St, Chatsworth (91311-4322)
PHONE....................818 885-0928
EMP: 10 **EST:** 2013
SALES (est): 1MM **Privately Held**
SIC: 3961

▲ = Import ▼=Export
◆ =Import/Export

(P-22987)
KULAYFUL SILICONE BRACELETS
2267 Joshua Tree Way, West Covina (91791-4331)
PHONE..........................626 610-3816
Chris Angeles, *President*
EMP: 20 **EST:** 2013
SALES (est): 838.5K **Privately Held**
SIC: 3961 Bracelets, except precious metal

(P-22988)
LIZ PALACIOS DESIGNS LTD
1 Stanton Way, Mill Valley (94941-1421)
PHONE..........................628 444-3339
Liz Palacios, *President*
Mingyu Fang, *Office Mgr*
EMP: 29
SQ FT: 7,500
SALES (est): 3.5MM **Privately Held**
WEB: www.lizpalacios.com
SIC: 3961 Costume jewelry

(P-22989)
LOUNGEFLY LLC
Also Called: Lounge Fly
20310 Plummer St, Chatsworth (91311-5371)
PHONE..........................818 718-5600
Trevor Schultz,
Dale Schultz, *Natl Sales Mgr*
Ramona Krueger, *Accounts Mgr*
▲ **EMP:** 25
SQ FT: 2,500
SALES (est): 5.6MM **Privately Held**
WEB: www.loungefly.com
SIC: 3961 Costume jewelry

(P-22990)
NEW ORIGINS ACCESSORIES INC (PA)
Also Called: Charming Hawaii
3980 Valley Blvd Ste D, Walnut (91789-1530)
PHONE..........................909 869-7559
Vinod Kumar, *President*
Manju Kumar, *Admin Sec*
▲ **EMP:** 12
SQ FT: 2,400
SALES (est): 1.4MM **Privately Held**
SIC: 3961 Costume jewelry, ex. precious metal & semiprecious stones

(P-22991)
NOVELA DESIGNS INC
643 S Olive St Ste 421, Los Angeles (90014-3608)
PHONE..........................213 505-4092
Alejandro Fuentes, *President*
EMP: 10
SQ FT: 1,200
SALES (est): 500K **Privately Held**
SIC: 3961 Costume jewelry

(P-22992)
PEARL ROVE INC
9570 Ridgehaven Ct Ste B, San Diego (92123-1667)
PHONE..........................858 869-1827
Pnina Gruver, *Admin Sec*
EMP: 12
SQ FT: 2,300
SALES (est): 603.9K **Privately Held**
SIC: 3961 5632 Costume jewelry, ex. precious metal & semiprecious stones; costume jewelry

(P-22993)
PIN CRAFT INC
Also Called: Pin Concepts
7933 Ajay Dr, Sun Valley (91352-5315)
PHONE..........................818 248-0077
Vahe Asatourian, *President*
Kellie Torio, *Assistant*
Linna Kazanchian, *Supervisor*
◆ **EMP:** 27
SALES (est): 647.6K **Privately Held**
WEB: www.pincraft.com
SIC: 3961 Pins (jewelry), except precious metal

(P-22994)
SAMS TRADE DEVELOPMENT CORP
818 S Main St, Los Angeles (90014-2002)
PHONE..........................213 225-0188
Sam Chu, *President*
▲ **EMP:** 24
SALES (est): 2.4MM **Privately Held**
SIC: 3961 Costume jewelry, ex. precious metal & semiprecious stones

(P-22995)
SHARP PERFORMANCE USA INC (PA)
16029 Arrow Hwy Ste D, Baldwin Park (91706-2066)
PHONE..........................626 888-1190
Grant Stoddart, *CEO*
Diana Chen, *President*
Josh Cochran, *Sales Mgr*
▲ **EMP:** 11
SALES (est): 1.5MM **Privately Held**
SIC: 3961 2386 3951 Keychains, except precious metal; garments, leather; pens & mechanical pencils

(P-22996)
SPORT PINS INTERNATIONAL INC
888 Berry Ct Ste A, Upland (91786-8445)
PHONE..........................909 985-4549
Connie Bivens, *President*
John Bivens, *CFO*
Michael Bivens, *Treasurer*
Jeff Bivens, *Admin Sec*
Nancy Elliott, *Bookkeeper*
◆ **EMP:** 14
SQ FT: 2,300
SALES (est): 2.2MM **Privately Held**
WEB: www.sportpins.net
SIC: 3961 2395 3499 Pins (jewelry), except precious metal; emblems, embroidered; novelties & giftware, including trophies

(P-22997)
V & V MANUFACTURING INC
15320 Proctor Ave, City of Industry (91745-1023)
PHONE..........................626 330-0641
Everett C Visk, *President*
Everett Visk, *President*
Steve Visk, *Vice Pres*
EMP: 12
SQ FT: 3,500
SALES: 800K **Privately Held**
SIC: 3961 Costume jewelry, ex. precious metal & semiprecious stones

---
3965 Fasteners, Buttons, Needles & Pins

(P-22998)
BECKMAN INDUSTRIES
701 Del Nrte Blvd Ste 205, Oxnard (93030)
P.O. Box 2307, Agoura Hills (91376-2307)
PHONE..........................805 375-3003
Robert Becker, *President*
Danny Becker, *Vice Pres*
Warren Venet, *Purch Mgr*
EMP: 16
SQ FT: 19,248
SALES (est): 3.4MM **Privately Held**
WEB: www.beckmanindustries.com
SIC: 3965 5072 Fasteners; hardware

(P-22999)
CATAME INC (PA)
Also Called: Ucan Zippers
1930 Long Beach Ave, Los Angeles (90058-1020)
PHONE..........................213 749-2610
Liz H Lai, *CEO*
Malan Lai, *Managing Prtnr*
Paul Lai, *CFO*
Floyd Lai, *Admin Sec*
▲ **EMP:** 28 **EST:** 1995
SQ FT: 50,000
SALES (est): 4.8MM **Privately Held**
WEB: www.catameinc.com
SIC: 3965 5131 Zipper; zippers

(P-23000)
ENGINEERING MATERIALS CO INC
2055 W Cowles St, Long Beach (90813-1087)
PHONE..........................562 436-0063
Edward Rickter, *President*
Susan J Brackett, *Treasurer*
Cynthia Ann Russell, *Admin Sec*
EMP: 20 **EST:** 1951
SQ FT: 24,000
SALES (est): 1.9MM **Privately Held**
SIC: 3965 Fasteners

(P-23001)
FASTENER TECHNOLOGY CORP
7415 Fulton Ave, North Hollywood (91605-4116)
PHONE..........................818 764-6467
Dennis Suedkamp, *CEO*
Saul Bautista, *Engineer*
Margarita Szabo, *Human Res Mgr*
EMP: 89 **EST:** 1979
SQ FT: 24,000
SALES (est): 13MM **Privately Held**
WEB: www.ftc-usa.com
SIC: 3965 3452 Fasteners; bolts, nuts, rivets & washers

(P-23002)
GIST INC
Also Called: Gist Silversmiths
4385 Pleasant Valley Rd, Placerville (95667-8430)
PHONE..........................530 644-8000
Gary Gist, *President*
Jennifer Folsom, *Vice Pres*
Wende Heinen, *Sales Staff*
▲ **EMP:** 85
SQ FT: 15,000
SALES (est): 12.9MM **Privately Held**
WEB: www.gistsilversmiths.com
SIC: 3965 3911 Buckles & buckle parts; jewelry apparel

(P-23003)
HENWAY INC
Also Called: Anatase Products
1314 Goodrick Dr, Tehachapi (93561-1508)
PHONE..........................661 822-6873
David Benhan, *Vice Pres*
Scott D Baker, *Corp Secy*
Johnathan Harris, *Sales Staff*
Kevin Steinmetz, *Manager*
EMP: 18
SQ FT: 18,500
SALES (est): 2MM **Privately Held**
WEB: www.aircraftbolts.com
SIC: 3965 3452 Fasteners; bolts, nuts, rivets & washers

(P-23004)
L & P BUTTON & TRIMMING CO
2477 Ridgeway Rd, San Marino (91108-2118)
PHONE..........................626 796-0903
Patty P Chan, *President*
Leon Tsay, *Vice Pres*
▲ **EMP:** 10
SALES (est): 1.3MM **Privately Held**
SIC: 3965 Buttons & parts

(P-23005)
LABELTEX MILLS INC (PA)
6100 Wilmington Ave, Los Angeles (90001-1826)
PHONE..........................323 582-0228
Torag Pourshamtobi, *CEO*
Shahrokh Shamtobi, *President*
Ben Younessi, *Vice Pres*
Rebecca Cocco, *Executive*
Mishel Imani, *Executive*
▲ **EMP:** 200
SQ FT: 135,000
SALES (est): 27.5MM **Privately Held**
WEB: www.labeltexmills.com
SIC: 3965 2253 2241 Fasteners, buttons, needles & pins; collar & cuff sets, knit; labels, woven

(P-23006)
MORTON GRINDING INC
Also Called: Morton Manufacturing
201 E Avenue K15, Lancaster (93535-4572)
PHONE..........................661 298-0895
Yolanda A Morton, *Ch of Bd*
Frank Morton, *President*
Wallace Morton, *President*
Dale Ray, *COO*
Patrick Dansby, *Corp Secy*
EMP: 110
SQ FT: 45,000
SALES (est): 26.7MM **Privately Held**
SIC: 3965 3769 3452 Fasteners; guided missile & space vehicle parts & auxiliary equipment; bolts, nuts, rivets & washers

(P-23007)
PAIHO NORTH AMERICA CORP
16051 El Prado Rd, Chino (91708-9144)
PHONE..........................661 257-6611
Yi Ming Lin, *President*
Catherine Hsieh, *CFO*
Shu-Ching Hsieh, *CFO*
▲ **EMP:** 22
SQ FT: 52,000
SALES (est): 8.3MM **Privately Held**
SIC: 3965 Fasteners, hooks & eyes

(P-23008)
SHORELINE PRODUCTS INC
Also Called: Sola Products
120 Calle Iglesia Ste A, San Clemente (92672-7543)
PHONE..........................949 388-1919
Cassandra House, *President*
Steven House, *Director*
▲ **EMP:** 10
SALES (est): 1.8MM **Privately Held**
SIC: 3965 3949 Fasteners; surfboards

(P-23009)
SPS TECHNOLOGIES LLC
Also Called: Aerospace Fasteners Group
1224 E Warner Ave, Santa Ana (92705-5414)
PHONE..........................714 545-9311
Mike Kleene, *Branch Mgr*
Debbie Lupascu, *Technology*
Karen Alexander, *Sales Mgr*
Ofelia Tapia, *Sales Mgr*
Michael Harhen, *Director*
EMP: 500
SQ FT: 40,000
SALES (corp-wide): 225.3B **Publicly Held**
WEB: www.spst.com
SIC: 3965 3728 3452 3714 Fasteners; aircraft parts & equipment; bolts, nuts, rivets & washers; motor vehicle parts & accessories; machine tool accessories; iron & steel forgings
HQ: Sps Technologies, Llc
301 Highland Ave
Jenkintown PA 19046
215 572-3000

(P-23010)
SPS TECHNOLOGIES LLC
Cherry Aerospace Div
1224 E Warner Ave, Santa Ana (92705-5414)
PHONE..........................714 371-1925
Michael Harhen, *Branch Mgr*
EMP: 500
SALES (corp-wide): 225.3B **Publicly Held**
WEB: www.spst.com
SIC: 3965 3452 Fasteners; bolts, nuts, rivets & washers
HQ: Sps Technologies, Llc
301 Highland Ave
Jenkintown PA 19046
215 572-3000

(P-23011)
TOLEETO FASTENER INTERNATIONAL
1580 Jayken Way, Chula Vista (91911-4644)
PHONE..........................619 662-1355
David Deavenport, *President*
Tom V Oss, *Vice Pres*
Sara Davenport, *Principal*
EMP: 26
SQ FT: 10,000
SALES: 1.8MM **Privately Held**
WEB: www.toleeto.com
SIC: 3965 Fasteners

(P-23012)
TOMARCO CONTRACTOR SPC INC
Also Called: Tamarco Contractor Specialties
9372 Cabot Dr, San Diego (92126-4311)
PHONE 858 547-0700
Patrick Armstrong, *Manager*
EMP: 10
SALES (corp-wide): 68.6MM **Privately Held**
WEB: www.tomarco.com
SIC: 3965 Fasteners; eyelets, metal: clothing, fabrics, boots or shoes; buckles & buckle parts
PA: Tomarco Contractor Specialties, Inc.
14848 Northam St
La Mirada CA 90638
714 523-1771

(P-23013)
TVS DISTRIBUTORS INC
Also Called: Tts Products
2822 E Olympic Blvd, Los Angeles (90023-3412)
PHONE 323 268-1347
Vera Sapp, *President*
▲ EMP: 12
SQ FT: 8,000
SALES (est): 1.8MM **Privately Held**
SIC: 3965 Fasteners

(P-23014)
TWO LADS INC (PA)
5001 Hampton St, Vernon (90058-2133)
P.O. Box 58572, Los Angeles (90058-0572)
PHONE 323 584-0064
Lee R Adams, *President*
David Scharf, *Corp Secy*
Linda Gold, *Sales Mgr*
▼ EMP: 30
SQ FT: 6,300
SALES (est): 3.4MM **Privately Held**
SIC: 3965 5131 2241 Buttons & parts; buttons; narrow fabric mills

(P-23015)
WCBM COMPANY (PA)
Also Called: West Coast Button Mfg Co
1812 W 135th St, Gardena (90249-2520)
PHONE 323 262-3274
Keith Tanabe, *CEO*
Grace Kadoya, *CFO*
▲ EMP: 32
SQ FT: 19,000
SALES (est): 2.2MM **Privately Held**
SIC: 3965 Buttons & parts

(P-23016)
WEST COAST AEROSPACE INC (PA)
220 W E St, Wilmington (90744-5502)
PHONE 310 518-3167
Kenneth L Wagner Jr, *President*
Thomas Lieb, *Vice Pres*
Jeannie Vassor, *Administration*
Tom Nyikos, *Engineer*
Ryan Wagner, *Human Res Dir*
▲ EMP: 90
SQ FT: 7,200
SALES (est): 17.6MM **Privately Held**
WEB: www.westcoastaerospace.com
SIC: 3965 3452 Fasteners; bolts, nuts, rivets & washers

(P-23017)
WEST COAST AEROSPACE INC
3017 E Las Hermanas St, Compton (90221)
PHONE 310 632-2064
Chris Brumby, *Manager*
EMP: 10
SALES (corp-wide): 17.6MM **Privately Held**
WEB: www.westcoastaerospace.com
SIC: 3965 Fasteners
PA: West Coast Aerospace, Inc.
220 W E St
Wilmington CA 90744
310 518-3167

(P-23018)
YKK (USA) INC
Also Called: Y K K U S A
5001 E La Palma Ave, Anaheim (92807-1926)
PHONE 714 701-1200
Mike Blunt, *Manager*
Dennis Smith, *Regl Sales Mgr*
EMP: 150 **Privately Held**
SIC: 3965 5131 Fasteners; hooks, crochet; zipper; fasteners, hooks & eyes; zippers
HQ: Ykk (U.S.A.), Inc.
1300 Cobb Industrial Dr
Marietta GA 30066
770 427-5521

3991 Brooms & Brushes

(P-23019)
A & B BRUSH MFG CORP
1150 3 Ranch Rd, Duarte (91010-2751)
PHONE 626 303-8856
Donn Anawalt Jr, *President*
Tom Derto, *Manager*
▲ EMP: 15
SQ FT: 26,500
SALES (est): 2.4MM **Privately Held**
SIC: 3991 Brushes, household or industrial

(P-23020)
AMERICAN ROTARY BROOM CO INC (PA)
181 Pawnee St Ste B, San Marcos (92078-2555)
PHONE 760 591-4025
James Wagner, *President*
Mary M Wagner, *Corp Secy*
Joe Baeskens, *Vice Pres*
EMP: 10 EST: 1955
SQ FT: 9,720
SALES (est): 2MM **Privately Held**
WEB: www.americanrotarybroom.com
SIC: 3991 Street sweeping brooms, hand or machine

(P-23021)
AMERICAN ROTARY BROOM CO INC
688 New York Dr, Pomona (91768-3311)
PHONE 909 629-9117
Joe Baeskens, *Vice Pres*
Clayton Trejo, *Sales Executive*
EMP: 26
SALES (corp-wide): 2MM **Privately Held**
WEB: www.americanrotarybroom.com
SIC: 3991 3711 4959 Brooms; motor vehicles & car bodies; sweeping service: road, airport, parking lot, etc.
PA: American Rotary Broom Co., Inc.
181 Pawnee St Ste B
San Marcos CA 92078
760 591-4025

(P-23022)
BRUSH RESEARCH MFG CO
Also Called: Brm Manufacturing
4642 Floral Dr, Los Angeles (90022-1288)
PHONE 323 261-2193
Tara L Rands, *CEO*
Grant Fowlie, *President*
Heather Jones, *Treasurer*
Robert Fowlie, *Officer*
Mike Miller, *Vice Pres*
▲ EMP: 130 EST: 1962
SALES (est): 21.9MM **Privately Held**
WEB: www.brushresearch.com
SIC: 3991 Brushes, household or industrial

(P-23023)
BUTLER HOME PRODUCTS LLC
9409 Buffalo Ave, Rancho Cucamonga (91730-6012)
PHONE 909 476-3884
Paul Anton, *Branch Mgr*
EMP: 13
SALES (corp-wide): 337.5MM **Privately Held**
WEB: www.mrcleantools.com
SIC: 3991 2392 Brooms; mops, floor & dust

HQ: Butler Home Products, Llc
2 Cabot Rd Ste 1
Hudson MA 01749
508 597-8000

(P-23024)
CT OLDENKAMP LLC
Also Called: Martin Sweeping
78380 Clarke Ct, La Quinta (92253-2213)
PHONE 760 200-9510
Curtis Oldenkamp, *Principal*
EMP: 10
SALES (est): 1.3MM **Privately Held**
SIC: 3991 Street sweeping brooms, hand or machine

(P-23025)
ENVIRO-COMMERCIAL SWEEPING
210 San Jose Ave Ste 5, Chico (95927)
PHONE 408 920-0274
Michael P Delucchi, *President*
Romy Salgado, *Treasurer*
Rebecca Rossi, *Admin Sec*
EMP: 15
SALES (est): 1.4MM **Privately Held**
WEB: www.envirocommercial.com
SIC: 3991 7538 Street sweeping brooms, hand or machine; general automotive repair shops

(P-23026)
FOAMPRO MFG INC
Also Called: Foampro Manufacturing
1781 Langley Ave, Irvine (92614-5621)
P.O. Box 18888 (92623-8888)
PHONE 949 252-0112
Gregory Isaac, *Ch of Bd*
Chad Coil, *Vice Pres*
▲ EMP: 80 EST: 1952
SQ FT: 25,000
SALES (est): 11.6MM **Privately Held**
WEB: www.foampromfg.com
SIC: 3991 Paint rollers; paint brushes

(P-23027)
GORDON BRUSH MFG CO INC (PA)
3737 Capitol Ave, City of Industry (90601-1732)
PHONE 323 724-7777
Kenneth L Rakusin, *President*
William E Loitz, *Vice Pres*
Denis Valentine, *Design Engr*
William Loitz, *Engineer*
Connie Faundez, *Accounting Mgr*
▲ EMP: 60 EST: 1951
SQ FT: 51,600
SALES (est): 15.1MM **Privately Held**
WEB: www.gordonbrush.net
SIC: 3991 Brushes, household or industrial

(P-23028)
KINGSOLVER INC
Also Called: Supreme Enterprise
8417 Secura Way, Santa Fe Springs (90670-2215)
P.O. Box 3106 (90670-0106)
PHONE 562 945-7590
Keith Kingsolver, *President*
Christina Kingsolver, *Admin Sec*
▲ EMP: 19
SQ FT: 22,000
SALES (est): 2.7MM **Privately Held**
WEB: www.kingsolver.com
SIC: 3991 5199 Brooms; broom, mop & paint handles

(P-23029)
LAKIM INDUSTRIES INCORPORATED (PA)
Also Called: Quali-Tech Manufacturing
389 Rood Rd, Calexico (92231-9763)
PHONE 310 637-8900
Song B Kim, *CEO*
Juhyun Kim, *CFO*
Hector Herrera, *Opers Staff*
Soyoung Kim, *Sales Staff*
Erica Gomez, *Accounts Mgr*
▲ EMP: 30
SALES (est): 6.4MM **Privately Held**
WEB: www.quali-techmfg.com
SIC: 3991 Paint rollers; paint brushes

(P-23030)
PASCO INDUSTRIES INC
2040 Redondo Pl, Fullerton (92835-3306)
PHONE 714 992-2051
Carl G Cantonis, *CEO*
George Cantonis, *President*
Cynthia C Cantonis-Finn, *Vice Pres*
Anne Cantonis, *Admin Sec*
EMP: 15 EST: 1951
SQ FT: 28,000
SALES: 900K **Privately Held**
SIC: 3991 5199 Paint rollers; paint brushes; sponges (animal); chamois leather

(P-23031)
UNITED ROTARY BRUSH CORP
688 New York Dr, Pomona (91768-3311)
PHONE 909 629-9117
Joe Baeskens, *Branch Mgr*
EMP: 37
SALES (corp-wide): 47.1MM **Privately Held**
SIC: 3991 Brushes, household or industrial
PA: United Rotary Brush Corporation
15607 W 100th Ter
Lenexa KS 66219
913 888-8450

(P-23032)
UNITED ROTARY BRUSH CORP
160 Enterprise Ct Ste B, Galt (95632-8179)
PHONE 913 888-8450
Jim Olvera, *Manager*
EMP: 25
SALES (corp-wide): 47.1MM **Privately Held**
WEB: www.united-rotary.com
SIC: 3991 Brushes, household or industrial
PA: United Rotary Brush Corporation
15607 W 100th Ter
Lenexa KS 66219
913 888-8450

(P-23033)
WESTCOAST BRUSH MFG INC
1330 Philadelphia St, Pomona (91766-5563)
PHONE 909 627-7170
Heriberto Guerrero, *President*
Concepcion Guerrero, *Vice Pres*
▲ EMP: 22
SQ FT: 20,000
SALES (est): 3.3MM **Privately Held**
WEB: www.westcoastbrush.com
SIC: 3991 Brushes, household or industrial

(P-23034)
WORLD TREND INC (PA)
1920 W Holt Ave, Pomona (91768-3351)
PHONE 909 620-9945
Barnabas C Chen, *President*
▲ EMP: 15
SQ FT: 22,000
SALES (est): 1.4MM **Privately Held**
WEB: www.worldtrend.com
SIC: 3991 Toothbrushes, except electric; brushes, except paint & varnish

---

3993 Signs & Advertising Displays

(P-23035)
A GOOD SIGN & GRAPHICS CO
2110 S Susan St, Santa Ana (92704-4417)
PHONE 714 444-4466
Babak Richard Abedi, *CEO*
Ted Howard, *Sales Staff*
Thang MAI, *Manager*
EMP: 20 EST: 2008
SALES (est): 2.5MM **Privately Held**
WEB: www.agoodsign.com
SIC: 3993 Signs, not made in custom sign painting shops

(P-23036)
A PLUS SIGNS INC
4270 N Brawley Ave, Fresno (93722-3979)
PHONE 559 275-0700
Chris Pacheco, *President*
Jeff Ashlock, *Vice Pres*
Lauren Gibson, *Project Mgr*
EMP: 47
SQ FT: 12,000

SALES (est): 4MM **Privately Held**
WEB: www.a-plussigns.com
SIC: 3993 7389 2399 Electric signs;
signs, not made in custom sign painting
shops; sign painting & lettering shop; banners, pennants & flags

(P-23037)
AAHS ENTERPRISES INC
Also Called: Aahs Graphics Signs & Engrv
6600 Telegraph Rd, Commerce
(90040-3210)
PHONE.....................323 838-9130
Gurmeet Sawhney, *President*
EMP: 16
SALES: 1.8MM **Privately Held**
SIC: 3993 Signs & advertising specialties

(P-23038)
AARONS SIGNS & PRINTING
3770 Van Buren Blvd, Riverside
(92503-4250)
PHONE.....................951 352-7303
Gary Kerrington, *Principal*
EMP: 30
SALES (est): 1.8MM **Privately Held**
WEB: www.aaronssigns.com
SIC: 3993 Signs & advertising specialties

(P-23039)
ABIS SIGNS INC
14240 Don Julian Rd Ste E, City of Industry
(91746-3040)
PHONE.....................626 818-4329
Eddie Takahashi, *Principal*
EMP: 14
SALES (corp-wide): 729.2K **Privately
Held**
SIC: 3993 Neon signs
PA: Abis Signs Inc
12223 Highland Ave 106-21
Rancho Cucamonga CA 91739
626 818-4303

(P-23040)
ABSOLUTE SIGN INC
10655 Humbolt St, Los Alamitos
(90720-2447)
PHONE.....................562 592-5838
Patricia Scialampo, *President*
Gregory Benedict, *Vice Pres*
EMP: 15
SALES (est): 1.9MM **Privately Held**
WEB: www.absolutesign.com
SIC: 3993 Electric signs; neon signs

(P-23041)
ACT NOW INSTANT SIGNS INC
Also Called: Act Now Signs
550 W Cienega Ave Ste B, San Dimas
(91773-2977)
PHONE.....................909 394-7818
James R Kuhlman, *President*
Kathy Kuhlman, *Vice Pres*
Lili Jurado, *Sales Staff*
EMP: 10
SQ FT: 5,000
SALES (est): 857.4K **Privately Held**
SIC: 3993 Signs, not made in custom sign
painting shops

(P-23042)
AD ART INC (PA)
Also Called: Ad Art Sign Company
150 Executive Park Blvd # 2100, San Fran-
cisco (94134-3364)
PHONE.....................415 869-6460
Terry J Long, *CEO*
Robert Kiereczyk, *President*
Doug Head, *Exec VP*
Duane Contento, *Senior VP*
David Esajian, *Vice Pres*
▲ EMP: 70
SQ FT: 4,000
SALES: 27MM **Privately Held**
WEB: www.adart.com
SIC: 3993 Electric signs

(P-23043)
ADTEK MEDIA INC
Also Called: Pumptop TV
13841 West St, Garden Grove
(92843-3912)
PHONE.....................949 680-4200
Richard Paulsen, *President*
Mitchell Phan, *CFO*

Richard Nelson, *Vice Pres*
Roy Reeves, *Vice Pres*
EMP: 30
SQ FT: 10,000
SALES: 5MM **Privately Held**
SIC: 3993 Signs & advertising specialties

(P-23044)
ADTI MEDIA LLC
Also Called: Advanced Digital Tech Intl
1257 Simpson Way, Escondido
(92029-1403)
PHONE.....................951 795-4446
James P Martingale, *President*
Joe Milkovits, *Vice Pres*
Rick Baldacci,
Lawrence F De George,
▲ EMP: 30
SALES (est): 5.3MM **Privately Held**
SIC: 3993 Signs & advertising specialties

(P-23045)
AHR SIGNS INCORPORATED
Also Called: Ampersand Contract Signing Grp
3400 N San Fernando Rd, Los Angeles
(90065-1419)
PHONE.....................323 255-1102
Rouben Varozian, *President*
EMP: 13
SQ FT: 15,000
SALES (est): 1.7MM **Privately Held**
WEB: www.ampersandsigns.com
SIC: 3993 Signs, not made in custom sign
painting shops

(P-23046)
AINOR SIGNS INC
5443 Stationers Way, Sacramento
(95842-1900)
PHONE.....................916 348-4370
Joseph Ainor, *President*
Catherine Bettencourt, *Admin Sec*
Christie Lawrence, *Controller*
Joe Morano, *Director*
EMP: 12 EST: 2006
SQ FT: 1,500
SALES (est): 2.4MM **Privately Held**
SIC: 3993 Signs, not made in custom sign
painting shops

(P-23047)
AMERICAN ACRYLIC DISPLAY INC
1061 S Leslie St, La Habra (90631-6843)
PHONE.....................714 738-7990
Mario Herrera, *President*
Francisco Rivera, *Vice Pres*
EMP: 11
SQ FT: 7,000
SALES (est): 1.4MM **Privately Held**
WEB: www.acrylicdisplayinc.com
SIC: 3993 3089 Displays & cutouts, win-
dow & lobby; plastic processing

(P-23048)
AMERICAN FLEET & RET GRAPHICS
Also Called: Amgraph
2091 Del Rio Way, Ontario (91761-8038)
PHONE.....................909 937-7570
Kristin Stewart, *CEO*
Brian Stewart, *President*
Dawn Miltenberger, *Department Mgr*
Marlene Marrero, *Admin Asst*
EMP: 37
SALES (est): 7.6MM **Privately Held**
SIC: 3993 Signs & advertising specialties

(P-23049)
ANDERSON SIGNS
Also Called: Anderson's Signs & Crane
1240 N Filbert St, Stockton (95205-3813)
P.O. Box 336, Victor (95253-0336)
PHONE.....................209 367-0120
Steve Anderson, *Owner*
EMP: 10
SALES (est): 760.3K **Privately Held**
WEB: www.thelouisvillechannel.com
SIC: 3993 Signs & advertising specialties

(P-23050)
APEX UNIVERSAL INC (PA)
11033 Forest Pl, Santa Fe Springs
(90670-3935)
PHONE.....................562 944-8878
Frank Fei, *President*

Janet Yang, *General Mgr*
▲ EMP: 14
SQ FT: 7,500
SALES (est): 2.1MM **Privately Held**
WEB: www.apexuniversal.com
SIC: 3993 3669 Signs & advertising spe-
cialties; transportation signaling devices

(P-23051)
ARCHITECTURAL DESIGN SIGNS INC (PA)
Also Called: Ad/S Companies
1160 Railroad St, Corona (92882-1835)
PHONE.....................951 278-0680
Sean L Solomon, *President*
EMP: 95
SQ FT: 630,000
SALES (est): 25.6MM **Privately Held**
WEB: www.ad-s.com
SIC: 3993 Signs & advertising specialties

(P-23052)
ARCHITECTURAL S WEIDNER
Also Called: WEIDNERCA
5001 24th St, Sacramento (95822-2201)
PHONE.....................800 561-7446
Mark Douglas Copeland, *CEO*
Edwin F Weidner III, *President*
Edwin F Weidner Jr, *Chairman*
Kathy Weidner, *Treasurer*
Arie Korver, *Vice Pres*
EMP: 47
SQ FT: 20,450
SALES: 12.3MM **Privately Held**
WEB: www.weidnersignage.com
SIC: 3993 2759 7389 Signs & advertising
specialties; screen printing; sign painting
& lettering shop

(P-23053)
ARROW SIGN CO (PA)
Also Called: Arrow Sign Company
1051 46th Ave, Oakland (94601-4436)
PHONE.....................209 931-5522
Charles Sterne, *President*
Jeremy Blackburn, *Project Mgr*
Dan Jetke, *Project Mgr*
Michael Bennett, *Engineer*
Tina Mowdy, *Credit Mgr*
EMP: 48 EST: 1958
SQ FT: 119,375
SALES (est): 12.3MM **Privately Held**
WEB: www.arrowsigncompany.com
SIC: 3993 Electric signs

(P-23054)
ARROW SIGN CO
3133 N Ad Art Rd, Stockton (95215-2217)
PHONE.....................209 931-7852
Chuck Sterne, *Branch Mgr*
EMP: 27
SALES (corp-wide): 12.3MM **Privately
Held**
WEB: www.arrowsigncompany.com
SIC: 3993 Electric signs
PA: Arrow Sign Co.
1051 46th Ave
Oakland CA 94601
209 931-5522

(P-23055)
ART & SIGN PRODUCTION INC
3651 E Chevy Chase Dr, Glendale
(91206-1211)
PHONE.....................818 245-6945
Chris Ghantous, *President*
Armand Ghantous, *Treasurer*
Gill Ghantous, *Vice Pres*
Gisele Ghantous, *Admin Sec*
EMP: 10
SQ FT: 15,000
SALES (est): 1.3MM **Privately Held**
WEB: www.artandsign.com
SIC: 3993 7374 Signs & advertising spe-
cialties; computer graphics service

(P-23056)
ART SIGNWORKS INC
41785 Elm St Ste 302, Murrieta
(92562-9276)
PHONE.....................951 698-8484
Paul Williamson, *President*
Cheryl Burnette, *Principal*
Christie Valenzuela, *Principal*
Kevin Cohn, *Production*
EMP: 10

SQ FT: 5,000
SALES: 700K **Privately Held**
SIC: 3993 Signs & advertising specialties

(P-23057)
ASTRO DISPLAY COMPANY INC
4247 E Airport Dr, Ontario (91761-1565)
PHONE.....................909 605-2875
Thomas Andric, *Ch of Bd*
EMP: 20
SQ FT: 16,000
SALES: 1.5MM **Privately Held**
SIC: 3993 7319 3089 Displays & cutouts,
window & lobby; display advertising serv-
ice; plastic processing

(P-23058)
B & H SIGNS INC
926 S Primrose Ave, Monrovia
(91016-3440)
PHONE.....................626 359-6643
William Henry, *President*
EMP: 56
SQ FT: 7,000
SALES (est): 6.8MM **Privately Held**
SIC: 3993 Signs, not made in custom sign
painting shops

(P-23059)
BEELINE GROUP LLC
31023 Huntwood Ave, Hayward
(94544-7007)
P.O. Box 757, Carthage MO (64836-0757)
PHONE.....................510 477-5400
Josh Roberts, *CEO*
Wayne Kimball, *CFO*
Julie Stier, *Exec Dir*
Kurt Harvey, *Info Tech Dir*
Mario Orsi, *Controller*
EMP: 57
SQ FT: 27,000
SALES (est): 15.3MM **Privately Held**
SIC: 3993 Signs & advertising specialties

(P-23060)
BK SIGNS INC
1028 W Kirkwall Rd, Azusa (91702-5126)
PHONE.....................626 334-5600
Brian Scott Kanner, *CEO*
EMP: 18
SQ FT: 16,000
SALES (est): 2.9MM **Privately Held**
WEB: www.bksigns.com
SIC: 3993 1731 Signs & advertising spe-
cialties; advertising artwork; general elec-
trical contractor

(P-23061)
BLACKCOFFEE FABRICATORS INC
Also Called: Blackcoffee Sign Fabricators
777 W Mill St, San Bernardino
(92410-3355)
PHONE.....................909 974-4499
Erin Foley, *President*
Dale Foley, *Vice Pres*
Jim Foley, *Vice Pres*
Maria Foley, *Admin Sec*
EMP: 14
SALES (est): 1.7MM **Privately Held**
SIC: 3993 Signs & advertising specialties

(P-23062)
BLAKE SIGN COMPANY INC
11661 Seaboard Cir, Stanton (90680-3427)
PHONE.....................714 891-5682
John A Blake, *President*
Devin Blake, *Shareholder*
Mike Blake, *Shareholder*
Dan Blake, *Vice Pres*
Joan Blake, *Vice Pres*
EMP: 17
SQ FT: 5,400
SALES (est): 2.4MM **Privately Held**
WEB: www.blakesigns.com
SIC: 3993 Signs, not made in custom sign
painting shops

(P-23063)
BLANCHARD SIGNS
6750 Central Ave Ste A, Riverside
(92504-1447)
PHONE.....................951 354-5050
Ron Blanchard, *Partner*
Carol Blanchard, *Partner*
EMP: 11

SALES: 600K **Privately Held**
SIC: **3993** Signs, not made in custom sign painting shops

(P-23064)
BLAZER EXHIBITS & GRAPHICS INC
4227 Technology Dr, Fremont (94538-6339)
PHONE..................408 263-7000
David Graham, *CEO*
Loren Ellis, *President*
Susan Graham, *Treasurer*
Vanessa Ellis, *Vice Pres*
Daniel Thomas, *Executive*
EMP: 15
SQ FT: 20,000
SALES (est): 2.1MM **Privately Held**
WEB: www.blazergraphics.com
SIC: **3993** Signs & advertising specialties

(P-23065)
BRAILLE SIGNS INC
16782 Von Karman Ave # 30, Irvine (92606-2419)
PHONE..................949 797-1570
Steve Corum, *President*
Ruth Corum, *Vice Pres*
Jason Chuang, *Supervisor*
▲ EMP: 13
SQ FT: 3,000
SALES (est): 1.9MM **Privately Held**
WEB: www.braillesignsinc.com
SIC: **3993** Signs, not made in custom sign painting shops

(P-23066)
BRIGHTSIGN LLC
983 University Ave Bldg A, Los Gatos (95032-7637)
PHONE..................408 852-9263
Anthony Wood,
Bryan Kennedy, *President*
Frank Pisano, *Vice Pres*
Julian Sinai, *Sr Software Eng*
Jordan Duval, *Technical Staff*
▲ EMP: 88
SQ FT: 19,362
SALES (est): 2.7MM **Privately Held**
SIC: **3993** Signs & advertising specialties

(P-23067)
BRITE-LITE NEON CORP
17242 Goya St, Granada Hills (91344-1206)
PHONE..................818 763-4798
Philip Mastopietro, *President*
Mark Mastopietro, *Corp Secy*
Rick Cincis, *Vice Pres*
EMP: 15
SALES: 1.3MM **Privately Held**
WEB: www.briteliteneon.com
SIC: **3993** 7629 Neon signs; electrical repair shops

(P-23068)
CAL-SIGN WHOLESALE INC
5260 Jerusalem Ct, Modesto (95356-9219)
PHONE..................209 523-7446
Greg Johnson, *President*
Roger Johnson, *Corp Secy*
Mark Johnson, *Vice Pres*
Rhonda Shafer, *Admin Asst*
EMP: 17
SQ FT: 4,050
SALES (est): 2.2MM **Privately Held**
WEB: www.calsignwholesale.com
SIC: **3993** Electric signs

(P-23069)
CALIFORNIA NEON PRODUCTS
Also Called: C N P Signs & Graphics
2555 Cmino Del Rio S Ste, San Diego (92108)
PHONE..................619 283-2191
Peter McCarter, *CEO*
Richard McCarter, *Corp Secy*
Robert McCarter, *Vice Pres*
Steve Cregan, *Project Mgr*
EMP: 70 EST: 1939
SALES (est): 17.9MM **Privately Held**
WEB: www.cnpsigns.com
SIC: **3993** 1799 Electric signs; sign installation & maintenance

(P-23070)
CALIFORNIA SIGNS INC
Also Called: CA Signs
10280 Glenoaks Blvd, Pacoima (91331-1604)
PHONE..................818 899-1888
Matthew Miller, *President*
Yvette Miller, *Admin Sec*
Justin Miooer, *Opers Staff*
EMP: 35
SQ FT: 21,000
SALES (est): 6.1MM **Privately Held**
WEB: www.casigns.com
SIC: **3993** Signs, not made in custom sign painting shops

(P-23071)
CANZONE AND COMPANY
Also Called: C & C Signs
1345 W Cowles St, Long Beach (90813-2734)
PHONE..................714 537-8175
Chris Canzone, *President*
Jessica Canzone, *Treasurer*
EMP: 20
SQ FT: 4,800
SALES (est): 2.6MM **Privately Held**
SIC: **3993** Signs, not made in custom sign painting shops

(P-23072)
CAPITOL NEON
5920 Rosebud Ln Ste 1, Sacramento (95841-2980)
PHONE..................916 349-1800
Michael L Durfee, *Partner*
Rocky Morino, *Partner*
Ron Underwood, *Partner*
Jennifer Sissney, *Manager*
EMP: 14
SQ FT: 16,000
SALES (est): 1.6MM **Privately Held**
WEB: www.capitolneon.com
SIC: **3993** Neon signs

(P-23073)
CARREON DEVELOPMENT INC
Also Called: South Bay Neon
4286 Powderhorn Dr, San Diego (92154-1719)
PHONE..................619 690-4973
Isaac S Carreon, *President*
EMP: 11 EST: 1982
SQ FT: 4,000
SALES (est): 770K **Privately Held**
SIC: **3993** Electric signs

(P-23074)
CELLOTAPE INC (HQ)
39611 Eureka Dr, Newark (94560-4806)
PHONE..................510 651-5551
Toll Free:..................888 -
Pete Offermann, *Ch of Bd*
Renee Rhodes, *Executive*
Eric Lomas, *Admin Sec*
Cellotape Smart, *Products*
Nick Testanero, *Director*
EMP: 102
SQ FT: 55,000
SALES (est): 24.6MM
SALES (corp-wide): 238MM **Privately Held**
SIC: **3993** 2675 2672 2759 Signs & advertising specialties; die-cut paper & board; coated & laminated paper; labels & seals; printing
PA: Resource Label Group, Llc
147 Seaboard Ln
Franklin TN 37067
615 661-5900

(P-23075)
CHANDLER SIGNS LLC
3220 Executive Rdg # 250, Vista (92081-8573)
PHONE..................760 734-1708
Chuck Riffe, *Vice Pres*
EMP: 100
SALES (corp-wide): 74MM **Privately Held**
WEB: www.chandlersigns.com
SIC: **3993** Electric signs
PA: Chandler Signs, Llc
14201 Sovereign Rd 101
Fort Worth TX 76155
214 902-2000

(P-23076)
CHIEF NEON SIGN CO INC
15027 S Maple Ave, Gardena (90248-1939)
PHONE..................310 327-1317
Alan D Paulson, *President*
Alan M Paulson, *President*
Armeta Paulson, *Corp Secy*
Lisa Paila, *Office Mgr*
EMP: 12
SQ FT: 12,400
SALES (est): 970K **Privately Held**
WEB: www.chiefneonsign.com
SIC: **3993** Signs, not made in custom sign painting shops

(P-23077)
CLEGG INDUSTRIES INC
Also Called: Clegg Promo
19032 S Vermont Ave, Gardena (90248-4412)
PHONE..................310 225-3800
Timothy P Clegg, *CEO*
Kevin Clegg, *President*
Michael Amar, *Senior VP*
Michael Bistocchi, *Senior VP*
Los Angeles, *Vice Pres*
▲ EMP: 175
SQ FT: 31,000
SALES (est): 25.1MM **Privately Held**
WEB: www.cleggonline.com
SIC: **3993** 3648 2542 Advertising novelties; lighting equipment; partitions & fixtures, except wood

(P-23078)
COAST SIGN INCORPORATED
Also Called: Coast Sign Display
1500 W Embassy St, Anaheim (92802-1016)
PHONE..................714 520-9144
Afshan Alemi, *CEO*
S Charlie Alemi, *President*
Jagadish Kariyappa, *Vice Pres*
Theresa Heitkamp, *Project Mgr*
Michelle Hoffman, *Project Mgr*
▲ EMP: 250
SQ FT: 130,000
SALES: 50MM **Privately Held**
WEB: www.coastsign.com
SIC: **3993** Signs, not made in custom sign painting shops

(P-23079)
CONTINENTAL SIGNS INC
7541 Santa Rita Cir Ste D, Stanton (90680-3498)
PHONE..................714 894-2011
Joseph Artinger, *President*
Edward Artinger, *Vice Pres*
Tim Shevlin, *Sales Associate*
EMP: 24
SQ FT: 7,800
SALES: 1.6MM **Privately Held**
WEB: www.continentalsigns.com
SIC: **3993** 1731 Signs, not made in custom sign painting shops; general electrical contractor

(P-23080)
CORNERSTONE DISPLAY GROUP INC
28606 Livingston Ave, Valencia (91355-4186)
PHONE..................661 705-1700
Tom Hester, *Principal*
Kip Kirkpatrick, *Partner*
Maritza Cardenas, *Purch Agent*
Albert Guerra, *Sales Mgr*
Brent Jacobson, *Art Dir*
▲ EMP: 45
SQ FT: 20,000
SALES (est): 8.5MM **Privately Held**
WEB: www.cornerstonedisplay.com
SIC: **3993** Advertising artwork; displays & cutouts, window & lobby

(P-23081)
CORPORATE SIGN SYSTEMS INC
2464 De La Cruz Blvd, Santa Clara (95050-2923)
PHONE..................408 292-1600
Danny Moran, *CEO*
Phil Wyatt, *Vice Pres*
Aaron Froke, *Technology*
Becky Augustine, *Accounting Mgr*
Stephanie Weitzenkamp, *Opers Staff*
EMP: 20 EST: 1961
SQ FT: 7,000
SALES (est): 3.6MM **Privately Held**
WEB: www.corporatesigns.com
SIC: **3993** 7389 Signs & advertising specialties; sign painting & lettering shop

(P-23082)
COWBOY DIRECT RESPONSE
Also Called: Synergy Direct Response
130 E Alton Ave, Santa Ana (92707-4415)
PHONE..................714 824-3780
Cynthia Rogers, *CEO*
John T Rogers, *CEO*
Brenda Manos, *Business Dir*
Erin Anderson, *Executive Asst*
Norm Shepherd, *Admin Sec*
EMP: 35
SQ FT: 10,000
SALES (est): 7MM **Privately Held**
WEB: www.synergydr.com
SIC: **3993** 8999 2759 Advertising artwork; advertising copy writing; promotional printing

(P-23083)
CREATIVE SIGN INC
17922 Lyons Cir, Huntington Beach (92647-7167)
PHONE..................714 842-4343
Thomas Morrison, *President*
Patricia Morrison, *Vice Pres*
EMP: 10
SQ FT: 10,000
SALES: 900K **Privately Held**
SIC: **3993** Advertising artwork

(P-23084)
CUMMINGS RESOURCES LLC
1495 Columbia Ave, Riverside (92507-2021)
PHONE..................951 248-1130
Jim Mole, *Plant Mgr*
EMP: 24
SQ FT: 50,000
SALES (corp-wide): 863.9MM **Privately Held**
SIC: **3993** Signs & advertising specialties
HQ: Cummings Resources Llc
15 Century Blvd Ste 200
Nashville TN 37214

(P-23085)
D N G CUMMINGS INC
Also Called: Action Sign Systems
3580 Haven Ave Ste 1, Redwood City (94063-4639)
PHONE..................650 593-8974
Dorothy Cummings, *President*
Greg Cummings, *Vice Pres*
Richard Cummings, *Vice Pres*
Gregory Patrick, *General Mgr*
EMP: 20
SQ FT: 9,600
SALES (est): 2.1MM **Privately Held**
SIC: **3993** Signs, not made in custom sign painting shops

(P-23086)
D3 LED LLC (PA)
Also Called: Dynamic Digital Displays
11370 Sunrise Park Dr, Rancho Cordova (95742-6542)
PHONE..................916 669-7408
George Pappas, *Mng Member*
Jason Barak, *Managing Prtnr*
Bryan Robertus, *Exec VP*
Eric Bland, *Vice Pres*
Debby John-Shadle, *Vice Pres*
◆ EMP: 20
SQ FT: 60,000
SALES (est): 12.4MM **Privately Held**
WEB: www.d3led.com
SIC: **3993** Signs & advertising specialties

(P-23087)
DEE SIGN CO
Also Called: Go Logo
16250 Stagg St, Van Nuys (91406-1715)
PHONE..................818 988-1000
Brad Hunefeld, *President*
EMP: 61

▲ = Import ▼=Export
◆ =Import/Export

SALES (corp-wide): 8.6MM **Privately Held**
WEB: www.dee-sign.com
SIC: 3993 Signs & advertising specialties
PA: Dee Sign Co.
6163 Allen Rd
West Chester OH 45069
513 779-3333

(P-23088)
DG DISPLAYS LLC
355 Parkside Dr, San Fernando
(91340-3036)
PHONE..........................877 358-5976
Robert Blumenfeld,
Zachary Blumenfeld,
EMP: 30
SALES (est): 802.2K **Privately Held**
SIC: 3993 Signs & advertising specialties

(P-23089)
DUNBAR ELECTRIC SIGN COMPANY
Also Called: City Crane
4020 Rosedale Hwy, Bakersfield
(93308-6131)
P.O. Box 10717 (93389-0717)
PHONE..........................661 323-2600
Clayton Dunbar, *CEO*
EMP: 22
SALES (est): 2.5MM **Privately Held**
WEB: www.cityneon.com
SIC: 3993 7629 5999 1799 Electric
signs; neon signs; electrical equipment
repair services; banners; sign installation
& maintenance

(P-23090)
DUNCAN DESIGN INC
860 Scenic Ave, Santa Rosa (95407-8348)
PHONE..........................707 636-2300
Greg Duncan, *President*
EMP: 10
SALES (est): 700K **Privately Held**
WEB: www.duncandesigninc.com
SIC: 3993 Signs & advertising specialties

(P-23091)
DYNAMITE SIGN GROUP INC
Also Called: TNT Electric Signs Co
3080 E 29th St, Long Beach (90806-2317)
PHONE..........................562 595-7725
William Henigsman, *President*
Michael Gray, *Vice Pres*
EMP: 30
SQ FT: 7,500
SALES (est): 5.1MM **Privately Held**
WEB: www.tntelectricsign.com
SIC: 3993 Neon signs

(P-23092)
EAGLE SIGNS INC
1028 E Acacia St, Ontario (91761-4553)
PHONE..........................909 923-3034
Robert Kneevers, *President*
Christopher Kneevers, *Partner*
Drew Solome, *Opers Mgr*
EMP: 11
SQ FT: 6,700
SALES (est): 775K **Privately Held**
WEB: www.eaglesigns.net
SIC: 3993 Signs & advertising specialties

(P-23093)
EDELMANN USA INC (DH)
Also Called: Bert-Co. of Ontario CA
2150 S Parco Ave, Ontario (91761-5768)
P.O. Box 4150 (91761-1068)
PHONE..........................323 669-5700
Rose Van Der Zanden, *Controller*
Analia Torres, *Sales Staff*
EMP: 20
SALES (est): 237.6K
SALES (corp-wide): 361.2MM **Privately Held**
SIC: 3993 Signs & advertising specialties
HQ: Edelmann Gmbh
Steinheimer Str. 45
Heidenheim An Der Brenz 89518
732 134-00

(P-23094)
EGADS LLC
42191 Sarah Way, Temecula (92590-3415)
PHONE..........................951 695-9050
EMP: 11

SALES (corp-wide): 42.6MM **Privately Held**
SIC: 3993
PA: E.Gads, Llc
3235 Polaris Ave
Las Vegas NV 89102
702 314-7777

(P-23095)
EGGLESTON SIGNS
Also Called: Sign Post, The
1558 Juliesse Ave Ste S, Sacramento
(95815-1827)
PHONE..........................916 920-1750
Jeam Basben, *Owner*
EMP: 14
SQ FT: 6,000
SALES (est): 1MM **Privately Held**
SIC: 3993 6512 Signs & advertising specialties; commercial & industrial building operation

(P-23096)
ELRO MANUFACTURING COMPANY (PA)
Also Called: Elro Sign Company
400 W Walnut St, Gardena (90248-3137)
PHONE..........................310 380-7444
Max R Rhodes, *CEO*
Frank J Rhodes, *Treasurer*
EMP: 37 EST: 1948
SQ FT: 18,000
SALES (est): 6.2MM **Privately Held**
WEB: www.elrosigns.com
SIC: 3993 Electric signs

(P-23097)
ENCORE IMAGE INC
303 W Main St, Ontario (91762-3843)
P.O. Box 9297 (91762-9297)
PHONE..........................909 986-4632
Mark Haist, *President*
EMP: 20 EST: 1945
SQ FT: 30,000
SALES (est): -3.1MM
SALES (corp-wide): 29.5MM **Privately Held**
WEB: www.ontarioneon.com
SIC: 3993 1799 Electric signs; sign installation & maintenance
PA: Encore Image Group, Inc.
1445 Sepulveda Blvd
Torrance CA 90501
310 534-7500

(P-23098)
ENCORE IMAGE GROUP INC (PA)
1445 Sepulveda Blvd, Torrance
(90501-5004)
PHONE..........................310 534-7500
Kozell Boren, *Ch of Bd*
Tom Johnson, *President*
Tommy K Boren, *VP Opers*
▲ EMP: 90 EST: 1959
SQ FT: 70,000
SALES (est): 29.5MM **Privately Held**
WEB: www.gotsign.com
SIC: 3993 Electric signs

(P-23099)
ENHANCE AMERICA INC
3463 Grapevine St, Jurupa Valley
(91752-3504)
PHONE..........................951 361-3000
Jackson Ling, *President*
Thomas Dobmeier, *Vice Pres*
Heidi Mann, *Regl Sales Mgr*
Heather Mullen, *Regl Sales Mgr*
◆ EMP: 20
SALES (est): 3.1MM **Privately Held**
SIC: 3993 Signs & advertising specialties

(P-23100)
EVANS MANUFACTURING INC (PA)
7422 Chapman Ave, Garden Grove
(92841-2106)
P.O. Box 5669 (92846-0669)
PHONE..........................714 379-6100
Alan Vaught, *CEO*
James Schneiderman, *Human Res Dir*
Malia Weaver, *Buyer*
Sarah Masloski, *Sales Staff*
Jennifer Jacobson, *Manager*

▲ EMP: 185
SQ FT: 17,000
SALES (est): 40.3MM **Privately Held**
WEB: www.evans-mfg.com
SIC: 3993 Signs & advertising specialties; injection molding of plastics

(P-23101)
EVERBRITE WEST LLC
Also Called: Fluoresco Lighting & Sign
2778 Pomona Blvd, Pomona (91768-3222)
PHONE..........................909 592-0870
Ladd Kleiman, *Branch Mgr*
EMP: 68
SALES (corp-wide): 244.9MM **Privately Held**
SIC: 3993 Signs & advertising specialties
HQ: Everbrite West Llc
5505 S Nogales Hwy
Tucson AZ 85706
520 623-7953

(P-23102)
EVERBRITE WEST LLC
2733 Via Orange Way, Spring Valley
(91978-1717)
PHONE..........................619 444-9000
Ken Christianson, *Branch Mgr*
James Subers, *Sales Staff*
EMP: 10
SALES (corp-wide): 244.9MM **Privately Held**
SIC: 3993 1731 7629 3648 Electric
signs; lighting contractor; electrical repair
shops; lighting equipment; commercial indusl & institutional electric lighting fixtures
HQ: Everbrite West Llc
5505 S Nogales Hwy
Tucson AZ 85706
520 623-7953

(P-23103)
EXHIBIT WORKS INC
Also Called: Ewi Worldwide
19531 Pauling, Foothill Ranch
(92610-2623)
PHONE..........................949 470-0850
Dominic Silvio, *Branch Mgr*
Ron Landwehr, *Plant Mgr*
Adam Lewis, *Accounts Mgr*
EMP: 15
SALES (corp-wide): 94.7MM **Privately Held**
SIC: 3993 7389 Displays & cutouts, window & lobby; advertising, promotional & trade show services
PA: Exhibit Works, Inc.
27777 Inkster Rd Ste 200
Farmington Hills MI 48334
734 525-9010

(P-23104)
EXPO-3 INTERNATIONAL INC
12350 Edison Way 60, Garden Grove
(92841-2810)
PHONE..........................714 379-8383
Daniel J Mills, *Ch of Bd*
Chris Smith, *President*
John Cooper, *Technology*
EMP: 20
SQ FT: 60,000
SALES (est): 2.7MM **Privately Held**
WEB: www.expo3.com
SIC: 3993 Displays & cutouts, window & lobby

(P-23105)
EXPRESS SIGN AND NEON
1720 W Slauson Ave, Los Angeles
(90047-1119)
PHONE..........................323 291-3333
Frank Bang, *Owner*
▲ EMP: 15
SALES (est): 1.4MM **Privately Held**
SIC: 3993 Signs, not made in custom sign painting shops

(P-23106)
FAIRMONT SIGN COMPANY
850 S Guild Ave, Lodi (95240-3170)
PHONE..........................209 365-6490
Garry Seafreed, *Branch Mgr*
Melissa Devaney, *Accounts Mgr*
EMP: 45

SALES (corp-wide): 7.2MM **Privately Held**
SIC: 3993 Signs, not made in custom sign painting shops
PA: Fairmont Sign Company
3750 E Outer Dr
Detroit MI 48234
313 368-4000

(P-23107)
FAN FAVE INC
Also Called: Fanfave
285 S Dupont Ave Ste 104, Ontario
(91761-1597)
PHONE..........................909 975-4999
Gary Arnett, *CEO*
Jeff Arnett, *President*
EMP: 20
SQ FT: 17,000
SALES: 800K **Privately Held**
SIC: 3993 Advertising artwork

(P-23108)
FAST AD INC
224 S Center St, Santa Ana (92703-4302)
PHONE..........................714 835-9353
Guy W Barnes, *President*
Kathleen Barnes, *Corp Secy*
EMP: 60
SQ FT: 12,000
SALES (est): 2.5MM **Privately Held**
WEB: www.fastad.com
SIC: 3993 Signs & advertising specialties

(P-23109)
FASTSIGNS
650 Harrison St, San Francisco
(94107-1311)
PHONE..........................415 537-6900
Jason Moline, *Owner*
Bruce Vaughn, *Vice Pres*
Richard Jongordon, *Admin Sec*
EMP: 11
SQ FT: 7,000
SALES: 1MM **Privately Held**
SIC: 3993 Signs & advertising specialties

(P-23110)
FASTSIGNS
2130 S El Camino Real, San Mateo
(94403-1800)
PHONE..........................650 345-0900
David Skromme, *Owner*
Linda Skromme, *Co-Owner*
EMP: 10
SQ FT: 4,000
SALES (est): 992.3K **Privately Held**
SIC: 3993 Signs & advertising specialties

(P-23111)
FEDERAL HEATH SIGN COMPANY LLC
4602 North Ave, Oceanside (92056-3509)
PHONE..........................760 941-0715
Tim O'Donald, *Branch Mgr*
Stew Edinger, *Vice Pres*
Dee Wallace, *Executive*
Lora Madec, *Project Mgr*
Toni Miller, *Project Mgr*
EMP: 120
SALES (corp-wide): 457.2MM **Privately Held**
WEB: www.zimsign.com
SIC: 3993 Neon signs
HQ: Federal Heath Sign Company, Llc
2300 St Hwy 121
Euless TX 76039

(P-23112)
FEDERAL HEATH SIGN COMPANY LLC
3609 Ocean Ranch Blvd # 204, Oceanside
(92056-8601)
PHONE..........................760 901-7447
Kevin Stotmeister, *Manager*
Deborah Trusty, *President*
Rick Foreman, *Vice Pres*
Amy Potter, *Project Mgr*
James Tebelman, *Project Mgr*
EMP: 12
SALES (corp-wide): 457.2MM **Privately Held**
SIC: 3993 Electric signs

HQ: Federal Heath Sign Company, Llc
2300 St Hwy 121
Euless TX 76039

(P-23113)
FEDERAL PRISON INDUSTRIES
Also Called: Unicor
3901 Klein Blvd, Lompoc (93436-2706)
PHONE..............................805 735-2771
Steve Southall, *Manager*
EMP: 25 **Publicly Held**
SIC: 3993 2759 3315 2521 Signs & advertising specialties; commercial printing; cable, steel: insulated or armored; wood office furniture; correctional institutions; ; miscellaneous fabricated wire products
HQ: Federal Prison Industries, Inc
320 1st St Nw
Washington DC 20534
202 305-3500

(P-23114)
FLYNN SIGNS AND GRAPHICS INC
Also Called: Flynn Signs and Letters
1345 Coronado Ave, Long Beach (90804-2806)
PHONE..............................562 498-6655
David Flynn, *President*
EMP: 13
SQ FT: 16,150
SALES (est): 1.8MM **Privately Held**
WEB: www.flynnsigns.com
SIC: 3993 Signs, not made in custom sign painting shops

(P-23115)
FOVELL ENTERPRISES INC
Also Called: Southwest Sign Company
1852 Pomona Rd, Corona (92880-1777)
PHONE..............................951 734-6275
Jack Fovell, *CEO*
▲ EMP: 26
SQ FT: 12,500
SALES (est): 4.3MM **Privately Held**
WEB: www.southwestsign.com
SIC: 3993 Electric signs

(P-23116)
FRESNO NEON SIGN CO INC
5901 E Clinton Ave, Fresno (93727-8641)
PHONE..............................559 292-2944
William Kratt, *President*
Kimberly Kratt Rutiaga, *Vice Pres*
Phyllis Kratt, *Admin Sec*
Rosie Robles, *Administration*
EMP: 12
SQ FT: 22,000
SALES (est): 1.6MM **Privately Held**
WEB: www.fresnoneon.com
SIC: 3993 1799 Electric signs; neon signs; scoreboards, electric; sign installation & maintenance

(P-23117)
FUSION SIGN & DESIGN INC (PA)
680 Columbia Ave, Riverside (92507-2144)
PHONE..............................877 477-8777
Loren Hanson, *CEO*
Alex Smith, *President*
Mark Breininger, *Vice Pres*
Rachel Otero, *Vice Pres*
Brian Johnson, *Division Mgr*
▲ EMP: 117
SALES (est): 28.9MM **Privately Held**
SIC: 3993 Electric signs

(P-23118)
G M P C LLC
Also Called: Econscious
2180 S Mcdowell Blvd, Petaluma (94954-6974)
PHONE..............................707 766-9504
EMP: 15
SALES (corp-wide): 16.3MM **Privately Held**
SIC: 3993 7336 Advertising novelties; commercial art & graphic design
PA: G M P C, Llc
11390 W Olym Blvd Ste 400
Los Angeles CA 90064
310 392-4070

(P-23119)
GARNETT SIGNS LLC
Also Called: Garnett Sign Studio
441 Victory Ave, South San Francisco (94080-6312)
PHONE..............................650 871-9518
Stephen Savoy, *President*
Maggie Cox, *Office Mgr*
Masaki Kitamori, *Graphic Designe*
Clifford Kane, *Manager*
EMP: 15
SQ FT: 13,250
SALES: 1.5MM **Privately Held**
WEB: www.garnettsign.com
SIC: 3993 3479 Signs, not made in custom sign painting shops; name plates: engraved, etched, etc.

(P-23120)
GARYS SIGNS AND SCREEN PRTG
Also Called: Gary's Signs & Screen Printing
1620 Ackerman Dr, Lodi (95240-6334)
PHONE..............................209 369-8592
Gary Markle, *President*
Robyn Markle, *Admin Sec*
EMP: 11 EST: 1972
SQ FT: 3,750
SALES (est): 880K **Privately Held**
SIC: 3993 2759 Electric signs; screen printing

(P-23121)
GEORGE P JOHNSON COMPANY
18500 Crenshaw Blvd, Torrance (90504-5055)
PHONE..............................310 965-4300
John Capano, *Branch Mgr*
Greg Buteyn, *Vice Pres*
Patrick Santy, *Vice Pres*
Mike Gottschalk, *Engineer*
Taylor Bukolt, *Sales Staff*
EMP: 100
SALES (corp-wide): 285.9MM **Privately Held**
SIC: 3993 Signs & advertising specialties
HQ: George P Johnson Company
3600 Giddings Rd
Auburn Hills MI 48326
248 475-2500

(P-23122)
GMPC LLC
Also Called: Big Accessories
2180 S Mcdowell Blvd, Petaluma (94954-6974)
PHONE..............................707 766-1702
Steve Wegner,
Bridget Mc Coy, *CFO*
Rich Knight, *Executive*
EMP: 17
SALES (corp-wide): 16.3MM **Privately Held**
SIC: 3993 7336 Advertising novelties; commercial art & graphic design
PA: G M P C, Llc
11390 W Olym Blvd Ste 400
Los Angeles CA 90064
310 392-4070

(P-23123)
GPO DISPLAY
7685 Hawthorn Ave, Livermore (94550-7121)
PHONE..............................510 659-9855
EMP: 11
SALES (est): 1.1MM **Privately Held**
SIC: 3993 Signs & advertising specialties

(P-23124)
GRADE A SIGN LLC
529 N La Cienega Blvd # 300, West Hollywood (90048-2001)
PHONE..............................310 652-9700
EMP: 20
SALES (est): 1.3MM **Privately Held**
SIC: 3993

(P-23125)
GREGORY M FINK
Also Called: G. Fink & Associates
23182 Alcalde Dr Ste H, Laguna Hills (92653-1450)
PHONE..............................949 305-4242

Greg Fink, *Owner*
Phillip Cohen, *Med Doctor*
▲ EMP: 12
SALES: 1.2MM **Privately Held**
SIC: 3993 Electric signs

(P-23126)
HARBOR SIGNS INC
850 N Union St, Stockton (95205-4152)
PHONE..............................209 463-8686
Malcolm Fortune, *President*
Laura Fortune, *Corp Secy*
Kurt Loewen, *Vice Pres*
EMP: 12
SQ FT: 10,000
SALES (est): 1.2MM **Privately Held**
WEB: www.harborsignsinc.com
SIC: 3993 Signs, not made in custom sign painting shops

(P-23127)
HERITAGE DESIGN
32382 Del Obispo St B1, San Juan Capistrano (92675-4029)
PHONE..............................949 248-1300
Claudia Martinez, *President*
EMP: 10
SALES (est): 830.1K **Privately Held**
SIC: 3993 Signs & advertising specialties

(P-23128)
HOKE OUTDOOR ADVERTISING INC
1955 N Main St, Orange (92865-4101)
P.O. Box 1666, Canyon Country (91386-1666)
PHONE..............................714 637-3610
Robert H Hoke, *President*
Lisa Manuz, *Manager*
EMP: 40
SQ FT: 5,200
SALES (est): 403.2K **Privately Held**
WEB: www.hokeoutdoor.com
SIC: 3993 7312 Signs, not made in custom sign painting shops; displays & cutouts, window & lobby; billboard advertising

(P-23129)
HUPP SIGNS & LIGHTING INC
70 Loren Ave, Chico (95928-7433)
P.O. Box 7730 (95927-7730)
PHONE..............................530 345-7078
Joe Hupp,
EMP: 30
SQ FT: 18,000
SALES (est): 4.3MM **Privately Held**
WEB: www.huppneon.com
SIC: 3993 Neon signs

(P-23130)
ILLUMINATED CREATIONS INC
Also Called: Ellis and Ellis Sign
1111 Joellis Way, Sacramento (95815-3914)
PHONE..............................916 924-1936
Bret E Ellis, *CEO*
Sydney Ellis, *President*
Sharon Ellis, *Corp Secy*
Brad Edward Ellis, *Vice Pres*
Robert Hana, *Project Mgr*
EMP: 40
SQ FT: 60,000
SALES (est): 7.6MM **Privately Held**
WEB: www.ellissigns.com
SIC: 3993 Signs, not made in custom sign painting shops

(P-23131)
IMAGINE THAT UNLIMITED
Also Called: Charlaine Graphics
13100 Kirkham Way Ste 211, Poway (92064-7128)
PHONE..............................858 566-8868
Carol Honeysett, *President*
Sue Rudolph, *CFO*
Susan Rudolph, *CFO*
EMP: 10
SQ FT: 3,500
SALES (est): 1.2MM **Privately Held**
SIC: 3993 Electric signs

(P-23132)
INFINITY WATCH CORPORATION
Also Called: Iwcus
21078 Commerce Point Dr, Walnut (91789-3051)
PHONE..............................626 289-9878
Patrick Tam, *President*
Brenda Tam, *Vice Pres*
▲ EMP: 25
SQ FT: 12,000
SALES (est): 2.8MM **Privately Held**
WEB: www.infinitywatch.com
SIC: 3993 Signs & advertising specialties

(P-23133)
INFLATABLE ADVERTISING CO INC
1600 W Olympic Blvd, Los Angeles (90015-3802)
PHONE..............................213 387-6839
Susan Talesnick, *President*
Michel Rimolos, *Treasurer*
William H Neusteter, *Admin Sec*
EMP: 12
SALES (est): 609.8K **Privately Held**
SIC: 3993 Advertising novelties

(P-23134)
INFLATABLE DESIGN GROUP INC
Also Called: Idg
1080 W Bradley Ave Ste B, El Cajon (92020-1500)
PHONE..............................619 596-6100
Shawn McEachern, *President*
Carlos Orjuela, *Vice Pres*
▲ EMP: 16
SQ FT: 32,000
SALES (est): 1.8MM **Privately Held**
SIC: 3993 Advertising novelties

(P-23135)
INLAND SIGNS INC
1715 S Bon View Ave, Ontario (91761-4410)
PHONE..............................909 581-0699
Klodian Gjoka, *President*
Filip Gjoka, *Principal*
EMP: 22 EST: 2002
SALES: 9MM **Privately Held**
WEB: www.inlandsigns.com
SIC: 3993 Electric signs

(P-23136)
INTEGRATED SIGN ASSOCIATES
1160 Pioneer Way Ste M, El Cajon (92020-1944)
PHONE..............................619 579-2229
Aaron Coippinger, *President*
Matt Sheredy, *Project Mgr*
Joe Hoffman, *Sales Mgr*
Tony Asano, *Art Dir*
Curt Bauer, *Accounts Exec*
EMP: 30
SQ FT: 15,000
SALES (est): 4.5MM **Privately Held**
WEB: www.isasign.com
SIC: 3993 Neon signs

(P-23137)
J S HACKL ARCHI SIGNA INC
1999 Alpine Way, Hayward (94545-1701)
PHONE..............................510 940-2608
John Hackley, *President*
EMP: 17
SQ FT: 20,000
SALES (est): 2MM **Privately Held**
WEB: www.hackley.net
SIC: 3993 Signs & advertising specialties

(P-23138)
JACK B MARTIN
Also Called: Jack Martin Signworks
109 E 5th St, Hanford (93230-5130)
PHONE..............................559 583-1175
Jack Martin, *Owner*
EMP: 10
SALES: 1.4MM **Privately Held**
SIC: 3993 Signs & advertising specialties

(P-23139)
JAR VENTURES INC
Also Called: Sign-A-Rama
1355 Hartnell Ave, Redding (96002-2227)
PHONE..............................530 224-9655

▲ = Import ▼=Export
◆ =Import/Export

John Robbins, *President*
EMP: 21
SALES (est): 2.7MM **Privately Held**
SIC: 3993 Signs & advertising specialties

(P-23140)
JEFF FRANK
Also Called: Northwest Signs
120 Encinal St, Santa Cruz (95060-2111)
PHONE.............................831 469-8208
Jeff Frank, *Owner*
Nancy Burk, *Manager*
EMP: 15
SQ FT: 5,000
SALES (est): 1.1MM **Privately Held**
WEB: www.cyclo-x.com
SIC: 3993 7349 Signs & advertising specialties; lighting maintenance service

(P-23141)
JOHN BISHOP DESIGN INC
Also Called: J B3d
731 N Main St, Orange (92868-1105)
PHONE.............................714 744-2300
John Bishop, *President*
Lisa Bishop, *Corp Secy*
EMP: 38
SQ FT: 1,000
SALES (est): 5.6MM **Privately Held**
WEB: www.jb3d.com
SIC: 3993 Signs & advertising specialties

(P-23142)
JOHNSON UNITED INC (PA)
Also Called: United Sign Systems
5201 Pentecost Dr, Modesto (95356-9271)
PHONE.............................209 543-1320
Darryl Johnson, *CEO*
Andy Soares, *Principal*
Mike Noordewier, *Admin Sec*
Robert Cain, *Project Mgr*
April Depew, *Project Mgr*
▼ EMP: 31
SQ FT: 23,000
SALES: 7.5MM **Privately Held**
SIC: 3993 Signs & advertising specialties

(P-23143)
JSJ ELECTRICAL DISPLAY CORP
340 Via Palo Linda, Fairfield (94534-1528)
PHONE.............................707 747-5595
Brian Schneider, *President*
Jeff Jensen, *Managing Prtnr*
EMP: 18
SALES: 2.5MM **Privately Held**
WEB: www.jsjdisplay.com
SIC: 3993 Neon signs

(P-23144)
JUSTIPHER INC
Also Called: Fastsigns
1248 W Winton Ave, Hayward (94545-1406)
PHONE.............................510 918-6800
Linda Fong, *Branch Mgr*
EMP: 15 **Privately Held**
SIC: 3993 Signs & advertising specialties
PA: Justipher, Inc.
1901 Franklin St
Oakland CA 94612

(P-23145)
K S DESIGNS INC
Also Called: Cal West Designs
9515 Sorensen Ave, Santa Fe Springs (90670-2650)
PHONE.............................562 929-3973
Robin Shelton, *President*
EMP: 32
SQ FT: 49,000
SALES: 1.8MM **Privately Held**
SIC: 3993 Displays & cutouts, window & lobby

(P-23146)
LEDPAC LLC
9850 Siempre Viva Rd # 5, San Diego (92154-7247)
PHONE.............................760 489-8067
Jacques Dubord,
Amy Dubord,
EMP: 52

SALES (est): 585.6K **Privately Held**
SIC: 3993 3646 Signs & advertising specialties; fluorescent lighting fixtures, commercial

(P-23147)
LEOTEK ELECTRONICS USA LLC
1955 Lundy Ave, San Jose (95131-1848)
PHONE.............................408 380-1788
James C Hwang, *CEO*
Chen-Ho Wu, *President*
Chris Berumen, *Regional Mgr*
Pushun Sheth, *Engineer*
Joanne Cheng, *Accountant*
◆ EMP: 23
SQ FT: 10,000
SALES (est): 4.8MM **Privately Held**
WEB: www.leotek.com
SIC: 3993 5046 Electric signs; signs, electrical
PA: Lite-On Technology Corporation
22f, 392, Ruey Kuang Rd.,
Taipei City TAP 11492

(P-23148)
LIVING WAY INDUSTRIES INC
Also Called: Creative Graphic Services
20734 Centre Pointe Pkwy, Santa Clarita (91350-2966)
PHONE.............................661 298-3200
Ronald Niner, *President*
Charlene E Niner, *Corp Secy*
Willie Niner, *Human Res Mgr*
EMP: 18 EST: 1970
SQ FT: 22,500
SALES (est): 3.2MM **Privately Held**
SIC: 3993 Signs & advertising specialties

(P-23149)
LOCAL NEON CO INC
12536 Chadron Ave, Hawthorne (90250-4850)
PHONE.............................310 978-2000
Scott Blakely, *President*
Cassius C Blakely, *Shareholder*
Jeanne Blakely, *Admin Sec*
EMP: 50 EST: 1953
SQ FT: 20,000
SALES (est): 4.3MM **Privately Held**
SIC: 3993 Signs & advertising specialties

(P-23150)
LOREN INDUSTRIES
Also Called: Loren Electric Sign & Lighting
12226 Coast Dr, Whittier (90601-1607)
PHONE.............................562 699-1122
Daniel Marc Lorenzon, *CEO*
Michelle Lornezon, *Vice Pres*
Christopher Reiff, *Sales Staff*
Dave Palmgren, *Manager*
EMP: 45
SQ FT: 8,000
SALES (est): 7.5MM **Privately Held**
WEB: www.luxorindustries.com
SIC: 3993 3648 1799 Electric signs; outdoor lighting equipment; street lighting fixtures; sign installation & maintenance

(P-23151)
MANERI SIGN CO INC
1928 W 135th St, Gardena (90249-2452)
PHONE.............................310 327-6261
Don Nicholas, *President*
Jamie Austin, *Sales Staff*
EMP: 35
SQ FT: 20,000
SALES: 6MM
SALES (corp-wide): 81.9MM **Privately Held**
WEB: www.manerisign.net
SIC: 3993 Signs & advertising specialties
PA: Traffic Solutions Corporation
4000 Westerly Pl Ste 100
Newport Beach CA 92660
949 553-8272

(P-23152)
MARK EASE PRODUCTS INC
132 S Aurora St, Stockton (95202-3121)
P.O. Box 607 (95201-0607)
PHONE.............................209 462-8632
Karl Gassner, *President*
Laura Gassner, *Corp Secy*
EMP: 20

SQ FT: 8,000
SALES (est): 1.9MM **Privately Held**
WEB: www.markease.com
SIC: 3993 3953 Signs, not made in custom sign painting shops; marking devices

(P-23153)
MARKETSHARE INC (PA)
2001 Tarob Ct, Milpitas (95035-6825)
PHONE.............................408 262-0677
Frederick Wilhelm, *CEO*
Alexis Bybel, *CFO*
John Lovell, *Vice Pres*
James Gochnauer, *Opers Staff*
Shawn Oliver, *Marketing Staff*
EMP: 99
SQ FT: 16,000
SALES (est): 14.9MM **Privately Held**
WEB: www.marketlineonline.com
SIC: 3993 7312 Electric signs; billboard advertising

(P-23154)
MARTINELLI ENVMTL GRAPHICS
Also Called: Martinelli Envmtl Graphics
1829 Egbert Ave, San Francisco (94124-2519)
PHONE.............................415 468-4000
Jack Martinelli, *President*
Patty Martinelli, *Treasurer*
EMP: 15
SQ FT: 8,000
SALES: 1.3MM **Privately Held**
WEB: www.martinelli-graphics.com
SIC: 3993 Electric signs

(P-23155)
MAXWELL ALARM SCREEN MFG INC
Also Called: Maxwell Sign and Decal Div
20327 Nordhoff St, Chatsworth (91311-6128)
PHONE.............................818 773-5533
Michael A Kagen, *CEO*
Patty Kagen, *Treasurer*
Rita Cortes, *Office Mgr*
A J Rowedder, *Sales Staff*
EMP: 28
SQ FT: 28,000
SALES (est): 4.1MM **Privately Held**
SIC: 3993 3442 Signs & advertising specialties; screens, window, metal

(P-23156)
MCHALE SIGN COMPANY INC
3707 Electro Way, Redding (96002-9346)
PHONE.............................530 223-2030
Patrick Corey, *President*
Bernice Corey, *Corp Secy*
Kevin Corey, *Technology*
EMP: 12
SQ FT: 14,000
SALES: 619.8K **Privately Held**
WEB: www.mchalesign.com
SIC: 3993 Electric signs

(P-23157)
MEDIA NATION ENTERPRISES LLC
15271 Barranca Pkwy, Irvine (92618-2201)
PHONE.............................714 371-9494
Navin Narang, *Branch Mgr*
EMP: 30
SALES (corp-wide): 3.7MM **Privately Held**
SIC: 3993 Signs & advertising specialties
PA: Media Nation Enterprises, Llc
15271 Barranca Pkwy
Irvine CA

(P-23158)
MEGA SIGN INC
Also Called: Mega Led Technology
6500 Flotilla St, Commerce (90040-1714)
PHONE.............................888 315-7446
David Park, *President*
Joseph Kim, *Asst Director*
▲ EMP: 22 EST: 2007
SQ FT: 30,000
SALES (est): 4.1MM **Privately Held**
SIC: 3993 Electric signs

(P-23159)
METAL ART OF CALIFORNIA INC
Also Called: Sign Mart Retail Store
640 N Cypress St, Orange (92867-6604)
PHONE.............................714 532-7100
Gene S Sobel, *Manager*
EMP: 90
SALES (corp-wide): 19.8MM **Privately Held**
WEB: www.sign-mart.com
SIC: 3993 7389 2759 Signs & advertising specialties; engraving service; screen printing
PA: Metal Art Of California, Inc.
640 N Cypress St
Orange CA 92867
714 532-7100

(P-23160)
METAL ART OF CALIFORNIA INC (PA)
Also Called: Sign Mart
640 N Cypress St, Orange (92867-6604)
PHONE.............................714 532-7100
Gene S Sobel, *President*
Calvin Larson, *Vice Pres*
Tori Agathakis, *General Mgr*
April Flett, *Manager*
▲ EMP: 91 EST: 1974
SQ FT: 22,000
SALES (est): 19.8MM **Privately Held**
WEB: www.sign-mart.com
SIC: 3993 Signs & advertising specialties

(P-23161)
MINA-TREE SIGNS INCORPORATED (PA)
1233 E Ronald St, Stockton (95205-3331)
P.O. Box 8406 (95208-0406)
PHONE.............................209 941-2921
Harold Leroy Minatre, *President*
EMP: 37
SALES (est): 4.6MM **Privately Held**
WEB: www.mina-treesigns.com
SIC: 3993 Electric signs; advertising novelties

(P-23162)
MONOGRAPHX INC
1052 251st St, Harbor City (90710-2418)
PHONE.............................310 325-6780
Paul Kuljis, *CEO*
EMP: 10 EST: 1978
SALES: 1.5MM **Privately Held**
WEB: www.monographx.com
SIC: 3993 Displays & cutouts, window & lobby

(P-23163)
MORRIS ROBERTS LLC
20251 Sw Acacia St # 120, Newport Beach (92660-0768)
PHONE.............................800 672-3974
John Morris,
EMP: 24
SALES (est): 1.2MM **Privately Held**
SIC: 3993 Signs & advertising specialties

(P-23164)
MOTIVATIONAL SYSTEMS INC
11437 Sunrise Gold Cir A, Rancho Cordova (95742-7206)
PHONE.............................916 635-0234
Debra Bennett, *Manager*
EMP: 30
SALES (corp-wide): 28.1MM **Privately Held**
WEB: www.motivationalsystems.com
SIC: 3993 7336 Signs, not made in custom sign painting shops; commercial art & graphic design
PA: Motivational Systems, Inc.
2200 Cleveland Ave
National City CA 91950
619 474-8246

(P-23165)
NATIONAL SIGN & MARKETING CORP
13580 5th St, Chino (91710-5113)
P.O. Box 2409 (91708-2409)
PHONE.............................909 591-4742
John J Kane, *President*
Rhonda Robinson, *Project Mgr*

PRODUCTS & SVCS

Carmen Gomez, *Human Res Dir*
EMP: 70
SQ FT: 46,000
SALES (est): 14MM **Privately Held**
SIC: 3993 Neon signs

(P-23166)
NATIONAL STOCK SIGN COMPANY
Also Called: Nassco
1040 El Dorado Ave, Santa Cruz (95062-2825)
PHONE..................................831 476-2020
Lorie Kurt Patrick, *President*
Henrietta Cooper, *President*
Robert Cooper, *Corp Secy*
EMP: 10
SQ FT: 10,000
SALES (est): 1.3MM **Privately Held**
SIC: 3993 Signs, not made in custom sign painting shops

(P-23167)
NEIMAN/HOELLER INC
Also Called: Neiman & Company
6842 Valjean Ave, Van Nuys (91406-4712)
PHONE..................................818 781-8600
Harry J Neiman, *CEO*
Robert R Hoeller III, *President*
Will Raksin, *Sr Project Mgr*
EMP: 56
SQ FT: 17,000
SALES (est): 7.8MM **Privately Held**
WEB: www.neimanandco.com
SIC: 3993 3646 Electric signs; ornamental lighting fixtures, commercial

(P-23168)
NEON IDEAS
1635 Buena Vista St, Ventura (93001-2214)
PHONE..................................805 648-7681
Larry Gieskeing, *Owner*
EMP: 10
SALES (est): 420K **Privately Held**
SIC: 3993 Neon signs

(P-23169)
OKI DOKI SIGNS
Also Called: Od Signs
1680 W Winton Ave Ste 7, Hayward (94545-1333)
PHONE..................................510 940-7446
Kin So, *Owner*
▲ **EMP:** 12 EST: 1994
SQ FT: 1,750
SALES (est): 1.5MM **Privately Held**
WEB: www.odsigns.com
SIC: 3993 Signs & advertising specialties

(P-23170)
OPTEC DISPLAYS INC
1700 S De Soto Pl Ste A, Ontario (91761-8060)
PHONE..................................626 369-7188
Shu Hwa Wu, *President*
David Pratt, *Exec Dir*
Wenny Tsay, *General Mgr*
Be Salazar, *Administration*
Yifeng Liang, *Software Dev*
◆ **EMP:** 64
SALES (est): 11.4MM **Privately Held**
WEB: www.optecdisplays.com
SIC: 3993 Signs & advertising specialties

(P-23171)
ORANGE CNTY NAME PLATE CO INC
13201 Arctic Cir, Santa Fe Springs (90670-5509)
P.O. Box 2764 (90670-0764)
PHONE..................................714 522-7693
Elias Rodriguez, *President*
Sam Rodriguez, *Corp Secy*
Ben L Rodriguez, *Vice Pres*
Ben Rodriguez, *Vice Pres*
Mike Rodriguez, *Purchasing*
EMP: 85
SQ FT: 31,000
SALES (est): 14.3MM **Privately Held**
WEB: www.counterman.org
SIC: 3993 Name plates: except engraved, etched, etc.: metal

(P-23172)
OUSSOREN EPPEL CORPORATION
Also Called: Gateway Marketing Concepts
12232 Thatcher Ct, Poway (92064-6876)
P.O. Box 231666, Encinitas (92023-1666)
PHONE..................................858 483-6770
Judith Oussoren Eppel, *President*
▲ **EMP:** 10
SALES (est): 1.6MM **Privately Held**
WEB: www.qualitybadges.com
SIC: 3993 2396 2754 Signs, not made in custom sign painting shops; automotive & apparel trimmings; promotional printing, gravure

(P-23173)
OUTDOOR SIGN SYSTEM INC (PA)
22603 La Palma Ave # 309, Yorba Linda (92887-6709)
PHONE..................................714 692-2052
Edward J Hoke, *Principal*
EMP: 15
SALES (est): 2.2MM **Privately Held**
SIC: 3993 Electric signs

(P-23174)
P&P ENTERPRISES
1246 W 7th St, Los Angeles (90017-2362)
PHONE..................................213 802-0890
Carlos A Paredes, *Owner*
EMP: 10
SQ FT: 3,500
SALES: 750K **Privately Held**
SIC: 3993 Signs & advertising specialties

(P-23175)
PACIFIC NEON
2939 Academy Way, Sacramento (95815-1802)
P.O. Box 15100 (95851-0100)
PHONE..................................916 927-0527
Oleta Lambert, *Ch of Bd*
John Drury, *President*
Bill Dickson, *Design Engr*
Karen Dalke, *Project Mgr*
Candace Groomes, *Project Mgr*
EMP: 40
SQ FT: 65,000
SALES (est): 8.1MM **Privately Held**
WEB: www.pacificneon.com
SIC: 3993 1799 7359 Electric signs; sign installation & maintenance; sign rental

(P-23176)
PD GROUP
Also Called: Sign-A-Rama
41945 Boardwalk Ste L, Palm Desert (92211-9099)
PHONE..................................760 674-3028
Jeff Gracy, *President*
Terrance Flannagan, *Vice Pres*
Terry Flanagan, *Info Tech Mgr*
Ed Landen, *Sales Staff*
EMP: 25
SQ FT: 11,500
SALES (est): 1.5MM **Privately Held**
SIC: 3993 7389 5999 Signs & advertising specialties; sign painting & lettering shop; banners

(P-23177)
PELICAN SIGN SERVICE INC
1565 Lafayette St, Santa Clara (95050-3978)
PHONE..................................408 246-3833
Frank Pleican, *CEO*
Frank E Pelican Jr, *President*
Merie Stineman, *Manager*
EMP: 11 EST: 1975
SQ FT: 6,200
SALES (est): 1.3MM **Privately Held**
WEB: www.pelicansigns.com
SIC: 3993 Signs & advertising specialties

(P-23178)
PRIMUS INC
Also Called: Western Highway Products
17901 Jamestown Ln, Huntington Beach (92647-7138)
P.O. Box 534 (92648-0534)
PHONE..................................714 527-2261
Steve Ellsworth, *President*
Timothy M Riordan, *Vice Pres*

Barbara Echevarria, *Cust Mgr*
▲ **EMP:** 80
SQ FT: 120,000
SALES (est): 11.3MM **Privately Held**
WEB: www.couchandphilippi.com
SIC: 3993 Signs, not made in custom sign painting shops

(P-23179)
PRO-LITE INC
Also Called: Advanced Products
3505 Cadillac Ave Ste D, Costa Mesa (92626-1464)
PHONE..................................714 668-9988
Kuo-Fong Kaoh, *President*
Daravon Chanthapadith, *Executive Asst*
▲ **EMP:** 17
SQ FT: 7,200
SALES (est): 3MM **Privately Held**
WEB: www.pro-lite.com
SIC: 3993 Signs & advertising specialties

(P-23180)
PV LABELS INC (PA)
1100 S Linwood Ave Ste B, Santa Ana (92705-4345)
PHONE..................................760 241-8900
Steve Stearns, *President*
Nikkos Arredondo, *Marketing Staff*
▼ **EMP:** 10
SALES (est): 1.9MM **Privately Held**
SIC: 3993 3231 Name plates: except engraved, etched, etc.: metal; reflector glass beads, for highway signs or reflectors

(P-23181)
QUIEL BROS ELC SIGN SVC CO INC
272 S I St, San Bernardino (92410-2408)
PHONE..................................909 885-4476
Larry R Quiel, *President*
Raymond Quiel, *Chairman*
Gary Quiel, *Vice Pres*
Jerry Quiel, *Vice Pres*
David Northchutt, *Technology*
▲ **EMP:** 40
SQ FT: 8,000
SALES (est): 6.3MM **Privately Held**
WEB: www.quielsigns.com
SIC: 3993 7353 7331 7629 Electric signs; cranes & aerial lift equipment, rental or leasing; general electrical contractor; electrical equipment repair, high voltage

(P-23182)
R&M DEESE INC
Also Called: Electro-Tech's
1875 Sampson Ave, Corona (92879-6009)
P.O. Box 2317 (92878-2317)
PHONE..................................951 734-7342
Raymond Deese, *President*
Mary Deese, *Treasurer*
Ray Deese, *Executive*
▲ **EMP:** 22
SQ FT: 20,000
SALES (est): 2.8MM **Privately Held**
SIC: 3993 3679 Signs & advertising specialties; liquid crystal displays (LCD)

(P-23183)
RAGO NEON INC
235 Laurel Ave, Hayward (94541-3822)
PHONE..................................510 537-1903
Antone F Rago II, *President*
EMP: 16
SQ FT: 9,600
SALES (est): 1.8MM **Privately Held**
WEB: www.ragoneon.com
SIC: 3993 Neon signs

(P-23184)
RAPID DISPLAYS INC
33195 Lewis St, Union City (94587-2201)
PHONE..................................510 471-6955
Bruce Watson, *President*
Kris Ziakas, *Info Tech Dir*
Mitra Azaripour, *Accountant*
EMP: 300
SALES (corp-wide): 296.3MM **Privately Held**
WEB: www.rapiddisplays.com
SIC: 3993 Displays & cutouts, window & lobby

HQ: Rapid Displays, Inc.
4300 W 47th St
Chicago IL 60632
773 927-5000

(P-23185)
REICHERT ENTERPRISES INC
Also Called: Reichert's Signs
2720 S Harbor Blvd, Santa Ana (92704-5822)
PHONE..................................714 513-9199
Dan Demell, *President*
EMP: 40
SQ FT: 5,800
SALES (est): 3.8MM **Privately Held**
WEB: www.rsisigns.com
SIC: 3993 5999 Signs & advertising specialties; banners, flags, decals & posters

(P-23186)
RICHARDS NEON SHOP INC
Also Called: RNS Channel Letters
4375 Prado Rd Ste 102, Corona (92880-7444)
PHONE..................................951 279-6767
Richard Pando, *President*
EMP: 24
SALES (est): 3.8MM **Privately Held**
WEB: www.richardsneon.com
SIC: 3993 Electric signs

(P-23187)
ROSS NAME PLATE COMPANY
2 Red Plum Cir, Monterey Park (91755-7486)
PHONE..................................323 725-6812
Michael Ross, *President*
EMP: 37
SQ FT: 25,000
SALES (est): 5.1MM **Privately Held**
WEB: www.rossnameplate.com
SIC: 3993 2754 Name plates: except engraved, etched, etc.: metal; labels: gravure printing

(P-23188)
S2K GRAPHICS INC
Also Called: S 2 K
9255 Deering Ave, Chatsworth (91311-5804)
PHONE..................................818 885-3900
Dan C Pulos, *CEO*
Jack Wilson, *Ch of Bd*
Dana Rosellini, *Corp Secy*
Michelle Lindberg, *Executive*
Michelle O'Briant, *Executive*
EMP: 35
SALES (est): 8.6MM
SALES (corp-wide): 3B **Privately Held**
WEB: www.s2kgraphics.com
SIC: 3993 7532 2759 Signs & advertising specialties; truck painting & lettering; screen printing
HQ: Franke Usa Holding, Inc.
1105 N Market St Ste 1300
Wilmington DE 19801

(P-23189)
SAFEWAY SIGN COMPANY
9875 Yucca Rd, Adelanto (92301-2282)
PHONE..................................760 246-7070
Michael F Moore, *President*
Andrea M Gutierrez, *Vice Pres*
David C Moore, *Vice Pres*
Mina Alvarez, *Sales Staff*
Kolby Moore, *Facilities Mgr*
EMP: 49 EST: 1948
SQ FT: 60,000
SALES (est): 12.1MM **Privately Held**
WEB: www.safewaysign.com
SIC: 3993 Signs, not made in custom sign painting shops

(P-23190)
SALES OFFICE ACCESSORIES INC
11562 Knott St Ste 8, Garden Grove (92841-1823)
PHONE..................................714 896-9600
Kenneth J Morelli, *President*
EMP: 10
SALES (est): 1MM **Privately Held**
WEB: www.soainc.com
SIC: 3993 Signs & advertising specialties

▲ = Import ▼=Export
◆ =Import/Export

(P-23191)
SAN DIEGO ELECTRIC SIGN INC
1890 Cordell Ct Ste 105, El Cajon (92020-0913)
P.O. Box 103, Bonita (91908-0103)
PHONE.................................619 258-1775
Greg Ballard, *President*
Jayne Ballard, *Vice Pres*
Janie Ballard, *General Mgr*
Lelsie Crosby, *Admin Sec*
EMP: 17
SALES (est): 2.2MM **Privately Held**
SIC: 3993 Electric signs

(P-23192)
SAN PEDRO SIGN COMPANY
701 Lakme Ave, Wilmington (90744-5943)
PHONE.................................310 549-4661
Gus Navarro, *President*
Margarita Bautista, *Controller*
Rosario Miranda,
EMP: 20 **EST:** 1976
SQ FT: 7,000
SALES (est): 3.2MM **Privately Held**
WEB: www.spesco.com
SIC: 3993 Electric signs

(P-23193)
SC WORKS
Also Called: Signworks
1805 Contra Costa St A, Seaside (93955-3010)
PHONE.................................831 332-5311
Steven Caldeira, *President*
EMP: 13 **EST:** 2016
SALES (est): 643.4K **Privately Held**
SIC: 3993 Electric signs

(P-23194)
SCHEA HOLDINGS INC
Also Called: Signgroup/Karman
9812 Independence Ave, Chatsworth (91311-4319)
PHONE.................................818 888-3818
Michael Schackne, *President*
Kathy Schackne, *Vice Pres*
EMP: 22
SQ FT: 10,000
SALES: 2MM **Privately Held**
WEB: www.asigngroup.net
SIC: 3993 Electric signs

(P-23195)
SHYE WEST INC (PA)
Also Called: Imagine This
43 Corporate Park Ste 102, Irvine (92606-5137)
PHONE.................................949 486-4598
Patrick Papaccio, *President*
Craig Perkins, *President*
Shawn Keep, *Vice Pres*
Chris Tipton, *Vice Pres*
Gretchen Krebs, *Executive*
▲ **EMP:** 27
SQ FT: 6,000
SALES (est): 8.9MM **Privately Held**
WEB: www.promogiant.com
SIC: 3993 5099 Advertising novelties; novelties, durable

(P-23196)
SIGN ART CO
423 S California St, San Gabriel (91776-2527)
PHONE.................................626 287-2512
Eddy Hsieh, *President*
EMP: 10
SQ FT: 2,800
SALES (est): 540K **Privately Held**
SIC: 3993 Electric signs

(P-23197)
SIGN DESIGNS INC
Also Called: Macdonald Screen Print
204 Campus Way, Modesto (95350-5845)
P.O. Box 4590 (95352-4590)
PHONE.................................209 524-4484
David Johnston, *President*
Pete Michelini, *CFO*
Doug Smith, *Vice Pres*
EMP: 44
SQ FT: 35,000
SALES (est): 6.7MM **Privately Held**
WEB: www.signdesigns.com
SIC: 3993 Electric signs

(P-23198)
SIGN EXCELLENCE LLC
8515 Telfair Ave, Sun Valley (91352-3928)
PHONE.................................818 308-1044
Jose D Gutierrez, *Mng Member*
EMP: 12
SALES (est): 1.4MM **Privately Held**
SIC: 3993 Signs & advertising specialties

(P-23199)
SIGN INDUSTRIES INC
2101 Carrillo Privado, Ontario (91761-7600)
PHONE.................................909 930-0303
Maria Saavedra, *President*
Enrique Saavedra, *Admin Sec*
Priscilla Saavedra, *Graphic Designe*
Joe Rhodes, *Human Res Dir*
Mark Chavez, *Accounts Exec*
▲ **EMP:** 30
SQ FT: 4,500
SALES (est): 7.5MM **Privately Held**
WEB: www.signindustries.com
SIC: 3993 Neon signs

(P-23200)
SIGN SOLUTIONS INC
Also Called: Artsigns
532 Mercury Dr, Sunnyvale (94085-4018)
PHONE.................................408 245-7133
Fax: 408 245-1389
EMP: 14
SQ FT: 7,600
SALES (est): 1.8MM **Privately Held**
WEB: www.artsigns.net
SIC: 3993

(P-23201)
SIGN SOURCE INC
Also Called: Signsource
204 W Carleton Ave Ste A, Orange (92867-3632)
PHONE.................................714 979-9979
John Mearns, *President*
Doug Odwyer, *General Mgr*
Cynthia Best, *Admin Sec*
Israel Pizarro, *Prdtn Mgr*
EMP: 15
SQ FT: 23,000
SALES (est): 2.2MM **Privately Held**
WEB: www.signsource.net
SIC: 3993 Signs & advertising specialties

(P-23202)
SIGN SPECIALISTS CORPORATION
111 W Dyer Rd Ste F, Santa Ana (92707-3425)
PHONE.................................714 641-0064
Garrick Batt, *CEO*
Tariq Shaikh, *Vice Pres*
Jeff Sherman, *General Mgr*
Jaime Colchado, *Project Mgr*
Tony Wilbanks, *Graphic Designe*
EMP: 22 **EST:** 2001
SALES (est): 4MM **Privately Held**
WEB: www.sign-specialists.com
SIC: 3993 Signs, not made in custom sign painting shops

(P-23203)
SIGN TECHNOLOGY INC
Also Called: Signtech
1700 Entp Blvd Ste F, West Sacramento (95691)
PHONE.................................916 372-1200
Michael Wilmer, *CEO*
Dallas Dorn, *Sales Staff*
EMP: 30
SQ FT: 11,660
SALES (est): 4.5MM **Privately Held**
WEB: www.signtechnology.com
SIC: 3993 Signs, not made in custom sign painting shops

(P-23204)
SIGNAGE SOLUTIONS CORPORATION
2231 S Dupont Dr, Anaheim (92806-6105)
PHONE.................................714 491-0299
Chris Deruyter, *CEO*
Jim Gledhill, *Vice Pres*
Josh De Ruyter, *Executive*
Austin Betty, *Project Mgr*
Rene Camarena, *Project Mgr*

EMP: 30
SQ FT: 14,000
SALES (est): 5MM **Privately Held**
WEB: www.signage-solutions.com
SIC: 3993 7389 Signs & advertising specialties; sign painting & lettering shop

(P-23205)
SIGNQUEST
13040 Cerise Ave, Hawthorne (90250-5523)
PHONE.................................310 355-0528
Ramy Nicholas, *Principal*
EMP: 20
SALES (est): 1.4MM **Privately Held**
SIC: 3993 Signs & advertising specialties

(P-23206)
SIGNS AND SERVICES COMPANY
10980 Boatman Ave, Stanton (90680-2602)
PHONE.................................714 761-8200
Jacob Deryuyter, *CEO*
Matt De Ruyter, *President*
Henry Hu, *Controller*
Jerry Kranz, *Opers Mgr*
Larry Pokras, *Accounts Exec*
EMP: 33
SQ FT: 16,000
SALES: 4.5MM **Privately Held**
SIC: 3993 Signs, not made in custom sign painting shops

(P-23207)
SIGNS OF SUCCESS INC
2350 Skyway Dr Ste 10, Santa Maria (93455-1532)
PHONE.................................805 925-7545
Stephen Sheppard, *President*
Glenda Sheppard, *Treasurer*
EMP: 16
SQ FT: 3,600
SALES: 500K **Privately Held**
WEB: www.signsofsuccess.net
SIC: 3993 7389 5999 Signs & advertising specialties; sign painting & lettering shop; decals

(P-23208)
SIGNTECH ELECTRICAL ADVG INC
4444 Federal Blvd, San Diego (92102-2505)
PHONE.................................619 527-6100
Harold E Schauer Jr, *CEO*
David E Schauer, *President*
Kimra Schauer, *CFO*
Art Navarro, *Vice Pres*
Patty Soria, *Vice Pres*
EMP: 120
SQ FT: 25,000
SALES (est): 26.7MM **Privately Held**
WEB: www.signtechusa.com
SIC: 3993 1799 Electric signs; sign installation & maintenance

(P-23209)
SIGNWORLD AMERICA INC (PA)
12023 Arrow Rte, Rancho Cucamonga (91739-9219)
PHONE.................................844 900-7446
Yangchi Chung, *CEO*
◆ **EMP:** 17
SALES (est): 2.5MM **Privately Held**
SIC: 3993 5199 5999 Signs & advertising specialties; advertising specialties; banners

(P-23210)
SIMPLY SMASHING INC
Also Called: Fruehe Design
4790 W Jacquelyn Ave, Fresno (93722-6406)
PHONE.................................559 658-2367
Tim Fruehe, *President*
EMP: 20
SALES (est): 3.1MM **Privately Held**
SIC: 3993 7336 Advertising novelties; graphic arts & related design

(P-23211)
SKYLINE DIGITAL IMAGES INC
10420 Pioneer Blvd, Santa Fe Springs (90670-3734)
PHONE.................................562 944-1677

Jerilyn Benson, *Manager*
▲ **EMP:** 25
SALES (est): 2.1MM **Privately Held**
SIC: 3993 Displays & cutouts, window & lobby

(P-23212)
SKYWAY SIGNS LLC
Also Called: Wesco Sign
2400 W Carson St Ste 115, Torrance (90501-3174)
PHONE.................................505 401-5270
Mohammed Quraishi, *Mng Member*
EMP: 14
SALES (est): 1.8MM **Privately Held**
SIC: 3993 Signs & advertising specialties

(P-23213)
SOTELEO SALVADAR
Also Called: S S Sign Electric
620 Imperial St, Los Angeles (90021-1310)
PHONE.................................213 621-2040
Salvador Sotelo, *Owner*
EMP: 20
SQ FT: 10,000
SALES (est): 883.1K **Privately Held**
SIC: 3993 1731 1542 1521 Signs, not made in custom sign painting shops; general electrical contractor; commercial & office building, new construction; new construction, single-family houses; multi-family dwelling construction

(P-23214)
SPECIALIZED GRAPHICS INC
3951 Industrial Way Ste A, Concord (94520-8552)
PHONE.................................925 680-0265
Michael Gratton, *CEO*
EMP: 20
SQ FT: 3,500
SALES (est): 2MM **Privately Held**
WEB: www.sgsignage.com
SIC: 3993 Electric signs

(P-23215)
STANDARDVISION LLC
3370 N San Fernando Rd # 206, Los Angeles (90065-1437)
PHONE.................................323 222-3630
Adrian Velicescu, *CEO*
Kevin Bartanian, *Exec VP*
Grif Palmer, *Vice Pres*
Jeremiah Montoya, *Software Engr*
Maya Bartur, *Project Mgr*
▲ **EMP:** 34
SQ FT: 25,000
SALES: 31.2MM **Privately Held**
SIC: 3993 7336 Signs & advertising specialties; commercial art & graphic design

(P-23216)
STANFORD SIGN & AWNING INC (PA)
2556 Faivre St, Chula Vista (91911-4604)
PHONE.................................619 423-6200
David Lesage, *President*
Richie Del Gatto, *Opers Staff*
Steve Aretz, *Sales Staff*
Todd Gordon, *Sales Staff*
Carlos Davila, *Manager*
EMP: 85
SQ FT: 35,000
SALES (est): 11.9MM **Privately Held**
WEB: www.stansign.com
SIC: 3993 2394 Electric signs; canvas awnings & canopies

(P-23217)
STATEWIDE SAFETY & SIGNS INC
40 S G St, Arcata (95521-6654)
PHONE.................................707 825-6927
Scott St John, *Manager*
EMP: 31 **Privately Held**
SIC: 3993 Signs & advertising specialties
HQ: Statewide Safety & Signs, Inc.
522 Lindon Ln
Nipomo CA 93444
805 929-5070

(P-23218)
STOP-LOOK SIGN CO INTL INC
Also Called: Stop Look Plastics Inc
401 Commercial Way, La Habra
(90631-6168)
PHONE.....................................562 690-7576
Larry Dobkin, *President*
Mike Dougherty, *Treasurer*
Christine Dougherty, *Vice Pres*
Janet Dobkin, *Admin Sec*
▲ EMP: 15 EST: 1960
SQ FT: 8,000
SALES (est): 3.6MM **Privately Held**
WEB: www.stoplooksign.com
SIC: 3993 Signs & advertising specialties

(P-23219)
STREET GRAPHICS INC
Also Called: Delta Signs
1834 W Euclid Ave, Stockton (95204-2911)
PHONE.....................................209 948-1713
EMP: 20
SQ FT: 12,000
SALES (est): 2.5MM **Privately Held**
WEB: www.deltasigns.net
SIC: 3993

(P-23220)
SUNSET SIGNS AND PRINTING
2981 E White Star Ave, Anaheim
(92806-2630)
PHONE.....................................714 255-9104
Tracy Eschenbrenner, *CEO*
EMP: 16
SALES (est): 3.2MM **Privately Held**
SIC: 3993 Signs & advertising specialties

(P-23221)
SUPERIOR ELECTRICAL ADVG (PA)
1700 W Anaheim St, Long Beach
(90813-1102)
PHONE.....................................562 495-3808
Jim Sterk, *CEO*
Patti Skoglundadams, *President*
Stan Janocha, *COO*
Doug Tokeshi, *CFO*
Steve Feist, *Division Mgr*
▲ EMP: 85 EST: 1962
SQ FT: 100,000
SALES: 15.7MM **Privately Held**
SIC: 3993 7629 Electric signs; electrical
equipment repair services

(P-23222)
SUPERIOR ELECTRICAL ADVG
125 Houston Ln, Lodi (95240-2422)
PHONE.....................................209 334-3337
David Coberly, *Finance Mgr*
EMP: 10
SALES (est): 772.3K
SALES (corp-wide): 15.7MM **Privately Held**
SIC: 3993 7629 Electric signs; electrical
equipment repair services
PA: Superior Electrical Advertising
1700 W Anaheim St
Long Beach CA 90813
562 495-3808

(P-23223)
SUPERSONIC ADS INC
17 Bluxome St, San Francisco
(94107-1605)
PHONE.....................................650 825-6010
Gil Shoham, *CEO*
Adam David, *Vice Pres*
Daphne Saragosti, *Vice Pres*
Giles Davis, *Business Dir*
Guy Ferber, *Business Dir*
EMP: 20
SALES (est): 2.7MM **Privately Held**
SIC: 3993 Advertising artwork

(P-23224)
T D I SIGNS
1419 Seabright Ave, Long Beach
(90813-1100)
PHONE.....................................562 436-5188
Arthur Rivas, *President*
EMP: 25
SQ FT: 10,000
SALES (est): 3.8MM **Privately Held**
WEB: www.tdisigns.com
SIC: 3993 Electric signs

(P-23225)
TAE GWANG INC
4922 S Figueroa St, Los Angeles
(90037-3344)
PHONE.....................................323 233-2882
Sammy Chu, *President*
EMP: 15
SQ FT: 3,401
SALES (est): 1.5MM **Privately Held**
WEB: www.taegwang.com
SIC: 3993 Signs & advertising specialties

(P-23226)
TFN ARCHITECTURAL SIGNAGE INC (PA)
Also Called: Third Floor North Company
3411 W Lake Center Dr, Santa Ana
(92704-6925)
PHONE.....................................714 556-0990
Brian L Burnett, *President*
Catherine Burnett, *Shareholder*
Jeff Burnett, *Shareholder*
Jim Clark, *CFO*
Teresa Burnett, *Treasurer*
EMP: 45
SQ FT: 8,800
SALES (est): 6.7MM **Privately Held**
SIC: 3993 Signs, not made in custom sign
painting shops

(P-23227)
THOMAS-SWAN SIGN COMPANY INC
2717 Goodrick Ave, Richmond
(94801-1109)
PHONE.....................................415 621-1511
Allen E Thomas, *CEO*
Michael Roberts, *President*
John Soares, *CFO*
Donna Thomas, *Treasurer*
Stacy Roberts, *Vice Pres*
EMP: 35 EST: 1877
SQ FT: 40,000
SALES (est): 6.4MM **Privately Held**
WEB: www.thomasswan.com
SIC: 3993 Electric signs; neon signs

(P-23228)
TIMLIN INDUSTRIES INC
6777 Nancy Ridge Dr, San Diego
(92121-2231)
PHONE.....................................541 947-6771
Tim Kloos, *President*
Kaye Warner, *Admin Sec*
EMP: 40
SQ FT: 4,800
SALES: 3.8MM **Privately Held**
SIC: 3993 5199 5947 Advertising novel-
ties; advertising specialties; novelties

(P-23229)
TO INDUSTRIES INC
Also Called: Quantam Signs & Graphics
23180 Del Lago Dr, Lake Forest (92630)
PHONE.....................................949 454-6078
Keith To, *President*
EMP: 12
SALES (est): 1.5MM **Privately Held**
WEB: www.quantum-signs.com
SIC: 3993 Signs, not made in custom sign
painting shops

(P-23230)
TORTOLANI INC
1313 Mirasol St, Los Angeles
(90023-3108)
PHONE.....................................323 268-1488
Robin Tortolani, *President*
Robin Tortolani Italia, *President*
EMP: 14 EST: 1997
SALES: 800K **Privately Held**
WEB: www.tortolani.com
SIC: 3993 5944 Advertising novelties; jew-
elry stores

(P-23231)
TRADENET ENTERPRISE INC
Also Called: Vantage Led
1580 Magnolia Ave, Corona (92879-2073)
PHONE.....................................888 595-3956
Chris MA, *CEO*
Yuusuke Arimura, *COO*
Ricky Chai, *Vice Pres*
Steven Lopes, *Software Dev*
Leo Mares, *Technical Staff*

▲ EMP: 60
SALES (est): 10.5MM **Privately Held**
SIC: 3993 Electric signs

(P-23232)
TRAFFIC CONTROL & SAFETY CORP
13755 Blaisdell Pl, Poway (92064-6837)
PHONE.....................................858 679-7292
David Nicholas, *Branch Mgr*
EMP: 11 **Privately Held**
WEB: www.statewidesafety.com
SIC: 3993 5088 7359 5082 Signs, not
made in custom sign painting shops;
transportation equipment & supplies; work
zone traffic equipment (flags, cones, bar-
rels, etc.); contractors' materials
PA: Traffic Control And Safety Corporation
1100 Main St
Irvine CA 92614

(P-23233)
ULTRANEON SIGN CORP
Also Called: Ultraneon Sign Company
5458 Complex St Ste 401, San Diego
(92123-1118)
PHONE.....................................858 569-6716
Gus Hadaya, *President*
EMP: 40
SQ FT: 22,000
SALES: 5MM **Privately Held**
SIC: 3993 Neon signs; scoreboards, elec-
tric

(P-23234)
UNIVERSAL CUSTOM DISPLAY
Also Called: Universal Custom Design
9104 Elkmont Dr Ste 100, Elk Grove
(95624-9724)
PHONE.....................................916 714-2505
Daniel Hayes, *President*
Don Almeda, *Vice Pres*
Charles Dickenson, *Vice Pres*
Jeanne Hayes, *Admin Mgr*
Brett Jones, *Info Tech Dir*
▲ EMP: 175
SQ FT: 120,000
SALES (est): 42.7MM **Privately Held**
WEB: www.universalcustomdisplay.com
SIC: 3993 2541 Signs & advertising spe-
cialties; display fixtures, wood

(P-23235)
UNIVERSAL MERCANTILE EXCHANGE
Also Called: Umx
21128 Commerce Point Dr, Walnut
(91789-3053)
PHONE.....................................909 839-0556
Hs Che Wang, *President*
William Huang, *Vice Pres*
Fred Saelor, *HR Admin*
▲ EMP: 15
SQ FT: 8,026
SALES (est): 2MM **Privately Held**
WEB: www.umei.com
SIC: 3993 5091 5099 Signs & advertising
specialties; golf & skiing equipment &
supplies; fire extinguishers

(P-23236)
VISIBLE GRAPHICS INC
9736 Eton Ave, Chatsworth (91311-4305)
PHONE.....................................818 787-0477
Janine Kendall, *CEO*
Ken Kendall, *CFO*
EMP: 16 EST: 2002
SALES: 6.6MM **Privately Held**
WEB: www.visiblegraphics.com
SIC: 3993 Signs & advertising specialties

(P-23237)
VISIONEERED IMAGE SYSTEMS INC
444 W Ocean Blvd Ste 1400, Long Beach
(90802-4522)
PHONE.....................................818 613-7600
Anthony Materna, *President*
Karl Boldt, *Senior VP*
EMP: 16
SALES (est): 1.2MM **Privately Held**
SIC: 3993 Electric signs

(P-23238)
VOGUE SIGN INC
715 Commercial Ave, Oxnard
(93030-7233)
PHONE.....................................805 487-7222
Jack Woodruff, *President*
Christian Muldoon, *Project Mgr*
Dave Jones, *Prdtn Mgr*
Kirk Hamilton, *Sales Mgr*
Ron Wilkinson, *Manager*
EMP: 12
SQ FT: 11,000
SALES (est): 1.9MM **Privately Held**
WEB: www.voguesigns.com
SIC: 3993 Electric signs

(P-23239)
VOMELA SPECIALTY COMPANY
Corporate Identity Systems
1342 San Mateo Ave, South San Francisco
(94080-6501)
PHONE.....................................650 877-8000
Robert Pietila, *Branch Mgr*
EMP: 27
SALES (corp-wide): 128.5MM **Privately Held**
SIC: 3993 2759 Signs & advertising spe-
cialties; screen printing
PA: Vomela Specialty Company
845 Minnehaha Ave E
Saint Paul MN 55106
651 228-2200

(P-23240)
VPRO INC
Also Called: Sticker City
4638 Van Nuys Blvd, Sherman Oaks
(91403-2915)
PHONE.....................................818 905-5678
Andisne Soleimanpour, *President*
Idin Soleimanpour, *Admin Sec*
Dean Soleimani, *Sales Executive*
Alexa Solano, *Sales Staff*
EMP: 11
SALES (est): 193.4K **Privately Held**
SIC: 3993 Signs & advertising specialties

(P-23241)
WESTERN ELECTRICAL ADVG CO
Also Called: Southwest Sign Systems
853 Dogwood Ave, El Centro (92243)
P.O. Box 587 (92244-0587)
PHONE.....................................760 352-0471
Dennis Berg, *President*
Vernon I Berg, *Chairman*
Glenna L Berg, *Corp Secy*
EMP: 25
SALES: 802K **Privately Held**
SIC: 3993 1731 Electric signs; signs, not
made in custom sign painting shops; gen-
eral electrical contractor

(P-23242)
WESTERN SIGN COMPANY INC
6221a Enterprise Dr Ste A, Diamond
Springs (95619-9398)
PHONE.....................................916 933-3765
David Brazelton, *President*
Todd Johnston, *Vice Pres*
Keith Wills, *Vice Pres*
Cindy Brazelton, *Admin Sec*
Wendie Denham, *Opers Mgr*
EMP: 20 EST: 1959
SQ FT: 12,000
SALES (est): 3.2MM **Privately Held**
WEB: www.westernsign.com
SIC: 3993 1799 Electric signs; neon signs;
sign installation & maintenance

(P-23243)
WESTERN SIGN SYSTEMS INC
261 S Pacific St, San Marcos
(92078-2429)
PHONE.....................................760 736-6070
David Lesage, *President*
Mike Leon, *Graphic Designe*
Tiffany Del Gatto, *Human Res Dir*
Joe Mayerchik, *Prdtn Mgr*
EMP: 25
SQ FT: 6,000
SALES (est): 3MM **Privately Held**
SIC: 3993 Signs & advertising specialties

(P-23244)
WILLIAMS SIGN CO
111 S Huntington St, Pomona
(91766-1436)
PHONE......................909 622-5304
Chad Bruce, *President*
Justin M Williams, *President*
Sharon Willison, *Treasurer*
Marcelle Williams, *Vice Pres*
EMP: 10
SQ FT: 4,700
SALES (est): 1.2MM **Privately Held**
SIC: 3993 1799 Neon signs; sign installa-
tion & maintenance

(P-23245)
WOLFPACK INC
Also Called: Wolfpack Sign Group
2440 Grand Ave Ste B, Vista (92081-7829)
P.O. Box 3620 (92085-3620)
PHONE......................760 736-4500
Carolyn Wolf, *CEO*
Peter Wolf, *Corp Secy*
Ryan Meyer, *Vice Pres*
EMP: 20
SQ FT: 15,000
SALES (est): 3.2MM **Privately Held**
WEB: www.wolfpacksigns.com
SIC: 3993 Signs, not made in custom sign
painting shops

(P-23246)
**XPERT MARKETING GROUP
INC**
Also Called: Mycustomerdata
32 Alicante, Trabuco Canyon (92679-4149)
P.O. Box 80100, Rcho STA Marg (92688-
0100)
PHONE......................949 309-6300
Kevin Bone, *CEO*
Tom Virden, *President*
Jim Yanco, *President*
Dan Beres, *Exec VP*
EMP: 50
SALES (est): 4.4MM **Privately Held**
SIC: 3993 Signs & advertising specialties

(P-23247)
**YOUNG ELECTRIC SIGN
COMPANY**
Also Called: Yesco
875 National Dr Ste 107, Sacramento
(95834-1162)
PHONE......................916 419-8101
Rachel Williamson, *Branch Mgr*
EMP: 35
SALES (corp-wide): 331.2MM **Privately
Held**
SIC: 3993 5999 1799 Electric signs;
awnings; sign installation & maintenance
PA: Young Electric Sign Company Inc
2401 S Foothill Dr
Salt Lake City UT 84109
801 464-4600

(P-23248)
**YOUNG ELECTRIC SIGN
COMPANY**
Also Called: Yesco
10235 Bellegrave Ave, Jurupa Valley
(91752-1919)
PHONE......................909 923-7668
Duane Wardle, *Branch Mgr*
Megan Hornsby, *Office Mgr*
Dale Ingraham, *Manager*
EMP: 100
SQ FT: 8,500
SALES (corp-wide): 331.2MM **Privately
Held**
SIC: 3993 1799 Electric signs; sign instal-
lation & maintenance
PA: Young Electric Sign Company Inc
2401 S Foothill Dr
Salt Lake City UT 84109
801 464-4600

(P-23249)
**YOUNG ELECTRIC SIGN
COMPANY**
Also Called: Yesco
46750 Fremont Blvd # 101, Fremont
(94538-6573)
PHONE......................510 877-7815
Kip Kitto, *Branch Mgr*
EMP: 27

SALES (corp-wide): 331.2MM **Privately
Held**
SIC: 3993 Signs & advertising specialties
PA: Young Electric Sign Company Inc
2401 S Foothill Dr
Salt Lake City UT 84109
801 464-4600

(P-23250)
ZUMAR INDUSTRIES INC
9719 Santa Fe Springs Rd, Santa Fe
Springs (90670-2919)
PHONE......................562 941-4633
Benn Limcke, *President*
Lee Young, *CFO*
Tj Thibert, *Info Tech Mgr*
Pamela Foster, *Accounts Mgr*
EMP: 56 **EST:** 1947
SQ FT: 30,000
SALES (est): 6.4MM
SALES (corp-wide): 30MM **Privately
Held**
WEB: www.zumar.com
SIC: 3993 Signs & advertising specialties
PA: Zumar Industries, Inc.
12015 Steele St S
Tacoma WA 98444
253 536-7740

3995 Burial Caskets

(P-23251)
**PETTIGREW & SONS CASKET
CO**
6151 Power Inn Rd, Sacramento
(95824-2343)
PHONE......................916 383-0777
Fay Pettigrew, *President*
Althea Pettigrew, *Treasurer*
Donald Pettigrew, *Vice Pres*
James Pettigrew, *Vice Pres*
Barbara Hart, *Admin Sec*
▼**EMP:** 20
SQ FT: 25,000
SALES (est): 2.5MM **Privately Held**
WEB: www.pettigrewcaskets.com
SIC: 3995 Burial caskets

(P-23252)
UNIVERSAL MEDITECH INC
1320 E Fortune Ave # 102, Fresno
(93725-1958)
PHONE......................559 366-7798
Zhaoyan Wang, *President*
EMP: 45 **EST:** 2015
SALES (est): 1MM **Privately Held**
SIC: 3995 2835 Casket linings; pregnancy
test kits

3996 Linoleum & Hard Surface Floor Coverings, NEC

(P-23253)
ALTRO USA INC
Also Called: Compass Flooring
12648 Clark St, Santa Fe Springs
(90670-3950)
PHONE......................562 944-8292
Al Boegh, *Principal*
EMP: 57
SALES (corp-wide): 19.8MM **Privately
Held**
SIC: 3996 5023 Hard surface floor cover-
ings; resilient floor coverings: tile or sheet
PA: Altro Usa, Inc.
80 Industrial Way Ste 1
Wilmington MA 01887
800 583-4244

(P-23254)
HOVEY TILE ART
1221 Opal Ave, Mentone (92359-1272)
PHONE......................909 794-3815
Dean Hovey, *Owner*
EMP: 21
SALES (est): 1.5MM **Privately Held**
SIC: 3996 Tile, floor: supported plastic

(P-23255)
RENOS FLOOR COVERING INC
1515 Solano Ave, Vallejo (94590-5736)
P.O. Box 503, NAPA (94559-0503)
PHONE......................415 459-1403
Carolyn Reno, *President*
John Norman, *Vice Pres*
EMP: 16
SALES (est): 2.7MM **Privately Held**
SIC: 3996 Asphalted-felt-base floor cover-
ings: linoleum, carpet

(P-23256)
WILLIAM A SHUBECK
10961 Desert Lawn Dr # 102, Calimesa
(92320-2232)
PHONE......................909 795-6970
William A Shubeck, *Owner*
EMP: 4
SALES (est): 1MM **Privately Held**
SIC: 3996 Hard surface floor coverings

3999 Manufacturing Industries, NEC

(P-23257)
1254 INDUSTRIES
1444 Alpine Pl, San Marcos (92078-3801)
PHONE......................760 798-8531
▲**EMP:** 13
SALES (est): 1.6MM **Privately Held**
SIC: 3999 Barber & beauty shop equip-
ment

(P-23258)
5 STAR REDEMPTION INC
Also Called: Planet Star
8803 Shirley Ave, Northridge (91324-3412)
PHONE......................818 709-0875
William B Faith, *President*
▲**EMP:** 20 **EST:** 1996
SALES (est): 2.1MM **Privately Held**
WEB: www.fivestarredemption.com
SIC: 3999 Coin-operated amusement ma-
chines

(P-23259)
**A & A JEWELRY TOOLS
FINDINGS**
Also Called: A&A Jewelry Tools & Supplies
319 W 6th St, Los Angeles (90014-1703)
PHONE......................213 627-8004
Gene Adem, *Partner*
Robert Adem, *Partner*
Fouad Farah, *Partner*
Naim Farah, *Partner*
Philp Farah, *Partner*
▲**EMP:** 18
SQ FT: 3,000
SALES (est): 2MM **Privately Held**
WEB: www.aajewelry.com
SIC: 3999 5944 Atomizers, toiletry; jew-
elry, precious stones & precious metals

(P-23260)
A S G CORPORATION
Also Called: Smith & Company
1361 Newton St, Los Angeles
(90021-2723)
PHONE......................213 748-6361
Albert Weiss, *President*
William Weiss, *Vice Pres*
Esther Weiss, *Admin Sec*
◆**EMP:** 15
SALES (est): 1.9MM **Privately Held**
SIC: 3999 7929 Lamp shade frames; en-
tertainers & entertainment groups

(P-23261)
**ABOVE & BEYOND BALLOONS
INC**
Also Called: Above and Beyond
16661 Jamboree Rd, Irvine (92606-5118)
PHONE......................949 586-8470
Michael Chaklos, *CEO*
Karen Chaklos, *Vice Pres*
▲**EMP:** 44
SQ FT: 25,000
SALES: 6MM **Privately Held**
WEB: www.advertisingballons.com
SIC: 3999 Advertising display products

(P-23262)
**ACCURATE STAGING MFG INC
(PA)**
13900 S Figueroa St, Los Angeles
(90061-1028)
PHONE......................310 324-1040
Alfredo Gomez, *CEO*
Jose Cantu, *President*
EMP: 29
SQ FT: 18,000
SALES (est): 6.2MM **Privately Held**
WEB: www.accuratestaging.com
SIC: 3999 Stage hardware & equipment,
except lighting

(P-23263)
**ADVANCED BUILDING SYSTEMS
INC**
11905 Regentview Ave, Downey
(90241-5515)
PHONE......................818 652-4252
Alex Youssef, *President*
EMP: 20
SALES (est): 504.6K **Privately Held**
SIC: 3999 Manufacturing industries

(P-23264)
**ADVANCED COSMETIC RES
LABS INC**
Also Called: Acrl
20550 Prairie St, Chatsworth (91311-6006)
PHONE......................818 709-9945
Kitty Hunter, *President*
Celeste Guillen, *Research*
Fred Radvinsky, *Purchasing*
Richard Garza, *Sr Project Mgr*
▲**EMP:** 50
SQ FT: 48,000
SALES (est): 7.3MM **Privately Held**
WEB: www.advancedcosmeticlabs.com
SIC: 3999 2844 Barber & beauty shop
equipment; toilet preparations

(P-23265)
ADVANCED MOBILITY INC
7720 Sepulveda Blvd, Van Nuys
(91405-1018)
PHONE......................818 780-1788
Scott Deacon, *President*
Linda V Winkle, *Treasurer*
Linda Van Winkle, *Corp Secy*
Bill Deacon, *Vice Pres*
EMP: 19 **EST:** 1975
SQ FT: 12,000
SALES (est): 1MM **Privately Held**
SIC: 3999 5531 Wool pulling; automotive
accessories

(P-23266)
AEGIS PRINCIPIA LLC
12165 Ojeda Ct, Tustin (92782-1284)
PHONE......................714 731-2283
Brando Balarezo,
EMP: 10
SALES (est): 508.1K **Privately Held**
SIC: 3999 Novelties, bric-a-brac & hobby
kits

(P-23267)
AKON INCORPORATED
2135 Ringwood Ave, San Jose
(95131-1725)
PHONE......................408 432-8039
Surya Sareen, *President*
Louis Seieroe, *Business Dir*
Preeti Kotha, *Project Engr*
Ajay Dalal, *Engineer*
Sylvia Van, *Controller*
EMP: 60
SQ FT: 35,000
SALES (est): 11.8MM **Privately Held**
SIC: 3999 Slot machines

(P-23268)
ALL AMERICAN FABRICATION
1328 Burton Ave Ste B10, Salinas
(93901-4437)
PHONE......................831 676-3490
Ahumberto Abalos, *Owner*
EMP: 12
SALES (est): 51.3K **Privately Held**
SIC: 3999 Manufacturing industries

(P-23269)
ALL POWER MANUFACTURING CO
13141 Molette St, Santa Fe Springs (90670-5500)
PHONE...................................562 802-2640
Michael J Hartnett, *Principal*
J Lucas, *Administration*
Martha Lopez, *Info Tech Mgr*
EMP: 14
SALES (corp-wide): 702.5MM **Publicly Held**
SIC: **3999** Atomizers, toiletry
HQ: All Power Manufacturing Co
1 Tribiology Ctr
Oxford CT 06478
562 802-2640

(P-23270)
ALLIED FEATHER & DOWN CORP (PA)
6905 W Acco St Ste A, Montebello (90640-5448)
PHONE...................................323 581-5677
Steve Uretsky, *CEO*
Nate Hascalovici, *CFO*
Fion Huang, *Vice Pres*
Marylou Ramirez, *Admin Asst*
Jonathan Uretsky, *VP Opers*
◆ EMP: 50
SQ FT: 12,000
SALES (est): 8.6MM **Privately Held**
WEB: www.alliedfeather.com
SIC: **3999** 5719 Down (feathers); bedding (sheets, blankets, spreads & pillows)

(P-23271)
ALOHA BAY
Also Called: Bright Lights Candle Company
16275 A Main St, Lower Lake (95457)
P.O. Box 539 (95457-0539)
PHONE...................................707 994-3267
Bernard S Burger, *CEO*
Roy Dixon, *Principal*
Tom Closser, *Marketing Staff*
▲ EMP: 35
SQ FT: 1,500
SALES (est): 4.1MM **Privately Held**
WEB: www.brightlightscandles.com
SIC: **3999** 5199 Candles; candles

(P-23272)
AMARETTO ORCHARDS LLC
Also Called: Famoso Nut
32331 Famoso Woody Rd, Mc Farland (93250-9771)
PHONE...................................661 399-9697
Bruce Baretta,
David Delis, *Controller*
Dominique Camou, *Prdtn Mgr*
Jose Jaime, *Foreman/Supr*
◆ EMP: 20
SALES (est): 2.9MM **Privately Held**
SIC: **3999** 2068 Nut shells, grinding, from purchased nuts; salted & roasted nuts & seeds

(P-23273)
AMERICAN STRAW COMPANY LLC
1697 Woods Dr, Los Angeles (90069-1633)
PHONE...................................213 304-1095
Carolyn Chen,
EMP: 15
SALES (est): 436.7K **Privately Held**
SIC: **3999** Straw goods

(P-23274)
AMGEN MANUFACTURING LIMITED
1 Amgen Center Dr, Newbury Park (91320-1799)
PHONE...................................787 656-2000
Victoria H Blatter, *Principal*
EMP: 12
SALES (est): 45K
SALES (corp-wide): 23.7B **Publicly Held**
SIC: **3999** Atomizers, toiletry
PA: Amgen Inc.
1 Amgen Center Dr
Thousand Oaks CA 91320
805 447-1000

(P-23275)
ANIMA INTERNATIONAL CORP
19502 Avenida Del Campo, Walnut (91789-1607)
PHONE...................................626 723-4960
MEI LI, *President*
Benjamin MA, *Vice Pres*
▲ EMP: 12
SALES (est): 1.2MM **Privately Held**
WEB: www.animainternational.com
SIC: **3999** Pet supplies

(P-23276)
ANTHONYS CHRISTMAS TREES
Also Called: Anthonys Chistmas Tree
510 Alston Rd, Santa Barbara (93108-2304)
PHONE...................................805 966-6668
Anthony Dal Bello, *President*
Maria Dal Bello, *Admin Sec*
EMP: 50
SALES (est): 4.9MM **Privately Held**
WEB: www.anthonyschristmastrees.com
SIC: **3999** 5199 Wreaths, artificial; Christmas trees, including artificial; Christmas novelties

(P-23277)
ARRIVE-AI INC
16751 Millikan Ave, Irvine (92606-5009)
PHONE...................................949 221-0166
Jose Vasquez, *President*
EMP: 10
SALES (est): 283.1K **Privately Held**
SIC: **3999** Manufacturing industries

(P-23278)
ARTEFFEX CONCEPTIONEERING
911 Mayo St, Los Angeles (90042-3122)
PHONE...................................818 506-5358
Dan O'Quinn, *Owner*
EMP: 10
SALES (est): 430K **Privately Held**
SIC: **3999** Puppets & marionettes

(P-23279)
ARTIFCIAL GRASS RECYCLERS CORP
25800 Washington Ave, Murrieta (92562-9748)
PHONE...................................714 635-7000
EMP: 40
SALES (corp-wide): 6.6MM **Privately Held**
SIC: **3999** Grasses, artificial & preserved
PA: Artificial Grass Recyclers Corporation
42505 Rio Nedo
Temecula CA 92590
855 409-4247

(P-23280)
ARTIFICIAL GRASS LIQUIDATORS
Also Called: Agl
42505 Rio Nedo, Temecula (92590-3726)
PHONE...................................951 677-3377
Dillon Georgian, *President*
EMP: 30 EST: 2015
SALES (est): 1.4MM **Privately Held**
SIC: **3999** Grasses, artificial & preserved

(P-23281)
ATA BOY INC
3171 Los Feliz Blvd # 205, Los Angeles (90039-1536)
PHONE...................................323 644-0117
Alan Cushman, *President*
Judy Albright, *CFO*
Alex Perez, *Natl Sales Mgr*
▲ EMP: 31
SQ FT: 4,000
SALES (est): 3.3MM **Privately Held**
WEB: www.ata-boy.com
SIC: **3999** 5947 Novelties, bric-a-brac & hobby kits; gift shop

(P-23282)
ATLAS MATCH LLC
1337 Limerick Dr, Placentia (92870-3410)
PHONE...................................714 993-3328
EMP: 60
SALES (est): 2.2MM **Privately Held**
SIC: **3999**

(P-23283)
BADGE CO
Also Called: The Badge Company
18261 Enterprise Ln Ste D, Huntington Beach (92648-1245)
PHONE...................................714 842-3037
David J Bowen, *President*
Kimberly A Ramsey, *General Mgr*
EMP: 17 EST: 1979
SQ FT: 6,000
SALES (est): 1.6MM **Privately Held**
WEB: www.badge.com
SIC: **3999** Badges, metal: policemen, firemen, etc.

(P-23284)
BALSAM HILL LLC
50 Woodside Plz Ste 11, Redwood City (94061-2500)
PHONE...................................888 552-2572
Thomas Harman, *Mng Member*
Bernie Leas, *Opers Staff*
Carl Winter, *Manager*
▲ EMP: 18
SALES (est): 2.5MM **Privately Held**
SIC: **3999** Christmas trees, artificial

(P-23285)
BART MANUFACTURING INC (PA)
3787 Spinnaker Ct, Fremont (94538-6537)
PHONE...................................408 320-4373
Dave Weissbart, *CEO*
Trevor Weissbart, *Finance Mgr*
Edward Lloyd, *Manager*
EMP: 69
SALES (est): 19.3MM **Privately Held**
SIC: **3999** Chairs, hydraulic, barber & beauty shop

(P-23286)
BEAD SHOPPE
2030 Douglas Blvd Ste 42, Roseville (95661-3857)
PHONE...................................916 782-8642
Ester Morse, *Owner*
Steve Ruckels, *Admin Sec*
Christian Speck, *Real Est Agnt*
▲ EMP: 12
SALES (est): 571K **Privately Held**
WEB: www.thebeadshoppe.com
SIC: **3999** 5094 Stringing beads; beads

(P-23287)
BERG MANUFACTURING INC
408 Aldo Ave, Santa Clara (95054-2301)
PHONE...................................408 727-2374
Doug Berg, *CEO*
Jamie Berg, *President*
EMP: 10
SALES (est): 1.4MM **Privately Held**
SIC: **3999** Barber & beauty shop equipment

(P-23288)
BRIGHT GLOW CANDLE COMPANY INC (PA)
110 Erie St, Pomona (91768-3342)
PHONE...................................909 469-0119
Richard Alcedo, *President*
◆ EMP: 39
SQ FT: 64,000
SALES (est): 7.6MM **Privately Held**
WEB: www.brightglowcandle.com
SIC: **3999** Candles

(P-23289)
BRITE INDUSTRIES INC
Also Called: Brite Labs
1746 13th St, Oakland (94607-1510)
PHONE...................................510 250-9330
Brian Brown, *CEO*
EMP: 96
SALES (est): 259.5K **Privately Held**
SIC: **3999** 5159 ;

(P-23290)
CA937 AFJROTC
12431 Roscoe Blvd Ste 300, Sun Valley (91352-3723)
PHONE...................................818 394-3600
EMP: 99 EST: 2013
SALES (est): 3.1MM **Privately Held**
SIC: **3999**

(P-23291)
CAESAR HARDWARE INTL LTD
4985 Hallmark Pkwy, San Bernardino (92407-1870)
PHONE...................................800 306-3829
Chao Xu, *CEO*
EMP: 13
SALES: 15MM
SALES (corp-wide): 310.2K **Privately Held**
SIC: **3999** 3429 Atomizers, toiletry; fireplace equipment, hardware: andirons, grates, screens
PA: Yuyao Super Wing Foreign Trade Co., Ltd
Room 1401, Yangguang International Mansion, No.55, Yuli Road
Yuyao
574 626-2691

(P-23292)
CALIFORNIA ACRYLIC INDS INC (HQ)
Also Called: Cal Spas
1462 E 9th St, Pomona (91766-3833)
PHONE...................................909 623-8781
Casey Loyd, *President*
Sheba Nobel, *CFO*
Buzz Loyd, *Admin Sec*
▲ EMP: 37
SQ FT: 300,000
SALES (est): 21.4MM **Privately Held**
SIC: **3999** 3949 Hot tubs; billiard & pool equipment & supplies, general

(P-23293)
CALIFORNIA EXOTIC NOVLT LLC
1455 E Francis St, Ontario (91761-8329)
P.O. Box 50400 (91761-1078)
PHONE...................................909 606-1950
Susan Colvin, *CEO*
Josh Leduff, *Chief Mktg Ofcr*
Jackie White, *Vice Pres*
Aaron Buden, *Technology*
Robbie Eich, *Graphic Designe*
▲ EMP: 80
SQ FT: 66,000
SALES (est): 35.4MM **Privately Held**
WEB: www.calexotics.com
SIC: **3999** 5947 Novelties, bric-a-brac & hobby kits; novelties

(P-23294)
CALIFORNIA INDUSTIRAL MFG LLC (PA)
1221 Independence Pl, Gridley (95948-9341)
P.O. Box 830, Durham (95938-0830)
PHONE...................................530 846-9960
EMP: 15
SALES (est): 3.3MM **Privately Held**
SIC: **3999** Manufacturing industries

(P-23295)
CAMBRO MANUFACTURING COMPANY
21558 Ferrero, City of Industry (91789-5216)
PHONE...................................909 354-8962
EMP: 12
SALES (corp-wide): 307.8MM **Privately Held**
SIC: **3999** Barber & beauty shop equipment
PA: Cambro Manufacturing Company Inc
5801 Skylab Rd
Huntington Beach CA 92647
714 848-1555

(P-23296)
CANDAMAR DESIGNS INC
520 E Jamie Ave, La Habra (90631-6842)
PHONE...................................714 871-6190
Carla E Martin, *President*
▲ EMP: 30 EST: 1970
SQ FT: 12,500
SALES (est): 2.4MM **Privately Held**
WEB: www.candamar.com
SIC: **3999** 5949 Sewing kits, novelty; sewing, needlework & piece goods

(P-23297)
CANDLEBAY CO
3440 W Warner Ave Ste Cd, Santa Ana
(92704-5320)
PHONE....................................949 307-1807
Craig Dualba, *President*
▲ EMP: 10
SALES (est): 1.1MM **Privately Held**
WEB: www.candlebay.com
SIC: 3999 Candles

(P-23298)
CANNALOGIC
5404 Whitsett Ave 219, Valley Village
(91607-1615)
PHONE....................................619 458-0775
Jasmine Savoy, *President*
EMP: 17
SALES (est): 440.7K **Privately Held**
SIC: 3999 Manufacturing industries

(P-23299)
CARBERRY LLC (HQ)
17130 Muskrat Ave Ste B, Adelanto
(92301-2473)
PHONE....................................800 564-0842
Roy McFarland, *Director*
EMP: 24 EST: 2017
SQ FT: 12,000
SALES (est): 1.5MM
SALES (corp-wide): 1.1MM **Privately
Held**
SIC: 3999 2064 ; chewing candy, not
chewing gum
PA: Plus Products Holdings Inc.
2174 Waverley St
Palo Alto CA 94301
800 564-0842

(P-23300)
CCL LABEL INC
21481 8th St E, Sonoma (95476-9291)
PHONE....................................707 938-7800
Michelle Clayworth, *Comptroller*
John Arters, *Graphic Designe*
John Kunz, *Accountant*
Michael Giuliana, *Controller*
Tim Jones, *Opers Mgr*
EMP: 12
SALES (corp-wide): 3.9B **Privately Held**
SIC: 3999 Barber & beauty shop equip-
ment
HQ: Ccl Label, Inc.
161 Worcester Rd Ste 603
Framingham MA 01701
508 872-4511

(P-23301)
CDM COMPANY INC
12 Corporate Plaza Dr # 200, Newport
Beach (92660-7986)
PHONE....................................949 644-2820
Mitch Junkins, *President*
Mia Brown, *Vice Pres*
Wendy Diehl, *Vice Pres*
Dana Pescrillo, *Project Mgr*
Steve Giordano, *Manager*
▲ EMP: 23
SQ FT: 7,000
SALES (est): 3.1MM **Privately Held**
WEB: www.thecdmco.com
SIC: 3999 3944 8742 5112 Novelties,
bric-a-brac & hobby kits; games, toys &
children's vehicles; marketing consulting
services; pens &/or pencils

(P-23302)
CERTIFIX INC
Also Called: Certifix Live Scan
1950 W Corporate Way, Anaheim
(92801-5373)
PHONE....................................714 496-3850
Helmy El Mangoury, *CEO*
Helmy El-Mangoury, *Manager*
Alexa Paredes, *Accounts Mgr*
Justin Lowe, *Supervisor*
EMP: 14 EST: 2007
SALES (est): 1.1MM **Privately Held**
WEB: www.certifixlivescan.com
SIC: 3999 7381 7389 Fingerprint equip-
ment; fingerprint service; mailbox rental &
related service

(P-23303)
CES ELECTRONICS MFG INC
14731 Franklin Ave Ste E, Tustin
(92780-7221)
PHONE....................................714 505-3441
Nicolae Stafan, *Principal*
EMP: 11
SALES (est): 1.2MM **Privately Held**
SIC: 3999 Manufacturing industries

(P-23304)
CLAMP SWING PRICING CO INC
8386 Capwell Dr, Oakland (94621-2114)
PHONE....................................510 567-1600
Benjamin Garfinkle, *President*
Wilma Garfinkle, *Ch of Bd*
◆ EMP: 30
SQ FT: 47,000
SALES (est): 4.4MM **Privately Held**
WEB: www.clampswing.com
SIC: 3999 Identification plates

(P-23305)
CONSOLIDATED TRAINING LLC
144 Holm Rd Spc 47, Watsonville
(95076-2428)
PHONE....................................831 768-8888
EMP: 22
SALES: 15MM **Privately Held**
SIC: 3999

(P-23306)
COUNTRY FLORAL SUPPLY INC
6909 Las Positas Rd Ste F, Livermore
(94551-5113)
PHONE....................................925 960-9823
Michelle Luke, *Manager*
EMP: 53
SALES (corp-wide): 48.5MM **Privately
Held**
SIC: 3999 5193 Artificial trees & flowers;
artificial flowers
PA: Country Floral Supply, Inc.
3802 Weatherly Cir
Westlake Village CA 91361
805 520-8026

(P-23307)
CRP SPORTS LLC
3191 Red Hill Ave Ste 250, Costa Mesa
(92626-3495)
PHONE....................................949 395-7759
EMP: 10
SALES (est): 614.4K **Privately Held**
SIC: 3999 Manufacturing industries

(P-23308)
CRYOPACIFIC INCORPORATED
641 S Palm St Ste G, La Habra
(90631-5784)
P.O. Box 626 (90633-0626)
PHONE....................................562 697-7904
Randy Reynoso, *Principal*
Derek Green, *Engineer*
EMP: 10
SALES (est): 990.8K **Privately Held**
SIC: 3999 Manufacturing industries

(P-23309)
**D&H MANUFACTURING
COMPANY**
Also Called: D&H / R&D
49235 Milmont Dr, Fremont (94538-7349)
PHONE....................................510 770-5100
EMP: 15 EST: 2015
SALES (est): 1.6MM **Privately Held**
SIC: 3999 Manufacturing industries

(P-23310)
DANGEROUS COFFEE CO LLC
3644 Midway Dr, San Diego (92110-5201)
PHONE....................................619 405-8291
Quentin Sponselee,
EMP: 10
SALES (est): 364.9K **Privately Held**
SIC: 3999 Manufacturing industries

(P-23311)
DARYLS PET SHOP
208 E State St, Redlands (92373-5233)
PHONE....................................909 793-1788
Leslie Triplette, *President*
EMP: 15

SALES (est): 848K **Privately Held**
SIC: 3999 Pet supplies; boat models, except toy; models, general, except toy; railroad models, except toy

(P-23312)
DB STUDIOS INC
17032 Murphy Ave, Irvine (92614-5914)
PHONE....................................949 833-0100
Darin Rasmussen, *President*
Mark Bense, *CFO*
Mike Mikyska, *Vice Pres*
John Riley, *Vice Pres*
Eric Weintraub, *Opers Staff*
▲ EMP: 35
SQ FT: 22,500
SALES (est): 4.6MM
SALES (corp-wide): 1.1B **Publicly Held**
WEB: www.displayboys.com
SIC: 3999 3993 7389 7319 Advertising
display products; signs & advertising spe-
cialties; advertising, promotional & trade
show services; display advertising serv-
ice; commercial art & graphic design
PA: Innerworkings, Inc.
203 N Lasalle St Ste 1800
Chicago IL 60601
312 642-3700

(P-23313)
DESERT SHADES INC
5014 W Jefferson Blvd, Los Angeles
(90016-3925)
PHONE....................................323 731-5000
Benny Nadal, *Regional Mgr*
Marlene Nadal, *Admin Sec*
▲ EMP: 14 EST: 1979
SQ FT: 4,400
SALES (est): 1.3MM **Privately Held**
SIC: 3999 Shades, lamp or candle

(P-23314)
DEVELOPLUS INC
1575 Magnolia Ave, Corona (92879-2073)
PHONE....................................951 738-8595
Deorao K Agrey, *CEO*
▲ EMP: 70
SQ FT: 40,000
SALES (est): 15.4MM **Privately Held**
SIC: 3999 5087 Hair & hair-based prod-
ucts; beauty parlor equipment & supplies

(P-23315)
DKP DESIGNS INC
110 Maryland St, El Segundo (90245-4115)
PHONE....................................310 322-6000
Deborah P Koppel, *President*
Brad Koppel, *Vice Pres*
Maria Defilippo, *Production*
Matthew Koppel, *Marketing Staff*
Trevor Koppel, *Director*
▲ EMP: 15 EST: 1996
SQ FT: 4,000
SALES (est): 2.1MM **Privately Held**
WEB: www.dkpdesigns.com
SIC: 3999 Advertising display products

(P-23316)
DO IT RIGHT PRODUCTS LLC
1838 N Case St, Orange (92865-4233)
PHONE....................................714 998-8152
Elana Sherve, *Branch Mgr*
EMP: 12
SALES (corp-wide): 2.3MM **Privately
Held**
SIC: 3999 Models, general, except toy
PA: Do It Right Products Llc
44321 62nd St W
Lancaster CA 93536
661 722-9664

(P-23317)
DOLPHIN SPAS INC
701 W Foothill Blvd, Azusa (91702-2348)
PHONE....................................626 334-0099
Kareem Azizeh, *President*
EMP: 11
SQ FT: 27,000
SALES: 2MM **Privately Held**
WEB: www.dolphinspas.com
SIC: 3999 5999 Hot tubs; spas & hot tubs

(P-23318)
E-LIQ CUBE INC (PA)
13515 Alondra Blvd, Santa Fe Springs
(90670-5602)
PHONE....................................562 537-9454
▲ EMP: 18
SALES: 1MM **Privately Held**
SIC: 3999

(P-23319)
EATYOURMEALSCOM LLC
4418 Deer Ridge Rd, Danville
(94506-6017)
PHONE....................................925 984-5452
Michael Hughes,
EMP: 12
SALES (est): 329.6K **Privately Held**
SIC: 3999 Manufacturing industries

(P-23320)
ECO-SHELL INC
5230 Grange Rd, Corning (96021-9239)
PHONE....................................530 824-8794
Charles R Crain Jr, *CEO*
◆ EMP: 22 EST: 1996
SQ FT: 60,000
SALES (est): 4.4MM **Privately Held**
WEB: www.ecoshell.com
SIC: 3999 Nut shells, grinding, from pur-
chased nuts

(P-23321)
ECOLIGHT INC
Also Called: Stone Candles
1660 Lincoln Blvd, Santa Monica
(90404-3712)
PHONE....................................310 450-7444
Daniel Wainer, *President*
Michael Wainer, *Manager*
EMP: 13
SALES: 1.1MM **Privately Held**
SIC: 3999 5199 5999 Candles; candles;
candle shops

(P-23322)
ED JONES COMPANY
2834 8th St, Berkeley (94710-2707)
PHONE....................................510 704-0704
Chester F Stegman, *President*
Krista Stegman, *Treasurer*
Jonathan Bloom, *Vice Pres*
Janet Johnson, *Office Mgr*
Elisabeth Rusca, *Admin Sec*
EMP: 10
SQ FT: 5,000
SALES (est): 910.7K **Privately Held**
WEB: www.edjonesco.com
SIC: 3999 5199 Badges, metal: police-
men, firemen, etc.; badges

(P-23323)
**EDGATE CORRELATION SVCS
LLC**
5473 Krny Vlla Rd Ste 300, San Diego
(92123)
PHONE....................................858 712-9341
Sara Schiff,
Rick Wells,
EMP: 25
SALES: 950K **Privately Held**
SIC: 3999 Education aids, devices & sup-
plies

(P-23324)
**EDWARDS LIFESCIENCE FING
LLC**
1 Edwards Way, Irvine (92614-5688)
PHONE....................................949 250-3480
Mike Mussaollem, *President*
EMP: 13
SALES (est): 1.2MM
SALES (corp-wide): 3.7B **Publicly Held**
SIC: 3999 Advertising curtains
PA: Edwards Lifesciences Corp
1 Edwards Way
Irvine CA 92614
949 250-2500

(P-23325)
EG WEAR INC
4512 Harlin Dr Ste A, Sacramento
(95826-9719)
PHONE....................................916 361-1508
Mark Wolfgram, *Principal*
EMP: 11

PRODUCTS & SVCS

SALES (est): 1.2MM **Privately Held**
SIC: 3999 2759 Embroidery kits; screen printing

(P-23326)
ELAFREE INC
Also Called: Creations Salon
17779 Main St Ste F&G, Irvine (92614-4796)
PHONE...................................949 724-9390
Aaron Gaskin, *President*
Kimberly C Gaskin, *Corp Secy*
EMP: 12
SQ FT: 2,000
SALES: 410K **Privately Held**
SIC: 3999 Hair & hair-based products

(P-23327)
ETTORE PRODUCTS CO
2100 N Loop Rd, Alameda (94502-8010)
P.O. Box 2164, Oakland (94621-0064)
PHONE...................................510 748-4130
Michael A Smahlik, *Principal*
Rufus Bunch, *COO*
Diane Smahlik, *Corp Secy*
Alma Bryant, *Accounting Mgr*
Waylon Lee, *QC Mgr*
▲ **EMP:** 85
SQ FT: 30,000
SALES (est): 17.8MM **Privately Held**
WEB: www.ettore.com
SIC: 3999 Window squeegees

(P-23328)
EVO MANUFACTURING INC
1829 W Commonwealth Ave, Fullerton (92833-3013)
PHONE...................................714 879-8913
EMP: 10
SALES (est): 822K **Privately Held**
SIC: 3999 Manufacturing industries

(P-23329)
EXHART ENVMTL SYSTEMS INC
20364 Plummer St, Chatsworth (91311-5371)
PHONE...................................818 576-9628
Isaac Weiser, *President*
Michael Weiser, *Exec VP*
Shari Weiser, *Exec VP*
Margaret Weiser, *Vice Pres*
◆ **EMP:** 17 EST: 1989
SALES (est): 2.1MM **Privately Held**
WEB: www.exhart.com
SIC: 3999 Lawn ornaments

(P-23330)
FAMILY INDUSTRIES LLC
1700 N Spring St, Los Angeles (90012-1929)
PHONE...................................619 306-1035
Alexander Barry Meiners,
EMP: 10
SALES (est): 1MM **Privately Held**
SIC: 3999 Barber & beauty shop equipment

(P-23331)
FANCY MODELS CORP
48888 Fremont Blvd # 150, Fremont (94538-6557)
PHONE...................................510 683-0819
Ching Yu, *President*
EMP: 10
SALES (est): 791.6K **Privately Held**
WEB: www.fancymodels.com
SIC: 3999 3944 Models, general, except toy; games, toys & children's vehicles

(P-23332)
FLAME & WAX INC
Also Called: Voluspa
2900 Mccabe Way, Irvine (92614-6239)
PHONE...................................949 752-4000
Troy Arntsen, *President*
Erika Roybal, *Executive Asst*
Jennifer Hicks, *Purch Mgr*
Frank Munoz, *Mfg Staff*
Teresa Savastano, *Sales Staff*
▲ **EMP:** 31
SALES (est): 6.5MM **Privately Held**
SIC: 3999 2844 Candles; toilet preparations

(P-23333)
FLAME OUT INC
Also Called: Deist Safety
2623 N San Fernando Rd, Los Angeles (90065-1316)
PHONE...................................323 221-0000
James F Deist, *President*
▲ **EMP:** 20
SQ FT: 8,000
SALES (est): 1.1MM **Privately Held**
WEB: www.flameout.net
SIC: 3999 Fire extinguishers, portable

(P-23334)
FOLKMANIS INC
1219 Park Ave, Emeryville (94608-3607)
PHONE...................................510 658-7677
Atis Folkmanis, *President*
Dan Folkmanis, *Vice Pres*
Judy Folkmanis, *Vice Pres*
Elaine Kollias, *Mktg Dir*
Wendy Morton, *Marketing Mgr*
◆ **EMP:** 40
SALES (est): 4.8MM **Privately Held**
WEB: www.folkmanis.com
SIC: 3999 3942 Puppets & marionettes; dolls & stuffed toys

(P-23335)
FORRESTER EASTLAND CORPORATION
Also Called: Versa Stage
1320 Storm Pkwy, Torrance (90501-5041)
PHONE...................................310 784-2464
Clive Forrester, *CEO*
Erik Eastland, *President*
EMP: 27
SQ FT: 17,900
SALES (est): 6.4MM **Privately Held**
WEB: www.allaccessinc.com
SIC: 3999 7819 Stage hardware & equipment, except lighting; equipment & prop rental, motion picture production

(P-23336)
FOSS LAMPSHADE STUDIOS INC (PA)
1357 International Blvd, Oakland (94606-4303)
P.O. Box 1795, San Leandro (94577-0179)
PHONE...................................510 534-4133
Mark Foss, *President*
EMP: 12
SALES (est): 881.6K **Privately Held**
SIC: 3999 3645 Lamp shade frames; residential lighting fixtures

(P-23337)
FOUNTAINHEAD INDUSTRIES
700 N San Vicente Blvd G910, West Hollywood (90069-5060)
PHONE...................................310 248-2444
Hal Kline, *President*
EMP: 20
SALES (est): 536.3K **Privately Held**
SIC: 3999 Chairs, hydraulic, barber & beauty shop

(P-23338)
FRINGE STUDIO LLC
17909 Fitch, Irvine (92614-6016)
P.O. Box 3663, Culver City (90231-3663)
PHONE...................................949 387-9680
Scott Kingsland, *Mng Member*
Todd Kirshner,
▲ **EMP:** 10
SALES (est): 4.3MM **Privately Held**
SIC: 3999 Candles; shades, lamp or candle
PA: Punch Studio, Llc
6025 W Slauson Ave
Culver City CA 90230

(P-23339)
GALAXY ENTERPRISES INC
Also Called: Galaxy Medical
5411 Sheila St, Commerce (90040-2103)
PHONE...................................323 728-3980
Henry Talei, *Principal*
Agnes Putzer, *Export Mgr*
▲ **EMP:** 25 EST: 1949
SQ FT: 40,000

SALES (est): 3.3MM **Privately Held**
WEB: www.galaxymfg.com
SIC: 3999 3843 3841 Barber & beauty shop equipment; dental chairs; medical instruments & equipment, blood & bone work

(P-23340)
GARMON CORPORATION
Also Called: Naturvet
27461 Via Industria, Temecula (92590-3752)
PHONE...................................951 296-6308
Scott J Garmon, *President*
Laura Silva, *Human Res Dir*
Jodi Hoefler, *VP Mktg*
Sim Salles, *Sales Staff*
▲ **EMP:** 120 EST: 1979
SQ FT: 18,500
SALES (est): 36.5K **Privately Held**
WEB: www.naturvet.com
SIC: 3999 Pet supplies

(P-23341)
GEMINI INDUSTRIES INC
1910 E Warner Ave Ste G, Santa Ana (92705-5548)
PHONE...................................949 553-4255
Sebastian Musco, *Vice Pres*
Makhan Panesar, *Manager*
EMP: 12
SALES (est): 1.1MM **Privately Held**
SIC: 3999 Barber & beauty shop equipment

(P-23342)
GENERAL WAX CO INC (PA)
Also Called: General Wax & Candle Co
6863 Beck Ave, North Hollywood (91605-6206)
P.O. Box 9398 (91609-1398)
PHONE...................................818 765-5800
Carol Lazar, *CEO*
Mike Tapp, *President*
Colton Lazar, *Corp Secy*
Jerry Baker, *Executive*
Martha Smith, *Office Mgr*
◆ **EMP:** 85
SQ FT: 120,000
SALES (est): 21.4MM **Privately Held**
WEB: www.genwax.com
SIC: 3999 Candles

(P-23343)
GERMAINS SEED TECHNOLOGY INC
8333 Swanston Ln, Gilroy (95020-4517)
PHONE...................................408 848-8120
Paul Mullan, *CEO*
Patrick Clode, *Treasurer*
Catherine Farr, *Admin Sec*
▲ **EMP:** 39
SALES (est): 6MM
SALES (corp-wide): 19.8B **Privately Held**
SIC: 3999 Seeds, coated or treated, from purchased seeds
HQ: Germain's(U.K.)Limited
Hansa Road
King's Lynn
155 377-4012

(P-23344)
GLOBAL ENTERPRISE MFG INC
1560 S Harris Ct, Anaheim (92806-5931)
P.O. Box 590, La Mirada (90637-0590)
PHONE...................................657 234-1150
Jacob Bahbah, *President*
Andrew J Bahbah, *Vice Pres*
EMP: 22
SALES (est): 661.1K **Privately Held**
SIC: 3999 Manufacturing industries

(P-23345)
GLOBAL UXE INC
Also Called: Aquiesse
405 Science Dr, Moorpark (93021-2247)
PHONE...................................805 583-4600
Michael Joseph Horn, *President*
▲ **EMP:** 20
SALES (est): 1.3MM **Privately Held**
SIC: 3999 Candles

(P-23346)
GLOBALUXE INC
Also Called: Candle Crafters
405 Science Dr, Moorpark (93021-2247)
PHONE...................................805 583-4600
Michael Joseph Horn, *CEO*
▲ **EMP:** 20
SALES (est): 3MM **Privately Held**
WEB: www.globaluxe.com
SIC: 3999 5199 5999 Candles; candles; candle shops

(P-23347)
GOLD LEAF & METALLIC POWDERS
6001 Santa Monica Blvd, Los Angeles (90038-1807)
PHONE...................................323 769-4888
Scott Holland, *Manager*
Salvador Castillo, *Purchasing*
EMP: 50
SALES (est): 1.6MM **Privately Held**
WEB: www.glandmp.com
SIC: 3999 3497 Manufacturing industries; metal foil & leaf

(P-23348)
GOLDEN SUPREME INC
12304 Mccann Dr, Santa Fe Springs (90670-3333)
PHONE...................................562 903-1063
Ross Stillwagon, *President*
Ricardo J Fischbach, *Shareholder*
Fernando Fischbach, *Treasurer*
▲ **EMP:** 30
SQ FT: 13,000
SALES (est): 3.3MM **Privately Held**
WEB: www.goldensupreme.com
SIC: 3999 5087 Hair curlers, designed for beauty parlors; beauty parlor equipment & supplies

(P-23349)
H & H SPECIALTIES INC
14850 Don Julian Rd Ste B, City of Industry (91746-3122)
PHONE...................................626 575-0776
Reid Neslage, *Owner*
Mary Louise Higgins, *Principal*
EMP: 31
SQ FT: 30,000
SALES (est): 4.5MM **Privately Held**
WEB: www.hhspecialties.com
SIC: 3999 3625 Stage hardware & equipment, except lighting; relays & industrial controls

(P-23350)
H P GROUP
5070 Lindsay Ct, Chino (91710-5746)
PHONE...................................909 364-1069
Tim Zhu, *Owner*
EMP: 10 EST: 2001
SALES (est): 509K **Privately Held**
SIC: 3999 Candles

(P-23351)
HAIR BY COUTURE INC
1010 W Magnolia Blvd, Burbank (91506-1649)
PHONE...................................310 848-7676
Olga Oks, *President*
Victor Susanin, *President*
Irina Khlebopros, *CFO*
Vanessa Lopez, *CFO*
Kirill Kizyuk, *Senior VP*
◆ **EMP:** 12
SQ FT: 2,000
SALES (est): 81.3K **Privately Held**
SIC: 3999 Hair & hair-based products

(P-23352)
HIGH TECH PET PRODUCTS INC
2111 Portola Rd A, Ventura (93003-7723)
PHONE...................................805 644-1797
Nicholas Donge, *President*
Adele Bonge, *Graphic Designe*
▲ **EMP:** 44 EST: 1980
SALES (est): 4.6MM **Privately Held**
WEB: www.hitecpet.com
SIC: 3999 Pet supplies

(P-23353)
HOGAN MFG INC (PA)
19527 Mchenry Ave, Escalon (95320-9613)
P.O. Box 398 (95320-0398)
PHONE..............................209 838-7323
Mark Hogan, *President*
Jeff Hogan, *Vice Pres*
Paul Reichmuth, *Vice Pres*
Jan Consoli, *Executive*
Bernice Hogan, *Admin Sec*
▲ EMP: 275 EST: 1944
SQ FT: 43,000
SALES (est): 48MM Privately Held
WEB: www.hoganmfg.com
SIC: 3999 3441 3443 1791 Wheelchair
lifts; fabricated structural metal; fabricated
plate work (boiler shop); structural steel
erection

(P-23354)
HOGAN MFG INC
Lift-U
1520 1st St, Escalon (95320-1703)
P.O. Box 398 (95320-0398)
PHONE..............................209 838-2400
Paul Riechmuth, *Admin Mgr*
Jon Durham, *Manager*
EMP: 150
SALES (corp-wide): 48MM Privately
Held
WEB: www.hoganmfg.com
SIC: 3999 3842 3714 3534 Wheelchair
lifts; surgical appliances & supplies; motor
vehicle parts & accessories; elevators &
moving stairways
PA: Hogan Mfg., Inc.
19527 Mchenry Ave
Escalon CA 95320
209 838-7323

(P-23355)
HOLIDAY FOLIAGE INC
2592 Otay Center Dr, San Diego
(92154-7611)
PHONE..............................619 661-9094
Kristine Vanzutphen, *CEO*
William Vanzutphen Jr, *CFO*
Juanita Keller, *Vice Pres*
▲ EMP: 50
SQ FT: 18,000
SALES (est): 7.6MM Privately Held
WEB: www.holidayfoliage.com
SIC: 3999 Artificial trees & flowers; flowers,
artificial & preserved; wreaths, artificial

(P-23356)
HOLO INC
2461 Peralta St, Oakland (94607-1703)
PHONE..............................510 221-4177
Arian Aghababaie, *CEO*
Hal Zarem, *COO*
Hany Eitouni, *Vice Pres*
Michael Smith, *VP Opers*
Brian Adzima, *Director*
EMP: 30
SALES (est): 3MM Privately Held
SIC: 3999 Manufacturing industries

(P-23357)
HSE USA INC (PA)
5832 E 61st St, Commerce (90040-3412)
PHONE..............................323 278-0888
Nelson Yip, *President*
EMP: 10
SQ FT: 30,000
SALES (est): 3MM Privately Held
SIC: 3999 Candles

(P-23358)
HUDSON INDUSTRIES INC
Also Called: Hudson Construction
11107 Lake Blvd, Felton (95018-9800)
P.O. Box 67365, Scotts Valley (95067-
7365)
PHONE..............................831 335-4431
Nathan Hudson, *President*
EMP: 10 EST: 2011
SALES (est): 25K Privately Held
SIC: 3999 Manufacturing industries

(P-23359)
HUNTCO INDUSTRIES LLC
22536 La Quilla Dr, Chatsworth
(91311-1221)
P.O. Box 4026 (91313-4026)
PHONE..............................818 700-1600

David C Hunt, *Principal*
David Hunt, *Principal*
EMP: 11
SALES (est): 969.3K Privately Held
SIC: 3999 Manufacturing industries

(P-23360)
**HUNTER/GRATZNER
INDUSTRIES**
4107 Redwood Ave, Los Angeles
(90066-5603)
PHONE..............................310 578-9929
Ian Hunter, *President*
Shannon Gans, *CFO*
Matthew Gratzner, *Admin Sec*
EMP: 10
SQ FT: 7,500
SALES: 2MM Privately Held
WEB: www.newdealstudios.com
SIC: 3999 Models, except toy

(P-23361)
ICON LINE INC
Also Called: I.C.O.N. Salon
20600 Ventura Blvd Ste C, Woodland Hills
(91364-6691)
PHONE..............................818 709-4266
Chiara Scudieri, *President*
Michelle Lepire, *Director*
▲ EMP: 12
SQ FT: 1,800
SALES (est): 1.2MM Privately Held
WEB: www.iconproducts.com
SIC: 3999 5999 Hair, dressing of, for the
trade; hair care products

(P-23362)
**INNOVATIVE CASEWORK MFG
INC**
12261 Industry St, Garden Grove
(92841-2815)
PHONE..............................714 890-9100
Valerie Perez, *Principal*
EMP: 25 EST: 2017
SALES (est): 607.8K Privately Held
SIC: 3999 Manufacturing industries

(P-23363)
**INTEGRATED MFG SOLUTIONS
LLC**
2590 Pioneer Ave Ste C, Vista
(92081-8427)
PHONE..............................760 599-4300
EMP: 24 EST: 2007
SQ FT: 2,000
SALES (est): 3MM Privately Held
SIC: 3999

(P-23364)
INTERCONTINENTAL N MAS
Also Called: Inp
11492 Refinement Rd, Rancho Cordova
(95742-7300)
PHONE..............................916 631-1674
Lana MA, *President*
John MA, *Vice Pres*
▲ EMP: 20
SALES (est): 2.2MM Privately Held
WEB: www.intercontinentalnail.com
SIC: 3999 Fingernails, artificial

(P-23365)
**INTERNATIONAL DECORATIVES
CO**
Also Called: Koala Kountry Folage
27220 N Lake Wohlford Rd, Valley Center
(92082-6721)
P.O. Box 2064, Grand Lake CO (80447-
2064)
PHONE..............................760 749-2682
Fax: 760 749-3671
EMP: 25
SQ FT: 2,000
SALES (est): 2.4MM Privately Held
WEB: www.intdecco.com
SIC: 3999 5193

(P-23366)
INTERSTATE CABINET INC
Also Called: Interstate Design Industry
1631 Pomona Rd Ste B, Corona
(92880-6927)
PHONE..............................951 736-0777
James L Fago, *President*
Nancy Fago-Fleer, *Admin Sec*

▲ EMP: 30 EST: 1975
SQ FT: 56,000
SALES (est): 2.8MM Privately Held
WEB: www.interstatedesignind.com
SIC: 3999 Barber & beauty shop equip-
ment

(P-23367)
IRVINE & JACHENS INC
6700 Mission St, Daly City (94014-2031)
PHONE..............................650 755-4715
Richard Stegman, *President*
EMP: 10
SQ FT: 4,500
SALES (est): 739.5K Privately Held
WEB: www.irvineandjachensbadges.com
SIC: 3999 3429 3965 Badges, metal: po-
licemen, firemen, etc.; saddlery hardware;
buckles & buckle parts

(P-23368)
J & A JEFFERY INC
Also Called: Western Stabilization
395 Industrial Way Ste B, Dixon
(95620-9787)
P.O. Box 1022 (95620-1022)
PHONE..............................707 678-0369
John Jordan, *CEO*
Judy Jeffery, *President*
Ashley Jeffery, *Vice Pres*
EMP: 50
SQ FT: 16,000
SALES (est): 12.2MM Privately Held
WEB: www.wstabilization.com
SIC: 3999 0711 Custom pulverizing &
grinding of plastic materials; soil prepara-
tion services

(P-23369)
J C INDUSTRIES INC
3977 Camino Ranchero, Camarillo
(93012-5066)
PHONE..............................805 389-4040
▼ EMP: 15
SQ FT: 12,000
SALES (est): 980K Privately Held
WEB: www.jcind.com
SIC: 3999

(P-23370)
JACUZZI BRANDS LLC
Also Called: Sundance Spas
13925 City Center Dr, Chino Hills
(91709-5437)
P.O. Box 2900, Chino (91708-2900)
PHONE..............................909 606-1416
Diana Fox, *Manager*
EMP: 50 Privately Held
SIC: 3999 Hot tubs
HQ: Jacuzzi Brands Llc
13925 City Center Dr # 200
Chino Hills CA 91709
909 606-1416

(P-23371)
JNJ OPERATIONS LLC
Also Called: Jackandjillkidscom
859 E Sepulveda Blvd, Carson
(90745-6130)
PHONE..............................855 525-6545
EMP: 20
SALES (est): 504.6K Privately Held
SIC: 3999

(P-23372)
JOANN LAMMENS
Also Called: Gina T Interior Accents
2152 Bonita Ave, La Verne (91750-4915)
PHONE..............................909 593-8478
Joann Lammens, *Owner*
EMP: 12
SQ FT: 4,000
SALES (est): 1.3MM Privately Held
SIC: 3999 5193 Artificial flower arrange-
ments; artificial flowers

(P-23373)
JOE BLASCO ENTERPRISES INC
Also Called: Joe Blasco Cosmetics
1285 N Valdivia Way A, Palm Springs
(92262-5428)
PHONE..............................323 467-4949
Joseph D Blasco, *President*
▲ EMP: 52
SQ FT: 13,788

SALES (est): 3.4MM Privately Held
WEB: www.joeblasco.com
SIC: 3999 7231 2844 Barber & beauty
shop equipment; cosmetology school; toilet preparations
PA: Joe Blasco Make-Up Center West, Inc.
1285 N Valdivia Way A
Palm Springs CA 92262
323 467-4949

(P-23374)
JT MANUFACTURING INC (PA)
1122 Wrigley Way, Milpitas (95035-5418)
PHONE..............................408 674-4338
Joe V Tran, *Principal*
EMP: 12
SALES (est): 3.5MM Privately Held
SIC: 3999 Manufacturing industries

(P-23375)
JUUL LABS INC (PA)
560 20th St, San Francisco (94107-4344)
PHONE..............................415 829-2336
Kc Crosthwaite, *CEO*
Guy Cartwright, *CFO*
Charles Lam, *Manager*
EMP: 277
SALES (est): 281.8MM Privately Held
SIC: 3999 Cigarette & cigar products & ac-
cessories

(P-23376)
K-TOPS PLASTIC MFG INC
15051 Don Julian Rd, City of Industry
(91746-3302)
PHONE..............................626 575-9679
▲ EMP: 22 EST: 2005
SALES (est): 3.1MM Privately Held
SIC: 3999

(P-23377)
K9 BALLISTICS INC
708 Via Alondra, Camarillo (93012-8713)
PHONE..............................805 233-8103
Jenny Chickasawah, *Human Resources*
Sean Farley, *CEO*
EMP: 16
SQ FT: 20,000
SALES (est): 1.3MM Privately Held
SIC: 3999 Pet supplies

(P-23378)
KAHOOTS INC
6525 Bisby Lake Ave, San Diego
(92119-2600)
PHONE..............................619 337-0825
EMP: 10 Privately Held
SIC: 3999 Pet supplies
PA: Kahoots, Inc.
947 Main St
Ramona CA 92065

(P-23379)
KDR PET TREATS LLC
Also Called: Plato Pet Treats
2676 S Maple Ave, Fresno (93725-2108)
PHONE..............................559 485-4316
Bob Montgomery,
Nichole Nonini, *Mktg Dir*
Dana Montgomery,
Kent Watts,
▲ EMP: 12
SALES (est): 2.9MM Privately Held
WEB: www.platopettreats.com
SIC: 3999 Pet supplies

(P-23380)
KDS NAIL PRODUCTS
Also Called: Texchem Chemical
8580 Younger Creek Dr, Sacramento
(95828-1000)
PHONE..............................916 381-9358
Dat Vinh MA, *Principal*
▲ EMP: 13
SALES (est): 1.1MM Privately Held
SIC: 3999 2899 Fingernails, artificial;
chemical preparations; oils & essential
oils

(P-23381)
KERBER INDUSTRIES INC
166 San Lorenzo St, Pomona
(91766-2334)
PHONE..............................909 319-0877
Jeff Kerber, *President*

EMP: 22
SALES (est): 1MM Privately Held
SIC: 3999 Atomizers, toiletry

(P-23382)
KIMBALL NELSON INC
Also Called: Heaven or Las Vegas
7740 Lemona Ave, Van Nuys (91405-1136)
PHONE.............................310 636-0081
David Kip Smith, *President*
Nina Lazutin, *Vice Pres*
EMP: 15
SQ FT: 6,000
SALES: 900K Privately Held
WEB: www.rentneon.com
SIC: 3999 Theatrical scenery

(P-23383)
KITANICA MANUFACTURING
867 Newton Carey Jr Way, Oakland
(94607-1596)
PHONE.............................707 272-7286
Leonard Riccio, *Principal*
EMP: 18
SALES (est): 226.4K Privately Held
SIC: 3999 Manufacturing industries

(P-23384)
**KNORR BEESWAX PRODUCTS
INC**
14906 Via De La Valle, Del Mar
(92014-4304)
PHONE.............................760 431-2007
Steven C Knorr, *President*
Susan Prickett, *Manager*
▲ EMP: 13
SQ FT: 5,000
SALES: 900K Privately Held
WEB: www.knorrbeeswax.com
SIC: 3999 Candles

(P-23385)
KNT MANUFACTURING INC
39760 Eureka Dr, Newark (94560-4808)
PHONE.............................510 896-1699
Keith Ngo, *CEO*
Javier De La Torre, *Director*
EMP: 32
SALES (est): 6.6MM Privately Held
SIC: 3999 Barber & beauty shop equip-
ment

(P-23386)
KS INDUSTRIES
3160 Camino Del Rio S # 116, San Diego
(92108-8933)
PHONE.............................858 344-1146
Krystle Moore, *CEO*
EMP: 10 EST: 2014
SALES (est): 794.7K Privately Held
SIC: 3999 Manufacturing industries

(P-23387)
KYMERA INDUSTRIES INC
14735 Manzanita Dr, Fontana
(92335-2586)
PHONE.............................909 228-7194
Jennifer Hatch, *CEO*
EMP: 10
SALES (est): 214K Privately Held
SIC: 3999 Manufacturing industries

(P-23388)
L & B LABORATORIES INC
1660 Mabury Rd, San Jose (95133-1032)
PHONE.............................408 251-7888
Viet Le, *Principal*
EMP: 18
SALES (est): 2.1MM Privately Held
SIC: 3999 Barber & beauty shop equip-
ment

(P-23389)
LA RUTAN
Also Called: Emily's Classic Beauty Salon
6284 Long Beach Blvd, Long Beach
(90805-2160)
P.O. Box 21398 (90801-4398)
PHONE.............................310 940-7956
Emily Fields, *President*
Aleaha Fields, *Vice Pres*
▲ EMP: 20
SQ FT: 600

SALES (est): 1.5MM Privately Held
SIC: 3999 2678 2676 2842 Hair, dressing of, for the trade; wigs, including doll
wigs, toupees or wiglets; memorandum
books, notebooks & looseleaf filler paper;
sanitary paper products; specialty cleaning preparations; beauty shops

(P-23390)
LANSING INDUSTRIES INC
12671 High Bluff Dr # 150, San Diego
(92130-3018)
PHONE.............................858 523-0719
Benjamin Weiss, *Administration*
EMP: 11 EST: 2010
SALES (est): 1.1MM Privately Held
SIC: 3999 Manufacturing industries

(P-23391)
LB MANUFACTURING LLC
1403 S Coast Hwy, Oceanside
(92054-5353)
PHONE.............................413 222-2857
Eric Banach,
EMP: 10
SALES (est): 283.1K Privately Held
SIC: 3999 Manufacturing industries

(P-23392)
LEARNERS DIGEST INTL LLC
450 N Brand Blvd Ste 900, Glendale
(91203-2397)
PHONE.............................818 240-7500
Fred Studier, *CEO*
Brendan McLoughlin, *Chief Mktg Ofcr*
Lon Osmond, *Vice Pres*
John Paul Uva, *Vice Pres*
Desiree Micale, *Admin Asst*
▲ EMP: 120
SQ FT: 35,000
SALES: 12.6MM
SALES (corp-wide): 4.8B Privately Held
WEB: www.audiodigest.com
SIC: 3999 Education aids, devices & sup-
plies
HQ: Wolters Kluwer Health, Inc.
   2001 Market St Ste 5
   Philadelphia PA 19103
   215 521-8300

(P-23393)
LEARNING RESOURCES INC
Also Called: Educational Insights
152 W Walnut St Ste 201, Gardena
(90248-3147)
PHONE.............................800 995-4436
Julie Cho, *Sales Mgr*
EMP: 20
SALES (corp-wide): 30.9MM Privately
Held
SIC: 3999 3944 Education aids, devices &
supplies; games, toys & children's vehi-
cles
PA: Learning Resources, Inc.
   380 N Fairway Dr
   Vernon Hills IL 60061
   847 573-8400

(P-23394)
LEXOR INC
7400 Hazard Ave, Westminster
(92683-5031)
PHONE.............................714 444-4144
Marianna Magos, *CEO*
Christopher L Long, *President*
Sonali Bandaranayake, *Graphic Designe*
Tracy Pham, *Human Res Mgr*
Ken Tran, *Sales Associate*
▲ EMP: 90
SALES (est): 15.5MM Privately Held
SIC: 3999 Chairs, hydraulic, barber &
beauty shop

(P-23395)
LIN MAI INC
Also Called: Promotion West
6333 San Fernando Rd, Glendale
(91201-2413)
PHONE.............................818 890-1220
Michael Todd, *President*
Lynn Fliegelman, *Co-President*
▲ EMP: 30

SALES (est): 2.7MM Privately Held
WEB: www.prowest.net
SIC: 3999 3993 2542 2541 Advertising
display products; signs & advertising specialties; partitions & fixtures, except wood;
wood partitions & fixtures

(P-23396)
LINPENG INTERNATIONAL INC
1939 S Campus Ave, Ontario (91761-5410)
PHONE.............................909 923-9881
Fisher Lin, *President*
Fiona Lin, *Manager*
▲ EMP: 10
SQ FT: 3,000
SALES: 600K Privately Held
SIC: 3999 5094 Stringing beads; beads

(P-23397)
LIXIT CORPORATION (PA)
Also Called: Equitex
100 Coombs St, NAPA (94559-3941)
P.O. Box 2580 (94558-0525)
PHONE.............................800 358-8254
Linda Parks, *President*
Elizabeth Dennis, *COO*
Janette Brooks, *CFO*
Laurie Corona, *Vice Pres*
Howard Pickens, *Vice Pres*
▲ EMP: 86
SQ FT: 50,000
SALES (est): 14.6MM Privately Held
WEB: www.lixit.com
SIC: 3999 Pet supplies

(P-23398)
LNT P/M INC
11711 Monarch St, Garden Grove
(92841-1830)
PHONE.............................714 552-7245
Viktor Samarov, *President*
EMP: 10
SALES (est): 364.8K Privately Held
SIC: 3999 Manufacturing industries

(P-23399)
LOST ART LIQUIDS LLC
Also Called: Lost Art Liquids
155 W Washington Blvd, Los Angeles
(90015-3552)
PHONE.............................213 816-2988
Ryan Thomas, *CFO*
EMP: 16
SQ FT: 9,500
SALES (est): 10MM Privately Held
SIC: 3999 Cigarette & cigar products & ac-
cessories

(P-23400)
MA CHER (USA) INC (DH)
1518 Abbot Kinney Blvd, Venice
(90291-3743)
PHONE.............................310 581-5222
Derek Hydon, *President*
Martin Zoland, *Vice Pres*
▲ EMP: 12
SQ FT: 5,000
SALES (est): 1.5MM Privately Held
WEB: www.macher.com
SIC: 3999 Handbag & luggage frames &
handles

(P-23401)
MACS LIFT GATE INC (PA)
2801 E South St, Long Beach
(90805-3736)
PHONE.............................562 634-5962
Richard Mac Donald, *President*
Mike Macdonald, *CFO*
Gerald J Mac Donald, *Vice Pres*
Lawrence Mac Donald, *Vice Pres*
EMP: 25
SALES (est): 3.1MM Privately Held
SIC: 3999 5013 Wheelchair lifts; motor ve-
hicle supplies & new parts

(P-23402)
MASTER INDS WORLDWIDE LLC
1001 S Linwood Ave, Santa Ana
(92705-4323)
PHONE.............................949 660-0644
Barbara Johnson, *Mng Member*
▲ EMP: 11
SALES (est): 1.3MM Privately Held
SIC: 3999 2426 Manufacturing industries;
blanks, wood: bowling pins, handles, etc.

(P-23403)
**MCCALLS COUNTRY CANNING
INC (PA)**
41735 Cherry St, Murrieta (92562-9186)
P.O. Box 1375 (92564-1375)
PHONE.............................951 461-2277
EMP: 15
SQ FT: 40,000
SALES (est): 1.3MM Privately Held
WEB: www.mccallscandles.com
SIC: 3999 Candles

(P-23404)
MEDIC IDS
Also Called: Medic I D'S Internatl
20350 Ventura Blvd # 140, Woodland Hills
(91364-2484)
PHONE.............................818 705-0595
Michael Silverstein, *Owner*
EMP: 10
SQ FT: 2,000
SALES (est): 846.2K Privately Held
WEB: www.medicid.com
SIC: 3999 Identification tags, except paper

(P-23405)
**MEDICAL BREAKTHROUGH
MASSAGE**
28016 Industry Dr, Valencia (91355-4191)
PHONE.............................408 677-7702
Max Lun, *CEO*
Patrick O'Malley, *Opers Mgr*
EMP: 21
SQ FT: 40,000
SALES: 12MM Privately Held
SIC: 3999 Massage machines, electric:
barber & beauty shops

(P-23406)
MEGIDDO GLOBAL LLC
153 W Rosecrans Ave, Gardena
(90248-1829)
PHONE.............................818 267-6686
Omer Nissani,
EMP: 10
SALES (est): 342.6K Privately Held
SIC: 3999 Manufacturing industries

(P-23407)
MELLO SALES GROUP INC
141a Silverado Trl, NAPA (94559-4017)
PHONE.............................707 257-6451
James S Mello, *CEO*
Kevin Mello, *President*
Julie Hutchings, *Vice Pres*
EMP: 10
SALES (est): 503.6K Privately Held
SIC: 3999 Pet supplies

(P-23408)
MERCADO LATINO INC
Continental Candle Company
1420 W Walnut St, Compton (90220-5013)
PHONE.............................310 537-1062
Andy Sly, *Engineer*
EMP: 40
SALES (corp-wide): 227.6MM Privately
Held
WEB: www.mercadolatinoinc.com
SIC: 3999 3641 7699 3645 Candles;
electric lamps; restaurant equipment re-
pair; residential lighting fixtures
PA: Mercado Latino, Inc.
   245 Baldwin Park Blvd
   City Of Industry CA 91746
   626 333-6862

(P-23409)
MFI INC
363 San Miguel Dr Ste 200, Newport Beach
(92660-7891)
PHONE.............................949 887-8691
Steven Bandawat, *Principal*
▲ EMP: 12 EST: 2014
SALES (est): 1.1MM Privately Held
SIC: 3999 Manufacturing industries

(P-23410)
**MGR DESIGN INTERNATIONAL
INC**
1950 Williams Dr, Oxnard (93036-2695)
PHONE.............................805 981-6400
Michelle Bechard, *CEO*
Rony Havive, *President*
Anne Morreghan, *Director*

▲ = Import ▼ =Export
◆ =Import/Export

◆ **EMP:** 200
SQ FT: 80,000
SALES (est): 28.3MM **Privately Held**
SIC: 3999 Potpourri; candles

(P-23411)
MICHAELS STORES INC
15228 Summit Ave, Fontana (92336-0231)
PHONE..................................909 646-9656
Judy Jauregui, *General Mgr*
EMP: 34
SALES (corp-wide): 5.2B **Publicly Held**
SIC: 3999 Barber & beauty shop equipment
HQ: Michaels Stores, Inc.
8000 Bent Branch Dr
Irving TX 75063
972 409-1300

(P-23412)
MID VALLEY GRINDING CO INC
616 Irving Ave, Glendale (91201-2029)
PHONE..................................818 764-1086
Anthony Cagno, *President*
Don Schumacher, *Vice Pres*
EMP: 12
SALES: 973.9K **Privately Held**
SIC: 3999 3469 Custom pulverizing & grinding of plastic materials; machine parts, stamped or pressed metal

(P-23413)
MINO INDUSTRY USA INC (PA)
38 Executive Park Ste 250, Irvine
(92614-4747)
PHONE..................................949 943-8070
Jun Sugimoto, *CEO*
Koji Toyota, *CFO*
Toyota Koji, *Principal*
EMP: 12
SALES (est): 3MM **Privately Held**
SIC: 3999 Atomizers, toiletry

(P-23414)
MOBILITY SPECIALISTS INC
490 Capricorn St, Brea (92821-3203)
PHONE..................................714 674-0480
Vince Fabozzi, *President*
Steve Duncan, *General Mgr*
EMP: 10
SALES (corp-wide): 3.4MM **Privately Held**
WEB: www.mobilityspecialists.net
SIC: 3999 Wheelchair lifts
PA: The Mobility Specialists Inc
4040 Sorrento Valley Blvd
San Diego CA 92121
858 450-9589

(P-23415)
MOSAIC BRANDS INC
Also Called: Hair ACC By Mia Minnelli
3266 Buskirk Ave, Pleasant Hill
(94523-4315)
P.O. Box 585, Alamo (94507-0585)
PHONE..................................925 322-8700
Mia Minnelli, *President*
▲ **EMP:** 25
SQ FT: 20,000
SALES (est): 1.6MM **Privately Held**
SIC: 3999 3069 Hair & hair-based products; rubber hair accessories

(P-23416)
MOTHER PLUCKER FEATHER CO INC
2511 W 3rd St Ste 102, Los Angeles
(90057-1946)
P.O. Box 57160 (90057-0160)
PHONE..................................213 637-0411
William Zelowitz, *President*
Steven Landerth, *CEO*
Lelan Berner, *Production*
EMP: 11
SQ FT: 16,000
SALES (est): 1.4MM **Privately Held**
WEB: www.motherplucker.com
SIC: 3999 5159 Trimmings, feather; feathers

(P-23417)
MULTIS INC
766 S 12th St, San Jose (95112-2304)
PHONE..................................510 441-2653
Sean Keenan, *President*
Stan Wilkison, *Vice Pres*

EMP: 50
SALES (est): 3.2MM **Privately Held**
SIC: 3999 Atomizers, toiletry

(P-23418)
NAILS 2000 INTERNATIONAL INC
10892 Forbes Ave Ste A2, Garden Grove
(92843-6505)
PHONE..................................714 265-1983
MAI Vo, *President*
▲ **EMP:** 16
SQ FT: 11,000
SALES (est): 2MM **Privately Held**
WEB: www.nails2000.com
SIC: 3999 Fingernails, artificial

(P-23419)
NAPA INDUSTRIES INC
1379 Beckwith Ave, Los Angeles
(90049-3615)
PHONE..................................310 293-1209
Amir Ali Jandaghi, *CEO*
EMP: 10
SALES (est): 1MM **Privately Held**
SIC: 3999 Atomizers, toiletry

(P-23420)
NATO LLC
38 Laurel Mountain Rd, Mammoth Lakes
(93546-6007)
P.O. Box 1415 (93546-1415)
PHONE..................................760 934-8677
Charles Byrne, *Co-Owner*
Jose Luis Andreu, *Co-Owner*
▲ **EMP:** 50
SQ FT: 3,000
SALES (est): 3.1MM **Privately Held**
SIC: 3999 Pet supplies

(P-23421)
NATURE ZONE PET PRODUCTS
265 Boeing Ave, Chico (95973-9003)
PHONE..................................530 343-5199
Fern Benson, *Owner*
EMP: 23
SQ FT: 10,000
SALES (est): 500K **Privately Held**
WEB: www.naturezonepet.com
SIC: 3999 Pet supplies

(P-23422)
NATUREMAKER INC
6225 El Camino Real, Carlsbad
(92009-1604)
PHONE..................................760 438-4244
Gary Hanick, *President*
Bennett Abrams, *Vice Pres*
EMP: 30
SQ FT: 40,000
SALES (est): 4.1MM **Privately Held**
WEB: www.naturemaker.com
SIC: 3999 Artificial trees & flowers

(P-23423)
NESTLE PURINA PETCARE COMPANY
Also Called: Nestle Purina Factory
1710 Golden Cat Rd, Maricopa (93252)
PHONE..................................661 769-8261
Mike Ashmore, *Manager*
Dave Brown, *General Mgr*
Ruth Jared, *Administration*
Paula Harris, *Human Res Dir*
EMP: 60
SALES (corp-wide): 92B **Privately Held**
SIC: 3999 Pet supplies
HQ: Nestle Purina Petcare Company
1 Checkerboard Sq
Saint Louis MO 63164
314 982-1000

(P-23424)
NEW DIMENSION ONE SPAS INC (DH)
1819 Aston Ave Ste 105, Carlsbad
(92008-7338)
PHONE..................................800 345-7727
Robert Hallam, *President*
Linda Hallam, *Ch of Bd*
Terry Hauser, *Vice Pres*
Phil Sandner, *Vice Pres*
Sam Sims, *Vice Pres*
◆ **EMP:** 160
SQ FT: 125,000

SALES (est): 23.7MM **Privately Held**
WEB: www.d1spas.com
SIC: 3999 3088 Hot tubs; plastics plumbing fixtures
HQ: Jacuzzi Brands Llc
13925 City Center Dr # 200
Chino Hills CA 91709
909 606-1416

(P-23425)
NEW METHOD FUR DRESSING CO
131 Beacon St, South San Francisco
(94080-6985)
PHONE..................................650 583-9881
Charles Crocker, *President*
Moe Malek, *Vice Pres*
EMP: 30
SQ FT: 22,000
SALES (est): 1.9MM **Privately Held**
SIC: 3999 3111 Furs, dressed: bleached, curried, scraped, tanned or dyed; leather tanning & finishing

(P-23426)
NEWTEX INDUSTRIES INC
Also Called: Thermostatic Industries
9654 Hermosa Ave, Rancho Cucamonga
(91730-5812)
PHONE..................................323 277-0900
Jerry Joliet, *Principal*
Sudhakar Dixit, *Principal*
Jerome Joliet, *Principal*
EMP: 75 EST: 2016
SALES (est): 2.1MM **Privately Held**
SIC: 3999 Manufacturing industries

(P-23427)
NFI INDUSTRIES
11888 Mission Blvd, Jurupa Valley
(91752-1003)
PHONE..................................951 681-6455
EMP: 13 EST: 2017
SALES (est): 1.4MM **Privately Held**
SIC: 3999 Atomizers, toiletry

(P-23428)
NORMAL CENTRIX INC
14101 Valleyheart Dr # 104, Sherman Oaks
(91423-2885)
PHONE..................................310 715-9977
Jay Wilder, *CEO*
EMP: 11
SQ FT: 1,200
SALES: 1.5MM **Privately Held**
SIC: 3999 Education aids, devices & supplies

(P-23429)
NORTH VALLEY CANDLE MOLDS
6928 Danyeur Rd, Redding (96001-5343)
PHONE..................................530 247-0447
Don Sletner, *Partner*
Robert Irving, *Partner*
Barbara Sletner, *Partner*
▼ **EMP:** 20
SQ FT: 5,000
SALES (est): 1.6MM **Privately Held**
WEB: www.moldman.com
SIC: 3999 3544 Candles; special dies, tools, jigs & fixtures

(P-23430)
NU VISIONS DE MEXICO SA DE CV
9355 Airway Rd, San Diego (92154-7931)
PHONE..................................619 987-0518
▲ **EMP:** 160
SALES (est): 9.8MM **Privately Held**
SIC: 3999

(P-23431)
OLD AN INC
17651 Armstrong Ave, Irvine (92614-5727)
PHONE..................................949 263-1400
Tina Rocca-Lundstrom, *President*
Tina Rocca Lundstrom, *President*
Steven Lundstrom, *Vice Pres*
◆ **EMP:** 30
SQ FT: 15,000
SALES (est): 2.5MM **Privately Held**
WEB: www.aromanaturals.com
SIC: 3999 Candles

(P-23432)
OPTIMIZED FUEL TECHNOLOGIES
Also Called: Optec
5858 Dryden Pl Ste 238, Carlsbad
(92008-6518)
PHONE..................................760 444-5556
Henry Delaune, *Principal*
EMP: 12
SALES (est): 362.6K **Privately Held**
SIC: 3999 Manufacturing industries

(P-23433)
ORIENTAL ODYSSEYS INC
Also Called: O O Campbell
14557 Griffith St, San Leandro
(94577-6703)
PHONE..................................510 357-6100
Sylvia White, *President*
Paul Fisher, *Vice Pres*
EMP: 30
SQ FT: 10,000
SALES (est): 2.3MM **Privately Held**
WEB: www.orientalodysseys.com
SIC: 3999 Candles

(P-23434)
ORIGIN LLC (HQ)
119 E Graham Pl, Burbank (91502-2028)
PHONE..................................818 848-1648
Craig Lutes, *CEO*
John L Alvarez,
▲ **EMP:** 35
SQ FT: 25,000
SALES (est): 13.5MM
SALES (corp-wide): 80MM **Privately Held**
WEB: www.originpop.com
SIC: 3999 Advertising display products
PA: Ideal Box Co.
4800 S Austin Ave
Chicago IL 60638
708 594-3100

(P-23435)
ORTEGA MANUFACTURING INC
3960 Industrial Ave, Hemet (92545-9790)
P.O. Box 959, Wildomar (92595-0959)
PHONE..................................951 766-9363
Tony Ortega, *President*
Cindy Ortega, *Vice Pres*
EMP: 12
SQ FT: 12,000
SALES: 800K **Privately Held**
SIC: 3999 Novelties, bric-a-brac & hobby kits

(P-23436)
OSI INDUSTRIES LLC
1155 Mt Vernon Ave, Riverside
(92507-1830)
PHONE..................................951 684-4500
Holly Botos, *CIO*
Gary Born, *Controller*
Edlin Herrera, *Receptionist*
Susie Miller, *Assistant*
Martin Garcia, *Supervisor*
▲ **EMP:** 26
SALES (est): 3.9MM **Privately Held**
SIC: 3999 Atomizers, toiletry

(P-23437)
OWEN MAGIC SUPREME INC
734 N Mckeever Ave, Azusa (91702-2394)
PHONE..................................626 969-4519
Leslie Smith, *President*
EMP: 19
SQ FT: 12,000
SALES: 200K **Privately Held**
WEB: www.owenmagic.com
SIC: 3999 Magic equipment, supplies & props

(P-23438)
PACIFIC LASERTEC INC
3821 Sienna St, Oceanside (92056-7283)
PHONE..................................760 450-4095
Lynn Strickland, *President*
EMP: 20
SQ FT: 19,000
SALES (est): 578.7K **Privately Held**
SIC: 3999 Barber & beauty shop equipment

(P-23439)
PACIFIC SUNSHINE ENTERPRISES
857 Gray Ave Ste B, Yuba City (95991-3652)
PHONE..................530 673-1888
Billie Fa-Chun Lo, *President*
Shirley Chou, *Vice Pres*
▲ EMP: 11 EST: 1974
SQ FT: 10,000
SALES (est): 1.1MM **Privately Held**
SIC: 3999 Flowers, artificial & preserved

(P-23440)
PACIFIC TESTTRONICS INC
5983 Smithway St, Commerce (90040-1607)
PHONE..................323 721-1077
William Hartfield, *Principal*
Patrick Bowers, *Shareholder*
Paul Huff, *Shareholder*
James Hartfield, *Treasurer*
EMP: 10
SALES: 88K **Privately Held**
WEB: www.hkfinc.com
SIC: 3999 Barber & beauty shop equipment

(P-23441)
PACMIN INCORPORATED (PA)
Also Called: Pacific Miniatures
2021 Raymer Ave, Fullerton (92833-2664)
PHONE..................714 447-4478
Frederick Ouweleen Jr, *President*
Flora Ouweleen, *Treasurer*
Daniel Ouweleen, *Exec VP*
Tracy Campbell, *Executive*
Tom Toomey, *Director*
▲ EMP: 96
SQ FT: 35,400
SALES (est): 13.5MM **Privately Held**
SIC: 3999 Models, general, except toy

(P-23442)
PARADIGM CONTRACT MFG LLC
5531 Belle Ave, Cypress (90630-4550)
PHONE..................714 889-7074
Scott Penin, *Partner*
Faith Stancliff, *Partner*
EMP: 15
SALES: 1.5MM **Privately Held**
SIC: 3999 Atomizers, toiletry

(P-23443)
PARYLENE USA INC
23 Spectrum Pointe Dr # 201, Lake Forest (92630-2272)
PHONE..................949 452-0770
David Stiles, *President*
EMP: 10 EST: 2017
SALES (est): 283.1K **Privately Held**
SIC: 3999 Manufacturing industries

(P-23444)
PDMA VENTURES INC
22951 La Palma Ave, Yorba Linda (92887-6701)
PHONE..................714 777-8770
Charles Platt, *President*
EMP: 35
SALES: 5MM **Privately Held**
SIC: 3999 Manufacturing industries

(P-23445)
PENINSULA PACKAGING LLC (DH)
Also Called: Peninsula Packaging Company
1030 N Anderson Rd, Exeter (93221-9341)
PHONE..................559 594-6813
John McKernan, *CEO*
Mark Kubishta, *Project Mgr*
Jamie Fife, *Technology*
Stephen Day, *VP Opers*
▲ EMP: 70
SALES (est): 117.7MM **Privately Held**
SALES (corp-wide): 5.3B **Publicly Held**
WEB: www.penpack.net
SIC: 3999 3085 Atomizers, toiletry; plastics bottles
HQ: Sonoco Plastics, Inc.
1 N 2nd St
Hartsville SC 29550
843 383-7000

(P-23446)
PET PARTNERS INC (PA)
Also Called: North American Pet Products
450 N Sheridan St, Corona (92880-2020)
PHONE..................951 279-9888
Keith Bonner, *CEO*
Ronald Bonner, *President*
Gloria Bonner, *Admin Sec*
Gordan Thulemeyer, *VP Sales*
▲ EMP: 170
SQ FT: 120,000
SALES: 35MM **Privately Held**
SIC: 3999 Pet supplies

(P-23447)
PETSPORT USA INC
1160 Railroad Ave, Pittsburg (94565-2642)
PHONE..................925 439-9243
Eden Hass, *CEO*
Eden G Hass, *CEO*
Erick Gonzalez, *Research*
Bret Ballinger, *QC Mgr*
▲ EMP: 14 EST: 1995
SQ FT: 18,000
SALES: 6MM **Privately Held**
WEB: www.petsportusa.com
SIC: 3999 Pet supplies

(P-23448)
PHIARO INCORPORATED
9016 Research Dr, Irvine (92618-4215)
PHONE..................949 727-1261
Takeichiro Iwasaki, *President*
Takuya Nishimura, *Exec Dir*
Tajima Wakako, *Sales Executive*
Yosuke Inoue, *Manager*
▲ EMP: 32
SQ FT: 35,000
SALES: 6MM **Privately Held**
SIC: 3999 Models, general, except toy
PA: Phiaro Corporation, Inc.
8-2-3, Nobitome
Niiza STM 352-0
-

(P-23449)
PIERCO INCORPORATED
680 Main St, Riverside (92501-1034)
PHONE..................909 251-7100
Erik Flemming, *CEO*
John Caron, *Managing Dir*
EMP: 15
SALES (est): 1.5MM **Privately Held**
SIC: 3999 3089 Beekeepers' supplies; air mattresses, plastic

(P-23450)
POMMES FRITES CANDLE CO
Also Called: Pf Candle Co
7300 E Slauson Ave, Commerce (90040-3627)
PHONE..................213 488-2016
Kristen Pumphrey, *CEO*
Thomas Neuberger, *General Mgr*
EMP: 30
SALES (est): 373.5K **Privately Held**
SIC: 3999 5149 5199 5999 Candles; flavourings & fragrances; candles; candle shops

(P-23451)
PRIDE INDUSTRIES ONE INC
10030 Foothills Blvd, Roseville (95747-7102)
P.O. Box 1200, Rocklin (95677-7200)
PHONE..................916 788-2100
Michael Ziegler, *CEO*
Pete Berghuis, *COO*
Jeff Dern, *CFO*
EMP: 4300
SALES (est): 228.8MM
SALES (corp-wide): 290.6MM **Privately Held**
SIC: 3999 Barber & beauty shop equipment
PA: Pride Industries
10030 Foothills Blvd
Roseville CA 95747
916 788-2100

(P-23452)
PRIMARCH MANUFACTURING INC
1211 Liberty Way, Vista (92081-8307)
PHONE..................760 730-8572
Douglas Smith, *CEO*

Jack Hartmann, *Manager*
EMP: 10
SALES (est): 1.5MM **Privately Held**
SIC: 3999 Boutiquing: decorating gift items with sequins, fruit, etc.

(P-23453)
PROJEX INTERNATIONAL INC
9555 Hierba Rd, Santa Clarita (91390-4564)
PHONE..................661 268-0999
Richard Graham, *President*
Evan Greenberg, *Principal*
EMP: 15
SALES (est): 1.3MM **Privately Held**
SIC: 3999 Theatrical scenery

(P-23454)
PRYSM INC (PA)
180 Baytech Dr Ste 200, San Jose (95134-2304)
PHONE..................408 586-1100
Amit Jain, *President*
Don Williams, *President*
Jasbir Singh, *CFO*
Paige O'Neill, *Chief Mktg Ofcr*
Tushar Kothari, *Exec VP*
▲ EMP: 70
SQ FT: 25,000
SALES (est): 35.1MM **Privately Held**
SIC: 3999 Advertising display products

(P-23455)
QUALITY RESOURCES DIST LLC
16254 Beaver Rd, Adelanto (92301-3906)
PHONE..................510 378-6861
Wesley Staley, *Mng Member*
EMP: 21 EST: 2018
SALES (est): 1.1MM **Privately Held**
SIC: 3999

(P-23456)
RADA INDUSTRY
1060 S Ditman Ave, Los Angeles (90023-2405)
PHONE..................323 265-3727
Bassam Rada El Reda, *Principal*
EMP: 10
SALES (est): 1.4MM **Privately Held**
SIC: 3999 Manufacturing industries

(P-23457)
RAPID MANUFACTURING (PA)
9724 Eton Ave, Chatsworth (91311-4305)
PHONE..................818 899-4377
EMP: 14
SALES (est): 4.2MM **Privately Held**
SIC: 3999 Barber & beauty shop equipment

(P-23458)
RARE ELEMENTS HAIR CARE
Also Called: Amato Beverly Hills
8950 W Olympic Blvd 641, Beverly Hills (90211-3561)
PHONE..................310 277-6524
John Amato, *Owner*
EMP: 10
SALES: 300K **Privately Held**
SIC: 3999 Hair & hair-based products

(P-23459)
REEL EFX INC
5539 Riverton Ave, North Hollywood (91601-2816)
PHONE..................818 762-1710
Jim Gill, *President*
Rosy Romano, *CFO*
Susan Gill, *Vice Pres*
Susan Milliken, *Vice Pres*
EMP: 25
SQ FT: 34,000
SALES: 2.7MM **Privately Held**
WEB: www.reelefx.com
SIC: 3999 Stage hardware & equipment, except lighting

(P-23460)
RELAX MEDICAL SYSTEMS INC
Also Called: RMS
3260 E Willow St, Signal Hill (90755-2309)
PHONE..................800 405-7677
Leon Press, *CEO*
◆ EMP: 15

SALES (est): 1MM **Privately Held**
SIC: 3999 5083 5261 Hydroponic equipment; hydroponic equipment & supplies; hydroponic equipment & supplies

(P-23461)
RESQ MANUFACTURING
11365 Sunrise Park Dr # 200, Rancho Cordova (95742-6556)
PHONE..................916 638-6786
Martin Szegedy, *CEO*
EMP: 45 EST: 2012
SALES: 4.7MM **Privately Held**
SIC: 3999 Airplane models, except toy

(P-23462)
RICON CORP (HQ)
1135 Aviation Pl, San Fernando (91340-1460)
PHONE..................818 267-3000
William Baldwin, *President*
Raymond T Betler, *CEO*
Dave Chaimwitz, *CFO*
Stanton Saucier, *Vice Pres*
Jason Moore, *General Mgr*
◆ EMP: 105 EST: 1971
SQ FT: 225,000
SALES (est): 22.2MM
SALES (corp-wide): 4.3B **Publicly Held**
WEB: www.riconcorp.com
SIC: 3999 Wheelchair lifts
PA: Westinghouse Air Brake Technologies Corporation
30 Isabella St
Pittsburgh PA 15212
412 825-1000

(P-23463)
ROLENN MANUFACTURING INC
1549 Marlborough Ave, Riverside (92507-2029)
PHONE..................951 682-1185
Thomas Accatino, *Principal*
EMP: 20
SALES (corp-wide): 6MM **Privately Held**
SIC: 3999 Atomizers, toiletry
PA: Rolenn Manufacturing, Inc.
2065 Roberta St
Riverside CA 92507
951 682-1185

(P-23464)
RUCCI INC
6700 11th Ave, Los Angeles (90043-4730)
PHONE..................323 778-9000
Ramin Lavian, *President*
Elsie Lavian, *Vice Pres*
▲ EMP: 19
SQ FT: 17,000
SALES (est): 2.3MM **Privately Held**
WEB: www.rucci.com
SIC: 3999 5087 Barber & beauty shop equipment; beauty parlor equipment & supplies

(P-23465)
SAN DIEGO AFR AMRCN GNLOGY RSC
5148 Market St, San Diego (92114-2209)
P.O. Box 740240 (92174-0240)
PHONE..................619 231-5810
Margaret Lewis, *Principal*
Felix Green, *Principal*
EMP: 45
SALES (est): 1.3MM **Privately Held**
SIC: 3999 Education aids, devices & supplies

(P-23466)
SAUNDERS MANUFACTURING SVCS
15330 Fairfield Ranch Rd G, Chino Hills (91709-8823)
P.O. Box 10 (91709-0001)
PHONE..................714 961-8492
Dennis Saunders, *President*
▼ EMP: 10
SQ FT: 10,000
SALES (est): 1MM **Privately Held**
WEB: www.smsproducts.com
SIC: 3999 Advertising display products

▲ = Import ▼=Export
◆ =Import/Export

(P-23467)
SCAFCO CORPORATION
Also Called: Scafco Steel Stud Mfg
2177 Jerrold Ave, San Francisco
(94124-1009)
PHONE..................................415 852-7974
EMP: 18
SALES (corp-wide): 160.5MM **Privately Held**
SIC: 3999 Barber & beauty shop equipment
PA: Scafco Corporation
2800 E Main Ave
Spokane WA 99202
509 343-9000

(P-23468)
SCAFCO CORPORATION
2525 S Airport Way, Stockton
(95206-3521)
PHONE..................................209 670-8053
Erick King, Branch Mgr
EMP: 36
SALES (corp-wide): 160.5MM **Privately Held**
SIC: 3999 Barber & beauty shop equipment
PA: Scafco Corporation
2800 E Main Ave
Spokane WA 99202
509 343-9000

(P-23469)
SCHWARZKOPF INC (DH)
600 Corporate Pointe # 400, Culver City
(90230-7681)
PHONE..................................310 641-0990
Hans C Schwarzkopf, President
Heinz Bieler, President
◆ EMP: 20
SQ FT: 5,566
SALES (est): 8.3MM
SALES (corp-wide): 22.7B **Privately Held**
WEB: www.hansschwarzkopf.com
SIC: 3999 5122 Barber & beauty shop equipment; hair preparations
HQ: Henkel Us Operations Corporation
1 Henkel Way
Rocky Hill CT 06067
860 571-5100

(P-23470)
SCOR INDUSTRIES
2321 S Willow Ave, Bloomington
(92316-2972)
PHONE..................................909 820-5046
EMP: 13
SALES (est): 1.6MM **Privately Held**
SIC: 3999 Manufacturing industries

(P-23471)
SCRIPTO-TOKAI CORPORATION (DH)
2055 S Haven Ave, Ontario (91761-0736)
PHONE..................................909 930-5000
Tomoyuki Kurata, President
Tokiharu Murofushi, CFO
Fred Ashley, Admin Sec
▲ EMP: 80
SQ FT: 120,000
SALES (est): 10.4MM **Privately Held**
WEB: www.scriptousa.com
SIC: 3999 3951 Cigarette lighters, except precious metal; ball point pens & parts; fountain pens & fountain pen desk sets; pencils & pencil parts, mechanical

(P-23472)
SEGA OF AMERICA INC (DH)
6400 Oak Cyn Ste 100, Irvine
(92618-5204)
PHONE..................................949 788-0455
Tatsuyuki Miyazaki, CEO
Hayao Nakayama, Ch of Bd
Ian Curran, President
Howell Ivy, President
Yukio Aoyama, Senior VP
▲ EMP: 45
SQ FT: 9,000
SALES: 144MM **Privately Held**
SIC: 3999 5092 Coin-operated amusement machines; video games

(P-23473)
SENTIMENTS INC (PA)
Also Called: Best Friends By Sheri
5635 Smithway St, Commerce
(90040-1545)
PHONE..................................323 843-2080
Shohreh Dadbin, CEO
John Dadbin, Treasurer
Benjamin Dadbin, Vice Pres
Diana Hernandez, Executive Asst
▲ EMP: 15
SALES (est): 5.1MM **Privately Held**
SIC: 3999 Pet supplies

(P-23474)
SGPS INC
Also Called: Show Group Production Services
15823 S Main St, Gardena (90248-2548)
PHONE..................................310 538-4175
Barrie Owen, CEO
Mike Estill, General Mgr
Katy Marx, General Mgr
Jesse Sugimoto, Project Mgr
EMP: 85
SQ FT: 40,000
SALES (est): 14.5MM **Privately Held**
WEB: www.sgps.net
SIC: 3999 Theatrical scenery

(P-23475)
SHELLPRO INC
18378 Atkins Rd, Lodi (95240-9649)
P.O. Box 2680 (95241-2680)
PHONE..................................209 334-2081
Calvin Suess, President
Virgil Suess, Vice Pres
Beth McCarty, Bookkeeper
EMP: 30
SQ FT: 225,000
SALES (est): 347K **Privately Held**
WEB: www.shellpro.net
SIC: 3999 Nut shells, grinding, from purchased nuts

(P-23476)
SILVESTRI STUDIO INC (PA)
Also Called: Silvester California
8125 Beach St, Los Angeles (90001-3426)
P.O. Box 512198 (90051-0198)
PHONE..................................323 277-4420
E Alain Levi, CEO
▲ EMP: 80
SQ FT: 130,000
SALES (est): 16.7MM **Privately Held**
SIC: 3999 2542 3993 Mannequins; office & store showcases & display fixtures; signs & advertising specialties

(P-23477)
SKY GLOBAL SERVICES INC
23 Corporate Plaza Dr # 100, Newport Beach (92660-7942)
PHONE..................................949 291-5511
William Harrison, CEO
EMP: 10
SALES: 500K **Privately Held**
SIC: 3999 Manufacturing industries

(P-23478)
SMALL WNDERS HNDCRFTED MNTURES
7033 Canoga Ave Ste 5, Canoga Park
(91303-3118)
PHONE..................................818 703-7450
Zarin Huda, President
Omar Huda, Vice Pres
EMP: 15
SALES (est): 1MM **Privately Held**
SIC: 3999 Miniatures

(P-23479)
SOCIAL BRANDS LLC
6575 Simson St, Oakland (94605-2271)
PHONE..................................415 728-1761
Benjamin Seabury, Mng Member
EMP: 20
SALES (est): 544.3K **Privately Held**
SIC: 3999 Manufacturing industries

(P-23480)
SOFTUB INC (PA)
24700 Avenue Rockefeller, Valencia
(91355-3465)
PHONE..................................858 602-1920
Tom Thornbury, Chairman

Joe Ellard, District Mgr
Inez Frank, Technology
Lisa Decanio, Asst Controller
Monica Montoya, Human Resources
▲ EMP: 85
SALES (est): 31.9MM **Privately Held**
WEB: www.softub.com
SIC: 3999 Hot tubs

(P-23481)
SPA LA LA INC
Also Called: Making Scents
21430 Strathern St Unit I, Canoga Park
(91304-4183)
PHONE..................................605 321-1276
Edith Sullivan, President
EMP: 12
SQ FT: 1,800
SALES (est): 920K **Privately Held**
SIC: 3999 Heating pads, nonelectric

(P-23482)
SPECTRUM BRANDS INC
Also Called: United Pet Group
5144 N Commerce Ave Ste A, Moorpark
(93021-7135)
PHONE..................................805 222-3611
EMP: 107
SALES (corp-wide): 3.1B **Publicly Held**
SIC: 3999 Pet supplies
HQ: Spectrum Brands, Inc.
3001 Deming Way
Middleton WI 53562
608 275-3340

(P-23483)
SPRAGG INDUSTRIES INC
20049 Crestview Dr, Canyon Country
(91351-5754)
PHONE..................................661 424-9673
Melinda Spragg, CEO
EMP: 10
SALES (est): 1.1MM **Privately Held**
SIC: 3999 Barber & beauty shop equipment

(P-23484)
STANG INDUSTRIES INC
Also Called: Stang Industrial Products
2616 Research Dr Ste B, Corona
(92882-6978)
PHONE..................................714 556-0222
Charles Stang, CEO
Abdul Kashif, CFO
▲ EMP: 19
SQ FT: 20,000
SALES (est): 2.9MM **Privately Held**
WEB: www.stangindustrial.com
SIC: 3999 3492 3561 Fire extinguishers, portable; control valves, aircraft: hydraulic & pneumatic; pumps & pumping equipment

(P-23485)
STEELDECK INC
13147 S Western Ave, Gardena
(90249-1921)
PHONE..................................323 290-2100
Phil Parsons, President
Adrian Funnell, Vice Pres
Pete Varela, MIS Dir
▲ EMP: 25
SALES (est): 4.3MM **Privately Held**
WEB: www.steeldeck.com
SIC: 3999 2541 2531 Stage hardware & equipment, except lighting; partitions for floor attachment, prefabricated: wood; theater furniture

(P-23486)
SUBLIME MACHINING INC
2537 Willow St, Oakland (94607-1723)
PHONE..................................858 349-2445
Alexander Fang, Principal
EMP: 21
SALES (est): 2.7MM **Privately Held**
SIC: 3999 5159 7699 ; ; industrial machinery & equipment repair

(P-23487)
SUN BADGE CO
2248 S Baker Ave, Ontario (91761-7710)
PHONE..................................909 930-1444
Rick Hamilton, President
Chris Hamilton, Vice Pres
Ed Killoren, Executive

Benjamin Dawson, Marketing Staff
▲ EMP: 35
SQ FT: 24,000
SALES (est): 3.9MM **Privately Held**
WEB: www.sunbadgeco.com
SIC: 3999 Badges, metal: policemen, firemen, etc.

(P-23488)
SUN VALLEY FLORAL GROUP LLC
3160 Upper Bay Rd, Arcata (95521-9690)
PHONE..................................707 826-8700
Lane Devries, CEO
Doug Dobecki, Manager
▲ EMP: 750
SALES (est): 72.9MM **Privately Held**
SIC: 3999 Flowers, artificial & preserved

(P-23489)
SUNDANCE SPAS INC (DH)
13925 City Center Dr # 200, Chino Hills
(91709-5437)
PHONE..................................909 606-7733
Bob Rowan, CEO
Jonathan Clark, Principal
Paul V Slyke, VP Finance
Maggy Mendoza, Buyer
◆ EMP: 60
SALES (est): 21.3MM **Privately Held**
SIC: 3999 1799 5999 Hot tubs; swimming pool construction; spas & hot tubs
HQ: Jacuzzi Brands Llc
13925 City Center Dr # 200
Chino Hills CA 91709
909 606-1416

(P-23490)
SUNDERSTORM LLC
1146 N Central Ave, Glendale
(91202-2506)
PHONE..................................818 605-6682
Cameron Clark, CEO
Keith Cich, President
EMP: 17
SALES (est): 1.3MM **Privately Held**
SIC: 3999

(P-23491)
SUNFUSION ENERGY SYSTEMS INC
9020 Kenamar Dr Ste 204, San Diego
(92121-2431)
PHONE..................................800 544-0282
Walter Ellard, Principal
EMP: 20
SALES (est): 504.6K **Privately Held**
SIC: 3999 Manufacturing industries

(P-23492)
SUNSTAR SPA COVERS INC (HQ)
26074 Avenue Hall Ste 13, Valencia
(91355-3445)
PHONE..................................858 602-1950
Tom Thornbury, Ch of Bd
Edward McGarry, President
▲ EMP: 40
SALES (est): 15.9MM
SALES (corp-wide): 31.9MM **Privately Held**
WEB: www.spatop.com
SIC: 3999 Hot tub & spa covers
PA: Softub, Inc.
24700 Avenue Rockefeller
Valencia CA 91355
858 602-1920

(P-23493)
SUPERIOR-STUDIO SPC INC
2239 Yates Ave, Commerce (90040-1913)
PHONE..................................323 278-0100
Jean-Pierre Fournier, President
Lauren Ward, Sales Staff
◆ EMP: 20
SQ FT: 60,000
SALES (est): 2.4MM **Privately Held**
SIC: 3999 Advertising display products

(P-23494)
SUTTONS FOREST PRODUCTS
8222 Hallwood Blvd, Marysville
(95901-9406)
P.O. Box 1250 (95901-0035)
PHONE..................................530 741-2747

PRODUCTS & SVCS

Gerry Sutton, *President*
Mary Sutton, *Admin Sec*
EMP: 11
SQ FT: 2,000
SALES (est): 1.1MM **Privately Held**
SIC: 3999 Flowers, artificial & preserved

(P-23495)
SWISSDIGITAL USA CO LTD
11533 Slater Ave Ste H, Fountain Valley
(92708-5418)
PHONE..................626 351-1999
Hunter Li, *CEO*
EMP: 10
SALES: 100K **Privately Held**
SIC: 3999 5099 Handles, handbag & luggage; luggage

(P-23496)
T-REX PRODUCTS INCORPORATED
7920 Airway Rd Ste A6, San Diego
(92154-8311)
PHONE..................619 482-4424
Alan Botterman, *President*
David Hanono, *CFO*
▲ **EMP:** 15
SQ FT: 14,000
SALES: 5.9MM **Privately Held**
WEB: www.t-rexproducts.com
SIC: 3999 Pet supplies

(P-23497)
T3 MICRO INC (PA)
228 Main St Ste 12, Venice (90291-5203)
PHONE..................310 452-2888
Kent Yu, *President*
Amanda Afeiche, *Finance*
Jennifer Arruda, *Accountant*
Daryl Thomas, *Sales Staff*
Antonia Peterson, *Manager*
▲ **EMP:** 20
SALES (est): 5.2MM **Privately Held**
SIC: 3999 Hair & hair-based products

(P-23498)
TAG TOYS INC
1810 S Acacia Ave, Compton (90220-4927)
PHONE..................310 639-4566
Lawrence Mestyanek, *CEO*
Barbara Villafana, *CFO*
Judy Mestyanek, *Vice Pres*
EMP: 65
SQ FT: 60,000
SALES (est): 6.9MM **Privately Held**
WEB: www.tagtoys.com
SIC: 3999 8351 3944 Education aids, devices & supplies; child day care services; games, toys & children's vehicles

(P-23499)
TAKT MANUFACTURING INC
1300 E Victor Rd, Lodi (95240-0800)
PHONE..................408 250-4975
Trevor Weissbart, *Principal*
EMP: 15
SALES (est): 397K **Privately Held**
SIC: 3999 Manufacturing industries

(P-23500)
TANDEM DESIGN INC
Also Called: Tandem Exhibit
1846 W Sequoia Ave, Orange
(92868-1018)
PHONE..................714 978-7272
Maury Bonas, *President*
Susan Bonas, *Vice Pres*
Stephen Gann, *Prdtn Mgr*
EMP: 23
SQ FT: 20,000
SALES (est): 2.2MM **Privately Held**
WEB: www.tandemdesigninc.com
SIC: 3999 Preparation of slides & exhibits

(P-23501)
TECHNICAL MANUFACTURING W LLC
24820 Avenue Tibbitts, Valencia
(91355-3404)
PHONE..................661 295-7226
Brad Topper,
Johnny Valadez,
EMP: 23
SALES (est): 4MM **Privately Held**
SIC: 3999 Barber & beauty shop equipment

(P-23502)
THC DESIGN LLC
1346 Elwood St, Los Angeles
(90021-2413)
PHONE..................562 980-0056
Ryan Jennemann,
EMP: 12
SALES (est): 1.4MM **Privately Held**
SIC: 3999

(P-23503)
THERMOPLAQUE COMPANY INC
14928 Calvert St, Van Nuys (91411-2698)
PHONE..................818 988-1080
Gregory Floor, *President*
C Luke Floor, *Vice Pres*
Kathleen M Floor, *Admin Sec*
EMP: 10
SQ FT: 6,300
SALES (est): 1MM **Privately Held**
SIC: 3999 Plaques, picture, laminated

(P-23504)
TIBBAN MANUFACTURING INC
12593 Highline Dr, Apple Valley
(92308-5047)
P.O. Box 2675 (92307-0051)
PHONE..................760 961-1160
James A Tibban, *CEO*
Tony Tibban, *Principal*
◆ **EMP:** 17
SALES (est): 2.1MM **Privately Held**
SIC: 3999 Barber & beauty shop equipment

(P-23505)
TLK INDUSTRIES INC
23650 Via Del Rio, Yorba Linda
(92887-2714)
PHONE..................714 692-9373
Timothy Rose, *Principal*
EMP: 10 **EST:** 2012
SALES (est): 1MM **Privately Held**
SIC: 3999 Advertising curtains

(P-23506)
TOM LEONARD INVESTMENT CO INC
Also Called: Peak Seasons
7240 Sycamore Canyon Blvd, Riverside
(92508-2331)
PHONE..................951 351-7778
Tom Leonard, *CEO*
Greg Szuba, *Vice Pres*
Arlene Leonard, *Admin Sec*
Desiree Menjivar, *Supervisor*
▲ **EMP:** 40
SQ FT: 35,000
SALES (est): 5.2MM **Privately Held**
WEB: www.peakseasons.com
SIC: 3999 3399 Christmas tree ornaments, except electrical & glass; paste, metal

(P-23507)
TOYKIDZ INC
100 S Doheny Dr Ph 10, Los Angeles
(90048-2998)
P.O. Box 2035, Beverly Hills (90213-2035)
PHONE..................213 688-2999
Trith B Dadlani, *CEO*
▲ **EMP:** 15 **EST:** 2008
SALES (est): 852.2K **Privately Held**
SIC: 3999 3944 Advertising display products; games, toys & children's vehicles

(P-23508)
TPC INDUSTRIES LLC
5920 W Birch Ave, Fresno (93722-2878)
PHONE..................310 849-9574
Charles Powell, *Mng Member*
Kathi Feliciano, *CFO*
EMP: 20
SALES (est): 1MM **Privately Held**
SIC: 3999 Manufacturing industries

(P-23509)
TRANS FX INC
Also Called: T F X
2361 Eastman Ave, Oxnard (93030-8136)
PHONE..................805 485-6110
Allen Pike, *President*
Rick Bordonaro, *Exec VP*
Hollis Hedrich, *Executive*
EMP: 15

SQ FT: 25,000
SALES (est): 2.7MM **Privately Held**
WEB: www.transfx.com
SIC: 3999 3711 7389 3812 Models, except toy; automobile assembly, including specialty automobiles; design services; acceleration indicators & systems components, aerospace

(P-23510)
TRAXX CORPORATION
1201 E Lexington Ave, Pomona
(91766-5520)
PHONE..................909 623-8032
Craig Silvers, *CEO*
Jon Hall, *Chairman*
Mark Johnson, *Natl Sales Mgr*
Pat Summerville, *Sales Mgr*
▲ **EMP:** 100
SQ FT: 52,000
SALES (est): 17.8MM **Privately Held**
SIC: 3999 Carpet tackles

(P-23511)
TREK ARMOR INCORPORATED
41795 Elm St Ste 401, Murrieta
(92562-9278)
PHONE..................951 319-4008
Mitchell P Walk, *CEO*
EMP: 16
SALES (est): 1.7MM **Privately Held**
SIC: 3999 Manufacturing industries

(P-23512)
TRNLWB LLC
Also Called: Trinity Lighweight
17410 Lockwood Valley Rd, Frazier Park
(93225-9318)
PHONE..................661 245-3736
EMP: 5005
SALES (corp-wide): 13.7MM **Privately Held**
SIC: 3999 Barber & beauty shop equipment
PA: Trnlwb, Llc
1112 E Cpeland Rd Ste 500
Arlington TX 76011
800 581-3117

(P-23513)
URETHANE MASTERS INCORPORATED
455 54th St, San Diego (92114-2220)
PHONE..................651 357-8821
Gayle McEnroe, *President*
EMP: 15
SALES (est): 397K **Privately Held**
SIC: 3999 Manufacturing industries

(P-23514)
USA SOLAR TECHNOLOGY INC
28381 Vincent Moraga Dr, Temecula
(92590-3653)
PHONE..................714 356-8360
Michael Douthwaite, *Principal*
EMP: 10
SALES (est): 311.4K **Privately Held**
SIC: 3999 Manufacturing industries

(P-23515)
USCPS
Also Called: US Composite Pipe South
3009 N Laurel Ave, Rialto (92377-3725)
PHONE..................909 434-1888
Nabil Shehade, *Principal*
Pati Page, *Admin Asst*
James Knight, *Engineer*
Deanna Morrison, *Analyst*
Patrick Martin, *Manager*
EMP: 60
SALES (est): 950K **Privately Held**
SIC: 3999 Manufacturing industries

(P-23516)
VERNON MACHINE AND FOUNDRY
5420 S Santa Fe Ave, Vernon
(90058-3522)
PHONE..................323 277-0550
Bob Bouse, *President*
EMP: 12
SALES: 500K **Privately Held**
SIC: 3999 Manufacturing industries

(P-23517)
VISTA PRIME MANAGEMENT LLC
7895 Convoy Ct Ste 17, San Diego
(92111-1215)
PHONE..................858 256-9221
George Sadler, *President*
EMP: 13
SALES (est): 1.6MM **Privately Held**
SIC: 3999 5159 8741 ; ; management services

(P-23518)
VITALHUE
2036 Nevada City Hwy # 188, Grass Valley
(95945-7700)
PHONE..................323 646-8775
Uri Egozi, *President*
EMP: 14 **EST:** 2017
SALES (est): 403.9K **Privately Held**
SIC: 3999 Manufacturing industries

(P-23519)
VITAVET LABS INC
Also Called: Nuvet Labs
5717 Corsa Ave, Westlake Village
(91362-4001)
PHONE..................818 865-2600
Blake Kirschbaum, *President*
Matt Simpson, *COO*
Dr Raymond Kirschbaum, *CFO*
Martha Padilla, *Cust Mgr*
Krista Bellini, *Manager*
▼ **EMP:** 20 **EST:** 1997
SALES (est): 2.5MM **Privately Held**
WEB: www.nuvetlabs.com
SIC: 3999 Pet supplies

(P-23520)
VIVIGLO TECHNOLOGIES INC
620 Lunar Ave Ste B, Brea (92821-3131)
PHONE..................949 933-9738
Leslie Groll, *President*
EMP: 40
SQ FT: 15,000
SALES: 10MM **Privately Held**
WEB: www.viviglo.com
SIC: 3999 Models, except toy

(P-23521)
VOLTA INDUSTRIES LLC (PA)
144 King St, San Francisco (94107-1905)
PHONE..................917 838-3590
Christopher Wendel, *Principal*
Ross Hatamiya, *Vice Pres*
Cole Shelton, *VP Bus Dvlpt*
Chuck Richmond, *Project Mgr*
Scott Mercer,
EMP: 16
SALES (est): 7.5MM **Privately Held**
SIC: 3999 Barber & beauty shop equipment

(P-23522)
WATKINS MANUFACTURING CORP (HQ)
Also Called: Watkins Wellness
1280 Park Center Dr, Vista (92081-8398)
PHONE..................760 598-6464
Steve Hammock, *President*
Sandra Shuda, *VP Human Res*
◆ **EMP:** 277
SQ FT: 430,000
SALES (est): 125.2MM
SALES (corp-wide): 8.3B **Publicly Held**
WEB: www.ownaspa.com
SIC: 3999 Hot tubs
PA: Masco Corporation
17450 College Pkwy
Livonia MI 48152
313 274-7400

(P-23523)
WBT GROUP LLC
Also Called: Wbt Industries
1401 S Shamrock Ave, Monrovia
(91016-4246)
PHONE..................323 735-1201
Lisa Stanislawski,
▲ **EMP:** 40
SALES (est): 4.3MM **Privately Held**
SIC: 3999 Buttons: Red Cross, union, identification

▲ = Import ▼=Export
◆ =Import/Export

(P-23524)
WELLAND INDUSTRIES LLC
3860 Prospect Ave, Yorba Linda
(92886-1724)
PHONE.....................714 528-9900
Yanbing Hou, *Principal*
▲ **EMP:** 10
SALES (est) 826.3K **Privately Held**
SIC: 3999 Manufacturing industries

(P-23525)
WHITEFISH ENTERPRISES INC
14557 Griffith St, San Leandro
(94577-6703)
PHONE.....................510 357-6100
Sylvia T White, *President*
▲ **EMP:** 14
SALES (est): 1.5MM **Privately Held**
SIC: 3999 Candles

(P-23526)
WHITESTONE INDUSTRIES INC
2076 White Ln Spc 283, Bakersfield
(93304-7608)
PHONE.....................888 567-2234
Carlos Corado Garcia, *Administration*
EMP: 10 EST: 2015
SALES (est): 926.8K **Privately Held**
SIC: 3999 Manufacturing industries

(P-23527)
WOODEN WICK CO
1440 S Coast Hwy Ste A, Laguna Beach
(92651-3107)
PHONE.....................714 594-7790
EMP: 12
SALES (est): 43.6K **Privately Held**
SIC: 3999 Candles

(P-23528)
WOODFORD WICKS LLC
Also Called: Woodford Wicks Candle Company
302 Williams Way, Hayward (94541-4388)
PHONE.....................614 554-8474
Brett Butler,
Barbara J Blake,
Lowell F Blake,
Dorene S Butler,
George L Butler,
▲ **EMP:** 10
SQ FT: 2,500
SALES (est): 840.8K **Privately Held**
SIC: 3999 Candles

(P-23529)
XOLAR CORPORATION
Also Called: Hot Spring Spa
1012 E Bidwell St Ste 600, Folsom
(95630-5561)
PHONE.....................916 983-6301
Ellen Fredman, *Branch Mgr*
EMP: 29
SALES (corp-wide): 7.4MM **Privately Held**
SIC: 3999 Hot tubs
PA: Xolar Corporation
2200 Mercury Way
Santa Rosa CA 95407
707 526-2380

(P-23530)
ZAZZIE FOODS INC
1398 University Ave, Berkeley
(94702-1711)
PHONE.....................510 526-7664
Cassandra Chen, *CEO*
EMP: 10
SALES (est): 650K **Privately Held**
SIC: 3999 Manufacturing industries

(P-23531)
ZMB INDUSTRIES LLC
Also Called: Zombie Industries
12925 Brookprinter Pl # 400, Poway
(92064-8822)
PHONE.....................858 842-1000
Roger Davis, *President*
EMP: 10 EST: 2011
SQ FT: 12,500
SALES (est): 1.1MM **Privately Held**
SIC: 3999 Barber & beauty shop equipment

(P-23532)
ZYMED LABORATORIES
458 Carlton Ct, South San Francisco
(94080-2012)
PHONE.....................650 952-0110
Bean Paso, *CEO*
EMP: 40
SALES (est): 1.6MM **Privately Held**
SIC: 3999 Manufacturing industries

7372 Prepackaged Software

(P-23533)
15FIVE INC
3053 Fillmore St Ste 279, San Francisco
(94123-4009)
PHONE.....................208 816-4225
David Hassell, *CEO*
Rahul Reddy, *Partner*
Brad McGinity, *Officer*
Shane Metcalf, *Vice Pres*
Stacey Hurst, *Executive Asst*
EMP: 11
SALES (est): 1.1MM **Privately Held**
SIC: 7372 7389 Application computer software; business oriented computer software;

(P-23534)
1ON1 LLC
12015 Waterfront Dr # 261, Playa Vista
(90094-2536)
PHONE.....................310 448-5376
Susan Josephson, *Mng Member*
Todd Cherniawsky,
Nicole David,
Lorri Goddard,
Stephane Medam,
EMP: 50
SQ FT: 5,000
SALES (est): 20MM **Privately Held**
SIC: 7372 Application computer software

(P-23535)
24X7SAAS INC
2307 Larkspur Canyon Dr, San Jose
(95138-2467)
PHONE.....................408 391-6205
Srinivas Burli, *CEO*
EMP: 15 EST: 2012
SALES (est): 898.7K **Privately Held**
SIC: 7372 Prepackaged software

(P-23536)
3BECOM INC (PA)
2400 Lincoln Ave Ste 216, Altadena
(91001-5436)
PHONE.....................818 726-0007
Bob Ntoya, *President*
Brian Jones, *COO*
Brennon Neff, *CFO*
Adam Gerber, *Principal*
Simon Wise, *Principal*
EMP: 15
SALES (est): 2.1MM **Privately Held**
SIC: 7372 Prepackaged software

(P-23537)
3DGROUNDWORKS LLC
350 Rhode Island St # 240, San Francisco
(94103-5188)
PHONE.....................415 964-0060
Thorsten Froemming, *Principal*
EMP: 11
SALES (est): 1.1MM **Privately Held**
SIC: 7372 Prepackaged software

(P-23538)
500FRIENDS INC (DH)
Also Called: Merkle Loyalty Solutions
77 Geary St Fl 5, San Francisco
(94108-5703)
PHONE.....................800 818-8356
Justin Yoshimura, *CEO*
Michael Hemsey, *President*
Matt Gilbert, *COO*
Geoffrey Smalling, *CTO*
EMP: 20
SALES (est): 62MM
SALES (corp-wide): 6.3B **Privately Held**
SIC: 7372 7371 Business oriented computer software; computer software development & applications

HQ: Merkle Inc.
7001 Columbia Gateway Dr
Columbia MD 21046
443 542-4000

(P-23539)
7 GENERATION GAMES INC
2111 7th St Apt 8, Santa Monica
(90405-1279)
PHONE.....................260 402-1172
Annmaria De Mars, *CEO*
Maria Burns Ortiz, *COO*
Diana Sanchez, *Project Mgr*
Dennis De Mars, *Chief Engr*
EMP: 12
SALES (est): 1MM **Privately Held**
SIC: 7372 Educational computer software

(P-23540)
ABAQUS INC
2297 Saint Francis Dr, Palo Alto
(94303-3134)
PHONE.....................415 496-9436
Shailendra Jain, *CEO*
Ayush Kapahi, *Partner*
EMP: 12 EST: 2007
SALES (est): 705.8K **Privately Held**
SIC: 7372 5734 Business oriented computer software; software, business & non-game

(P-23541)
ABB ENTERPRISE SOFTWARE INC
60 Spear St, San Francisco (94105-1506)
PHONE.....................415 527-2850
Greg Dukat, *Branch Mgr*
EMP: 175
SALES (corp-wide): 36.4B **Privately Held**
WEB: www.indusinternational.com
SIC: 7372 Business oriented computer software
HQ: Abb Enterprise Software Inc.
305 Gregson Dr
Cary NC 27511
919 856-2360

(P-23542)
ABF DATA SYSTEMS INC
Also Called: Direct Systems Support
2801 Townsgate Rd Ste 111, Westlake Village (91361-3028)
PHONE.....................818 591-8307
Robert Hedge, *Vice Pres*
EMP: 15
SALES (est): 905.8K
SALES (corp-wide): 36.1MM **Privately Held**
WEB: www.abf-dss.com
SIC: 7372 Prepackaged software
PA: Abf Data Systems, Inc.
9020 Kenamar Dr Ste 201
San Diego CA 92121
858 547-8300

(P-23543)
ABLE HEALTH INC
1516 Folsom St, San Francisco
(94103-3721)
P.O. Box 225310 (94122-5310)
PHONE.....................617 529-6264
Rachel Katz, *CEO*
Steven Daniels, *President*
Emily Richmond, *Vice Pres*
Meryl Grant, *Project Dir*
EMP: 12
SQ FT: 800
SALES (est): 263.1K **Privately Held**
SIC: 7372 Business oriented computer software

(P-23544)
ABLE SOFTWARE INC
20251 Sw Acacia St # 220, Newport Beach
(92660-1716)
PHONE.....................949 274-8321
Ming LI, *President*
Sing Lee, *Manager*
EMP: 39
SALES (est): 2.4MM **Privately Held**
WEB: www.able-soft.com
SIC: 7372 Prepackaged software

(P-23545)
ACCELA INC (PA)
2633 Camino Ramon Ste 500, San Ramon
(94583-9149)
PHONE.....................925 659-3200
Gary Kovacs, *CEO*
Mark Jung, *Ch of Bd*
Maury Blackman, *CEO*
Ed Daihl, *CEO*
Jeffrey Toung, *COO*
EMP: 150
SALES (est): 80MM **Privately Held**
WEB: www.accela.com
SIC: 7372 Business oriented computer software

(P-23546)
ACCORDENT TECHNOLOGIES INC
1846 Schooldale Dr, San Jose
(95124-1136)
PHONE.....................310 374-7491
EMP: 16
SALES (corp-wide): 856.9MM **Publicly Held**
SIC: 7372
HQ: Accordent Technologies, Inc.
300 N Cntntl Blvd Ste 200
El Segundo CA
310 374-7491

(P-23547)
ACCOUNTANTS EDGE SOFTWARE SVCS (PA)
35436 Panorama Dr, Yucaipa
(92399-3532)
PHONE.....................800 689-6932
Renae Smith, *Principal*
EMP: 10
SALES (est): 1.7MM **Privately Held**
SIC: 7372 Prepackaged software

(P-23548)
ACCOUNTMATE SOFTWARE CORP (PA)
1445 Technology Ln Ste A5, Petaluma
(94954-7613)
PHONE.....................707 774-7500
David Dierke, *Principal*
David Render, *COO*
Tommy Tan, *CTO*
Larry Villamor, *Software Dev*
Rosemarie Dasig, *Applctn Conslt*
▲ **EMP:** 45
SQ FT: 8,700
SALES: 4.2MM **Privately Held**
WEB: www.accountmate.com
SIC: 7372 Business oriented computer software

(P-23549)
ACM STUDENT CHAPTER AT UCR
446 Winston St Vincent, Riverside (92507)
PHONE.....................951 389-0713
John Tham, *President*
EMP: 15
SALES (est): 305.2K **Privately Held**
SIC: 7372 Educational computer software

(P-23550)
ACME DATA INC
2400 Camino Ramon Ste 180, San Ramon
(94583-4211)
P.O. Box 2973, Danville (94526-7973)
PHONE.....................925 913-4591
Thomas Brennan, *President*
Steven Kleinmann, *Vice Pres*
EMP: 19
SALES (est): 1.2MM **Privately Held**
WEB: www.stalworth.com
SIC: 7372 Business oriented computer software

(P-23551)
ACQUIS INC
16795 Lark Ave Ste 102, Los Gatos
(95032-7691)
PHONE.....................408 402-5367
Audrey McKeown, *President*
EMP: 10
SQ FT: 2,000

SALES (est): 783.1K **Privately Held**
SIC: **7372** 7371 7379 Prepackaged software; custom computer programming services; computer software development; data processing consultant

(P-23552)
ACTIVISION BLIZZARD INC
4 Hamilton Landing, Novato (94949-8256)
PHONE................................415 881-9100
EMP: 209
SALES (corp-wide): 7.5B **Publicly Held**
SIC: **7372** Home entertainment computer software
PA: Activision Blizzard, Inc.
    3100 Ocean Park Blvd
    Santa Monica CA 90405
    310 255-2000

(P-23553)
ACTIVISION BLIZZARD INC (PA)
3100 Ocean Park Blvd, Santa Monica (90405-3032)
PHONE................................310 255-2000
Robert A Kotick, *CEO*
Brian Kelly, *Ch of Bd*
Dennis Durkin, *President*
Collister Johnson, *President*
Rob Kostich, *President*
EMP: 333
SQ FT: 152,431
SALES: 7.5B **Publicly Held**
WEB: www.blizzard.com
SIC: **7372** Home entertainment computer software

(P-23554)
ACTIVISION BLIZZARD INC
Blizzard Entertainment
3 Blizzard, Irvine (92618-3628)
P.O. Box 18979 (92623-8979)
PHONE................................949 955-1380
Frank Pearce, *Principal*
Michael Maggio, *Engineer*
Stephen Raub, *Engineer*
Luke Tomlinson, *Engineer*
Rob Tomson, *Engineer*
EMP: 85
SALES (corp-wide): 7.5B **Publicly Held**
WEB: www.blizzard.com
SIC: **7372** Prepackaged software
PA: Activision Blizzard, Inc.
    3100 Ocean Park Blvd
    Santa Monica CA 90405
    310 255-2000

(P-23555)
ACTIVISION PUBLISHING INC (HQ)
3100 Ocean Park Blvd, Santa Monica (90405-3032)
PHONE................................310 255-2000
Michael Griffith, *President*
Dave Cowling, *President*
Dan Rosensweig, *President*
Colin Schiller, *President*
Eric Hirshberg, *CEO*
▲ EMP: 1306
SALES (est): 98.4MM
SALES (corp-wide): 7.5B **Publicly Held**
SIC: **7372** Home entertainment computer software
PA: Activision Blizzard, Inc.
    3100 Ocean Park Blvd
    Santa Monica CA 90405
    310 255-2000

(P-23556)
ACTUATE CORPORATION (HQ)
951 Mariners Island Blvd # 7, San Mateo (94404-1561)
PHONE................................650 645-3000
Mark J Barrenechea, *President*
John Doolittle, *CFO*
Adam Howatson, *Chief Mktg Ofcr*
Gordon A Davies, *Officer*
Gordon Davies, *Exec VP*
EMP: 15
SQ FT: 58,000
SALES: 134.5MM
SALES (corp-wide): 2.8B **Privately Held**
WEB: www.actuate.com
SIC: **7372** Prepackaged software

PA: Open Text Corporation
    275 Frank Tompa Dr
    Waterloo ON N2L 0
    519 888-7111

(P-23557)
ACUREO INC
Also Called: Propertyradar.com
12242 Bus Park Dr Ste 20, Truckee (96161-3327)
P.O. Box 837 (96160-0837)
PHONE................................530 550-8801
Sean O'Toole, *CEO*
David Laplante, *Chief Mktg Ofcr*
Susan Heninger, *Info Tech Mgr*
Madeline Schnapp, *Research*
Josh Hess, *Opers Mgr*
EMP: 13 EST: 2008
SALES (est): 1.3MM **Privately Held**
SIC: **7372** Business oriented computer software

(P-23558)
AD HOC LABS INC
Also Called: Burner App
2898 Rowena Ave Ste 100, Los Angeles (90039-2020)
PHONE................................323 800-4927
EMP: 10 EST: 2012
SQ FT: 2,000
SALES (est): 657.8K **Privately Held**
SIC: **7372**

(P-23559)
ADAPTIVE INC (PA)
65 Enterprise Ste E475, Aliso Viejo (92656-2705)
P.O. Box 305, Chesterfield VA (23832-0005)
PHONE................................888 399-4621
Jeff Goins, *President*
Sandra Foster, *Partner*
Joe Stefaniak, *Vice Pres*
Paul Koerber, *Sr Software Eng*
EMP: 18
SQ FT: 5,000
SALES (est): 4.8MM **Privately Held**
WEB: www.adaptive.com
SIC: **7372** Prepackaged software

(P-23560)
ADAPTIVE INSGHTS LLC A WORKDAY (HQ)
2300 Geng Rd Ste 100, Palo Alto (94303-3352)
PHONE................................650 528-7500
Thomas F Bogan, *CEO*
Amy Reichanadter, *Officer*
Melanie D Vinson, *Admin Sec*
Bob McDiarmid, *Software Dev*
Ravinder Redd Rallagudam, *Software Dev*
EMP: 200
SALES: 106.5MM
SALES (corp-wide): 2.8B **Publicly Held**
WEB: www.adaptiveplanning.com
SIC: **7372** Business oriented computer software
PA: Workday, Inc.
    6110 Stoneridge Mall Rd
    Pleasanton CA 94588
    925 951-9000

(P-23561)
ADDING TECHNOLOGY (PA)
27 W Anapamu St, Santa Barbara (93101-3107)
PHONE................................805 252-6971
Natalie Browne, *Principal*
EMP: 11
SALES (est): 2.1MM **Privately Held**
SIC: **7372** Prepackaged software

(P-23562)
ADDVOCATE INC
599 3rd St Apt 103, San Francisco (94107-3800)
PHONE................................415 797-7620
Piers Cooper, *CEO*
John Flynn, *Vice Pres*
Lida Tohidi, *Opers Staff*
EMP: 12
SQ FT: 25,000
SALES (est): 848.8K **Privately Held**
SIC: **7372** Business oriented computer software

(P-23563)
ADEXA INC (PA)
5777 W Century Blvd # 1100, Los Angeles (90045-5643)
PHONE................................310 642-2100
Khosrow Cyrus Hadavi, *CEO*
Kameron Hadavi, *Vice Pres*
John Hosford, *Vice Pres*
William Green, *VP Business*
Tim Field, *CTO*
EMP: 50
SQ FT: 31,000
SALES (est): 18MM **Privately Held**
WEB: www.adexa.com
SIC: **7372** Business oriented computer software

(P-23564)
ADMI INC
18525 Sutter Blvd Ste 290, Morgan Hill (95037-8102)
PHONE................................408 776-0060
Allen D Moyer, *President*
Michael Collins, *Manager*
Jordan Ferguson, *Manager*
EMP: 23 EST: 2007
SALES (est): 2.9MM **Privately Held**
SIC: **7372** Operating systems computer software

(P-23565)
ADOBE INC
601 And 625 Townsend St, San Francisco (94103)
PHONE................................415 832-2000
Les Schmidt, *Vice Pres*
EMP: 1000
SALES (corp-wide): 9B **Publicly Held**
SIC: **7372** Prepackaged software
PA: Adobe Inc.
    345 Park Ave
    San Jose CA 95110
    408 536-6000

(P-23566)
ADOBE INC
321 Park Ave, San Jose (95110-2704)
PHONE................................408 536-6000
Jess Walker, *Software Engr*
EMP: 34
SALES (corp-wide): 9B **Publicly Held**
SIC: **7372** Prepackaged software
PA: Adobe Inc.
    345 Park Ave
    San Jose CA 95110
    408 536-6000

(P-23567)
ADOBE INC (PA)
345 Park Ave, San Jose (95110-2704)
PHONE................................408 536-6000
Shantanu Narayen, *Ch of Bd*
Ann Lewnes, *Chief Mktg Ofcr*
Scott Belsky,
Bryan Lamkin, *Exec VP*
Donna Morris, *Exec VP*
EMP: 600
SQ FT: 989,000
SALES: 9B **Publicly Held**
WEB: www.adobe.com
SIC: **7372** Application computer software

(P-23568)
ADOBE MACROMEDIA SOFTWARE LLC (HQ)
601 Townsend St, San Francisco (94103-5247)
PHONE................................415 832-2000
Bruce R Chizen,
Murray Demo,
Shantanu Narayen,
EMP: 20
SQ FT: 210,000
SALES (est): 35.8MM
SALES (corp-wide): 9B **Publicly Held**
WEB: www.macromedia.com
SIC: **7372** Prepackaged software; publishers' computer software; educational computer software; home entertainment computer software
PA: Adobe Inc.
    345 Park Ave
    San Jose CA 95110
    408 536-6000

(P-23569)
ADS SOLUTIONS
10 Commercial Blvd # 208, Novato (94949-6107)
PHONE................................415 897-3700
Kenneth Levin, *President*
Ann Grace, *Software Dev*
Greg Tognoli, *Sales Staff*
EMP: 19
SALES (est): 1.8MM **Privately Held**
WEB: www.amplexus.com
SIC: **7372** Application computer software; business oriented computer software

(P-23570)
ADVANCED PUBLISHING TECH INC (PA)
123 S Victory Blvd, Burbank (91502-2347)
PHONE................................818 557-3035
David Kraai, *President*
Ken Barber, *Vice Pres*
David Bridges, *Vice Pres*
Jeff Sie, *Vice Pres*
Bryan Fowler, *Engineer*
EMP: 47
SALES (est): 3.5MM **Privately Held**
WEB: www.advpubtech.com
SIC: **7372** Publishers' computer software

(P-23571)
ADVANCED TECHNOLOGIES
2001 Columbus St, Bakersfield (93305-2312)
PHONE................................661 872-4807
Tawna Johnson, *Owner*
Ron Johnson, *Co-Owner*
EMP: 16
SQ FT: 4,000
SALES (est): 1.1MM **Privately Held**
WEB: www.atsecure.net
SIC: **7372** Prepackaged software

(P-23572)
ADVENT RESOURCES INC
235 W 7th St, San Pedro (90731-3321)
PHONE................................310 241-1500
Ysidro Salinas, *Ch of Bd*
Timothy Gill, *CEO*
Vishal Ghelani, *Vice Pres*
Benjamin Gill, *Vice Pres*
Mitch Stahl, *Exec Dir*
EMP: 80
SQ FT: 22,000
SALES (est): 12.2MM **Privately Held**
WEB: www.adventresources.com
SIC: **7372** Prepackaged software

(P-23573)
ADVISOR SOFTWARE INC (PA)
2175 N Calif Blvd Ste 400, Walnut Creek (94596-7103)
PHONE................................925 299-7778
Andrew Rudd, *CEO*
Neal Ringquist, *President*
Neil Osborne, *CFO*
Erik Jepson, *Officer*
Mark Harper, *Administration*
EMP: 25
SQ FT: 5,500
SALES (est): 7.7MM **Privately Held**
WEB: www.advisorsoftware.com
SIC: **7372** Business oriented computer software

(P-23574)
ADVISYS INC
16969 Von Karman Ave # 125, Irvine (92606-4915)
PHONE................................949 752-4927
Kenneth Kerr, *CEO*
Richard M Kettley, *Ch of Bd*
Gregg Janes, *Vice Pres*
Dane Parker, *Vice Pres*
Sherelyn Kettley, *Admin Sec*
EMP: 28
SQ FT: 5,000
SALES (est): 4.5MM **Privately Held**
WEB: www.kettley.com
SIC: **7372** Application computer software

(P-23575)
AELLA DATA INC
4701 Patrick Henry Dr, Santa Clara (95054-1819)
PHONE................................408 391-4430
Changming Liu, *CEO*

Paul Jespersen, *Vice Pres*
Jared Hufferd, *VP Sales*
EMP: 12 **EST:** 2015
SALES (est): 200K **Privately Held**
SIC: 7372 Business oriented computer
software

(P-23576)
AFFECTLAYER INC
Also Called: Chorus.ai
465 California St Ste 600, San Francisco
(94104-1816)
PHONE....................650 924-1082
Roy Raanani, *CEO*
EMP: 11
SALES (est): 350.1K **Privately Held**
SIC: 7372 Application computer software

(P-23577)
AFRESH TECHNOLOGIES INC
2948 20th St Apt 302, San Francisco
(94110-2870)
PHONE....................805 551-9245
Matthew Schwartz, *CEO*
Nathan Fenner, *COO*
Volodymyr Kuleshov, *CTO*
EMP: 10
SQ FT: 1,400
SALES (est): 221.8K **Privately Held**
SIC: 7372 Business oriented computer
software

(P-23578)
AGENCYCOM LLC
5353 Grosvenor Blvd, Los Angeles
(90066-6913)
PHONE....................415 817-3800
Chan Suh, *CEO*
Jordan Warren, *President*
Rob Elliott, *CFO*
EMP: 400
SQ FT: 130,000
SALES (est): 20.2MM
SALES (corp-wide): 15.2B **Publicly Held**
WEB: www.agency.com
SIC: 7372 Application computer software
PA: Omnicom Group Inc.
437 Madison Ave
New York NY 10022
212 415-3600

(P-23579)
AGGRIGATOR INC
30 E San Joaquin St # 202, Salinas
(93901-2947)
PHONE....................650 245-5117
Gerard Rego, *CEO*
Doug Peterson, *Bd of Directors*
Margarita Quihuis, *Bd of Directors*
Benjamin Warr, *Bd of Directors*
EMP: 10 **EST:** 2014
SALES (est): 700.3K **Privately Held**
SIC: 7372 Business oriented computer
software

(P-23580)
AGILEPOINT INC (PA)
1916 Old Middlefield Way, Mountain View
(94043-2555)
PHONE....................650 968-6789
Jesse Shiah, *President*
Bryan Chandler, *COO*
Leonard Ducharme, *Officer*
EMP: 26
SQ FT: 2,000
SALES (est): 11.1MM **Privately Held**
WEB: www.ascentn.com
SIC: 7372 Business oriented computer
software

(P-23581)
AGILOFT INC
460 Seaport Ct Ste 200, Redwood City
(94063-5548)
PHONE....................650 587-8615
Colin Earl, *CEO*
May Quock, *Vice Pres*
Christian Thun, *Vice Pres*
Tina Quema, *Admin Asst*
David Bauman, *Administration*
EMP: 46
SQ FT: 3,200
SALES (est): 5.8MM **Privately Held**
WEB: www.supportwizard.com
SIC: 7372 Business oriented computer
software

(P-23582)
AGRICULTURAL DATA SYSTEMS INC
Also Called: ADS
24331 Los Arboles Dr, Laguna Niguel
(92677-2196)
PHONE....................949 363-5353
Carl Gennaro, *President*
Jeff Brumit, *CFO*
EMP: 12
SQ FT: 2,000
SALES (est): 2.6MM **Privately Held**
WEB: www.touchmemory.com
SIC: 7372 Prepackaged software

(P-23583)
AHA LABS INC
20 Gloria Cir, Menlo Park (94025-3556)
PHONE....................650 575-1425
Brian De Haaff, *CEO*
Melissa Hopkins, *Surgery Dir*
Ron Yang, *Surgery Dir*
Susie Boyer, *Senior Mgr*
Jamey Iaccino, *Senior Mgr*
EMP: 10 **EST:** 2013
SALES (est): 604.5K **Privately Held**
SIC: 7372 Business oriented computer
software

(P-23584)
AIRA TECH CORP
4225 Executive Sq Ste 400, La Jolla
(92037-1499)
PHONE....................619 271-9152
Suman Kanuganti, *Co-Owner*
Troy Otilio, *COO*
Anne Bohn, *CFO*
Scott Minick, *Principal*
Josh Wolfe, *Principal*
EMP: 20 **EST:** 2015
SALES (est): 1MM **Privately Held**
SIC: 7372 Application computer software

(P-23585)
AKAMAI TECHNOLOGIES INC
1400 Fashion Island Blvd # 15, San Mateo
(94404-2060)
PHONE....................617 444-3000
Jerry Trash, *Branch Mgr*
Steve Sosik, *Software Dev*
Dante Delucia, *Data Proc Staff*
Christine Santo, *Facilities Mgr*
Kristin Nelson-Patel, *Manager*
EMP: 38
SALES (corp-wide): 2.7B **Publicly Held**
SIC: 7372 Prepackaged software
PA: Akamai Technologies, Inc.
150 Broadway Ste 100
Cambridge MA 02142
617 444-3000

(P-23586)
AKIMBO SYSTEMS INC
411 Borel Ave Ste 100, San Mateo
(94402-3516)
PHONE....................650 292-3330
Thomas F Frank, *President*
Robert Hammer, *CFO*
EMP: 24 **EST:** 1995
SQ FT: 4,000
SALES (est): 2MM **Privately Held**
SIC: 7372 Application computer software

(P-23587)
AKTANA INC
207 Powell St Ste 800, San Francisco
(94102-2230)
PHONE....................888 707-3125
David Ehrlich, *President*
Clay Hausmann, *Chief Mktg Ofcr*
Marc Cohen, *Officer*
Schultz John, *Vice Pres*
Kelly Morhig, *Executive Asst*
EMP: 20
SALES (est): 1.7MM **Privately Held**
SIC: 7372 Prepackaged software

(P-23588)
AKUPARA GAMES LLC
17336 Boswell Pl, Granada Hills
(91344-1024)
PHONE....................747 998-2193
David Logan, *Manager*
EMP: 10

SALES (est): 290.4K **Privately Held**
SIC: 7372 Home entertainment computer
software

(P-23589)
ALATION INC (PA)
3 Lagoon Dr Ste 300, Redwood City
(94065-1567)
P.O. Box 1216 (94064-1216)
PHONE....................650 779-4440
Satyen Sangani, *CEO*
Max Ochoa, *CFO*
Aaron Kalb, *Officer*
Raj Gossain, *Senior VP*
Tephanie McReynolds, *Senior VP*
EMP: 35
SALES (est): 10.8MM **Privately Held**
SIC: 7372 Application computer software

(P-23590)
ALEKS CORPORATION (PA)
Also Called: Aleks Educational Systems
15640 Laguna Canyon Rd, Irvine (92618)
PHONE....................714 245-7191
R G Wilmot Lampros, *President*
Jean-Claude Falmagne, *Chairman*
Melissa Deveikis, *Marketing Staff*
Raymond Ramos, *Sales Staff*
Jimmy Bartlett, *Education*
EMP: 13 **EST:** 1998
SQ FT: 50,000
SALES (est): 10.2MM **Privately Held**
WEB: www.aris.ss.uci.edu
SIC: 7372 Educational computer software

(P-23591)
ALERTENTERPRISE INC
4350 Starboard Dr, Fremont (94538-6434)
PHONE....................510 440-0840
Jasvir Gill, *CEO*
Kaval Kaur, *COO*
Ehsan Hameed, *Vice Pres*
Srini Kakkera, *Vice Pres*
Willem Ryan, *Vice Pres*
EMP: 140
SQ FT: 24,000
SALES (est): 15.6MM **Privately Held**
SIC: 7372 Prepackaged software

(P-23592)
ALIENVAULT INC (HQ)
1100 Park Pl Ste 300, San Mateo
(94403-7108)
PHONE....................650 713-3333
Barmak Meftah, *President*
Marcus Bragg, *COO*
Andy Johnson, *CFO*
Ron Dovich, *Senior VP*
Russell Spitler, *Senior VP*
EMP: 12 **EST:** 2012
SALES (est): 37.8MM
SALES (corp-wide): 170.7B **Publicly
Held**
SIC: 7372 Business oriented computer
software
PA: At&T Inc.
208 S Akard St
Dallas TX 75202
210 821-4105

(P-23593)
ALIENVAULT LLC (DH)
1100 Park Pl Ste 300, San Mateo
(94403-7108)
PHONE....................650 713-3333
Barmak Meftah, *President*
J Alberto Yepez, *Ch of Bd*
Chris Murphy, *President*
Brian Robins, *CFO*
Rita Selvaggi, *Chief Mktg Ofcr*
EMP: 56
SALES (est): 37.8MM
SALES (corp-wide): 170.7B **Publicly
Held**
SIC: 7372 Business oriented computer
software
HQ: Alienvault, Inc.
1100 Park Pl Ste 300
San Mateo CA 94403
650 713-3333

(P-23594)
ALIVECOR INC (PA)
444 Castro St Ste 600, Mountain View
(94041-2058)
PHONE....................650 396-8650

Priya Abani, *CEO*
Jacqueline Shreibati, *Officer*
Daniel Treiman, *Sr Software Eng*
Sharon Tracy, *VP Sales*
Brian Clarke, *General Counsel*
EMP: 41
SALES (est): 4MM **Privately Held**
SIC: 7372 Application computer software

(P-23595)
ALLDATA LLC
9650 W Taron Dr Ste 100, Elk Grove
(95757-8197)
PHONE....................916 684-5200
Stephen Odland,
Bob Olsen,
EMP: 76
SQ FT: 35,000
SALES (est): 43.3MM
SALES (corp-wide): 11.8B **Publicly Held**
WEB: www.alldata.com
SIC: 7372 Business oriented computer
software
PA: Autozone, Inc.
123 S Front St
Memphis TN 38103
901 495-6500

(P-23596)
ALLDIGITAL HOLDINGS INC
1405 Warner Ave Ste A, Tustin
(92780-6405)
PHONE....................949 250-7340
Michael Linos, *President*
Brad Eisenstein, *CFO*
Steve Smith, *Vice Pres*
EMP: 15
SQ FT: 3,769
SALES (est): 3.8MM **Privately Held**
SIC: 7372 Prepackaged software

(P-23597)
ALTIUM LLC
4275 Executive Sq Ste 825, La Jolla
(92037-1478)
PHONE....................800 544-4186
Aram Mirkazemi,
Martin Ive, *Treasurer*
EMP: 75
SALES (est): 2.2MM **Privately Held**
SIC: 7372 Prepackaged software

(P-23598)
AMERICAN ISRAEL PUBLIC AFFAIRS
Also Called: Aipac
1801 Century Park E # 600, Los Angeles
(90067-2302)
PHONE....................323 937-1184
Andy Trilling, *Director*
Kimberly Pellman, *Program Dir*
Pedro Cavallero, *Director*
EMP: 10
SALES (corp-wide): 88.5MM **Privately
Held**
SIC: 7372 Application computer software
PA: American Israel Public Affairs Commit-
tee (Inc)
251 H St Nw
Washington DC 20001
202 639-5200

(P-23599)
ANALYTIC AND COMPUTATIONAL RES
Also Called: Acri
1931 Stradella Rd, Los Angeles
(90077-2320)
PHONE....................310 471-3023
Akshai K Runchal, *President*
Chanchal Runchal, *Treasurer*
EMP: 10 **EST:** 1979
SALES: 1MM **Privately Held**
WEB: www.acri.net
SIC: 7372 5045 8742 Prepackaged soft-
ware; computers, peripherals & software;
industry specialist consultants

(P-23600)
ANDROMEDA SOFTWARE INC
2965 Potter Ave, Thousand Oaks
(91360-6422)
PHONE....................805 379-4109
Sumeet Pasricha, *President*
Donn Gladstone, *CEO*
EMP: 12

SALES (est): 1.1MM **Privately Held**
WEB: www.andromedasoftware.com
SIC: 7372 7371 Prepackaged software;
custom computer programming services

(P-23601)
ANGELLIST LLC
90 Gold St, San Francisco (94133-5103)
PHONE..................................415 857-0840
Naval Ravikant, *CEO*
EMP: 12 EST: 2010
SALES (est): 608.6K **Privately Held**
SIC: 7372 Business oriented computer
software

(P-23602)
ANSYS INC
2645 Zanker Rd, San Jose (95134-2136)
PHONE..................................408 457-2000
Dave Logie, *Software Dev*
Aleksandra Egelja-Maruszew, *Technical Staff*
Yue Cao, *Engineer*
Doug Kaufman, *Engineer*
Matt Stephanson, *Engineer*
EMP: 12
SALES (corp-wide): 1.2B **Publicly Held**
SIC: 7372 Prepackaged software
PA: Ansys, Inc.
2600 Ansys Dr
Canonsburg PA 15317
884 462-6797

(P-23603)
APEX COMMUNICATIONS INC (DH)
21700 Oxnard St Ste 1060, Woodland Hills (91367-7571)
PHONE..................................818 379-8400
Ben Levy, *President*
EMP: 15
SQ FT: 7,500
SALES (est): 2.7MM
SALES (corp-wide): 449.4K **Privately Held**
WEB: www.apexvoice.com
SIC: 7372 Application computer software
HQ: Dialogic Inc.
4 Gatehall Dr Ste 9
Parsippany NJ 07054
973 967-6000

(P-23604)
APPBACKR INC
2251 Yale St, Palo Alto (94306-1427)
P.O. Box 268 (94302-0268)
PHONE..................................650 272-6129
Trevor Cornwell, *CEO*
Johanna Casao, *Corp Comm Staff*
EMP: 10
SALES (est): 792.3K **Privately Held**
WEB: www.appbackr.com
SIC: 7372 Application computer software

(P-23605)
APPDIRECT INC (PA)
650 California St Fl 25, San Francisco (94108-2606)
PHONE..................................415 852-3924
Nicolas Desmarais, *Ch of Bd*
Daniel Saks, *President*
Michael Difilippo, *CFO*
Mark Beebe, *Vice Pres*
Francois Duquette, *Sr Software Eng*
EMP: 59
SQ FT: 10,000
SALES (est): 28.4MM **Privately Held**
SIC: 7372 7371 Application computer software; computer software development & applications

(P-23606)
APPDYNAMICS INC (HQ)
303 2nd St Fl 8, San Francisco (94107-1366)
PHONE..................................415 442-8400
David Wadhwani, *President*
Daniel J Wright, *Senior VP*
Arpit Patel, *Vice Pres*
Keith Scott, *Executive*
Kurt Thompson, *Executive*
EMP: 148
SQ FT: 83,500
SALES: 150.5MM
SALES (corp-wide): 51.9B **Publicly Held**
SIC: 7372 Prepackaged software

PA: Cisco Systems, Inc.
170 W Tasman Dr
San Jose CA 95134
408 526-4000

(P-23607)
APPETIZE TECHNOLOGIES INC
6601 Center Dr W Ste 700, Los Angeles (90045-1545)
PHONE..................................877 559-4225
Max Roper, *CEO*
Jason Pratts, *COO*
Dan Machock, *CFO*
Mark Eastwood, *Officer*
Kevin Anderson, *Senior VP*
EMP: 110 EST: 2011
SALES (est): 257.6K **Privately Held**
SIC: 7372 Application computer software

(P-23608)
APPFOLIO INC (PA)
50 Castilian Dr Ste 101, Goleta (93117-5578)
PHONE..................................805 364-6093
Jason Randall, *President*
Andreas Von Blottnitz, *Ch of Bd*
Ida Kane, *CFO*
Janet Kerr, *Bd of Directors*
James Peters, *Bd of Directors*
EMP: 139
SQ FT: 79,200
SALES: 190MM **Publicly Held**
SIC: 7372 Business oriented computer software

(P-23609)
APPFOLIO INC
Also Called: Mycase
9201 Spectrum, San Diego (92123)
PHONE..................................866 648-1536
Troy Alford, *Engineer*
EMP: 573
SALES (corp-wide): 190MM **Publicly Held**
SIC: 7372 Prepackaged software
PA: Appfolio, Inc.
50 Castilian Dr Ste 101
Goleta CA 93117
805 364-6093

(P-23610)
APPFORMIX INC
Also Called: Acelio
4 N 2nd St Ste 595, San Jose (95113-1325)
PHONE..................................408 899-2240
Sumeet Singh, *CEO*
George Youhana, *Manager*
EMP: 15
SQ FT: 4,000
SALES (est): 1MM **Privately Held**
SIC: 7372 Utility computer software

(P-23611)
APPLIED BUSINESS SOFTWARE INC
Also Called: A B S
2847 Gundry Ave, Signal Hill (90755-1812)
PHONE..................................562 426-2188
Jerry Delgado, *President*
Elizabeth Morales, *Chief Mktg Ofcr*
Eddy Delgado, *Vice Pres*
Gerardo Delgado, *Vice Pres*
Edimia Delgado, *Admin Sec*
EMP: 15 EST: 1979
SQ FT: 7,200
SALES (est): 2.1MM **Privately Held**
WEB: www.abstmo.com
SIC: 7372 5045 5734 Prepackaged software; computers, peripherals & software; computer & software stores

(P-23612)
APPLIED EXPERT SYSTEMS INC
Also Called: AES
999 Commercial St Ste 201, Palo Alto (94303-4909)
P.O. Box 50927 (94303-0673)
PHONE..................................650 617-2400
Catherine H Liu, *President*
David Cheng, *Vice Pres*
Ming Jia, *Software Engr*
Mark Nguyen, *Research*
David Billing, *Technology*
▲ EMP: 38

SALES (est): 3.4MM **Privately Held**
WEB: www.aesclever.com
SIC: 7372 Business oriented computer software

(P-23613)
APPLIED STATISTICS & MGT INC
Also Called: Md-Staff
32848 Wolf Store Rd Ste A, Temecula (92592-8277)
P.O. Box 891329 (92589-1329)
PHONE..................................951 699-4600
Trung Phan, *President*
Nickolaus Phan, *COO*
Mahabubul Alam, *Software Engr*
Charles Ringger, *Software Engr*
Mark Ashley, *Legal Staff*
EMP: 45
SQ FT: 4,000
SALES (est): 5MM **Privately Held**
WEB: www.mdstaff.com
SIC: 7372 7371 Prepackaged software; computer software systems analysis & design, custom

(P-23614)
APPOINTY SOFTWARE INC
16 Corning Ave Ste 136, Milpitas (95035-5343)
PHONE..................................408 634-4141
Nemesh Singh, *President*
EMP: 25 EST: 2016
SALES (est): 552K **Privately Held**
SIC: 7372 Business oriented computer software

(P-23615)
APPORTO CORPORATION
200 Hamilton Ave, Palo Alto (94301-2529)
PHONE..................................650 326-0920
Anthony Awaida, *CEO*
EMP: 20 EST: 2011
SALES (est): 721.1K **Privately Held**
SIC: 7372 Prepackaged software

(P-23616)
APPVANCE INC
3080 Olcott St Ste B240, Santa Clara (95054-3278)
PHONE..................................408 871-0122
Kevin Surace, *CEO*
John Hubinger, *Ch of Bd*
EMP: 24
SALES (est): 1.9MM **Privately Held**
SIC: 7372 Prepackaged software

(P-23617)
APPWARE INC
Also Called: Eteam Technologies
65 Enterprise, Aliso Viejo (92656-2705)
PHONE..................................415 732-9298
Thomas Cornelius, *President*
EMP: 25
SALES (est): 528.6K **Privately Held**
SIC: 7372 Prepackaged software

(P-23618)
APPZEN INC (PA)
4699 Old Ironsides Dr # 430, Santa Clara (95054-1824)
PHONE..................................408 647-5253
Anant Kale, *Director*
Meena Chockalingam, *Associate Dir*
Kunal Verma, *CTO*
Debashis Saha, *VP Engrg*
James Qian, *Senior Mgr*
EMP: 14
SALES (est): 4.7MM **Privately Held**
SIC: 7372 Business oriented computer software

(P-23619)
APTEAN INC
2361 Rosecrans Ave # 375, El Segundo (90245-4916)
PHONE..................................310 536-6080
Rebecca Goco, *Manager*
EMP: 10
SALES (corp-wide): 462MM **Privately Held**
SIC: 7372 Prepackaged software
PA: Aptean, Inc.
4325 Alexander Dr Ste 100
Alpharetta GA 30022
770 351-9600

(P-23620)
APTELIGENT INC
1100 La Avenida St Ste A, Mountain View (94043-1453)
PHONE..................................415 371-1402
Pat Gelsinger, *CEO*
Scott Bajtos, *COO*
Sanjay Poonen, *COO*
Raghu Raghuram, *COO*
Rajiv Ramaswami, *COO*
EMP: 60
SALES (est): 4.2MM
SALES (corp-wide): 90.6B **Publicly Held**
SIC: 7372 Prepackaged software
HQ: Vmware, Inc.
3401 Hillview Ave
Palo Alto CA 94304
650 427-5000

(P-23621)
APTIV DIGITAL LLC
2160 Gold St, San Jose (95002-3700)
PHONE..................................818 295-6789
Neil Jones, *President*
Christine Otto, *Director*
EMP: 85
SALES (est): 3.5MM
SALES (corp-wide): 695.8MM **Publicly Held**
WEB: www.tvguideinc.com
SIC: 7372 Home entertainment computer software
HQ: Rovi Guides, Inc.
2233 N Ontario St Ste 100
Burbank CA 91504

(P-23622)
ARCTIC WOLF NETWORKS INC (PA)
111 W Evelyn Ave Ste 115, Sunnyvale (94086-6131)
PHONE..................................408 610-3263
Brian Nesmith, *CEO*
Kim Tremblay, *Vice Pres*
Dom Arseneault, *Engineer*
Brad Bierman, *Engineer*
Karen Hamilton, *Finance*
EMP: 11 EST: 2012
SALES (est): 3.1MM **Privately Held**
SIC: 7372 7371 Business oriented computer software; computer software systems analysis & design, custom

(P-23623)
ARENA SOLUTIONS INC
Also Called: Omnify Software
989 E Hillsdale Blvd # 250, Foster City (94404-4201)
PHONE..................................978 988-3800
Brad Paul, *Treasurer*
EMP: 50
SALES (corp-wide): 19.6MM **Privately Held**
SIC: 7372 Prepackaged software
PA: Arena Solutions, Inc.
989 E Hillsdale Blvd # 250
Foster City CA 94404
650 513-3500

(P-23624)
ARIBA INC (DH)
3420 Hillview Ave Bldg 3, Palo Alto (94304-1355)
PHONE..................................650 849-4000
Alex Atzberger, *CEO*
Marc Malone, *CFO*
Alicia Tillman, *Chief Mktg Ofcr*
Brad Brubaker, *Admin Sec*
Kimberly Truong, *Administration*
EMP: 105
SQ FT: 86,000
SALES (est): 384.4MM
SALES (corp-wide): 28.2B **Privately Held**
WEB: www.ariba.com
SIC: 7372 Business oriented computer software
HQ: Sap America, Inc.
3999 West Chester Pike
Newtown Square PA 19073
610 661-1000

▲ = Import ▼=Export
◆ =Import/Export

(P-23625)
ARISTAMD INC
11099 N Torrey Pines Rd # 290, La Jolla
(92037-1029)
PHONE.................................858 750-4777
Brooke Levasseur, *CEO*
Dereck Tatman, *President*
Adam Darkins, *Officer*
Rebecca Dofina, *Principal*
Suhayla Karawan, *Opers Mgr*
EMP: 10
SALES (est): 1MM **Privately Held**
SIC: 7372 Operating systems computer
software

(P-23626)
ARXIS TECHNOLOGY INC
2468 Tapo Canyon Rd, Simi Valley
(93063-2361)
PHONE.................................805 306-7890
Christopher L Hamilton, *CEO*
Mark Severance, *Sales Staff*
Janna Crowther, *Sr Consultant*
Marc Hall, *Sr Consultant*
Betsy Quis, *Manager*
EMP: 32
SALES (est): 4.4MM **Privately Held**
SIC: 7372 Prepackaged software

(P-23627)
ASCERT LLC (PA)
Also Called: Softsell Business Systems
759 Bridgeway, Sausalito (94965-2102)
PHONE.................................415 339-8500
Rob Walker,
Andrew Mould,
EMP: 12
SQ FT: 3,000
SALES (est): 1.8MM **Privately Held**
WEB: www.ascert.com
SIC: 7372 7371 Prepackaged software;
computer software development & appli-
cations

(P-23628)
ASPECT SOFTWARE INC
101 Academy Ste 130, Irvine (92617-3081)
PHONE.................................408 595-5002
James Foy, *Owner*
EMP: 50
SALES (corp-wide): 303.2MM **Privately
Held**
SIC: 7372 Prepackaged software
HQ: Aspect Software, Inc.
2325 E Camelback Rd # 700
Phoenix AZ 85016
978 250-7900

(P-23629)
ASSET GENERAL INC
Also Called: Metrofeed
5363 Aurora Summit Trl, San Diego
(92130-5066)
P.O. Box 2861, La Jolla (92038-2861)
PHONE.................................800 753-2556
Don Senerath, *President*
EMP: 25
SQ FT: 2,000
SALES (est): 1MM **Privately Held**
SIC: 7372 7371 7379 7374 Business oriented computer software; computer software development & applications;
computer software development; computer related maintenance services; computer related consulting services; service
bureau, computer; software training, computer

(P-23630)
ASSET SCIENCE LLC
17150 Via Del Campo # 200, San Diego
(92127-2110)
PHONE.................................858 255-7982
John Sheeran, *CEO*
Terence Howard, *President*
EMP: 35 **EST:** 2010
SALES (est): 1.3MM **Privately Held**
SIC: 7372 Application computer software

(P-23631)
ASTEA INTERNATIONAL INC
8 Hughes, Irvine (92618-2072)
PHONE.................................949 784-5000
Carl Smith, *Branch Mgr*
EMP: 30

SALES (corp-wide): 27.4MM **Publicly
Held**
WEB: www.astea.com
SIC: 7372 Business oriented computer
software
PA: Astea International Inc.
240 Gibraltar Rd Ste 300
Horsham PA 19044
215 682-2500

(P-23632)
**ASTERA SOFTWARE
CORPORATION**
310 N Westlake Blvd # 140, Westlake Vil-
lage (91362-7064)
PHONE.................................805 579-0004
Ibrahim Surani, *CEO*
Munira Surani, *Admin Sec*
Cyrus Hashtpari, *Accounts Mgr*
Rich Steen, *Accounts Exec*
EMP: 12
SALES (est): 1.3MM **Privately Held**
WEB: www.astera.com
SIC: 7372 Application computer software

(P-23633)
ASTRO TECHNOLOGY INC
3335 Birch St, Palo Alto (94306-2808)
PHONE.................................650 533-5087
Andy Pflaum, *CEO*
EMP: 28
SQ FT: 150
SALES (est): 188.8K
SALES (corp-wide): 400.5MM **Publicly
Held**
SIC: 7372 Application computer software
PA: Slack Technologies, Inc.
500 Howard St Ste 100
San Francisco CA 94105
415 902-5526

(P-23634)
ATHOC INC (DH)
3001 Bishop Dr Ste 400, San Ramon
(94583-5005)
PHONE.................................925 242-5660
Guy Miasnik, *President*
Douglas Doyle, *Officer*
Aviv Siegel, *Exec VP*
Ly Tran, *Exec VP*
Karen Garavatti, *Vice Pres*
EMP: 61
SALES (est): 15.3MM
SALES (corp-wide): 904MM **Privately
Held**
WEB: www.athoc.com
SIC: 7372 Prepackaged software
HQ: Blackberry Corporation
3001 Bishop Dr
San Ramon CA 94583
972 650-6126

(P-23635)
ATLANTIS COMPUTING INC (PA)
900 Glenneyre St, Laguna Beach
(92651-2707)
PHONE.................................650 917-9471
Jason Donahue, *CEO*
Timm Hoyt, *Partner*
Richard Van Hoesen, *CFO*
David Cumberworth, *Vice Pres*
Ruben Spruijt, *CTO*
EMP: 35
SQ FT: 5,000
SALES (est): 6.6MM **Privately Held**
SIC: 7372 Business oriented computer
software

(P-23636)
ATLASSIAN INC (DH)
350 Bush St Ste 13, San Francisco
(94104-2879)
PHONE.................................415 701-1110
Scott Farquhar, *CEO*
Jeff Diana,
Carilu Dietrich, *Vice Pres*
Audra Eng, *Vice Pres*
Daniel Freeman, *Vice Pres*
EMP: 101
SALES (est): 43.3MM
SALES (corp-wide): 873.9MM **Privately
Held**
WEB: www.atlassian.com
SIC: 7372 Business oriented computer
software

(P-23637)
ATYPON SYSTEMS LLC (PA)
5201 Great America Pkwy # 215, Santa
Clara (95054-1177)
PHONE.................................408 988-1240
Georgios Papadopoulos, *CEO*
Colin Caprani, *Partner*
Chao Zhang, *Partner*
Joshua Pyle, *President*
Gordon Tibbitts, *President*
EMP: 60
SQ FT: 6,000
SALES (est): 12.3MM **Privately Held**
WEB: www.atypon.com
SIC: 7372 Application computer software

(P-23638)
**AUDATEX NORTH AMERICA INC
(DH)**
Also Called: Audaexplore
15030 Ave Of, San Diego (92128)
PHONE.................................858 946-1900
Don Tartre, *Vice Pres*
Jack Pearlstein, *CFO*
Ryan Hager, *Vice Pres*
Richard Palmer, *Vice Pres*
Steve Poeschl, *Software Engr*
EMP: 200
SQ FT: 35,000
SALES (est): 130MM
SALES (corp-wide): 849MM **Privately
Held**
SIC: 7372 Business oriented computer
software

(P-23639)
AUTODESK INC
1 Market St, San Francisco (94105-1420)
PHONE.................................415 356-0700
Chris Bradshaw, *Branch Mgr*
Yvonne Cekel, *Partner*
Wes Hamerstadt, *Partner*
Lisa Campbell, *Chief Mktg Ofcr*
Lee Pisacano, *Vice Pres*
EMP: 61
SALES (corp-wide): 2.5B **Publicly Held**
WEB: www.autodesk.com
SIC: 7372 Application computer software
PA: Autodesk, Inc.
111 Mcinnis Pkwy
San Rafael CA 94903
415 507-5000

(P-23640)
AUTODESK INC (PA)
111 Mcinnis Pkwy, San Rafael
(94903-2700)
PHONE.................................415 507-5000
Andrew Anagnost, *President*
Stacy J Smith, *Ch of Bd*
R Scott Herren, *CFO*
Pascal W Di Fronzo,
Carmel Galvin, *Officer*
◆ **EMP:** 400 **EST:** 1982
SQ FT: 189,000
SALES: 2.5B **Publicly Held**
WEB: www.autodesk.com
SIC: 7372 Application computer software

(P-23641)
AUTODESK INC
3950 Civic Center Dr, San Rafael
(94903-5901)
PHONE.................................415 507-5000
Kathryn Najafi-Tagol, *Manager*
Thomas Georgens, *Bd of Directors*
EMP: 250
SALES (corp-wide): 2.5B **Publicly Held**
WEB: www.autodesk.com
SIC: 7372 Application computer software
PA: Autodesk, Inc.
111 Mcinnis Pkwy
San Rafael CA 94903
415 507-5000

(P-23642)
AVAST SOFTWARE INC (PA)
2625 Broadway St, Redwood City
(94063-1532)
PHONE.................................844 340-9251
Vincent Wayne Steckler, *CEO*
Julianne Marsello, *Partner*
Lorne Somerville, *Managing Prtnr*
Wendy Thompson, *Treasurer*
Robin Selden, *Chief Mktg Ofcr*
EMP: 18

SALES (est): 43MM **Privately Held**
SIC: 7372 Application computer software

(P-23643)
AVATIER CORPORATION (PA)
4733 Chabot Dr Ste 201, Pleasanton
(94588-3971)
P.O. Box 12124 (94588-2124)
PHONE.................................925 217-5170
Nelson Cicchitto, *CEO*
Nelson A Cicchitto, *CEO*
Steven Yeffa, *CFO*
Eric Havens, *Software Engr*
Jami Cox, *Opers Staff*
EMP: 21
SQ FT: 5,500
SALES (est): 12.5MM **Privately Held**
WEB: www.avatier.com
SIC: 7372 7373 Business oriented com-
puter software; systems software devel-
opment services

(P-23644)
AVAYA HOLDINGS CORP (PA)
4655 Great America Pkwy, Santa Clara
(95054-1236)
PHONE.................................908 953-6000
Charles H Giancarlo, *Ch of Bd*
Dino Di Palma, *Partner*
Drew Thomas, *Partner*
Kevin J Kennedy, *President*
Ed Nalbandian, *President*
EMP: 46
SALES: 2.2B **Publicly Held**
SIC: 7372 3661 Prepackaged software;
telephones & telephone apparatus

(P-23645)
AXCELEON INC
1947 Overlook Rd, Fullerton (92831-1020)
PHONE.................................714 960-5200
Michael Duffy, *President*
Mary Keogh, *CEO*
EMP: 15
SALES (est): 1.5MM **Privately Held**
WEB: www.axceleon.com
SIC: 7372 Prepackaged software

(P-23646)
AXIA TECHNOLOGIES LLC
4183 State St, Santa Barbara
(93110-1817)
PHONE.................................855 376-2942
Randal Clark, *CEO*
Kevin Falconer, *COO*
Mike Sheffey, *CTO*
Dan Berger, *Sales Staff*
Travis Davis, *Director*
EMP: 21 **EST:** 2016
SALES (est): 1.2MM **Privately Held**
SIC: 7372 Prepackaged software

(P-23647)
AZUL SYSTEMS INC (PA)
385 Moffett Park Dr # 115, Sunnyvale
(94089-1217)
PHONE.................................650 230-6500
Scott Sellers, *President*
Anya Chernyak, *Vice Pres*
Michael J Field, *Vice Pres*
George W Gould, *Vice Pres*
George Gould, *Vice Pres*
EMP: 65
SALES (est): 21.7MM **Privately Held**
WEB: www.azulsystems.com
SIC: 7372 Operating systems computer
software

(P-23648)
BADGER MAPS INC
539 Broadway, San Francisco
(94133-4521)
PHONE.................................415 592-5909
Steven Benson, *CEO*
Timothy Jernigan, *Marketing Staff*
Anna Bolender, *Relations*
EMP: 40
SQ FT: 1,000
SALES (est): 1.1MM **Privately Held**
SIC: 7372 Application computer software

(P-23649)
BADGEVILLE INC
805 Veterans Blvd Ste 307, Redwood City
(94063-1737)
PHONE.................................650 323-6668

Jon Shalowitz, *President*
Stephanie Vinella, *CFO*
Karen Hsu, *Vice Pres*
Andy Pederson, *Vice Pres*
Roel Stalman, *Vice Pres*
EMP: 45 **EST:** 2010
SALES (est): 9.2MM **Privately Held**
SIC: 7372 Prepackaged software

(P-23650)
BAFFLE INC
2811 Mission College Blvd, Santa Clara
(95054-1884)
PHONE..................408 663-6737
Ameesh Divatia, *CEO*
EMP: 10 **EST:** 2015
SQ FT: 10,000
SALES (est): 357.3K **Privately Held**
SIC: 7372 Application computer software

(P-23651)
BANJO INC (PA)
833 Main St, Redwood City (94063-1901)
PHONE..................650 425-6376
Damien Patton, *CEO*
Ryan Johnson, *Vice Pres*
Kor Esta, *Office Mgr*
Katie Vellucci, *Executive Asst*
Leung Kw Justin, *Engineer*
EMP: 15 **EST:** 2010
SALES (est): 1.7MM **Privately Held**
SIC: 7372 Prepackaged software

(P-23652)
BARRA LLC (HQ)
Also Called: Msci Barra
2100 Milvia St, Berkeley (94704-1861)
PHONE..................510 548-5442
Kamal Duggirala, *CEO*
Andrew Rudd, *Ch of Bd*
Aamir Sheikh, *President*
Greg Stockett, *CFO*
Susan Gledhill, *General Mgr*
▲ **EMP:** 280
SQ FT: 35,000
SALES (est): 29MM **Publicly Held**
WEB: www.barra.com
SIC: 7372 8741 6282 Business oriented
computer software; financial management
for business; investment advisory service

(P-23653)
BARRACUDA NETWORKS INC (HQ)
3175 Winchester Blvd, Campbell
(95008-6557)
PHONE..................408 342-5400
William D Jenkins Jr, *President*
Dustin Driggs, *CFO*
Erin Hintz, *Chief Mktg Ofcr*
Zachary Levow, *Exec VP*
Fleming Shi, *Technology*
EMP: 225
SQ FT: 61,400
SALES: 352.6MM
SALES (corp-wide): 44.8MM **Privately Held**
WEB: www.barracudanetworks.com
SIC: 7372 7373 Prepackaged software;
computer integrated systems design
PA: Barracuda Holdings, Llc
3175 Winchester Blvd
Campbell CA 95008
408 342-5400

(P-23654)
BASE CRM
1019 Market St Fl 1, San Francisco
(94103-1637)
PHONE..................773 796-6266
Uzi Shmilovici, *Principal*
Michael Logan, *Vice Pres*
Jeremy Barber, *Engineer*
Lindsey Bly, *Marketing Staff*
Josh Bean, *Manager*
EMP: 13
SALES (est): 1MM **Privately Held**
SIC: 7372 Prepackaged software

(P-23655)
BCG/MANAGEMENT RESOURCES
Also Called: Beck Consulting
1320 Willow Pass Rd # 60, Concord
(94520-5232)
PHONE..................800 456-8474

Bruno Johansson, *CEO*
Dirk Manders, *President*
Jude Enoch, *Consultant*
▲ **EMP:** 12
SQ FT: 4,000
SALES (est): 1.1MM
SALES (corp-wide): 462MM **Privately Held**
WEB: www.beckconsulting.com
SIC: 7372 Business oriented computer
software
PA: Aptean, Inc.
4325 Alexander Dr Ste 100
Alpharetta GA 30022
770 351-9600

(P-23656)
BEATS MUSIC LLC
235 2nd St, San Francisco (94105-3124)
PHONE..................415 590-5104
Timothy Cook, *CEO*
EMP: 95
SALES (est): 8.5MM
SALES (corp-wide): 260.1B **Publicly Held**
SIC: 7372 Prepackaged software
PA: Apple Inc.
1 Apple Park Way
Cupertino CA 95014
408 996-1010

(P-23657)
BEEKEE CORP
5882 Bolsa Ave Ste 210, Huntington Beach
(92649-5700)
PHONE..................949 275-5861
Thomas Markel, *CEO*
Kaveh Mahjoob, *CTO*
EMP: 10
SALES: 500K **Privately Held**
SIC: 7372 Prepackaged software

(P-23658)
BEHAVIOSEC INC
535 Mission St Fl 14, San Francisco
(94105-3253)
PHONE..................833 248-6732
Neil Costigan, *President*
Olov Renberg, *Vice Pres*
EMP: 15
SALES (est): 579.7K **Privately Held**
SIC: 7372 Application computer software

(P-23659)
BENEFIT SOFTWARE INCORPORATED
212 Cottage Grove Ave A, Santa Barbara
(93101-3450)
PHONE..................805 679-6200
Larry S Dubois, *President*
EMP: 30
SQ FT: 5,105
SALES (est): 2.4MM **Privately Held**
WEB: www.benefits4us.com
SIC: 7372 Prepackaged software

(P-23660)
BENTO TECHNOLOGIES INC
Also Called: Bento Merge Enterprises
221 Main St Ste 1325, San Francisco
(94105-1946)
P.O. Box 190608 (94119-0608)
PHONE..................415 887-2028
Farhan Ahmad, *CEO*
Sean Anderson, *CFO*
Jonathan Su, *Vice Pres*
Renato Steinberg, *CTO*
Grace Tang, *Opers Staff*
EMP: 11 **EST:** 2014
SQ FT: 2,628
SALES (est): 937K **Privately Held**
SIC: 7372 Business oriented computer
software

(P-23661)
BETHEBEAST INC
3738 W 181st St, Torrance (90504-3921)
PHONE..................424 206-1081
Michael Mahoney, *President*
Steve Brodzinski, *Director*
EMP: 27
SALES (est): 709.7K **Privately Held**
SIC: 7372 Educational computer software

(P-23662)
BETTERCOMPANY INC
621 Sansome St, San Francisco
(94111-2395)
PHONE..................415 501-9692
Thomas Williams, *CEO*
Colin Putney, *CTO*
Blake Egan, *Director*
EMP: 10
SQ FT: 2,500
SALES (est): 501.6K **Privately Held**
SIC: 7372 Business oriented computer
software

(P-23663)
BETTERWORKS SYSTEMS INC
999 Main St, Redwood City (94063-2152)
PHONE..................650 656-9013
Doug Dennerline, *CEO*
Diane Strohfus, *Officer*
Karen Richter, *Vice Pres*
Mathew Geist, *Software Engr*
Justin Huang, *Software Engr*
EMP: 75
SALES: 8MM **Privately Held**
SIC: 7372 Publishers' computer software

(P-23664)
BGL DEVELOPMENT INC
Also Called: The Bristol Group
3070 Kerner Blvd Ste H, San Rafael
(94901-5419)
P.O. Box 2399 (94912-2399)
PHONE..................415 256-2525
Peter R Harris, *President*
Nicole Letaw, *COO*
David Nakabayashi, *Creative Dir*
Andrew Guynn, *Principal*
Kevin Clark, *Info Tech Dir*
EMP: 10
SQ FT: 2,600
SALES (est): 1MM **Privately Held**
WEB: www.bg.com
SIC: 7372 Prepackaged software

(P-23665)
BIDCHAT INC
14570 Benefit St Unit 302, Sherman Oaks
(91403-5510)
PHONE..................818 631-6212
Zachary Ein, *CEO*
EMP: 10
SALES: 5MM **Privately Held**
SIC: 7372 Business oriented computer
software

(P-23666)
BIG SWITCH NETWORKS INC (PA)
3111 Coronado Dr Bldg A, Santa Clara
(95054-3206)
PHONE..................650 322-6510
Douglas Murray, *CEO*
Jeffrey Wang, *President*
Seamus Hennessy, *CFO*
Wendell Laidley, *CFO*
Gregg Holzrichter, *Chief Mktg Ofcr*
EMP: 58
SALES (est): 42.8MM **Privately Held**
SIC: 7372 Prepackaged software

(P-23667)
BILLCOM INC
1810 Embarcadero Rd, Palo Alto
(94303-3308)
PHONE..................650 353-3301
Rene Lacerte, *CEO*
Jennifer Mohoney, *Partner*
Becky Riffis, *Partner*
Mark Orttung, *COO*
John Rettig, *CFO*
EMP: 140
SALES (est): 40.9MM **Privately Held**
SIC: 7372 Application computer software

(P-23668)
BIMARIAN INC
3350 Scott Blvd, Santa Clara (95054-3104)
PHONE..................408 520-2666
Siva Pullabhotla, *CEO*
EMP: 25 **EST:** 2012
SQ FT: 1,500
SALES (est): 876.4K **Privately Held**
SIC: 7372 Business oriented computer
software

(P-23669)
BINTI INC
1212 Broadway Ste 200, Oakland
(94612-1805)
PHONE..................844 424-6844
Felicia Curcuru, *CEO*
EMP: 23
SALES (est): 126.2K **Privately Held**
SIC: 7372 7389 Business oriented com-
puter software;

(P-23670)
BIOTA TECHNOLOGY INC
Also Called: Uc2
11095 Flintkote Ave Ste B, San Diego
(92121-1214)
PHONE..................650 888-6512
Jay Kshatriya, *CEO*
Ajay Kshatriya, *General Mgr*
EMP: 15
SALES (est): 109K **Privately Held**
SIC: 7372 Business oriented computer
software

(P-23671)
BIOWARE AUSTIN LLC
209 Redwood Shores Pkwy, Redwood City
(94065-1175)
PHONE..................650 628-1500
John Riccitiello, *Principal*
EMP: 17 **EST:** 2010
SALES (est): 542.7K **Privately Held**
SIC: 7372 Prepackaged software

(P-23672)
BITZER MOBILE INC
4230 Leonard Stocking Dr, Santa Clara
(95054-1777)
PHONE..................866 603-8392
Naeem Zafar, *President*
Ali Ahmed, *CTO*
EMP: 40
SQ FT: 2,000
SALES (est): 2.1MM
SALES (corp-wide): 39.5B **Publicly Held**
SIC: 7372 Business oriented computer
software
PA: Oracle Corporation
500 Oracle Pkwy
Redwood City CA 94065
650 506-7000

(P-23673)
BIZ PERFORMANCE SOLUTIONS INC
Also Called: Bizps
840 Loma Vista St, Moss Beach
(94038-9721)
PHONE..................408 844-4284
David Mosher, *CEO*
Ken Matusow, *COO*
EMP: 15
SALES: 1MM **Privately Held**
SIC: 7372 8711 Application computer soft-
ware; consulting engineer

(P-23674)
BIZMATICS INC (PA)
4010 Moorpark Ave Ste 222, San Jose
(95117-1843)
PHONE..................408 873-3030
Vinay Deshpande, *CEO*
Chris Ferguson, *President*
Sneha Baing, *Executive*
Parag Deshpande, *Analyst*
Cheri Yeung, *Accountant*
EMP: 250
SQ FT: 2,000
SALES: 5.9MM **Privately Held**
SIC: 7372 Business oriented computer
software

(P-23675)
BLACKBERRY CORPORATION (HQ)
3001 Bishop Dr, San Ramon (94583-5005)
PHONE..................972 650-6126
John Chen, *CEO*
Rashad Munawar, *Senior Mgr*
Coray Runge, *Manager*
▲ **EMP:** 79

▲ = Import ▼=Export
◆ =Import/Export

SALES (est): 268.2MM
SALES (corp-wide): 904MM **Privately Held**
WEB: www.osgcorp.com
SIC: 7372 Prepackaged software
PA: Blackberry Limited
2200 University Ave E
Waterloo ON N2K 0
519 888-7465

(P-23676)
BLACKLINE SYSTEMS INC (HQ)
21300 Victory Blvd Fl 12, Woodland Hills (91367-7734)
PHONE....................................877 777-7750
Therese Tucker, *CEO*
Jennifer T Pottle, *Partner*
Dorothy Scofield, *Partner*
Charles Best, *CFO*
Mark Partin, *CFO*
EMP: 108
SQ FT: 66,447
SALES (est): 99.6MM
SALES (corp-wide): 227.7MM **Publicly Held**
WEB: www.blackline.com
SIC: 7372 Business oriented computer software
PA: Blackline, Inc.
21300 Victory Blvd Fl 12
Woodland Hills CA 91367
818 223-9008

(P-23677)
BLIND SQUIRREL GAMES INC
1251 E Dyer Rd Ste 200, Santa Ana (92705-5655)
PHONE....................................714 460-0860
Bradford Hendricks, *CEO*
Patrick Ghiocel, *Sr Software Eng*
Ron Bitzer, *Info Tech Dir*
Jonathan Rucker, *Prgrmr*
Jason Neal, *Engineer*
EMP: 23 EST: 2010
SQ FT: 27,000
SALES (est): 4.4MM **Privately Held**
WEB: www.blindsquirrelgames.com
SIC: 7372 Home entertainment computer software

(P-23678)
BLIZZARD ENTERTAINMENT INC (HQ)
1 Blizzard, Irvine (92618-3628)
P.O. Box 18979 (92623-8979)
PHONE....................................949 955-1380
Mike Morhaime, *President*
Paul Sams, *President*
Frank Pearce, *Exec VP*
Chris Metzen, *Senior VP*
Robert Bridenbecker, *Vice Pres*
▲ EMP: 85
SALES (est): 74.5MM
SALES (corp-wide): 7.5B **Publicly Held**
SIC: 7372 5734 7819 Prepackaged software; software, computer games; reproduction services, motion picture production
PA: Activision Blizzard, Inc.
3100 Ocean Park Blvd
Santa Monica CA 90405
310 255-2000

(P-23679)
BLUE COAT LLC
350 Ellis St, Mountain View (94043-2202)
PHONE....................................408 220-2200
Michael Fey, *President*
Thomas Seifert, *CFO*
Fran Rosch, *Exec VP*
Scott Taylor, *Exec VP*
Balaji Yelamanchili, *Exec VP*
EMP: 1583
SALES (est): 96.8MM
SALES (corp-wide): 4.7B **Publicly Held**
SIC: 7372 Prepackaged software
PA: Nortonlifelock Inc.
60 E Rio Salado Pkwy # 1
Tempe AZ 85281
650 527-8000

(P-23680)
BLUE COAT SYSTEMS LLC (HQ)
350 Ellis St, Mountain View (94043-2202)
PHONE....................................650 527-8000
Michael Fey, *President*

Donald W Alford, *President*
David Yntemai, *President*
Nicholas R Noviello, *CFO*
Thomas Seifert, *CFO*
▲ EMP: 81
SQ FT: 234,000
SALES (est): 35.1MM
SALES (corp-wide): 4.7B **Publicly Held**
WEB: www.cacheflow.com
SIC: 7372 Prepackaged software
PA: Nortonlifelock Inc.
60 E Rio Salado Pkwy # 1
Tempe AZ 85281
650 527-8000

(P-23681)
BLUE IRON NETWORK INC
5811 Mcfadden Ave, Huntington Beach (92649-1323)
PHONE....................................714 901-1456
Robert McCandless, *CEO*
Cari McCandless, *CFO*
EMP: 25
SQ FT: 11,000
SALES (est): 1.7MM **Privately Held**
SIC: 7372 Business oriented computer software

(P-23682)
BLUERUN VENTURES LP
545 Middlefield Rd # 210, Menlo Park (94025-3400)
PHONE....................................650 462-7250
John Malloy, *CEO*
Jui Tan, *Partner*
Jemu Park, *Analyst*
Jennifer Yu, *Controller*
EMP: 15
SALES (est): 2.2MM **Privately Held**
SIC: 7372 Operating systems computer software

(P-23683)
BLUESNAP INC
5201 Great America Pkwy # 320, Santa Clara (95054-1122)
PHONE....................................866 475-4687
Hagai Tal, *Branch Mgr*
EMP: 25 **Privately Held**
SIC: 7372 Application computer software
PA: Bluesnap, Inc.
800 South St Ste 640
Waltham MA 02453

(P-23684)
BLUESTACK SYSTEMS INC
2105 S Bascom Ave Ste 380, Campbell (95008-3278)
PHONE....................................408 412-9439
Rosen Sharma, *President*
Hue Harguindeguy, *CFO*
Jay Vaishnav, *Senior VP*
James Sunderland, *Software Engr*
Stephen Johnston, *Controller*
EMP: 26
SALES (est): 2.4MM **Privately Held**
SIC: 7372 Application computer software

(P-23685)
BONAFIDE MANAGEMENT SYSTEMS
241 Lombard St, Thousand Oaks (91360-5807)
PHONE....................................805 777-7666
Larry Lai, *CEO*
Andres Baudry, *Ch of Bd*
EMP: 12
SQ FT: 4,000
SALES (est): 1.4MM **Privately Held**
WEB: www.bonafide.com
SIC: 7372 7371 Utility computer software; custom computer programming services

(P-23686)
BONSAI AI INC
2150 Shattuck Ave # 1200, Berkeley (94704-1357)
PHONE....................................510 900-1112
EMP: 42
SQ FT: 1,445
SALES (est): 49.3K
SALES (corp-wide): 110.3B **Publicly Held**
SIC: 7372

PA: Microsoft Corporation
1 Microsoft Way
Redmond WA 98052
425 882-8080

(P-23687)
BOOKETTE SOFTWARE CO INC
12795 Corte Cordillera, Salinas (93908-8942)
PHONE....................................831 484-9250
Ronald Loiacono, *President*
EMP: 14
SALES (est): 1.1MM **Privately Held**
SIC: 7372 Prepackaged software

(P-23688)
BORLAND SOFTWARE CORPORATION
951 Mariners Isl Blvd # 460, San Mateo (94404-1558)
PHONE....................................650 286-1900
Gina Rosenberger, *Branch Mgr*
Anil Peres-Da-Silva, *Senior Mgr*
EMP: 100 **Privately Held**
WEB: www.borland.com
SIC: 7372 Business oriented computer software
HQ: Borland Software Corporation
8310 N Cpitl Of Texas Hwy
Austin TX 78731
512 340-2200

(P-23689)
BOX INC (PA)
900 Jefferson Ave, Redwood City (94063-1837)
PHONE....................................877 729-4269
Aaron Levie, *Ch of Bd*
Chase Roberts, *Partner*
Stephanie Carullo, *COO*
Dylan Smith, *CFO*
Daniel Levin, *Bd of Directors*
EMP: 148 EST: 2005
SQ FT: 340,000
SALES: 608.3MM **Publicly Held**
SIC: 7372 Application computer software

(P-23690)
BPO MANAGEMENT SERVICES INC (HQ)
8175 E Kaiser Blvd 100, Anaheim (92808-2214)
PHONE....................................714 974-2670
Patrick Dolan, *Ch of Bd*
James Cortens, *President*
Don Rutherford, *CFO*
Koushik Dutta, *CTO*
EMP: 15
SQ FT: 3,500
SALES (est): 12.9MM
SALES (corp-wide): 28.1MM **Privately Held**
WEB: www.netguru.com
SIC: 7372 7371 Prepackaged software; custom computer programming services
PA: Bpo Management Services, Inc
8175 E Kaiser Blvd 100
Anaheim CA 92808
714 972-2670

(P-23691)
BPO SYSTEMS INC (PA)
1700 Ygnacio Valley Rd # 205, Walnut Creek (94598-3191)
PHONE....................................925 478-4299
Rambabu V Yarlagadda, *CEO*
EMP: 38 EST: 2000
SQ FT: 4,000
SALES (est): 4MM **Privately Held**
WEB: www.bposystems.com
SIC: 7372 Prepackaged software

(P-23692)
BQE SOFTWARE INC
3825 Del Amo Blvd Trrance Torrance, Torrance (90503)
PHONE....................................310 602-4020
Shafat Qazi, *CEO*
Sharone Strauss, *Vice Pres*
Kari Weinberger, *Marketing Staff*
Jason Burkley, *Sales Staff*
Humza Khan, *Sales Staff*
EMP: 95
SQ FT: 20,000

SALES (est): 13.1MM **Privately Held**
WEB: www.billquick.com
SIC: 7372 5734 Application computer software; software, business & non-game

(P-23693)
BRAINCHIP INC (HQ)
65 Enterprise, Aliso Viejo (92656-2705)
PHONE....................................949 330-6750
Louis Dinardo, *CEO*
Thomas Stengel, *Vice Pres*
Peter Van Der Made, *CTO*
EMP: 26 EST: 2014
SQ FT: 2,500
SALES (est): 3.4MM **Privately Held**
SIC: 7372 Prepackaged software

(P-23694)
BRAINS OUT MEDIA INC
2629 Foothill Blvd # 111, La Crescenta (91214-3511)
PHONE....................................818 296-1036
Fermin Iglesias, *President*
EMP: 15 EST: 2014
SALES: 850K **Privately Held**
SIC: 7372 7374 Application computer software; computer graphics service

(P-23695)
BRANCH MESSENGER INC
130 W Union St, Pasadena (91103-3628)
PHONE....................................323 300-4063
Atif Siddiqi, *President*
EMP: 10 EST: 2014
SALES (est): 244K **Privately Held**
SIC: 7372 Application computer software

(P-23696)
BRENDAN TECHNOLOGIES INC
1947 Camino Vida Roble # 21, Carlsbad (92008-6540)
PHONE....................................760 929-7500
John R Dunn II, *Ch of Bd*
George Dunn, *COO*
Lowell W Giffhorn, *CFO*
Lowell Giffhorn, *CFO*
EMP: 20
SQ FT: 3,988
SALES: 521.3K **Privately Held**
WEB: www.brendan.com
SIC: 7372 Business oriented computer software; utility computer software; application computer software

(P-23697)
BRIGHTIDEA INCORPORATED
255 California St # 1100, San Francisco (94111-4927)
PHONE....................................415 814-1387
Luis Ostdiek, *Branch Mgr*
Mike Xu, *President*
Brian Benson, *Consultant*
EMP: 25
SALES (corp-wide): 8.6MM **Privately Held**
SIC: 7372 Prepackaged software
PA: Brightidea Incorporated
25 Pacific Ave
San Francisco CA
415 814-3817

(P-23698)
BRILLIANT WORLDWIDE INC
200 Pine St Fl 8, San Francisco (94104-2707)
PHONE....................................650 468-2966
Sue Khim, *CEO*
Suyeon Khim, *CEO*
EMP: 25
SALES (est): 73.2K **Privately Held**
SIC: 7372 Educational computer software

(P-23699)
BROADLY INC
409 13th St Fl 3, Oakland (94612-2606)
PHONE....................................510 400-6039
Joshua Melick, *CEO*
Chris Deianni, *Business Mgr*
Matt Baker, *Opers Staff*
Laura Nelson, *Marketing Staff*
Kim Olson, *Sales Staff*
EMP: 30
SALES (est): 184.4K **Privately Held**
SIC: 7372 Business oriented computer software

PRODUCTS & SVCS

(P-23700)
BROADVISION INC (PA)
460 Seaport Ct Ste 102, Redwood City
(94063-5548)
PHONE.....................650 331-1000
Pehong Chen, *Ch of Bd*
Sandra Adams, *Vice Pres*
Lisheng Zhang, *Engineer*
May He, *Accounting Mgr*
Combi Serena, *Finance*
EMP: 95
SQ FT: 16,399
SALES: 5MM **Publicly Held**
WEB: www.broadvision.com
SIC: 7372 Prepackaged software

(P-23701)
BTRADE LLC
655 N Central Ave # 1460, Glendale
(91203-1422)
PHONE.....................818 334-4433
Steve Zapata, *Mng Member*
Don Miller, *COO*
Clifton Gonsalves, *Vice Pres*
Teresa Perez, *Vice Pres*
Theresa Perez, *Administration*
EMP: 25
SALES: 3MM **Privately Held**
SIC: 7372 Business oriented computer
software

(P-23702)
BUILDING ROBOTICS INC
Also Called: Comfy
300 Frank H, Oakland (94612)
PHONE.....................510 761-6482
Andrew Krioukov, *CEO*
Chitra Nayak, *COO*
Nick Colburn, *CFO*
Amip Shah, *Vice Pres*
Stephen Dawson-Haggerty, *CTO*
EMP: 15
SALES (est): 616.9K **Privately Held**
SIC: 7372 Application computer software

(P-23703)
BUOY LABS INC
Also Called: Resideo Buoy
125 Mcpherson St, Santa Cruz
(95060-5883)
PHONE.....................855 481-7112
Keri Waters, *CEO*
EMP: 16
SALES (est): 1.5MM
SALES (corp-wide): 4.8B **Publicly Held**
SIC: 7372 Prepackaged software
PA: Resideo Technologies, Inc.
1985 Douglas Dr N
Golden Valley MN 55422
763 954-5204

(P-23704)
C3AI INC (PA)
Also Called: C3 Iot
1300 Seaport Blvd Ste 500, Redwood City
(94063-5592)
PHONE.....................650 503-2200
Thomas M Siebel, *CEO*
Ed Abbo, *President*
Jordan Marchetto, *Software Dev*
Dylan Ferris, *Software Engr*
EMP: 122
SQ FT: 35,000
SALES (est): 55.3MM **Privately Held**
SIC: 7372 Business oriented computer
software

(P-23705)
CA INC
3965 Freedom Cir Fl 6, Santa Clara
(95054-1286)
PHONE.....................800 225-5224
EMP: 166
SALES (corp-wide): 20.8B **Publicly Held**
SIC: 7372 Business oriented computer
software
HQ: Ca, Inc.
520 Madison Ave
New York NY 10022
800 225-5224

(P-23706)
CA INC
3013 Douglas Blvd Ste 120, Roseville
(95661-3842)
PHONE.....................800 405-5540

Larry Lynch, *Manager*
EMP: 20
SALES (corp-wide): 20.8B **Publicly Held**
WEB: www.cai.com
SIC: 7372 Business oriented computer
software
HQ: Ca, Inc.
520 Madison Ave
New York NY 10022
800 225-5224

(P-23707)
CADENCE DESIGN SYSTEMS INC
707 California St, Mountain View
(94041-2005)
PHONE.....................408 943-1234
EMP: 45
SALES (corp-wide): 2.1B **Publicly Held**
SIC: 7372 Prepackaged software
PA: Cadence Design Systems, Inc.
2655 Seely Ave Bldg 5
San Jose CA 95134
408 943-1234

(P-23708)
CADENCE DESIGN SYSTEMS INC
7505 Irvine Center Dr # 250, Irvine
(92618-3078)
PHONE.....................949 788-6080
EMP: 34
SALES (corp-wide): 1.9B **Publicly Held**
SIC: 7372
PA: Cadence Design Systems, Inc.
2655 Seely Ave Bldg 5
San Jose CA 95134
408 943-1234

(P-23709)
CADENCE DESIGN SYSTEMS INC (PA)
2655 Seely Ave Bldg 5, San Jose
(95134-1931)
PHONE.....................408 943-1234
Lip-Bu Tan, *CEO*
John B Shoven, *Ch of Bd*
Anirudh Devgan, *President*
John M Wall, *CFO*
Thomas P Beckley, *Senior VP*
▲ EMP: 700
SALES: 2.1B **Publicly Held**
WEB: www.cadence.com
SIC: 7372 Prepackaged software; applica-
tion computer software

(P-23710)
CADENCE DESIGN SYSTEMS INC
2150 Shattuck Ave Fl 10, Berkeley
(94704-1345)
PHONE.....................510 647-2800
Ted Vucurezich, *Branch Mgr*
EMP: 18
SALES (corp-wide): 2.1B **Publicly Held**
WEB: www.cadence.com
SIC: 7372 Application computer software
PA: Cadence Design Systems, Inc.
2655 Seely Ave Bldg 5
San Jose CA 95134
408 943-1234

(P-23711)
CADENCE DESIGN SYSTEMS INC
6700 Koll Center Pkwy # 160, Pleasanton
(94566-7060)
PHONE.....................925 895-3202
Matt Depretis, *Branch Mgr*
Aditya Mainkar, *Manager*
EMP: 10
SALES (corp-wide): 2.1B **Publicly Held**
WEB: www.cadence.com
SIC: 7372 Application computer software
PA: Cadence Design Systems, Inc.
2655 Seely Ave Bldg 5
San Jose CA 95134
408 943-1234

(P-23712)
CADENCE US INC (PA)
2655 Seely Ave, San Jose (95134-1931)
PHONE.....................408 943-1234
James Lico, *Vice Pres*
CHI-Ping Hsu, *Vice Pres*

Tina Jones, *Vice Pres*
Nimish Modi, *Vice Pres*
Neil Zaman, *Vice Pres*
EMP: 10
SALES (est): 1.3MM **Privately Held**
SIC: 7372 Application computer software

(P-23713)
CALEB ENTERPRISES INC
5857 Owens Ave Ste 300, Carlsbad
(92008-5507)
PHONE.....................760 683-8787
Matthew Menotti, *CEO*
EMP: 15
SALES (est): 305.2K **Privately Held**
SIC: 7372 Prepackaged software

(P-23714)
CALYPTO DESIGN SYSTEMS INC
2099 Gateway Pl Ste 550, San Jose
(95110-1051)
PHONE.....................408 850-2300
Sanjiv Kaul, *President*
Chris Mausler, *CFO*
Richard Langridge, *Info Tech Dir*
Bala Sethuraman, *Research*
EMP: 17
SALES (est): 2.2MM **Privately Held**
WEB: www.calypto.com
SIC: 7372 Business oriented computer
software

(P-23715)
CANARY TECHNOLOGIES CORP
450 9th St, San Francisco (94103-4411)
PHONE.....................415 578-1414
Satjot Sawhney, *CEO*
Harman Narula, *Administration*
EMP: 22 EST: 2017
SALES (est): 500.7K **Privately Held**
SIC: 7372 Business oriented computer
software

(P-23716)
CANTO SOFTWARE INC (PA)
625 Market St Ste 600, San Francisco
(94105-3308)
PHONE.....................415 495-6545
Jack McGannon, *CEO*
Hans D Schaedel, *CFO*
Jonathan De Jesus, *Sales Staff*
Andreas Mockenhaupt, *Director*
EMP: 15 EST: 1993
SALES (est): 5MM **Privately Held**
WEB: www.canto.com
SIC: 7372 Prepackaged software

(P-23717)
CAREVAULT CORPORATION
182 Exbourne Ave Ste 200, San Carlos
(94070-1828)
PHONE.....................714 333-0556
Avanish Sahai, *CEO*
EMP: 10 EST: 2011
SALES (est): 654.7K **Privately Held**
SIC: 7372 Prepackaged software

(P-23718)
CARGO CHIEF INC
10 Rollins Rd Ste 202, Millbrae
(94030-3129)
PHONE.....................650 560-5001
Russell Jones, *CEO*
Abtin Hamidi, *Vice Pres*
Kyle Wilson, *Director*
EMP: 12
SALES: 4MM **Privately Held**
SIC: 7372 Business oriented computer
software

(P-23719)
CARPARTS TECHNOLOGIES
32122 Camn Capistrano # 100, San Juan
Capistrano (92675-3734)
PHONE.....................949 488-8860
Charles Ruban, *CEO*
Cynthia Robbins, *President*
EMP: 163 EST: 2004
SQ FT: 1,400
SALES (est): 6.3MM **Privately Held**
WEB: www.crcs.com
SIC: 7372 Prepackaged software

(P-23720)
CASEMAKER INC
1680 Civic Center Dr Frnt, Santa Clara
(95050-4146)
PHONE.....................408 261-8265
Jui-Long Liu, *President*
Linda Franklin, *Director*
EMP: 14
SQ FT: 11,000
SALES (est): 1.8MM **Privately Held**
WEB: www.casemaker.com
SIC: 7372 7371 Application computer soft-
ware; custom computer programming
services

(P-23721)
CASPIAN RESEARCH & TECH LLC
1434 Westwood Blvd Ste 14, Los Angeles
(90024-4939)
PHONE.....................310 474-3244
Amir Tarighat, *Director*
EMP: 10
SALES (est): 221.8K **Privately Held**
SIC: 7372 7382 Operating systems com-
puter software; security systems services

(P-23722)
CASPIO INC (PA)
2953 Bunker Hill Ln # 201, Santa Clara
(95054-1131)
PHONE.....................650 691-0900
Frank Zamani, *CEO*
Spring Babb, *Admin Sec*
EMP: 23 EST: 2000
SQ FT: 4,000
SALES (est): 3.8MM **Privately Held**
SIC: 7372 Business oriented computer
software

(P-23723)
CATALYST DEVELOPMENT CORP
56925 Yucca Trl, Yucca Valley
(92284-7913)
PHONE.....................760 228-9653
Cary Harwin, *President*
Brian Rich, *Managing Prtnr*
Mike Stefanik, *Senior VP*
Kapil Desai, *Analyst*
Samantha Lexton, *Sr Associate*
EMP: 50
SALES (est): 3MM **Privately Held**
WEB: www.catalyst.com
SIC: 7372 Business oriented computer
software

(P-23724)
CATAPULT COMMUNICATIONS CORP (DH)
26601 Agoura Rd, Calabasas
(91302-1959)
PHONE.....................818 871-1800
Richard A Karp, *Ch of Bd*
David Mayfield, *President*
Chris Stephenson, *CFO*
Terry Eastham, *Vice Pres*
Barbara J Fairhurst, *Vice Pres*
▲ EMP: 25
SQ FT: 39,000
SALES (est): 13.9MM
SALES (corp-wide): 3.8B **Publicly Held**
WEB: www.catapult.com
SIC: 7372 3661 Application computer soft-
ware; telephone & telegraph apparatus
HQ: Ixia
26601 Agoura Rd
Calabasas CA 91302
818 871-1800

(P-23725)
CELIGO INC (PA)
1820 Gateway Dr Ste 260, San Mateo
(94404-4068)
PHONE.....................650 579-0210
Jan K Arendtsz, *CEO*
Mark Simon, *Vice Pres*
Lisa Lorenz, *Office Mgr*
Laura Sherman, *Administration*
Swapna Vemparala, *Software Engr*
EMP: 50
SALES (est): 14.8MM **Privately Held**
SIC: 7372 Business oriented computer
software

▲ = Import ▼=Export
◆ =Import/Export

(P-23726)
CELLFUSION INC
1115 Lorne Way, Sunnyvale (94087-5158)
PHONE......................650 347-4000
Kersten Ellerbrock, *Manager*
EMP: 11 **Privately Held**
SIC: 7372 Prepackaged software
PA: Cellfusion, Inc.
2033 Gateway Pl Fl 5
San Jose CA 95110
-

(P-23727)
CEREGO INC
433 California St # 1030, San Francisco
(94104-2014)
PHONE......................415 518-3926
Andrew Smith Lewis, *Mng Member*
Tsai Brian, *COO*
Justin Pimcar, *Engineer*
Kyle Stewart, *Engineer*
Alex Volkovitsky, *Engineer*
EMP: 12
SALES (est): 1.5MM **Privately Held**
SIC: 7372 7379 Educational computer
software;

(P-23728)
CERNER CORPORATION
Also Called: Cerner Life Sciences
9100 Wilshire Blvd 655e, Beverly Hills
(90212-3442)
PHONE......................310 247-7700
Gloria Shulman, *Vice Pres*
Matthew Rosenbaum, *Applctn Conslt*
Ann Donahue, *Sr Consultant*
EMP: 42
SALES (corp-wide): 5.3B **Publicly Held**
WEB: www.cerner.com
SIC: 7372 Business oriented computer
software
PA: Cerner Corporation
2800 Rock Creek Pkwy
Kansas City MO 64117
816 201-1024

(P-23729)
CERTAIN INC (PA)
75 Hawthorne St Ste 550, San Francisco
(94105-3938)
PHONE......................415 353-5330
Peter Micciche, *CEO*
Brian Bailard, *Officer*
Lesa Barker, *Admin Mgr*
Shawn Bruce, *Technology*
Jason Bradfield, *Analyst*
EMP: 38 **EST:** 1994
SALES (est): 10.7MM **Privately Held**
SIC: 7372 Prepackaged software

(P-23730)
CFORIA SOFTWARE INC
4333 Park Terrace Dr # 201, Westlake Village (91361-5656)
PHONE......................818 871-9687
Dave McIntyre, *President*
Chris Caparon, *President*
Desirae McArdle, *Prgrmr*
EMP: 22
SQ FT: 4,000
SALES (est): 3.8MM **Privately Held**
WEB: www.cforia.com
SIC: 7372 Business oriented computer
software

(P-23731)
CFS TAX SOFTWARE
Also Called: CFS Income Tax
1445 E Los Angeles Ave # 214, Simi Valley
(93065-2828)
P.O. Box 941659 (93094-1659)
PHONE......................805 522-1157
Ted Sullivan, *President*
Duy Tran, *Vice Pres*
Tyler Monroe, *Software Dev*
Juliana Caizzo, *MIS Staff*
Greg Hatfield, *Prgrmr*
EMP: 60
SALES (est): 6MM **Privately Held**
WEB: www.taxtools.com
SIC: 7372 8721 Business oriented computer software; accounting, auditing & bookkeeping

(P-23732)
CHANGYOUCOM (US) LLC
1654 Hollenbeck Ave # 14, Sunnyvale
(94087-5474)
PHONE......................408 889-9866
EMP: 45 **EST:** 2009
SALES (est): 3.4MM **Privately Held**
SIC: 7372 Publishers' computer software

(P-23733)
CHECK POINT SOFTWARE TECH INC (HQ)
959 Skyway Rd Ste 300, San Carlos
(94070-2723)
PHONE......................650 628-2000
John Slavitt, *CEO*
Eyal Deshen, *CFO*
Julie Parrish, *Chief Mktg Ofcr*
Asheem Chandna, *Vice Pres*
Dorit Dor, *Vice Pres*
▲ **EMP:** 120
SALES (est): 247.1MM
SALES (corp-wide): 517.3MM **Privately Held**
WEB: www.checkpoint.com
SIC: 7372 Operating systems computer software
PA: Check Point Software Technologies Ltd.
5 Shlomo Kaplan
Tel Aviv-Jaffa 67891
375 345-55

(P-23734)
CHEMSW INC
2480 Burskirk Ste 300, Pleasant Hill
(94523)
PHONE......................707 864-0845
Brian Stafford, *President*
Patrick Spink, *Vice Pres*
EMP: 16
SQ FT: 2,600
SALES (est): 293.7K
SALES (corp-wide): 1.8B **Privately Held**
WEB: www.chemsw.com
SIC: 7372 Prepackaged software
HQ: Dassault Systemes Biovia Corp.
5005 Wateridge Vista Dr # 2
San Diego CA 92121

(P-23735)
CHOWNOW INC
12181 Bluff Creek Dr # 200, Playa Vista
(90094-2992)
PHONE......................888 707-2469
Eric Jaffe, *President*
Christopher Schnack, *Executive*
Mike Wang, *Executive*
Ha Lam, *Software Engr*
Tom Pumilia, *Sales Mgr*
EMP: 100
SQ FT: 25,000
SALES (est): 2.1MM **Privately Held**
SIC: 7372 Business oriented computer software

(P-23736)
CIMMARON SOFTWARE INC
16885 W Bernardo Dr # 345, San Diego
(92127-1618)
PHONE......................858 385-1291
Richard Lidstrom, *CEO*
Goran Stijacic, *President*
EMP: 20
SQ FT: 5,000
SALES (est): 1.7MM **Privately Held**
WEB: www.cimmaronsoftware.com
SIC: 7372 7371 5734 Prepackaged software; custom computer programming services; software, business & non-game

(P-23737)
CIPHERCLOUD INC (PA)
2581 Junction Ave Ste 200, San Jose
(95134-1923)
PHONE......................408 519-6930
Pravin Kothari, *CEO*
Stanley Chan, *Vice Pres*
Paul Culpepper, *Vice Pres*
Harnish Kanani, *Vice Pres*
Ramesh Rathi, *Vice Pres*
EMP: 90
SQ FT: 21,800

SALES (est): 36MM **Privately Held**
SIC: 7372 Business oriented computer software

(P-23738)
CIRCA 1605 INC
1475 Folsom St Ste 200, San Francisco
(94103-3761)
PHONE......................217 899-3512
Matthew Galligan, *CEO*
Ben Huh, *Co-Owner*
Arsenio Santos, *Co-Owner*
EMP: 20
SQ FT: 3,000
SALES (est): 1.2MM **Privately Held**
SIC: 7372 Application computer software

(P-23739)
CIRRENT INC
2 E 3rd Ave Ste 100, San Mateo
(94401-4011)
P.O. Box 809 (94401-0809)
PHONE......................650 569-1135
Robert Conant, *CEO*
EMP: 10
SALES (est): 431.3K **Privately Held**
SIC: 7372 Application computer software

(P-23740)
CISCO IRONPORT SYSTEMS LLC (HQ)
170 W Tasman Dr, San Jose (95134-1706)
PHONE......................650 989-6500
Scott Weiss, *CEO*
Renee Kremer, *Partner*
Tom Peterson, *President*
Craig Collins, *CFO*
Bob Kavner, *Chairman*
EMP: 260
SALES (est): 50.6MM
SALES (corp-wide): 51.9B **Publicly Held**
WEB: www.ironport.com
SIC: 7372 5045 Prepackaged software; computers, peripherals & software
PA: Cisco Systems, Inc.
170 W Tasman Dr
San Jose CA 95134
408 526-4000

(P-23741)
CITRIX SYSTEMS INC
4988 Great America Pkwy, Santa Clara
(95054-1200)
PHONE......................408 790-8000
Klaus Oerstermann, *Principal*
Huzaifah Saifee, *Partner*
Rajiv Sinha, *Vice Pres*
Gil Rosario, *Executive*
Daljit Singh, *Principal*
EMP: 95
SALES (corp-wide): 2.9B **Publicly Held**
WEB: www.citrix.com
SIC: 7372 Prepackaged software
PA: Citrix Systems, Inc.
851 W Cypress Creek Rd
Fort Lauderdale FL 33309
954 267-3000

(P-23742)
CITRIX SYSTEMS INC
7414 Hollister Ave Goleta, Los Angeles
(90074-0001)
PHONE......................800 424-8749
EMP: 17
SALES (corp-wide): 2.9B **Publicly Held**
SIC: 7372 Prepackaged software
PA: Citrix Systems, Inc.
851 W Cypress Creek Rd
Fort Lauderdale FL 33309
954 267-3000

(P-23743)
CLASSDOJO INC
735 Tehama St, San Francisco
(94103-3822)
PHONE......................650 646-8235
Usamah Chaudhary, *President*
Chris Koakiettaveecha, *Sr Software Eng*
April Ablon, *Software Engr*
Elisette Weiss, *Opers Staff*
Manoj Lamba, *Marketing Staff*
EMP: 12
SQ FT: 2,000
SALES (est): 1MM **Privately Held**
SIC: 7372 Educational computer software

(P-23744)
CLASSY INC
350 10th Ave Ste 1300, San Diego
(92101-8703)
PHONE......................619 961-1892
Scot P Chisholm, *CEO*
Adam Aarons, *President*
Todd Crutchfield, *COO*
Carilu Dietrich, *Chief Mktg Ofcr*
Neena Gupta Needel,
EMP: 21
SALES (est): 2.2MM **Privately Held**
SIC: 7372 Prepackaged software

(P-23745)
CLEARSLIDE INC (DH)
45 Fremont St Fl 32, San Francisco
(94105-2258)
PHONE......................877 360-3366
Dustin Grosse, *CEO*
Jim Benton, *Officer*
Sandra Wright, *Vice Pres*
Bobby Schluter, *Executive*
Lawrence Bruhmuller, *Engineer*
EMP: 84
SALES (est): 27.5MM
SALES (corp-wide): 303.2MM **Privately Held**
SIC: 7372 Business oriented computer software
HQ: Corel Corporation
1600 Carling Ave Suite 100
Ottawa ON K1Z 8
613 728-8200

(P-23746)
CLEARWELL SYSTEMS INC
350 Ellis St, Mountain View (94043-2202)
PHONE......................877 253-2793
Aaref Hilaly, *CEO*
Anup Singh, *CFO*
Venkat Rangan, *CTO*
▼ **EMP:** 110
SQ FT: 17,000
SALES (est): 9.1MM
SALES (corp-wide): 4.7B **Publicly Held**
WEB: www.clearwellsystems.com
SIC: 7372 Business oriented computer software
PA: Nortonlifelock Inc.
60 E Rio Salado Pkwy # 1
Tempe AZ 85281
650 527-8000

(P-23747)
CLIPCALL INC
645 Harrison St Ste 200, San Francisco
(94107-3624)
PHONE......................650 285-7597
Daniel Shaked, *CEO*
Einat Har, *CFO*
EMP: 15
SALES (est): 108.8K **Privately Held**
SIC: 7372 Business oriented computer software

(P-23748)
CLOCKWARE
548 Market St, San Francisco
(94104-5401)
PHONE......................650 556-8880
Ronald Kfoury, *President*
EMP: 15
SALES (est): 1.2MM **Privately Held**
WEB: www.clockware.com
SIC: 7372 Application computer software

(P-23749)
CLONETAB INC
1660 W Linne Rd Ste 214, Tracy
(95377-8027)
PHONE......................209 292-5663
Hema Meka, *CEO*
Bharathi Meka, *CFO*
Samantha Dalton, *Executive*
EMP: 39
SALES (est): 173.7K **Privately Held**
SIC: 7372 Prepackaged software

(P-23750)
CLOUDCAR INC
2550 Great America Way # 301, Santa Clara (95054-1161)
PHONE......................650 946-1236
Philipp Popov, *CEO*
Bruce Leak, *COO*

Albert Jordan, *Vice Pres*
Irene Tang, *Program Mgr*
Samson Roopkumar, *Info Tech Mgr*
EMP: 30
SALES: 1MM **Privately Held**
SIC: 7372 Prepackaged software

(P-23751)
CLOUDFLARE INC (PA)
101 Townsend St, San Francisco
(94107-1934)
PHONE.............................888 993-5273
Matthew Prince, *Ch of Bd*
EMP: 129
SALES: 192.6MM **Publicly Held**
SIC: 7372 Prepackaged software

(P-23752)
CLOUDNCO INC
Also Called: CLOud&co
300 Beale St Apt 613, San Francisco
(94105-2096)
PHONE.............................408 605-8755
Matthieu Dejardins, *CEO*
EMP: 16
SALES (est): 426.9K **Privately Held**
SIC: 7372 Application computer software;
business oriented computer software

(P-23753)
CLOUDPIC INC
19925 Stevens Creek Blvd, Cupertino
(95014-2300)
PHONE.............................408 786-1098
Richard Chuang, *CEO*
EMP: 10
SQ FT: 300
SALES (est): 590.9K **Privately Held**
SIC: 7372 Application computer software

(P-23754)
CLOUDSHIELD TECHNOLOGIES LLC
212 Gibraltar Dr, Sunnyvale (94089-1324)
PHONE.............................408 331-6640
Randy Brumfield, *Senior VP*
Timothy Laehy, *CFO*
Todd Beine, *CTO*
EMP: 21
SQ FT: 35,000
SALES (est): 9.5MM
SALES (corp-wide): 44.5MM **Privately Held**
WEB: www.cloudshield.com
SIC: 7372 8741 8742 Prepackaged software; business management; business consultant
PA: Lookingglass Cyber Solution, Inc.
10740 Parkridge Blvd # 200
Reston VA 20191
703 351-1000

(P-23755)
CLUB SPEED LLC
549 Queensland Cir # 101, Corona
(92879-1397)
PHONE.............................951 817-7073
Romir Bosu, *CEO*
Caleb Everett, *President*
EMP: 42
SALES (est): 3.4MM **Privately Held**
SIC: 7372 Prepackaged software

(P-23756)
COBALT LABS INC
575 Market St Fl 4, San Francisco
(94105-5818)
PHONE.............................415 651-7028
Esben Friis Jensen, *Founder*
Jacob Hansen, *CEO*
Chris Tilton, *Vice Pres*
Tim Bilbro, *Executive*
Scott Marcelo, *Executive*
EMP: 20 **EST:** 2017
SALES (est): 633.2K **Privately Held**
SIC: 7372 Prepackaged software

(P-23757)
CODEFAST INC
21170 Canyon Oak Way, Cupertino
(95014-6572)
PHONE.............................408 687-4700
Nick Barens, *President*
EMP: 11

SALES (est): 528.5K
SALES (corp-wide): 3.1B **Publicly Held**
WEB: www.codefast.com
SIC: 7372 Business oriented computer software
HQ: Coverity Llc
185 Berry St Ste 6500
San Francisco CA 94107
415 321-5200

(P-23758)
COLLABRATIVE DRG DISCOVERY INC
Also Called: Molecular Databank
1633 Bayshore Hwy Ste 342, Burlingame
(94010-1515)
PHONE.............................650 204-3084
Barry Bunin, *President*
Lixin Liu, *Accountant*
Frank Cole, *Sales Staff*
Sylvia Ernst, *Director*
EMP: 11
SALES (est): 1MM **Privately Held**
SIC: 7372 Prepackaged software

(P-23759)
COLORTOKENS INC
2101 Tasman Dr Ste 201, Santa Clara
(95054-1020)
PHONE.............................408 341-6030
Rajesh Parekh, *President*
EMP: 50
SALES (est): 1.3MM **Privately Held**
SIC: 7372 Business oriented computer software

(P-23760)
COMMAAI INC
Also Called: Comma.ai
1441 State St, San Diego (92101-3421)
PHONE.............................415 712-8205
Ricardo Biasina, *CEO*
Viviane Ford, *COO*
EMP: 11
SALES (est): 1MM **Privately Held**
SIC: 7372 Prepackaged software

(P-23761)
COMMERCE VELOCITY LLC
1 Technology Dr Ste J725, Irvine
(92618-2353)
PHONE.............................949 756-8950
Umesh Verma,
Ajay Chopra,
EMP: 50
SQ FT: 5,000
SALES (est): 16MM
SALES (corp-wide): 7.5B **Publicly Held**
WEB: www.cvelocity.com
SIC: 7372 Business oriented computer software
PA: Fidelity National Financial, Inc.
601 Riverside Ave Fl 4
Jacksonville FL 32204
904 854-8100

(P-23762)
COMPATIBLE SOFTWARE SYSTEMS
10966 Bigge St, San Leandro
(94577-1121)
PHONE.............................510 562-1172
Marvin McClendon, *Owner*
EMP: 10
SQ FT: 1,400
SALES (est): 982.9K **Privately Held**
WEB: www.ctswest.com
SIC: 7372 Prepackaged software

(P-23763)
COMPOSITE SOFTWARE LLC (HQ)
755 Sycamore Dr, Milpitas (95035-7411)
PHONE.............................800 553-6387
Jim Green, *CEO*
Jon Bode, *CFO*
Marc Breissinger, *Exec VP*
Robert Eve, *Exec VP*
Che Wijesinghe, *Exec VP*
EMP: 74
SQ FT: 14,000
SALES (est): 17.7MM
SALES (corp-wide): 51.9B **Publicly Held**
WEB: www.compositesw.com
SIC: 7372 Prepackaged software

PA: Cisco Systems, Inc.
170 W Tasman Dr
San Jose CA 95134
408 526-4000

(P-23764)
COMPUGROUP MEDICAL INC
25 B Tech Dr Ste 200, Irvine (92618)
PHONE.............................949 789-0500
John Tangredi, *COO*
EMP: 19
SALES (corp-wide): 45MM **Privately Held**
SIC: 7372 Prepackaged software
PA: Compugroup Medical, Inc.
3838 N Central Ave # 1600
Phoenix AZ 85012
855 270-6700

(P-23765)
COMPULINK BUSINESS SYSTEMS INC (PA)
Also Called: Compulink Healthcare Solutions
1100 Business Center Cir, Newbury Park
(91320-1124)
PHONE.............................805 446-2050
Link Wilson, *President*
Mark Young, *COO*
Aundria Hyer, *Vice Pres*
Cole Galbarith, *Info Tech Mgr*
Jose Melendez, *Technology*
EMP: 54
SQ FT: 15,000
SALES (est): 13.5MM **Privately Held**
WEB: www.compulink-software.com
SIC: 7372 Business oriented computer software

(P-23766)
COMPULINK MANAGEMENT CTR INC
Also Called: Laserfiche Document Imaging
3545 Long Beach Blvd, Long Beach
(90807-3941)
PHONE.............................562 988-1688
Nien-Ling Wacker, *President*
Henk Eisner, *CFO*
Hedy Aref, *Vice Pres*
Karl Chan, *Vice Pres*
Jim Haney, *Vice Pres*
▲ **EMP:** 170
SQ FT: 30,000
SALES (est): 36.9MM **Privately Held**
WEB: www.laserfiche.com
SIC: 7372 Business oriented computer software

(P-23767)
COMPUTERS AND STRUCTURES INC
Also Called: C S I
1646 N Calif Blvd Ste 600, Walnut Creek
(94596-7456)
PHONE.............................510 649-2200
Ashraf Habibullah, *President*
Marilyn Wilkes, *Vice Pres*
Atif Habibullah, *Director*
EMP: 14
SQ FT: 4,000
SALES (est): 2.4MM **Privately Held**
WEB: www.csiberkeley.com
SIC: 7372 Application computer software

(P-23768)
CONDECO SOFTWARE INC (HQ)
2105 S Bascom Ave Ste 150, Campbell
(95008-3276)
PHONE.............................917 677-7600
Martin Brooker, *CEO*
Craig Goldberg, *Technical Staff*
EMP: 37
SALES (est): 7.7MM
SALES (corp-wide): 41.3MM **Privately Held**
SIC: 7372 Business oriented computer software
PA: Condeco Group Limited
8th Floor Exchange Tower
London E14 9
207 001-2020

(P-23769)
CONFIDENT TECHNOLOGIES INC
3830 Vly Cntre Dr Ste 705, San Diego
(92130)
PHONE.............................858 345-5640
William Goldbach, *Exec VP*
EMP: 11 **EST:** 2010
SQ FT: 1,600
SALES (est): 692.7K **Privately Held**
SIC: 7372 Business oriented computer software

(P-23770)
CONFLUENT INC (PA)
101 University Ave # 111, Palo Alto
(94301-1679)
PHONE.............................650 453-5860
Jay Kreps, *CEO*
Erica Schultz, *President*
Cheryl Dalrymple, *CFO*
Luanne Dauber, *Chief Mktg Ofcr*
Chuck Faris, *Vice Pres*
EMP: 35 **EST:** 2014
SQ FT: 6,000
SALES (est): 10.3MM **Privately Held**
SIC: 7372 Application computer software;
business oriented computer software; utility computer software

(P-23771)
CONSILIO - A FIRST ADVANTAGE
605 E Huntington Dr # 211, Monrovia
(91016-6352)
PHONE.............................626 921-1600
EMP: 35
SALES (corp-wide): 7.6MM **Privately Held**
SIC: 7372 Application computer software
PA: Consilio, Llc
1828 L St Nw Ste 1070
Washington DC 20036
202 822-6222

(P-23772)
CONTACTUAL INC
810 W Maude Ave, Sunnyvale
(94085-2910)
PHONE.............................650 292-4408
Mansour Salame, *CEO*
David Sohm, *President*
David Chen, *Vice Pres*
Dani Shomron, *Vice Pres*
Richard W Southwick, *Vice Pres*
EMP: 50
SQ FT: 5,000
SALES (est): 3.3MM
SALES (corp-wide): 352.5MM **Publicly Held**
WEB: www.contactual.com
SIC: 7372 Prepackaged software
PA: 8x8, Inc.
2125 Onel Dr
San Jose CA 95131
408 727-1885

(P-23773)
CONTRACT WRANGLER INC
922 S Claremont St, San Mateo
(94402-1834)
PHONE.............................310 266-3373
John Gengarella, *CEO*
Harry Register, *Chairman*
Brian Ascher, *Director*
Neil Peretz, *Director*
EMP: 35
SQ FT: 2,000
SALES (est): 39.6K **Privately Held**
SIC: 7372 Prepackaged software

(P-23774)
CONVERSIONPOINT HOLDINGS INC
840 Newport Center Dr # 450, Newport
Beach (92660-6384)
PHONE.............................888 706-6764
Robert Tallack, *President*
Jonathan Gregg, *President*
Don Walker Barrett III, *COO*
Raghu Kilambi, *CFO*
Tom Furukawa, *CTO*
EMP: 85
SALES (est): 1.2MM **Privately Held**
SIC: 7372 Prepackaged software

(P-23775)
COPPER CRM INC (PA)
301 Howard St Ste 600, San Francisco (94105-6600)
PHONE.................................415 231-6360
Jonathan Lee, *CEO*
Charles Ashworth,
Steve Holm, *Vice Pres*
Jun Hu, *Vice Pres*
Oberbauer Justin, *Vice Pres*
EMP: 104 **EST:** 2011
SQ FT: 15,000
SALES (est): 41.6MM **Privately Held**
SIC: 7372 Application computer software

(P-23776)
CORCEN DATA INTERNATIONAL INC
17341 Irvine Blvd Ste 205, Tustin (92780-3010)
PHONE.................................714 251-6110
Han OH, *President*
Michelle OH, *General Mgr*
EMP: 12
SQ FT: 21,000
SALES (est): 765.7K **Privately Held**
WEB: www.corcen.com
SIC: 7372 7371 5734 Business oriented computer software; custom computer programming services; software, business & non-game

(P-23777)
CORNERSTONE ONDEMAND INC (PA)
1601 Cloverf Blvd 620s, Santa Monica (90404-4178)
PHONE.................................310 752-0200
Adam L Miller, *CEO*
Jeffrey Lautenbach, *President*
Brian L Swartz, *CFO*
Adrianna Burrows, *Chief Mktg Ofcr*
Adam Weiss, *Officer*
EMP: 148
SQ FT: 94,000
SALES: 537.8MM **Publicly Held**
WEB: www.cornerstoneondemand.com
SIC: 7372 Business oriented computer software

(P-23778)
CORRUGATED TECHNOLOGIES INC
Also Called: C T I
15150 Avenue Of Science, San Diego (92128-3405)
PHONE.................................858 578-3550
EMP: 30
SALES (est): 4.4MM **Privately Held**
WEB: www.corrtech.com
SIC: 7372

(P-23779)
COSMI FINANCE LLC
1635 Chelsea Rd Ste A, San Marino (91108-2456)
PHONE.................................310 603-5800
Edward O Lanchantin, *Mng Member*
S Amos Smith,
EMP: 12
SQ FT: 2,000
SALES (est): 2MM **Privately Held**
SIC: 7372 Prepackaged software

(P-23780)
COUNTERPOINT SOFTWARE INC
24528 Palermo Dr, Calabasas (91302-2501)
PHONE.................................818 222-7777
James Foley, *President*
Anna Dow, *Vice Pres*
Dick Levine, *Vice Pres*
Darlene Hosaka, *Principal*
Mary Nelson, *Principal*
EMP: 13
SALES (est): 1.3MM **Privately Held**
WEB: www.counterpoint.net
SIC: 7372 Application computer software

(P-23781)
COUPA SOFTWARE INCORPORATED (PA)
1855 S Grant St, San Mateo (94402-7016)
PHONE.................................650 931-3200
Robert Bernshteyn, *Ch of Bd*
Steven Winter, *Risk Mgmt Dir*
EMP: 148
SQ FT: 69,220
SALES: 260.3MM **Publicly Held**
WEB: www.coupa.com
SIC: 7372 Business oriented computer software

(P-23782)
CROSSROADS SOFTWARE INC
210 W Birch St Ste 207, Brea (92821-4504)
PHONE.................................714 990-6433
Jeff Cullen, *President*
EMP: 13
SQ FT: 1,000
SALES (est): 1MM **Privately Held**
WEB: www.crossroadssoftware.com
SIC: 7372 Prepackaged software

(P-23783)
CROWDSTRIKE HOLDINGS INC (PA)
150 Mathilda Pl Ste 300, Sunnyvale (94086-6012)
PHONE.................................888 512-8906
George Kurtz, *President*
Gerhard Watzinger, *Ch of Bd*
Michael Carpenter, *President*
Shawn Henry, *President*
Colin Black, *COO*
EMP: 120
SQ FT: 30,331
SALES: 249.8MM **Publicly Held**
SIC: 7372 7379 Prepackaged software; computer related maintenance services

(P-23784)
CRYSTAL DYNAMICS INC (DH)
1400a Saport Blvd Ste 300, Redwood City (94063)
PHONE.................................650 421-7600
Philip Rogers, *CEO*
John Miller, *President*
Kun Chen, *Info Tech Mgr*
Santiago Velez, *Software Engr*
Grant Ricks, *Project Mgr*
EMP: 90
SQ FT: 26,000
SALES (est): 13.1MM **Privately Held**
WEB: www.crystald.com
SIC: 7372 Business oriented computer software
HQ: Square Enix Limited
240 Blackfriars Road
London SE1 8
208 636-3000

(P-23785)
CUADRA ASSOCIATES INC (PA)
3415 S Sepulveda Blvd # 3, Los Angeles (90034-6060)
PHONE.................................310 591-2490
Phillip Green, *Principal*
Ron Aspe, *President*
Marius Alban, *Recruiter*
EMP: 10
SQ FT: 3,500
SALES (est): 2.5MM **Privately Held**
WEB: www.cuadra.com
SIC: 7372 5045 Business oriented computer software; computers, peripherals & software

(P-23786)
CULTURE AMP INC (HQ)
13949 Ventura Blvd, Sherman Oaks (91423-3584)
PHONE.................................415 326-8453
Didier Raoul Elzinga, *CEO*
Douglas Mark English, *CFO*
Rodney James Hamilton, *Admin Sec*
Stacey Nordwall, *Opers Staff*
Barbra Gago, *Marketing Staff*
EMP: 40
SALES (est): 44.6K **Privately Held**
SIC: 7372 Prepackaged software

(P-23787)
CUMULUS NETWORKS INC (PA)
185 E Dana St, Mountain View (94041-1507)
PHONE.................................650 383-6700
Jame Rivers, *CEO*
Nolan Leake, *Co-Owner*
Reza Malekzadeh, *Vice Pres*
Edward Leake, *Principal*
Elizabeth Seamans, *Software Engr*
EMP: 124
SALES (est): 26.7MM **Privately Held**
SIC: 7372 7371 Publishers' computer software; computer software development

(P-23788)
CVPS INC
9514 Glenhaven Dr, Glenhaven (95443)
P.O. Box 638 (95443-0638)
PHONE.................................707 998-9364
Kai Schuette, *President*
Andy Preas, *Vice Pres*
EMP: 33
SALES (est): 3.4MM **Privately Held**
WEB: www.cvps.net
SIC: 7372 Application computer software

(P-23789)
CYBER MDIA SOLUTIONS LTD LBLTY
25361 Commercentre Dr # 250, Lake Forest (92630-8811)
PHONE.................................877 480-8255
Allan E Gindi, *Mng Member*
Allan Gindi, *Mng Member*
EMP: 25 **EST:** 2003
SALES (est): 943.7K **Privately Held**
SIC: 7372 8742 Business oriented computer software; marketing consulting services

(P-23790)
CYBERINC CORPORATION (HQ)
Also Called: Aurionpro
4000 Executive Pkwy # 250, San Ramon (94583-4257)
PHONE.................................925 242-0777
Samir Shah, *CEO*
Nirav Shah, *COO*
Romi Randhawa, *Security Dir*
EMP: 30
SQ FT: 3,000
SALES: 6.1MM
SALES (corp-wide): 46.8MM **Privately Held**
WEB: www.aurionprosolutions.com
SIC: 7372 7371 Business oriented computer software; custom computer programming services

(P-23791)
CYBERLINKCOM CORP
1073 S Winchester Blvd, San Jose (95128-3702)
PHONE.................................408 217-1850
Shing Wong, *President*
Hilda Peng, *Senior Mgr*
Christina Tao, *Manager*
EMP: 12
SALES (est): 1.7MM **Privately Held**
WEB: www.pixartech.com
SIC: 7372 Application computer software

(P-23792)
CYBREX CONSULTING INC
4470 W Sunset Blvd, Los Angeles (90027-6302)
PHONE.................................513 999-2109
James Whitmore, *Managing Dir*
EMP: 100 **EST:** 2010
SQ FT: 1,000
SALES: 2MM **Privately Held**
SIC: 7372 8742 Prepackaged software; real estate consultant

(P-23793)
CYLANCE INC (DH)
400 Spectrum Center Dr, Irvine (92618-4934)
PHONE.................................949 375-3380
Stuart McClure, *CEO*
Rick Stojak, *Partner*
Daniel Doimo, *President*
Felix Marquardt, *President*
Brian Robins, *CFO*
EMP: 148

SALES: 200MM
SALES (corp-wide): 904MM **Privately Held**
SIC: 7372 Application computer software
HQ: Blackberry Corporation
3001 Bishop Dr
San Ramon CA 94583
972 650-6126

(P-23794)
CYMMETRIA INC
2557 Park Blvd Apt L106, Palo Alto (94306-1937)
PHONE.................................415 568-6870
Ilya Levtov, *CEO*
Jonathan Braverman,
EMP: 24 **EST:** 2014
SALES (est): 711.5K **Privately Held**
SIC: 7372 Business oriented computer software

(P-23795)
CYTOBANK INC
3945 Freedom Cir Ste 540, Santa Clara (95054-1225)
PHONE.................................650 918-7966
Nikesh Kotecha, *CEO*
Angela Landrigan, *Products*
EMP: 12
SALES (est): 16.1K **Privately Held**
SIC: 7372 7371 Application computer software; computer software systems analysis & design, custom

(P-23796)
D3PUBLISHER OF AMERICA INC
Also Called: D3 Go
15910 Ventura Blvd # 800, Encino (91436-2810)
PHONE.................................310 268-0820
Yoji Takenaka, *President*
Yuji ITOH, *Ch of Bd*
Hidetaka Tachibana, *CFO*
Arthur Kawamoto, *Manager*
EMP: 63
SQ FT: 6,129
SALES (est): 8.4MM **Privately Held**
SIC: 7372 Home entertainment computer software
HQ: D3 Publisher Inc.
1-9-5, Dogenzaka
Shibuya-Ku TKY 150-0
-

(P-23797)
DASSAULT SYSTEMES BIOVIA CORP
5005 Wtrdge Vista Dr Fl 2 Flr 2, San Diego (92121)
PHONE.................................858 799-5000
Scipio Carnecchia, *Branch Mgr*
James Shin, *Vice Pres*
Lindsey Lodi, *Executive Asst*
Jacquie Stead, *Executive Asst*
Jason Gregory, *Sr Software Eng*
EMP: 39
SALES (corp-wide): 1.8B **Privately Held**
SIC: 7372 Prepackaged software
HQ: Dassault Systemes Biovia Corp.
5005 Wateridge Vista Dr # 2
San Diego CA 92121

(P-23798)
DASSAULT SYSTEMES BIOVIA CORP (DH)
Also Called: Accelrys Inc.
5005 Wateridge Vista Dr # 2, San Diego (92121-5784)
PHONE.................................858 799-5000
Max Carnecchia, *CEO*
Jason Gray, *Senior VP*
Mathew Hahn, *Senior VP*
Judith Ohrn Hicks, *Senior VP*
Scott Hiraoka, *Senior VP*
EMP: 45
SQ FT: 68,436
SALES: 75.3MM
SALES (corp-wide): 1.8B **Privately Held**
WEB: www.accelrys.com
SIC: 7372 Application computer software; business oriented computer software

---

(PA)=Parent Co (HQ)=Headquarters (DH)=Div Headquarters
✪ = New Business established in last 2 years

HQ: 3ds Acquisition Corp.
175 Wyman St
Waltham MA 02451
781 810-5011

(P-23799)
DATA ADVANTAGE GROUP INC
145 Natoma St Fl 5, San Francisco
(94105-3733)
PHONE...............................415 947-0400
Geoffrey Rayner, *CEO*
Gregory Blumstein, *President*
EMP: 15
SQ FT: 2,200
SALES (est): 1.9MM **Privately Held**
WEB: www.dataag.com
SIC: 7372 Prepackaged software

(P-23800)
DATA AGENT LLC
1349 Josephine St, Berkeley (94703-1113)
PHONE...............................800 772-8314
EMP: 12
SALES: 1.1MM **Privately Held**
WEB: www.DataAgent.com
SIC: 7372

(P-23801)
DATA LINKAGE SOFTWARE INC
2421 W 205th St Ste D207, Torrance
(90501-1469)
PHONE...............................310 781-3056
Marwan Dajani, *President*
▲ **EMP:** 15
SQ FT: 1,900
SALES: 1.5MM **Privately Held**
SIC: 7372 Business oriented computer
software

(P-23802)
DATABASE WORKS INC
500 S Kraemer Blvd # 110, Brea
(92821-6766)
PHONE...............................714 203-8800
Terry Young, *President*
EMP: 13
SQ FT: 2,500
SALES: 1.5MM **Privately Held**
WEB: www.dbworks.com
SIC: 7372 3577 Business oriented com-
puter software; application computer soft-
ware; optical scanning devices

(P-23803)
DATAFOX INTELLIGENCE INC
475 Sansome St Fl 15, San Francisco
(94111-3166)
PHONE...............................415 969-2144
Bastiaan Janmaat, *CEO*
Michael Dorsey, *COO*
Kelly Chris, *Executive*
Stacy Huang, *Software Engr*
Samantha Paras, *Software Engr*
EMP: 18
SALES (est): 2.2MM **Privately Held**
SIC: 7372 Business oriented computer
software

(P-23804)
DATAGENICS SOFTWARE INC
5527 Satsuma Ave, North Hollywood
(91601-2841)
PHONE...............................818 487-3900
Michael Vandemore, *President*
Pamela Vandemere, *Vice Pres*
EMP: 10
SQ FT: 2,500
SALES: 1MM **Privately Held**
WEB: www.datagenics.com
SIC: 7372 Business oriented computer
software

(P-23805)
DATAGUISE INC
39650 Liberty St Ste 400, Fremont
(94538-2261)
PHONE...............................510 824-1036
Manmeet S Bhasin, *President*
Adrian Booth, *Vice Pres*
Christopher Glover, *Vice Pres*
EMP: 32
SALES (est): 3.5MM **Privately Held**
SIC: 7372 Prepackaged software

(P-23806)
DATERA INC
2811 Mission College Blvd, Santa Clara
(95054-1884)
PHONE...............................650 384-6366
Marc Fleischmann, *CEO*
EMP: 37 **EST:** 2016
SALES (est): 6.8MM **Privately Held**
SIC: 7372 Prepackaged software

(P-23807)
DAVID CORPORATION
925 Highland Pointe Dr # 180, Roseville
(95678-5423)
PHONE...............................916 762-8688
H Alex Aminian, *Branch Mgr*
Karen Davis, *Accountant*
Mary Rose, *Marketing Mgr*
EMP: 10
SALES (corp-wide): 7MM **Privately Held**
SIC: 7372 5734 7373 Prepackaged soft-
ware; software, business & non-game;
value-added resellers, computer systems
PA: David Corporation
301 Edgewater Pl Ste 116
Wakefield MA 01880
781 587-3008

(P-23808)
DCATALOG INC
2635 N 1st St Ste 102, San Jose
(95134-2031)
PHONE...............................408 824-5648
Michael Raviv, *President*
EMP: 20 **EST:** 2012
SALES: 300K **Privately Held**
SIC: 7372 Application computer software

(P-23809)
DE NOVO SOFTWARE
400 N Brand Blvd Ste 850, Glendale
(91203-9709)
PHONE...............................213 814-1240
David Novo, *President*
EMP: 10
SQ FT: 2,000
SALES (est): 1.4MM **Privately Held**
SIC: 7372 Prepackaged software

(P-23810)
DECISIONINSITE LTD LBLTY CO
101 Pacifica Ste 380, Irvine (92618-3330)
PHONE...............................877 204-1392
Michael B Regele, *President*
Ron Van Orden, *Business Dir*
Kyle Gilbert, *Info Tech Dir*
Ryan Mack, *Technology*
EMP: 20
SALES (est): 1.4MM
SALES (corp-wide): 18.1MM **Privately
Held**
SIC: 7372 Educational computer software
PA: Hoonuit, Llc
118 Wood St 105
Little Falls MN 56345
320 631-5900

(P-23811)
DECISIONLOGIC LLC
13500 Evening Creek Dr N # 600, San
Diego (92128-8125)
PHONE...............................858 586-0202
David Evans, *President*
Adam Little, *CFO*
Vlad Arutunian, *Vice Pres*
Mandi Wooledge, *Vice Pres*
Wade Worthington, *Info Tech Dir*
EMP: 23
SALES (est): 3.2MM **Privately Held**
SIC: 7372 Business oriented computer
software

(P-23812)
DEEM INC (DH)
642 Harrison St Fl 2, San Francisco
(94107-1323)
PHONE...............................415 590-8300
John F Rizzo, *President*
David Shiba, *CFO*
Eddie Bridgers, *Senior VP*
Todd Kaiser, *Senior VP*
Neil Markey, *Senior VP*
▲ **EMP:** 65
SQ FT: 133,000

SALES (est): 90.3MM
SALES (corp-wide): 4.5B **Privately Held**
WEB: www.reardencommerce.com
SIC: 7372 Prepackaged software
HQ: Enterprise Holdings, Inc.
600 Corporate Park Dr
Saint Louis MO 63105
314 512-5000

(P-23813)
DEL MAR DATATRAC INC
Also Called: Del Mar Database
10509 Vista Sorrento Pkwy # 400, San
Diego (92121-2707)
PHONE...............................858 550-8810
Jeb S Spencer, *President*
EMP: 35
SALES (est): 2.6MM
SALES (corp-wide): 41.6MM **Privately
Held**
WEB: www.delmardb.com
SIC: 7372 Prepackaged software
HQ: Ellie Mae, Inc.
4420 Rosewood Dr Ste 500
Pleasanton CA 94588
855 224-8572

(P-23814)
DELPHIX CORP (PA)
1400 Saport Blvd Ste 200a, Redwood City
(94063)
PHONE...............................650 494-1645
Chris Cook, *CEO*
Stewart Grierson, *CFO*
Monika Saha, *Chief Mktg Ofcr*
Jedidiah Yueh, *Officer*
Jason Binder, *Vice Pres*
EMP: 50
SQ FT: 18,000
SALES (est): 28.9MM **Privately Held**
SIC: 7372 Business oriented computer
software

(P-23815)
DEMANDBASE INC
680 Folsom St Ste 400, San Francisco
(94107-2159)
PHONE...............................415 683-2660
Chris Golec, *CEO*
Peter Isaacson, *Chief Mktg Ofcr*
Alan Fletcher, *Officer*
Fatima Khan, *Officer*
Mike Hilts, *Vice Pres*
EMP: 251
SALES (est): 50.6MM **Privately Held**
WEB: www.demandbase.com
SIC: 7372 Business oriented computer
software

(P-23816)
DENALI SOFTWARE INC (HQ)
2655 Seely Ave, San Jose (95134-1931)
PHONE...............................408 943-1234
Sanjay Srivastava, *President*
R Mark Gogolewski, *CFO*
EMP: 36
SQ FT: 10,000
SALES: 4.4MM
SALES (corp-wide): 2.1B **Publicly Held**
WEB: www.denali.com
SIC: 7372 Application computer software
PA: Cadence Design Systems, Inc.
2655 Seely Ave Bldg 5
San Jose CA 95134
408 943-1234

(P-23817)
DINCLOUD INC
27520 Hawthorne Blvd # 185, Rllng HLS
Est (90274-3576)
PHONE...............................310 929-1101
Mark Briggs, *CEO*
Mike L Chase, *Exec VP*
Ali M Dincmo, *Vice Pres*
David Graffia, *Vice Pres*
Alex Orton, *Consultant*
EMP: 53
SQ FT: 1,500
SALES: 4MM
SALES (corp-wide): 43.1MM **Privately
Held**
SIC: 7372 Business oriented computer
software

PA: Premier Bpo, Inc.
128 N 2nd St Ste 210
Clarksville TN 37040
931 551-8888

(P-23818)
DISTILLERY INC
90 Heron Ct, San Quentin (94964)
PHONE...............................415 505-5446
Adrian Szwarcburg, *President*
EMP: 55
SALES (est): 1.9MM **Privately Held**
SIC: 7372 Prepackaged software

(P-23819)
DM SOFTWARE INC
1842 Park Skyline Rd, Santa Ana
(92705-3120)
PHONE...............................714 953-2653
Bill Parson, *Owner*
EMP: 10
SALES (corp-wide): 1.9MM **Privately
Held**
WEB: www.oxford.com.pl
SIC: 7372 Prepackaged software
PA: Dm Software Inc
654 Jack Cir
Stateline NV 89449
775 589-6049

(P-23820)
DO DINE INC
Also Called: Multani Logistics
24052 Mission Blvd, Hayward
(94544-1017)
PHONE...............................510 583-7546
Bikramjit Singh, *CEO*
EMP: 15
SQ FT: 5,000
SALES: 1.4MM **Privately Held**
SIC: 7372 Business oriented computer
software

(P-23821)
DOCSEND INC
351 California St # 1200, San Francisco
(94104-2416)
PHONE...............................888 258-5951
Russell Heddleston, *CEO*
Anthony Cassanego, *CFO*
David Koslow, *Admin Sec*
Sonja Jacob, *Marketing Staff*
Ryan Oconnor, *Sales Staff*
EMP: 16
SALES (est): 384.8K **Privately Held**
SIC: 7372 Business oriented computer
software

(P-23822)
DOCTOR ON DEMAND INC
275 Battery St Ste 650, San Francisco
(94111-3332)
PHONE...............................415 935-4447
Adam Jackson, *CEO*
Robin Cherry Glass, *President*
Jennifer Nuckles, *Chief Mktg Ofcr*
Barry Becker, *Vice Pres*
David Deane, *Vice Pres*
EMP: 100
SALES (est): 328.6K **Privately Held**
SIC: 7372 Application computer software

(P-23823)
DOCUSIGN INC (PA)
221 Main St Ste 1550, San Francisco
(94105-1947)
PHONE...............................415 489-4940
Daniel D Springer, *President*
Michael J Sheridan, *CFO*
Kirsten O Wolberg, *Officer*
Ben Chuba, *Vice Pres*
Pedro Martins, *Vice Pres*
EMP: 300
SQ FT: 146,000
SALES: 700.9MM **Publicly Held**
WEB: www.docusign.com
SIC: 7372 Prepackaged software

(P-23824)
DOMICO SOFTWARE
1220 Oakland Blvd Ste 300, Walnut Creek
(94596-8409)
PHONE...............................510 841-4155
Glenn Hunter, *President*
EMP: 15
SQ FT: 4,000

SALES (est): 1.6MM **Privately Held**
WEB: www.domico.com
SIC: 7372 7371 Prepackaged software;
custom computer programming services

(P-23825)
DOMINO DATA LAB INC (PA)
548 4th St, San Francisco (94107-1621)
P.O. Box 78062 (94107-8062)
PHONE.................................415 570-2425
Nick Elprin, *CEO*
John Joo, *Engineer*
Aaron Read, *Engineer*
Adriene Young, *Finance*
Dan Enthoven, *Sales Staff*
EMP: 34
SALES (est): 2.5MM **Privately Held**
SIC: 7372 Business oriented computer
software

(P-23826)
DORADO NETWORK SYSTEMS CORP
Also Called: Corelogic Dorado
555 12th St Ste 1100, Oakland
(94607-4049)
PHONE.................................650 227-7300
Dain Ehring, *CEO*
Karen Camp, *CFO*
Adam Springer, *Vice Pres*
Dave Parker, *VP Bus Dvlpt*
Rob Carpenter PHD, *CTO*
EMP: 140
SQ FT: 19,000
SALES (est): 11.7MM
SALES (corp-wide): 1.7B **Publicly Held**
WEB: www.dorado.com
SIC: 7372 Application computer software
PA: Corelogic, Inc.
40 Pacifica Ste 900
Irvine CA 92618
949 214-1000

(P-23827)
DOUBLE-TAKE SOFTWARE INC (HQ)
15300 Barranca Pkwy, Irvine (92618-2200)
PHONE.................................949 253-6500
Erik Price, *Technical Staff*
Erik Yoder, *Engineer*
Eva Ullmann, *Manager*
Reggie Payne, *Consultant*
EMP: 26
SALES (est): 25.2MM
SALES (corp-wide): 296.4MM **Publicly Held**
WEB: www.nsisw.com
SIC: 7372 7373 5045 7371 Prepackaged
software; computer-aided system serv-
ices; computer software; custom com-
puter programming services
PA: Carbonite, Inc.
2 Avenue De Lafayette # 6
Boston MA 02111
617 587-1100

(P-23828)
DOUBLEDUTCH INC (PA)
350 Rhode Island St # 375, San Francisco
(94103-5181)
PHONE.................................800 748-9024
Bryan Parker, *CEO*
Brad Roberts, *CFO*
Lawrence Coburn, *Officer*
Lucian Beebe, *Vice Pres*
Taylor McLoughlin, *Program Mgr*
EMP: 65
SALES: 28MM **Privately Held**
SIC: 7372 Application computer software

(P-23829)
DOVE TREE CANYON SOFTWARE INC
707 Broadway Ste 1240, San Diego
(92101-5322)
PHONE.................................619 236-8895
Charles William Woo, *President*
Dyana Woo, *Vice Pres*
EMP: 10
SALES: 840K **Privately Held**
WEB: www.dovetree.com
SIC: 7372 Business oriented computer
software

(P-23830)
DRAFTDAY FANTASY SPORTS INC
690 5th St Ste 105, San Francisco
(94107-1517)
PHONE.................................310 306-1828
Todd Greene, *CEO*
EMP: 20
SALES (corp-wide): 4.5MM **Publicly Held**
SIC: 7372 8742 Prepackaged software;
marketing consulting services
PA: X Function Inc
45 W 89th St Apt 4a
New York NY 10024
212 231-0092

(P-23831)
DRAFTDAY FANTASY SPORTS INC
2058 Broadway Ofc, Santa Monica
(90404-2910)
PHONE.................................310 306-1828
EMP: 21
SQ FT: 3,200
SALES (corp-wide): 4.5MM **Publicly Held**
SIC: 7372 7371 Prepackaged software;
custom computer programming services
PA: X Function Inc
45 W 89th St Apt 4a
New York NY 10024
212 231-0092

(P-23832)
DRIVEAI INC
365 Ravendale Dr, Mountain View
(94043-5217)
P.O. Box 57, Los Altos (94023-0057)
PHONE.................................408 693-0765
Sameep Tandon, *CEO*
Swati Dube, *Co-Owner*
Brody Huval, *Co-Owner*
Jeff Kinske, *Co-Owner*
Joel Pazhayampallil, *Co-Owner*
EMP: 150 **EST:** 2015
SALES (est): 368.1K **Privately Held**
SIC: 7372 Prepackaged software

(P-23833)
DRIVESCALE INC
1230 Midas Way Ste 210, Sunnyvale
(94085-4068)
PHONE.................................408 849-4651
Gene Banman, *CEO*
Denise Shiffman, *Officer*
Sk Vinod, *Vice Pres*
Alvin Eugene Banman, *Principal*
Satya Nishtala, *Principal*
EMP: 10 **EST:** 2013
SALES (est): 816.1K **Privately Held**
SIC: 7372 Application computer software

(P-23834)
DROPBOX INC (PA)
1800 Owens St Ste 200, San Francisco
(94158-2381)
PHONE.................................415 857-6800
Andrew W Houston, *Ch of Bd*
EMP: 148
SALES: 1.3B **Publicly Held**
SIC: 7372 Prepackaged software

(P-23835)
DRUVA INC (HQ)
800 W California Ave # 100, Sunnyvale
(94086-3608)
PHONE.................................650 241-3501
Jaspreet Singh, *CEO*
Mahesh Patel, *CFO*
Thomas Been, *Chief Mktg Ofcr*
Sherry Lowe, *Chief Mktg Ofcr*
Wynn White, *Chief Mktg Ofcr*
EMP: 58
SALES (est): 23.5MM **Privately Held**
SIC: 7372 Business oriented computer
software

(P-23836)
DUDA MOBILE INC
577 College Ave, Palo Alto (94306-1433)
PHONE.................................855 790-0003
Itia Sadan, *CEO*
Adam Ferris, *Partner*
Sarah Carpenter, *CFO*
Russell Jeffery, *Technical Mgr*
Joann Avina, *Accountant*

EMP: 35
SALES (est): 4.2MM **Privately Held**
SIC: 7372 Application computer software

(P-23837)
DWA NOVA LLC
1000 Flower St, Glendale (91201-3007)
PHONE.................................818 695-5000
Lincoln Wallen, *CEO*
Derek Chan, *COO*
EMP: 75
SQ FT: 10,000
SALES (est): 1.4MM **Privately Held**
SIC: 7372 Business oriented computer
software

(P-23838)
E-FREIGHT TECHNOLOGY INC
2225 W Cromwell Ave, Alhambra (91803)
PHONE.................................626 943-8418
Chen-Hsin MA, *President*
EMP: 30
SQ FT: 2,000
SALES (est): 2.3MM **Privately Held**
WEB: www.efreightech.com
SIC: 7372 Prepackaged software

(P-23839)
E-TRANSACTIONS SOFTWARE TECH
21195 Grenola Dr, Cupertino (95014-1625)
PHONE.................................408 873-9100
Srinivasa Reddy, *President*
Vedavathi Reddy, *Director*
EMP: 18 **EST:** 1998
SALES: 2.5MM **Privately Held**
WEB: www.etst.com
SIC: 7372 Prepackaged software

(P-23840)
EBIX INC
Also Called: Benefits Software
212 Cottage Ave, Santa Barbara (93101)
PHONE.................................805 568-0240
William Smith, *Manager*
Fred Walton, *Manager*
EMP: 20
SALES (corp-wide): 497.8MM **Publicly Held**
SIC: 7372 7371 Prepackaged software;
computer software development & appli-
cations
PA: Ebix, Inc.
1 Ebix Way
Duluth GA 30097
678 281-2020

(P-23841)
ECRIO INC
19925 Stevens Creek Blvd # 100, Cuper-
tino (95014-2300)
PHONE.................................408 973-7290
Randy Granovetter, *CEO*
Tad Bogdan, *COO*
Nagesh Challa, *Officer*
Ted Goldstein, *Officer*
Lina Martin, *Vice Pres*
EMP: 90
SALES (est): 6.5MM **Privately Held**
WEB: www.ecrio.com
SIC: 7372 Prepackaged software

(P-23842)
EDCAST INC (PA)
1901 Old Middlefield Way # 21, Mountain
View (94043-2556)
PHONE.................................650 823-3511
Karl Mehta, *CEO*
John Otoole, *Managing Dir*
Ramin Mahmoodi, *Engineer*
Ling Gee, *Manager*
Martin Neuberger, *Manager*
EMP: 27
SALES (est): 5.9MM **Privately Held**
SIC: 7372 Educational computer software

(P-23843)
EDMODO INC
777 Mariners Island Blvd # 510, San Mateo
(94404-5048)
PHONE.................................310 614-6868
Nic Borg, *CEO*
Mollie Carter, *Vice Pres*
Marianne Biskup, *Social Dir*
Stephen Fisico, *Software Engr*
Hsuanwei Fan, *Teacher*

EMP: 36 **EST:** 2009
SALES (est): 5.9MM **Privately Held**
SIC: 7372 Educational computer software

(P-23844)
EDUCATION ELEMENTS INC
999 Skyway Rd Ste 325, San Carlos
(94070-2725)
PHONE.................................650 336-0660
Anthony Kim, *CEO*
Amy Jenkins, *Vice Pres*
Arthur Svider, *Vice Pres*
Richard Luong, *Engineer*
Jenni Tonti, *Finance*
EMP: 28
SALES (est): 3.3MM **Privately Held**
SIC: 7372 Educational computer software

(P-23845)
EDUTONE CORPORATION (PA)
Also Called: Global Grid For Learning
1101 Marina Village Pkwy # 201, Alameda
(94501-6472)
PHONE.................................888 904-9773
Robert Iskander, *President*
Julian Mobbs, *CEO*
Wallace Reeves, *Vice Pres*
Larry Smith, *Vice Pres*
EMP: 11
SALES: 5MM **Privately Held**
SIC: 7372 Educational computer software

(P-23846)
EEYE INC (HQ)
Also Called: Eeye Digital Security
65 Enterprise Ste 100, Aliso Viejo
(92656-2503)
PHONE.................................949 333-1900
Kevin Hickey, *CEO*
Tyler Hanson, *CFO*
Marc Maiffret, *CTO*
EMP: 28 **EST:** 1998
SALES (est): 8.3MM
SALES (corp-wide): 57.1MM **Privately Held**
WEB: www.eeye.com
SIC: 7372 Business oriented computer
software
PA: Beyondtrust Software, Inc.
5090 N 40th St Ste 400
Phoenix AZ 85018
623 455-6499

(P-23847)
EGAIN CORPORATION (PA)
1252 Borregas Ave, Sunnyvale
(94089-1309)
PHONE.................................408 636-4500
Ashutosh Roy, *Ch of Bd*
Eric Smit, *CFO*
Promod Narang, *Senior VP*
Todd Woodstra, *Senior VP*
Chris Krystalowich, *Vice Pres*
EMP: 111
SQ FT: 42,541
SALES: 67.2MM **Publicly Held**
WEB: www.egain.com
SIC: 7372 7371 Prepackaged software;
application computer software; custom
computer programming services

(P-23848)
EGAIN CORPORATION
455 W Maude Ave, Sunnyvale
(94085-3540)
PHONE.................................408 212-3400
Don Paulson, *CEO*
Gary Marzik, *Partner*
EMP: 17
SALES (corp-wide): 67.2MM **Publicly Held**
SIC: 7372 Application computer software
PA: Egain Corporation
1252 Borregas Ave
Sunnyvale CA 94089
408 636-4500

(P-23849)
EIS GROUP INC
731 Sansome St Fl 4, San Francisco
(94111-1723)
PHONE.................................415 402-2622
Alec Miloslavsky, *CEO*
Sergiy Synyanskyy, *CFO*
Mary A Gillespie, *Exec VP*
Slava Kritov, *Senior VP*

Grosso Anthony, *Vice Pres*
EMP: 128
SQ FT: 16,803
SALES (est): 22.7MM **Privately Held**
SIC: 7372 Business oriented computer
  software

(P-23850)
ELECTRONIC ARTS INC (PA)
Also Called: EA
209 Redwood Shores Pkwy, Redwood City
(94065-1175)
PHONE......................650 628-1500
Andrew Wilson, *CEO*
Lawrence F Probst III, *Ch of Bd*
Blake Jorgensen, *COO*
Christopher Bruzzo, *Chief Mktg Ofcr*
Patrick Sderlund, *Officer*
▲ **EMP:** 475
SQ FT: 660,000
SALES: 4.9B **Publicly Held**
WEB: www.ea.com
SIC: 7372 Home entertainment computer
  software

(P-23851)
ELECTRONIC ARTS INC
Also Called: Electronic Arts Los Angeles
5510 Lincoln Blvd Ste 100, Los Angeles
(90094-2035)
PHONE......................310 754-7000
John Batter, *Branch Mgr*
EMP: 10
SALES (corp-wide): 4.9B **Publicly Held**
WEB: www.ea.com
SIC: 7372 Home entertainment computer
  software
PA: Electronic Arts Inc.
  209 Redwood Shores Pkwy
  Redwood City CA 94065
  650 628-1500

(P-23852)
ELEKTA INC
100 Mathilda Pl Fl 5, Sunnyvale
(94086-6017)
PHONE......................408 830-8000
Derek Lane, *Software Dev*
John Whitmer, *Software Engr*
John Weston, *Engineer*
Mona Lee, *Regl Sales Mgr*
Ellen Hurd, *Lic Prac Nurse*
EMP: 40
SALES (corp-wide): 1.3B **Privately Held**
SIC: 7372 7373 Business oriented com-
  puter software; computer integrated sys-
  tems design
HQ: Elekta, Inc.
  400 Perimeter Center Ter
  Atlanta GA 30346
  770 300-9725

(P-23853)
ELEVATE INC
180 Avenida La Pata, San Clemente
(92673-6300)
PHONE......................949 276-5428
Wright W Thurston, *CEO*
Rod Place, *COO*
Bryan Ferre, *Chief Mktg Ofcr*
Alexander Chester, *Officer*
EMP: 21
SALES (est): 1.7MM **Privately Held**
SIC: 7372 Prepackaged software

(P-23854)
ELLIE MAE INC (HQ)
4420 Rosewood Dr Ste 500, Pleasanton
(94588-3059)
PHONE......................855 224-8572
Jonathan Corr, *President*
Dan Madden, *CFO*
Susan Chenoweth Beermann, *Chief Mktg
  Ofcr*
Selim Aissi, *Officer*
Brian Brown, *Exec VP*
EMP: 148 **EST:** 1997
SQ FT: 280,680
SALES: 480.2MM
SALES (corp-wide): 41.6MM **Privately
Held**
WEB: www.elliemae.com
SIC: 7372 7371 Prepackaged software;
  computer software systems analysis &
  design, custom; computer software devel-
  opment & applications

PA: Em Eagle Purchaser, Llc
  4420 Rosewood Dr Ste 500
  Pleasanton CA 94588
  855 224-8572

(P-23855)
ELLIPSIS HEALTH INC
535 Mission St Fl 25, San Francisco
(94105-3225)
PHONE......................650 906-6117
Mainul Islam, *CEO*
EMP: 12
SALES (est): 866.5K **Privately Held**
SIC: 7372 Application computer software

(P-23856)
EMPOWER SOFTWARE TECH LLC
28999 Old Town Front St # 203, Temecula
(92590-5806)
PHONE......................951 672-6257
Thomas V Smith, *Partner*
Ed Power,
Jeff Power,
Julie Smith,
EMP: 12
SALES (est): 1.5MM **Privately Held**
WEB: www.storagecommander.com
SIC: 7372 Business oriented computer
  software

(P-23857)
EMX DIGITAL LLC
Also Called: Breal Time
600 California St Fl 11, San Francisco
(94108-2727)
PHONE......................212 792-6810
EMP: 22
SALES (corp-wide): 6.8MM **Privately
Held**
SIC: 7372 Prepackaged software
PA: Emx Digital, Llc
  261 Madison Ave Fl 4
  New York NY 10016
  212 792-6810

(P-23858)
ENABLENCE SYSTEMS INC (HQ)
Also Called: Pannaway
2933 Bayview Dr, Fremont (94538-6520)
PHONE......................510 226-8900
Gary Davis, *President*
Robert Monaco, *COO*
Boris Grek, *Vice Pres*
EMP: 21
SALES (est): 9.6MM
SALES (corp-wide): 3.3MM **Privately
Held**
WEB: www.pannaway.com
SIC: 7372 Application computer software
PA: Enablence Technologies Inc
  390 March Rd Suite 119
  Kanata ON K2K 0
  613 656-2850

(P-23859)
ENERGY EXEMPLAR LLC (DH)
3013 Douglas Blvd Ste 120, Roseville
(95661-3842)
PHONE......................916 722-1484
Louise Drayton, *CFO*
Glenn Drayton, *CTO*
EMP: 10
SQ FT: 1,400
SALES: 3.5MM **Privately Held**
SIC: 7372 8748 Utility computer software;
  business consulting

(P-23860)
ENGAGIO INC
181 2nd Ave Ste 200, San Mateo
(94401-3816)
PHONE......................650 265-2264
Jon Miller, *CEO*
Heidi Bullock, *Chief Mktg Ofcr*
Cheryl Chavez, *Officer*
Inger Rarick, *Vice Pres*
Corey Marcel, *Executive*
EMP: 50 **EST:** 2015
SALES: 531K **Privately Held**
SIC: 7372 Business oriented computer
  software

(P-23861)
ENGRADE INC
1337 3rd Street Promenade # 300, Santa
Monica (90401-1379)
PHONE......................800 305-1367
Zach Posner, *CEO*
Christopher Orlando, *Director*
Andrew Foglia, *Manager*
Jenny Kroening, *Accounts Mgr*
EMP: 12
SALES (est): 1.1MM **Privately Held**
SIC: 7372 Educational computer software

(P-23862)
ENPIRION
101 Innovation Dr, San Jose (95134-1941)
PHONE......................408 904-2800
Juinn Chen, *Vice Pres*
EMP: 12
SALES (est): 630K **Privately Held**
SIC: 7372 Prepackaged software

(P-23863)
ENTCO LLC (DH)
Also Called: Autonomy Interwoven
1140 Enterprise Way, Sunnyvale
(94089-1412)
PHONE......................312 580-9100
Jeremy K Cox,
John E Calonico Jr, *Senior VP*
Mercedes De Luca, *VP Info Sys*
Rishi Varma,
EMP: 329
SQ FT: 110,000
SALES (est): 44.4MM **Privately Held**
WEB: www.iwov.com
SIC: 7372 Business oriented computer
  software
HQ: Micro Focus (Us), Inc.
  700 King Farm Blvd # 125
  Rockville MD 20850
  301 838-5000

(P-23864)
ENTERPRISE INFORMATICS INC
10052 Mesa Ridge Ct Ste 1, San Diego
(92121-2971)
PHONE......................858 625-3000
John W Low, *CFO*
David Dorries, *President*
Pierre De Wet, *VP Opers*
Glenn Cox, *VP Mktg*
Hilmar Retief, *Manager*
EMP: 26
SQ FT: 12,192
SALES (est): 1.5MM
SALES (corp-wide): 558.9MM **Privately
Held**
WEB: www.altris.com
SIC: 7372 Prepackaged software
PA: Bentley Systems, Incorporated
  685 Stockton Dr
  Exton PA 19341
  610 458-5000

(P-23865)
ENTERPRISE SERVICES LLC
333 N Lantana St Ste 287, Camarillo
(93010-9009)
PHONE......................805 388-8000
EMP: 10
SALES (corp-wide): 11.5B **Publicly Held**
WEB: www.eds.com
SIC: 7372 Prepackaged software
HQ: Perspecta Enterprise Solutions Llc
  13600 Eds Dr A3s
  Herndon VA 20171
  703 245-9675

(P-23866)
ENTERPRISE SIGNAL INC
Also Called: Kloudgin
440 N Wolfe Rd, Sunnyvale (94085-3869)
PHONE......................877 256-8303
Vikram Takru, *CEO*
Dharnesh Sethi, *CFO*
Vikas Bansal, *CTO*
Pushkala Venkateswaran, *Director*
Julie Stafford, *Manager*
EMP: 65
SALES (est): 155.9K **Privately Held**
SIC: 7372 Business oriented computer
  software

(P-23867)
ENVIZIO INC
Also Called: Enviz.io
2400 Country Dr, Fremont (94536-5329)
PHONE......................650 814-4302
Youriy Drozd, *Bd of Directors*
EMP: 24
SALES (est): 1.3MM **Privately Held**
SIC: 7372 Application computer software;
  operating systems computer software

(P-23868)
EOS SOFTWARE INC
900 E Hamilton Ave # 100, Campbell
(95008-0664)
PHONE......................855 900-4876
Mohit Doshi, *CEO*
EMP: 10
SQ FT: 500
SALES (est): 621.6K **Privately Held**
SIC: 7372 Business oriented computer
  software

(P-23869)
EPICOR SOFTWARE CORPORATION
4120 Dublin Blvd Ste 300, Dublin
(94568-7759)
PHONE......................925 361-9900
Pervez Qureshi, *Branch Mgr*
EMP: 101 **Publicly Held**
SIC: 7372 Prepackaged software
HQ: Epicor Software Corporation
  804 Las Cimas Pkwy # 200
  Austin TX 78746

(P-23870)
EPIGNOSIS LLC
315 Montgomery St Fl 9, San Francisco
(94104-1858)
PHONE......................646 797-2799
Dimitrios Tsigkos,
Chris Mathiopoulos, *Accounts Mgr*
EMP: 25 **EST:** 2012
SALES (est): 1.2MM **Privately Held**
SIC: 7372 Application computer software

(P-23871)
EPIRUS INC
2100 E Grand Ave Ste 330, El Segundo
(90245-5149)
P.O. Box 3927, Redondo Beach (90277-
1725)
PHONE......................310 487-5016
Nathan Mintz, *CEO*
Joseph Lonsdale, *Ch of Bd*
Max Mednik, *COO*
John Tenet, *Vice Ch Bd*
Daniel Thompson, *Vice Pres*
EMP: 10
SALES: 1MM **Privately Held**
SIC: 7372 7373 0781 1771 Prepackaged
  software; computer integrated systems
  design; landscape counseling & planning;
  stucco, gunite & grouting contractors;
  commercial physical research

(P-23872)
EQ TECHNOLOGIC INC
600 Anton Blvd, Costa Mesa (92626-7221)
PHONE......................215 891-9010
Dinesh Khaladkar, *Branch Mgr*
Joseph Garay,
Deshpande Pallavi, *Manager*
EMP: 20
SALES (corp-wide): 32.4MM **Privately
Held**
SIC: 7372 Business oriented computer
  software
PA: Eq Technologic, Inc.
  500 Office Center Dr # 400
  Fort Washington PA 19034
  215 891-9010

(P-23873)
EQUIMINE
26457 Rancho Pkwy S, Lake Forest
(92630-8326)
PHONE......................877 437-8464
Rabih Zahr, *President*
Nedal Mackarem, *Vice Pres*
Richard Borchard, *Technology*
EMP: 15

SALES: 4MM **Privately Held**
SIC: **7372** 3429 Business oriented computer software; keys, locks & related
hardware

(P-23874)
ERIDE INC
1 Letterman Dr Ste 310, San Francisco
(94129-1411)
PHONE....................................415 848-7800
Arthur Woo, *President*
Gary L Fischer, *CFO*
W Bradley Stewart, *Vice Pres*
Paul McBurney, *CTO*
EMP: 30
SQ FT: 5,000
SALES (est): 2.2MM **Privately Held**
WEB: www.eride-inc.com
SIC: **7372** Business oriented computer
software
PA: Furuno Electric Co., Ltd.
9-52, Ashiharacho
Nishinomiya HYO 662-0

(P-23875)
ESMART SOURCE INC
Also Called: Rfid4u
5159 Commercial Cir Ste H, Concord
(94520-8503)
P.O. Box 5366 (94524-0366)
PHONE....................................408 739-3500
Sanjiv Dua, *CEO*
EMP: 15
SALES (est): 1.9MM **Privately Held**
SIC: **7372** 7373 Business oriented com-
puter software; local area network (LAN)
systems integrator

(P-23876)
ESQ BUSINESS SERVICES INC
(PA)
Also Called: E S Q
20660 Stevens, Cupertino (95014)
PHONE....................................925 734-9800
Iqbal S Sandhu, *Director*
Joe Haggarty, *President*
Neil Butani, *Officer*
Maria Mendoza, *Business Dir*
Shridhar Venkatraman, *CTO*
EMP: 95
SQ FT: 300
SALES (est): 11.4MM **Privately Held**
WEB: www.esq.com
SIC: **7372** 7379 Prepackaged software;
computer related consulting services

(P-23877)
EVENT FARM INC (HQ)
3103 Neilson Way Ste B, Santa Monica
(90405-5355)
PHONE....................................888 444-8162
Ryan Costello, *CEO*
EMP: 28
SALES (est): 6.5MM **Privately Held**
SIC: **7372** Business oriented computer
software
PA: Membersuite, Inc.
47 Perimeter Ctr E # 300
Atlanta GA 30346
678 606-0310

(P-23878)
EVENTURE INTERACTIVE INC
3420 Bristol St Fl 6, Costa Mesa
(92626-1996)
PHONE....................................855 986-5669
Gannon Giguiere, *Ch of Bd*
Jason Harvey, *CEO*
Michael D Rountree, *CFO*
EMP: 13
SQ FT: 2,000
SALES (est): 923.2K **Privately Held**
SIC: **7372** Application computer software

(P-23879)
EVOLPHIN SOFTWARE INC (PA)
2410 Camino Ramon Ste 228, San Ramon
(94583-4323)
PHONE....................................888 386-4114
Brian Ahearn, *CEO*
Brad Christus, *Vice Pres*
Rahul Bhargava, *CTO*
Tomas Sudnius, *Finance Mgr*
EMP: 15
SQ FT: 20,000

SALES (est): 3.1MM **Privately Held**
SIC: **7372** Business oriented computer
software

(P-23880)
EVOLUTION ROBOTICS INC
1055 E Colo Blvd Ste 320, Pasadena
(91106)
PHONE....................................626 993-3300
Paolo Pirjanian, *CEO*
Bill Gross, *President*
Doug McPherson, *Asst Sec*
EMP: 40
SALES (est): 4.2MM **Publicly Held**
WEB: www.evolution.com
SIC: **7372** Application computer software
PA: Irobot Corporation
8 Crosby Dr
Bedford MA 01730

(P-23881)
EVOLV TECHNOLOGY
SOLUTIONS INC
611 Mission St Fl 6, San Francisco
(94105-3536)
PHONE....................................415 444-9040
Michael Scharff, *CEO*
EMP: 33
SALES (est): 567.6K **Privately Held**
SIC: **7372** Prepackaged software

(P-23882)
EXACTUALS LLC
1100 Glendon Ave Fl 17, Los Angeles
(90024-3588)
PHONE....................................310 689-7491
Michael Hurst, *CEO*
Bryan Walley, *COO*
Andrew Mauritzen, *CFO*
Ilie Ardelean,
Suneela Gandrothu, *Sr Software Eng*
EMP: 15
SALES (est): 381.1K
SALES (corp-wide): 21.4B **Privately Held**
SIC: **7372** Prepackaged software
HQ: City National Bank
555 S Flower St Fl 21
Los Angeles CA 90071
310 888-6000

(P-23883)
EXADEL INC (PA)
1340 Treat Blvd, Walnut Creek
(94597-2101)
PHONE....................................925 363-9510
Fima Katz, *President*
Lev Shur, *President*
Alex Kreymer, *COO*
Dmitry Binunsky, *Vice Pres*
Jonathan Fries, *Vice Pres*
EMP: 62
SALES (est): 22.5MM **Privately Held**
WEB: www.exadel.com
SIC: **7372** Application computer software

(P-23884)
EXPANDABLE SOFTWARE INC
(PA)
900 Lafayette St Ste 400, Santa Clara
(95050-4925)
PHONE....................................408 261-7880
Bob Swedroe, *CEO*
David Kearney, *Treasurer*
Gerald Lass, *Vice Pres*
Vern Marschke, *Vice Pres*
Tony Nevshemal, *Vice Pres*
EMP: 40
SQ FT: 10,000
SALES (est): 6.7MM **Privately Held**
WEB: www.expandable.com
SIC: **7372** 7371 Prepackaged software;
custom computer programming services

(P-23885)
EXPERT REPUTATION LLC
Also Called: Review Concierge
101 N Acacia Ave Ste 105, Solana Beach
(92075-1198)
PHONE....................................866 407-6020
Eric Januszko,
David Engel,
EMP: 13
SQ FT: 1,000
SALES (est): 1MM **Privately Held**
SIC: **7372** Application computer software

(P-23886)
EYVO INC
775 E Blithedale Ave, Mill Valley
(94941-1554)
PHONE....................................888 237-9801
Michael Petter, *CEO*
EMP: 15
SQ FT: 1,500
SALES (est): 705.1K **Privately Held**
SIC: **7372** Prepackaged software

(P-23887)
EZ 2000 INC
Also Called: EZ 2000 1 Rated Dental Sftwr
1800 Century Park E # 600, Los Angeles
(90067-1501)
PHONE....................................800 273-5033
Mark Shainberg, *President*
EMP: 10
SALES (est): 876.3K **Privately Held**
SIC: **7372** Prepackaged software

(P-23888)
EZBOARD INC
Also Called: Yuku.com
607 Market St Fl 5, San Francisco
(94105-3319)
PHONE....................................415 773-0400
Robert Labatt, *President*
EMP: 14
SQ FT: 1,400
SALES (est): 1.1MM **Privately Held**
WEB: www.ezboard.com
SIC: **7372** Application computer software

(P-23889)
EZOIC INC (PA)
6023 Innovation Way # 200, Carlsbad
(92009-1789)
PHONE....................................760 444-4995
Dwayne Lafleur, *President*
John Cole, *Principal*
Mark Evans, *Principal*
Jenny Hay, *Accounts Exec*
EMP: 10
SALES (est): 2MM **Privately Held**
SIC: **7372** Application computer software

(P-23890)
FACEFIRST INC
15821 Ventura Blvd # 425, Encino
(91436-4776)
PHONE....................................805 482-8428
Joseph Rosenkrantz, *CEO*
Dara Riordan, *Officer*
Roger Angarita, *Vice Pres*
Michelle Tutino, *Executive Asst*
Gary Brown, *Director*
EMP: 28
SQ FT: 6,500
SALES (est): 1.3MM **Privately Held**
SIC: **7372** 7371 Business oriented com-
puter software; computer software devel-
opment

(P-23891)
FACILITRON INC (PA)
485 Alberto Way Ste 210, Los Gatos
(95032-5476)
PHONE....................................800 272-2962
Jeff Benjamin, *CEO*
Hao Liu, *Manager*
EMP: 13 EST: 2014
SQ FT: 3,000
SALES (est): 3.2MM **Privately Held**
SIC: **7372** Business oriented computer
software

(P-23892)
FAIR ISAAC INTERNATIONAL
CORP (HQ)
200 Smith Ranch Rd, San Rafael
(94903-5551)
PHONE....................................415 446-6000
Thomas G Grudnowski, *President*
Cheryl St John, *Cust Svc Dir*
EMP: 600
SALES (est): 51.2MM
SALES (corp-wide): 1B **Publicly Held**
SIC: **7372** Business oriented computer
software
PA: Fair Isaac Corporation
181 Metro Dr Ste 700
San Jose CA 95110
408 535-1500

(P-23893)
FAMSOFT CORP
44946 Osgood Rd, Fremont (94539-6110)
PHONE....................................408 452-1550
Fareeha Fahim-Rahman, *President*
Scott Frick, *Associate*
EMP: 10 EST: 2007
SALES (est): 1.2MM **Privately Held**
SIC: **7372** Operating systems computer
software

(P-23894)
FAMSOFT CORPORATION
44946 Osgood Rd, Fremont (94539-6110)
PHONE....................................510 683-3940
Fahim Rahman, *CEO*
Fareeha Rahman, *President*
EMP: 20
SQ FT: 2,500
SALES (est): 1.4MM **Privately Held**
WEB: www.famsoft.com
SIC: **7372** 7361 8243 7373 Prepackaged
software; employment agencies; data pro-
cessing schools; computer integrated sys-
tems design; custom computer
programming services

(P-23895)
FIELDCENTRIX INC
8 Hughes, Irvine (92618-2072)
PHONE....................................949 784-5000
Renee Labran, *President*
Helen Fuerst, *Office Admin*
Mark Borgeson, *Sr Software Eng*
Joyce Cambell, *Info Tech Mgr*
Stephen Omnus, *Project Mgr*
EMP: 30 EST: 1994
SALES (est): 2.4MM **Privately Held**
WEB: www.fieldcentrix.com
SIC: **7372** Business oriented computer
software

(P-23896)
FILETRAIL INC
1990 The Alameda, San Jose
(95126-1432)
PHONE....................................408 289-1300
Darrell Mervau, *President*
Meghan Bofenkamp, *Manager*
EMP: 23
SQ FT: 2,000
SALES: 4.7MM **Privately Held**
WEB: www.filetrail.com
SIC: **7372** Utility computer software

(P-23897)
FINIX PAYMENTS INC
408 2nd St Ste 202, San Francisco
(94107)
PHONE....................................714 417-2727
Richie Serna, *CEO*
Sean Donovan, *COO*
EMP: 11
SALES (est): 846.8K **Privately Held**
SIC: **7372** Business oriented computer
software

(P-23898)
FIORANO SOFTWARE INC
230 California Ave # 103, Palo Alto
(94306-1637)
PHONE....................................650 326-1136
Atul Saini, *CEO*
Madhav Vodnala, *President*
Anjali Saini, *CFO*
William La Forge, *Vice Pres*
Tony George, *Manager*
◆ EMP: 85
SALES (est): 8.2MM **Privately Held**
SIC: **7372** 7371 Prepackaged software;
custom computer programming services;
computer software development

(P-23899)
FIREEYE INC (PA)
601 Mccarthy Blvd, Milpitas (95035-7932)
PHONE....................................408 321-6300
Kevin R Mandia, *CEO*
William T Robbins, *Exec VP*
EMP: 148
SQ FT: 190,000
SALES: 830.9MM **Publicly Held**
WEB: www.fireeye.com
SIC: **7372** 3577 Prepackaged software;
computer peripheral equipment

(P-23900)
FIRST ADVANTAGE TALENT MANAGEM
Also Called: Findly
98 Battery St Ste 400, San Francisco
(94111-5512)
PHONE..................415 446-3930
Rob Stubblefield, CFO
David Sanchez, Vice Pres
EMP: 26 EST: 2007
SQ FT: 4,000
SALES (est): 3.1MM Privately Held
SIC: 7372 Prepackaged software

(P-23901)
FIVE9 INC (PA)
4000 Executive Pkwy # 400, San Ramon
(94583-4206)
PHONE..................925 201-2000
Rowan Trollope, CEO
Michael Burkland, Ch of Bd
Daniel Burkland, President
Barry Zwarenstein, CFO
David Milam, Chief Mktg Ofcr
EMP: 148
SQ FT: 79,600
SALES (est): 257.6MM Publicly Held
WEB: www.five9.com
SIC: 7372 7374 Prepackaged software; data processing & preparation

(P-23902)
FLASH CODE SOLUTIONS LLC
4727 Wilshire Blvd # 302, Los Angeles
(90010-3806)
PHONE..................800 633-7467
James B Davis, Principal
EMP: 17
SQ FT: 2,600
SALES (est): 616.2K Privately Held
SIC: 7372 Application computer software

(P-23903)
FLIPAGRAM INC
916 Silver Spur Rd # 310, Rlng HLS Est
(90274-3810)
PHONE..................415 827-8373
Farhad Mohit, CEO
EMP: 16 EST: 2007
SALES (est): 1.4MM Privately Held
SIC: 7372 7389 Prepackaged software;

(P-23904)
FLIPCAUSE INC
283 4th St Ste 101, Oakland (94607-4320)
PHONE..................800 523-1950
Emerson Valiao, CEO
EMP: 15
SQ FT: 2,000
SALES: 3.5MM Privately Held
SIC: 7372 Prepackaged software

(P-23905)
FLOOR COVERING SOFT
221 E Walnut St Ste 110, Pasadena
(91101-1554)
PHONE..................626 683-9188
Steven Wang, CEO
Alicia Pollerana, Sales Staff
▼EMP: 15
SQ FT: 2,500
SALES (est): 1.7MM Privately Held
SIC: 7372 Prepackaged software

(P-23906)
FLYWHEEL SOFTWARE INC
816 Hamilton St, Redwood City
(94063-1624)
PHONE..................650 260-1700
Steve Humphreys, CEO
Sachin Kansal, Chief Engr
Mark Towfiq, Chief Engr
Anagha Dutt, Controller
Brogan Keane, Marketing Staff
EMP: 30
SALES (est): 5.8MM Privately Held
SIC: 7372 Application computer software

(P-23907)
FOCUS POINT OF SALE
Also Called: Focus Pos
48 Waterworks Way, Irvine (92618-3107)
PHONE..................949 336-7500
Julie Sharpe, Owner
Karrie Wermes, Owner

EMP: 12 EST: 2013
SQ FT: 3,900
SALES (est): 991.9K Privately Held
SIC: 7372 7373 Application computer software; office computer automation systems integration

(P-23908)
FOODLINK ONLINE LLC
475 Alberto Way Ste 100, Los Gatos
(95032-5480)
PHONE..................408 395-7280
EMP: 20
SQ FT: 5,000
SALES (est): 2.7MM Privately Held
WEB: www.foodlinkonline.com
SIC: 7372

(P-23909)
FORECROSS CORPORATION (PA)
505 Montgomery St Fl 11, San Francisco
(94111-2585)
PHONE..................415 543-1515
Kim O Jones, President
Bernadette C Castello, CFO
EMP: 12
SALES: 5MM Publicly Held
WEB: www.forecross.com
SIC: 7372 Business oriented computer software

(P-23910)
FORESITE SYSTEMS LIMITED (PA)
19925 Stevens Creek Blvd, Cupertino
(95014-2300)
PHONE..................408 855-8600
Lance Allison, CEO
Graham Margetson, President
Travis Miller, Vice Pres
EMP: 11
SALES (est): 3.3MM Privately Held
SIC: 7372 7379 Prepackaged software; computer related consulting services

(P-23911)
FORGE GLOBAL INC (PA)
415 Mission St Ste 5510, San Francisco
(94105-2615)
PHONE..................415 881-1612
Kelly Rodriques, Ch of Bd
Samvit Ramadurgam, President
Mark Lee, CEO
Javier Avalos, Director
John Zic, Director
EMP: 10 EST: 2015
SALES (est): 1.5MM Privately Held
SIC: 7372 Business oriented computer software

(P-23912)
FORGEROCK US INC (HQ)
201 Mission St, San Francisco
(94105-1831)
PHONE..................415 599-1100
John Fernandez, CFO
Pola Lobello, Partner
Robert Humphrey, Chief Mktg Ofcr
Lasse Andresen, CTO
EMP: 73
SQ FT: 15,744
SALES: 14MM
SALES (corp-wide): 89.9MM Privately Held
SIC: 7372 5045 Prepackaged software; computer software
PA: Forgerock, Inc.
201 Mission St Ste 2900
San Francisco CA 94105
415 599-1100

(P-23913)
FORMATION INC
Also Called: Formation Systems
35 Stillman St, San Francisco
(94107-1361)
PHONE..................650 257-2277
Christian Hansen, CEO
Christian Selchau-Hansen, CEO
Ammon Haggerty, Vice Pres
EMP: 87
SQ FT: 10,000
SALES (est): 1.3MM Privately Held
SIC: 7372 Business oriented computer software

(P-23914)
FORMTRAN INC
26501 Rancho Pkwy S # 103, Lake Forest
(92630-8359)
PHONE..................949 829-5822
Mike Stuhley, President
Randy Woodward, Technical Mgr
EMP: 10
SQ FT: 2,500
SALES (est): 1.3MM Privately Held
WEB: www.formtran.com
SIC: 7372 Business oriented computer software

(P-23915)
FORTANIX INC (PA)
444 Castro St Ste 305, Mountain View
(94041-2076)
PHONE..................628 400-2043
Ambuj Kumar, CEO
Andy Leiserson, Chief
EMP: 21
SALES (est): 6.4MM Privately Held
SIC: 7372 Prepackaged software

(P-23916)
FOUNDATION 9 ENTERTAINMENT INC (PA)
30211 A De Las Bandera200, Rancho
Santa Margari (92688)
PHONE..................949 698-1500
James N Hearn, CEO
John Goldman, Ch of Bd
David Mann, President
EMP: 200
SALES (est): 38.1MM Privately Held
SIC: 7372 Home entertainment computer software

(P-23917)
FOUNDSTONE INC
27201 Puerta Real Ste 400, Mission Viejo
(92691-8517)
PHONE..................949 297-5600
George Kurtz, CEO
Stuart McClure, President
Larry McIntosh, Chief Mktg Ofcr
William Chan, Vice Pres
Chris Prosise, Vice Pres
EMP: 80
SQ FT: 15,000
SALES (est): 4.9MM Privately Held
WEB: www.foundstone.com
SIC: 7372 Application computer software
HQ: Mcafee, Llc
2821 Mission College Blvd
Santa Clara CA 95054
888 847-8766

(P-23918)
FRAGMOB LLC
9655 Granite Ridge Dr # 200, San Diego
(92123-2674)
PHONE..................858 587-6659
Jade Charles, CEO
Jonathan Shapiro, President
EMP: 18
SALES (est): 1.7MM Privately Held
SIC: 7372 Publishers' computer software

(P-23919)
FRANZ INC
2201 Broadway Ste 715, Oakland
(94612-3024)
PHONE..................510 452-2000
Jans Aasman, CEO
Kevin Layer, COO
Lada Smirnova, CFO
John Foderar, Treasurer
Craig Norvell, Vice Pres
EMP: 25
SQ FT: 5,000
SALES (est): 4.6MM Privately Held
WEB: www.franz.com/
SIC: 7372 7371 Prepackaged software; computer software development

(P-23920)
FREEZE TAG INC (PA)
18062 Irvine Blvd Ste 103, Tustin
(92780-3328)
PHONE..................714 210-3850
Craig Holland, Officer
Mick Donahoo, COO
Tamara Sahagun, Contractor
John Holman, Associate

EMP: 14
SQ FT: 900
SALES (est): 2.1MM Publicly Held
WEB: www.freezetag.com
SIC: 7372 Prepackaged software

(P-23921)
FREIGHTGATE INC
Also Called: Edi Ideas
10055 Slater Ave Ste 231, Fountain Valley
(92708-4722)
PHONE..................714 799-2833
Martin Hubert, President
Sascha Hack, CTO
Nathan Huang, Software Engr
EMP: 26
SALES (est): 3.2MM
SALES (corp-wide): 2.9MM Privately Held
WEB: www.freightgate.com
SIC: 7372 7371 Application computer software; utility computer software; computer software development & applications
PA: Edi Ideas Inc
16051 Springdale St # 111
Huntington Beach CA 92649
714 841-2833

(P-23922)
FRONTAPP INC
525 Brannan St Ste 300, San Francisco
(94107-1632)
PHONE..................415 680-3048
Mathilde Collin, CEO
Laurent Perrin, CTO
EMP: 71
SQ FT: 11,000
SALES: 5MM Privately Held
SIC: 7372 Application computer software

(P-23923)
FUJISOFT AMERICA INC
1710 S Amphlett Blvd # 215, San Mateo
(94402-2705)
PHONE..................650 235-9422
James Prenton, Administration
Renhong Sun, CEO
Rei Atluri, Engineer
EMP: 12
SQ FT: 2,700 Privately Held
SIC: 7372 Prepackaged software
PA: Fujisoft Service Bureau Incorporated
2-19-7, Kotobashi
Sumida-Ku TKY 130-0

(P-23924)
FUZEBOX SOFTWARE CORPORATION (HQ)
150 Spear St Ste 900, San Francisco
(94105-5118)
PHONE..................415 692-4800
David Obrand, CEO
Charlie Newark-French, President
Mark Stubbs, CFO
Jeffrey Henley, Bd of Directors
Manuel Rivelo, Bd of Directors
EMP: 17
SQ FT: 16,000
SALES (est): 16MM
SALES (corp-wide): 122.9MM Privately Held
WEB: www.callwave.com
SIC: 7372 Application computer software
PA: Fuze, Inc.
2 Copley Pl Ste 700
Boston MA 02116
800 890-1553

(P-23925)
G7 PRODUCTIVITY SYSTEMS
Also Called: Versacheck
16885 W Bernardo Dr # 290, San Diego
(92127-1618)
P.O. Box 270459 (92198-2459)
PHONE..................858 675-1095
Thomas Priebus, President
Teri Pfarr, COO
Jim Danforth, CFO
EMP: 60
SQ FT: 18,000
SALES (est): 3.9MM Privately Held
WEB: www.g7ps.com
SIC: 7372 Prepackaged software

▲ = Import ▼=Export
◆ =Import/Export

(P-23926)
GAMECLOUD STUDIOS INC
30111 Tech Dr Ste 110, Murrieta (92563)
PHONE..................................951 677-2345
EMP: 20 EST: 2010
SALES (est): 1.2MM **Privately Held**
SIC: 7372

(P-23927)
GAMEMINE LLC
2341 Wilson Ave, Venice (90291-4738)
PHONE..................................310 310-3105
Flaviu Rus, *Mng Member*
Daneil Starr,
EMP: 35 EST: 2017
SALES: 50MM **Privately Held**
SIC: 7372 Publishers' computer software

(P-23928)
GATE-OR-DOOR INC
14811 Leroy Ave, Ripon (95366-9417)
PHONE..................................209 751-4881
James Bickle, *Principal*
EMP: 21
SALES (est): 3MM **Privately Held**
SIC: 7372 Operating systems computer
software

(P-23929)
GATHERAPP INC
301 Bryant St Apt 201, San Francisco
(94107-4170)
PHONE..................................415 409-9476
Abraham Shafi, *CEO*
EMP: 10
SALES (est): 221.8K **Privately Held**
SIC: 7372 Application computer software

(P-23930)
GE DIGITAL LLC (HQ)
2623 Camino Ramon, San Ramon
(94583-9130)
PHONE..................................925 242-6200
Vineet Shrivastava, *Surgery Dir*
Luke Tresnicky, *Technical Staff*
Shirley D'Souza, *Opers Staff*
Lili Mokhtari, *Manager*
EMP: 67
SALES (est): 46.3MM
SALES (corp-wide): 121.6B **Publicly
Held**
SIC: 7372 Business oriented computer
software
PA: General Electric Company
41 Farnsworth St
Boston MA 02210
617 443-3000

(P-23931)
GENERAL ELECTRIC COMPANY
2623 Camino Ramon, San Ramon
(94583-9130)
PHONE..................................925 242-6200
Holly Gilthorpe, *Ch Credit Ofcr*
Rebecca Lawson, *Vice Pres*
Jennifer Schulze, *Vice Pres*
Ashima Puri, *Program Mgr*
Lavanya Mallikharjuna, *Software Engr*
EMP: 72
SALES (corp-wide): 121.6B **Publicly
Held**
SIC: 7372 Business oriented computer
software
PA: General Electric Company
41 Farnsworth St
Boston MA 02210
617 443-3000

(P-23932)
**GENERAL MEDIA SYSTEMS
LLC**
611 K St Ste B202, San Diego
(92101-7090)
PHONE..................................818 210-4236
Michael Cardona,
Gregory Aouiverate,
Steve Matthyssen,
EMP: 10
SQ FT: 8,000
SALES: 25MM **Privately Held**
SIC: 7372 Application computer software

(P-23933)
**GENESIS GROUP SFTWR
DEVELOPERS**
Also Called: Ggsdi
16027 Brookhurst St Ste G, Fountain Valley
(92708-1562)
PHONE..................................714 630-4297
EMP: 25
SALES (est): 2.2MM **Privately Held**
WEB: www.ggsdi.com
SIC: 7372 7371

(P-23934)
**GENESYS TELECOM LABS INC
(HQ)**
Also Called: Genesys Telecom Labs
2001 Junipero Serra Blvd, Daly City
(94014-3891)
PHONE..................................650 466-1100
Tony Bates, *CEO*
Rex Lofland, *Partner*
Tom Eggemeier, *President*
Paul Segre, *Chairman*
David Sudbey, *Ch Credit Ofcr*
EMP: 450
SQ FT: 156,000
SALES (est): 622.6MM
SALES (corp-wide): 34.6MM **Privately
Held**
WEB: www.genesyslabs.com
SIC: 7372 Business oriented computer
software
PA: Permira Advisers Llp
80 Pall Mall
London SW1Y
207 632-1000

(P-23935)
**GEOGRAPHIC DATA MGT
SOLUTIONS**
Also Called: Gdms
42140 10th St W, Lancaster (93534-7004)
PHONE..................................661 949-1025
Brian Glidden, *President*
Lisa Aitken, *Vice Pres*
Daniel Stanton, *Director*
EMP: 10
SALES (est): 982.2K **Privately Held**
SIC: 7372 5045 Business oriented com-
puter software; computers, peripherals &
software

(P-23936)
GET AHEAD LEARNING LLC
70 S Lake Ave Ste 1000, Pasadena
(91101-4995)
PHONE..................................626 796-8500
Walter B Rose,
EMP: 10
SALES (est): 511.5K **Privately Held**
WEB: www.getaheadlearning.com
SIC: 7372 Educational computer software

(P-23937)
GETGOING INC
610 Bridgeport Ln, Foster City
(94404-3606)
PHONE..................................415 608-7474
Alek Vernitsky, *CEO*
Alek Strygin, *COO*
Nilesh Lakhani, *Principal*
Fred Reid, *Principal*
Ilya Gluhovsky, *Chief Engr*
EMP: 18 EST: 2011
SALES (est): 1.9MM **Privately Held**
SIC: 7372 7371 Application computer soft-
ware; business oriented computer soft-
ware; computer software development

(P-23938)
GIGAMON INC (HQ)
3300 Olcott St, Santa Clara (95054-3005)
PHONE..................................408 831-4000
Paul A Hooper, *CEO*
Michelle Hodges, *Partner*
Shane Buckley, *President*
Dave Arkley, *CFO*
Karl Van Den Bergh, *Chief Mktg Ofcr*
▲ EMP: 145
SQ FT: 105,600
SALES: 310.8MM **Privately Held**
WEB: www.gigamon.com
SIC: 7372 3577 Prepackaged software;
computer peripheral equipment

PA: Ginsberg Holdco, Inc.
3300 Olcott St
Santa Clara CA 95054
408 831-4000

(P-23939)
GILDEDTREE INC
251 Lafayette Cir Ste 310, Lafayette
(94549-4388)
PHONE..................................925 246-5624
Yariv Lioz, *President*
Barry Weinstein, *Vice Pres*
EMP: 15
SALES (est): 663.6K **Privately Held**
SIC: 7372 Educational computer software

(P-23940)
GITACLOUD INC
5791 Athenour Ct, Pleasanton
(94588-9678)
PHONE..................................925 519-5965
Ashutosh Bansal,
EMP: 12
SALES (est): 256K **Privately Held**
SIC: 7372 7389 Prepackaged software;

(P-23941)
GLASSLÁB INC
209 Redwood Shores Pkwy, Redwood City
(94065-1175)
PHONE..................................415 244-5584
Jessica Lindl, *Exec Dir*
Granetta Blevins, *CFO*
Michael John, *Managing Dir*
Michelle Riconscente, *Managing Dir*
Rose Abernathy, *Prgrmr*
EMP: 24 EST: 2014
SALES: 4.2MM **Privately Held**
SIC: 7372 8748 Educational computer
software; educational consultant

(P-23942)
GLOBAL EDGE LLC
5230 Las Virgenes Rd # 265, Calabasas
(91302-3459)
PHONE..................................888 315-2692
EMP: 30 **Privately Held**
SIC: 7372 8721
PA: Global Edge, Llc
5230 Las Virgenes Rd # 265
Calabasas CA

(P-23943)
GLOBAL INFOVISION INC
2290 Ardemore Dr, Fullerton (92833-4819)
PHONE..................................714 738-4465
Prem Gupta, *President*
EMP: 10
SALES (est): 940K **Privately Held**
WEB: www.globalinfovision.net
SIC: 7372 Prepackaged software

(P-23944)
**GLOBAL MICRO SOLUTIONS
INC**
21250 Hawthorne Blvd # 540, Torrance
(90503-5506)
PHONE..................................310 218-5678
Mike Uesugi, *President*
Angela Uesugi, *Vice Pres*
EMP: 10
SQ FT: 1,500
SALES (est): 1MM **Privately Held**
SIC: 7372 7371 Prepackaged software;
computer software systems analysis &
design, custom

(P-23945)
GLOBAL WAVE GROUP LLC
8a Journey Ste 100, Aliso Viejo (92656)
PHONE..................................949 916-9800
Zubin Mehta, *Mng Member*
Randy M Ruckle, *COO*
Rhett Rowe, *Senior VP*
EMP: 10 EST: 2007
SALES (est): 938.6K **Privately Held**
SIC: 7372 Prepackaged software

(P-23946)
GOALSR INC
3139 Independence Dr, Livermore
(94551-7595)
PHONE..................................650 453-5844
Vidyadhar Handragal, *President*
Divya Krishnaswamy, *CEO*

EMP: 47
SQ FT: 1,000
SALES: 500K **Privately Held**
SIC: 7372 7371 Application computer software; computer software systems analysis & design, custom; computer software
development; computer software development & applications

(P-23947)
GOENGINEER INC
6400 Canoga Ave Ste 121, Woodland Hills
(91367-7781)
PHONE..................................818 716-1650
Ken Coburn, *Branch Mgr*
Alexandra Slyngman, *Office Mgr*
EMP: 11
SALES (corp-wide): 54.2MM **Privately
Held**
SIC: 7372 Prepackaged software
PA: Goengineer, Inc.
1787 E Fort Union Blvd # 100
Salt Lake City UT 84121
801 359-6100

(P-23948)
GOODCO INC
543 Howard St Fl 4, San Francisco
(94105-3015)
PHONE..................................415 425-1012
Samar Birwadker, *CEO*
Subbu Balakrishinan, *CTO*
EMP: 10
SALES (est): 620K **Privately Held**
SIC: 7372 Business oriented computer
software

(P-23949)
GOODRX INC (PA)
233 Wilshire Blvd Ste 990, Santa Monica
(90401-1248)
PHONE..................................310 500-6544
Douglass Hirsch, *CEO*
Mike Darrow, *Exec VP*
Mark Ensley, *Vice Pres*
Trevor Dezdek, *Principal*
Tom Zoch, *District Mgr*
EMP: 16
SALES (est): 4.8MM **Privately Held**
SIC: 7372 Application computer software

(P-23950)
GOVERNMENTJOBSCOM INC
Also Called: Neogov
300 Continental Blvd # 565, El Segundo
(90245-5042)
PHONE..................................310 426-6304
Damir Davidovic, *CEO*
Scott Letourneau, *President*
Chris Rosenberger, *Info Tech Mgr*
George Gerbi, *Software Dev*
Ashish Srivastava, *Software Dev*
EMP: 130
SQ FT: 5,000
SALES (est): 20.8MM **Privately Held**
WEB: www.governmentjobs.com
SIC: 7372 Prepackaged software

(P-23951)
GRADESCOPE INC
2054 University Ave # 600, Berkeley
(94704-1076)
P.O. Box 11691 (94712-2691)
PHONE..................................702 985-7442
Arjun Singh, *CEO*
EMP: 10
SQ FT: 1,600
SALES (est): 294K
SALES (corp-wide): 5.5B **Privately Held**
SIC: 7372 Educational computer software
HQ: Turnitin, Llc
2101 Webster St Ste 1800
Oakland CA 94612
866 816-5046

(P-23952)
GRANITE SOFTWARE INC
7590 N Glenoaks Blvd # 102, Burbank
(91504-1011)
PHONE..................................818 252-1950
Elmer Vasquez, *President*
Christopher Negron, *Prgrmr*
Gloria McClain, *Supervisor*
EMP: 15 EST: 1999

SALES (est): 1.2MM **Privately Held**
WEB: www.iclosingsdirect.com
SIC: 7372 Prepackaged software

(P-23953)
GRAYPAY LLC
6345 Balboa Blvd Ste 115, Encino
(91316-1517)
PHONE..................................818 387-6735
Marc Geolina, *Mng Member*
Bryan Rainey,
Jaimie Smith, *Manager*
EMP: 60 EST: 2015
SALES (est): 2.4MM **Privately Held**
SIC: 7372 Business oriented computer
software

(P-23954)
GREAT LAKES DATA SYSTEMS INC
Also Called: G L D S
5954 Priestly Dr, Carlsbad (92008-8812)
PHONE..................................760 602-1900
Doug Ganske, *Manager*
Jeff Dew, *Info Tech Dir*
Sandi Kruger, *Manager*
Marco Ortiz, *Manager*
EMP: 10
SQ FT: 6,360
SALES (corp-wide): 8.5MM **Privately Held**
WEB: www.cablebilling.com
SIC: 7372 Prepackaged software
PA: Great Lakes Data Systems, Inc.
306 Seippel Blvd
Beaver Dam WI 53916
920 887-7651

(P-23955)
GREEN HILLS SOFTWARE LLC (HQ)
30 W Sola St, Santa Barbara (93101-2599)
PHONE..................................805 965-6044
Daniel O Dowd, *CEO*
Dave Kleidermacher, *President*
Michael W Liacko, *President*
Daniel O'Dowd, *CEO*
Matt Fechtman, *CFO*
EMP: 105
SALES (est): 77.1MM
SALES (corp-wide): 23.4MM **Privately Held**
WEB: www.ghs.com
SIC: 7372 Prepackaged software
PA: Ghs Holding Company
30 W Sola St
Santa Barbara CA 93101
805 965-6044

(P-23956)
GREMLIN INC
55 S Market St Ste 1205, San Jose
(95113-2324)
PHONE..................................408 214-9885
Kolton Andrus, *CEO*
Matthew Fornaciari, *Shareholder*
EMP: 40
SALES (est): 5MM **Privately Held**
SIC: 7372 8742 Prepackaged software;
management consulting services

(P-23957)
GREYHELLER LLC
111 Deerwood Rd Ste 200, San Ramon
(94583-4445)
PHONE..................................925 415-5053
Hendrix Bodden, *CEO*
Greg Wendt, *Exec Dir*
Keith Waggoner, *Engineer*
Jim Henderson, *Sales Dir*
Mark Martin, *Manager*
EMP: 12
SQ FT: 1,500
SALES (est): 1.3MM **Privately Held**
SIC: 7372 Prepackaged software

(P-23958)
GRIDGAIN SYSTEMS INC (PA)
1065 E Hillsdale Blvd, Foster City
(94404-1613)
PHONE..................................650 241-2281
Abe Kleinfeld, *President*
Eoin Connor, *CFO*
Andy Sacks, *Exec VP*
Terry Erisman, *Vice Pres*
Jon Webster, *VP Bus Dvlpt*

EMP: 54
SALES (est): 17.8MM **Privately Held**
SIC: 7372 Prepackaged software

(P-23959)
GROWDIARIES LLC
8605 Santa Monica Blvd, West Hollywood
(90069-4109)
PHONE..................................626 354-8935
Egor Prilukov,
EMP: 10
SALES (est): 221.8K **Privately Held**
SIC: 7372 Application computer software

(P-23960)
GUARDIAN ANALYTICS INC
2465 Latham St Ste 200, Mountain View
(94040-4792)
PHONE..................................650 383-9200
Laurent Pacalin, *President*
Vinny Alvino, *COO*
Hue Harguindeguy, *CFO*
Dennis Concannon, *Vice Pres*
Prashanth Shetty, *Vice Pres*
EMP: 27
SALES (est): 7.5MM **Privately Held**
WEB: www.guardiananalytics.com
SIC: 7372 Prepackaged software

(P-23961)
GUAVUS INC (HQ)
2125 Zanker Rd, San Jose (95131-2109)
PHONE..................................650 243-3400
Anukool Lakhina, *CEO*
Michael Crane, *President*
Ty Nam, *COO*
Anupam Rastogi, *CTO*
EMP: 53
SALES (est): 25.6MM
SALES (corp-wide): 262.1MM **Privately Held**
WEB: www.guavus.com
SIC: 7372 7371 Prepackaged software;
computer software development & applications
PA: Thales
Tour Carpe Diem Esplanade Nord
Courbevoie 92400
157 778-000

(P-23962)
GUCK ARIBA
807 Eleventh Ave, Sunnyvale
(94089-4731)
PHONE..................................650 390-1445
Chris Cavanaugh, *Vice Pres*
Leigh Interihal, *Vice Pres*
Dave Johnston, *Vice Pres*
Brian Krieger, *Vice Pres*
Darlene French, *Executive*
EMP: 147
SALES (est): 7MM **Privately Held**
SIC: 7372 Business oriented computer
software

(P-23963)
GUIDANCE SOFTWARE INC (HQ)
1055 E Colo Blvd Ste 400, Pasadena
(91106)
PHONE..................................626 229-9191
Patrick Dennis, *President*
Barry Plaga, *COO*
Michael Harris, *Chief Mktg Ofcr*
Alfredo Gomez, *Senior VP*
Michael Macguire, *Vice Pres*
EMP: 215 EST: 1997
SQ FT: 90,000
SALES: 110.5MM
SALES (corp-wide): 2.8B **Privately Held**
WEB: www.guidancesoftware.com
SIC: 7372 3572 Business oriented computer software; computer storage devices
PA: Open Text Corporation
275 Frank Tompa Dr
Waterloo ON N2L 0
519 888-7111

(P-23964)
GUIDANCE SOFTWARE INC
215 N Marengo Ave Ste 250, Pasadena
(91101-1532)
PHONE..................................626 229-9199
EMP: 32
SALES (est): 1.6MM **Privately Held**
SIC: 7372 Prepackaged software

(P-23965)
GUIDEWIRE SOFTWARE INC (PA)
2850 S Del St Ste 400, San Mateo (94403)
PHONE..................................650 357-9100
Mike Rosenbaum, *President*
Marcus S Ryu, *Ch of Bd*
Priscilla Hung, *COO*
Curtis Smith, *CFO*
Ali Kheirolomoom, *Officer*
EMP: 148
SQ FT: 97,674
SALES: 719.5MM **Publicly Held**
WEB: www.guidewire.com
SIC: 7372 Business oriented computer
software

(P-23966)
GUPSHUP INC
38350 Fremont Blvd # 203, Fremont
(94536-6060)
PHONE..................................415 506-9095
EMP: 19
SALES (corp-wide): 2.3MM **Privately Held**
SIC: 7372 Prepackaged software
PA: Gupshup, Inc.
415 Jackson St
San Francisco CA 94111
415 506-9095

(P-23967)
H2 WELLNESS INCORPORATED
15414 Milldale Dr, Los Angeles
(90077-1601)
PHONE..................................310 362-1888
Hooman Fakki, *CEO*
Houman Arasteh, *COO*
Russ Nash, *Bd of Directors*
EMP: 55
SALES (est): 3.6MM **Privately Held**
SIC: 7372 Application computer software

(P-23968)
HABLA INCORPORATED
Also Called: Olark
548 Market St, San Francisco
(94104-5401)
PHONE..................................703 867-0135
Ben Congleton, *CEO*
EMP: 30 EST: 2015
SALES (est): 1MM **Privately Held**
SIC: 7372 Business oriented computer
software

(P-23969)
HAZELCAST INC (PA)
2 W 5th Ave Ste 300, San Mateo
(94402-2002)
PHONE..................................650 521-5453
Kelly Herrell, *CEO*
Kevin Cox, *Vice Pres*
Morgan Dioli, *Vice Pres*
Paul Salazar, *Principal*
Greg Luck, *CTO*
EMP: 28 EST: 2012
SALES (est): 6.2MM **Privately Held**
SIC: 7372 7371 Publishers' computer software; computer software systems analysis & design, custom

(P-23970)
HEALTH GORILLA INC (PA)
185 N Wolfe Rd, Sunnyvale (94086-5212)
PHONE..................................844 446-7455
Steven Yaskin, *CEO*
Sergio Wagner, *Vice Pres*
Heena Shah, *Manager*
EMP: 14
SALES (est): 4MM **Privately Held**
SIC: 7372 Application computer software

(P-23971)
HEALTHLINE SYSTEMS LLC (HQ)
9605 Scranton Rd Ste 200, San Diego
(92121-1768)
P.O. Box 420399 (92142-0399)
PHONE..................................858 673-1700
Dan E Littrell, *President*
EMP: 27
SQ FT: 20,800

SALES (est): 7.5MM
SALES (corp-wide): 231.6MM **Publicly Held**
WEB: www.healthlinesystem.com
SIC: 7372 7371 Business oriented computer software; computer software development
PA: Healthstream, Inc.
500 11th Ave N Ste 1000
Nashville TN 37203
615 301-3100

(P-23972)
HEALTHSTREAM INC
Also Called: Echo, A Healthstream Company
9605 Scranton Rd Ste 200, San Diego
(92121-1768)
PHONE..................................800 733-8737
Robert A Frist Jr, *Ch of Bd*
EMP: 193
SALES (corp-wide): 231.6MM **Publicly Held**
SIC: 7372 7371 Prepackaged software;
custom computer programming services
PA: Healthstream, Inc.
500 11th Ave N Ste 1000
Nashville TN 37203
615 301-3100

(P-23973)
HEALTHYWEALTHYHACK INC
Also Called: Fintech Platform
16979 Frank Ave, Los Gatos (95032-3453)
PHONE..................................669 225-3745
Sachin Piplani, *CEO*
EMP: 12
SALES (est): 500K **Privately Held**
SIC: 7372 Business oriented computer
software

(P-23974)
HEARSAY SOCIAL INC (PA)
185 Berry St Ste 3800, San Francisco
(94107-1725)
PHONE..................................888 990-3777
Clara Shih, *CEO*
Michael H Lock, *President*
Steve Garrity, *COO*
William Salisbury, *CFO*
Dave Peterson, *Chief Mktg Ofcr*
EMP: 60
SALES (est): 13.5MM **Privately Held**
SIC: 7372 Publishers' computer software

(P-23975)
HEAT SOFTWARE INTERMEDIATE INC
2590 N 1st St Ste 360, San Jose
(95131-1057)
PHONE..................................408 601-2800
Jon Temple, *CEO*
Cary Baker, *CFO*
David Puglia, *Chief Mktg Ofcr*
Roberto Casetta, *Vice Pres*
Fred Johannessen, *Vice Pres*
EMP: 383
SALES (est): 10.2MM **Privately Held**
SIC: 7372 7371 Prepackaged software;
computer software systems analysis & design, custom

(P-23976)
HEIRLOOM COMPUTING INC
3000 Dnville Blvd Ste 148, Alamo (94507)
PHONE..................................510 709-7245
Gary Crook, *President*
Kevin Moultrup, *COO*
Edward Abbati, *CFO*
Mark Haynie, *Senior Mgr*
EMP: 10
SALES (est): 211.4K **Privately Held**
SIC: 7372 Prepackaged software

(P-23977)
HELLO NETWORK INC
2 Mint Plz Apt 1004, San Francisco
(94103-1875)
PHONE..................................408 891-4727
Orkut Buyukkokten, *CEO*
John Murphy, *COO*
EMP: 10
SALES (est): 667.6K **Privately Held**
SIC: 7372 Application computer software

(P-23978)
HEROKU INC
1 Market St Ste 300, San Francisco (94105-1315)
PHONE..................650 704-6107
Tod Nielsen, *CEO*
Brad Gyger, *Vice Pres*
Michael Schiff, *Vice Pres*
Loren Fraser, *Executive*
Jordanee Key, *Administration*
EMP: 30
SALES (est): 3.4MM
SALES (corp-wide): 13.2B **Publicly Held**
SIC: 7372 Application computer software
PA: Salesforce.Com, Inc.
415 Mission St Fl 3
San Francisco CA 94105
415 901-7000

(P-23979)
HEWLETT PACKARD ENTERPRISE CO
1140 Enterprise Way, Sunnyvale (94089-1412)
PHONE..................312 580-9100
Rick Smith, *President*
Randy Van Sickle, *Network Enginr*
Tony Trotter, *Engineer*
Blake Kimura, *Marketing Staff*
Greg Giles, *Director*
EMP: 34
SALES (corp-wide): 30.8B **Publicly Held**
SIC: 7372 Business oriented computer software
PA: Hewlett Packard Enterprise Company
6280 America Center Dr
San Jose CA 95002
650 687-5817

(P-23980)
HEWLETT PACKARD ENTERPRISE CO (PA)
Also Called: Hpe
6280 America Center Dr, San Jose (95002-2563)
PHONE..................650 687-5817
Antonio F Neri, *President*
Patricia F Russo, *Ch of Bd*
Philip Davis, *President*
Keerti Melkote, *President*
Tarek A Robbiati, *CFO*
EMP: 148 **EST:** 1939
SALES: 30.8B **Publicly Held**
SIC: 7372 7379 3572 Business oriented computer software; computer related maintenance services; computer storage devices

(P-23981)
HEXACORP LTD
Also Called: Orfium
201 Ocean Ave Unit 1108p, Santa Monica (90402-1452)
PHONE..................760 815-0904
Roberts Wells, *CEO*
Christopher Mohoney, *President*
Drew Delis, *COO*
EMP: 20 **EST:** 2014
SALES: 200K **Privately Held**
SIC: 7372 7389 Prepackaged software;

(P-23982)
HIGHER ONE PAYMENTS INC
Also Called: Cashnet
80 Swan Way Ste 200, Oakland (94621-1439)
PHONE..................510 769-9888
Dan Peterson, *President*
Chuck Haddock, *Senior VP*
Mark Tancil, *Vice Pres*
EMP: 45
SQ FT: 4,500
SALES (est): 2.7MM
SALES (corp-wide): 157.9MM **Privately Held**
WEB: www.cashnet.com
SIC: 7372 Business oriented computer software
HQ: Higher One, Inc.
115 Munson St
New Haven CT 06511

(P-23983)
HOLLYWOOD SOFTWARE INC
5000 Van Nuys Blvd # 460, Van Nuys (91403-1854)
PHONE..................818 205-2121
Carol Dibattiste, *CEO*
Karl Anderson, *COO*
Kim Lockhart, *Senior VP*
Larry McCourt, *Senior VP*
Susan Wells, *Senior VP*
EMP: 19 **EST:** 1997
SALES (est): 2MM **Privately Held**
SIC: 7372 Operating systems computer software

(P-23984)
HOOJOOK
1754 Tech Dr Ste 132, San Jose (95148)
PHONE..................408 596-9427
Shauli Chaudhuri, *CEO*
Surendra Arora, *Vice Pres*
EMP: 12
SQ FT: 1,000
SALES (est): 760K **Privately Held**
SIC: 7372 Application computer software

(P-23985)
HOOPLA SOFTWARE INC
84 W Santa Clara St # 460, San Jose (95113-1815)
PHONE..................408 498-9600
Michael Smalls, *CEO*
Cathleen Candia, *Executive Asst*
Matthias Blankenhaus, *Engineer*
Christine Hao, *Engineer*
Julie Williamson, *Opers Mgr*
EMP: 38
SALES (est): 3.5MM **Privately Held**
SIC: 7372 Application computer software

(P-23986)
HORTONWORKS INC (HQ)
5470 Great America Pkwy, Santa Clara (95054-3644)
PHONE..................408 916-4121
Scott Aronson, *Risk Mgmt Dir*
Linda Morales, *Partner*
Sean Roberts, *Partner*
Scott Davidson, *CFO*
Jim Frankola, *CFO*
EMP: 725
SQ FT: 92,000
SALES (est): 221.8MM
SALES (corp-wide): 479.9MM **Publicly Held**
SIC: 7372 Application computer software
PA: Cloudera, Inc.
395 Page Mill Rd Ste 300
Palo Alto CA 94306
650 362-0488

(P-23987)
HOST ANALYTICS INC (HQ)
555 Twin Dolphin Dr # 400, Redwood City (94065-2132)
PHONE..................650 249-7100
Grant Halloran, *CEO*
Jim Eberlin, *President*
Ian Halifax, *CFO*
Ben Plummer, *Chief Mktg Ofcr*
Lance Walter, *Chief Mktg Ofcr*
EMP: 25 **EST:** 2000
SALES (est): 17.5MM **Privately Held**
WEB: www.hostanalytics.com
SIC: 7372 Application computer software

(P-23988)
HOWARDSOFT
7854 Ivanhoe Ave A, La Jolla (92037-4501)
P.O. Box 8432 (92038-8432)
PHONE..................858 454-0121
James Howard, *Owner*
Maril Sowell, *General Mgr*
EMP: 10 **EST:** 1980
SALES (est): 844.9K **Privately Held**
WEB: www.howardsoft.com
SIC: 7372 8721 Prepackaged software; accounting, auditing & bookkeeping

(P-23989)
HPE ENTERPRISES LLC (HQ)
6280 America Center Dr, San Jose (95002-2563)
PHONE..................650 857-5817
Sheena Campbell, *Partner*
Joseph Cioppa, *Partner*

Ian Reid, *Officer*
Alain Andreoli, *Senior VP*
Scott Anderson, *Vice Pres*
EMP: 30 **EST:** 2015
SALES (est): 14.9MM
SALES (corp-wide): 30.8B **Publicly Held**
SIC: 7372 7379 3572 Prepackaged software; computer related maintenance services; computer storage devices
PA: Hewlett Packard Enterprise Company
6280 America Center Dr
San Jose CA 95002
650 687-5817

(P-23990)
HR CLOUD INC
222 N Pacific Coast Hwy, El Segundo (90245-5648)
PHONE..................510 909-1993
Damir Davidovic, *Principal*
EMP: 20 **EST:** 2016
SQ FT: 10,000
SALES (est): 1.5MM **Privately Held**
SIC: 7372 Business oriented computer software

(P-23991)
HUMANCONCEPTS LLC
3 Harbor Dr Ste 200, Sausalito (94965-1491)
PHONE..................650 581-2500
Martin Sacks,
Hanif Ismail,
Kathleen Jensen,
Luis Rivera,
EMP: 40 **EST:** 2000
SQ FT: 6,500
SALES (est): 2.5MM
SALES (corp-wide): 177MM **Privately Held**
WEB: www.orgplus.com
SIC: 7372 Prepackaged software
PA: Saba Software, Inc.
4120 Dublin Blvd Ste 200
Dublin CA 94568
877 722-2101

(P-23992)
HYSTERICAL SOFTWARE INC
2874 Hillside Dr, Burlingame (94010-5968)
PHONE..................415 793-5785
Donna Pribble, *President*
EMP: 10
SALES (est): 196.7K **Privately Held**
SIC: 7372 Prepackaged software

(P-23993)
HYTRUST INC (PA)
1975 W El Camino Real # 203, Mountain View (94040-2218)
PHONE..................650 681-8100
John De Santis, *CEO*
Eric Chiu, *President*
Mercy Caprara, *CFO*
Fred Kost, *Senior VP*
Ashwin Krishnan, *Senior VP*
EMP: 44
SQ FT: 12,000
SALES (est): 4.4MM **Privately Held**
SIC: 7372 Educational computer software

(P-23994)
I T M SOFTWARE CORP
1030 W Maude Ave, Sunnyvale (94085-2812)
PHONE..................650 864-2500
Kenneth Coleman, *CEO*
Tom Niermann, *Founder*
Steve O'Conner, *Vice Pres*
Christina Ellwood, *Principal*
Jorge Helmer, *VP Finance*
EMP: 30
SQ FT: 18,600
SALES (est): 2.1MM **Privately Held**
WEB: www.itm-software.com
SIC: 7372 Prepackaged software

(P-23995)
IAC/INTERACTIVECORP
8800 W Sunset Blvd, West Hollywood (90069-2105)
PHONE..................212 314-7300
Phillip Marlock, *Branch Mgr*
EMP: 13

SALES (corp-wide): 4.2B **Publicly Held**
SIC: 7372 7375 5961 Prepackaged software; information retrieval services; on-line data base information retrieval; catalog & mail-order houses
PA: Iac/Interactivecorp
555 W 18th St
New York NY 10011
212 314-7300

(P-23996)
IAR SYSTEMS SOFTWARE INC (HQ)
1065 E Hillsdale Blvd # 420, Foster City (94404-1615)
PHONE..................650 287-4250
Stefan Skarin, *CEO*
Mike Skrtic, *Partner*
Nadim Shehayed, *President*
Dannielle Burgard, *Admin Mgr*
Aaron Bauch, *Engineer*
EMP: 10
SALES (est): 2.1MM
SALES (corp-wide): 42.7MM **Privately Held**
WEB: www.iar.com
SIC: 7372 Application computer software
PA: I.A.R. Systems Group Ab
Strandbodgatan 1
Uppsala 753 2
841 092-000

(P-23997)
ICEBREAKER HEALTH INC
Also Called: Lemonaid Health
150 Spear St Ste 350, San Francisco (94105-1747)
PHONE..................415 926-5818
Ian Van Every, *President*
EMP: 12
SQ FT: 1,270
SALES (est): 500.5K **Privately Held**
SIC: 7372 Business oriented computer software

(P-23998)
IFWE INC (HQ)
848 Battery St, San Francisco (94111-1504)
PHONE..................415 946-1850
Dash Gopinath, *CEO*
Greg Tseng, *CEO*
Nick Hermansaker, *Vice Pres*
Misha Nasledov, *Sr Software Eng*
Johann Schleier Smith, *CTO*
EMP: 87
SQ FT: 13,000
SALES (est): 30.7MM
SALES (corp-wide): 178.6MM **Publicly Held**
WEB: www.tagged.com
SIC: 7372 Application computer software
PA: The Meet Group Inc
100 Union Square Dr
New Hope PA 18938
215 862-1162

(P-23999)
IGRAD INC
2163 Newcastle Ave # 100, Cardiff By The Sea (92007-1871)
PHONE..................858 705-2917
Rob Labreche, *President*
Kevin Soehner, *Opers Staff*
Jennifer Kelly, *Director*
EMP: 22
SQ FT: 2,000
SALES (est): 1.9MM **Privately Held**
SIC: 7372 Business oriented computer software

(P-24000)
ILLUMINATE EDUCATION INC (PA)
6531 Irvine Center Dr # 100, Irvine (92618-2145)
PHONE..................949 656-3133
Christine Willig, *CEO*
Dick Davidson, *CFO*
Jane Snyder, *Chief Mktg Ofcr*
Shawn Mahoney, *Officer*
Spencer Kerrigan, *Vice Pres*
EMP: 65 **EST:** 2009
SALES (est): 15.4MM **Privately Held**
SIC: 7372 Educational computer software

(P-24001)
IMAGEWARE SYSTEMS INC (PA)
13500 Evening Creek Dr N # 550, San Diego (92128-8125)
PHONE..............................858 673-8600
S James Miller Jr, *Ch of Bd*
Wayne Wetherell, *CFO*
David Harding, *Senior VP*
David Somerville, *Senior VP*
EMP: 96
SQ FT: 8,511
SALES: 4.4MM **Publicly Held**
WEB: www.iwsinc.com
SIC: 7372 3699 Business oriented computer software; security control equipment & systems

(P-24002)
IMAGINE THAT INC
6830 Via Del Oro Ste 230, San Jose (95119-1390)
PHONE..............................408 365-0305
Bob Diamond, *President*
Pat Diamond, *CFO*
Kathi Hansen, *Marketing Staff*
EMP: 10
SQ FT: 45,000
SALES (est): 1.5MM **Privately Held**
WEB: www.imaginethatinc.com
SIC: 7372 Business oriented computer software

(P-24003)
IMPAC MEDICAL SYSTEMS INC (HQ)
Also Called: Elekta / Impac Medical Systems
100 Mathilda Pl Fl 5, Sunnyvale (94086-6017)
PHONE..............................408 830-8000
Fax: 408 830-8003
EMP: 40
SQ FT: 35,000
SALES (est): 61.6MM
SALES (corp-wide): 1.3B **Privately Held**
WEB: www.impac.com
SIC: 7372 7373
PA: Elekta Ab (Publ)
Kungstensgatan 18
Stockholm 113 5
858 725-400

(P-24004)
IMPLY DATA INC
1633 Old Bayshore Hwy # 232, Burlingame (94010-1533)
PHONE..............................415 685-8187
Fang Jin Yang, *CEO*
John Hartley, *Exec VP*
Gian Merlino, *Exec VP*
Vadim Ogievetsky, *Exec VP*
EMP: 10 EST: 2015
SQ FT: 1,000
SALES (est): 393K **Privately Held**
SIC: 7372 Business oriented computer software

(P-24005)
IN SYNC COMPUTER SOLUTIONS INC
Also Called: Insync Computer Solutions
23282 Mill Creek Dr, Laguna Hills (92653-1658)
PHONE..............................949 837-5000
Frank Halsema, *CEO*
Karen Bessette, *CFO*
EMP: 11
SQ FT: 3,000
SALES (est): 2.1MM **Privately Held**
WEB: www.insynclh.com
SIC: 7372 Prepackaged software

(P-24006)
INBENTA TECHNOLOGIES INC (PA)
1065 E Hillsdale Blvd # 425, Foster City (94404-1639)
PHONE..............................408 213-8771
Jordi Torras, *CEO*
Patrick Cassady, *Exec VP*
Rochelle Reed, *Business Mgr*
Irene Estrada, *Cust Mgr*
Leah Clark, *Director*
EMP: 22 EST: 2011

SALES: 3MM **Privately Held**
SIC: 7372 Application computer software

(P-24007)
INCANDESCENT INC
350 Sansome St, San Francisco (94104-1304)
PHONE..............................415 464-7975
Michael De, *CEO*
EMP: 11
SALES (est): 357.8K **Privately Held**
SIC: 7372 Prepackaged software

(P-24008)
INDIUM SOFTWARE INC
1250 Oakmead Pkwy Ste 210, Sunnyvale (94085-4035)
PHONE..............................408 501-8844
Harsha Nutalapati, *CEO*
Vijay Shankar Balaji, *President*
Shailesh Khanapur, *Assoc VP*
Bala S Selva, *Senior VP*
EMP: 250
SALES (est): 10.4MM **Privately Held**
WEB: www.indiumsoft.com
SIC: 7372 Prepackaged software
HQ: Indium Software (India) Limited
2nd Floor Vds House,
Chennai TN 60008

(P-24009)
INDIVIDUAL SOFTWARE INC
2301 Armstrong St Ste 101, Livermore (94551-9349)
PHONE..............................925 734-6767
Jo-L Hendrickson, *President*
Diane Dietzler, *Vice Pres*
EMP: 48 EST: 1981
SALES (est): 6.3MM **Privately Held**
WEB: www.individualsoftware.com
SIC: 7372 7371 Prepackaged software; custom computer programming services

(P-24010)
INDUSTRIOUS SOFTWARE SOLUTION
Also Called: Industrious Software Solutions
8901 S La Cienega Blvd # 202, Inglewood (90301-7414)
PHONE..............................310 672-8700
Stephen Ryza, *President*
Gina Lynn Tan, *Controller*
EMP: 17
SQ FT: 10,000
SALES (est): 1.5MM **Privately Held**
SIC: 7372 5112 Business oriented computer software; business forms

(P-24011)
INFINISIM INC
2860 Zanker Rd Ste 202, San Jose (95134-2133)
PHONE..............................408 934-9777
Samia Rashid, *President*
Zakir Syed, *CTO*
EMP: 12
SALES (est): 786.4K **Privately Held**
SIC: 7372 Business oriented computer software

(P-24012)
INFOR (US) INC
Also Called: MAI Systems
26250 Entp Way Ste 220, Lake Forest (92630)
PHONE..............................678 319-8000
Barbara Nolan, *President*
Marvin Perkins, *Sales Staff*
Christine Greiner, *Manager*
EMP: 190
SALES (corp-wide): 3.1B **Privately Held**
SIC: 7372 Business oriented computer software
HQ: Infor (Us), Inc.
13560 Morris Rd Ste 4100
Alpharetta GA 30004
678 319-8000

(P-24013)
INFOR (US) INC
Also Called: Hansen Information Tech
11000 Olson Dr Ste 201, Rancho Cordova (95670-5642)
PHONE..............................916 921-0324
Charles Hansen, *Manager*

EMP: 225
SALES (corp-wide): 3.1B **Privately Held**
SIC: 7372 Application computer software
HQ: Infor (Us), Inc.
13560 Morris Rd Ste 4100
Alpharetta GA 30004
678 319-8000

(P-24014)
INFOR PUBLIC SECTOR INC (DH)
11092 Sun Center Dr, Rancho Cordova (95670-6109)
PHONE..............................916 921-0883
Charles Hansen, *CEO*
Mark Watts, *President*
Bob Benstead, *Principal*
EMP: 160
SQ FT: 28,000
SALES (est): 22.2MM
SALES (corp-wide): 3.1B **Privately Held**
SIC: 7372 Application computer software
HQ: Infor (Us), Inc.
13560 Morris Rd Ste 4100
Alpharetta GA 30004
678 319-8000

(P-24015)
INFORM DECISIONS
30162 Tomas 101, Rcho STA Marg (92688-2124)
PHONE..............................949 709-5838
Dan Forester, *President*
EMP: 13
SALES (est): 1.4MM **Privately Held**
WEB: www.informdecision.com
SIC: 7372 Business oriented computer software

(P-24016)
INFORM SOLUTION INCORPORATED
201 Mentor Dr, Santa Barbara (93111-3337)
PHONE..............................805 879-6000
Rey Hugh, *President*
EMP: 11
SALES (est): 567.2K
SALES (corp-wide): 81.5B **Publicly Held**
WEB: www.informsolutions.com
SIC: 7372 Prepackaged software
HQ: Mentor Worldwide Llc
31 Technology Dr Ste 200
Irvine CA 92618
800 636-8678

(P-24017)
INFORMATICA LLC (PA)
2100 Seaport Blvd, Redwood City (94063-5596)
PHONE..............................650 385-5000
Anil Chakravarthy, *CEO*
Maryanne Cotrone, *Partner*
Monie Tenbroeck, *Partner*
Nick Voll, *Partner*
Chris Sortzi, *President*
EMP: 148
SQ FT: 290,000
SALES (est): 801.2MM **Privately Held**
WEB: www.metadataexchange.com
SIC: 7372 Prepackaged software

(P-24018)
INFORMATION INTEGRATION GROUP
457 Palm Dr Ste 200, Glendale (91202-4339)
PHONE..............................818 956-3744
Alec Baghdasaryan, *President*
Gohar Hovhannisyan, *Technical Staff*
Mark Ayes, *Marketing Mgr*
Alenoush Baghdasaryan, *Fmly & Gen Dent*
EMP: 21
SALES (est): 3.4MM **Privately Held**
WEB: www.iigservices.com
SIC: 7372 7371 Prepackaged software; computer software development

(P-24019)
INFORMATION RESOURCES INC
400 N Johnson St, Visalia (93291-6005)
PHONE..............................559 732-0324
Ken Weber, *Branch Mgr*
Ray Stradley, *Consultant*

EMP: 30
SQ FT: 6,000
SALES (corp-wide): 364.2MM **Privately Held**
WEB: www.infores.com
SIC: 7372 8732 Prepackaged software; market analysis or research
PA: Information Resources, Inc
150 N Clinton St
Chicago IL 60661
312 726-1221

(P-24020)
INKTOMI CORPORATION (HQ)
701 First Ave, Sunnyvale (94089-1019)
PHONE..............................650 653-2800
David Peterschmidt, *Ch of Bd*
Randy Gottfried, *CFO*
EMP: 25
SQ FT: 177,000
SALES (est): 19.7MM **Privately Held**
WEB: www.inktomi.com
SIC: 7372 7371 Application computer software; custom computer programming services

(P-24021)
INLAND TEK INC
7364 Oxford Pl, Rancho Cucamonga (91730-8282)
PHONE..............................909 900-8457
Ahammad Akbar Khan, *President*
EMP: 10
SALES (est): 221.8K **Privately Held**
SIC: 7372 Prepackaged software

(P-24022)
INMAGE SYSTEMS INC
1065 La Avenida St, Mountain View (94043-1421)
PHONE..............................408 200-3840
Debbie Button, *CEO*
John Ferraro, *President*
Marty Bradford, *CFO*
EMP: 23
SALES (est): 8.3MM
SALES (corp-wide): 125.8B **Publicly Held**
SIC: 7372 Business oriented computer software
PA: Microsoft Corporation
1 Microsoft Way
Redmond WA 98052
425 882-8080

(P-24023)
INNFINITY SOFTWARE SYSTEMS LLC
600 B St Ste 300, San Diego (92101-4505)
PHONE..............................619 798-3915
Beverly McCabe, *CEO*
Jon Miller, *COO*
Richard Koppert, *CFO*
Colleen Fitzpatrick, *Sales Executive*
EMP: 15
SALES (est): 2.8MM **Privately Held**
SIC: 7372 Prepackaged software

(P-24024)
INNOVATE LABS LLC
553 S Fair Oaks Ave 592, Pasadena (91105)
PHONE..............................917 753-2673
Adam Fisk,
EMP: 14 EST: 2015
SALES (est): 68.4K **Privately Held**
SIC: 7372 7389 Application computer software;

(P-24025)
INNOVYZE INC (DH)
605 E Huntington Dr # 205, Monrovia (91016-6353)
PHONE..............................626 568-6868
Paul F Boulos, *President*
Mark Cuny, *CFO*
Angela R Shirrell, *Admin Sec*
Patrick Moore, *Engineer*
EMP: 15
SALES (est): 2.4MM
SALES (corp-wide): 3.2B **Privately Held**
WEB: www.mwhsoftinc.com
SIC: 7372 Prepackaged software

HQ: Mwh Americas, Inc.
370 Interlocken Blvd
Broomfield CO 80021
303 410-4000

(P-24026)
INSIDEVIEW TECHNOLOGIES INC
444 De Haro St Ste 210, San Francisco
(94107-2398)
PHONE.....................415 728-9309
Umberto Milletti, *CEO*
Jim Lightsey, *CFO*
Tracy Eiler, *Chief Mktg Ofcr*
Lisa Bailey, *Vice Pres*
Marc Perramond, *Vice Pres*
EMP: 150
SALES (est): 26.3MM **Privately Held**
SIC: 7372 Business oriented computer
software

(P-24027)
INSIGHT SOLUTIONS INC
13095 Paramount Ct, Saratoga
(95070-4209)
PHONE.....................408 725-0213
Raghav Sherma, *President*
EMP: 40
SALES (est): 2.4MM **Privately Held**
WEB: www.insightsol.com
SIC: 7372 8748 Application computer soft-
ware; business consulting

(P-24028)
INTEGRAL DEVELOPMENT CORP (PA)
Also Called: Integral Engineering
850 Hansen Way, Palo Alto (94304-1017)
PHONE.....................650 424-4500
Harpal Sandhu, *President*
Albert Yau, *CFO*
Vikas Srivastava, *Officer*
Patrick Barkhordarian, *Vice Pres*
Ian Doull, *Vice Pres*
EMP: 200
SQ FT: 35,000
SALES (est): 31.5MM **Privately Held**
WEB: www.integral.com
SIC: 7372 Business oriented computer
software

(P-24029)
INTERNET STRATEGY INC
Also Called: One Park Place
10875 Rancho Bernardo Rd # 100, San
Diego (92127-2115)
PHONE.....................858 673-6022
Jill Ewing, *President*
Steve Hundley, *CEO*
EMP: 14
SQ FT: 10,000
SALES (est): 1.2MM **Privately Held**
SIC: 7372 Prepackaged software

(P-24030)
INTERNET SYSTEMS CNSORTIUM INC (PA)
950 Charter St, Redwood City
(94063-3110)
PHONE.....................650 423-1300
Jeff Osborn, *Exec Dir*
EMP: 15
SQ FT: 10,000
SALES: 357K **Privately Held**
SIC: 7372 Prepackaged software

(P-24031)
INTERSHOP COMMUNICATIONS INC
461 2nd St Apt 151, San Francisco
(94107-1498)
PHONE.....................415 844-1500
Jochen Moll, *CEO*
Peter Mark Droste, *Ch of Bd*
Eckhard Pfeiffer, *Chairman*
Hans W Gutsch, *Treasurer*
Brian McGlynn, *Vice Pres*
EMP: 20
SQ FT: 2,700
SALES (est): 3.1MM
SALES (corp-wide): 35.7MM **Privately Held**
WEB: www.inter-shop.org
SIC: 7372 7375 Prepackaged software; in-
formation retrieval services

PA: Intershop Communications Ag
Intershop Tower
Jena 07740
364 150-0

(P-24032)
INTERWORKING LABS INC
Also Called: Iwl
230 Mount Hermon Rd # 208, Scotts Valley
(95066-4034)
P.O. Box 66190 (95067-6190)
PHONE (831 460-7010
Christine K Wellens, *President*
Shantel Marie Jordan, *Marketing Staff*
EMP: 10
SQ FT: 2,000
SALES (est): 973.6K **Privately Held**
WEB: www.iwl.com
SIC: 7372 Application computer software

(P-24033)
INTOUCH TECHNOLOGIES INC (PA)
Also Called: Intouch Health
7402 Hollister Ave, Goleta (93117-2583)
PHONE.....................805 562-8686
Yulun Wang, *CEO*
Susan Wang, *Shareholder*
David Adornetto, *COO*
Stephen L Wilson, *CFO*
Paul Evans, *Exec VP*
EMP: 148
SQ FT: 1,600
SALES (est): 90.1MM **Privately Held**
WEB: www.intouchhealth.com
SIC: 7372 Business oriented computer
software

(P-24034)
INTUIT INC
7535 Torrey Santa Fe Rd, San Diego
(92129-5704)
PHONE.....................858 215-8726
EMP: 36
SALES (corp-wide): 4.6B **Publicly Held**
SIC: 7372
PA: Intuit Inc.
2700 Coast Ave
Mountain View CA 94043
650 944-6000

(P-24035)
INTUIT INC (PA)
2700 Coast Ave, Mountain View
(94043-1140)
P.O. Box 7850 (94039-7850)
PHONE.....................650 944-6000
Brad D Smith, *Ch of Bd*
Michelle M Clatterbuck, *CFO*
Scott D Cook, *Chairman*
Laura A Fennell, *Exec VP*
Laura Fennell, *Exec VP*
EMP: 70
SQ FT: 712,000
SALES: 6.7B **Publicly Held**
WEB: www.intuit.com
SIC: 7372 Business oriented computer
software

(P-24036)
INTUIT INC
2700 Coast Ave Bldg 7, Mountain View
(94043-1140)
PHONE.....................650 944-6000
Brad Smith, *Branch Mgr*
EMP: 128
SALES (corp-wide): 6.7B **Publicly Held**
WEB: www.intuit.com
SIC: 7372 Business oriented computer
software
PA: Intuit Inc.
2700 Coast Ave
Mountain View CA 94043
650 944-6000

(P-24037)
INTUIT INC
2650 Casey Ave, Mountain View
(94043-1141)
P.O. Box 7850 (94039-7850)
PHONE.....................650 944-6000
Stephen Bennett, *President*
Michele Sanyal, *Business Anlyst*
EMP: 13

SALES (corp-wide): 6.7B **Publicly Held**
SIC: 7372 Business oriented computer
software
PA: Intuit Inc.
2700 Coast Ave
Mountain View CA 94043
650 944-6000

(P-24038)
INTUIT INC
2535 Garcia Ave, Mountain View
(94043-1111)
PHONE.....................650 944-6000
Connie Berg, *Branch Mgr*
Jeff Brewer, *Vice Pres*
Brian Curran, *Executive*
Adam Reed, *Creative Dir*
Nita Acosta, *Executive Asst*
EMP: 128
SALES (corp-wide): 6.7B **Publicly Held**
WEB: www.intuit.com
SIC: 7372 Business oriented computer
software
PA: Intuit Inc.
2700 Coast Ave
Mountain View CA 94043
650 944-6000

(P-24039)
INTUIT INC
141 Corona Way, Portola Valley
(94028-7437)
PHONE.....................650 944-2840
EMP: 136
SALES (corp-wide): 6.7B **Publicly Held**
WEB: www.intuit.com
SIC: 7372 Business oriented computer
software
PA: Intuit Inc.
2700 Coast Ave
Mountain View CA 94043
650 944-6000

(P-24040)
INTUIT INC
180 Jefferson Dr, Menlo Park (94025-1115)
PHONE.....................650 944-6000
Brad Smith, *Branch Mgr*
Jason Yip, *Business Anlyst*
Betsy Kha, *Marketing Staff*
Lisa Leib, *Manager*
EMP: 128
SALES (corp-wide): 6.7B **Publicly Held**
WEB: www.intuit.com
SIC: 7372 Business oriented computer
software
PA: Intuit Inc.
2700 Coast Ave
Mountain View CA 94043
650 944-6000

(P-24041)
INTUIT INC
Also Called: Turbotax
7545 Torrey Santa Fe Rd, San Diego
(92129-5704)
PHONE.....................858 215-8000
Jason Jackson, *Branch Mgr*
Manny Ruiz, *Sr Software Eng*
Sheri Dombrow, *Software Dev*
Wolf Paulus, *Software Engr*
Elizabeth Trinh, *Database Admin*
EMP: 300
SALES (corp-wide): 6.7B **Publicly Held**
WEB: www.intuit.com
SIC: 7372 Business oriented computer
software
PA: Intuit Inc.
2700 Coast Ave
Mountain View CA 94043
650 944-6000

(P-24042)
INVOICE2GO INC (PA)
2317 Broadway St Fl 2, Redwood City
(94063-1674)
PHONE.....................650 300-5180
Gregory Waldorf, *CEO*
Mark Bartels, *CFO*
Madeleine Lux, *Office Mgr*
Sarah Stone, *Office Mgr*
Bryan Chung, *Consultant*
EMP: 49
SALES: 10.2MM **Privately Held**
SIC: 7372 Prepackaged software

(P-24043)
INVOTECH SYSTEMS INC
20951 Burbank Blvd Ste B, Woodland Hills
(91367-6696)
PHONE.....................818 461-9800
Harvey Welles, *President*
Robert Andrews, *Technical Staff*
Kerri Merchan, *Sales Mgr*
Oswald Lares, *Sales Staff*
Chad Slining, *Manager*
EMP: 15
SQ FT: 10,000
SALES (est): 2.7MM **Privately Held**
WEB: www.invo.com
SIC: 7372 Business oriented computer
software

(P-24044)
IPAYABLES INC (PA)
95 Argonaut Ste 270, Aliso Viejo
(92656-4140)
PHONE.....................949 215-9122
Kenneth L Virgin, *CEO*
Robert L Ripley, *COO*
Jon Titel, *CTO*
Ryan Gibson, *Info Tech Dir*
EMP: 63
SALES (est): 1MM **Privately Held**
WEB: www.ipayables.com
SIC: 7372 Business oriented computer
software

(P-24045)
IPOLIPO INC
Also Called: Jifflenow
440 N Wolfe Rd, Sunnyvale (94085-3869)
PHONE.....................408 916-5290
Hari Shetty, *President*
Arun Kumar, *Administration*
Chopra Anil, *Software Dev*
Nayak Anusha, *Software Dev*
Francis Arun, *Software Dev*
EMP: 75 EST: 2006
SALES (est): 3.6MM **Privately Held**
SIC: 7372 Application computer software

(P-24046)
IPRESSROOM INC
Also Called: Ipr Software
16501 Ventura Blvd # 424, Encino
(91436-2007)
PHONE.....................310 499-0544
Chris Bechtel, *President*
Tom Madden, *Chairman*
Vadim Derkach, *Director*
EMP: 20
SQ FT: 10,000
SALES (est): 1.6MM **Privately Held**
WEB: www.ipressroom.com
SIC: 7372 Application computer software

(P-24047)
IQMS (HQ)
2231 Wisteria Ln, Paso Robles
(93446-9820)
PHONE.....................805 227-1122
Gary Nemmers, *President*
Matt Ouska, *CFO*
Steve Bieszczat, *Chief Mktg Ofcr*
Shannon Holloway, *Officer*
Rocky Morrison, *Exec VP*
EMP: 130
SQ FT: 60,000
SALES: 37MM
SALES (corp-wide): 1.8B **Privately Held**
WEB: www.iqms.com
SIC: 7372 Prepackaged software
PA: Dassault Systemes
10 Rue Marcel Dassault
Velizy-Villacoublay 78140
161 623-000

(P-24048)
ISOLUTECOM INC (PA)
9 Northam Ave, Newbury Park
(91320-3323)
PHONE.....................805 498-6259
Byron Nutley, *Ch of Bd*
Don Hyun, *President*
Thomas Mangle, *CFO*
Michael Brown, *CTO*
EMP: 50
SALES (est): 5.1MM **Privately Held**
WEB: www.isolute.com
SIC: 7372 Business oriented computer
software

(P-24049)
IT RETAIL INC
191 W Big Springs Rd, Riverside (92507-4737)
PHONE..................951 683-4950
Martin E Goodwin, *President*
Kristin Henry, *Executive*
Tom Xu, *Software Dev*
Richard Sutton, *Technical Staff*
Donna Armstrong, *Director*
EMP: 12
SALES: 2MM **Privately Held**
SIC: 7372 Business oriented computer software

(P-24050)
ITC SFTWARE SLUTIONS GROUP LLC (PA)
Also Called: Itcssg
201 Sandpointe Ave # 305, Santa Ana (92707-5778)
PHONE..................877 248-2774
Ray Jandga, *President*
Guru Gurumoorthy, *Vice Pres*
Arulselvam Venkatasubbu, *Recruiter*
Del Hussain, *Consultant*
EMP: 32
SQ FT: 3,000
SALES (est): 10MM **Privately Held**
SIC: 7372 7371 7373 Prepackaged software; computer software systems analysis & design, custom; systems software development services

(P-24051)
ITTAVI INC
Also Called: Supportpay
1631 Alhambra Blvd # 120, Sacramento (95816-7054)
PHONE..................866 246-4408
Sheri Atwood, *CEO*
EMP: 25
SALES (est): 996.5K **Privately Held**
SIC: 7372 7373 7371 8748 Business oriented computer software; systems software development services; custom computer programming services; systems engineering consultant, ex. computer or professional

(P-24052)
IVANTI INC
150 Mathilda Pl Ste 302, Sunnyvale (94086-6012)
PHONE..................408 343-8181
Scott Arnold, *Branch Mgr*
William Myrhang, *Marketing Staff*
EMP: 12
SALES (corp-wide): 24.9MM **Privately Held**
SIC: 7372 Application computer software
HQ: Ivanti, Inc.
698 W 10000 S Ste 500
South Jordan UT 84095
801 208-1500

(P-24053)
IVYDOCTORS INC
555 Bryant St, Palo Alto (94301-1704)
PHONE..................415 890-3937
William Lard, *Principal*
EMP: 12
SALES (est): 256K **Privately Held**
SIC: 7372 Application computer software

(P-24054)
IXSYSTEMS INC (PA)
2490 Kruse Dr, San Jose (95131-1234)
PHONE..................408 943-4100
Mike Lauth, *CEO*
Andrew Madrid, *COO*
Brett Davis, *Exec VP*
Morgan Littlewood, *Senior VP*
Jeff Kaminsky, *General Mgr*
EMP: 60
SQ FT: 20,000
SALES (est): 21.4MM **Privately Held**
WEB: www.ixsystems.com
SIC: 7372 Operating systems computer software

(P-24055)
J F K & ASSOCIATES INC
1100 Moraga Way Ste 202, Moraga (94556-1155)
PHONE..................925 388-0255

Jack Keane, *President*
EMP: 20
SALES (est): 3MM **Privately Held**
WEB: www.jfkcorp.com
SIC: 7372 Prepackaged software

(P-24056)
JAMIS SOFTWARE CORPORATION
4909 Murphy Canyon Rd # 460, San Diego (92123-7301)
PHONE..................858 300-5542
Don Hanson, *President*
Susan Wills, *Vice Pres*
Katie Hill, *Office Mgr*
Bob Sanger, *Software Engr*
Greg Dimase, *Programmer Anys*
EMP: 14
SALES (est): 1.4MM
SALES (corp-wide): 3.8B **Privately Held**
SIC: 7372 Application computer software
PA: The Gores Group Llc
9800 Wilshire Blvd
Beverly Hills CA 90212
310 209-3010

(P-24057)
JAUNT INC
Also Called: Jaunt Xr
951 Mariners Island Blvd # 500, San Mateo (94404-1589)
PHONE..................650 618-6579
George Kliavkoff, *CEO*
Fabrice Cantou, *CFO*
Mitzi Reaugh, *Vice Pres*
Jean-Paul Colaco, *Risk Mgmt Dir*
Arthur Van Hoff, *CTO*
EMP: 37
SALES (est): 5.2MM **Privately Held**
SIC: 7372 7371 Application computer software; business oriented computer software; computer software development & applications

(P-24058)
JEMSTEP INC
5150 El Camino Real B16, Los Altos (94022-1550)
PHONE..................650 966-6500
Kevin Cimring, *CEO*
Simon Roy, *President*
Matthew Rennie, *Engineer*
Mark Richards, *Products*
EMP: 20
SALES (est): 1.7MM
SALES (corp-wide): 5.3B **Publicly Held**
SIC: 7372 Business oriented computer software
HQ: Invesco North American Holdings Inc
1555 Peachtree St Ne # 1800
Atlanta GA 30309
404 892-0896

(P-24059)
JESTA DIGITAL ENTRMT INC (HQ)
15303 Ventura Blvd # 900, Sherman Oaks (91403-3199)
PHONE..................323 648-4200
Jason Aintabi, *CEO*
Mark Anderson, *COO*
EMP: 12
SALES (est): 2.8MM **Privately Held**
WEB: www.jestadigital.com
SIC: 7372 Prepackaged software

(P-24060)
JETLORE LLC
1528 S El Camino Real # 101, San Mateo (94402-3067)
PHONE..................650 485-1822
Eldar Sadikov, *CEO*
Brian Yamasaki, *President*
Montse Medina, *COO*
Thomas Lai, *Officer*
EMP: 24
SQ FT: 6,700
SALES (est): 597.7K
SALES (corp-wide): 15.4B **Publicly Held**
SIC: 7372 Prepackaged software
PA: Paypal Holdings, Inc.
2211 N 1st St
San Jose CA 95131
408 967-1000

(P-24061)
JML CONNECTION INC
1372 Wilson St, Los Angeles (90021-2838)
PHONE..................213 519-2000
Xufang Pan, *Manager*
EMP: 10
SALES (corp-wide): 5MM **Privately Held**
SIC: 7372 Application computer software
PA: Jml Connection, Inc
18459 Pines Blvd Ste 313
Pembroke Pines FL 33029
305 974-5989

(P-24062)
JTEA INC
Also Called: Zigzagzoom
1421 Valane Dr, Glendale (91208-1741)
PHONE..................847 878-2226
Thomas Kang, *CEO*
EMP: 20
SALES (est): 1MM **Privately Held**
SIC: 7372 Home entertainment computer software; publishers' computer software

(P-24063)
JUMIO SOFTWARE & DEV LLC
1971 Landings Dr, Mountain View (94043-0806)
PHONE..................650 388-0264
EMP: 30
SALES (est): 1.2MM
SALES (corp-wide): 16.9MM **Privately Held**
SIC: 7372
PA: Jumio Inc
268 Lambert Ave
Palo Alto CA
650 424-8545

(P-24064)
JUNIPER SQUARE INC
351 California St # 1450, San Francisco (94104-2415)
PHONE..................415 841-2722
Alex Robinson, *Principal*
Porras Elizabeth, *Director*
EMP: 12
SALES (est): 1.6MM **Privately Held**
SIC: 7372 Prepackaged software

(P-24065)
JUST LIGHT TECHNOLOGY INC
46560 Fremont Blvd # 105, Fremont (94538-6484)
PHONE..................510 585-5652
Jerome Tang, *CEO*
Roger Chen, *Sales Staff*
EMP: 10
SALES (est): 295.2K **Privately Held**
SIC: 7372 5074 Business oriented computer software; heating equipment & panels, solar

(P-24066)
JUSTENOUGH SOFTWARE CORP INC (HQ)
15440 Laguna Canyon Rd # 100, Irvine (92618-2138)
PHONE..................949 706-5400
Malcolm Buxton, *President*
Wikus Van Dyk, *Development*
Tonya Nicholls, *Human Res Dir*
Justin Aggelakos, *Director*
Keith Whaley, *Retailers*
EMP: 30
SALES (est): 11.3MM
SALES (corp-wide): 17.2MM **Privately Held**
SIC: 7372 Prepackaged software
PA: Mi9 Retail Inc.
12000 Biscayne Blvd # 600
North Miami FL 33181
647 849-1101

(P-24067)
K & M SOFTWARE DESIGN LLC
2828 Cochran St Ste 351, Simi Valley (93065-2780)
PHONE..................805 583-0403
EMP: 10 EST: 1997
SQ FT: 1,500
SALES (est): 760K **Privately Held**
SIC: 7372

(P-24068)
KAAZING CORPORATION (PA)
2107 N 1st St Ste 660, San Jose (95131-2005)
PHONE..................650 960-8148
Vikram Mehta, *CEO*
Jonas Jacobi, *President*
Sheila Dahlgren, *Chief Mktg Ofcr*
Simon Negus, *Officer*
Sidda Eraiah, *Vice Pres*
EMP: 19
SQ FT: 8,400
SALES: 871.9K **Privately Held**
SIC: 7372 Business oriented computer software

(P-24069)
KAI OS TECHNOLOGIES SFTWR INC
7310 Miramar Rd Ste 440, San Diego (92126-4222)
PHONE..................858 547-3940
Sebastien A J Codeville, *President*
EMP: 10
SALES (est): 500K **Privately Held**
SIC: 7372 Operating systems computer software

(P-24070)
KANA SOFTWARE INC (HQ)
Also Called: Verint
2550 Walsh Ave Ste 120, Santa Clara (95051-1345)
PHONE..................650 614-8300
Mark Duffell, *CEO*
Brett White, *President*
Jeff Wylie, *CFO*
James Norwood, *Chief Mktg Ofcr*
Jim Bureau, *Senior VP*
EMP: 100
SQ FT: 40,000
SALES (est): 79.7MM **Publicly Held**
SIC: 7372 Application computer software

(P-24071)
KATANA SOFTWARE INC
333 W Broadway Ste 105, Long Beach (90802-4438)
PHONE..................562 495-1366
Robert Woodward, *President*
Melissa Gordon, *COO*
Andy Johnstone, *Sr Software Eng*
Mark Goles, *CTO*
Sherri Clifford, *Software Engr*
EMP: 10
SALES (est): 869.7K **Privately Held**
WEB: www.katanasoftware.com
SIC: 7372 Business oriented computer software

(P-24072)
KAZUHM INC
6450 Lusk Blvd Ste E208, San Diego (92121-2778)
PHONE..................858 771-3861
Tim O'Neal, *CEO*
EMP: 20
SALES (est): 62.1K **Privately Held**
SIC: 7372 Business oriented computer software

(P-24073)
KBA2 INC
Also Called: Crowdoptic
55 New Montgomery St # 606, San Francisco (94105-3433)
PHONE..................415 528-5500
Jon Fisher, *CEO*
Jim Kovach, *COO*
Richard Smith, *Vice Pres*
Nandini Swaroop, *Software Engr*
Luke Harris, *Engineer*
EMP: 15
SQ FT: 2,500
SALES (est): 1.2MM **Privately Held**
SIC: 7372 Application computer software

(P-24074)
KHAN ACADEMY INC
1200 Villa St Ste 200, Mountain View (94041-2922)
P.O. Box 1630 (94042-1630)
PHONE..................650 336-5426
Salman Khan, *Exec Dir*
Shantanu Sinha, *President*
Esther Cho, *Executive Asst*

Nada Abdelhamid, *Software Engr*
Joe Raedle, *Software Engr*
EMP: 85
SALES: 27.9MM **Privately Held**
SIC: 7372 Educational computer software

(P-24075)
KHOROS LLC (PA)
1 Pier Ste 1a, San Francisco (94111-2003)
PHONE....................415 757-3100
Jack Blaha, *CEO*
Jim Cox, *CFO*
Sam Monti, *CFO*
Katherine Calvert, *Chief Mktg Ofcr*
Scott Shepherd,
EMP: 50
SALES (est): 76.2MM **Privately Held**
WEB: www.lithium.com
SIC: 7372 Business oriented computer
software

(P-24076)
KIANA ANALYTICS INC
440 N Wolfe Rd W050, Sunnyvale
(94085-3869)
PHONE....................650 575-3871
Sebastian Andreatta, *Vice Pres*
EMP: 12
SALES (est): 409.7K **Privately Held**
SIC: 7372 Business oriented computer
software

(P-24077)
KINETIC FARM INC
210 Industrial Rd Ste 102, San Carlos
(94070-2395)
PHONE....................650 503-3279
EMP: 17 **EST:** 2010
SALES (est): 1.2MM **Privately Held**
SIC: 7372

(P-24078)
KINGCOM(US) LLC (HQ)
3100 Ocean Park Blvd, Santa Monica
(90405-3032)
PHONE....................424 744-5697
EMP: 200
SALES (est): 17.7MM
SALES (corp-wide): 7.5B **Publicly Held**
SIC: 7372 Home entertainment computer
software
PA: Activision Blizzard, Inc.
3100 Ocean Park Blvd
Santa Monica CA 90405
310 255-2000

(P-24079)
KINTERA INC (HQ)
Also Called: Blackbaud Internet Solutions
9605 Scranton Rd Ste 200, San Diego
(92121-1768)
PHONE....................858 795-3000
Marc E Chardon, *CEO*
Alfred R Berkeley III, *Ch of Bd*
Richard Labarbera, *President*
Richard Davidson, *CFO*
Richard R Davidson, *Treasurer*
EMP: 68
SQ FT: 38,000
SALES (est): 34.2MM
SALES (corp-wide): 848.6MM **Publicly
Held**
WEB: www.kintera.org
SIC: 7372 Prepackaged software
PA: Blackbaud, Inc.
2000 Daniel Island Dr
Daniel Island SC 29492
843 216-6200

(P-24080)
KLOOMA HOLDINGS INC
113 N San Vicente Blvd, Beverly Hills
(90211-2329)
PHONE....................305 747-3315
Gary Merisier, *CEO*
EMP: 20
SALES (est): 382.7K **Privately Held**
SIC: 7372 Application computer software

(P-24081)
KNO INC
2200 Mission College Blvd, Santa Clara
(95054-1537)
PHONE....................408 844-8120
Ronald D Dickel, *CEO*
Babur Habib, *CTO*

EMP: 70
SQ FT: 35,000
SALES (est): 9MM
SALES (corp-wide): 70.8B **Publicly Held**
SIC: 7372 Educational computer software
PA: Intel Corporation
2200 Mission College Blvd
Santa Clara CA 95054
408 765-8080

(P-24082)
KOFAX LIMITED (DH)
15211 Laguna Canyon Rd, Irvine
(92618-3146)
PHONE....................949 783-1000
Reynolds C Bish, *CEO*
James Arnold Jr, *CFO*
Grant Johnson, *Chief Mktg Ofcr*
Bradford Weller, *Exec VP*
Anthony Macciola, *CTO*
EMP: 38
SQ FT: 91,000
SALES (est): 112.2MM
SALES (corp-wide): 441.3K **Privately
Held**
SIC: 7372 Business oriented computer
software
HQ: Lexmark International Inc.
740 W New Circle Rd
Lexington KY 40511
859 232-2000

(P-24083)
KONAMI DIGITAL ENTRMT INC (DH)
2381 Rosecrans Ave # 200, El Segundo
(90245-4922)
PHONE....................310 220-8100
Tomohiro Uesugi, *President*
Takahiro Azuma, *Vice Pres*
Chris Bartee, *Principal*
Kazumi Kitaue, *Principal*
Cesar Pardini, *Info Tech Dir*
▲ **EMP:** 68
SQ FT: 53,596
SALES (est): 34.5MM **Privately Held**
SIC: 7372 Home entertainment computer
software

(P-24084)
KPISOFT INC
50 California St Ste 1500, San Francisco
(94111-4612)
PHONE....................415 439-5228
Ravee Ramamoothie, *CEO*
EMP: 80
SQ FT: 4,000
SALES (est): 2.9MM **Privately Held**
SIC: 7372 Prepackaged software

(P-24085)
KRANEM CORPORATION
560 S Winchester Blvd, San Jose
(95128-2560)
PHONE....................650 319-6743
Ajay Batheja, *Ch of Bd*
Edward Miller, *CFO*
Luigi Caramico, *Vice Pres*
Christopher L Rasmussen, *Admin Sec*
EMP: 190
SALES (est): 8.3MM **Privately Held**
SIC: 7372 Business oriented computer
software

(P-24086)
KRATOS TECH TRNING SLTIONS INC (HQ)
10680 Treena St Fl 6, San Diego
(92131-2487)
PHONE....................858 812-7300
Eric M Demarco, *President*
Kenneth Reagan, *President*
Deanna H Lund, *CFO*
Laura L Siegal, *Treasurer*
Jane Judd, *Bd of Directors*
EMP: 139
SQ FT: 25,000
SALES (est): 94.3MM **Publicly Held**
WEB: www.sys.com
SIC: 7372 Business oriented computer
software

(P-24087)
KRONOS INCORPORATED
240 Commerce, Irvine (92602-5004)
PHONE....................800 580-7374

Kaylee Uribe, *Branch Mgr*
Richard Bak, *Software Engr*
Glen Gerber, *Software Engr*
EMP: 56
SALES (corp-wide): 1B **Privately Held**
SIC: 7372 Business oriented computer
software
HQ: Kronos Incorporated
900 Chelmsford St # 312
Lowell MA 01851
978 250-9800

(P-24088)
KWAN SOFTWARE ENGINEERING INC
Also Called: Veripic
1879 Lundy Ave Ste 286, San Jose
(95131-1884)
PHONE....................408 496-1200
John Kwan, *President*
Kellie Sanker, *Executive*
EMP: 32 **EST:** 1997
SALES (est): 5.3MM **Privately Held**
SIC: 7372 Business oriented computer
software

(P-24089)
KYRIBA CORP (PA)
9620 Towne Cntre Dr 200, San Diego
(92121)
PHONE....................858 210-3560
Jean-Luc Robert, *CEO*
Timothy Ray, *President*
Didier Martineau, *COO*
Fabrice Lvy, *CFO*
Remy Dubois, *Exec VP*
EMP: 50
SALES (est): 75.6MM **Privately Held**
WEB: www.kyriba.com
SIC: 7372 Prepackaged software

(P-24090)
LASERBEAM SOFTWARE LLC
1647 Willow Pass Rd, Concord
(94520-2611)
PHONE....................925 459-2595
Patrick Durall, *CEO*
Larry Nelson, *Director*
EMP: 26
SALES (est): 1.2MM **Privately Held**
WEB: www.laserbeamsoftware.com
SIC: 7372 Application computer software

(P-24091)
LASTLINE INC
6950 Hollister Ave # 101, Goleta
(93117-2896)
PHONE....................805 456-7075
EMP: 168 **Privately Held**
SIC: 7372 Prepackaged software
PA: Lastline, Inc.
203 Redwood Shores Pkwy
Redwood City CA 94065

(P-24092)
LASTLINE INC (PA)
203 Redwood Shores Pkwy, Redwood City
(94065-1198)
PHONE....................805 456-7075
John Dilullo, *CEO*
Ananth Avva, *CFO*
Claire Trimble, *Chief Mktg Ofcr*
Christopher Kruegel, *Officer*
Bert Rankin, *Officer*
EMP: 52
SALES (est): 43.3MM **Privately Held**
SIC: 7372 Prepackaged software

(P-24093)
LATTICE DATA INC
801 El Camino Real, Menlo Park
(94025-4807)
PHONE....................650 800-7262
Andy Jacques, *CEO*
EMP: 20
SQ FT: 5,700
SALES (est): 330.7K
SALES (corp-wide): 260.1B **Publicly
Held**
SIC: 7372 Business oriented computer
software
PA: Apple Inc.
1 Apple Park Way
Cupertino CA 95014
408 996-1010

(P-24094)
LAWINFOCOM INC
5901 Priestly Dr Ste 200, Carlsbad
(92008-8825)
PHONE....................800 397-3743
Gunter Enz, *President*
Cara Mae Harrison, *COO*
EMP: 68 **EST:** 1989
SQ FT: 10,000
SALES: 4.6MM **Privately Held**
WEB: www.lawinfo.com
SIC: 7372 8111 7375 Publishers' com-
puter software; legal services; information
retrieval services

(P-24095)
LCPTRACKER INC
117 E Chapman Ave, Orange
(92866-1401)
P.O. Box 187 (92856-6187)
PHONE....................714 669-0052
Mark Douglas, *President*
Loren Doll, *Vice Pres*
Colin Hamilton, *Project Mgr*
Kelli Hardge, *Project Mgr*
Parker Douglas, *Technology*
EMP: 20
SQ FT: 1,500
SALES (est): 3.1MM **Privately Held**
SIC: 7372 Business oriented computer
software

(P-24096)
LCR-DIXON CORPORATION
2048 Union St Apt 4, San Francisco
(94123-4118)
P.O. Box 812, Bel Air MD (21014-0812)
PHONE....................404 307-1695
Suzy SOO, *CEO*
Jeffrey Bleachler, *COO*
Laura Sherinsky, *Office Mgr*
Amy Eller, *Manager*
EMP: 16
SALES (est): 503.2K **Privately Held**
SIC: 7372 Application computer software

(P-24097)
LEADS360 LLC
207 Hindry Ave, Inglewood (90301-1519)
PHONE....................888 843-1777
Nick Hedges, *CEO*
David Nachman, *President*
Darian Hong, *CFO*
Darian Sj Hong, *CFO*
Josh Evans, *Senior VP*
EMP: 30
SALES (est): 6.6MM **Privately Held**
WEB: www.leads360.com
SIC: 7372 7371 Prepackaged software;
computer software development

(P-24098)
LEARNERS GUILD LTD
492 9th St, Oakland (94607-4055)
PHONE....................415 448-7054
Shereef Bishay, *CEO*
EMP: 13
SQ FT: 7,500
SALES (est): 363K **Privately Held**
SIC: 7372 Educational computer software

(P-24099)
LEEYO SOFTWARE INC (HQ)
2841 Junction Ave Ste 201, San Jose
(95134-1938)
PHONE....................408 988-5800
Jagan Reddy, *CEO*
Jeffery Pickett, *Ch of Bd*
Michael Compton, *CFO*
Karthikeyan Ramamoorthy, *Vice Pres*
Sudarsan Umashankar, *Vice Pres*
EMP: 41
SALES (est): 16MM **Publicly Held**
WEB: www.leeyotech.com
SIC: 7372 Business oriented computer
software

(P-24100)
LEVEL LABS LP
Also Called: Unshackled
530 Lytton Ave Lbby, Palo Alto
(94301-1539)
PHONE....................408 499-6839
Manan Mehta, *Managing Prtnr*
Nitin Pachisia, *Mng Member*
Maria Salamanca, *Associate*

PRODUCTS & SVCS

EMP: 30
SALES (est): 128.3K **Privately Held**
SIC: 7372 Application computer software

(P-24101)
LIGHTSPEED SOFTWARE
1800 19th St, Bakersfield (93301-4315)
PHONE....................661 716-7600
Greg Funk, *Vice Pres*
Max Hardy, *Administration*
Bradley White, *Sr Ntwrk Engine*
Andrew Hecht, *Software Dev*
Jason Isaac, *Software Dev*
EMP: 14
SALES (est): 1.5MM **Privately Held**
SIC: 7372 Prepackaged software

(P-24102)
LINE EURO-AMERICAS CORP
5750 Wilshire Blvd # 640, Los Angeles
(90036-3697)
PHONE....................323 591-0380
Jeanie Han, *CEO*
Jinyeop Yoo, *Finance Mgr*
EMP: 15
SQ FT: 6,000
SALES (est): 1.4MM **Privately Held**
SIC: 7372 Prepackaged software

(P-24103)
LIVEACTION INC (PA)
3500 W Bayshore Rd, Palo Alto
(94303-4228)
PHONE....................415 837-3303
Darren Kimura, *CEO*
Rodney Caines, *Partner*
R Brooks Borcherding, *President*
Dana Matsunaga, *President*
Wendy Iwanski, *CFO*
EMP: 35
SQ FT: 3,000
SALES: 5.7MM **Privately Held**
SIC: 7372 Business oriented computer
software

(P-24104)
LIVEOFFICE LLC
Also Called: Advisorsquare
900 Corporate Pointe, Culver City
(90230-7609)
PHONE....................877 253-2793
Alexander Rusich,
Matt Hardy,
Jeffrey W Hausman,
Nikhil Menta,
Matt Smith,
EMP: 77
SQ FT: 15,000
SALES (est): 5.5MM
SALES (corp-wide): 4.7B **Publicly Held**
WEB: www.advisorsquare.com
SIC: 7372 Prepackaged software
PA: Nortonlifelock Inc.
60 E Rio Salado Pkwy # 1
Tempe AZ 85281
650 527-8000

(P-24105)
LIVETIME SOFTWARE INC
276 Avocado St Apt C102, Costa Mesa
(92627-7302)
PHONE....................415 905-4009
Darren Williams, *President*
EMP: 50
SALES (est): 2.7MM **Privately Held**
SIC: 7372 Prepackaged software

(P-24106)
LOANHERO INC
750 B St Ste 1410, San Diego
(92101-8190)
PHONE....................888 912-4376
Zalman Vitenson, *CEO*
Derek Barclay, *President*
Steve Connolly, *COO*
Olaf Janke, *CFO*
Mikel Sides, *Exec VP*
EMP: 10
SALES (est): 221.8K
SALES (corp-wide): 1.5MM **Privately
Held**
SIC: 7372 Business oriented computer
software

PA: Lendingpoint Llc
1201 Roberts Blvd Nw # 200
Kennesaw GA 30144
678 324-6864

(P-24107)
LOGICOOL INC
1825 De La Cruz Blvd # 201, Santa Clara
(95050-3012)
PHONE....................408 907-1344
EMP: 30
SALES (est): 2.9MM **Privately Held**
SIC: 7372

(P-24108)
LOGINEXT SOLUTIONS INC
5002 Spring Crest Ter, Fremont
(94536-6525)
PHONE....................339 244-0380
Dhruvil Sanghvi, *CEO*
Manisha Raisinghani, *Chief Engr*
EMP: 100
SALES (est): 124.1K **Privately Held**
SIC: 7372 7371 7379 8243 Prepackaged
software; computer software systems
analysis & design, custom; computer software development & applications; software programming applications; computer
related consulting services; software
training, computer

(P-24109)
LOTUSFLARE INC
530 Lakeside Dr Ste 130, Sunnyvale
(94085-4055)
PHONE....................626 695-5634
Surendra Gadodia, *CEO*
Nick Thakkar, *Principal*
EMP: 15
SALES (est): 686.4K **Privately Held**
SIC: 7372 Business oriented computer
software

(P-24110)
LOYYAL CORPORATION
44 Tehama St Fl 5, San Francisco
(94105-3110)
PHONE....................415 419-9590
Gregory Simon, *CEO*
EMP: 10
SALES: 1.9MM **Privately Held**
SIC: 7372 Application computer software

(P-24111)
LPA INSURANCE AGENCY INC
Also Called: Sat
3800 Watt Ave Ste 147, Sacramento
(95821-2676)
PHONE....................916 286-7850
Michael Winkel, *President*
EMP: 56
SALES (est): 3.4MM
SALES (corp-wide): 8.4B **Publicly Held**
WEB: www.sungard.com
SIC: 7372 Application computer software
HQ: Fis Data Systems Inc.
200 Campus Dr
Collegeville PA 19426
484 582-2000

(P-24112)
LUNA IMAGING INC
2702 Media Center Dr, Los Angeles
(90065-1733)
PHONE....................323 908-1400
Marlo Lee, *President*
Lori Richmeier, *Admin Mgr*
Drake Zabriskie, *CTO*
Michelle De, *Project Mgr*
Robert Amesbury, *Finance*
EMP: 15
SQ FT: 6,000
SALES (est): 1.7MM **Privately Held**
WEB: www.lunaimaging.com
SIC: 7372 7373 Publishers' computer soft-
ware; computer integrated systems de-
sign

(P-24113)
LW CONSULTING SERVICES LLC
13292 Rhoda Dr, Los Altos Hills
(94022-2531)
PHONE....................650 919-3001
Lung-Lon Wey,
EMP: 10

SALES: 200K **Privately Held**
SIC: 7372 7389 Prepackaged software;

(P-24114)
LYNX SOFTWARE TECHNOLOGIES INC (PA)
855 Embedded Way, San Jose
(95138-1030)
PHONE....................408 979-3900
Inder Singh, *Chairman*
Gurjot Singh, *President*
Will Keegan, *CTO*
Ingrid Osborne, *Controller*
Lee Cresswell, *Sales Dir*
EMP: 52
SQ FT: 30,000
SALES (est): 15.6MM **Privately Held**
WEB: www.lynuxworks.com
SIC: 7372 Business oriented computer
software

(P-24115)
LYRIS INC
4 N 2nd St Fl 11, San Jose (95113-1305)
PHONE....................800 768-2929
Scott Knies, *Principal*
EMP: 35
SALES (corp-wide): 48.7MM **Privately
Held**
WEB: www.jlhalsey.com
SIC: 7372 Business oriented computer
software
HQ: Lyris, Inc.
401 Congress Ave Ste 2650
Austin TX 78701
512 201-8287

(P-24116)
M D SOFTWARE INC
Also Called: MD Software Enterprise
1226 E 42nd Pl, San Bernardino
(92404-1525)
PHONE....................909 881-7599
Ralph Mallinger, *President*
EMP: 12
SALES (est): 900K **Privately Held**
SIC: 7372 Prepackaged software

(P-24117)
M NEXON INC
Also Called: Nexon America
222 N Pacific Coast Hwy # 300, El Se-
gundo (90245-5614)
PHONE....................213 858-5930
John Robinson, *CEO*
EMP: 30 **EST:** 2011
SALES (est): 209.3K **Privately Held**
SIC: 7372 5092 Application computer soft-
ware; video games
PA: Nexon Co.,Ltd.
1-4-5, Roppongi
Minato-Ku TKY 106-0

(P-24118)
M29 TECHNOLOGY AND DESIGN
133 Bridge St Ste B, Arroyo Grande
(93420-3366)
PHONE....................805 489-9402
John Herlihy, *Owner*
Corey Aufang, *Software Dev*
EMP: 12
SQ FT: 1,200
SALES (est): 750K **Privately Held**
WEB: www.m29.com
SIC: 7372 7371 Prepackaged software;
custom computer programming services

(P-24119)
MADCAP SOFTWARE INC (PA)
9191 Towne Centre Dr # 150, San Diego
(92122-1261)
PHONE....................858 320-0387
Anthony Oliver, *CEO*
Taunya Conte, *CFO*
Francis Novak, *Vice Pres*
John Golding, *Sr Software Eng*
Gregory Chan, *Software Dev*
EMP: 18
SALES (est): 2.8MM **Privately Held**
SIC: 7372 Prepackaged software

(P-24120)
MAGELLAN WEST LLC
1580 Oakland Rd Ste C107, San Jose
(95131-2441)
PHONE....................408 324-0620
Damien Hessian,
EMP: 30
SQ FT: 35,000
SALES (est): 2MM **Privately Held**
WEB: www.magellanworld.com
SIC: 7372 5045 7371 3695 Prepackaged
software; computers, peripherals & soft-
ware; computer software development &
applications; computer software tape &
disks: blank, rigid & floppy

(P-24121)
MAGIC SOFTWARE ENTERPRISES INC
24422 Avenida De La Carlo, Laguna Hills
(92653-3636)
PHONE....................949 250-1718
Eyal Karny, *CEO*
Asaf Berenstin, *CFO*
Fred Esquillo, *Vice Pres*
Glenn Johnson, *Vice Pres*
Brian Pitoniak, *Vice Pres*
EMP: 20
SQ FT: 7,000
SALES (est): 3MM
SALES (corp-wide): 76.7MM **Privately
Held**
SIC: 7372 7379 7371 Prepackaged soft-
ware; computer related consulting serv-
ices; custom computer programming
services
PA: Magic Software Enterprises Ltd.
5 Haplada
Or Yehuda 60218
353 893-89

(P-24122)
MAGIC TOUCH SOFTWARE INTL
330 Rancheros Dr Ste 258, San Marcos
(92069-2979)
PHONE....................800 714-6490
Gary Bagheri, *President*
George Peiov, *Vice Pres*
EMP: 14 **EST:** 2007
SQ FT: 1,500
SALES: 850K **Privately Held**
SIC: 7372 Business oriented computer
software

(P-24123)
MAGNET SYSTEMS INC
2300 Geng Rd Ste 100, Palo Alto
(94303-3352)
P.O. Box 320805, Los Gatos (95032-0113)
PHONE....................650 329-5904
Alfred Chuang, *CEO*
Elizabeth Vera, *Executive Asst*
EMP: 30
SALES (est): 5.6MM **Privately Held**
SIC: 7372 Application computer software

(P-24124)
MAKO LABS LLC
Also Called: Injekt
169 Saxony Rd Ste 107, Encinitas
(92024-6779)
P.O. Box 908, Cardiff By The Sea (92007-
0908)
PHONE....................619 786-3618
Steve Iverson, *CEO*
Matt Gurren, *Vice Pres*
EMP: 20
SALES (est): 2.8MM **Privately Held**
SIC: 7372 Application computer software

(P-24125)
MALIKCO LLC
2121 N Calif Blvd Ste 290, Walnut Creek
(94596-7351)
PHONE....................925 974-3555
Stephynie R Malik, *CEO*
Dennis J Dunnigan, *Director*
Ragean Kennedy, *Accounts Exec*
EMP: 50
SQ FT: 1,000
SALES (est): 4.8MM **Privately Held**
WEB: www.malikco.com
SIC: 7372 Operating systems computer
software

▲ = Import ▼=Export
◆ =Import/Export

(P-24126)
MAPBOX INC
50 Beale St Ste 900, San Francisco
(94105-1863)
PHONE....................202 250-3633
Eric Gundersen, *CEO*
Roy Ng, *COO*
Ali Anthes, *Vice Pres*
Alex Barth, *Vice Pres*
Dave Cole, *Vice Pres*
EMP: 10
SALES (est): 1.2MM **Privately Held**
SIC: 7372 Application computer software

(P-24127)
MARKETING PRO CONSULTING INC
Also Called: Mortgageplannercrm
1230 Columbia St Ste 500, San Diego
(92101-8520)
P.O. Box 3480 (92163-1480)
PHONE....................619 233-8591
Michael Gulitz, *President*
Juliana S Krijan, *Vice Pres*
EMP: 13
SALES (est): 955.1K **Privately Held**
SIC: 7372 8742 Application computer software; marketing consulting services

(P-24128)
MARKZWARE
Also Called: Markzware Software
1805 E Dyer Rd Ste 101, Santa Ana
(92705-5742)
PHONE....................949 756-5100
Patrick Marchese, *President*
Ron Crandall, *Vice Pres*
Valerie Consalvi, *Info Tech Dir*
David Peterson, *Info Tech Mgr*
Doug Rosen, *Project Mgr*
EMP: 11
SQ FT: 5,000
SALES (est): 1.2MM **Privately Held**
WEB: www.markzware.com
SIC: 7372 Business oriented computer software

(P-24129)
MATCHPOINT SOLUTIONS (PA)
3875 Hopyard Rd Ste 325, Pleasanton
(94588-8526)
PHONE....................925 829-4455
Cindy Everson, *President*
Michael Turk, *Senior VP*
Pooja Kulkarni, *Technical Mgr*
Jay Maddala, *Tech Recruiter*
John Zukoski, *Accounting Dir*
EMP: 10
SALES (est): 2.1MM **Privately Held**
SIC: 7372 Educational computer software

(P-24130)
MATRIX LOGIC CORPORATION
1380 East Ave Ste 124240, Chico
(95926-7349)
PHONE....................415 893-9897
Stephen C Page, *President*
Roberto Villongco, *Engineer*
Frank Rayner, *Sr Consultant*
EMP: 11
SQ FT: 1,500
SALES (est): 1.2MM **Privately Held**
WEB: www.matrix-logic.com
SIC: 7372 Business oriented computer software

(P-24131)
MAXIMUS HOLDINGS INC
2475 Hanover St, Palo Alto (94304-1114)
PHONE....................650 935-9500
Dominic Gallello, *CEO*
Jim Johnson, *CFO*
Anshul Singh, *Executive*
EMP: 1006
SALES (est): 21.9MM
SALES (corp-wide): 604.2MM **Privately Held**
SIC: 7372 Prepackaged software
PA: Symphony Technology Group, L.L.C.
428 University Ave
Palo Alto CA 94301
650 935-9500

(P-24132)
MAXXESS SYSTEMS INC (PA)
22661 Old Canal Rd, Yorba Linda
(92887-4601)
PHONE....................714 772-1000
Kevin Charles Daly, *CEO*
Nancy Islas, *President*
Joel Slutzky, *Chairman*
EMP: 25
SQ FT: 12,000
SALES (est): 3.4MM **Privately Held**
WEB: www.maxxesssystems.com
SIC: 7372 Business oriented computer software

(P-24133)
MAYSOFT INC
Also Called: The Mayflower Group
1727 Santa Barbara St, Santa Barbara
(93101-1024)
PHONE....................978 635-1700
Frank Paolino, *President*
EMP: 10
SALES (est): 1MM **Privately Held**
WEB: www.maysoft.com
SIC: 7372 7371 Word processing computer software; computer software systems analysis & design, custom; computer software development

(P-24134)
MCAFEE INC
6707 Barnhurst Dr, San Diego
(92117-4208)
PHONE....................858 967-2342
EMP: 82 **Privately Held**
SIC: 7372 Prepackaged software
HQ: Mcafee, Llc
2821 Mission College Blvd
Santa Clara CA 95054
888 847-8766

(P-24135)
MCAFEE LLC (HQ)
2821 Mission College Blvd, Santa Clara
(95054-1838)
PHONE....................888 847-8766
Christopher Young, *CEO*
Jean-Claude Broido, *President*
Tom Miglis, *President*
Michael Berry, *CFO*
Thomas Gann, *Officer*
▲ **EMP:** 148
SQ FT: 208,000
SALES (est): 1.5B **Privately Held**
WEB: www.mcafee.com
SIC: 7372 Application computer software

(P-24136)
MCAFEE FINANCE 2 LLC
2821 Mission College Blvd, Santa Clara
(95054-1838)
PHONE....................888 847-8766
EMP: 1129
SALES (est): 10.3MM
SALES (corp-wide): 277.9MM **Privately Held**
SIC: 7372 Prepackaged software
HQ: Mcafee Finance 1, Llc
2821 Mission College Blvd
Santa Clara CA 95054
888 847-8766

(P-24137)
MCAFEE SECURITY LLC
2821 Mission College Blvd, Santa Clara
(95054-1838)
PHONE....................866 622-3911
Michael Decesare, *President*
Bob Kelly, *CFO*
Edward Hayden, *Senior VP*
Louis Riley, *Senior VP*
EMP: 5030 **EST:** 2006
SQ FT: 208,000
SALES (est): 98.4MM **Privately Held**
SIC: 7372 Application computer software
HQ: Mcafee, Llc
2821 Mission College Blvd
Santa Clara CA 95054
888 847-8766

(P-24138)
MEDALLIA INC (PA)
575 Market St Ste 1850, San Francisco
(94105-5803)
PHONE....................650 321-3000

Leslie J Stretch, *President*
Borge Hald, *Ch of Bd*
Roxanne M Oulman, *CFO*
Jimmy C Duan, *Ch Credit Ofcr*
Mikael J Ottosson, *Exec VP*
EMP: 145
SALES (est): 376.3MM **Publicly Held**
WEB: www.medallia.com
SIC: 7372 8732 Business oriented computer software; market analysis, business & economic research

(P-24139)
MEDATA INC (PA)
5 Peters Canyon Rd # 250, Irvine
(92606-1793)
PHONE....................714 918-1310
Cy King, *CEO*
Tom Herndon, *President*
Thomas Herndon, *COO*
Bryan Lowe, *CFO*
T Don Theis, *Senior VP*
EMP: 51 **EST:** 1975
SQ FT: 17,192
SALES (est): 114.3MM **Privately Held**
WEB: www.medata.com
SIC: 7372 6411 Business oriented computer software; medical insurance claim processing, contract or fee basis

(P-24140)
MEDIA GOBBLER INC
6427 W Sunset Blvd, Los Angeles
(90028-7314)
PHONE....................323 203-3222
Chris Kantrowitz, *CEO*
Phil Kinkade, *President*
Olivier Albin, *Office Mgr*
Heather Rafter, *Consultant*
EMP: 14
SALES (est): 1.5MM **Privately Held**
SIC: 7372 Application computer software

(P-24141)
MEDICAL DATA RECOVERY INC
17310 Red Hill Ave # 270, Irvine
(92614-5637)
P.O. Box 16634 (92623-6634)
PHONE....................949 251-0073
Michael Mackenzie, *President*
EMP: 10
SQ FT: 2,500
SALES (est): 2.3MM **Privately Held**
SIC: 7372 Prepackaged software

(P-24142)
MEDICAL TRANSCRIPTION BILLING
405 Kenyon St Ste 300, San Diego (92110)
PHONE....................800 869-3700
EMP: 561
SALES (corp-wide): 50.5MM **Publicly Held**
SIC: 7372 Prepackaged software
PA: Medical Transcription Billing, Corp.
7 Clyde Rd
Somerset NJ 08873
732 873-5133

(P-24143)
MEDITAB SOFTWARE INC
2233 Watt Ave Ste 360, Sacramento
(95825-0569)
P.O. Box 255687 (95865-5687)
PHONE....................510 673-1838
Kunal Shah, *President*
Paragi Patel, *CFO*
Ronak Kotecha, *Regl Sales Mgr*
Hemang Bhatt, *Manager*
EMP: 10
SALES (est): 170.7K **Privately Held**
SIC: 7372 Business oriented computer software
PA: Meditab Software (India) Private Limited
Officeno. 219/A, 2nd Floor,
Ahmedabad GJ 38006

(P-24144)
MEDITAB SOFTWARE INC
333 Hegenberger Rd # 800, Oakland
(94621-1416)
PHONE....................510 632-2021
Mike Patel, *President*
Kal Patel, *COO*

Marc Beaniza, *Executive*
Sumair Sidhu, *Info Tech Dir*
Jigar Varmora, *Prgrmr*
EMP: 250
SQ FT: 10,000
SALES (est): 27.9MM **Privately Held**
SIC: 7372 Business oriented computer software

(P-24145)
MEDRIO INC (PA)
345 California St Ste 325, San Francisco
(94104-2658)
PHONE....................415 963-3700
Michael Richard Novotny, *CEO*
Nathan Weems, *CFO*
Richard H Scheller, *Exec VP*
Ryan Lacey, *Director*
Nicholas Labounty, *Manager*
EMP: 30
SALES: 10.6MM **Privately Held**
SIC: 7372 Business oriented computer software

(P-24146)
MELIAN LABS INC (PA)
Also Called: Mytime
881 Corbett Ave Apt 3, San Francisco
(94131-1658)
PHONE....................888 423-1944
Ethan Anderson, *CEO*
EMP: 16
SALES (est): 3.1MM **Privately Held**
SIC: 7372 4813 5044 Application computer software; ; calculating machines

(P-24147)
MENTOR GRAPHICS CORPORATION
12255 El Camino Real # 150, San Diego
(92130-4000)
PHONE....................858 523-2600
Polly Partolan, *Principal*
Lucas Lee, *Consultant*
EMP: 36
SALES (corp-wide): 95B **Privately Held**
SIC: 7372 Prepackaged software
HQ: Mentor Graphics Corporation
8005 Sw Boeckman Rd
Wilsonville OR 97070
503 685-7000

(P-24148)
MENTOR GRAPHICS CORPORATION
18301 Von Karman Ave # 760, Irvine
(92612-0137)
PHONE....................949 790-3200
Scott Mackerras, *Manager*
Bill Keller, *Technology*
Della Felton, *Sales Staff*
EMP: 15
SALES (corp-wide): 95B **Privately Held**
WEB: www.mentor.com
SIC: 7372 Business oriented computer software
HQ: Mentor Graphics Corporation
8005 Sw Boeckman Rd
Wilsonville OR 97070
503 685-7000

(P-24149)
METRICSTREAM INC (PA)
Also Called: Complianceonline
2479 E Byshore Rd Ste 260, Palo Alto
(94303)
PHONE....................650 620-2900
Mikael Hagstroem, *CEO*
Gaurave Kapoor, *COO*
Steven R Springsteel, *CFO*
Gunjan Sinha, *Chairman*
Venky Yerrapotu, *Exec VP*
EMP: 150
SALES (est): 214.3MM **Privately Held**
SIC: 7372 Application computer software

(P-24150)
METRONOME SOFTWARE LLC
25241 Paseo De Alicia # 200, Laguna Hills
(92653-4643)
PHONE....................949 273-5190
Chieu Nguyen, *Mng Member*
Huy Nguyen, *General Mgr*
David Lim, *CTO*
Wou Kuo, *Software Engr*
Samantha Keith, *Controller*

EMP: 12
SQ FT: 6,500
SALES (est): 1.1MM **Privately Held**
SIC: 7372 Prepackaged software

(P-24151)
MICRO FOCUS LLC (DH)
Also Called: Entit Software, LLC
4555 Great America Pkwy # 401, Santa
Clara (95054-1243)
PHONE.........................801 861-7000
Christopher P Hsu,
Allen Chen, *Sales Mgr*
EMP: 14 **EST:** 2007
SALES (est): 3MM **Privately Held**
SIC: 7372 Operating systems computer
software
HQ: Micro Focus (Us), Inc.
700 King Farm Blvd # 125
Rockville MD 20850
301 838-5000

(P-24152)
MICROMEGA SYSTEMS INC
2 Fifer Ave Ste 120, Corte Madera
(94925-1153)
PHONE.........................415 924-4700
Charles Bornheim, *President*
EMP: 12
SQ FT: 3,300
SALES (est): 1.2MM **Privately Held**
WEB: www.micromegasystems.com
SIC: 7372 7371 7379 Business oriented
computer software; custom computer pro-
gramming services; computer software
development; computer related consulting
services

(P-24153)
MICROS SYSTEMS INC
5805 Owens Dr, Pleasanton (94588-3939)
PHONE.........................443 285-8000
Jeff Wooden, *Branch Mgr*
EMP: 25
SALES (corp-wide): 39.5B **Publicly Held**
WEB: www.micros.com
SIC: 7372 Prepackaged software
HQ: Micros Systems, Inc.
7031 Columbia Gateway Dr # 1
Columbia MD 21046
443 285-6000

(P-24154)
MICROSOFT CORPORATION
75 Enterprise Ste 100, Aliso Viejo
(92656-2628)
PHONE.........................949 680-3000
Shobhit Mishra, *Branch Mgr*
Maria Dalal, *Sr Software Eng*
Dorion Whitlock, *Technical Staff*
EMP: 35
SALES (corp-wide): 125.8B **Publicly
Held**
SIC: 7372 Prepackaged software
PA: Microsoft Corporation
1 Microsoft Way
Redmond WA 98052
425 882-8080

(P-24155)
MICROSOFT CORPORATION
9255 Towne Centre Dr # 400, San Diego
(92121-3037)
PHONE.........................858 909-3800
Stephanie McCarron, *Manager*
Devon Morris, *Program Mgr*
Scott Pigman, *Technical Staff*
Dan Morwood, *Sales Staff*
Elizabeth Stephens, *Director*
EMP: 40
SALES (corp-wide): 125.8B **Publicly
Held**
WEB: www.microsoft.com
SIC: 7372 Application computer software
PA: Microsoft Corporation
1 Microsoft Way
Redmond WA 98052
425 882-8080

(P-24156)
MICROSOFT CORPORATION
1085 La Avenida St, Mountain View
(94043-1421)
PHONE.........................650 964-7200
Susan Peletta, *Executive*
Jeff Asis, *Partner*

Jim Hogan, *Vice Pres*
John Stevans, *Program Mgr*
Zulfi Alam, *General Mgr*
EMP: 76
SALES (corp-wide): 125.8B **Publicly
Held**
SIC: 7372 Prepackaged software
PA: Microsoft Corporation
1 Microsoft Way
Redmond WA 98052
425 882-8080

(P-24157)
MICROSOFT CORPORATION
7007 Friars Rd, San Diego (92108-1148)
PHONE.........................619 849-5872
EMP: 100
SALES (corp-wide): 125.8B **Publicly
Held**
SIC: 7372 Application computer software
PA: Microsoft Corporation
1 Microsoft Way
Redmond WA 98052
425 882-8080

(P-24158)
MICROSOFT CORPORATION
1415 L St Ste 200, Sacramento
(95814-3962)
PHONE.........................916 369-3600
James Waterman, *Manager*
Lucas Correa, *Manager*
Ram Nagaraja, *Manager*
Mitch Pierce, *Manager*
Kristi Verma, *Manager*
EMP: 20
SALES (corp-wide): 125.8B **Publicly
Held**
WEB: www.microsoft.com
SIC: 7372 Application computer software;
operating systems computer software
PA: Microsoft Corporation
1 Microsoft Way
Redmond WA 98052
425 882-8080

(P-24159)
MICROSOFT CORPORATION
1020 Entp Way Bldg B, Sunnyvale (94089)
PHONE.........................650 693-1009
William H Gates III, *Branch Mgr*
Swathi Shenoy, *Software Engr*
EMP: 103
SALES (corp-wide): 125.8B **Publicly
Held**
SIC: 7372 Prepackaged software
PA: Microsoft Corporation
1 Microsoft Way
Redmond WA 98052
425 882-8080

(P-24160)
MICROSOFT CORPORATION
3 Park Plz Ste 1800, Irvine (92614-8541)
PHONE.........................949 263-3000
Sandy Thomas, *General Mgr*
Rohit Malhotra, *Software Engr*
Juliet Helms, *Technical Staff*
Amine Brahimi, *Engineer*
Pouya Torabi, *Senior Mgr*
EMP: 125
SALES (corp-wide): 125.8B **Publicly
Held**
WEB: www.microsoft.com
SIC: 7372 Application computer software
PA: Microsoft Corporation
1 Microsoft Way
Redmond WA 98052
425 882-8080

(P-24161)
MICROSOFT CORPORATION
13031 W Jefferson Blvd # 200, Playa Vista
(90094-7001)
PHONE.........................213 806-7300
Evelyn Morgan, *Manager*
Adam Foxman, *Software Dev*
Matthew Fraser, *Software Dev*
Pratap Ladhani, *Software Dev*
Josette Huang, *Software Engr*
EMP: 100
SALES (corp-wide): 125.8B **Publicly
Held**
WEB: www.microsoft.com
SIC: 7372 Application computer software

PA: Microsoft Corporation
1 Microsoft Way
Redmond WA 98052
425 882-8080

(P-24162)
MICROSOFT CORPORATION
555 California St Ste 200, San Francisco
(94104-1504)
PHONE.........................415 972-6400
Teeka Miller, *Branch Mgr*
Vance Frankiewicz, *Technical Staff*
Vandan Kaushik, *Technical Staff*
Rupert Scammell, *Engineer*
Paulo Viralhadas, *Engineer*
EMP: 160
SALES (corp-wide): 125.8B **Publicly
Held**
WEB: www.microsoft.com
SIC: 7372 Application computer software
PA: Microsoft Corporation
1 Microsoft Way
Redmond WA 98052
425 882-8080

(P-24163)
MICROSOFT CORPORATION
2045 Lafayette St, Santa Clara
(95050-2901)
PHONE.........................408 987-9608
Jim Brown, *President*
EMP: 100
SALES (corp-wide): 125.8B **Publicly
Held**
WEB: www.microsoft.com
SIC: 7372 Application computer software
PA: Microsoft Corporation
1 Microsoft Way
Redmond WA 98052
425 882-8080

(P-24164)
MICROTELEMATICS INC
Also Called: Carmine
1500 Quail St Ste 280, Newport Beach
(92660-2734)
PHONE.........................949 537-3636
Reza Fategh, *President*
Miles Herrera, *Accounts Exec*
EMP: 10
SALES: 1MM
SALES (corp-wide): 177.9K **Privately
Held**
SIC: 7372 Business oriented computer
software
PA: Persepolis Holding B.V.
Marten Meesweg 8
Rotterdam
887 127-160

(P-24165)
**MICROVISION DEVELOPMENT
INC**
1734 Oriole Ct, Carlsbad (92011-4052)
PHONE.........................760 438-7781
James Harley Mayall, *CEO*
John Gaby, *Vice Pres*
EMP: 23
SALES (est): 2.8MM **Privately Held**
WEB: www.mvd.com
SIC: 7372 Business oriented computer
software

(P-24166)
MIDRANGE SOFTWARE INC
12716 Riverside Dr, Studio City
(91607-3383)
PHONE.........................818 762-8539
Jacques Ohana, *President*
Simon Ohana, *Vice Pres*
EMP: 20
SQ FT: 10,000
SALES (est): 2.3MM **Privately Held**
WEB: www.midrangesoftware.com
SIC: 7372 Prepackaged software

(P-24167)
MINDSAI INC
101 Cooper St Ste 218, Santa Cruz
(95060-4526)
PHONE.........................831 239-4644
Sumit Sanyal, *CEO*
EMP: 12
SALES (est): 281.6K **Privately Held**
SIC: 7372 Business oriented computer
software

(P-24168)
MINDSNACKS INC
1479 Folsom St, San Francisco
(94103-3734)
PHONE.........................415 875-9817
Jesse Pickard, *CEO*
Bryan Schreier, *Principal*
Aydin Senkut, *Principal*
EMP: 30 **EST:** 2010
SQ FT: 5,250
SALES (est): 2.3MM **Privately Held**
SIC: 7372 Application computer software

(P-24169)
MINT SOFTWARE INC
280 Hope St, Mountain View (94041-1308)
P.O. Box 7850 (94039-7850)
PHONE.........................650 944-6000
Aaron T Patzer, *President*
Rob Hayes, *Partner*
David K Michaels, *President*
EMP: 12
SQ FT: 5,000
SALES (est): 1MM
SALES (corp-wide): 6.7B **Publicly Held**
SIC: 7372 Business oriented computer
software
PA: Intuit Inc.
2700 Coast Ave
Mountain View CA 94043
650 944-6000

(P-24170)
MIRTH CORPORATION
611 Anton Blvd Ste 500, Costa Mesa
(92626-1934)
PHONE.........................714 389-1200
Jon Teichrow, *President*
Samuel Sippl, *CFO*
Gary Teichrow, *Vice Pres*
Andrew Thorson, *Vice Pres*
Shelly Larrimore MBA, *Sales Staff*
EMP: 35
SQ FT: 10,000
SALES (est): 4.2MM
SALES (corp-wide): 529.1MM **Publicly
Held**
WEB: www.webreachinc.com
SIC: 7372 Business oriented computer
software
PA: Nextgen Healthcare, Inc.
18111 Von Karman Ave # 8
Irvine CA 92612
949 255-2600

(P-24171)
MITRATECH HOLDINGS INC
5900 Wilshire Blvd # 1500, Los Angeles
(90036-5031)
PHONE.........................323 964-0000
Laura Paynter, *Hum Res Coord*
Jeff Drury, *Opers Staff*
Tomas Medina, *Manager*
EMP: 13
SALES (corp-wide): 78.3MM **Privately
Held**
SIC: 7372 Business oriented computer
software
PA: Mitratech Holdings, Inc.
5001 Plz On
Austin TX 78746
512 382-7322

(P-24172)
MIXAMO INC
2415 3rd St Ste 239, San Francisco
(94107-3177)
PHONE.........................415 255-7455
EMP: 25
SALES (est): 1.6MM
SALES (corp-wide): 7.3B **Publicly Held**
SIC: 7372
PA: Adobe Systems Incorporated
345 Park Ave
San Jose CA 95110
408 536-6000

(P-24173)
MJUS LLC (FKA MINDJET LLC)
275 Battery St Ste 1000, San Francisco
(94111-3333)
PHONE.........................415 229-4344
Scott Raskin, *CEO*
Teresa Vegher, *Partner*
Steve Glass, *President*
Steve Anderson, *CFO*

Amy Melton, *Sr Software Eng*
EMP: 40
SQ FT: 15,140
SALES (est): 6.9MM
SALES (corp-wide): 145.9MM **Privately Held**
SIC: 7372 Business oriented computer software; educational computer software
HQ: Spigit Holdings Corporation
12301 Res Blvd Ste 5-101
Austin TX 78759
415 229-4400

(P-24174)
MOBILEIRON INC (PA)
401 E Middlefield Rd, Mountain View (94043-4005)
PHONE...................650 919-8100
Simon Biddiscombe, *President*
Tae Hea Nahm, *Ch of Bd*
Scott D Hill, *CFO*
Kenneth Klein, *Bd of Directors*
James Tolonen, *Bd of Directors*
EMP: 148
SQ FT: 78,000
SALES: 193.1MM **Publicly Held**
SIC: 7372 Prepackaged software

(P-24175)
MOBILEOPS CORPORATION
1422 Wright Ave, Sunnyvale (94087-4017)
PHONE...................408 203-0243
Rajiv Taori, *CEO*
EMP: 10 **EST:** 2012
SALES (est): 702.9K **Privately Held**
SIC: 7372 Business oriented computer software

(P-24176)
MOD2 INC
Also Called: Mod 2
3317 S Broadway, Los Angeles (90007-4114)
PHONE...................213 747-8424
Javid Nia, *President*
Ronald Bantayan, *Manager*
EMP: 15
SQ FT: 12,000
SALES (est): 1.2MM **Privately Held**
WEB: www.mod2.com
SIC: 7372 7371 Business oriented computer software; application computer software; computer software systems analysis & design, custom

(P-24177)
MODE ANALYTICS INC
208 Utah St Ste 400, San Francisco (94103-4881)
PHONE...................415 271-7599
Derek Steer, *CEO*
Thomas Van Steyn, *Sales Staff*
EMP: 14
SALES (est): 873.8K **Privately Held**
SIC: 7372 Business oriented computer software

(P-24178)
MODEL MATCH INC
209 Avnida Fbrcnte Ste 15, San Clemente (92672)
PHONE...................949 525-9405
Kirk Waldfogel, *Principal*
Eric Levin, *Principal*
Eric Petersen, *Principal*
Steve Rennie, *Principal*
Drew Waterhouse, *Principal*
EMP: 18
SQ FT: 3,400
SALES (est): 228.4K **Privately Held**
SIC: 7372 Application computer software

(P-24179)
MONITISE INC
1 Embarcadero Ctr Ste 900, San Francisco (94111-3754)
PHONE...................650 286-1059
Lisa Stanton, *General Mgr*
EMP: 12
SQ FT: 1,939
SALES: 1.8MM
SALES (corp-wide): 5.8B **Publicly Held**
SIC: 7372 Prepackaged software

HQ: Monitise Group Limited
Medius House, 2 Sheraton Street
London W1F 8

(P-24180)
MSCSOFTWARE CORPORATION (HQ)
4675 Macarthur Ct Ste 900, Newport Beach (92660-1845)
PHONE...................714 540-8900
Dominic Gallello, *President*
Hugues Jeancolas, *Vice Pres*
Leo Kilfoy, *General Mgr*
Celia Arcos, *Office Admin*
Hiroko Shirai, *Executive Asst*
EMP: 245 **EST:** 1963
SALES (est): 146.4MM
SALES (corp-wide): 4.3B **Privately Held**
WEB: www.mscsoftware.com
SIC: 7372 Business oriented computer software
PA: Hexagon Ab
Lilla Bantorget 15
Stockholm 111 2
860 126-20

(P-24181)
MULESOFT INC
50 Fremont St Ste 300, San Francisco (94105-2231)
PHONE...................415 229-2009
Greg Schott, *CEO*
Matt Langdon, *CFO*
Vidya Peters, *Chief Mktg Ofcr*
Mark Dao, *Officer*
Brent Grimes, *Vice Pres*
EMP: 841
SQ FT: 41,500
SALES: 296.4MM
SALES (corp-wide): 13.2B **Publicly Held**
WEB: www.mulesoft.com
SIC: 7372 7371 Prepackaged software; computer software development
PA: Salesforce.Com, Inc.
415 Mission St Fl 3
San Francisco CA 94105
415 901-7000

(P-24182)
MUNKYFUN INC
1 Embarcadero Ctr Ste 500, San Francisco (94111-3610)
PHONE...................415 281-3837
Nicholas Pavis, *CEO*
Kameron Beck, *Technical Staff*
Stephanie Mahnke, *Human Res Mgr*
Lynn Taylor, *Opers Mgr*
EMP: 44 **EST:** 2008
SALES (est): 5MM **Privately Held**
SIC: 7372 Application computer software

(P-24183)
MURSION INC (PA)
303 2nd St Ste 460, San Francisco (94107-1366)
PHONE...................415 746-9631
Mark Atkinson, *CEO*
Dovid Gurevich, *CFO*
Arjun Nagendran, *Vice Pres*
Greg Ayers, *Training Spec*
EMP: 54
SALES (est): 8.3MM **Privately Held**
SIC: 7372 Educational computer software; publishers' computer software

(P-24184)
MUSICMATCH INC
16935 W Bernardo Dr # 270, San Diego (92127-1634)
PHONE...................858 485-4300
Dennis Mudd, *CEO*
Peter Csathy, *President*
Gary Acord, *CFO*
Chris Allen, *Senior VP*
Don Leigh, *Senior VP*
EMP: 140
SQ FT: 20,000
SALES (est): 6.9MM **Privately Held**
WEB: www.musicmatch.com
SIC: 7372 5734 Prepackaged software; software, business & non-game
PA: Altaba Inc.
140 E 45th St Ste 15a
New York NY 10017

(P-24185)
MY EYE MEDIA LLC
2211 N Hollywood Way, Burbank (91505-1113)
PHONE...................818 559-7200
Michael Kadenacy, *President*
Rodd Feingold, *CFO*
Jane C Hawley, *Senior VP*
EMP: 43
SQ FT: 20,000
SALES (est): 13.2MM
SALES (corp-wide): 866.9K **Privately Held**
WEB: www.myeyemedia.com
SIC: 7372 Business oriented computer software
HQ: Eurofins Product Testing Us Holdings, Inc.
11720 N Creek Pkwy N # 400
Bothell WA 98011
800 383-0085

(P-24186)
MYENERSAVE INC
Also Called: Bidgely
440 N Wolfe Rd, Sunnyvale (94085-3869)
PHONE...................408 464-6385
Abhay Gupta, *CEO*
Lior Matkovitch, *Manager*
EMP: 11
SALES (est): 635K **Privately Held**
SIC: 7372 Utility computer software

(P-24187)
MYWAY LEARNING COMPANY INC
47 Laurel Ave, Larkspur (94939-1910)
PHONE...................415 937-1722
John Mayerhofer, *CEO*
EMP: 10
SALES (est): 260.9K **Privately Held**
SIC: 7372 Educational computer software

(P-24188)
NAZCA SOLUTIONS INC
4 First American Way, Santa Ana (92707-5913)
PHONE...................612 279-6100
Robert Karraa, *President*
Ted Mondale, *Vice Pres*
EMP: 20
SQ FT: 45,000
SALES (est): 897.9K **Publicly Held**
WEB: www.nazcainc.com
SIC: 7372 Application computer software
PA: First American Financial Corporation
1 First American Way
Santa Ana CA 92707

(P-24189)
NC INTERACTIVE LLC
1900 S Norfolk St Ste 125, San Mateo (94403-1175)
PHONE...................650 393-2200
Songyee Yoon, *CEO*
Eric Garay, *CFO*
Janet Lin, *General Counsel*
EMP: 99 **EST:** 2016
SQ FT: 16,692
SALES (est): 1.4MM **Privately Held**
SIC: 7372 Prepackaged software

(P-24190)
NCOUP INC
825 Corporate Way, Fremont (94539-6115)
PHONE...................510 739-4010
John S McLlwain, *President*
Kamar Aulakh, *COO*
Amar Chahal, *Exec VP*
Gabriel Romero, *Technical Mgr*
Avinash Yadav, *Engineer*
EMP: 40
SALES (est): 6.3MM **Privately Held**
WEB: www.velos.com
SIC: 7372 Publishers' computer software

(P-24191)
NEATPOCKET LLC
8033 W Sunset Blvd, West Hollywood (90046-2401)
PHONE...................323 632-7440
Aidan Marus, *CEO*
EMP: 12

SALES (est): 309.8K **Privately Held**
SIC: 7372 Business oriented computer software

(P-24192)
NET OPTICS INC
Also Called: Ixia
5301 Stevens Creek Blvd, Santa Clara (95051-7201)
PHONE...................408 737-7777
Thomas B Miller, *CEO*
Robert Shaw, *President*
Dennis Omanoff, *COO*
Burt Podbere, *CFO*
Nadine Matityahu, *Corp Secy*
EMP: 85
SQ FT: 39,000
SALES (est): 9MM
SALES (corp-wide): 3.8B **Publicly Held**
WEB: www.netoptics.com
SIC: 7372 Operating systems computer software
HQ: Ixia
26601 Agoura Rd
Calabasas CA 91302
818 871-1800

(P-24193)
NETAPHOR SOFTWARE INC
15510 Rockfield Blvd C100, Irvine (92618-2726)
PHONE...................949 470-7955
Rakesh Mahajan, *CEO*
Shripathi Kamath, *Officer*
Robert Russell, *Manager*
EMP: 11
SQ FT: 2,700
SALES (est): 950K **Privately Held**
WEB: www.netaphor.com
SIC: 7372 Business oriented computer software

(P-24194)
NETCUBE SYSTEMS INC
1275 Arbor Ave, Los Altos (94024-5330)
PHONE...................650 862-7858
Mallikarjuna Reddy, *President*
EMP: 75
SQ FT: 1,000
SALES: 35MM **Privately Held**
SIC: 7372 7379 7371 7361 Application computer software; computer related consulting services; custom computer programming services; employment agencies

(P-24195)
NETSARANG INC
4701 P Henry Dr 137, Santa Clara (95054)
PHONE...................669 204-3301
Andrew Wonik Chang, *Vice Pres*
EMP: 12
SALES: 400K **Privately Held**
SIC: 7372 Prepackaged software

(P-24196)
NETSOL TECHNOLOGIES INC (PA)
23975 Park Sorrento # 250, Calabasas (91302-4016)
PHONE...................818 222-9197
Najeeb Ghauri, *Ch of Bd*
Johannes Riedl, *Partner*
Umar Qadri, *COO*
Boo Ali, *CFO*
Roger Almond, *CFO*
EMP: 41
SQ FT: 5,000
SALES: 60.9MM **Publicly Held**
WEB: www.netsoltech.com
SIC: 7372 7373 7299 Business oriented computer software; computer integrated systems design; personal document & information services

(P-24197)
NETSUITE INC (DH)
Also Called: Oracle
2955 Campus Dr Ste 100, San Mateo (94403-2539)
PHONE...................650 627-1000
Dorian Daley, *President*
Erica Prado, *President*
Evan Goldberg, *Exec VP*
Jim McGeever, *Exec VP*
Gary Wiessinger, *Exec VP*

(PA)=Parent Co (HQ)=Headquarters (DH)=Div Headquarters
✪ = New Business established in last 2 years

EMP: 148
SQ FT: 165,000
SALES: 741.1MM
SALES (corp-wide): 39.5B **Publicly Held**
SIC: 7372 Business oriented computer
software
HQ: Oc Acquisition Llc
500 Oracle Pkwy
Redwood City CA 94065
650 506-7000

(P-24198)
NETWORK AUTOMATION INC
3530 Wilshire Blvd # 1800, Los Angeles
(90010-2335)
PHONE...................................213 738-1700
Dustin Snell, *CEO*
Graham Taylor, *CTO*
Carmiel Banasky, *Marketing Staff*
Esther Suh, *Agent*
EMP: 50
SQ FT: 9,000
SALES (est): 3.6MM
SALES (corp-wide): 79.8MM **Privately
Held**
WEB: www.networkautomation.com
SIC: 7372 Business oriented computer
software
PA: Help/Systems, Llc
6455 City West Pkwy
Eden Prairie MN 55344
952 933-0609

(P-24199)
NETWORK VIGILANCE LLC
12121 Scripps Summit Dr # 320, San Diego
(92131-4608)
PHONE...................................858 695-8676
Peter Bybee,
Gayle Bybee,
EMP: 18
SQ FT: 4,000
SALES (est): 3.9MM **Privately Held**
SIC: 7372 7375 Application computer soft-
ware; information retrieval services

(P-24200)
NETWRIX CORPORATION (PA)
300 Spectrum Center Dr # 200, Irvine
(92618-4925)
PHONE...................................888 638-9749
Steve Dickson, *CEO*
Ryan Schertzer, *Vice Pres*
Oleg Lalaev, *Technical Staff*
Paul Trufanoff, *Technical Staff*
Bob Cordisco, *Engineer*
EMP: 38
SQ FT: 12,000
SALES (est): 10.6MM **Privately Held**
SIC: 7372 Business oriented computer
software

(P-24201)
NEW BI US GAMING LLC
10920 Via Frontera # 420, San Diego
(92127-1729)
PHONE...................................858 592-2472
Ian Bonner, *CEO*
Kimberly Armstrong, *Vice Pres*
Russell Schechter, *Vice Pres*
EMP: 92 EST: 2012
SALES (est): 6MM **Privately Held**
SIC: 7372 Prepackaged software

(P-24202)
NEW CAM COMMERCE SOLUTIONS LLC
5555 Garden Grove Blvd # 100, Westmin-
ster (92683-8227)
PHONE...................................714 338-0200
Doug Roberson, *Mng Member*
EMP: 77
SQ FT: 26,000
SALES (est): 5.9MM
SALES (corp-wide): 21.3MM **Privately
Held**
SIC: 7372 Business oriented computer
software
PA: Celerant Technology Corp.
4830 Arthur Kill Rd Ste 3
Staten Island NY 10309
718 351-2000

(P-24203)
NEW GENERATION SOFTWARE INC
Also Called: N G S
3835 N Freeway Blvd # 200, Sacramento
(95834-1954)
PHONE...................................916 920-2200
Bernard B Gough, *CEO*
John O'Sullivan, *Executive*
Eric Bassett, *Technology*
Jeff Pearson, *Manager*
EMP: 45
SQ FT: 10,000
SALES (est): 6.2MM **Privately Held**
WEB: www.ngsi.com
SIC: 7372 Application computer software;
utility computer software

(P-24204)
NEW RELIC INC (PA)
188 Spear St Ste 1200, San Francisco
(94105-1750)
PHONE...................................650 777-7600
Lewis Cirne, *CEO*
Ana Valarezo, *Partner*
Peter Fenton, *Ch of Bd*
Mark Sachleben, *CFO*
Matthew Flaming, *Vice Pres*
EMP: 148
SQ FT: 73,391
SALES: 479.2MM **Publicly Held**
SIC: 7372 Application computer software

(P-24205)
NEWERA SOFTWARE INC
18625 Sutter Blvd Ste 950, Morgan Hill
(95037-8122)
P.O. Box 1797 (95038-1797)
PHONE...................................408 520-7100
Glen Bagsby, *President*
EMP: 14
SQ FT: 650
SALES (est): 1.7MM **Privately Held**
SIC: 7372 Business oriented computer
software

(P-24206)
NEXTGEN HEALTHCARE INC (PA)
18111 Von Karman Ave # 8, Irvine
(92612-0199)
PHONE...................................949 255-2600
John R Frantz, *President*
Craig A Barbarosh, *Vice Ch Bd*
Jeffrey D Linton, *Exec VP*
David A Metcalfe, *Exec VP*
Bailey Bachman, *Executive*
EMP: 148
SQ FT: 83,100
SALES: 529.1MM **Publicly Held**
WEB: www.qsii.com
SIC: 7372 7373 Prepackaged software;
computer integrated systems design

(P-24207)
NGMOCO INC
185 Berry St Ste 2400, San Francisco
(94107-1750)
PHONE...................................415 375-3170
Clive Downie, *CEO*
Neil Young, *President*
Joanna Drake Earl, *COO*
Joseph Keene, *CFO*
Michael Staskin, *Chief Mktg Ofcr*
EMP: 10
SALES (est): 2MM **Privately Held**
SIC: 7372 Prepackaged software
PA: Dena Co., Ltd.
2-21-1, Shibuya
Shibuya-Ku TKY 150-0
-

(P-24208)
NIGHTINGALE VANTAGEMED CORP (HQ)
10670 White Rock Rd, Rancho Cordova
(95670-6095)
PHONE...................................916 638-4744
Steven Curd, *COO*
Mark Cameron, *COO*
Liesel Loesch, *CFO*
Richard Altinger, *Vice Pres*
Jennifer Bentley, *VP Mktg*
EMP: 55

SALES (est): 10.6MM **Privately Held**
WEB: www.vantagemed.com
SIC: 7372 Business oriented computer
software
PA: Nexia Health Technologies Inc
15 Allstate Prkwy 6th Fl
Markham ON L3R 5
905 415-3063

(P-24209)
NIS AMERICA INC
4 Hutton Cntre Dr Ste 650, Santa Ana
(92707)
PHONE...................................714 540-1199
Souhei Niikawa, *CEO*
Harusato Akenaga, *President*
Johanna Hirota, *CFO*
Mitsuharu Hiraoka, *Vice Pres*
Mizuki Nishida, *Production*
▲ EMP: 40
SQ FT: 1,000
SALES (est): 5MM **Privately Held**
WEB: www.nisamerica.com
SIC: 7372 Publishers' computer software
PA: Nipponichi K.K.
1-8-4, Nihombashihoridomecho
Chuo-Ku TKY
-

(P-24210)
NOK NOK LABS INC
2890 Zanker Rd Ste 203, San Jose
(95134-2118)
PHONE...................................650 433-1300
Phil Dunkelberger, *CEO*
Jonas Lamis, *Vice Pres*
David Wiener, *Vice Pres*
Matthew Lourie, *Surgery Dir*
Heather Cowper, *Administration*
EMP: 16
SALES (est): 1.9MM **Privately Held**
SIC: 7372 Business oriented computer
software

(P-24211)
NOMINUM INC
3355 Scott Blvd Fl 3, Santa Clara
(95054-3127)
PHONE...................................650 381-6000
Garry Messiana, *CEO*
Gopala Tumuluri, *COO*
Bob Verheecke, *CFO*
Pete Wisowaty, *Exec VP*
Srini Avirneni, *Senior VP*
EMP: 50
SQ FT: 15,000
SALES (est): 26.9MM
SALES (corp-wide): 2.7B **Publicly Held**
WEB: www.nominum.com
SIC: 7372 Prepackaged software
PA: Akamai Technologies, Inc.
150 Broadway Ste 100
Cambridge MA 02142
617 444-3000

(P-24212)
NOVASTOR CORPORATION (PA)
29209 Canwood St Ste 200, Agoura Hills
(91301-1908)
PHONE...................................805 579-6700
Peter Means, *President*
Martin Albert, *Chairman*
EMP: 30
SQ FT: 7,800
SALES (est): 5.6MM **Privately Held**
WEB: www.no-panic.com
SIC: 7372 7371 5734 Business oriented
computer software; custom computer pro-
gramming services; software, business &
non-game

(P-24213)
NPHASE INC
323 Neptune Ave, Encinitas (92024-2521)
PHONE...................................805 750-8580
Scott A Climes, *CEO*
EMP: 20 EST: 2014
SALES (est): 421K **Privately Held**
SIC: 7372 Business oriented computer
software

(P-24214)
NTN BUZZTIME INC (PA)
1800 Aston Ave Ste 100, Carlsbad
(92008-7399)
PHONE...................................760 438-7400

Allen Wolff, *CEO*
Gregg Thomas, *Ch of Bd*
Steve Mitgang, *Bd of Directors*
Sandra Gurrola, *VP Finance*
▲ EMP: 137
SQ FT: 28,000
SALES: 23.3MM **Publicly Held**
WEB: www.ntnwireless.com
SIC: 7372 7922 7929 7359 Application
computer software; entertainment promo-
tion; entertainment service; equipment
rental & leasing

(P-24215)
NTRUST INFOTECH INC
230 Commerce Ste 180, Irvine
(92602-1336)
PHONE...................................562 207-1600
Srikanth Ramachandran, *CEO*
Kevin C Harrigan, *Vice Pres*
Manoj Kumar, *Vice Pres*
Ramesh Narayanan, *Vice Pres*
Sameer Sarvate, *Vice Pres*
EMP: 65 EST: 2003
SALES (est): 6.5MM **Privately Held**
SIC: 7372 7371 Business oriented com-
puter software; computer software devel-
opment & applications
PA: Ntrust Infotech Private Limited
3rd Floor Ganesh Towers
Chennai TN 60000

(P-24216)
NUMECENT INC
530 Technology Dr Ste 375, Irvine
(92618-3505)
PHONE...................................949 833-2800
Tom Lagatta, *CEO*
Osman Kent, *Ch of Bd*
Ed Corrente, *CFO*
Hildy Shandell, *CFO*
EMP: 30 EST: 2012
SALES (est): 3.6MM **Privately Held**
SIC: 7372 Application computer software

(P-24217)
NUORDER INC (PA)
1901 Avenue Of The Stars, Los Angeles
(90067-6001)
PHONE...................................310 954-1313
Heath Wells, *CEO*
Adam Schneider, *COO*
Danny Essner, *Senior VP*
Kevin Sagarchi, *Executive*
Brittany Worthy, *Executive*
EMP: 20
SALES (est): 5.6MM **Privately Held**
SIC: 7372 Application computer software

(P-24218)
NURSESBOND INC
26386 Primrose Way, Moreno Valley
(92555-2239)
P.O. Box 9258 (92552-9258)
PHONE...................................951 286-8537
Chibunna Nwaobia, *CEO*
EMP: 10
SALES: 250K **Privately Held**
SIC: 7372 8299 Application computer soft-
ware; educational service; nondegree
granting: continuing educ.

(P-24219)
NWP SERVICES CORPORATION (HQ)
535 Anton Blvd Ste 1100, Costa Mesa
(92626-7699)
P.O. Box 19661, Irvine (92623-9661)
PHONE...................................949 253-2500
Ron Reed, *President*
Lana Reeve,
Mike Haviken, *Exec VP*
Monique Black, *Human Resources*
Bob Smolarski, *Opers Staff*
EMP: 141
SQ FT: 21,171
SALES (est): 48.8MM
SALES (corp-wide): 869.4MM **Publicly
Held**
WEB: www.nwpco.com
SIC: 7372 8721 Utility computer software;
billing & bookkeeping service

▲ = Import ▼=Export
◆ =Import/Export

PA: Realpage, Inc.
2201 Lakeside Blvd
Richardson TX 75082
972 820-3000

(P-24220)
NYANSA INC
430 Cowper St Ste 250, Palo Alto
(94301-1579)
PHONE...................................650 446-7818
Abe Ankumah, *CEO*
Daniel Kan, *Vice Pres*
Anand Srinivas, *CTO*
David Callisch, *VP Mktg*
Jason Reese, *VP Sales*
EMP: 45
SALES: 3MM **Privately Held**
SIC: 7372 Application computer software

(P-24221)
ODDWORLD INHABITANTS INC
869 Monterey St, San Luis Obispo
(93401-3224)
PHONE...................................805 503-3000
Sherry McKenna, *CEO*
Lorne Lanning, *President*
Maurice Konkle, *COO*
Raymond Swanland, *Production*
EMP: 60
SQ FT: 15,000
SALES (est): 2.4MM **Privately Held**
WEB: www.oddworld.com
SIC: 7372 Application computer software

(P-24222)
OKTA INC (PA)
100 1st St Ste 600, San Francisco
(94105-2634)
PHONE...................................888 722-7871
Todd McKinnon, *Ch of Bd*
Natasha Bhargava, *Partner*
Charles Race, *President*
J Frederic Kerrest, *COO*
William E Losch, *CFO*
EMP: 148
SQ FT: 207,066
SALES: 399.2MM **Publicly Held**
SIC: 7372 7371 Prepackaged software;
software programming applications

(P-24223)
OKTA INC
Also Called: Stormpath
172 Lakeshore Dr, San Mateo
(94402-3624)
PHONE...................................650 348-2620
EMP: 16
SALES (corp-wide): 399.2MM **Publicly
Held**
SIC: 7372 Business oriented computer
software
PA: Okta, Inc.
100 1st St Ste 600
San Francisco CA 94105
888 722-7871

(P-24224)
OMNITRACS MIDCO LLC (PA)
9276 Scranton Rd Ste 200, San Diego
(92121-7703)
PHONE...................................858 651-5812
EMP: 33
SALES (est): 102MM **Privately Held**
SIC: 7372 Business oriented computer
software

(P-24225)
**OMNIVORE TECHNOLOGIES
INC**
1191 B St, Hayward (94541)
PHONE...................................800 293-4058
Mike Wior, *CEO*
Andrew Hyde, *CFO*
Andy Hyde, *CFO*
Shane Wheatland, *Chief Mktg Ofcr*
Matt Haselhoff, *Vice Pres*
EMP: 30
SQ FT: 3,500
SALES (est): 165K **Privately Held**
SIC: 7372 Business oriented computer
software

(P-24226)
ON24 INC (PA)
50 Beale St Ste 800, San Francisco
(94105-1863)
PHONE...................................877 202-9599
Sharat Sharan, *President*
Ian Halifax, *CFO*
Joe Hyland, *Chief Mktg Ofcr*
Mike Badgis, *Vice Pres*
Mahesh Kheny, *Vice Pres*
EMP: 350
SQ FT: 28,353
SALES (est): 81.9MM **Privately Held**
WEB: www.on24.com
SIC: 7372 Business oriented computer
software

(P-24227)
ONC HOLDINGS INC
Also Called: Gobeme
832 Folsom St Ste 1001, San Francisco
(94107-1142)
PHONE...................................415 243-3343
David Kochbeck, *CEO*
Jim Bertoldi, *CFO*
Christian Mackey, *Director*
Dominic Rotondi, *Director*
EMP: 12 EST: 2013
SALES (est): 739.4K **Privately Held**
SIC: 7372 Educational computer software

(P-24228)
**OPEN DMAIN SPHINX SLTIONS
CORP**
3871 Piedmont Ave 300, Oakland
(94611-5378)
PHONE...................................510 420-0846
Ernst-Dietrich Wecker, *President*
EMP: 12
SALES (est): 326.9K **Privately Held**
WEB: www.odsphinx.com
SIC: 7372 7371 Prepackaged software;
computer software development & appli-
cations

(P-24229)
OPENCLOVIS SOLUTIONS INC
765 Baywood Dr Ste 336, Petaluma
(94954-5507)
PHONE...................................707 981-7120
Hong Lu, *President*
Vk Budhraja, *CEO*
EMP: 26
SALES (est): 1.5MM **Privately Held**
SIC: 7372 Business oriented computer
software

(P-24230)
OPENPRO INC
Also Called: Openpro Erp Software
10061 Talbert Ave Ste 228, Fountain Valley
(92708-5159)
PHONE...................................714 378-4600
James Clark, *CEO*
Thomas Vinje, *Partner*
Shannon G Clark, *CFO*
Jason Park, *Accounts Mgr*
EMP: 12
SQ FT: 2,500
SALES (est): 1.3MM **Privately Held**
WEB: www.openpro.com
SIC: 7372 Business oriented computer
software

(P-24231)
OPENTV INC (DH)
Also Called: Nagra
275 Sacramento St Ste Sl1, San Francisco
(94111-3831)
PHONE...................................415 962-5000
Yves Pitton, *CEO*
Andr Kudelski, *CEO*
Wesley O Hoffman, *COO*
Pamela Creamer, *CFO*
Shum Mukherjee, *CFO*
EMP: 150
SALES (est): 78.6MM
SALES (corp-wide): 919.6MM **Privately
Held**
SIC: 7372 Prepackaged software

(P-24232)
OPENWAVE MOBILITY INC (PA)
400 Seaport Ct Ste 104, Redwood City
(94063-2799)
PHONE...................................650 480-7200

John Paul Giere, *President*
Poh Sim Gan, *CFO*
Aman Brar, *Vice Pres*
Dean Liming, *Vice Pres*
Thao Ly, *Technical Staff*
EMP: 35
SALES (est): 9.6MM **Privately Held**
SIC: 7372 Prepackaged software

(P-24233)
OPERA COMMERCE LLC
1875 S Grant St Ste 800, San Mateo
(94402-7014)
PHONE...................................650 625-1262
Sameer Merchant,
Nadine Jarrard, *Vice Pres*
Daniel Nordberg, *Business Dir*
Benjamin Kaufman, *Principal*
Melissa Coleman, *Sales Dir*
EMP: 10
SALES (est): 614.1K
SALES (corp-wide): 264.1MM **Privately
Held**
SIC: 7372 Prepackaged software
PA: Otello Corporation Asa
Gjerdrums Vei 19
Oslo 0484
236 924-00

(P-24234)
**OPERA SOFTWARE AMERICAS
LLC**
1875 S Grant St Ste 750, San Mateo
(94402-2670)
PHONE...................................650 625-1262
Lars Boilesen, *CEO*
John Metzger, *President*
Erik C Harrell, *CFO*
Mahi De Silva, *Exec VP*
Meghan Oshea, *Sales Staff*
EMP: 13
SALES (est): 1.6MM **Privately Held**
SIC: 7372 Prepackaged software
PA: Opera Limited
Maples Corporate Services Limited
George Town GR CAYMAN

(P-24235)
OPSVEDA INC
4030 Moorpark Ave Ste 107, San Jose
(95117-1848)
PHONE...................................408 628-0461
Sanjiv Gupta, *President*
Harsh Vardhan Pant, *Vice Pres*
Dinesh Somani, *Vice Pres*
EMP: 19 EST: 2010
SALES (est): 6.5MM **Privately Held**
SIC: 7372 7371 Business oriented com-
puter software; computer software devel-
opment

(P-24236)
OPTIMIS SERVICES INC
225 Mantua Rd, Pacific Palisades
(90272-3349)
PHONE...................................310 230-2780
Alan Morelli, *President*
EMP: 22
SALES (est): 730.9K **Privately Held**
SIC: 7372 Business oriented computer
software

(P-24237)
**OPTIMUM SOLUTIONS GROUP
LLC**
419 Ponderosa Ct, Lafayette (94549-1812)
PHONE...................................415 954-7100
G John Houtary,
Lisa Massman,
EMP: 109
SQ FT: 3,300
SALES (est): 4.6MM
SALES (corp-wide): 3.3B **Privately Held**
WEB: www.optimumsolutions.com
SIC: 7372 7371 8243 7374 Prepackaged
software; computer software systems
analysis & design, custom; data process-
ing schools; computer graphics service
PA: Kpmg Llp
345 Park Ave Lowr Ll4
New York NY 10154
212 758-9700

(P-24238)
ORACLE AMERICA INC
Also Called: Sun Microsystems
4220 Network Cir, Santa Clara
(95054-1780)
PHONE...................................408 276-4300
Mark Toliver, *President*
Daniele Knab, *Technical Staff*
Peter Lam, *Technical Staff*
Valerie Peng, *Technical Staff*
Hang Vo, *Technical Staff*
EMP: 187
SALES (corp-wide): 39.5B **Publicly Held**
SIC: 7372 Prepackaged software
HQ: Oracle America, Inc.
500 Oracle Pkwy
Redwood City CA 94065
650 506-7000

(P-24239)
ORACLE AMERICA INC
Also Called: Sun Microsystems
1001 Sunset Blvd, Rocklin (95765-3702)
PHONE...................................303 272-6473
Mark Kulaga, *Branch Mgr*
Chris Wilson, *Branch Mgr*
Arieh Markel, *Software Engr*
Joe Darschewski, *Project Mgr*
EMP: 15
SALES (corp-wide): 39.5B **Publicly Held**
SIC: 7372 Prepackaged software
HQ: Oracle America, Inc.
500 Oracle Pkwy
Redwood City CA 94065
650 506-7000

(P-24240)
ORACLE AMERICA INC
475 Sansome St Fl 15, San Francisco
(94111-3166)
PHONE...................................415 908-3609
EMP: 58
SALES (corp-wide): 39.5B **Publicly Held**
SIC: 7372 Prepackaged software
HQ: Oracle America, Inc.
500 Oracle Pkwy
Redwood City CA 94065
650 506-7000

(P-24241)
ORACLE AMERICA INC
600 Oracle Pkwy, Redwood City
(94065-1603)
PHONE...................................408 702-5945
EMP: 17
SALES (corp-wide): 39.5B **Publicly Held**
SIC: 7372 Prepackaged software
HQ: Oracle America, Inc.
500 Oracle Pkwy
Redwood City CA 94065
650 506-7000

(P-24242)
ORACLE AMERICA INC
4120 Network Cir, Santa Clara
(95054-1778)
PHONE...................................408 276-3331
Scott G McNealy, *Ch of Bd*
Ashok Krishnamurthi, *CEO*
Karen Willem, *CFO*
Rick Fabiano, *Principal*
Mark Leslie, *Principal*
EMP: 150
SALES (est): 16.3MM **Privately Held**
WEB: www.xsigo.com
SIC: 7372 Prepackaged software

(P-24243)
ORACLE AMERICA INC
Also Called: Sun Microsystems
5815 Owens Dr, Pleasanton (94588-3939)
PHONE...................................925 694-3314
Terri Beck, *Manager*
EMP: 75
SALES (corp-wide): 39.5B **Publicly Held**
SIC: 7372 Prepackaged software
HQ: Oracle America, Inc.
500 Oracle Pkwy
Redwood City CA 94065
650 506-7000

P
R
O
D
U
C
T
S

&

S
V
C
S

(P-24244)
ORACLE AMERICA INC
Also Called: Sun Microsystems
15821 Ventura Blvd # 270, Encino
(91436-2915)
PHONE..........................818 905-0200
Stephen McKenna, *Technical Staff*
Card Pregozen, *Engineer*
EMP: 21
SALES (corp-wide): 39.5B **Publicly Held**
SIC: 7372 Prepackaged software
HQ: Oracle America, Inc.
    500 Oracle Pkwy
    Redwood City CA 94065
    650 506-7000

(P-24245)
ORACLE AMERICA INC
Also Called: Sun Microsystems
9540 Towne Centre Dr, San Diego
(92121-1988)
PHONE..........................858 625-5044
Steven Nathan, *Manager*
EMP: 77
SALES (corp-wide): 39.5B **Publicly Held**
SIC: 7372 Prepackaged software
HQ: Oracle America, Inc.
    500 Oracle Pkwy
    Redwood City CA 94065
    650 506-7000

(P-24246)
ORACLE AMERICA INC
Also Called: Sun Microsystems
3401 Centre Lake Dr # 410, Ontario
(91761-1201)
PHONE..........................909 605-0222
Clyde Johnston, *Branch Mgr*
EMP: 15
SALES (corp-wide): 39.5B **Publicly Held**
SIC: 7372 Prepackaged software
HQ: Oracle America, Inc.
    500 Oracle Pkwy
    Redwood City CA 94065
    650 506-7000

(P-24247)
ORACLE AMERICA INC
Also Called: Sun Microsystems
4230 Leonard Stocking Dr, Santa Clara
(95054-1777)
PHONE..........................408 276-7534
Denise Shiffman, *VP Mktg*
Larry Williams, *COO*
Joe Fuentes, *Comms Mgr*
Michael Connaughton, *General Mgr*
William H Howard, *CIO*
EMP: 250
SALES (corp-wide): 39.5B **Publicly Held**
SIC: 7372 Prepackaged software
HQ: Oracle America, Inc.
    500 Oracle Pkwy
    Redwood City CA 94065
    650 506-7000

(P-24248)
ORACLE CORPORATION
279 Barnes Rd, Tustin (92782-3748)
PHONE..........................713 654-0919
John Czapko, *Branch Mgr*
EMP: 191
SALES (corp-wide): 39.5B **Publicly Held**
SIC: 7372 Business oriented computer
    software
PA: Oracle Corporation
    500 Oracle Pkwy
    Redwood City CA 94065
    650 506-7000

(P-24249)
ORACLE CORPORATION
475 Sansome St Fl 15, San Francisco
(94111-3166)
PHONE..........................415 834-9731
Lisa Schwarz, *Director*
Niraj Hegdekar, *Software Engr*
Hang Du, *Technical Staff*
Gaurang Mavadiya, *Technical Staff*
Peter Yap, *Technical Staff*
EMP: 32
SALES (corp-wide): 39.5B **Publicly Held**
SIC: 7372 Prepackaged software
PA: Oracle Corporation
    500 Oracle Pkwy
    Redwood City CA 94065
    650 506-7000

(P-24250)
ORACLE CORPORATION
214 Clarence Ave, Sunnyvale
(94086-5907)
PHONE..........................650 607-5402
Jitendra Chinthakindi, *Principal*
EMP: 302
SALES (corp-wide): 39.5B **Publicly Held**
SIC: 7372 Business oriented computer
    software
PA: Oracle Corporation
    500 Oracle Pkwy
    Redwood City CA 94065
    650 506-7000

(P-24251)
ORACLE CORPORATION
1408 Antigua Ln, Foster City (94404-3970)
PHONE..........................650 678-3612
ARA Michaelian, *Principal*
EMP: 302
SALES (corp-wide): 39.5B **Publicly Held**
SIC: 7372 Business oriented computer
    software
PA: Oracle Corporation
    500 Oracle Pkwy
    Redwood City CA 94065
    650 506-7000

(P-24252)
ORACLE CORPORATION
1490 Newhall St, Santa Clara
(95050-6135)
PHONE..........................408 421-2890
Stephanie Camarda, *Principal*
EMP: 302
SALES (corp-wide): 39.5B **Publicly Held**
SIC: 7372 Business oriented computer
    software
PA: Oracle Corporation
    500 Oracle Pkwy
    Redwood City CA 94065
    650 506-7000

(P-24253)
ORACLE CORPORATION
231 Kerry Dr, Santa Clara (95050-6603)
PHONE..........................408 276-5552
Annie Van Dalen, *Principal*
Abhijit Kumar, *Technology*
EMP: 302
SALES (corp-wide): 39.5B **Publicly Held**
SIC: 7372 Business oriented computer
    software
PA: Oracle Corporation
    500 Oracle Pkwy
    Redwood City CA 94065
    650 506-7000

(P-24254)
ORACLE CORPORATION
3084 Thurman Dr, San Jose (95148-3143)
PHONE..........................408 276-3822
Alasdair Rendall, *Principal*
Mehdi Syed, *Software Engr*
EMP: 302
SALES (corp-wide): 39.5B **Publicly Held**
SIC: 7372 Business oriented computer
    software
PA: Oracle Corporation
    500 Oracle Pkwy
    Redwood City CA 94065
    650 506-7000

(P-24255)
ORACLE CORPORATION
9890 Towne Centre Dr # 150, San Diego
(92121-1999)
PHONE..........................858 202-0648
EMP: 191
SALES (corp-wide): 39.5B **Publicly Held**
SIC: 7372 Business oriented computer
    software
PA: Oracle Corporation
    500 Oracle Pkwy
    Redwood City CA 94065
    650 506-7000

(P-24256)
ORACLE CORPORATION
3532 Eastin Pl, Santa Clara (95051-2600)
PHONE..........................650 506-9864
Maneesh Jain, *Principal*
Gia Nguyen, *Senior Engr*
EMP: 302

(P-24257)
SALES (corp-wide): 39.5B **Publicly Held**
SIC: 7372 Business oriented computer
    software
PA: Oracle Corporation
    500 Oracle Pkwy
    Redwood City CA 94065
    650 506-7000

(P-24257)
ORACLE CORPORATION
372 Calero Ave, San Jose (95123-4315)
PHONE..........................408 390-8623
Aileen F Casanave, *Principal*
EMP: 302
SALES (corp-wide): 39.5B **Publicly Held**
SIC: 7372 Business oriented computer
    software
PA: Oracle Corporation
    500 Oracle Pkwy
    Redwood City CA 94065
    650 506-7000

(P-24258)
ORACLE CORPORATION
525 Market St, San Francisco
(94105-2708)
PHONE..........................415 402-7200
Victor Coskey, *Principal*
Rafiul Ahad, *Vice Pres*
Trey Parsons, *Vice Pres*
Sivarami Pothula, *Administration*
Eric Tran, *Administration*
EMP: 191
SALES (corp-wide): 39.5B **Publicly Held**
SIC: 7372 Business oriented computer
    software
PA: Oracle Corporation
    500 Oracle Pkwy
    Redwood City CA 94065
    650 506-7000

(P-24259)
ORACLE CORPORATION
6224 Hummingbird Ln, Rocklin
(95765-5929)
P.O. Box 3442 (95677-8469)
PHONE..........................916 435-8342
Richard Gless, *Principal*
Elishia Duran, *Analyst*
EMP: 302
SALES (corp-wide): 39.5B **Publicly Held**
SIC: 7372 Business oriented computer
    software
PA: Oracle Corporation
    500 Oracle Pkwy
    Redwood City CA 94065
    650 506-7000

(P-24260)
ORACLE CORPORATION
5805 Owens Dr, Pleasanton (94588-3939)
PHONE..........................877 767-2253
Bor R Fu, *Senior VP*
Clement Sciammas, *Vice Pres*
Kevin Zhou, *Sr Software Eng*
David Laux, *Technical Staff*
Meena Palani, *Technical Staff*
EMP: 315
SALES (corp-wide): 39.5B **Publicly Held**
SIC: 7372 Business oriented computer
    software
PA: Oracle Corporation
    500 Oracle Pkwy
    Redwood City CA 94065
    650 506-7000

(P-24261)
ORACLE CORPORATION
3925 Emerald Isle Ln, San Jose
(95135-1708)
PHONE..........................925 694-6258
Johnson Aremu, *Principal*
EMP: 306
SALES (corp-wide): 39.5B **Publicly Held**
SIC: 7372 Business oriented computer
    software
PA: Oracle Corporation
    500 Oracle Pkwy
    Redwood City CA 94065
    650 506-7000

(P-24262)
ORACLE CORPORATION
5863 Carmel Way, Union City
(94587-5170)
PHONE..........................510 471-6971

Renzo Zagni, *Principal*
Terry Bowen, *Software Engr*
Roger Chan, *Software Engr*
Mark Chaney, *Software Engr*
John Holder, *Software Engr*
EMP: 302
SALES (corp-wide): 39.5B **Publicly Held**
SIC: 7372 Business oriented computer
    software
PA: Oracle Corporation
    500 Oracle Pkwy
    Redwood City CA 94065
    650 506-7000

(P-24263)
ORACLE CORPORATION
200 Crprate Pinte Ste 200, Culver City
(90230)
PHONE..........................310 258-7500
EMP: 302
SALES (corp-wide): 39.5B **Publicly Held**
SIC: 7372 Business oriented computer
    software
PA: Oracle Corporation
    500 Oracle Pkwy
    Redwood City CA 94065
    650 506-7000

(P-24264)
ORACLE CORPORATION
200 N Pacific Coast Hwy # 400, El Se-
gundo (90245-5628)
PHONE..........................310 343-7405
EMP: 306
SALES (corp-wide): 39.5B **Publicly Held**
SIC: 7372 Business oriented computer
    software
PA: Oracle Corporation
    500 Oracle Pkwy
    Redwood City CA 94065
    650 506-7000

(P-24265)
ORACLE CORPORATION
1001 Sunset Blvd, Rocklin (95765-3702)
PHONE..........................916 315-3500
Chris Wilson, *Branch Mgr*
Liz Brock, *Administration*
Pavel Buenitsky, *Info Tech Dir*
Steve Fitzgerald, *Info Tech Dir*
Marion Smith, *Info Tech Dir*
EMP: 500
SALES (corp-wide): 39.5B **Publicly Held**
SIC: 7372 7371 Business oriented com-
    puter software; custom computer pro-
    gramming services
PA: Oracle Corporation
    500 Oracle Pkwy
    Redwood City CA 94065
    650 506-7000

(P-24266)
ORACLE CORPORATION
475 Sansome St Fl 15, San Francisco
(94111-3166)
P.O. Box 44471 (94144-0001)
PHONE..........................650 506-7000
Brian Sheth, *Vice Pres*
Mark Han, *Principal*
Tanya Fitzgerald, *Admin Asst*
Sangheon Kim, *Sr Software Eng*
Ranju Rajan, *Info Tech Mgr*
EMP: 24
SALES (corp-wide): 39.5B **Publicly Held**
SIC: 7372 Prepackaged software
PA: Oracle Corporation
    500 Oracle Pkwy
    Redwood City CA 94065
    650 506-7000

(P-24267)
ORACLE SYSTEMS
CORPORATION
200 Crprate Pinte Ste 200, Culver City
(90230)
PHONE..........................818 817-2900
Elizabeth Deitz, *General Mgr*
Ram Ramachandran, *Sr Software Eng*
Kamal Fazah, *Technical Staff*
Lisa Schwartz, *Marketing Staff*
EMP: 70
SALES (corp-wide): 39.5B **Publicly Held**
WEB: www.forcecapital.com
SIC: 7372 Prepackaged software

HQ: Oracle Systems Corporation
500 Oracle Pkwy
Redwood City CA 94065
650 506-7000

(P-24268)
ORACLE SYSTEMS CORPORATION
102 Santa Barbara Ave, Daly City
(94014-1045)
PHONE...............................650 506-8648
EMP: 92
SALES (corp-wide): 39.5B **Publicly Held**
WEB: www.forcecapital.com
SIC: 7372 Prepackaged software
HQ: Oracle Systems Corporation
500 Oracle Pkwy
Redwood City CA 94065
650 506-7000

(P-24269)
ORACLE SYSTEMS CORPORATION
301 Island Pkwy, Belmont (94002-4109)
PHONE...............................650 654-7606
EMP: 304
SALES (corp-wide): 39.5B **Publicly Held**
SIC: 7372 Prepackaged software
HQ: Oracle Systems Corporation
500 Oracle Pkwy
Redwood City CA 94065
650 506-7000

(P-24270)
ORACLE SYSTEMS CORPORATION
500 Oracle Pkwy, San Mateo (94403)
PHONE...............................650 506-6780
Sayekumar Arumugam, *Principal*
EMP: 108
SALES (corp-wide): 39.5B **Publicly Held**
WEB: www.forcecapital.com
SIC: 7372 Prepackaged software
HQ: Oracle Systems Corporation
500 Oracle Pkwy
Redwood City CA 94065
650 506-7000

(P-24271)
ORACLE SYSTEMS CORPORATION
501 Island Pkwy, Belmont (94002-4153)
PHONE...............................650 506-5062
Michael Rocha, *Branch Mgr*
Scott Forten, *IT/INT Sup*
Sunil Pinto, *Technical Staff*
Seo Takeshi, *Technical Staff*
Shawn Woo, *Sales Staff*
EMP: 16
SALES (corp-wide): 39.5B **Publicly Held**
WEB: www.forcecapital.com
SIC: 7372 Prepackaged software
HQ: Oracle Systems Corporation
500 Oracle Pkwy
Redwood City CA 94065
650 506-7000

(P-24272)
ORACLE SYSTEMS CORPORATION
10 Twin Dolphin Dr, Redwood City
(94065-1035)
PHONE...............................650 506-0300
EMP: 252
SALES (corp-wide): 39.5B **Publicly Held**
WEB: www.forcecapital.com
SIC: 7372 Prepackaged software
HQ: Oracle Systems Corporation
500 Oracle Pkwy
Redwood City CA 94065
650 506-7000

(P-24273)
ORACLE SYSTEMS CORPORATION
Also Called: PeopleSoft
1840 Gateway Dr Ste 250, San Mateo
(94404-4027)
PHONE...............................650 378-1351
Martine Riente, *Manager*
Norma Robertson, *Administration*
EMP: 10
SALES (corp-wide): 39.5B **Publicly Held**
WEB: www.forcecapital.com
SIC: 7372 Prepackaged software

HQ: Oracle Systems Corporation
500 Oracle Pkwy
Redwood City CA 94065
650 506-7000

(P-24274)
ORACLE SYSTEMS CORPORATION
300 Oracle Pkwy, Redwood City
(94065-1667)
PHONE...............................650 506-5887
Sam Mohamad, *Vice Pres*
Azeez Zackriah, *Program Mgr*
Anupama Kartha, *Project Leader*
Sailen Saha, *Technical Staff*
Rishabh Jain, *Engineer*
EMP: 35
SALES (corp-wide): 39.5B **Publicly Held**
WEB: www.forcecapital.com
SIC: 7372 Prepackaged software
HQ: Oracle Systems Corporation
500 Oracle Pkwy
Redwood City CA 94065
650 506-7000

(P-24275)
ORACLE SYSTEMS CORPORATION
5840 Owens Dr, Pleasanton (94588-3900)
PHONE...............................925 694-3000
Apu Gupta, *Principal*
Peter Chen, *Manager*
Daniel Wright, *Consultant*
EMP: 252
SALES (corp-wide): 39.5B **Publicly Held**
WEB: www.forcecapital.com
SIC: 7372 5734 Prepackaged software;
software, business & non-game
HQ: Oracle Systems Corporation
500 Oracle Pkwy
Redwood City CA 94065
650 506-7000

(P-24276)
ORACLE SYSTEMS CORPORATION
2010 Main St Ste 450, Irvine (92614-7260)
PHONE...............................949 224-1000
Dawn Lotez, *Manager*
Jeff Hollenshead, *Network Enginr*
EMP: 100
SALES (corp-wide): 39.5B **Publicly Held**
WEB: www.forcecapital.com
SIC: 7372 Prepackaged software
HQ: Oracle Systems Corporation
500 Oracle Pkwy
Redwood City CA 94065
650 506-7000

(P-24277)
ORACLE SYSTEMS CORPORATION
17901 Von Karman Ave # 800, Irvine
(92614-6297)
PHONE...............................949 623-9460
EMP: 275
SALES (corp-wide): 39.5B **Publicly Held**
WEB: www.forcecapital.com
SIC: 7372 5045 Prepackaged software;
computers, peripherals & software
HQ: Oracle Systems Corporation
500 Oracle Pkwy
Redwood City CA 94065
650 506-7000

(P-24278)
ORACLE TALEO LLC
4140 Dublin Blvd Ste 400, Dublin
(94568-7757)
PHONE...............................925 452-3000
Dorian Daley, *President*
Eric Ball, *CFO*
Guy Gauvin, *Exec VP*
Neil Hudspith, *Exec VP*
Jason Blessing, *Senior VP*
EMP: 1164
SQ FT: 47,500
SALES (est): 95MM
SALES (corp-wide): 39.5B **Publicly Held**
WEB: www.taleo.com
SIC: 7372 Business oriented computer
software

PA: Oracle Corporation
500 Oracle Pkwy
Redwood City CA 94065
650 506-7000

(P-24279)
ORANGEGRID LLC
145 S State College Blvd # 350, Brea
(92821-5851)
PHONE...............................657 220-1519
Todd Mobraten, *Mng Member*
Owens Barry, *Vice Pres*
Werts Ryan, *Chief*
EMP: 28 **EST:** 2014
SALES (est): 2.4MM **Privately Held**
SIC: 7372 Prepackaged software

(P-24280)
OSR ENTERPRISES INC
1910 E Stowell Rd, Santa Maria
(93454-8002)
PHONE...............................805 925-1831
James O Rice, *CEO*
Owen S Rice, *Ch of Bd*
Betty E Rice, *Vice Pres*
EMP: 45
SQ FT: 1,500
SALES (est): 8.6MM **Privately Held**
WEB: www.osrent.com
SIC: 7372 Publishers' computer software

(P-24281)
OUTPUT INC
1418 N Spring St Ste 102, Los Angeles
(90012-1924)
PHONE...............................310 795-6099
Gregg Lehrmann, *President*
EMP: 18
SALES (est): 968.9K **Privately Held**
SIC: 7372 Application computer software

(P-24282)
OUTSYSTEMS INC
2603 Camino Ramon Ste 210, San Ramon
(94583-9136)
PHONE...............................925 804-6189
Paulo Rosado, *CEO*
EMP: 10
SALES (est): 836.4K
SALES (corp-wide): 177.9K **Privately Held**
SIC: 7372 Application computer software
HQ: Outsystems - Software Em Rede, S.A.
Rua Do Central Park, Edificio 2 2oa
Linda A Velha 2795-
214 153-730

(P-24283)
OWL TERRITORY INC
Also Called: Docrun
227 Broadway Ste 303, Santa Monica
(90401-3441)
PHONE...............................800 607-0677
EMP: 12 **EST:** 2011
SQ FT: 1,200
SALES (est): 820K **Privately Held**
SIC: 7372

(P-24284)
PACIOLAN LLC (DH)
Also Called: Ticketswest
5291 California Ave # 100, Irvine
(92617-3220)
PHONE...............................866 722-4652
Dave Butler, *CEO*
Jane Kleinberger, *Ch of Bd*
Kimberly Boren, *CFO*
Steve Shaw, *CFO*
Teri Clark, *Admin Sec*
EMP: 85 **EST:** 1980
SALES (est): 28.5MM **Privately Held**
WEB: www.paciolan.com
SIC: 7372 5045 Business oriented com-
puter software; computers
HQ: Learfield Communications, Llc
2400 Dallas Pkwy Ste 510
Plano TX 75093
336 464-0224

(P-24285)
PAGERDUTY INC (PA)
600 Townsend St Ste 200e, San Francisco
(94103-5690)
PHONE...............................844 800-3889
Jennifer G Tejada, *Ch of Bd*
Howard Wilson, *CFO*

Steven Chung, *Senior VP*
Stacey A Giamalis, *Senior VP*
Jonathan Rende, *Senior VP*
EMP: 143
SQ FT: 59,000
SALES: 117.8MM **Publicly Held**
WEB: www.pagerduty.com
SIC: 7372 Prepackaged software

(P-24286)
PAKEDGE DEVICE & SOFTWARE INC
17011 Beach Blvd Ste 600, Huntington
Beach (92647-5962)
PHONE...............................714 880-4511
Dusan Jankov, *Branch Mgr*
EMP: 22 **Privately Held**
SIC: 7372 Application computer software
HQ: Pakedge Device & Software Inc.
11734 S Election Rd # 200
Draper UT 84020
650 385-8700

(P-24287)
PANORAMIC SOFTWARE CORPORATION
Also Called: Panosoft
9650 Research Dr, Irvine (92618-4666)
PHONE...............................877 558-8526
Jeff Von Waldburg, *President*
EMP: 17
SQ FT: 1,500
SALES: 325MM **Privately Held**
SIC: 7372 7371 Prepackaged software;
custom computer programming services

(P-24288)
PASPORT SOFTWARE PROGRAMS INC
Also Called: Pasport Communications
307 Bridgeway, Sausalito (94965-2451)
PHONE...............................415 331-2606
Jon Gornstei, *President*
EMP: 10
SALES (est): 548.8K **Privately Held**
SIC: 7372 8742 Prepackaged software;
marketing consulting services

(P-24289)
PATIENTPOP INC
214 Wilshire Blvd, Santa Monica
(90401-1202)
PHONE...............................844 487-8399
Travis Schneider, *CEO*
Jason Gardner, *CFO*
Luke Kervin, *Co-CEO*
Jeb Burrows, *Vice Pres*
Thomas Le Blan, *Vice Pres*
EMP: 51 **EST:** 2015
SALES (est): 1.1MM **Privately Held**
SIC: 7372 Business oriented computer
software

(P-24290)
PATRON SOLUTIONS LLC
5171 California Ave # 200, Irvine
(92617-3068)
PHONE...............................949 823-1700
Steve Shaw, *Owner*
EMP: 245
SALES (est): 17.4MM **Privately Held**
SIC: 7372 Application computer software

(P-24291)
PAXATA INC
1800 Seaport Blvd 1, Redwood City
(94063-5543)
PHONE...............................650 542-7897
Prakasa Nanduri, *CEO*
David Brewster, *Co-Owner*
John Botros, *CFO*
Nenshad Bardoliwalla, *Vice Pres*
Manu Chadha, *Vice Pres*
EMP: 90
SALES (est): 10.6MM **Privately Held**
SIC: 7372 Business oriented computer
software

(P-24292)
PAYLOCITY HOLDING CORPORATION
2107 Livingston St, Oakland (94606-5218)
PHONE...............................847 956-4850
Lisa Formicola, *Director*
Janine Howard, *Manager*

EMP: 498
SALES (corp-wide): 467.6MM **Publicly Held**
SIC: 7372 Prepackaged software
PA: Paylocity Holding Corporation
1400 American Ln
Schaumburg IL 60173
847 463-3200

(P-24293)
PEOPLE CENTER INC
Also Called: Rippling
2443 Fillmore St 380-7, San Francisco (94115-1814)
PHONE..................................781 864-1232
Parker Conrad, *CEO*
Persona Sankaranarayana, *CTO*
Oscar London, *Sales Staff*
EMP: 50
SQ FT: 4,000
SALES: 1MM **Privately Held**
SIC: 7372 Business oriented computer software

(P-24294)
PHANTOM CYBER CORPORATION
2479 E Byshore Rd Ste 185, Palo Alto (94303)
PHONE..................................650 208-5151
Oliver Friedrichs, *CEO*
Eric Hoffman, *Partner*
Jackie Kruger, *Partner*
Dave Dewalt, *Vice Chairman*
Tim Driscoll, *CFO*
EMP: 30 EST: 2014
SALES (est): 2.4MM
SALES (corp-wide): 1.8B **Publicly Held**
SIC: 7372 7371 Prepackaged software; computer software development & applications
PA: Splunk Inc.
270 Brannan St
San Francisco CA 94107
415 848-8400

(P-24295)
PHOENIX TECHNOLOGIES LTD (HQ)
150 S Los Robles Ave # 500, Pasadena (91101-2441)
PHONE..................................408 570-1000
Rich Geruson, *President*
Debasish N Biswas, *President*
Steven S Chan, *President*
Brian Stein, *CFO*
Richard Arnold, *Exec VP*
◆ EMP: 20
SQ FT: 47,000
SALES: 54.9MM **Privately Held**
WEB: www.phoenix.com
SIC: 7372 6794 Prepackaged software; patent owners & lessors

(P-24296)
PHOTOBACKS LLC
40 Paseo Montecillo, Palm Desert (92260-3126)
PHONE..................................760 582-2550
Evan Aberman, *Director*
EMP: 10 EST: 2011
SALES (est): 289.8K **Privately Held**
SIC: 7372 Application computer software

(P-24297)
PICTRON INC
1250 Oakmead Pkwy Ste 210, Sunnyvale (94085-4035)
PHONE..................................408 725-8888
Darwin Kuan, *Exec VP*
EMP: 12
SQ FT: 3,000
SALES (est): 1.1MM **Privately Held**
WEB: www.pictron.com
SIC: 7372 Business oriented computer software

(P-24298)
PIERRY INC (PA)
557 Grand St, Redwood City (94062-2065)
PHONE..................................800 860-7953
Josh Pierry, *CEO*
Ben Lee, *Chief Mktg Ofcr*
Benjamin Lee, *Chief Mktg Ofcr*
Robert Bell, *Officer*
Jeff Green, *Vice Pres*

EMP: 10 EST: 2014
SALES (est): 7.5MM **Privately Held**
SIC: 7372 7311 Prepackaged software; advertising agencies

(P-24299)
PILOT SOFTWARE INC
3410 Hillview Ave, Palo Alto (94304-1395)
PHONE..................................650 230-2830
Jonathan D Becher, *President*
EMP: 15
SQ FT: 4,100
SALES: 3MM **Privately Held**
SIC: 7372 Business oriented computer software

(P-24300)
PIPELINER CRM
15243 La Cruz Dr Unit 492, Pacific Palisades (90272-5328)
PHONE..................................424 280-6445
Nikoluas Kimla, *CEO*
Gerald Toumayan, *COO*
John Golden, *Officer*
Don Araldi, *Exec VP*
Colleen Toumayan, *Corp Comm Staff*
EMP: 20
SALES (est): 1MM **Privately Held**
SIC: 7372 Business oriented computer software

(P-24301)
PLANGRID INC (HQ)
Also Called: Loupe
2111 Mission St Ste 400, San Francisco (94110-6349)
PHONE..................................800 646-0796
Tracy Young, *CEO*
Douglas Leone, *Managing Prtnr*
Kevin Halter, *President*
Michael Galvin, *CFO*
David Cain, *Chief Mktg Ofcr*
EMP: 76
SQ FT: 16,000
SALES (est): 16.4MM
SALES (corp-wide): 2.5B **Publicly Held**
SIC: 7372 Application computer software
PA: Autodesk, Inc.
111 Mcinnis Pkwy
San Rafael CA 94903
415 507-5000

(P-24302)
PLANIT SOLUTIONS
1240 Commerce Ave, Woodland (95776-5910)
PHONE..................................530 666-6647
Jeff Welge, *Manager*
EMP: 15
SALES (est): 809.2K **Privately Held**
WEB: www.planitsolutions.com
SIC: 7372 Prepackaged software

(P-24303)
PLUGG ME LNC
18100 Von Karman Ave # 850, Irvine (92612-0169)
PHONE..................................949 705-4472
Clarissa Watkins, *CEO*
EMP: 25
SALES (est): 456.2K **Privately Held**
SIC: 7372 Application computer software

(P-24304)
PLX TECHNOLOGY INC
1320 Ridder Park Dr, San Jose (95131-2313)
PHONE..................................408 435-7400
Hock Tan, *President*
Anthony Maslowski, *CFO*
Charlie Kawwas, *Senior VP*
Boon Chye Ooi, *Senior VP*
Andy Nallappan, *Vice Pres*
▲ EMP: 157
SQ FT: 55,000
SALES (est): 12.4MM
SALES (corp-wide): 20.8B **Publicly Held**
WEB: www.plxtech.com
SIC: 7372 3674 Business oriented computer; integrated circuits, semiconductor networks, etc.
HQ: Avago Technologies Wireless (U.S.A.) Manufacturing Llc
4380 Ziegler Rd
Fort Collins CO 80525
970 288-2575

(P-24305)
PMS SYSTEMS CORPORATION
Also Called: Assetsmart
31355 Oak Crest Dr # 100, Westlake Village (91361-4680)
P.O. Box 997, Pacific Palisades (90272-0997)
PHONE..................................310 450-2566
Phillip T Chase, *Chairman*
Christopher Campbell, *President*
Phillip Chase, *COO*
Judith A Chase, *Treasurer*
Jeff Taggart, *Software Dev*
EMP: 12
SALES: 3MM **Privately Held**
WEB: www.assetsmart.com
SIC: 7372 7371 Prepackaged software; computer software development

(P-24306)
POLARION SOFTWARE INC
1001 Marina Village Pkwy # 403, Alameda (94501-6401)
PHONE..................................877 572-4005
Frank Schrder, *CEO*
George Briner, *CFO*
Stefano Rizzo, *Senior VP*
Nikolay Entin, *Vice Pres*
Jiri Walek, *Vice Pres*
EMP: 90
SALES (est): 7.2MM **Privately Held**
SIC: 7372 Prepackaged software

(P-24307)
PORT 80 SOFTWARE INC
Also Called: I I S Mechanics
2105 Garnet Ave Ste E, San Diego (92109-3670)
PHONE..................................858 274-4497
Thomas Powell, *CEO*
EMP: 20
SALES (est): 1.8MM **Privately Held**
WEB: www.port80software.com
SIC: 7372 Prepackaged software

(P-24308)
PORTELLUS INC
2522 Chambers Rd Ste 100, Tustin (92780-6962)
PHONE..................................949 250-9600
John Le, *President*
EMP: 80
SALES: 3.6MM **Privately Held**
WEB: www.portellus.com
SIC: 7372 Prepackaged software

(P-24309)
POTENTIA LABS INC
2870 4th Ave Apt 212, San Diego (92103-6272)
PHONE..................................951 603-3531
Dustin Milner, *President*
Eric Lenhardt, *Vice Pres*
EMP: 15
SALES (est): 701K **Privately Held**
SIC: 7372 Business oriented computer software

(P-24310)
POWERSCHOOL GROUP LLC (HQ)
150 Parkshore Dr, Folsom (95630-4710)
PHONE..................................916 288-1636
Hardeep Gulati, *CEO*
Mark Oldemeyer, *CFO*
Edward Dedic, *Vice Pres*
SAI Rangarajan, *Vice Pres*
Mike Rhein, *Vice Pres*
EMP: 148
SALES (est): 84.2MM
SALES (corp-wide): 5B **Privately Held**
SIC: 7372 Prepackaged software
PA: Vista Equity Partners Management, Llc
4 Embarcadero Ctr Fl 20
San Francisco CA 94111
415 765-6500

(P-24311)
POWWOW INC
71 Stevenson St Ste 400, San Francisco (94105-0908)
PHONE..................................877 800-4381
Jonathan Kaplan, *CEO*
EMP: 24

SALES (est): 613K
SALES (corp-wide): 76.7MM **Privately Held**
SIC: 7372 Business oriented computer software
PA: Magic Software Enterprises Ltd.
5 Haplada
Or Yehuda 60218
353 893-89

(P-24312)
PREDPOL INC
920 41st Ave Ste D, Santa Cruz (95062-4457)
P.O. Box 2870 (95063-2870)
PHONE..................................831 331-4550
Brian Macdonald, *CEO*
Christine Bottomley, *CFO*
Matt Houseman, *Vice Pres*
Denis Haskin, *Software Dev*
EMP: 10
SALES (est): 682K **Privately Held**
SIC: 7372 Application computer software

(P-24313)
PREZI INC (PA)
450 Bryant St, San Francisco (94107-1303)
PHONE..................................415 398-8012
Peter Arvai, *CEO*
Jim Szafranski, *COO*
Narayan Menon, *CFO*
Daniel Klein, *Executive*
Claudia Ramirez, *Admin Sec*
EMP: 30 EST: 2009
SQ FT: 1,600
SALES (est): 13.5MM **Privately Held**
WEB: www.prezi.com
SIC: 7372 Business oriented computer software

(P-24314)
PRISM SOFTWARE CORPORATION
15500 Rockfield Blvd C, Irvine (92618-2700)
PHONE..................................949 855-3100
Carl S Von Bibra, *Chairman*
David Ayres, *President*
Michael Cheever, *Treasurer*
Conrad Von Bibra, *Admin Sec*
EMP: 25
SALES (est): 3.7MM **Privately Held**
WEB: www.prism-software.com
SIC: 7372 Publishers' computer software; utility computer software; word processing computer software; operating systems computer software

(P-24315)
PROCEDE SOFTWARE LP
6815 Flanders Dr Ste 200, San Diego (92121-3914)
PHONE..................................858 450-4800
Peter Kneale, *General Ptnr*
Phillip Mossy, *Partner*
Grady Bolte, *Applctn Conslt*
Jason Edwards, *Applctn Conslt*
Eric Liddell, *Director*
EMP: 20
SALES (est): 3.3MM **Privately Held**
WEB: www.procedesoftware.com
SIC: 7372 Business oriented computer software

(P-24316)
PRODUCTPLAN LLC
10 E Yanonali St Ste 2a, Santa Barbara (93101-1878)
PHONE..................................805 618-2975
James Semick,
Mark Barbir, *Senior VP*
Greg Goodman,
EMP: 20 EST: 2013
SALES (est): 560.4K **Privately Held**
SIC: 7372 Business oriented computer software

(P-24317)
PROJECTORIS INC
Also Called: Screenmeet.com
50 Fremont St Ste 2275, San Francisco (94105-2263)
PHONE..................................917 972-5553
Ben Lilienthal, *President*
Lou Guercia, *COO*

EMP: 15
SALES (est): 790K **Privately Held**
SIC: 7372 Prepackaged software

(P-24318)
PROSPRING INC
101 Atlantic Ave Ste 103, Long Beach
(90802-5175)
PHONE.....................562 726-1800
John Molisani, *President*
John Molisani Jr, *President*
Suzanne Nabliba, *Vice Pres*
EMP: 12
SALES: 1.5MM **Privately Held**
WEB: www.prospring.net
SIC: 7372 7379 Publishers' computer software; computer related consulting services

(P-24319)
PROVIDENET COMMUNICATIONS CORP
20 Great Oaks Blvd, San Jose
(95119-1002)
PHONE.....................408 398-6335
Greg McNab, *President*
EMP: 29
SQ FT: 6,000
SALES (est): 3.8MM **Privately Held**
WEB: www.cdumail.com
SIC: 7372 4813 Prepackaged software; telephone communication, except radio

(P-24320)
PROXIMEX CORPORATION
300 Santana Row Ste 200, San Jose
(95128-2443)
PHONE.....................408 215-9000
Jack Smith, *CEO*
James A Barth, *CFO*
Diane M Z Robinette, *Vice Pres*
Ken Prayoon Cheng, *CTO*
EMP: 16
SALES (est): 4.5MM **Privately Held**
WEB: www.proximex.com
SIC: 7372 Business oriented computer software
HQ: Johnson Controls Security Solutions
Llc
6600 Congress Ave
Boca Raton FL 33487
561 264-2071

(P-24321)
PS SUPPORT INC
800 W El Camin Real, Mountain View
(94040)
PHONE.....................301 351-9366
Qiang Du, *CEO*
EMP: 11
SALES: 1MM **Privately Held**
SIC: 7372 Application computer software

(P-24322)
PUBINNO INC
1040 Mariposa St, San Francisco
(94107-2520)
PHONE.....................669 251-6538
Can Algul, *CEO*
Emre Ilke Cosar, *COO*
Necdet Alpmen, *CTO*
EMP: 13
SALES (est): 300K **Privately Held**
SIC: 7372 Prepackaged software

(P-24323)
PUNCHH INC
1875 S Grant St Ste 810, San Mateo
(94402-7048)
PHONE.....................415 623-4466
Jitendra Gupta, *CEO*
Kim Decarolis, *Vice Pres*
EMP: 17
SALES (est): 2.1MM **Privately Held**
SIC: 7372 Prepackaged software

(P-24324)
PUSHTOTEST INC
1735 Tech Dr Ste 820, San Jose (95110)
PHONE.....................408 436-8203
EMP: 10
SALES (est): 957.4K **Privately Held**
SIC: 7372

(P-24325)
QAD INC (PA)
100 Innovation Pl, Santa Barbara
(93108-2268)
PHONE.....................805 566-6000
Anton Chilton, *CEO*
Pamela M Lopker, *Ch of Bd*
Daniel Lender, *CFO*
John Neale, *Treasurer*
Kara Bellamy, *Senior VP*
EMP: 148
SQ FT: 120,000
SALES: 333MM **Publicly Held**
WEB: www.qad.com
SIC: 7372 7371 Business oriented computer software; custom computer programming services

(P-24326)
QAD INC
6450 Via Real, Carpinteria (93013-2903)
PHONE.....................805 684-6614
Mark Rasmussen, *Vice Pres*
Daniel N Lender, *CFO*
Murray Ray, *Exec VP*
Kara Bellamy, *Vice Pres*
Evan M Bishop, *Vice Pres*
EMP: 17
SALES (corp-wide): 333MM **Publicly Held**
SIC: 7372 Prepackaged software
PA: Qad Inc.
100 Innovation Pl
Santa Barbara CA 93108
805 566-6000

(P-24327)
QED SOFTWARE LLC
Also Called: Trinium Technologies
304 Tejon Pl, Palos Verdes Estates
(90274-1204)
PHONE.....................310 214-3118
Michael Thomas, *CEO*
Barry Assadi, *CTO*
EMP: 27
SQ FT: 2,500
SALES (est): 4.5MM **Privately Held**
WEB: www.triniumtech.com
SIC: 7372 Business oriented computer software
PA: Wisetech Global Limited
U 3 72 O'riordan St
Alexandria NSW 2015

(P-24328)
QSI 2011 INC (PA)
Also Called: Questys Solutions
2302 Martin Ste 475, Irvine (92612-7402)
PHONE.....................949 855-6885
Rodney Anderson, *President*
Michael Richard, *CFO*
Dylan Tan, *Technical Staff*
Laura Lechien, *Sales Mgr*
Vickie McGee, *Corp Comm Staff*
EMP: 18 EST: 1980
SQ FT: 5,050
SALES (est): 2MM **Privately Held**
WEB: www.questysolutions.com
SIC: 7372 Business oriented computer software

(P-24329)
QUADBASE SYSTEMS INC
990 Linden Dr Ste 230, Santa Clara
(95050-6175)
PHONE.....................408 982-0835
Fred Luk, *President*
EMP: 15
SALES (est): 1.6MM **Privately Held**
WEB: www.quadbase.com
SIC: 7372 7371 Application computer software; custom computer programming services

(P-24330)
QUALCOMM INNOVATION CENTER INC (HQ)
4365 Executive Dr # 1100, San Diego
(92121-2123)
PHONE.....................858 587-1121
Rob Chandhok, *President*
Ahmad Jalali, *Vice Pres*
Steven Mair, *Program Mgr*
Christie Partch, *Admin Asst*
Raj Kushwaha, *Sr Software Eng*

EMP: 43 EST: 2009
SALES (est): 6.1MM
SALES (corp-wide): 24.2B **Publicly Held**
SIC: 7372 Prepackaged software
PA: Qualcomm Incorporated
5775 Morehouse Dr
San Diego CA 92121
858 587-1121

(P-24331)
QUANTAL INTERNATIONAL INC
455 Market St Ste 1200, San Francisco
(94105-2441)
PHONE.....................415 644-0754
Terry Marsh, *President*
Jeff Rogers, *COO*
Paul Pfleiderer, *CFO*
Indro Fedrigo, *Vice Pres*
Lawrence Tint,
EMP: 26
SQ FT: 7,000
SALES (est): 2.7MM **Privately Held**
WEB: www.quantal.com
SIC: 7372 6282 Business oriented computer software; investment advisory service

(P-24332)
QUEST SOFTWARE INC
Packettrap Networks
118 2nd St Fl 6, San Francisco
(94105-3620)
PHONE.....................415 373-2222
Steven M Goodman, *President*
EMP: 65
SALES (corp-wide): 1.5B **Privately Held**
SIC: 7372 Prepackaged software
HQ: Quest Software, Inc.
4 Polaris Way
Aliso Viejo CA 92656
949 754-8000

(P-24333)
QUEST SOFTWARE INC
5450 Great America Pkwy, Santa Clara
(95054-3644)
PHONE.....................408 899-3823
EMP: 15
SALES (corp-wide): 1.5B **Privately Held**
SIC: 7372 Prepackaged software
HQ: Quest Software, Inc.
4 Polaris Way
Aliso Viejo CA 92656
949 754-8000

(P-24334)
QUEST SOFTWARE INC
Also Called: Cloud Automation Division
4 Polaris Way, Aliso Viejo (92656-5356)
PHONE.....................949 754-8000
Angela Morales, *Partner*
Katherine Tate, *Officer*
Doug Wright, *Surgery Dir*
Mark Lomas, *Admin Mgr*
Pierre Nguyen, *Administration*
EMP: 80
SALES (corp-wide): 1.5B **Privately Held**
SIC: 7372 Prepackaged software
HQ: Quest Software, Inc.
4 Polaris Way
Aliso Viejo CA 92656
949 754-8000

(P-24335)
QUESTIVITY INC
1680 Civic Center Dr # 209, Santa Clara
(95050-4660)
PHONE.....................408 615-1781
Humayun Sohel, *President*
Muhammad Jafri, *Network Enginr*
Ahmed Zwink, *Recruiter*
Ralph Forrest, *Manager*
Ameen Syed, *Consultant*
EMP: 15
SQ FT: 1,180
SALES (est): 5MM **Privately Held**
WEB: www.questivity.com
SIC: 7372 7361 Prepackaged software; employment agencies

(P-24336)
QUMU INC (HQ)
1100 Grundy Ln Ste 110, San Bruno
(94066-3072)
PHONE.....................650 396-8530
Jim Stewart, *CFO*

Taimur Mirza, *Sr Software Eng*
David Higuera, *Info Tech Mgr*
Naureen Moon, *Software Engr*
David Bukhan, *VP Engrg*
EMP: 56
SQ FT: 13,000
SALES (est): 8.5MM
SALES (corp-wide): 25MM **Publicly Held**
WEB: www.mediapublisher.com
SIC: 7372 Business oriented computer software
PA: Qumu Corporation
510 1st Ave N Ste 305
Minneapolis MN 55403
612 638-9100

(P-24337)
QWILT INC (PA)
275 Shoreline Dr Ste 510, Redwood City
(94065-1413)
PHONE.....................866 824-8009
Alon Maor, *CEO*
Yoni Mizrahi, *CFO*
Yuval Shahar, *Chairman*
Yoav Gressel, *Vice Pres*
Jesper Knutsson, *Vice Pres*
EMP: 25 EST: 2010
SALES (est): 5.3MM **Privately Held**
SIC: 7372 Business oriented computer software

(P-24338)
RAKSHAK
2518 Alvin St, Mountain View (94043-2708)
PHONE.....................404 513-5867
Rajan K Singh, *Principal*
EMP: 20
SALES (est): 869K **Privately Held**
WEB: www.rakshak.com
SIC: 7372 Prepackaged software

(P-24339)
READ CORP
16012a Flintlock Rd, Cupertino
(95014-5401)
PHONE.....................408 705-2123
Ione Benford, *CEO*
Thomas Benford, *Chairman*
EMP: 35
SALES (est): 1.7MM **Privately Held**
WEB: www.read-ink.com
SIC: 7372 Operating systems computer software

(P-24340)
READ IT LATER INC
Also Called: Pocket
233 Sansome St Ste 1200, San Francisco
(94104-2300)
PHONE.....................415 692-6111
Nathan Weiner, *CEO*
Blake Boznanski, *Partner*
EMP: 34
SALES: 5MM
SALES (corp-wide): 421.2MM **Privately Held**
SIC: 7372 Application computer software
HQ: Mozilla Corporation
331 E Evelyn Ave
Mountain View CA 94041
650 903-0800

(P-24341)
READYTECH CORPORATION
2201 Broadway Ste 725, Oakland
(94612-3024)
PHONE.....................510 834-3344
John K Woodward, *President*
Sue Ray, *CFO*
Ryan Armstrong, *Administration*
Felipe Cabezas, *Info Tech Dir*
Candice Cheng, *Technology*
EMP: 14
SALES (est): 2.1MM **Privately Held**
SIC: 7372 Educational computer software

(P-24342)
REAL SOFTWARE SYSTEMS LLC (PA)
21255 Burbank Blvd # 220, Woodland Hills
(91367-6610)
PHONE.....................818 313-8000
Kent Sahin, *Mng Member*
Jenny Gonzales, *Consultant*
EMP: 60

SALES (est): 8MM **Privately Held**
WEB: www.realsoftwaresystems.com
SIC: 7372 Business oriented computer software

(P-24343)
REALIZATION TECHNOLOGIES INC
440 N Wolfe Rd 52, Sunnyvale (94085-3869)
PHONE..................................408 271-1720
Sanjeev Gupta, *President*
Ravi Radhakrishnan, *Admin Sec*
Chris Dailey, *Project Mgr*
EMP: 20 EST: 1999
SALES (est): 2.4MM **Privately Held**
WEB: www.realization.com
SIC: 7372 Application computer software

(P-24344)
REALPAGE INC
Also Called: Ops Technology
333 3rd St, San Francisco (94107-1240)
PHONE..................................415 222-6996
Tony Howard, *Branch Mgr*
EMP: 22
SALES (corp-wide): 869.4MM **Publicly Held**
SIC: 7372 7371 Prepackaged software; custom computer programming services
PA: Realpage, Inc.
　　2201 Lakeside Blvd
　　Richardson TX 75082
　　972 820-3000

(P-24345)
REALSCOUT INC
480 Ellis St Ste 203, Mountain View (94043-2204)
PHONE..................................650 397-6500
Arthur Kaneko, *CEO*
Andrew S Flanchner, *President*
Betty Kayton, *CFO*
Winkler Helena, *Vice Pres*
Anna Morales, *Executive*
EMP: 15
SQ FT: 500
SALES (est): 1.5MM **Privately Held**
SIC: 7372 Business oriented computer software

(P-24346)
REALWARE INC
444 Haas Ave, San Leandro (94577-2926)
PHONE..................................510 382-9045
David Bennett, *President*
EMP: 10 EST: 1998
SALES: 1MM **Privately Held**
WEB: www.realwareinc.com
SIC: 7372 Prepackaged software

(P-24347)
REALWISE INC
Also Called: Avm Technologies
28042 Avenue Stanford E, Valencia (91355-1157)
PHONE..................................661 295-9399
Steve Sturgeon, *President*
EMP: 10
SALES (est): 907.7K **Privately Held**
WEB: www.realwise.com
SIC: 7372 5734 Business oriented computer software; personal computers

(P-24348)
REBOL TECHNOLOGIES INC
301 S State St, Ukiah (95482-4906)
P.O. Box 1510 (95482-1510)
PHONE..................................707 485-0599
Tom Coull, *President*
Cynthia Sassenrath, *COO*
Carl Sassenrath, *CTO*
EMP: 17 EST: 1997
SALES (est): 1MM **Privately Held**
WEB: www.rebol.com
SIC: 7372 Application computer software

(P-24349)
RECEIVD INC
Also Called: Kicksend
655 Castro St Ste 2, Mountain View (94041-2019)
PHONE..................................650 336-5817
Pradeep Elankumaran, *CEO*
Brendan Lim, *Bd of Directors*
EMP: 10 EST: 2011

SALES (est): 643.3K **Privately Held**
SIC: 7372 Application computer software

(P-24350)
RED GATE SOFTWARE INC
144 W Colo Blvd Ste 200, Pasadena (91105)
PHONE..................................626 993-3949
Tom Curtis, *President*
Jason Young, *Sales Mgr*
EMP: 23
SQ FT: 5,500
SALES (est): 2.9MM
SALES (corp-wide): 58.6MM **Privately Held**
SIC: 7372 Business oriented computer software
HQ: Red Gate Software Limited
　　Newnham House
　　Cambridge CAMBS CB4 0
　　122 342-0397

(P-24351)
RED HAT INC
444 Castro St Ste 1200, Mountain View (94041-2050)
PHONE..................................650 567-9039
Alex Daly, *Manager*
EMP: 15
SALES (corp-wide): 79.5B **Publicly Held**
WEB: www.apacheweek.com
SIC: 7372 Operating systems computer software
HQ: Red Hat, Inc.
　　100 E Davie St
　　Raleigh NC 27601
　　-

(P-24352)
REDCORT SOFTWARE INC
619 Woodworth Ave Ste 200, Clovis (93612-1872)
P.O. Box 25764, Fresno (93729-5764)
PHONE..................................559 434-8544
Keith Delong, *CEO*
EMP: 10
SALES (est): 1MM **Privately Held**
WEB: www.redcort.com
SIC: 7372 Business oriented computer software

(P-24353)
REDSEAL INC
1600 Technology Dr Fl 4, San Jose (95110-1382)
PHONE..................................408 641-2200
Ray Rothrock, *CEO*
Greg Straughn, *CFO*
Gordon Adams, *Officer*
Jay Miller, *Vice Pres*
Sundar Raj, *Vice Pres*
EMP: 100
SQ FT: 6,500
SALES (est): 22.1MM **Privately Held**
WEB: www.redseal.net
SIC: 7372 Prepackaged software

(P-24354)
REDWOOD APPS INC
805 Veterans Blvd Ste 322, Redwood City (94063-1737)
PHONE..................................408 348-3808
Benkat Supramanian, *President*
Markus Hummel, *Vice Pres*
EMP: 10 EST: 2016
SQ FT: 1,000
SALES (est): 268.4K **Privately Held**
SIC: 7372 Prepackaged software

(P-24355)
RELATIONAL CENTER
2717 S Robertson Blvd # 1, Los Angeles (90034-2442)
PHONE..................................323 935-1807
Traci Bivens Davis, *Principal*
EMP: 21 EST: 2008
SALES (est): 721.1K **Privately Held**
SIC: 7372 Prepackaged software

(P-24356)
RELOADED TECHNOLOGIES INC
17011 Beach Blvd Ste 320, Huntington Beach (92647-7420)
PHONE..................................949 870-3123
Bjorn Book-Larsson, *CEO*

EMP: 10 EST: 2013
SALES (est): 415.6K **Privately Held**
SIC: 7372 Publishers' computer software

(P-24357)
RETAIL SOLUTIONS INCORPORATED (PA)
100 Century Center Ct # 800, San Jose (95112-4537)
PHONE..................................650 390-6100
Bert Clement, *CEO*
Peter Rieman, *COO*
Patrick U Di Chiro, *Officer*
Jonathan Golovin, *Officer*
Dr Shantaha Moham, *Senior VP*
EMP: 30
SALES (est): 37.6MM **Privately Held**
WEB: www.retailsolutions.com
SIC: 7372 Business oriented computer software

(P-24358)
RETROSPECT INC
44 Westwind Rd, Lafayette (94549-2116)
PHONE..................................888 376-1078
Mihir Shah, *CEO*
Brian Dunagan, *Vice Pres*
JG Heithcock, *General Mgr*
EMP: 20
SALES (est): 5.4MM
SALES (corp-wide): 41MM **Privately Held**
SIC: 7372 Prepackaged software
PA: Storcentric, Inc.
　　1289 Anvilwood Ave
　　Sunnyvale CA 94089
　　408 454-4200

(P-24359)
REVJET
981 Industrial Rd Ste F, San Carlos (94070-4150)
PHONE..................................650 508-2215
Patrick McNenny, *Vice Pres*
Bradley McKeon, *Vice Pres*
David Mackay, *Risk Mgmt Dir*
Andriy Gusyev, *Engrg Dir*
Derek Gavigan, *Sales Dir*
EMP: 110 EST: 2017
SALES (est): 2.3MM **Privately Held**
SIC: 7372 Application computer software

(P-24360)
REYNEN COURT LLC
2 Blair Ave, Piedmont (94611-4102)
PHONE..................................917 588-0746
Andrew Klein, *CEO*
EMP: 12
SALES (est): 256K **Privately Held**
SIC: 7372 Business oriented computer software

(P-24361)
RFL GLOBAL INC
732 E Jefferson Blvd, Los Angeles (90011-2435)
PHONE..................................323 235-2580
EMP: 15 EST: 2014
SALES (est): 690K **Privately Held**
SIC: 7372

(P-24362)
RIFFYN INC (PA)
484 9th St, Oakland (94607-4048)
PHONE..................................510 542-9868
Timothy Gardner, *CEO*
John F Conway, *Ch Credit Ofcr*
Tom Bourgoin, *Vice Pres*
Lili Nader, *CTO*
Alistair McLean, *Software Engr*
EMP: 10
SALES (est): 1.5MM **Privately Held**
SIC: 7372 Business oriented computer software

(P-24363)
RIVERMEADOW SOFTWARE INC
2107 N 1st St Ste 660, San Jose (95131-2005)
PHONE..................................408 217-6498
Richard Scannell, *Exec VP*
Denise Maher, *Executive Asst*
Srinivasa Vegeraju, *Sr Software Eng*
John Merryman, *Director*
Norem Soriano, *Manager*
EMP: 10 EST: 2013

SALES (est): 831.5K **Privately Held**
SIC: 7372 Business oriented computer software

(P-24364)
ROBLOX CORPORATION
970 Park Pl, San Mateo (94403-1907)
PHONE..................................888 858-2569
David Baszucki, *CEO*
Michael Poon, *CFO*
Scott Rubin, *Vice Pres*
Andrew Francis, *Sr Software Eng*
Dinghao LI, *Software Engr*
EMP: 500
SALES (est): 4MM **Privately Held**
SIC: 7372 Prepackaged software

(P-24365)
ROLLAPP INC (PA)
530 Lytton Ave Fl 2, Palo Alto (94301-1541)
PHONE..................................650 617-3372
Dmitry Dakhnovsky, *Principal*
Ivan Poyda, *COO*
Dima Malenko, *CTO*
EMP: 13 EST: 2012
SALES (est): 3.7MM **Privately Held**
SIC: 7372 Prepackaged software

(P-24366)
RONIN CONTENT SERVICES INC
Also Called: Ronin Content
5900 Smiley Dr, Culver City (90232-7319)
P.O. Box 3241 (90231-3241)
PHONE..................................323 445-5945
Joshua Otten, *CEO*
EMP: 10
SALES (est): 221.8K **Privately Held**
SIC: 7372 Application computer software

(P-24367)
ROSE BUSINESS SOLUTIONS INC
875 Chelsea Ln, Encinitas (92024-6675)
PHONE..................................858 794-9401
K Linda Rose, *President*
Glen Medwid, *CFO*
EMP: 20
SALES: 2.7MM **Privately Held**
WEB: www.rosebizinc.com
SIC: 7372 Prepackaged software

(P-24368)
RUNA INC
2 W 5th Ave Ste 300, San Mateo (94402-2002)
PHONE..................................508 253-5000
Ashok Narasimhan, *CEO*
EMP: 15
SALES (est): 789.9K **Privately Held**
SIC: 7372 Business oriented computer software
HQ: Staples, Inc.
　　500 Staples Dr
　　Framingham MA 01702
　　508 253-5000

(P-24369)
RYPPLE
577 Howard St Fl 3, San Francisco (94105-4635)
PHONE..................................888 479-7753
EMP: 15
SALES (est): 1.1MM **Privately Held**
SIC: 7372

(P-24370)
S-MATRIX CORPORATION
1594 Myrtle Ave, Eureka (95501-1454)
PHONE..................................707 441-0404
Richard Verseput, *President*
George Cooney, *Vice Pres*
EMP: 14
SALES (est): 1.6MM **Privately Held**
WEB: www.s-matrix-corp.com
SIC: 7372 7371 Business oriented computer software; software programming applications

(P-24371)
SABA SOFTWARE INC (PA)
4120 Dublin Blvd Ste 200, Dublin (94568-7759)
PHONE..................................877 722-2101

▲ = Import ▼=Export
◆ =Import/Export

Phil Saunders, *President*
Allison Wudel, *Partner*
Pete Low, *CFO*
Debbie Shotwell,
Paige Newcombe, *Officer*
EMP: 100
SQ FT: 36,000
SALES (est): 177MM **Privately Held**
WEB: www.saba.com
SIC: 7372 7371 Application computer software; computer software development & applications

(P-24372)
SAFETYCHAIN SOFTWARE INC (PA)
7599 Redwood Blvd Ste 205, Novato (94945-7706)
PHONE....................................415 233-9474
Walter Smith, *Principal*
David Detweiler, *Vice Pres*
Brian Sharp, *Vice Pres*
Kanti Keislar, *Business Anlyst*
Sean Fisher, *Project Mgr*
EMP: 21
SALES (est): 6.4MM **Privately Held**
SIC: 7372 Business oriented computer software

(P-24373)
SAGE SOFTWARE INC
1380 Tatan Trail Rd, Burlingame (94010)
PHONE....................................650 579-3628
Mau Chung Chang, *Branch Mgr*
EMP: 245
SALES (corp-wide): 2.3B **Privately Held**
SIC: 7372 Business oriented computer software
HQ: Sage Software, Inc.
271 17th St Nw Ste 1100
Atlanta GA 30363
866 996-7243

(P-24374)
SAGE SOFTWARE HOLDINGS INC (HQ)
6561 Irvine Center Dr, Irvine (92618-2118)
PHONE....................................866 530-7243
Stev Swenson, *CEO*
Mack Lout, *CFO*
Bill Feder, *Vice Pres*
Doug Meyer, *Vice Pres*
Dion Diroma, *IT/INT Sup*
EMP: 400
SALES (est): 464.7MM
SALES (corp-wide): 2.3B **Privately Held**
SIC: 7372 7371 Business oriented computer software; custom computer programming services
PA: The Sage Group Plc.
North Park Avenue
Newcastle-Upon-Tyne NE13
191 294-3000

(P-24375)
SALESFORCECOM INC
50 Fremont St Ste 300, San Francisco (94105-2231)
PHONE....................................415 323-8685
Charlene Kahler, *Principal*
Aseem Gupta, *Counsel*
Kathleen McKinnon, *Manager*
Rachel Christu, *Advisor*
EMP: 21
SALES (corp-wide): 13.2B **Publicly Held**
SIC: 7372 Business oriented computer software
PA: Salesforce.Com, Inc.
415 Mission St Fl 3
San Francisco CA 94105
415 901-7000

(P-24376)
SALESFORCECOM INC
1 Market Ste 300, San Francisco (94105-5188)
PHONE....................................703 463-3300
John Devoe, *Administration*
Brian Demelo, *Partner*
John Coleman, *Vice Pres*
Bill Pessin, *Vice Pres*
Michael Quimby, *Vice Pres*
EMP: 14

SALES (corp-wide): 13.2B **Publicly Held**
SIC: 7372 7375 Business oriented computer software; information retrieval services
PA: Salesforce.Com, Inc.
415 Mission St Fl 3
San Francisco CA 94105
415 901-7000

(P-24377)
SALESFORCECOM INC (PA)
415 Mission St Fl 3, San Francisco (94105-2533)
PHONE....................................415 901-7000
Marc Benioff, *Ch of Bd*
Christina Kirkpatrick, *Partner*
Bob Stutz, *Partner*
Keith Block, *President*
Mark Hawkins, *President*
EMP: 600 **EST:** 1999
SALES: 13.2B **Publicly Held**
WEB: www.salesforce.com
SIC: 7372 7375 Business oriented computer software; information retrieval services

(P-24378)
SALESFORCECOM INC
1442 2nd St, Santa Monica (90401-2302)
PHONE....................................310 752-7000
Andy Demari, *Manager*
Paolo Bergamo, *Vice Pres*
Devon Prince, *IT/INT Sup*
EMP: 40
SALES (corp-wide): 13.2B **Publicly Held**
WEB: www.salesforce.com
SIC: 7372 Business oriented computer software
PA: Salesforce.Com, Inc.
415 Mission St Fl 3
San Francisco CA 94105
415 901-7000

(P-24379)
SAMSUNG SDS GLOBL SCL AMER INC
10509 Vista Sorrento Pkwy, San Diego (92121-2707)
PHONE....................................201 263-3000
EMP: 28 **Privately Held**
SIC: 7372 7371 Prepackaged software; computer software development
HQ: Samsung Sds Global Scl America, Inc.
100 Challenger Rd Ste 601
Ridgefield Park NJ 07660
201 229-4456

(P-24380)
SANTAN SOFTWARE SYSTEMS INC
19504 Ronald Ave, Torrance (90503-1239)
P.O. Box 34521, Los Angeles (90034-0521)
PHONE....................................310 836-2802
Barun Bamba, *President*
Varun Bamba, *President*
Bob Varun, *President*
Samita Bamba, *Admin Sec*
EMP: 21
SALES: 6MM **Privately Held**
WEB: www.santansoftwaresystems.com
SIC: 7372 Prepackaged software

(P-24381)
SAPERI SYSTEMS INC
9444 Waples St Ste 300, San Diego (92121-2942)
PHONE....................................858 381-0085
Emory Fry, *CEO*
Doug Burke, *President*
EMP: 11
SALES (est): 263K **Privately Held**
SIC: 7372 Prepackaged software
PA: Cognitive Medical Systems, Inc.
9444 Waples St Ste 200
San Diego CA 92121

(P-24382)
SARS SOFTWARE PRODUCTS INC
2175 Francisco Blvd E, San Rafael (94901-5510)
P.O. Box 653, Mill Valley (94942-0653)
PHONE....................................415 226-0040
Joanne Fields Doty, *President*

James Doty, *Vice Pres*
EMP: 15 **EST:** 1986
SQ FT: 2,000
SALES (est): 1.3MM **Privately Held**
SIC: 7372 Prepackaged software

(P-24383)
SAS INSTITUTE INC
Also Called: Post Montgomery Center
50 Post St Ste 50 # 50, San Francisco (94104-4552)
PHONE....................................415 421-2227
Bernard Doering, *Branch Mgr*
EMP: 33
SALES (corp-wide): 3B **Privately Held**
WEB: www.sas.com
SIC: 7372 Application computer software; business oriented computer software; educational computer software
PA: Sas Institute Inc.
100 Sas Campus Dr
Cary NC 27513
919 677-8000

(P-24384)
SAS INSTITUTE INC
2121 N 1st St Ste 100, San Jose (95131-2053)
PHONE....................................919 677-8000
Danny Parodi, *Manager*
EMP: 15
SALES (corp-wide): 3B **Privately Held**
WEB: www.sas.com
SIC: 7372 Application computer software; business oriented computer software; educational computer software
PA: Sas Institute Inc.
100 Sas Campus Dr
Cary NC 27513
919 677-8000

(P-24385)
SAS INSTITUTE INC
Salesstock.com
1148 N Lemon St, Orange (92867-4701)
PHONE....................................949 250-9999
Shawn Anthony Stiltz, *Vice Pres*
EMP: 56
SALES (corp-wide): 3B **Privately Held**
SIC: 7372 Application computer software; business oriented computer software; educational computer software
PA: Sas Institute Inc.
100 Sas Campus Dr
Cary NC 27513
919 677-8000

(P-24386)
SASS LABS INC
Also Called: Allyo
121 W Washington Ave # 209, Sunnyvale (94086-1101)
PHONE....................................404 731-7284
Ankit Somani, *President*
Sahil Sahni, *Vice Pres*
EMP: 20
SALES (est): 421K **Privately Held**
SIC: 7372 Application computer software

(P-24387)
SCENE 53 INC
800 E Charleston Rd Apt 7, Palo Alto (94303-4627)
PHONE....................................415 404-2461
Yonatan Maor, *CEO*
Hamutal Russo, *CFO*
EMP: 20
SALES (est): 993.2K **Privately Held**
SIC: 7372 Home entertainment computer software

(P-24388)
SCHOOL INNOVATIONS ACHIEVEMENT (PA)
5200 Golden Foothill Pkwy, El Dorado Hills (95762-9610)
PHONE....................................916 933-2290
Jeffrey C Williams, *CEO*
Gemma Ball, *Partner*
Susan Cook, *COO*
Joe Steele, *CFO*
Jerry Wooden, *Exec VP*
EMP: 95
SQ FT: 25,000

SALES: 14.8MM **Privately Held**
WEB: www.sia-us.com
SIC: 7372 8742 Prepackaged software; management consulting services

(P-24389)
SCIENTIFIC LEARNING CORP
300 Frank H Ogawa Plz # 600, Oakland (94612-2056)
PHONE....................................510 444-3500
Louise Dube, *Vice Pres*
Holly Koob, *Comms Mgr*
Joan Ferguson, *Program Mgr*
Steven Edwards, *Regional Mgr*
Vickie Bottero, *Executive Asst*
EMP: 25 **Publicly Held**
WEB: www.scilearn.com
SIC: 7372 7371 Prepackaged software; computer software development
PA: Scientific Learning Corporation
1956 Webster St Ste 200
Oakland CA 94612
-

(P-24390)
SCM ACCELERATORS LLC
2731 California St, San Francisco (94115-2513)
PHONE....................................415 595-8091
Scott Barrett, *President*
Chris Botha, *CEO*
Dejan Ahrens, *CTO*
Krish Ranganathan, *Sr Consultant*
EMP: 14
SALES: 9.8MM **Privately Held**
SIC: 7372 Business oriented computer software

(P-24391)
SCOPELY INC (PA)
3530 Hayden Ave Ste A, Culver City (90232-2413)
PHONE....................................323 400-6618
Walter Driver III, *President*
JC Bornaghi, *Vice Pres*
Eytan Elbaz, *Vice Pres*
Eric Futoran, *Vice Pres*
Divya Sankaran, *Sr Software Eng*
EMP: 200
SALES (est): 10.3MM **Privately Held**
SIC: 7372 Home entertainment computer software

(P-24392)
SCRIBE TECHNOLOGIES INC
739 Bryant St, San Francisco (94107-1014)
PHONE....................................415 746-9935
Rutika Muchhala, *Principal*
EMP: 12
SALES (est): 342.8K **Privately Held**
SIC: 7372 Application computer software

(P-24393)
SEAL SOFTWARE INC (PA)
1990 N Calif Blvd Ste 500, Walnut Creek (94596-3743)
PHONE....................................650 938-7325
Ulf Zetterberg, *CEO*
David Gingell, *Chief Mktg Ofcr*
Rich Bohne, *Risk Mgmt Dir*
Jim Wagner, *Security Dir*
EMP: 18
SALES (est): 5MM **Privately Held**
SIC: 7372 Prepackaged software

(P-24394)
SECURE COMPUTING CORPORATION (DH)
3965 Freedom Cir 4, Santa Clara (95054-1206)
PHONE....................................408 979-2020
Daniel Ryan, *President*
Richard Scott, *Ch of Bd*
Timothy J Steinkopf, *CFO*
Atri Chatterjee, *Senior VP*
Michael J Gallagher, *Senior VP*
EMP: 40
SQ FT: 10,895
SALES (est): 90.3MM **Privately Held**
WEB: www.securecomp.com
SIC: 7372 Prepackaged software
HQ: Mcafee, Llc
2821 Mission College Blvd
Santa Clara CA 95054
888 847-8766

(P-24395)
SECUREDATA INC
3255 Chnga Blvd W Ste 301, Los Angeles
(90068-1778)
PHONE...................424 363-8529
Dmitri Kardashev, *CEO*
EMP: 12
SALES: 3.3MM **Privately Held**
SIC: 7372 Application computer software

(P-24396)
SEMOTUS INC
Also Called: Hiplink Software
718 University Ave # 110, Los Gatos
(95032-7608)
PHONE...................408 667-2046
Anthony Lapine, *Chairman*
Pamela Lapine, *President*
Duke Swenson, *Controller*
Frank Williams, *Sales Mgr*
EMP: 25
SQ FT: 4,000
SALES (est): 2.2MM **Privately Held**
WEB: www.hiplink.com
SIC: 7372 7371 8243 Prepackaged soft-
ware; computer software systems analy-
sis & design, custom; operator training,
computer

(P-24397)
SENETUR LLC
399 Lakeside Dr Ste 400, Oakland (94612)
PHONE...................650 269-1023
Adrian Walker, *CEO*
EMP: 10
SQ FT: 500
SALES (est): 244K **Privately Held**
SIC: 7372 Business oriented computer
software

(P-24398)
SEPASOFT INC
1264 Hawks Flight Ct, El Dorado Hills
(95762-9348)
PHONE...................916 939-1684
Thomas Andrew Hechtman, *President*
Roxann Hechtman, *CFO*
Roxanna Hechtman, *CFO*
Byounghyun An, *Software Engr*
EMP: 15 EST: 2003
SQ FT: 2,955
SALES (est): 80.1K **Privately Held**
SIC: 7372 Prepackaged software

(P-24399)
SEQUENT SOFTWARE INC
4699 Old Ironsides Dr # 470, Santa Clara
(95054-1861)
PHONE...................650 419-2713
Andrew Weinstein, *CEO*
Robb Duffield, *CEO*
Lance Johnson, *Officer*
Hans Reisgies, *Senior VP*
Richard Nassar, *Vice Pres*
EMP: 17
SALES (est): 3.5MM **Privately Held**
SIC: 7372 Application computer software

(P-24400)
SERRA SYSTEMS INC (HQ)
126 Mill St, Healdsburg (95448-4438)
PHONE...................707 433-5104
Paul Deas, *President*
Pamela Deas, *Corp Secy*
Steven Deas, *Vice Pres*
EMP: 17
SQ FT: 7,000
SALES: 3.2MM
SALES (corp-wide): 78.4MM **Privately
Held**
WEB: www.serrasystems.com
SIC: 7372 Business oriented computer
software
PA: E & M Electric And Machinery, Inc.
126 Mill St
Healdsburg CA 95448
707 433-5578

(P-24401)
SERVICENOW INC
4810 Eastgate Mall, San Diego
(92121-1977)
PHONE...................858 720-0477
Dave Stephens, *Vice Pres*
Allie Zipp, *Executive Asst*
James Wilson, *Sr Ntwrk Engine*

Troy Prouty, *Senior Engr*
Bob Garland, *Director*
EMP: 10
SALES (corp-wide): 2.6B **Publicly Held**
SIC: 7372 Prepackaged software
PA: Servicenow, Inc.
2225 Lawson Ln
Santa Clara CA 95054
408 501-8550

(P-24402)
SESAME SOFTWARE INC
5201 Great America Pkwy # 320, Santa
Clara (95054-1122)
PHONE...................866 474-7575
Richard D Banister, *President*
Michael Hoydic, *Accounting Mgr*
Steven Hoydic, *Sales Staff*
Louis Linfoot, *Manager*
Scott O'Dell, *Manager*
EMP: 22
SALES: 1.7MM **Privately Held**
WEB: www.sesamesoftware.com
SIC: 7372 Business oriented computer
software

(P-24403)
SHAREDATA INC
Also Called: Sharedta/E Trade Bus Solutions
2465 Augustine Dr, Santa Clara (95054)
PHONE...................408 490-2500
Laura Fay, *President*
EMP: 53
SALES (est): 1.9MM **Privately Held**
SIC: 7372 Business oriented computer
software

(P-24404)
SHARPE SOFTWARE INC
925 Market St, Yuba City (95991-4210)
PHONE...................530 671-6499
Daniel Ontiveros, *President*
Fabiola Rodiles, *Office Mgr*
Brent Hooton, *Manager*
EMP: 10
SQ FT: 5,680
SALES (est): 1.1MM **Privately Held**
WEB: www.sharpesoft.com
SIC: 7372 Business oriented computer
software

(P-24405)
SHERBIT HEALTH INC
2200 Powell St Ste 460, Emeryville
(94608-2253)
PHONE...................925 683-8116
Alex Senemar, *CEO*
EMP: 12
SALES (est): 281.6K **Privately Held**
SIC: 7372 Business oriented computer
software

(P-24406)
SHORTCUTS SOFTWARE INC
7711 Center Ave Ste 550, Huntington
Beach (92647-3075)
PHONE...................714 622-6600
Rebecca Randall, *CEO*
Malcom Raward, *Treasurer*
Paul Tate, *Vice Pres*
Rebecca Stanley, *Opers Staff*
EMP: 30
SALES (est): 3.7MM **Privately Held**
WEB: www.shortcuts.com.au
SIC: 7372 Business oriented computer
software
HQ: Shortcuts Software Pty Ltd
L 2 South Tower 10 Browning St
South Brisbane QLD 4101
-

(P-24407)
SHOTSPOTTER INC
Also Called: SST
7979 Gateway Blvd Ste 210, Newark
(94560-1158)
PHONE...................510 794-3100
Ralph A Clark, *President*
Paul S Ames, *Senior VP*
Nasim Golzadeh, *Senior VP*
Joseph O Hawkins, *Senior VP*
Sonya L Strickler, *VP Finance*
EMP: 76
SQ FT: 12,020

SALES: 34.7MM **Privately Held**
WEB: www.shotspotter.com
SIC: 7372 7382 Prepackaged software;
security systems services

(P-24408)
SIEENA INC
Also Called: Definity First
1901 Avenue Of The Stars, Los Angeles
(90067-6001)
PHONE...................310 455-6188
Mauricio Galvan, *President*
Michael Abraham, *Officer*
Fernando Gutierrez, *Vice Pres*
Sergio Zuniga, *Vice Pres*
Hector Martinez, *Accounts Mgr*
EMP: 40
SALES (corp-wide): 660K **Privately Held**
SIC: 7372 Business oriented computer
software
PA: Sieena, Inc
12555 High Bluff Dr # 333
San Diego CA 92130
310 455-6188

(P-24409)
**SIEMENS PRODUCT LIFE MGMT
SFTW**
Also Called: Siemens PLM Software
2077 Gateway Pl Ste 400, San Jose
(95110-1085)
PHONE...................408 941-4600
Lorena Mendoza, *Branch Mgr*
Sied Langrudi, *VP Sales*
EMP: 49
SALES (corp-wide): 95B **Privately Held**
SIC: 7372 Business oriented computer
software
HQ: Siemens Industry Software Inc.
5800 Granite Pkwy Ste 600
Plano TX 75024
972 987-3000

(P-24410)
SIFTERY INC
49 Geary St Ste 530, San Francisco
(94108-5731)
PHONE...................415 484-8211
Vamshi Mokshagundam, *CEO*
Ayan Barua, *CTO*
EMP: 20 EST: 2012
SALES (est): 40.9K
SALES (corp-wide): 26.6MM **Privately
Held**
SIC: 7372 Business oriented computer
software
PA: G2 Crowd, Inc.
20 N Wacker Dr Ste 1800
Chicago IL 60606
847 748-7559

(P-24411)
SIGHT MACHINE INC
243 Vallejo St, San Francisco (94111-1511)
PHONE...................888 461-5739
Jon Sobel, *CEO*
John Stone, *President*
Syed Hoda, *Chief Mktg Ofcr*
Kurt Demaagd, *Vice Pres*
Brian Gillespie, *Vice Pres*
EMP: 60
SQ FT: 6,500
SALES (est): 2.4MM **Privately Held**
SIC: 7372 Business oriented computer
software

(P-24412)
SIMPLEFEED INC
289 S San Antonio Rd # 2, Los Altos
(94022-3758)
PHONE...................650 947-7445
Mark Carlson, *President*
Alik Elishberg, *Vice Pres*
Sequoia Capital, *Principal*
Yuriy Grinberg, *Chief Engr*
EMP: 15
SALES: 1.3MM **Privately Held**
SIC: 7372 Prepackaged software

(P-24413)
SIMPLELEGAL INC
488 Ellis St, Mountain View (94043-2204)
PHONE...................415 763-5366
Nathan Wenzel, *CEO*
Tina Fan, *Vice Pres*
David Lu, *VP Engrg*

Jasmine Tinkess, *Finance*
Wilson Yu, *Opers Staff*
EMP: 11
SALES (est): 350.1K **Privately Held**
SIC: 7372 Business oriented computer
software

(P-24414)
SIOS TECHNOLOGY CORP (HQ)
155 Bovet Rd Ste 476, San Mateo
(94402-3112)
PHONE...................650 645-7000
Rika Marrazzo, *Principal*
Kellymarie Silva, *Partner*
Kevin Williams, *Senior VP*
Michael Bilancieri, *Vice Pres*
Takashi Fukuda, *Principal*
EMP: 10
SQ FT: 4,400
SALES: 8MM **Privately Held**
WEB: www.steeleye.com
SIC: 7372 Business oriented computer
software

(P-24415)
SKYLIGHT SOFTWARE INC
3792 Bertini Ct Apt 1, San Jose
(95117-1906)
PHONE...................408 858-3933
Shabbir Khan, *President*
Sandhya Dalal, *Consultant*
EMP: 20
SQ FT: 1,400
SALES: 500K **Privately Held**
WEB: www.skylightsoftware.com
SIC: 7372 Prepackaged software

(P-24416)
**SLACK TECHNOLOGIES INC
(PA)**
500 Howard St Ste 100, San Francisco
(94105-3031)
PHONE...................415 902-5526
Stewart Butterfield, *Ch of Bd*
Allen Shim, *CFO*
Tamar Yehoshua,
Robert Frati, *Senior VP*
David Schellhase, *Admin Sec*
EMP: 148
SQ FT: 228,998
SALES: 400.5MM **Publicly Held**
SIC: 7372 Business oriented computer
software

(P-24417)
SMART ACTION COMPANY LLC
300 Continental Blvd # 350, El Segundo
(90245-5042)
PHONE...................310 776-9200
Tom Lewis, *CEO*
Brian Morin, *Chief Mktg Ofcr*
Michael Vanca, *Senior VP*
Louise Gold, *Vice Pres*
Peter E Voss, *Principal*
EMP: 26
SALES: 3.7MM **Privately Held**
SIC: 7372 Prepackaged software

(P-24418)
**SMART-TEK AUTOMATED SVCS
INC (HQ)**
11838 Bernardo Plaza Ct # 250, San Diego
(92128-2413)
PHONE...................858 798-1644
Kelly Mowrey, *COO*
Bryan Bonar, *CEO*
EMP: 17
SQ FT: 2,000
SALES (est): 27.7MM **Publicly Held**
SIC: 7372 Business oriented computer
software
PA: Trucept, Inc.
500 La Terraza Blvd # 150
Escondido CA 92025
866 961-5763

(P-24419)
SMARTDRAW SOFTWARE LLC
9909 Mira Mesa Blvd, San Diego
(92131-1056)
PHONE...................858 225-3300
Paul Stannard, *CEO*
J Anthony Patterson, *COO*
Jeff Anderson, *Vice Pres*
Dan Hoffman, *Vice Pres*
Linda Kaechele, *Vice Pres*

▲ = Import ▼=Export
◆ =Import/Export

EMP: 42
SQ FT: 14,567
SALES: 14.5MM **Privately Held**
WEB: www.smartdraw.com
SIC: 7372 Application computer software

(P-24420)
SMARTLOGIC SEMAPHORE INC
111 N Market St Ste 300, San Jose
(95113-1116)
PHONE................................408 213-9500
Rupert Bentley, *President*
EMP: 12
SALES (est): 1.2MM **Privately Held**
SIC: 7372 Business oriented computer
  software

(P-24421)
SMARTQED INC
421 37th Ave, San Mateo (94403-4328)
PHONE................................925 922-4618
Rishi Mukhopadhyay, *Principal*
Julie Basu, *CEO*
EMP: 10
SALES (est): 244K **Privately Held**
SIC: 7372 7389 Business oriented com-
  puter software;

(P-24422)
SNAPLOGIC INC (PA)
1825 S Grant St Ste 550, San Mateo
(94402-2719)
PHONE................................888 494-1570
Gaurav Dhillon, *CEO*
Bob Parker, *CFO*
Robert J Parker, *CFO*
David Downing, *Chief Mktg Ofcr*
Vaikom Krishnan, *Vice Pres*
EMP: 140
SALES (est): 30.4MM **Privately Held**
SIC: 7372 Business oriented computer
  software

(P-24423)
SNAPMD INC
121 W Lexington Dr # 412, Glendale
(91203-2203)
PHONE................................310 953-4800
Dave Skibinski, *CEO*
George Tierney, *COO*
Deric Frost, *Risk Mgmt Dir*
Douglas Campbell, *Principal*
EMP: 13
SQ FT: 2,200
SALES (est): 541.9K **Privately Held**
SIC: 7372 Business oriented computer
  software

(P-24424)
SO CAL SOFT-PAK INCORPORATED
Also Called: Soft Pak
8525 Gibbs Dr Ste 300, San Diego
(92123-1700)
PHONE................................619 283-2338
Brian Porter, *CEO*
Eddie Garratt, *Vice Pres*
Kevin Mohondro, *Prgrmr*
Norman Rowden, *Prgrmr*
EMP: 31
SQ FT: 5,000
SALES (est): 4.4MM **Privately Held**
WEB: www.soft-pak.com
SIC: 7372 8742 Business oriented com-
  puter software; management consulting
  services

(P-24425)
SOCIALIZE INC
450 Townsend St 102, San Francisco
(94107-1510)
PHONE................................415 529-4019
Daniel R Odio, *CEO*
Sean Shadmand, *President*
Isaac Mosquera, *CTO*
EMP: 50
SALES (est): 2.8MM
SALES (corp-wide): 11.9MM **Privately
Held**
SIC: 7372 Business oriented computer
  software
PA: Sharethis, Inc.
    3000 El Camino Real 5-150
    Palo Alto CA 94306
    650 641-0191

(P-24426)
SOFTWARE AG INC
Also Called: Software AG of Virginia
2901 Tasman Dr Ste 219, Santa Clara
(95054-1138)
PHONE................................408 490-5300
Karl-Heinz Streibich, *Branch Mgr*
EMP: 119
SALES (corp-wide): 991MM **Privately
Held**
SIC: 7372 Application computer software
HQ: Software Ag, Inc.
    11700 Plaza America Dr # 700
    Reston VA 20190
    703 860-5050

(P-24427)
SOFTWARE DEVELOPMENT INC
Also Called: Mi9
5000 Hopyard Rd Ste 160, Pleasanton
(94588-3352)
PHONE................................925 847-8823
Michael Burge, *President*
Jason Wilson, *Marketing Staff*
Barry Tyson, *Director*
Joshua Fischburg, *Manager*
EMP: 25
SQ FT: 8,400
SALES (est): 3.7MM
SALES (corp-wide): 161.2K **Privately
Held**
WEB: www.sdiretail.com
SIC: 7372 7379 Prepackaged software;
  computer related consulting services
PA: Mi9 Business Intelligence Systems Inc
    245 Yorkland Blvd Suite 301
    North York ON M2J 4
    416 491-1483

(P-24428)
SOFTWARE LICENSING CONSULTANTS
Also Called: SLC
1001 Shannon Ct Ste B, Livermore
(94550-9479)
PHONE................................925 371-1277
Edgardo Ramirez, *Vice Pres*
EMP: 35
SQ FT: 7,000
SALES (est): 2.9MM **Privately Held**
WEB: www.ekcos.com
SIC: 7372 5087 Prepackaged software;
  janitors' supplies

(P-24429)
SOFTWARE PARTNERS LLC
906 2nd St, Encinitas (92024-4410)
PHONE................................760 944-8436
Alean Kirnak, *President*
Dan Allen, *Exec VP*
EMP: 25
SALES (est): 1.6MM **Privately Held**
WEB: www.swpartners.com
SIC: 7372 Business oriented computer
  software

(P-24430)
SOLUTIONSOFT SYSTEMS INC
2350 Mission College Blvd, Santa Clara
(95054-1532)
PHONE................................408 346-1491
Paul Wang, *President*
Margaret Wang, *Principal*
Prasanna Mandaleeka, *Business Anlyst*
Aman Singha, *Opers Staff*
EMP: 20
SALES (est): 331.9K **Privately Held**
SIC: 7372 Operating systems computer
  software

(P-24431)
SOLV INC
Also Called: Swinerton Builders
16798 W Bernardo Dr, San Diego
(92127-1904)
PHONE................................858 622-4040
EMP: 124
SALES (corp-wide): 32MM **Privately
Held**
SIC: 7372 Prepackaged software
PA: Solv, Inc.
    260 Townsend St
    San Francisco CA 94107
    858 622-4040

(P-24432)
SONASOFT CORP (PA)
1735 N 1st St Ste 110, San Jose
(95112-4530)
PHONE................................408 583-1600
Frank Velasquez, *CEO*
Romesh K Japra, *Ch of Bd*
Paresh Mehta, *CFO*
Bilal Ahmed, *Vice Pres*
Neil Khanna, *Vice Pres*
EMP: 25
SALES: 771.7K **Publicly Held**
WEB: www.sonasoft.com
SIC: 7372 Prepackaged software

(P-24433)
SONIC SOLUTIONS HOLDINGS INC
2830 De La Cruz Blvd, Santa Clara
(95050-2619)
PHONE................................408 562-8400
EMP: 84
SALES (est): 120.6K
SALES (corp-wide): 695.8MM **Publicly
Held**
SIC: 7372 Home entertainment computer
  software
PA: Tivo Corporation
    2160 Gold St
    San Jose CA 95002
    408 519-9100

(P-24434)
SONIC STUDIO LLC
93 Madrone Rd, Fairfax (94930-2119)
P.O. Box 238 (94978-0238)
PHONE................................415 944-7642
Jonathan Reichbach, *President*
Madeleine Cortes, *CFO*
EMP: 11 EST: 2010
SALES (est): 704.8K **Privately Held**
SIC: 7372 7389 Home entertainment com-
  puter software;

(P-24435)
SONIC VR LLC
225 Broadway Ste 650, San Diego
(92101-5039)
PHONE................................206 227-8585
Jason Riggs, *CEO*
Jose Arjol Acebal, *COO*
Joy Lyons, *General Mgr*
David Carr, *Chief Engr*
EMP: 17
SQ FT: 6,000
SALES (est): 301.5K **Privately Held**
SIC: 7372 8731 Application computer soft-
  ware; commercial physical research

(P-24436)
SONOSIM INC
1738 Berkeley St Ste A, Santa Monica
(90404-4105)
PHONE................................323 473-3800
Eric Savitsky, *President*
Koren Bertolli, *COO*
Heidi Wienckowski, *Vice Pres*
Andres Luzio, *VP Engrg*
Nicole Durden, *Opers Staff*
EMP: 11
SQ FT: 900
SALES (est): 1.4MM **Privately Held**
SIC: 7372 7371 Educational computer
  software; computer software development
  & applications

(P-24437)
SPACE TIME INSIGHT INC (HQ)
1850 Gateway Dr Ste 125, San Mateo
(94404-4082)
P.O. Box 729, Bolton MA (01740-0729)
PHONE................................650 513-8550
Rob Schilling, *CEO*
Tony Tibshirani, *CEO*
William Tamblyn, *CFO*
Martin Aares, *Bd of Directors*
Gil Cogan, *Bd of Directors*
EMP: 41
SALES (est): 10MM
SALES (corp-wide): 25.8B **Privately Held**
SIC: 7372 Business oriented computer
  software
PA: Nokia Oyj
    Karakaari 7
    Espoo 02610
    104 488-000

(P-24438)
SPATIAL WAVE INC
23461 S Pointe Dr Ste 300, Laguna Hills
(92653-1523)
PHONE................................949 540-6400
Ali Diba, *President*
Meade Maleki, *Vice Pres*
Azaad Hamidi, *Engineer*
Jose Manaloto, *Controller*
Ferrer Sara, *Mktg Coord*
EMP: 10 EST: 2008
SALES (est): 50K **Privately Held**
SIC: 7372 Business oriented computer
  software

(P-24439)
SPECIALISTS IN CSTM SFTWR INC
2574 Wellesley Ave, Los Angeles
(90064-2738)
PHONE................................310 315-9660
Helen Russell, *President*
Melissa Vance, *Treasurer*
Helen Sassone, *Project Mgr*
David Wiser, *Project Mgr*
Dan Fraser, *Mktg Dir*
EMP: 44
SQ FT: 2,400
SALES (est): 7MM **Privately Held**
WEB: www.scs-mbs.com
SIC: 7372 Business oriented computer
  software

(P-24440)
SPIKE CHUNSOFT INC
5000 Airport Plaza Dr # 230, Long Beach
(90815-1271)
PHONE................................562 786-5080
Mitsutoshi Sakurai, *President*
Yasuhiro Iizuka, *CFO*
Yoko Marron, *Exec Dir*
EMP: 12
SQ FT: 2,400
SALES (est): 438K **Privately Held**
SIC: 7372 7373 Home entertainment com-
  puter software; systems software devel-
  opment services
HQ: Spike Chunsoft Co., Ltd.
    2-17-7, Akasaka
    Minato-Ku TKY 107-0
    -

(P-24441)
SPLUNK INC (PA)
270 Brannan St, San Francisco
(94107-2007)
PHONE................................415 848-8400
Douglas Merritt, *President*
Scott Morgan,
David Conte, *Senior VP*
Jacob Loomis, *Senior VP*
Timothy Tully, *Senior VP*
EMP: 160
SQ FT: 182,000
SALES: 1.8B **Publicly Held**
WEB: www.splunk.com
SIC: 7372 Business oriented computer
  software

(P-24442)
SPOTON COMPUTING INC
Also Called: Stanza
209 9th St Fl 3, San Francisco
(94103-3871)
PHONE................................650 293-7464
Smita Saxena, *CEO*
EMP: 28
SQ FT: 3,600
SALES (est): 248.2K **Privately Held**
SIC: 7372 Business oriented computer
  software

(P-24443)
SQUAMTECH INC
Also Called: Shiploop
2023 22nd St, San Francisco (94107-3203)
PHONE................................415 867-8300
Marco Buhlmann, *CEO*
EMP: 10
SALES (est): 440.1K **Privately Held**
SIC: 7372 Application computer software

PRODUCTS & SVCS

(P-24444)
SQUARE INC (PA)
1455 Market St Ste 600, San Francisco
(94103-1332)
PHONE..............................415 375-3176
Jack Dorsey, *Ch of Bd*
Ajmere Dale, *Officer*
Dj Ortua, *Trust Officer*
Tyler Doremus, *General Mgr*
Sarah Cook, *Executive Asst*
EMP: 50
SQ FT: 338,910
SALES: 3.3B **Publicly Held**
SIC: 7372 Prepackaged software

(P-24445)
SQUELCH INC
555 Twin Dolphin Dr # 170, Redwood City
(94065-2140)
PHONE..............................650 241-2700
Jayaram Bhat, *CEO*
Janette Schock, *CFO*
Giorgina Gottlied, *Vice Pres*
Dan Morris, *Vice Pres*
Ilan Raab, *Vice Pres*
EMP: 30 EST: 2017
SALES (est): 1.7MM **Privately Held**
SIC: 7372 Application computer software

(P-24446)
SRA OSS INC
5201 Great America Pkwy # 419, Santa
Clara (95054-1143)
PHONE..............................408 855-8200
RAO Papolu, *President*
EMP: 160
SQ FT: 5,000
SALES (est): 15.6MM **Privately Held**
WEB: www.sraoss.com
SIC: 7372 Publishers' computer software
HQ: Software Research Associates, Inc.
2-32-8, Minamiikebukuro
Toshima-Ku TKY 171-0
-

(P-24447)
SRSB INC
Also Called: Physicians Trust
5004 Cmino Escllo Ste 200, San Clemente
(92673)
PHONE..............................949 234-1881
Steve Rhodes, *President*
EMP: 17
SALES (est): 1.1MM **Privately Held**
SIC: 7372 Publishers' computer software

(P-24448)
STACKLA INC
33 New Mont, San Francisco (94105)
PHONE..............................415 789-3304
Damien Mahoney, *CEO*
Peter Cassaidy,
Mallory Walsh, *VP Mktg*
EMP: 65
SALES (est): 2.7MM **Privately Held**
SIC: 7372 Application computer software

(P-24449)
STACKROX INC (PA)
700 E El Camino Real # 200, Mountain
View (94040-2802)
PHONE..............................650 489-6769
Kamal Shah, *President*
WEI Dang, *Vice Pres*
Jillian McNerney, *Opers Staff*
I Michael, *Opers Staff*
Chris Klein, *Sales Staff*
EMP: 22
SALES (est): 6.2MM **Privately Held**
SIC: 7372 Application computer software

(P-24450)
STALKER SOFTWARE INC
Also Called: Communigate Systems
125 Park Pl Ste 210, Richmond
(94801-3980)
PHONE..............................415 569-2280
Vladimir Butenko, *President*
Philip Slater, *Engineer*
Naomi Nelson, *VP Opers*
Simon Obrien, *Marketing Staff*
Azdio Ballesteros, *Director*
EMP: 50

SALES (est): 5.6MM **Privately Held**
WEB: www.communigate.com
SIC: 7372 7371 Prepackaged software;
custom computer programming services

(P-24451)
**STANDARD COGNITION CORP
(PA)**
965 Mission St Fl 7, San Francisco
(94103-2955)
PHONE..............................201 707-7782
Jordan Fisher, *CEO*
Michael Suswal, *COO*
Anthony Lutz, *CFO*
EMP: 20
SALES: 2MM **Privately Held**
SIC: 7372 Business oriented computer
software

(P-24452)
STARVIEW INC
2841 Junction Ave Ste 110, San Jose
(95134-1921)
P.O. Box 2294, Kalispell MT (59903-2294)
PHONE..............................406 890-5910
Jerry Meerkatz, *CEO*
Steve Baunach, *Founder*
EMP: 34
SQ FT: 5,000
SALES (est): 1.7MM **Privately Held**
SIC: 7372 Business oriented computer
software

(P-24453)
STAT CLINICAL SYSTEMS INC
Also Called: Stat Systems
2560 9th St Ste 317, Berkeley
(94710-2500)
PHONE..............................510 705-8700
Frederick W Dietrich, *CEO*
EMP: 12 EST: 1998
SQ FT: 2,000
SALES (est): 909.4K **Privately Held**
WEB: www.statsystems.com
SIC: 7372 Business oriented computer
software

(P-24454)
STEALTH SECURITY INC
100 S Murphy Ave Ste 300, Sunnyvale
(94086-6118)
PHONE..............................844 978-3258
Larry Link, *President*
Rod Beckstrom, *Ch of Bd*
Tony McIlvenna, *Vice Pres*
Ameya Talwalkar, *Vice Pres*
David Weisman, *Vice Pres*
EMP: 13
SQ FT: 5,000
SALES (est): 117K **Privately Held**
SIC: 7372 Prepackaged software

(P-24455)
STEP MOBILE INC
2765 Sand Hill Rd Ste 201, Menlo Park
(94025-7098)
PHONE..............................203 913-9229
CJ McDonald, *CEO*
EMP: 10
SALES: 100K **Privately Held**
SIC: 7372 Application computer software

(P-24456)
STEPS MOBILE INC
231 3rd St 1, Davis (95616-4524)
PHONE..............................408 806-5178
Anthony Chang, *CEO*
Ron Yeng, *COO*
Bryan Vu, *CTO*
EMP: 10 EST: 2018
SALES: 500K **Privately Held**
SIC: 7372 7389 Application computer soft-
ware;

(P-24457)
STORM8 INC
Also Called: Storm8 Entertainment
2400 Bridge Pkwy 2, Redwood City
(94065-1166)
PHONE..............................650 596-8600
Perry Tam, *CEO*
Steve Parkis, *President*
Jeff Witt, *President*
Terence Fung, *Officer*
Tim Letourneau, *Officer*
EMP: 16

SALES (est): 4.3MM **Privately Held**
SIC: 7372 Prepackaged software

(P-24458)
STRATEGIC INFO GROUP INC
1953 San Elijo Ave # 201, Cardiff By The
Sea (92007-2348)
PHONE..............................760 697-1050
Douglas Novak, *CEO*
Ray Greenwood, *Senior VP*
John Graham, *Vice Pres*
Suzy Reno, *Vice Pres*
Suhas Tembe, *Technical Staff*
EMP: 28 EST: 1994
SALES (est): 4.8MM **Privately Held**
SIC: 7372 Educational computer software;
application computer software; business
oriented computer software

(P-24459)
STRATEGIC INSIGHTS INC
Also Called: Brightscope
9191 Towne Centre Dr # 401, San Diego
(92122-1225)
PHONE..............................858 452-7500
Chris Riggio, *Officer*
Jeremy Ross, *Exec VP*
David Gaunt, *Vice Pres*
Keith Sjgren, *Managing Dir*
Nicole Hoggar, *Executive Asst*
EMP: 65 **Privately Held**
SIC: 7372 Business oriented computer
software
PA: Strategic Insights, Inc.
805 3rd Ave
New York NY 10022
-

(P-24460)
STRATEGY COMPANION CORP
3240 El Camino Real # 120, Irvine
(92602-1384)
PHONE..............................714 460-8398
Robert Sterling, *President*
Eric Halverson, *Partner*
Grace Lin, *Office Admin*
Bill Tang, *Manager*
EMP: 70
SALES (est): 5.5MM **Privately Held**
SIC: 7372 Prepackaged software
PA: Strategy Companion Corp.
Scotia Centre 4th Floor
George Town GR CAYMAN

(P-24461)
**STREAMLINE DEVELOPMENT
LLC**
Also Called: Streamline Solutions
100 Smith Ranch Rd # 124, San Rafael
(94903-1900)
PHONE..............................415 499-3355
Laurence Snyder, *CEO*
Walter Franz, *CFO*
EMP: 25
SQ FT: 9,000
SALES (est): 4MM
SALES (corp-wide): 1B **Privately Held**
SIC: 7372 Prepackaged software
HQ: Electronics For Imaging, Inc.
6750 Dumbarton Cir
Fremont CA 94555
650 357-3500

(P-24462)
STREVUS INC
455 Market St Ste 1670, San Francisco
(94105-2472)
PHONE..............................415 704-8182
Ken Hoang, *CEO*
Gregg Loos, *President*
Dmitri Korablev, *Vice Pres*
Ken Price, *Vice Pres*
Jennifer Turcotte, *Vice Pres*
EMP: 60
SALES (est): 5MM **Privately Held**
SIC: 7372 7371 Business oriented com-
puter software; computer software devel-
opment

(P-24463)
STRYDER CORP (PA)
Also Called: Handshake
225 Bush St Fl 12, San Francisco
(94104-4254)
P.O. Box 40770 (94140-0770)
PHONE..............................415 981-8400
Garrett Lord, *Ch of Bd*
Randy Bitting, *Officer*
Ben Christensen, *Principal*
Scott Ringwelski, *Principal*
Jade Pathe, *Manager*
EMP: 29 EST: 2014
SALES (est): 13.4MM **Privately Held**
SIC: 7372 7371 7379 Educational com-
puter software; application computer soft-
ware; business oriented computer
software; computer software development
& applications; computer related consult-
ing services

(P-24464)
STUMBLEUPON INC (HQ)
535 Mission St Fl 11, San Francisco
(94105-3325)
PHONE..............................415 979-0640
Garrett Camp, *CEO*
Mark Bartels, *CFO*
Josh Smallman, *Vice Pres*
Ellen Edelman, *Executive*
Ankit Chaudhary, *Sr Software Eng*
EMP: 25
SALES (est): 6MM **Privately Held**
WEB: www.STUMBLEUPON.com
SIC: 7372 Application computer software
PA: Mix Tech, Inc
535 Mission St Fl 11
San Francisco CA 94105
415 940-2055

(P-24465)
SUGARSYNC INC
Also Called: Sharpcast
6922 Hollywood Blvd # 500, Los Angeles
(90028-6125)
PHONE..............................650 571-5105
Laura Yecies, *President*
Peter Chantel, *CFO*
Fred Huey, *CFO*
Samir S Mehta, *General Mgr*
Abha Chaudhary, *Software Engr*
EMP: 30
SQ FT: 11,000
SALES (est): 7MM **Privately Held**
WEB: www.sugarsync.com
SIC: 7372 Business oriented computer
software

(P-24466)
SUMOPTI
742 Moreno Ave, Palo Alto (94303-3617)
PHONE..............................650 331-1126
EMP: 10
SQ FT: 1,500
SALES (est): 45.8K **Privately Held**
SIC: 7372

(P-24467)
SUN MICROSYSTEMS TECH LTD
4150 Network Cir, Santa Clara
(95054-1778)
PHONE..............................650 960-1300
Safra A Catz, *CEO*
John Fowler, *Officer*
Michael E Lehman, *Exec VP*
Brian Sutphin, *Exec VP*
Ron Huizen, *Vice Pres*
EMP: 36
SALES (est): 3.1MM **Privately Held**
SIC: 7372 Prepackaged software

(P-24468)
SUPER BINGE MEDIA INC
530 Bush St Ste 600, San Francisco
(94108-3634)
PHONE..............................714 688-6231
Nicholas Talarico, *President*
Yigeng Sun, *Officer*
George Zeloom, *Officer*
EMP: 13
SALES: 500K **Privately Held**
SIC: 7372 Application computer software
PA: Super Lucky Casino Inc.
530 Bush St Ste 600
San Francisco CA 94108
-

(P-24469)
SUPERIOR SOFTWARE INC
16055 Ventura Blvd # 650, Encino
(91436-2601)
PHONE.....................................818 990-1135
EMP: 10
SQ FT: 200
SALES (est): 708.9K **Privately Held**
SIC: 7372 8111 5734

(P-24470)
SUPPORT TECHNOLOGIES INC
1939 Deere Ave, Irvine (92606-4818)
PHONE.....................................949 442-2957
Tayo Daramole, *President*
Ian Yhap, *Engineer*
George Yu, *Manager*
EMP: 15
SQ FT: 2,000
SALES (est): 715.1K **Privately Held**
WEB: www.alexusinfo.com
SIC: 7372 Prepackaged software

(P-24471)
SUPPORTCOM INC
1200 Crossman Ave Ste 240, Sunnyvale
(94089-1106)
PHONE.....................................516 393-6759
Roop K Lakkaraju, *Exec VP*
Elena Fintzi, *Vice Pres*
Charles Myers, *Marketing Staff*
Ernest Maupin, *Director*
Ryan Newell, *Director*
EMP: 11
SALES (corp-wide): 69.5MM **Publicly Held**
SIC: 7372 Prepackaged software
PA: Support.Com, Inc.
    1200 Crossman Ave Ste 210
    Sunnyvale CA 94089
    650 556-9440

(P-24472)
SWIFTSTACK INC (PA)
660 Market St Ste 500, San Francisco
(94104-5021)
PHONE.....................................415 625-0293
Don Jaworski, *CEO*
Anders Tjernlund, *COO*
Randall Jackson, *Vice Pres*
Timur Alperovich, *Sr Software Eng*
Andrew Boring, *Engineer*
EMP: 34
SALES (est): 8.5MM **Privately Held**
SIC: 7372 Business oriented computer
    software; application computer software

(P-24473)
SWIFTSTACK INC
1054 S De Anza Blvd, San Jose
(95129-3553)
PHONE.....................................408 642-1865
Don Jaworski, *CEO*
EMP: 37
SALES (corp-wide): 8.5MM **Privately Held**
SIC: 7372 Prepackaged software
PA: Swiftstack, Inc.
    660 Market St Ste 500
    San Francisco CA 94104
    415 625-0293

(P-24474)
SYAPSE INC
303 2nd St Ste N500, San Francisco
(94107-3639)
PHONE.....................................650 924-1461
Gary J Kurtzman MD, *CEO*
Jonathan Hirsch, *President*
Fletcher Payne, *CFO*
Dennis Shin, *Ch Credit Ofcr*
Thomas D Brown, *Chief Mktg Ofcr*
EMP: 180
SALES (est): 4.3MM **Privately Held**
SIC: 7372 Prepackaged software

(P-24475)
SYMPHONYRM INC
530 University Ave, Palo Alto (94301-1900)
PHONE.....................................650 336-8430
Michael Linnert, *CEO*
Vipul Vyas, *Vice Pres*
EMP: 12
SALES (est): 536.2K **Privately Held**
SIC: 7372 Business oriented computer
    software

(P-24476)
SYNERGEX INTERNATIONAL CORP
2355 Gold Meadow Way # 200, Gold River
(95670-6326)
PHONE.....................................916 635-7300
Michele C Wong, *CEO*
Serena Channel, *Partner*
Vigfus A Asmundson, *Shareholder*
Georgia Petersen, *Shareholder*
Thomas J Powers, *Shareholder*
EMP: 55
SALES (est): 7.9MM **Privately Held**
WEB: www.synergex.com
SIC: 7372 Business oriented computer
    software

(P-24477)
SYNERGY GLOBAL INC
4 Embarcadero Ctr # 1400, San Francisco
(94111-4106)
PHONE.....................................415 766-3540
EMP: 10 EST: 2011
SALES (est): 710K **Privately Held**
SIC: 7372

(P-24478)
SYNOPSYS INC (PA)
690 E Middlefield Rd, Mountain View
(94043-4033)
PHONE.....................................650 584-5000
Aart J De Geus, *Ch of Bd*
Trac Pham, *CFO*
Joseph W Logan, *Officer*
John F Runkel Jr, *Admin Sec*
EMP: 500
SQ FT: 341,000
SALES: 3.1B **Publicly Held**
WEB: www.synopsys.com
SIC: 7372 7371 Prepackaged software;
    computer software development

(P-24479)
SYNOPSYS INC
199 S Los Robles Ave # 400, Pasadena
(91101-4634)
PHONE.....................................626 795-9101
George Bayz, *CEO*
Daren Reid, *Research*
Qingran Zheng, *Research*
Padma Kolli, *Engineer*
EMP: 90
SALES (corp-wide): 3.1B **Publicly Held**
SIC: 7372 8711 Application computer soft-
    ware; engineering services
PA: Synopsys, Inc.
    690 E Middlefield Rd
    Mountain View CA 94043
    650 584-5000

(P-24480)
SYNPLICITY INC (HQ)
690 E Middlefield Rd, Mountain View
(94043-4010)
PHONE.....................................650 584-5000
Gary Meyers, *President*
Alisa Yaffa, *Ch of Bd*
Andrew Dauman, *President*
John J Hanlon, *CFO*
Roy Vallee, *Bd of Directors*
EMP: 160
SQ FT: 66,212
SALES (est): 17.8MM
SALES (corp-wide): 3.1B **Publicly Held**
WEB: www.synplicity.com
SIC: 7372 Prepackaged software
PA: Synopsys, Inc.
    690 E Middlefield Rd
    Mountain View CA 94043
    650 584-5000

(P-24481)
SYNTEST TECHNOLOGIES INC
4320 Stevens Creek Blvd # 100, San Jose
(95129-1285)
PHONE.....................................408 720-9956
Laung-Terng Wang, *CEO*
Ravi Apte, *Senior VP*
Renay Chang, *Admin Asst*
EMP: 10
SQ FT: 5,000
SALES (est): 892.1K **Privately Held**
WEB: www.syntest.com
SIC: 7372 Business oriented computer
    software

(P-24482)
SYSOP TOOLS INC
815 Moraga Dr, Los Angeles (90049-1633)
PHONE.....................................310 598-3885
Kurt D Lewis, *President*
David Martin, *CFO*
EMP: 10
SQ FT: 2,000
SALES (est): 936.1K **Privately Held**
SIC: 7372 Business oriented computer
    software

(P-24483)
TAKIPI INC
797 Bryant St, San Francisco
(94107-1027)
PHONE.....................................408 203-9585
Tal Weiss, *CEO*
Limor Wilks, *Vice Pres*
David Boyle, *VP Sales*
Ophir Primat, *Marketing Staff*
Chen Harel, *Manager*
EMP: 10
SQ FT: 500
SALES (est): 741.9K
SALES (corp-wide): 3.4MM **Privately Held**
SIC: 7372 Application computer software
PA: Takipi Ltd
    72 Rosen Pinchas
    Tel Aviv-Jaffa 69512
    360 431-88

(P-24484)
TALISMAN SYSTEMS GROUP INC
1111 Oak St, San Francisco (94117-2216)
PHONE.....................................415 357-1751
Michael Varnum, *President*
William Hatfield, *Shareholder*
Monique Knox, *Shareholder*
William Yu, *Shareholder*
Jason Yan, *Info Tech Dir*
EMP: 12
SALES (est): 1.7MM **Privately Held**
WEB: www.talisys.com
SIC: 7372 7371 Business oriented com-
    puter software; custom computer pro-
    gramming services

(P-24485)
TALIX INC
660 3rd St Ste 302, San Francisco
(94107-1921)
PHONE.....................................628 220-3885
Derek Gordon, *President*
Bob Hetchler, *Senior VP*
Paul Clip, *Vice Pres*
Shahyan Currimbhoy, *Vice Pres*
Tim England, *Vice Pres*
EMP: 70
SALES (est): 2.2MM **Privately Held**
SIC: 7372 8099 Application computer soft-
    ware; blood related health services

(P-24486)
TALKDESK INC (PA)
535 Mission St Fl 12, San Francisco
(94105-3225)
PHONE.....................................888 743-3044
Ben McCarthy, *Administration*
Gadi Shamia, *COO*
Michael Reed, *Senior VP*
Jon Heaps, *Vice Pres*
Derris Vandivort, *Technical Staff*
EMP: 34 EST: 2011
SALES (est): 8.4MM **Privately Held**
SIC: 7372 Application computer software

(P-24487)
TALLYGO INC (PA)
4133 Redwood Ave # 1015, Los Angeles
(90066-5627)
PHONE.....................................510 858-1969
Thomas Scaramellino, *CEO*
Matt Triplett,
EMP: 10
SALES (est): 819.8K **Privately Held**
SIC: 7372 Application computer software

(P-24488)
TANGOE US INC
9920 Pcf Hts Blvd Ste 200, San Diego
(92121)
PHONE.....................................858 452-6800
Sandy Jimenez, *Branch Mgr*

EMP: 100
SALES (corp-wide): 491.5MM **Privately Held**
SIC: 7372 Application computer software
HQ: Tangoe Us, Inc.
    1 Waterview Dr Ste 200
    Shelton CT 06484
    973 257-0300

(P-24489)
TAPINGO INC (HQ)
39 Stillman St, San Francisco
(94107-1309)
PHONE.....................................415 283-5222
Daniel Almog, *CEO*
Sweta Desai, *Partner*
Ryann Starks, *Partner*
Jeff Macdonald, *Finance Mgr*
Leanne Reis, *Pub Rel Mgr*
EMP: 48
SQ FT: 4,300
SALES (est): 11.8MM
SALES (corp-wide): 1B **Publicly Held**
SIC: 7372 Prepackaged software
PA: Grubhub Inc.
    111 W Washington St # 2100
    Chicago IL 60602
    877 585-7878

(P-24490)
TAPONIX INC
Also Called: Tapclicks
5300 Stevens Creek Blvd, San Jose
(95129-1032)
PHONE.....................................408 725-2942
Babak Hedayati, *CEO*
Syed Ahmed, *President*
Noah Jacobson, *President*
Michael Mertz, *Vice Pres*
Ryan Adcock, *Legal Staff*
EMP: 12
SQ FT: 3,192
SALES (est): 1.3MM **Privately Held**
SIC: 7372 Business oriented computer
    software

(P-24491)
TDO SOFTWARE INC
6235 Lusk Blvd, San Diego (92121-2731)
PHONE.....................................858 558-3696
Luiz Motta, *General Mgr*
Sean Doonan, *Web Dvlpr*
Jared Ardine, *Technical Staff*
Cheryl Hall, *Technical Staff*
EMP: 25
SQ FT: 3,600
SALES (est): 1.9MM **Privately Held**
WEB: www.tdosoftware.com
SIC: 7372 Prepackaged software
PA: Sonendo, Inc.
    26061 Merit Cir Ste 102
    Laguna Hills CA 92653

(P-24492)
TEAMIFIER INC
514 Live Oak Ln, Emerald Hills
(94062-3415)
PHONE.....................................408 591-9872
Steven Ganz, *CEO*
EMP: 10 EST: 2015
SALES (est): 38.6K **Privately Held**
SIC: 7372 7371 Application computer soft-
    ware; custom computer programming
    services

(P-24493)
TECH4LEARNING INC (PA)
6160 Mission, San Diego (92120)
PHONE.....................................619 563-5348
David Wagner, *President*
Dallas Jones, *CFO*
Rodger Cook, *Vice Pres*
Melinda Kolk, *Vice Pres*
Carolyn Daly, *Regional Mgr*
EMP: 16
SQ FT: 2,839
SALES (est): 2MM **Privately Held**
WEB: www.tech4learning.com
SIC: 7372 Educational computer software

PRODUCTS & SVCS

(P-24494)
TECHMO ENTERTAINMENT INC
3191 17 Mile Dr, Pebble Beach
(93953-3605)
P.O. Box 828 (93953-0828)
PHONE..................................408 309-3039
Thomas Williams, *CEO*
EMP: 12
SALES (est): 682.9K **Privately Held**
SIC: 7372 Business oriented computer
software

(P-24495)
**TECHNICAL SALES INTL LLC
(HQ)**
910 Pleasant Grove Blvd # 120, Roseville
(95678-6193)
PHONE..................................866 493-6337
Tammy Ford, *CEO*
Brenda Brill, *Accountant*
Cedric Green, *Opers Mgr*
Nathan Moore, *Regl Sales Mgr*
Bill Whitney, *Sales Staff*
EMP: 11
SALES (est): 2.8MM **Privately Held**
WEB: www.technicalsalesinternational.com
SIC: 7372 Application computer software

(P-24496)
TEKEVER CORPORATION
5201 Great America Pkwy, Santa Clara
(95054-1122)
PHONE..................................408 730-2617
Michael L Margolis, *CEO*
Robert Whitehouse, *Business Dir*
EMP: 70
SALES (est): 3.3MM **Privately Held**
WEB: www.tekever.com
SIC: 7372 Prepackaged software

(P-24497)
TELESIGN HOLDINGS INC (DH)
13274 Fiji Way Ste 600, Marina Del Rey
(90292-7293)
PHONE..................................310 740-9700
Ryan Disraeli, *CEO*
Philipp Gast, *CFO*
Justin Hart, *Chief Mktg Ofcr*
Tom Powledge, *Officer*
Joe Amadea, *Sales Staff*
EMP: 30 **EST:** 2016
SALES: 7.8MM **Privately Held**
SIC: 7372 Prepackaged software

(P-24498)
TELLUS SOLUTIONS INC
3350 Scott Blvd Bldg 34a, Santa Clara
(95054-3105)
PHONE..................................408 850-2942
Sara Jain, *President*
Jinesh Jain, *Vice Pres*
Mary Alvarez, *Tech Recruiter*
Mohit Ghosh, *Tech Recruiter*
Manoj Kumar, *Tech Recruiter*
EMP: 38
SALES (est): 3MM **Privately Held**
SIC: 7372 7371 7373 Prepackaged soft-
ware; custom computer programming
services; computer integrated systems
design

(P-24499)
**TESELAGEN BIOTECHNOLOGY
INC**
1501 Mariposa St Ste 312, San Francisco
(94107-2367)
PHONE..................................650 387-5932
Michael John Fero, *CEO*
Tom Baruch, *Bd of Directors*
Nathan Hillson, *Security Dir*
Eduardo Abeliuk, *CTO*
EMP: 10
SALES (est): 1MM **Privately Held**
SIC: 7372 Prepackaged software

(P-24500)
THEBRAIN TECHNOLOGIES LP
11522 W Washington Blvd, Los Angeles
(90066-5914)
PHONE..................................310 751-5000
Harlan Hugh, *General Ptnr*
Shelley Hayduk, *Partner*
EMP: 15
SQ FT: 2,850

SALES (est): 1.4MM **Privately Held**
WEB: www.thebrain.com
SIC: 7372 Business oriented computer
software; home entertainment computer
software

(P-24501)
THERMEON CORPORATION (PA)
1175 Warner Ave, Tustin (92780-6458)
PHONE..................................714 731-9191
Rollo S Pickford, *Ch of Bd*
Scott Sampson, *President*
Sharon Miller, *CFO*
Scott Porter, *Technology*
EMP: 14
SQ FT: 5,000
SALES (est): 2.8MM **Privately Held**
WEB: www.thermeon.com
SIC: 7372 7373 5045 Prepackaged soft-
ware; computer systems analysis & de-
sign; computers, peripherals & software

(P-24502)
THINKSMART LLC
530 Jackson St Fl 3, San Francisco
(94133-5132)
PHONE..................................888 489-4284
Paul Hirner, *CEO*
Peter Cernak, *Software Dev*
Dani Dayan, *Accountant*
Dillon Knowlton, *Production*
Kelli Negro, *Marketing Staff*
EMP: 12 **EST:** 2013
SALES (est): 679.5K
SALES (corp-wide): 78.3MM **Privately
Held**
SIC: 7372 Business oriented computer
software
PA: Mitratech Holdings, Inc.
5001 Plz On
Austin TX 78746
512 382-7322

(P-24503)
THIRDMOTION INC
795 Folsom St Fl 1, San Francisco
(94107-4226)
PHONE..................................415 848-2724
Roel Pieper, *CEO*
Alexander Dailey,
Randy Fish, *CTO*
EMP: 14
SALES: 250K **Privately Held**
SIC: 7372 Application computer software

(P-24504)
THIRDROCK SOFTWARE
7098 Chiala Ln, San Jose (95129-2856)
PHONE..................................408 777-2910
Subrata Dasgupta, *Owner*
EMP: 15 **EST:** 1995
SALES (est): 952.4K **Privately Held**
SIC: 7372 Prepackaged software

(P-24505)
THOUGHTSPOT INC
910 Hermosa Ct, Sunnyvale (94085-4199)
PHONE..................................800 508-7008
Sudheesh Nair, *CEO*
Ajeet Singh, *Ch of Bd*
David Freeman, *Senior VP*
Brian McCarthy, *Senior VP*
Chris Brozek, *Vice Pres*
EMP: 452
SALES (est): 4.3MM **Privately Held**
SIC: 7372 Business oriented computer
software

(P-24506)
THOUSANDEYES INC (PA)
201 Mission St Ste 1700, San Francisco
(94105-8102)
PHONE..................................415 513-4526
Mohit Lad, *CEO*
Paul Kizakevich, *Vice Pres*
Prabha Krishna, *Vice Pres*
David Stokey, *Vice Pres*
Craig Thomas, *Vice Pres*
EMP: 75
SALES (est): 18.9MM **Privately Held**
SIC: 7372 Business oriented computer
software

(P-24507)
THRIO INC
5230 Las Virgenes Rd, Calabasas
(91302-3448)
PHONE..................................747 258-4201
Rose Sinicrope, *COO*
EMP: 20
SALES (est): 508.2K **Privately Held**
SIC: 7372 Prepackaged software

(P-24508)
TI LIMITED LLC (PA)
20335 Ventura Blvd, Woodland Hills
(91364-2444)
PHONE..................................323 877-5991
ARI Daniels,
Alberto Gamez,
EMP: 52 **EST:** 2016
SQ FT: 9,000
SALES: 9MM **Privately Held**
SIC: 7372 8748 Business oriented com-
puter software; business consulting

(P-24509)
TIBCO SOFTWARE INC
575 Market St Fl 15, San Francisco
(94105-5815)
PHONE..................................415 344-0339
Vivek Ranadiv, *Branch Mgr*
EMP: 15
SALES (corp-wide): 885.6MM **Privately
Held**
SIC: 7372 Prepackaged software
HQ: Tibco Software Inc.
3307 Hillview Ave
Palo Alto CA 94304

(P-24510)
TIMELY DATA RESOURCES INC
107 Washburn Ave, Capitola (95010-3743)
PHONE..................................831 462-2510
Robert Weissberg, *President*
Yvonne Brill, *Vice Pres*
EMP: 10
SQ FT: 2,000
SALES (est): 1.1MM **Privately Held**
WEB: www.tdrweb.com
SIC: 7372 Publishers' computer software

(P-24511)
TIMEVALUE SOFTWARE
22 Mauchly, Irvine (92618-2306)
P.O. Box 50250 (92619-0250)
PHONE..................................949 727-1800
Michael Applegate, *President*
Linda Applegate, *Vice Pres*
Randy Fleury, *Vice Pres*
Charles Miller, *Vice Pres*
Jim Rey, *Vice Pres*
EMP: 25
SQ FT: 18,000
SALES: 2.5MM **Privately Held**
WEB: www.timevalue.com
SIC: 7372 7371 Prepackaged software;
computer software development

(P-24512)
TIPESTRY INC
940 Stewart Dr 203, Sunnyvale
(94085-3912)
PHONE..................................650 421-1344
David Davies, *CEO*
EMP: 11
SALES: 1MM **Privately Held**
SIC: 7372 Prepackaged software

(P-24513)
TIVIX INC (PA)
2845 California St, San Francisco
(94115-2515)
PHONE..................................415 680-1299
Bret Waters, *President*
Francis Cleary, *Web Dvlpr*
Dariusz Fryta, *Software Engr*
Flavio Zhingri, *Software Engr*
Bill Conneely, *Director*
EMP: 11
SALES (est): 1.7MM **Privately Held**
SIC: 7372 Application computer software

(P-24514)
TMX
5882 Fullerton Ave Apt 3, Buena Park
(90621-2001)
PHONE..................................657 325-1756

Jorge Zamora, *General Ptnr*
Curtis Heath, *Manager*
EMP: 43
SALES: 376K **Privately Held**
SIC: 7372 7389 Application computer soft-
ware;

(P-24515)
TOKBOX INC (DH)
501 2nd St Ste 310, San Francisco
(94107-4191)
PHONE..................................415 284-4688
J Scott Lomond, *CEO*
Jana Munyon, *Office Mgr*
Tiffany Walsh, *Sr Software Eng*
Badri Rajasekar, *VP Engrg*
Christian Bennstrom, *Engineer*
EMP: 10
SALES (est): 2.6MM
SALES (corp-wide): 1B **Publicly Held**
SIC: 7372 Application computer software
HQ: Telefonica Digital, Inc.
501 2nd St Ste 310
San Francisco CA 94107
650 967-4357

(P-24516)
TOPGUEST INC
Also Called: Ezrez Software
601 Montgomery St Fl 17, San Francisco
(94111-2621)
PHONE..................................646 415-9402
Geoff Lewis, *CEO*
EMP: 20
SALES (est): 1MM **Privately Held**
SIC: 7372 Business oriented computer
software
PA: Switchfly, Inc
500 3rd St Ste 440
San Francisco CA 94107

(P-24517)
TOPI SYSTEMS INC
20650 4th St Apt 2, Saratoga (95070-5893)
PHONE..................................408 807-5124
EMP: 10
SALES (est): 570K **Privately Held**
SIC: 7372 Prepackaged software

(P-24518)
TOPLINE GAME LABS LLC
10351 Santa Monica Blvd # 410, Los Ange-
les (90025-6937)
PHONE..................................310 461-0350
David Geller, *CEO*
Elon Spar, *Ch of Bd*
Joshua Small, *COO*
EMP: 17
SQ FT: 2,500
SALES (est): 1.5MM **Privately Held**
SIC: 7372 Home entertainment computer
software

(P-24519)
TOPPAGE INC
3101 Whipple Rd Ste 28, Union City
(94587-1223)
PHONE..................................510 471-6366
Frank Gabrielli, *President*
Kent Toussaint, *Manager*
EMP: 10
SALES (est): 606.3K **Privately Held**
SIC: 7372 Prepackaged software

(P-24520)
TORIAN GROUP INC
519 W Center Ave, Visalia (93291-6019)
PHONE..................................559 733-1940
Tim Torian, *President*
Jose Lucatero, *Network Tech*
EMP: 10
SALES (est): 1.8MM **Privately Held**
WEB: www.torian.com
SIC: 7372 Application computer software

(P-24521)
**TOTAL CMMNICATOR
SOLUTIONS INC**
Also Called: Spark Compass
11150 Santa Monica Blvd # 600, Los Ange-
les (90025-3380)
PHONE..................................619 277-1488
Brent Erik Bjojegard, *CEO*
EMP: 95

▲ = Import ▼=Export
◆ =Import/Export

SALES: 5MM **Privately Held**
SIC: 7372 Application computer software

(P-24522)
TOUCHPOINT SOLUTIONS
18426 Brookhurst St # 207, Fountain Valley
(92708-6778)
PHONE..............................714 740-7242
Brett Greathouse, *President*
Mark Mortensen, *COO*
Michael Moss, *Administration*
Renee Rice, *Sales Staff*
EMP: 10 EST: 2013
SALES (est): 504.9K **Privately Held**
SIC: 7372 Application computer software

(P-24523)
TOUTAPP INC
901 Mariners Island Blvd # 500, San Mateo
(94404-1592)
PHONE..............................866 548-1927
Tawheed Kader, *CEO*
David Hauser, *Engineer*
Jessica Green, *Sales Staff*
EMP: 17
SALES (est): 2MM
SALES (corp-wide): 9B **Publicly Held**
SIC: 7372 Application computer software
HQ: Marketo, Inc.
901 Mariners Island Blvd # 200
San Mateo CA 94404
-

(P-24524)
TRANSPLANT CONNECT INC
Also Called: I Transplant Enterprise Tech
2701 Ocean Park Blvd # 222, Santa Monica
(90405-5212)
PHONE..............................310 392-1400
John Piano, *CEO*
Brian Buroker, *Partner*
Lucia Lopez, *Admin Asst*
Renu Varghese, *Software Dev*
Jerome Depotter, *Software Engr*
EMP: 28
SALES (est): 3.4MM **Privately Held**
WEB: www.transplantconnect.com
SIC: 7372 7371 Prepackaged software;
custom computer programming services

(P-24525)
**TRAVEL COMPUTER SYSTEMS
INC**
Also Called: Travcom
1990 Westwood Blvd # 310, Los Angeles
(90025-8426)
PHONE..............................310 558-3130
Jack Revel, *President*
Marsha N Revel, *Admin Sec*
Lydia Appelius, *Manager*
EMP: 16
SQ FT: 1,200
SALES: 1.5MM **Privately Held**
WEB: www.travcom.com
SIC: 7372 Business oriented computer
software

(P-24526)
TRIBEWORX LLC
4 San Joaquin Plz Ste 150, Newport Beach
(92660-5934)
PHONE..............................800 949-3432
EMP: 75
SQ FT: 10,000
SALES (est): 4.9MM **Privately Held**
SIC: 7372

(P-24527)
TRILIBIS INC (PA)
Also Called: Trilibis Mobile
66 Bovet Rd Ste 285, San Mateo
(94402-3128)
P.O. Box 19170, Sacramento (95819-0170)
PHONE..............................650 646-2400
Alex Panelli, *President*
Tom Burke, *CFO*
EMP: 12
SALES (est): 1.8MM **Privately Held**
SIC: 7372 Application computer software

(P-24528)
TRIZIC INC
60 E Sir Francis Drake Bl, Larkspur
(94939-1713)
PHONE..............................415 366-6583
Andrew Sievers, *CEO*

Steve Lewczyk, *Officer*
Vanessa Torney, *Office Mgr*
Jennifer Wu, *VP Mktg*
EMP: 40
SALES (est): 527.5K **Privately Held**
SIC: 7372 Business oriented computer
software

(P-24529)
TROV INC (PA)
347 Hartz Ave, Danville (94526-3307)
PHONE..............................925 478-5500
Scott Walchek, *CEO*
Sean O'Donoghue, *General Mgr*
Michael Pearson, *Admin Sec*
David Canavan, *Controller*
EMP: 21 EST: 2012
SQ FT: 4,972
SALES (est): 4MM **Privately Held**
SIC: 7372 Application computer software

(P-24530)
TUBEMOGUL INC
1250 53rd St Ste 1, Emeryville
(94608-2965)
PHONE..............................510 653-0126
Brett Wilson, *President*
Robert Gatto, *COO*
Ron Will, *CFO*
Keith Eadie, *Chief Mktg Ofcr*
Paul Joachim, *Officer*
EMP: 68
SQ FT: 49,000
SALES: 180.7MM
SALES (corp-wide): 9B **Publicly Held**
SIC: 7372 Application computer software
PA: Adobe Inc.
345 Park Ave
San Jose CA 95110
408 536-6000

(P-24531)
TUKKO GROUP LLC
Also Called: Tukko Labs
530 Alameda Del Prado, Novato
(94949-9810)
PHONE..............................408 598-1251
Ashton B Wolfson, *CEO*
EMP: 20
SALES (est): 846.7K **Privately Held**
SIC: 7372 Prepackaged software

(P-24532)
TURBOTOOLS CORPORATION
2190 31st Ave, San Francisco
(94116-1637)
PHONE..............................415 759-5599
Alex H Chernyak, *CEO*
Michael Savransky, *Vice Pres*
EMP: 15
SALES (est): 846.3K **Privately Held**
WEB: www.turbotools.com
SIC: 7372 Prepackaged software

(P-24533)
TYLER TECHNOLOGIES INC
Also Called: Tyler Camera Systems
14218 Aetna St, Van Nuys (91401-3433)
PHONE..............................818 989-4420
Nelson Tyler, *Owner*
EMP: 15
SALES (corp-wide): 935.2MM **Publicly
Held**
SIC: 7372 Prepackaged software
PA: Tyler Technologies, Inc.
5101 Tennyson Pkwy
Plano TX 75024
972 713-3700

(P-24534)
TZ HOLDINGS LP
567 San Nicolas Dr # 120, Newport Beach
(92660-6513)
PHONE..............................949 719-2200
Regina Paolillo, *Principal*
EMP: 2000
SALES (est): 46.9MM **Privately Held**
SIC: 7372 Prepackaged software

(P-24535)
**ULTIMATE SOFTWARE GROUP
INC**
5 Hutton Centre Dr # 130, Santa Ana
(92707-8738)
PHONE..............................949 214-2710
John Stauffer, *Vice Pres*

Danny Pyo, *Accounts Mgr*
Norma Digerlando, *Consultant*
EMP: 44
SALES (corp-wide): 1.1B **Privately Held**
SIC: 7372 Application computer software
PA: The Ultimate Software Group Inc
2000 Ultimate Way
Weston FL 33326
954 331-7000

(P-24536)
UNDERGROUND LABS INC
1114 Oakwood Cir, Clayton (94517-1700)
PHONE..............................925 297-5333
Jeff Annison, *CEO*
EMP: 10
SALES (est): 696.5K **Privately Held**
SIC: 7372 7371 Application computer soft-
ware; computer software development &
applications

(P-24537)
UNIFI SOFTWARE INC
1810 Gateway Dr Ste 380, San Mateo
(94404-4063)
PHONE..............................732 614-9522
Matt Mosman, *CEO*
Rob Carlson, *President*
Intekhab Nazeer, *CFO*
Chris Selland, *Vice Pres*
Nitasha Uprit, *Vice Pres*
EMP: 25
SALES: 1.6MM **Privately Held**
SIC: 7372 Business oriented computer
software

(P-24538)
UNIFYID INC
603 Jefferson Ave, Redwood City
(94063-1705)
PHONE..............................650 561-2202
John Whaley, *CEO*
Kurt Somerville, *COO*
EMP: 10 EST: 2015
SQ FT: 2,900
SALES (est): 121.1K **Privately Held**
SIC: 7372 Utility computer software

(P-24539)
UNION SOLUTIONS INC
15355 Bittern Ct, San Leandro
(94579-2757)
PHONE..............................510 483-1222
Xuan James, *Admin Sec*
Paula E Bailey, *CFO*
EMP: 14
SQ FT: 1,500
SALES (est): 560.2K **Privately Held**
WEB: www.unionsolutions.com
SIC: 7372 Prepackaged software

(P-24540)
UNISOFT CORPORATION
10 Rollins Rd Ste 118, Millbrae
(94030-3128)
PHONE..............................650 259-1290
Audrey Ruelas, *President*
Guy Hadland, *CEO*
EMP: 19 EST: 1981
SALES (est): 2.1MM **Privately Held**
WEB: www.unisoft.com
SIC: 7372 5045 Operating systems com-
puter software; utility computer software;
computer software

(P-24541)
**UNIVERSAL MCLOUD USA
CORP**
580 California St, San Francisco
(94104-1000)
PHONE..............................613 222-5904
Russ McMeekin, *CEO*
Michael Sicuro, *CFO*
Gino Lander, *Officer*
Darren Anderson, *Exec VP*
EMP: 15
SALES (est): 305.2K
SALES (corp-wide): 657.9K **Privately
Held**
SIC: 7372 Business oriented computer
software
PA: Universal Mcloud Corp
550-510 Burrard St
Vancouver BC V6C 3
866 420-1781

(P-24542)
UNTANGLE HOLDINGS INC
100 W San Fernando St # 565, San Jose
(95113-1787)
PHONE..............................408 598-4299
Scott Devens, *CEO*
Lori Booroojian, *CFO*
Amy Abatangle, *Chief Mktg Ofcr*
Dirk Morris, *Officer*
Timur Kovalev, *CTO*
EMP: 32
SALES (est): 1.3MM **Privately Held**
SIC: 7372 Prepackaged software

(P-24543)
UPGUARD INC (PA)
723 N Shoreline Blvd, Mountain View
(94043-3208)
PHONE..............................888 882-3223
Alan Sharp-Paul, *CEO*
Mike Baukes, *CFO*
Paul McCarthy, *CTO*
Patrick Harlan, *Technical Staff*
Christopher Pollot, *Sales Staff*
EMP: 30
SQ FT: 13,800
SALES (est): 8.9MM **Privately Held**
SIC: 7372 Business oriented computer
software

(P-24544)
UPSTANDING LLC
Also Called: Mobilityware
440 Exchange Ste 100, Irvine
(92602-1390)
PHONE..............................949 788-9900
Dave Yonamine,
Claudia Avitabile, *Office Mgr*
Carrie Collins, *Admin Asst*
Lee H McElroy, *Finance*
John Libby,
EMP: 180
SQ FT: 48,000
SALES (est): 2.5MM **Privately Held**
WEB: www.upstanding.com
SIC: 7372 Business oriented computer
software

(P-24545)
**URBAN TRADING SOFTWARE
INC**
21227 Foothill Blvd, Hayward
(94541-1517)
PHONE..............................877 633-6171
Soufyan Abouahmed, *Principal*
EMP: 50
SALES (est): 1.2MM **Privately Held**
SIC: 7372 Prepackaged software

(P-24546)
VALIANTICA INC (PA)
940 Saratoga Ave Ste 108, San Jose
(95129-3409)
PHONE..............................408 694-3803
Peiwei Mi, *President*
Richard Crandall, *Human Res Mgr*
Radhika Jagtap, *Human Res Mgr*
Pooja Jadhav, *Human Resources*
EMP: 15
SALES (est): 2.3MM **Privately Held**
WEB: www.valiantica.com
SIC: 7372 Business oriented computer
software

(P-24547)
VANTIQ INC
1990 N Calif Blvd Ste 400, Walnut Creek
(94596-7249)
PHONE..............................303 377-2882
Marty Sprinzen, *CEO*
Miguel Nhuch, *Risk Mgmt Dir*
Paul Butterworth, *CTO*
EMP: 13 EST: 2014
SQ FT: 3,500
SALES (est): 302.5K **Privately Held**
SIC: 7372 Application computer software

(P-24548)
VARMOUR NETWORKS INC (PA)
270 3rd St, Los Altos (94022-3617)
PHONE..............................650 564-5100
Jia-Jyi Roger Lian, *CEO*
Amy Staas, *CFO*
Demetrios Lazarikos, *Officer*
Keith Stewart, *Vice Pres*
Eva Tsai, *Vice Pres*

EMP: 48
SALES (est): 14.4MM **Privately Held**
SIC: 7372 Prepackaged software

(P-24549)
VEEVA SYSTEMS INC (PA)
4280 Hacienda Dr, Pleasanton
(94588-2719)
PHONE.....................925 452-6500
Peter P Gassner, *CEO*
Gordon Ritter, *Ch of Bd*
Matthew J Wallach, *President*
Timothy S Cabral, *CFO*
E Nitsa Zuppas, *Chief Mktg Ofcr*
EMP: 145
SALES: 862.2MM **Publicly Held**
SIC: 7372 7371 7379 Prepackaged software; software programming applications; computer related consulting services

(P-24550)
VELTI INC (HQ)
Also Called: Velti USA
150 California St Fl 10, San Francisco
(94111-4556)
PHONE.....................415 362-2077
Alex Moukas, *CEO*
Sally Rau, *President*
Wilson W Cheung, *CFO*
EMP: 32
SALES (est): 9.6MM
SALES (corp-wide): 571K **Privately Held**
WEB: www.adinfuse.com
SIC: 7372 Prepackaged software

(P-24551)
VERA SECURITY INC
777 California Ave, Palo Alto (94304-1102)
PHONE.....................844 438-8372
Carlos Delatorre, *CEO*
Sam Wolff, *CFO*
Ramon Peypoch, *Senior VP*
Ajay Arora, *Security Dir*
Mitch Mikkelsen, *Office Mgr*
EMP: 36
SALES (est): 584K **Privately Held**
SIC: 7372 Business oriented computer software

(P-24552)
VERB TECHNOLOGY COMPANY INC (PA)
2210 Newport Blvd Ste 200, Newport Beach (92663-4321)
PHONE.....................855 250-2300
Rory J Cutaia, *Ch of Bd*
Jeffrey R Clayborne, *CFO*
Jimmy Geiskopf, *Bd of Directors*
Tal Golan, *Security Dir*
EMP: 13 **EST:** 2012
SQ FT: 4,900
SALES: 32K **Publicly Held**
SIC: 7372 Prepackaged software

(P-24553)
VERBIO INC
2225 E Byshore Rd Ste 200, Palo Alto (94303)
PHONE.....................650 862-8935
Carlos Puigjaner, *CEO*
Antonio Terradas, *Vice Pres*
EMP: 32 **EST:** 2014
SALES (est): 892.3K **Privately Held**
SIC: 7372 Business oriented computer software

(P-24554)
VERILOGIX INC
960 Knox St Bldg A, Torrance
(90502-1086)
P.O. Box 3472, Pls Vrds Pnsl (90274-9472)
PHONE.....................310 527-5100
Tom Christy, *President*
EMP: 18
SALES (est): 1.2MM **Privately Held**
WEB: www.verilogix.com
SIC: 7372 3674 Educational computer software; semiconductors & related devices

(P-24555)
VERITAS SOFTWARE GLOBAL LLC
1600 Plymouth St, Mountain View
(94043-1203)
PHONE.....................650 335-8000

EMP: 15 **EST:** 2011
SALES (est): 1.3MM **Privately Held**
SIC: 7372

(P-24556)
VEROS SOFTWARE INC
2333 N Broadway Ste 350, Santa Ana
(92706-1651)
PHONE.....................714 415-6300
Darius Bozorgi, *President*
Shirley Glowa, *President*
Adrienne Ainbinder, *Vice Pres*
Kashyap Deliwala, *Vice Pres*
Farnaz Calafi, *Executive Asst*
EMP: 20
SALES (est): 4MM **Privately Held**
SIC: 7372 Application computer software

(P-24557)
VERSA NETWORKS INC (PA)
6001 America Center Dr # 400, San Jose
(95002-2562)
PHONE.....................408 385-7660
Kulvinder Ahuja, *CEO*
Kelly Ahuja, *CEO*
Apurva Mehta, *Founder*
Kumar B Mehta, *Founder*
Jim Goetz, *Principal*
EMP: 44
SQ FT: 37,000
SALES (est): 43.8MM **Privately Held**
SIC: 7372 Application computer software

(P-24558)
VERSANT CORPORATION (HQ)
500 Arguello St Ste 200, Redwood City
(94063-1567)
PHONE.....................650 232-2400
Bernhard Woebker, *President*
Keiron McCammon, *COO*
EMP: 17
SQ FT: 6,800
SALES (est): 6.5MM
SALES (corp-wide): 107MM **Privately Held**
SIC: 7372 Prepackaged software
PA: Actian Corporation
2300 Geng Rd Ste 150
Palo Alto CA 94303
650 587-5500

(P-24559)
VGW US INC
442 Post St Fl 9, San Francisco
(94102-1510)
PHONE.....................415 240-0498
Derek Brinkman, *President*
EMP: 12
SALES (est): 256K **Privately Held**
SIC: 7372 Home entertainment computer software

(P-24560)
VIDEOAMP INC (PA)
2229 S Carmelina Ave, Los Angeles
(90064-1001)
PHONE.....................949 294-0351
Ross McCray, *CEO*
Nick Chakalos, *Senior VP*
Luis Manrique, *Vice Pres*
Kenny Rogers, *Engineer*
Jessica Levine, *Sales Staff*
EMP: 17
SALES (est): 6.5MM **Privately Held**
SIC: 7372 Prepackaged software

(P-24561)
VINDICIA INC
2988 Campus Dr Ste 300, San Mateo
(94403-2531)
PHONE.....................650 264-4700
Kris Nagel, *CEO*
Mark Elrod, *Exec VP*
Jack Bullock, *Senior VP*
Hurst Arthur, *Vice Pres*
Charles Breed, *Vice Pres*
EMP: 135
SQ FT: 9,000
SALES (est): 15.3MM **Privately Held**
SIC: 7372 Business oriented computer software
HQ: Amdocs, Inc.
1390 Tmberlake Manor Pkwy
Chesterfield MO 63017
314 212-7000

(P-24562)
VINTELLUS INC
19918 Wellington Ct, Saratoga
(95070-3813)
PHONE.....................510 972-4710
Sivakumar Sundaresan, *CEO*
EMP: 16
SALES (est): 409.9K **Privately Held**
SIC: 7372 Business oriented computer software

(P-24563)
VIRSEC SYSTEMS INC
226 Airport Pkwy Ste 350, San Jose
(95110-1026)
PHONE.....................978 274-7260
Satya Gupta, *CTO*
Atiq Raza, *CEO*
Raymond Demeo, *COO*
Tom Miller, *Senior VP*
Saurabh Sharma, *Vice Pres*
EMP: 10
SALES (est): 927.2K **Privately Held**
WEB: www.virsec.com
SIC: 7372 Utility computer software

(P-24564)
VISAGE SOFTWARE INC
5151 California Ave # 230, Irvine
(92617-3205)
PHONE.....................949 614-0759
Jason Lankow, *CEO*
Jake Burkett, *Shareholder*
Ross Crooks, *Shareholder*
Jonsen Carmack, *Marketing Mgr*
EMP: 11
SQ FT: 5,000
SALES (est): 740.2K **Privately Held**
SIC: 7372 Business oriented computer software

(P-24565)
VISIER INC (PA)
550 S Wnchester Blvd # 620, San Jose
(95128-2545)
PHONE.....................888 277-9331
John Schwarz, *CEO*
Ryan Wong, *President*
Steve Bamberger, *Officer*
Adam Binnie, *Officer*
Dave Weisbeck, *Officer*
EMP: 17
SALES (est): 3.3MM **Privately Held**
SIC: 7372 Business oriented computer software

(P-24566)
VISUALON INC
2590 N 1st St Ste 100, San Jose
(95131-1021)
PHONE.....................408 645-6618
Andy Lin, *President*
Bill Lin, *Senior VP*
Sean Torsney, *Senior VP*
Shawn O'Farrell, *Vice Pres*
Judy LI, *Finance*
EMP: 120
SALES (est): 25MM **Privately Held**
WEB: www.visualon.com
SIC: 7372 Prepackaged software

(P-24567)
VIV LABS INC
60 S Market St Ste 900, San Jose
(95113-2372)
PHONE.....................650 268-9837
Dag Kittlaus, *CEO*
EMP: 17
SALES (est): 722K **Privately Held**
SIC: 7372 Utility computer software
PA: Samsung Electronics Co., Ltd.
129 Samsung-Ro, Yeongtong-Gu
Suwon 16677

(P-24568)
VMWARE INC (DH)
3401 Hillview Ave, Palo Alto (94304-1383)
PHONE.....................650 427-5000
Patrick Gelsinger, *CEO*
Jared Byrd, *Partner*
Suzanne Hensley, *Partner*
Michael Dell, *Ch of Bd*
Sanjay Poonen, *COO*
▲ **EMP:** 148
SQ FT: 1,604,769

SALES: 8.9B
SALES (corp-wide): 90.6B **Publicly Held**
SIC: 7372 Prepackaged software
HQ: Emc Corporation
176 South St
Hopkinton MA 01748
508 435-1000

(P-24569)
VNOMIC INC
1250 Oakmead Pkwy Ste 210, Sunnyvale
(94085-4035)
PHONE.....................408 890-2220
Alle Bannon, *CEO*
Derek Palma, *Vice Pres*
EMP: 15
SALES: 5.2MM **Privately Held**
SIC: 7372 Application computer software

(P-24570)
VOYANT INTERNATIONAL CORP
Also Called: Voyant Aviation Broadband
444 Castro St Ste 318, Mountain View
(94041-2059)
PHONE.....................800 710-6637
Dana R Waldman, *CEO*
Mark M Laisure, *Ch of Bd*
David R Wells, *CFO*
Scott Fairbairn, *CTO*
EMP: 10
SALES (est): 584.8K **Privately Held**
WEB: www.voyant.net
SIC: 7372 Business oriented computer software

(P-24571)
VYAKAR INC
830 Stewart Dr Ste 228, Sunnyvale
(94085-4513)
PHONE.....................844 321-5323
Deepak Kumar, *President*
EMP: 14
SALES: 500K **Privately Held**
SIC: 7372 Business oriented computer software

(P-24572)
WAGGL INC (PA)
3 Harbor Dr Ste 200, Sausalito
(94965-1491)
PHONE.....................415 399-9949
Michael Papay, *CEO*
Meghan Gehle, *Office Mgr*
Mila Stoupnikova, *Controller*
EMP: 12 **EST:** 2014
SQ FT: 2,000
SALES (est): 309.3K **Privately Held**
SIC: 7372 Application computer software

(P-24573)
WANADA INVESTMENTS LLC
Also Called: LLC Lindero Learning Center
2010 Fox Hills Dr, Los Angeles
(90025-6046)
PHONE.....................818 292-8627
John Andrew Adams, *Mng Member*
Lora Malvani, *Exec Dir*
EMP: 20
SALES: 205K **Privately Held**
SIC: 7372 Educational computer software

(P-24574)
WEBCLOAK LLC
2 Park Plz Ste 700, Irvine (92614-8517)
PHONE.....................949 417-9940
William Shopoff, *CEO*
Martin Dawson, *Officer*
EMP: 10 **EST:** 2014
SALES (est): 468.6K **Privately Held**
SIC: 7372 Application computer software

(P-24575)
WEBEDOCTOR INC
231 Imperial Hwy Ste 104a, Fullerton
(92835-1046)
PHONE.....................714 990-3999
Anwer Siddiqi, *CEO*
Tanwer Siddiqi, *Marketing Mgr*
EMP: 26
SALES (est): 2.5MM **Privately Held**
WEB: www.webedoctor.com
SIC: 7372 Application computer software

▲ = Import ▼=Export
◆ =Import/Export

(P-24576)
WEMO MEDIA INC
550 Rose Ave, Venice (90291-2606)
PHONE.................................310 399-8058
Neville Spiteri, *CEO*
EMP: 10
SALES (est): 785.3K **Privately Held**
SIC: 7372 Application computer software

(P-24577)
WEST COAST CONSULTING LLC
9233 Research Dr Ste 200, Irvine (92618-4294)
PHONE.................................949 250-4102
Rajat Khurana,
Puja Budhani, *Tech Recruiter*
Yogesh Tomar, *Tech Recruiter*
Karam Singh, *Technical Staff*
Reena Rawat, *Business Mgr*
EMP: 125
SALES (est): 11.7MM **Privately Held**
WEB: www.westcoastllc.com
SIC: 7372 Prepackaged software

(P-24578)
WESTEND SOFTWARE INC (PA)
1905 Speyer Ln, Redondo Beach (90278-4816)
PHONE.................................310 370-0367
Zeljko Rakocevic, *President*
EMP: 10
SALES (est): 2.6MM **Privately Held**
SIC: 7372 Business oriented computer software

(P-24579)
WHAMCLOUD INC
696 San Ramon Valley Blvd, Danville (94526-4022)
PHONE.................................925 452-7599
Brent Gorda, *CEO*
EMP: 23
SALES (est): 1.1MM **Privately Held**
SIC: 7372 Application computer software

(P-24580)
WILLOW TECHNOLOGY INC (PA)
215 Cummins Ln, McKinleyville (95519-9243)
PHONE.................................360 393-4962
Gary Clueit, *President*
Susan Clueit, *CFO*
Sarah Clueit, *Admin Sec*
EMP: 30
SALES (est): 3MM **Privately Held**
WEB: www.willowtech.com
SIC: 7372 Prepackaged software

(P-24581)
WIND RIVER SYSTEMS INC (HQ)
500 Wind River Way, Alameda (94501-1162)
PHONE.................................510 748-4100
Jim Douglas, *CEO*
Scot Morrision, *President*
Barry R Mainz, *COO*
Jane Bon, *CFO*
Richard Kraber, *CFO*
EMP: 148
SQ FT: 273,000
SALES (est): 325.9MM **Privately Held**
WEB: www.windriver.com
SIC: 7372 7373 Application computer software; systems software development services

(P-24582)
WIND RIVER SYSTEMS INC
10505 Sorrento Valley Rd, San Diego (92121-1618)
PHONE.................................858 824-3100
Brad Murdoch, *Vice Pres*
Michelle Moselina, *Analyst*
EMP: 100 **Privately Held**
WEB: www.windriver.com
SIC: 7372 Prepackaged software
HQ: Wind River Systems, Inc.
500 Wind River Way
Alameda CA 94501
510 748-4100

(P-24583)
WIRELESS GLUE NETWORKS INC
4185 Blackhawk Plaza Cir # 220, Danville (94506-4622)
PHONE.................................925 310-4561
Peter McCabe, *President*
Matthew Dowling, *Officer*
Robert Fries, *Senior VP*
Rich Pappas, *VP Bus Dvlpt*
John Lin, *CTO*
EMP: 11
SQ FT: 2,000
SALES (est): 1MM **Privately Held**
SIC: 7372 3575 7371 Application computer software; computer terminals, monitors & components; computer software development

(P-24584)
WME BI LLC
17075 Camino, San Diego (92127)
PHONE.................................877 592-2472
EMP: 60
SALES (est): 1.4MM **Privately Held**
SIC: 7372 Operating systems computer software

(P-24585)
WONDERGROVE LLC
17563 Ventura Blvd Fl 1, Encino (91316-3836)
PHONE.................................800 889-7249
Terrance Thoren,
Jason Richards,
EMP: 19
SALES (est): 801.6K **Privately Held**
SIC: 7372 Educational computer software

(P-24586)
WORDSMART CORPORATION
10025 Mesa Rim Rd, San Diego (92121-2913)
P.O. Box 366, La Jolla (92038-0366)
PHONE.................................858 565-8068
David Kay, *CEO*
Subhash Katbamna, *Controller*
EMP: 70
SQ FT: 12,375
SALES (est): 9.4MM **Privately Held**
WEB: www.wordsmart.com
SIC: 7372 Educational computer software

(P-24587)
WORKSHARE TECHNOLOGY INC
650 California St Fl 7, San Francisco (94108-2737)
PHONE.................................415 590-7700
Brad Anthony Foy, *CEO*
Thomas C Hoster, *CFO*
Nick Thomson, *Officer*
Barrie Hadfield, *Vice Pres*
Billy Lucas, *Executive*
EMP: 140
SQ FT: 15,000
SALES (est): 21.3MM
SALES (corp-wide): 23.4MM **Privately Held**
WEB: www.workshare.com
SIC: 7372 Prepackaged software
HQ: Workshare Limited
10-20 Fashion Street, Whitechapel
London E1 6P
207 426-0000

(P-24588)
WORKSPOT INC (PA)
1901 S Bascom Ave Ste 900, Campbell (95008-2250)
PHONE.................................888 426-8113
Amitabh Sinha, *President*
Maryam Alexandrian-Adams, *COO*
Michele Borovac, *Chief Mktg Ofcr*
Richard Lo, *Officer*
Ty Wang, *Vice Pres*
EMP: 19
SALES (est): 4.6MM **Privately Held**
SIC: 7372 Business oriented computer software

(P-24589)
WORLDFLASH SOFTWARE INC
3853 Marcasel Ave Ste 101, Los Angeles (90066-4613)
PHONE.................................310 745-0632
Sharone Levinson, *President*
Gabrielle Frig, *CFO*
EMP: 25
SALES (est): 1.1MM **Privately Held**
WEB: www.worldflash.com
SIC: 7372 7371 Prepackaged software; computer software development & applications

(P-24590)
WORLDLINK MEDIA
38 Keyes Ave Ste 17, San Francisco (94129-1716)
PHONE.................................415 561-2141
Kirk Bergstrom, *President*
Jessica Docter, *Executive*
EMP: 10
SALES (est): 367.1K **Privately Held**
WEB: www.goworldlink.com
SIC: 7372 Educational computer software

(P-24591)
XAVIENT DIGITAL LLC
Also Called: Xavient Info Systems Inc
21700 Oxnard St Ste 1700, Woodland Hills (91367-7590)
PHONE.................................805 955-4111
Rajeev Tandon, *CEO*
Saif Ahmad, *President*
Arshad Majeed, *Exec VP*
Kurt Eltz, *Senior VP*
Matt Dimarsico, *Vice Pres*
EMP: 1800
SALES (corp-wide): 10.6B **Privately Held**
SIC: 7372 Business oriented computer software
HQ: Telus International (U.S) Corp.
2251 S Decatur Blvd
Las Vegas NV 89102
702 238-7900

(P-24592)
XCELMOBILITY INC
2225 E Byshore Rd Ste 200, Palo Alto (94303)
PHONE.................................650 320-1728
Zhixiong WEI, *Ch of Bd*
LI Ouyang, *CFO*
Ying Yang, *Admin Sec*
EMP: 98
SALES: 384.5K **Privately Held**
SIC: 7372 7999 Business oriented computer software; gambling & lottery services

(P-24593)
XL DYNAMICS INC
18303 Gridley Rd, Cerritos (90703-5401)
P.O. Box 1052, Artesia (90702-1052)
PHONE.................................562 916-1402
Pavan Agarwal, *CEO*
EMP: 20
SALES (est): 1.4MM **Privately Held**
WEB: www.mortgagesoftonline.com
SIC: 7372 Prepackaged software

(P-24594)
XLSOFT CORPORATION (PA)
12 Mauchly Ste K, Irvine (92618-6304)
PHONE.................................949 453-2781
Mitsutoshi Watanabe, *President*
Nanako Watanabe, *CFO*
EMP: 14
SQ FT: 7,000
SALES (est): 1.9MM **Privately Held**
WEB: www.xlsoft.com
SIC: 7372 7371 Publishers' computer software; custom computer programming services

(P-24595)
XPANSIV DATA SYSTEMS INC
2 Bryant St, San Francisco (94105-1640)
PHONE.................................415 915-5124
Joe Madden, *CEO*
John Melby, *President*
Michael Burstein, *CFO*
Jason Libersky, *CTO*
EMP: 49
SALES (est): 37.2K **Privately Held**
SIC: 7372 Prepackaged software

PA: Xpansiv Cbl Holding Group Limited
Se 19 L 5 58 Pitt St
Sydney NSW 2000
-

(P-24596)
Y-CHANGE INC
43575 Mission Blvd 416, Fremont (94539-5831)
PHONE.................................510 573-2205
Alan Leeds, *President*
EMP: 15
SALES (est): 950K **Privately Held**
WEB: www.ychange.com
SIC: 7372 Application computer software

(P-24597)
YAYYO INC
433 N Camden Dr Ste 600, Beverly Hills (90210-4416)
PHONE.................................310 926-2643
Ramy El-Batrawi, *CEO*
Laurie Digionanni, *COO*
Kevin F Pickard, *CFO*
EMP: 10
SALES: 235.6K
SALES (corp-wide): 838.5K **Publicly Held**
SIC: 7372 Prepackaged software
PA: X Llc
433 N Camden Dr Ste 600
Beverly Hills CA 90210
310 926-2643

(P-24598)
YELLOW MAGIC INCORPORATED
41571 Date St, Murrieta (92562-7086)
P.O. Box 3033, Fallbrook (92088-3033)
PHONE.................................951 506-4005
Ronald G Mintle, *CEO*
Beverly Mintle, *Treasurer*
Sam Pretorius, *Vice Pres*
James Snyder, *Vice Pres*
EMP: 15
SALES (est): 2MM **Privately Held**
SIC: 7372 7389 Home entertainment computer software; educational computer software;

(P-24599)
YOURPEOPLE INC
Also Called: Zenefits
50 Beale St, San Francisco (94105-1813)
PHONE.................................888 249-3263
Parker Conrad, *CEO*
Jessica Hoffman, *Partner*
Avinash Anand, *President*
David Sacks, *CEO*
Laks Srini, *Officer*
EMP: 700 EST: 2004
SALES: 158.4MM **Privately Held**
SIC: 7372 8741 6411 Business oriented computer software; administrative management; insurance brokers

(P-24600)
YUJA INC
84 W Santa Clara St # 690, San Jose (95113-1809)
PHONE.................................888 257-2278
Ajit Singh, *President*
Nannette Don, *Sales Staff*
Boudreau Kline, *Manager*
Smith Isaac, *Accounts Mgr*
Zayn Mashat, *Accounts Mgr*
EMP: 125
SALES (est): 1MM **Privately Held**
SIC: 7372 Prepackaged software

(P-24601)
ZENDESK INC (PA)
1019 Market St, San Francisco (94103-1612)
PHONE.................................415 418-7506
Mikkel Svane, *Ch of Bd*
Adrian McDermott, *President*
Elena Gomez, *CFO*
Inamarie Johnson,
John Geschke, *Senior VP*
EMP: 148
SQ FT: 18,000
SALES: 598.7MM **Publicly Held**
SIC: 7372 Business oriented computer software

PRODUCTS & SVCS

(P-24602)
ZENPAYROLL INC (PA)
Also Called: Gusto
525 20th St, San Francisco (94107-4345)
PHONE..............................800 936-0383
Joshua D Reeves, *CEO*
Katharine Kinney, *Partner*
Ashley Prince, *Partner*
Tom Roberts, *Partner*
Nate Watson, *Partner*
EMP: 250
SALES (est): 74.9MM **Privately Held**
SIC: 7372 Business oriented computer
software

(P-24603)
ZENTERA SYSTEMS INC
97 E Brokaw Rd Ste 360, San Jose
(95112-1031)
PHONE..............................408 436-4811
Jaushin Lee, *CEO*
Belinda Shih, *Opers Mgr*
Nancy Lam, *Accounts Exec*
EMP: 16 EST: 2012
SQ FT: 2,834
SALES (est): 1.7MM **Privately Held**
SIC: 7372 Business oriented computer
software

(P-24604)
ZENYX INC
2870 Zanker Rd Ste 210, San Jose
(95134-2133)
PHONE..............................415 741-0170
Srikant Sharma, *CEO*
Derek Pignatelli, *Director*
EMP: 10
SALES (est): 494.2K **Privately Held**
SIC: 7372 Business oriented computer
software

(P-24605)
ZINIO SYSTEMS INC
114 Sansome St Fl 4, San Francisco
(94104-3803)
PHONE..............................415 494-2700
Rusty Lewis, *CEO*
Michelle Bottomley, *President*
Richard A Maggiotto, *President*
Virendra Vase, *COO*
Tom Nofziger, *CFO*
EMP: 75 EST: 2000
SALES (est): 8MM **Privately Held**
WEB: www.zinio.com
SIC: 7372 Publishers' computer software

(P-24606)
ZOHO CORPORATION (HQ)
4141 Hacienda Dr, Pleasanton
(94588-8566)
P.O. Box 742760, Los Angeles (90074-
2760)
PHONE..............................925 924-9500
Sridhar Vembu, *CEO*
Tony Thomas, *Ch of Bd*
Sridhar Iyengar, *Vice Pres*
Rex Antony, *Technical Staff*
Darin Arundale, *Engineer*
EMP: 14
SQ FT: 10,000
SALES (est): 199.2MM **Privately Held**
SIC: 7372 Application computer software

(P-24607)
ZULIP INC
185 Berry St Ste 400, San Francisco
(94107-1725)
PHONE..............................617 945-7653
Jeff Arnold, *CEO*
EMP: 12
SALES (est): 524.8K **Privately Held**
SIC: 7372 Prepackaged software

(P-24608)
ZYE LABS LLC
310 S Twin Oaks Valley Rd, San Marcos
(92078-4303)
PHONE..............................904 800-9935
John Ringgold, *CEO*
EMP: 10 EST: 2014
SQ FT: 700
SALES (est): 463K **Privately Held**
SIC: 7372 Application computer software

(P-24609)
ZYNGA INC
650 Townsend St, San Francisco
(94103-5646)
PHONE..............................415 621-2391
Zachary Zynga, *Branch Mgr*
EMP: 19
SALES (corp-wide): 907.2MM **Publicly
Held**
SIC: 7372 Prepackaged software
PA: Zynga Inc.
699 8th St
San Francisco CA 94103
855 449-9642

(P-24610)
ZYRION INC
440 N Wolfe Rd, Sunnyvale (94085-3869)
PHONE..............................408 524-7424
EMP: 75
SQ FT: 6,000
SALES (est): 4.7MM **Privately Held**
SIC: 7372
PA: Kaseya Global Ireland Limited
Commerzbank House
Dublin
-

7692 Welding Repair

(P-24611)
A & M WELDING INC
16935 S Broadway, Gardena (90248-3111)
PHONE..............................310 329-2700
Tom A Jorgenson, *President*
Linda Jorgenson, *Vice Pres*
EMP: 18 EST: 1952
SQ FT: 25,000
SALES (est): 1.6MM **Privately Held**
WEB: www.ammetalforming.com
SIC: 7692 Welding repair

(P-24612)
ADAMS WELDING INC
6352 Apache Rd, Westminster
(92683-2051)
PHONE..............................714 412-7684
Gary Adams, *CEO*
Rebecca Adams, *Vice Pres*
EMP: 12
SALES (est): 1.5MM **Privately Held**
SIC: 7692 7389 Welding repair;

(P-24613)
AEROSPACE WELDING INC
2035 Granville Ave, Los Angeles
(90025-6103)
PHONE..............................310 914-0324
Edward Sutter, *President*
Craig Ittner, *Treasurer*
Gary Ittner, *Admin Sec*
Carmelita Sutter, *Controller*
EMP: 19
SQ FT: 20,000
SALES (est): 1.7MM **Privately Held**
WEB: www.aerospace-welding.com
SIC: 7692 Welding repair

(P-24614)
AG-WELD INC
1236 G St, Wasco (93280-2359)
P.O. Box 637 (93280-0637)
PHONE..............................661 758-3061
Jeff Mehlberg, *CEO*
Bedi Mehlberg, *Vice Pres*
Patty Mehlberg, *Controller*
▲ EMP: 15 EST: 1980
SQ FT: 20,000
SALES (est): 1.6MM **Privately Held**
SIC: 7692 Welding repair

(P-24615)
AGNALDOS WELDING INC
828 S Burnett Rd, Tipton (93272)
P.O. Box 154 (93272-0154)
PHONE..............................559 752-4254
Agnaldo Tamariz, *President*
Delores Tamariz, *Treasurer*
James Tamariz, *Director*
EMP: 12
SALES: 838.4K **Privately Held**
SIC: 7692 7699 5083 Welding repair;
farm machinery repair; farm equipment
parts & supplies

(P-24616)
**ARCMATIC WELDING SYSTEMS
INC (PA)**
1175 Nimitz Ave Ste 240, Vallejo
(94592-1003)
PHONE..............................707 643-5517
William L Bong, *President*
Bill Bong, *President*
Twila Nixon, *Controller*
▲ EMP: 11
SALES (est): 1.2MM **Privately Held**
SIC: 7692 Welding repair

(P-24617)
B W PADILLA INC
Also Called: Brian's Welding
197 Ryland St, San Jose (95110-2241)
PHONE..............................408 275-9834
Brian Wade Padilla, *CEO*
Diana Padilla, *Vice Pres*
EMP: 24
SALES (est): 2.2MM **Privately Held**
WEB: www.brianswelding.com
SIC: 7692 Welding repair

(P-24618)
**BRIGHTLIGHT WELDING & MFG
INC**
3395a Edward Ave, Santa Clara
(95054-2310)
PHONE..............................408 988-0418
Steve Condos, *President*
Anthony Condos, *Corp Secy*
Cindi Bogue, *Office Mgr*
Rick Wittrock, *Project Mgr*
EMP: 20
SQ FT: 8,000
SALES (est): 2.2MM **Privately Held**
WEB: www.brightlightwelding.com
SIC: 7692 Welding repair

(P-24619)
BROTHERS ENTERPRISES INC
Also Called: Heritage Truck Painting
7380 Mission Gorge Rd, San Diego
(92120-1224)
PHONE..............................619 229-8003
Carlos Osnaya, *President*
Victor Osnaya, *Vice Pres*
EMP: 10 EST: 2004
SQ FT: 3,000
SALES (est): 1.1MM **Privately Held**
WEB: www.heritagetruck-painting.com
SIC: 7692 7532 Automotive welding; colli-
sion shops, automotive

(P-24620)
C L P INC (PA)
Also Called: Rick's Hitches & Welding
1546 E Main St, El Cajon (92021-5901)
PHONE..............................619 444-3105
Richard Preston, *President*
Betty Preston, *Vice Pres*
EMP: 30
SQ FT: 23,500
SALES (est): 1.8MM **Privately Held**
SIC: 7692 7533 7699 Welding repair;
muffler shop, sale or repair & installation;
recreational vehicle repair services

(P-24621)
CALIFORNIA IRON DESIGN
8906 Lankershim Blvd, Sun Valley
(91352-1915)
PHONE..............................818 767-6690
Alvaro Maron, *Owner*
EMP: 12
SALES (est): 279.5K **Privately Held**
SIC: 7692 1799 Welding repair; special
trade contractors

(P-24622)
CAMBERO METAL WORKS INC
210 Agostino Rd, San Gabriel
(91776-2503)
PHONE..............................626 309-5315
Angel Cambero, *President*
Virginia Cambero, *Vice Pres*
Nick Cambero, *Foreman/Supr*
EMP: 13 EST: 2015
SALES (est): 1.9MM **Privately Held**
SIC: 7692 3316 3444 Welding repair;
sheet, steel, cold-rolled: from purchased
hot-rolled; awnings, sheet metal

(P-24623)
**CAMERON WELDING SUPPLY
(PA)**
11061 Dale Ave, Stanton (90680-3247)
P.O. Box 266 (90680-0266)
PHONE..............................714 530-9353
Elizabeth Perry, *CEO*
Joseph Churilla, *President*
Robert Rodriguez, *Branch Mgr*
Maria Mangaya, *General Mgr*
Geno Sanchez, *Store Mgr*
▲ EMP: 36
SQ FT: 4,500
SALES: 20MM **Privately Held**
WEB: www.cameronwelding.com
SIC: 7692 5999 Welding repair; welding
supplies

(P-24624)
CAMLAND INC
3152 Canopy Dr, Camarillo (93012-7763)
PHONE..............................805 485-9242
Darlene Camarillo, *CEO*
Dave Green, *Vice Pres*
EMP: 16 EST: 1999
SQ FT: 15,000
SALES (est): 923K **Privately Held**
WEB: www.camland.com
SIC: 7692 3713 Welding repair; truck &
bus bodies

(P-24625)
CHIAPA WELDING INC (PA)
276 E Grand Ave, Porterville (93257-2401)
PHONE..............................559 784-3400
Art Chiapa, *President*
EMP: 10
SQ FT: 3,000
SALES (est): 616.6K **Privately Held**
SIC: 7692 1799 1791 Welding repair;
welding on site; ornamental metal work;
iron work, structural

(P-24626)
**COMPLETE CUTNG & WLDG
SUPS INC (PA)**
Also Called: Complete Welding Supplies
806 E Holt Ave, Pomona (91767-5717)
PHONE..............................909 868-9292
Guillermo Gallardo, *President*
Rose Amaya, *Principal*
▲ EMP: 15 EST: 1996
SQ FT: 11,000
SALES (est): 2.6MM **Privately Held**
SIC: 7692 Welding repair

(P-24627)
CONSOL ENTERPRISES
918 Mission Rock Rd B1, Santa Paula
(93060-9796)
PHONE..............................805 648-3486
Craig Brown, *President*
EMP: 10
SALES (est): 1MM **Privately Held**
SIC: 7692 Welding repair

(P-24628)
CW WELDING SERVICE INC (PA)
1735 Santa Fe Ave, Long Beach
(90813-1242)
PHONE..............................562 432-5421
Craig Wildvank, *President*
Jason Rodriguez, *Project Mgr*
Branden Wildvank, *Project Mgr*
EMP: 49
SQ FT: 22,000
SALES (est): 7.8MM **Privately Held**
WEB: www.cwservices.us
SIC: 7692 Welding repair

(P-24629)
**DEANS CERTIFIED WELDING
INC**
27645 Commerce Center Dr, Temecula
(92590-2521)
PHONE..............................951 676-0242
Michael W Deam, *CEO*
Elizabeth Scott, *Office Mgr*
EMP: 14 EST: 2015
SALES (est): 1.5MM **Privately Held**
SIC: 7692 Welding repair

▲ = Import ▼=Export
◆ =Import/Export

(P-24630)
DENTONIS WELDING WORKS INC (PA)
Also Called: Dentonis Spring and Suspension
801 S Airport Way, Stockton (95205-6901)
PHONE...................................209 464-4930
David B Dentoni II, *CEO*
Donna Dentoni, *Treasurer*
Dan Dentoni, *Vice Pres*
Debbie Townley, *Human Resources*
Anthony Miranda, *Sales Mgr*
EMP: 45
SQ FT: 1,000
SALES (est): 12.6MM **Privately Held**
WEB: www.dentoni.com
SIC: 7692 3599 5531 7539 Welding repair; machine shop, jobbing & repair; automotive parts; automotive springs, rebuilding & repair

(P-24631)
DIP BRAZE INC
9131 De Garmo Ave, Sun Valley (91352-2696)
PHONE...................................818 768-1555
Gail Brown, *President*
Robert Gebo, *President*
Robert Gilmore, *Technology*
EMP: 35 **EST:** 1956
SQ FT: 10,500
SALES (est): 3.8MM **Privately Held**
WEB: www.dipbraze.com
SIC: 7692 3398 Brazing; metal heat treating

(P-24632)
DOUG DELEO WELDING INC
249 N Ashland Ave, Lindsay (93247-2430)
P.O. Box 878 (93247-0878)
PHONE...................................559 562-3700
Doug Deleo, *CEO*
Pam Deleo, *Vice Pres*
EMP: 13
SQ FT: 9,600
SALES (est): 2.4MM **Privately Held**
SIC: 7692 1799 Welding repair; welding on site

(P-24633)
ELECTRON BEAM ENGINEERING INC
1425 S Allec St, Anaheim (92805-6306)
PHONE...................................714 491-5990
Richard Trillwood, *CEO*
Grant Trillwood, *General Mgr*
Hilary Hurt, *Admin Sec*
Patricia Trillwood, *Director*
EMP: 14
SQ FT: 17,000
SALES: 2.4MM **Privately Held**
WEB: www.ebeinc.com
SIC: 7692 3548 Welding repair; welding apparatus

(P-24634)
GALAXY BRAZING CO INC
10015 Freeman Ave, Santa Fe Springs (90670-3405)
PHONE...................................562 946-9039
John Mc Gee, *President*
Donna Mc Gee, *Treasurer*
EMP: 24 **EST:** 1961
SQ FT: 13,144
SALES (est): 2.6MM **Privately Held**
WEB: www.galaxybrazing.com
SIC: 7692 3398 1799 Brazing; metal heat treating; welding on site

(P-24635)
GHAZARIAN WLDG FABRICATION INC
Also Called: Ghazarian Welding & Repair
2903 E Annadale Ave, Fresno (93725-1944)
P.O. Box 28416 (93729-8416)
PHONE...................................559 233-1210
Ghazar Ghazarian, *Owner*
EMP: 10
SQ FT: 6,000
SALES (est): 1.7MM **Privately Held**
WEB: www.ghazarianwelding.com
SIC: 7692 Automotive welding

(P-24636)
GK WELDING INC
1150 Hensley St, Richmond (94801-2119)
PHONE...................................510 233-0133
George Kassab, *President*
EMP: 10 **EST:** 1996
SQ FT: 2,000
SALES (est): 266.2K **Privately Held**
SIC: 7692 Welding repair

(P-24637)
HAGIST WELDING
34895 Kruse Ranch Rd, Cazadero (95421-9783)
PHONE...................................707 847-3362
Fritz Hagist, *Owner*
EMP: 12
SALES (est): 580.9K **Privately Held**
SIC: 7692 Cracked casting repair

(P-24638)
HANSENS WELDING INC
358 W 168th St, Gardena (90248-2733)
PHONE...................................310 329-6888
Gary D Hansen, *CEO*
Robert Hansen, *Vice Pres*
Shauna Hansen, *Admin Sec*
EMP: 25
SQ FT: 26,000
SALES (est): 5.2MM **Privately Held**
WEB: www.hansenswelding.com
SIC: 7692 Welding repair

(P-24639)
HAYES WELDING INC (PA)
Also Called: Valew Welding & Fabrication
12522 Violet Rd, Adelanto (92301-2704)
P.O. Box 310 (92301-0310)
PHONE...................................760 246-4878
Roger L Hayes, *CEO*
Velma D Hayes, *President*
Vernon L Hayes, *Vice Pres*
Keseloff Manya, *Clerk*
▲ **EMP:** 86
SQ FT: 45,000
SALES (est): 14.5MM **Privately Held**
WEB: www.valew.com
SIC: 7692 3465 3714 3713 Welding repair; automotive stampings; body parts, automobile: stamped metal; fenders, automobile: stamped or pressed metal; fuel systems & parts, motor vehicle; truck & bus bodies; fabricated plate work (boiler shop)

(P-24640)
HAYES WELDING INC
Also Called: Valew Welding & Fabrication
11746 Mariposa Rd Ste 100, Hesperia (92345-1624)
PHONE...................................760 246-4878
EMP: 14
SALES (corp-wide): 14.5MM **Privately Held**
SIC: 7692 Welding repair
PA: Hayes Welding, Inc.
12522 Violet Rd
Adelanto CA 92301
760 246-4878

(P-24641)
IRON WORKS & CUSTOM RACKS
15337 Illinois Ave, Paramount (90723-4108)
P.O. Box 1977 (90723-1977)
PHONE...................................323 581-2222
Roberto Gonzalez, *Owner*
EMP: 12
SALES (est): 421.4K **Privately Held**
SIC: 7692 Welding repair

(P-24642)
IV WELDING & MECHANICAL INC
185 S 3rd St, El Centro (92243-2521)
PHONE...................................760 482-9353
Fred R Baeza, *President*
EMP: 10
SQ FT: 11,000
SALES (est): 650K **Privately Held**
SIC: 7692 Welding repair

(P-24643)
J MCDOWELL WLDG FRM MCHY INC
29820 County Road 25, Winters (95694-9706)
P.O. Box 1210 (95694-1210)
PHONE...................................530 661-6006
Jack A McDowell, *President*
EMP: 13 **EST:** 2011
SALES (est): 647.2K **Privately Held**
SIC: 7692 7699 Welding repair; farm machinery repair

(P-24644)
JABIL SILVER CREEK INC (HQ)
Also Called: Wolfe Engineering, Inc.
5981 Optical Ct, San Jose (95138-1400)
PHONE...................................669 255-2900
John P Wolfe, *CEO*
Rita Wolfe, *Vice Pres*
▲ **EMP:** 115
SQ FT: 76,000
SALES (est): 25.7MM
SALES (corp-wide): 25.2B **Publicly Held**
WEB: www.wolfe-engr.com
SIC: 7692 8711 3674 3317 Welding repair; engineering services; semiconductors & related devices; steel pipe & tubes; fabricated pipe & fittings
PA: Jabil Inc.
10560 Dr Mrtn Lther King
Saint Petersburg FL 33716
727 577-9749

(P-24645)
JETI INC (PA)
Also Called: Jet I
14578 Hawthorne Ave, Fontana (92335-2507)
PHONE...................................909 357-2966
John Lowery, *President*
Jose Gradilla, *Vice Pres*
EMP: 13
SQ FT: 10,000
SALES (est): 851.3K **Privately Held**
SIC: 7692 Welding repair

(P-24646)
JON STEEL ERECTORS INC
1431 S Gage St, San Bernardino (92408-2835)
PHONE...................................909 799-0005
Octavio Arellano, *President*
EMP: 22
SALES (est): 671.4K **Privately Held**
SIC: 7692 5082 1791 Welding repair; general construction machinery & equipment; structural steel erection

(P-24647)
K C WELDING INC
1549 Dogwood Rd, El Centro (92243-9605)
PHONE...................................760 352-3832
C Mostrong, *Principal*
EMP: 13
SALES (est): 1.2MM **Privately Held**
SIC: 7692 Welding repair

(P-24648)
LA HABRA WELDING INC
10819 Koontz Ave, Santa Fe Springs (90670-4409)
PHONE...................................562 923-2229
Ira Smith, *President*
Steven Smith, *Vice Pres*
Jerry Wachel, *Admin Sec*
EMP: 12 **EST:** 1966
SQ FT: 30,900
SALES (est): 1.7MM **Privately Held**
WEB: www.lhwinc.com
SIC: 7692 Welding repair

(P-24649)
LAZESTAR
6956 Preston Ave, Livermore (94551-9545)
PHONE...................................925 443-5293
Daniel P Schwertfeger, *President*
EMP: 25
SALES (est): 2MM **Privately Held**
WEB: www.lazestar.com
SIC: 7692 Welding repair

(P-24650)
MARLEON INC
Also Called: Hanley Welding
3202 W Rosecrans Ave, Hawthorne (90250-8225)
PHONE...................................310 679-1242
Leon Hanley, *President*
EMP: 26
SQ FT: 3,000
SALES (est): 2.9MM **Privately Held**
SIC: 7692 2431 Welding repair; staircases, stairs & railings

(P-24651)
MIKES PRECISION WELDING INC
28073 Diaz Rd Ste D, Temecula (92590-3464)
P.O. Box 891929 (92589-1929)
PHONE...................................951 676-4744
Michael Prunty, *President*
Jeanette Prunty, *Admin Sec*
EMP: 11
SQ FT: 3,000
SALES (est): 1.1MM **Privately Held**
SIC: 7692 Welding repair

(P-24652)
MORRIS WELDING CO INC
11210 Socrates Mine Rd, Middletown (95461)
P.O. Box 567 (95461-0567)
PHONE...................................707 987-1114
Sonnie Young, *President*
Judy Morris, *Corp Secy*
EMP: 11 **EST:** 1971
SQ FT: 6,000
SALES (est): 2.4MM **Privately Held**
SIC: 7692 1623 Welding repair; water, sewer & utility lines

(P-24653)
NEVADA HEAT TREATING LLC (PA)
Also Called: California Brazing
37955 Central Ct Ste D, Newark (94560-3466)
PHONE...................................510 790-2300
Richard T Penrose, *Corp Secy*
Pat McKenna, *Vice Pres*
Jeffrey Ager, *General Mgr*
Mark Leonard, *Mfg Staff*
Ben Tayebi, *Maintence Staff*
◆ **EMP:** 37
SQ FT: 45,000
SALES (est): 13.3MM **Privately Held**
WEB: www.californiabrazing.com
SIC: 7692 3398 3599 Brazing; metal heat treating; air intake filters, internal combustion engine, except auto

(P-24654)
OTTO ARC SYSTEMS INC
3921 Sandstone Dr Ste 1, El Dorado Hills (95762-9343)
PHONE...................................916 939-3400
Alan S Avis Jr, *President*
▲ **EMP:** 10
SALES (est): 950K **Privately Held**
SIC: 7692 Welding repair

(P-24655)
PACIFIC WELDING & FABRICATION
1535 Tidelands Ave Ste F, National City (91950-4239)
PHONE...................................619 336-1758
Carlos Frias, *President*
EMP: 10
SALES (est): 461.4K **Privately Held**
SIC: 7692 Welding repair

(P-24656)
PERFORMANCE WELDING
2540 S Sarah St, Fresno (93706-5033)
PHONE...................................559 233-0042
Fax: 559 233-0046
EMP: 10
SALES (est): 1.1MM **Privately Held**
SIC: 7692

P
R
O
D
U
C
T
S

&

S
V
C
S

(P-24657)
PHILLIPS MACHINE & WLDG CO INC
16125 Gale Ave, City of Industry (91745-1709)
PHONE.................................626 855-4600
Don McKenna, *Branch Mgr*
EMP: 22
SALES (corp-wide): 12.3MM **Privately Held**
SIC: 7692 Welding repair
PA: Phillip's Machine And Welding Company, Inc.
　　16125 Gale Ave
　　City Of Industry CA 91745
　　626 855-4600

(P-24658)
PT WELDING INC
1960 E Main St, Woodland (95776-6202)
PHONE.................................530 406-0267
Patrick Trafician, *CEO*
EMP: 12
SALES (est): 1.7MM **Privately Held**
SIC: 7692 Welding repair

(P-24659)
R B WELDING INC
155 E Redondo Beach Blvd, Gardena (90248-2347)
PHONE.................................310 324-8680
Nabil Abeskharoun, *President*
EMP: 15
SQ FT: 2,500
SALES (est): 2.6MM **Privately Held**
SIC: 7692 3441 Welding repair; fabricated structural metal

(P-24660)
RANDY NIX CSTM WLDG & MFG INC
22700 Road 196, Lindsay (93247-9832)
P.O. Box 730, Strathmore (93267-0730)
PHONE.................................559 562-1958
Guy Randy Nix, *President*
Traci L Nix, *Corp Secy*
EMP: 15
SQ FT: 74,880
SALES: 1.5MM **Privately Held**
SIC: 7692 3556 Welding repair; packing house machinery

(P-24661)
RETTIG MACHINE INC
301 Kansas St, Redlands (92373-8153)
P.O. Box 7460 (92375-0460)
PHONE.................................909 793-7811
Franz A Rettig Sr, *President*
Susan L Rettig, *Corp Secy*
Franz A Rettig Jr, *Vice Pres*
Robert A Rettig, *Vice Pres*
Susan Rettig, *Executive*
EMP: 25
SQ FT: 37,000
SALES: 1.6MM **Privately Held**
WEB: www.rettigmachine.com
SIC: 7692 3599 Welding repair; machine shop, jobbing & repair

(P-24662)
ROMEROS WELDING & MAR SVCS INC
519 Waterfront Ave, Vallejo (94592)
PHONE.................................925 550-0518
Jesus G Romero, *President*
Edith Romero, *Admin Sec*
EMP: 13
SQ FT: 15,000
SALES: 1.6MM **Privately Held**
SIC: 7692 7699 Welding repair; boat repair

(P-24663)
SELKEN ENTERPRISES INC
Also Called: Sel-Tech
108 Boeing Ave, Chico (95973-9011)
PHONE.................................530 891-4200
Jerry Selken, *President*
Erik Rust, *General Mgr*
Laura Swainston, *Admin Asst*
EMP: 14
SQ FT: 25,000

SALES (est): 2.5MM **Privately Held**
WEB: www.sel-tech.com
SIC: 7692 3728 3721 3444 Welding repair; aircraft parts & equipment; aircraft body & wing assemblies & parts; aircraft assemblies, subassemblies & parts; aircraft; hoppers, sheet metal

(P-24664)
SHANNON SIDE WELDING INC
620 Villa St, Daly City (94014-3032)
PHONE.................................415 680-6101
Patrick Sheedy, *Branch Mgr*
EMP: 10
SALES (corp-wide): 1.2MM **Privately Held**
SIC: 7692 Welding repair
PA: Shannon Side Welding, Inc.
　　214 Shaw Rd Ste I
　　South San Francisco CA 94080
　　415 408-3219

(P-24665)
SO CAL TRACTOR SALES CO INC
30517 The Old Rd, Castaic (91384-3709)
PHONE.................................818 252-1900
Utz James, *President*
EMP: 23
SQ FT: 26,000
SALES (est): 2MM **Privately Held**
SIC: 7692 7549 1799 Welding repair; high performance auto repair & service; steam cleaning of building exteriors

(P-24666)
SOUTHCOAST WELDING & MFG LLC
2591 Faivre St Ste 1, Chula Vista (91911-7146)
PHONE.................................619 429-1337
Patrick Shoup, *President*
Leo Mathieu, *CFO*
Jay Parast, *Vice Pres*
David Lerma, *Admin Sec*
Gary Cathcart, *Controller*
EMP: 270
SQ FT: 82,000
SALES (est): 30.7MM **Privately Held**
SIC: 7692 Welding repair

(P-24667)
STAINLESS TECHNOLOGIES LLC
19425 W Grove Ave, Visalia (93291)
PHONE.................................559 651-0460
Robert Krikorian, *President*
Manny Hoy, *CFO*
Freddy Perales, *General Mgr*
Clay Kitchner, *Project Mgr*
EMP: 16 **EST:** 2007
SQ FT: 5,000
SALES (est): 772K **Privately Held**
SIC: 7692 Welding repair

(P-24668)
STAINLESS WORKS INC
201 E Owens Ave, Tulare (93274-5434)
PHONE.................................559 688-4310
Richard Perales, *President*
Margaret Perales, *Treasurer*
David Munoz, *Vice Pres*
Judy Munoz, *Admin Sec*
Ryan Walsh, *Engineer*
EMP: 12 **EST:** 1998
SQ FT: 2,200
SALES (est): 900K **Privately Held**
SIC: 7692 Welding repair

(P-24669)
SULZER PUMP SERVICES (US) INC
Also Called: Sulzer Bingham Pumps
9856 Jordan Cir, Santa Fe Springs (90670-3303)
P.O. Box 3904 (90670-1904)
PHONE.................................562 903-1000
Tim Voyles, *Manager*
EMP: 29
SQ FT: 18,968
SALES (corp-wide): 3.3B **Privately Held**
WEB: www.sulzerpumps.com
SIC: 7692 Welding repair

HQ: Sulzer Pump Services (Us) Inc.
　　101 Old Underwood Rd G
　　La Porte TX 77571
　　281 417-7110

(P-24670)
TC STEEL
464 Sonoma Mountain Rd, Petaluma (94954-9579)
PHONE.................................707 773-2150
Tom Cleary, *President*
Kim Cleary, *CFO*
EMP: 40 **EST:** 1989
SALES (est): 3.9MM **Privately Held**
SIC: 7692 3449 5051 7389 Welding repair; miscellaneous metalwork; structural shapes, iron or steel; scrap steel cutting

(P-24671)
TERRI BELL
Also Called: Alpine Metals
2152 Ruth Ave Ste 4, South Lake Tahoe (96150-4336)
PHONE.................................530 541-4180
Terri Bell, *Owner*
EMP: 12
SQ FT: 13,000
SALES (est): 700K **Privately Held**
WEB: www.alpinemetals.com
SIC: 7692 1799 Welding repair; welding on site

(P-24672)
THOMAS MANUFACTURING CO LLC
1308 W 8th Ave, Chico (95926-3002)
PHONE.................................530 893-8940
Carolyn Dauterman,
Thomas Dauterman,
▲ **EMP:** 25
SQ FT: 55,000
SALES (est): 2.9MM **Privately Held**
SIC: 7692 5083 3599 Welding repair; agricultural machinery & equipment; machine shop, jobbing & repair

(P-24673)
THOMAS WELDING & MCH SP INC
1308 W 8th Ave, Chico (95926-3002)
PHONE.................................530 893-8940
Thomas Danterman, *CEO*
Carolyn Sue Dauterman, *Vice Pres*
EMP: 25
SQ FT: 55,000
SALES (est): 2.5MM **Privately Held**
SIC: 7692 5083 3599 Welding repair; agricultural machinery & equipment; machine shop, jobbing & repair

(P-24674)
TIKOS TANKS INC
Also Called: Rte Welding
14561 Hawthorne Ave, Fontana (92335-2508)
PHONE.................................951 757-8014
Ruben Gutierrez III, *Founder*
Ruben Alonso, *Asst Mgr*
Chris Loya, *Parts Mgr*
EMP: 45
SALES (est): 7.4MM **Privately Held**
SIC: 7692 Welding repair

(P-24675)
TITAN STEEL FABRICATORS INC
1069 E Bradley Ave, El Cajon (92021-1232)
P.O. Box 2057 (92021-0057)
PHONE.................................619 449-1271
Allan W Jones, *President*
Timothy Jackman, *Vice Pres*
EMP: 10
SALES (est): 1.7MM **Privately Held**
SIC: 7692 Welding repair

(P-24676)
TOMS METAL SPECIALISTS INC
Also Called: Toms Welding & Fabrication
1416 Wallace Ave, San Francisco (94124-3318)
P.O. Box 24385 (94124-0385)
PHONE.................................415 822-7971
Tom Chang, *CEO*
George Chang, *Office Mgr*
EMP: 33
SQ FT: 4,000

SALES (est): 6.6MM **Privately Held**
WEB: www.tomsmetal.com
SIC: 7692 Welding repair

(P-24677)
VETPOWERED LLC
2970 Main St, San Diego (92113-3730)
PHONE.................................619 269-7116
Hernan Luis Y Prado,
Rachel Luis Y Prado, *Vice Pres*
EMP: 16
SQ FT: 32,000
SALES: 2MM **Privately Held**
WEB: www.lypindustries.com
SIC: 7692 7359 3599 7699 Automotive welding; home cleaning & maintenance equipment rental services; machine shop, jobbing & repair; industrial machinery & equipment repair; commercial cooking & foodwarming equipment; ballistic missiles, complete

(P-24678)
WELDLOGIC INC
2651 Lavery Ct, Newbury Park (91320-1502)
PHONE.................................805 375-1670
Robert Elizarraz, *President*
Jack Froschauer, *Vice Pres*
Rick Heminuk, *Vice Pres*
▲ **EMP:** 65
SQ FT: 25,000
SALES (est): 11.6MM **Privately Held**
WEB: www.weldlogic.com
SIC: 7692 Welding repair

(P-24679)
WEST COAST WELDING & CNSTR
390 S Del Norte Blvd, Oxnard (93030-7914)
PHONE.................................805 604-1222
Micheal Edward Barbey, *CEO*
Tamara Barbey, *CFO*
Stella Delgado, *Admin Sec*
John Bricker, *Superintendent*
EMP: 15
SALES (est): 2.2MM **Privately Held**
SIC: 7692 Welding repair

(P-24680)
WYMORE INC
697 S Dogwood Rd, El Centro (92243-9747)
P.O. Box 2618 (92244-2618)
PHONE.................................760 352-2045
Marla Wymore Stilwell, *President*
Michael Mouser, *Treasurer*
Richard C Wymore, *Director*
Thomas A Wymore, *Director*
EMP: 30 **EST:** 1947
SQ FT: 25,200
SALES (est): 5.3MM **Privately Held**
SIC: 7692 3599 5251 5085 Welding repair; machine shop, jobbing & repair; tools; tools

7694 Armature Rewinding Shops

(P-24681)
ALLIED ELECTRIC MOTOR SVC INC
2635 S Sierra Vista Ave, Fresno (93725-2103)
PHONE.................................559 486-4222
Salvatore Rome, *Director*
EMP: 13
SALES (corp-wide): 43.9MM **Privately Held**
WEB: www.alliedelectric.net
SIC: 7694 Electric motor repair
PA: Allied Electric Motor Service, Inc.
　　4690 E Jensen Ave
　　Fresno CA 93725
　　559 486-4222

(P-24682)
ALSOP PUMP
Also Called: Alsop Electric Motor Shop
1508 Abbott St, Salinas (93901-4507)
PHONE.................................831 424-3946
Steve Allison, *Owner*
EMP: 12

▲ = Import ▼=Export
◆ =Import/Export

SQ FT: 2,250
SALES: 389.2K **Privately Held**
SIC: **7694** 5063 Electric motor repair; motors, electric

(P-24683)
ARROW ELECTRIC MOTOR SERVICE
645 Broadway St, Fresno (93721-2890)
PHONE..............................559 266-0104
Larry Kragh, *President*
Geri Kragh, *Corp Secy*
Cathy Knott, *Office Mgr*
Jeff Kragh, *Sales Staff*
Janice Sanders, *Manager*
EMP: 11
SQ FT: 25,000
SALES (est): 2MM **Privately Held**
WEB: www.arrowelectricmotor.com
SIC: **7694** Electric motor repair

(P-24684)
AUL CORP (PA)
1250 Main St Ste 300, NAPA (94559-2622)
PHONE..............................707 257-9700
Jimmy Atkinson, *President*
Glenn Schreuder, *Treasurer*
Jason Garner, *Senior VP*
Paul McCarthy, *Senior VP*
Craig Bertenshaw, *Vice Pres*
EMP: 40
SQ FT: 8,500
SALES (est): 4.6MM **Privately Held**
WEB: www.aulcorp.com
SIC: **7694** 7549 Motor repair services; automotive maintenance services

(P-24685)
BAKERSFIELD ELC MTR REPR INC
Also Called: B E M R
121 W Sumner St, Bakersfield (93301-4137)
PHONE..............................661 327-3583
Michael Wayne Langston, *President*
Jerry Endicott, *President*
Nina Endicott, *Vice Pres*
EMP: 13 **EST:** 1949
SQ FT: 12,350
SALES: 3.6MM **Privately Held**
SIC: **7694** 5063 Rewinding services; electric motor repair; motors, electric

(P-24686)
DEMARIA ELECTRIC INC
Also Called: Demaria Electric Motor Svcs
7048 Marcelle St, Paramount (90723-4839)
PHONE..............................310 549-4980
Daniel Demaria, *President*
Gary Demaria, *Information Mgr*
EMP: 30 **EST:** 1977
SQ FT: 6,500
SALES (est): 2.4MM **Privately Held**
WEB: www.demariaelectric.com
SIC: **7694** 7699 Electric motor repair; engine repair & replacement, non-automotive

(P-24687)
E & L ELECTRIC INC
12322 Los Nietos Rd, Santa Fe Springs (90670-2912)
PHONE..............................562 903-9272
Mike Fitch, *President*
Adam Fitch, *Sales Staff*
EMP: 17
SQ FT: 10,000
SALES (est): 4.5MM **Privately Held**
SIC: **7694** 5063 Electric motor repair; motors, electric

(P-24688)
ELECTRIC MOTOR WORKS INC
803 Inyo St, Bakersfield (93305-5127)
P.O. Box 3349 (93385-3349)
PHONE..............................661 327-4271
L B Thomasl B Thomas, *President*
Chuck Thomas, *Vice Pres*
Austin Schwebel, *General Mgr*
Melody Alther, *Office Mgr*
Mike Anderson, *Sales Mgr*
EMP: 20
SQ FT: 7,600

SALES: 2MM **Privately Held**
SIC: **7694** 5063 Electric motor repair; motors, electric

(P-24689)
EURTON ELECTRIC COMPANY INC
9920 Painter Ave, Santa Fe Springs (90670)
P.O. Box 2113 (90670-0113)
PHONE..............................562 946-4477
John Buchanan, *President*
Heather Buchanan, *Vice Pres*
Rick Arellano, *General Mgr*
Julie Galaviz, *Office Mgr*
Julie Galaviz-Macias, *Office Mgr*
▲ EMP: 35
SQ FT: 10,000
SALES (est): 5.1MM **Privately Held**
SIC: **7694** 5063 Rewinding services; electrical supplies

(P-24690)
EVANS ELECTRIC SERVICE (PA)
531 Fulton St, Fresno (93721-2811)
P.O. Box 11456 (93773-1456)
PHONE..............................559 268-4704
Evan W Hammer Sr, *President*
Jacqueline L Hammer, *Vice Pres*
EMP: 40 **EST:** 1955
SQ FT: 20,000
SALES (est): 1.8MM **Privately Held**
WEB: www.evans-electric.com
SIC: **7694** Electric motor repair; rebuilding motors, except automotive; rewinding stators

(P-24691)
G POWELL ELECTRIC
Also Called: GP Electric
1020 Price Ave, Pomona (91767-5739)
PHONE..............................909 865-2291
Geepi Powell, *President*
EMP: 25
SQ FT: 19,000
SALES (est): 3MM **Privately Held**
WEB: www.gpelectric.com
SIC: **7694** 5063 Electric motor repair; motors, electric

(P-24692)
GENERAL LINEAR SYSTEMS
4332 Artesia Ave, Fullerton (92833-2523)
PHONE..............................714 994-4822
Garrett Hartney, *President*
Annette Hartney, *Treasurer*
James Mynatt, *Vice Pres*
Maria Ortega, *Office Mgr*
Bill Hartnet, *Sales Staff*
EMP: 16
SQ FT: 4,000
SALES (est): 1.3MM **Privately Held**
WEB: www.coilwinder.com
SIC: **7694** Coil winding service

(P-24693)
GRECH MOTORS LLC (PA)
6915 Arlington Ave, Riverside (92504-1905)
PHONE..............................951 688-8347
Edward P Grech, *Mng Member*
Sue Reagan, *Executive Asst*
David Reagan, *Research*
Chris Hoo, *Controller*
John Beck, *VP Opers*
EMP: 48
SALES (est): 7.9MM **Privately Held**
SIC: **7694** Electric motor repair

(P-24694)
R A REED ELECTRIC COMPANY (PA)
Also Called: Reed Electric & Field Service
5503 S Boyle Ave, Vernon (90058-3932)
PHONE..............................323 587-2284
John A Richard Jr, *President*
Alex Wong, *CFO*
Dorothy J Richard, *Treasurer*
Tim Durnil, *Sales Staff*
John Carter, *Accounts Mgr*
EMP: 29
SQ FT: 55,000
SALES (est): 6.1MM **Privately Held**
SIC: **7694** 5063 Electric motor repair; motors, electric

(P-24695)
R P M ELECTRIC MOTORS
11352 Westminster Ave, Garden Grove (92843-3655)
PHONE..............................714 638-4174
Bon Pham, *Owner*
EMP: 10
SQ FT: 6,000
SALES (est): 1.6MM **Privately Held**
SIC: **7694** 5063 Electric motor repair; motors, electric

(P-24696)
STANLEY ELECTRIC MOTOR CO INC
1520 E Miner Ave, Stockton (95205-4537)
PHONE..............................209 464-7321
Bradley Oneto, *President*
Pete Mamalis, *Controller*
Keota Sounthone, *Purchasing*
EMP: 27
SQ FT: 92,500
SALES (est): 9.3MM **Privately Held**
WEB: www.stanleyelectric.com
SIC: **7694** 5063 Electric motor repair; motors, electric

(P-24697)
SULZER ELECTRO-MECHANICAL SERV
620 S Rancho Ave, Colton (92324-3243)
PHONE..............................909 825-7971
Gary Patton, *Branch Mgr*
EMP: 50
SALES (corp-wide): 3.3B **Privately Held**
SIC: **7694** 5063 Electric motor repair; motors, electric
HQ: Sulzer Electro-Mechanical Services (Us) Inc.
1910 Jasmine Dr
Pasadena TX 77503
713 473-3231

(P-24698)
SUPERIOR ELECTRIC MTR SVC INC
4622 Alcoa Ave, Vernon (90058-2416)
PHONE..............................323 583-1040
Vicky Marachelian, *President*
Art Marachelian, *Vice Pres*
Christopher Marachelian, *Vice Pres*
EMP: 18
SQ FT: 12,000
SALES (est): 4.5MM **Privately Held**
SIC: **7694** 5063 Electric motor repair; motors, electric

(P-24699)
TOM GARCIA INC
Also Called: Union Electric Motor Service
2777 Newton Ave, San Diego (92113-3713)
PHONE..............................619 232-4881
Tom Garcia Jr, *CEO*
▲ EMP: 10
SQ FT: 18,000
SALES (est): 1.8MM **Privately Held**
WEB: www.tomgarcia.com
SIC: **7694** 5999 Electric motor repair; electronic parts & equipment

(P-24700)
VALLEJO ELECTRIC MOTOR INC
925 Maine St, Vallejo (94590-6311)
PHONE..............................707 552-7488
Larry Lightman, *President*
William Cygan, *Treasurer*
Dillon Lightman, *Admin Sec*
EMP: 12
SQ FT: 7,000
SALES (est): 1.2MM **Privately Held**
SIC: **7694** Electric motor repair

(P-24701)
VINCENT ELECTRIC COMPANY (PA)
Also Called: Vincent Electic Motor Company
8383 Baldwin St, Oakland (94621-1925)
PHONE..............................510 639-4500
Ronald Vincent, *Ch of Bd*
Thomas R Marvin, *President*
Sarah Beckwich, *Treasurer*
Nancy Vincent Marvin, *Admin Sec*

John Piekar, *Human Res Mgr*
EMP: 30
SQ FT: 27,000
SALES (est): 4.1MM **Privately Held**
WEB: www.vincentelectric.com
SIC: **7694** 5063 Electric motor repair; motors, electric

(P-24702)
VISALIA ELECTRIC MOTOR SP INC
Also Called: Visalia Electric Motor Service
7515 W Sunnyview Ave, Visalia (93291-9602)
PHONE..............................559 651-0606
Gene Quesnoy, *President*
EMP: 15
SQ FT: 30,000
SALES (est): 1.9MM **Publicly Held**
WEB: www.visaliaelectric.com
SIC: **7694** Electric motor repair
HQ: Magnetech Industrial Services, Inc.
800 Nave Rd Se
Massillon OH 44646
330 830-3500

ALPHABETIC SECTION

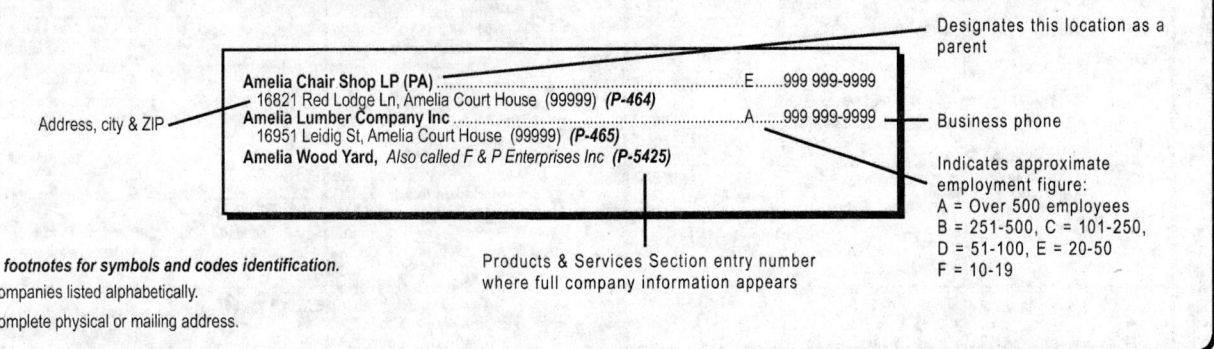

See footnotes for symbols and codes identification.
* Companies listed alphabetically.
* Complete physical or mailing address.

Products & Services Section entry number where full company information appears

---

.com, Lake Elsinore *Also called Roadracing World Publishing* **(P-6019)**

101 Apparel Inc ....F......714 454-8988
1802 N Glassell St Orange (92865) **(P-2983)**

101 Roofing & Sheet Metal Co ....F......415 695-0101
1390 Wallace Ave San Francisco (94124) **(P-12074)**

101 Vertical Fabrication Inc ....E......909 428-6000
10255 Beech Ave Fontana (92335) **(P-11726)**

10100 Holdings Inc (PA) ....F......310 552-0705
10100 Santa Monica Blvd # 1050 Los Angeles (90067) **(P-4437)**

10x Genomics Inc (PA) ....C......925 401-7300
6230 Stoneridge Mall Rd Pleasanton (94588) **(P-21157)**

1254 Industries ....F......760 798-8531
1444 Alpine Pl San Marcos (92078) **(P-23257)**

12th Street By Cynthia Vincent, Los Angeles *Also called Green Mochi LLC* **(P-3229)**

15five Inc ....F......208 816-4225
3053 Fillmore St Ste 279 San Francisco (94123) **(P-23533)**

18 Media Inc (PA) ....F......650 324-1818
873 Santa Cruz Ave # 206 Menlo Park (94025) **(P-5872)**

18 Rabbits Inc (PA) ....F......415 922-6006
995 Market St Fl 2 San Francisco (94103) **(P-1353)**

180 Snacks (PA) ....E......714 238-1192
1173 N Armando St Anaheim (92806) **(P-1418)**

1891 Alton A California Co ....F......949 261-6402
1891 Alton Pkwy Ste A Irvine (92606) **(P-16871)**

1le California Inc ....E......209 846-7541
3224 Mchenry Ave Ste F Modesto (95350) **(P-17003)**

1on1 LLC ....E......310 448-5376
12015 Waterfront Dr # 261 Playa Vista (90094) **(P-23534)**

1perfectchoice ....F......909 594-8855
21908 Valley Blvd Walnut (91789) **(P-5045)**

1st Choice Fertilizer Inc ....F......800 504-5699
1515 Aurora Dr San Leandro (94577) **(P-8787)**

1st Responder Fire Protection, Northridge *Also called First Responder Fire* **(P-14817)**

2 Awesome International, Calabasas *Also called Solid 21 Incorporated* **(P-22572)**

2 Impact Group, Fontana *Also called Harvest Asia Inc* **(P-22679)**

2 S 2 Inc ....F......760 599-9225
1357 Rocky Point Dr Oceanside (92056) **(P-18803)**

2 Spec Mfg, San Jose *Also called Michael T Mingione* **(P-4991)**

2-G Enterprises, Mountain View *Also called Applied Physics Systems Inc* **(P-21434)**

2.95 Guys, Poway *Also called Smoothreads Inc* **(P-3815)**

2016 Montgomery Inc ....F......323 316-6886
755 E 14th Pl Los Angeles (90021) **(P-2662)**

2100 Freedom Inc (HQ) ....D......714 796-7000
625 N Grand Ave Santa Ana (92701) **(P-5542)**

220 Laboratories Inc ....C......951 683-2912
2321 3rd St Riverside (92507) **(P-8430)**

220 Laboratories Inc (PA) ....C......951 683-2912
2375 3rd St Riverside (92507) **(P-8431)**

23 Bottles of Beer LLC ....E......707 545-2337
725 4th St Santa Rosa (95404) **(P-1488)**

24/7 Studio Equipment Inc ....D......818 840-8247
3111 N Kenwood St Burbank (91505) **(P-17432)**

24x7saas Inc ....F......408 391-6205
2307 Larkspur Canyon Dr San Jose (95138) **(P-23535)**

253 Inc ....F......650 737-5670
245 E Harris Ave South San Francisco (94080) **(P-12075)**

260 Resource Management LLC ....F......866 700-1031
100 Bayview Cir Ste 505 Newport Beach (92660) **(P-149)**

2bb Unlimited Inc ....E......213 253-9810
724 E 1st St Ste 300 Los Angeles (90012) **(P-2958)**

2j Antennas USA ....F......858 866-1072
7420 Carroll Rd Ste D San Diego (92121) **(P-17433)**

2m Machine Corporation ....F......562 404-4225
13171 Rosecrans Ave Santa Fe Springs (90670) **(P-15643)**

2m Machining & Mfg Co ....F......323 564-9388
8630 Santa Fe Ave South Gate (90280) **(P-20979)**

2nd Gen Productions Inc ....F......800 877-6282
400 El Sobrante Rd Corona (92879) **(P-8356)**

2xwireless Inc ....D......877 581-8002
1065 Marauder St Chico (95973) **(P-17434)**

3 Badge Beverage Corporation ....F......707 343-1167
32 Patten St Sonoma (95476) **(P-1573)**

3 Ball Co, La Mirada *Also called Twpm Inc* **(P-5318)**

3 D Studios ....F......510 535-1809
800 51st Ave Oakland (94601) **(P-11727)**

3 Gen Inc ....F......949 481-6384
31521 Rancho Viejo Rd # 104 San Juan Capistrano (92675) **(P-21567)**

3 Ink Productions Inc ....F......559 275-4565
4790 W Jacquelyn Ave Fresno (93722) **(P-2720)**

3 Point Distribution LLC ....E......949 266-2700
170 Technology Dr Irvine (92618) **(P-3060)**

3-D Polymers ....F......310 324-7694
13026 S Normandie Ave Gardena (90249) **(P-9274)**

3-D Precision Machine Inc ....E......951 296-5449
42132 Remington Ave Temecula (92590) **(P-19940)**

3-V Fastener Co Inc ....D......951 734-4391
320 Reed Cir Corona (92879) **(P-12663)**

32 Bar Blues LLC ....F......805 962-6665
1015 Cindy Ln B Carpinteria (93013) **(P-3535)**

360 Manufacturing Solutions, Santa Clara *Also called Erb Investment Company LLC* **(P-15935)**

360 Systems ....F......818 991-0360
3281 Grande Vista Dr Newbury Park (91320) **(P-17178)**

360,, Jurupa Valley *Also called Roller Derby Skate Corp* **(P-22875)**

365 Printing Inc ....F......714 752-6990
14747 Artesia Blvd Ste 3a La Mirada (90638) **(P-6388)**

3b Machining Co Inc ....F......408 719-9237
2292 Trade Zone Blvd 1a San Jose (95131) **(P-15644)**

3becom Inc (PA) ....F......818 726-0007
2400 Lincoln Ave Ste 216 Altadena (91001) **(P-23536)**

3d Detailing Products For The, Santa Clarita *Also called 3d International LLC* **(P-8357)**

3d Instruments LP (HQ) ....E......714 399-9200
4990 E Hunter Ave Anaheim (92807) **(P-20824)**

3d International LLC ....E......661 250-2020
20724 Cntre Pnte Pkwy Uni Santa Clarita (91350) **(P-8357)**

3d Machine Co Inc ....E......714 777-8985
4790 E Wesley Dr Anaheim (92807) **(P-15645)**

3d Robotics Inc (PA) ....D......415 599-1404
1608 4th St Ste 410 Berkeley (94710) **(P-19244)**

3d Systems Inc ....F......803 280-7777
16550 W Bernardo Dr # 5 San Diego (92127) **(P-14875)**

3d/International Inc ....D......661 250-2020
20724 Centre Pointe Pkwy # 1 Santa Clarita (91350) **(P-8358)**

3dcd ....F......805 383-3837
3233 Mission Oaks Blvd Camarillo (93012) **(P-19208)**

3dconnexion Inc ....D......510 713-6000
6505 Kaiser Dr Fremont (94555) **(P-15139)**

3deo Inc ....F......844 496-3825
14000 Van Ness Ave Ste C Gardena (90249) **(P-13963)**

3dgroundworks LLC ....F......415 964-0060
350 Rhode Island St # 240 San Francisco (94103) **(P-23537)**

3g Rebar Inc ....F......661 588-0294
6400 Price Way Bakersfield (93308) **(P-12582)**

3h Communication Systems Inc ....E......949 529-1583
4000 Barranca Pkwy # 250 Irvine (92604) **(P-20526)**

3M Company ....C......951 737-3441
18750 Minnesota Rd Corona (92881) **(P-10965)**

3M Company ....F......818 882-0606
8357 Canoga Ave Canoga Park (91304) **(P-16582)**

3M Company ....F......949 863-1360
2111 Mcgaw Ave Irvine (92614) **(P-22129)**

3M Company ....E......626 358-0136
1601 S Shamrock Ave Monrovia (91016) **(P-9275)**

3M Company ....B......818 341-1300
19901 Nordhoff St Northridge (91324) **(P-7706)**

3M Unitek Corporation ....B......626 445-7960
2724 Peck Rd Monrovia (91016) **(P-22130)**

3par Inc (HQ) ....C......510 445-1046
4209 Technology Dr Fremont (94538) **(P-14876)**

3y Power Technology Inc ....F......949 450-0152
80 Bunsen Irvine (92618) **(P-18804)**

4 Flight, Rancho Cucamonga *Also called Safran Cabin Inc* **(P-20216)**

4 Over LLC (HQ) ....B......818 246-1170
5900 San Fernando Rd D Glendale (91202) **(P-6967)**

4 Over LLC ....F......818 246-1170
1225 Los Angeles St Glendale (91204) **(P-6968)**

4 What Its Worth Inc (PA) ....F......323 728-4503
5815 Smithway St Commerce (90040) **(P-3133)**

4 You Apparel Inc ....F......323 583-4242
2944 E 44th St Vernon (90058) **(P-3209)**

Employee Codes: A=Over 500 employees, B=251-500
C=101-250, D=51-100, E=20-50, F=10-19

2020 California
Manfacturers Register

© Mergent Inc. 1-800-342-5647

1003

4-D Engineering Inc … E … 310 532-2384
1635 W 144th St Gardena (90247) ***(P-15646)***

402 Shoes Inc … E … 323 655-5437
402 N La Cienega Blvd West Hollywood (90048) ***(P-3437)***

4505 Meats Inc … E … 415 255-3094
548 Market St San Francisco (94104) ***(P-2314)***

478826 Limited … E … 916 933-5280
5050 Hillsdale Cir El Dorado Hills (95762) ***(P-15647)***

4excelsior, Anaheim *Also called Excelsior Nutrition Inc* ***(P-7659)***

4x Development Inc … F … 562 424-2225
2650 E 28th St Signal Hill (90755) ***(P-12753)***

5 Ball Inc … F … 310 830-0630
200 Broad Ave Wilmington (90744) ***(P-6064)***

5 I Sciences Inc … F … 858 943-4566
16885 Via Del Campo Ct # 130 San Diego (92127) ***(P-21568)***

5 Star Redemption Inc … E … 818 709-0875
8803 Shirley Ave Northridge (91324) ***(P-23258)***

5-Stars Engineering Assoc Inc … E … 408 380-4849
3393 De La Cruz Blvd Santa Clara (95054) ***(P-14261)***

500friends Inc (HQ) … E … 800 818-8356
77 Geary St Fl 5 San Francisco (94108) ***(P-23538)***

515 W Seventh LLC … F … 323 278-8116
430 S Pecan St Los Angeles (90033) ***(P-17004)***

55 Degree Wine … F … 323 662-5556
3111 Glendale Blvd Ste 2 Los Angeles (90039) ***(P-1574)***

5800 Sunset Productions Inc … F … 323 460-3987
5800 W Sunset Blvd Los Angeles (90028) ***(P-5543)***

5h Sheet Metal Fabrication Inc … F … 714 633-7544
1826 W Business Center Dr Orange (92867) ***(P-12076)***

5th Axis Inc … D … 858 505-0432
7140 Engineer Rd San Diego (92111) ***(P-15648)***

6480 Corporation … E … 818 765-9670
7230 Coldwater Canyon Ave North Hollywood (91605) ***(P-6969)***

6f Resolution Inc … D … 209 467-0490
5100 W Goldleaf Cir Los Angeles (90056) ***(P-19561)***

7 & 8 LLC … F … 707 963-9425
4028 Spring Mountain Rd Saint Helena (94574) ***(P-1575)***

7 Generation Games Inc … F … 260 402-1172
2111 7th St Apt 8 Santa Monica (90405) ***(P-23539)***

7 U P RC Bottling Company … D … 714 974-8560
1300 W Taft Ave Orange (92865) ***(P-14692)***

7 Up, Stockton *Also called Varni Brothers Corporation* ***(P-2181)***

7 Up / R C Bottling Co, Vernon *Also called American Bottling Company* ***(P-2033)***

7-Up, Orange *Also called 7 U P RC Bottling Company* ***(P-14692)***

7x7, San Francisco *Also called Hartle Media Ventures LLC* ***(P-5948)***

800total Gym Commercial LLC … F … 858 586-6080
5225 Avd Encinas Ste C Carlsbad (92008) ***(P-22729)***

860, Shameless, Hot Wire, Los Angeles *Also called JT Design Studio Inc* ***(P-3350)***

89bio Inc … F … 415 500-4614
535 Mission St Fl 14 San Francisco (94105) ***(P-7707)***

9 To 5 Seating, Hawthorne *Also called D3 Inc* ***(P-4831)***

909 Magazine, Upland *Also called 909 Media Group Inc* ***(P-5873)***

909 Media Group Inc … F … 909 608-7426
100 N Euclid Ave Ste 202 Upland (91786) ***(P-5873)***

A & A Aerospace Inc … F … 562 901-6803
1442 Hayes Ave Long Beach (90813) ***(P-19993)***

A & A Aerospace Inc … F … 562 901-6803
1987 W 16th St Long Beach (90813) ***(P-19994)***

A & A Concrete Supply, Chico *Also called A & A Ready Mixed Concrete Inc* ***(P-10674)***

A & A Custom Shutters … F … 818 383-1819
10465 San Fernando Rd # 8 Pacoima (91331) ***(P-11925)***

A & A Electronic Assembly, San Fernando *Also called Signature Tech Group Inc* ***(P-19081)***

A & A Fabrication & Polsg Corp … F … 562 696-0441
12031 Philadelphia St Whittier (90601) ***(P-11728)***

A & A Jewelry Tools Findings … F … 213 627-8004
319 W 6th St Los Angeles (90014) ***(P-23259)***

A & A Machine & Dev Co Inc … F … 310 532-7706
16625 Gramercy Pl Gardena (90247) ***(P-15649)***

A & A Ready Mix Concrete, Newport Beach *Also called Lebata Inc* ***(P-10779)***

A & A Ready Mixed Concrete Inc … F … 209 830-5070
10250 W Linne Rd Tracy (95377) ***(P-10670)***

A & A Ready Mixed Concrete Inc … E … 310 515-0933
134 W Redondo Beach Blvd Gardena (90248) ***(P-10671)***

A & A Ready Mixed Concrete Inc (PA) … E … 949 253-2800
4621 Teller Ave Ste 130 Newport Beach (92660) ***(P-10672)***

A & A Ready Mixed Concrete Inc … F … 530 671-1220
1201 Market St Yuba City (95991) ***(P-10673)***

A & A Ready Mixed Concrete Inc … E … 530 342-5989
3578 Esplanade A Chico (95973) ***(P-10674)***

A & A Ready Mixed Concrete Inc … E … 707 399-0682
3809 Bithell Ln Suisun City (94585) ***(P-10675)***

A & A Ready Mixed Concrete Inc … F … 562 923-7281
9645 Washburn Rd Downey (90241) ***(P-10676)***

A & A Ready Mixed Concrete Inc … E … 209 546-1950
4035 E Mariposa Rd Stockton (95215) ***(P-10677)***

A & A Ready Mixed Concrete Inc … F … 949 580-1844
25901 Towne Centre Dr Foothill Ranch (92610) ***(P-10678)***

A & A Ready Mixed Concrete Inc … E … 916 383-3756
8272 Berry Ave Sacramento (95828) ***(P-10679)***

A & B Aerospace Inc … E … 626 334-2976
612 S Ayon Ave Azusa (91702) ***(P-15650)***

A & B Brush Mfg Corp … F … 626 303-8856
1150 3 Ranch Rd Duarte (91010) ***(P-23019)***

A & B Die Casting Co Inc … E … 877 708-0009
900 Alfred Nobel Dr Hercules (94547) ***(P-11328)***

A & B Diecasting, Hercules *Also called Benda Tool & Model Works Inc* ***(P-14022)***

A & B Sandblast Co, Los Angeles *Also called Rosenkranz Enterprises Inc* ***(P-13090)***

A & C Imports & Exports, Burlingame *Also called A & C Trade Consultants Inc* ***(P-11651)***

A & C Trade Consultants Inc … F … 650 375-7000
1 Edwards Ct Ste 101 Burlingame (94010) ***(P-11651)***

A & D Plating Inc … F … 760 480-4580
2265 Micro Pl Ste A Escondido (92029) ***(P-12894)***

A & D Precision Machining Inc … E … 510 657-6781
4155 Business Center Dr Fremont (94538) ***(P-15651)***

A & D Precision Mfg Inc … E … 714 779-2714
4751 E Hunter Ave Anaheim (92807) ***(P-15652)***

A & D Rubber Products Co Inc (PA) … E … 209 941-0100
1438 Bourbon St Stockton (95204) ***(P-9212)***

A & E Anodizing Inc … F … 408 297-5910
652 Charles St Ste A San Jose (95112) ***(P-12895)***

A & F Metal Products … F … 805 346-2040
520 Farnel Rd Ste L Santa Maria (93458) ***(P-12754)***

A & G Electropolish, Fountain Valley *Also called Lakin Industries Inc* ***(P-13040)***

A & G Industries Inc … F … 760 891-0323
341 Enterprise St San Marcos (92078) ***(P-12077)***

A & G Instr Svc & Calibration … F … 714 630-7400
1227 N Tustin Ave Anaheim (92807) ***(P-13286)***

A & H Engineering & Mfg Inc … E … 562 623-9717
17109 Edwards Rd Cerritos (90703) ***(P-15653)***

A & H Tool Engineering, Cerritos *Also called A & H Engineering & Mfg Inc* ***(P-15653)***

A & H Wire EDM, San Dimas *Also called Alfredo Hernandez* ***(P-15717)***

A & J Enterprises Inc … F … 323 654-5902
7925 Santa Monica Blvd West Hollywood (90046) ***(P-6389)***

A & J Industries Inc … F … 310 216-2170
1430 240th St Harbor City (90710) ***(P-4327)***

A & J Machining Inc … F … 903 566-0304
16305 Vineyard Blvd Ste B Morgan Hill (95037) ***(P-15654)***

A & J Manufacturing, Harbor City *Also called A & J Industries Inc* ***(P-4327)***

A & J Manufacturing Company … E … 714 544-9570
70 Icon Foothill Ranch (92610) ***(P-12755)***

A & J Precision Sheetmetal Inc … D … 408 885-9134
1161 N 4th St San Jose (95112) ***(P-12078)***

A & L Engineering, Hawthorne *Also called Acuna Dionisio Able* ***(P-15689)***

A & L Ready-Mix, Sonora *Also called L K Lehman Trucking* ***(P-10595)***

A & M Electronics Inc … E … 661 257-3680
25018 Avenue Kearny Valencia (91355) ***(P-17797)***

A & M Engineering Inc … D … 626 813-2020
15854 Salvatiera St Irwindale (91706) ***(P-15655)***

A & M Printing, Pleasanton *Also called Leo Lam Inc* ***(P-6698)***

A & M Sculpture Lighting, Los Angeles *Also called A & M Sculptured Metals LLC* ***(P-12079)***

A & M Sculptured Metals LLC … E … 323 263-2221
1781 N Indiana St Los Angeles (90063) ***(P-12079)***

A & M Welding Inc … F … 310 329-2700
16935 S Broadway Gardena (90248) ***(P-24611)***

A & R Doors Inc … F … 831 637-8139
41 5th St Frnt Hollister (95023) ***(P-3988)***

A & R Engineering Co Inc … E … 310 603-9060
1053 E Bedmar St Carson (90746) ***(P-15656)***

A & R Powder Coating Inc … F … 714 630-0709
1198 N Grove St Ste B Anaheim (92806) ***(P-13131)***

A & R Pre-Hung Door, Hollister *Also called A & R Doors Inc* ***(P-3988)***

A & S Mold & Die Corp … D … 818 341-5393
9705 Eton Ave Chatsworth (91311) ***(P-9599)***

A & V Engineering Inc … F … 310 637-9906
1155 W Mahalo Pl Compton (90220) ***(P-15657)***

A A A Engineering & Mfg Co … E … 626 447-5029
2118 Huntington Dr San Marino (91108) ***(P-15658)***

A A A Sign & Banner Mfg Co, Los Angeles *Also called AAA Flag & Banner Mfg Co Inc* ***(P-3828)***

A A Cater Truck Mfg Co Inc … D … 323 233-2343
750 E Slauson Ave Los Angeles (90011) ***(P-4679)***

A A E Aerospace & Coml Tech, Huntington Beach *Also called American Automated Engrg Inc* ***(P-20472)***

A A Label Inc (PA) … E … 925 803-5709
6958 Sierra Ct Dublin (94568) ***(P-5488)***

A A P, Gardena *Also called American Aircraft Products Inc* ***(P-12104)***

A A Prezant Discount Rbr Bands, San Mateo *Also called Prezant Company* ***(P-14312)***

A A Trader, Santa Clara *Also called America Asia Trade Promotion* ***(P-3599)***

A Alpha Wave Guide Co (PA) … F … 310 322-3487
1217 E El Segundo Blvd El Segundo (90245) ***(P-2663)***

A Alpha Waveguide Tube Co, El Segundo *Also called A Alpha Wave Guide Co* ***(P-2663)***

A and C Electronics … F … 818 886-8900
18153 Napa St Northridge (91325) ***(P-17798)***

A and G Inc … C … 714 756-0400
1501 E Cerritos Ave Anaheim (92805) ***(P-2741)***

A and G Inc (HQ) … A … 714 765-0400
11296 Harrel St Jurupa Valley (91752) ***(P-3061)***

A and G News Papers, Hayward *Also called Daily Review* ***(P-5611)***

A and M Ornamental Iron & Wldg … F … 951 734-6730
1611 Railroad St Corona (92880) ***(P-12440)***

A B, Sylmar *Also called Advanced Bionics LLC* ***(P-21972)***

A B Boyd Co (PA) … E … 209 236-1111
600 S Mcclure Rd Modesto (95357) ***(P-9276)***

A B C Plastic Fabrication,, Chatsworth *Also called A B C Plastics Inc* ***(P-9435)***

A B C Plastics Inc … F … 818 775-0065
9132 De Soto Ave Chatsworth (91311) ***(P-9435)***

A B C Press, Signal Hill *Also called Floyd Dennee* ***(P-7066)***

A B C Restaurant Equipment Co, South El Monte *Also called Master Enterprises Inc* ***(P-12280)***

A B C-Clio Inc (PA) … C … 805 968-1911
147 Castilian Dr Goleta (93117) ***(P-6065)***

A B G Instruments & Engrg … F … 805 238-6262
604 30th St Paso Robles (93446) ***(P-14006)***

A B S, Signal Hill *Also called Applied Business Software Inc* ***(P-23611)***

Mergent e-mail: customerrelations@mergent.com
1004
2020 California
Manufacturers Register
(P-0000) Products & Services Section entry number
(PA)=Parent Co (HQ)=Headquarters (DH)=Div Headquarters

A Better Trap, Fresno *Also called Better World Manufacturing Inc* ***(P-9663)***
A C D, Santa Ana *Also called Acd LLC* ***(P-11990)***
A C L, Santa Clara *Also called Advanced Component Labs Inc* ***(P-18064)***
A C M, Burlingame *Also called Advanced Components Mfg* ***(P-15693)***
A C Manufacturing Inc ....F....760 745-3717
3023 Mount Whitney Rd Escondido (92029) ***(P-15659)***
A C Plating, Bakersfield *Also called U M S Inc* ***(P-13121)***
A C T, La Mirada *Also called Advanced Charging Tech Inc* ***(P-16773)***
A C T, Ontario *Also called Aerospace and Coml Tooling Inc* ***(P-13901)***
A C U Precision Sheet Metal, Perris *Also called American Coffee Urn Mfg Co Inc* ***(P-12105)***
A Career Apparel, Burlingame *Also called School Apparel Inc* ***(P-3277)***
A Chemblock, Burlingame *Also called Advanced Chemblocks Inc* ***(P-7729)***
A Commom Thread, Los Angeles *Also called Dda Holdings Inc* ***(P-3314)***
A Company In Development Stage, South San Francisco *Also called Aclara Biosciences Inc* ***(P-21427)***
A D Machine, Anaheim *Also called Sam Machining Inc* ***(P-16383)***
A D S Environmental Srvs, Huntington Beach *Also called ADS LLC* ***(P-20827)***
A D S Gold Inc ....F....714 632-1888
3843 E Eagle Dr Anaheim (92807) ***(P-11187)***
A Development Stage Company, Beverly Hills *Also called Stratos Renewables Corporation* ***(P-8778)***
A Division Acorn Engrg Co, City of Industry *Also called Whitehall Manufacturing Inc* ***(P-22126)***
A Division Continental Can Co, Santa Ana *Also called Consolidated Container Co LP* ***(P-9517)***
A Division of Metagenics, Aliso Viejo *Also called Catalina Lifesciences Inc* ***(P-7834)***
A E M, Hawthorne *Also called Advanced Engine Management Inc* ***(P-19568)***
A E T C O Inc ....E....909 593-2521
2825 Metropolitan Pl Pomona (91767) ***(P-4488)***
A F B Systems Inc ....F....818 775-0151
20400 Prairie St Unit B Chatsworth (91311) ***(P-19941)***
A F C Hydraulic Seals ....F....323 585-9110
4926 S Boyle Ave Vernon (90058) ***(P-9213)***
A F E Industries Inc (PA) ....D....562 944-6889
13233 Barton Cir Whittier (90605) ***(P-6970)***
A F M Engineering Inc ....F....714 547-0194
1313 E Borchard Ave Santa Ana (92705) ***(P-15660)***
A Fab, Lake Forest *Also called American Deburring Inc* ***(P-15738)***
A G Artwear Inc ....F....714 898-3636
15564 Producer Ln Huntington Beach (92649) ***(P-22977)***
A G I, Riverside *Also called Aleph Group Inc* ***(P-21589)***
A Good Sign & Graphics Co ....E....714 444-4466
2110 S Susan St Santa Ana (92704) ***(P-23035)***
A H K Electronic Shtmtl Inc ....E....408 778-3901
875 Jarvis Dr Ste 120 Morgan Hill (95037) ***(P-12080)***
A H Machine Inc ....F....310 672-0016
214 N Cedar Ave Inglewood (90301) ***(P-15661)***
A H Plating, Valencia *Also called Sunvair Overhaul Inc* ***(P-20241)***
A H Systems Inc ....F....818 998-0223
9710 Cozycroft Ave Chatsworth (91311) ***(P-20980)***
A I M, El Segundo *Also called Active Interest Media Inc* ***(P-5874)***
A I S, Irvine *Also called American Indus Systems Inc* ***(P-18815)***
A J Fasteners Inc ....E....714 630-1556
2800 E Miraloma Ave Anaheim (92806) ***(P-12664)***
A K M, San Jose *Also called Akm Semiconductor Inc* ***(P-18075)***
A Lot To Say Inc ....F....925 964-5079
1541 S Vineyard Ave Ontario (91761) ***(P-3826)***
A Lot To Say Inc (PA) ....F....877 366-8448
4155 Blackhawk Danville (94506) ***(P-3827)***
A M Cabinets Inc (PA) ....D....310 532-1919
239 E Gardena Blvd Gardena (90248) ***(P-4778)***
A M I, Panorama City *Also called ARC Machines Inc* ***(P-14238)***
A M T, San Jose *Also called Advance Modular Technology Inc* ***(P-15148)***
A M T Metal Fabricators Inc ....E....510 236-1414
211 Parr Blvd Richmond (94801) ***(P-11729)***
A N Tool & Die Inc ....F....626 795-3238
518 S Fair Oaks Ave Pasadena (91105) ***(P-15662)***
A P C, Santa Fe Springs *Also called Associated Plating Company* ***(P-12936)***
A P S, Santa Clarita *Also called Applied Polytech Systems Inc* ***(P-4457)***
A P Seedorff & Company Inc ....F....714 252-5330
1338 N Knollwood Cir Anaheim (92801) ***(P-16692)***
A Plus Cabinets Inc ....F....760 322-5262
83930 Dr Carreon Blvd Indio (92201) ***(P-4160)***
A Plus Label Incorporated ....E....714 229-9811
3215 W Warner Ave Santa Ana (92704) ***(P-5489)***
A Plus Signs Inc ....E....559 275-0700
4270 N Brawley Ave Fresno (93722) ***(P-23036)***
A Q Pharmaceuticals Inc ....E....714 903-1000
11555 Monarch St Ste C Garden Grove (92841) ***(P-7708)***
A R Electronics Inc ....E....760 343-1200
31290 Plantation Dr Thousand Palms (92276) ***(P-18805)***
A R P, Ventura *Also called Automotive Racing Products Inc* ***(P-11565)***
A R P, Santa Paula *Also called Automotive Racing Products Inc* ***(P-11566)***
A R S Mechanical ....F....408 288-8822
1205 N 5th St Frnt Frnt San Jose (95112) ***(P-12081)***
A Rudin Inc (PA) ....D....323 589-5547
6062 Alcoa Ave Vernon (90058) ***(P-4627)***
A Rudin Designs, Vernon *Also called A Rudin Inc* ***(P-4627)***
A S A Engineering Inc ....E....949 460-9911
8 Hammond Ste 105 Irvine (92618) ***(P-14877)***
A S Batle Company ....F....415 864-3300
224 Mississippi St San Francisco (94107) ***(P-10994)***
A S G Corporation ....F....213 748-6361
1361 Newton St Los Angeles (90021) ***(P-23260)***
A S I, North Hollywood *Also called Asi Semiconductor Inc* ***(P-18129)***
A S I, North Hollywood *Also called Advanced Semiconductor Inc* ***(P-18067)***
A S I, San Pablo *Also called Analytcal Scentific Instrs Inc* ***(P-21171)***
A S P, Irvine *Also called Advanced Sterlization* ***(P-21584)***
A T A, Paso Robles *Also called Applied Technologies Assoc Inc* ***(P-21435)***
A T E, Oceanside *Also called Advanced Thrmlforming Entp Inc* ***(P-9613)***
A T Parker Inc (PA) ....E....818 755-1700
10866 Chandler Blvd North Hollywood (91601) ***(P-19245)***
A T S, Burbank *Also called Accratronics Seals Corporation* ***(P-18806)***
A T T, Orange *Also called Air Tube Transfer Systems Inc* ***(P-13813)***
A Taste of Denmark ....E....510 420-8889
3401 Telegraph Ave Oakland (94609) ***(P-1133)***
A Teichert & Son Inc ....E....530 587-3811
13879 Butterfield Dr Truckee (96161) ***(P-321)***
A Teichert & Son Inc ....E....209 832-4150
36314 S Bird Rd Tracy (95304) ***(P-322)***
A Teichert & Son Inc ....E....530 661-4290
35030 County Road 20 Woodland (95695) ***(P-323)***
A Teichert & Son Inc ....E....916 991-8170
7466 Pacific Ave Pleasant Grove (95668) ***(P-10680)***
A Teichert & Son Inc ....F....530 885-4244
2601 State Highway 49 Cool (95614) ***(P-324)***
A Teichert & Son Inc ....E....916 386-6974
8609 Jackson Rd Sacramento (95826) ***(P-10681)***
A Teichert & Son Inc ....E....530 749-1230
3331 Walnut Ave Marysville (95901) ***(P-325)***
A Teichert & Son Inc ....E....530 743-6111
4249 Hmmnton Smrtville Rd Marysville (95901) ***(P-326)***
A Teichert & Son Inc ....E....916 783-7132
721 Berry St Roseville (95678) ***(P-10682)***
A Teichert & Son Inc ....E....916 351-0123
3417 Grant Line Rd Rancho Cordova (95742) ***(P-327)***
A Teichert & Son Inc ....E....916 386-6900
8760 Kiefer Blvd Sacramento (95826) ***(P-328)***
A Terrycable California Corp ....E....760 244-9351
17376 Eucalyptus St Hesperia (92345) ***(P-19562)***
A Thanks Million Inc ....F....858 432-7744
8195 Mercury Ct Ste 140 San Diego (92111) ***(P-3472)***
A V Poles and Lighting Inc ....E....661 945-2731
43827 Division St Lancaster (93535) ***(P-17005)***
A World of Moulding ....E....714 361-9308
3041 S Main St Santa Ana (92707) ***(P-3989)***
A&A Concrete Supply, Yuba City *Also called A & A Ready Mixed Concrete Inc* ***(P-10673)***
A&A Concrete Supply, Stockton *Also called A & A Ready Mixed Concrete Inc* ***(P-10677)***
A&A Concrete Supply, Sacramento *Also called A & A Ready Mixed Concrete Inc* ***(P-10679)***
A&A Engineering Inc ....F....805 685-4882
158 Santa Felicia Dr Goleta (93117) ***(P-15663)***
A&A Global Imports Inc ....E....323 767-5990
3359 E 50th St Vernon (90058) ***(P-9600)***
A&A Jewelry Supply, Los Angeles *Also called Adfa Incorporated* ***(P-13135)***
A&A Jewelry Tools & Supplies, Los Angeles *Also called A & A Jewelry Tools Findings* ***(P-23259)***
A&A Metal Finishing Entps LLC ....E....916 442-1063
8290 Alpine Ave Sacramento (95826) ***(P-12896)***
A&A Plating, Riverside *Also called Arturo Campos* ***(P-12935)***
A&D Fire Sprinklers Inc ....F....714 634-3923
1601 W Orangewood Ave Orange (92868) ***(P-14792)***
A&G Machine Shop Inc ....F....831 759-2261
1352 Burton Ave Ste B Salinas (93901) ***(P-15664)***
A&M Products Manufacturing Co (HQ) ....E....510 271-7000
1221 Broadway Ste 51 Oakland (94612) ***(P-10966)***
A&M Timber Inc ....F....530 515-1740
4002 Alta Mesa Dr Redding (96002) ***(P-3869)***
A&R Lighting Co ....F....562 927-8617
7644 Emil Ave Bell (90201) ***(P-17096)***
A&T Precision Machining ....F....408 363-1198
330 Piercy Rd San Jose (95138) ***(P-15665)***
A&W Precision Machining Inc ....F....310 527-7242
17907 S Figueroa St Ste C Gardena (90248) ***(P-15666)***
A-1 Engraving Co Inc ....F....562 861-2216
8225 Phlox St Downey (90241) ***(P-13132)***
A-1 Estrn-Home-Made Pickle Inc ....E....323 223-1141
1832 Johnston St Los Angeles (90031) ***(P-878)***
A-1 Grit Co, Riverside *Also called Newman Bros California Inc* ***(P-4094)***
A-1 Jays Machining Inc (PA) ....D....408 262-1845
2228 Oakland Rd San Jose (95131) ***(P-15667)***
A-1 Machine Manufacturing Inc (PA) ....C....408 727-0880
490 Gianni St Santa Clara (95054) ***(P-15668)***
A-1 Metal Products Inc ....E....323 721-3334
2707 Supply Ave Commerce (90040) ***(P-12082)***
A-1 Ornamental Ironworks Inc ....F....559 251-1447
4637 E White Ave Fresno (93702) ***(P-12700)***
A-1 Plastics Incorporated ....F....619 444-9442
618 W Bradley Ave El Cajon (92020) ***(P-14297)***
A-Aztec Rents & Sells Inc (PA) ....C....310 347-3010
2665 Columbia St Torrance (90503) ***(P-3671)***
A-H Plating Inc ....D....818 845-6243
28079 Avenue Stanford Valencia (91355) ***(P-12897)***
A-Info Inc ....E....949 346-7326
60 Tesla Irvine (92618) ***(P-19995)***
A-L-L Magnetics ....F....714 632-1754
2831 E Via Martens Anaheim (92806) ***(P-13493)***
A-List, Commerce *Also called Just For Wraps Inc* ***(P-3351)***
A-W Engineering Company Inc ....E....562 945-1041
8528 Dice Rd Santa Fe Springs (90670) ***(P-12756)***
A-Z Mfg Inc ....E....714 444-4446
3101 W Segerstrom Ave Santa Ana (92704) ***(P-15669)***
A.A.C. Forearm Forklift, Baldwin Park *Also called Above All Co Forearm Forklift* ***(P-13854)***

ALPHABETIC

A.B.S. By Allen Schwartz, Los Angeles *Also called ABs Clothing Collection Inc* ***(P-3282)***
A.C.T., Sacramento *Also called Aluminum Coating Tech Inc* ***(P-12924)***
A/C Folding Gates F 909 629-3026
1374 E 9th St Pomona (91766) ***(P-12441)***
A/D Enterprises, Fountain Valley *Also called Adrienne Designs LLC* ***(P-22488)***
A1 Carton Co, Los Angeles *Also called Best Box Company Inc* ***(P-5200)***
A2, Sunnyvale *Also called Westak Inc* ***(P-18049)***
AA Laboratory Eggs Inc (PA) F 714 893-5675
15075 Weststate St Westminster (92683) ***(P-2187)***
Aa Leasing, Los Angeles *Also called Vahe Enterprises Inc* ***(P-19560)***
AA Portable Power Corporation E 510 525-2328
825 S 19th St Richmond (94804) ***(P-19150)***
AA Production Services Inc (PA) E 530 668-7525
433 2nd St Ste 103 Woodland (95695) ***(P-150)***
AA Production Services Inc E 530 982-0123
8032 County Road 61 Princeton (95970) ***(P-81)***
AAA Air Support F 310 538-1377
13723 Harvard Pl Gardena (90249) ***(P-19996)***
AAA Flag & Banner Mfg Co Inc C 310 836-3341
8966 National Blvd Los Angeles (90034) ***(P-3828)***
AAA Garments & Lettering Inc F 916 363-4590
9309 La Riviera Dr Ste C Sacramento (95826) ***(P-3717)***
AAA Pallet Recycling & Mfg Inc E 951 681-7748
23120 Oleander Ave Perris (92570) ***(P-4344)***
AAA Plating & Inspection Inc D 323 979-8930
424 E Dixon St Compton (90222) ***(P-12898)***
AAA Printing By Wizard E 310 285-0505
8961 W Sunset Blvd Ste 1d West Hollywood (90069) ***(P-3718)***
AAA Stamping Inc E 909 947-4151
1630 Shearwater St Ontario (91761) ***(P-12757)***
Aaagolddesigns, Los Angeles *Also called Modern Gold Design Inc* ***(P-22550)***
Aab Garage Door Inc F 310 530-3637
25333 Pennsylvania Ave Lomita (90717) ***(P-3990)***
AAC, Irvine *Also called American Audio Component Inc* ***(P-18814)***
Aaero Swiss F 714 692-0558
22347 La Palma Ave # 105 Yorba Linda (92887) ***(P-15670)***
AAF Steel Structural, Lake Elsinore *Also called Afakori Inc* ***(P-11738)***
Aahs Enterprises Inc F 323 838-9130
6600 Telegraph Rd Commerce (90040) ***(P-23037)***
Aahs Graphics Signs & Engrv, Commerce *Also called Aahs Enterprises Inc* ***(P-23037)***
Aamp of America F 805 338-6800
2500 E Francis St Ontario (91761) ***(P-19246)***
Aamstamp Machine Company LLC F 661 272-0500
38960 Trade Center Dr B Palmdale (93551) ***(P-13450)***
Aap Division, Inglewood *Also called Engineered Magnetics Inc* ***(P-16785)***
Aard Industries Inc E 951 296-0844
42075 Avenida Alvarado Temecula (92590) ***(P-13369)***
Aard Spring & Stamping, Temecula *Also called Aard Industries Inc* ***(P-13369)***
Aardvark Clay & Supplies Inc (PA) E 714 541-4157
1400 E Pomona St Santa Ana (92705) ***(P-22937)***
Aaren Scientific Inc (HQ) D 909 937-1033
1040 S Vintage Ave Ste A Ontario (91761) ***(P-21329)***
Aaron Bennett, Santa Clara *Also called Tmk Manufacturing Inc* ***(P-14203)***
Aaron Corporation C 323 235-5959
1820 E 41st St Vernon (90058) ***(P-3279)***
Aaron Dutt Enterprises Inc F 714 632-7035
1140 N Kraemer Blvd Ste M Anaheim (92806) ***(P-12758)***
Aarons Signs & Printing E 951 352-7303
3770 Van Buren Blvd Riverside (92503) ***(P-23038)***
Aasc, Stockton *Also called Applied Arospc Structures Corp* ***(P-20037)***
Aatech E 909 854-3200
6666 Box Springs Blvd Riverside (92507) ***(P-15477)***
AB & I Foundry, Oakland *Also called McWane Inc* ***(P-11147)***
AB Manufacturing Inc F 408 972-5085
115 Red River Way San Jose (95136) ***(P-22399)***
AB Mauri Food Inc F 562 483-4619
12604 Hiddencreek Way A Cerritos (90703) ***(P-2387)***
AB Medical Technologies Inc F 530 605-2522
20272 Skypark Dr Redding (96002) ***(P-21569)***
AB Sciex LLC (HQ) D 877 740-2129
1201 Radio Rd Redwood City (94065) ***(P-21158)***
AB&r Inc E 323 727-0007
5849 Smithway St Commerce (90040) ***(P-3280)***
Abacus Powder Coating E 626 443-7556
1829 Tyler Ave South El Monte (91733) ***(P-13133)***
Abacus Printing & Graphics Inc F 818 929-6740
23806 Strathern St West Hills (91304) ***(P-6390)***
Abacus Prtg & Digital Graphics, West Hills *Also called Abacus Printing & Graphics Inc* ***(P-6390)***
Abad Foam Inc E 714 994-2223
6560 Caballero Blvd Buena Park (90620) ***(P-9498)***
Abalquiga, Los Angeles *Also called La Princesita Tortilleria* ***(P-2512)***
Abaqus Inc F 415 496-9436
2297 Saint Francis Dr Palo Alto (94303) ***(P-23540)***
Abaxis Inc (HQ) C 510 675-6500
3240 Whipple Rd Union City (94587) ***(P-21426)***
ABB Enterprise Software Inc D 510 987-7111
1321 Harbor Bay Pkwy # 101 Alameda (94502) ***(P-16538)***
ABB Enterprise Software Inc C 415 527-2850
60 Spear St San Francisco (94105) ***(P-23541)***
ABB Motors and Mechanical Inc F 510 785-9900
21056 Forbes Ave Hayward (94545) ***(P-16625)***
Abba Roller LLC (HQ) E 909 947-1244
1351 E Philadelphia St Ontario (91761) ***(P-9277)***
Abbott, Sunnyvale *Also called St Jude Medical LLC* ***(P-21915)***
Abbott Diabetes Care Inc (HQ) C 510 749-5400
1420 Harbor Bay Pkwy Alameda (94502) ***(P-8198)***
Abbott Diagnostics Division, Santa Clara *Also called Abbott Laboratories* ***(P-21570)***
Abbott Laboratories E 818 493-2388
15900 Valley View Ct Sylmar (91342) ***(P-7709)***
Abbott Laboratories B 408 330-0057
4551 Great America Pkwy Santa Clara (95054) ***(P-21570)***
Abbott Laboratories E 951 914-3000
41888 Motor Car Pkwy Temecula (92591) ***(P-7710)***
Abbott Laboratories A 408 845-3000
3200 Lakeside Dr Santa Clara (95054) ***(P-21571)***
Abbott Nutrition F 707 399-1100
2302 Courage Dr Fairfield (94533) ***(P-7711)***
Abbott Nutrition Mfg Inc (HQ) C 707 399-1100
2351 N Watney Way Ste C Fairfield (94533) ***(P-7712)***
Abbott Technologies Inc E 818 504-0644
8203 Vineland Ave Sun Valley (91352) ***(P-16539)***
Abbott Vascular, Santa Clara *Also called Abbott Laboratories* ***(P-21571)***
Abbott Vascular Inc B 951 941-2400
26531 Ynez Rd Temecula (92591) ***(P-7713)***
Abbott Vascular Inc (HQ) B 408 845-3000
3200 Lakeside Dr Santa Clara (95054) ***(P-21572)***
Abbott Vascular Inc E 951 914-2400
42301 Zevo Dr Ste D Temecula (92590) ***(P-21573)***
Abbott Vascular Inc C 408 845-3186
30590 Cochise Cir Murrieta (92563) ***(P-21574)***
Abbs Vision Systems Inc F 805 642-0499
4848 Colt St Ste 14 Ventura (93003) ***(P-22337)***
Abby Precision Mfg, Cloverdale *Also called Dyna-King Inc* ***(P-22792)***
ABC - Clio LLC F 800 368-6868
147 Castilian Dr Goleta (93117) ***(P-6066)***
ABC Assembly Inc F 408 293-3560
43006 Osgood Rd Fremont (94539) ***(P-17799)***
ABC Custom Wood Shutters Inc E 949 595-0300
20561 Pascal Way Lake Forest (92630) ***(P-3991)***
ABC Imaging of Washington E 949 419-3728
17240 Red Hill Ave Irvine (92614) ***(P-6971)***
ABC Printing Inc F 408 263-1118
1090 S Milpitas Blvd Milpitas (95035) ***(P-6391)***
ABC Sheet Metal, Anaheim *Also called Steeldyne Industries* ***(P-12388)***
ABC Sun Control LLC F 818 982-6989
7241 Ethel Ave North Hollywood (91605) ***(P-3672)***
ABC-Clio, Goleta *Also called A B C-Clio Inc* ***(P-6065)***
Abco Laboratories Inc (PA) D 707 427-1818
2450 S Watney Way Fairfield (94533) ***(P-7714)***
Abcron Corporation F 714 730-9988
3002 Dow Ave Ste 408 Tustin (92780) ***(P-17179)***
Abd El & Larson Holdings LLC (PA) E 510 656-1600
48205 Warm Springs Blvd Fremont (94539) ***(P-16583)***
Abekas Inc F 650 470-0900
1233 Midas Way Sunnyvale (94085) ***(P-17435)***
Abel Automatics Inc E 805 484-8789
165 N Aviador St Camarillo (93010) ***(P-12614)***
Abel Reels, Camarillo *Also called Abel Automatics Inc* ***(P-12614)***
Aberdeen LLC E 562 903-1500
9808 Alburtis Ave Santa Fe Springs (90670) ***(P-15000)***
Abex Display Systems Inc (PA) C 800 537-0231
355 Parkside Dr San Fernando (91340) ***(P-5193)***
Abex Exhibit Systems, San Fernando *Also called Abex Display Systems Inc* ***(P-5193)***
ABF Data Systems Inc F 818 591-8307
2801 Townsgate Rd Ste 111 Westlake Village (91361) ***(P-23542)***
ABG Communications, Jurupa Valley *Also called Luce Communications LLC* ***(P-6711)***
Abis Signs Inc F 626 818-4329
14240 Don Julian Rd Ste E City of Industry (91746) ***(P-23039)***
Abisco Products Co E 562 906-9330
5925 E Washington Blvd Commerce (90040) ***(P-7301)***
Abl Aero Inc E 661 257-2500
25032 Anza Dr Valencia (91355) ***(P-19997)***
Abl Space Systems Company F 650 996-8214
224 Oregon St El Segundo (90245) ***(P-20527)***
Able Aerospace Adhesives, Valencia *Also called Abl Aero Inc* ***(P-19997)***
Able Card LLC E 626 969-1888
1388 W Foothill Blvd Azusa (91702) ***(P-6972)***
Able Card Corporation, Irwindale *Also called Million Corporation* ***(P-7143)***
Able Design and Fabrication, Rancho Dominguez *Also called Adf Incorporated* ***(P-12447)***
Able Health Inc F 617 529-6264
1516 Folsom St San Francisco (94103) ***(P-23543)***
Able Industrial Products Inc (PA) E 909 930-1585
2006 S Baker Ave Ontario (91761) ***(P-9214)***
Able Iron Works E 909 397-5300
222 Hershey St Pomona (91767) ***(P-12442)***
Able Metal Plating Inc E 510 569-6539
932 86th Ave Oakland (94621) ***(P-12899)***
Able Sheet Metal Inc (PA) E 323 269-2181
614 N Ford Blvd Los Angeles (90022) ***(P-12083)***
Able Software Inc E 949 274-8321
20251 Sw Acacia St # 220 Newport Beach (92660) ***(P-23544)***
Able Wire EDM Inc F 714 255-1967
440 Atlas St Ste A Brea (92821) ***(P-15671)***
ABN Industrial Co Inc (PA) F 714 521-9211
5940 Dale St Buena Park (90621) ***(P-15672)***
Above & Beyond Balloons Inc E 949 586-8470
16661 Jamboree Rd Irvine (92606) ***(P-23261)***
Above All Co Forearm Forklift E 626 962-2990
14832 Arrow Hwy Baldwin Park (91706) ***(P-13854)***
Above and Beyond, Irvine *Also called Above & Beyond Balloons Inc* ***(P-23261)***
Abraham Steel Fabrication Inc F 805 544-8610
2741 Mcmillan Ave Ste B San Luis Obispo (93401) ***(P-11730)***
Abrams Electronics Inc E 831 758-6400
420 W Market St Salinas (93901) ***(P-16872)***
Abrasive Finishing Co E 310 323-7175
14920 S Main St Gardena (90248) ***(P-11427)***

Mergent e-mail: customerrelations@mergent.com
1006
2020 California
Manufacturers Register
(P-0000) Products & Services Section entry number
(PA)=Parent Co (HQ)=Headquarters (DH)=Div Headquarters

Abrasive Wheels Inc F 626 935-8800
17841 E Valley Blvd City of Industry (91744) ***(P-10939)***

Abraxis Bioscience Inc D 310 883-1300
2730 Wilshire Blvd # 110 Santa Monica (90403) ***(P-7715)***

Abraxis Bioscience LLC (HQ) C 800 564-0216
11755 Wilshire Blvd Fl 20 Los Angeles (90025) ***(P-7716)***

Abrisa Glass & Coating, Santa Paula *Also called Abrisa Industrial Glass Inc **(P-10259)***

Abrisa Industrial Glass Inc (HQ) D 805 525-4902
200 Hallock Dr Santa Paula (93060) ***(P-10259)***

Abrisa Technologies E 805 525-4902
200 Hallock Dr Santa Paula (93060) ***(P-21330)***

ABS By Allen Schwartz, Los Angeles *Also called Aquarius Rags LLC **(P-3214)***

ABS By Allen Schwartz LLC (HQ) E 213 895-4400
1218 S Santa Fe Ave Los Angeles (90021) ***(P-3281)***

ABs Clothing Collection Inc F 213 895-4400
1218 S Santa Fe Ave Los Angeles (90021) ***(P-3282)***

ABS Manufacturers Inc F 408 295-5984
519 Horning St San Jose (95112) ***(P-12443)***

Absinthe Group Inc E 530 823-8527
2043 Airpark Ct Ste 30 Auburn (95602) ***(P-753)***

Absolute Aquasystems, Northridge *Also called Pure Water Centers Inc **(P-15563)***

Absolute Board Co Inc E 760 295-2201
4040 Calle Platino # 102 Oceanside (92056) ***(P-22730)***

Absolute EDM, Carlsbad *Also called Diligent Solutions Inc **(P-15898)***

Absolute Graphic Tech USA Inc E 909 597-1133
235 Jason Ct Corona (92879) ***(P-16693)***

Absolute Machine E 530 242-6840
5020 Mountain Lakes Blvd Redding (96003) ***(P-15673)***

Absolute Machining F 818 709-7367
20622 Superior St Unit 4 Chatsworth (91311) ***(P-11731)***

Absolute Pro Music, Los Angeles *Also called Absolute Usa Inc **(P-17180)***

Absolute Screen Graphics Inc F 909 923-1227
2131 S Hellman Ave Ste A Ontario (91761) ***(P-3765)***

Absolute Screenprint Inc C 714 529-2120
333 Cliffwood Park St Brea (92821) ***(P-3766)***

Absolute Sign Inc F 562 592-5838
10655 Humbolt St Los Alamitos (90720) ***(P-23040)***

Absolute Technologies, Anaheim *Also called D & D Gear Incorporated **(P-20080)***

Absolute Turnkey Services Inc E 408 850-7530
555 Aldo Ave Santa Clara (95054) ***(P-17800)***

Absolute Usa Inc E 213 744-0044
1800 E Washington Blvd Los Angeles (90021) ***(P-17180)***

Absolute Woods Products, Goleta *Also called Madera Concepts **(P-4514)***

Absolution Brewing Company (PA) F 310 787-9563
2878 Columbia St Torrance (90503) ***(P-1489)***

Abzena (san Diego) Inc F 858 550-4094
8810 Rehco Rd Ste E San Diego (92121) ***(P-8266)***

AC Air Technology Inc F 855 884-7222
13832 Magnolia Ave Chino (91710) ***(P-12740)***

AC Photonics Inc E 408 986-9838
2701 Northwestern Pkwy Santa Clara (95051) ***(P-14416)***

AC Products Inc E 714 630-7311
9930 Painter Ave Whittier (90605) ***(P-8851)***

AC Propulsion E 909 592-5399
446 Borrego Ct San Dimas (91773) ***(P-16626)***

AC Pumping Unit Repair Inc E 562 492-1300
2625 Dawson Ave Signal Hill (90755) ***(P-151)***

AC Tech, Garden Grove *Also called Advanced Chemistry & Tech Inc **(P-8852)***

AC&a Enterprises LLC (HQ) D 949 716-3511
25671 Commercentre Dr Lake Forest (92630) ***(P-19942)***

Academic Cap & Gown, Chatsworth *Also called Academic Ch Choir Gwns Mfg Inc **(P-3536)***

Academic Ch Choir Gwns Mfg Inc E 818 886-8697
20644 Superior St Chatsworth (91311) ***(P-3536)***

Academic Therapy Publications, Novato *Also called Arena Press **(P-6187)***

Academy Awning Inc E 800 422-9646
1501 Beach St Montebello (90640) ***(P-3719)***

Acadia Pharmaceuticals Inc (PA) B 858 558-2871
3611 Valley Centre Dr # 300 San Diego (92130) ***(P-7717)***

Acapulco Mexican Deli Inc E 323 266-0267
929 S Kern Ave Los Angeles (90022) ***(P-2315)***

ACC Precision Inc F 805 278-9801
321 Hearst Dr Oxnard (93030) ***(P-15674)***

Acca Recording Products, La Habra *Also called Keyin Inc **(P-19222)***

Accel Manufacturing Inc F 408 727-5883
1709 Grant St Santa Clara (95050) ***(P-13899)***

Accel-Rf Corporation F 858 278-2074
4380 Viewridge Ave Ste D San Diego (92123) ***(P-20981)***

Accela Inc (PA) C 925 659-3200
2633 Camino Ramon Ste 500 San Ramon (94583) ***(P-23545)***

Accelerated Cnstr & Met LLC F 209 846-7998
2955 Farrar Ave Modesto (95354) ***(P-11732)***

Accelerated Memory Prod Inc E 714 460-9800
1317 E Edinger Ave Santa Ana (92705) ***(P-18059)***

Accelrys Inc., San Diego *Also called Dassault Systemes Biovia Corp **(P-23798)***

Accent Awnings, Santa Ana *Also called Accent Industries Inc **(P-11926)***

Accent Industries Inc (PA) E 714 708-1389
1600 E Saint Gertrude Pl Santa Ana (92705) ***(P-11926)***

Accent Manufacturing Inc E 408 846-9993
105 Leavesley Rd Bldg 3d Gilroy (95020) ***(P-5046)***

Accent Plastics Inc (PA) D 951 273-7777
1925 Elise Cir Corona (92879) ***(P-9601)***

Accent Plastics Inc E 951 273-7777
1915 Elise Cir Corona (92879) ***(P-9602)***

Accepted Co F 310 815-9553
2229 S Canfield Ave Los Angeles (90034) ***(P-6173)***

Acces I/O Products Inc F 858 550-9559
10623 Roselle St San Diego (92121) ***(P-15140)***

Access Closure Inc B 408 610-6500
5452 Betsy Ross Dr Santa Clara (95054) ***(P-21575)***

Access Marketing, San Luis Obispo *Also called ITW Global Tire Repair Inc **(P-9168)***

Access Mfg Inc F 530 795-0720
1805 Railroad Ave Winters (95694) ***(P-19515)***

Access Professional Inc F 858 571-4444
1955 Cordell Ct Ste 104 El Cajon (92020) ***(P-12444)***

Access Professional Systems, El Cajon *Also called Access Professional Inc **(P-12444)***

Access Scientific Inc E 858 354-8761
1042 N El Camino Real Encinitas (92024) ***(P-21576)***

Access Systems Inc F 916 941-8099
4947 Hillsdale Cir El Dorado Hills (95762) ***(P-21159)***

Acclaim Lighting LLC F 323 213-4626
6122 S Eastern Ave Commerce (90040) ***(P-17006)***

Acclarent Inc B 650 687-5888
31 Technology Dr Ste 200 Irvine (92618) ***(P-21577)***

Acco Brands USA LLC D 650 572-2700
1500 Fashion Island Blvd # 300 San Mateo (94404) ***(P-15117)***

Acco Brands USA LLC E 562 941-0505
14430 Best Ave Garden Grove (92841) ***(P-9603)***

Acco Engineered Systems Inc F 661 631-1975
3121 N Sillect Ave # 104 Bakersfield (93308) ***(P-15406)***

Accordent Technologies Inc F 310 374-7491
1846 Schooldale Dr San Jose (95124) ***(P-23546)***

Accountants Edge Software Svcs (PA) F 800 689-6932
35436 Panorama Dr Yucaipa (92399) ***(P-23547)***

Accountmate Software Corp (PA) E 707 774-7500
1445 Technology Ln Ste A5 Petaluma (94954) ***(P-23548)***

Accounts Payable, Sunnyvale *Also called Mellanox Technologies Inc **(P-18381)***

Accracutt Cabinets F 951 685-7322
2238 S Phoenix Ave Ontario (91761) ***(P-4161)***

Accratronics Seals Corporation D 818 843-1500
2211 Kenmere Ave Burbank (91504) ***(P-18806)***

Accriva Dgnostics Holdings Inc (HQ) B 858 404-8203
6260 Sequence Dr San Diego (92121) ***(P-21578)***

Accriva Diagnostics, San Diego *Also called International Technidyne Corp **(P-21748)***

Accsys Technology Inc E 925 462-6949
1177 Quarry Ln Pleasanton (94566) ***(P-19247)***

Accu Machine Inc E 408 855-8835
440 Aldo Ave Santa Clara (95054) ***(P-15675)***

Accu Rack, Yorba Linda *Also called M B S Inc **(P-19170)***

Accu-Blend Corporation F 626 334-7744
364 Malbert St Perris (92570) ***(P-9036)***

Accu-Gage & Thread Grinding Co F 626 568-2932
40 S San Gabriel Blvd Pasadena (91107) ***(P-20825)***

Accu-Glass Products Inc F 818 365-4215
25047 Anza Dr Valencia (91355) ***(P-18807)***

Accu-Seal Sencorpwhite Inc F 760 591-9800
225 Bingham Dr Ste B San Marcos (92069) ***(P-14693)***

Accu-Sembly Inc D 626 357-3447
1835 Huntington Dr Duarte (91010) ***(P-17801)***

Accu-Swiss Inc (PA) F 209 847-1016
544 Armstrong Way Oakdale (95361) ***(P-12615)***

Accu-Tech Laser Processing Inc F 760 744-6692
550 S Pacific St Ste A100 San Marcos (92078) ***(P-15676)***

Accu-Tek, Ontario *Also called Excel Industries Inc **(P-12802)***

Accucrome Plating Co Inc F 310 327-8268
115 W 154th St Gardena (90248) ***(P-12900)***

Accudyne Engineering & Eqp, Bell *Also called West Coast-Accudyne Inc **(P-13999)***

Accufab Inc F 909 930-1751
1326 E Francis St Ontario (91761) ***(P-15677)***

Accuracy Screw Machine Pdts, San Carlos *Also called Pencom Accuracy Inc **(P-12646)***

Accurate Always Inc E 650 728-9428
127 Ocean Ave Half Moon Bay (94019) ***(P-14878)***

Accurate Anodizing Inc F 310 637-0349
1801 W El Segundo Blvd Compton (90222) ***(P-12901)***

Accurate Circuit Engrg Inc D 714 546-2162
3019 Kilson Dr Santa Ana (92707) ***(P-17802)***

Accurate Dial & Nameplate Inc (PA) F 323 245-9181
329 Mira Loma Ave Glendale (91204) ***(P-13134)***

Accurate Double Disc Grinding, Pacoima *Also called Westcoast Grinding Corporation **(P-16519)***

Accurate Engineering Inc E 818 768-3919
8710 Telfair Ave Sun Valley (91352) ***(P-17803)***

Accurate Grinding and Mfg Corp E 951 479-0909
807 E Parkridge Ave Corona (92879) ***(P-19943)***

Accurate Heating & Cooling Inc E 209 858-4125
3515 Yosemite Ave Lathrop (95330) ***(P-12084)***

Accurate Laminated Pdts Inc E 714 632-2773
1826 Dawns Way Fullerton (92831) ***(P-4960)***

Accurate Manufacturing Company, Glendale *Also called McCoppin Enterprises **(P-16183)***

Accurate Metal Products Inc F 951 360-3594
4276 Campbell St Riverside (92509) ***(P-11733)***

Accurate Moulding Mirror Work, Sunnyvale *Also called MRr Moulding Industries Inc **(P-4091)***

Accurate Plating Company E 323 268-8567
2811 Alcazar St Los Angeles (90033) ***(P-12902)***

Accurate Prfmce Machining Inc E 714 434-7811
2255 S Grand Ave Santa Ana (92705) ***(P-15678)***

Accurate Screen Processing F 818 957-3965
3538 Foothill Blvd La Crescenta (91214) ***(P-3767)***

Accurate Solutions Inc F 760 753-6524
2273 Wales Dr Cardiff By The Sea (92007) ***(P-17775)***

Accurate Staging Mfg Inc (PA) E 310 324-1040
13900 S Figueroa St Los Angeles (90061) ***(P-23262)***

Accurate Steel Treating Inc E 562 927-6528
10008 Miller Way South Gate (90280) ***(P-11428)***

Accurate Technology, Anaheim *Also called Gledhill/Lyons Inc **(P-20115)***

Accurate Technology Mfg Inc D 408 733-4344
930 Thompson Pl Sunnyvale (94085) ***(P-15679)***

Employee Codes: A=Over 500 employees, B=251-500
C=101-250, D=51-100, E=20-50, F=10-19
2020 California
Manfacturers Register
© Mergent Inc. 1-800-342-5647
1007

Accurate Tube Bending Inc E 510 790-6500
37770 Timber St Newark (94560) ***(P-13454)***

Accurate Wire & Display Inc E 310 532-7821
3600 Oak Cliff Dr Fallbrook (92028) ***(P-13393)***

Accuray Incorporated (PA) C 408 716-4600
1310 Chesapeake Ter Sunnyvale (94089) ***(P-21579)***

Accuride International Inc (PA) E 562 903-0200
12311 Shoemaker Ave Santa Fe Springs (90670) ***(P-11557)***

Accurite Technologies Inc F 408 395-7100
15732 Los Gatos Blvd Los Gatos (95032) ***(P-15141)***

Accusplit (PA) E 925 290-1900
1262 Quarry Ln Ste B Pleasanton (94566) ***(P-22475)***

Accutech LLC E 760 599-6555
2641 La Mirada Dr Vista (92081) ***(P-21580)***

Accutek Packaging Equipment Co (PA) E 760 734-4177
2980 Scott St Vista (92081) ***(P-14694)***

Accuturn Corporation E 951 656-6621
7189 Old 215 Frontage Rd Moreno Valley (92553) ***(P-20528)***

Accuvac Technology Division, Benicia *Also called Turnkey Technologies Inc* ***(P-16478)***

Acd LLC (HQ) C 949 261-7533
2321 Pullman St Santa Ana (92705) ***(P-11990)***

Ace, Anaheim *Also called Anaheim Custom Extruders Inc* ***(P-9630)***

Ace, Santa Ana *Also called Accurate Circuit Engrg Inc* ***(P-17802)***

Ace Air Manufacturing F 310 323-7246
1430 W 135th St Gardena (90249) ***(P-19998)***

Ace Aviation Service Inc F 760 721-2804
3239 Roymar Rd Ste B Oceanside (92058) ***(P-19999)***

Ace Bindery Inc F 714 220-0232
10549 Dale Ave Stanton (90680) ***(P-7325)***

Ace Calendering Enterprises (PA) F 909 937-1901
1311 S Wanamaker Ave Ontario (91761) ***(P-9278)***

Ace Clearwater Enterprises Inc (PA) D 310 323-2140
19815 Magellan Dr Torrance (90502) ***(P-20000)***

Ace Clearwater Enterprises Inc F 310 538-5380
1614 Kona Dr Compton (90220) ***(P-14007)***

Ace Commercial Inc E 562 946-6664
10310 Pioneer Blvd Ste 1 Santa Fe Springs (90670) ***(P-6392)***

Ace Composites Inc D 530 743-1885
1394 Sky Harbor Dr Olivehurst (95961) ***(P-9604)***

Ace Graphics Inc F 213 746-5100
5351 Bonsai Ave Moorpark (93021) ***(P-6393)***

Ace Heaters LLC E 951 738-2230
130 Klug Cir Corona (92880) ***(P-15407)***

Ace Holdings Inc C 213 972-2100
650 S Hill St Ste 510 Los Angeles (90014) ***(P-22487)***

Ace Industries Inc E 619 482-2700
738 Design Ct Ste 302 Chula Vista (91911) ***(P-15680)***

Ace Iron Inc C 510 324-3300
929 Howard St Marina Del Rey (90292) ***(P-12445)***

Ace Machine Shop Inc D 310 608-2277
11200 Wright Rd Lynwood (90262) ***(P-15681)***

Ace Pleating & Stitching Inc E 323 582-8213
2351 E 49th St Vernon (90058) ***(P-3720)***

Ace Precision Mold Co Inc F 562 921-8999
14701 Carmenita Rd Norwalk (90650) ***(P-9605)***

Ace Products Enterprises Inc E 707 765-1500
3920 Cypress Dr Ste B Petaluma (94954) ***(P-10186)***

Ace Products Group, Petaluma *Also called Ace Products Enterprises Inc* ***(P-10186)***

Ace Sushi, Torrance *Also called Asiana Cuisine Enterprises Inc* ***(P-2397)***

Ace Trailer Co E 559 442-1500
2285 E Date Ave Fresno (93706) ***(P-19812)***

Acecad Inc F 831 655-1900
791 Foam St Ste 200 Monterey (93940) ***(P-15142)***

Acelio, San Jose *Also called Appformix Inc* ***(P-23610)***

Acells Corp F 760 727-6666
1351 Dist Way Ste 1 Vista (92081) ***(P-21160)***

Acelrx Pharmaceuticals Inc D 650 216-3500
351 Galveston Dr Redwood City (94063) ***(P-7718)***

Acer American Holdings Corp (HQ) F 408 533-7700
333 W San Carlos St # 1500 San Jose (95110) ***(P-15143)***

Acg Ecopack, Ontario *Also called Advanced Color Graphics* ***(P-6397)***

Achaogen Inc (PA) C 650 800-3636
1 Tower Pl Ste 400 South San Francisco (94080) ***(P-7719)***

Achronix Semiconductor Corp D 408 889-4100
2903 Bunker Hill Ln # 200 Santa Clara (95054) ***(P-18060)***

Aci Supplies LLC E 714 989-1821
425 N Berry St Brea (92821) ***(P-22959)***

Acker Stone Industries Inc (HQ) E 951 674-0047
13296 Temescal Canyon Rd Corona (92883) ***(P-10526)***

Ackley Metal Products Inc F 714 979-7431
1311 E Saint Gertrude Pl B Santa Ana (92705) ***(P-15682)***

Aclara Biosciences Inc D 800 297-2728
345 Oyster Point Blvd South San Francisco (94080) ***(P-21427)***

Acm Machining Inc E 916 804-9489
240 State Highway 16 # 18 Plymouth (95669) ***(P-15683)***

Acm Machining Inc (PA) E 916 852-8600
11390 Gold Dredge Way Rancho Cordova (95742) ***(P-15684)***

Acm Research Inc C 510 445-3700
42307 Osgood Rd Ste I Fremont (94539) ***(P-15478)***

Acm Student Chapter At Ucr F 951 389-0713
446 Winston St Vincent Riverside (92507) ***(P-23549)***

Acme Auto Headlining, Long Beach *Also called Acme Headlining Co* ***(P-19563)***

Acme Awning & Canvas Co, San Diego *Also called Guardian Corporate Services* ***(P-3685)***

Acme Bag Co Inc (PA) F 530 662-6130
440 N Pioneer Ave Ste 300 Woodland (95776) ***(P-5432)***

Acme Bread Co D 650 938-2978
362 E Grand Ave South San Francisco (94080) ***(P-1134)***

Acme Bread Co Div II, Berkeley *Also called Doughtronics Inc* ***(P-1192)***

Acme Bread Company, Berkeley *Also called Doughtronics Inc* ***(P-1191)***

Acme Castings Inc E 323 583-3129
6009 Santa Fe Ave Huntington Park (90255) ***(P-11392)***

Acme Cryogenics Inc E 805 981-4500
531 Sandy Cir Oxnard (93036) ***(P-14417)***

Acme Data Inc F 925 913-4591
2400 Camino Ramon Ste 180 San Ramon (94583) ***(P-23550)***

Acme Divac Industries, Newport Beach *Also called C & H Hydraulics Inc* ***(P-20060)***

Acme Headlining Co D 562 432-0281
550 W 16th St Long Beach (90813) ***(P-19563)***

Acme Machine Products, Modesto *Also called Steven Varrati* ***(P-16423)***

Acme Portable Machines Inc E 626 610-1888
1330 Mountain View Cir Azusa (91702) ***(P-14879)***

Acme Press Inc D 925 682-1111
2312 Stanwell Dr Concord (94520) ***(P-6394)***

Acme Screw Products Inc E 323 581-8611
7950 S Alameda St Huntington Park (90255) ***(P-12583)***

Acme United Corporation E 714 557-2001
630 Young St Santa Ana (92705) ***(P-5096)***

Acme Vial & Glass Co E 805 239-2666
1601 Commerce Way Paso Robles (93446) ***(P-10282)***

Acme Wiping Materials, Los Angeles *Also called Max Fischer & Sons Inc* ***(P-3626)***

Aco Pacific Inc F 650 595-8588
2604 Read Ave Belmont (94002) ***(P-21428)***

Acologix Inc E 510 512-7200
3960 Point Eden Way Hayward (94545) ***(P-7720)***

Acom Data, Ontario *Also called Dura Micro Inc* ***(P-15023)***

Acorn Engineering Company (PA) A 800 488-8999
15125 Proctor Ave City of Industry (91746) ***(P-12525)***

Acorn Newspaper Inc E 818 706-0266
30423 Canwood St Ste 108 Agoura Hills (91301) ***(P-5544)***

Acorn Plastics Inc (HQ) D 909 591-8461
13818 Oaks Ave Chino (91710) ***(P-9606)***

Acorn Vac, Chino *Also called Acornvac Inc* ***(P-11652)***

Acorn-Gencon Plastics LLC D 909 591-8461
13818 Oaks Ave Chino (91710) ***(P-9607)***

Acornvac Inc E 909 902-1141
13818 Oaks Ave Chino (91710) ***(P-11652)***

Acosta Sheet Metal Mfg Co, San Jose *Also called Sal J Acsta Sheetmetal Mfg Inc* ***(P-12366)***

Acoustic Guitar Magazine, Richmond *Also called String Letter Publishing Inc* ***(P-6349)***

Acoustical Interiors Inc (PA) F 650 728-9441
123 Princeton Ave El Granada (94018) ***(P-10979)***

Acp Composites, Livermore *Also called Aerospace Composite Products* ***(P-20020)***

Acp Noxtat Inc E 714 547-5477
1112 E Washington Ave Santa Ana (92701) ***(P-7539)***

Acp Ventures F 925 297-0100
3340 Mt Diablo Blvd Ste B Lafayette (94549) ***(P-6395)***

Acpt, Huntington Beach *Also called Advanced Cmpsite Pdts Tech Inc* ***(P-9611)***

Acquis Inc F 408 402-5367
16795 Lark Ave Ste 102 Los Gatos (95032) ***(P-23551)***

Acra Enterprises Inc F 805 964-4757
5760 Thornwood Dr Goleta (93117) ***(P-15685)***

Acri, Los Angeles *Also called Analytic and Computational Res* ***(P-23599)***

Acrl, Chatsworth *Also called Advanced Cosmetic RES Labs Inc* ***(P-23264)***

Acro-Spec Grinding Co Inc F 951 736-1199
4134 Indus Way Riverside (92503) ***(P-15686)***

Acroamatics Inc E 805 967-9909
7230 Hollister Ave Goleta (93117) ***(P-17436)***

Acrometrix Corporation E 707 746-8888
46500 Kato Rd Fremont (94538) ***(P-8199)***

Acromil LLC (HQ) C 626 964-2522
18421 Railroad St City of Industry (91748) ***(P-20001)***

Acromil LLC D 951 808-9929
1168 Sherborn St Corona (92879) ***(P-20002)***

Acromil Corporation (PA) C 626 964-2522
18421 Railroad St City of Industry (91748) ***(P-20003)***

Acrontos Manufacturing Inc E 714 850-9133
1641 E Saint Gertrude Pl Santa Ana (92705) ***(P-12759)***

Acroscope LLC F 408 727-6896
3501 Thomas Rd Ste 7 Santa Clara (95054) ***(P-15687)***

Acrylic Designs Inc F 714 630-1370
1221 N Barsten Way Anaheim (92806) ***(P-9608)***

Acrylic Distribution Corp D 818 767-8448
8501 Lankershim Blvd Sun Valley (91352) ***(P-4759)***

Acrylicore Inc F 310 515-4846
15902 S Broadway Gardena (90248) ***(P-9436)***

ACS, Antioch *Also called Allied Container Systems Inc* ***(P-12527)***

ACS Co Ltd C 408 981-7162
6341 San Ignacio Ave San Jose (95119) ***(P-13900)***

ACS Controls Corporation F 916 640-8800
4704 Roseville Rd Ste 101 North Highlands (95660) ***(P-20780)***

ACS Instrumentation Valves Inc D 510 262-1880
3065 Richmond Pkwy # 106 Richmond (94806) ***(P-20826)***

Acsco Products Inc E 818 953-2240
313 N Lake St Burbank (91502) ***(P-19564)***

Act Inc Dmand Kontrols Systems, Costa Mesa *Also called Advanced Conservation Technolo* ***(P-11689)***

Act Now Instant Signs Inc F 909 394-7818
550 W Cienega Ave Ste B San Dimas (91773) ***(P-23041)***

Act Now Signs, San Dimas *Also called Act Now Instant Signs Inc* ***(P-23041)***

Actagro LLC (PA) E 559 369-2222
677 W Palmdon Dr Ste 108 Fresno (93704) ***(P-8810)***

Actavalon Inc F 949 244-5684
3210 Merryfield Row San Diego (92121) ***(P-7721)***

Actavis LLC F 951 493-5582
132 Business Center Dr Corona (92880) ***(P-7722)***

Actavis LLC D 909 270-1400
311 Bonnie Cir Corona (92880) ***(P-7723)***

Mergent e-mail: customerrelations@mergent.com
1008
2020 California Manufacturers Register
(P-0000) Products & Services Section entry number
(PA)=Parent Co (HQ)=Headquarters (DH)=Div Headquarters

Actelion Phrmaceuticals US Inc (HQ) ....E......650 624-6900
5000 Shoreline Ct Ste 200 South San Francisco (94080) *(P-7724)*

Acti Corporation Inc ....E......949 753-0352
3 Jenner Ste 160 Irvine (92618) *(P-17181)*

Actiance Inc ....E......650 631-6300
1400 Seaport Blvd Redwood City (94063) *(P-12446)*

Action Bag & Cover Inc ....D......714 965-7777
18401 Mount Langley St Fountain Valley (92708) *(P-3652)*

Action Color Card, Eastvale *Also called Jim Perry (P-7336)*

Action Electronic Assembly Inc ....E......760 510-0003
2872 S Santa Fe Ave San Marcos (92069) *(P-17804)*

Action Embroidery Corp (PA) ....C......909 983-1359
1315 Brooks St Ontario (91762) *(P-3829)*

Action Enterprises Inc ....F......714 978-0333
1911 S Betmor Ln Anaheim (92805) *(P-9609)*

Action Graphic Arts Inc ....F......626 443-3113
13065 Raintree Pl Chino (91710) *(P-7367)*

Action Innovations Inc ....E......714 978-0333
1911 S Betmor Ln Anaheim (92805) *(P-9610)*

Action Laminates LLC ....F......510 259-6217
3400 Investment Blvd Hayward (94545) *(P-4779)*

Action Mold and Tool Co, Anaheim *Also called Action Innovations Inc (P-9610)*

Action Plastics, Santa Ana *Also called Smiths Action Plastic Inc (P-9596)*

Action Sign Systems, Redwood City *Also called D N G Cummings Inc (P-23085)*

Action Stamping Inc ....E......626 914-7466
517 S Glendora Ave Glendora (91741) *(P-12760)*

Actionmold, Anaheim *Also called Action Enterprises Inc (P-9609)*

Actionpac Scales & Automation, Oxnard *Also called Coastal Cnting Indus Scale Inc (P-14147)*

Activa Global Spt & Entrmt LLC ....E......949 265-8260
30950 Rncho Viejo Rd 125 San Juan Capistrano (92675) *(P-22731)*

Active ID LLC ....E......408 782-3900
845 Embedded Way San Jose (95138) *(P-13855)*

Active Interest Media Inc (PA) ....D......310 356-4100
300 Continental Blvd # 650 El Segundo (90245) *(P-5874)*

Active Knitwear Resources Inc ....F......626 308-1328
322 S Date Ave Alhambra (91803) *(P-3134)*

Active Plating Inc ....E......714 547-0356
1411 E Pomona St Santa Ana (92705) *(P-12903)*

Active Window Products ....D......323 245-5185
5431 W San Fernando Rd Los Angeles (90039) *(P-11927)*

Activeapparel Inc (PA) ....F......951 361-0060
11076 Venture Dr Jurupa Valley (91752) *(P-3062)*

Activeon Inc (PA) ....F......858 798-3300
10905 Technology Pl San Diego (92127) *(P-17182)*

Activewire Inc ....F......650 465-4000
1799 Silacci Dr Campbell (95008) *(P-15144)*

Activision Blizzard Inc ....C......415 881-9100
4 Hamilton Landing Novato (94949) *(P-23552)*

Activision Blizzard Inc (PA) ....B......310 255-2000
3100 Ocean Park Blvd Santa Monica (90405) *(P-23553)*

Activision Blizzard Inc ....D......949 955-1380
3 Blizzard Irvine (92618) *(P-23554)*

Activision Publishing Inc (HQ) ....A......310 255-2000
3100 Ocean Park Blvd Santa Monica (90405) *(P-23555)*

Acton Inc ....F......323 250-0685
2400 Lincoln Ave Ste 238 Altadena (91001) *(P-16627)*

Actron Manufacturing Inc ....D......951 371-0885
1841 Railroad St Corona (92880) *(P-11558)*

Actsolar Inc ....F......408 721-5000
2900 Semiconductor Dr Santa Clara (95051) *(P-21429)*

Actuate Corporation (HQ) ....E......650 645-3000
951 Mariners Island Blvd # 7 San Mateo (94404) *(P-23556)*

Acu Spec Inc ....F......408 748-8600
990 Richard Ave Ste 103 Santa Clara (95050) *(P-15688)*

Acuant Inc (HQ) ....E......213 867-2621
6080 Center Dr Ste 850 Los Angeles (90045) *(P-15145)*

Acufast Aircraft Products Inc ....E......818 365-7077
12445 Gladstone Ave Sylmar (91342) *(P-20004)*

Acuity Brands Lighting Inc ....E......510 845-2760
55 Harrison St 200 Oakland (94607) *(P-17007)*

Aculon Inc ....F......858 350-9474
11839 Sorrento Valley Rd # 901 San Diego (92121) *(P-8704)*

Acuna Dionisio Able ....F......310 978-4741
12629 Prairie Ave Hawthorne (90250) *(P-15689)*

Acuprint, Los Angeles *Also called Ink & Color Inc (P-6637)*

Acuprint.com, Carlsbad *Also called Continuous Cartridge (P-22411)*

Acureo ....F......530 550-8801
12242 Bus Park Dr Ste 20 Truckee (96161) *(P-23557)*

Acushnet Company ....B......760 804-6500
2819 Loker Ave E Carlsbad (92010) *(P-22732)*

Acutek Adhesive Specialties ....E......310 419-0190
540 N Oak St Inglewood (90302) *(P-9279)*

Acutus Medical Inc ....F......858 673-1621
2210 Faraday Ave Ste 100 Carlsbad (92008) *(P-21968)*

Acxess Spring, Colton *Also called Alfonso Jaramillo (P-13372)*

Ad Art Inc (PA) ....D......415 869-6460
150 Executive Park Blvd # 2100 San Francisco (94134) *(P-23042)*

Ad Art Company, Vernon *Also called RJ Acquisition Corp (P-7201)*

Ad Art Sign Company, San Francisco *Also called Ad Art Inc (P-23042)*

Ad Hoc Labs Inc ....F......323 800-4927
2898 Rowena Ave Ste 100 Los Angeles (90039) *(P-23558)*

Ad Industries LLC (PA) ....F......818 765-4200
14071 Peyton Dr Unit 2170 Chino Hills (91709) *(P-7302)*

Ad Review, Albany *Also called Mingo Enterprises Inc (P-5989)*

Ad Special TS EMB Screen Prtg ....F......707 452-7272
202 Bella Vista Rd Ste B Vacaville (95687) *(P-3768)*

Ad-De-Pro Inc ....F......562 862-1915
8276 Phlox St Downey (90241) *(P-12616)*

Ad/S Companies, Corona *Also called Architectural Design Signs (P-23051)*

Adam Nutrition, A Division Ivc, Mira Loma *Also called International Vitamin Corp (P-7957)*

Adama Minerals, South San Francisco *Also called Zion Health Inc (P-8612)*

Adamant Enterprise Inc ....E......626 934-3399
2326 Jurado Ave Hacienda Heights (91745) *(P-5381)*

Adamas Pharmaceuticals Inc (PA) ....D......510 450-3500
1900 Powell St Ste 1000 Emeryville (94608) *(P-7725)*

Adamation, Hacienda Heights *Also called Barhena Inc (P-15491)*

Adamis Pharmaceuticals Corp (PA) ....E......858 997-2400
11682 El Cmino Real Ste 3 San Diego (92130) *(P-7726)*

Adams and Brooks Inc ....D......213 392-8700
4345 Hallmark Pkwy San Bernardino (92407) *(P-1354)*

Adams Business Media, Palm Springs *Also called Adams Trade Press LP (P-5875)*

Adams Label Company LLC (PA) ....F......925 371-5393
6052 Industrial Way Ste G Livermore (94551) *(P-6973)*

Adams Rite Aerospace, Fullerton *Also called Zmp Aquisition Corporation (P-16772)*

Adams Rite Aerospace Inc (HQ) ....C......714 278-6500
4141 N Palm St Fullerton (92835) *(P-20005)*

Adams Trade Press LP (PA) ....E......760 318-7000
420 S Palm Canyon Dr Palm Springs (92262) *(P-5875)*

Adams Welding Inc ....F......714 412-7684
6352 Apache Rd Westminster (92683) *(P-24612)*

Adams-Campbell Company Ltd ....E......626 330-3425
15323 Proctor Ave City of Industry (91745) *(P-12085)*

Adaps Photonics Inc ....E......650 521-6390
97 E Brokaw Rd San Jose (95112) *(P-17341)*

Adapt Automation Inc ....E......714 662-4454
1661 Palm St Ste A Santa Ana (92701) *(P-14262)*

Adaptive Aerospace Corporation ....F......661 822-2850
20304 W Valley Blvd Ste H Tehachapi (93561) *(P-20006)*

Adaptive Digital Systems Inc ....E......949 955-3116
20322 Sw Acacia St # 200 Newport Beach (92660) *(P-17437)*

Adaptive Electronics, San Jose *Also called Infiniti Solutions Usa Inc (P-17900)*

Adaptive Inc (PA) ....F......888 399-4621
65 Enterprise Ste E475 Aliso Viejo (92656) *(P-23559)*

Adaptive Insghts LLC A Workday (HQ) ....C......650 528-7500
2300 Geng Rd Ste 100 Palo Alto (94303) *(P-23560)*

Adaptive Shelters LLC ....E......949 923-5444
427 E 17th St Ste F268 Costa Mesa (92627) *(P-4453)*

Adara Power Inc ....F......844 223-2969
15466 Los Gatos Blvd # 109351 Los Gatos (95032) *(P-19151)*

ADB Industries ....D......310 679-9193
1400 Manhattan Ave Fullerton (92831) *(P-11429)*

ADC Enterprises Inc ....F......714 538-3102
633 W Katella Ave Ste T Orange (92867) *(P-15690)*

Adco Manufacturing ....C......559 875-5563
2170 Academy Ave Sanger (93657) *(P-14695)*

Adco Products, Valencia *Also called Amzr Inc (P-3832)*

Adco Products Inc ....D......937 339-6267
23091 Mill Creek Dr Laguna Hills (92653) *(P-18808)*

Adcon Lab Inc ....E......408 531-9187
6110 Running Springs Rd San Jose (95135) *(P-14418)*

Adcotech Corporation ....D......408 943-9999
1980 Tarob Ct Milpitas (95035) *(P-14419)*

Adcraft Products Co Inc ....E......714 776-1230
1230 S Sherman St Anaheim (92805) *(P-6974)*

Add-On Computer Peripheral Inc ....C......949 546-8200
15775 Gateway Cir Tustin (92780) *(P-15146)*

Addice Inc ....F......626 617-7779
19977 Harrison Ave City of Industry (91789) *(P-15147)*

Adding Technology (PA) ....F......805 252-6971
27 W Anapamu St Santa Barbara (93101) *(P-23561)*

Addison Engineering, San Jose *Also called Addison Technology Inc (P-17805)*

Addison Technology Inc ....E......408 749-1000
150 Nortech Pkwy San Jose (95134) *(P-17805)*

Addition Mfg Tech CA Inc ....E......760 597-5220
1391 Specialty Dr Ste A Vista (92081) *(P-13964)*

Addvocate Inc ....F......415 797-7620
599 3rd St Apt 103 San Francisco (94107) *(P-23562)*

Adegbesan Adefemi ....E......310 663-0789
1525 254th St Harbor City (90710) *(P-14880)*

Adel Park LLC ....F......213 321-2030
1432 Edinger Ave Ste 120 Tustin (92780) *(P-13701)*

Adel Wiggins Group, Commerce *Also called Transdigm Inc (P-20252)*

Adelaide Marine Services LLC ....F......619 852-8722
100 W 35th St Unit Lm National City (91950) *(P-9128)*

Adelanto Elementary School Dst ....E......760 530-7680
14350 Bellflower St Adelanto (92301) *(P-2388)*

Adem LLC ....E......408 727-8955
1040 Di Giulio Ave # 160 Santa Clara (95050) *(P-15691)*

Adenna LLC ....F......909 510-6999
2151 Michelson Dr Ste 260 Irvine (92612) *(P-21969)*

Adept Med International Inc (PA) ....F......530 621-1220
665 Pleasant Valley Rd Diamond Springs (95619) *(P-21581)*

Adept Process Services Inc ....E......619 434-3194
1505 Cleveland Ave National City (91950) *(P-20310)*

Adesa International LLC ....E......909 321-8240
1440 S Vineyard Ave Ontario (91761) *(P-716)*

Adesto Technologies Corp (PA) ....D......408 400-0578
3600 Peterson Way Santa Clara (95054) *(P-18061)*

Adex Electronics Inc ....F......949 597-1772
3 Watson Irvine (92618) *(P-18062)*

Adex Medical Inc ....E......951 653-9122
6101 Quail Valley Ct D Riverside (92507) *(P-21970)*

Adexa Inc (PA) ....E......310 642-2100
5777 W Century Blvd # 1100 Los Angeles (90045) *(P-23563)*

Adeza Biomedical Corporation ....C......408 745-6491
1240 Elko Dr Sunnyvale (94089) *(P-8200)*

Adf Incorporated ....E......310 669-9700
1550 W Mahalo Pl Rancho Dominguez (90220) *(P-12447)*

A
L
P
H
A
B
E
T
I
C

Adfa Incorporated ....E 213 627-8004
319 W 6th St Los Angeles (90014) *(P-13135)*

Adhara Inc (PA) ....F 619 661-9901
9465 Customhouse Plz H1 San Diego (92154) *(P-12904)*

Adhesves Sealants Coatings Div, Roseville *Also called HB Fuller Company (P-8871)*

ADI, Compton *Also called American Dawn Inc (P-2922)*

ADI, Valencia *Also called Aerospace Dynamics Intl Inc (P-20021)*

ADI American Def Interconnect, Chatsworth *Also called Newvac LLC (P-17790)*

Adiana Inc ....E 650 421-2900
1240 Elko Dr Sunnyvale (94089) *(P-7727)*

Adidas North America Inc ....E 707 446-1070
378 Nut Tree Rd Vacaville (95687) *(P-3063)*

Adidas Outlet Store Vacaville, Vacaville *Also called Adidas North America Inc (P-3063)*

Adina For Life Inc ....E 415 285-9300
660 York St Ste 205 San Francisco (94110) *(P-2188)*

ADM, Colton *Also called Archer-Daniels-Midland Company (P-989)*

ADM, Los Angeles *Also called Archer-Daniels-Midland Company (P-990)*

ADM, Los Angeles *Also called Archer-Daniels-Midland Company (P-992)*

ADM, Lodi *Also called Archer-Daniels-Midland Company (P-993)*

ADM Milling Co ....D 530 476-2662
1603 Old Hwy 99 W Arbuckle (95912) *(P-987)*

ADM Works LLC ....E 714 245-0536
1343 E Wilshire Ave Santa Ana (92705) *(P-11362)*

Admail West Inc ....D 916 554-5755
800 N 10th St Ste F Sacramento (95811) *(P-5286)*

Admail-Express Inc ....E 510 471-6200
31640 Hayman St Hayward (94544) *(P-6396)*

Admi Inc ....E 408 776-0060
18525 Sutter Blvd Ste 290 Morgan Hill (95037) *(P-23564)*

Admin - Shafter Admin Office, Shafter *Also called Cemex Cnstr Mtls PCF LLC (P-10726)*

Administrative Services, San Francisco *Also called City & County of San Francisco (P-7023)*

Adobe Inc ....A 415 832-2000
601 And 625 Townsend St San Francisco (94103) *(P-23565)*

Adobe Inc ....E 408 536-6000
321 Park Ave San Jose (95110) *(P-23566)*

Adobe Inc (PA) ....A 408 536-6000
345 Park Ave San Jose (95110) *(P-23567)*

Adobe Macromedia Software LLC (HQ) ....E 415 832-2000
601 Townsend St San Francisco (94103) *(P-23568)*

Adolf Goldfarb ....F 310 451-1211
1434 6th St Ste 10 Santa Monica (90401) *(P-22656)*

Adomani Inc ....F 951 407-9860
4740 Green River Rd Corona (92880) *(P-19565)*

Adrienne Designs LLC ....E 714 558-1209
17150 Newhope St Ste 514 Fountain Valley (92708) *(P-22488)*

Adrienne Dresses Inc ....F 213 622-8557
719 S Los Angeles St # 827 Los Angeles (90014) *(P-3210)*

ADS, Laguna Niguel *Also called Agricultural Data Systems Inc (P-23582)*

ADS LLC ....E 714 379-9778
15205 Springdale St Huntington Beach (92649) *(P-20827)*

ADS Solutions ....F 415 897-3700
10 Commercial Blvd # 208 Novato (94949) *(P-23569)*

ADS Water Inc ....F 415 448-6266
12 N Altadena Dr Pasadena (91107) *(P-15479)*

Adtec Technology Inc ....F 510 226-5766
48625 Warm Springs Blvd Fremont (94539) *(P-18694)*

Adtech Optics, City of Industry *Also called Adtech Photonics Inc (P-21331)*

Adtech Photonics Inc ....E 626 956-1000
18007 Cortney Ct City of Industry (91748) *(P-21331)*

Adtech Tool Engrg Corporations ....F 310 515-1717
13620 Cimarron Ave Gardena (90249) *(P-14128)*

Adtek Inc ....E 209 634-0300
1460 Ellerd Dr Turlock (95380) *(P-11734)*

Adtek Media Inc ....E 949 680-4200
13841 West St Garden Grove (92843) *(P-23043)*

Adti Media LLC ....E 951 795-4446
1257 Simpson Way Escondido (92029) *(P-23044)*

Adult Video News, Chatsworth *Also called Avn Media Network Inc (P-6073)*

Adultfriendfinder, Campbell *Also called Medleycom Incorporated (P-5749)*

Adura Led Solutions LLC ....F 714 660-2944
511 Princeland Ct Corona (92879) *(P-17806)*

Aduro Biotech Inc (PA) ....D 510 848-4400
740 Heinz Ave Berkeley (94710) *(P-7728)*

Advance Adapters Inc ....E 805 238-7000
4320 Aerotech Center Way Paso Robles (93446) *(P-19566)*

Advance Aqua Tanks, Los Angeles *Also called Alan Lem & Co Inc (P-10336)*

Advance Architectural, Fountain Valley *Also called Advanced Architectural Frames (P-11929)*

Advance Carbon Products Inc ....E 510 293-5930
2036 National Ave Hayward (94545) *(P-16679)*

Advance Elctro Polishing, Santa Clara *Also called Process Stainless Lab Inc (P-13079)*

Advance Electronic Service ....E 510 490-1065
44141 Fremont Blvd Fremont (94538) *(P-17807)*

Advance Engineering & Tech Co ....F 213 250-8338
717 W Temple St Ste 203 Los Angeles (90012) *(P-20745)*

Advance Fabrication, Grass Valley *Also called Barger & Associates (P-9289)*

Advance Finishing ....F 323 754-2889
11645 S Broadway Los Angeles (90061) *(P-13136)*

Advance Lab Instr & Sups, Los Angeles *Also called Advance Engineering & Tech Co (P-20745)*

Advance Latex Products Inc ....E 310 559-8300
6915 Woodley Ave B Van Nuys (91406) *(P-3438)*

Advance Modular Technology Inc ....F 408 453-9880
2075 Bering Dr Ste C San Jose (95131) *(P-15148)*

Advance Overhead Door Inc ....E 818 781-5590
15829 Stagg St Van Nuys (91406) *(P-11928)*

Advance Pacific Tank, Placentia *Also called Keesee Tank Company (P-12024)*

Advance Paper Box Company ....C 323 750-2550
6100 S Gramercy Pl Los Angeles (90047) *(P-5194)*

Advance Pipe Bending & Fabg Co, Huntington Park *Also called B F Mc Gilla Inc (P-13459)*

Advance Plastics, National City *Also called B and P Plastics Inc (P-9649)*

Advance Screen Graphic ....F 323 724-9910
5720 Union Pacific Ave Commerce (90022) *(P-6975)*

Advance Storage Products, Huntington Beach *Also called JCM Industries Inc (P-4985)*

Advanced Adbag Packaging Inc ....F 650 591-1625
597 Quarry Rd San Carlos (94070) *(P-5382)*

Advanced Aerospace ....C 714 265-6200
10781 Forbes Ave Garden Grove (92843) *(P-15408)*

Advanced Aircraft Seal, Riverside *Also called Sphere Alliance Inc (P-7614)*

Advanced Analogic Tech Inc ....E 408 330-1400
2740 Zanker Rd San Jose (95134) *(P-18063)*

Advanced Architectural Frames ....E 424 209-6018
17102 Newhope St Fountain Valley (92708) *(P-11929)*

Advanced Arm Dynamics (PA) ....E 310 372-3050
123 W Torrance Blvd # 203 Redondo Beach (90277) *(P-21971)*

Advanced Assemblies Inc ....F 408 988-1016
990 Richard Ave Ste 109 Santa Clara (95050) *(P-18809)*

Advanced Biocatalytics Corp ....F 949 442-0880
18010 Sky Park Cir # 130 Irvine (92614) *(P-8334)*

Advanced Biohealing.com, San Diego *Also called Shire Rgenerative Medicine Inc (P-8130)*

Advanced Bionics LLC (HQ) ....B 661 362-1400
12740 San Fernando Rd Sylmar (91342) *(P-21972)*

Advanced Bionics Corporation (HQ) ....C 661 362-1400
28515 Westinghouse Pl Valencia (91355) *(P-21973)*

Advanced Building Systems Inc ....E 818 652-4252
11905 Regentview Ave Downey (90241) *(P-23263)*

Advanced Ceramic Technology ....F 714 538-2524
803 W Angus Ave Orange (92868) *(P-15692)*

Advanced Charging Tech Inc ....E 877 228-5922
16855 Knott Ave La Mirada (90638) *(P-16773)*

Advanced Chemblocks Inc ....F 650 692-2368
849 Mitten Rd Ste 101 Burlingame (94010) *(P-7729)*

Advanced Chemical Tech Inc ....E 800 527-9607
8728 Utica Ave Rancho Cucamonga (91730) *(P-7466)*

Advanced Chemistry & Tech Inc (HQ) ....E 714 373-8118
7341 Anaconda Ave Garden Grove (92841) *(P-8852)*

Advanced Chip Magnetics Inc ....F 310 370-8188
4225 Spencer St Torrance (90503) *(P-18695)*

Advanced Circuits Inc ....D 415 602-6834
1602 Tacoma Way Redwood City (94063) *(P-17808)*

Advanced Clutch Technology Inc ....E 661 940-7555
206 E Avenue K4 Lancaster (93535) *(P-19567)*

Advanced Cmpsite Pdts Tech Inc ....E 714 895-5544
15602 Chemical Ln Huntington Beach (92649) *(P-9611)*

Advanced Color Graphics ....D 909 930-1500
1921 S Business Pkwy Ontario (91761) *(P-6397)*

Advanced Component Labs Inc ....E 408 327-0200
990 Richard Ave Ste 118 Santa Clara (95050) *(P-18064)*

Advanced Components Mfg ....E 650 344-6272
1415 N Carolan Ave Burlingame (94010) *(P-15693)*

Advanced Composites Engrg, Temecula *Also called Advanced Composites Engrg LLC (P-9612)*

Advanced Composites Engrg LLC ....F 951 694-3055
42245 Sarah Way Temecula (92590) *(P-9612)*

Advanced Conservation Technolo ....F 714 668-1200
3176 Pullman St Ste 119 Costa Mesa (92626) *(P-11689)*

Advanced Cosmetic RES Labs Inc ....E 818 709-9945
20550 Prairie St Chatsworth (91311) *(P-23264)*

Advanced Cutting Tools Inc ....E 714 842-9376
17741 Metzler Ln Huntington Beach (92647) *(P-11520)*

Advanced Dealer Services, Fremont *Also called Advanced Enterprises LLC (P-17438)*

Advanced Design Engrg & Mfg, Santa Clara *Also called Adem LLC (P-15691)*

Advanced Digital Research Inc ....F 949 252-1055
1813 E Dyer Rd Ste 410 Santa Ana (92705) *(P-15118)*

Advanced Digital Tech Intl, Escondido *Also called Adti Media LLC (P-23044)*

Advanced Display Systems Inc ....F 714 995-2200
8614 Central Ave Stanton (90680) *(P-20502)*

Advanced Drainage Systems Inc ....E 559 674-4989
1025 Commerce Dr Madera (93637) *(P-9462)*

Advanced Electromagnetics Inc ....E 619 449-9492
1320 Air Wing Rd Ste 101 San Diego (92154) *(P-20828)*

Advanced Engine Management Inc (PA) ....C 310 484-2322
2205 W 126th St Ste A Hawthorne (90250) *(P-19568)*

Advanced Engineering & EDM Inc ....F 858 679-6800
13007 Kirkham Way Ste A Poway (92064) *(P-15694)*

Advanced Enginering and EDM ....E 858 679-6800
13007 Kirkham Way Ste A Poway (92064) *(P-15695)*

Advanced Enterprises LLC ....F 408 923-5000
48511 Warm Springs Blvd # 202 Fremont (94539) *(P-17438)*

Advanced Enviromental ....F 310 782-9400
2420 W Carson St Torrance (90501) *(P-14008)*

Advanced Equipment Corporation (PA) ....E 714 635-5350
2401 W Commonwealth Ave Fullerton (92833) *(P-4961)*

Advanced Flow Engineering Inc (PA) ....D 951 493-7155
252 Granite St Corona (92879) *(P-19569)*

Advanced Foam Inc ....E 310 515-0728
1745 W 134th St Gardena (90249) *(P-9499)*

Advanced Global Tech Group ....E 714 281-8020
8015 E Treeview Ct Anaheim (92808) *(P-18749)*

Advanced Ground Systems (HQ) ....E 562 906-9300
10805 Painter Ave Santa Fe Springs (90670) *(P-19944)*

Advanced H2o, Ontario *Also called Advanced Refreshment LLC (P-2022)*

Advanced Honeycomb Tech ....E 760 744-3200
1015 Linda Vista Dr Ste C San Marcos (92078) *(P-12761)*

Advanced Hpc Inc ....F 858 716-8262
8228 Mercury Ct Ste 100 San Diego (92111) *(P-15001)*

Mergent e-mail: customerrelations@mergent.com 2020 California (P-0000) Products & Services Section entry number
1010 Manufacturers Register (PA)=Parent Co (HQ)=Headquarters (DH)=Div Headquarters

Advanced Indus Coatings Inc .... D 209 234-2700
950 Industrial Dr Stockton (95206) (P-13137)
Advanced Industrial Ceramics .... E 408 955-9990
2449 Zanker Rd San Jose (95131) (P-14420)
Advanced Industrial Services, Bakersfield Also called CL Knox Inc (P-184)
Advanced Inst of Skin Care .... F 818 765-2606
7225 Fulton Ave North Hollywood (91605) (P-8432)
Advanced Instruments, Pomona Also called Analytical Industries Inc (P-20834)
Advanced Intl Tech LLC .... E 858 566-2945
9909 Hibert St Ste A San Diego (92131) (P-15696)
Advanced Keyboard Tech Inc .... F 805 237-2055
2501 Golden Hill Rd # 200 Paso Robles (93446) (P-14881)
Advanced Laser & Wtr Jet Cutng, Santa Clara Also called Advanced Laser Cutting
Inc (P-15697)
Advanced Laser Cutting Inc .... F 408 486-0700
820 Comstock St Santa Clara (95054) (P-15697)
Advanced Laser Dies Inc .... F 562 949-0081
9629 Beverly Rd Pico Rivera (90660) (P-14303)
Advanced Lgs LLC .... F 818 652-4252
11905 Regentview Ave Downey (90241) (P-11735)
Advanced Lighting Concepts Inc .... E 888 880-1880
11235 W Bernardo Ct # 102 San Diego (92127) (P-17008)
Advanced Linear Devices Inc .... E 408 747-1155
415 Tasman Dr Sunnyvale (94089) (P-18065)
Advanced Machine Programming, Morgan Hill Also called AMP III LLC (P-14131)
Advanced Machining Tooling Inc .... E 858 486-9050
13535 Danielson St Poway (92064) (P-14009)
Advanced Manufacturing Tech .... C 714 238-1488
3140a E Coronado St Anaheim (92806) (P-19248)
Advanced Materials Inc (HQ) .... F 310 537-5444
20211 S Susana Rd Compton (90221) (P-9500)
Advanced Materials Analysis .... F 650 391-4190
740 Sierra Vista Ave D Mountain View (94043) (P-9391)
Advanced McHning Solutions Inc .... E 619 671-3055
3523 Main St Ste 606 Chula Vista (91911) (P-15698)
Advanced McHning Tchniques Inc .... E 408 778-4500
16205 Vineyard Blvd Morgan Hill (95037) (P-15699)
Advanced Metal Finishing LLC .... E 530 888-7772
2130 March Rd Roseville (95747) (P-12905)
Advanced Metal Forming Inc .... F 619 239-9437
2618 National Ave San Diego (92113) (P-11736)
Advanced Metal Mfg Inc .... E 805 322-4161
49 Strathearn Pl Simi Valley (93065) (P-12086)
Advanced Metal Works Inc .... F 559 237-2332
1560 H St Fresno (93721) (P-12087)
Advanced Mfg & Dev Inc .... C 707 459-9451
200 N Lenore Ave Willits (95490) (P-12088)
Advanced Micro Devices Inc (PA) .... B 408 749-4000
2485 Augustine Dr Santa Clara (95054) (P-18066)
Advanced Micro Instruments Inc .... E 714 848-5533
225 Paularino Ave Costa Mesa (92626) (P-21161)
Advanced Microtechnology Inc .... F 408 945-9191
480 Vista Way Milpitas (95035) (P-20982)
Advanced Microwave Inc .... F 408 739-4214
333 Moffett Park Dr Sunnyvale (94089) (P-18810)
Advanced Mobility Inc .... F 818 780-1788
7720 Sepulveda Blvd Van Nuys (91405) (P-23265)
Advanced Mold Technology Inc .... F 714 990-0144
1560 Moonstone Brea (92821) (P-14010)
Advanced Motion Controls, Camarillo Also called Barta-Schoenewald Inc (P-16632)
Advanced Mtls Joining Corp (PA) .... E 626 449-2696
2858 E Walnut St Pasadena (91107) (P-20007)
Advanced Orthopaedic Solutions .... E 310 533-9966
3203 Kashiwa St Torrance (90505) (P-21974)
Advanced Orthotic Designs .... F 951 710-1640
9351 Narnia Dr Riverside (92503) (P-21975)
Advanced Oxygen Therapy Inc (HQ) .... F 760 431-4700
3512 Seagate Way Ste 100 Oceanside (92056) (P-21582)
Advanced Packaging & Crating .... F 714 892-1702
15432 Electronic Ln Huntington Beach (92649) (P-4410)
Advanced Packaging Tech Amer, San Diego Also called Apta Group Inc (P-18119)
Advanced Pattern & Mold .... F 909 930-3444
1720 S Balboa Ave Ontario (91761) (P-11177)
Advanced Photonix, Camarillo Also called OSI Optoelectronics Inc (P-18461)
Advanced Power & Controls LLC .... F 714 540-9010
605 E Alton Ave Ste A Santa Ana (92705) (P-16628)
Advanced Prcsion Machining Inc .... F 949 650-6113
1649 Monrovia Ave Costa Mesa (92627) (P-15700)
Advanced Precision Spring .... F 408 436-6595
1754 Junction Ave Ste A San Jose (95112) (P-13370)
Advanced Pressure Technology .... D 707 259-0102
687 Technology Way NAPA (94558) (P-20829)
Advanced Process Services Inc .... E 323 278-6530
4350 E Washington Blvd Commerce (90023) (P-13287)
Advanced Products, Costa Mesa Also called Pro-Lite Inc (P-23179)
Advanced Publishing Tech Inc .... F 818 557-3035
1105 N Hollywood Way Burbank (91505) (P-6174)
Advanced Publishing Tech Inc (PA) .... E 818 557-3035
123 S Victory Blvd Burbank (91502) (P-23570)
Advanced Refractive Tech .... F 949 940-1300
12518 Cavallo St San Diego (92130) (P-21583)
Advanced Refreshment LLC (HQ) .... F 425 746-8100
2560 E Philadelphia St Ontario (91761) (P-2022)
Advanced Results Company Inc .... F 408 986-0123
18760 Afton Ave Saratoga (95070) (P-14557)
Advanced Rtrcraft Trining Svcs .... E 650 967-6300
938 W Evelyn Ave Unit B Sunnyvale (94086) (P-19249)
Advanced Safety Devices LLC .... F 818 701-9200
21430 Strathern St Unit M Canoga Park (91304) (P-20983)

Advanced Sealing (HQ) .... D 562 802-7782
15500 Blackburn Ave Norwalk (90650) (P-9215)
Advanced Semiconductor Inc (PA) .... D 818 982-1200
7525 Ethel Ave Ste I North Hollywood (91605) (P-18067)
Advanced Skin & Hair Inc .... F 310 442-9700
12121 Wilshire Blvd # 1012 Los Angeles (90025) (P-8433)
Advanced Spectral Tech Inc .... E 805 527-7657
94 W Cochran St Ste A Simi Valley (93065) (P-21332)
Advanced Sterlization (HQ) .... E 800 595-0200
33 Technology Dr Irvine (92618) (P-21584)
Advanced Structural Tech Inc .... C 805 204-9133
950 Richmond Ave Oxnard (93030) (P-12701)
Advanced Surface Finishing Inc .... F 408 275-9718
1181 N 4th St Ste 50 San Jose (95112) (P-12906)
Advanced Tactics Inc .... F 310 701-3659
3339 Airport Dr Torrance (90505) (P-19845)
Advanced Tech Plating .... E 714 630-7093
1061 N Grove St Anaheim (92806) (P-12907)
Advanced Technologies .... F 661 872-4807
2001 Columbus St Bakersfield (93305) (P-23571)
Advanced Technology Co, Pasadena Also called Advanced Mtls Joining Corp (P-20007)
Advanced Technology Machining .... F 661 257-2313
28210 Avenue Crocker # 301 Valencia (91355) (P-15701)
Advanced Thermal Sciences .... F 714 688-4200
3355 E La Palma Ave Anaheim (92806) (P-18068)
Advanced Thrmlforming Entp Inc .... F 760 722-4400
3750 Oceanic Way Oceanside (92056) (P-9613)
Advanced Uv Inc .... E 562 407-0299
16350 Manning Way Cerritos (90703) (P-15480)
Advanced Vision Science Inc .... E 805 683-3851
5743 Thornwood Dr Goleta (93117) (P-22338)
Advanced Viticulture Inc .... F 707 838-3805
930 Shiloh Rd Bldg 44-E Windsor (95492) (P-1576)
Advanced Vsual Image Dsign LLC .... C 951 279-2138
229 N Sherman Ave Irvine (92614) (P-6976)
Advanced Web Offset Inc .... D 760 727-1700
2260 Oak Ridge Way Vista (92081) (P-6977)
Advancedcath Technologies LLC (HQ) .... E 408 433-9505
176 Component Dr San Jose (95131) (P-21585)
Advanex Americas Inc (HQ) .... D 714 995-4519
5780 Cerritos Ave Cypress (90630) (P-13371)
Advaning, Garden Grove Also called Airflex5d LLC (P-4680)
Advantage Adhesives Inc .... E 909 204-4990
8345 White Oak Ave Rancho Cucamonga (91730) (P-8853)
Advantage Business Forms Inc .... F 909 875-7163
102 N Riverside Ave Rialto (92376) (P-6978)
Advantage Custom Fixtures, Los Angeles Also called American Furniture Systems
Inc (P-4827)
Advantage Engineering Corp .... E 805 216-9920
301 Bernoulli Cir Oxnard (93030) (P-22733)
Advantage Engrg & Chemistry, Santa Ana Also called AEC Group Inc (P-19571)
Advantage Homes, Stanton Also called Inception Homes Inc (P-4452)
Advantage Metal Products, Livermore Also called Segundo Metal Products Inc (P-12371)
Advantage Pharmaceuticals .... F 916 630-4960
4363 Pacific St Rocklin (95677) (P-7730)
Advantage Truss Company LLC .... E 831 635-0377
2025 San Juan Rd Hollister (95023) (P-4285)
Advantec Mfs Inc .... F 925 479-0625
6723 Sierra Ct Ste A Dublin (94568) (P-14643)
Advantest America Inc (HQ) .... D 408 456-3600
3061 Zanker Rd San Jose (95134) (P-18069)
Advantest Test Solutions Inc .... E 949 523-6900
4 Goodyear Irvine (92618) (P-18070)
Advanti Racing Usa LLC (HQ) .... E 951 272-5930
10721 Business Dr Ste 1 Fontana (92337) (P-19570)
Advent Resources Inc .... D 310 241-1500
235 W 7th St San Pedro (90731) (P-23572)
Adventure Medical Kits, Alameda Also called Tender Corporation (P-22108)
Adventures In Personal Cmpt, Vacaville Also called Joseph Charles Whitson (P-6262)
Advertiser Perceptions .... E 925 648-3902
3009 Deer Meadow Dr Danville (94506) (P-5545)
Advertiser, The, Oakdale Also called Morris Publications (P-5763)
Advertising Services .... E 714 522-2781
7697 9th St Buena Park (90621) (P-6398)
Advertising Solutions, San Diego Also called AT&T Corp (P-6192)
Adverum Biotechnologies Inc .... D 650 272-6269
1035 Obrien Dr Ste A Menlo Park (94025) (P-8267)
Advin Systems Inc .... F 408 243-7000
11693 Vineyard Spring Ct Cupertino (95014) (P-18071)
Advisor Software Inc (PA) .... E 925 299-7778
2175 N Calif Blvd Ste 400 Walnut Creek (94596) (P-23573)
Advisorsquare, Culver City Also called Liveoffice LLC (P-24104)
Advisys Inc .... E 949 752-4927
16969 Von Karman Ave # 125 Irvine (92606) (P-23574)
Adwear Inc .... F 213 629-2535
850 S Broadway Ste 400 Los Angeles (90014) (P-3022)
Adwest Technologies Inc (HQ) .... E 714 632-8595
4222 E La Palma Ave Anaheim (92807) (P-14644)
Aea Ribbon Mics .... F 626 798-9128
1029 N Allen Ave Pasadena (91104) (P-17183)
Aea Technology Inc .... F 760 931-8979
5933 Sea Lion Pl Ste 112 Carlsbad (92010) (P-20984)
AEC Group Inc .... E 714 444-1395
3600 W Carriage Dr Santa Ana (92704) (P-19571)
Aechelon Technology Inc (PA) .... E 415 255-0120
888 Brannan St Ste 210 San Francisco (94103) (P-14882)
AEG Industries Inc .... E 707 575-0697
1219 Briggs Ave Santa Rosa (95401) (P-20008)

Employee Codes: A=Over 500 employees, B=251-500
C=101-250, D=51-100, E=20-50, F=10-19

2020 California
Manfacturers Register

© Mergent Inc. 1-800-342-5647
1011

A
L
P
H
A
B
E
T
I
C

Aegis Industries Inc .... F 805 922-2700
2360 Thompson Way Ste A Santa Maria (93455) ***(P-8615)***
Aegis Its, Fremont *Also called Team Econolite* ***(P-17768)***
Aegis Principia LLC .... F 714 731-2283
12165 Ojeda Ct Tustin (92782) ***(P-23266)***
Aehr Test Systems (PA) .... D 510 623-9400
400 Kato Ter Fremont (94539) ***(P-20985)***
Aei Communications Corp .... E 650 552-9416
1001 Broadway Ste 2d Millbrae (94030) ***(P-17342)***
Aei Electech Corp .... F 510 489-5088
33485 Western Ave Union City (94587) ***(P-18811)***
Aei Manufacturing Inc .... F 818 407-5400
9452 De Soto Ave Chatsworth (91311) ***(P-16873)***
Aella Data Inc .... F 408 391-4430
4701 Patrick Henry Dr Santa Clara (95054) ***(P-23575)***
Aem (holdings) Inc .... D 858 481-0210
6610 Cobra Way San Diego (92121) ***(P-16584)***
Aem Electronics (usa) Inc .... E 858 481-0210
6610 Cobra Way San Diego (92121) ***(P-18696)***
Aemetis Advnced Fels Keyes Inc .... E 209 632-4511
4209 Jessup Rd Ceres (95307) ***(P-8705)***
Aemi, San Diego *Also called Advanced Electromagnetics Inc* ***(P-20828)***
AEP Cali, San Diego *Also called Soncell North America Inc* ***(P-20725)***
AEP Span, Fontana *Also called ASC Profiles LLC* ***(P-11744)***
Aep-California LLC .... F 619 596-1925
10729 Wheatlands Ave C Santee (92071) ***(P-19572)***
Aera Energy, Rio Vista *Also called Dick Brown Technical Services* ***(P-90)***
Aera Energy LLC (HQ) .... A 661 665-5000
10000 Ming Ave Bakersfield (93311) ***(P-82)***
Aera Energy LLC .... E 661 665-4400
59231 Main Camp Rd Mc Kittrick (93251) ***(P-83)***
Aera Energy LLC .... D 661 665-3200
29235 Highway 33 Maricopa (93252) ***(P-84)***
Aera Energy LLC .... E 559 935-7418
29010 Shell Rd Coalinga (93210) ***(P-13763)***
Aera Energy South Midway, Maricopa *Also called Aera Energy LLC* ***(P-84)***
Aercap Los Angeles, Los Angeles *Also called Aercap US Global Aviation LLC* ***(P-19846)***
Aercap US Global Aviation LLC (HQ) .... E 310 788-1999
10250 Constellation Blvd Los Angeles (90067) ***(P-19846)***
Aero Bending Company .... E 661 948-2363
560 Auto Center Dr Ste A Palmdale (93551) ***(P-12089)***
Aero Chip Inc .... E 562 404-6300
13563 Freeway Dr Santa Fe Springs (90670) ***(P-15702)***
Aero Chip Intgrted Systems Inc .... F 310 329-8600
13565 Freeway Dr Santa Fe Springs (90670) ***(P-20529)***
Aero Chrome Plating, Panorama City *Also called TMW Corporation* ***(P-13118)***
Aero Component Engineering, Valencia *Also called Pacific Aero Components Inc* ***(P-20191)***
Aero Corporation .... E 562 598-2281
3061 Quail Run Rd Los Alamitos (90720) ***(P-19847)***
Aero Dynamic Machining Inc .... D 714 379-1073
11841 Monarch St Garden Grove (92841) ***(P-20009)***
Aero Engineering Inc .... F 714 879-6200
1020 E Elm Ave Fullerton (92831) ***(P-15703)***
Aero Engineering & Mfg Co Cal .... E 661 295-0875
28217 Avenue Crocker Valencia (91355) ***(P-20010)***
Aero Industries LLC .... E 805 688-6734
139 Industrial Way Buellton (93427) ***(P-15704)***
Aero Manufacturing & Pltg Co .... E 818 241-2844
927 Thompson Ave Glendale (91201) ***(P-12908)***
Aero Mechanism Precision Inc .... E 818 886-1855
21700 Marilla St Chatsworth (91311) ***(P-15705)***
Aero Pacific Corporation (PA) .... D 714 961-9200
588 Porter Way Placentia (92870) ***(P-20011)***
Aero Pacific Corporation .... E 714 961-9200
7100 Belgrave Ave Garden Grove (92841) ***(P-20012)***
Aero Performance, Corona *Also called Irwin Aviation Inc* ***(P-20141)***
Aero Powder Coating Inc .... E 323 264-6405
710 Monterey Pass Rd Monterey Park (91754) ***(P-13138)***
Aero Precision Engineering Inc .... E 310 642-9747
11300 Hindry Ave Los Angeles (90045) ***(P-12090)***
Aero Precision Industries LLC (PA) .... C 925 455-9900
201 Lindbergh Ave Livermore (94551) ***(P-20013)***
Aero Products Co., Los Angeles *Also called Coating Specialties Inc* ***(P-20072)***
Aero Sense Inc .... F 661 257-1608
26074 Avenue Hall Ste 18 Valencia (91355) ***(P-20014)***
Aero Space Composites, Stanton *Also called Cynthia Garcia* ***(P-20079)***
Aero Turbine Inc .... D 209 983-1112
6800 Lindbergh St Stockton (95206) ***(P-19945)***
Aero-Clas Heat Tran Prod Inc .... F 909 596-1630
1677 Curtiss Ct La Verne (91750) ***(P-11991)***
Aero-Craft Hydraulics Inc .... E 951 736-4690
392 N Smith Ave Corona (92880) ***(P-20015)***
Aero-Electric Connector Inc (PA) .... D 310 618-3737
2280 W 208th St Torrance (90501) ***(P-16874)***
Aero-k Inc .... E 626 350-5125
10764 Lower Azusa Rd El Monte (91731) ***(P-15706)***
Aero-Mechanical Engrg Inc .... F 714 891-2423
5945 Engineer Dr Huntington Beach (92649) ***(P-15707)***
Aeroantenna Technology Inc .... C 818 993-3842
20732 Lassen St Chatsworth (91311) ***(P-20530)***
Aerocraft Heat Treating Co Inc .... D 562 674-2400
15701 Minnesota Ave Paramount (90723) ***(P-11430)***
Aerodynamic Engineering Inc .... E 714 891-2651
15495 Graham St Huntington Beach (92649) ***(P-15708)***
Aerodynamic Plating Co .... D 310 329-7959
13620 S Saint Andrews Pl Gardena (90249) ***(P-12909)***
Aerodyne Prcsion Machining Inc .... E 714 891-1311
5471 Argosy Ave Huntington Beach (92649) ***(P-15709)***
Aerofab Corporation .... F 714 635-0902
4001 E Leaverton Ct Anaheim (92807) ***(P-11737)***
Aerofit LLC .... C 714 521-5060
1425 S Acacia Ave Fullerton (92831) ***(P-13455)***
Aerofoam Industries Inc .... D 951 245-4429
31855 Corydon St Lake Elsinore (92530) ***(P-4851)***
Aerojet Rcketdyne Holdings Inc (PA) .... D 310 252-8100
222 N Pacific Coast Hwy # 50 El Segundo (90245) ***(P-20531)***
Aerojet Rocketdyne Inc (HQ) .... A 916 355-4000
2001 Aerojet Rd Rancho Cordova (95742) ***(P-20016)***
Aerojet Rocketdyne Inc .... F 916 355-4000
1180 Iron Point Rd # 350 Folsom (95630) ***(P-20017)***
Aerojet Rocketdyne De Inc (HQ) .... C 818 586-1000
8900 De Soto Ave Canoga Park (91304) ***(P-8706)***
Aerojet Rocketdyne De Inc .... C 818 586-9629
8495 Carla Ln West Hills (91304) ***(P-8707)***
Aerojet Rocketdyne De Inc .... C 818 586-1000
9001 Lurline Ave Chatsworth (91311) ***(P-8708)***
Aerol Co Inc (PA) .... E 310 762-2660
19560 S Rancho Way Rancho Dominguez (90220) ***(P-11363)***
Aeroliant Manufacturing Inc .... E 310 257-1903
1613 Lockness Pl Torrance (90501) ***(P-15710)***
Aerometals Inc (PA) .... D 916 939-6888
3920 Sandstone Dr El Dorado Hills (95762) ***(P-20018)***
Aeroshear Aviation Svcs Inc (PA) .... E 818 779-1650
7701 Woodley Ave 200 Van Nuys (91406) ***(P-20019)***
Aerospace and Coml Tooling Inc .... F 909 930-5780
1866 S Lake Pl Ontario (91761) ***(P-13901)***
Aerospace Composite Products (PA) .... E 925 443-5900
78 Lindbergh Ave Livermore (94551) ***(P-20020)***
Aerospace Dynamics Intl Inc .... B 661 257-3535
25540 Rye Canyon Rd Valencia (91355) ***(P-20021)***
Aerospace Engineering Corp .... D 714 996-8178
2632 Saturn St Brea (92821) ***(P-20022)***
Aerospace Facilities Group Inc .... F 702 513-8336
1590 Raleys Ct Ste 30 West Sacramento (95691) ***(P-14793)***
Aerospace Fasteners Group, Santa Ana *Also called SPS Technologies LLC* ***(P-23009)***
Aerospace Parts Holdings Inc .... A 949 877-3630
3150 E Miraloma Ave Anaheim (92806) ***(P-20023)***
Aerospace Seals & Gaskets .... E 951 256-8380
1478 Davril Cir Ste A Corona (92880) ***(P-9216)***
Aerospace Systems, Redondo Beach *Also called Northrop Grumman Systems Corp* ***(P-19921)***
Aerospace Tool Grinding .... F 562 802-3339
14020 Shoemaker Ave Norwalk (90650) ***(P-13902)***
Aerospace Welding Inc .... F 310 914-0324
2035 Granville Ave Los Angeles (90025) ***(P-24613)***
Aerostar Engineering & Mfg Inc .... F 310 326-5098
25514 Frampton Ave Harbor City (90710) ***(P-15711)***
Aerosysng Inc .... F 714 633-1901
1112 W Barkley Ave Orange (92868) ***(P-19848)***
Aerosystems Engineering, Orange *Also called Aerosysng Inc* ***(P-19848)***
Aerotec Alloys Inc .... E 562 809-1378
10632 Alondra Blvd Norwalk (90650) ***(P-11329)***
Aerotech News and Review Inc (PA) .... E 520 623-9321
220 E Avenue K4 Ste 7 Lancaster (93535) ***(P-5876)***
Aerovironment Inc .... D 626 357-9983
1610 S Magnolia Ave Monrovia (91016) ***(P-19849)***
Aerovironment Inc (PA) .... D 805 581-2187
900 Innovators Way Simi Valley (93065) ***(P-19850)***
Aerovironment Inc .... F 626 357-9983
1725 Peck Rd Monrovia (91016) ***(P-19851)***
Aerovironment Inc .... E 626 357-9983
222 E Huntington Dr # 118 Monrovia (91016) ***(P-19852)***
Aerovironment Inc .... F 626 357-9983
2290 Agate Ct Simi Valley (93065) ***(P-19853)***
Aerovironment Inc .... E 626 357-9983
825 S Myrtle Ave Monrovia (91016) ***(P-19854)***
Aerowind Corporation .... F 619 569-1960
1959 John Towers Ave El Cajon (92020) ***(P-20471)***
AES, Palo Alto *Also called Applied Expert Systems Inc* ***(P-23612)***
AES, San Diego *Also called Automotive Exch & Sup of Cal* ***(P-19587)***
Aeswave.com, Fresno *Also called Automotive Electronics Svcs* ***(P-13396)***
Aethercomm Inc .... C 760 208-6002
3205 Lionshead Ave Carlsbad (92010) ***(P-17439)***
AF Gomes Inc .... E 408 453-7300
901 Commercial St Ste 140 San Jose (95112) ***(P-12091)***
AF Machine & Tool Co Inc .... F 310 674-1919
950 W Hyde Park Blvd D Inglewood (90302) ***(P-15712)***
Afakori Inc .... E 949 859-4277
29390 Hunco Way Lake Elsinore (92530) ***(P-11738)***
Afc Finishing Systems .... E 530 533-8907
250 Airport Pkwy Oroville (95965) ***(P-12526)***
Afco, Gardena *Also called Abrasive Finishing Co* ***(P-11427)***
Afco, Alhambra *Also called Alhambra Foundry Company Ltd* ***(P-11140)***
Afco, Huntington Park *Also called Aircraft Foundry Co Inc* ***(P-11364)***
Afe Power, Corona *Also called Advanced Flow Engineering Inc* ***(P-19569)***
Affectlayer Inc .... F 650 924-1082
465 California St Ste 600 San Francisco (94104) ***(P-23576)***
Affinity Flavors, Corona *Also called Fischler Investments Inc* ***(P-2208)***
Affluent Living Publication, Anaheim *Also called Affluent Target Marketing Inc* ***(P-5877)***
Affluent Target Marketing Inc .... E 714 446-6280
3855 E La Palma Ave # 250 Anaheim (92807) ***(P-5877)***
Affordable Goods .... F 916 514-1049
131 Cognac Cir Sacramento (95835) ***(P-14883)***
Affymetrix Inc .... D 408 731-5000
3380 Central Expy Santa Clara (95051) ***(P-21162)***
Affymetrix Inc .... C 858 642-2058
5893 Oberlin Dr San Diego (92121) ***(P-21163)***

Mergent e-mail: customerrelations@mergent.com
1012
2020 California
Manufacturers Register
(P-0000) Products & Services Section entry number
(PA)=Parent Co (HQ)=Headquarters (DH)=Div Headquarters

Affymetrix Inc.......D.......408 731-5000
3450 Central Expy Santa Clara (95051) ***(P-21164)***
Affymetrix Inc (HQ).......B.......408 731-5000
3380 Central Expy Santa Clara (95051) ***(P-21165)***
Affymetrix Anatrace.......F.......408 731-5756
3380 Central Expy Santa Clara (95051) ***(P-21166)***
Afg Insulating Riverside Plant, Riverside *Also called Poma GL Specialty Windows Inc* ***(P-10273)***
Afi, Santa Clara *Also called Acu Spec Inc* ***(P-15688)***
Afn Services LLC.......E.......408 364-1564
368 E Campbell Ave Campbell (95008) ***(P-5047)***
AFP Advanced Food Products LLC.......C.......559 627-2070
1211 E Noble Ave Visalia (93292) ***(P-717)***
Afr Apparel International Inc.......D.......818 773-5000
19401 Business Center Dr Northridge (91324) ***(P-3439)***
Afresh Technologies Inc.......F.......805 551-9245
2948 20th St Apt 302 San Francisco (94110) ***(P-23577)***
Aft Corporation.......E.......310 576-1007
1815c Centinela Ave Santa Monica (90404) ***(P-7368)***
Aftco Mfg Co Inc.......D.......949 660-8757
2400 S Garnsey St Santa Ana (92707) ***(P-22734)***
After Capture, Los Angeles *Also called Rangefinder Publishing Co Inc* ***(P-6013)***
After Hours.......F.......562 925-5737
7310 Adams St Ste F Paramount (90723) ***(P-17184)***
Aftermarket Parts Company LLC.......B.......951 681-2751
10293 Birtcher Dr Jurupa Valley (91752) ***(P-19449)***
Aftermaster Inc (PA).......F.......310 657-4886
6671 W Sunset Blvd # 1520 Hollywood (90028) ***(P-22400)***
AG Global Products LLC.......E.......323 334-2900
15301 Blackburn Ave Norwalk (90650) ***(P-16824)***
AG Machining Inc.......D.......805 531-9555
609 Science Dr Moorpark (93021) ***(P-11739)***
AG Millworks, Ventura *Also called Art Glass Etc Inc* ***(P-3999)***
AG Neovo Technology Corp.......F.......408 321-8210
2362 Qume Dr Ste A San Jose (95131) ***(P-15119)***
AG Ray Inc.......F.......209 334-1999
20400 N Kennefick Rd Acampo (95220) ***(P-13604)***
AG Spraying.......F.......559 698-9507
5815 S Calaveras Ave Tranquillity (93668) ***(P-13494)***
Ag-Weld Inc.......F.......661 758-3061
1236 G St Wasco (93280) ***(P-24614)***
AGA Precision Systems Inc.......F.......714 540-3163
122 E Dyer Rd Santa Ana (92707) ***(P-15713)***
Age Incorporated.......E.......562 483-7300
14831 Spring Ave Santa Fe Springs (90670) ***(P-16585)***
Age Logistics Corporation.......F.......626 243-5253
426 E Duarte Rd Monrovia (91016) ***(P-13843)***
Agencycom LLC.......B.......415 817-3800
5353 Grosvenor Blvd Los Angeles (90066) ***(P-23578)***
Agent 18, West Hollywood *Also called Sargam International Inc* ***(P-17280)***
Agents West Inc.......E.......949 614-0293
6 Hughes Ste 210 Irvine (92618) ***(P-19250)***
Aggregate - Cache Creek S&G, Madison *Also called Cemex Cnstr Mtls PCF LLC* ***(P-10728)***
Aggregate - Lemon Cove Quarry, Woodlake *Also called Cemex Cnstr Mtls PCF LLC* ***(P-10717)***
Aggregate - Red Hill Quarry, Little Lake *Also called Kiewit Corporation* ***(P-309)***
Aggregate -Eliot Quarry, Pleasanton *Also called Cemex Cnstr Mtls PCF LLC* ***(P-10712)***
Aggregate -Patterson Quarry, Sheridan *Also called Cemex Cnstr Mtls PCF LLC* ***(P-10715)***
Aggregate -Sunol Quarry, Sunol *Also called Cemex Cnstr Mtls PCF LLC* ***(P-10410)***
Aggregate Mining Products LLC.......F.......951 277-1267
21780 Temescal Canyon Rd Corona (92883) ***(P-14558)***
Aggregate Products Inc (PA).......F.......760 395-5312
100 Brawley Ave Thermal (92274) ***(P-311)***
Aggregate West Coast, Thermal *Also called West Coast Aggregate Supply* ***(P-368)***
Aggrigator Inc.......F.......650 245-5117
30 E San Joaquin St # 202 Salinas (93901) ***(P-23579)***
Agi Publishing Inc (PA).......E.......559 251-8888
1850 N Gateway Blvd # 152 Fresno (93727) ***(P-6175)***
Agi Publishing Inc.......C.......559 251-8888
1850 N Gateway Blvd # 152 Fresno (93727) ***(P-6176)***
Agile Technologies Inc.......F.......949 454-8030
2 Orion Aliso Viejo (92656) ***(P-18072)***
Agilent Labs, Santa Clara *Also called Agilent Technologies Inc* ***(P-20994)***
Agilent Tech World Trade Inc (HQ).......F.......408 345-8886
5301 Stevens Creek Blvd Santa Clara (95051) ***(P-20986)***
Agilent Technologies Inc.......B.......510 794-1234
39201 Cherry St Newark (94560) ***(P-20987)***
Agilent Technologies Inc.......C.......916 985-7888
91 Blue Ravine Rd Folsom (95630) ***(P-20988)***
Agilent Technologies Inc.......F.......805 566-6655
1170 Mark Ave Carpinteria (93013) ***(P-20989)***
Agilent Technologies Inc.......A.......408 345-8886
5301 Stevens Creek Blvd Santa Clara (95051) ***(P-20990)***
Agilent Technologies Inc.......B.......858 373-6300
11011 N Torrey Pines Rd La Jolla (92037) ***(P-20991)***
Agilent Technologies Inc.......D.......877 424-4536
395 Page Mill Rd Palo Alto (94306) ***(P-20992)***
Agilent Technologies Inc (PA).......B.......408 345-8886
5301 Stevens Creek Blvd Santa Clara (95051) ***(P-20993)***
Agilent Technologies Inc.......A.......408 345-8886
5301 Stevens Creek Blvd Santa Clara (95051) ***(P-20994)***
Agilent Technologies Inc.......A.......408 553-7777
3175 Bowers Ave Santa Clara (95054) ***(P-20995)***
Agilent Technologies Inc.......A.......408 345-8886
30721 Russell Ranch Rd Westlake Village (91362) ***(P-20996)***
Agilent Technologies Inc.......B.......858 373-6300
11011 N Torrey Pines Rd La Jolla (92037) ***(P-20997)***
Agilepoint Inc (PA).......E.......650 968-6789
1916 Old Middlefield Way Mountain View (94043) ***(P-23580)***
Agility Fuel Systems LLC (HQ).......C.......949 236-5520
1815 Carnegie Ave Santa Ana (92705) ***(P-19573)***
Agility Fuel Systems LLC.......F.......256 831-6155
3335 Susan St Ste 100 Costa Mesa (92626) ***(P-13583)***
Agiloft Inc.......E.......650 587-8615
460 Seaport Ct Ste 200 Redwood City (94063) ***(P-23581)***
Agilone Inc (PA).......E.......877 769-3047
771 Vaqueros Ave Sunnyvale (94085) ***(P-21167)***
Agl, Temecula *Also called Artificial Grass Liquidators* ***(P-23280)***
Agnaldos Welding Inc.......F.......559 752-4254
828 S Burnett Rd Tipton (93272) ***(P-24615)***
Agoura Music.......F.......818 991-8316
625 N Sycamore Ave # 313 Los Angeles (90036) ***(P-22604)***
Agouron Pharmaceuticals Inc (HQ).......E.......858 622-3000
10777 Science Center Dr San Diego (92121) ***(P-7731)***
Agra Trading LLC.......F.......530 894-1782
60 Independence Cir # 203 Chico (95973) ***(P-8788)***
Agra-Farm Foods Inc.......F.......626 443-2335
2223 Seaman Ave El Monte (91733) ***(P-1014)***
Agraquest Inc (HQ).......D.......866 992-2937
890 Embarcadero Dr West Sacramento (95605) ***(P-7732)***
Agri Cel Inc.......D.......661 792-2107
401 Road 192 Delano (93215) ***(P-9501)***
Agri Service, Oceanside *Also called Mary Matava* ***(P-8834)***
Agribag Inc.......E.......510 533-2388
3925 Alameda Ave Oakland (94601) ***(P-2920)***
Agricultural Data Systems Inc.......F.......949 363-5353
24331 Los Arboles Dr Laguna Niguel (92677) ***(P-23582)***
Agricultural Manufacturing.......F.......559 485-1662
4106 S Cedar Ave Fresno (93725) ***(P-13702)***
Agriculture Bag Manufacturing,, Oakland *Also called Agriculture Bag Mfg USA Inc* ***(P-2721)***
Agriculture Bag Mfg USA Inc (PA).......E.......510 632-5637
960 98th Ave Oakland (94603) ***(P-2721)***
Agrifim Irrigation Pdts Inc.......F.......559 443-6680
2855 S East Ave Fresno (93725) ***(P-13605)***
Agron Inc.......D.......310 473-7223
2440 S Sepulveda Blvd # 201 Los Angeles (90064) ***(P-3460)***
Agse, Santa Fe Springs *Also called Advanced Ground Systems* ***(P-19944)***
Agt, Corona *Also called Absolute Graphic Tech USA Inc* ***(P-16693)***
Agua Dulce Vineyards LLC.......E.......661 268-7402
9640 Sierra Hwy Agua Dulce (91390) ***(P-1577)***
Aguda Wilson Ramos.......F.......209 942-2446
5409 Asbury Way Stockton (95219) ***(P-17440)***
Aguilar Williams Inc.......F.......562 693-2736
7635 Baldwin Pl Whittier (90602) ***(P-12910)***
Agusa.......E.......559 924-4785
1055 S 19th Ave Lemoore (93245) ***(P-840)***
Ah Wines Inc.......F.......209 625-8170
27 E Vine St Lodi (95240) ***(P-1578)***
Aha Labs Inc.......F.......650 575-1425
20 Gloria Cir Menlo Park (94025) ***(P-23583)***
Ahead Magnetics Inc.......D.......408 226-9800
6410 Via Del Oro San Jose (95119) ***(P-18812)***
Aheadtek, San Jose *Also called Ahead Magnetics Inc* ***(P-18812)***
Ahf-Ducommun Incorporated (HQ).......C.......310 380-5390
268 E Gardena Blvd Gardena (90248) ***(P-20024)***
Ahlborn Structural Steel Inc.......E.......707 573-0742
1230 Century Ct Santa Rosa (95403) ***(P-11740)***
Ahn Enterprises LLC.......F.......408 734-1878
1240 Birchwood Dr Ste 2 Sunnyvale (94089) ***(P-18697)***
Ahr Signs Incorporated.......F.......323 255-1102
3400 N San Fernando Rd Los Angeles (90065) ***(P-23045)***
Ai Industries LLC (PA).......D.......650 366-4099
1725 E Byshore Rd Ste 101 Redwood City (94063) ***(P-12911)***
Aidells Sausage Company Inc.......A.......510 614-5450
2411 Baumann Ave San Lorenzo (94580) ***(P-434)***
Aih LLC (HQ).......E.......760 930-4600
5810 Van Allen Way Carlsbad (92008) ***(P-16629)***
Aii Beauty, Commerce *Also called American Intl Inds Inc* ***(P-8435)***
Aim Mail Centers, Woodland *Also called American International Mfg Co* ***(P-13609)***
Aimmune Therapeutics Inc.......C.......650 614-5220
8000 Marina Blvd Ste 300 Brisbane (94005) ***(P-7733)***
Ainor Signs Inc.......F.......916 348-4370
5443 Stationers Way Sacramento (95842) ***(P-23046)***
Aip Aerospace Holdings, Irvine *Also called Coast Composites LLC* ***(P-15856)***
Aipac, Los Angeles *Also called American Israel Public Affairs* ***(P-23598)***
Air & Gas Tech Inc.......E.......619 557-8373
3191 Commercial St San Diego (92113) ***(P-20311)***
Air Bearing Technology, Hayward *Also called KLA Tencor* ***(P-14787)***
Air Blast Inc.......F.......626 576-0144
2050 Pepper St Alhambra (91801) ***(P-14645)***
Air Combat Systems, Palmdale *Also called Northrop Grumman Systems Corp* ***(P-19918)***
Air Craftors Engineering Inc.......F.......909 900-0635
4040 Cheyenne Ct Chino (91710) ***(P-15714)***
Air Distribution Products, San Pedro *Also called Kesclo Financial Inc* ***(P-12490)***
Air Dreams Mattresses.......F.......626 573-5733
3266 Rosemead Blvd El Monte (91731) ***(P-4709)***
Air Dry Co of America LLC.......E.......805 238-2840
1740 Commerce Way Paso Robles (93446) ***(P-20781)***
Air Electro, Chatsworth *Also called Aei Manufacturing Inc* ***(P-16873)***
Air Factors Inc.......F.......925 579-0040
4771 Arroyo Vis Ste D Livermore (94551) ***(P-14646)***
Air Filter Sales, Hayward *Also called Purolator Pdts A Filtration Co* ***(P-14674)***
Air Flow Research Heads Inc.......E.......661 257-8124
28611 Industry Dr Valencia (91355) ***(P-19574)***

ALPHABETIC

Air Frame Forming Inc......F......562 663-1662
15717 Colorado Ave Paramount (90723) ***(P-13965)***
Air Link International, Anaheim *Also called D & B Supply Corp* ***(P-13820)***
Air Liquid Healthcare......E......909 899-4633
12460 Arrow Rte Rancho Cucamonga (91739) ***(P-7393)***
Air Liquide Electronics US LP......E......510 624-4338
46401 Landing Pkwy Fremont (94538) ***(P-7467)***
Air Logistics Corporation (PA)......E......626 633-0294
146 Railroad Ave Monrovia (91016) ***(P-9614)***
Air Marketing......F......562 208-3990
516 E 7th St Long Beach (90813) ***(P-6177)***
Air Monitor Corporation (PA)......D......707 544-2706
1050 Hopper Ave Santa Rosa (95403) ***(P-20782)***
Air O Fan, Reedley *Also called Air-O Fan Products Corporation* ***(P-13606)***
Air Products, Vernon *Also called Evonik Corporation* ***(P-8966)***
Air Products and Chemicals Inc......E......562 944-3873
8934 Dice Rd Santa Fe Springs (90670) ***(P-7394)***
Air Products and Chemicals Inc......F......310 847-7300
23300 S Alameda St Carson (90810) ***(P-7395)***
Air Products and Chemicals Inc......E......562 437-0462
901 W 12th St Long Beach (90813) ***(P-7396)***
Air Products and Chemicals Inc......F......949 474-1860
400 Macarthur Blvd Newport Beach (92660) ***(P-7397)***
Air Products and Chemicals Inc......C......760 931-9555
1969 Palomar Oaks Way Carlsbad (92011) ***(P-7398)***
Air Products and Chemicals Inc......E......310 952-9172
700 N Henry Ford Ave Wilmington (90744) ***(P-7399)***
Air Solutions LLC......F......510 573-6474
37310 Cedar Blvd Ste J Newark (94560) ***(P-15409)***
Air Source Industries......F......562 426-4017
3976 Cherry Ave Long Beach (90807) ***(P-7400)***
Air Transport Manufacturing......F......818 504-3300
2629 Foothill Blvd La Crescenta (91214) ***(P-12092)***
Air Tube Transfer Systems Inc......E......714 363-0700
715 N Cypress St Orange (92867) ***(P-13813)***
Air-O Fan Products Corporation (PA)......F......559 638-6546
507 E Dinuba Ave Reedley (93654) ***(P-13606)***
Air-Trak......F......858 677-9950
15090 Avenue Of Science # 103 San Diego (92128) ***(P-17441)***
Air-Vol Block Inc......E......805 543-1314
1 Suburban Rd San Luis Obispo (93401) ***(P-10498)***
Aira Tech Corp......E......619 271-9152
4225 Executive Sq Ste 400 La Jolla (92037) ***(P-23584)***
Airbolt Industries Inc......F......818 767-5600
25334 Stanford Ave Unit B Valencia (91355) ***(P-11407)***
Airborne Components, Carson *Also called Stanford Mu Corporation* ***(P-20480)***
Airborne Systems N Amer CA Inc......C......714 662-1400
3100 W Segerstrom Ave Santa Ana (92704) ***(P-3830)***
Airborne Technologies Inc......D......805 389-3700
999 Avenida Acaso Camarillo (93012) ***(P-20025)***
Aircoat Inc......F......310 527-2258
13405 S Broadway Los Angeles (90061) ***(P-13139)***
Aircraft Covers Inc......D......408 738-3959
18850 Adams Ct Morgan Hill (95037) ***(P-2664)***
Aircraft Foundry Co Inc......F......323 587-3171
5316 Pacific Blvd Huntington Park (90255) ***(P-11364)***
Aircraft Hinge Inc......E......661 257-3434
28338 Constellation Rd # 970 Santa Clarita (91355) ***(P-20026)***
Aircraft Stamping Company Inc......E......323 283-1239
1285 Paseo Alicia San Dimas (91773) ***(P-12093)***
Aircraft Technical Publishers (PA)......D......415 330-9500
2000 Sierra Point Pkwy # 501 Brisbane (94005) ***(P-6178)***
Airdyne Refrigeration, Cerritos *Also called Refrigerator Manufacturers LLC* ***(P-15452)***
Airdyne Refrigeration, Cerritos *Also called ARI Industries Inc* ***(P-15413)***
Airex, Anaheim *Also called Emitcon Inc* ***(P-20968)***
Airflex5d LLC......F......855 574-0158
12282 Knott St Garden Grove (92841) ***(P-4680)***
Airgain Inc (PA)......C......760 579-0200
3611 Valley Centre Dr # 150 San Diego (92130) ***(P-17442)***
Airgard Inc (PA)......E......408 573-0701
1755 Mccarthy Blvd Milpitas (95035) ***(P-14647)***
Airgas Inc......F......714 521-4789
15116 Canary Ave La Mirada (90638) ***(P-8789)***
Airgas Usa LLC......F......650 873-4212
315 Harbor Way South San Francisco (94080) ***(P-7401)***
Airgas Usa LLC......E......760 744-1472
1415 Grand Ave San Marcos (92078) ***(P-7402)***
Airgas Usa LLC......E......562 946-8394
9810 Jordan Cir Santa Fe Springs (90670) ***(P-7403)***
Airgas Usa LLC......D......510 429-4200
700 Decoto Rd Union City (94587) ***(P-7404)***
Airgas Usa LLC......F......925 969-0419
1750 Clinton Dr Concord (94521) ***(P-7405)***
Airgas Usa LLC......E......562 945-1383
8832 Dice Rd Santa Fe Springs (90670) ***(P-7406)***
Airgas Usa LLC......F......818 787-6010
7254 Coldwater Canyon Ave North Hollywood (91605) ***(P-7407)***
Airgas Usa LLC......E......510 624-4000
46409 Landing Pkwy Fremont (94538) ***(P-7408)***
Airgas Usa LLC......E......562 906-8700
9756 Santa Fe Springs Rd Santa Fe Springs (90670) ***(P-7409)***
Airgas Usa LLC......E......661 201-8107
311 Kentucky St Bakersfield (93305) ***(P-7410)***
Airgas Usa LLC......F......909 899-4670
12550 Arrow Rte Rancho Cucamonga (91739) ***(P-7411)***
Airo Industries Company......E......818 838-1008
429 Jessie St San Fernando (91340) ***(P-4852)***
Airparts Express Inc......D......714 308-2764
3420 W Macarthur Blvd G Santa Ana (92704) ***(P-20027)***
Airpoint Precision Inc......F......530 622-0510
6221 Enterprise Dr Ste D Diamond Springs (95619) ***(P-15715)***
Airsoft Megastore, Arcadia *Also called Airsoft Zone Corporation* ***(P-22735)***
Airsoft Zone Corporation (PA)......E......818 495-6502
138 E Longden Ave Arcadia (91006) ***(P-22735)***
Airspace Seal and Gasket Corp......E......951 256-8380
1476 Davril Cir Corona (92880) ***(P-9217)***
Airspace Systems Inc......E......310 704-7155
1933 Davis St Ste 229 San Leandro (94577) ***(P-16694)***
Airstream of Orange County, Midway City *Also called Lin Consulting LLC* ***(P-20489)***
Airtech Advanced Mtls Group, Huntington Beach *Also called Airtech International Inc* ***(P-20028)***
Airtech International Inc (PA)......C......714 899-8100
5700 Skylab Rd Huntington Beach (92647) ***(P-20028)***
Airtronics Metal Products Inc (PA)......C......408 977-7800
140 San Pedro Ave Morgan Hill (95037) ***(P-12094)***
Airware, San Francisco *Also called Unmanned Innovation Inc* ***(P-19936)***
Airworthy Cabin Solutions LLC......F......714 901-0660
1560 S Harris Ct Anaheim (92806) ***(P-11559)***
Aisin Electronics Inc......C......209 983-4988
199 Frank West Cir Stockton (95206) ***(P-16695)***
Aisling Industries, Calexico *Also called Creation Tech Calexico Inc* ***(P-17856)***
Aitech Defense Systems Inc......E......818 700-2000
19756 Prairie St Chatsworth (91311) ***(P-19251)***
Aitech Rugged Group Inc (PA)......E......818 700-2000
19756 Prairie St Chatsworth (91311) ***(P-19252)***
Aixtron Inc......C......669 228-3759
1700 Wyatt Dr Ste 15 Santa Clara (95054) ***(P-18073)***
Aja Video Systems Inc (PA)......E......530 274-2048
180 Litton Dr Grass Valley (95945) ***(P-17443)***
Ajax, Union City *Also called Ichor Systems Inc* ***(P-9833)***
Ajax - Untd Pttrns & Molds Inc......C......510 476-8000
34585 7th St Union City (94587) ***(P-9615)***
Ajax Custom Manufacturing, Union City *Also called Ajax - Untd Pttrns & Molds Inc* ***(P-9615)***
Ajax Forge Company (PA)......E......323 582-6307
1956 E 48th St Vernon (90058) ***(P-12702)***
Ajax Forge Company......E......323 582-6307
1960 E 48th St Vernon (90058) ***(P-12703)***
Ajg Inc......E......323 346-0171
7220 E Slauson Ave Commerce (90040) ***(P-3506)***
Ajile Systems Inc (PA)......E......408 557-0829
920 Saratoga Ave Ste 104 San Jose (95129) ***(P-18074)***
Ajinomoto Bio-Pharma Services, San Diego *Also called Althea Ajinomoto Inc* ***(P-21594)***
Ajinomoto Foods North Amer Inc......F......510 293-1838
2395 American Ave Hayward (94545) ***(P-936)***
Ajinomoto Foods North Amer Inc......C......909 477-4700
4200 Concours Ste 100 Ontario (91764) ***(P-937)***
Ajinomoto Foods North Amer Inc (HQ)......D......909 477-4700
4200 Concours Ste 100 Ontario (91764) ***(P-938)***
Ajinomoto Windsor Inc......C......323 277-7000
6711 S Alameda St Los Angeles (90001) ***(P-939)***
AJW Construction......E......510 568-2300
966 81st Ave Oakland (94621) ***(P-9086)***
AK Darcy, Costa Mesa *Also called Darcy AK Corporation* ***(P-15879)***
AK Industries, Compton *Also called Allan Kidd* ***(P-16875)***
AK Mak Bakeries Division, Sanger *Also called Soojians Inc* ***(P-1330)***
Akamai Technologies Inc......E......617 444-3000
1400 Fashion Island Blvd # 15 San Mateo (94404) ***(P-23585)***
Akaranta Inc......F......909 989-9800
8661 Baseline Rd Rancho Cucamonga (91730) ***(P-7734)***
Akas Manufacturing Corporation......E......510 786-3200
3200 Investment Blvd Hayward (94545) ***(P-12095)***
Aker International Inc......E......619 423-5182
2248 Main St Ste 4 Chula Vista (91911) ***(P-10244)***
Aker Leather Products, Chula Vista *Also called Aker International Inc* ***(P-10244)***
Akido Printing Inc......F......510 357-0238
2096 Merced St San Leandro (94577) ***(P-6399)***
Akimbo Systems Inc......E......650 292-3330
411 Borel Ave Ste 100 San Mateo (94402) ***(P-23586)***
Akira Seiki U S A Inc......F......925 443-1200
255 Capitol St Livermore (94551) ***(P-13903)***
Akm Fire Inc......E......818 343-8208
18322 Oxnard St Tarzana (91356) ***(P-14794)***
Akm Semiconductor Inc......E......408 436-8580
1731 Tech Dr Ste 500 San Jose (95110) ***(P-18075)***
Akn Holdings LLC (PA)......F......310 432-7100
10250 Constellation Blvd Los Angeles (90067) ***(P-5878)***
Akon Incorporated......D......408 432-8039
2135 Ringwood Ave San Jose (95131) ***(P-23267)***
Akra Plastic Products Inc......E......909 930-1999
1504 E Cedar St Ontario (91761) ***(P-9616)***
Akt, Paso Robles *Also called Advanced Keyboard Tech Inc* ***(P-14881)***
Akt America Inc (HQ)......B......408 563-5455
3101 Scott Blvd Bldg 91 Santa Clara (95054) ***(P-19253)***
Aktana Inc......E......888 707-3125
207 Powell St Ste 800 San Francisco (94102) ***(P-23587)***
Akupara Games LLC......F......747 998-2193
17336 Boswell Pl Granada Hills (91344) ***(P-23588)***
Akzo Nobel Inc......E......714 966-0934
3010 Bristol St Costa Mesa (92626) ***(P-8709)***
Akzo Nobel Inc......E......760 743-7374
735 N Escondido Blvd Escondido (92025) ***(P-8710)***
Al & Krla Pipe Fabricators Inc......F......619 448-0060
8047 Wing Ave El Cajon (92020) ***(P-13456)***
Al Fresco Concepts Inc......F......408 497-1579
16875 Joleen Way Unit 170 Morgan Hill (95037) ***(P-18076)***
Al Industries, Santa Ana *Also called Acrontos Manufacturing Inc* ***(P-12759)***
Al Johnson Company, Camarillo *Also called Gc International Inc* ***(P-17324)***

ALPHABETIC SECTION

Align Aerospace LLC (HQ)

Al Kramp Specialties ....E....209 464-7539
1707 El Pinal Dr Stockton (95205) ***(P-17097)***
Al Shellco LLC (HQ) ....C....570 296-6444
9330 Scranton Rd Ste 600 San Diego (92121) ***(P-17185)***
Al's Machine Shop, Ontario *Also called Portable Spndle Repr Spcialist* ***(P-14292)***
Al-Mag Heat Treat ....F....626 442-8570
9735 Alpaca St South El Monte (91733) ***(P-11431)***
Alabama Metal Industries Corp ....E....909 350-9280
11093 Beech Ave Fontana (92337) ***(P-12448)***
Alaco Ladder Company, Chino *Also called B E & P Enterprises LLC* ***(P-4492)***
Alaco Ladder Company ....E....909 591-7561
5167 G St Chino (91710) ***(P-4489)***
Alameda Construction Svcs Inc ....E....310 635-3277
2528 E 125th St Compton (90222) ***(P-329)***
Alameda Directory Inc ....F....510 747-1060
1416 Park Ave Alameda (94501) ***(P-6179)***
Alameda Newspapers Inc (HQ) ....C....510 783-6111
22533 Foothill Blvd Hayward (94541) ***(P-5546)***
Alameda Newspapers Inc ....D....650 348-4321
1080 S Amphlett Blvd San Mateo (94402) ***(P-5547)***
Alamillo Radolfo ....F....323 773-9614
4901 Patata St Ste 404 Cudahy (90201) ***(P-10295)***
Alan Hamilton Industries ....D....818 885-5121
21020 Lassen St Chatsworth (91311) ***(P-6400)***
Alan Johnson Prfmce Engrg Inc ....E....805 922-1202
1097 Foxen Canyon Rd Santa Maria (93454) ***(P-19450)***
Alan Lem & Co Inc ....E....310 538-4282
515 W 130th St Los Angeles (90061) ***(P-10336)***
Alan Pre-Fab Building Corp ....F....310 538-0333
17817 Evelyn Ave Gardena (90248) ***(P-4454)***
Alan Wofsy Fine Arts LLC ....F....415 292-6500
1109 Geary Blvd San Francisco (94109) ***(P-6067)***
Alannas Engineer Manufacturing, Chatsworth *Also called Perez Severino* ***(P-13538)***
Alard Machine Products, Gardena *Also called GT Precision Inc* ***(P-12633)***
Alarin Aircraft Hinge Inc ....E....323 725-1666
6231 Randolph St Commerce (90040) ***(P-11560)***
Alasco Rubber & Plastics Corp ....F....707 823-5270
1250 Enos Ave Sebastopol (95472) ***(P-9280)***
Alation Inc (PA) ....E....650 779-4440
3 Lagoon Dr Ste 300 Redwood City (94065) ***(P-23589)***
Alatus Aerosystems (PA) ....C....610 251-1000
17055 Gale Ave City of Industry (91745) ***(P-20029)***
Alatus Aerosystems ....D....626 498-7376
9301 Mason Ave Chatsworth (91311) ***(P-20030)***
Albanay Aquatic Center, Albany *Also called Albany Swimming Pool* ***(P-22736)***
Albany Swimming Pool ....E....510 559-6640
1311 Portland Ave Albany (94706) ***(P-22736)***
Albers Dairy Equipment. Inc, Chino *Also called Albers Mfg Co Inc* ***(P-13607)***
Albers Mfg Co Inc (PA) ....E....909 597-5537
14323 Albers Way Chino (91710) ***(P-13607)***
Albert Goyenetche Dairy ....F....661 764-6176
6041 Brandt Rd Buttonwillow (93206) ***(P-682)***
Albion Knitting Mills Inc ....E....213 624-7740
2152 Sacramento St Los Angeles (90021) ***(P-3283)***
ALC, Fresno *Also called Auernheimer Labs Inc* ***(P-17197)***
Alcast Mfg Inc (PA) ....E....310 542-3581
7355 E Slauson Ave Commerce (90040) ***(P-11365)***
Alcast Mfg Inc ....E....310 542-3581
2910 Fisk Ln Redondo Beach (90278) ***(P-11351)***
Alcatel-Lucent USA, San Jose *Also called Nokia of America Corporation* ***(P-17390)***
Alcatel-Lucent USA Inc ....F....310 297-2620
2361 Rosecrans Ave # 150 El Segundo (90245) ***(P-15149)***
Alcatel-Lucent USA Inc ....E....510 475-5000
30971a San Benito St Hayward (94544) ***(P-17343)***
Alcatel-Lucent USA Inc ....B....408 878-6500
701 E Middlefield Rd Mountain View (94043) ***(P-18077)***
Alcatel-Lucent USA Inc ....E....818 880-3500
26801 Agoura Rd Calabasas (91301) ***(P-17344)***
Alcine Gazette, El Cajon *Also called East County Gazette* ***(P-5623)***
Alco Designs, Gardena *Also called Vege-Mist Inc* ***(P-15470)***
Alco Engrg & Tooling Corp ....E....714 556-6060
3001 Oak St Santa Ana (92707) ***(P-12096)***
Alco Manufacturing Inc ....F....714 549-5007
207 E Alton Ave Santa Ana (92707) ***(P-14011)***
Alco Metal Fab, Santa Ana *Also called Alco Engrg & Tooling Corp* ***(P-12096)***
Alco Plating Corp (PA) ....C....213 749-7561
1400 Long Beach Ave Los Angeles (90021) ***(P-12912)***
Alco Tech Inc ....F....818 503-9209
12750 Raymer St Unit 2 North Hollywood (91605) ***(P-12762)***
Alcoa, Newbury Park *Also called Arconic Inc* ***(P-11178)***
Alcoa, Fullerton *Also called Arconic Inc* ***(P-11179)***
Alcoa, Fullerton *Also called Arconic Inc* ***(P-11180)***
Alcoa, Torrance *Also called Arconic Inc* ***(P-11181)***
Alcoa, Sylmar *Also called Arconic Inc* ***(P-11182)***
Alcon Lensx Inc (HQ) ....D....949 753-1393
15800 Alton Pkwy Irvine (92618) ***(P-21586)***
Alcon Manufacturing Ltd (PA) ....F....949 753-1393
15800 Alton Pkwy Irvine (92618) ***(P-7735)***
Alcon Surgical, Irvine *Also called Alcon Vision LLC* ***(P-21587)***
Alcon Vision LLC ....A....949 753-6488
15800 Alton Pkwy Irvine (92618) ***(P-21587)***
Alcotrevi Inc ....F....818 244-0400
1133 S Central Ave 1 Glendale (91204) ***(P-21588)***
Alder & Co LLC ....F....661 326-0320
412 Wallace St Bakersfield (93307) ***(P-4545)***
Alder Creek Millwork ....E....916 379-9831
8409 Rovana Cir Ste 7 Sacramento (95828) ***(P-4162)***
Alderman Logging, Sonora *Also called Alderman Timber Company Inc* ***(P-3870)***
Alderman Timber Company Inc ....F....209 532-9636
17180 Alderman Rd Sonora (95370) ***(P-3870)***
Aldetec Inc ....E....916 453-3382
3560 Business Dr Ste 100 Sacramento (95820) ***(P-17444)***
Aldila Inc (HQ) ....D....858 513-1801
1945 Kellogg Ave Carlsbad (92008) ***(P-22737)***
Aldila Inc ....C....858 513-1801
13450 Stowe Dr Poway (92064) ***(P-22738)***
Aldila De Poway, Poway *Also called Aldila Inc* ***(P-22738)***
Aldila Golf Corp ....C....858 513-1801
13450 Stowe Dr Poway (92064) ***(P-22739)***
Aldila Golf Corp (HQ) ....D....858 513-1801
1945 Kellogg Ave Carlsbad (92008) ***(P-22740)***
Aldila Materials Technology (HQ) ....E....858 513-1801
13450 Stowe Dr Poway (92064) ***(P-8940)***
Aldo Fragale ....F....310 324-0050
17813 S Main St Ste 111 Gardena (90248) ***(P-15716)***
Aldran Chemical Inc ....E....650 347-8242
1313 N Carolan Ave Burlingame (94010) ***(P-8359)***
Ale USA Inc ....A....818 878-4816
26801 Agoura Rd Calabasas (91301) ***(P-17445)***
Alectro Inc ....F....909 590-9521
6770 Central Ave Ste B Riverside (92504) ***(P-16540)***
Aleeda Wetsuits, Huntington Beach *Also called Sgt Boardriders Inc* ***(P-9371)***
Alegacy Foodservice Products ....D....562 320-3100
12683 Corral Pl Santa Fe Springs (90670) ***(P-5048)***
Aleks Corporation (PA) ....F....714 245-7191
15640 Laguna Canyon Rd Irvine (92618) ***(P-23590)***
Aleks Educational Systems, Irvine *Also called Aleks Corporation* ***(P-23590)***
Alemad Inc ....E....530 661-1697
2061 Freeway Dr Ste C Woodland (95776) ***(P-4878)***
Alembic Inc ....F....707 523-2611
3005 Wiljan Ct Ste A Santa Rosa (95407) ***(P-22605)***
Aleph Group Inc ....E....951 213-4815
1900 E Alessndro Blvd # 105 Riverside (92508) ***(P-19451)***
Aleph Group Inc ....F....951 213-4815
6920 Sycamore Canyon Blvd Riverside (92507) ***(P-21589)***
Aleratec Inc ....E....818 678-6900
9851 Owensmouth Ave Chatsworth (91311) ***(P-14884)***
Alere Connect LLC ....E....888 876-3327
9975 Summers Ridge Rd San Diego (92121) ***(P-22227)***
Alere Inc ....B....510 732-7200
6465 National Dr Livermore (94550) ***(P-8201)***
Alere San Diego Inc ....A....858 455-4808
9975 Summers Ridge Rd San Diego (92121) ***(P-8202)***
Alert Plating Company ....E....818 771-9304
9939 Glenoaks Blvd Sun Valley (91352) ***(P-12913)***
Alertenterprise Inc ....C....510 440-0840
4350 Starboard Dr Fremont (94538) ***(P-23591)***
Alex Design Inc ....F....916 386-8020
8541 Younger Creek Dr # 400 Sacramento (95828) ***(P-4163)***
Alex Tronix, Fresno *Also called GNA Industries Inc* ***(P-16719)***
Alex Velvet Inc ....E....323 255-6900
3334 Eagle Rock Blvd Los Angeles (90065) ***(P-22489)***
Alexander Business Supplies ....F....818 346-1820
21500 Wyandotte St # 110 Canoga Park (91303) ***(P-6401)***
Alexander Color Printing, Canoga Park *Also called Alexander Business Supplies* ***(P-6401)***
Alexander Valley Gourmet LLC ....E....707 473-0116
140 Grove Ct B Healdsburg (95448) ***(P-2389)***
Alexander Valley Vineyards, Healdsburg *Also called AVV Winery Co LLC* ***(P-1586)***
Alexander's Costumes, San Bernardino *Also called Alexanders Textile Pdts Inc* ***(P-3537)***
Alexanders Textile Pdts Inc ....F....951 276-2500
200 N D St San Bernardino (92401) ***(P-3537)***
Alfa Scientific Designs Inc ....D....858 513-3888
13200 Gregg St Poway (92064) ***(P-8203)***
Alfonso Jaramillo ....F....951 276-2777
2225 E Cooley Dr Colton (92324) ***(P-13372)***
Alfred Domaine ....F....805 541-9463
7525 Orcutt Rd San Luis Obispo (93401) ***(P-1579)***
Alfred Music Group Inc (PA) ....E....818 891-5999
16320 Roscoe Blvd Ste 100 Van Nuys (91406) ***(P-6068)***
Alfred Picon ....F....562 928-2561
7644 Emil Ave Bell (90201) ***(P-4962)***
Alfred's Machining, Plymouth *Also called Acm Machining Inc* ***(P-15683)***
Alfredo Hernandez ....F....909 971-9320
474 W Arrow Hwy Ste K San Dimas (91773) ***(P-15717)***
Alger Alternative Energy LLC ....F....317 493-5289
1536 Jones St Brawley (92227) ***(P-10967)***
Alger International, Los Angeles *Also called Alger-Triton Inc* ***(P-16958)***
Alger Precision Machining LLC ....C....909 986-4591
724 S Bon View Ave Ontario (91761) ***(P-12617)***
Alger-Triton Inc ....E....310 229-9500
5600 W Jefferson Blvd Los Angeles (90016) ***(P-16958)***
Algonquin Power Sanger LLC ....E....559 875-0800
1125 Muscat Ave Sanger (93657) ***(P-16541)***
Alhambra Foundry Company Ltd ....E....626 289-4294
1147 S Meridian Ave Alhambra (91803) ***(P-11140)***
Alice G Fink-Painter, Santa Fe Springs *Also called Spec Tool Company* ***(P-20727)***
Alien Technology LLC (PA) ....E....408 782-3900
845 Embedded Way San Jose (95138) ***(P-17446)***
Alienvault Inc (HQ) ....F....650 713-3333
1100 Park Pl Ste 300 San Mateo (94403) ***(P-23592)***
Alienvault LLC (HQ) ....D....650 713-3333
1100 Park Pl Ste 300 San Mateo (94403) ***(P-23593)***
Align Aerospace Holding Inc (HQ) ....F....818 727-7800
21123 Nordhoff St Chatsworth (91311) ***(P-11152)***
Align Aerospace LLC (HQ) ....C....818 727-7800
9401 De Soto Ave Chatsworth (91311) ***(P-20031)***

ALPHABETIC

Employee Codes: A=Over 500 employees, B=251-500
C=101-250, D=51-100, E=20-50, F=10-19

2020 California
Manfacturers Register

© Mergent Inc. 1-800-342-5647
1015

Align Technology Inc (PA)...B......408 470-1000
2820 Orchard Pkwy San Jose (95134) ***(P-22131)***
Alinabal Inc...E......661 877-9356
29101 The Old Rd Valencia (91355) ***(P-11477)***
Alion Energy Inc...D......510 965-0868
2200 Central St D Richmond (94801) ***(P-18078)***
Alios Biopharma, Inc., South San Francisco *Also called Janssen Biopharma Inc* ***(P-7968)***
Alisa Michelle Designs, Studio City *Also called Michelle Alisa Designs Inc* ***(P-22549)***
Alive & Radiant Foods Inc...E......510 238-0128
2921 Adeline St Emeryville (94608) ***(P-2316)***
Alivecor Inc (PA)...E......650 396-8650
444 Castro St Ste 600 Mountain View (94041) ***(P-23594)***
Alj, Camarillo *Also called Gc International Inc* ***(P-17323)***
All About Printing, Canoga Park *Also called Barrys Printing Inc* ***(P-6436)***
All Access Apparel Inc (PA)...C......323 889-4300
1515 Gage Rd Montebello (90640) ***(P-3473)***
All Access Stging Prdctons Inc (PA)...D......310 784-2464
1320 Storm Pkwy Torrance (90501) ***(P-17098)***
All Ameri Injec Moldi Servi, Temecula *Also called TST Molding LLC* ***(P-10095)***
All American Cabinetry Inc...D......818 376-0500
13901 Saticoy St Van Nuys (91402) ***(P-4879)***
All American Fabrication...F......831 676-3490
1328 Burton Ave Ste B10 Salinas (93901) ***(P-23268)***
All American Frame & Bedg Corp...E......323 773-7415
4641 Ardine St Cudahy (90201) ***(P-4681)***
All American Label, Dublin *Also called A A Label Inc* ***(P-5488)***
All American Label...E......213 622-2222
1700 Wall St Los Angeles (90015) ***(P-2749)***
All American Modular LLC...F......209 744-0400
750 Spaans Dr Ste F Galt (95632) ***(P-4455)***
All American Pipe Bending, Santa Ana *Also called Saf-T-Co Supply* ***(P-16954)***
All American Plastic & Packg, National City *Also called Ghazal & Sons Inc* ***(P-5397)***
All American Racers Inc...C......714 557-2116
2334 S Broadway Santa Ana (92707) ***(P-20380)***
All American Sterile Coat, Van Nuys *Also called All American Cabinetry Inc* ***(P-4879)***
All Bay Pallet Company Inc (PA)...E......510 636-4131
24993 Tarman Ave Hayward (94544) ***(P-4345)***
All City Printing Inc...F......415 861-8088
1061 Howard St San Francisco (94103) ***(P-6402)***
All Diameter Grinding Inc...E......714 744-1200
725 N Main St Orange (92868) ***(P-15718)***
All Energy Inc...F......619 988-7030
3401 Adams Ave A28 San Diego (92116) ***(P-17099)***
All Forms Express...F......714 596-8641
17572 Griffin Ln Huntington Beach (92647) ***(P-6979)***
All Good Pallets Inc...E......209 467-7000
1055 Diamond St Stockton (95205) ***(P-4346)***
All Label Inc...F......626 964-6744
17989 Arenth Ave City of Industry (91748) ***(P-5490)***
All Manufacturers Inc...E......951 280-4200
2900 Palisades Dr Corona (92880) ***(P-21590)***
All Metal Fabrication...F......626 449-6191
617 S Raymond Ave Pasadena (91105) ***(P-12097)***
All Metals Inc (PA)...E......408 200-7000
705 Reed St Santa Clara (95050) ***(P-11197)***
All Metals Proc San Diego Inc...C......714 828-8238
8401 Standustrial St Stanton (90680) ***(P-12914)***
All New Stamping Co...C......626 443-8813
10801 Lower Azusa Rd El Monte (91731) ***(P-12763)***
All One God Faith Inc (PA)...C......844 937-2551
1335 Park Center Dr Vista (92081) ***(P-8335)***
All Power Manufacturing Co...F......562 802-2640
13141 Molette St Santa Fe Springs (90670) ***(P-23269)***
All Pure Pool Service, Yucaipa *Also called SCC Chemical Corporation* ***(P-7392)***
All Quality & Services Inc...C......510 249-5800
47817 Fremont Blvd Fremont (94538) ***(P-17809)***
All Sales Manufacturing Inc...E......916 933-0236
5121 Hillsdale Cir El Dorado Hills (95762) ***(P-19575)***
All Sensors Corporation...E......408 776-9434
16035 Vineyard Blvd Morgan Hill (95037) ***(P-18079)***
All Source Coatings Inc...E......858 586-0903
10625 Scripps Ranch Blvd D San Diego (92131) ***(P-13140)***
All Spec Sheet Metal Inc...F......925 427-4900
547 Bliss Ave Pittsburg (94565) ***(P-12098)***
All Sports Services Inc...F......909 885-4626
1814 Commercecenter W Ste G San Bernardino (92408) ***(P-6980)***
All Star Clothing Inc...F......323 233-7773
4507 Staunton Ave Vernon (90058) ***(P-3135)***
All Star Precision...E......909 944-8373
8739 Lion St Rancho Cucamonga (91730) ***(P-15719)***
All Stars Packaging Inc...F......626 664-3797
13851 Roswell Ave Ste H Chino (91710) ***(P-5155)***
All Stars Packaging & Display, Chino *Also called All Stars Packaging Inc* ***(P-5155)***
All Strong Industry (usa) Inc (PA)...E......909 598-6494
326 Paseo Tesoro Walnut (91789) ***(P-5013)***
All Technology Machine, Irvine *Also called Lubrication Scientifics Inc* ***(P-13312)***
All Time Machine Inc...F......909 673-1899
2050 Del Rio Way Ontario (91761) ***(P-15720)***
All Weather Inc...D......916 928-1000
1065 National Dr Ste 1 Sacramento (95834) ***(P-21430)***
All Weather Insulated Panels, Vacaville *Also called Pre-Insulated Metal Tech Inc* ***(P-12570)***
All Weld Mch & Fabrication Co, San Jose *Also called O-S Inc* ***(P-16254)***
All West Container, San Francisco *Also called Packageone Inc* ***(P-5252)***
All West Fabricators Inc...E......510 623-1200
44875 Fremont Blvd Fremont (94538) ***(P-11741)***
All West Plastics Inc...E......714 894-9922
5451 Argosy Ave Huntington Beach (92649) ***(P-9427)***
All-American Mfg Co...E......323 581-6293
2201 E 51st St Vernon (90058) ***(P-11653)***
All-Battery.com, Fremont *Also called Tenergy Corporation* ***(P-19175)***
All-Star Lettering Inc...E......562 404-5995
9419 Ann St Santa Fe Springs (90670) ***(P-6981)***
All-Star Logo, Inglewood *Also called All-Star Mktg & Promotions Inc* ***(P-3721)***
All-Star Mktg & Promotions Inc...F......323 582-4880
8715 Aviation Blvd Inglewood (90301) ***(P-3721)***
All-Tech Machine & Engrg Inc...E......510 353-2000
2700 Prune Ave Fremont (94539) ***(P-15721)***
All-Truss Inc...E......707 938-5595
22700 Broadway Sonoma (95476) ***(P-4286)***
All-Ways Metal Inc...E......310 217-1177
401 E Alondra Blvd Gardena (90248) ***(P-12099)***
Allakos Inc...E......650 597-5002
975 Island Dr Ste 201 Redwood City (94065) ***(P-7736)***
Allan Aircraft Supply Co LLC...E......818 765-4992
11643 Vanowen St North Hollywood (91605) ***(P-13344)***
Allan Copley Designs, Chula Vista *Also called DStyle Inc* ***(P-13517)***
Allan Kidd...E......310 762-1600
3115 E Las Hermanas St Compton (90221) ***(P-16875)***
Allbirds Inc...C......888 963-8944
730 Montgomery St San Francisco (94111) ***(P-10157)***
Allblack Co Inc...E......562 946-2955
13090 Park St Santa Fe Springs (90670) ***(P-12915)***
Allbrite Car Care Products...F......714 666-8683
1201 N Las Brisas St Anaheim (92806) ***(P-8360)***
Alldata LLC...D......916 684-5200
9650 W Taron Dr Ste 100 Elk Grove (95757) ***(P-23595)***
Alldigital Holdings Inc...F......949 250-7340
1405 Warner Ave Ste A Tustin (92780) ***(P-23596)***
Allegra...F......415 824-9610
434 9th St San Francisco (94103) ***(P-6403)***
Allegra Print & Imaging, San Diego *Also called JA Ferrari Print Imaging LLC* ***(P-6659)***
Allegro, South Gate *Also called Conair Corporation* ***(P-16807)***
Allegro Copy & Print, Lafayette *Also called Acp Ventures* ***(P-6395)***
Allegro Pacific Corporation...F......323 724-0101
7250 Oxford Way Commerce (90040) ***(P-10231)***
Allen Industrial Inc...F......951 849-4966
960 S Hathaway St Banning (92220) ***(P-12916)***
Allen Mold Inc...F......714 538-6517
1100 W Katella Ave Ste N Orange (92867) ***(P-9617)***
Allen Morgan...F......714 538-7492
1233 W Collins Ave Orange (92867) ***(P-14752)***
Allen Reed Company Inc...F......310 575-8704
25000 Avenue Stanford # 208 Valencia (91355) ***(P-5097)***
Allen Sarah &...E......415 242-0906
560 Crestlake Dr San Francisco (94132) ***(P-15150)***
Allergan Inc...C......512 527-6688
735 Workman Mill Rd Whittier (90601) ***(P-7737)***
Allergan Sales LLC...E......408 376-3001
503 Vandell Way Ste A Campbell (95008) ***(P-7738)***
Allergan Sales LLC...E......714 246-2288
18655a Teller Ave Irvine (92612) ***(P-7739)***
Allergan Sales LLC (HQ)...A......862 261-7000
2525 Dupont Dr Irvine (92612) ***(P-7740)***
Allergan Spclty Thrpeutics Inc...A......714 246-4500
2525 Dupont Dr Irvine (92612) ***(P-7741)***
Allergan Usa Inc...A......714 427-1900
18581 Teller Ave Irvine (92612) ***(P-7742)***
Allergy Research Group LLC...E......510 263-2000
2300 N Loop Rd Alameda (94502) ***(P-7743)***
Allhealth Inc...C......213 538-0762
515 S Figueroa St # 1300 Los Angeles (90071) ***(P-14885)***
Alliance Air Products Llc...C......619 428-9688
2285 Michael Faraday Dr San Diego (92154) ***(P-15410)***
Alliance Analytical Inc...E......800 916-5600
355 Fairview Way Milpitas (95035) ***(P-8268)***
Alliance Apparel Inc...E......323 888-8900
3422 Garfield Ave Commerce (90040) ***(P-3136)***
Alliance Chemical & Envmtl...F......805 385-3330
1721 Ives Ave Oxnard (93033) ***(P-12917)***
Alliance Display & Packaging, Burbank *Also called Westrock Rkt Company* ***(P-5281)***
Alliance Fiber Optic Pdts Inc...D......408 736-6900
275 Gibraltar Dr Sunnyvale (94089) ***(P-10296)***
Alliance Finishing and Mfg, Oxnard *Also called Alliance Chemical & Envmtl* ***(P-12917)***
Alliance Hose & Extrusions Inc...E......714 202-8500
533 W Collins Ave Orange (92867) ***(P-8711)***
Alliance Medical Products Inc...C......949 768-4690
9342 9292 Jeronimo Rd Irvine (92618) ***(P-21591)***
Alliance Memory Inc...F......650 610-6800
511 Taylor Way San Carlos (94070) ***(P-18080)***
Alliance Metal Products Inc...C......818 709-1204
20844 Plummer St Chatsworth (91311) ***(P-12100)***
Alliance Multimedia LLC...F......760 522-3455
2033 San Elijo Ave Ste 20 Cardiff (92007) ***(P-6982)***
Alliance Ready Mix Inc (PA)...E......805 343-0360
915 Sheridan Rd Arroyo Grande (93420) ***(P-10683)***
Alliance Spacesystems LLC...C......714 226-1400
4398 Corporate Center Dr Los Alamitos (90720) ***(P-16680)***
Alliance Tags...E......858 549-7297
9235 Trade Pl San Diego (92126) ***(P-6983)***
Alliance Technical Svcs Inc...F......805 606-3020
1785 Utah Ave Lompoc (93437) ***(P-20276)***
Alliance Trutrus, San Diego *Also called Commercial Truss Co* ***(P-4296)***
Alliance Welding Supplies, San Jose *Also called Tech Air Northern Cal LLC* ***(P-7451)***
Alliance Welding Supplies, Livermore *Also called Tech Air Northern Cal LLC* ***(P-7452)***
Alliance Welding Supplies, Oakland *Also called Tech Air Northern Cal LLC* ***(P-7456)***

Mergent e-mail: customerrelations@mergent.com
1016
2020 California
Manufacturers Register
(P-0000) Products & Services Section entry number
(PA)=Parent Co (HQ)=Headquarters (DH)=Div Headquarters

Alliant Tchsystems Oprtons LLC......F......408 513-3271
151 Martinvale Ln Ste 150 San Jose (95119) *(P-13274)*
Alliant Tchsystems Oprtons LLC......F......818 887-8195
9401 Corbin Ave Northridge (91324) *(P-20532)*
Allied Bio Medical, Ventura *Also called Implantech Associates Inc (P-22029)*
Allied Coatings Inc......F......800 630-2375
1125 Linda Vista Dr # 104 San Marcos (92078) *(P-8616)*
Allied Components Intl......E......949 356-1780
19671 Descartes Foothill Ranch (92610) *(P-18698)*
Allied Concrete & Supply Co......E......209 524-3177
440 Mitchell Rd Ste B Modesto (95354) *(P-10684)*
Allied Concrete Rdymx Svcs LLC......F......415 282-8117
450 Amador St San Francisco (94124) *(P-10685)*
Allied Container Systems Inc......C......925 944-7600
511 Wilbur Ave Ste B4 Antioch (94509) *(P-12527)*
Allied Disc Grinding......F......209 339-0333
2478 Maggio Cir Ste A Lodi (95240) *(P-15722)*
Allied Dvbe Inc......F......619 690-4900
260 Bonita Glen Dr Apt V3 Chula Vista (91910) *(P-2984)*
Allied Dvbe Supply, Chula Vista *Also called Allied Dvbe Inc (P-2984)*
Allied Electric Motor Svc Inc......F......559 486-4222
2635 S Sierra Vista Ave Fresno (93725) *(P-24681)*
Allied Electronic Services......F......714 245-2500
1342 E Borchard Ave Santa Ana (92705) *(P-17810)*
Allied Engrg & Consulting, Bakersfield *Also called Tringen Corporation (P-273)*
Allied Feather & Down Corp (PA)......E......323 581-5677
6905 W Acco St Ste A Montebello (90640) *(P-23270)*
Allied Harbor Aerospace Fas, Corona *Also called All Manufacturers Inc (P-21590)*
Allied Litho Products, Los Angeles *Also called Allied Pressroom Products Inc (P-22938)*
Allied Mdular Bldg Systems Inc (PA)......E......714 516-1188
642 W Nicolas Ave Orange (92868) *(P-12528)*
Allied Mechanical Products, Ontario *Also called Tower Mechanical Products Inc (P-20733)*
Allied Mechanical Products, Ontario *Also called Tower Industries Inc (P-16462)*
Allied Pressroom Products Inc......F......323 266-6250
3546 Emery St Los Angeles (90023) *(P-22938)*
Allied Printing Company......F......916 442-1373
1912 O St Sacramento (95811) *(P-6404)*
Allied Signal Aerospace, Torrance *Also called Alliedsignal Arospc Svc Corp (P-11408)*
Allied Telesis Inc......D......408 519-6700
468 S Abbott Ave Milpitas (95035) *(P-15151)*
Allied Telesis Inc......E......408 519-8700
3041 Orchard Pkwy San Jose (95134) *(P-15152)*
Allied Telesis Inc......E......408 519-8700
3041 Orchard Pkwy San Jose (95134) *(P-15153)*
Allied West Paper Corp......D......909 349-0710
11101 Etiwanda Ave # 100 Fontana (92337) *(P-5457)*
Alliedsignal Arospc Svc Corp (HQ)......E......310 323-9500
2525 W 190th St Torrance (90504) *(P-11408)*
Allison-Kaufman Co......D......818 373-5100
7640 Haskell Ave Van Nuys (91406) *(P-22490)*
Allman Products Inc......E......818 715-0093
21251 Deering Ct Canoga Park (91304) *(P-9502)*
Alloy De Casting Co, Buena Park *Also called Alloy Die Casting Co (P-11330)*
Alloy Die Casting Co......B......714 521-9800
6550 Caballero Blvd Buena Park (90620) *(P-11330)*
Alloy Machining and Honing Inc......F......323 726-8248
2808 Supply Ave Commerce (90040) *(P-15723)*
Alloy Machining Services Inc......F......323 725-2545
2808 Supply Ave Commerce (90040) *(P-15724)*
Alloy Metal Products, Livermore *Also called Fred Matter Inc (P-15975)*
Alloy Processing, Compton *Also called Kens Spray Equipment Inc (P-13197)*
Alloy Tech Electropolishing......F......714 434-6604
2220 S Huron Dr Santa Ana (92704) *(P-12918)*
Allstar Microelectronics Inc......F......949 546-0888
30191 Avenida De Las Rancho Santa Margari (92688) *(P-15002)*
Allstarshop.com, Rancho Santa Margari *Also called Allstar Microelectronics Inc (P-15002)*
Allstate Plastics LLC......F......510 783-9600
1763 Sabre St Hayward (94545) *(P-5383)*
Alltec Integrated Mfg Inc......E......805 595-3500
2240 S Thornburg St Santa Maria (93455) *(P-9618)*
Allteq Industries Inc......F......925 833-7666
215 Rustic Pl San Ramon (94582) *(P-18081)*
Allura Printing Inc......F......714 433-0200
185 Paularino Ave Ste B Costa Mesa (92626) *(P-6405)*
Allure Labs Inc......E......510 489-8896
30901 Wiegman Ct Hayward (94544) *(P-8434)*
Alluxa Inc......E......707 284-1040
3660 N Laughlin Rd Santa Rosa (95403) *(P-21333)*
Allvia Inc......E......408 720-3333
657 N Pastoria Ave Sunnyvale (94085) *(P-18082)*
Ally Enterprises......E......661 412-9933
5001 E Commercecenter Dr # 260 Bakersfield (93309) *(P-152)*
Allyn James Inc......F......925 828-5530
6575 Trinity Ct Ste B Dublin (94568) *(P-6406)*
Allyo, Sunnyvale *Also called Sass Labs Inc (P-24386)*
Alm Chrome......E......714 545-3540
654 Young St Santa Ana (92705) *(P-12919)*
Alm Media Holdings Inc......E......415 490-1054
1035 Market St Ste 500 San Francisco (94103) *(P-5879)*
Alma Rosa Winery Vineyards LLC (PA)......F......805 688-9090
181 Industrial Way Ste C Buellton (93427) *(P-1580)*
Almac Felt Co, Granada Hills *Also called Almac Fixture & Supply Co (P-2921)*
Almac Fixture & Supply Co......E......818 360-1706
12932 Jolette Ave Granada Hills (91344) *(P-2921)*
Almack Liners Inc......E......818 718-5878
9541 Cozycroft Ave Chatsworth (91311) *(P-3211)*
Almaden, Santa Clara *Also called Stone Publishing Inc (P-7230)*
Almatron Electronics Inc......E......714 557-6000
644 Young St Santa Ana (92705) *(P-17811)*
Almond Company......D......559 665-4405
22782 Road 9 Chowchilla (93610) *(P-1419)*
Almond Valley Nut Co......E......209 480-7300
11255 E Whitmore Ave Denair (95316) *(P-1420)*
Almore Dye House Inc......E......818 506-5444
6850 Tujunga Ave North Hollywood (91605) *(P-2850)*
Alms Company, Gold River *Also called Markes International Inc (P-21259)*
Alna Envelope Company Inc......E......323 235-3161
1567 E 25th St Los Angeles (90011) *(P-6951)*
Aloha, Fremont *Also called Air Liquide Electronics US LP (P-7467)*
Aloha Bay......E......707 994-3267
16275 A Main St Lower Lake (95457) *(P-23271)*
Alon Asphalt Bakersfield, Bakersfield *Also called Alon Usa LP (P-9037)*
Alon Usa LP......F......661 392-3630
1201 China Grade Loop Bakersfield (93308) *(P-9037)*
Alona Apparel Inc......F......323 232-1548
1651 Mateo St Los Angeles (90021) *(P-3064)*
Alor International Ltd......E......858 454-0011
11696 Sorrento Valley Rd # 101 San Diego (92121) *(P-22491)*
Alpargatas Usa Inc......E......646 277-7171
513 Boccaccio Ave Venice (90291) *(P-10166)*
Alpase, Chino *Also called Tst Inc (P-11212)*
Alpena Sausage Inc......F......818 505-9482
5329 Craner Ave North Hollywood (91601) *(P-435)*
Alpha Alarm & Audio Inc......F......707 452-8334
1400 Belden Ct Dixon (95620) *(P-17186)*
Alpha and Omega Semicdtr Inc (HQ)......C......408 789-0008
475 Oakmead Pkwy Sunnyvale (94085) *(P-18083)*
Alpha Aviation Components Inc (PA)......E......818 894-8801
16772 Schoenborn St North Hills (91343) *(P-15725)*
Alpha Aviation Components Inc......F......818 894-8468
16774 Schoenborn St North Hills (91343) *(P-15726)*
Alpha Corporation of Tennessee......D......951 657-5161
19991 Seaton Ave Perris (92570) *(P-7540)*
Alpha Dental of Utah Inc......E......562 467-7759
12898 Towne Center Dr Cerritos (90703) *(P-22132)*
Alpha Dyno Nobel......F......661 824-1356
1682 Sabovich St 30a Mojave (93501) *(P-8903)*
Alpha Ems Corporation......C......510 498-8788
44193 S Grimmer Blvd Fremont (94538) *(P-17812)*
Alpha Explosives, Mojave *Also called Alpha Dyno Nobel (P-8903)*
Alpha Grinding Inc......F......562 803-1509
12402 Benedict Ave Downey (90242) *(P-15727)*
Alpha I Publishing Inc......F......909 862-9572
28400 Coachman Ln Highland (92346) *(P-6180)*
Alpha Impressions Inc......F......323 234-8221
4161 S Main St Los Angeles (90037) *(P-3769)*
Alpha Laser......F......951 582-0285
302 Elizabeth Ln Corona (92880) *(P-19254)*
Alpha Machine Company Inc......F......831 462-7400
933 Chittenden Ln Ste A Capitola (95010) *(P-15728)*
Alpha Magnetics Inc......F......510 732-6698
23453 Bernhardt St Hayward (94545) *(P-13495)*
Alpha Materials Inc......E......951 788-5150
6170 20th St Riverside (92509) *(P-10686)*
Alpha Omega Swiss Inc......E......714 692-8009
23305 La Palma Ave Yorba Linda (92887) *(P-12618)*
Alpha Omega Winery LLC......F......707 963-9999
1155 Mee Ln Saint Helena (94574) *(P-1581)*
Alpha Polishing Corporation (PA)......D......323 263-7593
1313 Mirasol St Los Angeles (90023) *(P-12920)*
Alpha Printing & Graphics Inc......E......626 851-9800
12758 Schabarum Ave Irwindale (91706) *(P-6407)*
Alpha Productions Incorporated......E......310 559-1364
5830 W Jefferson Blvd Los Angeles (90016) *(P-12101)*
Alpha Products Inc......E......805 981-8666
351 Irving Dr Oxnard (93030) *(P-18750)*
Alpha Publishing Corporation......E......909 464-0500
337 N Vineyard Ave # 240 Ontario (91764) *(P-6069)*
Alpha Research & Tech Inc......D......916 431-9340
5175 Hillsdale Cir # 100 El Dorado Hills (95762) *(P-14886)*
Alpha Sensors Inc......E......949 250-6578
125 S Tremont St Ste 100 Oceanside (92054) *(P-20830)*
Alpha Technics, Oceanside *Also called Alpha Sensors Inc (P-20830)*
Alpha Technics Inc......C......949 250-6578
125 S Tremont St Ste 100 Oceanside (92054) *(P-20831)*
Alpha Technologies Group Inc (PA)......B......310 566-4005
11990 San Vicente Blvd # 350 Los Angeles (90049) *(P-11992)*
Alpha Wire Corporation......A......310 639-9473
1048 E Burgrove St Carson (90746) *(P-11285)*
Alpha-Owens Corning, Perris *Also called Alpha Corporation of Tennessee (P-7540)*
Alphabet Lighting......F......714 259-0990
15774 Gateway Cir Tustin (92780) *(P-17009)*
Alphacast Foundry Inc......F......213 624-7156
826 S Santa Fe Ave Los Angeles (90021) *(P-11331)*
Alphacoat Finishing LLC......E......949 748-7796
9350 Cabot Dr San Diego (92126) *(P-12921)*
AlphaGraphics, Sunnyvale *Also called Jsl Partners Inc (P-6670)*
AlphaGraphics, San Francisco *Also called Integrated Digital Media (P-6646)*
AlphaGraphics, San Francisco *Also called Integrated Digital Media (P-6647)*
AlphaGraphics, San Rafael *Also called Califrnia Integrated Media Inc (P-6469)*
AlphaGraphics, Modesto *Also called Batchlder Bus Cmmnications Inc (P-6437)*
AlphaGraphics, Brea *Also called Herrick Retail Corporation Th (P-6612)*
AlphaGraphics, Roseville *Also called Print & Mail Solutions Inc (P-6794)*
Alphalogix Inc......D......714 901-1456
5811 Mcfadden Ave Huntington Beach (92649) *(P-19209)*

Employee Codes: A=Over 500 employees, B=251-500
C=101-250, D=51-100, E=20-50, F=10-19
2020 California
Manfacturers Register
© Mergent Inc. 1-800-342-5647
1017

Alphatec Holdings Inc ....F......760 431-9286
2150 Palomar Airport Rd Carlsbad (92011) *(P-21976)*
Alphatec Holdings Inc (PA) ....E......760 431-9286
5818 El Camino Real Carlsbad (92008) *(P-21592)*
Alphatec Spine Inc (HQ) ....C......760 494-6610
5818 El Camino Real Carlsbad (92008) *(P-21977)*
Alphena Technologies ....F......626 961-6098
414 Cloverleaf Dr Ste B Baldwin Park (91706) *(P-9619)*
Alpine Biomed Corp 650 802-0400
1501 Industrial Rd San Carlos (94070) *(P-21593)*
Alpine Industries ....F......530 926-2460
5820 Serrano Dr Mount Shasta (96067) *(P-12764)*
Alpine Meats Inc ....E......209 477-2691
9850 Lower Sacramento Rd Stockton (95210) *(P-436)*
Alpine Metals, South Lake Tahoe Also called Terri Bell *(P-24671)*
Alpinestars USA ....F......310 891-0222
2780 W 237th St Torrance (90505) *(P-3023)*
Alro Cstm Drapery Installation 650 847-4343
809 San Antonio Rd Ste 1 Palo Alto (94303) *(P-5014)*
Alros Label Co Inc ....F......818 781-2403
14200 Aetna St Van Nuys (91401) *(P-6984)*
Alros Lebel Co, Van Nuys Also called Alros Label Co Inc *(P-6984)*
Als Garden Art Inc (PA) ....B......909 424-0221
311 W Citrus St Colton (92324) *(P-10995)*
Alsop Electric Motor Shop, Salinas Also called Alsop Pump *(P-24682)*
Alsop Pump ....F......831 424-3946
1508 Abbott St Salinas (93901) *(P-24682)*
Alstom Signaling Operation LLC ....C......951 343-9699
7337 Central Ave Riverside (92504) *(P-17713)*
Alston Tascom Inc 909 517-3660
5171 Edison Ave Ste C Chino (91710) *(P-17345)*
Alstyle AP & Activewear MGT Co ....F......714 765-0400
1501 E Cerritos Ave Anaheim (92805) *(P-2771)*
Alstyle Apparel, Jurupa Valley Also called A and G Inc *(P-3061)*
Alstyle Apparel LLC ....A......714 765-0400
1501 E Cerritos Ave Anaheim (92805) *(P-2665)*
Alstyle Dyeing & Finishing, Anaheim Also called A and G Inc *(P-2741)*
Alstyle Dyeing & Finishing, Anaheim Also called Alstyle AP & Activewear MGT Co *(P-2771)*
Alta Advanced Technologies Inc ....E......909 983-2973
760 E Sunkist St Ontario (91761) *(P-8269)*
Alta Design and Manufacturing ....F......408 450-5394
885 Auzerais Ave San Jose (95126) *(P-15729)*
Alta Devices Inc ....C......408 988-8600
545 Oakmead Pkwy Sunnyvale (94085) *(P-18084)*
Alta Manufacturing Inc ....E......510 668-1870
47650 Westinghouse Dr Fremont (94539) *(P-17813)*
Alta Properties Inc 805 683-1431
879 Ward Dr Santa Barbara (93111) *(P-19255)*
Alta Properties Inc ....B......805 683-2575
869 Ward Dr Santa Barbara (93111) *(P-20998)*
Alta Properties Inc ....B......805 690-5382
879 Ward Dr Santa Barbara (93111) *(P-19256)*
Alta Properties Inc 805 967-0171
839 Ward Dr Santa Barbara (93111) *(P-10473)*
Alta Properties Inc (PA) ....C......805 967-0171
879 Ward Dr Santa Barbara (93111) *(P-10474)*
Alta Solutions Inc ....F......858 668-5200
12580 Stowe Dr Poway (92064) *(P-20999)*
Alta-Dena Certified Dairy LLC ....C......805 685-8328
123 Aero Camino Goleta (93117) *(P-683)*
Alta-Dena Certified Dairy LLC ....C......800 395-7004
17851 Railroad St City of Industry (91748) *(P-684)*
Alta-Dena Certified Dairy LLC (HQ) ....B......626 964-6401
17637 E Valley Blvd City of Industry (91744) *(P-685)*
Altaflex ....D......408 727-6614
336 Martin Ave Santa Clara (95050) *(P-17814)*
Altair Lighting, Compton Also called Jimway Inc *(P-17137)*
Altair Technologies Inc ....E......650 508-8700
41970 Christy St Fremont (94538) *(P-14421)*
Altamont Manufacturing Inc ....F......925 371-5401
241 Rickenbacker Cir Livermore (94551) *(P-15730)*
Altasens Inc (HQ) ....E......818 338-9400
2201 E Dominguez St Long Beach (90810) *(P-18085)*
Altaviz LLC (PA) 949 656-4003
13766 Alton Pkwy Ste 143 Irvine (92618) *(P-7744)*
Altec Industries Inc ....F......707 678-0800
1450 N 1st St Dixon (95620) *(P-13703)*
Altec Industries Inc ....D......707 678-0800
325 Industrial Way Dixon (95620) *(P-13704)*
Altemp Alloys Inc ....F......714 279-0249
330 W Taft Ave Orange (92865) *(P-11024)*
Altera Corporation (HQ) ....B......408 544-7000
101 Innovation Dr San Jose (95134) *(P-18086)*
Alterg Inc ....D......510 270-5900
48368 Milmont Dr Fremont (94538) *(P-22741)*
Altergy Systems ....E......916 458-8590
140 Blue Ravine Rd Folsom (95630) *(P-16774)*
Alternators Starters Etc ....F......408 559-3540
1360 White Oaks Rd Ste H Campbell (95008) *(P-19184)*
Altest Corporation ....E......408 436-9900
898 Faulstich Ct San Jose (95112) *(P-15731)*
Althea Ajinomoto Inc ....C......858 882-0123
11040 Roselle St San Diego (92121) *(P-21594)*
Altia Systems Inc ....E......408 996-9710
10020 N De Anza Blvd Cupertino (95014) *(P-22401)*
Altierre Corporation ....E......408 435-7343
1980 Concourse Dr San Jose (95131) *(P-18087)*
Altigen Communications Inc ....C......408 597-9000
670 N Mccarthy Blvd Milpitas (95035) *(P-17346)*

Altinex Inc ....E......714 990-0877
500 S Jefferson St Placentia (92870) *(P-17447)*
Altium LLC ....D......800 544-4186
4275 Executive Sq Ste 825 La Jolla (92037) *(P-23597)*
Altmans Products LLC (HQ) ....E......310 559-4093
7136 Kittyhawk Ave Apt 4 Los Angeles (90045) *(P-11646)*
Alto Rey, North Hollywood Also called Lookout Enterprises Inc *(P-2337)*
Altro Usa Inc ....D......562 944-8292
12648 Clark St Santa Fe Springs (90670) *(P-23253)*
Alts Tool & Machine Inc (PA) ....D......619 562-6653
10926 Woodside Ave N Santee (92071) *(P-15732)*
Alturdyne Power Systems Inc ....E......619 343-3204
1405 N Johnson Ave El Cajon (92020) *(P-13559)*
Altus Positioning Systems Inc ....F......310 541-8139
20725 S Wstn Ave Ste 100 Torrance (90501) *(P-21431)*
Alu Menziken, Anaheim Also called Universal Alloy Corporation *(P-11250)*
Alum-A-Coat, El Monte Also called Santoshi Corporation *(P-13097)*
Alum-A-Therm, Westminster Also called Bodycote Imt Inc *(P-11434)*
Alum-Alloy Coinc ....E......909 986-0410
603 S Hope Ave Ontario (91761) *(P-12728)*
Aluma USA Inc ....F......707 545-9344
435 Tesconi Cir Santa Rosa (95401) *(P-22492)*
Alumafab 562 630-6440
14335 Iseli Rd Santa Fe Springs (90670) *(P-17010)*
Alumatec Inc ....D......818 609-7460
18411 Sherman Way Reseda (91335) *(P-85)*
Alumatherm Incorporated ....F......510 832-2819
1717 Kirkham St Oakland (94607) *(P-11930)*
Alumawall Inc ....D......408 275-7165
1701 S 7th St Ste 9 San Jose (95112) *(P-12529)*
Alumax Building Products, Sun City Also called Omnimax International Inc *(P-11974)*
Alumen-8, Oceanside Also called Amerillum LLC *(P-17102)*
Alumflam North America ....E......562 926-9520
16604 Edwards Rd Cerritos (90703) *(P-12922)*
Alumin-Art Plating Co Inc ....E......909 983-1866
803 W State St Ontario (91762) *(P-12923)*
Aluminum Casting Company, Santa Fe Springs Also called Employee Owned Pacific Cast PR *(P-11380)*
Aluminum Coating Tech Inc ....E......916 442-1063
8290 Alpine Ave Sacramento (95826) *(P-12924)*
Aluminum Die Casting Co Inc ....D......951 681-3900
10775 San Sevaine Way Jurupa Valley (91752) *(P-11332)*
Aluminum Precision Pdts Inc ....C......805 488-4401
1001 Mcwane Blvd Oxnard (93033) *(P-12729)*
Aluminum Precision Pdts Inc ....D......714 549-4075
502 E Alton Ave Santa Ana (92707) *(P-12730)*
Aluminum Pros Inc ....F......310 366-7696
13917 S Main St Los Angeles (90061) *(P-14343)*
Aluminum Seating Inc ....F......909 884-9449
555 Tennis Court Ln San Bernardino (92408) *(P-4853)*
Aluminum Tube Railings, Pomona Also called Atr Technologies Incorporated *(P-12453)*
Alumistar Inc ....E......562 633-6673
12711 Imperial Hwy Santa Fe Springs (90670) *(P-11366)*
Aluratek Inc ....E......949 468-2046
15241 Barranca Pkwy Irvine (92618) *(P-17187)*
Alva Manufacturing Inc ....E......714 237-0925
236 E Orangethorpe Ave Placentia (92870) *(P-12619)*
Alvarado Alta Calidad LLC ....E......323 222-0038
2907 Humboldt St Los Angeles (90031) *(P-4760)*
Alvarado Alta Clidad Cstm Furn, Los Angeles Also called Alvarado Alta Calidad LLC *(P-4760)*
Alvarado Dye & Knitting Mill ....E......510 324-8892
30542 Union City Blvd Union City (94587) *(P-3024)*
Alvarado Manufacturing Co Inc ....D......909 591-8431
12660 Colony Ct Chino (91710) *(P-21432)*
Alvarado Micro Precision Inc ....F......760 598-0186
2389 La Mirada Dr Ste 9 Vista (92081) *(P-15733)*
Alvarez Refinishing Inc ....E......714 780-0171
23 W Romneya Dr Anaheim (92801) *(P-2842)*
Alvellan Inc ....E......925 689-2421
1030 Shary Ct Concord (94518) *(P-15734)*
Alvin D Troyer and Associates ....F......650 574-0167
310 Shaw Rd Ste F South San Francisco (94080) *(P-11561)*
Alyn Industries Inc ....D......818 988-7696
16028 Arminta St Van Nuys (91406) *(P-18813)*
Alza Corporation (HQ) ....A......707 453-6400
700 Eubanks Dr Vacaville (95688) *(P-7745)*
Alza Corporation ....A......650 564-5000
1010 Joaquin Rd Mountain View (94043) *(P-21168)*
Alza Corporation ....A......707 453-6400
700 Eubanks Dr Vacaville (95688) *(P-21169)*
Alza Pharmaceuticals, Vacaville Also called Alza Corporation *(P-7745)*
AM Castenada Inc ....F......951 686-3966
1450 University Ave Ste P Riverside (92507) *(P-22592)*
AM Retail Group Inc ....C......323 728-8996
100 Citadel Dr Commerce (90040) *(P-3212)*
Am-Par Manufacturing Co Inc ....F......530 671-1800
959 Von Geldern Way Yuba City (95991) *(P-15735)*
Am-Tek Engineering Inc ....F......909 673-1633
1180 E Francis St Ste C Ontario (91761) *(P-15736)*
AMA Plastics (PA) ....B......951 734-5600
1100 Citrus St Riverside (92507) *(P-9620)*
Amada Miyachi America Inc (HQ) ....C......626 303-5676
1820 S Myrtle Ave Monrovia (91016) *(P-14236)*
Amada Miyachi America Inc ....E......626 303-5676
245 E El Norte St Monrovia (91016) *(P-21595)*
Amador Transit Mix Inc ....E......209 223-0406
12480 Ridge Rd Sutter Creek (95685) *(P-10687)*

Mergent e-mail: customerrelations@mergent.com
1018
2020 California
Manufacturers Register
(P-0000) Products & Services Section entry number
(PA)=Parent Co (HQ)=Headquarters (DH)=Div Headquarters

Amag Technology Inc (HQ)....E....310 518-2380
20701 Manhattan Pl Torrance (90501) *(P-15154)*
Amanet, Canoga Park *Also called American Mfg Netwrk Inc (P-15739)*
Amaral Industries Common Law....D....510 569-8669
20993 Foothill Blvd 144 Hayward (94541) *(P-4490)*
Amaretto Orchards LLC....E....661 399-9697
32331 Famoso Woody Rd Mc Farland (93250) *(P-23272)*
Amarillo Wind Machine LLC....F....559 592-4256
20513 Avenue 256 Exeter (93221) *(P-13608)*
Amark Industries Inc (PA)....C....951 654-7351
600 W Esplanade Ave San Jacinto (92583) *(P-14753)*
Amato Beverly Hills, Beverly Hills *Also called Rare Elements Hair Care (P-23458)*
Amays Bakery & Noodle Co Inc (PA)....D....213 626-2713
837 E Commercial St Los Angeles (90012) *(P-1300)*
Amazing Facts International....D....916 434-3880
6615 Sierra College Blvd Roseville (95746) *(P-6070)*
Amazing Facts Ministries, Roseville *Also called Amazing Facts International (P-6070)*
Amazing Steel, Montclair *Also called Mitchell Fabrication (P-11846)*
Amazing Steel Company....E....909 590-0393
4564 Mission Blvd Montclair (91763) *(P-11742)*
Amazon Environmental Inc (PA)....E....951 588-0206
779 Palmyrita Ave Riverside (92507) *(P-8617)*
Amazon Paint, Riverside *Also called Amazon Environmental Inc (P-8617)*
Amazon Prsrvation Partners Inc....E....415 775-6355
1501a Vermont St San Francisco (94107) *(P-754)*
Ambarella Inc....A....408 734-8888
3101 Jay St Santa Clara (95054) *(P-18088)*
Ambassador Industries....F....213 383-1171
2754 W Temple St Los Angeles (90026) *(P-5015)*
Ambay Circuits Inc....F....818 786-8241
16117 Leadwell St Van Nuys (91406) *(P-17815)*
Amber Steel Co., Rialto *Also called H Wayne Lewis Inc (P-12591)*
Ambiance Apparel, Los Angeles *Also called Ambiance USA Inc (P-3284)*
Ambiance USA Inc (PA)....D....323 587-0007
2415 E 15th St Los Angeles (90021) *(P-3284)*
Ambios Technology Inc (PA)....E....831 427-1160
1 Technology Dr Milpitas (95035) *(P-21170)*
Ambit Biosciences Corporation....D....858 334-2100
10201 Wtridge Cir Ste 200 San Diego (92121) *(P-7746)*
Ambrit Engineering Corporation....D....714 557-1074
2640 Halladay St Santa Ana (92705) *(P-14012)*
Ambrit Industries Inc....E....818 243-1224
432 Magnolia Ave Glendale (91204) *(P-13966)*
Ambrx Inc....D....858 875-2400
10975 N Torrey Pines Rd # 100 La Jolla (92037) *(P-7747)*
AMC, Stanton *Also called All Metals Proc San Diego Inc (P-12914)*
AMC Machining Inc....E....805 238-5452
1540 Commerce Way Paso Robles (93446) *(P-12584)*
Amcan Beverages Inc....C....707 557-0500
1201 Commerce Blvd American Canyon (94503) *(P-2023)*
Amcan Usa LLC....F....858 587-1032
8970 Crestmar Pt San Diego (92121) *(P-15003)*
Amcc Sales, Santa Clara *Also called Applied Micro Circuits Corp (P-18117)*
Amcells, Vista *Also called Acells Corp (P-21160)*
Amcor Flexibles LLC....C....707 257-6481
5425 Broadway St American Canyon (94503) *(P-5321)*
Amcor Flexibles LLC....C....323 721-6777
5416 Union Pacific Ave Commerce (90022) *(P-5322)*
Amcor Industries Inc....E....323 585-2852
2011 E 49th St Vernon (90058) *(P-19576)*
Amcor Manufacturing Inc....E....209 581-9687
500 Winmoore Way Modesto (95358) *(P-7468)*
Amcor Rigid Packaging Usa LLC....F....520 746-0737
14270 Ramona Ave Chino (91710) *(P-9621)*
Amcor Rigid Packaging Usa LLC....C....909 517-2700
14270 Ramona Ave Chino (91710) *(P-9480)*
AMD International Sls Svc Ltd (HQ)....E....408 749-4000
1 Amd Pl Sunnyvale (94085) *(P-18089)*
AMD International Tech LLC....E....909 985-8300
1725 S Campus Ave Ontario (91761) *(P-12102)*
AMD Ventures LLC....C....408 749-4000
1 Amd Pl Sunnyvale (94085) *(P-18090)*
Amedica Biotech Inc....F....510 785-5980
28301 Industrial Blvd K Hayward (94545) *(P-21596)*
Ameditech Inc....C....858 535-1968
9940 Mesa Rim Rd San Diego (92121) *(P-21597)*
Amerasia Furniture Components....E....310 638-0570
2772 Norton Ave Lynwood (90262) *(P-4628)*
Amergence Technology Inc....E....909 859-8400
295 Brea Canyon Rd Walnut (91789) *(P-14422)*
Ameri-Fax, Orange *Also called Positive Concepts Inc (P-5522)*
America Asia Trade Promotion....F....408 970-8868
4633 Old Ironsides Dr # 400 Santa Clara (95054) *(P-3599)*
America Asian Trade Assn Prom....D....408 588-0008
4633 Old Ironside Ste 308 Santa Rosa (95404) *(P-17011)*
America Manufacturing, Rancho Cucamonga *Also called Mape Engineering Inc (P-19971)*
America Mountain Wldg Inds Inc....F....626 698-8066
1613 Chelsea Rd Ste 208 San Marino (91108) *(P-14237)*
America Printing, Burlingame *Also called Asia America Enterprise Inc (P-6421)*
America Techcode Semicdtr Inc....E....408 910-2028
10456 San Fernando Ave Cupertino (95014) *(P-18091)*
America Wood Finishes Inc....F....323 232-8256
728 E 59th St Los Angeles (90001) *(P-8618)*
American & Efird LLC....D....323 724-6884
6098 Rickenbacker Rd Commerce (90040) *(P-2889)*
American Acrylic Display Inc....F....714 738-7990
1061 S Leslie St La Habra (90631) *(P-23047)*
American Activated Carbon Corp....F....310 491-2842
7310 Deering Ave Canoga Park (91303) *(P-16681)*
American Aerospace Pdts Inc....F....714 662-7620
1720 S Santa Fe St Santa Ana (92705) *(P-12103)*
American Air Liquide Inc (HQ)....D....510 624-4000
46409 Landing Pkwy Fremont (94538) *(P-7412)*
American Aircraft Products Inc....D....310 532-7434
15411 S Broadway Gardena (90248) *(P-12104)*
American Alupack Inds LLC....E....805 485-1500
1201 N Rice Ave Unit B Oxnard (93030) *(P-11215)*
American Amplifier Tech LLC....F....530 574-3474
7889 Lichen Dr 360 Citrus Heights (95621) *(P-21000)*
American AP Dyg & Finshg Inc....D....310 644-4001
747 Warehouse St Los Angeles (90021) *(P-2742)*
American Apparel, Los Angeles *Also called App Winddown LLC (P-3541)*
American Apparel (usa) LLC....F....213 488-0226
747 Warehouse St Los Angeles (90021) *(P-3538)*
American Apparel ACC Inc (PA)....E....626 350-3828
10160 Olney St El Monte (91731) *(P-9622)*
American Apparel Retail Inc (HQ)....E....213 488-0226
747 Warehouse St Los Angeles (90021) *(P-2666)*
American Arium Inc....E....949 623-7090
17791 Fitch Irvine (92614) *(P-18092)*
American Audio Component Inc....E....909 596-3788
20 Fairbanks Ste 198 Irvine (92618) *(P-18814)*
American Automated Engrg Inc....D....714 898-9951
5382 Argosy Ave Huntington Beach (92649) *(P-20472)*
American Bath Factory, Corona *Also called Le Elegant Bath Inc (P-9591)*
American Battery Charging LLC....E....401 231-5227
15272 Newsboy Cir Huntington Beach (92649) *(P-16775)*
American Best Car Parts, Anaheim *Also called American Fabrication Corp (P-19579)*
American Bicycle Security Co, Santa Paula *Also called Turtle Storage Ltd (P-5008)*
American Biodiesel Inc....F....209 466-4823
809 Snedeker Ave Ste C Stockton (95203) *(P-8712)*
American Bioscience, Santa Monica *Also called Abraxis Bioscience Inc (P-7715)*
American Blast Systems Inc....E....949 244-6859
16182 Gothard St Ste H Huntington Beach (92647) *(P-11025)*
American Blinds and Drap Inc....E....510 487-3500
30776 Huntwood Ave Hayward (94544) *(P-3586)*
American Board Assembly Inc....C....805 523-0274
5456 Endeavour Ct Moorpark (93021) *(P-17816)*
American Bottling Company....C....951 341-7500
1188 Mt Vernon Ave Riverside (92507) *(P-2024)*
American Bottling Company....E....707 766-9750
2210 S Mcdowell Blvd Ext Petaluma (94954) *(P-2025)*
American Bottling Company....F....707 462-8871
100 Wabash Ave Ukiah (95482) *(P-2026)*
American Bottling Company....E....661 323-7921
230 E 18th St Bakersfield (93305) *(P-2027)*
American Bottling Company....D....559 442-1553
2012 S Pearl St Fresno (93721) *(P-2028)*
American Bottling Company....F....707 840-9727
1555 Heartwood Dr McKinleyville (95519) *(P-2029)*
American Bottling Company....D....925 938-8777
1981 N Broadway Ste 215 Walnut Creek (94596) *(P-2030)*
American Bottling Company....C....818 898-1471
1166 Arroyo St San Fernando (91340) *(P-2031)*
American Bottling Company....E....805 928-1001
618 Hanson Way Santa Maria (93458) *(P-2032)*
American Bottling Company....B....323 268-7779
3220 E 26th St Vernon (90058) *(P-2033)*
American Bottling Company....F....916 929-3575
2720 Land Ave Sacramento (95815) *(P-2034)*
American Bottling Company....D....916 929-7777
2670 Land Ave Sacramento (95815) *(P-2035)*
American Bottling Company....D....831 632-0777
11205 Commercial Pkwy Castroville (95012) *(P-2036)*
American Bottling Company....D....925 251-3001
6160 Stoneridge Mall Rd # 280 Pleasanton (94588) *(P-2037)*
American Bow Thruster, Rohnert Park *Also called Arcturus Marine Systems (P-13560)*
American Brass & Alum Fndry Co....E....800 545-9988
2060 Garfield Ave Commerce (90040) *(P-11654)*
American Capacitor Corporation....E....626 814-4444
5367 3rd St Irwindale (91706) *(P-18675)*
American Carousel, Laguna Niguel *Also called S & S Woodcarver Inc (P-4529)*
American Carports Inc (PA)....F....866 730-9865
1415 Clay St Colusa (95932) *(P-12530)*
American Carrier Equipment, Fresno *Also called Ace Trailer Co (P-19812)*
American Carrier Systems....D....559 442-1500
2285 E Date Ave Fresno (93706) *(P-19452)*
American Casting Co, Hollister *Also called Reed Manufacturing Inc (P-11167)*
American Casuals, Torrance *Also called Pmp Products Inc (P-10203)*
American Cellar Wine Club, Westlake Village *Also called American Clubs LLC (P-6181)*
American Ceramic Technology (PA)....F....619 992-3104
12909 Lomas Verdes Dr Poway (92064) *(P-21978)*
American Chain & Gear Company....F....323 581-9131
3370 Paseo Halcon San Clemente (92672) *(P-14738)*
American Circuit Tech Inc (PA)....E....714 777-2480
5330 E Hunter Ave Anaheim (92807) *(P-17817)*
American City Bus Journals Inc....E....916 447-7661
555 Capitol Mall Ste 200 Sacramento (95814) *(P-5548)*
American Cleaner and Laundry....E....805 925-1571
2230 S Depot St Ste D Santa Maria (93455) *(P-15402)*
American Clubs LLC....F....805 496-1218
4550 E Thousand Oaks Blvd Westlake Village (91362) *(P-6181)*
American Cnc Inc....F....818 890-3400
12430 Montague St Ste 207 Pacoima (91331) *(P-15737)*
American Coffee Urn Mfg Co Inc....F....951 943-1495
5178 Western Way Perris (92571) *(P-12105)*
American Compaction Eqp Inc....E....949 661-2921
29380 Hunco Way Lake Elsinore (92530) *(P-13705)*

ALPHABETIC

American Concrete Products, Morgan Hill *Also called US Concrete Inc (P-10662)*
American Consumer Products LLC....E....310 443-3330
2845 E 26th St Vernon (90058) *(P-8941)*
American Containers Inc....E....209 460-1127
813 W Luce St Ste B Stockton (95203) *(P-5195)*
American Costume Corp....F....818 432-4350
12980 Raymer St North Hollywood (91605) *(P-3539)*
American Craftsmen Corporation....F....626 793-3329
273 N Hill Ave Pasadena (91106) *(P-4546)*
American Crcuit Card Retainers....F....714 738-6194
2310 E Orangethorpe Ave Anaheim (92806) *(P-14887)*
American Custom Coach Inc....F....909 796-4747
1255 W Colton Ave Redlands (92374) *(P-19516)*
American Custom Meats LLC....D....209 839-8800
4276 N Tracy Blvd Tracy (95304) *(P-437)*
American Cylinder Head Inc....F....510 261-1590
499 Lesser St Oakland (94601) *(P-19577)*
American Cylndr Hd RPR/Excg....F....510 536-1764
499 Lesser St Oakland (94601) *(P-19578)*
American Dart Lines, Santa Maria *Also called Bottelsen Dart Co Inc (P-22663)*
American Dawn Inc (PA)....D....310 223-2000
401 W Artesia Blvd Compton (90220) *(P-2922)*
American Deburring Inc....E....949 457-9790
20742 Linear Ln Lake Forest (92630) *(P-15738)*
American Decal Company, Fountain Valley *Also called Tape Factory Inc (P-5376)*
American Design Inc....F....619 429-1995
1672 Industrial Blvd Chula Vista (91911) *(P-9623)*
American Designs, Los Angeles *Also called Kesmor Associates (P-22534)*
American Die & Rollforming....F....916 652-7667
3495 Swetzer Rd Loomis (95650) *(P-14013)*
American Die Casting Inc....E....909 356-7768
14576 Fontlee Ln Fontana (92335) *(P-11352)*
American Electronics, Carson *Also called Ducommun Labarge Tech Inc (P-20094)*
American Elements, Los Angeles *Also called Merelex Corporation (P-7505)*
American Emperor Inc....F....713 478-5973
888 Doolittle Dr San Leandro (94577) *(P-11562)*
American Etal Technology, Fremont *Also called Axt Inc (P-18140)*
American Etching & Mfg....E....323 875-3910
13730 Desmond St Pacoima (91331) *(P-13141)*
American Fabrication, Bakersfield *Also called Russell Fabrication Corp (P-13484)*
American Fabrication Corp (PA)....C....714 632-1709
2891 E Via Martens Anaheim (92806) *(P-19579)*
American Fashion Group Inc (PA)....F....213 748-2100
1430 E Washington Blvd Los Angeles (90021) *(P-3065)*
American Fine Arts Foundry LLC....E....818 848-7593
2520 N Ontario St Ste A Burbank (91504) *(P-11393)*
American Fleet & Ret Graphics....E....909 937-7570
2091 Del Rio Way Ontario (91761) *(P-23048)*
American Foam Fiber & Sups Inc....D....626 969-7268
255 S 7th Ave Ste A City of Industry (91746) *(P-2923)*
American Foil & Embosing Inc....F....949 580-0080
35 Musick Irvine (92618) *(P-6985)*
American Food Ingredients Inc....E....760 967-6287
4021 Avenida Plata 501 Oceanside (92056) *(P-841)*
American Fruits & Flavors LLC (HQ)....C....818 899-9574
10725 Sutter Ave Pacoima (91331) *(P-2189)*
American Fruits & Flavors LLC....E....323 264-7791
1547 Knowles Ave Los Angeles (90063) *(P-2190)*
American Furniture Aliance Inc....F....323 804-5242
9141 Arrow Rte Rancho Cucamonga (91730) *(P-4761)*
American Furniture Systems Inc....E....626 457-9900
14105 Avalon Blvd Los Angeles (90061) *(P-4827)*
American Garage Decor Inc....F....760 975-9148
10883 Thornmint Rd San Diego (92127) *(P-9624)*
American Garment Company....F....562 483-8300
16230 Manning Way Cerritos (90703) *(P-3540)*
American Garment Finishing....E....310 962-1929
17941 Lost Canyon Rd # 6 Canyon Country (91387) *(P-2722)*
American Gasket & Die Company....F....408 441-6200
2275 Paragon Dr San Jose (95131) *(P-9218)*
American General Tool Group....E....760 745-7993
929 Poinsettia Ave # 101 Vista (92081) *(P-9163)*
American Giant Inc....F....415 529-2429
161 Natoma St Fl 2 San Francisco (94105) *(P-3025)*
American Graphic Board Inc....E....323 721-0585
5880 E Slauson Ave Commerce (90040) *(P-5491)*
American Grip Inc....E....818 768-8922
8468 Kewen Ave Sun Valley (91352) *(P-17100)*
American Handgunner and Guns, Poway *Also called Publishers Development Corp (P-6008)*
American Hi-Tech Petro & Chem, Richmond *Also called Amtecol Inc (P-9129)*
American Highway Technology, Modesto *Also called Dayton Superior Corporation (P-13871)*
American Histology Reagent Co, Lodi *Also called American Mstr Tech Scntfic Inc (P-21598)*
American Historic Inns Inc....F....949 499-8070
249 Forest Ave Laguna Beach (92651) *(P-6182)*
American Horse Products....F....949 248-5300
31896 Plaza Dr Ste C4 San Juan Capistrano (92675) *(P-3831)*
American Household Company, Los Angeles *Also called Housewares International Inc (P-9830)*
American HX Auto Trade Inc....D....909 484-1010
9455 Hyssop Dr Rancho Cucamonga (91730) *(P-19453)*
American Imex, Irvine *Also called J F Fong Inc (P-21764)*
American Index and Files LLC....F....714 630-3360
2900 E Miraloma Ave Ste B Anaheim (92806) *(P-5492)*
American Induction Tech Inc....F....714 456-1122
310 N Palm St Ste B Brea (92821) *(P-14754)*
American Indus Systems Inc....E....888 485-6688
1768 Mcgaw Ave Irvine (92614) *(P-18815)*
American Industrial Corp....F....714 680-4763
1624 N Orangethorpe Way Anaheim (92801) *(P-14014)*
American Industrial Pump, Antioch *Also called Tomiko Inc (P-14600)*
American Ingredients Inc....F....714 630-6000
2929 E White Star Ave Anaheim (92806) *(P-7644)*
American Innotek Inc (PA)....D....760 741-6600
2655 Vsta Pcf Drv Ocnside Oceanside Oceanside (92056) *(P-9625)*
American International Mfg Co....E....530 666-2446
1230 Fortna Ave Woodland (95776) *(P-13609)*
American International Racing....F....626 969-7733
1132 W Kirkwall Rd Azusa (91702) *(P-19580)*
American Intl Inds Inc....A....323 728-2999
2220 Gaspar Ave Commerce (90040) *(P-8435)*
American Israel Public Affairs....F....323 937-1184
1801 Century Park E # 600 Los Angeles (90067) *(P-23598)*
American Lab and Systems, Los Angeles *Also called Mjw Inc (P-14591)*
American Label Co, Cerritos *Also called American Non Stop Label Corp (P-6986)*
American Lawyer Media, San Francisco *Also called Alm Media Holdings Inc (P-5879)*
American Licorice Company....B....510 487-5500
2477 Liston Way Union City (94587) *(P-1355)*
American Linen Rental, Santa Maria *Also called American Cleaner and Laundry (P-15402)*
American Liquid Packaging Syst (PA)....E....408 524-7474
440 N Wolfe Rd Sunnyvale (94085) *(P-7541)*
American Lithium Energy Corp....F....760 599-7388
2261 Rutherford Rd Carlsbad (92008) *(P-7469)*
American Lithographers Inc....D....916 441-5392
2629 5th St Sacramento (95818) *(P-6408)*
American Mailing & Prtg Svc, Anaheim *Also called Sharon Havriluk (P-7316)*
American Maple Inc....F....310 515-8881
14020 S Western Ave Gardena (90249) *(P-22742)*
American Marble, Vista *Also called Kammerer Enterprises Inc (P-10912)*
American Marble & Granite Co (PA)....F....323 268-7979
4084 Whittier Blvd Los Angeles (90023) *(P-10887)*
American Marble & Onyx Coinc....E....323 776-0900
10321 S La Cienega Blvd Los Angeles (90045) *(P-10888)*
American Medical Sales Inc....E....310 471-8900
218 Bronwood Ave Los Angeles (90049) *(P-22207)*
American Metal Bearing Company....E....714 892-5527
7191 Acacia Ave Garden Grove (92841) *(P-14608)*
American Metal Enterprises Inc....F....714 894-6810
15855 Chemical Ln Huntington Beach (92649) *(P-21979)*
American Metal Filter Company....F....619 628-1917
611 Marsat Ct Chula Vista (91911) *(P-14648)*
American Metal Processing....E....619 444-6171
390 Front St El Cajon (92020) *(P-12106)*
American Mfg Netwrk Inc....F....818 786-1113
7001 Eton Ave Canoga Park (91303) *(P-15739)*
American Modular Systems Inc....D....209 825-1921
787 Spreckels Ave Manteca (95336) *(P-4456)*
American Mstr Tech Scntfic Inc....C....209 368-4031
1330 Thurman St Lodi (95240) *(P-21598)*
American Nail Plate Ltg Inc....D....909 982-1807
9044 Del Mar Ave Montclair (91763) *(P-16959)*
American National Mfg Inc....C....951 273-7888
252 Mariah Cir Corona (92879) *(P-4710)*
American Naturals Company LLC....E....323 201-6891
3737 Longridge Ave Sherman Oaks (91423) *(P-2390)*
American Non Stop Label Corp....F....562 921-9437
16221 Arthur St Cerritos (90703) *(P-6986)*
American Ornamental Studio....F....650 589-0561
1 Fairview Pl Millbrae (94030) *(P-10527)*
American Pacific Truss Inc....E....949 363-1691
24265 Rue De Cezanne Laguna Niguel (92677) *(P-4287)*
American PCF Prtrs College Inc....E....949 250-3212
17931 Sky Park Cir Irvine (92614) *(P-6409)*
American Performance Engi....F....661 256-7309
7347 W Rosamond Blvd Rosamond (93560) *(P-20381)*
American Plant Services Inc (PA)....D....562 630-1773
6242 N Paramount Blvd Long Beach (90805) *(P-11026)*
American Plastic Card Co....C....818 784-4224
21550 Oxnard St Ste 300 Woodland Hills (91367) *(P-9626)*
American Plastic Products Inc....D....818 504-1073
9243 Glenoaks Blvd Sun Valley (91352) *(P-14015)*
American Pneumatic Tools Inc....F....562 204-1555
1000 S Grand Ave Santa Ana (92705) *(P-13967)*
American Poly-Foam Company Inc....E....510 786-3626
1455 Crocker Ave Hayward (94544) *(P-9503)*
American Power Solutions Inc....E....714 626-0300
14355 Industry Cir La Mirada (90638) *(P-17101)*
American Prcision Grinding Mch....F....626 357-6610
456 Gerona Ave San Gabriel (91775) *(P-15740)*
American Precision Gear Co....E....650 627-8060
365 Foster City Blvd Foster City (94404) *(P-14739)*
American Precision Hydraulics....E....714 903-8610
5601 Research Dr Huntington Beach (92649) *(P-13968)*
American Precision Sheet Metal, Chatsworth *Also called Keith E Archambeau Sr Inc (P-12262)*
American Precision Spring....E....408 986-1020
1513 Arbuckle Ct Santa Clara (95054) *(P-13373)*
American Premier Corp....E....909 923-7070
1531 S Carlos Ave Ontario (91761) *(P-22743)*
American Pride Inc....E....909 591-7688
12285 Colony Ave Chino (91710) *(P-10187)*
American Printing & Copy Inc....F....650 325-2322
1100 Obrien Dr Menlo Park (94025) *(P-6410)*
American Printing & Design....E....310 287-0460
14622 Ventura Blvd # 102 Sherman Oaks (91403) *(P-6411)*
American Printworks, Vernon *Also called P&Y T-Shrts Silk Screening Inc (P-14290)*
American Probe & Tech Inc....F....408 263-3356
1795 Grogan Ave Merced (95341) *(P-21001)*
American Production Co Inc....D....650 368-5334
2734 Spring St Redwood City (94063) *(P-11492)*

Mergent e-mail: customerrelations@mergent.com 2020 California Manufacturers Register (P-0000) Products & Services Section entry number
1020 (PA)=Parent Co (HQ)=Headquarters (DH)=Div Headquarters

American Publishing Corp E 909 390-7548
2143 E Convention Center Ontario (91764) ***(P-6071)***
American Qualex Inc F 949 492-8298
920 Calle Negocio Ste A San Clemente (92673) ***(P-10297)***
American Qualex International F 949 492-8298
920a Calle Negocio Ste A San Clemente (92673) ***(P-8942)***
American Quality Tools Inc E 951 280-4700
12650 Magnolia Ave Ste B Riverside (92503) ***(P-14129)***
American Quilting Company Inc E 323 233-2500
1540 Calzona St Los Angeles (90023) ***(P-3722)***
American Range Corporation C 818 897-0808
13592 Desmond St Pacoima (91331) ***(P-12107)***
American Ready Mix, Escondido *Also called Superior Ready Mix Concrete LP* ***(P-10850)***
American Ready Mix Inc F 760 446-4556
1141 W Graaf Ave Ridgecrest (93555) ***(P-10688)***
American Relays Inc E 562 926-2837
15537 Blackburn Ave Norwalk (90650) ***(P-16696)***
American Reliance Inc E 626 443-6818
12941 Ramona Blvd Ste F Baldwin Park (91706) ***(P-14888)***
American Rice Inc D 530 438-2265
1 Comet Ln Maxwell (95955) ***(P-1034)***
American Rim Supply Inc E 760 431-3666
1955 Kellogg Ave Carlsbad (92008) ***(P-19581)***
American River Packaging, Sacramento *Also called Pk1 Inc* ***(P-5258)***
American Rotary Broom Co Inc (PA) F 760 591-4025
181 Pawnee St Ste B San Marcos (92078) ***(P-23020)***
American Rotary Broom Co Inc E 909 629-9117
688 New York Dr Pomona (91768) ***(P-23021)***
American Rotoform, South San Francisco *Also called Barrango* ***(P-15774)***
American Rv, Santa Clarita *Also called Stiers Rv Centers LLC* ***(P-20522)***
American Scale Co Inc F 323 269-0305
4338 E Washington Blvd Commerce (90023) ***(P-15639)***
American Scence Tech As T Corp (PA) C 415 251-2800
50 California St Fl 21 San Francisco (94111) ***(P-19855)***
American Scence Tech As T Corp D 310 773-1978
2372 Morse Ave Ste 571 Irvine (92614) ***(P-19856)***
American SD Power Inc F 909 947-0673
14181 Fern Ave Chino (91710) ***(P-16630)***
American Security Educators F 562 928-1847
8734 Cleta St Ste E Downey (90241) ***(P-6183)***
American Security Products Co C 951 685-9680
11925 Pacific Ave Fontana (92337) ***(P-13496)***
American Sheet Metal, El Cajon *Also called Asm Construction Inc* ***(P-12118)***
American Sheet Metal Inc F 714 780-0155
1430 N Daly St Anaheim (92806) ***(P-12108)***
American Single Sheets, Redlands *Also called Continental Datalabel Inc* ***(P-5502)***
American Skynet Electronics, Milpitas *Also called Silicon Vly World Trade Corp* ***(P-16615)***
American Society of Composers E 323 883-1000
7920 W Sunset Blvd # 300 Los Angeles (90046) ***(P-6184)***
American Solar Advantage Inc E 951 496-1075
7056 Archibald St 102-432 Corona (92880) ***(P-18093)***
American Sport Bags Inc E 714 547-8013
1485 E Warner Ave Santa Ana (92705) ***(P-3653)***
American Spring Inc F 310 324-2181
321 W 135th St Los Angeles (90061) ***(P-13335)***
American Steel & Stairways Inc E 408 848-2992
8525 Forest St Ste A Gilroy (95020) ***(P-12449)***
American Steel Masters Inc E 626 333-3375
15050 Proctor Ave City of Industry (91746) ***(P-11743)***
American Straw Company LLC F 213 304-1095
1697 Woods Dr Los Angeles (90069) ***(P-23273)***
American Sugar Refining Inc B 510 787-6763
830 Loring Ave Crockett (94525) ***(P-1349)***
American Supply, Ontario *Also called Castillo Maritess* ***(P-3679)***
American System Publications E 323 259-1867
3018 Carmel St Los Angeles (90065) ***(P-6185)***
American Technical Molding Inc C 909 982-1025
2052 W 11th St Upland (91786) ***(P-9627)***
American Thermoform Corp (PA) F 909 593-6711
1758 Brackett St La Verne (91750) ***(P-14313)***
American Tooth Industries D 805 487-9868
1200 Stellar Dr Oxnard (93033) ***(P-22133)***
American Trck Trlr Bdy Co Inc (PA) E 209 836-8985
100 W Valpico Rd Ste D Tracy (95376) ***(P-19517)***
American Truck Dismantling F 909 429-2166
15303 Arrow Blvd Fontana (92335) ***(P-153)***
American Truss, Laguna Niguel *Also called American Pacific Truss Inc* ***(P-4287)***
American Ultraviolet West Inc E 310 784-2930
23555 Telo Ave Torrance (90505) ***(P-13814)***
American Underwater Products (HQ) D 800 435-3483
2002 Davis St San Leandro (94577) ***(P-22744)***
American Vangaurd, Newport Beach *Also called Amvac Chemical Corporation* ***(P-8820)***
American Vanguard Corporation (PA) D 949 260-1200
4695 Macarthur Ct Newport Beach (92660) ***(P-8818)***
American Wire Inc F 909 884-9990
784 S Lugo Ave San Bernardino (92408) ***(P-13394)***
AMERICAN WIRE SALES, Rancho Dominguez *Also called Standard Wire & Cable Co* ***(P-11320)***
American Wood Fibers Inc F 530 741-3700
4560 Skyway Dr Marysville (95901) ***(P-3923)***
American Yeast Corporation E 661 834-1050
5455 District Blvd Bakersfield (93313) ***(P-2391)***
American Zabin Intl Inc E 213 746-3770
3933 S Hill St Los Angeles (90037) ***(P-6987)***
American Zinc Enterprises, Walnut *Also called Sea Shield Marine Products* ***(P-11348)***
Americana Sports Inc E 626 914-0238
422 S Vermont Ave Glendora (91741) ***(P-22745)***
Americas Best Beverage Inc E 800 723-8808
600 50th Ave Oakland (94601) ***(P-2274)***
Americas Finest Products E 310 450-6555
1639 9th St Santa Monica (90404) ***(P-8336)***
Americas Gold Inc E 213 688-4904
650 S Hill St Ste 224 Los Angeles (90014) ***(P-22493)***
Americas Gold - Amrcas Damonds, Los Angeles *Also called Americas Gold Inc* ***(P-22493)***
Americas Styrenics LLC F 424 488-3757
305 Crenshaw Blvd Torrance (90503) ***(P-7470)***
Americawear, Commerce *Also called RDD Enterprises Inc* ***(P-2974)***
Americh Corporation (PA) C 818 982-1711
13212 Saticoy St North Hollywood (91605) ***(P-21980)***
Americhip Inc (PA) D 310 323-3697
19032 S Vermont Ave Gardena (90248) ***(P-6412)***
Americon F 805 987-0412
900 Flynn Rd Camarillo (93012) ***(P-4780)***
Americore Inc E 209 632-5679
19705 August Ave Hilmar (95324) ***(P-12531)***
Ameriflex Inc D 951 737-5557
2390 Railroad St Corona (92880) ***(P-13457)***
Amerillum LLC D 760 727-7675
3728 Maritime Way Oceanside (92056) ***(P-17102)***
Amerimade Technology Inc E 925 243-9090
449 Mountain Vista Pkwy Livermore (94551) ***(P-9628)***
Amerimax, Anaheim *Also called Euramax Holdings Inc* ***(P-11216)***
Ameripec Inc C 714 690-9191
6965 Aragon Cir Buena Park (90620) ***(P-2038)***
Ameripharma, Orange *Also called Harpers Pharmacy Inc* ***(P-7934)***
Amerisink Inc (PA) F 510 667-9998
835 Fremont Ave San Leandro (94577) ***(P-11655)***
Ameritex International, Los Angeles *Also called Amtex California Inc* ***(P-3587)***
Ameron International Corp C 425 258-2616
1020 B St Fillmore (93015) ***(P-10528)***
Ameron International Corp C 209 836-5050
10100 W Linne Rd Tracy (95377) ***(P-13345)***
Ameron International Corp D 805 524-0223
1020 B St Fillmore (93015) ***(P-10529)***
Ameron International Corp E 714 256-7755
201 N Berry St Brea (92821) ***(P-22339)***
Amertex International Inc E 626 570-9409
2108 Orange St Alhambra (91803) ***(P-3137)***
Ames Fire Waterworks D 530 666-2493
1485 Tanforan Ave Woodland (95776) ***(P-16697)***
Ames Industrial, Los Angeles *Also called Ames Rubber Mfg Co Inc* ***(P-9281)***
Ames Rubber Mfg Co Inc E 818 240-9313
4516 Brazil St Los Angeles (90039) ***(P-9281)***
Amest Corporation F 949 766-9692
30394 Esperanza Rcho STA Marg (92688) ***(P-18094)***
Ametek Inc D 949 642-2400
17032 Armstrong Ave Irvine (92614) ***(P-16631)***
Ametek Ameron LLC E 626 337-4640
4750 Littlejohn St Baldwin Park (91706) ***(P-20533)***
Ametek Ameron LLC (HQ) D 626 856-0101
4750 Littlejohn St Baldwin Park (91706) ***(P-20832)***
Ametek HCC, Rosemead *Also called Hermetic Seal Corporation* ***(P-18935)***
Ametek Programmable Power Inc (HQ) C 858 450-0085
9250 Brown Deer Rd San Diego (92121) ***(P-21002)***
Amex Manufacturing Inc F 619 391-7412
2307 Avenida Costa Este San Diego (92154) ***(P-12450)***
Amex Plating Incorporated E 408 986-8222
3333 Woodward Ave Santa Clara (95054) ***(P-12925)***
AMF, Roseville *Also called Advanced Metal Finishing LLC* ***(P-12905)***
AMF Pharma LLC E 909 930-9599
1931 S Lynx Ave Ontario (91761) ***(P-7748)***
AMF Support Surfaces Inc (HQ) C 951 549-6800
1691 N Delilah St Corona (92879) ***(P-4711)***
Amfab, Anaheim *Also called Evert Hancock Incorporated* ***(P-12202)***
Amflex Plastics Incorporated F 760 643-1756
4039 Calle Platino Ste G Oceanside (92056) ***(P-9629)***
AMG Employee Management Inc F 323 254-7448
3235 N San Fernando Rd 1d Los Angeles (90065) ***(P-22476)***
AMG Torrance LLC (HQ) D 310 515-2584
5401 Business Dr Huntington Beach (92649) ***(P-20032)***
Amgen Inc (PA) A 805 447-1000
1 Amgen Center Dr Thousand Oaks (91320) ***(P-8270)***
Amgen Inc F 805 499-0512
1909 Oak Terrace Ln Newbury Park (91320) ***(P-7749)***
Amgen Inc E 650 244-2000
1120 Veterans Blvd South San Francisco (94080) ***(P-7750)***
Amgen Inc D 805 447-1000
1840 De Havilland Dr Newbury Park (91320) ***(P-7751)***
Amgen Manufacturing Limited F 787 656-2000
1 Amgen Center Dr Newbury Park (91320) ***(P-23274)***
Amgen USA Inc (HQ) D 805 447-1000
1 Amgen Center Dr Thousand Oaks (91320) ***(P-8271)***
Amgraph, Ontario *Also called American Fleet & Ret Graphics* ***(P-23048)***
Amh International Inc F 805 388-2082
1270 Avenida Acaso Ste J Camarillo (93012) ***(P-15741)***
AMI, El Dorado Hills *Also called All Sales Manufacturing Inc* ***(P-19575)***
AMI, Costa Mesa *Also called Advanced Micro Instruments Inc* ***(P-21161)***
AMI/Coast Magnetics Inc E 323 936-6188
5333 W Washington Blvd Los Angeles (90016) ***(P-18699)***
Amiad Filtration Systems, Oxnard *Also called Amiad USA Inc* ***(P-15481)***
Amiad USA Inc E 805 988-3323
1251 Maulhardt Ave Oxnard (93030) ***(P-15481)***
Amico - Diamond Perforated, Visalia *Also called Diamond Perforated Metals Inc* ***(P-12793)***
Amico Fontana, Fontana *Also called Alabama Metal Industries Corp* ***(P-12448)***
Amigo Custom Screen Prints LLC E 760 525-5593
6351 Yarrow Dr Ste A&B Carlsbad (92011) ***(P-6988)***

Employee Codes: A=Over 500 employees, B=251-500
C=101-250, D=51-100, E=20-50, F=10-19
2020 California
Manfacturers Register
© Mergent Inc. 1-800-342-5647
1021

Amimon Inc..........F......650 641-3191
2350 Mission College Blvd # 190 Santa Clara (95054) ***(P-5156)***
Aminco International USA Inc (PA)..........E......949 457-3261
20571 Crescent Bay Dr Lake Forest (92630) ***(P-22494)***
Amino Technologies (us) LLC (HQ)..........D......408 861-1400
20823 Stevens Creek Blvd Cupertino (95014) ***(P-17448)***
Amiri, Los Angeles *Also called Atelier Luxury Group LLC* ***(P-3771)***
Amish Country Gazebos Inc..........F......800 700-1777
739 E Francis St Ontario (91761) ***(P-4547)***
Amity Rubberized Pen Company..........E......626 969-0863
612 N Commercial Ave Covina (91723) ***(P-22932)***
Amity Washer & Stamping Co..........E......562 941-1259
10926 Painter Ave Santa Fe Springs (90670) ***(P-12765)***
Amko Restaurant Furniture Inc..........E......323 234-0388
5833 Avalon Blvd Los Angeles (90003) ***(P-5049)***
Amkor Technology Inc..........D......858 320-6280
5465 Morehouse Dr Ste 210 San Diego (92121) ***(P-18095)***
Amkor Technology Inc..........E......949 724-9370
3 Corporate Park Ste 230 Irvine (92606) ***(P-18096)***
Amlogic Inc..........E......408 850-9688
2518 Mission College Blvd Santa Clara (95054) ***(P-18097)***
Ammi Publishing Inc..........F......415 435-2652
1550 Tiburon Blvd Ste D Belvedere Tiburon (94920) ***(P-5549)***
Ammiel Enterprise Inc..........F......213 973-5032
1100 S San Pedro St C01 Los Angeles (90015) ***(P-3213)***
AMO Corporation..........F......916 791-2001
9580 Oak Avenue Pkwy # 9 Folsom (95630) ***(P-14130)***
AMO Usa Inc..........C......714 247-8200
1700 E Saint Andrew Pl Santa Ana (92705) ***(P-21599)***
Amobee Inc..........F......858 638-1515
10201 Wtridge Cir Ste 200 San Diego (92121) ***(P-20833)***
Amoretti, Oxnard *Also called Noushig Inc* ***(P-1251)***
Amos Art Studio, Northridge *Also called Emanuel Morez Inc* ***(P-4568)***
AMP, Santa Ana *Also called Accelerated Memory Prod Inc* ***(P-18059)***
AMP III LLC..........D......408 779-2927
465 Woodview Ave Morgan Hill (95037) ***(P-14131)***
AMP Plus Inc..........D......323 231-2600
2042 E Vernon Ave Vernon (90058) ***(P-17087)***
AMP Research, Tustin *Also called Lund Motion Products Inc* ***(P-19708)***
Ampac Analytical, El Dorado Hills *Also called Ampac Fine Chemicals LLC* ***(P-7753)***
Ampac Fine Chemicals LLC (HQ)..........B......916 357-6880
Highway 50 And Hazel Ave Rancho Cordova (95741) ***(P-7752)***
Ampac Fine Chemicals LLC..........F......916 245-6500
1100 Windfield Way El Dorado Hills (95762) ***(P-7753)***
Ampac USA, Montclair *Also called Nef Tech Inc* ***(P-15548)***
Ampac Usa Inc..........F......707 571-1754
3343 Industrial Dr Ste 2 Santa Rosa (95403) ***(P-8436)***
Ampersand Contract Signing Grp, Los Angeles *Also called Ahr Signs Incorporated* ***(P-23045)***
Ampersand Ice Cream LLC..........F......559 264-8000
1940 N Echo Ave Fresno (93704) ***(P-628)***
Ampersand Publishing LLC (PA)..........E......805 564-5200
715 Anacapa St Santa Barbara (93101) ***(P-5550)***
Ampertech Inc..........E......714 523-4068
636 S State College Blvd Fullerton (92831) ***(P-14132)***
Ampex Data Systems Corporation (HQ)..........D......650 367-2011
26460 Corporate Ave Hayward (94545) ***(P-15004)***
Amphastar Pharmaceuticals Inc (PA)..........C......909 980-9484
11570 6th St Rancho Cucamonga (91730) ***(P-7754)***
Amphenol Corporation..........F......805 378-6464
5069 Maureen Ln Ste B Moorpark (93021) ***(P-18751)***
Amphenol DC Electronics Inc..........B......408 947-4500
1870 Little Orchard St San Jose (95125) ***(P-16876)***
Amphion, Rancho Cucamonga *Also called Executive Safe and SEC Corp* ***(P-13522)***
Ampine LLC..........C......209 223-1690
11610 Ampine Fibreform Rd Sutter Creek (95685) ***(P-4781)***
Amplifier Technologies Inc..........E......323 278-0001
1749 Chapin Rd Montebello (90640) ***(P-17449)***
Ampligraphix..........F......661 321-3150
1768 Glenwood Dr Bakersfield (93306) ***(P-6413)***
Ampro Adlink Technology Inc..........D......408 360-0200
5215 Hellyer Ave Ste 110 San Jose (95138) ***(P-14889)***
Ampro Computers, Inc., San Jose *Also called Ampro Adlink Technology Inc* ***(P-14889)***
Ampro Systems Inc..........E......510 624-9000
1000 Page Ave Fremont (94538) ***(P-17818)***
Amq Solutions LLC (HQ)..........F......877 801-0370
764 Walsh Ave Santa Clara (95050) ***(P-4782)***
AMR Industries Enterprises Inc..........E......415 860-5566
2131 19th Ave Ste 203 San Francisco (94116) ***(P-13764)***
Amrapur Overseas Incorporated (PA)..........E......714 893-8808
1560 E 6th St Ste 101 Corona (92879) ***(P-2924)***
Amrel, Baldwin Park *Also called American Reliance Inc* ***(P-14888)***
Amrep Inc (HQ)..........C......909 923-0430
1555 S Cucamonga Ave Ontario (91761) ***(P-8361)***
Amrex Electrotherapy Equipment, Paramount *Also called Amrex-Zetron Inc* ***(P-19257)***
Amrex-Zetron Inc..........E......310 527-6868
7034 Jackson St Paramount (90723) ***(P-19257)***
Amrich Energy Inc..........F......805 354-0830
1160 Marsh St Ste 105 San Luis Obispo (93401) ***(P-8713)***
Amro Fabricating Corporation..........E......951 842-6140
17101 Heacock St Moreno Valley (92551) ***(P-20033)***
Amro Fabricating Corporation (PA)..........C......626 579-2200
1430 Adelia Ave South El Monte (91733) ***(P-20034)***
Amron International Inc (PA)..........D......760 208-6500
1380 Aspen Way Vista (92081) ***(P-22746)***
Amron Manufacturing Inc..........F......714 278-9204
635 Gregory Cir Corona (92881) ***(P-20035)***
Amron Urethane Products, Corona *Also called Amron Manufacturing Inc* ***(P-20035)***
AMS, Manteca *Also called American Modular Systems Inc* ***(P-4456)***
AMS Drilling..........F......949 232-1149
120 Tustin Ave Ste C Newport Beach (92663) ***(P-86)***
Amscan Inc..........D......714 972-2626
804 W Town And Country Rd Orange (92868) ***(P-5306)***
Amsco US Inc..........C......562 630-0333
15341 Texaco Ave Paramount (90723) ***(P-18816)***
Amsec, Fontana *Also called American Security Products Co* ***(P-13496)***
Amtec, Anaheim *Also called Applied Manufacturing Tech Inc* ***(P-14315)***
Amtec Human Capital Inc..........E......949 472-0396
21661 Audubon Way El Toro (92630) ***(P-14016)***
Amtech Microelectronics Inc..........E......408 612-8888
485 Cochrane Cir Morgan Hill (95037) ***(P-17819)***
Amtecol Inc..........E......510 235-7979
810 Wright Ave Richmond (94804) ***(P-9129)***
Amtek, Poway *Also called United Security Products Inc* ***(P-19428)***
Amtek Electronic Inc..........E......408 971-8787
1150 N 5th St San Jose (95112) ***(P-14890)***
Amtex California Inc..........E......323 859-2200
113 S Utah St Los Angeles (90033) ***(P-3587)***
Amtrend Corporation..........D......714 630-2070
1458 Manhattan Ave Fullerton (92831) ***(P-4880)***
Amundson Tom Tmber Flling Cntr..........F......530 529-0504
14615 River Oaks Dr Red Bluff (96080) ***(P-3871)***
Amvac Chemical Corporation (HQ)..........E......323 264-3910
4695 Macarthur Ct # 1200 Newport Beach (92660) ***(P-8819)***
Amvac Chemical Corporation..........F......949 260-1212
4695 Macarthur Ct # 1200 Newport Beach (92660) ***(P-8820)***
Amylin Pharmaceuticals LLC..........D......858 552-2200
9373 Twn Cntr Dr 150 San Diego (92101) ***(P-7755)***
Amyris Inc (PA)..........B......510 450-0761
5885 Hollis St Ste 100 Emeryville (94608) ***(P-8714)***
Amys Kitchen Inc..........E......707 568-4500
1650 Corp Cir Ste 200 Petaluma (94954) ***(P-940)***
Amys Kitchen Inc (PA)..........A......707 578-7188
2330 Northpoint Pkwy Santa Rosa (95407) ***(P-941)***
Amzart Inc..........F......323 404-9372
3260 Casitas Ave Los Angeles (90039) ***(P-2392)***
Amzr Inc..........C......800 541-2326
29115 Avenue Valleyview Valencia (91355) ***(P-3832)***
An Environmental Inks..........F......909 930-9656
1920 S Quaker Ridge Pl Ontario (91761) ***(P-8909)***
Ana Global LLC..........A......619 482-9990
2360 Marconi Ct San Diego (92154) ***(P-4752)***
Anabolic Incorporated..........D......949 863-0340
17802 Gillette Ave Irvine (92614) ***(P-7756)***
Anabolic Laboratories Inc..........F......949 863-0340
26021 Commercentre Dr Lake Forest (92630) ***(P-7757)***
Anacapa Boatyard, Newport Beach *Also called Anacapa Marine Services* ***(P-20312)***
Anacapa Marine Services (PA)..........F......805 985-1818
151 Shipyard Way Ste 5 Newport Beach (92663) ***(P-20312)***
Anaco Inc..........C......951 372-2732
1001 El Camino Ave Corona (92879) ***(P-14780)***
Anacom Inc..........E......408 519-2062
1961 Concourse Dr San Jose (95131) ***(P-17450)***
Anacom General Corporation..........E......714 774-8484
1240 S Claudina St Anaheim (92805) ***(P-17188)***
Anacom Medtek, Anaheim *Also called Anacom General Corporation* ***(P-17188)***
Anacor Pharmaceuticals Inc..........E......650 543-7500
1020 E Meadow Cir Palo Alto (94303) ***(P-7758)***
Anacrown Inc..........F......310 530-1165
25835 Narbonne Ave # 250 Lomita (90717) ***(P-13497)***
Anadite Cal Restoration Tr..........E......562 861-2205
10647 Garfield Ave South Gate (90280) ***(P-12926)***
Anaheim Automation Inc..........E......714 992-6990
4985 E Landon Dr Anaheim (92807) ***(P-16698)***
Anaheim Custom Extruders Inc..........E......714 693-8508
4640 E La Palma Ave Anaheim (92807) ***(P-9630)***
Anaheim Embroidery Inc..........E......714 563-5220
1230 N Jefferson St Ste C Anaheim (92807) ***(P-3723)***
Anaheim Plant, Anaheim *Also called Stepan Company* ***(P-7615)***
Anaheim Precision Shtmtl Mfg, Orange *Also called APM Manufacturing* ***(P-19857)***
Anaheim Wire Products Inc (PA)..........E......714 563-8300
1009 E Vermont Ave Anaheim (92805) ***(P-13395)***
Anajet LLC..........E......714 662-3200
1100 Valencia Ave Tustin (92780) ***(P-14314)***
Analog Bits..........E......650 279-9323
945 Stewart Dr Sunnyvale (94085) ***(P-18098)***
Analog Devices Inc..........B......408 727-9222
1530 Buckeye Dr Milpitas (95035) ***(P-18099)***
Analog Devices Inc..........E......714 641-9391
940 S Coast Dr Ste 230 Costa Mesa (92626) ***(P-18100)***
Analogix Semiconductor Inc..........E......408 988-8848
3211 Scott Blvd Ste 100 Santa Clara (95054) ***(P-18101)***
Analytcal Scentific Instrs Inc..........E......510 669-2250
3023 Research Dr San Pablo (94806) ***(P-21171)***
Analytic and Computational Res..........F......310 471-3023
1931 Stradella Rd Los Angeles (90077) ***(P-23599)***
Analytic Endodontics, Orange *Also called Sybron Dental Specialties Inc* ***(P-22194)***
Analytical Industries Inc..........E......909 392-6900
2855 Metropolitan Pl Pomona (91767) ***(P-20834)***
Analytical Sciences, Irvine *Also called Allergan Sales LLC* ***(P-7739)***
Analytik Jena US LLC (HQ)..........D......909 946-3197
2066 W 11th St Upland (91786) ***(P-21172)***
Anaplex Corporation..........E......714 522-4481
15547 Garfield Ave Paramount (90723) ***(P-12927)***
Anasys Instruments Corp..........F......805 730-3310
325 Chapala St Santa Barbara (93101) ***(P-21173)***
Anatase Products, Tehachapi *Also called Henway Inc* ***(P-23003)***

Mergent e-mail: customerrelations@mergent.com
1022
2020 California
Manufacturers Register
(P-0000) Products & Services Section entry number
(PA)=Parent Co (HQ)=Headquarters (DH)=Div Headquarters

Anatesco Inc.....F.....661 399-6990
128 Bedford Way Bakersfield (93308) *(P-154)*
Anatometal Inc.....E.....831 454-9880
165 Dubois St Santa Cruz (95060) *(P-22495)*
Anatomic Global Inc.....C.....800 874-7237
1241 Old Temescal Rd # 103 Corona (92881) *(P-3600)*
Anc Technology LLC.....D.....805 530-3958
10195 Stockton Rd Moorpark (93021) *(P-17820)*
Anchen Pharmaceuticals Inc.....F.....949 639-8100
5 Goodyear Irvine (92618) *(P-7759)*
Anchor Audio Inc.....D.....760 827-7100
5931 Darwin Ct Carlsbad (92008) *(P-17189)*
Anchor Distilling Company.....E.....415 863-8350
1705 Mariposa St San Francisco (94107) *(P-1582)*
Anchored Prints Inc.....E.....714 929-9317
635 N Eckhoff St Ste Q Orange (92868) *(P-6414)*
Anco International Inc.....E.....909 887-2521
19851 Cajon Blvd San Bernardino (92407) *(P-13346)*
Ancra International LLC (HQ).....C.....626 765-4800
601 S Vincent Ave Azusa (91702) *(P-13856)*
Anda Networks Inc (PA).....F.....408 519-4900
1100 La Avenida St Ste A Mountain View (94043) *(P-17347)*
Andalou Naturals.....F.....415 446-9470
1470 Cader Ln Petaluma (94954) *(P-8437)*
Andari Fashion Inc.....C.....626 575-2759
9626 Telstar Ave El Monte (91731) *(P-3066)*
Andeavor.....F.....310 847-5705
2350 E 223rd St Carson (90810) *(P-21)*
Anderco Inc.....E.....714 446-9508
540 Airpark Dr Fullerton (92833) *(P-3992)*
Andersen Industries Inc.....E.....760 246-8766
17079 Muskrat Ave Adelanto (92301) *(P-19813)*
Anderson Bat Company LLC.....D.....714 524-7500
236 E Orangethorpe Ave Placentia (92870) *(P-22747)*
Anderson Bros Artistic Iron Co.....F.....951 898-6880
310 Elizabeth Ln Corona (92880) *(P-13498)*
Anderson Desk Inc.....B.....619 671-1040
7510 Airway Rd Ste 7 San Diego (92154) *(P-4783)*
Anderson Logging Inc.....D.....707 964-2770
1296 N Main St Fort Bragg (95437) *(P-3872)*
Anderson Moulds Incorporated.....F.....209 943-1145
3131 E Anita St Stockton (95205) *(P-9631)*
Anderson Signs.....F.....209 367-0120
1240 N Filbert St Stockton (95205) *(P-23049)*
Anderson Valley Brewing Inc.....E.....707 895-2337
17700 Hwy 253 Boonville (95415) *(P-1490)*
Anderson Valley Brewing Co, Boonville *Also called Anderson Valley Brewing Inc (P-1490)*
Anderson's Carpet & Linoleum, Oakland *Also called Linoleum Sales Co Inc (P-10271)*
Anderson's Signs & Crane, Stockton *Also called Anderson Signs (P-23049)*
Andre-Boudin Bakeries Inc.....F.....925 935-4375
67 Broadwalk Ln Walnut Creek (94596) *(P-1135)*
Andre-Boudin Bakeries Inc.....F.....408 249-4101
2855 Stevens Crk 2451 San Jose (95128) *(P-1136)*
Andrea Zee Corporation.....F.....209 462-1700
711 S San Joaquin St Stockton (95203) *(P-10889)*
Andresen, Burlingame *Also called Clic LLC (P-6488)*
Andresen Digital Pre-Press, Santa Monica *Also called Aft Corporation (P-7368)*
Andretti Winery, NAPA *Also called Awg Ltd Inc (P-1587)*
Andrew Alexander Inc.....D.....323 752-0066
1306 S Alameda St Compton (90221) *(P-10136)*
Andrew LLC.....F.....909 270-9356
1710 S Grove Ave Ste A&B Ontario (91761) *(P-988)*
Andrew Morgan Furniture, Escondido *Also called California Cstm Furn & Uphl Co (P-3778)*
Andrews Electronics, Valencia *Also called Partsearch Technologies Inc (P-19046)*
Andrews Powder Coating Inc.....E.....818 700-1030
10138 Canoga Ave Chatsworth (91311) *(P-13142)*
Andromeda Software Inc.....F.....805 379-4109
2965 Potter Ave Thousand Oaks (91360) *(P-23600)*
Androp Packaging Inc.....E.....909 605-8842
4400 E Francis St Ontario (91761) *(P-5196)*
Andrus Sheet Metal Inc.....E.....510 232-8687
5021 Seaport Ave Richmond (94804) *(P-12109)*
Anemostat Products, Carson *Also called Mestek Inc (P-15445)*
Ang Newspaper Group Inc (HQ).....F.....650 359-6666
1301 Grant Ave B Novato (94945) *(P-5551)*
Angel Manufacturing, Los Angeles *Also called Angels Garments (P-3067)*
Angeleno Magazine, San Francisco *Also called Modern Luxury Media LLC (P-5991)*
Angell & Giroux Inc.....D.....323 269-8596
2727 Alcazar St Los Angeles (90033) *(P-4828)*
Angellist LLC.....F.....415 857-0840
90 Gold St San Francisco (94133) *(P-23601)*
Angels, Los Angeles *Also called Hip & Hip Inc (P-3337)*
Angels Garments.....F.....213 748-0581
525 E 12th St Ste 107 Los Angeles (90015) *(P-3067)*
Angels Sheet Metal Inc.....F.....209 736-0911
320 N Main St Angels Camp (95222) *(P-12110)*
Angels Young Inc.....F.....213 614-0742
514 S Broadway Los Angeles (90013) *(P-2959)*
Angelus Aluminum Foundry Co.....F.....323 268-0145
3479 E Pico Blvd Los Angeles (90023) *(P-11367)*
Angelus Block Co Inc.....E.....805 485-1137
4575 E Vineyard Ave Oxnard (93036) *(P-10499)*
Angelus Block Co Inc.....D.....714 637-8594
1705 N Main St Orange (92865) *(P-10500)*
Angelus Formulations, Santa Fe Springs *Also called Angelus Shoe Polish Co Inc (P-8362)*
Angelus Plating Works.....F.....310 516-1883
1713 W 134th St Gardena (90249) *(P-19582)*
Angelus Sheet Metal & Plbg Sup, Los Angeles *Also called Angelus Sheet Metal Mfg Co (P-12111)*
Angelus Sheet Metal Mfg Co.....F.....323 221-4191
1355 Carroll Ave Los Angeles (90026) *(P-12111)*
Angelus Shoe Polish Co Inc.....F.....562 941-4242
12060 Florence Ave Santa Fe Springs (90670) *(P-8362)*
Angry Horse Brewing, Montebello *Also called Desert Brothers Craft (P-1520)*
Angular Machining Inc.....E.....408 954-8326
2040 Hartog Dr San Jose (95131) *(P-15742)*
Anheuser-Busch LLC.....C.....818 989-5300
15800 Roscoe Blvd Van Nuys (91406) *(P-1491)*
Anheuser-Busch LLC.....C.....858 581-7000
5959 Santa Fe St San Diego (92109) *(P-1492)*
Anheuser-Busch LLC.....C.....800 622-2667
2800 S Reservoir St Pomona (91766) *(P-1493)*
Aniise Skin Care, Los Angeles *Also called Global Sales Inc (P-8500)*
Anillo Industries Inc (PA).....E.....714 637-7000
2090 N Glassell St Orange (92865) *(P-12665)*
Anima International Corp.....F.....626 723-4960
19502 Avenida Del Campo Walnut (91789) *(P-23275)*
Animal Nutrition Inds Inc.....F.....949 583-2920
5602 E La Palma Ave Anaheim (92807) *(P-7645)*
Anitas Mexican Foods Corp (PA).....C.....909 884-8706
3454 N Mike Daley Dr San Bernardino (92407) *(P-2317)*
Anivive Lifesciences Inc.....F.....714 931-7810
3250 Airflite Way 400 Long Beach (90807) *(P-7760)*
Anki Inc (PA).....E.....877 721-2654
333 S Grand Ave Ste 4100 Los Angeles (90071) *(P-22657)*
Anlin Industries.....C.....800 287-7996
1665 Tollhouse Rd Clovis (93611) *(P-3993)*
Anlin Window Systems, Clovis *Also called Anlin Industries (P-3993)*
Anmar Precision Components.....F.....818 764-0901
7424 Greenbush Ave North Hollywood (91605) *(P-20036)*
Ann Lilli Corp (PA).....D.....415 482-9444
1010 B St Ste 209 San Rafael (94901) *(P-3262)*
Annabelle Candy Inc.....D.....510 783-2900
27211 Industrial Blvd Hayward (94545) *(P-1356)*
Annianna, Commerce *Also called Siho Corporation (P-3406)*
Annieglass Inc (PA).....E.....831 761-2041
310 Harvest Dr Watsonville (95076) *(P-10298)*
Annies Inc (HQ).....D.....510 558-7500
1610 5th St Berkeley (94710) *(P-2393)*
Annies Baking LLC (HQ).....E.....510 558-7500
1610 5th St Berkeley (94710) *(P-1137)*
Annmar Industries Inc.....F.....714 630-5443
990 S Jay Cir Anaheim (92808) *(P-9632)*
Annona Company LLC.....F.....858 299-4238
444 S Cedros Ave Ste 175 Solana Beach (92075) *(P-1015)*
Ano-Tech Metal Finishing, Clovis *Also called Atmf Inc (P-12938)*
Anocote.....F.....858 566-1015
7550 Trade St San Diego (92121) *(P-12928)*
Anodizing Industries Inc.....E.....323 227-4916
5222 Alhambra Ave Los Angeles (90032) *(P-12929)*
Anodyne Inc.....E.....714 549-3321
2230 S Susan St Santa Ana (92704) *(P-12930)*
Anokiwave Inc (PA).....E.....858 792-9910
11236 El Camino Real # 100 San Diego (92130) *(P-18102)*
Anoroc Precision Shtmtl Inc.....E.....310 515-6015
19122 S Santa Fe Ave Compton (90221) *(P-12112)*
Anoto Incorporated.....F.....510 777-0071
7677 Oakport St Ste 1200 Oakland (94621) *(P-22933)*
Anova Microsystems Inc.....F.....408 941-1888
173 Santa Rita Ct Los Altos (94022) *(P-15155)*
Anozira Incorporated.....F.....925 771-8400
2415 San Ramon Vly Blvd San Ramon (94583) *(P-10530)*
Anp Lighting, Montclair *Also called American Nail Plate Ltg Inc (P-16959)*
Anritsu Company, Morgan Hill *Also called Anritsu US Holding Inc (P-21003)*
Anritsu Company (HQ).....B.....800 267-4878
490 Jarvis Dr Morgan Hill (95037) *(P-17451)*
Anritsu Instruments Company.....E.....315 797-4449
490 Jarvis Dr Morgan Hill (95037) *(P-10299)*
Anritsu US Holding Inc (HQ).....B.....408 778-2000
490 Jarvis Dr Morgan Hill (95037) *(P-21003)*
Anschutz Film Group LLC (HQ).....E.....310 887-1000
1888 Century Park E # 1400 Los Angeles (90067) *(P-22402)*
Ansell Sndel Med Solutions LLC.....E.....818 534-2500
9301 Oakdale Ave Ste 300 Chatsworth (91311) *(P-21981)*
Ansons Transportation Inc.....E.....559 892-1867
438 E Shaw Ave Ste 434 Fresno (93710) *(P-13857)*
Ansys Inc.....F.....408 457-2000
2645 Zanker Rd San Jose (95134) *(P-23602)*
Antaeus Fashions Group Inc.....E.....626 452-0797
2400 Chico Ave South El Monte (91733) *(P-3068)*
Antaky Quilting Company, Los Angeles *Also called American Quilting Company Inc (P-3722)*
Antcom Corporation.....E.....310 782-1076
367 Van Ness Way Ste 602 Torrance (90501) *(P-17452)*
Antec Inc.....E.....510 770-1200
47681 Lakeview Blvd Fremont (94538) *(P-15156)*
Antelope Valley Newspapers Inc.....E.....661 940-1000
44939 10th St W Lancaster (93534) *(P-5552)*
Antelope Valley Press, Lancaster *Also called Antelope Valley Newspapers Inc (P-5552)*
Antenna Works, Long Beach *Also called Metra Electronics Corporation (P-19718)*
Anterra Group Inc.....F.....949 215-0658
25255 Cabot Rd Ste 215 Laguna Hills (92653) *(P-8425)*
Antex Knitting Mills, Los Angeles *Also called Tenenblatt Corporation (P-2813)*
Antex Knitting Mills, Los Angeles *Also called Matchmaster Dyg & Finshg Inc (P-2856)*
Antex Knitting Mills, Los Angeles *Also called Guru Knits Inc (P-3164)*
Anthem Music & Media Fund LLC.....F.....310 286-6600
5750 Wilshire Blvd Fl 4th Los Angeles (90036) *(P-6072)*

A L P H A B E T I C

Employee Codes: A=Over 500 employees, B=251-500
C=101-250, D=51-100, E=20-50, F=10-19
2020 California
Manfacturers Register
© Mergent Inc. 1-800-342-5647
1023

Anthony California Inc (PA)....E.......909 627-0351
14485 Monte Vista Ave Chino (91710) ***(P-16960)***
Anthony Doors Inc....B.......818 365-9451
12812 Arroyo St Sylmar (91342) ***(P-10337)***
Anthony Doors Inc (HQ)....A.......818 365-9451
12391 Montero Ave Sylmar (91342) ***(P-15411)***
Anthony International, Sylmar *Also called Anthony Doors Inc* ***(P-10337)***
Anthony International, Sylmar *Also called Anthony Doors Inc* ***(P-15411)***
Anthony Jones....F.......714 894-3483
14161 Beach Blvd Westminster (92683) ***(P-22748)***
Anthony Welded Products Inc (PA)....E.......661 721-7211
1447 S Lexington St Delano (93215) ***(P-13858)***
Anthonys Chistmas Tree, Santa Barbara *Also called Anthonys Christmas Trees* ***(P-23276)***
Anthonys Christmas Trees....E.......805 966-6668
510 Alston Rd Santa Barbara (93108) ***(P-23276)***
Anthonys Rdymx & Bldg Sups Inc (PA)....F.......310 542-9400
4500 Manhattan Beach Blvd Lawndale (90260) ***(P-10689)***
Antibodies Incorporated....F.......800 824-8540
25242 County Road 95 Davis (95616) ***(P-8204)***
Antica NAPA Valley, NAPA *Also called Antinori California* ***(P-1583)***
Antigen Discovery Inc., Irvine *Also called Immport Therapeutics Inc* ***(P-22214)***
Antinori California....E.......707 265-8866
3149 Soda Canyon Rd NAPA (94558) ***(P-1583)***
Antioch Building Materials Co....E.......925 634-3541
6823 Brentwood Blvd Brentwood (94513) ***(P-10690)***
Antique Apparatus Company, Torrance *Also called Rock-Ola Manufacturing Corp* ***(P-17277)***
Antique Designs, Inglewood *Also called Glp Designs Inc* ***(P-5062)***
Antique Designs Ltd Inc....E.......310 671-5400
916 W Hyde Park Blvd Inglewood (90302) ***(P-4784)***
Anto Offset Printing....F.......510 843-8454
1101 5th St Berkeley (94710) ***(P-6415)***
Antonina's Bakery, Manteca *Also called Pin Hsiao & Associates LLC* ***(P-1262)***
Antypas & Associates Inc....F.......650 961-4311
749 Thorsen Ct Los Altos (94024) ***(P-17453)***
Anura Plastic Engineerign....D.......626 814-9684
5050 Rivergrade Rd Baldwin Park (91706) ***(P-9633)***
Anvil Arts Inc....F.......714 630-2870
1137 N Fountain Way Anaheim (92806) ***(P-4682)***
Anvil Cases Inc....C.......626 968-4100
1242 E Edna Pl Unit B Covina (91724) ***(P-10188)***
Anvil International LLC....F.......909 418-3233
551 N Loop Dr Ontario (91761) ***(P-13458)***
Anwright Corporation....E.......818 896-2465
10225 Glenoaks Blvd Pacoima (91331) ***(P-12620)***
Any Budget Printing & Mailing....F.......858 278-3151
8170 Ronson Rd Ste L San Diego (92111) ***(P-6416)***
Ao Sky Corporation....F.......415 717-9901
4989 Pedro Hill Rd Pilot Hill (95664) ***(P-20534)***
Ao Winery, Saint Helena *Also called Alpha Omega Winery LLC* ***(P-1581)***
Aoc LLC....D.......951 657-5161
19991 Seaton Ave Perris (92570) ***(P-2894)***
AOC California Plant, Perris *Also called Aoc LLC* ***(P-2894)***
Aoclsc Inc....C.......813 248-1988
8015 Paramount Blvd Pico Rivera (90660) ***(P-9130)***
Aoclsc Inc....E.......562 776-4000
3365 E Slauson Ave Vernon (90058) ***(P-9131)***
Aocusa, Pico Rivera *Also called Aoclsc Inc* ***(P-9130)***
Aocusa, Vernon *Also called Aoclsc Inc* ***(P-9131)***
Aoptix Technologies Inc....D.......408 558-3300
695 Campbell Tech Pkwy # 100 Campbell (95008) ***(P-19258)***
Aos, Torrance *Also called Advanced Orthopaedic Solutions* ***(P-21974)***
Aot Electronics Inc....E.......949 600-6335
23172 Alcalde Dr Ste E Laguna Hills (92653) ***(P-15157)***
AP Plastics....F.......951 782-0705
4025 Garner Rd Riverside (92501) ***(P-9634)***
AP Precision Metals Inc....F.......619 628-0003
1215 30th St San Diego (92154) ***(P-12113)***
AP Tech, NAPA *Also called Advanced Pressure Technology* ***(P-20829)***
Apama Medical Inc....F.......408 903-4094
745 Camden Ave Ste A Campbell (95008) ***(P-21600)***
Apartment Directory of L A....F.......310 832-0354
2515 S Western Ave Ste 13 San Pedro (90732) ***(P-6186)***
Apartment Drctry L A-South Bay, San Pedro *Also called Apartment Directory of L A* ***(P-6186)***
APC By Scheineder Electric, Costa Mesa *Also called Schneider Electric It Usa* ***(P-19078)***
Apct Inc (PA)....D.......408 727-6442
3495 De La Cruz Blvd Santa Clara (95054) ***(P-17821)***
Apem Inc....D.......760 598-2518
970 Park Center Dr Vista (92081) ***(P-18817)***
Aperia Technologies Inc....E.......415 494-9624
1616 Rollins Rd Burlingame (94010) ***(P-14423)***
Aperio, Vista *Also called Leica Biosystems Imaging Inc* ***(P-21773)***
Apex Brewing Supply....F.......916 250-7950
3237 Rippey Rd Ste 600 Loomis (95650) ***(P-14344)***
Apex Communications Inc (HQ)....F.......818 379-8400
21700 Oxnard St Ste 1060 Woodland Hills (91367) ***(P-23603)***
Apex Container Services, Commerce *Also called Apex Drum Company Inc* ***(P-4411)***
Apex Conveyor Corp....E.......951 304-7808
41674 Corning Pl Murrieta (92562) ***(P-13815)***
Apex Conveyor Systems Inc....F.......951 304-7808
41674 Corning Pl Murrieta (92562) ***(P-13816)***
Apex Design Technology, Anaheim *Also called Apex Technology Holdings Inc* ***(P-20535)***
Apex Die Corporation....D.......650 592-6350
840 Cherry Ln San Carlos (94070) ***(P-5446)***
Apex Digital Inc....F.......909 366-2028
4401 Eucalyptus Ave # 110 Chino (91710) ***(P-16961)***
Apex Door & Frame, Hesperia *Also called Apex Specialty Cnstr Entps* ***(P-3995)***
Apex Drum Company Inc....F.......323 721-8994
6226 Ferguson Dr Commerce (90022) ***(P-4411)***
Apex Enterprises Inc....F.......530 871-0732
687 Oro Dam Blvd E 4 Oroville (95965) ***(P-3873)***
Apex Interior Source Inc....E.......760 343-1919
30555 Roseview Ln Thousand Palms (92276) ***(P-3994)***
Apex Precision Tech Inc....E.......317 821-1000
23622 Calabasas Rd # 323 Calabasas (91302) ***(P-19583)***
Apex Specialty Cnstr Entps....F.......714 334-1118
17461 Poplar St Hesperia (92345) ***(P-3995)***
Apex Technology Holdings Inc....C.......714 688-7188
2850 E Coronado St Anaheim (92806) ***(P-20535)***
Apex Universal Inc (PA)....F.......562 944-8878
11033 Forest Pl Santa Fe Springs (90670) ***(P-23050)***
Apexigen Inc....E.......650 931-6236
75 Shoreway Rd Ste C San Carlos (94070) ***(P-7761)***
Apffels Coffee Inc....E.......562 309-0400
12115 Pacific St Santa Fe Springs (90670) ***(P-2275)***
Aphex Systems Ltd....E.......818 767-2929
3500 N San Fernando Blvd Burbank (91505) ***(P-17454)***
API, North Hollywood *Also called Architectural Plywood Inc* ***(P-4273)***
API Marketing....F.......916 632-1946
13020 Earhart Ave Auburn (95602) ***(P-6417)***
Apic Corporation....D.......310 642-7975
5800 Uplander Way Culver City (90230) ***(P-18103)***
Apical Instruments Inc....F.......650 967-1030
2971 Spring St Redwood City (94063) ***(P-21433)***
Aplus Flash Technology Inc....F.......408 382-1100
780 Montague Expy Ste 103 San Jose (95131) ***(P-18104)***
APM Manufacturing (HQ)....C.......714 453-0100
1738 N Neville St Orange (92865) ***(P-19857)***
Apnea Sciences Corporation....F.......949 226-4421
17 Brownsbury Rd Laguna Niguel (92677) ***(P-9282)***
Apoc, Long Beach *Also called Asphalt Products Oil Corp* ***(P-9109)***
Apogee Electronics Corporation....E.......310 584-9394
1715 Berkeley St Santa Monica (90404) ***(P-17190)***
Apollo Instruments Inc....E.......949 756-3111
55 Peters Canyon Rd Irvine (92606) ***(P-21334)***
Apollo Manufacturing Services....F.......858 271-8009
10360 Sorrento Valley Rd A San Diego (92121) ***(P-16776)***
Apollo Med Extrusion Tech Inc....F.......760 453-2944
3508 Seagate Way Ste 170 Oceanside (92056) ***(P-21601)***
Apollo Metal Spinning Co Inc....F.......562 634-5141
15315 Illinois Ave Paramount (90723) ***(P-12741)***
Apollo Printing & Graphics, Anaheim *Also called Tajen Graphics Inc* ***(P-6884)***
Apollo Sprayers Intl Inc....F.......760 727-8300
1030 Joshua Way Vista (92081) ***(P-14621)***
App Winddown LLC (HQ)....E.......213 488-0226
747 Warehouse St Los Angeles (90021) ***(P-3541)***
Apparel Enterprises Co Inc....E.......619 474-6916
1900 Wilson Ave Ste B National City (91950) ***(P-3285)***
Apparel House USA, Gardena *Also called Stanzino Inc* ***(P-2714)***
Apparel Limited Inc....D.......323 859-2430
3011 E Pico Blvd Los Angeles (90023) ***(P-3286)***
Apparel News Group....E.......213 327-1002
110 E 9th St Ste A777 Los Angeles (90079) ***(P-5880)***
Apparel Newsgroup, The, Los Angeles *Also called Mnm Corporation* ***(P-5990)***
Apparel Prod Svcs Globl LLC....E.......818 700-3700
8954 Lurline Ave Chatsworth (91311) ***(P-3287)***
Apparel Unified LLC....F.......562 639-7233
12136 Del Vista Dr La Mirada (90638) ***(P-6989)***
Apparelway Inc....F.......323 581-5888
4516 Loma Vista Ave Vernon (90058) ***(P-2902)***
Appbackr Inc....F.......650 272-6129
2251 Yale St Palo Alto (94306) ***(P-23604)***
Appdirect Inc (PA)....D.......415 852-3924
650 California St Fl 25 San Francisco (94108) ***(P-23605)***
Appdynamics Inc (HQ)....C.......415 442-8400
303 2nd St Fl 8 San Francisco (94107) ***(P-23606)***
Apperson Inc (PA)....D.......562 356-3333
17315 Studebaker Rd # 209 Cerritos (90703) ***(P-7279)***
Appetize Technologies Inc....C.......877 559-4225
6601 Center Dr W Ste 700 Los Angeles (90045) ***(P-23607)***
Appfolio Inc (PA)....C.......805 364-6093
50 Castilian Dr Ste 101 Goleta (93117) ***(P-23608)***
Appfolio Inc....A.......866 648-1536
9201 Spectrum San Diego (92123) ***(P-23609)***
Appformix Inc....F.......408 899-2240
4 N 2nd St Ste 595 San Jose (95113) ***(P-23610)***
Apple Blossom Mould Mill Work, San Ramon *Also called Blossom Apple Moulding & Mllwk* ***(P-4003)***
Apple Inc (PA)....A.......408 996-1010
1 Apple Park Way Cupertino (95014) ***(P-17455)***
Apple Paper Converting Inc....E.......714 632-3195
3800 E Miraloma Ave Anaheim (92806) ***(P-5493)***
Apple Tree International Corp....F.......626 679-7025
10700 Business Dr Ste 200 Fontana (92337) ***(P-14891)***
Apple Valley News, Hesperia *Also called Hesperia Resorter* ***(P-5662)***
Applecore....F.......310 567-6768
1200 Harkness St Manhattan Beach (90266) ***(P-3770)***
Applica Inc....E.......818 565-0011
11651 Vanowen St North Hollywood (91605) ***(P-17456)***
Applied Anodize Inc....D.......408 435-9191
622 Charcot Ave Ste D San Jose (95131) ***(P-12931)***
Applied Arospc Structures Corp (PA)....C.......209 982-0160
3437 S Airport Way Stockton (95206) ***(P-20037)***
Applied Business Software Inc....F.......562 426-2188
2847 Gundry Ave Signal Hill (90755) ***(P-23611)***
Applied Cardiac Systems Inc....D.......949 855-9366
1 Hughes Ste A Irvine (92618) ***(P-21602)***

Applied Ceramics Inc (PA) .... F 510 249-9700
48630 Milmont Dr Fremont (94538) ***(P-18105)***
Applied Cmpsite Structures Inc (HQ) .... C 714 990-6300
1195 Columbia St Brea (92821) ***(P-20038)***
Applied Coatings & Linings .... E 626 280-6354
3224 Rosemead Blvd El Monte (91731) ***(P-13143)***
Applied Control Electronics .... F 530 626-5181
5480 Merchant Cir Placerville (95667) ***(P-16699)***
Applied Engineering, San Jose *Also called Electronic Interface Co Inc* ***(P-19304)***
Applied Expert Systems Inc .... E 650 617-2400
999 Commercial St Ste 201 Palo Alto (94303) ***(P-23612)***
Applied Films Corporation .... E 408 727-5555
3050 Bowers Ave Santa Clara (95054) ***(P-18106)***
Applied Instrument Tech Inc .... E 909 204-3700
2121 Aviation Dr Upland (91786) ***(P-20835)***
Applied Liquid Polymer .... F 562 402-6300
17213 Roseton Ave Artesia (90701) ***(P-10501)***
Applied Manufacturing LLC .... A 949 713-8000
22872 Avenida Empresa Rcho STA Marg (92688) ***(P-21603)***
Applied Manufacturing Tech Inc .... F 714 630-9530
1464 N Hundley St Anaheim Anaheim (92806) ***(P-14315)***
Applied Materials Inc .... E 408 727-5555
3320 Scott Blvd Santa Clara (95054) ***(P-18107)***
Applied Materials Inc .... E 949 244-1600
4675 Macarthur Ct Newport Beach (92660) ***(P-18108)***
Applied Materials Inc .... E 406 752-2107
1285 Walsh Ave Santa Clara (95050) ***(P-18109)***
Applied Materials Inc .... E 408 727-5555
380 Fairview Way Milpitas (95035) ***(P-18110)***
Applied Materials Inc (PA) .... A 408 727-5555
3050 Bowers Ave Santa Clara (95054) ***(P-14424)***
Applied Materials Inc .... D 408 727-5555
3340 Scott Blvd Santa Clara (95054) ***(P-18111)***
Applied Materials Inc .... F 512 272-3692
3101 Scott Blvd Santa Clara (95054) ***(P-18112)***
Applied Materials Inc .... F 916 786-3900
9000 Foothills Blvd Roseville (95747) ***(P-14425)***
Applied Materials Inc .... E 408 727-5555
3535 Garrett Dr Bldg 100 Santa Clara (95054) ***(P-18113)***
Applied Materials Inc .... E 408 727-5555
974 E Arques Ave Sunnyvale (94085) ***(P-14426)***
Applied Materials Inc .... E 510 687-8018
44050 Fremont Blvd Fremont (94538) ***(P-18114)***
Applied Materials Inc .... D 408 727-5555
2821 Scott Blvd Bldg 17 Santa Clara (95050) ***(P-18115)***
Applied Materials Inc .... F 408 727-5555
3330 Scott Blvd Bldg 6 Santa Clara (95054) ***(P-5881)***
Applied Medical Corporation (PA) .... C 949 713-8000
22872 Avenida Empresa Rcho STA Marg (92688) ***(P-21604)***
Applied Medical Distribution, Rcho STA Marg *Also called Applied Medical Resources Corp* ***(P-21605)***
Applied Medical Resources, Rcho STA Marg *Also called Applied Medical Corporation* ***(P-21604)***
Applied Medical Resources Corp (HQ) .... B 949 713-8000
22872 Avenida Empresa Rcho STA Marg (92688) ***(P-21605)***
Applied Membranes Inc .... D 760 727-3711
2450 Business Park Dr Vista (92081) ***(P-15482)***
Applied Micro Circuits Corp (HQ) .... C 408 542-8600
4555 Great America Pkwy # 601 Santa Clara (95054) ***(P-18116)***
Applied Micro Circuits Corp .... E 408 523-1000
455 W Maude Ave Sunnyvale (94085) ***(P-15005)***
Applied Micro Circuits Corp .... E 408 542-8600
4555 Great America Pkwy # 601 Santa Clara (95054) ***(P-18117)***
Applied Microstructures Inc .... F 408 907-2885
2381 Bering Dr San Jose (95131) ***(P-21004)***
Applied Photon Technology Inc .... E 510 780-9500
3346 Arden Rd Hayward (94545) ***(P-16856)***
Applied Physics Systems Inc (PA) .... D 650 965-0500
425 Clyde Ave Mountain View (94043) ***(P-21434)***
Applied Polytech Systems Inc .... E 818 504-9261
26000 Springbrook Ave # 102 Santa Clarita (91350) ***(P-4457)***
Applied Powdercoat Inc .... E 805 981-1991
3101 Camino Del Sol Oxnard (93030) ***(P-13144)***
Applied Process Equipment .... F 650 365-6895
2620 Bay Rd Redwood City (94063) ***(P-15743)***
Applied Products Inc .... F 800 274-9801
8670 23rd Ave Sacramento (95826) ***(P-8854)***
Applied Science Inc (PA) .... F 530 273-8299
983 Golden Gate Ter Grass Valley (95945) ***(P-21606)***
Applied Sewing Resources Inc .... E 707 748-1614
6440 Goodyear Rd Benicia (94510) ***(P-2667)***
Applied Silicone Company LLC .... D 805 525-5657
1050 Cindy Ln Carpinteria (93013) ***(P-8715)***
Applied Silicone Corporation, Carpinteria *Also called Applied Silicone Company LLC* ***(P-8715)***
Applied Silver Inc .... F 888 939-4747
26254 Eden Landing Rd Hayward (94545) ***(P-4491)***
Applied Statistics & MGT Inc .... E 951 699-4600
32848 Wolf Store Rd Ste A Temecula (92592) ***(P-23613)***
Applied Systems LLC .... F 951 842-6300
6666 Box Sprng Blvd Rvrsi Riverside Riverside (92507) ***(P-11993)***
Applied Technologies Assoc Inc (HQ) .... C 805 239-9100
3025 Buena Vista Dr Paso Robles (93446) ***(P-21435)***
Applied Thin-Film Products (PA) .... C 510 661-4287
3620 Yale Way Fremont (94538) ***(P-18818)***
Applied Thin-Film Products .... F 510 661-4287
3439 Edison Way Fremont (94538) ***(P-18819)***
Applied Wireless Inc .... F 805 383-9600
1250 Avenida Acaso Ste F Camarillo (93012) ***(P-18118)***

Appointy Software Inc .... E 408 634-4141
16 Corning Ave Ste 136 Milpitas (95035) ***(P-23614)***
Apporto Corporation .... E 650 326-0920
200 Hamilton Ave Palo Alto (94301) ***(P-23615)***
Appress, Berkeley *Also called Apress L P* ***(P-5882)***
Appro International Inc (HQ) .... E 408 941-8100
220 Devcon Dr San Jose (95112) ***(P-15006)***
Approved Aeronautics LLC .... F 951 200-3730
1240 Graphite Dr Corona (92881) ***(P-20039)***
Approved Networks Inc (PA) .... D 800 590-9535
6 Orchard Ste 150 Lake Forest (92630) ***(P-10996)***
Approved Optics, Lake Forest *Also called Approved Networks Inc* ***(P-10996)***
Approved Turbo Components .... F 559 627-3600
1545 E Acequia Ave Visalia (93292) ***(P-19946)***
Appvance Inc .... E 408 871-0122
3080 Olcott St Ste B240 Santa Clara (95054) ***(P-23616)***
Appware Inc .... E 415 732-9298
65 Enterprise Aliso Viejo (92656) ***(P-23617)***
Appzen Inc (PA) .... F 408 647-5253
4699 Old Ironsides Dr # 430 Santa Clara (95054) ***(P-23618)***
APR Engineering Inc .... E 562 983-3800
1812 W 9th St Long Beach (90813) ***(P-20277)***
Apress L P .... F 510 549-5930
2588 Telegraph Ave Berkeley (94704) ***(P-5882)***
Apricorn .... E 858 513-2000
12191 Kirkham Rd Poway (92064) ***(P-15158)***
Apricot Designs Inc .... E 626 966-3299
677 Arrow Grand Cir Covina (91722) ***(P-21607)***
April Instrument .... F 650 964-8379
1401 Fallen Leaf Ln Los Altos (94024) ***(P-21005)***
APS Global, Chatsworth *Also called Apparel Prod Svcs Globl LLC* ***(P-3287)***
APS Marine, National City *Also called Adept Process Services Inc* ***(P-20310)***
APT, Santa Ana *Also called American Pneumatic Tools Inc* ***(P-13967)***
APT Electronics Inc .... C 714 687-6760
241 N Crescent Way Anaheim (92801) ***(P-17822)***
APT Metal Fabricators Inc .... E 818 896-7478
11164 Bradley Ave Pacoima (91331) ***(P-12766)***
Apta Group Inc (PA) .... E 619 710-8170
7580 Britannia Ct San Diego (92154) ***(P-18119)***
Aptan Corp .... F 213 748-5271
2000 S Main St Los Angeles (90007) ***(P-2668)***
Aptco LLC (PA) .... E 661 792-2107
31381 Pond Rd Bldg 2 Mc Farland (93250) ***(P-7542)***
Aptean Inc .... F 310 536-6080
2361 Rosecrans Ave # 375 El Segundo (90245) ***(P-23619)***
Apteligent Inc .... D 415 371-1402
1100 La Avenida St Ste A Mountain View (94043) ***(P-23620)***
Aptiv Digital LLC .... D 818 295-6789
2160 Gold St San Jose (95002) ***(P-23621)***
Aptiv Services 3 (us) LLC (HQ) .... F 949 458-3100
30 Corporate Park Ste 303 Irvine (92606) ***(P-19584)***
Apton Biosystems Inc .... F 650 284-6992
24245 Elise Ct Los Altos Hills (94024) ***(P-21174)***
Aptos Coffee Roasting Co, Aptos *Also called Santa Cruz Coffee Roasting Co* ***(P-2310)***
Apx Manufacturing, Tustin *Also called Apx Technology Corporation* ***(P-14133)***
Apx Technology Corporation .... F 714 838-8501
14831 Myford Rd Tustin (92780) ***(P-14133)***
Aq Transportation .... F 626 143-4552
326 Boyd St Ste C Los Angeles (90013) ***(P-20366)***
Aqs, Fremont *Also called All Quality & Services Inc* ***(P-17809)***
Aqua Backflow and Chlorination .... F 909 598-7251
1060 Northgate St Ste C Riverside (92507) ***(P-17776)***
Aqua Logic Inc .... E 858 292-4773
9558 Camino Ruiz San Diego (92126) ***(P-15412)***
Aqua Man Inc (PA) .... F 805 499-5707
2568 Turquoise Cir Newbury Park (91320) ***(P-15483)***
Aqua Man Service, Newbury Park *Also called Aqua Man Inc* ***(P-15483)***
Aqua Measure Instrument Co .... F 909 941-7776
9567 Arrow Rte Ste E Rancho Cucamonga (91730) ***(P-21436)***
Aqua Mix Inc .... D 951 256-3040
250 Benjamin Dr Corona (92879) ***(P-8363)***
Aqua Prieta Tees LLC .... F 714 719-2000
33398 Paseo El Lazo San Juan Capistrano (92675) ***(P-6990)***
Aqua Products Inc .... E 714 670-0691
6860 Oran Cir Ste 6351 Buena Park (90621) ***(P-15395)***
Aqua-Lung America Inc (HQ) .... C 760 597-5000
2340 Cousteau Ct Vista (92081) ***(P-20536)***
Aquadyne Computer Corporation .... F 858 495-1040
9434 Chesapeake Dr # 1204 San Diego (92123) ***(P-16700)***
Aquafine Corporation (HQ) .... D 661 257-4770
29010 Avenue Paine Valencia (91355) ***(P-15484)***
Aquahydrate Inc .... D 310 559-5058
5870 W Jefferson Blvd D Los Angeles (90016) ***(P-2039)***
Aquamar Inc .... C 909 481-4700
10888 7th St Rancho Cucamonga (91730) ***(P-2236)***
Aquaneering Inc .... E 858 578-2028
7960 Stromesa Ct San Diego (92126) ***(P-13610)***
Aquantia Corp (HQ) .... D 408 228-8300
91 E Tasman Dr Ste 100 San Jose (95134) ***(P-18120)***
Aquarian Accessories Corp .... E 714 632-0230
1140 N Tustin Ave Anaheim (92807) ***(P-22606)***
Aquarian Coatings Corp .... E 714 632-0230
1140 N Tustin Ave Anaheim (92807) ***(P-12932)***
Aquarian Drumheads, Anaheim *Also called Aquarian Accessories Corp* ***(P-22606)***
Aquarius Rags LLC (PA) .... F 213 895-4400
1218 S Santa Fe Ave Los Angeles (90021) ***(P-3214)***
Aquastar Pool Productions, Ventura *Also called Aquastar Pool Products Inc* ***(P-14559)***
Aquastar Pool Products Inc .... F 877 768-2717
2340 Palma Dr Ste 104 Ventura (93003) ***(P-14559)***

ALPHABETIC

Employee Codes: A=Over 500 employees, B=251-500
C=101-250, D=51-100, E=20-50, F=10-19
2020 California
Manfacturers Register
© Mergent Inc. 1-800-342-5647
1025

Aquasyn LLC F 818 350-0423
9525 Owensmouth Ave Ste E Chatsworth (91311) ***(P-13288)***

Aquatec International Inc D 949 225-2200
17422 Pullman St Irvine (92614) ***(P-14560)***

Aquatec Water Systems, Irvine *Also called Aquatec International Inc* ***(P-14560)***

Aquatic Av Inc F 408 559-1668
282 Kinney Dr San Jose (95112) ***(P-17191)***

Aquatic Co C 714 993-1220
8101 E Kaiser Blvd # 200 Anaheim (92808) ***(P-9580)***

Aquatic Co (HQ) D 714 993-1220
1700 N Delilah St Corona (92879) ***(P-9581)***

Aquatic Industries Inc C 800 877-2005
8101 E Kaiser Blvd # 200 Anaheim (92808) ***(P-9582)***

Aqueos Corporation D 805 676-4330
2550 Eastman Ave Ventura (93003) ***(P-13765)***

Aqueos Corporation (PA) C 805 364-0570
418 Chapala St Ste E&F Santa Barbara (93101) ***(P-13766)***

Aqueous Technologies Corp E 909 944-7771
1678 N Maple St Corona (92880) ***(P-15485)***

Aqueous Vets F 951 764-9384
288 Jasmine Way Danville (94506) ***(P-15486)***

Aquest Inc E 831 622-9296
4120 Pine Meadows Way Pebble Beach (93953) ***(P-11656)***

Aquiesse, Moorpark *Also called Global Uxe Inc* ***(P-23345)***

Aquila Space Inc F 650 224-8559
Nasa Ames Research Park Moffett Field (94035) ***(P-17457)***

AR Casting Inc F 818 765-1202
7240 Coldwater Canyon Ave B North Hollywood (91605) ***(P-22496)***

AR Square F 909 985-5995
8757 Lanyard Ct Ste 150 Rancho Cucamonga (91730) ***(P-10189)***

AR Wilson Quarry, Aromas *Also called Granite Rock Co* ***(P-342)***

AR-Ce Inc F 310 771-1960
141 E 162nd St Gardena (90248) ***(P-22939)***

ARA Technology E 408 734-8131
1286 Anvilwood Ave Sunnyvale (94089) ***(P-12933)***

Araca Merchandise LP E 818 743-5400
459 Park Ave San Fernando (91340) ***(P-6991)***

Aradigm Corporation (PA) E 510 265-9000
39655 Eureka Dr Newark (94560) ***(P-7762)***

Aram Precision Tool Die Inc F 818 998-1000
9758 Cozycroft Ave Chatsworth (91311) ***(P-15744)***

Aranda Tooling Inc D 714 379-6565
13950 Yorba Ave Chino (91710) ***(P-15745)***

Arandas Tortilla Company Inc E 209 464-8675
1318 E Scotts Ave Stockton (95205) ***(P-2394)***

Arandas Woodcraft Inc E 310 538-9945
137 W 157th St Gardena (90248) ***(P-4164)***

Aras Power Technologies (PA) F 408 935-8877
371 Fairview Way Milpitas (95035) ***(P-18700)***

Arbiter Systems Incorporated (PA) E 805 237-3831
1324 Vendels Cir Ste 121 Paso Robles (93446) ***(P-21006)***

Arbo Box Inc E 562 404-2726
2900 Supply Ave Commerce (90040) ***(P-4328)***

Arbo Inc E 510 658-3700
1205 Stanford Ave Oakland (94608) ***(P-1301)***

Arbor Fence Inc E 707 938-3133
22725 8th St E Ste C Sonoma (95476) ***(P-12451)***

Arbor Snowboards Inc E 310 577-1120
102 Washington Blvd Marina Del Rey (90292) ***(P-22749)***

ARC Machines Inc (HQ) D 818 896-9556
14320 Arminta St Panorama City (91402) ***(P-14238)***

ARC Plastics Inc E 562 802-3299
14010 Shoemaker Ave Norwalk (90650) ***(P-9635)***

ARC Products, San Diego *Also called Ssco Manufacturing Inc* ***(P-14255)***

Arcade Belts Inc (PA) E 530 580-8089
150 Alpine Meadows Rd Alpine Meadows (96146) ***(P-3526)***

Arcadia Inc E 310 665-0490
2323 Firestone Blvd South Gate (90280) ***(P-11931)***

Arcadia Inc E 916 375-1478
2324 Del Monte St West Sacramento (95691) ***(P-11255)***

Arcadia Inc (PA) C 323 269-7300
2301 E Vernon Ave Vernon (90058) ***(P-11256)***

Arcadia Norcal, Vernon *Also called Arcadia Inc* ***(P-11256)***

Arch Foods Inc E 510 868-6000
610 85th Ave Oakland (94621) ***(P-11511)***

Arch Foods Inc (PA) E 510 331-8352
25817 Clawiter Rd Hayward (94545) ***(P-11512)***

Arch-Rite Inc F 714 630-9305
1062 N Armando St Anaheim (92806) ***(P-3996)***

Archangel Investments LLC F 707 944-9261
6236 Silverado Trl NAPA (94558) ***(P-1584)***

Archer-Daniels-Midland Company F 909 783-7574
455 N 6th St Colton (92324) ***(P-989)***

Archer-Daniels-Midland Company E 323 266-2750
1543 Calada St Los Angeles (90023) ***(P-990)***

Archer-Daniels-Midland Company C 510 346-3309
2282 Davis Ct Hayward (94545) ***(P-991)***

Archer-Daniels-Midland Company F 323 269-8175
3691 Noakes St Los Angeles (90023) ***(P-992)***

Archer-Daniels-Midland Company C 209 339-1252
350 N Guild Ave Lodi (95240) ***(P-993)***

Archeyy & Friends LLC E 703 579-7649
3630 Andrews Dr Apt 114 Pleasanton (94588) ***(P-1066)***

Archigraphics, Norwalk *Also called Architectural Cathode Lighting* ***(P-17103)***

Archion, La Verne *Also called Postvision Inc* ***(P-15075)***

Archipelago Inc C 213 743-9200
2440 E 38th St Vernon (90058) ***(P-8438)***

Archipelago Botanicals, Vernon *Also called Archipelago Inc* ***(P-8438)***

Architctral Mllwk Slutions Inc F 760 510-6440
2565 Progress St Vista (92081) ***(P-3997)***

Architctral Mllwk Snta Barbara E 805 965-7011
8 N Nopal St Santa Barbara (93103) ***(P-3998)***

Architctural Facades Unlimited D 408 846-5350
600 E Luchessa Ave Gilroy (95020) ***(P-10531)***

Architectural Blomberg LLC E 916 428-8060
1453 Blair Ave Sacramento (95822) ***(P-11932)***

Architectural Cathode Lighting F 323 581-8800
12123 Pantheon St Norwalk (90650) ***(P-17103)***

Architectural Design Signs Inc (PA) D 951 278-0680
1160 Railroad St Corona (92882) ***(P-23051)***

Architectural Enterprises Inc E 323 268-4000
5821 Randolph St Commerce (90040) ***(P-12452)***

Architectural Foam Products F 707 544-2779
3237 Santa Rosa Ave Santa Rosa (95407) ***(P-9504)***

Architectural Foamstone Inc F 818 767-4500
9757 Glenoaks Blvd Sun Valley (91352) ***(P-5447)***

Architectural Plastics Inc E 707 765-9898
1299 N Mcdowell Blvd Petaluma (94954) ***(P-9636)***

Architectural Plywood Inc E 818 255-1900
7104 Case Ave North Hollywood (91605) ***(P-4273)***

Architectural S Weidner E 800 561-7446
5001 24th St Sacramento (95822) ***(P-23052)***

Architectural Wood Design Inc E 559 292-9104
5672 E Dayton Ave Fresno (93727) ***(P-4165)***

Architectural Woodworking Co D 626 570-4125
582 Monterey Pass Rd Monterey Park (91754) ***(P-4881)***

Archrock Inc F 661 321-0271
3333 Gibson St Bakersfield (93308) ***(P-155)***

Archwood Mfg Group Inc F 818 781-7673
15058 Delano St Van Nuys (91411) ***(P-288)***

Arcline Investment MGT LP (PA) F 415 801-4570
4 Embarcadero Ctr # 3460 San Francisco (94111) ***(P-7634)***

Arcmate Manufacturing Corp F 760 489-1140
911 S Andreasen Dr Escondido (92029) ***(P-11563)***

Arcmatic Welding Systems Inc (PA) F 707 643-5517
1175 Nimitz Ave Ste 240 Vallejo (94592) ***(P-24616)***

Arconic Fastening Systems, Carson *Also called Huck International Inc* ***(P-12681)***

Arconic Fastening Systems, Sylmar *Also called Valley-Todeco Inc* ***(P-12699)***

Arconic Fstening Systems Rings, Fontana *Also called Forged Metals Inc* ***(P-12709)***

Arconic Fstening Systems Rings, Sylmar *Also called JW Manufacturing Inc* ***(P-12684)***

Arconic Global Fas & Rings Inc D 714 871-1550
800 S State College Blvd Fullerton (92831) ***(P-11153)***

Arconic Inc B 805 262-4230
1300 Rancho Conejo Blvd Newbury Park (91320) ***(P-11178)***

Arconic Inc B 714 871-1550
800 S State College Blvd Fullerton (92831) ***(P-11179)***

Arconic Inc B 714 278-8981
801 S Placentia Ave Fullerton (92831) ***(P-11180)***

Arconic Inc B 212 836-2674
3016 Lomita Blvd Torrance (90505) ***(P-11181)***

Arconic Inc B 818 367-2261
12975 Bradley Ave Sylmar (91342) ***(P-11182)***

Arctic Fox, San Marcos *Also called Boinca Inc* ***(P-8449)***

Arctic Glacier California Inc D 209 524-3128
1440 Coldwell Ave Modesto (95350) ***(P-2349)***

Arctic Glacier USA Inc C 310 638-0321
17011 Central Ave Carson (90746) ***(P-2350)***

Arctic Silver Incorporated F 559 740-0912
9826 W Legacy Ave Visalia (93291) ***(P-9132)***

Arctic Wolf Networks Inc (PA) F 408 610-3263
111 W Evelyn Ave Ste 115 Sunnyvale (94086) ***(P-23622)***

Arctic Zero Inc E 619 342-1423
1345 Broadway El Cajon (92021) ***(P-629)***

Arcturus Marine Systems D 707 586-3155
517a Martin Ave Rohnert Park (94928) ***(P-13560)***

Arcturus Uav Inc F 707 206-9372
1035 N Mcdowell Blvd Petaluma (94954) ***(P-20442)***

Ardagh Glass Inc E 559 675-4700
24441 Avenue 12 Madera (93637) ***(P-10283)***

Ardax Systems Inc F 650 591-2656
1669 Industrial Rd San Carlos (94070) ***(P-17458)***

Ardella's, Carson *Also called Richandre Inc* ***(P-977)***

Ardelyx Inc D 510 745-1700
34175 Ardenwood Blvd Fremont (94555) ***(P-7763)***

Arden & Howe Printing Inc F 916 444-7154
430 17th St Sacramento (95811) ***(P-6418)***

Arden Engineering Inc (HQ) E 949 877-3642
3130 E Miraloma Ave Anaheim (92806) ***(P-20040)***

Arden Engineering Inc E 714 998-6410
1878 N Main St Orange (92865) ***(P-20041)***

Arden/Paradise Manufacturing, Victorville *Also called Paradise Manufacturing Co Inc* ***(P-3698)***

Ardent Mills LLC E 951 201-1170
2020 E Steel Rd Colton (92324) ***(P-994)***

Ardent Mills LLC F 323 725-0771
5471 Ferguson Dr Commerce (90022) ***(P-995)***

Ardent Mills LLC E 909 887-3407
19684 Cajon Blvd San Bernardino (92407) ***(P-996)***

Ardent Systems Inc E 408 526-0100
2040 Ringwood Ave San Jose (95131) ***(P-17823)***

Ardian Inc F 650 417-6500
1380 Shorebird Way Mountain View (94043) ***(P-21608)***

Ardica Technologies Inc F 415 568-9270
2325 3rd St Ste 424 San Francisco (94107) ***(P-18121)***

Arecont Vision Costar LLC D 818 937-0700
400 N Brand Blvd Ste 860 Glendale (91203) ***(P-16777)***

Areesys Corporation E 510 979-9601
4055 Clipper Ct Fremont (94538) ***(P-19259)***

Aremac Associates Inc E 626 303-8795
2004 S Myrtle Ave Monrovia (91016) ***(P-15746)***

Aremac Heat Treating Inc..........E.......626 333-3898
330 S 9th Ave City of Industry (91746) *(P-11432)*
Arena Pharmaceuticals Inc (PA)..........D.......858 453-7200
6154 Nancy Ridge Dr San Diego (92121) *(P-7764)*
Arena Press..........F.......415 883-3314
20 Leveroni Ct Novato (94949) *(P-6187)*
Arena Solutions Inc..........E.......978 988-3800
989 E Hillsdale Blvd # 250 Foster City (94404) *(P-23623)*
Arens Brothers Logging, Pollock Pines *Also called Dan Arens and Son Inc* *(P-3879)*
Arete Therapeutics Inc..........F.......650 737-4600
52 Buena Vista Ter San Francisco (94117) *(P-7765)*
Arevalo Tortilleria Inc..........E.......323 888-1711
3033 Supply Ave Commerce (90040) *(P-2395)*
Arevalo Tortilleria Inc (PA)..........C.......323 888-1711
1537 W Mines Ave Montebello (90640) *(P-2396)*
Arga Controls Inc..........F.......626 799-3314
10410 Trademark St Rancho Cucamonga (91730) *(P-20836)*
Arga Controls A Unit, Rancho Cucamonga *Also called Electro Switch Corp* *(P-18897)*
Argee Mfg Co San Diego Inc..........D.......619 449-5050
9550 Pathway St Santee (92071) *(P-9637)*
Argen Corporation..........F.......858 455-7900
8515 Miralani Dr San Diego (92126) *(P-22134)*
Argen Corporation (PA)..........C.......858 455-7900
5855 Oberlin Dr San Diego (92121) *(P-11188)*
Argo Spring Mfg Co Inc..........D.......800 252-2740
13930 Shoemaker Ave Norwalk (90650) *(P-13336)*
Argonaut..........E.......310 822-1629
5355 Mcconnell Ave Los Angeles (90066) *(P-5553)*
Arguello Inc..........E.......805 567-1632
17100 Clle Mariposa Reina Goleta (93117) *(P-109)*
Argus Courier, Petaluma *Also called St Louis Post-Dispatch LLC* *(P-5838)*
Argyle Precision, Orange *Also called ISI Detention Contg Group Inc* *(P-16056)*
ARI Industries Inc..........D.......714 993-3700
17018 Edwards Rd Cerritos (90703) *(P-15413)*
Aria Technologies Inc..........E.......925 292-1616
102 Wright Brothers Ave Livermore (94551) *(P-11286)*
Arias Industries Inc..........E.......310 532-9737
275 Roswell Ave Long Beach (90803) *(P-19585)*
Arias Pistons, Long Beach *Also called Arias Industries Inc* *(P-19585)*
Ariat International Inc (PA)..........C.......510 477-7000
3242 Whipple Rd Union City (94587) *(P-10245)*
Ariba Inc (HQ)..........C.......650 849-4000
3420 Hillview Ave Bldg 3 Palo Alto (94304) *(P-23624)*
Aridis Pharmaceuticals Inc..........E.......408 385-1742
5941 Optical Ct San Jose (95138) *(P-7766)*
Aries 33 LLC..........E.......310 355-8330
3400 S Main St Los Angeles (90007) *(P-3069)*
Aries Prepared Beef Company..........E.......818 771-0181
11850 Sheldon St Sun Valley (91352) *(P-1067)*
Aries Research Inc..........F.......925 818-1078
46750 Fremont Blvd # 107 Fremont (94538) *(P-15159)*
Aries Solutions, Fremont *Also called Aries Research Inc* *(P-15159)*
Arista Foods Corporation..........F.......714 666-1001
1240 N Barsten Way Anaheim (92806) *(P-942)*
Aristamd Inc..........F.......858 750-4777
11099 N Torrey Pines Rd # 290 La Jolla (92037) *(P-23625)*
Ariza Cheese Co Inc..........E.......562 630-4144
7602 Jackson St Paramount (90723) *(P-541)*
Arizona Portland Cement, Glendora *Also called Calportland Company* *(P-10408)*
Ark Newspaper, The, Belvedere Tiburon *Also called Ammi Publishing Inc* *(P-5549)*
Arkema Coating Resins, Torrance *Also called Arkema Inc* *(P-7383)*
Arkema Inc..........C.......310 214-5327
19206 Hawthorne Blvd Torrance (90503) *(P-7383)*
Arktura LLC (PA)..........E.......310 532-1050
18225 S Figueroa St Gardena (90248) *(P-4762)*
Arlo Technologies Inc (PA)..........D.......408 890-3900
3030 Orchard Pkwy San Jose (95134) *(P-17192)*
Arlon EMD, Rancho Cucamonga *Also called EMD Specialty Materials LLC* *(P-17869)*
Arlon Graphics LLC..........C.......714 985-6300
200 Boysenberry Ln Placentia (92870) *(P-9392)*
Arlon LLC..........C.......714 540-2811
2811 S Harbor Blvd Santa Ana (92704) *(P-9638)*
Arm Inc (HQ)..........B.......408 576-1500
150 Rose Orchard Way San Jose (95134) *(P-18122)*
Arm Electronics Inc..........E.......916 787-1100
8860 Industrial Ave # 140 Roseville (95678) *(P-19260)*
Arm Inc..........C.......858 453-1900
5375 Mira Sorrento Pl # 540 San Diego (92121) *(P-18123)*
Armanino Foods Distinction Inc..........E.......510 441-9300
30588 San Antonio St Hayward (94544) *(P-943)*
Armata Pharmaceuticals Inc (PA)..........D.......310 655-2928
4503 Glencoe Ave Marina Del Rey (90292) *(P-8272)*
Armenco Catrg Trck Mfg Co Inc..........F.......818 768-0400
11819 Vose St North Hollywood (91605) *(P-19518)*
Arminak Solutions LLC..........E.......626 385-5858
1361 Mountain View Cir Azusa (91702) *(P-8439)*
Armite Laboratories Inc..........F.......949 646-9035
1560 Superior Ave Ste A4 Costa Mesa (92627) *(P-9133)*
Armo Biosciences Inc..........E.......650 779-5075
575 Chesapeake Dr Redwood City (94063) *(P-7767)*
Armona Frozen Food Lockers..........F.......559 584-3948
10870 14th Ave Armona (93202) *(P-438)*
Armorcast Products Company Inc..........E.......909 390-1365
500 S Dupont Ave Ontario (91761) *(P-9639)*
Armored Group Inc..........E.......818 767-3030
11555 Cantara St North Hollywood (91605) *(P-4329)*
Armored Mobility Inc..........E.......831 430-9899
5610 Scotts Valley Dr B332 Scotts Valley (95066) *(P-9437)*
Armorstruxx LLC..........E.......209 365-9400
850 Thurman St Lodi (95240) *(P-20042)*
Arms Precision Inc..........F.......951 273-1800
169 Radio Rd Corona (92879) *(P-15747)*
Armstrong Petroleum Corp (PA)..........E.......949 650-4000
1080 W 17th St Costa Mesa (92627) *(P-22)*
Armstrong Technology Inc..........E.......530 888-6262
12780 Earhart Ave Auburn (95602) *(P-15748)*
Armtec Countermeasures Co (HQ)..........F.......760 398-0143
85901 Avenue 53 Coachella (92236) *(P-20537)*
Armtec Defense Products Co (HQ)..........B.......760 398-0143
85901 Avenue 53 Coachella (92236) *(P-13281)*
Arna Trading Inc (PA)..........F.......760 940-2775
2892 S Santa Fe Ave # 109 San Marcos (92069) *(P-5090)*
Arnies Supply Service Ltd (PA)..........E.......323 263-1696
1541 N Ditman Ave Los Angeles (90063) *(P-4347)*
Arnold & Egan Manufacturing Co..........E.......415 822-2700
1515 Griffith St San Francisco (94124) *(P-4882)*
Arnold Electronics Inc..........F.......714 646-8343
1907 Nancita Cir Placentia (92870) *(P-17824)*
Arnold-Gonsalves Engrg Inc..........E.......909 465-1579
5731 Chino Ave Chino (91710) *(P-15749)*
Aromyx Corporation..........F.......650 430-8100
319 Bernardo Ave Mountain View (94043) *(P-20783)*
Aronson Manufacturing, Van Nuys *Also called Nat Aronson & Associates Inc* *(P-9200)*
Arrhenius, Santa Clara *Also called Prodigy Surface Tech Inc* *(P-13080)*
Arrive Technologies Inc (PA)..........F.......888 864-6959
3693 Westchester Dr Roseville (95747) *(P-18124)*
Arrive-Ai Inc..........F.......949 221-0166
16751 Millikan Ave Irvine (92606) *(P-23277)*
Arrk Product Dev Group USA Inc..........C.......858 552-1587
1949 Palomar Oaks Way A Carlsbad (92011) *(P-12114)*
Arrow Abrasive Company Inc..........F.......562 869-2282
12033 1/2 Regentview Ave Downey (90241) *(P-10940)*
Arrow Diecasting Inc..........F.......323 245-8439
4031 Goodwin Ave Los Angeles (90039) *(P-11333)*
Arrow Electric Motor Service..........F.......559 266-0104
645 Broadway St Fresno (93721) *(P-24683)*
Arrow Engineering..........E.......626 960-2806
4946 Azusa Canyon Rd Irwindale (91706) *(P-15750)*
Arrow Head Regional Med Ctr, Colton *Also called County of San Bernardino* *(P-20752)*
Arrow Industries, Buellton *Also called Gavial Holdings Inc* *(P-18922)*
Arrow Screw Products Inc..........E.......805 928-2269
941 W Mccoy Ln Santa Maria (93455) *(P-15751)*
Arrow Sign Co (PA)..........E.......209 931-5522
1051 46th Ave Oakland (94601) *(P-23053)*
Arrow Sign Co..........E.......209 931-7852
3133 N Ad Art Rd Stockton (95215) *(P-23054)*
Arrow Sign Company, Oakland *Also called Arrow Sign Co* *(P-23053)*
Arrow Steel Products Inc..........F.......909 349-1032
13171 Santa Ana Ave Fontana (92337) *(P-11117)*
Arrow Transit Mix..........E.......661 945-7600
507 E Avenue L12 Lancaster (93535) *(P-10691)*
Arrow Truck Bodies & Equipment..........E.......909 947-3991
1639 S Campus Ave Ontario (91761) *(P-19519)*
Arrow Truck Sales Incorporated..........F.......909 829-2365
10175 Cherry Ave Fontana (92335) *(P-19520)*
Arrowhead Brass & Plumbing LLC..........D.......323 221-9137
4900 Valley Blvd Los Angeles (90032) *(P-11657)*
Arrowhead Ice, Torrance *Also called Southern California Ice Co* *(P-2363)*
Arrowhead Pharmaceuticals Inc (PA)..........F.......626 304-3400
225 S Lake Ave Ste 1050 Pasadena (91101) *(P-7768)*
Arrowhead Press Inc..........E.......626 358-1168
220 W Maple Ave Ste B Monrovia (91016) *(P-6419)*
Arrowhead Products Corporation..........A.......714 828-7770
4411 Katella Ave Los Alamitos (90720) *(P-20043)*
Arroyo Grande Mushroom Farm, Arroyo Grande *Also called Spawn Mate Inc* *(P-8804)*
Arroyo Seco Racquet Club..........F.......323 258-4178
920 Lohman Ln South Pasadena (91030) *(P-9283)*
Arroyo Seco Rock, King City *Also called Wm J Clark Trucking Svc Inc* *(P-370)*
ARS, Burbank *Also called Hutchinson Arospc & Indust Inc* *(P-20129)*
ARS Enterprises (PA)..........F.......562 946-3505
15554 Minnesota Ave Paramount (90723) *(P-21982)*
Arsenic Inc..........F.......310 701-7559
530 S Hewitt St Unit 119 Los Angeles (90013) *(P-5883)*
Arsh Incorporated..........F.......408 971-2722
2300 Stevens Creek Blvd San Jose (95128) *(P-6420)*
Arsys Inc..........F.......714 654-7681
1428 S Grand Ave Santa Ana (92705) *(P-14427)*
Art, El Dorado Hills *Also called Alpha Research & Tech Inc* *(P-14886)*
Art & Sign Production Inc..........F.......818 245-6945
3651 E Chevy Chase Dr Glendale (91206) *(P-23055)*
Art Brand Studios LLC (PA)..........E.......408 201-5000
18715 Madrone Pkwy Morgan Hill (95037) *(P-6188)*
Art Bronze Inc..........E.......818 897-2222
11275 San Fernando Rd San Fernando (91340) *(P-11394)*
Art Craft Staturary Inc..........E.......510 633-1411
10441 Edes Ave Oakland (94603) *(P-10890)*
Art Glass Etc Inc..........E.......805 644-4494
3111 Golf Course Dr Ventura (93003) *(P-3999)*
Art Impressions Inc..........F.......818 591-0105
23586 Calabasas Rd # 210 Calabasas (91302) *(P-6189)*
Art Manufacturers Inc..........E.......714 540-9125
623 Young St Santa Ana (92705) *(P-16962)*
Art Masterpiece Gallery..........F.......323 277-9448
4950 S Santa Fe Ave Vernon (90058) *(P-3601)*
Art Microelectronics Corp..........F.......626 447-7503
5917 Oak Ave Ste 201 Temple City (91780) *(P-18125)*

ALPHABETIC

Employee Codes: A=Over 500 employees, B=251-500
C=101-250, D=51-100, E=20-50, F=10-19
2020 California
Manfacturers Register
© Mergent Inc. 1-800-342-5647
1027

Art Mold Die Casting Inc ....E......818 767-6464
11872 Sheldon St Sun Valley (91352) ***(P-14017)***
Art of Muse LLC ....E......510 644-1870
2222 5th St Berkeley (94710) ***(P-4548)***
Art Plates, Rancho Cucamonga *Also called Pitbull Gym Incorporated* ***(P-9961)***
Art Robbins Instruments LLC ....E......408 734-8400
1293 Mountain View Alviso Sunnyvale (94089) ***(P-21175)***
Art Services Melrose ....F......310 247-1452
626 N Almont Dr West Hollywood (90069) ***(P-9640)***
Art Signworks Inc ....F......951 698-8484
41785 Elm St Ste 302 Murrieta (92562) ***(P-23056)***
Artcrafters Cabinets Inc ....E......818 752-8960
5446 Cleon Ave North Hollywood (91601) ***(P-4166)***
Arte De Mexico Inc (PA) ....D......818 753-4559
1000 Chestnut St Burbank (91506) ***(P-4829)***
Arte De Mexico Inc ....E......818 753-4510
5506 Riverton Ave North Hollywood (91601) ***(P-17012)***
Artech Industries Inc ....E......951 276-3331
1966 Keats Dr Riverside (92501) ***(P-18820)***
Arteez ....F......916 631-0473
3600 Sunrise Blvd Ste 4 Rancho Cordova (95742) ***(P-6992)***
Arteffex Conceptioneering ....F......818 506-5358
911 Mayo St Los Angeles (90042) ***(P-23278)***
Artehouse, San Rafael *Also called One Bella Casa Inc* ***(P-3630)***
Artemis Pet Food Company Inc ....F......818 771-0700
18010 S Figueroa St Gardena (90248) ***(P-1084)***
Arteris Inc ....E......408 470-7300
595 Millich Dr Ste 200 Campbell (95008) ***(P-18126)***
Arteris Holdings Inc ....E......408 470-7300
591 W Hamilton Ave # 250 Campbell (95008) ***(P-18127)***
Artesa Winery, NAPA *Also called Codorniu Napa Inc* ***(P-1643)***
Artesia Sawdust Products Inc ....E......909 947-5983
13434 S Ontario Ave Ontario (91761) ***(P-3924)***
Artesian Home Products, Granite Bay *Also called New Cal Metals Inc* ***(P-12312)***
Arthrex Inc ....D......805 964-8104
460 Ward Dr Ste C Santa Barbara (93111) ***(P-21609)***
Arthur Dogswell LLC (PA) ....E......888 559-8833
11301 W Olympic Blvd Los Angeles (90064) ***(P-1068)***
Arthur P Lamarre & Sons Inc ....F......209 667-6557
1918 Paulson Rd Ste 101 Turlock (95380) ***(P-12115)***
Arthurmade Plastics Inc ....D......323 721-7325
2131 Garfield Ave Commerce (90040) ***(P-9641)***
Artifact Puzzles ....F......650 283-0589
180 Constitution Dr Ste 6 Menlo Park (94025) ***(P-22658)***
Artifacts International, Chula Vista *Also called Califrnia Furn Collections Inc* ***(P-4764)***
Artifcial Grass Recyclers Corp ....E......714 635-7000
25800 Washington Ave Murrieta (92562) ***(P-23279)***
Artificial Grass Liquidators ....E......951 677-3377
42505 Rio Nedo Temecula (92590) ***(P-23280)***
Artisan Brewers LLC ....E......510 567-4926
1933 Davis St Ste 177 San Leandro (94577) ***(P-1494)***
Artisan Crust ....E......323 759-7000
754 E Florence Ave Los Angeles (90001) ***(P-1138)***
Artisan House Inc ....E......818 767-7476
8238 Lankershim Blvd North Hollywood (91605) ***(P-13499)***
Artisan Moss LLC ....F......833 667-7278
3450 Palmer Dr Ste 4 Cameron Park (95682) ***(P-1451)***
Artisan Nameplate Awards Corp ....E......714 556-6222
2730 S Shannon St Santa Ana (92704) ***(P-6993)***
Artisan Screen Printing Inc ....C......626 815-2700
1055 W 5th St Azusa (91702) ***(P-6994)***
Artisan Vehicle Systems Inc ....D......805 512-9955
2385 Pleasant Valley Rd Camarillo (93012) ***(P-19454)***
Artissimo Designs LLC (HQ) ....E......310 906-3700
2100 E Grand Ave Ste 400 El Segundo (90245) ***(P-5494)***
Artistic Concepts ....F......323 257-8101
3293 N San Fernando Rd Los Angeles (90065) ***(P-4785)***
Artistic Coverings Inc ....E......562 404-9343
14135 Artesia Blvd Cerritos (90703) ***(P-9505)***
Artistic Plastics Inc ....F......951 808-9700
725 E Harrison St Corona (92879) ***(P-9642)***
Artistic Pltg & Met Finshg Inc ....D......619 661-1691
2801 E Miraloma Ave Anaheim (92806) ***(P-12934)***
Artistic Welding Inc ....D......310 515-4922
505 E Gardena Blvd Gardena (90248) ***(P-12116)***
Artistry In Motion Inc ....E......818 994-7388
19411 Londelius St Northridge (91324) ***(P-5495)***
Artiva USA Inc ....E......562 298-8968
12866 Ann St Ste 1 Santa Fe Springs (90670) ***(P-16963)***
Artiva USA Inc (PA) ....E......909 628-1388
13901 Magnolia Ave Chino (91710) ***(P-16964)***
Arto Brick and Cal Pavers, Gardena *Also called Arto Brick Veneer Mfgco* ***(P-10430)***
Arto Brick Veneer Mfgco ....E......310 768-8500
15209 S Broadway Gardena (90248) ***(P-10430)***
Arts, Sunnyvale *Also called Advanced Rtrcraft Trining Svcs* ***(P-19249)***
Arts & Crafts Press, San Diego *Also called Rush Press Inc* ***(P-6850)***
Arts Custom Cabinets Inc ....F......559 562-2766
897 E Tulare Rd Lindsay (93247) ***(P-4549)***
Arts Elegance Inc ....E......626 793-4794
154 W Bellevue Dr Pasadena (91105) ***(P-22497)***
Artsigns, Sunnyvale *Also called Sign Solutions Inc* ***(P-23200)***
Artsons Manufacturing Company ....E......323 773-3469
11121 Garfield Ave South Gate (90280) ***(P-11027)***
Arturo Campos ....F......951 300-2111
796 Palmyrita Ave Ste B Riverside (92507) ***(P-12935)***
Aruba Networks Inc (HQ) ....B......408 227-4500
3333 Scott Blvd Santa Clara (95054) ***(P-15160)***
Aruba Networks Inc ....E......408 227-4500
392 Acoma Way Fremont (94539) ***(P-17459)***
Aruba Networks Inc ....F......408 227-4500
390 W Caribbean Dr Sunnyvale (94089) ***(P-17460)***
Aruba Networks Cafe, Santa Clara *Also called Aruba Networks Inc* ***(P-15160)***
Arvato Services, Valencia *Also called Bertelsmann Inc* ***(P-6075)***
Arvi Manufacturing Inc ....F......408 734-4776
1256 Birchwood Dr Ste B Sunnyvale (94089) ***(P-13500)***
Arvinyl Laminates LP ....E......951 371-7800
233 N Sherman Ave Corona (92882) ***(P-9393)***
Arxis Technology Inc ....E......805 306-7890
2468 Tapo Canyon Rd Simi Valley (93063) ***(P-23626)***
Aryzta Holdings IV LLC (HQ) ....C......310 417-4700
6080 Center Dr Ste 900 Los Angeles (90045) ***(P-1302)***
Aryzta LLC ....C......909 472-3500
1220 S Baker Ave Ontario (91761) ***(P-1303)***
Aryzta LLC ....C......949 261-7400
2350 Pullman St Santa Ana (92705) ***(P-1304)***
Aryzta LLC (HQ) ....C......310 417-4700
6080 Center Dr Ste 900 Los Angeles (90045) ***(P-1305)***
Aryzta US Holdings I Corp ....A......800 938-1900
14490 Catalina St San Leandro (94577) ***(P-1306)***
Arz Tech Inc ....F......714 642-9954
1407 N Batavia St Ste 115 Orange (92867) ***(P-9643)***
Arzy Company Inc ....F......213 627-7344
650 S Hill St Ste 915 Los Angeles (90014) ***(P-22498)***
Arzy Company Fine Jewelry, Los Angeles *Also called Arzy Company Inc* ***(P-22498)***
AS Match Dyeing Co Inc ....C......323 277-0470
2522 E 37th St Vernon (90058) ***(P-2821)***
Asa, Oxnard *Also called Advanced Structural Tech Inc* ***(P-12701)***
Asa Corporation ....F......530 305-3720
3111 Sunset Blvd Ste V Rocklin (95677) ***(P-21176)***
Asante Technologies Inc (PA) ....E......408 435-8388
2223 Oakland Rd San Jose (95131) ***(P-15161)***
Asante Technologies Inc ....F......408 435-8388
673 S Milpitas Blvd # 100 Milpitas (95035) ***(P-15162)***
Asante Technologies Inc ....E......408 435-8388
47341 Bayside Pkwy Fremont (94538) ***(P-15163)***
Asbury Graphite Inc California ....F......510 799-3636
2855 Franklin Canyon Rd Rodeo (94572) ***(P-9038)***
ASC Group Inc ....C......818 896-1101
12243 Branford St Sun Valley (91352) ***(P-18128)***
ASC Process Systems Inc ....C......818 833-0088
28402 Livingston Ave Valencia (91355) ***(P-14755)***
ASC Profiles LLC ....E......916 376-2899
5001 Bailey Loop McClellan (95652) ***(P-12532)***
ASC Profiles LLC ....C......909 823-0401
10905 Beech Ave Fontana (92337) ***(P-11744)***
Ascap, Los Angeles *Also called American Society of Composers* ***(P-6184)***
Ascendis Pharma Inc ....F......650 352-8389
500 Emerson St Palo Alto (94301) ***(P-7769)***
Ascent Manufacturing LLC ....E......714 540-6414
2545 W Via Palma Anaheim (92801) ***(P-12767)***
Ascent Technology Inc ....E......408 213-1080
838 Jury Ct San Jose (95112) ***(P-12117)***
Ascent Tooling Group LLC ....A......949 455-0665
1395 S Lyon St Santa Ana (92705) ***(P-20538)***
Ascert LLC (PA) ....F......415 339-8500
759 Bridgeway Sausalito (94965) ***(P-23627)***
Asclemed Usa Inc ....F......310 218-4146
379 Van Ness Ave Ste 1403 Torrance (90501) ***(P-7770)***
Asco Automatic Switch ....F......714 937-0811
333 City Blvd W Ste 2140 Orange (92868) ***(P-13289)***
Asco Automatic Switch Co, Orange *Also called Asco Automatic Switch* ***(P-13289)***
Asco Sintering Co ....E......323 725-3550
2750 Garfield Ave Commerce (90040) ***(P-11564)***
Ascor Inc (HQ) ....F......925 328-4650
4650 Norris Canyon Rd San Ramon (94583) ***(P-16701)***
Asd, Canoga Park *Also called Advanced Safety Devices LLC* ***(P-20983)***
Asdak International ....F......714 449-0733
1809 1/2 N Orngethorpe Pa Anaheim (92801) ***(P-10484)***
Asea Power Systems ....E......714 896-9695
15272 Newsboy Cir Huntington Beach (92649) ***(P-18821)***
Aseptic Innovations Inc ....E......714 584-2110
4940 E Landon Dr Anaheim (92807) ***(P-10284)***
Aseptic Sltons USA Vntures LLC ....C......951 736-9230
484 Alcoa Cir Corona (92880) ***(P-2040)***
Aseptic Solutions USA-Corona, Corona *Also called Aseptic Sltons USA Vntures LLC* ***(P-2040)***
Aseptic Technology LLC ....D......714 694-0168
24855 Corbit Pl Yorba Linda (92887) ***(P-10285)***
Ashford Textiles LLC ....E......310 327-4670
1535 W 139th St Gardena (90249) ***(P-2925)***
Ashka Print LLC ....E......323 980-6008
600 E Wash Blvd Ste W4 Los Angeles (90015) ***(P-6995)***
Ashtel Dental, Ontario *Also called Ashtel Studios Inc* ***(P-22208)***
Ashtel Studios Inc ....E......909 434-0911
1610 E Philadelphia St Ontario (91761) ***(P-22208)***
Asi Semiconductor Inc ....E......818 982-1200
7525 Ethel Ave North Hollywood (91605) ***(P-18129)***
Asi Tooling LLC ....F......760 744-2520
1780 La Costa Meadows Dr # 103 San Marcos (92078) ***(P-14134)***
Asi/Silica Machinery LLC (PA) ....E......818 920-1962
6404 Independence Ave Woodland Hills (91367) ***(P-11395)***
Asia America Enterprise Inc ....E......650 348-2333
1321 N Carolan Ave Burlingame (94010) ***(P-6421)***
Asia Food Inc ....F......626 284-1328
566 Monterey Pass Rd Monterey Park (91754) ***(P-395)***
Asia Pacific California Inc (PA) ....F......650 513-6189
1648 Gilbreth Rd Burlingame (94010) ***(P-5554)***

Mergent e-mail: customerrelations@mergent.com
1028
2020 California
Manufacturers Register
(P-0000) Products & Services Section entry number
(PA)=Parent Co (HQ)=Headquarters (DH)=Div Headquarters

Asia Pacific California Inc ....E.......626 281-8500
923 E Valley Blvd Ste 203 San Gabriel (91776) *(P-5555)*
Asia Plastics Inc ....E.......626 448-8100
9347 Rush St South El Monte (91733) *(P-5384)*
Asian America Business Journal, San Diego *Also called Vangie L Cortes (P-5857)*
Asian Week (PA) ....F.......415 397-0220
809 Sacramento St San Francisco (94108) *(P-5556)*
Asiana Cuisine Enterprises Inc ....A.......310 327-2223
22771 S Wstn Ave Ste 100 Torrance (90501) *(P-2397)*
Asias Finest ....F.......619 297-0800
407 Camino Del Rio S San Diego (92108) *(P-11513)*
Asic Advantage Inc ....D.......408 541-8686
3850 N 1st St San Jose (95134) *(P-18130)*
Asigma Corporation ....F.......760 966-3103
2930 San Luis Rey Rd Oceanside (92058) *(P-15752)*
Askgene Pharma Inc ....F.......805 807-9868
5217 Verdugo Way Ste A Camarillo (93012) *(P-7771)*
Asm Construction Inc ....E.......619 449-1966
1947 John Towers Ave El Cajon (92020) *(P-12118)*
Asm Precision Inc ....F.......707 584-7950
613 Martin Ave Ste 106 Rohnert Park (94928) *(P-12119)*
Asml USA, San Diego *Also called Cymer LLC (P-19286)*
ASPE Inc ....F.......951 296-2595
42295 Avnida Alvrado Unit Temecula (92590) *(P-14316)*
Aspect Software Inc ....E.......408 595-5002
101 Academy Ste 130 Irvine (92617) *(P-23628)*
Aspen Brands Corporation ....F.......702 946-9430
1305 E Wakeham Ave Santa Ana (92705) *(P-4550)*
Aspen Medical Products LLC ....D.......949 681-0200
6481 Oak Cyn Irvine (92618) *(P-21610)*
Asphalt Fabric and Engrg Inc ....D.......562 997-4129
2683 Lime Ave Signal Hill (90755) *(P-22750)*
Asphalt Products Oil Corp (HQ) ....F.......562 423-6471
5903 N Paramount Blvd Long Beach (90805) *(P-9109)*
Asrc Aerospace Corp ....E.......650 604-5946
Nasa Ames Research Ctr Mountain View (94035) *(P-20539)*
Asrock America Inc ....E.......909 590-8308
13848 Magnolia Ave Chino (91710) *(P-17825)*
Assa Abloy Entrance Sys US Inc ....F.......916 686-4116
9733 Kent St 100 Elk Grove (95624) *(P-19261)*
Assa Abloy Entrance Systems US ....D.......714 578-0526
1520 S Sinclair St Anaheim (92806) *(P-19262)*
Assali Hulling & Shelling ....F.......209 883-4263
8618 E Whitmore Ave Hughson (95326) *(P-1421)*
Assault Industries Inc ....F.......714 799-6711
12691 Monarch St Garden Grove (92841) *(P-20503)*
Assembly Automation Industries ....E.......626 303-2777
1849 Business Center Dr Duarte (91010) *(P-14263)*
Assembly Biosciences Inc ....F.......415 978-2163
331 Oyster Point Blvd South San Francisco (94080) *(P-7772)*
Assembly Technologies Co LLC ....F.......714 979-4400
2921 W Central Ave Ste B Santa Ana (92704) *(P-17826)*
Asset General Inc ....E.......800 753-2556
5363 Aurora Summit Trl San Diego (92130) *(P-23629)*
Asset Science LLC ....E.......858 255-7982
17150 Via Del Campo # 200 San Diego (92127) *(P-23630)*
Assetsmart, Westlake Village *Also called PMS Systems Corporation (P-24305)*
Assisvis Inc ....E.......909 628-2031
10780 Mulberry Ave Fontana (92337) *(P-9463)*
Assoc Students University CA ....E.......510 590-7874
112 Hearst Gym Rm 4520 Berkeley (94720) *(P-6190)*
Associated Desert Newspaper (HQ) ....E.......760 337-3400
205 N 8th St El Centro (92243) *(P-5557)*
Associated Desert Shoppers (HQ) ....D.......760 346-1729
73400 Highway 111 Palm Desert (92260) *(P-6191)*
Associated Electrics Inc ....E.......949 544-7500
21062 Bake Pkwy Ste 100 Lake Forest (92630) *(P-22659)*
Associated Gear, Santa Fe Springs *Also called Quality Gears Inc (P-14747)*
Associated Microbreweries Inc ....D.......858 587-2739
9675 Scranton Rd San Diego (92121) *(P-1495)*
Associated Microbreweries Inc ....D.......714 546-2739
901 S Coast Dr Ste A Costa Mesa (92626) *(P-1496)*
Associated Microbreweries Inc (PA) ....E.......858 273-2739
5985 Santa Fe St San Diego (92109) *(P-1497)*
Associated Microbreweries Inc ....C.......619 234-2739
1157 Columbia St San Diego (92101) *(P-1498)*
Associated Plating Company ....E.......562 946-5525
9636 Ann St Santa Fe Springs (90670) *(P-12936)*
Associated Ready Mix Con Inc (PA) ....E.......949 253-2800
4621 Teller Ave Ste 130 Newport Beach (92660) *(P-10692)*
Associated Ready Mix Concrete, Baldwin Park *Also called Standard Concrete Products (P-10843)*
Associated Ready Mix Concrete ....E.......818 504-3100
8946 Bradley Ave Sun Valley (91352) *(P-10693)*
Associated Ready Mixed Con, Gardena *Also called A & A Ready Mixed Concrete Inc (P-10671)*
Associated Rebar Inc ....E.......831 758-1820
1095 Madison Ln Salinas (93907) *(P-11745)*
Associated Students UCLA ....C.......310 825-2787
308 Westwood Plz Ste 118 Los Angeles (90095) *(P-5558)*
Associated Wire Rope & Rigging ....E.......310 448-5444
910 Mahar Ave Wilmington (90744) *(P-2905)*
Assoluto Inc ....F.......213 748-1116
215 S Santa Fe Ave Apt 5 Los Angeles (90012) *(P-3288)*
AST Power LLC ....E.......949 226-2275
54 Coral Reef Newport Coast (92657) *(P-19185)*
AST Sportswear Inc (PA) ....D.......714 223-2030
2701 E Imperial Hwy Brea (92821) *(P-3474)*
Asta Construction Co Inc (PA) ....E.......707 374-6472
1090 Saint Francis Way Rio Vista (94571) *(P-87)*
Astea International Inc ....E.......949 784-5000
8 Hughes Irvine (92618) *(P-23631)*
Astec International Holding, Carlsbad *Also called Aih LLC (P-16629)*
Asteelflash USA Corp (HQ) ....C.......510 440-2840
4211 Starboard Dr Fremont (94538) *(P-17827)*
Astera Software Corporation ....F.......805 579-0004
310 N Westlake Blvd # 140 Westlake Village (91362) *(P-23632)*
Asteres Inc (PA) ....E.......858 777-8600
4110 Sorrento Valley Blvd San Diego (92121) *(P-15371)*
Astex Pharmaceuticals Inc (HQ) ....D.......925 560-0100
4420 Rosewood Dr Ste 200 Pleasanton (94588) *(P-7773)*
Asthmatx Inc ....D.......408 419-0100
888 Ross Dr Ste 100 Sunnyvale (94089) *(P-21611)*
Asti Winery, Cloverdale *Also called Treasury Wine Estates Americas (P-1968)*
Astor Manufacturing ....E.......661 645-5585
779 Anita St Ste B Chula Vista (91911) *(P-20044)*
Astourian Jewelry Mfg Inc ....F.......213 683-0436
635 S Hill St Ste 407 Los Angeles (90014) *(P-22499)*
Astra Communications Inc ....F.......818 859-7305
1101 Chestnut St Burbank (91506) *(P-17461)*
Astraeus Aerospace LLC ....F.......310 907-9205
16255 Ventura Blvd # 625 Encino (91436) *(P-19858)*
Astrazeneca Pharmaceuticals LP ....E.......650 305-2600
200 Cardinal Way Redwood City (94063) *(P-7774)*
Astro Aerospace ....C.......805 684-6641
2601 Camino Del Sol Oxnard (93030) *(P-20540)*
Astro Aluminum Treating Co Inc ....D.......562 923-4344
11040 Palmer Ave South Gate (90280) *(P-11433)*
Astro Chrome and Polsg Corp ....E.......818 781-1463
8136 Lankershim Blvd North Hollywood (91605) *(P-12937)*
Astro Display Company Inc ....E.......909 605-2875
4247 E Airport Dr Ontario (91761) *(P-23057)*
Astro Haven Enterprises Inc ....F.......949 215-3777
555 Anton Blvd Ste 150 Costa Mesa (92626) *(P-21437)*
Astro Machine Co Inc ....F.......310 679-8291
3734 W 139th St Hawthorne (90250) *(P-15753)*
Astro Packaging, Anaheim *Also called Reliable Packaging Systems Inc (P-8891)*
Astro Seal Inc ....E.......951 787-6670
827 Palmyrita Ave Ste B Riverside (92507) *(P-18822)*
Astro Technology Inc ....E.......650 533-5087
3335 Birch St Palo Alto (94306) *(P-23633)*
Astro-Tek Industries LLC ....D.......714 238-0022
1198 N Kraemer Blvd Anaheim (92806) *(P-20045)*
Astrochef LLC ....D.......213 627-9860
1111 Mateo St Los Angeles (90021) *(P-944)*
Astrofoam Molding Company Inc ....F.......805 482-7276
4117 Calle Tesoro Camarillo (93012) *(P-9506)*
Astrologie California, Commerce *Also called Ajg Inc (P-3506)*
Astron Corporation ....E.......949 458-7277
9 Autry Irvine (92618) *(P-18701)*
Astronic ....C.......949 454-1180
2 Orion Aliso Viejo (92656) *(P-17828)*
Astronics Company, Pasadena *Also called Sabrin Corporation (P-12364)*
Astronics Test Systems Inc (HQ) ....C.......800 722-2528
4 Goodyear Irvine (92618) *(P-21007)*
Astrophysics Inc (PA) ....C.......909 598-5488
21481 Ferrero City of Industry (91789) *(P-22209)*
Astura Medical ....F.......760 814-8047
3186 Lionshead Ave # 100 Carlsbad (92010) *(P-21612)*
Asturies Manufacturing Co Inc ....E.......951 270-1766
310 Cessna Cir Corona (92880) *(P-20046)*
Asucla Publications, Los Angeles *Also called Associated Students UCLA (P-5558)*
Asv Wines Inc (PA) ....E.......661 792-3159
1998 Road 152 Delano (93215) *(P-1585)*
At Mobile Bottling Line LLC ....F.......707 257-3757
413 Saint Andrews Dr NAPA (94558) *(P-2041)*
At Systems Technologies Inc ....E.......317 591-2616
301 N Lake Ave Ste 600 Pasadena (91101) *(P-15372)*
AT&T Corp ....C.......619 521-6100
8954 Rio San Diego Dr # 604 San Diego (92108) *(P-6192)*
AT&T Corp ....B.......415 542-9000
370 3rd St Rm 714 San Francisco (94107) *(P-6193)*
Ata Boy Inc ....E.......323 644-0117
3171 Los Feliz Blvd # 205 Los Angeles (90039) *(P-23281)*
Atara Biotherapeutics Inc (PA) ....C.......650 278-8930
611 Gateway Blvd Ste 900 South San Francisco (94080) *(P-8273)*
Atara Biotherapeutics Inc ....F.......805 623-4211
2380 Conejo Spectrum St # 200 Newbury Park (91320) *(P-7775)*
Atara Biotherapeutics Inc ....F.......805 309-9534
2430 Conejo Spectrum St Thousand Oaks (91320) *(P-8274)*
Atc, Santa Ana *Also called Assembly Technologies Co LLC (P-17826)*
Ate Micrographics Inc ....F.......510 475-5882
3101 Whipple Rd Ste 22 Union City (94587) *(P-21177)*
Atech Manufacturing, San Jose *Also called T&S Manufacturing Tech LLC (P-11895)*
Atelier Luxury Group LLC ....E.......310 751-2444
1330 Channing St Los Angeles (90021) *(P-3771)*
Athanor Group Inc ....C.......909 467-1205
921 E California St Ontario (91761) *(P-12621)*
Athoc Inc (HQ) ....D.......925 242-5660
3001 Bishop Dr Ste 400 San Ramon (94583) *(P-23634)*
Athos Works, Redwood City *Also called Mad Apparel Inc (P-3106)*
ATI Flat Rlled Pdts Hldngs LLC ....F.......562 654-3900
8570 Mercury Ln Pico Rivera (90660) *(P-11028)*
ATI Forged Products, Irvine *Also called Chen-Tech Industries Inc (P-21663)*
ATI Solutions Inc (PA) ....F.......818 772-7900
18425 Napa St Northridge (91325) *(P-17714)*
ATI Windows, Riverside *Also called Nevada Window Supply Inc (P-4093)*
ATI Windows, Riverside *Also called San Joaquin Window Inc (P-11981)*

ALPHABETIC

Employee Codes: A=Over 500 employees, B=251-500
C=101-250, D=51-100, E=20-50, F=10-19
2020 California
Manfacturers Register
© Mergent Inc. 1-800-342-5647
1029

Atieva Usa Inc (HQ)..........B.......510 648-3553
7373 Gateway Blvd Newark (94560) ***(P-19455)***
Atk Mission Research, Goleta *Also called Mission Research Corporation* ***(P-19915)***
Atk Space Systems Inc (HQ)..........E.......323 722-0222
6033 Bandini Blvd Commerce (90040) ***(P-20541)***
Atk Space Systems Inc..........D.......805 685-2262
600 Pine Ave Goleta (93117) ***(P-20542)***
Atk Space Systems Inc..........A.......310 343-3799
1960 E Grand Ave Ste 1150 El Segundo (90245) ***(P-20543)***
Atlantic Representations Inc..........E.......562 903-9550
10018 Santa Fe Springs Rd Santa Fe Springs (90670) ***(P-4683)***
Atlantis Computing Inc (PA)..........E.......650 917-9471
900 Glenneyre St Laguna Beach (92651) ***(P-23635)***
Atlas Carpet Mills Inc..........C.......323 724-7930
3201 S Susan St Santa Ana (92704) ***(P-2865)***
Atlas Computer Centers, Santa Maria *Also called Aegis Industries Inc* ***(P-8615)***
Atlas Copco Compressors LLC..........F.......510 413-5200
6094 Stewart Ave Fremont (94538) ***(P-14622)***
Atlas Copco Compressors LLC..........E.......866 545-4999
12827 Telegraph Rd Santa Fe Springs (90670) ***(P-14623)***
Atlas Copco Compressors LLC..........F.......510 413-5200
48434 Milmont Dr Fremont (94538) ***(P-14624)***
Atlas Copco Mafi-Trench Co LLC (HQ)..........C.......805 352-0112
3037 Industrial Pkwy Santa Maria (93455) ***(P-14649)***
Atlas Foam Products..........F.......818 837-3626
12836 Arroyo St Sylmar (91342) ***(P-9507)***
Atlas Galvanizing LLC..........E.......323 587-6247
2639 Leonis Blvd Vernon (90058) ***(P-13145)***
Atlas Granite & Stone..........F.......916 638-7100
2560 Grennan Ct Rancho Cordova (95742) ***(P-4883)***
Atlas Magnetics Inc..........F.......714 632-9718
1121 N Kraemer Pl Anaheim (92806) ***(P-18823)***
Atlas Match LLC..........D.......714 993-3328
1337 Limerick Dr Placentia (92870) ***(P-23282)***
Atlas Pacific Engineering Co..........D.......559 233-4500
3115 S Willow Ave Fresno (93725) ***(P-14345)***
Atlas Pacific Engineering Co..........E.......209 574-9884
4500 N Star Way Modesto (95356) ***(P-14346)***
Atlas Pallet Corp..........F.......925 432-6261
600 Industry Rd Pittsburg (94565) ***(P-4348)***
Atlas Screw Machine Pdts Co..........F.......415 621-6737
560 Natoma St San Francisco (94103) ***(P-12622)***
Atlas Sheet Metal Inc..........F.......949 600-8787
19 Musick Irvine (92618) ***(P-12120)***
Atlas Shower Door Co, Sacramento *Also called Atlas Specialties Corporation* ***(P-10338)***
Atlas Specialties Corporation (PA)..........E.......503 636-8182
4337 Astoria St Sacramento (95838) ***(P-10338)***
Atlas Sponge Rubber Company..........F.......626 359-5391
114 E Pomona Ave Monrovia (91016) ***(P-9284)***
Atlas Spring Mfgcorp..........C.......310 532-6200
10635 Santa Monica Blvd Los Angeles (90025) ***(P-13374)***
Atlas Survival Shelters LLC..........E.......323 727-7084
7407 Telegraph Rd Montebello (90640) ***(P-4684)***
Atlassian Inc (HQ)..........C.......415 701-1110
350 Bush St Ste 13 San Francisco (94104) ***(P-23636)***
Atm Plus Inc..........F.......619 575-3278
2232 Verus St Ste F San Diego (92154) ***(P-9285)***
Atm Skateboards, Oceanside *Also called Speedskins Inc* ***(P-22894)***
Atmf Inc..........E.......559 299-6836
807 Lincoln Ave Clovis (93612) ***(P-12938)***
Atmos Engineering Inc..........F.......650 879-1674
443 Dearborn Park Rd Pescadero (94060) ***(P-21438)***
Atomera Incorporated..........F.......408 442-5248
750 University Ave # 280 Los Gatos (95032) ***(P-18131)***
Atomic Aquatics Inc (PA)..........F.......714 375-1433
3585 Cadillac Ave Ste A Costa Mesa (92626) ***(P-22751)***
Atomic Monkey Industries Inc..........F.......949 415-8846
946 Calle Amanecer San Clemente (92673) ***(P-3772)***
Atp, Brisbane *Also called Aircraft Technical Publishers* ***(P-6178)***
Atp, Fremont *Also called Applied Thin-Film Products* ***(P-18818)***
Atp Electronics Inc..........E.......408 732-5000
2590 N 1st St Ste 150 San Jose (95131) ***(P-15007)***
Atr Sales Inc..........E.......714 432-8411
110 E Garry Ave Santa Ana (92707) ***(P-14781)***
Atr Technologies Incorporated..........F.......909 399-9724
805 Towne Center Dr Pomona (91767) ***(P-12453)***
Atra International Traders Inc..........E.......562 864-3885
3301 Leonis Blvd Vernon (90058) ***(P-5323)***
Atra-Flex, Santa Ana *Also called Atr Sales Inc* ***(P-14781)***
Atreca Inc..........D.......650 595-2595
500 Saginaw Dr Redwood City (94063) ***(P-8275)***
Atrevete Inc..........F.......323 277-5551
2055 E 51st St Vernon (90058) ***(P-3138)***
Ats International, Los Angeles *Also called Parts Out Inc* ***(P-19199)***
Ats Products Inc (PA)..........E.......510 234-3173
2785 Goodrick Ave Richmond (94801) ***(P-9644)***
Ats Systems, Rcho STA Marg *Also called Ats Workholding Inc* ***(P-14135)***
Ats Tool Inc..........E.......949 888-1744
30222 Esperanza Rcho STA Marg (92688) ***(P-14018)***
Ats Workholding, Rcho STA Marg *Also called Ats Tool Inc* ***(P-14018)***
Ats Workholding Inc..........D.......800 321-1833
30222 Esperanza Rcho STA Marg (92688) ***(P-14135)***
Attends Healthcare Pdts Inc..........C.......909 392-1200
1941 N White Ave La Verne (91750) ***(P-5098)***
Attilas Byshore Art Studio LLC..........F.......415 282-2815
2207 Quesada Ave San Francisco (94124) ***(P-10997)***
Atx Networks (san Diego) Corp (HQ)..........D.......858 546-5050
8880 Rehco Rd San Diego (92121) ***(P-17462)***
Atxco Inc..........E.......650 334-2079
3030 Bunker Hill St # 325 San Diego (92109) ***(P-7776)***
Atypon Systems LLC (PA)..........D.......408 988-1240
5201 Great America Pkwy # 215 Santa Clara (95054) ***(P-23637)***
Atyr Pharma Inc..........E.......858 731-8389
3545 John Hopkins Ct # 2 San Diego (92121) ***(P-8276)***
Auberry Forest Products Inc..........F.......559 855-6255
32177 Auberry Rd Auberry (93602) ***(P-3874)***
Aubin Industries Inc..........F.......800 324-0051
23833 S Chrisman Rd Tracy (95304) ***(P-9579)***
Auburn Journal Inc (HQ)..........E.......530 885-5656
1030 High St Auburn (95603) ***(P-5559)***
Auburn Journal Inc..........D.......530 346-2232
1030 High St Auburn (95603) ***(P-5560)***
Auburn Printers and Mfg, Auburn *Also called API Marketing* ***(P-6417)***
Auburn Tile Inc..........F.......909 984-2841
545 W Main St Ontario (91762) ***(P-10532)***
Audaexplore, San Diego *Also called Audatex North America Inc* ***(P-23638)***
Audatex North America Inc (HQ)..........C.......858 946-1900
15030 Ave Of San Diego (92128) ***(P-23638)***
Audentes Therapeutics Inc (PA)..........C.......415 818-1001
600 California St Fl 17 San Francisco (94108) ***(P-8277)***
Audeze LLC (PA)..........F.......714 581-8010
3410 S Susan St Santa Ana (92704) ***(P-17193)***
Audience Inc (HQ)..........D.......650 254-2800
331 Fairchild Dr Mountain View (94043) ***(P-18132)***
Audience Inc..........E.......323 413-2370
5670 Wilshire Blvd # 100 Los Angeles (90036) ***(P-6194)***
Audio 2000's, Moorpark *Also called H&F Technologies Inc* ***(P-17235)***
Audio Dynamix Inc..........F.......714 549-5100
2770 S Harbor Blvd Ste D Santa Ana (92704) ***(P-17194)***
Audio Fx LLC..........F.......916 929-2100
1415 Howe Ave Sacramento (95825) ***(P-17195)***
Audio Fx Home Theater, Sacramento *Also called Audio Fx LLC* ***(P-17195)***
Audio Images, Tustin *Also called Henrys Adio Vsual Slutions Inc* ***(P-17240)***
Audio Impressions Inc..........F.......818 532-7360
6592 Oak Springs Dr Oak Park (91377) ***(P-22607)***
Audio Partners Publishing..........F.......530 888-7803
131 E Placer St Auburn (95603) ***(P-17310)***
Audio Video Color Corporation (PA)..........D.......424 213-7500
17707 S Santa Fe Ave Compton (90221) ***(P-5324)***
Audiolink, Thousand Palms *Also called A R Electronics Inc* ***(P-18805)***
Audionics System Inc..........E.......818 345-9599
21541 Nordhoff St Ste C Chatsworth (91311) ***(P-17196)***
Audrey 3plus1, Vernon *Also called Three Plus One Inc* ***(P-3199)***
Auernheimer Labs Inc..........F.......559 442-1048
4561 E Florence Ave Fresno (93725) ***(P-17197)***
Auger Industries Inc..........F.......714 577-9350
390 E Crowther Ave Placentia (92870) ***(P-15754)***
August Accessories, Camarillo *Also called August Hat Company Inc* ***(P-3461)***
August Hat Company Inc (PA)..........E.......805 983-4651
850 Calle Plano Ste M Camarillo (93012) ***(P-3461)***
AUL Corp (PA)..........E.......707 257-9700
1250 Main St Ste 300 NAPA (94559) ***(P-24684)***
Aurafin Oroamerica, Burbank *Also called Richline Group Inc* ***(P-22563)***
Auric Blends, Santa Rosa *Also called Teh-Pari International* ***(P-9029)***
Aurident Inc..........E.......714 870-1851
610 S State College Blvd Fullerton (92831) ***(P-22135)***
Aurionpro, San Ramon *Also called Cyberinc Corporation* ***(P-23790)***
Auris Health Inc (HQ)..........C.......650 610-0750
150 Shoreline Dr Redwood City (94065) ***(P-21613)***
Auritec Pharmaceuticals Inc..........F.......424 272-9501
2285 E Foothill Blvd Pasadena (91107) ***(P-7777)***
Auro Pharmaceuticals Inc..........F.......562 352-9630
511 S Harbor Blvd Ste F La Habra (90631) ***(P-7778)***
Auro Pharmacies Inc..........E.......562 352-9630
511 S Harbor Blvd Ste F La Habra (90631) ***(P-7779)***
Aurora Casting & Engrg Inc..........D.......805 933-2761
1790 E Lemonwood Dr Santa Paula (93060) ***(P-11409)***
Aurum Assembly Plus Inc..........E.......858 578-8710
8829 Production Ave San Diego (92121) ***(P-17829)***
Auspex Pharmaceuticals Inc..........E.......858 558-2400
3333 N Torrey Pines Ct La Jolla (92037) ***(P-7780)***
Austn Creek Materials, Santa Rosa *Also called Bohan Cnlis - Astin Creek Rdym* ***(P-312)***
Auto Club Enterprises..........B.......714 885-2376
3333 Fairview Rd Costa Mesa (92626) ***(P-5884)***
Auto Doctor, Temecula *Also called Thompson Magnetics Inc* ***(P-19118)***
Auto Edge Solutions, Pacoima *Also called Moc Products Company Inc* ***(P-9002)***
Auto Lectrics, Campbell *Also called Alternators Starters Etc* ***(P-19184)***
Auto Scrubber, Thousand Oaks *Also called Thousands Oaks Hand Wash* ***(P-15591)***
Auto Trend Products, Vernon *Also called Punch Press Products Inc* ***(P-14099)***
Auto Wash Concepts Inc..........F.......562 948-2575
11769 Telegraph Rd Santa Fe Springs (90670) ***(P-15487)***
Auto-Chlor System Wash Inc..........F.......818 376-0940
16141 Hart St Van Nuys (91406) ***(P-8364)***
Autoanything Inc..........C.......858 569-8111
6602 Convoy Ct Ste 200 San Diego (92111) ***(P-19456)***
Autoanything.com, San Diego *Also called Autoanything Inc* ***(P-19456)***
Autobahn Construction Inc..........F.......714 769-7025
933 N Batavia St Ste A Orange (92867) ***(P-13706)***
Autodesk Inc..........D.......415 356-0700
1 Market St San Francisco (94105) ***(P-23639)***
Autodesk Inc (PA)..........B.......415 507-5000
111 Mcinnis Pkwy San Rafael (94903) ***(P-23640)***
Autodesk Inc..........C.......415 507-5000
3950 Civic Center Dr San Rafael (94903) ***(P-23641)***
Autoflow Products Co..........F.......310 515-2866
15915 S San Pedro St Gardena (90248) ***(P-20837)***

Autoliv Safety Technology Inc.....A.....619 662-8000
2475 Paseo D Las Amrcs San Diego (92154) ***(P-3833)***
Automated Bldg Components Inc.....F.....559 485-8232
2853 S Orange Ave Fresno (93725) ***(P-4288)***
Automated Packg Systems Inc.....F.....562 941-1476
10440 Ontiveros Pl Ste 1 Santa Fe Springs (90670) ***(P-13758)***
Automatic Control Engrg Corp.....E.....510 293-6040
20788 Corsair Blvd Hayward (94545) ***(P-21439)***
Automatic Switch Company.....F.....714 283-4000
120 S Chaparral Ct # 200 Anaheim (92808) ***(P-13290)***
Automation & Entertainment Inc (PA).....F.....408 353-4223
25870 Soquel San Jose Rd Los Gatos (95033) ***(P-13291)***
Automation Electronics, Chatsworth *Also called RJA Industries Inc* ***(P-19069)***
Automation Gt, Carlsbad *Also called Laurelwood Industries Inc* ***(P-16141)***
Automation Plating, Glendale *Also called Aero Manufacturing & Pltg Co* ***(P-12908)***
Automation Plating Corporation.....E.....323 245-4951
927 Thompson Ave Glendale (91201) ***(P-12939)***
Automation Printing Co (PA).....E.....213 488-1230
1230 Long Beach Ave Los Angeles (90021) ***(P-7354)***
Automation Technical Svcs Inc.....F.....619 302-6970
10459 Roselle St Ste C San Diego (92121) ***(P-14428)***
Automation West Inc.....F.....714 556-7381
1605 E Saint Gertrude Pl Santa Ana (92705) ***(P-15755)***
Autometrix Inc.....F.....530 477-5065
12098 Charles Dr Grass Valley (95945) ***(P-14287)***
Automoco LLC.....D.....707 544-4761
9142 Independence Ave Chatsworth (91311) ***(P-19586)***
Automotive Electronics Svcs.....F.....559 292-7851
5465 E Hedges Ave Fresno (93727) ***(P-13396)***
Automotive Engineered Pdts Inc.....D.....619 229-7797
7149 Mission Gorge Rd San Diego (92120) ***(P-13969)***
Automotive Exch & Sup of Cal (PA).....E.....619 282-3207
4354 Twain Ave Ste G San Diego (92120) ***(P-19587)***
Automotive Lease Guide Alg Inc.....E.....424 258-8026
120 Broadway Ste 200 Santa Monica (90401) ***(P-6195)***
Automotive Racing Products Inc (PA).....D.....805 339-2200
1863 Eastman Ave Ventura (93003) ***(P-11565)***
Automotive Racing Products Inc.....D.....805 525-1497
1760 E Lemonwood Dr Santa Paula (93060) ***(P-11566)***
Auton Motorized Systems, Valencia *Also called Virgil Walker Inc* ***(P-11912)***
Auton Motorized Systems, Valencia *Also called Virgil Walker Inc* ***(P-18686)***
Autonomy Interwoven, Sunnyvale *Also called Entco LLC* ***(P-23863)***
Autosplice Inc (PA).....C.....858 535-0077
10431 Wtridge Cir Ste 110 San Diego (92121) ***(P-16877)***
Autotechbizcom Inc.....F.....949 245-7033
23551 Commerce Center Dr I Laguna Hills (92653) ***(P-14429)***
Autumn Express, Berkeley *Also called Autumn Press Inc* ***(P-6422)***
Autumn Milling Co Inc.....E.....310 635-0703
621 26th St Manhattan Beach (90266) ***(P-3925)***
Autumn Press Inc (PA).....E.....510 654-4545
945 Camelia St Berkeley (94710) ***(P-6422)***
Auxin Solar Inc.....E.....408 225-4380
6835 Via Del Oro San Jose (95119) ***(P-18133)***
AV Now Inc.....E.....831 425-2500
225 Technology Cir Scotts Valley (95066) ***(P-17198)***
Ava James, Commerce *Also called C-Quest Inc* ***(P-3147)***
Avago Technologies US Inc.....F.....408 433-4068
1730 Fox Dr San Jose (95131) ***(P-18134)***
Avago Technologies US Inc (HQ).....B.....800 433-8778
1320 Ridder Park Dr San Jose (95131) ***(P-18135)***
Avail Medsystems Inc.....E.....650 772-1529
380 Portage Ave Palo Alto (94306) ***(P-21614)***
Avalanche Technology Inc.....E.....510 438-0148
3450 W Warren Ave Fremont (94538) ***(P-18136)***
Avalco Inc.....F.....310 676-3057
2029 Verdugo Blvd Ste 710 Montrose (91020) ***(P-13292)***
Avalon Apparel LLC (PA).....C.....323 581-3511
2520 W 6th St Los Angeles (90057) ***(P-3475)***
Avalon Communications, Hawthorne *Also called Technology Training Corp* ***(P-6886)***
Avalon Glass & Mirror Company.....D.....323 321-8806
642 Alondra Blvd Carson (90746) ***(P-10339)***
Avalon Mfg Co Incoirporated.....F.....951 340-0280
509 Bateman Cir Corona (92880) ***(P-14347)***
Avalon Shutters Inc.....C.....909 937-4900
3407 N Perris Blvd Perris (92571) ***(P-4000)***
Avanir Pharmaceuticals Inc (HQ).....C.....949 389-6700
30 Enterprise Ste 400 Aliso Viejo (92656) ***(P-7781)***
Avant Enterprises Inc (PA).....E.....866 300-3311
18457 Railroad St City of Industry (91748) ***(P-11521)***
Avantec Manufacturing Inc.....E.....714 532-6197
1811 N Case St Orange (92865) ***(P-17830)***
Avantec Vascular Corporation.....E.....408 329-5400
870 Hermosa Ave Sunnyvale (94085) ***(P-21615)***
Avantis Medical Systems Inc.....E.....408 733-1901
2367 Bering Dr San Jose (95131) ***(P-22228)***
Avanzato Technology Corp.....E.....312 509-0506
5335 Mcconnell Ave Los Angeles (90066) ***(P-14430)***
Avast Software Inc (PA).....F.....844 340-9251
2625 Broadway St Redwood City (94063) ***(P-23642)***
Avatar Machine LLC.....E.....949 817-7728
18100 Mount Washington St Fountain Valley (92708) ***(P-15756)***
Avatier Corporation (PA).....E.....925 217-5170
4733 Chabot Dr Ste 201 Pleasanton (94588) ***(P-23643)***
Avaya Holdings Corp (PA).....E.....908 953-6000
4655 Great America Pkwy Santa Clara (95054) ***(P-23644)***
Avc, Compton *Also called Audio Video Color Corporation* ***(P-5324)***
AVC Specialists Inc.....E.....513 458-2600
5146 N Commerce Ave Ste G Moorpark (93021) ***(P-20784)***
Avcorp Cmpsite Fabrication Inc.....B.....310 970-5658
1600 W 135th St Gardena (90249) ***(P-20047)***
Avcorp Cmpstes Fabrication Inc.....F.....310 527-0700
1551 W 139th St Gardena (90249) ***(P-20048)***
Avd, Newport Beach *Also called American Vanguard Corporation* ***(P-8818)***
Ave Jewelry Design Mfg, North Hollywood *Also called Ave Jewelry Inc* ***(P-22500)***
Ave Jewelry Inc.....F.....213 488-0097
13127 Ebell St North Hollywood (91605) ***(P-22500)***
Aveox Inc.....E.....805 915-0200
2265 Ward Ave Ste A Simi Valley (93065) ***(P-16778)***
Avermedia Technologies Inc.....F.....510 403-0006
4038 Clipper Ct Fremont (94538) ***(P-15164)***
Avery Dennison Corporation (PA).....B.....626 304-2000
207 N Goode Ave Glendale (91203) ***(P-5349)***
Avery Dennison Corporation.....B.....714 674-8500
50 Pointe Dr Brea (92821) ***(P-5350)***
Avery Dennison Corporation.....C.....626 938-7239
751 N Todd Ave Azusa (91702) ***(P-5351)***
Avery Dennison Corporation.....C.....909 987-4631
11195 Eucalyptus St Rancho Cucamonga (91730) ***(P-5352)***
Avery Dennison Corporation.....C.....909 428-4238
10721 Jasmine St Fontana (92337) ***(P-5353)***
Avery Dennison Corporation.....C.....626 304-2000
2900 Bradley St Pasadena (91107) ***(P-5354)***
Avery Dennison Corporation.....C.....323 728-8888
5819 Telegraph Rd Commerce (90040) ***(P-5355)***
Avery Dennison Corporation.....C.....626 304-2000
2743 Thompson Creek Rd Pomona (91767) ***(P-5356)***
Avery Plastics Inc.....D.....619 696-1230
4070 Goldfinch St Ste A San Diego (92103) ***(P-9645)***
Avery Products Corporation.....E.....619 671-1022
6987 Calle De Linea # 101 San Diego (92154) ***(P-5478)***
Avery Products Corporation (HQ).....B.....714 675-8500
50 Pointe Dr Brea (92821) ***(P-5479)***
Avet Industries Inc.....F.....818 576-9895
9687 Topanga Canyon Pl Chatsworth (91311) ***(P-22752)***
Avet Reels, Chatsworth *Also called Avet Industries Inc* ***(P-22752)***
AVI.....F.....760 451-9379
431 Janemar Rd Fallbrook (92028) ***(P-18824)***
Aviat Networks Inc (PA).....C.....408 941-7100
860 N Mccarthy Blvd # 20 Milpitas (95035) ***(P-17463)***
Aviat US Inc (HQ).....B.....408 941-7100
860 N Mccarthy Blvd # 200 Milpitas (95035) ***(P-17464)***
Aviate Enterprises Inc.....E.....916 993-4000
5844 Price Ave McClellan (95652) ***(P-15414)***
Aviation and Indus Dev Corp.....F.....310 373-6057
23870 Hawthorne Blvd Torrance (90505) ***(P-9394)***
Aviation Equipment Processing, Costa Mesa *Also called Flare Group* ***(P-20104)***
Aviator Systems Inc.....F.....949 677-2461
37440 Calle De Lobo Murrieta (92562) ***(P-20049)***
Avibank Mfg Inc (HQ).....C.....818 392-2100
11500 Sherman Way North Hollywood (91605) ***(P-20050)***
Avibank Mfg Inc.....D.....661 257-2329
25323 Rye Canyon Rd Valencia (91355) ***(P-11567)***
Avid Bioservices Inc (PA).....C.....714 508-6000
2642 Michelle Dr Ste 200 Tustin (92780) ***(P-7782)***
Avid Idntification Systems Inc (PA).....D.....951 371-7505
3185 Hamner Ave Norco (92860) ***(P-18137)***
Avid Ink, Irvine *Also called Advanced Vsual Image Dsign LLC* ***(P-6976)***
Avid Lyfe Inc.....F.....888 510-2517
3133 Tiger Run Ct Ste 109 Carlsbad (92010) ***(P-3289)***
Avid Systems Inc (HQ).....C.....650 526-1600
280 Bernardo Ave Mountain View (94043) ***(P-17465)***
Avid Technology Inc.....B.....510 486-8302
2600 10th St Ste 100 Berkeley (94710) ***(P-22403)***
Avid Technology Inc.....E.....818 557-2520
101 S 1st St Ste 200 Burbank (91502) ***(P-22404)***
Avid Technology Inc.....C.....818 779-7860
14007 Runnymede St Van Nuys (91405) ***(P-22405)***
Avilas Garden Art (PA).....C.....909 350-4546
14608 Merrill Ave Fontana (92335) ***(P-10533)***
Avinger Inc.....D.....650 241-7900
400 Chesapeake Dr Redwood City (94063) ***(P-21616)***
Avion Graphics Inc.....E.....949 472-0438
27192 Burbank Foothill Ranch (92610) ***(P-6423)***
Avion Tl Mfg Machining Ctr Inc.....F.....661 257-2915
29035 The Old Rd Valencia (91355) ***(P-15757)***
Avis Roto Die Co.....E.....323 255-7070
1560 N San Fernando Rd Los Angeles (90065) ***(P-14019)***
Avista Technologies Inc.....F.....760 744-0536
140 Bosstick Blvd San Marcos (92069) ***(P-8943)***
Avita Beverage Company Inc (PA).....F.....213 477-1979
18401 Burbank Blvd # 121 Tarzana (91356) ***(P-2042)***
Aviva Biosciences Corporation.....E.....858 552-0888
7700 Ronson Rd Ste 100 San Diego (92111) ***(P-19263)***
Avm Technologies, Valencia *Also called Realwise Inc* ***(P-24347)***
Avn Media Network Inc.....E.....818 718-5788
9400 Penfield Ave Chatsworth (91311) ***(P-6073)***
Avogy Inc.....E.....408 684-5200
677 River Oaks Pkwy San Jose (95134) ***(P-18138)***
Avoy Corp.....F.....510 295-8055
114 Greenbank Ave Piedmont (94611) ***(P-6424)***
Avoy Corp (PA).....F.....510 832-7746
2406 Webster St Oakland (94612) ***(P-6425)***
Avp Technology LLC.....E.....510 683-0157
4140 Business Center Dr Fremont (94538) ***(P-14696)***
Avr Global Technologies Inc (PA).....F.....949 391-1180
500 La Terraza Blvd Escondido (92025) ***(P-18825)***
AVV Winery Co LLC.....E.....707 433-7209
8644 Highway 128 Healdsburg (95448) ***(P-1586)***

ALPHABETIC

Employee Codes: A=Over 500 employees, B=251-500
C=101-250, D=51-100, E=20-50, F=10-19
2020 California
Manfacturers Register
© Mergent Inc. 1-800-342-5647
1031

AVX Antenna Inc (HQ)......E......858 550-3820
5501 Oberlin Dr Ste 100 San Diego (92121) ***(P-17466)***
AVX Filters Corporation......D......818 767-6770
11144 Penrose St Ste 7 Sun Valley (91352) ***(P-14795)***
Aw Industries Inc......D......909 629-1500
1810 S Reservoir St Pomona (91766) ***(P-4551)***
Awake Inc......D......818 365-9361
10711 Walker St Cypress (90630) ***(P-3215)***
Award Packaging Spc Corp......E......323 727-1200
12855 Midway Pl Cerritos (90703) ***(P-5197)***
Aware Products Inc......E......818 206-6700
9250 Mason Ave Chatsworth (91311) ***(P-8440)***
Aware Products LLC......C......818 206-6700
9250 Mason Ave Chatsworth (91311) ***(P-8441)***
Awcc Corporation......F......949 497-6313
434 N Coast Hwy Laguna Beach (92651) ***(P-3507)***
Awesome Products Inc (PA)......C......714 562-8873
6370 Altura Blvd Buena Park (90620) ***(P-8365)***
Aweta-Autoline Inc (PA)......E......559 244-8340
4516 E Citron Fresno (93725) ***(P-13611)***
Awg Ltd Inc......F......707 259-6777
4162 Big Ranch Rd NAPA (94558) ***(P-1587)***
AWI, Sacramento *Also called All Weather Inc* ***(P-21430)***
Awnings, Fresno *Also called Pacific Tent and Awning* ***(P-3696)***
Awo, Vista *Also called Advanced Web Offset Inc* ***(P-6977)***
Ax II Inc......E......310 292-6523
13921 S Figueroa St Los Angeles (90061) ***(P-2750)***
Axceleon Inc......F......714 960-5200
1947 Overlook Rd Fullerton (92831) ***(P-23645)***
Axcelis Technologies Inc......B......949 477-5160
1360 Reynolds Ave Ste 106 Irvine (92614) ***(P-21440)***
Axcelis Technologies Inc......B......510 979-1970
5673 W Las Positas Blvd # 205 Pleasanton (94588) ***(P-21441)***
Axel Johnson Metals, Vallejo *Also called Nl Industries Inc* ***(P-11193)***
Axelgaard Manufacturing Co Ltd (PA)......D......760 723-7554
520 Industrial Way Fallbrook (92028) ***(P-22229)***
Axelgaard Manufacturing Co Ltd......E......760 723-7554
329 W Aviation Rd Fallbrook (92028) ***(P-22230)***
Axent Corporation Limited......E......949 900-4349
3 Musick Irvine (92618) ***(P-5458)***
Axent USA, Irvine *Also called Axent Corporation Limited* ***(P-5458)***
Axeon Water Technologies......D......760 723-5417
40980 County Center Dr # 110 Temecula (92591) ***(P-15488)***
Axess Products Corp......F......818 785-4000
9409 Owensmouth Ave Chatsworth (91311) ***(P-17199)***
Axia Technologies LLC......E......855 376-2942
4183 State St Santa Barbara (93110) ***(P-23646)***
Axial Industries Inc......C......408 977-7800
1991 Senter Rd San Jose (95112) ***(P-12121)***
Axiom Industries Inc......E......559 276-1310
4202 W Sierra Madre Ave Fresno (93722) ***(P-21983)***
Axiom Label Group, Compton *Also called Kmr Label LLC* ***(P-6957)***
Axiom Materials Inc......E......949 623-4400
2320 Pullman St Santa Ana (92705) ***(P-8855)***
Axis Group Inc......F......510 487-7393
1220 Whipple Rd Union City (94587) ***(P-18139)***
Axium Plastics LLC......D......909 969-0766
5701 Clark St Ontario (91761) ***(P-9646)***
Axl Musical Instruments Ltd......C......415 508-1398
31067 San Clemente St Hayward (94544) ***(P-22608)***
Axles Now, Anaheim *Also called Friedl Corporation* ***(P-19662)***
Axp Technology Inc......F......510 683-1180
41041 Trimboli Way # 1761 Fremont (94538) ***(P-17013)***
Axt Inc......E......510 683-5900
4311 Solar Way Fremont (94538) ***(P-18140)***
Axt Inc (PA)......E......510 438-4700
4281 Technology Dr Fremont (94538) ***(P-18141)***
Axxcelera Brdband Wireless Inc (HQ)......F......805 968-9621
82 Coromar Dr Santa Barbara (93117) ***(P-17467)***
Axxis Corporation......E......951 436-9921
1535 Nandina Ave Perris (92571) ***(P-15758)***
Axygen Inc (HQ)......E......510 494-8900
33210 Central Ave Union City (94587) ***(P-9647)***
Axygen Scientific, Union City *Also called Axygen Inc* ***(P-9647)***
Ayala and Son Pallets, Sanger *Also called Triple A Pallets Inc* ***(P-4402)***
Ayantra Inc......F......510 623-7526
47873 Fremont Blvd Fremont (94538) ***(P-17348)***
Ayca Furniture, Corona *Also called Crescent Woodworking Co Ltd* ***(P-4562)***
Aymar Engineering......F......619 562-1121
9434 Abraham Way Santee (92071) ***(P-12122)***
AZ Displays Inc......E......949 831-5000
75 Columbia Aliso Viejo (92656) ***(P-18826)***
AZ Manufacturing, Santa Ana *Also called A-Z Mfg Inc* ***(P-15669)***
Az-Iz Case Co, Vernon *Also called Procases Inc* ***(P-4342)***
Aza Industries Inc (PA)......E......760 560-0440
1410 Vantage Ct Vista (92081) ***(P-22753)***
Azaa Investments Inc (PA)......F......858 569-8111
6602 Convoy Ct Ste 200 San Diego (92111) ***(P-19457)***
Azachorok Contract Svcs LLC......F......661 951-6566
320 Grand Cypress Ave # 502 Palmdale (93551) ***(P-12123)***
Azazie Inc......F......650 963-9420
148 E Brokaw Rd San Jose (95112) ***(P-3216)***
Azimuth Electronics Inc......F......949 492-6481
2605 S El Camino Real San Clemente (92672) ***(P-21008)***
Azimuth Industrial Co Inc......E......510 441-6000
30593 Un Cy Blvd Ste 110 Union City (94587) ***(P-18142)***
Azimuth Semiconductor Assembly, Union City *Also called Azimuth Industrial Co Inc* ***(P-18142)***

Azitex Knitting Mills, Los Angeles *Also called Azitex Trading Corp* ***(P-2816)***
Azitex Trading Corp......D......213 745-7072
1850 E 15th St Los Angeles (90021) ***(P-2816)***
Azpire Print & Mediaworks LLC......F......310 736-5952
10555 Clarkson Rd Los Angeles (90064) ***(P-6426)***
Aztec Containers, Vista *Also called Aztec Technology Corporation* ***(P-11746)***
Aztec Machine Co Inc......F......916 638-4894
3156 Fitzgerald Rd Ste A Rancho Cordova (95742) ***(P-15759)***
Aztec Perlite Company Inc......F......760 741-1733
1518 Simpson Way Escondido (92029) ***(P-10968)***
Aztec Technology Corporation (PA)......E......760 727-2300
2550 S Santa Fe Ave Vista (92084) ***(P-11746)***
Aztec Technology Corporation......F......909 350-8830
14022 Slover Ave Fontana (92337) ***(P-4349)***
Aztec Tents, Torrance *Also called A-Aztec Rents & Sells Inc* ***(P-3671)***
Azteca Jeans Inc......E......323 758-7721
6600 Avalon Blvd Los Angeles (90003) ***(P-3290)***
Azteca News......F......714 972-9912
1532 E Wellington Ave Santa Ana (92701) ***(P-5561)***
Azteca Ornamental Iron Works, Rosemead *Also called Azteca Ornamental Metals* ***(P-12454)***
Azteca Ornamental Metals......F......626 280-2822
2738 Stingle Ave Rosemead (91770) ***(P-12454)***
Aztech Products International......E......858 481-8412
326 10th St Del Mar (92014) ***(P-19264)***
Azul Systems Inc (PA)......D......650 230-6500
385 Moffett Park Dr # 115 Sunnyvale (94089) ***(P-23647)***
Azuma Foods Internatl, Hayward *Also called Azuma Foods Intl Inc USA* ***(P-2256)***
Azuma Foods Intl Inc USA (HQ)......D......510 782-1112
20201 Mack St Hayward (94545) ***(P-2256)***
Azumex Corp......E......619 710-8855
9295 Siempre Viva Rd A San Diego (92154) ***(P-1348)***
Azure Biosystems Inc......E......925 307-7127
6747 Sierra Ct Ste A Dublin (94568) ***(P-8278)***
Azure Microdynamics Inc......D......949 699-3344
19652 Descartes Foothill Ranch (92610) ***(P-15760)***
Azusa Engineering Inc......F......626 966-4071
1542 W Industrial Park St Covina (91722) ***(P-19588)***
Azusa Rock LLC (HQ)......F......858 530-9444
3901 Fish Canyon Rd Azusa (91702) ***(P-297)***
Azusa Rock Inc......F......619 440-2363
3605 Dehesa Rd El Cajon (92019) ***(P-298)***
Azusa Rock Inc......E......209 826-5066
22101 Sunset Dr Los Banos (93635) ***(P-10694)***
B & B Battery (usa) Inc (PA)......E......323 278-1900
6415 Randolph St Commerce (90040) ***(P-19178)***
B & B Doors and Windows Inc......E......818 837-8480
11455 Ilex Ave San Fernando (91340) ***(P-11933)***
B & B Enameling Inc......F......714 848-0044
17591 Sampson Ln Huntington Beach (92647) ***(P-13146)***
B & B Jewelry Mfg, Los Angeles *Also called Nationwide Jewelry Mfrs Inc* ***(P-22553)***
B & B Label Inc......F......805 922-0332
2357 Thompson Way Santa Maria (93455) ***(P-6996)***
B & B Manufacturing Co (PA)......C......661 257-2161
27940 Beale Ct Santa Clarita (91355) ***(P-15761)***
B & B Pipe and Tool Co (PA)......E......562 424-0704
3035 Walnut Ave Long Beach (90807) ***(P-15762)***
B & B Pipe and Tool Co......F......661 323-8208
2301 Parker Ln Bakersfield (93308) ***(P-15763)***
B & B Red-I-Mix Concrete Inc......E......626 359-8371
590 Live Oak Ave Baldwin Park (91706) ***(P-10695)***
B & B Refractories Inc......F......562 946-4535
12121 Los Nietos Rd Santa Fe Springs (90670) ***(P-10459)***
B & B Rv Inc......E......530 365-7043
3750 Auto Mall Dr Anderson (96007) ***(P-19840)***
B & B Services, Baldwin Park *Also called B & B Red-I-Mix Concrete Inc* ***(P-10695)***
B & B Specialties Inc (PA)......C......714 985-3000
4321 E La Palma Ave Anaheim (92807) ***(P-11568)***
B & C Industries, Anaheim *Also called B & Cawnings Inc* ***(P-12124)***
B & C Painting Solutions Inc......E......209 982-0422
107 Val Dervin Pkwy Stockton (95206) ***(P-13147)***
B & C Plating Co......E......323 263-6757
1507 S Sunol Dr Los Angeles (90023) ***(P-12940)***
B & Cawnings Inc......E......714 632-3303
3082 E Miraloma Ave Anaheim (92806) ***(P-12124)***
B & D Litho Group Inc......E......909 390-0903
325 N Ponderosa Ave Ontario (91761) ***(P-6427)***
B & E Enterprises......F......714 630-3731
1380 N Mccan St Anaheim (92806) ***(P-20382)***
B & E Manufacturing Co Inc......E......714 898-2269
12151 Monarch St Garden Grove (92841) ***(P-20051)***
B & G Aerospace Metals......E......951 738-8133
1801 Railroad St Corona (92880) ***(P-11410)***
B & G Electronic Assembly Inc......F......909 608-2077
10350 Regis Ct Rancho Cucamonga (91730) ***(P-18827)***
B & G House of Printing, Gardena *Also called Matsuda House Printing Inc* ***(P-6719)***
B & G Metal Inc......F......626 444-8566
9408 Gidley St Temple City (91780) ***(P-12125)***
B & G Millworks......F......562 944-4599
12522 Lakeland Rd Santa Fe Springs (90670) ***(P-4001)***
B & G Precision Inc......F......510 438-9785
45450 Industrial Pl Ste 9 Fremont (94538) ***(P-15764)***
B & H Engineering Company, San Carlos *Also called Begovic Industries Inc* ***(P-15782)***
B & H Labeling Systems, Ceres *Also called B & H Manufacturing Co Inc* ***(P-14697)***
B & H Manufacturing Co Inc (PA)......C......209 537-5785
3461 Roeding Rd Ceres (95307) ***(P-14697)***
B & H Signs Inc......D......626 359-6643
926 S Primrose Ave Monrovia (91016) ***(P-23058)***
B & H Technical Ceramics Inc......F......650 637-1171
390 Industrial Rd San Carlos (94070) ***(P-15765)***

B & H Tool Company, San Marcos *Also called Neville Industries Inc* ***(P-14084)***
B & I Fender Trims Inc..........D.......718 326-4323
1401 Air Wing Rd San Diego (92154) ***(P-19589)***
B & L Casing Service LLC..........F.......661 589-9080
21054 Kratzmeyer Rd Bakersfield (93314) ***(P-156)***
B & M Machine Inc..........F.......909 355-0998
8439 Cherry Ave Fontana (92335) ***(P-15766)***
B & M Racing & Prfmce Pdts, Chatsworth *Also called Automoco LLC* ***(P-19586)***
B & M Upholstery..........F.......415 621-7447
2525 16th St Ste 201 San Francisco (94103) ***(P-2669)***
B & R Accessories Inc..........F.......213 688-8727
7508 Deering Ave Ste D Canoga Park (91303) ***(P-22978)***
B & R Farms LLC..........E.......831 637-9168
5280 Fairview Rd Hollister (95023) ***(P-842)***
B & R Mold Inc..........F.......805 526-8665
4564 E Los Angeles Ave C Simi Valley (93063) ***(P-14020)***
B & R Vinyards Inc..........F.......408 842-5649
4350 Monterey Rd Gilroy (95020) ***(P-1588)***
B & S Plastics Inc..........A.......805 981-0262
2200 Sturgis Rd Oxnard (93030) ***(P-9648)***
B & W Precision Inc..........F.......714 447-0971
1260 Pioneer St Ste A Brea (92821) ***(P-15767)***
B & Y Global Sourcing LLC..........F.......213 891-1112
801 S Grand Ave Ste 475 Los Angeles (90017) ***(P-3217)***
B & Y Machine Co..........F.......909 795-8588
1060 5th St Calimesa (92320) ***(P-15611)***
B and P Plastics Inc..........E.......619 477-1893
225 W 30th St National City (91950) ***(P-9649)***
B and Z Printing Inc..........E.......714 892-2000
1300 E Wakeham Ave B Santa Ana (92705) ***(P-6428)***
B B C, San Jose *Also called Babbitt Bearing Co Inc* ***(P-15772)***
B Braun Medical Inc..........A.......610 691-5400
2525 Mcgaw Ave Irvine (92614) ***(P-21617)***
B Brays Card Inc..........F.......760 265-4720
12053 Mariposa Rd Victorville (92394) ***(P-6429)***
B C H Manufacturing Co Inc..........F.......510 569-6586
10012 Denny St Oakland (94603) ***(P-13707)***
B C I, San Diego *Also called Brehm Communications Inc* ***(P-6458)***
B C Lighting, Compton *Also called California Metal Group Inc* ***(P-12146)***
B C M, Chula Vista *Also called Bellama Cstm Met Fbrcators Inc* ***(P-12130)***
B C Song International Inc..........D.......510 785-8383
2509 Technology Dr Hayward (94545) ***(P-9039)***
B C T, Laguna Hills *Also called Raintree Business Products* ***(P-6832)***
B C Yellow Pages..........F.......530 876-8616
1001 Bille Rd Paradise (95969) ***(P-6196)***
B Cumming Company A Corp..........F.......818 504-2571
9990 Glenoaks Blvd Ste B Sun Valley (91352) ***(P-9286)***
B D L, Brea *Also called Belt Drives Ltd* ***(P-20384)***
B D Pharmingen Inc (HQ)..........F.......858 812-8800
10975 Torreyana Rd San Diego (92121) ***(P-8205)***
B Dazzle Inc..........F.......310 374-3000
500 Meyer Ln Redondo Beach (90278) ***(P-22660)***
B E & P Enterprises LLC (PA)..........E.......909 591-7561
5167 G St Chino (91710) ***(P-4492)***
B E M R, Bakersfield *Also called Bakersfield Elc Mtr Repr Inc* ***(P-24685)***
B F, Riverside *Also called Brenner-Fiedler & Associates* ***(P-21444)***
B F I Labels, Yorba Linda *Also called Beckers Fabrication Inc* ***(P-5357)***
B F Mc Gilla Inc..........E.......323 581-8288
2020 E Slauson Ave Huntington Park (90255) ***(P-13459)***
B F S Printing Bulk Mail Etc, Yuba City *Also called Business Fulfillment Svcs Inc* ***(P-6462)***
B Gone Bird Inc (PA)..........F.......949 387-5662
15375 Barranca Pkwy Ste D Irvine (92618) ***(P-9428)***
B H Tank Works Inc..........F.......323 221-1579
1919 N San Fernando Rd Los Angeles (90065) ***(P-11994)***
B I A S, Petaluma *Also called Berkley Integrated Audio Softw* ***(P-19210)***
B J Bindery..........D.......714 835-7342
833 S Grand Ave Santa Ana (92705) ***(P-7326)***
B J Embroidery & Screenprint..........F.......707 463-2767
272 E Smith St Ukiah (95482) ***(P-3724)***
B K Harris Inc..........F.......714 630-8780
3574 E Enterprise Dr Anaheim (92807) ***(P-6430)***
B M B, Rancho Cordova *Also called Bmb Metal Products Corporation* ***(P-12132)***
B M I, El Segundo *Also called Bundy Manufacturing Inc* ***(P-15803)***
B M S, Poway *Also called Broadcast Microwave Services* ***(P-17474)***
B Metal Fabrication Inc..........E.......650 615-7705
318 S Maple Ave South San Francisco (94080) ***(P-12126)***
B O A Inc..........E.......714 256-8960
580 W Lambert Rd Ste L Brea (92821) ***(P-3070)***
B P I Corp..........F.......408 988-7888
1208 Norman Ave Ste B Santa Clara (95054) ***(P-15768)***
B P John Hauling, Murrieta *Also called B P John Recycle Inc* ***(P-3926)***
B P John Recycle Inc..........E.......951 696-1144
38875 Avenida La Cresta Murrieta (92562) ***(P-3926)***
B P W, Santa Fe Springs *Also called Brown-Pacific Inc* ***(P-11030)***
B R & F Spray Inc..........F.......408 988-7582
3380 De La Cruz Blvd Santa Clara (95054) ***(P-13148)***
B S A, Fremont *Also called Ball Screws & Actuators Co Inc* ***(P-14782)***
B S K T Inc..........E.......818 349-1566
8447 Canoga Ave Canoga Park (91304) ***(P-15769)***
B Stephen Cooperage Inc..........F.......909 591-2929
10746 Vernon Ave Ontario (91762) ***(P-11508)***
B T E Deltec Inc..........C.......619 291-4211
2727 Kurtz St San Diego (92110) ***(P-18828)***
B T I, City of Industry *Also called Battery Technology Inc* ***(P-19152)***
B T I Areospace & Electronics, Chino *Also called Bti Aerospace & Electronics* ***(P-15800)***
B W I, Anaheim *Also called Bud Wil Inc* ***(P-9510)***
B W Implement Co..........E.......661 764-5254
288 W Front St Buttonwillow (93206) ***(P-13612)***
B W Padilla Inc..........E.......408 275-9834
197 Ryland St San Jose (95110) ***(P-24617)***
B&A Health Products Co, Brea *Also called Lifebloom Corporation* ***(P-7992)***
B&B Hardware Inc..........E.......805 683-6700
5370 Hollister Ave Ste 2 Santa Barbara (93111) ***(P-12666)***
B&B Pallet Company, Compton *Also called Bruce Iversen* ***(P-4352)***
B&B Rv Center, Anderson *Also called B & B Rv Inc* ***(P-19840)***
B&B Spring Co, Cerritos *Also called Clio Inc* ***(P-13379)***
B&F Fedelini Inc (PA)..........E.......213 628-3901
1301 S Main St Ste 226 Los Angeles (90015) ***(P-2926)***
B&F Fedelini Inc..........E.......213 628-3901
305 E 9th St Los Angeles (90015) ***(P-2927)***
B&G Machine Shop, Bakersfield *Also called Mc Cain & Mc Cain Inc* ***(P-16181)***
B&K Precision Corporation (PA)..........E.......714 921-9095
22820 Savi Ranch Pkwy Yorba Linda (92887) ***(P-21009)***
B&W Custom Restaurant Eqp..........E.......714 578-0332
541 E Jamie Ave La Habra (90631) ***(P-15489)***
B&Z Manufacturing Company Inc..........E.......408 943-1117
1478 Seareel Ln San Jose (95131) ***(P-15770)***
B-Bridge International Inc..........E.......408 252-6200
3350 Scott Blvd Bldg 29 Santa Clara (95054) ***(P-8279)***
B-Efficient Inc..........E.......209 663-9199
11545 W Bernardo Ct # 209 San Diego (92127) ***(P-17014)***
B-Flat Publishing LLC..........F.......510 639-7170
9616 Macarthur Blvd Oakland (94605) ***(P-6197)***
B-J Machine Inc..........F.......714 685-0712
1763 N Batavia St Orange (92865) ***(P-12768)***
B-K Lighting Inc..........D.......559 438-5800
40429 Brickyard Dr Madera (93636) ***(P-16965)***
B.R. Cohn, Glen Ellen *Also called Vintage Wine Estates Inc* ***(P-1991)***
B.T.i Tool Engineering, Santee *Also called T I B Inc* ***(P-14109)***
B/E Aerospace Inc..........D.......951 278-4563
350 W Rincon St Corona (92880) ***(P-20052)***
B/E Aerospace Inc..........D.......714 896-9001
7155 Fenwick Ln Westminster (92683) ***(P-15771)***
B/E Aerospace Inc..........C.......714 896-9001
7155 Fenwick Ln Westminster (92683) ***(P-20053)***
B/E Aerospace Inc..........B.......714 688-4200
3355 E La Palma Ave Anaheim (92806) ***(P-20054)***
B2 Apparel Inc..........F.......323 233-0044
219 E 32nd St Los Angeles (90011) ***(P-3542)***
BA Holdings (HQ)..........E.......951 684-5110
3016 Kansas Ave Bldg 1 Riverside (92507) ***(P-11995)***
Baatz Enterprises Inc..........F.......323 660-4866
2223 W San Bernardino Rd West Covina (91790) ***(P-19458)***
Bab Hydraulics, Fontana *Also called Bab Steering Hydraulics* ***(P-19590)***
Bab Steering Hydraulics (PA)..........E.......208 573-4502
14554 Whittram Ave Fontana (92335) ***(P-19590)***
Baba Foods Slo LLC..........F.......805 439-2250
3889 Long St Ste 100 San Luis Obispo (93401) ***(P-945)***
Baba Small Batch, San Luis Obispo *Also called Baba Foods Slo LLC* ***(P-945)***
Babbitt Bearing Co Inc..........E.......408 298-1101
1170 N 5th St San Jose (95112) ***(P-15772)***
Babcock & Wilcox Company..........E.......707 259-1122
710 Airpark Rd NAPA (94558) ***(P-13561)***
Babcock and Wilcox, NAPA *Also called Babcock & Wilcox Company* ***(P-13561)***
Babette (PA)..........E.......510 625-8500
867 Newton Carey Jr Way Oakland (94607) ***(P-3291)***
Baby Box Company Inc (PA)..........F.......844 422-2926
1601 Vine St Los Angeles (90028) ***(P-5459)***
Baby Guess Inc..........E.......213 765-3100
1444 S Alameda St Los Angeles (90021) ***(P-3492)***
Babylon Printing Inc..........E.......408 519-5000
1800 Dobbin Dr San Jose (95133) ***(P-6431)***
Bacchus Press Inc (PA)..........E.......510 420-5800
1287 66th St Emeryville (94608) ***(P-6432)***
Bace Manufacturing Inc (HQ)..........A.......714 630-6002
3125 E Coronado St Anaheim (92806) ***(P-9650)***
Bace Manufacturing Inc..........D.......510 657-5800
45581 Northport Loop W Fremont (94538) ***(P-9651)***
Bachem Americas Inc (HQ)..........C.......310 784-4440
3132 Kashiwa St Torrance (90505) ***(P-8280)***
Bachem Americas Inc..........F.......888 422-2436
1271 Avenida Chelsea Vista (92081) ***(P-7783)***
Bachem Bioscience Inc..........E.......310 784-7322
3132 Kashiwa St Torrance (90505) ***(P-8281)***
Bachem California, Torrance *Also called Bachem Americas Inc* ***(P-8280)***
Bachem Vista BSD, Vista *Also called Bachem Americas Inc* ***(P-7783)***
Bachur & Associates..........F.......408 988-5861
1950 Homestead Rd Santa Clara (95050) ***(P-6433)***
Back Support Systems Inc..........F.......760 329-1472
67688 San Andreas St Desert Hot Springs (92240) ***(P-9508)***
Backflow Apparatus & Valve..........E.......310 639-5231
20435 S Susana Rd Long Beach (90810) ***(P-13347)***
Backstage Equipment Inc..........F.......818 504-6026
8052 Lankershim Blvd North Hollywood (91605) ***(P-12585)***
Backstage Studio Equip, North Hollywood *Also called Backstage Equipment Inc* ***(P-12585)***
Backstage West..........E.......323 525-2356
5055 Wilshire Blvd 5 Los Angeles (90036) ***(P-5885)***
Backyard Unlimited (PA)..........F.......916 630-7433
4765 Pacific St Rocklin (95677) ***(P-4412)***
Bacon Adhesives, Irvine *Also called Royal Adhesives & Sealants LLC* ***(P-8893)***
Bactrack, San Francisco *Also called Khn Solutions Inc* ***(P-21497)***
Badge Co..........F.......714 842-3037
18261 Enterprise Ln Ste D Huntington Beach (92648) ***(P-23283)***

Employee Codes: A=Over 500 employees, B=251-500
C=101-250, D=51-100, E=20-50, F=10-19
2020 California
Manfacturers Register
© Mergent Inc. 1-800-342-5647
1033

Badger Maps Inc .... E 415 592-5909
539 Broadway San Francisco (94133) ***(P-23648)***
Badgeville Inc .... E 650 323-6668
805 Veterans Blvd Ste 307 Redwood City (94063) ***(P-23649)***
Bae Systems Controls Inc .... C 323 642-5000
5140 W Goldleaf Cir G100 Los Angeles (90056) ***(P-13562)***
Bae Systems Imging Sltions Inc .... C 408 433-2500
1841 Zanker Rd Ste 50 San Jose (95112) ***(P-18143)***
Bae Systems Info & Elec Sys .... C 858 592-5000
10920 Technology Pl San Diego (92127) ***(P-21010)***
Bae Systems Land Armaments LP .... A 408 289-0111
6331 San Ignacio Ave San Jose (95119) ***(P-20544)***
Bae Systems Land Armaments LP .... D 408 289-0111
6331 San Ignacio Ave San Jose (95119) ***(P-20496)***
Bae Systems San Diego .... A 619 238-1000
2205 Belt St San Diego (92113) ***(P-20278)***
Bae Systems Tech Sol Srvc Inc .... F 858 278-3042
9650 Chesapeake Dr San Diego (92123) ***(P-20545)***
Baems, Patterson *Also called Bay Area Ems Solutions LLC* ***(P-17832)***
Baf Industries (PA) .... E 714 258-8055
1451 Edinger Ave Ste F Tustin (92780) ***(P-8366)***
Baffle Inc .... F 408 663-6737
2811 Mission College Blvd Santa Clara (95054) ***(P-23650)***
Bagcraftpapercon I LLC .... D 626 961-6766
515 Turnbull Canyon Rd City of Industry (91745) ***(P-5433)***
Bagelry Inc (PA) .... E 831 429-8049
320 Cedar St Ste A Santa Cruz (95060) ***(P-1139)***
Bagmasters, Corona *Also called CTA Manufacturing Inc* ***(P-3656)***
Baguette World, Los Angeles *Also called Kobi Katz Inc* ***(P-22536)***
Bahne and Company Inc .... F 760 753-8847
585 Westlake St Ste A Encinitas (92024) ***(P-22754)***
Bahne Single Ski, Encinitas *Also called Bahne and Company Inc* ***(P-22754)***
Baier Marine Company Inc .... E 800 455-3917
2920 Airway Ave Costa Mesa (92626) ***(P-11569)***
Bailey Essel William Jr .... F 707 341-3391
1373 Lincoln Ave Calistoga (94515) ***(P-1589)***
Bailey 44 LLC .... E 213 228-1930
4700 S Boyle Ave Vernon (90058) ***(P-3139)***
Bailey Industries Inc .... F 949 461-0807
25256 Terreno Dr Mission Viejo (92691) ***(P-20055)***
Bailey Valve Inc .... E 559 434-2838
264 W Fallbrook Ave # 105 Fresno (93711) ***(P-13293)***
Baise Enterprises Inc .... F 916 446-0167
3258 Stockton Blvd Sacramento (95820) ***(P-6434)***
Baja Designs, San Marcos *Also called Bestop Baja LLC* ***(P-19592)***
Baja Onyx & Marble Intl, San Ysidro *Also called Betty Stillwell* ***(P-10894)***
Baja Products, Ontario *Also called Chladni & Jariwala Inc* ***(P-13297)***
Bajasys LLC .... F 619 661-0748
9923 Via De La Amistad # 105 San Diego (92154) ***(P-15165)***
Bakakers Specialty Foods Inc .... F 209 234-5935
2619 Lycoming St Ste 200 Stockton (95206) ***(P-997)***
Bake R Us Inc .... F 310 630-5873
13400 S Western Ave Gardena (90249) ***(P-1140)***
Bakemark USA LLC (PA) .... B 562 949-1054
7351 Crider Ave Pico Rivera (90660) ***(P-1055)***
Bakemark USA LLC .... E 510 487-8188
32621 Central Ave Union City (94587) ***(P-2398)***
Baker Atlas, Bakersfield *Also called Baker Hghes Olfld Oprtions LLC* ***(P-157)***
Baker Commodities Inc (PA) .... C 323 268-2801
4020 Bandini Blvd Vernon (90058) ***(P-1452)***
Baker Commodities Inc .... E 559 237-4320
16801 W Jensen Ave Kerman (93630) ***(P-1453)***
Baker Commodities Inc .... E 559 686-4797
7480 Hanford Armona Rd Hanford (93230) ***(P-1454)***
Baker Commodities Inc .... E 323 318-8260
3001 Sierra Pine Ave Vernon (90058) ***(P-1455)***
Baker Coupling Company Inc .... E 323 583-3444
2929 S Santa Fe Ave Vernon (90058) ***(P-13460)***
Baker Filtration, South Gate *Also called Bakercorp* ***(P-16682)***
Baker Filtration .... E 925 252-2400
2700 California Ave Pittsburg (94565) ***(P-15490)***
Baker Furnace Inc .... F 714 223-7262
2680 Orbiter St Brea (92821) ***(P-14756)***
Baker Hghes Olfld Oprtions LLC .... F 661 831-5200
4730 Armstrong Rd Bakersfield (93313) ***(P-157)***
Baker Hghes Olfld Oprtions LLC .... D 714 893-8511
5421 Argosy Ave Huntington Beach (92649) ***(P-158)***
Baker Hghes Olfld Oprtions LLC .... F 714 891-8544
15421 Assembly Ln Huntington Beach (92649) ***(P-159)***
Baker Hghes Olfld Oprtions LLC .... E 661 834-9654
5700 Doolittle Ave Shafter (93263) ***(P-160)***
Baker Hughes, Santa Paula *Also called Baker Petrolite LLC* ***(P-169)***
Baker Hughes A GE Company LLC .... D 714 893-8511
5421 Argosy Ave Huntington Beach (92649) ***(P-161)***
Baker Hughes A GE Company LLC .... E 661 834-9654
3901 Fanucchi Way Shafter (93263) ***(P-162)***
Baker Hughes A GE Company LLC .... D 661 387-1010
1127 Carrier Parkway Ave Bakersfield (93308) ***(P-163)***
Baker Hughes A GE Company LLC .... D 800 229-7447
5145 Boylan St Bakersfield (93308) ***(P-164)***
Baker Hughes A GE Company LLC .... D 661 834-9654
6117 Schirra Ct Bakersfield (93313) ***(P-13767)***
Baker Hughes A GE Company LLC .... F 661 391-0794
19433 Colombo St Bakersfield (93308) ***(P-165)***
Baker Interiors Furniture Co .... E 415 626-1414
101 Henry Adams St # 350 San Francisco (94103) ***(P-4763)***
Baker Oil Tools, Huntington Beach *Also called Baker Hghes Olfld Oprtions LLC* ***(P-159)***
Baker Petrolite LLC .... F 925 682-3313
2280 Bates Ave Ste A Concord (94520) ***(P-166)***
Baker Petrolite LLC .... D 661 325-4138
5125 Boylan St Bakersfield (93308) ***(P-167)***
Baker Petrolite LLC .... F 562 406-7090
11808 Bloomfield Ave Santa Fe Springs (90670) ***(P-168)***
Baker Petrolite LLC .... E 805 525-4404
265 Quail Ct Santa Paula (93060) ***(P-169)***
Baker Tanks, Pittsburg *Also called Baker Filtration* ***(P-15490)***
Bakercorp .... F 562 904-3680
5500 Rawlings Ave South Gate (90280) ***(P-16682)***
Bakersfield Elc Mtr Repr Inc .... F 661 327-3583
121 W Sumner St Bakersfield (93301) ***(P-24685)***
Bakersfield Machine Company .... D 661 709-1992
5605 N Chester Ave Ext Bakersfield (93308) ***(P-15773)***
Bakersfield Well Casing LLC .... F 661 399-2976
17876 Zerker Rd Bakersfield (93308) ***(P-88)***
Bakersfield Woodworks Inc .... F 661 282-8492
3416 Big Trail Ave Bakersfield (93313) ***(P-4002)***
Bakersfield Yard Asp & Rdymx, Bakersfield *Also called Legacy Vulcan LLC* ***(P-10784)***
Bakery Depot Inc .... F 323 261-8388
4489 Bandini Blvd Vernon (90058) ***(P-1141)***
Bal Seal Engineering Inc (PA) .... B 949 460-2100
19650 Pauling Foothill Ranch (92610) ***(P-13375)***
Balaji Trading Inc .... D 909 444-7999
4850 Eucalyptus Ave Chino (91710) ***(P-17349)***
Balboa Boat Yard Inc .... F 949 673-6834
2414 Newport Blvd Newport Beach (92663) ***(P-20313)***
Balboa Manufacturing Co LLC (PA) .... E 858 715-0060
9401 Waples St Ste 120 San Diego (92121) ***(P-2772)***
Balboa Water Group LLC (PA) .... C 714 384-0384
3030 Airway Ave Ste B Costa Mesa (92626) ***(P-16702)***
Balda C Brewer Inc (HQ) .... C 714 630-6810
4501 E Wall St Ontario (91761) ***(P-9652)***
Balda HK Plastics Inc .... D 760 757-1100
3229 Roymar Rd Oceanside (92058) ***(P-12623)***
Baldacci Family Vineyard, NAPA *Also called Archangel Investments LLC* ***(P-1584)***
Baldwin Brass, Foothill Ranch *Also called Baldwin Hardware Corporation* ***(P-11570)***
Baldwin Hardware Corporation (HQ) .... A 949 672-4000
19701 Da Vinci Foothill Ranch (92610) ***(P-11570)***
Balita Media Inc .... E 818 552-4503
2629 Foothill Blvd La Crescenta (91214) ***(P-5562)***
Ball Corporation .... B 209 848-6500
300 Greger St Oakdale (95361) ***(P-11493)***
Ball Metal Beverage Cont Corp .... C 707 437-7516
2400 Huntington Dr Fairfield (94533) ***(P-11494)***
Ball of Cotton Inc .... E 323 888-9448
6400 E Washington Blvd Commerce (90040) ***(P-2773)***
Ball Plastic Container, Chino *Also called Amcor Rigid Packaging Usa LLC* ***(P-9480)***
Ball Screws & Actuators Co Inc (HQ) .... D 510 770-5932
48767 Kato Rd Fremont (94538) ***(P-14782)***
Ball TEC, Los Angeles *Also called Micro Surface Engr Inc* ***(P-11481)***
Ballard & Tighe Publishers, Brea *Also called Educational Ideas Incorporated* ***(P-6099)***
Ballast Point Brewing, San Diego *Also called Ballast Point Spirits LLC* ***(P-1499)***
Ballast Point Spirits LLC .... C 858 695-2739
9045 Carroll Way San Diego (92121) ***(P-1499)***
Ballast Pt Brewing & Spirits, San Diego *Also called Home Brew Mart Inc* ***(P-1537)***
Balletto Vineyards, Santa Rosa *Also called Laguna Oaks Vnyards Winery Inc* ***(P-1791)***
Balsam Hill LLC .... F 888 552-2572
50 Woodside Plz Ste 11 Redwood City (94061) ***(P-23284)***
Baltic Ltvian Unvrsal Elec LLC .... E 818 879-5200
5706 Corsa Ave Ste 102 Westlake Village (91362) ***(P-17200)***
Baltimore Aircoil Company Inc .... C 559 673-9231
15341 Road 28 1/2 Madera (93638) ***(P-15415)***
Balut Pateros, Westminster *Also called AA Laboratory Eggs Inc* ***(P-2187)***
Bambacigno Steel Company .... E 209 524-9681
4930 Mchenry Ave Modesto (95356) ***(P-11029)***
Bambeck Systems Inc (PA) .... F 949 250-3100
1921 Carnegie Ave Ste 3a Santa Ana (92705) ***(P-20838)***
Bamberger Polymers Inc .... F 714 672-4740
145 S State College Blvd # 100 Brea (92821) ***(P-7543)***
Bamboosa, Culver City *Also called M Group Inc* ***(P-10199)***
Bamford Equipment, Oroville *Also called J W Bamford Inc* ***(P-3889)***
Bananafish Productions Inc .... F 714 956-2129
1536 W Embassy St Anaheim (92802) ***(P-10340)***
Banbury Precision, Santa Clara *Also called B P I Corp* ***(P-15768)***
Band-It Rubber Company Inc .... F 951 735-5072
1711 N Delilah St Corona (92879) ***(P-9287)***
Bandag Licensing Corporation .... D 562 531-3880
2500 E Thompson St Long Beach (90805) ***(P-9288)***
Bandai America Incorporated (HQ) .... D 714 816-9751
2120 Park Pl Ste 120 El Segundo (90245) ***(P-22661)***
Bandel Mfg Inc .... E 818 246-7493
4459 Alger St Los Angeles (90039) ***(P-12769)***
Bandmerch LLC .... E 818 736-4800
3120 W Empire Ave Burbank (91504) ***(P-3773)***
Bandy Manufacturing LLC .... D 818 846-9020
3420 N San Fernando Blvd Burbank (91504) ***(P-20056)***
Banh An Binh .... E 408 935-8950
1965 Stonewood Ln San Jose (95132) ***(P-18829)***
Banh MI & Che Cali .... E 714 534-6987
13838 Brookhurst St Garden Grove (92843) ***(P-1142)***
Banjo Inc (PA) .... F 650 425-6376
833 Main St Redwood City (94063) ***(P-23651)***
Bank C Plating Co, Los Angeles *Also called We Five-R Corporation* ***(P-13129)***
Banks Power Products, Azusa *Also called Gale Banks Engineering* ***(P-13596)***
Banner Solutions, Anaheim *Also called Mid-West Wholesale Hardware Co* ***(P-11611)***
Bar Manufacturing Inc .... D 916 939-0551
3921 Sandstone Dr Ste 1 El Dorado Hills (95762) ***(P-18144)***

Mergent e-mail: customerrelations@mergent.com
1034
2020 California
Manufacturers Register
(P-0000) Products & Services Section entry number
(PA)=Parent Co (HQ)=Headquarters (DH)=Div Headquarters

Bar Media Inc...F.......415 861-5019
44 Gough St Ste 204 San Francisco (94103) *(P-5563)*
Bar None Inc...F.......714 259-8450
1302 Santa Fe Dr Tustin (92780) *(P-2009)*
Bar-S Foods Co...B.......408 941-9958
392 Railroad Ct Milpitas (95035) *(P-439)*
Bar-S Foods Co...B.......323 589-3600
4919 Alcoa Ave Vernon (90058) *(P-440)*
Bar-S Foods Co. Los Angeles, Vernon *Also called Bar-S Foods Co (P-440)*
Barbara Lesser, Los Angeles *Also called Wearable Integrity Inc (P-3434)*
Barbee Valve & Supply Inc (HQ)...F.......619 585-8484
745 Main St Anaheim (92805) *(P-13294)*
Barber-Webb Company Inc (PA)...E.......541 488-4821
3833 Medford St Los Angeles (90063) *(P-9653)*
Barbosa Cabinets Inc...B.......209 836-2501
2020 E Grant Line Rd Tracy (95304) *(P-4167)*
Barbour Vineyards LLC...D.......707 257-1829
104 Camino Dorado NAPA (94558) *(P-1590)*
Barco Inc...F.......510 490-1005
1421 Mccarthy Blvd Milpitas (95035) *(P-15120)*
Barco Uniforms Inc...C.......310 323-7315
350 W Rosecrans Ave Gardena (90248) *(P-2960)*
Bare Nothings Inc (PA)...E.......714 848-8532
17705 Sampson Ln Huntington Beach (92647) *(P-3292)*
Barebottle Brewing Company Inc...F.......415 926-8617
1525 Cortland Ave # 6 San Francisco (94110) *(P-1500)*
Barefoot Cellars, Santa Rosa *Also called Grape Links Inc (P-1734)*
Bargain Mart Classifieds, North Hollywood *Also called Hughes Price & Sharp Inc (P-5668)*
Bargas Bindery...F.......510 357-7901
1658 Scenicview Dr San Leandro (94577) *(P-7327)*
Barger & Associates...E.......530 271-5424
400 Crown Point Cir Grass Valley (95945) *(P-9289)*
Bargueiras Rene Inc...F.......818 500-8288
621 S Victory Blvd Burbank (91502) *(P-22501)*
Barhena Inc...E.......888 383-8800
1085 Bixby Dr Hacienda Heights (91745) *(P-15491)*
Barkens Hardchrome Inc...E.......310 632-2000
239 E Greenleaf Blvd Compton (90220) *(P-14431)*
Barker-Canoga Inc...F.......760 246-4777
16528 Koala Rd Ste A Adelanto (92301) *(P-14136)*
Barkerblue Inc...E.......650 696-2100
363 N Amphlett Blvd San Mateo (94401) *(P-7355)*
Barkevs Inc...F.......800 227-7321
707 S Broadway Ste 415 Los Angeles (90014) *(P-22502)*
Barksdale Inc (HQ)...C.......323 583-6243
3211 Fruitland Ave Vernon (90058) *(P-21442)*
Barlow and Sons Printing Inc...F.......707 664-9773
481 Aaron St Cotati (94931) *(P-6435)*
Barlow Printing, Cotati *Also called Barlow and Sons Printing Inc (P-6435)*
Barnana, Santa Monica *Also called Wholesome Valley Foods (P-2647)*
Barnes Plastics Inc...E.......310 329-6301
18903 Anelo Ave Gardena (90248) *(P-9654)*
Barnett Performance Products, Ventura *Also called Barnett Tool & Engineering (P-20383)*
Barnett Tool & Engineering...D.......805 642-9435
2238 Palma Dr Ventura (93003) *(P-20383)*
Barney & Co California LLC...F.......559 442-1752
2925 S Elm Ave Ste 101 Fresno (93706) *(P-2399)*
Barns and Buildings Inc...D.......951 678-4571
23100 Baxter Rd Wildomar (92595) *(P-12533)*
Barns By Harrahs...F.......530 824-4611
3489 S 99w Corning (96021) *(P-12534)*
Baron & Baron, Huntington Beach *Also called License Frame Inc (P-13200)*
Baron Brand Spices, Fairfield *Also called Abco Laboratories Inc (P-7714)*
Baron Usa LLC...E.......931 528-8476
350 Baron Cir Woodland (95776) *(P-14796)*
Barra LLC (HQ)...B.......510 548-5442
2100 Milvia St Berkeley (94704) *(P-23652)*
Barracuda Networks Inc...F.......408 342-5400
5225 Hellyer Ave Ste 150 San Jose (95138) *(P-15166)*
Barracuda Networks Inc (HQ)...C.......408 342-5400
3175 Winchester Blvd Campbell (95008) *(P-23653)*
Barranca Diamond Products, Torrance *Also called Barranca Holdings Ltd (P-14137)*
Barranca Holdings Ltd...F.......310 523-5867
22815 Frampton Ave Torrance (90501) *(P-14137)*
Barrango (PA)...F.......650 737-9206
391 Forbes Blvd South San Francisco (94080) *(P-15774)*
Barrel Merchants, Saint Helena *Also called Red River Lumber Co (P-4425)*
Barrel Ten Qarter Cir Land Inc (HQ)...E.......707 258-0550
6342 Bystrum Rd Ceres (95307) *(P-1591)*
Barrett Engineering Inc...F.......858 256-9194
1725 Burton St San Diego (92111) *(P-19186)*
Barricade Co & Traffic Sup Inc (PA)...F.......707 523-2350
3963 Santa Rosa Ave Santa Rosa (95407) *(P-13501)*
Barrick Gold Corporation...D.......707 995-6070
26775 Morgan Valley Rd Lower Lake (95457) *(P-1)*
Barrier Systems Sales & Svc, Rio Vista *Also called Lindsay Trnsp Solutions Inc (P-10599)*
Barrot Corporation...E.......949 852-1640
1881 Kaiser Ave Irvine (92614) *(P-14021)*
Barrx Medical Inc...D.......408 328-7300
540 Oakmead Pkwy Sunnyvale (94085) *(P-22231)*
Barry Avenue Plating Co Inc...D.......310 478-0078
2210 Barry Ave Los Angeles (90064) *(P-12941)*
Barry Callebaut USA LLC...F.......707 642-8200
1175 Commerce Blvd Ste D American Canyon (94503) *(P-1406)*
Barry Controls Aerospace, Burbank *Also called Hutchinson Arospc & Indust Inc (P-9320)*
Barry Costello...F.......530 265-3300
319 Broad St Nevada City (95959) *(P-3508)*
Barrys Cultured Marble Inc...F.......707 745-3444
866 Teal Dr Benicia (94510) *(P-10891)*
Barrys Printing Inc...E.......818 998-8600
9005 Eton Ave Ste D Canoga Park (91304) *(P-6436)*
Bart Manufacturing Inc (PA)...D.......408 320-4373
3787 Spinnaker Ct Fremont (94538) *(P-23285)*
Barta-Schoenewald Inc (PA)...C.......805 389-1935
3805 Calle Tecate Camarillo (93012) *(P-16632)*
Bartholomew Park Winery, Sonoma *Also called Vineburg Wine Company Inc (P-1987)*
Bartolini Guitars...F.......386 517-6823
2133 Research Dr Ste 16 Livermore (94550) *(P-18830)*
Bartolini Pickups, Livermore *Also called Bartolini Guitars (P-18830)*
Barton Perreira LLC (PA)...E.......949 305-5360
459 Wald Irvine (92618) *(P-22340)*
Barzillai Manufacturing Co...F.......909 947-4200
1410 S Cucamonga Ave Ontario (91761) *(P-12127)*
BAS Recycling Inc...E.......951 214-6590
14050 Day St Moreno Valley (92553) *(P-9164)*
Basalite Building Products LLC (HQ)...E.......707 678-1901
2150 Douglas Blvd Ste 260 Roseville (95661) *(P-10534)*
Basalite Building Products LLC...C.......209 833-3670
11888 W Linne Rd Tracy (95377) *(P-10502)*
Basalite Building Products LLC...E.......209 333-6161
104 E Turner Rd Lodi (95240) *(P-10535)*
Basalite-Tracy, Tracy *Also called Basalite Building Products LLC (P-10502)*
Basaw Manufacturing Inc (PA)...E.......818 765-6650
7300 Varna Ave North Hollywood (91605) *(P-4330)*
Basaw Services Inc...E.......818 765-6650
7300 Varna Ave North Hollywood (91605) *(P-4331)*
Basaw Services Inc...E.......818 765-6650
13340 Raymer St North Hollywood (91605) *(P-4332)*
Base Crm...F.......773 796-6266
1019 Market St Fl 1 San Francisco (94103) *(P-23654)*
Base Hockey LP (PA)...F.......805 405-3650
581 Calle Arroyo Thousand Oaks (91360) *(P-22755)*
Base Lite Corporation...E.......909 444-2776
12260 Eastend Ave Chino (91710) *(P-16966)*
Baselite, Chino *Also called Base Lite Corporation (P-16966)*
BASF Catalysts LLC...F.......510 490-2150
46820 Fremont Blvd Fremont (94538) *(P-8716)*
BASF Corporation...E.......714 921-1430
138 E Meats Ave Orange (92865) *(P-8717)*
BASF Corporation...F.......510 796-9911
38403 Cherry St Newark (94560) *(P-8718)*
BASF Enzymes LLC (HQ)...F.......858 431-8520
3550 John Hopkins Ct San Diego (92121) *(P-8719)*
BASF Venture Capital Amer Inc...F.......510 445-6140
46820 Fremont Blvd Fremont (94538) *(P-8720)*
Bashoura Inc...F.......626 963-7600
539 S Glenwood Ave Glendora (91741) *(P-22503)*
Basic American Inc (PA)...D.......925 472-4438
2999 Oak Rd Ste 800 Walnut Creek (94597) *(P-843)*
Basic American Foods, Walnut Creek *Also called Basic American Inc (P-843)*
Basic Business Forms Inc...E.......805 278-4551
561 Kinetic Dr Ste A Oxnard (93030) *(P-6997)*
Basic Electronics Inc...E.......714 530-2400
11371 Monarch St Garden Grove (92841) *(P-18831)*
Basic Energy Services Inc...E.......714 530-0855
12891 Nelson St Garden Grove (92840) *(P-170)*
Basic Energy Services Inc...E.......661 588-3800
6710 Stewart Way Bakersfield (93308) *(P-171)*
Basic Microcom Inc...F.......951 708-1268
38595 Rancho Christina Rd Temecula (92592) *(P-16703)*
Basin Marine Inc...F.......949 673-0360
829 Harbor Island Dr A Newport Beach (92660) *(P-20314)*
Basin Marine Shipyard, Newport Beach *Also called Basin Marine Inc (P-20314)*
Basmat Inc (PA)...D.......310 325-2063
1531 240th St Harbor City (90710) *(P-12128)*
Basque French Bakery, Fresno *Also called Fresno French Bread Bakery Inc (P-1207)*
Bass Angler...F.......925 362-3190
2500 Shadow Mountain Ct San Ramon (94583) *(P-5886)*
Bass Angler Magazine, San Ramon *Also called Bass Angler (P-5886)*
Bassani Exhaust, Anaheim *Also called Bassani Manufacturing (P-13461)*
Bassani Manufacturing...E.......714 630-1821
2900 E La Jolla St Anaheim (92806) *(P-13461)*
Bastan Corporation...F.......619 424-3416
2260 Main St Ste 17 Chula Vista (91911) *(P-718)*
Batchlder Bus Cmmnications Inc...F.......209 577-2222
2900 Standiford Ave Ste 5 Modesto (95350) *(P-6437)*
Bates Industries Inc...F.......562 426-8668
3671 Industry Ave Ste C5 Lakewood (90712) *(P-3509)*
Bates Leathers, Lakewood *Also called Bates Industries Inc (P-3509)*
Bath Petals Inc...F.......310 532-4532
15620 S Figueroa St Gardena (90248) *(P-8442)*
Bath Promotions, Gardena *Also called Bath Petals Inc (P-8442)*
Batida Inc...F.......714 557-4597
3187 Airway Ave Ste B Costa Mesa (92626) *(P-6438)*
Baton Lock & Hardware Co Inc...E.......714 265-3636
14275 Commerce Dr Garden Grove (92843) *(P-11571)*
Baton Security, Garden Grove *Also called Baton Lock & Hardware Co Inc (P-11571)*
Battery Hut, Burbank *Also called Pro Power Products Inc (P-16794)*
Battery Technology Inc (PA)...D.......626 336-6878
16651 E Johnson Dr City of Industry (91745) *(P-19152)*
Battery-Biz Inc...D.......805 437-7777
1380 Flynn Rd Camarillo (93012) *(P-19187)*
Batth Dehydrator LLC...E.......559 864-3501
4624 W Nebraska Ave Caruthers (93609) *(P-844)*
Bau Furniture Manufacturing (PA)...E.......949 643-2729
23811 Aliso Creek Rd # 134 Laguna Niguel (92677) *(P-4552)*
Bauer Industries (PA)...F.......916 648-9200
708 Alhambra Blvd Ste 2 Sacramento (95816) *(P-11572)*

Employee Codes: A=Over 500 employees, B=251-500
C=101-250, D=51-100, E=20-50, F=10-19
2020 California
Manfacturers Register
© Mergent Inc. 1-800-342-5647
1035

Bauer International Corp....F....714 259-9800
9251 Irvine Blvd Irvine (92618) ***(P-15492)***
Bauers & Collins....F....818 983-1281
6765 Lankershim Blvd North Hollywood (91606) ***(P-21984)***
Baughn Engineering Inc....F....909 392-0933
2815 Metropolitan Pl Pomona (91767) ***(P-21011)***
Baumann Engineering Inc....D....909 621-4181
212 S Cambridge Ave Claremont (91711) ***(P-15775)***
Bausch & Lomb Incorporated....D....949 788-6000
50 Technology Dr Irvine (92618) ***(P-7784)***
Bausch & Lomb Incorporated....C....949 788-6000
50 Technology Dr Irvine (92618) ***(P-22341)***
Bausch & Lomb Surgical Div, Irvine *Also called Eyeonics Inc* ***(P-22358)***
Bausch Health Americas Inc....F....800 548-5100
50 Technology Dr Irvine (92618) ***(P-7785)***
Bausch Health Americas Inc....C....707 793-2600
1330 Redwood Way Ste C Petaluma (94954) ***(P-21178)***
Bausman and Company Inc (PA)....C....909 947-0139
1500 Crafton Ave Bldg 124 Mentone (92359) ***(P-4786)***
Bavco, Long Beach *Also called Backflow Apparatus & Valve* ***(P-13347)***
Baxalta Incorporated....A....818 240-5600
4501 Colorado Blvd Los Angeles (90039) ***(P-7786)***
Baxalta US Inc....B....805 498-8664
1700 Rancho Conejo Blvd Thousand Oaks (91320) ***(P-21618)***
Baxalta US Inc....D....818 947-5600
15903 Strathern St Van Nuys (91406) ***(P-7787)***
Baxalta US Inc....F....805 375-6807
1455 Lawrence Dr Thousand Oaks (91320) ***(P-7788)***
Baxstra Inc....D....323 770-4171
1224 W 132nd St Gardena (90247) ***(P-3968)***
Baxter Healthcare Corporation....C....303 222-6837
4551 E Philadelphia St Ontario (91761) ***(P-7789)***
Baxter Healthcare Corporation....C....949 474-6301
17511 Armstrong Ave Irvine (92614) ***(P-21619)***
Baxter Healthcare Corporation....D....949 250-2500
1402 Alton Pkwy Irvine (92606) ***(P-21620)***
Baxter International Inc....F....510 723-2000
2024 W Winton Ave Hayward (94545) ***(P-7790)***
Baxter Medication Delivery, Irvine *Also called Baxter Healthcare Corporation* ***(P-21619)***
Bay AR Yellow Pages....F....650 558-8888
46292 Warm Springs Blvd Fremont (94539) ***(P-6198)***
Bay Area Canvas Inc....F....408 727-4314
2362 De La Cruz Blvd Santa Clara (95050) ***(P-3673)***
Bay Area Circuits Inc....E....510 933-9000
44358 Old Warm Sprng Blvd Fremont (94538) ***(P-17831)***
Bay Area Coffee Inc....E....707 745-1320
4201 Industrial Way Benicia (94510) ***(P-2276)***
Bay Area Drilling Inc....F....925 427-7574
1860 Loveridge Rd Pittsburg (94565) ***(P-330)***
Bay Area Ems Solutions LLC....F....408 753-3651
147 Walker Ranch Pkwy Patterson (95363) ***(P-17832)***
Bay Area Indus Filtration Inc....E....510 562-6373
6355 Coliseum Way Oakland (94621) ***(P-14797)***
Bay Area Mch & Mar Repr Inc....F....510 815-2339
1305 S 51st St Richmond (94804) ***(P-15776)***
Bay Area Pallette Company, Antioch *Also called Chep (usa) Inc* ***(P-4356)***
Bay Area Reporter, San Francisco *Also called Bar Media Inc* ***(P-5563)***
Bay Associates Wire Tech Corp (HQ)....D....510 988-3800
46840 Lakeview Blvd Fremont (94538) ***(P-2906)***
Bay Central Printing Inc....F....510 429-9111
33401 Western Ave Union City (94587) ***(P-6439)***
Bay Cities Container Corp (PA)....C....562 948-3751
5138 Industry Ave Pico Rivera (90660) ***(P-5198)***
Bay Cities Italian Bakery Inc....F....310 608-1881
1120 W Mahalo Pl Compton (90220) ***(P-1143)***
Bay Cities Metal Products, Gardena *Also called Bay Cities Tin Shop Inc* ***(P-12129)***
Bay Cities Tin Shop Inc....E....310 660-0351
301 E Alondra Blvd Gardena (90248) ***(P-12129)***
Bay City Marine Inc (PA)....E....619 477-3991
1625 Cleveland Ave National City (91950) ***(P-11747)***
Bay City Marine Inc....E....619 477-3991
1625 Cleveland Ave National City (91950) ***(P-20279)***
Bay Classifieds Inc....E....510 636-1867
433 Hegenberger Rd # 205 Oakland (94621) ***(P-14317)***
Bay Elctrnic Spport Trnics Inc....C....408 432-3222
2090 Fortune Dr San Jose (95131) ***(P-17833)***
Bay Equipment Co Inc....F....510 226-8800
44221 S Grimmer Blvd Fremont (94538) ***(P-12704)***
Bay Guardian Company....D....415 255-3100
135 Micaicaippi St San Francisco (94107) ***(P-5564)***
Bay Leaf Spice Company....E....925 330-1918
21c Orinda Way 363 Orinda (94563) ***(P-2400)***
Bay Marine Boatworks Inc....E....510 237-0140
310 W Cutting Blvd Richmond (94804) ***(P-20315)***
Bay Ornamental Iron Inc....E....949 548-1015
757 Newton Way Costa Mesa (92627) ***(P-12455)***
Bay Precision Machining Inc....E....650 365-3010
815 Sweeney Ave Ste D Redwood City (94063) ***(P-15777)***
Bay Ship & Yacht Co (PA)....C....510 337-9122
2900 Main St Ste 2100 Alameda (94501) ***(P-20280)***
Bay Standard Manufacturing Inc (PA)....E....925 634-1181
24485 Marsh Creek Rd Brentwood (94513) ***(P-12667)***
Bay Tech Manufacturing Inc....F....510 783-0660
23334 Bernhardt St Hayward (94545) ***(P-15778)***
Bay Valve Service & Engrg LLC....E....707 748-7166
3948 Teal Ct Benicia (94510) ***(P-5050)***
Baycorr Packaging LLC (PA)....C....925 449-1148
6850 Brisa St Livermore (94550) ***(P-5199)***
Bayer Corporation....B....510 705-5000
820 Parker St Berkeley (94710) ***(P-21621)***
Bayer Cropscience, West Sacramento *Also called Agraquest Inc* ***(P-7732)***
Bayer Diabetes Care, Sunnyvale *Also called Bayer Healthcare LLC* ***(P-7797)***
Bayer Healthcare LLC....B....415 437-5800
455 Mission Bay Blvd S # 493 San Francisco (94158) ***(P-7791)***
Bayer Healthcare LLC....C....510 597-6150
5885 Hollis St Emeryville (94608) ***(P-7792)***
Bayer Healthcare LLC....C....510 705-7545
800 Dwight Way Berkeley (94710) ***(P-7793)***
Bayer Healthcare LLC....B....510 705-7539
717 Potter St Street-2 Berkeley (94710) ***(P-7794)***
Bayer Healthcare LLC....C....510 705-4421
747 Grayson St Berkeley (94710) ***(P-7795)***
Bayer Healthcare LLC....C....510 705-4914
2448 6th St Berkeley (94710) ***(P-7796)***
Bayer Healthcare LLC....D....408 499-0606
510 Oakmead Pkwy Sunnyvale (94085) ***(P-7797)***
Bayer Hlthcare Phrmcticals Inc....B....510 262-5000
455 Mission Bay Blvd S San Francisco (94158) ***(P-7798)***
Bayfab Metals Inc....E....510 568-8950
870 Doolittle Dr San Leandro (94577) ***(P-11934)***
Bayless Engineering Inc....C....661 257-3373
26100 Ave Hall Valencia Valencia (91355) ***(P-15779)***
Bayless Engineering & Mfg, Valencia *Also called Bayless Engineering Inc* ***(P-15779)***
Bayline, Union City *Also called Compro Packaging LLC* ***(P-5211)***
Bayliss Botanicals LLC....F....530 868-5466
17 W Rio Bonito Rd Biggs (95917) ***(P-7799)***
Bayshore Lights, San Francisco *Also called Ijk & Co Inc* ***(P-19322)***
Bayside Shutters....F....714 628-9994
1464 N Batavia St Orange (92867) ***(P-11935)***
Bayspec Inc....E....408 512-5928
1101 Mckay Dr San Jose (95131) ***(P-21179)***
Bayview Plastic Solutions Inc....E....510 360-0001
43651 S Grimmer Blvd Fremont (94538) ***(P-9655)***
Baywa R.E.renewable Energy, Irvine *Also called Baywa RE Solar Projects LLC* ***(P-18145)***
Baywa RE Solar Projects LLC....E....949 398-3915
17901 Von Karman Ave # 1050 Irvine (92614) ***(P-18145)***
Baywood Cellars Inc....E....415 606-4640
5573 W Woodbridge Rd Lodi (95242) ***(P-1592)***
Bazz Houston Co, Garden Grove *Also called Houston Bazz Co* ***(P-12817)***
Bb Apparel, Los Angeles *Also called B2 Apparel Inc* ***(P-3542)***
Bb Co Inc....E....213 747-4701
1753 E 21st St Los Angeles (90058) ***(P-3293)***
BBC Corp....E....530 677-4009
4286 N Star Dr Shingle Springs (95682) ***(P-6440)***
Bbe Sound Inc (PA)....E....714 897-6766
2548 Fender Ave Ste D Fullerton (92831) ***(P-22609)***
Bbk Specialties Inc....F....661 255-2857
24147 Del Monte Dr # 297 Valencia (91355) ***(P-10465)***
Bbs Manufacturing Inc....F....760 798-8011
1905 Diamond St Ste A San Marcos (92078) ***(P-22756)***
Bbt, Los Angeles *Also called Bhaktivedanta Book Tr Intl Inc* ***(P-6078)***
Bcbg Maxazria Entrmt LLC....F....323 277-4713
2761 Fruitland Ave Vernon (90058) ***(P-3294)***
Bcg/Management Resources....F....800 456-8474
1320 Willow Pass Rd # 60 Concord (94520) ***(P-23655)***
BCI Inc....F....626 579-4234
1822 Belcroft Ave South El Monte (91733) ***(P-15780)***
Bcj Sand and Rock Inc....F....707 544-0303
3388 Regional Pkwy Ste A Santa Rosa (95403) ***(P-371)***
Bcs International, Hayward *Also called B C Song International Inc* ***(P-9039)***
Bcsi, Sonora *Also called Birchwood Cabinets Sonora Inc* ***(P-4169)***
Bd Biscnces Systems Rgents Inc....C....408 518-5024
2350 Qume Dr San Jose (95131) ***(P-7471)***
Bd Carefusion, San Diego *Also called Carefusion Corporation* ***(P-22237)***
BD Classic Enterprizes Inc....F....562 944-6177
12903 Sunshine Ave Santa Fe Springs (90670) ***(P-7544)***
Bd Impotex LLC....F....323 521-1500
2623 S San Pedro St Los Angeles (90011) ***(P-3218)***
Bdfco Inc....D....714 228-2900
1926 Kauai Dr Costa Mesa (92626) ***(P-17715)***
Bdm Engineering Inc....E....714 558-6129
1031 S Linwood Ave Santa Ana (92705) ***(P-13708)***
BDR Industries Inc....E....818 341-2112
9700 Owensmouth Ave Lbby Chatsworth (91311) ***(P-15167)***
BDS, Brea *Also called Blower Drive Service Co* ***(P-19594)***
BDS Natural Products Inc (PA)....D....310 518-2227
14824 S Main St Gardena (90248) ***(P-2401)***
Be Beauty, Garden Grove *Also called Cali Chem Inc* ***(P-8454)***
Beach Reporter, Rllng HLS Est *Also called National Media Inc* ***(P-5772)***
Beach Reporter, The, Hermosa Beach *Also called National Media Inc* ***(P-5773)***
Beacon Concrete Inc....E....323 889-7775
1597 S Bluff Rd Montebello (90640) ***(P-10696)***
Beacon Media Inc....F....626 301-1010
125 E Chestnut Ave Monrovia (91016) ***(P-5565)***
Bead Shoppe....F....916 782-8642
2030 Douglas Blvd Ste 42 Roseville (95661) ***(P-23286)***
Beam Dynamics Inc....F....408 764-4805
5100 Patrick Henry Dr Santa Clara (95054) ***(P-14138)***
Beam On Technology Corporation....E....408 982-0161
317 Brokaw Rd Santa Clara (95050) ***(P-14798)***
Beam Suntory, Irvine *Also called Jim Beam Brands Co* ***(P-2014)***
Beam Wine Estates, Healdsburg *Also called Constellation Brands US Oprs* ***(P-1648)***
Bear Brothers Enterprises Ltd....E....914 588-6885
777 E Tahqtz Cyn Way # 200 Palm Springs (92262) ***(P-5887)***
Bear Creek Winery, Lodi *Also called Goldstone Land Company LLC* ***(P-1731)***
Bear Industrial Holdings Inc....E....562 926-3000
9971 Muirlands Blvd Irvine (92618) ***(P-9464)***
Bear Industrial Supply & Mfg, Irvine *Also called Bear Industrial Holdings Inc* ***(P-9464)***

Bear Label Machines, Gold River *Also called Kirk A Schliger* ***(P-14667)***
Bear Republic Brewing Co Inc (PA)....C....707 894-2722
110 Sandholm Ln Ste 10 Cloverdale (95425) ***(P-1501)***
Bear Republic Brewing Co Inc....F....707 433-2337
345 Healdsburg Ave Healdsburg (95448) ***(P-1502)***
Beard Seats, Newport Beach *Also called Redart Corporation* ***(P-4870)***
Beards Custom Cabinets, Redding *Also called David Beard* ***(P-4187)***
Bears For Humanity Inc....E....866 325-1668
841 Ocean View Ave San Mateo (94401) ***(P-8721)***
Beats By Dr. Dre, Culver City *Also called Beats Electronics LLC* ***(P-18832)***
Beats By Dre, Culver City *Also called Beats Electronics LLC* ***(P-17201)***
Beats Electronics LLC (PA)....F....424 268-3055
8600 Hayden Pl Culver City (90232) ***(P-18832)***
Beats Electronics LLC (HQ)....D....424 326-4679
8600 Hayden Pl Culver City (90232) ***(P-17201)***
Beats Music LLC....D....415 590-5104
235 2nd St San Francisco (94105) ***(P-23656)***
Beaudry International LLC....F....213 623-5025
3835 E Thousand Oaks Blvd Westlake Village (91362) ***(P-22593)***
Beaulieu Vineyard, Rutherford *Also called Diageo North America Inc* ***(P-2013)***
Beaumont DC 52, Beaumont *Also called Wolverine World Wide Inc* ***(P-10165)***
Beaumont Juice Inc....D....951 769-7171
550 B St Beaumont (92223) ***(P-755)***
Beauty & Health International (PA)....E....714 903-9730
7541 Anthony Ave Garden Grove (92841) ***(P-7800)***
Beauty Craft Furniture Corp....E....916 428-2238
3316 51st Ave Sacramento (95823) ***(P-4553)***
Bebop Sensors Inc....E....510 848-3231
970 Miller Ave Berkeley (94708) ***(P-2901)***
Bechhold & Son Flasher & Lure....F....530 367-6650
616 Keller St Petaluma (94952) ***(P-22757)***
Bechler Cams Inc....F....714 774-5150
1313 S State College Pkwy Anaheim (92806) ***(P-21443)***
Beck Consulting, Concord *Also called Bcg/Management Resources* ***(P-23655)***
Becker Automotive Design USA, Oxnard *Also called Becker Automotive Designs Inc* ***(P-19459)***
Becker Automotive Designs Inc....E....805 487-5227
1711 Ives Ave Oxnard (93033) ***(P-19459)***
Becker Specialty Corporation....F....909 356-1095
15310 Arrow Blvd Fontana (92335) ***(P-18702)***
Becker Surfboards Inc....F....310 372-6554
301 Pier Ave Hermosa Beach (90254) ***(P-22758)***
Becker Woodworking....F....323 564-2441
847 E 108th St Los Angeles (90059) ***(P-3969)***
Beckers Fabrication Inc....E....714 692-1600
22465 La Palma Ave Yorba Linda (92887) ***(P-5357)***
Beckman Coulter Inc....D....909 597-3967
15989 Cypress Ave Chino (91708) ***(P-21180)***
Beckman Coulter Inc....C....559 784-0800
167 W Poplar Ave Porterville (93257) ***(P-21181)***
Beckman Coulter Inc....C....760 438-9151
2470 Faraday Ave Carlsbad (92010) ***(P-21182)***
Beckman Coulter Inc....D....916 374-3511
2040 Enterprise Blvd West Sacramento (95691) ***(P-21183)***
Beckman Coulter Inc....C....818 970-2161
250 S Kraemer Blvd Brea (92821) ***(P-21622)***
Beckman Industries....F....805 375-3003
701 Del Nrte Blvd Ste 205 Oxnard (93030) ***(P-22998)***
Beckman Instruments Inc....E....714 871-4848
2500 N Harbor Blvd Fullerton (92835) ***(P-8206)***
Beckmanns Old World Bakery Ltd....C....831 423-9242
104 Bronson St Ste 6 Santa Cruz (95062) ***(P-1144)***
Beco Baby Carrier, Costa Mesa *Also called Caperon Designs Inc* ***(P-22667)***
Becs Pacific Ltd....F....661 397-9400
19456 Colombo St Ste B Bakersfield (93308) ***(P-12742)***
Becton Dickinson and Company....B....858 812-8800
10975 Torreyana Rd San Diego (92121) ***(P-21623)***
Becton Dickinson and Company....B....408 432-9475
2350 Qume Dr San Jose (95131) ***(P-21624)***
Becton Dickinson and Company....F....888 876-4287
3750 Torrey View Ct San Diego (92130) ***(P-21625)***
Bed Time Originals, El Segundo *Also called Lambs & Ivy Inc* ***(P-3623)***
Bedard Machine Inc....F....714 990-4846
141 Viking Ave Brea (92821) ***(P-15781)***
Bedford Winery....F....805 344-2107
448 Bell St Los Alamos (93440) ***(P-1593)***
Bee Darlin Inc (PA)....D....213 749-2116
1875 E 22nd St Los Angeles (90058) ***(P-3219)***
Bee Darlin and Be Smart, Los Angeles *Also called Bee Darlin Inc* ***(P-3219)***
Bee Wire & Cable Inc....E....909 923-5800
2850 E Spruce St Ontario (91761) ***(P-11287)***
Beef Jerky Factory, Colton *Also called Hawa Corporation* ***(P-463)***
Beejay LLC....F....619 220-8697
3450 Kurtz St Ste C San Diego (92110) ***(P-22662)***
Beekee Corp....F....949 275-5861
5882 Bolsa Ave Ste 210 Huntington Beach (92649) ***(P-23657)***
Beeline Group LLC....D....510 477-5400
31023 Huntwood Ave Hayward (94544) ***(P-23059)***
Beemak Plastics LLC....D....310 886-5880
16711 Knott Ave La Mirada (90638) ***(P-9656)***
Beemak-Idl Display Products, La Mirada *Also called Beemak Plastics LLC* ***(P-9656)***
Before Butcher Inc....F....858 265-9511
2550 Britannia Blvd San Diego (92154) ***(P-441)***
Bega Supply Inc....F....310 719-1252
1613 W 134th St Ste 3 Gardena (90249) ***(P-17202)***
Bega Video Supplies, Gardena *Also called Bega Supply Inc* ***(P-17202)***
Bega/Us Inc....D....805 684-0533
1000 Bega Way Carpinteria (93013) ***(P-17104)***
Begovic Industries Inc....E....650 594-2861
1725 Old County Rd San Carlos (94070) ***(P-15782)***
Behaviosec Inc....F....833 248-6732
535 Mission St Fl 14 San Francisco (94105) ***(P-23658)***
Behr Holdings Corporation (HQ)....A....714 545-7101
3400 W Segerstrom Ave Santa Ana (92704) ***(P-8619)***
Behr Paint Company, Santa Ana *Also called Behr Process Corporation* ***(P-8621)***
Behr Paint Corp., Santa Ana *Also called Behr Sales Inc* ***(P-8626)***
Behr Process Corporation....E....714 545-7101
1603 W Alton Ave Santa Ana (92704) ***(P-8620)***
Behr Process Corporation (HQ)....A....714 545-7101
1801 E Saint Andrew Pl Santa Ana (92705) ***(P-8621)***
Behr Process Corporation....D....714 545-7101
3400 W Garry Ave Santa Ana (92704) ***(P-8622)***
Behr Process Corporation....D....714 545-7101
3130 S Harbor Blvd # 400 Santa Ana (92704) ***(P-8623)***
Behr Process Corporation....F....714 545-7101
3500 W Segerstrom Ave Santa Ana (92704) ***(P-8624)***
Behr Process Corporation....D....714 545-7101
1995 S Standard Ave Santa Ana (92707) ***(P-8625)***
Behr Sales Inc (HQ)....C....714 545-7101
3400 W Segerstrom Ave Santa Ana (92704) ***(P-8626)***
BEI Industrial Encoders, Thousand Oaks *Also called Sensata Technologies Inc* ***(P-15332)***
BEI Industrial Encoders, Thousand Oaks *Also called Carros Sensors Systems Co LLC* ***(P-18853)***
BEI North America LLC (HQ)....F....805 716-0642
1461 Lawrence Dr Thousand Oaks (91320) ***(P-18833)***
Beko Radiator Cores Inc....E....925 671-2975
2322 Bates Ave Ste A Concord (94520) ***(P-19591)***
Bel Aire Bridal Inc....E....310 325-8160
23002 Mariposa Ave Torrance (90502) ***(P-3774)***
Bel Aire Bridal Accessories, Torrance *Also called Bel Aire Bridal Inc* ***(P-3774)***
Bel Power Solutions Inc....A....866 513-2839
2390 Walsh Ave Santa Clara (95051) ***(P-18703)***
Bel-Air Cases, Ontario *Also called California Quality Plas Inc* ***(P-9688)***
Bel-Air Machining Co....F....714 953-6616
151 E Columbine Ave Santa Ana (92707) ***(P-15783)***
Belagio Enterprises Inc....E....323 731-6934
4801 W Jefferson Blvd Los Angeles (90016) ***(P-2670)***
Belco Cabinets Inc....F....209 334-5437
1109 Black Diamond Way Lodi (95240) ***(P-11936)***
Belco Packaging Systems Inc....E....626 357-9566
910 S Mountain Ave Monrovia (91016) ***(P-14698)***
Belden Inc....F....510 438-9071
47823 Westinghouse Dr Fremont (94539) ***(P-11288)***
Belding Golf Bag Company, The, Oxnard *Also called Illah Sports Inc A Corporation* ***(P-22827)***
Belkin Inc....C....800 223-5546
12045 Waterfront Dr Playa Vista (90094) ***(P-17203)***
Bell Enterprise, San Bernardino *Also called Kendra Group Inc* ***(P-17740)***
Bell Foundry Co (PA)....D....323 564-5701
5310 Southern Ave South Gate (90280) ***(P-22759)***
Bell Powder Coating Inc....F....805 658-2233
4747 Mcgrath St Ventura (93003) ***(P-13149)***
Bell Sports Inc (HQ)....D....469 417-6600
5550 Scotts Valley Dr Scotts Valley (95066) ***(P-22760)***
Bell-Carter Foods Inc....B....530 528-4820
1012 2nd St Corning (96021) ***(P-879)***
Bell-Carter Foods Inc....E....209 549-5939
4207 Finch Rd Modesto (95357) ***(P-756)***
Bell-Carter Foods LLC (PA)....B....209 549-5939
590 Ygnacio Valley Rd # 300 Walnut Creek (94596) ***(P-757)***
Bell-Carter Olive Company, Walnut Creek *Also called Bell-Carter Foods LLC* ***(P-757)***
Bell-Carter Packaging, Modesto *Also called Bell-Carter Foods Inc* ***(P-756)***
Bell-Carterolive Company, Corning *Also called Bell-Carter Foods Inc* ***(P-879)***
Bella Notte Linens Inc....E....415 883-3434
60 Galli Dr Ste 2 Novato (94949) ***(P-2723)***
Bella Vineyards LLC....F....707 473-9171
9711 W Dry Creek Rd Healdsburg (95448) ***(P-1594)***
Bellacanvas, Los Angeles *Also called Color Image Apparel Inc* ***(P-2779)***
Bellama Cstm Met Fbrcators Inc....F....619 585-3351
3129 Main St Chula Vista (91911) ***(P-12130)***
Bellasposa Wedding Center....F....909 758-0176
11450 4th St Ste 103 Rancho Cucamonga (91730) ***(P-3220)***
Bellaterra Home LLC....F....916 896-3188
8372 Tiogawoods Dr # 180 Sacramento (95828) ***(P-4168)***
Bellavuos....F....626 653-0121
417 N Azusa Ave West Covina (91791) ***(P-8443)***
Bellou Publishing, San Jose *Also called Times Media Inc* ***(P-5850)***
Bellows Mfg & RES Inc....F....818 838-1333
13596 Vaughn St San Fernando (91340) ***(P-15784)***
Belmar Company, San Francisco *Also called B & M Upholstery* ***(P-2669)***
Belmont Publications Inc....F....714 825-1234
3621 S Harbor Blvd # 265 Santa Ana (92704) ***(P-5888)***
Belovac LLC....F....951 427-4299
435 E Lincoln St Ste A Banning (92220) ***(P-14432)***
Belport Company Inc (PA)....E....805 484-1051
4825 Calle Alto Camarillo (93012) ***(P-22136)***
Belt Drives Ltd....E....714 693-1313
505 W Lambert Rd Brea (92821) ***(P-20384)***
Belts By Simon Inc....D....714 573-0303
14382 Chambers Rd Tustin (92780) ***(P-3527)***
Bema Electronic Mfg Inc....D....510 490-7770
4545 Cushing Pkwy Fremont (94538) ***(P-18834)***
Bemco Inc (PA)....E....805 583-4970
2255 Union Pl Simi Valley (93065) ***(P-21184)***
Beme International LLC....E....858 751-0580
7333 Ronson Rd San Diego (92111) ***(P-3602)***
Ben Davis, San Rafael *Also called Ben F Davis Company* ***(P-3026)***

A L P H A B E T I C

Employee Codes: A=Over 500 employees, B=251-500
C=101-250, D=51-100, E=20-50, F=10-19
2020 California
Manfacturers Register
© Mergent Inc. 1-800-342-5647
1037

Ben F Davis Company (PA)....F....415 382-1000
3140 Kerner Blvd Ste G San Rafael (94901) *(P-3026)*
Bench 2 Bench Technologies, Fullerton *Also called Winonics Inc* *(P-18052)*
Bench Depot, Tecate *Also called Benchpro Inc* *(P-5052)*
Bench-Craft Inc....F....714 523-3322
4005 Artesia Ave Fullerton (92833) *(P-5051)*
Bench-Tek Solutions Llc....F....408 653-1100
525 Aldo Ave Santa Clara (95054) *(P-4830)*
Benchmark Elec Mfg Sltions Inc (HQ)....D....805 222-1303
5550 Hellyer Ave San Jose (95138) *(P-17834)*
Benchmark Elec Mfg Sol Moorpk....A....805 532-2800
200 Science Dr Moorpark (93021) *(P-18835)*
Benchmark Elec Phoenix Inc....B....619 397-2402
1659 Gailes Blvd San Diego (92154) *(P-17835)*
Benchmark Electronics Inc....D....510 360-2800
42701 Christy St Fremont (94538) *(P-17836)*
Benchmark Electronics Inc....B....925 363-1151
2301 Arnold Ind Way Ste G Concord (94520) *(P-17837)*
Benchmark Engineering Div of, Santa Fe Springs *Also called K Metal Products Inc* *(P-13420)*
Benchmark Thermal, Grass Valley *Also called Manufacturers Coml Fin LLC* *(P-11705)*
Benchmark Thermal Corporation....D....530 477-5011
13185 Nevada City Ave Grass Valley (95945) *(P-11690)*
Benchpro Inc....C....619 478-9400
23949 Tecate Mission Rd Tecate (91980) *(P-5052)*
Bend-Tek Inc....D....714 210-8966
2205 S Yale St Santa Ana (92704) *(P-12131)*
Benda Tool & Model Works Inc....E....510 741-3170
900 Alfred Nobel Dr Hercules (94547) *(P-14022)*
Bender Ccp Inc....D....707 745-9970
2150 E 37th St Vernon Vernon (90058) *(P-15785)*
Bender US, Vernon *Also called Bender Ccp Inc* *(P-15785)*
Bendick Precision Inc....F....626 445-0217
56 La Porte St Arcadia (91006) *(P-15786)*
Bendpak Inc....C....805 933-9970
1645 E Lemonwood Dr Santa Paula (93060) *(P-14433)*
Benefit Software Incorporated....E....805 679-6200
212 Cottage Grove Ave A Santa Barbara (93101) *(P-23659)*
Benefits Software, Santa Barbara *Also called Ebix Inc* *(P-23840)*
Benen Manufacturing LLC....F....408 573-7252
2266 Trade Zone Blvd San Jose (95131) *(P-14139)*
Benicia Fabrication & Mch Inc....C....707 745-8111
101 E Channel Rd Benicia (94510) *(P-11996)*
Benicia Herald, Benicia *Also called Gibson Printing & Publishing* *(P-5645)*
Benigna....F....323 262-2484
4630 Floral Dr Los Angeles (90022) *(P-2985)*
Benjamin Lewis Inc....F....949 859-5119
23042 Alcalde Dr Ste C Laguna Hills (92653) *(P-6441)*
Benjamin Litho Inc....F....408 232-3800
1810 Oakland Rd Ste F San Jose (95131) *(P-6442)*
Benmar Marine Electronics Inc....F....714 540-5120
2225 S Huron Dr Santa Ana (92704) *(P-20546)*
Bennett Industries Inc....F....415 482-9000
4304 Redwood Hwy 200 San Rafael (94903) *(P-6443)*
Bennett's Bakery, Sacramento *Also called Bennetts Baking Company* *(P-1338)*
Bennett's Honey Farm, Fillmore *Also called Honey Bennetts Farm Inc* *(P-2480)*
Bennetts Baking Company....F....916 481-3349
2530 Tesla Way Sacramento (95825) *(P-1338)*
Bens Alternative Foods....F....510 614-6745
2712 Marina Blvd Ste 36 San Leandro (94577) *(P-946)*
Bent Fir Company....F....707 274-6628
3598 Manzanita Ave Nice (95464) *(P-4554)*
Bent Manufacturing Co Bdaa Inc....F....714 842-0600
15442 Chemical Ln Huntington Beach (92649) *(P-9657)*
Bentec Medical Opco LLC....E....530 406-3333
1380 E Beamer St Woodland (95776) *(P-21626)*
Bentec Scientific LLC....E....530 406-3333
1380 E Beamer St Woodland (95776) *(P-21627)*
Bentek Corporation....D....408 954-9600
1991 Senter Rd San Jose (95112) *(P-18836)*
Bentek Solar, San Jose *Also called Bentek Corporation* *(P-18836)*
Bentley Management Corporation....F....323 653-8060
8060 Melrose Ave Ste 210 Los Angeles (90046) *(P-5889)*
Bentley Mills Inc....F....800 423-4709
315 S 7th Ave City of Industry (91746) *(P-2866)*
Bentley Mills Inc (PA)....C....626 333-4585
14641 Don Julian Rd City of Industry (91746) *(P-2867)*
Bentley Prtg & Graphics Inc....F....714 636-1622
1608 Sierra Madre Cir Placentia (92870) *(P-6444)*
Bentley-Simonson Inc....D....805 650-2794
1746 S Victoria Ave Ste F Ventura (93003) *(P-23)*
Bento Merge Enterprises, San Francisco *Also called Bento Technologies Inc* *(P-23660)*
Bento Technologies Inc....F....415 887-2028
221 Main St Ste 1325 San Francisco (94105) *(P-23660)*
Benziger Family Winery, Glen Ellen *Also called Bfw Associates LLC* *(P-1598)*
Beonca Machine Inc....F....909 392-9991
1680 Curtiss Ct La Verne (91750) *(P-15787)*
Beranek Inc....E....310 328-9094
2340 W 205th St Torrance (90501) *(P-20057)*
Berber Food Manufacturing Inc....C....510 553-0444
425 Hester St San Leandro (94577) *(P-2402)*
Berenice 2 AM Corp....F....858 255-8693
8008 Girard Ave Ste 150 La Jolla (92037) *(P-630)*
Bereshith Inc (PA)....F....213 749-7304
1015 Crocker St Los Angeles (90021) *(P-3140)*
Berg Manufacturing Inc....F....408 727-2374
408 Aldo Ave Santa Clara (95054) *(P-23287)*
Berg-Nelson Company Inc....F....562 432-3491
1633 W 17th St Long Beach (90813) *(P-9197)*
Bergandi Machinery Company, Ontario *Also called Bmci Inc* *(P-14264)*
Berger Modular....F....209 329-9368
350 Crescent Dr Galt (95632) *(P-4438)*
Bergin Glass Impressions Inc....E....707 224-0111
938 Kaiser Rd NAPA (94558) *(P-10341)*
Bericap LLC....D....909 390-5518
1671 Champagne Ave Ste B Ontario (91761) *(P-9658)*
Bering Technology Inc....E....408 364-6500
1608 W Campbell Ave 328 Campbell (95008) *(P-15168)*
Beringer Vineyards, Saint Helena *Also called Treasury Wine Estates Americas* *(P-1965)*
Beringer Vinyards, Saint Helena *Also called Treasury Wine Estates Americas* *(P-1966)*
Berkeley Design Automation Inc....E....408 496-6600
46871 Bayside Pkwy Fremont (94538) *(P-18146)*
Berkeley Farms LLC....E....916 689-7613
7444 Reese Rd Sacramento (95828) *(P-686)*
Berkeley Farms LLC (HQ)....B....510 265-8600
25500 Clawiter Rd Hayward (94545) *(P-687)*
Berkeley Forge & Tool Inc....D....510 525-5117
1331 Eastshore Hwy Berkeley (94710) *(P-12705)*
Berkeley Mills, Berkeley *Also called Berkeley Mllwk & Furn Co Inc* *(P-4555)*
Berkeley Mllwk & Furn Co Inc....E....510 549-2854
2830 7th St Berkeley (94710) *(P-4555)*
Berkeley Nutritional Mfg Corp....D....925 243-6300
1852 Rutan Dr Livermore (94551) *(P-7801)*
Berkeley Scientific....F....510 525-1945
21 Westminster Ave Kensington (94708) *(P-18837)*
Berkley Integrated Audio Softw....E....707 782-1866
121 H St Petaluma (94952) *(P-19210)*
Berlex Bioscience, San Francisco *Also called Bayer Hlthcare Phrmcticals Inc* *(P-7798)*
Berlin Food & Lab Equipment Co....E....650 589-4231
43 S Linden Ave South San Francisco (94080) *(P-20746)*
Bermad Inc (PA)....E....877 577-4283
3816 S Willow Ave Ste 101 Fresno (93725) *(P-13348)*
Bermad Control Valves, Fresno *Also called Bermad Inc* *(P-13348)*
Bermingham Controls Inc A (PA)....E....562 860-0463
11144 Business Cir Cerritos (90703) *(P-13295)*
Bernardo Winery Inc (PA)....E....858 487-1866
13330 Pseo Del Vrano Nrte San Diego (92128) *(P-1595)*
Bernardus LLC (PA)....E....831 659-1900
5 W Carmel Valley Rd Carmel Valley (93924) *(P-1596)*
Bernardus Winery, Carmel Valley *Also called Bernardus LLC* *(P-1596)*
Bernell Hydraulics Inc (PA)....E....909 899-1751
8810 Etiwanda Ave Rancho Cucamonga (91739) *(P-15626)*
Berney-Karp Inc....D....323 260-7122
3350 E 26th St Vernon (90058) *(P-10485)*
Bernhardt & Bernhardt Inc....F....714 544-0708
14771 Myford Rd Ste D Tustin (92780) *(P-13904)*
Bernman Mold and Engineering....F....909 930-3844
1219 S Bon View Ave Ontario (91761) *(P-14023)*
Berns Bros Inc....F....562 437-0471
1250 W 17th St Long Beach (90813) *(P-15788)*
Berrett-Koehler Publishers Inc (PA)....E....510 817-2277
1333 Broadway Ste 1000 Oakland (94612) *(P-6074)*
Berri Pro Inc....F....781 929-8288
929 Colorado Ave Santa Monica (90401) *(P-2191)*
Berry Global Inc....F....714 751-2920
3030 S Susan St Santa Ana (92704) *(P-9659)*
Berry Global Inc....F....714 777-5200
4875 E Hunter Ave Anaheim (92807) *(P-9660)*
Berry Global Inc....C....909 465-9055
14000 Monte Vista Ave Chino (91710) *(P-9661)*
Berry Global Inc....E....800 462-3843
13335 Orden Dr Santa Fe Springs (90670) *(P-9662)*
Berry Global Films LLC....C....909 517-2872
14000 Monte Vista Ave Chino (91710) *(P-9395)*
Berry Petroleum Company LLC....F....661 255-6066
25121 Sierra Hwy Newhall (91321) *(P-24)*
Berry Petroleum Company LLC....E....661 769-8820
28700 Hovey Hills Rd Taft (93268) *(P-25)*
Berry Petroleum Company LLC (HQ)....D....661 616-3900
5201 Truxtun Ave Ste 100 Bakersfield (93309) *(P-26)*
Berry Petroleum Company LLC....F....805 984-0053
5713 W Gonzales Rd Oxnard (93036) *(P-27)*
Bert & Rockys Cream Co Inc....F....909 625-1852
242 Yale Ave Claremont (91711) *(P-631)*
Bert-Co Industries Inc....F....323 669-5700
2150 S Parco Ave Ontario (91761) *(P-6998)*
Bert-Co Industries Inc (PA)....C....323 669-5700
2150 S Parco Ave Ontario (91761) *(P-6445)*
Bert-Co. of Ontario CA, Ontario *Also called Edelmann Usa Inc* *(P-23093)*
Bertagna Orchards Inc....F....530 343-8014
3329 Hegan Ln Chico (95928) *(P-1597)*
Bertelsmann Inc....B....661 702-2700
29011 Commerce Center Dr Valencia (91355) *(P-6075)*
Bertolin Engineering Corp....F....408 988-0166
485 Robert Ave Santa Clara (95050) *(P-12770)*
Beryl Lockhart Enterprises, Sun Valley *Also called Ble Inc* *(P-89)*
Bes Concrete Products, Tracy *Also called Bescal Inc* *(P-10536)*
Besam Entrance Solutions, Elk Grove *Also called Assa Abloy Entrance Sys US Inc* *(P-19261)*
Besam Entrance Solutions, Anaheim *Also called Assa Abloy Entrance Systems US* *(P-19262)*
Bescal Inc....E....209 836-3492
10304 W Linne Rd Tracy (95377) *(P-10536)*
Bespoke Coachworks Inc....F....818 571-9900
7641 Burnet Ave Van Nuys (91405) *(P-19460)*
Besser Company, Compton *Also called Concrete Mold Corporation* *(P-14038)*
Best Box Company Inc....F....323 589-6088
8011 Beach St Los Angeles (90001) *(P-5200)*

Best Data Products Inc ....D....818 534-1414
21541 Blythe St Canoga Park (91304) ***(P-15169)***
Best Engineering, North Hollywood *Also called Karapet Engineering Inc* ***(P-16107)***
Best Express Foods Inc ....B....510 782-5338
1742 Sabre St Hayward (94545) ***(P-1145)***
Best Formulations Inc ....C....626 912-9998
17758 Rowland St City of Industry (91748) ***(P-2403)***
Best Friends By Sheri, Commerce *Also called Sentiments Inc* ***(P-23473)***
Best Industrial Supply ....F....626 279-5090
9711 Rush St South El Monte (91733) ***(P-13859)***
Best Ink and Thread, Ontario *Also called Medrano Raymundo* ***(P-2892)***
Best Living International Inc ....F....626 625-2911
12234 Florence Ave Santa Fe Springs (90670) ***(P-4685)***
Best Marble Co ....E....510 614-0155
2446 Teagarden St San Leandro (94577) ***(P-10892)***
Best Quality Furniture Mfg Inc ....D....909 230-6440
5400 E Francis St Ontario (91761) ***(P-4629)***
Best Redwood, San Diego *Also called Rtmex Inc* ***(P-3984)***
Best Roll-Up Door Inc ....E....562 802-2233
13202 Arctic Cir Santa Fe Springs (90670) ***(P-11937)***
Best Sanitizers Inc ....D....530 265-1800
310 Prvdnce Mine Rd # 120 Nevada City (95959) ***(P-8367)***
Best Slip Cover Company, Studio City *Also called Harmony Infinite Inc* ***(P-5063)***
Best USA, West Sacramento *Also called Tomra Sorting Inc* ***(P-14406)***
Best Value Textbooks LLC ....E....530 222-5980
410 Hemsted Dr Ste 100 Redding (96002) ***(P-6076)***
Best Way Marble, Los Angeles *Also called Best-Way Marble & Tile Co Inc* ***(P-10893)***
Best- In- West ....E....909 947-6507
2279 Eagle Glen Pkwy Corona (92883) ***(P-3725)***
Best-In-West Emblem Co, Corona *Also called Best- In- West* ***(P-3725)***
Best-Way Marble & Tile Co Inc ....E....323 266-6794
5037 Telegraph Rd Los Angeles (90022) ***(P-10893)***
Bestek Manufacturing Inc ....E....408 321-8834
675 Sycamore Dr Milpitas (95035) ***(P-15170)***
Bestest International ....F....714 974-8837
181 W Orangethorpe Ave C Placentia (92870) ***(P-20839)***
Bestest Medical, Placentia *Also called Bestest International* ***(P-20839)***
Bestforms Inc ....E....805 388-0503
1135 Avenida Acaso Camarillo (93012) ***(P-7280)***
Bestop Baja LLC ....E....760 560-2252
185 Bosstick Blvd San Marcos (92069) ***(P-19592)***
Bestronics, San Jose *Also called Bay Elctrnic Spport Trnics Inc* ***(P-17833)***
Bestronics Holdings Inc (PA) ....E....408 385-7777
2090 Fortune Dr San Jose (95131) ***(P-18676)***
Bestway Hydraulics Co Inc ....E....310 639-2507
1518 S Santa Fe Ave Compton (90221) ***(P-14561)***
Beta Box Inc ....F....323 383-9820
12021 Wilshire Blvd Los Angeles (90025) ***(P-17204)***
Bethebeast Inc ....E....424 206-1081
3738 W 181st St Torrance (90504) ***(P-23661)***
Better Bar Manufacturing LLC ....E....951 525-3111
6975 Arlington Ave Riverside (92503) ***(P-579)***
Better Beverages Inc (PA) ....E....562 924-8321
10624 Midway Ave Cerritos (90703) ***(P-2192)***
Better Built Truss Inc ....E....209 869-4545
251 E 4th St Ripon (95366) ***(P-4289)***
Better Chinese LLC ....F....650 384-0902
150 W Iowa Ave Ste 104 Sunnyvale (94086) ***(P-6077)***
Better Cleaning Systems Inc ....E....559 673-5700
1122 Maple St Madera (93637) ***(P-16843)***
Better Instant Copy ....F....323 782-6934
512 S San Vicente Blvd # 1 Los Angeles (90048) ***(P-6446)***
Better Mens Clothes, Los Angeles *Also called Hirsh Inc* ***(P-208)***
Better Nutritionals LLC ....D....310 502-2277
17120 S Figueroa St Ste B Gardena (90248) ***(P-580)***
Better Way Grinding, Santa Fe Springs *Also called Better-Way & Lovell Grinding* ***(P-15789)***
Better World Manufacturing Inc (PA) ....F....559 291-4276
3535 N Sabre Dr Fresno (93727) ***(P-9663)***
Better-Way & Lovell Grinding ....F....562 693-8722
8333 Chetle Ave Santa Fe Springs (90670) ***(P-15789)***
Bettercompany Inc ....F....415 501-9692
621 Sansome St San Francisco (94111) ***(P-23662)***
Betterline Products Inc ....E....760 535-5030
1101 E Elm Ave Fullerton (92831) ***(P-15790)***
Betterworks Systems Inc ....D....650 656-9013
999 Main St Redwood City (94063) ***(P-23663)***
Betts Company (PA) ....D....559 498-3304
2843 S Maple Ave Fresno (93725) ***(P-13376)***
Betts Company ....E....559 498-8624
2867 S Maple Ave Fresno (93725) ***(P-19521)***
Betts Company ....F....909 427-9988
10771 Almond Ave Ste B Fontana (92337) ***(P-13377)***
Betts Spring Manufacturing, Fresno *Also called Betts Company* ***(P-13376)***
Betts Truck Parts, Fontana *Also called Betts Company* ***(P-13377)***
Betty Clark's Confections, El Monte *Also called California Treats Inc* ***(P-760)***
Betty Stillwell ....D....619 428-2001
524 W Calle Primera # 1004 San Ysidro (92173) ***(P-10894)***
Beu Industries Inc ....E....310 885-9626
2937 E Maria St E Rncho Dmngz (90221) ***(P-5325)***
Beveled Edge Inc ....F....408 467-9900
1740 Junction Ave Ste D San Jose (95112) ***(P-10342)***
Beveragefactory.com, San Diego *Also called Cydea Inc* ***(P-1517)***
Beverly Hillcrest Oil Corp ....F....949 598-7300
27241 Burbank El Toro (92610) ***(P-28)***
Beverly Hills Courier Inc ....E....310 278-1322
499 N Canon Dr Ste 100 Beverly Hills (90210) ***(P-5566)***
Bey-Berk International (PA) ....E....818 773-7534
9145 Deering Ave Chatsworth (91311) ***(P-13502)***
Beynon Sports Surfaces Inc ....E....559 237-2590
4668 N Sonora Ave Ste 101 Fresno (93722) ***(P-22761)***
Beyond Green LLC ....F....800 983-7221
2 Rancho Cir Lake Forest (92630) ***(P-9664)***
Beyond Meat Inc (PA) ....E....866 756-4112
119 Standard St El Segundo (90245) ***(P-947)***
Beyond Meat Inc ....E....310 567-3323
1325 E El Segundo Blvd El Segundo (90245) ***(P-948)***
Beyond Seating Inc ....F....323 633-5359
2120 Edwards Ave South El Monte (91733) ***(P-11573)***
Beyond Ultimate LLC ....F....626 330-9777
360 S 9th Ave City of Industry (91746) ***(P-5091)***
Bez Ambar Inc ....E....213 629-9191
611 Wilshire Blvd Ste 607 Los Angeles (90017) ***(P-22504)***
BF Suma Pharmaceuticals Inc ....F....626 285-8366
5077 Walnut Grove Ave San Gabriel (91776) ***(P-581)***
Bfw Associates LLC (HQ) ....E....707 935-3000
1883 London Ranch Rd Glen Ellen (95442) ***(P-1598)***
Bgl Development Inc ....F....415 256-2525
3070 Kerner Blvd Ste H San Rafael (94901) ***(P-23664)***
Bgm Installation Inc ....F....310 830-3113
528 E D St Wilmington (90744) ***(P-9165)***
Bh-Tech Inc ....A....858 694-0900
7841 Balboa Ave Ste 208 San Diego (92111) ***(P-9665)***
Bhaktivedanta Book Tr Intl Inc ....F....310 837-5284
9701 Venus Blvd Ste A Los Angeles (90034) ***(P-6078)***
BHC Industries Inc ....E....310 632-2000
239 E Greenleaf Blvd Compton (90220) ***(P-12942)***
Bhk Inc ....E....909 983-2973
760 E Sunkist St Ontario (91761) ***(P-16857)***
Bhogart LLC ....E....855 553-3887
1919 Monterey Hwy Ste 80 San Jose (95112) ***(P-14348)***
Bhu Food, San Diego *Also called Lauras Original Boston* ***(P-1231)***
Bi Cmos Foundry, Santa Clara *Also called Onspec Technology Partners Inc* ***(P-18454)***
Bi Nutraceuticals Inc (HQ) ....E....310 669-2100
2384 E Pacifica Pl Rancho Dominguez (90220) ***(P-2193)***
Bi Technologies Corporation ....E....714 447-2402
413 Rood Rd Ste 7 Calexico (92231) ***(P-18838)***
Bi-Search International Inc ....E....714 258-4500
17550 Gillette Ave Irvine (92614) ***(P-18839)***
Biale Estate ....F....707 257-7555
4038 Big Ranch Rd NAPA (94558) ***(P-1599)***
Bibbero Systems Inc (HQ) ....E....800 242-2376
1300 N Mcdowell Blvd Petaluma (94954) ***(P-6447)***
Bico Inc ....F....818 842-7179
3116 W Valhalla Dr Burbank (91505) ***(P-20747)***
Bico-Braun International, Burbank *Also called Bico Inc* ***(P-20747)***
Bicycle Music Co, The, Los Angeles *Also called Anthem Music & Media Fund LLC* ***(P-6072)***
Bidchat Inc ....F....818 631-6212
14570 Benefit St Unit 302 Sherman Oaks (91403) ***(P-23665)***
Bidgely, Sunnyvale *Also called Myenersave Inc* ***(P-24186)***
Bidu Inc ....F....213 748-4433
756 E Wash Blvd Ste B Los Angeles (90021) ***(P-3295)***
Bien Air Usa Inc ....F....949 477-6050
8861 Research Dr Ste 100 Irvine (92618) ***(P-22137)***
Bien Padre Foods Inc ....E....707 442-4585
1459 Railroad St Eureka (95501) ***(P-719)***
Big 5 Electronics Inc ....E....562 941-4669
13452 Alondra Blvd Cerritos (90703) ***(P-17205)***
Big Accessories, Petaluma *Also called Gmpc LLC* ***(P-23122)***
Big Bang Clothing, Vernon *Also called All Star Clothing Inc* ***(P-3135)***
Big Bang Clothing Inc (PA) ....F....323 233-7773
4507 Staunton Ave Vernon (90058) ***(P-3296)***
Big Bang Clothing Co, Vernon *Also called Big Bang Clothing Inc* ***(P-3296)***
Big D Products, Fairfield *Also called Drake Enterprises Incorporated* ***(P-3837)***
Big Five Electronics, Cerritos *Also called Big 5 Electronics Inc* ***(P-17205)***
Big Front Uniforms, Los Angeles *Also called Bunkerhill Indus Group Inc* ***(P-3027)***
Big Gun Inc ....F....714 970-0423
190 Business Center Dr B Corona (92880) ***(P-19593)***
Big Gun Exhaust, Corona *Also called Big Gun Inc* ***(P-19593)***
Big GZ Pallets ....F....209 465-0351
1181 S Wilson Way Stockton (95205) ***(P-4350)***
Big Heart Pet Brands ....F....209 547-7200
18284 S Harlan Rd Lathrop (95330) ***(P-758)***
Big Heart Pet Brands ....C....310 519-3791
24700 Main St Carson (90745) ***(P-759)***
Big Heart Pet Brands Inc (HQ) ....B....415 247-3000
1 Maritime Plz Fl 2 San Francisco (94111) ***(P-1069)***
Big Hill Logging & Rd Building (PA) ....E....530 673-4155
680 Sutter St Yuba City (95991) ***(P-3875)***
Big Ink Printing ....F....408 624-1204
1711 Branham Ln Ste A5 San Jose (95118) ***(P-6448)***
Big Nickel, Palm Desert *Also called Daniels Inc* ***(P-6220)***
Big Oak Hardwood Floor Co Inc ....D....650 591-8651
1731 Leslie St San Mateo (94402) ***(P-3970)***
Big Shine Los Angeles Inc ....F....818 346-0770
27211 Branbury Ct Valencia (91354) ***(P-17468)***
Big Sleep Futon Inc ....E....800 647-2671
760 S Vail Ave Montebello (90640) ***(P-4712)***
Big Studio Inc ....F....562 989-2444
1247 E Hill St Long Beach (90755) ***(P-2822)***
Big Switch Networks Inc (PA) ....D....650 322-6510
3111 Coronado Dr Bldg A Santa Clara (95054) ***(P-23666)***
Big Tex Trailer Mfg Inc ....F....951 845-5344
1425 E Sixth St Beaumont (92223) ***(P-13613)***
Big Time Digital ....F....714 752-5959
1250 E 223rd St Ste 111 Carson (90745) ***(P-6449)***
Big Tree Big Sleep, Montebello *Also called Big Sleep Futon Inc* ***(P-4712)***

ALPHABETIC

Employee Codes: A=Over 500 employees, B=251-500
C=101-250, D=51-100, E=20-50, F=10-19
2020 California
Manfacturers Register
© Mergent Inc. 1-800-342-5647
1039

Big Tree Furniture & Inds Inc (PA) .... E......310 894-7500
  760 S Vail Ave Montebello (90640) *(P-4556)*
Big Valley Metals .... F......916 372-2383
  620 Houston St Ste 1 West Sacramento (95691) *(P-11748)*
Big Valley Pallet .... E......209 632-7687
  2512 Paulson Rd Turlock (95380) *(P-4351)*
Big3d .... E......559 233-3380
  2794 N Larkin Ave Fresno (93727) *(P-6450)*
Big3d.com, Fresno Also called Big3d *(P-6450)*
Bigfogg Inc (PA) .... F......951 587-2460
  42095 Zevo Dr Ste A2 Temecula (92590) *(P-15416)*
Bijan Rad Inc .... E......818 902-1606
  16125 Cantlay St Van Nuys (91406) *(P-14434)*
Bikernet.com, Wilmington Also called 5 Ball Inc *(P-6064)*
Bill Williams Welding Co .... E......562 432-5421
  1735 Santa Fe Ave Long Beach (90813) *(P-11749)*
Bill Wood Lathing .... E......909 628-1733
  12188 Central Ave Pmb 621 Chino (91710) *(P-13397)*
Billcom .... C......650 353-3301
  1810 Embarcadero Rd Palo Alto (94303) *(P-23667)*
Billet Industries, Gilroy Also called Nice Rack Tower Accessories *(P-19728)*
Billington Welding & Mfg Inc .... D......209 526-0846
  1442 N Emerald Ave Modesto (95351) *(P-14349)*
Bills Pipes Inc .... F......951 371-1329
  226 N Maple St Corona (92880) *(P-20385)*
Billy Beez Usa LLC .... F......661 383-0050
  24201 Valencia Blvd Santa Clarita (91355) *(P-22762)*
Billy Beez Usa LLC .... F......408 300-9547
  925 Blossom Hill Rd # 1397 San Jose (95123) *(P-22763)*
Billy Blues, Commerce Also called AB&r Inc *(P-3280)*
Bimarian Inc .... E......408 520-2666
  3350 Scott Blvd Santa Clara (95054) *(P-23668)*
Bimbo Bakeries U.S.A., Montebello Also called Bimbo Bakeries Usa Inc *(P-1149)*
Bimbo Bakeries Usa Inc .... F......209 538-6170
  1749 Reliance St Modesto (95358) *(P-1146)*
Bimbo Bakeries Usa Inc .... D......805 544-7687
  3580 Sueldo St San Luis Obispo (93401) *(P-1147)*
Bimbo Bakeries Usa Inc .... F......951 280-9044
  385 N Sherman Ave Corona (92882) *(P-1148)*
Bimbo Bakeries Usa Inc .... F......323 720-6099
  480 S Vale Ave Montebello (90640) *(P-1149)*
Bimbo Bakeries Usa Inc .... F......916 456-3863
  3495 Swetzer Rd Loomis (95650) *(P-1150)*
Bimbo Bakeries Usa Inc .... E......916 681-8069
  7601 Wilbur Way Sacramento (95828) *(P-1151)*
Bimbo Bakeries Usa Inc .... A......916 732-4733
  3231 6th Ave Sacramento (95817) *(P-1152)*
Bimbo Bakeries Usa Inc .... F......760 737-7700
  2069 Aldergrove Ave Escondido (92029) *(P-1153)*
Bimbo Bakeries Usa Inc .... D......858 677-0573
  4000 Ruffin Rd Ste B San Diego (92123) *(P-1154)*
Bimbo Bakeries Usa Inc .... F......559 498-3632
  1836 G St Fresno (93706) *(P-1155)*
Bimbo Bakeries Usa Inc .... F......510 614-4500
  14388 Washington Ave San Leandro (94578) *(P-1156)*
Bimbo Bakeries Usa Inc .... E......650 583-5828
  264 S Spruce Ave South San Francisco (94080) *(P-1157)*
Bimbo Bakeries Usa Inc .... D......714 634-8068
  1220 Howell St Anaheim (92805) *(P-1158)*
Bimbo Bakeries Usa Inc .... D......209 532-5185
  116 Ponderosa Dr Sonora (95370) *(P-1159)*
Bimbo Bakeries Usa Inc .... F......661 274-8458
  38960 Trade Center Dr A Palmdale (93551) *(P-2404)*
Bimbo Bakeries Usa Inc .... E......323 913-7214
  1771 Blake Ave Los Angeles (90031) *(P-1160)*
Bimbo Bakeries Usa Inc .... E......650 583-3259
  475 S Canal St South San Francisco (94080) *(P-1161)*
Bimbo Bakeries Usa Inc .... F......805 384-1059
  333 Dawson Dr Ste A Camarillo (93012) *(P-1162)*
Bimbo Bakeries Usa Inc .... F......831 465-1214
  2740 Soquel Ave Santa Cruz (95062) *(P-1163)*
Bimbo Bakeries Usa Inc .... E......916 922-1307
  1201 El Camino Ave Sacramento (95815) *(P-1164)*
Bimbo Bakeries Usa Inc .... C......510 436-5350
  3525 Arden Rd Ste 300 Hayward (94545) *(P-1165)*
Bimbo Bakeries Usa Inc .... E......650 291-3213
  2380 N Clovis Ave Fresno (93727) *(P-1166)*
Bimbo Bakeries Usa Inc .... E......714 533-9436
  1215 Alek St Anaheim (92805) *(P-2405)*
Bimbo Bakeries Usa Inc .... C......559 489-0980
  3292 S Willow Ave Ste 101 Fresno (93725) *(P-1167)*
Bimeda Inc .... F......626 815-1680
  5539 Ayon Ave Irwindale (91706) *(P-7802)*
Bindel Bros Grading & .... E......831 754-1490
  1104 Madison Ln Salinas (93907) *(P-13709)*
Binder Metal Products Inc .... E......626 602-3824
  14909 S Broadway Gardena (90248) *(P-12771)*
Binders Express Inc .... F......310 329-4811
  13800 Gramercy Pl Gardena (90249) *(P-7303)*
Bindery , The, San Diego Also called D A M Bindery Inc *(P-7329)*
Bingo Publishers Incorporated .... E......949 581-5410
  24881 Alicia Pkwy Ste E Laguna Hills (92653) *(P-6199)*
Binh-Nhan D Ngo .... F......408 641-1721
  1751 Fortune Dr Ste F San Jose (95131) *(P-17838)*
Binti Inc .... E......844 424-6844
  1212 Broadway Ste 200 Oakland (94612) *(P-23669)*
Bio Check, Inc., South San Francisco Also called Biocheck Inc *(P-21631)*
Bio Creative Enterprises .... F......714 352-3600
  350 Kalmus Dr Costa Mesa (92626) *(P-8444)*
Bio Creative Labs, Costa Mesa Also called Bio Creative Enterprises *(P-8444)*

Bio Cybernetics International .... F......909 447-7050
  2701 Kimball Ave Pomona (91767) *(P-21985)*
Bio-Medical Devices Inc .... E......949 752-9642
  17171 Daimler St Irvine (92614) *(P-21628)*
Bio-Medical Devices Intl Inc .... F......800 443-3842
  17171 Daimler St Irvine (92614) *(P-21629)*
Bio-Nutraceuticals Inc .... D......818 727-0246
  21820 Marilla St Chatsworth (91311) *(P-7803)*
Bio-Nutritional RES Group Inc (PA) .... D......714 427-6990
  6 Morgan Ste 100 Irvine (92618) *(P-582)*
Bio-RAD Laboratories Inc (PA) .... B......510 724-7000
  1000 Alfred Nobel Dr Hercules (94547) *(P-22232)*
Bio-RAD Laboratories Inc .... A......510 741-6916
  225 Linus Pauling Dr Hercules (94547) *(P-21185)*
Bio-RAD Laboratories Inc .... B......949 789-0685
  21 Technology Dr Irvine (92618) *(P-21186)*
Bio-RAD Laboratories Inc .... C......949 598-1200
  9500 Jeronimo Rd Irvine (92618) *(P-7646)*
Bio-RAD Laboratories Inc .... C......510 741-1000
  2000 Alfred Nobel Dr Hercules (94547) *(P-21187)*
Bio-RAD Laboratories Inc .... C......510 741-6709
  4000 Alfred Nobel Dr Hercules (94547) *(P-21188)*
Bio-RAD Laboratories Inc .... A......510 232-7000
  2000 Alfred Nobel Dr Hercules (94547) *(P-21189)*
Bio-RAD Laboratories Inc .... B......510 741-6715
  6000 James Watson Dr Hercules (94547) *(P-21190)*
Bio-RAD Laboratories Inc .... B......510 741-6999
  2000 Alfred Nobel Dr Hercules (94547) *(P-21191)*
Bio-RAD Laboratories Inc .... B......510 232-7000
  3110 Regatta Ave Richmond (94804) *(P-21192)*
Bio-RAD Laboratories Inc .... E......510 741-5790
  5400 E 2nd St Benicia (94510) *(P-21193)*
Bio-RAD Laboratories Inc .... B......510 724-7000
  2500 Atlas Rd Richmond (94806) *(P-21194)*
Bio-RAD Labs, Richmond Also called Bio-RAD Laboratories Inc *(P-21192)*
Bio-Zone Laboratories, Pittsburg Also called Biozone Laboratories Inc *(P-7814)*
BIO2, Westminster Also called Biolargo Inc *(P-7472)*
Biocalth International Inc .... F......909 267-3988
  1920 Wright Ave La Verne (91750) *(P-7804)*
Biocare Medical LLC .... C......925 603-8000
  60 Berry Dr Pacheco (94553) *(P-21630)*
Biocentury Publications Inc (PA) .... E......650 595-5333
  1235 Radio Rd Ste 100 Redwood City (94065) *(P-5567)*
Biocheck Inc .... E......650 573-1968
  425 Eccles Ave South San Francisco (94080) *(P-21631)*
Biodico Westside LLC .... F......805 683-8103
  426 Donze Ave Santa Barbara (93101) *(P-8722)*
Biodot Inc (PA) .... E......949 440-3685
  2852 Alton Pkwy Irvine (92606) *(P-20840)*
Bioelectron Technology Corp (PA) .... E......650 641-9200
  350 Bernardo Ave Mountain View (94043) *(P-7805)*
Biofilm Inc .... D......760 727-9030
  3225 Executive Rdg Vista (92081) *(P-21632)*
Biogeneral Inc .... F......858 453-4451
  9925 Mesa Rim Rd San Diego (92121) *(P-21633)*
Biogenex Laboratories (PA) .... E......510 824-1400
  49026 Milmont Dr Fremont (94538) *(P-21634)*
Bioinitiatives Inc .... E......916 780-9100
  7641 Galilee Rd Ste 110 Roseville (95678) *(P-21635)*
Biokey Inc .... E......510 668-0881
  44370 Old Warm Springs Bl Fremont (94538) *(P-7806)*
Biolargo Inc (PA) .... F......949 643-9540
  14921 Chestnut St Westminster (92683) *(P-7472)*
Biolase Inc (PA) .... C......949 361-1200
  4 Cromwell Irvine (92618) *(P-22138)*
Biolegend Inc (PA) .... C......858 455-9588
  8999 Biolegend Way San Diego (92121) *(P-8282)*
Biolog Inc .... E......510 785-2564
  21124 Cabot Blvd Hayward (94545) *(P-21195)*
Biom LLC .... F......858 717-2995
  9655 Gran Rdge Dr Ste 200 San Diego (92123) *(P-21986)*
Biomarin Pharmaceutical Inc (PA) .... B......415 506-6700
  770 Lindaro St San Rafael (94901) *(P-7807)*
Biomarin Pharmaceutical Inc .... F......415 506-3258
  21 Pimentel Ct Novato (94949) *(P-7808)*
Biomarin Pharmaceutical Inc .... F......415 218-7386
  79 Digital Dr Novato (94949) *(P-7809)*
Biomechanical Analysis & .... E......714 990-5932
  20509 Earlgate St Walnut (91789) *(P-21987)*
Biomechanical Services, Walnut Also called Biomechanical Analysis & *(P-21987)*
Biomed Instruments Inc .... F......714 459-5716
  1511 Alto Ln Fullerton (92831) *(P-22233)*
Biomer Technology LLC .... F......925 426-0787
  1233 Quarry Ln 135 Pleasanton (94566) *(P-8283)*
Biomerica Inc (PA) .... E......949 645-2111
  17571 Von Karman Ave Irvine (92614) *(P-21636)*
Biomet San Diego LLC .... F......760 942-2786
  1540 Rubenstein Ave Cardiff By The Sea (92007) *(P-21988)*
Biometric Solutions LLC .... F......408 625-7763
  41829 Albrae St Unit 110 Fremont (94538) *(P-15171)*
Biomicrolab Inc .... E......925 689-1200
  2500 Dean Lesher Dr Ste A Concord (94520) *(P-15640)*
Bionano Genomics Inc (PA) .... D......858 888-7600
  9540 Twne Cntre Dr Ste 10 San Diego (92121) *(P-21196)*
Bioness Inc .... C......661 362-4850
  25103 Rye Canyon Loop Valencia (91355) *(P-22234)*
Bionicsound Inc .... F......714 300-4809
  390 Spar Ave Ste 104 San Jose (95117) *(P-21989)*
Bionikear.com, San Jose Also called Bionicsound Inc *(P-21989)*

Bionorica LLC......F......949 361-4900
903 Calle Amanecer # 110 San Clemente (92673) ***(P-7810)***
Biopac Systems Inc......E......805 685-0066
42 Aero Camino Goleta (93117) ***(P-21197)***
Biopharmx Corporation (PA)......E......650 889-5020
115 Nicholson Ln San Jose (95134) ***(P-7811)***
Biorad Inc......E......949 598-1200
9500 Jeronimo Rd Irvine (92618) ***(P-21198)***
Biorx Laboratories, Commerce *Also called Biorx Pharmaceuticals Inc* ***(P-7812)***
Biorx Pharmaceuticals Inc......E......323 725-3100
6465 Corvette St Commerce (90040) ***(P-7812)***
Bioscience Laboratories, Campbell *Also called Allergan Sales LLC* ***(P-7738)***
Bioscience Research Reagents, Temecula *Also called EMD Millipore Corporation* ***(P-8296)***
Bioseal......E......714 528-4695
167 W Orangethorpe Ave Placentia (92870) ***(P-21637)***
Biosearch Technologies Inc (HQ)......C......415 883-8400
2199 S Mcdowell Blvd Petaluma (94954) ***(P-8284)***
Biosense Webster Inc (HQ)......C......909 839-8500
33 Technology Dr Irvine (92618) ***(P-22235)***
Bioserv, San Diego *Also called Nextpharma Tech USA Inc* ***(P-8037)***
Bioserv Corporation......E......917 817-1326
5340 Eastgate Mall San Diego (92121) ***(P-8207)***
Bioserve, San Diego *Also called Bioserv Corporation* ***(P-8207)***
Biosig Technologies Inc......E......310 620-9320
12424 Wilshire Blvd # 745 Los Angeles (90025) ***(P-21638)***
Biosource International Inc......C......805 659-5759
5791 Van Allen Way Carlsbad (92008) ***(P-8208)***
Biospacific Inc (HQ)......F......510 652-6155
5980 Horton St Ste 360 Emeryville (94608) ***(P-8209)***
Biospherical Instruments Inc......F......619 686-1888
5340 Riley St San Diego (92110) ***(P-20547)***
Biosynthetic Technologies LLC (HQ)......F......949 390-5910
2 Park Plz Ste 200 Irvine (92614) ***(P-14350)***
Biosys Healthcare, Yorba Linda *Also called Viasys Respiratory Care Inc* ***(P-21957)***
Biota Technology Inc......F......650 888-6512
11095 Flintkote Ave Ste B San Diego (92121) ***(P-23670)***
Biotage LLC......F......408 267-7214
3670 Charter Park Dr B San Jose (95136) ***(P-21199)***
Biotech Energy of America......F......714 904-7844
30 Castro Ave San Rafael (94901) ***(P-8723)***
Biotherm Hydronic Inc......F......707 794-9660
476 Primero Ct Cotati (94931) ***(P-11691)***
Biotium Inc......F......510 265-1027
46117 Landing Pkwy Fremont (94538) ***(P-8697)***
Biotix Inc (HQ)......E......858 875-7696
10636 Scripps Summit Ct # 130 San Diego (92131) ***(P-8724)***
Biovail Technologies Ltd......C......703 995-2400
1 Enterprise Aliso Viejo (92656) ***(P-7813)***
Bioware Austin LLC......F......650 628-1500
209 Redwood Shores Pkwy Redwood City (94065) ***(P-23671)***
Biozone Laboratories Inc (HQ)......F......925 473-1000
580 Garcia Ave Pittsburg (94565) ***(P-7814)***
Biozone Laboratories Inc......E......925 431-1010
701 Willow Pass Rd Ste 8 Pittsburg (94565) ***(P-7815)***
Bipolarics Inc......E......408 372-7574
45920 Sentinel Pl Fremont (94539) ***(P-18147)***
Birchwood Cabinets Sonora Inc......F......209 532-1417
14375 Cuesta Ct Sonora (95370) ***(P-4169)***
Birchwood Lighting Inc......E......714 550-7118
3340 E La Palma Ave Anaheim (92806) ***(P-17105)***
Birdcage Press LLC......F......650 462-6300
2320 Bowdoin St Palo Alto (94306) ***(P-6200)***
Birdeye Inc (PA)......E......800 561-3357
250 Cambridge Ave Ste 103 Palo Alto (94306) ***(P-6201)***
Biscomerica Corp......C......909 877-5997
565 W Slover Ave Rialto (92377) ***(P-1307)***
Biscotti and Kate Mack, Oakland *Also called Mack & Reiss Inc* ***(P-3494)***
Biscotti House, Clovis *Also called Rosettis Fine Foods Inc* ***(P-1269)***
Bish Inc......E......619 660-6220
2820 Via Orange Way Ste G Spring Valley (91978) ***(P-20058)***
Bishamon Industries Corp......E......909 390-0055
5651 E Francis St Ontario (91761) ***(P-13860)***
Bishop-Wisecarver Corporation (PA)......D......925 439-8272
2104 Martin Way Pittsburg (94565) ***(P-13503)***
Bison Engineering Company......F......562 408-1525
15535 Texaco Ave Paramount (90723) ***(P-15791)***
Bit Group Usa Inc (PA)......D......858 613-1200
15870 Bernardo Center Dr San Diego (92127) ***(P-21639)***
Bit Medtech, San Diego *Also called Bit Group Usa Inc* ***(P-21639)***
Bitchin Inc......E......760 224-7447
6211 Yarrow Dr Ste C Carlsbad (92011) ***(P-2406)***
Bitchin Sauce, Carlsbad *Also called Bitchin Inc* ***(P-2406)***
Bitmax LLC (PA)......E......323 978-7878
6255 W Sunset Blvd # 1515 Los Angeles (90028) ***(P-17716)***
Bitmicro Networks Inc (PA)......F......510 743-3124
47929 Fremont Blvd Fremont (94538) ***(P-15008)***
Bitzer Mobile Inc......E......866 603-8392
4230 Leonard Stocking Dr Santa Clara (95054) ***(P-23672)***
Bivar Inc......E......949 951-8808
4 Thomas Irvine (92618) ***(P-18840)***
Bixby Knolls Prtg & Graphics, Fullerton *Also called Fullerton Printing Inc* ***(P-6588)***
Bixolon America Inc......F......858 764-4580
13705 Cimarron Ave Gardena (90249) ***(P-15172)***
Biz Launchers Inc......F......760 744-6604
1075 Linda Vista Dr San Marcos (92078) ***(P-6451)***
Biz Performance Solutions Inc......F......408 844-4284
840 Loma Vista St Moss Beach (94038) ***(P-23673)***
Bizinkcom LLC......F......818 676-0766
9822 Independence Ave Chatsworth (91311) ***(P-6999)***
Bizlink Technology Inc (HQ)......D......510 252-0786
47211 Bayside Pkwy Fremont (94538) ***(P-16878)***
Bizmatics Inc (PA)......C......408 873-3030
4010 Moorpark Ave Ste 222 San Jose (95117) ***(P-23674)***
Bizps, Moss Beach *Also called Biz Performance Solutions Inc* ***(P-23673)***
Bjb Enterprises Inc......E......714 734-8450
14791 Franklin Ave Tustin (92780) ***(P-7545)***
Bjc......F......310 977-6068
1356 Lomita Blvd Apt 1 Harbor City (90710) ***(P-2659)***
BJs Ukiah Embroidery......F......707 463-2767
272 E Smith St Ukiah (95482) ***(P-7000)***
BJS&t Enterprises Inc......F......619 448-7795
1702 N Magnolia Ave # 101 El Cajon (92020) ***(P-13150)***
Bk Sems Usa Inc......F......949 390-7120
4 Executive Park Ste 270 Irvine (92614) ***(P-4493)***
BK Signs Inc......F......626 334-5600
1028 W Kirkwall Rd Azusa (91702) ***(P-23060)***
Bkon Interior Soution......F......562 408-1655
15330 Allen St Paramount (90723) ***(P-4787)***
Black & Decker (us) Inc......F......562 925-7551
9020 Alondra Blvd Bellflower (90706) ***(P-14215)***
Black & Decker Corporation......F......909 390-5548
3949 E Guasti Rd Ste A Ontario (91761) ***(P-14216)***
Black Diamond Blade Company (PA)......E......800 949-9014
234 E O St Colton (92324) ***(P-13710)***
Black Diamond Manufacturing Co......F......925 439-9160
755 Bliss Ave Pittsburg (94565) ***(P-15792)***
Black Diamond Video Inc......D......510 439-4500
503 Canal Blvd Richmond (94804) ***(P-15173)***
Black Gold Pump & Supply Inc......F......323 298-0077
2459 Lewis Ave Signal Hill (90755) ***(P-172)***
Black Hills Nanosystems Corp......F......605 341-3641
1941 Jackson St 9 Oakland (94612) ***(P-18148)***
Black Media News, Winnetka *Also called Life Media Inc* ***(P-5977)***
Black N Gold, Paramount *Also called Kum Kang Trading USAinC* ***(P-8528)***
Black Oxide Industries Inc......E......714 870-9610
1745 N Orangethorpe Park Anaheim (92801) ***(P-12943)***
Black Oxide Service Inc......F......760 744-8692
1070 Linda Vista Dr Ste A San Marcos (92078) ***(P-12944)***
Black Phoenix Inc......F......818 506-9404
12120 Sherman Way North Hollywood (91605) ***(P-8445)***
Black Phoenix Alchemy Lab, North Hollywood *Also called Black Phoenix Inc* ***(P-8445)***
Black Point Products Inc......E......510 232-7723
2700 Rydin Rd Ste G Richmond (94804) ***(P-17350)***
Black Radio Exclusive Magazine, Sherman Oaks *Also called Sidney Millers Black Radio Ex* ***(P-6027)***
Black Silver Enterprises Inc (PA)......F......858 623-9220
6024 Paseo Delicias Rancho Santa Fe (92067) ***(P-3297)***
Black Stallion Winery LLC......F......707 253-1400
4089 Silverado Trl NAPA (94558) ***(P-1600)***
Black's Irrigation Systems, Chowchilla *Also called Blacks Irrigations Systems* ***(P-10537)***
Blackbaud Internet Solutions, San Diego *Also called Kintera Inc* ***(P-24079)***
Blackberry Corporation (HQ)......D......972 650-6126
3001 Bishop Dr San Ramon (94583) ***(P-23675)***
Blackburn Alton Invstments LLC......E......714 731-2000
700 E Alton Ave Santa Ana (92705) ***(P-7001)***
Blackcoffee Fabricators Inc......F......909 974-4499
777 W Mill St San Bernardino (92410) ***(P-23061)***
Blackcoffee Sign Fabricators, San Bernardino *Also called Blackcoffee Fabricators Inc* ***(P-23061)***
Blackline Manufacturing, Chico *Also called Mtech Inc* ***(P-9915)***
Blackline Systems Inc (HQ)......C......877 777-7750
21300 Victory Blvd Fl 12 Woodland Hills (91367) ***(P-23676)***
Blacklion Enterprises Inc (PA)......F......951 328-0400
1731 Bonita Vista Dr San Bernardino (92404) ***(P-12456)***
Blacks Irrigations Systems......F......559 665-4891
144 N Chowchilla Blvd Chowchilla (93610) ***(P-10537)***
Blackseries Campers Inc......E......626 579-1069
19501 E Walnut Dr S City of Industry (91748) ***(P-19814)***
Blacktalon Industries Inc......F......707 256-1812
481 Technology Way NAPA (94558) ***(P-13398)***
Blackthorn Therapeutics Inc......E......415 548-5401
780 Brannan St San Francisco (94103) ***(P-8210)***
Blacoh Fluid Controls Inc (PA)......F......951 342-3100
601 Columbia Ave Ste D Riverside (92507) ***(P-11997)***
Blaga Precision Inc......F......714 891-9509
11650 Seaboard Cir Stanton (90680) ***(P-15793)***
Blaha Oldrih......F......760 789-9791
114 10th St Ramona (92065) ***(P-14140)***
Blair Adhesive Products......F......562 946-6004
11034 Lockport Pl Santa Fe Springs (90670) ***(P-8856)***
Blairs Metal Polsg Pltg Co Inc......F......562 860-7106
17760 Crusader Ave Cerritos (90703) ***(P-12945)***
Blake Manufacturing, City of Industry *Also called Turnham Corporation* ***(P-14207)***
Blake Manufacturing Co, City of Industry *Also called Turnham Corporation* ***(P-14206)***
Blake Sign Company Inc......F......714 891-5682
11661 Seaboard Cir Stanton (90680) ***(P-23062)***
Blake Wire & Cable Corp......F......818 781-8300
16134 Runnymede St Van Nuys (91406) ***(P-11289)***
Blanchard Signs......F......951 354-5050
6750 Central Ave Ste A Riverside (92504) ***(P-23063)***
Blanco Basura Beverage Inc......C......888 705-7225
5776 Stoneridge Mall Rd # 338 Pleasanton (94588) ***(P-1503)***
Blank and Cables Inc......F......415 648-3842
3100 E 10th St Oakland (94601) ***(P-4557)***
Blanks Plus, Los Angeles *Also called Mj Blanks Inc* ***(P-2798)***
Blast Structures, Huntington Beach *Also called American Blast Systems Inc* ***(P-11025)***

ALPHABETIC

Employee Codes: A=Over 500 employees, B=251-500
C=101-250, D=51-100, E=20-50, F=10-19
2020 California
Manfacturers Register
© Mergent Inc. 1-800-342-5647
1041

Blasted Wood Products Inc ....F....714 237-1600
7108 Santa Rita Cir Buena Park (90620) ***(P-3927)***

Blastrac NA ....F....800 256-3440
5220 Gaines St San Diego (92110) ***(P-13711)***

Blastronix Inc ....F....209 795-0738
999 W Highway 4 Murphys (95247) ***(P-15174)***

Blazar Communications Corp ....F....949 336-7115
17951 Sky Park Cir Ste K Irvine (92614) ***(P-7304)***

Blazar Mailing Solutions, Irvine *Also called Blazar Communications Corp* ***(P-7304)***

Blazer Exhibits & Graphics Inc ....F....408 263-7000
4227 Technology Dr Fremont (94538) ***(P-23064)***

Blc Wc Inc (PA) ....C....562 926-1452
13260 Moore St Cerritos (90703) ***(P-7002)***

Blc Wc Inc ....E....510 489-5400
2900 Faber St Union City (94587) ***(P-14699)***

Blc Wc Inc ....E....510 471-4100
2935 Whipple Rd Union City (94587) ***(P-5358)***

Ble Inc ....F....818 504-9577
11360 Goss St Sun Valley (91352) ***(P-89)***

Blentech Corporation ....D....707 523-5949
2899 Dowd Dr Santa Rosa (95407) ***(P-14351)***

Blick Industries LLC ....F....949 499-5026
2245 Laguna Canyon Rd Laguna Beach (92651) ***(P-14700)***

Blind Squirrel Games Inc ....E....714 460-0860
1251 E Dyer Rd Ste 200 Santa Ana (92705) ***(P-23677)***

Blinking Owl Distillery ....F....949 370-4688
210 N Bush St Santa Ana (92701) ***(P-1504)***

Bliss Holdings LLC ....E....626 506-8696
745 S Vinewood St Escondido (92029) ***(P-17106)***

Blisslights Inc ....E....888 868-4603
100 E San Marcos Blvd # 308 San Marcos (92069) ***(P-19265)***

Blisslights LLC ....E....888 868-4603
100 E San Marcos Blvd # 308 San Marcos (92069) ***(P-17107)***

Blisterpak Inc ....E....323 728-5555
3020 Supply Ave Commerce (90040) ***(P-9666)***

Blitzers Premium Frozen Yogurt ....F....951 679-7709
29101 Newport Rd Menifee (92584) ***(P-632)***

Blitzz Technology Inc ....E....949 380-7709
53 Parker Irvine (92618) ***(P-17469)***

Blizzard Entertainment Inc (HQ) ....D....949 955-1380
1 Blizzard Irvine (92618) ***(P-23678)***

Block Alternatives ....F....661 729-2800
604 W Avenue L Ste 101 Lancaster (93534) ***(P-22764)***

Block Tops Inc (PA) ....E....714 978-5080
1321 S Sunkist St Anaheim (92806) ***(P-4884)***

Blocks Wearables Inc ....F....650 307-9557
1800 Century Park E Fl 10 Los Angeles (90067) ***(P-22477)***

Blomberg Building Materials (PA) ....D....916 428-8060
1453 Blair Ave Sacramento (95822) ***(P-11938)***

Blomberg Glass, Sacramento *Also called Blomberg Windows Systems* ***(P-10343)***

Blomberg Window Systems, Sacramento *Also called Blomberg Building Materials* ***(P-11938)***

Blomberg Window Systems, Sacramento *Also called Architectural Blomberg LLC* ***(P-11932)***

Blomberg Windows Systems ....C....916 428-8060
1453 Blair Ave Sacramento (95822) ***(P-10343)***

Blommer Chocolate Co Cal Inc ....C....510 471-4300
1515 Pacific St Union City (94587) ***(P-1407)***

Blommer Chocolate Company ....E....510 471-3401
1515 Pacific St Union City (94587) ***(P-1357)***

Bloom Energy Corporation (PA) ....B....408 543-1500
4353 N 1st St San Jose (95134) ***(P-18149)***

Bloomers Metal Stampings Inc ....E....661 257-2955
28615 Braxton Ave Valencia (91355) ***(P-12772)***

Bloomfield Bakers ....A....626 610-2253
10711 Bloomfield St Los Alamitos (90720) ***(P-1308)***

Blossom Apple Moulding & Mllwk ....E....925 820-2345
2411 Old Crow Canyon Rd L San Ramon (94583) ***(P-4003)***

Blossom Valley Foods Inc ....E....408 848-5520
20 Casey Ln Gilroy (95020) ***(P-2194)***

Blow Molded Products Inc ....E....951 360-6055
4720 Felspar St Riverside (92509) ***(P-9667)***

Blower Drive Service Co ....E....562 693-4302
1280 W Lambert Rd Ste B Brea (92821) ***(P-19594)***

Blower-Dempsay Corporation ....D....714 547-9266
4044 W Garry Ave Santa Ana (92704) ***(P-5201)***

Blowout Tools Inc ....F....661 746-1700
19484 Broken Ct Shafter (93263) ***(P-173)***

Bltee LLC ....E....213 802-1736
7101 Telegraph Rd Montebello (90640) ***(P-3141)***

Blu Heaven, Commerce *Also called Alliance Apparel Inc* ***(P-3136)***

Blue Book Publishers Inc (PA) ....D....858 454-7939
9820 Willow Creek Rd # 410 San Diego (92131) ***(P-6202)***

Blue California Company, Rcho STA Marg *Also called Phyto Tech Corp* ***(P-8076)***

Blue Can Water (PA) ....F....818 450-3290
8309 Laurel Cny Blvd 219 Sun Valley (91352) ***(P-2043)***

Blue Cedar Networks Inc ....E....415 329-0401
325 Pacific Ave Fl 1 San Francisco (94111) ***(P-15175)***

Blue Circle Corp ....F....562 531-2711
7520 Monroe St Paramount (90723) ***(P-12668)***

Blue Coat LLC ....A....408 220-2200
350 Ellis St Mountain View (94043) ***(P-23679)***

Blue Coat Systems LLC (HQ) ....D....650 527-8000
350 Ellis St Mountain View (94043) ***(P-23680)***

Blue Cross Beauty Products Inc ....E....818 896-8681
557 Jessie St San Fernando (91340) ***(P-8446)***

Blue Cross Laboratories Inc (PA) ....C....661 255-0955
20950 Centre Pointe Pkwy Santa Clarita (91350) ***(P-8368)***

Blue Danube Systems Inc (PA) ....F....650 316-5010
3131 Jay St Ste 201 Santa Clara (95054) ***(P-17470)***

Blue Desert International Inc ....D....951 273-7575
510 N Sheridan St Ste A Corona (92880) ***(P-15493)***

Blue Diamond, Turlock *Also called Blue Diamond Growers* ***(P-2408)***

Blue Diamond Growers ....C....916 446-8464
1701 C St Sacramento (95811) ***(P-2407)***

Blue Diamond Growers ....C....559 251-4044
10840 E Mckinley Ave Sanger (93657) ***(P-1422)***

Blue Diamond Growers ....D....209 604-1501
1300 N Washington Rd Turlock (95380) ***(P-2408)***

Blue Eagle Stucco Products ....F....559 485-4100
1407 N Clark St Fresno (93703) ***(P-10998)***

Blue Engravers, Long Beach *Also called Midonna Inc* ***(P-7142)***

Blue Iron Network Inc ....E....714 901-1456
5811 Mcfadden Ave Huntington Beach (92649) ***(P-23681)***

Blue Lake Roundstock Co LLC ....F....530 515-7007
19195 Latona Rd Anderson (96007) ***(P-4471)***

Blue Microphone, Westlake Village *Also called Baltic Ltvian Unvrsal Elec LLC* ***(P-17200)***

Blue Microphones LLC ....F....818 879-5200
5706 Corsa Ave Ste 102 Westlake Village (91362) ***(P-17206)***

Blue Mtn Ctr of Meditation Inc ....E....707 878-2369
3600 Tomales Rd Tomales (94971) ***(P-6079)***

Blue Nalu Inc ....F....858 703-8703
6197 Cornerstone Ct E San Diego (92121) ***(P-14352)***

Blue PCF Flvors Fragrances Inc ....E....626 934-0099
1354 Marion Ct City of Industry (91745) ***(P-2195)***

Blue Ribbon Cont & Display Inc ....F....562 944-1217
11106 Shoemaker Ave Santa Fe Springs (90670) ***(P-5202)***

Blue Ribbon Sheepskin, San Diego *Also called Motorlamb International Acc* ***(P-3850)***

Blue Rock Networks LLC ....F....415 577-8004
1160 Battery St Ste 100 San Francisco (94111) ***(P-21012)***

Blue Sky Energy Inc ....F....760 597-1642
2598 Fortune Way Ste K Vista (92081) ***(P-16779)***

Blue Sky Home & ACC Inc ....E....909 930-6200
1360 E Locust St Ontario (91761) ***(P-377)***

Blue Sky Remediation Svcs Inc ....F....626 961-5736
14000 Valley Blvd La Puente (91746) ***(P-17717)***

Blue Sky Research Incorporated (PA) ....E....408 941-6068
510 Alder Dr Milpitas (95035) ***(P-21335)***

Blue Sphere Inc ....E....714 953-7555
10869 Portal Dr Los Alamitos (90720) ***(P-2961)***

Blue Squirrel Inc ....D....858 268-0717
8295 Aero Pl San Diego (92123) ***(P-17718)***

Blue-White Industries Ltd (PA) ....D....714 893-8529
5300 Business Dr Huntington Beach (92649) ***(P-20961)***

Bluebarry Enterprises Inc ....F....818 956-0912
16525 Sherman Way Ste C11 Van Nuys (91406) ***(P-6452)***

Bluefield Associates Inc ....E....909 476-6027
14900 Hilton Dr Fontana (92336) ***(P-8447)***

Bluefrog Embroidery, San Leandro *Also called Double V Industries* ***(P-3737)***

Bluegate Surface Works Inc ....F....562 630-9005
15936 Downey Ave Paramount (90723) ***(P-4170)***

Bluenalu, San Diego *Also called Blue Nalu Inc* ***(P-14352)***

Bluerun Ventures LP ....F....650 462-7250
545 Middlefield Rd # 210 Menlo Park (94025) ***(P-23682)***

Bluescope Buildings N Amer Inc ....C....559 651-5300
7440 W Doe Ave Visalia (93291) ***(P-12535)***

Bluesnap Inc ....E....866 475-4687
5201 Great America Pkwy # 320 Santa Clara (95054) ***(P-23683)***

Bluestack Systems Inc ....E....408 412-9439
2105 S Bascom Ave Ste 380 Campbell (95008) ***(P-23684)***

Bluetone Muffler Mfg Co ....E....626 442-1073
9366 Klingerman St South El Monte (91733) ***(P-19595)***

Bluewater Publishing LLC ....F....925 634-0880
9040 Brentwood Blvd Ste B Brentwood (94513) ***(P-6203)***

Bluewater Wear, Santa Ana *Also called Aftco Mfg Co Inc* ***(P-22734)***

Blum Construction Co Inc ....F....408 629-3740
404 Umbarger Rd Ste A San Jose (95111) ***(P-11939)***

Bluprint Clothing Corp ....D....323 780-4347
5600 Bandini Blvd Bell (90201) ***(P-3142)***

Blur Leather, Los Angeles *Also called Luna Mora LLC* ***(P-3798)***

Blurb Inc ....D....415 364-6300
580 California St Fl 3 San Francisco (94104) ***(P-6080)***

Blvd, Los Angeles *Also called Boulevard Style Inc* ***(P-3143)***

Blythe Energy Inc ....F....760 922-9950
385 N Buck Blvd Blythe (92225) ***(P-79)***

Bmb Metal Products Corporation ....E....916 631-9120
11460 Elks Cir Rancho Cordova (95742) ***(P-12132)***

BMC East LLC ....F....818 842-8139
161 W Cypress Ave Burbank (91502) ***(P-4004)***

BMC Industries, Bakersfield *Also called Bakersfield Machine Company* ***(P-15773)***

Bmci Inc ....E....951 361-8000
1689 S Parco Ave Ontario (91761) ***(P-14264)***

Bmi, Temecula *Also called Bomatic Inc* ***(P-9669)***

Bmi Products Northern Cal Inc ....F....408 293-4008
990 Ames Ave Milpitas (95035) ***(P-10999)***

Bmp, Riverside *Also called Blow Molded Products Inc* ***(P-9667)***

BMW Precision Machining Inc ....E....760 439-6813
2379 Industry St Oceanside (92054) ***(P-15794)***

Bni, Chatsworth *Also called Bio-Nutraceuticals Inc* ***(P-7803)***

Bnk Petroleum (us) Inc ....E....805 484-3613
760 Paseo Camarillo # 350 Camarillo (93010) ***(P-110)***

Bnl Technologies Inc ....E....310 320-7272
20525 Manhattan Pl Torrance (90501) ***(P-15009)***

BNP Enterprises LLC ....F....949 770-5438
22902 Roebuck St Lake Forest (92630) ***(P-19596)***

Bnrg, Irvine *Also called Bio-Nutritional RES Group Inc* ***(P-582)***

Bo Dean Co Inc (PA) ....E....707 576-8205
1060 N Dutton Ave Santa Rosa (95401) ***(P-289)***

Bo-Sherrel Corporation ....F....510 744-3525
3340 Tree Swallow Pl Fremont (94555) ***(P-15176)***

Boardhouse, Gardena *Also called L&F Wood LLC* ***(P-4073)***

Boardriders Inc (HQ) ....C....714 889-2200
5600 Argosy Ave Ste 100 Huntington Beach (92649) ***(P-3071)***
Boards On Nord Inc ....F....530 513-3922
14822 Meridian Meadows Ln Chico (95973) ***(P-22765)***
Boardwalk Solutions, Gardena *Also called Ocean Direct LLC* ***(P-2267)***
Boatworks ....F....805 374-9455
2251 Townsgate Rd Westlake Village (91361) ***(P-20316)***
Boatyard-Channel Islands, The, Oxnard *Also called Tbyci LLC* ***(P-20359)***
Bob Lewis Machine Company Inc ....F....310 538-9406
1324 W 135th St Gardena (90247) ***(P-15795)***
Bob Martin Co, South El Monte *Also called Robert P Martin Company* ***(P-11105)***
Bobboi Natural Gelato, La Jolla *Also called Berenice 2 AM Corp* ***(P-630)***
Bobby Salazar Corporate, Fowler *Also called Bobby Slzars Mxcan Fd Pdts Inc* ***(P-720)***
Bobby Slzars Mxcan Fd Pdts Inc (PA) ....E....559 834-4787
2810 San Antonio Dr Fowler (93625) ***(P-720)***
Bobbys Metal Finishing ....F....818 837-1928
12423 Gladstone Ave # 25 Sylmar (91342) ***(P-12946)***
Bobs Iron Inc ....E....510 567-8983
740 Kevin Ct Oakland (94621) ***(P-11750)***
Bobster Eyewear, San Diego *Also called Balboa Manufacturing Co LLC* ***(P-2772)***
Boc Gases, Richmond *Also called Messer LLC* ***(P-7423)***
Bocchi Laboratories, Santa Clarita *Also called Shadow Holdings LLC* ***(P-8578)***
Bocchi Laboratories, Santa Clarita *Also called Shadow Holdings LLC* ***(P-8579)***
Bock Machine Company Inc ....F....909 947-7250
2141 S Parco Ave Ontario (91761) ***(P-15796)***
Bode Concrete LLC ....D....415 920-7100
755 Stockton Ave San Jose (95126) ***(P-10697)***
Body Care Resort Inc ....F....310 328-8888
22125 S Vermont Ave Torrance (90502) ***(P-16825)***
Body Dope, Berkeley *Also called Two Star Dog Inc* ***(P-3202)***
Body Flex Sports, Walnut *Also called Hupa International Inc* ***(P-22823)***
Body Flex Sports Inc (PA) ....F....909 598-9876
21717 Ferrero Walnut (91789) ***(P-22766)***
Body Glove International LLC ....F....310 374-3441
6255 W Sunset Blvd # 650 Hollywood (90028) ***(P-3072)***
Bodycote Imt Inc ....D....714 893-6561
7474 Garden Grove Blvd Westminster (92683) ***(P-11434)***
Bodycote Thermal Proc Inc ....F....323 264-0111
2900 S Sunol Dr Vernon (90058) ***(P-11435)***
Bodycote Thermal Proc Inc ....E....310 604-8000
515 W Apra St Ste A Compton (90220) ***(P-11436)***
Bodycote Thermal Proc Inc ....D....714 893-6561
7474 Garden Grove Blvd Westminster (92683) ***(P-11437)***
Bodycote Thermal Proc Inc ....D....323 583-1231
3370 Benedict Way Huntington Park (90255) ***(P-12947)***
Bodycote Thermal Proc Inc ....E....562 693-3135
11845 Burke St Santa Fe Springs (90670) ***(P-11438)***
Bodycote Thermal Proc Inc ....E....510 492-4200
4240 Technology Dr Fremont (94538) ***(P-11439)***
Bodycote Thermal Proc Inc ....E....562 946-1717
9921 Romandel Ave Santa Fe Springs (90670) ***(P-11440)***
Bodycote Usa Inc ....F....323 264-0111
2900 S Sunol Dr Vernon (90058) ***(P-11441)***
Boeger Winery Inc ....E....530 622-8094
1709 Carson Rd Placerville (95667) ***(P-1601)***
Boeing Company ....E....559 998-8260
Lemoore Nval Base Hnger 1 Lemoore (93245) ***(P-19859)***
Boeing Company ....A....310 662-7286
22308 Harbor Ridge Ln Torrance (90502) ***(P-19860)***
Boeing Company ....B....714 896-3311
5301 Bolsa Ave Huntington Beach (92647) ***(P-20443)***
Boeing Company ....A....562 797-5831
2201 Seal Beach Blvd Seal Beach (90740) ***(P-19861)***
Boeing Company ....A....714 952-1509
5463 Plumeria Ln Cypress (90630) ***(P-19862)***
Boeing Company ....A....949 452-0259
24172 Via Madrugada Mission Viejo (92692) ***(P-19863)***
Boeing Company ....E....559 998-8214
210 Reeves Blvd Bldg 210 # 210 Lemoore (93246) ***(P-20548)***
Boeing Company ....A....661 810-4686
122 E Jones Rd Bldg 151 Edwards (93524) ***(P-19864)***
Boeing Company ....A....714 317-1070
3521 E Spring St Long Beach (90806) ***(P-19865)***
Boeing Company ....A....562 593-6668
2400 E Wardlow Rd Long Beach (90807) ***(P-19866)***
Boeing Company ....A....562 944-6583
12203 Hillwood Dr Whittier (90604) ***(P-19867)***
Boeing Company ....A....562 425-3613
3460 Cherry Ave Bldg 56 Long Beach (90807) ***(P-19868)***
Boeing Company ....A....760 246-0273
18310 Readiness St Victorville (92394) ***(P-19869)***
Boeing Company ....E....310 662-9000
900 N Pacific Coast Hwy El Segundo (90245) ***(P-17471)***
Boeing Company ....A....714 934-9801
15400 Graham St Ste 101 Huntington Beach (92649) ***(P-19870)***
Boeing Company ....D....310 426-4100
222 N Pacific Coast Hwy # 2050 El Segundo (90245) ***(P-19871)***
Boeing Company ....A....714 372-5361
2201 Seal Beach Blvd Seal Beach (90740) ***(P-17472)***
Boeing Company ....A....714 896-3311
5301 Bolsa Ave Huntington Beach (92647) ***(P-19872)***
Boeing Company ....E....562 593-5511
3855 N Lakewood Blvd D35-0072 Long Beach (90846) ***(P-20549)***
Boeing Company ....A....562 496-1000
4000 N Lakewood Blvd Long Beach (90808) ***(P-19873)***
Boeing Company ....A....714 896-1301
5301 Bolsa Ave Huntington Beach (92647) ***(P-19874)***
Boeing Company ....B....661 212-0024
1500 E Avenue M Palmdale (93550) ***(P-20550)***
Boeing Company ....A....562 593-5511
4000 N Lakewood Blvd Long Beach (90808) ***(P-19875)***
Boeing Company ....A....714 896-1670
14441 Astronautics Ln Huntington Beach (92647) ***(P-19876)***
Boeing Company ....A....707 437-8574
451 1st St Travis Afb (94535) ***(P-19877)***
Boeing Company ....A....714 896-1839
5301 Bolsa Ave Huntington Beach (92647) ***(P-19878)***
Boeing Company ....E....714 896-3311
5222 Rancho Rd Huntington Beach (92647) ***(P-19879)***
Boeing Company ....A....310 416-9319
1700 E Imperial Ave El Segundo (90245) ***(P-19880)***
Boeing Company ....A....818 428-1154
8900 De Soto Ave Canoga Park (91304) ***(P-19881)***
Boeing Company ....A....951 571-0122
5250 Tanker Way March ARB (92518) ***(P-19882)***
Boeing Intellectual ....E....562 797-2020
3501 Bolsa Ave Huntington Beach (92647) ***(P-19883)***
Boeing Satellite Systems ....D....310 364-5088
2060 E Imperial Hwy Fl 1 El Segundo (90245) ***(P-20551)***
Boeing Satellite Systems Inc ....F....310 568-2735
2300 E Imperial Hwy El Segundo (90245) ***(P-19884)***
Boeing Satellite Systems Inc ....E....310 364-6444
1950 E Imperial Hwy El Segundo (90245) ***(P-19885)***
Boeing Satellite Systems Inc (HQ) ....E....310 791-7450
900 N Pacific Coast Hwy El Segundo (90245) ***(P-17473)***
Bogner Amplification ....F....818 765-8929
11411 Vanowen St North Hollywood (91605) ***(P-17207)***
Bohan Cnlis - Astin Creek Rdym ....F....707 632-5296
1528 Copperhill Pkwy F Santa Rosa (95403) ***(P-312)***
Bohns Printing ....F....661 948-8081
656 W Lancaster Blvd Lancaster (93534) ***(P-6453)***
Boinca Inc (PA) ....F....714 809-6313
15000 S Avalon Blvd Ste F Gardena (90248) ***(P-8448)***
Boinca Inc ....F....619 398-7252
1611 S Rancho Santa Fe Rd San Marcos (92078) ***(P-8449)***
Boise Cascade Company ....E....209 983-4114
12030 S Harlan Rd Lathrop (95330) ***(P-5099)***
Bojer Inc ....E....626 334-1711
177 S Peckham Rd Azusa (91702) ***(P-3603)***
Bolcof Plstic Mtls Stheast Inc ....F....800 621-2681
960 W 10th St Azusa (91702) ***(P-7546)***
Bolcof Port Polymers, Azusa *Also called Bolcof Plstic Mtls Stheast Inc* ***(P-7546)***
Bold Data Technology Inc ....E....510 490-8296
47540 Seabridge Dr Fremont (94538) ***(P-14892)***
Bolero Inds Inc A Cal Corp ....E....562 693-3000
11850 Burke St Santa Fe Springs (90670) ***(P-9668)***
Bolero Plastics, Santa Fe Springs *Also called Bolero Inds Inc A Cal Corp* ***(P-9668)***
Bolide International, San Dimas *Also called Bolide Technology Group Inc* ***(P-19266)***
Bolide Technology Group Inc ....D....909 305-8889
468 S San Dimas Ave San Dimas (91773) ***(P-19266)***
Bolttech Mannings Inc ....D....310 604-9500
16926 Keegan Ave Carson (90746) ***(P-14217)***
Bolttech Mannings Inc ....D....707 751-0157
475 Industrial Way Benicia (94510) ***(P-14218)***
Bomark Inc ....E....626 968-1666
601 S 6th Ave La Puente (91746) ***(P-8910)***
Bomatic Inc (HQ) ....E....909 947-3900
43225 Business Park Dr Temecula (92590) ***(P-9669)***
Bomatic Inc ....E....909 947-3900
2181 E Francis St Ontario (91761) ***(P-9670)***
Bombardier Transportation ....D....323 224-3461
1555 N San Fernando Rd Los Angeles (90065) ***(P-20367)***
Bon Appetit Bakery, Vernon *Also called Bon Appetit Danish Inc* ***(P-1168)***
Bon Appetit Danish Inc ....D....323 584-9500
4525 District Blvd Vernon (90058) ***(P-1168)***
Bonafide Management Systems ....F....805 777-7666
241 Lombard St Thousand Oaks (91360) ***(P-23685)***
Bond Furs Inc ....F....626 471-9912
114 W Lime Ave Monrovia (91016) ***(P-3498)***
Bond Manufacturing Co Inc (PA) ....D....925 252-1135
2516 Verne Roberts Cir H3 Antioch (94509) ***(P-10538)***
Bonded Fiberloft Inc ....B....323 726-7820
2748 Tanager Ave Commerce (90040) ***(P-2671)***
Bonded Window Coverings Inc ....E....858 974-7700
7831 Ostrow St San Diego (92111) ***(P-5016)***
Bondline Elctrnic Adhsive Corp ....E....408 830-9200
777 N Pastoria Ave Sunnyvale (94085) ***(P-8857)***
Bonehead Composites, Perris *Also called J F Christopher Inc* ***(P-22833)***
Bonelli Enterprises ....E....650 873-3222
330 Corey Way South San Francisco (94080) ***(P-11940)***
Bonelli Fine Food Inc ....F....650 906-9896
3525 Del Mar Heights Rd San Diego (92130) ***(P-536)***
Bonelli Windows and Doors, South San Francisco *Also called Bonelli Enterprises* ***(P-11940)***
Bonneau Wines LLC ....F....707 996-0420
75 Bonneau Rd Sonoma (95476) ***(P-1602)***
Bonner Metal Processing LLC ....E....925 455-3833
6052 Industrial Way Ste A Livermore (94551) ***(P-12586)***
Bonner Processing Inc ....E....925 455-3833
6052 Industrial Way Ste A Livermore (94551) ***(P-12948)***
Bonnier Corporation ....D....760 707-0100
15255 Alton Pkwy Irvine (92618) ***(P-5890)***
Bonny Doon Vineyard (PA) ....F....831 425-3625
328 Ingalls St Santa Cruz (95060) ***(P-1603)***
Bonny Doon Winery Inc ....D....831 425-3625
328 Ingalls St Santa Cruz (95060) ***(P-1604)***
Bonsai Ai Inc ....E....510 900-1112
2150 Shattuck Ave # 1200 Berkeley (94704) ***(P-23686)***
Bonsal American Inc ....E....714 523-1530
16005 Phoebe Ave La Mirada (90638) ***(P-10539)***

ALPHABETIC

Employee Codes: A=Over 500 employees, B=251-500
C=101-250, D=51-100, E=20-50, F=10-19
2020 California
Manfacturers Register
© Mergent Inc. 1-800-342-5647
1043

Boochcraft, Chula Vista *Also called Boochery Inc* ***(P-2010)***
Boochery Inc ..... F 619 738-1008
684 Anita St Ste F Chula Vista (91911) ***(P-2010)***
Book Binders, Pico Rivera *Also called Kater-Crafts Incorporated* ***(P-7338)***
Bookette Software Co Inc ..... F 831 484-9250
12795 Corte Cordillera Salinas (93908) ***(P-23687)***
Bookpack Inc ..... F 510 601-8301
3286 Adeline St Ste 1 Berkeley (94703) ***(P-6204)***
Boom Industrial Inc ..... D 909 495-3555
167 University Pkwy Pomona (91768) ***(P-14435)***
Boom Movement LLC ..... D 410 358-3600
1 Viper Way Ste 3 Vista (92081) ***(P-17208)***
Boone Printing & Graphics Inc ..... D 805 683-2349
70 S Kellogg Ave Ste 8 Goleta (93117) ***(P-7003)***
Boosted Inc (PA) ..... E 650 933-5151
82 Pioneer Way Ste 200 Mountain View (94041) ***(P-22767)***
Boosted Boards, Mountain View *Also called Boosted Inc* ***(P-22767)***
Boostpower USA Inc ..... F 805 376-6077
2560 Calcite Cir Newbury Park (91320) ***(P-13584)***
Boozak Inc ..... E 951 245-6045
508 Chaney St Ste A Lake Elsinore (92530) ***(P-12133)***
Boral Roofing LLC ..... E 209 982-1473
9508 S Harlan Rd French Camp (95231) ***(P-10540)***
Boral Roofing LLC ..... D 209 983-1600
342 Roth Rd Lathrop (95330) ***(P-10541)***
Boral Roofing LLC ..... D 909 822-4407
3511 N Riverside Ave Rialto (92377) ***(P-10542)***
Bordeaux, Los Angeles *Also called Jamm Industries Corp* ***(P-3342)***
Borden Decal Company Inc ..... E 415 431-1587
870 Harrison St Unit 101 San Francisco (94107) ***(P-7004)***
Borden Lighting ..... E 510 357-0171
2355 Verna Ct San Leandro (94577) ***(P-17015)***
Borden Manufacturing ..... E 530 347-6642
3314 Pacific Trl Cottonwood (96022) ***(P-13970)***
Bordenaves, San Rafael *Also called Bordenaves Marin Baking* ***(P-1169)***
Bordenaves Marin Baking ..... D 415 453-2957
1512 4th St San Rafael (94901) ***(P-1169)***
Border Precast Inc ..... F 760 351-1233
615 Us Highway 111 Brawley (92227) ***(P-10543)***
Bore-Max, El Monte *Also called GAI Manufacturing Co LLC* ***(P-13800)***
Boresha International Inc ..... E 925 676-1400
7041 Koll Center Pkwy # 100 Pleasanton (94566) ***(P-2277)***
Borett Automation Technologies ..... F 818 597-8664
3824 Bowsprit Cir Westlake Village (91361) ***(P-14799)***
Borga Stl Bldngs Cmponents Inc ..... E 559 834-5375
300 W Peach St Fowler (93625) ***(P-12134)***
Borges Rock Product, Sun Valley *Also called Over & Over Ready Mix Inc* ***(P-10619)***
Borin Manufacturing Inc ..... E 310 822-1000
5741 Buckingham Pkwy B Culver City (90230) ***(P-14562)***
Boring Thrading Bars Unlimited, Vista *Also called Alvarado Micro Precision Inc* ***(P-15733)***
Boris Bs Frms Vtrnary Svcs Inc ..... D 916 730-4225
9245 Laguna Springs Dr Elk Grove (95758) ***(P-1085)***
Borland Software Corporation ..... D 650 286-1900
951 Mariners Isl Blvd # 460 San Mateo (94404) ***(P-23688)***
Borsos Engineering Inc ..... E 760 930-0296
5924 Balfour Ct Ste 102 Carlsbad (92008) ***(P-14893)***
Bos, San Marcos *Also called Black Oxide Service Inc* ***(P-12944)***
Bosch Diagnostics, Santa Barbara *Also called Robert Bosch LLC* ***(P-21882)***
Bosch Enrgy Stor Solutions LLC ..... F 650 320-2933
4005 Miranda Ave Ste 200 Palo Alto (94304) ***(P-16633)***
Boscogen Inc ..... E 949 380-4317
8 Chrysler Irvine (92618) ***(P-7816)***
Boss, Commerce *Also called Norstar Office Products Inc* ***(P-4812)***
Boss Litho Inc ..... E 626 912-7088
2380 Peck Rd City of Industry (90601) ***(P-6454)***
Boss Printing Inc ..... F 714 545-2677
3403 W Macarthur Blvd Santa Ana (92704) ***(P-6455)***
Bostik Inc ..... D 951 296-6425
27460 Bostik Ct Temecula (92590) ***(P-8858)***
Boston Scientific - Valencia, Valencia *Also called Boston Scientific Corporation* ***(P-21641)***
Boston Scientific Corporation ..... B 661 645-6668
28460 Avenue Stanford Valencia (91355) ***(P-21640)***
Boston Scientific Corporation ..... C 408 935-3400
150 Baytech Dr San Jose (95134) ***(P-21990)***
Boston Scientific Corporation ..... E 800 678-2575
25155 Rye Canyon Loop Valencia (91355) ***(P-21641)***
Boston Scntfic Nrmdlation Corp ..... F 661 949-4869
25129 Rye Canyon Loop Valencia (91355) ***(P-21991)***
Boston Scntfic Nrmdlation Corp (HQ) ..... B 661 949-4310
25155 Rye Canyon Loop Valencia (91355) ***(P-21992)***
Bot N Bot Inc ..... F 562 906-4873
13005 Los Nietos Rd Santa Fe Springs (90670) ***(P-2318)***
Botanas Mexico Inc ..... F 626 279-1512
11122 Rush St South El Monte (91733) ***(P-2409)***
Botanicalabs Inc ..... F 818 466-5639
21900 Plummer St Chatsworth (91311) ***(P-8450)***
Botanx LLC ..... E 714 854-1601
3357 E Miraloma Ave # 156 Anaheim (92806) ***(P-8451)***
Botner Manufacturing Inc ..... F 510 569-2943
900 Aladdin Ave San Leandro (94577) ***(P-12135)***
Bottelsen Dart Co Inc ..... F 805 922-4519
945 W Mccoy Ln Santa Maria (93455) ***(P-22663)***
Bottle Coatings, Sun Valley *Also called Sundial Powder Coatings Inc* ***(P-13257)***
Bottlemate Inc ..... E 323 887-9009
2095 Leo Ave Commerce (90040) ***(P-9671)***
Bottlers Unlimited Inc ..... E 707 255-0595
753 Jefferson St NAPA (94559) ***(P-2044)***
Bottling Group LLC ..... F 559 485-5050
1150 E North Ave Fresno (93725) ***(P-2045)***
Bottling Group LLC ..... E 951 697-3200
6659 Sycamore Canyon Blvd Riverside (92507) ***(P-2046)***
Bouchaine Vineyards Inc ..... F 707 252-9065
1075 Buchli Station Rd NAPA (94559) ***(P-1605)***
Bouchaine Winery, NAPA *Also called Bouchaine Vineyards Inc* ***(P-1605)***
Boudin Souerdough BAKery& Cafe, San Jose *Also called Andre-Boudin Bakeries Inc* ***(P-1136)***
Boudoir Spirits Inc ..... F 909 714-6644
7197 Boulder Ave Ste 12 Highland (92346) ***(P-2011)***
Boudoir Vodka, Highland *Also called Boudoir Spirits Inc* ***(P-2011)***
Boulder Creek Guitars Inc ..... F 408 842-0222
5810 Obata Way Ste 1 Gilroy (95020) ***(P-22610)***
Boulevard Style Inc ..... F 213 749-1551
1680 E 40th Pl Los Angeles (90011) ***(P-3143)***
Boulevard Style Inc (PA) ..... F 213 749-1551
1015 Crocker St Ste 27 Los Angeles (90021) ***(P-3144)***
Bourns Inc (PA) ..... C 951 781-5500
1200 Columbia Ave Riverside (92507) ***(P-18704)***
Bourns Inc ..... C 951 781-5690
1200 Columbia Ave Riverside (92507) ***(P-21013)***
Bourns Inc ..... F 951 781-5360
8662 Siempre Viva Rd San Diego (92154) ***(P-21014)***
Bowen Enterprises, El Cajon *Also called Bowen Printing Inc* ***(P-5496)***
Bowen Printing Inc ..... F 619 440-8605
380 Coogan Way El Cajon (92020) ***(P-5496)***
Bowers & Kelly Products Inc ..... E 714 630-1285
4572 E Eisenhower Cir Anaheim (92807) ***(P-9509)***
Bowers Machining, Anaheim *Also called Aaron Dutt Enterprises Inc* ***(P-12758)***
Bowman Plating Co Inc ..... C 310 639-4343
2631 E 126th St Compton (90222) ***(P-12949)***
Bowtie Inc ..... D 949 855-8822
3 Burroughs Irvine (92618) ***(P-5891)***
Box Inc (PA) ..... C 877 729-4269
900 Jefferson Ave Redwood City (94063) ***(P-23689)***
Box Co Inc ..... F 619 661-8090
7575 Britannia Park Pl San Diego (92154) ***(P-6456)***
Box Master ..... E 661 298-2666
17000 Sierra Hwy Canyon Country (91351) ***(P-12773)***
Boxes R Us Inc ..... D 626 820-5410
15051 Don Julian Rd City of Industry (91746) ***(P-5311)***
Boyd, Modesto *Also called LTI Holdings Inc* ***(P-7632)***
Boyd & Boyd Industries (PA) ..... F 661 631-8400
3500 Chester Ave Bakersfield (93301) ***(P-14701)***
Boyd Construction, Yorba Linda *Also called Boyd Corporation* ***(P-11751)***
Boyd Corporation (PA) ..... F 714 533-2375
5832 Ohio St Yorba Linda (92886) ***(P-11751)***
Boyd Corporation (HQ) ..... E 209 236-1111
5960 Inglewood Dr Ste 115 Pleasanton (94588) ***(P-8859)***
Boyd Corporation ..... C 888 244-6931
600 S Mcclure Rd Modesto (95357) ***(P-8860)***
Boyd Lighting Fixture Co (PA) ..... E 415 778-4300
30 Liberty Ship Way # 3150 Sausalito (94965) ***(P-17016)***
Boyd Specialties LLC ..... D 909 219-5120
1016 E Cooley Dr Ste N Colton (92324) ***(P-442)***
Boyer Inc ..... E 831 724-0123
105 Thompson Rd Watsonville (95076) ***(P-8790)***
BP Castrol, Richmond *Also called BP Lubricants USA Inc* ***(P-9134)***
BP Lubricants USA Inc ..... E 510 236-6312
801 Wharf St Richmond (94804) ***(P-9134)***
BP West Coast Products LLC ..... B 310 816-8787
22600 Wilmington Ave Carson (90745) ***(P-29)***
BP West Coast Products LLC ..... B 510 231-4724
1306 Canal Blvd Richmond (94804) ***(P-30)***
Bpi Records, Commerce *Also called Bridge Publications Inc* ***(P-6081)***
Bpo Management Services Inc (HQ) ..... F 714 974-2670
8175 E Kaiser Blvd 100 Anaheim (92808) ***(P-23690)***
Bpo Systems Inc (PA) ..... E 925 478-4299
1700 Ygnacio Valley Rd # 205 Walnut Creek (94598) ***(P-23691)***
Bps Tactical Inc ..... F 909 794-2435
2165 E Colton Ave Mentone (92359) ***(P-2986)***
BQE Software Inc ..... D 310 602-4020
3825 Del Amo Blvd Trrance Torrance Torrance (90503) ***(P-23692)***
Bracton Beer Line Cleaners, Anaheim *Also called Bracton Sosafe Inc* ***(P-8369)***
Bracton Sosafe Inc ..... F 714 632-8499
1061 N Shepard St Ste E Anaheim (92806) ***(P-8369)***
Brad Barry Company Ltd ..... E 909 591-9493
14020 Central Ave Ste 580 Chino (91710) ***(P-2278)***
Bradfield Manufacturing Inc ..... F 714 543-8348
2633 E Mardi Gras Ave Anaheim (92806) ***(P-12457)***
Bradford Canning Stahl Inc ..... F 209 257-1535
250 Scottsville Blvd Jackson (95642) ***(P-15797)***
Bradley Corp ..... F 909 481-7255
5556 Ontario Mills Pkwy Ontario (91764) ***(P-11658)***
Bradley Manufacturing Co Inc ..... E 562 923-5556
9130 Firestone Blvd Downey (90241) ***(P-9672)***
Bradley Tchnologies-California ..... E 310 538-0714
447 E Rosecrans Ave Gardena (90248) ***(P-8861)***
Bradley's Plastic Bag Co, Downey *Also called Bradley Manufacturing Co Inc* ***(P-9672)***
Bradshaw Kirchofer Home Furn ..... F 310 325-0010
22926 Mariposa Ave Torrance (90502) ***(P-4558)***
Brady Sheet Metal Inc ..... F 818 846-4043
320 N Victory Blvd Burbank (91502) ***(P-12136)***
Bragel International Inc ..... E 909 598-8808
3383 Pomona Blvd Pomona (91768) ***(P-3451)***
Braid Logistics, Mountain View *Also called Hansen Medical Inc* ***(P-21731)***
Braiform Enterprises Inc ..... D 714 526-0257
576 N Gilbert St Fullerton (92833) ***(P-9673)***
Braille Signs Inc ..... F 949 797-1570
16782 Von Karman Ave # 30 Irvine (92606) ***(P-23065)***

Mergent e-mail: customerrelations@mergent.com
1044
2020 California
Manufacturers Register
(P-0000) Products & Services Section entry number
(PA)=Parent Co (HQ)=Headquarters (DH)=Div Headquarters

Brainchip Inc (HQ) ....E....949 330-6750
65 Enterprise Aliso Viejo (92656) ***(P-23693)***
Brains Out Media Inc ....F....818 296-1036
2629 Foothill Blvd # 111 La Crescenta (91214) ***(P-23694)***
Brainstormproducts LLC ....F....760 871-1135
1011 S Andreasen Dr # 100 Escondido (92029) ***(P-22664)***
Brambila's Draperies, Los Angeles *Also called Juan Brambila Sr* ***(P-4580)***
Brampton Mthesen Fabr Pdts Inc ....E....510 483-7771
1688 Abram Ct San Leandro (94577) ***(P-3674)***
Branan Medical Corporation (PA) ....E....949 598-7166
9940 Mesa Rim Rd San Diego (92121) ***(P-21642)***
Branch Messenger Inc ....F....323 300-4063
130 W Union St Pasadena (91103) ***(P-23695)***
Brand Identity Inc ....F....916 553-0000
9520 Flintridge Way Orangevale (95662) ***(P-6457)***
Brand Ink Inc ....E....760 721-4465
3801 Oceanic Dr Ste 103 Oceanside (92056) ***(P-7005)***
Brand X Hurarches ....E....510 658-9006
4228 Telegraph Ave Oakland (94609) ***(P-10158)***
Branded Spirits USA Ltd ....F....415 813-5045
500 Sansome St Ste 600 San Francisco (94111) ***(P-2012)***
Brandelli Arts Inc ....E....714 537-0969
1250 Shaws Flat Rd Sonora (95370) ***(P-11000)***
Branding Irons Unlimited, Canoga Park *Also called Infinity Stamps Inc* ***(P-12821)***
Brandmd Skin Care, Chatsworth *Also called Samuel Raoof* ***(P-8574)***
Brandnew Industries Inc ....F....805 964-8251
375 Pine Ave Ste 22 Santa Barbara (93117) ***(P-22948)***
Brandt Consolidated Inc ....F....559 499-2100
3654 S Willow Ave Fresno (93725) ***(P-8811)***
Brandt Electronics Inc ....E....408 240-0014
1971 Tarob Ct Milpitas (95035) ***(P-18841)***
Brantner and Associates Inc (HQ) ....C....619 562-7070
1700 Gillespie Way El Cajon (92020) ***(P-18752)***
Brass Tech, Santa Ana *Also called Newport Metal Finishing Inc* ***(P-13211)***
Brasscraft Corona, Corona *Also called Brasscraft Manufacturing Co* ***(P-13349)***
Brasscraft Manufacturing Co ....D....951 735-4375
215 N Smith Ave Corona (92880) ***(P-13349)***
Brasstech Inc (HQ) ....C....949 417-5207
2001 Carnegie Ave Santa Ana (92705) ***(P-11659)***
Brava, Pomona *Also called Bragel International Inc* ***(P-3451)***
Brava Home Inc ....E....408 675-2569
312 Chestnut St Redwood City (94063) ***(P-16826)***
Bravo Communications Inc ....E....408 297-8700
3463 Meadowlands Ln San Jose (95135) ***(P-15177)***
Bravo Design Inc ....F....818 563-1385
150 E Olive Ave Ste 304 Burbank (91502) ***(P-7006)***
Bravo Fono, Palo Alto *Also called Fono Unlimited Inc* ***(P-645)***
Bravo Sports ....E....858 408-0083
4370 Jutland Dr San Diego (92117) ***(P-22768)***
Bravo Sports (HQ) ....D....562 484-5100
12801 Carmenita Rd Santa Fe Springs (90670) ***(P-22769)***
Bravo Support, Commerce *Also called S Bravo Systems Inc* ***(P-12049)***
Braxton Caribbean Mfg Co Inc ....D....714 508-3570
2641 Walnut Ave Tustin (92780) ***(P-12774)***
Brazeau Thoroughbred Farms LP ....F....951 925-8957
30500 State St Hemet (92543) ***(P-13614)***
Brea Canon Oil Co Inc ....F....310 326-4002
23903 Normandie Ave Harbor City (90710) ***(P-31)***
Bread Basket, Daly City *Also called Westlake Bakery Inc* ***(P-1295)***
Bread Los Angeles ....E....323 201-3953
1527 Beach St Montebello (90640) ***(P-1309)***
Breakaway Press Inc ....E....818 727-7388
9620 Topanga Canyon Pl A Chatsworth (91311) ***(P-7007)***
Breal Time, San Francisco *Also called Emx Digital LLC* ***(P-23857)***
Breathe Technologies Inc ....E....949 988-7700
15091 Bake Pkwy Irvine (92618) ***(P-21993)***
Bree Engineering Corp ....E....760 510-4950
1275 Stone Dr Ste A San Marcos (92078) ***(P-18842)***
Breezaire Products Co ....F....858 566-7465
8610 Production Ave Ste A San Diego (92121) ***(P-11998)***
Breg Inc (HQ) ....C....760 599-3000
2885 Loker Ave E Carlsbad (92010) ***(P-21643)***
Brehm Communications Inc (PA) ....E....858 451-6200
16644 W Bernardo Dr # 300 San Diego (92127) ***(P-6458)***
Brehm Communications Inc ....F....916 985-2581
921 Sutter St Folsom (95630) ***(P-5568)***
Breitburn Energy Partners I LP ....E....213 225-5900
707 Wilshire Blvd # 4600 Los Angeles (90017) ***(P-32)***
Breitburn GP LLC ....A....213 225-5900
707 Wilshire Blvd # 4600 Los Angeles (90017) ***(P-33)***
Brendan Technologies Inc ....E....760 929-7500
1947 Camino Vida Roble # 21 Carlsbad (92008) ***(P-23696)***
Brenner-Fiedler & Associates (PA) ....E....562 404-2721
4059 Flat Rock Dr Riverside (92505) ***(P-21444)***
Brent Engineering Inc ....F....949 679-5630
81 Shield Irvine (92618) ***(P-13712)***
Brent-Wood Products Inc ....E....800 400-7335
777 E Rosecrans Ave Los Angeles (90059) ***(P-4494)***
Brentwood Appliances Inc ....F....323 266-4600
3088 E 46th St Vernon (90058) ***(P-16847)***
Brentwood Home LLC (PA) ....C....562 949-3759
701 Burning Tree Rd Ste A Fullerton (92833) ***(P-4713)***
Brentwood Home LLC ....F....213 457-7626
2301 E 7th St Ste 417 Los Angeles (90023) ***(P-4714)***
Brentwood News, Antioch *Also called Contra Costa Newspapers Inc* ***(P-5602)***
Brentwood Originals Inc (PA) ....A....310 637-6804
20639 S Fordyce Ave Carson (90810) ***(P-3604)***
Brentwood Press & Pubg LLC ....E....925 516-4757
248 Oak St Brentwood (94513) ***(P-5569)***
Brentwood Readymix, Brentwood *Also called Antioch Building Materials Co* ***(P-10690)***
Brentwood Yellow Pages, Brentwood *Also called Brentwood Press & Pubg LLC* ***(P-5569)***
Brett Corp ....E....858 292-4919
8316 Clairemont Mesa Blvd # 105 San Diego (92111) ***(P-7008)***
Brevet Industries, Irvine *Also called Brewer Irvine Inc* ***(P-9674)***
Brew Building, Fort Bragg *Also called North Coast Brewing Co Inc* ***(P-1550)***
Brew4u LLC ....F....415 516-8211
935 Washington St San Carlos (94070) ***(P-1505)***
Brewer Irvine Inc ....D....949 474-7000
16661 Jamboree Rd Irvine (92606) ***(P-9674)***
Brewmaster Inc ....E....415 642-3371
1195 Evans Ave San Francisco (94124) ***(P-1506)***
Brewster Foods, Reseda *Also called Test Laboratories Inc* ***(P-2624)***
Brg Sports, Scotts Valley *Also called Vista Outdoor Inc* ***(P-22921)***
Brian Klaas Inc ....F....818 394-9881
11101 Tuxford St Sun Valley (91352) ***(P-4963)***
Brian's Welding, San Jose *Also called B W Padilla Inc* ***(P-24617)***
Brice Manufacturing Co Inc ....E....818 896-2938
10262 Norris Ave Pacoima (91331) ***(P-20059)***
Brice Tool & Stamping ....F....714 630-6400
1170 N Van Horne Way Anaheim (92806) ***(P-12775)***
Brickschain Cnstr Blockchain ....F....833 274-2572
511 Olive St Santa Barbara (93101) ***(P-10431)***
Brickstone Group Inc ....F....310 991-4747
15425 Antioch St Unit 304 Pacific Palisades (90272) ***(P-2410)***
Bridge Publications Inc (PA) ....E....323 888-6200
5600 E Olympic Blvd Commerce (90022) ***(P-6081)***
Bridge USA Inc ....E....310 532-5921
20817 S Western Ave Torrance (90501) ***(P-5892)***
Bridgebio Pharma Inc ....C....650 391-9740
421 Kipling St Palo Alto (94301) ***(P-7817)***
Bridgelux Inc ....D....925 583-8400
46430 Fremont Blvd Fremont (94538) ***(P-18150)***
Bridgeport Products Inc ....D....949 348-8800
26895 Aliso Creek Rd B Aliso Viejo (92656) ***(P-10190)***
Bridgewave Communications Inc ....E....408 567-6900
17034 Camino San Bernardo San Diego (92127) ***(P-11290)***
Bridgford Foods Corporation (HQ) ....B....714 526-5533
1308 N Patt St Anaheim (92801) ***(P-1056)***
Bridlewood Winery ....E....805 688-9000
3555 Roblar Ave Santa Ynez (93460) ***(P-1606)***
Brief Relief, Oceanside *Also called American Innotek Inc* ***(P-9625)***
Briggs & Sons ....F....707 938-4325
1225 E Macarthur St Sonoma (95476) ***(P-4885)***
Bright Business Media LLC ....F....415 339-9355
475 Gate 5 Rd Ste 235 Sausalito (94965) ***(P-5893)***
Bright Glow Candle Company Inc (PA) ....E....909 469-0119
110 Erie St Pomona (91768) ***(P-23288)***
Bright Lights Candle Company, Lower Lake *Also called Aloha Bay* ***(P-23271)***
Bright People Foods Inc (PA) ....E....530 669-6870
1640 Tide Ct Woodland (95776) ***(P-2411)***
Bright Shark Powder Coating ....F....909 591-1385
4530 Schaefer Ave Chino (91710) ***(P-13151)***
Brightidea Incorporated ....E....415 814-1387
255 California St # 1100 San Francisco (94111) ***(P-23697)***
Brightlight Welding & Mfg Inc ....E....408 988-0418
3395a Edward Ave Santa Clara (95054) ***(P-24618)***
Brighton Collectibles LLC ....F....925 932-1500
1195 Broadway Plz Walnut Creek (94596) ***(P-3543)***
Brighton Collectibles LLC ....F....650 838-0086
180 El Camino Real Millbrae (94030) ***(P-10217)***
Brighton Collectibles LLC ....E....626 961-9381
10250 Santa Monica Blvd Los Angeles (90067) ***(P-3528)***
Brightscope, San Diego *Also called Strategic Insights Inc* ***(P-24459)***
Brightsign LLC ....D....408 852-9263
983 University Ave Bldg A Los Gatos (95032) ***(P-23066)***
Brightwater Medical Inc ....F....951 290-3410
42580 Rio Nedo Temecula (92590) ***(P-21644)***
Briles Aerospace Inc ....F....310 701-2087
1559 W 135th St Gardena (90249) ***(P-12669)***
Brilliant Home Technology Inc ....F....650 539-5320
155 Bovet Rd Ste 500 San Mateo (94402) ***(P-16586)***
Brilliant Instruments Inc ....F....408 866-0426
1622 W Campbell Ave 107 Campbell (95008) ***(P-20841)***
Brilliant Solutions, Irvine *Also called Meguiars Inc* ***(P-8396)***
Brilliant Worldwide Inc ....E....650 468-2966
200 Pine St Fl 8 San Francisco (94104) ***(P-23698)***
Bristol Omega Inc ....E....909 794-6862
9441 Opal Ave Ste 2 Mentone (92359) ***(P-4886)***
Bristol Sounds Elec Whse, Santa Ana *Also called Bristol Sounds Electronics* ***(P-17209)***
Bristol Sounds Electronics ....F....714 549-5923
2604 S Bristol St Santa Ana (92704) ***(P-17209)***
Bristolite, Santa Ana *Also called Sundown Liquidating Corp* ***(P-10277)***
Britcan Inc ....E....760 722-2300
3809 Ocean Ranch Blvd # 110 Oceanside (92056) ***(P-4964)***
Brite Industries Inc ....D....510 250-9330
1746 13th St Oakland (94607) ***(P-23289)***
Brite Labs, Oakland *Also called Brite Industries Inc* ***(P-23289)***
Brite Lite Enterprises ....F....310 363-7120
11661 San Vicente Blvd Los Angeles (90049) ***(P-17210)***
Brite Plating Co Inc ....D....323 263-7593
1313 Mirasol St Los Angeles (90023) ***(P-12950)***
Brite Vue Div, Visalia *Also called Kawneer Company Inc* ***(P-12489)***
Brite-Lite Neon Corp ....F....818 763-4798
17242 Goya St Granada Hills (91344) ***(P-23067)***
Britelab ....D....650 961-0671
6341 San Ignacio Ave San Jose (95119) ***(P-20962)***
British American Tl & Die LLC ....C....714 776-8995
2273 E Via Burton Anaheim (92806) ***(P-11522)***

ALPHABETIC

Employee Codes: A=Over 500 employees, B=251-500
C=101-250, D=51-100, E=20-50, F=10-19
2020 California
Manfacturers Register
© Mergent Inc. 1-800-342-5647
1045

Britz Fertilizers Inc........E.......559 582-0942
12498 11th Ave Hanford (93230) *(P-13615)*
Brixen & Sons Inc........E.......714 566-1444
2100 S Fairview St Santa Ana (92704) *(P-7009)*
Brk Group LLC........E.......562 949-4394
8357 Loch Lomond Dr Pico Rivera (90660) *(P-2928)*
Brm Manufacturing, Los Angeles *Also called Brush Research Mfg Co (P-23022)*
Broach Masters Inc........E.......530 885-1939
1605 Industrial Dr Auburn (95603) *(P-14141)*
Broadata Communications Inc........F.......310 530-1416
2545 W 237th St Ste K Torrance (90505) *(P-11291)*
Broadcast Microwave Services (PA)........C.......858 391-3050
12305 Crosthwaite Cir Poway (92064) *(P-17474)*
Broadcom, San Jose *Also called LSI Corporation (P-18359)*
Broadcom Corporation........E.......408 922-7000
250 Innovation Dr San Jose (95134) *(P-18151)*
Broadcom Corporation (HQ)........B.......408 433-8000
1320 Ridder Park Dr San Jose (95131) *(P-18152)*
Broadcom Corporation........A.......858 385-8800
16340 W Bernardo Dr A San Diego (92127) *(P-18153)*
Broadcom Inc (PA)........F.......408 433-8000
1320 Ridder Park Dr San Jose (95131) *(P-18154)*
Broadley-James-Corporation........D.......949 829-5555
19 Thomas Irvine (92618) *(P-20842)*
Broadlight Inc........F.......408 982-4210
2901 Tasman Dr Ste 218 Santa Clara (95054) *(P-18155)*
Broadly Inc........E.......510 400-6039
409 13th St Fl 3 Oakland (94612) *(P-23699)*
Broadvision Inc (PA)........D.......650 331-1000
460 Seaport Ct Ste 102 Redwood City (94063) *(P-23700)*
Broadvision Rcao Broadvisi........F.......650 261-5100
585 Broadway St Redwood City (94063) *(P-6205)*
Broadway Knitting Mills Corp........E.......559 456-0955
1766 N Helm Ave Ste 101 Fresno (93727) *(P-2774)*
Broadway Pl, Los Angeles *Also called Promises Promises Inc (P-3251)*
Broan-Nutone LLC........C.......262 673-8795
622 Emery Rd Tecate (91980) *(P-11692)*
Brocade Cmmnctions Systems LLC (HQ)........A.......408 333-8000
130 Holger Way San Jose (95134) *(P-15178)*
Brochure Holders 4u, Santa Ana *Also called Clear-Ad Inc (P-9710)*
Brocks Trailers Inc........E.......661 363-5038
6901 E Brundage Ln Bakersfield (93307) *(P-13616)*
Brodhead Grating Products LLC........F.......562 598-4314
3651 Sausalito St Los Alamitos (90720) *(P-12458)*
Brodhead Steel Products Co (PA)........E.......650 871-8251
7550 Alpine Rd La Honda (94020) *(P-12459)*
Broken Earth Winery........F.......805 239-2562
5625 E Highway 46 Paso Robles (93446) *(P-1607)*
Broken Token........F.......760 294-1923
541 N Quince St Ste 1 Escondido (92025) *(P-22665)*
Bromack, Los Angeles *Also called LA Cabinet & Millwork Inc (P-4919)*
Bromwell Company (PA)........F.......800 683-2626
8605 Santa Monica Blvd Los Angeles (90069) *(P-10470)*
Broncs Inc........C.......714 705-4377
12691 Pala Dr Ste A Garden Grove (92841) *(P-2672)*
Bronze-Way Plating Corporation (PA)........E.......323 266-6933
3301 E 14th St Los Angeles (90023) *(P-12951)*
Brookhurst Mill........F.......951 688-3511
3315 Van Buren Blvd Riverside (92503) *(P-1086)*
Brooks Automation Inc........D.......510 498-8745
46702 Bayside Pkwy Fremont (94538) *(P-15417)*
Brooks Automation Inc........F.......858 527-7000
13915 Danielson St # 103 Poway (92064) *(P-14436)*
Brooks Millwork Company........F.......562 920-3000
13551 Yorba Ave Chino (91710) *(P-4005)*
Brooks Polycold Systems, Fremont *Also called Brooks Automation Inc (P-15417)*
Brooks Products, Ontario *Also called Heitman Brooks II LLC (P-10584)*
Brooks Street Baking Company, Montclair *Also called Brooks Street Companies (P-1170)*
Brooks Street Companies........C.......909 983-6090
5560 Brooks St Montclair (91763) *(P-1170)*
Brookshire Innovations LLC........E.......916 786-7601
502 Giuseppe Ct Ste 7 Roseville (95678) *(P-20386)*
Brookshire Tool & Mfg Co Inc........F.......562 861-2567
10654 Garfield Ave South Gate (90280) *(P-15798)*
Brothers Enterprises Inc........F.......619 229-8003
7380 Mission Gorge Rd San Diego (92120) *(P-24619)*
Brothers Intl Desserts........C.......949 655-0080
2727 S Susan St Santa Ana (92704) *(P-633)*
Brothers Machine & Tool Inc........E.......951 361-9454
11095 Inland Ave Jurupa Valley (91752) *(P-13971)*
Brothers Machine & Tool Inc (PA)........F.......951 361-2909
11098 Inland Ave Jurupa Valley (91752) *(P-13972)*
Brothers Optical Laboratory........D.......714 639-9852
870 N Eckhoff St Orange (92868) *(P-22342)*
Brown & Honeycutt Truss Systms........E.......760 244-8887
16775 Smoke Tree St Hesperia (92345) *(P-4290)*
Brown Estate Vineyard LLC........F.......707 963-2435
3233 Sage Canyon Rd Saint Helena (94574) *(P-1608)*
Brown Wood Products Inc........E.......650 593-9875
310 Devonshire Blvd San Carlos (94070) *(P-4413)*
Brown-Pacific Inc........E.......562 921-3471
13639 Bora Dr Santa Fe Springs (90670) *(P-11030)*
Brownie Baker Inc........D.......559 277-7070
4870 W Jacquelyn Ave Fresno (93722) *(P-1310)*
Browntrout Publishers Inc (PA)........E.......424 290-6122
201 Continental Blvd # 200 El Segundo (90245) *(P-6206)*
Bruce Eicher Inc (PA)........F.......310 657-4630
8755 Melrose Ave Los Angeles (90069) *(P-16967)*
Bruce Iversen........E.......310 537-4168
439 E Carlin Ave Compton (90222) *(P-4352)*
Bruce's Custom Covers, Morgan Hill *Also called Aircraft Covers Inc (P-2664)*
Bruck Braid Company........E.......213 627-7611
1200 S Santa Fe Ave Los Angeles (90021) *(P-3775)*
Brud Inc........F.......310 806-2283
837 N Spring St Ste 101 Los Angeles (90012) *(P-6207)*
Bruder Industry........D.......916 939-6888
3920 Sandstone Dr El Dorado Hills (95762) *(P-15799)*
Bruin Biometrics LLC........F.......310 268-9494
10877 Wilshire Blvd # 1600 Los Angeles (90024) *(P-21645)*
Bruker Biosciences Cad, San Jose *Also called Bruker Biospin Corporation (P-21200)*
Bruker Biospin Corporation........E.......510 683-4300
61 Daggett Dr San Jose (95134) *(P-21200)*
Bruker Corporation........E.......408 376-4040
1717 Dell Ave Campbell (95008) *(P-15179)*
Bruker Nano Inc........F.......805 967-2700
112 Robin Hill Rd Santa Barbara (93117) *(P-21201)*
Brunette Printing, Los Angeles *Also called Brunettes Printing Service (P-6459)*
Brunettes Printing Service........F.......213 749-7441
742 E Washington Blvd Los Angeles (90021) *(P-6459)*
Brunton Enterprises Inc........C.......562 945-0013
8815 Sorensen Ave Santa Fe Springs (90670) *(P-11752)*
Brush Dance Inc........F.......415 491-4950
165 N Redwood Dr Ste 200 San Rafael (94903) *(P-5497)*
Brush Research Mfg Co........C.......323 261-2193
4642 Floral Dr Los Angeles (90022) *(P-23022)*
Brush Wellman, Fremont *Also called Materion Brush Inc (P-13452)*
Brushy Peak Winery, Livermore *Also called Cedar Mountain Winery Inc (P-1623)*
Brutocao Cellars (PA)........F.......707 744-1066
1400 Highway 175 Hopland (95449) *(P-1609)*
Brutocao Vineyards........E.......707 744-1320
1400 Highway 175 Hopland (95449) *(P-1610)*
Brutocaosellers.com, Hopland *Also called Brutocao Vineyards (P-1610)*
Bruvado Imports, Pleasanton *Also called Blanco Basura Beverage Inc (P-1503)*
Bryan Edwards Publishing Co........F.......714 634-0264
2185 N Orange Olive Rd # 3 Orange (92865) *(P-6082)*
Bryan Press Inc........F.......626 961-9257
1011 S Stimson Ave City of Industry (91745) *(P-6460)*
Bryant Rubber Corp (PA)........E.......310 530-2530
1112 Lomita Blvd Harbor City (90710) *(P-9219)*
Bryant Rubber Corp........D.......310 530-2530
1083 W 251st St Bellflower (90706) *(P-9220)*
Bryngelson Prints, Redlands *Also called Duden Enterprises Inc (P-3738)*
Bsh Home Appliances Corp (HQ)........C.......949 440-7100
1901 Main St Ste 600 Irvine (92614) *(P-16848)*
Bsmi, Brentwood *Also called Bay Standard Manufacturing Inc (P-12667)*
Bsr, Berkeley *Also called Assoc Students University CA (P-6190)*
Bsst LLC........F.......626 593-4500
5462 Irwindale Ave Ste A Irwindale (91706) *(P-19597)*
BT Screw Products, Los Angeles *Also called Crellin Machine Company (P-12626)*
BT Sheet Metal Inc........F.......949 481-5715
1031 Calle Trepadora D San Clemente (92673) *(P-12137)*
Bti Aerospace & Electronics........E.......909 465-1569
13546 Vintage Pl Chino (91710) *(P-15800)*
Btm-Beartech Manufacturing........F.......714 550-1700
910 S Placentia Ave Ste A Placentia (92870) *(P-12624)*
Btrade LLC........E.......818 334-4433
655 N Central Ave # 1460 Glendale (91203) *(P-23701)*
Bu LLC........F.......951 277-7470
9073 Pulsar Ct Ste A Corona (92883) *(P-1507)*
Bubblegum USA, Los Angeles *Also called Komex International Inc (P-3172)*
Bucate Plata Importing Co, Oakland *Also called Brand X Hurarches (P-10158)*
Buchanans Spoke & Rim........E.......626 969-4655
805 W 8th St Azusa (91702) *(P-20387)*
Buchbinder, Jay Industries, Compton *Also called Jbi LLC (P-4692)*
Bucy Die Casting........F.......818 843-5044
633 S Glenwood Pl Burbank (91506) *(P-14024)*
Bud Wil Inc........E.......714 630-1242
1170 N Red Gum St Anaheim (92806) *(P-9510)*
Buddha Teas, Carlsbad *Also called Living Wellness Partners LLC (P-2531)*
Buddy Bar Casting Corporation........D.......562 861-9664
10801 Sessler St South Gate (90280) *(P-11368)*
Budget Enterprises Inc........E.......949 697-9544
9301 Research Dr Irvine (92618) *(P-10260)*
Buds Cotton Inc........E.......714 223-7800
1240 N Fee Ana St Anaheim (92807) *(P-8452)*
Buds Ice Cream San Francisco, Hayward *Also called Berkeley Farms LLC (P-687)*
Buds Polishing & Metal Finshg........F.......714 632-0121
1156 N Kraemer Pl Anaheim (92806) *(P-12952)*
Buellton Advanced Materials, Buellton *Also called Lockheed Martin Corporation (P-20609)*
Buena Park Anaheim Independent........E.......714 952-8505
9551 Valley View St Cypress (90630) *(P-5570)*
Buena Park Tool & Engineering........F.......714 843-6215
7661 Windfield Dr Huntington Beach (92647) *(P-15801)*
Buff and Shine Mfg Inc........E.......310 886-5111
2139 E Del Amo Blvd Rancho Dominguez (90220) *(P-10941)*
Buffalo Bills Brewery, Hayward *Also called Steinbeck Brewing Company (P-1566)*
Buffalo Distribution Inc........E.......510 324-3800
30750 San Clemente St Hayward (94544) *(P-16587)*
Build At Home LLC........F.......909 949-1601
273 N Benson Ave Upland (91786) *(P-22770)*
Build Your Own Garment, Dublin *Also called Print Ink Inc (P-7182)*
Build-In C & C, Hollister *Also called C & C Built-In Inc (P-4171)*
Builder & Developer Magazines........F.......949 631-0308
1602 Monrovia Ave Newport Beach (92663) *(P-5894)*
Builders Concrete Inc (HQ)........E.......559 225-3667
3664 W Ashlan Ave Fresno (93722) *(P-10698)*
Builders Concrete Inc Npp........F.......559 229-6643
15821 Ventura Blvd Ste 47 Encino (91436) *(P-10699)*

Builders Drapery Service Inc .... E 408 263-3300
1494 Gladding Ct Milpitas (95035) *(P-2673)*
Building Components .... F 310 274-6516
3148 Abington Dr Beverly Hills (90210) *(P-9675)*
Building Robotics Inc .... F 510 761-6482
300 Frank H Oakland (94612) *(P-23702)*
Buildit Engineering Co Inc .... F 818 244-6666
3074 N Lima St Burbank (91504) *(P-11226)*
Buildmat Plus Investments Inc .... F 909 823-7663
15435 Arrow Blvd Bldg A Fontana (92335) *(P-10544)*
Buk Optics Inc .... E 714 384-9620
3600 W Moore Ave Santa Ana (92704) *(P-21336)*
Bulb Star, Alhambra *Also called K Live (P-18331)*
Buldoor LLC .... F 877 388-1366
647 Camino De Los San Clemente (92673) *(P-11574)*
Bull Hn Info Systems Inc .... E 310 337-3600
6077 Bristol Pkwy Culver City (90230) *(P-14894)*
Bulldog Reporter .... F 510 596-9300
124 Linden St Oakland (94607) *(P-5571)*
Bullet Guard Corporation .... F 800 233-5632
3963 Commerce Dr West Sacramento (95691) *(P-13504)*
Bulletproof Brands Co Inc .... F 916 635-3718
1704 Halifax Way El Dorado Hills (95762) *(P-2047)*
Bullfrog Printing and Graphics .... F 714 641-0220
1261 S Wright St Santa Ana (92705) *(P-6461)*
Bulls-Eye Marketing Inc .... F 707 745-5278
6610 Goodyear Rd Benicia (94510) *(P-19598)*
Bullseye, Lancaster *Also called Aerotech News and Review Inc (P-5876)*
Bullseye Leak Detection Inc .... F 916 760-8944
4015 Seaport Blvd West Sacramento (95691) *(P-15802)*
Bullzeye Mfg .... F 209 482-5626
13625 Clements Rd Lodi (95240) *(P-11085)*
Bulthaup Corp .... F 310 288-3875
153 S Robertson Blvd Los Angeles (90048) *(P-4686)*
Bumble Bee, San Diego *Also called Bumble Bee Foods LLC (P-2238)*
Bumble Bee Capital Corp .... C 858 715-4000
280 10th Ave San Diego (92101) *(P-2237)*
Bumble Bee Foods LLC (HQ) .... B 858 715-4000
280 10th Ave San Diego (92101) *(P-2238)*
Bumble Bee Holdings Inc (HQ) .... B 858 715-4000
280 10th Ave San Diego (92101) *(P-443)*
Bumble Bee Plastics Inc .... F 562 903-0833
10140 Shoemaker Ave Santa Fe Springs (90670) *(P-9676)*
Bumble Bee Seafoods LP .... D 858 715-4000
280 10th Ave San Diego (92101) *(P-2239)*
Bumble Bee Seafoods Inc .... E 858 715-4000
280 10th Ave San Diego (92101) *(P-2240)*
Bumble Bee Seafoods Inc .... A 858 715-4068
280 10th Ave San Diego (92101) *(P-2241)*
Bumble Bee Seafoods LLC .... E 562 483-7474
13100 Arctic Cir Santa Fe Springs (90670) *(P-2242)*
Bumbleride Inc .... F 619 615-0475
2345 Kettner Blvd Ste B San Diego (92101) *(P-22666)*
Bumjin America Inc (PA) .... F 619 671-0386
2177 Britannia Blvd # 204 San Diego (92154) *(P-9677)*
Bundy and Sons Inc .... E 530 246-3868
15196 Mountain Shadows Dr Redding (96001) *(P-3876)*
Bundy Manufacturing Inc .... E 323 772-3273
507 S Douglas St El Segundo (90245) *(P-15803)*
Bunge North America, Modesto *Also called Bunge Oils Inc (P-1448)*
Bunge North America Inc .... D 530 666-1691
845 Kentucky Ave Woodland (95695) *(P-1035)*
Bunge Oils Inc .... D 209 574-9981
436 S Mcclure Rd Modesto (95357) *(P-1448)*
Bunker Corp (PA) .... D 949 361-3935
1131 Via Callejon San Clemente (92673) *(P-19599)*
Bunkerhill Indus Group Inc .... F 323 227-4222
4535 Huntington Dr S Los Angeles (90032) *(P-3027)*
Buoy Labs Inc .... F 855 481-7112
125 Mcpherson St Santa Cruz (95060) *(P-23703)*
Burbank Plating Service Corp .... F 818 899-1157
13561 Desmond St Pacoima (91331) *(P-12953)*
Burbank Steel Treating Inc .... E 818 842-0975
415 S Varney St Burbank (91502) *(P-11442)*
Burgess Cellars Inc .... F 707 963-4766
1108 Deer Park Rd Saint Helena (94574) *(P-1611)*
Burke Display Systems Inc .... E 949 248-0091
55 S Peak Laguna Niguel (92677) *(P-4965)*
Burke Industries Inc (HQ) .... C 408 297-3500
2250 S 10th St San Jose (95112) *(P-9290)*
Burke Industries Inc .... C 408 297-3500
2250 S 10th St San Jose (95112) *(P-9110)*
Burlingame Htg Ventilation Inc .... F 650 697-9142
821 Malcolm Rd Burlingame (94010) *(P-12138)*
Burlingame Industries Inc .... C 909 355-7000
2352 N Locust Ave Rialto (92377) *(P-11001)*
Burlington Engineering Inc .... E 714 921-4045
220 W Grove Ave Orange (92865) *(P-12954)*
Burner App, Los Angeles *Also called Ad Hoc Labs Inc (P-23558)*
Burnet Machining Inc .... F 805 964-6321
330 S Kellogg Ave Ste N Goleta (93117) *(P-15804)*
Burnett & Son Meat Co Inc .... D 626 357-2165
1420 S Myrtle Ave Monrovia (91016) *(P-396)*
Burnett Fine Foods, Monrovia *Also called Burnett & Son Meat Co Inc (P-396)*
Burning Beard Brewing Company .... F 619 456-9185
785 Vernon Way El Cajon (92020) *(P-1508)*
Burning Torch Inc .... E 323 733-7700
1738 Cordova St Los Angeles (90007) *(P-3298)*
Burns Stainless LLC .... F 949 631-5120
1041 W 18th St Ste B104 Costa Mesa (92627) *(P-19600)*
Burton Ching Ltd .... F 415 522-5520
432 N Canal St Ste 5 South San Francisco (94080) *(P-3605)*
Burton James Inc .... D 626 961-7221
428 Turnbull Canyon Rd City of Industry (91745) *(P-4630)*
Burtree Inc .... E 818 786-4276
13513 Sherman Way Van Nuys (91405) *(P-15805)*
Bus Services Corporation .... E 562 231-1770
6801 Suva St Bell Gardens (90201) *(P-19601)*
Bush Polishing & Chrome .... F 714 537-7440
2236 W 2nd St Santa Ana (92703) *(P-12955)*
Bushman Products, Torrance *Also called Momentum Management LLC (P-9339)*
Bushnell Industries Inc .... F 559 651-9039
7449 Avenue 304 Visalia (93291) *(P-8370)*
Bushnell Ribbon Corporation .... D 562 948-1410
300 W Brookdale Pl Fullerton (92832) *(P-22960)*
Business Extension Bureau .... E 650 737-5700
500 S Airport Blvd South San Francisco (94080) *(P-5895)*
Business Fulfillment Svcs Inc .... F 530 671-7006
791 Plumas St Yuba City (95991) *(P-6462)*
Business Journal .... E 559 490-3400
1315 Van Ness Ave Ste 200 Fresno (93721) *(P-5896)*
Business Jrnl Publications Inc .... E 408 295-3800
125 S Market St 11 San Jose (95113) *(P-5572)*
Business Jrnl Publications Inc .... E 415 989-2522
275 Battery St Ste 600 San Francisco (94111) *(P-5573)*
Business Point Impressions, Concord *Also called Hnc Printing Services LLC (P-6615)*
Business With Pleasure .... F 831 430-9711
1 Victor Sq Scotts Valley (95066) *(P-6463)*
Busseto Foods Inc (PA) .... C 559 485-9882
1351 N Crystal Ave Fresno (93728) *(P-444)*
Butane Propane News Inc .... F 626 357-2168
338 E Foothill Blvd Arcadia (91006) *(P-5897)*
Butler Home Products LLC .... F 909 476-3884
9409 Buffalo Ave Rancho Cucamonga (91730) *(P-23023)*
Butler Inc .... F 310 323-3114
1600 W 166th St Gardena (90247) *(P-12670)*
Butler Manufacturing, Visalia *Also called Bluescope Buildings N Amer Inc (P-12535)*
Butte Sand and Gravel .... E 530 755-0225
10373 S Butte Rd Sutter (95982) *(P-331)*
Buttonwood Farm Winery Inc .... F 805 688-3032
1500 Alamo Pintado Rd Solvang (93463) *(P-1612)*
Buxcon Sheetmetal Inc .... F 619 937-0001
11222 Woodside Ave N Santee (92071) *(P-12139)*
Buy and Sell Press Inc .... F 209 223-3333
605 Broadway Jackson (95642) *(P-6208)*
Buy Insta Slim Inc .... F 949 263-2301
17831 Sky Park Cir Ste C Irvine (92614) *(P-3028)*
Buzz Converting Inc .... F 209 948-1341
4343 E Fremont St Stockton (95215) *(P-5157)*
Buzzworks Inc .... F 415 863-5964
365 11th St San Francisco (94103) *(P-1509)*
BV WILMS, Indio *Also called M F G Eurotec Inc (P-4588)*
Bvp Designs Inc .... F 818 280-2900
21354 Nordhoff St Ste 101 Chatsworth (91311) *(P-15396)*
BVT Publishing, Redding *Also called Best Value Textbooks LLC (P-6076)*
Bway Corporation .... E 951 361-4100
11440 Pacific Ave Fontana (92337) *(P-11495)*
Bwm, Modesto *Also called Billington Welding & Mfg Inc (P-14349)*
Byd Energy LLC .... E 661 949-2918
1800 S Figueroa St Los Angeles (90015) *(P-19188)*
Byd Motors LLC (HQ) .... E 213 748-3980
1800 S Figueroa St Los Angeles (90015) *(P-19602)*
Byer California (PA) .... A 415 626-7844
66 Potrero Ave San Francisco (94103) *(P-3145)*
Byer California .... D 925 245-0184
3740 Livermore Outlets Dr Livermore (94551) *(P-3146)*
Byer California .... B 323 780-7615
1201 Rio Vista Ave Los Angeles (90023) *(P-2775)*
Byington Steel Treating Inc (PA) .... E 408 727-6630
1225 Memorex Dr Santa Clara (95050) *(P-11443)*
Byrnes & Kiefer Co .... D 714 554-4000
501 Airpark Dr Fullerton (92833) *(P-2196)*
Byrum Technologies Inc .... E 760 744-6692
550 S Pacific St Ste 100 San Marcos (92078) *(P-19267)*
Byton North America Corp .... C 408 966-5078
4201 Burton Dr Santa Clara (95054) *(P-19461)*
C & A Transducers Inc .... E 714 554-9188
14329 Commerce Dr Garden Grove (92843) *(P-18843)*
C & C Built-In Inc .... E 831 635-5880
2000 Lana Way Hollister (95023) *(P-4171)*
C & C Die Engraving .... F 562 944-3399
12510 Mccann Dr Santa Fe Springs (90670) *(P-15806)*
C & C Signs, Long Beach *Also called Canzone and Company (P-23071)*
C & D Aerospace, Garden Grove *Also called Safran Cabin Inc (P-20221)*
C & D Precision Components .... F 626 799-7109
969 S Raymond Ave Pasadena (91105) *(P-15807)*
C & D Prescision Machining Inc .... E 408 383-1888
2031 Concourse Dr San Jose (95131) *(P-15808)*
C & D Semiconductor Svcs Inc (PA) .... E 408 383-1888
2031 Concourse Dr San Jose (95131) *(P-14437)*
C & F Foods Inc (PA) .... D 626 723-1000
15620 E Valley Blvd City of Industry (91744) *(P-2412)*
C & G Mercury Plastics, Sylmar *Also called C & G Plastics (P-9678)*
C & G Plastics .... E 818 837-3773
12729 Foothill Blvd Sylmar (91342) *(P-9678)*
C & Gtool Inc .... F 916 614-9114
3247 Back Cir Sacramento (95821) *(P-14142)*
C & H Enterprises, Fremont *Also called Colleen & Herb Enterprises Inc (P-15858)*

ALPHABETIC

Employee Codes: A=Over 500 employees, B=251-500
C=101-250, D=51-100, E=20-50, F=10-19
2020 California
Manfacturers Register
© Mergent Inc. 1-800-342-5647
1047

C & H Hydraulics Inc ....F....949 646-6230
1585 Monrovia Ave Newport Beach (92663) ***(P-20060)***
C & H Letterpress Inc ....F....714 438-1350
3400 W Castor St Santa Ana (92704) ***(P-7010)***
C & H Machine Inc ....D....760 746-6459
943 S Andrsen Dr Escndido Escondido Escondido (92029) ***(P-15620)***
C & H Metal Products, Ontario *Also called Daaze Inc* ***(P-12171)***
C & H Molding Incorporated ....E....951 361-5030
11160 Thurston Ln Jurupa Valley (91752) ***(P-14025)***
C & H Testing Service Inc (PA) ....E....661 589-4030
6224 Price Way Bakersfield (93308) ***(P-174)***
C & J Industries, Santa Fe Springs *Also called Custom Steel Fabrication Inc* ***(P-11778)***
C & J Metal Prducts, Paramount *Also called Jeffrey Fabrication LLC* ***(P-12254)***
C & J Metal Products Inc ....E....562 634-3101
6323 Alondra Blvd Paramount (90723) ***(P-12140)***
C & L Tool and Die Inc ....F....619 270-8385
8684 Avenida De La Fuente # 12 San Diego (92154) ***(P-14026)***
C & M Spring & Engineering Co ....E....909 597-2030
5244 Las Flores Dr Chino (91710) ***(P-13378)***
C & M Wood Industries ....C....760 949-3292
17229 Lemon St Ste D Hesperia (92345) ***(P-5017)***
C & R Extrusions Inc ....F....626 642-0244
2618 River Ave Rosemead (91770) ***(P-9396)***
C & R Molds Inc ....E....805 658-7098
2737 Palma Dr Ventura (93003) ***(P-9679)***
C & S Assembly Inc ....F....866 779-8939
1150 N Armando St Anaheim (92806) ***(P-18844)***
C & S Plastics ....F....818 896-2489
12621 Foothill Blvd Sylmar (91342) ***(P-9680)***
C & S Products CA Inc (PA) ....F....909 218-8971
1345 S Parkside Pl Ontario (91761) ***(P-8371)***
C & Y Investment Inc ....F....323 267-9000
946 E 29th St Los Angeles (90011) ***(P-3299)***
C A Botana International Inc (PA) ....E....858 450-1717
9365 Waples St Ste A San Diego (92121) ***(P-8453)***
C A Buchen Corp ....E....818 767-5408
9231 Glenoaks Blvd Sun Valley (91352) ***(P-11753)***
C A E, Azusa *Also called Casella Aluminum Extrusions* ***(P-11227)***
C A N Enterprises ....D....925 939-9736
291 Kinross Dr Walnut Creek (94598) ***(P-2776)***
C A P S, Santa Fe Springs *Also called Central Admxture Phrm Svcs Inc* ***(P-7837)***
C A Schroeder Inc (PA) ....E....818 365-9561
1318 1st St San Fernando (91340) ***(P-10980)***
C and R Pavers, Escondido *Also called Regina F Barajas* ***(P-13744)***
C and R Sales Inc ....F....951 686-6864
3750 S Riverside Ave Colton (92324) ***(P-11754)***
C and T Machining, Palmdale *Also called Sharkey Technology Group Inc* ***(P-16399)***
C B Concrete Construction ....F....408 354-3484
641 University Ave Los Gatos (95032) ***(P-10700)***
C B Machine Products Inc ....F....909 517-1828
13735 Iroquois Pl Chino (91710) ***(P-15809)***
C B S, San Marcos *Also called Falmat Inc* ***(P-11302)***
C B S Fasteners Inc ....E....714 779-6368
1345 N Brasher St Anaheim (92807) ***(P-12671)***
C B Sheets Inc ....E....562 921-1223
13901 Carmenita Rd Santa Fe Springs (90670) ***(P-5158)***
C Brewer Company, Ontario *Also called Balda C Brewer Inc* ***(P-9652)***
C C I, Orange *Also called Coastal Component Inds Inc* ***(P-18869)***
C C I Mling-Shipping Eqp Suppl, Ventura *Also called CCI Mail & Shipping Systems* ***(P-4969)***
C C M D Inc ....F....310 673-5532
700 Centinela Ave Inglewood (90302) ***(P-12956)***
C C T C North America, Monterey *Also called China Circuit Tech Corp N Amer* ***(P-17845)***
C C T Laser Services Inc ....F....209 833-1110
25421 S Schulte Rd Tracy (95377) ***(P-19268)***
C Case Company Inc ....E....559 867-3912
7010 W Cerini Ave Riverdale (93656) ***(P-175)***
C D International Tech Inc ....F....408 986-0725
695 Pinnacle Pl Livermore (94550) ***(P-18845)***
C D S, Canyon Country *Also called Commercial Display Systems LLC* ***(P-15419)***
C D Video, Santa Ana *Also called CD Video Manufacturing Inc* ***(P-19212)***
C E I, Oakhurst *Also called Control Enterprises Inc* ***(P-13325)***
C Enterprises Inc ....D....760 599-5111
2445 Cades Way Vista (92081) ***(P-15180)***
C Enterprises, L.P., Vista *Also called C Enterprises Inc* ***(P-15180)***
C F Manufacturing ....F....818 504-9899
11867 Sheldon St Sun Valley (91352) ***(P-19603)***
C F W Research & Dev Co ....F....805 489-8750
338 S 4th St Grover Beach (93433) ***(P-11213)***
C Gonshor Fine Jewelry Inc ....F....213 629-1075
640 S Hill St Ste 546a Los Angeles (90014) ***(P-22505)***
C H K Manufacturing Inc ....E....510 632-5637
960 98th Ave Oakland (94603) ***(P-5385)***
C J Precision Industries Inc ....F....562 426-3708
2817 Cherry Ave Signal Hill (90755) ***(P-15810)***
C K Tool Company Inc ....F....650 968-0261
1033 Wright Ave Mountain View (94043) ***(P-15811)***
C L E, Downey *Also called Can Lines Engineering Inc* ***(P-14702)***
C L Hann Industries Inc ....F....408 293-4800
1020 Timothy Dr San Jose (95133) ***(P-15812)***
C L P Inc (PA) ....E....619 444-3105
1546 E Main St El Cajon (92021) ***(P-24620)***
C M Automotive Systems Inc (PA) ....E....909 869-7912
120 Commerce Way Walnut (91789) ***(P-14625)***
C M C, Ontario *Also called California Mfg Cabinetry Inc* ***(P-4888)***
C M C, Fremont *Also called Content Management Corporation* ***(P-7034)***
C M D Products, Roseville *Also called Cmd Products* ***(P-9515)***
C M H Records Inc ....E....323 663-8098
2898 Rowena Ave Ste 201 Los Angeles (90039) ***(P-17311)***
C M I, Corona *Also called Corona Magnetics Inc* ***(P-18709)***
C M Machine Inc ....F....951 654-6019
560 S Grand Ave San Jacinto (92582) ***(P-15813)***
C M P, San Leandro *Also called Peggy S Lane Inc* ***(P-9595)***
C M Sport, Walnut Creek *Also called C A N Enterprises* ***(P-2776)***
C Magazine, Santa Monica *Also called C Publishing LLC* ***(P-6209)***
C Mondavi & Family (PA) ....D....707 967-2200
2800 Main St Saint Helena (94574) ***(P-1613)***
C N C, San Diego *Also called Howco Inc* ***(P-19684)***
C N C Machining Inc ....F....805 681-8855
510 S Fairview Ave Goleta (93117) ***(P-15814)***
C N P Signs & Graphics, San Diego *Also called California Neon Products* ***(P-23069)***
C NC Noodle Co ....F....510 732-1318
1787 Sabre St Hayward (94545) ***(P-2367)***
C P Auto Products Inc ....E....323 266-3850
3901 Medford St Los Angeles (90063) ***(P-12957)***
C P I, El Cajon *Also called Combustion Parts Inc* ***(P-13566)***
C P I, Agoura Hills *Also called Chatsworth Products Inc* ***(P-13509)***
C P P, Pomona *Also called Consolidated Foundries Inc* ***(P-11157)***
C P Products, Long Beach *Also called Diamond-U Products Inc* ***(P-13327)***
C P Shades Inc (PA) ....F....415 331-4581
403 Coloma St Sausalito (94965) ***(P-3300)***
C Pallets From Bkersfield Call ....F....661 833-2801
2508 E Brundage Ln Bakersfield (93307) ***(P-4353)***
C Preme Limited LLC ....F....310 355-0498
1250 E 223rd St Carson (90745) ***(P-22771)***
C Publishing LLC ....E....310 393-3800
1543 7th St Ste 202 Santa Monica (90401) ***(P-6209)***
C R Laurence Co Inc (HQ) ....B....323 588-1281
2503 E Vernon Ave Vernon (90058) ***(P-19604)***
C R M, Newport Beach *Also called Crm Co LLC* ***(P-9261)***
C R W Distributors Inc ....E....310 463-4577
1223 Wilshire Blvd Santa Monica (90403) ***(P-445)***
C S America Inc (HQ) ....E....323 583-7627
13365 Estelle St Corona (92879) ***(P-2887)***
C S Bio Co (PA) ....F....650 322-1111
20 Kelly Ct Menlo Park (94025) ***(P-7818)***
C S C, Poway *Also called Advanced Machining Tooling Inc* ***(P-14009)***
C S Dash Cover Inc ....F....562 790-8300
14020 Paramount Blvd Paramount (90723) ***(P-3776)***
C S I, Walnut Creek *Also called Computers and Structures Inc* ***(P-23767)***
C S I, Santa Ana *Also called Color Science Inc* ***(P-8699)***
C S L, Santa Clara *Also called Csl Operating LLC* ***(P-12981)***
C S M, Poway *Also called Toray Membrane Usa Inc* ***(P-15594)***
C S T, Thousand Oaks *Also called Custom Sensors & Tech Inc* ***(P-18882)***
C S T I, San Jose *Also called Chemical Safety Technology Inc* ***(P-14439)***
C T I, San Diego *Also called Corrugated Technologies Inc* ***(P-23778)***
C T L Printing Inds Inc ....E....714 635-2980
1741 W Lincoln Ave Ste A Anaheim (92801) ***(P-7011)***
C T R, Healdsburg *Also called Cooling Tower Resources Inc* ***(P-4498)***
C T V Inc ....F....408 378-1606
481 Vandell Way Campbell (95008) ***(P-6464)***
C W Cole & Company Inc ....E....626 443-2473
2560 Rosemead Blvd South El Monte (91733) ***(P-17017)***
C W Enterprises Inc ....F....951 786-9999
2111 Iowa Ave Ste D Riverside (92507) ***(P-17108)***
C W McGrath Inc ....F....619 443-3811
13080 Highway 8 Business El Cajon (92021) ***(P-308)***
C W Moss Auto Parts Inc ....F....714 639-3083
402 W Chapman Ave Orange (92866) ***(P-12743)***
C&C Building Automation Co Inc ....E....650 292-7450
390 Swift Ave Ste 22 South San Francisco (94080) ***(P-21445)***
C&C Metal Form & Tooling Inc ....E....562 861-9554
10654 Garfield Ave South Gate (90280) ***(P-12776)***
C&D Aerodesign, San Diego *Also called Safran Cabin Inc* ***(P-20222)***
C&D Precision Machining, San Jose *Also called C & D Semiconductor Svcs Inc* ***(P-14437)***
C&F WIRE PRODUCTS, Stanton *Also called Stecher Enterprises Inc* ***(P-13389)***
C&H Sugar, Crockett *Also called C&H Sugar Company Inc* ***(P-1350)***
C&H Sugar Company, Crockett *Also called American Sugar Refining Inc* ***(P-1349)***
C&H Sugar Company Inc ....A....510 787-2121
830 Loring Ave Crockett (94525) ***(P-1350)***
C&J Fab Center Inc ....F....310 323-0970
1415 W 135th St Gardena (90249) ***(P-12141)***
C&M Fine Pack, San Bernardino *Also called D&W Fine Pack LLC* ***(P-9745)***
C&O Manufacturing Company Inc ....D....562 692-7525
9640 Beverly Rd Pico Rivera (90660) ***(P-12142)***
C&S Global Foods Inc ....F....209 392-2223
20110 State Highway 33 Dos Palos (93620) ***(P-2413)***
C&T Publishing Inc ....E....925 677-0377
1651 Challenge Dr Concord (94520) ***(P-6210)***
C-Cure, Huntington Beach *Also called Custom Building Products Inc* ***(P-8864)***
C-Cure, Ontario *Also called Western States Wholesale Inc* ***(P-10525)***
C-Fab ....E....949 646-2616
932 W 17th St Costa Mesa (92627) ***(P-11575)***
C-Pak Industries Inc ....E....909 880-6017
4925 Hallmark Pkwy San Bernardino (92407) ***(P-9681)***
C-Preme, Carson *Also called C Preme Limited LLC* ***(P-22771)***
C-Quest Inc ....D....323 980-1400
1439 S Herbert Ave Commerce (90023) ***(P-3147)***
C-Thru Sunrooms, Corona *Also called Stell Industries Inc* ***(P-12575)***
C. R. C, Santa Clara *Also called Component Re-Engineering Inc* ***(P-18170)***
C.E.C., Colton *Also called Computerized Embroidery Co* ***(P-3735)***
C.P.s Fine Gems Jwly Collectn, Monrovia *Also called CPS Gem Corporation* ***(P-22508)***

Mergent e-mail: customerrelations@mergent.com
1048
2020 California
Manufacturers Register
(P-0000) Products & Services Section entry number
(PA)=Parent Co (HQ)=Headquarters (DH)=Div Headquarters

C2 Publishing, Costa Mesa *Also called Chet Cooper* ***(P-5903)***
C3 Iot, Redwood City *Also called C3ai Inc* ***(P-23704)***
C3-Ilex LLC (PA)...............E.......510 659-8300
46609 Fremont Blvd Fremont (94538) ***(P-20785)***
C3ai Inc (PA)...............C.......650 503-2200
1300 Seaport Blvd Ste 500 Redwood City (94063) ***(P-23704)***
C4 Litho...............F.......714 259-1073
27020 Daisy Cir Yorba Linda (92887) ***(P-6465)***
C8 Medisensors Inc...............E.......408 623-7281
6375 San Ignacio Ave San Jose (95119) ***(P-7819)***
Ca Inc...............C.......800 225-5224
3965 Freedom Cir Fl 6 Santa Clara (95054) ***(P-23705)***
Ca Inc...............E.......800 405-5540
3013 Douglas Blvd Ste 120 Roseville (95661) ***(P-23706)***
CA Signs, Pacoima *Also called California Signs Inc* ***(P-23070)***
CA Skyhook Inc...............E.......619 229-2169
4149 Cartagena Dr Ste B San Diego (92115) ***(P-4006)***
CA-Te LP...............F.......559 539-1530
33230 La Colina Dr Springville (93265) ***(P-12536)***
Ca-WA Corp...............E.......909 868-0630
1360 W 1st St Pomona (91766) ***(P-9291)***
Ca75 Atk, San Diego *Also called Northrop Grumman Innovation* ***(P-20466)***
Ca937 Afjrotc...............D.......818 394-3600
12431 Roscoe Blvd Ste 300 Sun Valley (91352) ***(P-23290)***
Caban Systems Inc...............F.......650 270-0113
858 Stanton Rd Burlingame (94010) ***(P-19153)***
Cabeau Inc...............E.......877 962-2232
21700 Oxnard St Ste 900 Woodland Hills (91367) ***(P-3834)***
Cabinet & Millwork Installers, Santa Clarita *Also called Door & Hardware Installers Inc* ***(P-4036)***
Cabinet Company Inc...............F.......530 273-7533
416 Crown Point Cir Ste 7 Grass Valley (95945) ***(P-4887)***
Cabinet Concepts...............F.......909 599-9191
131 S Eucla Ave San Dimas (91773) ***(P-4172)***
Cabinet Crafters, Lockeford *Also called John Hewitt* ***(P-4212)***
Cabinet Home, Alhambra *Also called Home Paradise LLC* ***(P-12816)***
Cabinet Master & Son Inc...............F.......626 332-0300
667 E Edna Pl Covina (91723) ***(P-4173)***
Cabinets & Doors Direct Inc...............F.......909 629-3388
858 E 1st St Pomona (91766) ***(P-4174)***
Cabinets 2000 LLC...............C.......562 868-0909
11100 Firestone Blvd Norwalk (90650) ***(P-4175)***
Cabinets 2000, Inc., Norwalk *Also called Cabinets 2000 LLC* ***(P-4175)***
Cabinets By Andy Inc...............F.......707 839-0220
2411 Central Ave McKinleyville (95519) ***(P-4176)***
Cabinets Galore Oc, San Diego *Also called Cabinets Galore Orange County* ***(P-3928)***
Cabinets Galore Orange County...............E.......858 586-0555
9279 Cabot Dr Ste D San Diego (92126) ***(P-3928)***
Cable Aml Inc (PA)...............F.......310 222-5599
2271 W 205th St Ste 101 Torrance (90501) ***(P-17475)***
Cable Builders Inc...............F.......760 308-0042
846 Robert Ln Encinitas (92024) ***(P-2907)***
Cable Car Classics Inc...............F.......707 433-6810
3239 Rio Lindo Ave Healdsburg (95448) ***(P-20368)***
Cable Connection Inc...............D.......510 249-9000
1035 Mission Ct Fremont (94539) ***(P-16879)***
Cable Devices Incorporated (HQ)...............C.......714 554-4370
3008 S Croddy Way Santa Ana (92704) ***(P-15181)***
Cable Exchange, Santa Ana *Also called Cable Devices Incorporated* ***(P-15181)***
Cable Harness Systems Inc...............E.......714 841-9650
7462 Talbert Ave Huntington Beach (92648) ***(P-18846)***
Cable Manufacturing Tech...............F.......925 687-3700
2455 Bates Ave Ste E Concord (94520) ***(P-2908)***
Cable Moore Inc (PA)...............E.......510 436-8000
4700 Coliseum Way Oakland (94601) ***(P-13399)***
Cable Strand, Long Beach *Also called Cablestrand Corp* ***(P-13400)***
Cable-Cisco, San Francisco *Also called Carpenter Group* ***(P-13844)***
Cableco, Santa Fe Springs *Also called Carpenter Group* ***(P-13403)***
Cableco...............E.......562 942-8076
13100 Firestone Blvd Santa Fe Springs (90670) ***(P-2909)***
Cablestrand Corp...............F.......562 595-4527
2660 Signal Pkwy Long Beach (90755) ***(P-13400)***
Cabletek Inc...............F.......310 523-5000
525 Finney Ct Gardena (90248) ***(P-16880)***
Cabo Gear, Carlsbad *Also called Cabo International Inc* ***(P-2674)***
Cabo International Inc...............F.......760 597-9199
3512 Celinda Dr Carlsbad (92008) ***(P-2674)***
Caborca Leather LLC...............E.......707 463-7607
4275 Peaceful Glen Rd Vacaville (95688) ***(P-3529)***
Cabrac Inc...............E.......818 834-0177
13250 Paxton St Pacoima (91331) ***(P-12777)***
Cac Inc...............F.......949 587-3328
20322 Windrow Dr Ste 100 Lake Forest (92630) ***(P-18847)***
Cac Fabrication Inc...............F.......818 882-2626
9710 Owensmouth Ave Ste C Chatsworth (91311) ***(P-11755)***
Cacciatore Fine Wns & Olv Oil (PA)...............F.......559 757-9463
1875 S Elm St Pixley (93256) ***(P-1614)***
Cachcach, Santa Ana *Also called Funny-Bunny Inc* ***(P-3085)***
Cache Creek Foods LLC...............F.......530 662-1764
411 N Pioneer Ave Woodland (95776) ***(P-2414)***
Cache Phlow Enterprise...............F.......925 609-8649
1894 Lynwood Dr Apt D Concord (94519) ***(P-7305)***
Cacique Inc (PA)...............C.......626 961-3399
800 Royal Oaks Dr Ste 200 Monrovia (91016) ***(P-542)***
Cacique Cheese, Monrovia *Also called Cacique Inc* ***(P-542)***
Caco-Pacific Corporation (PA)...............C.......626 331-3361
813 N Cummings Rd Covina (91724) ***(P-14027)***
Cactus Tape, Irwindale *Also called V Himark (usa) Inc* ***(P-8901)***
Cad Manufacturing Inc...............F.......562 408-1113
7320 Adams St Paramount (90723) ***(P-20061)***
Cad Works Inc...............E.......626 336-5491
16366 E Valley Blvd La Puente (91744) ***(P-15815)***
Cade Corporation...............D.......310 539-2508
609 Deep Valley Dr Rllng HLS Est (90274) ***(P-8944)***
Caden Concepts LLC...............F.......323 651-1190
13412 Ventura Blvd # 300 Sherman Oaks (91423) ***(P-3726)***
Cadence Acoustics, City of Industry *Also called H&N Brothers Co Ltd* ***(P-17236)***
Cadence Aerospace, Anaheim *Also called Aerospace Parts Holdings Inc* ***(P-20023)***
Cadence Aerospace LLC (PA)...............E.......949 877-3630
3150 E Miraloma Ave Anaheim (92806) ***(P-20062)***
Cadence Design Systems Inc...............E.......408 943-1234
707 California St Mountain View (94041) ***(P-23707)***
Cadence Design Systems Inc...............E.......949 788-6080
7505 Irvine Center Dr # 250 Irvine (92618) ***(P-23708)***
Cadence Design Systems Inc (PA)...............A.......408 943-1234
2655 Seely Ave Bldg 5 San Jose (95134) ***(P-23709)***
Cadence Design Systems Inc...............F.......510 647-2800
2150 Shattuck Ave Fl 10 Berkeley (94704) ***(P-23710)***
Cadence Design Systems Inc...............F.......925 895-3202
6700 Koll Center Pkwy # 160 Pleasanton (94566) ***(P-23711)***
Cadence Gourmet LLC...............E.......951 272-5949
155 Klug Cir Corona (92880) ***(P-2415)***
Cadence Gourmet Involve Foods, Corona *Also called Cadence Gourmet LLC* ***(P-2415)***
Cadence US Inc (PA)...............F.......408 943-1234
2655 Seely Ave San Jose (95134) ***(P-23712)***
Cadillac Plating Inc...............F.......714 639-0342
1147 W Struck Ave Orange (92867) ***(P-12958)***
Cae Automation and Test LLC...............F.......408 204-0006
44368 Warm Springs Blvd Fremont (94538) ***(P-15816)***
Caer Inc...............E.......415 879-9864
129 N Laurel Ave Los Angeles (90048) ***(P-721)***
Caesar Hardware Intl Ltd...............F.......800 306-3829
4985 Hallmark Pkwy San Bernardino (92407) ***(P-23291)***
Cafe Champagne, Temecula *Also called Thornton Winery* ***(P-1956)***
Cafe Fanny, Berkeley *Also called Le Barbocce Inc* ***(P-1029)***
Cafe Niebaum Coppola, San Francisco *Also called Niebam-Cppola Estate Winery LP* ***(P-1841)***
Cafe Virtuoso LLC...............F.......619 550-1830
1622 National Ave San Diego (92113) ***(P-2279)***
Cafecito Organico Oc LLC...............F.......213 537-8367
2916 Heathercliff Rd Malibu (90265) ***(P-2280)***
Caffe Cardinale Cof Roasting...............F.......831 626-2095
246 The Crossroads Blvd Carmel (93923) ***(P-2281)***
Caffe Clabria Cof Roasters LLC...............E.......619 683-7787
3933 30th St San Diego (92104) ***(P-2282)***
Caffe Classico Foods Inc...............F.......925 602-5400
2500 Annalisa Dr Concord (94520) ***(P-2283)***
Caffe D'Vita, Chino *Also called Brad Barry Company Ltd* ***(P-2278)***
Caffe Del Mar, Solana Beach *Also called Future Wave Technologies Inc* ***(P-2294)***
Cain Cellars Inc...............E.......707 963-1616
3800 Langtry Rd Saint Helena (94574) ***(P-1615)***
Cain Vineyard & Winery, Saint Helena *Also called Cain Cellars Inc* ***(P-1615)***
Caitac Garment Processing Inc...............B.......310 217-9888
14725 S Broadway Gardena (90248) ***(P-2823)***
Cake Cafe Bar LLC...............F.......530 615-4126
131 Mill St Ste 1 Grass Valley (95945) ***(P-1171)***
Cakebread Cellar Vineyards, Rutherford *Also called Cakebread Cellars* ***(P-1616)***
Cakebread Cellars...............D.......707 963-5221
8300 Saint Helena Hwy Rutherford (94573) ***(P-1616)***
Cal Best Ceilings Inc...............F.......909 946-1565
979 Seaboard Ct Upland (91786) ***(P-17018)***
Cal Bind...............E.......626 338-3699
4700 Littlejohn St Baldwin Park (91706) ***(P-7328)***
Cal Central Catering Trailers, Modesto *Also called Golden Valley & Associates Inc* ***(P-13874)***
Cal Coast Acidizing Co...............F.......805 934-2411
6226 Dominion Rd Santa Maria (93454) ***(P-176)***
Cal Coast Acidizing Service, Santa Maria *Also called Cal Coast Acidizing Co* ***(P-176)***
Cal Coast Stucco...............F.......818 767-0115
10932 Tuxford St Sun Valley (91352) ***(P-11002)***
Cal Coil Magnetics Inc...............E.......626 455-0011
2523 Seaman Ave El Monte (91733) ***(P-18705)***
Cal Door, Salinas *Also called California Kit Cab Door Corp* ***(P-4010)***
Cal Fiber Inc...............F.......323 268-0191
1360 S Beverly Glen Blvd # 401 Los Angeles (90024) ***(P-2929)***
Cal Flex, San Fernando *Also called California Flex Corporation* ***(P-9685)***
Cal LLC Breakwater Intl...............F.......310 518-1718
327 Lecouvreur Ave Wilmington (90744) ***(P-20281)***
Cal Moto...............F.......650 966-1183
2490 Old Middlefield Way Mountain View (94043) ***(P-20388)***
Cal Nor Design Inc (PA)...............F.......925 829-7722
14126 Washington Ave San Leandro (94578) ***(P-14028)***
Cal Nor Embroidery & Spc...............F.......916 786-3131
4208 Douglas Blvd Ste 100 Granite Bay (95746) ***(P-3727)***
Cal Nor Powder Coating Inc...............F.......707 462-0217
265 E Clay St Ukiah (95482) ***(P-13152)***
Cal Pac Sheet Metal Inc...............E.......714 979-2733
2720 S Main St Ste B Santa Ana (92707) ***(P-12143)***
Cal Pacific Dyeing & Finishing...............D.......310 327-3792
233 E Gardena Blvd Gardena (90248) ***(P-2851)***
Cal Partitions Inc...............F.......310 539-1911
23814 President Ave Harbor City (90710) ***(P-4966)***
Cal Pipe Manufacturing Inc (PA)...............E.......562 803-4388
19440 S Dminguez Hills Dr Compton (90220) ***(P-13462)***
Cal Plate (PA)...............D.......562 403-3000
17110 Jersey Ave Artesia (90701) ***(P-14318)***

A
L
P
H
A
B
E
T
I
C

Employee Codes: A=Over 500 employees, B=251-500
C=101-250, D=51-100, E=20-50, F=10-19
2020 California
Manfacturers Register
© Mergent Inc. 1-800-342-5647
1049

Cal Portland Cement Co...E...909 423-0436
695 S Rancho Ave Colton (92324) ***(P-10701)***
Cal Precision Inc...F...951 273-9901
1680 Commerce St Corona (92880) ***(P-15817)***
Cal Printing, San Jose *Also called Four Colorcom* ***(P-6582)***
Cal Quake Construction Inc...E...323 931-2969
636 N Formosa Ave Los Angeles (90036) ***(P-177)***
Cal Saw Canada, San Francisco *Also called Sawbird Inc* ***(P-11555)***
Cal Sheets LLC...D...209 234-3300
1212 Performance Dr Stockton (95206) ***(P-5203)***
Cal Signal Corp...F...650 343-6100
384 Beach Rd Burlingame (94010) ***(P-17719)***
Cal Simba Inc (PA)...E...805 240-1177
1680 Universe Cir Oxnard (93033) ***(P-22588)***
Cal Southern Braiding Inc...D...562 927-5531
7450 Scout Ave Bell Gardens (90201) ***(P-18848)***
Cal Southern Graphics Corp...D...310 559-3600
8432 Steller Dr Culver City (90232) ***(P-6466)***
Cal Spas, Pomona *Also called California Acrylic Inds Inc* ***(P-23292)***
Cal Springs LLC...D...562 943-5599
6250 N Irwindale Ave Irwindale (91702) ***(P-7012)***
Cal Star Systems Group Inc...E...818 922-2000
6613 Valjean Ave Van Nuys (91406) ***(P-19269)***
Cal State Rubber, Santa Fe Springs *Also called Duro Roller Company Inc* ***(P-9303)***
Cal Stitch Embroidery Inc...F...909 465-5448
2057 Hunter Rd Chino Hills (91709) ***(P-3728)***
Cal Tape & Label, Anaheim *Also called C T L Printing Inds Inc* ***(P-7011)***
Cal Tech Precision Inc...D...714 992-4130
1830 N Lemon St Anaheim (92801) ***(P-20063)***
Cal Traders...F...530 566-1405
1260 Muir Ave Chico (95973) ***(P-1423)***
Cal Trend Automotive Products, Santa Ana *Also called Cal Trends Accessories LLC* ***(P-3835)***
Cal Trends Accessories LLC...E...714 708-5115
2121 S Anne St Santa Ana (92704) ***(P-3835)***
Cal Vsta Erosion Ctrl Pdts LLC...E...530 476-0706
459 Country Rd 99w 99 W Arbuckle (95912) ***(P-13713)***
Cal West Construction Inc...F...559 217-3306
4670 N Wilson Ave Fresno (93704) ***(P-14029)***
Cal West Designs, Santa Fe Springs *Also called K S Designs Inc* ***(P-23145)***
Cal West Spcialty Coatings Inc...F...408 720-7440
1058 W Evelyn Ave Ste 10 Sunnyvale (94086) ***(P-8627)***
Cal Yuba Investments, Olivehurst *Also called Yuba River Moulding Mllwk Inc* ***(P-4159)***
Cal-Asia Truss Inc...E...916 685-5648
10547 E Stockton Blvd Elk Grove (95624) ***(P-4291)***
Cal-Aurum Industries...E...714 898-0996
15632 Container Ln Huntington Beach (92649) ***(P-12959)***
Cal-Coast Dairy Systems Inc...E...209 634-9026
424 S Tegner Rd Turlock (95380) ***(P-13617)***
Cal-Coast Pkg & Crating Inc...E...310 518-7215
2040 E 220th St Carson (90810) ***(P-4333)***
Cal-Comp USA (san Diego) Inc...C...858 587-6900
1940 Camino Vida Roble Carlsbad (92008) ***(P-17839)***
Cal-Draulics, Corona *Also called Johnson Caldraul Inc* ***(P-20147)***
Cal-India Foods International...E...909 613-1660
13591 Yorba Ave Chino (91710) ***(P-8725)***
Cal-June Inc (PA)...E...323 877-4164
5238 Vineland Ave North Hollywood (91601) ***(P-11576)***
Cal-Mil Plastic Products Inc (PA)...E...800 321-9069
4079 Calle Platino Oceanside (92056) ***(P-9682)***
Cal-Mold Incorporated...C...951 361-6400
3900 Hamner Ave Eastvale (91752) ***(P-9683)***
Cal-Monarch, Corona *Also called California Wire Products Corp* ***(P-13401)***
Cal-Pac Chemical Co Inc...F...323 585-2178
6231 Maywood Ave Huntington Park (90255) ***(P-7473)***
Cal-Sensors Inc (PA)...E...707 303-3837
1260 Calle Suerte Camarillo (93012) ***(P-20552)***
Cal-Sign Wholesale Inc...F...209 523-7446
5260 Jerusalem Ct Modesto (95356) ***(P-23068)***
Cal-Tron Corporation...E...760 873-8491
2290 Dixon Ln Bishop (93514) ***(P-9684)***
Cal-Tron Plating Inc...E...562 945-1181
11919 Rivera Rd Santa Fe Springs (90670) ***(P-12960)***
Cal-Weld Inc...C...510 226-0100
4308 Solar Way Fremont (94538) ***(P-13505)***
Cal-West Machining Inc...F...714 637-4161
1734 W Sequoia Ave Orange (92868) ***(P-15621)***
Calamp Corp (PA)...C...949 600-5600
15635 Alton Pkwy Ste 250 Irvine (92618) ***(P-17476)***
Calamp Corp...F...760 438-9010
2231 Rutherford Rd # 110 Carlsbad (92008) ***(P-17477)***
Calaveras Enterprise, San Andreas *Also called Calaveras First Co Inc* ***(P-5574)***
Calaveras First Co Inc...E...209 754-3861
15 Main St San Andreas (95249) ***(P-5574)***
Calaveras Materials Inc (HQ)...E...209 883-0448
1100 Lowe Rd Hughson (95326) ***(P-10702)***
Calaveras Materials Inc...F...209 883-0448
1100 Lowe Rd Hughson (95326) ***(P-10545)***
Calavo Growers Inc (PA)...B...805 525-1245
1141 Cummings Rd Ste A Santa Paula (93060) ***(P-2416)***
Calbiotech Inc...E...619 660-6162
1935 Cordell Ct El Cajon (92020) ***(P-21646)***
Calchef Foods LLC...E...888 638-7083
4221 E Mariposa Rd Ste B Stockton (95215) ***(P-880)***
Calco Supply Inc...E...415 760-7793
1460 Yosemite Ave San Francisco (94124) ***(P-17109)***
Calcon Steel Construction...E...310 768-8094
1226 W 196th St Torrance (90502) ***(P-11756)***
Calcraft Company, Rialto *Also called Calcraft Corporation* ***(P-11757)***
Calcraft Corporation...F...909 879-2900
1426 S Willow Ave Rialto (92376) ***(P-11757)***
Caldera Medical Inc...D...818 879-6555
5171 Clareton Dr Agoura Hills (91301) ***(P-21647)***
Caldigit Inc...F...714 572-6668
1941 E Miraloma Ave Ste B Placentia (92870) ***(P-15010)***
Caldyn, Los Angeles *Also called California Dynamics Corp* ***(P-21446)***
Caleb Enterprises Inc...F...760 683-8787
5857 Owens Ave Ste 300 Carlsbad (92008) ***(P-23713)***
Caleb Technology Corporation...E...310 257-4780
2905 Lomita Blvd Torrance (90505) ***(P-19154)***
Calera Corporation...E...831 731-6000
11500 Dolan Rd Moss Landing (95039) ***(P-8726)***
Calex Mfg Co Inc...E...925 687-4411
2401 Stanwell Dr Frnt Concord (94520) ***(P-18849)***
Calfabco (PA)...F...323 265-1205
1432 Chico Ave South El Monte (91733) ***(P-12778)***
Calgon Carbon Corporation...F...707 668-5637
501 Hatchery Rd Blue Lake (95525) ***(P-7474)***
Calgren Renewable Fuels, Pixley *Also called Gfp Ethanol LLC* ***(P-8740)***
Calhoun & Poxon Company Inc...F...323 225-2328
5330 Alhambra Ave Los Angeles (90032) ***(P-16588)***
Cali Chem Inc...E...714 265-3740
14271 Corp Dr Ste B Garden Grove (92843) ***(P-8454)***
Cali Today Daily Newspaper...F...408 297-8271
1310 Tully Rd Ste 105 San Jose (95122) ***(P-5575)***
Cali-Fame Los Angeles Inc...D...310 747-5263
20934 S Santa Fe Ave Carson (90810) ***(P-3462)***
Caliame, Sebastopol *Also called Marimar Torres Estate Corp* ***(P-1811)***
Caliber Screenprinting Inc...F...760 353-3499
1101 S Hope St El Centro (92243) ***(P-3777)***
Caliber Sealing Solutions Inc (PA)...F...949 461-0555
2780 Palisades Dr Corona (92882) ***(P-9221)***
Calico Tag & Label Inc...F...562 944-6889
13233 Barton Cir Whittier (90605) ***(P-7013)***
Calidad Inc...E...909 947-3937
1730 S Balboa Ave Ontario (91761) ***(P-11369)***
Calient Technologies Inc (PA)...E...805 562-5500
25 Castilian Dr Goleta (93117) ***(P-17351)***
Caliente Systems Inc...D...510 790-0300
6821 Central Ave Newark (94560) ***(P-11999)***
Calif Frut and Tmto Ktchn LLC...F...530 666-6600
1785 Ashby Rd Merced (95348) ***(P-2417)***
Calif Silk Screen, Torrance *Also called California Silkscreen* ***(P-3779)***
Califia Farms LLC...E...661 679-1000
33374 Lerdo Hwy Bakersfield (93308) ***(P-2048)***
Califoam Products Inc...F...909 364-1600
10775 Silicon Ave Montclair (91763) ***(P-9292)***
California Acrylic Inds Inc (HQ)...E...909 623-8781
1462 E 9th St Pomona (91766) ***(P-23292)***
California Acti, Irvine *Also called Acti Corporation Inc* ***(P-17181)***
California Amforge Corporation...D...626 334-4931
750 N Vernon Ave Azusa (91702) ***(P-11031)***
California Apparel News, Los Angeles *Also called Apparel News Group* ***(P-5880)***
California Art Products Co, North Hollywood *Also called Capco/Psa* ***(P-9693)***
California Audio Video Distrg, South San Francisco *Also called Cav Distributing Corporation* ***(P-17312)***
California Bag, Woodland *Also called Acme Bag Co Inc* ***(P-5432)***
California Bedrooms Inc...E...559 233-7050
95 Santa Fe Ave Fresno (93721) ***(P-4559)***
California Bio-Productex Inc...E...559 582-5308
13220 Crown Ave Hanford (93230) ***(P-8727)***
California Blimps...F...949 650-1183
738 W 17th St Ste D Costa Mesa (92627) ***(P-19886)***
California Blind Company, North Hollywood *Also called Carl Nersesian* ***(P-4015)***
California Bottling Company...E...916 772-1000
8250 Industrial Ave Roseville (95678) ***(P-2049)***
California Box II...E...909 944-9202
8949 Toronto Ave Rancho Cucamonga (91730) ***(P-5204)***
California Brazing, Newark *Also called Nevada Heat Treating LLC* ***(P-24653)***
California Broach Company...F...323 260-4812
4815 Telegraph Rd Los Angeles (90022) ***(P-15818)***
California Button, Anaheim *Also called United Paper Box Inc* ***(P-5319)***
California Cab & Store Fix...E...916 386-1340
8472 Carbide Ct Sacramento (95828) ***(P-4007)***
California Cage Co, San Diego *Also called Specialty Steel Products Inc* ***(P-13436)***
California Calendar, Chino Hills *Also called Ad Industries LLC* ***(P-7302)***
California Candy, South El Monte *Also called California Snack Foods Inc* ***(P-1358)***
California Carbon Company Inc...F...562 436-1962
2825 E Grant St Wilmington (90744) ***(P-7475)***
California Cart Builder LLC...F...951 245-1114
29375 Hunco Way Lake Elsinore (92530) ***(P-19815)***
California Cascade Industries...C...916 736-3353
7512 14th Ave Sacramento (95820) ***(P-4472)***
California Cascade-Woodland...F...530 666-1261
1492 Churchill Downs Ave Woodland (95776) ***(P-4473)***
California Cedar Products Co (PA)...E...209 932-5002
2385 Arch Airport Rd # 500 Stockton (95206) ***(P-4495)***
California Churros Corporation...C...909 370-4777
751 Via Lata Colton (92324) ***(P-1172)***
California Classics, Santa Clarita *Also called California Millworks Corp* ***(P-4011)***
California Clock Co (PA)...F...714 545-4321
16060 Abajo Cir Fountain Valley (92708) ***(P-22478)***
California Coast Clothing LLC...F...323 923-3870
3690 S Santa Fe Ave Vernon (90058) ***(P-2675)***
California Coating Lab...E...510 357-1800
670 Mccormick St San Leandro (94577) ***(P-22343)***

California Cocktails Inc .....F......714 990-0982
345 Oak Pl Brea (92821) *(P-2197)*
California Combining Corp .....E......323 589-5727
5607 S Santa Fe Ave Vernon (90058) *(P-2895)*
California Commercial Asp Corp (PA) .....F......858 513-0611
4211 Ponderosa Ave Ste C San Diego (92123) *(P-9087)*
California Community News LLC (HQ) .....B......626 472-5297
5091 4th St Irwindale (91706) *(P-5576)*
California Compactor Svc Inc .....F......661 298-5556
17000 Sierra Hwy Canyon Country (91351) *(P-13506)*
California Composite Cont Corp .....E......951 940-9343
22770 Perry St Perris (92570) *(P-5287)*
California Composite Container, Perris *Also called Green Products Packaging Corp (P-5293)*
California Composites MGT Inc .....E......714 258-0405
1935 E Occidental St Santa Ana (92705) *(P-20064)*
California Concentrate Company .....E......209 334-9112
18678 N Highway 99 Acampo (95220) *(P-905)*
California Concrete Pipe Corp .....F......209 466-4212
2960 S Highway 99 Stockton (95215) *(P-10546)*
California Costume Int'l, Los Angeles *Also called Califrnia Cstume Cllctions Inc (P-3544)*
California Countertop Inc (PA) .....E......619 460-0205
7811 Alvarado Rd La Mesa (91942) *(P-4967)*
California Cstm Frt & Flavors, Irwindale *Also called California Custom Fruits (P-2198)*
California Cstm Furn & Uphl Co .....E......760 727-1444
3325 San Pasqual Trl Escondido (92025) *(P-3778)*
California Custom Caps .....E......626 454-1766
2319 Sastre Ave South El Monte (91733) *(P-3463)*
California Custom Fruits (PA) .....D......626 736-4130
15800 Tapia St Irwindale (91706) *(P-2198)*
California Dairies Inc (PA) .....D......559 625-2200
2000 N Plaza Dr Visalia (93291) *(P-688)*
California Dairies Inc .....D......559 233-5154
755 F St Fresno (93706) *(P-689)*
California Dairies Inc .....D......562 809-2595
11709 Artesia Blvd Artesia (90701) *(P-690)*
California Dairies Inc .....D......209 656-1942
475 S Tegner Rd Turlock (95380) *(P-537)*
California Decor .....E......310 603-9944
541 E Pine St Compton (90222) *(P-4008)*
California Deluxe Window Indus (PA) .....E......818 349-5566
20735 Superior St Chatsworth (91311) *(P-4009)*
California Dental Group, North Hollywood *Also called Airgas Usa LLC (P-7407)*
California Designers Choice .....E......805 987-5820
547 Constitution Ave F Camarillo (93012) *(P-4177)*
California Die Casting Inc .....E......909 947-9947
1820 S Grove Ave Ontario (91761) *(P-11353)*
California Digital Inc (PA) .....D......310 217-0500
6 Saddleback Rd Rolling Hills (90274) *(P-15182)*
California Door, Morgan Hill *Also called California Kit Cab Door Corp (P-4178)*
California Dried Fruit Inc .....E......559 233-0970
9145 W Herndon Ave Fresno (93723) *(P-845)*
California Dynamics Corp (PA) .....E......323 223-3882
5572 Alhambra Ave Los Angeles (90032) *(P-21446)*
California Dynasty, Los Angeles *Also called MGT Industries Inc (P-3373)*
California Economizer .....E......714 898-9963
5622 Engineer Dr Huntington Beach (92649) *(P-16704)*
California Electric Steel .....E......209 736-0465
250 Monte Verda Angels Camp (95222) *(P-11169)*
California Electric Supply, Anaheim *Also called Ced Anaheim 018 (P-19271)*
California Embroidery, Fresno *Also called Holcomb Products Inc (P-3745)*
California Etching Inc .....F......707 224-9966
1952 Iroquois St NAPA (94559) *(P-13153)*
California Exotic Novlt LLC .....D......909 606-1950
1455 E Francis St Ontario (91761) *(P-23293)*
California Expanded Met Pdts (PA) .....D......626 369-3564
13191 Crosrds Pkwy N 32 City of Industry (91746) *(P-12144)*
California Expanded Met Pdts .....E......925 473-9340
1001a Pttsburg Antoch Hwy Pittsburg (94565) *(P-12537)*
California Family Foods LLC .....D......530 476-3326
6550 Struckmeyer Rd Arbuckle (95912) *(P-1036)*
California Farm Equipment Mag .....F......661 589-0435
17045 S Central Vly Hwy Shafter (93263) *(P-13618)*
California Fashion Club Inc (PA) .....F......626 575-1838
207 S 9th Ave La Puente (91746) *(P-3263)*
California Faucets .....F......657 400-1639
5231 Argosy Ave Huntington Beach (92649) *(P-11660)*
California Faucets Inc (PA) .....D......714 890-0450
5271 Argosy Ave Huntington Beach (92649) *(P-11661)*
California Feather Inds Inc .....F......323 585-5800
2241 E 49th St Vernon (90058) *(P-3606)*
California Flex Corporation (PA) .....F......818 361-1169
1318 1st St San Fernando (91340) *(P-9685)*
California Flexrake Corp .....E......626 443-4026
9620 Gidley St Temple City (91780) *(P-11523)*
California Frames, Los Angeles *Also called Ronald D Teson Inc (P-3983)*
California Fruit Basket, Sanger *Also called Melkonian Enterprises Inc (P-854)*
California Gasket and Rbr Corp (PA) .....E......310 323-4250
533 W Collins Ave Orange (92867) *(P-9293)*
California Glass & Mirror Div, Santa Ana *Also called Twed-Dells Inc (P-10396)*
California Glass Bending Corp .....E......310 549-5255
2100 W 139th St Gardena (90249) *(P-10344)*
California Gold Bars Inc (PA) .....F......510 848-9292
1041 Folger Ave Berkeley (94710) *(P-1408)*
California Heating Equipment, Anaheim *Also called Energy Reconnaissance Inc (P-14761)*
California Heavy Oil Inc .....E......888 848-4754
10889 Wilshire Blvd Los Angeles (90024) *(P-111)*
California Heritage Mills Inc .....E......530 438-2100
1 Comet Ln Maxwell (95955) *(P-1037)*

California Hot Springs Water .....F......661 548-6582
42231 Hot Springs Dr Calif Hot Spg (93207) *(P-2050)*
California House, Sacramento *Also called Beauty Craft Furniture Corp (P-4553)*
California Hydroforming Co Inc .....F......626 912-0036
850 Lawson St City of Industry (91748) *(P-12145)*
California Industrial Mfg LLC (PA) .....F......530 846-9960
1221 Independence Pl Gridley (95948) *(P-23294)*
California Industrial Fabrics .....E......619 661-7166
2325 Marconi Ct San Diego (92154) *(P-2743)*
California Industrial Rbr Co .....E......530 674-2444
1690 Sierra Ave Yuba City (95993) *(P-7626)*
California Insulated Wire & .....D......818 569-4930
3050 N California St Burbank (91504) *(P-11292)*
California Integration Coordin .....F......530 626-6168
6048 Enterprise Dr Diamond Springs (95619) *(P-17840)*
California Interfill Inc .....F......951 351-2619
8178 Mar Vista Ct Riverside (92504) *(P-8455)*
California Iron Design .....F......818 767-6690
8906 Lankershim Blvd Sun Valley (91352) *(P-24621)*
California Jig Grinding Co .....F......323 723-4017
861 N Holly Glen Dr Long Beach (90815) *(P-15819)*
California Kit Cab Door Corp .....C......831 784-5142
1800 Abbott St Salinas (93901) *(P-4010)*
California Kit Cab Door Corp (PA) .....D......408 782-5700
400 Cochrane Cir Morgan Hill (95037) *(P-4178)*
California Leisure Products .....F......707 462-2106
265 Thomas St Ukiah (95482) *(P-4458)*
California Lithographers, Concord *Also called Acme Press Inc (P-6394)*
California Machine Specialties, Chino *Also called Young Machine Inc (P-16535)*
California Master Printers .....F......626 812-8930
796 N Todd Ave Azusa (91702) *(P-6467)*
California Metal Group Inc .....F......310 609-1400
1205 S Alameda St Compton (90220) *(P-12146)*
California Metal Processing Co .....E......323 753-2247
1518 W Slauson Ave # 1530 Los Angeles (90047) *(P-12961)*
California Mfg & Engrg Co LLC .....C......559 842-1500
1401 S Madera Ave Kerman (93630) *(P-13714)*
California Mfg Cabinetry Inc .....F......909 930-3632
1474 E Francis St Ontario (91761) *(P-4888)*
California Micro Devices Corp (HQ) .....E......408 542-1051
3001 Stender Way Santa Clara (95054) *(P-18689)*
California Milling Co, Los Angeles *Also called Grain Craft Inc (P-1004)*
California Millworks Corp .....E......661 294-2345
27772 Avenue Scott Santa Clarita (91355) *(P-4011)*
California Mini Truck Inc .....F......661 398-9585
12539 Jomani Dr Bakersfield (93312) *(P-19605)*
California Motor Controls Inco .....F......707 746-6255
3070 Bay Vista Ct Benicia (94510) *(P-16705)*
California Natural Color, Modesto *Also called E & J Gallo Winery (P-1678)*
California Natural Products .....C......209 858-2525
1250 Lathrop Rd Lathrop (95330) *(P-2418)*
California Natural Vitamins .....E......818 772-8441
9044 Independence Ave Canoga Park (91304) *(P-7820)*
California Neon Products .....D......619 283-2191
2555 Cmino Del Rio S Ste San Diego (92108) *(P-23069)*
California New Foods LLC .....E......831 444-1872
11165 Commercial Pkwy Castroville (95012) *(P-2419)*
California Newspapers Inc .....A......415 883-8600
150 Alameda Del Prado Novato (94949) *(P-5577)*
California Newspapers Partnr (PA) .....C......408 920-5333
4 N 2nd St Ste 800 San Jose (95113) *(P-5578)*
California Nuggets Inc .....E......209 599-7131
23073 S Frederick Rd Ripon (95366) *(P-2319)*
California Olive and Vine LLC .....F......530 763-7921
1670 Poole Blvd Yuba City (95993) *(P-1467)*
California Olive Ranch Inc (PA) .....E......530 846-8000
1367 E Lassen Ave Ste A1 Chico (95973) *(P-1468)*
California Pak Intl Inc .....E......310 223-2500
1700 S Wilmington Ave Compton (90220) *(P-16542)*
California Panel Systems LLP .....E......619 562-7010
1020 N Marshall Ave El Cajon (92020) *(P-12147)*
California Paper Bag Inc .....F......818 240-6717
1829 Dana St Ste A Glendale (91201) *(P-5434)*
California Paperboard, Santa Clara *Also called Caraustar Industries Inc (P-5290)*
California Performance Packg .....B......909 390-4422
33200 Lewis St Union City (94587) *(P-9511)*
California Pharmaceuticals LLC .....F......805 482-3737
768 Calle Plano Camarillo (93012) *(P-7821)*
California Pipe Fabricators .....E......707 678-3069
7277 Chevron Way Dixon (95620) *(P-13463)*
California Plasteck, Ontario *Also called Paramount Panels Inc (P-9953)*
California Plasteck, Ontario *Also called Paramount Panels Inc (P-20194)*
California Plastic Cntrs Inc .....F......562 423-3900
2210 E Artesia Blvd Long Beach (90805) *(P-9686)*
California Plastics, Riverside *Also called Consolidated Cont Holdings LLC (P-9718)*
California Plastics Inc .....F......805 483-8188
1611 S Rose Ave Oxnard (93033) *(P-9687)*
California Plastix Inc .....E......909 629-8288
1319 E 3rd St Pomona (91766) *(P-5386)*
California Portland Cement, Mojave *Also called Calportland Company (P-10404)*
California Pot & Tile Works, Los Angeles *Also called SMD Enterprises Inc (P-10450)*
California Pot & Tile Works, Los Angeles *Also called California Potteries Inc (P-10437)*
California Potteries Inc .....E......323 235-4151
859 E 60th St Los Angeles (90001) *(P-10437)*
California Poultry, Los Angeles *Also called Western Supreme Inc (P-531)*
California Precision Pdts Inc .....D......858 638-7300
6790 Flanders Dr San Diego (92121) *(P-12148)*

Employee Codes: A=Over 500 employees, B=251-500
C=101-250, D=51-100, E=20-50, F=10-19

2020 California
Manfacturers Register

© Mergent Inc. 1-800-342-5647

1051

California Premium Incentives, Lake Forest *Also called Aminco International USA Inc* ***(P-22494)***
California Pro-Specs Inc ....E....916 455-9890
2240 15th Ave Sacramento (95822) ***(P-3971)***
California Prtg Solutions Inc....E....909 307-2032
1950 W Park Ave Redlands (92373) ***(P-7014)***
California Quality Plas Inc....E....909 930-5667
2104 S Cucamonga Ave Ontario (91761) ***(P-9688)***
California Ramp Works Inc ....E....909 949-1601
273 N Benson Ave Upland (91786) ***(P-12538)***
California Reamer Company Inc....F....562 946-6377
12747 Los Nietos Rd Santa Fe Springs (90670) ***(P-14143)***
California Resources Corp....E....661 763-6107
1320 4th St Los Osos (93402) ***(P-34)***
California Resources Corp....E....661 395-8000
5000 Stockdale Hwy Bakersfield (93309) ***(P-35)***
California Resources Corp....F....661 412-5222
900 Old River Rd Bakersfield (93311) ***(P-112)***
California Resources Corp (PA) ....C....888 848-4754
27200 Tourney Rd Ste 200 Santa Clarita (91355) ***(P-36)***
California Resources Corp....D....562 624-3400
111 W Ocean Blvd Ste 800 Long Beach (90802) ***(P-37)***
California Resources Corp....F....707 374-4109
2692 Amerada Rd Rio Vista (94571) ***(P-113)***
California Resources Corp....F....805 641-5566
3055 Pacific Coast Hwy Ventura (93001) ***(P-114)***
California Resources Corp....E....310 208-8800
270 Quail Ct Ste 100 Santa Paula (93060) ***(P-38)***
California Resources Prod Corp ....D....805 483-8017
3450 E 5th St Oxnard (93033) ***(P-39)***
California Resources Prod Corp ....E....530 671-8201
855 Harter Pkwy Ste 200 Yuba City (95993) ***(P-40)***
California Resources Prod Corp (HQ) ....C....661 869-8000
900 Old River Rd Bakersfield (93311) ***(P-41)***
California Respiratory Care....D....818 379-9999
16055 Ventura Blvd # 715 Encino (91436) ***(P-8945)***
California Ribbon Carbn Co Inc ....D....323 724-9100
10914 Thienes Ave South El Monte (91733) ***(P-22961)***
California Scene Publishing....F....858 635-9400
8360 Juniper Creek Ln San Diego (92126) ***(P-6468)***
California Screw Products Corp....C....562 633-6626
14957 Gwenchris Ct Paramount (90723) ***(P-11577)***
California Sensor Corporation....E....760 438-0525
2075 Corte Del Nogal P Carlsbad (92011) ***(P-21447)***
California Shellfish Co Inc (PA) ....F....415 923-7400
818 E Broadway C San Gabriel (91776) ***(P-2257)***
California Signs Inc ....E....818 899-1888
10280 Glenoaks Blvd Pacoima (91331) ***(P-23070)***
California Silica Products LLC....F....909 947-0028
12808 Rancho Rd Adelanto (92301) ***(P-7476)***
California Silkscreen....F....310 320-5111
1507 Plaza Del Amo Torrance (90501) ***(P-3779)***
California Smart Foods ....E....415 826-0449
2565 3rd St Ste 342 San Francisco (94107) ***(P-1173)***
California Snack Foods Inc....E....626 444-4508
2131 Tyler Ave South El Monte (91733) ***(P-1358)***
California Specialty Farms, Los Angeles *Also called Worldwide Specialties Inc* ***(P-2649)***
California St UNI Channel Isla ....E....805 437-2670
45 Rincon Dr Unit 104a Camarillo (93012) ***(P-16543)***
California Stairs, Gilroy *Also called Northern California Stair* ***(P-4097)***
California Stamp Company, San Diego *Also called On-Line Stampco Inc* ***(P-22954)***
California Stay Co Inc....F....310 839-7236
2600 Overland Ave Apt 219 Los Angeles (90064) ***(P-10147)***
California Steel Inds Inc (PA)....B....909 350-6300
14000 San Bernardino Ave Fontana (92335) ***(P-11032)***
California Steel Inds Inc ....A....909 350-6300
1 California Steel Way Fontana (92335) ***(P-11033)***
California Steel Products ....F....310 603-5645
10851 Drury Ln Lynwood (90262) ***(P-12587)***
California Stl Stair Rail Mfr....E....209 824-1785
587 Carnegie St Manteca (95337) ***(P-11034)***
California Stone Coating....F....510 284-2554
37911 Von Euw Cmn Fremont (94536) ***(P-13715)***
California Sulphur Company ....E....562 437-0768
2250 E Pacific Coast Hwy Wilmington (90744) ***(P-7477)***
California Supertrucks Inc ....E....951 656-2903
14385 Veterans Way Moreno Valley (92553) ***(P-19522)***
California Surveying & Draftin....F....707 293-9449
411 Russell Ave Santa Rosa (95403) ***(P-15183)***
California Surveying & Draftin (PA)....E....916 344-0232
4733 Auburn Blvd Sacramento (95841) ***(P-15184)***
California Swatch Dyers Inc....E....213 748-8425
776 E Washington Blvd Los Angeles (90021) ***(P-2843)***
California Technical Pltg Corp....E....818 365-8205
11533 Bradley Ave San Fernando (91340) ***(P-12962)***
California Technology, Springville *Also called CA-Te LP* ***(P-12536)***
California Tool & Die, Azusa *Also called Mc William & Son Inc* ***(P-12841)***
California Trade Converters....E....818 899-1455
13299 Louvre St Pacoima (91331) ***(P-5159)***
California Treats Inc ....D....626 454-4099
2131 Tyler Ave El Monte (91733) ***(P-760)***
California Trusframe LLC....B....951 657-7491
144 Commerce Way Sanger (93657) ***(P-4292)***
California Trusframe LLC....C....951 657-7491
23665 Cajalco Rd Perris (92570) ***(P-4293)***
California Trusframe LLC (PA)....C....951 350-4880
25220 Hancock Ave Ste 350 Murrieta (92562) ***(P-4294)***
California Truss Company ....E....209 883-8000
2800 Tully Rd Hughson (95326) ***(P-4295)***
California Turbo Inc ....F....909 854-2800
10721 Business Dr Fontana (92337) ***(P-14650)***
California Webbing Mills Inc....F....323 753-0260
6920 Stanford Ave Los Angeles (90001) ***(P-2930)***
California Wire Products Corp....E....951 371-7730
1316 Railroad St Corona (92882) ***(P-13401)***
California Woodworking Inc ....E....805 982-9090
1726 Ives Ave Oxnard (93033) ***(P-4179)***
Californian, The, San Diego *Also called North County Times* ***(P-5782)***
Califrnia Anlytical Instrs Inc ....D....714 974-5560
1312 W Grove Ave Orange (92865) ***(P-20843)***
Califrnia Cstume Cllctions Inc (PA)....E....323 262-8383
210 S Anderson St Los Angeles (90033) ***(P-3544)***
Califrnia Furn Collections Inc....C....619 621-2455
150 Reed Ct Ste A Chula Vista (91911) ***(P-4764)***
Califrnia Indus Rfrgn Mchs Inc ....F....951 361-0040
3197 Cornerstone Dr Mira Loma (91752) ***(P-15418)***
Califrnia Integrated Media Inc (PA)....F....415 627-8310
3000 Kerner Blvd San Rafael (94901) ***(P-6469)***
Califrnia Mantel Fireplace Inc (PA)....E....916 925-5775
4141 N Freeway Blvd Sacramento (95834) ***(P-4012)***
Califrnia Nwspapers Ltd Partnr (HQ)....B....626 962-8811
605 E Huntington Dr # 100 Monrovia (91016) ***(P-5579)***
Califrnia Nwspapers Ltd Partnr....B....909 987-6397
9616 Archibald Ave # 100 Rancho Cucamonga (91730) ***(P-5580)***
Califrnia Nwspapers Ltd Partnr....E....909 793-3221
19 E Citrus Ave Ste 102 Redlands (92373) ***(P-5581)***
Califrnia Nwspapers Ltd Partnr....C....530 877-4413
5399 Clark Rd Paradise (95969) ***(P-5582)***
Califrnia PCF Rice Mil A CA LP....C....530 661-1923
194 W Main St Woodland (95695) ***(P-1038)***
Califrnia Rsrces Elk Hills LLC....B....661 412-5000
900 Old River Rd Bakersfield (93311) ***(P-115)***
Califrnia Rsurces Long Bch Inc....C....562 624-3204
111 W Ocean Blvd Ste 800 Long Beach (90802) ***(P-178)***
Calimesa News Mirror ....E....909 795-8145
1007 Calimesa Blvd Ste D Calimesa (92320) ***(P-5583)***
Calimmune Inc....F....310 806-6240
129 N Hill Ave Ste 105 Pasadena (91106) ***(P-7822)***
Calimmune Inc (HQ)....F....310 806-6240
35 N Lake Ave Ste 600 Pasadena (91101) ***(P-7823)***
Calipaso Winery LLC ....E....805 226-9296
4230 Buena Vista Dr Paso Robles (93446) ***(P-1617)***
Calison Inc....E....626 448-3328
2447 Leef Ave South El Monte (91733) ***(P-2764)***
Calistoga Roastery, The, Calistoga *Also called Coffee Guys Inc* ***(P-2284)***
Calithera Biosciences Inc ....E....650 870-1000
343 Oyster Point Blvd South San Francisco (94080) ***(P-7824)***
Calix Inc (PA)....B....408 514-3000
2777 Orchard Pkwy San Jose (95134) ***(P-17478)***
Callaway Golf Company....A....760 804-4502
5858 Dryden Pl Carlsbad (92008) ***(P-22772)***
Callaway Golf Company....A....760 345-4653
44500 Indian Wells Ln Indian Wells (92210) ***(P-22773)***
Callaway Golf Company (PA)....B....760 931-1771
2180 Rutherford Rd Carlsbad (92008) ***(P-22774)***
Callaway Vineyard & Winery....D....951 676-4001
32720 Rancho Cal Rd Temecula (92591) ***(P-1618)***
Callisto Shoes Rolling Hills, Torrance *Also called J & A Shoe Company Inc* ***(P-10171)***
Calmar Laser, Palo Alto *Also called Calmar Optcom Inc* ***(P-17352)***
Calmar Optcom Inc....E....408 733-7800
951 Commercial St Palo Alto (94303) ***(P-17352)***
Calmat Co (HQ)....C....818 553-8821
500 N Brand Blvd Ste 500 # 500 Glendale (91203) ***(P-9088)***
Calmat Co ....E....661 858-2673
16101 Hwy 156 Maricopa (93252) ***(P-299)***
Calmax Technology Inc (PA)....E....408 748-8660
526 Laurelwood Rd Santa Clara (95054) ***(P-15820)***
Calmex Fireplace Equip Mfg, Santa Fe Springs *Also called Calmex Fireplace Equipment Mfg* ***(P-11578)***
Calmex Fireplace Equipment Mfg....F....716 645-2901
13629 Talc St Santa Fe Springs (90670) ***(P-11578)***
Calmini Products Inc ....F....661 398-9500
6951 Mcdivitt Dr Bakersfield (93313) ***(P-19606)***
Calmont Engineering & Elec (PA)....E....714 549-0336
420 E Alton Ave Santa Ana (92707) ***(P-11293)***
Calmont Wire & Cable, Santa Ana *Also called Calmont Engineering & Elec* ***(P-11293)***
Calmoseptine Inc ....F....714 848-2949
16602 Burke Ln Huntington Beach (92647) ***(P-7825)***
Calmut Industrial Asphalt, Glendale *Also called Huntmix Inc* ***(P-9095)***
Calnetix Technologies LLC....D....562 293-1660
16323 Shoemaker Ave Cerritos (90703) ***(P-16634)***
Calogic LLC (PA)....F....510 656-2900
237 Whitney Pl Fremont (94539) ***(P-21015)***
Calor Apparel Group Intl Corp....E....949 548-9095
884 W 16th St Newport Beach (92663) ***(P-3440)***
Calpaco Papers Inc (PA) ....C....323 767-2800
3155 Universe Dr Jurupa Valley (91752) ***(P-5498)***
Calpak Usa Inc ....E....310 937-7335
2110 Artesia Blvd B202 Redondo Beach (90278) ***(P-17841)***
Calperf Inc (PA) ....F....408 829-7779
1810 Richard Ave Santa Clara (95050) ***(P-397)***
Calpi Inc....F....661 589-5648
7141 Downing Ave Bakersfield (93308) ***(P-179)***
Calpico Inc....E....650 588-2241
1387 San Mateo Ave South San Francisco (94080) ***(P-16881)***
Calpipe Security Bollards, Compton *Also called Cal Pipe Manufacturing Inc* ***(P-13462)***
Calplant I LLC....E....530 570-0542
6101 State Highway 162 Willows (95988) ***(P-4483)***

Mergent e-mail: customerrelations@mergent.com
1052
2020 California
Manufacturers Register
(P-0000) Products & Services Section entry number
(PA)=Parent Co (HQ)=Headquarters (DH)=Div Headquarters

Calplant I Holdco LLC (PA) ....E....530 570-0542
6101 State Highway 162 Willows (95988) ***(P-4484)***
Calportland, Colton *Also called Cal Portland Cement Co* ***(P-10701)***
Calportland ....F....760 343-3403
2025 E Financial Way Glendora (91741) ***(P-332)***
Calportland ....F....760 343-3126
72200 Vista Chino Thousand Palms (92276) ***(P-333)***
Calportland Company ....D....805 345-3400
219 Tank Farm Rd San Luis Obispo (93401) ***(P-10403)***
Calportland Company ....C....661 824-2401
9350 Oak Creek Rd Mojave (93501) ***(P-10404)***
Calportland Company ....E....909 825-4260
695 S Rancho Ave Colton (92324) ***(P-10405)***
Calportland Company ....F....760 245-5321
19409 National Trails Hwy Oro Grande (92368) ***(P-10406)***
Calportland Company ....F....209 469-0109
2201 W Washington St # 6 Stockton (95203) ***(P-10407)***
Calportland Company (HQ) ....D....626 852-6200
2025 E Financial Way Glendora (91741) ***(P-10408)***
Calportland Company ....E....818 767-0508
8981 Bradley Ave Sun Valley (91352) ***(P-10409)***
Calportland Company ....F....626 334-3226
1030 W Gladstone St Azusa (91702) ***(P-10703)***
Calportland Company ....D....626 691-2596
590 Live Oak Ave Irwindale (91706) ***(P-10704)***
Calram LLC ....F....805 987-6205
829 Via Alondra Camarillo (93012) ***(P-13507)***
Calspray Inc ....F....650 325-0096
1905 Bay Rd East Palo Alto (94303) ***(P-13154)***
Calstar Products Inc ....D....262 752-9131
3945 Freedom Cir Ste 560 Santa Clara (95054) ***(P-10432)***
Calstone Company ....F....408 686-9627
13755 Llagas Ave San Martin (95046) ***(P-10503)***
Calstone Company ....E....209 745-2981
421 Crystal Way Galt (95632) ***(P-10504)***
Calstrip Industries Inc (PA) ....E....323 726-1345
3030 Dulles Dr Jurupa Valley (91752) ***(P-11118)***
Calstrip Steel Corporation (HQ) ....D....323 838-2097
3030 Dulles Dr Jurupa Valley (91752) ***(P-11444)***
Caltex Plastics Inc (PA) ....E....800 584-7303
2380 E 51st St Vernon (90058) ***(P-5387)***
Caltoy, Buena Park *Also called Dream International Usa Inc* ***(P-22647)***
Calva Products Co Inc ....E....209 339-1516
4351 E Winery Rd Acampo (95220) ***(P-1087)***
Calwest Galvanizing Corp ....D....310 549-2200
2226 E Dominguez St Carson (90810) ***(P-13155)***
Calypto Design Systems Inc ....F....408 850-2300
2099 Gateway Pl Ste 550 San Jose (95110) ***(P-23714)***
Calysta Inc (PA) ....E....650 492-6880
1140 Obrien Dr Ste B Menlo Park (94025) ***(P-8728)***
Calzyme Laboratories Inc (PA) ....F....805 541-5754
3443 Miguelito Ct San Luis Obispo (93401) ***(P-8729)***
CAM, Fullerton *Also called Consolidated Aerospace Mfg LLC* ***(P-20559)***
CAM-Tech, Irvine *Also called Computer Asssted Mfg Tech Corp* ***(P-15860)***
Cambero Metal Works Inc ....F....626 309-5315
210 Agostino Rd San Gabriel (91776) ***(P-24622)***
Cambria Winery, Santa Maria *Also called Jackson Family Wines Inc* ***(P-1767)***
Cambridge Laser Laboratories ....F....510 651-0110
853 Brown Rd Fremont (94539) ***(P-10345)***
Cambro Manufacturing Company (PA) ....B....714 848-1555
5801 Skylab Rd Huntington Beach (92647) ***(P-9689)***
Cambro Manufacturing Company ....F....909 354-8962
21558 Ferrero City of Industry (91789) ***(P-23295)***
Cambro Manufacturing Company ....B....714 848-1555
7601 Clay Ave Huntington Beach (92648) ***(P-9690)***
Cambro Manufacturing Company ....B....714 848-1555
5801 Skylab Rd Huntington Beach (92647) ***(P-9691)***
Camco Furnace, San Carlos *Also called Concepts & Methods Co Inc* ***(P-14758)***
Camelbak Acquisition Corp ....C....707 792-9700
2000 S Mcdowell Blvd Petaluma (94954) ***(P-22775)***
Camelbak Products LLC (HQ) ....D....707 792-9700
2000 S Mcdowell Blvd Petaluma (94954) ***(P-22776)***
Camelia City Millwork Inc ....F....916 451-2454
7831 Clifton Rd Sacramento (95826) ***(P-4013)***
Cameo Crafts ....E....513 381-1480
4995 Hillsdale Cir El Dorado Hills (95762) ***(P-7015)***
Camera Ready Cars, Fountain Valley *Also called Gaffoglio Fmly Mtlcrafters Inc* ***(P-10361)***
Cameron International Corp ....F....661 323-8183
4315 Yeager Way Bakersfield (93313) ***(P-13768)***
Cameron International Corp ....E....707 752-8800
535 Getty Ct Ste A Benicia (94510) ***(P-13769)***
Cameron International Corp ....D....530 242-6965
562 River Park Dr Redding (96003) ***(P-13770)***
Cameron International Corp ....D....510 928-1480
1282 Bayview Farm Rd Pinole (94564) ***(P-180)***
Cameron Metal Cutting, Santa Ana *Also called Automation West Inc* ***(P-15755)***
Cameron Micro Drill Presses, Sonora *Also called Treat Manufacturing Inc* ***(P-13959)***
Cameron Technologies Us Inc ....D....562 222-8440
4040 Capitol Ave Whittier (90601) ***(P-20844)***
Cameron Welding Supply (PA) ....E....714 530-9353
11061 Dale Ave Stanton (90680) ***(P-24623)***
Cameron West Coast (PA) ....F....909 355-8995
9452 Resenda Ave Fontana (92335) ***(P-13771)***
Cameron's Measurement Systems, Whittier *Also called Cameron Technologies Us Inc* ***(P-20844)***
Cameroncompany, Petaluma *Also called Robert W Cameron & Co Inc* ***(P-6142)***
Camfil USA Inc ....D....559 992-5118
500 Industrial Ave Corcoran (93212) ***(P-14651)***
Camino Neurocare ....D....858 455-1115
5955 Pacific Center Blvd San Diego (92121) ***(P-21648)***
Camino Real Foods Inc (PA) ....C....323 585-6599
2638 E Vernon Ave Vernon (90058) ***(P-949)***
Camino Real Kitchens, Vernon *Also called Camino Real Foods Inc* ***(P-949)***
Camisasca Automotive Mfg Inc ....E....949 452-0195
20341 Hermana Cir Lake Forest (92630) ***(P-12779)***
Camisasca Automotive Mfg Inc (PA) ....E....949 452-0195
20352 Hermana Cir Lake Forest (92630) ***(P-12780)***
Camland Inc ....F....805 485-9242
3152 Canopy Dr Camarillo (93012) ***(P-24624)***
Camlever Inc ....F....909 629-9669
954 S East End Ave Pomona (91766) ***(P-13716)***
Camp Bow Wow Temecula, Temecula *Also called M & L Haight LLC* ***(P-10248)***
Camp Smidgemore Inc (HQ) ....E....323 634-0333
3641 10th Ave Los Angeles (90018) ***(P-3301)***
Campbell & Loftin Inc ....F....714 871-1950
1560 N Missile Way Anaheim (92801) ***(P-12149)***
Campbell Certified Inc (PA) ....E....760 722-9353
1629 Ord Way Oceanside (92056) ***(P-11758)***
Campbell Engineering Inc ....E....949 859-3306
20412 Barents Sea Cir Lake Forest (92630) ***(P-14144)***
Campbell Graphics Inc ....E....408 371-6411
156 N 2nd St Campbell (95008) ***(P-6470)***
Campbell Grinding Inc ....F....209 339-8838
1003 E Vine St Lodi (95240) ***(P-15821)***
Campbell Pump Co, Fresno *Also called Lily Pond Products* ***(P-14492)***
Camserv, Pinole *Also called Cameron International Corp* ***(P-180)***
Camsoft Corporation ....E....951 674-8100
32295 Mission Trl Ste 8 Lake Elsinore (92530) ***(P-19211)***
Camtek LLC ....F....626 508-1700
2645 Nina St Pasadena (91107) ***(P-7826)***
Camtek Usa Inc ....E....510 624-9905
48389 Fremont Blvd # 112 Fremont (94538) ***(P-18156)***
Camtron US, Anaheim *Also called Jeico Security Inc* ***(P-19335)***
Can Lines Engineering Inc (PA) ....D....562 861-2996
9839 Downey Norwalk Rd Downey (90241) ***(P-14702)***
Canaan Company, Fresno *Also called DV Kap Inc* ***(P-3614)***
Canadas Finest Foods Inc ....D....951 296-1040
26090 Ynez Rd Temecula (92591) ***(P-906)***
Canadian Solar (usa) Inc ....F....925 807-7499
3000 Oak Rd Ste 400 Walnut Creek (94597) ***(P-18157)***
Canady Manufacturing Co Inc ....F....818 365-9181
500 5th St San Fernando (91340) ***(P-15822)***
Canam Technology Inc ....F....562 856-0178
5318 E 2nd St Ste 700 Long Beach (90803) ***(P-17479)***
Canandaigua Wine Company Inc ....A....559 673-7071
12667 Road 24 Madera (93637) ***(P-1619)***
Canari, Vista *Also called Leemarc Industries LLC* ***(P-3101)***
Canary Communications Inc ....F....408 365-0609
6040 Hellyer Ave Ste 150 San Jose (95138) ***(P-17480)***
Canary Medical USA LLC ....F....760 448-5066
2710 Loker Ave W Ste 350 Carlsbad (92010) ***(P-21649)***
Canary Technologies Corp ....E....415 578-1414
450 9th St San Francisco (94103) ***(P-23715)***
Canay Manufacturing Inc ....F....661 295-0205
26140 Avenue Hall Valencia (91355) ***(P-13156)***
Cancer Genetics Inc ....C....323 224-3900
1640 Marengo St Ste 7 Los Angeles (90033) ***(P-8211)***
Candamar Designs Inc ....E....714 871-6190
520 E Jamie Ave La Habra (90631) ***(P-23296)***
Candella Lighting Co Inc ....F....323 798-1091
430 S Pecan St Los Angeles (90033) ***(P-17019)***
Candella Lighting Company, Los Angeles *Also called 515 W Seventh LLC* ***(P-17004)***
Candies Tolteca ....E....559 266-9193
2139 N Pleasant Ave Fresno (93705) ***(P-1359)***
Candle Crafters, Moorpark *Also called Globaluxe Inc* ***(P-23346)***
Candlebay Co ....F....949 307-1807
3440 W Warner Ave Ste Cd Santa Ana (92704) ***(P-23297)***
Candlelight Press Inc ....E....323 299-3798
26752 Oak Ave Ste F Canyon Country (91351) ***(P-6471)***
Candlewick-Porterville, Porterville *Also called Tdg Operations LLC* ***(P-2885)***
Candroy Embroidery, San Diego *Also called Epicson Inc* ***(P-7058)***
Candu Graphics ....F....310 822-1620
5737 Kanan Rd Ste 132 Agoura Hills (91301) ***(P-6472)***
Canidae Corporation ....F....909 599-5190
1975 Tandem Norco (92860) ***(P-1070)***
Canidae Pet Foods, Norco *Also called Canidae Corporation* ***(P-1070)***
Canine Caviar Pet Foods Inc ....E....714 223-1800
4131 Tigris Way Riverside (92503) ***(P-1088)***
Canine Caviar Pet Foods De Inc ....F....714 223-1800
4131 Tigris Way Riverside (92503) ***(P-1071)***
Cannalink Inc ....F....310 921-1955
110 W C St Ste 1300 San Diego (92101) ***(P-20845)***
Cannalogic ....F....619 458-0775
5404 Whitsett Ave 219 Valley Village (91607) ***(P-23298)***
Cannon Gasket Inc ....F....909 355-1547
7784 Edison Ave Fontana (92336) ***(P-9222)***
Cannon Sleep Products, Fresno *Also called Pleasant Mattress Inc* ***(P-4737)***
Cano Architecture, Ontario *Also called Precast Repair* ***(P-10628)***
Canoga Perkins Corporation (HQ) ....D....818 718-6300
20600 Prairie St Chatsworth (91311) ***(P-17720)***
Canoo Inc ....C....318 849-6327
19951 Mariner Ave Torrance (90503) ***(P-19462)***
Cantabio Pharmaceuticals Inc ....F....408 501-8893
1250 Oakmead Pkwy Ste 210 Sunnyvale (94085) ***(P-7827)***
Canterbury Designs Inc ....E....323 936-7111
6195 Maywood Ave Huntington Park (90255) ***(P-12460)***

ALPHABETIC

Employee Codes: A=Over 500 employees, B=251-500
C=101-250, D=51-100, E=20-50, F=10-19
2020 California
Manfacturers Register
© Mergent Inc. 1-800-342-5647
1053

Canterbury International, Huntington Park *Also called Canterbury Designs Inc (P-12460)*
Canto Software Inc (PA)............F.......415 495-6545
625 Market St Ste 600 San Francisco (94105) *(P-23716)*
Canvas Awning Co Inc............F.......909 447-5100
325 W Main St Ontario (91762) *(P-3675)*
Canvas Concepts, San Diego *Also called Masterpiece Artist Canvas LLC (P-2703)*
Canvas Concepts Inc............F.......619 424-3428
649 Anita St Ste A2 Chula Vista (91911) *(P-3676)*
Canvas Specialty Inc............E.......323 722-1156
1309 S Eastern Ave Commerce (90040) *(P-3677)*
Canyon Composites Incorporated............E.......714 991-8181
1548 N Gemini Pl Anaheim (92801) *(P-20065)*
Canyon Engineering Pdts Inc............D.......661 294-0084
28909 Avenue Williams Valencia (91355) *(P-20066)*
Canyon Graphics Inc............D.......858 646-0444
6680 Cobra Way San Diego (92121) *(P-4014)*
Canyon Plastics Inc............D.......800 350-2275
28455 Livingston Ave Valencia (91355) *(P-9692)*
Canyon Road Winery, Healdsburg *Also called Geyser Peak Winery (P-1722)*
Canyon Rock & Asphalt, San Diego *Also called Superior Ready Mix Concrete LP (P-10848)*
Canyon Rock Co Inc............E.......707 887-2207
7525 Hwy 116 Forestville (95436) *(P-334)*
Canyon Steel Fabricators Inc............E.......951 683-2352
8314 Sultana Ave Fontana (92335) *(P-11759)*
Canzone and Company............E.......714 537-8175
1345 W Cowles St Long Beach (90813) *(P-23071)*
Capax Technologies Inc............E.......661 257-7666
24842 Avenue Tibbitts Valencia (91355) *(P-16780)*
Capco/Psa............E.......818 762-4276
11125 Vanowen St North Hollywood (91605) *(P-9693)*
Capella Microsystems Inc............E.......408 988-8000
2201 Laurelwood Rd Santa Clara (95054) *(P-17842)*
Caperon Designs Inc............F.......714 552-3201
1733 Monrovia Ave Ste N Costa Mesa (92627) *(P-22667)*
Capistrano Labs Inc............E.......949 492-0390
150 Calle Iglesia Ste B San Clemente (92672) *(P-21650)*
Capital Cooking Equipment............E.......562 903-1168
13211 Florence Ave Santa Fe Springs (90670) *(P-11693)*
Capital Corrugated and Carton, Sacramento *Also called Capital Corrugated LLC (P-5205)*
Capital Corrugated LLC............D.......916 388-7848
8333 24th Ave Sacramento (95826) *(P-5205)*
Capitol Beverage Packers............D.......916 929-7777
2670 Land Ave Sacramento (95815) *(P-2051)*
Capitol Components, Sacramento *Also called Capitol Store Fixtures (P-4788)*
Capitol Iron Works Inc............E.......916 381-1554
7009 Power Inn Rd Sacramento (95828) *(P-11760)*
Capitol Machine Co, Santa Ana *Also called M & W Machine Corporation (P-16159)*
Capitol Neon............F.......916 349-1800
5920 Rosebud Ln Ste 1 Sacramento (95841) *(P-23072)*
Capitol Steel Fabricators Inc............E.......323 721-5460
3565 Greenwood Ave Commerce (90040) *(P-11761)*
Capitol Steel Products............F.......916 383-3368
6331 Power Inn Rd Ste B Sacramento (95824) *(P-10942)*
Capitol Store Fixtures............E.......916 646-9096
4220 Pell Dr Ste C Sacramento (95838) *(P-4788)*
Capitol Tarpaulin Co, Sacramento *Also called Philip A Stitt Agency (P-3699)*
Caplugs, Rancho Dominguez *Also called Protective Industries Inc (P-9999)*
Capna Fabrication............E.......888 416-6777
15148 Bledsoe St Sylmar (91342) *(P-14353)*
Capna Systems, Sylmar *Also called Capna Fabrication (P-14353)*
Capo Industries Division, El Cajon *Also called Senior Operations LLC (P-16396)*
Cappac Plastic Products............E.......323 721-7542
5835 S Malt Ave Commerce (90040) *(P-9512)*
Capricor Therapeutics Inc (PA)............F.......310 358-3200
8840 Wilshire Blvd Fl 2 Beverly Hills (90211) *(P-7828)*
Caps, Irvine *Also called Central Admxture Phrm Svcs Inc (P-7836)*
Caps & Tabs Inc............E.......619 285-5400
3111 Camino Del Rio N # 400 San Diego (92108) *(P-583)*
Capsa Solutions LLC............E.......800 437-6633
14000 S Broadway Los Angeles (90061) *(P-15011)*
Capstan California Inc (PA)............B.......310 366-5999
16100 S Figueroa St Gardena (90248) *(P-13508)*
Capstan Permaflow............F.......310 366-5999
16110 S Figueroa St Gardena (90248) *(P-15823)*
Capstone Fire Management Inc (PA)............E.......760 839-2290
2240 Auto Park Way Escondido (92029) *(P-14800)*
Capstone Turbine Corporation (PA)............C.......818 734-5300
16640 Stagg St Van Nuys (91406) *(P-13563)*
Captek Softgel Intl Inc (HQ)............B.......562 921-9511
16218 Arthur St Cerritos (90703) *(P-7829)*
Captive Ocean Reef Enterprises............F.......949 581-8888
34135 Moongate Ct Dana Point (92629) *(P-14801)*
Captive Plastics LLC............D.......209 858-9188
601 Tesla Dr A Lathrop (95330) *(P-9694)*
Captive-Aire Systems Inc............F.......951 231-5102
2510 Cloudcrest Way Riverside (92507) *(P-12150)*
Captive-Aire Systems Inc............C.......530 351-7150
6856 Lockheed Dr Redding (96002) *(P-12151)*
CAr Enterprises Inc............F.......760 947-6411
13100 Main St Hesperia (92345) *(P-15373)*
Car Sound Exhaust System Inc............D.......949 858-5900
22961 Arroyo Vis Rcho STA Marg (92688) *(P-19607)*
Car Sound Exhaust System Inc (PA)............E.......949 858-5900
1901 Corporate Ctr Oceanside (92056) *(P-19608)*
Car Sound Exhaust System Inc............E.......949 888-1625
1901 Corporate Ctr Oceanside (92056) *(P-7478)*
Car Sound Exhaust System Inc............D.......949 858-5900
30142 Ave De Las Bndra Rcho STA Marg (92688) *(P-19609)*
Car Sound Exhaust System Inc............E.......949 858-5900
23201 Antonio Pkwy Rcho STA Marg (92688) *(P-19610)*
Caracal Enterprises LLC............E.......707 773-3373
1260 Holm Rd Ste A Petaluma (94954) *(P-15397)*
Caran Precision Engrg Mfg Corp............D.......714 447-5400
2830 Orbiter St Brea (92821) *(P-12781)*
Carando Technologies Inc............E.......209 948-6500
345 N Harrison St Stockton (95203) *(P-13973)*
Caraustar Industries Inc............C.......209 464-6590
800b W Church St Stockton (95203) *(P-5288)*
Caraustar Industries Inc............E.......951 685-5544
4502 E Airport Dr Ontario (91761) *(P-5289)*
Caraustar Industries Inc............C.......408 845-7600
525 Mathew St Santa Clara (95050) *(P-5290)*
Caravan Bakery Inc............E.......510 487-2600
33300 Western Ave Union City (94587) *(P-1174)*
Caravan Canopy Intl Inc............E.......714 367-3000
14600 Alondra Blvd La Mirada (90638) *(P-3678)*
Caravan Manufacturing Co Inc............F.......714 220-9722
10814 Los Vaqueros Cir Los Alamitos (90720) *(P-9695)*
Caravan Trading Company............D.......510 487-8090
33300 Western Ave Union City (94587) *(P-1175)*
Carberry LLC (HQ)............E.......800 564-0842
17130 Muskrat Ave Ste B Adelanto (92301) *(P-23299)*
Carbide Company LLC............D.......760 477-1000
2470 Ash St Ste 1 Vista (92081) *(P-11524)*
Carbide Products Co Inc............F.......310 320-7910
22711 S Western Ave Torrance (90501) *(P-10943)*
Carboline Company............E.......909 459-1090
5533 Brooks St Montclair (91763) *(P-8628)*
Carbomer Inc............D.......858 552-0992
6324 Ferris Sq Ste B San Diego (92121) *(P-7479)*
Carbon Inc............C.......650 285-6307
1089 Mills Way Redwood City (94063) *(P-15185)*
Carbon By Design LLC............D.......760 643-1300
1491 Poinsettia Ave # 136 Vista (92081) *(P-20067)*
Carbon California Company LLC............F.......805 933-1901
270 Quail Ct Ste 201 Santa Paula (93060) *(P-42)*
Carbon Recycling Incorporated............F.......619 491-9200
7938 Ivanhoe Ave Ste B La Jolla (92037) *(P-8730)*
Carbon Recycling Inernational, La Jolla *Also called Carbon Recycling Incorporated (P-8730)*
Carbon Solutions Inc............F.......909 234-2738
5094 Victoria Hill Dr Riverside (92506) *(P-16683)*
Carbonyte Systems Incorporated............F.......916 387-0316
3 Wayne Ct Ste A Sacramento (95829) *(P-8629)*
Carbro Corporation............E.......310 643-8400
15724 Condon Ave Lawndale (90260) *(P-14145)*
Card Nale Tasting Room,, Oakville *Also called Jackson Family Wines Inc (P-1764)*
Card Scanning Solutions, Los Angeles *Also called Acuant Inc (P-15145)*
Cardenas Enterprises Inc............F.......323 588-0137
339 W Norman Ave Arcadia (91007) *(P-4968)*
Cardiaq Valve Technologies Inc, Irvine *Also called Edwards Lfsciences Cardiaq LLC (P-21696)*
Cardic Machine Products Inc............F.......310 884-3400
17000 Keegan Ave Carson (90746) *(P-15824)*
Cardigan Road Productions............E.......310 289-1442
1999 Ave Of The Sts 110 Los Angeles (90067) *(P-18850)*
Cardinal C G, Moreno Valley *Also called Cardinal Glass Industries Inc (P-10261)*
Cardinal Cg Company, Los Angeles *Also called Cardinal Glass Industries Inc (P-10346)*
Cardinal Glass Industries Inc............D.......951 485-9007
24100 Cardinal Ave Moreno Valley (92551) *(P-10261)*
Cardinal Glass Industries Inc............E.......323 319-0070
1125 E Lanzit Ave Los Angeles (90059) *(P-10346)*
Cardinal Health 414 LLC............E.......714 572-9900
640 S Jefferson St Placentia (92870) *(P-7830)*
Cardinal Industrial Finishes (PA)............D.......626 444-9274
1329 Potrero Ave South El Monte (91733) *(P-8630)*
Cardinal Laboratories Inc............D.......626 610-1200
710 S Ayon Ave Azusa (91702) *(P-8456)*
Cardinal Paint and Powder Inc............C.......626 937-6767
15010 Don Julian Rd City of Industry (91746) *(P-8631)*
Cardinal Paint and Powder Inc............E.......408 452-8522
890 Commercial St San Jose (95112) *(P-8632)*
Cardinal Sheet Metal Inc............F.......951 788-8800
3184 Durahart St Riverside (92507) *(P-12152)*
Cardiovascular Systems, Tustin *Also called Terumo Americas Holding Inc (P-21301)*
Cardiva Medical Inc............C.......408 470-7100
1615 Wyatt Dr Santa Clara (95054) *(P-21651)*
Cardlogix............F.......949 380-1312
16 Hughes Ste 100 Irvine (92618) *(P-15186)*
Cardona Manufacturing Corp............E.......818 841-8358
1869 N Victory Pl Burbank (91504) *(P-20068)*
Care Fusion............A.......858 617-2000
10020 Pacific Mesa Blvd San Diego (92121) *(P-21652)*
Care Fusion Products, San Diego *Also called Becton Dickinson and Company (P-21625)*
Care Innovations LLC............E.......800 450-0970
950 Iron Point Rd Ste 160 Folsom (95630) *(P-22236)*
Care Tex Industries Inc (PA)............D.......323 567-5074
4583 Firestone Blvd South Gate (90280) *(P-2777)*
Career Cap Corporation............E.......619 575-2277
1680 Industrial Blvd Chula Vista (91911) *(P-3464)*
Career Tech Circuit Services, Chatsworth *Also called Circuit Services Llc (P-17849)*
Carefusion 207 Inc............B.......760 778-7200
1100 Bird Center Dr Palm Springs (92262) *(P-21653)*
Carefusion 211 Inc............A.......714 283-2228
22745 Savi Ranch Pkwy Yorba Linda (92887) *(P-21654)*
Carefusion 213 LLC (HQ)............B.......800 523-0502
3750 Torrey View Ct San Diego (92130) *(P-21655)*

Mergent e-mail: customerrelations@mergent.com
1054
2020 California
Manufacturers Register
(P-0000) Products & Services Section entry number
(PA)=Parent Co (HQ)=Headquarters (DH)=Div Headquarters

Carefusion Corporation (HQ)....B....858 617-2000
3750 Torrey View Ct San Diego (92130) ***(P-22237)***
Carefusion Corporation....F....760 778-7200
1100 Bird Center Dr Palm Springs (92262) ***(P-7831)***
Carefusion Corporation....E....800 231-2466
22745 Savi Ranch Pkwy Yorba Linda (92887) ***(P-21656)***
Careray USA, Santa Clara *Also called Compass Innovations Inc* ***(P-9398)***
Caretex Inc....D....323 567-5074
4581 Firestone Blvd South Gate (90280) ***(P-8698)***
Carevault Corporation....F....714 333-0556
182 Exbourne Ave Ste 200 San Carlos (94070) ***(P-23717)***
Cargill Incorporated....D....714 449-6708
600 N Gilbert St Fullerton (92833) ***(P-7647)***
Cargill Incorporated....E....323 588-2274
566 N Gilbert St Fullerton (92833) ***(P-1469)***
Cargill Flour Milling Division, San Bernardino *Also called Ardent Mills LLC* ***(P-996)***
Cargill Meat Solutions Corp....C....559 875-2232
2350 Academy Ave Sanger (93657) ***(P-398)***
Cargill Meat Solutions Corp....E....909 476-3120
10602 N Trademark Pkwy # 500 Rancho Cucamonga (91730) ***(P-399)***
Cargill Meat Solutions Corp....C....559 268-5586
3115 S Fig Ave Fresno (93706) ***(P-400)***
Cargill Molasses, Stockton *Also called Westway Feed Products LLC* ***(P-1132)***
Cargo Chief Inc....F....650 560-5001
10 Rollins Rd Ste 202 Millbrae (94030) ***(P-23718)***
Cargo Data Corporation....F....805 650-5922
1502 Eastman Ave Ste A Ventura (93003) ***(P-21448)***
Caribbean Coffee Company Inc....F....805 692-2200
495 Pine Ave Ste A Goleta (93117) ***(P-1016)***
Carl & Irving Printers Inc....F....559 686-8354
161 N N St Tulare (93274) ***(P-6473)***
Carl Nersesian....F....818 888-0111
13415 Saticoy St North Hollywood (91605) ***(P-4015)***
Carl Zeiss Inc....E....925 557-4100
5160 Hacienda Dr Dublin (94568) ***(P-21337)***
Carl Zeiss Meditec Inc (HQ)....B....925 557-4100
5160 Hacienda Dr Dublin (94568) ***(P-21338)***
Carl Zeiss Meditec Inc....E....858 716-0661
5160 Hacienda Dr Dublin (94568) ***(P-21339)***
Carl Zeiss Meditec Prod LLC....D....877 644-4657
1040 S Vintage Ave Ste A Ontario (91761) ***(P-21657)***
Carl Zeiss Meditec,, Ontario *Also called Aaren Scientific Inc* ***(P-21329)***
Carl Zeiss Ophthalmic Systems....C....925 557-4100
5160 Hacienda Dr Dublin (94568) ***(P-21658)***
Carl Zeiss Vision Inc (HQ)....D....858 790-7700
12121 Scripps Summit Dr San Diego (92131) ***(P-22344)***
Carl Ziss X-Ray Microscopy Inc....D....925 701-3600
4385 Hopyard Rd Ste 100 Pleasanton (94588) ***(P-22210)***
Carley Inc (PA)....B....310 325-8474
1502 W 228th St Torrance (90501) ***(P-10300)***
Carlisle Interconnect, El Segundo *Also called Tri-Star Electronics Intl Inc* ***(P-16936)***
Carlisle Interconnect Tech Inc....E....951 788-0252
4200 Garner Rd Riverside (92501) ***(P-11086)***
Carlos Shower Doors Inc....F....661 327-5594
300 Kentucky St Bakersfield (93305) ***(P-10347)***
Carlsbad Manufacturing, Carlsbad *Also called Stone Yard Inc* ***(P-4774)***
Carlsbad Technology Inc (HQ)....D....760 431-8284
5922 Farnsworth Ct # 102 Carlsbad (92008) ***(P-7832)***
Carlsbad Technology Inc....D....760 431-8284
5923 Balfour Ct Carlsbad (92008) ***(P-7833)***
Carlson & Beauloye Air Pwr Inc....F....619 232-5719
2143 Newton Ave San Diego (92113) ***(P-15825)***
Carlson & Beauloye Mach Sp Inc....F....619 232-5719
2141 Newton Ave San Diego (92113) ***(P-15826)***
Carlson Wireless Tech Inc....F....707 443-0100
3134 Jacobs Ave Ste C Eureka (95501) ***(P-17481)***
Carlstar Group LLC....F....909 829-1703
10730 Production Ave Fontana (92337) ***(P-19611)***
Carlstar Group LLC....C....310 816-1015
1990 S Vintage Ave Ontario (91761) ***(P-9166)***
Carlyle Glasgow Wldg Svcs Inc....F....909 902-1814
4747 E State St Ste A Ontario (91762) ***(P-11762)***
Carmel Communications Inc....F....831 274-8593
734 Lighthouse Ave Pacific Grove (93950) ***(P-5584)***
Carmel Instruments LLC....F....408 866-0426
1622 W Campbell Ave Campbell (95008) ***(P-20846)***
Carmel Pine Cone, The, Pacific Grove *Also called Carmel Communications Inc* ***(P-5584)***
Carmen Abato Enterprises....F....714 895-1887
11258 Monarch St Ste G Garden Grove (92841) ***(P-11294)***
Carmenet Vineyards, Sonoma *Also called Treasury Chateau & Estates* ***(P-1962)***
Carmi Flavors, Commerce *Also called Carmi Flvr & Fragrance Co Inc* ***(P-2199)***
Carmi Flvr & Fragrance Co Inc (PA)....E....323 888-9240
6030 Scott Way Commerce (90040) ***(P-2199)***
Carmine, Newport Beach *Also called Microtelematics Inc* ***(P-24164)***
Carneros Ranching Inc....F....707 253-9464
1134 Dealy Ln NAPA (94559) ***(P-1620)***
Carnevale & Lohr Inc....E....562 927-8311
6521 Clara St Bell Gardens (90201) ***(P-10895)***
Caro Nut Company....E....559 439-2365
2885 S Cherry Ave Fresno (93706) ***(P-846)***
Carol Anderson Inc (PA)....E....310 638-3333
18700 S Laurel Park Rd Rancho Dominguez (90220) ***(P-3221)***
Carol Anderson By Invitation, Rancho Dominguez *Also called Carol Anderson Inc* ***(P-3221)***
Carol Wior Inc....D....562 927-0052
7533 Garfield Ave Bell (90201) ***(P-3302)***
Carolina Lquid Chmistries Corp....F....336 722-8910
510 W Central Ave Ste C Brea (92821) ***(P-21659)***
Carols Roman Shades Inc....E....925 674-9622
130 Mason Cir Ste K Concord (94520) ***(P-5018)***

Caron Compactor Co....E....800 448-8236
1204 Ullrey Ave Escalon (95320) ***(P-13717)***
Carousel USA, Fontana *Also called JE Thomson & Company LLC* ***(P-13878)***
Carparts Technologies....C....949 488-8860
32122 Camn Capistrano # 100 San Juan Capistrano (92675) ***(P-23719)***
Carpenter Co....B....951 354-7550
7809 Lincoln Ave Riverside (92504) ***(P-9513)***
Carpenter E R Co, Riverside *Also called Carpenter Co* ***(P-9513)***
Carpenter Group (PA)....E....415 285-1954
222 Napoleon St San Francisco (94124) ***(P-13844)***
Carpenter Group....F....707 562-3543
112 Bgley St Crnr Of Rlro Corner Of Railro Vallejo (94592) ***(P-13402)***
Carpenter Group....F....562 942-8076
13100 Firestone Blvd Santa Fe Springs (90670) ***(P-13403)***
Carpenter Specialty Alloys, Rancho Cucamonga *Also called Carpenter Technology Corp* ***(P-11035)***
Carpenter Technology Corp....E....909 476-4000
8250 Milliken Ave Rancho Cucamonga (91730) ***(P-11035)***
Carpentry Millwork, Fresno *Also called Architectural Wood Design Inc* ***(P-4165)***
Carpod Inc....F....818 395-8676
12132 Gothic Ave Granada Hills (91344) ***(P-9696)***
Carr Corporation (PA)....E....310 587-1113
1547 11th St Santa Monica (90401) ***(P-22211)***
Carr Management Inc....D....951 277-4800
22324 Temescal Canyon Rd Corona (92883) ***(P-9697)***
Carr Manufacturing Company Inc....F....949 215-7952
19675 Descartes Foothill Ranch (92610) ***(P-16882)***
Carr Pattern Co Inc....F....951 719-1068
27419 Via Industria Temecula (92590) ***(P-12744)***
Carreon Development Inc....F....619 690-4973
4286 Powderhorn Dr San Diego (92154) ***(P-23073)***
Carrera Construction Inc....F....831 728-3299
1961 Main St Ste 261 Watsonville (95076) ***(P-181)***
Carriercomm Inc....E....805 968-9621
82 Coromar Dr Goleta (93117) ***(P-17482)***
Carris Reels California Inc (HQ)....E....559 674-0804
2100 W Almond Ave Madera (93637) ***(P-4496)***
Carroll Metal Works Inc....D....619 477-9125
740 W 16th St National City (91950) ***(P-11763)***
Carros Americas Inc....E....805 267-7176
2945 Townsgate Rd Ste 200 Westlake Village (91361) ***(P-18851)***
Carros Sensors Systems Co LLC....C....925 979-4400
355 Lennon Ln Walnut Creek (94598) ***(P-18852)***
Carros Sensors Systems Co LLC (HQ)....C....805 968-0782
1461 Lawrence Dr Thousand Oaks (91320) ***(P-18853)***
Carryout Bags Inc (PA)....F....626 279-7000
3592 Rosemead Blvd # 513 Rosemead (91770) ***(P-5326)***
Carryoutsupplies.com, Duarte *Also called S W C Group Inc* ***(P-5309)***
Carson Valley Inc....F....562 906-0062
13215 Barton Cir Whittier (90605) ***(P-12153)***
Carson's Coatings, Galt *Also called Carsons Inc* ***(P-12782)***
Carsons Inc....E....209 745-2387
550 Industrial Dr Ste 200 Galt (95632) ***(P-12782)***
Cartel Industries LLC....E....949 474-3200
17152 Armstrong Ave Irvine (92614) ***(P-12154)***
Carter Holt Harvey Holdings....D....951 272-8180
1230 Railroad St Corona (92882) ***(P-11036)***
Carter Plating Inc....F....818 842-1325
1842 N Keystone St Burbank (91504) ***(P-12963)***
Carter Pump & Machine Inc....F....661 393-8620
635 G St Wasco (93280) ***(P-15827)***
Carton Design, Pico Rivera *Also called CD Container Inc* ***(P-5206)***
Carttronics LLC....E....888 696-2278
8 Studebaker Irvine (92618) ***(P-19270)***
Carturner Inc (PA)....F....760 598-7448
3444 Tripp Ct Ste B San Diego (92121) ***(P-21449)***
Caruthers Raisin Pkg Co Inc (PA)....D....559 864-9448
12797 S Elm Ave Caruthers (93609) ***(P-847)***
Carvalho Family Winery LLC....F....916 744-1615
35265 Willow Ave Clarksburg (95612) ***(P-1621)***
Carving Ice, Placentia *Also called R&Js Business Group Inc* ***(P-2361)***
Casa Agria....F....805 485-1454
701 Del Norte Blvd Oxnard (93030) ***(P-1510)***
Casa De Hermandad (PA)....E....310 477-8272
11750 W Pico Blvd Los Angeles (90064) ***(P-22777)***
Casa Grande Woodworks....E....805 226-2040
4230 Cloud Way Paso Robles (93446) ***(P-4016)***
Casa Herrera Inc (PA)....C....909 392-3930
2655 Pine St Pomona (91767) ***(P-14354)***
Casa Mexico Enterprises Inc....F....888 411-9530
3156 Foothill Blvd Ste G La Crescenta (91214) ***(P-7016)***
Casa Sanchez Foods, Hayward *Also called Fante Inc* ***(P-2322)***
Cascade Optical Coating Inc....F....714 543-9777
1225 E Hunter Ave Santa Ana (92705) ***(P-21340)***
Cascade Pump Company....D....562 946-1414
10107 Norwalk Blvd Santa Fe Springs (90670) ***(P-14563)***
Casco Mfg, San Fernando *Also called C A Schroeder Inc* ***(P-10980)***
Case Automation Corporation....F....951 493-6666
208 Jason Ct Corona (92879) ***(P-13817)***
Case Club, Anaheim *Also called Foam Plastics & Rbr Pdts Corp* ***(P-9535)***
Case Hardigg Center....F....413 665-2163
651 Barrington Ave Ste A Ontario (91764) ***(P-4334)***
Case World Co....F....626 330-1000
301 S Doubleday Ave Ontario (91761) ***(P-10232)***
Case's Oil, Riverdale *Also called C Case Company Inc* ***(P-175)***
Casella, Sacramento *Also called Clarus Lighting LLC* ***(P-17111)***
Casella Aluminum Extrusions....F....714 961-8322
824 N Todd Ave Azusa (91702) ***(P-11227)***

Employee Codes: A=Over 500 employees, B=251-500
C=101-250, D=51-100, E=20-50, F=10-19

2020 California
Manfacturers Register

© Mergent Inc. 1-800-342-5647
1055

Casemaker Inc......F......408 261-8265
1680 Civic Center Dr Frnt Santa Clara (95050) ***(P-23720)***
Caseworx Inc......E......909 799-8550
1130 Research Dr Redlands (92374) ***(P-4789)***
Casey Printing Inc......E......831 385-3221
398 E San Antonio Dr King City (93930) ***(P-6474)***
Cashnet, Oakland *Also called Higher One Payments Inc* ***(P-23982)***
Casmari Inc......F......818 727-1856
9035 Eton Ave Ste C Canoga Park (91304) ***(P-2778)***
Cason Engineering Inc......E......916 939-9311
4952 Windplay Dr Ste D El Dorado Hills (95762) ***(P-15828)***
Caspers, San Leandro *Also called Spar Sausage Co* ***(P-499)***
Caspian Research & Tech LLC......F......310 474-3244
1434 Westwood Blvd Ste 14 Los Angeles (90024) ***(P-23721)***
Caspio Inc (PA)......E......650 691-0900
2953 Bunker Hill Ln # 201 Santa Clara (95054) ***(P-23722)***
Cast Parts Inc (HQ)......C......909 595-2252
4200 Valley Blvd Walnut (91789) ***(P-11154)***
Cast Parts Inc......C......626 937-3444
16800 Chestnut St City of Industry (91748) ***(P-11155)***
Cast-Rite Corporation......D......310 532-2080
515 E Airline Way Gardena (90248) ***(P-14030)***
Cast-Rite International Inc (PA)......D......310 532-2080
515 E Airline Way Gardena (90248) ***(P-11411)***
Castaic Brick, Castaic *Also called Clay Castaic Manufacturing Co* ***(P-10434)***
Castaic Clay Products LLC......D......661 259-3066
32201 Castaic Lake Dr Castaic (91384) ***(P-10433)***
Castaic Lake R V Park Inc......F......661 257-3340
31540 Ridge Route Rd Castaic (91384) ***(P-4439)***
Castaic R V Park, Castaic *Also called Castaic Lake R V Park Inc* ***(P-4439)***
Castaic Truck Stop Inc......E......661 295-1374
31611 Castaic Rd Castaic (91384) ***(P-9040)***
Castello Diamorosa, Calistoga *Also called Villa Amorosa* ***(P-1984)***
Castillo Maritess......F......949 216-0468
1490 S Vineyard Ave Ste G Ontario (91761) ***(P-3679)***
Castle & Cooke Inc......D......951 245-2460
28251 Lake St Lake Elsinore (92530) ***(P-13718)***
Castle Hill Holdings Inc......F......925 943-1119
3161 Putnam Blvd Pleasant Hill (94523) ***(P-21994)***
Castle Importing Inc......F......909 428-9200
14550 Miller Ave Fontana (92336) ***(P-543)***
Castlelite Block LLC (PA)......E......707 678-3465
8615 Robben Rd Dixon (95620) ***(P-10505)***
Castor Engineering Inc......F......562 690-4036
450 Commercial Way La Habra (90631) ***(P-13296)***
Castoro Cellars (PA)......E......805 467-2002
1315 N Bethel Rd Templeton (93465) ***(P-1622)***
Casual Fridays Inc......E......858 433-1442
3990 Old Town Ave A203 San Diego (92110) ***(P-6211)***
Casualway Home & Garden, Oxnard *Also called Casualway Usa LLC* ***(P-4687)***
Casualway Usa LLC......D......805 660-7408
1623 Lola Way Oxnard (93030) ***(P-4687)***
Catalina Carpet Mills Inc (PA)......D......562 926-5811
14418 Best Ave Santa Fe Springs (90670) ***(P-2868)***
Catalina Cylinders Inc (PA)......E......714 890-0999
7300 Anaconda Ave Garden Grove (92841) ***(P-12000)***
Catalina Home, Santa Fe Springs *Also called Catalina Carpet Mills Inc* ***(P-2868)***
Catalina Industries Inc......F......818 772-8888
8814 Reseda Blvd Northridge (91324) ***(P-8633)***
Catalina Lifesciences Inc......E......800 898-6888
25 Enterprise Ste 200 Aliso Viejo (92656) ***(P-7834)***
Catalina Pacific Concrete, Sun Valley *Also called Calportland Company* ***(P-10409)***
Catalina Pacific Concrete, Azusa *Also called Calportland Company* ***(P-10703)***
Catalina Pacific Concrete......E......310 532-4600
19030 Normandie Ave Torrance (90502) ***(P-10705)***
Catalina Paint Stores, Northridge *Also called Catalina Industries Inc* ***(P-8633)***
Catalina Spas, Murrieta *Also called Vortex Whirlpool Systems Inc* ***(P-9597)***
Catalina Tempering Inc (PA)......E......323 789-7800
1125 E Lanzit Ave Los Angeles (90059) ***(P-11525)***
Catalina Yachts Inc (PA)......C......818 884-7700
21200 Victory Blvd Woodland Hills (91367) ***(P-20317)***
Catalyst Biosciences Inc (PA)......F......650 266-8674
611 Gateway Blvd Ste 710 South San Francisco (94080) ***(P-7835)***
Catalyst Development Corp......E......760 228-9653
56925 Yucca Trl Yucca Valley (92284) ***(P-23723)***
Catalytic Solutions Inc (HQ)......D......805 486-4649
1700 Fiske Pl Oxnard (93033) ***(P-20786)***
Catame Inc (PA)......E......213 749-2610
1930 Long Beach Ave Los Angeles (90058) ***(P-22999)***
Catapult Communications Corp (HQ)......E......818 871-1800
26601 Agoura Rd Calabasas (91302) ***(P-23724)***
Catawba County Schools, Camarillo *Also called Microsemi Communications Inc* ***(P-18399)***
Catch Surfboard Co LLC......F......949 218-0428
201 Calle Pintoresco San Clemente (92672) ***(P-22778)***
Cater Line , The, City of Industry *Also called CH Image Inc* ***(P-6479)***
Caterpillar Inc......F......310 921-9811
17364 Hawthorne Blvd Torrance (90504) ***(P-13719)***
Caterpillar Inc......B......909 390-9035
5101 E Airport Dr Ontario (91761) ***(P-13720)***
Caterpillar Pwr Gnrtn Sys......E......858 694-6629
2200 Pacific Hwy San Diego (92101) ***(P-13564)***
Cathera Inc......F......650 388-5088
627 National Ave Mountain View (94043) ***(P-21660)***
Cathy Ireland Home, Chino *Also called Omnia Leather Motion Inc* ***(P-3629)***
Cattaneo Bros Inc......E......805 543-7188
769 Caudill St San Luis Obispo (93401) ***(P-446)***
Caulipower LLC......E......844 422-8544
16200 Ventura Blvd # 400 Encino (91436) ***(P-950)***
Cav Distributing Corporation......F......650 588-2228
389 Oyster Point Blvd # 6 South San Francisco (94080) ***(P-17312)***
Cavallo & Cavallo Inc......F......909 428-6994
14955 Hilton Dr Fontana (92336) ***(P-15829)***
Cavanaugh Machine Works Inc......E......562 437-1126
1540 Santa Fe Ave Long Beach (90813) ***(P-15830)***
Cavco Industries Inc......C......951 688-5353
7007 Jurupa Ave Riverside (92504) ***(P-4440)***
Cavern Club LLC......F......323 837-9800
1708 Aeros Way Montebello (90640) ***(P-3148)***
Cavins Oil Well Tools, Signal Hill *Also called Dawson Enterprises* ***(P-13773)***
Cavins Oil Well Tools, Taft *Also called Dawson Enterprises* ***(P-188)***
Cavium LLC (HQ)......B......408 222-2500
5488 Marvell Ln Santa Clara (95054) ***(P-18158)***
Cavium Networks Intl Inc (HQ)......F......650 625-7000
2315 N 1st St San Jose (95131) ***(P-18159)***
Cavium, Inc., Santa Clara *Also called Cavium LLC* ***(P-18158)***
Cavotec Dabico US Inc......E......714 947-0005
5665 Corporate Ave Cypress (90630) ***(P-20069)***
Cavotec Inet US Inc......D......714 947-0005
5665 Corporate Ave Cypress (90630) ***(P-13721)***
CB Mill Inc......F......415 386-5309
1232 Connecticut St San Francisco (94107) ***(P-4560)***
Cbc Steel Buildings LLC......C......209 858-2425
1700 E Louise Ave Lathrop (95330) ***(P-12539)***
Cbd Axis, National City *Also called Pro Team Axis LLC* ***(P-7684)***
Cbec, San Diego *Also called Clear Blue Energy Corp* ***(P-17112)***
Cbj LP......F......818 676-1750
21550 Oxnard St Woodland Hills (91367) ***(P-5898)***
Cbj LP......E......323 549-5225
5700 Wilshire Blvd # 170 Los Angeles (90036) ***(P-5899)***
Cbj LP......E......858 277-6359
4909 Murphy Canyon Rd # 200 San Diego (92123) ***(P-5900)***
Cbj LP......E......949 833-8373
18500 Von Karman Ave # 150 Irvine (92612) ***(P-5901)***
Cbrite Inc......F......805 722-1121
421 Pine Ave Goleta (93117) ***(P-20847)***
CBS Scientific Co Inc (PA)......E......858 755-4959
10805 Vista Sorrento Pkwy # 100 San Diego (92121) ***(P-21450)***
Ccbcc Operations LLC......C......661 723-0714
1123 W Avenue L14 Lancaster (93534) ***(P-2052)***
Ccd, Los Angeles *Also called I T I Electro-Optic Corp* ***(P-20886)***
Ccd, Anaheim *Also called Craftsman Cutting Dies Inc* ***(P-11526)***
Ccda Waters LLC......D......714 991-7031
2121 E Winston Rd Anaheim (92806) ***(P-10286)***
CCI Industries Inc (PA)......E......714 662-3879
350 Fischer Ave Ste A Costa Mesa (92626) ***(P-9698)***
CCI Mail & Shipping Systems......F......805 658-9123
369 Estrella St Ventura (93003) ***(P-4969)***
CCL Label Inc......F......707 938-7800
21481 8th St E Sonoma (95476) ***(P-23300)***
CCL Label Inc......C......909 608-2655
576 College Commerce Way Upland (91786) ***(P-7017)***
CCL Label (delaware) Inc......C......909 608-2260
576 College Commerce Way Upland (91786) ***(P-7018)***
CCL Tube Inc (HQ)......C......310 635-4444
2250 E 220th St Carson (90810) ***(P-9699)***
CCM Assembly & Mfg Inc......E......760 560-1310
2275 Michael Faraday Dr # 6 San Diego (92154) ***(P-18854)***
CCM Enterprises......F......619 562-2605
9366 Abraham Way Santee (92071) ***(P-4889)***
CCM Enterprises (PA)......D......619 562-2605
10848 Wheatlands Ave Santee (92071) ***(P-4890)***
Ccoi Gate & Fence, Hollister *Also called Gregory Patterson* ***(P-12478)***
Ccpu, San Diego *Also called Continuous Computing Corp* ***(P-14901)***
CD Alexander LLC......E......949 250-3306
2802 Willis St Santa Ana (92705) ***(P-15187)***
CD Container Inc......D......562 948-1910
7343 Paramount Blvd Pico Rivera (90660) ***(P-5206)***
CD Video Manufacturing Inc......D......714 265-0770
12650 Westminster Ave Santa Ana (92706) ***(P-19212)***
Cdc Data LLC......F......818 350-5070
9735 Lurline Ave Chatsworth (91311) ***(P-15188)***
Cdeq......E......818 767-5143
9421 Telfair Ave Sun Valley (91352) ***(P-10301)***
Cdg Technology LLC......F......530 243-4451
779 Twin View Blvd Redding (96003) ***(P-16684)***
Cdh Painting Inc......F......707 443-4429
802 Harris St Eureka (95503) ***(P-8634)***
CDI, Irvine *Also called Concept Development Llc* ***(P-17855)***
CDM Company Inc......E......949 644-2820
12 Corporate Plaza Dr # 200 Newport Beach (92660) ***(P-23301)***
Cdr Graphics Inc (PA)......E......310 474-7600
2299 Westwood Blvd Los Angeles (90064) ***(P-6475)***
Cds California LLC......F......818 766-5000
3330 Chnga Blvd W Ste 200 Los Angeles (90068) ***(P-22406)***
Cdti Advanced Materials Inc (PA)......E......805 639-9458
1700 Fiske Pl Oxnard (93033) ***(P-7480)***
Cebe Co, Paramount *Also called Robert W Wiesmantel* ***(P-16364)***
CEC Print Solutions Inc......F......510 670-0160
30971 San Benito St Hayward (94544) ***(P-6476)***
Cecilias Designs Inc......E......323 584-6151
6862 Vanscoy Ave North Hollywood (91605) ***(P-3729)***
Ceco, Oxnard *Also called Component Equipment Coinc* ***(P-18755)***
Ceco Environmental Corp......E......760 530-1409
4222 E La Palma Ave Anaheim (92807) ***(P-9700)***
Ced Anaheim 018......F......714 956-5156
1304 S Allec St Anaheim (92805) ***(P-19271)***
Cedar Lane North, South San Francisco *Also called Cedarlane Natural Foods North* ***(P-2421)***

Mergent e-mail: customerrelations@mergent.com
1056
2020 California
Manufacturers Register
(P-0000) Products & Services Section entry number
(PA)=Parent Co (HQ)=Headquarters (DH)=Div Headquarters

Cedar Mountain Winery Inc ....F....925 373-6636
 10843 Reuss Rd Livermore (94550) *(P-1623)*
Cedarlane Natural Foods Inc (PA) ....D.....310 886-7720
 1135 E Artesia Blvd Carson (90746) *(P-2420)*
Cedarlane Natural Foods Inc ....A....310 527-7833
 717 E Artesia Blvd Carson (90746) *(P-951)*
Cedarlane Natural Foods North ....E....650 742-0444
 150 Airport Blvd South San Francisco (94080) *(P-2421)*
Cee -Jay Research & Sales LLC ....E....626 815-1530
 920 W 10th St Azusa (91702) *(P-7019)*
Cee Baileys Aircraft Plas Inc ....E....323 721-4900
 6900 W Acco St Montebello (90640) *(P-20389)*
Cee Sportswear ....E....323 726-8158
 6409 Gayhart St Commerce (90040) *(P-3303)*
Ceenee Inc ....E....408 890-5018
 683 River Oaks Pkwy San Jose (95134) *(P-17211)*
Celamark Corp ....E....415 883-3386
 8 Digital Dr Ste 100 Novato (94949) *(P-20848)*
Celebration Cellars LLC ....F....951 506-5500
 33410 Rancho Cal Rd Temecula (92591) *(P-1624)*
Celerinos Pallets ....F....626 923-4182
 1320 Mateo St Los Angeles (90021) *(P-4354)*
Celeros Corp ....E....650 325-6900
 559 Clyde Ave Ste 220 Mountain View (94043) *(P-15012)*
Celesco Transducer Products ....E....818 701-2701
 20630 Plummer St Chatsworth (91311) *(P-18855)*
Celestial Lighting, Santa Fe Springs *Also called Shimada Enterprises Inc (P-17161)*
Celestica Aerospace Tech Corp ....C....512 310-7540
 895 S Rockefeller Ave Ontario (91761) *(P-17843)*
Celestica LLC ....C....510 770-5100
 49235 Milmont Dr Fremont (94538) *(P-18856)*
Celestica LLC ....B....760 357-4880
 280 Campillo St Ste G Calexico (92231) *(P-16883)*
Celestica LLC ....C....408 574-6000
 5325 Hellyer Ave San Jose (95138) *(P-18160)*
Celestica Prcsion McHining Ltd ....E....510 252-2100
 40725 Encyclopedia Cir Fremont (94538) *(P-15831)*
Celestica-Aerospace, Ontario *Also called Celestica Aerospace Tech Corp (P-17843)*
Celestron Acquisition LLC ....D....310 328-9560
 2835 Columbia St Torrance (90503) *(P-21341)*
Celestron LLC ....E....310 328-9560
 2835 Columbia St Torrance (90503) *(P-21342)*
Celigo Inc (PA) ....E....650 579-0210
 1820 Gateway Dr Ste 260 San Mateo (94404) *(P-23725)*
Celite Corporation ....F....805 736-1221
 2500 San Miguelito Rd Lompoc (93436) *(P-384)*
Cell Marque Corporation ....E....916 746-8900
 6600 Sierra College Blvd Rocklin (95677) *(P-8212)*
Cellco Partnership ....E....714 775-0600
 3770 W Mcfadden Ave Ste H Santa Ana (92704) *(P-17483)*
Cellesta Inc ....F....858 552-0888
 10554 Caminito Alvarez San Diego (92126) *(P-8213)*
Cellfusion Inc ....F....650 347-4000
 1115 Lorne Way Sunnyvale (94087) *(P-23726)*
Cello Jeans, Los Angeles *Also called Hidden Jeans Inc (P-2691)*
Cellotape Inc (HQ) ....C....510 651-5551
 39611 Eureka Dr Newark (94560) *(P-23074)*
Cellphone-Mate Inc ....D....510 770-0469
 48346 Milmont Dr Fremont (94538) *(P-17484)*
Cellscope Inc ....F....510 282-0674
 5537 Claremont Ave Apt 1 Oakland (94618) *(P-17353)*
Celltron Inc ....F....620 783-1333
 19860 Plummer St Chatsworth (91311) *(P-18857)*
Cellu-Con Inc ....E....559 568-0190
 19994 Meredith Dr Strathmore (93267) *(P-8821)*
Cellulo Co Division, Fresno *Also called Gusmer Enterprises Inc (P-14823)*
Celprogen Inc ....F....310 542-8822
 3914 Del Amo Blvd Ste 901 Torrance (90503) *(P-8285)*
Cem - Long Bch Terminal, Long Beach *Also called Cemex Cnstr Mtls PCF LLC (P-10710)*
Cem - Sacramento Terminal, Sacramento *Also called Cemex Cnstr Mtls PCF LLC (P-10721)*
Cemco, City of Industry *Also called California Expanded Met Pdts (P-12144)*
Cemco, Pittsburg *Also called California Expanded Met Pdts (P-12537)*
Cemcoat Inc ....E....323 733-0125
 4928 W Jefferson Blvd Los Angeles (90016) *(P-12964)*
Cemex, Pleasanton *Also called RMC Pacific Materials Inc (P-10429)*
Cemex (PA) ....E....916 941-2800
 5180 Gldn Fthl Pkwy # 200 El Dorado Hills (95762) *(P-10706)*
Cemex Inc ....F....925 606-2200
 7633 Southfront Rd 250 Livermore (94551) *(P-10707)*
Cemex Inc ....E....909 974-5500
 4120 Jurupa St Ste 202 Ontario (91761) *(P-10708)*
Cemex Cement Inc ....E....805 529-1355
 9035 Happy Camp Rd Moorpark (93263) *(P-10709)*
Cemex Cnstr Mtls PCF LLC ....E....562 435-0195
 601 Pier D Ave Long Beach (90802) *(P-10710)*
Cemex Cnstr Mtls PCF LLC ....F....951 377-9657
 3221 N Riverside Ave Rialto (92377) *(P-10711)*
Cemex Cnstr Mtls PCF LLC ....E....925 846-2824
 1544 Stanley Blvd Pleasanton (94566) *(P-10712)*
Cemex Cnstr Mtls PCF LLC ....E....530 626-3590
 5481 Davidson Rd El Dorado (95623) *(P-10713)*
Cemex Cnstr Mtls PCF LLC ....E....209 835-1454
 30350 S Tracy Blvd Tracy (95377) *(P-10714)*
Cemex Cnstr Mtls PCF LLC ....E....707 422-2520
 1601 Cement Hill Rd Fairfield (94533) *(P-10547)*
Cemex Cnstr Mtls PCF LLC ....E....916 645-1949
 8705 Camp Far West Rd Sheridan (95681) *(P-10715)*
Cemex Cnstr Mtls PCF LLC ....F....714 637-9470
 1730 N Main St Orange (92865) *(P-10716)*

Cemex Cnstr Mtls PCF LLC ....F....559 597-2397
 24325 Lomitas Dr Woodlake (93286) *(P-10717)*
Cemex Cnstr Mtls PCF LLC ....E....916 364-2470
 9751 Kiefer Blvd Sacramento (95827) *(P-10718)*
Cemex Cnstr Mtls PCF LLC ....E....925 858-4344
 333 23rd Ave Oakland (94606) *(P-10719)*
Cemex Cnstr Mtls PCF LLC ....E....925 688-1025
 3951 Laura Alice Way Concord (94520) *(P-10720)*
Cemex Cnstr Mtls PCF LLC ....F....916 383-0526
 8251 Power Ridge Rd Sacramento (95826) *(P-10721)*
Cemex Cnstr Mtls PCF LLC ....E....661 725-1819
 1100 Garzoli Ave Delano (93215) *(P-10722)*
Cemex Cnstr Mtls PCF LLC ....F....909 335-3105
 8203 Alabama Ave Highland (92346) *(P-10723)*
Cemex Cnstr Mtls PCF LLC ....F....916 686-8310
 10286 Waterman Rd Elk Grove (95624) *(P-10724)*
Cemex Cnstr Mtls PCF LLC ....E....661 396-0510
 11638 Old River Rd Bakersfield (93311) *(P-10725)*
Cemex Cnstr Mtls PCF LLC ....F....661 746-3423
 131 Vultee Ave Shafter (93263) *(P-10726)*
Cemex Cnstr Mtls PCF LLC ....E....209 862-0182
 3407 W Stuhr Rd Newman (95360) *(P-10727)*
Cemex Cnstr Mtls PCF LLC ....E....530 666-2137
 30288 Highway 16 Madison (95653) *(P-10728)*
Cemex Cnstr Mtls PCF LLC ....E....707 422-2520
 1601 Cement Hill Rd Fairfield (94533) *(P-10506)*
Cemex Cnstr Mtls PCF LLC ....F....707 580-3138
 7059 Tremont Rd Dixon (95620) *(P-10507)*
Cemex Cnstr Mtls PCF LLC ....F....925 862-2201
 6527 Calaveras Rd Sunol (94586) *(P-10410)*
Cemex Cnstr Mtls PCF LLC ....E....909 594-0105
 20903 Currier Rd Walnut (91789) *(P-10729)*
Cemex Cnstr Mtls PCF LLC ....F....909 355-8754
 13200 Santa Ana Ave Fontana (92337) *(P-10730)*
Cemex Cnstr Mtls PCF LLC ....E....805 529-1544
 9035 Roseland Ave Moorpark (93021) *(P-10731)*
Cemex Cnstr Mtls PCF LLC ....E....209 524-6322
 318 Beard Ave Modesto (95354) *(P-10732)*
Cemex Cnstr Mtls PCF LLC ....F....310 603-9122
 2722 N Alameda St Compton (90222) *(P-10733)*
Cemex Cnstr Mtls PCF LLC ....E....323 221-1828
 625 Lamar St Los Angeles (90031) *(P-10734)*
Cemex Cnstr Mtls PCF LLC ....E....323 466-4928
 1000 N La Brea Ave West Hollywood (90038) *(P-10735)*
Cemex Materials LLC ....E....707 678-4311
 7059 Tremont Rd Dixon (95620) *(P-10736)*
Cemex Materials LLC ....E....510 234-3616
 401 Wright Ave Richmond (94804) *(P-10737)*
Cemex Materials LLC ....F....707 448-7121
 1601 Cement Hill Rd Fairfield (94533) *(P-10738)*
Cemex Materials LLC ....E....707 255-3035
 385 Tower Rd NAPA (94558) *(P-10739)*
Cemex Materials LLC ....E....559 275-2241
 4150 N Brawley Ave Fresno (93722) *(P-10740)*
Cemex Materials LLC ....E....909 825-1500
 1205 S Rancho Ave Colton (92324) *(P-10741)*
Cemex USA Inc ....C....909 798-1144
 8731 Orange St Redlands (92374) *(P-10742)*
Cemtrol Inc ....F....714 666-6606
 3035 E La Jolla St Anaheim (92806) *(P-14895)*
Cen Cal Rock & Ready Mix, Ripon *Also called Ken Anderson (P-10776)*
Cencal Cnc Inc ....E....559 897-8706
 2491 Simpson St Kingsburg (93631) *(P-15832)*
Cencal Recycling LLC ....F....209 546-8000
 501 Port Road 22 Stockton (95203) *(P-5092)*
Cenergy Solutions Inc ....E....510 474-7593
 40967 Albrae St Fremont (94538) *(P-19612)*
Cengage Learning Inc ....E....951 719-1878
 40880 County Center Dr G Temecula (92591) *(P-6083)*
Cenic Ntwrk Operations Website ....F....714 220-3494
 5757 Plaza Dr Ste 205 Cypress (90630) *(P-20444)*
Centent Company ....E....714 979-6491
 3879 S Main St Santa Ana (92707) *(P-14896)*
Center For Cllbrtive Classroom ....D....510 533-0213
 1001 Marina Village Pkwy # 110 Alameda (94501) *(P-6084)*
Center Health Services ....F....619 692-2077
 2313 El Cajon Blvd San Diego (92104) *(P-21202)*
Center Line Performance Wheels, Newport Beach *Also called Center Line Wheel Corporation (P-19613)*
Center Line Wheel Corporation ....D....562 921-9637
 23 Corporate Plaza Dr # 150 Newport Beach (92660) *(P-19613)*
Center Thatre Group Costume Sp, Los Angeles *Also called Center Thtre Group Los Angeles (P-3545)*
Center Thtre Group Los Angeles ....E....213 972-3751
 2856 E 11th St Los Angeles (90023) *(P-3545)*
Centerline Engineering, Fullerton *Also called Centerline Manufacturing Inc (P-18858)*
Centerline Manufacturing Inc ....F....714 525-9890
 1234 E Ash Ave Ste D Fullerton (92831) *(P-18858)*
Centerline Precision Inc ....F....408 988-4380
 2265 Calle Del Mundo Santa Clara (95054) *(P-8286)*
Centerpoint Mfg Co Inc ....E....818 842-2147
 2625 N San Fernando Blvd Burbank (91504) *(P-15833)*
Centersource Systems LLC ....F....707 838-1061
 60 Commerce Ln Ste D Cloverdale (95425) *(P-6085)*
Centon Electronics Inc (PA) ....D....949 855-9111
 27412 Aliso Viejo Pkwy Aliso Viejo (92656) *(P-15013)*
Central Admxture Phrm Svcs Inc (HQ) .....F....949 660-2000
 2525 Mcgaw Ave Irvine (92614) *(P-7836)*
Central Admxture Phrm Svcs Inc ....E....562 941-9595
 10370 Slusher Dr Ste 6 Santa Fe Springs (90670) *(P-7837)*

Employee Codes: A=Over 500 employees, B=251-500
C=101-250, D=51-100, E=20-50, F=10-19

2020 California
Manfacturers Register

© Mergent Inc. 1-800-342-5647
1057

Central Admxture Phrm Svcs Inc ... E ... 858 578-1380
7935 Dunbrook Rd Ste C San Diego (92126) *(P-7838)*
Central Blower Co ... E ... 626 330-3182
211 S 7th Ave City of Industry (91746) *(P-14652)*
Central Business Forms Inc ... F ... 650 548-0918
289 Foster City Blvd B Foster City (94404) *(P-6477)*
Central Cal Metals, Fresno *Also called Robert J Alandt & Sons (P-11876)*
Central California Cnstr Inc ... F ... 661 978-8230
7221 Downing Ave Bakersfield (93308) *(P-182)*
Central California Cont Mfg ... E ... 559 665-7611
800 Commerce Dr Chowchilla (93610) *(P-9701)*
Central Coast Cabinets ... F ... 831 724-2992
111a Lee Rd Watsonville (95076) *(P-4790)*
Central Coast Printing, Grover Beach *Also called David B Anderson (P-6533)*
Central Coast Water Authority ... F ... 805 463-2122
5250 Annlope Rd Cholame (93461) *(P-15494)*
Central Coast Wine Services, Santa Maria *Also called Central Coast Wine Warehouse (P-1625)*
Central Coast Wine Warehouse (PA) ... E ... 805 928-9210
2717 Aviation Way Ste 101 Santa Maria (93455) *(P-1625)*
Central Concrete Supply Coinc (HQ) ... D ... 408 293-6272
755 Stockton Ave San Jose (95126) *(P-10743)*
Central Drugs, La Habra *Also called Auro Pharmacies Inc (P-7779)*
Central Grease Company Inc ... F ... 559 846-9607
17771 W Gettysburg Ave Kerman (93630) *(P-8426)*
Central Machine & Sheet Metal, San Jose *Also called Henry Ll (P-12235)*
Central Marble Supply Inc ... F ... 619 595-1800
3754 Main St Ste B San Diego (92113) *(P-10896)*
Central Pallets ... F ... 209 462-3019
1881 E Market St Stockton (95205) *(P-4355)*
Central Plastics and Mfg, Tracy *Also called Mother Lode Plas Molding Inc (P-9914)*
Central Precast Concrete Inc ... E ... 925 417-6854
3500 Boulder St Pleasanton (94566) *(P-10548)*
Central Printing & Graphics, Bakersfield *Also called Ampligraphix (P-6413)*
Central Printing Group, Foster City *Also called Central Business Forms Inc (P-6477)*
Central Tech Inc ... F ... 408 955-0919
2271 Ringwood Ave San Jose (95131) *(P-19272)*
Central Tent, Santa Clarita *Also called Frametent Inc (P-3683)*
Central Valley AG Grinding Inc (PA) ... E ... 209 869-1721
5509 Langworth Rd Oakdale (95361) *(P-998)*
Central Valley Cabinet Mfg ... F ... 559 584-8441
10739 14th Ave Armona (93202) *(P-4180)*
Central Valley Machining Inc ... E ... 559 291-7749
5820 E Harvard Ave Fresno (93727) *(P-11764)*
Central Valley Meat Co Inc (PA) ... C ... 559 583-9624
10431 8 3/4 Ave Hanford (93230) *(P-401)*
Central Valley Prof Svcs, Oakdale *Also called Central Valley Professional SE (P-5388)*
Central Valley Professional SE ... F ... 209 847-7832
8207 Mondo Ln Oakdale (95361) *(P-5388)*
Central Valley Tank of Cal ... F ... 559 456-3500
4752 E Carmen Ave Fresno (93703) *(P-12001)*
Central Vly Assembly Packg Inc ... E ... 559 486-4260
5515 E Lamona Ave 103 Fresno (93727) *(P-11662)*
Centric Parts Inc ... C ... 626 961-5775
14528 Bonelli St City of Industry (91746) *(P-19463)*
Centron Industries Inc ... E ... 310 324-6443
441 W Victoria St Gardena (90248) *(P-17485)*
Centurion, Merced *Also called Fineline Industries Inc (P-20331)*
Centurum Information Tech Inc ... E ... 619 224-1100
4250 Pacific Hwy Ste 105 San Diego (92110) *(P-11295)*
Century Blinds Inc ... D ... 951 734-3762
300 S Promenade Ave Corona (92879) *(P-5019)*
Century Industries, Orange *Also called Century Precision Machine Inc (P-15836)*
Century Pallets, Lynwood *Also called Roger R Caruso Enterprises Inc (P-4397)*
Century Parts Inc ... F ... 310 328-0281
913 W 223rd St Torrance (90502) *(P-15834)*
Century Pattern Co Inc ... F ... 562 402-1707
15526 Domart Ave Norwalk (90650) *(P-14001)*
Century Precision Engrg Inc ... E ... 310 538-0015
2141 W 139th St Gardena (90249) *(P-15835)*
Century Precision Machine Inc ... F ... 714 637-3691
1130 W Grove Ave Orange (92865) *(P-15836)*
Century Publishing ... F ... 951 849-4586
218 N Murray St Banning (92220) *(P-7020)*
Century Rubber Company Inc ... F ... 661 366-7009
719 Rooster Dr Bakersfield (93307) *(P-9294)*
Century Sewing Co ... E ... 626 289-0533
421 S Raymond Ave Alhambra (91803) *(P-3222)*
Century Spring, Commerce *Also called Matthew Warren Inc (P-13340)*
Century Technology Inc ... F ... 650 583-8908
3020 26th Ave San Francisco (94132) *(P-17844)*
Century Wire & Cable Inc ... D ... 213 236-8879
7400 E Slauson Ave Commerce (90040) *(P-11296)*
Cenveo Worldwide Limited ... C ... 323 262-6000
6250 S Boyle Ave Vernon (90058) *(P-5499)*
Cenveo Worldwide Limited ... D ... 415 821-7171
665 3rd St Ste 505 San Francisco (94107) *(P-6478)*
Cenveo Worldwide Limited ... D ... 323 261-7171
150 N Myers St Los Angeles (90033) *(P-5468)*
Cepheid ... F ... 408 541-4191
904 E Caribbean Dr Sunnyvale (94089) *(P-21203)*
Cepheid ... F ... 408 548-9104
632 E Caribbean Dr Sunnyvale (94089) *(P-8214)*
Cepheid (HQ) ... B ... 408 541-4191
904 E Caribbean Dr Sunnyvale (94089) *(P-21204)*
Cequal Products Inc ... F ... 310 458-0441
1328 16th St Santa Monica (90404) *(P-6086)*
Cera Inc ... E ... 626 814-2688
14180 Live Oak Ave Ste I Baldwin Park (91706) *(P-20748)*
Ceradyne Inc (HQ) ... B ... 949 862-9600
1922 Barranca Pkwy Irvine (92606) *(P-11003)*
Ceradyne Inc ... F ... 949 756-0642
17466 Daimler St Irvine (92614) *(P-11004)*
Ceramic Tech Inc ... E ... 510 252-8500
46211 Research Ave Fremont (94539) *(P-15837)*
Ceratizit Los Angeles LLC ... D ... 310 464-8050
1401 W Walnut St Rancho Dominguez (90220) *(P-13905)*
Cercacor Laboratories Inc ... F ... 949 679-6100
40 Parker Irvine (92618) *(P-21451)*
Cerebrotech Medical Systems (PA) ... F ... 925 399-5392
1048 Serpentine Ln # 301 Pleasanton (94566) *(P-21661)*
Cerego Inc ... F ... 415 518-3926
433 California St # 1030 San Francisco (94104) *(P-23727)*
Cerner Corporation ... E ... 310 247-7700
9100 Wilshire Blvd 655e Beverly Hills (90212) *(P-23728)*
Cerner Life Sciences, Beverly Hills *Also called Cerner Corporation (P-23728)*
Cernex Inc ... E ... 408 541-9226
1710 Zanker Rd Ste 103 San Jose (95112) *(P-18859)*
Certain Inc (PA) ... E ... 415 353-5330
75 Hawthorne St Ste 550 San Francisco (94105) *(P-23729)*
Certainteed Corona Inc ... C ... 951 272-1300
235 Radio Rd Corona (92879) *(P-9702)*
Certainteed Corporation ... D ... 510 490-0890
6400 Stevenson Blvd Fremont (94538) *(P-9111)*
Certainteed Corporation ... C ... 209 365-7500
300 S Beckman Rd Lodi (95240) *(P-7547)*
Certainteed Corporation ... B ... 559 665-4831
17775 Avenue 23 1/2 Chowchilla (93610) *(P-10981)*
Certance LLC (HQ) ... B ... 949 856-7800
141 Innovation Dr Irvine (92617) *(P-15014)*
Certified Distribution Svcs, Santa Fe Springs *Also called Contract Transportation Sys Co (P-8638)*
Certified Enameling Inc ... D ... 323 264-4403
3342 Emery St Los Angeles (90023) *(P-13157)*
Certified Meat Products Inc ... E ... 559 256-1433
4586 E Commerce Ave Fresno (93725) *(P-402)*
Certified Metal Craft Inc ... E ... 619 593-3636
877 Vernon Way El Cajon (92020) *(P-11445)*
Certified Stainless Svc Inc ... F ... 209 356-3300
441 Business Park Way Atwater (95301) *(P-12002)*
Certified Stainless Svc Inc (PA) ... C ... 209 537-4747
2704 Railroad Ave Ceres (95307) *(P-12003)*
Certified Stainless Svc Inc ... E ... 209 537-4747
581 Industry Way Atwater (95301) *(P-12004)*
Certified Steel Treating Corp ... E ... 323 583-8711
2454 E 58th St Vernon (90058) *(P-12965)*
Certified Thermoplastics Inc, Santa Clarita *Also called Certified Thermoplastics LLC (P-9703)*
Certified Thermoplastics LLC ... E ... 661 222-3006
26381 Ferry Ct Santa Clarita (91350) *(P-9703)*
Certifix Inc ... F ... 714 496-3850
1950 W Corporate Way Anaheim (92801) *(P-23302)*
Certifix Live Scan, Anaheim *Also called Certifix Inc (P-23302)*
Certis USA LLC ... E ... 661 758-8471
720 5th St Wasco (93280) *(P-8822)*
Cerus Corporation (PA) ... C ... 925 288-6000
2550 Stanwell Dr Ste 300 Concord (94520) *(P-8287)*
Ces Electronics Mfg Inc ... F ... 714 505-3441
14731 Franklin Ave Ste E Tustin (92780) *(P-23303)*
Cesca Therapeutics, Rancho Cordova *Also called Thermogenesis Holdings Inc (P-20776)*
Ceterix Orthopaedics Inc ... E ... 650 241-1748
6500 Kaiser Dr Ste 120 Fremont (94555) *(P-21662)*
Cevians LLC ... D ... 714 619-5135
3128 Red Hill Ave Costa Mesa (92626) *(P-10262)*
CF, Van Nuys *Also called Consolidated Fabricators Corp (P-12009)*
CF&b Manufacturing Inc ... E ... 714 744-8361
1405 N Manzanita St Orange (92867) *(P-5389)*
Cfarms Inc ... E ... 916 375-3000
1244 E Beamer St Woodland (95776) *(P-2422)*
Cfkba Inc (PA) ... D ... 650 847-3900
150 Jefferson Dr Menlo Park (94025) *(P-11297)*
Cforia Software Inc ... E ... 818 871-9687
4333 Park Terrace Dr # 201 Westlake Village (91361) *(P-23730)*
CFS Income Tax, Simi Valley *Also called CFS Tax Software (P-23731)*
CFS Tax Software ... D ... 805 522-1157
1445 E Los Angeles Ave # 214 Simi Valley (93065) *(P-23731)*
Cfw Precision Metal Components, Grover Beach *Also called C F W Research & Dev Co (P-11213)*
Cfx Battery, Irwindale *Also called Contour Energy Systems Inc (P-19156)*
Cg Financial LLC ... F ... 619 656-2919
7020 Alamitos Ave Ste B San Diego (92154) *(P-722)*
Cg Manufacturing Inc ... F ... 818 886-1191
21021 Osborne St Canoga Park (91304) *(P-12155)*
CG Motor Sports Inc ... F ... 909 628-1440
5150 Eucalyptus Ave Ste A Chino (91710) *(P-9704)*
Cg Roxane LLC ... D ... 530 225-1260
1400 Marys Dr Weed (96094) *(P-2053)*
Cg Roxane LLC (PA) ... D ... 760 764-2885
1210 State Hwy 395 Olancha (93549) *(P-2054)*
Cg Roxane Shasta, Weed *Also called Cg Roxane LLC (P-2053)*
CGB, Gardena *Also called California Glass Bending Corp (P-10344)*
Cgm Inc ... E ... 818 609-7088
19611 Ventura Blvd # 211 Tarzana (91356) *(P-22594)*
Cgm Findings, Tarzana *Also called Cgm Inc (P-22594)*
Cgnfm, Valencia *Also called Creations Grdn Natural Fd Mkts (P-7651)*

Mergent e-mail: customerrelations@mergent.com
1058
2020 California
Manufacturers Register
(P-0000) Products & Services Section entry number
(PA)=Parent Co (HQ)=Headquarters (DH)=Div Headquarters

Cgr/Thompson Industries Inc....................D....714 678-4200
7155 Fenwick Ln Westminster (92683) **(P-16544)**
CH Image Inc....................F....626 336-6063
15350 Valley Blvd City of Industry (91746) **(P-6479)**
Ch Industrial Technology Inc....................F....559 485-8011
3160 E California Ave Fresno (93702) **(P-11765)**
CH Laboratories Inc (PA)....................E....310 516-8273
1243 W 130th St Gardena (90247) **(P-7839)**
Ch Products, Vista Also called Apem Inc **(P-18817)**
Cha Bio & Diostech Co Ltd....................D....213 487-3211
3731 Wilshire Blvd # 850 Los Angeles (90010) **(P-7840)**
Cha Industries Inc....................E....510 683-8554
4201 Business Center Dr Fremont (94538) **(P-14438)**
Cha Vacuum Technology, Fremont Also called Cha Industries Inc **(P-14438)**
Chad Empey....................F....707 762-1900
1329 Scott St Ste G Petaluma (94954) **(P-10263)**
Chad Industries Incorporated....................E....714 938-0080
1565 S Sinclair St Anaheim (92806) **(P-14802)**
Chagall Design Limited....................F....310 537-9530
20625 Belshaw Ave Carson (90746) **(P-3546)**
Chalgren Enterprises....................F....408 847-3994
380 Tomkins Ct Gilroy (95020) **(P-22238)**
Challenge Graphics Inc....................E....818 892-0123
16611 Roscoe Pl North Hills (91343) **(P-6480)**
Challenge Publications Inc....................F....818 700-6868
21835 Nordhoff St Chatsworth (91311) **(P-5902)**
Challenger Ornamental Ir Works....................F....818 507-7030
437 W Palmer Ave Glendale (91204) **(P-12461)**
Chambers & Chambers Inc....................F....818 995-6961
14011 Ventura Blvd 210e Sherman Oaks (91423) **(P-1626)**
Chambers Chmbers Wine Mrchants, Sherman Oaks Also called Chambers & Chambers Inc **(P-1626)**
Chameleon Beverage Company Inc (PA)....................D....323 724-8223
6444 E 26th St Commerce (90040) **(P-2055)**
Chameleon Books & Journals, Gilroy Also called Chameleon Like Inc **(P-7306)**
Chameleon Like Inc....................E....408 847-3661
345 Kishimura Dr Gilroy (95020) **(P-7306)**
Chamisal Vineyards LLC....................F....866 808-9463
7525 Orcutt Rd San Luis Obispo (93401) **(P-1627)**
Champ Co, Campbell Also called Consoldted Hnge Mnfctured Pdts **(P-15864)**
Champion Discs Incorporated....................F....800 408-8449
950 S Dupont Ave Ontario (91761) **(P-22779)**
Champion Installs Inc....................F....916 627-0929
9631 Elk Grove Florin Rd Elk Grove (95624) **(P-4181)**
Champion Laboratories Inc....................F....951 275-0715
740 Palmyrita Ave Ste A Riverside (92507) **(P-19614)**
Champion Newspapers, Chino Also called Champion Pblications Chino Inc **(P-5585)**
Champion Pblications Chino Inc....................E....909 628-5501
13179 9th St Chino (91710) **(P-5585)**
Champion-Arrowhead LLC....................D....323 221-9137
5147 Alhambra Ave Los Angeles (90032) **(P-11663)**
Champions Choice Inc....................F....714 635-4491
1910 E Via Burton Anaheim (92806) **(P-9135)**
Champs Sports, Newark Also called Foot Locker Retail Inc **(P-10179)**
Chandler Aggregates Inc (PA)....................E....951 277-1341
24867 Maitri Rd Corona (92683) **(P-290)**
Chandler Signs LLC....................D....760 734-1708
3220 Executive Rdg # 250 Vista (92081) **(P-23075)**
Chandler Wire Products, La Verne Also called Dhl Wire Products **(P-11091)**
Changyoucom (us) LLC....................E....408 889-9866
1654 Hollenbeck Ave # 14 Sunnyvale (94087) **(P-23732)**
Channel Isl Opto Mech....................F....805 644-2153
1595 Walter St Ste 1 Ventura (93003) **(P-15838)**
Channel Islands Surfboards Inc....................F....805 745-2823
1115 Mark Ave Carpinteria (93013) **(P-22780)**
Channel Microwave, Thousand Oaks Also called Smiths Interconnect Inc **(P-19084)**
Channel Systems Inc....................E....510 568-7170
74 98th Ave Oakland (94603) **(P-10549)**
Channel Technologies Group, Santa Barbara Also called International Tranducer Corp **(P-21055)**
Channel Vision Technology, Costa Mesa Also called Djh Enterprises **(P-17503)**
Channell Commercial Corp (PA)....................D....951 719-2600
33380 Ziders Rd Temecula (92591) **(P-17354)**
Chantilly....................E....949 494-7702
202 Park Ave Laguna Beach (92651) **(P-634)**
Chantilly Bakery Inc....................F....858 693-3300
12714 Chandon Ct San Diego (92130) **(P-1176)**
Chantilly Ice Cream, Laguna Beach Also called Chantilly **(P-634)**
Chapala Iron & Manufacturing....................F....805 654-9803
1301 Callens Rd Ventura (93003) **(P-11037)**
Chapman Designs Inc....................E....562 698-4600
8333 Secura Way Santa Fe Springs (90670) **(P-3929)**
Chapman Engineering Corp....................E....714 542-1942
2321 Cape Cod Way Santa Ana (92703) **(P-15839)**
Chapmn-Wlters Intrcoastal Corp....................E....949 448-9940
141 Via Lampara Rcho STA Marg (92688) **(P-22781)**
Chappellet Vineyard....................E....707 286-4219
1581 Sage Canyon Rd Saint Helena (94574) **(P-1628)**
Chappellet Winery Inc (PA)....................E....707 286-4268
1581 Sage Canyon Rd Saint Helena (94574) **(P-1629)**
Charades, City of Industry Also called Diamond Collection LLC **(P-3551)**
Charades LLC (PA)....................C....626 435-0077
14438 Don Julian Rd City of Industry (91746) **(P-3547)**
Chargepoint Inc (PA)....................B....408 841-4500
254 E Hacienda Ave Campbell (95008) **(P-16781)**
Chargetek Inc....................E....805 444-7792
409 Calle San Pablo # 104 Camarillo (93012) **(P-16782)**
Charlaine Graphics, Poway Also called Imagine That Unlimited **(P-23131)**

Charles Gemeiner Cabinets....................E....323 299-8696
3225 Exposition Pl Los Angeles (90018) **(P-4017)**
Charles Jj Inc....................E....559 264-6664
4115 S Orange Ave Fresno (93725) **(P-4474)**
Charles Krug Winery, Saint Helena Also called C Mondavi & Family **(P-1613)**
Charles Ligeti Co....................E....213 612-0831
611 Wilshire Blvd Ste 801 Los Angeles (90017) **(P-22506)**
Charles Meisner Inc....................E....909 946-8216
201 Sierra Pl Ste A Upland (91786) **(P-14031)**
Charlies Beer Company USA LLC....................F....909 980-0436
9581 Bus Ctr Dr Ste G Rancho Cucamonga (91730) **(P-1511)**
Charlois Cooperage USA....................F....707 224-2377
1285 S Foothill Blvd Cloverdale (95425) **(P-3986)**
Charm America, Glendale Also called Saks Styling Incorporated **(P-22568)**
Charman Manufacturing Inc....................E....213 489-7000
5681 S Downey Rd Vernon (90058) **(P-11123)**
Charming Hawaii, Walnut Also called New Origins Accessories Inc **(P-22990)**
Chart Inc....................E....408 371-3303
46441 Landing Pkwy Fremont (94538) **(P-12005)**
Chase Corporation....................F....626 395-7706
132 E Colorado Blvd Pasadena (91105) **(P-16941)**
Chase Corporation....................F....714 964-6268
20001 Brookhurst St Huntington Beach (92646) **(P-16942)**
Chase-Durer Ltd (PA)....................F....310 550-7280
8455 Ftn Ave Unit 515 West Hollywood (90069) **(P-22479)**
Chateau Diana LLC (PA)....................F....707 433-6992
6195 Dry Creek Rd Healdsburg (95448) **(P-1630)**
Chateau Masson LLC....................E....408 741-7002
14831 Pierce Rd Saratoga (95070) **(P-1631)**
Chateau Montelena Winery....................F....707 942-5105
1429 Tubbs Ln Calistoga (94515) **(P-1632)**
Chateau Potelle Inc....................E....707 255-9440
528 Coombs St NAPA (94559) **(P-1633)**
Chateau Potelle Holdings LLC....................F....707 255-9440
1200 Dowdell Ln Saint Helena (94574) **(P-1634)**
Chateau St Jean, Kenwood Also called Treasury Wine Estates Americas **(P-1967)**
Chatsworth Products Inc (PA)....................E....818 735-6100
29899 Agoura Rd Ste 120 Agoura Hills (91301) **(P-13509)**
Chatsworth Products Inc....................C....818 882-8595
9353 Winnetka Ave Chatsworth (91311) **(P-13510)**
Chauhan Industries Inc....................F....805 484-1616
32 Wood Rd Ste A Camarillo (93010) **(P-9705)**
Chavers Gasket Corporation....................E....949 472-8118
23325 Del Lago Dr Laguna Hills (92653) **(P-9223)**
Chavez Welding & Machining....................E....408 247-4658
1115 Campbell Ave 1a San Jose (95126) **(P-15840)**
Chawk Technology Intl Inc (PA)....................D....510 330-5299
31033 Huntwood Ave Hayward (94544) **(P-9706)**
CHE Precision Inc....................F....805 499-8885
2640 Lavery Ct Ste C Newbury Park (91320) **(P-15841)**
Checchi Enterprises Inc....................F....530 378-1207
19849 Riverside Ave Anderson (96007) **(P-6481)**
Check It Out, Los Angeles Also called Nexxen Apparel Inc **(P-3376)**
Check Point Software Tech Inc (HQ)....................C....650 628-2000
959 Skyway Rd Ste 300 San Carlos (94070) **(P-23733)**
Check Yourself Inc....................F....805 967-6190
5785 Thornwood Dr Goleta (93117) **(P-15842)**
Check Yourself Machining, Goleta Also called Check Yourself Inc **(P-15842)**
Checkerspot Inc....................F....510 239-7921
740 Heinz Ave Berkeley (94710) **(P-8288)**
Checkworks Inc....................D....626 333-1444
315 Cloverleaf Dr Ste J Baldwin Park (91706) **(P-7307)**
Cheek Engineering & Stamping....................F....714 832-9480
1732 Mcgaw Ave Irvine (92614) **(P-12783)**
Cheek Machine Corp....................E....714 279-9486
1312 S Allec St Anaheim (92805) **(P-15843)**
Cheerpak....................E....818 922-5451
7778 Varna Ave North Hollywood (91605) **(P-1017)**
Cheese Administrative Corp Inc....................E....209 826-3744
429 H St Los Banos (93635) **(P-544)**
Cheese Cake City Inc....................F....510 524-9404
1225 4th St Berkeley (94710) **(P-1177)**
Cheesecake Factory Bakery Inc (HQ)....................B....818 880-9323
26950 Agoura Rd Agoura Hills (91301) **(P-1178)**
Chef Brand Foods....................F....559 651-1696
8637 W Doe Ave Visalia (93291) **(P-1179)**
Chef Brands, Visalia Also called Chef Brand Foods **(P-1179)**
Chef Merito Inc (PA)....................D....818 787-0100
7915 Sepulveda Blvd Van Nuys (91405) **(P-2423)**
Chefmaster....................E....714 554-4000
501 Airpark Dr Fullerton (92833) **(P-2424)**
Chella, Camarillo Also called Mosaic Distributors LLC **(P-8541)**
Chella Professional Skin Care, Camarillo Also called Mosaic Marketing Partners LLC **(P-8542)**
Chem Arrow Corp....................E....626 358-2255
13643 Live Oak Ln Irwindale (91706) **(P-9136)**
Chem-Mark of Orange County, Cerritos Also called Better Beverages Inc **(P-2192)**
Chem-Tainer Industries Inc....................E....310 635-5400
135 E Stanley St Compton (90220) **(P-9707)**
Chemat Technology Inc....................E....818 727-9786
9036 Winnetka Ave Northridge (91324) **(P-20749)**
Chemat Vision, Northridge Also called Chemat Technology Inc **(P-20749)**
Chemco Products Company, Paramount Also called LMC Enterprises **(P-8393)**
Chemcor Chemical Corporation....................F....909 590-7234
13770 Benson Ave Chino (91710) **(P-8372)**
Chemdiv Inc....................E....858 794-4860
12760 High Bluff Dr # 370 San Diego (92130) **(P-8946)**
Chemeor Inc....................E....626 966-3808
727 Arrow Grand Cir Covina (91722) **(P-8427)**

Employee Codes: A=Over 500 employees, B=251-500
C=101-250, D=51-100, E=20-50, F=10-19

2020 California
Manfacturers Register

© Mergent Inc. 1-800-342-5647

1059

Chemetry, Moss Landing *Also called Calera Corporation* ***(P-8726)***

Chemical & Material Technology............E......408 354-2656
229 Creekside Village Dr Los Gatos (95032) ***(P-21343)***

Chemical Diversity Labs, San Diego *Also called Chemdiv Inc* ***(P-8946)***

Chemical Methods Assoc LLC (HQ)............D......714 898-8781
12700 Knott St Garden Grove (92841) ***(P-15495)***

Chemical Safety Technology Inc............E......408 263-0984
2461 Autumnvale Dr San Jose (95131) ***(P-14439)***

Chemical Systems Div, San Jose *Also called United Technologies Corp* ***(P-19987)***

Chemical Technologies Intl Inc............F......916 638-1315
2747 Merc Dr Ste 200 Rancho Cordova (95742) ***(P-15496)***

Chemicals Incorporated............F......951 681-9697
13560 Colombard Ct Fontana (92337) ***(P-8947)***

Chemocentryx Inc (PA)............D......650 210-2900
850 Maude Ave Mountain View (94043) ***(P-7841)***

Chemseal, Pacoima *Also called Flamemaster Corporation* ***(P-8967)***

Chemsw Inc............F......707 864-0845
2480 Burskirk Ste 300 Pleasant Hill (94523) ***(P-23734)***

Chemtainer Industries, Compton *Also called Chem-Tainer Industries Inc* ***(P-9707)***

Chemtex International, Sunnyvale *Also called American Liquid Packaging Syst* ***(P-7541)***

Chemtex Print USA Inc............E......310 900-1818
3061 E Maria St Compton (90221) ***(P-7021)***

Chemtool Incorporated............E......661 823-7190
1300 Goodrick Dr Tehachapi (93561) ***(P-9137)***

Chemtrade Chemicals US LLC............E......925 458-7300
501 Nichols Rd Bay Point (94565) ***(P-7481)***

Chemtrade Chemicals US LLC............E......510 232-7193
525 Castro St Richmond (94801) ***(P-7482)***

Chemtreat Inc............E......804 935-2000
8885 Rehco Rd San Diego (92121) ***(P-8948)***

CHEMTROL, Santa Barbara *Also called Santa Barbara Control Systems* ***(P-20932)***

Chen-Tech Industries Inc (HQ)............E......949 855-6716
9 Wrigley Irvine (92618) ***(P-21663)***

Chenbro Micom (usa) Inc............E......909 937-0100
2800 Jurupa St Ontario (91761) ***(P-15015)***

Cheol Lee, Los Angeles *Also called Noahs Ark International Inc* ***(P-3184)***

Chep (usa) Inc............D......925 234-4970
2276 Wilbur Ln Antioch (94509) ***(P-4356)***

Cherokee Uniform, Chatsworth *Also called Strategic Partners Inc* ***(P-10163)***

Cherry Pit............F......707 449-8378
812 E Monte Vista Ave Vacaville (95688) ***(P-9138)***

Cherry Valley Sheet Metal............F......951 845-1578
39638 Avenida Sonrisa Cherry Valley (92223) ***(P-13619)***

Chet Cooper............F......949 854-8700
1001 W 17th St Costa Mesa (92627) ***(P-5903)***

Chevron Captain Company LLC (HQ)............C......925 842-1000
6001 Bollinger Canyon Rd San Ramon (94583) ***(P-9041)***

Chevron Corporation............F......805 733-5174
3602 Harris Grade Rd Lompoc (93436) ***(P-43)***

Chevron Global Energy Inc (HQ)............D......925 842-1000
6001 Bollinger Canyon Rd San Ramon (94583) ***(P-9042)***

Chevron Global Lubricants, San Ramon *Also called Chevron Global Energy Inc* ***(P-9042)***

Chevron Mining Inc............B......760 856-7625
67750 Bailey Rd Mountain Pass (92366) ***(P-15)***

Chevron Oronite Company LLC (HQ)............E......713 432-2500
6001 Bollinger Canyon Rd San Ramon (94583) ***(P-8949)***

Chevron Phillips Chem Co LP............D......909 420-5500
6001 Bollinger Canyon Rd San Ramon (94583) ***(P-9465)***

Chevron Products Company, San Ramon *Also called Chevron Captain Company LLC* ***(P-9041)***

Chh Lp............E......951 506-5800
28134 Jefferson Ave Temecula (92590) ***(P-2425)***

CHI Fung Plastics Inc............F......510 532-4835
1000 54th Ave Oakland (94601) ***(P-9481)***

CHI-AM Comics Daily Inc............F......626 281-2989
673 Monterey Pass Rd Monterey Park (91754) ***(P-6212)***

Chiapa Welding Inc (PA)............F......559 784-3400
276 E Grand Ave Porterville (93257) ***(P-24625)***

Chicago Brothers, Vernon *Also called Overhill Farms Inc* ***(P-972)***

Chick Publications Inc............E......909 987-0771
8780 Archibald Ave Rancho Cucamonga (91730) ***(P-6087)***

Chico Community Publishing (PA)............E......530 894-2300
353 E 2nd St Chico (95928) ***(P-5586)***

Chico Community Publishing............D......916 498-1234
1124 Del Paso Blvd Sacramento (95815) ***(P-5587)***

Chico Custom Counter............F......530 894-8123
3080 Thorntree Dr Ste 45 Chico (95973) ***(P-4891)***

Chico Enterprise Record, Chico *Also called Gatehouse Media LLC* ***(P-5642)***

Chico Metal Finishing Inc............F......530 534-7308
3151 Richter Ave Oroville (95966) ***(P-12966)***

Chicobag, Chico *Also called Chicoeco Inc* ***(P-3654)***

Chicoeco Inc............E......530 342-4426
747 Fortress St Chico (95973) ***(P-3654)***

Chicwrap, Valencia *Also called Allen Reed Company Inc* ***(P-5097)***

Chief Neon Sign Co Inc............F......310 327-1317
15027 S Maple Ave Gardena (90248) ***(P-23076)***

Child Evngelism Fellowship Inc............E......661 873-9032
2201 Mount Vernon Ave Bakersfield (93306) ***(P-6482)***

Children's Choice, Danville *Also called Choice Foodservices Inc* ***(P-11370)***

Chili Bar LLC............E......530 622-3325
11380 State Highway 193 Placerville (95667) ***(P-313)***

Chili Bar Slate, Placerville *Also called Chili Bar LLC* ***(P-313)***

Chili's, Santa Maria *Also called Impo International LLC* ***(P-10170)***

Chill Spot Inc............F......818 762-0041
11706 Moorpark St Studio City (91604) ***(P-635)***

Chimes Printing Incorporated............F......510 235-2388
1065 Hensley St Richmond (94801) ***(P-6483)***

China Circuit Tech Corp N Amer............F......831 646-2194
11 Thomas Owens Way Monterey (93940) ***(P-17845)***

China Custom Manufacturing Ltd............A......510 979-1920
44843 Fremont Blvd Fremont (94538) ***(P-9708)***

China Loco Szhou Precise Indus............E......510 429-3700
4125 Business Center Dr Fremont (94538) ***(P-18753)***

China Master USA Entrmt Co............F......626 810-9372
17890 Castleton St # 230 City of Industry (91748) ***(P-11005)***

China Press............F......626 281-8500
2121 W Mission Rd Ste 103 Alhambra (91803) ***(P-5588)***

China Press, The, Burlingame *Also called Asia Pacific California Inc* ***(P-5554)***

Chinecherem Eze Inc............F......310 806-1807
13052 Hawthorne Los Angeles (90001) ***(P-10167)***

Chinecherem Eze Foundation, Los Angeles *Also called Chinecherem Eze Inc* ***(P-10167)***

Chinese Consumer Yellow Pages, Fremont *Also called Chinese Overseas Mktg Svc Corp* ***(P-6214)***

Chinese Consumer Yellow Pages, Rosemead *Also called Chinese Overseas Mktg Svc Corp* ***(P-6215)***

Chinese Overseas Mktg Svc Corp............E......510 476-0880
33420 Alvarado Niles Rd Union City (94587) ***(P-6213)***

Chinese Overseas Mktg Svc Corp............E......626 280-8588
46292 Warm Springs Blvd Fremont (94539) ***(P-6214)***

Chinese Overseas Mktg Svc Corp (PA)............D......626 280-8588
3940 Rosemead Blvd Rosemead (91770) ***(P-6215)***

Chinese Times, San Francisco *Also called Gum Sun Times Inc* ***(P-5650)***

Chinese-La Daily News, El Monte *Also called LAweb Offset Printing Inc* ***(P-7117)***

Chino Ice Service LLC............E......909 628-2105
3640 Francis Ave Chino (91710) ***(P-2351)***

Chiodo Candy Co............D......510 464-2977
2923 Adeline St Oakland (94608) ***(P-1360)***

Chip-Makers Tooling Supply Inc............F......562 698-5840
7352 Whittier Ave Whittier (90602) ***(P-14032)***

Chipco Manufacturing Co Inc............F......530 751-8150
623 Bridge St Yuba City (95991) ***(P-15844)***

Chipmasters Manufacturing Inc (PA)............F......626 804-8178
798 N Coney Ave Azusa (91702) ***(P-15845)***

Chipton-Ross Inc............D......310 414-7800
420 Culver Blvd Playa Del Rey (90293) ***(P-19887)***

Chiquita Brands Intl Inc............F......510 732-9500
3586 Arden Rd Hayward (94545) ***(P-907)***

Chladni & Jariwala Inc............E......909 947-5227
1120 E Locust St Ontario (91761) ***(P-13297)***

Chlor Alkali Products & Vinyls, Santa Fe Springs *Also called Olin Chlor Alkali Logistics* ***(P-7391)***

Choice Food Products Inc............F......559 266-1674
1822 W Hedges Ave Fresno (93728) ***(P-447)***

Choice Foodservices Inc............D......925 837-0104
569 San Ramon Valley Blvd Danville (94526) ***(P-11370)***

Choice Lithographics, Buena Park *Also called Cyu Lithographics Inc* ***(P-6528)***

Chol Enterprises Inc............E......310 516-1328
12831 S Figueroa St Los Angeles (90061) ***(P-20070)***

Cholestech, Livermore *Also called Alere Inc* ***(P-8201)***

Chooljian & Sons Inc............D......559 888-2031
Del Rey Ave Del Rey (93616) ***(P-14355)***

Choon Inc (PA)............E......213 225-2500
520 Mateo St Los Angeles (90013) ***(P-3223)***

Choose Manufacturing Co LLC............E......714 327-1698
1638 E Edinger Ave Ste A Santa Ana (92705) ***(P-17846)***

Chorus.ai, San Francisco *Also called Affectlayer Inc* ***(P-23576)***

Chosen Foods LLC (PA)............F......877 674-2244
1747 Hancock St Ste A San Diego (92101) ***(P-8950)***

Chownow Inc............D......888 707-2469
12181 Bluff Creek Dr # 200 Playa Vista (90094) ***(P-23735)***

Chris French Metal Inc............F......510 238-9339
2500 Union St Oakland (94607) ***(P-11766)***

Chrislie, Azusa *Also called Arminak Solutions LLC* ***(P-8439)***

Christian Music Today Inc............F......408 377-9232
80 Gilman Ave Ste 2 Campbell (95008) ***(P-5589)***

Christian Science Church............E......805 966-6661
120 E Valerio St Santa Barbara (93101) ***(P-5590)***

Christian Today Inc............F......323 931-0505
354 S Normandie Ave # 101 Los Angeles (90020) ***(P-5591)***

Christie Digital Systems Inc (HQ)............E......714 236-8610
10550 Camden Dr Cypress (90630) ***(P-22407)***

Christine Alexander Inc............E......213 488-1114
110 E 9th St Ste B336 Los Angeles (90079) ***(P-3730)***

Christine Milne............F......415 485-5658
1133 Francisco Blvd E H San Rafael (94901) ***(P-1339)***

Christy Vault Company (PA)............E......650 994-1378
1000 Collins Ave Colma (94014) ***(P-10550)***

Chroma Systems Solutions Inc (HQ)............D......949 297-4848
19772 Pauling Foothill Ranch (92610) ***(P-21016)***

Chromacode Inc............E......442 244-4369
2330 Faraday Ave Ste 100 Carlsbad (92008) ***(P-20750)***

Chromadex Corporation (PA)............D......949 419-0288
10005 Muirlands Blvd G Irvine (92618) ***(P-7648)***

Chromal Plating & Grinding, Los Angeles *Also called Chromal Plating Company* ***(P-12967)***

Chromal Plating Company............E......323 222-0119
1748 Workman St Los Angeles (90031) ***(P-12967)***

Chromatic Inc Lithographers............E......818 242-5785
127 Concord St Glendale (91203) ***(P-6484)***

Chrome Craft, Sacramento *Also called Mencarini & Jarwin Inc* ***(P-13048)***

Chrome Hearts LLC (PA)............E......323 957-7544
921 N Mansfield Ave Los Angeles (90038) ***(P-3510)***

Chromologic LLC............E......626 381-9974
1225 S Shamrock Ave Monrovia (91016) ***(P-21664)***

Chron Trol, San Diego *Also called Chrontrol Corporation* ***(P-16589)***

Mergent e-mail: customerrelations@mergent.com
1060
2020 California
Manufacturers Register
(P-0000) Products & Services Section entry number
(PA)=Parent Co (HQ)=Headquarters (DH)=Div Headquarters

Chronicle Books LLC ....C....415 537-4200
680 2nd St San Francisco (94107) *(P-6088)*
Chronix Biomedical Inc (PA) ....F....408 960-2306
5941 Optical Ct Ste 203e San Jose (95138) *(P-8215)*
Chronomite Laboratories Inc ....E....310 534-2300
17451 Hurley St City of Industry (91744) *(P-20787)*
Chrontel Inc (PA) ....C....408 383-9328
2210 Otoole Ave Ste 100 San Jose (95131) *(P-18161)*
Chrontrol Corporation (PA) ....F....619 282-8686
6611 Jackson Dr San Diego (92119) *(P-16589)*
Chua & Sons Inc ....E....323 588-8044
3300 E 50th St Vernon (90058) *(P-2751)*
Chubby Gorilla Inc (PA) ....E....844 365-5218
10425 Slusher Dr Santa Fe Springs (90670) *(P-9709)*
Chuck L Logging Inc ....E....530 459-3842
6527 Big Springs Rd Montague (96064) *(P-3877)*
Chulada Inc ....E....818 841-6536
640 S Flower St Burbank (91502) *(P-7649)*
Chulada Spices Herbs & Snacks, Burbank *Also called Chulada Inc (P-7649)*
Chunma America, Vernon *Also called Chunma Usa Inc (P-10191)*
Chunma Usa Inc ....F....323 846-0077
2000 E 25th St Vernon (90058) *(P-10191)*
Chup Corporation ....F....949 455-0676
2990 Airway Ave Ste A Costa Mesa (92626) *(P-6485)*
Church & Dwight Co Inc ....E....559 661-2790
31266 Avenue 12 Madera (93638) *(P-7384)*
Church Scientology Intl ....D....323 960-3500
6331 Hollywood Blvd # 801 Los Angeles (90028) *(P-7022)*
Churchill Aerospace LLC ....C....909 266-3116
5091 G St Chino (91710) *(P-14219)*
Churm Publishing Inc (PA) ....E....714 796-7000
1451 Quail St Ste 201 Newport Beach (92660) *(P-5904)*
Chus Packaging Supplies Inc ....E....562 944-6411
10011 Santa Fe Springs Rd Santa Fe Springs (90670) *(P-9224)*
Ci, Mather *Also called Construction Innovations LLC (P-19278)*
Ci Management LLC ....F....650 654-8900
2039 Seabrook Ct Redwood City (94065) *(P-10148)*
Cianna Medical Inc ....F....949 360-0059
6 Journey Ste 125 Aliso Viejo (92656) *(P-9260)*
Ciao Wireless Inc ....D....805 389-3224
4000 Via Pescador Camarillo (93012) *(P-18860)*
Ciasons Industrial Inc ....E....714 259-0838
1615 Boyd St Santa Ana (92705) *(P-9225)*
Cicon Engineering Inc ....E....818 909-6060
8345 Canoga Ave Canoga Park (91304) *(P-18861)*
Cicon Engineering Inc ....F....818 882-6508
21421 Schoenborn St Canoga Park (91304) *(P-18862)*
Cicon Engineering Inc (PA) ....C....818 909-6060
6633 Odessa Ave Van Nuys (91406) *(P-18863)*
Cicon Engineering Inc ....E....818 909-6060
9300 Mason Ave Chatsworth (91311) *(P-18864)*
Cidara Therapeutics Inc (PA) ....D....858 752-6170
6310 Nncy Rdge Dr Ste 101 San Diego (92121) *(P-8289)*
Cii, Santee *Also called Compucraft Industries Inc (P-20075)*
Cilajet LLC ....E....310 320-8000
16425 Ishida Ave Gardena (90248) *(P-8373)*
Cim, Compton *Also called Circle Industrial Mfg Corp (P-13974)*
Cim Services, Compton *Also called Circle Industrial Mfg Corp (P-14757)*
Cimc Intermodal Equipment LLC (HQ) ....D....562 904-8600
10530 Sessler St South Gate (90280) *(P-19816)*
Cimc Reefer Trailer Inc (PA) ....F....951 218-1414
22101 Alessandro Blvd Moreno Valley (92553) *(P-13861)*
Cimmaron Software Inc ....E....858 385-1291
16885 W Bernardo Dr # 345 San Diego (92127) *(P-23736)*
Cimrmaan Ivo ....F....858 693-1536
7550 Trade St San Diego (92121) *(P-12784)*
Cine Mechanics Inc ....F....818 701-7944
20610 Plummer St Chatsworth (91311) *(P-22408)*
Cinemag Inc ....F....818 993-4644
4487 Ish Dr Simi Valley (93063) *(P-18865)*
Cinemills Corporation (PA) ....F....818 843-4560
2021 N Lincoln St Burbank (91504) *(P-17110)*
Cintas Corporation ....F....916 375-8633
1679 Entp Blvd Ste 10 West Sacramento (95691) *(P-3029)*
Cinton ....E....714 961-8808
620 Richfield Rd Placentia (92870) *(P-5359)*
Ciphercloud Inc (PA) ....D....408 519-6930
2581 Junction Ave Ste 200 San Jose (95134) *(P-23737)*
Ciphertex LLC ....F....818 773-8989
9301 Jordan Ave Ste 105a Chatsworth (91311) *(P-15189)*
Ciphertex Data Security, Chatsworth *Also called Ciphertex LLC (P-15189)*
Circa 1605 Inc ....E....217 899-3512
1475 Folsom St Ste 200 San Francisco (94103) *(P-23738)*
Circle Industrial Mfg Corp (PA) ....E....310 638-5101
1613 W El Segundo Blvd Compton (90222) *(P-14757)*
Circle Industrial Mfg Corp ....F....310 638-5101
2727 N Slater Ave Compton (90222) *(P-13974)*
Circle Racing Wheels Inc (PA) ....F....800 959-2100
14955 Don Julian Rd City of Industry (91746) *(P-19615)*
Circle Seal Controls, Corona *Also called Circor Aerospace Inc (P-13298)*
Circle W Enterprises Inc ....E....661 257-2400
27737 Avenue Hopkins Valencia (91355) *(P-13404)*
Circlemaster Inc ....F....858 578-3900
7777 Alvarado Rd Ste 320 La Mesa (91942) *(P-12156)*
Circor Aerospace Inc ....B....951 270-6200
2301 Wardlow Cir Corona (92880) *(P-20071)*
Circor Aerospace Inc (HQ) ....C....951 270-6200
2301 Wardlow Cir Corona (92880) *(P-13298)*
Circor Aerospace Inc ....D....951 270-6200
15148 Bledsoe St Sylmar (91342) *(P-11579)*
Circor Aerospace Machining Ctr, Sylmar *Also called Circor Aerospace Inc (P-11579)*
Circor Aerospace Pdts Group ....B....951 270-6200
2301 Wardlow Cir Corona (92880) *(P-11156)*
Circuit Assembly Corp (PA) ....E....949 855-7887
3 Vanderbilt Ste A Irvine (92618) *(P-18754)*
Circuit Automation Inc ....F....714 763-4180
5292 System Dr Huntington Beach (92649) *(P-18866)*
Circuit Bd Test & Insptn Sls, Irvine *Also called Teradyne Inc (P-21140)*
Circuit Check Inc ....D....408 263-7444
1764 Houret Ct Milpitas (95035) *(P-21017)*
Circuit Connections ....E....408 955-9505
2310 Lundy Ave San Jose (95131) *(P-17847)*
Circuit Express Inc ....F....805 581-2172
67 W Easy St Ste 129 Simi Valley (93065) *(P-17848)*
Circuit Services Llc ....E....818 701-5391
9134 Independence Ave Chatsworth (91311) *(P-17849)*
Circuit Spectrum Inc ....F....408 946-8484
988 Morse St San Jose (95126) *(P-17850)*
Cirexx Corporation ....E....408 988-3980
791 Nuttman St Santa Clara (95054) *(P-17851)*
Cirexx International Inc (PA) ....C....408 988-3980
791 Nuttman St Santa Clara (95054) *(P-17852)*
Cirrent Inc ....F....650 569-1135
2 E 3rd Ave Ste 100 San Mateo (94401) *(P-23739)*
Cirrus Logic Inc ....D....510 226-1204
45630 Northport Loop E Fremont (94538) *(P-18162)*
Cirtec Medical LLC ....D....408 395-0443
101b Cooper Ct Los Gatos (95032) *(P-21665)*
CIS, Santa Ana *Also called Creative Intgrated Systems Inc (P-18185)*
Cisc Semiconductor Corp ....F....847 553-4204
800 W El Camino Real Mountain View (94040) *(P-18163)*
Cisco & Brothers Designs, Los Angeles *Also called Cisco Bros Corp (P-4632)*
Cisco Bros Corp ....F....323 778-8612
938 E 60th St Los Angeles (90001) *(P-4631)*
Cisco Bros Corp (PA) ....C....323 778-8612
5955 S Western Ave Los Angeles (90047) *(P-4632)*
Cisco Ironport Systems LLC (HQ) ....B....650 989-6500
170 W Tasman Dr San Jose (95134) *(P-23740)*
Cisco Mfg Inc ....E....510 584-9626
3185 De La Cruz Blvd Santa Clara (95054) *(P-15846)*
Cisco Systems Inc ....A....408 526-7939
325 E Tasman Dr San Jose (95134) *(P-15190)*
Cisco Systems Inc ....A....408 570-9149
771 Alder Dr Milpitas (95035) *(P-15191)*
Cisco Systems Inc ....F....415 837-6261
500 Terry A Francois Blvd San Francisco (94158) *(P-15192)*
Cisco Systems Inc ....F....714 434-2100
3500 Hyland Ave Costa Mesa (92626) *(P-15193)*
Cisco Systems Inc ....A....408 526-4000
121 Theory Irvine (92617) *(P-15194)*
Cisco Systems Inc ....A....408 225-5248
11 Great Oaks Blvd San Jose (95119) *(P-15195)*
Cisco Systems Inc ....A....408 526-4000
510 Mccarthy Blvd Milpitas (95035) *(P-15196)*
Cisco Systems Inc ....A....408 526-6698
3650 Cisco Way Bldg 17 San Jose (95134) *(P-15197)*
Cisco Systems Inc ....A....925 223-1006
4460 Rosewood Dr Ste 100 Pleasanton (94588) *(P-15198)*
Cisco Systems Inc (PA) ....A....408 526-4000
170 W Tasman Dr San Jose (95134) *(P-15199)*
Cisco Systems Inc ....A....408 434-1903
3600 Cisco Way San Jose (95134) *(P-15200)*
Cisco Systems Inc ....A....408 424-4050
110 W Tasman Dr San Jose (95134) *(P-15201)*
Cisco Systems Inc ....A....408 526-5999
3700 Cisco Way San Jose (95134) *(P-15202)*
Cisco Technology Inc (HQ) ....F....408 526-4000
170 W Tasman Dr San Jose (95134) *(P-15203)*
Ciscos Shop ....F....657 230-9158
2911 E Miraloma Ave # 17 Anaheim (92806) *(P-11664)*
Citizens of Humanity LLC (PA) ....D....323 923-1240
5715 Bickett St Huntington Park (90255) *(P-3304)*
Citragen Pharmaceuticals Inc ....F....510 249-9066
3789 Spinnaker Ct Fremont (94538) *(P-7842)*
Citrix Systems Inc ....D....408 790-8000
4988 Great America Pkwy Santa Clara (95054) *(P-23741)*
Citrix Systems Inc ....F....800 424-8749
7414 Hollister Ave Goleta Los Angeles (90074) *(P-23742)*
City & County of San Francisco ....E....415 557-5251
875 Stevenson St Ste 125 San Francisco (94103) *(P-7023)*
City Baking Company ....D....650 589-8128
1373 Lowrie Ave South San Francisco (94080) *(P-1180)*
City Canvas ....F....408 287-2688
1381 N 10th St San Jose (95112) *(P-3680)*
City Crane, Bakersfield *Also called Dunbar Electric Sign Company (P-23089)*
City Industrial Tool & Die (PA) ....F....310 530-1234
25524 Frampton Ave Harbor City (90710) *(P-11038)*
City of Delano ....E....661 721-3352
1107 Lytle Ave Delano (93215) *(P-15497)*
City of Industry, Chino *Also called Balaji Trading Inc (P-17349)*
City of Riverside ....D....951 351-6140
5950 Acorn St Riverside (92504) *(P-15498)*
City of San Diego ....E....619 758-2310
2392 Kincaid Rd San Diego (92101) *(P-21205)*
City of Santa Fe Springs ....F....562 868-8761
11641 Florence Ave Santa Fe Springs (90670) *(P-22782)*
City of Santa Monica Wtr Trtmn, Los Angeles *Also called Santa Monica City of (P-15574)*
City Paper Box Co ....F....323 231-5990
652 E 61st St Los Angeles (90001) *(P-5207)*

ALPHABETIC

Employee Codes: A=Over 500 employees, B=251-500
C=101-250, D=51-100, E=20-50, F=10-19
2020 California
Manfacturers Register
© Mergent Inc. 1-800-342-5647
1061

City Steel Heat Treating Inc ... F ... 562 789-7373
1221 W Struck Ave Orange (92867) ***(P-11446)***

City Triangles, Los Angeles *Also called Jodi Kristopher LLC* ***(P-3235)***

Ciuti International Inc ... F ... 909 484-1414
8790 Rochester Ave Ste A Rancho Cucamonga (91730) ***(P-1470)***

Civic Center News Inc ... E ... 213 481-1448
1264 W 1st St Los Angeles (90026) ***(P-5592)***

CJ Enterprises ... E ... 714 898-8558
11530 Western Ave Stanton (90680) ***(P-14033)***

CJ Foods Manufacturing Corp ... E ... 714 888-3500
500 S State College Blvd Fullerton (92831) ***(P-2426)***

CJ Products Inc ... F ... 760 444-4217
4087 Calle Platino Oceanside (92056) ***(P-3607)***

Cjd Construction Services Inc ... E ... 626 335-1116
416 S Vermont Ave Glendora (91741) ***(P-183)***

Cji Process Systems Inc ... D ... 562 777-0614
12000 Clark St Santa Fe Springs (90670) ***(P-12006)***

Cjs Toffee & Toppings LLC ... F ... 415 929-7852
2269 Chestnut St 298 San Francisco (94123) ***(P-1361)***

CK Steel Inc ... F ... 310 638-0855
19826 S Alameda St Compton (90221) ***(P-11767)***

CK Technologies Inc (PA) ... E ... 805 987-4801
3629 Vista Mercado Camarillo (93012) ***(P-20849)***

Ckcc Inc ... E ... 213 629-0939
2125 Bay St Los Angeles (90021) ***(P-3780)***

Ckd Industries Inc ... F ... 714 871-5600
501 E Jamie Ave La Habra (90631) ***(P-12785)***

Cks Solution Incorporated ... E ... 714 292-6307
556 Vanguard Way Ste C Brea (92821) ***(P-18867)***

Ckt, Camarillo *Also called CK Technologies Inc* ***(P-20849)***

CL Knox Inc ... D ... 661 837-0477
34933 Imperial St Bakersfield (93308) ***(P-184)***

Cl-One Corporation ... D ... 949 364-2895
29582 Spotted Bull Ln San Juan Capistrano (92675) ***(P-2056)***

Clama Products Inc ... F ... 714 258-8606
1993 Ritchey St Santa Ana (92705) ***(P-14034)***

Clamp Swing Pricing Co Inc ... E ... 510 567-1600
8386 Capwell Dr Oakland (94621) ***(P-23304)***

Clamshell Buildings, Oxnard *Also called Clamshell Structures Inc* ***(P-12540)***

Clamshell Structures Inc ... F ... 805 988-1340
1101 Maulhardt Ave Oxnard (93030) ***(P-12540)***

Clarcor Air Filtration Pdts ... D ... 951 272-1850
1295 E Ontario Ave # 102 Corona (92881) ***(P-14653)***

Clarcor Industrial Air, Sacramento *Also called Pecofacet (us) Inc* ***(P-14849)***

Claremont Courier ... E ... 909 621-4761
114 Olive St Claremont (91711) ***(P-5593)***

Claremont Institute Statesmans (PA) ... E ... 909 981-2200
1317 W Foothill Blvd # 120 Upland (91786) ***(P-7024)***

CLAREMONT INSTITUTE, THE, Upland *Also called Claremont Institute Statesmans* ***(P-7024)***

Clariant Corporation ... E ... 909 825-1793
926 S 8th St Colton (92324) ***(P-5360)***

Clariant Corporation ... C ... 650 494-1749
3350 W Bayshore Rd Palo Alto (94303) ***(P-7548)***

Clariant Corporation ... E ... 661 763-5192
801 W 14th St Long Beach (90813) ***(P-8731)***

Clariant Plas Coatings USA LLC ... F ... 909 606-1325
14355 Ramona Ave Chino (91710) ***(P-8732)***

Clarify Medical Inc ... E ... 877 738-6041
10505 Sorrento Valley Rd # 450 San Diego (92121) ***(P-22239)***

Clariphy Communications Inc (HQ) ... D ... 949 861-3074
7585 Irvine Center Dr # 100 Irvine (92618) ***(P-18164)***

Clarity H2o LLC ... F ... 619 993-4780
752 Pomelo Dr Vista (92081) ***(P-15499)***

Clark - Pacific Corporation ... D ... 626 962-8751
131 Los Angeles St Irwindale (91706) ***(P-10551)***

Clark - Pacific Corporation ... C ... 909 823-1433
13592 Slover Ave Fontana (92337) ***(P-10552)***

Clark - Pacific Corporation ... D ... 925 746-7176
3478 Buskirk Ave Ste 1039 Pleasant Hill (94523) ***(P-10553)***

Clark Steel Fabricators Inc ... E ... 619 390-1502
12610 Vigilante Rd Lakeside (92040) ***(P-12462)***

Clarkdietrich Building Systems, Riverside *Also called Clarkwestern Dietrich Building* ***(P-12157)***

Clarke Engineering Inc ... F ... 818 768-0690
8058 Lankershim Blvd North Hollywood (91605) ***(P-14740)***

Clarke Pb & Associates Inc ... E ... 714 835-3022
2500 E Francis St Ontario (91761) ***(P-17212)***

Clarkwestern Dietrich Building ... F ... 951 360-3500
6510 General Rd Riverside (92509) ***(P-12157)***

Clarmil Manufacturing Corp (PA) ... D ... 510 476-0700
30865 San Clemente St Hayward (94544) ***(P-2427)***

Clarus Lighting LLC ... F ... 916 363-2888
10183 Croydon Way Ste C Sacramento (95827) ***(P-17111)***

Clary Corporation ... E ... 626 359-4486
150 E Huntington Dr Monrovia (91016) ***(P-18868)***

Class A Powdercoat Inc ... E ... 916 681-7474
7506 Henrietta Dr Sacramento (95822) ***(P-13158)***

Classdojo Inc ... F ... 650 646-8235
735 Tehama St San Francisco (94103) ***(P-23743)***

Classic Components Inc (PA) ... F ... 714 619-5690
3420 W Fordham Ave Santa Ana (92704) ***(P-12968)***

Classic Components Inc ... E ... 714 619-5690
7651 Whitney Dr Huntington Beach (92647) ***(P-12969)***

Classic Containers Inc ... B ... 909 930-3610
1700 S Hellman Ave Ontario (91761) ***(P-9482)***

Classic Cosmetics Inc ... F ... 818 773-9042
9601 Irondale Ave Chatsworth (91311) ***(P-8457)***

Classic Cosmetics Inc (PA) ... C ... 818 773-9042
9530 De Soto Ave Chatsworth (91311) ***(P-8458)***

Classic Graphix ... F ... 562 940-0806
12152 Woodruff Ave Downey (90241) ***(P-3731)***

Classic Innovations, Cloverdale *Also called Classic Mill & Cabinet* ***(P-4182)***

Classic Litho & Design Inc ... E ... 310 224-5200
340 Maple Ave Torrance (90503) ***(P-6486)***

Classic Mill & Cabinet ... E ... 707 894-9800
590 Santana Dr Cloverdale (95425) ***(P-4182)***

Classic Quilting ... F ... 714 558-8312
1471 E Warner Ave Santa Ana (92705) ***(P-3732)***

Classic Salads LLC ... E ... 928 726-6196
100 Harrington Rd Royal Oaks (95076) ***(P-2428)***

Classic Slipcover Inc ... E ... 323 583-0804
4300 District Blvd Vernon (90058) ***(P-3608)***

Classic Soft Trim Central Cal, Madera *Also called Muscle Road Inc* ***(P-19725)***

Classic Tees Inc ... E ... 626 607-0255
4915 Walnut Grove Ave San Gabriel (91776) ***(P-3305)***

Classic Vinegar, Ceres *Also called Classic Wine Vinegar Co Inc* ***(P-2429)***

Classic Wine Vinegar Co Inc ... F ... 209 538-7600
4110 Brew Master Dr Ceres (95307) ***(P-2429)***

Classic Wire Cut Company Inc ... C ... 661 257-0558
28210 Constellation Rd Valencia (91355) ***(P-15847)***

Classified Flea Market, Oakland *Also called Bay Classifieds Inc* ***(P-14317)***

Classy Inc ... E ... 619 961-1892
350 10th Ave Ste 1300 San Diego (92101) ***(P-23744)***

Clausen Meat Company Inc ... E ... 209 667-8690
19455 W Clausen Rd Turlock (95380) ***(P-403)***

Clay Castaic Manufacturing Co ... D ... 661 259-3066
32201 Castaic Lake Dr Castaic (91384) ***(P-10434)***

Clay Designs Inc ... E ... 562 432-3991
6435 Green Valley Cir # 112 Culver City (90230) ***(P-10486)***

Clay Laguna Co (HQ) ... C ... 626 330-0631
14400 Lomitas Ave City of Industry (91746) ***(P-10969)***

Clay Mix LLC ... F ... 559 485-0065
1003 N Abby St Fresno (93701) ***(P-10744)***

Clayborn Lab, Truckee *Also called Horvath Holdings Inc* ***(P-2754)***

Clayton Homes Inc ... F ... 916 363-2681
9998 Old Placerville Rd Sacramento (95827) ***(P-4441)***

Clayton Homes Inc ... C ... 951 657-1611
3100 N Perris Blvd Perris (92571) ***(P-4442)***

Clayton Industries, City of Industry *Also called Clayton Manufacturing Company* ***(P-14803)***

Clayton Manufacturing Company (PA) ... C ... 626 443-9381
17477 Hurley St City of Industry (91744) ***(P-14803)***

Clayton Manufacturing Inc (HQ) ... D ... 626 443-9381
17477 Hurley St City of Industry (91744) ***(P-14804)***

CLC Work Gear, South Gate *Also called Custom Leathercraft Mfg LLC* ***(P-10246)***

Cleaire Advanced Emission (PA) ... F ... 510 347-6103
1001 42nd St Emeryville (94608) ***(P-9043)***

Clean America Inc ... F ... 562 694-5990
1400 Pioneer St Brea (92821) ***(P-19273)***

Clean Cut Technologies LLC ... D ... 714 864-3500
1145 N Ocean Cir Anaheim (92806) ***(P-9514)***

Clean Sciences Inc ... F ... 510 440-8660
301 Whitney Pl Fremont (94539) ***(P-12970)***

Clean Water Technology Inc (HQ) ... D ... 310 380-4648
151 W 135th St Los Angeles (90061) ***(P-15500)***

Clean Wave Management Inc ... F ... 949 488-2922
1291 Puerta Del Sol San Clemente (92673) ***(P-19888)***

Clean Wave Management Inc ... E ... 949 361-5356
1291 Puerta Del Sol San Clemente (92673) ***(P-14609)***

Cleanflame, Gridley *Also called Wax Box Firelog Corporation* ***(P-11724)***

Cleanlogic LLC ... E ... 310 261-3001
4051 S Broadway Los Angeles (90037) ***(P-8374)***

Cleanpartset Inc ... E ... 408 886-3300
3530 Bassett St Santa Clara (95054) ***(P-14440)***

Cleanroom Film & Bags, Orange *Also called CF&b Manufacturing Inc* ***(P-5389)***

Cleansmart Solutions Inc ... E ... 650 871-9123
47422 Kato Rd Fremont (94538) ***(P-5469)***

Cleantech Group, San Francisco *Also called Ctg I LLC* ***(P-6218)***

Cleanworld ... F ... 916 635-7300
2330 Gold Meadow Way Gold River (95670) ***(P-22783)***

Clear Blue Energy Corp ... D ... 858 451-1549
17150 Via Del Ca San Diego (92127) ***(P-17112)***

Clear Channel Radio Sales, Los Angeles *Also called Katz Millennium Sls & Mktg Inc* ***(P-17552)***

Clear Image Inc (PA) ... E ... 916 933-4700
4949 Windplay Dr Ste 100 El Dorado Hills (95762) ***(P-5390)***

Clear Image Printing Inc ... E ... 818 547-4684
12744 San Fernando Rd # 200 Sylmar (91342) ***(P-6487)***

Clear Path Technologies Inc ... F ... 951 278-3520
561 W Rincon St Corona (92880) ***(P-19274)***

Clear Skies Solutions Inc ... F ... 925 570-4471
2345 Mirada Ct Tracy (95377) ***(P-20788)***

Clear View LLC ... F ... 408 271-2734
1650 Las Plumas Ave Ste A San Jose (95133) ***(P-11941)***

Clear Water Corporation Inc ... F ... 818 765-8293
7848 San Fernando Rd B Sun Valley (91352) ***(P-15501)***

Clear-Ad Inc ... E ... 877 899-1002
2410 W 3rd St Santa Ana (92703) ***(P-9710)***

Clear-Com Communications, Alameda *Also called Clear-Com LLC* ***(P-17486)***

Clear-Com LLC ... A ... 510 337-6600
1301 Marina Vil Pkwy 10 Alameda (94501) ***(P-17486)***

Clearbags, El Dorado Hills *Also called Clear Image Inc* ***(P-5390)***

Clearchem Diagnostics Inc ... F ... 714 734-8041
1710 E Grevillea Ct Ontario (91761) ***(P-7483)***

Clearflow Inc (PA) ... E ... 714 916-5010
140 Technology Dr Ste 100 Irvine (92618) ***(P-21666)***

Clearlake Lava Inc ... F ... 707 995-1515
13329 Point Lakeview Rd Lower Lake (95457) ***(P-10745)***

Clearlight Diagnostics LLC F 928 525-4290
428 Oakmead Pkwy Sunnyvale (94085) *(P-8216)*
Clearslide Inc (HQ) D 877 360-3366
45 Fremont St Fl 32 San Francisco (94105) *(P-23745)*
Clearwater Paper Corporation A 925 947-4700
1320 Willow Pass Rd # 550 Concord (94520) *(P-5100)*
Clearwell Systems Inc C 877 253-2793
350 Ellis St Mountain View (94043) *(P-23746)*
Cleasby Manufacturing Co Inc (PA) E 415 822-6565
1414 Bancroft Ave San Francisco (94124) *(P-13722)*
Cleatech LLC E 714 754-6668
2106 N Glassell St Orange (92865) *(P-20751)*
Clegg Industries Inc C 310 225-3800
19032 S Vermont Ave Gardena (90248) *(P-23077)*
Clegg Promo, Gardena *Also called Clegg Industries Inc (P-23077)*
Clendenen Lindquist Vintners F 805 937-9801
4665 Santa Maria Mesa Rd Santa Maria (93454) *(P-1635)*
Cleophus Quealy Beer Company F 510 463-4534
448 Hester St San Leandro (94577) *(P-1512)*
Cli Liquidating Corporation D 510 354-0300
47266 Benicia St Fremont (94538) *(P-22240)*
Clic LLC F 415 421-2900
855 Stanton Rd 300 Burlingame (94010) *(P-6488)*
Clickscanshare Inc E 925 283-1400
3631 Mt Diablo Blvd Ste C Lafayette (94549) *(P-15204)*
Clickscanshare Inc (PA) F 619 461-5880
8055 Clairemont Mesa Blvd # 101 San Diego (92111) *(P-15205)*
Cliff Digital F 310 323-5600
14700 S Main St Gardena (90248) *(P-7025)*
Cliff Vine Winery Inc F 707 944-2388
7400 Silverado Trl NAPA (94558) *(P-1636)*
Cliffdale LLC F 818 885-0300
20409 Prairie St Chatsworth (91311) *(P-20445)*
Cliffdale Manufacturing LLC C 818 341-3344
20409 Prairie St Chatsworth (91311) *(P-20473)*
Clinch-On Cornerbead Company, Orange *Also called Continuous Coating Corp (P-12979)*
Clinical Formula LLC F 949 631-0149
888 W 16th St Newport Beach (92663) *(P-7843)*
Cliniqa Corporation (HQ) D 760 744-1900
495 Enterprise St San Marcos (92078) *(P-8290)*
Clint Precision Mfg Inc F 858 271-4041
7665 Formula Pl Ste A San Diego (92121) *(P-15848)*
Clio Inc E 562 926-3724
12981 166th St Cerritos (90703) *(P-13379)*
Clipcall Inc F 650 285-7597
645 Harrison St Ste 200 San Francisco (94107) *(P-23747)*
Clipper Windpower PLC A 805 690-3275
6305 Carpinteria Ave # 300 Carpinteria (93013) *(P-13565)*
Clique Brands Inc (PA) E 323 648-5619
750 N San Vicnte Blvd Re800 West Hollywood (90069) *(P-5905)*
Clo Systems LLC F 626 939-4226
15312 Valley Blvd City of Industry (91746) *(P-16635)*
Clockware F 650 556-8880
548 Market St San Francisco (94104) *(P-23748)*
Clonetab Inc E 209 292-5663
1660 W Linne Rd Ste 214 Tracy (95377) *(P-23749)*
Clorox Company (PA) B 510 271-7000
1221 Broadway Ste 1300 Oakland (94612) *(P-8375)*
Clorox Company F 209 234-1094
11940 S Harlan Rd Lathrop (95330) *(P-8376)*
Clorox Company F 925 368-6000
4900 Johnson Dr Pleasanton (94588) *(P-8377)*
Clorox Company Voluntary F 510 271-7000
1221 Broadway Ste 1300 Oakland (94612) *(P-7385)*
Clorox International Company (HQ) D 510 271-7000
1221 Broadway Fl 13 Oakland (94612) *(P-8823)*
Clorox Manufacturing Company (HQ) C 510 271-7000
1221 Broadway Oakland (94612) *(P-8378)*
Clorox Products Mfg Co, Oakland *Also called Clorox Manufacturing Company (P-8378)*
Clorox Products Mfg Co D 707 437-1051
2600 Huntington Dr Fairfield (94533) *(P-8379)*
Clorox Products Mfg Co D 909 307-2756
2300 W San Bernardino Ave Redlands (92374) *(P-8380)*
Clorox Sales Company E 760 432-8362
530 Idaho Ave Escondido (92025) *(P-7386)*
Clos De La Tech LLC F 650 722-3038
575 Eastview Way Woodside (94062) *(P-1637)*
Clos Du Bois Wines Inc E 707 857-1651
19410 Geyserville Ave Geyserville (95441) *(P-1638)*
Clos Du Val Wine Company Ltd E 707 259-2200
5330 Silverado Trl NAPA (94558) *(P-1639)*
Clos La Chance Wines Inc E 408 686-1050
1 Hummingbird Ln San Martin (95046) *(P-1640)*
Clos Pegase Winery Inc E 707 942-4981
1060 Dunaweal Ln Calistoga (94515) *(P-1641)*
Closetmaid LLC F 909 590-4444
5150 Edison Ave Ste C Chino (91710) *(P-13405)*
Closets By Design Inc C 562 699-9945
3860 Capitol Ave City of Industry (90601) *(P-4892)*
Clothing By Frenzii Inc F 213 670-0265
905 Mateo St Los Angeles (90021) *(P-3149)*
Clothing Illustrated Inc (PA) E 213 403-9950
2014 E 15th St Los Angeles (90021) *(P-3306)*
Cloud Automation Division, Aliso Viejo *Also called Quest Software Inc (P-24334)*
Cloud Company (PA) E 805 549-8093
4855 Morabito Pl San Luis Obispo (93401) *(P-14805)*
Cloud Engines Inc E 415 738-8076
77 Geary St Ste 500 San Francisco (94108) *(P-15016)*
Cloud Nine Comforts, Torrance *Also called Universal Cushion Company Inc (P-3647)*
CLOud&co, San Francisco *Also called Cloudnco Inc (P-23752)*
Cloudburst Inc E 805 986-4125
707 E Hueneme Rd Oxnard (93033) *(P-14654)*
Cloudcar Inc E 650 946-1236
2550 Great America Way # 301 Santa Clara (95054) *(P-23750)*
Cloudflare Inc (PA) C 888 993-5273
101 Townsend St San Francisco (94107) *(P-23751)*
Cloudminds Technology Inc F 650 391-6817
4500 Great America Pkwy # 2 Santa Clara (95054) *(P-13818)*
Cloudnco Inc F 408 605-8755
300 Beale St Apt 613 San Francisco (94105) *(P-23752)*
Cloudpic Inc F 408 786-1098
19925 Stevens Creek Blvd Cupertino (95014) *(P-23753)*
Cloudscaling Group, San Francisco *Also called EMC Corporation (P-15025)*
Cloudshield Technologies LLC E 408 331-6640
212 Gibraltar Dr Sunnyvale (94089) *(P-23754)*
Clougherty Packing LLC (HQ) B 323 583-4621
3049 E Vernon Ave Vernon (90058) *(P-404)*
Clougherty Packing LLC F 559 992-8421
3922 Avenue 120 Corcoran (93212) *(P-448)*
Clover Garments Inc D 415 826-6909
2565 3rd St Ste 232 San Francisco (94107) *(P-3307)*
Clover Technologies Group LLC E 760 357-9277
315 Weakley St Calexico (92231) *(P-22409)*
Clovis Independent, Sacramento *Also called El Dorado Newspapers Inc (P-5627)*
Clp Apg LLC D 510 528-1444
1700 4th St Berkeley (94710) *(P-6089)*
Clp Apg, Inc., Berkeley *Also called Clp Apg LLC (P-6089)*
Clr Analytics Inc F 949 864-6696
25 Mauchly Ste 315 Irvine (92618) *(P-20504)*
Club Car LLC E 951 735-4675
1203 Hall Ave Riverside (92509) *(P-20505)*
Club Donatello Owners Assn E 415 474-7333
501 Post St San Francisco (94102) *(P-22480)*
Club Speed LLC E 951 817-7073
549 Queensland Cir # 101 Corona (92879) *(P-23755)*
Clutches New or Rebuilt, National City *Also called Southland Clutch Inc (P-19770)*
Clw Foods LLC (PA) E 559 639-6661
8765 E 3rd St Hanford (93230) *(P-2430)*
Clw Plastic Bag Mfg Co Inc F 562 903-8878
13060 Park St Santa Fe Springs (90670) *(P-5391)*
CM Brewing Technologies LLC F 888 391-9990
13681 Newport Ave 8-261 Tustin (92780) *(P-15502)*
CM Manufacturing Inc (HQ) C 408 284-7200
6321 San Ignacio Ave San Jose (95119) *(P-18165)*
CMA Dish Machines, Garden Grove *Also called Chemical Methods Assoc LLC (P-15495)*
Cmd Products F 916 434-0228
1130 Conroy Ln Ste 301 Roseville (95661) *(P-9515)*
CMH Manufacturing West, Sacramento *Also called Clayton Homes Inc (P-4441)*
CMI, Irvine *Also called Cooper Microelectronics Inc (P-18179)*
CMI, Hughson *Also called Calaveras Materials Inc (P-10702)*
CMI, Laguna Hills *Also called R L Bennett Engineering Inc (P-16334)*
CMI, San Clemente *Also called Composite Manufacturing Inc (P-21669)*
CMI Precision Machining, Placentia *Also called CMi Precision Machining LLC (P-15850)*
CMi Precision Machining LLC F 714 528-3000
527 Fee Ana St Placentia (92870) *(P-15849)*
CMi Precision Machining LLC F 714 528-3000
527 Fee Ana St Placentia (92870) *(P-15850)*
Cmmc, Long Beach *Also called Coastal Marine Maint Co LLC (P-20283)*
Cmos Sensor Inc F 408 366-2898
20045 Stevens Creek Blvd 1a Cupertino (95014) *(P-18166)*
Cmp Display Systems Inc D 805 499-3642
23301 Wilmington Ave Carson (90745) *(P-9711)*
Cmp Healthcare Media, San Francisco *Also called Ubm LLC (P-6048)*
CMr Marketing and RES Inc E 559 499-2100
3594 E Wawona Ave Fresno (93725) *(P-8824)*
CMS, Mission Viejo *Also called Community Merch Solutions LLC (P-15374)*
CMS Circuit Solutions Inc E 951 698-4452
41549 Cherry St Murrieta (92562) *(P-17853)*
CMS Engineering Inc F 714 899-6900
5702 Engineer Dr Huntington Beach (92649) *(P-15851)*
CMS Products Inc E 714 424-5520
12 Mauchly Ste E Irvine (92618) *(P-15017)*
Cmt, Los Gatos *Also called Chemical & Material Technology (P-21343)*
Cmt, Concord *Also called Cable Manufacturing Tech (P-2908)*
Cmt Sheet Metal F 949 679-9868
22732 Granite Way Ste C Laguna Hills (92653) *(P-12007)*
Cmy Image Corporation F 510 516-6668
33268 Central Ave Union City (94587) *(P-6489)*
Cmyk Enterprise Inc F 209 229-7230
1950 W Fremont St Stockton (95203) *(P-6490)*
Cmyk Prints and Promotions.com, Stockton *Also called Cmyk Enterprise Inc (P-6490)*
CN Publishing Group, Irvine *Also called Cycle News Inc (P-5604)*
Cnc Clothing, Compton *Also called Kim & Roy Co Inc (P-3040)*
Cnc Factory Corporation F 714 581-5999
4021 W Chandler Ave Santa Ana (92704) *(P-14146)*
Cnc Industries Inc F 909 445-0300
10635 Monte Vista Ave Montclair (91763) *(P-15852)*
Cnc Machining Service Inc F 559 732-5599
1130 E Acequia Ave Visalia (93292) *(P-15853)*
Cnc Machining Solutions Inc F 951 688-4267
12155 Magnolia Ave 10c Riverside (92503) *(P-22241)*
Cnc Manufacturing, Temecula *Also called Ralc Inc (P-16339)*
Cnc Noodle Corporation F 510 835-2269
325 Fallon St Oakland (94607) *(P-2431)*
Cnex Labs Inc E 408 695-1045
2880 Stevens Creek Blvd # 300 San Jose (95128) *(P-18167)*

Employee Codes: A=Over 500 employees, B=251-500
C=101-250, D=51-100, E=20-50, F=10-19
2020 California
Manfacturers Register
© Mergent Inc. 1-800-342-5647
1063

Cni Mfg Inc.....E.....626 962-6646
15627 Arrow Hwy Irwindale (91706) *(P-15854)*

Cnp Industries Inc.....F.....714 482-2320
351 Thor Pl Brea (92821) *(P-16849)*

Cns Aviation Inc.....F.....714 901-7072
1240 N Simon Cir Anaheim (92806) *(P-19889)*

Co-Color.....F.....909 394-7888
650 W Terrace Dr San Dimas (91773) *(P-6491)*

Co-West Commodities, San Bernardino *Also called Park West Enterprises (P-1464)*

Co/Color Division, San Dimas *Also called Co-Color (P-6491)*

Coach, Commerce *Also called Tapestry Inc (P-10228)*

Coach Inc.....F.....949 365-0771
3333 Bristol St Ste 2883 Costa Mesa (92626) *(P-10218)*

Coach Inc.....F.....805 496-9933
434 W Hillcrest Dr Thousand Oaks (91360) *(P-10219)*

Coachella Valley Rag Company, Lynwood *Also called Linens Exchange Inc (P-2944)*

Coachelle Valley Ice Co.....E.....760 347-3529
83796 Date Ave Indio (92201) *(P-2352)*

Coachworks Holdings Inc.....B.....951 684-9585
1863 Service Ct Riverside (92507) *(P-19464)*

Coadna Photonics Inc (HQ).....D.....408 736-1100
1012 Stewart Dr Sunnyvale (94085) *(P-17355)*

Coalign Innovations Inc.....E.....888 714-4440
2684 Middlefield Rd Ste A Redwood City (94063) *(P-21667)*

Coast 2 Coast Cables LLC.....F.....714 666-1062
3162 E La Palma Ave Ste D Anaheim (92806) *(P-11298)*

Coast Aerospace Mfg Inc.....E.....714 893-8066
950 Richfield Rd Placentia (92870) *(P-11768)*

Coast Air Supply Co Inc.....F.....310 472-5612
26501 Summit Cir Santa Clarita (91350) *(P-16884)*

Coast Color Printing Inc.....F.....310 352-3560
16301 S Broadway Gardena (90248) *(P-6492)*

Coast Composites LLC.....F.....949 455-0665
7 Burroughs Irvine (92618) *(P-15855)*

Coast Composites LLC (HQ).....D.....949 455-0665
5 Burroughs Irvine (92618) *(P-15856)*

Coast Creative Nameplates, San Jose *Also called Coast Engraving Companies (P-7369)*

Coast Custom Cable, Carson *Also called Alpha Wire Corporation (P-11285)*

Coast Cutters Co Inc.....F.....626 444-2965
2500 Royale Pl Fullerton (92833) *(P-11039)*

Coast Dance Shoes, Porter Ranch *Also called Jevin Enterprises Inc (P-9172)*

Coast Engraving Companies.....E.....408 297-2555
1097 N 5th St San Jose (95112) *(P-7369)*

Coast Flagstone Co.....D.....310 829-4010
1810 Colorado Ave Santa Monica (90404) *(P-10897)*

Coast Heat Treating Co.....E.....323 263-6944
1767 Industrial Way Los Angeles (90023) *(P-11447)*

Coast News.....E.....760 436-9737
315 S Coast Highway 101 W Encinitas (92024) *(P-5594)*

Coast Plating Inc.....F.....323 770-0240
417 W 164th St Gardena (90248) *(P-12971)*

Coast Seafoods Company.....E.....707 442-2947
25 Waterfront Dr Eureka (95501) *(P-2243)*

Coast Sheet Metal Inc.....E.....949 645-2224
990 W 17th St Costa Mesa (92627) *(P-12158)*

Coast Sign Display, Anaheim *Also called Coast Sign Incorporated (P-23078)*

Coast Sign Incorporated.....C.....714 520-9144
1500 W Embassy St Anaheim (92802) *(P-23078)*

Coast To Coast Circuits Inc (PA).....E.....714 891-9441
5331 Mcfadden Ave Huntington Beach (92649) *(P-17854)*

Coast To Coast Label Inc (PA).....F.....657 203-2583
18401 Bandilier Cir Fountain Valley (92708) *(P-5500)*

Coast To Coast Met Finshg Corp.....E.....626 282-2122
401 S Raymond Ave Alhambra (91803) *(P-12972)*

Coast To Coast Mfg LLC.....F.....909 798-5024
430 Nevada St Redlands (92373) *(P-9712)*

Coast Wood Preserving Inc (PA).....F.....209 632-9931
600 W Glenwood Ave Turlock (95380) *(P-4475)*

Coast/A C M, Torrance *Also called Coast/Dvnced Chip Mgnetics Inc (P-18706)*

Coast/Dvnced Chip Mgnetics Inc.....F.....310 370-8188
4225 Spencer St Torrance (90503) *(P-18706)*

Coastal Circuit, Redwood City *Also called Advanced Circuits Inc (P-17808)*

Coastal Cnting Indus Scale Inc.....F.....805 486-5754
1621 Fiske Pl Oxnard (93033) *(P-14147)*

Coastal Cocktails Inc (PA).....E.....949 250-3129
18011 Mitchell S Ste B Irvine (92614) *(P-2057)*

Coastal Component Inds Inc.....E.....714 685-6677
133 E Bristol Ln Orange (92865) *(P-18869)*

Coastal Connections.....E.....805 644-5051
2085 Sperry Ave Ste B Ventura (93003) *(P-17356)*

Coastal Container Inc.....E.....562 801-4595
8455 Loch Lomond Dr Pico Rivera (90660) *(P-5208)*

Coastal Decking Inc.....E.....619 477-0567
2050 Wilson Ave Ste A National City (91950) *(P-20282)*

Coastal Die Cutting Inc.....F.....619 677-3180
7100 Convoy Ct San Diego (92111) *(P-13975)*

Coastal Embroidery Inc.....F.....805 383-5593
2263 Pickwick Dr Camarillo (93010) *(P-3733)*

Coastal Enterprises, Fountain Valley *Also called Joy Products California Inc (P-22952)*

Coastal Enterprises.....E.....714 771-4969
1925 W Collins Ave Orange (92867) *(P-7549)*

Coastal Graphics, San Diego *Also called Blue Book Publishers Inc (P-6202)*

Coastal Marine Maint Co LLC (PA).....F.....562 432-8066
250 W Wardlow Rd Long Beach (90807) *(P-20283)*

Coastal Products Company Inc.....F.....661 323-0487
2157 Mohawk St Bakersfield (93308) *(P-14564)*

Coastal PVA Opco LLC.....F.....530 406-3303
2929 Grandview St Placerville (95667) *(P-14897)*

Coastal Tag & Label Inc.....D.....562 946-4318
13233 Barton Cir Whittier (90605) *(P-7026)*

Coastal Vineyard Services LLC.....F.....805 441-4465
120 Callie Ct Arroyo Grande (93420) *(P-1642)*

Coastline High Prfmce Coatings.....F.....714 372-3263
7181 Orangewood Ave Garden Grove (92841) *(P-17487)*

Coastline International.....C.....888 748-7177
1207 Bangor St San Diego (92106) *(P-22242)*

Coastline Metal Finishing Corp.....D.....714 895-9099
7061 Patterson Dr Garden Grove (92841) *(P-12973)*

Coastwide Tag & Label Co.....E.....323 721-1501
7647 Industry Ave Pico Rivera (90660) *(P-7027)*

Coates Incorporated.....F.....530 832-1533
73816 S Delleker Rd Portola (96122) *(P-19616)*

Coating Services Group LLC.....F.....619 596-7444
11649 Rverside Dr Ste 139 Lakeside (92040) *(P-13159)*

Coating Specialties Inc.....F.....310 639-6900
815 E Rosecrans Ave Los Angeles (90059) *(P-20072)*

Coatings By Sandberg Inc.....F.....714 538-0888
856 N Commerce St Orange (92867) *(P-13160)*

Coatings Resource, Huntington Beach *Also called Laird Coatings Corporation (P-8653)*

Cobalt Labs Inc.....E.....415 651-7028
575 Market St Fl 4 San Francisco (94105) *(P-23756)*

Cobalt Robotics Inc.....D.....650 781-3626
4019 Transport St Ste De Palo Alto (94303) *(P-14898)*

Cobel Technologies Inc.....E.....626 332-2100
822 N Grand Ave Covina (91724) *(P-16590)*

Cobham Adv Elec Sol Inc.....C.....858 560-1301
9404 Chesapeake Dr San Diego (92123) *(P-20553)*

Cobham Adv Elec Sol Inc.....B.....408 624-3000
5300 Hellyer Ave San Jose (95138) *(P-20554)*

Cobham Trivec-Avant Inc.....E.....714 841-4976
17831 Jamestown Ln Huntington Beach (92647) *(P-17488)*

Cobra Engineering Inc.....D.....714 692-8180
23801 La Palma Ave Yorba Linda (92887) *(P-19617)*

Cobra Performance Boats Inc.....F.....909 482-0047
5109 Holt Blvd Montclair (91763) *(P-20318)*

Cobra Systems.....F.....714 688-7992
3521 E Enterprise Dr Anaheim (92807) *(P-6216)*

Coc Inc, Los Angeles *Also called Colon Manufacturing Inc (P-3150)*

Coca Cola Btlg of Eureka Cal.....F.....707 443-2796
1335 Albee St Eureka (95501) *(P-2058)*

Coca-Cola, Lancaster *Also called Ccbcc Operations LLC (P-2052)*

Coca-Cola, Eureka *Also called Coca Cola Btlg of Eureka Cal (P-2058)*

Coca-Cola, Santa Maria *Also called Tognazzini Beverage Service (P-2176)*

Coca-Cola Company.....C.....909 975-5200
1650 S Vintage Ave Ontario (91761) *(P-2059)*

Coca-Cola Company.....E.....626 855-4440
13255 Amar Rd City of Industry (91746) *(P-2060)*

Coca-Cola Company.....C.....949 250-5961
3 Park Plz Ste 600 Irvine (92614) *(P-2061)*

Coca-Cola Company.....E.....714 991-7031
2121 E Winston Rd Anaheim (92806) *(P-2062)*

Coca-Cola Company.....D.....909 975-5200
1650 S Vintage Ave Ontario (91761) *(P-2200)*

Coca-Cola Company.....C.....510 476-7048
2025 Pike Ave San Leandro (94577) *(P-2063)*

Coca-Cola Refreshments USA Inc.....C.....805 644-2211
5335 Walker St Ventura (93003) *(P-2064)*

Coca-Cola Refreshments USA Inc.....D.....760 435-7111
3900 Ocean Ranch Blvd Oceanside (92056) *(P-2065)*

Coco Delice.....F.....510 601-1394
1555 Park Ave Ste A Emeryville (94608) *(P-1409)*

Coco Dry, Ontario *Also called C & S Products CA Inc (P-8371)*

Coco Products LLC.....F.....909 218-8971
1345 S Parkside Pl Ontario (91761) *(P-8381)*

Coconut Secret, Petaluma *Also called Leslies Organics LLC (P-8751)*

Cod USA Inc.....E.....949 381-7367
25954 Commercentre Dr Lake Forest (92630) *(P-4854)*

Coda Automotive Inc.....E.....310 820-3611
12101 W Olympic Blvd Los Angeles (90064) *(P-19618)*

Coda Automotive Inc.....D.....619 291-2040
1441 Camino Del Rio S San Diego (92108) *(P-19619)*

Coda Automotive Inc.....D.....949 830-7000
14 Auto Center Dr Irvine (92618) *(P-19620)*

Coda Energy Holdings LLC.....E.....626 775-3900
111 N Artsakh St Ste 300 Glendale (91206) *(P-19275)*

Codan US Corporation.....C.....714 430-1300
3511 W Sunflower Ave Santa Ana (92704) *(P-9713)*

Codar Ocean Sensors Ltd (PA).....F.....408 773-8240
1914 Plymouth St Mountain View (94043) *(P-20555)*

Code-In-Motion LLC.....F.....949 361-2633
232 Avenida Fabricante # 103 San Clemente (92672) *(P-14806)*

Codefast Inc.....F.....408 687-4700
21170 Canyon Oak Way Cupertino (95014) *(P-23757)*

Codexis Inc (PA).....C.....650 421-8100
200 Penobscot Dr Redwood City (94063) *(P-7484)*

Codorniu Napa Inc.....D.....707 254-2148
1345 Henry Rd NAPA (94559) *(P-1643)*

Cody Cylinder Services.....E.....951 786-3650
1393 Dodson Way Ste A Riverside (92507) *(P-15857)*

Coe Orchard Equipment Inc.....D.....530 695-5121
3453 Riviera Rd Live Oak (95953) *(P-13620)*

Coen Company Inc (HQ).....E.....650 522-2100
951 Mariners Island Blvd San Mateo (94404) *(P-11694)*

Coffee Guys Inc (PA).....E.....707 942-5747
975 Silverado Trl Calistoga (94515) *(P-2284)*

Coffee Klatch, Rancho Cucamonga *Also called Klatch Coffee Inc (P-2304)*

Coffee Works Inc.....F.....916 452-1086
3418 Folsom Blvd Sacramento (95816) *(P-2285)*

Cognella Inc ... D ... 858 552-1120
3970 Sorrento Valley Blvd # 500 San Diego (92121) ***(P-6090)***
Coh-Fb LLC ... E ... 323 923-1240
5715 Bickett St Huntington Park (90255) ***(P-3030)***
Cohbar Inc ... F ... 650 446-7888
1455 Adams Dr Ste 2050 Menlo Park (94025) ***(P-7844)***
Coherent Inc ... A ... 408 764-4000
5100 Patrick Henry Dr Santa Clara (95054) ***(P-19276)***
Coherent Inc (PA) ... A ... 408 764-4000
5100 Patrick Henry Dr Santa Clara (95054) ***(P-21206)***
Coherent Asia Inc ... D ... 408 764-4000
5100 Patrick Henry Dr Santa Clara (95054) ***(P-18870)***
Coherent Auburn Group, The, Santa Clara *Also called Coherent Inc* ***(P-19276)***
Coherus Analytical Laboratory, Camarillo *Also called Coherus Biosciences Inc* ***(P-8291)***
Coherus Biosciences Inc ... D ... 805 445-7051
4014 Cmino Ranchero Ste A Camarillo (93012) ***(P-8291)***
Cohu Inc (PA) ... C ... 858 848-8100
12367 Crosthwaite Cir Poway (92064) ***(P-21018)***
Cohuhd Costar LLC ... D ... 858 391-1800
7330 Trade St San Diego (92121) ***(P-17213)***
Coi Ceramics Inc ... E ... 858 621-5700
7130 Miramar Rd Ste 100b San Diego (92121) ***(P-20073)***
Coi Rubber Products Inc ... B ... 626 965-9966
19255 San Jose Ave City of Industry (91748) ***(P-7627)***
Coic, San Diego *Also called Coi Ceramics Inc* ***(P-20073)***
Coil Winding Specialist Inc ... F ... 714 279-9010
353 W Grove Ave Orange (92865) ***(P-18707)***
Coin Dealer Newsletter Inc ... F ... 310 515-7369
2034 262nd St Lomita (90717) ***(P-5906)***
Coin Gllery of San Frncsco Inc ... F ... 510 236-8882
951 Hensley St Richmond (94801) ***(P-4970)***
Colbrit Manufacturing Co Inc ... E ... 818 709-3608
9666 Owensmouth Ave Ste G Chatsworth (91311) ***(P-14035)***
Colby Pharmaceutical Company (PA) ... F ... 650 333-3150
1095 Colby Ave Ste C Menlo Park (94025) ***(P-7845)***
Cold Creek Compost Inc ... F ... 707 485-5966
6000 Potter Valley Rd Ukiah (95482) ***(P-8812)***
Cold Jet LLC ... F ... 513 831-3211
10281 Trademark St Ste A Rancho Cucamonga (91730) ***(P-14441)***
Cold Pack System Inc ... F ... 858 586-0800
9020 Activity Rd Ste A San Diego (92126) ***(P-9516)***
Cold Spring Granite Company ... E ... 559 689-3257
36772 Road 606 Raymond (93653) ***(P-10898)***
Cold Spring Granite Company ... E ... 559 438-2100
802 W Pinedale Ave # 102 Fresno (93711) ***(P-10899)***
Coldstone Creamery 256 ... F ... 951 304-9777
25395 Madison Ave 106d Murrieta (92562) ***(P-636)***
Coldstone Mira Mesa 114 ... F ... 858 695-9771
10716 Westview Pkwy San Diego (92126) ***(P-637)***
Cole Instrument Corp ... D ... 714 556-3100
2650 S Croddy Way Santa Ana (92704) ***(P-16636)***
Cole Lighting, South El Monte *Also called C W Cole & Company Inc* ***(P-17017)***
Cole Print & Marketing ... F ... 925 276-2344
2001 Salvio St Ste 25 Concord (94520) ***(P-6493)***
Colfax International ... E ... 408 730-2275
2805 Bowers Ave Ste 230 Santa Clara (95051) ***(P-14899)***
Colfax Record, Auburn *Also called Auburn Journal Inc* ***(P-5560)***
Colimatic Usa Inc ... F ... 949 600-6440
9272 Jeronimo Rd Ste 115 Irvine (92618) ***(P-14703)***
Collabrative DRG Discovery Inc ... F ... 650 204-3084
1633 Bayshore Hwy Ste 342 Burlingame (94010) ***(P-23758)***
Collard Rose Optical Lab, Orange *Also called J G Hernandez Company* ***(P-22364)***
Collaris Defense, Morgan Hill *Also called Collaris LLC* ***(P-18871)***
Collaris LLC ... D ... 510 825-9995
685 Jarvis Dr Ste C Morgan Hill (95037) ***(P-18871)***
Collection Development ... F ... 909 595-8588
710 Nogales St City of Industry (91748) ***(P-18168)***
Collection Led, City of Industry *Also called Collection Development* ***(P-18168)***
Colleen & Herb Enterprises Inc ... C ... 510 226-6083
46939 Bayside Pkwy Fremont (94538) ***(P-15858)***
Collicutt Energy Services Inc ... E ... 562 944-4413
12349 Hawkins St Santa Fe Springs (90670) ***(P-11665)***
Collidion Inc (PA) ... F ... 707 668-7600
1770 Corporate Cir Petaluma (94954) ***(P-7846)***
Collier O & P, Pleasant Hill *Also called Castle Hill Holdings Inc* ***(P-21994)***
Collimated Holes Inc ... E ... 408 374-5080
460 Division St Campbell (95008) ***(P-21344)***
Collins Aerospace, Chula Vista *Also called Rohr Inc* ***(P-20212)***
Collins Pine Company ... B ... 530 258-2111
500 Main St Chester (96020) ***(P-3930)***
Collins Technologies, Irvine *Also called Curtiss-Wright Flow Control* ***(P-13302)***
Collotype Labels USA Inc (HQ) ... D ... 707 603-2500
21 Executive Way NAPA (94558) ***(P-7028)***
Collotype Labels USA Inc ... F ... 707 931-7400
21684 8th St E Sonoma (95476) ***(P-7029)***
Colmol Inc ... E ... 858 693-7575
8517 Production Ave San Diego (92121) ***(P-7030)***
Colombaras Cabinet & Mllwk Inc ... F ... 530 662-2665
421 4th St Woodland (95695) ***(P-4791)***
Colon Manufacturing Inc (PA) ... F ... 213 749-6149
1100 S San Pedro St Los Angeles (90015) ***(P-3150)***
Colonel Lee's Enterprises, Vernon *Also called T & T Foods Inc* ***(P-747)***
Colonial Enterprises Inc ... E ... 909 822-8700
10620 Mulberry Ave Fontana (92337) ***(P-8459)***
Colonial Home Textiles, Corona *Also called Amrapur Overseas Incorporated* ***(P-2924)***
Colonnas Shipyard West LLC ... E ... 619 557-8373
105 S 31st St San Diego (92113) ***(P-20284)***
Color Inc ... E ... 818 240-1350
1600 Flower St Glendale (91201) ***(P-6494)***
Color Depot Inc ... F ... 818 500-9033
512 State St Glendale (91203) ***(P-7031)***
Color Design Laboratory ... E ... 818 341-5100
19151 Parthenia St Ste H Northridge (91324) ***(P-8460)***
Color Digit, Costa Mesa *Also called Chup Corporation* ***(P-6485)***
Color Image Apparel Inc ... E ... 855 793-3100
860 S Los Angeles St Los Angeles (90014) ***(P-2779)***
Color Marble Project Group Inc ... F ... 909 595-8858
20521 Earlgate St Walnut (91789) ***(P-335)***
Color ME Cotton, Los Angeles *Also called Jd/Cmc Inc* ***(P-3345)***
Color Science Inc ... F ... 714 434-1033
1230 E Glenwood Pl Santa Ana (92707) ***(P-8699)***
Color Service Inc ... E ... 323 283-4793
40 E Verdugo Ave Burbank (91502) ***(P-6495)***
Color Sky Inc ... F ... 626 338-8565
14439 Joanbridge St Baldwin Park (91706) ***(P-10900)***
Color TEC Industrial Finishing ... E ... 818 897-2669
11231 Ilex Ave Pacoima (91331) ***(P-13161)***
Color Tech Commercial Printing, Lake Forest *Also called Universal Printing Services* ***(P-6910)***
Color Tone Inc ... F ... 925 680-2695
2475 Estand Way Pleasant Hill (94523) ***(P-6496)***
Color-Box LLC ... E ... 559 674-1049
1275 S Granada Dr Madera (93637) ***(P-5209)***
Colorado's Bag Manufacture, Rancho Cucamonga *Also called AR Square* ***(P-10189)***
Colorcards 960 ... E ... 858 535-9311
6224 Via Regla San Diego (92122) ***(P-12974)***
Colorcom Inc ... F ... 323 246-4640
2437 S Eastern Ave Commerce (90040) ***(P-6497)***
Colored Solar, Simi Valley *Also called Gold Coast Solar LLC* ***(P-18254)***
Colorfast Dye & Print Hse Inc ... C ... 323 581-1656
5075 Pacific Blvd Vernon (90058) ***(P-6498)***
Colorful Products Corporation ... F ... 805 498-2195
996 Lawrence Dr Ste 301 Newbury Park (91320) ***(P-8461)***
Colorfx Inc ... E ... 818 767-7671
11050 Randall St Sun Valley (91352) ***(P-6499)***
Colormarx Corporation ... F ... 916 334-0334
4825 Auburn Blvd Sacramento (95841) ***(P-6500)***
Colormax Industries Inc (PA) ... E ... 213 748-6600
1627 Paloma St Los Angeles (90021) ***(P-2676)***
Colornet, Van Nuys *Also called Niknejad Inc* ***(P-6749)***
Coloron Jewelry Inc ... F ... 818 565-1100
7242 Valjean Ave Van Nuys (91406) ***(P-22979)***
Coloron Jewelry Manufacturing, Van Nuys *Also called Coloron Jewelry Inc* ***(P-22979)***
Colorplak.com, Temecula *Also called Custom Art Services Corp* ***(P-6526)***
Colorprint ... F ... 650 697-7611
1570 Gilbreth Rd Burlingame (94010) ***(P-6501)***
Colorstitch Inc ... F ... 714 754-4220
3100 S Croddy Way Santa Ana (92704) ***(P-3734)***
Colortech Label Inc ... F ... 714 999-5545
1230 S Sherman St Anaheim (92805) ***(P-5501)***
Colortokens Inc ... E ... 408 341-6030
2101 Tasman Dr Ste 201 Santa Clara (95054) ***(P-23759)***
Colortone, Whittier *Also called Windsor House Investments Inc* ***(P-5456)***
Colortone Digital, Pleasant Hill *Also called Color Tone Inc* ***(P-6496)***
Colorwen International Corp ... F ... 626 363-8855
951 Lawson St City of Industry (91748) ***(P-7457)***
Colour Drop ... F ... 415 353-5720
1388 Sutter St Ste 508 San Francisco (94109) ***(P-7032)***
Colt Group, Signal Hill *Also called Colt Services LP* ***(P-185)***
Colt Services LP ... F ... 562 988-2658
1399 E Burnett St Signal Hill (90755) ***(P-185)***
Colton Facilities, Colton *Also called Hydro Conduit of Texas LP* ***(P-10587)***
Colton Truck Terminal Garage, Colton *Also called Erf Enterprises Inc* ***(P-19532)***
Coltrin Inc ... F ... 323 266-6872
4466 Worth St Los Angeles (90063) ***(P-11124)***
Columbia Aluminum Products LLC ... D ... 323 728-7361
2565 Sampson Ave Corona (92879) ***(P-11228)***
Columbia Communications Inc ... F ... 203 533-0252
22480 Parrotts Ferry Rd Columbia (95310) ***(P-17489)***
Columbia Cosmetics Mfrs Inc (PA) ... D ... 510 562-5900
1661 Timothy Dr San Leandro (94577) ***(P-8462)***
Columbia Fabricating Co Inc ... E ... 818 247-4220
5079 Gloria Ave Encino (91436) ***(P-12463)***
Columbia Holding Corp ... B ... 310 327-4107
14400 S San Pedro St Gardena (90248) ***(P-11942)***
Columbia Products Co, Irvine *Also called Columbia Sanitary Products* ***(P-11666)***
Columbia Sanitary Products ... E ... 949 474-0777
1622 Browning Irvine (92606) ***(P-11666)***
Columbia Screw Products Inc ... F ... 714 549-1171
2901 Halladay St Santa Ana (92705) ***(P-12625)***
Columbia Showcase & Cab Co Inc ... C ... 818 765-9710
11034 Sherman Way Ste A Sun Valley (91352) ***(P-4893)***
Columbia Steel Inc ... D ... 909 874-8840
2175 N Linden Ave Rialto (92377) ***(P-11769)***
Columbia Stone Products ... F ... 760 737-3215
663 S Rancho Santa Fe Rd San Marcos (92078) ***(P-10944)***
Columbus Foods LLC ... B ... 510 921-3400
30977 San Antonio St Hayward (94544) ***(P-405)***
Columbus Manufacturing Inc (HQ) ... D ... 510 921-3423
30977 San Antonio St Hayward (94544) ***(P-449)***
Colvin-Friedman LLC ... E ... 707 769-4488
1311 Commerce St Petaluma (94954) ***(P-9714)***
Comac America Corporation ... F ... 760 616-9614
4350 Von Karman Ave # 400 Newport Beach (92660) ***(P-19890)***
Comant Industries Incorporated (HQ) ... E ... 714 870-2420
577 Burning Tree Rd Fullerton (92833) ***(P-20556)***

Employee Codes: A=Over 500 employees, B=251-500
C=101-250, D=51-100, E=20-50, F=10-19
2020 California
Manfacturers Register
© Mergent Inc. 1-800-342-5647
1065

Combimatrix Corporation (HQ).....E.....949 753-0624
310 Goddard Ste 150 Irvine (92618) ***(P-21207)***
Combustion Parts Inc.....E.....858 759-3320
1770 Gillespie Way # 111 El Cajon (92020) ***(P-13566)***
Comchoice, El Segundo *Also called Scenewise Inc* ***(P-19233)***
Comco Inc.....E.....818 333-8500
2151 N Lincoln St Burbank (91504) ***(P-15503)***
Comco Sheet Metal Company.....F.....510 832-6433
237 Southbrook Pl Clayton (94517) ***(P-12159)***
Comcore Opcital Communication, Fremont *Also called Comcore Technologies Inc* ***(P-21345)***
Comcore Technologies Inc.....E.....510 498-8858
48834 Kato Rd Ste 108a Fremont (94538) ***(P-21345)***
Comeback Brewing II Inc.....F.....510 526-1160
1404 4th St Berkeley (94710) ***(P-1513)***
Comet Technologies USA Inc.....E.....408 325-8770
2370 Bering Dr San Jose (95131) ***(P-21452)***
Comfort Industries Inc.....E.....562 692-8288
12266 Rooks Rd Whittier (90601) ***(P-2744)***
Comfort-Pedic Mattress USA.....F.....909 810-2600
9080 Charles Smith Ave Rancho Cucamonga (91730) ***(P-4715)***
Comfy, Oakland *Also called Building Robotics Inc* ***(P-23702)***
Cominco Advanced Material, Poway *Also called Teck Advanced Materials Inc* ***(P-18605)***
Comma.ai, San Diego *Also called Commaai Inc* ***(P-23760)***
Commaai Inc.....F.....415 712-8205
1441 State St San Diego (92101) ***(P-23760)***
Command Packaging LLC.....C.....323 980-0918
3840 E 26th St Vernon (90058) ***(P-5392)***
Commander Packaging West Inc.....E.....714 921-9350
602 S Rockefeller Ave D Ontario (91761) ***(P-5210)***
Commerce, Commerce *Also called Alarin Aircraft Hinge Inc* ***(P-11560)***
Commerce Foam Plant, Commerce *Also called Elite Comfort Solutions LLC* ***(P-9526)***
Commerce Printers Inc.....E.....714 549-5002
3201 Halladay St Santa Ana (92705) ***(P-6502)***
Commerce Velocity LLC.....E.....949 756-8950
1 Technology Dr Ste J725 Irvine (92618) ***(P-23761)***
Commercial and Security Labels, Valencia *Also called Quadriga USA Enterprises Inc* ***(P-5525)***
Commercial Casework Inc (PA).....D.....510 657-7933
41780 Christy St Fremont (94538) ***(P-4018)***
Commercial Clear Print Inc.....F.....818 709-1220
9025 Fullbright Ave Chatsworth (91311) ***(P-6503)***
Commercial Cstm Sting Uphl Inc.....D.....714 850-0520
12601 Western Ave Garden Grove (92841) ***(P-5053)***
Commercial Display Systems LLC.....E.....818 361-8160
17341 Sierra Hwy Canyon Country (91351) ***(P-15419)***
Commercial Electronics Pho, Newport Beach *Also called Macom Technology Solutions Inc* ***(P-17579)***
Commercial Energy California, Oakland *Also called Commercial Energy Montana Inc* ***(P-44)***
Commercial Energy Montana Inc.....E.....510 567-2700
7677 Oakport St Ste 525 Oakland (94621) ***(P-44)***
Commercial Furniture.....E.....714 350-7045
1261 N Lakeview Ave Anaheim (92807) ***(P-4792)***
Commercial Intr Resources Inc.....D.....562 926-5885
6077 Rickenbacker Rd Commerce (90040) ***(P-4633)***
Commercial Lbr & Pallet Co Inc (PA).....C.....626 968-0631
135 Long Ln City of Industry (91746) ***(P-4357)***
Commercial Manufacturing.....E.....559 237-1855
2432 S Railroad Ave Fresno (93706) ***(P-14356)***
Commercial Metal Forming Inc.....E.....714 532-6321
341 W Collins Ave Orange (92867) ***(P-12786)***
Commercial Metals Company.....F.....909 899-9993
12451 Arrow Rte Etiwanda (91739) ***(P-11040)***
Commercial Military Supply, Huntington Beach *Also called CMS Engineering Inc* ***(P-15851)***
Commercial Mill & Builders Sup, Milpitas *Also called Commercial Mtl & Door Sup Inc* ***(P-4019)***
Commercial Mtl & Door Sup Inc.....F.....408 432-3383
1210 Ames Ave Milpitas (95035) ***(P-4019)***
Commercial Patterns Inc.....F.....510 784-1014
3162 Baumberg Ave Ste H Hayward (94545) ***(P-9715)***
Commercial Sand Blast Company.....F.....323 581-8672
2678 E 26th St Vernon (90058) ***(P-12975)***
Commercial Sheet Metal Works.....E.....213 748-7321
1800 S San Pedro St Los Angeles (90015) ***(P-11770)***
Commercial Truss Co.....E.....858 693-1771
10731 Treena St Ste 207 San Diego (92131) ***(P-4296)***
Commex Corporation.....F.....510 887-4000
20408 Corsair Blvd Hayward (94545) ***(P-9397)***
Commnexus San Diego.....F.....888 926-3987
4225 Executive Sq # 1110 La Jolla (92037) ***(P-18169)***
Commodity Resource Envmtl Inc.....E.....661 824-2416
11847 United St Mojave (93501) ***(P-11189)***
Commodity Rsource Enviromental, Mojave *Also called Commodity Resource Envmtl Inc* ***(P-11189)***
Commsystems LLC.....F.....858 824-0056
12225 World Trade Dr I San Diego (92128) ***(P-17490)***
Communction Systms-Wst/Lnkabit, San Diego *Also called L3 Technologies Inc* ***(P-17566)***
Communicart.....F.....408 970-0922
1589 Laurelwood Rd Santa Clara (95054) ***(P-6504)***
Communication Arts, Menlo Park *Also called Coyne & Blanchard Inc* ***(P-5911)***
Communications & Pwr Inds LLC.....C.....650 846-3494
811 Hansen Way Palo Alto (94304) ***(P-17777)***
Communications & Pwr Inds LLC.....A.....650 846-3729
811 Hansen Way Palo Alto (94304) ***(P-17491)***
Communications & Pwr Inds LLC.....C.....650 846-2900
6385 San Ignacio Ave San Jose (95119) ***(P-17492)***
Communications & Pwr Inds LLC.....C.....650 846-2900
6385 San Ignacio Ave San Jose (95119) ***(P-18872)***
Communications & Pwr Inds LLC (HQ).....A.....650 846-2900
607 Hansen Way Palo Alto (94304) ***(P-17778)***
Communications & Pwr Inds LLC.....C.....650 846-2900
811 Hansen Way Palo Alto (94304) ***(P-17779)***
Communigate Systems, Richmond *Also called Stalker Software Inc* ***(P-24450)***
Community Adviser Newspaper, Banning *Also called Century Publishing* ***(P-7020)***
Community Close-Up Westminster.....D.....714 704-5811
1771 S Lewis St Anaheim (92805) ***(P-5595)***
Community Fuels, Stockton *Also called American Biodiesel Inc* ***(P-8712)***
Community Media Corporation.....D.....657 337-0200
19100 Crest Ave Apt 26 Castro Valley (94546) ***(P-5596)***
Community Media Corporation (PA).....F.....714 220-0292
5119 Ball Rd Cypress (90630) ***(P-5597)***
Community Merch Solutions LLC.....E.....877 956-9258
27201 Puerta Real Ste 120 Mission Viejo (92691) ***(P-15374)***
Community Printers Inc.....E.....831 426-4682
1827 Soquel Ave Santa Cruz (95062) ***(P-6505)***
Community Vision, North Hollywood *Also called Bauers & Collins* ***(P-21984)***
Compaction American, Lake Elsinore *Also called American Compaction Eqp Inc* ***(P-13705)***
Compactor Management Company, Fremont *Also called Lucio Family Enterprises Inc* ***(P-12268)***
Compandsave, Union City *Also called Cmy Image Corporation* ***(P-6489)***
Companion Medical Inc.....D.....858 522-0252
11011 Via Frontera Ste D San Diego (92127) ***(P-21668)***
Compass Components Inc (PA).....C.....510 656-4700
48133 Warm Springs Blvd Fremont (94539) ***(P-18873)***
Compass Flooring, Santa Fe Springs *Also called Altro Usa Inc* ***(P-23253)***
Compass Innovations Inc.....C.....408 418-3985
2352 Walsh Ave Santa Clara (95051) ***(P-9398)***
Compass Manufacturing Service, Fremont *Also called Compass Components Inc* ***(P-18873)***
Compass Water Solutions Inc (PA).....E.....949 222-5777
15542 Mosher Ave Tustin (92780) ***(P-15504)***
Compatible Software Systems.....F.....510 562-1172
10966 Bigge St San Leandro (94577) ***(P-23762)***
Competitor Golf & Tennis AP, Sacramento *Also called AAA Garments & Lettering Inc* ***(P-3717)***
Competitor Group Inc (HQ).....C.....858 450-6510
6420 Sequence Dr San Diego (92121) ***(P-5907)***
Competitor Magazine, San Diego *Also called Competitor Group Inc* ***(P-5907)***
Competitor Magazine.....E.....858 768-6800
10179 Hudiken St Ste 100 San Diego (92121) ***(P-5908)***
Complete Clothing Company (PA).....D.....323 277-1470
4950 E 49th St Vernon (90058) ***(P-3224)***
Complete Cutng & Wldg Sups Inc (PA).....F.....909 868-9292
806 E Holt Ave Pomona (91767) ***(P-24626)***
Complete Garment Inc.....E.....323 846-3731
2101 E 38th St Vernon (90058) ***(P-2780)***
Complete Kitchen & Bath, Grass Valley *Also called Cabinet Company Inc* ***(P-4887)***
Complete Metal Design.....F.....626 335-3636
154 S Valencia Ave Glendora (91741) ***(P-15859)***
Complete Metal Fabrication Inc.....F.....760 353-0260
596 E Main St El Centro (92243) ***(P-11771)***
Complete Truck Body Repair Inc.....F.....323 445-2675
1217 N Alameda St Compton Compton (90222) ***(P-19523)***
Complete Welding Supplies, Pomona *Also called Complete Cutng & Wldg Sups Inc* ***(P-24626)***
Compliance Poster, Monrovia *Also called Global Compliance Inc* ***(P-6243)***
Compliance Products Usa Inc.....F.....619 878-9696
650 Gateway Center Way D San Diego (92102) ***(P-21019)***
Compliance West USA, San Diego *Also called Compliance Products Usa Inc* ***(P-21019)***
Complianceonline, Palo Alto *Also called Metricstream Inc* ***(P-24149)***
Complyright Distribution Svcs.....E.....805 981-0992
3451 Jupiter Ct Oxnard (93030) ***(P-7281)***
Component Concepts LLC.....F.....760 722-9559
1732 Ord Way Oceanside (92056) ***(P-19155)***
Component Equipment Coinc.....D.....805 988-8004
3050 Camino Del Sol Oxnard (93030) ***(P-18755)***
Component Finishing, Rocklin *Also called Diverse McHning Fbrication LLC* ***(P-13514)***
Component Hsing Systems U S A, South Gate *Also called Tony Borges* ***(P-12579)***
Component Re-Engineering Inc.....F.....408 562-4000
3508 Bassett St Santa Clara (95054) ***(P-18170)***
Component Surfaces Inc.....F.....858 513-3656
11880 Cmnty Rd Ste 380 Poway (92064) ***(P-12976)***
Components For Automation Inc (PA).....F.....805 582-0065
1737 Lee St Simi Valley (93065) ***(P-13299)***
Componetics Inc.....F.....805 498-0939
2492 Turquoise Cir Newbury Park (91320) ***(P-18708)***
Composite Engineering, Inc., Sacramento *Also called Kratos Unmanned Aerial Systems* ***(P-9870)***
Composite Manufacturing Inc.....E.....949 361-7580
970 Calle Amanecer Ste D San Clemente (92673) ***(P-21669)***
Composite Plastic Systems Inc.....F.....805 354-1391
1701a River Rock Rd Santa Maria (93454) ***(P-20482)***
Composite Software LLC (HQ).....D.....800 553-6387
755 Sycamore Dr Milpitas (95035) ***(P-23763)***
Composite Support and Sltns In.....F.....310 514-3162
767 W Channel St San Pedro (90731) ***(P-5291)***
Composite Technology Intl, Sacramento *Also called Composite Technology Intl Inc* ***(P-4020)***
Composite Technology Intl Inc.....E.....916 551-1850
1730 I St Ste 100 Sacramento (95811) ***(P-4020)***
Composites Horizons LLC (HQ).....C.....626 331-0861
1629 W Industrial Park St Covina (91722) ***(P-20074)***
Compressed Air Concepts.....E.....310 537-1350
16207 Carmenita Rd Cerritos (90703) ***(P-14626)***

Comprhnsive Crdvsclar Spcalist (PA) ....E.......626 281-8663
220 S 1st St Ste 101 Alhambra (91801) ***(P-7847)***

Compro Packaging LLC ....E.......510 475-0118
1600 Atlantic St Union City (94587) ***(P-5211)***

Compserv Inc ....F.......415 331-4571
42 Golf Rd Pleasanton (94566) ***(P-18874)***

Compu Aire Inc ....C.......562 945-8971
8167 Byron Rd Whittier (90606) ***(P-15420)***

Compu Tech Lumber Products ....D.......707 437-6683
1980 Huntington Ct Fairfield (94533) ***(P-4297)***

Compu-Fire, Downey *Also called Engine Electronics Inc* ***(P-19191)***

Compucase Corporation ....A.......626 336-6588
16720 Chestnut St Ste C City of Industry (91748) ***(P-15018)***

Compucraft Industries Inc ....E.......619 448-0787
8787 Olive Ln Santee (92071) ***(P-20075)***

Compugraphics USA Inc (HQ) ....D.......510 249-2600
43455 Osgood Rd Fremont (94539) ***(P-18171)***

Compugroup Medical Inc ....F.......949 789-0500
25 B Tech Dr Ste 200 Irvine (92618) ***(P-23764)***

Compulink Business Systems Inc (PA) ....D.......805 446-2050
1100 Business Center Cir Newbury Park (91320) ***(P-23765)***

Compulink Healthcare Solutions, Newbury Park *Also called Compulink Business Systems Inc* ***(P-23765)***

Compulink Management Ctr Inc ....C.......562 988-1688
3545 Long Beach Blvd Long Beach (90807) ***(P-23766)***

Compulocks Brands Inc ....F.......562 201-2913
9115 Dice Rd Ste 18 Santa Fe Springs (90670) ***(P-19277)***

Computational Sensors Corp ....E.......805 962-1175
1042 Via Los Padres Santa Barbara (93111) ***(P-20557)***

Computational Systems Inc ....E.......661 832-5306
4301 Resnik Ct Bakersfield (93313) ***(P-21453)***

Computed Tool & Engineering ....F.......714 630-3911
2910 E Ricker Way Anaheim (92806) ***(P-14036)***

Computer Access Tech Corp ....D.......408 727-6600
3385 Scott Blvd Santa Clara (95054) ***(P-14900)***

Computer Asssted Mfg Tech Corp ....D.......949 263-8911
8710 Research Dr Irvine (92618) ***(P-15860)***

Computer Exchange, The, Sacramento *Also called Raymar Information Tech Inc* ***(P-17407)***

Computer Intgrted McHining Inc ....E.......619 596-9246
10940 Wheatlands Ave Santee (92071) ***(P-15861)***

Computer Metal Products Corp ....D.......805 520-6966
370 E Easy St Simi Valley (93065) ***(P-12160)***

Computer Plastics ....E.......510 785-3600
1914 National Ave Hayward (94545) ***(P-14037)***

Computer Prompting Service ....F.......818 563-3465
617 S Victory Blvd Burbank (91502) ***(P-22410)***

Computer Service Company ....E.......951 738-1444
210 N Delilah St Corona (92879) ***(P-17721)***

Computer-Nozzles, Irwindale *Also called Cni Mfg Inc* ***(P-15854)***

Computerized Embroidery Co ....F.......909 825-3841
673 E Cooley Dr Ste 101 Colton (92324) ***(P-3735)***

Computerized Fashion Svcs Inc ....F.......310 973-0106
3341 Jack Northrop Ave Hawthorne (90250) ***(P-3548)***

Computers and Structures Inc ....F.......510 649-2200
1646 N Calif Blvd Ste 600 Walnut Creek (94596) ***(P-23767)***

Computrus Inc ....E.......951 245-9103
250 Klug Cir Corona (92880) ***(P-12008)***

Compuvac Industries Inc ....F.......949 574-5085
18381 Mount Langley St Fountain Valley (92708) ***(P-14627)***

Comstar Industries Inc ....E.......714 556-1400
22465 La Palma Ave Yorba Linda (92887) ***(P-16706)***

Comstock Press ....E.......510 522-4115
2117 San Jose Ave Alameda (94501) ***(P-6506)***

Comstock Publishing Inc ....F.......916 364-1000
2335 American River Dr # 301 Sacramento (95825) ***(P-5909)***

Comstock's Magazine, Sacramento *Also called Comstock Publishing Inc* ***(P-5909)***

Comtech Xicom Technology Inc (HQ) ....C.......408 213-3000
3550 Bassett St Santa Clara (95054) ***(P-17493)***

Con Sol Enterprises, Santa Paula *Also called Trinity Steel Corporation* ***(P-11903)***

Con-Cise Contact Lens Co, Alameda *Also called Lens C-C Inc* ***(P-22368)***

Con-Fab California Corporation (PA) ....E.......209 249-4700
1910 Lathrop Rd Lathrop (95330) ***(P-10554)***

Con-Tech Plastics, Brea *Also called Ramtec Associates Inc* ***(P-10008)***

Conagra Brands Inc ....A.......209 847-0321
554 S Yosemite Ave Oakdale (95361) ***(P-2432)***

Conair Corporation ....D.......323 724-0101
9350 Rayo Ave South Gate (90280) ***(P-16807)***

Conamco SA De CV ....D.......760 586-4356
3008 Palm Hill Dr Vista (92084) ***(P-22139)***

Concannon Vineyard, Livermore *Also called Tesla Vineyards Lp* ***(P-1951)***

Concentric Analgesics Inc ....F.......415 771-5129
1824 Jackson St Apt A San Francisco (94109) ***(P-7848)***

Concentric Components Inc ....F.......209 529-4840
913 5th St Modesto (95351) ***(P-16637)***

Concentric Medical Inc ....E.......650 938-2100
47900 Bayside Pkwy Fremont (94538) ***(P-21670)***

Concept Development Llc ....E.......949 623-8000
1881 Langley Ave Irvine (92614) ***(P-17855)***

Concept Packaging Group, Ontario *Also called Southland Container Corp* ***(P-5269)***

Concept Part Solutions Inc ....E.......408 748-1244
2047 Zanker Rd San Jose (95131) ***(P-14148)***

Concept Studio Inc ....F.......949 759-0606
3195 Red Hill Ave Ste G Costa Mesa (92626) ***(P-10438)***

Concept Systems Mfg Inc ....F.......408 855-8595
2047 Zanker Rd San Jose (95131) ***(P-18172)***

Concept Transporters, Fresno *Also called Concept Vehicle Technologies* ***(P-19817)***

Concept Vehicle Technologies ....F.......559 233-1313
2695 S Cherry Ave Ste 120 Fresno (93706) ***(P-19817)***

Concepts & Methods Co Inc ....F.......650 593-1064
1017 Bransten Rd San Carlos (94070) ***(P-14758)***

Concepts & Wood, Huntington Park *Also called Plycraft Industries Inc* ***(P-4279)***

Concepts By J Inc ....E.......323 564-9988
834 E 108th St Los Angeles (90059) ***(P-4561)***

Concise Fabricators Inc ....E.......520 746-3226
7550 Panasonic Way San Diego (92154) ***(P-12161)***

Concisys Inc ....E.......858 292-5888
5452 Oberlin Dr San Diego (92121) ***(P-21020)***

Concord Music Group Inc (PA) ....D.......310 385-4455
5750 Wilshire Blvd # 450 Los Angeles (90036) ***(P-6091)***

Concord Sheet Metal, Pittsburg *Also called Levmar Inc* ***(P-12266)***

Concorde Battery Corp (PA) ....E.......626 813-1234
2009 W San Bernardino Rd West Covina (91790) ***(P-19179)***

Concrete Inc ....E.......209 830-1962
749 S Stanislaus St Stockton (95206) ***(P-10746)***

Concrete Inc ....F.......209 933-6999
10260 Waterman Rd Elk Grove (95624) ***(P-10747)***

Concrete Inc (HQ) ....D.......209 933-6999
400 S Lincoln St Stockton (95203) ***(P-10748)***

Concrete Mold Corporation ....E.......310 537-5171
2121 E Del Amo Blvd Compton (90220) ***(P-14038)***

Concrete Ready Mix Inc ....E.......408 224-2452
33 Hillsdale Ave San Jose (95136) ***(P-10749)***

Concreteaccessoriescom ....F.......714 871-9434
130 N Gilbert St Fullerton (92833) ***(P-12672)***

Condeco Software Inc (HQ) ....E.......917 677-7600
2105 S Bascom Ave Ste 150 Campbell (95008) ***(P-23768)***

Condor Electronics Inc ....E.......408 745-7141
990 San Antonio Rd Palo Alto (94303) ***(P-20850)***

Condor Outdoor Products Inc (PA) ....E.......626 358-3270
5268 Rivergrade Rd Baldwin Park (91706) ***(P-22784)***

Condor Pacific Inds Cal Inc ....E.......818 889-2150
905 Rancho Conejo Blvd Newbury Park (91320) ***(P-20076)***

Condor Reliability Services ....C.......408 486-9600
2175 De La Cruz Blvd # 8 Santa Clara (95050) ***(P-18173)***

Conductive Science Inc ....F.......858 699-1837
11643 Rverside Dr Ste 115 Lakeside (92040) ***(P-8635)***

Conesco Industries, Riverside *Also called Doka USA Ltd* ***(P-12186)***

Conesys Inc (PA) ....D.......310 618-3737
2280 W 208th St Torrance (90501) ***(P-18756)***

Conesys Inc ....F.......310 212-0065
548 Amapola Ave Torrance (90501) ***(P-18757)***

Conetech Custom Services LLC ....F.......707 823-2404
2191 Laguna Rd Santa Rosa (95401) ***(P-1644)***

Conexant Holdings Inc ....A.......415 983-2706
4000 Macarthur Blvd Newport Beach (92660) ***(P-18174)***

Conexant Systems LLC (HQ) ....E.......949 483-4600
1901 Main St Ste 300 Irvine (92614) ***(P-18175)***

Conexant Systems Worldwide Inc ....D.......949 483-4600
4000 Macarthur Blvd Newport Beach (92660) ***(P-18176)***

Confab, Lathrop *Also called Con-Fab California Corporation* ***(P-10554)***

Confident Technologies Inc ....F.......858 345-5640
3830 Vly Cntre Dr Ste 705 San Diego (92130) ***(P-23769)***

Confluent Inc (PA) ....E.......650 453-5860
101 University Ave # 111 Palo Alto (94301) ***(P-23770)***

Confluent Medical Tech Inc (PA) ....B.......510 683-2000
47533 Westinghouse Dr Fremont (94539) ***(P-21671)***

Conglas, Bakersfield *Also called Consolidated Fibrgls Pdts Co* ***(P-10982)***

Conklin & Conklin Incorporated ....E.......510 489-5500
34201 7th St Union City (94587) ***(P-12673)***

Conley's Mfg & Sales, Montclair *Also called John L Conley Inc* ***(P-12551)***

Connect Phillips Tech LLC (HQ) ....F.......800 423-4512
12012 Burke St Santa Fe Springs (90670) ***(P-20558)***

Connect Systems Inc ....E.......805 642-7184
1802 Eastman Ave Ste 116 Ventura (93003) ***(P-17494)***

Connectec Company Inc (PA) ....D.......949 252-1077
1701 Reynolds Ave Irvine (92614) ***(P-16885)***

Connectec Company Inc ....F.......949 252-1077
3901 S Main St Santa Ana (92707) ***(P-16886)***

Connected Apparel Company LLC (PA) ....E.......323 890-8000
6015 Bandini Blvd Commerce (90040) ***(P-3308)***

Connectedyard Inc ....E.......408 686-9466
1841 Zanker Rd Ste 10 San Jose (95112) ***(P-21208)***

Connection Enterprises Inc ....F.......951 688-8133
4130 Flat Rock Dr Ste 140 Riverside (92505) ***(P-16887)***

Connective Solutions LLC ....F.......800 241-2792
14252 Culver Dr Ste A343 Irvine (92604) ***(P-10302)***

Connector Kings Corporation ....F.......951 710-1180
2110 Mcallister St Riverside (92503) ***(P-18758)***

Connector Plating Corp ....F.......310 323-1622
327 W 132nd St Los Angeles (90061) ***(P-12977)***

Connectorkings.com, Riverside *Also called Connector Kings Corporation* ***(P-18758)***

Connectpv Inc ....F.......858 246-6140
13370 Kirkham Way Poway (92064) ***(P-21454)***

Connell Processing Inc ....E.......818 845-7661
3094 N Avon St Burbank (91504) ***(P-12978)***

Connelly Machine Works ....E.......714 558-6855
420 N Terminal St Santa Ana (92701) ***(P-15862)***

Conners Oro-Cal Mfg Co ....F.......530 533-5065
1720 Bird St Oroville (95965) ***(P-22507)***

Connor J Inc ....F.......626 358-3820
835 Meridian St Irwindale (91010) ***(P-21021)***

Connor Manufacturing Svcs Inc (PA) ....D.......650 591-2026
1710 S Amphlett Blvd # 318 San Mateo (94402) ***(P-15863)***

Conopco Inc ....C.......209 466-9580
1400 Waterloo Rd Stockton (95205) ***(P-8463)***

Conrad Wood Preserving Co ....F.......530 476-2894
7085 Eddy Rd Unit C Arbuckle (95912) ***(P-4476)***

Employee Codes: A=Over 500 employees, B=251-500
C=101-250, D=51-100, E=20-50, F=10-19
2020 California
Manfacturers Register

1067

Conroy & Knowlton Inc ....F....323 665-5288
320 S Montebello Blvd Montebello (90640) ***(P-9716)***
Consilience Converge, Los Olivos *Also called Escalera-Boulet LLC* ***(P-1691)***
Consilio - A First Advantage ....E....626 921-1600
605 E Huntington Dr # 211 Monrovia (91016) ***(P-23771)***
Consol Enterprises ....F....805 648-3486
918 Mission Rock Rd B1 Santa Paula (93060) ***(P-24627)***
Consoldted Hnge Mnfctured Pdts ....F....408 379-6550
1150b Dell Ave Campbell (95008) ***(P-15864)***
Consoldted Precision Pdts Corp ....C....323 773-2363
8333 Wilcox Ave Cudahy (90201) ***(P-11371)***
Consoldted Precision Pdts Corp ....C....805 488-6451
705 Industrial Way Port Hueneme (93041) ***(P-11372)***
Consolidated Aerospace Mfg LLC (PA) ....F....714 989-2797
1425 S Acacia Ave Fullerton (92831) ***(P-20559)***
Consolidated Aircraft Coatings, Riverside *Also called Poly-Fiber Inc* ***(P-8663)***
Consolidated Color Corporation ....E....562 420-7714
12316 Carson St Hawaiian Gardens (90716) ***(P-8636)***
Consolidated Cont Holdings LLC ....E....626 964-9657
17851 Railroad St City of Industry (91748) ***(P-9717)***
Consolidated Cont Holdings LLC ....E....951 340-9390
12165 Madera Way Riverside (92503) ***(P-9718)***
Consolidated Container Co LLC ....E....888 425-7343
1070 Samuelson St City of Industry (91748) ***(P-9719)***
Consolidated Container Co LLC ....D....626 856-2100
4516 Azusa Canyon Rd Irwindale (91706) ***(P-9720)***
Consolidated Container Co LLC ....C....209 820-1700
75 W Valpico Rd Tracy (95376) ***(P-9721)***
Consolidated Container Co LLC ....D....310 952-8736
1500 E 223rd St Carson (90745) ***(P-9483)***
Consolidated Container Co LLC ....F....909 390-6637
5772 Jurupa St Ste B Ontario (91761) ***(P-9484)***
Consolidated Container Co LLC ....D....209 531-9180
1620 Gobel Way Modesto (95358) ***(P-9485)***
Consolidated Container Co LP ....D....714 241-6640
1217 E Saint Gertrude Pl Santa Ana (92707) ***(P-9517)***
Consolidated Container Co LP ....E....909 590-7334
14312 Central Ave Chino (91710) ***(P-9722)***
Consolidated Fabricators Corp (PA) ....C....818 901-1005
14620 Arminta St Van Nuys (91402) ***(P-12009)***
Consolidated Fabricators Corp ....D....209 745-4604
901 Simmerhorn Rd Galt (95632) ***(P-12787)***
Consolidated Fibrgls Pdts Co ....D....661 323-6026
3801 Standard St Bakersfield (93308) ***(P-10982)***
Consolidated Foundries Inc ....E....909 595-2252
4200 W Valley Blvd Pomona (91769) ***(P-11157)***
Consolidated Geoscience Inc ....F....909 393-9700
14738 Central Ave Chino (91710) ***(P-116)***
Consolidated Graphics Inc ....D....323 460-4115
3550 Tyburn St Los Angeles (90065) ***(P-7033)***
Consolidated Laundry LLC ....E....323 232-2417
211 Erie St Pomona (91768) ***(P-15403)***
Consolidated Laundry Machinery, Pomona *Also called Consolidated Laundry LLC* ***(P-15403)***
Consolidated Printers Inc ....E....510 843-8524
2630 8th St Berkeley (94710) ***(P-6170)***
Consolidated Training LLC ....E....831 768-8888
144 Holm Rd Spc 47 Watsonville (95076) ***(P-23305)***
Consorzio, Berkeley *Also called NAPA Valley Kitchens Inc* ***(P-2562)***
Consteel Industrial Inc ....E....562 806-4575
15435 Woodcrest Dr Whittier (90604) ***(P-11772)***
Constellation Brands Inc ....E....415 912-3880
1255 Battery St San Francisco (94111) ***(P-1645)***
Constellation Brands Inc ....E....707 467-4840
2399 N State St Ukiah (95482) ***(P-1646)***
Constellation Brands US Oprs ....A....559 485-0141
12667 Road 24 Madera (93637) ***(P-1647)***
Constellation Brands US Oprs ....A....707 433-8268
349 Healdsburg Ave Healdsburg (95448) ***(P-1648)***
Constlltion Brnds US Oprations, Geyserville *Also called Clos Du Bois Wines Inc* ***(P-1638)***
Construction Electrical Pdts, Livermore *Also called R K Larrabee Company Inc* ***(P-16669)***
Construction Innovations LLC ....C....855 725-9555
10630 Mather Blvd Ste 200 Mather (95655) ***(P-19278)***
Construction Masters, Glendale *Also called Mold Masters Inc* ***(P-14079)***
Construction On Time Inc ....F....408 209-1799
5657 Meridian Ave San Jose (95118) ***(P-336)***
Construction Tl & Threading Co ....F....562 927-1326
8476 Garfield Ave Bell Gardens (90201) ***(P-12674)***
Contactual Inc ....E....650 292-4408
810 W Maude Ave Sunnyvale (94085) ***(P-23772)***
Contadina Foods, Woodland *Also called Pacific Coast Producers* ***(P-816)***
Container Components Inc (PA) ....E....818 882-4300
21947 Plummer St Chatsworth (91311) ***(P-9723)***
Container Decorating Inc ....F....510 489-9212
12 Homestead Ct Danville (94506) ***(P-3781)***
Container Graphics Corp ....D....209 577-0181
1137 Graphics Dr Modesto (95351) ***(P-14319)***
Container Options Inc ....F....909 478-0045
1493 E San Bernardino Ave San Bernardino (92408) ***(P-9724)***
Container Technology Inc (PA) ....E....805 683-5825
5454 San Patricio Dr Santa Barbara (93111) ***(P-9725)***
Containment Consultants Inc ....F....408 848-6998
110 Old Gilroy St Gilroy (95020) ***(P-12010)***
Containment Solutions Inc ....D....661 399-9556
2600 Pegasus Dr Bakersfield (93308) ***(P-12011)***
Contech Engnered Solutions Inc ....A....714 281-7883
950 S Coast Dr Ste 145 Costa Mesa (92626) ***(P-11125)***
Contech Engnered Solutions LLC ....E....530 243-1207
2245 Canyon Creek Rd Redding (96001) ***(P-12012)***
Contech Solutions Incorporated ....E....510 357-7900
631 Montague St San Leandro (94577) ***(P-18177)***
Contempo Window Fashions ....F....818 768-1773
5721 Newcastle Ave Encino (91316) ***(P-2677)***
Contemporary Bath.com, City of Industry *Also called Tonusa LLC* ***(P-4254)***
Contemporary Records, Berkeley *Also called Fantasy Inc* ***(P-17321)***
Content Management Corporation ....F....510 505-1100
4287 Technology Dr Fremont (94538) ***(P-7034)***
Contessa Premium Foods, Vernon *Also called F I O Imports Inc* ***(P-2454)***
Contex Inc ....F....818 788-5836
4505 Van Nuys Blvd Van Nuys (91403) ***(P-22345)***
Contex Inc Contact Lenses, Van Nuys *Also called Contex Inc* ***(P-22345)***
Context Engineering Co ....E....408 748-9112
1043 Di Giulio Ave Santa Clara (95050) ***(P-12788)***
Continental American Corp ....D....626 964-0164
1333 S Hillward Ave West Covina (91791) ***(P-9295)***
Continental Bdr Specialty Corp (PA) ....C....310 324-8227
407 W Compton Blvd Gardena (90248) ***(P-7308)***
Continental Coatings Inc ....F....909 355-1200
10938 Beech Ave Fontana (92337) ***(P-8637)***
Continental Colorcraft, Monterey Park *Also called Graphic Color Systems Inc* ***(P-6594)***
Continental Components LLC ....F....760 480-4420
243 S Escondido Blvd Escondido (92025) ***(P-4497)***
Continental Controls Corp ....E....858 453-9880
7720 Kenamar Ct Ste C San Diego (92121) ***(P-20851)***
Continental Data Graphics, El Segundo *Also called Continental Graphics Corp* ***(P-6510)***
Continental Datalabel Inc ....E....909 307-3600
211 Business Center Ct Redlands (92373) ***(P-5502)***
Continental Engineering Svcs, San Diego *Also called Continental Graphics Corp* ***(P-6507)***
Continental Enterprises, Fowler *Also called Pps Packaging Company* ***(P-5144)***
Continental Feature/ News Svc ....E....858 492-8696
501 W Broadway Ste C San Diego (92101) ***(P-5910)***
Continental Fiberglass Inc (PA) ....F....760 246-6480
17031 Muskrat Ave Adelanto (92301) ***(P-22785)***
Continental Forge Company (PA) ....D....310 603-1014
412 E El Segundo Blvd Compton (90222) ***(P-12731)***
Continental Graphics Corp ....B....858 552-6520
6910 Carroll Rd San Diego (92121) ***(P-6507)***
Continental Graphics Corp ....A....714 827-1752
4060 N Lakewood Blvd 8015fl Long Beach (90808) ***(P-6508)***
Continental Graphics Corp ....E....909 758-9800
9302 Pttsbrgh Ave Ste 100 Rancho Cucamonga (91730) ***(P-6509)***
Continental Graphics Corp ....E....310 662-2307
222 N Pacific Coast Hwy # 300 El Segundo (90245) ***(P-6510)***
Continental Graphix ....E....415 864-2345
166 Riviera Dr San Rafael (94901) ***(P-6511)***
Continental Heat Treating Inc ....D....562 944-8808
10643 Norwalk Blvd Santa Fe Springs (90670) ***(P-11448)***
Continental Industries, Anaheim *Also called International West Inc* ***(P-12249)***
Continental Intelligent Transp ....E....408 391-9008
3901 N 1st St San Jose (95134) ***(P-9167)***
Continental Machine Tool Co, Santa Ana *Also called Supreme Abrasives* ***(P-10955)***
Continental Maritime Inds Inc ....B....619 234-8851
1995 Bay Front St San Diego (92113) ***(P-20285)***
Continental Marketing Svc Inc ....F....626 626-8888
15381 Proctor Ave City of Industry (91745) ***(P-3655)***
Continental Security Inds ....F....661 251-8800
19425b Soledad Canyon Rd # 126 Canyon Country (91351) ***(P-17722)***
Continental Signs Inc ....E....714 894-2011
7541 Santa Rita Cir Ste D Stanton (90680) ***(P-23079)***
Continental Vitamin Co Inc ....D....323 581-0176
4510 S Boyle Ave Vernon (90058) ***(P-7849)***
Continential Data Graphics, Long Beach *Also called Continental Graphics Corp* ***(P-6508)***
Continntal Advnced Ldar Sltons ....F....805 318-2072
6307 Crpinteria Ave Ste A Santa Barbara (93103) ***(P-19621)***
Continuous Cartridge ....E....760 929-4808
5973 Avenida Encinas # 140 Carlsbad (92008) ***(P-22411)***
Continuous Coating Corp (PA) ....D....714 637-4642
520 W Grove Ave Orange (92865) ***(P-12979)***
Continuous Computing Corp ....E....858 882-8800
10431 Wtridge Cir Ste 110 San Diego (92121) ***(P-14901)***
Continuum Electro-Optics Inc ....D....408 727-3240
532 Gibraltar Dr Milpitas (95035) ***(P-21209)***
Continuum Estate, Saint Helena *Also called Tmr Wine Company* ***(P-1958)***
Contour Energy Systems Inc ....E....626 610-0660
1300 W Optical Dr Ste 100 Irwindale (91702) ***(P-19156)***
Contra Costa Metal Fabricators, Concord *Also called Monterey Mechanical Co* ***(P-12310)***
Contra Costa Newspapers Inc (HQ) ....A....925 935-2525
175 Lennon Ln Ste 100 Walnut Creek (94598) ***(P-5598)***
Contra Costa Newspapers Inc ....B....510 748-1683
1516 Oak St Alameda (94501) ***(P-5599)***
Contra Costa Newspapers Inc ....D....925 847-2123
127 Spring St Pleasanton (94566) ***(P-5600)***
Contra Costa Newspapers Inc ....C....925 977-8520
2205 Dean Lesher Dr Concord (94520) ***(P-5601)***
Contra Costa Newspapers Inc ....F....925 634-2125
1700 Cavallo Rd Antioch (94509) ***(P-5602)***
Contra Costa Times, Walnut Creek *Also called Contra Costa Newspapers Inc* ***(P-5598)***
Contraband Control Specialists ....F....661 322-3363
26 H St Bakersfield (93304) ***(P-8951)***
Contract Illumination ....E....714 771-5223
975 N Enterprise St Orange (92867) ***(P-17020)***
Contract Logging, Weed *Also called M & M Logging Inc* ***(P-3894)***
Contract Metal Products Inc ....E....510 979-4811
45535 Northport Loop W Fl Flr 1 Fremont (94538) ***(P-12162)***
Contract Resources, Commerce *Also called Commercial Intr Resources Inc* ***(P-4633)***
Contract Transportation Sys Co ....D....562 696-3262
12500 Slauson Ave Ste B2 Santa Fe Springs (90670) ***(P-8638)***
Contract Wrangler Inc ....E....310 266-3373
922 S Claremont St San Mateo (94402) ***(P-23773)***

Mergent e-mail: customerrelations@mergent.com
1068
2020 California
Manufacturers Register
(P-0000) Products & Services Section entry number
(PA)=Parent Co (HQ)=Headquarters (DH)=Div Headquarters

Contrctor Cmpliance Monitoring....E....619 472-9065
2343 Donnington Way San Diego (92139) ***(P-20789)***
Control Components Inc (HQ)....B....949 858-1877
22591 Avenida Empresa Rcho STA Marg (92688) ***(P-13300)***
Control Enterprises Inc....F....559 683-2044
40124 Highway 49 Oakhurst (93644) ***(P-13325)***
Control Switches Inc (PA)....F....562 498-7331
2425 Mira Mar Ave Long Beach (90815) ***(P-16707)***
Control Switches Intl Inc....E....562 498-7331
2425 Mira Mar Ave Long Beach (90815) ***(P-16708)***
Control Systems Intl Inc....E....949 238-4150
1 Sterling Irvine (92618) ***(P-13772)***
Controlled Entrances Inc....F....760 749-1212
27525 Valley Center Rd A Valley Center (92082) ***(P-19279)***
Controlmyspa, Costa Mesa *Also called Balboa Water Group LLC* ***(P-16702)***
Convaid Products Inc....D....310 618-0111
2830 California St Torrance (90503) ***(P-21995)***
Convergent Laser Technologies, Alameda *Also called Xintec Corporation* ***(P-22333)***
Convergent Manufacturing Tech....F....408 987-2770
966 Shulman Ave Santa Clara (95050) ***(P-15206)***
Convergent Mobile Inc....F....707 343-1200
870 Knight St Sonoma (95476) ***(P-18178)***
Converging Systems Inc....F....310 544-2628
32420 Nautilus Dr Ste 100 Pls Vrds Pnsl (90275) ***(P-15207)***
Convergint Technologies LLC....E....714 546-2780
1667 N Batavia St Orange (92867) ***(P-19280)***
Conversion Devices Inc....E....714 898-6551
15481 Electronic Ln Ste D Huntington Beach (92649) ***(P-22243)***
Conversion Technology Co Inc (PA)....E....805 378-0033
5360 N Commerce Ave Moorpark (93021) ***(P-22940)***
Conversionpoint Holdings Inc....D....888 706-6764
840 Newport Center Dr # 450 Newport Beach (92660) ***(P-23774)***
Convertly, San Jose *Also called Medianews Group Inc* ***(P-5743)***
Conveyor Concepts, Los Angeles *Also called Machine Building Specialties* ***(P-14383)***
Conveyor Group, Imperial *Also called Franklin Lee Enterprises LLC* ***(P-7069)***
Conveyor Mfg & Svc Inc....F....909 621-0406
771 Marylind Ave Claremont (91711) ***(P-13819)***
Conxtech Inc....C....510 264-9112
24493 Clawiter Rd Hayward (94545) ***(P-11773)***
Conxtech Inc (PA)....E....510 264-9111
6701 Koll Center Pkwy Pleasanton (94566) ***(P-11774)***
Cook and Cook Incorporated....E....714 680-6669
1000 E Elm Ave Fullerton (92831) ***(P-12013)***
Cook Concrete Products Inc....E....530 243-2562
5461 Eastside Rd Redding (96001) ***(P-10555)***
Cook Induction Heating Co Inc....E....323 560-1327
4925 Slauson Ave Maywood (90270) ***(P-11449)***
Cook King Inc....E....714 739-0502
15120 Desman Rd La Mirada (90638) ***(P-15505)***
Cooks Truck Body Mfg Inc....F....916 784-3220
9600 Del Rd Roseville (95747) ***(P-19524)***
Cool Curtain CCI, Costa Mesa *Also called CCI Industries Inc* ***(P-9698)***
Cool Jams Inc....F....858 566-6165
11206 Spencerport Way San Diego (92131) ***(P-3031)***
Cool Lumens Inc....F....831 471-8084
1334 Brommer St Ste B6 Santa Cruz (95062) ***(P-17021)***
Cool Things, Santa Ana *Also called Ecoolthing Corp* ***(P-13519)***
Cool Touch, Roseville *Also called Cooltouch Corporation* ***(P-22245)***
Cool-Pak LLC....D....805 981-2434
401 N Rice Ave Oxnard (93030) ***(P-9726)***
Coola LLC....E....760 940-2125
3200 Lionshead Ave Carlsbad (92010) ***(P-8464)***
Coola Suncare, Carlsbad *Also called Coola LLC* ***(P-8464)***
Coolhaus, Culver City *Also called Farchitecture Bb LLC* ***(P-642)***
Cooling Source Inc....C....925 292-1293
2021 Las Positas Ct # 101 Livermore (94551) ***(P-11334)***
Cooling Tower Resources Inc (PA)....E....707 433-3900
1470 Grove St Healdsburg (95448) ***(P-4498)***
Cooljet Systems, Brea *Also called Mkt Innovations* ***(P-16216)***
Coolsculpting, Pleasanton *Also called Zeltiq Aesthetics Inc* ***(P-21966)***
Coolssculpting, Dublin *Also called Zeltiq Aesthetics Inc* ***(P-21965)***
Coolsystems Inc (HQ)....C....888 426-3732
1800 Sutter St Ste 500 Concord (94520) ***(P-22244)***
Cooltec Refrigeration Corp....E....909 865-2229
1250 E Franklin Ave B Pomona (91766) ***(P-15421)***
Cooltouch, Roseville *Also called New Star Lasers Inc* ***(P-22288)***
Cooltouch Corporation....F....916 677-1975
9085 Foothills Blvd Roseville (95747) ***(P-22245)***
Cooper & Brain Inc....F....310 834-4411
655 E D St Wilmington (90744) ***(P-45)***
Cooper Bussmann LLC....F....925 924-8500
5735 W Las Positas Blvd # 100 Pleasanton (94588) ***(P-16783)***
Cooper Cameron Valves, Redding *Also called Cameron International Corp* ***(P-13770)***
Cooper Companies Inc (PA)....C....925 460-3600
6140 Stoneridge Mall Rd # 590 Pleasanton (94588) ***(P-22346)***
Cooper Crouse-Hinds LLC....C....805 484-0543
750 W Ventura Blvd Camarillo (93010) ***(P-18759)***
Cooper Crouse-Hinds LLC....C....805 484-0543
705 W Ventura Blvd Camarillo (93010) ***(P-9296)***
Cooper Crouse-Hinds LLC....C....805 484-0543
750 W Ventura Blvd Camarillo (93010) ***(P-9297)***
Cooper Interconnect Inc (HQ)....D....805 484-0543
750 W Ventura Blvd Camarillo (93010) ***(P-16888)***
Cooper Interconnect Inc....D....805 553-9632
750 W Ventura Blvd Camarillo (93010) ***(P-18760)***
Cooper Interconnect Inc....E....805 553-9632
750 W Ventura Blvd Camarillo (93010) ***(P-16943)***
Cooper Lighting LLC....E....909 605-6615
3350 Enterprise Dr Bloomington (92316) ***(P-17113)***
Cooper Microelectronics Inc....E....949 553-8352
1671 Reynolds Ave Irvine (92614) ***(P-18179)***
Coopervision Inc....D....925 251-6600
6150 Stoneridge Mall Rd # 370 Pleasanton (94588) ***(P-22347)***
Coordinated Wire Rope No. Ca., San Leandro *Also called Coordnted Wire Rope Rgging Inc* ***(P-2910)***
Coordnted Wire Rope Rgging Inc....F....510 569-6911
790 139th Ave Ste 1 San Leandro (94578) ***(P-2910)***
Coors Brewing Company....E....916 786-2666
3001 Douglas Blvd Ste 200 Roseville (95661) ***(P-1514)***
Coorstek Inc....D....805 644-5583
4544 Mcgrath St Ventura (93003) ***(P-14149)***
Coorstek Inc....C....805 644-5583
4544 Mcgrath St Ventura (93003) ***(P-14150)***
Coorstek Inc....D....510 492-6600
41348 Christy St Fremont (94538) ***(P-10475)***
Coorstek Vista Inc....C....760 542-7065
2065 Thibodo Rd Vista (92081) ***(P-10991)***
Cop Shopper, San Diego *Also called Krasnes Inc* ***(P-3519)***
Copain Wine Cellars LLC....F....707 836-8822
7800 Eastside Rd Healdsburg (95448) ***(P-1649)***
Copain Wine Sellers, Healdsburg *Also called Copain Wine Cellars LLC* ***(P-1649)***
Coplan & Coplan Inc....E....760 268-0583
2270 Camino Vida Roble H Carlsbad (92011) ***(P-14151)***
Copley Press Inc....F....760 752-6700
1152 Armorlite Dr San Marcos (92069) ***(P-5603)***
Copp Industrial Mfg Inc....E....909 593-7448
2837 Metropolitan Pl Pomona (91767) ***(P-12163)***
Coppa Woodworking Inc....F....310 548-4142
1231 Paraiso St San Pedro (90731) ***(P-4021)***
Copper Crm Inc (PA)....C....415 231-6360
301 Howard St Ste 600 San Francisco (94105) ***(P-23775)***
Copper Harbor Company Inc....F....510 639-4670
2300 Davis St San Leandro (94577) ***(P-8952)***
Copy 1 Inc....E....415 986-0111
77 Battery St Fl 2 San Francisco (94111) ***(P-6512)***
Copy Mill, San Francisco *Also called Ng John* ***(P-6748)***
Copy Shop & Printing Co, The, San Rafael *Also called Marin County Copy Shops Inc* ***(P-6714)***
Copy Solutions Inc....E....323 307-0900
919 S Fremont Ave Ste 398 Alhambra (91803) ***(P-6513)***
Copyland /Zip2print, San Jose *Also called Arsh Incorporated* ***(P-6420)***
Copymat, San Francisco *Also called Digital Mania Inc* ***(P-6540)***
Copymat Salinas LLC....F....831 753-0471
44 W Gabilan St Salinas (93901) ***(P-6514)***
Coraid Inc (PA)....D....650 517-9300
255 Shoreline Dr Ste 650 Redwood City (94065) ***(P-15019)***
Coral Head Inc (PA)....F....310 366-7712
1988 W 169th St Gardena (90247) ***(P-3073)***
Coral Reef Aquarium....E....310 538-4282
515 W 130th St Los Angeles (90061) ***(P-10348)***
Coral Reef Dive Center, Westminster *Also called Anthony Jones* ***(P-22748)***
Corasia Corp....F....408 321-8508
363 Fairview Way Milpitas (95035) ***(P-14704)***
Corazonas Foods Inc....F....800 388-8998
3780 Kilroy Airport Way # 430 Long Beach (90806) ***(P-2320)***
Corbell Products, Bloomington *Also called Westco Industries Inc* ***(P-12613)***
Corbett Canyon Vineyards....F....805 782-9463
2195 Corbett Canyon Rd Arroyo Grande (93420) ***(P-1650)***
Corbin Foods, Santa Ana *Also called Corbin-Hill Inc* ***(P-1181)***
Corbin Pacific Inc....E....408 633-2500
11445 Commercial Pkwy Castroville (95012) ***(P-20390)***
Corbin Pacific Inc (PA)....D....831 634-1100
2360 Technology Pkwy Hollister (95023) ***(P-20391)***
Corbin-Hill Inc....D....714 966-6695
2961 W Macarthur Blvd Santa Ana (92704) ***(P-1181)***
Corcen Data International Inc....F....714 251-6110
17341 Irvine Blvd Ste 205 Tustin (92780) ***(P-23776)***
Concept Therapeutics Inc....C....650 327-3270
149 Commonwealth Dr Menlo Park (94025) ***(P-7850)***
Corcoran Sawtelle Rosprim Inc....E....559 992-2117
542 Otis Ave Corcoran (93212) ***(P-11775)***
Cord Industries Inc....F....760 728-4590
541 Industrial Way Ste 2 Fallbrook (92028) ***(P-9727)***
Cord Intrnational/Hana Ola Rec....F....805 648-7881
1874 Terrace Dr Ventura (93001) ***(P-17313)***
Cordova Industries, Sylmar *Also called International Academy of Fin* ***(P-8745)***
Cordovan & Grey Ltd....E....562 699-8300
4826 Gregg Rd Pico Rivera (90660) ***(P-3002)***
Core Laboratories LP....E....661 325-5657
3437 Landco Dr Bakersfield (93308) ***(P-186)***
Core Supplement Technology....F....760 452-7364
4665 North Ave Oceanside (92056) ***(P-7851)***
Core Systems, Poway *Also called Rugged Systems Inc* ***(P-14970)***
Core Tech Products Inc....F....661 833-1572
1850 Sunnyside Ct Bakersfield (93308) ***(P-8465)***
Corefact Corporation....F....866 777-3986
20936 Cabot Blvd Hayward (94545) ***(P-6171)***
Corelogic Dorado, Oakland *Also called Dorado Network Systems Corp* ***(P-23826)***
Coreslab Structures La Inc....C....951 943-9119
150 W Placentia Ave Perris (92571) ***(P-10556)***
Coretest Systems Inc (PA)....F....408 778-3771
400 Woodview Ave Morgan Hill (95037) ***(P-21210)***
Coretex Products Inc (PA)....F....661 834-6805
1850 Sunnyside Ct Bakersfield (93308) ***(P-8466)***

A
L
P
H
A
B
E
T
I
C

Coretex USA Inc......E......877 247-8725
15110 Avenue O San Diego (92128) *(P-20560)*
Corium Inc (HQ)......C......650 298-8255
235 Constitution Dr Menlo Park (94025) *(P-7852)*
Corium International, Inc., Menlo Park *Also called Corium Inc (P-7852)*
Cork Pops......F......415 884-6000
7 Commercial Blvd Ste 3 Novato (94949) *(P-13511)*
Corn Maiden Foods Inc......D......310 784-0400
24201 Frampton Ave Harbor City (90710) *(P-723)*
Corn Products Development Inc (HQ)......F......209 982-1920
1021 Industrial Dr Stockton (95206) *(P-1060)*
Corn Products-Stockton Plant, Stockton *Also called Ingredion Incorporated (P-1061)*
Cornerstone Display Group Inc......E......661 705-1700
28606 Livingston Ave Valencia (91355) *(P-23080)*
Cornerstone Ondemand Inc (PA)......C......310 752-0200
1601 Cloverf Blvd 620s Santa Monica (90404) *(P-23777)*
Corningware Corelle & More, Eastvale *Also called Snapware Corporation (P-10061)*
Cornnuts Division of Planters, Fresno *Also called Kraft Heinz Foods Company (P-1431)*
Cornucopia Tool & Plastics Inc......E......805 238-7660
448 Sherwood Rd Paso Robles (93446) *(P-9728)*
Coroc, Bakersfield *Also called Weatherford International LLC (P-285)*
Corona Magnetics Inc......C......951 735-7558
201 Corporate Terrace St Corona (92879) *(P-18709)*
Corona Millworks Company (PA)......D......909 606-3288
5572 Edison Ave Chino (91710) *(P-4183)*
Corona Pathology......F......818 566-1891
4444 W Riverside Dr # 308 Burbank (91505) *(P-8733)*
Coronado Eagle, Coronado *Also called Eagle Newspapers LLC (P-5622)*
Coronado Equipment Sales......F......877 830-7447
2275 La Crosse Ave # 210 Colton (92324) *(P-13862)*
Coronado Leather Co Inc......F......619 238-0265
1961 Main St San Diego (92113) *(P-3511)*
Coronado Manufacturing Inc......E......818 768-5010
8991 Glenoaks Blvd Sun Valley (91352) *(P-20077)*
Coronado Stone Products, Fontana *Also called Creative Stone Mfg Inc (P-10557)*
Coronet Concrete Products (PA)......E......760 398-2441
83801 Avenue 45 Indio (92201) *(P-10750)*
Coronet Lighting, Gardena *Also called Dasol Inc (P-16859)*
Corp Couch, San Francisco *Also called Corporatecouch (P-18180)*
Corpak of Tulare, Tulare *Also called Westrock Cp LLC (P-5277)*
Corporate Graphics & Printing......F......805 529-5333
335 Science Dr Moorpark (93021) *(P-6515)*
Corporate Graphics Intl Inc......D......323 826-3440
4909 Alcoa Ave Vernon (90058) *(P-6516)*
Corporate Graphics West, Vernon *Also called Corporate Graphics Intl Inc (P-6516)*
Corporate Impressions La Inc......E......818 761-9295
10742 Burbank Blvd North Hollywood (91601) *(P-7035)*
Corporate Sign Systems Inc......E......408 292-1600
2464 De La Cruz Blvd Santa Clara (95050) *(P-23081)*
Corporatecouch......E......415 312-6078
260 Vicente St San Francisco (94127) *(P-18180)*
Corprint Incorporated......F......818 839-5316
4235 Mission Oaks Blvd Camarillo (93010) *(P-7036)*
Corralitos Market & Sausage Co......F......831 722-2633
569 Corralitos Rd Watsonville (95076) *(P-450)*
Correa Pallet Inc (PA)......E......559 757-1790
13036 Avenue 76 Pixley (93256) *(P-4358)*
Corrpro Companies Inc......E......562 944-1636
10260 Matern Pl Santa Fe Springs (90670) *(P-11176)*
Corru-Kraft IV......F......714 773-0124
1911 E Rosslynn Ave Fullerton (92831) *(P-5212)*
Corrugados De Baja California......A......619 662-8672
2475 Paseo De Las A San Diego (92154) *(P-5213)*
Corrugated and Packaging LLC......C......619 559-1564
951 Poinsettia Ave # 602 Vista (92081) *(P-9518)*
Corrugated Packaging Pdts Inc......E......650 615-9180
27403 Industrial Blvd Hayward (94545) *(P-5214)*
Corrugated Technologies Inc......E......858 578-3550
15150 Avenue Of Science San Diego (92128) *(P-23778)*
Corrwood Containers......E......559 651-0335
7182 Rasmussen Ave Visalia (93291) *(P-4414)*
Corsair Components Inc (PA)......C......510 657-8747
47100 Bayside Pkwy Fremont (94538) *(P-15208)*
Corsair Elec Connectors Inc......C......949 833-0273
17100 Murphy Ave Irvine (92614) *(P-18761)*
Corsair Memory Inc......C......510 657-8747
47100 Bayside Pkwy Fremont (94538) *(P-18181)*
Corsican Furniture, Gardena *Also called Victor Martin Inc (P-4707)*
Corte Custom Case, San Jacinto *Also called Wallace Wood Products (P-4954)*
Cortec Precision Shtmtl Inc (PA)......C......408 278-8540
2231 Will Wool Dr San Jose (95112) *(P-12164)*
Cortexyme Inc (PA)......F......415 910-5717
269 E Grand Ave South San Francisco (94080) *(P-7853)*
Cortez Furniture Mfg Inc......F......323 581-5935
2423 E 58th St Los Angeles (90058) *(P-4634)*
Cortima Co......E......760 347-5535
83778 Avenue 45 Indio (92201) *(P-10901)*
Cortina Systems Inc (HQ)......C......408 481-2300
2953 Bunker Hill Ln # 300 Santa Clara (95054) *(P-18182)*
Corvus Pharmaceuticals Inc......D......650 900-4520
863 Mitten Rd Ste 102 Burlingame (94010) *(P-7854)*
Cosa Marble Co......F......818 364-8800
13040 San Fernando Rd A Sylmar (91342) *(P-291)*
Cosco Home & Office Products, Ontario *Also called Dorel Juvenile Group Inc (P-9766)*
Cosemi Technologies Inc (PA)......F......949 623-9816
1370 Reynolds Ave Ste 100 Irvine (92614) *(P-18183)*
Cosentino Signature Wineries......E......707 921-2809
7415 St Helena Hwy Yountville (94599) *(P-1651)*
Cosentino Winery, Yountville *Also called Cosentino Signature Wineries (P-1651)*
Coskata Inc......F......630 657-5800
3945 Freedom Cir Ste 560 Santa Clara (95054) *(P-8734)*
Coskata Energy, Santa Clara *Also called Coskata Inc (P-8734)*
Cosmedica Skincare......F......800 922-5280
2208 Srra Madows Dr Ste A Rocklin (95677) *(P-8467)*
Cosmetic Enterprises Ltd......F......818 896-5355
12848 Pierce St Pacoima (91331) *(P-8468)*
Cosmetic Group Usa Inc......C......818 767-2889
8430 Tujunga Ave Sun Valley (91352) *(P-8469)*
Cosmetic Specialties Intl LLC......C......805 487-6698
550 E 3rd St Oxnard (93030) *(P-9729)*
Cosmi Finance LLC......F......310 603-5800
1635 Chelsea Rd Ste A San Marino (91108) *(P-23779)*
Cosmic Fog Vapors......D......949 266-1730
3115 Airway Ave Costa Mesa (92626) *(P-2651)*
Cosmic Plastics Inc (PA)......E......661 257-3274
28410 Industry Dr Valencia (91355) *(P-7550)*
Cosmo - Pharm Inc......E......818 764-0246
11751 Vose St Ste 53 North Hollywood (91605) *(P-7650)*
Cosmo Beauty Lab & Mfg, San Dimas *Also called Cosmobeauti Labs & Mfg Inc (P-8471)*
Cosmo Fiber Corporation (PA)......E......626 256-6098
1802 Santo Domingo Ave Duarte (91010) *(P-7037)*
Cosmo Import & Export LLC (PA)......E......916 209-5500
3919 Channel Dr West Sacramento (95691) *(P-4688)*
Cosmo International Corp......E......310 271-1100
9200 W Sunset Blvd # 401 West Hollywood (90069) *(P-8470)*
Cosmo International Fragrances, West Hollywood *Also called Cosmo International Corp (P-8470)*
Cosmobeauti Labs & Mfg Inc......F......909 971-9832
480 E Arrow Hwy San Dimas (91773) *(P-8471)*
Cosmodyne LLC......E......562 795-5990
3010 Old Ranch Pkwy # 300 Seal Beach (90740) *(P-14442)*
Cosmojet Inc......F......818 773-6544
9601 Cozycroft Ave Ste 2 Chatsworth (91311) *(P-6952)*
Cosmolara Inc......F......562 273-0348
8339 Allport Ave Santa Fe Springs (90670) *(P-8472)*
Cosmos Food Co Inc......E......323 221-9142
16015 Phoenix Dr City of Industry (91745) *(P-2433)*
Costal Brands, Manteca *Also called Delicato Vineyards (P-1659)*
Costco Wholesale Corporation......B......619 336-3360
1001 W 19th St Ste A National City (91950) *(P-21346)*
Cosway Company Inc......E......310 527-9135
14805 S Maple Ave Gardena (90248) *(P-8473)*
Cosway Company Inc (PA)......E......310 900-4100
20633 S Fordyce Ave Carson (90810) *(P-8474)*
Cots Journal Magazine, San Clemente *Also called R T C Group (P-6011)*
Cott Technologies Inc......F......626 961-3399
14923 Proctor Ave La Puente (91746) *(P-13464)*
Cotterman Company, Bakersfield *Also called Material Control Inc (P-13532)*
Cotton Generation Inc......E......323 581-8555
6051 Maywood Ave Huntington Park (90255) *(P-3476)*
Cotton Knits Trading......E......310 884-9600
3097 E Ana St Compton (90221) *(P-2817)*
Cotton Tale Designs Inc......E......714 435-9558
16291 Sierra Ridge Way Hacienda Heights (91745) *(P-3609)*
Cotty On, Vernon *Also called Cottyon Inc (P-2678)*
Cottyon Inc......E......323 589-1563
2202 E Anderson St Vernon (90058) *(P-2678)*
Cougar Biotechnology Inc......D......310 943-8040
10990 Wilshire Blvd # 1200 Los Angeles (90024) *(P-7855)*
Coughran Mechanical Services......F......707 374-2100
3053 Liberty Island Rd Rio Vista (94571) *(P-15865)*
Coulter Forge Technology Inc......F......510 420-3500
1494 67th St Emeryville (94608) *(P-12706)*
Coulter Steel and Forge, Emeryville *Also called Coulter Forge Technology Inc (P-12706)*
Council Oak Books LLC......F......415 931-7700
2822 Van Ness Ave San Francisco (94109) *(P-6092)*
Counter......E......310 406-3300
21209 Hawthorne Blvd B Torrance (90503) *(P-10149)*
Counterpart Automotive Inc......F......714 771-1732
420 W Brenna Ln Orange (92867) *(P-19622)*
Counterpoint Software Inc......F......818 222-7777
24528 Palermo Dr Calabasas (91302) *(P-23780)*
Countis Industries Inc......E......530 272-8334
12295 Charles Dr Grass Valley (95945) *(P-10476)*
Country Almanac, Palo Alto *Also called Embarcadero Publishing Company (P-5630)*
Country Floral Supply Inc......D......925 960-9823
6909 Las Positas Rd Ste F Livermore (94551) *(P-23306)*
Country House......F......714 505-8988
2852 Walnut Ave Ste C1 Tustin (92780) *(P-1362)*
Country Plastics Inc......F......559 597-2556
32501 Road 228 Woodlake (93286) *(P-9730)*
Country Weave, Santa Ana *Also called Newport Plastic Inc (P-9925)*
Countryman Associates Inc......F......650 364-9988
195 Constitution Dr Menlo Park (94025) *(P-17214)*
County of Alameda......E......510 272-6964
1225 Fallon St Ste G1 Oakland (94612) *(P-20963)*
County of Los Angeles......E......626 968-3312
14959 Proctor Ave La Puente (91746) *(P-13723)*
County of Los Angeles......F......310 456-8014
3637 Winter Canyon Rd Malibu (90265) *(P-13724)*
County of Marin......D......415 446-4414
3501 Civic Center Dr San Rafael (94903) *(P-4855)*
County of Monterey......F......831 755-4790
855 E Laurel Dr Ste C Salinas (93905) *(P-7038)*
County of NAPA......F......707 259-8620
804 1st St NAPA (94559) *(P-20852)*

County of San Bernardino ...... E......909 580-0015
400 N Pepper Ave Colton (92324) **(P-20752)**
Countywide Metal, El Cajon *Also called Mmix Technologies* **(P-12305)**
Coupa Software Incorporated (PA) ...... C......650 931-3200
1855 S Grant St San Mateo (94402) **(P-23781)**
Courage Production LLC ...... D......707 422-6300
2475 Courage Dr Fairfield (94533) **(P-451)**
Courtside Cellars LLC ...... E......805 467-2882
2425 Mission St San Miguel (93451) **(P-1652)**
Courtside Cellars LLC (PA) ...... E......805 782-0500
4910 Edna Rd San Luis Obispo (93401) **(P-1653)**
Covalent Metrology Svcs Inc ...... F......408 498-4611
921 Thompson Pl Sunnyvale (94085) **(P-20753)**
Covan Alarm Company, Livermore *Also called Covan Systems Inc* **(P-17215)**
Covan Systems Inc ...... F......510 226-9886
569 Leisure St Livermore (94551) **(P-17215)**
Cove Four-Slide Stamping Corp (PA) ...... C......516 379-4232
355 S Hale Ave Fullerton (92831) **(P-13406)**
Cove Four-Slide Stamping Corp. ...... E......714 525-2930
335 S Hale Ave Fullerton (92831) **(P-13407)**
Cove West Division, Fullerton *Also called Cove Four-Slide Stamping Corp* **(P-13406)**
Cove20 LLC ...... F......949 297-4930
15 Brookline Aliso Viejo (92656) **(P-18184)**
Cover King, Anaheim *Also called Shrin Corporation* **(P-19766)**
Coveris, Hanford *Also called Transcontinental US LLC* **(P-5425)**
Coveris, Ontario *Also called Transcontinental US LLC* **(P-5426)**
Covert Iron Works ...... F......323 560-2792
7821 Otis S Ave Huntington Park (90255) **(P-11150)**
Covia Holdings Corporation ...... E......925 634-3575
1300 Camino Diablo Rd Byron (94514) **(P-372)**
Covidien, Costa Mesa *Also called Newport Medical Instrs Inc* **(P-21838)**
Covidien, Sunnyvale *Also called Barrx Medical Inc* **(P-22231)**
Covidien Holding Inc ...... E......760 603-5020
2101 Faraday Ave Carlsbad (92008) **(P-21672)**
Covidien Holding Inc ...... A......619 690-8500
2475 Paseo De Las Amrcs A San Diego (92154) **(P-21673)**
Covidien Kenmex, San Diego *Also called Covidien Holding Inc* **(P-21673)**
Covidien LP ...... B......949 837-3700
9775 Toledo Way Irvine (92618) **(P-21674)**
Covina Welding & Shtmtl Inc ...... F......626 332-6293
473 E Front St Covina (91723) **(P-11776)**
Cowboy Direct Response ...... E......714 824-3780
130 E Alton Ave Santa Ana (92707) **(P-23082)**
Coy Industries Inc ...... D......310 603-2970
2970 E Maria St E Rncho Dmngz (90221) **(P-12165)**
Coyle Reproductions Inc (PA) ...... C......866 269-5373
2850 Orbiter St Brea (92821) **(P-6517)**
Coyne & Blanchard Inc ...... E......650 326-6040
110 Constitution Dr Menlo Park (94025) **(P-5911)**
Cozad Trailer Sales LLC ...... D......209 931-3000
4907 E Waterloo Rd Stockton (95215) **(P-19818)**
Cozza Inc ...... E......619 749-5663
9941 Prospect Ave Santee (92071) **(P-15866)**
Cozzia USA LLC ...... E......626 667-2272
861 S Oak Park Rd Covina (91724) **(P-19281)**
CP Kelco, San Diego *Also called Kelco Bio Polymers* **(P-8983)**
CP Kelco Us Inc ...... E......858 467-6542
2025 Harbor Dr San Diego (92113) **(P-8953)**
CP Kelco US Inc ...... E......858 292-4900
8355 Aero Dr San Diego (92123) **(P-8954)**
CP Kelco US Inc ...... F......858 292-4900
8225 Aero Dr San Diego (92123) **(P-8955)**
CP Manufacturing Inc (HQ) ...... C......619 477-3175
6795 Calle De Linea San Diego (92154) **(P-14443)**
CP Products, Anaheim *Also called Kiva Container Corporation* **(P-9554)**
Cp-Carrillo Inc ...... E......949 567-9000
17401 Armstrong Ave Irvine (92614) **(P-15612)**
Cp-Carrillo Inc (HQ) ...... C......949 567-9000
1902 Mcgaw Ave Irvine (92614) **(P-15613)**
Cpacket Networks Inc ...... E......650 969-9500
2130 Gold St 200 San Jose (95002) **(P-15209)**
CPC Fabrication Inc ...... E......714 549-2426
2904 Oak St Santa Ana (92707) **(P-12166)**
CPC Group Inc ...... F......626 350-8848
11223 Rush St I South El Monte (91733) **(P-9731)**
Cpd Industries ...... E......909 465-5596
4665 State St Montclair (91763) **(P-9519)**
Cpfilms Distribution Center, Anaheim *Also called Eastman Performance Films LLC* **(P-7557)**
CPI, Palo Alto *Also called Communications & Pwr Inds LLC* **(P-17491)**
CPI, Palo Alto *Also called Communications & Pwr Inds LLC* **(P-17778)**
CPI Advanced Inc ...... C......909 597-5533
14708 Central Ave Chino (91710) **(P-16545)**
CPI International Inc (PA) ...... F......650 846-2801
811 Hansen Way Palo Alto (94304) **(P-17780)**
CPI International Holding Inc ...... F......650 846-2900
811 Hansen Way Palo Alto (94304) **(P-18875)**
CPI Malibu Division ...... D......805 383-1829
3760 Calle Tecate Ste A Camarillo (93012) **(P-17495)**
Cpk Manufacturing Inc ...... F......408 971-4019
2188 Del Franco St Ste 70 San Jose (95131) **(P-15867)**
Cpp, Sunnyvale *Also called Myers-Briggs Company* **(P-6289)**
Cpp Cudahy, Cudahy *Also called Consoldted Precision Pdts Corp* **(P-11371)**
Cpp Ind ...... F......909 595-2252
16800 Chestnut St City of Industry (91748) **(P-20561)**
Cpp-Azusa, Azusa *Also called Magparts* **(P-11385)**
Cpp-City of Industry, City of Industry *Also called Cast Parts Inc* **(P-11155)**
Cpp-Pomona, Walnut *Also called Cast Parts Inc* **(P-11154)**

Cpp-Port Hueneme ...... C......805 488-6451
705 Industrial Way Port Hueneme (93041) **(P-11412)**
Cpp/Belwin Inc ...... E......818 891-5999
16320 Roscoe Blvd Ste 100 Van Nuys (91406) **(P-6093)**
Cppi, San Diego *Also called California Precision Pdts Inc* **(P-12148)**
Cprint Holdings LLC ...... F......213 488-0456
1901 E 7th Pl Los Angeles (90021) **(P-6518)**
CPS Gem Corporation ...... F......213 627-4019
1327 S Myrtle Ave Monrovia (91016) **(P-22508)**
CPS Printing ...... D......760 494-9000
2304 Faraday Ave Carlsbad (92008) **(P-6519)**
CPS Wood Works Inc ...... F......909 326-1102
1257 E 9th St Pomona (91766) **(P-4022)**
Cr & A Custom, Los Angeles *Also called CR & A Custom Apparel Inc* **(P-7039)**
CR & A Custom Apparel Inc ...... E......213 749-4440
312 W Pico Blvd Los Angeles (90015) **(P-7039)**
CR Laurence Co Inc ...... F......310 327-9300
14400 S San Pedro St Gardena (90248) **(P-11943)**
Cr Print, Westlake Village *Also called Earth Print Inc* **(P-6555)**
Cr Spotless, El Cajon *Also called Spotless Water Systems LLC* **(P-15584)**
Crabtree Glass Company Inc ...... F......818 765-1840
13203 Sherman Way North Hollywood (91605) **(P-12464)**
Craft Labor & Support Svcs LLC ...... D......619 336-9977
1545 Tidelands Ave Ste C National City (91950) **(P-20286)**
Craftech EDM Corporation ...... C......714 630-8117
2941 E La Jolla St Anaheim (92806) **(P-9732)**
Craftech Metal Forming Inc ...... E......951 940-6444
24100 Water Ave Ste B Perris (92570) **(P-11373)**
Crafted Metals Inc ...... F......619 464-1090
9220 Birch St Spring Valley (91977) **(P-13512)**
Crafters Companion ...... E......714 630-2444
2750 E Regal Park Dr Anaheim (92806) **(P-22668)**
Crafton Carton ...... E......510 441-5985
31790 Hayman St Hayward (94544) **(P-5312)**
Craftsman Cutting Dies Inc (PA) ...... E......714 776-8995
2273 E Via Burton Anaheim (92806) **(P-11526)**
Craftsman Lighting ...... F......626 330-8512
14266 Valley Blvd Ste A La Puente (91746) **(P-16968)**
Craftsman Printing, San Jose *Also called United Craftsmen Priniting* **(P-6909)**
Craftstones, Ramona *Also called Ramona Mining & Manufacturing* **(P-22599)**
Crafttech, Anaheim *Also called Craftech EDM Corporation* **(P-9732)**
Craic Technologies Inc ...... F......310 573-8180
948 N Amelia Ave San Dimas (91773) **(P-21211)**
Craig Kackert Design Tech, Simi Valley *Also called Jaxx Manufacturing Inc* **(P-18962)**
Craig Manufacturing Company (PA) ...... D......323 726-7355
8129 Slauson Ave Montebello (90640) **(P-19623)**
Craig Tools Inc ...... E......310 322-0614
142 Lomita St El Segundo (90245) **(P-14152)**
Crain Cutter Company Inc ...... D......408 946-6100
1155 Wrigley Way Milpitas (95035) **(P-11580)**
Cramer Engineering Inc ...... E......562 903-5556
302 Elizabeth Ln Corona (92880) **(P-15868)**
Crane Aerospace Inc ...... D......818 526-2600
3000 Winona Ave Burbank (91504) **(P-20562)**
Crane Co, Signal Hill *Also called Pacific Valves* **(P-13318)**
Crane Co ...... E......310 403-2820
13105 Saticoy St North Hollywood (91605) **(P-13326)**
Crane Co ...... F......707 748-7166
3948 Teal Ct Benicia (94510) **(P-18876)**
Crane Pro Services, Livermore *Also called Konecranes Inc* **(P-13849)**
Crane Valves Services Division, Benicia *Also called Crane Co* **(P-18876)**
Crane, John, Santa Fe Springs *Also called John Crane Inc* **(P-10973)**
Craneveyor Corp (PA) ...... D......626 442-1524
1524 Potrero Ave El Monte (91733) **(P-13845)**
Craneveyor Corp ...... E......909 627-6801
13730 Central Ave Chino (91710) **(P-12465)**
Craneworks Southwest Inc ...... E......760 735-9793
1312 E Barham Dr San Marcos (92078) **(P-13863)**
Crashcam Industries Corp ...... F......310 283-5379
19627 Vision Dr Topanga (90290) **(P-22412)**
Crate Modular Inc ...... D......310 405-0829
3025 E Dominguez St Carson (90810) **(P-12541)**
Cratex Manufacturing Co Inc ...... D......760 942-2877
328 Encinitas Blvd # 200 Encinitas (92024) **(P-10945)**
Crave Foods Inc ...... E......562 900-7272
2043 Imperial St Los Angeles (90021) **(P-952)**
Crawford Products Company Inc ...... F......323 721-6429
409 N Park Ave Montebello (90640) **(P-8639)**
Cray Cluster Solutions, San Jose *Also called Appro International Inc* **(P-15006)**
Crazy Industries ...... E......619 270-9090
8675 Avenida Costa Norte San Diego (92154) **(P-22786)**
CRC Marketing Inc ...... F......562 624-3400
111 W Ocean Blvd Ste 800 Long Beach (90802) **(P-46)**
CRC Services LLC ...... F......888 848-4754
9200 Oakdale Ave Fl 9 Chatsworth (91311) **(P-47)**
Crcm, Long Beach *Also called CRC Marketing Inc* **(P-46)**
Crd Mfg Inc ...... F......714 871-3300
1539 W Orange Grove Ave A Orange (92868) **(P-11581)**
Creaform USA Inc ...... F......855 939-4446
2031 Main St Irvine (92614) **(P-15210)**
Creamer Printing Co ...... F......310 671-9491
1413 N La Brea Ave Inglewood (90302) **(P-6520)**
Creation Tech Calexico (HQ) ...... C......760 336-8543
1778 Zinetta Rd Ste A Calexico (92231) **(P-17856)**
Creation Tech Santa Clara Inc ...... B......408 235-7500
2801 Northwestern Pkwy Santa Clara (95051) **(P-17857)**
Creations Grdn Natural Fd Mkts ...... C......661 877-4280
24849 Anza Dr Valencia (91355) **(P-7651)**

Employee Codes: A=Over 500 employees, B=251-500
C=101-250, D=51-100, E=20-50, F=10-19

2020 California
Manfacturers Register

© Mergent Inc. 1-800-342-5647

1071

A
L
P
H
A
B
E
T
I
C

Creations Salon, Irvine *Also called Elafree Inc (P-23326)*
Creative Age Publications Inc ....E....818 782-7328
7628 Densmore Ave Van Nuys (91406) *(P-5912)*
Creative Automation, Sun Valley *Also called Jack J Engel Manufacturing Inc (P-19331)*
Creative Color Printing Inc ....F....951 737-4551
1605 Railroad St Corona (92880) *(P-6521)*
Creative Computer Products ....F....858 458-1965
6369 Ncy Rdge Dr Ste 200 San Diego (92121) *(P-9733)*
Creative Concepts and Design ....F....707 812-9320
8460 Freedom Ln Winters (95694) *(P-4023)*
Creative Concepts Holdings LLC (HQ) ....F....949 705-6584
580 Garcia Ave Pittsburg (94565) *(P-2201)*
Creative Costuming Designs Inc ....E....714 895-0982
15402 Electronic Ln Huntington Beach (92649) *(P-2679)*
Creative Design Industries ....C....619 710-2525
2587 Otay Center Dr San Diego (92154) *(P-2987)*
Creative Electron Inc ....F....760 752-1192
201 Trade St San Marcos (92078) *(P-20563)*
Creative Extruded Products, West Covina *Also called Yogi Investments Inc (P-10134)*
Creative Foods LLC ....E....858 748-0070
12622 Poway Rd A Poway (92064) *(P-2434)*
Creative Graphic Services, Santa Clarita *Also called Living Way Industries Inc (P-23148)*
Creative Image Systems Inc ....F....909 947-8588
1921 E Acacia St Ontario (91761) *(P-8475)*
Creative Impressions Inc ....E....714 521-4441
7697 9th St Buena Park (90621) *(P-9399)*
Creative Industries, El Cajon *Also called Fuzetron Inc (P-14469)*
Creative Industry Handbooks, Toluca Lake *Also called Gmm Inc (P-6244)*
Creative Inflatables, South El Monte *Also called Promotonal Design Concepts Inc (P-9360)*
Creative Intgrated Systems Inc ....E....949 261-6577
1700 E Garry Ave Ste 112 Santa Ana (92705) *(P-18185)*
Creative Intl Pastries ....E....415 255-1128
950 Illinois St San Francisco (94107) *(P-1182)*
Creative Machine Technology, Corona *Also called Cremach Tech Inc (P-13906)*
Creative Machine Technology, Corona *Also called Cremach Tech Inc (P-13907)*
Creative Metal Products Corp ....F....408 281-0797
6284 San Ignacio Ave D San Jose (95119) *(P-15869)*
Creative Mfg Solutions ....E....408 327-0600
18400 Sutter Blvd Morgan Hill (95037) *(P-12167)*
Creative Outdoor Distrs USA, Lake Forest *Also called Cod USA Inc (P-4854)*
Creative Pathways Inc ....E....310 530-1965
20815 Higgins Ct Torrance (90501) *(P-14239)*
Creative Plastic Printing, San Diego *Also called Creative Computer Products (P-9733)*
Creative Press LLC ....D....714 774-5060
1600 E Ball Rd Anaheim (92805) *(P-6522)*
Creative Shower Door Corp ....F....510 623-9000
43652 S Grimmer Blvd Fremont (94538) *(P-9583)*
Creative Sign Inc ....F....714 842-4343
17922 Lyons Cir Huntington Beach (92647) *(P-23083)*
Creative Stone Mfg Inc (PA) ....C....909 357-8295
11191 Calabash Ave Fontana (92337) *(P-10557)*
Creative Teaching Press Inc (PA) ....D....714 799-2100
6262 Katella Ave Cypress (90630) *(P-6094)*
Creative Wood Products Inc ....C....510 635-5399
900 77th Ave Oakland (94621) *(P-4793)*
Credence Id LLC ....E....888 243-5452
5801 Christie Ave Ste 500 Emeryville (94608) *(P-17496)*
Creekside Managed Care ....F....707 578-0399
879 2nd St Santa Rosa (95404) *(P-7856)*
Creftcon Industries Inc ....C....203 377-5944
900 Ajax Ave City of Industry (91748) *(P-16944)*
Creganna - Tactx Medical, Campbell *Also called Tactx Medical Inc (P-21922)*
Crellin Machine Company ....E....323 225-8101
114 W Elmyra St Los Angeles (90012) *(P-12626)*
Cremach Tech Inc (PA) ....D....951 735-3194
369 Meyer Cir Corona (92879) *(P-13906)*
Cremach Tech Inc ....E....951 735-3194
400 E Parkridge Ave Corona (92879) *(P-13907)*
Cremax U S A Corporation ....F....626 956-8800
11740 Clark St Arcadia (91006) *(P-11582)*
Crenshaw Die and Mfg Corp ....D....949 475-5505
7432 Prince Dr Huntington Beach (92647) *(P-12789)*
Creo Inc ....F....530 756-1477
50 Fullerton Ct Ste 107 Sacramento (95825) *(P-7040)*
Crescent Inc ....E....714 992-6030
1196 N Osprey Cir Anaheim (92807) *(P-6523)*
Crescent Plastics Inc ....F....626 359-9248
1711 S California Ave Monrovia (91016) *(P-9734)*
Crescent Woodworking Co Ltd ....F....909 673-9955
400 Ramona Ave Ste 212 Corona (92879) *(P-4562)*
Cresco Manufacturing Inc ....E....714 525-2326
1614 N Orangethorpe Way Anaheim (92801) *(P-15870)*
Crescomfg.com, Anaheim *Also called Cresco Manufacturing Inc (P-15870)*
Crest Beverage LLC ....B....858 452-2300
8870 Liquid Ct San Diego (92121) *(P-691)*
Crest Coating Inc ....D....714 635-7090
1361 S Allec St Anaheim (92805) *(P-13162)*
Crestec Los Angeles, Long Beach *Also called Crestec Usa Inc (P-6524)*
Crestec Usa Inc ....E....310 327-9000
2410 Mira Mar Ave Long Beach (90815) *(P-6524)*
Crestmark Architectural Mill ....E....707 822-4034
5640 West End Rd Arcata (95521) *(P-4024)*
Crestone LLC ....E....323 588-8857
1852 E 46th St Vernon (90058) *(P-3477)*
Crew Knitwear LLC (PA) ....D....323 526-3888
660 S Myers St Los Angeles (90023) *(P-3309)*
Crew Wine Company LLC ....F....530 662-1032
12300 County Rd 92b Zamora (95698) *(P-1654)*

CRGsynergy ....E....415 497-0182
21 Commercial Blvd Ste 14 Novato (94949) *(P-20790)*
Cri 2000 LP (PA) ....D....619 542-1975
2245 San Diego Ave # 125 San Diego (92110) *(P-4499)*
Cri Sub 1 (HQ) ....F....310 537-1657
1715 S Anderson Ave Compton (90220) *(P-4794)*
Cricket Company LLC ....E....415 475-4150
68 Leveroni Ct Ste 200 Novato (94949) *(P-9298)*
Crimson Resource Management, Bakersfield *Also called Delta Trading LP (P-9089)*
Crimson Resource MGT Corp ....E....303 892-8878
5001 California Ave # 206 Bakersfield (93309) *(P-48)*
Crinetics Pharmaceuticals Inc ....E....858 450-6464
10222 Barnes Canyon Rd # 200 San Diego (92121) *(P-7857)*
Crisi Medical Systems Inc ....F....858 754-8640
9191 Towne Centre Dr # 330 San Diego (92122) *(P-7858)*
Crisol Metal Finishing ....F....310 516-1165
444 E Gardena Blvd C Gardena (90248) *(P-12980)*
Crispin Cider Works, The, Colfax *Also called Crispinian Inc (P-1515)*
Crispinian Inc ....E....530 346-8411
1213 S Auburn St Ste A Colfax (95713) *(P-1515)*
Crissair Inc ....C....661 367-3300
28909 Avenue Williams Valencia (91355) *(P-15627)*
Cristal Materials Inc ....F....323 855-1688
6825 Mckinley Ave Los Angeles (90001) *(P-4716)*
Cristek Interconnects Inc (PA) ....C....714 696-5200
5395 E Hunter Ave Anaheim (92807) *(P-18762)*
Criterion Automation Inc ....F....951 683-2400
1722 Production Cir Riverside (92509) *(P-11126)*
Criterion Composites Inc ....F....714 554-2717
14349 Commerce Dr Garden Grove (92843) *(P-20392)*
Critical Io LLC ....F....949 553-2200
36 Executive Park Ste 150 Irvine (92614) *(P-15211)*
Criticalpoint Capital LLC ....D....909 987-9533
9433 Hyssop Dr Rancho Cucamonga (91730) *(P-7628)*
Crittenden Publishing Inc (HQ) ....F....415 475-1522
45 Leveroni Ct Ste 204 Novato (94949) *(P-6217)*
Criveller California Corp ....F....707 431-2211
185 Grant Ave Healdsburg (95448) *(P-14357)*
Crl, Vernon *Also called C R Laurence Co Inc (P-19604)*
Crl Systems Inc ....D....510 351-3500
14798 Wicks Blvd San Leandro (94577) *(P-17497)*
Crm Co LLC (PA) ....E....949 263-9100
1301 Dove St Ste 940 Newport Beach (92660) *(P-9261)*
Crockett Graphics Inc (PA) ....D....805 987-8577
980 Avenida Acaso Camarillo (93012) *(P-5215)*
Crome Gallery, North Hollywood *Also called Alco Tech Inc (P-12762)*
Crookshanks Sales Co Inc ....E....559 992-5077
2375 Dairy Ave Corcoran (93212) *(P-10751)*
Crosno Construction Inc ....E....805 343-7437
819 Sheridan Rd Arroyo Grande (93420) *(P-12014)*
Crossbar Inc ....E....408 884-0281
3200 Patrick Henry Dr # 110 Santa Clara (95054) *(P-18186)*
Crossfield Products Corp (PA) ....E....310 886-9100
3000 E Harcourt St Compton (90221) *(P-7551)*
Crossing Automation Inc (HQ) ....E....510 661-5000
46702 Bayside Pkwy Fremont (94538) *(P-14444)*
Crossing Press, The, Emeryville *Also called Elaine Gill Inc (P-6100)*
Crossport Mocean ....F....949 646-1701
1611 Babcock St Newport Beach (92663) *(P-2962)*
Crossroads Recycled Lumber LLC ....F....559 877-3645
58500 Hancock Way North Fork (93643) *(P-3931)*
Crossroads Software Inc ....F....714 990-6433
210 W Birch St Ste 207 Brea (92821) *(P-23782)*
Crowdoptic, San Francisco *Also called Kba2 Inc (P-24073)*
Crowdstrike Holdings Inc (PA) ....C....888 512-8906
150 Mathilda Pl Ste 300 Sunnyvale (94086) *(P-23783)*
Crower Cams, San Diego *Also called Crower Engrg & Sls Co Inc (P-19624)*
Crower Engrg & Sls Co Inc ....C....619 690-7810
6180 Business Center Ct San Diego (92154) *(P-19624)*
Crown Carton Company Inc ....E....323 582-3053
1820 E 48th Pl Vernon (90058) *(P-5216)*
Crown Circuits Inc ....D....949 922-0144
6070 Avenida Encinas Carlsbad (92011) *(P-17858)*
Crown Citrus Company Inc ....F....760 344-1930
551 W Main St Brawley (92227) *(P-908)*
Crown Equipment Corporation ....E....559 585-8000
1355 E Fntana Ave Ste 102 Fresno (93725) *(P-13864)*
Crown Equipment Corporation ....D....626 968-0556
1300 Palomares St La Verne (91750) *(P-13865)*
Crown Equipment Corporation ....C....909 923-8357
4250 Greystone Dr Ontario (91761) *(P-13866)*
Crown Equipment Corporation ....E....510 471-7272
1400 Crocker Ave Hayward (94544) *(P-13867)*
Crown Equipment Corporation ....E....916 373-8980
1420 Enterprise Blvd West Sacramento (95691) *(P-13868)*
Crown Equipment Corporation ....D....310 952-6600
4061 Via Oro Ave Long Beach (90810) *(P-13869)*
Crown Fashion, Los Angeles *Also called Grand West Inc (P-2789)*
Crown Lift Trucks, La Verne *Also called Crown Equipment Corporation (P-13865)*
Crown Lift Trucks, Ontario *Also called Crown Equipment Corporation (P-13866)*
Crown Lift Trucks, Hayward *Also called Crown Equipment Corporation (P-13867)*
Crown Lift Trucks, West Sacramento *Also called Crown Equipment Corporation (P-13868)*
Crown Lift Trucks, Long Beach *Also called Crown Equipment Corporation (P-13869)*
Crown Mfg Co Inc ....E....510 742-8800
37625 Sycamore St Newark (94560) *(P-9735)*
Crown Micro, Fremont *Also called Bold Data Technology Inc (P-14892)*
Crown Pallet Company Inc ....E....626 937-6565
15151 Salt Lake Ave La Puente (91746) *(P-4359)*

ALPHABETIC SECTION Cummins Pacific LLC

Crown Paper Converting Inc....E....909 923-5226
1380 S Bon View Ave Ontario (91761) ***(P-5503)***

Crown Poly Inc....C....323 268-1298
5700 Bickett St Huntington Park (90255) ***(P-5393)***

Crown Printers, San Bernardino *Also called Shorett Printing Inc* ***(P-7212)***

Crown Printers Anaheim, San Bernardino *Also called Shorett Printing Inc* ***(P-6861)***

Crown Products Inc....E....760 471-1188
177 Newport Dr Ste A San Marcos (92069) ***(P-12168)***

Crown Steel, San Marcos *Also called Crown Products Inc* ***(P-12168)***

Crown Technical Systems....C....951 332-4170
13470 Philadelphia Ave Fontana (92337) ***(P-16591)***

CRP Sports LLC....F....949 395-7759
3191 Red Hill Ave Ste 250 Costa Mesa (92626) ***(P-23307)***

Crucial Power Products....F....323 721-5017
14000 S Broadway Los Angeles (90061) ***(P-18877)***

Crush Master Grinding Corp....E....909 595-2249
755 Penarth Ave Walnut (91789) ***(P-15871)***

Crydom Inc (HQ)....B....619 210-1590
2320 Paseo Delas Amer 2 San Diego (92154) ***(P-16709)***

Cryoatlanta, Irvine *Also called Cryognic Inds Svc Cmpanies LLC* ***(P-14565)***

Cryogenic Experts, Oxnard *Also called Acme Cryogenics Inc* ***(P-14417)***

Cryogenic Machinery Corp....F....818 765-6688
7306 Greenbush Ave North Hollywood (91605) ***(P-14445)***

Cryognic Inds Svc Cmpanies LLC (HQ)....F....949 261-7533
1851 Kaiser Ave Irvine (92614) ***(P-14565)***

Cryopacific Incorporated....F....562 697-7904
641 S Palm St Ste G La Habra (90631) ***(P-23308)***

Cryoport Systems Inc (HQ)....F....949 540-7204
17305 Daimler St Irvine (92614) ***(P-14446)***

Cryoquip LLC (HQ)....F....951 677-2060
25720 Jefferson Ave Murrieta (92562) ***(P-14447)***

Cryostar USA, Whittier *Also called Messer LLC* ***(P-7421)***

Cryostar USA LLC....E....562 903-1290
13117 Meyer Rd Whittier (90605) ***(P-14566)***

Cryoworks Inc....E....951 360-0920
3309 Grapevine St Mira Loma (91752) ***(P-13465)***

Cryptic Studios Inc....D....408 399-1969
980 University Ave Los Gatos (95032) ***(P-22669)***

Cryst Mark Inc A Swan Techno C....E....818 240-7520
613 Justin Ave Glendale (91201) ***(P-14448)***

Crystal Bottling Company Inc....D....916 568-3300
8631 Younger Creek Dr Sacramento (95828) ***(P-2066)***

Crystal Cal Lab Inc....E....714 991-1580
3981 E Miraloma Ave Anaheim (92806) ***(P-18878)***

Crystal Craft, La Verne *Also called Pf Plastics Inc* ***(P-4770)***

Crystal Cream & Butter Co (HQ)....D....916 444-7200
8340 Belvedere Ave Sacramento (95826) ***(P-692)***

Crystal Dynamics Inc (HQ)....D....650 421-7600
1400a Saport Blvd Ste 300 Redwood City (94063) ***(P-23784)***

Crystal Engineering Corp....E....805 595-5477
708 Fiero Ln Ste 9 San Luis Obispo (93401) ***(P-20853)***

Crystal Geyser Alpine Spring W, Olancha *Also called Cg Roxane LLC* ***(P-2054)***

Crystal Geyser Water Company....E....707 647-4410
5001 Fermi Dr Fairfield (94534) ***(P-2067)***

Crystal Geyser Water Company....E....661 323-6296
1233 E California Ave Bakersfield (93307) ***(P-2068)***

Crystal Geyser Water Company....F....661 321-0896
2351 E Brundage Ln Ste A Bakersfield (93307) ***(P-2069)***

Crystal Lighting Corp....F....562 944-0223
13182 Flores St Santa Fe Springs (90670) ***(P-17022)***

Crystal Mark, Glendale *Also called Cryst Mark Inc A Swan Techno C* ***(P-14448)***

Crystal Mining Corporation....F....386 479-5823
20380 Stevens Creek Blvd Cupertino (95014) ***(P-2)***

Crystal Mountain Springwater, Sacramento *Also called Crystal Bottling Company Inc* ***(P-2066)***

Crystal Technology, Fremont *Also called Gooch & Housego Palo Alto LLC* ***(P-18926)***

Crystal Tex Shoehorn, Downey *Also called Van Grace Quality Injection* ***(P-10109)***

Crystal Tip, Irvine *Also called Westside Resources Inc* ***(P-22206)***

Crystal Tips Holdings....E....800 944-3939
8850 Research Dr Irvine (92618) ***(P-9262)***

Crystal Vision Packg Systems, Torrance *Also called Aviation and Indus Dev Corp* ***(P-9394)***

Crystaliner Corp....E....949 548-0292
1626 Placentia Ave Costa Mesa (92627) ***(P-20319)***

Crystolon Inc....E....323 725-3482
7223 Sycamore St Commerce (90040) ***(P-4971)***

Cs Electronics, Irvine *Also called Cs Systems Inc* ***(P-15212)***

Cs Manfacturing Indus Svcs Inc (PA)....F....760 890-7746
619 Paulin Ave Ste 105 Calexico (92231) ***(P-18763)***

Cs Systems Inc....E....949 475-9100
16781 Noyes Ave Irvine (92606) ***(P-15212)***

CSC Ranch, Corcoran *Also called Crookshanks Sales Co Inc* ***(P-10751)***

Csdr International Inc....F....844 330-0664
7701 Woodley Ave Van Nuys (91406) ***(P-18187)***

CSDS, Sacramento *Also called California Surveying & Draftin* ***(P-15184)***

Csg, Lakeside *Also called Coating Services Group LLC* ***(P-13159)***

Csi Technologies Inc....F....760 682-2222
2540 Fortune Way Vista (92081) ***(P-18677)***

Csl Operating LLC....D....408 727-0893
529 Aldo Ave Santa Clara (95054) ***(P-12981)***

CSM Metal Fabricating & Engrg, Los Angeles *Also called Commercial Sheet Metal Works* ***(P-11770)***

Cspc Healthcare Inc....E....909 395-5272
1221 W State St Ontario (91762) ***(P-7859)***

Cspc Nutritionals, Ontario *Also called Cspc Healthcare Inc* ***(P-7859)***

Csr Technology Inc (HQ)....C....408 523-6500
1060 Rincon Cir San Jose (95131) ***(P-18879)***

CST Power and Construction Inc (HQ)....D....310 523-2322
879 W 190th St Ste 1100 Gardena (90248) ***(P-11257)***

CT Coachworks LLC....F....951 343-8787
9700 Indiana Ave Riverside (92503) ***(P-19841)***

CT Oldenkamp LLC....F....760 200-9510
78380 Clarke Ct La Quinta (92253) ***(P-23024)***

CTA Fixtures Inc....D....909 390-6744
5721 Santa Ana St Ste B Ontario (91761) ***(P-4894)***

CTA Manufacturing Inc....E....951 280-2400
1160 California Ave Corona (92881) ***(P-3656)***

Ctc Global Corporation (PA)....C....949 428-8500
2026 Mcgaw Ave Irvine (92614) ***(P-16889)***

Ctd Machines Inc....F....213 689-4455
7355 E Slauson Ave Commerce (90040) ***(P-13908)***

Ctf, Murrieta *Also called California Trusframe LLC* ***(P-4294)***

Ctg, Santa Barbara *Also called Alta Properties Inc* ***(P-10474)***

Ctg, Concord *Also called I3 Nanotec LLC* ***(P-14476)***

Ctg I LLC....F....415 233-9700
600 California St Fl 11 San Francisco (94108) ***(P-6218)***

CTI, Rancho Cordova *Also called Chemical Technologies Intl Inc* ***(P-15496)***

Cti-Controltech Inc....F....925 208-4250
22 Beta Ct San Ramon (94583) ***(P-16710)***

Ctra Industrial Machine....F....562 698-5188
11817 Slauson Ave Santa Fe Springs (90670) ***(P-14304)***

CTS Cement Manufacturing Corp (PA)....E....714 379-8260
12442 Knott St Garden Grove (92841) ***(P-8862)***

CTS Cement Manufacturing Corp....E....562 802-2660
13846 Firestone Blvd Santa Fe Springs (90670) ***(P-5435)***

CTS Cement Manufacturing Corp....F....310 472-4004
2077 Linda Flora Dr Los Angeles (90077) ***(P-8863)***

CTS Corporation....C....408 955-9001
2271 Ringwood Ave San Jose (95131) ***(P-17859)***

CTS Fabrication USA Inc....F....916 852-6303
11220 Pyrites Way Ste 300 Gold River (95670) ***(P-11214)***

CTS Printing....F....562 941-8420
9920 Jordan Cir Santa Fe Springs (90670) ***(P-6525)***

CTT Inc (PA)....D....408 541-0596
5870 Hellyer Ave Ste 70 San Jose (95138) ***(P-17498)***

Ctu Precast, Olivehurst *Also called Precast Con Tech Unlimited LLC* ***(P-10626)***

Cuadra Associates Inc (PA)....F....310 591-2490
3415 S Sepulveda Blvd # 3 Los Angeles (90034) ***(P-23785)***

Cuahutemoc Tortilleria....E....323 262-0410
3455 E 1st St Los Angeles (90063) ***(P-2435)***

Cubic Corporation (PA)....A....858 277-6780
9333 Balboa Ave San Diego (92123) ***(P-20564)***

Cubic Defense Applications Inc....C....858 505-2870
9333 Balboa Ave San Diego (92123) ***(P-19282)***

Cubic Defense Applications Inc (HQ)....A....858 277-6780
9333 Balboa Ave San Diego (92123) ***(P-19283)***

Cubic Trnsp Systems Inc (HQ)....A....858 268-3100
5650 Kearny Mesa Rd San Diego (92111) ***(P-21455)***

Cubic Trnsp Systems Inc....C....925 348-9163
1800 Sutter St Ste 900 Concord (94520) ***(P-21456)***

Cubic Zee Jewelry Inc....F....213 614-9800
728 S Hill St Ste 900 Los Angeles (90014) ***(P-22509)***

Cucamonga Division, Rancho Cucamonga *Also called Western Metal Dctg Co Coil Div* ***(P-6933)***

Cucina Holdings Inc....F....415 986-8688
4 Embarcadero Ctr Lbby 4 # 4 San Francisco (94111) ***(P-1183)***

Cuddly Toys....F....323 980-0572
1833 N Eastern Ave Los Angeles (90032) ***(P-22645)***

Cue Health Inc....E....256 651-1656
11175 Flintkote Ave San Diego (92121) ***(P-8217)***

Cuevas Mattress Inc....F....310 631-8382
3504 E Olympic Blvd Los Angeles (90023) ***(P-4717)***

Cuiti International, Rancho Cucamonga *Also called Ciuti International Inc* ***(P-1470)***

Culinary Brands Inc (PA)....D....626 289-3000
3280 E 44th St Vernon (90058) ***(P-953)***

Culinary Farms Inc....E....916 375-3000
1244 E Beamer St Woodland (95776) ***(P-848)***

Culinary International LLC (PA)....E....626 289-3000
3280 E 44th St Vernon (90058) ***(P-2436)***

Culinary Specialties Inc....D....760 744-8220
1231 Linda Vista Dr San Marcos (92078) ***(P-2437)***

Cult Cvlt....F....714 435-2858
1555 E Saint Gertrude Pl Santa Ana (92705) ***(P-20393)***

Culture AMP Inc (HQ)....E....415 326-8453
13949 Ventura Blvd Sherman Oaks (91423) ***(P-23786)***

Cultured Stone Corporation (HQ)....A....707 255-1727
Hwy 29 & Tower Rd NAPA (94559) ***(P-10558)***

Cummings Resources LLC....E....951 248-1130
1495 Columbia Ave Riverside (92507) ***(P-23084)***

Cummings Transportation, Shafter *Also called Cummings Vacuum Service Inc* ***(P-187)***

Cummings Vacuum Service Inc....D....661 746-1786
19605 Broken Ct Shafter (93263) ***(P-187)***

Cummins Aerospace, Anaheim *Also called Yeager Manufacturing Corp* ***(P-20272)***

Cummins Electrified Power NA (HQ)....F....408 624-1231
1181 Cadillac Ct Milpitas (95035) ***(P-19625)***

Cummins Pacific LLC....F....707 822-7392
5150 Boyd Rd Arcata (95521) ***(P-13585)***

Cummins Pacific LLC....F....530 244-6898
5125 Caterpillar Rd Redding (96003) ***(P-13586)***

Cummins Pacific LLC....E....916 371-0630
875 Riverside Pkwy West Sacramento (95605) ***(P-13587)***

Cummins Pacific LLC....E....866 934-4373
9520 Stewart And Gray Rd Downey (90241) ***(P-13588)***

Cummins Pacific LLC....E....909 877-0433
3061 S Riverside Ave Bloomington (92316) ***(P-13589)***

ALPHABETIC

Cummins Pacific LLC.....D.....559 277-6760
5333 N Cornelia Ave Fresno (93722) ***(P-13590)***
Cummins Pacific LLC.....E.....661 325-9404
4601 E Brundage Ln Bakersfield (93307) ***(P-13591)***
Cummins Pacific LLC (HQ).....D.....949 253-6000
1939 Deere Ave Irvine (92606) ***(P-13592)***
Cummins Pacific LLC.....E.....619 593-3093
310 N Johnson Ave El Cajon (92020) ***(P-13593)***
Cummins Pacific LLC.....E.....805 644-7281
3958 Transport St Ventura (93003) ***(P-13594)***
Cumulus Networks Inc (PA).....C.....650 383-6700
185 E Dana St Mountain View (94041) ***(P-23787)***
Cupertronix Inc.....F.....408 887-5455
2946 Via Torino Santa Clara (95051) ***(P-21212)***
Cura Medical Technologies LLC.....F.....949 939-4406
1365 S Acacia Ave Fullerton (92831) ***(P-22212)***
Curapharm Inc.....F.....619 449-7388
10054 Prospect Ave Ste A Santee (92071) ***(P-21675)***
Curation Foods Inc (HQ).....D.....800 454-1355
2811 Airpark Dr Santa Maria (93455) ***(P-2438)***
Curation Foods Inc.....F.....707 766-7511
1997 S Mcdwell Blvd Ste A Petaluma (94954) ***(P-2439)***
Curbell Plastics Inc.....E.....619 575-4633
1670 Brandywine Ave Ste B Chula Vista (91911) ***(P-9736)***
Cure Apparel LLC.....F.....562 927-7460
3338 S Malt Ave Commerce (90040) ***(P-3151)***
Cure Medical LLC (PA).....F.....800 570-1778
3471 Via Lido Ste 211 Newport Beach (92663) ***(P-21676)***
Curlin Healthcare Products Inc.....D.....714 893-2200
15751 Graham St Huntington Beach (92649) ***(P-15872)***
Curlin Medical Inc (HQ).....F.....714 897-9301
15662 Commerce Ln Huntington Beach (92649) ***(P-14567)***
Curran Engineering Company Inc.....E.....800 643-6353
28727 Industry Dr Valencia (91355) ***(P-12466)***
Current Ways Inc.....F.....619 596-3984
10221 Buena Vista Ave Santee (92071) ***(P-16784)***
Currie Enterprises.....E.....714 528-6957
382 N Smith Ave Corona (92880) ***(P-19626)***
Currie Machinery Co Inc.....D.....408 727-0422
1731 Cabana Dr San Jose (95125) ***(P-14358)***
Curry Graphics, Hayward *Also called Trade Only Screen Printing Inc* ***(P-7254)***
Curtco Media Group LLC.....F.....310 589-7700
29160 Heathercliff Rd # 1 Malibu (90265) ***(P-5913)***
Curtis Instruments Inc.....D.....925 961-1088
235 E Airway Blvd Livermore (94551) ***(P-20964)***
Curtis PMC, Livermore *Also called Curtis Instruments Inc* ***(P-20964)***
Curtis Technology Inc.....F.....858 453-5797
11391 Sorrento Valley Rd San Diego (92121) ***(P-18880)***
Curtis Winery, Los Olivos *Also called Firestone Vineyard LP* ***(P-1703)***
Curtiss-Wright Controls.....E.....714 982-1860
210 Ranger Ave Brea (92821) ***(P-21996)***
Curtiss-Wright Corporation.....E.....661 257-4430
28965 Avenue Penn Santa Clarita (91355) ***(P-13301)***
Curtiss-Wright Flow Control.....D.....949 271-7500
38 Executive Park Ste 350 Irvine (92614) ***(P-13302)***
Curtiss-Wright Flow Control.....C.....626 851-3100
28965 Avenue Penn Valencia (91355) ***(P-13303)***
Curve Line Metal Corporation.....F.....626 448-5956
9705 Klingerman St South El Monte (91733) ***(P-4689)***
Cushion Works.....F.....760 321-7808
68929 Perez Rd Ste B Cathedral City (92234) ***(P-3610)***
Cushion Works Inc.....F.....415 552-6220
3320 18th St San Francisco (94110) ***(P-3657)***
Custom AG Formulators Inc (PA).....D.....559 435-1052
3430 S Willow Ave Fresno (93725) ***(P-8825)***
Custom Aircraft Interiors Inc.....F.....562 426-5098
3701 Industry Ave Lakewood (90712) ***(P-20078)***
Custom Alloy Light Metals, City of Industry *Also called Custom Alloy Sales Inc* ***(P-11198)***
Custom Alloy Sales Inc (PA).....D.....626 369-3641
13191 Crssrds Pkwy N City of Industry (91746) ***(P-11198)***
Custom Art Services Corp.....F.....951 302-9889
37110 Mesa Rd Temecula (92592) ***(P-6526)***
Custom Aviation Supply, Chatsworth *Also called Custom Control Sensors LLC* ***(P-16592)***
Custom Blenders Corporation.....F.....510 635-4352
39 California Ave Ste 108 Pleasanton (94566) ***(P-8337)***
Custom Blow Molding, Escondido *Also called Pretium Packaging LLC* ***(P-9493)***
Custom Building Products Inc (HQ).....D.....800 272-8786
7711 Center Ave Ste 500 Huntington Beach (92647) ***(P-8864)***
Custom Building Products Inc.....D.....323 582-0846
6511 Salt Lake Ave Bell (90201) ***(P-8865)***
Custom Building Products Inc.....E.....209 983-8322
3525 Zephyr Ct Stockton (95206) ***(P-13725)***
Custom Characters Inc.....F.....818 507-5940
621 Thompson Ave Glendale (91201) ***(P-3549)***
Custom Chemical Formulators, Santa Fe Springs *Also called Morgan Gallacher Inc* ***(P-8397)***
Custom Chrome Manufacturing.....C.....408 825-5000
15750 Vineyard Blvd # 100 Morgan Hill (95037) ***(P-20394)***
Custom Coils Inc.....F.....707 752-8633
4000 Industrial Way Benicia (94510) ***(P-18710)***
Custom Control Sensors LLC (PA).....C.....818 341-4610
21111 Plummer St Chatsworth (91311) ***(P-16592)***
Custom Converting Inc.....F.....760 724-0664
2625 Temple Heights Dr C Oceanside (92056) ***(P-9520)***
Custom Cooperage Innerstave, Sonoma *Also called Innerstave LLC* ***(P-4416)***
Custom Crushing Industries.....F.....530 842-5544
2409 E Oberlin Rd Yreka (96097) ***(P-16)***
Custom Design Iron Works Inc.....F.....818 700-9182
9182 Kelvin Ave Chatsworth (91311) ***(P-11354)***
Custom Displays Inc.....E.....323 770-8074
411 W 157th St Gardena (90248) ***(P-4895)***
Custom Enamelers Inc.....E.....714 540-7884
18340 Mount Baldy Cir Fountain Valley (92708) ***(P-13163)***
Custom Engineering Plastics LP.....F.....858 452-0961
8558 Miramar Pl San Diego (92121) ***(P-9737)***
Custom Equipment Coinc.....F.....209 785-9891
90 Rock Creek Rd Ste 9 Copperopolis (95228) ***(P-13621)***
Custom Fabricated Metals LLC.....F.....909 822-8828
14580 Manzanita Dr Fontana (92335) ***(P-12588)***
Custom Fibreglass Mfg Co.....C.....562 432-5454
1711 Harbor Ave Long Beach (90813) ***(P-20483)***
Custom Foods, Santa Fe Springs *Also called J & J Processing Inc* ***(P-2217)***
Custom Framing Service, Van Nuys *Also called Kutzin & Kutzin Inc* ***(P-4511)***
Custom Furniture Design Inc.....E.....916 631-6300
3340 Sunrise Blvd Ste F Rancho Cordova (95742) ***(P-4184)***
Custom Goods Warehouse, Rancho Cucamonga *Also called Molex LLC* ***(P-18780)***
Custom Hardtops, Long Beach *Also called Custom Fibreglass Mfg Co* ***(P-20483)***
Custom Hardware Mfg Inc.....E.....714 547-7440
2112 E 4th St Ste 228g Santa Ana (92705) ***(P-11583)***
Custom Home Accessories, Rancho Cordova *Also called Penfield Products Inc* ***(P-12331)***
Custom Industries Inc.....E.....714 779-9101
1371 N Miller St Anaheim (92806) ***(P-10349)***
Custom Installations.....F.....619 445-0692
1452 Hawks Vista Ln Alpine (91901) ***(P-4185)***
Custom Label, Woodland *Also called Sachs Industries Inc* ***(P-5527)***
Custom Label and Decal LLC.....E.....510 876-0000
3392 Investment Blvd Hayward (94545) ***(P-7041)***
Custom Labeling & Btlg Corp.....F.....408 371-6171
15005 Concord Cir Morgan Hill (95037) ***(P-2070)***
Custom Leathercraft Mfg LLC (HQ).....E.....323 752-2221
10240 Alameda St South Gate (90280) ***(P-10246)***
Custom Lithograph.....E.....323 778-7751
7006 Stanford Ave Los Angeles (90001) ***(P-6527)***
Custom Marble & Onyx, Modesto *Also called Sharcar Enterprises Inc* ***(P-10930)***
Custom Mechanical Systems LLC.....F.....510 347-5500
1830 Embarcadero Ste 103 Oakland (94606) ***(P-15422)***
Custom Metal Finishing Corp.....E.....310 532-5075
17804 S Western Ave Gardena (90248) ***(P-14449)***
Custom Metal Works.....F.....714 953-5481
2233 W 2nd St Santa Ana (92703) ***(P-12467)***
Custom Mfg LLC.....F.....562 944-0245
12946 Los Nietos Rd Santa Fe Springs (90670) ***(P-12627)***
Custom Micro Machining Inc.....E.....510 651-9434
707 Brown Rd Fremont (94539) ***(P-15873)***
Custom Microwave Components.....F.....510 651-3434
44249 Old Warm Sprng Blvd Fremont (94538) ***(P-18881)***
Custom Molded Devices, Simi Valley *Also called Poly-Tainer Inc* ***(P-9492)***
Custom Muldings Sash Doors Inc.....F.....818 787-7367
7732 Densmore Ave Ste A Van Nuys (91406) ***(P-4025)***
Custom Pack Inc.....F.....714 534-2201
11621 Cardinal Cir Garden Grove (92843) ***(P-10287)***
Custom Packaging Design, Montclair *Also called Cpd Industries* ***(P-9519)***
Custom Pad and Partition Inc.....D.....408 970-9711
1100 Richard Ave Santa Clara (95050) ***(P-5217)***
Custom Paper Products.....D.....510 352-6880
2360 Teagarden St San Leandro (94577) ***(P-5187)***
Custom Pipe & Fabrication Inc (HQ).....D.....800 553-3058
10560 Fern Ave Stanton (90680) ***(P-13466)***
Custom Plastic Form Inc.....F.....818 765-2229
6868 Farmdale Ave North Hollywood (91605) ***(P-9738)***
Custom Plastics LLC (PA).....F.....909 984-0200
1305 Brooks St Ontario (91762) ***(P-9739)***
Custom Printing, Oxnard *Also called Pine Grove Industries Inc* ***(P-6782)***
Custom Quality Door & Trim Inc.....F.....951 278-0066
1116 Bradford Cir Corona (92882) ***(P-4026)***
Custom Quilting Inc.....E.....714 731-7271
2832 Walnut Ave Ste D Tustin (92780) ***(P-3611)***
Custom Sensors & Tech Inc (HQ).....D.....805 716-0322
1461 Lawrence Dr Thousand Oaks (91320) ***(P-18882)***
Custom Silicone Technologies, Pacoima *Also called Kdl Precision Molding Corp* ***(P-20477)***
Custom Source Design Inc.....F.....909 597-5221
15642 Dupont Ave Ste A Chino (91710) ***(P-11777)***
Custom Steel Fabrication Inc.....F.....562 907-2777
11966 Rivera Rd Santa Fe Springs (90670) ***(P-11778)***
Custom Tooling & Automation, Anaheim *Also called Custom Tooling & Stamping of O* ***(P-14039)***
Custom Tooling & Stamping of O.....F.....714 979-6782
1182 N Knollwood Cir Anaheim (92801) ***(P-14039)***
Custom Upholstered Furn Inc.....F.....323 731-3033
5000 W Jefferson Blvd Los Angeles (90016) ***(P-4635)***
Custom Wheels and ACC Inc.....F.....714 827-5200
41710 Reagan Way Murrieta (92562) ***(P-19627)***
Custom Window Design Inc.....E.....760 439-6213
3242 Production Ave Oceanside (92058) ***(P-4027)***
Custom Wire Products.....F.....619 469-2328
7580 North Ave Lemon Grove (91945) ***(P-13408)***
Custom Wood Products, Parlier *Also called John Daniel Gonzalez* ***(P-4418)***
Custom X Body Boards, Oceanside *Also called Superior Foam Products Inc* ***(P-22901)***
Customplanetcom Inc.....F.....760 508-2648
12180 Ridgecrest Rd # 314 Victorville (92395) ***(P-7042)***
Custopharm Inc (PA).....F.....760 683-0901
2325 Camino Vida Roble A Carlsbad (92011) ***(P-14450)***
Cut & Trim Inc.....F.....818 264-0101
20847 Betron St Woodland Hills (91364) ***(P-3152)***
Cut Loose (PA).....D.....415 822-2031
101 Williams Ave San Francisco (94124) ***(P-3310)***

Cutera Inc (PA)........C.......415 657-5500
3240 Bayshore Blvd Brisbane (94005) ***(P-22246)***
Cutie Pie Snack Pies, Lathrop *Also called Horizon Snack Foods Inc* ***(P-1343)***
Cutler-Hammer, Jurupa Valley *Also called Eaton Corporation* ***(P-19301)***
Cutter Lumber Products........E.......209 982-4477
4004 S El Dorado St Stockton (95206) ***(P-4360)***
Cutting Edge Creative LLC........D.......562 907-7007
8155 Byron Rd Whittier (90606) ***(P-4972)***
Cutting Edge Machining Inc (PA)........E.......408 738-8677
1331 Old County Rd Ste A Belmont (94002) ***(P-12628)***
Cutting Edge Supply, Colton *Also called Black Diamond Blade Company* ***(P-13710)***
Cutwater Spirits LLC........E.......858 672-3848
9750 Distribution Ave San Diego (92121) ***(P-8956)***
Cv Ice Company Inc........E.......760 347-3529
83796 Date Ave Indio (92201) ***(P-2353)***
Cv of Riverside, Riverside *Also called CV Wndows Dors Riverside Inc* ***(P-10350)***
Cv Sciences Inc (PA)........E.......866 290-2157
10070 Barnes Canyon Rd # 10 San Diego (92121) ***(P-7652)***
CV Wndows Dors Riverside Inc........E.......951 784-8766
6676 Lance Dr Riverside (92507) ***(P-10350)***
Cvag, Oakdale *Also called Central Valley AG Grinding Inc* ***(P-998)***
Cvc Audio & Video Supply Inc........F.......714 526-5725
3845 S Main St Santa Ana (92707) ***(P-19213)***
Cvc Specialties, Vernon *Also called Continental Vitamin Co Inc* ***(P-7849)***
Cvc Technologies Inc........E.......909 355-0311
10861 Business Dr Fontana (92337) ***(P-14705)***
Cvps Inc........E.......707 998-9364
9514 Glenhaven Dr Glenhaven (95443) ***(P-23788)***
Cvr Nitrogen LP (HQ)........F.......310 571-9800
10877 Wilshire Blvd Fl 10 Los Angeles (90024) ***(P-8791)***
Cw Industries........F.......562 432-5421
1735 Santa Fe Ave Long Beach (90813) ***(P-11779)***
CW Welding Service Inc (PA)........E.......562 432-5421
1735 Santa Fe Ave Long Beach (90813) ***(P-24628)***
Cwi Trading........F.......209 981-7023
714 Elaine Dr Stockton (95207) ***(P-16945)***
Cwic, Rcho STA Marg *Also called Chapmn-Wlters Intrcoastal Corp* ***(P-22781)***
Cwr Labs, San Jose *Also called Cpacket Networks Inc* ***(P-15209)***
Cws, Orange *Also called Coil Winding Specialist Inc* ***(P-18707)***
Cws Beverage........F.......805 286-2735
2732 Danley Ct Ste 101 Paso Robles (93446) ***(P-1516)***
CWT, Los Angeles *Also called Clean Water Technology Inc* ***(P-15500)***
Cxc Simulations LLC........F.......888 918-2010
3160 W El Segundo Blvd Hawthorne (90250) ***(P-19284)***
Cy Truss........E.......559 888-2160
10715 E American Ave Del Rey (93616) ***(P-4298)***
Cyber Mdia Solutions Ltd Lblty........E.......877 480-8255
25361 Commercentre Dr # 250 Lake Forest (92630) ***(P-23789)***
Cyber Medical Imaging Inc........E.......888 937-9729
11300 W Olympic Blvd # 710 Los Angeles (90064) ***(P-22140)***
Cyber Press, Santa Clara *Also called Nss Enterprises* ***(P-6754)***
Cyber Switching Inc........E.......408 595-3670
2050 Ringwood Ave Frnt San Jose (95131) ***(P-19285)***
Cyberdata Corporation........E.......831 373-2601
3 Justin Ct Monterey (93940) ***(P-15213)***
Cyberinc Corporation (HQ)........E.......925 242-0777
4000 Executive Pkwy # 250 San Ramon (94583) ***(P-23790)***
Cyberlinkcom Corp........F.......408 217-1850
1073 S Winchester Blvd San Jose (95128) ***(P-23791)***
Cybernet Manufacturing Inc........A.......949 600-8000
5 Holland Ste 201 Irvine (92618) ***(P-14902)***
Cybernetic Micro Systems Inc........F.......650 726-3000
3000 La Honda Rd San Gregorio (94074) ***(P-15121)***
Cybertech, Pomona *Also called Bio Cybernetics International* ***(P-21985)***
Cybertouch, Newbury Park *Also called Transparent Devices Inc* ***(P-15354)***
Cyberware Laboratory Inc........F.......831 484-1064
12835 Corte Cordillera Salinas (93908) ***(P-20854)***
Cybortronics Incorporated........F.......949 855-2814
470 Nibus Brea (92821) ***(P-21213)***
Cybrex Consulting Inc........D.......513 999-2109
4470 W Sunset Blvd Los Angeles (90027) ***(P-23792)***
Cycle House LLC........E.......310 358-0888
8511 Melrose Ave West Hollywood (90069) ***(P-22787)***
Cycle News Inc (PA)........E.......949 863-7082
17771 Mitchell N Irvine (92614) ***(P-5604)***
Cycle Shack Inc........D.......650 583-7014
816 Murchison Dr Millbrae (94030) ***(P-20395)***
Cycle World Magazine, Irvine *Also called Hearst Corporation* ***(P-5951)***
Cydea Inc........E.......800 710-9939
8510 Miralani Dr San Diego (92126) ***(P-1517)***
Cydwoq Inc........E.......818 848-8307
2102 Kenmere Ave Burbank (91504) ***(P-10150)***
Cygnet Aerospace Corp........F.......805 528-2376
1971 Fearn Ave Los Osos (93402) ***(P-11374)***
Cygnet Stampng & Fabrictng Inc........F.......818 240-7574
916 Western Ave Glendale (91201) ***(P-12790)***
Cygnet Stampng & Fabrictng Inc (PA)........E.......818 240-7574
613 Justin Ave Glendale (91201) ***(P-12791)***
Cylance Inc (HQ)........C.......949 375-3380
400 Spectrum Center Dr Irvine (92618) ***(P-23793)***
Cylinder Division, Corona *Also called Parker-Hannifin Corporation* ***(P-15634)***
Cylinder Head Exchange Inc........F.......818 364-2371
12677 San Fernando Rd Sylmar (91342) ***(P-19628)***
Cymabay Therapeutics Inc (PA)........E.......510 293-8800
7575 Gateway Blvd Ste 110 Newark (94560) ***(P-7860)***
Cymer LLC (HQ)........A.......858 385-7300
17075 Thornmint Ct San Diego (92127) ***(P-19286)***
Cymmetria Inc........E.......415 568-6870
2557 Park Blvd Apt L106 Palo Alto (94306) ***(P-23794)***
Cynergy3 Components Corp (PA)........F.......858 715-7200
2475 Pseo De Las Americas San Diego (92154) ***(P-16711)***
Cynthia Garcia........F.......714 897-4654
11782 Western Ave Ste 7 Stanton (90680) ***(P-20079)***
Cypress Furniture Inc........F.......510 723-4890
26602 Corporate Ave Hayward (94545) ***(P-4563)***
Cypress Grove Chevre Inc........D.......707 825-1100
1330 Q St Arcata (95521) ***(P-545)***
Cypress Magnetics Inc........F.......909 987-3570
8753 Industrial Ln Rancho Cucamonga (91730) ***(P-18711)***
Cypress Manufacturing LLC........F.......818 477-2777
25620 Rye Canyon Rd Ste B Valencia (91355) ***(P-9740)***
Cypress Ridge Winery, King City *Also called Delicato Vineyards* ***(P-1662)***
Cypress Semiconductor Corp........F.......408 943-2600
195 Champion Ct Bldg 2 San Jose (95134) ***(P-18188)***
Cypress Semiconductor Corp (PA)........A.......408 943-2600
198 Champion Ct San Jose (95134) ***(P-18189)***
Cypress Semiconductor Intl Inc (PA)........E.......408 943-2600
4001 N 1st St San Jose (95134) ***(P-18190)***
Cypress Sponge Rubber Products........F.......714 546-6464
301 Goetz Ave Santa Ana (92707) ***(P-9299)***
Cyron Inc........F.......818 772-1900
21029 Itasca St Ste C Chatsworth (91311) ***(P-17114)***
Cytec Aerospace Mtls CA Inc........C.......714 899-0400
851 W 18th St Costa Mesa (92627) ***(P-2896)***
Cytec Engineered Materials, Costa Mesa *Also called Cytec Aerospace Mtls CA Inc* ***(P-2896)***
Cytec Engineered Materials Inc........E.......714 632-8444
1191 N Hawk Cir Anaheim (92807) ***(P-7552)***
Cytec Engineered Materials Inc........C.......714 630-9400
645 N Cypress St Orange (92867) ***(P-7553)***
Cytec Engineered Materials Inc........C.......714 632-1174
1440 N Kraemer Blvd Anaheim (92806) ***(P-11375)***
Cytek Biosciences Inc (PA)........D.......510 657-0110
46107 Landing Pkwy Fremont (94538) ***(P-22247)***
Cytek Development Inc........F.......510 657-0102
4059 Clipper Ct Fremont (94538) ***(P-21214)***
Cytobank Inc........F.......650 918-7966
3945 Freedom Cir Ste 540 Santa Clara (95054) ***(P-23795)***
Cytokinetics Incorporated (PA)........C.......650 624-3000
280 E Grand Ave South San Francisco (94080) ***(P-7861)***
Cytomx Therapeutics Inc........C.......650 515-3185
151 Oyster Point Blvd # 40 South San Francisco (94080) ***(P-7862)***
Cytrx Corporation (PA)........E.......310 826-5648
11726 San Vicente Blvd # 650 Los Angeles (90049) ***(P-8292)***
Cytydel Plastics Inc........E.......310 523-2884
17813 S Main St Ste 117 Gardena (90248) ***(P-9741)***
Cyu Lithographics Inc........E.......888 878-9898
6951 Oran Cir Buena Park (90621) ***(P-6528)***
Cyvex Nutrition Inc........F.......949 622-9030
8141 E Kaiser Blvd # 180 Anaheim (92808) ***(P-584)***
D & B Precision Shtmtl Inc........F.......209 848-3030
693 Hi Tech Pkwy Oakdale (95361) ***(P-12169)***
D & B Supply Corp........F.......714 632-3020
1189 N Grove St Ste A Anaheim (92806) ***(P-13820)***
D & D Cbnets - Svage Dsgns Inc........E.......530 634-9713
1478 Sky Harbor Dr Olivehurst (95961) ***(P-4186)***
D & D Engineering, Turlock *Also called Donald H Binkley* ***(P-11786)***
D & D Gear Incorporated........C.......714 692-6570
4890 E La Palma Ave Anaheim (92807) ***(P-20080)***
D & D Gold Product Corp........F.......714 550-0372
11608 Quartz Ave Fl 2 Fountain Valley (92708) ***(P-999)***
D & D Motorcycle Service Inc........E.......323 567-9480
10401 Alameda St Lynwood (90262) ***(P-20396)***
D & D Plastics Incorporated........F.......310 515-1934
1632 W 139th St Gardena (90249) ***(P-9742)***
D & D Security Resources Inc (PA)........F.......800 453-4195
200 Mason Cir Ste C Concord (94520) ***(P-19287)***
D & D Technologies (usa) Inc........F.......714 677-1300
17531 Metzler Ln Huntington Beach (92647) ***(P-11584)***
D & D Technologies USA Inc........E.......949 852-5140
17531 Metzler Ln Huntington Beach (92647) ***(P-11087)***
D & F Standler Inc........F.......408 226-8188
195 Lewis Rd Ste 39 San Jose (95111) ***(P-15874)***
D & G Manufacturing, Signal Hill *Also called Flex-Mate Inc* ***(P-11529)***
D & H Trucking Equipment, San Diego *Also called Jjs Truck Equipment LLC* ***(P-19539)***
D & J Printing Inc........D.......661 775-4586
600 W Technology Dr Palmdale (93551) ***(P-6529)***
D & K Concrete Co, Fontana *Also called Dennie Manning Concrete Inc* ***(P-10752)***
D & L Moulding and Lumber Co........F.......626 444-0134
1044 N Soldano Ave Azusa (91702) ***(P-4028)***
D & L Pallet Company, Ontario *Also called Hannibal Lafayette* ***(P-4369)***
D & M Draperies Inc........F.......626 256-1993
323 W Maple Ave Monrovia (91016) ***(P-3588)***
D & M Manufacturing........F.......559 834-4668
5400 S Villa Ave Fresno (93725) ***(P-13622)***
D & M Precision, Oxnard *Also called Mjolnir Industries LLC* ***(P-14078)***
D & M Steel Inc........E.......818 896-2070
13020 Pierce St Pacoima (91331) ***(P-11780)***
D & R Brothers Inc........E.......213 747-4309
952 S Broadway 2 Los Angeles (90015) ***(P-3153)***
D & S Custom Plating Inc........F.......714 537-5411
11552 Anabel Ave Garden Grove (92843) ***(P-19629)***
D & S Industries Inc........F.......714 779-8074
4515 E Eisenhower Cir Anaheim (92807) ***(P-20081)***
D & T Fiberglass Inc........E.......916 383-9012
8900 Osage Ave Sacramento (95828) ***(P-9743)***
D & T Machining Inc........F.......408 486-6035
3360 Victor Ct Santa Clara (95054) ***(P-15875)***

Employee Codes: A=Over 500 employees, B=251-500
C=101-250, D=51-100, E=20-50, F=10-19
2020 California
Manfacturers Register
© Mergent Inc. 1-800-342-5647
1075

D A C, Carpinteria *Also called Development Assoc Contrls* ***(P-13913)***
D A C, Carpinteria *Also called Dac International Inc* ***(P-13910)***
D A M Bindery Inc F 858 621-7000
7949 Stromesa Ct Ste B San Diego (92126) ***(P-7329)***
D and J Marketing Inc E 310 538-1583
580 W 184th St Gardena (90248) ***(P-3782)***
D Benham Corporation F 619 448-8079
10969 Wheatlands Ave A Santee (92071) ***(P-6530)***
D Bindery, Sacramento *Also called Sacramental Color Coil* ***(P-7347)***
D D N, Chatsworth *Also called Datadirect Networks Inc* ***(P-15020)***
D D Office Products Inc E 323 582-3400
5025 Hampton St Vernon (90058) ***(P-5101)***
D D Wire Co Inc (PA) E 626 442-0459
4335 Temple City Blvd Temple City (91780) ***(P-11781)***
D D Wire Co Inc F 626 285-0298
4942 Encinita Ave Temple City (91780) ***(P-11782)***
D Davis Enterprise, Davis *Also called McNaughton Newspapers* ***(P-5737)***
D E I, Santa Fe Springs *Also called Dynamic Enterprises Inc* ***(P-15914)***
D F Stauffer Biscuit Co Inc E 714 546-6855
4041 W Garry Ave Santa Ana (92704) ***(P-1311)***
D G A Mch Sp Blnchard Grinding, Riverside *Also called DGA Machine Shop Inc* ***(P-15892)***
D G Industries F 714 990-3787
226 Viking Ave Brea (92821) ***(P-13909)***
D G U Trading Corporation E 909 469-1288
1999 W Holt Ave Pomona (91768) ***(P-10351)***
D Goldenwest Inc E 310 564-2641
2700 Pacific Coast Hwy # 2 Torrance (90505) ***(P-1184)***
D Hauptman Co Inc E 323 734-2507
4856 W Jefferson Blvd Los Angeles (90016) ***(P-22788)***
D I Printing, Hidden Valley Lake *Also called Jensen Graphics & Printing* ***(P-6665)***
D J Simpson Company (PA) F 650 225-9404
401 S Canal St A South San Francisco (94080) ***(P-8640)***
D K Environmental, Vernon *Also called Demenno/Kerdoon Holdings* ***(P-9139)***
D L B Pallets (PA) F 951 360-9896
4510 Rutile St Riverside (92509) ***(P-4361)***
D L Stoy Logging Co F 530 283-3292
17302 Mountain View Rd Greenville (95947) ***(P-3878)***
D Laurence Gates Ltd E 925 736-8176
2671 Crow Canyon Rd San Ramon (94583) ***(P-3932)***
D Mills Grnding Machining Inc E 951 697-6847
6131 Quail Valley Ct Riverside (92507) ***(P-15876)***
D N G Cummings Inc E 650 593-8974
3580 Haven Ave Ste 1 Redwood City (94063) ***(P-23085)***
D P I, Porterville *Also called Distributors Processing Inc* ***(P-2203)***
D S McGee Enterprises Inc E 951 378-8473
3240 Trade Center Dr Riverside (92507) ***(P-4029)***
D W I, Chino *Also called Diamond Wipes Intl Inc* ***(P-8483)***
D W Mack Co Inc E 626 969-1817
900 W 8th St Azusa (91702) ***(P-9744)***
D X Communications Inc E 323 256-3000
8160 Van Nuys Blvd Panorama City (91402) ***(P-17499)***
D&A Metal Fabrication Inc F 818 780-8231
16129 Runnymede St Van Nuys (91406) ***(P-12170)***
D&A Unlimited Inc E 562 336-1528
2700 Rose Ave Ste J Signal Hill (90755) ***(P-3311)***
D&D Security Enterprises, Concord *Also called D & D Security Resources Inc* ***(P-19287)***
D&H / R&D, Fremont *Also called D&H Manufacturing Company* ***(P-23309)***
D&H Manufacturing, Fremont *Also called Celestica LLC* ***(P-18856)***
D&H Manufacturing Company F 510 770-5100
49235 Milmont Dr Fremont (94538) ***(P-23309)***
D&S Brewing Solutions Inc E 650 207-4524
6148 E Oakbrook St Long Beach (90815) ***(P-1518)***
D&W Fine Pack LLC C 206 767-7777
4162 Georgia Blvd San Bernardino (92407) ***(P-9745)***
D'Ambrosio Bros, Sunnyvale *Also called Fullfillment Systems Inc* ***(P-458)***
D'Lido Bakery, Los Angeles *Also called Galdaza Food Corporation* ***(P-1213)***
D-1280-X Inc F 310 835-6909
126 N Marine Ave Wilmington (90744) ***(P-9044)***
D-Mac Inc E 714 808-3918
1105 E Discovery Ln Anaheim (92801) ***(P-4443)***
D-Tech Optoelectronics Inc (HQ) E 626 956-1100
18062 Rowland St City of Industry (91748) ***(P-17723)***
D-Tek Manufacturing E 408 588-1574
3245 Woodward Ave Santa Clara (95054) ***(P-18191)***
D.F. Industries, Chino *Also called Dick Farrell Industries Inc* ***(P-14759)***
D3 Inc (PA) C 310 223-2200
3211 Jack Northrop Ave Hawthorne (90250) ***(P-4831)***
D3 Go, Encino *Also called D3publisher of America Inc* ***(P-23796)***
D3 Led LLC (PA) E 916 669-7408
11370 Sunrise Park Dr Rancho Cordova (95742) ***(P-23086)***
D3publisher of America Inc D 310 268-0820
15910 Ventura Blvd # 800 Encino (91436) ***(P-23796)***
Da Global Energy Inc F 408 916-6303
548 Market St Ste 32810 San Francisco (94104) ***(P-16858)***
Da Vinci Fine Food, La Mesa *Also called Ritas Fine Food* ***(P-2600)***
Da Vita Tustin Dialysis Ctr E 714 835-2450
2090 N Tustin Ave Ste 100 Santa Ana (92705) ***(P-21677)***
Da-Ly Glass Corp E 323 589-5461
1193 W 2nd St Pomona (91766) ***(P-10352)***
Da/Pro Rubber Inc D 661 775-6290
28635 Braxton Ave Valencia (91355) ***(P-9300)***
Daa Draexlmaier Auto Amer LLC D 864 485-1000
801 Challenger St Livermore (94551) ***(P-19630)***
Daaze Inc F 626 442-4961
1714 S Grove Ave Ste B Ontario (91761) ***(P-12171)***
Dabmar Lighting Inc (PA) E 805 604-9090
320 Graves Ave Oxnard (93030) ***(P-17115)***
Dac International Inc (PA) E 805 684-8307
6390 Rose Ln Carpinteria (93013) ***(P-13910)***
Dacon Systems Inc F 951 735-2100
1891 N Delilah St Corona (92879) ***(P-11299)***
Dacon Systems Inc F 310 842-9933
12915 S Spring St Los Angeles (90061) ***(P-11300)***
Dacor D 626 799-1000
14425 Clark Ave City of Industry (91745) ***(P-16808)***
Dacor F 626 799-1000
14425 Clark Ave City of Industry (91745) ***(P-16809)***
Dacor Purchasing Industry, City of Industry *Also called Dacor* ***(P-16809)***
Dadee Manufacturing LLC E 602 276-4390
911 N Poinsettia St Santa Ana (92701) ***(P-19525)***
Dae Shin Usa Inc D 714 578-8900
610 N Gilbert St Fullerton (92833) ***(P-2724)***
Dahlhauser Manufacturing Co E 408 988-3717
1855 Russell Ave Santa Clara (95054) ***(P-13409)***
Daily Breeze, Torrance *Also called Medianews Group Inc* ***(P-5742)***
Daily Californian, Berkeley *Also called Indepndent Brkley Stdnt Pubg I* ***(P-5671)***
Daily Computing Solutions Inc F 818 240-5400
3521 Foxglove Rd Glendale (91206) ***(P-5605)***
Daily Democrat, The, Woodland *Also called Medianews Group Inc* ***(P-5745)***
Daily Doses LLC E 858 220-0076
13150 Saticoy St North Hollywood (91605) ***(P-5606)***
Daily Graphics, Los Angeles *Also called Daily Graphs Inc* ***(P-5914)***
Daily Graphs Inc E 310 448-6843
12655 Beatrice St Los Angeles (90066) ***(P-5914)***
Daily Journal E 650 344-5200
1720 S Amphlett Blvd # 123 San Mateo (94402) ***(P-5607)***
Daily Journal Corporation (PA) C 213 229-5300
915 E 1st St Los Angeles (90012) ***(P-5608)***
Daily Journal Corporation D 415 296-2400
44 Montgomery St Ste 500 San Francisco (94104) ***(P-5609)***
Daily Midway Driller, Taft *Also called St Louis Post-Dispatch LLC* ***(P-5839)***
Daily News, Woodland Hills *Also called Medianews Group Inc* ***(P-5741)***
Daily News, Menlo Park *Also called Medianews Group Inc* ***(P-5744)***
Daily News, Valencia *Also called Medianews Group Inc* ***(P-5746)***
Daily Offrngs Cof Roastery LLC F 805 423-7410
475 W Agua Caliente Rd Sonoma (95476) ***(P-2286)***
Daily Press, Victorville *Also called Lmg National Publishing Inc* ***(P-5701)***
Daily Recorder F 916 444-2355
901 H St Ste 312 Sacramento (95814) ***(P-5610)***
Daily Republic, Fairfield *Also called McNaughton Newspapers Inc* ***(P-5738)***
Daily Review E 510 783-6111
3317 Arden Rd Hayward (94545) ***(P-5611)***
Daily Sports Seoul Usa Inc E 213 487-9331
626 S Kingsley Dr Los Angeles (90005) ***(P-5612)***
Dailymedia Inc (PA) F 541 821-5207
8 E Figueroa St Ste 220 Santa Barbara (93101) ***(P-5613)***
Dairy Conveyor Corp E 714 891-0883
15212 Connector Ln Huntington Beach (92649) ***(P-13821)***
Dairy Farmers America Inc F 951 493-4900
170 N Maple St Ste 106 Corona (92880) ***(P-693)***
Dairy Farmers America Inc D 805 653-0042
4375 N Ventura Ave Ventura (93001) ***(P-694)***
Dairy Farmers America Inc D 209 667-9627
600 Trade Way Turlock (95380) ***(P-546)***
Dairymens Feed & Sup Coop Assn F 707 763-1585
323 E Washington St Petaluma (94952) ***(P-1089)***
Daisy Publishing Company Inc D 661 295-1910
25233 Anza Dr Santa Clarita (91355) ***(P-5915)***
Daisy Scout Publishing F 714 630-6611
1200 N Barsten Way Anaheim (92806) ***(P-6219)***
Dakota AG Welding, Ripon *Also called Jackrabbit* ***(P-13639)***
Dakota Press F 510 895-1300
14400 Doolittle Dr San Leandro (94577) ***(P-7356)***
Dakota Press Inc F 510 895-1300
14400 Doolittle Dr San Leandro (94577) ***(P-6531)***
Dakota Ultrasonics Corporation F 831 431-9722
1500 Green Hills Rd # 107 Scotts Valley (95066) ***(P-21457)***
Dakotahouse Industries Inc F 310 596-1100
5262 Cartwright Ave Apt 4 North Hollywood (91601) ***(P-385)***
Dal-Tile Corporation F 858 565-7767
7865 Ostrow St San Diego (92111) ***(P-7635)***
Dal-Tile Corporation E 818 787-3224
16201 Stagg St Van Nuys (91406) ***(P-7636)***
Dal-Tile Corporation F 323 257-7553
3550 Tyburn St Los Angeles (90065) ***(P-7637)***
Dale Brisco Inc F 559 834-5926
2132 S Temperance Ave Fowler (93625) ***(P-12172)***
Dale Chavez Company Inc F 951 303-0592
35165 La Bonita Donna Temecula (92592) ***(P-10137)***
Dale Grove Corporation E 408 251-7220
1501 Stone Creek Dr San Jose (95132) ***(P-14359)***
Dale's Welding & Fabrication, Salinas *Also called Dales Welding Inc* ***(P-13623)***
Dales Welding Inc F 831 424-6583
1112 Abbott St A Salinas (93901) ***(P-13623)***
Dallas Electronics Inc E 831 457-3610
2151 Delaware Ave Ste A Santa Cruz (95060) ***(P-17860)***
Damac, Costa Mesa *Also called Bdfco Inc* ***(P-17715)***
Dameron Alloy Foundries (PA) D 310 631-5165
6330 Gateway Dr Ste B Cypress (90630) ***(P-11170)***
Dan Arens and Son Inc F 530 644-6307
5780 Ridgeway Dr Pollock Pines (95726) ***(P-3879)***
Dan Copp Crushing Corp E 714 777-6400
22765 Savi Ranch Pkwy E Yorba Linda (92887) ***(P-337)***
Dan Gurneys All Amercn Racers, Santa Ana *Also called All American Racers Inc* ***(P-20380)***

Mergent e-mail: customerrelations@mergent.com
1076
2020 California
Manufacturers Register
(P-0000) Products & Services Section entry number
(PA)=Parent Co (HQ)=Headquarters (DH)=Div Headquarters

Dan M Swofford F 530 343-9994
728 Cherry St Chico (95928) ***(P-5916)***

Dan R Hunt Inc F 714 850-9383
2030 S Susan St Santa Ana (92704) ***(P-15877)***

Dan-Loc Bolt & Gasket, Carson *Also called Dan-Loc Group LLC* ***(P-9226)***

Dan-Loc Group LLC D 310 538-2822
20444 Tillman Ave Carson (90746) ***(P-9226)***

Dan-Mar Custom Draperies, Monrovia *Also called D & M Draperies Inc* ***(P-3588)***

Dana Creath Designs Ltd E 714 662-0111
3030 Kilson Dr Santa Ana (92707) ***(P-17116)***

Dana Innovations D 949 492-7777
991 Calle Amanecer San Clemente (92673) ***(P-17216)***

Danaher Corporation C 951 652-6811
3255 W Stetson Ave Hemet (92545) ***(P-20965)***

Danair Inc (PA) F 559 734-1961
1150 E Acequia Ave Visalia (93292) ***(P-13911)***

Danbee Inc F 323 780-0077
3360 E Pico Blvd Los Angeles (90023) ***(P-3225)***

Danchuk Manufacturing Inc D 714 540-4363
3201 S Standard Ave Santa Ana (92705) ***(P-19631)***

Danco Anodizing Inc (PA) E 626 445-3303
44 La Porte St Arcadia (91006) ***(P-12982)***

Danco Anodizing Inc E 909 923-0562
1750 E Monticello Ct Ontario (91761) ***(P-12983)***

Danco Machine, Santa Clara *Also called P M S D Inc* ***(P-16269)***

Danco Metal Surfacing, Arcadia *Also called Danco Anodizing Inc* ***(P-12982)***

Dang Tha F 714 898-0989
13050 Hoover St Westminster (92683) ***(P-4856)***

Dangerous Coffee Co LLC F 619 405-8291
3644 Midway Dr San Diego (92110) ***(P-23310)***

Daniel Loria Novartis E 510 655-8729
4560 Horton St Emeryville (94608) ***(P-7863)***

Daniel Voscloo Jr F 714 751-1401
2107 S Hathaway St Santa Ana (92705) ***(P-20082)***

Daniels Inc (PA) E 801 621-3355
74745 Leslie Ave Palm Desert (92260) ***(P-6220)***

Danisco US Inc (HQ) C 650 846-7500
925 Page Mill Rd Palo Alto (94304) ***(P-8218)***

Dannier Chemical Inc E 949 221-8660
2302 Martin Ste 450 Irvine (92612) ***(P-8957)***

Danoc Embroidery, Sacramento *Also called Danoc Manufacturing Corp Inc* ***(P-3264)***

Danoc Manufacturing Corp Inc F 916 455-2876
6015 Power Inn Rd Ste A Sacramento (95824) ***(P-3264)***

Danone Us LLC B 949 474-9670
3500 Barranca Pkwy # 240 Irvine (92606) ***(P-638)***

Danrich Welding Coinc F 562 634-4811
7001 Jackson St Paramount (90723) ***(P-12173)***

Danso Dental Lab, San Diego *Also called Light Mobile Inc* ***(P-22172)***

Dantel Inc E 559 292-1111
4210 N Brawley Ave 108 Fresno (93722) ***(P-17357)***

Danville Materials LLC E 714 399-0334
4020 E Leaverton Ct Anaheim (92807) ***(P-22141)***

Danville Materials LLC (HQ) E 760 743-7744
2875 Loker Ave E Carlsbad (92010) ***(P-22142)***

Danvo Machining Company, Santa Ana *Also called Daniel Voscloo Jr* ***(P-20082)***

Danworth Manufacturing Co F 510 487-8290
30991 Huntwood Ave # 401 Hayward (94544) ***(P-15878)***

Danza Del Sol Winery Inc F 951 302-6363
39050 De Portola Rd Temecula (92592) ***(P-1655)***

Dar-Ken Inc E 760 246-4010
10515 Rancho Rd Adelanto (92301) ***(P-9227)***

Darbo Manufacturing Company E 714 529-7693
363 Glenoaks St Brea (92821) ***(P-3312)***

Darcy AK Corporation F 949 650-5566
1760 Monrovia Ave Ste A22 Costa Mesa (92627) ***(P-15879)***

Dare Bioscience Inc F 858 926-7655
3655 Nobel Dr Ste 260 San Diego (92122) ***(P-7864)***

Dare Lithoworks Inc F 213 250-9062
13512 Vintage Pl Ste A Chino (91710) ***(P-6532)***

Dare Technologies Inc (HQ) F 714 634-5900
674 Via De La Valle # 100 Solana Beach (92075) ***(P-17358)***

Darioush Khaledi Winery LLC E 707 257-2345
4240 Silverado Trl NAPA (94558) ***(P-1656)***

Darko Precision Inc D 408 988-6133
470 Gianni St Santa Clara (95054) ***(P-15880)***

Darling Ingredients Inc D 415 647-4890
429 Amador St Pier 92 San Francisco (94124) ***(P-1456)***

Darling Ingredients Inc E 559 268-5325
795 W Belgravia Ave Fresno (93706) ***(P-1457)***

Darling Ingredients Inc D 323 583-6311
2626 E 25th St Los Angeles (90058) ***(P-1458)***

Darling Ingredients Inc F 209 620-7267
407 S Tegner Rd Turlock (95380) ***(P-1459)***

Darling International Inc E 209 667-9153
11946 Carpenter Rd Crows Landing (95313) ***(P-1460)***

Darmark Corporation D 858 679-3970
13225 Gregg St Poway (92064) ***(P-15881)***

Darnell Corporation D 626 912-1688
17915 Railroad St City of Industry (91748) ***(P-11585)***

Darnell-Rose Inc F 626 912-1688
1205 Via Roma Colton (92324) ***(P-11586)***

Darrell Zbrowski D 818 324-5961
8465 Vassar Ave Canoga Park (91304) ***(P-13870)***

Darrow, Manhattan Beach *Also called Dhy Inc* ***(P-3075)***

Dart Container Corp Calif, Lodi *Also called Dart Container Corp California* ***(P-9522)***

Dart Container Corp California (PA) B 951 735-8115
150 S Maple Ctr Corona (92880) ***(P-9521)***

Dart Container Corp California C 209 333-8088
1400 E Victor Rd Lodi (95240) ***(P-9522)***

Daryls Pet Shop F 909 793-1788
208 E State St Redlands (92373) ***(P-23311)***

Dasan Zhone Solutions Inc (HQ) C 510 777-7000
7195 Oakport St Oakland (94621) ***(P-17359)***

Dasco Engineering Corp C 310 326-2277
24747 Crenshaw Blvd Torrance (90505) ***(P-20083)***

Dash Sportswear E 323 846-2640
2624 Geraldine St Los Angeles (90011) ***(P-3313)***

Dash Sportwear, Los Angeles *Also called Dash Sportswear* ***(P-3313)***

Dasol Inc C 310 327-6700
16210 S Avalon Blvd Gardena (90248) ***(P-16859)***

Dassault Systemes Biovia Corp E 858 799-5000
5005 Wtrdge Vista Dr Fl 2 Flr 2 San Diego (92121) ***(P-23797)***

Dassault Systemes Biovia Corp (HQ) E 858 799-5000
5005 Wateridge Vista Dr # 2 San Diego (92121) ***(P-23798)***

Data Advantage Group Inc F 415 947-0400
145 Natoma St Fl 5 San Francisco (94105) ***(P-23799)***

Data Agent LLC F 800 772-8314
1349 Josephine St Berkeley (94703) ***(P-23800)***

Data Aire Inc (HQ) C 800 347-2473
230 W Blueridge Ave Orange (92865) ***(P-15423)***

Data Circle Inc F 949 260-6569
3333 Michelson Dr Ste 735 Irvine (92612) ***(P-18192)***

Data Device Corporation E 858 503-3300
13000 Gregg St Ste C Poway (92064) ***(P-20474)***

Data Electronic Services, Santa Ana *Also called Humberto Murillo Inc* ***(P-13026)***

Data Label Products Inc F 626 915-6478
840 N Cummings Rd Covina (91724) ***(P-5504)***

Data Linkage Software Inc F 310 781-3056
2421 W 205th St Ste D207 Torrance (90501) ***(P-23801)***

Data Physics Corporation E 408 216-8443
9031 Polsa Ct Corona (92883) ***(P-14451)***

Data Scale, Fremont *Also called Terry B Lowe* ***(P-14729)***

Data Solder Inc F 714 429-9866
2915 Kilson Dr Santa Ana (92707) ***(P-16890)***

Data Storm Inc F 818 352-4994
2001 Manistee Dr La Canada Flintridge (91011) ***(P-19288)***

Database Dynamics, Aliso Viejo *Also called Interactive Entertainment Inc* ***(P-22684)***

Database Works Inc F 714 203-8800
500 S Kraemer Blvd # 110 Brea (92821) ***(P-23802)***

Datadirect Networks Inc (PA) C 818 700-7600
9351 Deering Ave Chatsworth (91311) ***(P-15020)***

Datafox Intelligence Inc F 415 969-2144
475 Sansome St Fl 15 San Francisco (94111) ***(P-23803)***

Datagenics Software Inc F 818 487-3900
5527 Satsuma Ave North Hollywood (91601) ***(P-23804)***

Dataguise Inc E 510 824-1036
39650 Liberty St Ste 400 Fremont (94538) ***(P-23805)***

Datapage Inc F 323 725-7500
5577 Sheila St Commerce (90040) ***(P-7043)***

Dataray Incorporated F 530 472-1717
1675 Market St Redding (96001) ***(P-21215)***

Datatronics Romoland Inc D 951 928-7700
28151 Us Highway 74 Menifee (92585) ***(P-16546)***

Dateline Products LLC F 909 888-9785
1375 E Base Line St Ste B San Bernardino (92410) ***(P-4564)***

Datera Inc E 650 384-6366
2811 Mission College Blvd Santa Clara (95054) ***(P-23806)***

Datron Wrld Communications Inc (PA) C 760 597-1500
3055 Enterprise Ct Vista (92081) ***(P-17500)***

Datum Precision Inc F 530 272-8415
345 Crown Point Cir # 800 Grass Valley (95945) ***(P-20084)***

Datum Precision Machining, Anderson *Also called Dpm Inc* ***(P-15907)***

Dauntless Industries Inc E 626 966-4494
806 N Grand Ave Covina (91724) ***(P-14040)***

Dauntless Molds, Covina *Also called Dauntless Industries Inc* ***(P-14040)***

Dav Termite & Pest Inc F 619 829-8901
2005 Highland Ave National City (91950) ***(P-8826)***

Davco Enterprises Inc F 714 432-0600
3301 W Segerstrom Ave Santa Ana (92704) ***(P-8866)***

Dave Annala F 714 541-8383
1628 E Wilshire Ave Santa Ana (92705) ***(P-12174)***

Dave Humphrey Enterprises Inc F 209 835-2222
145 Gandy Dancer Dr Tracy (95377) ***(P-13726)***

Dave Richardson Trucking F 530 459-5088
8817 Lwer Lttle Shasta Rd Montague (96064) ***(P-3880)***

Dave Schneider's Fine Jewelry, Long Beach *Also called Schneiders Deisgn Studio Inc* ***(P-22570)***

Dave Whipple Sheet Metal Inc E 619 562-6962
1077 N Cuyamaca St El Cajon (92020) ***(P-12175)***

Dave's Donuts & Baking Co, Gardena *Also called Bake R Us Inc* ***(P-1140)***

Davenport International Corp E 818 765-6400
7230 Coldwater Canyon Ave North Hollywood (91605) ***(P-17217)***

Daves Interiors Inc E 714 998-5554
1579 N Main St Orange (92867) ***(P-4636)***

David A Neal Inc F 562 941-5626
9825 Bell Ranch Dr Santa Fe Springs (90670) ***(P-15882)***

David B Anderson E 805 489-0661
921 Huston St Grover Beach (93433) ***(P-6533)***

David Beard F 530 244-1248
821 Twin View Blvd Redding (96003) ***(P-4187)***

David Bruce Winery Inc F 408 354-4214
21439 Bear Creek Rd Los Gatos (95033) ***(P-1657)***

David Corporation F 916 762-8688
925 Highland Pointe Dr # 180 Roseville (95678) ***(P-23807)***

David Duley D 619 449-8556
700 La Cresta Blvd San Marcos (92079) ***(P-5188)***

David Engineering & Mfg, Corona *Also called Specialty Finance Inc* ***(P-12875)***

Employee Codes: A=Over 500 employees, B=251-500
C=101-250, D=51-100, E=20-50, F=10-19

2020 California
Manfacturers Register

© Mergent Inc. 1-800-342-5647
1077

David Garment Cutng Fusing Svc ....F......323 583-9885
5008 S Boyle Ave Vernon (90058) *(P-3032)*

David H Fell & Co Inc (PA) ....E......323 722-9992
6009 Bandini Blvd Los Angeles (90040) *(P-11199)*

David Haid ....E......323 752-8096
8619 Crocker St Los Angeles (90003) *(P-5054)*

David Kopf Instruments ....E......818 352-3274
7324 Elmo St Tujunga (91042) *(P-21678)*

David Kordansky Gallery Inc (PA) ....E......323 935-3030
5130 Edgewood Pl Los Angeles (90019) *(P-6095)*

David Pirrotta Dist Inc ....F......323 645-7456
7424 1/2 W Sunset Blvd # 5 Los Angeles (90046) *(P-8476)*

Davids Natural Toothpaste ....F......949 933-1185
40292 Rosewell Ct Temecula (92591) *(P-8477)*

Davidson Optronics Inc ....E......626 962-5181
9087 Arrow Rte Ste 180 Rancho Cucamonga (91730) *(P-21458)*

Davis Boats ....F......805 227-1170
2601 Engine Ave Paso Robles (93446) *(P-20320)*

Davis Gear & Machine Co ....F......310 337-9881
13625 S Normandie Ave Gardena (90249) *(P-15883)*

Davis Gregg Enterprises Inc ....F......619 449-4250
8525 Roland Acres Dr Santee (92071) *(P-12015)*

Davis Instruments Corporation ....D......510 732-9229
3465 Diablo Ave Hayward (94545) *(P-20565)*

Davis Shoe Therapeutics ....F......415 661-8705
3921 Judah St San Francisco (94122) *(P-10168)*

Davis Stone Inc ....E......760 745-7881
519 Venture St Escondido (92029) *(P-10902)*

Davis Wire Corporation (HQ) ....C......626 969-7651
5555 Irwindale Ave Irwindale (91706) *(P-11088)*

Davison Iron Works Inc ....E......916 381-2121
8845 Elder Creek Rd Ste A Sacramento (95828) *(P-11783)*

Davtron ....F......650 369-1188
427 Hillcrest Way Emerald Hills (94062) *(P-20566)*

Dawn Bakery Service Center, Union City *Also called Dawn Food Products Inc* ***(P-1185)***

Dawn Food Products Inc ....F......517 789-4400
2455 Tenaya Dr Modesto (95354) *(P-1312)*

Dawn Food Products Inc ....E......510 487-9007
2845 Faber St Union City (94587) *(P-1185)*

Dawn Sign Press Inc ....E......858 625-0600
6130 Nancy Ridge Dr San Diego (92121) *(P-6096)*

Dawn VME Products ....E......510 657-4444
47915 Westinghouse Dr Fremont (94539) *(P-18883)*

Dawson Enterprises (PA) ....E......562 424-8564
2853 Cherry Ave Signal Hill (90755) *(P-13773)*

Dawson Enterprises ....F......661 765-2181
815 Main St Taft (93268) *(P-188)*

Day Star Industries ....F......562 926-8800
13727 Excelsior Dr Santa Fe Springs (90670) *(P-4030)*

Day-Glo Color Corp ....F......323 560-2000
4615 Ardine St Cudahy (90201) *(P-7458)*

Daylight Solutions Inc (HQ) ....C......858 432-7500
16465 Via Esprillo # 100 San Diego (92127) *(P-18193)*

Daymar Corporation ....F......619 444-1155
460 Cypress Ln Ste B El Cajon (92020) *(P-2287)*

Daymar Select Fine Coffees, El Cajon *Also called Daymar Corporation* ***(P-2287)***

Daystar Technologies Inc ....D......408 582-7100
1010 S Milpitas Blvd Milpitas (95035) *(P-18194)*

Daytec Center LLC ....E......760 995-3515
17469 Lemon St Hesperia (92345) *(P-20397)*

Dayton Superior Corporation ....E......909 957-7271
10780 Mulberry Ave Fontana (92337) *(P-19891)*

Dayton Superior Corporation ....D......951 782-9517
6001 20th St Riverside (92509) *(P-11089)*

Dayton Superior Corporation ....E......209 869-1201
5300 Claus Rd Ste 7 Modesto (95357) *(P-13871)*

Dayton Superior Corporation ....E......909 820-0112
562 W Santa Ana Ave Bloomington (92316) *(P-11090)*

Daz Inc ....F......949 724-8800
2500 White Rd Ste B Irvine (92614) *(P-16593)*

Db Building Fasteners, Ontario *Also called DB Building Fasteners Inc* ***(P-12589)***

DB Building Fasteners Inc (PA) ....E......909 581-6740
5555 E Gibralter Ontario (91764) *(P-12589)*

Db Studios Inc ....E......949 833-0100
17032 Murphy Ave Irvine (92614) *(P-23312)*

DBC Printing Incorporated ....F......805 988-8855
220 Bernoulli Cir Oxnard (93030) *(P-6534)*

Dbg Subsidiary Inc ....C......323 837-3700
1500 N El Centro Ave # 150 Los Angeles (90028) *(P-3265)*

Dbv Inc ....E......562 404-9714
17120 Valley View Ave La Mirada (90638) *(P-7865)*

DC Electronics Inc ....F......408 947-4531
1870 Little Orchard St San Jose (95125) *(P-16891)*

DC Partners Inc (PA) ....E......714 558-9444
19329 Bryant St Northridge (91324) *(P-11376)*

DC Partners Inc ....E......818 718-1221
19408 Londelius St Northridge (91324) *(P-11377)*

DC Shades & Shutters Awnings ....F......818 597-9705
2370 Thunderbird Dr Thousand Oaks (91362) *(P-11944)*

DC Shoes Inc (HQ) ....D......714 889-4206
5600 Argosy Ave Ste 100 Huntington Beach (92649) *(P-3074)*

DC Valve Mfg & Precision Mchs, Morgan Hill *Also called Valvex Enterprises Inc* ***(P-16493)***

Dcatalog Inc ....E......408 824-5648
2635 N 1st St Ste 102 San Jose (95134) *(P-23808)*

Dcc General Engrg Contrs Inc ....D......760 480-7400
2180 Meyers Ave Escondido (92029) *(P-10559)*

Dcg Systems, Fremont *Also called Fei Efa Inc* ***(P-18768)***

DCI, Hayward *Also called Dielectric Coating Industries* ***(P-21348)***

DCI Hollow Metal On Demand, Fontana *Also called Door Components Inc* ***(P-11948)***

Dcl, Fremont *Also called Discopylabs* ***(P-17316)***

Dcl Productions ....F......415 826-2200
1284 Missouri St San Francisco (94107) *(P-3736)*

Dco Environmental & Recycl LLC ....F......573 204-3844
300 Montgomery St Ste 421 San Francisco (94104) *(P-9746)*

Dcor LLC (PA) ....D......805 535-2000
290 Maple Ct Ste 290 # 290 Ventura (93003) *(P-117)*

Dcx-Chol Enterprises Inc (PA) ....D......310 516-1692
12831 S Figueroa St Los Angeles (90061) *(P-17781)*

Dcx-Chol Enterprises Inc ....D......310 516-1692
12831 S Figueroa St Los Angeles (90061) *(P-17782)*

Dcx-Chol Enterprises Inc ....D......562 927-5531
7450 Scout Ave Bell (90201) *(P-18884)*

Dcx-Chol Enterprises Inc ....F......310 516-1692
12831 S Figueroa St Los Angeles (90061) *(P-17783)*

Dcx-Chol Enterprises Inc ....E......310 525-1205
12831 S Figueroa St Los Angeles (90061) *(P-17784)*

Dda Holdings Inc ....F......213 624-5200
834 S Broadway Ste 1100 Los Angeles (90014) *(P-3314)*

Ddh Enterprise Inc (PA) ....C......760 599-0171
2220 Oak Ridge Way Vista (92081) *(P-16892)*

DDS, Hayward *Also called Detention Device Systems* ***(P-15891)***

De Anza Manufacturing Svcs Inc ....D......408 734-2020
1271 Reamwood Ave Sunnyvale (94089) *(P-18885)*

De Anza Muffler Service, Riverside *Also called Vast National Inc* ***(P-11491)***

De Berns Company, Long Beach *Also called Berns Bros Inc* ***(P-15788)***

De La Cruz Products, Paramount *Also called Dlc Laboratories Inc* ***(P-7872)***

De Larshe Cabinetry LLC ....E......909 627-2757
2000 S Reservoir St Pomona (91766) *(P-4031)*

De Leon Entps Elec Spclist Inc ....E......818 252-6690
11934 Allegheny St Sun Valley (91352) *(P-17861)*

De Menno-Kerdoon Trading Co (HQ) ....C......310 537-7100
2000 N Alameda St Compton (90222) *(P-9045)*

De Nora Water Technologies Inc ....D......310 618-9700
1230 Rosecrans Ave # 300 Manhattan Beach (90266) *(P-15506)*

De Novo Software ....F......213 814-1240
400 N Brand Blvd Ste 850 Glendale (91203) *(P-23809)*

De Soto Clothing Inc ....F......858 578-6672
7584 Trade St San Diego (92121) *(P-3315)*

De Soto Sport, San Diego *Also called De Soto Clothing Inc* ***(P-3315)***

De Vries International Inc (PA) ....E......949 252-1212
17671 Armstrong Ave Irvine (92614) *(P-189)*

Dealzer Com ....F......818 429-1155
9250 Reseda Blvd Northridge (91324) *(P-8700)*

Deamco Corporation ....D......323 890-1190
6520 E Washington Blvd Commerce (90040) *(P-13822)*

Dean Distributors Inc ....E......323 587-8147
5015 Hallmark Pkwy San Bernardino (92407) *(P-2440)*

Dean Foods Company ....F......559 687-1927
605 N J St Tulare (93274) *(P-695)*

Dean Foods Company Cal Inc ....E......714 684-2160
6408 Regio Ave Buena Park (90620) *(P-696)*

Dean Socal LLC ....C......951 734-3950
17637 E Valley Blvd City of Industry (91744) *(P-697)*

Deans Certified Welding Inc ....F......951 676-0242
27645 Commerce Center Dr Temecula (92590) *(P-24629)*

Deanza Tool & Manufacturing, Riverside *Also called M G Deanza Acquisition Inc* ***(P-16161)***

Dear John American Classic, Arcadia *Also called Dear John Denim Inc* ***(P-2680)***

Dear John Denim Inc ....F......626 350-5100
12318 Lower Azusa Rd Arcadia (91006) *(P-2680)*

Debbies Delights Inc ....E......805 966-3504
233 E Gutierrez St Santa Barbara (93101) *(P-1340)*

Dec, Santa Ana *Also called Dynasty Electronic Company LLC* ***(P-17865)***

Dec Fabricators Inc ....F......562 403-3626
16916 Gridley Pl Cerritos (90703) *(P-13513)*

Deca International Corp ....E......714 367-5900
10700 Norwalk Blvd Santa Fe Springs (90670) *(P-20567)*

Decamilla Brothers LLC ....F......530 865-3379
717 Tehama St Orland (95963) *(P-1471)*

Decatur Electronics Inc (HQ) ....D......888 428-4315
15890 Bernardo Center Dr San Diego (92127) *(P-20568)*

Decatur Electronics Inc ....E......619 596-1925
10729 Wheatlands Ave C Santee (92071) *(P-20569)*

Decco Castings Inc ....E......619 444-9437
1596 Pioneer Way El Cajon (92020) *(P-11413)*

Decco Graphics Inc ....E......310 534-2861
24411 Frampton Ave Harbor City (90710) *(P-12792)*

Decco US Post-Harvest Inc (HQ) ....E......800 221-0925
1713 S California Ave Monrovia (91016) *(P-8827)*

Deccofelt Corporation ....E......626 963-8511
555 S Vermont Ave Glendora (91741) *(P-2931)*

Decision Medical, Poway *Also called Decision Sciences Med Co LLC* ***(P-22248)***

Decision Sciences Med Co LLC ....E......858 602-1600
12345 First American Way # 100 Poway (92064) *(P-22248)*

Decisioninsite Ltd Lblty Co ....E......877 204-1392
101 Pacifica Ste 380 Irvine (92618) *(P-23810)*

Decisionlogic LLC ....E......858 586-0202
13500 Evening Creek Dr N # 600 San Diego (92128) *(P-23811)*

Deck West Inc ....F......209 939-9700
1900 Sanguinetti Ln Stockton (95205) *(P-12176)*

Deckers Outdoor Corporation (PA) ....B......805 967-7611
250 Coromar Dr Goleta (93117) *(P-3550)*

Deco Enterprises Inc ....D......323 726-2575
2917 Vail Ave Commerce (90040) *(P-17023)*

Deco Lighting, Commerce *Also called Deco Enterprises Inc* ***(P-17023)***

Deco Plastics Inc ....F......619 448-6843
9530 Pathway St Ste 105 Santee (92071) *(P-9747)*

Decor Auto Inc ....F......323 733-9025
1709 W Washington Blvd Los Angeles (90007) *(P-3783)*

Decor Fabrics Inc ....E 323 752-2200
6515 Mckinley Ave Los Angeles (90001) *(P-4637)*
Decor International, Los Angeles *Also called Decor Fabrics Inc (P-4637)*
Decor Shower Door and Glass Co ....F 707 253-0622
1819 Tanen St Ste A NAPA (94559) *(P-10353)*
Decor Shower Enclosures, NAPA *Also called Decor Shower Door and Glass Co (P-10353)*
Decorative Construction ....F 626 862-6814
614 E Badillo St Covina (91723) *(P-4188)*
Decore Plating Company Inc ....F 310 324-6755
434 W 164th St Gardena (90248) *(P-12984)*
Decore-Ative Specialties (PA) ....A 626 254-9191
2772 Peck Rd Monrovia (91016) *(P-4032)*
Decore-Ative Specialties ....C 626 960-7731
4414 Azusa Canyon Rd Irwindale (91706) *(P-4033)*
Decore-Ative Specialties ....C 916 686-4700
104 Gate Eats Stock Blvd Elk Grove (95624) *(P-4034)*
Decra Roofing Systems Inc (HQ) ....D 951 272-8180
1230 Railroad St Corona (92882) *(P-12177)*
Decratek Inc ....E 760 747-1706
2875 Executive Pl Escondido (92029) *(P-11945)*
Decrevel Incorporated ....F 707 258-8065
1836 Soscol Ave NAPA (94559) *(P-14041)*
Dee Engineering Inc (PA) ....E 714 979-4990
3100 Airway Ave Ste 106 Costa Mesa (92626) *(P-19632)*
Dee Engineering Inc ....E 909 947-5616
1893 S Lake Pl Ontario (91761) *(P-19633)*
Dee Sign Co ....D 818 988-1000
16250 Stagg St Van Nuys (91406) *(P-23087)*
Deem Inc (HQ) ....D 415 590-8300
642 Harrison St Fl 2 San Francisco (94107) *(P-23812)*
Deep Foods Inc ....F 510 475-1900
4000 Whipple Rd Union City (94587) *(P-1313)*
Deep Ocean Engineering Inc ....F 408 436-1102
2403 Qume Dr San Jose (95131) *(P-20321)*
Deerfield Ranch Winery LLC ....F 707 833-5215
1310 Warm Springs Rd Glen Ellen (95442) *(P-1658)*
Deering Banjo Company Inc ....E 619 464-8252
3733 Kenora Dr Spring Valley (91977) *(P-22611)*
Deers Merchandise Inc ....F 909 869-8619
347 Enterprise Pl Pomona (91768) *(P-10487)*
Defense Solutions, Santa Clarita *Also called Curtiss-Wright Corporation (P-13301)*
Define Toys Inc ....F 626 330-8800
1255 Bixby Dr City of Industry (91745) *(P-22646)*
Definity First, Los Angeles *Also called Sieena Inc (P-24408)*
Defoe Furniture For Kids Inc ....F 909 947-4459
910 S Grove Ave Ontario (91761) *(P-4857)*
Deft Precision Machining, San Diego *Also called Cimrmaan Ivo (P-12784)*
Dehlinger Winery, Sebastopol *Also called Thomas Dehlinger (P-1953)*
Dei Headquarters Inc ....B 760 598-6200
3002 Wintergreen Dr Carlsbad (92008) *(P-17724)*
Dei Holdings Inc (HQ) ....C 760 598-6200
1 Viper Way Ste 3 Vista (92081) *(P-17725)*
Deiny Automotive Inc ....F 818 362-5865
13040 Bradley Ave Sylmar (91342) *(P-19465)*
Deist Engineering Inc ....E 818 240-7866
2623 N San Fernando Rd Los Angeles (90065) *(P-3033)*
Deist Safety, Los Angeles *Also called Flame Out Inc (P-23333)*
Deist Safety Equipment, Los Angeles *Also called Deist Engineering Inc (P-3033)*
Dejagers Inc ....E 760 775-4755
45846 Flower St Indio (92201) *(P-10903)*
Del Castillo Foods Inc ....E 209 369-2877
2346 Maggio Cir Lodi (95240) *(P-2441)*
Del Craft Plastics, Laguna Hills *Also called Rls Enterprises (P-10019)*
Del Dotto, NAPA *Also called Hedgeside Vintners (P-1751)*
Del Industries, San Luis Obispo *Also called Del Ozone Holding Company Inc (P-15507)*
Del Logging Inc ....E 530 294-5492
101 Punkin Center Rd Bieber (96009) *(P-3881)*
Del Mar Database, San Diego *Also called Del Mar Datatrac Inc (P-23813)*
Del Mar Datatrac Inc ....E 858 550-8810
10509 Vista Sorrento Pkwy # 400 San Diego (92121) *(P-23813)*
Del Mar Die Casting Co, Gardena *Also called Del Mar Industries (P-11355)*
Del Mar Food Products Corp ....B 831 722-3516
1720 Beach Rd Watsonville (95076) *(P-761)*
Del Mar Industries (PA) ....D 323 321-0600
12901 S Western Ave Gardena (90249) *(P-11355)*
Del Mar Industries ....E 310 327-2634
12901 S Western Ave Gardena (90249) *(P-11356)*
Del Mar Seafoods Inc (PA) ....C 831 763-3000
331 Ford St Watsonville (95076) *(P-2258)*
Del Monte Foods Inc ....D 559 419-9214
1509 Draper St Ste A Kingsburg (93631) *(P-762)*
Del Monte Foods Inc ....C 559 639-6160
10652 Jackson Ave Hanford (93230) *(P-763)*
Del Monte Foods Inc ....B 209 548-5509
4000 Yosemite Blvd Modesto (95357) *(P-764)*
Del Monte Foods Inc (HQ) ....C 925 949-2772
3003 Oak Rd Ste 600 Walnut Creek (94597) *(P-765)*
Del Monte Foods 48, Lathrop *Also called Big Heart Pet Brands (P-758)*
Del Ozone Holding Company Inc ....E 805 541-1601
3580 Sueldo St San Luis Obispo (93401) *(P-15507)*
Del Ray Packaging, Del Rey *Also called Chooljian & Sons Inc (P-14355)*
Del Real LLC (PA) ....C 951 681-0395
11041 Inland Ave Jurupa Valley (91752) *(P-954)*
Del Real Foods, Jurupa Valley *Also called Del Real LLC (P-954)*
Del Rey Enterprises Inc ....F 559 233-4452
8898 E Central Ave Del Rey (93616) *(P-849)*
Del Rey Juice Co ....D 559 888-8533
5286 S Del Rey Ave Del Rey (93616) *(P-909)*
Del Rio West Pallets ....E 209 983-8215
3845 S El Dorado St Stockton (95206) *(P-4362)*
Del West Engineering Inc (PA) ....C 661 295-5700
28128 Livingston Ave Valencia (91355) *(P-19634)*
Del West USA, Valencia *Also called Del West Engineering Inc (P-19634)*
Delafield Corporation (PA) ....C 626 303-0740
1520 Flower Ave Duarte (91010) *(P-15884)*
Delafield Fluid Technology, Duarte *Also called Delafield Corporation (P-15884)*
Delafoil Holdings Inc (PA) ....B 949 752-4580
18500 Von Karman Ave # 450 Irvine (92612) *(P-12178)*
Delallo Italian Foods, Oroville *Also called George Delallo Company Inc (P-771)*
Delamo Manufacturing Inc ....D 323 936-3566
7171 Telegraph Rd Montebello (90640) *(P-9748)*
Delaney Manufacturing Inc ....F 661 587-6681
6810 Downing Ave Bakersfield (93308) *(P-12179)*
Delano Growers Grape Products ....D 661 725-3255
32351 Bassett Ave Delano (93215) *(P-2202)*
Delano Waste Water Treatment, Delano *Also called City of Delano (P-15497)*
Delaware Systems Technology, San Bernardino *Also called Systems Technology Inc (P-14728)*
Delco Oheb Energy, Los Angeles *Also called Delco Operating Co LP (P-118)*
Delco Operating Co LP ....F 310 525-3535
1999 Avenue Of The Stars Los Angeles (90067) *(P-118)*
Delfin Design & Mfg Inc ....E 949 888-4644
15672 Producer Ln Huntington Beach (92649) *(P-9749)*
Delgado Brothers LLC ....E 323 233-9793
647 E 59th St Los Angeles (90001) *(P-4500)*
Delgau Spring, Corona *Also called Spring Delgau Inc (P-13388)*
Delicato Vineyards (PA) ....C 209 824-3600
12001 S Highway 99 Manteca (95336) *(P-1659)*
Delicato Vineyards ....E 707 265-1700
455 Devlin Rd Ste 201 NAPA (94558) *(P-1660)*
Delicato Vineyards ....E 707 253-1400
4089 Silverado Trl NAPA (94558) *(P-1661)*
Delicato Vineyards ....F 831 385-7587
51955 Oasis Rd King City (93930) *(P-1662)*
Delivery Zone LLC ....D 323 780-0888
120 S Anderson St Los Angeles (90033) *(P-2442)*
Dell Inc ....F 408 206-5466
5450 Great America Pkwy Santa Clara (95054) *(P-14903)*
Della Robbia Inc ....E 951 372-9199
796 E Harrison St Corona (92879) *(P-4718)*
Dellarise, Pasadena *Also called Pak Group LLC (P-1324)*
Dellarobbia Inc (PA) ....E 949 251-9532
119 Waterworks Way Irvine (92618) *(P-4638)*
Delmar Pharmaceutical Inc ....F 650 269-1984
3475 Edison Way Ste R Menlo Park (94025) *(P-7866)*
Delong Manufacturing Co Inc ....F 408 727-3348
967 Parker Ct Santa Clara (95050) *(P-15885)*
Delori Foods, City of Industry *Also called Delori Products Inc (P-2443)*
Delori Products Inc ....E 626 965-3006
17043 Green Dr City of Industry (91745) *(P-2443)*
Delphi Connection Systems LLC ....F 949 458-3155
8662 Siempre Viva Rd San Diego (92154) *(P-19635)*
Delphi Control Systems Inc ....F 909 593-8099
2806 Metropolitan Pl Pomona (91767) *(P-20855)*
Delphi Display Systems Inc ....D 714 825-3400
3550 Hyland Ave Costa Mesa (92626) *(P-15214)*
Delphix Corp (PA) ....E 650 494-1645
1400 Saport Blvd Ste 200a Redwood City (94063) *(P-23814)*
Delphon Industries LLC (PA) ....C 510 576-2220
31398 Huntwood Ave Hayward (94544) *(P-9750)*
Delray Lighting Inc ....E 818 767-3793
7545 N Lockheed Dr Burbank (91505) *(P-17117)*
Delstar Holding Corp ....E 619 258-1503
9225 Isaac St Santee (92071) *(P-9400)*
Delstar Technologies Inc ....E 619 258-1503
1306 Fayette St El Cajon (92020) *(P-9401)*
Delt Industries Inc ....F 805 579-0213
90 W Easy St Ste 2 Simi Valley (93065) *(P-11414)*
Delta Coast Beer LLC ....F 213 604-2428
2034 E Lincoln Ave Anaheim (92806) *(P-1519)*
Delta D V H Circuits Inc ....E 818 786-8241
16117 Leadwell St Van Nuys (91406) *(P-17862)*
Delta Design Inc (HQ) ....B 858 848-8000
12367 Crosthwaite Cir Poway (92064) *(P-14807)*
Delta Design Littleton Inc (HQ) ....F 858 848-8100
12367 Crosthwaite Cir Poway (92064) *(P-21022)*
Delta Door Company, Stockton *Also called Masonite International Corp (P-4082)*
Delta Dvh Circuits, Van Nuys *Also called Ambay Circuits Inc (P-17815)*
Delta Engineering and Mfg, Chino *Also called Delta Manufacturing Inc (P-15887)*
Delta Fabrication Inc ....D 818 407-4000
9600 De Soto Ave Chatsworth (91311) *(P-12180)*
Delta Group Electronics Inc ....D 858 569-1681
10180 Scripps Ranch Blvd San Diego (92131) *(P-18886)*
Delta Hi-Tech ....C 818 407-4000
9600 De Soto Ave Chatsworth (91311) *(P-15886)*
Delta Ironworks Inc ....F 831 663-1190
15420 Meridian Rd Salinas (93907) *(P-12468)*
Delta Lath & Plaster Inc ....E 916 383-6756
5451 Whse Way Ste 105 Sacramento (95826) *(P-13912)*
Delta Machine, San Jose *Also called Delta Matrix Inc (P-15888)*
Delta Manufacturing Inc ....E 909 590-4563
6260 Prescott Ct Chino (91710) *(P-15887)*
Delta Matrix Inc ....E 408 955-9140
2180 Oakland Rd San Jose (95131) *(P-15888)*
Delta Pacific Activewear Inc ....D 714 871-9281
331 S Hale Ave Fullerton (92831) *(P-2781)*

ALPHABETIC

Employee Codes: A=Over 500 employees, B=251-500
C=101-250, D=51-100, E=20-50, F=10-19
2020 California
Manfacturers Register
© Mergent Inc. 1-800-342-5647
1079

Delta Pacific Products, Union City *Also called Delta Yimin Technologies Inc* ***(P-9751)***
Delta Rebar Services Inc............F.......925 798-4220
2410 Bates Ave Concord (94520) ***(P-11784)***
Delta Signs, Stockton *Also called Street Graphics Inc* ***(P-23219)***
Delta Sportswear Inc............F.......714 568-1102
331 S Hale Ave Fullerton (92831) ***(P-3154)***
Delta Stag Manufacturing............D.......562 904-6444
1818 E Rosslynn Ave Fullerton (92831) ***(P-19526)***
Delta Tau Data Systems Inc Cal (HQ)............C.......818 998-2095
21314 Lassen St Chatsworth (91311) ***(P-14808)***
Delta Tau International Inc............F.......818 998-2095
21314 Lassen St Chatsworth (91311) ***(P-14809)***
Delta Tech Industries LLC............F.......909 673-1900
1901 S Vineyard Ave Ontario (91761) ***(P-17088)***
Delta Trading LP............E.......661 834-5560
17731 Millux Rd Bakersfield (93311) ***(P-9089)***
Delta Turnstile Controls, Concord *Also called Delta Turnstiles LLC* ***(P-19289)***
Delta Turnstiles LLC............F.......925 969-1498
1011 Detroit Ave Concord (94518) ***(P-19289)***
Delta Web Printing Inc............E.......916 375-0044
1871 Enterprise Blvd West Sacramento (95691) ***(P-7044)***
Delta Web Printing & Bindery, West Sacramento *Also called Delta Web Printing Inc* ***(P-7044)***
Delta Yimin Technologies Inc............E.......510 487-4411
33170 Central Ave Union City (94587) ***(P-9751)***
Delta-Stag Truck Body, Fullerton *Also called Delta Stag Manufacturing* ***(P-19526)***
Deltatrak Inc............E.......209 579-5343
1236 Doker Dr Modesto (95351) ***(P-21459)***
Deltatrak Inc (PA)............E.......925 249-2250
6140 Stoneridge Mall Rd # 180 Pleasanton (94588) ***(P-21460)***
Deltronic Corporation............D.......714 545-5800
3900 W Segerstrom Ave Santa Ana (92704) ***(P-21347)***
Deluxe Check Printers, Lancaster *Also called Deluxe Corporation* ***(P-7311)***
Deluxe Corporation............D.......408 370-8801
1551 Dell Ave Campbell (95008) ***(P-7309)***
Deluxe Corporation............B.......651 483-7100
2861 Mandela Pkwy Oakland (94608) ***(P-7310)***
Deluxe Corporation............B.......661 942-1144
42933 Business Ctr Pkwy Lancaster (93535) ***(P-7311)***
Deluxe Financial Services, Campbell *Also called Deluxe Corporation* ***(P-7309)***
Demag Cranes & Components Corp............E.......909 880-8800
13290 Sabre Blvd Victorville (92394) ***(P-13846)***
Demaiz Inc............F.......650 518-6268
77 S 28th St San Jose (95116) ***(P-724)***
Demandbase Inc............B.......415 683-2660
680 Folsom St Ste 400 San Francisco (94107) ***(P-23815)***
Demaria Electric Inc............E.......310 549-4980
7048 Marcelle St Paramount (90723) ***(P-24686)***
Demaria Electric Motor Svcs, Paramount *Also called Demaria Electric Inc* ***(P-24686)***
Demenno Kerdoon............C.......310 537-7100
2000 N Alameda St Compton (90222) ***(P-119)***
Demenno-Kerdoon, South Gate *Also called Demenno/Kerdoon Holdings* ***(P-9140)***
Demenno/Kerdoon Holdings............D.......323 268-3387
3650 E 26th St Vernon (90058) ***(P-9139)***
Demenno/Kerdoon Holdings (HQ)............D.......562 231-1550
9302 Garfield Ave South Gate (90280) ***(P-9140)***
Demes Gourmet Corporation............E.......714 870-6040
327 N State College Blvd Fullerton (92831) ***(P-452)***
Demetrius Pohl............F.......323 735-1027
2179 W 20th St Los Angeles (90018) ***(P-381)***
Demille Marble & Granite Inc............E.......760 341-7525
72091 Woburn Ct Ste D Thousand Palms (92276) ***(P-10904)***
Demptos NAPA Cooperage (HQ)............E.......707 257-2628
1050 Soscol Ferry Rd NAPA (94558) ***(P-4415)***
Demtech Services Inc............E.......530 621-3200
6414 Capitol Ave Diamond Springs (95619) ***(P-9752)***
Den-Mat Corporation (HQ)............B.......805 922-8491
236 S Broadway St Orcutt (93455) ***(P-8478)***
Den-Mat Corporation............E.......800 445-0345
21515 Vanowen St Ste 200 Canoga Park (91303) ***(P-8479)***
Den-Mat Holdings LLC (HQ)............F.......805 346-3700
1017 W Central Ave Lompoc (93436) ***(P-22143)***
Denali Software Inc (HQ)............E.......408 943-1234
2655 Seely Ave San Jose (95134) ***(P-23816)***
Denali Therapeutics Inc (PA)............C.......650 866-8548
161 Oyster Point Blvd South San Francisco (94080) ***(P-8293)***
Denali Water Solutions LLC............F.......714 799-0801
3031 Franklin Ave Riverside (92507) ***(P-9753)***
Denbeste Manufacturing Inc............F.......707 838-1407
810 Den Beste Ct Ste 107 Windsor (95492) ***(P-19527)***
Dendreon Pharmaceuticals Inc............F.......562 253-3931
1700 Saturn Way Seal Beach (90740) ***(P-7867)***
Dendreon Pharmaceuticals LLC (HQ)............E.......562 252-7500
1700 Saturn Way Seal Beach (90740) ***(P-7868)***
Denim-Tech LLC............D.......323 277-8998
2300 E 52nd St Vernon (90058) ***(P-15404)***
Denmac Industries Inc............E.......562 634-2714
7616 Rosecrans Ave Paramount (90723) ***(P-13164)***
Dennie Manning Concrete Inc............F.......909 823-7521
15815 Arrow Blvd Fontana (92335) ***(P-10752)***
Dennis Bolton Enterprises Inc............E.......818 982-1800
7285 Coldwater Canyon Ave North Hollywood (91605) ***(P-6535)***
Dennis Reeves Inc............F.......909 392-9999
1350 Palomares St Ste A La Verne (91750) ***(P-4896)***
Dennison Inc............E.......626 965-8917
17901 Railroad St City of Industry (91748) ***(P-12469)***
Denovo Dental Inc............E.......626 480-0182
5130 Commerce Dr Baldwin Park (91706) ***(P-22144)***
Denso International Amer Inc............F.......760 597-7400
2251 Rutherford Rd 100 Carlsbad (92008) ***(P-19636)***
Denso Pdts & Svcs Americas Inc............C.......951 698-3379
41673 Corning Pl Murrieta (92562) ***(P-19637)***
Dentium USA (HQ)............F.......714 226-0229
6731 Katella Ave Cypress (90630) ***(P-22145)***
Dentonis Spring and Suspension, Stockton *Also called Dentonis Welding Works Inc* ***(P-24630)***
Dentonis Welding Works Inc (PA)............E.......209 464-4930
801 S Airport Way Stockton (95205) ***(P-24630)***
Dentsply Sirona Inc............D.......909 795-2080
13553 Calimesa Blvd Yucaipa (92399) ***(P-22146)***
Denttio Inc............F.......323 254-1000
116 N Maryland Ave # 125 Glendale (91206) ***(P-22147)***
Deodar Brands LLC............E.......323 235-7303
4715 S Alameda St Vernon (90058) ***(P-2681)***
Dependable Furniture Mfg Co, San Leandro *Also called Van Sark Inc* ***(P-4676)***
Dependable Plas & Pattern Inc............E.......707 863-4900
4900 Fulton Dr Fairfield (94534) ***(P-9523)***
Dependable Precision Mfg Inc............F.......209 369-1055
1111 S Stockton St Ste A Lodi (95240) ***(P-12181)***
Dependble Incontinence Sup Inc............F.......626 812-0044
590 S Vincent Ave Azusa (91702) ***(P-5460)***
Depot 6, The, Apple Valley *Also called Valero Energy Corporation* ***(P-9081)***
Depuy Synthes Products Inc............F.......408 246-4300
130 Knowles Dr Ste E Los Gatos (95032) ***(P-21679)***
Derek and Constance Lee Corp (PA)............D.......909 595-8831
19355 San Jose Ave City of Industry (91748) ***(P-453)***
Derik Plastics Industries Inc............A.......626 371-7799
2540 Corp Pl Ste B100 Monterey Park (91754) ***(P-5160)***
Derma E, Simi Valley *Also called Stearns Corporation* ***(P-8588)***
Dermacare Neuroscience Inst............F.......323 780-2981
2580 Corporate Pl F109 Monterey Park (91754) ***(P-8480)***
Dermal Group, The, Carson *Also called Dermalogica LLC* ***(P-8481)***
Dermalogica LLC (HQ)............C.......310 900-4000
1535 Beachey Pl Carson (90746) ***(P-8481)***
Dermanew LLC (PA)............F.......626 442-2813
436 Smithwood Dr Beverly Hills (90212) ***(P-8482)***
Dermanew LLC............F.......310 276-0457
9461 Santa Monica Blvd Beverly Hills (90210) ***(P-21680)***
Dermanew Institute, Beverly Hills *Also called Dermanew LLC* ***(P-21680)***
Dermira Inc............B.......650 421-7200
275 Middlefield Rd # 150 Menlo Park (94025) ***(P-7869)***
Derosa Enterprises Inc............E.......760 743-5500
15935 Spring Oaks Rd # 1 El Cajon (92021) ***(P-12182)***
Desais Design Craft............F.......626 285-3189
408 S Gladys Ave San Gabriel (91776) ***(P-10303)***
Deschner Corporation............E.......714 557-1261
3211 W Harvard St Santa Ana (92704) ***(P-14810)***
Desco Manufacturing Company (PA)............F.......949 858-7400
23031 Arroyo Vis Ste A Rcho STA Marg (92688) ***(P-15889)***
Desert Block Co Inc............F.......661 824-2624
11374 Tuxford St Sun Valley (91352) ***(P-9090)***
Desert Brand, City of Industry *Also called Hill Brothers Chemical Company* ***(P-7389)***
Desert Brothers Craft............F.......323 530-0015
603 W Whittier Blvd Montebello (90640) ***(P-1520)***
Desert Grafics, Palm Springs *Also called Desert Publications Inc* ***(P-5917)***
Desert Microsystems Inc............E.......951 682-3867
3387 Chicago Ave Riverside (92507) ***(P-20856)***
Desert Publications Inc (PA)............E.......760 325-2333
303 N Indian Canyon Dr Palm Springs (92262) ***(P-5917)***
Desert Redi Mix, Indio *Also called Coronet Concrete Products* ***(P-10750)***
Desert Shades Inc............F.......323 731-5000
5014 W Jefferson Blvd Los Angeles (90016) ***(P-23313)***
Desert Shutters Inc............E.......949 388-8344
33907 Robles Dr Dana Point (92629) ***(P-3972)***
Desert Sky Machining Inc............E.......925 426-0400
1236 Quarry Ln Ste 104 Pleasanton (94566) ***(P-15890)***
Desert Sun Publishing Co (HQ)............C.......760 322-8889
750 N Gene Autry Trl Palm Springs (92262) ***(P-5614)***
Desert Sun The, Palm Springs *Also called Desert Sun Publishing Co* ***(P-5614)***
Desert Sun, The, Palm Springs *Also called Gannett Co Inc* ***(P-5638)***
Desert Trils Prpratory Academy, Adelanto *Also called Adelanto Elementary School Dst* ***(P-2388)***
Desiccare Inc............E.......909 444-8272
3400 Pomona Blvd Pomona (91768) ***(P-10970)***
Design Catapult Manufacturing............F.......949 522-6789
3609 W Macarthur Blvd # 805 Santa Ana (92704) ***(P-21681)***
Design Concepts Inc............F.......323 277-4771
4625 E 50th St Vernon (90058) ***(P-3316)***
Design Engineering, Canoga Park *Also called Infinity Precision Inc* ***(P-16044)***
Design Form Inc............F.......714 952-3700
8250 Electric Ave Stanton (90680) ***(P-12016)***
Design Imagery............F.......650 589-6464
3621 Ortega St San Francisco (94122) ***(P-4973)***
Design Industries Inc............F.......559 675-3535
17918 Brook Dr W Madera (93638) ***(P-10560)***
Design Journal Inc............F.......310 394-4394
1720 20th St Ste 201 Santa Monica (90404) ***(P-5918)***
Design La, Santa Monica *Also called Design Journal Inc* ***(P-5918)***
Design Octaves............E.......831 464-8500
2701 Research Park Dr Soquel (95073) ***(P-9754)***
Design Polymerics, Santa Ana *Also called Davco Enterprises Inc* ***(P-8866)***
Design Printing, Los Angeles *Also called Red Brick Corporation* ***(P-6839)***
Design Shapes In Steel Inc............E.......626 579-2032
10315 Rush St South El Monte (91733) ***(P-11041)***
Design Todays Inc (PA)............D.......213 745-3091
725 E Wash Blvd Fl 2nd Los Angeles (90021) ***(P-3317)***
Design Veronique, Richmond *Also called My True Image Mfg Inc* ***(P-22052)***

Design West Technologies Inc...D...714 731-0201
2701 Dow Ave Tustin (92780) *(P-9755)*
Design Workshops...F...510 434-0727
486 Lesser St Oakland (94601) *(P-4897)*
Designed By Scorpio Inc...F...213 612-4440
550 S Hill St Ste 1605 Los Angeles (90013) *(P-22510)*
Designed Metal Connections Inc (HQ)...B...310 323-6200
14800 S Figueroa St Gardena (90248) *(P-12629)*
Designer Drinks...E...760 444-2355
5050 Avenida Encinas Carlsbad (92008) *(P-2071)*
Designer Fashion Door, Temecula *Also called Designer Sash and Door Sys Inc (P-9756)*
Designer Printing Inc...F...415 989-0008
638 Washington St San Francisco (94111) *(P-6536)*
Designer Sash and Door Sys Inc...D...951 657-4179
45899 Via Tornado Temecula (92590) *(P-9756)*
Designer Sound SEC Systems...F...818 981-9249
13547 Ventura Blvd # 338 Sherman Oaks (91423) *(P-19290)*
Designerx Pharmaceuticals Inc...F...707 451-0441
4941 Allison Pkwy Ste B Vacaville (95688) *(P-7870)*
Designline Windows & Doors Inc...E...760 931-9422
5674 El Camino Real Ste K Carlsbad (92008) *(P-11946)*
Designs By Batya Inc...F...213 746-7844
1200 Santee St Ste 208 Los Angeles (90015) *(P-2963)*
Designs With Fabric, South San Francisco *Also called Magnolia Lane Soft HM Furn Inc (P-3624)*
Deskmakers Inc...E...323 264-2260
6525 Flotilla St Commerce (90040) *(P-4795)*
Desserts On US Inc...F...707 822-0160
57 Belle Falor Ct Arcata (95521) *(P-1186)*
Destiney Group Inc...F...323 581-4477
4800 District Blvd Vernon (90058) *(P-2682)*
Destiny Boutique, Murrieta *Also called Tuula Inc (P-8353)*
Destiny Tool, Santa Clara *Also called Step Tools Unlimited Inc (P-14199)*
Detention Device Systems...E...510 783-0771
25545 Seaboard Ln Hayward (94545) *(P-15891)*
Detoronics Corp...E...626 579-7130
13071 Rosecrans Ave Santa Fe Springs (90670) *(P-18764)*
Detroit Diesel Corporation...F...562 929-7016
10645 Studebaker Rd Fl 2 Downey (90241) *(P-13595)*
Deutstch Industrial Products, Banning *Also called Te Connectivity Corporation (P-18791)*
Deux Lux Inc (PA)...E...213 746-7040
11609 Vanowen St Ste B North Hollywood (91605) *(P-10233)*
Deva, Tustin *Also called Distribution Electrnics Vlued (P-19291)*
Developlus Inc...D...951 738-8595
1575 Magnolia Ave Corona (92879) *(P-23314)*
Development Assoc Contrls...E...805 684-8307
6390 Rose Ln Carpinteria (93013) *(P-13913)*
Devincenzi Metal Products Inc...D...650 692-5800
1809 Castenada Dr Burlingame (94010) *(P-12183)*
Devincnzi Archtctural Pdts Inc...F...650 692-5800
1717 Adrian Rd Burlingame (94010) *(P-12470)*
Devita Dialysis, Santa Ana *Also called Da Vita Tustin Dialysis Ctr (P-21677)*
Devoll Rubber Mfg Group, Victorville *Also called Devoll Rubber Mfg Group Inc (P-9301)*
Devoll Rubber Mfg Group Inc...F...760 246-0142
18626 Phantom St Victorville (92394) *(P-9301)*
Devon Furniture, San Gabriel *Also called R J Vincent Inc (P-4663)*
Devoto-Wade Llc...F...415 265-4461
655 Gold Ridge Rd Sebastopol (95472) *(P-1663)*
Dewalt Service Center 148, Bellflower *Also called Black & Decker (us) Inc (P-14215)*
Deweyl Tool Co Inc...E...707 765-5779
959 Transport Way Petaluma (94954) *(P-14153)*
Dex-O-Tex Division, Compton *Also called Crossfield Products Corp (P-7551)*
Dexcom Inc (PA)...B...858 200-0200
6340 Sequence Dr San Diego (92121) *(P-21682)*
Dexerials America Corporation...F...408 441-0846
2001 Gateway Pl Ste 455e San Jose (95110) *(P-20966)*
Dexin International Inc (PA)...C...626 859-7475
677 Arrow Grand Cir Covina (91722) *(P-17024)*
Dext Company, Santa Monica *Also called Reconserve Inc (P-1120)*
Dext Company of Maryland (HQ)...E...310 458-1574
2811 Wilshire Blvd # 410 Santa Monica (90403) *(P-1090)*
Dexta Corporation...D...707 255-2454
957 Enterprise Way NAPA (94558) *(P-22148)*
Dexter Axle Company...C...760 744-1610
135 Sunshine Ln San Marcos (92069) *(P-19819)*
Dexters Deli...E...760 720-7507
2508 El Cmino Real Ste B2 Carlsbad (92008) *(P-1072)*
Dezario Shoe Company, North Hollywood *Also called Meco-Nag Corporation (P-10172)*
Df Grafix Inc...F...858 866-0858
13871 Danielson St Poway (92064) *(P-6537)*
Dfine Inc (HQ)...D...408 321-9999
3047 Orchard Pkwy San Jose (95134) *(P-21683)*
Dg Displays LLC...E...877 358-5976
355 Parkside Dr San Fernando (91340) *(P-23088)*
Dg Engineering Corp (PA)...E...818 364-9024
13326 Ralston Ave Sylmar (91342) *(P-20570)*
Dg Mountz Associates, San Jose *Also called Mountz Inc (P-20906)*
DG Performance Spc Inc...D...714 961-8850
4100 E La Palma Ave Anaheim (92807) *(P-20506)*
DGA Machine Shop Inc...F...951 354-2113
5825 Ordway St Riverside (92504) *(P-15892)*
Dgb LLC...E...858 578-0414
8495 Commerce Ave San Diego (92121) *(P-22789)*
Dggr Packaging Crating & Foam, Anaheim *Also called JDC Development Group Inc (P-4417)*
Dharma Mudranalaya (PA)...E...707 847-3380
35788 Hauser Bridge Rd Cazadero (95421) *(P-6097)*
Dharma Publishing, Cazadero *Also called Dharma Mudranalaya (P-6097)*
Dhl Wire Products...F...909 596-2909
2325 1st St La Verne (91750) *(P-11091)*
Dhm Enterprises Inc...E...916 688-7767
7609 Wilbur Way Sacramento (95828) *(P-20507)*
DHm International Corp...D...323 263-3888
901 Monterey Pass Rd Monterey Park (91754) *(P-3318)*
Dhy Inc...E...310 376-7512
922 Duncan Ave Manhattan Beach (90266) *(P-3075)*
Diablo Clinical Research Inc...E...925 930-7267
2255 Ygnacio Valley Rd M Walnut Creek (94598) *(P-7871)*
Diablo Country Magazine Inc...E...925 943-1111
2520 Camino Diablo Walnut Creek (94597) *(P-5919)*
Diablo Custom Publishing, Walnut Creek *Also called Diablo Country Magazine Inc (P-5919)*
Diablo Molding & Trim Company...E...925 417-0663
5600 Sunol Blvd Ste C Pleasanton (94566) *(P-11947)*
Diablo Precision Inc...F...831 634-0136
500 Park Center Dr Ste 8 Hollister (95023) *(P-15893)*
Diageno Chateau & Estate Wines, NAPA *Also called Diageo North America Inc (P-1666)*
Diageo North America Inc...D...707 939-6200
21468 8th St E Ste 1 Sonoma (95476) *(P-1664)*
Diageo North America Inc...D...707 967-5200
1960 Saint Helena Hwy Rutherford (94573) *(P-2013)*
Diageo North America Inc...D...415 835-7300
1160 Battery St Ste 30 San Francisco (94111) *(P-1665)*
Diageo North America Inc...D...707 299-2600
555 Gateway Dr NAPA (94558) *(P-1666)*
Diagnostic Reagents, Los Angeles *Also called James Stewart (P-7967)*
Diagnostic Solutions Intl LLC...F...909 930-3600
2580 E Philadelphia St C Ontario (91761) *(P-20085)*
Diagnostics For Real World Ltd (PA)...F...408 773-1511
845 Embedded Way San Jose (95138) *(P-8219)*
Diagnostixx California Corp...E...909 482-0840
829 Towne Center Dr Pomona (91767) *(P-21684)*
Dial Precision Inc...D...760 947-3557
17235 Darwin Ave Hesperia (92345) *(P-15894)*
Dialact Corporation...F...510 659-8099
1111 Elko Dr Ste D Sunnyvale (94089) *(P-9402)*
Dialex, Sunnyvale *Also called Dialact Corporation (P-9402)*
Dialog Semiconductor, Campbell *Also called Iwatt Inc (P-18324)*
Dialog Semiconductor Inc (HQ)...E...408 845-8500
2560 Mission College Blvd # 110 Santa Clara (95054) *(P-18195)*
Dialogic Inc...D...800 755-4444
2890 Zanker Rd Ste 107 San Jose (95134) *(P-17360)*
Diamanti Inc...E...408 645-5111
111 N Market St Ste 800 San Jose (95113) *(P-15122)*
Diamatic Management Services, San Diego *Also called Global Polishing Solutions LLC (P-13730)*
Diamics Inc...F...415 883-0414
6 Hamilton Landing # 200 Novato (94949) *(P-21685)*
Diamodent Inc...F...888 281-8850
1580 N Harmony Cir Anaheim (92807) *(P-22149)*
Diamon Fusion Intl Inc...F...949 388-8000
9361 Irvine Blvd Irvine (92618) *(P-8958)*
Diamond Baseball Company Inc...E...800 366-2999
1880 E Saint Andrew Pl Santa Ana (92705) *(P-22790)*
Diamond Collection LLC...E...626 435-0077
14438 Don Julian Rd City of Industry (91746) *(P-3551)*
Diamond Creek Vineyard...F...707 942-6926
1500 Diamond Mountain Rd Calistoga (94515) *(P-1667)*
Diamond Crystal Brands Inc...E...559 651-7782
8700 W Doe Ave Visalia (93291) *(P-2444)*
Diamond Crystal Brands-Hormel, Visalia *Also called Diamond Crystal Brands Inc (P-2444)*
Diamond Doors, South Lake Tahoe *Also called Diamond Woodcraft (P-4035)*
Diamond Foods LLC (PA)...A...209 467-6000
1050 Diamond St Stockton (95205) *(P-1424)*
Diamond Foods LLC...F...209 467-6000
600 Montgomery St Fl 17 San Francisco (94111) *(P-1425)*
Diamond Gloves...E...714 667-0506
1100 S Linwood Ave Ste A Santa Ana (92705) *(P-21997)*
Diamond Ground Products Inc...E...805 498-3837
2651 Lavery Ct Newbury Park (91320) *(P-14240)*
Diamond Injection Molds Inc...F...909 390-2260
4365 E Lowell St Ste E Ontario (91761) *(P-14042)*
Diamond K2...E...310 539-6116
23911 Garnier St Ste C Torrance (90505) *(P-11551)*
Diamond Multimedia, Canoga Park *Also called Best Data Products Inc (P-15169)*
Diamond Multimedia Systems...B...408 868-9613
2880 Junction Ave San Jose (95134) *(P-17863)*
Diamond of California, Stockton *Also called Diamond Foods LLC (P-1424)*
Diamond Perforated Metals Inc...D...559 651-1889
7300 W Sunnyview Ave Visalia (93291) *(P-12793)*
Diamond Pet Food Processors O...E...209 983-4900
250 Roth Rd Lathrop (95330) *(P-1073)*
Diamond Precision Products, Placentia *Also called Foremost Precision Pdts Inc (P-15967)*
Diamond Sports, Santa Ana *Also called Diamond Baseball Company Inc (P-22790)*
Diamond Tech Incorporated...F...916 624-1118
4347 Pacific St Rocklin (95677) *(P-14220)*
Diamond Tool and Die Inc...E...510 534-7050
508 29th Ave Oakland (94601) *(P-15895)*
Diamond Truck Body Mfg Inc...F...209 943-1655
1908 E Fremont St Stockton (95205) *(P-19528)*
Diamond Truss...F...530 477-1477
12462 Charles Dr Grass Valley (95945) *(P-4299)*
Diamond Weld Industries Inc...F...559 268-9999
63 W North Ave Fresno (93706) *(P-14241)*
Diamond Wipes Intl Inc (PA)...D...909 230-9888
4651 Schaefer Ave Chino (91710) *(P-8483)*
Diamond Woodcraft...F...530 541-0866
2197 Ruth Ave Ste 1 South Lake Tahoe (96150) *(P-4035)*

ALPHABETIC

Employee Codes: A=Over 500 employees, B=251-500
C=101-250, D=51-100, E=20-50, F=10-19
2020 California
Manfacturers Register
© Mergent Inc. 1-800-342-5647
1081

Diamond-U Products Inc ....F....562 436-8245
515 W Cowles St Long Beach (90813) ***(P-13327)***
Diamonds By Design, Los Angeles *Also called Stardust Diamond Corp* ***(P-22601)***
Diamotec Inc ....F....310 539-4994
22104 S Vt Ave Ste 104 Torrance (90502) ***(P-14154)***
Dianas Mexican Food Pdts Inc (PA) ....E....562 926-5802
16330 Pioneer Blvd Norwalk (90650) ***(P-2445)***
Dianas Mexican Food Pdts Inc ....E....626 444-0555
2905 Durfee Ave El Monte (91732) ***(P-2446)***
Diane Markin Inc ....F....310 322-0200
112 Penn St El Segundo (90245) ***(P-10354)***
Diaring Inc ....F....213 489-3894
550 S Hill St Ste 990 Los Angeles (90013) ***(P-22511)***
Diasol Inc (PA) ....F....818 838-7077
1110 Arroyo St San Fernando (91340) ***(P-21686)***
Diasorin Molecular LLC ....C....562 240-6500
11331 Valley View St Cypress (90630) ***(P-8220)***
Diatomaceous Earth.com, Santa Barbara *Also called Esperer Webstores LLC* ***(P-586)***
Dicaperl Corporation (HQ) ....D....610 667-6640
23705 Crenshaw Blvd Torrance (90505) ***(P-386)***
Dicar Inc ....E....408 295-1106
1285 Alma Ct San Jose (95112) ***(P-11301)***
Dicarlo Concrete Inc ....F....909 261-4294
8657 Pecan Ave Ste 100 Rancho Cucamonga (91739) ***(P-17314)***
Dick Brown Technical Services ....F....707 374-2133
553 Airport Rd Ste B Rio Vista (94571) ***(P-90)***
Dick Farrell Industries Inc ....F....909 613-9424
5071 Lindsay Ct Chino (91710) ***(P-14759)***
Dicker & Dicker Beverly Hills, Beverly Hills *Also called Larry B LLC* ***(P-3500)***
Dickinson Corporation ....F....415 883-7147
31 Commercial Blvd Ste G Novato (94949) ***(P-20754)***
Dicon Fiberoptics Inc (PA) ....C....510 620-5000
1689 Regatta Blvd Bldg W1 Richmond (94804) ***(P-18887)***
Didi of California Inc ....E....323 256-4514
5816 Piedmont Ave Los Angeles (90042) ***(P-3155)***
Die & Tool Products Co Inc ....F....415 822-2888
1842 Sabre St Hayward (94545) ***(P-15896)***
Die Craft Engineering & Mfg Co ....F....562 777-8809
11975 Florence Ave Santa Fe Springs (90670) ***(P-14043)***
Die Craft Stamping Inc ....E....562 944-2395
10132 Norwalk Blvd Santa Fe Springs (90670) ***(P-13350)***
Die Shop ....F....562 630-4400
7302 Adams St Paramount (90723) ***(P-14044)***
Die-Namic Fabrication Inc ....F....909 350-2870
378 E Orange Show Rd San Bernardino (92408) ***(P-12794)***
Diecraft, Santa Fe Springs *Also called Die Craft Engineering & Mfg Co* ***(P-14043)***
Diecraft Corporation ....E....323 728-2601
5590 Naples Canal Long Beach (90803) ***(P-15897)***
Diego & Son Printing Inc ....E....619 233-5373
2277 National Ave San Diego (92113) ***(P-6538)***
Dielectric Coating Industries ....F....510 487-5980
30997 Huntwood Ave # 104 Hayward (94544) ***(P-21348)***
Diesel Injection Service, Colton *Also called Ostoich Diesel Service* ***(P-15631)***
Dietrich Industries Inc ....D....209 547-9066
2525 S Airport Way Stockton (95206) ***(P-11042)***
Dietzgen Corporation ....E....951 278-3259
1522 E Bentley Dr Corona (92879) ***(P-5505)***
Dig Corporation ....D....760 727-0914
1210 Activity Dr Vista (92081) ***(P-13624)***
Diggimac Inc DBA Ltg Element ....F....858 322-6000
16885 W Bernardo Dr # 380 San Diego (92127) ***(P-16893)***
Digi Group LLC ....F....800 521-8467
2421 W 205th St Ste D204 Torrance (90501) ***(P-17501)***
Digi Print Plus ....F....949 770-5000
9670 Research Dr Irvine (92618) ***(P-6539)***
Digicom Electronics Inc ....E....510 639-7003
7799 Pardee Ln Oakland (94621) ***(P-17864)***
Digilens Inc ....E....408 734-0219
1288 Hammerwood Ave Sunnyvale (94089) ***(P-21349)***
Digilock, Petaluma *Also called Security People Inc* ***(P-19080)***
Digital Check Technologies Inc ....E....909 204-4638
10231 Trademark St Ste A Rancho Cucamonga (91730) ***(P-15215)***
Digital Dynamics Inc ....E....831 438-4444
5 Victor Sq Scotts Valley (95066) ***(P-20857)***
Digital First Media LLC ....A....714 796-7000
625 N Grand Ave Santa Ana (92701) ***(P-5615)***
Digital Instruments Div, Goleta *Also called Veeco Process Equipment Inc* ***(P-21320)***
Digital Label Solutions Inc ....E....714 982-5000
22745 Old Canal Rd Yorba Linda (92887) ***(P-5506)***
Digital Loggers Inc ....E....408 330-5599
2695 Walsh Ave Santa Clara (95051) ***(P-16594)***
Digital Mania Inc ....E....415 896-0500
455 Market St Ste 180 San Francisco (94105) ***(P-6540)***
Digital Music Corporation ....F....707 545-0600
3165 Coffey Ln Santa Rosa (95403) ***(P-22612)***
Digital One Legal Solutions, San Francisco *Also called Copy 1 Inc* ***(P-6512)***
Digital One Printing Inc ....F....858 278-2228
13367 Kirkham Way 110 Poway (92064) ***(P-6541)***
Digital Periph Solutions Inc ....E....714 998-3440
160 S Old Springs Rd Anaheim (92808) ***(P-17218)***
Digital Power Corporation (HQ) ....E....510 657-2635
48430 Lakeview Blvd Fremont (94538) ***(P-18888)***
Digital Pre-Press Intl, South San Francisco *Also called Pre-Press International* ***(P-6789)***
Digital Printing Systems Inc (PA) ....D....626 815-1888
777 N Georgia Ave Azusa (91702) ***(P-6542)***
Digital Prototype Systems Inc ....E....559 454-1600
4955 E Yale Ave Fresno (93727) ***(P-17502)***
Digital Room Holdings Inc (PA) ....C....310 575-4440
8000 Haskell Ave Van Nuys (91406) ***(P-7045)***
Digital Signal Power Mfg, Ontario *Also called Dspm Inc* ***(P-18712)***
Digital Storm, Morgan Hill *Also called Hanaps Enterprises* ***(P-15238)***
Digital Surgery Systems Inc ....E....805 308-6909
315 Bollay Dr Goleta (93117) ***(P-21687)***
Digital Technology Lab Corp ....D....530 746-7400
3805 Faraday Ave Davis (95618) ***(P-14155)***
Digital Video Systems Inc (PA) ....E....650 938-8815
357 Castro St Ste 5 Mountain View (94041) ***(P-17219)***
Digital View Inc ....F....408 782-7773
18440 Tech Dr Ste 130 Morgan Hill (95037) ***(P-18889)***
Digitalpro Inc ....D....858 874-7750
13257 Kirkham Way Poway (92064) ***(P-7046)***
Digitran, Rancho Cucamonga *Also called Electro Switch Corp* ***(P-16597)***
Digivision Inc ....F....858 530-0100
9830 Summers Ridge Rd San Diego (92121) ***(P-20858)***
Dih Technologies Co ....F....858 768-9816
8920 Activity Rd Ste A San Diego (92126) ***(P-21688)***
Dilco Industrial Inc ....F....714 998-5266
205 E Bristol Ln Orange (92865) ***(P-14288)***
Diligent Solutions Inc ....E....760 814-8960
3240 Grey Hawk Ct Carlsbad (92010) ***(P-15898)***
Dillon Aircraft Deburring ....E....818 768-0801
11771 Sheldon St Sun Valley (91352) ***(P-12985)***
Dillon Precision Incorporated ....E....530 672-6794
3816 Maplewood Ln Placerville (95667) ***(P-15899)***
Dimad Enterprises Inc (PA) ....F....626 445-3303
44 La Porte St Arcadia (91006) ***(P-12986)***
Dimad Metal Finishing, Arcadia *Also called Dimad Enterprises Inc* ***(P-12986)***
Dimaxx Technologies LLC ....F....530 888-1942
11838 Kemper Rd Auburn (95603) ***(P-21350)***
Dime Racing, Huntington Beach *Also called Dime Research and Development* ***(P-19466)***
Dime Research and Development ....E....714 969-7879
5542 Research Dr Huntington Beach (92649) ***(P-19466)***
Dimensional Plastics Corp ....E....305 691-5961
6565 Crescent Park W # 111 Playa Vista (90094) ***(P-9757)***
Dimensions In Screen Printing, Irvine *Also called Tomorrows Look Inc* ***(P-2840)***
Dimensions of Dental Hygiene, Santa Ana *Also called Belmont Publications Inc* ***(P-5888)***
Dimensions Unlimited ....F....707 552-6800
1080 Nimitz Ave Ste 400 Vallejo (94592) ***(P-4898)***
Dimic Steel Tech Inc ....E....909 946-6767
145 N 8th Ave Upland (91786) ***(P-12184)***
Dimora Enterprises ....F....760 832-9070
1775 E Palm Canyon Dr # 105 Palm Springs (92264) ***(P-19467)***
Dimufidra Usa Inc ....D....323 651-3822
7356 Melrose Ave Los Angeles (90046) ***(P-1187)***
Dincloud Inc ....D....310 929-1101
27520 Hawthorne Blvd # 185 Rllng HLS Est (90274) ***(P-23817)***
Dinner On A Dollar Inc ....F....858 693-3939
10249 Caminito Pitaya San Diego (92131) ***(P-6221)***
Dinsmore & Associates Inc ....F....714 641-7111
1681 Kettering Irvine (92614) ***(P-9403)***
Dinuba Sentinel, Dinuba *Also called Sentinel Printing & Publishing* ***(P-5824)***
Dion Rostamian ....F....877 633-0293
1146 N Central Ave 227 Glendale (91202) ***(P-22413)***
Dionex Corporation (HQ) ....B....408 737-0700
1228 Titan Way Ste 1002 Sunnyvale (94085) ***(P-21216)***
Dionex Corporation ....D....408 737-0700
501 Mercury Dr Sunnyvale (94085) ***(P-21217)***
Dip Braze Inc ....E....818 768-1555
9131 De Garmo Ave Sun Valley (91352) ***(P-24631)***
Direct Chemicals, Huntington Beach *Also called Home & Body Company* ***(P-8389)***
Direct Drive Systems Inc ....D....714 872-5500
621 Burning Tree Rd Fullerton (92833) ***(P-16638)***
Direct Edge Screenworks Inc ....F....714 579-3686
430 W Collins Ave Orange (92867) ***(P-7047)***
Direct Label & Tag LLC ....E....562 948-4499
11909 Telegraph Rd Santa Fe Springs (90670) ***(P-6543)***
Direct Surplus Sales Inc ....F....530 533-9999
4801 Feather River Blvd # 3 Oroville (95965) ***(P-12185)***
Direct Systems Support, Westlake Village *Also called ABF Data Systems Inc* ***(P-23542)***
Dis, Azusa *Also called Dependble Incontinence Sup Inc* ***(P-5460)***
Disc Pumps, Santee *Also called Discflo Corporation* ***(P-14568)***
Disc Replicator Inc ....F....909 385-0118
21137 Commerce Point Dr Walnut (91789) ***(P-17315)***
Discflo Corporation ....E....619 596-3181
10850 Hartley Rd Santee (92071) ***(P-14568)***
Discopylabs (PA) ....E....510 651-5100
48641 Milmont Dr Fremont (94538) ***(P-17316)***
Discopylabs ....D....909 390-3800
4455 E Philadelphia St Ontario (91761) ***(P-17317)***
Discount Blind Center ....F....951 678-3980
16074 Grand Ave Lake Elsinore (92530) ***(P-5020)***
Discount Instant Printing ....F....213 622-4347
175 S Thurston Ave Los Angeles (90049) ***(P-6544)***
Discount Medical Supply, San Fernando *Also called Diasol Inc* ***(P-21686)***
Discount Merchant.com, San Diego *Also called MI Technologies Inc* ***(P-17926)***
Discount Outlet, Riverside *Also called Embroidery Outlet* ***(P-3743)***
Discounted Wheel Warehouse, Fullerton *Also called Wheel and Tire Club Inc* ***(P-11082)***
Disguise Inc (HQ) ....E....858 391-3600
12120 Kear Pl Poway (92064) ***(P-3552)***
Dishcraft Robotics Inc ....F....415 595-9671
611 Taylor Way Ste 1 San Carlos (94070) ***(P-14452)***
Disk Faktory, Tustin *Also called Innovative Diversfd Tech Inc* ***(P-15048)***
Disney Book Group LLC (HQ) ....F....818 560-1000
500 S Buena Vista St Burbank (91521) ***(P-6098)***
Disney Enterprises Inc ....D....407 397-6000
1313 S Harbor Blvd Anaheim (92802) ***(P-3553)***

Disney Publishing Worldwide (HQ)........D.......212 633-4400
500 S Buena Vista St Burbank (91521) ***(P-5920)***
Disorderly Kids, Los Angeles *Also called Avalon Apparel LLC* ***(P-3475)***
Dispatcher Newspaper........E.......415 775-0533
1188 Franklin St Fl 4 San Francisco (94109) ***(P-5616)***
Dispensing Dynamics Intl Inc (PA)........D.......626 961-3691
1020 Bixby Dr City of Industry (91745) ***(P-9758)***
Display Advertising Inc........F.......559 266-0231
1837 Van Ness Ave Fresno (93721) ***(P-7048)***
Display Fabrication Group Inc........E.......714 373-2100
1231 N Miller St Ste 100 Anaheim (92806) ***(P-3836)***
Display Integration Tech, Oceanside *Also called 2 S 2 Inc* ***(P-18803)***
Disposable Waste System, Santa Ana *Also called Jwc Environmental LLC* ***(P-15531)***
Distillery Inc........D.......415 505-5446
90 Heron Ct San Quentin (94964) ***(P-23818)***
Distinct Indulgence Inc........E.......818 546-1700
5018 Lante St Baldwin Park (91706) ***(P-1188)***
Distinctive Inds Texas Inc........E.......323 889-5766
9419 Ann St Santa Fe Springs (90670) ***(P-3512)***
Distinctive Inds Texas Inc........E.......512 491-3500
10618 Shoemaker Ave Santa Fe Springs (90670) ***(P-3513)***
Distinctive Industries........B.......800 421-9777
10618 Shoemaker Ave Santa Fe Springs (90670) ***(P-3784)***
Distinctive Metals By Angel S, Angels Camp *Also called Angels Sheet Metal Inc* ***(P-12110)***
Distinctive Plastics Inc........D.......760 599-9100
1385 Decision St Vista (92081) ***(P-9759)***
Distinctive Prpts NAPA Vly........D.......707 256-2251
1615 2nd St NAPA (94559) ***(P-5921)***
Distribution Center, San Bernardino *Also called Romeros Food Products Inc* ***(P-2604)***
Distribution Electrnics Vlued........E.......714 368-1717
2651 Dow Ave Tustin (92780) ***(P-19291)***
Distributors Processing Inc........F.......559 781-0297
17656 Avenue 168 Porterville (93257) ***(P-2203)***
Dita Inc (PA)........E.......949 599-2700
1787 Pomona Rd Corona (92880) ***(P-22348)***
Dita Eyewear, Corona *Also called Dita Inc* ***(P-22348)***
Ditec Co........F.......805 566-7800
1019 Mark Ave Carpinteria (93013) ***(P-21689)***
Ditec Mfg., Carpinteria *Also called Ditec Co* ***(P-21689)***
Ditech Networks Inc (HQ)........E.......408 883-3636
3099 N 1st St San Jose (95134) ***(P-17361)***
Diverse McHning Fbrication LLC........F.......916 672-6591
3620 Cincinnati Ave Ste A Rocklin (95765) ***(P-13514)***
Diverse Optics Inc........E.......909 593-9330
10310 Regis Ct Rancho Cucamonga (91730) ***(P-9760)***
Diversfied Mtllrgical Svcs Inc........E.......714 895-7777
12101 Industry St Garden Grove (92841) ***(P-11450)***
Diversfied Nano Solutions Corp........E.......858 924-1017
10531 4s Commons Dr San Diego (92127) ***(P-8911)***
Diversfied Tchncal Systems Inc (PA)........E.......562 493-0158
1720 Apollo Ct Seal Beach (90740) ***(P-18890)***
Diversified Construction, Oxnard *Also called Diversified Panels Systems Inc* ***(P-15424)***
Diversified Hangar Company........F.......805 239-8229
5905 Monterey Rd Paso Robles (93446) ***(P-11785)***
Diversified Images Inc........F.......661 702-0003
27955 Beale Ct Valencia (91355) ***(P-7049)***
Diversified Litho Services........F.......714 558-2995
4462 E Airport Dr Ontario (91761) ***(P-6545)***
Diversified Mfg Cal Inc........F.......760 599-9280
2555 Progress St Vista (92081) ***(P-15900)***
Diversified Mfg Tech Inc........F.......714 577-7000
931 S Via Rodeo Placentia (92870) ***(P-14045)***
Diversified Minerals Inc........E.......805 247-1069
1100 Mountain View Ave F Oxnard (93030) ***(P-10753)***
Diversified Nano Corporation (PA)........F.......858 673-0387
16885 W Bernardo Dr # 275 San Diego (92127) ***(P-15216)***
Diversified Packaging Inc........E.......714 850-9316
2221 S Anne St Santa Ana (92704) ***(P-9524)***
Diversified Panels Systems Inc........F.......805 487-9241
2345 Statham Blvd Oxnard (93033) ***(P-15424)***
Diversified Plastics Inc........E.......760 598-5333
1333 Keystone Way Vista (92081) ***(P-9761)***
Diversified Printers Inc........D.......714 994-3400
12834 Maxwell Dr Tustin (92782) ***(P-6222)***
Diversified Silicone, Santa Fe Springs *Also called Rogers Corporation* ***(P-9366)***
Diversified Spring Tech........F.......562 944-4049
9233 Santa Fe Springs Rd Santa Fe Springs (90670) ***(P-13380)***
Diversified Tool & Die........E.......760 598-9100
2585 Birch St Vista (92081) ***(P-12795)***
Diversitech Corporation........F.......760 246-4200
9252 Cassia Rd Adelanto (92301) ***(P-10561)***
Diversity In Steam, Irvine *Also called Diversitycomm Inc* ***(P-5922)***
Diversitycomm Inc........F.......949 825-5777
18 Technology Dr Ste 170 Irvine (92618) ***(P-5922)***
Divine Foods Inc........E.......800 440-6476
16752 Millikan Ave Irvine (92606) ***(P-1363)***
Divine Pasta Company........E.......213 542-3300
140 W Providencia Ave Burbank (91502) ***(P-2447)***
Diving Unlimited International........D.......619 236-1203
1148 Delevan Dr San Diego (92102) ***(P-22791)***
Divisadero 500 LLC........F.......415 572-6062
502 Divisadero St San Francisco (94117) ***(P-5055)***
Dixietruss Inc........F.......619 873-0440
12538 Vigilante Rd Lakeside (92040) ***(P-10562)***
Dixon Hard Chrome, Sun Valley *Also called Florence International Company* ***(P-13010)***
Dixon Tribune, Dixon *Also called Gibson Printing & Publishing* ***(P-5647)***
Dixon Tribune........F.......707 678-5594
145 E A St Dixon (95620) ***(P-5617)***
Diy Co........F.......844 564-6349
3360 20th St San Francisco (94110) ***(P-19292)***
Diy Drones, Berkeley *Also called 3d Robotics Inc* ***(P-19244)***
DJ Grey Company Inc........F.......707 431-2779
455 Allan Ct Healdsburg (95448) ***(P-18891)***
DJ Safety Inc........E.......323 221-0000
2623 N San Fernando Rd Los Angeles (90065) ***(P-3785)***
Djh Enterprises........E.......714 424-6500
234 Fischer Ave Costa Mesa (92626) ***(P-17503)***
Dji Service LLC........F.......818 235-0788
17301 Edwards Rd Cerritos (90703) ***(P-20086)***
Dji Technology Inc........E.......818 235-0789
201 S Victory Blvd Burbank (91502) ***(P-22414)***
DJM Suspension, Gardena *Also called D and J Marketing Inc* ***(P-3782)***
Djo LLC........F.......760 727-1280
3151 Scott St Vista (92081) ***(P-21998)***
Dkny, Commerce *Also called AM Retail Group Inc* ***(P-3212)***
Dkp Designs Inc........F.......310 322-6000
110 Maryland St El Segundo (90245) ***(P-23315)***
Dkp Inc........E.......559 266-2695
275 N Marks Ave Fresno (93706) ***(P-13625)***
Dkw Precision Machining Inc........E.......209 824-7899
17731 Ideal Pkwy Manteca (95336) ***(P-15901)***
Dl Tool and Mfg Co Inc........F.......818 837-3451
11828 Glenoaks Blvd San Fernando (91340) ***(P-14046)***
Dla Document Services........E.......805 982-4310
4231 San Pedro Rd Port Hueneme (93043) ***(P-6546)***
Dlc Laboratories Inc........F.......562 602-2184
7008 Marcelle St Paramount (90723) ***(P-7872)***
Dlive Inc........E.......650 491-9555
19450 Stevens Creek Blvd Cupertino (95014) ***(P-6223)***
DLS, Ontario *Also called Diversified Litho Services* ***(P-6545)***
Dlt Co, Los Angeles *Also called E J Y Corporation* ***(P-3739)***
Dm Collective Inc........E.......323 923-2400
4536 District Blvd Vernon (90058) ***(P-2782)***
Dm Luxury LLC........C.......858 366-9721
875 Prospect St Ste 300 La Jolla (92037) ***(P-7050)***
Dm Software Inc........F.......714 953-2653
1842 Park Skyline Rd Santa Ana (92705) ***(P-23819)***
Dmbm LLC........E.......714 321-6032
2445 E 12th St Ste C Los Angeles (90021) ***(P-3319)***
DMC Power Inc (PA)........D.......310 323-1616
623 E Artesia Blvd Carson (90746) ***(P-16894)***
Dmea MSC........E.......916 568-4087
5584 Patrol Rd Bldg 1069 McClellan (95652) ***(P-20087)***
Dmg Mori Manufacturing USA Inc (HQ)........E.......530 746-7400
3805 Faraday Ave Davis (95618) ***(P-13914)***
Dmg Mori Usa Inc........F.......562 430-3800
5740 Warland Dr Cypress (90630) ***(P-13915)***
Dmi Ready Mix, Oxnard *Also called Diversified Minerals Inc* ***(P-10753)***
Dmoc, Vista *Also called Diversified Mfg Cal Inc* ***(P-15900)***
Dmt, Placentia *Also called Diversified Mfg Tech Inc* ***(P-14045)***
Dn Tanks Inc (PA)........C.......619 440-8181
351 Cypress Ln El Cajon (92020) ***(P-20497)***
Dna Health Inst Cyrogenic Div, Ventura *Also called Dna Health Institute Llc* ***(P-8735)***
Dna Health Institute Llc........F.......805 654-9363
4562 Westinghouse St B Ventura (93003) ***(P-8735)***
Dnf Controls, Northridge *Also called Universal Ctrl Solutions Corp* ***(P-16763)***
Dnp America LLC........F.......408 616-1200
2099 Gateway Pl Ste 490 San Jose (95110) ***(P-18196)***
Do Dine Inc........F.......510 583-7546
24052 Mission Blvd Hayward (94544) ***(P-23820)***
Do It American Mfg Company LLC........F.......951 254-9204
137 Vander St Corona (92880) ***(P-13515)***
Do It Best, Pasadena *Also called George L Throop Co* ***(P-10580)***
Do It Right Products LLC (PA)........F.......661 722-9664
44321 62nd St W Lancaster (93536) ***(P-10563)***
Do It Right Products LLC........F.......714 998-8152
1838 N Case St Orange (92865) ***(P-23316)***
Do Well Laboratories Inc........F.......949 252-0001
14791 Myford Rd Tustin (92780) ***(P-585)***
Do-Nut Wheel Inc........F.......408 252-8193
10250 N De Anza Blvd Cupertino (95014) ***(P-1189)***
Doble Engineering Company........F.......909 923-9390
1520 S Hellman Ave Ontario (91761) ***(P-16595)***
Dockum Research Laboratory........F.......626 794-1821
844 E Mariposa St Altadena (91001) ***(P-22150)***
Docrun, Santa Monica *Also called Owl Territory Inc* ***(P-24283)***
Docsend Inc........F.......888 258-5951
351 California St # 1200 San Francisco (94104) ***(P-23821)***
Doctor On Demand Inc........D.......415 935-4447
275 Battery St Ste 650 San Francisco (94111) ***(P-23822)***
Doctors Signature Sales........E.......800 531-4877
495 Raleigh Ave El Cajon (92020) ***(P-7653)***
Document Capture Tech Inc (PA)........E.......408 436-9888
41332 Christy St Fremont (94538) ***(P-15217)***
Document Proc Solutions Inc........E.......925 839-1182
535 Main St Ste 317 Martinez (94553) ***(P-5102)***
Documotion Research Inc........F.......714 662-3800
2020 S Eastwood Ave Santa Ana (92705) ***(P-6547)***
Docupak Inc........E.......714 670-7944
17515 Valley View Ave Cerritos (90703) ***(P-7312)***
Docusign Inc (PA)........B.......415 489-4940
221 Main St Ste 1550 San Francisco (94105) ***(P-23823)***
Dodge - Wasmund Mfg Inc........F.......562 692-8104
4510 Manning Rd Pico Rivera (90660) ***(P-9762)***
Doerksen Precision Products........F.......831 476-1843
2725 Chanticleer Ave # 7 Santa Cruz (95065) ***(P-15902)***

Employee Codes: A=Over 500 employees, B=251-500
C=101-250, D=51-100, E=20-50, F=10-19
2020 California
Manfacturers Register
© Mergent Inc. 1-800-342-5647
1083

Dogeared Inc..........D.......310 846-4444
6053 Bristol Pkwy Culver City (90230) ***(P-22980)***
Dogg Digital, Cypress *Also called Tr Theater Research Inc* ***(P-17295)***
Dogpatch Wineworks..........F.......415 525-4440
170 Henry St San Francisco (94114) ***(P-1668)***
Doi Venture, Rancho Cucamonga *Also called Davidson Optronics Inc* ***(P-21458)***
Doka USA Ltd..........F.......951 509-0023
6901 Central Ave Riverside (92504) ***(P-12186)***
Dolby Laboratories Inc..........F.......408 730-5543
432 Lakeside Dr Sunnyvale (94085) ***(P-17504)***
Dolby Laboratories Inc..........E.......818 562-1101
1020 Chestnut St Burbank (91506) ***(P-17220)***
Dolby Laboratories Inc (PA)..........B.......415 558-0200
1275 Market St San Francisco (94103) ***(P-17221)***
Dolby Laboratories Inc..........D.......415 715-2500
175 S Hill Dr Brisbane (94005) ***(P-17505)***
Dolby Labs, Brisbane *Also called Dolby Laboratories Inc* ***(P-17505)***
Dolce Dolci LLC..........F.......818 343-8400
16745 Saticoy St Ste 112 Van Nuys (91406) ***(P-639)***
Dole Fresh Vegetables Inc (HQ)..........C.......831 422-8871
2959 Salinas Hwy Monterey (93940) ***(P-2448)***
Dole Packaged Foods LLC (HQ)..........A.......805 601-5500
3059 Townsgate Rd Ste 400 Westlake Village (91361) ***(P-910)***
Dole Packaged Foods LLC..........C.......559 875-3354
1117 K St Sanger (93657) ***(P-911)***
Dollar Shave Club Inc (HQ)..........E.......310 975-8528
13335 Maxella Ave Marina Del Rey (90292) ***(P-13916)***
Dolores Canning Coinc..........E.......323 263-9155
1020 N Eastern Ave Los Angeles (90063) ***(P-725)***
Dolphin Medical Inc (HQ)..........D.......800 448-6506
12525 Chadron Ave Hawthorne (90250) ***(P-22249)***
Dolphin Press Inc..........F.......650 873-9092
264 S Maple Ave South San Francisco (94080) ***(P-6548)***
Dolphin Spas Inc..........F.......626 334-0099
701 W Foothill Blvd Azusa (91702) ***(P-23317)***
Dolstra Automatic Products..........F.......714 894-2062
14441 Edwards St Westminster (92683) ***(P-15903)***
Domaine Chandon Inc (HQ)..........D.......707 944-8844
1 California Dr Yountville (94599) ***(P-1669)***
Domaine De La Terre Rouge..........F.......209 245-4277
10801 Dickson Rd Plymouth (95669) ***(P-1670)***
Domaine Saint Gregory, Redwood Valley *Also called Gregory Graziano* ***(P-1736)***
Domaine St George Winery, Healdsburg *Also called Pan Magna Group* ***(P-1854)***
Dome Printing and Lithograph, McClellan *Also called Meriliz Incorporated* ***(P-6725)***
Domico Software..........F.......510 841-4155
1220 Oakland Blvd Ste 300 Walnut Creek (94596) ***(P-23824)***
Domino Data Lab Inc (PA)..........E.......415 570-2425
548 4th St San Francisco (94107) ***(P-23825)***
Domino Plastics Mfg Inc..........E.......661 396-3744
601 Gateway Ct Bakersfield (93307) ***(P-9763)***
Dominus Estate Corporation..........F.......707 944-8954
2570 Napa Nook Rd Yountville (94599) ***(P-1671)***
Domries Enterprises Inc..........E.......559 485-4306
12281 Road 29 Madera (93638) ***(P-13626)***
Don Conibear..........F.......760 728-4590
541 Industrial Way Ste 2 Fallbrook (92028) ***(P-9764)***
Don Francisco Cheese, Modesto *Also called Rizo-Lopez Foods Inc* ***(P-570)***
Don Lee Farms, Inglewood *Also called Goodman Food Products Inc* ***(P-2474)***
Don Miguel Foods, Orange *Also called Don Miguel Mexican Foods Inc* ***(P-955)***
Don Miguel Mexican Foods Inc (HQ)..........E.......714 385-4500
333 S Anita Dr Ste 1000 Orange (92868) ***(P-955)***
Donal Machine Inc..........E.......707 763-6625
591 N Mcdowell Blvd Petaluma (94954) ***(P-15904)***
Donald H Binkley..........F.......209 664-9792
2901 Commerce Way Turlock (95380) ***(P-11786)***
Donald La Voie, San Jose *Also called La Voies of San Jose* ***(P-5030)***
Donaldson Company Inc..........D.......661 295-0800
26235 Technology Dr Valencia (91355) ***(P-19638)***
Dongbu Electronics Co..........F.......408 330-0330
2953 Bunker Hill Ln # 206 Santa Clara (95054) ***(P-18197)***
Dongbu Hi-Tech, Santa Clara *Also called Dongbu Electronics Co* ***(P-18197)***
Donn & Doff Inc (PA)..........F.......530 241-4040
2102 Civic Center Dr Redding (96001) ***(P-21999)***
Donnashi Enterprises Inc..........E.......760 200-3402
43644 Parkway Esplanade W La Quinta (92253) ***(P-20859)***
Donnelley Financial, Irvine *Also called RR Donnelley & Sons Company* ***(P-7204)***
Donnelley Financial, San Francisco *Also called R R Donnelley & Sons Company* ***(P-6963)***
Donoco Industries Inc..........E.......714 893-7889
5642 Research Dr Ste B Huntington Beach (92649) ***(P-10304)***
Donovan Aluminum Racing Engine, Torrance *Also called Donovan Engineering Corp* ***(P-19639)***
Donovan Engineering Corp..........F.......310 320-3772
2305 Border Ave Torrance (90501) ***(P-19639)***
Dony Corp..........F.......323 725-7697
1065 S Vail Ave Montebello (90640) ***(P-10192)***
Dony Trading Los Angeles, Montebello *Also called Dony Corp* ***(P-10192)***
Dool Fna Inc..........C.......562 483-4100
16220 Manning Way Cerritos (90703) ***(P-2725)***
Door & Glass Unique, Pomona *Also called D G U Trading Corporation* ***(P-10351)***
Door & Hardware Installers Inc..........E.......661 298-9383
14300 Davenport Rd Ste 1a Santa Clarita (91390) ***(P-4036)***
Door Components Inc..........C.......909 770-5700
7980 Redwood Ave Fontana (92336) ***(P-11948)***
Door Doctor, Anaheim *Also called R & S Overhead Door of So Cal* ***(P-11979)***
Door Service Company..........F.......760 320-0788
680 S Williams Rd Palm Springs (92264) ***(P-11092)***
Doorking Inc (PA)..........C.......310 645-0023
120 S Glasgow Ave Inglewood (90301) ***(P-19293)***
Doors Plus Inc..........F.......209 463-3667
314 N Main St Lodi (95240) ***(P-4037)***
Doors Unlimited..........F.......760 744-5590
1316 Armorlite Dr San Marcos (92069) ***(P-4189)***
Dorado Network Systems Corp..........C.......650 227-7300
555 12th St Ste 1100 Oakland (94607) ***(P-23826)***
Dorado Pkg, North Hollywood *Also called Corporate Impressions La Inc* ***(P-7035)***
Dorco Electronics Inc..........F.......562 623-1133
13540 Larwin Cir Santa Fe Springs (90670) ***(P-5292)***
Dorco Fiberglass Products, Santa Fe Springs *Also called Dorco Electronics Inc* ***(P-5292)***
Dorel Juvenile Group Inc..........C.......909 428-0295
9950 Calabash Ave Fontana (92335) ***(P-9765)***
Dorel Juvenile Group Inc..........C.......909 390-5705
5400 Shea Center Dr Ontario (91761) ***(P-9766)***
Doremi Cinema LLC..........E.......818 562-1101
1020 Chestnut St Burbank (91506) ***(P-22415)***
Doremi Labs, Burbank *Also called Dolby Laboratories Inc* ***(P-17220)***
Doringer Manufacturing Co Inc..........F.......310 366-7766
13400 Estrella Ave Gardena (90248) ***(P-13917)***
Dorris Lumber and Moulding Co (PA)..........C.......916 452-7531
3453 Ramona Ave Ste 5 Sacramento (95826) ***(P-4038)***
Dos Fashions..........E.......626 454-4558
2633 Troy Ave El Monte (91733) ***(P-2683)***
Dosa Inc..........E.......213 627-3672
850 S Broadway Ste 700 Los Angeles (90014) ***(P-3320)***
Dose Medical Corporation..........F.......949 367-9600
229 Avenida Fabricante San Clemente (92672) ***(P-21690)***
Dostal Studio..........F.......415 721-7080
898 Lincoln Ave San Rafael (94901) ***(P-22941)***
DOT Blue Safes Corporation..........E.......909 445-8888
2707 N Garey Ave Pomona (91767) ***(P-13516)***
DOT Copy Inc..........E.......818 341-6666
9655 De Soto Ave Chatsworth (91311) ***(P-6549)***
DOT Corp..........E.......714 708-5960
1801 S Standard Ave Santa Ana (92707) ***(P-6550)***
DOT Graphics, Chatsworth *Also called DOT Copy Inc* ***(P-6549)***
DOT Haizol Com..........F.......657 258-9027
500 S Kraemer Blvd # 205 Brea (92821) ***(P-14265)***
DOT Printer Inc (PA)..........C.......949 474-1100
2424 Mcgaw Ave Irvine (92614) ***(P-6551)***
Double K Industries, Chatsworth *Also called Invelop Inc* ***(P-13636)***
Double K Industries Inc..........E.......818 772-2887
9711 Mason Ave Chatsworth (91311) ***(P-13627)***
Double Precision Mfg..........E.......408 727-7726
2273 Calle De Luna Santa Clara (95054) ***(P-15905)***
Double V Industries..........E.......510 347-3764
717 Whitney St San Leandro (94577) ***(P-3737)***
Double-Take Software Inc (HQ)..........E.......949 253-6500
15300 Barranca Pkwy Irvine (92618) ***(P-23827)***
Doubleco Incorporated..........D.......909 481-0799
9444 9th St Rancho Cucamonga (91730) ***(P-12675)***
Doubledutch Inc (PA)..........D.......800 748-9024
350 Rhode Island St # 375 San Francisco (94103) ***(P-23828)***
Doublesight Displays Inc..........F.......949 253-1535
2882 Walnut Ave Ste A Tustin (92780) ***(P-15218)***
Douce De France..........F.......650 369-9644
686 Brdwy St Redwood City (94063) ***(P-1190)***
Doug Deleo Welding Inc..........F.......559 562-3700
249 N Ashland Ave Lindsay (93247) ***(P-24632)***
Doug Mockett & Company Inc..........E.......310 318-2491
1915 Abalone Ave Torrance (90501) ***(P-4565)***
Doug Trim Sub Contractor..........F.......661 944-2884
32010 Alaga Ave Pearblossom (93553) ***(P-13165)***
Doughpro, Perris *Also called Stearns Product Dev Corp* ***(P-14862)***
Doughtronics Inc (PA)..........E.......510 524-1327
1601 San Pablo Ave Berkeley (94702) ***(P-1191)***
Doughtronics Inc..........E.......510 843-2978
2730 9th St Berkeley (94710) ***(P-1192)***
Doughtronics Inc..........E.......415 288-2978
1 Ferry Building Ste 15 San Francisco (94111) ***(P-1193)***
Douglas & Sturgess Inc..........F.......510 235-8411
1023 Factory St Richmond (94801) ***(P-11006)***
Douglas Technologies Group Inc (PA)..........E.......760 758-5560
1340 N Melrose Dr Vista (92083) ***(P-19640)***
Douglas Wheel, Vista *Also called Douglas Technologies Group Inc* ***(P-19640)***
Douglass Truck Bodies Inc..........E.......661 327-0258
231 21st St Bakersfield (93301) ***(P-19529)***
Doval Industries Inc..........D.......323 226-0335
3961 N Mission Rd Los Angeles (90031) ***(P-11587)***
Doval Industries Co, Los Angeles *Also called Doval Industries Inc* ***(P-11587)***
Dove Tree Canyon Software Inc..........F.......619 236-8895
707 Broadway Ste 1240 San Diego (92101) ***(P-23829)***
Doves Jewelry Corporation..........E.......818 955-8886
2860 N Naomi St Burbank (91504) ***(P-22512)***
Dow Chemical Co Foundation..........E.......909 476-4127
11266 Jersey Blvd Rancho Cucamonga (91730) ***(P-7554)***
Dow Chemical Company..........C.......510 797-2281
7380 Morton Ave Newark (94560) ***(P-7485)***
Dow Chemical Company..........D.......925 432-3165
901 Loveridge Rd Pittsburg (94565) ***(P-7555)***
Dow Chemical Company..........C.......714 228-4700
14445 Alondra Blvd La Mirada (90638) ***(P-7486)***
Dow Chemical Company..........C.......510 786-0100
25500 Whitesell St Hayward (94545) ***(P-7556)***
Dow Frosini, San Francisco *Also called Alan Wofsy Fine Arts LLC* ***(P-6067)***
Dow Hydraulic Systems Inc..........F.......909 596-6602
2895 Metropolitan Pl Pomona (91767) ***(P-15628)***
Dow Hydraulic Systems Inc (PA)..........D.......909 596-6602
1835 Wright Ave La Verne (91750) ***(P-15906)***

Mergent e-mail: customerrelations@mergent.com
1084
2020 California
Manufacturers Register
(P-0000) Products & Services Section entry number
(PA)=Parent Co (HQ)=Headquarters (DH)=Div Headquarters

Dow Jones & Company Inc............E.......415 765-6131
201 California St Fl 13 San Francisco (94111) ***(P-5618)***
Dow Jones Lmg Stockton Inc............C.......209 943-6397
530 E Market St Stockton (95202) ***(P-5619)***
Dow Theory Letters Inc............F.......858 454-0481
7590 Fay Ave Ste 404 La Jolla (92037) ***(P-5923)***
Dow-Elco Inc............E.......323 723-1288
1313 W Olympic Blvd Montebello (90640) ***(P-16547)***
Dow-Key Microwave Corporation............C.......805 650-0260
4822 Mcgrath St Ventura (93003) ***(P-16712)***
Dowdys Sales and Services............F.......559 688-6973
15185 Avenue 224 Tulare (93274) ***(P-13628)***
Dowell Aluminum Foundry Inc............F.......323 877-9645
11342 Hartland St North Hollywood (91605) ***(P-11378)***
Dowling Magnets, Sonoma *Also called Sonoma International Inc* ***(P-22715)***
Down River, Stockton *Also called Signode Industrial Group LLC* ***(P-5531)***
Downey Grinding Co............E.......562 803-5556
12323 Bellflower Blvd Downey (90242) ***(P-13918)***
Downey Manufacturing Inc............F.......562 862-3311
11421 Downey Ave Downey (90241) ***(P-20088)***
Downey Patriot............F.......562 904-3668
8301 Florence Ave Ste 100 Downey (90240) ***(P-5620)***
Downhole Stabilization Inc............E.......661 631-1044
3515 Thomas Way Bakersfield (93308) ***(P-13774)***
Dp Print Services Inc............F.......310 600-5250
2331 Walling Ave La Habra (90631) ***(P-2852)***
Dp Products, San Jose *Also called Papadatos Enterprises Inc* ***(P-16278)***
Dpa Components International, Simi Valley *Also called Dpa Labs Inc* ***(P-18198)***
Dpa Labs Inc............E.......805 581-9200
2251 Ward Ave Simi Valley (93065) ***(P-18198)***
Dpi Direct, Poway *Also called Digitalpro Inc* ***(P-7046)***
DPI Labs Inc............E.......909 392-5777
1350 Arrow Hwy La Verne (91750) ***(P-20089)***
Dpm Inc............F.......530 378-3420
19641 Hirsch Ct Anderson (96007) ***(P-15907)***
Dps Telecom, Fresno *Also called Digital Prototype Systems Inc* ***(P-17502)***
Dpss Lasers Inc............E.......408 988-4300
2525 Walsh Ave Santa Clara (95051) ***(P-19294)***
Dr DBurr Inc............F.......310 323-6900
12943 S Budlong Ave Gardena (90247) ***(P-13919)***
Dr Earth Inc............F.......707 448-4676
4021 Devon Ct Vacaville (95688) ***(P-8792)***
Dr Heater USA, Burlingame *Also called Tlm International Inc* ***(P-16855)***
Dr J Skinclinic Inc............F.......562 474-8861
13834 Bettencourt St Cerritos (90703) ***(P-7873)***
Dr McDougall's Right Foods, Woodland *Also called Bright People Foods Inc* ***(P-2411)***
Dr Pepper Snapple Group, Riverside *Also called American Bottling Company* ***(P-2024)***
Dr Pepper/Seven Up Inc............D.......707 545-7797
1901 Russell Ave Santa Rosa (95403) ***(P-2072)***
DR Radon Boatbuilding Inc (PA)............F.......805 692-2170
67 Depot Rd Goleta (93117) ***(P-20322)***
Dr Smoothie Brands Inc............E.......714 449-9787
1730 Raymer Ave Fullerton (92833) ***(P-2204)***
Dr Smoothie Enterprises............E.......714 449-9787
1730 Raymer Ave Fullerton (92833) ***(P-2205)***
Dr. Bronners Magic Soaps, Vista *Also called All One God Faith Inc* ***(P-8335)***
Dr. J'S Natural, Garden Grove *Also called Premium Herbal USA LLC* ***(P-616)***
Dr. Jekyll's, Pasadena *Also called Nutraceutical Brews For Lf Inc* ***(P-1551)***
Dr. Shica's Healthy Surprises, Pasadena *Also called Vitafoods America LLC* ***(P-712)***
Draftday Fantasy Sports Inc............E.......310 306-1828
690 5th St Ste 105 San Francisco (94107) ***(P-23830)***
Draftday Fantasy Sports Inc............E.......310 306-1828
2058 Broadway Ofc Santa Monica (90404) ***(P-23831)***
Dragon Alliance Inc............E.......760 931-4900
971 Calle Amanecer San Clemente (92673) ***(P-22349)***
Dragon Herbs, Los Angeles *Also called Ron Teeguarden Enterprises Inc* ***(P-7687)***
Dragon Valves Inc (PA)............E.......562 921-6605
13457 Excelsior Dr Norwalk (90650) ***(P-13351)***
Drake Enterprises Incorporated............D.......707 864-3077
490 Watt Dr Fairfield (94534) ***(P-3837)***
Drake's Brewing Company, San Leandro *Also called Artisan Brewers LLC* ***(P-1494)***
Drapery Productions Inc............F.......650 340-8555
33 E 4th Ave San Mateo (94401) ***(P-2684)***
Drapes 4 Show Inc............E.......818 838-0852
12811 Foothill Blvd Sylmar (91342) ***(P-3612)***
Draw Tite, Commerce *Also called Scotch Paint Corporation* ***(P-8678)***
Dream Communications Inc............F.......619 275-9100
2431 Morena Blvd San Diego (92110) ***(P-5924)***
Dream Homes Magazine, San Diego *Also called Dream Communications Inc* ***(P-5924)***
Dream International Usa Inc............F.......714 521-6007
7001 Village Dr Ste 280 Buena Park (90621) ***(P-22647)***
Dream Products Incorporated............E.......818 773-4233
9754 Deering Ave Chatsworth (91311) ***(P-10220)***
Dreamctchers Empwerment Netwrk............E.......707 558-1775
2201 Tuolumne St Vallejo (94589) ***(P-18892)***
Dreamgear LLC............E.......310 222-5522
20001 S Western Ave Torrance (90501) ***(P-22670)***
Dreamplay Toys LLC............F.......424 208-7010
11755 Wilshire Blvd # 2000 Los Angeles (90025) ***(P-22671)***
Dreams Closets............F.......626 641-5070
13030 Ramona Blvd Unit 9 Baldwin Park (91706) ***(P-4190)***
Dreams Duvets & Bed Linens............F.......415 543-1800
921 Howard St San Francisco (94103) ***(P-3613)***
Dreams Duvets & Linens, San Francisco *Also called Dreams Duvets & Bed Linens* ***(P-3613)***
Dreamteam Business Group LLC............F.......559 430-7676
5261 E Kings Canyon Rd # 101 Fresno (93727) ***(P-7051)***
Dreamworks Knitting, Santa Ana *Also called Nutrade Inc* ***(P-2706)***
Drees Wood Products Inc............E.......562 633-7337
14020 Orange Ave Paramount (90723) ***(P-4039)***
Drees Wood Products Inc (PA)............E.......562 633-7337
14003 Orange Ave Paramount (90723) ***(P-4040)***
Dress To Kill Inc............F.......818 994-3890
15500 Erwin St Ste 1089 Van Nuys (91411) ***(P-3156)***
Dresser-Rand Company............E.......310 223-0600
18502 Dominguez Hill Dr Rancho Dominguez (90220) ***(P-14628)***
Dresser-Rand LLC............E.......925 356-5700
5159 Commercial Cir Ste D Concord (94520) ***(P-14629)***
Dresser-Rand Sales, Concord *Also called Dresser-Rand LLC* ***(P-14629)***
Dresses.com, Canoga Park *Also called Odette Christiane LLC* ***(P-3380)***
Dretloh Aircraft Supply Inc (PA)............F.......714 632-6982
2830 E La Cresta Ave Anaheim (92806) ***(P-20090)***
Dreyer's Grand Ice Cream, Bakersfield *Also called Nestle Dreyers Ice Cream Co* ***(P-662)***
Dreyer's Grand Ice Cream, Fresno *Also called Nestle Dreyers Ice Cream Co* ***(P-663)***
Drilling & Trenching Sup Inc (PA)............F.......510 895-1650
1458 Mariani Ct Tracy (95376) ***(P-14156)***
Drilling World, Tracy *Also called Drilling & Trenching Sup Inc* ***(P-14156)***
Driscoll Inc............E.......619 226-2500
2500 Shelter Island Dr San Diego (92106) ***(P-20323)***
Driscoll Boat Works, San Diego *Also called Driscoll Inc* ***(P-20323)***
Driscoll Mission Bay LLC............F.......619 223-5191
1500 Quivira Way Ste 2 San Diego (92109) ***(P-20324)***
Driveai Inc............C.......408 693-0765
365 Ravendale Dr Mountain View (94043) ***(P-23832)***
Driven Concepts Inc............F.......714 549-2170
4040 W Carriage Dr Santa Ana (92704) ***(P-3076)***
Driven Raceway and Family Ente............F.......707 585-3748
4601 Redwood Dr Rohnert Park (94928) ***(P-16946)***
Drivescale Inc............F.......408 849-4651
1230 Midas Way Ste 210 Sunnyvale (94085) ***(P-23833)***
Drj Organics, Cerritos *Also called Dr J Skinclinic Inc* ***(P-7873)***
Dropbox Inc (PA)............C.......415 857-6800
1800 Owens St Ste 200 San Francisco (94158) ***(P-23834)***
Drs Advanced Isr LLC............C.......714 220-3800
10600 Valley View St Cypress (90630) ***(P-18199)***
Drs Daylight Solutions, San Diego *Also called Daylight Solutions Inc* ***(P-18193)***
Drs Ntwork Imaging Systems LLC............D.......714 220-3800
10600 Valley View St Cypress (90630) ***(P-18200)***
Drs Own Inc (PA)............E.......760 804-0751
5923 Farnsworth Ct Carlsbad (92008) ***(P-22000)***
Drs Snsors Trgting Systems Inc, Cypress *Also called Drs Ntwork Imaging Systems LLC* ***(P-18200)***
Drug Product Services Lab, San Francisco *Also called Ucsf School of Pharmacy* ***(P-8172)***
Drum Magazine, San Jose *Also called Enter Music Publishing Inc* ***(P-5932)***
Drum Workshop Inc (PA)............D.......805 485-6999
3450 Lunar Ct Oxnard (93030) ***(P-22613)***
Druva Inc (HQ)............D.......650 241-3501
800 W California Ave # 100 Sunnyvale (94086) ***(P-23835)***
Dry Aged Denim LLC (PA)............F.......323 780-6206
1545 Rio Vista Ave Los Angeles (90023) ***(P-3003)***
Dry Creek Nutrition Inc............F.......209 341-5696
600 Yosemite Blvd Modesto (95354) ***(P-2206)***
Dry Creek Vineyard Inc............E.......707 433-1000
3770 Lambert Bridge Rd Healdsburg (95448) ***(P-1672)***
Dry Launch Light Co, Livermore *Also called Sierra Design Mfg Inc* ***(P-17092)***
Dry Vac Environmental Inc (PA)............E.......707 374-7500
864 Saint Francis Way Rio Vista (94571) ***(P-21218)***
Drymax Technologies Inc............F.......805 239-2555
9900 El Camino Real Atascadero (93422) ***(P-2765)***
Dryvit Systems Inc............E.......559 564-3591
354 S Acacia St Woodlake (93286) ***(P-8959)***
Drywired Defense LLC............E.......310 684-3891
9606 Santa Monica Blvd # 4 Beverly Hills (90210) ***(P-13166)***
Ds Cypress Magnetics Inc............F.......909 987-3570
8753 Industrial Ln Rancho Cucamonga (91730) ***(P-18765)***
Ds Fibertech Corp............E.......619 562-7001
11015 Mission Park Ct Santee (92071) ***(P-14760)***
Ds Services of America Inc............D.......323 551-5724
1449 N Avenue 46 Los Angeles (90041) ***(P-2073)***
DSB Enterprises Inc............E.......760 295-3500
425 S Melrose Dr Vista (92081) ***(P-1521)***
Dsj Printing Inc............F.......310 828-8051
1703 Stewart St Santa Monica (90404) ***(P-6552)***
DSM&t Co Inc............C.......909 357-7960
10609 Business Dr Fontana (92337) ***(P-19189)***
Dsp Group Inc (PA)............D.......408 986-4300
2055 Gateway Pl Ste 480 San Jose (95110) ***(P-18201)***
Dspm Inc............E.......714 970-2304
1921 S Quaker Ridge Pl Ontario (91761) ***(P-18712)***
Dss Networks Inc............F.......949 981-3473
24462 Redlen St Lake Forest (92630) ***(P-15219)***
Dss-Cctv Inc............F.......609 850-9498
1280 Activity Dr Ste A Vista (92081) ***(P-17506)***
Dssd Inc............F.......775 773-8665
4025 Bohannon Dr Menlo Park (94025) ***(P-15021)***
Dst Controls, Benicia *Also called Dusouth Industries* ***(P-20861)***
DStyle Inc............F.......619 662-0560
3451 Main St Ste 108 Chula Vista (91911) ***(P-13517)***
Dsy Educational Corporation............F.......805 684-8111
525 Maple St Carpinteria (93013) ***(P-3838)***
DT Mattson Enterprises Inc............E.......951 849-9781
201 W Lincoln St Banning (92220) ***(P-22672)***
Dtbm Inc............F.......626 579-7033
1825 Durfee Ave Ste C South El Monte (91733) ***(P-1194)***
DTE Stockton LLC............E.......209 467-3838
2526 W Washington St Stockton (95203) ***(P-190)***

Employee Codes: A=Over 500 employees, B=251-500
C=101-250, D=51-100, E=20-50, F=10-19

2020 California
Manfacturers Register

© Mergent Inc. 1-800-342-5647
1085

Dti Holdings Inc...........F.......949 485-1725
213 Technology Dr Irvine (92618) (P-19947)
DTL Mori Seiki, Davis Also called Digital Technology Lab Corp (P-14155)
DTL Research & Technical Ctr, Davis Also called Dmg Mori Manufacturing USA Inc (P-13914)
Dts LLC...........D.......818 436-1000
5220 Las Virgenes Rd Calabasas (91302) (P-17222)
Du-All Anodizing Corporation...........F.......408 275-6694
730 Chestnut St San Jose (95110) (P-12987)
Du-All Anodizing Inc...........E.......408 275-6694
730 Chestnut St San Jose (95110) (P-12988)
Du-All Safety LLC...........F.......510 651-8289
45950 Hotchkiss St Fremont (94539) (P-15908)
Dualcor Technologies Inc...........831 684-2457
1 Embarcadero Ctr Ste 500 San Francisco (94111) (P-15022)
Dub Custom Auto Show, Santa Fe Springs Also called Dub Publishing Inc (P-5925)
Dub Publishing Inc...........F.......626 336-3821
11803 Smith Ave Santa Fe Springs (90670) (P-5925)
Dubon & Sons Inc...........F.......213 923-1182
2852 E 11th St Los Angeles (90023) (P-956)
Duckhorn Wine Company...........E.......707 744-2800
14100 Mountain House Rd Hopland (95449) (P-1673)
Duckhorn Wine Company (HQ)...........F.......707 963-7108
1000 Lodi Ln Saint Helena (94574) (P-1674)
Duckhorn Wine Company...........F.......707 895-3202
9200 Highway 128 Philo (95466) (P-1675)
Ducommun Aerostructures Inc (HQ)...........B.......310 380-5390
268 E Gardena Blvd Gardena (90248) (P-19948)
Ducommun Aerostructures Inc...........E.......626 358-3211
801 Royal Oaks Dr Monrovia (91016) (P-20091)
Ducommun Aerostructures Inc...........E.......760 246-4191
4001 El Mirage Rd Adelanto (92301) (P-20092)
Ducommun Aerostructures Inc...........F.......714 637-4401
1885 N Batavia St Orange (92865) (P-19949)
Ducommun Aerostructures Inc...........E.......310 513-7200
23301 Wilmington Ave Carson (90745) (P-19950)
Ducommun Arostructures-Gardena, Gardena Also called Ahf-Ducommun Incorporated (P-20024)
Ducommun Incorporated (PA)...........C.......657 335-3665
200 Sandpointe Ave # 700 Santa Ana (92707) (P-20093)
Ducommun Incorporated...........E.......626 812-9666
1321 Mountain View Cir Azusa (91702) (P-18713)
Ducommun Labarge Tech Inc (HQ)...........C.......310 513-7200
23301 Wilmington Ave Carson (90745) (P-20094)
Duda Mobile Inc...........E.......855 790-0003
577 College Ave Palo Alto (94306) (P-23836)
Duden Enterprises Inc...........F.......909 795-0160
2025 W Park Ave Ste 4 Redlands (92373) (P-3738)
Dudes Brewing Company...........E.......424 271-2915
1840 W 208th St Somis (93066) (P-1522)
Duel Systems Inc...........408 453-9500
2025 Galeway Pl Ste 235 San Jose (95110) (P-18766)
Duff Bevill Vineyard Managmnt...........E.......707 433-6691
4724 Dry Creek Rd Healdsburg (95448) (P-1676)
Duffield Electric Boat Company, Costa Mesa Also called Duffield Marine Inc (P-20326)
Duffield Marine Inc...........F.......949 650-4633
16732 Pacific Coast Sunset Beach (90742) (P-20325)
Duffield Marine Inc (PA)...........E.......760 246-1211
670 W 17th St Ste E7 Costa Mesa (92627) (P-20326)
Duffield Marine Inc...........E.......949 645-6812
2001 W Coast Hwy Newport Beach (92663) (P-20327)
Duffy Electric Boat, Newport Beach Also called Duffield Marine Inc (P-20327)
Duffy Electric Boat Company, Sunset Beach Also called Duffield Marine Inc (P-20325)
Duke Empirical Inc...........D.......831 420-1104
2829 Mission St Santa Cruz (95060) (P-21691)
Duke Scientific Corporation...........650 424-1177
46360 Fremont Blvd Fremont (94538) (P-20755)
Dukers Appliance Co USA Ltd (HQ)...........F.......562 568-4060
2488 Peck Rd Whittier (90601) (P-15425)
Dukes Research and Mfg Inc...........E.......818 998-9811
9060 Winnetka Ave Northridge (91324) (P-19641)
Dulce Systems Inc...........818 435-6007
26893 Bouquet Canyon Rd L Santa Clarita (91350) (P-17726)
Dumont Printing Inc...........E.......559 485-6311
1333 G St Fresno (93706) (P-6553)
Dumont Printing & Mailing, Fresno Also called Dumont Printing Inc (P-6553)
Dunan Sensing LLC...........E.......408 613-1015
1953 Concourse Dr San Jose (95131) (P-19295)
Dunbar Electric Sign Company...........E.......661 323-2600
4020 Rosedale Hwy Bakersfield (93308) (P-23089)
Duncan Carter Corporation (PA)...........D.......805 964-9749
5427 Hollister Ave Santa Barbara (93111) (P-22614)
Duncan Design Inc...........F.......707 636-2300
860 Scenic Ave Santa Rosa (95407) (P-23090)
Duncan Enterprises (HQ)...........C.......559 291-4444
5673 E Shields Ave Fresno (93727) (P-8641)
Duncan McIntosh Company Inc (PA)...........E.......949 660-6150
18475 Bandilier Cir Fountain Valley (92708) (P-5926)
Duncan Press Inc...........F.......209 462-5245
25 W Lockeford St Lodi (95240) (P-6554)
Dunham Metal Processing Inc...........714 532-5551
936 N Parker St Orange (92867) (P-12989)
Dunlop Manufacturing Inc (PA)...........D.......707 745-2722
150 Industrial Way Benicia (94510) (P-22615)
Dunlop Manufacturing Inc...........E.......707 745-2709
649 Industrial Way Benicia (94510) (P-22616)
Dunnewood Vineyards, Ukiah Also called Constellation Brands Inc (P-1646)
Dunstan Enterprises Inc...........F.......562 630-6292
11821 Slauson Ave Santa Fe Springs (90670) (P-15909)

Dunweizer Machine Inc...........F.......562 698-7787
8338 Allport Ave Santa Fe Springs (90670) (P-12017)
Dunweizer Mch & Fabrication, Santa Fe Springs Also called Dunweizer Machine Inc (P-12017)
Duo Pane Industries...........F.......707 426-9696
2444 Trevino Way Fairfield (94534) (P-10355)
Duonetics...........F.......951 808-4903
809 E Parkridge Ave # 102 Corona (92879) (P-14569)
Dupaco Inc...........E.......760 758-4550
4144 Avenda De La Plata Oceanside (92056) (P-21692)
Duplan Industries...........E.......760 744-4047
1265 Stone Dr San Marcos (92078) (P-15910)
Dupont De Nemours Inc...........510 784-9105
2520 Barrington Ct Hayward (94545) (P-8828)
Dupree Inc...........F.......909 597-4889
14395 Ramona Ave Chino (91710) (P-12676)
Dur-Red Products...........E.......323 771-9000
4900 Cecilia St Cudahy (90201) (P-12187)
Dura Coat Products Inc (PA)...........D.......951 341-6500
5361 Via Ricardo Riverside (92509) (P-13167)
Dura Micro Inc...........E.......909 947-4590
901 E Cedar St Ontario (91761) (P-15023)
Dura Plastic Products Inc (PA)...........D.......951 845-3161
533 E Third St Beaumont (92223) (P-9767)
Dura Technologies Inc...........C.......909 877-8477
2720 S Willow Ave Ste A Bloomington (92316) (P-8642)
Dura-Chem Inc...........E.......951 245-7778
18327 Pasadena St Lake Elsinore (92530) (P-8960)
Durabag Company Inc...........D.......714 259-8811
1432 Santa Fe Dr Tustin (92780) (P-5394)
Duracite, Fairfield Also called Halabi Inc (P-10909)
Duracite...........F.......559 346-1181
2636 N Argyle Ave Fresno (93727) (P-4974)
Duracold Refrigeration Mfg LLC...........626 358-1710
1551 S Primrose Ave Monrovia (91016) (P-12542)
Duraflex, Chatsworth Also called Container Components Inc (P-9723)
Duraled Ltg Technolgies Corp...........F.......949 753-0162
15285 Alton Pkwy Ste 200 Irvine (92618) (P-16860)
Duralum Products Inc (PA)...........F.......916 452-7021
8269 Alpine Ave Sacramento (95826) (P-11258)
Duralum Products Inc...........F.......951 736-4500
2485 Railroad St Corona (92880) (P-11259)
Duramar Floor Inc...........F.......949 724-8800
2500 White Rd Ste B Irvine (92614) (P-10439)
Duramar Interior Surfaces, Irvine Also called Duramar Floor Inc (P-10439)
Duramar Interior Surfaces, Irvine Also called Daz Inc (P-16593)
Duramax Building Products, Montebello Also called US Polymers Inc (P-10104)
Durand-Wayland Machinery Inc (PA)...........E.......559 591-6904
1041 E Dinuba Ave Reedley (93654) (P-13629)
Durango Foods, Bell Also called Flores Brothers Inc (P-2460)
Duravent Inc (HQ)...........B.......800 835-4429
877 Cotting Ct Vacaville (95688) (P-12188)
Duray, Downey Also called J F Duncan Industries Inc (P-15528)
Durbin Rock Plant, Irwindale Also called Legacy Vulcan LLC (P-10781)
Durect Corporation (PA)...........D.......408 777-1417
10260 Bubb Rd Cupertino (95014) (P-7874)
Durect Corporation...........F.......408 777-1417
10240 Bubb Rd Cupertino (95014) (P-7875)
Durney Winery Corporation...........831 659-2690
18820 Cachagua Rd Carmel Valley (93924) (P-1677)
Duro Corporation...........F.......626 839-6541
17018 Evergreen Pl City of Industry (91745) (P-16810)
Duro Dyne West Corp...........B.......562 926-1774
10837 Commerce Way Ste D Fontana (92337) (P-15426)
Duro Flex Rubber Products Inc...........F.......562 946-5533
13215 Lakeland Rd Santa Fe Springs (90670) (P-9302)
Duro Roller Company Inc...........F.......562 944-8856
13006 Park St Santa Fe Springs (90670) (P-9303)
Duro-Sense Corp...........310 533-6877
869 Sandhill Ave Carson (90746) (P-20860)
Duron Incorporated...........F.......949 721-0900
4633 Camden Dr Corona Del Mar (92625) (P-14453)
Durston Manufacturing Company...........F.......909 593-1506
1395 Palomares St La Verne (91750) (P-11527)
Dusouth Industries...........E.......707 745-5117
651 Stone Rd Benicia (94510) (P-20861)
Dust Collector Services Inc...........E.......714 237-1690
1280 N Sunshine Way Anaheim (92806) (P-13518)
Dutek Incorporated...........E.......760 566-8888
2228 Oak Ridge Way Vista (92081) (P-19296)
Dutra Materials, Richmond Also called San Rafael Rock Quarry Inc (P-9105)
Dutra Materials, San Rafael Also called San Rafael Rock Quarry Inc (P-319)
DV Kap Inc...........E.......559 435-5575
426 W Bedford Ave Fresno (93711) (P-3614)
Dva Professsional Plastic, West Sacramento Also called Professional Plastics Inc (P-7600)
Dvbe Supply, San Diego Also called Tsf Construction Services Inc (P-2919)
Dvele Inc...........E.......909 796-2561
25525 Redlands Blvd Loma Linda (92354) (P-4444)
Dvele Omega Corporation...........D.......909 796-2561
25525 Redlands Blvd Loma Linda (92354) (P-4445)
Dvs Sciences Inc...........E.......408 900-7205
7000 Shoreline Ct Ste 100 South San Francisco (94080) (P-21219)
Dvtech Solution Corp...........F.......909 308-0358
13937 Magnolia Ave Chino (91710) (P-16596)
Dvxtreme, Chino Also called Dvtech Solution Corp (P-16596)
Dw Drum, Oxnard Also called Drum Workshop Inc (P-22613)
Dwa Alminum Composites USA Inc...........E.......818 998-1504
21100 Superior St Chatsworth (91311) (P-11379)

Mergent e-mail: customerrelations@mergent.com
1086
2020 California
Manufacturers Register
(P-0000) Products & Services Section entry number
(PA)=Parent Co (HQ)=Headquarters (DH)=Div Headquarters

Dwa Nova LLC .... D 818 695-5000
1000 Flower St Glendale (91201) ***(P-23837)***
Dwam, Carlsbad *Also called Denso International Amer Inc* ***(P-19636)***
Dwaynes Engineering & Cnstr .... D 661 762-7261
3655 Addie Ave Mc Kittrick (93251) ***(P-191)***
Dwell Home Inc .... F 877 864-5752
39962 Cedar Blvd Ste 277 Newark (94560) ***(P-4765)***
Dwell Life Inc (PA) .... E 415 373-5100
595 Pacific Ave 4 San Francisco (94133) ***(P-5927)***
Dwell Records, Los Angeles *Also called C M H Records Inc* ***(P-17311)***
Dwi Enterprises .... E 714 842-2236
11081 Winners Cir Ste 100 Los Alamitos (90720) ***(P-17223)***
Dxg Technology USA Inc .... E 626 820-0687
330 Turnbull Canyon Rd City of Industry (91745) ***(P-22416)***
Dxg USA, City of Industry *Also called Dxg Technology USA Inc* ***(P-22416)***
Dyell Machine (PA) .... E 909 350-4101
160 S Linden Ave Rialto (92376) ***(P-15911)***
Dyell Machine .... F 760 244-3333
17499 Alder St Hesperia (92345) ***(P-15912)***
Dyell Machine & Hydraulic Shop, Hesperia *Also called Dyell Machine* ***(P-15912)***
Dyk Incorporated (HQ) .... E 619 440-8181
351 Cypress Ln El Cajon (92020) ***(P-20498)***
Dyk Prestressed Tanks, El Cajon *Also called Dyk Incorporated* ***(P-20498)***
Dylern Incorporated .... E 530 470-8785
14444 Greenwood Cir Nevada City (95959) ***(P-15913)***
Dyln Inspired, Irvine *Also called Dyln Lifestyle LLC* ***(P-22589)***
Dyln Lifestyle LLC .... F 949 209-9401
18242 Mcdurmott W Ste A Irvine (92614) ***(P-22589)***
Dyna-King Inc .... F 707 894-5566
597 Santana Dr Ste A Cloverdale (95425) ***(P-22792)***
Dynabee USA, Anaheim *Also called Dynaflex International* ***(P-22793)***
Dynacast LLC .... C 949 707-1211
25952 Commercentre Dr Lake Forest (92630) ***(P-11357)***
Dynaflex International .... E 714 630-0909
1144 N Grove St Anaheim (92806) ***(P-22793)***
Dynaflex Products (PA) .... D 323 724-1555
6466 Gayhart St Commerce (90040) ***(P-19530)***
Dynalinear Technologies Inc .... F 408 376-5090
51 E Campbell Ave 108b Campbell (95008) ***(P-14454)***
Dynalloy Inc .... E 714 436-1206
1562 Reynolds Ave Irvine (92614) ***(P-18893)***
Dynamation Research, Los Angeles *Also called Gali Corporation* ***(P-20111)***
Dynamation Research Inc .... F 909 864-2310
2301 Pontius Ave Los Angeles (90064) ***(P-20095)***
Dynamet Incorporated .... E 714 375-3150
16052 Beach Blvd Ste 221 Huntington Beach (92647) ***(P-11270)***
Dynametric Inc .... F 626 358-2559
1715 Business Center Dr Duarte (91010) ***(P-17362)***
Dynamex Corporation .... E 310 329-0399
155 E Albertoni St Carson (90746) ***(P-2911)***
Dynamic Bindery Inc .... F 909 884-1296
170 S Arrowhead Ave San Bernardino (92408) ***(P-7330)***
Dynamic Cooking Systems Inc .... A 714 372-7000
695 Town Center Dr # 180 Costa Mesa (92626) ***(P-15508)***
Dynamic Digital Displays, Rancho Cordova *Also called D3 Led LLC* ***(P-23086)***
Dynamic E-Markets LLC .... F 619 327-4777
2335 Roll Dr Ste 5 San Diego (92154) ***(P-2652)***
Dynamic Engineering .... F 831 457-8891
150 Dubois St Ste C Santa Cruz (95060) ***(P-18202)***
Dynamic Enterprises Inc .... E 562 944-0271
10015 Greenleaf Ave Santa Fe Springs (90670) ***(P-15914)***
Dynamic Fabrication Inc .... F 714 662-2440
2615 S Hickory St Santa Ana (92707) ***(P-19297)***
Dynamic Intgrted Solutions LLC .... F 408 727-3400
1710 Fortune Dr San Jose (95131) ***(P-18203)***
Dynamic Intgrted Solutions LLC (PA) .... E 408 727-3400
3964 Rivermark Plz # 104 Santa Clara (95054) ***(P-18204)***
Dynamic Machine Inc .... F 323 585-0710
3470 Randolph St Huntington Park (90255) ***(P-15915)***
Dynamic Pre-Cast Co Inc .... F 707 573-1110
5300 Sebastopol Rd Santa Rosa (95407) ***(P-10564)***
Dynamic Sciences Intl Inc .... E 818 226-6262
9400 Lurline Ave Unit B Chatsworth (91311) ***(P-17507)***
Dynamic Services Inc .... F 949 458-2553
27091 Burbank El Toro (92610) ***(P-7052)***
Dynamic Solutions .... F 253 273-7936
631 W Rosecrans Ave # 23 Gardena (90248) ***(P-21461)***
Dynamics O&P, Los Angeles *Also called Dynamics Orthotics & Prostheti* ***(P-22001)***
Dynamics Orthotics & Prostheti .... E 213 383-9212
1830 W Olympic Blvd # 123 Los Angeles (90006) ***(P-22001)***
Dynamite Sign Group Inc .... E 562 595-7725
3080 E 29th St Long Beach (90806) ***(P-23091)***
Dynasty Electronic Company LLC .... D 714 550-1197
1790 E Mcfadden Ave Santa Ana (92705) ***(P-17865)***
Dynasty Import Co, San Francisco *Also called FML Inc* ***(P-22982)***
Dynatect Ro-Lab Inc .... E 262 786-1500
8830 W Linne Rd Tracy (95304) ***(P-9263)***
Dynatest Consulting Inc .... F 805 648-2230
165 S Chestnut St Ventura (93001) ***(P-21023)***
Dynatex International .... E 707 542-4227
5577 Skylane Blvd Santa Rosa (95403) ***(P-14157)***
Dynatrac Products Co Inc .... F 714 596-4461
7392 Count Cir Huntington Beach (92647) ***(P-19642)***
Dynavax Technologies Corp (PA) .... C 510 848-5100
2100 Powell St Ste 900 Emeryville (94608) ***(P-8294)***
Dytran Instruments Inc .... C 818 700-7818
21592 Marilla St Chatsworth (91311) ***(P-18894)***
Dz Tranz Group, Canoga Park *Also called Darrell Zbrowski* ***(P-13870)***
DZS, Oakland *Also called Dasan Zhone Solutions Inc* ***(P-17359)***

E & B Ntral Resources MGT Corp .... E 661 766-2501
1848 Perkins Rd New Cuyama (93254) ***(P-120)***
E & B Ntral Resources Mgt Corp (PA) .... D 661 679-1714
1600 Norris Rd Bakersfield (93308) ***(P-49)***
E & J Gallo Winery (PA) .... A 209 341-3111
600 Yosemite Blvd Modesto (95354) ***(P-1678)***
E & J Gallo Winery .... C 559 458-0807
5610 E Olive Ave Fresno (93727) ***(P-1679)***
E & J Gallo Winery .... D 559 458-2500
5631 E Olive Ave Fresno (93727) ***(P-1680)***
E & J Gallo Winery .... E 707 431-1946
3387 Dry Creek Rd Healdsburg (95448) ***(P-1681)***
E & J Gallo Winery .... F 209 341-3111
2101 Yosemite Blvd Modesto (95354) ***(P-1682)***
E & J Gallo Winery .... C 209 394-6215
18000 River Rd Livingston (95334) ***(P-1683)***
E & J Gallo Winery .... C 805 544-5855
2585 Biddle Ranch Rd San Luis Obispo (93401) ***(P-1684)***
E & J Gallo Winery .... B 323 720-6400
2650 Commerce Way Commerce (90040) ***(P-1685)***
E & J Gallo Winery .... E 707 963-2736
254 Saint Helena Hwy S Saint Helena (94574) ***(P-1686)***
E & J Gallo Winery .... F 209 341-7862
200 E Sandy Blvd Modesto (95354) ***(P-1687)***
E & L Electric Inc .... F 562 903-9272
12322 Los Nietos Rd Santa Fe Springs (90670) ***(P-24687)***
E & R Glass Contractors Inc .... E 909 624-1763
5369 Brooks St Montclair (91763) ***(P-10356)***
E & R Pallets Inc .... F 951 790-1212
4247 Campbell St Riverside (92509) ***(P-4363)***
E & S Precision Machine Inc .... F 209 545-6161
4631 Enterprise Way Modesto (95356) ***(P-15916)***
E & S Precision Sheetmetal Mfg .... F 760 329-1607
19298 Mclane St North Palm Springs (92258) ***(P-12189)***
E Alko Inc .... C 818 587-9700
8201 Woodley Ave Van Nuys (91406) ***(P-22962)***
E and B Natural Resources .... D 661 679-1700
1600 Norris Rd Bakersfield (93308) ***(P-121)***
E and J Gallo, Santa Ynez *Also called Bridlewood Winery* ***(P-1606)***
E D D Investment Co .... E 714 637-3040
2025 N Tustin St Orange (92865) ***(P-1195)***
E D I, South El Monte *Also called Engineering Design Inds Inc* ***(P-15934)***
E D Kilby Mfg & Farming .... E 530 846-5625
286 W Evans Reimer Rd Gridley (95948) ***(P-13630)***
E D M Sacramento Inc .... E 916 851-9285
11341 Sunrise Park Dr Rancho Cordova (95742) ***(P-15917)***
E E Systems Group Inc .... F 626 452-8988
12346 Valley Blvd Unit A El Monte (91732) ***(P-19298)***
E Enterprise Tech, San Jose *Also called Espace Enterprises Tech Inc* ***(P-14462)***
E F T Fast Quality Service .... F 714 751-1487
2328 S Susan St Santa Ana (92704) ***(P-12990)***
E G Meat and Provision Inc (PA) .... F 323 588-5333
4350 Alcoa Ave Vernon (90058) ***(P-454)***
E H Publishing Inc .... E 310 533-2400
3520 Challenger St Torrance (90503) ***(P-5928)***
E J Y Corporation .... E 213 748-1700
151 W 33rd St Los Angeles (90007) ***(P-3739)***
E K C Technology/Burmar Chem, Hayward *Also called Ekc Technology Inc* ***(P-8962)***
E L A Custom Architectural Div, City of Industry *Also called Environmental Ltg For Arch Inc* ***(P-17030)***
E L I, San Diego *Also called Energy Labs Inc* ***(P-15428)***
E M C, Moreno Valley *Also called Envirnmntal Mlding Cncepts LLC* ***(P-9305)***
E M E Inc .... C 310 639-1621
500 E Pine St Compton (90222) ***(P-12991)***
E M G Inc .... D 707 525-9941
675 Aviation Blvd Ste B Santa Rosa (95403) ***(P-22617)***
E O C, Compton *Also called Cri Sub 1* ***(P-4794)***
E P S Products, Palm Springs *Also called Xy Corp Inc* ***(P-14000)***
E Phocus Inc .... F 858 646-5462
10455 Pacific Center Ct San Diego (92121) ***(P-22417)***
E R C Company, E Rncho Dmngz *Also called Coy Industries Inc* ***(P-12165)***
E R G International, Oxnard *Also called Ergonom Corporation* ***(P-5059)***
E R Metals Inc .... F 760 948-2309
14407 Main St Hesperia (92345) ***(P-11396)***
E S M Plastics Inc .... F 909 591-7658
13575 Yorba Ave Chino (91710) ***(P-15918)***
E S Q, Cupertino *Also called Esq Business Services Inc* ***(P-23876)***
E S T, Carlsbad *Also called Electro Surface Tech Inc* ***(P-17866)***
E Sales, Garden Grove *Also called Elasco Inc* ***(P-7560)***
E Seek Inc .... F 714 832-7980
9471 Ridgehaven Ct Ste E San Diego (92123) ***(P-15220)***
E Vasquez Distributors Inc .... E 805 487-8458
4524 E Pleasant Valley Rd Oxnard (93033) ***(P-4364)***
E Virtual Corporation .... F 949 515-3670
192 22nd St Apt D Costa Mesa (92627) ***(P-17224)***
E W Smith Chemical Co .... F 909 590-9717
4738 Murietta St Chino (91710) ***(P-8961)***
E Z Buy E Z Sell Recycler Corp (HQ) .... C 310 886-7808
4954 Van Nuys Blvd # 201 Sherman Oaks (91403) ***(P-5621)***
E Z Martin Stick Labels Inc .... F 562 906-1577
12921 Sunnyside Pl Santa Fe Springs (90670) ***(P-7053)***
E-Band Communications LLC .... E 858 408-0660
17034 Camino San Bernardo San Diego (92127) ***(P-17508)***
E-Fab Inc .... E 408 727-5218
1075 Richard Ave Santa Clara (95050) ***(P-13168)***
E-Freight Technology Inc .... E 626 943-8418
2225 W Cromwell Ave Alhambra (91803) ***(P-23838)***

ALPHABETIC

Employee Codes: A=Over 500 employees, B=251-500
C=101-250, D=51-100, E=20-50, F=10-19
2020 California
Manfacturers Register
© Mergent Inc. 1-800-342-5647
1087

E-Fuel Corporation......E......408 267-2667
15466 Los Gatos Blvd 37 Los Gatos (95032) ***(P-19299)***
E-Liq Cube Inc (PA)......F......562 537-9454
13515 Alondra Blvd Santa Fe Springs (90670) ***(P-23318)***
E-M Manufacturing Inc......F......209 825-1800
1290 Dupont Ct Manteca (95336) ***(P-12190)***
E-Scepter, City of Industry *Also called Sceptre Inc* ***(P-19077)***
E-Solution Inc......F......714 589-2012
4081 E La Palma Ave Ste J Anaheim (92807) ***(P-13823)***
E-Transactions Software Tech......F......408 873-9100
21195 Grenola Dr Cupertino (95014) ***(P-23839)***
E-Z Haul Ready Mix Inc......E......559 233-6603
1538 N Blackstone Ave Fresno (93703) ***(P-10754)***
E-Z Mix Inc......E......909 874-7686
3355 Industrial Dr Bloomington (92316) ***(P-5436)***
E-Z Mix Inc (PA)......E......818 768-0568
11450 Tuxford St Sun Valley (91352) ***(P-5437)***
E-Z Mix Inc......E......510 782-8010
4125 Breakwater Ave Ste E Hayward (94545) ***(P-5438)***
E-Z Plastic Packaging Corp......E......323 887-0123
2051 Garfield Ave Commerce (90040) ***(P-5395)***
E-Z Up Directcom......E......909 426-0060
1900 2nd St Colton (92324) ***(P-3681)***
E-Z-Hook Test Products Div, Arcadia *Also called Tektest Inc* ***(P-18799)***
E. Force Sports, Vista *Also called Efgp Inc* ***(P-22796)***
E/G Electro-Graph Inc......D......760 438-9090
1491 Poinsettia Ave # 138 Vista (92081) ***(P-18205)***
E2e Mfg LLC......E......925 862-2057
7139 Koll Center Pkwy Pleasanton (94566) ***(P-12796)***
E8 Denim House LLC......F......310 386-4413
309 E 8th St Fl 5 Los Angeles (90014) ***(P-3077)***
EA, Redwood City *Also called Electronic Arts Inc* ***(P-23850)***
Ea Sports, Redwood City *Also called Electronic Arts Redwood Inc* ***(P-19215)***
Eagle Access Control Systems......E......818 837-7900
12953 Foothill Blvd Sylmar (91342) ***(P-16713)***
Eagle Creek Inc (HQ)......D......760 431-6400
5935 Darwin Ct Carlsbad (92008) ***(P-10193)***
Eagle Creek Travel Gear, Carlsbad *Also called Eagle Creek Inc* ***(P-10193)***
Eagle Dominion Energy Corp......E......805 272-9557
200 N Hayes Ave Oxnard (93030) ***(P-122)***
Eagle Dominion Trust, Oxnard *Also called Eagle Dominion Energy Corp* ***(P-122)***
Eagle Enterprises Inc......E......323 721-4741
604 W Whittier Blvd Montebello (90640) ***(P-19643)***
Eagle Iron Fabrication Inc......F......925 686-9510
100 Medburn St Ste A Concord (94520) ***(P-11787)***
Eagle Iron Works, Concord *Also called Eagle Iron Fabrication Inc* ***(P-11787)***
Eagle Laboratories, LLC, Rancho Cucamonga *Also called Eagle Labs LLC* ***(P-22350)***
Eagle Labs LLC......D......909 481-0011
10201a Trademark St Ste A Rancho Cucamonga (91730) ***(P-22350)***
Eagle Mold Technologies Inc......E......858 530-0888
12330 Crosthwaite Cir Poway (92064) ***(P-9768)***
Eagle Moulding Company 1 (PA)......E......530 673-6517
1625 Tierra Buena Rd Yuba City (95993) ***(P-4041)***
Eagle Newspapers LLC......E......619 437-8800
1224 10th St Ste 103 Coronado (92118) ***(P-5622)***
Eagle Products - Plast Indust......E......909 465-1548
10811 Fremont Ave Ontario (91762) ***(P-9769)***
Eagle Ridge Paper Ltd (HQ)......E......714 780-1799
100 S Anaheim Blvd # 250 Anaheim (92805) ***(P-5103)***
Eagle Rock Incorporated......F......530 623-4444
40029 La Grange Rd Junction City (96048) ***(P-13727)***
Eagle Roofing Products Co, Rialto *Also called Burlingame Industries Inc* ***(P-11001)***
Eagle Roofing Products Fla LLC......E......909 822-6000
3546 N Riverside Ave Rialto (92377) ***(P-10462)***
Eagle Signs Inc......F......909 923-3034
1028 E Acacia St Ontario (91761) ***(P-23092)***
Eagle Systems Inc......F......510 231-2686
1601 Atlas Rd Richmond (94806) ***(P-20369)***
Eagle Tech Manufacturing Inc......E......831 768-7467
841 Walker St Watsonville (95076) ***(P-20862)***
Eagle Valley Ginning LLC......E......209 826-5002
27480 S Bennett Rd Firebaugh (93622) ***(P-14455)***
Eaglemetric Corp......F......949 288-3363
98 Discovery Irvine (92618) ***(P-21462)***
Eagleridge Paper CA, Anaheim *Also called Eagle Ridge Paper Ltd* ***(P-5103)***
Eagleware Manufacturing Co Inc......E......562 320-3100
12683 Corral Pl Santa Fe Springs (90670) ***(P-12797)***
Eai-Jr286 Inc......F......310 297-6400
20100 S Vermont Ave Torrance (90502) ***(P-22794)***
Ear Charms Inc......F......949 494-4147
1855 Laguna Canyon Rd Laguna Beach (92651) ***(P-22513)***
Ear Gear, Laguna Beach *Also called Ear Charms Inc* ***(P-22513)***
Eargo Inc (PA)......D......650 996-9508
1600 Technology Dr Fl 6 San Jose (95110) ***(P-22002)***
Earl Hays Press......F......818 765-0700
10707 Sherman Way Sun Valley (91352) ***(P-7054)***
Earlens Corporation......F......650 366-9000
4045a Campbell Ave Menlo Park (94025) ***(P-22003)***
Early Bird Alert Inc......F......415 479-7902
70 Mitchell Blvd Ste 106 San Rafael (94903) ***(P-17363)***
Early Childhood Resources, San Diego *Also called Ecr4kids LP* ***(P-4858)***
Earnest Eats, Solana Beach *Also called Annona Company LLC* ***(P-1015)***
Earth & Vine Provisions Inc......F......916 434-8399
160 Flocchini Cir Lincoln (95648) ***(P-766)***
Earth Lab Inc......F......888 835-2276
5016 Maplewood Ave Apt B Los Angeles (90004) ***(P-8382)***
Earth Print Inc......F......818 879-6050
31115 Via Colinas Ste 301 Westlake Village (91362) ***(P-6555)***
Earthlite LLC (HQ)......C......760 599-1112
990 Joshua Way Vista (92081) ***(P-4690)***
Earthologytech LLC......E......619 435-5296
928 F Ave Coronado (92118) ***(P-13631)***
Earthpro Inc......E......408 294-1920
2010 El Camino Real Santa Clara (95050) ***(P-10508)***
Earthrise Nutritionals LLC......F......760 348-5027
113 E Hoober Rd Calipatria (92233) ***(P-2449)***
Earthsavers Erosion Ctrl LLC......F......530 662-7700
12972 County Road 102 Woodland (95776) ***(P-20791)***
Earthwise Packaging Inc......F......714 602-2169
12 Goddard Irvine (92618) ***(P-16895)***
Eascare Products USA, Fresno *Also called McGrayel Company Inc* ***(P-8997)***
Easic Corporation......E......408 855-9200
3940 Freedom Cir 100 Santa Clara (95054) ***(P-18206)***
East Bay Brass Foundry Inc......E......510 233-7171
1200 Chesley Ave Richmond (94801) ***(P-11335)***
East Bay Fixture Company......E......510 652-4421
941 Aileen St Oakland (94608) ***(P-4477)***
East Bay Glass Company Inc......F......510 834-2535
601 50th Ave Oakland (94601) ***(P-11949)***
East Bay Machine and Shtmtl, Concord *Also called Alvellan Inc* ***(P-15734)***
East County Gazette......F......619 444-5774
270 E Douglas Ave El Cajon (92020) ***(P-5623)***
East Electronics, Fremont *Also called Myntahl Corporation* ***(P-17387)***
East La Lamination Inc......F......323 881-9838
616 N Hazard Ave Los Angeles (90063) ***(P-9770)***
East Penn Manufacturing Co......F......916 374-9965
3701 Parkway Pl Ste B West Sacramento (95691) ***(P-19157)***
East Shore Garment Company LLC......E......323 923-4454
2015 E 48th St Vernon (90058) ***(P-2685)***
East West Printing......F......714 899-7885
7433 Lampson Ave Garden Grove (92841) ***(P-6556)***
East West Tea Company LLC......F......310 275-9891
1616 Preuss Rd Los Angeles (90035) ***(P-1018)***
Eastbay Express, Oakland *Also called Village Voice Media* ***(P-5860)***
Easterncctv (usa) LLC......D......626 961-8810
525 Parriott Pl W Hacienda Heights (91745) ***(P-19300)***
Eastman Kodak Company......D......949 306-9034
3 Santa Elena Rcho STA Marg (92688) ***(P-22418)***
Eastman Performance Films LLC......E......714 634-0900
4110 E La Palma Ave Anaheim (92807) ***(P-7557)***
Eastman Performance Films LLC......E......818 882-5744
21019 Osborne St Canoga Park (91304) ***(P-7558)***
Easton Bell Sports, Scotts Valley *Also called Bell Sports Inc* ***(P-22760)***
Eastwest Clothing Inc (PA)......E......323 980-1177
40 E Verdugo Ave Burbank (91502) ***(P-3157)***
Eastwood Machine LLC......F......619 873-3660
9346 Abraham Way Santee (92071) ***(P-15919)***
Easy Ad Incorporated......E......951 658-2244
155 S Harvard St Hemet (92543) ***(P-5624)***
Easy Ad Magazine, San Luis Obispo *Also called M G A Investment Co Inc* ***(P-6276)***
Easy Flex, Garden Grove *Also called Easyflex Inc* ***(P-11043)***
Easy Reader Inc......E......310 372-4611
832 Hermosa Ave Hermosa Beach (90254) ***(P-5625)***
Easydial Inc......D......949 916-5851
181 Technology Dr Ste 150 Irvine (92618) ***(P-21693)***
Easyflex Inc......E......888 577-8999
7423 Doig Dr Garden Grove (92841) ***(P-11043)***
Eat Like A Woman, Burbank *Also called Staness Jonekos Entps Inc* ***(P-2617)***
Eaton Aerospace LLC......E......818 550-4200
2905 Winona Ave Burbank (91504) ***(P-20571)***
Eaton Aerospace LLC......E......949 452-9500
9650 Jeronimo Rd Irvine (92618) ***(P-20572)***
Eaton Corporation......F......951 685-5788
11120 Philadelphia Ave Jurupa Valley (91752) ***(P-19301)***
Eaton Corporation......C......661 396-2557
200 New Stine Rd Bakersfield (93309) ***(P-16714)***
Eaton Industrial Corporation......B......949 425-9700
9650 Jeronimo Rd Irvine (92618) ***(P-20096)***
Eaton Leonard Tooling, Temecula *Also called Tube Form Solutions LLC* ***(P-14284)***
Eatyourmealscom LLC......F......925 984-5452
4418 Deer Ridge Rd Danville (94506) ***(P-23319)***
Eba Design Inc......F......714 417-9222
760 W 16th St Ste D Costa Mesa (92627) ***(P-8484)***
Eba Performance Makeup, Costa Mesa *Also called Eba Design Inc* ***(P-8484)***
Ebanista Inc (PA)......E......949 650-6397
2015 Newport Blvd Costa Mesa (92627) ***(P-4639)***
Ebara Technologies Inc (HQ)......D......916 920-5451
51 Main Ave Sacramento (95838) ***(P-14630)***
Ebatts.com, Camarillo *Also called Battery-Biz Inc* ***(P-19187)***
Ebix Inc......E......805 568-0240
212 Cottage Ave Santa Barbara (93101) ***(P-23840)***
Ebr Systems Inc (PA)......E......408 720-1906
480 Oakmead Pkwy Sunnyvale (94085) ***(P-22250)***
Ebs Products......F......714 896-6700
5082 Bolsa Ave Ste 112 Huntington Beach (92649) ***(P-14456)***
Ebsco Productions Inc......E......323 960-2599
1040 N Las Palmas Ave 1 Los Angeles (90038) ***(P-12798)***
Ebus Inc......E......562 904-3474
9250 Washburn Rd Downey (90242) ***(P-19531)***
Eca, Brea *Also called Energy Cnvrsion Applctions Inc* ***(P-16548)***
Eca Medical Instruments (HQ)......E......805 376-2509
1107 Tourmaline Dr Newbury Park (91320) ***(P-21694)***
Eca Medical Instruments......E......818 998-7284
21615 Parthenia St Canoga Park (91304) ***(P-21695)***
ECB Corp......E......916 492-8900
1650 Parkway Blvd West Sacramento (95691) ***(P-12191)***
Eccentric Jewelry, Tarzana *Also called Ggco Inc* ***(P-22520)***

Mergent e-mail: customerrelations@mergent.com
1088
2020 California
Manufacturers Register
(P-0000) Products & Services Section entry number
(PA)=Parent Co (HQ)=Headquarters (DH)=Div Headquarters

ALPHABETIC SECTION Edward Koehn Co Inc

Echelon Corporation (HQ) ....D....408 938-5200
3600 Peterson Way Santa Clara (95054) ***(P-21024)***
Echelon Fine Printing, Vernon *Also called The Ligature Inc* ***(P-6889)***
Echo, A Heatlhstream Company, San Diego *Also called Healthstream Inc* ***(P-23972)***
Eci Fuel Systems, Upland *Also called Exhaust Center Inc* ***(P-12205)***
Eckert Zegler Isotope Pdts Inc ....E....661 309-1010
1800 N Keystone St Burbank (91504) ***(P-21463)***
Eckert Zegler Isotope Pdts Inc (HQ) ....E....661 309-1010
24937 Avenue Tibbitts Valencia (91355) ***(P-21464)***
Eckert Zegler Isotope Pdts Inc ....E....661 309-1010
1800 N Keystone St Burbank (91504) ***(P-21465)***
Ecko Print & Packaging, Ontario *Also called Ecko Products Group LLC* ***(P-5218)***
Ecko Products Group LLC ....E....909 628-5678
740 S Milliken Ave Ste C Ontario (91761) ***(P-5218)***
Eclipse Chocolate Bar & Bistro ....F....619 578-2984
2145 Fern St San Diego (92104) ***(P-1410)***
Eclipse Data Technologies Inc ....F....925 224-8880
5139 Johnson Dr Pleasanton (94588) ***(P-19214)***
Eclipse Design Inc ....F....707 763-3104
427 Corona Rd Petaluma (94954) ***(P-12471)***
Eclipse Metal Fabrication Inc ....E....650 298-8731
2901 Spring St Redwood City (94063) ***(P-12192)***
Eclipse Microwave Inc ....F....408 526-1100
2095 Ringwood Ave Ste 60 San Jose (95131) ***(P-18895)***
Eclipse Prtg & Graphics LLC ....E....909 390-2452
4462 E Airport Dr Ontario (91761) ***(P-6557)***
Eclypse International Corp (PA) ....F....951 371-8008
265 N Joy St Ste 150 Corona (92879) ***(P-21025)***
Ecmm Services Inc ....C....714 988-9388
500 S Kraemer Blvd # 100 Brea (92821) ***(P-22963)***
Eco Global Solutions Inc ....F....707 254-9844
221 Gateway Rd W Ste 403 NAPA (94558) ***(P-20792)***
Eco Sensors, Newark *Also called Kwj Engineering Inc* ***(P-21498)***
Eco Services Operations Corp ....E....925 313-8224
100 Mococo Rd Martinez (94553) ***(P-7487)***
Eco Services Operations Corp ....D....310 885-6719
20720 S Wilmington Ave Long Beach (90810) ***(P-7488)***
Eco World USA LLC ....F....626 433-1333
9950 Baldwin Pl El Monte (91731) ***(P-17025)***
Eco-Gen Distributors Inc ....F....760 712-7460
340 Goddard Irvine (92618) ***(P-16639)***
Eco-Gen Energy Inc ....F....818 756-4700
7247 Hayvenhurst Ave A6 Van Nuys (91406) ***(P-16640)***
Eco-Shell Inc ....E....530 824-8794
5230 Grange Rd Corning (96021) ***(P-23320)***
Ecoatm LLC (HQ) ....C....858 999-3200
10121 Barnes Canyon Rd San Diego (92121) ***(P-17785)***
Ecolab Inc ....F....626 935-1212
18383 Railroad St City of Industry (91748) ***(P-8338)***
Ecolab Inc ....D....925 215-8008
3160 Crow Canyon Pl # 200 San Ramon (94583) ***(P-8339)***
Ecolight Inc ....F....310 450-7444
1660 Lincoln Blvd Santa Monica (90404) ***(P-23321)***
Ecolink Intelligent Tech Inc ....F....855 432-6546
2055 Corte Del Nogal Carlsbad (92011) ***(P-17225)***
Ecoly International Inc ....E....818 718-6982
5800 Bristol Pkwy Ste 700 Culver City (90230) ***(P-8485)***
Econ-O-Plate Inc ....F....310 342-5900
5760 Hannum Ave Culver City (90230) ***(P-6558)***
Econocold Refrigerators, Cerritos *Also called Refrigerator Manufacters Inc* ***(P-16822)***
Econoday Inc ....F....925 299-5350
3730 Mt Diablo Blvd # 340 Lafayette (94549) ***(P-6224)***
Econolite Control Products Inc (PA) ....C....714 630-3700
1250 N Tustin Ave Anaheim (92807) ***(P-17727)***
Economy Print & Image Inc ....F....619 295-4455
7515 Metropolitan Dr San Diego (92108) ***(P-6559)***
Economy Printing, San Diego *Also called Economy Print & Image Inc* ***(P-6559)***
Economy Printing ....F....858 679-8630
12642 Stoutwood St Poway (92064) ***(P-6560)***
Economy Printing Image, Poway *Also called Economy Printing* ***(P-6560)***
Economy Printing Service, Monterey *Also called Montero Printing Inc* ***(P-6738)***
Economy Stock Feed Company ....F....559 888-2187
10508 E Central Ave Del Rey (93616) ***(P-1091)***
Econotek Inc (PA) ....F....714 238-1131
2895 E Blue Star St Anaheim (92806) ***(P-22151)***
Econscious, Petaluma *Also called G M P C LLC* ***(P-23118)***
Ecoolthing Corp ....E....714 368-4791
1321 E Saint Gertrude Pl A Santa Ana (92705) ***(P-13519)***
Ecoplast Corporation Inc ....D....909 346-0450
13414 Slover Ave Fontana (92337) ***(P-9771)***
Ecosystem Aquarium, Dana Point *Also called Captive Ocean Reef Enterprises* ***(P-14801)***
Ecp Powder Coating ....F....619 448-3932
1835 John Towers Ave A El Cajon (92020) ***(P-13169)***
Ecr4kids LP ....E....619 323-2005
4370 Jutland Dr San Diego (92117) ***(P-4858)***
Ecrio Inc ....D....408 973-7290
19925 Stevens Creek Blvd # 100 Cupertino (95014) ***(P-23841)***
Ecs Refining, Santa Clara *Also called All Metals Inc* ***(P-11197)***
Ect News Network Inc ....F....818 461-9700
16133 Ventura Blvd # 700 Encino (91436) ***(P-6225)***
Ectec Inc ....F....661 451-1098
38638 Palms Pl Palmdale (93552) ***(P-20573)***
Ectron Corporation ....E....858 278-0600
8159 Engineer Rd San Diego (92111) ***(P-17509)***
Ecw Technology Inc ....F....310 373-0082
609 Deep Valley Dr Rllng HLS Est (90274) ***(P-14655)***
Ed Jones Company ....F....510 704-0704
2834 8th St Berkeley (94710) ***(P-23322)***
Edc-Biosystems Inc (PA) ....E....510 257-1500
49090 Milmont Dr Fremont (94538) ***(P-20863)***
Edcast Inc (PA) ....E....650 823-3511
1901 Old Middlefield Way # 21 Mountain View (94043) ***(P-23842)***
Edco Die Inc ....F....909 985-4417
2199 W Arrow Rte Upland (91786) ***(P-15920)***
Edco Plastics Inc ....E....714 772-1986
2110 E Winston Rd Anaheim (92806) ***(P-9772)***
Eddie Motorsports ....F....909 581-7398
11479 6th St Rancho Cucamonga (91730) ***(P-11588)***
Eddies Perfume & Cosmtc Co Inc ....E....818 341-1717
20929 Ventura Blvd Woodland Hills (91364) ***(P-8486)***
Eddy Pump Corporation (PA) ....F....619 258-7020
15405 Olde Highway 80 El Cajon (92021) ***(P-15629)***
Edelbrock LLC (HQ) ....B....310 781-2222
2700 California St Torrance (90503) ***(P-20398)***
Edelbrock Foundry Corp ....A....951 654-6677
1320 S Buena Vista St San Jacinto (92583) ***(P-11336)***
Edelbrock Holdings Inc ....C....310 781-2290
2301 Dominguez Way Torrance (90501) ***(P-19644)***
Edelbrock Holdings Inc ....C....951 654-6677
1380 S Buena Vista St San Jacinto (92583) ***(P-19645)***
Edelmann Usa Inc (HQ) ....E....323 669-5700
2150 S Parco Ave Ontario (91761) ***(P-23093)***
Eden Beauty Concepts Inc ....E....760 330-9941
3215 Executive Rdg Vista (92081) ***(P-8487)***
Eden Creamery LLC (PA) ....F....855 425-6867
4470 W Sunset Blvd # 90182 Los Angeles (90027) ***(P-640)***
Eden Equipment Company Inc ....F....909 629-2217
5670 Wilshire Blvd # 1400 Los Angeles (90036) ***(P-14811)***
Edeniq Inc ....D....559 302-1777
2505 N Shirk Rd Visalia (93291) ***(P-8736)***
Edessa Inc ....E....909 823-1377
11027 Cherry Ave Fontana (92337) ***(P-10565)***
Edey Door, Los Angeles *Also called Edey Manufacturing Co Inc* ***(P-11950)***
Edey Manufacturing Co Inc ....E....323 566-6151
2159 E 92nd St Los Angeles (90002) ***(P-11950)***
Edgate Correlation Svcs LLC ....E....858 712-9341
5473 Krny Vlla Rd Ste 300 San Diego (92123) ***(P-23323)***
Edge Compute Inc ....F....408 209-0368
5201 Great America Pkwy Santa Clara (95054) ***(P-18207)***
Edge Electronics Corporation ....E....510 614-7988
14670 Wicks Blvd San Leandro (94577) ***(P-12018)***
Edge Plastics Inc (PA) ....E....951 786-4750
3016 Kansas Ave Bldg 3 Riverside (92507) ***(P-9773)***
Edge Solutions Consulting Inc (PA) ....E....818 591-3500
2801 Townsgate Rd Ste 111 Westlake Village (91361) ***(P-14904)***
Edgewell Per Care Brands LLC ....B....949 466-0131
599 S Barranca Ave Covina (91723) ***(P-11514)***
Edgewood Press Inc ....F....714 516-2455
1130 N Main St Orange (92867) ***(P-6561)***
Edgington Oil Company LLC ....D....562 423-1465
2400 E Artesia Blvd Long Beach (90805) ***(P-9091)***
Edgy Soul ....F....310 800-2861
22337 Pacific Coast Hwy # 143 Malibu (90265) ***(P-22981)***
Edi Ideas, Fountain Valley *Also called Freightgate Inc* ***(P-23921)***
Edinburgh Instruments, Fremont *Also called Techcomp (usa) Inc* ***(P-21298)***
Edirect Publishing Inc ....F....760 602-8300
3451 Via Montebello # 192 Carlsbad (92009) ***(P-6226)***
Edison Opto USA Corporation ....F....909 284-9710
1809 Excise Ave Ste 201 Ontario (91761) ***(P-18208)***
Edition One Group ....F....510 705-1930
2080 2nd St Berkeley (94710) ***(P-6562)***
EDM International Logistics ....F....626 588-2299
2225 W Commwl Ave Ste 110 Alhambra (91803) ***(P-9525)***
EDM Performance Accessories, Brea *Also called Clean America Inc* ***(P-19273)***
Edmodo Inc ....E....310 614-6868
777 Mariners Island Blvd # 510 San Mateo (94404) ***(P-23843)***
Edmons Unque Furn Stone Gllery (PA) ....F....323 462-5787
5174 Melrose Ave Los Angeles (90038) ***(P-4566)***
Edmund A Gray Co (PA) ....D....213 625-0376
2277 E 15th St Los Angeles (90021) ***(P-13467)***
Edmund Kim International Inc (PA) ....E....310 604-1100
2880 E Ana St Compton (90221) ***(P-3078)***
Edna Valley Vineyard, San Luis Obispo *Also called E & J Gallo Winery* ***(P-1684)***
Ednas Inc ....F....805 541-3563
390 Buckley Rd Ste F San Luis Obispo (93401) ***(P-1196)***
Edner Corporation ....E....925 831-1248
528 Oakshire Pl Alamo (94507) ***(P-1197)***
Edo Rcnnssnce Srvllnce Systems, Van Nuys *Also called L3harris Technologies Inc* ***(P-20598)***
Edris Plastics Mfg Inc ....E....323 581-7000
4560 Pacific Blvd Vernon (90058) ***(P-9774)***
Edro Engineering Inc (HQ) ....D....909 594-5751
20500 Carrey Rd Walnut (91789) ***(P-14047)***
Edro Specialty Steels Inc ....F....800 368-3376
20500 Carrey Rd Walnut (91789) ***(P-14048)***
EDS, Tracy *Also called Encompass Dist Svcs LLC* ***(P-18216)***
EDS Wrap and Roll Foods LLC ....E....510 266-0888
2545 Barrington Ct Hayward (94545) ***(P-726)***
Education Elements Inc ....E....650 336-0660
999 Skyway Rd Ste 325 San Carlos (94070) ***(P-23844)***
Educational Ideas Incorporated ....E....714 990-4332
471 Atlas St Brea (92821) ***(P-6099)***
Educational Insights, Gardena *Also called Learning Resources Inc* ***(P-23393)***
Edutone Corporation (PA) ....F....888 904-9773
1101 Marina Village Pkwy # 201 Alameda (94501) ***(P-23845)***
Edward Koehn Co Inc ....F....510 843-0821
820 Folger Ave Berkeley (94710) ***(P-12630)***

ALPHABETIC

Employee Codes: A=Over 500 employees, B=251-500
C=101-250, D=51-100, E=20-50, F=10-19
2020 California
Manfacturers Register
© Mergent Inc. 1-800-342-5647
1089

Edward's Industries, Studio City *Also called Normel Inc* ***(P-7149)***
Edwards Assoc Cmmnications Inc (PA).....B.....805 658-2626
2277 Knoll Dr Ste A Ventura (93003) ***(P-5361)***
Edwards Industries, Studio City *Also called Kimdurla Inc* ***(P-10314)***
Edwards Label, Ventura *Also called Edwards Assoc Cmmnications Inc* ***(P-5361)***
Edwards Lfsciences Cardiaq LLC.....F.....949 387-2615
2 Jenner Ste 100 Irvine (92618) ***(P-21696)***
Edwards Lifescience Fing LLC.....F.....949 250-3480
1 Edwards Way Irvine (92614) ***(P-23324)***
Edwards Lifesciences Corp.....F.....949 250-3522
1402 Alton Pkwy Irvine (92606) ***(P-22004)***
Edwards Lifesciences Corp.....F.....949 250-3783
17192 Daimler St Irvine (92614) ***(P-21697)***
Edwards Lifesciences Corp (PA).....A.....949 250-2500
1 Edwards Way Irvine (92614) ***(P-22005)***
Edwards Lifesciences Corp.....E.....949 553-0611
1212 Alton Pkwy Irvine (92606) ***(P-22006)***
Edwards Lifesciences US Inc.....E.....949 250-2500
1 Edwards Way Irvine (92614) ***(P-22251)***
Edwards Sheet Metal Supply Inc.....E.....818 785-8600
7810 Burnet Ave Van Nuys (91405) ***(P-12193)***
EE Pauley Plastic Extrusion.....F.....760 240-3737
17177 Navajo Rd Apple Valley (92307) ***(P-9775)***
Eema Industries Inc.....E.....323 904-0200
5461 W Jefferson Blvd Los Angeles (90016) ***(P-17118)***
Eemus Manufacturing Corp.....F.....626 443-8841
11111 Rush St South El Monte (91733) ***(P-13170)***
Eep Holdings LLC (PA).....F.....909 597-7861
4626 Eucalyptus Ave Chino (91710) ***(P-9776)***
Eevelle LLC.....E.....760 434-2231
2270 Cosmos Ct Ste 100 Carlsbad (92011) ***(P-3839)***
Eeye Digital Security, Aliso Viejo *Also called Eeye Inc* ***(P-23846)***
Eeye Inc (HQ).....E.....949 333-1900
65 Enterprise Ste 100 Aliso Viejo (92656) ***(P-23846)***
Eezer Products Inc.....E.....559 255-4140
4734 E Home Ave Fresno (93703) ***(P-7559)***
Ef Composite Technologies LP.....F.....800 433-6723
2151 Las Palmas Dr Ste D Carlsbad (92011) ***(P-22795)***
Efaxcom (HQ).....D.....323 817-3207
6922 Hollywood Blvd Fl 5 Los Angeles (90028) ***(P-15221)***
Efaxcom.....E.....805 692-0064
5385 Hollister Ave # 208 Santa Barbara (93111) ***(P-15222)***
Eff Aero, Stockton *Also called Wkf (friedman Enterprises Inc* ***(P-19991)***
Effective Graphics Inc.....D.....310 323-2223
40 E Verdugo Ave Burbank (91502) ***(P-7370)***
Efgp Inc.....F.....760 692-3900
1384 Poinsettia Ave Ste E Vista (92081) ***(P-22796)***
Efi, Fremont *Also called Electronics For Imaging Inc* ***(P-7056)***
Efi Technology Inc.....E.....310 793-2505
2741 Plaza Del Amo # 211 Torrance (90503) ***(P-19646)***
Eg Systems LLC (PA).....E.....510 324-0126
6200 Village Pkwy Dublin (94568) ***(P-18209)***
Eg Wear Inc.....F.....916 361-1508
4512 Harlin Dr Ste A Sacramento (95826) ***(P-23325)***
Egads LLC.....F.....951 695-9050
42191 Sarah Way Temecula (92590) ***(P-23094)***
Egain Corporation (PA).....C.....408 636-4500
1252 Borregas Ave Sunnyvale (94089) ***(P-23847)***
Egain Corporation.....F.....408 212-3400
455 W Maude Ave Sunnyvale (94085) ***(P-23848)***
Egen, Vernon *Also called 4 You Apparel Inc* ***(P-3209)***
Eggleston Signs.....F.....916 920-1750
1558 Juliesse Ave Ste S Sacramento (95815) ***(P-23095)***
Eggs West LLC.....E.....661 758-9700
14460 Palm Ave Wasco (93280) ***(P-509)***
Eggtooth Originals Consulting.....F.....530 468-5131
13502 Graveyard Gulch Rd Fort Jones (96032) ***(P-22673)***
Egr Incorporated (HQ).....C.....909 923-7075
4000 Greystone Dr Ontario (91761) ***(P-19647)***
Egret, Sonoma *Also called Bonneau Wines LLC* ***(P-1602)***
EH Suda Inc (PA).....F.....650 622-9700
615 Industrial Rd San Carlos (94070) ***(P-15921)***
EH Suda Inc.....E.....530 778-9830
210 Texas Ave Lewiston (96052) ***(P-15922)***
Ei Corp.....E.....530 274-1240
13355 Grass Valley Ave A Grass Valley (95945) ***(P-17226)***
Ei-Lo Inc.....F.....949 200-6626
2102 Alton Pkwy Ste B Irvine (92606) ***(P-2988)***
Eibach Springs Inc.....D.....951 256-8300
264 Mariah Cir Corona (92879) ***(P-13337)***
Eico Inc (PA).....D.....408 945-9898
1054 Yosemite Dr Milpitas (95035) ***(P-21026)***
Eide Industries Inc.....D.....562 402-8335
16215 Piuma Ave Cerritos (90703) ***(P-3682)***
Eidon Inc.....F.....800 700-1169
12330 Stowe Dr Poway (92064) ***(P-7876)***
Eiger Biopharmaceuticals Inc (PA).....F.....650 272-6138
2155 Park Blvd Palo Alto (94306) ***(P-8295)***
Einflatables, Cerritos *Also called Funtastic Factory Inc* ***(P-15977)***
Einflatables, Buena Park *Also called Spn Investments Inc* ***(P-22895)***
Einstein Noah Rest Group Inc.....F.....714 847-4609
16304 Beach Blvd Westminster (92683) ***(P-547)***
Einstein Noah Rest Group Inc.....F.....408 358-5895
15996 Los Gatos Blvd Los Gatos (95032) ***(P-548)***
Eis Group Inc.....C.....415 402-2622
731 Sansome St Fl 4 San Francisco (94111) ***(P-23849)***
Eisel Enterprises Inc.....E.....714 993-1706
714 Fee Ana St Placentia (92870) ***(P-10566)***
Ej Diamonds Inc.....F.....213 623-2329
631 S Olive St Ste 201 Los Angeles (90014) ***(P-22514)***
EJ Lauren LLC.....E.....562 803-1113
9400 Hall Rd Downey (90241) ***(P-4640)***
Ej Usa Inc.....F.....562 528-0258
2020 W 14th St Long Beach (90813) ***(P-11141)***
Ejay Filtration Inc.....E.....951 683-0805
3036 Durahart St Riverside (92507) ***(P-13410)***
Ejays Machine Co Inc.....E.....714 879-0558
1108 E Valencia Dr Fullerton (92831) ***(P-15923)***
Ejl, Downey *Also called EJ Lauren LLC* ***(P-4640)***
EKA Designs, Westlake Village *Also called EKA Technologies Inc* ***(P-17510)***
EKA Technologies Inc.....E.....805 379-8668
2985 E Hillcrest Dr # 203 Westlake Village (91362) ***(P-17510)***
Ekc Technology Inc (HQ).....C.....510 784-9105
2520 Barrington Ct Hayward (94545) ***(P-8962)***
Ekko Material Hdlg Eqp Mfg Inc.....F.....909 212-1962
1761 W Holt Ave Pomona (91768) ***(P-20508)***
Eklavya LLC.....F.....925 443-3296
2021 Las Positas Ct # 141 Livermore (94551) ***(P-14812)***
Eklin Medical Systems Inc.....D.....760 918-9626
6359 Paseo Del Lago Carlsbad (92011) ***(P-21698)***
Eko Devices Inc.....F.....844 356-3384
2600 10th St Ste 260 Berkeley (94710) ***(P-22252)***
Ekso Bionics Inc (PA).....D.....510 984-1761
1414 Harbour Way S # 1201 Richmond (94804) ***(P-14457)***
Ekso Bionics Holdings Inc.....D.....510 984-1761
1414 Hrbour Way S Ste 120 Richmond (94804) ***(P-22007)***
El & El Wood Products Corp (PA).....C.....909 591-0339
6011 Schaefer Ave Chino (91710) ***(P-4042)***
El Burrito Mxican Fd Pdts Corp.....F.....626 369-7828
14944 Don Julian Rd City of Industry (91746) ***(P-767)***
El Cajon Plating, El Cajon *Also called Ecp Powder Coating* ***(P-13169)***
El Camino Machine & Wldg LLC (PA).....E.....831 758-8309
296 El Camino Real S Salinas (93901) ***(P-15924)***
El Camino Wood Products.....F.....310 768-3447
16816 S Broadway Gardena (90248) ***(P-4335)***
El Chavito Inc.....F.....844 424-2848
6020 Progressive Ave # 600 San Diego (92154) ***(P-1364)***
El Clasificado.....D.....323 278-5310
1125 Goodrich Blvd Commerce (90022) ***(P-6227)***
El Dorado Gold Panner Inc.....F.....530 626-5057
247 Placerville Dr Placerville (95667) ***(P-5626)***
El Dorado Mexican Food Pdts, Los Angeles *Also called Food-O-Mex Corporation* ***(P-2461)***
El Dorado Newspapers Inc (HQ).....C.....916 321-1826
2100 Q St Sacramento (95816) ***(P-5627)***
El Dorado Truss Coinc.....E.....530 622-1264
300 Industrial Dr Placerville (95667) ***(P-4300)***
El Gallito Market Inc.....E.....626 442-1190
12242 Valley Blvd El Monte (91732) ***(P-2450)***
El Indio Tortillas Fctry, Santa Ana *Also called El Indio Tortilleria* ***(P-2451)***
El Indio Tortilleria.....F.....714 542-3114
1502 W 5th St Santa Ana (92703) ***(P-2451)***
El Latino Newspaper, Chula Vista *Also called Latina & Associates Inc* ***(P-5695)***
El Metate Foods Inc.....F.....714 542-3913
125n Rancho Santiago Blvd Orange (92869) ***(P-1198)***
El Metate Foods Inc.....E.....949 646-9362
817 W 19th St Costa Mesa (92627) ***(P-1199)***
El Metate Market, Costa Mesa *Also called El Metate Foods Inc* ***(P-1199)***
El Metate Mercado, Orange *Also called El Metate Foods Inc* ***(P-1198)***
El Monte Plating Company.....F.....626 448-3607
11409 Stewart St El Monte (91731) ***(P-12992)***
El Observador Publications Inc.....F.....408 938-1700
1042 W Hedding St Ste 250 San Jose (95126) ***(P-5628)***
El Paraiso No 2.....E.....323 587-2073
1760 E Florence Ave Los Angeles (90001) ***(P-641)***
El Pelado LLC.....E.....707 938-2877
1180 Fremont Dr Sonoma (95476) ***(P-4365)***
El Popular Spanish Newspaper.....F.....661 325-7725
404 Truxtun Ave Bakersfield (93301) ***(P-5629)***
El Segundo Bread Bar LLC.....E.....310 615-9898
701 E El Segundo Blvd El Segundo (90245) ***(P-1200)***
El Sol, Modesto *Also called McClatchy Newspapers Inc* ***(P-5731)***
El Super Leon Pnchin Sncks Inc.....E.....619 426-2968
2545 Britannia Blvd Ste A San Diego (92154) ***(P-1365)***
Elafree Inc.....F.....949 724-9390
17779 Main St Ste F&G Irvine (92614) ***(P-23326)***
Elaine Gill Inc.....F.....510 559-1600
6001 Shellmound St Fl 4th Emeryville (94608) ***(P-6100)***
Elan Blanc, Palm Desert *Also called Equipment De Sport Usa Inc* ***(P-3744)***
Elanco Animal Health, Newbury Park *Also called Eli Lilly and Company* ***(P-7877)***
Elasco Inc.....D.....714 373-4767
11377 Markon Dr Garden Grove (92841) ***(P-7560)***
Elastomer Technologies Inc.....F.....951 272-5820
255 Glider Cir Corona (92880) ***(P-9228)***
Elation Lighting Inc.....D.....323 582-3322
6122 S Eastern Ave Commerce (90040) ***(P-17026)***
Elation Professional, Commerce *Also called Elation Lighting Inc* ***(P-17026)***
Elba Company, San Dimas *Also called Elba Jewelry Inc* ***(P-22515)***
Elba Jewelry Inc.....F.....909 394-5803
910 N Amelia Ave San Dimas (91773) ***(P-22515)***
Elco Lighting, Vernon *Also called AMP Plus Inc* ***(P-17087)***
Elco Rfrgn Solutions LLC.....A.....619 255-5251
2554 Commercial St San Diego (92113) ***(P-15427)***
Elcon Inc.....E.....408 292-7800
1009 Timothy Dr San Jose (95133) ***(P-18896)***
Elcon Power Conectr Pdts Group, Menlo Park *Also called Te Connectivity Corporation* ***(P-16931)***
Elcon Precision LLC.....E.....408 292-7800
1009 Timothy Dr San Jose (95133) ***(P-14158)***

Eldema Products....F....619 661-5113
10145 Via De La Amistad # 5 San Diego (92154) ***(P-17089)***
Eldorado National Cal Inc (HQ)....B....951 727-9300
9670 Galena St Riverside (92509) ***(P-19468)***
Eldorado Stone, North Hollywood *Also called Prime Building Material Inc* ***(P-10631)***
Eldorado Stone LLC (HQ)....E....800 925-1491
1370 Grand Ave Bldg B San Marcos (92078) ***(P-10567)***
Eldridge Products Inc....E....831 648-7777
465 Reservation Rd Marina (93933) ***(P-20864)***
Eleanor Rigby Leather Co....E....619 356-5590
4660 La Jolla Village Dr # 100 San Diego (92122) ***(P-10247)***
Elecraft Incorporated....E....831 763-4211
125 Westridge Dr Watsonville (95076) ***(P-21027)***
Electrasem Corp....F....951 371-6140
372 Elizabeth Ln Corona (92880) ***(P-20793)***
Electric Bike Company LLC....F....949 264-4080
519 Superior Ave Newport Beach (92663) ***(P-20399)***
Electric Designs, Gardena *Also called Gloria Lance Inc* ***(P-3161)***
Electric Gate Store Inc (PA)....C....818 504-2300
421 Park Ave San Fernando (91340) ***(P-19302)***
Electric Gate Store Inc....C....818 361-6872
15342 Chatsworth St Mission Hills (91345) ***(P-19303)***
Electric Motor Works Inc....E....661 327-4271
803 Inyo St Bakersfield (93305) ***(P-24688)***
Electric Visual Evolution LLC (PA)....E....949 940-9125
950 Calle Amanecer # 101 San Clemente (92673) ***(P-22351)***
Electrical Products Division, Fontana *Also called Southwire Inc* ***(P-11223)***
Electrical Products Rep, Irvine *Also called Agents West Inc* ***(P-19250)***
Electrical Rebuilders Sls Inc (PA)....D....323 249-7545
1559 W 134th St Gardena (90249) ***(P-19190)***
Electrical Systems, Corona *Also called Panel Shop Inc* ***(P-16605)***
Electriq Power Inc....F....408 393-7702
14451 Catalina St San Leandro (94577) ***(P-21028)***
Electrnic Cmbat Test Evluation, Palmdale *Also called Ectec Inc* ***(P-20573)***
Electro Adapter Inc....D....818 998-1198
20640 Nordhoff St Chatsworth (91311) ***(P-16896)***
Electro Component Assembly, Canoga Park *Also called Eca Medical Instruments* ***(P-21695)***
Electro Kinetics Division, Simi Valley *Also called Pacific Scientific Company* ***(P-20672)***
Electro Machine & Engrg Co, Compton *Also called E M E Inc* ***(P-12991)***
Electro Metal Finishing Corp (PA)....F....714 630-8940
1194 N Grove St Anaheim (92806) ***(P-13171)***
Electro Optical Industries....E....805 964-6701
320 Storke Rd Ste 100 Goleta (93117) ***(P-21351)***
Electro Plating Specialties....E....510 786-1881
2436 American Ave Hayward (94545) ***(P-12993)***
Electro Star Indus Coating Inc....F....530 527-5400
1945 Airport Blvd Red Bluff (96080) ***(P-13172)***
Electro Star Powder Coatings, Red Bluff *Also called Electro Star Indus Coating Inc* ***(P-13172)***
Electro Surface Tech Inc....D....760 431-8306
2281 Las Palmas Dr 101 Carlsbad (92011) ***(P-17866)***
Electro Switch Corp....C....909 581-0855
10410 Trademark St Rancho Cucamonga (91730) ***(P-16597)***
Electro Switch Corp....F....909 581-0855
10410 Trademark St Rancho Cucamonga (91730) ***(P-18897)***
Electro Tech Coatings Inc....E....760 746-0292
836 Rancheros Dr Ste A San Marcos (92069) ***(P-13173)***
Electro-Comm, Burbank *Also called Y B S Enterprises Inc* ***(P-17431)***
Electro-Mech Components Inc (PA)....F....626 442-7180
1826 Floradale Ave South El Monte (91733) ***(P-16598)***
Electro-Support Systems Corp....E....951 676-2751
27449 Colt Ct Temecula (92590) ***(P-18898)***
Electro-Tech Machining Div, Long Beach *Also called Kbr Inc* ***(P-16686)***
Electro-Tech Products Inc....E....909 592-1434
2001 E Gladstone St Ste A Glendora (91740) ***(P-18899)***
Electro-Tech's, Corona *Also called R&M Deese Inc* ***(P-23182)***
Electrochem Solutions Inc....F....510 476-1840
32500 Central Ave Union City (94587) ***(P-12994)***
Electrochem Solutions LLC....D....510 476-1840
32500 Central Ave Union City (94587) ***(P-12995)***
Electrocube Inc (PA)....D....909 595-1821
3366 Pomona Blvd Pomona (91768) ***(P-18900)***
Electrocut-Pacific, San Carlos *Also called Jerry Carroll Machinery Inc* ***(P-16081)***
Electrode Technologies Inc....E....714 549-3771
3110 W Harvard St Ste 14 Santa Ana (92704) ***(P-12996)***
Electrofilm Mfg Co LLC....D....661 257-2242
28150 Industry Dr Valencia (91355) ***(P-13328)***
Electroglas, Dublin *Also called Eg Systems LLC* ***(P-18209)***
Electrograph, Vista *Also called E/G Electro-Graph Inc* ***(P-18205)***
Electrolizing Inc....E....213 749-7876
1947 Hooper Ave Los Angeles (90011) ***(P-12997)***
Electrolurgy Inc (PA)....E....949 250-4494
1121 Duryea Ave Irvine (92614) ***(P-12998)***
Electrolurgy Inc....E....714 641-7488
1217 E Normandy Pl Santa Ana (92705) ***(P-13468)***
Electrolurgy Manufacturing, Santa Ana *Also called Electrolurgy Inc* ***(P-13468)***
Electromagnetics Division, Los Gatos *Also called Pulver Laboratories Inc* ***(P-16740)***
Electromatic Inc....F....818 765-3236
7351 Radford Ave North Hollywood (91605) ***(P-12999)***
Electromatic Inc (PA)....F....805 964-9880
789 S Kellogg Ave Goleta (93117) ***(P-13000)***
Electromatic Inc....F....562 623-9993
14025 Stage Rd Santa Fe Springs (90670) ***(P-13001)***
Electromax Inc....E....408 428-9474
1960 Concourse Dr San Jose (95131) ***(P-17867)***
Electron Beam Engineering Inc....F....714 491-5990
1425 S Allec St Anaheim (92805) ***(P-24633)***
Electron Imaging Incorporated....F....858 679-1569
14260 Garden Rd Ste A12 Poway (92064) ***(P-21220)***
Electron Plating III Inc....E....714 554-2210
13932 Enterprise Dr Garden Grove (92843) ***(P-13002)***
Electronic Arts Inc (PA)....B....650 628-1500
209 Redwood Shores Pkwy Redwood City (94065) ***(P-23850)***
Electronic Arts Inc....F....310 754-7000
5510 Lincoln Blvd Ste 100 Los Angeles (90094) ***(P-23851)***
Electronic Arts Los Angeles, Los Angeles *Also called Electronic Arts Inc* ***(P-23851)***
Electronic Arts Redwood Inc (HQ)....D....650 628-1500
209 Redwood Shores Pkwy Redwood City (94065) ***(P-19215)***
Electronic Auto Systems Inc....F....626 280-3855
9855 Joe Vargas Way South El Monte (91733) ***(P-17227)***
Electronic Chrome Grinding Co....E....562 946-6671
9128 Dice Rd Santa Fe Springs (90670) ***(P-13003)***
Electronic Cooling Solutions....F....408 738-8331
2344 Walsh Ave Ste B Santa Clara (95051) ***(P-14905)***
Electronic Interface Co Inc....D....408 286-2134
6341 San Ignacio Ave # 10 San Jose (95119) ***(P-19304)***
Electronic Manufacturing Tech, Irvine *Also called Sparton Irvine LLC* ***(P-19090)***
Electronic Mfg Leaders & Qlty, Simi Valley *Also called Emlinq LLC* ***(P-18905)***
Electronic Precision Spc Inc....E....714 256-8950
545 Mercury Ln Brea (92821) ***(P-13004)***
Electronic Prtg Solutions LLC....E....858 576-3000
4879 Ronson Ct Ste C San Diego (92111) ***(P-7055)***
Electronic Resources Network....F....530 758-0180
1950 5th St Davis (95616) ***(P-15223)***
Electronic Sensor Tech Inc....F....805 480-1994
1125 Bsneca Ctr Cir Ste B Newbury Park (91320) ***(P-21221)***
Electronic Source Company, Van Nuys *Also called Alyn Industries Inc* ***(P-18813)***
Electronic Stamping Corp....E....310 639-2120
19920 S Alameda St Compton (90221) ***(P-16599)***
Electronic Surfc Mounted Inds....E....858 455-1710
6731 Cobra Way San Diego (92121) ***(P-17868)***
Electronic Systems Co Esco, Sunnyvale *Also called Northrop Grumman Systems Corp* ***(P-19917)***
Electronic Systems Innovation....F....310 645-8400
5777 W Century Blvd # 1225 Los Angeles (90045) ***(P-14906)***
Electronic Theatre Contrls Inc....F....323 461-0216
1120 Scott Rd Burbank (91504) ***(P-17119)***
Electronic Waveform Lab Inc....E....714 843-0463
5702 Bolsa Ave Huntington Beach (92649) ***(P-21699)***
Electronics For Imaging Inc (HQ)....E....650 357-3500
6750 Dumbarton Cir Fremont (94555) ***(P-7056)***
Electrorack, Anaheim *Also called Ortronics Inc* ***(P-12319)***
Elegance Entries and Windows, Anaheim *Also called Elegance Entries Inc* ***(P-11951)***
Elegance Entries Inc....F....714 632-3667
1130 N Kraemer Blvd Ste G Anaheim (92806) ***(P-11951)***
Elegance Upholstery Inc....F....562 698-2584
11803 Slauson Ave Unit A Ontario (91762) ***(P-5056)***
Elekta Inc....E....408 830-8000
100 Mathilda Pl Fl 5 Sunnyvale (94086) ***(P-23852)***
Elekta / Impac Medical Systems, Sunnyvale *Also called Impac Medical Systems Inc* ***(P-24003)***
Elektron Technology Corp (HQ)....F....760 343-3650
11849 Telegraph Rd Santa Fe Springs (90670) ***(P-18210)***
Element Materials LLC....F....559 304-1008
4936 E Pontiac Way Fresno (93727) ***(P-7489)***
Element Santa Clara, Santa Clara *Also called Mission Park Hotel LP* ***(P-7506)***
Element Six Tech US Corp....F....408 986-8184
3901 Burton Dr Santa Clara (95054) ***(P-7490)***
Element Technica LLC....F....323 993-5329
4617 W Jefferson Blvd Los Angeles (90016) ***(P-22419)***
Elemental Led LLC (PA)....E....877 564-5051
1195 Park Ave Ste 211 Emeryville (94608) ***(P-17120)***
Elementcxi....E....408 935-8090
25 E Trimble Rd San Jose (95131) ***(P-18211)***
Elementis Specialties Inc....E....760 257-9112
31763 Mountain View Rd Newberry Springs (92365) ***(P-378)***
Elements....E....310 781-1384
20314a Gramercy Pl Torrance (90501) ***(P-22516)***
Elements Archtectural Surfaces, Redlands *Also called Fast Access Inc* ***(P-10571)***
Elements By Grapevine Inc....E....209 727-3711
18251 N Highway 88 Lockeford (95237) ***(P-4567)***
Elements Food Group Inc....D....909 983-2011
5560 Brooks St Montclair (91763) ***(P-1314)***
Elements Manufacturing Inc....E....831 421-9440
115 Harvey West Blvd C Santa Cruz (95060) ***(P-4899)***
Elephant Filmz & Music Inc....F....310 925-8712
3943 Irvine Blvd Ste 430 Irvine (92602) ***(P-22420)***
Elephant Flowers LLC....D....213 327-6323
3904 Gibraltar Ave Apt 8 Los Angeles (90008) ***(P-9777)***
Elevate Inc....E....949 276-5428
180 Avenida La Pata San Clemente (92673) ***(P-23853)***
Elevator Industries Inc....F....916 921-1495
110 Main Ave Sacramento (95838) ***(P-13798)***
Elevator Research & Mfg Co....D....213 746-1914
1417 Elwood St Los Angeles (90021) ***(P-13799)***
ELF Beauty Inc (PA)....E....510 210-8602
570 10th St Oakland (94607) ***(P-8488)***
Eli Lilly and Company....C....805 499-5475
63 Via Ricardo Newbury Park (91320) ***(P-7877)***
Elisid Magazine....E....619 990-9999
1450 University Ave F168 Riverside (92507) ***(P-5929)***
Elite 4 Print Inc....E....310 366-1344
851 E Walnut St Carson (90746) ***(P-6563)***
Elite Aviation Products Inc....E....949 536-7199
1641 Reynolds Ave Irvine (92614) ***(P-20574)***

ALPHABETIC

Employee Codes: A=Over 500 employees, B=251-500
C=101-250, D=51-100, E=20-50, F=10-19
2020 California
Manfacturers Register
© Mergent Inc. 1-800-342-5647
1091

Elite Cabinetry Inc....F....951 698-5050
25755 Jefferson Ave Murrieta (92562) *(P-5057)*
Elite Color Technologies Inc....F....310 324-3040
851 E Walnut St Carson (90746) *(P-7057)*
Elite Comfort Solutions LLC....F....909 390-6800
5440 E Francis St Ontario (91761) *(P-9304)*
Elite Comfort Solutions LLC....C....323 266-0422
4542 Dunham St Commerce (90040) *(P-9526)*
Elite E/M Inc....E....408 988-3505
340 Martin Ave Santa Clara (95050) *(P-12194)*
Elite Fashion Accessories Inc....F....559 435-0225
7141 N Warren Ave Fresno (93711) *(P-3530)*
Elite Generators Inc....F....818 718-0200
9007 De Soto Ave Canoga Park (91304) *(P-16641)*
Elite Global Solutions Inc....F....949 709-4872
19732 Descartes Foothill Ranch (92610) *(P-7561)*
Elite Lighting....C....323 888-1973
5424 E Slauson Ave Commerce (90040) *(P-17121)*
Elite Metal Fabrication Inc....E....408 433-9926
2299 Ringwood Ave Ste C1 San Jose (95131) *(P-15925)*
Elite Metal Finishing, Oceanside *Also called Rose Manufacturing Group Inc (P-13089)*
Elite Metal Finishing LLC (PA)....E....805 983-4320
540 Spectrum Cir Oxnard (93030) *(P-13005)*
Elite Metal Finishing LLC....D....805 983-4320
3430 Galaxy Pl Oxnard (93030) *(P-13006)*
Elite Mfg Corp....C....888 354-8356
12143 Altamar Pl Santa Fe Springs (90670) *(P-4832)*
Elite Modern, Santa Fe Springs *Also called Elite Mfg Corp (P-4832)*
Elite Optical, Compton *Also called Essilor Laboratories Amer Inc (P-22354)*
Elite Ready-Mix LLC....E....916 366-4627
6790 Bradshaw Rd Sacramento (95829) *(P-10755)*
Elite Service Experts Inc (PA)....F....916 275-3956
725 Del Paso Rd Sacramento (95834) *(P-14458)*
Elixir Industries....F....949 860-5000
24800 Chrisanta Dr # 100 Mission Viejo (92691) *(P-12799)*
Elixir Medical Corporation (PA)....F....408 636-2000
920 N Mccarthy Blvd Milpitas (95035) *(P-21700)*
Elizabeth Shutters Inc....E....909 825-1531
525 S Rancho Ave Colton (92324) *(P-11952)*
Elk Corporation of Texas....C....661 391-3900
6200 S Zerker Rd Shafter (93263) *(P-10568)*
Elk Grove Citizen, Elk Grove *Also called Herburger Publications Inc (P-5661)*
Elk Grove Milling Inc....E....916 684-2056
8320 Eschinger Rd Elk Grove (95757) *(P-1092)*
Elkay Interior Systems Inc....F....800 837-8373
225 Santa Monica Blvd Santa Monica (90401) *(P-5058)*
Elle Boutique....F....626 307-9882
200 E Garvey Ave Ste 105 Monterey Park (91755) *(P-3226)*
Ellegra Print & Imaging....F....562 432-2931
1419 Santa Fe Ave Long Beach (90813) *(P-6564)*
Ellen Lark Farm....F....805 272-8448
420 Bryant Cir Ste B Ojai (93023) *(P-1019)*
Ellensburg Lamb Company Inc....C....707 678-3091
7390 Rio Dixon Rd Dixon (95620) *(P-406)*
Ellensburg Lamb Company Inc (HQ)....F....530 758-3091
2530 River Plaza Dr # 200 Sacramento (95833) *(P-407)*
Ellex Iscience....F....510 291-1300
41316 Christy St Fremont (94538) *(P-21701)*
Ellex Itrack, Fremont *Also called Ellex Iscience (P-21701)*
Ellexar, Santa Ana *Also called Arsys Inc (P-14427)*
Ellie Mae Inc (HQ)....C....855 224-8572
4420 Rosewood Dr Ste 500 Pleasanton (94588) *(P-23854)*
Ellingson Inc....F....714 773-1923
119 W Santa Fe Ave Fullerton (92832) *(P-15926)*
Elliott Company....D....916 920-5451
51 Main Ave Sacramento (95838) *(P-14570)*
Elliott Manufacturing Company....F....559 233-6235
2664 S Cherry Ave Fresno (93706) *(P-15927)*
Ellipsis Health Inc....F....650 906-6117
535 Mission St Fl 25 San Francisco (94105) *(P-23855)*
Ellis and Ellis Sign, Sacramento *Also called Illuminated Creations Inc (P-23130)*
Ellis Truss Company, Hesperia *Also called Jim Ellis (P-4311)*
Ellison Biner....D....760 598-6500
2685 S Melrose Dr Vista (92081) *(P-14706)*
Ellison Educational Eqp Inc (PA)....D....949 598-8822
25862 Commercentre Dr Lake Forest (92630) *(P-14305)*
Elliston Vineyards Inc....D....925 862-2377
463 Kilkare Rd Sunol (94586) *(P-1688)*
Ellsworth Adhesive Systems, Irvine *Also called Ellsworth Corporation (P-8867)*
Ellsworth Corporation....F....949 341-9329
25 Hubble Irvine (92618) *(P-8867)*
Elm System Inc....F....408 694-2750
11622 El Carmino Real 1 San Diego (92130) *(P-19216)*
Elma Electronic Inc (HQ)....C....510 656-3400
44350 S Grimmer Blvd Fremont (94538) *(P-14907)*
Elmco & Assoc (PA)....F....916 383-0110
11225 Trade Center Dr # 100 Rancho Cordova (95742) *(P-9584)*
Elmech Inc....F....408 782-2990
195 San Pedro Ave Ste E15 Morgan Hill (95037) *(P-18901)*
Elro Manufacturing Company (PA)....E....310 380-7444
400 W Walnut St Gardena (90248) *(P-23096)*
Elro Sign Company, Gardena *Also called Elro Manufacturing Company (P-23096)*
Elsevier Inc....D....619 231-6616
525 B St Ste 1650 San Diego (92101) *(P-6228)*
Elson Alexander, Anaheim *Also called Universal Directory Publishing (P-6367)*
Eltron International, Agoura Hills *Also called Zebra Technologies Corporation (P-15369)*
Elwin Inc....E....714 752-6962
6910 8th St Buena Park (90620) *(P-5021)*

Ely Co Inc....E....310 539-5831
3046 Kashiwa St Torrance (90505) *(P-15928)*
Elyptol Inc....F....424 500-8099
2500 Broadway Ste F125 Santa Monica (90404) *(P-7654)*
Elysium Ceramics, Anaheim *Also called Elysium Mosaics Inc (P-10440)*
Elysium Jennings LLC....C....661 679-1700
1600 Norris Rd Bakersfield (93308) *(P-91)*
Elysium Mosaics Inc....F....714 991-7885
1180 N Anaheim Blvd Anaheim (92801) *(P-10440)*
Ema, City of Industry *Also called Engineering Model Associates (P-9780)*
Ema Textiles Inc....F....323 589-9800
2947 E 44th St Vernon (90058) *(P-2783)*
Emac Assembly Corp....F....818 882-2999
21615 Parthenia St Canoga Park (91304) *(P-18902)*
Emanuel Morez Inc....E....818 780-2787
8754 Yolanda Ave Northridge (91324) *(P-4568)*
Emazing Lights LLC....F....626 628-6482
240 S Loara St Anaheim (92802) *(P-17122)*
Embarcadero Publishing Company (PA)....C....650 964-6300
450 Cambridge Ave Palo Alto (94306) *(P-5630)*
Embedded Designs Inc....E....858 673-6050
16120 W Bernardo Dr Ste A San Diego (92127) *(P-20865)*
Embedded Systems Inc....E....805 624-6030
2250a Union Pl Simi Valley (93065) *(P-16715)*
Ember Acquisition Sub Inc (HQ)....C....626 293-3400
2015 Chestnut St Alhambra (91803) *(P-18903)*
Emberton Machine & Tool Inc....F....619 401-1870
1215 Pioneer Way Ste A El Cajon (92020) *(P-15929)*
Embolx Inc....F....408 990-2949
530 Lakeside Dr Ste 200 Sunnyvale (94085) *(P-21702)*
Embroidertex West Ltd (PA)....F....213 749-4319
435 E 16th St Los Angeles (90015) *(P-3740)*
Embroidery By P & J Inc....F....909 592-2622
301 E Arrow Hwy Ste 104 San Dimas (91773) *(P-3741)*
Embroidery One Corp....E....213 572-0280
1359 Channing St Los Angeles (90021) *(P-3742)*
Embroidery Outlet....F....951 687-1750
10460 Magnolia Ave Riverside (92505) *(P-3743)*
EMC Corporation....D....925 948-9000
6701 Koll Center Pkwy # 150 Pleasanton (94566) *(P-15024)*
EMC Corporation....E....877 636-8589
455 Market St Fl 4 San Francisco (94105) *(P-15025)*
EMC Corporation....D....949 794-9999
2201 Dupont Dr Ste 500 Irvine (92612) *(P-14908)*
EMC Corporation....D....925 600-6800
6801 Koll Center Pkwy Pleasanton (94566) *(P-15026)*
Emcor Group Inc....E....949 475-6020
2 Cromwell Irvine (92618) *(P-20967)*
Emcore Corporation....F....510 896-2139
8674 Thornton Ave Newark (94560) *(P-18212)*
Emcore Corporation (PA)....C....626 293-3400
2015 Chestnut St Alhambra (91803) *(P-18213)*
Emcore Corporation....C....626 293-3400
2015 Chestnut St Alhambra (91803) *(P-18214)*
EMD Millipore Corporation....C....510 576-1367
25801 Industrial Blvd B Hayward (94545) *(P-21222)*
EMD Millipore Corporation....F....760 788-9692
26578 Old Julian Hwy Ramona (92065) *(P-21223)*
EMD Millipore Corporation....C....951 676-8080
28835 Single Oak Dr Temecula (92590) *(P-21224)*
EMD Millipore Corporation....C....951 676-8080
28820 Single Oak Dr Temecula (92590) *(P-8296)*
EMD Specialty Materials LLC....F....909 987-9533
9433 Hyssop Dr Rancho Cucamonga (91730) *(P-17869)*
Emdin International Corp....F....626 813-3740
15841 Business Center Dr Irwindale (91706) *(P-22152)*
Eme Fan & Motor, Brea *Also called Sunon Inc (P-14680)*
Eme Technologies Inc....E....408 720-8817
3485 Victor St Santa Clara (95054) *(P-15930)*
Emerald Expositions LLC....D....949 226-5754
31910 Del Obispo St # 200 San Juan Capistrano (92675) *(P-5930)*
Emerald Expositions LLC....D....323 525-2000
5055 Wilshire Blvd # 600 Los Angeles (90036) *(P-5931)*
Emerald Kingdom Greenhouse LLC....E....530 215-5670
104 Masonic Ln Weaverville (96093) *(P-12543)*
Emerald Steel Inc....F....510 553-1386
727 66th Ave Oakland (94621) *(P-11788)*
Emergency Preparedness Pdts, Camarillo *Also called Recon 1 Inc (P-9180)*
Emergent Group Inc (HQ)....D....818 394-2800
10939 Pendleton St Sun Valley (91352) *(P-22008)*
Emerson Process Management....E....858 492-1069
5466 Complex St Ste 203 San Diego (92123) *(P-20866)*
Emerzian Woodworking Inc....E....559 292-2448
2555 N Argyle Ave Fresno (93727) *(P-4900)*
EMI Holding Inc (HQ)....F....310 214-0065
21250 Hawthorne Blvd B Torrance (90503) *(P-7878)*
EMI Solutions Inc....F....949 206-9960
13805 Alton Pkwy Ste B Irvine (92618) *(P-18904)*
Emiliomiti LLC....F....415 621-1171
2129 Harrison St San Francisco (94110) *(P-14360)*
Emily's Classic Beauty Salon, Long Beach *Also called La Rutan (P-23389)*
Emisense CA, Ladera Ranch *Also called Emisense Technologies LLC (P-18215)*
Emisense Technologies LLC (HQ)....F....949 502-8440
999 Corporate Dr Ste 100 Ladera Ranch (92694) *(P-18215)*
Emission Methods Inc....E....909 605-6800
1307 S Wanamaker Ave Ontario (91761) *(P-21466)*
Emitcon Inc....E....714 632-8595
1175 N Van Horne Way Anaheim (92806) *(P-20968)*
Emkay Mfg., Redwood City *Also called Bay Precision Machining Inc (P-15777)*

Mergent e-mail: customerrelations@mergent.com
1092
2020 California
Manufacturers Register
(P-0000) Products & Services Section entry number
(PA)=Parent Co (HQ)=Headquarters (DH)=Div Headquarters

Emlinq LLC..........D.......805 409-4807
2125 N Madera Rd Ste C Simi Valley (93065) ***(P-18905)***
Emmaus Medical Inc (HQ)..........F.......310 214-0065
21250 Hawthorne Blvd # 800 Torrance (90503) ***(P-7879)***
Emp Connectors Inc..........E.......310 533-6799
548 Amapola Ave Torrance (90501) ***(P-16897)***
Empire Container Corporation..........D.......310 537-8190
1161 E Walnut St Carson (90746) ***(P-5219)***
Empire Optical of California..........E.......818 997-6474
7633 Varna Ave North Hollywood (91605) ***(P-22352)***
Empire Pre Cast..........E.......951 609-1590
19473 Grand Ave Lake Elsinore (92530) ***(P-10569)***
Empire Sheet Metal Inc..........F.......909 923-2927
1215 S Bon View Ave Ontario (91761) ***(P-12195)***
Empire Shower Doors Inc..........F.......707 773-2898
1217 N Mcdowell Blvd Petaluma (94954) ***(P-10357)***
Empire West Inc..........E.......707 823-1190
9270 Graton Rd Graton (95444) ***(P-9778)***
Empire West Plastics, Graton *Also called Empire West Inc* ***(P-9778)***
Employee Owned Pacific Cast PR..........E.......562 633-6673
12711 Imperial Hwy Santa Fe Springs (90670) ***(P-11380)***
Employerware LLC..........E.......925 283-9735
3687 Mt Diablo Blvd 100a Lafayette (94549) ***(P-6229)***
Employment Screening Resources, Novato *Also called Integrity Support Services Inc* ***(P-8981)***
Emporium Di Sanarrey Corp..........F.......714 780-5474
631 S East St Anaheim (92805) ***(P-10905)***
Empower Rf Systems Inc (PA)..........D.......310 412-8100
316 W Florence Ave Inglewood (90301) ***(P-17511)***
Empower Software Tech LLC..........F.......951 672-6257
28999 Old Town Front St # 203 Temecula (92590) ***(P-23856)***
Emsolutions Inc..........F.......510 668-1118
2152 Zanker Rd San Jose (95131) ***(P-17870)***
Emtec Engineering..........F.......408 779-5800
16840 Joleen Way Ste F1 Morgan Hill (95037) ***(P-12196)***
Emx Digital LLC..........E.......212 792-6810
600 California St Fl 11 San Francisco (94108) ***(P-23857)***
Enaba-Kbw USA, Chino *Also called CPI Advanced Inc* ***(P-16545)***
Enablence Systems Inc (HQ)..........E.......510 226-8900
2933 Bayview Dr Fremont (94538) ***(P-23858)***
Enablence USA Components Inc..........D.......510 226-8900
2933 Bayview Dr Fremont (94538) ***(P-17364)***
Enaqua..........E.......760 599-2644
1350 Specialty Dr Ste D Vista (92081) ***(P-15509)***
Enas Media Inc..........E.......626 962-1115
1316 Michillinda Ave Arcadia (91006) ***(P-17318)***
Encinitas Oggis Inc..........F.......760 579-3211
305 Encinitas Blvd Encinitas (92024) ***(P-1523)***
Encompass, Sacramento *Also called Laser Recharge Inc* ***(P-22966)***
Encompass Dist Svcs LLC..........F.......925 249-0988
3502 Mars Way Ste 161 Tracy (95377) ***(P-18216)***
Encore Cases Inc..........E.......818 768-8803
8818 Lankershim Blvd Sun Valley (91352) ***(P-10194)***
Encore Fine Cabinetry Inc..........F.......559 822-4333
14748 Highway 41 Ste B Madera (93636) ***(P-4191)***
Encore Image Inc..........E.......909 986-4632
303 W Main St Ontario (91762) ***(P-23097)***
Encore Image Group Inc (PA)..........D.......310 534-7500
1445 Sepulveda Blvd Torrance (90501) ***(P-23098)***
Encore Industries..........E.......408 416-0501
597 Brennan St San Jose (95131) ***(P-12197)***
Encore Interiors Inc (HQ)..........C.......949 559-0930
5511 Skylab Rd Ste 101 Huntington Beach (92647) ***(P-20097)***
Encore Interiors Inc..........C.......562 344-1700
5511 Skylab Rd Ste 101 Huntington Beach (92647) ***(P-20098)***
Encore International..........C.......949 559-0930
5511 Skylab Rd Huntington Beach (92647) ***(P-19951)***
Encore Plastics, Huntington Beach *Also called Donoco Industries Inc* ***(P-10304)***
Encore Seating Inc..........D.......562 926-1969
5692 Fresca Dr La Palma (90623) ***(P-4833)***
Encore Seats Inc..........E.......949 559-0930
5511 Skylab Rd Huntington Beach (92647) ***(P-20099)***
End-Effectors Inc..........F.......408 727-0100
1230 Coleman Ave Santa Clara (95050) ***(P-13304)***
Endace USA Limited..........F.......877 764-5411
99 Almaden Blvd Ste 555 San Jose (95113) ***(P-14909)***
Endeavor Homes Inc..........E.......530 534-0300
655 Cal Oak Rd Oroville (95965) ***(P-13728)***
Endepo Inc..........F.......707 428-3245
2100 Geng Rd Ste 210 Palo Alto (94303) ***(P-11695)***
Enderle Fuel Injection..........E.......805 526-3838
1830 Voyager Ave Simi Valley (93063) ***(P-19648)***
Endodent Inc..........E.......626 359-5715
851 Meridian St Duarte (91010) ***(P-22153)***
Endologix Inc (PA)..........C.......949 595-7200
2 Musick Irvine (92618) ***(P-21703)***
Endotec Inc..........F.......714 681-6306
14525 Valley View Ave H Santa Fe Springs (90670) ***(P-22009)***
Endpak Packaging Inc..........D.......562 801-0281
9101 Perkins St Pico Rivera (90660) ***(P-5439)***
Endress & Hauser Conducta Inc..........E.......800 835-5474
4123 E La Palma Ave Anaheim (92807) ***(P-21225)***
Endress + Hauser Inc..........F.......714 577-5600
4123 E La Palma Ave # 200 Anaheim (92807) ***(P-20756)***
Endresshauser Conducta, Anaheim *Also called Endress & Hauser Conducta Inc* ***(P-21225)***
Endresshouser Conducta, Anaheim *Also called Endress + Hauser Inc* ***(P-20756)***
Endrun Technologies LLC..........F.......707 573-8633
2270 Northpoint Pkwy Santa Rosa (95407) ***(P-20757)***
Endura Technologies LLC..........F.......858 412-2135
7310 Miramar Rd Fl 5 San Diego (92126) ***(P-18217)***
Endural LLC..........F.......714 434-6533
1685 Scenic Ave Ste A Costa Mesa (92626) ***(P-9438)***
Endurance Ptc..........F.......415 445-9155
8 Madrona St Mill Valley (94941) ***(P-20400)***
Endurequest Corporation..........E.......559 783-9220
1813 Thunderbolt Dr Porterville (93257) ***(P-9779)***
Ener-Core Inc (PA)..........F.......949 732-4400
30100 Town Center Dr Laguna Niguel (92677) ***(P-16642)***
Ener-Core Power Inc (HQ)..........F.......949 428-3300
30100 Town Center Dr O Laguna Niguel (92677) ***(P-13567)***
Enerdyne Division, El Cajon *Also called Viasat Inc* ***(P-20742)***
Energent Corporation..........F.......949 885-0365
1831 Carnegie Ave Santa Ana (92705) ***(P-13568)***
Energetic Lighting, Chino *Also called Yankon Industries Inc* ***(P-17086)***
Energetix Solutions Inc..........F.......925 926-6412
2601 Cherry Ln Walnut Creek (94597) ***(P-8904)***
Energous Corporation..........D.......408 963-0200
3590 N 1st St Ste 210 San Jose (95134) ***(P-17512)***
Energy Absorption Systems Inc..........C.......916 645-8181
3617 Cincinnati Ave Rocklin (95765) ***(P-13520)***
Energy Cnvrsion Applctions Inc..........F.......714 256-2166
582 Explorer St Brea (92821) ***(P-16548)***
Energy Exemplar LLC (HQ)..........F.......916 722-1484
3013 Douglas Blvd Ste 120 Roseville (95661) ***(P-23859)***
Energy Labs Inc (HQ)..........B.......619 671-0100
1695 Cactus Rd San Diego (92154) ***(P-15428)***
Energy Lane Inc..........F.......323 962-5020
6767 W Sunset Blvd 8152 Los Angeles (90028) ***(P-7638)***
Energy Link Indus Svcs Inc..........E.......661 765-4444
11439 S Enos Ln Bakersfield (93311) ***(P-15931)***
Energy Management Group Inc (PA)..........F.......949 296-0764
1621 Browning Irvine (92606) ***(P-17123)***
Energy Operations Management..........F.......916 859-4700
2981 Gold Canal Dr Rancho Cordova (95670) ***(P-50)***
Energy Reconnaissance Inc..........F.......714 630-4491
1270 N Red Gum St Anaheim (92806) ***(P-14761)***
Energy Recovery Inc (PA)..........C.......510 483-7370
1717 Doolittle Dr San Leandro (94577) ***(P-14459)***
Energy Sales LLC (PA)..........F.......503 690-9000
2030 Ringwood Ave San Jose (95131) ***(P-19158)***
Energy Steel Corporation..........F.......925 685-5300
2043 Arnold Indus Way Concord (94520) ***(P-15932)***
Energy Suspension, San Clemente *Also called Bunker Corp* ***(P-19599)***
Energy Systems, Stockton *Also called Es West Coast LLC* ***(P-16643)***
Enersys..........F.......510 887-8080
30069 Ahern Ave Union City (94587) ***(P-19159)***
Enersys..........D.......909 464-8251
5580 Edison Ave Chino (91710) ***(P-19160)***
Enertron Technologies Inc..........E.......800 537-7649
3030 Enterprise Ct Ste D Vista (92081) ***(P-17027)***
Enervault Corporation..........F.......408 636-7519
1100 La Avenida St Ste A Mountain View (94043) ***(P-19161)***
Enevate Corporation..........E.......949 243-0399
101 Theory Ste 200 Irvine (92617) ***(P-19162)***
Enfora Inc..........D.......972 234-1689
9645 Scranton Rd Ste 205 San Diego (92121) ***(P-18906)***
Engage Communication Inc (PA)..........E.......831 688-1021
9565 Soquel Dr Ste 201 Aptos (95003) ***(P-17365)***
Engagio Inc..........E.......650 265-2264
181 2nd Ave Ste 200 San Mateo (94401) ***(P-23860)***
Engel & Gray Inc..........E.......805 925-2771
745 W Betteravia Rd Ste A Santa Maria (93455) ***(P-192)***
Engersall, Riverside *Also called Club Car LLC* ***(P-20505)***
Engine Electronics Inc..........F.......562 803-1700
12155 Pangborn Ave Downey (90241) ***(P-19191)***
Engine World LLC..........E.......510 653-4444
1487 67th St Emeryville (94608) ***(P-19649)***
Engineered Application LLC..........F.......323 585-2894
4727 E 49th St Vernon (90058) ***(P-13174)***
Engineered Coating Tech Inc..........F.......323 588-0260
2838 E 54th St Vernon (90058) ***(P-8643)***
Engineered Food Systems..........E.......714 921-9913
2490 Anselmo Dr Corona (92879) ***(P-15510)***
Engineered Lighting Products, El Monte *Also called R W Swarens Associates Inc* ***(P-17067)***
Engineered Magnetics Inc..........E.......310 649-9000
10524 S La Cienega Blvd Inglewood (90304) ***(P-16785)***
Engineered Outsource Solutions..........E.......408 617-2800
557 E California Ave Sunnyvale (94086) ***(P-18218)***
Engineered Plastic Division, San Jose *Also called Triad Tool & Engineering Inc* ***(P-10091)***
Engineered Products By Lee Ltd..........F.......818 352-3322
10444 Mcvine Ave Sunland (91040) ***(P-15933)***
Engineered Well Svc Intl Inc..........C.......866 913-6283
3120 Standard St Bakersfield (93308) ***(P-193)***
Engineering Design Inds Inc..........F.......626 443-7741
9649 Rush St South El Monte (91733) ***(P-15934)***
Engineering Jk Aerospace & Def..........F.......714 414-6722
23231 La Palma Ave Yorba Linda (92887) ***(P-20100)***
Engineering Materials Co Inc..........E.......562 436-0063
2055 W Cowles St Long Beach (90813) ***(P-23000)***
Engineering Model Associates (PA)..........E.......626 912-7011
1020 Wallace Way City of Industry (91748) ***(P-9780)***
Engineered Pnt Applications LLC..........F.......626 737-7400
1586 Franklin Ave Redlands (92373) ***(P-8644)***
English Ales Brewers Inc..........F.......831 883-3000
223 Reindollar Ave Ste A Marina (93933) ***(P-1524)***
Engrade Inc..........F.......800 305-1367
1337 3rd Street Promenade # 300 Santa Monica (90401) ***(P-23861)***
Enhance America Inc..........E.......951 361-3000
3463 Grapevine St Jurupa Valley (91752) ***(P-23099)***

Employee Codes: A=Over 500 employees, B=251-500
C=101-250, D=51-100, E=20-50, F=10-19
2020 California
Manfacturers Register
© Mergent Inc. 1-800-342-5647
1093

Enhanced Vision Systems Inc (HQ) ....D......800 440-9476
15301 Springdale St Huntington Beach (92649) *(P-21352)*
Enjoy Food, Colton Also called Saab Enterprises Inc *(P-494)*
Enjoy Haircare, Oceanside Also called USP Inc *(P-8599)*
Enki Technology Inc ....F......408 383-9034
1035 Walsh Ave Santa Clara (95050) *(P-7491)*
Enlighted Inc (PA) ....E......650 964-1094
930 Benecia Ave Sunnyvale (94085) *(P-17028)*
Enlink Geoenergy Services Inc ....E......424 242-1200
2630 Homestead Pl Rancho Dominguez (90220) *(P-15429)*
Ennis Inc ....C......805 238-1144
298 Sherwood Rd Paso Robles (93446) *(P-7282)*
Ennis Inc ....C......714 765-0400
1600 S Claudina Way Anaheim (92805) *(P-14049)*
Ennis-Flint Inc ....E......661 328-0503
200 2nd St Bakersfield (93304) *(P-8645)*
Enniss Inc ....E......619 561-1101
12535 Vigilante Rd Lakeside (92040) *(P-338)*
Enormarel Inc ....F......818 882-4666
9200 Mason Ave Chatsworth (91311) *(P-8489)*
Enova Engineering LLC (PA) ....F......209 538-3313
1088 Mt Clair Dr Ceres (95307) *(P-16947)*
Enova Solutions Inc ....F......661 327-2405
3553 Landco Dr Ste B Bakersfield (93308) *(P-8963)*
Enphase Energy Inc (PA) ....C......707 774-7000
47281 Bayside Pkwy Fremont (94538) *(P-18219)*
Enpirion ....F......408 904-2800
101 Innovation Dr San Jose (95134) *(P-23862)*
Enray Inc., Livermore Also called Truroots Inc *(P-2638)*
Ens Security, Hacienda Heights Also called Easterncctv (usa) LLC *(P-19300)*
Ensign US Drlg Cal Inc (HQ) ....D......661 589-0111
7001 Charity Ave Bakersfield (93308) *(P-13920)*
Ensign-Bickford Arospc Def Co ....F......805 292-4000
14370 White Sage Rd Moorpark (93021) *(P-20575)*
Ensphere Solutions Inc ....F......408 598-2441
2870 Briarwood Dr San Jose (95125) *(P-18220)*
Enstrom Mold & Engineering Inc ....E......760 744-1880
235 Trade St San Marcos (92078) *(P-14050)*
Entco LLC (HQ) ....B......312 580-9100
1140 Enterprise Way Sunnyvale (94089) *(P-23863)*
Entech Instruments Inc ....D......805 527-5939
2207 Agate Ct Simi Valley (93065) *(P-21226)*
Entegris Gp Inc ....E......805 541-9299
4175 Santa Fe Rd San Luis Obispo (93401) *(P-14813)*
Enter Music Publishing Inc ....F......408 971-9794
1346 The Alameda Ste 7 San Jose (95126) *(P-5932)*
Enterprise Arms, Irwindale Also called Entreprise Arms Inc *(P-13275)*
Enterprise Co, Santa Ana Also called G G C Inc *(P-14307)*
Enterprise Company, Santa Ana Also called G G C Inc *(P-14306)*
Enterprise Informatics Inc ....E......858 625-3000
10052 Mesa Ridge Ct Ste 1 San Diego (92121) *(P-23864)*
Enterprise Printing, Shingle Springs Also called BBC Corp *(P-6440)*
Enterprise Services LLC ....F......805 388-8000
333 N Lantana St Ste 287 Camarillo (93010) *(P-23865)*
Enterprise Signal Inc ....D......877 256-8303
440 N Wolfe Rd Sunnyvale (94085) *(P-23866)*
Enterprise Solutions Group, Santa Clara Also called Dell Inc *(P-14903)*
Entertainment Centers Plus, Rancho Cordova Also called Custom Furniture Design Inc *(P-4184)*
Entertainment Relations, Beverly Hills Also called Gibson Brands Inc *(P-22622)*
Entit Software, LLC, Santa Clara Also called Micro Focus LLC *(P-24151)*
Entra Health Systems LLC ....E......877 458-2646
1300 N Johnson Ave # 100 El Cajon (92020) *(P-21704)*
Entrepeneur Magazine, Irvine Also called Entrepreneur Media Inc *(P-5933)*
Entrepreneur Media Inc (PA) ....D......949 261-2325
18061 Fitch Irvine (92614) *(P-5933)*
Entreprise Arms Inc ....E......626 962-4692
15509 Arrow Hwy Irwindale (91706) *(P-13275)*
Entropic Communications LLC (HQ) ....E......858 768-3600
5966 La Place Ct Ste 100 Carlsbad (92008) *(P-18221)*
Entropy Enterprises LLC ....F......805 305-1400
170 Seacliff Dr Pismo Beach (93449) *(P-21705)*
Entrussed LLC ....F......916 753-5406
5065 Commercial Pl Sheridan (95681) *(P-4301)*
Envel Design Corporation ....F......805 376-8111
3579 Old Conejo Rd Newbury Park (91320) *(P-17029)*
Envelope Products Co. ....E......925 939-5173
2882 W Cromwell Ave Fresno (93711) *(P-5104)*
Envia Systems Inc ....E......510 509-1367
7979 Gateway Blvd Ste 101 Newark (94560) *(P-19305)*
Envion LLC ....D......818 217-2500
14724 Ventura Blvd Fl 200 Sherman Oaks (91403) *(P-14656)*
Enviormental Business Intl, San Diego Also called Informa Media Inc *(P-5964)*
Envirnmental Catalyst Tech LLC ....E......949 459-3870
3937 Ocean Ranch Blvd Oceanside (92056) *(P-7492)*
Envirnmental Pdts Applications, La Quinta Also called Vermillions Environmental *(P-20819)*
Envirnmntal Mlding Cncepts LLC ....F......951 214-6596
14050 Day St Moreno Valley (92553) *(P-9305)*
Enviro-Commercial Sweeping ....F......408 920-0274
210 San Jose Ave Ste 5 Chico (95927) *(P-23025)*
Enviro-Intercept Inc ....F......818 982-6063
7327 Varna Ave Unit 5 North Hollywood (91605) *(P-15430)*
Envirocare International Inc ....E......707 638-6800
507 Green Island Rd American Canyon (94503) *(P-14657)*
Envirokinetics Inc (PA) ....F......909 621-7599
101 S Milliken Ave Ontario (91761) *(P-14460)*
Environ Clean Technology, San Jose Also called Environ-Clean Technology Inc *(P-18222)*

Environ-Clean Technology Inc ....F......408 487-1770
1710 Ringwood Ave San Jose (95131) *(P-18222)*
Environmental Inks & Coatings, Ontario Also called An Environmental Inks *(P-8909)*
Environmental Lights, San Diego Also called Advanced Lighting Concepts Inc *(P-17008)*
Environmental Ltg For Arch Inc ....E......626 965-0821
17891 Arenth Ave City of Industry (91748) *(P-17030)*
Environmental Sampling Sup Inc ....F......510 465-4988
640 143rd Ave San Leandro (94578) *(P-9781)*
Environmental Technology Inc ....E......707 443-9323
300 S Bay Depot Rd Fields Landing (95537) *(P-7562)*
Enviroplex Inc ....D......209 466-8000
4777 Carpenter Rd Stockton (95215) *(P-12544)*
Envision Medical, Goleta Also called Linvatec Corporation *(P-21779)*
Envista Holdings Corporation ....A......714 817-7000
200 S Kraemer Blvd Bldg E Brea (92821) *(P-22154)*
Envita Labs LLC ....E......800 500-4376
1900 Carnegie Ave Ste A Santa Ana (92705) *(P-7655)*
Enviz.io, Fremont Also called Envizio Inc *(P-23867)*
Envizio Inc ....F......650 814-4302
2400 Country Dr Fremont (94536) *(P-23867)*
Envy Medical Inc (HQ) ....F......818 874-2700
9414 Eton Ave Chatsworth (91311) *(P-7880)*
Envy Wines LLC ....F......707 942-4670
1170 Tubbs Ln Calistoga (94515) *(P-1689)*
Eo Products, San Rafael Also called Small World Trading Co *(P-8582)*
Eoplex Inc ....F......408 638-5100
1321 Ridder Park Dr 10 San Jose (95131) *(P-19306)*
Eoplex Technologies Inc ....F......408 638-5100
2940 N 1st St San Jose (95134) *(P-19307)*
Eoplly Usa Inc ....F......650 225-9400
1670 S Amphlett Blvd # 140 San Mateo (94402) *(P-18223)*
Eos Estate Winery ....E......805 239-2562
2300 Airport Rd Paso Robles (93446) *(P-1690)*
Eos Software Inc ....F......855 900-4876
900 E Hamilton Ave # 100 Campbell (95008) *(P-23868)*
Ep Holdings LLC ....F......949 713-4600
30442 Esperanza Rcho STA Marg (92688) *(P-15027)*
Ep Memory, Rcho STA Marg Also called Ep Holdings Inc *(P-15027)*
Epac Technologies Inc (PA) ....C......510 317-7979
2561 Grant Ave San Leandro (94579) *(P-6565)*
EPC Power Corp ....E......858 748-5590
13250 Gregg St Ste A2 Poway (92064) *(P-16786)*
Epco, Fresno Also called Envelope Products Co *(P-5104)*
Epe Industries Usa Inc ....F......800 315-0336
17654 Newhope St Ste A Fountain Valley (92708) *(P-9527)*
Epe Industries Usa Inc (HQ) ....F......800 315-0336
17654 Newhope St Ste A Fountain Valley (92708) *(P-9528)*
Epe Industries USA Dallas, Fountain Valley Also called Epe Industries Usa Inc *(P-9527)*
Epe USA, Fountain Valley Also called Epe Industries Usa Inc *(P-9528)*
Epic Boats LLC (PA) ....F......760 542-6060
2755 Dos Aarons Way Ste A Vista (92081) *(P-20328)*
Epic Plastics, Lodi Also called Basalite Building Products LLC *(P-10535)*
Epic Printing Ink Corp ....F......909 598-6771
233 Pioneer Pl Pomona (91768) *(P-8912)*
Epic Technologies LLC (HQ) ....C......701 426-2192
9340 Owensmouth Ave Chatsworth (91311) *(P-17366)*
Epica Medical Innovations LLC ....E......949 238-6323
901 Calle Amanecer # 150 San Clemente (92673) *(P-21706)*
Epicor Software Corporation ....C......925 361-9900
4120 Dublin Blvd Ste 300 Dublin (94568) *(P-23869)*
Epicor Software Corporation ....D......949 585-4000
17320 Red Hill Ave # 250 Irvine (92614) *(P-15224)*
Epicson Inc ....E......858 558-5757
8250 Cmino Santa Fe Ste A San Diego (92121) *(P-7058)*
Epicuren Discovery ....D......949 588-5807
26081 Merit Cir Ste 116 Laguna Hills (92653) *(P-8221)*
Epidemic Ales ....F......925 566-8850
150 Mason Cir Concord (94520) *(P-1525)*
Epignosis LLC ....E......646 797-2799
315 Montgomery St Fl 9 San Francisco (94104) *(P-23870)*
Epilogue and Arrested, Los Angeles Also called Rhapsody Clothing Inc *(P-3398)*
Epinex Diagnostics Inc ....E......949 660-7770
14351 Myford Rd Ste J Tustin (92780) *(P-21707)*
Epirus Inc ....F......310 487-5016
2100 E Grand Ave Ste 330 El Segundo (90245) *(P-23871)*
Eplastics, San Diego Also called Ridout Plastics Company *(P-9418)*
Epmar Corporation ....E......562 946-8781
13210 Barton Cir Whittier (90605) *(P-8646)*
Epoca Yocool, South Gate Also called Win Soon Inc *(P-713)*
Epoch International Entps Inc ....C......510 556-1225
46583 Fremont Blvd Fremont (94538) *(P-14461)*
Epsilon Plastics Inc ....D......310 609-1320
3100 E Harcourt St Compton (90221) *(P-5396)*
Epson America Inc (HQ) ....A......800 463-7766
3840 Kilroy Airport Way Long Beach (90806) *(P-15225)*
Epson Electronics America Inc (HQ) ....E......408 922-0200
214 Devcon Dr San Jose (95112) *(P-18224)*
Eptronics Inc ....F......310 536-0700
19210 S Vermont Ave # 300 Gardena (90248) *(P-17031)*
Epworth Morehouse Cowles, Chino Also called Morehouse-Cowles LLC *(P-14501)*
Eq Technologic Inc ....E......215 891-9010
600 Anton Blvd Costa Mesa (92626) *(P-23872)*
Eqh Limited Inc ....E......310 736-4130
5440 Mcconnell Ave Los Angeles (90066) *(P-11528)*
Equestrian Designs LLC ....E......805 686-4455
91 2nd St Ste A Buellton (93427) *(P-3321)*
Equillium Inc ....E......858 412-5302
2223 Avenida De La Playa La Jolla (92037) *(P-8297)*

Mergent e-mail: customerrelations@mergent.com
1094
2020 California
Manufacturers Register
(P-0000) Products & Services Section entry number
(PA)=Parent Co (HQ)=Headquarters (DH)=Div Headquarters

Equimine.....F.....877 437-8464
26457 Rancho Pkwy S Lake Forest (92630) *(P-23873)*
Equipment & Tool Institute, Irvine *Also called Innova Electronics Corporation* *(P-19691)*
Equipment De Sport Usa Inc.....F.....760 772-5544
39301 Badger St Ste 500 Palm Desert (92211) *(P-3744)*
Equipment Design & Mfg Inc.....D.....909 594-2229
119 Explorer St Pomona (91768) *(P-12198)*
Equitex, NAPA *Also called Lixit Corporation* *(P-23397)*
Equity Ford Research.....F.....858 755-1327
11722 Sorrento Valley Rd I San Diego (92121) *(P-6230)*
Equus Products Inc.....E.....714 424-6779
17352 Von Karman Ave Irvine (92614) *(P-21029)*
ERA Products Inc.....F.....310 324-4908
1130 Benedict Canyon Dr Beverly Hills (90210) *(P-4859)*
Erb Investment Company LLC.....F.....408 727-6908
3501 Thomas Rd Ste 7 Santa Clara (95054) *(P-15935)*
Erba Organics, Chatsworth *Also called Erbaviva Inc* *(P-7656)*
Erbaviva Inc.....E.....818 998-7112
19831 Nordhoff Pl Ste 116 Chatsworth (91311) *(P-7656)*
ERC Concepts Co Inc.....E.....408 734-5345
1255 Birchwood Dr Sunnyvale (94089) *(P-12800)*
Ereplacements LLC.....E.....714 361-2652
16885 W Bernardo Dr # 370 San Diego (92127) *(P-19163)*
Erf Enterprises Inc.....F.....909 825-4080
863 E Valley Blvd Colton (92324) *(P-19532)*
Erg Aerospace Corporation.....D.....510 658-9785
964 Stanford Ave Oakland (94608) *(P-7493)*
Erg Materials and Aerospace, Oakland *Also called Erg Aerospace Corporation* *(P-7493)*
Erg Transit Systems (usa) Inc.....C.....925 686-8233
1800 Sutter St Ste 900 Concord (94520) *(P-15511)*
Erge Designs LLC.....F.....310 614-9197
4770 E 48th St Vernon (90058) *(P-3158)*
Ergo Baby Carrier Inc (HQ).....E.....213 283-2090
617 W 7th St Fl 10 Los Angeles (90017) *(P-22674)*
Ergodirect Inc.....F.....650 654-4300
1601 Old County Rd San Carlos (94070) *(P-4834)*
Ergonom Corporation.....D.....805 981-9978
361 Bernoulli Cir Oxnard (93030) *(P-5059)*
Ergononmic Comfort Design Inc.....F.....951 277-1558
9140 Stellar Ct Ste B Corona (92883) *(P-4835)*
Ericsson Inc.....E.....972 583-0000
1055 La Avenida St Mountain View (94043) *(P-17513)*
Ericsson Inc.....D.....949 721-6604
620 Newport Center Dr # 11 Newport Beach (92660) *(P-15226)*
Ericsson Inc.....E.....408 970-2000
250 Holger Way San Jose (95134) *(P-17514)*
Eride Inc.....E.....415 848-7800
1 Letterman Dr Ste 310 San Francisco (94129) *(P-23874)*
Erika Records Inc.....E.....714 228-5420
6300 Caballero Blvd Buena Park (90620) *(P-17319)*
Eriss.....F.....858 722-2177
1124 Glen Ellen Pl 201 San Marcos (92078) *(P-19217)*
Ermico Enterprises Inc.....D.....415 822-6776
1111 17th St Ste B San Francisco (94107) *(P-22797)*
Ermm Corporation.....E.....310 635-0524
5415 Martin Luther King Lynwood (90262) *(P-19820)*
Ernest Packaging Solutions (PA).....E.....800 757-4968
2825 S Elm Ave Ste 103 Fresno (93706) *(P-7494)*
Ernest Packaging Solutions.....E.....800 486-7222
8670 Fruitridge Rd # 300 Sacramento (95826) *(P-7495)*
Ernie Ball Inc (PA).....D.....805 544-7726
4117 Earthwood Ln San Luis Obispo (93401) *(P-22618)*
Ernie Ball Inc.....D.....800 543-2255
53973 Polk St Coachella (92236) *(P-22619)*
Ernst Mfg, Bakersfield *Also called Triple E Manufacturing Inc* *(P-14408)*
Erp Power LLC (PA).....F.....805 517-1300
893 Patriot Dr Ste E Moorpark (93021) *(P-21030)*
ES Kluft & Company Inc (PA).....C.....909 373-4211
11096 Jersey Blvd Ste 101 Rancho Cucamonga (91730) *(P-4719)*
Es West Coast LLC.....E.....209 870-1900
7100 Longe St Ste 300 Stockton (95206) *(P-16643)*
Es3 Prime Logistics Group Inc (PA).....F.....619 338-0380
550 W C St Ste 1630 San Diego (92101) *(P-19892)*
Esc, Compton *Also called Electronic Stamping Corp* *(P-16599)*
Escalera-Boulet LLC.....F.....805 691-1020
2923 Grand Ave Los Olivos (93441) *(P-1691)*
Escape Communications Inc.....F.....310 997-1300
2790 Skypark Dr Ste 203 Torrance (90505) *(P-17515)*
Eschaton Foundation (PA).....D.....831 423-1626
612 Ocean St Santa Cruz (95060) *(P-6566)*
Escient Pharmaceuticals Inc.....F.....858 617-8236
10578 Science Center Dr # 250 San Diego (92121) *(P-7881)*
Esco Industries Inc.....F.....951 782-2130
1755 Iowa Ave Bldg A Riverside (92507) *(P-12707)*
Escondido Sand & Gravel LLC.....F.....760 432-4690
500 N Tulip St Escondido (92025) *(P-9092)*
Ese, El Segundo *Also called Mod Electronics Inc* *(P-22481)*
Eshields LLC.....E.....909 305-8848
2307 Country Clb Vista St Glendora (91741) *(P-5327)*
Esi, Los Angeles *Also called Electronic Systems Innovation* *(P-14906)*
Esi Motion, Simi Valley *Also called Embedded Systems Inc* *(P-16715)*
Esilicon Corporation (PA).....C.....408 635-6300
2130 Gold St Ste 100 Alviso (95002) *(P-18225)*
Eska Inc.....E.....323 268-2134
3631 Union Pacific Ave Los Angeles (90023) *(P-3322)*
Esl Power Systems Inc.....D.....800 922-4188
2800 Palisades Dr Corona (92880) *(P-16898)*
ESM Aerospace Inc.....E.....818 841-3653
1203 W Isabel St Burbank (91506) *(P-12199)*

Esmart Massage Inc.....F.....657 341-0360
339 N Berry St Brea (92821) *(P-16827)*
Esmart Source Inc.....F.....408 739-3500
5159 Commercial Cir Ste H Concord (94520) *(P-23875)*
Esmi, San Diego *Also called Electronic Surfc Mounted Inds* *(P-17868)*
ESP Corp.....E.....310 639-2535
1175 W Victoria St Compton (90220) *(P-18907)*
ESP Safety Inc.....F.....408 886-9746
555 N 1st St San Jose (95112) *(P-22010)*
Espace Enterprises Tech Inc.....F.....408 844-8176
3010 N 1st St San Jose (95134) *(P-14462)*
Espana Metal Craft Inc.....F.....818 988-4988
7600 Ventura Canyon Ave Van Nuys (91402) *(P-12200)*
Espe Machine Work / Ver Mfg, San Jose *Also called Neodora LLC* *(P-14506)*
Especializados Del Aire, San Diego *Also called Alliance Air Products Llc* *(P-15410)*
Esperanzas Tortilleria Inc.....E.....760 743-5908
750 Rock Springs Rd Escondido (92025) *(P-2452)*
Esperer Holdings Inc (PA).....E.....805 880-4220
3820 State St Santa Barbara (93105) *(P-11200)*
Esperer Webstores LLC.....F.....805 880-1900
3820 State St Ste B Santa Barbara (93105) *(P-586)*
Esq Business Services Inc (PA).....D.....925 734-9800
20660 Stevens Cupertino (95014) *(P-23876)*
Ess Division, Milpitas *Also called Sandisk LLC* *(P-15090)*
Ess Technology Inc (HQ).....C.....408 643-8818
237 S Hillview Dr Milpitas (95035) *(P-18226)*
Essai Inc (PA).....C.....510 580-1700
48580 Kato Rd Fremont (94538) *(P-21031)*
Essence Imaging Inc.....E.....909 979-2116
20651 Golden Springs Dr Walnut (91789) *(P-22421)*
Essence Printing Inc (PA).....D.....650 952-5072
270 Oyster Point Blvd South San Francisco (94080) *(P-6567)*
Essence Water Inc.....F.....855 738-7426
12802 Knott St Garden Grove (92841) *(P-2074)*
Essential Pharmaceutical Corp.....E.....909 623-4565
1906 W Holt Ave Pomona (91768) *(P-7882)*
Essex Electronics Inc.....E.....805 684-7601
1130 Mark Ave Carpinteria (93013) *(P-18227)*
Essilor Laboratories Amer Inc.....E.....800 624-6672
801 N Burke St Visalia (93292) *(P-22353)*
Essilor Laboratories Amer Inc.....E.....310 604-8668
1450 W Walnut St Compton (90220) *(P-22354)*
Esslinger Engineering Inc.....E.....909 539-0544
5946 Freedom Dr Chino (91710) *(P-19650)*
Estam, Los Angeles *Also called Orbita Corp* *(P-3503)*
Estancia Estates.....D.....707 431-1975
980 Bryant Cyn Soledad (93960) *(P-1692)*
Estar Limited.....E.....310 989-6265
15216 Daphne Ave Gardena (90249) *(P-16861)*
Estate Cheese Group LLC (PA).....F.....707 996-1000
670 W Napa St Ste G Sonoma (95476) *(P-549)*
Estco Enterprises Inc.....F.....760 489-8745
1549 Simpson Way Escondido (92029) *(P-9306)*
Estephanian Originals Inc.....E.....626 358-7265
1550 E Mountain St Pasadena (91104) *(P-2824)*
Esys Energy Control Company.....E.....714 372-3322
12881 Knott St Ste 227 Garden Grove (92841) *(P-20867)*
ET Balancing Inc.....F.....310 538-9738
12823 Athens Way Los Angeles (90061) *(P-15936)*
Et Water Systems LLC.....F.....415 945-9383
384 Bel Marin Keys Blvd # 145 Novato (94949) *(P-21467)*
Eta USA, Morgan Hill *Also called US Eta Inc* *(P-19132)*
Etc, Burbank *Also called Electronic Theatre Contrls Inc* *(P-17119)*
Etched Media Corporation.....E.....408 374-6895
101 Gilman Ave Campbell (95008) *(P-13007)*
Etd Precision Ceramics Corp.....F.....408 577-0405
580 Charcot Ave San Jose (95131) *(P-18228)*
Eteam Technologies, Aliso Viejo *Also called Appware Inc* *(P-23617)*
Eternal Star Corporation.....E.....310 768-1945
17813 S Main St Ste 101 Gardena (90248) *(P-5480)*
Eternity Flooring, Pacoima *Also called LA Hardwood Flooring Inc* *(P-3977)*
Etha Natural Medicine, El Cajon *Also called Ethos Natural Medicine LLC* *(P-7657)*
Ethanol Energy Systems LLC.....F.....916 777-5654
406 Delta Ave Isleton (95641) *(P-8737)*
Ethernal Electric Company, San Diego *Also called Hi-Z Technology Inc* *(P-16787)*
Ethicon Inc.....B.....949 581-5799
33 Technology Dr Irvine (92618) *(P-22011)*
Ethos Natural Medicine LLC.....F.....858 267-7599
1950 Cordell Ct Ste 105 El Cajon (92020) *(P-7657)*
Ethosenergy Field Services LLC.....F.....707 399-0420
2485 Courage Dr Ste 100 Fairfield (94533) *(P-194)*
Ethosenergy Field Services LLC (HQ).....D.....310 639-3523
10455 Slusher Dr Bldg 12 Santa Fe Springs (90670) *(P-195)*
Ethosenergy Pwr Plant Svcs LLC.....E.....916 391-2993
3215 47th Ave Sacramento (95824) *(P-196)*
Eti, Fields Landing *Also called Environmental Technology Inc* *(P-7562)*
Eti B Si Professional, Huntington Park *Also called Eti Sound Systems Inc* *(P-17228)*
Eti Empire Direct, Anaheim *Also called Econotek Inc* *(P-22151)*
Eti Sound Systems Inc.....E.....323 835-6660
3383 E Gage Ave Huntington Park (90255) *(P-17228)*
Etm—Electromatic Inc (PA).....D.....510 797-1100
35451 Dumbarton Ct Newark (94560) *(P-17516)*
Etnies, Lake Forest *Also called Sole Technology Inc* *(P-10184)*
Eton Corporation.....E.....650 903-3866
1015 Corporation Way Palo Alto (94303) *(P-19308)*
Ets Express Inc (PA).....E.....805 278-7771
420 Lombard St Oxnard (93030) *(P-13175)*

Employee Codes: A=Over 500 employees, B=251-500
C=101-250, D=51-100, E=20-50, F=10-19
2020 California
Manfacturers Register
© Mergent Inc. 1-800-342-5647
1095

Ettore Products Co ...... D 510 748-4130
2100 N Loop Rd Alameda (94502) *(P-23327)*

Etude Wines Inc ...... F 707 257-5300
1250 Cuttings Wharf Rd NAPA (94559) *(P-1693)*

Eubanks Engineering Co (PA) ...... E 909 483-2456
1921 S Quaker Ridge Pl Ontario (91761) *(P-14266)*

Eufora, Vista Also called Eden Beauty Concepts Inc *(P-8487)*

Eugenios Sheet Metal Inc ...... F 909 923-2002
2151 Maple Privado Ontario (91761) *(P-12201)*

Eugenus Inc (HQ) ...... D 669 235-8244
677 River Oaks Pkwy San Jose (95134) *(P-21032)*

Euphonix Inc (HQ) ...... E 650 526-1600
280 Bernardo Ave Mountain View (94043) *(P-17517)*

Euramax Holdings Inc ...... F 714 563-8260
1411 N Daly St Anaheim (92806) *(P-11216)*

Euramco Safety Inc ...... F 619 670-9590
2746 Via Orange Way Spring Valley (91978) *(P-14658)*

Eureka Chemical Company (PA) ...... E 650 873-5374
234 Lawrence Ave South San Francisco (94080) *(P-8964)*

Eureka Record Works Inc (PA) ...... F 707 442-8121
210 C St Eureka (95501) *(P-17229)*

Eureka Times-Standard, Eureka Also called Pasadena Newspapers Inc *(P-5794)*

Euri Lighting, Torrance Also called Irtronix Inc *(P-16865)*

Euro Bello USA ...... E 213 446-2818
10660 Wilshire Blvd Los Angeles (90024) *(P-3514)*

Euro Machine Inc ...... F 818 998-5198
9627 Owensmouth Ave Ste 1 Chatsworth (91311) *(P-15937)*

Eurocraft Archtectural Met Inc ...... E 323 771-1323
5619 Watcher St Bell Gardens (90201) *(P-12472)*

Eurodesign Ltd (PA) ...... E 650 948-5160
62 Chester Cir Los Altos (94022) *(P-4569)*

Euroline Steel Windows ...... E 877 590-2741
22600 Savi Ranch Pkwy E Yorba Linda (92887) *(P-11953)*

Euroline Steel Windows & Doors, Yorba Linda Also called Euroline Steel Windows *(P-11953)*

European Elegance Woodwork ...... F 818 570-9401
12243 Foothill Blvd Sylmar (91342) *(P-4043)*

European Rolling Shutters, San Jose Also called Blum Construction Co Inc *(P-11939)*

European Services Group ...... F 714 898-0595
5062 Caspian Cir Huntington Beach (92649) *(P-11589)*

European Wholesale Counter ...... C 619 562-0565
10051 Prospect Ave Santee (92071) *(P-4901)*

European Woodwork ...... F 714 892-8831
7531 Suzi Ln Westminster (92683) *(P-4192)*

Europian Investment, Los Angeles Also called Hunter Digital Ltd *(P-15239)*

Eurostampa North America Inc ...... F 707 927-4848
2545 Napa Vly NAPA (94558) *(P-7059)*

Eurotec Seating, La Habra Also called Orbo Corporation *(P-4867)*

Eurotech Showers Inc ...... F 949 716-4099
23552 Commerce Center Dr A Laguna Hills (92653) *(P-9585)*

Eurton Electric Company Inc ...... E 562 946-4477
9920 Painter Ave Santa Fe Springs (90670) *(P-24689)*

Eurus Energy America Corp (HQ) ...... F 858 638-7115
9255 Towne Centre Dr # 840 San Diego (92121) *(P-16644)*

Euv Tech Inc ...... E 925 229-4388
2840 Howe Rd Ste A Martinez (94553) *(P-21227)*

Ev3 Neurovascular, Irvine Also called Micro Therapeutics Inc *(P-21819)*

Evalve Inc ...... D 650 330-8100
4045 Campbell Ave Menlo Park (94025) *(P-13352)*

Evan-Moor Corporation (HQ) ...... E 831 649-5901
18 Lower Ragsdale Dr Monterey (93940) *(P-6101)*

Evan-Moor Educational Publr, Monterey Also called Evan-Moor Corporation *(P-6101)*

Evans Electric Service (PA) ...... E 559 268-4704
531 Fulton St Fresno (93721) *(P-24690)*

Evans Food West Inc (PA) ...... F 909 947-3001
1920 S Augusta Ave Ontario (91761) *(P-2321)*

Evans Industries Inc ...... C 626 912-1688
17915 Railroad St City of Industry (91748) *(P-13521)*

Evans Manufacturing Inc (PA) ...... C 714 379-6100
7422 Chapman Ave Garden Grove (92841) *(P-23100)*

Evans Walker Enterprises ...... E 951 784-7223
2304 Fleetwood Dr Riverside (92509) *(P-19651)*

Evans, Walker Racing, Riverside Also called Evans Walker Enterprises *(P-19651)*

Evantec Corporation ...... F 949 632-2811
6120 Valley View St Buena Park (90620) *(P-9307)*

Evantec Scientific, Buena Park Also called Evantec Corporation *(P-9307)*

Evapco Inc ...... C 559 673-2207
1900 W Almond Ave Madera (93637) *(P-15431)*

Evapco West, Madera Also called Evapco Inc *(P-15431)*

Evden Enterprises Inc ...... F 707 462-0375
2000 Wellmar Dr Ukiah (95482) *(P-15938)*

Evensphere Incorporation ...... F 909 247-3030
1249 S Diamond Bar Blvd Diamond Bar (91765) *(P-18767)*

Event Farm Inc (HQ) ...... F 888 444-8162
3103 Neilson Way Ste B Santa Monica (90405) *(P-23877)*

Event Spice Wear, Los Angeles Also called Eska Inc *(P-3322)*

Eventure Interactive Inc ...... F 855 986-5669
3420 Bristol St Fl 6 Costa Mesa (92626) *(P-23878)*

Ever-Glory Intl Group Inc ...... F 626 859-6638
1009 Becklee Rd Glendora (91741) *(P-3323)*

Everbrands Inc ...... F 855 595-2999
10547 W Pico Blvd Los Angeles (90064) *(P-8490)*

Everbrite West LLC ...... D 909 592-0870
2778 Pomona Blvd Pomona (91768) *(P-23101)*

Everbrite West LLC ...... F 619 444-9000
2733 Via Orange Way Spring Valley (91978) *(P-23102)*

Eveready Pacific Corp, Riverside Also called Everpac *(P-14289)*

Everest Group Usa Inc ...... E 909 923-1818
1885 S Vineyard Ave Ste 3 Ontario (91761) *(P-2932)*

Everest Networks Inc ...... E 408 300-9236
205 Ravendale Dr Mountain View (94043) *(P-15227)*

Everett Charles Tech LLC (HQ) ...... D 909 625-5551
14570 Meyer Canyon Dr # 100 Fontana (92336) *(P-21033)*

Everett Charles Tech LLC ...... F 909 625-5551
14570 Meyer Canyon Dr # 100 Fontana (92336) *(P-21034)*

Everett Graphics Inc ...... D 510 577-6777
7300 Edgewater Dr Oakland (94621) *(P-5313)*

Everfilt, Mira Loma Also called Puri Tech Inc *(P-15564)*

Evergood Fine Foods, San Francisco Also called Evergood Sausage Co *(P-455)*

Evergood Sausage Co. ...... D 415 822-4660
1932 Van Dyke Ave San Francisco (94124) *(P-455)*

Evergreen Avionics Inc (PA) ...... F 805 445-6492
880 Calle Plano Ste J Camarillo (93012) *(P-18229)*

Evergreen Environmental Svcs, Gardena Also called Evergreen Oil Inc *(P-9142)*

Evergreen Holdings Inc (PA) ...... E 949 757-7770
18952 Macarthur Blvd # 410 Irvine (92612) *(P-9141)*

Evergreen Lighting, Pomona Also called Yawitz Inc *(P-17002)*

Evergreen Oil Inc (HQ) ...... E 949 757-7770
18025 S Broadway Gardena (90248) *(P-9142)*

Evergreen Systems Intl, Camarillo Also called Evergreen Avionics Inc *(P-18229)*

Everidge Inc ...... E 909 605-6419
8886 White Oak Ave Rancho Cucamonga (91730) *(P-15432)*

Everleigh, Huntington Park Also called J Heyri Inc *(P-3168)*

Everpac ...... D 951 774-3274
1499 Palmyrita Ave Riverside (92507) *(P-14289)*

Everson Spice Company Inc. ...... E 562 595-4785
2667 Gundry Ave Long Beach (90755) *(P-2453)*

Everspring Chemical Inc ...... D 310 707-1600
11577 W Olympic Blvd Los Angeles (90064) *(P-8965)*

Evert Hancock Incorporated ...... F 714 870-0376
1809 N National St Anaheim (92801) *(P-12202)*

Everything Mobile, Sunnyvale Also called Mobile Crossing Inc *(P-20632)*

Evissap Inc ...... E 408 432-7393
800 Charcot Ave San Jose (95131) *(P-17518)*

Evk Inc ...... E 617 335-3180
5235 Bandera St Montclair (91763) *(P-8868)*

Evo Manufacturing Inc ...... F 714 879-8913
1829 W Commonwealth Ave Fullerton (92833) *(P-23328)*

Evofem Inc ...... F 858 550-1900
12400 High Bluff Dr # 600 San Diego (92130) *(P-21708)*

Evofem Biosciences Inc (PA) ...... F 858 550-1900
12400 High Bluff Dr San Diego (92130) *(P-7883)*

Evolife Scientific Llc ...... F 888 750-0310
1452 E 33rd St Signal Hill (90755) *(P-7658)*

Evolphin Software Inc (PA) ...... F 888 386-4114
2410 Camino Ramon Ste 228 San Ramon (94583) *(P-23879)*

Evolus Inc (HQ) ...... D 949 284-4555
520 Nwport Ctr Dr Ste 120 Newport Beach (92660) *(P-7884)*

Evolution Design Lab Inc ...... E 626 960-8388
150 S Los Robles Ave # 100 Pasadena (91101) *(P-10169)*

Evolution Robotics Inc ...... E 626 993-3300
1055 E Colo Blvd Ste 320 Pasadena (91106) *(P-23880)*

Evolv Surfaces Inc ...... C 415 671-0635
1315 Armstrong Ave San Francisco (94124) *(P-4975)*

Evolv Technology Solutions Inc ...... F 415 444-9040
611 Mission St Fl 6 San Francisco (94105) *(P-23881)*

Evolva Inc ...... F 415 448-5451
80 E Sir Francis Drake Bl Larkspur (94939) *(P-8298)*

Evolve Dental Technologies Inc ...... F 949 713-0909
5 Vanderbilt Irvine (92618) *(P-22155)*

Evolve Manufacturing Tech Inc ...... E 650 968-9292
47300 Bayside Pkwy Fremont (94538) *(P-21709)*

Evonik Corporation ...... E 323 264-0311
3305 E 26th St Vernon (90058) *(P-8966)*

Evoqua Water Technologies ...... F 408 586-9745
960 Ames Ave Milpitas (95035) *(P-15512)*

Evoqua Water Technologies LLC ...... F 916 564-1222
199 Harris Ave Ste 1 Sacramento (95838) *(P-15513)*

Evy of California Inc (HQ) ...... C 213 746-4647
2042 Garfield Ave Commerce (90040) *(P-3478)*

Ew Corprtion Indus Fabricators (PA) ...... D 760 337-0020
1002 E Main St El Centro (92243) *(P-11789)*

Ew Packaging, Gardena Also called Ew Trading Inc *(P-9782)*

Ew Trading Inc ...... F 310 515-9898
17510 S Broadway Unit B Gardena (90248) *(P-9782)*

Ewi Worldwide, Foothill Ranch Also called Exhibit Works Inc *(P-23103)*

Exact Cnc Industries Inc ...... F 818 527-1908
20640 Bahama St Chatsworth (91311) *(P-12801)*

Exacta-Technology Inc ...... F 925 443-6200
378 Wright Brothers Ave Livermore (94551) *(P-15939)*

Exactacator Inc (PA) ...... E 209 464-8979
2237 Stagecoach Rd Stockton (95215) *(P-22798)*

Exactuals LLC ...... F 310 689-7491
1100 Glendon Ave Fl 17 Los Angeles (90024) *(P-23882)*

Exadel Inc (PA) ...... D 925 363-9510
1340 Treat Blvd Walnut Creek (94597) *(P-23883)*

Exam Room Supply LLC ...... E 805 298-3631
2419 Hrbour Blvd Unit 126 Ventura (93001) *(P-22253)*

Examiner Special Projects Div, Santa Monica Also called Hearst Corporation *(P-5950)*

Exar Corporation (HQ) ...... C 669 265-6100
1060 Rincon Cir San Jose (95131) *(P-18230)*

Exar Corporation ...... B 408 927-9975
48760 Kato Rd Fremont (94538) *(P-18231)*

Exatron Inc ...... E 408 629-7600
2842 Aiello Dr San Jose (95111) *(P-21035)*

Excaliber Systems Inc ...... E 805 376-1366
185 Los Vientos Dr Newbury Park (91320) *(P-7060)*

Excalibur Motorsports, Chino Also called Hua Rong International Corp *(P-20513)*

Excalibur Well Services Corp (PA)....D....661 589-5338
22034 Rosedale Hwy Bakersfield (93314) ***(P-92)***
Excavo LLC....F....310 823-7670
13428 Maxella Ave Ste 409 Marina Del Rey (90292) ***(P-3973)***
Excel Bridge Manufacturing Co., Santa Fe Springs *Also called Excel Sheet Metal Inc* ***(P-12203)***
Excel Cabinets Inc....E....951 279-4545
225 Jason Ct Corona (92879) ***(P-4193)***
Excel Cnc Machining Inc....E....408 970-9460
3185 De La Cruz Blvd Santa Clara (95054) ***(P-15940)***
Excel Industries Inc....E....909 947-4867
1601 Fremont Ct Ontario (91761) ***(P-12802)***
Excel Machining, Santa Clara *Also called Excel Cnc Machining Inc* ***(P-15940)***
Excel Manufacturing Inc....E....661 257-1900
20409 Prairie St Chatsworth (91311) ***(P-15941)***
Excel Precision Corp USA....E....408 727-4260
3350 Scott Blvd Bldg 62 Santa Clara (95054) ***(P-21036)***
Excel Sheet Metal Inc (PA)....D....562 944-0701
12001 Shoemaker Ave Santa Fe Springs (90670) ***(P-12203)***
Excelitas Technologies Corp....D....510 979-6500
44370 Christy St Fremont (94538) ***(P-17124)***
Excelitas Technologies Corp....C....626 967-6021
1330 E Cypress St Covina (91724) ***(P-21468)***
Excelity....E....818 767-1000
11127 Dora St Sun Valley (91352) ***(P-11415)***
Excellence Magazine Inc....F....415 382-0582
42 Digital Dr Ste 5 Novato (94949) ***(P-5934)***
Excellence Opto Inc....F....818 674-1921
20047 Tipico St Chatsworth (91311) ***(P-17728)***
Excelline Food Products LLC....C....818 701-7710
833 N Hollywood Way Burbank (91505) ***(P-957)***
Excelline Foods Inc....F....818 701-7710
833 N Hollywood Way Burbank (91505) ***(P-958)***
Excello Circuits Inc....E....714 993-0560
1924 Nancita Cir Placentia (92870) ***(P-17871)***
Excellon Acquisition LLC (HQ)....E....310 668-7700
20001 S Rancho Way Compton (90220) ***(P-14463)***
Excellon Automation Co, Compton *Also called Excellon Acquisition LLC* ***(P-14463)***
Excelpro Inc (PA)....F....323 415-8544
1630 Amapola Ave Torrance (90501) ***(P-550)***
Excelsior Machine Inc....F....559 291-7710
2964 Phillip Ave Clovis (93612) ***(P-15942)***
Excelsior Nutrition Inc....E....657 999-5188
1206 N Miller St Unit D Anaheim (92806) ***(P-7659)***
Excess Trading Inc....E....310 212-0020
12350 Montague St Ste L Pacoima (91331) ***(P-21469)***
Exchange, The, Seaside *Also called Monterey County Weekly* ***(P-5759)***
Exclara Inc....E....408 329-9319
4701 Patrick Henry Dr # 1701 Santa Clara (95054) ***(P-18232)***
Exclusive Powder Coatings Inc....F....661 294-9812
24922 Anza Dr Ste C Valencia (91355) ***(P-13176)***
Execuprint Inc....F....818 993-8184
9650 Topanga Canyon Pl E Chatsworth (91311) ***(P-7061)***
Executive Bus Solutions Inc....F....805 499-3290
21356 Nordhoff St Ste 108 Chatsworth (91311) ***(P-14320)***
Executive Safe and SEC Corp....E....909 947-7020
10722 Edison Ct Rancho Cucamonga (91730) ***(P-13522)***
Executive Tool Inc....E....714 996-1276
1220 N Richfield Rd Anaheim (92807) ***(P-12204)***
Exelixis Inc....C....650 837-8254
169 Harbor Way South San Francisco (94080) ***(P-7885)***
Exelixis Inc....B....650 837-7000
1851 Harbor Bay Pkwy Alameda (94502) ***(P-20969)***
Exelixis Inc....C....650 837-7000
1851 Harbor Bay Pkwy Alameda (94502) ***(P-7886)***
Exelixis Inc (PA)....D....650 837-7000
1851 Harbor Bay Pkwy Alameda (94502) ***(P-7887)***
Exemplis LLC....E....714 995-4800
6280 Artesia Blvd Buena Park (90620) ***(P-4836)***
Exemplis LLC....B....714 898-5500
6280 Artesia Blvd Buena Park (90620) ***(P-4837)***
Exemplis LLC (PA)....E....714 995-4800
6415 Katella Ave Cypress (90630) ***(P-4838)***
Exeter Mercantile Company....F....559 592-2121
258 E Pine St Exeter (93221) ***(P-13632)***
Exhart Envmtl Systems Inc....F....818 576-9628
20364 Plummer St Chatsworth (91311) ***(P-23329)***
Exhaust Center Inc....F....951 685-8602
1794 W 11th St Upland (91786) ***(P-12205)***
Exhaust Gas Technologies Inc....F....909 548-8100
15642 Dupont Ave Ste B Chino (91710) ***(P-19652)***
EXHAUST TECH, Commerce *Also called Dynaflex Products* ***(P-19530)***
Exhibit Works Inc....F....949 470-0850
19531 Pauling Foothill Ranch (92610) ***(P-23103)***
Exide Technologies....E....951 520-0677
345 Cessna Cir Ste 101 Corona (92880) ***(P-19164)***
Exin LLC....C....415 359-2600
1213 Evans Ave San Francisco (94124) ***(P-5631)***
Exit Light Co Inc....F....877 352-3948
3170 Scott St Vista (92081) ***(P-17032)***
Exit Sign Warehouse Inc....F....888 953-3948
16123 Cohasset St Van Nuys (91406) ***(P-17033)***
Exo Systems Inc....E....510 655-5033
333 Pali Ct Oakland (94611) ***(P-22254)***
Exodust Collectors LLC....F....562 808-0842
7045 Jackson St Paramount (90723) ***(P-14659)***
Exotic Silks Inc....F....650 948-8611
1959 Leghorn St Ste B Mountain View (94043) ***(P-2686)***
Exp Computer....F....408 530-8080
1296 Kifer Rd Ste 605 Sunnyvale (94086) ***(P-21470)***
Expandable Software Inc (PA)....E....408 261-7880
900 Lafayette St Ste 400 Santa Clara (95050) ***(P-23884)***
Expedite Precision Works Inc....E....408 437-1893
931 Berryessa Rd San Jose (95133) ***(P-15943)***
Experimental Aircraft Assn....F....818 705-2744
7026 Lasaine Ave Van Nuys (91406) ***(P-19893)***
Expert Assembly Services Inc....E....714 258-8880
14312 Chambers Rd Ste B Tustin (92780) ***(P-17872)***
Expert Coatings & Graphics LLC....F....714 476-2086
1570 S Lewis St Anaheim (92805) ***(P-13177)***
Expert Reputation LLC....F....866 407-6020
101 N Acacia Ave Ste 105 Solana Beach (92075) ***(P-23885)***
Expert Semiconductor Tech Inc....E....831 439-9300
10 Victor Sq Ste 100 Scotts Valley (95066) ***(P-14464)***
Expertech, Scotts Valley *Also called Expert Semiconductor Tech Inc* ***(P-14464)***
Exploding Kittens LLC....F....310 788-8699
101 S La Brea Ave A Los Angeles (90036) ***(P-22675)***
Exploramed Nc7 Inc....E....650 559-5805
1975 W El Camino Real Mountain View (94040) ***(P-22255)***
Expo Dyeing & Finishing Inc....C....714 220-9583
1365 N Knollwood Cir Anaheim (92801) ***(P-2853)***
Expo-3 International Inc....E....714 379-8383
12350 Edison Way 60 Garden Grove (92841) ***(P-23104)***
Expol Inc....F....408 567-9020
2122 Ronald St Santa Clara (95050) ***(P-15944)***
Exportech Worldwide LLC....F....909 278-9477
14310 Burning Tree Dr Victorville (92395) ***(P-14910)***
Express Business Systems Inc....E....858 549-9828
9155 Trade Pl San Diego (92126) ***(P-7062)***
Express Chipping....F....562 789-8058
418 Goetz Ave Santa Ana (92707) ***(P-6231)***
Express Container Inc....E....909 798-3857
560 Iowa St Redlands (92373) ***(P-5220)***
Express Folding....E....310 316-6762
21250 Hawthorne Blvd Torrance (90503) ***(P-6232)***
Express ID, Riverside *Also called J&C Tapocik Inc* ***(P-3559)***
Express It Delivers....E....626 855-1294
168 Mason Way Ste B5 City of Industry (91746) ***(P-6233)***
Express Lens Lab Inc....E....714 545-1024
17150 Newhope St Ste 305 Fountain Valley (92708) ***(P-22355)***
Express Machining, La Mirada *Also called United States Ball Corporation* ***(P-14619)***
Express Manufacturing Inc (PA)....C....714 979-2228
3519 W Warner Ave Santa Ana (92704) ***(P-18908)***
Express Pipe & Supply Co LLC (HQ)....E....310 204-7238
1235 S Lewis St Santa Monica (90404) ***(P-13469)***
Express Sheet Metal Product....F....562 925-9340
10131 Flora Vista St Bellflower (90706) ***(P-12206)***
Express Sign and Neon....F....323 291-3333
1720 W Slauson Ave Los Angeles (90047) ***(P-23105)***
Express Systems & Engrg Inc....E....951 461-1500
41357 Date St Murrieta (92562) ***(P-9783)***
Expression In Wood....F....909 596-8496
1738 Brackett St La Verne (91750) ***(P-4194)***
Expression Systems LLC (PA)....E....877 877-7421
2537 2nd St Davis (95618) ***(P-8299)***
Expressions Home Gallery, Santa Monica *Also called Express Pipe & Supply Co LLC* ***(P-13469)***
Exquisite Corporation....E....626 856-0200
5000 Rivergrade Rd Baldwin Park (91706) ***(P-8491)***
Exquisite Mfg & Filling Serv, Baldwin Park *Also called Exquisite Corporation* ***(P-8491)***
Extra Lite, Huntington Beach *Also called Pacific Link Corp* ***(P-21395)***
Extreme Group Holdings LLC....E....310 899-3200
1531 14th St Santa Monica (90404) ***(P-17320)***
Extreme Networks Inc (PA)....B....408 579-2800
6480 Via Del Oro San Jose (95119) ***(P-17367)***
Extreme Precision Inc....F....408 275-8365
1717 Little Orchard St B San Jose (95125) ***(P-15945)***
Extreme Precision LLC....F....949 459-1062
23266 Arroyo Vis Rcho STA Marg (92688) ***(P-15946)***
Extreme Production Music, Santa Monica *Also called Extreme Group Holdings LLC* ***(P-17320)***
Extron Contract Mfg Inc....C....510 353-0177
496 S Abbott Ave Milpitas (95035) ***(P-22676)***
Extron Contract Packaging, Milpitas *Also called Extron Contract Mfg Inc* ***(P-22676)***
Extron Electronics, Anaheim *Also called Rgb Systems Inc* ***(P-15322)***
Extrude Hone Abrsve Flw McHng, Paramount *Also called Extrude Hone Deburring Service* ***(P-15947)***
Extrude Hone Deburring Service....F....562 531-2976
8800 Somerset Blvd Paramount (90723) ***(P-15947)***
Extrumed Inc (HQ)....E....951 547-7400
547 Trm Cir Corona (92879) ***(P-9784)***
Exxel Media, Cardiff By The Sea *Also called Nutrition Resource Connection* ***(P-17332)***
Exxel Outdoors Inc....B....626 369-7278
343 Baldwin Park Blvd City of Industry (91746) ***(P-3840)***
Eye Care Network of Cal Inc (PA)....F....714 619-4660
345 Baker St Costa Mesa (92626) ***(P-21710)***
Eye Medical Group Santa Cruz....F....831 426-2550
515 Soquel Ave Santa Cruz (95062) ***(P-21711)***
Eyebrain Medical Inc....F....949 339-5157
3184 Airway Ave Ste C Costa Mesa (92626) ***(P-22356)***
Eyefluence Inc....E....408 586-8632
1600 Amphitheatre Pkwy Mountain View (94043) ***(P-22357)***
Eyeonics Inc....E....949 788-6000
50 Technology Dr Irvine (92618) ***(P-22358)***
Eyeshadow, Los Angeles *Also called Stony Apparel Corp* ***(P-3417)***
Eyvo Inc....F....888 237-9801
775 E Blithedale Ave Mill Valley (94941) ***(P-23886)***

ALPHABETIC

Employee Codes: A=Over 500 employees, B=251-500
C=101-250, D=51-100, E=20-50, F=10-19

2020 California
Manfacturers Register

© Mergent Inc. 1-800-342-5647
1097

EZ 2000 Inc ....F......800 273-5033
1800 Century Park E # 600 Los Angeles (90067) ***(P-23887)***
EZ 2000 1 Rated Dental Sftwr, Los Angeles *Also called EZ 2000 Inc* ***(P-23887)***
EZ Inflatables Inc ....E......626 480-9100
1410 Vineland Ave Baldwin Park (91706) ***(P-9308)***
EZ Lube LLC ....A......951 766-1996
532 W Florida Ave Hemet (92543) ***(P-9143)***
EZ Up Factory Store, Colton *Also called E-Z Up Directcom* ***(P-3681)***
Ezaki Glico USA Corp ....F......949 251-0144
18022 Cowan Ste 110 Irvine (92614) ***(P-1366)***
Ezboard Inc ....F......415 773-0400
607 Market St Fl 5 San Francisco (94105) ***(P-23888)***
Ezekiel, Irvine *Also called 3 Point Distribution LLC* ***(P-3060)***
Ezoic Inc (PA) ....F......760 444-4995
6023 Innovation Way # 200 Carlsbad (92009) ***(P-23889)***
Ezrez Software, San Francisco *Also called Topguest Inc* ***(P-24516)***
F & D Flores Enterprises Inc ....F......909 975-4853
761 E Francis St Ontario (91761) ***(P-21471)***
F & H Plating LLC ....F......818 765-1221
12023 Vose St Ste A North Hollywood (91605) ***(P-13008)***
F & L Tls Precision Machining, Corona *Also called F & L Tools Corporation* ***(P-20101)***
F & L Tools Corporation ....F......951 279-1555
245 Jason Ct Corona (92879) ***(P-20101)***
F C I, San Marcos *Also called Fluid Components Intl LLC* ***(P-20869)***
F Conrad Furlong Inc ....F......213 623-4191
550 S Hill St Ste 1620 Los Angeles (90013) ***(P-22517)***
F D M, Yorba Linda *Also called Fixture Design & Mfg Co* ***(P-5060)***
F E Trailers, Lakeside *Also called McQuaide Brothers Corporation* ***(P-19826)***
F E W Inc ....F......661 323-8319
420 30th St Bakersfield (93301) ***(P-15948)***
F G S Packing Services, Exeter *Also called Fruit Growers Supply Company* ***(P-5222)***
F Gavina & Sons Inc ....B......323 582-0671
2700 Fruitland Ave Vernon (90058) ***(P-2288)***
F I O Imports Inc ....C......323 263-5100
5980 Alcoa Ave Vernon (90058) ***(P-2454)***
F I T, Compton *Also called Fastener Innovation Tech Inc* ***(P-12631)***
F Korbel & Bros (PA) ....B......707 824-7000
13250 River Rd Guerneville (95446) ***(P-1694)***
F Korbel & Bros ....E......661 854-6120
15401 Bear Mtn Winery Rd Di Giorgio (93203) ***(P-1695)***
F M H, Irvine *Also called Fmh Aerospace Corp* ***(P-20107)***
F M I, Santa Ana *Also called Flexible Manufacturing LLC* ***(P-18769)***
F R Industries Inc ....F......818 503-9143
3157 Dona Susana Dr Studio City (91604) ***(P-2933)***
F T B & Son Inc ....E......714 891-8003
11551 Markon Dr Garden Grove (92841) ***(P-12207)***
F T I, Long Beach *Also called Fundamental Tech Intl Inc* ***(P-20874)***
F-J-E Inc ....E......562 437-7466
546 W Esther St Long Beach (90813) ***(P-4902)***
F-P Press, Union City *Also called Fricke-Parks Press Inc* ***(P-6585)***
F.K.a Trmph Strctrs-Los Angles, City of Industry *Also called Alatus Aerosystems* ***(P-20029)***
Faac ....F......800 221-8278
357 S Acacia Ave Unit 357 # 357 Fullerton (92831) ***(P-19309)***
Fab Tron ....F......714 996-4270
1358 N Jefferson St Anaheim (92807) ***(P-12208)***
Fabco Holdings Inc ....A......925 454-9500
151 Lawrence Dr Livermore (94551) ***(P-19653)***
Fabco Steel Fabrication Inc ....E......909 350-1535
14688 San Bernardino Ave Fontana (92335) ***(P-11790)***
Faber Enterprises Inc ....C......310 323-6200
14800 S Figueroa St Gardena (90248) ***(P-13329)***
Fable Inc ....F......650 598-9616
595 Quarry Rd San Carlos (94070) ***(P-12473)***
Fabnet, Anaheim *Also called Fabrication Network Inc* ***(P-12209)***
Fabri-Corp ....E......650 941-2076
25850 Vinedo Ln Los Altos Hills (94022) ***(P-15949)***
Fabri-Tech Components Inc ....F......510 249-2000
49038 Milmont Dr Fremont (94538) ***(P-18909)***
Fabric Brand, Huntington Park *Also called Coh-Fb LLC* ***(P-3030)***
Fabric Walls Inc ....F......415 863-2711
322 Harriet St San Francisco (94103) ***(P-3615)***
Fabrica Fine Carpet, Santa Ana *Also called Fabrica International Inc* ***(P-2869)***
Fabrica International Inc ....C......949 261-7181
3201 S Susan St Santa Ana (92704) ***(P-2869)***
Fabricast Inc (PA) ....E......626 443-3247
2517 Seaman Ave South El Monte (91733) ***(P-18910)***
Fabricated Components Corp ....C......714 974-8590
130 W Bristol Ln Orange (92865) ***(P-17873)***
Fabricated Extrusion Co LLC (PA) ....E......209 529-9200
2331 Hoover Ave Modesto (95354) ***(P-9785)***
Fabricated Glass Spc Inc ....F......707 429-6160
2350 S Watney Way Ste E Fairfield (94533) ***(P-10358)***
Fabrication Network Inc ....D......714 393-5282
5410 E La Palma Ave Anaheim (92807) ***(P-12209)***
Fabrication Tech Inds Inc ....D......619 477-4141
2200 Haffley Ave National City (91950) ***(P-11791)***
Fabricmate Systems Inc ....F......805 642-7470
2781 Golf Course Dr A Ventura (93003) ***(P-9786)***
Fabricor Products Inc ....F......760 373-8292
22512 Curtis Pl California City (93505) ***(P-12474)***
Fabricor Stamping, California City *Also called Fabricor Products Inc* ***(P-12474)***
Fabrique Delices, Hayward *Also called Sapar Usa Inc* ***(P-496)***
Fabritec Precision Inc (PA) ....F......209 529-8504
1060 Reno Ave Modesto (95351) ***(P-12210)***
Fabritex Inc ....F......213 747-1417
2301 E 7th St Ste D102 Los Angeles (90023) ***(P-2726)***
Fabrix, San Leandro *Also called Osumo Inc* ***(P-3805)***
Fabtex Inc ....C......714 538-0877
1202 W Struck Ave Orange (92867) ***(P-2727)***
Fabtron, San Carlos *Also called EH Suda Inc* ***(P-15921)***
Fabtron, Lewiston *Also called EH Suda Inc* ***(P-15922)***
Fabtron ....F......650 622-9700
615 Industrial Rd San Carlos (94070) ***(P-15950)***
Fabtronic Inc ....E......626 962-3293
5026 Calmview Ave Baldwin Park (91706) ***(P-12211)***
Face First Screen Print Inc ....E......949 443-9895
33049 Calle Aviador Ste C San Juan Capistrano (92675) ***(P-7063)***
Facefirst Inc ....E......805 482-8428
15821 Ventura Blvd # 425 Encino (91436) ***(P-23890)***
Facilitron Inc (PA) ....F......800 272-2962
485 Alberto Way Ste 210 Los Gatos (95032) ***(P-23891)***
Factory Direct Dist Corp ....F......619 435-3437
1001 B Ave Ste 100 San Diego (92118) ***(P-8383)***
Factory One Studio Inc ....D......323 752-1670
6700 Avalon Blvd Ste 101 Los Angeles (90003) ***(P-2687)***
Factory Reproductions ....F......909 590-5252
13353 Benson Ave Chino (91710) ***(P-19654)***
Factory Showroom Exchange, Los Angeles *Also called Sofa U Love* ***(P-4670)***
Factron Test Fixtures, Fontana *Also called Everett Charles Tech LLC* ***(P-21033)***
Fafco Inc (PA) ....E......530 332-2100
435 Otterson Dr Chico (95928) ***(P-11696)***
Fair Isaac International Corp (HQ) ....A......415 446-6000
200 Smith Ranch Rd San Rafael (94903) ***(P-23892)***
Fairchild Semicdtr Intl Inc (HQ) ....E......408 822-2000
1272 Borregas Ave Sunnyvale (94089) ***(P-18233)***
Fairmont Designs, Del Mar *Also called Fairmont Global LLC* ***(P-4903)***
Fairmont Global LLC (PA) ....F......415 320-2929
2010 Jimmy Durante Blvd Del Mar (92014) ***(P-4903)***
Fairmont Sign Company ....E......209 365-6490
850 S Guild Ave Lodi (95240) ***(P-23106)***
Fairway Import-Export Inc ....E......310 637-6162
2130 E Gladwick St Rancho Dominguez (90220) ***(P-22799)***
Fairway Injection Molds Inc ....D......909 595-2201
20109 Paseo Del Prado Walnut (91789) ***(P-14051)***
Fairway Trading Inc ....F......323 582-8111
5717 Ferguson Dr Commerce (90022) ***(P-2752)***
Faith Industries Inc ....E......951 351-1486
4117 Pearl St Lake Elsinore (92530) ***(P-4501)***
Faith Knight Inc ....F......213 488-1569
2340 Mountain Ave La Crescenta (91214) ***(P-22518)***
Falcon Abrasive Manufacturing ....F......909 598-3078
5490 Brooks St Montclair (91763) ***(P-10946)***
Falcon Automotive Inc ....E......714 569-1085
1305 E Wakeham Ave Santa Ana (92705) ***(P-3841)***
Falcon Electric, Baldwin Park *Also called Yutaka Electric Intl Inc* ***(P-16805)***
Falcon Electric Inc ....F......626 962-7770
5116 Azusa Canyon Rd Baldwin Park (91706) ***(P-16549)***
Falcon Iron ....F......209 845-8229
775 Wakefield Ct Oakdale (95361) ***(P-11792)***
Falcon Waterfree Tech LLC (HQ) ....E......310 209-7250
2255 Barry Ave Los Angeles (90064) ***(P-9309)***
Falkner Winery Inc ....D......951 676-6741
40620 Calle Contento Temecula (92591) ***(P-1696)***
Falkor Partners LLC ....D......714 721-8772
333 Mccormick Ave Costa Mesa (92626) ***(P-18234)***
Fallbrook Bonsall Village News, Temecula *Also called Villlage News Inc* ***(P-5861)***
Fallbrook Communications, Fallbrook *Also called Fallbrook Printing Corp* ***(P-6568)***
Fallbrook Industries Inc ....E......760 728-7229
323 Industrial Way Ste 1 Fallbrook (92028) ***(P-12803)***
Fallbrook Printing Corp ....F......760 731-2020
504 E Alvarado St Ste 110 Fallbrook (92028) ***(P-6568)***
Falltech, Compton *Also called Andrew Alexander Inc* ***(P-10136)***
Falmat Inc ....C......800 848-4257
1873 Diamond St San Marcos (92078) ***(P-11302)***
Falton Custom Cabinets Inc ....F......209 845-9823
667 High Tech Pkwy Oakdale (95361) ***(P-4195)***
Family Industries LLC ....F......619 306-1035
1700 N Spring St Los Angeles (90012) ***(P-23330)***
Family Loompya Corporation ....E......619 477-2125
2626 Southport Way Ste F National City (91950) ***(P-2455)***
Family Medicine Center Torr ....F......310 326-8600
2841 Lomita Blvd Ste 220 Torrance (90505) ***(P-7888)***
Famoso Nut, Mc Farland *Also called Amaretto Orchards LLC* ***(P-23272)***
Famous Amos Chclat Chip Cookie, Stockton *Also called Murray Biscuit Company LLC* ***(P-1322)***
Famsoft Corp ....F......408 452-1550
44946 Osgood Rd Fremont (94539) ***(P-23893)***
Famsoft Corporation ....E......510 683-3940
44946 Osgood Rd Fremont (94539) ***(P-23894)***
Fan Fave Inc ....E......909 975-4999
285 S Dupont Ave Ste 104 Ontario (91761) ***(P-23107)***
Fanboys Window Factory Inc (PA) ....E......626 280-8787
10750 Saint Louis Dr El Monte (91731) ***(P-11954)***
Fancy Models Corp ....F......510 683-0819
48888 Fremont Blvd # 150 Fremont (94538) ***(P-23331)***
Fancy Schmancy Art Frames, Canoga Park *Also called Vitale Home Designs Inc* ***(P-22486)***
Fanfave, Ontario *Also called Fan Fave Inc* ***(P-23107)***
Fanlight Corporation Inc ....F......909 868-6538
3992 Mission Blvd Montclair (91763) ***(P-16862)***
Fanlight Corporation Inc (PA) ....E......909 930-6868
2000 S Grove Ave Bldg B Ontario (91761) ***(P-16863)***
Fanno Saw Works ....F......530 895-1762
224 W 8th Ave Chico (95926) ***(P-11552)***
Fantasea Enterprises Inc ....F......949 673-8545
2901 W Coast Hwy Ste 160 Newport Beach (92663) ***(P-20329)***

Fantasia Distribution Inc......E......714 817-8300
1566 W Embassy St Anaheim (92802) ***(P-2660)***
Fantasia Hookah Tobacco, Anaheim *Also called Fantasia Distribution Inc* ***(P-2660)***
Fantasy Inc......D......510 486-2038
2600 10th St Ste 100 Berkeley (94710) ***(P-17321)***
Fantasy Activewear Inc (PA)......E......213 705-4111
5383 Alcoa Ave Vernon (90058) ***(P-2784)***
Fantasy Dyeing & Finishing Inc......D......323 983-9988
5383 Alcoa Ave Vernon (90058) ***(P-2785)***
Fantasy Manufacturing, Vernon *Also called Fantasy Activewear Inc* ***(P-2784)***
Fantasy Manufacturing Inc......F......707 838-7686
7716 Bell Rd Windsor (95492) ***(P-15951)***
Fante Inc (PA)......E......650 697-7525
2898 W Winton Ave Hayward (94545) ***(P-2322)***
Fantom Drives, Torrance *Also called Bnl Technologies Inc* ***(P-15009)***
Fanuc America Corporation......E......949 595-2700
25951 Commercentre Dr Lake Forest (92630) ***(P-14465)***
Fanuc Robotics West, Lake Forest *Also called Fanuc America Corporation* ***(P-14465)***
Fanuccicharter Oak Winery......F......707 963-2298
831 Charter Oak Ave Saint Helena (94574) ***(P-1697)***
Far Niente Wine Estates, Oakville *Also called Far Niente Winery Inc* ***(P-1698)***
Far Niente Winery Inc......D......707 944-2861
1350 Acacia Dr Oakville (94562) ***(P-1698)***
Far West Equipment Rentals......F......916 645-2929
649 7th St Lincoln (95648) ***(P-10756)***
Far West Meats, Highland *Also called Raemica Inc* ***(P-491)***
Far West Rice Inc......E......530 891-1339
3455 Nelson Rd Nelson (95958) ***(P-1039)***
Far West Technology Inc......F......805 964-3615
330 S Kellogg Ave Goleta (93117) ***(P-21472)***
Farallon Brands Inc (PA)......F......510 550-4299
33300 Central Ave Union City (94587) ***(P-3616)***
Farasis Energy Usa Inc......D......510 732-6600
21363 Cabot Blvd Hayward (94545) ***(P-16645)***
Farbotech Color Inc......F......909 596-9330
1630 Yeager Ave La Verne (91750) ***(P-8913)***
Farchitecture Bb LLC......E......917 701-2777
8588 Washington Blvd Culver City (90232) ***(P-642)***
Fargo Choice Foods LLC......E......510 774-0064
2885 Adeline St Oakland (94608) ***(P-1201)***
Farley Interlocking Pav Stones, Palm Desert *Also called Farley Paving Stone Co Inc* ***(P-10570)***
Farley Machine Inc......F......661 397-4987
1600 S Union Ave Bakersfield (93307) ***(P-13775)***
Farley Paving Stone Co Inc......D......760 773-3960
75135 Sheryl Ave Ste A Palm Desert (92211) ***(P-10570)***
Farlight LLC......F......310 830-0181
460 W 5th St San Pedro (90731) ***(P-17034)***
Farlows Scientific Glassblowing, Grass Valley *Also called Farlows Scntfic Glssblwing Inc* ***(P-10305)***
Farlows Scntfic Glssblwing Inc......E......530 477-5513
962 Golden Gate Ter Ste B Grass Valley (95945) ***(P-10305)***
Farmdale Creamery Inc......D......909 888-4938
1049 W Base Line St San Bernardino (92411) ***(P-698)***
Farmer Bros Co......E......858 292-7578
7855 Ostrow St Ste A San Diego (92111) ***(P-2289)***
Farmer Bros Co......F......510 638-1660
20671 Corsair Blvd Hayward (94545) ***(P-2290)***
Farmer Bros Co......F......661 663-9908
8802 Swigert Ct Bakersfield (93311) ***(P-2291)***
Farmer Bros Co......F......530 343-3165
480 Ryan Ave Ste 100 Chico (95973) ***(P-2292)***
Farmer Bros Co......E......209 466-0203
4243 Arch Rd Stockton (95215) ***(P-2293)***
Farmers Brothers Coffee, Hayward *Also called Farmer Bros Co* ***(P-2290)***
Farmers Brothers Coffee, Stockton *Also called Farmer Bros Co* ***(P-2293)***
Farmers International, Chico *Also called Cal Traders* ***(P-1423)***
Farmers Rice Cooperative (PA)......E......916 923-5100
2566 River Plaza Dr Sacramento (95833) ***(P-1040)***
Farmers Rice Cooperative......E......916 373-5549
1800 Terminal Rd Sacramento (95820) ***(P-1041)***
Farmers Rice Cooperative......C......916 373-5500
2224 Industrial Blvd West Sacramento (95691) ***(P-1042)***
Farmers Rice Cooperative......C......916 373-5500
2224 Industrial Blvd West Sacramento (95691) ***(P-1043)***
Farmhouse Culture Inc (PA)......E......831 466-0499
182 Lewis Rd Royal Oaks (95076) ***(P-7889)***
Farr West Fashions......F......831 661-5039
580 Cathedral Dr Aptos (95003) ***(P-3441)***
Farrar Grinding Company......F......323 678-4879
347 E Beach Ave Inglewood (90302) ***(P-20102)***
Farrell Brothers Holding Corp......F......714 630-3417
1137 N Armando St Anaheim (92806) ***(P-15952)***
Farsi Jewelry Mfg Co Inc......F......213 624-0043
631 Suth Olive St Ste 565 Los Angeles (90014) ***(P-22519)***
Farstone Technology Inc......C......949 336-4321
184 Technology Dr Ste 205 Irvine (92618) ***(P-19218)***
Fashion 1001 Nights, Los Angeles *Also called Night Fashion Inc* ***(P-3245)***
Fashion Blacksmith Inc......F......707 464-9219
121 Starfish Way Crescent City (95531) ***(P-20330)***
Fashion Camp......E......714 259-0946
2477 Park Ave Tustin (92782) ***(P-2934)***
Fashion Queen Mania Inc......E......213 788-7310
800 E 12th St Ste 428 Los Angeles (90021) ***(P-3266)***
Fashion Today Inc......E......213 744-1636
1100 S San Pedro St Ste A Los Angeles (90015) ***(P-3324)***
Fashion Today Inc (PA)......F......213 744-1636
3100 S Grand Ave Fl 3 Los Angeles (90007) ***(P-3325)***
Fast Access Inc......F......909 748-1245
1765 Howard Pl Redlands (92373) ***(P-10571)***
Fast Ad Inc......D......714 835-9353
224 S Center St Santa Ana (92703) ***(P-23108)***
Fast Sportswear Inc......D......323 720-1078
6400 E Washington Blvd Commerce (90040) ***(P-3326)***
Fast Turn Machining Inc......F......408 720-6888
3087 Lawrence Expy Santa Clara (95051) ***(P-15953)***
Fast Undercar, San Diego *Also called Atm Plus Inc* ***(P-9285)***
Fastec Imaging Corporation......E......858 592-2342
17150 Via Dl Cmpo 301 San Diego (92127) ***(P-22422)***
Fastener Depot Inc......F......530 621-3070
6166 Enterprise Dr Ste A Diamond Springs (95619) ***(P-12677)***
Fastener Innovation Tech Inc......D......310 538-1111
19300 S Susana Rd Compton (90221) ***(P-12631)***
Fastener Technology Corp......D......818 764-6467
7415 Fulton Ave North Hollywood (91605) ***(P-23001)***
Fastrak Manufacturing Svcs Inc......E......408 298-6414
1275 Alma Ct San Jose (95112) ***(P-18911)***
Fastramp, San Diego *Also called Stats Chippac Test Svcs Inc* ***(P-18580)***
Fastramp, Fremont *Also called Stats Chippac Test Svcs Inc* ***(P-18581)***
Fastsigns, Hayward *Also called Justipher Inc* ***(P-23144)***
Fastsigns......F......415 537-6900
650 Harrison St San Francisco (94107) ***(P-23109)***
Fastsigns......F......650 345-0900
2130 S El Camino Real San Mateo (94403) ***(P-23110)***
Fat Performance Inc......F......714 637-2889
1558 N Case St Orange (92867) ***(P-19655)***
Fat Wreck Chords Inc......F......415 284-1790
2196 Palou Ave San Francisco (94124) ***(P-17322)***
Fate Therapeutics Inc......F......858 875-1800
3535 General Atomics Ct # 20 San Diego (92121) ***(P-8300)***
Faust Printing Inc......E......909 980-1577
8656 Utica Ave Ste 100 Rancho Cucamonga (91730) ***(P-6569)***
Faustinos Chair Factory Inc......E......323 724-8055
2425 S Malt Ave Commerce (90040) ***(P-4796)***
Fax Star, Costa Mesa *Also called S E P E Inc* ***(P-14971)***
Fay & Quartermaine Machining, El Monte *Also called Fay and Qrtrmine McHining Corp* ***(P-14159)***
Fay and Qrtrmine McHining Corp......F......323 686-0224
2745 Seaman Ave El Monte (91733) ***(P-14159)***
Fay's Foods, North Hollywood *Also called Fayes Foods Inc* ***(P-2456)***
Fayes Foods Inc......E......818 508-8392
10650 Burbank Blvd North Hollywood (91601) ***(P-2456)***
FBproductions Inc......D......818 773-9337
12722 Rverside Dr Ste 204 Valley Village (91607) ***(P-6570)***
Fbs Floor Box Systems, Murrieta *Also called Jeluz Electric Ltd LLC* ***(P-19336)***
Fc Global Realty Incorporated......E......760 602-3300
2375 Camino Vida Roble B Carlsbad (92011) ***(P-21712)***
Fc Management Services......E......805 499-0050
2001 Anchor Ct Ste B Newbury Park (91320) ***(P-14466)***
Fca LLC......F......805 477-9901
3810 Transport St Ventura (93003) ***(P-4336)***
FCkingston Co......D......310 326-8287
23201 Normandie Ave Torrance (90501) ***(P-13305)***
Fcp Inc......D......951 678-4571
23100 Baxter Rd Wildomar (92595) ***(P-12545)***
Fcp Inc......E......805 684-1117
4125 Market St Ste 14 Ventura (93003) ***(P-12546)***
Fd, Newbury Park *Also called Follmer Development Inc* ***(P-7413)***
Fdc Aerofilter, El Dorado Hills *Also called Filtration Development Co LLC* ***(P-18715)***
FDS Manufacturing Company (PA)......C......909 591-1733
2200 S Reservoir St Pomona (91766) ***(P-5507)***
Fear of God LLC......E......310 466-9751
1200 S Santa Fe Ave Ste A Los Angeles (90021) ***(P-3079)***
Fear of God LLC (PA)......F......213 235-7985
3940 Lrl Cyn Blvd Ste 42 Studio City (91604) ***(P-3080)***
Feasible Inc......F......310 702-5803
1175 Park Ave Emeryville (94608) ***(P-18912)***
Feather Farm Inc......F......707 255-8833
1181 4th Ave NAPA (94559) ***(P-13411)***
Feather Publishing Company Inc (PA)......E......530 283-0800
287 Lawrence St Quincy (95971) ***(P-5632)***
Feather Publishing Company Inc......F......530 257-5321
100 Grand Ave Susanville (96130) ***(P-5633)***
Feather River Bulletin, Quincy *Also called Feather Publishing Company Inc* ***(P-5632)***
Feather River Concrete Product......F......530 532-7915
675 State Box Rd Oroville (95965) ***(P-10757)***
Featherock Inc (PA)......F......818 882-3888
20219 Bahama St Chatsworth (91311) ***(P-387)***
Featherrock, Chatsworth *Also called United States Pumice Company* ***(P-394)***
Fed Ex Kinkos Ofc & Print Ctr......F......805 604-6000
255 W Stanley Ave Ventura (93001) ***(P-6571)***
Federal Aviation ADM......E......310 640-9640
2250 E Imperial Hwy # 140 El Segundo (90245) ***(P-20103)***
Federal Buyers Guide Inc (PA)......F......805 963-7470
324 Palm Ave Santa Barbara (93101) ***(P-6234)***
Federal Custom Cable LLC......E......949 851-3114
1891 Alton Pkwy Ste A Irvine (92606) ***(P-18913)***
Federal Heath Sign Company LLC......C......760 941-0715
4602 North Ave Oceanside (92056) ***(P-23111)***
Federal Heath Sign Company LLC......F......760 901-7447
3609 Ocean Ranch Blvd # 204 Oceanside (92056) ***(P-23112)***
Federal Industries Inc......F......310 297-4040
645 Hawaii St El Segundo (90245) ***(P-13353)***
Federal Manufacturing Corp......E......818 341-9825
9825 De Soto Ave Chatsworth (91311) ***(P-12678)***
Federal Prison Industries......E......805 735-2771
3901 Klein Blvd Lompoc (93436) ***(P-23113)***

ALPHABETIC

Federal Prison Industries......C......805 736-4154
3600 Guard Rd Lompoc (93436) ***(P-4570)***
Federal Signal Corporation......E......714 871-3336
1108 E Raymond Way Anaheim (92801) ***(P-19469)***
Feedstuffs Processing Co......F......925 820-5454
112 Lark Ct Alamo (94507) ***(P-1093)***
Feemster Co Inc......E......909 621-9772
119 Yale Ave Claremont (91711) ***(P-1202)***
Feeney Inc......E......510 893-9473
2603 Union St Oakland (94607) ***(P-13412)***
Fei Efa Inc (HQ)......D......510 897-6800
3400 W Warren Ave Fremont (94538) ***(P-18768)***
Fei-Zyfer Inc (HQ)......E......714 933-4000
7321 Lincoln Way Garden Grove (92841) ***(P-17519)***
Feihe International Inc (PA)......A......626 757-8885
2275 Huntington Dr # 278 San Marino (91108) ***(P-587)***
Feit Electric Company Inc (PA)......C......562 463-2852
4901 Gregg Rd Pico Rivera (90660) ***(P-16969)***
Feitian Technologies Us Inc......F......408 352-5553
4677 Old Ironsides Dr # 312 Santa Clara (95054) ***(P-19310)***
Felbro Inc......C......323 263-8686
3666 E Olympic Blvd Los Angeles (90023) ***(P-4976)***
Felbro Food Products Inc......E......323 936-5266
5700 W Adams Blvd Los Angeles (90016) ***(P-2207)***
Felix Tool & Engineering......E......818 994-9401
14535 Bessemer St Van Nuys (91411) ***(P-14052)***
Fellyr International Inc......F......626 960-5111
13453 Brooks Dr Ste B Baldwin Park (91706) ***(P-3327)***
Fema Electronics Corporation......E......714 825-0140
22 Corporate Park Irvine (92606) ***(P-18914)***
Femco, Hollister *Also called Food Equipment Mfg Co* ***(P-14361)***
Femi Data Telecommunication, Harbor City *Also called Adegbesan Adefemi* ***(P-14880)***
Fence Factory......F......805 462-1362
2650 El Camino Real Atascadero (93422) ***(P-13413)***
Fence Factory......F......805 644-5482
1482 Callens Rd Ventura (93003) ***(P-12475)***
Fencer Enterprises LLC......F......916 635-1700
3469 Fitzgerald Rd Rancho Cordova (95742) ***(P-11093)***
Fenchem Inc (PA)......F......909 597-8880
15308 El Prado Rd Chino (91710) ***(P-8492)***
Fender Musical Instrs Corp......A......480 596-9690
301 Cessna Cir Corona (92880) ***(P-22620)***
Fenico Precision Castings Inc......D......562 634-5000
7805 Madison St Paramount (90723) ***(P-11416)***
Fenini, Baldwin Park *Also called Fellyr International Inc* ***(P-3327)***
Fenix International Inc......B......415 754-9222
30 Cleveland St San Francisco (94103) ***(P-16550)***
Fenix Space Inc......F......909 382-5677
294 S Leland San Bernardino (92408) ***(P-20446)***
Feral Productions LLC......E......510 791-5392
1935 N Macarthur Dr Tracy (95376) ***(P-15954)***
Ferco Color & Compounding Inc......E......909 930-0773
5498 Vine St Chino (91710) ***(P-7563)***
Ferco Plastic Products, Chino *Also called Ferco Color & Compounding Inc* ***(P-7563)***
Fermented Sciences Inc......F......805 798-2790
910 E Aliso St Ojai (93023) ***(P-1526)***
Ferminics Opto-Technology Corp......F......805 582-0155
4555 Runway St Simi Valley (93063) ***(P-17368)***
Fernqvist Labeling Solutions, Mountain View *Also called Fernqvist Retail Systems Inc* ***(P-6953)***
Fernqvist Retail Systems Inc (HQ)......F......650 428-0330
2544 Leghorn St Mountain View (94043) ***(P-6953)***
Ferraco Inc (HQ)......E......562 988-2414
2933 Long Beach Blvd Long Beach (90806) ***(P-22012)***
Ferrar-Crano Vnyrds Winery LLC (PA)......C......707 433-6700
8761 Dry Creek Rd Healdsburg (95448) ***(P-1699)***
Ferrari Intrcnnect Sltions Inc......F......951 684-8034
4385 E Lowell St Ste A Ontario (91761) ***(P-18915)***
Ferro Corporation......F......442 224-6100
1395 Aspen Way Vista (92081) ***(P-7496)***
Ferrosaur Inc......F......530 246-7843
4821 Mountain Lakes Blvd Redding (96003) ***(P-11793)***
Ferrotec (usa) Corporation......E......925 371-4170
4569 Las Positas Rd Ste C Livermore (94551) ***(P-9229)***
Ferrotec Temescal, Livermore *Also called Ferrotec (usa) Corporation* ***(P-9229)***
Fetish Group Inc (PA)......E......323 587-7873
1013 S Los Angeles St # 700 Los Angeles (90015) ***(P-3081)***
Fetters U.S.A., San Francisco *Also called Mr S Leather* ***(P-3520)***
Fetzer Production Facility, Paso Robles *Also called Fetzer Vineyards* ***(P-1701)***
Fetzer Vineyards (HQ)......C......707 744-1250
12901 Old River Rd Hopland (95449) ***(P-1700)***
Fetzer Vineyards......F......805 467-0192
8998 N River Rd Paso Robles (93446) ***(P-1701)***
Fhi Brands, Norwalk *Also called AG Global Products LLC* ***(P-16824)***
FI, El Segundo *Also called Federal Industries Inc* ***(P-13353)***
Fibco Composites Inc......F......714 269-1118
1220 Hearthside Ct Fullerton (92831) ***(P-20576)***
Fiber Care Baths Inc......B......760 246-0019
9832 Yucca Rd Ste A Adelanto (92301) ***(P-9586)***
Fiber Optic Cable Shop, Richmond *Also called Support Systems Intl Corp* ***(P-19097)***
Fiber Systems Inc......E......831 430-0700
380 Encinal St Ste 150 Santa Cruz (95060) ***(P-17369)***
Fiberglass Fabricators, Orange *Also called Lido Industries Inc* ***(P-9877)***
Fiberlite Centrifuge LLC......D......408 492-1109
422 Aldo Ave Santa Clara (95054) ***(P-21228)***
Fiberoptic Systems Inc......E......805 579-6600
60 Moreland Rd Ste A Simi Valley (93065) ***(P-11303)***
Fibersense & Signals Inc......F......408 941-1900
4423 Fortran Ct Ste 111 San Jose (95134) ***(P-17370)***
Fibreform Electronics Inc......E......714 898-9641
5341 Argosy Ave Huntington Beach (92649) ***(P-15955)***
Fibreform Precision Machining, Huntington Beach *Also called Fibreform Electronics Inc* ***(P-15955)***
Fibrogen Inc (PA)......C......415 978-1200
409 Illinois St San Francisco (94158) ***(P-7890)***
Ficcare, City of Industry *Also called Visionmax Inc* ***(P-3432)***
Field Applied Cmposite Systems, Monrovia *Also called Air Logistics Corporation* ***(P-9614)***
Field Foundation......E......562 921-3567
15306 Carmenita Rd Santa Fe Springs (90670) ***(P-197)***
Field Manufacturing Corp (PA)......E......310 781-9292
1751 Torrance Blvd Ste H Torrance (90501) ***(P-4977)***
Field Stone Winery & Vineyard......F......707 433-7266
10075 Highway 128 Healdsburg (95448) ***(P-1702)***
Field Support Services, Coronado *Also called Northrop Grumman Systems Corp* ***(P-20659)***
Field Time Target Training LLC......E......714 677-2841
8230 Electric Ave Stanton (90680) ***(P-13271)***
Field To Family Natural Foods......F......707 765-6756
224 Weller St Ste C Petaluma (94952) ***(P-510)***
Fieldcentrix Inc......E......949 784-5000
8 Hughes Irvine (92618) ***(P-23895)***
Fieldpiece Instruments Inc......F......714 634-1844
1636 W Collins Ave Orange (92867) ***(P-21037)***
Fierra Design CL Manufactures, Los Angeles *Also called Fierra Design Inc* ***(P-3082)***
Fierra Design Inc......E......213 622-2426
1359 Channing St Los Angeles (90021) ***(P-3082)***
Fierrito Metal Stamping......E......818 362-6136
12358 San Fernando Rd Sylmar (91342) ***(P-15956)***
Fierritos Inc......E......818 362-6136
12358 San Fernando Rd Sylmar (91342) ***(P-15957)***
Fiesta Concession, Vernon *Also called Mahar Manufacturing Corp* ***(P-22649)***
Fiesta Mexican Foods Inc......E......760 344-3580
979 G St Brawley (92227) ***(P-1203)***
Fife Metal Fabricating Inc......F......530 243-4696
4191 Eastside Rd Redding (96001) ***(P-11794)***
Figure 8, Torrance *Also called Nothing To Wear Inc* ***(P-3186)***
Filbur Manufacturing LLC......E......714 228-6000
20 Centerpointe Dr # 110 La Palma (90623) ***(P-14814)***
Filbur Pool & Spa Filtration, La Palma *Also called Filbur Manufacturing LLC* ***(P-14814)***
Filet Menu Inc......E......310 202-8000
1830 S La Cienega Blvd Los Angeles (90035) ***(P-6954)***
Filetrail Inc......E......408 289-1300
1990 The Alameda San Jose (95126) ***(P-23896)***
Filipino Channel, Stockton *Also called Aguda Wilson Ramos* ***(P-17440)***
Filmetrics Inc (PA)......E......858 573-9300
10655 Roselle St Ste 200 San Diego (92121) ***(P-21229)***
Filtec, Torrance *Also called Industrial Dynamics Co Ltd* ***(P-14478)***
Filter Concepts Incorporated......E......714 545-7003
22895 Eastpark Dr Yorba Linda (92887) ***(P-18714)***
Filter Pump Industries, Sun Valley *Also called Penguin Pumps Incorporated* ***(P-14593)***
Filthy Grill Inc......F......818 282-2017
70 N Dewey Ave Newbury Park (91320) ***(P-16811)***
Filtration Development Co LLC......F......415 884-0555
3920 Sandstone Dr El Dorado Hills (95762) ***(P-18715)***
Filtration Group LLC......D......707 525-8633
498 Aviation Blvd Santa Rosa (95403) ***(P-14660)***
Filtration Technology Group, Cerritos *Also called Ftg Inc* ***(P-19663)***
Filtronics Inc......F......714 630-5040
3726 E Miraloma Ave Anaheim (92806) ***(P-15514)***
Final Data Inc......E......818 835-9560
5950 Canoga Ave Ste 220 Woodland Hills (91367) ***(P-6235)***
Final Finish Inc......E......562 777-7774
10910 Norwalk Blvd Santa Fe Springs (90670) ***(P-2844)***
Finance Department, Hercules *Also called Bio-RAD Laboratories Inc* ***(P-21185)***
Finart Inc (PA)......F......714 957-1757
201 W Dyer Rd Ste C Santa Ana (92707) ***(P-15958)***
Finddoctr Inc......F......657 888-2629
9550 Bolsa Ave Ste 213 Westminster (92683) ***(P-6236)***
Findly, San Francisco *Also called First Advantage Talent Managem* ***(P-23900)***
Fine Electronic Assembly Inc......E......858 573-0887
4887 Mercury St San Diego (92111) ***(P-17874)***
Fine Ptch Elctrnic Assmbly LLC......E......626 337-2800
5106 Azusa Canyon Rd Irwindale (91706) ***(P-17875)***
Fine Quality Metal Finshg Inc......F......562 983-7425
1640 Daisy Ave Long Beach (90813) ***(P-13009)***
Fineline Architectural Mllwk, Costa Mesa *Also called Fineline Woodworking Inc* ***(P-4044)***
Fineline Carpentry Inc......E......650 592-2442
1297 Old County Rd Belmont (94002) ***(P-4196)***
Fineline Circuits & Technology......E......714 529-2942
594 Apollo St Ste A Brea (92821) ***(P-17876)***
Fineline Industries Inc (PA)......C......209 384-0255
2047 Grogan Ave Merced (95341) ***(P-20331)***
Fineline Woodworking Inc......D......714 540-5468
1139 Baker St Costa Mesa (92626) ***(P-4044)***
Finelite Inc (PA)......C......510 441-1100
30500 Whipple Rd Union City (94587) ***(P-17035)***
Finest Food Inc......F......858 699-4746
6491 Weathers Pl Ste A San Diego (92121) ***(P-2457)***
Finis Inc (PA)......E......925 454-0111
5849 W Schulte Rd Ste 104 Tracy (95377) ***(P-22800)***
Finis USA, Tracy *Also called Finis Inc* ***(P-22800)***
Finisar Corporation (HQ)......E......408 548-1000
1389 Moffett Park Dr Sunnyvale (94089) ***(P-17371)***
Finisar Corporation......F......408 548-1000
41762 Christy St Fremont (94538) ***(P-18235)***
Finish Renu Car Care, Corona *Also called Renu Chem Inc* ***(P-8414)***
Finishing Touch Moulding Inc......D......760 444-1019
6190 Corte Del Cedro Carlsbad (92011) ***(P-4197)***

Finix Payments Inc....F....714 417-2727
408 2nd St Ste 202 San Francisco (94107) *(P-23897)*
Finntech Inc....F....310 323-0790
1930 W 169th St Gardena (90247) *(P-15959)*
Fintech Platform, Los Gatos *Also called Healthywealthyhack Inc (P-23973)*
Fiola Development, Huntington Beach *Also called Fiolas Development LLC (P-10572)*
Fiolas Development LLC....F....714 893-7559
5362 Bolsa Ave Ste H Huntington Beach (92649) *(P-10572)*
Fiorano Software Inc....D....650 326-1136
230 California Ave # 103 Palo Alto (94306) *(P-23898)*
Fiore Di Pasta Inc....D....559 457-0431
4776 E Jensen Ave Fresno (93725) *(P-2458)*
Fiore Stone Inc....E....909 424-0221
19930 Jolora Ave Corona (92881) *(P-10573)*
Fiorellos Italian Ice Cream....F....415 459-8004
3100 Kerner Blvd Ste Hh San Rafael (94901) *(P-643)*
Firan Tech Group USA Corp (HQ)....F....818 407-4024
20750 Marilla St Chatsworth (91311) *(P-20577)*
Fire & Earth Ceramics....F....303 442-0245
418 Santander Dr San Ramon (94583) *(P-10441)*
Fire & Safety Electronics Inc....E....714 850-1320
3160 Pullman St Costa Mesa (92626) *(P-16716)*
Fire and Light Originals LP....F....707 825-7500
100 Ericson Ct Ste 100 # 100 Arcata (95521) *(P-10359)*
Fire Mountain Beverage....E....661 362-0716
27240 Turnberry Ln # 200 Valencia (91355) *(P-2075)*
Fire Windows and Doors, Redlands *Also called Coast To Coast Mfg LLC (P-9712)*
Fireblast Global Inc....E....951 277-8319
545 Monica Cir Corona (92880) *(P-14815)*
Firebrand Media LLC....E....949 715-4100
580 Broadway St Ste 301 Laguna Beach (92651) *(P-6572)*
Fireeye Inc (PA)....C....408 321-6300
601 Mccarthy Blvd Milpitas (95035) *(P-23899)*
Firefighter Gas Safety Pdts, Santa Ana *Also called Little Firefighter Corporation (P-13311)*
Firelight Glass, San Leandro *Also called Vitrico Corp (P-10332)*
Firequick Products Inc....F....760 371-4279
1137 Red Rock Inyokern Rd Inyokern (93527) *(P-14816)*
Firestone Vineyard LP....D....805 688-3940
5000 Zaca Station Rd Los Olivos (93441) *(P-1703)*
Firestone Walker Inc....E....805 254-4205
620 Mcmurray Rd Buellton (93427) *(P-1527)*
Firestone Walker Inc (PA)....C....805 225-5911
1400 Ramada Dr Paso Robles (93446) *(P-1528)*
Firestone Walker Brewing Co, Penn Valley *Also called Firestone Walker LLC (P-1529)*
Firestone Walker Brewing Co, Buellton *Also called Firestone Walker Inc (P-1527)*
Firestone Walker Brewing Co, Paso Robles *Also called Firestone Walker Inc (P-1528)*
Firestone Walker LLC....D....805 225-5911
10130 Commercial Ave Penn Valley (95946) *(P-1529)*
Firetide Inc (HQ)....F....408 399-7771
2105 S Bascom Ave Ste 220 Campbell (95008) *(P-15228)*
Firmenich....C....714 535-2871
424 S Atchison St Anaheim (92805) *(P-8738)*
First Advantage Talent Managem....E....415 446-3930
98 Battery St Ste 400 San Francisco (94111) *(P-23900)*
First American Building Svcs....F....415 299-7597
6 Commodore Dr Unit 530 Emeryville (94608) *(P-20794)*
First Choice International....F....310 537-1500
1201 W Artesia Blvd Compton (90220) *(P-21713)*
First Church Christ, Scientist, Santa Barbara *Also called Christian Science Church (P-5590)*
First Circuit Inc....F....760 560-0530
7701 Garboso Pl Carlsbad (92009) *(P-17877)*
First Class Foods, Hawthorne *Also called Firstclass Foods - Trojan Inc (P-408)*
First Class Packaging Inc....E....619 579-7166
280 Cypress Ln Ste D El Cajon (92020) *(P-5161)*
First Data Bank, South San Francisco *Also called First Databank Inc (P-6237)*
First Databank Inc (HQ)....D....800 633-3453
701 Gateway Blvd Ste 600 South San Francisco (94080) *(P-6237)*
First Energy Services Inc....E....661 387-1972
1031 Carrier Parkway Ave Bakersfield (93308) *(P-198)*
First Finish Inc....E....310 631-6717
11126 Wright Rd Lynwood (90262) *(P-2688)*
First Gold Corp....F....530 677-5974
3108 Ponte Morino Dr # 210 Cameron Park (95682) *(P-3)*
First Impressions Printing....E....510 784-0811
25030 Viking St Hayward (94545) *(P-6573)*
First Lithium LLC....F....310 489-6266
17244 S Main St Carson (90749) *(P-19165)*
First Press, North Hollywood *Also called 6480 Corporation (P-6969)*
First Responder Fire....F....562 842-6602
19146 Stare St Northridge (91324) *(P-14817)*
First Solar Inc....F....415 935-2500
135 Main St Fl 6 San Francisco (94105) *(P-18236)*
First Solar Electric, San Francisco *Also called First Solar Inc (P-18236)*
First Source Lighting, Auburn *Also called Gara Inc (P-17038)*
First Tactical LLC....A....855 665-3410
4300 Spyres Way Modesto (95356) *(P-2964)*
Firstclass Foods - Trojan Inc....C....310 676-2500
12500 Inglewood Ave Hawthorne (90250) *(P-408)*
Firstelement Fuel Inc....F....949 274-5701
2549 Eastbluff Dr 334 Newport Beach (92660) *(P-8739)*
Firth Rixson Inc....E....909 483-2200
11711 Arrow Rte Rancho Cucamonga (91730) *(P-12708)*
Fischer Cstm Cmmunications Inc (PA)....E....310 303-3300
19220 Normandie Ave B Torrance (90502) *(P-21038)*
Fischer Mold Incorporated....D....951 279-1140
393 Meyer Cir Corona (92879) *(P-9787)*
Fischler Investments Inc (HQ)....F....951 479-4682
2026 Cecilia Cir Corona (92881) *(P-2208)*

Fish Bowl, Los Angeles *Also called Second Generation Inc (P-3402)*
Fish House Foods Inc....B....760 597-1270
1263 Linda Vista Dr San Marcos (92078) *(P-2259)*
Fish On Rice LLC....F....619 696-6262
3250 Grey Hawk Ct Carlsbad (92010) *(P-1530)*
Fisher & Paykel, Costa Mesa *Also called Dynamic Cooking Systems Inc (P-15508)*
Fisher & Paykel Appliances Inc (HQ)....C....949 790-8900
695 Town Center Dr # 180 Costa Mesa (92626) *(P-16850)*
Fisher Graphic Inds A Cal Corp....B....209 577-0181
1137 Graphics Dr Modesto (95351) *(P-14321)*
Fisher Manufacturing Co Inc (PA)....E....559 685-5200
1900 S O St Tulare (93274) *(P-11667)*
Fisher Nut Company....F....209 527-0108
137 N Hart Rd Modesto (95358) *(P-2459)*
Fisher Printing Inc (PA)....C....714 998-9200
2257 N Pacific St Orange (92865) *(P-6574)*
Fisher Printing & Stamping Co....F....323 933-9193
5038 Venice Blvd Los Angeles (90019) *(P-7064)*
Fisher Sand & Gravel Co....F....602 619-0325
24560 Cooperstown Rd Oakdale (95361) *(P-339)*
Fishermans Pride Prcessors Inc....B....323 232-1980
4510 S Alameda St Vernon (90058) *(P-2260)*
Fisker Auto & Tech Group LLC....C....714 723-3247
3080 Airway Ave Costa Mesa (92626) *(P-19470)*
Fit-Line Inc....E....714 549-9091
2901 Tech Ctr Santa Ana (92705) *(P-9788)*
Fitbit Inc (PA)....B....415 513-1000
199 Fremont St Fl 14 San Francisco (94105) *(P-21473)*
Fitness Warehouse LLC (PA)....E....858 578-7676
9990 Alesmith Ct Ste 130 San Diego (92126) *(P-22801)*
Fitpro USA LLC....F....877 645-5776
1911 2nd St Livermore (94550) *(P-7660)*
Fittings That Fit Inc....F....909 248-2808
4628 Mission Blvd Montclair (91763) *(P-13414)*
Fitucci LLC....F....818 785-3841
14753 Oxnard St Van Nuys (91411) *(P-4198)*
Fitzgerald Designers & Mfrs, San Francisco *Also called J F Fitzgerald Company Inc (P-4647)*
Fitzgerald Formliners, Santa Ana *Also called Prime Forming & Cnstr Sups (P-10632)*
Five Corner Conservation Inc....F....818 792-1805
13654 Victory Blvd # 327 Van Nuys (91401) *(P-15960)*
Five Flavors Herbs....F....510 923-0178
344 40th St Oakland (94609) *(P-588)*
Five Keys Inc....E....209 358-7971
150 E Broadway Ave Atwater (95301) *(P-3083)*
Five Prime Therapeutics Inc....C....415 365-5600
111 Oyster Point Blvd South San Francisco (94080) *(P-7891)*
Five Star Food Containers Inc....D....626 437-6219
250 Eastgate Rd Barstow (92311) *(P-9529)*
Five Star Gourmet Foods Inc....A....909 390-0032
3880 Ebony St Ontario (91761) *(P-959)*
Five Star Juice, Torrance *Also called La Ejuice LLC (P-2661)*
Five Star Lumber Company LLC....E....831 422-4493
655 Brunken Ave Salinas (93901) *(P-4366)*
Five Star Lumber Company LLC (PA)....E....510 795-7204
6899 Smith Ave Newark (94560) *(P-4367)*
Five Star Pallet Co, Newark *Also called Five Star Lumber Company LLC (P-4367)*
Five Star Trailers Inc....F....559 498-0337
221 M St Fresno (93721) *(P-19821)*
Five-Star Graphics Inc....F....310 325-6881
2628 Woodbury Dr Torrance (90503) *(P-6575)*
Five9 Inc (PA)....C....925 201-2000
4000 Executive Pkwy # 400 San Ramon (94583) *(P-23901)*
Fixture Design & Mfg Co....E....714 776-3104
4848 Lakeview Ave Ste E Yorba Linda (92886) *(P-5060)*
Fixtures By Design LLC....F....714 572-5406
2951 Saturn St Ste Unitb Brea (92821) *(P-4904)*
Fixtures Unlimited, Gardena *Also called Tony Glazing Specialties Co (P-4950)*
Fizzy Color LLC....F....408 623-6705
3561 Homestead Rd Ste 231 Santa Clara (95051) *(P-6576)*
Fja Industries Inc....F....408 727-0100
1230 Coleman Ave Santa Clara (95050) *(P-14818)*
Flagcrafters Inc....E....619 585-1044
1120 Bay Blvd Ste E Chula Vista (91911) *(P-3842)*
Flame & Wax Inc....E....949 752-4000
2900 Mccabe Way Irvine (92614) *(P-23332)*
Flame Gard Inc....D....323 888-8707
6825 E Washington Blvd Los Angeles (90040) *(P-14819)*
Flame Out Inc....E....323 221-0000
2623 N San Fernando Rd Los Angeles (90065) *(P-23333)*
Flame-Spray Inc....E....619 283-2007
4674 Alvarado Canyon Rd San Diego (92120) *(P-13178)*
Flamemaster Corporation....E....818 890-1401
13576 Desmond St Pacoima (91331) *(P-8967)*
Flamestower Inc....D....415 699-8650
127 Kissling St San Francisco (94103) *(P-16646)*
Flanagan-Gorham Inc (PA)....F....818 279-2473
2029 Verdugo Blvd Ste 311 Montrose (91020) *(P-409)*
Flannery Inc (PA)....F....818 837-7585
300 Parkside Dr San Fernando (91340) *(P-10876)*
Flannigans Merchandising Inc....E....818 785-7428
15803 Stagg St Van Nuys (91406) *(P-7065)*
Flap Happy Inc....E....310 453-3527
2857 E 11th St Los Angeles (90023) *(P-3493)*
Flare Group....E....714 850-2080
1571 Macarthur Blvd Costa Mesa (92626) *(P-20104)*
Flarelink, Santa Ana *Also called Fit-Line Inc (P-9788)*
Flash Anatomy, Orange *Also called Bryan Edwards Publishing Co (P-6082)*
Flash Back USA....F....805 434-0321
1535 Templeton Rd Templeton (93465) *(P-8301)*

ALPHABETIC

Employee Codes: A=Over 500 employees, B=251-500
C=101-250, D=51-100, E=20-50, F=10-19
2020 California
Manfacturers Register
© Mergent Inc. 1-800-342-5647
1101

Flash Code Solutions LLC ......F......800 633-7467
4727 Wilshire Blvd # 302 Los Angeles (90010) ***(P-23902)***
Flashco Manufacturing Inc (PA) ......E......707 824-4448
150 Todd Rd Ste 400 Santa Rosa (95407) ***(P-11271)***
Flathers Precision Inc ......E......714 966-8505
1311 E Saint Gertrude Pl D Santa Ana (92705) ***(P-15961)***
Flaunt Magazine ......F......323 836-1044
1422 N Highland Ave Los Angeles (90028) ***(P-5935)***
Flavor House Inc ......E......760 246-9131
16378 Koala Rd Adelanto (92301) ***(P-2209)***
Flavorchem Corporation ......E......949 369-7900
271 Calle Pintoresco San Clemente (92672) ***(P-2210)***
Flavors Division, Los Angeles *Also called American Fruits & Flavors LLC* ***(P-2190)***
Fleenor Company Inc (PA) ......E......800 433-2531
2225 Harbor Bay Pkwy Alameda (94502) ***(P-5508)***
Fleenor Company Inc ......E......209 932-0329
4201 E Fremont St Stockton (95215) ***(P-5105)***
Fleenor Paper Company, Alameda *Also called Fleenor Company Inc* ***(P-5508)***
Fleet Management Solutions Inc ......E......800 500-6009
7391 Lincoln Way Garden Grove (92841) ***(P-17520)***
Fleetwood Continental Inc ......D......310 609-1477
19451 S Susana Rd Compton (90221) ***(P-11397)***
Fleetwood Enterprises Inc (HQ) ......C......951 354-3000
1351 Pomona Rd Ste 230 Corona (92882) ***(P-20509)***
Fleetwood Enterprises Inc ......B......951 750-1971
351 Corporate Terrace Cir Corona (92879) ***(P-4446)***
Fleetwood Homes, Riverside *Also called Fleetwood Motor Homes-Califinc* ***(P-19842)***
Fleetwood Homes, Riverside *Also called Cavco Industries Inc* ***(P-4440)***
Fleetwood Homes California Inc (HQ) ......E......951 351-2494
7007 Jurupa Ave Riverside (92504) ***(P-4447)***
Fleetwood Homes of Florida (HQ) ......F......909 261-4274
3125 Myers St Riverside (92503) ***(P-4448)***
Fleetwood Homes of Idaho Inc ......C......951 354-3000
3125 Myers St Riverside (92503) ***(P-4449)***
Fleetwood Homes of Kentucky (HQ) ......F......800 688-1745
1351 Pomona Rd Ste 230 Corona (92882) ***(P-4450)***
Fleetwood Homes of Virginia ......C......951 351-3500
3125 Myers St Riverside (92503) ***(P-4451)***
Fleetwood Motor Homes-Califinc (HQ) ......E......951 354-3000
3125 Myers St Riverside (92503) ***(P-19842)***
Fleetwood Travel Trlrs Ind Inc (HQ) ......F......951 354-3000
3125 Myers St Riverside (92503) ***(P-20484)***
Fleis Chmanns Vinegar, Cerritos *Also called AB Mauri Food Inc* ***(P-2387)***
Fleming Metal Fabricators ......E......323 723-8203
2810 Tanager Ave Commerce (90040) ***(P-19533)***
Fletcher Bldg Holdings USA Inc (HQ) ......D......951 272-8180
1230 Railroad St Corona (92882) ***(P-12212)***
Fletcher Coating Co ......E......714 637-4763
426 W Fletcher Ave Orange (92865) ***(P-13179)***
Flex Interconnect Tech Inc ......E......408 956-8204
1603 Watson Ct Milpitas (95035) ***(P-18916)***
Flex Products Inc ......C......707 525-6866
1402 Mariner Way Santa Rosa (95407) ***(P-21353)***
Flex Technologies Inc ......F......310 323-1801
15151 S Main St Gardena (90248) ***(P-7629)***
Flex-Mate Inc ......F......562 426-7169
1855 E 29th St Ste E Signal Hill (90755) ***(P-11529)***
Flexaust Company Inc (HQ) ......E......619 232-8429
1200 Prospect St Ste 325 La Jolla (92037) ***(P-15962)***
Flexco Inc ......E......562 927-2525
6855 Suva St Bell Gardens (90201) ***(P-20105)***
Flexcon Company Inc ......E......909 465-0408
12840 Reservoir St Chino (91710) ***(P-9404)***
Flexfirm Holdings LLC ......F......323 283-1173
2300 Chico Ave El Monte (91733) ***(P-2897)***
Flexi-Liner, Chino *Also called Liner Technologies Inc* ***(P-9878)***
Flexible Manufacturing LLC ......D......714 259-7996
1719 S Grand Ave Santa Ana (92705) ***(P-18769)***
Flexible Metal Inc (HQ) ......D......678 280-0127
1685 Brandywine Ave Chula Vista (91911) ***(P-13470)***
Flexible Video Systems, Marina Del Rey *Also called Sewer Rodding Equipment Co* ***(P-15576)***
Flexline Inc ......E......562 921-4141
15405 Cornet St Santa Fe Springs (90670) ***(P-7371)***
Flexo-Technologies Inc ......E......626 444-2595
145 Flowerfield Ln La Habra Heights (90631) ***(P-8914)***
Flexstar Technology, Inc, San Jose *Also called Neosem Technology Inc* ***(P-21089)***
Flexsystems Usa Inc ......E......619 401-1858
1308 N Magnolia Ave Ste J El Cajon (92020) ***(P-3843)***
Flextronics America LLC (HQ) ......C......408 576-7000
6201 America Center Dr San Jose (95002) ***(P-17878)***
Flextronics Corporation (HQ) ......B......803 936-5200
6201 America Center Dr Alviso (95002) ***(P-18917)***
Flextronics International Usa ......A......408 576-7000
260 S Milpitas Blvd # 15 Milpitas (95035) ***(P-17879)***
Flextronics Intl PA Inc ......F......408 577-2489
677 Gibraltar Dr Milpitas (95035) ***(P-12213)***
Flextronics Intl USA Inc ......F......510 814-7000
927 Gibraltar Dr Milpitas (95035) ***(P-15229)***
Flextronics Intl USA Inc ......F......408 678-3268
1177 Gibraltar Dr Bldg 9 Milpitas (95035) ***(P-17880)***
Flextronics Intl USA Inc ......B......408 577-2262
925 Lightpost Way Morgan Hill (95037) ***(P-17881)***
Flextronics Intl USA Inc ......A......408 576-7000
847 Gibraltar Dr Milpitas (95035) ***(P-17882)***
Flextronics Semiconductor (HQ) ......E......408 576-7000
2241 Lundy Ave Bldg 2 San Jose (95131) ***(P-18237)***
Flexy Foam, Chino *Also called Inter Packing Inc* ***(P-9552)***
Flight Environments Inc ......E......805 226-2912
570 Linne Rd Ste 100 Paso Robles (93446) ***(P-20106)***
Flight Metals LLC ......F......800 838-9047
879 W 190th St Ste 400 Gardena (90248) ***(P-20578)***
Flight Microwave Corporation ......E......310 607-9819
410 S Douglas St El Segundo (90245) ***(P-14467)***
Flight Standards District Off, El Segundo *Also called Federal Aviation ADM* ***(P-20103)***
Flint Group US LLC ......E......626 369-6900
650 Tamarack Ave Apt 1502 Brea (92821) ***(P-8915)***
Flint Group US LLC ......F......562 903-7976
14930 Marquardt Ave Santa Fe Springs (90670) ***(P-8916)***
Flint Ink North America Div, Brea *Also called Flint Group US LLC* ***(P-8915)***
Flipagram Inc ......F......415 827-8373
916 Silver Spur Rd # 310 Rllng HLS Est (90274) ***(P-23903)***
Flipcause Inc ......F......800 523-1950
283 4th St Ste 101 Oakland (94607) ***(P-23904)***
Flir Elctr-Ptcal Comp Bus Unit, Ventura *Also called Flir Eoc LLC* ***(P-21230)***
Flir Eoc LLC ......E......805 642-4645
2223 Eastman Ave Ste B Ventura (93003) ***(P-21230)***
Flir Motion Ctrl Systems Inc ......E......650 692-3900
6769 Hollister Ave Goleta (93117) ***(P-14468)***
Flir Systems Inc ......E......805 964-9797
6769 Hollister Ave # 100 Goleta (93117) ***(P-20579)***
Flo Stor Engineering Inc (PA) ......E......510 887-7179
21371 Cabot Blvd Hayward (94545) ***(P-13824)***
Flo TV Incorporated ......F......858 651-1645
5775 Morehouse Dr San Diego (92121) ***(P-17521)***
Flo-Kem, Compton *Also called LMC Enterprises* ***(P-8394)***
Flo-Mac Inc ......E......323 583-8751
1846 E 60th St Los Angeles (90001) ***(P-13471)***
Flolight, Campbell *Also called Prompter People Inc* ***(P-17628)***
Flood Ctrl Wtr Cnservation Dst, NAPA *Also called County of NAPA* ***(P-20852)***
Flood Ranch Company ......F......805 937-3616
6600 Foxen Canyon Rd Santa Maria (93454) ***(P-1704)***
Floor Covering Soft ......F......626 683-9188
221 E Walnut St Ste 110 Pasadena (91101) ***(P-23905)***
Flor De California ......E......909 673-1968
1930 S Bon View Ave # 18 Ontario (91761) ***(P-644)***
Flora Springs Wine Company ......F......707 963-5711
1978 Zinfandel Ln Saint Helena (94574) ***(P-1705)***
Florence & New Itln Art Co Inc ......E......510 785-9674
27735 Industrial Blvd Hayward (94545) ***(P-10574)***
Florence International Company ......E......818 767-9650
11645 Pendleton St Sun Valley (91352) ***(P-13010)***
Florence Macaroni Company ......F......310 548-5942
1312 W 2nd St San Pedro (90732) ***(P-2368)***
Flores Brothers Inc ......E......562 806-9128
7777 Scout Ave Bell (90201) ***(P-2460)***
Florestone Products Co (PA) ......E......559 661-4171
2851 Falcon Dr Madera (93637) ***(P-9587)***
Florian Industries Inc ......F......415 330-9000
151 Industrial Way Brisbane (94005) ***(P-11795)***
Floride Products LLC (PA) ......E......323 201-4363
2867 Vail Ave Commerce (90040) ***(P-7497)***
Flory Industries ......D......209 545-1167
4737 Toomes Rd Salida (95368) ***(P-13633)***
Flostor, Hayward *Also called Flo Stor Engineering Inc* ***(P-13824)***
Flotron Inc ......E......760 727-2700
2630 Progress St Vista (92081) ***(P-14053)***
Flour Fusion ......F......951 245-1166
133 N Main St Lake Elsinore (92530) ***(P-1204)***
Flow Control LLC ......F......949 608-3900
17942 Cowan Irvine (92614) ***(P-14571)***
Flow Dynamics Inc ......F......909 930-5522
1215 E Acacia St Ste 104 Ontario (91761) ***(P-11044)***
Flow N Control Inc ......F......818 330-7425
4452 Ocean View Blvd # 201 Montrose (91020) ***(P-13306)***
Flow Sports Inc (PA) ......E......949 361-5260
1011 Calle Sombra Ste 220 San Clemente (92673) ***(P-22802)***
Floway Pumps, Fresno *Also called Trillium Pumps Usa Inc* ***(P-14603)***
Flowers Baking Co Modesto LLC ......D......209 857-4600
736 Mariposa Rd Modesto (95354) ***(P-1205)***
Flowers Vineyard & Winery LLC ......F......707 847-3661
28500 Seaview Rd Cazadero (95421) ***(P-1706)***
Flowline Inc ......E......562 598-3015
10500 Humbolt St Los Alamitos (90720) ***(P-21474)***
Flowline Liquid Intelligence, Los Alamitos *Also called Flowline Inc* ***(P-21474)***
Flowmaster Inc ......C......916 371-2345
1500 Overland Ct West Sacramento (95691) ***(P-19656)***
Flowmaster Inc (HQ) ......E......707 544-4761
100 Stony Point Rd # 125 Santa Rosa (95401) ***(P-19657)***
Flowmetrics Inc ......E......818 407-3420
9201 Independence Ave Chatsworth (91311) ***(P-20868)***
Flowserve Corporation ......B......323 584-1890
2300 E Vernon Ave Stop 76 Vernon (90058) ***(P-14572)***
Flowserve Corporation ......E......310 667-4220
1909 E Cashdan St Compton (90220) ***(P-14573)***
Flowserve Corporation ......F......707 745-4710
6077 Egret Ct Benicia (94510) ***(P-14574)***
Flowserve Corporation ......C......951 296-2464
27455 Tierra Alta Way C Temecula (92590) ***(P-14575)***
Floyd Dennee ......F......562 595-6024
2780 Walnut Ave Signal Hill (90755) ***(P-7066)***
Fluid Components Intl LLC (PA) ......C......760 744-6950
1755 La Costa Meadows Dr A San Marcos (92078) ***(P-20869)***
Fluid Industrial Mfg Inc ......E......408 782-9900
374 S Milpitas Blvd Milpitas (95035) ***(P-15433)***
Fluid Line Technology Corp ......E......818 998-8848
9362 Eton Ave Ste A Chatsworth (91311) ***(P-21714)***
Fluid Lubrication & Chem Co ......F......800 826-2415
18400 S Broadway Gardena (90248) ***(P-9144)***

Mergent e-mail: customerrelations@mergent.com
1102
2020 California
Manufacturers Register
(P-0000) Products & Services Section entry number
(PA)=Parent Co (HQ)=Headquarters (DH)=Div Headquarters

Fluid Power Ctrl Systems Inc ......E......714 525-3727
1400 E Valencia Dr Fullerton (92831) ***(P-20870)***
Fluid Systems Division, Irvine *Also called Parker-Hannifin Corporation* ***(P-20195)***
Fluidigm Corporation (PA) ......C......650 266-6000
7000 Shoreline Ct Ste 100 South San Francisco (94080) ***(P-21231)***
Fluidix Inc (PA) ......F......760 935-2016
1422 Mammoth Tav Rd C6 Mammoth Lakes (93546) ***(P-14762)***
Fluidmaster Inc (PA) ......B......949 728-2000
30800 Rancho Viejo Rd San Juan Capistrano (92675) ***(P-11668)***
Fluorescent Supply Co Inc ......E......909 948-8878
9120 Center Ave Rancho Cucamonga (91730) ***(P-17036)***
Fluoresco Lighting & Sign, Pomona *Also called Everbrite West LLC* ***(P-23101)***
Flux Power Inc ......F......760 741-3589
2685 S Melrose Dr Vista (92081) ***(P-21039)***
Flux Power Holdings Inc (PA) ......D......877 505-3589
2685 S Melrose Dr Vista (92081) ***(P-19166)***
Fluxion Biosciences Inc ......E......650 241-4777
1600 Harbor Bay Pkwy # 150 Alameda (94502) ***(P-21715)***
Flydive Inc (PA) ......F......844 359-3483
3209 Midway Dr Unit 203 San Diego (92110) ***(P-22803)***
Flyer Defense LLC ......E......310 674-5030
151 W 135th St Los Angeles (90061) ***(P-19471)***
Flyers Energy LLC ......D......707 546-0766
444 Yolanda Ave Ste A Santa Rosa (95404) ***(P-14820)***
Flying Colors, Walnut *Also called Jakks Pacific Inc* ***(P-22686)***
Flying Embers, Ojai *Also called Fermented Sciences Inc* ***(P-1526)***
Flying Machine Factory, Compton *Also called Fmf Racing* ***(P-20401)***
Flyleaf Windows Inc ......E......925 344-1181
11040 Bollinger Canyon Rd San Ramon (94582) ***(P-10360)***
Flynn Signs and Graphics Inc ......F......562 498-6655
1345 Coronado Ave Long Beach (90804) ***(P-23114)***
Flynn Signs and Letters, Long Beach *Also called Flynn Signs and Graphics Inc* ***(P-23114)***
Flynt, Larry Publishing, Beverly Hills *Also called L F P Inc* ***(P-5971)***
Flythissim Technologies Inc ......F......844 746-2846
3534 Empleo St Ste B San Luis Obispo (93401) ***(P-19311)***
Flywheel Software Inc ......E......650 260-1700
816 Hamilton St Redwood City (94063) ***(P-23906)***
FM Industries, San Diego *Also called FM Plastics* ***(P-9789)***
FM Industries Inc ......C......510 673-0192
331 E Warren Ave Fremont (94539) ***(P-15963)***
FM Industries Inc (HQ) ......C......510 668-1900
221 E Warren Ave Fremont (94539) ***(P-15964)***
FM Plastics ......E......619 661-5929
9950 Marconi Dr Ste 106 San Diego (92154) ***(P-9789)***
FM Systems Inc ......F......714 979-0537
3877 S Main St Santa Ana (92707) ***(P-17522)***
FMC Corporation ......D......530 753-6718
201 Cousteau Pl Davis (95618) ***(P-7387)***
FMC Technologies Inc ......F......714 872-5574
621 Burning Tree Rd Fullerton (92833) ***(P-13776)***
Fmf Racing ......C......310 631-4363
18033 S Santa Fe Ave Compton (90221) ***(P-20401)***
Fmh Aerospace Corp ......D......714 751-1000
17072 Daimler St Irvine (92614) ***(P-20107)***
FMI, Chula Vista *Also called Flexible Metal Inc* ***(P-13470)***
Fmk Labs Inc ......E......951 736-1212
1690 N Delilah St Corona (92879) ***(P-8493)***
FML Inc ......F......415 864-5084
2765 16th St San Francisco (94103) ***(P-22982)***
Fmw Machine Shop ......F......650 363-1313
519 Claire St Hayward (94541) ***(P-15965)***
Fnc Medical Corporation ......E......805 644-7576
6000 Leland St Ventura (93003) ***(P-8494)***
Fntech ......F......714 429-1686
18107 Mount Washington St Fountain Valley (92708) ***(P-17125)***
Fntech ......F......714 429-7833
3000 W Segerstrom Ave Santa Ana (92704) ***(P-17126)***
Foam Concepts Inc ......E......714 693-1037
4729 E Wesley Dr Anaheim (92807) ***(P-9530)***
Foam Depot, La Puente *Also called Jona Global Trading Inc* ***(P-4725)***
Foam Depot, City of Industry *Also called American Foam Fiber & Sups Inc* ***(P-2923)***
Foam Design Center, Bakersfield *Also called Transdesign Inc* ***(P-4142)***
Foam Fabricators Inc ......F......310 537-5760
1810 S Santa Fe Ave Compton (90221) ***(P-9790)***
Foam Fabricators Inc ......F......209 523-7002
301 9th St Ste B Modesto (95351) ***(P-9531)***
Foam Factory Inc ......E......310 603-9808
17515 S Santa Fe Ave Compton (90221) ***(P-9532)***
Foam Injection Plastics Inc ......F......510 317-0218
2548 Grant Ave San Lorenzo (94580) ***(P-9791)***
Foam Molders and Specialties (PA) ......D......562 924-7757
11110 Business Cir Cerritos (90703) ***(P-9533)***
Foam Molders and Specialties ......E......562 924-7757
20004 State Rd Cerritos (90703) ***(P-9534)***
Foam Plastics & Rbr Pdts Corp ......F......714 779-0990
4765 E Bryson St Anaheim (92807) ***(P-9535)***
Foam Specialties, Cerritos *Also called Foam Molders and Specialties* ***(P-9533)***
Foam-Craft Inc ......C......714 459-9971
2441 Cypress Way Fullerton (92831) ***(P-9536)***
Foamation Inc ......F......818 837-6613
11852 Glenoaks Blvd San Fernando (91340) ***(P-9537)***
Foamex, San Leandro *Also called Fxi Inc* ***(P-9544)***
Foamex, Orange *Also called Fxi Inc* ***(P-9545)***
Foamex LP ......E......909 824-8981
1400 E Victoria Ave San Bernardino (92408) ***(P-9538)***
Foamordercom Inc ......F......415 503-1188
3455 Collins Ave Richmond (94806) ***(P-9539)***
Foampro Manufacturing, Irvine *Also called Foampro Mfg Inc* ***(P-23026)***
Foampro Mfg Inc ......D......949 252-0112
1781 Langley Ave Irvine (92614) ***(P-23026)***
Foamtec LLC ......F......916 851-8621
4420 Commodity Way Ste A Shingle Springs (95682) ***(P-10575)***
Focus Enhancements Inc (HQ) ......E......650 230-2400
931 Benecia Ave Sunnyvale (94085) ***(P-18238)***
Focus Enhncments Systems Group, Sunnyvale *Also called Focus Enhancements Inc* ***(P-18238)***
Focus Industries Inc ......D......949 830-1350
25301 Commercentre Dr Lake Forest (92630) ***(P-17037)***
Focus Landscape, Lake Forest *Also called Focus Industries Inc* ***(P-17037)***
Focus Point of Sale ......F......949 336-7500
48 Waterworks Way Irvine (92618) ***(P-23907)***
Focus Pos, Irvine *Also called Focus Point of Sale* ***(P-23907)***
Foh Group Inc (PA) ......E......323 466-5151
6255 W Sunset Blvd # 2212 Los Angeles (90028) ***(P-3452)***
Foilflex Products Inc ......F......661 702-0775
24963 Avenue Tibbitts Valencia (91355) ***(P-7067)***
Fold-A-Goal, Los Angeles *Also called D Hauptman Co Inc* ***(P-22788)***
Foldimate Inc ......E......805 876-4418
879 White Pine Ct Oak Park (91377) ***(P-16828)***
Folding Cartons, Camarillo *Also called Crockett Graphics Inc* ***(P-5215)***
Folex Co ......F......619 670-5588
2505 Folex Way Spring Valley (91978) ***(P-8340)***
Foley Family Wines Inc (HQ) ......D......707 708-7600
200 Concourse Blvd Paso Robles (93446) ***(P-1707)***
Foley Wine Group, Paso Robles *Also called Foley Family Wines Inc* ***(P-1707)***
Folgergraphics Inc ......E......510 293-2294
21093 Forbes Ave Hayward (94545) ***(P-7357)***
Folie A Deux Winery, Saint Helena *Also called Trinchero Family Estates Inc* ***(P-1971)***
Folkmanis Inc ......E......510 658-7677
1219 Park Ave Emeryville (94608) ***(P-23334)***
Follmer Development Inc ......E......805 498-4531
840 Tourmaline Dr Newbury Park (91320) ***(P-7413)***
Folsom Ready Mix Inc ......F......530 365-0191
19291 Latona Rd Anderson (96007) ***(P-10758)***
Folsom Ready Mix Inc (PA) ......E......916 851-8300
3401 Fitzgerald Rd Rancho Cordova (95742) ***(P-10576)***
Folsom Telegraph, Folsom *Also called Brehm Communications Inc* ***(P-5568)***
Fondo De Cultura Economica ......F......619 429-0455
2293 Verus St San Diego (92154) ***(P-6102)***
Fonegear LLC ......F......909 627-7999
14726 Ramona Ave Ste 208 Chino (91710) ***(P-17372)***
Fong Brothers Printing Inc (PA) ......C......415 467-1050
320 Valley Dr Brisbane (94005) ***(P-6577)***
Fong Fong Prtrs Lthgrphers Inc ......E......916 739-1313
3009 65th St Sacramento (95820) ***(P-6578)***
Fongs Graphics & Printing Inc ......E......626 307-1898
7743 Garvey Ave Rosemead (91770) ***(P-6955)***
Fono Unlimited Inc (PA) ......E......650 322-4664
99 Stanford Shopping Ctr Palo Alto (94304) ***(P-645)***
Fontal Controls Inc ......F......818 833-1127
12725 Encinitas Ave Sylmar (91342) ***(P-15966)***
Fontana Foundry Corporation ......E......909 822-6128
8306 Cherry Ave Fontana (92335) ***(P-11381)***
Fontana Paper Mills Inc ......D......909 823-4100
13733 Valley Blvd Fontana (92335) ***(P-9112)***
Food Equipment Mfg Co ......F......831 637-1624
175 Mitchell Rd Hollister (95023) ***(P-14361)***
Food Machinery Sales Inc ......D......559 651-2339
7020 W Sunnyview Ave Visalia (93291) ***(P-14707)***
Food Makers Bakery Eqp Inc ......E......626 358-1343
16019 Adelante St Irwindale (91702) ***(P-14362)***
Food Pharma, Santa Fe Springs *Also called Food Technology and Design LLC* ***(P-1367)***
Food Processing Equipment Co, Santa Fe Springs *Also called FPec Corporation A Cal Corp* ***(P-14365)***
Food Technology and Design LLC ......E......562 944-7821
10012 Painter Ave Santa Fe Springs (90670) ***(P-1367)***
Food-O-Mex Corporation ......D......323 225-1737
2928 N Main St Los Angeles (90031) ***(P-2461)***
Foodbeast Inc ......F......949 344-2634
305 W 4th St Santa Ana (92701) ***(P-6238)***
Foodlink Online LLC ......E......408 395-7280
475 Alberto Way Ste 100 Los Gatos (95032) ***(P-23908)***
Foodtools Consolidated Inc (PA) ......E......805 962-8383
315 Laguna St Santa Barbara (93101) ***(P-14363)***
Foot Imprint Inc ......E......626 991-4430
15373 Proctor Ave City of Industry (91745) ***(P-14322)***
Foot In Motion Inc ......F......312 752-0990
2239 Business Way Riverside (92501) ***(P-22013)***
Foot Locker Retail Inc ......F......510 797-5750
2059 Newpark Mall Fl 2 Newark (94560) ***(P-10179)***
Foote Axle & Forge LLC ......E......323 268-4151
3954 Whiteside St Los Angeles (90063) ***(P-19658)***
Foothill Instruments LLC ......F......818 952-5600
5011 Jarvis Ave La Canada (91011) ***(P-21475)***
Foothill Pritnig & Graphics/ C (PA) ......F......209 736-4332
2245 Highway 49 Angels Camp (95222) ***(P-6579)***
Foothill Ready Mix Inc ......E......530 527-2565
11415 State Highway 99w Red Bluff (96080) ***(P-10759)***
FOOTHILL VOCATIONAL OPPORTUNIT, Pasadena *Also called Fvo Solutions Inc* ***(P-13181)***
Foothills Advertiser, Exeter *Also called Foothills Sun-Gazette* ***(P-5634)***
Foothills Sun-Gazette ......E......559 592-3171
120 N E St Exeter (93221) ***(P-5634)***
Foppiano Vineyards, Healdsburg *Also called L Foppiano Wine Co* ***(P-1788)***
For Rent, Roseville *Also called United Advg Publications Inc* ***(P-6051)***
Forager Project LLC ......D......855 729-5253
235 Montgomery St Ste 730 San Francisco (94104) ***(P-912)***

A L P H A B E T I C

Employee Codes: A=Over 500 employees, B=251-500
C=101-250, D=51-100, E=20-50, F=10-19
2020 California
Manfacturers Register
© Mergent Inc. 1-800-342-5647
1103

Forbes Industries Div ... C ... 909 923-4559
1933 E Locust St Ontario (91761) ***(P-5061)***

Force Fabrication Inc ... F ... 805 754-2235
2233 Statham Blvd Oxnard (93033) ***(P-12214)***

Ford Logging Inc ... E ... 707 840-9442
1225 Central Ave Ste 11 McKinleyville (95519) ***(P-3882)***

Forderer Cornice Works ... F ... 415 431-4100
3364 Arden Rd Hayward (94545) ***(P-11955)***

Fordon Grind Industries, Torrance *Also called Aeroliant Manufacturing Inc* ***(P-15710)***

Foreal Spectrum Inc ... E ... 408 923-1675
2370 Qume Dr Ste A San Jose (95131) ***(P-21354)***

Forecast 3d, Carlsbad *Also called Product Slingshot Inc* ***(P-14098)***

Forecross Corporation (PA) ... F ... 415 543-1515
505 Montgomery St Fl 11 San Francisco (94111) ***(P-23909)***

Forem Manufacturing Inc ... F ... 510 577-9500
844 66th Ave Oakland (94621) ***(P-11190)***

Forem Metal, Oakland *Also called Forem Manufacturing Inc* ***(P-11190)***

Foremost Interiors Inc ... E ... 916 635-1423
2318 Gold River Rd Rancho Cordova (95670) ***(P-10906)***

Foremost Precision Pdts Inc ... F ... 714 961-0165
1940 Petra Ln Ste A Placentia (92870) ***(P-15967)***

Foremost Spring & Mfg, Santa Fe Springs *Also called Foremost Spring Company Inc* ***(P-13381)***

Foremost Spring Company Inc ... F ... 562 923-0791
11876 Burke St Santa Fe Springs (90670) ***(P-13381)***

Foreseeson Custom Displays Inc (PA) ... E ... 714 300-0540
2210 E Winston Rd Anaheim (92806) ***(P-15230)***

Foresite Systems Limited (PA) ... F ... 408 855-8600
19925 Stevens Creek Blvd Cupertino (95014) ***(P-23910)***

Forespar, Rcho STA Marg *Also called Light Composite Corporation* ***(P-11605)***

Forest Investment Group Inc ... F ... 415 459-2330
83 Hamilton Dr Ste 100 Novato (94949) ***(P-6580)***

Forest Laboratories LLC ... D ... 951 941-0024
12021 Dolly Way Moreno Valley (92555) ***(P-7892)***

Forest River Inc ... E ... 909 873-3777
255 S Pepper Ave Rialto (92376) ***(P-20485)***

Forester Communications Inc ... E ... 805 682-1300
2946 De La Vina St Santa Barbara (93105) ***(P-5936)***

Forever Young, Oakland *Also called Supernutrition* ***(P-8151)***

Forever Young ... E ... 650 355-5481
208 Palmetto Ave Pacifica (94044) ***(P-2462)***

Forge Global Inc (PA) ... F ... 415 881-1612
415 Mission St Ste 5510 San Francisco (94105) ***(P-23911)***

Forged Metals Inc ... C ... 909 350-9260
10685 Beech Ave Fontana (92337) ***(P-12709)***

Forgerock US Inc (HQ) ... D ... 415 599-1100
201 Mission St San Francisco (94105) ***(P-23912)***

Forgiato Inc ... D ... 818 771-9779
11915 Wicks St Sun Valley (91352) ***(P-19659)***

Form & Fusion Mfg Inc ... F ... 916 638-8576
11251 Trade Center Dr Rancho Cordova (95742) ***(P-12804)***

Form & Fusion Mfg Inc (PA) ... E ... 916 638-8576
11261 Trade Center Dr Rancho Cordova (95742) ***(P-12805)***

Form Factory Inc ... D ... 937 572-6126
2917 Santa Monica Blvd Santa Monica (90404) ***(P-589)***

Form Grind Corporation ... E ... 949 858-7000
30062 Aventura Rcho STA Marg (92688) ***(P-15968)***

Form Products, Rcho STA Marg *Also called Form Grind Corporation* ***(P-15968)***

Formalloy Technologies Inc ... F ... 619 377-9101
2810 Via Orange Way Ste A Spring Valley (91978) ***(P-14323)***

Formation Inc ... D ... 650 257-2277
35 Stillman St San Francisco (94107) ***(P-23913)***

Formation Systems, San Francisco *Also called Formation Inc* ***(P-23913)***

Formatop, Campbell *Also called Teammate Builders Inc* ***(P-5005)***

Formax Technologies Inc ... E ... 209 668-1001
305 S Soderquist Rd Turlock (95380) ***(P-19312)***

Formcraft, Fullerton *Also called Future Foam Inc* ***(P-9543)***

Formex LLC ... E ... 858 529-6600
11011 Torreyana Rd # 100 San Diego (92121) ***(P-7893)***

Formfactor Inc ... F ... 925 290-4000
7545 Longard Rd Livermore (94551) ***(P-18239)***

Formfactor Inc (PA) ... C ... 925 290-4000
7005 Southfront Rd Livermore (94551) ***(P-18240)***

Forming Specialties Inc ... E ... 310 639-1122
1309 W Walnut Pkwy Compton (90220) ***(P-20108)***

Formosa Meat Company Inc ... E ... 909 987-0470
10646 Fulton Ct Rancho Cucamonga (91730) ***(P-456)***

Forms Division, Irvine *Also called RR Donnelley & Sons Company* ***(P-7285)***

Formsolver Inc ... E ... 323 664-7888
3041 N North Coolidge Ave Los Angeles (90039) ***(P-4502)***

Formtran Inc ... F ... 949 829-5822
26501 Rancho Pkwy S # 103 Lake Forest (92630) ***(P-23914)***

Formula Plastics Inc ... B ... 866 307-1362
451 Tecate Rd Ste 2b Tecate (91980) ***(P-9792)***

Formulation Technology Inc ... E ... 209 847-0331
571 Armstrong Way Oakdale (95361) ***(P-7894)***

Formurex Inc ... F ... 209 931-2040
2470 Wilcox Rd Stockton (95215) ***(P-7895)***

Forrest Machining Inc ... C ... 661 257-0231
27756 Avenue Mentry Valencia (91355) ***(P-20109)***

Forrester Eastland Corporation ... E ... 310 784-2464
1320 Storm Pkwy Torrance (90501) ***(P-23335)***

Forrestmachining.com, Valencia *Also called Forrest Machining Inc* ***(P-20109)***

Forsythe Tech Worldwide ... F ... 818 710-8694
23924 Victory Blvd Woodland Hills (91367) ***(P-21716)***

Fort Bragg Advocate-News, Fort Bragg *Also called Gatehouse Media LLC* ***(P-5640)***

Fort Ord Works Inc ... E ... 831 275-1294
791 Neeson Rd Marina (93933) ***(P-20580)***

Fortanix Inc (PA) ... E ... 628 400-2043
444 Castro St Ste 305 Mountain View (94041) ***(P-23915)***

Fortasa Memory Systems Inc ... F ... 888 367-8588
1670 S Amphlett Blvd San Mateo (94402) ***(P-15028)***

Fortemedia Inc (PA) ... E ... 408 716-8028
4051 Burton Dr Santa Clara (95054) ***(P-18241)***

Fortemedia Inc ... D ... 408 716-8011
4051 Burton Dr Santa Clara (95054) ***(P-15029)***

Fortemedia Inc ... D ... 408 716-8028
19050 Pruneridge Ave Cupertino (95014) ***(P-15030)***

Fortemedia China, Santa Clara *Also called Fortemedia Inc* ***(P-15029)***

Forterra Pipe & Precast LLC ... F ... 661 746-3527
30781 San Diego St Shafter (93263) ***(P-12215)***

Forterra Pipe & Precast LLC ... D ... 916 379-9695
7020 Tokay Ave Sacramento (95828) ***(P-10577)***

Forterra Pipe & Precast LLC ... F ... 858 715-5600
9229 Harris Plant Rd San Diego (92145) ***(P-10578)***

Fortinet Inc (PA) ... B ... 408 235-7700
899 Kifer Rd Sunnyvale (94086) ***(P-15231)***

Fortner Eng & Mfg Inc ... D ... 818 240-7740
918 Thompson Ave Glendale (91201) ***(P-15969)***

Fortrend Engineering Corp ... E ... 408 734-9311
2220 Otoole Ave San Jose (95131) ***(P-20871)***

Fortress Inc ... E ... 909 593-8600
1721 Wright Ave La Verne (91750) ***(P-4797)***

Fortron/Source Corporation (PA) ... E ... 949 766-9240
23181 Antonio Pkwy Rcho STA Marg (92688) ***(P-16551)***

Fortuna Tortilla Factory ... F ... 209 394-3028
1425 C St Livingston (95334) ***(P-2463)***

Fortune Bakery, South El Monte *Also called Dtbm Inc* ***(P-1194)***

Fortune Brands Windows Inc ... C ... 707 446-7600
2019 E Monte Vista Ave Vacaville (95688) ***(P-9793)***

Fortune Casuals LLC (PA) ... C ... 310 733-2100
10119 Jefferson Blvd Culver City (90232) ***(P-3159)***

Fortune Drink Inc ... F ... 408 805-9526
19925 Stevens Creek Blvd # 100 Cupertino (95014) ***(P-2076)***

Fortune Swimwear LLC (HQ) ... E ... 310 733-2130
2340 E Olympic Blvd Ste A Los Angeles (90021) ***(P-2786)***

Forty Seven Inc ... D ... 650 352-4150
1490 Obrien Dr Ste A Menlo Park (94025) ***(P-7896)***

Forty-Niners Publication ... F ... 562 985-5568
1250 Bellflower Blvd Csul Long Beach (90840) ***(P-5937)***

Forward Integration Technology ... F ... 408 988-3330
444 Nelo St Santa Clara (95054) ***(P-11304)***

Forward Printing & Design ... F ... 510 535-2222
9331 Burr St Oakland (94605) ***(P-7068)***

Foss Lampshade Studios Inc (PA) ... F ... 510 534-4133
1357 International Blvd Oakland (94606) ***(P-23336)***

Foss Maritime Company ... F ... 562 437-6098
49 W Pier D St Long Beach (90802) ***(P-11796)***

Foster Commodities ... E ... 559 897-1081
1900 Kern St Kingsburg (93631) ***(P-1094)***

Foster Dairy Farms ... C ... 707 725-6182
572 State Highway 1 Fortuna (95540) ***(P-590)***

Foster Farms, Livingston *Also called Foster Poultry Farms* ***(P-511)***

Foster Farms, Waterford *Also called Foster Poultry Farms* ***(P-512)***

Foster Farms, Kingsburg *Also called Foster Commodities* ***(P-1094)***

Foster Farms, Livingston *Also called Foster Poultry Farms* ***(P-513)***

Foster Farms LLC ... E ... 559 897-1081
1900 Kern St Kingsburg (93631) ***(P-1095)***

Foster Planing Mill Co ... F ... 323 759-9156
1258 W 58th St Los Angeles (90037) ***(P-4503)***

Foster Poultry Farms (PA) ... C ... 209 394-6914
1000 Davis St Livingston (95334) ***(P-511)***

Foster Poultry Farms ... E ... 209 394-7901
1307 Ellenwood Rd Waterford (95386) ***(P-512)***

Foster Poultry Farms ... C ... 209 394-7901
1333 Swan St Livingston (95334) ***(P-513)***

Foster Poultry Farms ... E ... 209 394-7950
221 Stefani Ave Livingston (95334) ***(P-1096)***

Foster Poultry Farms ... D ... 209 668-5922
1033 S Center St Turlock (95380) ***(P-514)***

Foster Poultry Farms ... A ... 559 265-2000
900 W Belgravia Ave Fresno (93706) ***(P-515)***

Foster Poultry Farms ... B ... 559 793-5501
770 N Plano St Porterville (93257) ***(P-516)***

Foster Poultry Farms ... B ... 310 223-1499
1805 N Santa Fe Ave Compton (90221) ***(P-517)***

Foster Print, Santa Ana *Also called Blackburn Alton Invstments LLC* ***(P-7001)***

Foster Printing Company Inc ... D ... 714 731-2000
700 E Alton Ave Santa Ana (92705) ***(P-6581)***

Foster Sand & Gravel, Corona *Also called Werner Corporation* ***(P-10872)***

Foster Turkey Live Haul, Turlock *Also called Foster Poultry Farms* ***(P-514)***

Fotis and Son Imports Inc ... E ... 714 894-9022
15451 Electronic Ln Huntington Beach (92649) ***(P-14364)***

Found Image Press Inc ... F ... 619 282-3452
5225 Riley St San Diego (92110) ***(P-7295)***

Foundation 9 Entertainment Inc (PA) ... C ... 949 698-1500
30211 A De Las Bandera200 Rancho Santa Margari (92688) ***(P-23916)***

Foundation For Nat Progress ... E ... 415 321-1700
222 Sutter St Ste 600 San Francisco (94108) ***(P-5938)***

Foundry Med Innovations Inc ... F ... 888 445-2333
1965 Kellogg Ave Carlsbad (92008) ***(P-21717)***

Foundry Service & Supplies Inc ... E ... 909 284-5000
2029 S Parco Ave Ontario (91761) ***(P-11007)***

Foundstone Inc ... D ... 949 297-5600
27201 Puerta Real Ste 400 Mission Viejo (92691) ***(P-23917)***

Fountainhead Industries ... E ... 310 248-2444
700 N San Vicente Blvd G910 West Hollywood (90069) ***(P-23337)***

Mergent e-mail: customerrelations@mergent.com 2020 California (P-0000) Products & Services Section entry number
1104 Manufacturers Register (PA)=Parent Co (HQ)=Headquarters (DH)=Div Headquarters

Four Colorcom ....F....408 436-7574
2300 Stevens Creek Blvd San Jose (95128) *(P-6582)*
Four D Imaging ....F....510 290-3533
808 Gilman St Berkeley (94710) *(P-21476)*
Four Dimensions Inc ....F....510 782-1843
3140 Diablo Ave Hayward (94545) *(P-21040)*
Four In One Company, San Jose *Also called Lee Brothers Inc (P-888)*
Four M Studios ....D....415 249-2362
201 Mission St Fl 12 San Francisco (94105) *(P-6103)*
Four Oaks Farming, Hollister *Also called B & R Farms LLC (P-842)*
Four Seasons Design Inc (PA) ....C....619 761-5151
2451 Britannia Blvd San Diego (92154) *(P-3786)*
Four Seasons Restaurant Eqp ....E....951 278-9100
412 Jenks Cir Corona (92880) *(P-12216)*
Four Star Chemical, Vernon *Also called Starco Enterprises Inc (P-14539)*
Four Star Distribution ....D....949 369-4420
206 Calle Conchita San Clemente (92672) *(P-9171)*
Four Wheel Campers Inc ....E....530 666-1442
109 Pioneer Ave Woodland (95776) *(P-20486)*
Four-D Metal Finishing Inc ....E....408 730-5722
1065 Memorex Dr Santa Clara (95050) *(P-13011)*
Fourbro Inc ....F....714 277-3858
13772 A Better Way Garden Grove (92843) *(P-3084)*
Fourward Machine Inc ....F....858 272-0601
5111 Santa Fe St Ste J&I San Diego (92109) *(P-15970)*
Fovell Enterprises Inc ....E....951 734-6275
1852 Pomona Rd Corona (92880) *(P-23115)*
Foveon Inc ....E....408 855-6800
2249 Zanker Rd San Jose (95131) *(P-18242)*
Fowler Ensinger, Sanger *Also called Midvalley Publishing Inc (P-5755)*
Fowlers Machine Works Inc ....F....209 522-5146
300 S Riverside Dr Modesto (95354) *(P-15971)*
Fowlie Enterprises Inc ....E....805 583-2800
1143 Fern Oaks Dr Santa Paula (93060) *(P-1315)*
Fox Barrel Cider Company Inc ....E....530 346-9699
1213 S Auburn St Ste A Colfax (95713) *(P-1708)*
Fox Factory Holding Corp ....F....619 768-1800
750 Vernon Way El Cajon (92020) *(P-19660)*
Fox Factory Holding Corp (PA) ....E....831 274-6500
915 Disc Dr Scotts Valley (95066) *(P-20402)*
Fox Factory Inc (HQ) ....C....831 274-6500
915 Disc Dr Scotts Valley (95066) *(P-20403)*
Fox Factory Inc (HQ) ....C....831 274-6500
130 Hangar Way Watsonville (95076) *(P-19661)*
Fox Hills Industries ....E....714 893-1940
5831 Research Dr Huntington Beach (92649) *(P-11142)*
Fox Hills Machining Inc ....F....714 899-2211
7431 Belva Dr Ste 102 Huntington Beach (92647) *(P-15972)*
Fox Marble & Granite, San Francisco *Also called Evolv Surfaces Inc (P-4975)*
Fox Racing Shox, Scotts Valley *Also called Fox Factory Inc (P-20403)*
Fox Racing Shox, El Cajon *Also called Fox Factory Holding Corp (P-19660)*
Fox Racing Shox, Watsonville *Also called Fox Factory Inc (P-19661)*
Fox Thermal Instruments Inc ....E....831 384-4300
399 Reservation Rd Marina (93933) *(P-20872)*
Foxfury Lighting Solution, Oceanside *Also called Foxfury LLC (P-17127)*
Foxfury LLC ....E....760 945-4231
3528 Seagate Way Ste 100 Oceanside (92056) *(P-17127)*
Foxlink International Inc (HQ) ....E....714 256-1777
3010 Saturn St Ste 200 Brea (92821) *(P-16899)*
Foxlink World Circuit Tech ....E....714 256-0877
925 W Lambert Rd Ste C Brea (92821) *(P-17883)*
Foxsemicon Integrated Tech Inc ....F....408 383-9880
96 Bonaventura Dr San Jose (95134) *(P-18243)*
Fpc Graphics Inc ....E....951 686-0232
2682 Market St Riverside (92501) *(P-6583)*
FPec Corporation A Cal Corp (PA) ....F....562 802-3727
13623 Pumice St Santa Fe Springs (90670) *(P-14365)*
Fpg Oc Inc ....D....714 692-2950
24855 Corbit Pl Ste B Yorba Linda (92887) *(P-2211)*
Fra Mani LLC ....F....510 526-7000
1311 8th St Berkeley (94710) *(P-457)*
Fra' Mani Handcrafted Salumi, Berkeley *Also called Fra Mani LLC (P-457)*
Fragmob LLC ....F....858 587-6659
9655 Granite Ridge Dr # 200 San Diego (92123) *(P-23918)*
Fralock, Valencia *Also called Lockwood Industries LLC (P-18357)*
Framatic Company, Los Angeles *Also called Formsolver Inc (P-4502)*
Frametent Inc ....E....661 290-3375
26480 Summit Cir Santa Clarita (91350) *(P-3683)*
Framing Fabrics International, Los Angeles *Also called Frm USA LLC (P-13451)*
Frances Mary Accessories Inc ....A....925 962-2111
3732 Mt Diablo Blvd # 260 Lafayette (94549) *(P-10221)*
Franchise Services Inc (PA) ....E....949 348-5400
26722 Plaza Mission Viejo (92691) *(P-6584)*
Franchise Update Inc ....F....408 402-5681
6489 Camden Ave Ste 204 San Jose (95120) *(P-5939)*
Franchise Update Media Group, San Jose *Also called Franchise Update Inc (P-5939)*
Francis Ford Coppola Winery, Geyserville *Also called Francis Ford Cppola Prsnts LLC (P-1709)*
Francis Ford Cppola Prsnts LLC ....E....707 251-3200
300 Via Archimedes Geyserville (95441) *(P-1709)*
Franciscan Vineyards Inc ....C....707 933-2332
18701 Gehricke Rd Sonoma (95476) *(P-1710)*
Franciscan Vineyards Inc ....B....209 369-5861
5950 E Woodbridge Rd Acampo (95220) *(P-1711)*
Franciscan Vineyards Inc (HQ) ....D....707 963-7111
1178 Galleron Rd Saint Helena (94574) *(P-1712)*
Franciscan Vinyards Inc ....D....707 433-6981
16275 Healdsburg Ave Healdsburg (95448) *(P-1713)*
Franco American Corporation ....F....323 268-2345
1051 Monterey Pass Rd Monterey Park (91754) *(P-10961)*
Franco American Textile, Monterey Park *Also called Franco American Corporation (P-10961)*
Frank Russell Inc ....F....661 324-5575
341 Pacific Ave Shafter (93263) *(P-15973)*
Frank Stubbs Co Inc ....E....805 278-4300
1830 Eastman Ave Oxnard (93030) *(P-22014)*
Franklin Covey Co ....E....949 788-8102
3333 Michelson Dr Ste 400 Irvine (92612) *(P-6239)*
Franklin Lee Enterprises LLC ....F....760 355-1500
2419 Imprl Bus Park Dr Imperial (92251) *(P-7069)*
Franklin Logging, Burney *Also called Shasta Green Inc (P-3904)*
Franklin Logging Inc ....E....530 549-4924
11906 Wilson Way Redding (96003) *(P-3883)*
Franklin Wireless Corp ....D....858 623-0000
9707 Waples St Ste 150 San Diego (92121) *(P-17373)*
Franklins Inds San Diego Inc ....E....858 486-9399
12135 Dearborn Pl Poway (92064) *(P-15974)*
Franks Cabinet Shop Inc ....F....661 845-0781
11204 San Diego St Lamont (93241) *(P-4199)*
Frans Manufacturing Inc ....F....760 741-9135
126 N Vinewood St Escondido (92029) *(P-21718)*
Franz Inc ....E....510 452-2000
2201 Broadway Ste 715 Oakland (94612) *(P-23919)*
Franzia Winery, Ripon *Also called Franzia/Sanger Winery (P-1714)*
Franzia/Sanger Winery ....C....209 599-4111
17000 E State Highway 120 Ripon (95366) *(P-1714)*
Frase Enterprises ....E....510 856-3600
2261 Carion Ct Pittsburg (94565) *(P-16948)*
Frasinettis Winery & Rest, Sacramento *Also called James Frasinetti & Sons (P-1770)*
Fray Logging Inc ....E....209 984-5968
10619 Jim Brady Rd Jamestown (95327) *(P-3884)*
Frazier Aviation Inc ....E....818 898-1998
445 N Fox St San Fernando (91340) *(P-20110)*
Frc, Sacramento *Also called Farmers Rice Cooperative (P-1040)*
FReal Foods LLC ....D....800 483-3218
6121 Hollis St Ste 500 Emeryville (94608) *(P-591)*
Fred Matter Inc ....E....925 371-1234
7801 Las Positas Rd Livermore (94551) *(P-15975)*
Frederic Duclos, Huntington Beach *Also called A G Artwear Inc (P-22977)*
Fredi & Sons Inc ....F....818 881-1170
58 Calle Cabrillo Foothill Ranch (92610) *(P-10156)*
Free Motion Wakeboards, Carlsbad *Also called Liquid Force Wakeboards (P-22842)*
Freeberg Indus Fbrication Corp ....D....760 737-7614
2874 Progress Pl Escondido (92029) *(P-11797)*
Freedom Communications Inc ....E....949 454-7300
22481 Aspan St El Toro (92630) *(P-5635)*
Freedom Designs Inc ....C....805 582-0077
2241 N Madera Rd Simi Valley (93065) *(P-22015)*
Freedom Finishing, Los Angeles *Also called Freedom Wood Finishing Inc (P-2854)*
Freedom Innovations LLC (HQ) ....E....949 672-0032
3 Morgan Irvine (92618) *(P-22016)*
Freedom of Press Foundation ....F....510 995-0780
601 Van Ness Ave Ste E731 San Francisco (94102) *(P-5940)*
Freedom Photonics LLC ....E....805 967-4900
41 Aero Camino Santa Barbara (93117) *(P-19313)*
Freedom Wood Finishing Inc ....D....213 534-6620
600 Wilshire Blvd # 1200 Los Angeles (90017) *(P-2854)*
Freeform Research & Dev ....F....949 646-3217
1539 Monrovia Ave Ste 23 Newport Beach (92663) *(P-14160)*
Freeland Exceed Inc ....E....626 695-8031
1820 E Locust St Ontario (91761) *(P-17128)*
Freeline Design Surfboards, Santa Cruz *Also called Mel & Associates Inc (P-22852)*
Freemark Abbey Wnery Ltd Prtnr ....E....707 963-9694
3022 Saint Helena Hwy N Saint Helena (94574) *(P-1715)*
Freeport Bakery Inc ....E....916 442-4256
2966 Freeport Blvd Sacramento (95818) *(P-1206)*
Freeport-Mcmoran Oil & Gas LLC ....E....805 567-1601
760 W Hueneme Rd Oxnard (93033) *(P-123)*
Freeport-Mcmoran Oil & Gas LLC ....E....661 768-4831
3252 W Crocker Springs Rd Fellows (93224) *(P-51)*
Freeport-Mcmoran Oil & Gas LLC ....F....805 547-8969
1821 Price Canyon Rd San Luis Obispo (93401) *(P-124)*
Freeport-Mcmoran Oil & Gas LLC ....D....661 322-7600
1200 Discovery Dr Ste 500 Bakersfield (93309) *(P-52)*
Freeport-Mcmoran Oil & Gas LLC ....E....323 298-2200
5640 S Fairfax Ave Los Angeles (90056) *(P-53)*
Freestyle, Costa Mesa *Also called Sunburst Products Inc (P-22484)*
Freeway Machine & Welding Shop, Orange *Also called Lmm Enterprises (P-16148)*
Freewire Technologies Inc ....E....415 779-5515
1933 Davis St Ste 301a San Leandro (94577) *(P-16647)*
Freeze Tag Inc (PA) ....F....714 210-3850
18062 Irvine Blvd Ste 103 Tustin (92780) *(P-23920)*
Freightgate Inc ....E....714 799-2833
10055 Slater Ave Ste 231 Fountain Valley (92708) *(P-23921)*
Freixenet Sonoma Caves Inc ....E....707 996-4981
23555 Arnold Dr Sonoma (95476) *(P-1716)*
Fremarc Designs, City of Industry *Also called Fremarc Industries Inc (P-4571)*
Fremarc Industries Inc (PA) ....D....626 965-0802
18810 San Jose Ave City of Industry (91748) *(P-4571)*
Fremont Amgen Inc (HQ) ....B....510 284-6500
6397 Kaiser Dr Fremont (94555) *(P-7897)*
Fremont Package Express ....F....916 541-1812
734 Still Breeze Way Sacramento (95831) *(P-13872)*
French Custom Shutters Inc ....F....619 667-2636
9248 Olive Dr Spring Valley (91977) *(P-4045)*
French Tradition (PA) ....F....310 719-9977
13700 Crenshaw Blvd Gardena (90249) *(P-4572)*

A L P H A B E T I C

Employee Codes: A=Over 500 employees, B=251-500
C=101-250, D=51-100, E=20-50, F=10-19
2020 California
Manfacturers Register
© Mergent Inc. 1-800-342-5647
1105

Frequency Management Intl (PA) ....F....714 373-8100
15302 Bolsa Chica St Huntington Beach (92649) ***(P-18918)***
Fresco Plastics Inc ....E....831 625-9877
5680 Carmel Valley Rd Carmel (93923) ***(P-9794)***
Fresco Solar, Morgan Hill *Also called Al Fresco Concepts Inc* ***(P-18076)***
Fresenius Medical Care, Concord *Also called Fresenius Usa Inc* ***(P-7898)***
Fresenius Usa Inc (HQ) ....C....925 288-4218
4040 Nelson Ave Concord (94520) ***(P-7898)***
Fresh & Ready, San Fernando *Also called Lehman Foods Inc* ***(P-2526)***
Fresh & Ready Foods LLC ....D....818 837-7600
1145 Arroyo St Ste B San Fernando (91340) ***(P-2464)***
Fresh Creative Foods, Vista *Also called Rmjv LP* ***(P-14398)***
Fresh Express Incorporated ....E....831 424-2921
950 E Blanco Rd Salinas (93901) ***(P-2465)***
Fresh Innovations LLC ....E....805 483-2265
908 E 3rd St Oxnard (93030) ***(P-2354)***
Fresh Jive Manufacturing Inc ....E....213 748-0129
1317 S Olive St Los Angeles (90015) ***(P-2989)***
Fresh Packing Corporation ....E....213 612-0136
4333 S Maywood Ave Vernon (90058) ***(P-727)***
Fresh Peaches Incorporated (PA) ....E....909 980-0172
8423 Rochester Ave # 103 Rancho Cucamonga (91730) ***(P-2787)***
Fresh Peaches Swimwear, Rancho Cucamonga *Also called Fresh Peaches Incorporated* ***(P-2787)***
Fresh Start Bakeries, Ontario *Also called Aryzta LLC* ***(P-1303)***
Fresno Business Journal, Fresno *Also called Business Journal* ***(P-5896)***
Fresno D", Fresno *Also called Fresno Distributing Co* ***(P-17230)***
Fresno Distributing Co ....E....559 442-8800
2055 E Mckinley Ave Fresno (93703) ***(P-17230)***
Fresno Fab-Tech Inc ....E....559 875-9800
1035 K St Sanger (93657) ***(P-11798)***
Fresno French Bread Bakery Inc ....E....559 268-7088
2625 Inyo St Fresno (93721) ***(P-1207)***
Fresno Gem & Mineral Society ....F....559 486-7280
340 W Olive Ave Fresno (93728) ***(P-22595)***
Fresno Glass Plant, Fresno *Also called Vitro Flat Glass LLC* ***(P-10280)***
Fresno Neon Sign Co Inc ....F....559 292-2944
5901 E Clinton Ave Fresno (93727) ***(P-23116)***
Fresno Paper Express, Fresno *Also called Paper Pulp & Film* ***(P-5520)***
Fresno Precision Plastics Inc (PA) ....F....559 323-9595
998 N Temperance Ave Clovis (93611) ***(P-9795)***
Fresno Precision Plastics Inc ....F....916 689-5284
8456 Carbide Ct Sacramento (95828) ***(P-9796)***
Fresno Trade Bindery & Mailing, Fresno *Also called James Clark* ***(P-7335)***
Fresno Valves & Castings Inc (PA) ....C....559 834-2511
7736 E Springfield Ave Selma (93662) ***(P-11398)***
Freudenberg Medical LLC ....C....626 814-9684
5050 Rivergrade Rd Baldwin Park (91706) ***(P-22017)***
Freudenberg Medical LLC (HQ) ....B....805 684-3304
1110 Mark Ave Carpinteria (93013) ***(P-22018)***
Freudenberg-Nok General Partnr ....C....714 834-0602
2041 E Wilshire Ave Santa Ana (92705) ***(P-9230)***
Freund Baking, Commerce *Also called Oakhurst Industries Inc* ***(P-1252)***
Fricke-Parks Press Inc ....D....510 489-6543
33250 Transit Ave Union City (94587) ***(P-6585)***
Friday Flier, Canyon Lake *Also called Golding Publications* ***(P-7358)***
Friedl Corporation ....F....714 443-0122
1291 N Patt St Anaheim (92801) ***(P-19662)***
Fringe Studio LLC ....F....949 387-9680
17909 Fitch Irvine (92614) ***(P-23338)***
Frisco Baking Company Inc ....C....323 225-6111
621 W Avenue 26 Los Angeles (90065) ***(P-1208)***
Frito-Lay North America Inc ....B....909 941-6214
9535 Archibald Ave Rancho Cucamonga (91730) ***(P-2323)***
Frito-Lay North America Inc ....C....714 562-7260
16701 Trojan Way La Mirada (90638) ***(P-2324)***
Frito-Lay North America Inc ....E....209 824-3700
1190 Spreckels Rd Manteca (95336) ***(P-2325)***
Frito-Lay North America Inc ....E....925 689-4260
5045 Forni Dr Concord (94520) ***(P-2326)***
Frito-Lay North America Inc ....E....805 658-1668
4535 Dupont Ct Ventura (93003) ***(P-2327)***
Frito-Lay North America Inc ....F....858 576-3300
4953 Paramount Dr San Diego (92123) ***(P-2328)***
Frito-Lay North America Inc ....D....909 877-0902
635 W Valley Blvd Bloomington (92316) ***(P-2329)***
Frito-Lay North America Inc ....B....209 544-5400
600 Garner Rd Modesto (95357) ***(P-2330)***
Frito-Lay North America Inc ....A....661 328-6000
28801 Highway 58 Bakersfield (93314) ***(P-2331)***
Frm USA LLC ....E....323 469-9006
6001 Santa Monica Blvd Los Angeles (90038) ***(P-13451)***
Froglanders La Jolla ....F....858 459-3764
915 Pearl St Ste A La Jolla (92037) ***(P-699)***
Frogs Leap Winery ....E....707 963-4704
8815 Conn Creek Rd Rutherford (94573) ***(P-1717)***
Front Edge Technology Inc ....E....626 856-8979
13455 Brooks Dr Ste A Baldwin Park (91706) ***(P-19167)***
Frontapp Inc ....D....415 680-3048
525 Brannan St Ste 300 San Francisco (94107) ***(P-23922)***
Frontera Solutions Inc ....D....714 368-1631
1913 E 17th St Ste 210 Santa Ana (92705) ***(P-16685)***
Frontier AG Co Inc (PA) ....E....530 297-1020
46735 County Road 32b Davis (95618) ***(P-1097)***
Frontier Concrete Inc ....F....760 724-4483
717 Mercantile St Vista (92083) ***(P-10760)***
Frontier Electronics Corp ....F....805 522-9998
667 Cochran St Simi Valley (93065) ***(P-18716)***
Frontier Engrg & Mfg Tech Inc ....E....562 606-2655
800 W 16th St Long Beach (90813) ***(P-15976)***
Frontier Medicines ....E....650 457-1005
151 Oyster Point Blvd # 200 South San Francisco (94080) ***(P-7899)***
Frontier Semiconductor (PA) ....E....408 432-8338
165 Topaz St Milpitas (95035) ***(P-18244)***
Frontier Technologies, Long Beach *Also called Frontier Engrg & Mfg Tech Inc* ***(P-15976)***
Frontiers Magazine, Los Angeles *Also called Frontiers Media LLC* ***(P-6240)***
Frontiers Media LLC ....E....323 930-3220
5657 Wilshire Blvd # 470 Los Angeles (90036) ***(P-6240)***
Frontline Environmental TEC ....F....707 745-1116
3195 Park Rd Ste C Benicia (94510) ***(P-20873)***
Frontline Instrs & Contrls ....F....707 747-9766
3195 Park Rd Ste C Benicia (94510) ***(P-21477)***
Frontline Military Apparel, San Diego *Also called Textile 2000 Screen Printing* ***(P-7246)***
Frontline Technologies, Benicia *Also called Frontline Environmental TEC* ***(P-20873)***
Frontline Technologies, Benicia *Also called Frontline Instrs & Contrls* ***(P-21477)***
Frost Beacon, Chico *Also called Ultramar Inc* ***(P-9079)***
Frost Magnetics Incorporated ....E....559 642-2536
49643 Hartwell Rd Oakhurst (93644) ***(P-18717)***
Frozen Bean Inc ....E....855 837-6936
9238 Bally Ct Rancho Cucamonga (91730) ***(P-2212)***
Frt of America LLC ....F....408 261-2632
1101 S Winchester Blvd San Jose (95128) ***(P-14161)***
Fruehe Design, Fresno *Also called Simply Smashing Inc* ***(P-23210)***
Fruit Fillings Inc ....E....559 237-4715
2531 E Edgar Ave Fresno (93706) ***(P-768)***
Fruit Growers Supply Company (PA) ....E....661 290-8704
27770 N Entrmt Dr Fl 3 Flr 3 Valencia (91355) ***(P-5221)***
Fruit Growers Supply Company ....F....559 592-6550
674 E Myer Ave Exeter (93221) ***(P-5222)***
Fruiti Pops Inc ....F....562 404-2568
15418 Cornet St Santa Fe Springs (90670) ***(P-646)***
Fruitridge Prtg Lithograph Inc (PA) ....E....916 452-9213
3258 Stockton Blvd Sacramento (95820) ***(P-6586)***
Fruselva Usa LLC ....F....949 798-0061
4440 Von Karman Ave Newport Beach (92660) ***(P-769)***
Frutarom ....F....951 734-6620
790 E Harrison St Corona (92879) ***(P-2213)***
Frutstix Company, Santa Barbara *Also called Von Hoppen Ice Cream* ***(P-677)***
Frutstix Company, San Diego *Also called Von Hoppen Ice Cream* ***(P-678)***
Fry Reglet Corporation (PA) ....C....800 237-9773
14013 Marquardt Ave Santa Fe Springs (90670) ***(P-11229)***
Fs - Precision Tech Co LLC ....D....310 638-0595
3025 E Victoria St Compton (90221) ***(P-11417)***
FSA, Pleasanton *Also called Full Spectrum Group LLC* ***(P-21232)***
Fsc Lighting, Rancho Cucamonga *Also called Fluorescent Supply Co Inc* ***(P-17036)***
Fsm, Milpitas *Also called Frontier Semiconductor* ***(P-18244)***
Fsp Group USA Corp ....F....909 606-0960
14284 Albers Way Chino (91710) ***(P-18718)***
Ft Textiles, Orange *Also called Fabtex Inc* ***(P-2727)***
Ft3 Tactical, Stanton *Also called Field Time Target Training LLC* ***(P-13271)***
FTC - Forward Threat Control ....F....650 906-7917
234 Jason Way Mountain View (94043) ***(P-17729)***
Ftg Inc (PA) ....E....562 865-9200
12750 Center Court Dr S # 280 Cerritos (90703) ***(P-19663)***
Ftg Aerospace Inc (HQ) ....E....818 407-4024
20740 Marilla St Chatsworth (91311) ***(P-11358)***
Ftg Circuits Inc (HQ) ....D....818 407-4024
20750 Marilla St Chatsworth (91311) ***(P-17884)***
Fti, Turlock *Also called Formax Technologies Inc* ***(P-19312)***
Ftt Holdings Inc ....F....562 430-6262
3020 Old Ranch Pkwy Seal Beach (90740) ***(P-13777)***
Fudge Factory Farm, Placerville *Also called Sierra Foothills Fudge Factory* ***(P-1402)***
Fuel Injection Corporation ....F....925 371-6551
2246 N Macarthur Dr Tracy (95376) ***(P-19664)***
Fuel Injection Engineering, Aliso Viejo *Also called Hilborn Manufacturing Corp* ***(P-19681)***
Fuel Injection Engineering Co ....F....949 360-0909
22892 Glenwood Dr Aliso Viejo (92656) ***(P-19665)***
Fuelbox Inc ....F....919 949-9179
201 W Montecito St Santa Barbara (93101) ***(P-18919)***
Fuji Natural Foods Inc (HQ) ....D....909 947-1008
13500 S Hamner Ave Ontario (91761) ***(P-2466)***
Fuji Xerox, Palo Alto *Also called Xerox International Partners* ***(P-14342)***
Fujifilm Dimatix Inc (HQ) ....C....408 565-9150
2250 Martin Ave Santa Clara (95050) ***(P-15232)***
Fujifilm Irvine Scientific Inc ....C....949 261-7800
1830 E Warner Ave Santa Ana (92705) ***(P-8302)***
Fujifilm Ultra Pure Sltons Inc (HQ) ....E....831 632-2120
11225 Commercial Pkwy Castroville (95012) ***(P-8968)***
Fujifilm Wako Diagnostics US ....E....650 210-9153
1025 Terra Bella Ave A Mountain View (94043) ***(P-8222)***
Fujikin of America Inc (HQ) ....E....408 980-8269
454 Kato Ter Fremont (94539) ***(P-13330)***
Fujikura Composite America Inc ....E....760 598-6060
1819 Aston Ave Ste 101 Carlsbad (92008) ***(P-22804)***
Fujikuria Composits, Carlsbad *Also called Fujikura Composite America Inc* ***(P-22804)***
Fujisawa Bristol Corporation ....D....760 324-1488
69848 Highway 111 Rancho Mirage (92270) ***(P-7661)***
Fujisoft America Inc ....F....650 235-9422
1710 S Amphlett Blvd # 215 San Mateo (94402) ***(P-23923)***
Fujitsu Optical Co ....F....408 746-6000
1280 E Arques Ave Sunnyvale (94085) ***(P-10306)***
Fulcrum International Inc ....E....310 763-6823
993 S Firefly Dr Anaheim (92808) ***(P-2825)***
Fulcrum Microsystems Inc ....D....818 871-8100
26630 Agoura Rd Calabasas (91302) ***(P-18245)***

Mergent e-mail: customerrelations@mergent.com 2020 California Manufacturers Register (P-0000) Products & Services Section entry number
1106 (PA)=Parent Co (HQ)=Headquarters (DH)=Div Headquarters

Fulham Co Inc ....E.....323 779-2980
12705 S Van Ness Ave Hawthorne (90250) *(P-16552)*
Full Color Bus Cds & Flyers, Sacramento *Also called Full Color Business (P-6587)*
Full Color Business ....F.....916 218-7845
2620 El Camino Ave Sacramento (95821) *(P-6587)*
Full Spectrum Group LLC (PA) ....F.....925 485-9000
1252 Quarry Ln Pleasanton (94566) *(P-21232)*
Full Spectrum Omega Inc ....F.....714 866-0039
12832 Nutwood St Garden Grove (92840) *(P-8495)*
Full-Traction Suspension, Bakersfield *Also called California Mini Truck Inc (P-19605)*
Fullbloom Baking Company Inc ....B.....510 456-3638
6500 Overlake Pl Newark (94560) *(P-1209)*
Fuller Laboratories ....F.....714 525-7660
1312 E Valencia Dr Fullerton (92831) *(P-8223)*
Fuller Manufacturing Inc ....F.....209 267-5071
130 Ridge Rd Sutter Creek (95685) *(P-19314)*
Fullerton Printing Inc ....F.....714 870-7500
315 N Lemon St Fullerton (92832) *(P-6588)*
Fullfillment Systems Inc ....D.....408 745-7675
1228 Reamwood Ave Sunnyvale (94089) *(P-458)*
Fulltone Musical Products Inc ....F.....310 204-0155
11018 Washington Blvd Culver City (90232) *(P-22621)*
Fulton Acres Inc ....F.....707 762-2280
1330 Commerce St Ste A Petaluma (94954) *(P-3787)*
Fun o Cake ....F.....323 213-8684
2324 4th Ave Apt 201 Los Angeles (90018) *(P-1210)*
Fundamental Tech Intl Inc ....E.....562 595-0661
2900 E 29th St Long Beach (90806) *(P-20874)*
Fundex Investment Group, San Francisco *Also called Fundx Investment Group (P-6241)*
Fundx Investment Group ....F.....415 986-7979
235 Montgomery St # 1049 San Francisco (94104) *(P-6241)*
Fungs Village Inc ....E.....323 881-1600
5339 E Washington Blvd Commerce (90040) *(P-2369)*
Funktion Technologies Inc ....F.....310 937-7335
2110 Artesia Blvd B202 Redondo Beach (90278) *(P-20875)*
Funktion USA ....F.....760 473-4171
3465 Ann Dr Carlsbad (92008) *(P-12217)*
Funny-Bunny Inc (PA) ....D.....714 957-1114
1513b E Saint Gertrude Pl Santa Ana (92705) *(P-3085)*
Funtastic Factory Inc ....E.....562 777-1140
19703 Meadows Cir Cerritos (90703) *(P-15977)*
Fur Accents LLC ....F.....714 403-5286
349 W Grove Ave Orange (92865) *(P-3499)*
Furlong, Conrad, Los Angeles *Also called F Conrad Furlong Inc (P-22517)*
Furnace Pros, Orange *Also called Lochaber Cornwall Inc (P-14769)*
Furniture Technics Inc ....E.....562 802-0261
2900 Supply Ave Commerce (90040) *(P-4573)*
Furniture Techniques, Commerce *Also called Furniture Technics Inc (P-4573)*
Furniture Technologies Inc ....E.....760 246-9180
17227 Columbus St Adelanto (92301) *(P-3974)*
Furst, Los Angeles *Also called Lf Sportswear Inc (P-3174)*
Fusion 360 Inc ....F.....209 632-0139
677 E Olive Ave Turlock (95380) *(P-8303)*
Fusion Coatings Inc ....F.....925 443-8083
6589 Las Positas Rd Livermore (94551) *(P-13180)*
Fusion Diet Systems Inc (PA) ....F.....801 783-1194
620 Nwport Ctr Dr Ste 350 Newport Beach (92660) *(P-592)*
Fusion Food Factory ....E.....858 578-8001
9350 Trade Pl Ste A San Diego (92126) *(P-1211)*
Fusion Product Mfg Inc ....D.....619 819-5521
440 Industrial Rd Tecate (91980) *(P-14054)*
Fusion Sign & Design Inc (PA) ....C.....877 477-8777
680 Columbia Ave Riverside (92507) *(P-23117)*
Futek Advanced Sensor Tech Inc ....C.....949 465-0900
10 Thomas Irvine (92618) *(P-20876)*
Futon Express ....F.....626 443-8684
10309 Vacco St South El Monte (91733) *(P-4641)*
Futurama, San Mateo *Also called Bears For Humanity Inc (P-8721)*
Future Fibre Tech US Inc (HQ) ....F.....650 903-2222
800 W El Cam Mountain View (94040) *(P-19315)*
Future Fine Foods ....F.....805 682-9421
2615 De La Vina St Ste 1 Santa Barbara (93105) *(P-1212)*
Future Foam Inc ....E.....714 871-2344
2451 Cypress Way Fullerton (92831) *(P-9540)*
Future Foam Inc ....E.....209 832-1886
1000 E Grant Line Rd # 100 Tracy (95304) *(P-9541)*
Future Foam Inc ....C.....714 459-9971
2441 Cypress Way Fullerton (92831) *(P-9542)*
Future Foam Inc ....E.....714 459-9971
2441 Cypress Way Fullerton (92831) *(P-9543)*
Future Home, Los Angeles *Also called Home Portal LLC (P-16556)*
Future Molds Inc ....F.....909 989-7398
10349 Regis Ct Rancho Cucamonga (91730) *(P-14055)*
Future Tech Metals Inc ....E.....951 781-4801
719 Palmyrita Ave Riverside (92507) *(P-15978)*
Future Us Inc (HQ) ....D.....650 238-2400
1390 Market St Ste 200 San Francisco (94102) *(P-5941)*
Future Wave Technologies Inc ....E.....858 481-1112
1343 Camino Teresa Solana Beach (92075) *(P-2294)*
Futureflite Inc ....F.....818 653-2145
806 Calle Plano Camarillo (93012) *(P-4860)*
Futuris Automotive (ca) LLC ....B.....510 771-2300
6601 Overlake Pl Newark (94560) *(P-3788)*
Fuzebox Software Corporation (HQ) ....F.....415 692-4800
150 Spear St Ste 900 San Francisco (94105) *(P-23924)*
Fuzetron Inc ....F.....619 244-5141
2111 Paseo Grande El Cajon (92019) *(P-14469)*
Fvo Solutions Inc ....D.....626 449-0218
789 N Fair Oaks Ave Pasadena (91103) *(P-13181)*

Fxc Corporation ....D.....714 557-8032
3050 Red Hill Ave Costa Mesa (92626) *(P-3844)*
Fxc Corporation (PA) ....E.....714 556-7400
3050 Red Hill Ave Costa Mesa (92626) *(P-11590)*
Fxi Inc ....D.....510 357-2600
2451 Polvorosa Ave San Leandro (94577) *(P-9544)*
Fxi Inc ....C.....714 637-0110
2060 N Batavia St Orange (92865) *(P-9545)*
Fxp Technologies, Brea *Also called S&B Industry Inc (P-10038)*
Fyfe Co LLC (HQ) ....F.....858 444-2970
4995 Murphy Canyon Rd # 110 San Diego (92123) *(P-12590)*
Fziomed Inc (PA) ....E.....805 546-0610
231 Bonetti Dr San Luis Obispo (93401) *(P-21719)*
G & D Industries Inc ....F.....626 331-1250
1202 E Edna Pl Covina (91724) *(P-9797)*
G & F Horse Trailer Repair ....F.....909 820-4600
2175 S Willow Ave Bloomington (92316) *(P-20510)*
G & F White Wedding Carriages, Bloomington *Also called G & F Horse Trailer Repair (P-20510)*
G & G Quality Case Co Inc ....D.....323 233-2482
2025 E 25th St Vernon (90058) *(P-10195)*
G & H Precision Inc ....F.....818 982-3873
11950 Vose St North Hollywood (91605) *(P-15979)*
G & I Industries, Baldwin Park *Also called G & I Islas Industries Inc (P-14366)*
G & I Islas Industries Inc (PA) ....E.....626 960-5020
12860 Schabarum Ave Baldwin Park (91706) *(P-14366)*
G & L Musical Instruments, Fullerton *Also called Bbe Sound Inc (P-22609)*
G & L Tooling Inc ....F.....562 802-2857
14526 Carmenita Rd Norwalk (90650) *(P-13921)*
G & N Rubicon Gear Inc ....D.....951 356-3800
225 Citation Cir Corona (92880) *(P-12710)*
G & P Dntl Care Former Partnr, Oxnard *Also called Henry J Perez DDS (P-22159)*
G & P Group Inc ....F.....323 268-2686
13842 Bettencourt St Cerritos (90703) *(P-1426)*
G & S Enterprises, Stockton *Also called G & S Process Equipment Inc (P-15980)*
G & S Process Equipment Inc ....F.....209 466-3630
1700 N Broadway Ave Stockton (95205) *(P-15980)*
G A Doors Inc ....D.....714 739-1144
15140 Desman Rd La Mirada (90638) *(P-4046)*
G A Systems, Orange *Also called SA Serving Lines Inc (P-12363)*
G A Systems Inc ....F.....714 848-7529
226 W Carleton Ave Orange (92867) *(P-15515)*
G and H Vineyards, Rutherford *Also called Grgich Hills Cellar (P-1737)*
G and S Milling Co ....E.....707 459-0294
23205 Live Oak Rd Willits (95490) *(P-4047)*
G B Mold & Tool Design ....F.....408 254-3871
640 Giguere Ct San Jose (95133) *(P-14056)*
G B Remanufacturing Inc ....D.....562 272-7333
2040 E Cherry Indus Cir Long Beach (90805) *(P-9798)*
G By Guess, Santa Barbara *Also called Guess Inc (P-3006)*
G C S, Torrance *Also called Global Comm Semiconductors LLC (P-18252)*
G D M Electronic Assembly Inc ....D.....408 945-4100
2070 Ringwood Ave San Jose (95131) *(P-16900)*
G E Shell Core Co ....E.....323 773-4242
8346 Salt Lake Ave Cudahy (90201) *(P-14057)*
G F Cole Corporation (PA) ....F.....310 320-0601
21735 S Western Ave Torrance (90501) *(P-9231)*
G G C Inc (PA) ....E.....714 835-6530
2624 Rousselle St Santa Ana (92707) *(P-14306)*
G G C Inc ....E.....714 835-0551
2624 Rousselle St Santa Ana (92707) *(P-14307)*
G Girl, Vernon *Also called LAT LLC (P-3361)*
G Hartzell & Son Inc ....E.....925 798-2206
2372 Stanwell Cir Concord (94520) *(P-22156)*
G L D S, Carlsbad *Also called Great Lakes Data Systems Inc (P-23954)*
G L Mezzetta Inc ....D.....707 648-1050
105 Mezzetta Ct American Canyon (94503) *(P-770)*
G L O, Sunnyvale *Also called Glo-Usa Inc (P-18251)*
G M I, Anaheim *Also called Gear Manufacturing Inc (P-20113)*
G M P C LLC ....F.....707 766-9504
2180 S Mcdowell Blvd Petaluma (94954) *(P-23118)*
G M Quartz, Oakland *Also called GM Associates Inc (P-18925)*
G O Pallets Inc ....E.....909 823-4663
15642 Slover Ave Fontana (92337) *(P-4368)*
G P Manufacturing Inc ....F.....714 974-0288
541 W Briardale Ave Orange (92865) *(P-15981)*
G Powell Electric ....E.....909 865-2291
1020 Price Ave Pomona (91767) *(P-24691)*
G Printing Inc ....F.....818 246-1156
456 W Broadway Glendale (91204) *(P-7070)*
G Pucci & Sons Inc ....F.....415 468-0452
460 Valley Dr Brisbane (94005) *(P-22805)*
G R C, Chatsworth *Also called General Ribbon Corp (P-22964)*
G R Furniture Manufacturing, South El Monte *Also called Ramon Lopez (P-4664)*
G R J Fashions ....F.....323 537-5814
6750 Foster Bridge Blvd B Bell Gardens (90201) *(P-2890)*
G T Water Products Inc ....F.....805 529-2900
5239 N Commerce Ave Moorpark (93021) *(P-11669)*
G V Industries Inc ....E.....619 474-3013
1346 Cleveland Ave National City (91950) *(P-15982)*
G W, San Lorenzo *Also called Golden W Ppr Converting Corp (P-14708)*
G&A Apparel Group ....E.....323 234-1746
3610 S Broadway Los Angeles (90007) *(P-3789)*
G&A Bias Les, Los Angeles *Also called G&A Apparel Group (P-3789)*
G-G Distribution & Dev Co Inc ....C.....661 257-5700
28545 Livingston Ave Valencia (91355) *(P-13354)*
G-M Enterprises, Corona *Also called Jhawar Industries LLC (P-14767)*

Employee Codes: A=Over 500 employees, B=251-500
C=101-250, D=51-100, E=20-50, F=10-19

2020 California
Manfacturers Register

© Mergent Inc. 1-800-342-5647

1107

A
L
P
H
A
B
E
T
I
C

G. Fink & Associates, Laguna Hills *Also called Gregory M Fink* ***(P-23125)***
G/G Industries, Valencia *Also called G-G Distribution & Dev Co Inc* ***(P-13354)***
G2 Graphic Service Inc..........D.......818 623-3100
5510 Cleon Ave North Hollywood (91601) ***(P-7071)***
G2 Metal Fab..........E.......925 443-7903
6954 Preston Ave Livermore (94551) ***(P-11799)***
G7 Productivity Systems..........D.......858 675-1095
16885 W Bernardo Dr # 290 San Diego (92127) ***(P-23925)***
Gabels Cosmetics Inc..........F.......323 221-2430
126 S Avenue 18 Los Angeles (90031) ***(P-8496)***
Gabilan Welding Inc..........F.......831 637-3360
1091 San Felipe Rd Hollister (95023) ***(P-15983)***
Gabriel Container Co (PA)..........C.......562 699-1051
8844 Millergrove Dr Santa Fe Springs (90670) ***(P-5223)***
Gachupin Enterprises LLC..........E.......714 375-4111
5671 Engineer Dr Huntington Beach (92649) ***(P-7072)***
Gadia Polythylene Supplies Inc..........F.......818 775-0096
21141 Itasca St Chatsworth (91311) ***(P-9799)***
GAF Materials, Fontana *Also called Standard Industries Inc* ***(P-4487)***
Gaffoglio Fmly Mtlcrafters Inc (PA)..........C.......714 444-2000
11161 Slater Ave Fountain Valley (92708) ***(P-10361)***
Gage Wafco Co Inc..........F.......310 532-3106
16625 Gramercy Pl Gardena (90247) ***(P-14162)***
Gagne-Mulford Enterprises..........F.......925 671-7434
2490 Almond Ave Concord (94520) ***(P-9310)***
Gahh LLC (HQ)..........F.......800 722-2292
11128 Gault St North Hollywood (91605) ***(P-19666)***
Gail Materials Inc..........E.......951 667-6106
10060 Dawson Canyon Rd Corona (92883) ***(P-340)***
Gaines Manufacturing Inc..........E.......858 486-7100
12200 Kirkham Rd Poway (92064) ***(P-12218)***
Gaines Well Service Inc (PA)..........E.......916 687-6751
10063 Colony Rd Wilton (95693) ***(P-199)***
Gainey Ceramics Inc..........C.......909 596-4464
1200 Arrow Hwy La Verne (91750) ***(P-10488)***
GAI Manufacturing Co LLC..........F.......626 443-8616
3380 Gilman Rd El Monte (91732) ***(P-13800)***
Galaxy Bearing Company, Valencia *Also called Galaxy Die & Engineering Inc* ***(P-11399)***
Galaxy Brazing Co Inc..........E.......562 946-9039
10015 Freeman Ave Santa Fe Springs (90670) ***(P-24634)***
Galaxy Desserts..........C.......510 439-3160
1100 Marina Way S Ste D Richmond (94804) ***(P-1341)***
Galaxy Die & Engineering Inc..........E.......661 775-9301
24910 Avenue Tibbitts Valencia (91355) ***(P-11399)***
Galaxy Energy Systems Inc..........F.......760 778-4254
362 N Palm Canyon Dr Palm Springs (92262) ***(P-13569)***
Galaxy Enterprises Inc..........E.......323 728-3980
5411 Sheila St Commerce (90040) ***(P-23339)***
GALAXY ENTERPRISES INTERNATION, San Dimas *Also called Gei Inc* ***(P-14471)***
Galaxy Manufacturing Inc..........F.......408 654-4583
3200 Bassett St Santa Clara (95054) ***(P-12806)***
Galaxy Medical, Commerce *Also called Galaxy Enterprises Inc* ***(P-23339)***
Galaxy Pest Control, Malibu *Also called Games Production Company LLC* ***(P-22677)***
Galaxy Press, Concord *Also called Print-N-Stuff Inc* ***(P-6797)***
Galaxy Press Inc..........E.......323 399-3433
6115-6121 Malburg Way Vernon (90058) ***(P-6104)***
Galdaza Food Corporation..........E.......213 747-4025
1147 W Washington Blvd Los Angeles (90015) ***(P-1213)***
Gale Banks Engineering..........C.......626 969-9600
546 S Duggan Ave Azusa (91702) ***(P-13596)***
Galen Robotics Inc..........F.......408 502-5960
541 Jefferson Ave Ste 100 Redwood City (94063) ***(P-21720)***
Gali Corporation..........F.......310 477-1224
2301 Pontius Ave Los Angeles (90064) ***(P-20111)***
Galil Motion Control Inc..........E.......800 377-6329
270 Technology Way Rocklin (95765) ***(P-20877)***
Gallagher & Burk, Dublin *Also called Oliver De Silva Inc* ***(P-317)***
Gallagher Rental Inc..........E.......714 690-1559
15701 Heron Ave La Mirada (90638) ***(P-17129)***
Galleano Enterprises Inc..........D.......951 685-5376
4231 Wineville Ave Jurupa Valley (91752) ***(P-1718)***
Gallery, San Leandro *Also called Lindsay/Barnett Incorporated* ***(P-13530)***
Gallery Cabinet Connection..........F.......559 294-7007
5783 E Shields Ave Fresno (93727) ***(P-4200)***
Galleys Plus Custom Cabinets..........F.......951 278-4596
1432 E 6th St Corona (92879) ***(P-4201)***
Gallien Technology Inc (PA)..........D.......209 234-7300
2234 Industrial Dr Stockton (95206) ***(P-17231)***
Galliien Krueger, Stockton *Also called Gallien Technology Inc* ***(P-17231)***
Gallo Advertising, Modesto *Also called E & J Gallo Winery* ***(P-1687)***
Gallo Glass Company (HQ)..........A.......209 341-3710
605 S Santa Cruz Ave Modesto (95354) ***(P-10288)***
Gallo Global Nutrition LLC..........C.......209 394-7984
10561 Highway 140 Atwater (95301) ***(P-551)***
Gallo Os Sonoma, Healdsburg *Also called E & J Gallo Winery* ***(P-1681)***
Galt Herald, Galt *Also called Herburger Publications Inc* ***(P-5660)***
Galt Pipe Company..........F.......209 745-2936
321 Elm Ave Galt (95632) ***(P-13355)***
Galt Steel Foundry, Lodi *Also called Lodi Iron Works Inc* ***(P-11145)***
Galt Steel Foundry, Galt *Also called Lodi Iron Works Inc* ***(P-11146)***
Galtech Computer Corporation..........E.......805 376-1060
501 Flynn Rd Camarillo (93012) ***(P-4798)***
Galtech International, Camarillo *Also called Galtech Computer Corporation* ***(P-4798)***
Galvin Precision Machining Inc..........F.......707 526-5359
404 Yolanda Ave Santa Rosa (95404) ***(P-15984)***
Gambol Industries Inc..........E.......562 901-2470
1825 W Pier D St Long Beach (90802) ***(P-20332)***
Game Ready, Concord *Also called Coolsystems Inc* ***(P-22244)***
Gamecloud Studios Inc..........E.......951 677-2345
30111 Tech Dr Ste 110 Murrieta (92563) ***(P-23926)***
Gamemine LLC..........E.......310 310-3105
2341 Wilson Ave Venice (90291) ***(P-23927)***
Gamepro Magazine, Oakland *Also called Idg Games Media Group Inc* ***(P-5960)***
Games Production Company LLC..........F.......310 456-0099
21323 Pacific Coast Hwy Malibu (90265) ***(P-22677)***
Gaming Fund Group..........F.......510 532-8881
14507 Catalina St San Leandro (94577) ***(P-22256)***
Gamma, Vernon *Also called Rotax Incorporated* ***(P-3400)***
Gamma Alloys Inc..........F.......661 294-5291
28128 Livingston Ave Valencia (91355) ***(P-11183)***
Gamma Scientific Inc..........E.......858 635-9008
9925 Carroll Canyon Rd San Diego (92131) ***(P-21478)***
Gammell Industries Inc..........F.......562 634-6653
7535 Jackson St Paramount (90723) ***(P-11800)***
Gammon LLC..........F.......707 575-8282
1410 Neotomas Ave Ste 200 Santa Rosa (95405) ***(P-5942)***
Ganar Industries Inc..........F.......310 515-5683
13721 Harvard Pl Gardena (90249) ***(P-2935)***
Gander Publishing Inc..........F.......805 541-5523
450 Front St Avila Beach (93424) ***(P-6105)***
Gandona Inc A California Corp..........F.......707 967-5550
1535 Sage Canyon Rd Saint Helena (94574) ***(P-1719)***
Ganesh Industries LLC..........F.......818 349-9166
20869 Plummer St Chatsworth (91311) ***(P-14267)***
Gang Yan Diamond Products Inc..........F.......909 590-2255
4620 Mission Blvd Montclair (91763) ***(P-14163)***
Gann Products Company Inc..........F.......562 862-2337
9540 Stewart And Gray Rd Downey (90241) ***(P-9198)***
Gannett Co Inc..........E.......800 859-2091
1156 Aster Ave Ste C Sunnyvale (94086) ***(P-5943)***
Gannett Co Inc..........E.......310 444-2120
10960 Wilshire Blvd Los Angeles (90024) ***(P-5636)***
Gannett Co Inc..........C.......559 688-0521
330 N West St Tulare (93274) ***(P-5637)***
Gannett Co Inc..........D.......760 322-8889
750 N Gene Autry Trl Palm Springs (92262) ***(P-5638)***
Ganpac Distribution LLC..........E.......858 586-1868
7727 Formula Pl San Diego (92121) ***(P-1214)***
Gans Ink and Supply Co Inc (PA)..........E.......323 264-2200
1441 Boyd St Los Angeles (90033) ***(P-8917)***
Gantner Instruments Inc..........E.......858 537-2060
1550 Hotel Cir N San Diego (92108) ***(P-21041)***
Gar Enterprises..........E.......909 985-4575
1396 W 9th St Upland (91786) ***(P-18920)***
Gara Inc..........F.......530 887-1110
1730 Industrial Dr Auburn (95603) ***(P-17038)***
Garabedian Bros Inc (PA)..........E.......559 268-5014
2543 S Orange Ave Fresno (93725) ***(P-15985)***
Garage Doors Incorporated..........D.......408 293-7443
147 Martha St San Jose (95112) ***(P-4048)***
Garage Equipment Supply Inc..........F.......805 530-0027
646 Flinn Ave Ste A Moorpark (93021) ***(P-14470)***
Gard Inc..........E.......714 738-5891
524 E Walnut Ave Fullerton (92832) ***(P-12219)***
Garden Highway, Rancho Cordova *Also called Renaissance Food Group LLC* ***(P-2598)***
Garden Pals Inc..........E.......909 605-0200
1300 Valley Vista Dr # 209 Diamond Bar (91765) ***(P-11530)***
Gardena Sheet Metal, Gardena *Also called C&J Fab Center Inc* ***(P-12141)***
Gardena Specialized Processing, Chatsworth *Also called Gsp Acquisition Corporation* ***(P-13018)***
Gardena Textile Inc..........F.......310 327-5060
245 W 135th St Los Angeles (90061) ***(P-2788)***
Gardena Valley News Inc..........E.......310 329-6351
15005 S Vermont Ave Gardena (90247) ***(P-5639)***
Gardner Family Ltd Partnership..........E.......559 675-8149
300 Commerce Dr Madera (93637) ***(P-11591)***
Gardner Systems Inc..........F.......714 668-9018
3321 S Yale St Santa Ana (92704) ***(P-20758)***
Garfield Commercial Entps..........E.......714 690-5959
15977 Heron Ave La Mirada (90638) ***(P-4799)***
Garhauer Marine Corporation..........E.......909 985-9993
1062 W 9th St Upland (91786) ***(P-11592)***
Garlic Research Labs Inc..........F.......800 424-7990
624 Ruberta Ave Glendale (91201) ***(P-8829)***
Garlic Valley Farm, Glendale *Also called Garlic Research Labs Inc* ***(P-8829)***
Garlic Valley Farms Inc..........F.......818 247-9600
624 Ruberta Ave Glendale (91201) ***(P-881)***
Garlord Manufacturing Company, Ceres *Also called Enova Engineering LLC* ***(P-16947)***
Garmentprinter.com, Santa Fe Springs *Also called Stitch City Industries Inc* ***(P-14293)***
Garmon Corporation..........C.......951 296-6308
27461 Via Industria Temecula (92590) ***(P-23340)***
Garner Heat Treat Inc..........F.......510 568-0587
10001 Denny St Oakland (94603) ***(P-11451)***
Garner Holt Productions Inc..........E.......909 799-3030
1255 Research Dr Redlands (92374) ***(P-14911)***
Garner Products Inc..........F.......916 784-0200
10620 Industrial Ave # 100 Roseville (95678) ***(P-20581)***
Garnett Sign Studio, South San Francisco *Also called Garnett Signs LLC* ***(P-23119)***
Garnett Signs LLC..........F.......650 871-9518
441 Victory Ave South San Francisco (94080) ***(P-23119)***
Garratt-Callahan Company (PA)..........E.......650 697-5811
50 Ingold Rd Burlingame (94010) ***(P-8969)***
Garrett Precision Inc..........F.......949 855-9710
25082 La Suen Rd Laguna Hills (92653) ***(P-15986)***
Garry Electronics, Camarillo *Also called Cooper Crouse-Hinds LLC* ***(P-9296)***
Garvey Nut & Candy, Pico Rivera *Also called Genesis Foods Corporation* ***(P-1368)***
Garvey Nut and Candy, Vernon *Also called S & C Foods Inc* ***(P-1393)***

Mergent e-mail: customerrelations@mergent.com
1108
2020 California
Manufacturers Register
(P-0000) Products & Services Section entry number
(PA)=Parent Co (HQ)=Headquarters (DH)=Div Headquarters

Gary Bale Redi-Mix Con Inc....D....949 786-9441
16131 Construction Cir W Irvine (92606) ***(P-10761)***
Gary Doupnik Manufacturing Inc....D....916 652-9291
3237 Rippey Rd Loomis (95650) ***(P-4459)***
Gary Manufacturing Inc....E....619 429-4479
2626 Southport Way Ste E National City (91950) ***(P-9800)***
Gary Schroeder Enterprises....F....818 565-1133
158 W Verdugo Ave Burbank (91502) ***(P-19667)***
Gary's of California, Granada Hills *Also called Garys Leather Creations Inc* ***(P-10234)***
Gary's Signs & Screen Printing, Lodi *Also called Garys Signs and Screen Prtg* ***(P-23120)***
Garys Leather Creations Inc....D....818 831-9977
12644 Bradford Pl Granada Hills (91344) ***(P-10234)***
Garys Signs and Screen Prtg....F....209 369-8592
1620 Ackerman Dr Lodi (95240) ***(P-23120)***
Gas Recovery Systems LLC....F....949 718-1430
20662 Newport Coast Dr Irvine (92612) ***(P-200)***
Gasket Manufacturing Co....E....310 217-5600
18001 S Main St Gardena (90248) ***(P-9232)***
Gasket Specialties Inc....F....909 987-4724
8654 Helms Ave Rancho Cucamonga (91730) ***(P-9233)***
Gasketfab Division, Torrance *Also called Industrial Gasket and Sup Co* ***(P-9237)***
Gasser-Olds Inc....E....323 583-9031
1800 Highland Ave Manhattan Beach (90266) ***(P-11400)***
Gate-Or-Door Inc....E....209 751-4881
14811 Leroy Ave Ripon (95366) ***(P-23928)***
Gatehouse Media LLC....F....707 964-5642
690 S Main St Fort Bragg (95437) ***(P-5640)***
Gatehouse Media LLC....E....530 842-5777
309 S Broadway St Yreka (96097) ***(P-5641)***
Gatehouse Media LLC....D....530 891-1234
400 E Park Ave Chico (95928) ***(P-5642)***
Gatekeeper Systems Inc (PA)....E....949 268-1414
90 Icon Foothill Ranch (92610) ***(P-19316)***
Gateway Inc (HQ)....C....949 471-7000
7565 Irvine Center Dr # 150 Irvine (92618) ***(P-14912)***
Gateway Marketing Concepts, Poway *Also called Oussoren Eppel Corporation* ***(P-23172)***
Gateway Precision Inc....F....408 855-8849
2300 Calle De Luna Santa Clara (95054) ***(P-15987)***
Gateway US Retail Inc....C....949 471-7000
7565 Irvine Center Dr Irvine (92618) ***(P-14913)***
Gateworks Corporation....F....805 781-2000
3026 S Higuera St San Luis Obispo (93401) ***(P-20878)***
Gatherapp Inc....F....415 409-9476
301 Bryant St Apt 201 San Francisco (94107) ***(P-23929)***
Gator Machinery Company....F....909 823-1688
11020 Cherry Ave Fontana (92337) ***(P-13729)***
Gatsby Inc....F....408 573-8890
2106 Ringwood Ave San Jose (95131) ***(P-14308)***
Gavia, Vernon *Also called F Gavina & Sons Inc* ***(P-2288)***
Gavial Engineering & Mfg, Santa Maria *Also called Gavial Holdings Inc* ***(P-18921)***
Gavial Engineering & Mfg Inc (HQ)....E....805 614-0060
1435 W Mccoy Ln Santa Maria (93455) ***(P-17885)***
Gavial Holdings Inc (PA)....F....805 614-0060
1435 W Mccoy Ln Santa Maria (93455) ***(P-18921)***
Gavial Holdings Inc....E....805 688-6734
139 Industrial Way Buellton (93427) ***(P-18922)***
Gavial Itc LLC....D....805 614-0060
869 Ward Dr Santa Barbara (93111) ***(P-18923)***
Gayle Manufacturing Co Inc (PA)....C....530 662-0284
1455 E Kentucky Ave Woodland (95776) ***(P-11801)***
Gaylord's Meat Co, Fullerton *Also called Gaylords HRI Meats* ***(P-410)***
Gaylords HRI Meats....F....714 526-2278
1100 E Ash Ave Ste C Fullerton (92831) ***(P-410)***
Gaylords Inc (PA)....F....562 529-7543
13538 Excelsior Dr Santa Fe Springs (90670) ***(P-19534)***
Gayot Publications....E....323 965-3529
1744 Sunset Ave Santa Monica (90405) ***(P-6242)***
Gaze Inc....F....415 374-9193
1 Market Spear Twr San Francisco (94105) ***(P-18246)***
Gaze USA Inc....E....213 622-0022
1665 Mateo St Los Angeles (90021) ***(P-3328)***
Gaze USA Inc....F....213 622-0022
1665 Mateo St Los Angeles (90021) ***(P-3227)***
Gazette Media Co LLC....F....916 567-9654
770 L St Ste 950 Sacramento (95814) ***(P-5643)***
Gazette Newspapers....E....562 433-2000
5225 E 2nd St Long Beach (90803) ***(P-5644)***
Gb Industrial Spray Inc....F....209 825-7176
1140 Bessemer Ave Ste 1 Manteca (95337) ***(P-13182)***
Gb Sport Sf LLC....E....415 863-6171
200 Potrero Ave San Francisco (94103) ***(P-3515)***
GBF Enterprises Inc....E....714 979-7131
2709 Halladay St Santa Ana (92705) ***(P-15988)***
Gbm Manufacturing Inc....F....888 862-8397
1188 S Airport Way Stockton (95205) ***(P-10442)***
Gbt, South San Francisco *Also called Global Blood Therapeutics Inc* ***(P-7922)***
Gc Aero Inc....F....310 539-7600
21143 Hawth Blvd Ste 136 Torrance (90503) ***(P-11697)***
Gc International Inc (PA)....E....805 389-4631
4671 Calle Carga Camarillo (93012) ***(P-17323)***
Gc International Inc....E....805 389-4631
4671 Calle Carga Camarillo (93012) ***(P-17324)***
Gc Products Inc....E....916 645-3870
601 7th St Lincoln (95648) ***(P-10579)***
Gc Valves, Simi Valley *Also called Components For Automation Inc* ***(P-13299)***
Gcg Corporation....F....818 247-8508
608 Ruberta Ave Glendale (91201) ***(P-13012)***
Gcg Precision Metal Finishing, Glendale *Also called Gcg Corporation* ***(P-13012)***
GCI, San Diego *Also called Goto California Inc* ***(P-17233)***
Gcm Coating, Vernon *Also called Commercial Sand Blast Company* ***(P-12975)***
Gcm Medical & Oem Inc....D....510 475-0404
1350 Atlantic St Union City (94587) ***(P-12220)***
Gcn Supply LLC....E....909 643-4603
9070 Bridgeport Pl Rancho Cucamonga (91730) ***(P-12547)***
Gdas-Lincoln Inc....D....916 645-8961
1501 Aviation Blvd Lincoln (95648) ***(P-19894)***
Gdc, San Jose *Also called Dale Grove Corporation* ***(P-14359)***
Gdca Inc....E....925 456-9900
1799 Portola Ave Ste 1 Livermore (94551) ***(P-15233)***
Gdm Electronic & Medical, San Jose *Also called G D M Electronic Assembly Inc* ***(P-16900)***
Gdms, Lancaster *Also called Geographic Data Mgt Solutions* ***(P-23935)***
Gdsi, San Jose *Also called Grinding & Dicing Services Inc* ***(P-18256)***
GE Aviation Systems LLC....C....714 692-0200
23695 Via Del Rio Yorba Linda (92887) ***(P-20112)***
GE Digital LLC (HQ)....D....925 242-6200
2623 Camino Ramon San Ramon (94583) ***(P-23930)***
GE Health Care, San Diego *Also called GE Healthcare Inc* ***(P-7662)***
GE Healthcare Inc....E....858 279-9382
4877 Mercury St San Diego (92111) ***(P-7662)***
GE Nutrients Inc....F....949 502-5760
19700 Fairchild Ste 330 Irvine (92612) ***(P-7663)***
GE Vallecitos Nuclear Center, Sunol *Also called Ge-Hitachi Nuclear Energy* ***(P-7498)***
GE Ventures Inc....E....650 233-3900
2882 Sand Hill Rd Ste 240 Menlo Park (94025) ***(P-21721)***
GE Water & Process Tech, Bakersfield *Also called Suez Wts Usa Inc* ***(P-9027)***
GE Wind Energy LLC....C....661 823-6423
13681 Chantico Rd Tehachapi (93561) ***(P-13570)***
Ge-Hitachi Nuclear Energy....D....925 862-4382
6705 Vallecitos Rd Sunol (94586) ***(P-7498)***
Gea Farm Technologies Inc....E....559 497-5074
2717 S 4th St Fresno (93725) ***(P-8384)***
Gear Division, Shafter *Also called Lufkin Industries LLC* ***(P-12713)***
Gear Manufacturing Inc....E....714 792-2895
3701 E Miraloma Ave Anaheim (92806) ***(P-20113)***
Gear Technology, Rancho Cucamonga *Also called Marino Enterprises Inc* ***(P-20165)***
Gear Vendors Inc....E....619 562-0060
1717 N Magnolia Ave El Cajon (92020) ***(P-19668)***
Gebe Electronic Services Inc....E....323 731-2439
4112 W Jefferson Blvd Los Angeles (90016) ***(P-13183)***
Geeriraj Inc....E....760 244-6149
7042 Santa Fe Ave E A1 Hesperia (92345) ***(P-17886)***
Gefen LLC....E....818 772-9100
1800 S Mcdowell Blvd Ext Petaluma (94954) ***(P-19317)***
Gehr Industries Inc (HQ)....C....323 728-5558
7400 E Slauson Ave Commerce (90040) ***(P-11305)***
Gei Inc....F....909 592-2234
301 E Arrow Hwy Ste 108 San Dimas (91773) ***(P-14471)***
Geiger Manufacturing Inc....F....209 464-7746
1110 E Scotts Ave Stockton (95205) ***(P-15989)***
Geiger Plastics Inc....E....310 327-9926
16150 S Maple Ave A Gardena (90248) ***(P-9801)***
Gekkeikan Sake USAinC....E....916 985-3111
1136 Sibley St Folsom (95630) ***(P-1720)***
Gelateria Naia, Hercules *Also called Naia Inc* ***(P-661)***
Geltman Industries, Vernon *Also called Rezex Corporation* ***(P-2859)***
Gem Box of West....E....213 748-4875
2430 S Hill St Los Angeles (90007) ***(P-5224)***
Gem Enterprises LLC....E....760 746-6616
300 N Andreasen Dr Escondido (92029) ***(P-13013)***
Gem Mobile Treatment Svcs Inc (HQ)....E....562 595-7075
2525 Cherry Ave Ste 105 Signal Hill (90755) ***(P-20795)***
Gemfire Corporation....D....408 519-6015
2570 N 1st St Ste 440 San Jose (95131) ***(P-19318)***
Gemini - G E L....E....323 651-0513
8365 Melrose Ave Los Angeles (90069) ***(P-7372)***
Gemini Aluminum Corporation....E....909 595-7403
3255 Pomona Blvd Pomona (91768) ***(P-11230)***
Gemini Bio Products....F....916 471-3540
930 Riverside Pkwy Ste 50 Broderick (95605) ***(P-14783)***
Gemini Consultants Inc....F....925 866-8946
2303 Camino Ramon Ste 106 San Ramon (94583) ***(P-17887)***
Gemini Film & Bag Inc (PA)....E....323 582-0901
3574 Fruitland Ave Maywood (90270) ***(P-9802)***
Gemini Industries Inc....D....949 250-4011
2311 Pullman St Santa Ana (92705) ***(P-11201)***
Gemini Industries Inc....F....949 553-4255
1910 E Warner Ave Ste G Santa Ana (92705) ***(P-23341)***
Gemini Mfg & Engrg Inc....E....714 999-0010
1020 E Vermont Ave Anaheim (92805) ***(P-14058)***
Gemini Plastics, Maywood *Also called Gemini Film & Bag Inc* ***(P-9802)***
Gemma Creations, Los Angeles *Also called Gold Craft Jewelry Corp* ***(P-22524)***
Gems of Fruit Co, Placentia *Also called Packers Food Products Inc* ***(P-922)***
Gemsa Enterprises LLC....E....714 521-1736
14370 Gannet St La Mirada (90638) ***(P-1472)***
Gemsa Oils, La Mirada *Also called Gemsa Enterprises LLC* ***(P-1472)***
Gemtech Inds Good Earth Mfg....E....714 848-2517
2737 S Garnsey St Santa Ana (92707) ***(P-13184)***
Gemtech International, Santa Ana *Also called Gemtech Inds Good Earth Mfg* ***(P-13184)***
Gen-Probe Incorporated....D....858 410-8000
10210 Genetic Center Dr San Diego (92121) ***(P-8224)***
Genalyte Inc....F....858 956-1200
10520 Wateridge Cir San Diego (92121) ***(P-21722)***
Genasys Inc., San Diego *Also called Lrad Corporation* ***(P-17252)***
Genbio, San Diego *Also called Innominata* ***(P-8231)***
Gencor, Irvine *Also called GE Nutrients Inc* ***(P-7663)***
Gene Watson Construction A CA....A....661 763-5254
801 Kern St Taft (93268) ***(P-201)***

ALPHABETIC

Employee Codes: A=Over 500 employees, B=251-500
C=101-250, D=51-100, E=20-50, F=10-19
2020 California
Manfacturers Register
© Mergent Inc. 1-800-342-5647
1109

Geneforge Inc....F....650 219-9335
2699 Spring St Redwood City (94063) ***(P-21042)***
Genelabs Technologies Inc (HQ)....F....415 297-2901
505 Penobscot Dr Redwood City (94063) ***(P-7900)***
Genenco, Bakersfield *Also called James L Craft Inc* ***(P-16075)***
Genencor International, Palo Alto *Also called Danisco US Inc* ***(P-8218)***
Genentech Inc....E....707 454-1000
1000 New Horizons Way Vacaville (95688) ***(P-7901)***
Genentech Inc (HQ)....A....650 225-1000
1 Dna Way South San Francisco (94080) ***(P-7902)***
Genentech Inc....F....408 963-8759
465 E Grand Ave Ms432 South San Francisco (94080) ***(P-7903)***
Genentech Inc....B....760 231-2440
1 Antibody Way Oceanside (92056) ***(P-7904)***
Genentech Inc....B....650 216-2900
550 Broadway St Redwood City (94063) ***(P-7905)***
Genentech Inc....F....650 225-3214
431 Grandview Dr Bldg 27 South San Francisco (94080) ***(P-7906)***
Genentech Inc....C....650 225-1000
1 Dna Way South San Francisco (94080) ***(P-7907)***
Genentech Usa Inc....A....650 225-1000
1 Dna Way South San Francisco (94080) ***(P-7908)***
General Atomic Aeron....F....858 455-4560
14040 Danielson St Poway (92064) ***(P-19895)***
General Atomic Aeron....B....858 964-6700
13330 Evening Creek Dr N San Diego (92128) ***(P-19896)***
General Atomic Aeron....C....760 246-3660
9779 Yucca Rd Adelanto (92301) ***(P-19897)***
General Atomic Aeron....B....858 455-2810
3550 General Atomics Ct San Diego (92121) ***(P-19898)***
General Atomic Aeron....B....858 455-4309
16761 Via Del Campo Ct San Diego (92127) ***(P-19899)***
General Atomic Aeron....C....760 388-8208
73 El Mirage Airport Rd B Adelanto (92301) ***(P-19900)***
General Atomic Aeron (HQ)....B....858 312-2810
14200 Kirkham Way Poway (92064) ***(P-19901)***
General Atomic Aeron....B....858 312-2543
14115 Stowe Dr Poway (92064) ***(P-19902)***
General Carbon Company....F....323 588-9291
7542 Maie Ave Los Angeles (90001) ***(P-7459)***
General Coatings, Fresno *Also called Walton Industries Inc* ***(P-8692)***
General Coatings Mfg Corp....F....559 495-4004
1220 E North Ave Fresno (93725) ***(P-13185)***
General Connector, Camarillo *Also called Cooper Crouse-Hinds LLC* ***(P-18759)***
General Container....D....714 562-8700
5450 Dodds Ave Buena Park (90621) ***(P-5225)***
General Dynamics Corporation....E....619 544-3400
2798 Harbor Dr San Diego (92113) ***(P-20287)***
General Dynamics Mission....D....619 671-5400
7603 Saint Andrews Ave H San Diego (92154) ***(P-16717)***
General Dynamics Mission....B....408 908-7300
2688 Orchard Pkwy San Jose (95134) ***(P-17730)***
General Dynmics Mssion Systems....C....916 339-3852
5922 Roseville Rd Sacramento (95842) ***(P-14914)***
General Dynmics Mssion Systems....C....805 497-5042
112 S Lakeview Canyon Rd Westlake Village (91362) ***(P-17731)***
General Dynmics Mtion Ctrl LLC....F....619 671-5400
7603 Saint Andrews Ave H San Diego (92154) ***(P-16718)***
General Dynmics Ots Ncvlle Inc....D....707 473-9200
511 Grove St Healdsburg (95448) ***(P-15622)***
General Dynmics Ots Ncvlle Inc....D....916 355-7700
950 Iron Point Rd Ste 110 Folsom (95630) ***(P-20582)***
General Dynmics Stcom Tech Inc....D....408 955-1900
2205 Fortune Dr San Jose (95131) ***(P-17523)***
General Dynmics Stcom Tech Inc....D....310 539-6704
3111 Fujita St Torrance (90505) ***(P-17524)***
General Elec Assembly Inc....E....408 980-8819
1525 Atteberry Ln San Jose (95131) ***(P-17888)***
General Electric Company....D....925 242-6200
2623 Camino Ramon San Ramon (94583) ***(P-23931)***
General Electric Company....E....760 530-5200
18000 Phantom St Victorville (92394) ***(P-19903)***
General Electric Company....B....951 928-2829
26226 Antelope Rd Romoland (92585) ***(P-13571)***
General Electric Company....E....951 360-2400
11600 Philadelphia Ave Mira Loma (91752) ***(P-17039)***
General Engrg & Mch Works, San Francisco *Also called Robert E Blake Inc* ***(P-20303)***
General Forming Corporation....E....310 326-0624
2413 Moreton St Torrance (90505) ***(P-12221)***
General Foundry Service Corp....D....510 297-5040
1390 Business Center Pl San Leandro (94577) ***(P-11382)***
General Graphic Chemicals Co....F....510 832-4404
2525 Mandela Pkwy Ste 2 Oakland (94607) ***(P-8970)***
General Grinding & Mfg Co LLC....E....562 921-7033
15100 Valley View Ave La Mirada (90638) ***(P-15623)***
General Grinding Inc....E....510 261-5557
801 51st Ave Oakland (94601) ***(P-15990)***
General Industrial Repair....E....323 278-0873
7417 E Slauson Ave Commerce (90040) ***(P-15991)***
General Instrument, Santa Clara *Also called Ruckus Wireless Inc* ***(P-17647)***
General Linear Systems....F....714 994-4822
4332 Artesia Ave Fullerton (92833) ***(P-24692)***
General Media Systems LLC....F....818 210-4236
611 K St Ste B202 San Diego (92101) ***(P-23932)***
General Metal Engraving Inc....E....626 443-8961
9254 Garvey Ave South El Monte (91733) ***(P-22949)***
General Mills Inc....E....209 334-7061
2000 W Turner Rd Lodi (95242) ***(P-1020)***
General Mills Inc....D....818 553-6777
620 N Kenwood St Glendale (91206) ***(P-1021)***
General Mills Inc....E....323 584-3433
4309 Fruitland Ave Vernon (90058) ***(P-1000)***
General Mills Inc....E....310 605-6108
1055 Sandhill Ave Carson (90746) ***(P-700)***
General Mills Inc....D....951 685-7030
11618 Mulberry Ave Fontana (92337) ***(P-1022)***
General Monitors Inc (HQ)....C....949 581-4464
26776 Simpatica Cir Lake Forest (92630) ***(P-17732)***
General Nucleonics Inc....F....909 593-4985
2807 Metropolitan Pl Pomona (91767) ***(P-21479)***
General Photonics Corp....E....909 590-5473
14351 Pipeline Ave Chino (91710) ***(P-17374)***
General Plating, Los Angeles *Also called Alpha Polishing Corporation* ***(P-12920)***
General Production Services....F....818 365-4211
670 Arroyo St San Fernando (91340) ***(P-15992)***
General Ribbon Corp....B....818 709-1234
5775 E Ls Angls Ave Ste 2 Chatsworth (91311) ***(P-22964)***
General Sealants Inc....C....626 961-0211
300 Turnbull Canyon Rd City of Industry (91745) ***(P-8869)***
General Steel Fabricators Inc....F....818 897-1300
12179 Branford St Ste B Sun Valley (91352) ***(P-11802)***
General Truck Body Inc....D....323 276-1933
1130 S Vail Ave Montebello (90640) ***(P-19535)***
General Veneer Mfg Co....E....323 564-2661
8652 Otis St South Gate (90280) ***(P-4274)***
General Wax & Candle Co, North Hollywood *Also called General Wax Co Inc* ***(P-23342)***
General Wax Co Inc (PA)....D....818 765-5800
6863 Beck Ave North Hollywood (91605) ***(P-23342)***
Generation Alpha Inc (PA)....F....888 998-8881
853 Sandhill Ave Carson (90746) ***(P-16970)***
Generation Circuits LLC....E....760 743-7459
621 S Andreasen Dr Ste B Escondido (92029) ***(P-17889)***
Generic Manufacturing Corp....F....951 296-2838
27455 Bostik Ct Temecula (92590) ***(P-14367)***
Generitech Corporation....F....559 346-0233
4967 E Lansing Way Fresno (93727) ***(P-8497)***
Generon Igs Inc....E....925 431-1030
992 Arcy Ln Bldg 992 Pittsburg (94565) ***(P-14821)***
Genesis 2000, La Puente *Also called Genesis Tc Inc* ***(P-4642)***
Genesis Computer Systems Inc....E....714 632-3648
4055 E La Palma Ave Ste C Anaheim (92807) ***(P-14915)***
Genesis Foods Corporation (HQ)....D....323 890-5890
8825 Mercury Ln Pico Rivera (90660) ***(P-1368)***
Genesis Group Sftwr Developers....E....714 630-4297
16027 Brookhurst St Ste G Fountain Valley (92708) ***(P-23933)***
Genesis Mch & Fabrication Inc....F....661 324-4366
4321 Turcon Ave Bakersfield (93308) ***(P-15993)***
Genesis Natural Products, Chatsworth *Also called Nydr Holdings Inc* ***(P-2573)***
Genesis Printing....F....323 965-7935
5872 W Pico Blvd Los Angeles (90019) ***(P-6589)***
Genesis Supreme Rv Inc....E....951 337-0254
23129 Cajalco Rd Perris (92570) ***(P-20511)***
Genesis Tc Inc....F....626 968-4455
524 Hofgaarden St La Puente (91744) ***(P-4642)***
Genesys Telecom Labs, Daly City *Also called Genesys Telecom Labs Inc* ***(P-23934)***
Genesys Telecom Labs Inc (HQ)....B....650 466-1100
2001 Junipero Serra Blvd Daly City (94014) ***(P-23934)***
Genetix Usa Inc....F....408 719-6400
120 Baytech Dr San Jose (95134) ***(P-21233)***
Genetronics Inc....E....858 597-6006
11494 Sorrento Valley Rd A San Diego (92121) ***(P-20759)***
Genius Products Nt Inc....C....510 671-0219
6960 S Centinela Ave Culver City (90230) ***(P-2077)***
Genius Tools Americas Corp (PA)....E....909 230-9588
1440 E Cedar St Ontario (91761) ***(P-14164)***
Genmark Diagnostics Inc (PA)....C....760 448-4300
5964 La Place Ct Ste 100 Carlsbad (92008) ***(P-21723)***
Genoa Corporation....E....510 979-3000
41762 Christy St Fremont (94538) ***(P-18247)***
Genopis Inc....E....858 875-4700
10390 Pacific Center Ct San Diego (92121) ***(P-7909)***
Genovation Incorprated....F....949 833-3355
17741 Mitchell N Irvine (92614) ***(P-15234)***
Gensia Sicor Inc (HQ)....A....949 455-4700
19 Hughes Irvine (92618) ***(P-7910)***
Gentec Manufacturing Inc....F....408 432-6220
2241 Ringwood Ave San Jose (95131) ***(P-15994)***
Gentherm Incorporated....F....626 593-4500
5462 Irwindale Ave Ste A Irwindale (91706) ***(P-19669)***
Gentle Giants Products Inc....F....951 818-2512
4867 Pedley Ave Norco (92860) ***(P-1074)***
Gentry Golf Maintenance....E....714 630-3541
14893 Ball Rd Anaheim (92806) ***(P-22806)***
Gentry Magazine, Menlo Park *Also called 18 Media Inc* ***(P-5872)***
Genuine Parts Distributors, Ontario *Also called Tracy Industries Inc* ***(P-13600)***
Genzyme Corporation....D....800 255-1616
655 E Huntington Dr Monrovia (91016) ***(P-7911)***
Genzyme Genetics, Monrovia *Also called Genzyme Corporation* ***(P-7911)***
Geo A Diack Inc....E....626 961-2491
1250 S Johnson Dr City of Industry (91745) ***(P-11260)***
Geo Drilling Fluids Inc....E....916 383-2811
7268 Frasinetti Rd Sacramento (95828) ***(P-10971)***
Geo Labels Inc....F....909 923-6832
1180 E Francis St Ste G Ontario (91761) ***(P-7073)***
Geo M Martin Company (PA)....D....510 652-2200
1250 67th St Emeryville (94608) ***(P-14309)***
Geo Plastics....E....323 277-8106
2200 E 52nd St Vernon (90058) ***(P-9803)***
Geo Semiconductor Inc (PA)....E....408 638-0400
101 Metro Dr Ste 620 San Jose (95110) ***(P-18248)***

Mergent e-mail: customerrelations@mergent.com
1110
2020 California
Manufacturers Register
(P-0000) Products & Services Section entry number
(PA)=Parent Co (HQ)=Headquarters (DH)=Div Headquarters

Geodetics Inc ....E....858 729-0872
2649 Ariane Dr San Diego (92117) *(P-20583)*
Geographic Data Mgt Solutions ....F....661 949-1025
42140 10th St W Lancaster (93534) *(P-23935)*
Geolabs Westlake Village, Westlake Village *Also called R & R Services Corporation (P-9361)*
Geometrics Inc ....D....408 428-4244
2190 Fortune Dr San Jose (95131) *(P-21480)*
Georg Fischer Harvel LLC ....D....661 396-0653
7001 Schirra Ct Bakersfield (93313) *(P-9466)*
Georg Fischer Signet LLC ....D....626 571-2770
3401 Aero Jet Ave El Monte (91731) *(P-20879)*
George Coriaty ....E....562 698-7513
7240 Greenleaf Ave Whittier (90602) *(P-6590)*
George Delallo Company Inc ....E....530 533-3303
1800 Idora St Oroville (95966) *(P-771)*
George Fischer Inc (HQ) ....E....626 571-2770
3401 Aero Jet Ave El Monte (91731) *(P-15995)*
George Hood Inc ....E....408 295-6507
890 Faulstich Ct San Jose (95112) *(P-12222)*
George Industries ....B....323 264-6660
4116 Whiteside St Los Angeles (90063) *(P-13014)*
George Jue Mfg Co Inc ....D....562 634-8181
8140 Rosecrans Ave Paramount (90723) *(P-14221)*
George L Kovacs ....E....714 538-8026
1810 W Business Center Dr Orange (92867) *(P-14232)*
George L Throop Co ....E....626 796-0285
444 N Fair Oaks Ave Pasadena (91103) *(P-10580)*
George M Martin Co ....F....510 652-2200
910 Folger Ave Berkeley (94710) *(P-14310)*
George P Johnson Company ....D....310 965-4300
18500 Crenshaw Blvd Torrance (90504) *(P-23121)*
George Verhoeven Grain Inc (PA) ....F....909 605-1531
5355 E Airport Dr Ontario (91761) *(P-1098)*
Georgetown Precast Inc ....F....530 333-4404
2420 Georgia Slide Rd Georgetown (95634) *(P-10581)*
Georgia Pacific Holdings Inc ....A....626 926-1474
13208 Hadley St Apt 1 Whittier (90601) *(P-5461)*
Georgia-Pacific, Madera *Also called Color-Box LLC (P-5209)*
Georgia-Pacific LLC ....C....209 522-5201
2400 Lapham Dr Modesto (95354) *(P-5226)*
Georgia-Pacific LLC ....C....650 873-7800
249 E Grand Ave South San Francisco (94080) *(P-5227)*
Georgia-Pacific LLC ....C....925 757-2870
801 Minaker Dr Antioch (94509) *(P-10877)*
Georgia-Pacific LLC ....E....562 435-7094
1401 W Pier D St Long Beach (90802) *(P-10878)*
Georgia-Pacific LLC ....C....559 674-4685
24600 Avenue 13 Madera (93637) *(P-5228)*
Georgia-Pacific LLC ....C....559 485-4900
3630 E Wawona Ave Ste 104 Fresno (93725) *(P-5307)*
Georis Winery ....F....831 659-1050
4 Pilot Rd Carmel Valley (93924) *(P-1721)*
Gerald Gentellalli ....F....760 789-2094
19360 Camino Vista Rd Ramona (92065) *(P-22807)*
Gerard H Tanzi Inc ....F....209 532-0855
22555 Sawmill Flat Rd Columbia (95310) *(P-14368)*
Gerard Roof Products LLC (HQ) ....E....714 529-0407
721 Monroe Way Placentia (92870) *(P-12223)*
Gerard Roofing Technologies, Placentia *Also called Gerard Roof Products LLC (P-12223)*
Gerdau Rancho Cucamonga, Rancho Cucamonga *Also called Tamco (P-11077)*
Gergay and Associates ....E....415 431-4163
78 Delmar St San Francisco (94117) *(P-12807)*
Gerhardt Gear Co Inc ....E....818 842-6700
133 E Santa Anita Ave Burbank (91502) *(P-19670)*
Gerlinger Fndry Mch Works Inc (PA) ....D....530 243-1053
1527 Sacramento St Redding (96001) *(P-11803)*
Germains Seed Technology Inc ....E....408 848-8120
8333 Swanston Ln Gilroy (95020) *(P-23343)*
German Machine Products, Gardena *Also called German Machined Products Inc (P-15996)*
German Machined Products Inc ....E....310 532-4480
1415 W 178th St Gardena (90248) *(P-15996)*
Germanex Imports Inc ....F....818 700-0441
19015 Parthenia St Northridge (91324) *(P-19671)*
Geron Corporation (PA) ....E....650 473-7700
149 Commonwealth Dr # 2070 Menlo Park (94025) *(P-7912)*
Gerson's Machinery Co, Orange *Also called George L Kovacs (P-14232)*
Ges US (new England) Inc ....C....978 459-4434
1051 S East St Anaheim (92805) *(P-18924)*
Get ....F....562 989-5400
2030 W 17th St Long Beach (90813) *(P-15516)*
Get Ahead Learning LLC ....F....626 796-8500
70 S Lake Ave Ste 1000 Pasadena (91101) *(P-23936)*
Get Engineering Corp ....E....619 443-8295
9350 Bond Ave El Cajon (92021) *(P-20880)*
Getgoing Inc ....F....415 608-7474
610 Bridgeport Ln Foster City (94404) *(P-23937)*
Geyser Peak Winery ....E....707 857-9463
2306 Magnolia Dr Healdsburg (95448) *(P-1722)*
Gfbc Inc ....F....858 622-0085
6550 Mira Mesa Blvd San Diego (92121) *(P-1531)*
Gff Inc ....D....323 232-6255
145 Willow Ave City of Industry (91746) *(P-882)*
Gfmi Aerospace & Defense Inc ....E....714 361-4444
17375 Mount Herrmann St Fountain Valley (92708) *(P-20114)*
Gforce Corporation ....F....714 630-0909
1144 N Grove St Anaheim (92806) *(P-1215)*
Gfp Ethanol LLC ....E....559 757-3850
11704 Road 120 Pixley (93256) *(P-8740)*
Ggco Inc ....E....213 623-3636
18380 Ventura Blvd Tarzana (91356) *(P-22520)*
Ggf Marble & Supply Inc ....F....925 676-8385
1375 Franquette Ave Ste F Concord (94520) *(P-10907)*
Ggsdi, Fountain Valley *Also called Genesis Group Sftwr Developers (P-23933)*
Ggtw LLC ....E....619 423-3388
1470 Bay Blvd Chula Vista (91911) *(P-8971)*
Gh Foods Ca LLC (HQ) ....B....916 844-1140
8425 Carbide Ct Sacramento (95828) *(P-2467)*
Ghazal & Sons Inc (PA) ....D....619 474-6677
3020 Hoover Ave National City (91950) *(P-5397)*
Ghazarian Welding & Repair, Fresno *Also called Ghazarian Wldg Fabrication Inc (P-24635)*
Ghazarian Wldg Fabrication Inc ....F....559 233-1210
2903 E Annadale Ave Fresno (93725) *(P-24635)*
Ghiringhlli Spcialty Foods Inc ....C....707 561-7670
101 Benicia Rd Vallejo (94590) *(P-2468)*
Ghs Champion Inc ....E....650 326-8485
1090 Martin Ave Santa Clara (95050) *(P-1216)*
Giannelli Cabinet Mfg Co ....F....818 882-9787
8835 Shirley Ave Northridge (91324) *(P-4978)*
Giannini Garden Ornaments Inc ....E....650 873-4493
225 Shaw Rd South San Francisco (94080) *(P-10582)*
Gianno Co Ltd ....F....909 628-6928
13546 Vintage Pl Chino (91710) *(P-3160)*
Giant Horse Printing Inc ....F....650 875-7137
1336 San Mateo Ave South San Francisco (94080) *(P-6591)*
Giant Mgllan Tlscope Orgnztnal, Pasadena *Also called Gmto Corporation (P-21355)*
Giant Teddy, Anaheim *Also called Raykorvay Inc (P-22653)*
Gibbel Bros Inc ....E....323 875-1367
11145 Tuxford St Sun Valley (91352) *(P-10762)*
Gibbs Plastic & Rubber Co ....F....707 746-7300
3959 Teal Ct Benicia (94510) *(P-9311)*
Gibraltar Plastic Pdts Corp ....E....818 365-9318
12885 Foothill Blvd Sylmar (91342) *(P-9804)*
Gibson and Schaefer Inc (PA) ....E....619 352-3535
1126 Rock Wood Rd Heber (92249) *(P-10763)*
Gibson Brands Inc ....C....310 300-2369
9350 Civic Center Dr # 130 Beverly Hills (90210) *(P-22622)*
Gibson Exhaust Systems, Corona *Also called Gibson Performance Corporation (P-19672)*
Gibson Performance Corporation ....D....951 372-1220
1270 Webb Cir Corona (92879) *(P-19672)*
Gibson Printing & Publishing ....F....707 745-0733
820 1st St Benicia (94510) *(P-5645)*
Gibson Printing & Publishing ....F....925 228-6400
802 Alhambra Ave Martinez (94553) *(P-5646)*
Gibson Printing & Publishing ....F....707 678-5594
145 E A St Dixon (95620) *(P-5647)*
Gibson Radio and Publishing Co, Vallejo *Also called Luther E Gibson Inc (P-5981)*
Gibson Wine Company ....E....559 875-2505
1720 Academy Ave Sanger (93657) *(P-1723)*
Giga-Tronics Incorporated (PA) ....E....925 328-4650
5990 Gleason Dr Dublin (94568) *(P-21043)*
Gigamat Technologies Inc ....F....510 770-8008
47269 Fremont Blvd Fremont (94538) *(P-18249)*
Gigamem LLC ....F....949 461-9999
18375 Bandilier Cir Fountain Valley (92708) *(P-15031)*
Gigamon Inc (HQ) ....C....408 831-4000
3300 Olcott St Santa Clara (95054) *(P-23938)*
Gigavac, LLC, Carpinteria *Also called Sensata Technologies Inc (P-16753)*
Gigpeak Inc (HQ) ....C....408 546-3316
6024 Silver Creek Vly Rd San Jose (95138) *(P-18250)*
Gilbert Machine & Mfg, San Marcos *Also called Duplan Industries (P-15910)*
Gilbert Martin Wdwkg Co Inc (PA) ....E....800 268-5669
2345 Britannia Blvd San Diego (92154) *(P-4753)*
Gilbert Spray Coat Inc ....E....408 988-0747
300 Laurelwood Rd Santa Clara (95054) *(P-13186)*
Gildedtree Inc ....F....925 246-5624
251 Lafayette Cir Ste 310 Lafayette (94549) *(P-23939)*
Gilderfluke & Company Inc ....F....818 840-9484
205 S Flower St Burbank (91502) *(P-17232)*
Gilead Colorado Inc ....C....650 574-3000
333 Lakeside Dr Foster City (94404) *(P-7913)*
Gilead Palo Alto Inc ....B....909 394-4000
650 Cliffside Dr San Dimas (91773) *(P-7914)*
Gilead Palo Alto Inc (HQ) ....D....650 384-8500
333 Lakeside Dr Foster City (94404) *(P-7915)*
Gilead Sciences Inc ....F....760 945-7701
4049 Avenida De La Plata Oceanside (92056) *(P-8304)*
Gilead Sciences Inc (PA) ....B....650 574-3000
333 Lakeside Dr Foster City (94404) *(P-7916)*
Gilead Sciences Inc ....F....909 394-4090
542 W Covina Blvd San Dimas (91773) *(P-7917)*
Gilead Sciences Inc ....C....909 394-4000
650 Cliffside Dr San Dimas (91773) *(P-7918)*
Gilead Scientist, San Dimas *Also called Gilead Palo Alto Inc (P-7914)*
Gill Corporation (PA) ....C....626 443-6094
4056 Easy St El Monte (91731) *(P-9805)*
Gillette Company ....F....949 851-2222
19900 Macarthur Blvd Irvine (92612) *(P-11515)*
Gilli Inc ....F....213 744-9808
1100 S San Pedro St C07 Los Angeles (90015) *(P-3554)*
Gillig LLC ....B....510 785-1500
451 Discovery Dr Livermore (94551) *(P-19536)*
Gilwin Company ....E....209 522-9775
2354 Lapham Dr Modesto (95354) *(P-11956)*
Gim Factory, Santa Fe Springs *Also called Taokaenoi Usa Inc (P-2253)*
Gimelli Vineyards ....F....831 637-5445
403 Grass Valley Rd Hollister (95023) *(P-1724)*
Gin'l Fabrics, Los Angeles *Also called Ax II Inc (P-2750)*
Gina Designs ....F....707 967-1041
870 Sanitarium Rd Angwin (94576) *(P-22521)*

ALPHABETIC

Employee Codes: A=Over 500 employees, B=251-500
C=101-250, D=51-100, E=20-50, F=10-19
2020 California
Manfacturers Register
© Mergent Inc. 1-800-342-5647
1111

Gina T Interior Accents, La Verne *Also called Joann Lammens* ***(P-23372)***
Ginger Golden Products Inc ....E....323 838-1070
5860 Bandini Blvd Commerce (90040) ***(P-883)***
Gingi Pak, Camarillo *Also called Belport Company Inc* ***(P-22136)***
Gino Corporation ....F....323 234-7979
555 E Jefferson Blvd Los Angeles (90011) ***(P-2990)***
Ginza Collection Design Inc ....E....562 531-1116
6015 Obispo Ave Long Beach (90805) ***(P-3228)***
Giovanni Cosmetics Inc ....D....310 952-9960
2064 E University Dr Rancho Dominguez (90220) ***(P-8498)***
Giovanni Hair Care & Cosmetics, Rancho Dominguez *Also called Giovanni Cosmetics Inc* ***(P-8498)***
Girard Food Service, City of Industry *Also called Gff Inc* ***(P-882)***
Girl Talk Clothing, Los Angeles *Also called C & Y Investment Inc* ***(P-3299)***
Gist Inc ....D....530 644-8000
4385 Pleasant Valley Rd Placerville (95667) ***(P-23002)***
Gist Silversmiths, Placerville *Also called Gist Inc* ***(P-23002)***
Git America Inc ....F....714 433-2180
230 Commerce Ste 190 Irvine (92602) ***(P-8225)***
Gitacloud Inc ....F....925 519-5965
5791 Athenour Ct Pleasanton (94588) ***(P-23940)***
Giuliano's Bakery, Carson *Also called Giuliano-Pagano Corporation* ***(P-1217)***
Giuliano-Pagano Corporation ....D....310 537-7700
1264 E Walnut St Carson (90746) ***(P-1217)***
Giustos Specialty Foods LLC (PA) ....E....650 873-6566
344 Littlefield Ave South San Francisco (94080) ***(P-1001)***
Giustos Specialty Foods LLC ....E....650 873-6566
241 E Harris Ave South San Francisco (94080) ***(P-1002)***
Given Imaging Los Angeles LLC ....C....310 641-8492
5860 Uplander Way Culver City (90230) ***(P-22257)***
Giving Keys Inc ....D....213 935-8791
836 Traction Ave Los Angeles (90013) ***(P-22522)***
Gizmac Accessories LLC ....F....310 320-5563
4025 Spencer St Ste 102 Torrance (90503) ***(P-15235)***
GK Foods Inc ....E....760 752-5230
133 Mata Way Ste 101 San Marcos (92069) ***(P-1003)***
GK Welding Inc ....F....510 233-0133
1150 Hensley St Richmond (94801) ***(P-24636)***
GKM International Llc ....D....310 791-7092
1725 Burbury Way San Marcos (92078) ***(P-9806)***
GKN Aerospace Camarillo Inc ....F....805 383-6684
4680 Calle Carga Camarillo (93012) ***(P-12224)***
GKN Aerospace Chem-Tronics Inc ....F....619 258-5012
1148 Bert Acosta St El Cajon (92020) ***(P-19952)***
GKN Aerospace Chem-Tronics Inc (HQ) ....A....619 448-2320
1150 W Bradley Ave El Cajon (92020) ***(P-19953)***
GKN Arspace Trnsprncy Systems (HQ) ....C....714 893-7531
12122 Western Ave Garden Grove (92841) ***(P-9807)***
GL Woodworking Inc ....D....949 515-2192
14341 Franklin Ave Tustin (92780) ***(P-4504)***
Glacier Design Systems Inc (PA) ....F....714 897-2337
5405 Production Dr Huntington Beach (92649) ***(P-1532)***
Glacier Foods Division, Westlake Village *Also called Dole Packaged Foods LLC* ***(P-910)***
Glacier Foods Division, Sanger *Also called Dole Packaged Foods LLC* ***(P-911)***
Glacier Ice Company, Elk Grove *Also called Glacier Valley Ice Company LP* ***(P-2355)***
Glacier Valley Ice Company LP (PA) ....E....916 394-2939
8580 Laguna Station Rd Elk Grove (95758) ***(P-2355)***
Glad Products Company (HQ) ....C....510 271-7000
1221 Broadway Ste A Oakland (94612) ***(P-9405)***
Gladding McBean, Lincoln *Also called Pabco Clay Products LLC* ***(P-10435)***
Gladding McBean, Lincoln *Also called Pabco Building Products LLC* ***(P-10464)***
Glam and Glits Nail Design Inc ....D....661 393-4800
8700 Swigert Ct Unit 209 Bakersfield (93311) ***(P-8499)***
Glas Werk Inc ....E....949 766-1296
29710 Ave De Las Bndra Rcho STA Marg (92688) ***(P-10307)***
Glaser Designs Inc ....F....415 552-3188
1469 Pacific Ave San Francisco (94109) ***(P-10222)***
Glasman Shim & Stamping Inc ....F....951 278-8197
226 N Sherman Ave Ste B Corona (92882) ***(P-14822)***
Glaspro, Santa Fe Springs *Also called GP Merger Sub Inc* ***(P-10364)***
Glass Fabrication and Dist, Stanton *Also called Newport Industrial Glass Inc* ***(P-10381)***
Glass Shop of The North Bay, Petaluma *Also called Chad Empey* ***(P-10263)***
Glasslab Inc ....E....415 244-5584
209 Redwood Shores Pkwy Redwood City (94065) ***(P-23941)***
Glassplax ....E....951 677-4800
26605 Madison Ave Murrieta (92562) ***(P-10362)***
Glasswerks Group, South Gate *Also called Glasswerks La Inc* ***(P-10363)***
Glasswerks La Inc (HQ) ....B....888 789-7810
8600 Rheem Ave South Gate (90280) ***(P-10363)***
Glasswerks La Inc ....E....800 729-1324
42005 Zevo Dr Temecula (92590) ***(P-10264)***
Glastar Corporation ....E....818 341-0301
8425 Canoga Ave Canoga Park (91304) ***(P-14472)***
Glaukos Corporation (PA) ....C....949 367-9600
229 Avenida Fabricante San Clemente (92672) ***(P-21724)***
Glaxosmithkline Consumer ....D....559 650-1550
2020 E Vine Ave Fresno (93706) ***(P-7919)***
Glaxosmithkline LLC ....E....925 833-1551
11205 Creekside Ct Dublin (94568) ***(P-7920)***
Glaxosmithkline LLC ....E....619 863-0399
2399 Hummingbird St Chula Vista (91915) ***(P-7921)***
Glazier Steel Inc ....D....510 471-5300
650 Sandoval Way Hayward (94544) ***(P-11804)***
GLC General Inc ....F....714 870-9825
100 W Walnut Ave Fullerton (92832) ***(P-4505)***
Gleason Corporation (PA) ....F....310 470-6001
10474 Santa Monica Blvd # 400 Los Angeles (90025) ***(P-3658)***
Gledhill/Lyons Inc ....E....714 502-0274
1521 N Placentia Ave Anaheim (92806) ***(P-20115)***
Glen Ellen Carneros Winery, Sonoma *Also called Diageo North America Inc* ***(P-1664)***
Glen-Mac Swiss Co ....F....310 978-4555
12848 Weber Way Hawthorne (90250) ***(P-18770)***
Glenco Manufacturing Company ....E....909 984-3348
707 S Hope Ave Ontario (91761) ***(P-12632)***
Glencore Ltd ....E....562 427-6611
2020 Walnut Ave Long Beach (90806) ***(P-9046)***
Glendale Iron ....F....818 247-1098
4208 Chevy Chase Dr Los Angeles (90039) ***(P-12476)***
Glendale Ready-Mixed Concrete, Los Angeles *Also called Viking Ready Mix Co Inc* ***(P-10859)***
Glendale Stl & Orna Ironworks, Los Angeles *Also called Glendale Iron* ***(P-12476)***
Glendale Times, Glendale *Also called Los Angles Tmes Cmmnctions LLC* ***(P-5708)***
Glengarry Manufacturing Inc ....F....951 248-1111
1535 Marlborough Ave Riverside (92507) ***(P-15997)***
Glenn Engineering Inc ....F....209 667-4555
9850 3rd St Delhi (95315) ***(P-19822)***
Glenoaks Food Inc ....E....818 768-9091
11030 Randall St Sun Valley (91352) ***(P-459)***
Glentek Inc ....D....310 322-3026
208 Standard St El Segundo (90245) ***(P-16648)***
Glide-Write, Milpitas *Also called Marburg Technology Inc* ***(P-15283)***
Glima Inc ....F....818 980-9686
11133 Vanowen St Ste A North Hollywood (91605) ***(P-3329)***
Glimmer Gear ....F....619 399-9211
4337 Alabama St San Diego (92104) ***(P-22808)***
Glo-Usa Inc ....D....408 598-4400
1225 Bordeaux Dr Sunnyvale (94089) ***(P-18251)***
Global Aerospace Tech Corp ....E....818 407-5600
25109 Rye Canyon Loop Valencia (91355) ***(P-20116)***
Global Aerostructures ....F....909 987-4888
10291 Trademark St Ste C Rancho Cucamonga (91730) ***(P-20117)***
Global Billiard Mfg Co Inc ....E....310 764-5000
1141 Sandhill Ave Carson (90746) ***(P-22809)***
Global Blood Therapeutics Inc (PA) ....D....650 741-7700
171 Oyster Point Blvd # 30 South San Francisco (94080) ***(P-7922)***
Global Casuals Inc ....F....310 817-2828
18505 S Broadway Gardena (90248) ***(P-3086)***
Global Comm Semiconductors LLC (HQ) ....E....310 530-7274
23155 Kashiwa Ct Torrance (90505) ***(P-18252)***
Global Compliance Inc ....E....626 303-6855
438 W Chestnut Ave Ste A Monrovia (91016) ***(P-6243)***
Global Contract Manufacturing, Union City *Also called Gcm Medical & Oem Inc* ***(P-12220)***
Global Custom Security Inc ....F....818 889-6900
755 Lakefield Rd Ste B Westlake Village (91361) ***(P-19319)***
Global Diversified Inds Inc (PA) ....E....559 665-5800
1200 Airport Dr Chowchilla (93610) ***(P-4460)***
Global Doors Corp ....E....213 622-2003
1340 E 6th St Los Angeles (90021) ***(P-4049)***
Global Edge LLC ....E....888 315-2692
5230 Las Virgenes Rd # 265 Calabasas (91302) ***(P-23942)***
Global Elastomeric Pdts Inc ....D....661 831-5380
5551 District Blvd Bakersfield (93313) ***(P-13778)***
Global Electronics Intl, Rancho Cucamonga *Also called Mercury United Electronics Inc* ***(P-19012)***
Global Enterprise Mfg Inc ....E....657 234-1150
1560 S Harris Ct Anaheim (92806) ***(P-23344)***
Global Environmental Pdts Inc ....D....909 713-1600
5405 Industrial Pkwy San Bernardino (92407) ***(P-19472)***
Global Foundries, Santa Clara *Also called Globalfoundries US Inc* ***(P-14473)***
Global Future City Holding Inc ....F....949 769-3550
2 Park Plz Ste 400 Irvine (92614) ***(P-7923)***
Global Grid For Learning, Alameda *Also called Edutone Corporation* ***(P-23845)***
Global Infovision Inc ....F....714 738-4465
2290 Ardemore Dr Fullerton (92833) ***(P-23943)***
Global Link Sourcing Inc ....D....951 698-1977
41690 Corporate Center Ct Murrieta (92562) ***(P-5328)***
Global Marine Group Inc ....F....800 729-1665
6020 Progressive Ave # 800 San Diego (92154) ***(P-20333)***
Global Mfg Solutions LLC ....E....562 356-3222
2100 E Valencia Dr Ste D Fullerton (92831) ***(P-11306)***
Global Micro Solutions Inc ....F....310 218-5678
21250 Hawthorne Blvd # 540 Torrance (90503) ***(P-23944)***
Global Modular Inc (HQ) ....E....559 665-5800
1200 Airport Dr Chowchilla (93610) ***(P-4461)***
Global Motorsport Parts Inc ....C....408 778-0500
155 E Main Ave Ste 150 Morgan Hill (95037) ***(P-20404)***
Global Ocean Trading LLC ....F....626 281-0800
430 S Grfield Ave Ste 405 Alhambra (91801) ***(P-2244)***
Global Packaging Solutions Inc ....B....619 710-2661
6259 Progressive Dr # 200 San Diego (92154) ***(P-5229)***
Global Paper Solutions Inc ....E....714 687-6102
100 S Anaheim Blvd # 250 Anaheim (92805) ***(P-5106)***
Global Pcci (gpc) (PA) ....C....757 637-9000
2465 Campus Dr Ste 100 Irvine (92612) ***(P-12808)***
Global Plating Inc ....E....510 659-8764
44620 S Grimmer Blvd Fremont (94538) ***(P-13015)***
Global Polishing Solutions LLC (HQ) ....E....619 295-5505
5220 Gaines St San Diego (92110) ***(P-13730)***
Global Power Tech Group Inc ....F....949 273-4373
20692 Prism Pl Lake Forest (92630) ***(P-18253)***
Global Precision Manufacturing, Grass Valley *Also called Taylor Investments LLC* ***(P-14642)***
Global Precision Manufacturing ....F....831 239-9469
38 Hollins Dr Santa Cruz (95060) ***(P-13731)***
Global Printing Sourcing & Dev, San Rafael *Also called Goff Investment Group LLC* ***(P-6245)***
Global Pumice LLC ....F....760 240-3544
19968 Bear Valley Rd C Apple Valley (92308) ***(P-388)***

Mergent e-mail: customerrelations@mergent.com
1112
2020 California
Manufacturers Register
(P-0000) Products & Services Section entry number
(PA)=Parent Co (HQ)=Headquarters (DH)=Div Headquarters

Global Sales Inc ....E....310 474-7700
1732 Westwood Blvd Los Angeles (90024) ***(P-8500)***
Global Silicones Inc ....F....805 686-4500
49 Industrial Way Buellton (93427) ***(P-8741)***
Global Specialties Direct, Oakland *Also called Global Steel Products Corp* ***(P-4979)***
Global Steel Products Corp ....E....510 652-2060
936 61st St Oakland (94608) ***(P-4979)***
Global Sweeping Solutions, San Bernardino *Also called Global Environmental Pdts Inc* ***(P-19472)***
Global Tech Instruments Inc ....F....714 375-1811
18380 Enterprise Ln Huntington Beach (92648) ***(P-20584)***
Global Truss America LLC ....D....323 415-6225
4295 Charter St Vernon (90058) ***(P-11231)***
Global Unlimited Export LLC ....F....213 365-7051
3407 W 6th St Ste 802 Los Angeles (90020) ***(P-10223)***
Global Uxe Inc ....E....805 583-4600
405 Science Dr Moorpark (93021) ***(P-23345)***
Global Wave Group LLC ....F....949 916-9800
8a Journey Ste 100 Aliso Viejo (92656) ***(P-23945)***
Globalfoundries US Inc (HQ) ....B....408 462-3900
2600 Great America Way Santa Clara (95054) ***(P-14473)***
Globalscale Technologies Inc ....F....714 632-9239
1200 N Van Buren St Ste D Anaheim (92807) ***(P-15032)***
Globalux Lighting LLC ....F....909 591-7506
14750 Nelson Ave Unit B City of Industry (91744) ***(P-16971)***
Globaluxe Inc ....E....805 583-4600
405 Science Dr Moorpark (93021) ***(P-23346)***
Globalvision Systems Inc ....F....888 227-7967
9401 Oakdale Ave Ste 100 Chatsworth (91311) ***(P-15033)***
Globe Iron Foundry Inc ....D....323 723-8983
5649 Randolph St Commerce (90040) ***(P-11143)***
Globe Motors Inc ....C....408 935-8989
1507 Gladding Ct Milpitas (95035) ***(P-16649)***
Globe Plastics Inc ....E....909 464-1520
13477 12th St Chino (91710) ***(P-9808)***
Globe Rider Distribution, Vista *Also called Wax Research Inc* ***(P-9162)***
Glockworx, Oxnard *Also called Zev Technologies Inc* ***(P-13280)***
Gloria Ferrer Winery, Sonoma *Also called Freixenet Sonoma Caves Inc* ***(P-1716)***
Gloria Lance Inc (PA) ....D....310 767-4400
15616 S Broadway Gardena (90248) ***(P-3161)***
Gloriann Farms Inc ....C....209 221-7121
11104 W Tracy Blvd Tracy (95304) ***(P-9546)***
Glorious Empire LLC ....F....760 598-5000
2460 S Santa Fe Ave Ste B Vista (92084) ***(P-19673)***
Glovefit International Corp ....F....559 243-1110
4705 N Sonora Ave Ste 108 Fresno (93722) ***(P-9809)***
Glp Designs Inc ....F....310 652-6800
916 W Hyde Park Blvd Inglewood (90302) ***(P-5062)***
Gluesmith Industries ....F....626 282-9390
801 S Raymond Ave Ste 39 Alhambra (91803) ***(P-8870)***
Gluesmith, The, Alhambra *Also called Gluesmith Industries* ***(P-8870)***
Gluten Free Foods Mfg LLC (PA) ....F....909 823-8230
5010 Eucalyptus Ave Chino (91710) ***(P-2469)***
Glysens Incorporated ....E....858 638-7708
3931 Sorrento Valley Blvd San Diego (92121) ***(P-21725)***
GM Associates Inc ....D....510 430-0806
9824 Kitty Ln Oakland (94603) ***(P-18925)***
GM Marble & Granite Inc ....F....925 676-8385
1375 Franquette Ave Ste F Concord (94520) ***(P-314)***
GM Nameplate Inc ....C....408 435-1666
2095 Otoole Ave San Jose (95131) ***(P-5509)***
GME Mfg Inc ....F....909 989-4478
10641 Pullman Ct Rancho Cucamonga (91730) ***(P-20118)***
GMI, San Diego *Also called Groundmetrics Inc* ***(P-203)***
Gmj Woodworking ....E....760 294-7428
2365 Mountain View Dr Escondido (92027) ***(P-4050)***
Gmm Inc ....E....323 874-1600
10152 Riverside Dr Toluca Lake (91602) ***(P-6244)***
Gmp Global Nutrition Inc ....F....909 628-8889
13653 Central Ave Chino (91710) ***(P-7924)***
Gmp Laboratories America Inc ....D....714 630-2467
2931 E La Jolla St Anaheim (92806) ***(P-7925)***
Gmpc LLC ....F....707 766-1702
2180 S Mcdowell Blvd Petaluma (94954) ***(P-23122)***
Gms Elevator Services Inc ....E....909 599-3904
401 Borrego Ct San Dimas (91773) ***(P-13801)***
Gms Landscapes Inc ....D....805 402-3925
207 Camino Leon Camarillo (93012) ***(P-11670)***
Gms Molds (PA) ....F....310 684-1168
729 E 223rd St Carson (90745) ***(P-14059)***
Gmto Corporation ....D....626 204-0500
465 N Halstead St Ste 250 Pasadena (91107) ***(P-21355)***
GNA Industries Inc ....E....559 276-0953
4761 W Jacquelyn Ave Fresno (93722) ***(P-16719)***
GNB Corporation ....D....916 233-3543
3200 Dwight Rd Ste 100 Elk Grove (95758) ***(P-13922)***
GNB Vacuum Excellence Defined, Elk Grove *Also called GNB Corporation* ***(P-13922)***
Gnekow Family Winery LLC ....F....209 463-0697
17347 E Gawne Rd Stockton (95215) ***(P-1725)***
Gnosis International Llc ....E....858 254-6369
8008 Westbury Ave San Diego (92126) ***(P-8226)***
Go Green Mobile Power LLC ....F....877 800-4467
171 Pier Ave Ste 105 Santa Monica (90405) ***(P-16650)***
Go Logo, Van Nuys *Also called Dee Sign Co* ***(P-23087)***
Go Rhino, Brea *Also called Iddea California LLC* ***(P-19686)***
Goalsr Inc ....E....650 453-5844
3139 Independence Dr Livermore (94551) ***(P-23946)***
Gobble Inc ....C....888 405-7481
170 University St San Francisco (94134) ***(P-2470)***
Gobeme, San Francisco *Also called Onc Holdings Inc* ***(P-24227)***
Goddard Rotary Tool Co Inc ....F....760 743-6717
525 Opper St Escondido (92029) ***(P-13923)***
Goddess of Gadgets, South Pasadena *Also called Ximenez Icons* ***(P-3651)***
Goengineer Inc ....F....818 716-1650
6400 Canoga Ave Ste 121 Woodland Hills (91367) ***(P-23947)***
Goeppner Industries Inc ....F....310 784-2800
22924 Lockness Ave Torrance (90501) ***(P-15998)***
Goff Corporation ....E....415 526-1370
10 Paul Dr San Rafael (94903) ***(P-6106)***
Goff Investment Group LLC ....F....415 456-2934
135 3rd St Ste 150 San Rafael (94901) ***(P-6245)***
Goharddrive Inc ....F....626 593-9927
137 S 8th Ave Ste E La Puente (91746) ***(P-15034)***
Goharddrive.com, La Puente *Also called Goharddrive Inc* ***(P-15034)***
Gohz Inc ....E....800 603-1219
23555 Golden Springs Dr K1 Diamond Bar (91765) ***(P-16651)***
Gold Belt Line Inc ....F....619 424-5544
1547 Jayken Way Ste C Chula Vista (91911) ***(P-3034)***
Gold Coast Bakeries, Santa Ana *Also called Gold Coast Baking Company Inc* ***(P-1218)***
Gold Coast Baking Company Inc (PA) ....D....714 545-2253
1590 E Saint Gertrude Pl Santa Ana (92705) ***(P-1218)***
Gold Coast Ingredients Inc ....D....323 724-8935
2429 Yates Ave Commerce (90040) ***(P-2471)***
Gold Coast Ironworks ....F....805 485-6921
531 Montgomery Ave Oxnard (93036) ***(P-12477)***
Gold Coast Solar LLC ....E....310 351-7229
1975 Hillgate Way Apt G Simi Valley (93065) ***(P-18254)***
Gold Couture 22 K ....F....760 602-0690
6406 Kinglet Way Carlsbad (92011) ***(P-22523)***
Gold Craft Jewelry Corp (PA) ....F....213 623-8673
640 S Hill St Ste 650 Los Angeles (90014) ***(P-22524)***
Gold Craft Jewelry Corp ....E....213 623-8673
640 S Hill St Ste 650 Los Angeles (90014) ***(P-22525)***
Gold Crest Industries Inc ....E....909 930-9069
1018 E Acacia St Ontario (91761) ***(P-3659)***
Gold Leaf & Metallic Powders ....E....323 769-4888
6001 Santa Monica Blvd Los Angeles (90038) ***(P-23347)***
Gold Leaf Cigar Co, Azusa *Also called California Master Printers* ***(P-6467)***
Gold Panner, The, Placerville *Also called El Dorado Gold Panner Inc* ***(P-5626)***
Gold Prospectors Assn Amer, Murrieta *Also called Gold Prospectors Assn of Amer* ***(P-5944)***
Gold Prospectors Assn of Amer ....E....951 699-4749
25819 Jefferson Ave # 110 Murrieta (92562) ***(P-5944)***
Gold River Mills LLC (PA) ....D....530 661-1923
1620 E Kentucky Ave Woodland (95776) ***(P-1044)***
Gold Rush Kettle Korn Llc ....E....707 747-6773
4690 E 2nd St Ste 9 Benicia (94510) ***(P-1369)***
Gold Technologies Inc ....E....408 321-9568
1648 Mabury Rd Ste A San Jose (95133) ***(P-16901)***
Gold Venture Inc ....C....909 623-1810
1050 S State College Blvd Fullerton (92831) ***(P-9547)***
Goldak Inc ....E....818 240-2666
15835 Monte St Ste 104 Sylmar (91342) ***(P-20585)***
Golden Altos Corporation ....E....408 956-1010
402 S Hillview Dr Milpitas (95035) ***(P-21044)***
Golden Applexx Co Inc ....E....909 594-9788
19805 Harrison Ave Walnut (91789) ***(P-7074)***
Golden Bear Sportswear, San Francisco *Also called Gb Sport Sf LLC* ***(P-3515)***
Golden Bolt LLC ....F....818 626-8261
9361 Canoga Ave Chatsworth (91311) ***(P-12679)***
Golden Coast Sportswear Inc ....E....714 704-4655
1140 E Howell Ave Anaheim (92805) ***(P-3330)***
Golden Color Printing Inc ....E....626 455-0850
9353 Rush St South El Monte (91733) ***(P-6592)***
Golden Empire Concrete Co ....F....661 325-6833
8211 Gosford Rd Bakersfield (93313) ***(P-10764)***
Golden Empire Dental Lab Inc ....F....661 327-1888
929 21st St Bakersfield (93301) ***(P-22157)***
Golden Farms, Canoga Park *Also called Protemach Inc* ***(P-8766)***
Golden Fleece Designs Inc ....F....323 849-1901
441 S Victory Blvd Burbank (91502) ***(P-3684)***
Golden Gate Baldor, Hayward *Also called ABB Motors and Mechanical Inc* ***(P-16625)***
Golden Gate Freightliner Inc ....C....559 486-4310
2727 E Central Ave Fresno (93725) ***(P-13873)***
Golden Gate Hosiery Inc ....E....909 464-0805
14095 Laurelwood Pl Chino (91710) ***(P-2766)***
Golden Gate Litho ....F....510 568-5335
11144 Golf Links Rd Oakland (94605) ***(P-6593)***
Golden Gate Tofu Incorporated ....F....415 822-5613
1265 Griffith St San Francisco (94124) ***(P-1443)***
Golden Gate Truck Center, Fresno *Also called Golden Gate Freightliner Inc* ***(P-13873)***
Golden Island Jerky Co Inc (HQ) ....E....844 362-3222
10646 Fulton Ct Rancho Cucamonga (91730) ***(P-460)***
Golden Island Jerky Co Inc ....F....844 362-3222
9955 6th St Rancho Cucamonga (91730) ***(P-461)***
Golden Kraft Inc ....D....562 926-8888
15500 Valley View Ave La Mirada (90638) ***(P-5510)***
Golden Mattress Co Inc ....D....323 887-1888
4231 Firestone Blvd South Gate (90280) ***(P-4720)***
Golden Octagon Inc ....D....650 369-8573
2537 Middlefield Rd Redwood City (94063) ***(P-1219)***
Golden Office Trailers Inc ....E....951 678-2177
18257 Grand Ave Lake Elsinore (92530) ***(P-20487)***
Golden Pacific, Pomona *Also called Travelers Choice Travelware* ***(P-10213)***
Golden Pacific Seafoods Inc ....E....714 589-8888
700 S Raymond Ave Fullerton (92831) ***(P-14369)***
Golden Phoenix Bakery, San Leandro *Also called Triple C Foods Inc* ***(P-1334)***
Golden Plastics Corporation ....F....510 569-6465
8465 Baldwin St Oakland (94621) ***(P-9810)***

ALPHABETIC

Employee Codes: A=Over 500 employees, B=251-500
C=101-250, D=51-100, E=20-50, F=10-19
2020 California
Manfacturers Register
© Mergent Inc. 1-800-342-5647
1113

Golden Queen Mining Co LLC ....C....661 824-4300
2818 Silver Queen Rd Mojave (93501) ***(P-4)***
Golden Rule Bindery Inc ....E....760 471-2013
1315 Hot Springs Way # 102 Vista (92081) ***(P-7331)***
Golden Rule Packaging, Vista *Also called Golden Rule Bindery Inc* ***(P-7331)***
Golden Sheaf Bread Co Inc ....E....831 722-0179
125 Hangar Way Ste 230 Watsonville (95076) ***(P-1220)***
Golden Specialty Foods LLC ....E....562 802-2537
14605 Best Ave Norwalk (90650) ***(P-2472)***
Golden Star Silk Screen, Commerce *Also called Lucky Star Silkscreen LLC* ***(P-7127)***
Golden State Assembly Inc ....C....510 226-8155
47823 Westinghouse Dr Fremont (94539) ***(P-11217)***
Golden State Cider, Sebastopol *Also called Devoto-Wade Llc* ***(P-1663)***
Golden State Drilling Inc ....D....661 589-0730
3500 Fruitvale Ave Bakersfield (93308) ***(P-93)***
Golden State Engineering Inc ....C....562 634-3125
15338 Garfield Ave Paramount (90723) ***(P-14268)***
Golden State Fire Appratus Inc ....F....916 330-1638
7400 Reese Rd Sacramento (95828) ***(P-19473)***
Golden State Foods Corp (PA) ....E....949 247-8000
18301 Von Karman Ave # 1100 Irvine (92612) ***(P-2214)***
Golden State Foods Corp ....B....626 465-7500
640 S 6th Ave City of Industry (91746) ***(P-960)***
Golden State Mixing Inc ....E....209 632-3656
415 D St Turlock (95380) ***(P-701)***
Golden State Shutters, Dixon *Also called Victorian Shutters Inc* ***(P-4145)***
Golden State Steel & Stair Inc (PA) ....E....707 455-0400
479 Mason St Vacaville (95688) ***(P-11805)***
Golden State Vintners (PA) ....F....707 254-4900
4596 S Tracy Blvd Tracy (95377) ***(P-1726)***
Golden State Vintners ....E....707 254-1985
1075 Golden Gate Dr NAPA (94558) ***(P-1727)***
Golden State Vintners ....E....831 678-3991
1777 Metz Rd Soledad (93960) ***(P-1728)***
Golden State Vintners ....E....707 553-6480
1175 Commmerce Blvd Vallejo (94503) ***(P-1729)***
Golden Stone Group LLC ....F....714 723-1505
10862 Garden Grove Blvd Garden Grove (92843) ***(P-10443)***
Golden Supreme Inc ....E....562 903-1063
12304 Mccann Dr Santa Fe Springs (90670) ***(P-23348)***
Golden Temple, Los Angeles *Also called East West Tea Company LLC* ***(P-1018)***
Golden Textile Inc ....F....323 620-2612
2922 S Main St Los Angeles (90007) ***(P-2689)***
Golden Tiger, Los Angeles *Also called Ajinomoto Windsor Inc* ***(P-939)***
Golden Valley & Associates Inc ....E....209 549-1549
3511 Finch Rd A Modesto (95357) ***(P-13874)***
Golden Valley Dairy Products ....C....559 687-1188
1025 E Bardsley Ave Tulare (93274) ***(P-552)***
Golden Valley Industries Inc ....E....209 939-3370
960 Lone Palm Ave Modesto (95351) ***(P-411)***
Golden Vantage LLC ....F....626 255-3362
8807 Rochester Ave Rancho Cucamonga (91730) ***(P-4506)***
Golden Vly Grape Jice Wine LLC (PA) ....E....559 661-4657
11770 Road 27 1/2 Madera (93637) ***(P-1730)***
Golden W Ppr Converting Corp (PA) ....C....510 317-0646
2480 Grant Ave San Lorenzo (94580) ***(P-14708)***
Golden West Envelope Corp ....E....510 452-5419
1009 Morton St Alameda (94501) ***(P-5470)***
Golden West Food Group Inc (PA) ....E....888 807-3663
4401 S Downey Rd Vernon (90058) ***(P-412)***
Golden West Homes, Perris *Also called Clayton Homes Inc* ***(P-4442)***
Golden West Machine Inc ....E....562 903-1111
9930 Jordan Cir Santa Fe Springs (90670) ***(P-15999)***
Golden West Packg Group LLC (PA) ....B....404 345-8365
8333 24th Ave Sacramento (95826) ***(P-5230)***
Golden West Refining Company ....E....562 921-3581
13116 Imperial Hwy Santa Fe Springs (90670) ***(P-9047)***
Golden West Shutters, Lake Forest *Also called ABC Custom Wood Shutters Inc* ***(P-3991)***
Golden West Technology ....D....714 738-3775
1180 E Valencia Dr Fullerton (92831) ***(P-17890)***
Goldencorr Sheets LLC ....C....626 369-6446
13890 Nelson Ave City of Industry (91746) ***(P-5231)***
Goldeneye, Saint Helena *Also called Duckhorn Wine Company* ***(P-1674)***
Goldeneye Winery, Philo *Also called Duckhorn Wine Company* ***(P-1675)***
Goldenwood Truss Corporation ....D....805 659-2520
11032 Nardo St Ventura (93004) ***(P-4302)***
Goldfarb & Associates, Santa Monica *Also called Adolf Goldfarb* ***(P-22656)***
Goldilocks, Hayward *Also called Clarmil Manufacturing Corp* ***(P-2427)***
Goldilocks Bakeshop and Rest, Santa Fe Springs *Also called Goldilocks Corp California* ***(P-1221)***
Goldilocks Corp California (PA) ....E....562 946-9995
10329 Painter Ave Santa Fe Springs (90670) ***(P-1221)***
Golding Publications ....F....951 244-1966
31558 Railroad Canyon Rd Canyon Lake (92587) ***(P-7358)***
Goldman Global Greenfield Inc ....F....323 589-3444
2025 E 48th St Vernon (90058) ***(P-9811)***
Goldsign, Huntington Park *Also called Citizens of Humanity LLC* ***(P-3304)***
Goldstar Asphalt Products, Perris *Also called Npg Inc* ***(P-9098)***
Goldstone Land Company LLC ....E....209 368-3113
11900 Furry Rd Lodi (95240) ***(P-1731)***
Goldtec USA, San Jose *Also called Gold Technologies Inc* ***(P-16901)***
Golet Wine Estates, NAPA *Also called Clos Du Val Wine Company Ltd* ***(P-1639)***
Goleta Coffee Company, Goleta *Also called Grind Food Company Inc* ***(P-16005)***
Golf Apparel Brands Inc ....C....310 327-5188
3824 W 113th St Inglewood (90303) ***(P-3331)***
Golf Buddy, Santa Fe Springs *Also called Deca International Corp* ***(P-20567)***
Golf Design Inc ....D....714 899-4040
10523 Humbolt St Los Alamitos (90720) ***(P-22810)***
Golf Design USA, Los Alamitos *Also called Golf Design Inc* ***(P-22810)***
Golnex Inc ....E....510 490-6003
4259 Aplicella Ct Manteca (95337) ***(P-14269)***
Gomberg Fredrikson & Assoc, Woodside *Also called Wine Company of San Francisco* ***(P-2006)***
Gomen Furniture Mfg Inc ....E....310 635-4894
11612 Wright Rd Lynwood (90262) ***(P-4643)***
Gondola Skate Mvg Systems Inc (PA) ....F....619 222-6487
9941 Prospect Ave Santee (92071) ***(P-11045)***
Gonz's, Los Angeles *Also called Fresh Jive Manufacturing Inc* ***(P-2989)***
Gonzalez Feliciano ....F....909 236-1372
1583 E Grand Ave Pomona (91766) ***(P-4051)***
Gooch & Housego Palo Alto LLC (HQ) ....D....650 856-7911
44247 Nobel Dr Fremont (94538) ***(P-18926)***
Gooch and Housego Cal LLC ....D....805 529-3324
5390 Kazuko Ct Moorpark (93021) ***(P-21356)***
Good Feet, Carlsbad *Also called Drs Own Inc* ***(P-22000)***
Good Neighbor Pharmacy, Encino *Also called Zelzah Pharmacy Inc* ***(P-8194)***
Good Time Usa Inc ....F....213 741-0100
1100 S San Pedro St K04 Los Angeles (90015) ***(P-3555)***
Good View Future Group Inc ....F....408 834-5698
277 S B St San Mateo (94401) ***(P-2473)***
Good Worldwide LLC ....E....323 206-6495
6380 Wilshire Blvd # 1500 Los Angeles (90048) ***(P-6246)***
Good-West Rubber Corp (PA) ....D....909 987-1774
9615 Feron Blvd Rancho Cucamonga (91730) ***(P-9312)***
Goodall Guitars Inc ....F....707 962-1620
541 S Franklin St Fort Bragg (95437) ***(P-22623)***
Goodco Inc ....F....415 425-1012
543 Howard St Fl 4 San Francisco (94105) ***(P-23948)***
Goodman Food Products Inc (PA) ....C....310 674-3180
200 E Beach Ave Fl 1 Inglewood (90302) ***(P-2474)***
Goodrich Aerostructures, Chula Vista *Also called Goodrich Corporation* ***(P-20120)***
Goodrich Corporation ....F....562 906-7372
11120 Norwalk Blvd Santa Fe Springs (90670) ***(P-20119)***
Goodrich Corporation ....D....619 691-4111
850 Lagoon Dr Chula Vista (91910) ***(P-20120)***
Goodrich Corporation ....C....714 984-1461
2727 E Imperial Hwy Brea (92821) ***(P-20121)***
Goodrich Corporation ....E....707 422-1880
3530 Branscombe Rd Fairfield (94533) ***(P-20475)***
Goodrich Corporation ....D....562 944-4441
9920 Freeman Ave Santa Fe Springs (90670) ***(P-20122)***
Goodrx Inc (PA) ....F....310 500-6544
233 Wilshire Blvd Ste 990 Santa Monica (90401) ***(P-23949)***
Goodway Printing, Poway *Also called Streeter Printing* ***(P-6874)***
Goodwest Linings & Coatings, Rancho Cucamonga *Also called Goodwest Rubber Linings Inc* ***(P-9313)***
Goodwest Rubber Linings Inc ....E....888 499-0085
8814 Industrial Ln Rancho Cucamonga (91730) ***(P-9313)***
Goodwin Ammonia Company (PA) ....F....714 894-0531
12102 Industry St Garden Grove (92841) ***(P-8385)***
Goodyear Rbr Co Southern Cal, Rancho Cucamonga *Also called Good-West Rubber Corp* ***(P-9312)***
Goomby LLC ....F....323 556-0637
8350 Wilshire Blvd # 200 Beverly Hills (90211) ***(P-22811)***
Goomby Skateboarding, Beverly Hills *Also called Goomby LLC* ***(P-22811)***
Goorin Bros Inc (PA) ....E....415 431-9196
1890 Bryant St Ste 208 San Francisco (94110) ***(P-3465)***
Goorin Brosinc ....F
23787 Eichler St Ste E Hayward (94545) ***(P-3466)***
Goose Manufacturing Inc ....F....408 747-0940
1853 Little Orchard St San Jose (95125) ***(P-16000)***
Goosecross Cellars A Cal Corp ....F....707 944-1986
1119 State Ln Yountville (94599) ***(P-1732)***
Goosecross Cellars Coorstek ....F....707 944-1986
1119 State Ln Yountville (94599) ***(P-1733)***
Gopro Inc (PA) ....B....650 332-7600
3000 Clearview Way San Mateo (94402) ***(P-22423)***
Gordon Biersch Brewing Company ....D....408 792-1546
357 E Taylor St San Jose (95112) ***(P-1533)***
Gordon Brush Mfg Co Inc (PA) ....D....323 724-7777
3737 Capitol Ave City of Industry (90601) ***(P-23027)***
Gordon Laboratories Inc ....C....310 327-5240
751 E Artesia Blvd Carson (90746) ***(P-8501)***
Gores Radio Holdings LLC ....A....310 209-3010
10877 Wilshire Blvd # 1805 Los Angeles (90024) ***(P-19320)***
Gorilla Automotive Products, Vernon *Also called Amcor Industries Inc* ***(P-19576)***
Gorilla Circuits (PA) ....C....408 294-9897
1445 Oakland Rd San Jose (95112) ***(P-17891)***
Gorlitz Sewer & Drain Inc ....E....562 944-3060
10132 Norwalk Blvd Santa Fe Springs (90670) ***(P-15517)***
Gorlitz Sewer and Drain, Santa Fe Springs *Also called Die Craft Stamping Inc* ***(P-13350)***
Gospel Recordings Inc ....E....951 719-1650
41823 Enterprise Cir N Temecula (92590) ***(P-17325)***
Gosub 60 ....F....310 394-4760
1334 3rd Street Promenade # 309 Santa Monica (90401) ***(P-15236)***
Goto California Inc (HQ) ....C....619 691-8722
6120 Bus Ctr Ct Ste F200 San Diego (92154) ***(P-17233)***
Gould & Bass Company Inc ....E....909 623-6793
1431 W 2nd St Pomona (91766) ***(P-21045)***
Goulds Pumps ....E....562 949-2113
3951 Capitol Ave City of Industry (90601) ***(P-14576)***
Gourmet Coffee Warehouse Inc ....D....818 423-2626
11275 Chandler Blvd North Hollywood (91601) ***(P-2295)***

Mergent e-mail: customerrelations@mergent.com
1114
2020 California
Manufacturers Register
(P-0000) Products & Services Section entry number
(PA)=Parent Co (HQ)=Headquarters (DH)=Div Headquarters

Gourmet Coffee Warehouse Inc (PA) ....E....323 871-8930
920 N Formosa Ave Los Angeles (90046) ***(P-2296)***
Government Travel Directory, Santa Barbara *Also called Federal Buyers Guide Inc* ***(P-6234)***
Governmentjobscom Inc ....C....310 426-6304
300 Continental Blvd # 565 El Segundo (90245) ***(P-23950)***
GP Color Imaging Group, North Hollywood *Also called Wes Go Inc* ***(P-7267)***
GP Design Inc ....F....310 638-8737
1185 W Mahalo Pl Compton (90220) ***(P-3790)***
GP Electric, Pomona *Also called G Powell Electric* ***(P-24691)***
GP Industries Inc ....F....805 227-6565
3230 Rvrsid Ave Ste 110 Paso Robles (93446) ***(P-22812)***
GP Machining Inc ....E....805 686-0852
94 Commerce Dr Buellton (93427) ***(P-16001)***
GP Merger Sub Inc ....D....562 946-7722
9401 Ann St Santa Fe Springs (90670) ***(P-10364)***
GPde Slva Spces Incrporation ....D....562 407-2643
8531 Loch Lomond Dr Pico Rivera (90660) ***(P-2475)***
Gpo Display ....F....510 659-9855
7685 Hawthorn Ave Livermore (94550) ***(P-23123)***
Gpr Stabilizer LLC ....F....619 661-0101
8715 Dead Stick Rd San Diego (92154) ***(P-20405)***
Gps Logic LLC ....F....949 812-6942
1327 Calle Avanzado San Clemente (92673) ***(P-17525)***
Gps Metals Lab Inc ....E....858 433-6125
12396 World Trade Dr San Diego (92128) ***(P-11202)***
Grab Green, Camarillo *Also called Maddiebrit Products LLC* ***(P-8655)***
Graber Blinds, San Diego *Also called Springs Window Fashions LLC* ***(P-5041)***
Grace Communications Inc (PA) ....E....213 628-4384
210 S Spring St Los Angeles (90012) ***(P-5648)***
Grace Dvson Discovery Sciences, Hesperia *Also called W R Grace & Co-Conn* ***(P-21323)***
Grace Machine Co Inc ....E....323 771-6215
4540 Cecilia St Cudahy (90201) ***(P-16002)***
Gracie Collection, Rancho Santa Fe *Also called Black Silver Enterprises Inc* ***(P-3297)***
Grade A Sign LLC ....E....310 652-9700
529 N La Cienega Blvd # 300 West Hollywood (90048) ***(P-23124)***
Gradescope Inc ....F....702 985-7442
2054 University Ave # 600 Berkeley (94704) ***(P-23951)***
Grading and Excavating Mag, Santa Barbara *Also called Forester Communications Inc* ***(P-5936)***
Graffeo Leather Collection, San Carlos *Also called Meskin Khosrow Kay* ***(P-10241)***
Grafico Inc ....F....562 404-4976
15320 Cornet St Santa Fe Springs (90670) ***(P-7373)***
Graham Lee Associates Inc ....F....323 581-8203
8674 Atlantic Ave South Gate (90280) ***(P-4800)***
Graham Packaging Co Europe LLC ....C....909 989-5367
11555 Arrow Rte Rancho Cucamonga (91730) ***(P-9486)***
Graham Packaging Company LP ....D....714 979-1835
3300 W Segerstrom Ave Santa Ana (92704) ***(P-9812)***
Graham Packaging Company LP ....E....909 484-2900
9041 Pittsburgh Ave Rancho Cucamonga (91730) ***(P-9813)***
Graham Packaging Company LP ....D....209 578-1112
513 S Mcclure Rd Modesto (95357) ***(P-9814)***
Graham Webb International Inc (HQ) ....D....760 918-3600
6109 De Soto Ave Woodland Hills (91367) ***(P-8502)***
Grain Craft Inc ....E....323 585-0131
1861 E 55th St Los Angeles (90058) ***(P-1004)***
Grainless Goodness, Ojai *Also called Ellen Lark Farm* ***(P-1019)***
Gramberg Machine Inc ....F....805 278-4500
500 Spectrum Cir Oxnard (93030) ***(P-16003)***
Gramercy Aerospace Mfg LLC ....F....310 515-0576
17224 Gramercy Pl Gardena (90247) ***(P-20586)***
Gramic Enterprises Inc ....F....714 329-8627
21770 Deveron Cv Yorba Linda (92887) ***(P-1534)***
Gramicci Comfort Engineered, Agoura Hills *Also called Sole Survivor Corporation* ***(P-3409)***
Granatelli Motor Sports Inc ....E....805 486-6644
1000 Yarnell Pl Oxnard (93033) ***(P-19674)***
Granath & Granath Inc ....E....310 327-5740
1930 W Rosecrans Ave Gardena (90249) ***(P-13016)***
Granberg International, Pittsburg *Also called Granberg Pump and Meter Ltd* ***(P-14222)***
Granberg Pump and Meter Ltd ....F....707 562-2099
1051 Los Medanos St Pittsburg (94565) ***(P-14222)***
Grand American Millwork, La Mirada *Also called G A Doors Inc* ***(P-4046)***
Grand Cabinets and Stone Inc ....F....510 759-3268
1583 Entp Blvd Ste 20 West Sacramento (95691) ***(P-4202)***
Grand Casino On Main Inc ....E....310 253-9066
3826 Main St Culver City (90232) ***(P-1222)***
Grand Fusion Housewares Inc (PA) ....F....888 614-7263
12 Partridge Irvine (92604) ***(P-9815)***
Grand Fusion Housewares Inc ....E....909 292-5776
9375 Customhouse Plz San Diego (92154) ***(P-9816)***
Grand General Accessories LLC ....E....310 631-2589
1965 E Vista Bella Way Rancho Dominguez (90220) ***(P-16553)***
Grand Meadows Inc ....F....714 628-1690
1607 W Orange Grove Ave E Orange (92868) ***(P-7926)***
Grand Metals Inc ....F....310 327-5554
325 N Cota St Corona (92880) ***(P-11046)***
Grand Motif Records ....F....562 698-8538
8304 Enramada Ave Whittier (90605) ***(P-17326)***
Grand Pacific Fire Protection ....F....951 226-8304
13100 Red Corral Dr Corona (92883) ***(P-13689)***
Grand Packaging Pet Tech ....D....209 578-1112
513 S Mcclure Rd Modesto (95357) ***(P-9817)***
Grand Printing, Covina *Also called William J Hammett Inc* ***(P-6940)***
Grand Textile, Cerritos *Also called Dool Fna Inc* ***(P-2725)***
Grand West Inc (PA) ....F....323 235-2700
1441 E Adams Blvd Los Angeles (90011) ***(P-2789)***
Grand-Way Fabri-Graphic Inc ....E....818 206-8560
22550 Lamplight Pl Santa Clarita (91350) ***(P-13187)***
Grandesign Decor Inc ....E....408 436-9969
1727 N 1st St San Jose (95112) ***(P-11957)***
Grandis Metals Intl Corp ....F....949 459-2621
29752 Ave De Las Bndra Rcho STA Marg (92688) ***(P-11272)***
Grandis Titanium, Rcho STA Marg *Also called Grandis Metals Intl Corp* ***(P-11272)***
Granite Gold Inc ....F....858 499-8933
12780 Danielson Ct Ste A Poway (92064) ***(P-8386)***
Granite Kitchen Countertops, Concord *Also called GM Marble & Granite Inc* ***(P-314)***
Granite Rock Co (PA) ....D....831 768-2000
350 Technology Dr Watsonville (95076) ***(P-341)***
Granite Rock Co ....E....650 482-3800
365 Blomquist St Redwood City (94063) ***(P-9093)***
Granite Rock Co ....E....831 392-3700
1755 Del Monte Blvd Seaside (93955) ***(P-10765)***
Granite Rock Co ....D....831 768-2300
Quarry Rd Aromas (95004) ***(P-342)***
Granite Software Inc ....F....818 252-1950
7590 N Glenoaks Blvd # 102 Burbank (91504) ***(P-23952)***
Granitize Products Inc ....D....562 923-5438
11022 Vulcan St South Gate (90280) ***(P-8387)***
Grant Piston Rings, Anaheim *Also called Rtr Industries LLC* ***(P-15618)***
Grape Links Inc ....F....707 524-8000
420 Aviation Blvd Ste 106 Santa Rosa (95403) ***(P-1734)***
Grapheex, Simi Valley *Also called Pars Publishing Corp* ***(P-6770)***
Graphic Color Systems Inc ....D....323 283-3000
1166 W Garvey Ave Monterey Park (91754) ***(P-6594)***
Graphic Dies Inc ....F....562 946-1802
12335 Florence Ave Santa Fe Springs (90670) ***(P-7374)***
Graphic Film Group LLC (PA) ....F....310 887-6330
1901 Avenue Of The Stars Los Angeles (90067) ***(P-5945)***
Graphic Fox Inc ....F....530 895-1359
3124 Thorntree Dr Chico (95973) ***(P-6595)***
Graphic Packaging Intl LLC ....C....949 250-0900
1600 Barranca Pkwy Irvine (92606) ***(P-5162)***
Graphic Packaging Intl LLC ....C....559 651-3535
1600 Kelsey Rd Visalia (93291) ***(P-5107)***
Graphic Packaging Intl LLC ....C....530 533-1058
525 Airport Pkwy Oroville (95965) ***(P-7075)***
Graphic Prints Inc ....E....310 768-0474
1200 Kona Dr Compton (90220) ***(P-3791)***
Graphic Research Inc ....E....818 886-7340
9334 Mason Ave Chatsworth (91311) ***(P-17892)***
Graphic Sciences Inc ....F....909 947-3366
4663 E Guasti Rd Ste B Ontario (91761) ***(P-8918)***
Graphic Source, The, San Rafael *Also called Bennett Industries Inc* ***(P-6443)***
Graphic Systems, Lompoc *Also called Henry L Hudson* ***(P-6608)***
Graphic Systems ....F....805 686-0705
1693 Mission Dr Ste C101 Solvang (93463) ***(P-7076)***
Graphic Trends Incorporated ....E....562 531-2339
7301 Adams St Paramount (90723) ***(P-7077)***
Graphic Visions Inc ....E....818 845-8393
7119 Fair Ave North Hollywood (91605) ***(P-6596)***
Graphicpak Corporation ....F....323 306-3054
760 S Vail Ave Montebello (90640) ***(P-5232)***
Graphics Bindery ....F....818 886-2463
16611 Roscoe Pl North Hills (91343) ***(P-7332)***
Graphics Factory Inc ....F....818 727-9040
21344 Superior St Chatsworth (91311) ***(P-7078)***
Graphics Ink Lithography LLC ....F....760 438-9052
5531 Foxtail Loop Carlsbad (92010) ***(P-7079)***
Graphics United, Covina *Also called Shift Calendars Inc* ***(P-6860)***
Graphiq LLC ....C....805 335-2433
101a Innovation Pl Santa Barbara (93108) ***(P-6247)***
Graphix Press Inc ....E....818 834-8520
13814 Del Sur St San Fernando (91340) ***(P-6597)***
Graphtec America Inc (HQ) ....E....949 770-6010
17462 Armstrong Ave Irvine (92614) ***(P-20881)***
Grass Manufacturing Co Inc ....F....650 366-2556
2850 Bay Rd Redwood City (94063) ***(P-12809)***
Grass Valley Inc ....A....530 478-3000
125 Crown Point Ct Grass Valley (95945) ***(P-17526)***
Grass Valley Inc (HQ) ....D....530 265-1000
125 Crown Point Ct Grass Valley (95945) ***(P-17527)***
Grass Valley Usa LLC (HQ) ....B....800 547-8949
125 Crown Point Ct Grass Valley (95945) ***(P-17375)***
Grateful Naturals Corp ....F....323 379-4553
213 Walter Ave Newbury Park (91320) ***(P-8503)***
Grating Pacific Inc (PA) ....E....562 598-4314
3651 Sausalito St Los Alamitos (90720) ***(P-11806)***
Grau Design Inc ....F....323 461-4462
1133 N Highland Ave Los Angeles (90038) ***(P-3162)***
Gravity Boarding Company Inc ....F....760 591-4144
2211 S Hcnda Blvd Ste 201 Hacienda Heights (91745) ***(P-22813)***
Graybills Metal Polishing Inc ....F....626 967-5742
1212 E Puente Ave West Covina (91790) ***(P-13017)***
Grayd-A Prcsion Met Fbricators ....E....562 944-8951
13233 Florence Ave Santa Fe Springs (90670) ***(P-12225)***
Graypay LLC ....D....818 387-6735
6345 Balboa Blvd Ste 115 Encino (91316) ***(P-23953)***
Graysix Company ....E....510 845-5936
2427 4th St Berkeley (94710) ***(P-12226)***
Grayson Service Inc ....C....661 589-5444
1845 Greeley Rd Bakersfield (93314) ***(P-202)***
Great American Packaging ....E....323 582-2247
4361 S Soto St Vernon (90058) ***(P-5398)***
Great American Wineries Inc ....E....831 920-4736
2511 Garden Rd Ste B100 Monterey (93940) ***(P-1735)***
Great Lakes Data Systems Inc ....F....760 602-1900
5954 Priestly Dr Carlsbad (92008) ***(P-23954)***

Great Northern Corporation E 951 361-4770
12075 Cabernet Dr Fontana (92337) ***(P-5329)***
Great Northern Wheels Deals E 530 533-2134
810 Lake Blvd Ste C Redding (96003) ***(P-5649)***
Great River Food, City of Industry *Also called Derek and Constance Lee Corp **(P-453)***
Great Spaces USA, Merced *Also called Olde World Corporation **(P-4926)***
Great Western Litho, Van Nuys *Also called Investment Enterprises Inc **(P-7102)***
Great Western Packaging LLC D 818 464-3800
8230-8240 Haskell Ave Van Nuys (91406) ***(P-7080)***
Greatbatch Medical, San Diego *Also called Integer Holdings Corporation **(P-21745)***
Greatdad LLC F 415 572-8181
2337 Vallejo St San Francisco (94123) ***(P-5946)***
Greathouse Screen Printing F 858 279-4939
5644 Kearny Mesa Rd Ste E San Diego (92111) ***(P-7081)***
Grech Motors LLC (PA) E 951 688-8347
6915 Arlington Ave Riverside (92504) ***(P-24693)***
Greek Marble Inc F 323 221-6624
1600 N San Fernando Rd Los Angeles (90065) ***(P-10908)***
Green Acres Cannabis LLC E 415 657-3484
6256 3rd St San Francisco (94124) ***(P-7664)***
Green Circuits Inc C 408 526-1700
1130 Ringwood Ct San Jose (95131) ***(P-17893)***
Green Cures Inc E 818 773-3929
20201 Sherman Way Ste 101 Winnetka (91306) ***(P-7665)***
Green Dining Table F 626 782-7916
625 S Palm Ave Alhambra (91803) ***(P-462)***
Green Field Paper Company, San Diego *Also called Smithcorp Inc **(P-5152)***
Green Flash Brewing, San Diego *Also called Gfbc Inc **(P-1531)***
Green Hills Software LLC (HQ) C 805 965-6044
30 W Sola St Santa Barbara (93101) ***(P-23955)***
Green Lake Investors LLC E 707 577-1301
3310 Coffey Ln Santa Rosa (95403) ***(P-22950)***
Green Mattress Inc F 323 752-2026
6827 Mckinley Ave Los Angeles (90001) ***(P-2855)***
Green Mochi LLC F 213 225-2250
834 S Broadway Ste Mezz Los Angeles (90014) ***(P-3229)***
Green Products Packaging Corp F 951 940-9343
22770 Perry St Perris (92570) ***(P-5293)***
Green Rubber-Kennedy Ag LP (PA) E 831 753-6100
1310 Dayton St Salinas (93901) ***(P-9548)***
Green Sheet Inc F 707 284-1684
5830 Commerce Blvd Ste B Rohnert Park (94928) ***(P-7082)***
Green Soap Inc F 925 240-5546
450 E Grant Line Rd 1 Tracy (95376) ***(P-8341)***
Green Spot Packaging Inc E 909 625-8771
100 S Cambridge Ave Claremont (91711) ***(P-2078)***
Green Valley Foods Product F 760 964-1105
25684 Community Blvd Barstow (92311) ***(P-553)***
Green's Metal Cutoff, Santa Fe Springs *Also called Dunstan Enterprises Inc **(P-15909)***
Greenberg Teleprmpt F 714 633-1111
868 N Main St Orange (92868) ***(P-17376)***
Greenbox Art and Culture, San Diego *Also called No Boundaries Inc **(P-6750)***
Greenbroz Inc F 844 379-8746
955 Vernon Way El Cajon (92020) ***(P-13634)***
Greene Group, Oceanside *Also called Southwest Greene Intl Inc **(P-12874)***
Greener Printer, Richmond *Also called Tulip Pubg & Graphics Inc **(P-6903)***
Greenfields Outdoor Fitnes Inc F 888 315-9037
2617 W Woodland Dr Anaheim (92801) ***(P-22814)***
Greenform LLC F 310 331-1665
12900 Prairie Ave Hawthorne (90250) ***(P-13732)***
Greenheck Fan Corporation C 916 626-3400
170 Cyber Ct Rocklin (95765) ***(P-14661)***
Greenkraft Inc F 714 545-7777
2530 S Birch St Santa Ana (92707) ***(P-19474)***
Greenlee Textron Inc D 858 530-3100
7098 Miratech Dr Ste 130 San Diego (92121) ***(P-21046)***
Greenliant Systems Inc C 408 217-7400
3970 Freedom Cir Ste 100 Santa Clara (95054) ***(P-18255)***
Greenpower Motor Company Inc F 604 563-4144
1700 Hope Ave Porterville (93257) ***(P-19475)***
Greenscape Solutions Inc E 909 714-8333
7051 27th St Riverside (92509) ***(P-10509)***
Greenshine New Energy LLC D 949 609-9636
23661 Birtcher Dr Lake Forest (92630) ***(P-17130)***
Greenvity Communications Inc (PA) E 408 935-9358
2150 Trade Zone Blvd San Jose (95131) ***(P-14474)***
Greenvolts Inc D 415 963-4030
19200 Stevens Creek Blvd # 200 Cupertino (95014) ***(P-11698)***
Greenwich Biosciences Inc E 760 795-2200
5750 Fleet St Ste 200 Carlsbad (92008) ***(P-7927)***
Grefco Dicaperl, Torrance *Also called Dicaperl Corporation **(P-386)***
Greg Ian Islands Inc E 626 355-0019
123b E Montecito Ave B Sierra Madre (91024) ***(P-4905)***
Gregg Hammork Enterprizes Inc F 949 586-7902
23002 Alicia Pkwy Mission Viejo (92692) ***(P-54)***
Gregg's Mission Viejo Mobile, Mission Viejo *Also called Gregg Hammork Enterprizes Inc **(P-54)***
Gregor Inc F 559 441-7703
3565 N Hazel Ave Fresno (93722) ***(P-20334)***
Gregor Boat Co, Fresno *Also called Gregor Inc **(P-20334)***
Gregory Associates Inc E 408 446-5725
1233 Belknap Ct Cupertino (95014) ***(P-21047)***
Gregory Graziano F 707 485-9463
1170 Bel Arbres Dr Redwood Valley (95470) ***(P-1736)***
Gregory M Fink F 949 305-4242
23182 Alcalde Dr Ste H Laguna Hills (92653) ***(P-23125)***
Gregory Patterson E 831 636-1015
1741 Shelton Dr Hollister (95023) ***(P-12478)***

Greif Inc D 209 383-4396
2400 Cooper Ave Merced (95348) ***(P-5294)***
Greif Inc D 408 779-2161
235 San Pedro Ave Morgan Hill (95037) ***(P-5295)***
Greif Inc D 714 523-9580
5701 Fresca Dr La Palma (90623) ***(P-5296)***
Greif Inc E 909 350-2112
8250 Almeria Ave Fontana (92335) ***(P-11509)***
Greige Gods Boking PO AP Group, Vernon *Also called Softmax Inc **(P-3458)***
Greka Inc C 805 347-8700
1791 Sinton Rd Santa Maria (93458) ***(P-18)***
Greka Integrated Inc (PA) C 805 347-8700
1700 Sinton Rd Santa Maria (93458) ***(P-125)***
Greka Oil & Gas, Santa Maria *Also called Hvi Cat Canyon Inc **(P-211)***
Gremlin Inc E 408 214-9885
55 S Market St Ste 1205 San Jose (95113) ***(P-23956)***
Greneker Furniture E 323 263-9000
3110 E 12th St Los Angeles (90023) ***(P-4906)***
Greneker Solutions, Los Angeles *Also called Pacific Manufacturing MGT Inc **(P-4995)***
Grenfield Consulting E 310 286-0200
1801 Century Park E Fl 23 Los Angeles (90067) ***(P-126)***
Grey Studio Inc E 323 780-8111
629 S Clarence St Los Angeles (90023) ***(P-2690)***
Greyheller LLC F 925 415-5053
111 Deerwood Rd Ste 200 San Ramon (94583) ***(P-23957)***
Grgich Hills Cellar E 707 963-2784
1829 St Helena Hwy Rutherford (94573) ***(P-1737)***
Grico Precision Inc F 626 963-0368
128 S Valencia Ave Ste A Glendora (91741) ***(P-16004)***
Grid Modernization Division, San Jose *Also called Networked Energy Services Corp **(P-19364)***
Gridgain Systems Inc (PA) D 650 241-2281
1065 E Hillsdale Blvd Foster City (94404) ***(P-23958)***
Griff Industries Inc F 661 728-0111
4515 Runway Dr Lancaster (93536) ***(P-9818)***
Griffin Laboratories F 951 695-6727
43379 Bus Pk Dr Ste 300 Temecula (92590) ***(P-21726)***
Griffiths Printing, Anaheim *Also called Griffiths Services Inc **(P-6598)***
Griffiths Services Inc E 714 685-7700
121 S Old Springs Rd Anaheim (92808) ***(P-6598)***
Grifols Biologicals LLC (HQ) B 323 225-2221
2410 Lillyvale Ave Los Angeles (90032) ***(P-8305)***
Grimaud Farms California Inc (HQ) E 209 466-3200
1320 S Aurora St Ste A Stockton (95206) ***(P-518)***
Grimco Inc E 562 449-4964
13454 Imperial Hwy Santa Fe Springs (90670) ***(P-12810)***
Grind Food Company Inc F 805 964-8344
177 S Turnpike Rd Goleta (93111) ***(P-16005)***
Grinding & Dicing Services Inc E 408 451-2000
925 Berryessa Rd San Jose (95133) ***(P-18256)***
Griswold Controls LLC (PA) C 949 559-6000
2803 Barranca Pkwy Irvine (92606) ***(P-13356)***
Griswold Pump Company E 909 422-1700
22069 Van Buren St Grand Terrace (92313) ***(P-14577)***
Griswold Water Systems, Corona *Also called National Certified Fabricators **(P-18728)***
Gritstone Oncology Inc (PA) C 510 871-6100
5858 Horton St Ste 210 Emeryville (94608) ***(P-8306)***
Gro-Power Inc E 909 393-3744
15065 Telephone Ave Chino (91710) ***(P-8793)***
Gro-Tech Systems Inc F 530 432-7012
17282 Cattle Dr Rough and Ready (95975) ***(P-12548)***
Groskopf Warehouse & Logistics E 707 939-3100
20580 8th St E Sonoma (95476) ***(P-1738)***
Grossi Fabrication Inc E 209 883-2817
3200 Tully Rd Hughson (95326) ***(P-13415)***
Ground Control Systems Inc F 805 783-4600
3100 El Camino Real Atascadero (93422) ***(P-17528)***
Ground Fueling, Irvine *Also called Eaton Industrial Corporation **(P-20096)***
Ground Hog Inc E 909 478-5700
1470 Victoria Ct San Bernardino (92408) ***(P-13733)***
Groundmetrics Inc F 619 786-8023
3954 Murphy Canyon Rd D207 San Diego (92123) ***(P-203)***
Groundwork Coffee Company, North Hollywood *Also called Gourmet Coffee Warehouse Inc **(P-2295)***
Groundwork Coffee Company, Los Angeles *Also called Gourmet Coffee Warehouse Inc **(P-2296)***
Groundwork Coffee Roasters LLC C 818 506-6020
5457 Cleon Ave North Hollywood (91601) ***(P-2297)***
Group Five, Whittier *Also called Russ Bassett Corp **(P-4608)***
Group Manufacturing Services (PA) D 408 436-1040
1928 Hartog Dr San Jose (95131) ***(P-12227)***
Group Manufacturing Services F 916 858-3270
2751 Merc Dr Ste 900 Rancho Cordova (95742) ***(P-12228)***
Group Martin LLC Johnathon E 323 235-1555
3400 S Main St Los Angeles (90007) ***(P-3163)***
Grove Aircraft Co, El Cajon *Also called Robert Grove **(P-19927)***
Grover City Press, Arroyo Grande *Also called Politezer Newspaers Inc **(P-5799)***
Grover Manufacturing, Montebello *Also called Grover Smith Mfg Corp **(P-14578)***
Grover Products Co (PA) E 323 263-9981
3424 E Olympic Blvd Los Angeles (90023) ***(P-19675)***
Grover Products Co D 323 263-9981
3424 E Olympic Blvd Los Angeles (90023) ***(P-19676)***
Grover Smith Mfg Corp E 323 724-3444
620 S Vail Ave Montebello (90640) ***(P-14578)***
Grow More Inc D 310 515-1700
15600 New Century Dr Gardena (90248) ***(P-8830)***
Growdiaries LLC F 626 354-8935
8605 Santa Monica Blvd West Hollywood (90069) ***(P-23959)***

Mergent e-mail: customerrelations@mergent.com
1116
2020 California
Manufacturers Register
(P-0000) Products & Services Section entry number
(PA)=Parent Co (HQ)=Headquarters (DH)=Div Headquarters

Growers Ice Co....E....831 424-5781
1124 Abbott St Salinas (93901) *(P-2356)*
Growest Inc (PA)....F....951 638-1000
10490 Dawson Canyon Rd Corona (92883) *(P-1739)*
Growest Development, Corona *Also called Growest Inc (P-1739)*
Growthstock Inc....C....949 660-9473
2921 Daimler St Santa Ana (92705) *(P-18927)*
Gruber Systems Inc....E....661 257-0464
29083 The Old Rd Valencia (91355) *(P-14060)*
Gruma Corporation....F....858 673-5780
12316 World Trade Dr # 104 San Diego (92128) *(P-2332)*
Gruma Corporation....D....559 498-7820
2849 E Edgar Ave Fresno (93706) *(P-2333)*
Gruma Corporation....C....909 980-3566
11559 Jersey Blvd Ste A Rancho Cucamonga (91730) *(P-2334)*
Grundfos CBS Inc....F....510 512-1300
25568 Seaboard Ln Hayward (94545) *(P-14579)*
Grunion Gazette, Long Beach *Also called Gazette Newspapers (P-5644)*
Gryphon Mobile Electronics LLC....F....626 810-7770
159 W Orangethorpe Ave A Placentia (92870) *(P-17529)*
GS Cosmeceutical Usa Inc....E....925 371-5000
131 Pullman St Livermore (94551) *(P-8504)*
Gs Manufacturing....F....949 642-1500
985 W 18th St Costa Mesa (92627) *(P-14631)*
Gscm Ventures Inc....E....818 303-2600
12924 Pierce St Pacoima (91331) *(P-8505)*
Gsi Capital Partners LLC....F....760 745-1768
888 Rancheros Dr Ste A San Marcos (92069) *(P-22815)*
Gsi Technology Inc....D....408 980-8388
2360 Owen St Santa Clara (95054) *(P-18257)*
Gsi Technology Inc (PA)....D....408 331-8800
1213 Elko Dr Sunnyvale (94089) *(P-18258)*
Gsl Fine Lithographers....E....916 231-1410
8386 Rovana Cir Sacramento (95828) *(P-6599)*
Gsl Tech Inc....F....626 572-9617
3134 Maxson Rd El Monte (91732) *(P-593)*
Gsp, San Diego *Also called Greathouse Screen Printing (P-7081)*
Gsp Acquisition Corporation....E....310 532-9430
19745 Lassen St Chatsworth (91311) *(P-13018)*
Gsp Metal Finishing Inc....E....818 744-1328
16520 S Figueroa St Gardena (90248) *(P-13019)*
Gsp Precision Inc....E....818 845-2212
650 Town Center Dr # 950 Costa Mesa (92626) *(P-16006)*
Gst Inc....D....949 510-1142
3419 Via Lido Ste 164 Newport Beach (92663) *(P-15035)*
Gst Industries Inc....E....818 350-1900
9060 Winnetka Ave Northridge (91324) *(P-20123)*
Gt Advanced Technologies Inc....E....707 571-1911
1911 Airport Blvd Santa Rosa (95403) *(P-18259)*
GT Precision Inc....C....310 323-4374
1629 W 132nd St Gardena (90249) *(P-12633)*
Gt Sapphire Systems Group LLC....E....707 571-1911
1911 Airport Blvd Santa Rosa (95403) *(P-17377)*
GTC Manufacturing, Benicia *Also called Bulls-Eye Marketing Inc (P-19598)*
Gtr Enterprises Incorporated....E....760 931-1192
6352 Corte Del Abeto E Carlsbad (92011) *(P-16007)*
Gtran Inc (PA)....E....805 445-4500
829 Flynn Rd Camarillo (93012) *(P-18928)*
Gts Living Foods LLC....A....323 581-7787
4415 Bandini Blvd Vernon (90058) *(P-2079)*
Gtx Corp....F....213 489-3019
117 W 9th St Ste 1214 Los Angeles (90015) *(P-17530)*
Gu....E....510 527-4664
1204 10th St Berkeley (94710) *(P-7928)*
Guadalupe Associates Inc (PA)....F....415 387-2324
1348 10th Ave San Francisco (94122) *(P-6248)*
Guano Records LLC....F....714 263-5398
26298 Jaylene St Murrieta (92563) *(P-7083)*
Guard-Dogs, Ventura *Also called Abbs Vision Systems Inc (P-22337)*
Guardian Analytics Inc....E....650 383-9200
2465 Latham St Ste 200 Mountain View (94040) *(P-23960)*
Guardian Corporate Services....E....619 295-2646
2814 University Ave Frnt San Diego (92104) *(P-3685)*
Guardian Industries LLC....B....559 891-8867
11535 E Mountain View Ave Kingsburg (93631) *(P-10265)*
Guardian Industries Corp....D....559 891-8867
11535 E Mountain View Ave Kingsburg (93631) *(P-10266)*
Guardian Industries Corp....D....559 638-3588
11535 E Mountain View Ave Kingsburg (93631) *(P-10267)*
Guardian Survival Gear Inc....F....760 519-5643
1401 S Hicks Ave Commerce (90023) *(P-22019)*
Guardian-Kingsburg, Kingsburg *Also called Guardian Industries LLC (P-10265)*
Guardion Health Sciences Inc (PA)....F....858 605-9055
15150 Avenue Of Science # 20 San Diego (92128) *(P-7929)*
Guavus Inc (HQ)....D....650 243-3400
2125 Zanker Rd San Jose (95131) *(P-23961)*
Guck Ariba....C....650 390-1445
807 Eleventh Ave Sunnyvale (94089) *(P-23962)*
Guenoc Winery Inc....E....707 987-2385
200 Concourse Blvd Santa Rosa (95403) *(P-1740)*
Guernsey Coating Laboratory....F....805 642-1508
1788 Goodyear Ave Ventura (93003) *(P-13188)*
Guess Inc (PA)....A....213 765-3100
1444 S Alameda St Los Angeles (90021) *(P-3004)*
Guess Inc....E....626 856-5555
358 Plaza Dr West Covina (91790) *(P-3005)*
Guess Inc....F....805 963-9490
820 State St Santa Barbara (93101) *(P-3006)*
Guess Inc....E....408 847-3400
8300 Arroyo Cir Ste 270 Gilroy (95020) *(P-3087)*
Guess Inc....E....909 987-7776
1 Mills Cir Ste 313 Ontario (91764) *(P-3007)*
Guest Chex Inc....F....714 522-1860
7697 9th St Buena Park (90621) *(P-6600)*
Guestchex, Buena Park *Also called Guest Chex Inc (P-6600)*
Guidance Software Inc (HQ)....C....626 229-9191
1055 E Colo Blvd Ste 400 Pasadena (91106) *(P-23963)*
Guidance Software Inc....E....626 229-9199
215 N Marengo Ave Ste 250 Pasadena (91101) *(P-23964)*
Guidant Sales LLC....E....650 965-2634
825 E Middlefield Rd Mountain View (94043) *(P-21727)*
Guided Wave Inc....E....916 638-4944
3033 Gold Canal Dr Rancho Cordova (95670) *(P-21357)*
Guidetech Inc....E....408 733-6555
1300 Memorex Dr Santa Clara (95050) *(P-21048)*
Guidewire Software Inc (PA)....C....650 357-9100
2850 S Del St Ste 400 San Mateo (94403) *(P-23965)*
Guittard Chocolate Co....C....650 697-4427
10 Guittard Rd Burlingame (94010) *(P-1411)*
Gulbransen Inc....F....619 296-5760
2102 Hancock St San Diego (92110) *(P-22624)*
Gulf Enterprises, Chatsworth *Also called Mercury Magnetics Inc (P-18726)*
Gulf Streams....F....562 420-1818
4150 E Donald Douglas Dr Long Beach (90808) *(P-19904)*
Gulfstream Aerospace Corp GA....A....562 907-9300
9818 Mina Ave Whittier (90605) *(P-19905)*
Gulfstream California, Lincoln *Also called Gdas-Lincoln Inc (P-19894)*
Gulshan International Corp....F....408 745-6090
1355 Geneva Dr Sunnyvale (94089) *(P-18260)*
Gum Sun Times Inc (PA)....E....415 379-6788
625 Kearny St San Francisco (94108) *(P-5650)*
Gund Company Inc....F....909 890-9300
4701 E Airport Dr Ontario (91761) *(P-16949)*
Gundrill Tech Inc....E....562 946-9355
10030 Greenleaf Ave Santa Fe Springs (90670) *(P-16008)*
Gunnar Optiks LLC....E....858 769-2500
2236 Rutherford Rd # 123 Carlsbad (92008) *(P-22359)*
Gunnebo Entrance Control Inc (HQ)....F....707 748-0885
535 Getty Ct Ste F Benicia (94510) *(P-21481)*
Guntert Zmmerman Const Div Inc....E....209 599-0066
222 E 4th St Ripon (95366) *(P-13734)*
Gunthers Quality Ice Cream....F....916 457-3339
2801 Franklin Blvd Sacramento (95818) *(P-647)*
Gupshup Inc....F....415 506-9095
38350 Fremont Blvd # 203 Fremont (94536) *(P-23966)*
Guptill Gear Corporation....F....714 956-2170
874 S Rose Pl Anaheim (92805) *(P-16009)*
Guru Knits Inc....D....323 235-9424
225 W 38th St Los Angeles (90037) *(P-3164)*
GUSB Inc....F....323 233-0044
219 E 32nd St Los Angeles (90011) *(P-3165)*
Gusmer Enterprises Inc....D....908 301-1811
81 M St Fresno (93721) *(P-14823)*
Gustine Ready Mix, Gustine *Also called Legacy Vulcan LLC (P-10597)*
Gusto, San Francisco *Also called Zenpayroll Inc (P-24602)*
Gutierrez Grading....F....909 397-8717
1505 E Phillips Blvd Pomona (91766) *(P-7084)*
Gutterglove Inc....D....916 624-5000
8860 Industrial Ave # 140 Roseville (95678) *(P-12229)*
Guy Chaddock & Company (PA)....C....408 907-9200
1100 La Avenida St Mountain View (94043) *(P-4644)*
Guy G Veralrud....F....530 477-7323
10141 Evening Star Dr # 1 Grass Valley (95945) *(P-17234)*
Guzik Technical Enterprises....D....650 625-8000
2443 Wyandotte St Mountain View (94043) *(P-21049)*
Gw Crystal, Rancho Cucamonga *Also called Gw Partners International (P-10308)*
Gw Partners International....F....909 980-1010
8351 Elm Ave Ste 106 Rancho Cucamonga (91730) *(P-10308)*
Gw Services LLC (HQ)....E....760 560-1111
1385 Park Center Dr Vista (92081) *(P-15398)*
Gwla Acquisition Corp (PA)....F....323 789-7800
8600 Rheem Ave South Gate (90280) *(P-10268)*
Gym Parts Depot, Los Angeles *Also called Rtg Investment Group Inc (P-22878)*
Gypsy 05 Inc....E....323 265-2700
3200 Union Pacific Ave Los Angeles (90023) *(P-3332)*
Gypsy Heart, Alhambra *Also called Active Knitwear Resources Inc (P-3134)*
Gyrfalcon Technology Inc....E....408 944-9219
1900 Mccarthy Blvd # 208 Milpitas (95035) *(P-18261)*
Gyt San Diego Inc....F....619 661-2568
2253 Roll Paseo Dil Amer San Diego (92154) *(P-16010)*
H & B Sports Products Div, Ontario *Also called Hillerich & Bradsby Co (P-22821)*
H & H MANUFACTURING, Pomona *Also called Holland & Herring Mfg Inc (P-16033)*
H & H Specialties Inc....E....626 575-0776
14850 Don Julian Rd Ste B City of Industry (91746) *(P-23349)*
H & L Apparel Enterprise Inc....F....323 589-1563
2202 E Anderson St Vernon (90058) *(P-3166)*
H & L Tooth Company (PA)....D....323 721-5146
1540 S Greenwood Ave Montebello (90640) *(P-13735)*
H & M Cabinet Company....F....760 744-0559
1565 La Mirada Dr San Marcos (92078) *(P-4907)*
H & M Four-Slide Inc....F....951 461-8244
25779 Jefferson Ave Murrieta (92562) *(P-16011)*
H & M Precision Machining, Santa Clara *Also called H&M Precision Machining (P-12634)*
H & M Wrought Iron Factory....F....619 427-5682
2560 Main St Ste A Chula Vista (91911) *(P-12479)*
H & N Tool & Die Co Inc....F....951 372-9071
201 Jason Ct Ste B Corona (92879) *(P-13976)*
H A I, Placentia *Also called Hai Advnced Mtl Spcialists Inc (P-11478)*

ALPHABETIC

Employee Codes: A=Over 500 employees, B=251-500
C=101-250, D=51-100, E=20-50, F=10-19
2020 California
Manfacturers Register
© Mergent Inc. 1-800-342-5647
1117

H A Rider & Sons ....E......831 722-3882
2482 Freedom Blvd Watsonville (95076) *(P-2080)*
H and M Industries LLC ....F......805 499-5100
855 Rancho Conejo Blvd Newbury Park (91320) *(P-4908)*
H B R Industries Inc ....F......408 988-0800
2261 Fortune Dr Ste B San Jose (95131) *(P-18719)*
H C I, Rocklin *Also called Hugin Components Inc (P-12819)*
H C Muddox, Sacramento *Also called Pabco Clay Products LLC (P-10436)*
H Co Computer Products (PA) ....E......949 833-3222
16812 Hale Ave Irvine (92606) *(P-15036)*
H F Johnston Mfg Co, Vista *Also called H P Solutions Inc (P-14270)*
H Fam Engineering Inc ....F......909 930-5678
2131 S Hellman Ave Ste F Ontario (91761) *(P-16012)*
H I S C Inc ....F......949 492-8968
1009 Calle Recodo San Clemente (92673) *(P-10309)*
H J Harkins Company Inc ....E......805 929-1333
1400 W Grand Ave Ste F Grover Beach (93433) *(P-7930)*
H J S Graphics ....F......818 782-5490
3533 Old Conejo Rd # 104 Newbury Park (91320) *(P-6601)*
H K Lighting Group Inc ....F......805 480-4881
3529 Old Conejo Rd # 118 Newbury Park (91320) *(P-17131)*
H K Prcision Turning Machining, Oceanside *Also called Balda HK Plastics Inc (P-12623)*
H Lima Company Inc ....E......209 239-6787
704 E Yosemite Ave Manteca (95336) *(P-389)*
H M F, Anaheim *Also called Hitech Metal Fabrication Corp (P-11808)*
H M T, Madera *Also called Horn Machine Tools Inc (P-13977)*
H N Lockwood Inc ....E......650 366-9557
880 Sweeney Ave Redwood City (94063) *(P-9819)*
H N S, San Diego *Also called Hughes Network Systems LLC (P-17538)*
H P Applications ....F......323 585-2894
4727 E 49th St Vernon (90058) *(P-11452)*
H P Group ....F......909 364-1069
5070 Lindsay Ct Chino (91710) *(P-23350)*
H P M, Sunnyvale *Also called Horvath Precision Machining (P-16035)*
H P Solutions Inc ....E......760 727-2880
2475 Ash St Vista (92081) *(P-14270)*
H Q Machine Tech Inc ....E......714 956-3388
6900 8th St Buena Park (90620) *(P-16013)*
H Roberts Construction ....D......562 590-4825
2165 W Gaylord St Long Beach (90813) *(P-12549)*
H S N Consultants Inc ....F......805 684-8800
1110 Eugenia Pl Ste 100 Carpinteria (93013) *(P-5947)*
H Silani & Associates Inc ....F......310 623-4848
210 S Robertson Blvd Beverly Hills (90211) *(P-21358)*
H Starlet LLC ....F......323 235-8777
3447 S Main St Los Angeles (90007) *(P-3333)*
H V Food Products Company ....C......510 271-7612
1221 Broadway Oakland (94612) *(P-884)*
H Wayne Lewis Inc ....E......909 874-2213
312 S Willow Ave Rialto (92376) *(P-12591)*
H&F Technologies Inc ....F......805 523-2759
650 Flinn Ave Unit 4 Moorpark (93021) *(P-17235)*
H&H Imaging Inc ....F......415 431-4731
375 Alabama St Ste 150 San Francisco (94110) *(P-6602)*
H&H Platemakers, San Francisco *Also called H&H Imaging Inc (P-6602)*
H&M Logging ....F......707 964-2340
442 S Franklin St Fort Bragg (95437) *(P-3885)*
H&M Precision Machining ....F......408 982-9184
504 Robert Ave Santa Clara (95050) *(P-12634)*
H&N Brothers Co Ltd ....F......626 465-3383
918 Canada Ct City of Industry (91748) *(P-17236)*
H-Square Corporation ....E......408 732-1240
3100 Patrick Henry Dr Santa Clara (95054) *(P-18262)*
H.U.M.A.N. Healthy Vending, Culver City *Also called Nutrition Without Borders LLC (P-15399)*
H2 Cards Inc ....F......415 788-7888
638 Washington St San Francisco (94111) *(P-7085)*
H2 Co, Santa Clara *Also called H-Square Corporation (P-18262)*
H2 Environmental ....F......909 628-0369
13122 6th St Chino (91710) *(P-10962)*
H2 Wellness Incorporated ....D......310 362-1888
15414 Milldale Dr Los Angeles (90077) *(P-23967)*
H2o Engineering Inc ....F......805 542-9253
189 Granada Dr San Luis Obispo (93401) *(P-15518)*
H2o Plus LLC (PA) ....D......312 377-2132
111 Sutter St Fl 22 San Francisco (94104) *(P-8506)*
H2scan Corporation ....E......661 775-9575
27215 Turnberry Ln Unit A Valencia (91355) *(P-21482)*
H2w Technologies Inc ....F......661 291-1620
26380 Ferry Ct Santa Clarita (91350) *(P-16720)*
H3 High Security Solutions LLC ....E......310 373-2319
434 1/2 Palos Verdes Blvd Redondo Beach (90277) *(P-13270)*
Hab Enterprises Inc ....F......310 628-9000
15233 Ventura Blvd # 100 Sherman Oaks (91403) *(P-9234)*
Habla Incorporated ....E......703 867-0135
548 Market St San Francisco (94104) *(P-23968)*
Hacker Industries Inc (PA) ....F......949 729-3101
1600 Newport Dr 275 Newport Beach (92660) *(P-10879)*
Hackett Industries Inc ....E......209 955-8220
4445 E Fremont St Stockton (95215) *(P-14370)*
Hackrod Inc ....F......347 331-8919
2220 N Ventura Ave Ste A Ventura (93001) *(P-19476)*
Hadco Products Inc ....F......916 966-2409
3345 Sunrise Blvd Ste 5 Rancho Cordova (95742) *(P-5022)*
Haddads Fine Arts Inc ....F......714 996-2100
3855 E Miraloma Ave Anaheim (92806) *(P-8919)*
Hadley Media Inc ....F......800 270-2084
1665 S Ranch Santa Fe Rd San Marcos (92078) *(P-6249)*
Haeco Americas Cabin Solutions, Pacoima *Also called Brice Manufacturing Co Inc (P-20059)*
Haeger Incorporated (HQ) ....E......209 848-4000
811 Wakefield Dr Oakdale (95361) *(P-14271)*
Haemonetics Corporation ....B......530 774-2081
95 Declaration Dr Ste 3 Chico (95973) *(P-21728)*
Haemonetics Manufacturing Inc (HQ) ....E......626 339-7388
1630 W Industrial Park St Covina (91722) *(P-21729)*
Hagafen Cellars Inc ....F......707 252-0781
4160 Silverado Trl NAPA (94558) *(P-1741)*
Hagen-Renaker Inc (PA) ....C......909 599-2341
914 W Cienega Ave San Dimas (91773) *(P-10489)*
Hager Mfg Inc ....E......714 522-8870
14610 Industry Cir La Mirada (90638) *(P-20124)*
Hagist Welding ....F......707 847-3362
34895 Kruse Ranch Rd Cazadero (95421) *(P-24637)*
Hagle Lumber Company Inc ....E......805 987-3887
3100 Somis Rd Somis (93066) *(P-3933)*
Hahn Estate ....D......831 678-2132
37700 Foothill Rd Soledad (93960) *(P-1742)*
Hahnemann Homeopathic Pharmacy, San Rafael *Also called Hahnemann Labortories Inc (P-7931)*
Hahnemann Labortories Inc ....F......415 451-6978
1940 4th St San Rafael (94901) *(P-7931)*
Hai Advnced Mtl Spcialists Inc ....F......714 414-0575
1688 Sierra Madre Cir Placentia (92870) *(P-11478)*
Haig Precision Mfg Corp ....D......408 378-4920
3616 Snell Ave San Jose (95136) *(P-16014)*
Haigs Delicacies LLC ....E......510 782-6285
25673 Nickel Pl Hayward (94545) *(P-2476)*
Haimetal Duct Inc ....F......818 768-2315
625 Arroyo St San Fernando (91340) *(P-12230)*
Hain Celestial Group Inc ....F......310 945-4300
8468 Warner Dr Culver City (90232) *(P-5462)*
Hain Celestial Group Inc ....C......323 859-0553
5630 Rickenbacker Rd Bell (90201) *(P-8507)*
Hain Celestial Group Inc ....D......707 347-1200
2201 S Mcdowell Boulevard Petaluma (94954) *(P-8508)*
Hair ACC By Mia Minnelli, Pleasant Hill *Also called Mosaic Brands Inc (P-23415)*
Hair By Couture Inc ....F......310 848-7676
1010 W Magnolia Blvd Burbank (91506) *(P-23351)*
Hair Syndicut ....F......909 946-3200
565 N Central Ave Upland (91786) *(P-8972)*
Haisch Construction Co Inc ....F......530 378-6800
1800 S Barney Rd Anderson (96007) *(P-4303)*
Haizol Global, Brea *Also called DOT Haizol Com (P-14265)*
Halabi Inc (PA) ....C......707 402-1600
2100 Huntington Dr Fairfield (94533) *(P-10909)*
Halcore Group Inc ....D......626 575-0880
10941 Weaver Ave South El Monte (91733) *(P-19477)*
Halcyon Microelectronics Inc ....F......626 814-4688
5467 2nd St Irwindale (91706) *(P-18263)*
Haldex Brake Products Corp ....F......909 974-1200
291 Kettering Dr Ontario (91761) *(P-19677)*
Haldor Topsoe Inc ....F......714 621-3800
770 The Cy Dr S Ste 8400 Orange (92868) *(P-7499)*
Halex Corporation (HQ) ....E......909 629-6219
4200 Santa Ana St Ste A Ontario (91761) *(P-11531)*
Haley Bros, Riverside *Also called T M Cobb Company (P-4136)*
Haley Bros Inc (HQ) ....C......714 670-2112
6291 Orangethorpe Ave Buena Park (90620) *(P-4052)*
Haley Brothers, Stockton *Also called T M Cobb Company (P-4137)*
Haley Brothers, San Bernardino *Also called T M Cobb Company (P-4946)*
Haley Indus Ctings Linings Inc ....E......323 588-8086
2919 Tanager Ave Commerce (90040) *(P-13189)*
Half Moon Bay Review, Half Moon Bay *Also called Wick Communications Co (P-5867)*
Hall Associates Racg Pdts Inc ....F......310 326-4111
23104 Normandie Ave Torrance (90502) *(P-20512)*
Hall Health and Longevity Cntr ....F......310 566-6690
916 Main St Venice (90291) *(P-7666)*
Hall Letter Shop Inc ....F......661 327-3228
5200 Rosedale Hwy Bakersfield (93308) *(P-6603)*
Hall Machine, San Diego *Also called Rdl Machine Inc (P-16345)*
Hall Research Technologies LLC (PA) ....F......714 641-6607
1163 Warner Ave Tustin (92780) *(P-15237)*
Hall Wines LLC ....E......707 967-2626
401 Saint Helena Hwy S Saint Helena (94574) *(P-1743)*
Halle-Hopper LLC ....E......951 284-7373
630 Parkridge Ave Norco (92860) *(P-4053)*
Hallett Boats ....E......626 969-8844
180 S Irwindale Ave Azusa (91702) *(P-20335)*
Halliburton Company ....D......661 393-8111
34722 7th Standard Rd Bakersfield (93314) *(P-204)*
Hallmark Floors Inc (PA) ....E......909 947-7736
2360 S Archibald Ave Ontario (91761) *(P-3975)*
Hallmark Lighting LLC ....D......818 885-5010
9631 De Soto Ave Chatsworth (91311) *(P-17040)*
Hallmark Metals Inc ....E......626 335-1263
600 W Foothill Blvd Glendora (91741) *(P-12231)*
Hallmark Southwest, Loma Linda *Also called Dvele Omega Corporation (P-4445)*
Halo Neuro Inc ....F......415 851-3338
735 Market St Fl 4 San Francisco (94103) *(P-22258)*
Halo Neuroscience, San Francisco *Also called Halo Neuro Inc (P-22258)*
Halo Top, Los Angeles *Also called Eden Creamery LLC (P-640)*
Halo Top Creamery, West Hollywood *Also called Halo Top International LLC (P-648)*
Halo Top International LLC (PA) ....E......434 409-2057
1348 N Sierra Bonita Ave # 107 West Hollywood (90046) *(P-648)*
Halozyme Therapeutics Inc (PA) ....D......858 794-8889
11388 Sorrento Valley Rd # 200 San Diego (92121) *(P-8307)*

Mergent e-mail: customerrelations@mergent.com 2020 California Manufacturers Register (P-0000) Products & Services Section entry number
1118 (PA)=Parent Co (HQ)=Headquarters (DH)=Div Headquarters

Halsteel Inc (HQ) ....E....909 937-1001
4190 Santa Ana St Ste A Ontario (91761) *(P-11094)*
Halter Winery LLC ....E....805 226-9455
8910 Adelaida Rd Paso Robles (93446) *(P-1744)*
Hamar Wood Parquet Company ....E....562 944-8885
9303 Greenleaf Ave Santa Fe Springs (90670) *(P-3934)*
Hamax America Inc (PA) ....F....714 641-7528
660 Baker St Ste 405s Costa Mesa (92626) *(P-21234)*
Hambly Studios Inc ....E....408 496-1100
23980 Spalding Ave Los Altos (94024) *(P-3792)*
Hamilton & Associates, Chatsworth *Also called Alan Hamilton Industries (P-6400)*
Hamilton Iron Works, Torrance *Also called Calcon Steel Construction (P-11756)*
Hamilton Metalcraft Inc ....E....626 795-4811
848 N Fair Oaks Ave Pasadena (91103) *(P-12232)*
Hamilton Sundstrand Corp ....C....909 593-5300
960 Overland Ct San Dimas (91773) *(P-21235)*
Hamilton Sundstrand Spc Systms ....D....909 288-5300
960 Overland Ct San Dimas (91773) *(P-21483)*
Hamilton Technology Corp ....F....310 217-1191
14900 S Figueroa St Gardena (90248) *(P-17041)*
Hammer Collection Inc ....E....310 515-0276
14427 S Main St Gardena (90248) *(P-4645)*
Hammerhead Industries Inc ....F....805 658-9922
5720 Nicolle St Ventura (93003) *(P-9820)*
Hammitt Inc ....F....310 293-3787
2101 Pacific Coast Hwy A Hermosa Beach (90254) *(P-10196)*
Hammon Plating Corporation ....E....650 494-2691
890 Commercial St Palo Alto (94303) *(P-13020)*
Hammond Enterprises Inc ....E....925 432-3537
549 Garcia Ave Ste C Pittsburg (94565) *(P-16015)*
Hammond Power Solutions Inc ....E....310 537-4690
17715 S Susana Rd Compton (90221) *(P-16554)*
Hampton Fitness Products Ltd ....F....805 339-9733
1913 Portola Rd Ventura (93003) *(P-22816)*
Hampton-Brown Company LLC ....F....831 620-6001
1 Lower Ragsdale Dr # 1200 Monterey (93940) *(P-6172)*
Hamrock Inc ....C....562 944-0255
12521 Los Nietos Rd Santa Fe Springs (90670) *(P-11095)*
Hana Microelectronics Inc ....F....408 452-7474
3100 De La Cruz Blvd # 204 Santa Clara (95054) *(P-18264)*
Hanah Silk Inc ....F....707 442-0886
5155 Myrtle Ave Eureka (95503) *(P-2753)*
Hanaps Enterprises ....D....669 235-3810
865 Jarvis Dr Morgan Hill (95037) *(P-15238)*
Hancock Jaffe Laboratories Inc ....F....949 261-2900
70 Doppler Irvine (92618) *(P-21730)*
Hancor Inc ....D....661 366-1520
140 Vineland Rd Bakersfield (93307) *(P-9467)*
Hand & Nail Harmony Inc ....D....714 773-9758
1545 Moonstone Brea (92821) *(P-8509)*
Hand and Nail Harmony, Brea *Also called Hand & Nail Harmony Inc (P-8509)*
Hand Biomechanics Lab Inc ....F....916 923-5073
77 Scripps Dr Ste 104 Sacramento (95825) *(P-22020)*
Hand Crfted Dutchman Doors Inc ....E....209 833-7378
770 Stonebridge Dr Tracy (95376) *(P-4054)*
Hand Piece Parts and Products ....E....714 997-4331
707 W Angus Ave Orange (92868) *(P-22158)*
Handa Pharmaceuticals LLC ....F....510 354-2888
1732 N 1st St Ste 200 San Jose (95112) *(P-7932)*
Handbill Printers LP ....E....951 547-5910
820 E Parkridge Ave Corona (92879) *(P-6604)*
Handcraft Mattress Company ....F....714 241-8316
1131 Baker St Costa Mesa (92626) *(P-4721)*
Handcraft Tile Inc ....F....408 262-1140
786 View Dr Pleasanton (94566) *(P-10460)*
Handelman, Steven Studios, Santa Barbara *Also called Steven Handelman Studios (P-11151)*
Handley Cellars Ltd ....F....707 895-3876
3151 Highway 128 Philo (95466) *(P-1745)*
Handley Cellars Winery, Philo *Also called Handley Cellars Ltd (P-1745)*
Handshake, San Francisco *Also called Stryder Corp (P-24463)*
Handy Service Corporation ....F....714 632-7832
1043 S Melrose St Ste A Placentia (92870) *(P-7630)*
Hane & Hane Inc ....E....408 292-2140
650 University Ave San Jose (95110) *(P-13021)*
Hanergy Holding (america) LLC (HQ) ....F....650 288-3722
1350 Bayshore Hwy Burlingame (94010) *(P-18265)*
Hanford Ready-Mix Inc ....E....916 405-1918
9800 Kent St Elk Grove (95624) *(P-10766)*
Hanford Sand & Gravel Inc ....F....916 782-9150
9800 Kent St Elk Grove (95624) *(P-10767)*
Hanford Sentinel Inc ....D....559 582-0471
300 W 6th St Hanford (93230) *(P-5651)*
Hang-UPS Unlimited, Santa Monica *Also called Magna-Pole Products Inc (P-4989)*
Hanger ....F....323 238-7738
6099 Malburg Way Vernon (90058) *(P-22021)*
Hanger Inc ....F....949 408-3320
100 Pacifica Ste 270 Irvine (92618) *(P-22022)*
Hanger Clinic, Los Angeles *Also called Hanger Prsthetcs & Ortho Inc (P-22023)*
Hanger Clinic, Irvine *Also called Hanger Prsthetcs & Ortho Inc (P-22024)*
Hanger Prsthetcs & Ortho Inc ....D....323 866-2555
6300 Wilshire Blvd # 950 Los Angeles (90048) *(P-22023)*
Hanger Prsthetcs & Ortho Inc ....D....949 863-1951
18022 Cowan Ste 285 Irvine (92614) *(P-22024)*
Hanger Prsthetcs & Ortho Inc ....F....858 487-4516
15725 Pomerado Rd Poway (92064) *(P-22025)*
Hanger Prsthetcs & Ortho Inc ....F....925 371-5081
4659 Las Positas Rd Ste A Livermore (94551) *(P-22026)*
Hangers Randy West Coast Ctr ....F....323 728-2253
5350 Zambrano St Commerce (90040) *(P-11096)*
Hangtags.com, Huntington Beach *Also called Tri Print LLC (P-6900)*
Hank Player Inc ....F....818 856-6079
4303 Lemp Ave Studio City (91604) *(P-3334)*
Hanley Welding, Hawthorne *Also called Marleon Inc (P-24650)*
Hanmar LLC (PA) ....E....818 240-0170
11441 Bradley Ave Pacoima (91331) *(P-12811)*
Hanna Fuji Sushi, Santa Fe Springs *Also called Nikko Enterprise Corporation (P-2266)*
Hanna Winery Inc (PA) ....F....707 431-4310
9280 Highway 128 Healdsburg (95448) *(P-1746)*
Hannah Industries Inc ....F....714 939-7873
401 S Santa Fe St Santa Ana (92705) *(P-15519)*
Hannahmax Baking Inc ....C....310 380-6778
14601 S Main St Gardena (90248) *(P-1223)*
Hannan Products Corp (PA) ....F....951 735-1587
220 N Smith Ave Corona (92880) *(P-14709)*
Hannemann Fiberglass Inc ....F....626 969-7317
1132 W Kirkwall Rd Azusa (91702) *(P-19678)*
Hannibal Lafayette ....F....909 322-0600
10758 Fremont Ave Ontario (91762) *(P-4369)*
Hannibal Industries Inc (PA) ....C....323 513-1200
3851 S Santa Fe Ave Vernon (90058) *(P-11127)*
Hannibal Material Handling ....C....323 587-4060
2230 E 38th St Vernon (90058) *(P-4980)*
Hansen Bros Enterprises (PA) ....D....530 273-3100
11727 La Barr Meadows Rd Grass Valley (95949) *(P-343)*
Hansen Haulers Inc ....F....916 443-7755
1628 N C St 1630 Sacramento (95811) *(P-16016)*
Hansen Information Tech, Rancho Cordova *Also called Infor (us) Inc (P-24013)*
Hansen Machine Works, Sacramento *Also called Hansen Haulers Inc (P-16016)*
Hansen Medical Inc ....C....650 404-5800
800 E Middlefield Rd Mountain View (94043) *(P-21731)*
Hansens Oak Inc (PA) ....F....209 357-3424
166 E Broadway Ave Atwater (95301) *(P-4574)*
Hansens Welding Inc ....E....310 329-6888
358 W 168th St Gardena (90248) *(P-24638)*
Hanson Aggregates LLC ....E....408 996-4000
24001 Stevens Creek Blvd Cupertino (95014) *(P-344)*
Hanson Aggregates LLC ....D....805 485-3101
3555 E Vineyard Ave Oxnard (93036) *(P-10411)*
Hanson Aggregates LLC ....E....619 299-8640
5785 Mission Center Rd San Diego (92108) *(P-10412)*
Hanson Aggregates LLC ....E....626 856-6700
13550 Live Oak Ln Baldwin Park (91706) *(P-345)*
Hanson Aggregates LLC ....F....858 577-2727
9255 Camino Santa Fe San Diego (92121) *(P-10413)*
Hanson Aggregates LLC ....E....951 371-7625
19494 River Rock Rd Corona (92881) *(P-10414)*
Hanson Aggregates LLC ....F....805 934-4931
5325 Foxen Canyon Rd Santa Maria (93454) *(P-346)*
Hanson Aggregates LLC ....E....805 543-8100
131 Suburban Rd San Luis Obispo (93401) *(P-347)*
Hanson Aggregates LLC ....F....858 715-5600
12560 Highway 67 Lakeside (92040) *(P-9094)*
Hanson Aggregates LLC ....E....626 358-1811
13550 Live Oak Ln Irwindale (91706) *(P-10768)*
Hanson Aggrgtes Md-Pacific Inc ....F....805 928-3764
180 Atascadero Rd Morro Bay (93442) *(P-10769)*
Hanson Aggrgtes Md-Pacific Inc ....F....925 672-4955
Pine Hollow To Kaiser Rd Clayton (94517) *(P-10910)*
Hanson Brass Inc ....F....818 767-3501
7530 San Fernando Rd Sun Valley (91352) *(P-17132)*
Hanson Heat Lamps, Sun Valley *Also called Hanson Brass Inc (P-17132)*
Hanson Lab Furniture Inc ....E....805 498-3121
747 Calle Plano Camarillo (93012) *(P-20760)*
Hanson Lehigh Inc ....E....925 244-6500
12667 Alcosta Blvd # 400 San Ramon (94583) *(P-10415)*
Hanson Lehigh Inc ....E....972 653-5603
3000 Executive Pkwy # 240 San Ramon (94583) *(P-10770)*
Hanson Tank, Los Angeles *Also called Roy E Hanson Jr Mfg (P-12047)*
Hanson Truss Inc ....B....909 591-9256
13950 Yorba Ave Chino (91710) *(P-4304)*
Hanson Truss Components Inc ....D....530 740-7750
4476 Skyway Dr Olivehurst (95961) *(P-4305)*
Hantel Technologies Inc ....E....510 400-1164
3496 Breakwater Ct Hayward (94545) *(P-21732)*
Hantronix Inc ....E....408 252-1100
10080 Bubb Rd Cupertino (95014) *(P-14475)*
Hanwha Q Cells America Inc ....F....949 748-5996
400 Spectrum Center Dr # 1400 Irvine (92618) *(P-18266)*
Hanzell Vineyards ....F....707 996-3860
18596 Lomita Ave Sonoma (95476) *(P-1747)*
Happy Apple, Orosi *Also called Lochirco Fruit and Produce Inc (P-1384)*
Happy Company, The, Hayward *Also called Tender Loving Things Inc (P-8592)*
Happy Daze Rv's, Livermore *Also called Progressive Housing Inc (P-19745)*
Happy Girl Kitchen Co ....F....831 373-4475
173 Central Ave Pacific Grove (93950) *(P-772)*
Happy2ez Inc ....F....714 897-6100
14191 Beach Blvd Ste B Westminster (92683) *(P-9549)*
Harber All Natural Products ....F....347 921-1004
1440 3rd St Riverside (92507) *(P-8510)*
Harber Foods LLC (PA) ....F....347 921-1004
1440 3rd St Ste 25 Riverside (92507) *(P-8511)*
Harbison-Fischer Inc ....E....661 765-7792
116 E Main St Taft (93268) *(P-205)*
Harbison-Fischer Inc ....E....661 399-0628
200 Carver St Shafter (93263) *(P-13779)*

ALPHABETIC

Employee Codes: A=Over 500 employees, B=251-500
C=101-250, D=51-100, E=20-50, F=10-19
2020 California
Manfacturers Register
© Mergent Inc. 1-800-342-5647
1119

Harbison-Fischer Inc......E......661 387-0166
2801 Pegasus Dr Bakersfield (93308) ***(P-14580)***
Harbor Biosciences Inc (PA)......F......858 587-9333
9191 Towne Centre Dr # 409 San Diego (92122) ***(P-7933)***
Harbor Custom Canvas......F......562 436-7708
733 W Anaheim St Long Beach (90813) ***(P-3686)***
Harbor Electronics Inc (PA)......C......408 988-6544
3021 Kenneth St Santa Clara (95054) ***(P-18929)***
Harbor Furniture Manufacturing (PA)......E......323 636-1201
12508 Center St South Gate (90280) ***(P-4646)***
Harbor Green Grain LP......E......310 991-8089
13181 Crssroads Pkwy N City of Industry (91746) ***(P-1099)***
Harbor House, South Gate *Also called Harbor Furniture Manufacturing* ***(P-4646)***
Harbor Packaging, Poway *Also called Liberty Diversified Intl Inc* ***(P-5244)***
Harbor Products Inc......F......562 633-8184
15001 Lakewood Blvd Paramount (90723) ***(P-9314)***
Harbor Seal Incorporated......F......626 305-5754
909 S Myrtle Ave Monrovia (91016) ***(P-9235)***
Harbor Signs Inc......F......209 463-8686
850 N Union St Stockton (95205) ***(P-23126)***
Harbor Truck Bodies Inc......D......714 996-0411
255 Voyager Ave Brea (92821) ***(P-19537)***
Harbor Truck Body, Brea *Also called Harbor Truck Bodies Inc* ***(P-19537)***
Harcourt Trade Publishers, San Diego *Also called Houghton Mifflin Harcourt Pubg* ***(P-6111)***
Hardcore Racing Components LLC......F......661 294-5032
27717 Avenue Scott Valencia (91355) ***(P-22678)***
Hardcraft Industries Inc......D......408 432-8340
2221 Ringwood Ave San Jose (95131) ***(P-12233)***
Harding Containers Intl Inc......E......310 549-7272
4000 Santa Fe Ave Long Beach (90810) ***(P-4370)***
Hardware Imports Inc......F......909 595-6201
161 Commerce Way Walnut (91789) ***(P-19538)***
Hardware Specialties, Ontario *Also called F & D Flores Enterprises Inc* ***(P-21471)***
Hardy Frames Inc......D......951 245-9525
250 Klug Cir Corona (92880) ***(P-11047)***
Hardy Process Solutions......E......858 278-2900
9440 Carroll Park Dr # 150 San Diego (92121) ***(P-20882)***
Harkham Industries Inc (PA)......E......323 586-4600
857 S San Pedro St # 300 Los Angeles (90014) ***(P-3167)***
Harley Murray Inc......D......209 466-0266
1754 E Mariposa Rd Stockton (95205) ***(P-19823)***
Harman Envelopes, North Hollywood *Also called Harman Press* ***(P-6605)***
Harman Press......E......818 432-0570
6840 Vineland Ave North Hollywood (91605) ***(P-6605)***
Harman Professional Inc......B......951 242-2927
24950 Grove View Rd Moreno Valley (92551) ***(P-17237)***
Harman Professional Inc (HQ)......B......818 893-8411
8500 Balboa Blvd Northridge (91329) ***(P-17238)***
Harmless Harvest Inc (PA)......E......347 688-6286
712 Sansome St San Francisco (94111) ***(P-2477)***
Harmonic Design Inc......E......858 391-9085
13367 Krkrham Way Ste 110 Poway (92064) ***(P-16652)***
Harmonic Inc (PA)......B......408 542-2500
4300 N 1st St San Jose (95134) ***(P-17531)***
Harmonic Inc......F......408 542-2500
641 Baltic Way Sunnyvale (94089) ***(P-17532)***
Harmony Cellars......F......805 927-1625
3255 Harmony Valley Rd Harmony (93435) ***(P-1748)***
Harmony Infinite Inc......F......818 780-4569
12918 Bloomfield St Studio City (91604) ***(P-5063)***
Harmony Kids, San Fernando *Also called Newco International Inc* ***(P-4598)***
Haros Anodizing Specialist......F......408 980-0892
630 Walsh Ave Santa Clara (95050) ***(P-13022)***
Harper & Two Inc (PA)......F......562 424-3030
2937 Cherry Ave Signal Hill (90755) ***(P-18930)***
Harpercollins Publishers LLC......E......415 477-4400
353 Sacramento St Ste 500 San Francisco (94111) ***(P-6107)***
Harpers Pharmacy Inc......C......877 778-3773
132 S Anita Dr Ste 210 Orange (92868) ***(P-7934)***
Harrell Holdings (PA)......C......661 322-5627
1707 Eye St Ste 102 Bakersfield (93301) ***(P-5652)***
Harrington Hoists Inc......F......717 665-2000
2341 Pomona Rincon Rd # 103 Corona (92880) ***(P-13847)***
Harris & Bruno International, Roseville *Also called Harris & Bruno Machine Co Inc* ***(P-14324)***
Harris & Bruno Machine Co Inc (PA)......D......916 781-7676
8555 Washington Blvd Roseville (95678) ***(P-14324)***
Harris Corporation, Van Nuys *Also called L3harris Technologies Inc* ***(P-20597)***
Harris Corporation, San Diego *Also called L3harris Technologies Inc* ***(P-20898)***
Harris Industries Inc (PA)......D......714 898-8048
5181 Argosy Ave Huntington Beach (92649) ***(P-5362)***
Harris Organs Inc......E......562 693-3442
7047 Comstock Ave Whittier (90602) ***(P-22625)***
Harris Precision......F......408 866-4160
161 Lost Lake Ln Campbell (95008) ***(P-12234)***
Harris Precision Sheet Metal, Campbell *Also called Harris Precision* ***(P-12234)***
Harris Ranch Beef Company......A......559 896-3081
16277 S Mccall Ave Selma (93662) ***(P-413)***
Harris' Precision Products, Whittier *Also called Harris Organs Inc* ***(P-22625)***
Harrison Beverage Inc......F......626 757-1159
726 Arabian Ln Walnut (91789) ***(P-649)***
Harrison Group, Walnut *Also called Harrison Beverage Inc* ***(P-649)***
Harrow Health Inc (PA)......E......858 704-4040
12264 El Camino Real # 350 San Diego (92130) ***(P-7935)***
Harrys Dye and Wash Inc......E......714 446-0300
1015 E Orangethorpe Ave Anaheim (92801) ***(P-2826)***
Harsco Corporation......F......909 444-2527
5580 Cherry Ave Long Beach (90805) ***(P-12019)***
Harsco Distribution Center, Long Beach *Also called Harsco Corporation* ***(P-12019)***
Hart & Cooley Inc......E......559 875-1212
1121 Annadale Ave Sanger (93657) ***(P-12480)***
Hart Electronic Assembly Inc......D......818 709-2761
21726 Lassen St Chatsworth (91311) ***(P-18931)***
Harte Hanks Inc......E......714 577-4462
2830 Orbiter St Brea (92821) ***(P-5653)***
Harte Hanks Inc......F......626 251-4500
150 N Santa Anita Ave # 300 Arcadia (91006) ***(P-5654)***
Harten Jewelry Co Inc......E......562 652-5006
8213 Villaverde Dr Whittier (90605) ***(P-22526)***
Hartford Family Winery, Forestville *Also called Hartford Jackson LLC* ***(P-1749)***
Hartford Jackson LLC......F......707 887-1756
8075 Martinelli Rd Forestville (95436) ***(P-1749)***
Harthanks, Ontario *Also called Pennysaver* ***(P-5795)***
Hartle Media Ventures LLC......E......415 362-7797
680 2nd St San Francisco (94107) ***(P-5948)***
Hartley Company......E......949 646-9643
1987 Placentia Ave Costa Mesa (92627) ***(P-22934)***
Hartley-Racon, Costa Mesa *Also called Hartley Company* ***(P-22934)***
Hartman Slicer Div, Rancho Dominguez *Also called United Bakery Equipment Co Inc* ***(P-14732)***
Hartman Slices Division, Compton *Also called United Bakery Equipment Co Inc* ***(P-14410)***
Hartwell Corporation (HQ)......C......714 993-4200
900 Richfield Rd Placentia (92870) ***(P-11593)***
Hartwell Corporation......D......909 987-4616
9810 6th St Rancho Cucamonga (91730) ***(P-12812)***
Hartwick Combustion Tech Inc......F......562 922-8300
9426 Stewart And Gray Rd Downey (90241) ***(P-14824)***
Hartzell Aerospace, Valencia *Also called Electrofilm Mfg Co LLC* ***(P-13328)***
Harvard Card Systems, City of Industry *Also called Harvard Label LLC* ***(P-5108)***
Harvard Label LLC......C......626 333-8881
111 Baldwin Park Blvd City of Industry (91746) ***(P-5108)***
Harvatek International Corp......F......408 844-9698
3350 Scott Blvd Ste 4101 Santa Clara (95054) ***(P-17042)***
Harvest Asia Inc......F......888 800-3133
7888 Cherry Ave Ste G Fontana (92336) ***(P-22679)***
Harvest Container Company......E......559 562-1394
24476 Road 216 Lindsay (93247) ***(P-5233)***
Harvest Farms Inc......D......661 945-3636
45000 Yucca Ave Lancaster (93534) ***(P-961)***
Harvest Printing Company, Anderson *Also called Checchi Enterprises Inc* ***(P-6481)***
Harwil Precision Products......E......805 988-6800
541 Kinetic Dr Oxnard (93030) ***(P-18932)***
Hasa Inc......E......661 259-5848
1251 Loveridge Rd Pittsburg (94565) ***(P-7388)***
Hasala Engineering Inc......F......310 538-4268
125 W 155th St Gardena (90248) ***(P-16017)***
Hasbro Inc......B......909 393-3248
16047 Mountain Ave Chino (91708) ***(P-22680)***
Hasco, Placentia *Also called Hartwell Corporation* ***(P-11593)***
Hasco Fabrication Inc......F......909 627-0326
13370 Monte Vista Ave Chino (91710) ***(P-14710)***
Haskel International LLC (HQ)......C......818 843-4000
100 E Graham Pl Burbank (91502) ***(P-14581)***
Haskon, Div of, Brea *Also called Kirkhill Inc* ***(P-9241)***
Hastings Irrigation Pipe Co......F......559 675-1200
17619 Road 24 Madera (93638) ***(P-11232)***
Hatch Outdoors Inc......F......760 734-4343
961 Park Center Dr Vista (92081) ***(P-22817)***
Hathaway LLC......E......661 393-2004
4205 Atlas Ct Bakersfield (93308) ***(P-55)***
Haus of Grey LLC......F......562 270-4739
10930 Portal Dr Los Alamitos (90720) ***(P-3035)***
Hausenware Koyo LLC......F......412 897-3064
2111 Laughlin Rd Windsor (95492) ***(P-10310)***
Hauser & Sons Inc......F......510 234-8850
150 S 2nd St Richmond (94804) ***(P-5023)***
Hauser Shade, Richmond *Also called Hauser & Sons Inc* ***(P-5023)***
Hav Holdings & Subsidiaries, Sun Valley *Also called Hollywood Film Company* ***(P-22426)***
Havaianas, Venice *Also called Alpargatas Usa Inc* ***(P-10166)***
Havana Graphic Center Inc......E......818 841-3774
9250 Independence Ave # 109 Chatsworth (91311) ***(P-6606)***
Hawa Corporation......E......909 825-8882
125 E Laurel St Colton (92324) ***(P-463)***
Hawaii Kai, San Diego *Also called HK Enterprise Group Inc* ***(P-8974)***
Hawaii Pacific Teleport LP......F......707 938-7057
1145 Beasley Way Sonoma (95476) ***(P-17533)***
Hawaiian Host Candies La Inc......D......310 532-0543
15601 S Avalon Blvd Gardena (90248) ***(P-1370)***
Hawaiian Island Creations, Gardena *Also called Coral Head Inc* ***(P-3073)***
Hawk Crest, NAPA *Also called Stags Leap Wine Cellars* ***(P-1928)***
Haworth Inc......F......310 854-7633
144 N Robertson Blvd # 202 West Hollywood (90048) ***(P-4839)***
Hayden Industrial Products, San Bernardino *Also called Hayden Products LLC* ***(P-12020)***
Hayden Products LLC......D......951 736-2600
1393 E San Bernardino Ave San Bernardino (92408) ***(P-12020)***
Haydenshapes Surfboards......F......310 648-8268
209 Richmond St Apt D El Segundo (90245) ***(P-22818)***
Hayes Manufacturing Svcs LLC......E......408 730-5035
1178 Sonora Ct Sunnyvale (94086) ***(P-14061)***
Hayes Welding Inc (PA)......D......760 246-4878
12522 Violet Rd Adelanto (92301) ***(P-24639)***
Hayes Welding Inc......F......760 246-4878
11746 Mariposa Rd Ste 100 Hesperia (92345) ***(P-24640)***
Haymarket Worldwide Inc......E......949 417-6700
17030 Red Hill Ave Irvine (92614) ***(P-5949)***
Haynes Publications, Newbury Park *Also called Odcombe Press (nashville)* ***(P-6757)***

Mergent e-mail: customerrelations@mergent.com
1120
2020 California
Manufacturers Register
(P-0000) Products & Services Section entry number
(PA)=Parent Co (HQ)=Headquarters (DH)=Div Headquarters

Hayward Enterprises Inc ....F....707 261-5100
2700 Napa Valley Corp Dr NAPA (94558) ***(P-913)***
Hayward Gordon Us Inc ....E....760 246-3430
9351 Industrial Way Adelanto (92301) ***(P-14371)***
Hayward Quartz Machining Co, Fremont *Also called Hayward Quartz Technology* ***(P-18267)***
Hayward Quartz Technology ....C....510 657-9605
1700 Corporate Way Fremont (94539) ***(P-18267)***
Haze Bert and Assosiates ....F....714 557-1567
3188 Airway Ave Ste K1 Costa Mesa (92626) ***(P-206)***
Hazel Clothes, Vernon *Also called Crestone LLC* ***(P-3477)***
Hazelcast Inc (PA) ....E....650 521-5453
2 W 5th Ave Ste 300 San Mateo (94402) ***(P-23969)***
Haztech Systems Inc ....E....209 966-8088
4996 Gold Leaf Dr Mariposa (95338) ***(P-8701)***
HB Fuller Company ....D....916 787-6000
10500 Industrial Ave Roseville (95678) ***(P-8871)***
HB Products LLC ....E....714 799-6967
5671 Engineer Dr Huntington Beach (92649) ***(P-7086)***
Hbc Solutions Holdings LLC ....A....321 727-9100
10877 Wilshire Blvd Fl 18 Los Angeles (90024) ***(P-17534)***
Hbe Rental, Grass Valley *Also called Hansen Bros Enterprises* ***(P-343)***
Hbno, Camarillo *Also called IL Helth Buty Natural Oils Inc* ***(P-8977)***
HC Brill ....B....909 825-7343
2111 W Valley Blvd Colton (92324) ***(P-1342)***
HCC Industries Inc (HQ) ....F....626 443-8933
4232 Temple City Blvd Rosemead (91770) ***(P-18771)***
Hchd ....F....909 923-8889
1175 S Grove Ave Ste 104 Ontario (91761) ***(P-19478)***
Hci, San Marcos *Also called Hughes Circuits Inc* ***(P-17895)***
Hcl Labels Inc ....F....800 421-6710
1800 Green Hills Rd # 104 Scotts Valley (95066) ***(P-5511)***
Hco Holding I Corporation ....F....310 684-5320
2270 S Castle Harbour Pl Ontario (91761) ***(P-9113)***
Hco Holding II Corporation ....D....310 955-9200
999 N Pacific Coast Hwy El Segundo (90245) ***(P-9114)***
Hcp Industries Inc ....F....530 899-5591
415 Otterson Dr Ste 10 Chico (95928) ***(P-10466)***
HD Carry Inc ....F....949 831-6022
81 Columbia Ste 150 Aliso Viejo (92656) ***(P-9550)***
Hd Garment Solutions Inc ....E....323 581-6000
13351 Riverside Dr Sherman Oaks (91423) ***(P-3516)***
Hd Window Fashions Inc (HQ) ....B....213 749-6333
1818 Oak St Los Angeles (90015) ***(P-5024)***
HDD LLC ....F....707 433-9545
4035 Westside Rd Healdsburg (95448) ***(P-1750)***
Hdkaraoke Llc ....F....626 296-6200
2400 Lincoln Ave Altadena (91001) ***(P-17239)***
Hdp Holdings, San Diego *Also called Wd-40 Company* ***(P-9085)***
Head First Productions Inc ....F....714 522-3311
14848 Northam St La Mirada (90638) ***(P-14223)***
Headfirst Products, La Mirada *Also called Head First Productions Inc* ***(P-14223)***
Headgear Plus Promo, Petaluma *Also called Fulton Acres Inc* ***(P-3787)***
Headline Graphics Inc ....E....760 436-0133
2259 Flatiron Way San Marcos (92078) ***(P-7375)***
Headmaster Inc (PA) ....E....714 556-5244
3000 S Croddy Way Santa Ana (92704) ***(P-3467)***
Headrick Logging, Anderson *Also called James A Headrick Ii/Elizabeth* ***(P-3890)***
Headwaters Construction Inc ....E....714 523-1530
16005 Phoebe Ave La Mirada (90638) ***(P-10416)***
Headwaters Incorporated ....F....909 627-9066
1345 Philadelphia St Pomona (91766) ***(P-10583)***
Headway Technologies Inc ....F....408 935-1020
463 S Milpitas Blvd Milpitas (95035) ***(P-15037)***
Headway Technologies Inc (HQ) ....C....408 934-5300
682 S Hillview Dr Milpitas (95035) ***(P-15038)***
Headway Technologies Inc ....C....408 934-5300
497 S Hillview Dr Milpitas (95035) ***(P-15039)***
Headwinds ....F....626 359-8044
221 W Maple Ave Monrovia (91016) ***(P-20406)***
Health Breads Inc ....E....760 747-7390
155 Mata Way Ste 112 San Marcos (92069) ***(P-1224)***
Health Gorilla Inc (PA) ....F....844 446-7455
185 N Wolfe Rd Sunnyvale (94086) ***(P-23970)***
Health Naturals Inc ....F....714 259-1821
13 Navarre Irvine (92612) ***(P-7936)***
Healthline Media Inc ....B....415 281-3100
660 3rd St San Francisco (94107) ***(P-6250)***
Healthline Systems LLC (HQ) ....E....858 673-1700
9605 Scranton Rd Ste 200 San Diego (92121) ***(P-23971)***
Healthspecialty, Santa Fe Springs *Also called Cosmolara Inc* ***(P-8472)***
Healthstream Inc ....C....800 733-8737
9605 Scranton Rd Ste 200 San Diego (92121) ***(P-23972)***
Healthy Times ....F....858 513-1550
225 Broadway Ste 450 San Diego (92101) ***(P-2478)***
Healthywealthyhack Inc ....F....669 225-3745
16979 Frank Ave Los Gatos (95032) ***(P-23973)***
Healty Times Natural Products, San Diego *Also called Healthy Times* ***(P-2478)***
Hearsay Social Inc (PA) ....D....888 990-3777
185 Berry St Ste 3800 San Francisco (94107) ***(P-23974)***
Hearst Communications Inc ....B....916 725-8694
7916 Arcade Lake Ln Citrus Heights (95610) ***(P-5655)***
Hearst Communications Inc ....C....415 537-4200
680 2nd St San Francisco (94107) ***(P-5656)***
Hearst Corporation ....F....310 752-1040
3000 Ocean Park Blvd Santa Monica (90405) ***(P-5950)***
Hearst Corporation ....C....831 582-9605
224 Reindollar Ave Marina (93933) ***(P-5657)***
Hearst Corporation ....D....760 707-0100
15255 Alton Pkwy Ste 300 Irvine (92618) ***(P-5951)***
Hearst Corporation ....E....530 964-3131
1 Wyntoon Rd Mccloud (96057) ***(P-5952)***
Hearst Corporation ....F....415 777-0600
5 3rd St Ste 200 San Francisco (94103) ***(P-5658)***
HEARST CORPORATION THE, Marina *Also called Hearst Corporation* ***(P-5657)***
Heart Rate Inc ....E....714 850-9716
1411 E Wilshire Ave Santa Ana (92705) ***(P-22819)***
Heart Wood Manufacturing Inc ....D....408 848-9750
5860 Obata Way Gilroy (95020) ***(P-4203)***
Hearthco Inc ....E....530 622-3877
5781 Pleasant Valley Rd El Dorado (95623) ***(P-11594)***
Heartland Farms, City of Industry *Also called Sbm Dairies Inc* ***(P-2165)***
Hearts Delight ....E....805 648-7123
4035 N Ventura Ave Ventura (93001) ***(P-3335)***
Hearts For Long Beach Inc ....E....562 433-2000
5225 E 2nd St Long Beach (90803) ***(P-5659)***
Heartwood Cabinets, Gilroy *Also called Heart Wood Manufacturing Inc* ***(P-4203)***
Heat Factory Inc ....E....760 734-5300
2793 Loker Ave W Carlsbad (92010) ***(P-5399)***
Heat Software Intermediate Inc ....B....408 601-2800
2590 N 1st St Ste 360 San Jose (95131) ***(P-23975)***
Heateflex Corporation ....E....626 599-8566
405 E Santa Clara St Arcadia (91006) ***(P-11699)***
Heater Designs Inc ....E....909 421-0971
2211 S Vista Ave Bloomington (92316) ***(P-14763)***
Heath Ceramics Ltd ....D....415 361-5552
2900 18th St San Francisco (94110) ***(P-10490)***
Heatshield Products Inc ....E....760 751-0441
938 S Andreasen Dr Ste C Escondido (92029) ***(P-10992)***
Heatwave Labs Inc ....F....831 722-9081
195 Aviation Way Ste 100 Watsonville (95076) ***(P-17786)***
Heaven or Las Vegas, Van Nuys *Also called Kimball Nelson Inc* ***(P-23382)***
Heavy Duty Trucking, Irvine *Also called HIC Corporation* ***(P-5954)***
Heck Cellars, Di Giorgio *Also called F Korbel & Bros* ***(P-1695)***
Heco Inc ....F....916 372-5411
2350 Del Monte St West Sacramento (95691) ***(P-14741)***
Heco Pacific Manufacturing ....E....510 487-1155
1510 Pacific St Union City (94587) ***(P-13825)***
Hedgeside Vintners ....E....707 963-2134
540 Technology Way NAPA (94558) ***(P-1751)***
Hedman Hedders, Whittier *Also called Hedman Manufacturing* ***(P-19679)***
Hedman Manufacturing (PA) ....E....562 204-1031
12438 Putnam St Whittier (90602) ***(P-19679)***
Hee, Anaheim *Also called Ceco Environmental Corp* ***(P-9700)***
Heeger Inc ....F....323 728-5108
6446 Flotilla St Commerce (90040) ***(P-16653)***
HEI, San Diego *Also called Oggis Pizza & Brewing Co* ***(P-1553)***
Heidelberg Instruments Inc ....F....310 212-5071
2539 W 237th St Ste A Torrance (90505) ***(P-14325)***
Heiden's Foods, Anaheim *Also called Heidens Inc* ***(P-773)***
Heidens Inc ....F....714 525-3414
2900 E Blue Star St Anaheim (92806) ***(P-773)***
Heighten America Inc ....E....209 845-0455
1144 Post Rd Oakdale (95361) ***(P-16018)***
Heighten Manfacturing, Oakdale *Also called Heighten America Inc* ***(P-16018)***
Heinz Seeds, Stockton *Also called Kraft Heinz Foods Company* ***(P-1430)***
Heinz Weber Incorporated ....E....310 477-3561
13025 Park Pl Unit 402 Hawthorne (90250) ***(P-7376)***
Heirloom Computing Inc ....F....510 709-7245
3000 Dnville Blvd Ste 148 Alamo (94507) ***(P-23976)***
Heitman Brooks II LLC (PA) ....F....909 947-7470
1850 S Parco Ave Ontario (91761) ***(P-10584)***
Helados La Tapatia Inc ....E....559 441-1105
4495 W Shaw Ave Fresno (93722) ***(P-650)***
Helados Vallarta Inc ....F....559 709-1177
1418 G St Fresno (93706) ***(P-651)***
Helen Noble ....F....916 457-8990
2120 28th St Sacramento (95818) ***(P-5953)***
Helena Agri-Enterprises LLC ....E....559 582-0291
12218 11th Ave Hanford (93230) ***(P-8831)***
Helens Place Inc ....F....909 981-5715
893 W 9th St Upland (91786) ***(P-6607)***
Helfer Enterprises ....E....714 557-2733
3030 Oak St Santa Ana (92707) ***(P-16019)***
Helfer Tool Co, Santa Ana *Also called Helfer Enterprises* ***(P-16019)***
Helica Biosystems Inc ....F....714 578-7830
3310 W Macarthur Blvd Santa Ana (92704) ***(P-8227)***
Helical Products, Santa Maria *Also called Matthew Warren Inc* ***(P-13339)***
Helicopter Tech Co Ltd Partnr ....E....310 523-2750
12902 S Broadway Los Angeles (90061) ***(P-20125)***
Heliotrope Technologies Inc ....E....510 871-3980
850 Marina Village Pkwy Alameda (94501) ***(P-10269)***
Heliovolt Corporation ....D....512 767-6079
3945 Freedom Cir Ste 560 Santa Clara (95054) ***(P-18933)***
Helitek Company Ltd ....F....510 933-7688
4033 Clipper Ct Fremont (94538) ***(P-18268)***
Helix Medical, Carpinteria *Also called Freudenberg Medical LLC* ***(P-22018)***
Heller Seasoning, Modesto *Also called Newly Weds Foods Inc* ***(P-2568)***
Heller State, Carmel Valley *Also called Durney Winery Corporation* ***(P-1677)***
Hellman Properties LLC ....F....562 431-6022
711 First St Seal Beach (90740) ***(P-56)***
Hello Network Inc ....F....408 891-4727
2 Mint Plz Apt 1004 San Francisco (94103) ***(P-23977)***
Hellwig Products Company Inc ....E....559 734-7451
16237 Avenue 296 Visalia (93292) ***(P-19680)***
Hely & Weber Orthopedic, Santa Paula *Also called Weber Orthopedic Inc* ***(P-22123)***
Hemet Ready Mix, Hemet *Also called Superior Ready Mix Concrete LP* ***(P-10853)***

ALPHABETIC

Employee Codes: A=Over 500 employees, B=251-500 C=101-250, D=51-100, E=20-50, F=10-19
2020 California Manfacturers Register
© Mergent Inc. 1-800-342-5647
1121

Hemisphere Design & Mfg LLC....F....661 294-9500
28895 Industry Dr Valencia (91355) ***(P-4909)***
Hemodialysis Inc....E....626 792-0548
806 S Fair Oaks Ave Pasadena (91105) ***(P-21733)***
Hemosense Inc....D....408 719-1393
9975 Summers Ridge Rd San Diego (92121) ***(P-22259)***
Hemostat Laboratories Inc (PA)....E....707 678-9594
515 Industrial Way Dixon (95620) ***(P-8308)***
Hemosure Inc....E....888 436-6787
5358 Irwindale Ave Baldwin Park (91706) ***(P-8973)***
Henderson Services Inc....E....559 435-8874
6722 N Stonebridge Dr Fresno (93711) ***(P-20336)***
Henkel Electronic Mtls LLC....C....888 943-6535
14000 Jamboree Rd Irvine (92606) ***(P-8872)***
Henkel US Operations Corp....E....626 968-6511
15051 Don Julian Rd City of Industry (91746) ***(P-8873)***
Henkel US Operations Corp....C....310 764-4600
20021 S Susana Rd Compton (90221) ***(P-8428)***
Hennis Enterprises Inc....E....805 477-0257
2646 Palma Dr Ste 430 Ventura (93003) ***(P-7564)***
Henry Company, Ontario *Also called Hco Holding I Corporation* ***(P-9113)***
Henry Company LLC (HQ)....D....310 955-9200
999 N Pacific Coast Hwy El Segundo (90245) ***(P-9115)***
Henry J Perez DDS....F....805 983-6768
132 S A St Ste B Oxnard (93030) ***(P-22159)***
Henry L Hudson (PA)....F....805 736-2737
403 N G St Lompoc (93436) ***(P-6608)***
Henry Ll....F....408 944-9100
1020 Rock Ave San Jose (95131) ***(P-12235)***
Henry Plastic Molding Inc....C....510 490-7993
41703 Albrae St Fremont (94538) ***(P-9821)***
Henrys Adio Vsual Slutions Inc....E....714 258-7238
1582 Parkway Loop Ste F Tustin (92780) ***(P-17240)***
Henrys Metal Polishing Works....F....323 263-9701
9856 Rush St South El Monte (91733) ***(P-13023)***
Henway Inc....F....661 822-6873
1314 Goodrick Dr Tehachapi (93561) ***(P-23003)***
Hephaestus Innovations....F....831 254-8555
2661 W Bch St Ste 3b Suit Watsonville (95076) ***(P-14372)***
Heraeus Prcous Mtls N Amer LLC (HQ)....C....562 921-7464
15524 Carmenita Rd Santa Fe Springs (90670) ***(P-11203)***
Herald Printing Ltd (PA)....F....805 647-1870
1242 Los Angeles Ave Ventura (93004) ***(P-6609)***
Herb KAn Company Inc....F....831 438-9450
380 Encinal St Ste 100 Santa Cruz (95060) ***(P-7667)***
Herbal Science International....F....626 333-9998
205 Russell St City of Industry (91744) ***(P-7668)***
Herbalife Manufacturing LLC....D....949 457-0951
20481 Crescent Bay Dr Lake Forest (92630) ***(P-2215)***
Herbs Yeh Manufacturing Co....F....909 946-0794
195 N 2nd Ave Upland (91786) ***(P-594)***
Herburger Publications Inc (PA)....D....916 685-5533
604 N Lincoln Way Galt (95632) ***(P-5660)***
Herburger Publications Inc....F....916 685-3945
8970 Elk Grove Blvd Elk Grove (95624) ***(P-5661)***
Herdell Printing & Lithography....E....707 963-3634
340 Mccormick St Saint Helena (94574) ***(P-6610)***
Herff Jones LLC....F....951 541-3938
14321 Goose St Eastvale (92880) ***(P-22527)***
Heritage Bag Company....F....909 899-5554
12320 4th St Rancho Cucamonga (91730) ***(P-5400)***
Heritage Bronze, Hesperia *Also called E R Metals Inc* ***(P-11396)***
Heritage Cabinet Co Inc....F....818 786-4900
21740 Marilla St Chatsworth (91311) ***(P-4910)***
Heritage Carbide Inc....F....714 524-0222
901 S Via Rodeo Placentia (92870) ***(P-16020)***
Heritage Container Inc....D....951 360-1900
4777 Felspar St Riverside (92509) ***(P-5234)***
Heritage Design....F....949 248-1300
32382 Del Obispo St B1 San Juan Capistrano (92675) ***(P-23127)***
Heritage Distributing Company....E....626 333-9526
425 S 9th Ave City of Industry (91746) ***(P-595)***
Heritage Distributing Company (PA)....E....323 838-1225
5743 Smithway St Ste 105 Commerce (90040) ***(P-702)***
Heritage Leather Company Inc....E....323 983-0420
4011 E 52nd St Maywood (90270) ***(P-10138)***
Heritage Missional Community....F....530 605-1990
4302 Shasta Dam Blvd Shasta Lake (96019) ***(P-2298)***
Heritage Paper Co, Livermore *Also called Baycorr Packaging LLC* ***(P-5199)***
Heritage Paper Co....F....925 449-1148
17740 Shideler Pkwy Lathrop (95330) ***(P-6611)***
Heritage Paper Co (HQ)....D....714 540-9737
2400 S Grand Ave Santa Ana (92705) ***(P-5235)***
Heritage Products LLC....F....909 839-1866
20932c Currier Rd Unit C Walnut (91789) ***(P-9439)***
Heritage Roasting Company, Shasta Lake *Also called Heritage Missional Community* ***(P-2298)***
Heritage Truck Painting, San Diego *Also called Brothers Enterprises Inc* ***(P-24619)***
Heritage Woodworking Co Inc....E....530 243-7215
4633 Mountain Lakes Blvd Redding (96003) ***(P-4204)***
Herley Industries Inc....D....858 812-7300
4820 Estgate Mall Ste 200 San Diego (92121) ***(P-18934)***
Herman Engineering & Mfg Inc....F....909 483-1631
4501 E Airport Dr Ste B Ontario (91761) ***(P-9822)***
Herman Miller Inc....E....408 432-5730
2740 Zanker Rd Ste 150 San Jose (95134) ***(P-4801)***
Hermes-Microvision Inc....E....408 597-8600
1762 Automation Pkwy San Jose (95131) ***(P-18269)***
Hermetic Seal Corporation (HQ)....C....626 443-8931
4232 Temple City Blvd Rosemead (91770) ***(P-18935)***
Hernandez Zeferino....F....714 953-4010
1924 E Mcfadden Ave Santa Ana (92705) ***(P-8874)***
Hero Arts Rubber Stamps Inc....D....510 232-4200
1200 Hrbour Way S Ste 201 Richmond (94804) ***(P-22951)***
Hero Nutritional, Santa Ana *Also called Envita Labs LLC* ***(P-7655)***
Heroku Inc....E....650 704-6107
1 Market St Ste 300 San Francisco (94105) ***(P-23978)***
Heron Therapeutics Inc (PA)....C....858 251-4400
4242 Campus Point Ct # 200 San Diego (92121) ***(P-7937)***
Herotek Inc....E....408 941-8399
155 Baytech Dr San Jose (95134) ***(P-17535)***
Herrick Corporation (PA)....E....209 956-4751
3003 E Hammer Ln Stockton (95212) ***(P-11807)***
Herrick Corporation....C....209 956-4751
3003 E Hammer Ln Stockton (95212) ***(P-11048)***
Herrick Retail Corporation Th....F....714 256-9543
2923 Saturn St Ste D Brea (92821) ***(P-6612)***
Hershey Company....C....559 485-8110
2704 S Maple Ave Fresno (93725) ***(P-2370)***
Hertz Entertainment Services, Burbank *Also called 24/7 Studio Equipment Inc* ***(P-17432)***
Herzog Wine Cellars, Oxnard *Also called Royal Wine Corporation* ***(P-1900)***
Hesperia Resorter....E....760 244-0021
16925 Main St Ste A Hesperia (92345) ***(P-5662)***
Hesperia Unified School Dst....F....760 948-1051
11176 G Ave Hesperia (92345) ***(P-2479)***
Hesperia Usd Food Service, Hesperia *Also called Hesperia Unified School Dst* ***(P-2479)***
Hesperian Health Guides (PA)....E....510 845-1447
1919 Addison St Ste 304 Berkeley (94704) ***(P-6108)***
Hess Collection Import Co, NAPA *Also called Hess Collection Winery* ***(P-1752)***
Hess Collection Winery (HQ)....E....707 255-1144
4411 Redwood Rd NAPA (94558) ***(P-1752)***
Hess Precision Laser Inc....F....209 575-1634
4747 Stratos Way Ste D Modesto (95356) ***(P-19321)***
Hestan Commercial Corporation....C....714 869-2380
3375 E La Palma Ave Anaheim (92806) ***(P-16851)***
Hestan Smart Cooking Inc....F....773 710-1538
1 Meyer Plz Vallejo (94590) ***(P-12813)***
Hewitt Industries Los Angeles....E....714 891-9300
1455 Crenshaw Blvd # 290 Torrance (90501) ***(P-20883)***
Hewlett Packard Enterprise Co....E....312 580-9100
1140 Enterprise Way Sunnyvale (94089) ***(P-23979)***
Hewlett Packard Enterprise Co (PA)....C....650 687-5817
6280 America Center Dr San Jose (95002) ***(P-23980)***
Hexacorp Ltd....E....760 815-0904
201 Ocean Ave Unit 1108p Santa Monica (90402) ***(P-23981)***
Hexagon Metrology Inc....E....949 916-4490
7 Orchard Ste 102 Lake Forest (92630) ***(P-14165)***
Hexagon Metrology Inc....D....760 994-1401
3536 Seagate Way Oceanside (92056) ***(P-21050)***
Hexcel Corporation....D....925 551-4900
11711 Dublin Blvd Dublin (94568) ***(P-7565)***
Hexion Inc....F....714 971-0180
625 The City Dr S Ste 300 Orange (92868) ***(P-8742)***
Hexpol Compounding CA Inc....D....626 961-0311
491 Wilson Way City of Industry (91744) ***(P-9315)***
Hexpol Compounding LLC....E....562 464-4482
11841 Wakeman St Santa Fe Springs (90670) ***(P-9316)***
Hey Baby of California....E....818 504-2060
11238 Peoria St Ste C Sun Valley (91352) ***(P-3336)***
Heyday....F....510 549-3564
1808 San Pablo Ave Apt A Berkeley (94702) ***(P-6109)***
Heyday Books, Berkeley *Also called Heyday* ***(P-6109)***
Hf Group Inc (PA)....E....310 605-0755
203 W Artesia Blvd Compton (90220) ***(P-22424)***
Hgc Holdings Inc....C....323 567-2226
3303 Mrtn Lthr King Jr Bl Lynwood (90262) ***(P-1371)***
Hgst Inc....C....408 418-4148
5601 Great Oaks Pkwy San Jose (95119) ***(P-15040)***
Hgst Inc....F....408 801-2394
951 Sandisk Dr Milpitas (95035) ***(P-15041)***
Hgst Inc (HQ)....F....408 717-6000
5601 Great Oaks Pkwy San Jose (95119) ***(P-15042)***
Hl Performance Electric Vehicl....F....909 923-1973
620 S Magnolia Ave Ste B Ontario (91762) ***(P-16654)***
Hl Rel Connectors Inc....B....909 626-1820
760 Wharton Dr Claremont (91711) ***(P-16902)***
Hl Relblity McRelectronics Inc....E....408 764-5500
1804 Mccarthy Blvd Milpitas (95035) ***(P-18270)***
Hl Rez Digital Solutions....F....760 597-2650
1235 Activity Dr Ste E Vista (92081) ***(P-6613)***
Hl Tech Heat Treating Inc....F....310 532-3705
331 W 168th St Gardena (90248) ***(P-11453)***
Hl Tech Honeycomb Inc....C....858 974-1600
9355 Ruffin Ct San Diego (92123) ***(P-12814)***
Hl Tech Solder....F....714 572-1200
700 Monroe Way Placentia (92870) ***(P-11273)***
Hi-Craft Metal Products....E....310 323-6949
606 W 184th St Gardena (90248) ***(P-12236)***
Hi-Desert Publishing Company....E....909 797-9101
35154 Yucaipa Blvd Yucaipa (92399) ***(P-5663)***
Hi-Desert Publishing Company....E....909 336-3555
28200 Highway 189 O-1 Lake Arrowhead (92352) ***(P-5664)***
Hi-Desert Publishing Company (HQ)....D....760 365-3315
56445 29 Palms Hwy Yucca Valley (92284) ***(P-5665)***
Hi-Flo Corp....F....562 468-0800
5161 E El Cedral St Long Beach (90815) ***(P-14582)***
Hi-Grade Materials Co....E....661 533-3100
6500 E Avenue T Littlerock (93543) ***(P-10771)***
Hi-Line Industrial Saw and Sup....F....714 921-1600
179 Business Center Dr Corona (92880) ***(P-11553)***

Mergent e-mail: customerrelations@mergent.com
1122
2020 California
Manufacturers Register
(P-0000) Products & Services Section entry number
(PA)=Parent Co (HQ)=Headquarters (DH)=Div Headquarters

Hi-Lite Manufacturing Co Inc......D......909 465-1999
13450 Monte Vista Ave Chino (91710) *(P-17043)*
Hi-Plas, Jurupa Valley *Also called Highland Plastics Inc (P-9825)*
Hi-Precision Grinding, Santa Ana *Also called Deltronic Corporation (P-21347)*
Hi-Q Environmental Pdts Co Inc......F......858 549-2818
7386 Trade St San Diego (92121) *(P-21236)*
Hi-Rel Plastics & Molding Corp......E......951 354-0258
7575 Jurupa Ave Riverside (92504) *(P-9823)*
Hi-Shear Corporation (HQ)......A......310 784-4025
2600 Skypark Dr Torrance (90505) *(P-12680)*
HI-Shear Corporation......E......310 326-8110
2600 Skypark Dr Torrance (90505) *(P-11595)*
Hi-Tech Electronic Mfg Corp......D......858 657-0908
7420 Carroll Rd San Diego (92121) *(P-17894)*
Hi-Tech Engineering, Camarillo *Also called Hte Acquisition LLC (P-16036)*
Hi-Tech Iron Works, Commerce *Also called Architectural Enterprises Inc (P-12452)*
Hi-Tech Labels Incorporated (PA)......E......714 670-2150
8530 Roland St Buena Park (90621) *(P-16021)*
Hi-Tech Prcision Machining Inc......F......408 251-1269
1901 Las Plumas Ave # 50 San Jose (95133) *(P-16022)*
Hi-Tech Products, Buena Park *Also called Hi-Tech Labels Incorporated (P-16021)*
Hi-Tech Welding & Forming Inc......E......619 562-5929
1327 Fayette St El Cajon (92020) *(P-16023)*
Hi-Temp Forming Co Inc......D......714 529-6556
315 Arden Ave Ste 28 Glendale (91203) *(P-16024)*
Hi-Temp Insulation Inc......B......805 484-2774
4700 Calle Alto Camarillo (93012) *(P-12815)*
Hi-Torque Publications, Santa Clarita *Also called Daisy Publishing Company Inc (P-5915)*
Hi-Z Technology Inc......E......858 695-6660
7606 Miramar Rd Ste 7400 San Diego (92126) *(P-16787)*
Hi/Fn Inc (HQ)......F......408 778-2944
48720 Kato Rd Fremont (94538) *(P-18271)*
Hiatus, Los Angeles *Also called Crew Knitwear LLC (P-3309)*
Hibernia Woolen Mills, Manhattan Beach *Also called Stanton Carpet Corp (P-2880)*
HIC Corporation (PA)......F......949 261-1636
38 Executive Park Ste 300 Irvine (92614) *(P-5954)*
Hidden Jeans Inc (PA)......F......213 746-4223
1001 Towne Ave Ste 103 Los Angeles (90021) *(P-2691)*
Hiep Nguyen Corporation......E......408 451-9042
1641 Rogers Ave San Jose (95112) *(P-16025)*
High Camp Home, Truckee *Also called Recycled Spaces Inc (P-4772)*
High Connection Density Inc......E......408 743-9700
820 Kifer Rd Ste A Sunnyvale (94086) *(P-18772)*
High Country Water, Roseville *Also called California Bottling Company (P-2049)*
High End Seating Solutions LLC......E......714 259-0177
1919 E Occidental St Santa Ana (92705) *(P-20407)*
High Energy Sports Inc......F......714 632-3323
1081 N Shepard St Ste A Anaheim (92806) *(P-3845)*
High Fidelity Textiles, Los Angeles *Also called Padilla Remberto (P-2833)*
High Five Inc......E......714 847-2200
1452 Manhattan Ave Fullerton (92831) *(P-6614)*
High Precision Grinding......E......619 440-0303
1130 Pioneer Way El Cajon (92020) *(P-16026)*
High Sierra Electronics Inc......E......530 273-2080
155 Spring Hill Dr # 106 Grass Valley (95945) *(P-21237)*
High Sierra Plastics......F......760 873-5600
375 Joe Smith Rd Bishop (93514) *(P-9824)*
High Sierra Truss Company Inc......F......559 688-6611
1201 S K St Tulare (93274) *(P-4306)*
High Speed Cnc......F......408 492-0331
3324 Victor Ct Santa Clara (95054) *(P-16027)*
High Tech Etch (PA)......F......760 244-8916
17469 Lemon St Hesperia (92345) *(P-16028)*
High Tech Etch Research & Dev, Hesperia *Also called High Tech Etch (P-16028)*
High Tech Machine Shop S-Corp......F......909 356-5437
15149 Boyle Ave Fontana (92337) *(P-13597)*
High Tech Pet Products Inc......E......805 644-1797
2111 Portola Rd A Ventura (93003) *(P-23352)*
High-End Knitwear Inc......E......323 582-6061
1100 S Hope St Ph 202 Los Angeles (90015) *(P-2790)*
High-Tech Coatings Inc......F......714 547-2122
1724 S Santa Fe St Santa Ana (92705) *(P-13190)*
Highball Signal Inc......F......909 341-5367
6767 Di Carlo Pl Rancho Cucamonga (91739) *(P-17733)*
Higher One Payments Inc......E......510 769-9888
80 Swan Way Ste 200 Oakland (94621) *(P-23982)*
Highland Plastics Inc......C......951 360-9587
3650 Dulles Dr Jurupa Valley (91752) *(P-9825)*
Highland Technology......E......415 551-1700
650 Potrero Ave San Francisco (94110) *(P-21484)*
Highland Wholesale Foods Inc......E......209 933-0580
1604 Tillie Lewis Dr Stockton (95206) *(P-774)*
Highlander Harvesting Aid, Gonzales *Also called Ramsay Highlander Inc (P-13662)*
Highpoint Technologies Inc......F......408 942-5800
41650 Christy St Fremont (94538) *(P-15043)*
Hightower Metal Products......D......714 637-7000
2090 N Glassell St Orange (92865) *(P-16029)*
Hightower Metals, Orange *Also called Hightower Plating & Mfg Co (P-13024)*
Hightower Plating & Mfg Co......E......714 637-9110
2090 N Glassell St Orange (92865) *(P-13024)*
Highway Safety Control, NAPA *Also called Radiator Specialty Company (P-9018)*
Highways Magazine, Oxnard *Also called Tl Enterprises LLC (P-6042)*
Highwire Press Inc (PA)......E......650 721-6388
15575 Los Gatos Blvd A Los Gatos (95032) *(P-6251)*
Higuchi Inc., USA, Torrance *Also called Kabushiki Kisha Higuchi Shokai (P-16973)*
Hii San Diego Shipyard Inc......B......619 234-8851
1995 Bay Front St San Diego (92113) *(P-20288)*
Hilborn Fuel Injection Company, Aliso Viejo *Also called Fuel Injection Engineering Co (P-19665)*
Hilborn Manufacturing Corp......F......949 360-0909
22892 Glenwood Dr Aliso Viejo (92656) *(P-19681)*
Hilfiker Pipe Co......E......707 443-5091
1902 Hilfiker Ln Eureka (95503) *(P-10585)*
Hilfiker Retaining Walls, Eureka *Also called Hilfiker Pipe Co (P-10585)*
Hilkers Custom Cabinets Inc......F......951 487-7640
504 N Greco Ct San Jacinto (92582) *(P-4205)*
Hill Brothers Chemical Company......F......626 333-2251
15017 Clark Ave City of Industry (91745) *(P-7389)*
Hill Manufacturing Company LLC......E......408 988-4744
3363 Edward Ave Santa Clara (95054) *(P-12237)*
Hill Marine Products LLC......F......714 855-2986
2683 Halladay St Santa Ana (92705) *(P-16030)*
Hill Products Inc......F......818 877-9256
19160 Arminta St Reseda (91335) *(P-17241)*
Hill Top Winery, Valley Center *Also called Htr LLC (P-1756)*
Hiller Aircraft Corporation......E......559 659-5959
925 M St Firebaugh (93622) *(P-20126)*
Hillerich & Bradsby Co......E......916 652-4267
5960 Jetton Ln Loomis (95650) *(P-22820)*
Hillerich & Bradsby Co......D......800 282-2287
1800 S Archibald Ave Ontario (91761) *(P-22821)*
Hillholder Blocks By Modern......F......619 463-6344
3239 Bancroft Dr Spring Valley (91977) *(P-10586)*
Hillo America Inc......F......626 570-8899
10727 7th St Ste A Rancho Cucamonga (91730) *(P-17242)*
Hills Wldg & Engrg Contr Inc......D......661 746-5400
22038 Stockdale Hwy Bakersfield (93314) *(P-207)*
Hillshire Brands Company......B......909 481-0760
9357 Richmond Pl Ste 101 Rancho Cucamonga (91730) *(P-464)*
Hillshire Brands Company......B......510 276-1300
2411 Baumann Ave San Lorenzo (94580) *(P-465)*
Hillshire Brands Company......E......562 903-9260
10715 Springdale Ave # 5 Santa Fe Springs (90670) *(P-466)*
Hillside Capital Inc......C......650 367-2011
6222 Fallbrook Ave Woodland Hills (91367) *(P-17536)*
Hilltron Corporation......F......408 597-4424
2528 Qume Dr Ste 4 San Jose (95131) *(P-18936)*
Hilmar Cheese Company Inc......D......209 667-6076
3600 W Canal Dr Turlock (95380) *(P-554)*
Hilmar Cheese Company Inc (PA)......B......209 667-6076
8901 Lander Ave Hilmar (95324) *(P-555)*
Hilmar Ingredients, Hilmar *Also called Hilmar Cheese Company Inc (P-555)*
Hilmar Whey Protein Inc (PA)......B......209 667-6076
9001 Lander Ave Hilmar (95324) *(P-596)*
Hilmar Whey Protein Inc......D......209 667-6076
8901 Lander Ave Hilmar (95324) *(P-597)*
Hilz Cable Assemblies Inc......F......951 245-0499
31889 Corydon St Ste 110 Lake Elsinore (92530) *(P-21485)*
Hing WA Lee Inc......E......909 595-3500
19811 Colima Rd Walnut (91789) *(P-22596)*
Hinoichi Tofu, Garden Grove *Also called House Foods America Corp (P-2481)*
Hint Inc......E......415 513-4051
2124 Union St Ste D San Francisco (94123) *(P-2081)*
Hip & Hip Inc (PA)......E......310 494-6742
1100 S San Pedro St D07 Los Angeles (90015) *(P-3337)*
Hiplink Software, Los Gatos *Also called Semotus Inc (P-24396)*
Hire Elegance......F......858 740-7862
8333 Arjons Dr Ste E San Diego (92126) *(P-5064)*
Hirel Connectors, Claremont *Also called HI Rel Connectors Inc (P-16902)*
Hirok Inc......E......619 713-5066
5644 Kearny Mesa Rd Ste H San Diego (92111) *(P-13736)*
Hirsch Pipe & Supply Co Inc......F......949 487-7009
31920 Del Obispo St # 275 San Juan Capistrano (92675) *(P-11671)*
Hirsh Inc......E......213 622-9441
860 S Los Angeles St # 900 Los Angeles (90014) *(P-208)*
His Company Inc......F......951 493-0200
400 E Parkridge Ave # 101 Corona (92879) *(P-5363)*
His Company Inc......E......858 513-7748
2215 Pseo De Las Amrcas S San Diego (92154) *(P-16555)*
His Industries Inc......E......562 407-0512
1202 W Shelley Ct Orange (92868) *(P-14711)*
His Life Woodworks......E......310 756-0170
15107 S Main St Gardena (90248) *(P-4055)*
Hisco, San Diego *Also called His Company Inc (P-16555)*
Hispanic Business Inc......F......805 964-4554
5385 Hollister Ave # 204 Santa Barbara (93111) *(P-5955)*
Hispanic Business Magazine, Santa Barbara *Also called Hispanic Business Inc (P-5955)*
Hitachi Automotive Systems......D......310 212-0200
6200 Gateway Dr Cypress (90630) *(P-16655)*
Hitachi Chem Diagnostics Inc......C......650 961-5501
630 Clyde Ct Mountain View (94043) *(P-20761)*
Hitachi High-Technologies......F......818 280-0745
20770 Nordhoff St Chatsworth (91311) *(P-21238)*
Hitachi Home Elec Amer Inc (HQ)......C......619 591-5200
2420 Fenton St 200 Chula Vista (91914) *(P-17243)*
Hitachi Rail Usa Inc (PA)......F......415 397-7010
101 The Embarcadero # 210 San Francisco (94105) *(P-20370)*
Hitachi Vantara Corporation (HQ)......B......408 970-1000
2535 Augustine Dr Santa Clara (95054) *(P-15044)*
Hitachi Via Mechanics USA Inc, San Jose *Also called Via Mechanics (usa) Inc (P-15362)*
Hitech Metal Fabrication Corp......D......714 635-3505
1705 S Claudina Way Anaheim (92805) *(P-11808)*
Hitech Plastics and Molds, Valencia *Also called Cypress Manufacturing LLC (P-9740)*
Hitem, San Diego *Also called Hi-Tech Electronic Mfg Corp (P-17894)*
Hitex Dyeing & Finishing Inc......E......626 363-0160
355 Vineland Ave City of Industry (91746) *(P-3846)*

ALPHABETIC

Employee Codes: A=Over 500 employees, B=251-500
C=101-250, D=51-100, E=20-50, F=10-19
2020 California
Manfacturers Register
© Mergent Inc. 1-800-342-5647
1123

Hiti Digital America Inc....................E......909 594-0099
675 Brea Canyon Rd Ste 7 Walnut (91789) *(P-22425)*
Hits Magazine Inc (PA)....................F......323 946-7600
6906 Hollywood Blvd Fl 2 Los Angeles (90028) *(P-5956)*
Hitt Companies....................E......714 979-1405
3231 W Macarthur Blvd Santa Ana (92704) *(P-9317)*
Hitt Marking Devices I D Tech, Santa Ana *Also called Hitt Companies (P-9317)*
Hive Lighting Inc....................F......310 773-4362
525 S Hewitt St Los Angeles (90013) *(P-16972)*
Hixson Metal Finishing....................D......800 900-9798
829 Production Pl Newport Beach (92663) *(P-13025)*
Hizco Truck Body, Los Angeles *Also called A A Cater Truck Mfg Co Inc (P-4679)*
HK Canning Inc (PA)....................E......805 652-1392
130 N Garden St Ventura (93001) *(P-775)*
HK Enterprise Group Inc....................F......858 652-4400
6540 Lusk Blvd Ste C270 San Diego (92121) *(P-8974)*
Hka Elevator Consulting Inc....................F......949 348-9711
23211 S Pointe Dr Ste 101 Laguna Hills (92653) *(P-13802)*
Hlm, Vista *Also called Honor Life Medallions (P-10911)*
HMC Display, Madera *Also called Gardner Family Ltd Partnership (P-11591)*
HMcompany....................F......805 650-2651
4464 Mcgrath St Ste 111 Ventura (93003) *(P-16031)*
Hmr Building Systems LLC....................F......951 749-4700
620 Newport Center Dr # 12 Newport Beach (92660) *(P-3935)*
Hnc Parent Inc (PA)....................D......310 955-9200
999 N Pacific Coast Hwy El Segundo (90245) *(P-9116)*
Hnc Printing Services LLC....................F......925 771-2080
5125 Port Chicago Hwy Concord (94520) *(P-6615)*
Hni Corporation....................B......916 927-0400
3780 Pell Cir Sacramento (95838) *(P-4840)*
Ho Tai Printing & Book Store, San Francisco *Also called Ho Tai Printing Co Inc (P-6616)*
Ho Tai Printing Co Inc....................F......415 421-4218
723 Clay St Ste 725 San Francisco (94108) *(P-6616)*
Hobie Cat Company....................C......760 758-9100
4925 Oceanside Blvd Oceanside (92056) *(P-20337)*
Hockin Diversfd Holdings Inc....................F......760 787-0510
1672 Main St Ste E362 Ramona (92065) *(P-14662)*
Hocking International Labs Inc (PA)....................E......760 432-5277
980 Rancheros Dr San Marcos (92069) *(P-8388)*
Hodge Products Inc....................E......619 444-3147
7365 Mission Gorge Rd F San Diego (92120) *(P-11596)*
Hoefer Inc....................E......415 282-2307
760 National Ct Richmond (94804) *(P-21239)*
Hoefner Corporation....................E......626 443-3258
9722 Rush St South El Monte (91733) *(P-16032)*
Hoffman Magnetics Inc....................E......818 717-5095
19528 Ventura Blvd Tarzana (91356) *(P-19219)*
Hoffman Plastic Compounds Inc....................D......323 636-3346
16616 Garfield Ave Paramount (90723) *(P-7566)*
Hoffy, Vernon *Also called Square H Brands Inc (P-500)*
Hogan Co Inc....................E......909 421-0245
2741 S Lilac Ave Bloomington (92316) *(P-11097)*
Hogan Mfg Inc (PA)....................B......209 838-7323
19527 Mchenry Ave Escalon (95320) *(P-23353)*
Hogan Mfg Inc....................C......209 838-2400
1520 1st St Escalon (95320) *(P-23354)*
Hoist Fitness Systems, San Diego *Also called Fitness Warehouse LLC (P-22801)*
Hoist Fitness Systems Inc....................D......858 578-7676
11900 Community Rd Poway (92064) *(P-22822)*
Hoke Outdoor Advertising Inc....................E......714 637-3610
1955 N Main St Orange (92865) *(P-23128)*
Holcomb Products Inc....................F......559 822-2067
6751 N Blackstone Ave # 103 Fresno (93710) *(P-3745)*
Holiday Foliage Inc....................E......619 661-9094
2592 Otay Center Dr San Diego (92154) *(P-23355)*
Holland & Herring Mfg Inc....................E......909 469-4700
661 E Monterey Ave Pomona (91767) *(P-16033)*
Holland & Sherry Inc....................F......310 657-8550
8550 Melrose Ave West Hollywood (90069) *(P-2870)*
Hollands Custom Cabinets Inc....................E......619 443-6081
14511 Olde Highway 80 El Cajon (92021) *(P-4206)*
Holliday Rock Trucking Inc (PA)....................D......909 982-1553
1401 N Benson Ave Upland (91786) *(P-10772)*
Hollinger Metal Edge Inc....................E......323 721-7800
356 S Coyote Ln Anaheim (92808) *(P-5236)*
Hollister Brewing Company LLC....................E......805 968-2810
6980 Market Place Dr Goleta (93117) *(P-1535)*
Hollister Landscape Supply Inc (HQ)....................F......831 443-8644
520 Crazy Horse Canyon Rd A Salinas (93907) *(P-10773)*
Holloway House Publishing Co....................F......323 653-8060
8060 Melrose Ave Fl 3 Los Angeles (90046) *(P-6110)*
Holly Yashi Inc....................D......707 822-0389
1300 9th St Arcata (95521) *(P-22528)*
Hollywood Bed Spring Mfg Inc....................D......323 887-9500
5959 Corvette St Commerce (90040) *(P-11597)*
Hollywood Bike Racks, Los Angeles *Also called Hollywood Engineering Inc (P-11598)*
Hollywood Chairs....................F......760 471-6600
1880 Diamond St San Marcos (92078) *(P-4575)*
Hollywood Engineering Inc....................F......310 516-8600
12812 S Spring St Los Angeles (90061) *(P-11598)*
Hollywood Film Company....................D......818 683-1130
9265 Borden Ave Sun Valley (91352) *(P-22426)*
Hollywood Lamp & Shade Co....................F......323 585-3999
2928 Leonis Blvd Vernon (90058) *(P-16864)*
Hollywood Records Inc....................E......818 560-5670
500 S Buena Vista St Burbank (91521) *(P-17327)*
Hollywood Software Inc....................F......818 205-2121
5000 Van Nuys Blvd # 460 Van Nuys (91403) *(P-23983)*
Holman Ranch Corporation....................F......831 659-2640
19 E Carmel Valley Rd C Carmel Valley (93924) *(P-1753)*
Holo Inc....................E......510 221-4177
2461 Peralta St Oakland (94607) *(P-23356)*
Hologic Inc....................C......408 745-0975
1240 Elko Dr Sunnyvale (94089) *(P-22213)*
Hologic Inc....................E......858 410-8000
10210 Genetic Center Dr San Diego (92121) *(P-22260)*
Holsum Bakery Inc....................E......818 884-6562
21540 Blythe St Canoga Park (91304) *(P-1225)*
Holt Integrated Circuits, Mission Viejo *Also called W G Holt Inc (P-18651)*
Holt Tool & Machine Inc....................E......650 364-2547
2909 Middlefield Rd Redwood City (94063) *(P-11049)*
Holz Rubber Company Inc....................C......209 368-7171
1129 S Sacramento St Lodi (95240) *(P-9318)*
Holzinger Indus Shtmtl Inc....................F......562 944-6337
12440 Mccann Dr Santa Fe Springs (90670) *(P-12238)*
Home & Body Company (PA)....................E......714 842-8000
18352 Enterprise Ln Huntington Beach (92648) *(P-8389)*
Home Brew Mart Inc....................E......858 695-2739
9045 Carroll Way San Diego (92121) *(P-1536)*
Home Brew Mart Inc (HQ)....................C......858 790-6900
9045 Carroll Way San Diego (92121) *(P-1537)*
Home Collection Fine Furniture, Palm Desert *Also called Upholstery Factory Inc (P-4675)*
Home Paradise LLC....................F......626 284-9999
905 Westminster Ave G Alhambra (91803) *(P-12816)*
Home Portal LLC....................F......310 559-6100
3351 La Cienega Pl Los Angeles (90016) *(P-16556)*
Home-Flex, Valencia *Also called Valencia Pipe Company (P-9479)*
Homefacts Management LLC....................F......949 502-8300
1 Venture Ste 300 Irvine (92618) *(P-6252)*
Homefacts.com, Irvine *Also called Homefacts Management LLC (P-6252)*
Homegrown Naturals, Berkeley *Also called Annies Inc (P-2393)*
Homestead Fine Foods, South San Francisco *Also called Homestead Ravioli Company Inc (P-728)*
Homestead Publishing Inc....................E......307 733-6248
4388 17th St San Francisco (94114) *(P-6253)*
Homestead Ravioli Company Inc....................E......650 615-0750
315 S Maple Ave Ste 106 South San Francisco (94080) *(P-728)*
Homestead Sheet Metal....................E......619 469-4373
9031 Memory Ln Spring Valley (91977) *(P-11809)*
Hometex Corporation....................E......619 661-0400
1743 Continental Ln Escondido (92029) *(P-3617)*
Homewood Components Inc....................D......530 743-8855
5033 Feather River Blvd Marysville (95901) *(P-4307)*
Homewood Truss, Marysville *Also called Homewood Components Inc (P-4307)*
Homewood Winery....................F......707 996-6353
23120 Burndale Rd Sonoma (95476) *(P-1754)*
Hone & Strop Inc....................F......424 262-4474
1617 Franklin St Apt 6 Santa Monica (90404) *(P-8512)*
Honest Company Inc (PA)....................C......310 917-9199
12130 Millennium Ste 500 Playa Vista (90094) *(P-3442)*
Honey Bennetts Farm Inc....................E......805 521-1375
3176 Honey Ln Fillmore (93015) *(P-2480)*
Honey Punch, Los Angeles *Also called Klk Forte Industry Inc (P-3356)*
Honey Punch Inc (PA)....................F......323 800-3812
1535 Rio Vista Ave Los Angeles (90023) *(P-3338)*
Honeybee Robotics Ltd....................F......510 207-4555
398 W Washington Blvd Pasadena (91103) *(P-14825)*
Honeywell International Inc....................C......714 562-3000
22 Centerpointe Dr # 100 La Palma (90623) *(P-19954)*
Honeywell International Inc....................E......760 355-3420
510 W Aten Rd Imperial (92251) *(P-19682)*
Honeywell International Inc....................A......310 512-4237
6452 Morion Cir Huntington Beach (92647) *(P-19955)*
Honeywell International Inc....................C......408 954-1100
1804 Mccarthy Blvd Milpitas (95035) *(P-18272)*
Honeywell International Inc....................A......310 323-9500
2525 W 190th St Torrance (90504) *(P-19956)*
Honeywell International Inc....................A......951 500-6086
3105 Prince Valiant Ln Modesto (95350) *(P-19957)*
Honeywell International Inc....................A......949 425-3992
27831 Abadejo Mission Viejo (92692) *(P-19958)*
Honeywell International Inc....................A......209 323-8520
25 S Stockton St Ste C Lodi (95240) *(P-19959)*
Honeywell International Inc....................A......209 480-6733
2100 Geer Rd Ste C Turlock (95382) *(P-19960)*
Honeywell International Inc....................A......714 337-6864
22775 Savi Ranch Pkwy D Yorba Linda (92887) *(P-19961)*
Honeywell International Inc....................B......310 410-9605
6201 W Imperial Hwy Los Angeles (90045) *(P-19962)*
Honeywell International Inc....................D......408 962-2000
3500 Garrett Dr Santa Clara (95054) *(P-7500)*
Honeywell International Inc....................D......714 562-3016
6 Center Pt Ste 300 La Palma (90623) *(P-19963)*
Honeywell International Inc....................D......310 618-2140
325 Maple Ave Torrance (90503) *(P-17537)*
Honeywell International Inc....................C......619 671-5612
2055 Dublin Dr San Diego (92154) *(P-20796)*
Honeywell International Inc....................A......760 312-5300
233 Paulin Ave 8500 Calexico (92231) *(P-19964)*
Honeywell International Inc....................A......858 848-3187
13125 Danielson St Poway (92064) *(P-20884)*
Honeywell Safety Pdts USA Inc....................C......619 661-8383
7828 Waterville Rd San Diego (92154) *(P-22027)*
Hong Fat Dye Cutting Co....................F......626 452-0382
2103 Sastre Ave South El Monte (91733) *(P-7333)*
Hongene Biotech Corporation....................F......650 520-9678
29520 Kohoutek Way Union City (94587) *(P-8309)*
Honor Life, Vista *Also called Rayzist Photomask Inc (P-22972)*

Mergent e-mail: customerrelations@mergent.com
1124
2020 California
Manufacturers Register
(P-0000) Products & Services Section entry number
(PA)=Parent Co (HQ)=Headquarters (DH)=Div Headquarters

Honor Life Medallions .... F 760 727-8581
955 Park Center Dr Vista (92081) *(P-10911)*
Honor Plastics & Molding Inc .... E 909 594-7487
3270 Pomona Blvd Pomona (91768) *(P-9826)*
Honulua Surf Co, Irvine *Also called Veezee Inc (P-3207)*
Hood Manufacturing Inc .... D 714 979-7681
2621 S Birch St Santa Ana (92707) *(P-9827)*
Hoojook .... F 408 596-9427
1754 Tech Dr Ste 132 San Jose (95148) *(P-23984)*
Hook It Up .... C 714 600-0100
1513 S Grand Ave Santa Ana (92705) *(P-2653)*
Hook or Crook Cellars, Lodi *Also called Baywood Cellars Inc (P-1592)*
Hoopa Forest Industries .... E 530 625-4281
778 Marshall Ln Hoopa (95546) *(P-3886)*
Hoopla Software Inc .... E 408 498-9600
84 W Santa Clara St # 460 San Jose (95113) *(P-23985)*
Hoorsen Buhs LLC .... F 888 692-2997
2217 Main St Santa Monica (90405) *(P-22983)*
Hoosier Plstic Fabrication Inc .... C 951 272-3070
1152 California Ave Corona (92881) *(P-9828)*
Hop Kiln Winery, The, Healdsburg *Also called Overlook Vineyards LLC (P-1852)*
Hope Family Wines (PA) .... E 805 238-4112
1585 Live Oak Rd Paso Robles (93446) *(P-1755)*
Hope Plastic Co Inc .... E 818 769-5560
5353 Strohm Ave North Hollywood (91601) *(P-9829)*
Hopland Brewery, Hopland *Also called Mendocino Brewing Company Inc (P-1548)*
Horiba Automotive Test Systems, Irvine *Also called Horiba Instruments Inc (P-21240)*
Horiba Instruments Inc (HQ) .... C 949 250-4811
9755 Research Dr Irvine (92618) *(P-21240)*
Horiba Instruments Inc .... D 408 730-4772
430 Indio Way Sunnyvale (94085) *(P-21486)*
Horizon Cal Publications .... F 760 934-3929
452 Old Mammoth Rd Mammoth Lakes (93546) *(P-5666)*
Horizon Engineering Inc .... E 858 679-0785
13200 Kirkham Way Ste 109 Poway (92064) *(P-16034)*
Horizon Hobby LLC .... C 909 390-9595
4710 E Guasti Rd Ste A Ontario (91761) *(P-22681)*
Horizon International Ltd .... F 559 781-4640
1480 W Westfield Ave Porterville (93257) *(P-15520)*
Horizon Publications Inc .... F 760 873-3535
407 W Line St Ste 8 Bishop (93514) *(P-5667)*
Horizon Snack Foods Inc .... D 925 373-7700
197 Darcy Pkwy Lathrop (95330) *(P-1343)*
Horizon Well Logging Inc .... F 805 733-0972
711 Saint Andrews Way Lompoc (93436) *(P-209)*
Hormel Foods Corp Svcs LLC .... E 949 753-5350
2 Venture Ste 250 Irvine (92618) *(P-467)*
Horn Machine Tools Inc .... E 559 431-4131
40455 Brickyard Dr # 101 Madera (93636) *(P-13977)*
Horstman Manufacturing Co Inc .... E 760 598-2100
1970 Peacock Blvd Oceanside (92056) *(P-19683)*
Hortonworks Inc (HQ) .... A 408 916-4121
5470 Great America Pkwy Santa Clara (95054) *(P-23986)*
Horvath Holdings Inc .... E 530 587-4700
40173 Truckee Airport Rd Truckee (96161) *(P-2754)*
Horvath Precision Machining .... F 510 683-0810
930 Thompson Pl Sunnyvale (94085) *(P-16035)*
Hos, Vista *Also called Hruby Orbital Systems Inc (P-15521)*
Hospital Systems Inc .... D 925 427-7800
750 Garcia Ave Pittsburg (94565) *(P-22261)*
Hospitality Sleep Systems Inc .... F 909 387-9779
107 E Rialto Ave San Bernardino (92408) *(P-4722)*
Hospitality Wood Products Inc .... F 562 806-5564
7206 E Gage Ave Commerce (90040) *(P-4056)*
Host Analytics Inc (HQ) .... E 650 249-7100
555 Twin Dolphin Dr # 400 Redwood City (94065) *(P-23987)*
Hot Can Inc .... E 707 601-6013
10620 Treena St Ste 230 San Diego (92131) *(P-2299)*
Hot Chillys, San Luis Obispo *Also called Performance Apparel Corp (P-3385)*
Hot Shoppe Designs Inc .... F 949 487-2828
1323 Calle Avanzado San Clemente (92673) *(P-3088)*
Hot Spring Spa, Folsom *Also called Xolar Corporation (P-23529)*
Hot Topic Inc (HQ) .... A 626 839-4681
18305 San Jose Ave City of Industry (91748) *(P-3036)*
Hotech Corporation .... E 909 987-8828
9320 Santa Anita Ave # 100 Rancho Cucamonga (91730) *(P-18273)*
Hotlix (PA) .... E 805 473-0596
966 Griffin St Grover Beach (93433) *(P-1372)*
Hotlix .... F 805 773-1942
179 Pomeroy Ave Pismo Beach (93449) *(P-1373)*
Hotlix Candy, Grover Beach *Also called Hotlix (P-1372)*
Hotronic Inc .... E 408 378-3883
1875 Winchester Blvd # 100 Campbell (95008) *(P-17378)*
Houghton Mifflin Harcourt Pubg .... F 617 351-5000
525 B St Ste 1900 San Diego (92101) *(P-6111)*
House Foods America Corp (HQ) .... C 714 901-4350
7351 Orangewood Ave Garden Grove (92841) *(P-2481)*
House of Bagels Inc (PA) .... F 650 595-4700
1007 Washington St San Carlos (94070) *(P-1226)*
House of Print & Copy .... F 530 273-1000
1501 E Main St Grass Valley (95945) *(P-6617)*
House of Printing Inc .... E 626 793-7034
3336 E Colorado Blvd Pasadena (91107) *(P-6618)*
House of Quirky, Los Angeles *Also called Hq Brands LLC (P-3556)*
House of Uniforms, Chatsworth *Also called Warrens Department Store Inc (P-2982)*
Housewares International Inc .... E 323 581-3000
1933 S Broadway Ste 867 Los Angeles (90007) *(P-9830)*
Houston Bazz Co .... D 714 898-2666
12700 Western Ave Garden Grove (92841) *(P-12817)*

Houston Fearless 76, Compton *Also called Hf Group Inc (P-22424)*
Houston Rubber Co Inc .... F 818 899-1108
12623 Foothill Blvd Sylmar (91342) *(P-9319)*
Hovey Tile Art .... E 909 794-3815
1221 Opal Ave Mentone (92359) *(P-23254)*
How 2 Save Fuel LLC .... F 818 882-1189
18017 Chtswrth St Ste 166 Granada Hills (91344) *(P-8743)*
How2savefuel.com, Granada Hills *Also called How 2 Save Fuel LLC (P-8743)*
Howardsoft .... F 858 454-0121
7854 Ivanhoe Ave A La Jolla (92037) *(P-23988)*
Howco Inc .... F 619 275-1663
1221 W Morena Blvd San Diego (92110) *(P-19684)*
Howell Dick Hole Drilling Svc .... F 562 633-9898
2579 E 67th St Long Beach (90805) *(P-94)*
Howell Drilling, Long Beach *Also called Howell Dick Hole Drilling Svc (P-94)*
Howies Moulding Inc .... F 562 698-0261
8032 Allport Ave Santa Fe Springs (90670) *(P-4057)*
Howmedica Osteonics Corp .... E 714 557-5010
1947 W Collins Ave Orange (92867) *(P-21734)*
Hoya Corporation .... C 858 309-6050
4255 Ruffin Rd San Diego (92123) *(P-22360)*
Hoya Corporation USA .... F 408 654-2200
680 N Mccarthy Blvd # 120 Milpitas (95035) *(P-20587)*
Hoya Corporation USA (HQ) .... F 408 492-1069
680 N Mccarthy Blvd # 120 Milpitas (95035) *(P-21359)*
Hoya Holdings Inc .... D 626 739-5200
425 E Huntington Dr Monrovia (91016) *(P-21360)*
Hoya Holdings Inc (HQ) .... C 408 654-2300
680 N Mccarthy Blvd # 120 Milpitas (95035) *(P-22427)*
Hoya Optical Inc (PA) .... D 209 579-7739
1400 Carpenter Ln Modesto (95351) *(P-22361)*
Hoya San Diego, San Diego *Also called Hoya Corporation (P-22360)*
Hoya Surgical Optics Inc .... E 909 680-3900
15335 Fairfield Ranch Rd # 250 Chino Hills (91709) *(P-21735)*
Hp Inc (PA) .... A 650 857-1501
1501 Page Mill Rd Palo Alto (94304) *(P-14916)*
HP Core Co Inc .... F 323 582-1688
1843 E 58th Pl Los Angeles (90001) *(P-14002)*
HP Hood LLC .... B 916 379-9266
8340 Belvedere Ave Sacramento (95826) *(P-703)*
HP Inc .... A 650 857-1501
481 Cottonwood Dr Milpitas (95035) *(P-14917)*
HP Inc .... A 650 857-4946
1501 Page Mill Rd Palo Alto (94304) *(P-14918)*
HP Inc .... D 650 857-1501
130 Lytton Ave Palo Alto (94301) *(P-14919)*
HP Inc .... E 650 857-1501
3495 Deer Creek Rd Palo Alto (94304) *(P-14920)*
HP Inc .... D 415 979-3700
303 2nd St Ste S500 San Francisco (94107) *(P-14921)*
HP Precision Inc .... E 760 752-9377
288 Navajo St San Marcos (92078) *(P-12239)*
HP Water Systems Inc .... E 559 268-4751
9338 W Whites Bridge Ave Fresno (93706) *(P-14583)*
Hpcwire, San Diego *Also called Tabor Communications Inc (P-6356)*
Hpe, San Jose *Also called Hewlett Packard Enterprise Co (P-23980)*
Hpe Enterprises LLC (HQ) .... E 650 857-5817
6280 America Center Dr San Jose (95002) *(P-23989)*
Hpe Government Llc .... D 916 435-9200
46600 Landing Pkwy Fremont (94538) *(P-15123)*
Hpf Corporation (PA) .... F 858 566-9710
9920 Prospect Ave Ste 102 Santee (92071) *(P-22626)*
Hpi Cylinders, Santa Fe Springs *Also called Hydraulic Pneumatic Inc (P-15624)*
Hpi Federal LLC (HQ) .... F 650 857-1501
1501 Page Mill Rd Palo Alto (94304) *(P-14922)*
Hpl Contract Inc .... E 209 892-1717
525 Baldwin Rd Patterson (95363) *(P-4802)*
Hpmi, Fremont *Also called Henry Plastic Molding Inc (P-9821)*
Hpv Technologies Inc .... E 949 476-7000
301 E Alton Ave Santa Ana (92707) *(P-17244)*
Hq Brands LLC .... F 213 627-7922
860 S Los Angeles St # 326 Los Angeles (90014) *(P-3556)*
Hq Machine Tech LLC .... E 714 956-3388
6900 8th St Buena Park (90620) *(P-20127)*
Hr, Lodi *Also called Holz Rubber Company Inc (P-9318)*
Hr Cloud Inc .... E 510 909-1993
222 N Pacific Coast Hwy El Segundo (90245) *(P-23990)*
Hrh Door Corp .... E 916 928-0600
830 Prosessor Ln Sacramento (95834) *(P-11958)*
Hrk Pet Food Products Inc .... F 818 897-2521
12924 Pierce St Pacoima (91331) *(P-1100)*
Hruby Orbital Systems Inc .... F 760 936-8054
3275 Corporate Vw Vista (92081) *(P-15521)*
Hse Usa Inc (PA) .... F 323 278-0888
5832 E 61st St Commerce (90040) *(P-23357)*
HSG Manufacturing Inc .... F 909 902-5915
13346 Monte Vista Ave Chino (91710) *(P-12818)*
Hsi Mechanical Inc .... E 209 408-0183
1013 N Emerald Ave Modesto (95351) *(P-12240)*
Hsiao & Montano Inc .... E 626 588-2528
809 W Santa Anita Ave San Gabriel (91776) *(P-10197)*
Hsin Tung Yang Foods Company .... F 650 589-7689
405 S Airport Blvd South San Francisco (94080) *(P-468)*
Hsssi, San Dimas *Also called Hamilton Sundstrand Spc Systms (P-21483)*
Ht Multinational Inc .... E 626 964-2686
12851 Reservoir St Apt A Chino (91710) *(P-19685)*
Ht Window Fashions Corporation (PA) .... D 626 839-8866
770 Epperson Dr City of Industry (91748) *(P-5025)*
Hte, Folsom *Also called Wireless Innovation Inc (P-19143)*

Employee Codes: A=Over 500 employees, B=251-500
C=101-250, D=51-100, E=20-50, F=10-19

2020 California
Manfacturers Register

© Mergent Inc. 1-800-342-5647

1125

ALPHABETIC

Hte Acquisition LLC....................F.......805 987-5449
4610 Calle Quetzal Camarillo (93012) **(P-16036)**
Hti Turnkey Manufacturing Svcs....................E.......408 955-0807
2200 Zanker Rd Ste A San Jose (95131) **(P-18937)**
Htl Manufacturing Div, Simi Valley *Also called Meggitt Safety Systems Inc* **(P-20175)**
Htpmi Contract Manufacturing, San Jose *Also called Hi-Tech Prcision Machining Inc* **(P-16022)**
Htr LLC....................F.......760 297-4402
30803 Hilltop View Ct Valley Center (92082) **(P-1756)**
Hts Division, Lake Elsinore *Also called Mercury Metal Die & Letter Co* **(P-13206)**
Hts-Engineering Inc....................F.......760 631-2070
4079 Oceanside Blvd Ste J Oceanside (92056) **(P-12635)**
Hua Rong International Corp....................F.......909 591-8800
14020 Cent Ave Ste 530 Chino (91710) **(P-20513)**
Huang Qi....................F.......626 442-6808
4700 Miller Dr Ste H Temple City (91780) **(P-3230)**
Hub Construction Spc Inc....................D.......909 379-2100
5310 San Fernando Rd Glendale (91203) **(P-12241)**
Hub Construction Speciality, Glendale *Also called Hub Construction Spc Inc* **(P-12241)**
Hubbel Wiring Device Kellems, Ontario *Also called Hubbell Incorporated* **(P-16903)**
Hubbell Incorporated....................E.......909 390-8002
1392 Sarah Pl Ste A Ontario (91761) **(P-16903)**
Hubbell Incorporated....................E.......559 783-0470
1829 Thunderbolt Dr Porterville (93257) **(P-16904)**
Hubbell Lighting Inc....................D.......714 386-5550
17760 Rowland St Rowland Heights (91748) **(P-17044)**
Huck International Inc....................C.......310 830-8200
900 E Watson Center Rd Carson (90745) **(P-12681)**
HUD Industries....................F.......310 327-7110
2104 W Rosecrans Ave Gardena (90249) **(P-14373)**
Hudson & Company LLC....................E.......916 774-6465
100 Irene Ave Roseville (95678) **(P-3618)**
Hudson Construction, Felton *Also called Hudson Industries Inc* **(P-23358)**
Hudson Industries Inc....................F.......831 335-4431
11107 Lake Blvd Felton (95018) **(P-23358)**
Hudson Printing Inc....................E.......760 602-1260
2780 Loker Ave W Carlsbad (92010) **(P-7087)**
Hudson Valve Co Inc....................E.......661 831-6208
5630 District Blvd # 108 Bakersfield (93313) **(P-13307)**
Hues Metal Finishing Inc....................F.......760 744-5566
977 Linda Vista Dr San Marcos (92078) **(P-13191)**
Hufcor Airwall Since 1900, Long Beach *Also called Hufcor California Inc* **(P-4981)**
Hufcor California Inc (HQ)....................D.......562 634-3116
2380 E Artesia Blvd Long Beach (90805) **(P-4981)**
Huffman Logging Co Inc....................E.......707 725-4335
1155 Huffman Dr Fortuna (95540) **(P-3887)**
Huge Usa Inc....................F.......213 741-1707
1100 S San Pedro St J02 Los Angeles (90015) **(P-2692)**
Hugfun International, City of Industry *Also called Define Toys Inc* **(P-22646)**
Hughes Bros Aircrafters Inc....................E.......323 773-4541
11010 Garfield Pl South Gate (90280) **(P-14062)**
Hughes Circuits Inc (PA)....................E.......760 744-0300
546 S Pacific St San Marcos (92078) **(P-17895)**
Hughes Circuits Inc....................C.......760 744-0300
540 S Pacific St San Marcos (92078) **(P-17896)**
Hughes Network Systems LLC....................E.......858 455-9550
9605 Scranton Rd Ste 500 San Diego (92121) **(P-17538)**
Hughes Price & Sharp Inc....................E.......865 675-6278
5200 Lankershim Blvd # 850 North Hollywood (91601) **(P-5668)**
Hughson Nut Inc (HQ)....................D.......209 883-0403
1825 Verduga Rd Hughson (95326) **(P-1427)**
Hugin Components Inc....................F.......916 652-1070
4231 Pacific St Ste 23 Rocklin (95677) **(P-12819)**
Hugo Boss Usa Inc....................C.......310 260-0109
395 Santa Monica Pl # 162 Santa Monica (90401) **(P-2965)**
Hugo Engineering Co Inc....................F.......310 320-0288
837 Van Ness Ave Torrance (90501) **(P-20128)**
Huhtamaki Inc....................F.......916 688-4938
8450 Gerber Rd Sacramento (95828) **(P-5297)**
Huhtamaki Inc....................B.......323 269-0151
4209 Noakes St Commerce (90023) **(P-9551)**
Human Designs Pros/Ortho Lab, Long Beach *Also called Ferraco Inc* **(P-22012)**
Humanconcepts LLC....................E.......650 581-2500
3 Harbor Dr Ste 200 Sausalito (94965) **(P-23991)**
Humangear Inc....................F.......415 580-7553
636 Shrader St San Francisco (94117) **(P-9831)**
Humberto Murillo Inc....................E.......714 541-2628
410 Nantucket Pl Santa Ana (92703) **(P-13026)**
Humboldt Newspaper Inc....................A.......707 442-1711
930 6th St Eureka (95501) **(P-5669)**
Humidtech Inc....................F.......805 541-9500
1241 Johnson Ave Ste 345 San Luis Obispo (93401) **(P-22529)**
Huneeus Vintners LLC (PA)....................E.......707 286-2724
1040 Main St Ste 204 NAPA (94559) **(P-1757)**
Hung Tung....................F.......408 496-1818
3672 Bassett St Santa Clara (95054) **(P-16037)**
Hunkins Enterprises, El Segundo *Also called James Hunkins* **(P-19967)**
Hunnington Dialysis Center, Pasadena *Also called Hemodialysis Inc* **(P-21733)**
Hunt Enterprises, Santa Ana *Also called Dan R Hunt Inc* **(P-15877)**
Huntco Industries LLC....................F.......818 700-1600
22536 La Quilla Dr Chatsworth (91311) **(P-23359)**
Hunter Digital Ltd....................F.......310 471-5852
11999 San Vicente Blvd Los Angeles (90049) **(P-15239)**
Hunter Douglas Fabrications....................B.......408 435-8844
842 Charcot Ave San Jose (95131) **(P-5026)**
Hunter Industries Incorporated (PA)....................B.......760 744-5240
1940 Diamond St San Marcos (92078) **(P-9468)**
Hunter Technology Corporation (HQ)....................C.......408 957-1300
1940 Milmont Dr Milpitas (95035) **(P-18938)**
Hunter/Gratzner Industries....................F.......310 578-9929
4107 Redwood Ave Los Angeles (90066) **(P-23360)**
Huntford Printing....................E.......408 957-5000
275 Dempsey Rd Milpitas (95035) **(P-6619)**
Huntford Printing & Graphics, Milpitas *Also called Huntford Printing* **(P-6619)**
Hunting Energy Services Inc....................D.......661 633-4272
4900 California Ave 100a Bakersfield (93309) **(P-210)**
Hunting-Vinson, Bakersfield *Also called Hunting Energy Services Inc* **(P-210)**
Huntington Beach Machining, Huntington Beach *Also called Madsen Products Incorporated* **(P-16167)**
Huntington Company, North Hollywood *Also called John A Thomson PHD* **(P-7673)**
Huntington Mechanical Labs, Grass Valley *Also called Huntington Mechanical Labs Inc* **(P-14632)**
Huntington Mechanical Labs Inc....................E.......530 273-9533
13355 Nevada City Ave Grass Valley (95945) **(P-14632)**
Huntmix Inc....................C.......818 548-5200
500 N Brand Blvd Ste 500 Glendale (91203) **(P-9095)**
Huntsman Advanced Materials AM....................C.......818 265-7221
5121 W San Fernando Rd Los Angeles (90039) **(P-7567)**
Hupa International Inc....................E.......909 598-9876
21717 Ferrero Walnut (91789) **(P-22823)**
Hupalo Repasky Pipe Organs LLC....................F.......510 483-6905
2450 Alvarado St San Leandro (94577) **(P-22627)**
Hupp Signs & Lighting Inc....................E.......530 345-7078
70 Loren Ave Chico (95928) **(P-23129)**
Hurley International LLC....................F.......323 728-1821
100 Citadel Dr Ste 433 Commerce (90040) **(P-3089)**
Hurley International LLC....................C.......707 446-6300
321 Nut Tree Rd Vacaville (95687) **(P-3090)**
Hurley International LLC (HQ)....................C.......949 548-9375
1945g Placentia Ave Costa Mesa (92627) **(P-3091)**
Hurleys LP....................D.......707 944-2345
1516 King Ave NAPA (94559) **(P-5065)**
Hurleys Restaurant & Bar, NAPA *Also called Hurleys LP* **(P-5065)**
Hurst International, Chatsworth *Also called Labeling Hurst Systems LLC* **(P-7114)**
Husch Vineyards Inc (PA)....................E.......707 895-3216
4400 Highway 128 Philo (95466) **(P-1758)**
Husk-ITT Distributors Corp....................F.......951 340-4000
1580 Industrial Ave Norco (92860) **(P-9145)**
Huskey Specialty Lubricants, Norco *Also called Husk-ITT Distributors Corp* **(P-9145)**
Husks Unlimited (PA)....................E.......619 476-8301
1616 Silvas St Chula Vista (91911) **(P-914)**
Husky Injection Molding....................F.......714 545-8200
3505 Cadillac Ave Ste N4 Costa Mesa (92626) **(P-9832)**
Hussmann Corporation....................B.......909 590-4910
13770 Ramona Ave Chino (91710) **(P-15434)**
Hutchinson Arospc & Indust Inc....................C.......818 843-1000
4510 W Vanowen St Burbank (91505) **(P-20129)**
Hutchinson Arospc & Indust Inc....................C.......818 843-1000
4510 W Vanowen St Burbank (91505) **(P-9320)**
Hutchinson Seal Corporation (HQ)....................B.......248 375-4190
11634 Patton Rd Downey (90241) **(P-9236)**
Huy Fong Foods Inc....................E.......626 286-8328
4800 Azusa Canyon Rd Irwindale (91706) **(P-776)**
Hv Industries Inc....................F.......651 233-5676
13688 Newhope St Garden Grove (92843) **(P-3976)**
Hvi Cat Canyon Inc....................C.......805 621-5800
2617 E Clark Ave Santa Maria (93455) **(P-211)**
Hw Holdco LLC....................E.......714 540-8500
555 Anton Blvd Ste 950 Costa Mesa (92626) **(P-5957)**
Hwa In America Inc (PA)....................F.......619 567-4539
1541 Santiago Ridge Way San Diego (92154) **(P-18939)**
Hwe Mechanical, Bakersfield *Also called Hills Wldg & Engrg Contr Inc* **(P-207)**
HWF Construction Inc....................F.......661 587-3590
3685 Fruitvale Ave Bakersfield (93308) **(P-5958)**
Hy Jo Mfg Imports Corp....................E.......619 671-1018
7615 Siempre Viva Rd B San Diego (92154) **(P-13523)**
Hy-Tech Plating Inc....................E.......650 593-4566
1011 American St San Carlos (94070) **(P-13027)**
Hyatt Die Cast Engrg Corp - S....................E.......714 622-2131
12250 Industry St Garden Grove (92841) **(P-11337)**
Hyatt Die Cast Engrg Corp - S....................E.......408 523-7000
1250 Kifer Rd Sunnyvale (94086) **(P-11338)**
Hyatt Die Casting, Sunnyvale *Also called Hyatt Die Cast Engrg Corp - S* **(P-11338)**
Hybrid Kinetic Motors Corp....................F.......626 683-7330
800 E Colo Blvd Ste 880 Pasadena (91101) **(P-19479)**
Hybrinetics Inc....................D.......707 585-0333
225 Sutton Pl Santa Rosa (95407) **(P-16557)**
Hycor Biomedical LLC....................C.......714 933-3000
7272 Chapman Ave Ste A Garden Grove (92841) **(P-21736)**
Hyde, Vernon *Also called Streets Ahead Inc* **(P-3533)**
Hyde Printing and Graphics....................F.......925 686-4933
2748 Willow Pass Rd Concord (94519) **(P-6620)**
Hydra-Electric Company (PA)....................C.......818 843-6211
3151 N Kenwood St Burbank (91505) **(P-16600)**
Hydrabrush Inc....................F.......760 743-5160
701 S Andreasen Dr Ste C Escondido (92029) **(P-8513)**
Hydraforce Incorporated....................F.......951 689-3987
7383 Orangewood Dr Riverside (92504) **(P-14584)**
Hydralift, San Clemente *Also called Innovative Rv Technologies* **(P-212)**
Hydranautics (HQ)....................B.......760 901-2597
401 Jones Rd Oceanside (92058) **(P-8975)**
Hydrapak Inc....................E.......510 632-8318
6605 San Leandro St Oakland (94621) **(P-22824)**
Hydraulic Pneumatic Inc....................F.......562 926-1122
13766 Milroy Pl Santa Fe Springs (90670) **(P-15624)**
Hydraulic Shop Inc....................E.......909 875-9336
2753 S Vista Ave Bloomington (92316) **(P-13875)**

Hydraulic Technology Inc .... F 916 645-3317
3833 Cincinnati Ave Rocklin (95765) *(P-14585)*
Hydraulics International Inc (PA) .... B 818 998-1231
9201 Independence Ave Chatsworth (91311) *(P-20130)*
Hydraulics International Inc .... D 818 998-1236
9000 Mason Ave Chatsworth (91311) *(P-20131)*
Hydril Company .... B 661 588-9332
3237 Patton Way Bakersfield (93308) *(P-13780)*
Hydril USA Distribution LLC .... F 661 588-9332
3237 Patton Way Bakersfield (93308) *(P-13781)*
Hydrite Chemical Co .... E 559 651-3450
1603 Clancy Ct Visalia (93291) *(P-8976)*
Hydro Components and Tech, Vista *Also called Hydrocomponents & Tech Inc (P-15522)*
Hydro Conduit of Texas LP .... F 909 825-1500
1205 S Rancho Ave Colton (92324) *(P-10587)*
Hydro Extruder LLC .... B 626 964-3411
18111 Railroad St City of Industry (91748) *(P-11233)*
Hydro Fitting Mfg Corp .... E 626 967-5151
733 E Edna Pl Covina (91723) *(P-13357)*
Hydro Flow Filtration Sys LLC .... F 951 296-0904
42074 Remington Ave Temecula (92590) *(P-22965)*
Hydro Quip, Corona *Also called Blue Desert International Inc (P-15493)*
Hydro Systems Inc (PA) .... D 661 775-0686
29132 Avenue Paine Valencia (91355) *(P-11647)*
Hydro-Aire Inc (HQ) .... E 818 526-2600
3000 Winona Ave Burbank (91504) *(P-20132)*
Hydro-Logic Purification .... F 888 426-5644
370 Encinal St Ste 150 Santa Cruz (95060) *(P-14826)*
Hydrochempsc, Bakersfield *Also called PSC Industrial Outsourcing LP (P-252)*
Hydrocomponents & Tech Inc .... F 760 598-0189
1175 Park Center Dr Ste H Vista (92081) *(P-15522)*
Hydrofarm LLC (PA) .... E 707 765-9990
2249 S Mcdowell Blvd Ext Petaluma (94954) *(P-17133)*
Hydroform USA Incorporated .... C 310 632-6353
2848 E 208th St Carson (90810) *(P-20133)*
Hydrokleen Systems, Porterville *Also called Horizon International Ltd (P-15520)*
Hydrolynx Systems Inc .... F 916 374-1800
950 Riverside Pkwy Ste 10 West Sacramento (95605) *(P-21241)*
Hydromach Inc .... E 818 341-0915
20400 Prairie St Chatsworth (91311) *(P-20476)*
Hydropoint Data Systems Inc .... E 707 769-9696
1720 Corporate Cir Petaluma (94954) *(P-13635)*
Hygeia II Medical Group Inc .... E 714 515-7571
6241 Yarrow Dr Ste A Carlsbad (92011) *(P-22262)*
Hygenia, Camarillo *Also called Medical Packaging Corporation (P-22045)*
Hyghte Holdings, Carlsbad *Also called Astura Medical (P-21612)*
Hygieia Biological Labs (PA) .... E 530 661-1442
1785 E Main St Ste 4 Woodland (95776) *(P-8310)*
Hygiena LLC (PA) .... C 805 388-2383
941 Avenida Acaso Camarillo (93012) *(P-8228)*
Hyland Homeopathic, Gardena *Also called Standard Homeopathic Co (P-8143)*
Hyland's Homeopathic, Los Angeles *Also called Standard Homeopathic Co (P-8142)*
Hylete Inc .... E 858 225-8998
564 Stevens Ave Solana Beach (92075) *(P-3092)*
Hyperbaric Technologies Inc .... D 619 336-2022
3224 Hoover Ave National City (91950) *(P-22263)*
Hyperion Books For Children, Burbank *Also called Disney Book Group LLC (P-6098)*
Hyponex Corporation .... E 909 597-2811
15978 El Prado Rd Chino (91708) *(P-8794)*
Hyponex Corporation .... E 209 887-3845
23390 E Flood Rd Linden (95236) *(P-8795)*
Hypress Technologies Inc .... F 805 485-4060
340 Hearst Dr Oxnard (93030) *(P-13978)*
Hyspan Precision Products Inc (PA) .... D 619 421-1355
1685 Brandywine Ave Chula Vista (91911) *(P-14784)*
Hyspan Precision Products Inc .... D 619 421-1355
1683 Brandywine Ave Chula Vista (91911) *(P-13524)*
Hysterical Software Inc .... F 415 793-5785
2874 Hillside Dr Burlingame (94010) *(P-23992)*
Hytech Processing, Inglewood *Also called C C M D Inc (P-12956)*
Hytek R&D Inc (PA) .... E 408 761-5271
2044 Corporate Ct Milpitas (95035) *(P-17897)*
Hytron Mfg Co Inc .... E 714 903-6701
15582 Chemical Ln Huntington Beach (92649) *(P-16038)*
Hytrust Inc (PA) .... E 650 681-8100
1975 W El Camino Real # 203 Mountain View (94040) *(P-23993)*
Hyundai Translead (HQ) .... D 619 574-1500
8880 Rio San Diego Dr # 600 San Diego (92108) *(P-12021)*
Hyx Tech Corp .... F 951 907-3386
13620 Benson Ave Ste B Chino (91710) *(P-7088)*
I & A Inc .... E 408 432-8340
2221 Ringwood Ave San Jose (95131) *(P-12242)*
I & E Lath Mill Inc .... E 707 895-3380
8701 School Rd Philo (95466) *(P-3936)*
I & I Deburring Inc .... F 562 802-0058
14504 Carmenita Rd Ste A Norwalk (90650) *(P-13924)*
I & I Sports Supply Company (PA) .... E 310 715-6800
19751 Figueroa St Carson (90745) *(P-22825)*
I Amira Grand Foods Inc (PA) .... F 949 852-4468
1 Park Plz Ste 600 Irvine (92614) *(P-1045)*
I and E Cabinets Inc .... E 818 933-6480
14660 Raymer St Van Nuys (91405) *(P-4207)*
I B E, Sun Valley *Also called Industrial Battery Engrg Inc (P-19168)*
I B P Service Center, Brea *Also called Tyson Fresh Meats Inc (P-427)*
I C C, Fullerton *Also called Interntnal Cnnctors Cable Corp (P-17381)*
I Color Printing & Mailing Inc .... F 310 947-1452
1450 W 228th St Ste 12 Torrance (90501) *(P-6621)*
I Color Printing & Mailing Inc (PA) .... F 310 997-1452
13000 S Broadway Los Angeles (90061) *(P-6622)*
I D T, San Jose *Also called Integrated Device Tech Inc (P-18302)*
I D T, Pasadena *Also called Integrated Design Tools Inc (P-22430)*
I DES Inc .... E 707 374-7500
864 Saint Francis Way Rio Vista (94571) *(P-20885)*
I E P Full Service Printing .... F 415 648-6002
1501 Cortland Ave San Francisco (94110) *(P-7089)*
I E S, Corona *Also called Industrial Eqp Solutions Inc (P-14828)*
I I S Mechanics, San Diego *Also called Port 80 Software Inc (P-24307)*
I J Research Inc .... E 714 546-8522
2919 Tech Ctr Santa Ana (92705) *(P-18940)*
I Joah (PA) .... F 213 742-0500
1721 Wall St Los Angeles (90015) *(P-3339)*
I M B Electronic Products .... D 714 523-2110
1800 E Via Burton Anaheim (92806) *(P-18678)*
I O Interconnect Ltd (PA) .... E 714 564-1111
1202 E Wakeham Ave Santa Ana (92705) *(P-18773)*
I P, Chatsworth *Also called International Precision Inc (P-16053)*
I P C W, Commerce *Also called In Pro Car Wear Inc (P-17135)*
I P E, Norco *Also called Industrial Process Eqp Inc (P-14766)*
I R, El Segundo *Also called Infineon Tech Americas Corp (P-18282)*
I S G, Three Rivers *Also called Innovative Structural GL Inc (P-10366)*
I S G, Inyokern *Also called Intelligence Support Group Ltd (P-19326)*
I S I, Camarillo *Also called Interconnect Systems Inc (P-18313)*
I S T, Santa Clara *Also called Information Scan Tech Inc (P-21051)*
I Source Technical Svcs Inc .... F 949 453-1500
575 Rancho Cir Irvine (92618) *(P-18941)*
I Source Technical Svcs Inc (PA) .... F 949 453-1500
5 Rancho Cir Lake Forest (92630) *(P-18942)*
I T C, Buellton *Also called Infraredvision Technology Corp (P-20888)*
I T I Electro-Optic Corp (PA) .... E 310 445-8900
11500 W Olympic Blvd Los Angeles (90064) *(P-20886)*
I T I Electro-Optic Corp .... E 310 312-4526
1500 E Olympic Blvd # 400 Los Angeles (90021) *(P-20887)*
I T M Software Corp .... E 650 864-2500
1030 W Maude Ave Sunnyvale (94085) *(P-23994)*
I Transplant Enterprise Tech, Santa Monica *Also called Transplant Connect Inc (P-24524)*
I V C, Irvine *Also called International Vitamin Corp (P-7958)*
I V P, Canoga Park *Also called Interntnal Virtual PDT MGT Inc (P-17382)*
I-Coat Company LLC .... E 562 941-9989
12020 Mora Dr Ste 2 Santa Fe Springs (90670) *(P-21361)*
I-Flow LLC .... A 800 448-3569
43 Discovery Ste 100 Irvine (92618) *(P-21737)*
I-Tech Company Ltd Lblty Co .... F 510 226-9226
42978 Osgood Rd Fremont (94539) *(P-15045)*
I. C. O., Gualala *Also called Independent Coast Observer (P-5670)*
I.C.O.N. Salon, Woodland Hills *Also called ICON Line Inc (P-23361)*
I.E. Distribution, Huntington Beach *Also called Seven Wells LLC (P-4531)*
I.V. League Medical, Camarillo *Also called Western Mfg & Distrg LLC (P-20436)*
I/O Controls Corporation (PA) .... D 626 812-5353
1357 W Foothill Blvd Azusa (91702) *(P-16721)*
I/O Interconnect, Santa Ana *Also called I O Interconnect Ltd (P-18773)*
I/O Select Inc .... F 858 537-2060
9835 Carroll Centre Rd # 100 San Diego (92126) *(P-21487)*
I/Omagic Corporation (PA) .... E 949 707-4800
20512 Crescent Bay Dr Lake Forest (92630) *(P-15046)*
I2a Technologies Inc .... E 510 770-0322
3399 W Warren Ave Fremont (94538) *(P-18274)*
I3 Nanotec LLC .... F 510 594-2299
5040 Commercial Cir Ste A Concord (94520) *(P-14476)*
IAC Industries .... E 714 990-8997
3010 Saturn St Ste 205 Brea (92821) *(P-5066)*
Iac/Interactivecorp .... F 212 314-7300
8800 W Sunset Blvd West Hollywood (90069) *(P-23995)*
IaMplus LLC .... D 323 210-3852
809 N Cahuenga Blvd Los Angeles (90038) *(P-16788)*
Iar Systems Software Inc (HQ) .... F 650 287-4250
1065 E Hillsdale Blvd # 420 Foster City (94404) *(P-23996)*
Ibg Holdings Inc .... E 661 702-8680
24841 Avenue Tibbitts Valencia (91355) *(P-8514)*
Ibisworld Inc .... E 212 626-6794
11755 Wilshire Blvd # 1100 Los Angeles (90025) *(P-6254)*
IBM, Los Angeles *Also called International Bus Mchs Corp (P-14926)*
IC Ink Image Co Inc .... E 209 931-3040
4627 E Fremont St Stockton (95215) *(P-7090)*
Ic Sensors Inc .... D 510 498-1570
45738 Northport Loop W Fremont (94538) *(P-18275)*
Icad Inc .... D 408 419-2300
345 Potrero Ave Sunnyvale (94085) *(P-9264)*
Ice Link LLC .... F 714 771-6580
954 N Batavia St Orange (92867) *(P-14374)*
Ice Man Inc .... F 562 633-4423
8710 Park St Bellflower (90706) *(P-2357)*
Icebreaker Health Inc .... F 415 926-5818
150 Spear St Ste 350 San Francisco (94105) *(P-23997)*
ICEE Company (HQ) .... D 800 426-4233
1205 S Dupont Ave Ontario (91761) *(P-962)*
ICEE Company .... E 909 974-3518
4250 E Lowell St Ontario (91761) *(P-963)*
ICEE Company .... F 925 828-5807
6800 Sierra Ct Ste M Dublin (94568) *(P-2216)*
Ichia Usa Inc .... C 619 482-2222
509 Telegraph Canyon Rd Chula Vista (91910) *(P-18276)*
Ichor Systems Inc .... C 510 476-8000
34585 7th St Union City (94587) *(P-9833)*
Ichor Systems Inc (HQ) .... E 510 897-5200
3185 Laurelview Ct Fremont (94538) *(P-18277)*

ALPHABETIC

Employee Codes: A=Over 500 employees, B=251-500
C=101-250, D=51-100, E=20-50, F=10-19
2020 California
Manfacturers Register
© Mergent Inc. 1-800-342-5647
1127

ICI Architectural Millwork Inc.....F.....323 759-4993
6820 Brynhurst Ave Los Angeles (90043) *(P-4058)*
ICI Paints Store, Costa Mesa *Also called Akzo Nobel Inc (P-8709)*
ICI Paints Store, Escondido *Also called Akzo Nobel Inc (P-8710)*
Iclavis LLC.....F.....310 503-6847
8222 Allport Ave Santa Fe Springs (90670) *(P-6623)*
ICM Installations Inc.....F.....714 751-4026
1180 N Ftn Way Unit B Anaheim (92806) *(P-13525)*
Icolorprinting.net, Los Angeles *Also called I Color Printing & Mailing Inc (P-6622)*
Icon Aircraft Inc (PA).....D.....707 564-4000
2141 Icon Way Vacaville (95688) *(P-20134)*
Icon Apparel Group LLC.....E.....916 372-4266
2989 Promenade St Ste 100 West Sacramento (95691) *(P-2745)*
ICON Line Inc.....F.....818 709-4266
20600 Ventura Blvd Ste C Woodland Hills (91364) *(P-23361)*
Icon Screen Printing, Orange *Also called Icon Screening Inc (P-7091)*
Icon Screening Inc.....F.....714 630-4266
1108 W Grove Ave Orange (92865) *(P-7091)*
Iconn Inc.....E.....949 297-8448
8909 Irvine Center Dr Irvine (92618) *(P-18774)*
Iconn Technologies, Irvine *Also called Iconn Inc (P-18774)*
Icore International Inc.....C.....707 535-2700
3780 Flightline Dr Santa Rosa (95403) *(P-9834)*
ICP West, Buena Park *Also called Interntional Color Posters Inc (P-7101)*
Icpu, Santa Ana *Also called Industrial Cpu Systems Intl (P-14923)*
Icsh Parent Inc.....D.....323 724-8507
1540 S Greenwood Ave Montebello (90640) *(P-5298)*
Icsn Inc.....F.....951 687-2305
521 Princeland Ct Corona (92879) *(P-11339)*
Icu Medical Inc (PA).....B.....949 366-2183
951 Calle Amanecer San Clemente (92673) *(P-21738)*
Icu Medical Sales Inc (HQ).....F.....949 366-2183
951 Calle Amanecer San Clemente (92673) *(P-21739)*
Icy Dock USA, Arcadia *Also called Cremax U S A Corporation (P-11582)*
ID Supply.....F.....714 728-6478
15182 Triton Ln Ste 101 Huntington Beach (92649) *(P-7092)*
IDB Holdings Inc (HQ).....F.....909 390-5624
601 S Rockefeller Ave Ontario (91761) *(P-556)*
Iddea California LLC.....F.....714 257-7389
589 Apollo St Brea (92821) *(P-19686)*
Idea, Brea *Also called Instrument Design Eng Assoc I (P-18946)*
Idea Printing & Graphics Inc.....F.....559 733-4149
1921 E Main St Visalia (93292) *(P-6624)*
Idea Tooling & Engineering Inc.....D.....310 608-7488
13915 S Main St Los Angeles (90061) *(P-14063)*
Ideal Envmtl Pdts & Svcs, Gilroy *Also called Containment Consultants Inc (P-12010)*
Ideal Fasteners Inc.....E.....714 630-7840
3850 E Miraloma Ave Anaheim (92806) *(P-12682)*
Ideal Graphics Inc.....F.....714 632-3398
1458 N Hundley St Anaheim (92806) *(P-6625)*
Ideal Pallet System Inc.....F.....714 847-9657
7422 Cedar Dr Huntington Beach (92647) *(P-4371)*
Ideal Print Solutions, Oceanside *Also called Solution Box Inc (P-6964)*
Ideal Printing Co Inc.....E.....626 964-2019
17855 Maclaren St City of Industry (91744) *(P-6626)*
Ideal Products Inc.....E.....951 727-8600
4501 Etiwanda Ave Jurupa Valley (91752) *(P-4911)*
Ideas In Motion.....F.....760 635-1181
1435 Eolus Ave Encinitas (92024) *(P-22428)*
Ideaya Biosciences Inc.....D.....650 443-6209
7000 Shoreline Ct Ste 350 South San Francisco (94080) *(P-7938)*
Idemia America Corp.....C.....310 884-7900
3150 E Ana St Compton (90221) *(P-9835)*
Identiv Inc (PA).....B.....949 250-8888
2201 Walnut Ave Ste 100 Fremont (94538) *(P-15240)*
Ideon, Buena Park *Also called Exemplis LLC (P-4837)*
Idex Health & Science LLC (HQ).....D.....707 588-2000
600 Park Ct Rohnert Park (94928) *(P-20762)*
Idex Health & Science LLC.....C.....760 438-2131
2051 Palomar Airpt Rd # 200 Carlsbad (92011) *(P-21362)*
Idg, El Cajon *Also called Inflatable Design Group Inc (P-23134)*
Idg Consumer & Smb Inc (HQ).....C.....415 243-0500
501 2nd St San Francisco (94107) *(P-5959)*
Idg Games Media Group Inc.....E.....510 768-2700
555 12th St Oakland (94607) *(P-5960)*
IDM, Santa Ana *Also called International Disc Mfr Inc (P-17329)*
IDO Cabinet Inc.....F.....415 282-1683
1551 Minnesota St San Francisco (94107) *(P-4208)*
Idrive Inc.....F.....805 308-6094
249 N Turnpike Rd Santa Barbara (93111) *(P-19687)*
Idx Corporation.....C.....408 270-8094
5655 Silver Creek Vly Rd San Jose (95138) *(P-4982)*
Idx Los Angeles LLC.....C.....909 212-8333
5005 E Philadelphia St Ontario (91761) *(P-4059)*
Ied Group, Santa Ana *Also called International Electronic Desig (P-18952)*
Iee, Van Nuys *Also called Industrial Electronic Engineer (P-15245)*
Ieee Computer Society, Los Alamitos *Also called Institute of Electrical and El (P-6956)*
If Copack LLC.....E.....559 875-3354
1912 Industrial Way Sanger (93657) *(P-729)*
Ifco Systems North America Inc.....E.....909 356-0697
14750 Miller Ave Fontana (92336) *(P-4372)*
Ifco Systems Us LLC.....E.....909 484-4332
8950 Rochester Ave # 150 Rancho Cucamonga (91730) *(P-4373)*
Ifiber Optix Inc.....E.....714 665-9796
14450 Chambers Rd Tustin (92780) *(P-10311)*
Ifwe Inc (HQ).....D.....415 946-1850
848 Battery St San Francisco (94111) *(P-23998)*

Igenica Inc.....E.....650 231-4320
863 Mitten Rd Ste 102 Burlingame (94010) *(P-7939)*
Igi, Sierra Madre *Also called Greg Ian Islands Inc (P-4905)*
Igm Biosciences Inc.....D.....650 965-7873
325 E Middlefield Rd Mountain View (94043) *(P-7940)*
Ignatius Press, San Francisco *Also called Guadalupe Associates Inc (P-6248)*
Ignyta Inc (PA).....D.....858 255-5959
1 Dna Way South San Francisco (94080) *(P-7941)*
Igo Inc (PA).....F.....888 205-0093
6001 Oak Cyn Irvine (92618) *(P-17539)*
Igolping Inc.....F.....866 507-4440
43583 Greenhills Way Fremont (94539) *(P-22826)*
Igrad Inc.....E.....858 705-2917
2163 Newcastle Ave # 100 Cardiff By The Sea (92007) *(P-23999)*
Igraphics (PA).....E.....530 273-2200
165 Spring Hill Dr Grass Valley (95945) *(P-7093)*
Igraphix, San Francisco *Also called H2 Cards Inc (P-7085)*
Igraphix, San Francisco *Also called Designer Printing Inc (P-6536)*
Igs Inc.....F.....408 733-4621
916 E California Ave Sunnyvale (94085) *(P-10270)*
Ii-VI Optical Systems Inc.....D.....714 247-7100
14192 Chambers Rd Tustin (92780) *(P-21363)*
Ijk & Co Inc.....E.....415 826-8899
225 Industrial St San Francisco (94124) *(P-19322)*
Ijot Development Inc.....A.....925 258-9909
11360b Pleasant Valley Rd Penn Valley (95946) *(P-4861)*
Ikanos Communications Inc (HQ).....C.....858 587-1121
5775 Morehouse Dr San Diego (92121) *(P-18278)*
Ikegami Mold Corp America.....F.....619 858-6855
3570 Camino Del Rio N # 106 San Diego (92108) *(P-9836)*
Ikhana Aircraft Services, Murrieta *Also called Ikhana Group Inc (P-20135)*
Ikhana Group Inc.....C.....951 600-0009
37260 Sky Canyon Dr # 20 Murrieta (92563) *(P-20135)*
Ikong E-Commerce Inc.....F.....888 556-1522
385 S Lemon Ave Ste E429 Walnut (91789) *(P-14326)*
IL Canto, Santa Fe Springs *Also called Lanshon Inc (P-2967)*
IL Fiorello Olive Oil Co.....E.....707 864-1529
2625 Mankas Corner Rd Fairfield (94534) *(P-1473)*
IL Helth Buty Natural Oils Inc.....E.....805 384-0473
322 N Aviador St Camarillo (93010) *(P-8977)*
IL Pastaio Foods Inc.....F.....408 753-9220
1266 E Julian St San Jose (95116) *(P-2482)*
IL Pastaio Fresh Pasta Company, San Jose *Also called IL Pastaio Foods Inc (P-2482)*
Ilco Industries Inc.....E.....310 631-8655
1308 W Mahalo Pl Compton (90220) *(P-13472)*
Illah Sports Inc A Corporation.....E.....805 240-7790
1610 Fiske Pl Oxnard (93033) *(P-22827)*
Illinois Tool Works Inc.....E.....805 499-0335
1260 Calle Suerte Camarillo (93012) *(P-18279)*
Illinois Tool Works Inc.....C.....847 724-7500
1050 W 5th St Azusa (91702) *(P-9146)*
Illinois Tool Works Inc.....D.....800 762-7600
3200 Lakeville Hwy Petaluma (94954) *(P-15523)*
Illinois Tool Works Inc.....D.....916 939-4332
5000 Hillsdale Cir El Dorado Hills (95762) *(P-18280)*
Illumina Inc.....E.....800 809-4566
9885 Towne Centre Dr San Diego (92121) *(P-21242)*
Illumina Inc (PA).....B.....858 202-4500
5200 Illumina Way San Diego (92122) *(P-21243)*
Illumina Inc.....E.....510 670-9300
200 Lincoln Centre Dr Foster City (94404) *(P-21244)*
Illuminate Education Inc (PA).....D.....949 656-3133
6531 Irvine Center Dr # 100 Irvine (92618) *(P-24000)*
Illuminated Creations Inc.....E.....916 924-1936
1111 Joellis Way Sacramento (95815) *(P-23130)*
Ilona Draperies Inc.....E.....818 840-8811
19617 Bruces Pl Canyon Country (91351) *(P-3589)*
Ilos Corp.....F.....213 255-2060
1300 John Reed Ct Ste B City of Industry (91745) *(P-17134)*
Ilovetocreate A Duncan Entps, Fresno *Also called Duncan Enterprises (P-8641)*
Image Apparel For Business Inc.....E.....714 541-5247
1618 E Edinger Ave Santa Ana (92705) *(P-3037)*
Image Distribution Services.....F.....909 599-7680
3191 W Temple Ave Ste 180 Pomona (91768) *(P-6627)*
Image Distribution Services (PA).....E.....949 754-9000
60 Bunsen Irvine (92618) *(P-6628)*
Image Magazine Inc.....E.....949 608-5188
5001 Birch St Newport Beach (92660) *(P-5961)*
Image Micro Spare Parts Inc.....F.....562 776-9808
6301 Chalet Dr Commerce (90040) *(P-16656)*
Image Printing Solutions, Irvine *Also called Image Distribution Services (P-6628)*
Image Solutions Apparel Inc.....E.....310 464-8991
19571 Magellan Dr Torrance (90502) *(P-3038)*
Image Square Inc.....F.....310 586-2333
1627 Stanford St Santa Monica (90404) *(P-5109)*
Image Square Copy & Print, Santa Monica *Also called Image Square Inc (P-5109)*
Image Star LLC.....F.....415 883-5815
42 Digital Dr Ste 10 Novato (94949) *(P-3093)*
Image Technology, Palo Alto *Also called Suss McRtec Prcision Photomask (P-22460)*
Imagemover Inc.....F.....818 485-8840
10051 Bradley Ave Pacoima (91331) *(P-6629)*
Imagerlabs Inc.....F.....949 310-9560
1995 S Myrtle Ave Monrovia (91016) *(P-18281)*
Imageware Systems Inc (PA).....D.....858 673-8600
13500 Evening Creek Dr N # 550 San Diego (92128) *(P-24001)*
Imagex Inc.....F.....925 474-8100
5990 Stoneridge Dr # 112 Pleasanton (94588) *(P-6630)*
Imagictech, Victorville *Also called Exportech Worldwide LLC (P-14910)*

Mergent e-mail: customerrelations@mergent.com
1128
2020 California
Manufacturers Register
(P-0000) Products & Services Section entry number
(PA)=Parent Co (HQ)=Headquarters (DH)=Div Headquarters

Imaginary Fiber Glass Inc F 909 597-4110
15740 El Prado Rd Chino (91710) ***(P-2728)***
Imagine Communications Corp F 760 936-4000
1493 Poinsettia Ave # 143 Vista (92081) ***(P-17540)***
Imagine That Inc F 408 365-0305
6830 Via Del Oro Ste 230 San Jose (95119) ***(P-24002)***
Imagine That Unlimited F 858 566-8868
13100 Kirkham Way Ste 211 Poway (92064) ***(P-23131)***
Imagine This, Irvine *Also called Shye West Inc* ***(P-23195)***
Imaginery Fiberglass, Chino *Also called Imaginary Fiber Glass Inc* ***(P-2728)***
Imaging Technologies F 858 487-8944
15175 Innovation Dr San Diego (92128) ***(P-15241)***
Imatte Inc F 818 993-8007
20945 Plummer St Chatsworth (91311) ***(P-17245)***
IMC Networks Corp (PA) E 949 465-3000
25531 Commercentre Dr Lake Forest (92630) ***(P-15124)***
Imco, Sacramento *Also called Geo Drilling Fluids Inc* ***(P-10971)***
Imcsd, San Diego *Also called Integrated Microwave Corp* ***(P-18947)***
Imdex Technology Usa LLC E 805 540-2017
3474 Empresa Dr Ste 150 San Luis Obispo (93401) ***(P-21488)***
Imergy Power Systems Inc E 510 668-1485
3945 Freedom Cir Ste 560 Santa Clara (95054) ***(P-18943)***
Imerys Clays Inc F 805 737-2445
2500 Miguelito Rd Lompoc (93436) ***(P-376)***
Imerys Filtration Minerals, Lompoc *Also called Imerys Minerals California Inc* ***(P-382)***
Imerys Filtration Minerals Inc (HQ) E 805 562-0200
1732 N 1st St Ste 450 San Jose (95112) ***(P-390)***
Imerys Minerals California Inc B 805 736-1221
2500 Miguelito Canyon Rd Lompoc (93436) ***(P-382)***
Imerys Minerals California Inc (HQ) D 805 736-1221
2500 San Miguelito Rd Lompoc (93436) ***(P-391)***
Imerys Perlite Usa Inc F 760 745-5900
1450 Simpson Way Escondido (92029) ***(P-14827)***
Imesa, San Diego *Also called Leon Assembly Solutions Inc* ***(P-10478)***
IMG Companies LLC C 925 273-1100
225 Mountain Vista Pkwy Livermore (94551) ***(P-16039)***
IMI CCI, Rcho STA Marg *Also called Control Components Inc* ***(P-13300)***
Immco, El Monte *Also called Industrial Machine & Mfg Co* ***(P-11810)***
Immersion Corporation (PA) D 408 467-1900
50 Rio Robles San Jose (95134) ***(P-15242)***
Immport Therapeutics Inc F 949 679-4068
1 Technology Dr Ste E309 Irvine (92618) ***(P-22214)***
Immunalysis, Pomona *Also called Diagnostixx California Corp* ***(P-21684)***
Immune Design Corp E 650 225-0214
601 Gateway Blvd Ste 250 South San Francisco (94080) ***(P-7942)***
Immunic Inc F 858 673-6840
15222 Ave Of Science B San Diego (92128) ***(P-7943)***
Immuno Concepts Inc E 916 363-2649
9825 Goethe Rd Ste 350 Sacramento (95827) ***(P-21740)***
Immunoscience LLC F 925 400-6055
6780 Sierra Ct Ste M Dublin (94568) ***(P-8229)***
Imod Structures, Vallejo *Also called Intermodal Structures Inc* ***(P-4462)***
Imp International Inc (PA) E 909 321-1000
1905 S Lynx Ave Ontario (91761) ***(P-7669)***
Impac International, Ontario *Also called New Greenscreen Incorporated* ***(P-4992)***
Impac Medical Systems Inc (HQ) E 408 830-8000
100 Mathilda Pl Fl 5 Sunnyvale (94086) ***(P-24003)***
Impac Technologies Inc D 714 427-2000
3050 Red Hill Ave Costa Mesa (92626) ***(P-17541)***
Impact Bearing, San Clemente *Also called Clean Wave Management Inc* ***(P-19888)***
Impact Bearing, San Clemente *Also called Clean Wave Management Inc* ***(P-14609)***
Impact LLC E 714 546-6000
22521 Avenida Empresa # 107 Rcho STA Marg (92688) ***(P-18944)***
Impact Printing & Graphics E 909 614-1678
15150 Sierra Bonita Ln Chino (91710) ***(P-6631)***
Impact Project Management Inc E 760 747-6616
2872 S Santa Fe Ave San Marcos (92069) ***(P-17898)***
Impact-O-Graph Devices, Chatsworth *Also called Iog Products LLC* ***(P-18321)***
Impak Corporation F 323 277-4700
13700 S Broadway Los Angeles (90061) ***(P-9406)***
Impak Worldwide, Los Angeles *Also called Impak Corporation* ***(P-9406)***
Impakt Holdings LLC F 650 692-5800
490 Gianni St Santa Clara (95054) ***(P-12243)***
Impax Laboratories Inc D 510 240-6000
31047 Genstar Rd Hayward (94544) ***(P-7944)***
Impax Laboratories LLC (HQ) A 510 240-6000
30831 Huntwood Ave Hayward (94544) ***(P-7945)***
Impax Laboratories LLC E 510 240-6000
30831 Huntwood Ave Hayward (94544) ***(P-7946)***
Impax Laboratories LLC F 510 476-2000
30941 San Clemente St Hayward (94544) ***(P-7947)***
Impax Laboratories Usa LLC F 510 240-6000
30831 Huntwood Ave Hayward (94544) ***(P-7948)***
Impco Technologies Inc (HQ) C 714 656-1200
3030 S Susan St Santa Ana (92704) ***(P-19688)***
Impedimed Inc (HQ) E 760 585-2100
5900 Pasteur Ct Ste 125 Carlsbad (92008) ***(P-21741)***
Imperative Care Inc E 669 228-3814
1359 Dell Ave Campbell (95008) ***(P-22028)***
Imperial Cal Products Inc E 714 990-9100
425 Apollo St Brea (92821) ***(P-12820)***
Imperial Coml Cooking Eqp, Corona *Also called Imperial Manufacturing Co* ***(P-15524)***
Imperial Compost LLC F 760 351-1900
1698 Jones St Ste 5 Brawley (92227) ***(P-8832)***
Imperial Custom Cabinet Inc F 619 461-4093
8093 Lemon Grove Way Lemon Grove (91945) ***(P-4576)***
Imperial Designs, Sherman Oaks *Also called Western Imperial Trading Inc* ***(P-22584)***
Imperial Die Cutting Inc E 916 443-6142
800 Richards Blvd Sacramento (95811) ***(P-5448)***
Imperial Enterprises Inc E 818 886-5028
9666 Owensmouth Ave Ste A Chatsworth (91311) ***(P-10312)***
Imperial Manufacturing Co C 951 281-1830
1128 Sherborn St Corona (92879) ***(P-15524)***
Imperial Marking Systems, Cerritos *Also called Blc Wc Inc* ***(P-7002)***
Imperial Mfg Co, Corona *Also called Spenuzza Inc* ***(P-15582)***
Imperial Mfg Co, Duarte *Also called Spenuzza Inc* ***(P-15583)***
Imperial Pipe Services LLC E 951 682-3307
12375 Brown Ave Riverside (92509) ***(P-11128)***
Imperial Printers Inc (PA) F 760 352-4374
430 W Main St El Centro (92243) ***(P-6632)***
Imperial Printers Rocket Copy, El Centro *Also called Imperial Printers Inc* ***(P-6632)***
Imperial Printing, Campbell *Also called C T V Inc* ***(P-6464)***
Imperial Rubber Products Inc E 909 393-0528
5691 Gates St Chino (91710) ***(P-14327)***
Imperial Shade Venetian Blind, Los Angeles *Also called Imperial Shade Venetian Blind* ***(P-4983)***
Imperial Shade Venetian Blind F 323 233-4391
909 E 59th St Los Angeles (90001) ***(P-4983)***
Imperial Sugar Company C 760 344-3110
395 W Keystone Rd Brawley (92227) ***(P-1351)***
Imperial System, Union City *Also called Blc Wc Inc* ***(P-14699)***
Imperial Toy LLC (PA) C 818 536-6500
16641 Roscoe Pl North Hills (91343) ***(P-22682)***
Imperial Valley Foods Inc B 760 203-1896
1961 Buchanan Ave Calexico (92231) ***(P-915)***
Imperial Valley Press, El Centro *Also called Associated Desert Newspaper* ***(P-5557)***
Imperials Sand Dunes, Brea *Also called Worldwide Envmtl Pdts Inc* ***(P-20958)***
Impeva Labs Inc (PA) F 650 559-0103
2570 W El Cam Mountain View (94040) ***(P-19323)***
Implant Direct Sybron Intl LLC (HQ) F 818 444-3000
22715 Savi Ranch Pkwy Yorba Linda (92887) ***(P-22160)***
Implant Direct Sybron Mfg LLC C 818 444-3300
3050 E Hillcrest Dr Westlake Village (91362) ***(P-22161)***
Implantech Associates Inc E 805 289-1665
6025 Nicolle St Ste B Ventura (93003) ***(P-22029)***
Implantium, Cypress *Also called Dentium USA* ***(P-22145)***
Imply Data Inc F 415 685-8187
1633 Old Bayshore Hwy # 232 Burlingame (94010) ***(P-24004)***
Impo International LLC E 805 922-7753
3510 Black Rd Santa Maria (93455) ***(P-10170)***
Impossible Aerospace Corp F 707 293-9367
2222 Ronald St Santa Clara (95050) ***(P-19906)***
Impossible Foods Inc (PA) D 650 461-4385
400 Saginaw Dr Redwood City (94063) ***(P-2483)***
Impresa Aerospace LLC (PA) F 310 354-1200
344 W 157th St Gardena (90248) ***(P-20136)***
Impresa Aerospace LLC F 843 553-2021
344 W 157th St Gardena (90248) ***(P-20137)***
Impress Communications Inc D 818 701-8800
9320 Lurline Ave Chatsworth (91311) ***(P-6633)***
Impro Industries Usa Inc (HQ) F 909 396-6525
21660 Copley Dr Ste 100 Diamond Bar (91765) ***(P-11418)***
Impulse Enterprise E 858 565-7050
9855 Carroll Canyon Rd San Diego (92131) ***(P-16905)***
Impulse Enterprise D 858 565-7050
8254 Ronson Rd San Diego (92111) ***(P-16906)***
IMS, South El Monte *Also called Interntnal Mdction Systems Ltd* ***(P-7671)***
IMS, South El Monte *Also called Interntnal Mdction Systems Ltd* ***(P-7960)***
IMS, Chula Vista *Also called Integrated Marine Services Inc* ***(P-20289)***
IMS Products Inc F 951 653-7720
6240 Box Springs Blvd E Riverside (92507) ***(P-20408)***
IMS-Ess, Temecula *Also called Electro-Support Systems Corp* ***(P-18898)***
IMT, Milpitas *Also called Integrated Mfg Tech Inc* ***(P-16050)***
IMT Analytical, Goleta *Also called Innovative Micro Tech Inc* ***(P-18293)***
IMT International, Fremont *Also called Integrated Mfg Tech Inc* ***(P-13031)***
IMT Precision Inc E 510 324-8926
31902 Hayman St Hayward (94544) ***(P-16040)***
IMT-Stason Laboratories, Irvine *Also called Stason Pharmaceuticals Inc* ***(P-8144)***
Imtec Acculine LLC E 510 770-1800
49036 Milmont Dr Fremont (94538) ***(P-14477)***
In House Custom Decals F 909 613-1403
2300 S Reservoir St # 308 Pomona (91766) ***(P-7094)***
In House Stickers, Pomona *Also called In House Custom Decals* ***(P-7094)***
In Pro Car Wear Inc F 323 724-0568
6363 Corsair St Commerce (90040) ***(P-17135)***
In Style, Los Angeles *Also called Boulevard Style Inc* ***(P-3144)***
In Sync Computer Solutions Inc F 949 837-5000
23282 Mill Creek Dr Laguna Hills (92653) ***(P-24005)***
In To Ink F 858 271-6363
6959 Colorado Ave La Mesa (91942) ***(P-6634)***
In Win Development USA Inc E 909 348-0588
188 Brea Canyon Rd Walnut (91789) ***(P-15047)***
In-O-Vate Inc F 562 806-7515
9301 Garfield Ave South Gate (90280) ***(P-9117)***
Inaba Foods (usa) Inc F 310 818-2270
19301 Pcf Gtwy Dr Ste 120 Torrance (90502) ***(P-1075)***
Inari Medical Inc E 949 600-8433
9 Parker Ste 100 Irvine (92618) ***(P-21742)***
Inbenta Technologies Inc (PA) E 408 213-8771
1065 E Hillsdale Blvd # 425 Foster City (94404) ***(P-24006)***
Inboard Technology Inc F 844 846-2627
1347 Pacific Ave Ste 201 Santa Cruz (95060) ***(P-20409)***
Inc Polycarbon, Valencia *Also called Sgl Technic LLC* ***(P-10977)***

ALPHABETIC

Employee Codes: A=Over 500 employees, B=251-500
C=101-250, D=51-100, E=20-50, F=10-19

2020 California
Manfacturers Register

© Mergent Inc. 1-800-342-5647

1129

Inca One Corporation......E......310 808-0001
1632 1/2 W 134th St Gardena (90249) ***(P-18679)***
Inca Pallets Supply Inc......E......909 622-1414
1349 S East End Ave Pomona (91766) ***(P-4374)***
Inca Plastics Molding Co Inc......D......909 923-3235
948 E Belmont St Ontario (91761) ***(P-9837)***
Incal Technology Inc......E......510 657-8405
46420 Fremont Blvd Fremont (94538) ***(P-15243)***
Incandescent Inc......F......415 464-7975
350 Sansome St San Francisco (94104) ***(P-24007)***
Incarda Therapeutics Inc......E......510 422-5522
39899 Balentine Dr # 185 Newark (94560) ***(P-7949)***
Incelldx Inc......F......650 777-7630
1541 Industrial Rd San Carlos (94070) ***(P-21743)***
Inception Homes Inc......F......714 890-1883
12640 Beach Blvd Stanton (90680) ***(P-4452)***
Incharacter Costumes LLC......E......858 552-3600
4560 Alvarado Canyon Rd 1d San Diego (92120) ***(P-3557)***
Incipio Group, Irvine *Also called Incipio Technologies Inc* ***(P-15244)***
Incipio Technologies Inc (PA)......D......949 250-4929
3347 Michelson Dr Ste 100 Irvine (92612) ***(P-15244)***
Inclinator of California, San Fernando *Also called TL Shield & Associates Inc* ***(P-13810)***
Incredible Cheesecake, San Diego *Also called Princess Brandy Corp* ***(P-1264)***
Indel Engineering Inc......E......562 594-0995
6400 E Marina Dr Long Beach (90803) ***(P-20338)***
Independent Coast Observer......F......707 884-3501
38500 S Highway 1 Gualala (95445) ***(P-5670)***
Independent Forge Company......E......714 997-7337
692 N Batavia St Orange (92868) ***(P-12732)***
Independent Ink Inc......E......310 523-4657
13700 S Gramac Pl Gardena (90249) ***(P-8978)***
Independent Printing Co Inc (PA)......E......925 229-5050
1530 Franklin Canyon Rd Martinez (94553) ***(P-6635)***
Independent, The, Livermore *Also called Inland Valley Publising Co* ***(P-5675)***
Indepndent Brkley Stdnt Pubg I......D......510 548-8300
2483 Hearst Ave Berkeley (94709) ***(P-5671)***
Indepndent Flr Tstg Insptn Inc......F......925 676-7682
2300 Clayton Rd Ste 1240 Concord (94520) ***(P-10588)***
Index Printing Inc......F......209 862-2222
1021 Fresno St Newman (95360) ***(P-7095)***
Indi Molecular Inc......F......310 417-4999
6160 Bristol Pkwy Culver City (90230) ***(P-8230)***
India Journal, Santa Fe Springs *Also called Premier Media Inc* ***(P-5803)***
India Post, Fremont *Also called Rj Media* ***(P-5811)***
India-West Publications Inc (PA)......E......510 383-1140
933 Macarthur Blvd San Leandro (94577) ***(P-5672)***
Indian Head Industries Inc......D......707 894-3333
1184 S Cloverdale Blvd Cloverdale (95425) ***(P-19689)***
Indian Ink Screen Print......E......714 437-0882
1351 Logan Ave Ste A Costa Mesa (92626) ***(P-7096)***
Indian Summer, Rancho Cucamonga *Also called Mizkan Americas Inc* ***(P-2554)***
Indian Wells Brewery, Inyokern *Also called Indian Wells Companies* ***(P-1538)***
Indian Wells Companies......E......760 377-4290
2565 State Highway 14 Inyokern (93527) ***(P-1538)***
Indie Semiconductor......D......949 608-0854
32 Journey Ste 100 Aliso Viejo (92656) ***(P-2693)***
Indie Source Inc......E......424 200-2027
1933 S Broadway Ste 1168 Los Angeles (90007) ***(P-3039)***
Indigo Designs......F......909 997-0854
16607 Reed St Fontana (92336) ***(P-4209)***
Indio Products Inc......E......323 720-9117
5331 E Slauson Ave Commerce (90040) ***(P-8979)***
Indium Software Inc......C......408 501-8844
1250 Oakmead Pkwy Ste 210 Sunnyvale (94085) ***(P-24008)***
Individual Software Inc......E......925 734-6767
2301 Armstrong St Ste 101 Livermore (94551) ***(P-24009)***
Indtec Corporation......E......831 582-9388
3348 Paul Davis Dr # 109 Marina (93933) ***(P-17899)***
Indu Fashions......E......619 336-4638
220 W 25th St Ste B National City (91950) ***(P-3008)***
Indu-Electric North Amer Inc (PA)......E......310 578-2144
27756 Avenue Hopkins Valencia (91355) ***(P-14785)***
Induction Technology Corp......E......760 246-7333
22060 Bear Valley Rd Apple Valley (92308) ***(P-14764)***
Inductor Supply Inc......F......714 894-9050
11542 Knott St Ste 3 Garden Grove (92841) ***(P-18720)***
Induspac California Inc......F......909 390-4422
1550 Champagne Ave Ontario (91761) ***(P-7568)***
Induspac California Inc (HQ)......E......510 324-3626
21062 Forbes Ave Hayward (94545) ***(P-7569)***
Industrial Battery Engrg Inc......E......818 767-7067
9121 De Garmo Ave Sun Valley (91352) ***(P-19168)***
Industrial Coatings Division, Huntington Beach *Also called PPG Industries Inc* ***(P-8669)***
Industrial Components Div, Simi Valley *Also called Rexnord Industries LLC* ***(P-14396)***
Industrial Cpu Systems Intl......F......714 957-2815
2225 S Grand Ave Santa Ana (92705) ***(P-14923)***
Industrial Design Fabrication......F......209 937-9128
802 S San Joaquin St B Stockton (95206) ***(P-16041)***
Industrial Design Products......F......909 468-0693
2700 Pomona Blvd Pomona (91768) ***(P-13876)***
Industrial Dynamics Co Ltd (PA)......C......310 325-5633
3100 Fujita St Torrance (90505) ***(P-14478)***
Industrial Electric Mfg, Fremont *Also called New Iem LLC* ***(P-16604)***
Industrial Electric Mfg, Fremont *Also called Abd El & Larson Holdings LLC* ***(P-16583)***
Industrial Electronic Engineer......D......818 787-0311
7723 Kester Ave Van Nuys (91405) ***(P-15245)***
Industrial Eqp Solutions Inc......F......951 272-9540
301 N Smith Ave Corona (92880) ***(P-14828)***
Industrial Fire Sprnklr Co Inc......E......619 266-6030
3845 Imperial Ave San Diego (92113) ***(P-14829)***
Industrial Furnace & Insul Inc......F......909 947-2449
2090 S Hellman Ave Ontario (91761) ***(P-14765)***
Industrial Gasket and Sup Co......E......310 530-1771
23018 Normandie Ave Torrance (90502) ***(P-9237)***
Industrial Glass Products Inc......F......323 526-7125
4229 Union Pacific Ave Los Angeles (90023) ***(P-10365)***
Industrial Glass Service, Sunnyvale *Also called Igs Inc* ***(P-10270)***
Industrial Graphic, Yorba Linda *Also called Comstar Industries Inc* ***(P-16706)***
Industrial Insulations Inc (PA)......E......909 574-7433
10509 Business Dr Ste A Fontana (92337) ***(P-16950)***
Industrial Machine & Mfg Co......F......626 444-0181
2626 Seaman Ave El Monte (91733) ***(P-11810)***
Industrial Machining Co, Columbia *Also called Gerard H Tanzi Inc* ***(P-14368)***
Industrial Manufacturing Inc......F......562 941-5888
10110 Norwalk Blvd Santa Fe Springs (90670) ***(P-11700)***
Industrial Metal Finishing......F......714 628-8808
1941 Petra Ln Placentia (92870) ***(P-13028)***
Industrial Plating Co, Carlsbad *Also called Industrial Zinc Plating Corp* ***(P-13029)***
Industrial Power Products......E......530 893-0584
355 E Park Ave Chico (95928) ***(P-16042)***
Industrial Process Eqp Inc......F......714 447-0171
1700 Industrial Ave Norco (92860) ***(P-14766)***
Industrial SEC Allianc Ptnrs (PA)......F......619 232-7041
10350 Science Center Dr # 100 San Diego (92121) ***(P-22429)***
Industrial Sprockets Gears Inc......E......323 233-7221
13650 Rosecrans Ave Santa Fe Springs (90670) ***(P-14786)***
Industrial Tctnics Brings Corp (HQ)......D......310 537-3750
18301 S Santa Fe Ave E Rncho Dmngz (90221) ***(P-14610)***
Industrial Tool and Die Inc......F......714 549-1686
1330 E Saint Gertrude Pl Santa Ana (92705) ***(P-14064)***
Industrial Tools Inc......E......805 483-1111
1111 S Rose Ave Oxnard (93033) ***(P-14479)***
Industrial Tube Company LLC......D......661 295-4000
28150 Industry Dr Valencia (91355) ***(P-13331)***
Industrial Welding, Redding *Also called Ferrosaur Inc* ***(P-11793)***
Industrial Wiper & Supply Inc......E......408 286-4752
1025 98th Ave A Oakland (94603) ***(P-2755)***
Industrial Zinc Plating Corp......E......760 918-6877
7217 San Luis St Carlsbad (92011) ***(P-13029)***
Industrious Software Solution......F......310 672-8700
8901 S La Cienega Blvd # 202 Inglewood (90301) ***(P-24010)***
Industrious Software Solutions, Inglewood *Also called Industrious Software Solution* ***(P-24010)***
Industry Color Printing Inc......E......626 961-2403
11642 Washington Blvd Whittier (90606) ***(P-6636)***
Industry Terminal Us31, City of Industry *Also called Lhoist North America Ariz Inc* ***(P-10875)***
Inerfab, San Juan Capistrano *Also called American Horse Products* ***(P-3831)***
Inertech Supply Inc......D......626 282-2000
641 Monterey Pass Rd Monterey Park (91754) ***(P-9238)***
Inevit Inc......D......650 298-6001
541 Jefferson Ave Ste 100 Redwood City (94063) ***(P-19169)***
Infab Corporation......D......805 987-5255
1040 Avenida Acaso Camarillo (93012) ***(P-22030)***
Inficold Inc......F......408 464-8007
14654 Placida Ct Saratoga (95070) ***(P-14663)***
Infineon Tech Americas Corp (HQ)......A......310 726-8000
101 N Pacific Coast Hwy El Segundo (90245) ***(P-18282)***
Infineon Tech Americas Corp......A......310 726-8000
233 Kansas St El Segundo (90245) ***(P-18283)***
Infineon Tech Americas Corp......A......866 951-9519
640 N Mccarthy Blvd Milpitas (95035) ***(P-18284)***
Infineon Tech Americas Corp......A......951 375-6008
41915 Business Park Dr Temecula (92590) ***(P-15246)***
Infineon Tech Americas Corp......C......310 252-7116
1521 E Grand Ave El Segundo (90245) ***(P-18285)***
Infineon Tech N Amer Corp (HQ)......B......408 503-2642
640 N Mccarthy Blvd Milpitas (95035) ***(P-18286)***
Infineon Tech US Holdco Inc (HQ)......D......866 951-9519
640 N Mccarthy Blvd Milpitas (95035) ***(P-18287)***
Infineon Technologies AG, Milpitas *Also called Infineon Tech US Holdco Inc* ***(P-18287)***
Infinera Corporation (PA)......B......408 572-5200
140 Caspian Ct Sunnyvale (94089) ***(P-17379)***
Infinera Corporation......E......408 572-5200
1338 Bordeaux Dr Sunnyvale (94089) ***(P-18288)***
Infinisim Inc......F......408 934-9777
2860 Zanker Rd Ste 202 San Jose (95134) ***(P-24011)***
Infinite Electronics Inc (HQ)......E......949 261-1920
17792 Fitch Irvine (92614) ***(P-18945)***
Infinite Electronics Intl Inc (HQ)......C......949 261-1920
17792 Fitch Irvine (92614) ***(P-18775)***
Infinite Engineering Inc......F......714 534-4688
13682 Newhope St Garden Grove (92843) ***(P-16043)***
Infinite Optics Inc......E......714 557-2299
1712 Newport Cir Ste F Santa Ana (92705) ***(P-21364)***
Infiniter, Diamond Bar *Also called Quarton Usa Inc* ***(P-19387)***
Infiniti, Anaheim *Also called Jenson Custom Furniture Inc* ***(P-4648)***
Infiniti Plastic Technologies......F......310 618-8288
11150 Santa Monica Blvd # 1280 Los Angeles (90025) ***(P-9838)***
Infiniti Solutions Usa Inc (PA)......D......408 923-7300
3910 N 1st St San Jose (95134) ***(P-17900)***
Infinity Access Plus Inc......F......818 270-8172
12945 Sherman Way Ste 8 North Hollywood (91605) ***(P-12481)***
Infinity Aerospace Inc (PA)......D......818 998-9811
9060 Winnetka Ave Northridge (91324) ***(P-19965)***
Infinity Kitchen Products Inc......F......562 806-5771
7750 Scout Ave Bell Gardens (90201) ***(P-12244)***

Infinity Precision Inc ....F....818 447-3008
6919 Eton Ave Canoga Park (91303) *(P-16044)*
Infinity Stainless Products, Bell Gardens *Also called Infinity Kitchen Products Inc (P-12244)*
Infinity Stamps Inc ....F....818 576-1188
8577 Canoga Ave Canoga Park (91304) *(P-12821)*
Infinity Systems Inc ....F....714 692-1722
22715 La Palma Ave Yorba Linda (92887) *(P-16045)*
Infinity Textile ....F....562 777-9770
10638 Painter Ave Ste C Santa Fe Springs (90670) *(P-2936)*
Infinity Watch Corporation ....E....626 289-9878
21078 Commerce Point Dr Walnut (91789) *(P-23132)*
Inflatable Advertising Co Inc ....F....213 387-6839
1600 W Olympic Blvd Los Angeles (90015) *(P-23133)*
Inflatable Design Group Inc ....F....619 596-6100
1080 W Bradley Ave Ste B El Cajon (92020) *(P-23134)*
Inflatable Enterprises Inc ....F....818 482-6509
1418 Vineland Ave Baldwin Park (91706) *(P-9321)*
Inflight Entrmt & Connectivity, Irvine *Also called Thales Avionics Inc (P-20248)*
Inflight Warning Systems Inc ....F....714 993-9394
3910 Prospect Ave Unit P Yorba Linda (92886) *(P-20138)*
Infocus Jupiter, Hayward *Also called Jupiter Systems LLC (P-15126)*
Infofax Inc ....F....530 895-0431
305 Nord Ave Chico (95926) *(P-5962)*
Infoimage of California Inc (PA) ....D....650 473-6388
141 Jefferson Dr Menlo Park (94025) *(P-7097)*
Infokorea Inc ....E....213 487-1580
626 S Kingsley Dr Los Angeles (90005) *(P-5963)*
Infor (us) Inc ....C....678 319-8000
26250 Entp Way Ste 220 Lake Forest (92630) *(P-24012)*
Infor (us) Inc ....C....916 921-0883
11000 Olson Dr Ste 201 Rancho Cordova (95670) *(P-24013)*
Infor Public Sector Inc (HQ) ....C....916 921-0883
11092 Sun Center Dr Rancho Cordova (95670) *(P-24014)*
Inform Decisions ....F....949 709-5838
30162 Tomas 101 Rcho STA Marg (92688) *(P-24015)*
Inform Solution Incorporated ....F....805 879-6000
201 Mentor Dr Santa Barbara (93111) *(P-24016)*
Informa Business Media Inc ....E....949 252-1146
16815 Von Karman Ave # 150 Irvine (92606) *(P-6255)*
Informa Media Inc ....E....619 295-7685
4452 Park Blvd Ste 306 San Diego (92116) *(P-5964)*
Informa Media Inc ....D....301 755-0162
11500 W Olympic Blvd Los Angeles (90064) *(P-5965)*
Informatica LLC (PA) ....C....650 385-5000
2100 Seaport Blvd Redwood City (94063) *(P-24017)*
Information Integration Group ....E....818 956-3744
457 Palm Dr Ste 200 Glendale (91202) *(P-24018)*
Information Resources Inc ....E....559 732-0324
400 N Johnson St Visalia (93291) *(P-24019)*
Information Scan Tech Inc ....F....408 988-1908
487 Gianni St Santa Clara (95054) *(P-21051)*
Information Storage Dvcs Inc ....C....408 943-6666
2727 N 1st St San Jose (95134) *(P-18289)*
Informer Computer Systems ....F....714 899-2049
12711 Western Ave Garden Grove (92841) *(P-15125)*
Infoworld Media Group Inc (HQ) ....D....415 243-4344
501 2nd St Ste 500 San Francisco (94107) *(P-5966)*
Infrared Dynamics Inc ....E....714 572-4050
3830 Prospect Ave Yorba Linda (92886) *(P-11701)*
Infrared Industries Inc ....F....510 782-8100
25590 Seaboard Ln Hayward (94545) *(P-21245)*
Infraredvision Technology Corp ....E....805 686-8848
140 Industrial Way Buellton (93427) *(P-20888)*
Infrastructureworld LLC ....E....650 871-3950
1001 Bayhill Dr Ste 200 San Bruno (94066) *(P-21246)*
Infratab ....E....805 986-8880
4347 Raytheon Rd Unit 6 Oxnard (93033) *(P-8311)*
Ingalls Conveyors Inc ....E....323 837-9900
1005 W Olympic Blvd Montebello (90640) *(P-13826)*
Ingenu Inc (PA) ....E....858 201-6000
10301 Meanley Dr San Diego (92131) *(P-17542)*
Ingenue Inc ....D....323 726-8084
6114 Scott Way Commerce (90040) *(P-519)*
Ingenuity Brands, Burlingame *Also called Ingenuity Foods Inc (P-1023)*
Ingenuity Foods Inc ....F....650 562-7483
1564 Rollins Rd Ste 4 Burlingame (94010) *(P-1023)*
Ingla Rubber Products, Bellflower *Also called Bryant Rubber Corp (P-9220)*
Inglenook ....F....707 968-1100
1991 St Helena Hwy Rutherford (94573) *(P-1759)*
Ingomar Packing Company LLC (PA) ....D....209 826-9494
9950 S Ingomar Grade Los Banos (93635) *(P-777)*
Ingram Publisher Services LLC ....D....510 528-1444
1700 4th St Berkeley (94710) *(P-6256)*
Ingrasys Technology USA Inc ....E....863 271-8266
2025 Gateway Pl Ste 190 San Jose (95110) *(P-21052)*
Ingredients By Nature LLC ....E....909 230-6200
5555 Brooks St Montclair (91763) *(P-2484)*
Ingredion Incorporated ....D....209 982-1920
1021 Industrial Dr Stockton (95206) *(P-1061)*
Ingrersoll Rand Indus Refrig ....F....909 477-2037
13770 Ramona Ave Chino (91710) *(P-10151)*
Ingrezza, San Diego *Also called Neurocrine Biosciences Inc (P-8032)*
Ingrooves, San Francisco *Also called Isolation Network Inc (P-17246)*
Inhealth Technologies ....F....800 477-5969
1110 Mark Ave Carpinteria (93013) *(P-22031)*
Initiative Foods, Sanger *Also called If Copack LLC (P-729)*
Initiative Foods LLC ....C....559 875-3354
1912 Industrial Way Sanger (93657) *(P-730)*
Initio Corporation ....E....408 943-3189
2050 Ringwood Ave Ste A San Jose (95131) *(P-18290)*

Initium Aerospace LLC ....F....818 324-3684
4255 Ruffin Rd Ste 100 San Diego (92123) *(P-11158)*
Initium Eyewear Inc ....F....714 444-0866
412 Olive Ave Ste 218 Huntington Beach (92648) *(P-22362)*
Injection Molding, Acampo *Also called AG Ray Inc (P-13604)*
Injekt, Encinitas *Also called Mako Labs LLC (P-24124)*
Ink & Color Inc ....E....310 280-6060
5920 Bowcroft St Los Angeles (90016) *(P-6637)*
Ink 2000 Corp ....F....818 882-0168
19875 Nordhoff St Northridge (91324) *(P-8920)*
Ink Fx Corporation ....E....909 673-1950
2031 S Lynx Ave Ontario (91761) *(P-7098)*
Ink Makers Inc ....F....323 728-7500
2121 Yates Ave Commerce (90040) *(P-8921)*
Ink Spot Inc ....E....626 338-4500
9737 Bell Ranch Dr Santa Fe Springs (90670) *(P-6638)*
Ink Throwers, Encinitas *Also called R B T Inc (P-3809)*
Inkgrabber.com, Simi Valley *Also called Inkjetmadnesscom Inc (P-8922)*
Inkjetmadnesscom Inc ....F....805 583-7755
2205 1st St Ste 103 Simi Valley (93065) *(P-8922)*
Inkovation Inc (PA) ....E....800 465-4174
13659 Excelsior Dr Santa Fe Springs (90670) *(P-6639)*
Inktomi Corporation (HQ) ....E....650 653-2800
701 First Ave Sunnyvale (94089) *(P-24020)*
Inkwright LLC ....E....714 892-3300
5822 Research Dr Huntington Beach (92649) *(P-6640)*
Inland Artfl Limb & Brace Inc (PA) ....F....951 734-1835
680 Parkridge Ave Norco (92860) *(P-22032)*
Inland Color Graphics ....F....951 493-2999
2054 Tandem Norco (92860) *(P-7377)*
Inland Empire Cmnty Newspapers ....E....909 381-9898
1809 Commercenter W San Bernardino (92408) *(P-5673)*
Inland Empire Drive Line Svc (PA) ....F....909 390-3030
4035 E Guasti Rd Ste 301 Ontario (91761) *(P-19690)*
Inland Empire Foods Inc (PA) ....E....951 682-8222
5425 Wilson St Riverside (92509) *(P-850)*
Inland Empire Magazine, Riverside *Also called Inland Empire Media Group Inc (P-5967)*
Inland Empire Media Group Inc ....F....951 682-3026
3400 Central Ave Ste 160 Riverside (92506) *(P-5967)*
Inland Envelope Company ....D....909 622-2016
150 N Park Ave Pomona (91768) *(P-5471)*
Inland Group, Anaheim *Also called Inland Litho LLC (P-6641)*
Inland Litho LLC ....D....714 993-6000
4305 E La Palma Ave Anaheim (92807) *(P-6641)*
Inland Marine Industries Inc ....C....510 785-8555
3245 Depot Rd Hayward (94545) *(P-12245)*
Inland Metal Technologies, Hayward *Also called Inland Marine Industries Inc (P-12245)*
Inland PCF Resource Recovery ....E....619 390-1418
12650 Slughter Hse Cyn Rd Lakeside (92040) *(P-5093)*
Inland Powder Coating Corp ....C....909 947-1122
1656 S Bon View Ave Ste F Ontario (91761) *(P-13192)*
Inland Signs Inc ....E....909 581-0699
1715 S Bon View Ave Ontario (91761) *(P-23135)*
Inland Tek Inc ....F....909 900-8457
7364 Oxford Pl Rancho Cucamonga (91730) *(P-24021)*
Inland Truss Inc (PA) ....D....951 300-1758
275 W Rider St Perris (92571) *(P-4308)*
Inland Valley Daily Bulletin, Monrovia *Also called Califrnia Nwspapers Ltd Partnr (P-5579)*
Inland Valley Daily Bulletin, Rancho Cucamonga *Also called Califrnia Nwspapers Ltd Partnr (P-5580)*
Inland Valley News Inc ....F....909 949-3099
2009 Porter Field Way C Upland (91786) *(P-5674)*
Inland Valley Publising Co ....F....925 243-8000
2250 1st St Livermore (94550) *(P-5675)*
Inland Valley Truss Inc ....F....209 943-4710
150 N Sinclair Ave Stockton (95215) *(P-4309)*
Inline Plastics Inc ....E....909 923-1033
1950 S Baker Ave Ontario (91761) *(P-9839)*
Inmage Systems Inc ....E....408 200-3840
1065 La Avenida St Mountain View (94043) *(P-24022)*
Inmar Marine Group, San Diego *Also called Global Marine Group Inc (P-20333)*
Inmotion, Sonoma *Also called Monica Bruce Designs Inc (P-3802)*
Inneos LLC ....E....925 226-0138
5700 Stoneridge Dr # 200 Pleasanton (94588) *(P-21365)*
Innerspace Cases, North Hollywood *Also called Armored Group Inc (P-4329)*
Innerstave LLC ....E....707 996-8781
21660 8th St E Ste B Sonoma (95476) *(P-4416)*
Innerstep BSE (PA) ....D....831 461-5600
4742 Scotts Valley Dr Scotts Valley (95066) *(P-17901)*
Innespace Productions ....F....530 241-2800
20172 Charlanne Dr Redding (96002) *(P-20339)*
Innfinity Software Systems LLC ....F....619 798-3915
600 B St Ste 300 San Diego (92101) *(P-24023)*
Inno Tech Manufacturing Inc ....F....858 565-4556
10109 Carroll Canyon Rd San Diego (92131) *(P-16046)*
Innocor West LLC ....E....909 307-3737
300-310 S Tippecanoe Ave San Bernardino (92408) *(P-9322)*
Innodisk Usa Corporation ....E....510 770-9421
42996 Osgood Rd Fremont (94539) *(P-18291)*
Innominata ....F....858 592-9300
15222 Avenue Of Science A San Diego (92128) *(P-8231)*
Innophase Inc ....D....619 541-8280
6815 Flanders Dr Ste 150 San Diego (92121) *(P-18292)*
Innov8v, Irvine *Also called Innovative Tech & Engrg Inc (P-15247)*
Innova Champion Discs, Ontario *Also called Champion Discs Incorporated (P-22779)*
Innova Electronics Corporation ....E....714 241-6800
17352 Von Karman Ave Irvine (92614) *(P-19691)*

ALPHABETIC

Employee Codes: A=Over 500 employees, B=251-500
C=101-250, D=51-100, E=20-50, F=10-19
2020 California
Manfacturers Register
© Mergent Inc. 1-800-342-5647
1131

Innovacon Inc...D.....858 805-8900
9975 Summers Ridge Rd San Diego (92121) ***(P-8232)***
Innovalight Inc...E.....408 419-4400
965 W Maude Ave Sunnyvale (94085) ***(P-17136)***
Innovate Labs LLC...F.....917 753-2673
553 S Fair Oaks Ave 592 Pasadena (91105) ***(P-24024)***
Innovation Alley LLC...F.....559 453-6974
5473 E Hedges Ave Fresno (93727) ***(P-11811)***
Innovative Biosciences Corp...E.....760 603-0772
1849 Diamond St San Marcos (92078) ***(P-8515)***
Innovative Body Science, San Marcos *Also called Innovative Biosciences Corp* ***(P-8515)***
Innovative Casework Mfg Inc...E.....714 890-9100
12261 Industry St Garden Grove (92841) ***(P-23362)***
Innovative Circuits Engrg, San Jose *Also called Circuit Connections* ***(P-17847)***
Innovative Combustion Tech (PA)...F.....510 652-6000
5160 Fulton Dr Fairfield (94534) ***(P-11702)***
Innovative Control Systems Inc...E.....610 881-8061
20992 Bake Pkwy Ste 106 Lake Forest (92630) ***(P-15525)***
Innovative Cosmetic Labs Inc...F.....818 349-1121
9740 Cozycroft Ave Chatsworth (91311) ***(P-8516)***
Innovative Design and Sheet ME...F.....951 222-2270
616 Mrlbrugh Ave Unit S-1 Riverside (92507) ***(P-12246)***
Innovative Designs & Mfg Inc...F.....626 812-4422
1067 W 5th St Azusa (91702) ***(P-4691)***
Innovative Diversfd Tech Inc...E.....949 455-1701
18062 Irvine Blvd Ste 304 Tustin (92780) ***(P-15048)***
Innovative Earth Products...F.....888 588-5955
232 Avenida Fabricante San Clemente (92672) ***(P-22828)***
Innovative Emergency Equipment, Riverside *Also called Innovative Design and Sheet ME* ***(P-12246)***
Innovative Integration Inc...E.....805 520-3300
741 Flynn Rd Camarillo (93012) ***(P-20889)***
Innovative Machining Inc...E.....408 262-2270
845 Yosemite Way Milpitas (95035) ***(P-16047)***
Innovative Manufacturing Inc...F.....714 524-5246
1366 N Hundley St Anaheim (92806) ***(P-16048)***
Innovative Metal Inds Inc...D.....909 796-6200
1330 Riverview Dr San Bernardino (92408) ***(P-12592)***
Innovative Metal Products Inc...E.....760 734-1010
2443 Cades Way Ste 200 Vista (92081) ***(P-13526)***
Innovative Micro Tech Inc...C.....805 681-2807
75 Robin Hill Rd Goleta (93117) ***(P-18293)***
Innovative Molding (HQ)...D.....707 238-9250
1200 Valley House Dr # 100 Rohnert Park (94928) ***(P-9840)***
Innovative Mounts, Anaheim *Also called Innovative Manufacturing Inc* ***(P-16048)***
Innovative Organics Inc...E.....714 701-3900
4905 E Hunter Ave Anaheim (92807) ***(P-8744)***
Innovative Plastics Inc...F.....714 891-8800
5502 Buckingham Dr Huntington Beach (92649) ***(P-9440)***
Innovative Products Co, Temecula *Also called IPC Industries Inc* ***(P-20514)***
Innovative R Advanced (PA)...F.....949 273-8100
23101 Lake Center Dr # 100 Lake Forest (92630) ***(P-4723)***
Innovative R Advanced...E.....949 273-8100
3401 Etiwanda Ave Jurupa Valley (91752) ***(P-4724)***
Innovative Rv Technologies...E.....949 559-5372
205 Via Morada San Clemente (92673) ***(P-212)***
Innovative Stamping Inc...E.....310 537-6996
2068 E Gladwick St Compton (90220) ***(P-12822)***
Innovative Steel Structures, Modesto *Also called JR Daniels Commercial Bldrs* ***(P-12593)***
Innovative Structural GL Inc...E.....559 561-7000
40220 Pierce Dr Three Rivers (93271) ***(P-10366)***
Innovative Systems, Compton *Also called Innovative Stamping Inc* ***(P-12822)***
Innovative Tech & Engrg Inc...F.....949 955-2501
2691 Richter Ave Ste 124 Irvine (92606) ***(P-15247)***
Innovative Technology Inc...F.....805 571-8384
1501 Cook Pl Goleta (93117) ***(P-13193)***
Innovativetek Inc...E.....909 981-3401
1271 W 9th St Upland (91786) ***(P-19324)***
Innovista Sensors, Westlake Village *Also called Carros Americas Inc* ***(P-18851)***
Innoviva Inc (PA)...F.....650 238-9600
2000 Sierra Point Pkwy # 500 Brisbane (94005) ***(P-7950)***
Innovive LLC (PA)...E.....858 309-6620
10019 Waples Ct San Diego (92121) ***(P-13416)***
Innovtive Rttional Molding Inc...F.....559 673-4764
2300 W Pecan Ave Madera (93637) ***(P-9841)***
Innovyze Inc (HQ)...F.....626 568-6868
605 E Huntington Dr # 205 Monrovia (91016) ***(P-24025)***
Innowi Inc...E.....408 609-9404
3240 Scott Blvd Santa Clara (95054) ***(P-14924)***
Inogen Inc (PA)...C.....805 562-0500
326 Bollay Dr Goleta (93117) ***(P-21744)***
Inolux Corporation (PA)...F.....408 844-8734
3350 Scott Blvd Ste 4102 Santa Clara (95054) ***(P-18294)***
Inovate Roofing Products, South Gate *Also called In-O-Vate Inc* ***(P-9117)***
Inovio Pharmaceuticals Inc...E.....267 440-4200
10480 Wateridge Cir San Diego (92121) ***(P-7951)***
Inp, Rancho Cordova *Also called Intercontinental N Mas* ***(P-23364)***
Inphenix Inc...E.....925 606-8809
250 N Mines Rd Livermore (94551) ***(P-18295)***
Inphi Corporation (PA)...C.....408 217-7300
2953 Bunker Hill Ln # 300 Santa Clara (95054) ***(P-18296)***
Inphi International Pte Ltd...E.....805 719-2300
112 S Lakeview Canyon Rd Westlake Village (91362) ***(P-18297)***
Input/Output Technology Inc...E.....661 257-1000
28415 Industry Dr Ste 520 Valencia (91355) ***(P-15248)***
Inscopix Inc...F.....650 600-3886
2462 Embarcadero Way Palo Alto (94303) ***(P-21366)***
Inseat Solutions LLC...E.....562 447-1780
1871 Wright Ave La Verne (91750) ***(P-16829)***
Inserts & Kits Inc...F.....714 708-2888
1521 W Alton Ave Santa Ana (92704) ***(P-16049)***
Insideview Technologies Inc...C.....415 728-9309
444 De Haro St Ste 210 San Francisco (94107) ***(P-24026)***
Insieme Networks LLC...F.....408 424-1227
210 W Tasman Dr Bldg F San Jose (95134) ***(P-17380)***
Insight Editions LP...D.....415 526-1370
800 A St Ste B San Rafael (94901) ***(P-6112)***
Insight Management Corporation (PA)...E.....866 787-3588
1130 E Clark Ave Santa Maria (93455) ***(P-17328)***
Insight Mfg Services, Murphys *Also called Kaiser Enterprises Inc* ***(P-13474)***
Insight Solutions Inc...E.....408 725-0213
13095 Paramount Ct Saratoga (95070) ***(P-24027)***
Insight System Exchange, Santa Ana *Also called Limpus Prints Inc* ***(P-7121)***
Insignia, Buena Park *Also called Blasted Wood Products Inc* ***(P-3927)***
Insignia SC Holdings LLC (HQ)...A.....925 399-8900
1333 N Calif Blvd Ste 520 Walnut Creek (94596) ***(P-1374)***
Insilixa Inc...F.....408 809-3000
1000 Hamlin Ct Sunnyvale (94089) ***(P-18298)***
Insomniac Games Inc (PA)...D.....818 729-2400
2255 N Ontario St Ste 550 Burbank (91504) ***(P-22683)***
Inspired Properties LLC...E.....818 430-9634
14320 Ventura Blvd 181 Sherman Oaks (91423) ***(P-6113)***
Inspur Systems Inc (HQ)...E.....800 697-5893
47451 Fremont Blvd Fremont (94538) ***(P-14925)***
Inspyr Therapeutics Inc (PA)...F.....818 661-6302
31200 Via Colinas Ste 200 Westlake Village (91362) ***(P-7952)***
Instacure Healing Products...E.....818 222-9600
235 N Moorpark Rd # 2022 Thousand Oaks (91358) ***(P-7953)***
Instant Algae, Campbell *Also called Reed Mariculture Inc* ***(P-1121)***
Instant Asphalt Inc...F.....408 280-7733
365 Obata Ct Gilroy (95020) ***(P-8875)***
Instant Checkmate, San Diego *Also called Intelicare Direct Inc* ***(P-6648)***
Instant Imprints Franchising...E.....858 642-4848
6615 Flanders Dr Ste B San Diego (92121) ***(P-6642)***
Instant Tuck Inc...E.....310 955-8824
9663 Santa Monica Blvd Beverly Hills (90210) ***(P-3619)***
Instant Web LLC...C.....562 658-2020
7300 Flores St Downey (90242) ***(P-6643)***
Instantfigure, Irvine *Also called Buy Insta Slim Inc* ***(P-3028)***
Instathreads LLC...F.....661 470-7841
238 Lakeview Dr Palmdale (93551) ***(P-2891)***
Institute For Intl Studies, Stanford *Also called Leland Stanford Junior Univ* ***(P-6273)***
Institute of Electrical and El...D.....714 821-8380
10662 Los Vaqueros Cir Los Alamitos (90720) ***(P-6956)***
Institutional Real Estate (PA)...E.....925 933-4040
1475 N Broadway Ste 300 Walnut Creek (94596) ***(P-6257)***
Instrument & Valve Services Co...D.....562 633-0179
6851 Walthall Way A Paramount (90723) ***(P-20890)***
Instrument & Valve Services Co...F.....707 745-4664
531 Getty Ct Ste D Benicia (94510) ***(P-20891)***
Instrument Bearing Factory USA...E.....818 989-5052
19360 Rinaldi St Northridge (91326) ***(P-12683)***
Instrument Design Eng Assoc I...E.....714 525-3302
2923 Saturn St Ste F Brea (92821) ***(P-18946)***
Instrumentation Tech Systems...F.....818 886-2034
19360 Business Center Dr Northridge (91324) ***(P-15249)***
Instyle Printing Inc...E.....626 575-2725
2115 Central Ave South El Monte (91733) ***(P-3453)***
Insua Graphics Incorporated...E.....818 767-7007
9121 Glenoaks Blvd Sun Valley (91352) ***(P-6644)***
Insulated Products, Rancho Dominguez *Also called Simple Container Solutions Inc* ***(P-5173)***
Insulfab Inc...D.....805 482-2751
4725 Calle Alto Camarillo (93012) ***(P-10983)***
Insultech LLC (PA)...D.....714 384-0506
3530 W Garry Ave Santa Ana (92704) ***(P-8980)***
Insurance Journal, San Diego *Also called Wells Media Group Inc* ***(P-6057)***
Insync Computer Solutions, Laguna Hills *Also called In Sync Computer Solutions Inc* ***(P-24005)***
Inta Technologies Corporation...E.....408 748-9955
2281 Calle De Luna Santa Clara (95054) ***(P-13030)***
Intake Screens Inc...F.....916 665-2727
8417 River Rd Sacramento (95832) ***(P-13417)***
Integenx Inc (HQ)...D.....925 701-3400
5720 Stoneridge Dr # 300 Pleasanton (94588) ***(P-21247)***
Integer Holdings Corporation...F.....619 498-9448
8830 Siempre Viva Rd # 100 San Diego (92154) ***(P-21745)***
Integra Lfscnces Holdings Corp...E.....609 529-9748
5955 Pacific Center Blvd San Diego (92121) ***(P-21746)***
Integra Lifesciences, Carlsbad *Also called Seaspine Inc* ***(P-22081)***
Integra Tech Silicon Vly LLC (HQ)...C.....408 618-8700
1635 Mccarthy Blvd Milpitas (95035) ***(P-18299)***
Integra Technologies Inc...E.....310 606-0855
321 Coral Cir El Segundo (90245) ***(P-18300)***
Integra Technologies LLC...D.....408 923-7300
2006 Martin Ave Santa Clara (95050) ***(P-18301)***
Integral Aerospace LLC...C.....949 250-3123
2040 E Dyer Rd Santa Ana (92705) ***(P-20139)***
Integral Development Corp (PA)...C.....650 424-4500
850 Hansen Way Palo Alto (94304) ***(P-24028)***
Integral Engineering, Palo Alto *Also called Integral Development Corp* ***(P-24028)***
Integral Engrg Fabrication Inc...E.....626 369-0958
520 Hofgaarden St City of Industry (91744) ***(P-11812)***
Integrated Aqua Systems Inc...F.....760 745-2201
1235 Activity Dr Ste A Vista (92081) ***(P-15526)***
Integrated Business Network...F.....818 879-0670
28310 Roadside Dr Ste 136 Agoura Hills (91301) ***(P-7099)***
Integrated Communications Inc...E.....310 851-8066
1411 W 190th St Ste 110 Gardena (90248) ***(P-6645)***

Mergent e-mail: customerrelations@mergent.com
1132
2020 California
Manufacturers Register
(P-0000) Products & Services Section entry number
(PA)=Parent Co (HQ)=Headquarters (DH)=Div Headquarters

Integrated Design Tools Inc (PA) F 850 222-5939
1 W Mountain St Unit 3 Pasadena (91103) *(P-22430)*

Integrated Device Tech Inc (HQ) B 408 284-8200
6024 Silver Creek Vly Rd San Jose (95138) *(P-18302)*

Integrated Device Tech Inc B 408 284-1433
6024 Silver Creek Vly San Jose (95138) *(P-18303)*

Integrated Digital Media (PA) E 415 986-4091
840 Sansome St San Francisco (94111) *(P-6646)*

Integrated Digital Media E 415 882-9390
156 2nd St San Francisco (94105) *(P-6647)*

Integrated Dna Tech Inc F 858 410-6677
6828 Nncy Rdge Dr Ste 400 San Diego (92121) *(P-8312)*

Integrated Food Service, Gardena *Also called Lets Do Lunch (P-2528)*

Integrated Magnetics, Culver City *Also called Magnet Sales & Mfg Co Inc (P-10479)*

Integrated Magnetics Inc E 310 391-7213
11250 Playa Ct Culver City (90230) *(P-16657)*

Integrated Marine Services Inc D 619 429-0300
2320 Main St Chula Vista (91911) *(P-20289)*

Integrated Marketing Group LLC F 714 771-2401
528 W Briardale Ave Orange (92865) *(P-2694)*

Integrated Mfg Solutions LLC E 760 599-4300
2590 Pioneer Ave Ste C Vista (92081) *(P-23363)*

Integrated Mfg Tech Inc (HQ) F 408 934-5879
45473 Warm Springs Blvd Fremont (94539) *(P-13031)*

Integrated Mfg Tech Inc E 510 366-8793
1477 N Milpitas Blvd Milpitas (95035) *(P-16050)*

Integrated Microwave Corp D 858 259-2600
11353 Sorrento Valley Rd San Diego (92121) *(P-18947)*

Integrated Optical Svcs Corp E 408 982-9510
3270 Keller St Ste 109 Santa Clara (95054) *(P-8647)*

Integrated Polymer Inds Inc E 949 788-1050
9741 Irvine Center Dr Irvine (92618) *(P-8876)*

Integrated Sign Associates E 619 579-2229
1160 Pioneer Way Ste M El Cajon (92020) *(P-23136)*

Integrity Municpl Systems LLC F 858 486-1620
13135 Danielson St # 204 Poway (92064) *(P-15527)*

Integrity Security Svcs LLC F 805 965-6044
30 W Sola St Santa Barbara (93101) *(P-19325)*

Integrity Sheet Metal Inc F 909 608-0449
319 Mcarthur Way Ste 1 Upland (91786) *(P-12247)*

Integrity Support Services Inc F 415 898-0044
7110 Redwood Blvd Ste C Novato (94945) *(P-8981)*

Integrity Technology Corp E 270 812-8867
2505 Technology Dr Hayward (94545) *(P-18948)*

Integrted Polymr Solutions Inc (HQ) F 562 354-2920
3701 E Conant St Long Beach (90808) *(P-7639)*

Integrted Silicon Solution Inc (PA) D 408 969-6600
1623 Buckeye Dr Milpitas (95035) *(P-18304)*

Intel Americas Inc (HQ) D 408 765-8080
2200 Mission College Blvd Santa Clara (95054) *(P-15250)*

INTEL Corporation F 408 765-2508
3065 Bowers Ave Santa Clara (95054) *(P-15251)*

Intel Corporation D 916 943-6809
1200 Creekside Dr Folsom (95630) *(P-18305)*

Intel Corporation (PA) B 408 765-8080
2200 Mission College Blvd Santa Clara (95054) *(P-15252)*

Intel Corporation F 408 765-8080
530 Technology Dr Ste 100 Irvine (92618) *(P-18306)*

Intel Corporation C 408 425-8398
2300 Mission College Blvd Santa Clara (95054) *(P-15253)*

Intel Corporation A 408 544-7000
101 Innovation Dr San Jose (95134) *(P-15254)*

INTEL Corporation E 510 651-9841
44235 Nobel Dr Fremont (94538) *(P-18307)*

Intel Corporation D 916 356-8080
1900 Prairie City Rd Folsom (95630) *(P-18308)*

INTEL Corporation C 503 696-8080
2200 Mission College Blvd Santa Clara (95054) *(P-15255)*

Intel Federal LLC E 302 644-3756
2200 Mission College Blvd Santa Clara (95054) *(P-18309)*

INTEL International Limited (HQ) F 408 765-8080
2200 Mission College Blvd Santa Clara (95054) *(P-18310)*

Intel Network Systems Inc E 408 765-8080
3600 Juliette Ln Santa Clara (95054) *(P-18311)*

Intel Network Systems Inc F 858 877-4652
12220 Scrps Summit Dr # 300 San Diego (92131) *(P-15256)*

INTEL Puerto Rico Inc E 408 765-8080
2200 Mission College Blvd Santa Clara (95054) *(P-18312)*

Intelicare Direct Inc F 702 765-0867
9596 Chesapeake Dr Ste A San Diego (92123) *(P-6648)*

Intella Interventional Systems D 650 269-1375
605 W California Ave Sunnyvale (94086) *(P-21747)*

Intellgard Inventory Solutions, Carlsbad *Also called Meps Real-Time Inc (P-21505)*

Intelligence Support Group Ltd E 800 504-3341
7100 Monache Mtn Inyokern (93527) *(P-19326)*

Intelligent Barcode Systems F 626 576-8938
2190 Sherwood Rd San Marino (91108) *(P-21489)*

Intelligent Blends LP E 858 888-7937
5330 Eastgate Mall San Diego (92121) *(P-1024)*

Intelligent Cmpt Solutions Inc (PA) E 818 998-5805
8968 Fullbright Ave Chatsworth (91311) *(P-21053)*

Intelligent Energy Inc E 562 997-3600
1731 Tech Dr Ste 755 San Jose (95110) *(P-11599)*

Intelligent Peripherals F 415 564-4366
1123 Judah St San Francisco (94122) *(P-15257)*

Intelligent Photonics, San Francisco *Also called Invuity Inc (P-21758)*

Intelligent Quartz Solutions, Fremont *Also called Imtec Acculine LLC (P-14477)*

Intelligent Storage Solution C 408 428-0105
2073 Otoole Ave San Jose (95131) *(P-15049)*

Intelligent Technologies LLC C 858 458-1500
9454 Waples St San Diego (92121) *(P-16789)*

Intelligrated Systems Inc B 510 263-2300
5903 Christie Ave Emeryville (94608) *(P-13827)*

Intelligrated Systems Inc B 916 772-6800
3721 Douglas Blvd Ste 345 Roseville (95661) *(P-13828)*

Intellipower Inc D 714 921-1580
1746 N Saint Thomas Cir Orange (92865) *(P-18721)*

Intellisense Systems Inc C 310 320-1827
20600 Gramercy Pl Ste 101 Torrance (90501) *(P-20588)*

Intelmail USA Inc F 916 361-9300
9965 Horn Rd Ste D Sacramento (95827) *(P-15383)*

Intense Lighting LLC D 714 630-9877
3340 E La Palma Ave Anaheim (92806) *(P-17045)*

Intepro America LP (PA) E 714 953-2686
14662 Franklin Ave Ste E Tustin (92780) *(P-21054)*

Inter City Manufacturing Inc E 831 899-3636
507 Redwood Ave Seaside (93955) *(P-16051)*

Inter Color Plus Inter E 818 764-5034
13234 Sherman Way Ste 6 North Hollywood (91605) *(P-7100)*

Inter Mountain Truss & Girder F 209 847-9184
596 Armstrong Way Oakdale (95361) *(P-4310)*

Inter Packing Inc E 909 465-5555
12315 Colony Ave Chino (91710) *(P-9552)*

Inter-City Printing Co Inc F 510 451-4775
614 Madison St Oakland (94607) *(P-6649)*

Interactive Entertainment Inc F 714 460-2343
2 Enterprise Apt 7107 Aliso Viejo (92656) *(P-22684)*

Intercept Pharmaceuticals Inc F 646 747-1005
4760 Eastgate Mall San Diego (92121) *(P-7954)*

Intercity Centerless Grinding F 714 546-5644
11546 Coley River Cir Fountain Valley (92708) *(P-16052)*

Intercom Energy Inc F 619 863-9644
1330 Orange Ave 300-30 Coronado (92118) *(P-16558)*

Interconnect Solutions, Santa Ana *Also called Mx Electronics Mfg Inc (P-11309)*

Interconnect Solutions Gr F 323 691-5485
5855 Green Valley Cir # 2 Culver City (90230) *(P-16907)*

Interconnect Systems Inc (HQ) D 805 482-2870
741 Flynn Rd Camarillo (93012) *(P-18313)*

Intercontinental Cof Trdg LLC F 619 338-8335
110 W A St Ste 110 # 110 San Diego (92101) *(P-2300)*

Intercontinental Coffee Trdg, San Diego *Also called Intercontinental Cof Trdg LLC (P-2300)*

Intercontinental N Mas E 916 631-1674
11492 Refinement Rd Rancho Cordova (95742) *(P-23364)*

Interctive Dsplay Slutions Inc F 949 727-9493
490 Wald Irvine (92618) *(P-18949)*

Interface Masters Tech Inc E 408 441-9341
150 E Brokaw Rd San Jose (95112) *(P-18950)*

Intergen Inc F 408 245-2737
1145 Tasman Dr Sunnyvale (94089) *(P-19327)*

Interglobal Waste Management D 805 388-1588
820 Calle Plano Camarillo (93012) *(P-21248)*

Interhealth Nutraceuticals Inc E 800 783-4636
5451 Industrial Way Benicia (94510) *(P-7670)*

Interior Corner Usa Inc F 626 452-8833
2714 Stingle Ave Rosemead (91770) *(P-4984)*

Interior Wood Design Inc F 530 888-7707
334 Sacramento St Ste 1 Auburn (95603) *(P-4577)*

Interior Wood of San Diego E 619 295-6469
1215 W Nutmeg St San Diego (92101) *(P-4803)*

Interlink Inc D 714 905-7700
3845 E Coronado St Anaheim (92807) *(P-6650)*

Interlock Industries Inc D 530 668-5690
1326 Paddock Pl Woodland (95776) *(P-12248)*

Interlog Construction, Anaheim *Also called Interlog Corporation (P-18951)*

Interlog Corporation E 714 529-7808
1295 N Knollwood Cir Anaheim (92801) *(P-18951)*

Intermag Inc C 916 568-6744
1650 Santa Ana Ave Sacramento (95838) *(P-19220)*

Intermetro Industries Corp E 909 987-4731
9420 Santa Anita Ave Rancho Cucamonga (91730) *(P-13418)*

Intermodal Structures Inc F 415 887-2211
251 Bagley St Vallejo (94592) *(P-4462)*

Intermolecular Inc (HQ) C 408 582-5700
3011 N 1st St San Jose (95134) *(P-18314)*

Intermune Inc (HQ) C 415 466-4383
1 Dna Way South San Francisco (94080) *(P-7955)*

Internacional De Elevadores SA F 619 955-6180
9475 Nicola Tesla Ct San Diego (92154) *(P-13803)*

International Abrasive Mfg Co E 714 779-9970
1517 N Harmony Cir Anaheim (92807) *(P-8517)*

International Academy of Fin (PA) E 818 361-7724
13177 Foothill Blvd Sylmar (91342) *(P-8745)*

International Apparel, San Diego *Also called Pk Industries Inc (P-10202)*

International Baggyz, Los Angeles *Also called Krissy Op Shins USA Inc (P-3100)*

International Beauty Pdts LLC (PA) F 818 999-1222
8200 Remmet Ave Canoga Park (91304) *(P-8518)*

International Bus Mchs Corp A 310 412-8699
6033 W Century Blvd # 610 Los Angeles (90045) *(P-14926)*

International Bus Mchs Corp A 714 472-2237
600 Anton Blvd Ste 400 Costa Mesa (92626) *(P-14927)*

International Co-Packing Co, Fresno *Also called Lidestri Foods Inc (P-789)*

International Coatings Co Inc (PA) E 562 926-1010
13929 166th St Cerritos (90703) *(P-8877)*

International Daily News Inc (PA) E 323 265-1317
870 Monterey Pass Rd Monterey Park (91754) *(P-5676)*

International Decoratives Co E 760 749-2682
27220 N Lake Wohlford Rd Valley Center (92082) *(P-23365)*

International Disc Mfr Inc E 714 210-1780
4906 W 1st St Santa Ana (92703) *(P-17329)*

Employee Codes: A=Over 500 employees, B=251-500
C=101-250, D=51-100, E=20-50, F=10-19
2020 California
Manfacturers Register
© Mergent Inc. 1-800-342-5647
1133

International E-Z Up Inc (PA) .....D.....800 457-4233
1900 2nd St Norco (92860) ***(P-3687)***
International Electronic Desig (PA) .....F.....714 662-1018
2630 S Shannon St Santa Ana (92704) ***(P-18952)***
International Forming Tech Inc .....E.....805 278-8060
2331 Sturgis Rd Oxnard (93030) ***(P-13979)***
International Group Inc .....F.....510 232-8704
102 Cutting Blvd Richmond (94804) ***(P-9048)***
International Group Inc .....D.....510 232-8704
102 Cutting Blvd Richmond (94804) ***(P-9049)***
International Immunology Corp .....E.....951 677-5629
25549 Adams Ave Murrieta (92562) ***(P-8233)***
International Inboard Mar Inc .....E.....209 384-2566
2556 W 16th St Merced (95348) ***(P-20340)***
International Iron Products, San Diego *Also called Price Industries Inc* ***(P-11061)***
International Last Mfg Co .....E.....818 767-2045
5060 Densmore Ave Encino (91436) ***(P-9842)***
International Mercantile .....F.....760 438-2205
6102 Avenida Encinas Carlsbad (92011) ***(P-19692)***
International Mfg Tech Inc (HQ) .....E.....619 544-7741
2798 Harbor Dr San Diego (92113) ***(P-11050)***
International Molders, Van Nuys *Also called Advance Latex Products Inc* ***(P-3438)***
International Paper, Ontario *Also called New-Indy Containerboard LLC* ***(P-5136)***
International Paper, Visalia *Also called Graphic Packaging Intl LLC* ***(P-5107)***
International Paper Company .....E.....510 490-5887
42305 Albrae St Fremont (94538) ***(P-5110)***
International Paper Company .....C.....714 776-6060
601 E Ball Rd Anaheim (92805) ***(P-5237)***
International Paper Company .....C.....559 651-1416
900 N Plaza Dr Visalia (93291) ***(P-5111)***
International Paper Company .....D.....559 592-7279
1111 N Anderson Rd Exeter (93221) ***(P-5112)***
International Paper Company .....C.....209 526-4700
660 Mariposa Rd Modesto (95354) ***(P-5163)***
International Paper Company .....D.....916 685-9000
10268 Waterman Rd Elk Grove (95624) ***(P-5113)***
International Paper Company .....C.....714 736-0296
6211 Descanso Ave Buena Park (90620) ***(P-5114)***
International Paper Company .....C.....323 946-6100
11211 Greenstone Ave Santa Fe Springs (90670) ***(P-5238)***
International Paper Company .....D.....408 846-2060
6791 Alexander St Gilroy (95020) ***(P-5115)***
International Paper Company .....F.....805 933-4347
2000 Pleasant Valley Rd Camarillo (93010) ***(P-5116)***
International Paper Company .....F.....310 639-2310
19615 S Susana Rd Compton (90221) ***(P-5117)***
International Paper Company .....F.....559 875-3311
1000 Muscat Ave Sanger (93657) ***(P-5118)***
International Paper Company .....F.....562 404-1856
14150 Artesia Blvd Cerritos (90703) ***(P-5119)***
International Paper Company .....F.....714 889-4900
11205 Knott Ave Ste A Cypress (90630) ***(P-5120)***
International Paper Company .....F.....562 483-6680
12851 Alondra Blvd Norwalk (90650) ***(P-5121)***
International Paper Company .....F.....831 755-2100
1345 Harkins Rd Salinas (93901) ***(P-5122)***
International Paper Company .....D.....408 847-6400
6400 Jamieson Way Gilroy (95020) ***(P-5123)***
International Paper Company .....E.....916 371-4634
1714 Cebrian St West Sacramento (95691) ***(P-5124)***
International Paper Company .....C.....562 692-9465
9211 Norwalk Blvd Santa Fe Springs (90670) ***(P-5125)***
International Paper Company .....D.....909 605-2540
3551 E Francis St Ontario (91761) ***(P-5164)***
International Paper Company .....C.....310 549-5525
1350 E 223rd St Carson (90745) ***(P-5126)***
International Paper Company .....E.....209 931-9005
3550 Bozzano Rd Stockton (95215) ***(P-5239)***
International Paper Company .....D.....562 868-2246
6485 Descanso Ave Buena Park (90620) ***(P-5127)***
International Petroleum Produc .....F.....925 556-5530
7600 Dublin Blvd Ste 240 Dublin (94568) ***(P-9147)***
International Precision Inc .....E.....818 882-3933
9526 Vassar Ave Chatsworth (91311) ***(P-16053)***
International Printing & Typsg .....F.....818 787-6804
14535 Hamlin St Van Nuys (91411) ***(P-6651)***
International Processing Corp (HQ) .....E.....310 458-1574
233 Wilshire Blvd Ste 310 Santa Monica (90401) ***(P-1101)***
International Rectifier Corp (PA) .....E.....949 453-1008
17885 Von Karman Ave # 100 Irvine (92614) ***(P-18315)***
International RES Dev Corp Nev (PA) .....F.....858 488-9900
5212 Chelsea St La Jolla (92037) ***(P-19192)***
International Rite-Way Pdts, Ontario *Also called AMD International Tech LLC* ***(P-12102)***
International Rubber Pdts Inc (PA) .....D.....909 947-1244
1035 Calle Amanecer San Clemente (92673) ***(P-9323)***
International Sales Inc .....E.....760 722-1455
3210 Production Ave Ste B Oceanside (92058) ***(P-22829)***
International Seal Company, Santa Ana *Also called Freudenberg-Nok General Partnr* ***(P-9230)***
International Seals, Santa Ana *Also called Hernandez Zeferino* ***(P-8874)***
International Sensor Tech .....E.....949 452-9000
3 Whatney Ste 100 Irvine (92618) ***(P-21490)***
International Stem Cell Corp (PA) .....E.....760 940-6383
5950 Priestly Dr Carlsbad (92008) ***(P-7956)***
International Technidyne Corp (HQ) .....C.....858 263-2300
6260 Sequence Dr San Diego (92121) ***(P-21748)***
International Tents & Supplies .....F.....818 599-6258
1720 1st St San Fernando (91340) ***(P-3688)***
International Tranducer Corp .....C.....805 683-2575
869 Ward Dr Santa Barbara (93111) ***(P-21055)***
International Trend - 3 Corp .....E.....562 360-5185
7103 Marcelle St Paramount (90723) ***(P-3094)***
International Vitamin Corp .....C.....951 361-1120
11010 Hopkins St Ste B Mira Loma (91752) ***(P-7957)***
International Vitamin Corp (PA) .....B.....949 664-5500
1 Park Plz Ste 800 Irvine (92614) ***(P-7958)***
International West Inc .....D.....714 632-9190
1025 N Armando St Anaheim (92806) ***(P-12249)***
International Wind Inc (PA) .....E.....562 240-3963
137 N Joy St Corona (92879) ***(P-19966)***
International Wood Products, San Diego *Also called Jeld-Wen Inc* ***(P-4063)***
Internationally Delicious Inc (PA) .....F.....925 426-6155
174 Lawrence Dr Ste J Livermore (94551) ***(P-1344)***
Internet Industry Publishing .....E.....415 733-5400
315 Pacific Ave San Francisco (94111) ***(P-5968)***
Internet Machines Corporation (PA) .....D.....818 575-2100
30501 Agoura Rd Ste 203 Agoura Hills (91301) ***(P-15258)***
Internet Science Education Prj .....F.....415 806-3156
805 Chestnut St San Francisco (94133) ***(P-20464)***
Internet Strategy Inc .....F.....858 673-6022
10875 Rancho Bernardo Rd # 100 San Diego (92127) ***(P-24029)***
Internet Systems Cnsortium Inc (PA) .....F.....650 423-1300
950 Charter St Redwood City (94063) ***(P-24030)***
Interntional Color Posters Inc .....E.....949 768-1005
8081 Orangethorpe Ave Buena Park (90621) ***(P-7101)***
Interntional Photo Plates Corp .....E.....805 496-5031
2641 Townsgate Rd Ste 100 Westlake Village (91361) ***(P-13032)***
Interntional Thermal Instr Inc .....F.....858 755-4436
4511 Sun Valley Rd Del Mar (92014) ***(P-21249)***
Interntnal Assmbly Specialists, Aliso Viejo *Also called Shugart Corporation* ***(P-14974)***
Interntnal Cnnctors Cable Corp .....C.....888 275-4422
2100 E Valencia Dr Ste D Fullerton (92831) ***(P-17381)***
Interntnal Hmeopathic Mfg Dist .....F.....818 884-8040
7108 De Soto Ave Ste 105 Canoga Park (91303) ***(P-7959)***
Interntnal Indian Traty Cuncil .....F.....415 641-4482
2940 16th St Ste 305 San Francisco (94103) ***(P-22830)***
Interntnal Mdction Systems Ltd .....F.....626 459-5586
10642 El Poche St South El Monte (91733) ***(P-7671)***
Interntnal Mdction Systems Ltd .....A.....626 442-6757
1886 Santa Anita Ave South El Monte (91733) ***(P-7960)***
Interntnal Plymr Solutions Inc .....E.....949 458-3731
5 Studebaker Irvine (92618) ***(P-13308)***
Interntnal Veterinary Sciences, Anaheim *Also called Animal Nutrition Inds Inc* ***(P-7645)***
Interntnal Virtual PDT MGT Inc .....F.....818 812-9500
8957 De Soto Ave Canoga Park (91304) ***(P-17382)***
Interntonal Metallurgical Svcs .....F.....310 645-7300
6371 Arizona Cir Los Angeles (90045) ***(P-11454)***
Interntonal Thermoproducts Div, Santee *Also called Ds Fibertech Corp* ***(P-14760)***
Interocean Industries Inc .....E.....858 292-0808
3738 Ruffin Rd San Diego (92123) ***(P-20589)***
Interocean Systems, San Diego *Also called Interocean Industries Inc* ***(P-20589)***
Interocean Systems LLC .....E.....858 565-8400
3738 Ruffin Rd San Diego (92123) ***(P-20590)***
Interocean Systems, Inc., San Diego *Also called Interocean Systems LLC* ***(P-20590)***
Interorbital Systems .....F.....661 824-1662
1394 Barnes St Bldg 7 Mojave (93501) ***(P-11383)***
Interplastic, Ontario *Also called North American Composites Co* ***(P-7586)***
Interplastic Corporation .....E.....323 757-1801
12335 S Van Ness Ave Hawthorne (90250) ***(P-7570)***
Interplastic Corporation .....F.....209 932-0396
611 Gilmore Ave Ste C Stockton (95203) ***(P-7571)***
Interplex Nascal Inc .....D.....714 505-2900
15777 Gateway Cir Tustin (92780) ***(P-12823)***
Interpore Cross Intl Inc (HQ) .....D.....949 453-3200
181 Technology Dr Irvine (92618) ***(P-22033)***
Interpress Technologies Inc (HQ) .....E.....916 929-9771
1120 Del Paso Rd Sacramento (95834) ***(P-5165)***
Interscan Corporation .....E.....805 823-8301
4590 Ish Dr Ste 110 Simi Valley (93063) ***(P-20970)***
Intersect Ent Inc (PA) .....C.....650 641-2100
1555 Adams Dr Menlo Park (94025) ***(P-21749)***
Intershop Communications Inc .....E.....415 844-1500
461 2nd St Apt 151 San Francisco (94107) ***(P-24031)***
Intersil Design Center, San Diego *Also called Renesas Electronics Amer Inc* ***(P-18515)***
Intersil Quellan, Milpitas *Also called Quellan Inc* ***(P-18504)***
Interson Corp .....E.....925 462-4948
7150 Koll Center Pkwy Pleasanton (94566) ***(P-22264)***
Interspace Battery Inc (PA) .....F.....626 813-1234
2009 W San Bernardino Rd West Covina (91790) ***(P-11274)***
Interstate Cabinet Inc .....E.....951 736-0777
1631 Pomona Rd Ste B Corona (92880) ***(P-23366)***
Interstate Carports Corp .....F.....951 654-1750
1280 S Buena Vista St A San Jacinto (92583) ***(P-12550)***
Interstate Design Industry, Corona *Also called Interstate Cabinet Inc* ***(P-23366)***
Interstate Electronics Corp (HQ) .....B.....714 758-0500
602 E Vermont Ave Anaheim (92805) ***(P-21056)***
Interstate Electronics Corp .....E.....714 758-3395
604 E Vermont Ave Anaheim (92805) ***(P-17543)***
Interstate Meat Co Inc .....F.....323 838-9400
6114 Scott Way Commerce (90040) ***(P-14375)***
Interstate Rebar Inc .....F.....805 643-6892
2457 N Ventura Ave Ste L Ventura (93001) ***(P-11051)***
Interstate Steel Center Co .....E.....323 583-0855
7001 S Alameda St Los Angeles (90001) ***(P-11261)***
Intertex LLC .....E.....626 385-3300
550 S Ayon Ave Azusa (91702) ***(P-14664)***
Intertex, Inc., Azusa *Also called Intertex LLC* ***(P-14664)***
Intertool Innovative Tooling, San Leandro *Also called Leitch & Co Inc* ***(P-11535)***

Intertrade Aviation Corp........E.......714 895-3335
5722 Buckingham Dr Huntington Beach (92649) *(P-20140)*
Interworking Labs Inc........F.......831 460-7010
230 Mount Hermon Rd # 208 Scotts Valley (95066) *(P-24032)*
Intest Corporation........E.......408 678-9123
47777 Warm Springs Blvd Fremont (94539) *(P-18316)*
Intest Silicon Valley Corp........E.......408 678-9123
47777 Warm Springs Blvd Fremont (94539) *(P-18317)*
Intevac Inc (PA)........C.......408 986-9888
3560 Bassett St Santa Clara (95054) *(P-14480)*
Intevac Inc........E.......408 986-9888
3560 Bassett St Santa Clara (95054) *(P-14481)*
Intevac Photonics Inc (HQ)........F.......408 986-9888
3560 Bassett St Santa Clara (95054) *(P-21367)*
Intevac Photonics Inc........E.......760 476-0339
5909 Sea Lion Pl Ste A Carlsbad (92010) *(P-21368)*
Intevac Vision Systems, Carlsbad *Also called Intevac Photonics Inc (P-21368)*
Intex Forms Inc........E.......650 654-7855
1333 Old County Rd Belmont (94002) *(P-10313)*
Intimo Industry, Vernon *Also called Pjy Inc (P-2709)*
Intouch Health, Goleta *Also called Intouch Technologies Inc (P-24033)*
Intouch Technologies Inc (PA)........C.......805 562-8686
7402 Hollister Ave Goleta (93117) *(P-24033)*
Intra Aerospace LLC........E.......909 476-0343
10671 Civic Center Dr Rancho Cucamonga (91730) *(P-14742)*
Intraop Medical Services, Sunnyvale *Also called Mc Liquidation Inc (P-22278)*
Intri-Plex Technologies Inc (HQ)........C.......805 683-3414
751 S Kellogg Ave Goleta (93117) *(P-12824)*
Intro Designs, Anaheim *Also called Moreno Industries Inc (P-19723)*
Intubrite LLC........F.......760 727-1900
2460 Coral St Vista (92081) *(P-21750)*
Intuit Inc........E.......858 215-8726
7535 Torrey Santa Fe Rd San Diego (92129) *(P-24034)*
Intuit Inc (PA)........D.......650 944-6000
2700 Coast Ave Mountain View (94043) *(P-24035)*
Intuit Inc........C.......650 944-6000
2700 Coast Ave Bldg 7 Mountain View (94043) *(P-24036)*
Intuit Inc........F.......650 944-6000
2650 Casey Ave Mountain View (94043) *(P-24037)*
Intuit Inc........C.......650 944-6000
2535 Garcia Ave Mountain View (94043) *(P-24038)*
Intuit Inc........C.......650 944-2840
141 Corona Way Portola Valley (94028) *(P-24039)*
Intuit Inc........C.......650 944-6000
180 Jefferson Dr Menlo Park (94025) *(P-24040)*
Intuit Inc........B.......858 215-8000
7545 Torrey Santa Fe Rd San Diego (92129) *(P-24041)*
Intuitive Srgcal Oprations Inc........E.......408 523-2100
1020 Kifer Rd Sunnyvale (94086) *(P-21751)*
Intuitive Srgical Holdings LLC (HQ)........F.......408 523-2100
1020 Kifer Rd Sunnyvale (94086) *(P-21752)*
Intuitive Surgical Inc........E.......408 523-7314
1250 Kifer Rd Sunnyvale (94086) *(P-21753)*
Intuitive Surgical Inc........B.......408 523-2100
3410 Central Expy Santa Clara (95051) *(P-21754)*
Intuitive Surgical Inc (PA)........C.......408 523-2100
1020 Kifer Rd Sunnyvale (94086) *(P-21755)*
Intuity Medical Inc........D.......408 530-1700
3500 W Warren Ave Fremont (94538) *(P-21756)*
Invax Technologies, Sunnyvale *Also called Gulshan International Corp (P-18260)*
Invecas Inc........E.......408 758-5636
3385 Scott Blvd Santa Clara (95054) *(P-18318)*
Invelop Inc........E.......818 772-2887
9711 Mason Ave Chatsworth (91311) *(P-13636)*
Invenio Imaging Inc........F.......408 753-9147
2310 Walsh Ave Santa Clara (95051) *(P-21757)*
Invenios LLC........D.......805 962-3333
320 N Nopal St Santa Barbara (93103) *(P-10367)*
Invenlux Corporation........E.......626 277-4163
168 Mason Way Ste B5 City of Industry (91746) *(P-18319)*
Invensas Corporation........E.......408 324-5100
3025 Orchard Pkwy San Jose (95134) *(P-18320)*
Invensense Inc (HQ)........C.......408 501-2200
1745 Tech Dr Ste 200 San Jose (95110) *(P-20591)*
Inventive Resources Inc........F.......209 545-1663
5038 Salida Blvd Salida (95368) *(P-12250)*
Inverse Solutions Inc........E.......925 931-9500
3922 Valley Ave Ste A Pleasanton (94566) *(P-16054)*
Investment Enterprises Inc (PA)........E.......818 464-3800
8230 Haskell Ave Ste 8240 Van Nuys (91406) *(P-7102)*
Investment Land Appraisers........F.......310 819-8831
333 E 157th St Gardena (90248) *(P-7334)*
Investors Business Daily Inc (HQ)........C.......310 448-6000
12655 Beatrice St Los Angeles (90066) *(P-5677)*
Invia Robotics Inc (PA)........F.......818 597-1680
5701 Lindero Canyon Rd 3-100 Westlake Village (91362) *(P-14830)*
Invisalign, San Jose *Also called Align Technology Inc (P-22131)*
Invoice2go Inc (PA)........E.......650 300-5180
2317 Broadway St Fl 2 Redwood City (94063) *(P-24042)*
Invotech Systems Inc........F.......818 461-9800
20951 Burbank Blvd Ste B Woodland Hills (91367) *(P-24043)*
Invuity Inc........C.......415 665-2100
444 De Haro St Ste 110 San Francisco (94107) *(P-21758)*
Inwesco Incorporated (PA)........D.......626 334-7115
746 N Coney Ave Azusa (91702) *(P-11098)*
INX Digital Intl, San Leandro *Also called INX International Ink Co (P-8923)*
INX International Ink Co........F.......510 895-8001
2125 Williams St San Leandro (94577) *(P-8923)*
INX International Ink Co........F.......562 404-5664
13821 Marquardt Ave Santa Fe Springs (90670) *(P-8924)*
INX International Ink Co........F.......707 693-2990
1000 Business Park Dr Dixon (95620) *(P-8925)*
INX Prints Inc........D.......949 660-9190
1802 Kettering Irvine (92614) *(P-2845)*
Inyo Register, The, Bishop *Also called Horizon Publications Inc (P-5667)*
Io2 Technology LLC........F.......650 308-4216
310 Shaw Rd Ste G South San Francisco (94080) *(P-13282)*
Iog Products LLC........F.......818 350-5070
9737 Lurline Ave Chatsworth (91311) *(P-18321)*
Iogyn Inc........F.......408 996-2517
150 Baytech Dr San Jose (95134) *(P-22265)*
Iomic Inc........F.......714 564-1600
530 Technology Dr Ste 100 Irvine (92618) *(P-9324)*
Ionetix Corporation (PA)........E.......415 944-1440
101 The Embarcadero # 210 San Francisco (94105) *(P-19328)*
Ionis Pharmaceuticals Inc........E.......760 603-3567
2282 Faraday Ave Carlsbad (92008) *(P-7961)*
Ionis Pharmaceuticals Inc (PA)........B.......760 931-9200
2855 Gazelle Ct Carlsbad (92010) *(P-7962)*
Ios Optics, Santa Clara *Also called Integrated Optical Svcs Corp (P-8647)*
Iosafe Inc........F.......888 984-6723
10600 Industrial Ave # 120 Roseville (95678) *(P-15050)*
IOu International Inc........E.......323 846-0056
2624 Geraldine St Los Angeles (90011) *(P-2903)*
Iovance Biotherapeutics Inc (PA)........E.......650 260-7120
999 Skyway Rd Ste 150 San Carlos (94070) *(P-7963)*
Iowa Approach Inc........F.......650 422-3633
3715 Haven Ave Ste 110 Menlo Park (94025) *(P-21759)*
Ipac, Dublin *Also called International Petroleum Produc (P-9147)*
Ipac Inc........F.......925 556-5530
7600 Dublin Blvd Ste 240 Dublin (94568) *(P-9148)*
Iparis LLC........F.......866 293-2872
10120 Wexted Way Elk Grove (95757) *(P-14928)*
Ipart Automotive, Fontana *Also called Iparts Inc (P-9843)*
Iparts Inc........F.......909 587-6059
14975 Hilton Dr Fontana (92336) *(P-9843)*
Ipayables Inc (PA)........D.......949 215-9122
95 Argonaut Ste 270 Aliso Viejo (92656) *(P-24044)*
IPC Cal Flex Inc........E.......714 952-0373
13337 South St 307 Cerritos (90703) *(P-17902)*
IPC Industries Inc (PA)........F.......951 695-2720
27230 Madison Ave Ste C2 Temecula (92590) *(P-20514)*
Ipco Printing, Martinez *Also called Independent Printing Co Inc (P-6635)*
Ipex USA LLC........F.......209 368-7131
2395 Maggio Cir Lodi (95240) *(P-9469)*
Ipitek Group Inc........C.......760 438-8362
2330 Faraday Ave Carlsbad (92008) *(P-17544)*
Ipolipo Inc........D.......408 916-5290
440 N Wolfe Rd Sunnyvale (94085) *(P-24045)*
Ipolymer, Irvine *Also called Interntnal Plymr Solutions Inc (P-13308)*
Ipp Plastics Products Inc........F.......626 357-1178
4610 Littlejohn St Baldwin Park (91706) *(P-7572)*
Ipr Software, Encino *Also called Ipressroom Inc (P-24046)*
Ipressroom Inc........E.......310 499-0544
16501 Ventura Blvd # 424 Encino (91436) *(P-24046)*
Ips Corporation (HQ)........C.......310 898-3300
455 W Victoria St Compton (90220) *(P-8878)*
Ips Corporation........D.......310 516-7013
17110 S Main St Gardena (90248) *(P-8879)*
Ips Industries Inc........D.......562 623-2555
12641 166th St Cerritos (90703) *(P-9844)*
Ips Printing Inc........E.......916 442-8961
2020 K St Sacramento (95811) *(P-6652)*
Iq Textile Ind Inc........F.......213 745-2290
3003 S Hill St Los Angeles (90007) *(P-2937)*
Iq-Analog Corporation........E.......858 200-0388
12348 High Bluff Dr # 110 San Diego (92130) *(P-18322)*
Iqair North America Inc........E.......877 715-4247
14351 Firestone Blvd La Mirada (90638) *(P-14665)*
Iqd Frequency Products Inc........E.......760 318-2824
777 E Tahqtz Cyn Way # 200 Palm Springs (92262) *(P-18953)*
Iqinvision Inc........D.......949 369-8100
27127 Calle Arroyo # 1920 San Juan Capistrano (92675) *(P-22431)*
Iqms (HQ)........C.......805 227-1122
2231 Wisteria Ln Paso Robles (93446) *(P-24047)*
Ira Gold Group LLC........F.......800 984-6008
9107 Wilshire Blvd # 450 Beverly Hills (90210) *(P-11191)*
Ircamera LLC........E.......805 965-9650
30 S Calle Cesar Chavez Santa Barbara (93103) *(P-21369)*
IRD, La Jolla *Also called International RES Dev Corp Nev (P-19192)*
IRD Acquisitions LLC........F.......530 210-2966
12810 Earhart Ave Auburn (95602) *(P-22363)*
Irene Kasmer Inc........F.......310 553-8986
315 S Bedford Dr Beverly Hills (90212) *(P-3231)*
Irhythm Technologies Inc (PA)........E.......415 632-5700
650 Townsend St Ste 500 San Francisco (94103) *(P-22266)*
Iri, Salida *Also called Inventive Resources Inc (P-12250)*
Iridex, Mountain View *Also called Iris Medical Instruments Inc (P-22268)*
Iridex Corporation (PA)........C.......650 940-4700
1212 Terra Bella Ave Mountain View (94043) *(P-22267)*
Iris Group Inc........C.......760 431-1103
1675 Faraday Ave Carlsbad (92008) *(P-7103)*
Iris Medical Instruments Inc........C.......650 940-4700
1212 Terra Bella Ave Mountain View (94043) *(P-22268)*
Irisys LLC........E.......858 623-1520
6828 Nncy Rdge Dr Ste 100 San Diego (92121) *(P-7964)*
Irl-Mex Manufacturing Company........F.......818 246-7211
1436 Flower St Glendale (91201) *(P-12636)*
IRM, Madera *Also called Innovtive Rttional Molding Inc (P-9841)*

A L P H A B E T I C

Employee Codes: A=Over 500 employees, B=251-500
C=101-250, D=51-100, E=20-50, F=10-19
2020 California
Manfacturers Register
© Mergent Inc. 1-800-342-5647
1135

Iron and Resin, Ventura *Also called Streamline Dsign Slkscreen Inc* ***(P-7232)***
Iron Beds of America, Los Angeles *Also called Wesley Allen Inc* ***(P-4708)***
Iron Dog Fabrication Inc....F....707 579-7831
3450 Regional Pkwy Ste E Santa Rosa (95403) ***(P-11813)***
Iron Grip Barbell Company Inc....D....714 850-6900
4012 W Garry Ave Santa Ana (92704) ***(P-22831)***
Iron Master....F....818 361-4060
759 Arroyo St Ste D San Fernando (91340) ***(P-12482)***
Iron Shield Inc....F....626 287-4568
5926 Agnes Ave Temple City (91780) ***(P-12483)***
Iron Works & Custom Racks....F....323 581-2222
15337 Illinois Ave Paramount (90723) ***(P-24641)***
Iron Works Enterprises Inc....E....209 572-7450
801 S 7th St Modesto (95351) ***(P-19824)***
Ironclad Tool and Machine Inc....F....661 833-9990
120 Old Yard Dr Bakersfield (93307) ***(P-16055)***
Ironhead Studios Inc....F....818 901-7561
7616 Ventura Canyon Ave Van Nuys (91402) ***(P-3558)***
Ironies LLC....E....510 644-2100
2222 5th St Berkeley (94710) ***(P-4804)***
Ironridge Inc (HQ)....E....800 227-9523
28357 Industrial Blvd Hayward (94545) ***(P-11703)***
Ironwood Electric Inc....E....714 630-2350
1239 N Tustin Ave Anaheim (92807) ***(P-19329)***
Irp, San Clemente *Also called International Rubber Pdts Inc* ***(P-9323)***
Irritec Usa Inc....F....559 275-8825
1420 N Irritec Way Fresno (93703) ***(P-13637)***
Irrometer Company Inc....F....951 682-9505
1425 Palmyrita Ave Riverside (92507) ***(P-21491)***
Irtronix Inc....F....310 787-1100
20900 Normandie Ave B Torrance (90502) ***(P-16865)***
Irvine & Jachens Inc....F....650 755-4715
6700 Mission St Daly City (94014) ***(P-23367)***
Irvine Electronics Inc....D....949 250-0315
1601 Alton Pkwy Ste A Irvine (92606) ***(P-17903)***
Irvine Scientific, Santa Ana *Also called Fujifilm Irvine Scientific Inc* ***(P-8302)***
Irvine Sensors Corporation....E....714 444-8700
3000 Airway Ave Ste A1 Costa Mesa (92626) ***(P-18323)***
Irwin Aviation Inc....E....951 372-9555
225 Airport Cir Corona (92880) ***(P-20141)***
Isabelle Handbags Inc....E....323 277-9888
3155 Bandini Blvd Unit A Vernon (90058) ***(P-10224)***
Isap, San Diego *Also called Industrial SEC Allianc Ptnrs* ***(P-22429)***
ISC Engineering LLC....D....909 596-3315
4351 Schaefer Ave Chino (91710) ***(P-16790)***
Iscience Interventional Corp....D....650 421-2700
41316 Christy St Fremont (94538) ***(P-21760)***
Isec Incorporated....C....858 279-9085
5735 Krny Vlla Rd Ste 105 San Diego (92123) ***(P-20763)***
Isharya Inc....E....415 462-6294
4340 Stevens Creek Blvd San Jose (95129) ***(P-22530)***
ISI, Garden Grove *Also called Inductor Supply Inc* ***(P-18720)***
ISI, Oceanside *Also called International Sales Inc* ***(P-22829)***
ISI Detention Contg Group Inc....D....714 288-1770
577 N Batavia St Orange (92868) ***(P-16056)***
Isign Solutions Inc (PA)....F....650 802-7888
2033 Gateway Pl Ste 659 San Jose (95110) ***(P-15259)***
Isiqalo LLC....B....714 683-2820
5521 Schaefer Ave Chino (91710) ***(P-2791)***
Isis Pharmaceuticals....F....760 603-2631
1767 Avenida Segovia Oceanside (92056) ***(P-7965)***
Island Brewing Co....F....805 745-8272
5049 6th St Carpinteria (93013) ***(P-1539)***
Island Color Inc....F....714 352-5888
3972 Barranca Pkwy J521 Irvine (92606) ***(P-6653)***
Island Mountain Lumber, Willits *Also called G and S Milling Co* ***(P-4047)***
Island Powder Coating....E....626 279-2460
1830 Tyler Ave South El Monte (91733) ***(P-13194)***
Island Products, Buena Park *Also called Island Snacks Inc* ***(P-1375)***
Island Snacks Inc....E....714 994-1228
7650 Stage Rd Buena Park (90621) ***(P-1375)***
Ismart Alarm Inc....E....408 245-2551
120 San Lucar Ct Sunnyvale (94086) ***(P-17734)***
Isolatek International, San Bernardino *Also called United States Mineral Pdts Co* ***(P-10989)***
Isolation Network Inc (PA)....E....415 489-7000
55 Francisco St Ste 350 San Francisco (94133) ***(P-17246)***
Isolink Inc....E....408 946-1968
880 Yosemite Way Milpitas (95035) ***(P-18954)***
Isolutecom Inc (PA)....E....805 498-6259
9 Northam Ave Newbury Park (91320) ***(P-24048)***
Isomedia LLC....E....510 668-1656
41380 Christy St Fremont (94538) ***(P-17330)***
Isotope Products Lab, Valencia *Also called Eckert Zegler Isotope Pdts Inc* ***(P-21464)***
Isp Granule Products Inc....D....209 274-2930
1900 Hwy 104 Ione (95640) ***(P-10972)***
Issac, Tustin *Also called Trelleborg Sealing Solutions* ***(P-21936)***
ISU Petasys Corp....D....818 833-5800
12930 Bradley Ave Sylmar (91342) ***(P-17904)***
It Concepts LLC....F....925 401-0010
1244 Quarry Ln Ste B Pleasanton (94566) ***(P-21370)***
It Retail Inc....F....951 683-4950
191 W Big Springs Rd Riverside (92507) ***(P-24049)***
It's Delish, North Hollywood *Also called Mave Enterprises Inc* ***(P-1388)***
Italix Company Inc....F....408 988-2487
120 Mast St Ste A Morgan Hill (95037) ***(P-13195)***
Itc Nexus Holding Company, San Diego *Also called Accriva Dgnostics Holdings Inc* ***(P-21578)***
Itc Sftware Slutions Group LLC (PA)....E....877 248-2774
201 Sandpointe Ave # 305 Santa Ana (92707) ***(P-24050)***
Itcssg, Santa Ana *Also called Itc Sftware Slutions Group LLC* ***(P-24050)***
Itech, San Diego *Also called Intelligent Technologies LLC* ***(P-16789)***
Itech Medical Inc....F....714 841-2670
17011 Beach Blvd Ste 900 Huntington Beach (92647) ***(P-21761)***
Iteris Inc (PA)....C....949 270-9400
1700 Carnegie Ave Ste 100 Santa Ana (92705) ***(P-22432)***
Itouchless Housewares Pdts Inc....E....650 578-0578
777 Mariners Island Blvd # 125 San Mateo (94404) ***(P-9845)***
Its, Brea *Also called ITS Group Inc* ***(P-16722)***
Its, Northridge *Also called Instrumentation Tech Systems* ***(P-15249)***
ITS Group Inc....F....714 256-4100
266 Viking Ave Brea (92821) ***(P-16722)***
Itt LLC....C....707 523-2300
500 Tesconi Cir Santa Rosa (95401) ***(P-16908)***
ITT Aerospace Controls LLC....B....661 295-4000
28150 Industry Dr Valencia (91355) ***(P-20142)***
ITT Aerospace Controls LLC....E....661 295-4000
28150 Industry Dr Valencia (91355) ***(P-20143)***
ITT Corporation....B....714 557-4700
56 Technology Dr Irvine (92618) ***(P-16723)***
ITT LLC....D....562 908-4144
3951 Capitol Ave City of Industry (90601) ***(P-16724)***
ITT LLC....F....626 305-6100
1400 S Shamrock Ave Monrovia (91016) ***(P-16725)***
ITT LLC....F....559 265-4730
3878 S Willow Ave Ste 104 Fresno (93725) ***(P-14586)***
ITT Water & Wastewater USA Inc....E....707 422-9894
790 Chadbourne Rd Ste A Fairfield (94534) ***(P-14587)***
Ittavi Inc....E....866 246-4408
1631 Alhambra Blvd # 120 Sacramento (95816) ***(P-24051)***
Ituner Networks Corporation....F....510 226-6033
47801 Fremont Blvd Fremont (94538) ***(P-15260)***
ITW Alpine, Sacramento *Also called ITW Blding Cmponents Group Inc* ***(P-12022)***
ITW Blding Cmponents Group Inc....E....916 387-0116
8801 Folsom Blvd Ste 107 Sacramento (95826) ***(P-12022)***
ITW Global Tire Repair Inc....D....805 489-0490
125 Venture Dr Ste 210 San Luis Obispo (93401) ***(P-9168)***
ITW Plymers Salants N Amer Inc....E....714 898-0025
12271 Monarch St Garden Grove (92841) ***(P-7573)***
ITW Semisystems Inc....E....408 350-0244
625 Wool Creek Dr Ste G San Jose (95112) ***(P-11218)***
ITW-Opto Diode, Camarillo *Also called Illinois Tool Works Inc* ***(P-18279)***
IV Support Systems Inc....F....888 688-6822
12 Hughes Ste 105 Irvine (92618) ***(P-21762)***
IV Welding & Mechanical Inc....F....760 482-9353
185 S 3rd St El Centro (92243) ***(P-24642)***
Ivanti Inc....F....408 343-8181
150 Mathilda Pl Ste 302 Sunnyvale (94086) ***(P-24052)***
Ivar's Displays, Ontario *Also called Ivars Cabinet Shop Inc* ***(P-4912)***
Ivars Cabinet Shop Inc (PA)....C....909 923-2761
2314 E Locust Ct Ontario (91761) ***(P-4912)***
Ivera Medical Corporation, San Diego *Also called Ivera Medical LLC* ***(P-21763)***
Ivera Medical LLC....D....888 861-8228
10805 Rancho Bernardo Rd # 100 San Diego (92127) ***(P-21763)***
Iverson & Logging Inc....F....707 937-0028
41575 Little Lake Rd Mendocino (95460) ***(P-3888)***
IVEX Ontario, Ontario *Also called IVEX Protective Packaging Inc* ***(P-7574)***
IVEX Protective Packaging Inc....E....909 390-4422
1550 Champagne Ave Ontario (91761) ***(P-7574)***
Ivoprop Corporation....F....562 602-1451
15903 Lakewood Blvd # 103 Bellflower (90706) ***(P-20144)***
Ivydoctors Inc....F....415 890-3937
555 Bryant St Palo Alto (94301) ***(P-24053)***
Iwatt Inc (HQ)....E....408 374-4200
675 Campbell Tech Pkwy # 150 Campbell (95008) ***(P-18324)***
Iwco Direct - Downey, Downey *Also called Instant Web LLC* ***(P-6643)***
Iwcus, Walnut *Also called Infinity Watch Corporation* ***(P-23132)***
Iwen Naturals....F....510 589-8019
4150 Mystic View Ct Hayward (94542) ***(P-8519)***
Iwerks Entertainment Inc....D....661 678-1800
27509 Avenue Hopkins Santa Clarita (91355) ***(P-19330)***
Iwi, Sunnyvale *Also called Intella Interventional Systems* ***(P-21747)***
Iwl, Scotts Valley *Also called Interworking Labs Inc* ***(P-24032)***
Iws Predictive Technologies, Yorba Linda *Also called Inflight Warning Systems Inc* ***(P-20138)***
Ix Medical (PA)....F....877 902-6446
725 W Anaheim St Long Beach (90813) ***(P-22034)***
Ixi Technology, Yorba Linda *Also called Mc2 Sabtech Holdings Inc* ***(P-14940)***
Ixia, Santa Clara *Also called Net Optics Inc* ***(P-24192)***
Ixia (HQ)....B....818 871-1800
26601 Agoura Rd Calabasas (91302) ***(P-21057)***
Ixia....F....818 871-1800
26701 Agoura Rd Calabasas (91302) ***(P-21058)***
Ixia Communications, Calabasas *Also called Ixia* ***(P-21058)***
Ixsystems Inc (PA)....D....408 943-4100
2490 Kruse Dr San Jose (95131) ***(P-24054)***
Ixys LLC (HQ)....D....408 457-9000
1590 Buckeye Dr Milpitas (95035) ***(P-18325)***
Ixys Intgrtd Crcts Div AV Inc....E....949 831-4622
145 Columbia Aliso Viejo (92656) ***(P-18326)***
Ixys Long Beach Inc (HQ)....E....562 296-6584
2500 Mira Mar Ave Long Beach (90815) ***(P-18327)***
Izurieta Fence Company Inc....F....323 661-4759
3000 Gilroy St Los Angeles (90039) ***(P-11099)***
J & A Jeffery Inc....E....707 678-0369
395 Industrial Way Ste B Dixon (95620) ***(P-23368)***
J & A Pallet Accessory Inc....F....951 785-1594
6607 Doolittle Ave Ste A Riverside (92503) ***(P-4375)***

Mergent e-mail: customerrelations@mergent.com
1136
2020 California
Manufacturers Register
(P-0000) Products & Services Section entry number
(PA)=Parent Co (HQ)=Headquarters (DH)=Div Headquarters

ALPHABETIC SECTION
J S M Productions Inc

J & A Shoe Company Inc ....C....310 324-0139
960 Knox St Bldg A Torrance (90502) ***(P-10171)***

J & B Enterprises, Santa Clara *Also called J & B Refining Inc* ***(P-11192)***

J & B Manufacturing Corp ....C....760 846-6316
2780 La Mirada Dr Ste C Vista (92081) ***(P-10368)***

J & B Refining Inc ....F....408 988-7900
1650 Russell Ave Santa Clara (95054) ***(P-11192)***

J & C Apparel ....E....323 490-8260
757 Towne Ave Unit B Los Angeles (90021) ***(P-3009)***

J & C Custom Cabinets Inc ....E....916 638-3400
11451 Elks Cir Rancho Cordova (95742) ***(P-4805)***

J & D Business Forms Inc ....F....626 914-1777
650 W Terrace Dr San Dimas (91773) ***(P-6654)***

J & D Laboratories Inc ....B....844 453-5227
2710 Progress St Vista (92081) ***(P-7672)***

J & F Design Inc ....D....323 526-4444
2042 Garfield Ave Commerce (90040) ***(P-3340)***

J & F Machine Inc ....E....714 527-3499
6401 Global Dr Cypress (90630) ***(P-16057)***

J & H Drilling Co Inc ....F....714 994-0402
7431 Walnut Ave Buena Park (90620) ***(P-95)***

J & J Action Inc ....F....877 327-5268
3210 S Standard Ave Santa Ana (92705) ***(P-16830)***

J & J Co, Chatsworth *Also called J & J Products Inc* ***(P-13527)***

J & J Processing Inc ....E....562 926-2333
14715 Anson Ave Santa Fe Springs (90670) ***(P-2217)***

J & J Products Inc ....F....818 998-4250
9134 Independence Ave Chatsworth (91311) ***(P-13527)***

J & J Quality Door Inc ....E....209 948-5013
741 S Airport Way Stockton (95205) ***(P-4060)***

J & J Screen Printing, Rancho Cordova *Also called Arteez* ***(P-6992)***

J & J Snack Foods Corp Cal (HQ) ....C....323 581-0171
5353 S Downey Rd Vernon (90058) ***(P-1316)***

J & L Cstm Plstic Extrsons Inc ....E....626 442-0711
1532 Santa Anita Ave South El Monte (91733) ***(P-9846)***

J & L Digital Precision Inc ....F....650 592-0170
551 Taylor Way Ste 15 San Carlos (94070) ***(P-18955)***

J & L Imaging Center, Anaheim *Also called Jaguar Litho Incorporated* ***(P-7378)***

J & L Irrigation Company Inc ....F....559 237-2181
4264 W Jensen Ave Fresno (93706) ***(P-13638)***

J & L Metal Products ....F....951 278-0100
1121 Railroad St Ste 103 Corona (92882) ***(P-12251)***

J & L Tank Co, Lynwood *Also called Ermm Corporation* ***(P-19820)***

J & R Concrete Products Inc ....E....951 943-5855
440 W Markham St Perris (92571) ***(P-10589)***

J & R Machine Works ....E....661 945-8826
45420 60th St W Lancaster (93536) ***(P-16058)***

J & R Machining Inc ....F....408 365-7314
164 Martinvale Ln San Jose (95119) ***(P-16059)***

J & R Taylor Bros Assoc Inc ....D....626 334-9301
16321 Arrow Hwy Irwindale (91706) ***(P-1076)***

J & S Inc ....E....310 719-7144
229 E Gardena Blvd Gardena (90248) ***(P-16060)***

J & S Machine ....E....562 945-6419
8112 Freestone Ave Santa Fe Springs (90670) ***(P-16061)***

J & S Stakes Inc ....F....707 668-5647
3157 Greenwood Heights Dr Kneeland (95549) ***(P-4507)***

J A-Co Machine Works LLC ....E....877 429-8175
4 Carbonero Way Scotts Valley (95066) ***(P-16062)***

J and D Stl Fbrication Repr LP ....F....805 928-9674
2360 Westgate Rd Santa Maria (93455) ***(P-11814)***

J and S Machine, Santa Fe Springs *Also called J & S Machine* ***(P-16061)***

J B Enterprises, Sacramento *Also called John Boyd Enterprises Inc* ***(P-19696)***

J B I, La Habra *Also called JB Industries Corp* ***(P-12827)***

J B L Enterprises Inc ....F....760 754-2727
3219 Roymar Rd Oceanside (92058) ***(P-22832)***

J B Manufacturing Co, Adelanto *Also called Barker-Canoga Inc* ***(P-14136)***

J B Precision, Campbell *Also called Jessee Brothers Machine Sp Inc* ***(P-16082)***

J B Tool Inc ....F....714 993-7173
350 E Orngthrp Ave Ste 6 Placentia (92870) ***(P-16063)***

J B'S Private Label, Studio City *Also called Jbs Private Label Inc* ***(P-2792)***

J B3d, Orange *Also called John Bishop Design Inc* ***(P-23141)***

J Brand Inc ....D....213 749-3500
1318 E 7th St Ste 260 Los Angeles (90021) ***(P-2695)***

J Brand Jeans, Los Angeles *Also called J Brand Inc* ***(P-2695)***

J C Ford Company ....D....714 871-7361
901 S Leslie St La Habra (90631) ***(P-14376)***

J C Grinding (PA) ....F....562 944-3025
10923 Painter Ave Santa Fe Springs (90670) ***(P-13925)***

J C Industries Inc ....F....805 389-4040
3977 Camino Ranchero Camarillo (93012) ***(P-23369)***

J C Kitchen, South San Francisco *Also called Jesus Cabezas* ***(P-2488)***

J C Machining, Santa Fe Springs *Also called J C Grinding* ***(P-13925)***

J C Precision, Rancho Cucamonga *Also called JCPM Inc* ***(P-16078)***

J C Rack Systems, Arcadia *Also called Cardenas Enterprises Inc* ***(P-4968)***

J C S Volks Machine ....F....626 338-6003
15626 Cypress Ave Irwindale (91706) ***(P-19693)***

J C Trimming Company Inc ....E....323 235-4458
3800 S Hill St Los Angeles (90037) ***(P-3232)***

J D Heiskell Holdings LLC ....D....559 757-3135
11518 Road 120 Pixley (93256) ***(P-1102)***

J D Industries ....F....714 542-5517
1636 E Edinger Ave Ste P Santa Ana (92705) ***(P-16064)***

J Deluca Fish Company Inc (PA) ....E....310 684-5180
2194 Signal Pl San Pedro (90731) ***(P-2261)***

J E J Print Inc ....F....626 281-8989
673 Monterey Pass Rd Monterey Park (91754) ***(P-6655)***

J E S Disc Grinding Inc ....F....909 596-3823
2824 Metropolitan Pl Pomona (91767) ***(P-16065)***

J F Christopher Inc ....F....951 943-1166
3110 Indian Ave Ste D Perris (92571) ***(P-22833)***

J F Duncan Industries Inc (PA) ....D....562 862-4269
9301 Stewart And Gray Rd Downey (90241) ***(P-15528)***

J F Fitzgerald Company Inc ....F....415 648-6161
2750 19th St San Francisco (94110) ***(P-4647)***

J F Fong Inc ....F....949 553-8885
16520 Aston Irvine (92606) ***(P-21764)***

J F K & Associates Inc ....E....925 388-0255
1100 Moraga Way Ste 202 Moraga (94556) ***(P-24055)***

J F McCaughin Co ....E....626 573-3000
2628 River Ave Rosemead (91770) ***(P-22942)***

J F Shea Co Inc ....E....530 246-2200
17400 Clear Creek Rd Redding (96001) ***(P-10774)***

J Flying Machine Inc ....F....760 504-0323
701 S Andreasen Dr Ste C Escondido (92029) ***(P-16066)***

J Flying Manufacturing ....E....805 839-9229
11000 Brimhall Rd Ste E Bakersfield (93312) ***(P-9265)***

J G Hernandez Company ....E....800 242-2020
870 N Eckhoff St Orange (92868) ***(P-22364)***

J G Torres Company of Hawaii (PA) ....E....650 967-7219
825 Independence Ave Mountain View (94043) ***(P-10590)***

J H Castro, South El Monte *Also called Curve Line Metal Corporation* ***(P-4689)***

J H P & Associates Inc ....E....661 799-5888
28005 Smyth Dr Valencia (91355) ***(P-13572)***

J H Textiles Inc ....E....323 585-4124
2301 E 55th St Vernon (90058) ***(P-2938)***

J Hellman Frozen Foods Inc (PA) ....E....213 243-9105
1601 E Olympic Blvd # 200 Los Angeles (90021) ***(P-916)***

J Heyri Inc ....E....323 588-1234
6900 S Alameda St Huntington Park (90255) ***(P-3168)***

J J Engineering, Los Alamitos *Also called James Jackson* ***(P-16074)***

J J Foil Company Inc ....E....714 998-9920
650 W Freedom Ave Orange (92865) ***(P-5449)***

J K Lighting Systems, Stockton *Also called Al Kramp Specialties* ***(P-17097)***

J K Star Corp ....D....310 538-0185
1123 N Stanford Ave Los Angeles (90059) ***(P-3095)***

J L Cooper Electronics Inc ....E....310 322-9990
142 Arena St El Segundo (90245) ***(P-18956)***

J L Fisher Inc ....D....818 846-8366
1000 W Isabel St Burbank (91506) ***(P-22433)***

J L Industries, Commerce *Also called Samson Products Inc* ***(P-5001)***

J L Precision Sheet Metal, San Jose *Also called Laptalo Enterprises Inc* ***(P-12264)***

J L Shepherd and Associates ....E....818 898-2361
1010 Arroyo St San Fernando (91340) ***(P-21492)***

J L Wingert Company ....D....714 379-5519
11800 Monarch St Garden Grove (92841) ***(P-15529)***

J Lohr Viney, San Jose *Also called J Lohr Winery Corporation* ***(P-1760)***

J Lohr Winery Corporation (PA) ....E....408 288-5057
1000 Lenzen Ave San Jose (95126) ***(P-1760)***

J M A R Precision Systems, Chatsworth *Also called Pacific Precision Labs Inc* ***(P-21518)***

J M I, Union City *Also called Jenson Mechanical Inc* ***(P-16079)***

J M Mills Communications Inc (HQ) ....E....613 321-2100
4686 Mission Gorge Pl San Diego (92120) ***(P-17545)***

J M R Components, Chatsworth *Also called Jmr Electronics Inc* ***(P-15051)***

J M Smucker Company ....E....805 487-5483
800 Commercial Ave Oxnard (93030) ***(P-778)***

J Manufacturing, Grass Valley *Also called Vossloh Signaling Usa Inc* ***(P-12727)***

J McDowell Wldg Frm Mchy Inc ....F....530 661-6006
29820 County Road 25 Winters (95694) ***(P-24643)***

J Miller Canvas LLC ....E....714 641-0052
2429 S Birch St Santa Ana (92707) ***(P-2696)***

J Miller Co Inc ....E....818 837-0181
11537 Bradley Ave San Fernando (91340) ***(P-9239)***

J P B Jewelry Box Co (PA) ....F....323 225-0500
2428 Dallas St Los Angeles (90031) ***(P-4913)***

J P Gunite Inc ....E....619 938-0228
9458 New Colt Ct El Cajon (92021) ***(P-10775)***

J P L, Fresno *Also called J P Lamborn Co* ***(P-15435)***

J P Lamborn Co (PA) ....C....559 650-2120
3663 E Wawona Ave Fresno (93725) ***(P-15435)***

J P Specialties Inc ....F....951 763-7077
25811 Jefferson Ave Murrieta (92562) ***(P-9847)***

J P Sportswear, Vernon *Also called Aaron Corporation* ***(P-3279)***

J P Turgeon & Sons Inc ....E....323 773-3105
7758 Scout Ave Bell (90201) ***(P-13033)***

J P Weaver & Company Inc ....F....818 500-1740
941 Air Way Glendale (91201) ***(P-11008)***

J Pedroncelli Winery ....E....707 857-3531
1220 Canyon Rd Geyserville (95441) ***(P-1761)***

J R C Industries Inc ....D....562 698-0171
11804 Wakeman St Santa Fe Springs (90670) ***(P-5472)***

J R Rapid Print Inc ....F....909 947-4868
909 S Cucamonga Ave # 104 Ontario (91761) ***(P-6656)***

J R Schneider Co Inc ....F....707 745-0404
849 Jackson St Benicia (94510) ***(P-14831)***

J R U D E S Holdings LLC ....F....310 281-0800
9200 W Sunset Blvd Ph 2 West Hollywood (90069) ***(P-2966)***

J R V Products Inc ....F....714 259-9772
1314 N Harbor Blvd # 302 Santa Ana (92703) ***(P-18957)***

J Roberts Design, Brea *Also called M3 Products Inc* ***(P-4988)***

J RS Woodworks Inc ....F....707 588-8255
300 W Robles Ave Ste B Santa Rosa (95407) ***(P-4061)***

J S Hackl Archi Signa Inc ....F....510 940-2608
1999 Alpine Way Hayward (94545) ***(P-23137)***

J S M Productions Inc ....F....951 929-5771
537 E Florida Ave Hemet (92543) ***(P-6657)***

ALPHABETIC

Employee Codes: A=Over 500 employees, B=251-500
C=101-250, D=51-100, E=20-50, F=10-19
2020 California
Manfacturers Register
© Mergent Inc. 1-800-342-5647
1137

J S Paluch Co Inc....E....562 692-0484
9400 Norwalk Blvd Santa Fe Springs (90670) (P-6114)
J S West Milling Co Inc....E....209 529-4232
501 9th St Modesto (95354) (P-1103)
J Sheet Metal, Compton Also called Jaubin Sales & Mfg Corp (P-12252)
J Summitt Inc....E....562 236-5744
13834 Bettencourt St Cerritos (90703) (P-4062)
J T I, Pomona Also called Jacks Technologies & Inds Inc (P-14482)
J T Walker Industries Inc....E....909 481-1909
9322 Hyssop Dr Rancho Cucamonga (91730) (P-11959)
J Talley Corporation (PA)....E....951 654-2123
989 W 7th St San Jacinto (92582) (P-12484)
J W Bamford Inc....F....530 533-0732
4288 State Highway 70 Oroville (95965) (P-3889)
J W Floor Covering Inc....D....858 444-1214
3401 Enterprise Ave Hayward (94545) (P-2485)
J&B Mountain Holding, Irvine Also called Red Mountain Inc (P-20806)
J&C Tapocik Inc....F....951 351-4333
2941 Mcallister St Riverside (92503) (P-3559)
J&E Precision Machining Inc....F....408 281-1195
2814 Aiello Dr Ste A San Jose (95111) (P-16067)
J&J Products....F....805 544-4288
835 Capitolio Way Ste 4 San Luis Obispo (93401) (P-16068)
J&L Press Inc (PA)....F....818 549-8344
1218 W 163rd St Gardena (90247) (P-6658)
J&M Analytik AG....E....626 297-2930
141 California St Apt G Arcadia (91006) (P-21250)
J&M Manufacturing Inc....E....707 795-8223
430 Aaron St Cotati (94931) (P-18958)
J&S Goodwin Inc (HQ)....D....714 956-4040
5753 E Sta Ana Cyn G355 Anaheim (92807) (P-13877)
J&S Machine Works, Sylmar Also called Kay & James Inc (P-16109)
J&T Designs LLC....E....310 868-5190
1463 W El Segundo Blvd Compton (90222) (P-5067)
J-M Manufacturing Company Inc....D....951 657-7400
23711 Rider St Perris (92570) (P-7575)
J-M Manufacturing Company Inc (PA)....C....800 621-4404
5200 W Century Blvd Los Angeles (90045) (P-9470)
J-M Manufacturing Company Inc....D....909 822-3009
10990 Hemlock Ave Fontana (92337) (P-7576)
J-M Manufacturing Company Inc....C....209 982-1500
1051 Sperry Rd Stockton (95206) (P-7577)
J-Mark Company, Vista Also called J-Mark Manufacturing Inc (P-12825)
J-Mark Manufacturing Inc....E....760 727-6956
2480 Coral St Vista (92081) (P-12825)
J-T E C H....C....310 533-6700
548 Amapola Ave Torrance (90501) (P-18776)
J.L. Haley, Rancho Cordova Also called Vander-Bend Manufacturing Inc (P-16494)
J2 Global Communications, Santa Barbara Also called Efaxcom (P-15222)
J3 Associates Inc....F....408 281-4412
2751 Aiello Dr San Jose (95111) (P-16069)
JA Ferrari Print Imaging LLC....F....619 295-8307
7515 Metro Dr Ste 405 San Diego (92108) (P-6659)
Ja Solar USA Inc....F....408 586-0000
2570 N 1st St Ste 360 San Jose (95131) (P-18328)
JA Wouters Inc....F....805 221-5333
2305 Iron Stone Loop Templeton (93465) (P-96)
Jaann Inc....F....619 336-0584
225 W 15th St National City (91950) (P-11815)
Jaba USA, City of Industry Also called JC USA Trading Inc (P-2698)
Jabil Chad Automation, Anaheim Also called Jabil Inc (P-17906)
Jabil Circuit Inc....D....408 361-3200
1925 Lundy Ave San Jose (95131) (P-17905)
Jabil Inc....E....714 938-0080
1565 S Sinclair St Anaheim (92806) (P-17906)
Jabil Inc....B....408 361-3200
30 Great Oaks Blvd San Jose (95119) (P-17907)
Jabil Silver Creek Inc (HQ)....C....669 255-2900
5981 Optical Ct San Jose (95138) (P-24644)
Jack B Martin....F....559 583-1175
109 E 5th St Hanford (93230) (P-23138)
Jack Brain and Associates Inc....F....510 889-1360
20819 Nunes Ave Castro Valley (94546) (P-6258)
Jack C Drees Grinding Co Inc....E....818 764-8301
11815 Vose St B North Hollywood (91605) (P-16070)
Jack Frost Ice Service, Modesto Also called Arctic Glacier California Inc (P-2349)
Jack J Engel Manufacturing Inc....E....818 767-6220
11641 Pendleton St Sun Valley (91352) (P-19331)
Jack Martin Signworks, Hanford Also called Jack B Martin (P-23138)
Jack McMahon Landscape....F....707 942-1122
21 Miriam Dr Calistoga (94515) (P-3937)
Jack McMahon Landscraping Svcs, Calistoga Also called Jack McMahon Landscape (P-3937)
Jack West Cnc Inc....F....619 421-1695
3451 Main St Ste 111 Chula Vista (91911) (P-16071)
Jackandjillkidscom, Carson Also called Jnj Operations LLC (P-23371)
Jackrabbit (PA)....D....209 599-6118
471 Industrial Ave Ripon (95366) (P-13639)
Jacks Technologies & Inds Inc....F....909 865-2595
225 N Palomares St Pomona (91767) (P-14482)
JACKSAM CORP BLACKOUT, Rancho Santa Margari Also called Jacksam Corporation (P-14712)
Jacksam Corporation....E....800 605-3580
30191 Avenida De Las Rancho Santa Margari (92688) (P-14712)
Jackson Family Farms LLC (PA)....E....707 837-1000
425 Aviation Blvd Santa Rosa (95403) (P-1762)
Jackson Family Farms LLC....E....707 836-2047
5660 Skylane Blvd Santa Rosa (95403) (P-1763)
Jackson Family Wines Inc....E....707 948-2643
7600 Saint Helena Hwy Oakville (94562) (P-1764)
Jackson Family Wines Inc....E....707 528-6278
3690 Laughlin Rd Windsor (95492) (P-1765)
Jackson Family Wines Inc (PA)....D....707 544-4000
421 And 425 Aviation Blvd Santa Rosa (95403) (P-1766)
Jackson Family Wines Inc....E....805 938-7300
5475 Chardonnay Ln Santa Maria (93454) (P-1767)
Jackson Family Wines Inc....E....707 433-9463
7111 Highway 128 Healdsburg (95448) (P-1768)
Jackson-Mitchell Inc (PA)....E....209 667-0786
1240 South Ave Turlock (95380) (P-704)
Jaco Engineering....E....714 991-1680
879 S East St Anaheim (92805) (P-16072)
Jaco Machine Works, Scotts Valley Also called J A-Co Machine Works LLC (P-16062)
Jacobellis, Burbank Also called V J Provision Inc (P-428)
Jacobs Technology Inc....E....661 275-6100
8 Draco Dr Bldg 8350 Edwards (93524) (P-20447)
Jacobsen Trailer Inc....E....559 834-5971
1128 E South Ave Fowler (93625) (P-19825)
Jacobson Plastics Inc....D....562 433-4911
1401 Freeman Ave Long Beach (90804) (P-9848)
Jacquard Products, Healdsburg Also called Rupert Gibbon & Spider Inc (P-8677)
Jacuzzi Brands LLC (HQ)....E....909 606-1416
13925 City Center Dr # 200 Chino Hills (91709) (P-22035)
Jacuzzi Brands LLC....E....909 606-1416
13925 City Center Dr Chino Hills (91709) (P-23370)
Jacuzzi Family Vineyards LLC....F....707 931-7500
24724 Arnold Dr Sonoma (95476) (P-1769)
Jacuzzi Group Worldwide, Chino Hills Also called Jacuzzi Brands LLC (P-22035)
Jacuzzi Inc (HQ)....C....909 606-7733
14525 Monte Vista Ave Chino (91710) (P-15530)
Jacuzzi Inc....E....909 606-1416
13925 City Center Dr # 200 Chino Hills (91709) (P-9588)
Jacuzzi Outdoor Products, Chino Also called Jacuzzi Inc (P-15530)
Jacuzzi Products Co (HQ)....C....909 606-1416
13925 City Center Dr # 200 Chino Hills (91709) (P-9589)
Jacuzzi Products Co....B....909 548-7732
14525 Monte Vista Ave Chino (91710) (P-9590)
Jada Group Inc....D....626 810-8382
938 Hatcher Ave City of Industry (91748) (P-22685)
Jada Toys, City of Industry Also called Jada Group Inc (P-22685)
Jade Apparel Inc....E....323 867-9800
1625 S Greenwood Ave Montebello (90640) (P-3233)
Jade Products, Brea Also called Jade Range LLC (P-16812)
Jade Range LLC....C....714 961-2400
2650 Orbiter St Brea (92821) (P-16812)
Jade Spec LLC....F....310 933-4338
15932 Downey Ave Ste A Paramount (90723) (P-2697)
Jadespec, Paramount Also called Jade Spec LLC (P-2697)
Jaf International Inc....F....510 656-1718
2917 Bayview Dr Fremont (94538) (P-14929)
Jaffa Precision Engrg Inc....F....951 278-8797
12117 Madera Way Riverside (92503) (P-16073)
JAGUAR ANIMAL HEALTH, San Francisco Also called Jaguar Health Inc (P-7966)
Jaguar Health Inc (PA)....E....415 371-8300
201 Mission St Ste 2375 San Francisco (94105) (P-7966)
Jaguar Litho Incorporated....F....714 978-1821
1500 S Sunkist St Ste I Anaheim (92806) (P-7378)
Jain Irrigation Inc....C....559 485-7171
2851 E Florence Ave Fresno (93721) (P-13640)
Jake Stehelin Etienne....D....818 998-4250
8551 Canoga Ave Canoga Park (91304) (P-9849)
Jakks Pacific Inc....E....909 594-7771
21749 Baker Pkwy Walnut (91789) (P-22686)
Jakks Pacific Inc (PA)....C....424 268-9444
2951 28th St Santa Monica (90405) (P-22687)
Jal-Vue Window Company, Oakland Also called East Bay Glass Company Inc (P-11949)
Jam Design Inc....F....818 505-1680
5415 Cleon Ave North Hollywood (91601) (P-22984)
Jamac Steel Inc....E....909 983-7592
533 E Belmont St Ontario (91761) (P-11816)
Jamaco Enterprises Inc....F....818 991-2050
5331 Derry Ave Ste L Agoura Hills (91301) (P-5189)
James A Headrick Ii/Elizabeth....D....530 247-8000
7194 Bridge St Anderson (96007) (P-3890)
James Betts Enterprises Inc....E....530 581-1331
100 Sierra Terrace Rd Tahoe City (96145) (P-20341)
James Clark....F....559 456-3893
1766 N Helm Ave Ste 105 Fresno (93727) (P-7335)
James Frasinetti & Sons....E....916 383-2447
7395 Frasinetti Rd Sacramento (95828) (P-1770)
James Gang Company....F....619 225-1283
4851 Newport Ave San Diego (92107) (P-3793)
James Gang Custom Printing....F....619 225-1283
4851 Newport Ave San Diego (92107) (P-6660)
James Gang Graphics & Printing, San Diego Also called James Gang Custom Printing (P-6660)
James Hardie Building Pdts Inc....D....949 348-1800
26300 La Alameda Ste 400 Mission Viejo (92691) (P-10417)
James Hardie Trading Co Inc....C....949 582-2378
26300 La Alameda Ste 400 Mission Viejo (92691) (P-9118)
James Hunkins....F....310 640-8243
601 Lairport St El Segundo (90245) (P-19967)
James Jackson....F....562 493-1402
11021 Via El Mercado Los Alamitos (90720) (P-16074)
James Jeans, Los Angeles Also called Dry Aged Denim LLC (P-3003)
James Jones Company....C....909 418-2558
1470 S Vintage Ave Ontario (91761) (P-13309)

James Kim Young.......E.......310 605-5328
1215 W Walnut St Compton (90220) ***(P-3341)***
James L Craft Inc.......E.......661 323-8251
1101 33rd St Bakersfield (93301) ***(P-16075)***
James L Hall Co Incorporated (PA).......D.......707 547-0775
360 Tesconi Cir Ste B Santa Rosa (95401) ***(P-18959)***
James L Hall Co Incorporated.......D.......707 544-2436
218 Roberts Ave Santa Rosa (95401) ***(P-18722)***
James Litho, Ontario *Also called Eclipse Prtg & Graphics LLC* ***(P-6557)***
James P McNair Co Inc.......F.......415 681-2200
2236 Irving St San Francisco (94122) ***(P-11600)***
James Stewart.......E.......323 778-1687
8931 S Vermont Ave Los Angeles (90044) ***(P-7967)***
James Stout.......E.......408 988-8582
481 Gianni St Santa Clara (95054) ***(P-16076)***
James Tobin Cellars Inc.......E.......805 239-2204
8950 Union Rd Paso Robles (93446) ***(P-1771)***
James West Inc (PA).......F.......310 380-1510
13344 S Main St Ste B Los Angeles (90061) ***(P-3010)***
Jamis Software Corporation.......F.......858 300-5542
4909 Murphy Canyon Rd # 460 San Diego (92123) ***(P-24056)***
Jamm Industries Corp.......E.......213 622-0555
2425 E 12th St Los Angeles (90021) ***(P-3342)***
Jampro Antennas Inc.......D.......916 383-1177
6340 Sky Creek Dr Sacramento (95828) ***(P-17546)***
Jan-Al Cases, Los Angeles *Also called Jan-Al Innerprizes Inc* ***(P-4337)***
Jan-Al Innerprizes Inc.......E.......323 260-7212
3339 Union Pacific Ave Los Angeles (90023) ***(P-4337)***
Janco Airless Center, Berkeley *Also called Janco Chemical Corporation* ***(P-8648)***
Janco Chemical Corporation.......F.......510 527-9770
1235 5th St Berkeley (94710) ***(P-8648)***
Janda Company Inc.......E.......951 734-1935
226 N Sherman Ave Ste A Corona (92882) ***(P-14242)***
Jandy Pool Products, Carlsbad *Also called Zodiac Pool Systems LLC* ***(P-15610)***
Jane Mohr Design, Van Nuys *Also called Dress To Kill Inc* ***(P-3156)***
Janel Glass Company Inc.......E.......323 661-8621
2960 Marsh St Los Angeles (90039) ***(P-10369)***
Jano Graphics, Ventura *Also called National Graphics LLC* ***(P-6744)***
Jansen Ornamental Supply Co.......E.......626 442-0271
10926 Schmidt Rd El Monte (91733) ***(P-12485)***
Jansport Inc (HQ).......F.......510 814-7400
2601 Harbor Bay Pkwy Alameda (94502) ***(P-3660)***
Janssen Biopharma Inc.......E.......650 635-5500
260 E Grand Ave South San Francisco (94080) ***(P-7968)***
Janssen Research & Dev LLC.......C.......858 450-2000
3210 Merryfield Row San Diego (92121) ***(P-7969)***
Jantek Electronics Inc.......F.......626 350-4198
4820 Arden Dr Temple City (91780) ***(P-19332)***
Janteq Corp (PA).......E.......949 215-2603
9975 Toledo Way Ste 150 Irvine (92618) ***(P-17547)***
Janus International Group LLC.......E.......714 503-6120
2535 W La Palma Ave Anaheim (92801) ***(P-11960)***
Japan Engine Inc.......E.......510 532-7878
2131 Williams St San Leandro (94577) ***(P-19193)***
Japan Graphics Corp.......E.......310 222-8639
1820 W 220th St Ste 210 Torrance (90501) ***(P-6661)***
Japanese Truck Dismantling.......F.......310 835-3100
940 Alameda St Wilmington (90744) ***(P-19480)***
Japanese Weekend Inc (PA).......E.......415 621-0555
496 S Airport Blvd South San Francisco (94080) ***(P-3343)***
Japonesque LLC.......F.......925 866-6670
2420 Camino Ramon Ste 250 San Ramon (94583) ***(P-8520)***
Jar Ventures Inc.......E.......530 224-9655
1355 Hartnell Ave Redding (96002) ***(P-23139)***
Jarden Corporation.......D.......800 755-9520
23610 Banning Blvd Carson (90745) ***(P-9850)***
Jardine Performance Products, Corona *Also called Summit Industries Inc* ***(P-11890)***
Jari Electro Supply, Gilroy *Also called Chalgren Enterprises* ***(P-22238)***
Jariet Technologies Inc.......E.......310 698-1001
103 W Torrance Blvd Redondo Beach (90277) ***(P-20592)***
Jarrow Industries Inc.......C.......562 906-1919
12246 Hawkins St Santa Fe Springs (90670) ***(P-7970)***
Jarvis.......E.......707 255-5280
2970 Monticello Rd NAPA (94558) ***(P-1772)***
Jarvis Manufacturing Inc.......F.......408 226-2600
195 Lewis Rd Ste 36 San Jose (95111) ***(P-16077)***
Jarvis Winery, NAPA *Also called Jarvis* ***(P-1772)***
Jason Incorporated.......E.......562 921-9821
13006 Philadelphia St # 305 Whittier (90601) ***(P-10947)***
Jason Markk Inc.......E.......213 687-7060
329 E 2nd St Los Angeles (90012) ***(P-8390)***
Jason Tool & Engineering Inc.......E.......714 895-5067
7101 Honold Cir Garden Grove (92841) ***(P-9851)***
Jason's Natural, Bell *Also called Hain Celestial Group Inc* ***(P-8507)***
Jasper Display Corp.......E.......408 831-5788
2952 Bunker Hill Ln # 110 Santa Clara (95054) ***(P-14483)***
Jasper Electronics.......E.......714 917-0749
1580 N Kellogg Dr Anaheim (92807) ***(P-18960)***
Jasper Engine Exchange Inc.......F.......800 827-7455
1477 E Cedar St Ste D Ontario (91761) ***(P-19694)***
Jaton Corporation.......B.......510 933-8888
47677 Lakeview Blvd Fremont (94538) ***(P-17908)***
Jaubin Sales & Mfg Corp.......F.......310 631-8647
2006 E Gladwick St Compton (90220) ***(P-12252)***
Jaunt Inc.......E.......650 618-6579
951 Mariners Island Blvd # 500 San Mateo (94404) ***(P-24057)***
Jaunt Xr, San Mateo *Also called Jaunt Inc* ***(P-24057)***
Javad Ems Inc.......D.......408 770-1700
900 Rock Ave San Jose (95131) ***(P-18961)***
Javo Beverage Company Inc.......D.......760 560-5286
1311 Specialty Dr Vista (92081) ***(P-2218)***
Jawen Enterprises, San Diego *Also called Jay Brewer* ***(P-6662)***
Jaxx Manufacturing Inc.......E.......805 526-4979
1912 Angus Ave Simi Valley (93063) ***(P-18962)***
Jay Brewer.......F.......858 488-4871
926 Turquoise St Ste A San Diego (92109) ***(P-6662)***
Jay Gee Sales.......F.......818 365-1311
703 Arroyo St San Fernando (91340) ***(P-10491)***
Jay Manufacturing Corp.......F.......818 255-0500
7425 Fulton Ave North Hollywood (91605) ***(P-12826)***
Jay Mfg, North Hollywood *Also called Jay Manufacturing Corp* ***(P-12826)***
Jay-Cee Blouse Co Inc.......C.......213 622-0116
823 Maple Ave Ste 200 Los Angeles (90014) ***(P-3234)***
Jaya Apparel Group LLC (PA).......D.......323 584-3500
5175 S Soto St Vernon (90058) ***(P-3344)***
Jayco Hawaii California.......F.......510 601-9916
1468 66th St Emeryville (94608) ***(P-11262)***
Jayco Interface Technology Inc.......E.......951 738-2000
1351 Pico St Corona (92881) ***(P-18963)***
Jayco Mmi Inc.......E.......951 738-2000
1351 Pico St Corona (92881) ***(P-18964)***
Jayone Foods Inc.......E.......562 633-7400
7212 Alondra Blvd Paramount (90723) ***(P-2486)***
Jaz Distribution Inc.......F.......714 521-3888
8485 Artesia Blvd Ste B Buena Park (90621) ***(P-12711)***
Jaz Products, Santa Paula *Also called Westlake Engrg Roto Form* ***(P-10123)***
Jazz Imaging LLC.......F.......567 234-5299
800 Chartot Ave Ste 100 San Jose (95131) ***(P-22162)***
Jazz Pharmaceuticals Inc (HQ).......C.......650 496-3777
3170 Porter Dr Palo Alto (94304) ***(P-7971)***
Jazz Semiconductor, Newport Beach *Also called Newport Fab LLC* ***(P-18434)***
Jazz Semiconductor Inc (HQ).......A.......949 435-8000
4321 Jamboree Rd Newport Beach (92660) ***(P-18329)***
JB Britches Inc.......D.......818 898-4046
2279 Ward Ave Simi Valley (93065) ***(P-3011)***
JB Industries Corp.......F.......562 691-2105
451 Commercial Way La Habra (90631) ***(P-12827)***
JB Plastics Inc.......E.......714 541-8500
1921 E Edinger Ave Santa Ana (92705) ***(P-9852)***
JB Radiator Specialties, Sacramento *Also called John Boyd Enterprises Inc* ***(P-19695)***
JB&a Distribution, San Rafael *Also called Jeff Burgess & Associates Inc* ***(P-17247)***
Jbb Inc.......E.......888 538-9287
880 W Crowther Ave Placentia (92870) ***(P-19333)***
Jbi LLC (PA).......C.......310 886-8034
2650 E El Presidio St Long Beach (90810) ***(P-5068)***
Jbi LLC.......E.......310 537-2910
18521 S Santa Fe Ave Compton (90221) ***(P-4692)***
Jbi Interiors, Long Beach *Also called Jbi LLC* ***(P-5068)***
Jbr Inc (PA).......C.......916 258-8000
1731 Aviation Blvd Lincoln (95648) ***(P-2487)***
Jbr Gourmet Foods, Lincoln *Also called Jbr Inc* ***(P-2487)***
Jbs Case Ready, Riverside *Also called Swift Beef Company* ***(P-502)***
Jbs Private Label Inc.......E.......818 762-3736
4383 Irvine Ave Studio City (91604) ***(P-2792)***
Jbt Food Tech Madera, Madera *Also called John Bean Technologies Corp* ***(P-14377)***
JBW Precision Inc.......E.......805 499-1973
2650 Lavery Ct Newbury Park (91320) ***(P-12253)***
JC Ford, La Habra *Also called J C Ford Company* ***(P-14376)***
JC Hanscom Inc.......F.......562 789-9955
11830 Wakeman St Santa Fe Springs (90670) ***(P-4275)***
JC Industries, Los Angeles *Also called J C Trimming Company Inc* ***(P-3232)***
JC Metal Specialists Inc.......F.......650 827-1618
238 Michelle Ct South San Francisco (94080) ***(P-11817)***
JC Metal Specialists Inc (PA).......E.......415 822-3878
220 Michelle Ct San Francisco (94124) ***(P-11818)***
JC Pallet Co.......F.......661 393-2229
5800 State Rd Spc 13 Bakersfield (93308) ***(P-4376)***
JC USA Trading Inc.......F.......626 333-9990
159 N Sunset Ave City of Industry (91744) ***(P-2698)***
JC Window Fashions Inc.......E.......909 364-8888
6400 Fleet St Commerce (90040) ***(P-5027)***
Jc's Pie Pops, Chatsworth *Also called We The Pie People LLC* ***(P-679)***
Jci Jones Chemicals Inc.......E.......310 523-1629
1401 Del Amo Blvd Torrance (90501) ***(P-7390)***
Jci Metal Products (PA).......D.......619 229-8206
6540 Federal Blvd Lemon Grove (91945) ***(P-11819)***
JCM Industries Inc (PA).......E.......714 902-9000
15302 Pipeline Ln Huntington Beach (92649) ***(P-4985)***
JCPM Inc.......F.......909 484-9040
8576 Red Oak St Rancho Cucamonga (91730) ***(P-16078)***
Jcr Aircraft Deburring LLC.......E.......714 870-4427
221 Foundation Ave La Habra (90631) ***(P-13926)***
Jcr Deburring, La Habra *Also called Jcr Aircraft Deburring LLC* ***(P-13926)***
Jcs, Irwindale *Also called J C S Volks Machine* ***(P-19693)***
JD Business Solutions Inc.......E.......805 962-8193
1351 Holiday Hill Rd Goleta (93117) ***(P-6663)***
JD Printing and Mailing, San Dimas *Also called J & D Business Forms Inc* ***(P-6654)***
JD Processing Inc.......E.......714 972-8161
2220 Cape Cod Way Santa Ana (92703) ***(P-13034)***
Jd/Cmc Inc.......E.......818 767-2260
2834 E 11th St Los Angeles (90023) ***(P-3345)***
JDC Development Group Inc.......E.......714 575-1108
1321 N Blue Gum St Anaheim (92806) ***(P-4417)***
Jdh Pacific Inc (PA).......E.......562 926-8088
14821 Artesia Blvd La Mirada (90638) ***(P-11144)***
Jdi Display America Inc (PA).......F.......408 501-3720
1740 Tech Dr Ste 460 San Jose (95110) ***(P-18965)***

ALPHABETIC

Employee Codes: A=Over 500 employees, B=251-500
C=101-250, D=51-100, E=20-50, F=10-19
2020 California
Manfacturers Register
© Mergent Inc. 1-800-342-5647
1139

JDM Properties....E....209 632-0616
410 S Golden State Blvd Turlock (95380) ***(P-8746)***
Jds Technologies....F....858 486-8787
12200 Thatcher Ct Poway (92064) ***(P-18966)***
Jdsu, San Jose *Also called Viavi Solutions Inc* ***(P-19433)***
Jdsu Photonic Power (HQ)....F....408 546-5000
1768 Automation Pkwy San Jose (95131) ***(P-19334)***
JE Thomson & Company LLC....F....626 334-7190
15206 Ceres Ave Fontana (92335) ***(P-13878)***
Jeannine's Bakery, Santa Barbara *Also called Jeannines Bkg Co Santa Barbara* ***(P-1227)***
Jeannines Bkg Co Santa Barbara (PA)....F....805 966-1717
15 E Figueroa St Santa Barbara (93101) ***(P-1227)***
Jeb-PHI Inc....E....562 861-0863
10417 Lakewood Blvd Downey (90241) ***(P-6664)***
Jeff Burgess & Associates Inc (PA)....E....415 256-2800
1050 Northgate Dr Ste 200 San Rafael (94903) ***(P-17247)***
Jeff Frank....F....831 469-8208
120 Encinal St Santa Cruz (95060) ***(P-23140)***
Jeffrey Court Inc....D....951 340-3383
620 Parkridge Ave Norco (92860) ***(P-10444)***
Jeffrey Fabrication LLC....E....562 634-3101
6323 Alondra Blvd Paramount (90723) ***(P-12254)***
Jeffrey Rudes LLC....F....310 281-0800
9550 Heather Rd Beverly Hills (90210) ***(P-3096)***
Jeico Security Inc....F
1525 N Endeavor Ln Ste Q Anaheim (92801) ***(P-19335)***
Jejomi Designs Inc....E....323 584-4211
2626 Fruitland Ave Vernon (90058) ***(P-3517)***
Jeld-Wen Inc....E....800 468-3667
3760 Convoy St Ste 111 San Diego (92111) ***(P-4063)***
Jeld-Wen Inc....C....916 782-4900
3901 Cincinnati Ave Rocklin (95765) ***(P-4064)***
Jelenko, San Diego *Also called Argen Corporation* ***(P-11188)***
Jellco Container Inc....D....714 666-2728
1151 N Tustin Ave Anaheim (92807) ***(P-5240)***
Jelly Belly Candy Company (PA)....B....707 428-2800
1 Jelly Belly Ln Fairfield (94533) ***(P-1376)***
Jelly Belly Candy Company....E....707 428-2800
2400 N Watney Way Fairfield (94533) ***(P-1377)***
Jellypop, Pasadena *Also called Evolution Design Lab Inc* ***(P-10169)***
Jeluz Electric Ltd LLC....E....800 216-8307
25060 Hancock Ave Murrieta (92562) ***(P-19336)***
Jem America Corp....E....510 683-9234
3000 Laurelview Ct Fremont (94538) ***(P-21059)***
Jem Sportswear, Cypress *Also called Awake Inc* ***(P-3215)***
Jem-Hd Co Inc....D....619 710-1443
10030 Via De La Amistad F San Diego (92154) ***(P-9853)***
Jemstep Inc....E....650 966-6500
5150 El Camino Real B16 Los Altos (94022) ***(P-24058)***
Jemstone, Los Angeles *Also called Oak Apparel Inc* ***(P-3379)***
Jeneric/Pentron Incorporated (HQ)....C....203 265-7397
1717 W Collins Ave Orange (92867) ***(P-22163)***
Jenkins Beverage Inc....F....916 686-1800
3630 51st Ave Ste D Sacramento (95823) ***(P-15436)***
Jenkins Poultry Farms, Farmington *Also called Pleasant Valley Farms* ***(P-525)***
Jennings Aeronautics Inc....E....805 544-0932
3183 Duncan Ln Ste C San Luis Obispo (93401) ***(P-20593)***
Jennings Technology Co LLC (HQ)....D....408 292-4025
970 Mclaughlin Ave San Jose (95122) ***(P-18680)***
Jennis Group LLC....F....714 227-7972
1631 Placentia Ave Costa Mesa (92627) ***(P-6259)***
Jensen Door Systems Inc....F....760 736-4036
160 Vallecitos De Oro San Marcos (92069) ***(P-4065)***
Jensen Enterprises Inc....F....530 865-4277
7210 State Highway 32 Orland (95963) ***(P-10591)***
Jensen Enterprises Inc....B....909 357-7264
14221 San Bernardino Ave Fontana (92335) ***(P-10592)***
Jensen Graphics & Printing....F....707 987-8966
18270 Spyglass Rd Hidden Valley Lake (95467) ***(P-6665)***
Jensen Meat Company Inc....D....619 754-6400
2550 Britannia Blvd # 101 San Diego (92154) ***(P-469)***
Jensen Precast, Fontana *Also called Jensen Enterprises Inc* ***(P-10592)***
Jenson Custom Furniture Inc....D....714 634-8145
2161 S Dupont Dr Anaheim (92806) ***(P-4648)***
Jenson Mechanical Inc....E....510 429-8078
32420 Central Ave Union City (94587) ***(P-16079)***
Jentex Co Ltd....F....909 273-1088
1103 Bramford Ct Diamond Bar (91765) ***(P-2699)***
Jerames Industries Inc....E....619 334-2204
460 Cypress Ln Ste F El Cajon (92020) ***(P-16080)***
Jerames Tool & Mfg, El Cajon *Also called Jerames Industries Inc* ***(P-16080)***
Jeremiahs Pick Coffee Company....F....415 206-9900
1495 Evans Ave San Francisco (94124) ***(P-2301)***
Jeremywell International Inc....F....949 588-6888
14 Vanderbilt Irvine (92618) ***(P-14832)***
Jerome Russell, Canoga Park *Also called International Beauty Pdts LLC* ***(P-8518)***
Jerry Carroll Machinery Inc....F....650 591-3302
993 E San Carlos Ave San Carlos (94070) ***(P-16081)***
Jerry Melton & Sons Cnstr, Taft *Also called Jerry Melton & Sons Cnstr* ***(P-213)***
Jerry Melton & Sons Cnstr....D....661 765-5546
100 Jamison Ln Taft (93268) ***(P-213)***
Jerry Slmon Cstm Picture Frmng, Los Angeles *Also called Jerry Solomon Enterprises Inc* ***(P-4508)***
Jerry Solomon Enterprises Inc....E....323 556-2265
5221 W Jefferson Blvd Los Angeles (90016) ***(P-4508)***
Jess Howard....F....530 533-3888
2800 Richter Ave Oroville (95966) ***(P-9854)***
Jessee Brothers Machine Sp Inc....F....408 866-1755
1640 Dell Ave Campbell (95008) ***(P-16082)***
Jessica McClintock Inc (PA)....C....415 553-8200
2307 Broadway St San Francisco (94115) ***(P-3479)***
Jessie A Laurent, San Rafael *Also called Laurent Culinary Service* ***(P-2524)***
Jessie Steele Inc....F....510 204-0991
1020 The Alameda San Jose (95126) ***(P-3847)***
Jessies Grove Winery....F....209 368-0880
1973 W Turner Rd Lodi (95242) ***(P-1773)***
Jessop Industries....F....805 581-6976
4645 Industrial St Ste 2c Simi Valley (93063) ***(P-16083)***
Jesta Digital Entrmt Inc (HQ)....F....323 648-4200
15303 Ventura Blvd # 900 Sherman Oaks (91403) ***(P-24059)***
Jesus Cabezas....F....650 583-0469
145 Utah Ave South San Francisco (94080) ***(P-2488)***
Jet & Western Abrasives, Placentia *Also called Jet Abrasives Inc* ***(P-10948)***
Jet Abrasives Inc....E....323 588-1245
1891 E Miraloma Ave Placentia (92870) ***(P-10948)***
Jet Air Fbo LLC....E....619 448-5991
681 Kenney St El Cajon (92020) ***(P-20145)***
Jet Cutting Solutions Inc....F....909 948-2424
10853 Bell Ct Rancho Cucamonga (91730) ***(P-4463)***
Jet I, Fontana *Also called Jeti Inc* ***(P-24645)***
Jet Performance Products Inc....E....714 848-5500
17491 Apex Cir Huntington Beach (92647) ***(P-19194)***
Jet Plastics (PA)....D....323 268-6706
941 N Eastern Ave Los Angeles (90063) ***(P-9855)***
Jet Products, San Diego *Also called Senior Operations LLC* ***(P-16397)***
Jet Set California, San Leandro *Also called Jetset California Inc* ***(P-10418)***
Jet Transmission, Huntington Beach *Also called Jet Performance Products Inc* ***(P-19194)***
Jet/Brella Inc....E....818 786-5480
6849 Hayvenhurst Ave Van Nuys (91406) ***(P-19968)***
Jetair Technologies LLC....F....805 654-7000
1756 Eastman Ave Ste 100 Ventura (93003) ***(P-14666)***
Jetco, Irwindale *Also called Connor J Inc* ***(P-21021)***
Jetco Torque Tools LLC....F....626 359-2881
835 Meridian St Duarte (91010) ***(P-14743)***
Jeteffect Inc (PA)....F....562 989-8800
3250 Airflite Way Fl 3 Long Beach (90807) ***(P-19907)***
Jetfax, Los Angeles *Also called Efaxcom* ***(P-15221)***
Jeti Inc (PA)....F....909 357-2966
14578 Hawthorne Ave Fontana (92335) ***(P-24645)***
Jetlore LLC....E....650 485-1822
1528 S El Camino Real # 101 San Mateo (94402) ***(P-24060)***
Jetnexus LLC....E....800 568-9921
3201 Great America Pkwy Santa Clara (95054) ***(P-14930)***
Jetronics Company, Santa Rosa *Also called James L Hall Co Incorporated* ***(P-18722)***
Jetset California Inc....F....510 632-7800
2150 Edison Ave San Leandro (94577) ***(P-10418)***
Jetstream Trading Co....F....818 921-7158
1005 E Las Tunas Dr U356 San Gabriel (91776) ***(P-20146)***
Jevin Enterprises Inc....E....818 408-0488
11548 Apulia Ct Porter Ranch (91326) ***(P-9172)***
Jewel Date Company Inc....E....760 399-4474
84675 60th Ave Thermal (92274) ***(P-1378)***
Jewelry Club House Inc....F....213 362-7888
606 S Olive St Ste 2000 Los Angeles (90014) ***(P-22531)***
Jewelry Manufacturing, Los Angeles *Also called Gold Craft Jewelry Corp* ***(P-22525)***
Jewels By Angelo Inc....F....562 862-6293
9221 Rives Ave Downey (90240) ***(P-22532)***
JEWISH JOURNAL, THE, Los Angeles *Also called Tribe Media Corp* ***(P-5852)***
Jewish News, Sherman Oaks *Also called Phil Blazer Enterprises Inc* ***(P-5797)***
Jf Fixtures & Design, Long Beach *Also called F-J-E Inc* ***(P-4902)***
Jff Uniforms, Torrance *Also called Just For Fun* ***(P-2992)***
JG Boswell Tomato - Kern LLC....E....661 764-9000
36889 Hwy 58 Buttonwillow (93206) ***(P-779)***
JG Plastics Group LLC....E....714 751-4266
335 Fischer Ave Costa Mesa (92626) ***(P-9856)***
JGM Automotive Tooling Inc....E....714 895-7001
5355 Industrial Dr Huntington Beach (92649) ***(P-14484)***
JH Baxter A Cal Ltd Partnr (PA)....E....650 349-0201
1700 S El Camino Real San Mateo (94402) ***(P-4478)***
Jh Biotech Inc (PA)....E....805 650-8933
4951 Olivas Park Dr Ventura (93003) ***(P-8813)***
Jhawar Industries LLC....E....951 340-4646
525 Klug Cir Corona (92880) ***(P-14767)***
JIC Industrial Co Inc....F....408 935-9880
978 Hanson Ct Milpitas (95035) ***(P-18967)***
Jifco Inc (PA)....D....925 449-4665
571 Exchange Ct Livermore (94550) ***(P-13473)***
Jifco Fabaricated Piping, Livermore *Also called Jifco Inc* ***(P-13473)***
Jifflenow, Sunnyvale *Also called Ipolipo Inc* ***(P-24045)***
Jigmasters Tool & Gauge, Santa Ana *Also called Aluminum Precision Pdts Inc* ***(P-12730)***
Jigsaw Data Corporation....F....650 235-8400
900 Concar Dr San Mateo (94402) ***(P-6260)***
Jim & Lees Optical, Modesto *Also called Jims Optical* ***(P-21371)***
Jim Beam Brands Co....F....949 200-7200
17901 Von Karman Ave # 920 Irvine (92614) ***(P-2014)***
Jim Beauregard....D....831 423-9453
1661 Pine Flat Rd Santa Cruz (95060) ***(P-1774)***
Jim Ellis....F....760 244-8566
16797 Live Oak St Hesperia (92345) ***(P-4311)***
Jim Graham Inc....E....707 374-5114
4 Hill Ct Rio Vista (94571) ***(P-214)***
Jim James Enterprises Inc....F....818 772-8595
9148 Jordan Ave Chatsworth (91311) ***(P-12255)***
Jim Little Raymonds Print Shop, Fremont *Also called Raymonds Little Print Shop Inc* ***(P-6836)***

Jim Perry.......E.......909 947-0747
13611 Northlands Rd Eastvale (92880) *(P-7336)*
Jim Wheeler Logging, Miranda *Also called Wheeler Lumber Co Inc (P-3918)*
Jim's Machining, Camarillo *Also called Thiessen Products Inc (P-16455)*
Jim-Buoy, North Hollywood *Also called Cal-June Inc (P-11576)*
Jlmachine Company Inc.......E.......858 695-1787
9720 Distribution Ave San Diego (92121) *(P-16084)*
Jimenes Food Inc.......E.......562 602-2505
7046 Jackson St Paramount (90723) *(P-2489)*
Jimenez Mexican Foods Inc.......E.......951 351-0102
11010 Wells Ave Riverside (92505) *(P-731)*
Jiminys LLC.......F.......415 939-6314
2855 Mandela Pkwy Ste 11 Oakland (94608) *(P-1104)*
Jimo Enterprises.......E.......323 469-0805
6001 Santa Monica Blvd Los Angeles (90038) *(P-4509)*
Jims Optical.......F.......209 549-2517
5253 Jerusalem Ct Ste G Modesto (95356) *(P-21371)*
Jimway Inc.......D.......310 886-3718
20101 S Santa Fe Ave Compton (90221) *(P-17137)*
Jinelle, Los Angeles *Also called Rose Genuine Inc (P-3487)*
Jinkosolar (us) Inc.......F.......415 402-0502
595 Market St Ste 2200 San Francisco (94105) *(P-18330)*
Jinx Inc.......E.......818 399-4544
N Stanley Ave Los Angeles (90008) *(P-3346)*
Jishan Usa Inc.......F.......408 609-3286
15257 Don Julian Rd City of Industry (91745) *(P-17046)*
Jisoncase (usa) Limited.......F.......888 233-8880
9674 Telstar Ave Ste A El Monte (91731) *(P-10139)*
Jivago Inc (PA).......F.......310 205-5535
9454 Wilshire Blvd # 600 Beverly Hills (90212) *(P-8521)*
Jixing (usa) Inc.......F.......626 261-9539
11094 Brentwood Dr Rancho Cucamonga (91730) *(P-13358)*
Jj Lithographics Inc.......F.......562 698-0280
8607 Dice Rd Santa Fe Springs (90670) *(P-6666)*
Jj Printing, Santa Fe Springs *Also called Jj Lithographics Inc (P-6666)*
Jjs Truck Equipment LLC.......E.......858 566-1155
9685 Via Excelencia # 200 San Diego (92126) *(P-19539)*
Jkf Construction Inc.......F.......805 583-4228
460 E Easy St Ste 102 Simi Valley (93065) *(P-4210)*
JKL Components Corporation.......E.......818 896-0019
13343 Paxton St Pacoima (91331) *(P-17090)*
Jl Design Enterprises Inc.......D.......714 479-0240
1451 Edinger Ave Ste C Tustin (92780) *(P-2991)*
JL Haley Enterprises Inc.......C.......916 631-6375
3510 Luyung Dr Rancho Cordova (95742) *(P-16085)*
Jl Racing.com, Tustin *Also called Jl Design Enterprises Inc (P-2991)*
Jlcooper, El Segundo *Also called J L Cooper Electronics Inc (P-18956)*
Jlp Manufacturing Inc.......F.......909 931-7797
5609 Arrow Hwy Ste D Montclair (91763) *(P-11820)*
JM Eagle, Perris *Also called J-M Manufacturing Company Inc (P-7575)*
JM Eagle, Los Angeles *Also called J-M Manufacturing Company Inc (P-9470)*
JM Eagle, Los Angeles *Also called Pw Eagle Inc (P-9474)*
JM Kitchen Cabinets.......F.......323 752-6520
702 E Gage Ave Los Angeles (90001) *(P-4211)*
Jmg Machine Inc.......E.......714 522-6221
17037 Industry Pl La Mirada (90638) *(P-16086)*
Jmgj Group Inc.......F.......866 293-2872
10120 Wexted Way Elk Grove (95757) *(P-22985)*
Jmi Steel Inc.......E.......818 768-3955
8983 San Fernando Rd Sun Valley (91352) *(P-12486)*
Jml Connection Inc.......F.......213 519-2000
1372 Wilson St Los Angeles (90021) *(P-24061)*
Jml Textile Inc.......D.......323 584-2323
5801 S 2nd St Vernon (90058) *(P-2700)*
Jmp Electronics Inc.......F.......714 730-2086
2685 Dow Ave Ste A1 Tustin (92780) *(P-17909)*
Jmr Electronics Inc.......E.......818 993-4801
8968 Fullbright Ave Chatsworth (91311) *(P-15051)*
Jmt Inc.......F.......562 404-2014
14926 Bloomfield Ave Norwalk (90650) *(P-16087)*
Jmu Dental Inc.......F.......909 676-0000
150 E Lambert Rd Fullerton (92835) *(P-22164)*
Jmw Truss and Components, San Diego *Also called Trademark Construction Co Inc (P-19203)*
Jnc Machining.......F.......408 920-2520
1834 Stone Ave San Jose (95125) *(P-16088)*
JNJ Apparel Inc.......E.......323 584-9700
3838 S Santa Fe Ave Vernon (90058) *(P-3347)*
Jnj Operations LLC.......E.......855 525-6545
859 E Sepulveda Blvd Carson (90745) *(P-23371)*
Jns Industries Inc.......F.......909 923-8334
2320 S Vineyard Ave Ontario (91761) *(P-16089)*
Jo Sonjas Folk Art Studio.......F.......707 445-9306
2136 3rd St Eureka (95501) *(P-6115)*
Joa Corporation (PA).......E.......951 785-4411
7254 Magnolia Ave Riverside (92504) *(P-22036)*
Joanka Inc.......F.......310 326-8940
25510 Frampton Ave Harbor City (90710) *(P-11961)*
Joann Lammens.......F.......909 593-8478
2152 Bonita Ave La Verne (91750) *(P-23372)*
Joaos A Tin Fish Bar & Eatery.......E.......619 794-2192
2750 Dewey Rd San Diego (92106) *(P-11275)*
Joar Labs Inc.......E.......818 243-0700
4115 San Fernando Rd Glendale (91204) *(P-8522)*
Job Shop Managers, Valencia *Also called Skm Industries Inc (P-12873)*
Jobbers Meat Packing Co Inc.......F.......323 585-6328
3336 Fruitland Ave Vernon (90058) *(P-414)*
Jodel Enterprises.......F.......650 343-4510
340 Gateway Dr Apt 105 Pacifica (94044) *(P-17248)*
Jodi Kristopher LLC (PA).......C.......323 890-8000
1950 Naomi Ave Los Angeles (90011) *(P-3235)*
Jody Maronis Italian.......E.......310 822-5639
2011 Ocean Front Walk Venice (90291) *(P-470)*
Jody of California, Los Angeles *Also called Private Brand Mdsg Corp (P-3249)*
Joe Blasco Cosmetics, Palm Springs *Also called Joe Blasco Enterprises Inc (P-23373)*
Joe Blasco Enterprises Inc.......D.......323 467-4949
1285 N Valdivia Way A Palm Springs (92262) *(P-23373)*
Joe Montana Footwear.......D.......310 318-3100
228 Manhattan Beach Blvd Manhattan Beach (90266) *(P-9173)*
Joe's Jeans, Los Angeles *Also called Dbg Subsidiary Inc (P-3265)*
Joe's Trailer Repair, Fontana *Also called Wagonmasters Corporation (P-20524)*
Joes Custom Furn & Frames.......F.......323 721-1881
6402 Whittier Blvd Los Angeles (90022) *(P-4578)*
Johansing Iron Works Inc.......F.......707 361-8190
849 Jackson St Benicia (94510) *(P-12023)*
Johanson Dielectrics Inc (HQ).......C.......805 389-1166
4001 Calle Tecate Camarillo (93012) *(P-18681)*
Johanson Innovations Inc.......F.......805 544-4697
2975 Hawk Hill Ln San Luis Obispo (93405) *(P-21493)*
Johanson Technology Inc.......C.......805 389-1166
4001 Calle Tecate Camarillo (93012) *(P-18682)*
Johasee Rebar Inc.......E.......661 589-0972
18059 Rosedale Hwy Bakersfield (93314) *(P-11821)*
John A Thomson PHD.......E.......323 877-5186
12610 Saticoy St S North Hollywood (91605) *(P-7673)*
John B Campbell MD A Prof Corp.......F.......858 576-9960
9292 Chesapeake Dr # 100 San Diego (92123) *(P-8747)*
John B Sanfilippo & Son Inc.......B.......209 854-2455
29241 Cottonwood Rd Gustine (95322) *(P-1428)*
John Bean Technologies Corp.......C.......559 661-3200
2300 W Industrial Ave Madera (93637) *(P-14377)*
John Bean Technologies Corp.......E.......951 222-2300
1660 Iowa Ave Ste 100 Riverside (92507) *(P-14378)*
John Bean Technologies Corp.......C.......559 651-8300
9829 W Legacy Ave Visalia (93291) *(P-14379)*
John Bishop Design Inc.......E.......714 744-2300
731 N Main St Orange (92868) *(P-23141)*
John Boyd Enterprises Inc.......C.......916 504-3622
8441 Specialty Cir Sacramento (95828) *(P-19695)*
John Boyd Enterprises Inc (PA).......C.......916 381-4790
8401 Specialty Cir Sacramento (95828) *(P-19696)*
John Crane Inc.......E.......562 802-2555
12760 Florence Ave Santa Fe Springs (90670) *(P-10973)*
John Daniel Gonzalez.......E.......559 646-6621
13458 E Industrial Dr Parlier (93648) *(P-4418)*
John Deere Authorized Dealer, City of Industry *Also called Valley Power Systems Inc (P-13603)*
John Fitzpatrick & Sons.......F.......530 241-3216
1480 Beltline Rd Redding (96003) *(P-2082)*
John Henry Packaging West, Petaluma *Also called MPS Lansing Inc (P-5369)*
John Hewitt.......F.......209 727-9534
12759 E Brandt Rd Ste G Lockeford (95237) *(P-4212)*
John L Conley Inc.......D.......909 627-0981
4344 Mission Blvd Montclair (91763) *(P-12551)*
John L Perry Studio Inc.......E.......805 981-9665
3000 Paseo Mercado # 102 Oxnard (93036) *(P-9857)*
John L Staton Inc.......D.......510 527-3114
1214 5th St Berkeley (94710) *(P-4066)*
John List Corporation.......E.......818 882-7848
9732 Cozycroft Ave Chatsworth (91311) *(P-14233)*
John Lompa.......F.......510 965-6501
720 Harbour Way S Ste A Richmond (94804) *(P-7104)*
John M Phillips LLC.......F.......661 327-3118
2800 Gibson St Bakersfield (93308) *(P-215)*
John M Phillips Oil Field Eqp, Bakersfield *Also called John M Phillips LLC (P-215)*
John N Hansen Co Inc.......F.......650 652-9833
740 Southpoint Blvd Petaluma (94954) *(P-22688)*
John Pina Jr & Sons.......E.......707 944-2229
7960 Silverado Trl NAPA (94558) *(P-1775)*
John Russo Industrial Metal, Newark *Also called Jri Inc (P-12257)*
John Wheeler Logging Inc.......C.......530 527-2993
13570 State Highway 36 E Red Bluff (96080) *(P-3891)*
John Wiley & Sons Inc.......C.......415 433-1740
1 Montgomery St Ste 1200 San Francisco (94104) *(P-6116)*
Johnny Was Collection Inc (PA).......E.......323 231-8222
2423 E 23rd St Los Angeles (90058) *(P-3236)*
Johnny Was Showroom, Los Angeles *Also called Johnny Was Collection Inc (P-3236)*
Johns Formica Shop Inc.......F.......707 544-8585
2439 Piner Rd Santa Rosa (95403) *(P-4986)*
Johns Incredible Pizza Co.......D.......760 951-1111
14766 Bear Valley Rd Victorville (92395) *(P-2490)*
Johns Manville Corporation.......B.......530 934-6243
5916 County Road 49 Willows (95988) *(P-10984)*
Johns Manville Corporation.......D.......323 568-2220
4301 Firestone Blvd South Gate (90280) *(P-10985)*
Johnson & Johnson.......E.......408 273-4100
510 Cottonwood Dr Milpitas (95035) *(P-21765)*
Johnson & Johnson.......B.......909 839-8650
15715 Arrow Hwy Irwindale (91706) *(P-22037)*
Johnson & Johnson.......D.......650 237-4878
3509 Langdon Cmn Fremont (94538) *(P-5463)*
Johnson & Johnson (HQ).......B.......714 247-8200
1700 E Saint Andrew Pl Santa Ana (92705) *(P-22269)*
Johnson & Johnson.......E.......714 247-8200
2501 Pullman St Santa Ana (92705) *(P-21766)*
Johnson & Johnson Consumer Inc.......E.......310 642-1150
5760 W 96th St Los Angeles (90045) *(P-8523)*
Johnson & Johnson Vision, Milpitas *Also called Johnson & Johnson (P-21765)*

A L P H A B E T I C

Employee Codes: A=Over 500 employees, B=251-500
C=101-250, D=51-100, E=20-50, F=10-19
2020 California
Manfacturers Register
© Mergent Inc. 1-800-342-5647
1141

Johnson & Johnson Vision, Santa Ana *Also called Johnson & Johnson* ***(P-22269)***
Johnson Caldraul Inc..........E.......951 340-1067
220 N Delilah St Ste 101 Corona (92879) ***(P-20147)***
Johnson Contrls Authorized Dlr, Hayward *Also called Automatic Control Engrg Corp* ***(P-21439)***
Johnson Controls..........C.......858 633-9100
3568 Ruffin Rd San Diego (92123) ***(P-17735)***
Johnson Controls..........C.......925 273-0100
6952 Preston Ave Ste A Livermore (94551) ***(P-17736)***
Johnson Controls..........F.......530 893-0110
13504 Skypark Industrial Chico (95973) ***(P-17737)***
Johnson Controls..........D.......916 283-0300
4650 Beloit Dr Sacramento (95838) ***(P-17738)***
Johnson Controls Inc..........C.......562 799-8882
5770 Warland Dr Ste A Cypress (90630) ***(P-4862)***
Johnson Controls Inc..........B.......925 447-9200
6383 Las Positas Rd Livermore (94551) ***(P-19697)***
Johnson doc Enterprises..........E.......818 764-1543
11933 Vose St North Hollywood (91605) ***(P-9858)***
Johnson Farm Machinery Co Inc..........F.......530 662-1788
38574 Kentucky Ave Woodland (95695) ***(P-13641)***
Johnson Industrial Sheet Metal..........F.......916 927-8244
2131 Barstow St Sacramento (95815) ***(P-12256)***
Johnson Laminating Coating Inc..........D.......310 635-4929
20631 Annalee Ave Carson (90746) ***(P-9441)***
Johnson Leather Corporation (PA)..........F.......415 775-7393
1833 Polk St San Francisco (94109) ***(P-3518)***
Johnson Manufacturing, Woodland *Also called Johnson Farm Machinery Co Inc* ***(P-13641)***
Johnson Manufacturing Inc..........E.......714 903-0393
15201 Connector Ln Huntington Beach (92649) ***(P-16090)***
Johnson Marble Machinery Inc..........F.......818 764-6186
7325 Varna Ave North Hollywood (91605) ***(P-14485)***
Johnson Outdoors Inc..........E.......619 402-1023
1166 Fesler St Ste A El Cajon (92020) ***(P-22834)***
Johnson Precision Products Inc..........F.......714 824-6971
1308 E Wakeham Ave Santa Ana (92705) ***(P-16091)***
Johnson Racing, Santa Maria *Also called Alan Johnson Prfmce Engrg Inc* ***(P-19450)***
Johnson United Inc (PA)..........E.......209 543-1320
5201 Pentecost Dr Modesto (95356) ***(P-23142)***
Johnson Wilshire Inc..........E.......562 777-0088
17343 Freedom Way City of Industry (91748) ***(P-22038)***
Johnsons Orthopedic, Riverside *Also called Joa Corporation* ***(P-22036)***
Johnstons Trading Post Inc..........E.......530 661-6152
11 N Pioneer Ave Woodland (95776) ***(P-4419)***
Joico Laboratories Inc..........C.......626 321-4100
488 E Santa Clara St # 301 Arcadia (91006) ***(P-8524)***
Joint Technologies Limited..........F.......949 361-1158
5120 E La Palma Ave # 205 Anaheim (92807) ***(P-14931)***
Jolly Jumps Inc..........E.......805 484-0026
600 Via Alondra Camarillo (93012) ***(P-16092)***
Jolly Roger Games, Commerce *Also called Ultra Pro International LLC* ***(P-7320)***
Jolo Industries Inc..........E.......714 554-6840
10432 Brightwood Dr Santa Ana (92705) ***(P-18968)***
Jolyn Clothing Company LLC..........E.......714 794-2149
150 5th St Ste 100 Huntington Beach (92648) ***(P-3348)***
Jomar Machining Inc..........F.......650 324-2143
180 Constitution Dr Ste 8 Menlo Park (94025) ***(P-18969)***
Jon Brooks Inc (PA)..........C.......626 330-0631
14400 Lomitas Ave City of Industry (91746) ***(P-10974)***
Jon Steel Erectors Inc..........E.......909 799-0005
1431 S Gage St San Bernardino (92408) ***(P-24646)***
Jona Global Trading Inc..........F.......626 855-2588
245 S 8th Ave La Puente (91746) ***(P-4725)***
Jonathan Engnred Slutions Corp (PA)..........E.......714 665-4400
250 Commerce Ste 100 Irvine (92602) ***(P-11601)***
Jonathan Louis Intl Ltd..........B.......213 622-6114
12919 S Figueroa St Los Angeles (90061) ***(P-4649)***
Jonathan Louis Intl Ltd (PA)..........C.......323 770-3330
544 W 130th St Gardena (90248) ***(P-4650)***
Jonathan Martin, Los Angeles *Also called Harkham Industries Inc* ***(P-3167)***
Jondo Ltd (PA)..........D.......714 279-2300
22700 Savi Ranch Pkwy Yorba Linda (92887) ***(P-22434)***
Jonel Engineering..........E.......714 879-2360
500 E Walnut Ave Fullerton (92832) ***(P-15641)***
Jonell Oil Corporation..........F.......626 303-4691
13649 Live Oak Ln Irwindale (91706) ***(P-9149)***
Jones Glyn Productions Inc..........F.......760 431-8955
1945 Camino Vida Roble M Carlsbad (92008) ***(P-6261)***
Jones Iron Works..........F.......323 386-2368
2658 Griffith Park Blvd Los Angeles (90039) ***(P-12487)***
Joong-Ang Daily News Cal Inc (HQ)..........C.......213 368-2500
690 Wilshire Pl Los Angeles (90005) ***(P-5678)***
Joong-Ang Daily News Cal Inc..........F.......714 638-2341
8269 Garden Grove Blvd Garden Grove (92844) ***(P-5679)***
Joongang Dily Nwssan Francisco, Union City *Also called Korea Central Daily News* ***(P-5683)***
Jordan Vineyard & Winery, Healdsburg *Also called Jvw Corporation* ***(P-1778)***
Jordan Vineyard & Winery LP..........E.......707 431-5250
1474 Alexander Valley Rd Healdsburg (95448) ***(P-1776)***
Jorlind Enterprises Inc..........F.......949 364-2309
28570 Marguerite Pkwy # 108 Mission Viejo (92692) ***(P-6667)***
Jose Martinez..........F.......323 263-6230
1281 S Hicks Ave Los Angeles (90023) ***(P-1379)***
Jose Martinez Candy, Los Angeles *Also called Jose Martinez* ***(P-1379)***
Josef Mendelovitz..........F.......619 231-3555
11240 Explorer Rd La Mesa (91941) ***(P-6668)***
Joseph Charles Whitson..........F.......707 694-8806
154 Auburn Way Vacaville (95688) ***(P-6262)***
Joseph Company International..........E.......949 474-2200
1711 Langley Ave Irvine (92614) ***(P-11496)***
Joseph Farms, Atwater *Also called Gallo Global Nutrition LLC* ***(P-551)***
Joseph McCrink..........F.......760 489-1500
2802 Luciernaga St Carlsbad (92009) ***(P-11052)***
Joseph Phelps Vineyards, Saint Helena *Also called Stone Bridge Cellars Inc* ***(P-1936)***
Joslyn Sunbank Company LLC..........B.......805 238-2840
1740 Commerce Way Paso Robles (93446) ***(P-18777)***
Jossey-Bass Publishers, San Francisco *Also called John Wiley & Sons Inc* ***(P-6116)***
Jostens Inc..........C.......559 622-5200
231 S Kelsey St Visalia (93291) ***(P-22533)***
Jostens Printing & Publishing, Visalia *Also called Jostens Inc* ***(P-22533)***
Jot Engineering Inc..........F.......818 727-7572
8385 Canoga Ave Canoga Park (91304) ***(P-16093)***
Journal of Bocommunication Inc..........F.......310 475-4708
2772 Woodwardia Dr Los Angeles (90077) ***(P-5680)***
Journeyworks Publishing..........F.......831 423-1400
763 Chestnut St Santa Cruz (95060) ***(P-6263)***
Joy Active..........D.......310 660-0022
13324 Estrella Ave Gardena (90248) ***(P-3349)***
Joy of Cookies, Oakland *Also called Arbo Inc* ***(P-1301)***
Joy Processed Foods Inc..........E.......562 435-1106
1330 Seabright Ave Long Beach (90813) ***(P-2491)***
Joy Products California Inc..........F.......714 437-7250
17281 Mount Wynne Cir Fountain Valley (92708) ***(P-22952)***
Joy Signal Technology LLC..........E.......530 891-3551
1020 Marauder St Ste A Chico (95973) ***(P-16909)***
Joybird, Commerce *Also called Stitch Industries Inc* ***(P-4672)***
JP Graphics Inc..........E.......408 235-8821
3310 Woodward Ave Santa Clara (95054) ***(P-6669)***
JP Products LLC..........E.......310 237-6237
2054 Davie Ave Commerce (90040) ***(P-4579)***
Jpm Finishing Company, Hesperia *Also called Daytec Center LLC* ***(P-20397)***
JR Daniels Commercial Bldrs..........D.......209 545-6040
907 Maze Blvd Modesto (95351) ***(P-12593)***
Jr Grease Services..........E.......323 318-2096
5900 S Eastrn Ave Ste 104 Commerce (90040) ***(P-1461)***
JR Machine Company Inc..........E.......562 903-9477
13245 Florence Ave Santa Fe Springs (90670) ***(P-16094)***
JR Simplot Company..........E.......559 866-5681
12688 S Colorado Ave Helm (93627) ***(P-2492)***
JR Simplot Company..........D.......559 439-3900
12688 S Colorado Ave Fresno (93729) ***(P-917)***
JR Stephens Company..........E.......707 825-0100
5208 Boyd Rd Arcata (95521) ***(P-4213)***
JR Watkins LLC..........E.......415 477-8500
101 Mission St San Francisco (94105) ***(P-3620)***
Jr3 Inc..........F.......530 661-3677
22 Harter Ave Ste 1 Woodland (95776) ***(P-20892)***
Jrd Precision Machining Inc..........F.......408 246-9327
1158 Campbell Ave San Jose (95126) ***(P-16095)***
Jri Inc..........E.......510 494-5300
38021 Cherry St Newark (94560) ***(P-12257)***
Js Apparel Inc..........D.......310 631-6333
1751 E Del Amo Blvd Carson (90746) ***(P-3097)***
Js Glass Wholesale..........F.......213 746-5577
2035 E 37th St Vernon (90058) ***(P-10370)***
Js Manufacturing, Oceanside *Also called Schuman Enterprises Inc* ***(P-13545)***
Js Plastics Inc (PA)..........E.......619 672-5972
1283 E Main St Ste 112a El Cajon (92021) ***(P-9859)***
Js Trade Bindery Services Inc..........D.......650 486-1475
435 Harbor Blvd Belmont (94002) ***(P-7337)***
Jsdu, Santa Rosa *Also called Viavi Solutions Inc* ***(P-19432)***
Jsj Electrical Display Corp..........F.......707 747-5595
340 Via Palo Linda Fairfield (94534) ***(P-23143)***
Jsj Inc Corrugated..........F.......909 987-4746
10700 Jersey Blvd Rancho Cucamonga (91730) ***(P-5241)***
Jsl Foods Inc (PA)..........C.......323 223-2484
3550 Pasadena Ave Los Angeles (90031) ***(P-2493)***
Jsl Foods Inc..........D.......323 727-9999
2222 1/2 Davie Ave Commerce (90040) ***(P-2494)***
Jsl Partners Inc..........F.......408 747-9000
1294 Anvilwood Ct Sunnyvale (94089) ***(P-6670)***
Jsn Industries Inc..........D.......949 458-0050
9700 Jeronimo Rd Irvine (92618) ***(P-9860)***
Jsn Packaging Products Inc..........D.......949 458-0050
9700 Jeronimo Rd Irvine (92618) ***(P-9429)***
Jsr Micro Inc (HQ)..........C.......408 543-8800
1280 N Mathilda Ave Sunnyvale (94089) ***(P-8748)***
JT Design Studio Inc (PA)..........E.......213 891-1500
860 S Los Angeles St # 912 Los Angeles (90014) ***(P-3350)***
Jt Manufacturing Inc (PA)..........F.......408 674-4338
1122 Wrigley Way Milpitas (95035) ***(P-23374)***
Jtb Supply Company Inc..........F.......714 639-9558
1030 N Batavia St Ste A Orange (92867) ***(P-17739)***
Jtea Inc..........E.......847 878-2226
1421 Valane Dr Glendale (91208) ***(P-24062)***
Jts Modular Inc..........E.......661 835-9270
7001 Mcdivitt Dr Ste B Bakersfield (93313) ***(P-12552)***
Ju-Ju-Be Intl LLC (PA)..........E.......877 258-5823
15300 Barranca Pkwy # 100 Irvine (92618) ***(P-3661)***
Juan Brambila Sr..........F.......323 939-8312
5018 Venice Blvd Los Angeles (90019) ***(P-4580)***
Juanitas Foods..........C.......310 834-5339
645 Eubank Ave Wilmington (90744) ***(P-732)***
Judd Wire Inc..........F.......760 744-7720
870 Los Vallecitos Blvd San Marcos (92069) ***(P-11307)***
Judith Von Hopf Inc..........E.......909 481-1884
1525 W 13th St Ste H Upland (91786) ***(P-4914)***

Mergent e-mail: customerrelations@mergent.com
1142
2020 California
Manufacturers Register
(P-0000) Products & Services Section entry number
(PA)=Parent Co (HQ)=Headquarters (DH)=Div Headquarters

Judson Studios Inc....F....323 255-0131
200 S Avenue 66 Los Angeles (90042) *(P-10371)*
Judy Ann, Culver City *Also called Fortune Casuals LLC (P-3159)*
Judy O Productions Inc....E....323 938-8513
4858 W Pico Blvd Ste 331 Los Angeles (90019) *(P-6117)*
Juell Machine Coinc....F....909 594-8164
150 Pacific St Pomona (91768) *(P-16096)*
Juengermann Inc....E....805 644-7165
1899 Palma Dr Ste A Ventura (93003) *(P-13338)*
Juice Division, Pacoima *Also called American Fruits & Flavors LLC (P-2189)*
Juice Heads Inc....F....909 386-7933
735 E Base Line St San Bernardino (92410) *(P-780)*
Juicebot & Co LLC....F....651 270-8860
999 Corporate Dr Ste 100 Ladera Ranch (92694) *(P-14380)*
Juicy Couture Inc....C....888 824-8826
12723 Wentworth St Arleta (91331) *(P-2729)*
Juicy Whip Inc....E....909 392-7500
1668 Curtiss Ct La Verne (91750) *(P-14381)*
July Systems Inc (PA)....F....650 685-2460
533 Airport Blvd Ste 395 Burlingame (94010) *(P-19221)*
Jumio Software & Dev LLC....E....650 388-0264
1971 Landings Dr Mountain View (94043) *(P-24063)*
Jump Start Juice Bar....F....949 754-3120
8001 Irvine Center Dr # 40 Irvine (92618) *(P-918)*
Jumper Media LLC....D....831 333-6202
4747 Morena Blvd Ste 201 San Diego (92117) *(P-6264)*
Jumping Cracker Beans LLC....F....408 265-0658
1588 Camden Village Cir San Jose (95124) *(P-7296)*
Jumpstart Juice, Irvine *Also called Jump Start Juice Bar (P-918)*
June Precision Mfg Inc....F....949 855-9121
22276 Chestnut Ln Lake Forest (92630) *(P-12637)*
Juneshine Inc....F....619 501-8311
3052 El Cajon Blvd San Diego (92104) *(P-2495)*
Jungle Jumps, Pacoima *Also called Twin Peak Industries Inc (P-22914)*
Juniper Networks Inc (PA)....B....408 745-2000
1133 Innovation Way Sunnyvale (94089) *(P-15261)*
Juniper Networks (us) Inc....A....408 745-2000
1133 Innovation Way Sunnyvale (94089) *(P-15262)*
Juniper Square Inc....F....415 841-2722
351 California St # 1450 San Francisco (94104) *(P-24064)*
Juno Graphics....F....310 329-0126
16334 S Avalon Blvd Gardena (90248) *(P-6671)*
Junopacific Inc....C....831 462-1141
2840 Res Pk Dr Ste 160 Soquel (95073) *(P-9861)*
Jupiter Systems LLC....D....510 675-1000
31015 Huntwood Ave Hayward (94544) *(P-15126)*
Just Inc....C....844 423-6637
2000 Folsom St San Francisco (94110) *(P-885)*
Just Cellular Inc....E....818 701-3039
9327 Deering Ave Chatsworth (91311) *(P-17548)*
Just For Fun....E....310 320-1327
557 Van Ness Ave Torrance (90501) *(P-2992)*
Just For Kids, Redondo Beach *Also called Sunset Islandwear (P-2839)*
Just For Wraps Inc (PA)....C....213 239-0503
5745 Rickenbacker Rd Commerce (90040) *(P-3351)*
Just Light Technology Inc....F....510 585-5652
46560 Fremont Blvd # 105 Fremont (94538) *(P-24065)*
Just Off Melrose Inc....E....714 533-4566
1196 Montalvo Way Palm Springs (92262) *(P-1317)*
Just Saying Inc....F....888 512-5007
800 S Date Ave Alhambra (91803) *(P-3560)*
Justenough Software Corp Inc (HQ)....E....949 706-5400
15440 Laguna Canyon Rd # 100 Irvine (92618) *(P-24066)*
Justice Bros Dist Co Inc....E....626 359-9174
2734 Huntington Dr Duarte (91010) *(P-8429)*
Justice Bros-J B Car Care Pdts, Duarte *Also called Justice Bros Dist Co Inc (P-8429)*
Justin Inc....E....626 444-4516
2663 Lee Ave El Monte (91733) *(P-16559)*
Justin Vineyards & Winery LLC (HQ)....E....805 238-6932
11680 Chimney Rock Rd Paso Robles (93446) *(P-1777)*
Justipher Inc....F....510 918-6800
1248 W Winton Ave Hayward (94545) *(P-23144)*
Juul Labs Inc (PA)....B....415 829-2336
560 20th St San Francisco (94107) *(P-23375)*
Jvic Catalyst Services LLC....E....310 327-0991
18025 S Broadway Carson (90745) *(P-7501)*
Jvr Sheetmetal Fabrication Inc....E....714 841-2464
7101 Patterson Dr Garden Grove (92841) *(P-19908)*
Jvw Corporation....D....707 431-5250
1474 Alexander Valley Rd Healdsburg (95448) *(P-1778)*
JW Manufacturing Inc....D....805 498-4594
12989 Bradley Ave Sylmar (91342) *(P-12684)*
JW Molding Inc....F....805 499-2682
2523 Calcite Cir Newbury Park (91320) *(P-14065)*
JW Wireless....F....626 532-2511
846 E Valley Blvd Ste A San Gabriel (91776) *(P-17549)*
Jwc Carbide Inc....F....714 540-8870
33700 Calle Vis Temecula (92592) *(P-13927)*
Jwc Environmental LLC....D....714 662-5829
2600 S Garnsey St Santa Ana (92707) *(P-15531)*
JWP Manufacturing LLC....E....408 970-0641
3500 De La Cruz Blvd Santa Clara (95054) *(P-16097)*
K & B Foam Inc....C....619 661-1870
9335 Airway Rd Ste 100 San Diego (92154) *(P-9553)*
K & D Graphics....E....714 639-8900
1432 N Main St Ste C Orange (92867) *(P-5450)*
K & D Graphics Prtg & Packg, Orange *Also called K & D Graphics (P-5450)*
K & E Inc....F....310 675-3309
3906 W 139th St Hawthorne (90250) *(P-20148)*
K & E Manufacturing Inc....F....562 494-7570
1966 Freeman Ave Signal Hill (90755) *(P-12258)*
K & E Printing Ink, La Verne *Also called Farbotech Color Inc (P-8913)*
K & J Wire Products Corp....E....714 816-0360
1220 N Lance Ln Anaheim (92806) *(P-12488)*
K & K Laboratories Inc....E....760 758-2352
2160 Warmlands Ave Vista (92084) *(P-7972)*
K & L Precision Grinding Co....F....323 564-5151
9309 Atlantic Ave South Gate (90280) *(P-16098)*
K & M Meat Co, Vernon *Also called K & M Packing Co Inc (P-415)*
K & M Packing Co Inc....C....323 585-5318
2443 E 27th St Vernon (90058) *(P-415)*
K & M Software Design LLC....F....805 583-0403
2828 Cochran St Ste 351 Simi Valley (93065) *(P-24067)*
K & N Engineering Inc (PA)....A....951 826-4000
1455 Citrus St Riverside (92507) *(P-20410)*
K & S Enterprises, Adelanto *Also called Dar-Ken Inc (P-9227)*
K & W Manufacturing Co Inc....F....951 277-3300
23107 Temescal Canyon Rd Corona (92883) *(P-11602)*
K & Z Cabinet Co Inc....D....909 947-3567
1450 S Grove Ave Ontario (91761) *(P-4214)*
K A Tool & Technology Inc....E....408 957-9600
1700 Sango Ct Milpitas (95035) *(P-16099)*
K C A Engineered Plastics Inc (PA)....D....415 433-4494
580 California St Ste 22 San Francisco (94104) *(P-7578)*
K C B, Valencia *Also called Kcb Precision (P-16910)*
K C Hilites Inc....E....928 635-2607
13637 Cimarron Ave Gardena (90249) *(P-17091)*
K C Photo Engraving Company....F....626 795-4127
712 Arrow Grand Cir Covina (91722) *(P-14328)*
K C Sheetmetal Inc....F....408 441-6620
943 Berryessa Rd Ste B3 San Jose (95133) *(P-12259)*
K C Welding Inc....F....760 352-3832
1549 Dogwood Rd El Centro (92243) *(P-24647)*
K G Bags, San Rafael *Also called ONeil KG Bags (P-10201)*
K I C, San Diego *Also called Embedded Designs Inc (P-20865)*
K I K, Santa Fe Springs *Also called Kik-Socal Inc (P-8391)*
K I O Kables Inc....F....925 778-7500
2525 W 10th St Antioch (94509) *(P-13419)*
K K Molds Inc....F....818 548-8988
926 Western Ave Ste D Glendale (91201) *(P-11962)*
K Live....F....626 289-2885
300 W Valley Blvd 33 Alhambra (91803) *(P-18331)*
K M I, Anaheim *Also called Kanstul Musical Instrs Inc (P-22628)*
K Metal Products Inc....C....562 693-5425
11935 Baker Pl Santa Fe Springs (90670) *(P-13420)*
K P Graphics, Stockton *Also called Kp LLC (P-6684)*
K P I, Fremont *Also called Knightsbridge Plastics Inc (P-9868)*
K S Designs Inc....E....562 929-3973
9515 Sorensen Ave Santa Fe Springs (90670) *(P-23145)*
K S Equipment Inc....F....831 722-7173
17 Hangar Way Watsonville (95076) *(P-18970)*
K S Printing Inc....F....951 268-5180
710 E Parkridge Ave # 105 Corona (92879) *(P-7105)*
K S Telecom Inc....F....916 652-4735
2350 Humphrey Rd Penryn (95663) *(P-17383)*
K Short Inc....F....626 358-8511
126 W Walnut Ave Monrovia (91016) *(P-11822)*
K Squared Metals, Lake Elsinore *Also called Boozak Inc (P-12133)*
K Tech Telecommunications Inc....F....818 773-0333
9555 Owensmouth Ave Ste 2 Chatsworth (91311) *(P-17550)*
K Too....E....213 747-7766
800 E 12th St Ste 117 Los Angeles (90021) *(P-3169)*
K Tube Technologies, Poway *Also called K-Tube Corporation (P-11129)*
K V R Investment Group Inc....D....818 896-1102
12113 Branford St Sun Valley (91352) *(P-14486)*
K&K World Inc....E....714 234-6237
721 W Wedgewood Ln La Habra (90631) *(P-5069)*
K&M Jewellery, Burbank *Also called Makse Inc (P-22544)*
K-1 Packaging Group....E....626 964-9384
2001 W Mission Blvd Pomona (91766) *(P-6672)*
K-1 Packaging Group (PA)....D....626 964-9384
17989 Arenth Ave City of Industry (91748) *(P-6673)*
K-Bros, Canoga Park *Also called Cg Manufacturing Inc (P-12155)*
K-Cal Group Inc....F....626 922-1103
117 W Garvey Ave Monterey Park (91754) *(P-652)*
K-Fab, Santa Clara *Also called P M S D Inc (P-16270)*
K-Max Health Products Internat....F....909 455-0158
1468 E Mission Blvd Pomona (91766) *(P-598)*
K-P Engineering Corp....F....714 545-7045
2126 S Lyon St Ste A Santa Ana (92705) *(P-16100)*
K-Swiss Inc (HQ)....C....323 675-2700
523 W 6th St Ste 534 Los Angeles (90014) *(P-9174)*
K-Swiss Sales Corp....C....818 706-5100
31248 Oak Crest Dr # 150 Westlake Village (91361) *(P-9175)*
K-Tech Machine Inc....C....800 274-9424
1377 Armorlite Dr San Marcos (92069) *(P-16101)*
K-Tek, Vista *Also called M Klemme Technology Corp (P-17254)*
K-Too, Los Angeles *Also called K Too (P-3169)*
K-Tops Plastic Mfg Inc....E....626 575-9679
15051 Don Julian Rd City of Industry (91746) *(P-23376)*
K-Tube Corporation....D....858 513-9229
13400 Kirkham Way Frnt Poway (92064) *(P-11129)*
K-V Engineering Inc....E....714 229-9977
2411 W 1st St Santa Ana (92703) *(P-13928)*
K.G.S.electronics Inc., Upland *Also called Gar Enterprises (P-18920)*
K1 Packaging, City of Industry *Also called All Label Inc (P-5490)*

Employee Codes: A=Over 500 employees, B=251-500
C=101-250, D=51-100, E=20-50, F=10-19
2020 California
Manfacturers Register
© Mergent Inc. 1-800-342-5647
1143

K2 Pure Solutions LP D 925 203-1196
950 Loveridge Rd Pittsburg (94565) ***(P-15532)***
K2 Pure Solutions Nocal LP E 647 776-0273
950 Loveridge Rd Pittsburg (94565) ***(P-8982)***
K9 Ballistics Inc F 805 233-8103
708 Via Alondra Camarillo (93012) ***(P-23377)***
Kaar Drect Mail Flfillment LLC E 619 382-3670
1225 Expo Way Ste 160 San Diego (92154) ***(P-5681)***
Kaazing Corporation (PA) F 650 960-8148
2107 N 1st St Ste 660 San Jose (95131) ***(P-24068)***
Kabushiki Kisha Higuchi Shokai F 310 212-7234
2281 W 205th St Ste 107 Torrance (90501) ***(P-16973)***
Kacee Company F 916 348-3204
3570 Hiawatha North Highlands (95660) ***(P-16102)***
Kacee Discount Abrasives, North Highlands *Also called Kacee Company* ***(P-16102)***
Kadan Consultants Incorporated F 562 988-1165
5662 Research Dr Huntington Beach (92649) ***(P-16103)***
Kadbanou LLC F 818 409-0118
1951 Gardena Ave Glendale (91204) ***(P-781)***
Kadi Enterprises Inc F 818 556-3400
802 N Victory Blvd Burbank (91502) ***(P-471)***
Kafp, Foothill Ranch *Also called Kaiser Aluminum Fab Pdts LLC* ***(P-11219)***
Kaga (usa) Inc E 714 540-2697
2620 S Susan St Santa Ana (92704) ***(P-12828)***
Kaged Muscle LLC E 844 445-2433
101 Main St Ste 360 Huntington Beach (92648) ***(P-599)***
Kagome Inc (HQ) C 209 826-8850
333 Johnson Rd Los Banos (93635) ***(P-782)***
Kahoots Inc F 619 337-0825
6525 Bisby Lake Ave San Diego (92119) ***(P-23378)***
Kai Os Technologies Sftwr Inc F 858 547-3940
7310 Miramar Rd Ste 440 San Diego (92126) ***(P-24069)***
Kaic, Foothill Ranch *Also called Kaiser Aluminum Investments Co* ***(P-11220)***
Kainalu Blue Inc E 760 806-6400
4675 North Ave Oceanside (92056) ***(P-10986)***
Kainos Dental Technologies LLC (PA) E 800 331-4834
1844 San Miguel Dr 308b Walnut Creek (94596) ***(P-22165)***
Kaise Perma San Franc Medic Ce E 415 833-2000
2425 Geary Blvd San Francisco (94115) ***(P-22039)***
Kaiser Aluminum Corporation E 323 726-8011
6250 Bandini Blvd Commerce (90040) ***(P-11234)***
Kaiser Aluminum Corporation (PA) D 949 614-1740
27422 Portola Pkwy # 350 Foothill Ranch (92610) ***(P-11184)***
Kaiser Aluminum Fab Pdts LLC C 323 722-7151
6250 Bandini Blvd Commerce (90040) ***(P-11235)***
Kaiser Aluminum Fab Pdts LLC (HQ) A 949 614-1740
27422 Portola Pkwy # 200 Foothill Ranch (92610) ***(P-11219)***
Kaiser Aluminum Investments Co (HQ) C 949 614-1740
27422 Portola Pkwy # 350 Foothill Ranch (92610) ***(P-11220)***
Kaiser Enterprises Inc D 209 728-2091
798 Murphys Creek Rd Murphys (95247) ***(P-13474)***
Kakuichi America Inc D 310 539-1590
23540 Telo Ave Torrance (90505) ***(P-9471)***
Kal Machining Inc F 408 782-8989
18450 Sutter Blvd Morgan Hill (95037) ***(P-16104)***
Kal Plastics, Vernon *Also called Tom York Enterprises Inc* ***(P-10088)***
Kal-Cameron Manufacturing (HQ) D 626 338-7308
4265 Puente Ave Baldwin Park (91706) ***(P-11532)***
Kalanico Inc F 714 532-5770
1036 Chantilly Cir Santa Ana (92705) ***(P-4915)***
Kalila Medical Inc E 408 819-5175
1400 Dell Ave Ste C Campbell (95008) ***(P-21494)***
Kalman Manufacturing Inc E 408 776-7664
780 Jarvis Dr Ste 150 Morgan Hill (95037) ***(P-16105)***
Kaltec Electronics Inc (PA) F 813 888-9555
16220 Bloomfield Ave Cerritos (90703) ***(P-22435)***
Kaltec Enterprises, Cerritos *Also called Kaltec Electronics Inc* ***(P-22435)***
Kalypsys Inc C 858 552-0674
333 S Grand Ave Ste 4070 Los Angeles (90071) ***(P-7973)***
Kama Interconnect Inc F 818 713-9810
8030 Remmet Ave Ste 3 Canoga Park (91304) ***(P-18971)***
Kama Sutra, Thousand Oaks *Also called Kamsut Incorporated* ***(P-8525)***
Kama-Tech Corporation F 619 421-7858
3451 Main St Ste 109 Chula Vista (91911) ***(P-21372)***
Kamashian Engineering Inc F 562 920-9692
9128 Rose St Bellflower (90706) ***(P-14066)***
Kamet, Milpitas *Also called Khuus Inc* ***(P-16115)***
Kamikaze 7 Sushi Joint, Carlsbad *Also called Fish On Rice LLC* ***(P-1530)***
Kamiran Inc F 213 746-9161
1415 Maple Ave Ste 220 Los Angeles (90015) ***(P-3170)***
Kamm Industries Inc E 800 317-6253
43352 Business Park Dr Temecula (92590) ***(P-19698)***
Kammerer Enterprises Inc D 760 560-0550
1280 N Melrose Dr Vista (92083) ***(P-10912)***
Kamper Fabrication Inc E 209 599-7137
20107 N Ripon Rd Ripon (95366) ***(P-13642)***
Kamsut Incorporated E 805 495-7479
2151 Anchor Ct Thousand Oaks (91320) ***(P-8525)***
Kan Group Corp F 213 383-1236
3807 Wilshire Blvd # 518 Los Angeles (90010) ***(P-6265)***
Kana Software Inc (HQ) D 650 614-8300
2550 Walsh Ave Ste 120 Santa Clara (95051) ***(P-24070)***
Kanamax International Inc (PA) F 213 399-3398
10618 Rush St South El Monte (91733) ***(P-7974)***
Kandi Usa Inc F 909 941-4588
738 Epperson Dr City of Industry (91748) ***(P-19481)***
Kane Aerospace, Chino *Also called Kanetic Ltd LLC* ***(P-13035)***
Kanetic Ltd LLC F 505 228-5692
7000 Merrill Ave Chino (91710) ***(P-13035)***
Kanex E 714 332-1681
3 Pointe Dr Ste 300 Brea (92821) ***(P-19337)***
Kangol, Los Angeles *Also called Apparel Limited Inc* ***(P-3286)***
Kanstul Musical Instrs Inc E 714 563-1000
1501 E Lincoln Ave Anaheim (92805) ***(P-22628)***
Kap Manufacturing Inc E 909 599-2525
327 W Allen Ave San Dimas (91773) ***(P-16106)***
Kap Medical E 951 340-4360
1395 Pico St Corona (92881) ***(P-21495)***
Kapan - Kent Company Inc E 760 631-1716
2675 Vista Pacific Dr Oceanside (92056) ***(P-3794)***
Kapsch Trafficcom Usa Inc F 925 225-1600
4256 Hacienda Dr Ste 100 Pleasanton (94588) ***(P-16726)***
Kar Ice Service Inc (PA) F 760 256-2648
2521 Solar Way Barstow (92311) ***(P-2358)***
Karapet Engineering Inc F 818 255-0838
11455 Vanowen St North Hollywood (91605) ***(P-16107)***
Karbz Inc F 760 567-9953
77806 Flora Rd Ste E Palm Desert (92211) ***(P-19699)***
Kareem Cart Commissary & Mfg, Los Angeles *Also called Kareem Corporation* ***(P-22835)***
Kareem Corporation F 323 234-0724
4423 S Vermont Ave Los Angeles (90037) ***(P-22835)***
Karel Manufacturing, Calexico *Also called Lorenz Inc* ***(P-19348)***
Kargo Master Inc E 916 638-8703
11261 Trade Center Dr Rancho Cordova (95742) ***(P-12260)***
Karl Storz Endscpy-America Inc E 508 248-9011
2151 E Grand Ave Ste 100 El Segundo (90245) ***(P-21767)***
Karl Storz Endscpy-America Inc (HQ) B 424 218-8100
2151 E Grand Ave El Segundo (90245) ***(P-21768)***
Karl Storz Imaging Inc (HQ) B 805 968-5563
1 S Los Carneros Rd Goleta (93117) ***(P-21496)***
Karl Strauss Brewery & Rest, San Diego *Also called Associated Microbreweries Inc* ***(P-1498)***
Karl Strauss Brewery Garden, San Diego *Also called Associated Microbreweries Inc* ***(P-1497)***
Karl Strauss Brewing Company (PA) D 858 273-2739
5985 Santa Fe St San Diego (92109) ***(P-1540)***
Karl's Sash & Doors, Huntington Beach *Also called Karls Custom Sash and Doors* ***(P-4067)***
Karls Custom Sash and Doors E 714 842-7877
18292 Gothard St Huntington Beach (92648) ***(P-4067)***
Karma Automotive LLC F 949 722-7121
9950 Jeronimo Rd Irvine (92618) ***(P-19482)***
Karma Automotive LLC (HQ) B 714 723-3247
9950 Jeronimo Rd Irvine (92618) ***(P-19483)***
Karoun Cheese, San Fernando *Also called Karoun Dairies Inc* ***(P-558)***
Karoun Dairies Inc F 323 666-6222
5117 Santa Monica Blvd Los Angeles (90029) ***(P-557)***
Karoun Dairies Inc (PA) D 818 767-7000
13023 Arroyo St San Fernando (91340) ***(P-558)***
Karrior Electric Vehicles Inc F 310 515-7600
570 W 184th St Gardena (90248) ***(P-13879)***
Karrior Indus Elc Vehicles, Gardena *Also called Karrior Electric Vehicles Inc* ***(P-13879)***
Kasco Fab Inc D 559 442-1018
4529 S Chestnut Ave Lowr Fresno (93725) ***(P-11823)***
Kaser Corporation F 510 657-9002
39969 Paseo Padre Pkwy Fremont (94538) ***(P-14932)***
Kashiyama USA Inc F 510 979-0070
41432 Christy St Fremont (94538) ***(P-20893)***
Kastle Stair Inc (PA) E 714 596-2600
7422 Mountjoy Dr Huntington Beach (92648) ***(P-4068)***
Katadyn Desalination LLC E 415 526-2780
2220 S Mcdowell Blvd Ext Petaluma (94954) ***(P-16831)***
Katana Software Inc F 562 495-1366
333 W Broadway Ste 105 Long Beach (90802) ***(P-24071)***
Katch Precision Machining Inc F 310 676-4989
3953 W 139th St Hawthorne (90250) ***(P-16108)***
Katchall Fltration Systems LLC F 866 528-2425
263 W Fourth St Beaumont (92223) ***(P-15533)***
Kate Farms Inc C 805 845-2446
101 Innovation Pl Santa Barbara (93108) ***(P-2496)***
Kate Somerville Skincare LLC (HQ) D 323 655-7546
144 S Beverly Dr Ste 500 Beverly Hills (90212) ***(P-7975)***
Kateeva Inc B 510 953-7600
7015 Gateway Blvd Newark (94560) ***(P-17551)***
Kater-Crafts Incorporated E 562 692-0665
4860 Gregg Rd Pico Rivera (90660) ***(P-7338)***
Katerra Inc (PA) D 650 422-3572
2494 Sand Hill Rd Ste 100 Menlo Park (94025) ***(P-216)***
Katerra Inc B 623 236-5322
2302 Paradise Rd Tracy (95304) ***(P-4312)***
Katherine Baumann Collectibles, West Hollywood *Also called Kathrine Baumann Beverly Hills* ***(P-3237)***
Katherine Shih, Monterey Park *Also called CHI-AM Comics Daily Inc* ***(P-6212)***
Kathrine Baumann Beverly Hills E 310 274-7441
9040 W Sunset Blvd # 208 West Hollywood (90069) ***(P-3237)***
Kathryn M Ireland Inc (PA) E 323 965-9888
5285 W Washington Blvd Los Angeles (90016) ***(P-2701)***
Kathy Ireland Worldwide F 310 557-2700
39 Princeton Dr Rancho Mirage (92270) ***(P-3171)***
Katie K Inc F 323 589-3030
5601 Bickett St Vernon (90058) ***(P-3561)***
Katlan Industries Inc F 562 618-0940
3202 Blume Dr Los Alamitos (90720) ***(P-12829)***
Katolec Development Inc E 619 710-0075
6120 Business Center Ct San Diego (92154) ***(P-18972)***
Katz & Klein E 916 444-2024
9901 Horn Rd Ste D Sacramento (95827) ***(P-22365)***
Katz Millennium Sls & Mktg Inc D 323 966-5066
5700 Wilshire Blvd # 100 Los Angeles (90036) ***(P-17552)***
Katzirs Floor & HM Design Inc F 818 988-9663
14742 Calvert St Van Nuys (91411) ***(P-4069)***

Katzkin Leather Interiors Inc ....F.......323 725-1243
6868 W Acco St Montebello (90640) *(P-10235)*
Kav America Ag Inc ....E.......855 528-8721
422 Commercial Rd San Bernardino (92408) *(P-2302)*
Kavi Skin Solutions Inc (PA) ....E.......415 839-5156
700 Larkspur Landing Cir Larkspur (94939) *(P-7976)*
Kavlico Corporation (HQ) ....A.......805 523-2000
1461 Lawrence Dr Thousand Oaks (91320) *(P-18973)*
Kavlico Corporation ....E.......805 523-2000
2475 Pseo De Las Americas San Diego (92154) *(P-18974)*
Kawasaki Micro Elec Amer, San Jose *Also called Megachips Technology Amer Corp (P-18379)*
Kaweah Container Inc (HQ) ....D.......559 651-7846
7101 Avenue 304 Visalia (93291) *(P-5242)*
Kawneer Company Inc ....C.......559 651-4000
7200 W Doe Ave Visalia (93291) *(P-12489)*
Kay & James Inc ....D.......818 998-0357
14062 Balboa Blvd Sylmar (91342) *(P-16109)*
Kay and Associates Inc ....E.......559 410-0917
300 Reeves Blvd Lemoore (93246) *(P-19909)*
Kay Chesterfield Inc ....F.......510 533-5565
6365 Coliseum Way Oakland (94621) *(P-4651)*
Kaye Sandy Enterprises Inc ....E.......650 961-5334
1074 Independence Ave Mountain View (94043) *(P-20342)*
Kayo Corp (PA) ....F.......760 918-0405
6351 Yarrow Dr Ste D Carlsbad (92011) *(P-22836)*
Kayo of California (PA) ....E.......323 233-6107
161 W 39th St Los Angeles (90037) *(P-3267)*
Kayo of California ....F.......310 605-2693
11854 Alameda St Lynwood (90262) *(P-3352)*
Kayo Store, The, Carlsbad *Also called Kayo Corp (P-22836)*
Kazmere Entertainment ....F.......323 448-9009
400 N La Brea Ave Ste 500 Inglewood (90302) *(P-17249)*
Kazuhm Inc ....E.......858 771-3861
6450 Lusk Blvd Ste E208 San Diego (92121) *(P-24072)*
KB Delta Inc ....E.......310 530-1539
3340 Fujita St Torrance (90505) *(P-12830)*
KB Delta Comprsr Valve Parts, Torrance *Also called KB Delta Inc (P-12830)*
KB Design Enterprises, Anaheim *Also called Anaheim Embroidery Inc (P-3723)*
KB Sheetmetal Fabrication Inc ....E.......714 979-1780
17371 Mount Wynne Cir B Fountain Valley (92708) *(P-12261)*
KB Wines LLC ....E.......707 823-7430
220 Morris St Sebastopol (95472) *(P-1779)*
Kba Engineering LLC ....D.......661 323-0487
2157 Mohawk St Bakersfield (93308) *(P-13782)*
Kba Ltd of Kern County LLP ....F.......661 323-0487
2152 Mohawk St Bakersfield (93308) *(P-217)*
Kba2 Inc ....F.......415 528-5500
55 New Montgomery St # 606 San Francisco (94105) *(P-24073)*
Kbc Networks USA, Aliso Viejo *Also called Cove20 LLC (P-18184)*
Kbr Inc ....E.......562 436-9281
2000 W Gaylord St Long Beach (90813) *(P-16686)*
Kc Exclusive Inc (PA) ....D.......213 749-0088
1100 S San Pedro St Los Angeles (90015) *(P-3353)*
KC Metal Products Inc (PA) ....D.......408 436-8754
1960 Hartog Dr San Jose (95131) *(P-11824)*
Kc Metals, San Jose *Also called KC Metal Products Inc (P-11824)*
Kc Pharmaceuticals Inc (PA) ....D.......909 598-9499
3201 Producer Way Pomona (91768) *(P-7977)*
Kc Pharmaceuticals Inc ....E.......909 598-9499
3220 Producer Way Pomona (91768) *(P-7978)*
Kca Electronics Inc ....C.......714 239-2433
223 N Crescent Way Anaheim (92801) *(P-17910)*
Kcb Precision ....F.......661 295-5695
29009 Avenue Penn Valencia (91355) *(P-16910)*
Kdc-One, Chatsworth *Also called Thibiant International Inc (P-8593)*
KDF Inc ....E.......408 779-3731
15875 Concord Cir Morgan Hill (95037) *(P-20411)*
Kdl Precision Molding Corp ....D.......818 896-9899
11381 Bradley Ave Pacoima (91331) *(P-20477)*
Kdr Pet Treats LLC ....F.......559 485-4316
2676 S Maple Ave Fresno (93725) *(P-23379)*
Kds Ingredients LLC ....E.......760 310-5245
3460 Mrron Rd Ste 103-229 Oceanside (92056) *(P-2497)*
Kds Nail Products ....F.......916 381-9358
8580 Younger Creek Dr Sacramento (95828) *(P-23380)*
Kearneys Aluminum Foundry Inc (PA) ....E.......559 233-2591
2660 S Dearing Ave Fresno (93725) *(P-11340)*
KEBERT REPROGRAPHICS, Santee *Also called D Benham Corporation (P-6530)*
Kechika, Rcho STA Marg *Also called Point Conception Inc (P-3390)*
Keck & Schmidt Tool & Die Inc ....F.......626 579-3890
2610 Troy Ave El Monte (91733) *(P-14067)*
Keco Inc ....F.......619 546-9533
3475 Kurtz St San Diego (92110) *(P-15630)*
Keebler Company ....D.......714 228-1555
14000 183rd St La Palma (90623) *(P-1318)*
Keen-Kut Products Inc ....F.......510 785-5168
3190 Diablo Ave Hayward (94545) *(P-14166)*
Keene Engineering Inc (PA) ....F.......818 485-2681
20201 Bahama St Chatsworth (91311) *(P-14588)*
Keene Industries, Chatsworth *Also called Keene Engineering Inc (P-14588)*
Keepcup Ltd ....F.......310 957-2070
431 Colyton St Los Angeles (90013) *(P-9862)*
Keesee Tank Company ....F.......714 528-1814
721 S Melrose St Placentia (92870) *(P-12024)*
Kehoe Custom Wood Designs ....F.......714 993-0444
1320 N Miller St Ste D Anaheim (92806) *(P-4581)*
Keiser Corporation (PA) ....D.......559 256-8000
2470 S Cherry Ave Fresno (93706) *(P-22837)*
Keiser Sports Health Equipment, Fresno *Also called Keiser Corporation (P-22837)*
Keith E Archambeau Sr Inc ....E.......818 718-6110
20615 Plummer St Chatsworth (91311) *(P-12262)*
Keith Nichols ....E.......310 305-0397
8180 Manitoba St Apt 356 Playa Del Rey (90293) *(P-1780)*
Keithco Manufacturing Inc ....F.......714 258-8933
15031 Parkway Loop Ste C Tustin (92780) *(P-16110)*
Kelco, Oxnard *Also called Kim Laube & Company Inc (P-8527)*
Kelco Bio Polymers ....E.......619 595-5000
2025 Harbor Dr San Diego (92113) *(P-8983)*
Kelco Sales & Engineering, Norwalk *Also called Polley Inc (P-14852)*
Kelcourt Plastics Inc (HQ) ....D.......949 361-0774
1000 Calle Recodo San Clemente (92673) *(P-9430)*
Keller Classics Inc (PA) ....E.......805 524-1322
19628 Country Oaks St Tehachapi (93561) *(P-3268)*
Keller Engineering ....F.......310 532-0554
136 W 157th St Gardena (90248) *(P-16111)*
Keller Engineering Inc ....E.......310 326-6291
3203 Kashiwa St Torrance (90505) *(P-16112)*
Keller Entertainment Group Inc ....F.......310 443-2226
1093 Broxton Ave Ste 246 Los Angeles (90024) *(P-15263)*
Kellermyer Bergensons Svcs LLC (PA) ....F.......760 631-5111
1959 Avenida Plaza Real Oceanside (92056) *(P-15534)*
Kelley Blue Book Co Inc (HQ) ....D.......949 770-7704
195 Technology Dr Irvine (92618) *(P-5969)*
Kellogg Company ....B.......925 952-8423
2001 N Main St Ste 450 Walnut Creek (94596) *(P-1025)*
Kellogg Company ....C.......408 295-8656
475 Eggo Way San Jose (95116) *(P-1026)*
Kellogg Garden Product, Lockeford *Also called Kellogg Supply Inc (P-8796)*
Kellogg Sales Company ....E.......916 787-0414
300 Harding Blvd Ste 215 Roseville (95678) *(P-1027)*
Kellogg Supply Inc ....E.......209 727-3130
12686 Locke Rd Lockeford (95237) *(P-8796)*
Kelly & Thome ....E.......909 623-2559
228 San Lorenzo St Pomona (91766) *(P-16113)*
Kelly Computer Systems Inc ....E.......650 960-1010
1060 La Avenida St Mountain View (94043) *(P-15264)*
Kelly Network Solutions Inc ....F.......650 364-7201
22650 Alcalde Rd Cupertino (95014) *(P-21060)*
Kelly Pneumatics Inc ....F.......800 704-7552
711 W 17th St Ste F8 Costa Mesa (92627) *(P-19338)*
Kelly Teegarden Organics LLC ....F.......818 518-0707
6524 Platt Ave Ste 224 West Hills (91307) *(P-8526)*
Kelly Tool & Mfgcoinc ....F.......626 289-7962
433 S Palm Ave Alhambra (91803) *(P-12831)*
Kelly-Moore Paint Company Inc (PA) ....C.......650 592-8337
987 Commercial St San Carlos (94070) *(P-8649)*
Kelly-Moore Paint Company Inc ....E.......510 505-9834
3954 Decoto Rd Fremont (94555) *(P-8650)*
Kelly-Moore Paint Company Inc ....E.......650 595-0333
1075 Commercial St San Carlos (94070) *(P-8651)*
Kelly-Moore Paints, San Carlos *Also called Kelly-Moore Paint Company Inc (P-8649)*
Kelly-Moore Paints, Fremont *Also called Kelly-Moore Paint Company Inc (P-8650)*
Kelly-Moore Paints, San Carlos *Also called Kelly-Moore Paint Company Inc (P-8651)*
Kelmscott Communications LLC ....F.......949 475-1900
2485 Da Vinci Irvine (92614) *(P-6674)*
Kelpac Medical, San Clemente *Also called Kelcourt Plastics Inc (P-9430)*
Kelpac Medical ....D.......619 710-2550
2189 Britannia Blvd San Diego (92154) *(P-9431)*
Kelsey See Canyon Vineyards ....F.......805 595-9700
1945 See Canyon Rd San Luis Obispo (93405) *(P-1781)*
Kelytech Corporation ....E.......408 935-0888
1482 Gladding Ct Milpitas (95035) *(P-18975)*
Kemco, Ontario *Also called Kitchen Equipment Mfg Co Inc (P-12834)*
Kemeera Incorporated ....F.......510 281-9000
315 Jefferson St Oakland (94607) *(P-15265)*
Kemira Water Solutions Inc ....E.......909 350-5678
14000 San Bernardino Ave Fontana (92335) *(P-7502)*
Kemira Water Solutions Inc ....E.......909 350-5678
14000 San Bernardino Ave Fontana (92335) *(P-8984)*
Kemiron Pacific, Fontana *Also called Kemira Water Solutions Inc (P-8984)*
Kemper Enterprises Inc ....E.......909 627-6191
13595 12th St Chino (91710) *(P-11533)*
Kempton Machine Works Inc ....F.......714 990-0596
4070 E Leaverton Ct Anaheim (92807) *(P-14167)*
Ken Anderson ....E.......209 604-8579
904 Frontage Rd Ripon (95366) *(P-10776)*
Ken Hoffmann Inc ....E.......760 325-6012
345 Del Sol Rd Palm Springs (92262) *(P-13036)*
Ken Mason Tile Inc ....E.......562 432-7574
14600 S Western Ave Gardena (90249) *(P-10445)*
Ken-Wor Corp ....E.......714 554-6210
13962 Enterprise Dr Garden Grove (92843) *(P-11053)*
Kenco Engineering Inc ....E.......916 782-8494
2155 Pfe Rd Roseville (95747) *(P-13737)*
Kendall-Jackson Wine Estates (HQ) ....B.......707 544-4000
425 Aviation Blvd Santa Rosa (95403) *(P-1782)*
Kendra Group Inc ....F.......909 473-7206
2394 Saratoga Way San Bernardino (92407) *(P-17740)*
Keney Manufacturing Co (PA) ....F.......209 358-6474
586 Broadway Ave Atwater (95301) *(P-4215)*
Keney's Cabinets, Atwater *Also called Keney Manufacturing Co (P-4215)*
Kenjitsu USA Corp ....F.......619 734-5862
9830 Siempre Viva Rd # 14 San Diego (92154) *(P-18976)*
Kenlor Industries Inc ....F.......714 647-0770
1560 E Edinger Ave Ste A1 Santa Ana (92705) *(P-21769)*
Kennedy Athletics, Carson *Also called Cali-Fame Los Angeles Inc (P-3462)*

ALPHABETIC

Kennedy Engineered Products ...F ...661 272-1147
38830 17th St E Palmdale (93550) *(P-19700)*
Kennedy Hills Enterprises LLC ...F ...714 596-7444
19486 Woodlands Dr Huntington Beach (92648) *(P-17)*
Kennedy Hills Materials, Huntington Beach *Also called Kennedy Hills Enterprises LLC (P-17)*
Kennedy Name Plate Co Inc ...E ...323 585-0121
4501 Pacific Blvd Vernon (90058) *(P-13196)*
Kennerley-Spratling Inc (PA) ...C ...510 351-8230
2116 Farallon Dr San Leandro (94577) *(P-9863)*
Kennerley-Spratling Inc ...C ...408 944-9407
2308 Zanker Rd San Jose (95131) *(P-9864)*
Kenneth Cronon Inc ...F ...818 632-4972
10413 Haines Canyon Ave Tujunga (91042) *(P-3480)*
Kenneth Miller Clothing Inc ...E ...213 746-8866
210 E Olympic Blvd # 208 Los Angeles (90015) *(P-3354)*
Kenny Giannini Putters LLC ...F ...760 851-9475
74755 N Cove Dr Indian Wells (92210) *(P-22838)*
Kenny The Printer, Irvine *Also called American PCF Prtrs College Inc (P-6409)*
Kens Spray Equipment Inc (HQ) ...D ...310 635-9995
1900 W Walnut St Compton (90220) *(P-13197)*
Kens Stakes & Supplies ...F ...559 747-1313
193 S Mariposa Ave Visalia (93292) *(P-4510)*
Kensington Laboratories LLC (PA) ...F ...510 324-0126
6200 Village Pkwy Dublin (94568) *(P-16727)*
Kensington Protective Products ...F ...909 469-1240
151 N Reservoir St Pomona (91767) *(P-3689)*
Kenwalt Die Casting Company, Sun Valley *Also called Kenwalt Die Casting Corp (P-11341)*
Kenwalt Die Casting Corp ...E ...818 768-5800
8719 Bradley Ave Sun Valley (91352) *(P-11341)*
Kenwood Vineyards, Kenwood *Also called Pernod Ricard Usa LLC (P-1862)*
Kepner Plas Fabricators Inc ...E ...310 325-3162
3131 Lomita Blvd Torrance (90505) *(P-9865)*
Kerber Industries Inc ...E ...909 319-0877
166 San Lorenzo St Pomona (91766) *(P-23381)*
Keri Systems Inc (PA) ...D ...408 435-8400
302 Enzo Dr Ste 190 San Jose (95138) *(P-19339)*
Keriligthing, City of Industry *Also called Jishan Usa Inc (P-17046)*
Kern River Holding Inc ...F ...661 589-2507
7700 Downing Ave Bakersfield (93308) *(P-127)*
Kern Valley Sun, Lake Isabella *Also called Wick Communications Co (P-5866)*
Kerning Data Systems Inc ...F ...818 882-8712
9301 Jordan Ave Ste 102 Chatsworth (91311) *(P-14329)*
Kerr Corporation (HQ) ...C ...714 516-7400
1717 W Collins Ave Orange (92867) *(P-22166)*
Kerrock Countertops Inc (PA) ...E ...510 441-2300
1450 Dell Ave Ste C Campbell (95008) *(P-4582)*
Kerry Inc ...D ...760 396-2116
64405 Lincoln St Mecca (92254) *(P-600)*
Kerry Ingredients and Flavours, Commerce *Also called Mastertaste Inc (P-2220)*
Kersting Library Products, Fallbrook *Also called Accurate Wire & Display Inc (P-13393)*
Kesclo Financial Inc ...E ...800 322-8676
150 W 6th St Ste 205 San Pedro (90731) *(P-12490)*
Kesmor Associates ...E ...213 629-2300
610 S Broadway Ste 717 Los Angeles (90014) *(P-22534)*
Kett ...F ...714 974-8837
9581 Featherhill Dr Villa Park (92861) *(P-21251)*
Kett U S, Villa Park *Also called Kett (P-21251)*
Kettenbach LP ...F ...877 532-2123
16052 Beach Blvd Ste 221 Huntington Beach (92647) *(P-22167)*
Kettle Pop, Benicia *Also called Gold Rush Kettle Korn Llc (P-1369)*
Keurig Dr Pepper Inc ...D ...951 341-7500
1188 Mt Vernon Ave Riverside (92507) *(P-2083)*
Keurig Dr Pepper Inc ...E ...530 893-4501
306 Otterson Dr Chico (95928) *(P-2084)*
Keurig Dr Pepper Inc ...D ...925 938-8777
1981 N Broadway Walnut Creek (94596) *(P-2085)*
Kevin Orthopedic, Riverside *Also called Foot In Motion Inc (P-22013)*
Kevin Whaley ...E ...619 596-4000
9565 Pathway St Santee (92071) *(P-13421)*
Kevita Inc (HQ) ...D ...805 200-2250
2220 Celsius Ave Ste A Oxnard (93030) *(P-2086)*
Key Container, South Gate *Also called Liberty Container Company (P-5243)*
Key Energy Services Inc ...E ...661 334-8100
5080 California Ave # 150 Bakersfield (93309) *(P-218)*
Key Energy Services Inc ...E ...805 653-1300
3587 N Ventura Ave Ventura (93001) *(P-219)*
Key Item Sales Inc ...F ...818 885-0928
21037 Superior St Chatsworth (91311) *(P-22986)*
Key Line Litho, Gardena *Also called Keyline Lithography Inc (P-6675)*
Key Material Handling Inc ...F ...805 520-6007
4790 Alamo St Simi Valley (93063) *(P-13880)*
Key Source International (PA) ...F ...510 562-5000
7711 Oakport St Oakland (94621) *(P-15127)*
Key-Bak, Ontario *Also called West Coast Chain Mfg Co (P-19441)*
Keyfax Newmedia Inc ...F ...831 477-1205
911 Center St Ste A Santa Cruz (95060) *(P-17250)*
Keyin Inc ...F ...562 690-3888
511 S Harbor Blvd Ste C La Habra (90631) *(P-19222)*
Keyline Lithography Inc ...F ...310 538-8618
1726 W 180th St Gardena (90248) *(P-6675)*
Keys Cabinetry Inc ...F ...415 382-1466
20 Pimentel Ct Ste B14 Novato (94949) *(P-4916)*
Keysight Technologies Inc (PA) ...B ...800 829-4444
1400 Fountaingrove Pkwy Santa Rosa (95403) *(P-20894)*
Keysight Technologies Inc ...E ...408 553-3290
5301 Stevens Creek Blvd Santa Clara (95051) *(P-21061)*
Keysource Foods LLC ...E ...310 879-4888
2263 W 190th St Torrance (90504) *(P-2245)*
Keyssa Inc (PA) ...E ...408 637-2300
655 Campbell Technology P Campbell (95008) *(P-18332)*
Keyssa Systems Inc ...F ...408 637-2300
655 Campbell Technology P Campbell (95008) *(P-14487)*
Keystone Cabinetry Inc ...F ...818 565-3330
3110 N Clybourn Ave Burbank (91505) *(P-4216)*
Keystone Coffee Company ...F ...408 998-2221
2230 Will Wool Dr Ste 100 San Jose (95112) *(P-2303)*
Keystone Dental Inc ...E ...781 328-3382
13645 Alton Pkwy Ste A Irvine (92618) *(P-22168)*
Keystone Engineering Company (HQ) ...E ...562 497-3200
4401 E Donald Douglas Dr Long Beach (90808) *(P-16114)*
Kezar Life Sciences Inc ...E ...650 822-5600
4000 Shoreline Ct Ste 300 South San Francisco (94080) *(P-7979)*
Kf Fiberglass Inc (PA) ...E ...562 869-1536
8247 Phlox St Downey (90241) *(P-19701)*
KG Technologies Inc ...F ...888 513-1874
6028 State Farm Dr Rohnert Park (94928) *(P-18977)*
Kh Construction, Fresno *Also called Nevocal Enterprises Inc (P-353)*
Kh9100 LLC ...F ...818 972-2580
3073 N California St Burbank (91504) *(P-22366)*
Khan Academy Inc ...D ...650 336-5426
1200 Villa St Ste 200 Mountain View (94041) *(P-24074)*
Khmca, Oakland *Also called Kyoho Manufacturing California (P-12745)*
Khn Solutions Inc ...F ...877 334-6876
300 Broadway Ste 26 San Francisco (94133) *(P-21497)*
Khoros LLC (PA) ...E ...415 757-3100
1 Pier Ste 1a San Francisco (94111) *(P-24075)*
Khuus Inc ...D ...408 522-8000
1778 Mccarthy Blvd Milpitas (95035) *(P-16115)*
Khyber Foods Incorporated ...E ...714 879-0900
500 S Acacia Ave Fullerton (92831) *(P-2498)*
Kia Group, Poway *Also called Kia Incorporated (P-10180)*
Kia Incorporated (PA) ...E ...858 824-2999
13880 Stowe Dr Ste B Poway (92064) *(P-10180)*
Kiana Analytics Inc ...F ...650 575-3871
440 N Wolfe Rd W050 Sunnyvale (94085) *(P-24076)*
Kiara Sky Professional Nails, Bakersfield *Also called Glam and Glits Nail Design Inc (P-8499)*
Kibblwhite Precision Machining ...E ...650 359-4704
580 Crespi Dr Ste H Pacifica (94044) *(P-20412)*
Kicksend, Mountain View *Also called Receivd Inc (P-24349)*
Kiddo By Katie, Vernon *Also called Love Marks Inc (P-3176)*
Kieran Label Corp ...E ...619 449-4457
2321 Siempre Viva Ct # 101 San Diego (92154) *(P-7106)*
Kiewit Corporation ...E ...760 377-3117
Hwy 395 And Cinder Rd Little Lake (93542) *(P-309)*
Kifuki USA Co Inc (HQ) ...D ...626 334-8090
15547 1st St Irwindale (91706) *(P-520)*
Kik Custom Products, Torrance *Also called Prestone Products Corporation (P-9017)*
Kik Pool Additives Inc ...C ...909 390-9912
5160 E Airport Dr Ontario (91761) *(P-8985)*
Kik-Socal Inc ...A ...562 946-6427
9028 Dice Rd Santa Fe Springs (90670) *(P-8391)*
Kilby Mfg & Farming, Gridley *Also called E D Kilby Mfg & Farming (P-13630)*
Kilgore Machine Company Inc ...E ...714 540-3659
2312 S Susan St Santa Ana (92704) *(P-16116)*
Killion Industries Inc (PA) ...D ...760 727-5102
1380 Poinsettia Ave Vista (92081) *(P-4917)*
Kilovac, Carpinteria *Also called Te Connectivity Corporation (P-16761)*
Kim & Cami Productions Inc ...E ...323 584-1300
2950 Leonis Blvd Vernon (90058) *(P-3355)*
Kim & Roy Co Inc ...F ...310 762-1896
2924 E Ana St Compton (90221) *(P-3040)*
Kim and Cami, Vernon *Also called Kim & Cami Productions Inc (P-3355)*
Kim Laube & Company Inc ...E ...805 240-1300
2221 Statham Blvd Oxnard (93033) *(P-8527)*
Kim Seng Jewelry Inc ...F ...213 628-8566
818 N Broadway Ste 202 Los Angeles (90012) *(P-22597)*
Kim's Fence, Fullerton *Also called Kims Welding and Iron Works (P-12712)*
Kim's Jewelry Manufacturer, Los Angeles *Also called Y Y K Inc (P-22585)*
Kimball Electronics Indiana ...E ...669 234-1110
5215 Hellyer Ave Ste 130 San Jose (95138) *(P-21062)*
Kimball Nelson Inc ...F ...310 636-0081
7740 Lemona Ave Van Nuys (91405) *(P-23382)*
Kimberley Wine Vinegars, Acampo *Also called California Concentrate Company (P-905)*
Kimberly Lighting, Vernon *Also called Hollywood Lamp & Shade Co (P-16864)*
Kimberly Machine Inc ...E ...714 539-0151
12822 Joy St Garden Grove (92840) *(P-16117)*
Kimberly-Clark Corporation ...B ...714 578-0705
2001 E Orangethorpe Ave Fullerton (92831) *(P-5128)*
Kimberly-Clark Corporation ...F ...818 986-2430
15260 Ventura Blvd # 1410 Van Nuys (91403) *(P-5129)*
Kimdurla Inc ...E ...818 504-4041
12841 Blmfeld St Unit 104 Studio City (91604) *(P-10314)*
Kims Welding and Iron Works ...E ...714 680-7700
2331 E Orangethorpe Ave Fullerton (92831) *(P-12712)*
Kimzey Welding Works Inc ...F ...530 662-9331
164 Kentucky Ave Woodland (95695) *(P-16118)*
Kinamad, Camarillo *Also called VME Acquisition Corp (P-22121)*
Kinamed Inc ...E ...805 384-2748
820 Flynn Rd Camarillo (93012) *(P-22040)*
Kinary Inc ...E ...626 575-7873
2542 Troy Ave South El Monte (91733) *(P-3562)*
Kind Led Grow Lights, Santa Rosa *Also called Supercloset (P-11547)*
Kindred Biosciences Inc (PA) ...E ...650 701-7901
1555 Bayshore Hwy Ste 200 Burlingame (94010) *(P-7980)*

Kindred Litho Incorporated .... F.....909 944-4015
10833 Bell Ct Rancho Cucamonga (91730) *(P-6676)*
Kinematic Automation Inc .... D.....209 532-3200
21085 Longeway Rd Sonora (95370) *(P-21770)*
Kinematics Research Ltd (PA) .... F.....707 763-9993
55 Mitchell Blvd Ste 16 San Rafael (94903) *(P-13804)*
Kinestral Technologies Inc .... C.....650 416-5200
3955 Trust Way Hayward (94545) *(P-10372)*
Kinetic Electric Corporation .... E.....619 654-1157
944 Industrial Blvd 946 Chula Vista (91911) *(P-19340)*
Kinetic Farm Inc .... F.....650 503-3279
210 Industrial Rd Ste 102 San Carlos (94070) *(P-24077)*
Kinetico Quality Water Systems, Riverside Also called US Environmental *(P-9034)*
King Abrasives Inc .... F.....510 785-8100
1942 National Ave Hayward (94545) *(P-5364)*
King Graphics, San Diego Also called Colmol Inc *(P-7030)*
King Henrys Inc .... E.....661 295-5566
29124 Hancock Pkwy 1 Valencia (91355) *(P-2335)*
King Instrument Company Inc .... E.....714 891-0008
12700 Pala Dr Garden Grove (92841) *(P-20895)*
King Nutronics Corporation .... E.....818 887-5460
6421 Independence Ave Woodland Hills (91367) *(P-20896)*
King Plastics Inc .... D.....714 997-7540
840 N Elm St Orange (92867) *(P-9866)*
King Precision Inc .... E.....831 426-2704
111 Harrison Ct Santa Cruz (95062) *(P-12832)*
King Rustler .... E.....831 385-4880
522 Broadway St Ste A King City (93930) *(P-5682)*
King Shock Technology Inc .... D.....714 530-8701
12472 Edison Way Garden Grove (92841) *(P-19702)*
King's Printing, San Diego Also called Kings Printing Corp *(P-6677)*
Kingcom(us) LLC (HQ) .... C.....424 744-5697
3100 Ocean Park Blvd Santa Monica (90405) *(P-24078)*
Kingdom Matress Company, Gardena Also called Kingdom Mattress Inc *(P-4726)*
Kingdom Mattress Inc .... E.....562 630-5531
17920 S Figueroa St Gardena (90248) *(P-4726)*
Kingfa Global Inc .... F.....909 212-5413
1910 S Archibald Ave D Ontario (91761) *(P-12685)*
Kingman Industries Inc .... E.....951 698-1812
26370 Beckman Ct Ste A Murrieta (92562) *(P-8342)*
Kings Asian Gourmet Inc .... E.....415 222-6100
683 Brannan St Unit 304 San Francisco (94107) *(P-733)*
Kings Cabinet Systems .... F.....559 584-9662
426 Park Ave Hanford (93230) *(P-4806)*
Kings Crating Inc (PA) .... E.....619 590-1664
1364 Pioneer Way El Cajon (92020) *(P-19969)*
Kings Crating Inc .... E.....619 590-2631
1364 Pioneer Way El Cajon (92020) *(P-12833)*
Kings Printing Corp .... E.....619 297-6000
5401 Linda Vista Rd # 401 San Diego (92110) *(P-6677)*
Kings River Casting Inc .... F.....559 875-8250
1350 North Ave Sanger (93657) *(P-4863)*
Kings Way Sales and Mktg LLC .... F.....530 722-0272
6680 Lockheed Dr Redding (96002) *(P-14833)*
Kingsburg Cultivator Inc .... F.....559 897-3662
40190 Road 36 Kingsburg (93631) *(P-13643)*
Kingsford Products Company LLC (HQ) .... D.....510 271-7000
1221 Broadway Ste 1300 Oakland (94612) *(P-8696)*
Kingsley Mfg Co (PA) .... F.....949 645-4401
1984 Placentia Ave Costa Mesa (92627) *(P-22041)*
Kingsolver Inc .... F.....562 945-7590
8417 Secura Way Santa Fe Springs (90670) *(P-23028)*
Kingson Mold & Machine Inc .... E.....714 871-0221
1350 Titan Way Brea (92821) *(P-14068)*
Kingspan Insulated Panels Inc .... D.....209 531-9091
2000 Morgan Rd Modesto (95358) *(P-12553)*
Kingston Digital Inc (HQ) .... E.....714 435-2600
17600 Newhope St Fountain Valley (92708) *(P-15266)*
Kingston Technology Corp (PA) .... B.....714 445-3495
17600 Newhope St Fountain Valley (92708) *(P-15267)*
Kinkisharyo International LLC (HQ) .... F.....424 276-1803
1960 E Grand Ave Ste 1210 El Segundo (90245) *(P-20371)*
Kinsale Holdings Inc (PA) .... D.....415 400-2600
475 Sansome St Ste 570 San Francisco (94111) *(P-9325)*
Kintera Inc (HQ) .... D.....858 795-3000
9605 Scranton Rd Ste 200 San Diego (92121) *(P-24079)*
Kinwai USA Inc .... E.....510 780-9388
2265 Davis Ct Hayward (94545) *(P-4583)*
Kio Kables, Antioch Also called K I O Kables Inc *(P-13419)*
Kion Technology Inc .... E.....408 435-3008
2190 Oakland Rd San Jose (95131) *(P-13198)*
Kip Steel Inc .... E.....714 461-1051
1650 Valley Ln Fullerton (92833) *(P-11119)*
Kipe Molds Inc .... F.....714 572-9576
340 E Crowther Ave Placentia (92870) *(P-14069)*
Kirby Manufacturing Inc (PA) .... D.....209 723-0778
484 S St 59 Merced (95341) *(P-13644)*
Kirby Manufacturing Inc .... F.....559 686-1571
1478 N J St Tulare (93274) *(P-13645)*
Kirby-Tulare Manufacturing, Tulare Also called Kirby Manufacturing Inc *(P-13645)*
Kirk A Schliger .... F.....916 638-8433
11240 Pyrites Way Gold River (95670) *(P-14667)*
Kirk API Containers .... E.....323 278-5400
2131 Garfield Ave Commerce (90040) *(P-9867)*
Kirk Containers, Commerce Also called Arthurmade Plastics Inc *(P-9641)*
Kirkhill Inc .... D.....562 803-1117
12023 Woodruff Ave Downey (90241) *(P-9326)*
Kirkhill Inc (HQ) .... E.....714 529-4901
300 E Cypress St Brea (92821) *(P-7631)*

Kirkhill Inc .... A.....714 529-4901
300 E Cypress St Brea (92821) *(P-9240)*
Kirkhill Inc .... A.....714 529-4901
300 E Cypress St Brea (92821) *(P-9241)*
Kirsen Technologies Inc .... F.....510 540-5383
2041 Bancroft Way Ste 201 Berkeley (94704) *(P-17553)*
Kisca, Los Angeles Also called Komarov Enterprises Inc *(P-3269)*
Kisco Conformal Coating LLC (PA) .... F.....408 224-6533
6292 San Ignacio Ave C San Jose (95119) *(P-18333)*
Kiss Packaging Systems, Vista Also called Accutek Packaging Equipment Co *(P-14694)*
Kitanica Manufacturing .... F.....707 272-7286
867 Newton Carey Jr Way Oakland (94607) *(P-23383)*
Kitch Engineering Inc .... E.....818 897-7133
12320 Montague St Pacoima (91331) *(P-16119)*
Kitchen Cuts LLC .... E.....323 560-7415
6045 District Blvd Maywood (90270) *(P-472)*
Kitchen Equipment Mfg Co Inc .... E.....909 923-3153
2102 Maple Privado Ontario (91761) *(P-12834)*
Kitchen Post Inc .... F.....909 948-6768
8617 Baseline Rd Rancho Cucamonga (91730) *(P-4217)*
Kitchens Now Inc .... F.....916 229-8222
20 Blue Sky Ct Sacramento (95828) *(P-4218)*
Kitcor Corporation .... E.....323 875-2820
9959 Glenoaks Blvd Sun Valley (91352) *(P-12835)*
Kite Hill, Hayward Also called Lyrical Foods Inc *(P-2535)*
Kitsch LLC (PA) .... F.....424 240-5551
307 N New Hampshire Ave Los Angeles (90004) *(P-22535)*
Kittrich Corporation (PA) .... C.....714 736-1000
1585 W Mission Blvd Pomona (91766) *(P-5028)*
Kittyhawk Products, Garden Grove Also called Kpi Services Inc *(P-11455)*
Kiva Container Corporation .... E.....714 630-3850
2700 E Regal Park Dr Anaheim (92806) *(P-9554)*
Kiva Designs, Benicia Also called Applied Sewing Resources Inc *(P-2667)*
Kizanis Custom Cabinets, San Leandro Also called Steve and Cynthia Kizanis *(P-4250)*
Kizure Hair Products & Irons, Compton Also called Kizure Product Co Inc *(P-16832)*
Kizure Product Co Inc .... E.....310 604-0058
1950 N Central Ave Compton (90222) *(P-16832)*
Kjl Fasteners, Chilcoot Also called Pau Hana Group LLC *(P-11619)*
Kjm Enterprises Inc .... E.....858 537-2490
8148 Auberge Cir San Diego (92127) *(P-7107)*
Kk Audio Inc .... F.....818 765-2921
12620 Raymer St North Hollywood (91605) *(P-22436)*
Kk Graphics Inc .... F.....415 468-1057
1336 San Mateo Ave South San Francisco (94080) *(P-6678)*
Kl Electronics Inc .... E.....714 751-5611
3083 S Harbor Blvd Santa Ana (92704) *(P-17911)*
Kl-Megla America LLC .... E.....818 334-5311
2221 Celsius Ave Ste A Oxnard (93030) *(P-11603)*
KLA Corporation (PA) .... B.....408 875-3000
1 Technology Dr Milpitas (95035) *(P-21373)*
KLA Corporation .... D.....408 496-2055
3530 Bassett St Santa Clara (95054) *(P-21063)*
KLA Corporation .... D.....510 456-2490
850 Auburn Ct Fremont (94538) *(P-21064)*
KLA Tencor .... E.....510 887-2647
2260 American Ave Ste 1 Hayward (94545) *(P-14787)*
KLA-Tencor Asia-Pac Dist Corp .... E.....408 875-4144
1 Technology Dr Milpitas (95035) *(P-18334)*
Klatch Coffee Inc (PA) .... E.....909 981-4031
8767 Onyx Ave Rancho Cucamonga (91730) *(P-2304)*
Klean Kanteen Inc .... D.....530 592-4552
3960 Morrow Ln Chico (95928) *(P-11497)*
Kleen Maid Inc .... E.....323 581-3000
11450 Sheldon St Sun Valley (91352) *(P-3621)*
Kleenrite, Madera Also called Better Cleaning Systems Inc *(P-16843)*
Klein Bros Holdings Ltd .... E.....209 465-5033
1515 S Fresno Ave Stockton (95206) *(P-1429)*
Klein Bros Snacks, Stockton Also called Klein Bros Holdings Ltd *(P-1429)*
Klein Industries Inc .... F.....415 695-9117
2380 Jerrold Ave San Francisco (94124) *(P-16120)*
Klinky Manufacturing Co .... F.....818 766-6256
4000 W Magnolia Blvd D Burbank (91505) *(P-11604)*
Klippenstein Corporation .... E.....559 834-4258
5399 S Villa Ave Fresno (93725) *(P-14713)*
Klk Forte Industry Inc (PA) .... E.....323 415-9181
1535 Rio Vista Ave Los Angeles (90023) *(P-3356)*
Kln Precision Machining Corp .... D.....510 770-5001
40725 Encyclopedia Cir Fremont (94538) *(P-16121)*
Klooma Holdings Inc .... E.....305 747-3315
113 N San Vicente Blvd Beverly Hills (90211) *(P-24080)*
Kloudgin, Sunnyvale Also called Enterprise Signal Inc *(P-23866)*
Kls Doors LLC .... E.....909 605-6468
501 Kettering Dr Ontario (91761) *(P-4070)*
Klune Industries Inc (HQ) .... B.....818 503-8100
7323 Coldwater Canyon Ave North Hollywood (91605) *(P-20149)*
Km Printing Production Inc .... F.....626 821-0008
218 Longden Ave Irwindale (91706) *(P-6679)*
Kmb Foods Inc (PA) .... E.....626 447-0545
1010 S Sierra Way San Bernardino (92408) *(P-473)*
Kmg Chemicals Inc .... E.....800 956-7467
2340 Bert Dr Hollister (95023) *(P-8986)*
Kmg Electronic Chemicals Inc .... F.....831 636-5151
2340 Bert Dr Hollister (95023) *(P-8987)*
Kmic Technology Inc .... E.....408 240-3600
2095 Ringwood Ave Ste 10 San Jose (95131) *(P-17554)*
Kmp Numatech Pacific, Pomona Also called Numatech West (kmp) LLC *(P-5248)*
Kmr Label LLC .... E.....310 603-8910
1360 W Walnut Pkwy Compton (90220) *(P-6957)*

Employee Codes: A=Over 500 employees, B=251-500
C=101-250, D=51-100, E=20-50, F=10-19

2020 California
Manfacturers Register

© Mergent Inc. 1-800-342-5647

1147

Kmt International Inc ....E....510 713-1400
344 De Leon Ave Fremont (94539) ***(P-13783)***
KMW Communications, Fullerton *Also called KMW USA Inc* ***(P-18978)***
KMW USA Inc (HQ) ....E....714 515-1100
1818 E Orangethorpe Ave Fullerton (92831) ***(P-18978)***
Knauf Insulation Inc ....C....530 275-9665
3100 Ashby Rd Shasta Lake (96019) ***(P-10987)***
Knife River, Sutter Creek *Also called Amador Transit Mix Inc* ***(P-10687)***
Knight LLC (HQ) ....D....949 595-4800
15340 Barranca Pkwy Irvine (92618) ***(P-14834)***
Knight Publishing Corp ....E....323 653-8060
8060 Melrose Ave Ste 210 Los Angeles (90046) ***(P-5970)***
Knights Bridge Winery, Calistoga *Also called Bailey Essel William Jr* ***(P-1589)***
Knightsbridge Plastics Inc ....D....510 249-9722
3075 Osgood Ct Fremont (94539) ***(P-9868)***
Knightscope Inc ....F....650 924-1025
1070 Terra Bella Ave Mountain View (94043) ***(P-19341)***
Knit Fit Inc ....F....213 673-4731
112 W 9th St Ste 230 Los Angeles (90015) ***(P-3795)***
Knk Apparel Inc ....C....310 768-3333
223 W Rosecrans Ave Gardena (90248) ***(P-3041)***
Kno Inc ....D....408 844-8120
2200 Mission College Blvd Santa Clara (95054) ***(P-24081)***
Knoll Inc ....E....310 289-5800
555 W 5th St Ste 3100 Los Angeles (90013) ***(P-4807)***
Knorr Beeswax Products Inc ....F....760 431-2007
14906 Via De La Valle Del Mar (92014) ***(P-23384)***
Knorr Brake Company LLC ....F....510 475-0770
29471 Kohoutek Way Union City (94587) ***(P-20372)***
Knott's Berry Farm, Buena Park *Also called Knotts Berry Farm LLC* ***(P-2499)***
Knotts Berry Farm LLC (HQ) ....B....714 827-1776
8039 Beach Blvd Buena Park (90620) ***(P-2499)***
Knt Inc ....C....510 651-7163
39760 Eureka Dr Newark (94560) ***(P-16122)***
Knt Manufacturing, Newark *Also called Knt Inc* ***(P-16122)***
Knt Manufacturing Inc ....E....510 896-1699
39760 Eureka Dr Newark (94560) ***(P-23385)***
Koala Kountry Folage, Valley Center *Also called International Decoratives Co* ***(P-23365)***
Koam Knitech Inc ....E....310 515-1121
18118 S Broadway Gardena (90248) ***(P-2793)***
Kobelco Compressors Amer Inc ....D....951 739-3030
301 N Smith Ave Corona (92880) ***(P-14633)***
Kobelco Compressors Amer Inc (HQ) ....B....951 739-3030
1450 W Rincon St Corona (92880) ***(P-14634)***
Kobi Katz Inc ....D....213 689-9505
801 S Flower St Fl 3 Los Angeles (90017) ***(P-22536)***
Kobis Windows & Doors Mfg Inc ....E....818 764-6400
7326 Laurel Canyon Blvd North Hollywood (91605) ***(P-4219)***
Kobus Business Systems LLC ....F....559 595-1915
254 N Alta Ave Dinuba (93618) ***(P-15375)***
Kobus Harmse, Dinuba *Also called Kobus Business Systems LLC* ***(P-15375)***
Koch Feeds Inc ....E....209 725-8253
10916 Amsterdam Rd Winton (95388) ***(P-1105)***
Koch Filter Corporation ....F....951 361-9017
10290 Birtcher Dr Jurupa Valley (91752) ***(P-15437)***
Koco Motion Us LLC ....F....408 612-4970
335 Cochrane Cir Morgan Hill (95037) ***(P-20897)***
Koda Farms Inc ....E....209 392-2191
22540 Russell Ave South Dos Palos (93665) ***(P-1046)***
Koda Farms Milling Inc ....E....209 392-2191
22540 Russell Ave South Dos Palos (93665) ***(P-1047)***
Kodiak Cartoners Inc ....E....559 266-4844
2550 S East Ave Ste 101 Fresno (93706) ***(P-14714)***
Kodiak Precision Inc (PA) ....F....510 234-4165
444 S 1st St Richmond (94804) ***(P-16123)***
Kodiak Sciences Inc (PA) ....E....650 281-0850
2631 Hanover St Palo Alto (94304) ***(P-7981)***
Kofax Limited (HQ) ....E....949 783-1000
15211 Laguna Canyon Rd Irvine (92618) ***(P-24082)***
Kohler Co ....E....909 890-4291
701 S Arrowhead Ave San Bernardino (92408) ***(P-11648)***
Kois & Ponds Inc ....F....800 936-3638
4460 Brooks St Ste B Montclair (91763) ***(P-1106)***
Koito Aviation LLC ....F....661 257-2878
25011 Avenue Stanford D Valencia (91355) ***(P-20150)***
Kokatat Inc ....D....707 822-7621
5350 Ericson Way Arcata (95521) ***(P-3098)***
Kolkka John ....E....707 554-3660
1300 Green Island Rd Vallejo (94503) ***(P-4693)***
Kolkka Furniture Design & Mfg, Vallejo *Also called Kolkka John* ***(P-4693)***
Kollmorgen Corporation ....B....805 696-1236
33 S La Patera Ln Santa Barbara (93117) ***(P-16658)***
Koltov Inc (PA) ....E....805 764-0280
300 S Lewis Rd Ste A Camarillo (93012) ***(P-10236)***
Komag Incorporated ....F....408 576-2150
1710 Automation Pkwy San Jose (95131) ***(P-10477)***
Komar Apparel Supply, Los Angeles *Also called Mdc Interior Solutions LLC* ***(P-3570)***
Komarov Enterprises Inc ....D....213 244-7000
1936 Mateo St Los Angeles (90021) ***(P-3269)***
Komex International Inc ....E....323 233-9005
736 E 29th St Los Angeles (90011) ***(P-3172)***
Kona Bar LLC ....F....808 927-1934
2601 Ocean Park Blvd # 310 Santa Monica (90405) ***(P-1380)***
Konami Digital Entrmt Inc (HQ) ....D....310 220-8100
2381 Rosecrans Ave # 200 El Segundo (90245) ***(P-24083)***
Koncept Technologies Inc ....F....323 261-8999
429 E Huntington Dr Monrovia (91016) ***(P-16974)***
Konecranes Inc ....E....661 397-9700
2900 E Belle Ter Bldg A Bakersfield (93307) ***(P-13848)***
Konecranes Inc ....F....925 273-0140
5637 Blaribera St Livermore (94550) ***(P-13849)***
Kong Veterinary Products ....F....626 633-0077
16018 Adelante St Ste C Irwindale (91702) ***(P-21771)***
Kontech USA LLC ....F....626 622-1325
18045 Rowland St City of Industry (91748) ***(P-17047)***
Kontron America Inc ....D....800 822-7522
9477 Waples St Ste 150 San Diego (92121) ***(P-14933)***
Kontron America Incorporated (HQ) ....C....858 677-0877
9477 Waples St Ste 150 San Diego (92121) ***(P-14934)***
Kool Star, Long Beach *Also called Three Star Rfrgn Engrg Inc* ***(P-15455)***
Koolfog Inc (PA) ....F....760 321-9203
31290 Plantation Dr Thousand Palms (92276) ***(P-15438)***
Kopin Corporation ....E....831 636-5556
501 Tevis Trl Hollister (95023) ***(P-18335)***
Kopykake Enterprises Inc (PA) ....F....310 373-8906
3699 W 240th St Torrance (90505) ***(P-12836)***
Kor Water ....F....714 708-7567
200 Spectrum Center Dr # 300 Irvine (92618) ***(P-9327)***
Koral LLC ....E....323 391-1060
5124 Pacific Blvd Vernon (90058) ***(P-3099)***
Koral Active Wear, Vernon *Also called Koral LLC* ***(P-3099)***
Koral Industries LLC (PA) ....D....323 585-5343
5124 Pacific Blvd Vernon (90058) ***(P-3357)***
Koral Los Angeles, Vernon *Also called Koral Industries LLC* ***(P-3357)***
Korbel Champagne Cellers, Guerneville *Also called F Korbel & Bros* ***(P-1694)***
Korden Inc ....F....909 988-8979
611 S Palmetto Ave Ontario (91762) ***(P-4841)***
Kore Infrastructure LLC ....F....310 367-1003
200 N Pacific Coast Hwy # 340 El Segundo (90245) ***(P-8749)***
Kore Print Solutions Inc ....F....510 445-1638
20974 Corsair Blvd Hayward (94545) ***(P-6680)***
Korea Aerospace Industries Ltd ....F....714 868-8560
16700 Valley View Ave # 205 La Mirada (90638) ***(P-19910)***
Korea Central, Garden Grove *Also called Joong-Ang Daily News Cal Inc* ***(P-5679)***
Korea Central Daily News ....F....213 368-2500
33288 Central Ave Union City (94587) ***(P-5683)***
Korea Daily, Los Angeles *Also called Joong-Ang Daily News Cal Inc* ***(P-5678)***
Korea Daily News & Korea Times ....E....510 777-1111
8134 Capwell Dr Oakland (94621) ***(P-5684)***
Korea Times Los Angeles Inc ....E....510 777-1111
8134 Capwell Dr Oakland (94621) ***(P-5685)***
Korea Times Los Angeles Inc ....F....714 530-6001
9572 Garden Grove Blvd Garden Grove (92844) ***(P-5686)***
Korea Times San Francisco, The, Oakland *Also called Korea Times Los Angeles Inc* ***(P-5685)***
Koros USA Inc ....E....805 529-0825
610 Flinn Ave Moorpark (93021) ***(P-21772)***
Kortick Manufacturer Co, Pittsburg *Also called Frase Enterprises* ***(P-16948)***
Kosan Biosciences Incorporated ....D....650 995-7356
3832 Bay Center Pl Hayward (94545) ***(P-7982)***
Kosta Browne, Sebastopol *Also called KB Wines LLC* ***(P-1779)***
Kosta Browne Winery, Sebastopol *Also called Kosta Browne Wines LLC* ***(P-1783)***
Kosta Browne Wines LLC ....E....707 823-7430
220 Morris St Sebastopol (95472) ***(P-1783)***
Koto Inc ....F....310 327-7359
22857 Lockness Ave Torrance (90501) ***(P-22648)***
Koto Bukiya, Torrance *Also called Koto Inc* ***(P-22648)***
Kotonica Inc ....F....818 898-0978
3226 N Frederic St Burbank (91504) ***(P-9869)***
Kott Inc ....F....949 770-5055
27161 Burbank El Toro (92610) ***(P-8652)***
Kouzouian Custom Furniture, Granada Hills *Also called Kouzouians Fine Custom Furn* ***(P-5070)***
Kouzouians Fine Custom Furn ....E....818 772-1212
18586 Caspian Ct Granada Hills (91344) ***(P-5070)***
Kovin Corporation Inc ....E....858 558-0100
9240 Mira Este Ct San Diego (92126) ***(P-6681)***
Kozlowski Farms A Corporation ....E....707 887-1587
5566 Hwy 116 Forestville (95436) ***(P-783)***
Kozy Shack Enterprises LLC ....D....209 634-2131
600 S Tegner Rd Turlock (95380) ***(P-2500)***
Kp LLC (PA) ....D....510 346-0729
13951 Washington Ave San Leandro (94578) ***(P-6682)***
Kp LLC ....E....510 346-0729
13951 Washington Ave San Leandro (94578) ***(P-6683)***
Kp LLC ....E....209 466-6761
1134 Enterprise St Stockton (95204) ***(P-6684)***
Kpi Services Inc ....E....714 895-5024
11651 Monarch St Garden Grove (92841) ***(P-11455)***
Kpisoft Inc ....D....415 439-5228
50 California St Ste 1500 San Francisco (94111) ***(P-24084)***
Kraemer & Co Mfg Inc ....F....530 865-7982
3778 County Road 99w Orland (95963) ***(P-12554)***
Kraft Foods, Buena Park *Also called Mondelez Global LLC* ***(P-482)***
Kraft Foods, Fullerton *Also called Kraft Heinz Foods Company* ***(P-2501)***
Kraft Foods, Oakland *Also called Nestle Pizza Company Inc* ***(P-967)***
Kraft Foods, Ontario *Also called Kraft Heinz Foods Company* ***(P-784)***
Kraft Foods, Anaheim *Also called Mondelez Global LLC* ***(P-1245)***
Kraft Foods, Fresno *Also called Kraft Heinz Foods Company* ***(P-785)***
Kraft Heinz Foods Company ....C....209 942-0102
3735 Imperial Way Stockton (95215) ***(P-559)***
Kraft Heinz Foods Company ....E....209 832-4269
57 Stonebridge Ct Tracy (95376) ***(P-734)***
Kraft Heinz Foods Company ....B....714 870-8235
1500 E Walnut Ave Fullerton (92831) ***(P-2501)***

Mergent e-mail: customerrelations@mergent.com
1148
2020 California
Manufacturers Register
(P-0000) Products & Services Section entry number
(PA)=Parent Co (HQ)=Headquarters (DH)=Div Headquarters

Kraft Heinz Foods Company .... E 209 932-5700
6755 C E Dixon St Stockton (95206) *(P-1430)*
Kraft Heinz Foods Company .... F 909 605-7201
3971 E Airport Dr Ontario (91761) *(P-784)*
Kraft Heinz Foods Company .... B 559 441-8515
2494 S Orange Ave Fresno (93725) *(P-785)*
Kraft Heinz Foods Company .... F 925 242-4504
2603 Camino Ramon Ste 180 San Ramon (94583) *(P-786)*
Kraft Heinz Foods Company .... D 559 237-9206
4343 E Florence Ave Fresno (93725) *(P-1431)*
Kraft Heinz Foods Company .... B 209 552-6021
1905 Mchenry Ave Escalon (95320) *(P-787)*
Kraft Heinz Foods Company .... C 949 250-4080
2450 White Rd Irvine (92614) *(P-735)*
Kraft Tech Inc .... F 818 837-3520
661 Arroyo St San Fernando (91340) *(P-20413)*
Krallcast Inc .... F 626 333-0678
16205 Ward Way City of Industry (91745) *(P-11159)*
Kramarz Enterprises .... F 408 293-1187
1065 Delmas Ave San Jose (95125) *(P-16124)*
Kranem Corporation .... C 650 319-6743
560 S Winchester Blvd San Jose (95128) *(P-24085)*
Krasnes Inc .... D 619 232-2066
2222 Commercial St San Diego (92113) *(P-3519)*
Kratos Def & SEC Solutions Inc (PA) .... B 858 812-7300
10680 Treena St Ste 600 San Diego (92131) *(P-17555)*
Kratos Instruments LLC .... F 949 660-0666
2201 Alton Pkwy Irvine (92606) *(P-20594)*
Kratos Pressure Products, Irvine *Also called Kratos Instruments LLC (P-20594)*
Kratos Tech Trning Sltions Inc (HQ) .... C 858 812-7300
10680 Treena St Fl 6 San Diego (92131) *(P-24086)*
Kratos Unmanned Aerial Systems .... B 916 431-7977
5381 Raley Blvd Sacramento (95838) *(P-9870)*
Krave Jerky, Sonoma *Also called Krave Pure Foods Inc (P-474)*
Krave Pure Foods Inc .... D 707 939-9176
117 W Napa St Ste A Sonoma (95476) *(P-474)*
Krego Corporation .... F 818 837-1494
12971 Arroyo St San Fernando (91340) *(P-16601)*
Kretzschmar Steel, Colton *Also called C and R Sales Inc (P-11754)*
Krieger Speciality Products, Pico Rivera *Also called Metal Tite Products (P-11970)*
Krinos Foods LLC .... F 805 922-6700
1105 E Foster Rd Ste E Santa Maria (93455) *(P-886)*
Krisalis Inc .... F 209 286-1637
3366 Golden Gate Ct San Andreas (95249) *(P-16125)*
Krisalis Inc (PA) .... F 510 786-0858
28216 Industrial Blvd Hayward (94545) *(P-16126)*
Krisalis Precision Machining, Hayward *Also called Krisalis Inc (P-16126)*
Krissy Op Shins USA Inc .... D 213 747-2591
2408 S Broadway Los Angeles (90007) *(P-3100)*
Kristich-Monterey Pipe Co Inc .... F 831 724-4186
225 Salinas Rd Ste B Royal Oaks (95076) *(P-10593)*
Kritech Corporation (PA) .... F 310 538-9940
333 W 131st St Los Angeles (90061) *(P-18979)*
Kronos Incorporated .... D 800 580-7374
240 Commerce Irvine (92602) *(P-24087)*
Kruger Foods Inc .... C 209 941-8518
18362 E Highway 4 Stockton (95215) *(P-887)*
Krupp Brothers LLC .... F 707 226-2215
1345 Hestia Way NAPA (94558) *(P-1784)*
Kruse and Son Inc .... E 626 358-4536
235 Kruse Ave Monrovia (91016) *(P-475)*
Kryler Corp .... E 714 871-9611
1217 E Ash Ave Fullerton (92831) *(P-13037)*
Krytar Inc .... E 408 734-5999
1288 Anvilwood Ave Sunnyvale (94089) *(P-18980)*
KS Engineering Inc .... F 562 483-7788
14948 Shoemaker Ave Santa Fe Springs (90670) *(P-20151)*
KS Industries .... F 858 344-1146
3160 Camino Del Rio S # 116 San Diego (92108) *(P-23386)*
Ksc Industries Inc .... E 619 671-0110
9771 Clairemont Mesa Blvd E San Diego (92124) *(P-17251)*
KSD Inc .... F 951 849-7669
161 W Lincoln St Banning (92220) *(P-16127)*
Ksm Corp .... B 408 514-2400
1959 Concourse Dr San Jose (95131) *(P-18336)*
Ksm Structural Steel, Daly City *Also called Mah Kuo (P-11835)*
Ksm Vacuum Products Inc .... F 408 514-2400
1959 Concourse Dr San Jose (95131) *(P-12025)*
Ksu Corporation .... F 951 409-7055
3 Emmy Ln Ladera Ranch (92694) *(P-11825)*
KT Engineering Corporation .... F 310 537-3818
2016 E Vista Bella Way Rancho Dominguez (90220) *(P-16128)*
Kt Industries Inc .... F 323 255-7143
3203 Fletcher Dr Los Angeles (90065) *(P-16602)*
Kti Incorporated .... D 909 434-1888
3011 N Laurel Ave Rialto (92377) *(P-10594)*
Kto, West Hills *Also called Kelly Teegarden Organics LLC (P-8526)*
Kts Kitchens Inc .... C 310 764-0850
1065 E Walnut St Ste C Carson (90746) *(P-2502)*
Kuantum Brands LLC .... C 760 412-2432
1747 Hancock St Ste A San Diego (92101) *(P-2087)*
Kubota Authorized Dealer, Chico *Also called Industrial Power Products (P-16042)*
Kubota Tractor Corporation .... F 209 334-9910
1175 S Guild Ave Lodi (95240) *(P-13646)*
KUDos&co Inc .... E 650 799-9104
470 Ramona St Palo Alto (94301) *(P-6266)*
Kui Co Inc .... E 949 369-7949
266 Calle Pintoresco San Clemente (92672) *(P-5130)*
Kulayful Silicone Bracelets .... F 626 610-3816
2267 Joshua Tree Way West Covina (91791) *(P-22987)*

Kuleto Estate, Santa Rosa *Also called Kuleto Villa LLC (P-1785)*
Kuleto Villa LLC .... E 707 967-8577
200 Concourse Blvd Santa Rosa (95403) *(P-1785)*
Kulicke & Soffa Industries, Santa Ana *Also called Kulicke Sffa Wedge Bonding Inc (P-19342)*
Kulicke Sffa Wedge Bonding Inc .... C 949 660-0440
1821 E Dyer Rd Ste 200 Santa Ana (92705) *(P-19342)*
Kulthorn North America, San Diego *Also called Elco Rfrgn Solutions LLC (P-15427)*
Kum Kang Trading USA Inc .... F 562 531-6111
6433 Alondra Blvd Paramount (90723) *(P-8528)*
Kumi Kookoon .... F 310 515-8811
18018 S Western Ave Gardena (90248) *(P-3622)*
Kumjian Enterprises, South El Monte *Also called General Metal Engraving Inc (P-22949)*
Kuna Systems Corporation .... F 650 263-8257
883 Sneath Ln Ste 222 San Bruno (94066) *(P-14935)*
Kunde Enterprises Inc .... D 707 833-5501
9825 Sonoma Hwy Kenwood (95452) *(P-1786)*
Kunde Estate Winery, Kenwood *Also called Kunde Enterprises Inc (P-1786)*
Kunin Wines LLC .... F 805 963-9633
28 Anacapa St Ste A Santa Barbara (93101) *(P-1787)*
Kuprion Inc .... E 650 223-1600
4425 Fortran Dr San Jose (95134) *(P-8926)*
Kuraray America Inc .... F 949 476-9600
2 Park Plz Ste 480 Irvine (92614) *(P-7579)*
Kurdex Corporation .... F 408 734-8181
343 Gibraltar Dr Sunnyvale (94089) *(P-15268)*
Kurtz Family Corporation .... F 707 823-1213
1450 Industrial Ave Sebastopol (95472) *(P-9871)*
Kushwood Chair Inc .... C 909 930-2100
1290 E Elm St Ontario (91761) *(P-4584)*
Kuster Co Oil Well Services .... E 562 595-0661
2900 E 29th St Long Beach (90806) *(P-97)*
Kuster Company, Long Beach *Also called Kuster Co Oil Well Services (P-97)*
Kustom Lighting Products Inc .... E 626 443-0166
2107 Chico Ave South El Monte (91733) *(P-17138)*
Kustomer Kinetics Inc .... F 626 445-6161
136 E Saint Joseph St A Arcadia (91006) *(P-8529)*
Kuton Welding Inc .... F 818 771-0964
11380 Luddington St Sun Valley (91352) *(P-14243)*
Kutzin & Kutzin Inc .... F 818 994-0242
14726 Oxnard St Van Nuys (91411) *(P-4511)*
Kva Stainless, Carlsbad *Also called Joseph McCrink (P-11052)*
Kval Inc .... C 707 762-4363
825 Petaluma Blvd S Petaluma (94952) *(P-14298)*
Kval Machinery Co, Petaluma *Also called Kval Inc (P-14298)*
KVP, Irwindale *Also called Kong Veterinary Products (P-21771)*
KVP International Inc .... E 888 411-7387
13775 Ramona Ave Chino (91710) *(P-22042)*
Kw Automotive North Amer Inc .... E 800 445-3767
300 W Pontiac Way Clovis (93612) *(P-19703)*
Kw Plastics Recycling Division .... D 661 392-0500
1861 Sunnyside Ct Bakersfield (93308) *(P-9407)*
Kwan Software Engineering Inc .... E 408 496-1200
1879 Lundy Ave Ste 286 San Jose (95131) *(P-24088)*
Kwdz Manufacturing LLC (PA) .... D 323 526-3526
337 S Anderson St Los Angeles (90033) *(P-3481)*
Kween Foods LLC .... F 805 895-0003
429 S Sierra Ave Unit 130 Solana Beach (92075) *(P-1057)*
Kwik Kopy Printing, Mission Viejo *Also called Jorlind Enterprises Inc (P-6667)*
Kwikparts.com, Torrance *Also called Probe Racing Components Inc (P-15616)*
Kwj Engineering Inc (PA) .... E 510 794-4296
8430 Central Ave Ste C Newark (94560) *(P-21498)*
Kworld (usa) Computer Inc .... F 626 581-0867
499 Nibus Ste D Brea (92821) *(P-17556)*
Kyles Rock & Redi-Mix Inc .... E 916 681-4848
1221 San Simeon Dr Roseville (95661) *(P-10777)*
Kymera Industries Inc .... F 909 228-7194
14735 Manzanita Dr Fontana (92335) *(P-23387)*
Kymsta Corp .... E 213 380-8118
1506 W 12th St Los Angeles (90015) *(P-3358)*
Kyocera International Inc (HQ) .... C 858 492-1456
8611 Balboa Ave San Diego (92123) *(P-18337)*
Kyocharo USA LLC .... F 213 383-1236
3807 Wilshire Blvd # 518 Los Angeles (90010) *(P-5687)*
Kyoho Manufacturing California .... C 209 941-6200
809 Walker Ave Oakland (94610) *(P-12745)*
KYOLIC, Mission Viejo *Also called Wakunaga of America Co Ltd (P-625)*
Kyowa Kirin Phrm RES Inc (HQ) .... E 858 952-7000
9420 Athena Cir La Jolla (92037) *(P-7983)*
Kyriba Corp (PA) .... E 858 210-3560
9620 Towne Cntre Dr 200 San Diego (92121) *(P-24089)*
Kythera Biopharmaceuticals Inc .... E 818 587-4500
30930 Russell Ranch Rd # 3 Westlake Village (91362) *(P-7984)*
Kyung In Printing Inc .... C 619 662-3920
7920 Airway Rd Ste A8 San Diego (92154) *(P-6685)*
L & A Plastics, Yorba Linda *Also called Loritz & Associates Inc (P-9879)*
L & B Laboratories Inc .... F 408 251-7888
1660 Mabury Rd San Jose (95133) *(P-23388)*
L & H Industries .... F 714 635-1555
925 E Arlee Pl Anaheim (92805) *(P-919)*
L & H Iron Inc .... F 408 287-8797
1049 Felipe Ave San Jose (95122) *(P-12491)*
L & H Mold & Engineering Inc (PA) .... E 909 930-1547
140 Atlantic St Pomona (91768) *(P-9872)*
L & H Molds, Pomona *Also called L & H Mold & Engineering Inc (P-9872)*
L & L Custom Shutters Inc .... C 714 996-9539
3133 Yukon Ave Costa Mesa (92626) *(P-4071)*
L & L Louvers Inc .... E 951 735-9300
12355 Doherty St Riverside (92503) *(P-11963)*

Employee Codes: A=Over 500 employees, B=251-500
C=101-250, D=51-100, E=20-50, F=10-19

2020 California
Manfacturers Register

© Mergent Inc. 1-800-342-5647
1149

L & L Printers Carlsbad LLC ....E....760 477-0321
6200 Yarrow Dr Carlsbad (92011) ***(P-6686)***
L & L Printers Inc ....F....858 278-4300
6200 Yarrow Dr Carlsbad (92011) ***(P-6687)***
L & M Electronics ....F....650 341-1608
541 Taylor Way Ste 10 San Carlos (94070) ***(P-18338)***
L & M Machining Center Inc ....F....760 437-3810
1497 Poinsettia Ave # 156 Vista (92081) ***(P-16129)***
L & M Machining Corporation ....D....714 414-0923
550 S Melrose St Placentia (92870) ***(P-18778)***
L & N Fixtures Inc ....E....323 686-0041
2214 Tyler Ave El Monte (91733) ***(P-4918)***
L & P Button & Trimming Co ....F....626 796-0903
2477 Ridgeway Rd San Marino (91108) ***(P-23004)***
L & S Machine Inc ....F....562 924-9007
711 W 17th St Ste H2 Costa Mesa (92627) ***(P-12638)***
L & S Stone and Fireplace Shop, San Marcos *Also called L&S Stone LLC* ***(P-10913)***
L & T Precision Corporation ....C....858 513-7874
12105 Kirkham Rd Poway (92064) ***(P-12263)***
L & T Precision Engrg Inc ....E....408 441-1890
2395 Qume Dr San Jose (95131) ***(P-16130)***
L A Air Line Inc ....E....323 585-1088
3844 S Santa Fe Ave Vernon (90058) ***(P-2827)***
L A Japanese Daily News, Los Angeles *Also called Rafu Shimpo* ***(P-5806)***
L A Lighting, El Monte *Also called Los Angeles Ltg Mfg Co Inc* ***(P-17053)***
L A PRESS, Los Angeles *Also called LA Printing & Graphics Inc* ***(P-6690)***
L A S A M Inc ....F....323 586-8717
3844 S Santa Fe Ave Vernon (90058) ***(P-3482)***
L A Steel Craft Products (PA) ....E....626 798-7401
1975 Lincoln Ave Pasadena (91103) ***(P-22839)***
L A Supply Co ....E....949 470-9900
18005 Sky Park Cir Ste A Irvine (92614) ***(P-7108)***
L A Times Olympic Plant, Los Angeles *Also called Los Angles Tmes Cmmnctions LLC* ***(P-5714)***
L A Weekly, Los Angeles *Also called La Weekly* ***(P-5691)***
L C Miller Company ....E....323 268-3611
717 Monterey Pass Rd Monterey Park (91754) ***(P-14768)***
L C Pringle Sales Inc (PA) ....E....714 892-1524
12020 Western Ave Garden Grove (92841) ***(P-5029)***
L F P Inc (PA) ....D....323 651-3525
8484 Wilshire Blvd # 900 Beverly Hills (90211) ***(P-5971)***
L Foppiano Wine Co ....E....707 433-2736
12707 Old Redwood Hwy Healdsburg (95448) ***(P-1788)***
L J L Engineering Co, Santa Ana *Also called Laszlo J Lak* ***(P-16140)***
L J R Grinding Corp ....F....310 532-7232
445 W 164th St Gardena (90248) ***(P-16131)***
L J Smith Inc ....F....949 609-0544
25956 Commercentre Dr Lake Forest (92630) ***(P-4072)***
L K Lehman Trucking ....E....209 532-5586
19333 Industrial Dr Sonora (95370) ***(P-10595)***
L M I, Ontario *Also called Larry Mthvin Installations Inc* ***(P-10373)***
L N L Anodizing Inc ....E....818 768-9224
9900 Glenoaks Blvd Ste 3 Sun Valley (91352) ***(P-13038)***
L P Glassblowing Inc ....E....408 988-7561
2322 Calle Del Mundo Santa Clara (95054) ***(P-18981)***
L P McNear Brick Co Inc ....D....415 453-7702
1 Mcnear Brickyard Rd San Rafael (94901) ***(P-10510)***
L R Associates, Simi Valley *Also called Maury Razon* ***(P-3569)***
L Space, Irvine *Also called Lspace America LLC* ***(P-3177)***
L T C, Ukiah *Also called Liqua-Tech Corporation* ***(P-20971)***
L T Litho & Printing Co ....E....949 466-8584
16811 Noyes Ave Irvine (92606) ***(P-6688)***
L T S, City of Industry *Also called Lt Security Inc* ***(P-19350)***
L T Seroge Inc ....F....951 354-7141
7400 Jurupa Ave Riverside (92504) ***(P-19343)***
L Y A Group Inc ....F....213 683-1123
1317 S Grand Ave Los Angeles (90015) ***(P-3359)***
L Y Z Ltd (PA) ....F....415 445-9505
210 Post St San Francisco (94108) ***(P-3238)***
L&F Wood LLC ....F....310 400-5569
416 E Alondra Blvd Gardena (90248) ***(P-4073)***
L&H Enterprises ....F....760 230-2275
2111 Montgomery Ave Cardiff By The Sea (92007) ***(P-15269)***
L&S Machine Enterprises, Costa Mesa *Also called L & S Machine Inc* ***(P-12638)***
L&S Stone LLC (HQ) ....E....760 736-3232
1370 Grand Ave Ste B San Marcos (92078) ***(P-10913)***
L-3 Applied Technologies, Inc., San Diego *Also called L3 Applied Technologies Inc* ***(P-17558)***
L-3 Cmmnications Sonoma Eo Inc ....C....707 568-3000
428 Aviation Blvd Santa Rosa (95403) ***(P-22437)***
L-3 Communication, San Leandro *Also called L3 Technologies Inc* ***(P-17569)***
L-3 Communications Corporation ....F....858 694-7500
9020 Balboa Ave San Diego (92123) ***(P-17557)***
L-3 Communications Wescam ....E....707 568-3000
428 Aviation Blvd Ste 3l Santa Rosa (95403) ***(P-20595)***
L-3 Interstate Electronics, Anaheim *Also called Interstate Electronics Corp* ***(P-21056)***
L-3 Pacord, National City *Also called Pacord Inc* ***(P-20299)***
L-3 Telemetry & Rf Products, San Diego *Also called L3 Technologies Inc* ***(P-17560)***
L-G Wood Products, Pomona *Also called De Larshe Cabinetry LLC* ***(P-4031)***
L-Nutra Inc ....F....310 245-1724
8240 Zitola Ter Playa Del Rey (90293) ***(P-7985)***
L.A. Sleeve, Santa Fe Springs *Also called Los Angeles Sleeve Co Inc* ***(P-19706)***
L3 Applied Technologies Inc (HQ) ....D....858 404-7824
10180 Barnes Canyon Rd San Diego (92121) ***(P-17558)***
L3 Applied Technologies Inc ....C....858 404-7824
10180 Barnes Canyon Rd San Diego (92121) ***(P-17559)***
L3 Electron Devices Inc (HQ) ....A....310 517-6000
3100 Lomita Blvd Torrance (90505) ***(P-17787)***
L3 Technologies Inc ....B....858 279-0411
9020 Balboa Ave San Diego (92123) ***(P-17560)***
L3 Technologies Inc ....C....818 833-2500
15825 Roxford St Sylmar (91342) ***(P-20596)***
L3 Technologies Inc ....B....650 591-8411
3100 Lomita Blvd Torrance (90505) ***(P-17561)***
L3 Technologies Inc ....C....714 758-4222
602 E Vermont Ave Anaheim (92805) ***(P-17562)***
L3 Technologies Inc ....D....916 363-6581
9795 Bus Park Dr Ste K Sacramento (95827) ***(P-14936)***
L3 Technologies Inc ....C....916 351-4556
107 Woodmere Rd Folsom (95630) ***(P-17563)***
L3 Technologies Inc ....D....858 552-9716
10180 Barnes Canyon Rd San Diego (92121) ***(P-17564)***
L3 Technologies Inc ....C....760 431-6800
5957 Landau Ct Carlsbad (92008) ***(P-17741)***
L3 Technologies Inc ....D....805 584-1717
200 W Los Angeles Ave Simi Valley (93065) ***(P-17565)***
L3 Technologies Inc ....B....858 552-9500
9890 Towne Centre Dr # 100 San Diego (92121) ***(P-17566)***
L3 Technologies Inc ....C....650 326-9500
130 Constitution Dr Menlo Park (94025) ***(P-17567)***
L3 Technologies Inc ....C....818 367-0111
15825 Roxford St Sylmar (91342) ***(P-17568)***
L3 Technologies Inc ....C....858 499-0284
2700 Merced St San Leandro (94577) ***(P-17569)***
L3harris Technologies Inc ....B....818 901-2523
7821 Orion Ave Van Nuys (91406) ***(P-20597)***
L3harris Technologies Inc ....B....408 201-8000
7821 Orion Ave Van Nuys (91406) ***(P-20598)***
L3harris Technologies Inc ....E....619 684-7511
9201 Spectrum Center Blvd San Diego (92123) ***(P-20599)***
L3harris Technologies Inc ....C....619 296-6900
591 Camno De La Reina 5 San Diego (92108) ***(P-20898)***
La Aloe LLC ....E....888 968-2563
2301 E 7th St Ste A152 Los Angeles (90023) ***(P-920)***
La Barca Tortilleria Inc ....E....323 268-1744
3047 Whittier Blvd Los Angeles (90023) ***(P-2503)***
La Bath Vanity Inc ....F....909 303-3323
2222 Davie Ave Commerce (90040) ***(P-4220)***
La Blanca Swimwear, Cypress *Also called Manhattan Beachwear Inc* ***(P-3366)***
La Bonita, Norwalk *Also called Dianas Mexican Food Pdts Inc* ***(P-2445)***
La Bottleworks Inc ....E....323 724-4076
1605 Beach St Montebello (90640) ***(P-2088)***
La Boulangerie, Stockton *Also called Toufic Inc* ***(P-1287)***
La Boulangerie French Bky Cafe ....F....559 222-0555
730 W Shaw Ave Fresno (93704) ***(P-1228)***
La Brothers Enterprise Inc ....E....415 626-8818
57 Columbia Sq San Francisco (94103) ***(P-6689)***
LA Cabinet & Millwork Inc ....E....323 227-5000
3005 Humboldt St Los Angeles (90031) ***(P-4919)***
La Campana Tortilla Factory, Lodi *Also called Del Castillo Foods Inc* ***(P-2441)***
La Canada Valley Sun, La Canada Flintridge *Also called Los Angles Tmes Cmmnctions LLC* ***(P-5711)***
La Candelaria Furniture Mfr, Lynwood *Also called La Candelaria Manufacturing* ***(P-4585)***
La Candelaria Manufacturing ....F....310 763-0112
2790 M L King Jr Blvd Lynwood (90262) ***(P-4585)***
La Carreta Food Products ....F....909 825-0737
302 S La Cadena Dr Colton (92324) ***(P-2504)***
La Carreta Mexican Foods, Colton *Also called La Carreta Food Products* ***(P-2504)***
La Cascada Inc ....F....510 452-3663
1940 Union St Ste 10 Oakland (94607) ***(P-736)***
La Chapalita Inc (PA) ....E....626 443-8556
1724 Chico Ave El Monte (91733) ***(P-2505)***
La Chic, Vernon *Also called Rmla Inc* ***(P-3495)***
La Colonial, San Jose *Also called Robles Bros Inc* ***(P-2602)***
La Colonial Mexican Foods, Monterey Park *Also called La Colonial Tortilla Pdts Inc* ***(P-2506)***
La Colonial Tortilla Pdts Inc ....C....626 289-3647
543 Monterey Pass Rd Monterey Park (91754) ***(P-2506)***
La Crema Winery, Windsor *Also called Jackson Family Wines Inc* ***(P-1765)***
La Ejuice LLC ....E....310 531-3888
22871 Lockness Ave Torrance (90501) ***(P-2661)***
LA Envelope Incorporated ....E....323 838-9300
1053 S Vail Ave Montebello (90640) ***(P-5473)***
La Espanola Meats Inc ....E....310 539-0455
25020 Doble Ave Harbor City (90710) ***(P-476)***
La Estrellita Market & Deli, East Palo Alto *Also called La Estrellita Tizapan Mercado* ***(P-2507)***
La Estrellita Tizapan Mercado ....F....650 328-0799
2387 University Ave East Palo Alto (94303) ***(P-2507)***
La Famosa Manufacture Inc ....F....323 241-3100
6600 Mckinley Ave Los Angeles (90001) ***(P-4652)***
La Flora Del Sur, Los Angeles *Also called Walker Foods Inc* ***(P-837)***
La Follette Wines, Healdsburg *Also called Tandem Wines LLC* ***(P-1948)***
La Fortaleza Inc ....D....323 261-1211
525 N Ford Blvd Los Angeles (90022) ***(P-2508)***
LA Gauge Co Inc ....D....818 767-7193
7440 San Fernando Rd Sun Valley (91352) ***(P-16132)***
LA Gem and Jwly Design Inc ....D....213 488-1290
659 S Broadway Fl 7 Los Angeles (90014) ***(P-22537)***
La Gloria Flour Tortillas, Los Angeles *Also called La Gloria Foods Corp* ***(P-2510)***
La Gloria Foods Corp (PA) ....D....323 262-0410
3455 E 1st St Los Angeles (90063) ***(P-2509)***
La Gloria Foods Corp ....D....323 263-6755
3285 E Cesar E Chavez Ave Los Angeles (90063) ***(P-2510)***
La Gloria Tortilleria, Los Angeles *Also called La Gloria Foods Corp* ***(P-2509)***

La Habra Plating Co Inc....F....562 694-2704
900 S Cypress St La Habra (90631) ***(P-13039)***

La Habra Welding Inc....F....562 923-2229
10819 Koontz Ave Santa Fe Springs (90670) ***(P-24648)***

LA Hardwood Flooring Inc (PA)....F....818 361-0099
9880 San Fernando Rd Pacoima (91331) ***(P-3977)***

La Indiana Tamales Inc....E....323 262-4682
15268 Proctor Ave City of Industry (91745) ***(P-737)***

La Jolla Baking Co, San Diego *Also called Fusion Food Factory* ***(P-1211)***

La La Land Production & Design....E....323 267-8485
2155 E 7th St Ste 300 Los Angeles (90023) ***(P-10140)***

La Mamba LLC....E....323 526-3526
242 S Anderson St Los Angeles (90033) ***(P-3173)***

La Mano Tortilleria....F....626 350-4229
9529 Garvey Ave South El Monte (91733) ***(P-2511)***

La Mejor Restaurant, Farmersville *Also called Tortilleria La Mejor* ***(P-2631)***

La Mexicana LLC....E....323 277-3660
10615 Ruchti Rd South Gate (90280) ***(P-964)***

La Mode, Inglewood *Also called Golf Apparel Brands Inc* ***(P-3331)***

La Mousse....D....310 478-6051
11150 La Grange Ave Los Angeles (90025) ***(P-965)***

La Natura, Los Angeles *Also called New Fragrance Continental* ***(P-8547)***

La Opinion LP (HQ)....D....213 896-2196
915 Wilshire Blvd Ste 915 # 915 Los Angeles (90017) ***(P-5688)***

La Opinion LP....D....213 896-2222
210 E Washington Blvd Los Angeles (90015) ***(P-5689)***

La Palm Furnitures & ACC Inc (PA)....D....310 217-2700
1650 W Artesia Blvd Gardena (90248) ***(P-3746)***

La Parent Magazine (PA)....E....818 264-2222
5855 Topanga Canyon Blvd # 150 Woodland Hills (91367) ***(P-5972)***

La Paz Products Inc....F....714 990-0982
345 Oak Pl Brea (92821) ***(P-2219)***

La Princesita Tortilleria (PA)....E....323 267-0673
3432 E Cesar E Chavez Ave Los Angeles (90063) ***(P-2512)***

LA Printing & Graphics Inc....E....310 527-4526
13951 S Main St Los Angeles (90061) ***(P-6690)***

La Propoint Inc....E....818 767-6800
10870 La Tuna Canyon Rd Sun Valley (91352) ***(P-13528)***

La Rancherita Tortilla, Santa Ana *Also called M R S Foods Inc* ***(P-2537)***

La Reina, Los Angeles *Also called Old Pueblo Ranch Inc* ***(P-2575)***

La Rocks, Los Angeles *Also called LA Gem and Jwly Design Inc* ***(P-22537)***

La Rose of California, Los Angeles *Also called Jay-Cee Blouse Co Inc* ***(P-3234)***

La Rutan....E....310 940-7956
6284 Long Beach Blvd Long Beach (90805) ***(P-23389)***

La Sentinel Newspaper, Los Angeles *Also called Los Angeles Sentinel Inc* ***(P-5703)***

La Siciliana Dressmaking, Culver City *Also called La Siciliana Inc* ***(P-3239)***

La Siciliana Inc....E....323 870-4155
8674 Washington Blvd Culver City (90232) ***(P-3239)***

La Spec Industries Inc....F....323 588-8746
2315 E 52nd St Vernon (90058) ***(P-17048)***

La Tapatia - Norcal Inc....C....510 783-2045
23423 Cabot Blvd Hayward (94545) ***(P-2513)***

La Tapatia Tortilleria Inc....C....559 441-1030
104 E Belmont Ave Fresno (93701) ***(P-2514)***

La Terra Fina Usa Inc....D....510 404-5888
1300 Atlantic St Union City (94587) ***(P-2515)***

La Times....F....213 237-2279
202 W 1st St Ste 500 Los Angeles (90012) ***(P-5690)***

La Tortilla Factory Inc....E....707 586-4000
3645 Standish Ave Santa Rosa (95407) ***(P-2516)***

La Touch, Commerce *Also called Evy of California Inc* ***(P-3478)***

LA Triumph Inc....E....562 404-7657
13336 Alondra Blvd Cerritos (90703) ***(P-3042)***

LA Turbine (PA)....D....661 294-8290
28557 Industry Dr Valencia (91355) ***(P-13573)***

La Viena Ranch....E....559 674-6725
9408 Road 23 Madera (93637) ***(P-851)***

La Villeta De Sonoma....E....707 939-9392
23000 Arnold Dr Sonoma (95476) ***(P-12026)***

La Voies of San Jose....F....408 297-1285
2096 Lincoln Ave San Jose (95125) ***(P-5030)***

La Weekly....C....310 574-7100
724 S Spring St Ste 700 Los Angeles (90014) ***(P-5691)***

La Xpress Air & Heating Svcs....D....310 856-9678
6400 E Wash Blvd Ste 121 Commerce (90040) ***(P-6267)***

La Zamorana Candy....F....323 583-7100
7100 Wilson Ave Los Angeles (90001) ***(P-1381)***

La's Totally Awesome, Buena Park *Also called Awesome Products Inc* ***(P-8365)***

La- Rochelle, Livermore *Also called Steven Kent LLC* ***(P-1933)***

Lab Clear, Oakland *Also called Diamond Tool and Die Inc* ***(P-15895)***

Lab Ecx.com, Valencia *Also called Pharma Alliance Group Inc* ***(P-8071)***

Lab Surf Company....F....760 757-1975
3205 Production Ave Ste G Oceanside (92058) ***(P-22840)***

Lab Vision Corporation (HQ)....F....510 979-5000
46500 Kato Rd Fremont (94538) ***(P-21252)***

Lab, The, Burbank *Also called Kh9100 LLC* ***(P-22366)***

Lab-Clean LLC....E....714 689-0063
3627 Briggeman Dr Los Alamitos (90720) ***(P-8392)***

Labcon North America....C....707 766-2100
3700 Lakeville Hwy # 200 Petaluma (94954) ***(P-9873)***

Labeda Inline Wheels & Frames, Lake Elsinore *Also called Precision Sports Inc* ***(P-22865)***

Label Art of California, Oakland *Also called Tags & Labels* ***(P-6883)***

Label Art of California, Oakland *Also called Label Art-Easy Stik Labels* ***(P-7109)***

Label Art-Easy Stik Labels....E....510 465-1125
290 27th St Oakland (94612) ***(P-7109)***

Label Gallery, Los Angeles *Also called All American Label* ***(P-2749)***

Label House, Irvine *Also called L A Supply Co* ***(P-7108)***

Label Impressions Inc....E....714 634-3466
1831 W Sequoia Ave Orange (92868) ***(P-7110)***

Label Masters Inc....F....559 445-1208
3188 N Marks Ave Ste 112 Fresno (93722) ***(P-7111)***

Label Productions of Cal....F....951 296-1881
42068 Winchester Rd Temecula (92590) ***(P-7112)***

Label Service Inc....F....310 329-5605
20008 Normandie Ave Torrance (90502) ***(P-5365)***

Label Specialties Inc....F....714 961-8074
704 Dunn Way Placentia (92870) ***(P-7113)***

Labeling Hurst Systems LLC....F....818 701-0710
20747 Dearborn St Chatsworth (91311) ***(P-7114)***

Labeltex Mills Inc (PA)....C....323 582-0228
6100 Wilmington Ave Los Angeles (90001) ***(P-23005)***

Labeltronix LLC....D....800 429-4321
2419 E Winston Rd Anaheim (92806) ***(P-7115)***

Labl Holding Corporation....D....714 992-2574
531 Airpark Dr Fullerton (92833) ***(P-5512)***

Laboratorios Camacho Inc....F....818 764-2748
9349 Melvin Ave Ste 1 Northridge (91324) ***(P-7986)***

Labtronix, Hayward *Also called Akas Manufacturing Corporation* ***(P-12095)***

Labworks Inc....F....714 549-1981
2950 Airway Ave Ste A16 Costa Mesa (92626) ***(P-18982)***

Lac Bleu Inc....F....213 973-5335
3817 S Santa Fe Ave Vernon (90058) ***(P-3360)***

Lacey Milling Company Inc....F....559 584-6634
217 W 5th St Ste 231 Hanford (93230) ***(P-1005)***

Lackey Woodworking Inc....F....831 462-0528
2730 Chanticleer Ave Santa Cruz (95065) ***(P-4221)***

Laclede Inc....E....310 605-4280
2103 E University Dr Rancho Dominguez (90220) ***(P-22169)***

Laclede Research Center, Rancho Dominguez *Also called Laclede Inc* ***(P-22169)***

Ladera Foods Inc....F....650 823-7186
20 Coquito Ct Portola Valley (94028) ***(P-1028)***

Lady Jayne LP....F....
10833 Valley View St # 420 Cypress (90630) ***(P-5481)***

Laetitia Vineyard & Winery Inc....D....805 481-1772
453 Laetitia Vineyard Dr Arroyo Grande (93420) ***(P-1789)***

Laetitia Winery, Arroyo Grande *Also called Laetitia Vineyard & Winery Inc* ***(P-1789)***

Lafond Vineyard Inc....F....805 962-9303
114 E Haley St Ste M Santa Barbara (93101) ***(P-1790)***

Lagier Ranches Inc....F....209 982-5618
16161 Murphy Rd Escalon (95320) ***(P-7640)***

Lagun Engineering Solutions, Harbor City *Also called Republic Machinery Co Inc* ***(P-13943)***

Laguna Beach Ales & Lagers LLC....F....949 228-4496
31611 Florence Ave Laguna Beach (92651) ***(P-5692)***

Laguna Beach Magazine, Laguna Beach *Also called Firebrand Media LLC* ***(P-6572)***

Laguna Clay Company, City of Industry *Also called Jon Brooks Inc* ***(P-10974)***

Laguna Cookie Company Inc....D....714 546-6855
4041 W Garry Ave Santa Ana (92704) ***(P-1319)***

Laguna County Sanatation Dist....F....805 934-6282
3500 Black Rd Santa Maria (93455) ***(P-8988)***

Laguna Oaks Vnyards Winery Inc....F....707 568-2455
5700 Occidental Rd Santa Rosa (95401) ***(P-1791)***

Lagunitas Brewing Company (HQ)....C....707 322-4651
1280 N Mcdowell Blvd Petaluma (94954) ***(P-1541)***

Lahlouh Inc....C....650 692-6600
1649 Adrian Rd Burlingame (94010) ***(P-6691)***

Laila Jayde Dda, Cerritos *Also called American Garment Company* ***(P-3540)***

Laird Coatings Corporation....E....714 894-5252
15541 Commerce Ln Huntington Beach (92649) ***(P-8653)***

Laird Family Estate LLC (PA)....E....707 257-0360
5055 Solano Ave NAPA (94558) ***(P-1792)***

Laird Manufacturing, Merced *Also called Laird Mfg LLC* ***(P-13647)***

Laird Mfg LLC (PA)....E....209 722-4145
531 S State Highway 59 Merced (95341) ***(P-13647)***

Laird Mfg LLC....F....209 349-8918
1130 Stuart Dr Merced (95341) ***(P-13648)***

Laird R & F Products Inc (HQ)....E....760 916-9410
2091 Rutherford Rd Carlsbad (92008) ***(P-20600)***

Laird Technologies Inc....E....408 544-9500
2040 Fortune Dr Ste 102 San Jose (95131) ***(P-20899)***

Lake County Publishing Co (HQ)....D....707 263-5636
2150 S Main St Lakeport (95453) ***(P-5693)***

Lake County Record-Bee, Lakeport *Also called Lake County Publishing Co* ***(P-5693)***

Lake County Walnut Inc....F....707 279-1200
4545 Loasa Dr Kelseyville (95451) ***(P-1432)***

Lakeview Innovations Inc....F....212 502-6702
11391 Sunrise Gold Cir # 100 Rancho Cordova (95742) ***(P-3563)***

Lakim Industries Incorporated (PA)....E....310 637-8900
389 Rood Rd Calexico (92231) ***(P-23029)***

Lakin Industries Inc (PA)....F....714 968-6438
18330 Ward St Fountain Valley (92708) ***(P-13040)***

Lam Enterprises Inc....F....209 586-2217
824 S Center St Stockton (95206) ***(P-2517)***

Lam Research Corporation....E....408 434-6109
3590 N 1st St Ste 200 San Jose (95134) ***(P-18339)***

Lam Research Corporation....D....510 572-2186
3724 Dawn Cir Union City (94587) ***(P-14488)***

Lam Research Corporation (PA)....D....510 572-0200
4650 Cushing Pkwy Fremont (94538) ***(P-18340)***

Lam Research Corporation....E....510 572-8400
1 Portola Ave Livermore (94551) ***(P-18341)***

Lam Research Corporation....D....510 572-3200
46555 Landing Pkwy Fremont (94538) ***(P-14489)***

Lam Research Corporation....D....510 572-0200
4400 Cushing Pkwy Fremont (94538) ***(P-18342)***

Lam Research Intl Holdg Co (HQ)....F....510 572-0200
4650 Cushing Pkwy Fremont (94538) ***(P-14490)***

ALPHABETIC

Employee Codes: A=Over 500 employees, B=251-500
C=101-250, D=51-100, E=20-50, F=10-19

2020 California
Manfacturers Register

© Mergent Inc. 1-800-342-5647
1151

Lamar Tool and Die Casting Inc ....E....209 545-5525
4230 Technology Dr Modesto (95356) ***(P-11054)***
Lamart California Inc ....E....973 772-6262
33428 Alvarado Niles Rd Union City (94587) ***(P-10988)***
Lamart California Inc ....F....510 489-8100
7560 Bristow Ct Ste C San Diego (92154) ***(P-20152)***
Lamart Corporation ....C....510 489-8100
2600 Central Ave Ste E Union City (94587) ***(P-10963)***
Lamb Fuels Inc ....E....619 216-6940
725 Main St Ste B Chula Vista (91911) ***(P-8750)***
Lambda Research Optics Inc ....D....714 327-0600
1695 Macarthur Blvd Costa Mesa (92626) ***(P-21253)***
Lambert Bridge Winery Inc ....F....707 431-9600
4085 W Dry Creek Rd Healdsburg (95448) ***(P-1793)***
Lambs & Ivy Inc ....D....310 322-3800
2042 E Maple Ave El Segundo (90245) ***(P-3623)***
Lamer Street Kreations Corp ....F....909 305-4824
14589 Rancho Vista Dr Fontana (92335) ***(P-13529)***
Laminating Company of America, Lake Forest *Also called Tri-Star Laminates Inc* ***(P-18027)***
Laminating Company of America ....E....949 587-3300
20322 Windrow Dr Ste 100 Lake Forest (92630) ***(P-17912)***
Laminating Technologies, Anaheim *Also called Yti Enterprises Inc* ***(P-4544)***
Lamons Gasket Company ....F....310 886-1133
20009 S Rancho Way Compton (90220) ***(P-9242)***
Lamorenita Tortillera & Mt Mkt ....F....831 394-3770
1876 Fremont Blvd Seaside (93955) ***(P-2518)***
Lamps Plus Inc ....F....805 642-9007
4723 Telephone Rd Ventura (93003) ***(P-17049)***
Lamsco West Inc ....D....661 295-8620
29101 The Old Rd Santa Clarita (91355) ***(P-20153)***
Lancaster Estate, Santa Rosa *Also called Lancaster Vineyards Inc* ***(P-1794)***
Lancaster Vineyards Inc ....F....707 433-8178
200 Concourse Blvd Santa Rosa (95403) ***(P-1794)***
Lancer Orthodontics Inc (PA) ....E....760 744-5585
1493 Poinsettia Ave # 143 Vista (92081) ***(P-22170)***
Land N Top Cleaning Services ....E....760 624-8845
20953 Sioux Rd Apple Valley (92308) ***(P-2871)***
Land O'Lakes, Turlock *Also called Kozy Shack Enterprises LLC* ***(P-2500)***
Land OLakes Inc ....D....559 687-8287
400 S M St Tulare (93274) ***(P-560)***
Land OLakes Inc ....E....530 865-7626
3601 County Road C Orland (95963) ***(P-561)***
Landec Corporation (PA) ....D....650 306-1650
5201 Great America Pkwy # 232 Santa Clara (95054) ***(P-788)***
Landmark Label Manufacturing ....E....510 651-5551
39611 Eureka Dr Newark (94560) ***(P-7116)***
Landmark Lcds Inc ....F....408 386-4257
12453 Blue Meadow Ct Saratoga (95070) ***(P-18983)***
Landmark Luggage & Gifts, Sherman Oaks *Also called Safcor Inc* ***(P-10205)***
Landmark Mfg Inc ....E....760 941-6626
4112 Avenida De La Plata Oceanside (92056) ***(P-16133)***
Landmark Motor Cycle ACC, Oceanside *Also called Landmark Mfg Inc* ***(P-16133)***
Landmark Technology Inc ....E....408 435-8890
1660 Mckee Rd San Jose (95116) ***(P-18984)***
Landmark Vineyards, Kenwood *Also called Overlook Vineyards LLC* ***(P-1851)***
Landscape Communications Inc ....E....714 979-5276
14771 Plaza Dr Ste A Tustin (92780) ***(P-5973)***
Landscape Contract National, Tustin *Also called Landscape Communications Inc* ***(P-5973)***
Landscape Contractor, Salinas *Also called Uv Landscaping LLC* ***(P-10522)***
Lane Bennett Winery ....F....707 942-6684
3340 State Highway 128 Calistoga (94515) ***(P-1795)***
Lane International Trading Inc (PA) ....D....510 489-7364
33155 Transit Ave Union City (94587) ***(P-10159)***
Lane Winpak Inc (HQ) ....D....909 386-1762
998 S Sierra Way San Bernardino (92408) ***(P-14715)***
Lange Precision Inc ....F....714 870-5420
1106 E Elm Ave Fullerton (92831) ***(P-16134)***
Langetwins Wine Company Inc ....E....209 334-9780
1525 E Jahant Rd Acampo (95220) ***(P-1796)***
Langetwins Winery & Vineyards, Acampo *Also called Langetwins Wine Company Inc* ***(P-1796)***
Langills General Machine Inc ....E....916 452-0167
7850 14th Ave Sacramento (95826) ***(P-16135)***
Langley Hill Quarry ....F....650 851-0179
12 Langley Hill Rd Woodside (94062) ***(P-315)***
Langlois Company ....E....951 360-3900
10810 San Sevaine Way Jurupa Valley (91752) ***(P-1058)***
Langlois Flour Company, Jurupa Valley *Also called Langlois Company* ***(P-1058)***
Langston Companies Inc ....E....559 688-3839
2500 S K St Tulare (93274) ***(P-5440)***
Langtry Estates and Vineyards, Santa Rosa *Also called Guenoc Winery Inc* ***(P-1740)***
Language Los Angeles, Burbank *Also called Eastwest Clothing Inc* ***(P-3157)***
LANIC AEROSPACE, Rancho Cucamonga *Also called Lanic Engineering Inc* ***(P-20154)***
Lanic Engineering Inc (PA) ....E....877 763-0411
12144 6th St Rancho Cucamonga (91730) ***(P-20154)***
Lanpar Inc ....B....541 484-1962
1333 S Bon View Ave Ontario (91761) ***(P-4586)***
Lansair Corporation ....F....661 294-9503
25228 Anza Dr Santa Clarita (91355) ***(P-16136)***
Lansas Products, Lodi *Also called Vanderlans & Sons Inc* ***(P-15597)***
Lanshon Inc ....E....562 777-1688
12995 Los Nietos Rd Santa Fe Springs (90670) ***(P-2967)***
Lansing Industries Inc ....F....858 523-0719
12671 High Bluff Dr # 150 San Diego (92130) ***(P-23390)***
Lanstreetcom ....E....626 964-2000
17050 Evergreen Pl City of Industry (91745) ***(P-15128)***
Lantic Inc ....F....949 830-9951
27081 Burbank Foothill Ranch (92610) ***(P-9874)***
Lantic USA, Rancho Dominguez *Also called Fairway Import-Export Inc* ***(P-22799)***
Lantor, Lomita *Also called Anacrown Inc* ***(P-13497)***
Lantronix Inc (PA) ....C....949 453-3990
7535 Irvine Center Dr Irvine (92618) ***(P-15270)***
Lanty Inc ....C....626 582-8001
9660 Flair Dr El Monte (91731) ***(P-2519)***
Lanza Research International ....D....310 393-5227
429 Santa Monica Blvd # 510 Santa Monica (90401) ***(P-8530)***
Laperla Del Mayab, Santa Ana *Also called Laperla Spice Co Inc* ***(P-2520)***
Laperla Spice Co Inc ....F....714 543-5533
555 N Fairview St Santa Ana (92703) ***(P-2520)***
Laprensa San Diego ....F....619 425-7400
220 Glover Ave Apt E Chula Vista (91910) ***(P-5694)***
Laptalo Enterprises Inc ....D....408 727-6633
2360 Zanker Rd San Jose (95131) ***(P-12264)***
Laptop Lunches, Santa Cruz *Also called Obentec Inc* ***(P-4422)***
Lara Manufacturing Inc ....E....408 778-0811
16235 Vineyard Blvd Morgan Hill (95037) ***(P-12265)***
Lares Research ....E....530 345-1767
295 Lockheed Ave Chico (95973) ***(P-22171)***
Larin Corp ....E....909 464-0605
5651 Schaefer Ave Chino (91710) ***(P-11534)***
Laritech Inc ....C....805 529-5000
5898 Condor Dr Moorpark (93021) ***(P-17913)***
Larkin Precision Machining ....E....831 438-2700
175 El Pueblo Rd Ste 10 Scotts Valley (95066) ***(P-16137)***
Larosa Tortilla Factory ....D....831 728-5332
26 Menker St Watsonville (95076) ***(P-2521)***
Larry B LLC ....F....310 652-3877
215 S Robertson Blvd Beverly Hills (90211) ***(P-3500)***
Larry Mthvin Installations Inc (HQ) ....C....909 563-1700
501 Kettering Dr Ontario (91761) ***(P-10373)***
Larry Mthvin Installations Inc ....E....209 368-2105
128 N Cluff Ave Lodi (95240) ***(P-10374)***
Larry Schlussler ....F....707 822-9095
824 L St Ste 7 Arcata (95521) ***(P-16820)***
Larry Spun Products Inc ....E....323 881-6300
1533 S Downey Rd Los Angeles (90023) ***(P-12837)***
Larsens Inc ....F....831 476-3009
1041 17th Ave Ste A Santa Cruz (95062) ***(P-3690)***
Larson Al Boat Shop ....D....310 514-4100
1046 S Seaside Ave San Pedro (90731) ***(P-20290)***
Larson Brothers ....F....559 292-8161
5665 E Westover Ave # 101 Fresno (93727) ***(P-6268)***
Larson Electronic Glass Inc ....F....650 369-6734
2840 Bay Rd Redwood City (94063) ***(P-10315)***
Larson Family Winery Inc ....F....707 938-3031
23355 Millerick Rd Sonoma (95476) ***(P-1797)***
Larson Packaging Company LLC ....E....408 946-4971
1000 Yosemite Dr Milpitas (95035) ***(P-4338)***
Larson Picture Frames, Santa Fe Springs *Also called Larson-Juhl US LLC* ***(P-4512)***
Larson-Juhl US LLC ....E....562 946-6873
12206 Bell Ranch Dr Santa Fe Springs (90670) ***(P-4512)***
Larson-Juhl US LLC ....E....707 747-0555
5365 Industrial Way Benicia (94510) ***(P-4513)***
Lartech, San Jose *Also called L & H Iron Inc* ***(P-12491)***
Las Animas Con & Bldg Sup Inc ....E....831 425-4084
146 Encinal St Santa Cruz (95060) ***(P-10778)***
Las Colinas ....F....714 528-8100
600 S Jefferson St Ste M Placentia (92870) ***(P-15535)***
Las Cuatros Milpas ....F....909 885-3344
856 N Mount Vernon Ave San Bernardino (92411) ***(P-1229)***
Lasalle Intl Hldings Group Inc ....E....818 233-8000
9667 Owensmouth Ave Chatsworth (91311) ***(P-13784)***
Lasani-Felt Co ....E....323 233-5278
830 E 59th St Los Angeles (90001) ***(P-2939)***
Lasdos Victorias Candy Company, Rosemead *Also called Ldvc Inc* ***(P-1382)***
Laselva Beach Spice Co Inc ....F....831 724-4500
453 Mcquaide Dr Watsonville (95076) ***(P-2522)***
Laser Division, Santa Clara *Also called Spectra-Physics Inc* ***(P-19412)***
Laser Excel, Santa Rosa *Also called Green Lake Investors LLC* ***(P-22950)***
Laser Imaging International, Van Nuys *Also called E Alko Inc* ***(P-22962)***
Laser Industries Inc ....D....714 532-3271
1351 Manhattan Ave Fullerton (92831) ***(P-16138)***
Laser Operations LLC ....E....818 986-0000
15632 Roxford St Sylmar (91342) ***(P-18343)***
Laser Recharge Inc (PA) ....E....916 737-6360
9935 Horn Rd Ste A Sacramento (95827) ***(P-22966)***
Laser Reference Inc ....E....408 361-0220
151 Martinvale Ln San Jose (95119) ***(P-20764)***
Laser Tech, Riverside *Also called L T Seroge Inc* ***(P-19343)***
Laser Toner & Computer Supply ....F....805 529-3300
940 Enchanted Way Ste 106 Simi Valley (93065) ***(P-22967)***
Laserbeam Software LLC ....E....925 459-2595
1647 Willow Pass Rd Concord (94520) ***(P-24090)***
Lasercare Technologies Inc (PA) ....E....310 202-4200
3375 Robertson Pl Los Angeles (90034) ***(P-22968)***
Laserfiche Document Imaging, Long Beach *Also called Compulink Management Ctr Inc* ***(P-23766)***
Lasergraphics Inc ....E....949 753-8282
20 Ada Irvine (92618) ***(P-15271)***
Lasergraphics General Business, Irvine *Also called Lasergraphics Inc* ***(P-15271)***
Laserod Technologies LLC ....E....310 328-5869
20312 Gramercy Pl Torrance (90501) ***(P-19344)***
Lasertron Inc ....E....954 846-8600
909 Summit Way Laguna Beach (92651) ***(P-16139)***
Laspec Lighting, Vernon *Also called La Spec Industries Inc* ***(P-17048)***
Lassen County Times, Susanville *Also called Feather Publishing Company Inc* ***(P-5633)***

Lassen Forest Products Inc ....E....530 527-7677
22829 Casale Rd Red Bluff (96080) ***(P-4313)***
Lassonde Pappas and Co Inc ....D....909 923-4041
1755 E Acacia St Ontario (91761) ***(P-2523)***
Lastline Inc ....C....805 456-7075
6950 Hollister Ave # 101 Goleta (93117) ***(P-24091)***
Lastline Inc (PA) ....D....805 456-7075
203 Redwood Shores Pkwy Redwood City (94065) ***(P-24092)***
Laszlo J Lak ....F....714 850-0141
3621 W Moore Ave Santa Ana (92704) ***(P-16140)***
LAT LLC ....E....323 233-3017
2052 E Vernon Ave Vernon (90058) ***(P-3361)***
Lataz Product, Brea *Also called California Cocktails Inc* ***(P-2197)***
Latcham Granite Inc ....F....530 620-6642
2860 Omo Ranch Rd Somerset (95684) ***(P-1798)***
Latcham Vineyards, Somerset *Also called Latcham Granite Inc* ***(P-1798)***
Lathrop Engineering, Morgan Hill *Also called Paramit Corporation* ***(P-17952)***
Lathrop Woodworks, Lathrop *Also called Rafael Sandoval* ***(P-3942)***
Laticrete International Inc ....F....951 277-1776
22740 Temescal Canyon Rd Corona (92883) ***(P-10419)***
Latina & Associates Inc (PA) ....E....619 426-1491
1105 Broadway Chula Vista (91911) ***(P-5695)***
Latino Americanos Revista ....F....760 342-2312
82723 Miles Ave Indio (92201) ***(P-5974)***
Latitude 38 Publishing Company ....F....415 383-8200
15 Locust Ave Mill Valley (94941) ***(P-5975)***
Latourette Lift Services ....F....323 262-9111
4368 Bandini Blvd Vernon (90058) ***(P-13881)***
Lats International, Los Angeles *Also called Los Angles Tmes Cmmnctions LLC* ***(P-5713)***
Lattice Data Inc ....E....650 800-7262
801 El Camino Real Menlo Park (94025) ***(P-24093)***
Lattice Semiconductor Corp ....B....408 826-6000
2115 Onel Dr San Jose (95131) ***(P-18344)***
Laufer Media Inc ....F....818 291-8408
330 N Brand Blvd Ste 1150 Glendale (91203) ***(P-5976)***
Launchpoint Technologies Inc ....F....805 683-9659
5735 Hollister Ave Ste B Goleta (93117) ***(P-14788)***
Laundry By Shelli Segal, Commerce *Also called LCI Laundry Inc* ***(P-3241)***
Laura Chenels Chevre Inc ....D....707 996-4477
22085 Carneros Vinyrd Way Sonoma (95476) ***(P-562)***
Laura Scudders Company LLC ....E....714 444-3700
1537 E Mcfadden Ave Ste B Santa Ana (92705) ***(P-2336)***
Lauras French Baking Co Inc ....E....323 585-5144
722 S Oxford Ave Apt 107 Los Angeles (90005) ***(P-1230)***
Lauras Original Boston ....F....619 855-3258
1022 W Morena Blvd San Diego (92110) ***(P-1231)***
Laurelwood Industries Inc ....E....760 705-1649
1939 Palomar Oaks Way B Carlsbad (92011) ***(P-16141)***
Laurent Culinary Service ....F....415 485-1122
1945 Francisco Blvd E # 44 San Rafael (94901) ***(P-2524)***
Lava Cap Winery, Placerville *Also called Lava Springs Inc* ***(P-1799)***
Lava Products Inc ....E....949 951-7191
3168 Airway Ave Costa Mesa (92626) ***(P-6692)***
Lava Springs Inc ....E....530 621-0175
2221 Fruitridge Rd Placerville (95667) ***(P-1799)***
Lavang Tech Prcsion Sheet Mtls ....F....714 901-2782
14480 Hoover St Westminster (92683) ***(P-14272)***
Lavash Corporation ....E....323 663-5249
2835 Newell St Los Angeles (90039) ***(P-1232)***
Lavender Alley, Los Angeles *Also called S Sedghi Inc* ***(P-3489)***
Lavey Craft Prfmce Boats Inc ....F....951 273-9690
175 Vander St Corona (92880) ***(P-20343)***
Lavi Industries (PA) ....D....877 275-5284
27810 Avenue Hopkins Valencia (91355) ***(P-12492)***
Lavi Systems Inc ....F....818 373-5400
13731 Saticoy St Van Nuys (91402) ***(P-20155)***
Lavinder Inc ....F....310 278-2456
8687 Melrose Ave Ste B310 West Hollywood (90069) ***(P-2940)***
Lavish Clothing Inc ....F....213 745-5400
245 W 28th St Los Angeles (90007) ***(P-3240)***
LAweb Offset Printing Inc ....C....626 454-2469
9639 Telstar Ave El Monte (91731) ***(P-7117)***
Lawinfocom Inc ....D....800 397-3743
5901 Priestly Dr Ste 200 Carlsbad (92008) ***(P-24094)***
Lawleys Inc ....F....209 572-1700
4554 Qantas Ln Stockton (95206) ***(P-1107)***
Lawrence Equipment Inc (PA) ....C....626 442-2894
2034 Peck Rd El Monte (91733) ***(P-14382)***
Lawrence O Lawrence Ltd ....F....323 935-1100
8104 Beverly Blvd Los Angeles (90048) ***(P-2941)***
Lawrence of La Brea, Los Angeles *Also called Lawrence O Lawrence Ltd* ***(P-2941)***
Lawrence Roll Up Doors Inc (PA) ....E....626 962-4163
4525 Littlejohn St Baldwin Park (91706) ***(P-11964)***
Lawrence Roll Up Doors Inc ....F....818 837-1963
11035 Stranwood Ave Mission Hills (91345) ***(P-11965)***
Lawrence Roll Up Doors Inc ....F....626 338-6041
1406 Virginia Ave Ste 10 Baldwin Park (91706) ***(P-11966)***
Layne Laboratories Inc ....F....805 242-7918
4303 Huasna Rd Arroyo Grande (93420) ***(P-2942)***
Layton Printing & Mailing ....F....909 592-4419
1538 Arrow Hwy La Verne (91750) ***(P-6693)***
Lazestar ....E....925 443-5293
6956 Preston Ave Livermore (94551) ***(P-24649)***
Lb Manufacturing LLC ....F....413 222-2857
1403 S Coast Hwy Oceanside (92054) ***(P-23391)***
Lbi - USA, Chatsworth *Also called Lehrer Brllnprfktion Werks Inc* ***(P-9875)***
Lca Promotions Inc ....E....818 773-9170
9545 Cozycroft Ave Chatsworth (91311) ***(P-7118)***
LCD&d, Chatsworth *Also called Lighting Control & Design Inc* ***(P-17140)***
LCI Laundry Inc ....C....323 767-1900
5835 S Eastrn Ave Ste 100 Commerce (90040) ***(P-3241)***
Lcl Pacific, Los Angeles *Also called Precision Wire Products Inc* ***(P-11060)***
Lcoa, Lake Forest *Also called Laminating Company of America* ***(P-17912)***
Lcptracker Inc ....E....714 669-0052
117 E Chapman Ave Orange (92866) ***(P-24095)***
Lcr-Dixon Corporation ....F....404 307-1695
2048 Union St Apt 4 San Francisco (94123) ***(P-24096)***
Ld Smart Inc ....F....626 581-8887
15350 Stafford St La Puente (91744) ***(P-14937)***
Ldvc Inc ....E....626 448-4611
9606 Valley Blvd Rosemead (91770) ***(P-1382)***
Le Barbocce Inc ....E....510 526-7664
1328 6th St Frnt Frnt Berkeley (94710) ***(P-1029)***
Le Belge Chocolatier Inc ....E....707 258-9200
761 Skyway Ct NAPA (94558) ***(P-1383)***
Le Cache Premium Wine Cabinets, Petaluma *Also called Planet One Products Inc* ***(P-4932)***
Le Chef Costumier Inc ....E....818 242-0868
825 Western Ave Ste 21 Glendale (91201) ***(P-3564)***
Le Elegant Bath Inc ....C....951 734-0238
13405 Estelle St Corona (92879) ***(P-9591)***
Le Hung Tuan ....F....818 700-1008
20952 Itasca St Chatsworth (91311) ***(P-16142)***
Le Vu ....E....916 231-1594
4234 54th St McClellan (95652) ***(P-18985)***
Leach International Corp (HQ) ....B....714 736-7537
6900 Orangethorpe Ave Buena Park (90620) ***(P-18986)***
Leach International Corp ....B....714 739-0770
6900 Orangethorpe Ave Buena Park (90620) ***(P-16728)***
Leading Biosciences Inc ....F....858 395-6099
5800 Armada Dr Ste 210 Carlsbad (92008) ***(P-7987)***
Leadmasters ....F....760 949-6566
17229 Lemon St Ste E11 Hesperia (92345) ***(P-22841)***
Leadmmatic LLC ....E....310 857-4511
5154 Don Pio Dr Woodland Hills (91364) ***(P-6269)***
Leads360 LLC ....E....888 843-1777
207 Hindry Ave Inglewood (90301) ***(P-24097)***
Leaf Healthcare Inc ....F....925 621-1800
5994 W Las Positas Blvd Pleasanton (94588) ***(P-22270)***
Lean Manufacturing Group LLC ....F....661 702-9400
29170 Avenue Penn Valencia (91355) ***(P-13929)***
Leaner Creamer LLC ....F....818 621-5274
9107 Wilshire Blvd # 450 Beverly Hills (90210) ***(P-601)***
Leapfrog Enterprises Inc (HQ) ....B....510 420-5000
6401 Hollis St Ste 100 Emeryville (94608) ***(P-22689)***
Lear Baylor Inc ....E....714 799-9396
7215 Garden Grove Blvd C Garden Grove (92841) ***(P-20344)***
Learners Digest Intl LLC ....C....818 240-7500
450 N Brand Blvd Ste 900 Glendale (91203) ***(P-23392)***
Learners Guild Ltd ....F....415 448-7054
492 9th St Oakland (94607) ***(P-24098)***
Learning Resources Inc ....E....800 995-4436
152 W Walnut St Ste 201 Gardena (90248) ***(P-23393)***
Leather Cpr, Los Angeles *Also called Wonder Marketing Inc* ***(P-8695)***
Leather Pro Inc ....E....818 833-8822
12900 Bradley Ave Sylmar (91342) ***(P-10237)***
Leatherock International Inc ....E....619 299-7625
5285 Lovelock St San Diego (92110) ***(P-10141)***
Lebata Inc ....E....949 253-2800
4621 Teller Ave Ste 130 Newport Beach (92660) ***(P-10779)***
Lebec - Ncc CA Cement Company, Lebec *Also called National Cement Co Cal Inc* ***(P-10804)***
Lecroy Prtocol Solutions Group, Milpitas *Also called Teledyne Lecroy Inc* ***(P-21137)***
Led Engine, San Jose *Also called Osram Sylvania Inc* ***(P-18463)***
Led One Corporation (PA) ....F....510 770-1189
12437 Bellegrave Ave Eastvale (91752) ***(P-18345)***
Leda Corporation ....E....714 841-7821
7080 Kearny Dr Huntington Beach (92648) ***(P-20478)***
Leda Multimedia, Chino *Also called Shop4techcom* ***(P-15100)***
Ledconn Corp ....F....714 256-2111
301 Thor Pl Brea (92821) ***(P-18346)***
Ledengin Inc (PA) ....E....408 922-7200
651 River Oaks Pkwy San Jose (95134) ***(P-18347)***
Ledpac LLC ....D....760 489-8067
9850 Siempre Viva Rd # 5 San Diego (92154) ***(P-23146)***
Ledtronics Inc ....C....310 534-1505
23105 Kashiwa Ct Torrance (90505) ***(P-18348)***
Lee & Fields Publishing Inc ....F....213 380-5858
3731 Wilshire Blvd # 940 Los Angeles (90010) ***(P-6270)***
Lee Aerospace Products Inc ....F....805 527-1811
90 W Easy St Ste 5 Simi Valley (93065) ***(P-20156)***
Lee Augustyn Inc ....F....909 483-0688
9390 7th St Ste A Rancho Cucamonga (91730) ***(P-6694)***
Lee Brothers Inc ....E....650 964-9650
1011 Timothy Dr San Jose (95133) ***(P-888)***
Lee Brothers Truck Body Inc ....F....310 532-7980
18915 Roselle Ave Torrance (90504) ***(P-19540)***
Lee Central Cal Newspapers ....E....559 896-1976
2045 Grant St Selma (93662) ***(P-5696)***
Lee Enterprises Incorporated ....C....805 925-2691
3200 Skyway Dr Santa Maria (93455) ***(P-5697)***
Lee Fasteners Inc ....F....626 287-6848
3327 San Gabriel Blvd H Rosemead (91770) ***(P-11479)***
Lee Kum Kee (usa) Foods Inc ....D....626 709-1888
14455 Don Julian Rd City of Industry (91746) ***(P-2525)***
Lee Machine Products ....F....626 301-4105
2030 Central Ave Duarte (91010) ***(P-14070)***
Lee Maxton Inc ....F....909 483-0688
10844 Edison Ct Rancho Cucamonga (91730) ***(P-6695)***
Lee Pharmaceuticals ....D....626 442-3141
1434 Santa Anita Ave South El Monte (91733) ***(P-8531)***

ALPHABETIC

Employee Codes: A=Over 500 employees, B=251-500
C=101-250, D=51-100, E=20-50, F=10-19
2020 California
Manfacturers Register
© Mergent Inc. 1-800-342-5647
1153

Lee Ray Sandblasting, Santa Fe Springs *Also called Cji Process Systems Inc* ***(P-12006)***
Lee Sandusky Corporation ....E....661 854-5551
16125 Widmere Rd Arvin (93203) ***(P-4694)***
Lee Thomas Inc (PA)....E....310 532-7560
13800 S Figueroa St Los Angeles (90061) ***(P-3362)***
Leejay Industries, Los Alamitos *Also called Katlan Industries Inc* ***(P-12829)***
Leemah Corporation (PA)....C....415 394-1288
155 S Hill Dr Brisbane (94005) ***(P-17788)***
Leemarc Industries LLC....D....760 598-0505
2471 Coral St Vista (92081) ***(P-3101)***
Leemax International Inc....E....619 208-2355
1182 Via Escalante Chula Vista (91910) ***(P-3102)***
Leemco Inc (PA)....F....909 422-0088
360 S Mount Vernon Ave Colton (92324) ***(P-13310)***
Leeper's Stair Products, Corona *Also called Leepers Wood Turning Co Inc* ***(P-4074)***
Leepers Wood Turning Co Inc (PA)....D....562 422-6525
341 Bonnie Cir Ste 104 Corona (92880) ***(P-4074)***
Lees Concrete Materials Inc....F....559 486-2440
200 S Pine St Madera (93637) ***(P-10780)***
Lees Fashions Inc....E....760 753-2408
1157 Monterey Pl Encinitas (92024) ***(P-3242)***
Lees Imperial Welding Inc....C....510 657-4900
3300 Edison Way Fremont (94538) ***(P-11826)***
Lees Precision Tooling....F....562 926-1302
16751 Parkside Ave Cerritos (90703) ***(P-16143)***
Leeway Iron Works Inc....F....510 357-8637
565 Estabrook St San Leandro (94577) ***(P-11827)***
Leewood Press Inc....E....415 896-0513
1407 Indiana St San Francisco (94107) ***(P-6696)***
Leeyo Software Inc (HQ)....E....408 988-5800
2841 Junction Ave Ste 201 San Jose (95134) ***(P-24099)***
Left Coast Brewing Company....F....949 218-3961
1245 Puerta Del Sol San Clemente (92673) ***(P-1542)***
Leftbank Art, La Mirada *Also called Outlook Resources Inc* ***(P-3751)***
Lefton Technologies Inc....E....818 986-1728
1140 Brooklawn Dr Los Angeles (90077) ***(P-16729)***
Lefty Production Co LLC....F....323 515-9266
318 W 9th St Ste 1010 Los Angeles (90015) ***(P-3363)***
Legacy Bands Inc....F....818 890-2527
13261 Paxton St Pacoima (91331) ***(P-22538)***
Legacy Glass Studios, Menlo Park *Also called Legacy Us LLC* ***(P-10316)***
Legacy Graphics LLC....F....619 585-1044
1120 Bay Blvd Ste E Chula Vista (91911) ***(P-7119)***
Legacy Systems Incorporated....F....510 651-2312
4160 Technology Dr Ste E Fremont (94538) ***(P-14491)***
Legacy Us LLC....F....650 714-9750
1800 El Camino Real Ste D Menlo Park (94027) ***(P-10316)***
Legacy Vulcan LLC....E....626 856-6150
13000 Los Angeles St Irwindale (91706) ***(P-10781)***
Legacy Vulcan LLC....E....909 875-1150
2400 W Highland Ave San Bernardino (92407) ***(P-348)***
Legacy Vulcan LLC....F....626 856-6153
6232 Santos Diaz St Irwindale (91702) ***(P-349)***
Legacy Vulcan LLC....E....714 737-2922
Parkridge & Quarry Sts Corona (92877) ***(P-300)***
Legacy Vulcan LLC....E....818 983-1323
11447 Tuxford St Sun Valley (91352) ***(P-350)***
Legacy Vulcan LLC....E....661 822-4158
655 W Tehachapi Blvd Tehachapi (93561) ***(P-301)***
Legacy Vulcan LLC....F....925 284-4686
3195 Andreasen Dr Lafayette (94549) ***(P-302)***
Legacy Vulcan LLC....E....805 647-1161
6029 E Vineyard Ave Oxnard (93036) ***(P-10782)***
Legacy Vulcan LLC....E....626 633-4258
16001 1/2 E Foothill Blvd Irwindale (91702) ***(P-9096)***
Legacy Vulcan LLC....E....661 533-2127
6851 E Avenue T Littlerock (93543) ***(P-10783)***
Legacy Vulcan LLC....D....661 835-4800
8517 E Panama Ln Bakersfield (93307) ***(P-10784)***
Legacy Vulcan LLC....F....626 856-6148
16013 E Foothill Blvd Irwindale (91702) ***(P-10596)***
Legacy Vulcan LLC....E....909 875-5180
20350 Highland Ave Rialto (92377) ***(P-10785)***
Legacy Vulcan LLC....E....661 858-2673
Hwy W 166 Of Old Rver Rd Bakersfield (93313) ***(P-10786)***
Legacy Vulcan LLC....F....209 854-3088
28525 Bambouer Rd Gustine (95322) ***(P-10597)***
Legacy Vulcan LLC....F....760 439-0624
2925 Industry St Oceanside (92054) ***(P-10598)***
Legacy Vulcan LLC....D....559 434-1202
11599 Old Friant Rd Fresno (93730) ***(P-10787)***
Legacy Vulcan LLC....E....661 252-1010
13900 Lang Station Rd Canyon Country (91387) ***(P-10788)***
Legacy Vulcan LLC....E....858 566-2730
7220 Trade St Ste 200 San Diego (92121) ***(P-303)***
Legacy Vulcan LLC....F....916 682-0850
11501 Florin Rd Sacramento (95830) ***(P-10789)***
Legacy Vulcan LLC....E....626 856-6143
16001 E Foothill Blvd Irwindale (91702) ***(P-351)***
Legacy Vulcan LLC....E....925 373-1802
365 N Canyon Pkwy Livermore (94551) ***(P-10790)***
Legacy Vulcan LLC....E....661 533-2125
7107 E Avenue T Littlerock (93543) ***(P-10791)***
Legacy Vulcan LLC....E....818 983-0146
11401 Tuxford St Sun Valley (91352) ***(P-10792)***
Legal Vision Group LLC....E....310 945-5550
1880 Century Park E # 209 Los Angeles (90067) ***(P-6697)***
Legend Pump & Well Service Inc....E....909 384-1000
1324 W Rialto Ave San Bernardino (92410) ***(P-98)***
Legend Silicon Corp....E....408 735-9888
22 Stirling Way Hayward (94542) ***(P-17570)***
Legendary Headwear, San Diego *Also called Legendary Holdings Inc* ***(P-3468)***
Legendary Holdings Inc....E....619 872-6100
2295 Paseo De Las America San Diego (92154) ***(P-3468)***
Legends Apparel & I C Ink, Stockton *Also called IC Ink Image Co Inc* ***(P-7090)***
Leggett & Platt Incorporated....D....909 937-1010
1050 S Dupont Ave Ontario (91761) ***(P-4727)***
Leggett & Platt 0302, Valencia *Also called Leggett & Platt Incorporated* ***(P-4920)***
Leggett & Platt 0768, Poway *Also called Valley Metals LLC* ***(P-11138)***
Leggett & Platt Incorporated....D....562 945-2641
12352 Whittier Blvd Whittier (90602) ***(P-4728)***
Leggett & Platt Incorporated....E....661 775-8500
29120 Commerce Center Dr # 1 Valencia (91355) ***(P-4920)***
Legion Creative Group....E....323 498-1100
1680 Vine St Ste 700 Los Angeles (90028) ***(P-7120)***
Lehigh Hanson, Morro Bay *Also called Hanson Aggrgtes Md-Pacific Inc* ***(P-10769)***
Lehigh Hanson, Lakeside *Also called Hanson Aggregates LLC* ***(P-9094)***
Lehigh Southwest Cement Co....C....661 822-4445
13573 E Tehachapi Blvd Tehachapi (93561) ***(P-10420)***
Lehigh Southwest Cement Co....F....408 996-4271
24001 Stevens Creek Blvd Cupertino (95014) ***(P-10421)***
Lehigh Southwest Cement Co (HQ)....F....972 653-5500
2300 Clayton Rd Ste 300 Concord (94520) ***(P-10422)***
Lehigh Southwest Cement Co....C....530 275-1581
15390 Wonderland Blvd Redding (96003) ***(P-10793)***
Lehigh Southwest Cement Co....F....209 465-2624
2201 W Washington St Stockton (95203) ***(P-10794)***
Lehman Foods Inc....E....818 837-7600
1145 Arroyo St Ste B San Fernando (91340) ***(P-2526)***
Lehmans Manufacturing Co Inc....F....559 486-1700
4960 E Jensen Ave Fresno (93725) ***(P-11828)***
Lehrer Brllnprfktion Werks Inc (PA)....E....818 407-1890
20801 Nordhoff St Chatsworth (91311) ***(P-9875)***
Leica Biosystems Imaging Inc....C....760 539-1100
1360 Park Center Dr Vista (92081) ***(P-21773)***
Leica Geosystems Hds LLC....D....925 790-2300
5000 Executive Pkwy # 500 San Ramon (94583) ***(P-15272)***
Leidos Inc....E....619 524-2581
4025 Hancock St Ste 210 San Diego (92110) ***(P-15273)***
Leiner Health Products Inc....B....714 898-9936
7366 Orangewood Ave Garden Grove (92841) ***(P-7988)***
Leiner Health Products Inc....D....661 775-1422
27655b Avenue Hopkins Valencia (91355) ***(P-7989)***
Leisure Collective Inc....F....760 814-2840
6189 El Camino Real 101 Carlsbad (92009) ***(P-22367)***
Leisure Components, Cerritos *Also called Sedenquist-Fraser Entps Inc* ***(P-19764)***
Leitch & Co Inc....F....510 483-2323
1607 Abram Ct San Leandro (94577) ***(P-11535)***
Leiter's Compounding, San Jose *Also called Leiters Enterprises Inc* ***(P-7990)***
Leiters Enterprises Inc....D....800 292-6772
17 Great Oaks Blvd San Jose (95119) ***(P-7990)***
Leitz Tooling Systems LP....F....909 799-8494
1145 Orange Show Rd San Bernardino (92408) ***(P-13930)***
Lejon of California Inc....E....951 736-1229
1229 Railroad St Corona (92882) ***(P-3531)***
Lejon Tulliani, Corona *Also called Lejon of California Inc* ***(P-3531)***
Lekos Dye & Finishing Inc....D....310 763-0900
3131 E Harcourt St Compton (90221) ***(P-2746)***
Leland Stanford Junior Univ....E....650 723-9434
500 Broadway St Redwood City (94063) ***(P-5698)***
Leland Stanford Junior Univ....C....650 723-5553
557 Escondido Mall Stanford (94305) ***(P-6271)***
Leland Stanford Junior Univ....C....650 723-3052
424 Matison Ave Stanford (94305) ***(P-6272)***
Leland Stanford Junior Univ....D....650 723-4455
559 Nathan Abbott Way Stanford (94305) ***(P-6273)***
Lemonaid Health, San Francisco *Also called Icebreaker Health Inc* ***(P-23997)***
Lemor Trims Inc....F....213 741-1646
830 Venice Blvd Los Angeles (90015) ***(P-3796)***
Lengthwise Brewing Company....E....661 836-2537
7700 District Blvd Bakersfield (93313) ***(P-1543)***
Lennox....F....800 953-6669
4000 Hamner Ave Eastvale (91752) ***(P-15439)***
Lennox Industries Inc....C....805 288-8200
2221 Eastman Ave Oxnard (93030) ***(P-15440)***
Lenntek Corporation....E....310 534-2738
1610 Lockness Pl Torrance (90501) ***(P-17571)***
Lens C-C Inc (PA)....D....800 772-3911
1750 N Loop Rd Ste 150 Alameda (94502) ***(P-22368)***
Lens Technology I LLC....F....714 690-6470
45 Parker Ste 100 Irvine (92618) ***(P-21374)***
Lensvector Inc....D....408 542-0300
6203 San Ignacio Ave San Jose (95119) ***(P-22369)***
Lenus Handcrafted....F....619 200-4266
3323 Thorn St San Diego (92104) ***(P-8532)***
Lenz Precision Technology Inc....E....650 966-1784
355 Pioneer Way Ste A Mountain View (94041) ***(P-16144)***
Lenz Technology, Mountain View *Also called Lenz Precision Technology Inc* ***(P-16144)***
Leo Lam Inc....E....925 484-3690
3589 Nevada St Ste A Pleasanton (94566) ***(P-6698)***
Leo Molds....F....562 714-4807
125 W Victoria St Gardena (90248) ***(P-14071)***
Leoch Battery Corporation (PA)....E....949 588-5853
19751 Descartes Unit A Foothill Ranch (92610) ***(P-16659)***
Leon Assembly Solutions Inc....D....858 397-2826
10650 Scripps Ranch Blvd # 123 San Diego (92131) ***(P-10478)***
Leon Krous Drilling Inc....E....818 833-4654
9300 Borden Ave Sun Valley (91352) ***(P-99)***

Mergent e-mail: customerrelations@mergent.com 2020 California (P-0000) Products & Services Section entry number
1154 Manufacturers Register (PA)=Parent Co (HQ)=Headquarters (DH)=Div Headquarters

Leonard Craft Co LLC ....D....714 549-0678
3501 W Segerstrom Ave Santa Ana (92704) ***(P-22539)***
Leonards Carpet Service Inc (PA) ....D....714 630-1930
1121 N Red Gum St Anaheim (92806) ***(P-4921)***
Leonards Molded Products Inc ....E....661 253-2227
25031 Anza Dr Valencia (91355) ***(P-9328)***
Leonesse Cellars, Temecula *Also called Temecula Valley Winery MGT LLC* ***(P-1949)***
Leonesse Cellars LLC ....E....951 302-7601
38311 De Portola Rd Temecula (92592) ***(P-1800)***
Leons Powder Coating ....F....510 437-9224
834 49th Ave Oakland (94601) ***(P-13199)***
Leos Metal Polishing ....F....310 635-5257
10980 Alameda St Lynwood (90262) ***(P-13041)***
Leos Metal Polishing Works, Lynwood *Also called Leos Metal Polishing* ***(P-13041)***
Leotek Electronics USA LLC ....E....408 380-1788
1955 Lundy Ave San Jose (95131) ***(P-23147)***
Lepera Enterprises Inc ....E....818 767-5110
8207 Lankershim Blvd North Hollywood (91605) ***(P-20414)***
Leprino Foods Company ....B....209 835-8340
2401 N Macarthur Dr Tracy (95376) ***(P-563)***
Leprino Foods Company ....B....559 924-7722
490 F St Lemoore (93245) ***(P-564)***
Leprino Foods Company ....C....559 924-7939
351 Belle Haven Dr Lemoore (93245) ***(P-565)***
Lequios Japan Co Ltd ....F....410 629-8694
14241 Firestone Blvd La Mirada (90638) ***(P-2527)***
Lerexa Winery, Livingston *Also called E & J Gallo Winery* ***(P-1683)***
Les Schwab, Portola *Also called Coates Incorporated* ***(P-19616)***
Lesco, Torrance *Also called American Ultraviolet West Inc* ***(P-13814)***
Leslie Environmental Inds LLC ....F....209 840-1664
17617 Buttercup Cir Sonora (95370) ***(P-3892)***
Leslie-Locke, Carson *Also called Jarden Corporation* ***(P-9850)***
Leslies Organics LLC ....F....415 383-9800
1297 Dynamic St Petaluma (94954) ***(P-8751)***
Lester Box Inc ....F....562 437-5123
1470 Seabright Ave Long Beach (90813) ***(P-4420)***
Lester Box & Manufacturing, Long Beach *Also called Lester Box Inc* ***(P-4420)***
Lester Lithograph Inc ....E....714 491-3981
1128 N Gilbert St Anaheim (92801) ***(P-6699)***
Lets Do Lunch ....D....310 523-3664
310 W Alondra Blvd Gardena (90248) ***(P-2528)***
Lets Go Apparel Inc (PA) ....F....213 863-1767
1729 E Washington Blvd Los Angeles (90021) ***(P-3565)***
Letterhead Factory Inc ....F....310 538-3321
1007 E Dominguez St Ste H Carson (90746) ***(P-6700)***
Leucadia Pharmaceuticals, Carlsbad *Also called Custopharm Inc* ***(P-14450)***
Levac Specialties Inc ....F....916 362-3795
2305 Cemo Cir Gold River (95670) ***(P-20373)***
Levco Fab Inc ....F....909 465-0840
10757 Fremont Ave Ontario (91762) ***(P-13475)***
Levecke LLC ....D....951 681-8600
10810 Inland Ave Jurupa Valley (91752) ***(P-1801)***
Level 23 Fab ....F....714 979-2323
2117 S Anne St Santa Ana (92704) ***(P-11829)***
Level 5 Networks Inc ....E....408 245-9300
840 W California Ave Sunnyvale (94086) ***(P-18349)***
Level Labs LP ....E....408 499-6839
530 Lytton Ave Lbby Palo Alto (94301) ***(P-24100)***
Level Trek Corp ....F....626 689-4829
5670 Schaefer Ave Ste N Chino (91710) ***(P-9876)***
Levi Strauss & Co (PA) ....A....415 501-6000
1155 Battery St San Francisco (94111) ***(P-3012)***
Levi Strauss & Co ....F....310 246-9044
316 N Beverly Dr Beverly Hills (90210) ***(P-3013)***
Levi Strauss & Co ....F....951 674-2694
17600 Collier Ave Lake Elsinore (92530) ***(P-3014)***
Levi Strauss International (HQ) ....F....415 501-6000
1155 Battery St San Francisco (94111) ***(P-3103)***
Leviton Manufacturing Co Inc ....E....631 812-6041
3760 Kilroy Airport Way # 660 Long Beach (90806) ***(P-16911)***
Leviton Manufacturing Co Inc ....B....619 205-8600
6020 Progressive Ave # 500 San Diego (92154) ***(P-16912)***
Levmar Inc ....F....925 680-8723
1666 Willow Pass Rd Pittsburg (94565) ***(P-12266)***
Levolor, Costa Mesa *Also called Sampling International LLC* ***(P-3858)***
Lewis Barricade Inc ....E....661 363-0912
4000 Westerly Pl Ste 100 Newport Beach (92660) ***(P-9097)***
Lewis John Glass Studio ....F....510 635-4607
10229 Pearmain St Oakland (94603) ***(P-10317)***
Lewis-Goetz and Company Inc ....F....209 944-0791
4848 Frontier Way Ste C Stockton (95215) ***(P-9199)***
Lex Products LLC ....F....818 768-4474
12701 Van Nuys Blvd Ste Q Pacoima (91331) ***(P-21499)***
Lexington Quarry, Los Gatos *Also called Vulcan Aggregates Company LLC* ***(P-365)***
Lexisnexis Matthew Bender, San Francisco *Also called Relx Inc* ***(P-6017)***
Lexmark International Inc ....E....714 641-1007
575 Anton Blvd Fl 3 Costa Mesa (92626) ***(P-15274)***
Lexor Inc ....D....714 444-4144
7400 Hazard Ave Westminster (92683) ***(P-23394)***
Lexstar Inc (PA) ....E....845 947-1415
4959 Kalamis Way Oceanside (92056) ***(P-17050)***
Ley Grand Foods Corporation ....E....626 336-2244
287 S 6th Ave La Puente (91746) ***(P-1233)***
Leyvas Mexican Food ....E....626 350-6328
4032 Tyler Ave El Monte (91731) ***(P-1234)***
Lf Illumination LLC ....D....818 885-1335
9200 Deering Ave Chatsworth (91311) ***(P-17051)***
LF Industries Inc ....F....760 438-5711
6352 Corte Del Abeto G Carlsbad (92011) ***(P-16145)***
Lf Sportswear Inc (PA) ....E....310 437-4100
5333 Mcconnell Ave Los Angeles (90066) ***(P-3174)***
Lf Visuals Inc ....F....760 345-5571
39620 Entrepreneur Ln Palm Desert (92211) ***(P-2943)***
Lg Innotek Usa Inc (HQ) ....F....408 955-0364
2540 N 1st St Ste 400 San Jose (95131) ***(P-18987)***
Lg Nanoh2o Inc ....E....424 218-4000
21250 Hawthorne Blvd # 330 Torrance (90503) ***(P-8989)***
Lg-Ericsson USA Inc ....E....877 828-2673
20 Mason Irvine (92618) ***(P-17384)***
LGarde Inc ....E....714 259-0771
15181 Woodlawn Ave Tustin (92780) ***(P-15052)***
Lgc Biosearch Technologies, Petaluma *Also called Biosearch Technologies Inc* ***(P-8284)***
Lgc Wireless Inc ....C....408 952-2400
541 E Trimble Rd San Jose (95131) ***(P-17572)***
Lgphilips Lcd Amer Fin Corp ....E....408 350-7600
150 E Brokaw Rd San Jose (95112) ***(P-19345)***
Lhoist North America Ariz Inc ....F....626 336-4578
14931 Salt Lake Ave City of Industry (91746) ***(P-10875)***
Lhv Power Corporation (PA) ....E....619 258-7700
10221 Buena Vista Ave A Santee (92071) ***(P-18988)***
Lialee Inc ....F....213 765-7788
525 E 87th Pl Los Angeles (90003) ***(P-2794)***
Libby Laboratories Inc ....E....510 527-5400
1700 6th St Berkeley (94710) ***(P-8533)***
Liberty Cafe ....E....415 695-8777
410 Cortland Ave San Francisco (94110) ***(P-1235)***
Liberty Container Company ....C....323 564-4211
4224 Santa Ana St South Gate (90280) ***(P-5243)***
Liberty Diversified Intl Inc ....C....858 391-7302
13100 Danielson St Poway (92064) ***(P-5244)***
Liberty Industries ....F....626 575-3206
10754 Lower Azusa Rd El Monte (91731) ***(P-16146)***
Liberty Love, Commerce *Also called Cure Apparel LLC* ***(P-3151)***
Liberty Packg & Extruding Inc ....E....323 722-5124
3015 Supply Ave Commerce (90040) ***(P-5401)***
Liberty Paper, Vernon *Also called D D Office Products Inc* ***(P-5101)***
Liberty Printing Inc ....E....209 467-8800
2601 Teepee Dr Stockton (95205) ***(P-6701)***
Liberty School, Paso Robles *Also called Treana Winery LLC* ***(P-1961)***
Liberty Valley Doors Inc ....F....707 795-8040
6005 Gravenstein Hwy Cotati (94931) ***(P-4075)***
Liberty Vegetable Oil Company ....E....562 921-3567
15306 Carmenita Rd Santa Fe Springs (90670) ***(P-1474)***
Liboon Group Inc ....F....714 639-3639
1746 W Katella Ave Ste 6 Orange (92867) ***(P-13931)***
Libra Cable Technologies Inc ....F....310 618-8182
Monterey Business Park 27 Torrance (90503) ***(P-18989)***
Library Mosacis, Los Angeles *Also called Yenor Inc* ***(P-7277)***
Library Reproduction Service, Los Angeles *Also called The Microfilm Company of Cal* ***(P-6154)***
License Frame Inc ....E....714 903-7550
15462 Electronic Ln Huntington Beach (92649) ***(P-13200)***
Licher Direct Mail Inc ....E....626 795-3333
980 Seco St Pasadena (91103) ***(P-6702)***
Lida Childrens Wear Inc ....E....626 967-8868
3113 E California Blvd Pasadena (91107) ***(P-3483)***
Lidestri Foods Inc ....D....559 251-1000
568 S Temperance Ave Fresno (93727) ***(P-789)***
Lido Industries Inc ....F....714 633-3731
456 S Montgomery Way Orange (92868) ***(P-9877)***
Lieder Development Inc ....F....909 947-7722
1839 S Lake Pl Ontario (91761) ***(P-18990)***
Lief Labs, Valencia *Also called Lief Organics LLC* ***(P-7991)***
Lief Organics LLC ....E....661 775-2500
28901 28903 Ave Paine Valencia (91355) ***(P-7991)***
Life Force International, El Cajon *Also called Doctors Signature Sales* ***(P-7653)***
Life Line Packaging Inc ....F....619 444-2737
1250 Pierre Way El Cajon (92021) ***(P-5330)***
Life Line Products, El Cajon *Also called Life Line Packaging Inc* ***(P-5330)***
Life Media Inc ....E....800 201-9440
7657 Winnetka Ave Ste 504 Winnetka (91306) ***(P-5977)***
Life Paint Company (PA) ....E....562 944-6391
12927 Sunshine Ave Santa Fe Springs (90670) ***(P-8654)***
Life Science Outsourcing Inc ....D....714 672-1090
830 Challenger St Brea (92821) ***(P-21774)***
Life Style West, Orange *Also called Daves Interiors Inc* ***(P-4636)***
Life Technologies Corporation ....C....760 603-7200
500 Lincoln Centre Dr Foster City (94404) ***(P-21254)***
Life Technologies Corporation (HQ) ....C....760 603-7200
5781 Van Allen Way Carlsbad (92008) ***(P-8234)***
Life Technologies Corporation ....D....760 918-4259
5791 Van Allen Way Carlsbad (92008) ***(P-8313)***
Lifeaid Beverage Company LLC ....D....888 558-1113
2833 Mission St Santa Cruz (95060) ***(P-2089)***
Lifebloom Corporation ....E....562 944-6800
925 W Lambert Rd Ste B Brea (92821) ***(P-7992)***
Lifegas, Burbank *Also called Linde Gas North America LLC* ***(P-7414)***
Lifegas, City of Industry *Also called Linde Gas North America LLC* ***(P-7415)***
Lifekind Products Inc ....E....530 477-5395
333 Crown Point Cir # 225 Grass Valley (95945) ***(P-8343)***
Lifeline Food Co Inc ....F....831 899-5040
118 Cypress Lakes Ct Marina (93933) ***(P-566)***
Lifeline SEC & Automtn Inc ....D....916 285-9078
2081 Arena Blvd Ste 260 Sacramento (95834) ***(P-19346)***
Lifeline Systems Company ....C....831 755-0788
450 E Romie Ln Salinas (93901) ***(P-17742)***
Lifemed of California ....E....800 543-3633
13948 Mountain Ave Chino (91710) ***(P-21775)***

ALPHABETIC

Employee Codes: A=Over 500 employees, B=251-500
C=101-250, D=51-100, E=20-50, F=10-19
2020 California
Manfacturers Register
© Mergent Inc. 1-800-342-5647
1155

Lifeome Biolabs Inc ....F....619 302-0129
10054 Mesa Ridge Ct San Diego (92121) ***(P-8235)***

Lifescan Products LLC (HQ) ....D....408 719-8443
1000 Gibraltar Dr Milpitas (95035) ***(P-21776)***

Lifescience, Hercules *Also called Bio-RAD Laboratories Inc* ***(P-21191)***

Lifescience Plus Inc ....F....650 565-8172
2520 Wyandotte St Ste A Mountain View (94043) ***(P-21777)***

Lifesource Water Systems Inc (PA) ....E....626 792-9996
523 S Fair Oaks Ave Pasadena (91105) ***(P-15536)***

Lifetime Camper Shells Inc ....E....909 885-2814
1375 N E St San Bernardino (92405) ***(P-20488)***

Lifetime Memory Products Inc ....E....949 794-9000
2505 Da Vinci Ste A Irvine (92614) ***(P-17914)***

Lifetouch Nat Schl Studios Inc ....D....530 345-3993
2860 Fair St Chico (95928) ***(P-7313)***

Lifetrak Incorporated ....F....510 413-9030
8371 Central Ave Ste A Newark (94560) ***(P-22271)***

Lifi Labs Inc (PA) ....F....650 739-5563
350 Townsend St Ste 830 San Francisco (94107) ***(P-10318)***

Lifoam Industries LLC ....E....323 587-1934
2340 E 52nd St Vernon (90058) ***(P-9408)***

Lifoam Mfg, Vernon *Also called Lifoam Industries LLC* ***(P-9408)***

Lift By Encore, Huntington Beach *Also called Encore Interiors Inc* ***(P-20097)***

Lift By Encore, Huntington Beach *Also called Encore Seats Inc* ***(P-20099)***

Lift Off, San Diego *Also called Motsenbocker Advanced Developm* ***(P-8398)***

Lifx, San Francisco *Also called Lifi Labs Inc* ***(P-10318)***

Ligand Pharmaceuticals Inc ....E....858 550-7500
10275 Science Center Dr San Diego (92121) ***(P-7993)***

Ligand Pharmaceuticals Inc (PA) ....D....858 550-7500
3911 Sorrento Valley Blvd # 110 San Diego (92121) ***(P-7994)***

Light & Motion Industries ....D....831 645-1525
711 Neeson Rd Marina (93933) ***(P-17139)***

Light Composite Corporation ....D....949 858-8820
22322 Gilberto Rcho STA Marg (92688) ***(P-11605)***

Light Fixture Industries, Vista *Also called Exit Light Co Inc* ***(P-17032)***

Light Guard Systems Inc ....F....707 542-4547
2292 Airport Blvd Santa Rosa (95403) ***(P-16730)***

Light Labs Inc ....D....650 272-6942
725 Shasta St Redwood City (94063) ***(P-21375)***

Light Mobile Inc ....F....858 278-1750
7968 Arjons Dr Ste D San Diego (92126) ***(P-22172)***

Lightclub USA, Chatsworth *Also called Lightcraft Otdoor Environments* ***(P-16975)***

Lightcraft Otdoor Environments ....F....818 349-2663
9811 Owensmouth Ave Ste 1 Chatsworth (91311) ***(P-16975)***

Lightcross Inc ....E....626 236-4500
2630 Corporate Pl Monterey Park (91754) ***(P-18991)***

Lightech Fiberoptic Inc ....E....510 567-8700
1987 Adams Ave San Leandro (94577) ***(P-18992)***

Lightera, Sunnyvale *Also called Luminus Inc* ***(P-17057)***

Lighthouse Trucking, Montebello *Also called Beacon Concrete Inc* ***(P-10696)***

Lighting Company, The, Irvine *Also called Energy Management Group Inc* ***(P-17123)***

Lighting Control & Design Inc ....E....323 226-0000
9144 Deering Ave Chatsworth (91311) ***(P-17140)***

Lightning Dversion Systems LLC ....F....714 841-1080
16572 Burke Ln Huntington Beach (92647) ***(P-16913)***

Lightprint Labs, San Francisco *Also called Allen Sarah &* ***(P-15150)***

Lights Fantastic ....E....408 266-2787
2408 Lincoln Village Dr San Jose (95125) ***(P-6703)***

Lights of America Inc (PA) ....B....909 594-7883
611 Reyes Dr Walnut (91789) ***(P-16976)***

Lightspeed Software ....F....661 716-7600
1800 19th St Bakersfield (93301) ***(P-24101)***

Lightwave Laser, Santa Rosa *Also called Macon Industries Inc* ***(P-19352)***

Lightwave Pdl Inc ....F....909 548-3677
1246 E Lexington Ave Pomona (91766) ***(P-16977)***

Lightway Industries Inc ....E....661 257-0286
28435 Industry Dr Valencia (91355) ***(P-17052)***

Lignum Vitae Cabinet ....F....510 444-2030
1625 16th St Oakland (94607) ***(P-4808)***

Likom Caseworks USA Inc (HQ) ....E....210 587-7824
17890 Castleton St # 309 City of Industry (91748) ***(P-15129)***

Lili Butler Studio Inc ....F....707 793-0222
7950 Redwood Dr Ste 16 Cotati (94931) ***(P-3175)***

Lilly Biotechnology Center ....F....858 597-4990
10290 Campus Point Dr San Diego (92121) ***(P-7995)***

Lilly Ming International Inc ....F....949 266-4836
16 Trinity Irvine (92612) ***(P-7996)***

Lilly Tortilleria ....E....619 281-2890
4271 University Ave San Diego (92105) ***(P-2529)***

Lily Pond Products ....F....559 431-5203
351 W Cromwell Ave # 105 Fresno (93711) ***(P-14492)***

Lily Samii Collection, San Francisco *Also called L Y Z Ltd* ***(P-3238)***

Limited Access Unlimited Inc ....F....619 294-3682
5220 Anna Ave Ste A San Diego (92110) ***(P-13649)***

Limos By Tiffany Inc ....E....951 657-2680
23129 Cajalco Rd Perris (92570) ***(P-19541)***

Limpus Prints Inc ....F....714 545-5078
1820 S Santa Fe St Santa Ana (92705) ***(P-7121)***

Lin Consulting LLC ....F....714 650-8595
15086 Beach Blvd Midway City (92655) ***(P-20489)***

Lin Engineering Inc ....C....408 919-0200
16245 Vineyard Blvd Morgan Hill (95037) ***(P-16660)***

Lin Frank Distillers ....F....707 437-1092
2455 Huntington Dr Fairfield (94533) ***(P-2015)***

Lin MAI Inc ....E....818 890-1220
6333 San Fernando Rd Glendale (91201) ***(P-23395)***

Linabond Inc ....F....805 484-7373
1161 Avenida Acaso Camarillo (93012) ***(P-13201)***

Lincoln Iron Works ....E....310 684-2543
507 7th St Santa Monica (90402) ***(P-11055)***

Lind Marine Inc (PA) ....E....707 762-7251
100 E D St Petaluma (94952) ***(P-1108)***

Lindblade Metal Works, La Mirada *Also called Lindblade Metalworks Inc* ***(P-12493)***

Lindblade Metalworks Inc ....E....714 670-7172
14355 Macaw St La Mirada (90638) ***(P-12493)***

Linde Gas North America LLC ....F....626 855-8344
614 S Glenwood Pl Burbank (91506) ***(P-7414)***

Linde Gas North America LLC ....F....626 780-3104
680 Baldwin Park Blvd City of Industry (91746) ***(P-7415)***

Linden Nut, Linden *Also called Pearl Crop Inc* ***(P-2583)***

Lindgren Lumber Co ....F....707 822-6519
3851 W End Ct Arcata (95521) ***(P-3938)***

Lindquist Robert N & Assoc (PA) ....F....805 937-9801
4665 Santa Maria Mesa Rd Santa Maria (93454) ***(P-1802)***

Lindsay Trnsp Solutions Inc (HQ) ....D....707 374-6800
180 River Rd Rio Vista (94571) ***(P-10599)***

Lindsay/Barnett Incorporated ....F....510 483-6300
2194 Edison Ave Ste H San Leandro (94577) ***(P-13530)***

Lindsey Doors Inc ....E....760 775-1959
81101 Indio Blvd Ste D16 Indio (92201) ***(P-9442)***

Lindsey International Co., Azusa *Also called Lindsey Manufacturing Co* ***(P-12733)***

Lindsey Manufacturing Co ....C....626 969-3471
760 N Georgia Ave Azusa (91702) ***(P-12733)***

Lindsey Mfg, Indio *Also called Lindsey Doors Inc* ***(P-9442)***

Line Euro-Americas Corp ....F....323 591-0380
5750 Wilshire Blvd # 640 Los Angeles (90036) ***(P-24102)***

Line One Laboratories Inc USA ....E....818 886-2288
9600 Lurline Ave Chatsworth (91311) ***(P-9329)***

Line Publications Inc ....F....310 234-9501
9800 S La Cienega Blvd # 10 Inglewood (90301) ***(P-5978)***

Linea Pelle Inc (PA) ....F....310 231-9950
7107 Valjean Ave Van Nuys (91406) ***(P-10142)***

Lineage Cell Therapeutics Inc (PA) ....D....510 521-3390
2173 Salk Ave Ste 200 Carlsbad (92008) ***(P-8314)***

Linear Express, Milpitas *Also called Linear Technology Corporation* ***(P-18351)***

Linear Integrated Systems Inc ....F....510 490-9160
4042 Clipper Ct Fremont (94538) ***(P-18350)***

Linear Technology Corporation ....F....408 428-2050
720 Sycamore Dr Milpitas (95035) ***(P-18351)***

Linear Technology Corporation ....D....408 434-6237
1530 Buckeye Dr Milpitas (95035) ***(P-18352)***

Linear Technology LLC (HQ) ....A....408 432-1900
1630 Mccarthy Blvd Milpitas (95035) ***(P-18353)***

Linear Technology LLC ....D....805 965-6400
911 Olive St Santa Barbara (93101) ***(P-18354)***

Linear Technology LLC ....D....408 432-1900
5465 Morehouse Dr Ste 155 San Diego (92121) ***(P-18355)***

Linen Liners, Fullerton *Also called GLC General Inc* ***(P-4505)***

Linens Exchange Inc ....F....310 638-5507
3148 Martin Luther King Lynwood (90262) ***(P-2944)***

Liner Technologies Inc ....E....909 594-6610
4821 Chino Ave Chino (91710) ***(P-9878)***

Linfinity Microelectronics, Garden Grove *Also called Microsemi Corp-Analog* ***(P-18403)***

Link Depot, La Puente *Also called Ld Smart Inc* ***(P-14937)***

Link4 Corporation ....F....714 524-0004
175 E Freedom Ave Anaheim (92801) ***(P-20797)***

Links Medical Products Inc (PA) ....E....949 753-0001
9247 Research Dr Irvine (92618) ***(P-21778)***

Linmarr Associates Inc ....F....949 215-5466
8 Hammond Ste 108 Irvine (92618) ***(P-14611)***

Linnco LLC ....A....661 616-3900
5201 Truxtun Ave Bakersfield (93309) ***(P-57)***

Linoleum Sales Co Inc (PA) ....D....661 327-4053
1000 W Grand Ave Oakland (94607) ***(P-10271)***

Linpeng International Inc ....F....909 923-9881
1939 S Campus Ave Ontario (91761) ***(P-23396)***

Lintelle Engineering Inc ....E....831 439-8400
380 El Pueblo Rd Ste 105 Scotts Valley (95066) ***(P-19347)***

Linvatec Corporation ....D....805 571-8100
26 Castilian Dr Ste B Goleta (93117) ***(P-21779)***

Linx & More, Woodland Hills *Also called Linx Bracelets Inc* ***(P-22540)***

Linx Bracelets Inc ....F....818 224-4050
23147 Ventura Blvd # 250 Woodland Hills (91364) ***(P-22540)***

Lion Packing Co, Selma *Also called Lion Raisins Inc* ***(P-852)***

Lion Raisins Inc (PA) ....B....559 834-6677
9500 S De Wolf Ave Selma (93662) ***(P-852)***

Lion Semiconductor Inc ....F....415 462-4933
332 Townsend St San Francisco (94107) ***(P-18356)***

Lion Tank Line Inc ....E....323 726-1966
5801 Randolph St Commerce (90040) ***(P-9050)***

Lip Hing Metal Inc ....F....714 871-9220
738 Phillips Rowland Heights (91748) ***(P-13980)***

Lip Hing Metal Mfg Amer Inc ....F....626 810-8204
738 Phillips Rowland Heights (91748) ***(P-14273)***

Lippert Components Inc ....D....909 873-0061
168 S Spruce Ave Rialto (92376) ***(P-19484)***

Liqua-Tech Corporation ....F....800 659-3556
3501 N State St Ukiah (95482) ***(P-20971)***

Liqui-Box Corporation ....E....909 390-4646
5772 Jurupa St Ste C Ontario (91761) ***(P-9487)***

Liquid Bioscience Inc ....F....949 432-9559
26895 Aliso Creek Rd B800 Aliso Viejo (92656) ***(P-7997)***

Liquid Force Wakeboards ....E....760 943-8364
1815 Aston Ave Ste 105 Carlsbad (92008) ***(P-22842)***

Liquid Graphics Inc ....C....949 486-3588
2701 S Harbor Blvd Unit A Santa Ana (92704) ***(P-3104)***

Liquid Packaging, Paramount *Also called Vast Enterprises* ***(P-9157)***

Mergent e-mail: customerrelations@mergent.com
1156
2020 California
Manufacturers Register
(P-0000) Products & Services Section entry number
(PA)=Parent Co (HQ)=Headquarters (DH)=Div Headquarters

Liquid Robotics Inc (HQ)........D.......408 636-4200
1329 Moffett Park Dr Sunnyvale (94089) *(P-19704)*
Liquid Robotics Federal Inc........F.......408 636-4200
1329 Moffett Park Dr Sunnyvale (94089) *(P-21065)*
Liquid Technologies Inc........E.......909 393-9475
14425 Yorba Ave Chino (91710) *(P-8534)*
Liquidmetal Technologies Inc (PA)........E.......949 635-2100
20321 Valencia Cir Lake Forest (92630) *(P-11171)*
Liquidspring Technologies Inc........F.......562 941-4344
10400 Pioneer Blvd Ste 1 Santa Fe Springs (90670) *(P-20515)*
Lisa & Lesley Fashion ACC, Sherman Oaks *Also called Lisa and Lesley Co (P-3364)*
Lisa & ME, La Puente *Also called California Fashion Club Inc (P-3263)*
Lisa and Lesley Co........F.......323 877-9878
14140 Ventura Blvd # 101 Sherman Oaks (91423) *(P-3364)*
Lisac Construction, Campbell *Also called Kerrock Countertops Inc (P-4582)*
Lisi Aerospace, City of Industry *Also called Monadnock Company (P-11613)*
Lisi Aerospace North Amer Inc........A.......310 326-8110
2602 Skypark Dr Torrance (90505) *(P-11160)*
Lisi Medical Jeropa Inc (HQ)........D.......760 432-9785
950 Borra Pl Escondido (92029) *(P-13932)*
List Biological Labs Inc........E.......408 866-6363
540 Division St Campbell (95008) *(P-8315)*
List Labs, Campbell *Also called List Biological Labs Inc (P-8315)*
Lite Extrusions Manufacturing........E.......323 770-4298
15025 S Main St Gardena (90248) *(P-9443)*
Lite Line Frame Bags........E.......562 905-3150
535 N Puente St Brea (92821) *(P-10238)*
Lite Machines Corporation........F.......765 463-0959
2222 Faraday Ave Carlsbad (92008) *(P-20601)*
Lite On Technology Intl Inc (HQ)........E.......408 945-0222
720 S Hillview Dr Milpitas (95035) *(P-15275)*
Lite Stone Concrete LLC........F.......619 596-9151
12650 Highway 67 Ste B Lakeside (92040) *(P-10600)*
Litel Instruments Inc........E.......858 546-3788
10650 Scripps Ranch Blvd # 105 San Diego (92131) *(P-21066)*
Litepanels Inc........F.......818 752-7009
20600 Plummer St Chatsworth (91311) *(P-16866)*
Lites On West Soho, Oceanside *Also called Lexstar Inc (P-17050)*
Lith-O-Roll Corporation........E.......626 579-0340
9521 Telstar Ave El Monte (91731) *(P-14330)*
Lithiumstart Inc........E.......800 520-8864
865 Hinckley Rd Burlingame (94010) *(P-18993)*
Lithocraft Co, Anaheim *Also called Man-Grove Industries Inc (P-6713)*
Lithographix Inc (PA)........B.......323 770-1000
12250 Crenshaw Blvd Hawthorne (90250) *(P-6704)*
Lithographix Inc........D.......760 438-3456
6200 Yarrow Dr Carlsbad (92011) *(P-7122)*
Lithotech International LLC........E.......626 443-4210
9950 Baldwin Pl El Monte (91731) *(P-7123)*
Lithotechs Inc........F.......626 433-1333
9950 Baldwin Pl El Monte (91731) *(P-7124)*
Lithotype Company Inc (PA)........D.......650 871-1750
333 Point San Bruno Blvd South San Francisco (94080) *(P-6705)*
Lito........E.......323 260-4692
3730 Union Pacific Ave Los Angeles (90023) *(P-3443)*
Lito Childrens Wear Inc........E.......323 260-4692
3730 Union Pacific Ave Los Angeles (90023) *(P-2968)*
Liton Lighting, Los Angeles *Also called Eema Industries Inc (P-17118)*
Little Brothers Bakery LLC........D.......310 225-3790
320 W Alondra Blvd Gardena (90248) *(P-1236)*
Little Castle Furniture Co Inc........E.......805 278-4646
301 Todd Ct Oxnard (93030) *(P-4653)*
Little Digger Mining & Sup LLC........E.......626 856-3366
3524 Maine Ave Baldwin Park (91706) *(P-5)*
Little Einsteins LLC........F.......818 560-1000
500 S Buena Vista St Burbank (91521) *(P-6118)*
Little Firefighter Corporation........F.......714 834-0410
204 S Center St Santa Ana (92703) *(P-13311)*
Little Folk Visuals, Palm Desert *Also called Lf Visuals Inc (P-2943)*
Little Saigon News Inc........F.......714 265-0800
13861 Seaboard Cir Garden Grove (92843) *(P-5699)*
Live Journal Inc........E.......415 230-3600
6363 Skyline Blvd Oakland (94611) *(P-5700)*
Liveaction Inc (PA)........E.......415 837-3303
3500 W Bayshore Rd Palo Alto (94303) *(P-24103)*
Liveoffice LLC........D.......877 253-2793
900 Corporate Pointe Culver City (90230) *(P-24104)*
Liverpool Jeans, Montebello *Also called Cavern Club LLC (P-3148)*
Livetime Software Inc........E.......415 905-4009
276 Avocado St Apt C102 Costa Mesa (92627) *(P-24105)*
Livewire Innovation, Camarillo *Also called Livewire Test Labs Inc (P-21067)*
Livewire Test Labs Inc........F.......801 293-8300
808 Calle Plano Camarillo (93012) *(P-21067)*
Living Apothecary LLC........F.......917 951-2810
770 National Ct Richmond (94804) *(P-2090)*
Living Tree Community Foods........E.......510 526-7106
1455 5th St Berkeley (94710) *(P-2530)*
Living Waters Logging Inc........F.......707 822-3955
1159 Stromberg Ave Arcata (95521) *(P-3893)*
Living Way Industries Inc........F.......661 298-3200
20734 Centre Pointe Pkwy Santa Clarita (91350) *(P-23148)*
Living Wellness Partners LLC (PA)........E.......800 642-3754
3305 Tyler St Carlsbad (92008) *(P-2531)*
Livingstone Jewelry Co Inc........F.......213 683-1040
631 S Olive St Ste 340 Los Angeles (90014) *(P-22541)*
Livingstons Concrete Svc Inc (PA)........E.......916 334-4313
5416 Roseville Rd North Highlands (95660) *(P-10795)*
Livingstons Concrete Svc Inc........E.......916 334-4313
5416 Roseville Rd North Highlands (95660) *(P-10796)*
Livingstons Concrete Svc Inc........E.......916 334-4313
2915 Lesvos Ct Lincoln (95648) *(P-10797)*
Lixit Corporation (PA)........D.......800 358-8254
100 Coombs St NAPA (94559) *(P-23397)*
Liz Palacios Designs Ltd........E.......628 444-3339
1 Stanton Way Mill Valley (94941) *(P-22988)*
Ljr Blanchard Grinding, Gardena *Also called L J R Grinding Corp (P-16131)*
LL Baker Inc........F.......760 741-9899
431 N Hale Ave Escondido (92029) *(P-6706)*
Llamas Plastics Inc........C.......818 362-0371
12970 Bradley Ave Sylmar (91342) *(P-20157)*
LLC Baker Cummins........D.......925 732-9338
580 Garcia Ave Pittsburg (94565) *(P-8535)*
LLC Lindero Learning Center, Los Angeles *Also called Wanada Investments LLC (P-24573)*
LLC Lyons Magnus (PA)........B.......559 268-5966
3158 E Hamilton Ave Fresno (93702) *(P-790)*
LLC Marsh Perkins........F.......760 880-4558
80080 Via Pessaro La Quinta (92253) *(P-3566)*
Lloyd Design Corporation........D.......818 768-6001
19731 Nordhoff St Northridge (91324) *(P-19705)*
Lloyd E Hennessey Jr........E.......408 842-8437
7200 Alexander St Gilroy (95020) *(P-16147)*
Lloyd Mats, Northridge *Also called Lloyd Design Corporation (P-19705)*
LM Scofield Company (HQ)........E.......323 720-3000
12767 Imperial Hwy Santa Fe Springs (90670) *(P-8990)*
Lmb Heeger, Commerce *Also called Heeger Inc (P-16653)*
LMC Enterprises (PA)........D.......562 602-2116
6401 Alondra Blvd Paramount (90723) *(P-8393)*
LMC Enterprises........E.......310 632-7124
19402 S Susana Rd Compton (90221) *(P-8394)*
Lmg National Publishing Inc........D.......760 241-7744
13891 Park Ave Victorville (92392) *(P-5701)*
LMI, Lodi *Also called Larry Mthvin Installations Inc (P-10374)*
LMI Aerospace Inc........C.......760 597-7066
1351 Specialty Dr Vista (92081) *(P-20158)*
LMI Aerospace Inc........C.......760 599-4477
1377 Specialty Dr Vista (92081) *(P-20159)*
Lmm Enterprises........F.......714 543-8044
1348 E Sunview Dr Orange (92865) *(P-16148)*
LMS Reinforcing Steel Usa LP (PA)........F.......604 598-9930
18059 Rosedale Hwy Bakersfield (93314) *(P-12594)*
Lmw Enterprises LLC........E.......562 944-1969
12309 Telegraph Rd Santa Fe Springs (90670) *(P-15441)*
Lni Custom Manufacturing Inc........E.......310 978-2000
15542 Broadway Center St Gardena (90248) *(P-12494)*
Lnt P/M Inc........F.......714 552-7245
11711 Monarch St Garden Grove (92841) *(P-23398)*
Loaded Boards Inc........F.......310 839-1800
10575 Virginia Ave Culver City (90232) *(P-20415)*
Loanhero Inc........F.......888 912-4376
750 B St Ste 1410 San Diego (92101) *(P-24106)*
Loard's Ice Cream and Candies, San Leandro *Also called Loco Ventures Inc (P-653)*
Lob-Ster Inc (PA)........F.......818 764-6000
7340 Fulton Ave North Hollywood (91605) *(P-22843)*
Lobob Laboratories Inc........E.......408 324-0381
1440 Atteberry Ln San Jose (95131) *(P-7998)*
Lobster Sports, North Hollywood *Also called Lob-Ster Inc (P-22843)*
Lobue Laser & Eye Medical Ctrs........E.......951 696-1135
40740 California Oaks Rd Murrieta (92562) *(P-22272)*
Local Neon Co Inc........E.......310 978-2000
12536 Chadron Ave Hawthorne (90250) *(P-23149)*
Lochaber Cornwall Inc (PA)........F.......714 935-0302
675 N Eckhoff St Ste D Orange (92868) *(P-14769)*
Lochirco Fruit and Produce Inc........E.......559 528-4194
41899 Road 120 Orosi (93647) *(P-1384)*
Locix Inc........F.......650 231-2180
901 Sneath Ln 210 San Bruno (94066) *(P-16731)*
Lock America Inc........F.......951 277-5180
9168 Stellar Ct Corona (92883) *(P-11606)*
Lock-N-Stitch Inc........E.......209 632-2345
1015 S Soderquist Rd Turlock (95380) *(P-14168)*
Lock-Ridge Tool Company Inc........D.......909 865-8309
2000 Pomona Blvd Pomona (91768) *(P-12838)*
Lockhart Collection, Santa Fe Springs *Also called Lockhart Furniture Mfg Inc (P-4654)*
Lockhart Furniture Mfg Inc........D.......562 404-0561
13659 Rosecrans Ave Ste B Santa Fe Springs (90670) *(P-4654)*
Lockheed Martin (HQ)........E.......408 834-9741
1111 Lockheed Martin Way Sunnyvale (94089) *(P-19911)*
Lockheed Martin Aeronautics Co, Edwards *Also called Lockheed Martin Corporation (P-20614)*
Lockheed Martin Aeronautics Co, Palmdale *Also called Lockheed Martin Corporation (P-20618)*
Lockheed Martin Corporation........A.......831 425-6000
4203 Smith Grade Santa Cruz (95060) *(P-20602)*
Lockheed Martin Corporation........F.......619 542-3273
1330 30th St Ste A San Diego (92154) *(P-20603)*
Lockheed Martin Corporation........B.......408 756-1400
1523 Crom St Manteca (95337) *(P-20604)*
Lockheed Martin Corporation........F.......661 572-2974
1001 Lockheed Way Palmdale (93599) *(P-20605)*
Lockheed Martin Corporation........A.......408 734-4980
2770 De La Cruz Blvd Santa Clara (95050) *(P-20606)*
Lockheed Martin Corporation........B.......925 756-4594
4524 Chancery Ln Dublin (94568) *(P-20607)*
Lockheed Martin Corporation........D.......831 425-6000
16020 Empire Grade Santa Cruz (95060) *(P-20448)*
Lockheed Martin Corporation........B.......408 756-1868
1105 Remington Ct Sunnyvale (94087) *(P-20608)*

Lockheed Martin Corporation........B.......805 686-4069
153 Industrial Way Buellton (93427) ***(P-20609)***
Lockheed Martin Corporation........D.......408 756-5751
1111 Lockheed Martin Way Sunnyvale (94089) ***(P-20449)***
Lockheed Martin Corporation........A.......408 473-3000
3130 Zanker Rd San Jose (95134) ***(P-17573)***
Lockheed Martin Corporation........A.......650 424-2000
3251 Hanover St Palo Alto (94304) ***(P-20610)***
Lockheed Martin Corporation........B.......805 606-4860
Bldg 8310 Lompoc (93437) ***(P-17574)***
Lockheed Martin Corporation........F.......408 781-8570
266 Caspian Dr Sunnyvale (94089) ***(P-20611)***
Lockheed Martin Corporation........A.......408 473-7498
3100 Zanker Rd San Jose (95134) ***(P-20612)***
Lockheed Martin Corporation........B.......408 747-2626
160 E Tasman Dr San Jose (95134) ***(P-20450)***
Lockheed Martin Corporation........A.......805 614-3671
3201 Airpark Dr Ste 204 Santa Maria (93455) ***(P-20613)***
Lockheed Martin Corporation........A.......661 277-0691
225 N Flightline Rd Edwards (93524) ***(P-20614)***
Lockheed Martin Corporation........E.......408 742-6688
1111 Lockheed Martin Way Sunnyvale (94089) ***(P-20615)***
Lockheed Martin Corporation........A.......408 742-4321
1111 Lockheed Martin Way Sunnyvale (94089) ***(P-20451)***
Lockheed Martin Corporation........C.......858 740-5100
10325 Meanley Dr San Diego (92131) ***(P-20616)***
Lockheed Martin Corporation........E.......805 650-4600
2895 Golf Course Dr Ventura (93003) ***(P-20617)***
Lockheed Martin Corporation........A.......661 572-7428
1011 Lockheed Way Palmdale (93599) ***(P-20618)***
Lockheed Martin Corporation........D.......831 425-6375
16020 Empire Grade Santa Cruz (95060) ***(P-20619)***
Lockheed Martin Corporation........D.......805 571-2346
346 Bollay Dr Goleta (93117) ***(P-20620)***
Lockheed Martin Corporation........A.......408 756-5836
1111 Lockheed Martin Way Sunnyvale (94089) ***(P-20621)***
Lockheed Martin Corporation........C.......858 740-5100
10325 Meanley Dr San Diego (92131) ***(P-20622)***
Lockheed Martin Corporation........B.......661 572-7363
22630 Aguadero Pl Santa Clarita (91350) ***(P-20623)***
Lockheed Martin Corporation........B.......408 756-3008
2655 S Macarthur Dr Tracy (95376) ***(P-19912)***
Lockheed Martin Corporation........B.......408 756-4386
1643 Kitchener Dr Sunnyvale (94087) ***(P-20624)***
Lockheed Martin Corporation........F.......408 742-4321
1111 Lockheed Martin Way Sunnyvale (94089) ***(P-20625)***
Lockheed Martin Corporation........B.......408 742-5219
1374 Holland Ct San Jose (95118) ***(P-19913)***
Lockheed Martin Corporation........C.......760 446-1700
1121 W Reeves Ave Ridgecrest (93555) ***(P-20626)***
Lockheed Martin Corporation........B.......619 298-8453
1330 30th St Ste A San Diego (92154) ***(P-19914)***
Lockheed Martin Naval, Ridgecrest *Also called Lockheed Martin Corporation* ***(P-20626)***
Lockheed Martin Space Sys, Santa Cruz *Also called Lockheed Martin Corporation* ***(P-20619)***
Lockwood Industries LLC........C.......661 702-6999
28525 Industry Dr Valencia (91355) ***(P-18357)***
Lockwood Vineyard (PA)........F.......831 642-9566
9777 Blue Larkspur Ln # 101 Monterey (93940) ***(P-1803)***
Loco Ventures Inc........E.......510 351-0405
2000 Wayne Ave San Leandro (94577) ***(P-653)***
Lodestone LLC........F.......714 970-0900
4769 E Wesley Dr Anaheim (92807) ***(P-14244)***
Lodestone Pacific, Anaheim *Also called R H Barden Inc* ***(P-18737)***
Lodi Iron Works Inc (PA)........E.......209 368-5395
820 S Sacramento St Lodi (95240) ***(P-11145)***
Lodi Iron Works Inc........F.......209 368-5395
609 W Amador St Galt (95632) ***(P-11146)***
Lodi Mail Express, Lodi *Also called Lodi News Sentinel* ***(P-5702)***
Lodi News Sentinel........D.......209 369-2761
125 N Church St Lodi (95240) ***(P-5702)***
Log(n) LLC........F.......323 839-4538
5651 Dreyer Pl Oakland (94619) ***(P-6274)***
Logan Smith Machine Co........F.......916 632-2692
4190 Citrus Ave Rocklin (95677) ***(P-16149)***
Logi Graphics Incorporated........F.......714 841-3686
17592 Metzler Ln Huntington Beach (92647) ***(P-17915)***
Logic Beach Inc (PA)........F.......619 698-3300
8363 Center Dr Ste 6f La Mesa (91942) ***(P-20900)***
Logic Technology Inc (PA)........F.......408 530-1007
1138 W Evelyn Ave Sunnyvale (94086) ***(P-5366)***
Logico LLC........F.......619 600-5198
6020 Progressive Ave # 900 San Diego (92154) ***(P-11308)***
Logicool Inc........E.......408 907-1344
1825 De La Cruz Blvd # 201 Santa Clara (95050) ***(P-24107)***
Logicube Inc (PA)........E.......888 494-8832
19755 Nordhoff Pl Chatsworth (91311) ***(P-15276)***
Loginext Solutions Inc........D.......339 244-0380
5002 Spring Crest Ter Fremont (94536) ***(P-24108)***
Logisterra Inc........E.......619 280-9992
6190 Fairmount Ave Ste K San Diego (92120) ***(P-10198)***
Logistical Support LLC........C.......818 341-3344
20409 Prairie St Chatsworth (91311) ***(P-19970)***
Logitech Inc........E.......510 795-8500
3 Jenner Ste 180 Irvine (92618) ***(P-15277)***
Logitech Inc (HQ)........B.......510 795-8500
7700 Gateway Blvd Newark (94560) ***(P-15278)***
Logitech Streaming Media Inc........E.......510 795-8500
7600 Gateway Blvd Newark (94560) ***(P-18994)***
Logo Joes Inc........F.......951 461-0388
41695 Elm St Ste 101 Murrieta (92562) ***(P-3747)***
Logos Plus Inc........F.......562 634-3009
8130 Rosecrans Ave Paramount (90723) ***(P-3797)***
Lois A Valeskie........F.......415 641-2570
775 Congo St San Francisco (94131) ***(P-21500)***
Loleta Cheese Company Inc........F.......707 733-5470
252 Loleta Dr Loleta (95551) ***(P-567)***
Lollicup Tea Zone, Chino *Also called Lollicup USA Inc* ***(P-5308)***
Lollicup USA Inc (HQ)........E.......626 965-8882
6185 Kimball Ave Chino (91708) ***(P-5308)***
Loma Linda University........E.......909 558-4552
24951 Stewart St Loma Linda (92350) ***(P-6707)***
Loma Scientific International........E.......310 539-8655
3115 Kashiwa St Torrance (90505) ***(P-17575)***
Loma Vista Medical Inc........F.......650 490-4747
863a Mitten Rd Ste 100a Burlingame (94010) ***(P-21780)***
Lombard Enterprises Inc........E.......562 692-7070
3619 San Gbriel Rver Pkwy Pico Rivera (90660) ***(P-6708)***
Lombard Graphics, Pico Rivera *Also called Lombard Enterprises Inc* ***(P-6708)***
Lombard Medical Tech Inc (PA)........E.......949 379-3750
6440 Oak Cyn Ste 200 Irvine (92618) ***(P-21781)***
Lomeli's Gardens, Lockeford *Also called Lomelis Statuary Inc* ***(P-11009)***
Lomelis Statuary Inc (PA)........E.......209 367-1131
11921 E Brandt Rd Lockeford (95237) ***(P-11009)***
Lompoc Tortilla Shop, Lompoc *Also called Rodriguez Ismael* ***(P-2341)***
Long Bar Grinding Inc........F.......562 921-1983
13121 Arctic Cir Santa Fe Springs (90670) ***(P-16150)***
Long Beach Business Journal, Long Beach *Also called South Coast Publishing Inc* ***(P-5832)***
Long Beach City of, Long Beach *Also called Stearns Park* ***(P-4873)***
Long Beach Creamery LLC........F.......562 252-2730
4141 Long Beach Blvd Long Beach (90807) ***(P-654)***
Long Beach Enterprise Inc (PA)........E.......562 944-8945
12319 Florence Ave Santa Fe Springs (90670) ***(P-2262)***
Long Beach Navy Dispatch, San Diego *Also called Western States Weeklies Inc* ***(P-5865)***
Long Beach Seafoods Co........E.......562 432-7300
4643 Hackett Ave Lakewood (90713) ***(P-2263)***
Long Beach Woodworks LLC........F.......562 437-2293
1261 Highland Ave Glendale (91202) ***(P-4377)***
Long Machine Inc........E.......951 296-0194
27450 Colt Ct Temecula (92590) ***(P-16151)***
Long Pine Leathers, Vernon *Also called Jejomi Designs Inc* ***(P-3517)***
Longevity Global Inc........E.......877 566-4462
23591 Foley St Hayward (94545) ***(P-14245)***
Longi Solar Technology US Inc........F.......925 380-6084
2603 Camino Ramon Ste 423 San Ramon (94583) ***(P-18358)***
Lonix Pharmaceutical Inc........F.......626 287-4700
5001 Earle Ave Rosemead (91770) ***(P-602)***
Looka Patisserie, Pacifica *Also called The French Patisserie Inc* ***(P-1286)***
Looker Data Sciences Inc (PA)........D.......831 244-0340
101 Church St Fl 4 Santa Cruz (95060) ***(P-15053)***
Lookout Enterprises Inc........F.......323 969-0178
11468 Dona Teresa Dr North Hollywood (91604) ***(P-2337)***
Lopez Pallets Inc........F.......909 823-0865
11080 Redwood Ave Fontana (92337) ***(P-4378)***
Lopez Water Treatment Plant........F.......805 473-7152
2845 Lopez Dr Arroyo Grande (93420) ***(P-15537)***
Lor-Van Manufacturing LLC........E.......408 980-1045
3307 Edward Ave Santa Clara (95054) ***(P-12267)***
Loran Inc........E.......405 340-0660
1705 E Colton Ave Redlands (92374) ***(P-16560)***
Lorber Industries California........B.......310 275-1568
823 N Roxbury Dr Beverly Hills (90210) ***(P-2828)***
Lorber Industries of Claif, Beverly Hills *Also called Lorber Industries California* ***(P-2828)***
Lord Leviason Enterprises LLC........E.......818 453-8245
17337 Ventura Blvd Ste 10 Encino (91316) ***(P-1544)***
Loren Electric Sign & Lighting, Whittier *Also called Loren Industries* ***(P-23150)***
Loren Industries........E.......562 699-1122
12226 Coast Dr Whittier (90601) ***(P-23150)***
Lorenz Inc........B.......760 427-1815
1749 Stergios Rd Calexico (92231) ***(P-19348)***
Lorimar Communications, El Cajon *Also called Lorimar Group Inc* ***(P-17576)***
Lorimar Group Inc........F.......619 954-9300
1488 Pioneer Way Ste 14 El Cajon (92020) ***(P-17576)***
Loritz & Associates Inc........E.......714 694-0200
24895 La Palma Ave Yorba Linda (92887) ***(P-9879)***
Lormac Plastics Inc (PA)........F.......760 745-9115
2225 Meyers Ave Escondido (92029) ***(P-9880)***
Lorom West, Fremont *Also called Cable Connection Inc* ***(P-16879)***
Lorton's Fresh Squeezed Juices, San Bernardino *Also called Juice Heads Inc* ***(P-780)***
Lortz & Son Mfg Co........C.......281 241-9418
4042 Patton Way Bakersfield (93308) ***(P-13042)***
Lortz Manufacturing, Bakersfield *Also called Lortz & Son Mfg Co* ***(P-13042)***
Los Altos Town Crier, Los Altos *Also called Select Communications Inc* ***(P-6025)***
Los Angeles Ale Works LLC........F.......213 422-6569
12918 Cerise Ave Hawthorne (90250) ***(P-1545)***
Los Angeles Board Mills Inc........C.......323 685-8900
6027 S Eastern Ave Commerce (90040) ***(P-5166)***
Los Angeles Brass Products, Huntington Park *Also called Los Angles Pump Valve Pdts Inc* ***(P-14589)***
Los Angeles Bus Jurnl Assoc........E.......323 549-5225
5700 Wilshire Blvd # 170 Los Angeles (90036) ***(P-5979)***
Los Angeles Business Journal, Los Angeles *Also called Cbj LP* ***(P-5899)***
Los Angeles Downtown News, Los Angeles *Also called Civic Center News Inc* ***(P-5592)***
Los Angeles Fiber Co, Vernon *Also called Marspring Corporation* ***(P-4730)***
Los Angeles Galvanizing Co........D.......323 583-2263
2518 E 53rd St Huntington Park (90255) ***(P-13202)***
Los Angeles Ltg Mfg Co Inc........D.......626 454-8300
10141 Olney St El Monte (91731) ***(P-17053)***

Mergent e-mail: customerrelations@mergent.com
1158
2020 California
Manufacturers Register
(P-0000) Products & Services Section entry number
(PA)=Parent Co (HQ)=Headquarters (DH)=Div Headquarters

Los Angeles Mills Inc .... E....424 307-0075
2331 E 8th St Los Angeles (90021) *(P-2702)*
Los Angeles Plant, Cypress *Also called Hitachi Automotive Systems* *(P-16655)*
Los Angeles Poultry Co Inc .... D....323 232-1619
4816 Long Beach Ave Los Angeles (90058) *(P-521)*
Los Angeles Ppr Box & Bd Mills, Commerce *Also called Los Angeles Board Mills Inc (P-5166)*
Los Angeles Refining Co .... F....310 522-6000
2101 E Pacific Coast Hwy Wilmington (90744) *(P-9051)*
Los Angeles Sales Office-North, Simi Valley *Also called Weyerhaeuser Company (P-5285)*
Los Angeles Sentinel Inc .... D....323 299-3800
3800 Crenshaw Blvd Los Angeles (90008) *(P-5703)*
Los Angeles Sleeve Co Inc .... E....562 945-7578
12051 Rivera Rd Santa Fe Springs (90670) *(P-19706)*
Los Angeles Wraps, Torrance *Also called Sirena Incorporated* *(P-7215)*
Los Angles Pump Valve Pdts Inc .... E....323 277-7788
2528 E 57th St Huntington Park (90255) *(P-14589)*
Los Angles Tmes Cmmnctions LLC (PA) .... C....213 237-5000
2300 E Imperial Hwy El Segundo (90245) *(P-5704)*
Los Angles Tmes Cmmnctions LLC .... D....310 450-6666
1717 4th St Ste 100 Santa Monica (90401) *(P-5705)*
Los Angles Tmes Cmmnctions LLC .... C....213 237-7203
1245 S Longwood Ave Los Angeles (90019) *(P-5706)*
Los Angles Tmes Cmmnctions LLC .... B....714 966-5600
10540 Talbert Ave 300w Fountain Valley (92708) *(P-5707)*
Los Angles Tmes Cmmnctions LLC .... D....818 637-3203
1011 E Wilson Ave Fl 2 Glendale (91206) *(P-5708)*
Los Angles Tmes Cmmnctions LLC .... E....805 238-2720
705 Pine St Paso Robles (93446) *(P-5709)*
Los Angles Tmes Cmmnctions LLC .... F....415 274-9000
388 Market St Ste 1550 San Francisco (94111) *(P-5710)*
Los Angles Tmes Cmmnctions LLC .... E....818 790-8774
1061 Valley Sun Ln La Canada Flintridge (91011) *(P-5711)*
Los Angles Tmes Cmmnctions LLC .... E....951 683-6066
10427 San Sevaine Way E Jurupa Valley (91752) *(P-5712)*
Los Angles Tmes Cmmnctions LLC .... E....213 237-7987
145 S Spring St Los Angeles (90012) *(P-5713)*
Los Angles Tmes Cmmnctions LLC .... C....213 237-5691
2000 E 8th St Los Angeles (90021) *(P-5714)*
Los Angles Tmes Cmmnctions LLC .... F....310 638-9414
2001 E Cashdan St Compton (90220) *(P-5715)*
Los Banos Abattoir Co Inc .... E....209 826-2212
1312 W Pacheco Blvd Los Banos (93635) *(P-416)*
Los Banos Enterprise, Los Banos *Also called McClatchy Newspapers Inc* *(P-5732)*
Los Banos Rock and Ready Mix, Los Banos *Also called Azusa Rock Inc* *(P-10694)*
Los Cabos Mexican Foods, Santa Fe Springs *Also called M C I Foods Inc* *(P-2536)*
Los Gatos Tomato Products LLC (PA) .... E....559 945-2700
7041 N Van Ness Blvd Fresno (93711) *(P-791)*
Los Olivos Packaging Inc (PA) .... C....323 261-2218
929 Ridgecrest St Monterey Park (91754) *(P-792)*
Los Pericos Food Products LLC .... E....909 623-5625
2301 Valley Blvd Pomona (91768) *(P-2532)*
Lost Art Liquids, Los Angeles *Also called Lost Art Liquids LLC* *(P-23399)*
Lost Art Liquids LLC .... F....213 816-2988
155 W Washington Blvd Los Angeles (90015) *(P-23399)*
Lost Coast Brewery & Cafe, Eureka *Also called Table Bluff Brewing Inc* *(P-1568)*
Lost Dutchmans Minings Assn (HQ) .... E....951 699-4749
43445 Bus Pk Dr Ste 113 Temecula (92590) *(P-6)*
Lost International LLC .... F....949 600-6950
170 Technology Dr Irvine (92618) *(P-3105)*
Lotus Beverages .... F....213 216-1434
2542 San Gabriel Blvd Rosemead (91770) *(P-1804)*
Lotus Hygiene Systems Inc .... E....714 259-8805
1621 E Saint Andrew Pl Santa Ana (92705) *(P-10467)*
Lotus Labels, Brea *Also called President Enterprise Inc* *(P-7179)*
Lotus Orient Corp (PA) .... F....626 285-5796
411 S California St San Gabriel (91776) *(P-3243)*
Lotusflare Inc .... F....626 695-5634
530 Lakeside Dr Ste 130 Sunnyvale (94085) *(P-24109)*
Lotw Light of World .... F....805 278-4806
1301 Maulhardt Ave Oxnard (93030) *(P-18995)*
Lou Ana Foods, Brea *Also called Ventura Foods LLC* *(P-1485)*
Loud Mouth Inc .... E....619 743-0370
3840 Edna Pl Apt 1 San Diego (92116) *(P-22844)*
Louden Madelon, Vernon *Also called National Corset Supply House* *(P-3445)*
Louidar LLC .... E....951 676-5047
33820 Rancho Cal Rd Temecula (92591) *(P-1805)*
Louie Foods International .... F....559 264-2745
471 S Teilman Ave Fresno (93706) *(P-2533)*
Louis Levin & Son Inc .... F....562 802-8066
13550 Larwin Cir Santa Fe Springs (90670) *(P-13981)*
Louis M. Martini Winery, Saint Helena *Also called E & J Gallo Winery* *(P-1686)*
Louis Roesch Company .... F....650 212-2052
289 Foster City Blvd B Foster City (94404) *(P-6709)*
Louis Sardo Upholstery Inc (PA) .... D....310 327-0532
512 W Rosecrans Ave Gardena (90248) *(P-4864)*
Louis Vuitton US Mfg Inc .... F....909 599-2411
321 W Covina Blvd San Dimas (91773) *(P-10239)*
Louis W Osborn Co., La Mirada *Also called Headwaters Construction Inc* *(P-10416)*
Louise Green Millinery Co Inc .... F....310 479-1881
1616 Cotner Ave Los Angeles (90025) *(P-3469)*
Lounge Fly, Chatsworth *Also called Loungefly LLC* *(P-22989)*
Loungefly LLC .... E....818 718-5600
20310 Plummer St Chatsworth (91311) *(P-22989)*
Loupe, San Francisco *Also called Plangrid Inc* *(P-24301)*
Love In, Los Angeles *Also called Bereshith Inc* *(P-3140)*
Love Marks Inc (PA) .... F....323 859-8770
2050 E 51st St Vernon (90058) *(P-3176)*

Love Stitch, Los Angeles *Also called Clothing Illustrated Inc* *(P-3306)*
Lovestrength LLC .... F....760 481-9951
865 Arbor Glen Ln Vista (92081) *(P-3567)*
Low Voltage Architecture Inc .... E....310 573-7588
11715 San Vicente Blvd Los Angeles (90049) *(P-19349)*
Lowers Industrial Supply, Santa Fe Springs *Also called Lowers Wldg & Fabrication Inc (P-16152)*
Lowers Wldg & Fabrication Inc .... F....562 946-4521
10847 Painter Ave Santa Fe Springs (90670) *(P-16152)*
Lowpensky Moulding .... F....415 822-7422
900 Palou Ave San Francisco (94124) *(P-4076)*
Loyyal Corporation .... F....415 419-9590
44 Tehama St Fl 5 San Francisco (94105) *(P-24110)*
Lozano Enterprises, Los Angeles *Also called La Opinion LP* *(P-5688)*
Lpa Insurance Agency Inc .... D....916 286-7850
3800 Watt Ave Ste 147 Sacramento (95821) *(P-24111)*
Lpcc 6008, Ontario *Also called Leggett & Platt Incorporated* *(P-4727)*
Lpj Aerospace LLC .... F....310 834-5700
741 E 223rd St Carson (90745) *(P-20160)*
Lpn Wireless Inc .... F....707 781-9210
4170 Redwood Hwy San Rafael (94903) *(P-17577)*
Lps Agency Sales and Posting .... F....714 247-7500
3210 El Camino Real # 200 Irvine (92602) *(P-7125)*
LR Baggs Corporation .... E....805 929-3545
483 N Frontage Rd Nipomo (93444) *(P-22629)*
Lrad Corporation (PA) .... E....858 676-1112
16262 W Bernardo Dr San Diego (92127) *(P-17252)*
Lrb Millwork & Casework Inc .... F....951 328-0105
2760 S Iowa Ave Colton (92324) *(P-4077)*
Lrc Coil Company, Santa Fe Springs *Also called Lmw Enterprises LLC* *(P-15441)*
Lshuver Inc .... F....310 323-2326
3880 Redondo Beach Blvd Torrance (90504) *(P-6710)*
LSI Corporation (HQ) .... A....408 433-8000
1320 Ridder Park Dr San Jose (95131) *(P-18359)*
LSI Corporation .... E....619 312-0903
9745 Prospect Ave Santee (92071) *(P-18360)*
LSI Corporation .... E....800 372-2447
2 Park Plz Ste 440 Irvine (92614) *(P-18361)*
LSI Corporation .... F....408 436-8379
1310 Ridder Park Dr San Jose (95131) *(P-18362)*
LSI Logic, Irvine *Also called LSI Corporation* *(P-18361)*
LSI Products Inc .... D....951 343-9270
12885 Wildflower Ln Riverside (92503) *(P-19707)*
Lsl Instruments, Santa Clarita *Also called Manzanita* *(P-22630)*
Lso, San Diego *Also called Cri 2000 LP* *(P-4499)*
Lspace America LLC .... E....949 596-8726
9821 Irvine Center Dr Irvine (92618) *(P-3177)*
Lt Foods Americas Inc (HQ) .... E....562 340-4040
11130 Warland Dr Cypress (90630) *(P-1006)*
Lt Security Inc .... E....626 435-2838
18738 San Jose Ave City of Industry (91748) *(P-19350)*
Ltd Tech Inc .... F....805 480-1886
2630 Lavery Ct Ste B Newbury Park (91320) *(P-14274)*
LTI, Irvine *Also called Lens Technology I LLC* *(P-21374)*
LTI Boyd .... A....800 554-0200
600 S Mcclure Rd Modesto (95357) *(P-14275)*
LTI Holdings Inc (HQ) .... F....209 236-1111
600 S Mcclure Rd Modesto (95357) *(P-7632)*
Ltr, South Gate *Also called Lunday-Thagard Company* *(P-9160)*
Lubeco Inc .... E....562 602-1791
6859 Downey Ave Long Beach (90805) *(P-9150)*
Lubrication Scientifics Inc .... F....714 557-0664
17651 Armstrong Ave Irvine (92614) *(P-13312)*
Lubrication Scientifics LLC .... E....714 557-0664
17651 Armstrong Ave Irvine (92614) *(P-14835)*
Lubrigreen, Irvine *Also called Biosynthetic Technologies LLC* *(P-14350)*
LUBRIZOL ADVANCED MATERIALS, INC., Paso Robles *Also called Lubrizol Advanced Mtls Inc (P-8991)*
Lubrizol Advanced Mtls Inc .... D....805 239-1550
3115 Propeller Dr Paso Robles (93446) *(P-8991)*
Lubrizol Corporation .... F....925 352-4843
344 Clyde Dr Walnut Creek (94598) *(P-8992)*
Lubrizol Corporation .... F....949 212-1863
30211 Ave D Las Bandras Rancho Santa Margari (92688) *(P-8993)*
Luca International Group LLC (PA) .... F....510 498-8829
39650 Liberty St Ste 490 Fremont (94538) *(P-128)*
Lucas Labs, Gilroy *Also called Lucas/Signatone Corporation* *(P-21068)*
Lucas Oil Products Inc (PA) .... C....951 270-0154
302 N Sheridan St Corona (92880) *(P-9151)*
Lucas/Signatone Corporation (PA) .... E....408 848-2851
393 Tomkins Ct Ste J Gilroy (95020) *(P-21068)*
Luce Communications LLC .... E....951 361-7404
3810 Wabash Dr Jurupa Valley (91752) *(P-6711)*
Lucerne Foods Inc .... E....925 951-4724
5918 Stoneridge Mall Rd Pleasanton (94588) *(P-2534)*
Lucero Cables Inc .... C....408 536-0340
193 Stauffer Blvd San Jose (95125) *(P-18996)*
Lucid Motors, Newark *Also called Atieva Usa Inc* *(P-19455)*
Lucidport Technology Inc .... F....408 720-8800
19287 San Marcos Rd Saratoga (95070) *(P-16914)*
Lucio Family Enterprises Inc .... E....510 623-2323
2150 Prune Ave Fremont (94539) *(P-12268)*
Lucira Health Inc .... F....510 350-8071
1412 62nd St Emeryville (94608) *(P-21782)*
Lucite Intl Prtnr Holdings Inc .... E....760 929-0001
5441 Avd Encinas Ste B Carlsbad (92008) *(P-22845)*
Lucix Corporation (HQ) .... D....805 987-6645
800 Avenida Acaso Ste E Camarillo (93012) *(P-18997)*

Employee Codes: A=Over 500 employees, B=251-500
C=101-250, D=51-100, E=20-50, F=10-19

2020 California
Manfacturers Register

© Mergent Inc. 1-800-342-5647

1159

**A
L
P
H
A
B
E
T
I
C**

Lucky Brand Dungarees LLC (PA) ....D....213 443-5700
540 S Santa Fe Ave Los Angeles (90013) ***(P-3015)***
Lucky Brand Jeans, Los Angeles *Also called Lucky Brand Dungarees LLC* ***(P-3015)***
Lucky Devil LLC ....F....714 990-2237
431 Atlas St Brea (92821) ***(P-7126)***
Lucky Foods, San Francisco *Also called Sin MA Imports Company* ***(P-1062)***
Lucky Luke Brewing Company ....F....661 270-5588
610 W Avenue O Ste 104 Palmdale (93551) ***(P-1546)***
Lucky Star Silkscreen LLC ....E....323 728-4071
5767 E Washington Blvd Commerce (90040) ***(P-7127)***
Lucky Strike Entertainment Inc (PA) ....E....818 933-3752
15260 Ventura Blvd # 1110 Sherman Oaks (91403) ***(P-22846)***
Lucky-13 Apparel, Los Alamitos *Also called Blue Sphere Inc* ***(P-2961)***
Lucy Ann, Torrance *Also called Obatake Inc* ***(P-22556)***
Lufft Usa Inc ....F....805 335-8500
1110 Eugenia Pl Ste 200 Carpinteria (93013) ***(P-21501)***
Lufkin Industries LLC ....F....661 746-0792
3901 Fanucchi Way Shafter (93263) ***(P-12713)***
Luis Wtkins Cstm Wrught Ir LLC ....E....310 836-5655
3737 S Durango Ave Los Angeles (90034) ***(P-4695)***
Luma Comfort LLC ....E....855 963-9247
6600 Katella Ave Cypress (90630) ***(P-16833)***
Lumar Metals, Pomona *Also called Lur Inc* ***(P-12495)***
Lumascape USA Inc ....F....650 595-5862
1300 Industrial Rd Ste 19 San Carlos (94070) ***(P-17054)***
Lumasense Tech Holdings Inc (HQ) ....D....408 727-1600
3301 Leonard Ct Santa Clara (95054) ***(P-22273)***
Lumatronix Mfg Inc ....F....408 435-7820
1141 Ringwood Ct Ste 150 San Jose (95131) ***(P-16791)***
Lumenis, Livermore *Also called Rh Usa Inc* ***(P-21881)***
Lumenis Inc (HQ) ....C....408 764-3000
2077 Gateway Pl Ste 300 San Jose (95110) ***(P-21783)***
Lumens Audio Visual Inc ....F....970 988-6268
127 27th St Apt A Newport Beach (92663) ***(P-17743)***
Lumens Integration Inc ....F....510 657-8367
4116 Clipper Ct Fremont (94538) ***(P-22438)***
Lumenton Inc ....E....323 904-0202
5461 W Jefferson Blvd Los Angeles (90016) ***(P-17141)***
Lumenton Lighting, Los Angeles *Also called Lumenton Inc* ***(P-17141)***
Lumentum Holdings Inc (PA) ....C....408 546-5483
400 N Mccarthy Blvd Milpitas (95035) ***(P-17744)***
Lumentum Operations LLC (HQ) ....C....408 546-5483
400 N Mccarthy Blvd Milpitas (95035) ***(P-17745)***
Lumentum Operations LLC ....F....408 546-5483
1750 Automation Pkwy # 400 San Jose (95131) ***(P-21376)***
Lumenyte International Corp ....F....949 279-8687
535 4th St San Fernando (91340) ***(P-17142)***
Lumigrow Inc ....E....800 514-0487
6550 Vallejo St Ste 200 Emeryville (94608) ***(P-17055)***
Lumileds LLC (HQ) ....E....408 964-2900
370 W Trimble Rd San Jose (95131) ***(P-21069)***
Luminar Creations ....E....818 843-0010
420 N Moss St Burbank (91502) ***(P-22542)***
Lumination Lighting & Tech Inc ....C....855 283-1100
1515 240th St Harbor City (90710) ***(P-17056)***
Luminit LLC (PA) ....E....310 320-1066
1850 W 205th St Torrance (90501) ***(P-21377)***
Luminus Inc (HQ) ....C....408 708-7000
1145 Sonora Ct Sunnyvale (94086) ***(P-17057)***
Luminus Devices Inc ....E....978 528-8000
1145 Sonora Ct Sunnyvale (94086) ***(P-17143)***
Lumio Inc ....F....586 861-2408
6355 Topanga Canyon Blvd # 335 Woodland Hills (91367) ***(P-18363)***
Lumistar Inc (HQ) ....F....760 431-2181
2270 Camino Vida Roble L Carlsbad (92011) ***(P-17916)***
Luna Imaging Inc ....F....323 908-1400
2702 Media Center Dr Los Angeles (90065) ***(P-24112)***
Luna Mora LLC ....F....310 550-6979
1240 S Corning St Apt 306 Los Angeles (90035) ***(P-3798)***
Luna Sciences Corporation ....F....949 225-0000
18218 Mcdurmott E Ste A Irvine (92614) ***(P-16978)***
Luna Vineyards Inc ....E....707 255-2474
2921 Silverado Trl NAPA (94558) ***(P-1806)***
Lunas Sheet Metal Inc ....F....408 492-1260
3125 Molinaro St Ste 102 Santa Clara (95054) ***(P-12269)***
Lund Motion Products Inc ....E....949 221-0023
15651 Mosher Ave Tustin (92780) ***(P-19708)***
Lunday-Thagard Company (HQ) ....C....562 928-7000
9302 Garfield Ave South Gate (90280) ***(P-9160)***
Lunday-Thagard Company ....E....562 928-6990
9301 Garfield Ave South Gate (90280) ***(P-9119)***
Lundberg Designs, San Francisco *Also called Thomas Lundberg* ***(P-4703)***
Lundberg Family Farms, Richvale *Also called Wehah Farm Inc* ***(P-1054)***
Lundberg Studios Inc ....E....831 423-2532
131 Old Coast Rd Davenport (95017) ***(P-10375)***
Lundberg Survey Inc ....E....805 383-2400
911 Via Alondra Camarillo (93012) ***(P-5980)***
Lundia ....B....888 989-1370
449 Borrego Ct San Dimas (91773) ***(P-4587)***
Lupitas Bakery Inc (PA) ....F....323 752-2391
1848 W Florence Ave Los Angeles (90047) ***(P-1237)***
Luppen Holdings Inc (PA) ....E....323 581-8121
3050 Leonis Blvd Vernon (90058) ***(P-12839)***
Lur Inc ....F....909 623-4999
599 S East End Ave Pomona (91766) ***(P-12495)***
Luran Inc ....F....661 257-6303
24927 Avenue Tibbitts K Valencia (91355) ***(P-16153)***
Lusida Rubber Products ....F....323 446-0280
2540 Corp Pl Ste B103 Alhambra (91803) ***(P-9330)***
Lusk Quality Machine Products ....E....661 272-0630
39457 15th St E Palmdale (93550) ***(P-16154)***
Luster Cote Inc ....F....909 355-9995
10841 Business Dr Fontana (92337) ***(P-13203)***
Lustre-Cal Nameplate Corp ....D....209 370-1600
715 S Guild Ave Lodi (95240) ***(P-12595)***
Luther E Gibson Inc ....E....707 643-6104
544 Curtola Pkwy Vallejo (94590) ***(P-5981)***
Luus Family Corp ....E....209 466-1952
302 S San Joaquin St Stockton (95203) ***(P-522)***
Luxbright Inc ....F....323 871-4120
685 Cochran St Ste 200 Simi Valley (93065) ***(P-17058)***
Luxco Holdings LLC ....F....626 888-7688
6465 Lorena Ave Jurupa Valley (91752) ***(P-9881)***
Luxe Laboratory ....F....714 221-2330
7052 Orangewood Ave Ste 8 Garden Grove (92841) ***(P-22370)***
Luxfer Gas Cylinder, Riverside *Also called Luxfer Inc* ***(P-20161)***
Luxfer Inc (HQ) ....D....951 684-5110
3016 Kansas Ave Bldg 1 Riverside (92507) ***(P-20161)***
Luxfer Inc ....C....951 684-5110
1995 3rd St Riverside (92507) ***(P-11236)***
Luxfer Inc ....E....951 351-4100
6825 Jurupa Ave Riverside (92504) ***(P-12734)***
Luxfer-GTM Technologies LLC (PA) ....E....415 856-0570
1619 Shattuck Ave Berkeley (94709) ***(P-12027)***
Luxor Industries International ....E....909 469-4757
1250 E Franklin Ave Pomona (91766) ***(P-4078)***
Luxtera LLC ....C....760 448-3520
2320 Camino Vida Roble # 100 Carlsbad (92011) ***(P-18364)***
Luxtera, Inc., Carlsbad *Also called Luxtera LLC* ***(P-18364)***
Lvusm, San Dimas *Also called Louis Vuitton US Mfg Inc* ***(P-10239)***
Lw Consulting Services LLC ....F....650 919-3001
13292 Rhoda Dr Los Altos Hills (94022) ***(P-24113)***
Ly Brothers Corporation (PA) ....E....510 782-2118
1963 Sabre St Hayward (94545) ***(P-1238)***
Ly Brothers Corporation ....C....510 782-2118
20389 Corsair Blvd Hayward (94545) ***(P-1239)***
Lynam Industries Inc ....D....951 360-1919
13050 Santa Ana Ave Fontana (92337) ***(P-12270)***
Lyncean Technologies Inc ....F....650 320-8300
47633 Westinghouse Dr Fremont (94539) ***(P-22215)***
Lynch Ready Mix Concrete Co ....F....805 647-2817
11011 Azahar St Ste 4 Ventura (93004) ***(P-10798)***
Lynco Grinding Company Inc ....F....562 927-2631
5950 Clara St Bell (90201) ***(P-16155)***
Lyncole Grunding Solutions LLC ....E....310 214-4000
3547 Voyager St Ste 204 Torrance (90503) ***(P-16915)***
Lyncole Xit Grounding, Torrance *Also called Lyncole Grunding Solutions LLC* ***(P-16915)***
Lynde-Ordway Company Inc ....F....714 957-1311
3308 W Warner Ave Santa Ana (92704) ***(P-15384)***
Lynex Company Inc ....F....408 778-7884
375 Digital Dr Morgan Hill (95037) ***(P-8536)***
Lynn Products Inc ....A....310 530-5966
2645 W 237th St Torrance (90505) ***(P-15279)***
Lynwood Pattern Service Inc ....F....310 631-2225
2528 E 127th St Compton (90222) ***(P-11384)***
Lynx Enterprises Inc ....D....209 833-3400
724 E Grant Line Rd Ste B Tracy (95304) ***(P-12271)***
Lynx Grills Inc (HQ) ....F....323 722-4324
7300 Flores St Downey (90242) ***(P-16813)***
Lynx Phtnic Ntworks A Del Corp ....F....818 878-7500
6303 Owensmouth Ave Fl 10 Woodland Hills (91367) ***(P-17385)***
Lynx Software Technologies Inc (PA) ....D....408 979-3900
855 Embedded Way San Jose (95138) ***(P-24114)***
Lynx Studio Technology Inc ....F....714 545-4700
190 Mccormick Ave Costa Mesa (92626) ***(P-17253)***
Lyons Magnus Inc ....E....559 268-5966
1636 S 2nd St Fresno (93702) ***(P-793)***
Lyra Corporation ....F....415 668-2546
1802 Hays St San Francisco (94129) ***(P-6275)***
Lyric Culture LLC ....F....323 581-3511
2520 W 6th St Ste 250 Los Angeles (90057) ***(P-3178)***
Lyrical Foods Inc ....C....510 784-0955
3180 Corporate Pl Hayward (94545) ***(P-2535)***
Lyris Inc ....E....800 768-2929
4 N 2nd St Fl 11 San Jose (95113) ***(P-24115)***
Lyru Engineering Inc ....F....510 357-5951
965 San Leandro Blvd San Leandro (94577) ***(P-16156)***
Lyten Inc ....F....650 400-5635
933 Kifer Rd Ste B Sunnyvale (94086) ***(P-14493)***
Lytx Inc (PA) ....B....858 430-4000
9785 Towne Centre Dr San Diego (92121) ***(P-20627)***
M & A Custom Doors, Harbor City *Also called Joanka Inc* ***(P-11961)***
M & A Plastics Inc ....E....818 768-0479
11735 Sheldon St Sun Valley (91352) ***(P-9882)***
M & B Window Fashions, Los Angeles *Also called Hd Window Fashions Inc* ***(P-5024)***
M & G Custom Polishing ....F....714 995-0261
8356 Standustrial St Stanton (90680) ***(P-13043)***
M & H Creative Design Inc ....F....213 627-8881
550 S Hill St Ste 1030 Los Angeles (90013) ***(P-22543)***
M & H Type Composition & Fndry, San Francisco *Also called Lyra Corporation* ***(P-6275)***
M & J Precision, Morgan Hill *Also called Lara Manufacturing Inc* ***(P-12265)***
M & K Builders Inc ....F....209 478-7531
3212 Bixby Way Stockton (95209) ***(P-12555)***
M & L Haight LLC ....E....951 587-2267
42192 Sarah Way Temecula (92590) ***(P-10248)***
M & L Pharmaceuticals Inc ....F....909 890-0078
629 S Allen St San Bernardino (92408) ***(P-7999)***
M & L Precision Machining Inc (PA) ....E....408 436-3955
18665 Madrone Pkwy Morgan Hill (95037) ***(P-16157)***

M & M Logging Inc ....F....530 938-0745
7800 N Old Stage Rd Weed (96094) *(P-3894)*
M & M Machine & Tool, Auburn *Also called Mitchell-Duckett Corporation (P-16214)*
M & M Printed Bag Inc ....E....909 393-5537
5651 Kimball Ct Chino (91710) *(P-5402)*
M & M Sportswear Manufacturing ....F....209 984-5632
18267 4th Ave Jamestown (95327) *(P-2795)*
M & O Perry Industries Inc ....E....951 734-9838
412 N Smith Ave Corona (92880) *(P-14716)*
M & R Engineering Co ....F....714 991-8480
227 E Meats Ave Orange (92865) *(P-12639)*
M & R Plating Corporation ....F....818 896-2700
12375 Montague St Arleta (91331) *(P-13044)*
M & W Engineering Inc ....E....530 676-7185
3880 Dividend Dr Ste 100 Shingle Springs (95682) *(P-16158)*
M & W Machine Corporation ....F....714 541-2652
1642 E Edinger Ave Ste A Santa Ana (92705) *(P-16159)*
M and M Apparel, Chino *Also called M and M Sports (P-3748)*
M and M Cabinets Inc ....F....510 324-4034
33238 Central Ave Union City (94587) *(P-4222)*
M and M Sports ....F....909 548-3371
14288 Central Ave Ste A Chino (91710) *(P-3748)*
M and M Stamping Corp ....F....909 590-2704
13821 Oaks Ave Chino (91710) *(P-11830)*
M and W Glass ....E....909 517-3585
10745 Vernon Ave Ontario (91762) *(P-10376)*
M Argeso & Co Inc ....F....626 573-3000
2628 River Ave Rosemead (91770) *(P-9052)*
M B C Reprographics Inc ....E....858 541-1500
5560 Ruffin Rd Ste 5 San Diego (92123) *(P-7128)*
M B I Ready-Mix L L C ....E....530 346-2432
44 Central St Colfax (95713) *(P-10799)*
M B S Inc ....F....714 693-9952
18514 Yorba Linda Blvd Yorba Linda (92886) *(P-19170)*
M C C, Torrance *Also called Medical Chemical Corporation (P-8998)*
M C E, Salinas *Also called Magnetic Circuit Elements Inc (P-19001)*
M C E, Torrance *Also called Magnetic Component Engrg Inc (P-13531)*
M C I Foods Inc ....C....562 977-4000
13013 Molette St Santa Fe Springs (90670) *(P-2536)*
M C I Manufacturing Inc (PA) ....E....408 456-2700
1020 Rock Ave San Jose (95131) *(P-12272)*
M C Metal Inc ....F....415 822-2288
1347 Donner Ave San Francisco (94124) *(P-12496)*
M C O Inc ....F....909 627-3574
13925 Benson Ave Chino (91710) *(P-19709)*
M C Woodwork ....F....323 233-0954
747 E 60th St Los Angeles (90001) *(P-4379)*
M D D, Burbank *Also called US Steel Rule Dies Inc (P-14120)*
M D H Burner & Boiler Co Inc ....F....562 630-2875
12106 Center St South Gate (90280) *(P-14668)*
M D Software Inc ....F....909 881-7599
1226 E 42nd Pl San Bernardino (92404) *(P-24116)*
M DAmico Inc ....E....619 390-5858
12650 Highway 67 Ste E Lakeside (92040) *(P-5071)*
M E D Inc ....D....562 921-0464
14001 Marquardt Ave Santa Fe Springs (90670) *(P-19710)*
M E Hodge Inc ....F....909 393-0675
14598 Central Ave Chino (91710) *(P-16160)*
M E I, Santa Barbara *Also called Motion Engineering Inc (P-15292)*
M E T, Murrieta *Also called Medical Extrusion Tech Inc (P-9432)*
M F G Eurotec Inc ....E....760 863-0033
84464 Cabazon Center Dr Indio (92201) *(P-4588)*
M F G West, Adelanto *Also called Molded Fiber GL Companies - W (P-9906)*
M G A Investment Co Inc ....F....805 543-9050
3211 Broad St Ste 201 San Luis Obispo (93401) *(P-6276)*
M G Deanza Acquisition Inc ....F....951 683-3080
4010 Garner Rd Riverside (92501) *(P-16161)*
M G Generon, Pittsburg *Also called Generon Igs Inc (P-14821)*
M G Watanabe Inc ....F....562 402-8989
17031 Roseton Ave Artesia (90701) *(P-17578)*
M Group Inc ....E....843 221-7830
9808 Venice Blvd Ste 706 Culver City (90232) *(P-10199)*
M I E, Temecula *Also called Molding Intl & Engrg Inc (P-9908)*
M I P, Covina *Also called Moores Ideal Products LLC (P-22696)*
M I T Inc ....F....714 899-6066
15202 Pipeline Ln Huntington Beach (92649) *(P-14072)*
M K Products Inc ....D....949 798-1425
16882 Armstrong Ave Irvine (92606) *(P-14246)*
M Klemme Technology Corp ....F....760 727-0593
1384 Poinsettia Ave Ste F Vista (92081) *(P-17254)*
M L Interiors Inc ....E....949 723-5001
151 Shipyard Way Ste 4 Newport Beach (92663) *(P-3590)*
M L Z Inc ....F....562 436-3540
1800 W 9th St Long Beach (90813) *(P-12840)*
M M Book Bindery ....F....310 532-0780
1826 W 169th St Gardena (90247) *(P-7339)*
M M P, Long Beach *Also called Maruhide Marine Products Inc (P-2264)*
M M S, Claremont *Also called Micro Matrix Systems (P-12847)*
M N Enterprises, San Diego *Also called Mohammad Khan (P-9904)*
M N M Manufacturing Inc ....D....310 898-1099
3019 E Harcourt St Compton (90221) *(P-11967)*
M Nexon Inc ....E....213 858-5930
222 N Pacific Coast Hwy # 300 El Segundo (90245) *(P-24117)*
M O S Plastics, San Jose *Also called Kennerley-Spratling Inc (P-9864)*
M P A, Ione *Also called Mp Associates Inc (P-8905)*
M P C Industrial Products Inc ....E....949 863-0106
2150 Mcgaw Ave Irvine (92614) *(P-13045)*
M P C Industries, Irvine *Also called M P C Industrial Products Inc (P-13045)*
M P I, San Jose *Also called Micro-Probe Incorporated (P-21079)*
M P M Building Services Inc ....D....818 708-9676
7011 Hayvenhurst Ave F Van Nuys (91406) *(P-8395)*
M P S, Escondido *Also called Manufacturing & Prod Svcs Corp (P-19713)*
M R F Techniques Inc ....F....408 433-1941
2245b Fortune Dr Ste B San Jose (95131) *(P-18998)*
M R S Foods Inc (PA) ....E....714 554-2791
4408 W 5th St Santa Ana (92703) *(P-2537)*
M S E, Burbank *Also called Matthews Studio Equipment Inc (P-22439)*
M S E Media Solutions, Commerce *Also called MSE Media Solutions Inc (P-19226)*
M S F Inc ....F....650 592-0239
1100 Industrial Rd Ste 18 San Carlos (94070) *(P-4987)*
M Stevens Inc ....F....323 661-2147
1925 Blake Ave Los Angeles (90039) *(P-3365)*
M T S, Bakersfield *Also called MTS Stimulation Services Inc (P-226)*
M W Reid Welding Inc ....D....619 401-5880
781 Oconner St El Cajon (92020) *(P-11831)*
M Wave Design Corporation ....F....805 499-8825
94 W Cochran St Ste B Simi Valley (93065) *(P-18999)*
M&G Duravent, Inc., Vacaville *Also called Duravent Inc (P-12188)*
M&L Metals Inc ....F....510 732-1745
25362 Cypress Ave Hayward (94544) *(P-12273)*
M-5 Steel Mfg Inc (PA) ....E....323 263-9383
1450 Mirasol St Los Angeles (90023) *(P-12028)*
M-I LLC ....E....661 321-5400
4400 Fanucchi Way Shafter (93263) *(P-220)*
M-Pulse Microwave Inc ....E....408 432-1480
576 Charcot Ave San Jose (95131) *(P-18365)*
M-T Metal Fabrications Inc ....F....510 357-5262
536 Lewelling Blvd Ste A San Leandro (94579) *(P-12274)*
M.D. Resource, Livermore *Also called Medical Device Resource Corp (P-21797)*
M2 Antenna Systems Inc ....F....559 221-2271
4402 N Selland Ave Fresno (93722) *(P-19000)*
M2 Marketplace Inc ....F....310 354-3600
2555 W 190th St 201 Torrance (90504) *(P-14938)*
M29 Technology and Design ....F....805 489-9402
133 Bridge St Ste B Arroyo Grande (93420) *(P-24118)*
M3 Products Inc ....F....626 371-1900
335 N Puente St Ste E Brea (92821) *(P-4988)*
M360, San Francisco *Also called Medicines360 (P-8005)*
MA Cher (usa) Inc (HQ) ....F....310 581-5222
1518 Abbot Kinney Blvd Venice (90291) *(P-23400)*
Maas-Rowe Carillons Inc ....E....760 743-1311
2255 Meyers Ave Escondido (92029) *(P-19351)*
Mabel Baas Inc ....E....805 520-8075
3960 Royal Ave Simi Valley (93063) *(P-13204)*
Mabrey Products Inc ....F....530 895-3799
200 Ryan Ave Chico (95973) *(P-4079)*
Mabvax Thrpeutics Holdings Inc (PA) ....F....858 259-9405
11535 Sorrento Valley Rd San Diego (92121) *(P-8000)*
Mac Cal Company ....D....408 441-1435
1737 Junction Ave San Jose (95112) *(P-12275)*
Mac Cal Manufacturing, San Jose *Also called Mac Cal Company (P-12275)*
Mac Donald, Richard Galleries, Monterey *Also called Richard Macdonald Studios Inc (P-11020)*
Mac Engineering & Components ....F....408 286-3030
5122 Calle Del Sol Santa Clara (95054) *(P-11607)*
Mac M McCully Co, Moorpark *Also called Mc Cully Mac M Corporation (P-16662)*
Mac Performance Exhaust, Temecula *Also called MAC Products Inc (P-11056)*
MAC Products Inc ....D....951 296-3077
43214 Black Deer Loop # 113 Temecula (92590) *(P-11056)*
Mac Publishing LLC (HQ) ....E....415 243-0505
501 2nd St Ste 500 San Francisco (94107) *(P-5982)*
Macchia Inc ....F....209 333-2600
7099 E Peltier Rd Acampo (95220) *(P-1807)*
Macdermid Prtg Solutions LLC ....D....760 510-6277
260 S Pacific St San Marcos (92078) *(P-14331)*
Macdonald Carbide Co ....E....626 960-4034
4510 Littlejohn St Baldwin Park (91706) *(P-14073)*
Macdonald Screen Print, Modesto *Also called Sign Designs Inc (P-23197)*
Macgregor Yacht Corporation ....D....310 621-2206
1631 Placentia Ave Costa Mesa (92627) *(P-20345)*
Mach Oil Corp ....F....818 783-3567
17835 Ventura Blvd # 301 Encino (91316) *(P-9152)*
Machinables Inc ....F....415 216-9467
1101 Cowper St Berkeley (94702) *(P-15280)*
Machine Arts Incorporated ....F....805 965-5344
2105 S Hathaway St Santa Ana (92705) *(P-16162)*
Machine Building Specialties ....E....323 666-8289
1977 Blake Ave Los Angeles (90039) *(P-14383)*
Machine Control Tech Inc ....F....951 808-0973
210 Crouse Dr Corona (92879) *(P-21070)*
Machine Craft of San Diego ....E....858 642-0509
9822 Waples St San Diego (92121) *(P-16163)*
Machine Exprnce & Design Inc ....E....559 291-7710
2964 Phillip Ave Clovis (93612) *(P-16164)*
Machine Precision Components ....F....562 404-0500
14014 Dinard Ave Santa Fe Springs (90670) *(P-16165)*
Machine Vision Products Inc (PA) ....D....760 438-1138
3270 Corporate Vw Ste D Vista (92081) *(P-21378)*
Machinetek LLC ....F....760 438-6644
1985 Palomar Oaks Way Carlsbad (92011) *(P-20162)*
Machineworks Manufacturing ....F....818 527-1327
20540 Superior St Ste D Chatsworth (91311) *(P-20163)*
Machining and Frame Division, San Jose *Also called Mass Precision Inc (P-12279)*
Machining Specialist Corp ....E....714 847-1214
7125 Fenwick Ln Ste O Westminster (92683) *(P-16166)*
Machinist Cooperative, Gilroy *Also called Lloyd E Hennessey Jr (P-16147)*

Mack & Reiss Inc ..... D 510 434-9122
5601 San Leandro St Ste 3 Oakland (94621) ***(P-3494)***
Mack Wall Bed Systems, Petaluma *Also called McGunagle William H & Sons Mfg* ***(P-4590)***
Mackenzie Laboratories Inc ..... E 909 394-9007
1163 Nicole Ct Glendora (91740) ***(P-18366)***
Mackie International Inc (PA) ..... E 951 346-0530
7344 Magnolia Ave Ste 205 Riverside (92504) ***(P-655)***
Maclac Co, San Francisco *Also called R J McGlennon Company Inc* ***(P-8676)***
Macom Technology Solutions Inc ..... F 310 320-6160
4000 Macarthur Blvd # 101 Newport Beach (92660) ***(P-17579)***
Macon Industries Inc ..... F 707 566-2116
3186 Coffey Ln Santa Rosa (95403) ***(P-19352)***
Macpherson Oil Company ..... F 661 556-6096
24118 Round Mountain Rd Bakersfield (93308) ***(P-129)***
Macquarie Electronics Inc ..... F 408 965-3860
2153 Otoole Ave Ste 20 San Jose (95131) ***(P-18367)***
Macro Air Technologies, San Bernardino *Also called Macroair Technologies Inc* ***(P-14669)***
Macro Plastics Inc (HQ) ..... E 707 437-1200
2250 Huntington Dr Fairfield (94533) ***(P-9883)***
Macroair Technologies Inc (PA) ..... E 909 890-2270
794 S Allen St San Bernardino (92408) ***(P-14669)***
Macrogenics West Inc ..... F 650 624-2600
3280 Byshore Blvd Ste 200 Brisbane (94005) ***(P-8001)***
Macs Lift Gate Inc (PA) ..... E 562 634-5962
2801 E South St Long Beach (90805) ***(P-23401)***
Macs Lift Gate Inc ..... F 562 634-5962
2715 Seaboard Ln Long Beach (90805) ***(P-13882)***
Mactech Magazine, Westlake Village *Also called Xplain Corporation* ***(P-6062)***
Macworld Magazine, San Francisco *Also called Mac Publishing LLC* ***(P-5982)***
Mad Apparel Inc ..... E 800 714-9697
201 Arch St Redwood City (94062) ***(P-3106)***
Mad Engine LLC (PA) ..... E 858 558-5270
6740 Cobra Way Ste 100 San Diego (92121) ***(P-2829)***
Mad Hueys, The, Carlsbad *Also called Outdoor Lfstyle Collective LLC* ***(P-3188)***
Mad Will's Food Company, Auburn *Also called Nor Cal Food Solutions LLC* ***(P-891)***
Mad Zone, San Francisco *Also called Divisadero 500 LLC* ***(P-5055)***
Madcap Software Inc (PA) ..... F 858 320-0387
9191 Towne Centre Dr # 150 San Diego (92122) ***(P-24119)***
Maddiebrit Products LLC ..... F 818 483-0096
537 Constitution Ave B Camarillo (93012) ***(P-8655)***
Maddox Defense Inc ..... F 818 378-8246
6549 Mission Gorge Rd # 112 San Diego (92120) ***(P-3848)***
Madera Carports Inc ..... F 559 662-1815
17462 Baldwin St Madera (93638) ***(P-12556)***
Madera Concepts ..... F 805 692-0053
55b Depot Rd Goleta (93117) ***(P-4514)***
Madera Fina, Fremont *Also called Commercial Casework Inc* ***(P-4018)***
Madera Printing & Pubg Co Inc ..... E 559 674-2424
2890 Falcon Dr Madera (93637) ***(P-5716)***
Madison Inc of Oklahoma ..... D 918 224-6990
18000 Studebaker Rd Cerritos (90703) ***(P-11832)***
Madison Industries (HQ) ..... E 323 583-4061
18000 Studebaker Rd # 305 Cerritos (90703) ***(P-12557)***
Madison Industries Inc Arizona ..... E 602 252-3083
18000 Studebaker Rd # 305 Cerritos (90703) ***(P-11833)***
Madison Street Press, Oakland *Also called Inter-City Printing Co Inc* ***(P-6649)***
Madrid Inc ..... F 562 404-9941
7800 Industry Ave Pico Rivera (90660) ***(P-4276)***
Madrigal Vineyards, Calistoga *Also called Madrigal Vineyard Management* ***(P-1808)***
Madrigal Vineyard Management ..... E 707 942-8691
3718 Saint Helena Hwy Calistoga (94515) ***(P-1808)***
Madrone Hospice Inc ..... E 530 842-2547
217 W Miner St Yreka (96097) ***(P-10377)***
Madruga Iron Works Inc ..... E 209 832-7003
305 Gandy Dancer Dr Tracy (95377) ***(P-11834)***
Madsen Products Incorporated ..... F 714 894-1816
15321 Connector Ln Huntington Beach (92649) ***(P-16167)***
Maestro Cellers, Anaheim *Also called Two Blind Mice LLC* ***(P-1979)***
Maf Industries Inc (HQ) ..... D 559 897-2905
36470 Highway 99 Traver (93673) ***(P-14717)***
Mag Aerospace Industries Inc ..... B 310 631-3800
1500 Glenn Curtiss St Carson (90746) ***(P-11649)***
Mag High Tech ..... F 818 786-8366
14718 Arminta St Panorama City (91402) ***(P-12276)***
Mag Instrument Inc (PA) ..... B 909 947-1006
2001 S Hellman Ave Ontario (91761) ***(P-17144)***
Magazine Publishers Svc Inc ..... D 707 571-7610
350 E St Santa Rosa (95404) ***(P-5983)***
Magcomp Inc ..... F 714 532-3584
982 N Batavia St Orange (92867) ***(P-16561)***
Magellan Gold Corporation ..... E 707 884-3766
2010a Harbison Dr 312 Vacaville (95687) ***(P-10)***
Magellan International Corp ..... F 510 656-6661
4453 Enterprise St Fremont (94538) ***(P-11237)***
Magellan West LLC ..... E 408 324-0620
1580 Oakland Rd Ste C107 San Jose (95131) ***(P-24120)***
Magerack, Fremont *Also called Magellan International Corp* ***(P-11237)***
Magic Gumball International ..... E 818 716-1888
9310 Mason Ave Chatsworth (91311) ***(P-1385)***
Magic Plastics Inc ..... D 800 369-0303
25215 Avenue Stanford Santa Clarita (91355) ***(P-9884)***
Magic Software Enterprises Inc ..... E 949 250-1718
24422 Avenida De La Carlo Laguna Hills (92653) ***(P-24121)***
Magic Touch Software Intl ..... F 800 714-6490
330 Rancheros Dr Ste 258 San Marcos (92069) ***(P-24122)***
Magic-Flight General Mfg Inc ..... C 619 288-4638
3417 Hancock St San Diego (92110) ***(P-4515)***
Magicall Inc ..... E 805 484-4300
4550 Calle Alto Camarillo (93012) ***(P-16661)***
Magico LLC ..... E 510 649-9700
3170 Corporate Pl Hayward (94545) ***(P-17255)***
Magito & Company LLC ..... F 707 567-1521
1446 Industrial Ave Sebastopol (95472) ***(P-1809)***
Magma, Escondido *Also called One Stop Systems Inc* ***(P-15302)***
Magma Products Inc ..... D 562 627-0500
3940 Pixie Ave Lakewood (90712) ***(P-16814)***
Magna Charger Inc ..... D 805 642-8833
1990 Knoll Dr Ste A Ventura (93003) ***(P-3799)***
Magna Tool Inc ..... E 714 826-2500
5594 Market Pl Cypress (90630) ***(P-16168)***
Magna-Pole Products Inc (PA) ..... F 310 453-3806
1904 14th St Ste 107 Santa Monica (90404) ***(P-4989)***
Magnabiosciences LLC ..... D 858 481-4400
6325 Lusk Blvd San Diego (92121) ***(P-21784)***
Magnaflow, Oceanside *Also called Car Sound Exhaust System Inc* ***(P-19608)***
Magnamosis Inc ..... F 707 484-8774
953 Indiana St Rm 212 San Francisco (94107) ***(P-21785)***
Magnaslow, Rcho STA Marg *Also called Car Sound Exhaust System Inc* ***(P-19609)***
Magnebit Holding Corporation (PA) ..... F 858 573-0727
9590 Chesapeake Dr Ste 1 San Diego (92123) ***(P-21071)***
Magnell Associate Inc ..... F 626 271-1320
17708 Rowland St City of Industry (91748) ***(P-14939)***
Magnesium Alloy Pdts Co Inc ..... E 310 605-1440
2420 N Alameda St Compton (90222) ***(P-11401)***
Magnesium Alloy Products Co LP ..... E 323 636-2276
2420 N Alameda St Compton (90222) ***(P-11342)***
Magnet Sales & Mfg Co Inc (HQ) ..... D 310 391-7213
11248 Playa Ct Culver City (90230) ***(P-10479)***
Magnet Source Tm, The, Anaheim *Also called A-L-L Magnetics* ***(P-13493)***
Magnet Systems Inc ..... E 650 329-5904
2300 Geng Rd Ste 100 Palo Alto (94303) ***(P-24123)***
Magnetic Circuit Elements Inc ..... E 831 757-8752
1540 Moffett St Salinas (93905) ***(P-19001)***
Magnetic Coils Inc ..... E 707 459-5994
150 San Hedrin Cir Willits (95490) ***(P-18723)***
Magnetic Component Engrg Inc (PA) ..... D 310 784-3100
2830 Lomita Blvd Torrance (90505) ***(P-13531)***
Magnetic Design Labs Inc ..... F 714 558-3355
1636 E Edinger Ave Ste H Santa Ana (92705) ***(P-19002)***
Magnetic Metals Corporation ..... E 714 828-4625
2475 W La Palma Ave Anaheim (92801) ***(P-13982)***
Magnetic Moments, Goleta *Also called Launchpoint Technologies Inc* ***(P-14788)***
Magnetic Rcrding Solutions Inc ..... E 408 970-8266
3080 Oakmead Village Dr Santa Clara (95051) ***(P-21072)***
Magnetic Sensors Corp ..... E 714 630-8380
1365 N Mccan St Anaheim (92806) ***(P-19003)***
Magnetron Power Inventions Inc ..... F 310 462-6970
2226 W 232nd St Torrance (90501) ***(P-130)***
Magnitude Electronics LLC ..... F 650 551-1850
926 Bransten Rd San Carlos (94070) ***(P-19004)***
Magnolia Lane Soft HM Furn Inc ..... E 650 624-0700
187 Utah Ave South San Francisco (94080) ***(P-3624)***
Magnolia Pub & Brewery, San Francisco *Also called McLean Brewery Inc* ***(P-1547)***
Magnotek Manufacturing Inc ..... D 951 653-8461
6510 Box Springs Blvd Riverside (92507) ***(P-18724)***
Magnum Abrasives Inc ..... E 909 890-1100
758 S Allen St San Bernardino (92408) ***(P-10949)***
Magnum Data Inc ..... F 800 869-2589
28130 Avenue Crocker # 303 Valencia (91355) ***(P-22969)***
Magnum Semiconductor Inc ..... C 408 934-3700
6024 Silver Creek Vly Rd San Jose (95138) ***(P-18368)***
Magnuson Products LLC ..... E 805 642-8833
1990 Knoll Dr Ste A Ventura (93003) ***(P-19711)***
Magnuson Superchargers, Ventura *Also called Magnuson Products LLC* ***(P-19711)***
Magnussen Home Furnishings Inc ..... F 336 841-4424
2155 Excise Ave Ste B Ontario (91761) ***(P-4589)***
Magor Mold LLC ..... D 909 592-5729
420 S Lone Hill Ave San Dimas (91773) ***(P-14074)***
Magorian Mine Services (PA) ..... F 530 269-1960
10310 Sierra Hills Ln Auburn (95602) ***(P-352)***
Magparts (HQ) ..... D 626 334-7897
1545 W Roosevelt St Azusa (91702) ***(P-11385)***
Magtech & Power Conversion Inc ..... E 714 451-0106
1146 E Ash Ave Fullerton (92831) ***(P-18725)***
Magtek Inc ..... F 562 631-8602
20725 Annalee Ave Carson (90746) ***(P-18369)***
Magtek Inc (PA) ..... C 562 546-6400
1710 Apollo Ct Seal Beach (90740) ***(P-15281)***
Mah Kuo ..... F 805 766-2309
377 El Dorado Dr Daly City (94015) ***(P-11835)***
Mahar Manufacturing Corp (PA) ..... E 323 581-9988
2834 E 46th St Vernon (90058) ***(P-22649)***
Mahindra Genze, Fremont *Also called Mahindra Tractor Assembly Inc* ***(P-20416)***
Mahindra Tractor Assembly Inc (HQ) ..... E 650 779-5180
48016 Fremont Blvd Fremont (94538) ***(P-20416)***
Mahivr ..... F 949 559-5470
5405 Alton Pkwy Irvine (92604) ***(P-5441)***
Mahmood Izadi Inc ..... F 310 325-0463
3115 Lomita Blvd Torrance (90505) ***(P-14836)***
MAI Systems, Lake Forest *Also called Infor (us) Inc* ***(P-24012)***
Maidenform LLC ..... C 323 724-9558
100 Citadel Dr Ste 323 Commerce (90040) ***(P-3444)***
Maier Manufacturing Inc ..... E 530 272-9036
416 Crown Point Cir Ste 1 Grass Valley (95945) ***(P-20417)***
Maier Racing Enterprises Inc ..... F 510 581-7600
22215 Meekland Ave Hayward (94541) ***(P-19712)***
Mailrite Print & Mail Inc ..... E 916 927-6245
834 Striker Ave Ste C Sacramento (95834) ***(P-6712)***

Mailworks Inc ....E....619 670-2365
2513 Folex Way Spring Valley (91978) ***(P-5131)***
Main Steel LLC ....D....951 789-3010
3100 Jefferson St Riverside (92504) ***(P-13046)***
Main Street Banner, Carpinteria *Also called Dsy Educational Corporation* ***(P-3838)***
Main Street Kitchens ....F....925 944-0153
37 Quail Ct Ste 200 Walnut Creek (94596) ***(P-5513)***
Mainetti USA Inc ....F....562 741-2920
17511 S Susana Rd Compton (90221) ***(P-7129)***
Mainstreet Media Group LLC ....C....408 842-6400
6400 Monterey Rd Gilroy (95020) ***(P-5717)***
Maitlen & Benson Inc ....E....562 597-2200
1395 Obispo Ave Long Beach (90804) ***(P-14247)***
Majestic Garlic Inc ....F....951 677-0555
2222 Foothill Blvd Ste E La Canada (91011) ***(P-889)***
Make Beverage Holdings LLC ....E....949 923-8238
2569 Tea Leaf Ln Tustin (92782) ***(P-5072)***
Make Community LLC ....F....707 548-0833
708 Gravenstein Hwy N Sebastopol (95472) ***(P-5984)***
Makeit Inc ....F....626 470-7938
612 S Marengo Ave Alhambra (91803) ***(P-15282)***
Makerplace Inc ....F....619 435-1279
684 Margarita Ave Coronado (92118) ***(P-22690)***
Makers Usa Inc ....F....323 582-1800
5000 District Blvd Vernon (90058) ***(P-2999)***
Makerskit LLC ....E....213 973-7019
7600 Melrose Ave Ste E Los Angeles (90046) ***(P-22691)***
Makerskit.com, Los Angeles *Also called Makerskit LLC* ***(P-22691)***
Making It Big Inc ....E....707 795-1995
1375 Corp Ctr Pkwy Ste A Santa Rosa (95407) ***(P-3179)***
Making Scents, Canoga Park *Also called Spa La La Inc* ***(P-23481)***
Makino Inc ....E....714 444-4334
17800 Newhope St Ste K Fountain Valley (92708) ***(P-14169)***
Mako Inc ....E....323 262-2168
736 Monterey Pass Rd Monterey Park (91754) ***(P-2756)***
Mako Industries SC Inc ....E....714 632-1400
1280 N Red Gum St Anaheim (92806) ***(P-21255)***
Mako Labs LLC ....E....619 786-3618
169 Saxony Rd Ste 107 Encinitas (92024) ***(P-24124)***
Mako Overhead Door Inc ....F....714 998-0122
5618 E La Palma Ave Anaheim (92807) ***(P-11968)***
Makplate LLC ....F....408 842-7572
5780 Obata Way Gilroy (95020) ***(P-13047)***
Makse Inc ....F....213 622-5030
52 E Santa Anita Ave Burbank (91502) ***(P-22544)***
Mal, San Francisco *Also called Myanimelist LLC* ***(P-6288)***
Malakan Inc (PA) ....F....310 910-9270
412 1/2 S Central Ave Glendale (91204) ***(P-4277)***
Malco Manufacturing, Los Angeles *Also called Aluminum Pros Inc* ***(P-14343)***
Malcolm Demille Inc ....F....805 929-4353
650 S Frontage Rd Nipomo (93444) ***(P-22545)***
Malibu Ceramic Works ....E....310 455-2485
903 Fairbanks Ave Long Beach (90813) ***(P-10446)***
Malibu Enterprises Inc ....E....310 457-2112
28990 Pacific Coast Hwy # 108 Malibu (90265) ***(P-5718)***
Malibu Kitchen, Malibu *Also called Marys Country Kitchen* ***(P-1345)***
Malibu Times Inc ....F....310 456-5507
3864 Las Flores Canyon Rd Malibu (90265) ***(P-5719)***
Malikco LLC ....E....925 974-3555
2121 N Calif Blvd Ste 290 Walnut Creek (94596) ***(P-24125)***
Mallinckrodt Inc ....F....805 553-9303
3298 Morning Ridge Ave Thousand Oaks (91362) ***(P-21786)***
Mamma Lina Ravioli Co, San Diego *Also called Mamma Linas Incorporated* ***(P-2538)***
Mamma Linas Incorporated ....F....858 535-0620
10741 Roselle St San Diego (92121) ***(P-2538)***
Mammoth Media Inc ....D....310 393-3024
1447 2nd St Santa Monica (90401) ***(P-5720)***
Mammoth Times, Mammoth Lakes *Also called Horizon Cal Publications* ***(P-5666)***
Mammoth Water, Montebello *Also called Unix Packaging Inc* ***(P-2178)***
Man Fon Inc ....F....626 287-6043
421 S California St Ste C San Gabriel (91776) ***(P-2539)***
Man-Grove Industries Inc ....D....714 630-3020
1201 N Miller St Anaheim (92806) ***(P-6713)***
Manchester Feeds Inc (PA) ....F....714 637-7062
1520 E Barham Dr San Marcos (92078) ***(P-1109)***
Manchester Feeds San Marcos, San Marcos *Also called Manchester Feeds Inc* ***(P-1109)***
Mancias Steel Company Inc ....F....408 295-5096
519 Horning St San Jose (95112) ***(P-11836)***
Mandala, Carlsbad *Also called Oceanside Glasstile Company* ***(P-10447)***
Mandego Apparel, Hollister *Also called Mandego Inc* ***(P-2830)***
Mandego Inc ....F....831 637-5241
2300 Tech Pkwy Ste 2 Hollister (95023) ***(P-2830)***
Maneri Sign Co Inc ....E....310 327-6261
1928 W 135th St Gardena (90249) ***(P-23151)***
Manetti Group, Commerce *Also called Hangers Randy West Coast Ctr* ***(P-11096)***
Maney Aircraft Inc ....E....909 390-2500
1305 S Wanamaker Ave Ontario (91761) ***(P-20164)***
Mangia Inc ....F....949 581-1274
1 Marconi Ste F Irvine (92618) ***(P-794)***
Mango Materials Inc ....F....650 440-0430
800 Buchanan St Berkeley (94710) ***(P-7580)***
Manhattan Beachwear Inc (HQ) ....C....714 892-7354
10700 Valley View St Cypress (90630) ***(P-3366)***
Manhattan Beachwear Inc ....D....714 892-7354
10700 Valley View St Cypress (90630) ***(P-3367)***
Manhattan Components Inc ....F....714 761-7249
5920 Lakeshore Dr Cypress (90630) ***(P-9885)***
Manley Laboratories Inc ....E....909 627-4256
13880 Magnolia Ave Chino (91710) ***(P-17256)***

Manna Pro Feeds, Fresno *Also called Manna Pro Products LLC* ***(P-1110)***
Manna Pro Products LLC ....E....559 486-1810
2962 S Cedar Ave Fresno (93725) ***(P-1110)***
Manning Holoff Co Inc ....E....818 407-2500
15610 Moorpark St Apt 3 Encino (91436) ***(P-20901)***
Mannings Beef LLC ....D....562 908-1089
9531 Beverly Rd Pico Rivera (90660) ***(P-417)***
Mannis Communications Inc ....E....858 270-3103
1621 Grand Ave Ste C San Diego (92109) ***(P-5721)***
Mannis Communications Inc ....E....858 270-3103
4645 Caca St Fl 2 Flr 2 San Diego (92109) ***(P-5722)***
Mannkind Corporation (PA) ....C....818 661-5000
30930 Russell Ranch Rd # 300 Westlake Village (91362) ***(P-8002)***
Mansoor Amarna Corp ....F....818 894-8937
16923 Kinzie St Northridge (91343) ***(P-22943)***
Manta Instruments Inc ....F....844 633-2500
9755 Research Dr Irvine (92618) ***(P-21256)***
Manta Solar Corporation ....F....928 853-6216
5420 Fulton St San Francisco (94121) ***(P-11704)***
Manteca Bulletin, Manteca *Also called Morris Newspaper Corp Cal* ***(P-5762)***
Manti-Machine Co Inc ....F....714 902-1465
11782 Western Ave Ste 15 Stanton (90680) ***(P-16169)***
Manufacturer, Paramount *Also called Z-Tronix Inc* ***(P-19148)***
Manufacturers Coml Fin LLC ....E....530 477-5011
13185 Nevada City Ave Grass Valley (95945) ***(P-11705)***
Manufacturers Import & Export, San Jose *Also called Amtek Electronic Inc* ***(P-14890)***
Manufacturers of Wood Products, Santa Barbara *Also called Architctral Mllwk Snta Barbara* ***(P-3998)***
Manufacturers/Hyland Ltd ....F....408 748-1806
650 Reed St Santa Clara (95050) ***(P-10378)***
Manufacturing & Prod Svcs Corp ....F....760 796-4300
2222 Enterprise St Escondido (92029) ***(P-19713)***
Manufacturing USA Enterprises ....E....818 409-3070
4220 San Fernando Rd Glendale (91204) ***(P-22546)***
Manutech Mfg & Dist ....F....831 655-8794
2080 Sunset Dr Pacific Grove (93950) ***(P-13690)***
Manutronics Inc ....F....408 262-6579
736 S Hillview Dr Milpitas (95035) ***(P-19005)***
Manzana Products Co Inc ....E....707 823-5313
9141 Green Valley Rd Sebastopol (95472) ***(P-795)***
Manzanita ....F....818 785-1111
26559 Ruether Ave Santa Clarita (91350) ***(P-22630)***
Manzer Corporation ....E....619 295-6031
3801 30th St San Diego (92104) ***(P-3591)***
Map Masters, Poway *Also called Traylor Management Inc* ***(P-6362)***
Mapbox Inc ....F....202 250-3633
50 Beale St Ste 900 San Francisco (94105) ***(P-24126)***
Mape Engineering Inc ....F....626 338-7964
9840 6th St Rancho Cucamonga (91730) ***(P-19971)***
Mapei Corporation ....E....909 475-4100
5415 Industrial Pkwy San Bernardino (92407) ***(P-7581)***
Maple Consumer Foods, Fair Oaks *Also called Wholesome Harvest Baking Inc* ***(P-432)***
Maple Leaf Bakery, Richmond *Also called Wholesome Harvest Baking LLC* ***(P-1296)***
Maplegrove Gluten Free Foods ....E....909 334-7828
5010 Eucalyptus Ave Chino (91710) ***(P-2540)***
Maquet Medical Systems USA LLC ....A....408 635-3900
120 Baytech Dr San Jose (95134) ***(P-22274)***
Mar Cor Purification Inc ....E....800 633-3080
6351 Orangethorpe Ave Buena Park (90620) ***(P-15538)***
Mar Engineering Company ....E....818 765-4805
7350 Greenbush Ave North Hollywood (91605) ***(P-16170)***
Mar Vista Resources LLC ....F....559 992-4535
745 North Ave Corcoran (93212) ***(P-8797)***
Mar Vista Wood Products Inc ....F....562 698-2024
7343 Pierce Ave Whittier (90602) ***(P-4080)***
Maranti Networks Inc ....D....408 834-4000
1452 N Vasco Rd Livermore (94551) ***(P-15054)***
Marathon Machine Inc ....F....858 578-8670
7588 Trade St San Diego (92121) ***(P-16171)***
Marbil Industries Inc ....E....714 974-4032
2201 N Glassell St Orange (92865) ***(P-21257)***
Marble City Company Inc ....F....650 802-8189
611 Taylor Way Ste 6 San Carlos (94070) ***(P-10914)***
Marble Palace, Stockton *Also called Andrea Zee Corporation* ***(P-10889)***
Marble Shop Inc (PA) ....E....925 439-6910
180 Bliss Ave Pittsburg (94565) ***(P-10915)***
Marble Works of San Diego, San Diego *Also called Central Marble Supply Inc* ***(P-10896)***
Marburg Technology Inc ....C....408 262-8400
304 Turquoise St Milpitas (95035) ***(P-15283)***
Marcaflex Inc ....F....415 472-4423
2 Seville Dr San Rafael (94903) ***(P-5367)***
Marcea Inc ....F....213 746-5191
1742 Crenshaw Blvd Torrance (90501) ***(P-3368)***
Marcel Electronics Inc ....F....714 974-8590
240 W Bristol Ln Orange (92865) ***(P-17917)***
Marcel Electronics Inc ....F....714 974-8590
130 W Bristol Ln Orange (92865) ***(P-17918)***
March Vision Care Inc ....E....310 665-0975
6701 Center Dr W Ste 790 Los Angeles (90045) ***(P-22371)***
Marchem Solvay Group, Long Beach *Also called Solvay USA Inc* ***(P-7528)***
Marco Fine Arts ....D....310 615-1818
4860 W 147th St Hawthorne (90250) ***(P-7130)***
Marco Fine Furniture Inc ....E....415 285-3235
650 Potrero Ave San Francisco (94110) ***(P-4655)***
Marcoa Media LLC (PA) ....E....858 635-9627
9955 Black Mountain Rd San Diego (92126) ***(P-6277)***
Marcoa Quality Publishing LLC ....D....858 695-9600
9955 Black Mountain Rd San Diego (92126) ***(P-6278)***

Employee Codes: A=Over 500 employees, B=251-500
C=101-250, D=51-100, E=20-50, F=10-19
2020 California
Manfacturers Register
© Mergent Inc. 1-800-342-5647
1163

Mardian Equipment Co Inc..........E.......619 938-8071
  10168 Channel Rd Lakeside (92040) *(P-13883)*
Mare Island Dry Dock LLC..........D.......707 652-7356
  1180 Nimitz Ave Vallejo (94592) *(P-20291)*
Mareblu Naturals, Anaheim Also called 180 Snacks *(P-1418)*
Marelli North America Inc..........C.......949 855-8050
  9 Holland Irvine (92618) *(P-15442)*
Marflex, Vernon Also called Marspring Corporation *(P-2872)*
Margaret OLeary Inc (PA)..........D.......415 354-6663
  50 Dorman Ave San Francisco (94124) *(P-3369)*
Marge Carson Inc (PA)..........D.......626 571-1111
  1260 E Grand Ave Pomona (91766) *(P-4656)*
MARGEAUX AND LINDA'S VEGAN KIT, Los Angeles Also called Amzart Inc *(P-2392)*
Margus Automotive Elc Exch..........D.......323 232-5281
  165 E Jefferson Blvd Los Angeles (90011) *(P-19714)*
Maria Corporation..........F.......714 751-2460
  2760 S Harbor Blvd Ste C Santa Ana (92704) *(P-7131)*
Mariani Bros, Marysville Also called Mariani Packing Co Inc *(P-853)*
Mariani Packing Co Inc..........E.......530 749-6565
  9281 Highway 70 Marysville (95901) *(P-853)*
Mariani Winery, Saratoga Also called Savannah Chanelle Vineyards *(P-1907)*
Mariannes Ice Cream LLC..........E.......831 713-4746
  218 State Park Dr Aptos (95003) *(P-656)*
Mariannes Ice Cream LLC (PA)..........F.......831 457-1447
  2100 Delaware Ave Ste B Santa Cruz (95060) *(P-657)*
Mariba Corporation..........F.......626 963-6775
  158 N Glendora Ave Ste W Glendora (91741) *(P-4421)*
Marich Confectionery Co Inc..........C.......831 634-4700
  2101 Bert Dr Hollister (95023) *(P-1386)*
Marie Joann Designs Inc..........E.......714 996-0550
  630 S Jefferson St Ste H Placentia (92870) *(P-3849)*
Marietta Cellars Incorporated..........F.......707 433-2747
  22295 Chianti Rd Geyserville (95441) *(P-1810)*
Marietta Marketing, Geyserville Also called Marietta Cellars Incorporated *(P-1810)*
Marika LLC..........D.......323 888-7755
  5553-B Bandini Blvd Bell (90201) *(P-3370)*
Marimar Torres Estate Corp..........F.......707 823-4365
  11400 Graton Rd Sebastopol (95472) *(P-1811)*
Marimix Company Inc..........F.......714 633-7300
  987 N Enterprise St Orange (92867) *(P-1387)*
Marin County Copy Shops Inc..........F.......415 457-5600
  901 C St San Rafael (94901) *(P-6714)*
Marin Food Specialties Inc..........E.......925 634-6126
  14800 Byron Hwy Byron (94514) *(P-738)*
Marin French Cheese Company..........F.......707 762-6001
  7500 Red Hill Rd Petaluma (94952) *(P-568)*
Marin Independent Journal, Novato Also called California Newspapers Inc *(P-5577)*
Marin Magazine Inc..........E.......415 332-4800
  1 Harbor Dr Ste 208 Sausalito (94965) *(P-5985)*
Marin Manufacturing Inc..........F.......415 453-1825
  195 Mill St San Rafael (94901) *(P-11837)*
Marin Scope Incorporated..........E.......415 892-1516
  1301b Grant Ave Novato (94945) *(P-5723)*
Marin Scope Incorporated..........F.......415 892-1516
  700 Larkspur Landing Cir Larkspur (94939) *(P-5724)*
Marin Scope Newspapers, Novato Also called Marin Scope Incorporated *(P-5723)*
Marin USA..........E.......415 382-6000
  265 Bel Marin Keys Blvd Novato (94949) *(P-11608)*
Marina Industries, Los Angeles Also called Marina Sportswear Inc *(P-3371)*
Marina Shipyard, Long Beach Also called Indel Engineering Inc *(P-20338)*
Marina Sportswear Inc..........D.......323 232-2012
  3766 S Main St Los Angeles (90007) *(P-3371)*
Marine & Industrial Services..........F.......925 757-8791
  2391 W 10th St Antioch (94509) *(P-13476)*
Marine & Rest Fabricators Inc..........E.......619 232-7267
  3768 Dalbergia St San Diego (92113) *(P-12277)*
Marine Fenders Intl Inc..........E.......310 834-7037
  909 Mahar Ave Wilmington (90744) *(P-12746)*
Marine Group Boat Works LLC..........E.......619 427-6767
  997 G St Chula Vista (91910) *(P-20346)*
Marine Spill Response Corp..........E.......707 442-6087
  990 W Waterfront Dr Eureka (95501) *(P-21258)*
Marine Tech..........F.......619 225-0448
  1500 Quivira Way Ste 1 San Diego (92109) *(P-20347)*
Marinesync Corporation..........F.......619 578-2953
  3235 Hancock St San Diego (92110) *(P-20902)*
Marino Enterprises Inc..........E.......909 476-0343
  10671 Civic Center Dr Rancho Cucamonga (91730) *(P-20165)*
Marinpak..........F.......707 996-3931
  21684 8th St E Ste 100 Sonoma (95476) *(P-2541)*
Mariposa Gazette & Miner..........F.......209 966-2500
  5180 Hwy 140 Ste B Mariposa (95338) *(P-5725)*
Marisa Foods LLC..........E.......562 437-7775
  1401 Santa Fe Ave Long Beach (90813) *(P-477)*
Maritime Solutions LLC..........E.......619 234-2676
  1616 Newton Ave San Diego (92113) *(P-20348)*
Mark Crawford Logging Inc..........F.......530 496-3272
  26 Walker Creek Rd Seiad Valley (96086) *(P-3895)*
Mark Ease Products Inc..........E.......209 462-8632
  132 S Aurora St Stockton (95202) *(P-23152)*
Mark Levine Window Coverings, Newport Beach Also called M L Interiors Inc *(P-3590)*
Mark One Counter Top Designs, Fresno Also called Duracite *(P-4974)*
Mark Optics Inc..........E.......714 545-6684
  1424 E Saint Gertrude Pl Santa Ana (92705) *(P-21379)*
Mark Resources LLC (PA)..........F.......415 515-5540
  1962 22nd Ave San Francisco (94116) *(P-4842)*
Mark Sheffield Construction..........E.......661 589-8520
  9105 Langley Rd Bakersfield (93312) *(P-221)*
Mark V Products, Corona Also called 2nd Gen Productions Inc *(P-8356)*

Markap Inc..........E.......949 240-1418
  20382 Hermana Cir Lake Forest (92630) *(P-3532)*
Markes International Inc..........D.......513 745-0241
  2355 Gold Meadow Way # 120 Gold River (95670) *(P-21259)*
Marketing Bulletin Board..........F.......805 455-2255
  639 Olive Rd Santa Barbara (93108) *(P-5726)*
Marketing Bus Advantage Inc..........F.......925 933-3637
  1940 Olivera Rd Ste E Concord (94520) *(P-14494)*
Marketing Pro Consulting Inc..........E.......619 233-8591
  1230 Columbia St Ste 500 San Diego (92101) *(P-24127)*
Marketshare Inc (PA)..........D.......408 262-0677
  2001 Tarob Ct Milpitas (95035) *(P-23153)*
Marki Microwave Inc..........E.......408 778-4200
  215 Vineyard Ct Morgan Hill (95037) *(P-19006)*
Markland Industries Inc (PA)..........F.......714 245-2850
  1111 E Mcfadden Ave Santa Ana (92705) *(P-20418)*
Marko Foam Products Inc (PA)..........E.......800 862-7561
  2500 White Rd Ste A Irvine (92614) *(P-9555)*
Marksman Products, Santa Fe Springs Also called S/R Industries Inc *(P-22881)*
Markzware..........F.......949 756-5100
  1805 E Dyer Rd Ste 101 Santa Ana (92705) *(P-24128)*
Markzware Software, Santa Ana Also called Markzware *(P-24128)*
Marlee Manufacturing Inc..........E.......909 390-3222
  4711 E Guasti Rd Ontario (91761) *(P-21787)*
Marleon Inc..........E.......310 679-1242
  3202 W Rosecrans Ave Hawthorne (90250) *(P-24650)*
Marler Precision, San Andreas Also called Krisalis Inc *(P-16125)*
Marlin Designs LLC..........C.......949 637-7257
  1900 E Warner Ave Ste J Santa Ana (92705) *(P-4657)*
Marlin Machine Products..........F.......951 275-0050
  4071 Brewster Way Riverside (92501) *(P-16172)*
Marna Ro LLC..........E.......310 801-5788
  818 S Broadway Ste 800 Los Angeles (90014) *(P-3484)*
Maroney Company..........F.......818 882-2722
  9016 Winnetka Ave Northridge (91324) *(P-16173)*
Marples Gears Inc..........E.......626 570-1744
  808 W Santa Anita Ave San Gabriel (91776) *(P-14744)*
Marpo Kinetics Inc..........F.......925 606-6919
  1306 Stealth St Livermore (94551) *(P-22847)*
Marquez & Marquez Food PR, South Gate Also called Marquez Marquez Inc *(P-2338)*
Marquez Marquez Inc..........E.......562 408-0960
  11821 Industrial Ave South Gate (90280) *(P-2338)*
Marrone Bio Innovations Inc (PA)..........C.......530 750-2800
  1540 Drew Ave Davis (95618) *(P-8833)*
Marrs Printing Inc..........D.......909 594-9459
  860 Tucker Ln City of Industry (91789) *(P-6715)*
Mars Air Systems LLC..........D.......310 532-1555
  14716 S Broadway Gardena (90248) *(P-14670)*
MArs Engineering Company Inc..........E.......510 483-0541
  699 Montague St San Leandro (94577) *(P-12640)*
Mars Food Us LLC (HQ)..........B.......310 933-0670
  2001 E Cashdan St Ste 201 Rancho Dominguez (90220) *(P-2542)*
Mars Food Us LLC..........B.......562 616-7347
  6875 Pacific View Dr Los Angeles (90068) *(P-1048)*
Mars Medical Ride Corp..........F.......310 518-1024
  23702 Main St Carson (90745) *(P-19485)*
Mars Petcare Us Inc..........E.......909 887-8131
  2765 Lexington Way San Bernardino (92407) *(P-1077)*
Mars Petcare Us Inc..........E.......760 261-7900
  13243 Nutro Way Victorville (92395) *(P-1078)*
Mars Printing and Packaging, City of Industry Also called Marrs Printing Inc *(P-6715)*
Marsal Packaging & Rfrgn..........F.......714 812-6775
  931 S Cypress St La Habra (90631) *(P-15443)*
Marsha Vicki Originals Inc..........E.......714 895-6371
  5292 Production Dr Huntington Beach (92649) *(P-2969)*
Marshall & Swift/Boeckh LLC..........E.......213 683-9000
  777 S Figueroa St Fl 12 Los Angeles (90017) *(P-6119)*
Marshall Genuine Products LLC..........F.......619 754-4099
  616 Marsat Ct Chula Vista (91911) *(P-14170)*
Marspring Corporation (PA)..........E.......323 589-5637
  4920 S Boyle Ave Vernon (90058) *(P-2872)*
Marspring Corporation..........E.......800 522-5252
  4920 S Boyle Ave Vernon (90058) *(P-4729)*
Marspring Corporation..........E.......310 484-6849
  5190 S Santa Fe Ave Vernon (90058) *(P-4730)*
Martek Power, Torrance Also called Sure Power Inc *(P-19098)*
Martellotto Inc..........F.......619 567-9244
  12934 Francine Ter Poway (92064) *(P-1812)*
Marteq Process Solutions Inc..........F.......714 495-4275
  1721 S Grand Ave Santa Ana (92705) *(P-18370)*
Martha Olsons Great Foods Inc..........F.......209 234-5935
  4407 Giannecchini Ln Stockton (95206) *(P-1320)*
Martha's All Natural, Stockton Also called Martha Olsons Great Foods Inc *(P-1320)*
Martha's All Natural, Stockton Also called Bakakers Specialty Foods Inc *(P-997)*
Martin Aerospace Corporation..........F.......310 231-0055
  11150 Tennessee Ave 1b Los Angeles (90064) *(P-13332)*
Martin Archery, Los Angeles Also called Martin Sports Inc *(P-22848)*
Martin Brass Foundry..........D.......951 698-7041
  22427 Bear Creek Dr N Murrieta (92562) *(P-11402)*
Martin Company, The, Los Angeles Also called Martin Aerospace Corporation *(P-13332)*
Martin Engineering Inc..........F.......626 960-5153
  5454 2nd St Irwindale (91706) *(P-14384)*
Martin Enterprises, Highland Also called Tj Composites Inc *(P-12408)*
Martin Erattrud Co, Gardena Also called Baxstra Inc *(P-3968)*
Martin Fischer Logging Inc..........F.......209 293-4847
  1165 Skull Flat Rd West Point (95255) *(P-3896)*
Martin Furniture, San Diego Also called Gilbert Martin Wdwkg Co Inc *(P-4753)*
Martin Marietta Materials Inc..........951 682-0918
  1500 Rubidoux Blvd Riverside (92509) *(P-310)*

Mergent e-mail: customerrelations@mergent.com
1164

2020 California
Manufacturers Register

(P-0000) Products & Services Section entry number
(PA)=Parent Co (HQ)=Headquarters (DH)=Div Headquarters

ALPHABETIC SECTION
Material Supply Inc (PA)

Martin Purefoods Corporation......F.......909 865-4440
1713 W 2nd St Pomona (91766) ***(P-478)***
Martin Sports Inc (PA)......E.......509 529-2554
1100 Glendon Ave Ste 920 Los Angeles (90024) ***(P-22848)***
Martin Sprocket & Gear Inc......E.......916 441-7172
1199 Vine St Sacramento (95811) ***(P-14745)***
Martin Sprocket & Gear Inc......F.......323 728-8117
5920 Triangle Dr Commerce (90040) ***(P-14746)***
Martin Sweeping, La Quinta *Also called CT Oldenkamp LLC* ***(P-23024)***
Martin-Chandler Inc......F.......323 321-5119
122 E Alondra Blvd Gardena (90248) ***(P-16174)***
Martin/Brattrud Inc......D.......323 770-4171
1224 W 132nd St Gardena (90247) ***(P-4658)***
Martinek Manufacturing......E.......510 438-0357
42650 Osgood Rd Fremont (94539) ***(P-16175)***
Martinelli Envmtl Graphics, San Francisco *Also called Martinelli Envmtl Graphics* ***(P-23154)***
Martinelli Envmtl Graphics......F.......415 468-4000
1829 Egbert Ave San Francisco (94124) ***(P-23154)***
Martinez & Turek, Rialto *Also called Martinez and Turek Inc* ***(P-16176)***
Martinez and Turek Inc......C.......909 820-6800
300 S Cedar Ave Rialto (92376) ***(P-16176)***
Martinez News Gazette, Martinez *Also called Gibson Printing & Publishing* ***(P-5646)***
Martinez Pallet Services LLC......F.......209 968-1393
671 Mariposa Rd Modesto (95354) ***(P-4380)***
Martini Prati Winery, Santa Rosa *Also called Conetech Custom Services LLC* ***(P-1644)***
Marton Precision Mfg LLC......E.......714 808-6523
1365 S Acacia Ave Fullerton (92831) ***(P-19972)***
Martronic Engineering Inc (PA)......F.......805 583-0808
874 Patriot Dr Unit D Moorpark (93021) ***(P-19353)***
Maruchan Inc (HQ)......B.......949 789-2300
15800 Laguna Canyon Rd Irvine (92618) ***(P-2543)***
Maruchan Inc......C.......949 789-2300
1902 Deere Ave Irvine (92606) ***(P-2371)***
Maruhachi Ceramics America Inc......E.......800 736-6221
1985 Sampson Ave Corona (92879) ***(P-10463)***
Maruhide Marine Products Inc......D.......562 435-6509
2145 W 17th St Long Beach (90813) ***(P-2264)***
Maruichi American Corporation......D.......562 903-8600
11529 Greenstone Ave Santa Fe Springs (90670) ***(P-11130)***
Marukan Vinegar U S A Inc (HQ)......C.......562 630-6060
16203 Vermont Ave Paramount (90723) ***(P-2544)***
Marukome USA Inc......F.......949 863-0110
17132 Pullman St Irvine (92614) ***(P-2545)***
Marvac Scientific Mfg Co......F.......925 825-4636
3231 Monument Way Ste I Concord (94518) ***(P-20765)***
Marvell Semiconductor Inc......F.......949 614-7700
15485 Sand Canyon Ave Irvine (92618) ***(P-18371)***
Marvell Semiconductor Inc......E.......408 855-8839
5450 Bayfront Plz Santa Clara (95054) ***(P-21073)***
Marvell Semiconductor Inc (HQ)......A.......408 222-2500
5488 Marvell Ln Santa Clara (95054) ***(P-18372)***
Marvin Engineering Co Inc (PA)......A.......310 674-5030
261 W Beach Ave Inglewood (90302) ***(P-20166)***
Marvin Group The, Inglewood *Also called Marvin Land Systems Inc* ***(P-19486)***
Marvin Group, The, Inglewood *Also called Marvin Engineering Co Inc* ***(P-20166)***
Marvin Land Systems Inc......E.......310 674-5030
261 W Beach Ave Inglewood (90302) ***(P-19486)***
Marvin Test Solutions Inc......D.......949 263-2222
1770 Kettering Irvine (92614) ***(P-21074)***
Marway Power Solutions, Santa Ana *Also called Marway Power Systems Inc* ***(P-15284)***
Marway Power Systems Inc (PA)......E.......714 917-6200
1721 S Grand Ave Santa Ana (92705) ***(P-15284)***
Marwell Corporation......F.......909 794-4192
1094 Wabash Ave Mentone (92359) ***(P-16603)***
Marx Digital Cnc Machine Shop, Santa Clara *Also called Marx Digital Mfg Inc* ***(P-16177)***
Marx Digital Mfg Inc (PA)......E.......408 748-1783
3551 Victor St Santa Clara (95054) ***(P-16177)***
Mary Anns Baking Co Inc......C.......916 681-7444
8371 Carbide Ct Sacramento (95828) ***(P-1240)***
Mary Matava......F.......760 439-9920
3210 Oceanside Blvd Oceanside (92056) ***(P-8834)***
Marybelle Farms Inc......E.......916 645-8568
3761 Nicolaus Rd Lincoln (95648) ***(P-1111)***
Marys Country Kitchen......F.......310 456-7845
3900 Cross Creek Rd Ste 3 Malibu (90265) ***(P-1345)***
Marzetti West, Milpitas *Also called Tmarzetti Company* ***(P-902)***
Mas Metals Inc......F.......510 259-1426
32410 Central Ave Union City (94587) ***(P-12497)***
Masco Corporation......D.......313 274-7400
19914 Via Baron Way Rancho Dominguez (90220) ***(P-11672)***
Mascorro Leather Inc......D.......323 724-6759
1303 S Gerhart Ave Commerce (90022) ***(P-10240)***
Mashindustries Inc......E.......714 736-9600
7150 Village Dr Buena Park (90621) ***(P-5073)***
Masimo Americas Inc......F.......949 297-7000
52 Discovery Irvine (92618) ***(P-21788)***
Masimo Corporation......E.......949 297-7000
9600 Jeronimo Rd Irvine (92618) ***(P-22275)***
Masimo Corporation (PA)......B.......949 297-7000
52 Discovery Irvine (92618) ***(P-22276)***
Masimo Semiconductor Inc......E.......603 595-8900
52 Discovery Irvine (92618) ***(P-18373)***
Mask Technology Inc......E.......714 557-3383
2601 Oak St Santa Ana (92707) ***(P-19007)***
Mask U S Inc......F.......619 476-9041
3121 Main St Ste F Chula Vista (91911) ***(P-3568)***
Mask-Off Company Inc......F.......626 303-8015
345 W Maple Ave Monrovia (91016) ***(P-8880)***
Maskell Fusion Tech Services, Riverside *Also called Maskell Rigging & Equipment* ***(P-11131)***
Maskell Rigging & Equipment (PA)......F.......951 900-7460
6650 Doolittle Ave Riverside (92503) ***(P-11131)***
Maskless Lithography Inc......F.......408 433-1864
2550 Zanker Rd San Jose (95131) ***(P-6716)***
Mason Electric Co......B.......818 361-3366
13955 Balboa Blvd Sylmar (91342) ***(P-20167)***
Masonite Entry Door Corp......F.......951 243-2261
25100 Globe St Moreno Valley (92551) ***(P-4081)***
Masonite International Corp......E.......209 948-0637
433 W Scotts Ave Stockton (95203) ***(P-4082)***
Masonry Fireplace Inds LLC......F.......714 542-5397
6391 Jurupa Ave Riverside (92504) ***(P-10601)***
Mass Group......E.......310 214-2000
1959 Kingsdale Ave Redondo Beach (90278) ***(P-6717)***
Mass Precision Inc......C.......408 954-0200
46555 Landing Pkwy Fremont (94538) ***(P-12278)***
Mass Precision Inc (PA)......B.......408 954-0200
2110 Oakland Rd San Jose (95131) ***(P-12279)***
Mass Press, Redondo Beach *Also called Mass Group* ***(P-6717)***
Mass Systems, Baldwin Park *Also called Ametek Ameron LLC* ***(P-20832)***
Mast Biosurgery USA Inc......E.......858 550-8050
6749 Top Gun St Ste 108 San Diego (92121) ***(P-21789)***
Masten Space Systems Inc......F.......661 824-3423
1570 Sabovich St 25 Mojave (93501) ***(P-20452)***
Master Arts Engraving, Anaheim *Also called Master Arts Inc* ***(P-7379)***
Master Arts Inc......F.......714 240-4550
3737 E Miraloma Ave Anaheim (92806) ***(P-7379)***
Master Builders LLC......E.......909 987-1758
9060 Haven Ave Rancho Cucamonga (91730) ***(P-8994)***
Master Enterprises Inc......E.......626 442-1821
2025 Lee Ave South El Monte (91733) ***(P-12280)***
Master Fab Inc......F.......951 277-4772
9210 Stellar Ct Corona (92883) ***(P-12281)***
Master Inds Worldwide LLC......F.......949 660-0644
1001 S Linwood Ave Santa Ana (92705) ***(P-23402)***
Master Industries Inc......E.......949 660-0644
1001 S Linwood Ave Santa Ana (92705) ***(P-22849)***
Master Link Sausage, Fullerton *Also called Demes Gourmet Corporation* ***(P-452)***
Master Machine Products, Riverside *Also called Metric Machining* ***(P-13935)***
Master Metal Products Company......F.......408 275-1210
495 Emory St San Jose (95110) ***(P-12282)***
Master Metal Works Inc......E.......626 444-8818
1805 Potrero Ave South El Monte (91733) ***(P-12498)***
Master Plastics Incorporated......E.......707 451-3168
820 Eubanks Dr Ste I Vacaville (95688) ***(P-9886)***
Master Powder Coating Inc......E.......562 863-4135
13721 Bora Dr Santa Fe Springs (90670) ***(P-8656)***
Master Precision Machining......E.......408 727-0185
2199 Ronald St Santa Clara (95050) ***(P-16178)***
Master Productions Inc......F.......858 677-0037
8310 Miramar Mall Ste A San Diego (92121) ***(P-6718)***
Master Research & Mfg Inc......D.......562 483-8789
13528 Pumice St Norwalk (90650) ***(P-20168)***
Master Washer Stamping Svc Co......F.......323 722-0969
80899 Camino San Lucas Indio (92203) ***(P-14075)***
Master-Halco Inc......E.......909 350-4740
8008 Church Ave Highland (92346) ***(P-11100)***
Masterbrand Cabinets Inc......E.......951 686-3614
3700 S Riverside Ave Colton (92324) ***(P-4223)***
Mastering Lab Inc......F.......805 640-2900
911 Bryant Pl Ojai (93023) ***(P-17331)***
Masterite Division, Los Angeles *Also called Dcx-Chol Enterprises Inc* ***(P-17783)***
Masterpiece Artist Canvas LLC......E.......619 710-2500
1401 Air Wing Rd San Diego (92154) ***(P-2703)***
Masterpiece Cookies, Livermore *Also called Internationally Delicious Inc* ***(P-1344)***
Masterpiece Leaded Windows......E.......858 391-3344
11651 Rverside Dr Ste 143 Lakeside (92040) ***(P-10379)***
Masters In Metal Inc......E.......805 988-1992
131 Lombard St Oxnard (93030) ***(P-10471)***
Mastertaste Inc......D.......323 727-2100
1916 S Tubeway Ave Commerce (90040) ***(P-2220)***
Mastey De Paris Inc......E.......661 257-4814
25413 Rye Canyon Rd Valencia (91355) ***(P-8537)***
Mastini Designs......F.......800 979-4848
9454 Wilshire Blvd # 600 Beverly Hills (90212) ***(P-22547)***
Mat Cactus Mfg Co......E.......626 969-0444
930 W 10th St Azusa (91702) ***(P-2873)***
Mat Mat......F.......818 678-9392
21029 Itasca St Chatsworth (91311) ***(P-11498)***
Matanzas Creek Winery......E.......707 528-6464
6097 Bennett Valley Rd Santa Rosa (95404) ***(P-1813)***
Matchless LLC......E.......310 473-5100
8423 Wilshire Blvd Beverly Hills (90211) ***(P-17580)***
Matchmaster Dyg & Finshg Inc (PA)......C.......323 232-2061
3750 S Broadway Los Angeles (90007) ***(P-2856)***
Matchmaster Dyg & Finshg Inc......D.......323 232-2061
3750 Broadway Pl Los Angeles (90007) ***(P-2811)***
Matchpoint Solutions (PA)......F.......925 829-4455
3875 Hopyard Rd Ste 325 Pleasanton (94588) ***(P-24129)***
Materia Inc (PA)......C.......626 584-8400
60 N San Gabriel Blvd Pasadena (91107) ***(P-7503)***
Material Control Inc......E.......661 617-6033
6901 District Blvd Ste A Bakersfield (93313) ***(P-13532)***
Material Handling Division, Victorville *Also called Demag Cranes & Components Corp* ***(P-13846)***
Material Sciences Corporation......E.......562 699-4550
3730 Capitol Ave City of Industry (90601) ***(P-11221)***
Material Supply Inc (PA)......C.......951 801-5004
11700 Industry Ave Fontana (92337) ***(P-12283)***

ALPHABETIC

Employee Codes: A=Over 500 employees, B=251-500
C=101-250, D=51-100, E=20-50, F=10-19
2020 California
Manfacturers Register
© Mergent Inc. 1-800-342-5647
1165

Materials Development Corp (PA) ....F....818 700-8290
21541 Nordhoff St Ste B Chatsworth (91311) ***(P-21075)***
Materials Innovation, Sunnyvale *Also called Jsr Micro Inc* ***(P-8748)***
Materion Brush Inc ....E....510 623-1500
44036 S Grimmer Blvd Fremont (94538) ***(P-13452)***
Matheson Tri-Gas Inc ....E....626 334-2905
16125 Ornelas St Irwindale (91706) ***(P-7416)***
Matheson Tri-Gas Inc ....F....510 714-3026
6925 Central Ave Newark (94560) ***(P-7417)***
Matheson Tri-Gas Inc ....E....909 758-5464
8800 Utica Ave Rancho Cucamonga (91730) ***(P-7418)***
Matheson Tri-Gas Inc ....D....510 793-2559
6775 Central Ave Newark (94560) ***(P-7419)***
Matheson Tri-Gas Inc ....F....323 773-2777
5555 District Blvd Vernon (90058) ***(P-7420)***
Mathews Ready Mix LLC ....E....530 671-2400
249 Lamon St Yuba City (95991) ***(P-10800)***
Mathews Readymix, Yuba City *Also called Mathews Ready Mix LLC* ***(P-10800)***
Mathews Readymix Inc ....F....530 893-8856
1619 Skyway Chico (95928) ***(P-10801)***
Mathy Machine Inc ....E....619 448-0404
9315 Wheatlands Rd Santee (92071) ***(P-13983)***
Matician Inc ....F....650 504-9181
430 Sherman Ave Ste 100 Palo Alto (94306) ***(P-14837)***
Matko, San Bernardino *Also called Mkkr Inc* ***(P-14175)***
Matrix Cab Parts Inc ....F....818 782-7022
7950 Woodley Ave Ste B Van Nuys (91406) ***(P-4083)***
Matrix Document Imaging Inc ....D....626 966-9959
527 E Rowland St Ste 214 Covina (91723) ***(P-7132)***
Matrix Logic Corporation ....F....415 893-9897
1380 East Ave Ste 124240 Chico (95926) ***(P-24130)***
Matrix Millwork, Van Nuys *Also called Matrix Cab Parts Inc* ***(P-4083)***
Matrix Stream Technologies Inc ....F....650 292-4982
1840 Gateway Dr Ste 200 San Mateo (94404) ***(P-17257)***
Matrix USA Inc ....E....714 825-0404
2730 S Main St Santa Ana (92707) ***(P-17919)***
Matsmatsmats.com, Woodland Hills *Also called Tinyinklingcom LLC* ***(P-9380)***
Matsuda House Printing Inc ....E....310 532-1533
1825 W 169th St Ste A Gardena (90247) ***(P-6719)***
Matsui International Co Inc ....C....310 767-7812
1501 W 178th St Gardena (90248) ***(P-8995)***
Matsun America Corp ....F....909 930-0779
4070 Greystone Dr Ste B Ontario (91761) ***(P-3043)***
Matsusada Precision Inc ....F....650 877-0151
299 Harbor Way South San Francisco (94080) ***(P-22216)***
Mattco Forge Inc (PA) ....D....562 634-8635
16443 Minnesota Ave Paramount (90723) ***(P-12714)***
Matte Grey, Los Alamitos *Also called Haus of Grey LLC* ***(P-3035)***
Mattel Inc (PA) ....A....310 252-2000
333 Continental Blvd El Segundo (90245) ***(P-22650)***
Mattel Inc ....F....909 382-3780
1456 E Harry Shepard Blvd San Bernardino (92408) ***(P-22692)***
Mattel Direct Import Inc (HQ) ....F....310 252-2000
333 Continental Blvd El Segundo (90245) ***(P-22693)***
Matteo LLC ....E....213 617-2813
1000 E Cesar E Chavez Ave Los Angeles (90033) ***(P-3625)***
Matterhorn Filter Corporation ....F....310 329-8073
125 W Victoria St Gardena (90248) ***(P-7504)***
Matterhorn Ice Cream Inc ....D....208 287-8916
1221 66th St Sacramento (95819) ***(P-658)***
Matternet Inc (PA) ....E....650 260-2727
161 E Evelyn Ave Mountain View (94041) ***(P-20169)***
Matthew Warren Inc ....E....805 928-3851
901 W Mccoy Ln Santa Maria (93455) ***(P-13339)***
Matthew Warren Inc ....D....800 237-5225
5959 Triumph St Commerce (90040) ***(P-13340)***
Matthews International Corp ....E....951 537-6615
442 W Esplanade Ave 105 San Jacinto (92583) ***(P-11403)***
Matthews Manufacturing Inc ....E....323 980-4373
3301 E 14th St Los Angeles (90023) ***(P-12284)***
Matthews Skyline Logging Inc ....E....707 743-2890
10100 East Rd Potter Valley (95469) ***(P-3897)***
Matthews Studio Equipment Inc ....E....818 843-6715
4520 W Valerio St Burbank (91505) ***(P-22439)***
Matthey Johnson Inc ....C....858 716-2400
12205 World Trade Dr San Diego (92128) ***(P-11204)***
Matthey Johnson Inc ....E....408 727-2221
1070 Coml St Ste 110 San Jose (95112) ***(P-21790)***
Matthias Rath Inc (HQ) ....F....408 567-5000
1260 Memorex Dr Santa Clara (95050) ***(P-603)***
Mattson Technology Inc (HQ) ....C....510 657-5900
47131 Bayside Pkwy Fremont (94538) ***(P-18374)***
Matz Rubber Co Inc ....E....323 849-5170
1209 Chestnut St Burbank (91506) ***(P-9331)***
Maui Imaging Inc ....F....408 744-1127
70 Las Colinas Ln San Jose (95119) ***(P-22277)***
Maui Toys ....E....330 747-4333
2951 28th St Ste 1000 Santa Monica (90405) ***(P-22850)***
Maul Mfg Inc (PA) ....E....714 641-0727
3041 S Shannon St Santa Ana (92704) ***(P-16179)***
Maurer Marine Inc ....F....949 645-7673
873 W 17th St Costa Mesa (92627) ***(P-20349)***
Maurice & Maurice Engrg Inc ....E....760 949-5151
17579 Mesa St Ste B4 Hesperia (92345) ***(P-11185)***
Maurice Carrie Winery ....E....951 676-1711
34225 Rancho Cal Rd Temecula (92591) ***(P-1814)***
Maurice Landstrass ....E....650 355-5532
1667 Rosita Rd Pacifica (94044) ***(P-21076)***
Maury Microwave Inc ....C....909 987-4715
2900 Inland Empire Blvd Ontario (91764) ***(P-19008)***
Maury Razon ....F....818 989-6246
74 W Cochran St Ste A Simi Valley (93065) ***(P-3569)***
Mave Enterprises Inc ....E....818 767-4533
11555 Cantara St Ste B-E North Hollywood (91605) ***(P-1388)***
Mavens Creamery LLC ....E....408 216-9270
1701 S 7th St Ste 7 San Jose (95112) ***(P-659)***
Maverick Abrasives Corporation ....D....714 854-9531
4340 E Miraloma Ave Anaheim (92807) ***(P-10950)***
Maverick Aerospace Inc ....F....714 578-1700
3718 Capitol Ave City of Industry (90601) ***(P-20170)***
Maverick Aerospace LLC ....E....714 578-1700
3718 Capitol Ave City of Industry (90601) ***(P-20171)***
Maverick Enterprises Inc ....C....707 463-5591
751 E Gobbi St Ukiah (95482) ***(P-11222)***
Max Fischer & Sons Inc ....E....213 624-8756
1327 Palmetto St Los Angeles (90013) ***(P-3626)***
Max Leon Inc (PA) ....D....626 797-6886
3100 New York Dr Pasadena (91107) ***(P-3372)***
Max Precision Machine Inc ....F....408 956-8986
2467 Autumnvale Dr San Jose (95131) ***(P-16180)***
Max Q, Ontario *Also called Maximum Quality Metal Pdts Inc* ***(P-12285)***
Max Smt Corp ....F....877 589-9422
5675 Kimball Ct Chino (91710) ***(P-14635)***
Max Studio.com, Pasadena *Also called Max Leon Inc* ***(P-3372)***
Maxair Systems, Irvine *Also called Bio-Medical Devices Inc* ***(P-21628)***
Maxco Supply Inc ....D....559 638-8449
2059 E Olsen Ave Reedley (93654) ***(P-5167)***
Maxford Technology LLC ....F....408 855-8288
2225 Calle De Luna Santa Clara (95054) ***(P-11010)***
Maxim Integrated Products Inc (PA) ....A....408 601-1000
160 Rio Robles San Jose (95134) ***(P-18375)***
Maxim Lighting Intl Inc (PA) ....C....626 956-4200
253 Vineland Ave City of Industry (91746) ***(P-16979)***
Maxim Lighting Intl Inc ....D....626 956-4200
247 Vineland Ave City of Industry (91746) ***(P-16980)***
Maxim-Dallas Direct Inc ....F....800 659-5909
120 San Gabriel Dr Sunnyvale (94086) ***(P-18376)***
Maxima Racing Oils, Santee *Also called South West Lubricants Inc* ***(P-9156)***
Maximum Quality Metal Pdts Inc ....E....909 902-5018
1017 E Acacia St Ontario (91761) ***(P-12285)***
Maximus Holdings Inc ....A....650 935-9500
2475 Hanover St Palo Alto (94304) ***(P-24131)***
Maxit Designs Inc ....F....916 489-1023
4044 Wayside Ln Ste A Carmichael (95608) ***(P-2796)***
Maxlinear Inc (PA) ....E....760 692-0711
5966 La Place Ct Ste 100 Carlsbad (92008) ***(P-18377)***
Maxlite Inc ....D....714 678-5000
1148 N Ocean Cir Anaheim (92806) ***(P-17059)***
Maxon Auto Corporation ....F....626 400-6464
8599 Enterprise Way Chino (91710) ***(P-5168)***
Maxon Crs LLC ....E....424 236-4660
5400 W Rosecrans Ave # 105 Hawthorne (90250) ***(P-20292)***
Maxon Industries Inc ....D....562 464-0099
11921 Slauson Ave Santa Fe Springs (90670) ***(P-19715)***
Maxstraps Inc ....D....707 829-3000
925 Gravenstein Ave Sebastopol (95472) ***(P-2757)***
Maxtor Corporation (HQ) ....D....831 438-6550
4575 Scotts Valley Dr Scotts Valley (95066) ***(P-15055)***
Maxtrol Corporation ....E....714 245-0506
1701 E Edinger Ave Ste B6 Santa Ana (92705) ***(P-17920)***
Maxus Group, Walnut *Also called Prophecy Technology LLC* ***(P-15313)***
Maxwell Alarm Screen Mfg Inc ....E....818 773-5533
20327 Nordhoff St Chatsworth (91311) ***(P-23155)***
Maxwell Sign and Decal Div, Chatsworth *Also called Maxwell Alarm Screen Mfg Inc* ***(P-23155)***
Maxwell Technologies Inc (HQ) ....B....858 503-3300
3888 Calle Fortunada San Diego (92123) ***(P-19195)***
Maxxess Systems Inc (PA) ....E....714 772-1000
22661 Old Canal Rd Yorba Linda (92887) ***(P-24132)***
Maxxon Company, City of Industry *Also called Dennison Inc* ***(P-12469)***
Maya Steels Fabrication Inc ....D....310 532-8830
301 E Compton Blvd Gardena (90248) ***(P-11838)***
Mayer Baking Co, Torrance *Also called Kopykake Enterprises Inc* ***(P-12836)***
Mayoni Enterprises ....D....818 896-0026
10320 Glenoaks Blvd Pacoima (91331) ***(P-12286)***
Maysoft Inc ....F....978 635-1700
1727 Santa Barbara St Santa Barbara (93101) ***(P-24133)***
Mazzei Injector Company LLC ....E....661 363-6500
500 Rooster Dr Bakersfield (93307) ***(P-15539)***
MB Sports Inc ....E....209 357-4153
280 Airpark Rd Atwater (95301) ***(P-20350)***
Mb2 Raceway Clovis Inc (PA) ....F....559 298-7223
1200 Shaw Ave Clovis (93612) ***(P-16951)***
MBA Electronics, Fremont *Also called William Ho* ***(P-15366)***
MBC Mattress Co Inc ....E....951 371-8044
19270 Envoy Ave Corona (92881) ***(P-4731)***
Mbf Interiors Inc ....E....858 565-2944
7831 Ostrow St San Diego (92111) ***(P-3592)***
Mbf Transportation LLC ....F....562 282-0540
13610 Imperial Hwy Ste 6 Santa Fe Springs (90670) ***(P-20374)***
MBK Enterprises Inc ....E....818 998-1477
9959 Canoga Ave Chatsworth (91311) ***(P-22043)***
MBK Tape Solutions, Chatsworth *Also called MBK Enterprises Inc* ***(P-22043)***
Mbtechnology ....E....559 233-2181
188 S Teilman Ave Fresno (93706) ***(P-9120)***
Mc Allister Industries Inc (PA) ....E....858 755-0683
731 S Highway 101 Ste 2 Solana Beach (92075) ***(P-6958)***
Mc Cain & Mc Cain Inc ....F....661 322-7764
3801 Gilmore Ave Bakersfield (93308) ***(P-16181)***

Mc Clellan Bottling Group .... F 530 241-2600
4712 Mountain Lakes Blvd Redding (96003) ***(P-2091)***

Mc Cully Mac M Corporation .... E 805 529-0661
12012 Hertz Ave Moorpark (93021) ***(P-16662)***

Mc Electronics LLC .... B 831 637-1651
1891 Airway Dr Hollister (95023) ***(P-19009)***

Mc Intyre Coil, San Leandro *Also called Edge Electronics Corporation* ***(P-12018)***

Mc Lane Manufacturing Inc .... D 562 633-8158
6814 Foster Bridge Blvd Bell Gardens (90201) ***(P-13691)***

Mc Laughlin Mine, Lower Lake *Also called Barrick Gold Corporation* ***(P-1)***

Mc Liquidation Inc .... E 408 636-1020
570 Del Rey Ave Sunnyvale (94085) ***(P-22278)***

Mc Products Inc .... F 949 888-7100
23331 Antonio Pkwy Rcho STA Marg (92688) ***(P-8996)***

Mc William & Son Inc .... F 626 969-1821
421 S Irwindale Ave Azusa (91702) ***(P-12841)***

Mc-Dowell-Craig Mfgco (PA) .... F 714 521-7170
13146 Firestone Blvd Santa Fe Springs (90670) ***(P-4843)***

Mc2 Sabtech Holdings Inc .... E 714 221-5000
22705 Savi Ranch Pkwy Yorba Linda (92887) ***(P-14940)***

McAero LLC .... F 310 787-9911
12711 Imperial Hwy Santa Fe Springs (90670) ***(P-16182)***

McAfee Inc .... D 858 967-2342
6707 Barnhurst Dr San Diego (92117) ***(P-24134)***

McAfee LLC (HQ) .... C 888 847-8766
2821 Mission College Blvd Santa Clara (95054) ***(P-24135)***

McAfee Finance 2 LLC .... A 888 847-8766
2821 Mission College Blvd Santa Clara (95054) ***(P-24136)***

McAfee Security LLC .... A 866 622-3911
2821 Mission College Blvd Santa Clara (95054) ***(P-24137)***

McC Controls LLC .... E 218 847-1317
859 Cotting Ct Ste G Vacaville (95688) ***(P-15540)***

McCain Manufacturing Inc .... D 760 295-9290
2633 Progress St Vista (92081) ***(P-11839)***

McCalls Country Canning Inc (PA) .... F 951 461-2277
41735 Cherry St Murrieta (92562) ***(P-23403)***

McCarthy Ranch .... F 408 356-2300
15425 Los Gatos Blvd # 102 Los Gatos (95032) ***(P-4464)***

McCarthys Draperies Inc .... E 916 422-0155
6955 Luther Dr Sacramento (95823) ***(P-3593)***

McCash Manufacturing Inc .... E 408 748-8991
1256 Washoe Dr San Jose (95120) ***(P-21791)***

McClatchy Company (PA) .... C 916 321-1844
2100 Q St Sacramento (95816) ***(P-5727)***

McClatchy Newspapers Inc (HQ) .... A 916 321-1855
2100 Q St Sacramento (95816) ***(P-5728)***

McClatchy Newspapers Inc .... B 559 441-6111
1626 E St Fresno (93706) ***(P-5729)***

McClatchy Newspapers Inc .... F 305 740-8440
948 11th St 300 Modesto (95354) ***(P-5730)***

McClatchy Newspapers Inc .... B 209 238-4636
1325 H St Modesto (95354) ***(P-5731)***

McClatchy Newspapers Inc .... D 209 826-3831
907 6th St Los Banos (93635) ***(P-5732)***

McClatchy Newspapers Inc .... C 209 722-1511
1190 W Olive Ave Ste F Merced (95348) ***(P-5733)***

McClatchy Newspapers Inc .... B 209 587-2250
948 11th St Ste 30 Modesto (95354) ***(P-5734)***

McClatchy Newspapers Inc .... D 408 200-1000
4 N 2nd St Ste 800 San Jose (95113) ***(P-5735)***

McClatchy Newspapers Inc .... C 805 781-7800
3825 S Higuera St San Luis Obispo (93401) ***(P-5736)***

McCoppin Enterprises .... E 818 240-4840
6641 San Fernando Rd Glendale (91201) ***(P-16183)***

McCormacks Guides Inc .... F 925 229-1869
3211 Elmquist Ct Martinez (94553) ***(P-6279)***

McCormick & Company Inc .... D 714 685-0934
180 N Riverview Dr Anaheim (92808) ***(P-2546)***

McCormick & Company Inc .... D 831 775-3350
340 El Cam Ste 20 Salinas (93901) ***(P-2547)***

McCormick & Company Inc .... C 831 758-2411
340 El Camino Real S # 20 Salinas (93901) ***(P-2548)***

McCormick Fresh Herbs LLC .... D 323 278-9750
1575 W Walnut Pkwy Compton (90220) ***(P-2549)***

McCrometer Inc .... C 951 652-6811
3255 W Stetson Ave Hemet (92545) ***(P-20972)***

McCullough Aero Company, Santa Fe Springs *Also called McAero LLC* ***(P-16182)***

McDaniel Inc .... F 909 591-8353
10807 Monte Vista Ave Montclair (91763) ***(P-11161)***

McDaniel Manufacturing Inc .... F 530 626-6336
6180 Enterprise Dr Ste D Diamond Springs (95619) ***(P-11609)***

McDowell & Craig Off Systems .... D 562 921-4441
13146 Firestone Blvd Norwalk (90650) ***(P-4844)***

McDowell Craig, Santa Fe Springs *Also called Mc-Dowell-Craig Mfgco* ***(P-4843)***

McDowell Publishers, Ontario *Also called Alpha Publishing Corporation* ***(P-6069)***

McDowell-Craig Office Furn, Norwalk *Also called McDowell & Craig Off Systems* ***(P-4844)***

McE, Rancho Cordova *Also called Nidec Motor Corporation* ***(P-13806)***

McElroy Metal Mill Inc .... E 760 246-5545
17031 Koala Rd Adelanto (92301) ***(P-12558)***

McEvoy of Marin LLC .... D 707 778-2307
5935 Red Hill Rd Petaluma (94952) ***(P-1475)***

McEvoy Properties LLC .... C 415 537-4200
680 2nd St San Francisco (94107) ***(P-6120)***

McEvoy Ranch, Petaluma *Also called McEvoy of Marin LLC* ***(P-1475)***

McGrath Rentcorp .... C 951 360-6600
11450 Mission Blvd Jurupa Valley (91752) ***(P-12559)***

McGrayel Company Inc .... E 559 299-7660
5361 S Villa Ave Fresno (93725) ***(P-8997)***

McGuire Furniture, San Francisco *Also called Baker Interiors Furniture Co* ***(P-4763)***

McGunagle William H & Sons Mfg (PA) .... F 707 762-7900
971 Transport Way Ste B Petaluma (94954) ***(P-4590)***

McHale Sign Company Inc .... F 530 223-2030
3707 Electro Way Redding (96002) ***(P-23156)***

McIntire Tool Die & Machine (PA) .... F 909 888-0440
308 S Mountain View Ave San Bernardino (92408) ***(P-12842)***

McIntyre Industries, San Leandro *Also called Optimization Corporation* ***(P-14672)***

McKeague Patpatrick .... F 805 541-4593
1339 Marsh St San Luis Obispo (93401) ***(P-6121)***

McKeever Danlee Confectionary .... E 626 334-8964
760 N Mckeever Ave Azusa (91702) ***(P-1389)***

McKenna Boiler Works Inc .... F 323 221-1171
1510 N Spring St Los Angeles (90012) ***(P-12029)***

McKenna Labs Inc (PA) .... E 714 687-6888
1601 E Orangethorpe Ave Fullerton (92831) ***(P-8003)***

McKenzie Machining Inc .... F 408 748-8885
481 Perry Ct Santa Clara (95054) ***(P-16184)***

McKinnon Enterprises .... E 858 571-1818
4577 Viewridge Ave San Diego (92123) ***(P-5986)***

McLean Brewery Inc .... E 415 864-7468
1398 Haight St San Francisco (94117) ***(P-1547)***

McLellan Equipment Inc (PA) .... D 650 873-8100
251 Shaw Rd South San Francisco (94080) ***(P-19542)***

McLellan Equipment Inc .... D 559 582-8100
13221 Crown Ave Hanford (93230) ***(P-19543)***

McLellan Industries Inc .... D 650 873-8100
13221 Crown Ave Hanford (93230) ***(P-19544)***

McLeod Racing LLC .... F 714 630-2764
1570 Lakeview Loop Anaheim (92807) ***(P-19716)***

McMahon Steel Company Inc .... C 619 671-9700
1880 Nirvana Ave Chula Vista (91911) ***(P-11610)***

McMillin Mfg Corp .... D 323 981-8585
40 E Verdugo Ave Burbank (91502) ***(P-12287)***

McMillin Wire Products, Burbank *Also called McMillin Mfg Corp* ***(P-12287)***

McMurtrie & Mcmurtrie Inc .... D 626 815-0177
915 W 5th St Azusa (91702) ***(P-3978)***

McNab Ridge Winery, Ukiah *Also called Plc LLC* ***(P-1868)***

McNab Ridge Winery LLC .... F 707 462-2423
2350 Mcnab Ranch Rd Ukiah (95482) ***(P-1815)***

McNaughton Newspapers .... D 530 756-0800
315 G St Davis (95616) ***(P-5737)***

McNaughton Newspapers Inc (PA) .... D 707 425-4646
1250 Texas St Fairfield (94533) ***(P-5738)***

McNeal Enterprises Inc .... D 408 922-7290
2031 Ringwood Ave San Jose (95131) ***(P-9887)***

McNear Brick & Block, San Rafael *Also called L P McNear Brick Co Inc* ***(P-10510)***

McNeilus Truck and Mfg Inc .... E 909 370-2100
401 N Pepper Ave Colton (92324) ***(P-19545)***

MCP Industries Inc (PA) .... F 951 736-1881
708 S Temescal St Ste 101 Corona (92879) ***(P-9332)***

MCP Industries Inc .... E 951 736-1313
1660 Leeson Ln Corona (92879) ***(P-11673)***

McPrint Corp .... F 714 632-9966
327 E Commercial St Pomona (91767) ***(P-6720)***

McPrint Direct, Pomona *Also called McPrint Corp* ***(P-6720)***

McQuaide Brothers Corporation .... F 619 444-9932
11919 Woodside Ave Lakeside (92040) ***(P-19826)***

McRoskey Mattress, San Francisco *Also called Pleasant Mattress Inc* ***(P-4736)***

McStarlite, Harbor City *Also called Basmat Inc* ***(P-12128)***

McUbe Inc (PA) .... E 408 637-5503
2570 N 1st St Ste 300 San Jose (95131) ***(P-14941)***

McV Microwave, San Diego *Also called McV Technologies Inc* ***(P-17581)***

McV Technologies Inc .... F 858 450-0468
6349 Nancy Ridge Dr San Diego (92121) ***(P-17581)***

McWane Inc (PA) .... C 510 632-3467
7825 San Leandro St Oakland (94621) ***(P-11147)***

McWhirter Steel Inc .... F 661 951-8998
42211 7th St E Lancaster (93535) ***(P-11840)***

MD Engineering Inc .... E 951 736-5390
1550 Consumer Cir Corona (92880) ***(P-16185)***

MD Manufacturing Inc .... F 661 283-7550
34970 Mcmurtrey Ave Bakersfield (93308) ***(P-15541)***

MD Software Enterprise, San Bernardino *Also called M D Software Inc* ***(P-24116)***

MD Stainless Services .... E 562 904-7022
8241 Phlox St Downey (90241) ***(P-13477)***

Md-Staff, Temecula *Also called Applied Statistics & MGT Inc* ***(P-23613)***

Mda Cmmunications Holdings LLC .... A 650 852-4000
3825 Fabian Way Palo Alto (94303) ***(P-17582)***

Mdc Interior Solutions LLC .... D 800 621-4006
6900 E Washington Blvd Los Angeles (90040) ***(P-3570)***

Mdc Vacuum Products LLC (PA) .... D 510 265-3500
30962 Santana St Hayward (94544) ***(P-18378)***

Mdc Vacuum Products LLC .... D 510 265-3500
23874b Cabot Blvd Hayward (94545) ***(P-13313)***

Mdi, Riverside *Also called Molded Devices Inc* ***(P-9905)***

Mdi East Inc (HQ) .... E 951 509-6918
6918 Ed Perkic St Riverside (92504) ***(P-9888)***

Mds, Tarzana *Also called Universal Merchandise Inc* ***(P-2981)***

ME & ME Costumes Inc .... F 323 876-4432
1052 N Cahuenga Blvd Los Angeles (90038) ***(P-22440)***

Meade Instruments Corp .... D 949 451-1450
27 Hubble Irvine (92618) ***(P-21380)***

Meadow Decor Inc .... F 909 923-2558
1477 E Cedar St Ste A Ontario (91761) ***(P-4766)***

Meadow Farms Sausage Co Inc .... F 323 752-2300
6215 S Western Ave Los Angeles (90047) ***(P-479)***

Meadows Mechanical, Gardena *Also called Meadows Sheet Metal and AC Inc* ***(P-12288)***

Meadows Sheet Metal and AC Inc .... E 310 615-1125
333 Crown Vista Dr Gardena (90248) ***(P-12288)***

ALPHABETIC

Employee Codes: A=Over 500 employees, B=251-500
C=101-250, D=51-100, E=20-50, F=10-19

2020 California
Manfacturers Register

© Mergent Inc. 1-800-342-5647
1167

Mealenders, San Francisco *Also called Willpower Labs Inc* ***(P-8188)***
Mean Well Usa Inc......F......510 683-8886
44030 Fremont Blvd Fremont (94538) ***(P-19010)***
Means Engineering Inc......D......760 931-9452
5927 Geiger Ct Carlsbad (92008) ***(P-21260)***
Measurement Specialties Inc......D......818 701-2750
9131 Oakdale Ave Ste 170 Chatsworth (91311) ***(P-21502)***
Measurement Specialties Inc......D......530 273-4608
424 Crown Point Cir Grass Valley (95945) ***(P-21077)***
Meat Packers Butchers Sup Inc......F......323 268-8514
2820 E Washington Blvd Los Angeles (90023) ***(P-14385)***
Mec Corona Summit III LLC......C......951 739-6200
1 Monster Way Corona (92879) ***(P-2092)***
Mechancal Systm-Rial Refueling, Yorba Linda *Also called GE Aviation Systems LLC* ***(P-20112)***
Mechanical and Mch Repr Svcs......F......909 625-8705
10584 Silicon Ave Montclair (91763) ***(P-16186)***
Mechanical Bookbinding, Baldwin Park *Also called Cal Bind* ***(P-7328)***
Mechanix Wear LLC (PA)......D......800 222-4296
28525 Witherspoon Pkwy Valencia (91355) ***(P-3502)***
Mechanized Engineering Systems......F......310 830-9763
737 E 223rd St Carson (90745) ***(P-13884)***
Mechanized Enterprises Inc......F......714 630-5512
1140 N Kraemer Blvd Ste M Anaheim (92806) ***(P-16187)***
Mechanized Science Seals Inc......E......714 898-5602
5322 Mcfadden Ave Huntington Beach (92649) ***(P-21503)***
Meco-Nag Corporation......D......818 764-2020
7306 Laurel Canyon Blvd North Hollywood (91605) ***(P-10172)***
Mecoptron Inc......E......510 226-9966
3115 Osgood Ct Fremont (94539) ***(P-16188)***
Mecpro Inc......E......408 727-9757
980 George St Santa Clara (95054) ***(P-16189)***
Mectec Molds Inc......F......909 981-3636
1525 Howard Access Rd D Upland (91786) ***(P-14076)***
Med, Clovis *Also called Machine Exprnce & Design Inc* ***(P-16164)***
Med-Fit Systems Inc......C......760 723-3618
3553 Rosa Way Fallbrook (92028) ***(P-22851)***
Med-Pharmex Inc......F......909 593-7875
2727 Thompson Creek Rd Pomona (91767) ***(P-8004)***
Med-Safe Systems Inc......C......855 236-2772
10975 Torreyana Rd San Diego (92121) ***(P-21792)***
Medallia Inc (PA)......C......650 321-3000
575 Market St Ste 1850 San Francisco (94105) ***(P-24138)***
Medallion Therapeutics Inc......E......661 621-6122
25134 Rye Canyon Loop # 200 Valencia (91355) ***(P-21793)***
Medata Inc (PA)......D......714 918-1310
5 Peters Canyon Rd # 250 Irvine (92606) ***(P-24139)***
Medconx Inc......E......408 330-0003
2901 Tasman Dr Ste 211 Santa Clara (95054) ***(P-9333)***
Mededge Inc......F......310 745-2290
11965 Venice Blvd Ste 407 Los Angeles (90066) ***(P-21794)***
Medegen LLC (HQ)......E......909 390-9080
4501 E Wall St Ontario (91761) ***(P-9889)***
Medeia Inc......F......800 433-4609
7 W Figueroa St Ste 215 Santa Barbara (93101) ***(P-21795)***
Medelita LLC......F......949 542-4100
23456 S Pointe Dr Ste A Laguna Hills (92653) ***(P-2970)***
Medennium Inc (PA)......E......949 789-9000
9 Parker Ste 150 Irvine (92618) ***(P-22372)***
Medgear, Cerritos *Also called LA Triumph Inc* ***(P-3042)***
Medi Kid Company......F......951 925-8800
448 S Palm Ave Ste A Hemet (92543) ***(P-22044)***
Media Blast & Abrasive Inc......F......714 257-0484
591 Apollo St Brea (92821) ***(P-15542)***
Media Gobbler Inc......F......323 203-3222
6427 W Sunset Blvd Los Angeles (90028) ***(P-24140)***
Media King Inc......E......626 288-4558
140 W Valley Blvd 201a San Gabriel (91776) ***(P-19354)***
Media Nation Enterprises LLC......E......714 371-9494
15271 Barranca Pkwy Irvine (92618) ***(P-23157)***
Media News, Paradise *Also called Califrnia Nwspapers Ltd Partnr* ***(P-5582)***
Media News Group......F......707 459-4643
77 W Commercial St Willits (95490) ***(P-5739)***
Media News Groups, Vacaville *Also called Reporter* ***(P-5809)***
Medianews Group Inc......D......562 435-1161
300 Oceangate Ste 150 Long Beach (90802) ***(P-5740)***
Medianews Group Inc......A......818 713-3000
21860 Burbank Blvd # 200 Woodland Hills (91367) ***(P-5741)***
Medianews Group Inc......C......310 540-5511
5215 Torrance Blvd Torrance (90503) ***(P-5742)***
Medianews Group Inc......B......408 920-5713
4 N 2nd St Ste 800 San Jose (95113) ***(P-5743)***
Medianews Group Inc......C......650 391-1000
255 Constitution Dr Menlo Park (94025) ***(P-5744)***
Medianews Group Inc......E......530 662-5421
711 Main St Woodland (95695) ***(P-5745)***
Medianews Group Inc......C......661 257-5200
24800 Ave Rockefeller Valencia (91355) ***(P-5746)***
Medianews Group Inc......C......707 994-6656
14913 Lakeshore Dr Clearlake (95422) ***(P-5747)***
Medianews Group Inc......E......530 527-2151
728 Main St Red Bluff (96080) ***(P-5748)***
Mediapointe Inc......F......805 480-3700
3952 Camino Ranchero Camarillo (93012) ***(P-17258)***
Mediatek USA Inc (PA)......C......408 526-1899
2840 Junction Ave San Jose (95134) ***(P-14942)***
Mediatek USA Inc......F......408 526-1899
96 Corporate Park Ste 300 Irvine (92606) ***(P-14943)***
Medic I D'S Internatl, Woodland Hills *Also called Medic Ids* ***(P-23404)***
Medic Ids......F......818 705-0595
20350 Ventura Blvd # 140 Woodland Hills (91364) ***(P-23404)***
Medical Aesthetics Menlo Park......F......650 336-3358
885 Oak Grove Ave Ste 101 Menlo Park (94025) ***(P-21796)***
Medical Analysis Systems Inc (HQ)......C......510 979-5000
46360 Fremont Blvd Fremont (94538) ***(P-8236)***
Medical Breakthrough Massage......E......408 677-7702
28016 Industry Dr Valencia (91355) ***(P-23405)***
Medical Chemical Corporation......E......310 787-6800
19250 Van Ness Ave Torrance (90501) ***(P-8998)***
Medical Data Recovery Inc......F......949 251-0073
17310 Red Hill Ave # 270 Irvine (92614) ***(P-24141)***
Medical Device Manufacturing, Brea *Also called Life Science Outsourcing Inc* ***(P-21774)***
Medical Device Resource Corp......F......510 732-9950
5981 Graham Ct Livermore (94550) ***(P-21797)***
Medical Extrusion Tech Inc (PA)......E......951 698-4346
26608 Pierce Cir Ste A Murrieta (92562) ***(P-9432)***
Medical Instr Dev Labs Inc......E......510 357-3952
557 Mccormick St San Leandro (94577) ***(P-21798)***
Medical Packaging Corporation......D......805 388-2383
941 Avenida Acaso Camarillo (93012) ***(P-22045)***
Medical Tactile Inc......F......310 641-8228
5500 W Rosecrans Ave A Hawthorne (90250) ***(P-21799)***
Medical Transcription Billing......A......800 869-3700
405 Kenyon St Ste 300 San Diego (92110) ***(P-24142)***
Medicines360 (PA)......F......415 951-8700
353 Sacramento St Ste 300 San Francisco (94111) ***(P-8005)***
Medicool Inc......F......310 782-2200
20460 Gramercy Pl Torrance (90501) ***(P-21800)***
Medifarm So Cal Inc......E......855 447-6967
2040 Main St Ste 225 Irvine (92614) ***(P-13650)***
Medigreens, Huntington Beach *Also called Mgfso LLC* ***(P-8013)***
Medika Health Care, Fremont *Also called Medika Therapeutics Inc* ***(P-21801)***
Medika Therapeutics Inc......F......510 377-0898
4046 Clipper Ct Fremont (94538) ***(P-21801)***
Mediland Corporation......D......562 630-9696
7027 Motz St Paramount (90723) ***(P-10272)***
Medimmune LLC......B......650 603-2000
297 Bernardo Ave Mountain View (94043) ***(P-8006)***
Medimmune Vaccines, Mountain View *Also called Medimmune LLC* ***(P-8006)***
Medina Medical Inc......F......650 396-7756
39684 Eureka Dr Newark (94560) ***(P-21802)***
Medina Wood Products Inc......F......209 832-4523
26342 S Banta Rd Tracy (95304) ***(P-4381)***
Medisense, Alameda *Also called Abbott Diabetes Care Inc* ***(P-8198)***
Meditab Software Inc......F......510 673-1838
2233 Watt Ave Ste 360 Sacramento (95825) ***(P-24143)***
Meditab Software Inc......C......510 632-2021
333 Hegenberger Rd # 800 Oakland (94621) ***(P-24144)***
Medium Entertainment Inc......E......469 951-2688
501 Folsom St Fl 1 San Francisco (94105) ***(P-22694)***
Medius, San Jose *Also called Babylon Printing Inc* ***(P-6431)***
Medivation Inc (HQ)......C......415 543-3470
525 Market St Ste 3600 San Francisco (94105) ***(P-8007)***
Medivision Inc......F......714 563-2772
4883 E La Palma Ave # 503 Anaheim (92807) ***(P-22279)***
Medivision Optics, Anaheim *Also called Medivision Inc* ***(P-22279)***
Medleycom Incorporated......F......408 745-5418
910 E Hamilton Ave Fl 6 Campbell (95008) ***(P-5749)***
Medlin & Sons, Whittier *Also called Medlin and Son Engineering Svc* ***(P-16190)***
Medlin and Son Engineering Svc......E......562 464-5889
12484 Whittier Blvd Whittier (90602) ***(P-16190)***
Medlin Ramps......F......562 229-1991
14903 Marquardt Ave Santa Fe Springs (90670) ***(P-13984)***
Medline Industires, Temecula *Also called Medline Industries Inc* ***(P-22046)***
Medline Industries Inc......F......951 296-2600
42500 Winchester Rd Temecula (92590) ***(P-22046)***
Medplast Group Inc......C......510 657-5800
45581 Northport Loop W Fremont (94538) ***(P-9890)***
Medrano Raymundo......E......909 947-5507
1752 S Bon View Ave Ontario (91761) ***(P-2892)***
Medrio Inc (PA)......E......415 963-3700
345 California St Ste 325 San Francisco (94104) ***(P-24145)***
Medtronic Inc......B......949 798-3934
1659 Gailes Blvd San Diego (92154) ***(P-21803)***
Medtronic Inc......C......510 985-9670
2200 Powell St Emeryville (94608) ***(P-21804)***
Medtronic Inc......F......805 571-3769
125 Cremona Dr Goleta (93117) ***(P-22280)***
Medtronic Inc......C......300 646-4633
18000 Devonshire St Northridge (91325) ***(P-21805)***
Medtronic Inc......D......707 541-3281
3576 Unocal Pl Bldg B Santa Rosa (95403) ***(P-22047)***
Medtronic Inc......E......949 837-3700
9775 Toledo Way Irvine (92618) ***(P-21806)***
Medtronic Inc......E......707 541-3144
5345 Skyllane Blvd Santa Rosa (95403) ***(P-21807)***
Medtronic Inc......D......949 474-3943
1851 E Deere Ave Santa Ana (92705) ***(P-21808)***
Medtronic Inc......E......408 548-6618
1860 Barber Ln Milpitas (95035) ***(P-21809)***
Medtronic Inc......E......951 332-3600
11811 Landon Dr Eastvale (91752) ***(P-21810)***
Medtronic Ats Medical Inc......E......949 380-9333
1851 E Deere Ave Santa Ana (92705) ***(P-21811)***
Medtronic Minimed Inc (HQ)......A......800 646-4633
18000 Devonshire St Northridge (91325) ***(P-22281)***
Medtronic PS Medical Inc (HQ)......C......805 571-3769
125 Cremona Dr Goleta (93117) ***(P-21812)***

Mergent e-mail: customerrelations@mergent.com
1168
2020 California
Manufacturers Register
(P-0000) Products & Services Section entry number
(PA)=Parent Co (HQ)=Headquarters (DH)=Div Headquarters

Medtronic Spine LLC.....C.....408 548-6500
1221 Crossman Ave Sunnyvale (94089) *(P-21813)*
Medwaves Inc.....E.....858 946-0015
16760 W Bernardo Dr San Diego (92127) *(P-21814)*
Medway Plastics Corporation.....C.....562 630-1175
2250 E Cherry Indus Cir Long Beach (90805) *(P-9891)*
Medweb, San Francisco *Also called Nexsys Electronics Inc (P-15297)*
Mee Audio, City of Industry *Also called S2e Inc (P-17279)*
Mee Industries Inc (PA).....F.....626 359-4550
16021 Adelante St Irwindale (91702) *(P-15444)*
Meeder Equipment Company (PA).....E.....559 485-0979
3495 S Maple Ave Fresno (93725) *(P-14495)*
Meerkat Inc.....F.....909 877-0093
434 S Yucca Ave Rialto (92376) *(P-16191)*
Meese Inc.....E.....714 739-4005
16404 Knott Ave La Mirada (90638) *(P-9892)*
Meese Obitron Dunn Co, La Mirada *Also called Meese Inc (P-9892)*
Mega Force Corporation.....E.....408 956-9989
2035 Otoole Ave San Jose (95131) *(P-15285)*
Mega Led Technology, Commerce *Also called Mega Sign Inc (P-23158)*
Mega Machinery Inc.....F.....951 300-9300
6688 Doolittle Ave Riverside (92503) *(P-14496)*
Mega Plus Pcb Incorporated.....F.....714 550-0265
1479 E Warner Ave Santa Ana (92705) *(P-17921)*
Mega Precision O Rings Inc.....F.....310 530-1166
23206 Normandie Ave Ste 5 Torrance (90502) *(P-16192)*
Mega Sign Inc.....E.....888 315-7446
6500 Flotilla St Commerce (90040) *(P-23158)*
Megachips Technology Amer Corp (HQ).....E.....408 570-0555
2755 Orchard Pkwy San Jose (95134) *(P-18379)*
Megacycle Cams, San Rafael *Also called Megacycle Engineering Inc (P-20419)*
Megacycle Engineering Inc.....F.....415 472-3195
90 Mitchell Blvd San Rafael (94903) *(P-20419)*
Megaforce, San Jose *Also called Mega Force Corporation (P-15285)*
Megaprint Digital Prtg Corp.....F.....650 517-0200
1404 Old County Rd Belmont (94002) *(P-6721)*
Megavision, Goleta *Also called Transcendent Imaging LLC (P-22465)*
Meggitt.....C.....877 666-0712
1785 Voyager Ave Ste 100 Simi Valley (93063) *(P-20172)*
Meggitt (orange County) Inc (HQ).....C.....949 493-8181
14600 Myford Rd Irvine (92606) *(P-21504)*
Meggitt (orange County) Inc.....F.....408 739-3533
355 N Pastoria Ave Sunnyvale (94085) *(P-20628)*
Meggitt (san Diego) Inc (HQ).....C.....858 824-8976
6650 Top Gun St San Diego (92121) *(P-20173)*
Meggitt Aerospace, Sunnyvale *Also called Meggitt (orange County) Inc (P-20628)*
Meggitt Airdynamics Inc (HQ).....E.....951 734-0070
2616 Research Dr Corona (92882) *(P-14671)*
Meggitt Arcft Braking Systems, Gardena *Also called Nasco Aircraft Brake Inc (P-20185)*
Meggitt Control Systems, Simi Valley *Also called Meggitt Safety Systems Inc (P-19355)*
Meggitt Control Systems, North Hollywood *Also called Meggitt North Hollywood Inc (P-13314)*
Meggitt Defense Systems Inc.....B.....949 465-7700
9801 Muirlands Blvd Irvine (92618) *(P-20174)*
Meggitt North Hollywood Inc (HQ).....C.....818 765-8160
12838 Saticoy St North Hollywood (91605) *(P-13314)*
Meggitt Polymers & Composites, Simi Valley *Also called Meggitt-Usa Inc (P-20176)*
Meggitt Polymers & Composites, San Diego *Also called Meggitt (san Diego) Inc (P-20173)*
Meggitt Safety Systems Inc.....D.....805 584-4100
1785 Voyager Ave Simi Valley (93063) *(P-20175)*
Meggitt Safety Systems Inc (HQ).....C.....805 584-4100
1785 Voyager Ave Simi Valley (93063) *(P-19355)*
Meggitt Safety Systems Inc.....C.....805 584-4100
1785 Voyager Ave Simi Valley (93063) *(P-20629)*
Meggitt Sensing Systems, Irvine *Also called Meggitt (orange County) Inc (P-21504)*
Meggitt-Usa Inc (HQ).....C.....805 526-5700
1955 Surveyor Ave Simi Valley (93063) *(P-20176)*
Megiddo Global LLC.....F.....818 267-6686
153 W Rosecrans Ave Gardena (90248) *(P-23406)*
Meguiars Inc (HQ).....E.....949 752-8000
17991 Mitchell S Irvine (92614) *(P-8396)*
MEI Pharma Inc.....E.....858 369-7100
3611 Vly Cntre Dr Ste 500 San Diego (92130) *(P-8008)*
Meisei Corporation.....F.....805 497-2626
948 Tourmaline Dr Newbury Park (91320) *(P-14224)*
Meister Eye & Laser, Citrus Heights *Also called Nvision Laser Eye Centers Inc (P-22374)*
Meivac Incorporated.....E.....408 362-1000
5830 Hellyer Ave San Jose (95138) *(P-18380)*
Mek Denim, Vernon *Also called Deodar Brands LLC (P-2681)*
Mekong Printing Inc.....E.....714 558-9595
2421 W 1st St Santa Ana (92703) *(P-6722)*
Mel & Associates Inc (PA).....F.....831 476-2950
821 41st Ave Santa Cruz (95062) *(P-22852)*
Melamed International Inc (PA).....F.....310 271-8585
113 N Palm Dr Beverly Hills (90210) *(P-3107)*
Melcast, Cerritos *Also called Molino Company (P-6734)*
Melco Engineering Corporation.....F.....818 591-1000
3605 Avenida Cumbre Calabasas (91302) *(P-21815)*
Melco Steel Inc.....E.....626 334-7875
1100 W Foothill Blvd Azusa (91702) *(P-12030)*
Melfred Borzall Inc.....F.....562 946-7524
12115 Shoemaker Ave Santa Fe Springs (90670) *(P-16193)*
Melfred Borzall Inc.....E.....805 614-4344
2712 Airpark Dr Santa Maria (93455) *(P-13933)*
Melian Labs Inc (PA).....F.....888 423-1944
881 Corbett Ave Apt 3 San Francisco (94131) *(P-24146)*
Melkes Machine Inc.....E.....626 448-5062
9928 Hayward Way South El Monte (91733) *(P-16194)*
Melkonian Enterprises Inc.....E.....559 485-6191
2730 S De Wolf Ave Sanger (93657) *(P-854)*
Mellace Family Brands Inc.....C.....760 448-1940
6195 El Camino Real Carlsbad (92009) *(P-1433)*
Mellanox Technologies Inc.....E.....408 970-3400
350 Oakmead Pkwy Ste 100 Sunnyvale (94085) *(P-18381)*
Mellanox Technologies Inc (HQ).....B.....408 970-3400
350 Oakmead Pkwy Sunnyvale (94085) *(P-18382)*
Melles Griot Inc.....F.....760 438-2131
2072 Corte Del Nogal Carlsbad (92011) *(P-21381)*
Melling Sintered Metals, Gardena *Also called Melling Tool Rush Metals LLC (P-11480)*
Melling Tool Rush Metals LLC.....D.....580 725-3295
16100 S Figueroa St Gardena (90248) *(P-11480)*
Mello Sales Group Inc.....F.....707 257-6451
141a Silverado Trl NAPA (94559) *(P-23407)*
Melmarc Products Inc.....B.....714 549-2170
752 S Campus Ave Ontario (91761) *(P-3749)*
Melrose Bakery, Los Angeles *Also called Dimufidra Usa Inc (P-1187)*
Melrose Mac Inc.....F.....818 840-8466
2400 W Olive Ave Burbank (91506) *(P-14944)*
Melrose Metal Products Inc.....E.....510 657-8771
44533 S Grimmer Blvd Fremont (94538) *(P-12289)*
Melrose Nameplate Label Co Inc (PA).....E.....510 732-3100
26575 Corporate Ave Hayward (94545) *(P-13205)*
Melville Winery LLC.....F.....805 735-7030
5185 E Highway 246 Lompoc (93436) *(P-1816)*
Membrane Switch and Panel Inc.....F.....714 957-6905
3198 Arprt Loop Dr Ste K Costa Mesa (92626) *(P-19011)*
Memjet Labels Inc (HQ).....F.....858 673-3300
10920 Via Frontera # 120 San Diego (92127) *(P-15286)*
Memjet Labels Inc.....E.....858 798-3061
10918 Technology Pl San Diego (92127) *(P-15287)*
Memory Experts Intl USA Inc (HQ).....E.....714 258-3000
1651 E Saint Andrew Pl Santa Ana (92705) *(P-15056)*
Memory Glass LLC.....F.....805 682-6469
325 Rutherford St Ste E Goleta (93117) *(P-10319)*
Memory Threads.....F.....818 837-7070
506 E Washington Ave A Santa Ana (92701) *(P-2730)*
Memry Corporation.....C.....650 463-3400
4065 Campbell Ave Menlo Park (94025) *(P-21816)*
Menasha Packaging Company LLC.....E.....951 374-5281
305 Resource Dr Ste 100 Bloomington (92316) *(P-5245)*
Menasha Packaging Company LLC.....D.....562 698-3705
8110 Sorensen Ave Santa Fe Springs (90670) *(P-5246)*
Mencarini & Jarwin Inc.....F.....916 383-1660
5950 88th St Sacramento (95828) *(P-13048)*
Menches Tool & Die Inc.....E.....650 592-2328
30995 San Benito St Hayward (94544) *(P-16195)*
Mendias Imports, Rosemead *Also called Lotus Beverages (P-1804)*
Mendicino Wine Company, Ukiah *Also called Parducci Wine Estates LLC (P-1857)*
Mendo Litho, Fort Bragg *Also called Mendocino Lithographers (P-6723)*
Mendocino Brewing Company Inc.....E.....707 744-1015
13351 S Highway 101 Hopland (95449) *(P-1548)*
Mendocino Lithographers.....F.....707 964-0062
100 N Franklin St Fort Bragg (95437) *(P-6723)*
Menezes Hay Co.....F.....209 394-3111
5030 Dwight Way Livingston (95334) *(P-1112)*
Menlo Energy LLC.....E.....415 762-8200
555 California St # 4600 San Francisco (94104) *(P-8752)*
Menlo Microsystems Inc.....E.....949 771-0277
49 Discovery Ste 150 Irvine (92618) *(P-18383)*
Menlo Therapeutics Inc.....E.....650 486-1416
200 Cardinal Way Ste 200 # 200 Redwood City (94063) *(P-8009)*
Mens Wearhouse.....E.....510 657-9821
6100 Stevenson Blvd Fremont (94538) *(P-3044)*
Mensi, Carson *Also called Mechanized Engineering Systems (P-13884)*
Mentor Graphics Corporation.....E.....858 523-2600
12255 El Camino Real # 150 San Diego (92130) *(P-24147)*
Mentor Graphics Corporation.....F.....949 790-3200
18301 Von Karman Ave # 760 Irvine (92612) *(P-24148)*
Mentor Worldwide LLC (HQ).....C.....800 636-8678
31 Technology Dr Ste 200 Irvine (92618) *(P-22048)*
Mentzer Electronics.....E.....650 697-2642
858 Stanton Rd Burlingame (94010) *(P-22282)*
Menu Services, Buena Park *Also called Advertising Services (P-6398)*
Mepco Label Systems.....D.....209 946-0201
1313 S Stockton St Lodi (95240) *(P-7133)*
Meps Real-Time Inc.....E.....760 448-9500
6451 El Camino Real Ste C Carlsbad (92009) *(P-21505)*
Mer-Mar Electronics, Hesperia *Also called Geeriraj Inc (P-17886)*
Mercado Latino Inc.....E.....310 537-1062
1420 W Walnut St Compton (90220) *(P-23408)*
Merced County Times, Merced *Also called Mid Valley Publication (P-5753)*
Merced Screw Products Inc.....E.....209 723-7706
1861 Grogan Ave Merced (95341) *(P-12641)*
Merced Sun Star, Merced *Also called McClatchy Newspapers Inc (P-5733)*
Mercer Foods LLC.....F.....209 529-0150
1836 Lapham Dr Modesto (95354) *(P-855)*
Merchandising Systems Inc.....E.....510 477-9100
381 Claire Pl Menlo Park (94025) *(P-4990)*
Merchants Metals LLC.....F.....916 381-8243
6829 Mccomber St Sacramento (95828) *(P-13422)*
Merchants Metals LLC.....F.....951 686-1888
6466 Mission Blvd Riverside (92509) *(P-11101)*
Merck & Co Inc.....D.....650 496-6400
901 California Ave Palo Alto (94304) *(P-8010)*
Merck Sharp & Dohme Corp.....D.....619 292-4900
8355 Aero Dr San Diego (92123) *(P-8011)*
Merco Manufacturing Co, Placentia *Also called Aero Pacific Corporation (P-20011)*

ALPHABETIC

Employee Codes: A=Over 500 employees, B=251-500
C=101-250, D=51-100, E=20-50, F=10-19
2020 California
Manfacturers Register
© Mergent Inc. 1-800-342-5647
1169

Mercotac Inc....F.......760 431-7723
6195 Corte Del Cedro # 100 Carlsbad (92011) *(P-16916)*
Mercury Broach Company Inc....F.......626 443-5904
2546 Seaman Ave El Monte (91733) *(P-14171)*
Mercury Engineering Corp....F.......562 861-7816
5630 Imperial Hwy South Gate (90280) *(P-16196)*
Mercury Magnetics Inc....E.......818 998-7791
10050 Remmet Ave Chatsworth (91311) *(P-18726)*
Mercury Metal Die & Letter Co (PA)....F.......951 674-8717
600 3rd St Ste A Lake Elsinore (92530) *(P-13206)*
Mercury Networks LLC....F.......408 859-1345
1800 Wyatt Dr Ste 2 Santa Clara (95054) *(P-17583)*
Mercury Plastics Inc....D.......323 264-2400
2939 E Washington Blvd Los Angeles (90023) *(P-9409)*
Mercury Plastics Inc (PA)....B.......626 961-0165
14825 Salt Lake Ave City of Industry (91746) *(P-5403)*
Mercury Security Products LLC....F.......562 986-9105
2355 Mira Mar Ave Long Beach (90815) *(P-19356)*
Mercury Systems Inc....C.......805 388-1345
1000 Avenida Acaso Camarillo (93012) *(P-17922)*
Mercury Systems Inc....F.......669 226-5800
85 Nicholson Ln San Jose (95134) *(P-17923)*
Mercury Systems - Trsted Mssio, Fremont *Also called Mercury Systems - Trsted Mssio (P-14945)*
Mercury Systems - Trsted Mssio (HQ)....D.......510 252-0870
47200 Bayside Pkwy Fremont (94538) *(P-14945)*
Mercury United Electronics Inc....E.......909 466-0427
9804 Cres Ctr Dr Ste 603 Rancho Cucamonga (91730) *(P-19012)*
Meredith Publishing, San Francisco *Also called Four M Studios (P-6103)*
Merelex Corporation....E.......310 208-0551
10884 Weyburn Ave Los Angeles (90024) *(P-7505)*
Merex Inc....F.......805 446-2700
1283 Flynn Rd Camarillo (93012) *(P-21078)*
Meri Gol Products Limited, Palmdale *Also called Park-Rand Enterprises Inc (P-8404)*
Meridian Gold Inc....C.......209 785-3222
4461 Rock Creek Rd Copperopolis (95228) *(P-7)*
Meridian Graphics Inc....D.......949 833-3500
2652 Dow Ave Tustin (92780) *(P-6724)*
Meridian Jewelry & Design Inc....F.......510 428-2095
3814 La Cresta Ave Oakland (94602) *(P-22548)*
Meridian Rapid Def Group LLC....F.......720 616-7795
177 E Colo Blvd Ste 200 Pasadena (91105) *(P-12290)*
Meridian Technical Sales Inc....E.......408 526-2000
520 Alder Dr Milpitas (95035) *(P-6122)*
Meriliz Incorporated (PA)....C.......916 923-3663
2031 Dome Ln McClellan (95652) *(P-6725)*
Merit Aluminum Inc (PA)....D.......951 735-1770
2480 Railroad St Corona (92880) *(P-11238)*
Merit Cables Incorporated....E.......714 547-3054
830 N Poinsettia St Santa Ana (92701) *(P-21817)*
Merit Printing Ink Company....F.......323 268-1807
1451 S Lorena St Los Angeles (90023) *(P-8927)*
Meritek Electronics Corp (PA)....D.......626 373-1728
5160 Rivergrade Rd Baldwin Park (91706) *(P-14497)*
Merito.com, Van Nuys *Also called Chef Merito Inc (P-2423)*
Meritor Specialty Products LLC (HQ)....F.......248 435-1000
151 Lawrence Dr Livermore (94551) *(P-19717)*
Meritronics Inc (PA)....E.......408 969-0888
500 Yosemite Dr Ste 108 Milpitas (95035) *(P-17924)*
Meritronics Materials Inc....F.......408 390-5642
500 Yosemite Dr Ste 112 Milpitas (95035) *(P-17925)*
Merkle Loyalty Solutions, San Francisco *Also called 500friends Inc (P-23538)*
Merle Norman Cosmetics Inc (PA)....B.......310 641-3000
9130 Bellanca Ave Los Angeles (90045) *(P-8538)*
Merlex Stucco Inc....E.......877 547-8822
2911 N Orange Olive Rd Orange (92865) *(P-11011)*
Merlex Stucco Mfg, Orange *Also called Merlex Stucco Inc (P-11011)*
Merlin Solar Technologies Inc....E.......650 740-1160
5891 Rue Ferrari San Jose (95138) *(P-18384)*
Merlin-Alltec Mold Making Inc....F.......562 529-5050
15543 Minnesota Ave Paramount (90723) *(P-9893)*
Merrick Engineering Inc (PA)....C.......951 737-6040
1275 Quarry St Corona (92879) *(P-9894)*
Merrill Corporation....D.......213 253-5900
350 S Grand Ave Ste 3000 Los Angeles (90071) *(P-7134)*
Merrill Corporation....D.......714 690-2200
10716 Reagan St Los Alamitos (90720) *(P-7135)*
Merrill Corporation....E.......650 493-1400
1731 Embarcadero Rd # 100 Palo Alto (94303) *(P-7136)*
Merrill Corporation....D.......858 623-0300
8899 University Center Ln # 200 San Diego (92122) *(P-7137)*
Merrill Corporation....F.......831 759-9300
14500 Reservation Rd Salinas (93908) *(P-7138)*
Merrill Corporation....F.......949 252-9449
1900 Avenue Of The Stars # 1200 Los Angeles (90067) *(P-7139)*
Merrill Corporation Inc....E.......310 552-5288
10635 Santa Monica Blvd # 350 Los Angeles (90025) *(P-7140)*
Merrill's Packaging Supply, Burlingame *Also called Merrills Packaging Inc (P-9410)*
Merrill/Orange County, Los Angeles *Also called Merrill Corporation (P-7139)*
Merrills Packaging Inc....D.......650 259-5959
1529 Rollins Rd Burlingame (94010) *(P-9410)*
Merryvale Vineyards LLC....E.......707 963-2225
1000 Main St Saint Helena (94574) *(P-1817)*
Meru Networks Inc (HQ)....D.......408 215-5300
894 Ross Dr Sunnyvale (94089) *(P-17746)*
Mesa Label Express Inc....F.......858 668-2820
13257 Kirkham Way Poway (92064) *(P-7141)*
Mesa Reprographics, San Diego *Also called M B C Reprographics Inc (P-7128)*
Mesa Safe Company Inc....E.......714 202-8000
337 W Freedom Ave Orange (92865) *(P-13533)*
Mesa/Boogie Limited (PA)....D.......707 765-1805
1317 Ross St Petaluma (94954) *(P-17259)*
Mesgona Corporation....F.......310 926-3238
12534 Moorpark St Apt H Studio City (91604) *(P-6280)*
Meskin Khosrow Kay....E.......650 595-3090
661 Laurel St San Carlos (94070) *(P-10241)*
Mesmerize, Los Angeles *Also called Kamiran Inc (P-3170)*
Mesotech International Inc....F.......916 368-2020
4531 Harlin Dr Sacramento (95826) *(P-21261)*
Messana Inc....F.......855 729-6244
4105 Soquel Dr Ste B Soquel (95073) *(P-14770)*
Messana Radiant Cooling, Soquel *Also called Messana Inc (P-14770)*
Messer LLC....F.......562 903-1290
13117 Meyer Rd Whittier (90605) *(P-7421)*
Messer LLC....E.......310 533-8394
2535 Del Amo Blvd Torrance (90503) *(P-7422)*
Messer LLC....F.......510 233-8911
731 W Cutting Blvd Richmond (94804) *(P-7423)*
Messer LLC....E.......916 381-1606
5858 88th St Sacramento (95828) *(P-7424)*
Messer LLC....E.......925 371-4170
4569 Las Positas Rd Ste C Livermore (94551) *(P-7425)*
Messer LLC....D.......626 855-8366
660 Baldwin Park Blvd City of Industry (91746) *(P-7426)*
Messer LLC....D.......408 496-1177
2041 Mission College Blvd Santa Clara (95054) *(P-14590)*
Messer Logging Inc....E.......559 855-3160
32111 Rock Hill Ln Auberry (93602) *(P-3898)*
Mestek Inc....C.......310 835-7500
1220 E Watson Center Rd Carson (90745) *(P-15445)*
Metabasis Therapeutics Inc....F.......858 550-7500
11085 N Torrey Pines Rd # 300 La Jolla (92037) *(P-8012)*
Metacrylics, Gilroy *Also called Instant Asphalt Inc (P-8875)*
Metal Art of California Inc....D.......714 532-7100
640 N Cypress St Orange (92867) *(P-23159)*
Metal Art of California Inc (PA)....D.......714 532-7100
640 N Cypress St Orange (92867) *(P-23160)*
Metal Building Components Mbci, Atwater *Also called Nci Group Inc (P-12567)*
Metal Cast Inc....E.......714 285-9792
2002 W Chestnut Ave Santa Ana (92703) *(P-11172)*
Metal Chem Inc....E.......818 727-9951
21514 Nordhoff St Chatsworth (91311) *(P-13049)*
Metal Coaters, Rancho Cucamonga *Also called Nci Group Inc (P-12566)*
Metal Coaters California Inc....D.......909 987-4681
9123 Center Ave Rancho Cucamonga (91730) *(P-13207)*
Metal Coaters System, Rancho Cucamonga *Also called Metal Coaters California Inc (P-13207)*
Metal Container Corporation....C.......951 354-0444
7155 Central Ave Riverside (92504) *(P-11499)*
Metal Container Corporation....C.......951 360-4500
10980 Inland Ave Jurupa Valley (91752) *(P-11500)*
Metal Engineering Inc....E.......626 334-1819
1642 S Sacramento Ave Ontario (91761) *(P-12291)*
Metal Engineering & Mfg....F.......626 334-5271
1031b W Kirkwall Rd Azusa (91702) *(P-12292)*
Metal Etch Services Inc....E.......760 510-9476
1165 Linda Vista Dr # 106 San Marcos (92078) *(P-21262)*
Metal Fabrication and Art LLC....F.......323 980-9595
3499 E 15th St Los Angeles (90023) *(P-11841)*
Metal Fd Hhld Pdts Pckging Div, Oakdale *Also called Ball Corporation (P-11493)*
Metal Finishing Division, South Gate *Also called Anadite Cal Restoration Tr (P-12926)*
Metal Finishing Solutions Inc....F.......408 988-8642
870 Comstock St Santa Clara (95054) *(P-12293)*
Metal Improvement Company LLC....E.......323 585-2168
2588 Industry Way A Lynwood (90262) *(P-11456)*
Metal Improvement Company LLC....D.......818 983-1952
6940 Farmdale Ave North Hollywood (91605) *(P-11457)*
Metal Improvement Company LLC....E.......949 855-8010
35 Argonaut Ste A1 Laguna Hills (92656) *(P-11458)*
Metal Improvement Company LLC....D.......818 407-6280
20751 Superior St Chatsworth (91311) *(P-11459)*
Metal Improvement Company LLC....E.......925 960-1090
7655 Longard Rd Bldg A Livermore (94551) *(P-11460)*
Metal Improvement Company LLC....F.......714 546-4160
2151 S Hathaway St Santa Ana (92705) *(P-11461)*
Metal Improvement Company LLC....F.......323 563-1533
2588a Industry Way Lynwood (90262) *(P-11462)*
Metal Manufacturing Co Inc....E.......916 922-3484
2240 Evergreen St Sacramento (95815) *(P-11969)*
Metal Master Inc....E.......858 292-8880
4611 Overland Ave San Diego (92123) *(P-12294)*
Metal Preparations....E.......213 628-5176
1000 E Ocean Blvd # 416 Long Beach (90802) *(P-13050)*
Metal Products Engineering, Vernon *Also called Luppen Holdings Inc (P-12839)*
Metal Products Engineering....E.......323 581-8121
3050 Leonis Blvd Vernon (90058) *(P-11463)*
Metal Sales Manufacturing Corp....F.......909 829-8618
14213 Whittram Ave Fontana (92335) *(P-12295)*
Metal Supply LLC....D.......562 634-9940
11810 Center St South Gate (90280) *(P-11842)*
Metal Surfaces Inc....C.......562 927-1331
6060 Shull St Bell Gardens (90201) *(P-13051)*
Metal Tek Engineering Inc....E.......909 821-4158
7426 Cherry Ave Ste 210 Fontana (92336) *(P-4084)*
Metal Tite Products (PA)....D.......562 695-0645
4880 Gregg Rd Pico Rivera (90660) *(P-11970)*
Metal Works Supply, Oroville *Also called Smb Industries Inc (P-11881)*

Mergent e-mail: customerrelations@mergent.com
1170
2020 California
Manufacturers Register
(P-0000) Products & Services Section entry number
(PA)=Parent Co (HQ)=Headquarters (DH)=Div Headquarters

Metal X Direct Inc F 949 336-0055
1555 Mesa Verde Dr E 11g Costa Mesa (92626) *(P-12499)*
Metal-Fab Services Industries E 714 630-7771
2500 E Miraloma Way Anaheim (92806) *(P-12296)*
Metalcast, Santa Ana *Also called Metal Cast Inc (P-11172)*
Metalfab, Santa Clara *Also called Sutter P Dahlglen Entps Inc (P-16433)*
Metalfx, Willits *Also called Advanced Mfg & Dev Inc (P-12088)*
Metalite Manufacturing, Pacoima *Also called Hanmar LLC (P-12811)*
Metalite Manufacturing Company E 818 890-2802
11441 Bradley Ave Pacoima (91331) *(P-12843)*
Metalite Mfg Companys, Pacoima *Also called Metalite Manufacturing Company (P-12843)*
Metalore Inc E 310 643-0360
750 S Douglas St El Segundo (90245) *(P-16197)*
Metalpro Industries Inc E 661 294-0764
28064 Avenue Stanford H Santa Clarita (91355) *(P-12297)*
Metals Direct Inc E 530 605-1931
6771 Eastside Rd Redding (96001) *(P-12298)*
Metals USA Building Pdts LP D 714 522-7852
6450a Caballero Blvd Buena Park (90620) *(P-11843)*
Metals USA Building Pdts LP (HQ) A 713 946-9000
955 Columbia St Brea (92821) *(P-11263)*
Metals USA Building Pdts LP E 800 325-1305
1951 S Parco Ave Ste C Ontario (91761) *(P-11264)*
Metals USA Building Pdts LP E 916 635-2245
11340 White Rock Rd Ste B Rancho Cordova (95742) *(P-11265)*
Metals USA Building Pdts LP E 714 529-0407
955 Columbia St Brea (92821) *(P-11266)*
Metalset Inc E 510 233-9998
1200 Hensley St Richmond (94801) *(P-11844)*
Metamaterial Tech USA Inc F 650 993-9223
5880 W Las Positas Blvd Pleasanton (94588) *(P-21382)*
Metco Fourslide Manufacturing, Gardena *Also called Metco Manufacturing Inc (P-12844)*
Metco Manufacturing Inc E 310 516-6547
17540 S Denver Ave Gardena (90248) *(P-12844)*
Metech Recycling Inc E 408 848-3050
6200 Engle Way Gilroy (95020) *(P-11205)*
Meteor Lighting, City of Industry *Also called Ilos Corp (P-17134)*
Method Home Products F 415 568-4600
637 Commercial St Fl 3 San Francisco (94111) *(P-5132)*
Metlsaw Systems Inc E 707 746-6200
2950 Bay Vista Ct Benicia (94510) *(P-13934)*
Metra Biosystems Inc (HQ) E 408 616-4300
2981 Copper Rd Santa Clara (95051) *(P-8237)*
Metra Electronics Corporation F 562 470-6601
3201 E 59th St Long Beach (90805) *(P-19718)*
Metrex Valve Corp E 626 335-4027
505 S Vermont Ave Glendora (91741) *(P-13315)*
Metric Design & Manufacturing F 408 378-4544
217 E Hacienda Ave Campbell (95008) *(P-14077)*
Metric Machining (PA) E 909 947-9222
3263 Trade Center Dr Riverside (92507) *(P-13935)*
Metric Precision, Huntington Beach *Also called AMG Torrance LLC (P-20032)*
Metric Products Inc (PA) E 310 815-9000
4630 Leahy St Culver City (90232) *(P-3454)*
Metric Systems Corporation F 760 560-0348
2091 Las Palmas Dr Ste D Carlsbad (92011) *(P-17584)*
Metricstream Inc (PA) C 650 620-2900
2479 E Byshore Rd Ste 260 Palo Alto (94303) *(P-24149)*
Metro Digital Printing Inc E 714 545-8400
3311 W Macarthur Blvd Santa Ana (92704) *(P-6726)*
Metro Novelty & Pleating Co D 213 748-1201
906 Thayer Ave Los Angeles (90024) *(P-3800)*
Metro Poly Corporation E 510 357-9898
1651 Aurora Dr San Leandro (94577) *(P-5404)*
Metro Publishing Inc F 831 457-9000
1205 Pacific Ave Ste 301 Santa Cruz (95060) *(P-5750)*
Metro Publishing Inc F 707 527-1200
847 5th St Santa Rosa (95404) *(P-5751)*
Metro Ready Mix F 661 829-7851
1635 James Rd Bakersfield (93308) *(P-10802)*
Metro Roof Products, Oceanside *Also called Metrotile Manufacturing LLC (P-9121)*
Metro Santa Cruz Newspaper, Santa Cruz *Also called Metro Publishing Inc (P-5750)*
Metro Truck Body Incorporated E 310 532-5570
1201 W Jon St Torrance (90502) *(P-19546)*
Metro World Plastics Inc F 415 255-8515
344348 Shell St San Francisco (94102) *(P-9411)*
Metrofeed, San Diego *Also called Asset General Inc (P-23629)*
Metrolaser Inc F 949 553-0688
22941 Mill Creek Dr Laguna Hills (92653) *(P-21263)*
Metroll, Fontana *Also called Buildmat Plus Investments Inc (P-10544)*
Metromedia Technologies Inc E 818 552-6500
19401 S Vt Ave Ste E100 Torrance (90502) *(P-15288)*
Metronome Software LLC F 949 273-5190
25241 Paseo De Alicia # 200 Laguna Hills (92653) *(P-24150)*
Metrophones Unlimited Inc E 650 630-5400
15675 La Jolla Ct Morgan Hill (95037) *(P-17386)*
Metropolitan News Company, Los Angeles *Also called Grace Communications Inc (P-5648)*
Metropolitan News Company E 951 369-5890
3540 12th St Riverside (92501) *(P-5752)*
Metrosa, Santa Rosa *Also called Metro Publishing Inc (P-5751)*
Metrotech Corporation (PA) D 408 734-3880
3251 Olcott St Santa Clara (95054) *(P-20630)*
Metrotile Manufacturing LLC E 760 435-9842
3093 Industry St Ste A Oceanside (92054) *(P-9121)*
Mettler Electronics Corp E 714 533-2221
1333 S Claudina St Anaheim (92805) *(P-21818)*
Mettler-Toledo Rainin LLC (HQ) C 510 564-1600
7500 Edgewater Dr Oakland (94621) *(P-21506)*
Mevsa, Cypress *Also called Mitsubishi Electric Visual (P-19021)*
Mexapparel Inc (PA) F 323 364-8600
2344 E 38th St Vernon (90058) *(P-3045)*
Meyco Machine and Tool Inc E 714 435-1546
11579 Martens River Cir Fountain Valley (92708) *(P-14172)*
Meyenburg Goat Milk Products, Turlock *Also called Jackson-Mitchell Inc (P-704)*
Meyer Cookware Industries Inc E 707 551-2800
1 Meyer Plz Vallejo (94590) *(P-12845)*
Meyer Corporation US (HQ) D 707 551-2800
1 Meyer Plz Vallejo (94590) *(P-12846)*
Meyer Sound Laboratories Inc (PA) C 510 486-1166
2832 San Pablo Ave Berkeley (94702) *(P-17260)*
Meyer Sound Labs, Berkeley *Also called Meyer Sound Laboratories Inc (P-17260)*
Meyer Wines, Vallejo *Also called Meyer Corporation US (P-12846)*
Meyers Publishing Inc F 805 445-8881
799 Camarillo Springs Rd Camarillo (93012) *(P-5987)*
Meyers Sheet Metal Box Inc F 650 873-8889
138 W Harris Ave South San Francisco (94080) *(P-12299)*
Meza Pallet Inc F 909 829-0223
14619 Merrill Ave Fontana (92335) *(P-4339)*
Meziere Enterprises Inc E 800 208-1755
220 S Hale Ave Ste A Escondido (92029) *(P-16198)*
Mf Inc C 213 627-2498
2010 E 15th St Los Angeles (90021) *(P-3180)*
Mfb Worldwide Inc (PA) F 323 562-2339
4901 Patata St 201-204 Cudahy (90201) *(P-2945)*
Mfg Packaging Products F 714 984-2300
3200 Enterprise St Brea (92821) *(P-14718)*
Mfi Inc F 949 887-8691
363 San Miguel Dr Ste 200 Newport Beach (92660) *(P-23409)*
Mflex, Irvine *Also called Multi-Fineline Electronix Inc (P-17928)*
Mgb Industries Inc F 619 247-9284
679 Anita St Ste B Chula Vista (91911) *(P-20177)*
MGF Graphics, Northridge *Also called N M H Inc (P-6742)*
Mgfso LLC F 949 500-7645
7372 Siena Dr Huntington Beach (92648) *(P-8013)*
MGM Brakes, Cloverdale *Also called Indian Head Industries Inc (P-19689)*
MGM Brakes D 707 894-3333
1184 S Cloverdale Blvd Cloverdale (95425) *(P-19719)*
MGM Data Inc F 213 747-3282
155 W Wash Blvd 105los Los Angeles (90015) *(P-15057)*
MGM Transformer Co D 323 726-0888
5701 Smithway St Commerce (90040) *(P-16562)*
Mgp Caliper Covers, Chula Vista *Also called Marshall Genuine Products LLC (P-14170)*
Mgr Design International Inc C 805 981-6400
1950 Williams Dr Oxnard (93036) *(P-23410)*
MGT Industries Inc (PA) C 310 516-5900
13889 S Figueroa St Los Angeles (90061) *(P-3373)*
Mhb Group Inc E 408 744-1011
1240 Mountain Vw Alviso C Sunnyvale (94089) *(P-5988)*
Ml Rancho Tortilla Inc D 559 299-3183
801 Purvis Ave Clovis (93612) *(P-2550)*
Ml Rancho Tortilla Factory, San Leandro *Also called Berber Food Manufacturing Inc (P-2402)*
Ml Technologies Inc C 619 710-2637
2215 Pseo De Las Americas San Diego (92154) *(P-17926)*
Mi9, Pleasanton *Also called Software Development Inc (P-24427)*
Miasole B 408 919-5700
2590 Walsh Ave Santa Clara (95051) *(P-18385)*
Miasole Hi-Tech Corp (HQ) C 408 919-5700
2590 Walsh Ave Santa Clara (95051) *(P-18386)*
Mic Labs F 925 822-2847
7643 Corrinne Pl San Ramon (94583) *(P-222)*
Michael and Company, Lockeford *Also called Woodside Investment Inc (P-13558)*
Michael BS LLC E 310 320-0141
22625 S Western Ave Torrance (90501) *(P-739)*
Michael D Wilson Inc F 559 568-1115
19774 Orange Belt Dr Strathmore (93267) *(P-13534)*
Michael Hagan E 909 213-5916
17858 Laurel Dr Fontana (92336) *(P-22853)*
Michael T Mingione F 408 365-1544
2885 Aiello Dr Ste D San Jose (95111) *(P-4991)*
Michaels Furniture Company Inc B 916 381-9086
15 Koch Rd Ste J Corte Madera (94925) *(P-4591)*
Michaels Stores Inc E 909 646-9656
15228 Summit Ave Fontana (92336) *(P-23411)*
Michel-Schlmberger Partners LP E 707 433-7427
4155 Wine Creek Rd Healdsburg (95448) *(P-1818)*
Michel-Schlumberger Fine Wine, Healdsburg *Also called Michel-Schlmberger Partners LP (P-1818)*
Michelle Alisa Designs Inc F 818 501-9300
4528 Van Noord Ave Studio City (91604) *(P-22549)*
Michelsen Packaging California, Fresno *Also called Michelsen Packaging Co Cal (P-5331)*
Michelsen Packaging Co Cal E 559 237-3819
4165 S Cherry Ave Fresno (93706) *(P-5331)*
Michigan Metal Partitions, Anaheim *Also called Weis/Robart Partitions Inc (P-12521)*
Micile Inc F 626 381-9974
1225 S Shamrock Ave Monrovia (91016) *(P-14946)*
Micrel LLC A 408 944-0800
2180 Fortune Dr San Jose (95131) *(P-18387)*
Micrel LLC C 408 944-0800
1849 Fortune Dr San Jose (95131) *(P-18388)*
Micrel LLC C 408 944-0800
1931 Fortune Dr San Jose (95131) *(P-18389)*
Micrel Semiconductor, San Jose *Also called Micrel LLC (P-18388)*
Micro Analog Inc C 909 392-8277
1861 Puddingstone Dr La Verne (91750) *(P-18390)*
Micro Chips of America Inc E 818 577-9543
5302 Comercio Ln Apt 1 Woodland Hills (91364) *(P-19013)*

ALPHABETIC

Employee Codes: A=Over 500 employees, B=251-500
C=101-250, D=51-100, E=20-50, F=10-19
2020 California
Manfacturers Register
© Mergent Inc. 1-800-342-5647
1171

Micro Connectors Inc .... E 510 266-0299
2700 Mccone Ave Hayward (94545) *(P-15289)*

Micro Express, Irvine *Also called A S A Engineering Inc* *(P-14877)*

Micro Filtration Systems, Dublin *Also called Advantec Mfs Inc* *(P-14643)*

Micro Focus LLC (HQ) .... F 801 861-7000
4555 Great America Pkwy # 401 Santa Clara (95054) *(P-24151)*

Micro Gage Inc .... E 626 443-1741
9537 Telstar Ave Ste 131 El Monte (91731) *(P-18391)*

Micro Grow Greenhouse Systems .... F 951 296-3340
42065 Zevo Dr Ste B1 Temecula (92590) *(P-20798)*

Micro Lambda Wireless Inc .... E 510 770-9221
46515 Landing Pkwy Fremont (94538) *(P-19014)*

Micro Lithography Inc .... C 408 747-1769
1247 Elko Dr Sunnyvale (94089) *(P-20903)*

Micro Matic Usa Inc .... E 818 701-9765
19761 Bahama St 19791 Northridge (91324) *(P-15446)*

Micro Matic Usa Inc .... E 818 882-8012
19791 Bahama St Northridge (91324) *(P-13316)*

Micro Matrix Systems (PA) .... E 909 626-8544
1899 Salem Ct Claremont (91711) *(P-12847)*

Micro Plastics Inc .... E 818 882-0244
20821 Dearborn St Chatsworth (91311) *(P-16917)*

Micro Semicdtr Researches LLC .... E 408 492-1369
805 Aldo Ave Ste 101 Santa Clara (95054) *(P-18392)*

Micro Space Products, Hawthorne *Also called K & E Inc* *(P-20148)*

Micro Steel Inc .... E 818 348-8701
7850 Alabama Ave Canoga Park (91304) *(P-20479)*

Micro Surface Engr Inc (PA) .... E 323 582-7348
1550 E Slauson Ave Los Angeles (90011) *(P-11481)*

Micro Tech Systems, Fremont *Also called Mt Systems Inc* *(P-14503)*

Micro Therapeutics (HQ) .... E 949 837-3700
9775 Toledo Way Irvine (92618) *(P-21819)*

Micro Tool & Manufacturing Inc .... E 619 582-2884
6494 Federal Blvd Lemon Grove (91945) *(P-14173)*

Micro Trim Inc .... F 714 241-7046
3613 W Macarthur Blvd # 605 Santa Ana (92704) *(P-11239)*

Micro-DOT, Santa Clarita *Also called Zada Graphics Inc* *(P-6947)*

Micro-Metric Inc. .... F 408 452-8505
1050 Commercial St San Jose (95112) *(P-21507)*

Micro-Mode Products Inc. .... C 619 449-3844
1870 John Towers Ave El Cajon (92020) *(P-17585)*

Micro-OHM Corporation .... E 626 357-5377
1088 Hamilton Rd Duarte (91010) *(P-18690)*

Micro-Probe Incorporated (HQ) .... D 408 457-3900
617 River Oaks Pkwy San Jose (95134) *(P-21079)*

Micro-TEC, Chatsworth *Also called Wallace E Miller Inc* *(P-16509)*

Micro-Tech Scientific Inc .... F 760 597-9088
3059 Palm Hill Dr Vista (92084) *(P-21264)*

Micro-Tracers Inc .... F 415 822-1100
1370 Van Dyke Ave San Francisco (94124) *(P-8999)*

Micro-Tronics, Sonora *Also called O M Jones Inc* *(P-19033)*

Micro-Vu Corp California (PA) .... D 707 838-6272
7909 Conde Ln Windsor (95492) *(P-21383)*

Micro/Sys Inc. .... E 818 244-4600
3730 Park Pl Montrose (91020) *(P-14947)*

Microbar Inc .... B 510 659-9770
45473 Warm Springs Blvd Fremont (94539) *(P-14498)*

Microbiotic Health Foods Inc .... F 858 273-5775
4901 Morena Blvd Ste 403 San Diego (92117) *(P-1321)*

Microchip Technology Inc .... C 408 735-9110
450 Holger Way San Jose (95134) *(P-18393)*

Microcool .... F 760 322-1111
72216 Northshore St # 103 Thousand Palms (92276) *(P-20904)*

Microcosm Inc. .... E 310 219-2700
3111 Lomita Blvd Torrance (90505) *(P-20465)*

Microdyn-Nadir Us Inc (HQ) .... D 805 964-8003
93 S La Patera Ln Goleta (93117) *(P-15543)*

Microdyne Plastics Inc .... D 909 503-4010
1901 E Cooley Dr Colton (92324) *(P-9895)*

Microfab Manufacturing Inc .... F 760 744-7240
220 Distribution St San Marcos (92078) *(P-12300)*

Microfab Mfg Shtmtl Pdts, San Marcos *Also called Microfab Manufacturing Inc* *(P-12300)*

Microfabrica Inc .... E 888 964-2763
7911 Haskell Ave Van Nuys (91406) *(P-19015)*

Microflex Technologies LLC .... F 714 937-1507
430 W Collins Ave Orange (92867) *(P-18394)*

Microform Precision LLC .... D 916 419-0580
4244 S Market Ct Ste A Sacramento (95834) *(P-12301)*

Microlux Inc .... F 408 435-1700
1065 Asbury St San Jose (95126) *(P-19357)*

Micromega Systems Inc .... F 415 924-4700
2 Fifer Ave Ste 120 Corte Madera (94925) *(P-24152)*

Micrometals Inc (PA) .... D 714 970-9400
5615 E La Palma Ave Anaheim (92807) *(P-19016)*

Micrometals/Texas Inc. .... E 325 677-8753
5615 E La Palma Ave Anaheim (92807) *(P-19017)*

Micromold Inc. .... F 951 684-7130
2100 Iowa Ave Riverside (92507) *(P-9896)*

Micron Consumer Pdts Group Inc (HQ) .... F 669 226-3000
540 Alder Dr Fremont (94538) *(P-15058)*

Micron Instruments, Simi Valley *Also called Piezo-Metrics Inc* *(P-18469)*

Micron Machine Company .... E 858 486-5900
12530 Stowe Dr Poway (92064) *(P-16199)*

Micron Technology Inc .... E 408 855-4000
570 Alder Dr Bldg 2 Milpitas (95035) *(P-18395)*

Micron Technology Inc .... A 916 458-3003
2235 Iron Point Rd Folsom (95630) *(P-18396)*

Micronas USA Inc .... C 408 625-1200
560 S Winchester Blvd San Jose (95128) *(P-17261)*

Micronova Manufacturing Inc .... E 310 784-6990
3431 Lomita Blvd Torrance (90505) *(P-3627)*

Microplate, Inglewood *Also called Multichrome Company Inc* *(P-13056)*

Microplex Inc .... F 714 630-8220
1070 Ortega Way Placentia (92870) *(P-18397)*

Micropoint Bioscience Inc .... E 408 588-1682
3521 Leonard Ct Santa Clara (95054) *(P-8238)*

Microprint Inc .... E 626 369-1950
133 Puente Ave City of Industry (91746) *(P-6727)*

Micros Systems Inc .... C 443 285-8000
5805 Owens Dr Pleasanton (94588) *(P-24153)*

Microscale Industries Inc .... F 714 593-1422
18435 Bandilier Cir Fountain Valley (92708) *(P-6728)*

Microsemi Communications Inc .... E 805 388-3700
11861 Western Ave Garden Grove (92841) *(P-18398)*

Microsemi Communications Inc (HQ) .... C 805 388-3700
4721 Calle Carga Camarillo (93012) *(P-18399)*

Microsemi Corp - Pwr Prdts Grp. .... F 408 986-8031
3000 Oakmead Village Dr Santa Clara (95051) *(P-18400)*

Microsemi Corp - Santa Ana, Garden Grove *Also called Microsemi Corporation* *(P-18404)*

Microsemi Corp- Rf Integrated (HQ) .... C 916 850-8640
105 Lake Forest Way Folsom (95630) *(P-18401)*

Microsemi Corp-Analog .... E 408 643-6000
3850 N 1st St San Jose (95134) *(P-18402)*

Microsemi Corp-Analog (HQ) .... D 714 898-8121
11861 Western Ave Garden Grove (92841) *(P-18403)*

Microsemi Corp-Power MGT Group .... C 714 994-6500
11861 Western Ave Garden Grove (92841) *(P-16732)*

Microsemi Corporation .... B 714 898-7112
11861 Western Ave Garden Grove (92841) *(P-18404)*

Microsemi Corporation (HQ) .... E 949 380-6100
1 Enterprise Aliso Viejo (92656) *(P-18405)*

Microsemi Corporation .... C 707 568-5900
3843 Brickway Blvd # 100 Santa Rosa (95403) *(P-18406)*

Microsemi Corporation .... F 408 643-6000
3850 N 1st St San Jose (95134) *(P-18407)*

Microsemi Corporation .... D 650 318-4200
3870 N 1st St San Jose (95134) *(P-18408)*

Microsemi Frequency Time Corp .... D 707 528-1230
3750 Westwind Blvd Santa Rosa (95403) *(P-18409)*

Microsemi Frequency Time Corp .... E 805 465-1700
802 Calle Plano Camarillo (93012) *(P-18410)*

Microsemi Frequency Time Corp .... F 408 433-0910
2300 Orchard Pkwy San Jose (95131) *(P-18411)*

Microsemi Rfis, Folsom *Also called Microsemi Corp- Rf Integrated* *(P-18401)*

Microsemi Semiconductor US Inc .... D 707 568-5900
3843 Brickway Blvd # 100 Santa Rosa (95403) *(P-19018)*

Microsemi Soc Corp (HQ) .... D 408 643-6000
3870 N 1st St San Jose (95134) *(P-18412)*

Microsemi Soc Corp .... E 650 318-4200
2051 Stierlin Ct Mountain View (94043) *(P-18413)*

Microsemi Stor Solutions Inc (HQ) .... D 408 239-8000
1380 Bordeaux Dr Sunnyvale (94089) *(P-18414)*

Microsemi Stor Solutions Inc. .... F 916 788-3300
101 Creekside Ridge Ct # 100 Roseville (95678) *(P-18415)*

Microsoft Corporation .... E 949 680-3000
75 Enterprise Ste 100 Aliso Viejo (92656) *(P-24154)*

Microsoft Corporation .... E 858 909-3800
9255 Towne Centre Dr # 400 San Diego (92121) *(P-24155)*

Microsoft Corporation .... D 650 964-7200
1085 La Avenida St Mountain View (94043) *(P-24156)*

Microsoft Corporation .... E 619 849-5872
7007 Friars Rd San Diego (92108) *(P-24157)*

Microsoft Corporation .... E 916 369-3600
1415 L St Ste 200 Sacramento (95814) *(P-24158)*

Microsoft Corporation .... C 650 693-1009
1020 Entp Way Bldg B Sunnyvale (94089) *(P-24159)*

Microsoft Corporation .... C 650 693-4000
680 Vaqueros Ave Sunnyvale (94085) *(P-15290)*

Microsoft Corporation .... C 949 263-3000
3 Park Plz Ste 1800 Irvine (92614) *(P-24160)*

Microsoft Corporation .... D 213 806-7300
13031 W Jefferson Blvd # 200 Playa Vista (90094) *(P-24161)*

Microsoft Corporation .... F 415 972-6400
555 California St Ste 200 San Francisco (94104) *(P-24162)*

Microsoft Corporation .... D 408 987-9608
2045 Lafayette St Santa Clara (95050) *(P-24163)*

Microsource Inc .... D 925 328-4650
5990 Gleason Dr Dublin (94568) *(P-21080)*

Microtech LLC .... E 714 966-1645
17260 Newhope St Fountain Valley (92708) *(P-22173)*

Microtech Scientific, Vista *Also called Micro-Tech Scientific Inc* *(P-21264)*

Microtech Systems Inc .... F 650 596-1900
5619 Scotts Valley Dr # 160 Scotts Valley (95066) *(P-19223)*

Microtelematics Inc .... F 949 537-3636
1500 Quail St Ste 280 Newport Beach (92660) *(P-24164)*

Microvention Inc (HQ) .... B 714 258-8000
35 Enterprise Aliso Viejo (92656) *(P-21820)*

Microvention Terumo, Aliso Viejo *Also called Microvention Inc* *(P-21820)*

Microvision Development Inc .... E 760 438-7781
1734 Oriole Ct Carlsbad (92011) *(P-24165)*

Microvoice Corporation .... E 805 389-2922
345 Willis Ave Camarillo (93010) *(P-17586)*

Microvoice Systems, Camarillo *Also called Microvoice Corporation* *(P-17586)*

Microwave Dynamics .... F 949 679-7788
16541 Scientific Irvine (92618) *(P-17587)*

Microwave Power Products Div, Palo Alto *Also called Communications & Pwr Inds LLC* *(P-17779)*

Microwave Technology Inc (HQ) .... E 510 651-6700
4268 Solar Way Fremont (94538) *(P-19019)*

Micrus Endovascular LLC (HQ) ... C ... 408 433-1400
821 Fox Ln San Jose (95131) ***(P-21821)***
Mid Century Imports Inc ... F ... 818 509-3050
5333 Cahuenga Blvd North Hollywood (91601) ***(P-4592)***
Mid Labs, San Leandro *Also called Medical Instr Dev Labs Inc* ***(P-21798)***
Mid Michigan Trading Post Ltd ... D ... 517 323-9020
5200 Lankershim Blvd # 350 North Hollywood (91601) ***(P-6281)***
Mid Ohio Field Services LLC ... F ... 614 755-5067
4686 Ontario Mills Pkwy Ontario (91764) ***(P-223)***
Mid Valley Dairy, Turlock *Also called Super Store Industries* ***(P-669)***
Mid Valley Grinding Co Inc ... F ... 818 764-1086
616 Irving Ave Glendale (91201) ***(P-23412)***
Mid Valley Mfg Inc ... F ... 559 864-9441
2039 W Superior Ave Caruthers (93609) ***(P-16200)***
Mid Valley Milk Co ... F ... 661 721-8419
10786 Avenue 144 Tipton (93272) ***(P-705)***
Mid Valley Publication ... E ... 209 383-0433
2221 K St Merced (95340) ***(P-5753)***
Mid Valley Publications, Winton *Also called Winton Times* ***(P-5868)***
Mid-State Concrete Products ... E ... 805 928-2855
1625 E Donovan Rd Ste C Santa Maria (93454) ***(P-10602)***
Mid-Valley Tarp Service, Modesto *Also called Modesto Tent and Awning Inc* ***(P-3691)***
Mid-West Fabricating Co ... E ... 562 698-9615
8623 Dice Rd Santa Fe Springs (90670) ***(P-19720)***
Mid-West Wholesale Hardware Co ... E ... 714 630-4751
1274 N Grove St Anaheim (92806) ***(P-11611)***
Midas Technology Inc ... E ... 818 937-4774
2552 White Rd Ste A Irvine (92614) ***(P-17262)***
Middle East Baking Co ... E ... 650 348-7200
1380 Marsten Rd Burlingame (94010) ***(P-1241)***
Middle Sales, Woodland *Also called Interlock Industries Inc* ***(P-12248)***
Midern Computer Inc ... E ... 626 964-8682
18005 Cortney Ct City of Industry (91748) ***(P-14948)***
Midonna Inc ... F ... 562 983-5140
1375 Caspian Ave Long Beach (90813) ***(P-7142)***
Midrange Software Inc ... E ... 818 762-8539
12716 Riverside Dr Studio City (91607) ***(P-24166)***
Midthrust Imports Inc ... E ... 213 749-6651
830 E 14th Pl Los Angeles (90021) ***(P-2818)***
Midvalley Publishing Inc ... E ... 559 638-2244
1130 G St Reedley (93654) ***(P-5754)***
Midvalley Publishing Inc ... E ... 559 875-2511
740 N St Sanger (93657) ***(P-5755)***
Midway Farms, Fresno *Also called California Dried Fruit Inc* ***(P-845)***
Midwest Rubber, Ontario *Also called Ace Calendering Enterprises* ***(P-9278)***
Midwestern Pipeline Svcs Inc (PA) ... F ... 707 557-6633
160 Klamath Ct American Canyon (94503) ***(P-9122)***
Mighty Networks Inc ... F ... 323 464-1050
2690 N Beachwood Dr Fl 2 Los Angeles (90068) ***(P-6282)***
Mighty Soy Inc ... F ... 323 266-6969
1227 S Eastern Ave Los Angeles (90022) ***(P-14386)***
Miholin Inc ... F ... 213 820-8225
1500 S Bradshawe Ave Monterey Park (91754) ***(P-3108)***
Mikailian Meat Product Inc ... F ... 661 257-1055
25310 Avenue Stanford Santa Clarita (91355) ***(P-480)***
Mikawaya, Vernon *Also called Mochi Ice Cream Company* ***(P-1244)***
Mike Fellows ... E ... 707 938-0278
28913 Arnold Dr Sonoma (95476) ***(P-3801)***
Mike Kenney Tool Inc ... E ... 714 577-9262
2900 Saturn St Ste A Brea (92821) ***(P-16201)***
Mike Murach & Associates ... F ... 559 440-9071
4340 N Knoll Ave Fresno (93722) ***(P-6123)***
Mike Printer Inc ... F ... 818 902-9922
6933 Woodley Ave Van Nuys (91406) ***(P-6729)***
Mikelson Machine Shop Inc ... E ... 626 448-3920
2546 Merced Ave South El Monte (91733) ***(P-20178)***
Mikes Metal Works Inc ... F ... 619 440-8804
3552 Fowler Canyon Rd Jamul (91935) ***(P-11057)***
Mikes Micro Parts Inc ... E ... 626 443-0675
1901 Potrero Ave South El Monte (91733) ***(P-16202)***
Mikes Precision Welding Inc ... F ... 951 676-4744
28073 Diaz Rd Ste D Temecula (92590) ***(P-24651)***
Mikes Sheet Metal Products ... E ... 916 348-3800
3315 Elkhorn Blvd North Highlands (95660) ***(P-12302)***
Mikhail Darafeev Inc (PA) ... E ... 909 613-1818
5075 Edison Ave Chino (91710) ***(P-4593)***
Mikron Products Inc ... D ... 909 545-8600
1251 E Belmont St Ontario (91761) ***(P-9266)***
Mikroscan Technologies Inc ... F ... 760 893-8095
2764 Gateway Rd 100 Carlsbad (92009) ***(P-21822)***
Mikuni Color USA Inc ... F ... 916 572-0704
855 Riverside Pkwy Ste 80 West Sacramento (95605) ***(P-16687)***
Mil-Spec Magnetics Inc ... E ... 909 598-8116
169 Pacific St Pomona (91768) ***(P-18727)***
Mila Usa Inc ... E ... 415 734-8540
11 Laurel Ave Belvedere Tiburon (94920) ***(P-16834)***
Milco Waterjet, Huntington Beach *Also called Milco Wire Edm Inc* ***(P-16203)***
Milco Wire Edm Inc ... F ... 714 373-0098
15221 Connector Ln Huntington Beach (92649) ***(P-16203)***
Milcomm Inc ... F ... 626 523-8305
10291 Trademark St Ste C Rancho Cucamonga (91730) ***(P-20179)***
Mildara Blass Inc ... C ... 707 836-5000
205 Concourse Blvd Santa Rosa (95403) ***(P-1819)***
Mildef Inc (PA) ... F ... 703 224-8835
630 W Lambert Rd Brea (92821) ***(P-14949)***
Milestone AV Technologies LLC ... F ... 800 266-7225
11150 Inland Ave Ste A Jurupa Valley (91752) ***(P-12303)***
Milestones Products Inc ... F ... 323 728-3434
1965 S Tubeway Ave Commerce (90040) ***(P-8539)***
Milgard Manufacturing Inc ... C ... 805 581-6325
355 E Easy St Simi Valley (93065) ***(P-10380)***
Milgard Manufacturing Inc ... F ... 480 763-6000
26879 Diaz Rd Temecula (92590) ***(P-9897)***
Milgard Manufacturing Inc ... C ... 916 387-0700
6050 88th St Sacramento (95828) ***(P-11971)***
Milgard Windows, Temecula *Also called Milgard Manufacturing Inc* ***(P-9897)***
Milgard Windows, Sacramento *Also called Milgard Manufacturing Inc* ***(P-11971)***
Milgard-Simi Valley, Simi Valley *Also called Milgard Manufacturing Inc* ***(P-10380)***
Military Aircraft Parts ... E ... 916 635-8010
11265 Sunrise Gold Cir G Rancho Cordova (95742) ***(P-16204)***
Military Aircraft Parts (PA) ... E ... 916 635-8010
116 Oxburough Dr Folsom (95630) ***(P-16205)***
Military Magazine, Sacramento *Also called Helen Noble* ***(P-5953)***
Milky Mama LLC ... F ... 877 886-4559
10722 Arrow Rte Ste 104 Rancho Cucamonga (91730) ***(P-1242)***
Mill 42 Inc ... F ... 714 979-4200
3711 Long Beach Blvd # 500 Long Beach (90807) ***(P-2797)***
Mill At Kings River LLC ... E ... 559 875-7800
15111 E Goodfellow Ave Sanger (93657) ***(P-1476)***
Mill Creek Vneyards Winery Inc ... F ... 707 433-4788
1401 Westside Rd Healdsburg (95448) ***(P-1820)***
Millbrook Kitchens Inc ... F ... 310 684-3366
15960 Downey Ave Paramount (90723) ***(P-4224)***
Millcraft Inc ... D ... 714 632-9621
2850 E White Star Ave Anaheim (92806) ***(P-4085)***
Millennial Brands LLC ... E ... 925 230-0617
126 W 9th St Los Angeles (90015) ***(P-10173)***
Millennium Automation ... F ... 510 683-5942
1300 Fulton Pl Fremont (94539) ***(P-14838)***
Millennium Graphics Inc ... F ... 925 602-0635
3443 Park Pl Pleasanton (94588) ***(P-6959)***
Millennium Metalcraft Inc ... E ... 510 657-4700
3201 Osgood Cmn Fremont (94539) ***(P-12304)***
Millennium Space Systems Inc (HQ) ... E ... 310 683-5840
2265 E El Segundo Blvd El Segundo (90245) ***(P-20631)***
Millenworks ... D ... 714 426-5500
1361 Valencia Ave Tustin (92780) ***(P-19487)***
Miller & Pidskalny Cstm Wdwrk ... F ... 949 250-8508
1940 Blair Ave Santa Ana (92705) ***(P-4594)***
Miller Castings Inc (PA) ... D ... 562 695-0461
2503 Pacific Park Dr Whittier (90601) ***(P-11162)***
Miller Castings Inc ... F ... 562 695-0461
12251 Coast Dr Whittier (90601) ***(P-11163)***
Miller Cnc, San Diego *Also called Miller Machine Works LLC* ***(P-16207)***
Miller Electric Mfg Co ... C ... 805 520-7494
2523 Ellington Ct Simi Valley (93063) ***(P-14248)***
Miller Gasket Co, San Fernando *Also called J Miller Co Inc* ***(P-9239)***
Miller Hot Dogs, Lodi *Also called Miller Packing Company* ***(P-481)***
Miller Machine Inc ... E ... 814 723-5700
4055 Calle Platino # 200 Oceanside (92056) ***(P-16206)***
Miller Machine Works LLC ... F ... 619 501-9866
1905 Broadway San Diego (92102) ***(P-16207)***
Miller Manufacturing Inc ... F ... 707 584-9528
165 Cascade Ct Rohnert Park (94928) ***(P-5031)***
Miller Marine ... E ... 619 791-1500
2275 Manya St San Diego (92154) ***(P-20293)***
Miller Milling Company LLC ... E ... 559 441-8133
2908 S Maple Ave Fresno (93725) ***(P-1007)***
Miller Packing Company ... E ... 209 339-2310
1122 Industrial Way Lodi (95240) ***(P-481)***
Miller Products Inc ... D ... 209 467-2470
2315 Station Dr Stockton (95215) ***(P-5368)***
Miller Woodworking Inc ... E ... 310 257-6806
1429 259th St Harbor City (90710) ***(P-4086)***
Millercoors LLC ... D ... 626 969-6811
15801 1st St Irwindale (91706) ***(P-1549)***
Millers American Honey Inc ... E ... 909 825-1722
1455 Riverview Dr San Bernardino (92408) ***(P-2551)***
Millers Fab & Weld Corp ... E ... 951 359-3100
6100 Industrial Ave Riverside (92504) ***(P-11845)***
Millers Woodworking, Tustin *Also called GL Woodworking Inc* ***(P-4504)***
Millerton Builders Inc ... E ... 559 252-0490
4714 E Home Ave Fresno (93703) ***(P-5032)***
Million Corporation ... D ... 626 969-1888
1300 W Optical Dr Ste 600 Irwindale (91702) ***(P-7143)***
Millipart Inc (PA) ... F ... 626 963-4101
412 W Carter Dr Glendora (91740) ***(P-16208)***
Millpledge North America Inc ... F ... 310 215-0400
5310 Derry Ave Ste S&T Agoura Hills (91301) ***(P-8239)***
Mills ASAP Reprographics (PA) ... F ... 805 772-2019
495 Morro Bay Blvd Morro Bay (93442) ***(P-5482)***
Mills Iron Works ... D ... 323 321-6520
14834 S Maple Ave Gardena (90248) ***(P-13359)***
Millwood Cabinet Co Inc ... E ... 661 327-0371
2321 Virginia Ave Bakersfield (93307) ***(P-4225)***
Millwork Co ... F ... 760 788-1533
607 Brazos St Ste C Ramona (92065) ***(P-4087)***
Millwork Div, Oroville *Also called Setzer Forest Products Inc* ***(P-3949)***
Millworks Etc Inc ... E ... 805 499-3400
2586 Calcite Cir Newbury Park (91320) ***(P-11972)***
Millworks By Design Inc ... E ... 818 597-1326
2248 Townsgate Rd Ste 1 Westlake Village (91361) ***(P-4088)***
Millworx Prcsion Machining Inc ... E ... 951 371-2683
506 Malloy Ct Corona (92880) ***(P-16209)***
Milners Anodizing ... F ... 707 584-1188
3330 Mcmaude Pl Santa Rosa (95407) ***(P-13052)***
Milo Engineering, Torrance *Also called Milo Machining Inc* ***(P-16210)***

Employee Codes: A=Over 500 employees, B=251-500
C=101-250, D=51-100, E=20-50, F=10-19
2020 California
Manfacturers Register
© Mergent Inc. 1-800-342-5647
1173

Milo Machining Inc......F......310 530-0925
2675 Skypark Dr Ste 304 Torrance (90505) ***(P-16210)***
Milodon Incorporated......E......805 577-5950
2250 Agate Ct Simi Valley (93065) ***(P-19721)***
Milpitas Post Newspapers Inc......F......408 262-2454
59 Marylinn Dr Milpitas (95035) ***(P-5756)***
Miltons Baking Company LLC......E......858 350-9696
5875 Avenida Encinas Carlsbad (92008) ***(P-1243)***
Milwright, Sebastopol *Also called Kurtz Family Corporation* ***(P-9871)***
Mimi Chica (PA)......F......323 264-9278
161 W 33rd St Los Angeles (90007) ***(P-3374)***
Mimi Chica Design, Los Angeles *Also called Mimi Chica* ***(P-3374)***
Mimo, Los Angeles *Also called 2bb Unlimited Inc* ***(P-2958)***
Min-E-Con LLC......D......949 250-0087
17312 Eastman Irvine (92614) ***(P-18779)***
Mina Product Development Inc......F......714 966-2150
3020 Red Hill Ave Costa Mesa (92626) ***(P-9898)***
Mina-Tree Signs Incorporated (PA)......E......209 941-2921
1233 E Ronald St Stockton (95205) ***(P-23161)***
Minachee Inc......F......213 745-8100
1248 S Flower St Los Angeles (90015) ***(P-3046)***
Minatronic Inc......F......805 239-8864
1139 13th St Paso Robles (93446) ***(P-19020)***
Mindjolt......F......415 543-7800
144 2nd St Fl 4 San Francisco (94105) ***(P-22695)***
Mindray Ds Usa Inc......F......650 230-2800
2100 Gold St San Jose (95002) ***(P-8240)***
Mindray Innvtion Ctr Slcon Vly, San Jose *Also called Mindray Ds Usa Inc* ***(P-8240)***
Mindrum Precision Inc......E......909 989-1728
10000 4th St Rancho Cucamonga (91730) ***(P-20973)***
Mindrum Precision Products, Rancho Cucamonga *Also called Mindrum Precision Inc* ***(P-20973)***
Mindsai Inc......F......831 239-4644
101 Cooper St Ste 218 Santa Cruz (95060) ***(P-24167)***
Mindsnacks Inc......E......415 875-9817
1479 Folsom St San Francisco (94103) ***(P-24168)***
Mindspeed Technologies LLC (HQ)......D......949 579-3000
4000 Macarthur Blvd Newport Beach (92660) ***(P-18416)***
Mindspeed Technologies, Inc., Newport Beach *Also called Mindspeed Technologies LLC* ***(P-18416)***
Mineral Essence, North Hollywood *Also called Advanced Inst of Skin Care* ***(P-8432)***
Mineral King Minerals Inc (PA)......F......559 582-9228
7600 N Ingram Ave Ste 105 Fresno (93711) ***(P-8798)***
Minerva Surgical Inc......F......650 399-1770
101 Saginaw Dr Redwood City (94063) ***(P-21823)***
Minestone......F......818 775-5999
17739 Valley Vista Blvd Encino (91316) ***(P-292)***
Mingo Enterprises Inc......F......510 528-3044
1209 Solano Ave Ste B Albany (94706) ***(P-5989)***
Mini Vac Inc......F......818 244-6777
634 E Colorado St Glendale (91205) ***(P-16844)***
Mini-Flex Corporation......F......805 644-1474
2472 Eastman Ave Ste 29 Ventura (93003) ***(P-16211)***
Miniature Precision Inc......F......530 244-4131
4488 Mountain Lakes Blvd Redding (96003) ***(P-16212)***
Minitouch Inc......F......510 651-5000
47853 Warm Springs Blvd Fremont (94539) ***(P-21824)***
Mino Industry USA Inc (PA)......F......949 943-8070
38 Executive Park Ste 250 Irvine (92614) ***(P-23413)***
Minsley Inc......E......909 458-1100
989 S Monterey Ave Ontario (91761) ***(P-2552)***
Mint Grips, Benicia *Also called Gibbs Plastic & Rubber Co* ***(P-9311)***
Mint Software Inc......F......650 944-6000
280 Hope St Mountain View (94041) ***(P-24169)***
Minton-Spidell Inc (PA)......F......310 836-0403
8467 Steller Dr Culver City (90232) ***(P-4595)***
Mintronix Inc......F......805 482-1298
6090 Cielo Vista Ct Camarillo (93012) ***(P-14950)***
Minus K Technology Inc......C......310 348-9656
460 Hindry Ave Ste C Inglewood (90301) ***(P-18417)***
Minute Man Envmtl Systems Inc......E......949 637-5446
830 W 16th St Costa Mesa (92627) ***(P-6730)***
Minuteman Press, Monterey *Also called Rapid Printers Inc* ***(P-6835)***
Minuteman Press, Van Nuys *Also called Printcom Inc* ***(P-6798)***
Minuteman Press, Rancho Cucamonga *Also called Lee Maxton Inc* ***(P-6695)***
Minuteman Press Oakland, Oakland *Also called Avoy Corp* ***(P-6425)***
Mio Technology, Fremont *Also called Mitac Usa Inc* ***(P-14951)***
Mips Tech Inc (HQ)......D......408 530-5000
300 Orchard Cy Dr Ste 170 Campbell (95008) ***(P-18418)***
Mir Printing & Graphics......F......818 313-9333
21333 Deering Ct Canoga Park (91304) ***(P-6731)***
Miracle Bedding Corporation......E......562 908-2370
3700 Capitol Ave City of Industry (90601) ***(P-4732)***
Miracle Cover (PA)......F......714 842-8863
20721 Goshawk Ln Huntington Beach (92646) ***(P-8657)***
Miracle Greens Inc......C......800 521-5867
8477 Steller Dr Culver City (90232) ***(P-604)***
Miradry Inc......E......408 940-8700
2790 Walsh Ave Santa Clara (95051) ***(P-22049)***
Mirage Sprtfshng & Commrcl......F......805 983-0975
1810 Kapalua Dr Oxnard (93036) ***(P-22854)***
Miramar Labs, Inc., Santa Clara *Also called Miradry Inc* ***(P-22049)***
Miramonte Winery, Temecula *Also called Celebration Cellars LLC* ***(P-1624)***
Miranda, Grass Valley *Also called Grass Valley Inc* ***(P-17527)***
Mirati Therapeutics Inc......F......858 332-3410
9393 Twne Cntre Dr Ste 20 San Diego (92121) ***(P-8014)***
Mirion Technologies Inc (PA)......C......925 543-0800
3000 Executive Pkwy # 518 San Ramon (94583) ***(P-21508)***
Mirth Corporation......E......714 389-1200
611 Anton Blvd Ste 500 Costa Mesa (92626) ***(P-24170)***
Mirum Pharmaceuticals Inc......E......650 667-4085
950 Tower Ln Ste 1050 Foster City (94404) ***(P-8015)***
Misa Los Angeles, Los Angeles *Also called T-Bags LLC* ***(P-3420)***
Miss Cristina, Los Angeles *Also called Miss Kim Inc* ***(P-3244)***
Miss Kim Inc......F......213 747-4011
1015 San Julian St Los Angeles (90015) ***(P-3244)***
Mission AG Resources LLC......E......559 591-3333
6801 Avenue 430 Unit A Reedley (93654) ***(P-605)***
Mission Bell Mfg Co Inc......E......209 229-7280
25656 Schulte Ct Tracy (95377) ***(P-4226)***
Mission Bell Winery, Madera *Also called Constellation Brands US Oprs* ***(P-1647)***
Mission Concrete Products, Gilroy *Also called Quinn Development Co* ***(P-10514)***
Mission Crtical Composites LLC......E......714 831-2100
15400 Graham St Ste 102 Huntington Beach (92649) ***(P-20180)***
Mission Custom Extrusion Inc......E......909 822-1581
10904 Beech Ave Fontana (92337) ***(P-9899)***
Mission Flavors Fragrances Inc......F......949 461-3344
25882 Wright El Toro (92610) ***(P-2221)***
Mission Foods, Fresno *Also called Gruma Corporation* ***(P-2333)***
Mission Foods, Rancho Cucamonga *Also called Gruma Corporation* ***(P-2334)***
Mission Foods Dc60, San Diego *Also called Gruma Corporation* ***(P-2332)***
Mission Hill Audio Video, San Diego *Also called Mission Hills Radio/Tv Inc* ***(P-13423)***
Mission Hills Radio/Tv Inc......F......858 277-1100
9474 Chesapeake Dr # 906 San Diego (92123) ***(P-13423)***
Mission Hockey Company (PA)......F......949 585-9390
12 Goodyear Ste 100 Irvine (92618) ***(P-22855)***
Mission Kleensweep Prod Inc......D......323 223-1405
13644 Live Oak Ln Baldwin Park (91706) ***(P-8344)***
Mission Laboratories, Baldwin Park *Also called Mission Kleensweep Prod Inc* ***(P-8344)***
Mission Microwave Tech LLC......E......951 893-4925
9924 Norwalk Blvd Santa Fe Springs (90670) ***(P-17588)***
Mission Park Hotel LP......E......408 809-3838
1950 Wyatt Dr Santa Clara (95054) ***(P-7506)***
Mission Plastics Inc......C......909 947-7287
1930 S Parco Ave Ontario (91761) ***(P-9900)***
Mission Ready Mix, Ventura *Also called Lynch Ready Mix Concrete Co* ***(P-10798)***
Mission Research Corporation (HQ)......F......805 690-2447
6750 Navigator Way # 200 Goleta (93117) ***(P-19915)***
Mission Rubber, Corona *Also called MCP Industries Inc* ***(P-11673)***
Mission Rubber Co, Corona *Also called MCP Industries Inc* ***(P-9332)***
Mission Tool and Mfg Co Inc......E......510 782-8383
3440 Arden Rd Hayward (94545) ***(P-16213)***
Mission Truss, Lakeside *Also called Dixietruss Inc* ***(P-10562)***
Mission Valley Regional Occu......E......510 657-1865
5019 Stevenson Blvd Fremont (94538) ***(P-9000)***
Mist & Cool LLC......F......805 986-4125
707 E Hueneme Rd Oxnard (93033) ***(P-16835)***
Mist Incorporated......E......818 678-5619
9006 Fullbright Ave Chatsworth (91311) ***(P-14174)***
Mistras Group Inc......E......310 793-7173
3551 Voyager St Ste 104 Torrance (90503) ***(P-21509)***
Misyd Corp (PA)......D......213 742-1800
30 Fremont Pl Los Angeles (90005) ***(P-3485)***
Mitac Information Systems......E......510 668-3679
39889 Eureka Dr Newark (94560) ***(P-15291)***
Mitac Information Systems Corp (HQ)......C......510 284-3000
39889 Eureka Dr Newark (94560) ***(P-15059)***
Mitac Usa Inc (HQ)......E......510 661-2800
47988 Fremont Blvd Fremont (94538) ***(P-14951)***
Mitann Inc (HQ)......E......408 782-2500
400 Jarvis Dr Ste A Morgan Hill (95037) ***(P-9001)***
Mitchell Dean Collins......F......714 894-6767
12771 Monarch St Garden Grove (92841) ***(P-4227)***
Mitchell Fabrication......E......909 590-0393
4564 Mission Blvd Montclair (91763) ***(P-11846)***
Mitchell Instruments, Vista *Also called Mitchell Test & Safety Inc* ***(P-21510)***
Mitchell Instruments Co Inc......F......760 744-2690
2875 Scott St Ste 101 Vista (92081) ***(P-21081)***
Mitchell Processing LLC......E......909 519-5759
2778 Pomona Blvd Pomona (91768) ***(P-9334)***
Mitchell Repair Info Co LLC (HQ)......E......858 391-5000
14145 Danielson St Ste A Poway (92064) ***(P-6283)***
Mitchell Rubber Products LLC (PA)......C......951 681-5655
10220 San Sevaine Way Jurupa Valley (91752) ***(P-9335)***
Mitchell Rubber Products LLC......D......951 681-5655
10220 San Sevaine Way Jurupa Valley (91752) ***(P-9336)***
Mitchell Test & Safety Inc......F......760 744-2690
2875 Scott St Ste 101-103 Vista (92081) ***(P-21510)***
Mitchell-Duckett Corporation......F......530 268-2112
10074 Streeter Rd Ste B Auburn (95602) ***(P-16214)***
Mitchell1, Poway *Also called Mitchell Repair Info Co LLC* ***(P-6283)***
Mitchellamazing, Montclair *Also called Amazing Steel Company* ***(P-11742)***
Mitco Industries Inc (PA)......E......909 877-0800
2235 S Vista Ave Bloomington (92316) ***(P-16215)***
Mitrani USA Corp......F......818 888-9994
7451 Westcliff Dr West Hills (91307) ***(P-9592)***
Mitratech Holdings Inc......F......323 964-0000
5900 Wilshire Blvd # 1500 Los Angeles (90036) ***(P-24171)***
Mitsubishi Cement Corporation......C......760 248-7373
5808 State Highway 18 Lucerne Valley (92356) ***(P-10423)***
Mitsubishi Chemical Advncd Mtr......E......209 464-2701
3837 Imperial Way Stockton (95215) ***(P-9901)***
Mitsubishi Chemical Crbn Fbr......C......800 929-5471
1822 Reynolds Ave Irvine (92614) ***(P-8881)***
Mitsubishi Chemical Crbn Fbr (HQ)......C......916 386-1733
5900 88th St Sacramento (95828) ***(P-16688)***

Mitsubishi Electric Visual C 800 553-7278
10833 Valley View St # 300 Cypress (90630) *(P-19021)*
Mitxpc Inc F 510 226-6883
45437 Warm Springs Blvd Fremont (94539) *(P-14952)*
Mitxpc Embedded Sys Solutions, Fremont *Also called Mitxpc Inc (P-14952)*
Miwa Inc E 510 261-5999
5733 San Leandro St Ofc Oakland (94621) *(P-13424)*
Mix Garden Inc F 707 433-4327
1083 Vine St Healdsburg (95448) *(P-10803)*
Mixamo Inc E 415 255-7455
2415 3rd St Ste 239 San Francisco (94107) *(P-24172)*
Mixed Bag Designs Inc D 650 239-5358
1744 Rollins Rd Burlingame (94010) *(P-5405)*
Mixed Chicks LLC F 818 888-4008
21218 Vanowen St Canoga Park (91303) *(P-8540)*
Mixed Nuts Inc E 323 587-6887
7909 Crossway Dr Pico Rivera (90660) *(P-1434)*
Mixmor Inc F 323 664-1941
3131 Casitas Ave Los Angeles (90039) *(P-13738)*
Mixonic F 866 838-5067
1145 Polk St Ste A San Francisco (94109) *(P-7144)*
Miyako Oriental Foods Inc F 626 962-9633
4287 Puente Ave Baldwin Park (91706) *(P-1444)*
Miyokos Kitchen D 415 521-5313
2086 Marina Ave Petaluma (94954) *(P-538)*
Mizkan Americas Inc F 831 728-2061
46 Walker St Watsonville (95076) *(P-2553)*
Mizkan Americas Inc E 909 484-8743
10037 8th St Rancho Cucamonga (91730) *(P-2554)*
Mizu Inc (PA) F 307 690-3219
2225 Faraday Ave Ste E Carlsbad (92008) *(P-9337)*
Mizuho Orthopedic Systems Inc (HQ) B 510 429-1500
30031 Ahern Ave Union City (94587) *(P-21825)*
Mizuho OSI, Union City *Also called Mizuho Orthopedic Systems Inc (P-21825)*
Mj Blanks Inc E 213 629-0006
1155 S Grand Ave Apt 614 Los Angeles (90015) *(P-2798)*
Mjc Engineering and Tech Inc F 714 890-0618
15401 Assembly Ln Huntington Beach (92649) *(P-13985)*
Mjck Corporation E 888 992-8437
3222 E Washington Blvd Vernon (90058) *(P-2799)*
Mjd Cabinets, Lakeside *Also called M DAmico Inc (P-5071)*
MJM Expert Pipe Fbrcation Wldg E 661 330-8698
3404 Wrenwood St Bakersfield (93309) *(P-11847)*
Mjolnir Industries LLC F 805 488-3550
5701 Perkins Rd Oxnard (93033) *(P-14078)*
Mjus LLC (fka Mindjet Llc) E 415 229-4344
275 Battery St Ste 1000 San Francisco (94111) *(P-24173)*
Mjw Inc D 323 778-8900
1328 W Slauson Ave Los Angeles (90044) *(P-14591)*
Mk Diamond Products Inc (PA) C 310 539-5221
1315 Storm Pkwy Torrance (90501) *(P-14225)*
Mk Digital Direct Inc F 619 661-0628
861 Harold Pl Ste 209 Chula Vista (91914) *(P-21265)*
Mk Magnetics Inc D 760 246-6373
17030 Muskrat Ave Adelanto (92301) *(P-11102)*
Mk Manufacturing, Irvine *Also called M K Products Inc (P-14246)*
Mk Printing, Santa Ana *Also called Mekong Printing Inc (P-6722)*
Mk Tool and Abrasive Inc F 562 776-8818
4710 S Eastern Ave Los Angeles (90040) *(P-10951)*
Mkkr Inc F 909 890-5994
430 E Parkcenter Cir N San Bernardino (92408) *(P-14175)*
Mkm Customs, Roseville *Also called Sinister Mfg Company Inc (P-19768)*
Mks Color Composite, Compton *Also called Permalite Plastics Corp (P-8703)*
Mkt Innovations, Brea *Also called Mike Kenney Tool Inc (P-16201)*
Mkt Innovations D 714 524-7668
2900 Saturn St Ste A Brea (92821) *(P-16216)*
ML Kishigo Mfg Co LLC D 949 852-1963
2901 Daimler St Santa Ana (92705) *(P-3571)*
Mlabs, Lakeport *Also called Mountain Lake Labs (P-20636)*
Mlim LLC A 619 299-3131
350 Camino De La Reina San Diego (92108) *(P-5757)*
Mline Transportation Company E 916 729-1053
6621 Clear Creek Ct Citrus Heights (95610) *(P-1445)*
Mmi Services Inc C 661 589-9366
4042 Patton Way Bakersfield (93308) *(P-224)*
Mmix Technologies F 619 631-6644
1348 Pioneer Way El Cajon (92020) *(P-12305)*
Mmp Sheet Metal Inc E 562 691-1055
501 Commercial Way La Habra (90631) *(P-12306)*
MMR Technologies Inc (PA) F 650 962-9620
41 Daggett Dr San Jose (95134) *(P-14499)*
Mmw Operation, South El Monte *Also called Master Metal Works Inc (P-12498)*
MNC Bliss Enterprises Inc F 916 483-1167
1715 Fulton Ave Sacramento (95825) *(P-17145)*
Mng Newspapers, San Jose *Also called California Newspapers Partnr (P-5578)*
Mnm Corporation (PA) E 213 627-3737
110 E 9th St Ste A777 Los Angeles (90079) *(P-5990)*
Mobile Crossing Inc F 916 485-2773
1230 Oakmead Pkwy Ste 304 Sunnyvale (94085) *(P-20632)*
Mobile Designs Inc F 530 244-1050
4650 Caterpillar Rd Redding (96003) *(P-11240)*
Mobile Equipment Appraisers, Bakersfield *Also called Mobile Equipment Company (P-13850)*
Mobile Equipment Company E 661 327-8476
3610 Gilmore Ave Bakersfield (93308) *(P-13850)*
Mobile Home Park Magazines, Sunnyvale *Also called Mhb Group Inc (P-5988)*
Mobile Management, Jurupa Valley *Also called McGrath Rentcorp (P-12559)*
Mobile Mini Inc F 510 252-9326
44580 Old Warm Sprng Blvd Fremont (94538) *(P-12560)*
Mobile Mini Inc E 209 858-9300
16351 Mckinley Ave Lathrop (95330) *(P-12561)*
Mobile Mini Inc C 909 356-1690
42207 3rd St E Lancaster (93535) *(P-12562)*
Mobile Mini Inc E 858 578-9222
12345 Crosthwaite Cir Poway (92064) *(P-12563)*
Mobile Mini Storage, Poway *Also called Mobile Mini Inc (P-12563)*
Mobile Tone Inc F 323 939-6928
5430 Westhaven St Los Angeles (90016) *(P-17589)*
Mobile Wireless Tech Llc F 714 239-1535
125 W Cerritos Ave Anaheim (92805) *(P-17747)*
Mobileiron Inc (PA) C 650 919-8100
401 E Middlefield Rd Mountain View (94043) *(P-24174)*
Mobileops Corporation F 408 203-0243
1422 Wright Ave Sunnyvale (94087) *(P-24175)*
Mobility Specialists Inc F 714 674-0480
490 Capricorn St Brea (92821) *(P-23414)*
Mobilityware, Irvine *Also called Upstanding LLC (P-24544)*
Mobis Parts America LLC B 949 450-0014
10550 Talbert Ave 4 Fountain Valley (92708) *(P-19722)*
Mobius Photonics Inc F 408 496-1084
110 Pioneer Way Ste A Mountain View (94041) *(P-19358)*
Mobiveil Inc F 408 791-2977
890 Hillview Ct Ste 250 Milpitas (95035) *(P-18419)*
Moc Products Company Inc (PA) D 818 794-3500
12306 Montague St Pacoima (91331) *(P-9002)*
Mochi Ice Cream Company (PA) E 323 587-5504
5563 Alcoa Ave Vernon (90058) *(P-1244)*
Mockingbird Networks D 408 342-5300
10040 Bubb Rd Cupertino (95014) *(P-14953)*
Mod 2, Los Angeles *Also called Mod2 Inc (P-24176)*
Mod Electronics Inc E 310 322-2136
142 Sierra St El Segundo (90245) *(P-22481)*
Mod Shop E 310 523-1008
15610 S Main St Gardena (90248) *(P-4596)*
Mod2 Inc F 213 747-8424
3317 S Broadway Los Angeles (90007) *(P-24176)*
Moda Enterprises Inc F 714 484-0076
1334 N Knollwood Cir Anaheim (92801) *(P-19488)*
Mode Analytics Inc F 415 271-7599
208 Utah St Ste 400 San Francisco (94103) *(P-24177)*
Model Match Inc F 949 525-9405
209 Avnida Fbrcnte Ste 15 San Clemente (92672) *(P-24178)*
Modem Graphic Inc D 626 912-7088
18600 San Jose Ave City of Industry (91748) *(P-6732)*
Modern Aire Ventilating, North Hollywood *Also called Modern-Aire Ventilating Inc (P-12307)*
Modern Bamboo Incorporated F 925 820-2804
5853 Virmar Ave Oakland (94618) *(P-4597)*
Modern Blind Factory, San Diego *Also called Mbf Interiors Inc (P-3592)*
Modern Ceramics Mfg Inc E 408 383-0554
2240 Lundy Ave San Jose (95131) *(P-10320)*
MODERN COMBAT SOLUTIONS, Vista *Also called Real Action Paintball Inc (P-22870)*
Modern Concepts Inc D 310 637-0013
3121 E Ana St E Rncho Dmngz (90221) *(P-9902)*
Modern Custom Fabrication E 559 264-4741
2421 E California Ave Fresno (93721) *(P-12031)*
Modern Engine Inc E 818 409-9494
701 Sonora Ave Glendale (91201) *(P-16217)*
Modern Gold Design Inc E 213 614-1818
650 S Hill St Ste 509 Los Angeles (90014) *(P-22550)*
Modern Gourmet Foods, Irvine *Also called Coastal Cocktails Inc (P-2057)*
Modern Luxury Media LLC (HQ) E 404 443-0004
243 Vallejo St San Francisco (94111) *(P-5991)*
Modern Manufacturing Inc E 714 254-0156
4110 E La Palma Ave Anaheim (92807) *(P-16218)*
Modern Metal Installations F 916 316-0997
4400 Shady Oak Way Fair Oaks (95628) *(P-12500)*
Modern Metals Industries Inc E 800 437-6633
14000 S Broadway Los Angeles (90061) *(P-21826)*
Modern Plating, Los Angeles *Also called Alco Plating Corp (P-12912)*
Modern Postcard, Carlsbad *Also called Iris Group Inc (P-7103)*
Modern Stairways Inc F 619 466-1484
3239 Bancroft Dr Spring Valley (91977) *(P-10603)*
Modern Studio Equipment Inc F 818 764-8574
7414 Bellaire Ave North Hollywood (91605) *(P-22441)*
Modern Wall Graphics LLC E 760 787-0346
2191 W Esplanade Ave San Jacinto (92582) *(P-9412)*
Modern Woodworks, Canoga Park *Also called Mww Inc (P-4518)*
Modern-Aire Ventilating Inc E 818 765-9870
7319 Lankershim Blvd North Hollywood (91605) *(P-12307)*
Modernpro LLC F 949 232-2148
15 Woodcrest Ln Aliso Viejo (92656) *(P-6284)*
Modesto Bee Circulation, Modesto *Also called McClatchy Newspapers Inc (P-5734)*
Modesto Bee, The, Modesto *Also called McClatchy Newspapers Inc (P-5730)*
Modesto Pltg & Powdr Coating F 209 526-2696
436 Mitchell Rd Ste D Modesto (95354) *(P-13053)*
Modesto Tent and Awning Inc F 209 545-1607
4448 Sisk Rd Modesto (95356) *(P-3691)*
Modified Plastics Inc (PA) E 714 546-4667
1240 E Glenwood Pl Santa Ana (92707) *(P-9903)*
Moducom, Los Angeles *Also called Modular Communications Systems (P-17590)*
Modular Communications Systems E 818 764-1333
373 N Western Ave Ste 15 Los Angeles (90004) *(P-17590)*
Modular Metal Fabricators Inc C 951 242-3154
24600 Nandina Ave Moreno Valley (92551) *(P-12308)*
Modular Office Solutions Inc D 909 476-4200
11701 6th St Rancho Cucamonga (91730) *(P-4845)*

ALPHABETIC

Employee Codes: A=Over 500 employees, B=251-500
C=101-250, D=51-100, E=20-50, F=10-19
2020 California
Manfacturers Register
© Mergent Inc. 1-800-342-5647
1175

Modular Process Tech Corp.......F.......408 325-8640
1675 Walsh Ave Ste E Santa Clara (95050) ***(P-14771)***
Modulus Inc.......F.......408 457-3712
518 Sycamore Dr Milpitas (95035) ***(P-17927)***
Modus Advanced Inc.......E.......925 962-5943
1575 Greenville Rd Livermore (94550) ***(P-9338)***
Modutek Corp.......E.......408 362-2000
6387 San Ignacio Ave San Jose (95119) ***(P-20905)***
Moeller Mfg & Sup Inc, Anaheim *Also called Moeller Mfg & Sup LLC* ***(P-11612)***
Moeller Mfg & Sup LLC.......E.......714 999-5551
805 E Cerritos Ave Anaheim (92805) ***(P-11612)***
Moen Industries.......E.......562 946-6381
10330 Pioneer Blvd # 235 Santa Fe Springs (90670) ***(P-14311)***
Mogan David Wine, Ripon *Also called Wine Group Inc* ***(P-2007)***
Mohammad Khan.......F.......619 231-1664
2606 Imperial Ave San Diego (92102) ***(P-9904)***
Mohawk Industries Inc.......D.......909 357-1064
9687 Transportation Way Fontana (92335) ***(P-2874)***
Mohawk Industries Inc.......C.......510 440-8790
41490 Boyce Rd Fremont (94538) ***(P-2875)***
Mohawk Laboratories Division, Sunnyvale *Also called Nch Corporation* ***(P-7511)***
Mohawk Land & Cattle Co Inc.......D.......408 436-1800
1660 Old Bayshore Hwy San Jose (95112) ***(P-418)***
Mohawk Western Plastics Inc.......E.......909 593-7547
1496 Arrow Hwy La Verne (91750) ***(P-5406)***
Moisture Register Products, Rancho Cucamonga *Also called Aqua Measure Instrument Co* ***(P-21436)***
Mojado Bros, Placentia *Also called Soft Touch Inc* ***(P-7218)***
Mojave Copy & Printing Inc.......F.......760 241-7898
12402 Industrial Blvd E10 Victorville (92395) ***(P-6733)***
Mojave Foods Corporation.......C.......323 890-8900
6200 E Slauson Ave Commerce (90040) ***(P-2555)***
Moki International (usa) Inc.......E.......205 208-0179
21700 Oxnard St Ste 850 Woodland Hills (91367) ***(P-17263)***
Mold Masters Inc.......F.......323 999-2599
715 Ruberta Ave Glendale (91201) ***(P-14079)***
Mold USA.......F.......310 823-6653
322 Culver Blve Apt 6 Playa Del Rey (90293) ***(P-14080)***
Mold Vision Inc.......F.......951 245-8020
18351 Pasadena St Lake Elsinore (92530) ***(P-16219)***
Molded Devices, Riverside *Also called Mdi East Inc* ***(P-9888)***
Molded Devices Inc (PA).......E.......480 785-9100
6918 Ed Perkic St Riverside (92504) ***(P-9905)***
Molded Fiber GL Companies - W.......D.......760 246-4042
9400 Holly Rd Adelanto (92301) ***(P-9906)***
Molded Interconnect Industries, Foothill Ranch *Also called Lantic Inc* ***(P-9874)***
Moldex-Metric Inc.......B.......310 837-6500
10111 Jefferson Blvd Culver City (90232) ***(P-22050)***
Molding Acquisition Corp.......F.......209 723-5000
2651 Cooper Ave Merced (95348) ***(P-7582)***
Molding Company.......E.......408 748-6968
1987 Russell Ave Santa Clara (95054) ***(P-4516)***
Molding Corporation America.......E.......818 890-7877
10349 Norris Ave Pacoima (91331) ***(P-9907)***
Molding Intl & Engrg Inc.......D.......951 296-5010
42136 Avenida Alvarado Temecula (92590) ***(P-9908)***
Molding Solutions Inc (PA).......D.......707 575-1218
3225 Regional Pkwy Santa Rosa (95403) ***(P-9909)***
Moldings Plus Inc.......E.......909 947-3310
1856 S Grove Ave Ontario (91761) ***(P-4089)***
Molecular Bio Products, San Diego *Also called Thermo Fisher Scientific Inc* ***(P-21310)***
Molecular Bioproducts Inc (HQ).......C.......858 453-7551
9389 Waples St San Diego (92121) ***(P-21266)***
Molecular Bioproducts Inc.......C.......707 762-6689
2200 S Mcdowell Blvd Ext Petaluma (94954) ***(P-21267)***
Molecular Databank, Burlingame *Also called Collabrative DRG Discovery Inc* ***(P-23758)***
Molecular Devices LLC (HQ).......C.......408 747-1700
3860 N 1st St San Jose (95134) ***(P-21268)***
Molecule Labs Inc.......E.......925 473-8200
524 Stone Rd Ste A Benicia (94510) ***(P-8753)***
Moleculum.......F.......714 619-5139
3128 Red Hill Ave Costa Mesa (92626) ***(P-9053)***
Molekule Inc (PA).......F.......352 871-3803
1301 Folsom St San Francisco (94103) ***(P-20799)***
Moles Farm.......D.......559 444-0324
9503 S Hughes Ave Fresno (93706) ***(P-856)***
Molex LLC.......E.......909 803-1362
12200 Arrow Rte Rancho Cucamonga (91739) ***(P-18780)***
Molinari Salami Co, San Francisco *Also called P G Molinari & Sons Inc* ***(P-485)***
Molino Company.......D.......323 726-1000
13712 Alondra Blvd Cerritos (90703) ***(P-6734)***
Moller International Inc.......F.......530 756-5086
1855 N 1st St Unit C Dixon (95620) ***(P-19916)***
Molly Max, Los Angeles *Also called Assoluto Inc* ***(P-3288)***
Molly's Custom Silver, Riverside *Also called Paradise Ranch* ***(P-3573)***
Mom Enterprises Inc.......F.......415 526-2710
1003 W Cutting Blvd # 110 Richmond (94804) ***(P-8016)***
Momeni Engineering LLC.......E.......714 897-9301
15662 Commerce Ln Huntington Beach (92649) ***(P-16220)***
Momentum Management LLC.......F.......310 329-2599
1206 W Jon St Torrance (90502) ***(P-9339)***
Mon Amie, Los Angeles *Also called Fashion Today Inc* ***(P-3324)***
Mon Amie, Los Angeles *Also called Fashion Today Inc* ***(P-3325)***
Monaco Sheet Metal.......F.......858 272-0297
5131 Santa Fe St Ste A San Diego (92109) ***(P-12309)***
Monadnock Company.......C.......626 964-6581
16728 Gale Ave City of Industry (91745) ***(P-11613)***
Monaero Engineering Inc.......F.......714 994-5463
17011 Industry Pl La Mirada (90638) ***(P-20181)***
Monarch Art & Frame Inc.......E.......818 373-6180
7700 Gloria Ave Van Nuys (91406) ***(P-4517)***
Monarch Litho Inc (PA).......E.......323 727-0300
1501 Date St Montebello (90640) ***(P-6735)***
Monarch Precision Deburring.......F.......714 258-0342
1514 E Edinger Ave Ste C Santa Ana (92705) ***(P-13936)***
Monarchy Diamond Inc.......B.......213 924-1161
550 S Hill St Ste 1088 Los Angeles (90013) ***(P-392)***
Monco Products Inc.......E.......714 891-2788
7562 Acacia Ave Garden Grove (92841) ***(P-9910)***
Mondelez Global LLC.......A.......714 690-7428
6201 Knott Ave Buena Park (90620) ***(P-482)***
Mondelez Global LLC.......E.......714 634-2773
1220 Howell St Anaheim (92805) ***(P-1245)***
Mongabayorg Corporation.......E.......209 315-5573
37 W Summit Dr Emerald Hills (94062) ***(P-6285)***
Monica Bruce Designs Inc.......F.......707 938-0277
28913 Arnold Dr Sonoma (95476) ***(P-3802)***
Monier Lifetile, Lathrop *Also called Boral Roofing LLC* ***(P-10541)***
Monier Lifetile, Rialto *Also called Boral Roofing LLC* ***(P-10542)***
Monitise Inc.......F.......650 286-1059
1 Embarcadero Ctr Ste 900 San Francisco (94111) ***(P-24179)***
Mono Engineering Corp.......E.......818 772-4998
20977 Knapp St Chatsworth (91311) ***(P-16221)***
Monobind Inc (PA).......E.......949 951-2665
100 N Pointe Dr Lake Forest (92630) ***(P-21827)***
Monogram Aerospace Fas Inc (HQ).......C.......323 722-4760
3423 Garfield Ave Commerce (90040) ***(P-11614)***
Monogram Biosciences Inc.......B.......650 635-1100
345 Oyster Point Blvd South San Francisco (94080) ***(P-8241)***
Monogram Systems, Carson *Also called Zodiac Wtr Waste Aero Systems* ***(P-20274)***
Monogram Systems, Carson *Also called Mag Aerospace Industries Inc* ***(P-11649)***
Monogram Systems.......F.......801 400-7944
1500 Glenn Curtiss St Carson (90746) ***(P-20182)***
Monographx Inc.......F.......310 325-6780
1052 251st St Harbor City (90710) ***(P-23162)***
Monolith Materials Inc.......E.......650 933-4957
1700 Seaport Blvd Ste 110 Redwood City (94063) ***(P-7507)***
Monopole Inc.......F.......818 500-8585
4661 Alger St Los Angeles (90039) ***(P-8658)***
Monopoly Music, Whittier *Also called Grand Motif Records* ***(P-17326)***
Monrow Inc.......E.......213 741-6007
1404 S Main St Ste C Los Angeles (90015) ***(P-3181)***
Monsanto Company.......C.......831 623-7016
500 Lucy Brown Rd San Juan Bautista (95045) ***(P-8835)***
Monson Machine Inc.......F.......951 736-6615
1802 Pomona Rd Corona (92880) ***(P-16222)***
Monster Beverage Company.......A.......866 322-4466
1990 Pomona Rd Corona (92880) ***(P-2093)***
Monster Beverage Corporation (PA).......D.......951 739-6200
1 Monster Way Corona (92879) ***(P-2094)***
Monster City Studios.......F.......559 498-0540
411 S West Ave Fresno (93706) ***(P-9556)***
Monster Gardens, Rohnert Park *Also called Sonoma Plant Works Inc* ***(P-13696)***
Monster Route Inc.......F.......650 368-1628
3559 Haven Ave Ste A Menlo Park (94025) ***(P-11848)***
Monster Tool Company, Vista *Also called Carbide Company LLC* ***(P-11524)***
Mont St John Cellars Inc.......F.......707 255-8864
5400 Old Sonoma Rd NAPA (94559) ***(P-1821)***
Montage Technology Inc.......F.......408 982-2788
101 Metro Dr Ste 500 San Jose (95110) ***(P-18420)***
Montague Company.......C.......510 785-8822
1830 Stearman Ave Hayward (94545) ***(P-15544)***
Montblanc North America LLC.......F.......408 241-5188
2855 Stevens Creek Blvd Santa Clara (95050) ***(P-22551)***
Montblanc Santa Clara, Santa Clara *Also called Montblanc North America LLC* ***(P-22551)***
Montbleau & Associates Inc (PA).......D.......619 263-5550
555 Raven St San Diego (92102) ***(P-4809)***
Montclair Bronze Inc (PA).......E.......909 986-2664
5621 State St Montclair (91763) ***(P-11404)***
Montclair Machine Shop Inc.......F.......909 986-2664
5621 State St Montclair (91763) ***(P-16223)***
Montclair Wood Corporation.......C.......909 985-0302
545 N Mountain Ave # 104 Upland (91786) ***(P-3979)***
Monte Allen Interiors Inc.......E.......310 380-4640
1505 W 139th St Gardena (90249) ***(P-4659)***
Monte De Oro Winery.......F.......951 491-6551
35820 Rancho Cal Rd Temecula (92591) ***(P-1822)***
Montebello Container Co LLC.......D.......714 994-2351
14333 Macaw St La Mirada (90638) ***(P-5247)***
Montebello Plastics LLC.......E.......323 728-6814
601 W Olympic Blvd Montebello (90640) ***(P-9413)***
Monterey Bay Beverage Co Inc.......E.......818 784-4885
14535 Benefit St Unit 4 Sherman Oaks (91403) ***(P-796)***
Monterey Bay Office Pdts Inc.......F.......408 727-4627
1700 Wyatt Dr Santa Clara (95054) ***(P-6960)***
Monterey Bay Rebar Inc (PA).......F.......831 724-3013
547 Airport Blvd Watsonville (95076) ***(P-11849)***
Monterey Canyon LLC (PA).......D.......213 741-0209
1515 E 15th St Los Angeles (90021) ***(P-3375)***
Monterey Coast Brewing LLC.......F.......831 758-2337
165 Main St Salinas (93901) ***(P-14387)***
Monterey Coun Graphic Comm, Salinas *Also called County of Monterey* ***(P-7038)***
Monterey County Herald Company (HQ).......E.......831 372-3311
2200 Garden Rd 101 Monterey (93940) ***(P-5758)***
Monterey County Weekly.......E.......831 393-3348
668 Williams Ave Seaside (93955) ***(P-5759)***

Monterey Design Systems Inc ....C....408 747-7370
2171 Landings Dr Mountain View (94043) ***(P-19224)***
Monterey Foam Company Inc ....F....408 279-6756
1716 Stone Ave Ste A San Jose (95125) ***(P-11012)***
Monterey Graphics Inc ....F....310 787-3370
23505 Crenshaw Blvd # 137 Torrance (90505) ***(P-6736)***
Monterey Herald, Monterey *Also called Monterey County Herald Company* ***(P-5758)***
Monterey Machine Products ....F....626 967-2242
1504 W Industrial Park St Covina (91722) ***(P-16224)***
Monterey Mechanical Co ....F....925 689-6670
1126 Landini Ln Concord (94520) ***(P-12310)***
Monterey Signs Inc ....F....831 632-0490
555 Broadway Ave Seaside (93955) ***(P-6737)***
Montero Printing Inc ....E....831 655-5511
2 Harris Ct Ste A6 Monterey (93940) ***(P-6738)***
Montery Wine Company LLC ....F....831 386-1100
1010 Industrial Way King City (93930) ***(P-1823)***
Montesquieu Winery, San Diego *Also called WG Best Weinkellerei Inc* ***(P-1997)***
Montevina Winery, Plymouth *Also called Sierra Sunrise Vineyard Inc* ***(P-1916)***
Monticello Cellars Inc ....F....707 253-2802
4242 Big Ranch Rd NAPA (94558) ***(P-1824)***
Montoya & Jaramillo Inc ....F....408 727-5776
1161 Richard Ave Santa Clara (95050) ***(P-13054)***
Monty Ventsam Inc ....F....818 768-6424
9495 San Fernando Rd Sun Valley (91352) ***(P-4090)***
Moo Time, San Diego *Also called Nadolife Inc* ***(P-660)***
Moog Aircraft Group, Torrance *Also called Moog Inc* ***(P-20635)***
Moog Inc ....C....818 341-5156
21339 Nordhoff St Chatsworth (91311) ***(P-20633)***
Moog Inc ....B....805 618-3900
7406 Hollister Ave Goleta (93117) ***(P-20634)***
Moog Inc ....B....310 533-1178
1218 W Jon St Torrance (90502) ***(P-16733)***
Moog Inc ....B....310 533-1178
20263 S Western Ave Torrance (90501) ***(P-20635)***
Moog Jon Street Warehouse, Torrance *Also called Moog Inc* ***(P-16733)***
Mooney Industries ....F....818 998-0199
8744 Remmet Ave Canoga Park (91304) ***(P-16225)***
Mooney International, Chino *Also called Soaring America Corporation* ***(P-19931)***
Moonshine Ink ....E....530 587-3607
10137 Riverside Dr Truckee (96161) ***(P-5760)***
Moore Business Forms, Vacaville *Also called R R Donnelley & Sons Company* ***(P-6828)***
Moore Epitaxial Inc ....E....209 833-0100
1422 Harding Ave Tracy (95376) ***(P-14500)***
Moore Farms Inc ....F....661 854-5588
916 S Derby St Arvin (93203) ***(P-2556)***
Moore Quality Galvanizing Inc ....E....559 673-2822
3001 Falcon Dr Madera (93637) ***(P-13208)***
Moore Quality Galvanizing LP ....E....559 673-2822
3001 Falcon Dr Madera (93637) ***(P-13209)***
Moore Technologies, Tracy *Also called Moore Epitaxial Inc* ***(P-14500)***
Moore Tool Co ....E....760 949-4142
16701 Chestnut St Ste 8 Hesperia (92345) ***(P-11615)***
Moores Ideal Products LLC ....F....626 339-9007
830 W Golden Grove Way Covina (91722) ***(P-22696)***
Moose Boats Inc ....F....707 778-9828
1175 Nimitz Ave Ste 115 Vallejo (94592) ***(P-20351)***
Mophie Inc (HQ) ....E....888 866-7443
15495 Sand Canyon Ave # 4 Irvine (92618) ***(P-17591)***
Moquin Press Inc ....D....650 592-0575
555 Harbor Blvd Belmont (94002) ***(P-6739)***
Moran Tools ....E....760 801-3570
2515 Bella Vista Dr Vista (92084) ***(P-13986)***
Moravek Biochemicals Inc (PA) ....E....714 990-2018
577 Mercury Ln Brea (92821) ***(P-7508)***
Moreau Wetzel Engineering Co ....F....310 830-5479
24424 Main St Ste 604 Carson (90745) ***(P-14081)***
Morehouse Foods Inc ....E....626 854-1655
760 Epperson Dr City of Industry (91748) ***(P-890)***
Morehouse-Cowles LLC ....E....909 627-7222
13930 Magnolia Ave Chino (91710) ***(P-14501)***
Morena Tile, San Juan Capistrano *Also called Suntile Inc* ***(P-10453)***
Moreno Industries Inc ....F....714 229-9696
1225 N Knollwood Cir Anaheim (92801) ***(P-19723)***
Morgan Advanced Ceramics Inc ....C....530 823-3401
13079 Earhart Ave Auburn (95602) ***(P-7509)***
Morgan Gallacher Inc ....E....562 695-1232
8707 Millergrove Dr Santa Fe Springs (90670) ***(P-8397)***
Morgan Hill Plastics Inc ....E....408 779-2118
8118 Arroyo Cir Gilroy (95020) ***(P-9911)***
Morgan Hill Precision Inc ....F....408 778-7895
15500 Concord Cir Ste 100 Morgan Hill (95037) ***(P-16226)***
Morgan Manufacturing Inc ....F....707 763-6848
521 2nd St Petaluma (94952) ***(P-11536)***
Morgan Marine, Woodland Hills *Also called Catalina Yachts Inc* ***(P-20317)***
Morgan Medesign Inc ....F....707 568-2929
7700 Bell Rd Ste B Windsor (95492) ***(P-21828)***
Morgan Polymer Seals LLC (PA) ....E....858 679-4946
2475 A Paseo De Las San Diego (92154) ***(P-9243)***
Morgan Products Inc ....F....661 257-3022
28103 Avenue Stanford Santa Clarita (91355) ***(P-16227)***
Morgan Technical Ceramics Inc ....F....510 491-1100
2425 Whipple Rd Hayward (94544) ***(P-11013)***
Morgan Winery Inc (PA) ....F....831 751-7777
590 Brunken Ave Ste C Salinas (93901) ***(P-1825)***
Morin Corp ....E....909 428-3747
10707 Commerce Way Fontana (92337) ***(P-12564)***
Morin Industrial Technology, Huntington Beach *Also called M I T Inc* ***(P-14072)***
Morin West, Fontana *Also called Morin Corp* ***(P-12564)***
Morinaga Nutritional Foods Inc ....F....310 787-0200
3838 Del Amo Blvd Ste 201 Torrance (90503) ***(P-2557)***
Morning Star Company ....D....209 827-2724
13448 Volta Rd Los Banos (93635) ***(P-797)***
Morning Star Packing, Los Banos *Also called Morning Star Company* ***(P-797)***
Morning Star Packing Co LP ....E....209 826-8000
12045 Ingomar Grade Los Banos (93635) ***(P-798)***
Morning Star Packing Co LP ....E....530 473-3642
2211 Old Highway 99 Williams (95987) ***(P-799)***
Morningstar Foods, Gustine *Also called Saputo Dairy Foods Usa LLC* ***(P-709)***
Morrell's Metal Finishing, Compton *Also called Morrells Electro Plating Inc* ***(P-13055)***
Morrells Electro Plating Inc ....E....310 639-1024
432 E Euclid Ave Compton (90222) ***(P-13055)***
Morrill Industries Inc ....D....209 838-2550
24754 E River Rd Escalon (95320) ***(P-13360)***
Morris Enterprises Inc ....E....818 894-9103
16799 Schoenborn St North Hills (91343) ***(P-9912)***
Morris Group International, City of Industry *Also called Acorn Engineering Company* ***(P-12525)***
Morris Group International (PA) ....F....626 336-4561
15125 Proctor Ave City of Industry (91746) ***(P-12565)***
Morris Kitchen Inc ....F....646 413-5186
2525 Kenilworth Ave Los Angeles (90039) ***(P-2558)***
Morris Multimedia Inc ....D....661 259-1234
24000 Creekside Rd Santa Clarita (91355) ***(P-5761)***
Morris Newspaper Corp Cal (HQ) ....D....209 249-3500
531 E Yosemite Ave Manteca (95336) ***(P-5762)***
Morris Publications (PA) ....E....209 847-3021
122 S 3rd Ave Oakdale (95361) ***(P-5763)***
Morris Roberts LLC ....E....800 672-3974
20251 Sw Acacia St # 120 Newport Beach (92660) ***(P-23163)***
Morris Welding Co Inc ....F....707 987-1114
11210 Socrates Mine Rd Middletown (95461) ***(P-24652)***
Morrison Mar & Intermodal Inc ....E....925 362-4599
753 Tunbridge Rd Ste A150 Danville (94526) ***(P-20294)***
Morrissey Bros Printers Inc ....E....323 233-7197
929 E Slauson Ave Los Angeles (90011) ***(P-7145)***
Mortan Industries Inc ....E....951 682-2215
880 Columbia Ave Ste 2 Riverside (92507) ***(P-9340)***
Mortech Manufacturing Co Inc ....E....626 334-1471
411 N Aerojet Dr Azusa (91702) ***(P-4865)***
Mortgage Company, The, Poway *Also called Eidon Inc* ***(P-7876)***
Mortgageplannercrm, San Diego *Also called Marketing Pro Consulting Inc* ***(P-24127)***
Morton Grinding Inc ....C....661 298-0895
201 E Avenue K15 Lancaster (93535) ***(P-23006)***
Morton Manufacturing, Lancaster *Also called Morton Grinding Inc* ***(P-23006)***
Morton Salt Inc ....F....510 797-2281
7380 Morton Ave Newark (94560) ***(P-9003)***
Morton Salt Inc ....F....562 437-0071
1050 Pier F Ave Long Beach (90802) ***(P-379)***
Morts Custom Sheetmetal ....F....530 241-7013
18121 Clear Creek Rd Redding (96001) ***(P-12311)***
Mosaic Brands Inc ....E....925 322-8700
3266 Buskirk Ave Pleasant Hill (94523) ***(P-23415)***
Mosaic Distributors LLC ....F....805 383-7711
507 Calle San Pablo Camarillo (93012) ***(P-8541)***
Mosaic Marketing Partners LLC ....F....805 383-7711
507 Calle San Pablo Camarillo (93012) ***(P-8542)***
Mosaic Vineyards & Winery Inc ....F....707 857-2000
2001 Highway 128 Geyserville (95441) ***(P-1826)***
Moseley Associates Inc (HQ) ....C....805 968-9621
82 Coromar Dr Goleta (93117) ***(P-17592)***
Mosier Bros ....F....559 564-3304
19580 Avenue 344 Woodlake (93286) ***(P-12032)***
MOSplastics Inc ....C....408 944-9407
2308 Zanker Rd San Jose (95131) ***(P-9913)***
Moss Landing Cement Co LLC ....F....831 731-6000
7697 Highway 1 Moss Landing (95039) ***(P-10424)***
Mosys Inc ....D....408 418-7500
2309 Bering Dr San Jose (95131) ***(P-18421)***
Mota Group Inc (PA) ....E....408 370-1248
60 S Market St Ste 1100 San Jose (95113) ***(P-19225)***
Motec USA, Huntington Beach *Also called JGM Automotive Tooling Inc* ***(P-14484)***
Motek Industries ....F....626 960-6005
14434 Joanbridge St Baldwin Park (91706) ***(P-16228)***
Mother Jones Magazine, San Francisco *Also called Foundation For Nat Progress* ***(P-5938)***
Mother Lode Plas Molding Inc ....E....209 532-5146
1905 N Macarthur Dr # 100 Tracy (95376) ***(P-9914)***
Mother Lode Printing & Pubg Co ....D....530 344-5030
2889 Ray Lawyer Dr Placerville (95667) ***(P-5764)***
Mother Plucker Feather Co Inc ....F....213 637-0411
2511 W 3rd St Ste 102 Los Angeles (90057) ***(P-23416)***
Motherly Inc ....E....917 860-9926
1725 Oakdell Dr Menlo Park (94025) ***(P-6286)***
Moticont ....E....818 785-1800
6901 Woodley Ave Van Nuys (91406) ***(P-19359)***
Motion Engineering Inc (HQ) ....D....805 696-1200
33 S La Patera Ln Santa Barbara (93117) ***(P-15292)***
Motionloft Inc ....E....415 580-7671
550 15th St Ste 29 San Francisco (94103) ***(P-21269)***
Motiv Design Group Inc ....F....408 441-0611
430 Perrymont Ave San Jose (95125) ***(P-16229)***
Motivational Systems Inc ....E....916 635-0234
11437 Sunrise Gold Cir A Rancho Cordova (95742) ***(P-23164)***
Motoart LLC ....F....310 375-4531
21809 S Western Ave Torrance (90501) ***(P-11014)***
Motor Technology Inc ....E....951 270-6200
2301 Wardlow Cir Corona (92880) ***(P-16663)***

Employee Codes: A=Over 500 employees, B=251-500
C=101-250, D=51-100, E=20-50, F=10-19
2020 California
Manfacturers Register
© Mergent Inc. 1-800-342-5647
1177

Motorcar Parts of America Inc (PA) ....A 310 212-7910
2929 California St Torrance (90503) ***(P-19724)***
Motorlamb International Acc ....F 858 569-8111
8055 Clairemont Mesa Blvd # 108 San Diego (92111) ***(P-3850)***
Motorola Mobility LLC ....D 206 383-7785
1633 Bayshore Hwy Burlingame (94010) ***(P-17593)***
Motorola Mobility LLC ....D 847 576-5000
809 Eleventh Ave Bldg 4 Sunnyvale (94089) ***(P-17594)***
Motorola Solutions Inc ....C 510 217-7400
1101 Marina Village Pkwy # 200 Alameda (94501) ***(P-17595)***
Motorola Solutions Inc ....E 213 362-6706
725 S Figueroa St # 1855 Los Angeles (90017) ***(P-17596)***
Motorola Solutions Inc ....F 858 541-2163
9665 Chesapeake Dr # 220 San Diego (92123) ***(P-18422)***
Motorola Solutions Inc ....C 954 723-4730
6101 W Century Blvd Los Angeles (90045) ***(P-17597)***
Motorola Solutions Inc ....E 510 420-7400
6001 Shellmound St Fl 4th Emeryville (94608) ***(P-15130)***
Motorola Solutions Inc ....D 650 318-3200
805 E Middlefield Rd Mountain View (94043) ***(P-17598)***
Motorshield LLC ....F 323 396-9200
3364 Garfield Ave Commerce (90040) ***(P-8659)***
Motoshieldpro, Commerce *Also called Motorshield LLC* ***(P-8659)***
Motran Industries Inc ....F 661 257-4995
3037 Golf Course Dr Ste 4 Ventura (93003) ***(P-16664)***
Motsenbocker Advanced Developm (PA) ....F 858 581-0222
4901 Morena Blvd Ste 806 San Diego (92117) ***(P-8398)***
Motu Global LLC ....F 801 471-7800
924 W 9th St Upland (91786) ***(P-800)***
Mount Palomar Winery, Temecula *Also called Louidar LLC* ***(P-1805)***
Mount Rose Publishing Co Inc ....F 530 587-6061
10775 Pioneer Trl Truckee (96161) ***(P-5765)***
Mount Rose Publishing Co Inc (PA) ....F 530 583-3487
395 N Lake Blvd Ste A Tahoe City (96145) ***(P-5766)***
Mount Seven, Atwater *Also called Five Keys Inc* ***(P-3083)***
Mountain Democrat, Placerville *Also called Mother Lode Printing & Pubg Co* ***(P-5764)***
Mountain Lake Labs ....F 707 331-3297
2675 Lands End Dr Lakeport (95453) ***(P-20636)***
Mountain Life, Mariposa *Also called Mariposa Gazette & Miner* ***(P-5725)***
Mountain News & Shopper, Lake Arrowhead *Also called Hi-Desert Publishing Company* ***(P-5664)***
Mountain View Voice ....E 650 326-8210
450 Cambridge Ave Palo Alto (94306) ***(P-5767)***
Mountain Winery, Saratoga *Also called Chateau Masson LLC* ***(P-1631)***
Mountz Inc (PA) ....E 408 292-2214
1080 N 11th St San Jose (95112) ***(P-20906)***
Mouse Graphics, Costa Mesa *Also called Orange Coast Reprographics Inc* ***(P-6761)***
Mousepad Designs, Cerritos *Also called Mpd Holdings Inc* ***(P-15294)***
Mova Stone Inc ....E 916 922-2080
4361 Pell Dr Ste 100 Sacramento (95838) ***(P-10916)***
Moveel Fuel LLC ....F 213 748-1444
15000 S Avalon Blvd Ste K Gardena (90248) ***(P-8754)***
Movement Products Inc ....F 949 206-0000
22365 El Toro Rd Ste 295 Lake Forest (92630) ***(P-20420)***
Movie Star, Los Angeles *Also called Foh Group Inc* ***(P-3452)***
Movieline Magazine, Inglewood *Also called Line Publications Inc* ***(P-5978)***
Moving Image Technologies LLC ....E 714 751-7998
17760 Newhope St Ste B Fountain Valley (92708) ***(P-22442)***
Movits, Carson *Also called O W I Inc* ***(P-17267)***
Moxa Americas Inc ....E 714 528-6777
601 Valencia Ave Ste 100 Brea (92823) ***(P-15293)***
Moz Designs Inc ....E 510 632-0853
711 Kevin Ct Oakland (94621) ***(P-12501)***
Mozaik LLC ....F 562 207-1900
2330 Artesia Ave Ste B Fullerton (92833) ***(P-5190)***
Mp Associates Inc ....C 209 274-4715
6555 Jackson Valley Rd Ione (95640) ***(P-8905)***
Mp Mine Operations LLC ....C 702 277-0848
67750 Bailey Rd Mountain Pass (92366) ***(P-383)***
MP Tool Inc ....F 661 294-7711
28110 Avenue Stanford E Valencia (91355) ***(P-16230)***
MPA, Torrance *Also called Motorcar Parts of America Inc* ***(P-19724)***
Mpb Furniture Corporation ....F 760 375-4800
414 W Ridgecrest Blvd Ridgecrest (93555) ***(P-4660)***
Mpbs Industries, Los Angeles *Also called Meat Packers Butchers Sup Inc* ***(P-14385)***
Mpc Networkcom Inc ....F 949 873-1002
440 Fair Dr Ste 233 Costa Mesa (92626) ***(P-6287)***
Mpd Holdings Inc ....E 562 777-1051
16200 Commerce Way Cerritos (90703) ***(P-15294)***
Mpi, Newbury Park *Also called Multilayer Prototypes Inc* ***(P-17929)***
Mpi Label Systems, Stockton *Also called Miller Products Inc* ***(P-5368)***
Mpj Recycling LLC ....F 916 761-5740
2100 21st St Ste B Sacramento (95818) ***(P-14502)***
MPK Sonoma, Sonoma *Also called Marinpak* ***(P-2541)***
Mpl Brands Inc (PA) ....E 888 513-3022
71 Liberty Ship Way Sausalito (94965) ***(P-1827)***
Mpl Brands Inc ....F 415 515-3536
2280 Union St San Francisco (94123) ***(P-1828)***
Mplus Motors Corp ....F 510 259-8435
15375 Barranca Pkwy Ste K Irvine (92618) ***(P-20421)***
Mpm & Associates, Van Nuys *Also called M P M Building Services Inc* ***(P-8395)***
Mpo Videotronics Inc (PA) ....D 805 499-8513
5069 Maureen Ln Moorpark (93021) ***(P-22443)***
MPS Industries Incorporated (PA) ....E 310 325-1043
19210 S Vermont Ave # 405 Gardena (90248) ***(P-16563)***
MPS International Ltd ....A 408 826-0600
79 Great Oaks Blvd San Jose (95119) ***(P-18423)***
MPS Lansing Inc ....E 707 778-1250
101 H St Ste M Petaluma (94952) ***(P-5369)***
MPS Medical Inc ....E 714 672-1090
830 Challenger St Ste 200 Brea (92821) ***(P-21829)***
Mr Gears Inc ....F 650 364-7793
428 Stanford Ave Redwood City (94063) ***(P-16231)***
Mr Lock, Corona *Also called Lock America Inc* ***(P-11606)***
MR Mold & Engineering Corp ....E 714 996-5511
2700 E Imperial Hwy Ste C Brea (92821) ***(P-14082)***
Mr S Leather ....E 415 863-7764
385 8th St San Francisco (94103) ***(P-3520)***
Mr T Transport ....F 562 602-5536
15535 Garfield Ave Paramount (90723) ***(P-225)***
Mr Tortilla Inc ....F 818 307-7414
1112 Arroyo St San Fernando (91340) ***(P-2559)***
Mr Washerman, South El Monte *Also called Calfabco* ***(P-12778)***
Mr. Nature, Cerritos *Also called G & P Group Inc* ***(P-1426)***
Mri, San Fernando *Also called Simon Harrison* ***(P-21539)***
Mri Interventions Inc ....E 949 900-6833
5 Musick Irvine (92618) ***(P-21830)***
Mrp Holdings Corp., City of Industry *Also called Hexpol Compounding CA Inc* ***(P-9315)***
MRr Moulding Industries Inc ....F 510 794-8116
125 N Mary Ave Spc 42 Sunnyvale (94086) ***(P-4091)***
Mrs Appletree's Bakery, Baldwin Park *Also called Distinct Indulgence Inc* ***(P-1188)***
Mrs Baird's Bakeries, Los Angeles *Also called Bimbo Bakeries Usa Inc* ***(P-1160)***
Mrs Grossmans Paper Company ....D 707 763-1700
3810 Cypress Dr Petaluma (94954) ***(P-5483)***
Mrs Redds Pie Co Inc ....E 909 825-4800
150 S La Cadena Dr Colton (92324) ***(P-1246)***
Mrv Systems LLC ....E 800 645-7114
6370 Lusk Blvd Ste F100 San Diego (92121) ***(P-21082)***
MS Aerospace Inc ....B 818 833-9095
13928 Balboa Blvd Sylmar (91342) ***(P-12686)***
Ms Bellows, Huntington Beach *Also called Mechanized Science Seals Inc* ***(P-21503)***
Ms Cast Stone Inc ....E 760 754-9697
235 Via Del Monte Oceanside (92058) ***(P-10604)***
MS Intertrade Inc (PA) ....E 707 837-8057
2221 Bluebell Dr Ste A Santa Rosa (95403) ***(P-2265)***
Ms2 Technologies LLC ....F 310 277-4110
2448 E 25th St Vernon (90058) ***(P-11276)***
MSA West LLC ....E 213 536-9880
16161 Ventura Blvd C326 Encino (91436) ***(P-3455)***
MSC-La, City of Industry *Also called Material Sciences Corporation* ***(P-11221)***
Msci Barra, Berkeley *Also called Barra LLC* ***(P-23652)***
Mscsoftware Corporation (HQ) ....C 714 540-8900
4675 Macarthur Ct Ste 900 Newport Beach (92660) ***(P-24180)***
MSE Media Solutions Inc ....E 323 721-1656
5533 E Slauson Ave Commerce (90040) ***(P-19226)***
MSI Hvac, Fontana *Also called Material Supply Inc* ***(P-12283)***
MSP Group Inc ....E 310 660-0022
206 W 140th St Los Angeles (90061) ***(P-2704)***
Msquared, Fresno *Also called M2 Antenna Systems Inc* ***(P-19000)***
Mt, Oxnard *Also called Travis Mike Inc* ***(P-12884)***
Mt Shasta Btlg Distrg Co Inc ....F 530 926-3121
302 Chestnut St Mount Shasta (96067) ***(P-2095)***
Mt Systems Inc ....F 510 651-5277
49040 Milmont Dr Fremont (94538) ***(P-14503)***
Mtech Inc ....F 530 894-5091
1072 Marauder St Ste 210 Chico (95973) ***(P-9915)***
MTI De Baja Inc ....E 951 654-2333
42941 Madio St Ste 2 Indio (92201) ***(P-20637)***
MTI Laboratory Inc ....E 310 955-3700
201 Continental Blvd # 300 El Segundo (90245) ***(P-17599)***
MTI Technology Corporation (PA) ....C 949 251-1101
15461 Red Hill Ave # 200 Tustin (92780) ***(P-15060)***
Mtil, El Segundo *Also called MTI Laboratory Inc* ***(P-17599)***
Mtm Industrial Inc ....F 760 967-1346
3230 Production Ave Ste B Oceanside (92058) ***(P-16232)***
MTS Stimulation Services Inc (PA) ....E 661 589-5804
7131 Charity Ave Bakersfield (93308) ***(P-226)***
Mu Gallery Makers, Vernon *Also called Makers Usa Inc* ***(P-2999)***
Mueller Gages Company ....F 626 287-2911
318 Agostino Rd San Gabriel (91776) ***(P-14176)***
Mufich Engineering Inc ....E 714 283-0599
341 W Blueridge Ave Orange (92865) ***(P-16233)***
Muhlhauser Enterprises Inc (PA) ....E 909 877-2792
25825 Adams Ave Murrieta (92562) ***(P-11850)***
Muhlhauser Steel, Murrieta *Also called Muhlhauser Enterprises Inc* ***(P-11850)***
Muhlhauser Steel Inc ....E 909 877-2792
25825 Adams Ave Murrieta (92562) ***(P-11851)***
Muirsis Inc ....F 714 579-1555
2841 Saturn St Ste J Brea (92821) ***(P-11674)***
Mulesoft Inc ....A 415 229-2009
50 Fremont St Ste 300 San Francisco (94105) ***(P-24181)***
Mulfat LLC ....E 818 367-0149
15835 Monte St Ste 103 Sylmar (91342) ***(P-14954)***
Mulgrew Arcft Components Inc ....D 626 256-1375
1810 S Shamrock Ave Monrovia (91016) ***(P-20183)***
Mulherin Monumental Inc ....F 760 353-7717
1000 S 2nd St El Centro (92243) ***(P-10917)***
Mulholland Brothers (PA) ....E 415 824-5995
1710 4th St Berkeley (94710) ***(P-4661)***
Mullen Technologies Inc (PA) ....E 714 613-1900
1405 Pioneer St Brea (92821) ***(P-19489)***
Muller Company ....F 858 587-9955
3366 N Torrey Pines Ct # 140 La Jolla (92037) ***(P-22051)***
Multani Logistics, Hayward *Also called Do Dine Inc* ***(P-23820)***

Mergent e-mail: customerrelations@mergent.com
1178
2020 California
Manufacturers Register
(P-0000) Products & Services Section entry number
(PA)=Parent Co (HQ)=Headquarters (DH)=Div Headquarters

ALPHABETIC SECTION N2 Aero, Glendale

Multi Packaging Solutions Inc E 818 638-0216
2350 W Empire Ave 150 Burbank (91504) ***(P-6740)***

Multi Power Products Inc F 415 883-6300
47931 Westinghouse Dr Fremont (94539) ***(P-19360)***

Multi-Color NAPA, NAPA *Also called Collotype Labels USA Inc* ***(P-7028)***

Multi-Fineline Electronix Inc (HQ) A 949 453-6800
101 Academy Ste 250 Irvine (92617) ***(P-17928)***

Multi-Link International Corp E 562 941-5380
12235 Los Nietos Rd Santa Fe Springs (90670) ***(P-9557)***

Multibeam Corporation E 408 980-1800
3951 Burton Dr Santa Clara (95054) ***(P-14504)***

Multichrome Company Inc (PA) E 310 216-1086
1013 W Hillcrest Blvd Inglewood (90301) ***(P-13056)***

Multicoat Products Inc F 949 888-7100
23331 Antonio Pkwy Rcho STA Marg (92688) ***(P-8660)***

Multicolor, Sonoma *Also called Collotype Labels USA Inc* ***(P-7029)***

Multilayer Prototypes Inc F 805 498-9390
2513 Teller Rd Newbury Park (91320) ***(P-17929)***

Multimedia Led Inc (PA) F 951 280-7500
4225 Prado Rd Ste 108 Corona (92880) ***(P-19022)***

Multimek Inc E 408 653-1300
357 Reed St Santa Clara (95050) ***(P-17930)***

Multimetrixs LLC F 510 527-6769
1025 Solano Ave Albany (94706) ***(P-16792)***

Multiquip Industries Corp F 888 996-7267
22605 La Palma Ave # 507 Yorba Linda (92887) ***(P-11973)***

Multis Inc E 510 441-2653
766 S 12th St San Jose (95112) ***(P-23417)***

Multitest Elctrnic Systems Inc (HQ) B 408 988-6544
3021 Kenneth St Santa Clara (95054) ***(P-21083)***

Multivitamin Direct Inc E 408 573-7276
2178 Paragon Dr San Jose (95131) ***(P-7674)***

Mumm NAPA Valley, Rutherford *Also called Pernod Ricard Usa LLC* ***(P-1863)***

Munchkin Inc (PA) C 818 893-5000
7835 Gloria Ave Van Nuys (91406) ***(P-9488)***

Municon Consultants, San Francisco *Also called Lois A Valeskie* ***(P-21500)***

Munkyfun Inc E 415 281-3837
1 Embarcadero Ctr Ste 500 San Francisco (94111) ***(P-24182)***

Munselle Vineyards LLC F 707 857-9988
3660 Highway 128 Geyserville (95441) ***(P-1829)***

Murad LLC (HQ) C 310 726-0600
2121 Park Pl Fl 1 El Segundo (90245) ***(P-8017)***

Murray Biscuit Company LLC E 209 472-3718
5250 Claremont Ave Stockton (95207) ***(P-1322)***

Murray Trailers, Stockton *Also called Harley Murray Inc* ***(P-19823)***

Murrey International Inc E 310 532-6091
25701 Weston Dr Laguna Niguel (92677) ***(P-22856)***

Mursion Inc (PA) D 415 746-9631
303 2nd St Ste 460 San Francisco (94107) ***(P-24183)***

Muscardini Cellars LLC F 707 933-9305
9380 Sonoma Hwy Kenwood (95452) ***(P-1830)***

Muscle Dynamics Corporation F 562 926-3232
14133 Freeway Dr Santa Fe Springs (90670) ***(P-22857)***

Muscle Road Inc F 559 499-6888
28838 Ave 15 One Half Madera (93638) ***(P-19725)***

Musclepharm Corporation (PA) D 303 396-6100
4400 W Vanowen St Burbank (91505) ***(P-606)***

Musco Family Olive Co, Tracy *Also called Olive Musco Products Inc* ***(P-812)***

Music Connection Inc F 818 995-0101
16130 Ventura Blvd # 540 Encino (91436) ***(P-5992)***

Music Connection Magazine, Encino *Also called Music Connection Inc* ***(P-5992)***

Music Market Update, Los Angeles *Also called Hits Magazine Inc* ***(P-5956)***

Musicmatch Inc C 858 485-4300
16935 W Bernardo Dr # 270 San Diego (92127) ***(P-24184)***

Mustang Hills LLC E 661 888-5810
16409 K St Mojave (93501) ***(P-2888)***

Mustard Seed Technologies Inc C 714 556-7007
3000 W Warner Ave Santa Ana (92704) ***(P-19023)***

Muth Machine Works (HQ) E 714 527-2239
8042 Katella Ave Stanton (90680) ***(P-16234)***

Mutt Lynch Winery Inc F 707 473-8080
3451 Airway Dr Ste C Santa Rosa (95403) ***(P-1831)***

Muzik Inc (PA) E 973 615-1223
9220 W Sunset Blvd # 112 West Hollywood (90069) ***(P-19024)***

Mv Excel F 619 223-7493
2838 Garrison St San Diego (92106) ***(P-22858)***

Mvm Products LLC D 949 366-1470
946 Calle Amanecer Ste E San Clemente (92673) ***(P-22444)***

Mvp Rv Inc E 951 848-4288
40 E Verdugo Ave Burbank (91502) ***(P-20490)***

Mw McWong International Inc E 916 371-8080
1921 Arena Blvd Sacramento (95834) ***(P-17146)***

MWsausse & Co Inc (PA) D 661 257-3311
28744 Witherspoon Pkwy Valencia (91355) ***(P-16734)***

Mww Inc E 800 575-3475
7945 Deering Ave Canoga Park (91304) ***(P-4518)***

Mx Electronics Mfg Inc D 714 258-0200
1651 E Saint Andrew Pl Santa Ana (92705) ***(P-11309)***

MXF Designs Inc D 323 266-1451
1601 Perrino Pl Ste A Los Angeles (90023) ***(P-3182)***

My Burbankcom Inc F 818 842-2140
10061 Rverside Dr Ste 520 Toluca Lake (91602) ***(P-5768)***

My Eye Media LLC E 818 559-7200
2211 N Hollywood Way Burbank (91505) ***(P-24185)***

My Fruity Faces LLC F 877 358-9210
2400 Lincoln Ave Altadena (91001) ***(P-1477)***

My Machine Inc F 626 214-9223
5140 Commerce Dr Baldwin Park (91706) ***(P-16235)***

My Michelle, La Puente *Also called Mymichelle Company LLC* ***(P-3183)***

My Sign Design LLC F 818 384-0800
4821 Lankershim Blvd F145 North Hollywood (91601) ***(P-6741)***

My Tech USA, Corona *Also called Hardy Frames Inc* ***(P-11047)***

My True Image Mfg Inc D 510 970-7990
999 Marina Way S Richmond (94804) ***(P-22052)***

My World Styles LLC F 800 355-4008
16 Dutton Ave San Leandro (94577) ***(P-8543)***

Mya International Inc F 619 429-6012
3517 Main St Ste 304 Chula Vista (91911) ***(P-8018)***

Myanimelist LLC F 714 423-8289
505 Howard St Ste 201 San Francisco (94105) ***(P-6288)***

Myc Direct Inc F 909 287-9919
19977 Harrison Ave Walnut (91789) ***(P-20766)***

Mycase, San Diego *Also called Appfolio Inc* ***(P-23609)***

Mycustomerdata, Trabuco Canyon *Also called Xpert Marketing Group Inc* ***(P-23246)***

Mydax Inc F 530 888-6662
12260 Shale Ridge Ln # 4 Auburn (95602) ***(P-15447)***

Mydyer.com, Long Beach *Also called Providence Industries LLC* ***(P-3048)***

Mye Technologies Inc E 661 964-0217
28460 Westinghouse Pl Valencia (91355) ***(P-19361)***

Myenersave Inc F 408 464-6385
440 N Wolfe Rd Sunnyvale (94085) ***(P-24186)***

Myers & Sons Hi-Way Safety Inc E 909 591-1781
520 W Grand Ave Escondido (92025) ***(P-17748)***

Myers & Sons Hi-Way Safety Inc (PA) C 909 591-1781
13310 5th St Chino (91710) ***(P-17749)***

Myers Container LLC E 800 406-9377
21508 Ferrero B Walnut (91789) ***(P-11510)***

Myers Mixers LLC E 323 560-4723
8376 Salt Lake Ave Cudahy (90201) ***(P-14839)***

Myers Wine Cntry Kitchens LLC E 707 252-9463
511 Alexis Ct NAPA (94558) ***(P-10289)***

Myers-Briggs Company (PA) D 650 969-8901
185 N Wolfe Rd Sunnyvale (94086) ***(P-6289)***

Mygrant Glass Company Inc E 858 455-8022
10220 Camino Santa Fe San Diego (92121) ***(P-19726)***

Mylan Pharmaceuticals Inc D 650 631-3100
150 Industrial Rd San Carlos (94070) ***(P-8019)***

Mymichelle Company LLC (HQ) B 626 934-4166
13077 Temple Ave La Puente (91746) ***(P-3183)***

Myntahl Corporation E 510 413-0002
48273 Lakeview Blvd Fremont (94538) ***(P-17387)***

Myogenix Incorporated F 800 950-0348
2309 A St Santa Maria (93455) ***(P-8020)***

Myojo USA Inc F 909 464-1411
6220 Prescott Ct Chino (91710) ***(P-2372)***

Myokardia Inc (PA) D 650 741-0900
333 Allerton Ave South San Francisco (94080) ***(P-8021)***

Myosci Technologies Inc F 760 433-5376
1211 Liberty Way Ste B Vista (92081) ***(P-607)***

Myotek Industries Incorporated (PA) D 949 502-3776
1278 Glenneyre St Ste 431 Laguna Beach (92651) ***(P-19196)***

Myricom Inc E 626 821-5555
3871 E Colo Blvd Ste 101 Pasadena (91107) ***(P-14955)***

Myron L Company D 760 438-2021
2450 Impala Dr Carlsbad (92010) ***(P-20907)***

Mytee Products Inc E 858 679-1191
13655 Stowe Dr Poway (92064) ***(P-15545)***

Mytek America, La Canada Flintridge *Also called Data Storm Inc* ***(P-19288)***

Mytime, San Francisco *Also called Melian Labs Inc* ***(P-24146)***

Mytrex Inc F 949 800-9725
4070 N Palm St Ste 707 Fullerton (92835) ***(P-13651)***

Myvoicegig LLC F 714 702-6006
12517 Wedgwood Cir Tustin (92780) ***(P-6290)***

Myway Learning Company Inc F 415 937-1722
47 Laurel Ave Larkspur (94939) ***(P-24187)***

Mywi Fabricators Inc F 626 279-6994
2115-2119 Edwards Ave South El Monte (91733) ***(P-11852)***

N A Suez E 310 414-0183
1935 S Hughes Way El Segundo (90245) ***(P-20908)***

N A T C O, Glendale *Also called North American Textile Co LLC* ***(P-3804)***

N C Industries F 951 296-9603
42147 Roick Dr Temecula (92590) ***(P-16236)***

N C W G Inc F 530 265-9463
321 Spring St Nevada City (95959) ***(P-1832)***

N D E Inc E 408 727-3955
3301 Keller St Santa Clara (95054) ***(P-17931)***

N D Industries, Santa Fe Springs *Also called ND Industries Inc* ***(P-12687)***

N G S, Sacramento *Also called New Generation Software Inc* ***(P-24203)***

N H Research Incorporated D 949 474-3900
16601 Hale Ave Irvine (92606) ***(P-21084)***

N J P Sports Inc F 818 247-3914
548 Arden Ave Glendale (91203) ***(P-3692)***

N M H Inc F 818 843-8522
19426 Londelius St Northridge (91324) ***(P-6742)***

N S Ceramic Molding Co E 909 947-3231
1336 E Francis St Unit 1 Ontario (91761) ***(P-14083)***

N V Cast Stone LLC D 707 261-6615
1111 Green Island Rd Vallejo (94503) ***(P-10605)***

N W D T, Hayward *Also called Keen-Kut Products Inc* ***(P-14166)***

N Z Pump Co Inc F 626 458-8023
801 S Palm Ave Alhambra (91803) ***(P-14592)***

N-Synch Technologies F 949 218-7761
30100 Town Center Dr 0-204 Laguna Niguel (92677) ***(P-15131)***

N-Tek Inc E 408 735-8442
823 Kifer Rd Sunnyvale (94086) ***(P-14505)***

N/S Corporation (PA) D 310 412-7074
235 W Florence Ave Inglewood (90301) ***(P-15546)***

N2 Aero, Glendale *Also called N2 Development Inc* ***(P-20184)***

ALPHABETIC

Employee Codes: A=Over 500 employees, B=251-500
C=101-250, D=51-100, E=20-50, F=10-19
2020 California
Manfacturers Register
© Mergent Inc. 1-800-342-5647
1179

N2 Development Inc....F....323 210-3251
1819 Dana St Ste A Glendale (91201) ***(P-20184)***
Nabolom Bakery....F....510 845-2253
2708 Russell St Berkeley (94705) ***(P-1247)***
Nabors Well Services Co....D....805 648-2731
2567 N Ventura Ave C Ventura (93001) ***(P-227)***
Nabors Well Services Co....C....661 588-6140
1025 Earthmover Ct Bakersfield (93314) ***(P-228)***
Nabors Well Services Co....B....661 589-3970
7515 Rosedale Hwy Bakersfield (93308) ***(P-229)***
Nabors Well Services Co....C....310 639-7074
19431 S Santa Fe Ave Compton (90221) ***(P-230)***
Nabors Well Services Co....D....661 392-7668
1954 James Rd Bakersfield (93308) ***(P-231)***
Nac Mfg Inc....E....909 472-3033
601 Kettering Dr Ontario (91761) ***(P-8799)***
Nada Appraisal Guide, Costa Mesa *Also called National Appraisal Guides Inc* ***(P-6291)***
Nadalie USA, Calistoga *Also called Tonnellerie Francaise French C* ***(P-4430)***
Nadin Company....E....818 500-8908
1815 Flower St Glendale (91201) ***(P-8022)***
Nadolife Inc....D....619 522-6890
2709 Newton Ave San Diego (92113) ***(P-660)***
Nady Systems Inc....E....510 652-2411
3341 Vincent Rd Pleasant Hill (94523) ***(P-17264)***
Nafhc, Santa Maria *Also called North American Fire Hose Corp* ***(P-9201)***
Nafm LLC....F....951 738-1114
1521 Pomona Rd Ste A Corona (92880) ***(P-14719)***
Nafm Engineering Service, Corona *Also called Nafm LLC* ***(P-14719)***
Naftex Westside Partners Limit....E....310 277-9004
1900 Avenue Of The Stars Los Angeles (90067) ***(P-58)***
Naggiar Vineyards LLC....F....530 268-9059
18125 Rosemary Ln Grass Valley (95949) ***(P-1833)***
Nagles Veal Inc....E....909 383-7075
1411 E Base Line St San Bernardino (92410) ***(P-419)***
Nagra, San Francisco *Also called Opentv Inc* ***(P-24231)***
Nai, Carlsbad *Also called Natural Alternatives Intl Inc* ***(P-8025)***
Naia Inc....E....510 724-2479
736 Alfred Nobel Dr Hercules (94547) ***(P-661)***
Nailpro, Van Nuys *Also called Creative Age Publications Inc* ***(P-5912)***
Nails 2000 International Inc....F....714 265-1983
10892 Forbes Ave Ste A2 Garden Grove (92843) ***(P-23418)***
Nakagawa Manufacturing USA Inc....E....510 782-0197
8652 Thornton Ave Newark (94560) ***(P-5133)***
Nakamura-Beeman Inc....E....562 696-1400
8520 Wellsford Pl Santa Fe Springs (90670) ***(P-4810)***
Naked Princess Worldwide LLC (PA)....F....310 271-1199
11766 Wilshire Blvd Fl 9 Los Angeles (90025) ***(P-8544)***
Nalco Champion, Bakersfield *Also called Nalco Company LLC* ***(P-7510)***
Nalco Company LLC....F....661 864-7955
4900 California Ave 420b Bakersfield (93309) ***(P-9004)***
Nalco Company LLC....F....661 834-0454
6321 District Blvd Bakersfield (93313) ***(P-7510)***
Nalco Company LLC....F....800 798-2247
1000 Burnett Ave Ste 430 Concord (94520) ***(P-9005)***
Nalco Company LLC....F....805 584-9950
980 Enchanted Way Ste 203 Simi Valley (93065) ***(P-9006)***
Nalco Wtr Prtrtment Sltons LLC....E....714 792-0708
704 Richfield Rd Placentia (92870) ***(P-15547)***
Nally & Millie, Los Angeles *Also called MXF Designs Inc* ***(P-3182)***
Nana's Cookie Company, San Diego *Also called Microbiotic Health Foods Inc* ***(P-1321)***
Nancys Specialty Foods....B....510 494-1100
2400 Olympic Blvd Ste 8 Walnut Creek (94595) ***(P-2560)***
Nancys Tortilleria & Mini Mkt....E....909 629-5889
348 S Towne Ave Pomona (91766) ***(P-2561)***
Nanka Seimen Co....F....323 585-9967
3030 Leonis Blvd Vernon (90058) ***(P-2373)***
Nankai Enviro-Tech Corporation....C....619 754-2250
2320 Paseo De Las America San Diego (92154) ***(P-9916)***
Nannette Keller, Tehachapi *Also called Keller Classics Inc* ***(P-3268)***
Nanofilm, Westlake Village *Also called Interntional Photo Plates Corp* ***(P-13032)***
Nanoflowx LLC....E....323 396-9200
3364 Garfield Ave Commerce (90040) ***(P-13210)***
Nanoimaging Services Inc....F....888 675-8261
4940 Carroll Canyon Rd # 115 San Diego (92121) ***(P-21270)***
Nanometer Technologies Inc....F....805 226-7332
2985 Theatre Dr Ste 3 Paso Robles (93446) ***(P-17388)***
Nanoprecision Products Inc....E....310 597-4991
802 Calle Plano Camarillo (93012) ***(P-12848)***
Nanoscale Combinatorial....E....408 987-2000
3100 Central Expy Santa Clara (95051) ***(P-9007)***
Nanosilicon Inc....E....408 263-7341
2461 Autumnvale Dr San Jose (95131) ***(P-18424)***
Nanostim Inc....F....408 530-0700
776 Palomar Ave Sunnyvale (94085) ***(P-22283)***
Nanosyn, Santa Clara *Also called Nanoscale Combinatorial* ***(P-9007)***
Nanosys Inc....C....408 240-6700
233 S Hillview Dr Milpitas (95035) ***(P-18425)***
Nanotronics Automation, Hollister *Also called Nanotronics Imaging Inc* ***(P-19362)***
Nanotronics Imaging Inc....F....831 630-0700
777 Flynn Rd Hollister (95023) ***(P-19362)***
Nanovea Inc (PA)....F....949 461-9292
6 Morgan Ste 156 Irvine (92618) ***(P-21271)***
Nantkwest Inc....F....858 633-0300
9920 Jefferson Blvd Culver City (90232) ***(P-8316)***
Nantkwest Inc (HQ)....E....805 633-0300
3530 John Hopkins Ct San Diego (92121) ***(P-8317)***
NAPA Beaucanon Estate....F....707 254-1460
1006 Monticello Rd NAPA (94558) ***(P-1834)***
NAPA Desktop Publishing, NAPA *Also called NAPA Printing & Graphics Ctr* ***(P-6743)***
NAPA Industries Inc....F....310 293-1209
1379 Beckwith Ave Los Angeles (90049) ***(P-23419)***
NAPA Printing & Graphics Ctr (PA)....F....707 257-6555
630 Airpark Rd Ste D NAPA (94558) ***(P-6743)***
NAPA Register, NAPA *Also called NAPA Valley Publishing Co* ***(P-5770)***
NAPA Valley Cast Stone, Vallejo *Also called N V Cast Stone LLC* ***(P-10605)***
NAPA Valley Coffee Roasting Co (PA)....F....707 224-2233
948 Main St NAPA (94559) ***(P-2305)***
NAPA Valley Kitchens Inc....D....510 558-7500
1610 5th St Berkeley (94710) ***(P-2562)***
NAPA Valley Publishing Co....D....707 226-3711
1615 Soscol Ave NAPA (94559) ***(P-5769)***
NAPA Valley Publishing Co (PA)....E....707 226-3711
1615 Soscol Ave NAPA (94559) ***(P-5770)***
NAPA Valley Register, NAPA *Also called NAPA Valley Publishing Co* ***(P-5769)***
NAPA Wine Company LLC....E....707 944-8669
7830 St Helena Hwy 40 Oakville (94562) ***(P-1835)***
Napro, Los Alamitos *Also called North American Petroleum* ***(P-9010)***
Naprotek Inc....D....408 830-5000
90 Rose Orchard Way San Jose (95134) ***(P-17932)***
Naptech Test Equipment Inc....F....707 995-7145
9781 Pt Lkeview Rd Unit 3 Kelseyville (95451) ***(P-21085)***
Narayan Corporation....E....310 719-7330
13432 Estrella Ave Gardena (90248) ***(P-9489)***
Narcotics Anonymous World Serv....E....818 773-9999
19737 Nordhoff Pl Chatsworth (91311) ***(P-6124)***
Nareg Jewelry Inc....E....213 683-1660
640 S Hill St Ste 542a Los Angeles (90014) ***(P-22552)***
Nasco Aircraft Brake Inc....D....310 532-4430
13300 Estrella Ave Gardena (90248) ***(P-20185)***
Nasco Gourmet Foods Inc....D....714 279-2100
22720 Savi Ranch Pkwy Yorba Linda (92887) ***(P-801)***
Nasco Petroleum LLC....F....949 461-5212
20532 El Toro Rd Ste 102 Mission Viejo (92692) ***(P-232)***
Nashua Corporation....D....323 583-8828
13341 Cambridge St Santa Fe Springs (90670) ***(P-5134)***
Nasmyth Tmf Inc....D....818 954-9504
29102 Hancock Pkwy Valencia (91355) ***(P-13057)***
Naso Industries Corporation....E....805 650-1231
3007 Bunsen Ave Ste Q Ventura (93003) ***(P-17933)***
Naso Technologies, Ventura *Also called Naso Industries Corporation* ***(P-17933)***
Nassco, San Diego *Also called National Stl & Shipbuilding Co* ***(P-20295)***
Nassco, Santa Cruz *Also called National Stock Sign Company* ***(P-23166)***
Nassco, San Diego *Also called International Mfg Tech Inc* ***(P-11050)***
Nat Aronson & Associates Inc....F....818 787-5160
7640 Gloria Ave Ste J Van Nuys (91406) ***(P-9200)***
Natel Energy Inc....F....510 342-5269
2401 Monarch St Alameda (94501) ***(P-13574)***
Natel Engineering, Chatsworth *Also called Epic Technologies LLC* ***(P-17366)***
Natel Engineering Company LLC (PA)....C....818 495-8617
9340 Owensmouth Ave Chatsworth (91311) ***(P-18426)***
Natel Engineering Company Inc....E....818 734-6552
9340 Owensmouth Ave Chatsworth (91311) ***(P-17934)***
Natel Engineering Company Inc....C....408 228-5462
2243 Lundy Ave San Jose (95131) ***(P-17935)***
Natel Engineering Company Inc....C....760 737-6777
2066 Aldergrove Ave Escondido (92029) ***(P-17936)***
Nates Fine Foods LLC....E....310 897-2690
8880 Industrial Ave # 100 Roseville (95678) ***(P-966)***
Nathan Anthony Furniture, Vernon *Also called Yen-Nhai Inc* ***(P-4678)***
Nathan Kimmel Company LLC....F....213 627-8556
4880 Valley Blvd Los Angeles (90032) ***(P-3693)***
National Appraisal Guides Inc....E....714 556-8511
3186 Airway Ave Ste K Costa Mesa (92626) ***(P-6291)***
National Band Saw Company....F....661 294-9552
1055 W Avenue L12 Lancaster (93534) ***(P-14388)***
National Bedding Company LLC....C....925 373-1350
6818 Patterson Pass Rd Livermore (94550) ***(P-4733)***
National Bevpak, Hayward *Also called Shasta Beverages Inc* ***(P-2171)***
National Bright Lighting Inc....E....909 818-9188
1480 Adelia Ave South El Monte (91733) ***(P-17147)***
National Cement Co Cal Inc....F....661 248-6733
5 Miles East Of I 5 Ofc H Lebec (93243) ***(P-10804)***
National Cement Co Cal Inc (HQ)....E....818 728-5200
15821 Ventura Blvd # 475 Encino (91436) ***(P-10805)***
National Cement Company Inc (HQ)....E....818 728-5200
15821 Ventura Blvd # 475 Encino (91436) ***(P-10425)***
National Certified Fabricators....F....951 278-8992
1525 E 6th St Corona (92879) ***(P-18728)***
National Cnstr Rentals Inc....F....323 838-1800
1045 S Greenwood Ave Montebello (90640) ***(P-233)***
National Copy Cartridge, El Cajon *Also called US Print & Toner Inc* ***(P-22975)***
National Corset Supply House (PA)....D....323 261-0265
3240 E 26th St Vernon (90058) ***(P-3445)***
National Diamond Lab Cal....F....818 240-5770
4650 Alger St Los Angeles (90039) ***(P-14177)***
National Directory Services....E....530 268-8636
19698 View Forever Ln Grass Valley (95945) ***(P-6125)***
National Diversified Sales Inc (HQ)....C....559 562-9888
21300 Victory Blvd # 215 Woodland Hills (91367) ***(P-9917)***
National Dragster Magazine, Glendora *Also called National Hot Rod Association* ***(P-5771)***
National Dyeing, Vernon *Also called AS Match Dyeing Co Inc* ***(P-2821)***
National Emblem Inc (PA)....C....310 515-5055
3925 E Vernon St Long Beach (90815) ***(P-3750)***
National Ewp Inc....F....510 236-6282
1961 Meeker Ave Richmond (94804) ***(P-11)***
National Ewp Inc....E....909 931-4014
5566 Arrow Hwy Montclair (91763) ***(P-12)***

Mergent e-mail: customerrelations@mergent.com
1180
2020 California
Manufacturers Register
(P-0000) Products & Services Section entry number
(PA)=Parent Co (HQ)=Headquarters (DH)=Div Headquarters

National Explrtion Wells Pumps, Montclair *Also called National Ewp Inc* ***(P-12)***
National Filter Media Corp ....D....760 246-4551
17130 Muskrat Ave Ste B Adelanto (92301) ***(P-14840)***
National Graphics LLC ....E....805 644-9212
4893 Mcgrath St Ventura (93003) ***(P-6744)***
National Hardwood Flooring & M, Van Nuys *Also called Katzirs Floor & HM Design Inc* ***(P-4069)***
National Hot Rod Association ....E....626 250-2300
2220 E Route 66 Glendora (91740) ***(P-5771)***
National Instruments Corp ....B....408 610-6800
4600 Patrick Henry Dr Santa Clara (95054) ***(P-21086)***
National Law Digest Inc ....E....310 791-9975
23844 Hawthorne Blvd # 200 Torrance (90505) ***(P-6126)***
National Media Inc (HQ) ....E....310 377-6877
609 Deep Valley Dr # 200 Rllng HLS Est (90274) ***(P-5772)***
National Media Inc ....E....310 372-0388
2615 Pcf Cast Hwy Ste 329 Hermosa Beach (90254) ***(P-5773)***
National Medical Products Inc ....F....949 768-1147
57 Parker Unit A Irvine (92618) ***(P-9918)***
National Metal Fabricators ....E....510 887-6231
28435 Century St Hayward (94545) ***(P-11853)***
National Metal Stampings Inc ....D....661 945-1157
42110 8th St E Lancaster (93535) ***(P-12849)***
National Mustang Racers Assn, Santa Ana *Also called Promedia Companies* ***(P-6007)***
National O Rings, Downey *Also called Hutchinson Seal Corporation* ***(P-9236)***
National Oilwell Varco Inc ....E....714 978-1900
1701 W Sequoia Ave Orange (92868) ***(P-13785)***
National Oilwell Varco Inc ....E....760 357-0970
220 Weakley St Calexico (92231) ***(P-13786)***
National Oilwell Varco Inc ....F....661 387-9316
1320 E Los Angeles Ave Shafter (93263) ***(P-234)***
National Oilwell Varco Inc ....F....530 682-0571
1438b Ohm Rd Arbuckle (95912) ***(P-235)***
National Oilwell Varco Inc ....E....714 978-1900
759 N Eckhoff St Orange (92868) ***(P-13787)***
National Oilwell Varco Inc ....F....714 456-1244
743 N Eckhoff St Orange (92868) ***(P-100)***
National Oilwell Varco Inc ....E....714 978-1900
752 N Poplar St Orange (92868) ***(P-13788)***
National Packaging Products, Commerce *Also called Yavar Manufacturing Co Inc* ***(P-5320)***
National Pen Co LLC (HQ) ....C....866 388-9850
12121 Scripps Summit Dr # 200 San Diego (92131) ***(P-22935)***
National Raisin Company, Fowler *Also called Sunshine Raisin Corporation* ***(P-1403)***
National Ready Mix, Duarte *Also called Viking Ready Mix Co Inc* ***(P-10866)***
National Ready Mixed Con Co ....F....323 245-5539
4549 Brazil St Los Angeles (90039) ***(P-10806)***
National Ready Mixed Con Co ....F....818 884-0893
6969 Deering Ave Canoga Park (91303) ***(P-10807)***
National Ready Mixed Con Co (HQ) ....E....818 728-5200
15821 Ventura Blvd # 475 Encino (91436) ***(P-10808)***
National Ready Mixed Con Co ....F....562 865-6211
11725 Artesia Blvd Artesia (90701) ***(P-10809)***
National Recycling Corporation ....F....510 268-1022
1312 Kirkham St Oakland (94607) ***(P-5514)***
National Sales Inc ....F....916 912-2894
825 F St Ste 600 West Sacramento (95605) ***(P-5135)***
National Scientific Sup Co Inc ....F....909 621-4585
260 York Pl Claremont (91711) ***(P-9919)***
National Semiconductor Corp (HQ) ....A....408 721-5000
2900 Semiconductor Dr Santa Clara (95051) ***(P-18427)***
National Sign & Marketing Corp ....D....909 591-4742
13580 5th St Chino (91710) ***(P-23165)***
National Signal Inc ....E....714 441-7707
2440 Artesia Ave Fullerton (92833) ***(P-20516)***
National Stabilizers Inc ....F....626 969-5700
611 S Duggan Ave Azusa (91702) ***(P-2563)***
National Stl & Shipbuilding Co (HQ) ....B....619 544-3400
2798 Harbor Dr San Diego (92113) ***(P-20295)***
National Stock Sign Company ....F....831 476-2020
1040 El Dorado Ave Santa Cruz (95062) ***(P-23166)***
National Sweetwater Inc ....F....951 303-0999
43394 Calle De Velardo Temecula (92592) ***(P-9008)***
National Wholesale Lumber, Pixley *Also called Correa Pallet Inc* ***(P-4358)***
Nations Petroleum Cal LLC ....D....661 387-6402
9600 Ming Ave Ste 300 Bakersfield (93311) ***(P-131)***
Nationwide Boiler Incorporated (PA) ....D....510 490-7100
42400 Christy St Fremont (94538) ***(P-12033)***
Nationwide Jewelry Mfrs Inc ....F....213 489-1215
631 S Olive St Ste 790 Los Angeles (90014) ***(P-22553)***
Nationwide Plastic Products ....E....310 366-7585
16809 Gramercy Pl Gardena (90247) ***(P-9414)***
Nationwide Printing Svcs Inc ....F....714 258-7899
400 Camino Vista Verde San Clemente (92673) ***(P-7146)***
Native American Media ....F....310 475-6845
10806 1/2 Wilshire Blvd Los Angeles (90024) ***(P-5993)***
Native Canadian Media, Los Angeles *Also called Native American Media* ***(P-5993)***
Native Kjalii Foods Inc ....E....415 592-8670
1474 29th Ave San Francisco (94122) ***(P-740)***
Nato LLC ....E....760 934-8677
38 Laurel Mountain Rd Mammoth Lakes (93546) ***(P-23420)***
Natren Inc ....D....805 371-4737
3105 Willow Ln Thousand Oaks (91361) ***(P-2564)***
Natrol LLC (HQ) ....C....818 739-6000
21411 Prairie St Chatsworth (91311) ***(P-8023)***
Natura-Genics Inc ....F....909 597-6676
6952 Buckeye St Chino (91710) ***(P-8024)***
Natural Alternatives Intl Inc (PA) ....E....760 736-7700
1535 Faraday Ave Carlsbad (92008) ***(P-8025)***
Natural Balance Pet Foods Inc (HQ) ....E....800 829-4493
100 N First St Ste 200 Burbank (91502) ***(P-1113)***
Natural Decadence LLC ....F....707 444-2629
3750 Harris St Eureka (95503) ***(P-1346)***
Natural Elements, Vernon *Also called L A S A M Inc* ***(P-3482)***
Natural Envmtl Protection Co ....E....909 620-8028
750 S Reservoir St Pomona (91766) ***(P-7583)***
Natural Medicine Intl, Upland *Also called Herbs Yeh Manufacturing Co* ***(P-594)***
Natural Pest Controls & Firewd (PA) ....F....916 726-0855
8864 Little Creek Dr Orangevale (95662) ***(P-8836)***
Natural Std RES Collaboration ....E....617 591-3300
3120 W March Ln Fl 1 Stockton (95219) ***(P-6127)***
Natural Wonders Ca Inc ....F....818 593-2001
7240 Eton Ave Canoga Park (91303) ***(P-7675)***
Naturalife Eco Vite Labs ....D....310 370-1563
20433 Earl St Torrance (90503) ***(P-608)***
Naturas Foods California Inc ....F....909 594-7838
334 Paseo Sonrisa Walnut (91789) ***(P-741)***
Nature Creation, Canoga Park *Also called Natural Wonders Ca Inc* ***(P-7675)***
Nature Zone Pet Products ....E....530 343-5199
265 Boeing Ave Chico (95973) ***(P-23421)***
Nature's Baby Organics, Rancho Mirage *Also called Natures Baby Products Inc* ***(P-8545)***
Nature's Bounty, Anaheim *Also called Nbty Manufacturing LLC* ***(P-8027)***
Nature's Flavors, Orange *Also called Newport Flavors & Fragrances* ***(P-2222)***
Nature's Glory, North Hollywood *Also called Cosmo - Pharm Inc* ***(P-7650)***
Nature-Cide, Canoga Park *Also called Pacific Shore Holdings Inc* ***(P-8061)***
Naturemaker Inc ....E....760 438-4244
6225 El Camino Real Carlsbad (92009) ***(P-23422)***
Naturener Usa LLC (HQ) ....E....415 217-5500
435 Pacific Ave Fl 4 San Francisco (94133) ***(P-16665)***
Natures Baby Products Inc ....F....818 521-5054
58 Dartmouth Dr Rancho Mirage (92270) ***(P-8545)***
Natures Bounty Co ....F....310 952-7107
901 E 233rd St Carson (90745) ***(P-7676)***
Natures Bounty Co ....F....714 898-9936
7366 Orangewood Ave Garden Grove (92841) ***(P-7677)***
Naturestar Bio Tech Inc ....F....909 930-1878
1175 S Grove Ave Ste 101 Ontario (91761) ***(P-8026)***
Naturvet, Temecula *Also called Garmon Corporation* ***(P-23340)***
Natus Medical Incorporated ....E....303 962-1800
1501 Industrial Rd San Carlos (94070) ***(P-22284)***
Natus Medical Incorporated ....D....858 260-2590
5955 Pacific Center Blvd San Diego (92121) ***(P-22285)***
Natus Medical Incorporated (PA) ....B....925 223-6700
6701 Koll Center Pkwy # 12 Pleasanton (94566) ***(P-22286)***
Natutac, Cerritos *Also called Winning Laboratories Inc* ***(P-7705)***
Natvar, City of Industry *Also called Tekni-Plex Inc* ***(P-5537)***
Nautilus Seafood, San Pedro *Also called J Deluca Fish Company Inc* ***(P-2261)***
Navajo Concrete Inc ....F....805 238-0955
2484 Ramada Dr Paso Robles (93446) ***(P-10810)***
Navajo Rock & Block, Paso Robles *Also called Navajo Concrete Inc* ***(P-10810)***
Naval Maint Training Group, Port Hueneme *Also called United States Dept of Navy* ***(P-20264)***
Navarro Vineyard, Philo *Also called Navarro Winery* ***(P-1836)***
Navarro Winery ....D....707 895-3686
5601 Highway 128 Philo (95466) ***(P-1836)***
Navcom Defense Electronics Inc (PA) ....D....951 268-9205
9129 Stellar Ct Corona (92883) ***(P-20638)***
Navcom Technology Inc (HQ) ....E....310 381-2000
20780 Madrona Ave Torrance (90503) ***(P-17600)***
Navigational Services Inc ....F....619 477-1564
34 E 17th St Ste C National City (91950) ***(P-20296)***
Navigator Yachts and Pdts Inc ....C....951 657-2117
364 Malbert St Perris (92570) ***(P-20352)***
Navistar Inc ....D....818 907-0129
14651 Ventura Blvd Sherman Oaks (91403) ***(P-19490)***
Naylor Corp ....E....415 421-1789
Spc 112 Pier 39 San Francisco (94133) ***(P-1412)***
Nazca Solutions Inc ....E....612 279-6100
4 First American Way Santa Ana (92707) ***(P-24188)***
Nbp, Claremont *Also called New Bedford Panoramex Corp* ***(P-17148)***
Nbty Manufacturing LLC ....C....714 765-8323
5115 E La Palma Ave Anaheim (92807) ***(P-8027)***
NC Dynamics Incorporated ....C....562 634-7392
6925 Downey Ave Long Beach (90805) ***(P-20186)***
NC Dynamics LLC ....C....562 634-7392
3401 E 69th St Long Beach (90805) ***(P-16237)***
NC Engineering Inc ....F....310 532-4810
13439 S Budlong Ave Gardena (90247) ***(P-16238)***
NC Interactive LLC ....D....650 393-2200
1900 S Norfolk St Ste 125 San Mateo (94403) ***(P-24189)***
Nca Laboratories Inc ....F....916 852-7029
11305 Sunrise Gold Cir D Rancho Cordova (95742) ***(P-17265)***
Ncdi, Long Beach *Also called NC Dynamics Incorporated* ***(P-20186)***
Nch Corporation ....F....972 438-0211
932 Kifer Rd Sunnyvale (94086) ***(P-7511)***
Nci Group Inc ....D....909 987-4681
9123 Center Ave Rancho Cucamonga (91730) ***(P-12566)***
Nci Group Inc ....C....209 357-1000
550 Industry Way Atwater (95301) ***(P-12567)***
Ncla Inc ....F....562 926-6252
1388 W Foothill Blvd Azusa (91702) ***(P-5515)***
Ncoup Inc ....E....510 739-4010
825 Corporate Way Fremont (94539) ***(P-24190)***
ND Industries Inc ....E....562 926-3321
13929 Dinard Ave Santa Fe Springs (90670) ***(P-12687)***
Nds, Woodland Hills *Also called National Diversified Sales Inc* ***(P-9917)***
Nds, Fresno *Also called Agrifim Irrigation Pdts Inc* ***(P-13605)***
Ndsp Crp, San Jose *Also called Ndsp Delaware Inc* ***(P-18428)***

ALPHABETIC

Employee Codes: A=Over 500 employees, B=251-500
C=101-250, D=51-100, E=20-50, F=10-19
2020 California
Manfacturers Register
© Mergent Inc. 1-800-342-5647
1181

Ndsp Delaware Inc......D......408 626-1640
224 Airport Pkwy Ste 400 San Jose (95110) ***(P-18428)***
NDT Systems Inc......E......714 893-2438
5542 Buckingham Dr Ste A Huntington Beach (92649) ***(P-21511)***
Nea Electronics Inc......E......805 292-4010
14370 White Sage Rd Moorpark (93021) ***(P-18781)***
Neal Family Vineyards LLC......F......707 965-2800
716 Liparita Ave Angwin (94508) ***(P-1837)***
Neal Feay Company......D......805 967-4521
133 S La Patera Ln Goleta (93117) ***(P-11241)***
Nearfield Systems Inc......D......310 525-7000
19730 Magellan Dr Torrance (90502) ***(P-21087)***
Neato Robotics Inc (HQ)......D......510 795-1351
8100 Jarvis Ave Ste 100 Newark (94560) ***(P-14276)***
Neatpocket LLC......F......323 632-7440
8033 W Sunset Blvd West Hollywood (90046) ***(P-24191)***
Neb Cal Printing, San Diego *Also called Kovin Corporation Inc* ***(P-6681)***
Nebia Inc......F......203 570-6222
375 Alabama St Ste 200 San Francisco (94110) ***(P-9341)***
Neclec......E......559 797-0103
5945 E Harvard Ave Fresno (93727) ***(P-13058)***
Nectave Inc......F......714 393-0144
6700 Caballero Blvd Buena Park (90620) ***(P-2565)***
Nef Tech Inc......F......909 548-4900
5255 State St Montclair (91763) ***(P-15548)***
Nefab Packaging Inc......D......408 678-2500
8477 Central Ave Newark (94560) ***(P-4340)***
Nefful USA Inc......F......626 839-6657
18563 Gale Ave City of Industry (91748) ***(P-3446)***
Nei Systems, Fremont *Also called New England Interconnect Syste* ***(P-11311)***
Neighboring LLC......F......818 271-0640
2427 Sentinel Ln San Marcos (92078) ***(P-22174)***
Neil A Kjos Music Company (PA)......E......858 270-9800
4382 Jutland Dr San Diego (92117) ***(P-6292)***
Neil Jones Food Company......D......831 637-0573
711 Sally St Hollister (95023) ***(P-802)***
Neil Jones Food Company......E......559 659-5100
2502 N St Firebaugh (93622) ***(P-803)***
Neil Patel Digital LLC......E......619 356-8119
750 B St Ste 2600 San Diego (92101) ***(P-6293)***
Neill Aircraft Co......B......562 432-7981
1260 W 15th St Long Beach (90813) ***(P-20187)***
Neilmed Pharmaceuticals Inc......B......707 525-3784
601 Aviation Blvd Santa Rosa (95403) ***(P-8028)***
Neiman & Company, Van Nuys *Also called Neiman/Hoeller Inc* ***(P-23167)***
Neiman/Hoeller Inc......D......818 781-8600
6842 Valjean Ave Van Nuys (91406) ***(P-23167)***
Neko World Inc......E......301 649-1188
21041 S Wstn Ave Ste 200 Torrance (90501) ***(P-22697)***
Nektar Therapeutics......E......650 622-1790
150 Industrial Rd San Carlos (94070) ***(P-8029)***
Nektar Therapeutics (PA)......B......415 482-5300
455 Mission Bay Blvd S San Francisco (94158) ***(P-8030)***
Nektar Therapeutics Al Corp......D......256 512-9200
455 Mission Bay Blvd S San Francisco (94158) ***(P-8755)***
Nelco Products Inc (HQ)......C......714 879-4293
1100 E Kimberly Ave Anaheim (92801) ***(P-9444)***
Nelgo Industries Inc......E......760 433-6434
3265 Production Ave Ste A Oceanside (92058) ***(P-16239)***
Nelgo Manufacturing, Oceanside *Also called Nelgo Industries Inc* ***(P-16239)***
Nellson Nutraceutical Inc (PA)......B......626 812-6522
5115 E La Palma Ave Anaheim (92807) ***(P-1390)***
Nellson Nutraceutical LLC (PA)......B......714 765-7000
5115 E La Palma Ave Anaheim (92807) ***(P-1391)***
Nelson & Sons Inc......E......707 462-3755
550 Nelson Ranch Rd Ukiah (95482) ***(P-1838)***
Nelson Banner Inc......E......707 585-9942
5720 Labath Ave Rohnert Park (94928) ***(P-5407)***
Nelson Case Corporation......F......714 528-2215
650 S Jefferson St Ste A Placentia (92870) ***(P-4341)***
Nelson Engineering Llc......E......714 893-7999
11600 Monarch St Garden Grove (92841) ***(P-16240)***
Nelson Family Vineyard, Ukiah *Also called Nelson & Sons Inc* ***(P-1838)***
Nelson Jewellery (usa) Inc......F......213 489-3323
631 S Olive St Ste 300 Los Angeles (90014) ***(P-22598)***
Nelson Name Plate Company (PA)......C......323 663-3971
2800 Casitas Ave Los Angeles (90039) ***(P-7147)***
Nelson Sports Inc......E......562 944-8081
10528 Pioneer Blvd Santa Fe Springs (90670) ***(P-10181)***
Nelson Stud Welding Inc......F......909 468-2105
20621 Valley Blvd Ste B Walnut (91789) ***(P-12688)***
Nelson Thread Grinding Inc......F......818 768-2578
8205 Lankershim Blvd North Hollywood (91605) ***(P-16241)***
Nelson-Miller, Los Angeles *Also called Nelson Name Plate Company* ***(P-7147)***
Nemco, Irvine *Also called Suntsu Electronics Inc* ***(P-19096)***
Nemco Electronics Corp......C......650 571-1234
40 Roan Pl Woodside (94062) ***(P-18683)***
Neo Pacific Holdings Inc......E......818 786-2900
14940 Calvert St Van Nuys (91411) ***(P-9920)***
Neo Tech Aqua Solutions Inc......F......858 571-6590
3853 Calle Fortunada San Diego (92123) ***(P-9009)***
Neo Tech Natel Epic Oncore, Chatsworth *Also called Oncore Manufacturing Svcs Inc* ***(P-17945)***
Neoconix Inc......E......408 530-9393
4020 Moorpark Ave Ste 108 San Jose (95117) ***(P-18429)***
Neodora LLC......E......650 283-3319
1545 Berger Dr San Jose (95112) ***(P-14506)***
Neogen Corporation......E......209 664-1683
1355 Paulson Rd Turlock (95380) ***(P-8399)***
Neogov, El Segundo *Also called Governmentjobscom Inc* ***(P-23950)***
Neology Inc (HQ)......E......858 391-0260
13520 Evening Creek Dr N S San Diego (92128) ***(P-21088)***
Neomen, Palm Springs *Also called Pleros LLC* ***(P-8563)***
Neomend Inc......D......949 783-3300
60 Technology Dr Irvine (92618) ***(P-21831)***
Neon Ideas......F......805 648-7681
1635 Buena Vista St Ventura (93001) ***(P-23168)***
Neonode Inc (PA)......D......408 496-6722
2880 Zanker Rd Ste 362 San Jose (95134) ***(P-21272)***
Neophotonics Corporation......F......408 232-9200
40931 Encyclopedia Cir Fremont (94538) ***(P-18430)***
Neophotonics Corporation (PA)......B......408 232-9200
2911 Zanker Rd San Jose (95134) ***(P-18431)***
Neoplast Inc......F......951 300-9300
1350 Citrus St Riverside (92507) ***(P-9921)***
Neosem Technology Inc (HQ)......E......408 643-7000
1965 Concourse Dr San Jose (95131) ***(P-21089)***
Neotech, Chatsworth *Also called Natel Engineering Company LLC* ***(P-18426)***
Neotract Inc (HQ)......F......925 401-0700
4155 Hopyard Rd Pleasanton (94588) ***(P-21832)***
Nepco, Pomona *Also called Natural Envmtl Protection Co* ***(P-7583)***
Neptec Optical Solutions, Fremont *Also called Neptec Os Inc* ***(P-11310)***
Neptec Optical Solutions Inc......E......510 687-1101
48603 Warm Springs Blvd Fremont (94539) ***(P-10321)***
Neptec Os Inc......E......510 687-1101
48603 Warm Springs Blvd Fremont (94539) ***(P-11310)***
Neptune Foods, Vernon *Also called Fishermans Pride Prcessors Inc* ***(P-2260)***
Neptune Trading Inc......F......909 923-0236
4021 Greystone Dr Ontario (91761) ***(P-11516)***
Nerdist Channel LLC......E......818 333-2705
2525 N Naomi St Burbank (91504) ***(P-17601)***
Nerdist Industries, Burbank *Also called Nerdist Channel LLC* ***(P-17601)***
Nerveda Inc......D......858 705-2365
3888 Quarter Mile Dr San Diego (92130) ***(P-8031)***
Nest Environments Inc......F......714 979-5500
530 E Dyer Rd Santa Ana (92707) ***(P-4092)***
Nestle Confections Factory, Modesto *Also called Nestle Usa Inc* ***(P-610)***
Nestle Dist Ctr & Logistics, Jurupa Valley *Also called Nestle Usa Inc* ***(P-968)***
Nestle Dreyers Ice Cream Co......F......661 398-5448
7301 District Blvd Bakersfield (93313) ***(P-662)***
Nestle Dreyers Ice Cream Co......F......559 834-2554
4065 E Therese Ave Fresno (93725) ***(P-663)***
Nestle Dsd, Fresno *Also called Nestle Usa Inc* ***(P-609)***
Nestle Pizza Company Inc......F......510 261-8001
2530 E 11th St Oakland (94601) ***(P-967)***
Nestle Purina Factory, Maricopa *Also called Nestle Purina Petcare Company* ***(P-23423)***
Nestle Purina Petcare Company......D......661 769-8261
1710 Golden Cat Rd Maricopa (93252) ***(P-23423)***
Nestle Purina Petcare Company......C......314 982-1000
800 N Brand Blvd Fl 5 Glendale (91203) ***(P-1079)***
Nestle Refrigerated Food Co......B......818 549-6000
800 N Brand Blvd Fl 5 Glendale (91203) ***(P-2374)***
Nestle Usa Inc......F......559 834-2554
4065 E Therese Ave Fresno (93725) ***(P-609)***
Nestle Usa Inc......D......209 574-2000
736 Garner Rd Modesto (95357) ***(P-610)***
Nestle Usa Inc......F......951 360-7200
3450 Dulles Dr Jurupa Valley (91752) ***(P-968)***
Net Optics Inc......D......408 737-7777
5301 Stevens Creek Blvd Santa Clara (95051) ***(P-24192)***
Net Shapes Inc......C......909 947-3231
1336 E Francis St Ste B Ontario (91761) ***(P-11164)***
Netaphor Software Inc......F......949 470-7955
15510 Rockfield Blvd C100 Irvine (92618) ***(P-24193)***
Netapp Inc (PA)......A......408 822-6000
1395 Crossman Ave Sunnyvale (94089) ***(P-15061)***
Netcube Systems Inc......D......650 862-7858
1275 Arbor Ave Los Altos (94024) ***(P-24194)***
Netflix Inc (PA)......C......408 540-3700
100 Winchester Cir Los Gatos (95032) ***(P-6294)***
Netgear Inc (PA)......C......408 907-8000
350 E Plumeria Dr San Jose (95134) ***(P-17389)***
Nethra Imaging Inc (PA)......F......408 257-5880
2855 Bowers Ave Santa Clara (95051) ***(P-18432)***
Netlist Inc (PA)......D......949 435-0025
175 Technology Dr Ste 150 Irvine (92618) ***(P-18433)***
Netmarble Us Inc......F......714 276-1196
600 Wilshire Blvd # 1100 Los Angeles (90017) ***(P-6295)***
Netsarang Inc......F......669 204-3301
4701 P Henry Dr 137 Santa Clara (95054) ***(P-24195)***
Netsol Technologies Inc (PA)......E......818 222-9197
23975 Park Sorrento # 250 Calabasas (91302) ***(P-24196)***
Netsuite Inc (HQ)......C......650 627-1000
2955 Campus Dr Ste 100 San Mateo (94403) ***(P-24197)***
Network Automation Inc......E......213 738-1700
3530 Wilshire Blvd # 1800 Los Angeles (90010) ***(P-24198)***
Network Chemistry Inc......F......650 858-3120
1804 Embarcadero Rd # 201 Palo Alto (94303) ***(P-19363)***
Network Pcb Inc......E......408 943-8760
1914 Otoole Way San Jose (95131) ***(P-17937)***
Network Printing & Copy Center......F......858 695-8221
12155 Flint Pl Poway (92064) ***(P-6745)***
Network Vigilance LLC......F......858 695-8676
12121 Scripps Summit Dr # 320 San Diego (92131) ***(P-24199)***
Networked Energy Services Corp (HQ)......E......408 622-9900
5215 Hellyer Ave Ste 150 San Jose (95138) ***(P-19364)***
Networks Electronic Co LLC......E......818 341-0440
9750 De Soto Ave Chatsworth (91311) ***(P-13283)***

Netwrix Corporation (PA) ....E....888 638-9749
300 Spectrum Center Dr # 200 Irvine (92618) **(P-24200)**
Neural Analytics Inc ....F....818 317-4999
2440 S Sepulveda Blvd # 115 Los Angeles (90064) **(P-21833)**
Neural Id LLC ....F....650 394-8800
203 Redwood Shr Pkwy # 250 Redwood City (94065) **(P-19227)**
Neurocrine Biosciences Inc (PA) ....C....858 617-7600
12780 El Camino Real # 100 San Diego (92130) **(P-8032)**
Neurohacker Collective LLC ....F....855 281-2328
5938 Priestly Dr Ste 200 Carlsbad (92008) **(P-611)**
Neurolenses, Costa Mesa *Also called Eyebrain Medical Inc* **(P-22356)**
Neuroptics Inc ....F....949 250-9792
23041 Ave D L Carlota 1 Laguna Hills (92653) **(P-21834)**
Neurosmith LLC ....E....562 296-1100
1000 N Studebaker Rd # 3 Long Beach (90815) **(P-22698)**
Neurostructures Inc ....F....800 352-6103
199 Technology Dr Ste 110 Irvine (92618) **(P-22053)**
Neutraderm Inc ....E....818 534-3190
20660 Nordhoff St Chatsworth (91311) **(P-8546)**
Neutrogena, Los Angeles *Also called Johnson & Johnson Consumer Inc* **(P-8523)**
Neutron Plating Inc ....D....714 632-9241
2993 E Blue Star St Anaheim (92806) **(P-13059)**
Neutronic Stamping & Plating ....E....714 964-8900
100 Business Center Dr Corona (92880) **(P-13060)**
Nevada City Winery, Nevada City *Also called N C W G Inc* **(P-1832)**
Nevada County Publishing Co ....A....530 273-9561
464 Sutton Way Grass Valley (95945) **(P-5774)**
Nevada Heat Treating LLC (PA) ....E....510 790-2300
37955 Central Ct Ste D Newark (94560) **(P-24653)**
Nevada Window Supply Inc ....F....951 300-0100
1455 Columbia Ave Riverside (92507) **(P-4093)**
Neville Industries Inc ....F....760 471-8949
285 Pawnee St Ste D San Marcos (92078) **(P-14084)**
Nevion Usa Inc ....D....805 247-8575
400 W Ventura Blvd # 155 Camarillo (93010) **(P-17602)**
Nevocal Enterprises Inc ....D....559 277-0700
5320 N Barcus Ave Fresno (93722) **(P-353)**
Nevro Corp ....C....650 251-0005
411 Acacia Ave Palo Alto (94306) **(P-21835)**
Nevro Corp (PA) ....C....650 251-0005
1800 Bridge Pkwy Redwood City (94065) **(P-21836)**
Nevwest Inc ....E....619 420-8100
1225 S Expo Way Ste 140 San Diego (92154) **(P-20639)**
New Age Enclosures, Santa Maria *Also called Alltec Integrated Mfg Inc* **(P-9618)**
New Age Metal Finishing LLC ....E....559 498-8585
2169 N Pleasant Ave Fresno (93705) **(P-13061)**
New Bedford Panoramex Corp ....E....909 982-9806
1480 N Claremont Blvd Claremont (91711) **(P-17148)**
New Bi US Gaming LLC ....D....858 592-2472
10920 Via Frontera # 420 San Diego (92127) **(P-24201)**
New Brunswick Industries Inc ....E....619 448-4900
1850 Gillespie Way El Cajon (92020) **(P-17938)**
New Cal Metals Inc ....F....916 652-7424
3495 Swetzer Rd Granite Bay (95746) **(P-12312)**
New CAM Commerce Solutions LLC ....D....714 338-0200
5555 Garden Grove Blvd # 100 Westminster (92683) **(P-24202)**
New Century Gold LLC ....F....818 936-2676
6303 Owensmouth Ave Fl 10 Woodland Hills (91367) **(P-22554)**
New Century Industries Inc ....E....562 634-9551
7231 Rosecrans Ave Paramount (90723) **(P-19727)**
New Century Machine Tools Inc ....F....562 906-8455
9641 Santa Fe Springs Rd Santa Fe Springs (90670) **(P-13937)**
New Century Snacks, Commerce *Also called Snak Club LLC* **(P-1438)**
New Chef Fashion Inc ....D....323 581-0300
3223 E 46th St Vernon (90058) **(P-2971)**
New Cntury Mtals Southeast Inc ....F....562 356-6804
15723 Shoemaker Ave Norwalk (90650) **(P-11277)**
New Dimension Electronics, Santa Clara *Also called N D E Inc* **(P-17931)**
New Dimension One Spas Inc (HQ) ....C....800 345-7727
1819 Aston Ave Ste 105 Carlsbad (92008) **(P-23424)**
New Direction Silk Screen ....F....916 971-3939
2328 Auburn Blvd Ste 2 Sacramento (95821) **(P-7148)**
New England Interconnect Syste ....B....603 355-3515
46840 Lakeview Blvd Fremont (94538) **(P-11311)**
New Fragrance Continental ....F....323 766-0060
5033 Exposition Blvd Los Angeles (90016) **(P-8547)**
New Generation Software Inc ....E....916 920-2200
3835 N Freeway Blvd # 200 Sacramento (95834) **(P-24203)**
New Generation Sourcing, Carlsbad *Also called Designer Drinks* **(P-2071)**
New Global Food ....F....562 404-9953
13577 Larwin Cir Santa Fe Springs (90670) **(P-2566)**
New Gold Manufacturing Inc ....D....818 847-1020
2150 N Lincoln St Burbank (91504) **(P-22555)**
New Gordon Industries LLC ....E....562 483-7378
13750 Rosecrans Ave Santa Fe Springs (90670) **(P-12850)**
New Green Day LLC ....E....323 566-7603
1710 E 111th St Los Angeles (90059) **(P-5094)**
New Greenscreen Incorporated ....E....951 685-9660
11445 Pacific Ave Fontana (92337) **(P-12313)**
New Greenscreen Incorporated ....E....800 767-9378
5500 Jurupa St Ontario (91761) **(P-4992)**
New Harbinger Publications Inc (PA) ....E....510 652-0215
5674 Shattuck Ave Oakland (94609) **(P-6128)**
New Haven Companies Inc ....D....213 749-8181
13571 Vaughn St Unit E San Fernando (91340) **(P-2946)**
New Hong Kong Noodle Co Inc ....E....650 588-6425
360 Swift Ave Ste 22 South San Francisco (94080) **(P-2375)**
New Horizon, South San Francisco *Also called Hsin Tung Yang Foods Company* **(P-468)**
New Horizon Foods Inc ....E....510 489-8600
33440 Western Ave Union City (94587) **(P-2567)**
New Iem LLC ....D....510 656-1600
48205 Warm Springs Blvd Fremont (94539) **(P-16604)**
New Image Foam Products LLC ....E....916 388-0741
6835 Power Inn Rd Sacramento (95828) **(P-9558)**
New Incorporation Now ....F....562 484-3020
12323 Imperial Hwy Norwalk (90650) **(P-5775)**
New Logic Research Inc ....D....510 655-7305
5040 Commercial Cir Ste A Concord (94520) **(P-14507)**
New Maverick Desk Inc ....C....310 217-1554
15100 S Figueroa St Gardena (90248) **(P-4811)**
New Method Fur Dressing Co ....E....650 583-9881
131 Beacon St South San Francisco (94080) **(P-23425)**
New Ngc Inc ....C....562 435-4465
1850 Pier B St Long Beach (90813) **(P-10880)**
New Origins Accessories Inc (PA) ....F....909 869-7559
3980 Valley Blvd Ste D Walnut (91789) **(P-22990)**
New Paradise, South El Monte *Also called CPC Group Inc* **(P-9731)**
New Printing, Van Nuys *Also called Digital Room Holdings Inc* **(P-7045)**
New Product Integration Solutn ....D....408 944-9178
685 Jarvis Dr Ste A Morgan Hill (95037) **(P-11103)**
New Quantum Living, Arcadia *Also called Quantum Corporation* **(P-15080)**
New Relic Inc (PA) ....C....650 777-7600
188 Spear St Ste 1200 San Francisco (94105) **(P-24204)**
New Rise Brand Holdings LLC ....E....323 233-9005
801 S Figueroa St # 1000 Los Angeles (90017) **(P-3016)**
New Source Technology LLC ....F....925 462-6888
6678 Owens Dr Ste 105 Pleasanton (94588) **(P-22287)**
New Star Lasers Inc ....E....916 677-1900
8331 Sierra College Blvd # 204 Roseville (95661) **(P-22288)**
New Technology Plastics Inc ....E....562 941-6034
7110 Fenwick Ln Westminster (92683) **(P-7584)**
New Times Media Group, San Luis Obispo *Also called Slo New Times Inc* **(P-5829)**
New Vision Display Inc (HQ) ....E....916 786-8111
1430 Blue Oaks Blvd # 100 Roseville (95747) **(P-19025)**
New Wave Industries Ltd (PA) ....F....800 882-8854
3315 Orange Grove Ave North Highlands (95660) **(P-15549)**
New Wave Research Incorporated (HQ) ....C....510 249-1550
48660 Kato Rd Fremont (94538) **(P-19365)**
New World Library, Novato *Also called Whatever Publishing Inc* **(P-6162)**
New World Machining Inc ....E....408 227-3810
2799 Aiello Dr San Jose (95111) **(P-16242)**
New World Manufacturing Inc ....F....707 894-5257
27627 Dutcher Creek Rd Cloverdale (95425) **(P-9342)**
New World Medical Incorporated ....F....909 466-4304
10763 Edison Ct Rancho Cucamonga (91730) **(P-21837)**
New York Frozen Foods Inc ....E....626 338-3000
5100 Rivergrade Rd Baldwin Park (91706) **(P-1248)**
New York Toy Exchange Inc ....F....626 327-4547
11955 Jack Benny Dr Ste 1 Rancho Cucamonga (91739) **(P-22699)**
New Zealand Pump Company, Alhambra *Also called N Z Pump Co Inc* **(P-14592)**
New-Indy Containerboard, Ontario *Also called New-Indy Ontario LLC* **(P-5137)**
New-Indy Containerboard, Oxnard *Also called New-Indy Oxnard LLC* **(P-5138)**
New-Indy Containerboard LLC (HQ) ....D....909 296-3400
3500 Porsche Way Ste 150 Ontario (91764) **(P-5136)**
New-Indy Ontario LLC ....C....909 390-1055
5100 Jurupa St Ontario (91761) **(P-5137)**
New-Indy Oxnard LLC ....C....805 986-3881
5936 Perkins Rd Oxnard (93033) **(P-5138)**
Newage Pavilions LLC ....F....818 701-9600
9360 Penfield Ave Chatsworth (91311) **(P-19366)**
Neways Inc ....E....949 264-1542
28202 Cabot Rd Ste 100 Laguna Niguel (92677) **(P-19026)**
Newbasis West LLC ....C....951 787-0600
2626 Kansas Ave Riverside (92507) **(P-10606)**
Newbold Cleaners ....F....916 481-1130
4211 Arden Way Ste A Sacramento (95864) **(P-15405)**
Newby Rubber Inc ....E....661 327-5137
320 Industrial St Bakersfield (93307) **(P-9343)**
Newco International Inc ....B....818 834-7100
13600 Vaughn St San Fernando (91340) **(P-4598)**
Newcomb Spring Corp ....E....714 995-5341
8380 Cerritos Ave Stanton (90680) **(P-13382)**
Newcomb Spring of California, Stanton *Also called Newcomb Spring Corp* **(P-13382)**
Newegg.com, City of Industry *Also called Magnell Associate Inc* **(P-14939)**
Newell Brands Inc ....F....760 246-2700
17182 Nevada St Victorville (92394) **(P-9922)**
Newera Software Inc ....F....408 520-7100
18625 Sutter Blvd Ste 950 Morgan Hill (95037) **(P-24205)**
Newfield Technology Corp (PA) ....E....909 931-4405
4230 E Airport Dr Ste 105 Ontario (91761) **(P-19491)**
Newhall Signal, Santa Clarita *Also called Signal* **(P-5826)**
Newhouse Upholstery ....E....626 444-1370
2309 Edwards Ave El Monte (91733) **(P-4866)**
Newhouse Upholstery Mfg, El Monte *Also called Newhouse Upholstery* **(P-4866)**
Newlight Technologies Inc ....E....714 556-4500
14382 Astronautics Ln Huntington Beach (92647) **(P-9923)**
Newline Rubber Company ....F....408 214-0359
13165 Monterey Hwy # 100 San Martin (95046) **(P-9344)**
Newlon Rouge LLC ....F....310 458-7737
1640 5th St Ste 218 Santa Monica (90401) **(P-5776)**
Newly Weds Foods Inc ....E....209 491-7777
437 S Mcclure Rd Modesto (95357) **(P-2568)**
Newman and Sons Inc (PA) ....E....805 522-1646
2655 1st St Ste 210 Simi Valley (93065) **(P-10607)**
Newman Bros California Inc (PA) ....E....951 782-0102
1901 Massachusetts Ave Riverside (92507) **(P-4094)**
Newman Flange & Fitting Co ....D....209 862-2977
1649 L St Newman (95360) **(P-12715)**

Employee Codes: A=Over 500 employees, B=251-500
C=101-250, D=51-100, E=20-50, F=10-19
2020 California
Manfacturers Register
© Mergent Inc. 1-800-342-5647
1183

Newmatic Engineering Inc (PA) ....F....415 824-2664
355 Goddard Ste 250 Irvine (92618) ***(P-20800)***
Newnex Technology Corp ....F....408 986-9988
3041 Olcott St Santa Clara (95054) ***(P-15295)***
Newpacket Wireless Corporation ....F....408 747-1003
1600 Wyatt Dr Ste 10 Santa Clara (95054) ***(P-15296)***
Newport Brass, Santa Ana *Also called Brasstech Inc* ***(P-11659)***
Newport Corporation (HQ) ....B....949 863-3144
1791 Deere Ave Irvine (92606) ***(P-20767)***
Newport Corporation ....A....408 980-4300
3635 Peterson Way Santa Clara (95054) ***(P-19367)***
Newport Energy LLC ....E....408 230-7545
19200 Von Karman Ave # 400 Irvine (92612) ***(P-132)***
Newport Fab LLC ....D....949 435-8000
4321 Jamboree Rd Newport Beach (92660) ***(P-18434)***
Newport Fish, South San Francisco *Also called Tardio Enterprises Inc* ***(P-2273)***
Newport Flavors & Fragrances ....E....714 771-2200
833 N Elm St Orange (92867) ***(P-2222)***
Newport Glass Works Ltd ....F....714 484-8100
10564 Fern Ave Stanton (90680) ***(P-21384)***
Newport Glassworks, Stanton *Also called Newport Optical Industries* ***(P-21385)***
Newport Industrial Glass Inc ....E....714 484-7500
8610 Central Ave Stanton (90680) ***(P-10381)***
Newport Laminates Inc ....E....714 545-8335
3121 W Central Ave Santa Ana (92704) ***(P-9924)***
Newport Medical Instrs Inc ....D....949 642-3910
1620 Sunflower Ave Costa Mesa (92626) ***(P-21838)***
Newport Mesa Usd Campus C ....F....714 424-8939
2985 Bear St Costa Mesa (92626) ***(P-6746)***
Newport Metal Finishing Inc ....D....714 556-8411
3230 S Standard Ave Santa Ana (92705) ***(P-13211)***
Newport Optical Industries (PA) ....E....714 484-8100
10564 Fern Ave Stanton (90680) ***(P-21385)***
Newport Plastic Inc ....E....714 549-1955
1525 E Edinger Ave Santa Ana (92705) ***(P-9925)***
Newport Plastics LLC (PA) ....E....800 854-8402
1525 E Edinger Ave Santa Ana (92705) ***(P-9926)***
Newport Thin Film Lab Inc ....F....909 591-0276
13824 Magnolia Ave Chino (91710) ***(P-9927)***
Newport Vessels, Monrovia *Also called Torero Specialty Products LLC* ***(P-22909)***
News Media Corporation ....D....831 761-7300
21 Brennan St Ste 18 Watsonville (95076) ***(P-5777)***
News Media Inc ....E....805 237-6060
502 First St Paso Robles (93446) ***(P-5778)***
News Publishers' Press, Glendale *Also called P E N Inc* ***(P-7164)***
News Review, The, Ridgecrest *Also called Sierra View Inc* ***(P-5825)***
Newtex Industries Inc ....D....323 277-0900
9654 Hermosa Ave Rancho Cucamonga (91730) ***(P-23426)***
Newton Heat Treating Company ....D....626 964-6528
19235 E Walnut Dr N City of Industry (91748) ***(P-11464)***
Newton Vineyard LLC (HQ) ....E....707 963-9000
2555 Madrona Ave Saint Helena (94574) ***(P-1839)***
Newvac LLC (HQ) ....C....310 525-1205
9330 De Soto Ave Chatsworth (91311) ***(P-16918)***
Newvac LLC ....C....310 990-0401
9330 Desoto Ave Chatsworth (91311) ***(P-17789)***
Newvac LLC ....F....310 990-0401
9330 De Soto Ave Chatsworth (91311) ***(P-17790)***
Newvac LLC ....D....310 516-1692
9330 Desoto Ave Chatsworth (91311) ***(P-17791)***
Newvac LLC ....E....310 525-1205
9330 De Soto Ave Chatsworth (91311) ***(P-19027)***
Newvac Division, Chatsworth *Also called Newvac LLC* ***(P-17789)***
Nexcoil Steel LLC ....F....209 900-1919
1265 Shaw Rd Stockton (95215) ***(P-11120)***
Nexfon Corporation ....F....925 200-2233
7172 Regional St Dublin (94568) ***(P-10322)***
Nexgen Pharma Inc (PA) ....C....949 863-0340
46 Corporate Park Ste 100 Irvine (92606) ***(P-8033)***
Nexgen Pharma Inc ....E....949 260-3702
17802 Gillette Ave Irvine (92614) ***(P-8034)***
Nexgen Pharma Inc ....F....949 863-0340
17802 Gillette Ave Irvine (92614) ***(P-8035)***
Nexgen Power Systems Inc ....E....408 230-7698
2010 El Camino Real Santa Clara (95050) ***(P-18435)***
Nexlogic Technologies Inc ....D....408 436-8150
2085 Zanker Rd San Jose (95131) ***(P-17939)***
Nexon America, El Segundo *Also called M Nexon Inc* ***(P-24117)***
Nexrange Industries, City of Industry *Also called Duro Corporation* ***(P-16810)***
Nexsan Technologies Inc (HQ) ....E....408 724-9809
325 E Hillcrest Dr # 150 Thousand Oaks (91360) ***(P-15062)***
Nexsan Technologies Inc ....E....760 745-3550
302 Enterprise St Escondido (92029) ***(P-15063)***
Nexstar Pharmaceutical, San Dimas *Also called Gilead Sciences Inc* ***(P-7918)***
Nexsteppe Seeds Inc ....E....650 887-5700
400 E Jamie Ct Ste 202 South San Francisco (94080) ***(P-8756)***
Nexsun Corp ....E....213 382-2220
3250 Wilshire Blvd # 1410 Los Angeles (90010) ***(P-8757)***
Nexsys Electronics Inc (PA) ....F....415 541-9980
70 Zoe St Ste 100 San Francisco (94107) ***(P-15297)***
Next Day Flyers, Van Nuys *Also called Postcard Press Inc* ***(P-7178)***
Next Day Frame Inc ....D....310 886-0851
11560 Wright Rd Lynwood (90262) ***(P-4767)***
Next Day Printed Tees ....F....619 420-8618
3523 Main St Ste 601 Chula Vista (91911) ***(P-3803)***
Next ERA, Vernon *Also called Peter K Inc* ***(P-3386)***
Next Generation, Commerce *Also called J & F Design Inc* ***(P-3340)***
Next Intent Inc ....E....805 781-6755
865 Via Esteban San Luis Obispo (93401) ***(P-16243)***
Next Level Elevator Inc ....F....888 959-6010
2199 N Batavia St Ste S Orange (92865) ***(P-13805)***
Next Level Warehouse Solutions ....F....916 922-7225
555 Display Way Sacramento (95838) ***(P-13829)***
Next Pharmaceuticals Inc ....E....831 621-8712
360 Espinosa Rd Salinas (93907) ***(P-8036)***
Next Phase Solar, Berkeley *Also called Sunsystem Technology LLC* ***(P-18594)***
Next System Inc ....E....661 257-1600
20605 Soledad Canyon Rd # 222 Canyon Country (91351) ***(P-2876)***
Next Up, Commerce *Also called Connected Apparel Company LLC* ***(P-3308)***
Nextag Inc (PA) ....D....650 645-4700
555 Twin Dolphin Dr # 370 Redwood City (94065) ***(P-6296)***
Nextclientcom Inc ....F....661 222-7755
25012 Avenue Kearny Valencia (91355) ***(P-6297)***
Nextec Microwave & Rf Inc ....F....408 727-1189
3010 Scott Blvd Santa Clara (95054) ***(P-17603)***
Nextest Systems Corporation ....C....408 960-2400
875 Embedded Way San Jose (95138) ***(P-21090)***
Nextest Systems Teradyne Co, San Jose *Also called Nextest Systems Corporation* ***(P-21090)***
Nextev, San Jose *Also called Nio Usa Inc* ***(P-19492)***
NEXTEX INTERNATIONAL, South Gate *Also called Nextrade Inc* ***(P-2947)***
Nextgen Healthcare Inc (PA) ....C....949 255-2600
18111 Von Karman Ave # 8 Irvine (92612) ***(P-24206)***
Nextinput Inc (PA) ....F....408 770-9293
980 Linda Vista Ave Mountain View (94043) ***(P-16735)***
Nextivity Inc (PA) ....D....858 485-9442
16550 W Bernardo Dr # 550 San Diego (92127) ***(P-17604)***
Nextpharma Tech USA Inc ....E....858 450-3123
5340 Eastgate Mall San Diego (92121) ***(P-8037)***
Nextrade Inc (PA) ....E....562 944-9950
12411 Industrial Ave South Gate (90280) ***(P-2947)***
Nextsport Inc ....F....510 601-8802
106 Linden St Ste 201 Oakland (94607) ***(P-22700)***
Nexus Automation, Livermore *Also called Eklavya LLC* ***(P-14812)***
Nexus California Inc ....F....909 937-1000
4551 Brickell Privado St Ontario (91761) ***(P-9415)***
Nexus Dx Inc ....E....858 410-4600
6759 Mesa Ridge Rd San Diego (92121) ***(P-21839)***
Nexxen Apparel Inc (PA) ....F....323 267-9900
1555 Los Palos St Los Angeles (90023) ***(P-3376)***
Nexyn Corporation ....F....408 962-0895
1287 Forgewood Ave Sunnyvale (94089) ***(P-19028)***
Neyenesch Printers Inc ....D....619 297-2281
2750 Kettner Blvd San Diego (92101) ***(P-6747)***
NFC Innovation Center, San Jose *Also called Thin Film Electronics Inc* ***(P-19117)***
Nfi Industries ....F....951 681-6455
11888 Mission Blvd Jurupa Valley (91752) ***(P-23427)***
Nflash Inc ....F....949 678-9411
23142 Alcalde Dr Ste A Laguna Hills (92653) ***(P-15064)***
Ng John ....F....415 929-7188
780 Van Ness Ave San Francisco (94102) ***(P-6748)***
Ngcodec Inc ....E....408 766-4382
440 N Wolfe Rd Ste 2187 Sunnyvale (94085) ***(P-18436)***
Ngd Systems Inc ....E....949 870-9148
355 Goddard Ste 200 Irvine (92618) ***(P-15065)***
NGK Spark Plugs (usa) Inc ....E....949 580-2639
68 Fairbanks Irvine (92618) ***(P-19197)***
Ngm Biopharmaceuticals Inc ....C....650 243-5555
333 Oyster Point Blvd South San Francisco (94080) ***(P-8038)***
NGMBIO, South San Francisco *Also called Ngm Biopharmaceuticals Inc* ***(P-8038)***
Ngmoco Inc ....F....415 375-3170
185 Berry St Ste 2400 San Francisco (94107) ***(P-24207)***
Nguoi Viet Newspaper, Westminster *Also called Nguoi Vietnamese People Inc* ***(P-5779)***
Nguoi Vietnamese People Inc (PA) ....E....714 892-9414
14771 Moran St Westminster (92683) ***(P-5779)***
Nhk Laboratories (PA) ....D....562 903-5835
12230 Florence Ave Santa Fe Springs (90670) ***(P-8039)***
Nhs Inc ....D....831 459-7800
104 Bronson St Ste 9 Santa Cruz (95062) ***(P-22859)***
Ni Industries Inc ....E....309 283-3355
7300 E Slauson Ave Commerce (90040) ***(P-12596)***
Ni Microwave Components, Santa Clara *Also called National Instruments Corp* ***(P-21086)***
Nia Energy LLC ....F....818 422-8000
23679 Calabasas Rd Calabasas (91302) ***(P-16867)***
Niagara Bottling LLC ....F....909 230-5000
1401 Alder Ave Rialto (92376) ***(P-2096)***
Niagara Bottling LLC ....F....209 983-8436
811 Zephyr St Stockton (95206) ***(P-2097)***
Niagara Bottling LLC (PA) ....F....909 230-5000
1440 Bridgegate Dr Diamond Bar (91765) ***(P-2098)***
Niagara Drinking Water, Diamond Bar *Also called Niagara Bottling LLC* ***(P-2098)***
Nibco Inc ....C....951 737-5599
1375 Sampson Ave Corona (92879) ***(P-13535)***
Nic Protection Inc ....F....818 249-2539
7135 Foothill Blvd Tujunga (91042) ***(P-16981)***
Nice Rack Tower Accessories ....F....408 846-1919
8850 Muraoka Dr Gilroy (95020) ***(P-19728)***
Nicholas Michael Designs Inc ....C....714 562-8101
2330 Raymer Ave Fullerton (92833) ***(P-4768)***
Nichols Farms, Hanford *Also called Nichols Pistachio* ***(P-1435)***
Nichols Lumber, Baldwin Park *Also called Survey Stake and Marker Inc* ***(P-4537)***
Nichols Manufacturing Inc ....F....408 945-0911
913 Hanson Ct Milpitas (95035) ***(P-16244)***
Nichols Pistachio ....C....559 584-6811
13762 1st Ave Hanford (93230) ***(P-1435)***
Nichols Winery & Cellars, Playa Del Rey *Also called Keith Nichols* ***(P-1780)***
Nicholson Ranch LLC ....E....707 938-8822
4200 Napa Rd Sonoma (95476) ***(P-1840)***

Nick Sciabica & Sons A Corp.......E.......209 577-5067
2150 Yosemite Blvd Modesto (95354) *(P-1478)*
Nick's Cabinet Doors, Azusa *Also called Nicks Doors Inc (P-4095)*
Nicks Doors Inc.......F.......626 812-6491
1052 W Kirkwall Rd Azusa (91702) *(P-4095)*
Nicksons Machine Shop Inc.......E.......805 925-2525
914 W Betteravia Rd Santa Maria (93455) *(P-16245)*
Nico Nat Mfg Corp.......E.......323 721-1900
2624 Yates Ave Commerce (90040) *(P-4922)*
Nicola, Commerce *Also called Protrend Ltd (P-3252)*
Nicole Fullerton.......F.......661 257-0406
27821 Pine Crest Pl Castaic (91384) *(P-3572)*
Niconat Manufacturing, Commerce *Also called Nico Nat Mfg Corp (P-4922)*
Nidec Motor Corporation.......B.......916 463-9200
11380 White Rock Rd Rancho Cordova (95742) *(P-13806)*
Niebam-Cppola Estate Winery LP.......E.......415 291-1700
916 Kearny St San Francisco (94133) *(P-1841)*
Niebam-Cppola Estate Winery LP (PA).......C.......707 968-1100
1991 St Helena Hwy Rutherford (94573) *(P-1842)*
Nieco Corporation.......D.......707 838-3226
7950 Cameron Dr Windsor (95492) *(P-15550)*
Niedwick Corporation.......E.......714 771-9999
967 N Eckhoff St Orange (92867) *(P-16246)*
Niedwick Machine Co, Orange *Also called Niedwick Corporation (P-16246)*
Night Fashion Inc.......E.......213 747-8740
628 W 30th St Ofc C Los Angeles (90007) *(P-3245)*
Night Optics Usa Inc.......F.......714 899-4475
605 Oro Dam Blvd E Oroville (95965) *(P-17750)*
Nightingale Vantagemed Corp (HQ).......D.......916 638-4744
10670 White Rock Rd Rancho Cordova (95670) *(P-24208)*
Nightscaping Outdoor Lighting, Redlands *Also called Loran Inc (P-16560)*
Nihon Kohden Orangemed Inc.......F.......949 502-6448
15375 Barranca Pkwy C109 Irvine (92618) *(P-22289)*
Nike Inc.......E.......310 736-3800
3505 Hayden Ave Culver City (90232) *(P-9176)*
Nike Inc.......F.......949 768-4000
20001 Ellipse Foothill Ranch (92610) *(P-3470)*
Nike Inc.......E.......310 670-6770
222 E Redondo Beach Blvd C Gardena (90248) *(P-9177)*
Nikkel Iron Works Corporation.......F.......661 746-4904
17045 S Central Vly Hwy Shafter (93263) *(P-13652)*
Nikko Enterprise Corporation.......E.......562 941-6080
13168 Sandoval St Santa Fe Springs (90670) *(P-2266)*
Niknejad Inc.......E.......310 478-8363
6855 Hayvenhurst Ave Van Nuys (91406) *(P-6749)*
Nikon Research Corp America.......E.......800 446-4566
1399 Shoreway Rd Belmont (94002) *(P-21091)*
NILGIRI PRESS, Tomales *Also called Blue Mtn Ctr of Meditation Inc (P-6079)*
Nils Inc (PA).......F.......714 755-1600
3151 Airway Ave Ste V Costa Mesa (92626) *(P-3377)*
Nils Skiwear, Costa Mesa *Also called Nils Inc (P-3377)*
Nilson Report, The, Carpinteria *Also called H S N Consultants Inc (P-5947)*
Nimble Storage Inc (HQ).......C.......408 432-9600
211 River Oaks Pkwy San Jose (95134) *(P-15066)*
Nimbus Data Inc.......E.......650 276-4500
5151 California Ave # 100 Irvine (92617) *(P-15067)*
Nimbus Water Systems.......F.......951 984-2800
42445 Avenida Alvarado Temecula (92590) *(P-15551)*
Nina Mia Inc.......D.......714 773-5588
826 Enterprise Way Fullerton (92831) *(P-2569)*
Nina Religion, Huntington Park *Also called Saydel Inc (P-8577)*
Ninas Mexican Foods Inc.......E.......909 468-5888
20631 Valley Blvd Ste A Walnut (91789) *(P-2570)*
Niner Wine Estates LLC.......F.......805 239-2233
2400 W Highway 46 Paso Robles (93446) *(P-1843)*
Ninja Jump Inc.......D.......323 255-5418
3221 N San Fernando Rd Los Angeles (90065) *(P-22701)*
Ninth Avenue Foods, City of Industry *Also called Heritage Distributing Company (P-595)*
Nio Usa Inc.......D.......408 518-7000
3200 N 1st St San Jose (95134) *(P-19492)*
Nippon Carbide Inds USA Inc.......F.......562 777-1810
13856 Bettencourt St Cerritos (90703) *(P-7512)*
Nippon Industries Inc.......E.......707 427-3127
2430 S Watney Way Fairfield (94533) *(P-969)*
Nippon Trends Food Service Inc.......D.......408 214-0511
631 Giguere Ct Ste A1 San Jose (95133) *(P-2571)*
Niron Inc.......E.......909 598-1526
20541 Earlgate St Walnut (91789) *(P-14085)*
Nis America Inc.......E.......714 540-1199
4 Hutton Cntre Dr Ste 650 Santa Ana (92707) *(P-24209)*
Nishiba Industries Corporation.......A.......619 661-8866
2360 Marconi Ct San Diego (92154) *(P-9928)*
Nissi Trim, Los Angeles *Also called Ckcc Inc (P-3780)*
Nissin Foods USA Company Inc (HQ).......C.......310 327-8478
2001 W Rosecrans Ave Gardena (90249) *(P-2376)*
Niterider Technical Lighting &.......E.......858 268-9316
12255 Crosthwaite Cir A Poway (92064) *(P-17149)*
Nitinol Development Corp.......A.......510 683-2000
47533 Westinghouse Dr Fremont (94539) *(P-22373)*
Nitinol Devices & Components, Fremont *Also called Nitinol Development Corp (P-22373)*
Nitro 2 Go Inc.......E.......909 864-4886
1420 Richardson St San Bernardino (92408) *(P-7678)*
Nitto Americas Inc (HQ).......C.......510 445-5400
48500 Fremont Blvd Fremont (94538) *(P-5370)*
Nittobo America Inc.......D.......951 677-5629
25549 Adams Ave Murrieta (92562) *(P-8318)*
Nivagen Pharmaceuticals Inc.......E.......916 364-1662
3050 Fite Cir Ste 100 Sacramento (95827) *(P-8040)*

Nix Mouthwash.......E.......888 909-9088
19925 Stevens Creek Blvd Cupertino (95014) *(P-8548)*
Nixsys Inc.......F.......714 435-9610
34 Mauchly Ste B Irvine (92618) *(P-14956)*
Nkok Inc.......F.......626 330-1988
5354 Irwindale Ave Ste A Irwindale (91706) *(P-22702)*
Nl Industries Inc.......E.......707 552-4850
403 Ryder St Vallejo (94590) *(P-11193)*
NL&a Collections Inc.......E.......323 277-6266
6323 Maywood Ave Huntington Park (90255) *(P-16982)*
Nlp Furniture Industries Inc.......C.......619 661-5170
1425 Corporate Center Dr # 200 San Diego (92154) *(P-5074)*
Nls, San Diego *Also called Non-Linear Systems (P-20909)*
NM Laser Products Inc.......F.......408 227-8299
337 Piercy Rd San Jose (95138) *(P-19368)*
NM Machining Inc.......E.......408 972-8978
175 Lewis Rd Ste 25 San Jose (95111) *(P-16247)*
No Boundaries Inc.......E.......619 266-2349
789 Gateway Center Way San Diego (92102) *(P-6750)*
No Lift Nails Inc.......F.......714 897-0070
3211 S Shannon St Santa Ana (92704) *(P-7585)*
No Second Thoughts Inc.......D.......619 428-5992
1333 30th St Ste D San Diego (92154) *(P-2972)*
No Starch Press Inc.......F.......415 863-9900
245 8th St San Francisco (94103) *(P-6298)*
No Static Pro Audio Inc.......F.......818 729-8554
2070 Floyd St Burbank (91504) *(P-17266)*
Noah's, Los Gatos *Also called Einstein Noah Rest Group Inc (P-548)*
Noah's New York Bagels, Westminster *Also called Einstein Noah Rest Group Inc (P-547)*
Noahs Ark International Inc.......F.......714 521-1235
2319 E 8th St Los Angeles (90021) *(P-3184)*
Noahs Bottled Water.......E.......209 526-2945
416 Hosmer Ave Modesto (95351) *(P-2099)*
Nobbe Orthopedics Inc.......F.......805 687-7508
3010 State St Santa Barbara (93105) *(P-22054)*
Nobel Biocare Usa LLC.......B.......714 282-4800
22715 Savi Ranch Pkwy Yorba Linda (92887) *(P-22175)*
Noble Concrete Plants, Tracy *Also called Dave Humphrey Enterprises Inc (P-13726)*
Noble Energy, Seal Beach *Also called Samedan Oil Corporation (P-65)*
Noble Metals, San Diego *Also called Matthey Johnson Inc (P-11204)*
Noble Methane Inc.......F.......530 668-7961
104 Matmor Rd Woodland (95776) *(P-236)*
Nod, Calabasas *Also called Nova-One Diagnostics LLC (P-8242)*
Noel Burt.......E.......925 439-7030
880 Howe Rd Ste F Martinez (94553) *(P-15614)*
Noel Technologies, Campbell *Also called Semi Automation & Tech Inc (P-18530)*
Noels Lighting Inc.......E.......562 908-6181
9335 Stephens St Unit I Pico Rivera (90660) *(P-17060)*
Nok Nok Labs Inc.......F.......650 433-1300
2890 Zanker Rd Ste 203 San Jose (95134) *(P-24210)*
Nokia of America Corporation.......F.......408 363-5906
5390 Hellyer Ave San Jose (95138) *(P-17390)*
Nokia Slutions Networks US LLC.......F.......650 623-2767
701 E Middlefield Rd Mountain View (94043) *(P-17391)*
Noll Inc.......F.......805 543-3602
390 Buckley Rd Frnt San Luis Obispo (93401) *(P-13987)*
Noll/Norwesco LLC.......C.......209 234-1600
1320 Performance Dr Stockton (95206) *(P-12314)*
Nolo.......C.......510 549-1976
950 Parker St Berkeley (94710) *(P-6129)*
Nology Engineering Inc.......F.......760 591-0888
1333 Keystone Way Vista (92081) *(P-19729)*
Noma Bearing Corporation.......F.......310 329-1800
1555 W Rosecrans Ave Gardena (90249) *(P-14612)*
Nominum Inc.......E.......650 381-6000
3355 Scott Blvd Fl 3 Santa Clara (95054) *(P-24211)*
Non-Linear Systems.......F.......619 521-2161
4561 Mission Gorge Pl F San Diego (92120) *(P-20909)*
Nonstop Printing Inc.......F.......323 464-1640
6226 Santa Monica Blvd Los Angeles (90038) *(P-6751)*
Noodle Theory.......F.......510 595-6988
6099 Claremont Ave Oakland (94618) *(P-2377)*
Noodoe Inc.......F.......909 468-1118
829 S Lemon Ave Ste A-11c Walnut (91789) *(P-16666)*
Nooshin Inc.......F.......310 559-5766
555 Chalette Dr Beverly Hills (90210) *(P-3378)*
Nooshin Blanque, Beverly Hills *Also called Nooshin Inc (P-3378)*
Nor Cal Food Solutions LLC.......F.......530 823-8527
2043 Airpark Ct Auburn (95602) *(P-891)*
Nor Cal Truck Sales & Mfg.......F.......925 787-9735
200 Industrial Way Benicia (94510) *(P-13885)*
Nor Car Truck Sales, Benicia *Also called Nor Cal Truck Sales & Mfg (P-13885)*
Nor-Cal Beverage Co Inc.......E.......916 372-1700
1375 Terminal St West Sacramento (95691) *(P-2100)*
Nor-Cal Metal Fabricators.......D.......510 350-0121
1121 3rd St Oakland (94607) *(P-12315)*
Nor-Cal Products Inc (HQ).......C.......530 842-4457
1967 S Oregon St Yreka (96097) *(P-13361)*
Nor-Cal Smokeshop.......F.......831 645-9021
765 Lighthouse Ave Monterey (93940) *(P-22860)*
Nor-Cal Vans Inc.......F.......530 892-0150
1300 Nord Ave Chico (95926) *(P-19547)*
Norac Inc (PA).......B.......626 334-2907
405 S Motor Ave Azusa (91702) *(P-8758)*
Norac Pharma, Azusa *Also called S&B Pharma Inc (P-7690)*
Norberg Crushing Inc.......F.......619 390-4200
592 Tyrone St El Cajon (92020) *(P-316)*
Norberts Athletic Products.......F.......310 830-6672
354 W Gardena Blvd Gardena (90248) *(P-22861)*

Employee Codes: A=Over 500 employees, B=251-500
C=101-250, D=51-100, E=20-50, F=10-19
2020 California
Manfacturers Register
© Mergent Inc. 1-800-342-5647
1185

Norcal Printing Inc (PA)....F....415 282-8856
1555 Yosemite Ave Ste 28 San Francisco (94124) ***(P-6752)***
Norcal Recycled Rock Aggregate (PA)....F....707 459-9636
291a Shell Ln Willits (95490) ***(P-10811)***
Norcal Respiratory Inc....E....530 246-1200
3075 Crossroads Dr Ste A Redding (96003) ***(P-22290)***
Norcal Waste Equipment Co....E....510 568-8336
299 Park St San Leandro (94577) ***(P-19548)***
Norchem Corporation (PA)....D....323 221-0221
5649 Alhambra Ave Los Angeles (90032) ***(P-14508)***
Norco Injection Molding Inc....D....909 393-4000
14325 Monte Vista Ave Chino (91710) ***(P-9929)***
Norco Plastics, Chino *Also called Norco Injection Molding Inc* ***(P-9929)***
Norco Plastics Inc....D....909 393-4000
14325 Monte Vista Ave Chino (91710) ***(P-9930)***
Norco Printing Inc....F....510 569-2200
440 Hester St San Leandro (94577) ***(P-7359)***
Norden Millimeter Inc....E....530 642-9123
5441 Merchant Cir Ste C Placerville (95667) ***(P-17605)***
Nordic Naturals Inc (PA)....C....800 662-2544
111 Jennings Way Watsonville (95076) ***(P-1462)***
Nordic Saw & Tool Mfrs....E....209 634-9015
2114 Divanian Dr Turlock (95382) ***(P-11554)***
Nordson Asymtek, Carlsbad *Also called Nordson California Inc* ***(P-19228)***
Nordson Asymtek Inc....F....760 727-2880
2475 Ash St Vista (92081) ***(P-20910)***
Nordson Asymtek Inc (HQ)....C....760 431-1919
2747 Loker Ave W Carlsbad (92010) ***(P-20911)***
Nordson California Inc....D....760 918-8490
2747 Loker Ave W Carlsbad (92010) ***(P-19228)***
Nordson Dage Inc....E....440 985-4496
2747 Loker Ave W Carlsbad (92010) ***(P-22217)***
Nordson Med Design & Dev Inc....F....603 707-8753
610 Palomar Ave Sunnyvale (94085) ***(P-21840)***
Nordson Medical (ca) LLC....D....657 215-4200
7612 Woodwind Dr Huntington Beach (92647) ***(P-21841)***
Nordson Yestech Inc....E....949 361-2714
2747 Loker Ave W Carlsbad (92010) ***(P-21386)***
Norell Prsthtics Orthotics Inc (PA)....F....510 770-9010
5466 Complex St Ste 207 San Diego (92123) ***(P-22055)***
Norm Harboldt....E....714 596-4242
17592 Gothard St Huntington Beach (92647) ***(P-13212)***
Norm Tessier Cabinets Inc....E....909 987-8955
11989 6th St Rancho Cucamonga (91730) ***(P-4228)***
Normal Centrix Inc....F....310 715-9977
14101 Valleyheart Dr # 104 Sherman Oaks (91423) ***(P-23428)***
Norman & Globus Inc....F....510 222-2638
4128 Lakeside Dr Richmond (94806) ***(P-6130)***
Norman International, Vernon *Also called Norman Paper and Foam Co Inc* ***(P-5332)***
Norman Paper and Foam Co Inc....E....323 582-7132
4501 S Santa Fe Ave Vernon (90058) ***(P-5332)***
Norman Wireline Service Inc....F....661 399-5697
1301 James Rd Bakersfield (93308) ***(P-237)***
Normandie Country Bakery Inc (PA)....E....323 939-5528
3022 S Cochran Ave Los Angeles (90016) ***(P-1249)***
Normandy Refinishers Inc....E....626 792-9202
355 S Rosemead Blvd Pasadena (91107) ***(P-13062)***
Normel Inc....F....818 504-4041
12841 Blmfeld St Unit 104 Studio City (91604) ***(P-7149)***
Norotos Inc....C....714 662-3113
201 E Alton Ave Santa Ana (92707) ***(P-16248)***
Norpak, Hayward *Also called Norton Packaging Inc* ***(P-9931)***
Norquist Salvage Corp Inc....E....916 454-0435
5005 Stockton Blvd Ste B Sacramento (95820) ***(P-3109)***
Norquist Salvage Corp Inc....E....916 922-9942
410 El Camino Ave Sacramento (95815) ***(P-3110)***
Norsal Printing Inc....F....818 886-4164
20255 Prairie St Chatsworth (91311) ***(P-6753)***
Norsco Inc....F....209 845-2327
1816 Ackley Cir Oakdale (95361) ***(P-12642)***
Norstar Office Products Inc (PA)....E....323 262-1919
5353 Jillson St Commerce (90040) ***(P-4812)***
Nortek Security & Control LLC....F....760 438-7000
12471 Riverside Dr Eastvale (91752) ***(P-19369)***
North America Pwr & Infra....E....562 403-4337
19112 Gridley Rd 2001 Cerritos (90703) ***(P-10426)***
North American Composites, Stockton *Also called Interplastic Corporation* ***(P-7571)***
North American Composites Co....E....909 605-8977
4990 Vanderbilt St Ontario (91761) ***(P-7586)***
North American Fire Hose Corp....D....805 922-7076
910 Noble Way Santa Maria (93454) ***(P-9201)***
North American Foam & Packg, Fullerton *Also called Gold Venture Inc* ***(P-9547)***
North American Pet Products, Corona *Also called Pet Partners Inc* ***(P-23446)***
North American Petroleum....E....562 598-6671
11072 Via El Mercado Los Alamitos (90720) ***(P-9010)***
North American Textile Co LLC (PA)....E....818 409-0019
346 W Cerritos Ave Glendale (91204) ***(P-3804)***
North Amrcn Specialty Pdts LLC....F....209 365-7500
300 S Beckman Rd Lodi (95240) ***(P-7587)***
North Area News (PA)....F....916 486-1248
2612 El Camino Ave Sacramento (95821) ***(P-5780)***
North Atlantic Books, Berkeley *Also called Society For The Study Ntiv Art* ***(P-6147)***
North Bay Industries, Rohnert Park *Also called North Bay Rhblitation Svcs Inc* ***(P-3851)***
North Bay Industries, Monterey *Also called North Bay Rhblitation Svcs Inc* ***(P-3185)***
North Bay Plywood Inc....E....707 224-7849
510 Northbay Dr NAPA (94559) ***(P-4096)***
North Bay Rhblitation Svcs Inc (PA)....C....707 585-1991
649 Martin Ave Rohnert Park (94928) ***(P-3851)***
North Bay Rhblitation Svcs Inc....E....831 372-4094
875 Airport Rd Monterey (93940) ***(P-3185)***
North Cal Wood Products Inc....E....707 462-0686
700 Kunzler Ranch Rd Ukiah (95482) ***(P-3939)***
North Coast Brewing Co Inc (PA)....D....707 964-2739
455 N Main St Fort Bragg (95437) ***(P-1550)***
North Coast Industries, Sausalito *Also called Tony Marterie & Associates* ***(P-3256)***
North Coast Journal Inc....F....707 442-1400
310 F St Eureka (95501) ***(P-5781)***
North County Polishing....E....760 480-0847
220 S Hale Ave Ste A Escondido (92029) ***(P-13063)***
North County Sand and Grav Inc....F....951 928-2881
26227 Sherman Rd Sun City (92585) ***(P-354)***
North County Times (HQ)....C....800 533-8830
350 Camino De La Reina San Diego (92108) ***(P-5782)***
North County Times....E....951 676-4315
28441 Rancho California R Temecula (92590) ***(P-5783)***
North Face, The, Alameda *Also called Vf Outdoor LLC* ***(P-3128)***
North Face, The, San Francisco *Also called Vf Outdoor LLC* ***(P-22918)***
North Hollywood Uniform Group, North Hollywood *Also called North Hollywood Uniform Inc* ***(P-3270)***
North Hollywood Uniform Inc....F....818 503-5931
7328 Laurel Canyon Blvd North Hollywood (91605) ***(P-3270)***
North Pacific International....F....909 628-2224
5944 Sycamore Ct Chino (91710) ***(P-13453)***
North Sails Group LLC....D....619 226-1415
4630 Santa Fe St San Diego (92109) ***(P-3694)***
North Sails One Design, San Diego *Also called North Sails Group LLC* ***(P-3694)***
North State Rendering Co Inc....E....530 343-6076
15 Shippee Rd Oroville (95965) ***(P-1463)***
North Valley Candle Molds....E....530 247-0447
6928 Danyeur Rd Redding (96001) ***(P-23429)***
North Valley Newspapers Inc....F....530 365-2797
2676 Gateway Dr Anderson (96007) ***(P-5784)***
North Valley Rain Gutters....F....530 894-3347
27 Freight Ln Ste C Chico (95973) ***(P-12316)***
Northbay Stone Wrks Cntertops....F....415 898-0200
849 Sweetser Ave Novato (94945) ***(P-4923)***
Northern Aggregates Inc....E....707 459-3929
500 Cropley Ln Willits (95490) ***(P-355)***
Northern Cal Pet Imaging Ctr....F....916 737-3211
3195 Folsom Blvd Ste 110 Sacramento (95816) ***(P-22218)***
Northern California Labels Inc....F....562 802-8528
12809 Marquardt Ave Santa Fe Springs (90670) ***(P-7150)***
Northern California Stair....F....408 847-0106
7150 Alexander St Gilroy (95020) ***(P-4097)***
Northern Quinoa Prod Corp....E....806 535-8118
200 Kansas St Ste 215 San Francisco (94103) ***(P-1030)***
Northland Process Piping Inc....D....559 925-9724
400 E St Lemoore (93245) ***(P-11058)***
Northrdge Tr-Mdlity Imging Inc....F....818 709-2468
9457 De Soto Ave Chatsworth (91311) ***(P-20768)***
Northrop Grumman Corporation....A....626 812-2842
14099 Champlain Ct Fontana (92336) ***(P-20640)***
Northrop Grumman Corporation....A....818 715-3264
9736 Trigger Pl Chatsworth (91311) ***(P-20641)***
Northrop Grumman Corporation....C....310 332-1000
1 Hornet Way El Segundo (90245) ***(P-20642)***
Northrop Grumman Corporation....A....858 967-1221
18701 Caminito Pasadero San Diego (92128) ***(P-20643)***
Northrop Grumman Corporation....A....310 332-0412
28063 Liana Ln Valencia (91354) ***(P-20644)***
Northrop Grumman Corporation....A....310 332-6653
17311 Santa Barbara St Fountain Valley (92708) ***(P-20645)***
Northrop Grumman Corporation....A....310 764-3000
18701 Wilmington Ave Carson (90746) ***(P-20646)***
Northrop Grumman Corporation....A....858 618-7617
10806 Willow Ct San Diego (92127) ***(P-20647)***
Northrop Grumman Corporation....A....858 514-9259
4010 Sorrento Valley Blvd San Diego (92121) ***(P-20648)***
Northrop Grumman Corporation....E....310 812-4321
4020 Redondo Beach Ave Redondo Beach (90278) ***(P-20649)***
Northrop Grumman Corporation....F....818 715-2383
21050 Burbank Blvd Woodland Hills (91367) ***(P-20650)***
Northrop Grumman Innovation....B....858 621-5700
9617 Distribution Ave San Diego (92121) ***(P-20466)***
Northrop Grumman Innovation....B....818 887-8100
9401 Corvin Ave Woodland Hills (91367) ***(P-20651)***
Northrop Grumman Innovation....D....951 520-7300
250 Klug Cir Corona (92880) ***(P-20467)***
Northrop Grumman Innovation....D....805 961-8600
6750 Navigator Way # 200 Goleta (93117) ***(P-20652)***
Northrop Grumman Intl Trdg Inc....A....818 715-3607
21240 Burbank Blvd Woodland Hills (91367) ***(P-20653)***
Northrop Grumman Mar Systems, Sunnyvale *Also called Northrop Grumman Systems Corp* ***(P-19920)***
Northrop Grumman Space, San Diego *Also called Northrop Grumman Systems Corp* ***(P-20667)***
Northrop Grumman Systems Corp....B....408 735-2241
401 E Hendy Ave Sunnyvale (94086) ***(P-19917)***
Northrop Grumman Systems Corp....C....310 812-5149
1 Space Park Blvd Redondo Beach (90278) ***(P-17606)***
Northrop Grumman Systems Corp....A....818 715-4040
21240 Burbank Blvd Ms29 Woodland Hills (91367) ***(P-20654)***
Northrop Grumman Systems Corp....B....310 632-1846
1 Hornet Way Dept Mt00w5 El Segundo (90245) ***(P-20655)***
Northrop Grumman Systems Corp....B....661 272-7000
3520 E Avenue M Palmdale (93550) ***(P-19918)***

Northrop Grumman Systems Corp .... A....805 278-2074
2700 Camino Del Sol Oxnard (93030) (P-20656)
Northrop Grumman Systems Corp .... F....858 514-9020
9112 Spectrum Center Blvd San Diego (92123) (P-20657)
Northrop Grumman Systems Corp .... E....818 715-2597
21200 Burbank Blvd Woodland Hills (91367) (P-20658)
Northrop Grumman Systems Corp .... E....619 437-4231
N Island Naval A Sta Coronado (92118) (P-20659)
Northrop Grumman Systems Corp .... F....818 249-5252
2550 Honolulu Ave Montrose (91020) (P-20660)
Northrop Grumman Systems Corp .... A....858 618-4349
17066 Goldentop Rd San Diego (92127) (P-20661)
Northrop Grumman Systems Corp .... C....626 812-1000
1100 W Hollyvale St Azusa (91702) (P-20662)
Northrop Grumman Systems Corp .... B....661 540-0446
3520 E Avenue M Palmdale (93550) (P-20663)
Northrop Grumman Systems Corp .... E....916 570-4454
5441 Luce Ave McClellan (95652) (P-20664)
Northrop Grumman Systems Corp .... B....310 812-4321
2477 Manhattan Beach Blvd Redondo Beach (90278) (P-20665)
Northrop Grumman Systems Corp .... B....626 812-1464
1111 W 3rd St Azusa (91702) (P-20666)
Northrop Grumman Systems Corp .... C....858 514-9000
9326 Spectrum Center Blvd San Diego (92123) (P-20667)
Northrop Grumman Systems Corp .... C....310 332-1000
1 Hornet Way El Segundo (90245) (P-19919)
Northrop Grumman Systems Corp .... A....408 735-3011
401 E Hendy Ave Ms33-3 Sunnyvale (94086) (P-19920)
Northrop Grumman Systems Corp .... B....310 812-1089
1 Space Park Blvd Redondo Beach (90278) (P-19921)
Northrop Grumman Systems Corp .... B....310 812-4321
1 Space Park Blvd D Redondo Beach (90278) (P-19922)
Norths Bakery California Inc .... E....818 761-2892
5430 Satsuma Ave North Hollywood (91601) (P-1250)
Northwest Circuits Corp .... D....619 661-1701
8660 Avenida Costa Blanca San Diego (92154) (P-17940)
Northwest Pallets, Woodland Also called Ricardo Ochoa (P-5262)
Northwest Pipe Company .... B....760 246-3191
12351 Rancho Rd Adelanto (92301) (P-11132)
Northwest Signs, Santa Cruz Also called Jeff Frank (P-23140)
Northwest Skyline Logging Inc .... F....530 493-5150
725 Lower Airport Rd Happy Camp (96039) (P-3899)
Northwestern Converting Co 800 959-3402
2395 Railroad St Corona (92880) (P-3628)
Northwood Design Partners Inc .... E....510 731-6505
1550 Atlantic St Union City (94587) (P-4813)
Norton Company, Fullerton Also called Penhall Diamond Products Inc (P-14181)
Norton Packaging Inc (PA) 510 786-1922
20670 Corsair Blvd Hayward (94545) (P-9931)
Norton Packaging Inc .... D....323 588-6167
5800 S Boyle Ave Vernon (90058) (P-9932)
Nortra Cables Inc .... D....408 942-1106
570 Gibraltar Dr Milpitas (95035) (P-19029)
Norwesco Inc .... F....559 585-1668
13241 11th Ave Hanford (93230) (P-9933)
Norwich Aero Products Inc (HQ) .... E....607 336-7636
6900 Orangethorpe Ave B Buena Park (90620) (P-20668)
Not Only Jeans Inc .... E....213 765-9725
3004 S Main St Los Angeles (90007) (P-2705)
Nothing To Wear Inc (PA) .... E....310 328-0408
630 Maple Ave Torrance (90503) (P-3186)
Nothwest Pipe Company, Tracy Also called Nwpc LLC (P-12034)
Noticiero Semanal Advertising .... D....559 784-5000
115 E Oak Ave Porterville (93257) (P-5785)
Notron Manufacturing Inc .... F....818 247-7739
801 Milford St Glendale (91203) (P-16249)
Noushig Inc .... E....805 983-2903
451 Lombard St Oxnard (93030) (P-1251)
Nov, Orange Also called National Oilwell Varco Inc (P-13785)
Nov Orange Warehouse, Orange Also called National Oilwell Varco Inc (P-13788)
Nova, Huntington Park Also called NL&a Collections Inc (P-16982)
Nova Care Orthtics Prosthetics, Poway Also called Hanger Prsthetcs & Ortho Inc (P-22025)
Nova Drilling Services Inc .... E....408 732-6682
1500 Buckeye Dr Milpitas (95035) (P-17941)
Nova Lifestyle Inc (PA) .... E....323 888-9999
6565 E Washington Blvd Commerce (90040) (P-4599)
Nova Measuring Instruments Inc .... E....408 200-4344
3342 Gateway Blvd Fremont (94538) (P-21092)
Nova Mobile Systems Inc .... F....800 734-9885
2888 Loker Ave E Ste 311 Carlsbad (92010) (P-18782)
Nova Print Inc .... F....951 525-4040
2100 S Fairview St Santa Ana (92704) (P-3246)
Nova Tool Co .... F....925 828-7172
27736 Industrial Blvd Hayward (94545) (P-22953)
Nova-One Diagnostics LLC .... D....818 348-1543
22287 Mulholland Hwy Calabasas (91302) (P-8242)
Novabay Pharmaceuticals Inc .... E....510 899-8800
2000 Powell St Ste 1150 Emeryville (94608) (P-8041)
Novacart .... E....510 215-8999
512 W Ohio Ave Richmond (94804) (P-5139)
Novacart USA, Richmond Also called Novacart (P-5139)
Novanta Corporation .... E....510 770-1417
4575 Cushing Pkwy Fremont (94538) (P-19030)
Novanta Corporation .... E....408 754-4176
5750 Hellyer Ave San Jose (95138) (P-19031)
Novaray Medical Inc. .... F....510 619-9200
39655 Eureka Dr Newark (94560) (P-22219)
Novartis Biophrmctcl Ops-Vcvll, Vacaville Also called Novartis Pharmaceuticals Corp (P-8243)

Novartis Corporation .... D....858 812-1741
3115 Merryfield Row San Diego (92121) (P-8042)
Novartis Corporation .... D....510 879-9500
5300 Chiron Way Emeryville (94608) (P-8837)
Novartis Inst For Biomedical R .... F....510 923-4248
5300 Chiron Way Emeryville (94608) (P-8043)
Novartis Pharmaceuticals Corp .... E....707 452-8081
2010 Cessna Dr Vacaville (95688) (P-8243)
Novastor Corporation (PA) .... E....805 579-6700
29209 Canwood St Ste 200 Agoura Hills (91301) (P-24212)
Novato Advance Newspaper, Novato Also called St Louis Post-Dispatch LLC (P-5837)
Novatorque Inc .... E....510 933-2700
281 Greenoaks Dr Atherton (94027) (P-16667)
Novela Designs Inc .... F....213 505-4092
643 S Olive St Ste 421 Los Angeles (90014) (P-22991)
Novipax Inc (HQ) .... D....909 392-1750
1941 N White Ave La Verne (91750) (P-5516)
Novtek Inc .... F....408 441-9934
7018 Mariposa St Santee (92071) (P-21093)
Novtek Test Systems, Santee Also called Novtek Inc (P-21093)
Novus Therapeutics Inc. .... F....949 238-8090
19900 Macarthur Blvd # 550 Irvine (92612) (P-8044)
Novvi LLC (PA) .... E....281 488-0833
5885 Hollis St Ste 100 Emeryville (94608) (P-9054)
Novx Corporation .... E....408 998-5555
1750 N Loop Rd Ste 100 Alameda (94502) (P-21094)
Npc Firewood, Orangevale Also called Natural Pest Controls & Firewd (P-8836)
Npg Inc (PA) .... D....951 940-0200
1354 Jet Way Perris (92571) (P-9098)
Nphase Inc .... E....805 750-8580
323 Neptune Ave Encinitas (92024) (P-24213)
Npi Services Inc .... F....714 850-0550
1580 Corporate Dr Ste 124 Costa Mesa (92626) (P-17942)
Npi Solutions, Morgan Hill Also called New Product Integration Solutn (P-11103)
Npms Natural Products Mil Svcs, Gardena Also called BDS Natural Products Inc (P-2401)
Nq Engineering Inc .... F....209 836-3255
1852 W 11th St Pmb 532 Tracy (95376) (P-16250)
NRC Manufacturing Inc .... F....510 438-9400
47690 Westinghouse Dr Fremont (94539) (P-19032)
NRC USA Inc .... F....213 325-2780
3700 Wilshire Blvd # 300 Los Angeles (90010) (P-16852)
NRG Energy Services LLC .... D....702 815-2023
100302 Yates Well Rd Nipton (92364) (P-16564)
NS Wash Systems, Inglewood Also called N/S Corporation (P-15546)
Nsd Industries Inc .... F....626 813-2001
5027 Gayhurst Ave Baldwin Park (91706) (P-16251)
Nsi Architectural, Anaheim Also called Onesolution Light and Control (P-17150)
NSK Prec Amer Santa Fe Springs, Cerritos Also called NSK Precision America Inc (P-14613)
NSK Precision America Inc .... F....562 968-1000
13921 Bettencourt St Cerritos (90703) (P-14613)
Nss Enterprises .... E....408 970-9200
3380 Viso Ct Santa Clara (95054) (P-6754)
Nst, San Diego Also called No Second Thoughts Inc (P-2972)
Ntek, Sunnyvale Also called N-Tek Inc (P-14505)
NTL Precision Machining Inc .... F....408 298-6650
1355 Vander Way San Jose (95112) (P-16252)
NTN Buzztime Inc (PA) .... C....760 438-7400
1800 Aston Ave Ste 100 Carlsbad (92008) (P-24214)
Ntrust Infotech Inc .... D....562 207-1600
230 Commerce Ste 180 Irvine (92602) (P-24215)
Nu Engineering .... E....714 894-1206
12121 Bartlett St Garden Grove (92845) (P-16253)
Nu Health Products, Walnut Also called Nu-Health Products Co (P-7679)
Nu TEC Powdercoating .... F....714 632-5045
2990 E Blue Star St Anaheim (92806) (P-13213)
Nu Venture Diving Co .... E....805 815-4044
1600 Beacon Pl Oxnard (93033) (P-14636)
Nu Visions De Mexico SA De Cv .... C....619 987-0518
9355 Airway Rd San Diego (92154) (P-23430)
Nu-Health California LLC .... F....800 806-0519
16910 Cherie Pl Carson (90746) (P-804)
Nu-Health Products Co .... E....909 869-0666
20875 Currier Rd Walnut (91789) (P-7679)
Nu-Hope Laboratories Inc .... E....818 899-7711
12640 Branford St Pacoima (91331) (P-22056)
Nubile, Los Angeles Also called Semore Inc (P-3019)
Nubs Plastics Inc .... E....760 598-2525
991 Park Center Dr Vista (92081) (P-9934)
Nucast Industries Inc. .... F....951 277-8888
23220 Park Canyon Dr Corona (92883) (P-10608)
Nucleus Enterprises LLC .... D....619 517-8747
888 Prospect St Ste 200 La Jolla (92037) (P-9935)
Nuconic Packaging LLC .... E....323 588-9033
4889 Loma Vista Ave Vernon (90058) (P-9936)
Nugeneration Technologies LLC (PA) .... F....707 820-4080
1155 Park Ave Emeryville (94608) (P-9011)
Nugentec, Emeryville Also called Nugeneration Technologies LLC (P-9011)
Nugentec Oilfield Chem LLC .... E....707 891-3012
1155 Park Ave Emeryville (94608) (P-8345)
Nugier Hydraulics, Gardena Also called Nugier Press Company Inc (P-13988)
Nugier Press Company Inc .... F....310 515-6025
18031 La Salle Ave Gardena (90248) (P-13988)
Numano Sake Company, Berkeley Also called Takara Sake USA Inc (P-2020)
Numatech West (kmp) LLC .... D....909 706-3627
1201 E Lexington Ave Pomona (91766) (P-5248)
Numecent Inc .... E....949 833-2800
530 Technology Dr Ste 375 Irvine (92618) (P-24216)

Employee Codes: A=Over 500 employees, B=251-500
C=101-250, D=51-100, E=20-50, F=10-19

2020 California
Manfacturers Register

© Mergent Inc. 1-800-342-5647

1187

Numotech Inc...D.......818 772-1579
9420 Reseda Blvd Ste 504 Northridge (91324) ***(P-21842)***
Nuorder Inc (PA)...E.......310 954-1313
1901 Avenue Of The Stars Los Angeles (90067) ***(P-24217)***
Nuphoton Technologies Inc...F.......951 696-8366
41610 Corning Pl Murrieta (92562) ***(P-19370)***
Nupla LLC...C.......818 768-6800
11912 Sheldon St Sun Valley (91352) ***(P-11537)***
Nuprodx Inc...F.......925 292-0866
161 S Vasco Rd Ste G Livermore (94551) ***(P-22057)***
Nuro Inc...F.......650 476-2687
1300 Terra Bella Ave # 100 Mountain View (94043) ***(P-14509)***
Nursery Supplies Inc...E.......714 538-0251
534 W Struck Ave Orange (92867) ***(P-9937)***
Nursesbond Inc...F.......951 286-8537
26386 Primrose Way Moreno Valley (92555) ***(P-24218)***
Nurseweek Publishing, Sunnyvale *Also called Gannett Co Inc* ***(P-5943)***
Nuset Inc...E.......626 246-1668
1364 Marion Ct City of Industry (91745) ***(P-11616)***
Nusil Silicone Technology, Carpinteria *Also called Nusil Technology LLC* ***(P-7588)***
Nusil Technology LLC...D.......805 684-8780
1000 Cindy Ln Carpinteria (93013) ***(P-7588)***
Nusil Technology LLC...D.......661 391-4750
2343 Pegasus Dr Bakersfield (93308) ***(P-9345)***
Nusil Technology LLC...D.......805 684-8780
1150 Mark Ave Carpinteria (93013) ***(P-9346)***
Nustar Logistics LP...F.......925 427-6880
1100 Willow Pass Rd Pittsburg (94565) ***(P-59)***
Nut Case Helmets, Santa Fe Springs *Also called Nutcase Inc* ***(P-22862)***
Nutcase Inc...F.......503 243-4570
12801 Carmenita Rd Santa Fe Springs (90670) ***(P-22862)***
Nutec Rehab, Sacramento *Also called Tri Quality Inc* ***(P-22112)***
Nutiva...D.......510 255-2700
213 W Cutting Blvd Richmond (94804) ***(P-2572)***
Nutra Blend LLC...D.......559 661-6161
2140 W Industrial Ave Madera (93637) ***(P-1114)***
Nutraceutical Brews For Lf Inc...F.......310 273-8339
825 Cambridge Ct Pasadena (91107) ***(P-1551)***
Nutrade Inc...E.......949 477-2300
2808 Willis St Santa Ana (92705) ***(P-2706)***
Nutrawise Corporation, Irvine *Also called Nutrawise Health & Beauty Corp* ***(P-8045)***
Nutrawise Health & Beauty Corp (PA)...D.......949 900-2400
9600 Toledo Way Irvine (92618) ***(P-8045)***
Nutri Granulations Inc...D.......714 994-7855
16024 Phoebe Ave La Mirada (90638) ***(P-612)***
Nutribiotic, Lakeport *Also called Nutrition Resource Inc* ***(P-8046)***
Nutricology, Alameda *Also called Allergy Research Group LLC* ***(P-7743)***
Nutrien AG Solutions Inc...F.......805 488-3646
2150 Eastman Ave Oxnard (93030) ***(P-8800)***
Nutrien AG Solutions Inc...E.......209 551-1424
3348 Claus Rd Modesto (95355) ***(P-8814)***
Nutrition Resource Inc (PA)...F.......707 263-0411
865 Parallel Dr Lakeport (95453) ***(P-8046)***
Nutrition Resource Connection...F.......760 803-8234
254 May Ct Cardiff By The Sea (92007) ***(P-17332)***
Nutrition Without Borders LLC...F.......310 845-7745
4641 Leahy St Culver City (90232) ***(P-15399)***
Nutritional Engineering Inc...F.......760 599-5200
1208 Avenida Chelsea Vista (92081) ***(P-8047)***
Nutrius LLC...E.......559 897-5862
39494 Clarkson Dr Kingsburg (93631) ***(P-1115)***
Nuvair, Oxnard *Also called Nu Venture Diving Co* ***(P-14636)***
Nuvasive Inc (PA)...D.......858 909-1800
7475 Lusk Blvd San Diego (92121) ***(P-21843)***
Nuvasive Spclzed Orthpdics Inc...D.......949 837-3600
101 Enterprise Ste 100 Aliso Viejo (92656) ***(P-21844)***
Nuvet Labs, Westlake Village *Also called Vitavet Labs Inc* ***(P-23519)***
Nuvora Inc...E.......408 856-2200
3350 Scott Blvd Ste 502 Santa Clara (95054) ***(P-8549)***
Nuwest Milling LLC...F.......209 883-1163
4636 Geer Rd Hughson (95326) ***(P-1116)***
Nuzee Inc...E.......760 295-2408
2865 Scott St Ste 107 Vista (92081) ***(P-2306)***
Nvent Thermal LLC (HQ)...B.......650 474-7414
899 Broadway St Redwood City (94063) ***(P-20801)***
Nvidia Corporation (PA)...B.......408 486-2000
2788 San Tomas Expy Santa Clara (95051) ***(P-18437)***
Nvidia Corporation...F.......408 566-5364
2001 Walsh Ave Santa Clara (95050) ***(P-18438)***
Nvidia Development Inc...E.......408 486-2000
2701 San Tomas Expy Santa Clara (95050) ***(P-18439)***
Nvidia US Investment Company...A.......408 615-2500
2701 San Tomas Expy Santa Clara (95050) ***(P-17607)***
Nvision Laser Eye Centers Inc...F.......916 723-7400
5959 Greenback Ln Ste 310 Citrus Heights (95621) ***(P-22374)***
Nwe Technology Inc...C.......408 919-6100
1688 Richard Ave Santa Clara (95050) ***(P-15068)***
Nwp Services Corporation (HQ)...C.......949 253-2500
535 Anton Blvd Ste 1100 Costa Mesa (92626) ***(P-24219)***
Nwpc LLC...D.......209 836-5050
10100 W Linne Rd Tracy (95377) ***(P-12034)***
Nxedge San Carlos LLC...F.......650 422-2269
1000 Commercial St San Carlos (94070) ***(P-18440)***
Nxp Usa Inc...D.......408 518-5500
2680 Zanker Rd Ste 200 San Jose (95134) ***(P-18441)***
Nxp Usa Inc...B.......408 518-5500
411 E Plumeria Dr San Jose (95134) ***(P-18442)***
Nxp Usa Inc...E.......408 991-2700
690 E Arques Ave Sunnyvale (94085) ***(P-18443)***
Nxp Usa Inc...E.......408 991-2000
440 N Wolfe Rd Sunnyvale (94085) ***(P-18444)***
Nxp Usa Inc...F.......949 399-4000
9 Cushing Ste 100 Irvine (92618) ***(P-18445)***
Nyabenga Llc...F.......925 418-4221
9020 Brentwood Blvd Ste A Brentwood (94513) ***(P-6299)***
Nyansa Inc...E.......650 446-7818
430 Cowper St Ste 250 Palo Alto (94301) ***(P-24220)***
Nycetek Inc...F.......714 671-3860
555 W Lambert Rd Ste F Brea (92821) ***(P-4924)***
Nydr Holdings Inc...F.......818 626-8174
9525 Cozycroft Ave Ste M Chatsworth (91311) ***(P-2573)***
Nylok LLC...E.......714 635-3993
313 N Euclid Way Anaheim (92801) ***(P-12689)***
Nylok Western Fastener, Anaheim *Also called Nylok LLC* ***(P-12689)***
Nypro Healthcare Baja, Chula Vista *Also called Nypro Inc* ***(P-9938)***
Nypro Inc...D.......619 498-9250
505 Main St Rm 107 Chula Vista (91911) ***(P-9938)***
Nypro San Diego Inc...D.......619 482-7033
505 Main St Chula Vista (91911) ***(P-9939)***
Nyx Industries Inc...F.......909 937-3923
9452 Resenda Ave Fontana (92335) ***(P-13653)***
O & S California Inc...B.......619 661-1800
9731 Siempre Viva Rd E San Diego (92154) ***(P-19371)***
O and Y Precision Inc...F.......408 362-1333
312 Piercy Rd San Jose (95138) ***(P-14178)***
O C M, Los Angeles *Also called Old Country Millwork Inc* ***(P-14234)***
O D I, Riverside *Also called Edge Plastics Inc* ***(P-9773)***
O H I Company...E.......209 466-8921
820 S Pershing Ave Stockton (95206) ***(P-14389)***
O Industries Corporation...F.......310 719-2289
1930 W 139th St Gardena (90249) ***(P-3980)***
O K Color America Corporation...F.......310 320-9343
578 Amapola Ave Torrance (90501) ***(P-9940)***
O M Jones Inc...E.......209 532-1008
18897 Microtronics Way Sonora (95370) ***(P-19033)***
O M Y A, Lucerne Valley *Also called Omya California Inc* ***(P-7513)***
O O Campbell, San Leandro *Also called Oriental Odysseys Inc* ***(P-23433)***
O Olive Oil & Vinegar, Petaluma *Also called Curation Foods Inc* ***(P-2439)***
O P F, Oxnard *Also called Oxnard Prcsion Fabrication Inc* ***(P-12320)***
O W I Inc...F.......310 515-1900
17141 Kingsview Ave Carson (90746) ***(P-17267)***
O'Brien Iron Works, Concord *Also called Energy Steel Corporation* ***(P-15932)***
O'Neil Data Systems, Inc., Los Angeles *Also called ONeil Capital Management* ***(P-6961)***
O-S Inc...F.......408 946-5890
541 W Capitol Expy Ste 10 San Jose (95136) ***(P-16254)***
O.C. Metro Magazine, Newport Beach *Also called Churm Publishing Inc* ***(P-5904)***
Oak Apparel Inc...F.......213 489-9766
1363 Elwood St Los Angeles (90021) ***(P-3379)***
Oak Design Corporation...E.......909 628-9597
13272 6th St Chino (91710) ***(P-4814)***
Oak Land Company, Chula Vista *Also called Oak Land Furniture* ***(P-4696)***
Oak Land Furniture...F.......619 424-8758
2462 Main St Ste D Chula Vista (91911) ***(P-4696)***
Oak Manufacturing Company Inc...F.......323 581-8087
2850 E Vernon Ave Vernon (90058) ***(P-15400)***
Oak Ridge Winery LLC...E.......209 369-4768
6100 E Hwy 12 Victor Rd Lodi (95240) ***(P-1844)***
Oak Tree Furniture Inc...D.......562 944-0754
13681 Newport Ave Ste 8 Tustin (92780) ***(P-4600)***
Oak-It Inc...E.......951 735-5973
143 Business Center Dr Corona (92880) ***(P-4098)***
Oak-It Inc...E.......310 719-3999
845 Sandhill Ave Carson (90746) ***(P-4925)***
Oakdale Cheese & Specialties...F.......209 848-3139
10040 State Highway 120 Oakdale (95361) ***(P-569)***
Oakhurst Industries Inc (PA)...C.......323 724-3000
2050 S Tubeway Ave Commerce (90040) ***(P-1252)***
Oakland Magazine, Alameda *Also called Alameda Directory Inc* ***(P-6179)***
Oakland Production Center, Oakland *Also called Kemeera Incorporated* ***(P-15265)***
Oakland Tribune Inc...A.......510 208-6300
600 Grand Ave 308 Oakland (94610) ***(P-5786)***
Oakley Inc...D.......949 672-6849
20081 Ellipse Foothill Ranch (92610) ***(P-22375)***
Oakley Inc (HQ)...A.......949 951-0991
1 Icon Foothill Ranch (92610) ***(P-3187)***
Oakley Sales Corp...F.......949 951-0991
1 Icon El Toro (92610) ***(P-22376)***
Oakmead Prtg & Reproduction...E.......408 734-5505
233 E Weddell Dr Ste G Sunnyvale (94089) ***(P-6755)***
Oakridge, Oxnard *Also called Scully Sportswear Inc* ***(P-3522)***
Oakwood Interiors, Ontario *Also called Lanpar Inc* ***(P-4586)***
Oasis Alloy Wheels Inc...F.......714 533-3286
400 S Lemon St Anaheim (92805) ***(P-11386)***
Oasis Breads, San Marcos *Also called Health Breads Inc* ***(P-1224)***
Oasis Date Garden Inc...E.......760 399-5665
59111 Grapefruit Blvd Thermal (92274) ***(P-2574)***
Oasis Foods Inc...E.......209 382-0263
10881 Toews Ave Le Grand (95333) ***(P-805)***
Oasis Materials Company LP...E.......858 486-8846
12131 Community Rd Ste D Poway (92064) ***(P-19034)***
Oasis Medical Inc (PA)...D.......909 305-5400
510-528 S Vermont Ave Glendora (91741) ***(P-22377)***
Oasis Metal Works, Anaheim *Also called Oasis Alloy Wheels Inc* ***(P-11386)***
Oasis Structures & Water Works...F.......707 839-1683
273 Anker Ln McKinleyville (95519) ***(P-15552)***
Oatey Co...E.......800 321-9532
6600 Smith Ave Newark (94560) ***(P-8882)***

Obagi Cosmeceuticals LLC (PA) ....D.......800 636-7546
3760 Kilroy Airport Way Long Beach (90806) ***(P-8048)***
Obagi Medical, Long Beach *Also called Obagi Cosmeceuticals LLC* ***(P-8048)***
Obalon Therapeutics Inc ....C.......760 795-6558
5421 Avd Encinas Ste F Carlsbad (92008) ***(P-21845)***
Obatake Inc ....E.......310 782-2730
20309 Gramercy Pl Ste A Torrance (90501) ***(P-22556)***
Obentec Inc ....F.......831 457-0301
500 Chestnut St Ste 225 Santa Cruz (95060) ***(P-4422)***
Oberon Co ....D.......408 227-3730
7216 Via Colina San Jose (95139) ***(P-19035)***
Oberon Fuels Inc (PA) ....F.......619 255-9361
2159 India St Ste 200 San Diego (92101) ***(P-9055)***
Observables Inc ....F.......805 272-9255
117 N Milpas St Santa Barbara (93103) ***(P-19372)***
Observer Newspaper ....E.......310 452-9900
1844 Lincoln Blvd Santa Monica (90404) ***(P-5787)***
Oc Baking Company ....D.......714 998-2253
1960 N Glassell St Orange (92865) ***(P-1253)***
Oc Fleet Service Inc ....F.......714 460-8069
8270 Monroe Ave Stanton (90680) ***(P-20297)***
Oc Glass, Irvine *Also called USA Fire Glass* ***(P-10399)***
Oc Metals Inc ....E.......714 668-0783
2720 S Main St Ste B Santa Ana (92707) ***(P-12317)***
Oc Waterjet ....F.......714 685-0851
2280 N Batavia St Orange (92865) ***(P-11854)***
Occam Networks Inc (HQ) ....E.......805 692-2900
6868 Cortona Dr Santa Barbara (93117) ***(P-17392)***
Occidental Manufacturing Inc ....E.......707 824-2560
4200 Ross Rd Sebastopol (95472) ***(P-10249)***
Oce Dsplay Grphics Systems Inc ....D.......773 714-8500
2811 Orchard Pkwy San Jose (95134) ***(P-14332)***
Ocean Aero Inc ....E.......858 945-3768
10350 Sorrento Valley Rd San Diego (92121) ***(P-20669)***
Ocean Avenue Brewing Co ....E.......949 497-3381
237 Ocean Ave Laguna Beach (92651) ***(P-1552)***
Ocean Beauty Seafoods LLC ....C.......213 624-2101
629 S Central Ave Los Angeles (90021) ***(P-2246)***
Ocean Blue Inc ....E.......909 478-9910
494 Commercial Rd San Bernardino (92408) ***(P-9559)***
Ocean Brewing Company, Laguna Beach *Also called Ocean Avenue Brewing Co* ***(P-1552)***
Ocean Direct LLC (PA) ....E.......424 266-9300
13771 Gramercy Pl Gardena (90249) ***(P-2267)***
Ocean Divers USA LLC ....F.......760 599-6898
975 Park Center Dr Vista (92081) ***(P-9941)***
Ocean Fresh LLC (PA) ....E.......707 964-1389
350 N Main St Fort Bragg (95437) ***(P-2247)***
Ocean Fresh Seafood Products, Fort Bragg *Also called Ocean Fresh LLC* ***(P-2247)***
Ocean Heat Inc ....F.......951 208-1923
13610 Imperial Hwy Ste 4 Santa Fe Springs (90670) ***(P-22058)***
Ocean Protecta Incorporated ....E.......714 891-2628
10743 Progress Way Cypress (90630) ***(P-20353)***
Ocean Technology Systems, Santa Ana *Also called Undersea Systems Intl Inc* ***(P-19427)***
Oceania Inc ....E.......562 926-8886
14209 Gannet St La Mirada (90638) ***(P-9416)***
Oceania International LLC ....E.......949 407-8904
23661 Birtcher Dr Lake Forest (92630) ***(P-11278)***
Oceanic, San Leandro *Also called American Underwater Products* ***(P-22744)***
Oceans Flavor Foods LLC ....F.......619 793-5269
4492 Camino De La Plz San Ysidro (92173) ***(P-9012)***
Oceanscience, Poway *Also called Tern Design Ltd* ***(P-20947)***
Oceanside Glasstile Company (PA) ....B.......760 929-4000
5858 Edison Pl Carlsbad (92008) ***(P-10447)***
Oceanside Marine Center Inc (PA) ....F.......760 722-1833
1550 Harbor Dr N Oceanside (92054) ***(P-20354)***
Oceanside Plastic Enterprises ....F.......760 433-0779
3038 Industry St Ste 108 Oceanside (92054) ***(P-14086)***
Oceanside Ready Mix, Oceanside *Also called Legacy Vulcan LLC* ***(P-10598)***
Oceanwide Repairs, Long Beach *Also called APR Engineering Inc* ***(P-20277)***
Ocg Inc ....D.......714 375-4024
17952 Lyons Cir Huntington Beach (92647) ***(P-19036)***
Oci, Santa Fe Springs *Also called Office Chairs Inc* ***(P-4815)***
Oclaro Inc (HQ) ....D.......408 383-1400
400 N Mccarthy Blvd Milpitas (95035) ***(P-18446)***
Oclaro (north America) Inc (HQ) ....B.......408 383-1400
252 Charcot Ave San Jose (95131) ***(P-17393)***
Oclaro Fiber Optics Inc (HQ) ....E.......408 383-1400
400 N Mccarthy Blvd Milpitas (95035) ***(P-18447)***
Oclaro Photonics Inc (HQ) ....D.......408 383-1400
400 N Mccarthy Blvd Milpitas (95035) ***(P-21387)***
Oclaro Subsystems Inc ....C.......408 383-1400
400 N Mccarthy Blvd Milpitas (95035) ***(P-17394)***
Oclaro Technology Inc (HQ) ....D.......408 383-1400
400 N Mccarthy Blvd Milpitas (95035) ***(P-17395)***
Ocli, Santa Rosa *Also called Optical Coating Laboratory LLC* ***(P-13215)***
OCP Group Inc ....E.......858 279-7400
7130 Engineer Rd San Diego (92111) ***(P-15132)***
Ocpc Inc ....D.......949 475-1900
2485 Da Vinci Irvine (92614) ***(P-6756)***
Oct Medical Imaging Inc ....F.......949 701-6656
1002 Health Sciences Rd Irvine (92617) ***(P-21846)***
Octillion Power Systems Inc ....F.......510 397-5952
721 Sandoval Way Hayward (94544) ***(P-19730)***
Oculeve Inc ....F.......415 745-3784
4410 Rosewood Dr Pleasanton (94588) ***(P-8049)***
Ocunexus Therapeutics Inc ....F.......858 480-2403
12481 High Bluff Dr D San Diego (92130) ***(P-8050)***
Od Signs, Hayward *Also called Oki Doki Signs* ***(P-23169)***

Odcombe Press (nashville) ....E.......615 793-5414
859 Lawrence Dr Newbury Park (91320) ***(P-6757)***
Oddbox Holdings Inc ....F.......949 474-9222
16842 Hale Ave Irvine (92606) ***(P-7151)***
Oddworld Inhabitants Inc ....D.......805 503-3000
869 Monterey St San Luis Obispo (93401) ***(P-24221)***
Odette Christiane LLC ....F.......818 883-0410
21521 Blythe St Canoga Park (91304) ***(P-3380)***
Odonate Therapeutics Inc ....C.......858 731-8180
4747 Executive Dr Ste 510 San Diego (92121) ***(P-8051)***
ODonnell Manufacturing Inc ....F.......562 944-9671
14811 Via Defrancesco Ave Riverside (92508) ***(P-16255)***
Odusa, Vista *Also called Ocean Divers USA LLC* ***(P-9941)***
Odwalla Inc ....E.......310 342-3920
700 Isis Ave Inglewood (90301) ***(P-806)***
Odwalla Inc ....E.......408 254-5800
1805 Las Plumas Ave San Jose (95133) ***(P-807)***
Odyssey Innovative Designs, San Gabriel *Also called Hsiao & Montano Inc* ***(P-10197)***
OEM Materials & Supplies Inc ....E.......714 564-9600
1500 Ritchey St Santa Ana (92705) ***(P-5140)***
Oepic Semiconductors Inc ....E.......408 747-0388
1231 Bordeaux Dr Sunnyvale (94089) ***(P-18448)***
Off Broadway, La Verne *Also called Fortress Inc* ***(P-4797)***
Off Dock USA Inc ....F.......310 522-4400
22700 S Alameda St Carson (90810) ***(P-13886)***
Off Lead Inc ....F.......209 931-6909
9751 N Highway 99 Stockton (95212) ***(P-10250)***
Off Price Network LLC ....E.......213 477-8205
10544 Dunleer Dr Los Angeles (90064) ***(P-3271)***
Offenhauser Sales Corp ....F.......323 225-1307
5300 Alhambra Ave Los Angeles (90032) ***(P-19731)***
Offerman Industries ....F.......951 676-5016
43154 Via Dos Picos Ste F Temecula (92590) ***(P-16256)***
Office Chairs Inc ....D.......562 802-0464
14815 Radburn Ave Santa Fe Springs (90670) ***(P-4815)***
Office Master Inc ....D.......909 392-5678
1110 Mildred St Ontario (91761) ***(P-4846)***
Officelocale Inc ....F.......805 777-8866
275 E Hillcrest Dr # 160 Thousand Oaks (91360) ***(P-7152)***
Offline Inc (PA) ....E.......213 742-9001
2250 Maple Ave Los Angeles (90011) ***(P-3456)***
Ofs Brands Holdings Inc ....F.......714 903-2257
5559 Mcfadden Ave Huntington Beach (92649) ***(P-4816)***
Oggi Corp, Anaheim *Also called Asdak International* ***(P-10484)***
Oggi's Pizza & Brewing Co, Vista *Also called DSB Enterprises Inc* ***(P-1521)***
Oggis Pizza & Brewing Co ....E.......858 481-7883
12840 Carmel Country Rd San Diego (92130) ***(P-1553)***
Ogio International Inc ....D.......801 619-4100
2180 Rutherford Rd Carlsbad (92008) ***(P-10200)***
Ogletree's, Saint Helena *Also called Ronald F Ogletree Inc* ***(P-12358)***
OH Juice Inc ....F.......619 318-0207
5631 Palmer Way Ste A Carlsbad (92010) ***(P-808)***
Ohadi Management Corporation ....F.......909 625-2000
11088 Elm Ave Rancho Cucamonga (91730) ***(P-21847)***
Ohanyan's Deli, Fresno *Also called Ohanyans Inc* ***(P-483)***
Ohanyans Inc (PA) ....F.......559 225-4290
3296 W Sussex Way Fresno (93722) ***(P-483)***
OHara Metal Products ....E.......707 863-9090
4949 Fulton Dr Ste E Fairfield (94534) ***(P-13341)***
Oheck LLC ....C.......323 923-2700
5830 Bickett St Huntington Park (90255) ***(P-3521)***
Ohio Inc ....F.......415 647-6446
630 Treat Ave San Francisco (94110) ***(P-4817)***
Ohno America Inc ....E.......770 773-3820
18781 Winnwood Ln Santa Ana (92705) ***(P-2877)***
Oil Country Manufacturing ....C.......805 643-1200
300 W Stanley Ave Ventura (93001) ***(P-13789)***
Oil Well Service Company (PA) ....C.......562 612-0600
10840 Norwalk Blvd Santa Fe Springs (90670) ***(P-238)***
Oil Well Service Company ....E.......661 746-4809
10255 Enos Ln Shafter (93263) ***(P-239)***
Oil Well Service Company ....E.......805 525-2103
1015 Mission Rock Rd Santa Paula (93060) ***(P-240)***
Oil-Dri Corporation America ....F.......661 765-7194
950 Petroleum Club Rd Taft (93268) ***(P-8400)***
Ojo De Agua Produce, Dos Palos *Also called C&S Global Foods Inc* ***(P-2413)***
Oki Doki Signs ....F.......510 940-7446
1680 W Winton Ave Ste 7 Hayward (94545) ***(P-23169)***
Oki Graphics Inc ....F.......408 451-9294
2148 Zanker Rd San Jose (95131) ***(P-7153)***
Okonite Company ....C.......805 922-6682
2900 Skyway Dr Santa Maria (93455) ***(P-11312)***
Okta Inc (PA) ....C.......888 722-7871
100 1st St Ste 600 San Francisco (94105) ***(P-24222)***
Okta Inc ....F.......650 348-2620
172 Lakeshore Dr San Mateo (94402) ***(P-24223)***
Ola Corporate Services Inc ....F.......323 655-1005
6404 Wilshire Blvd # 525 Los Angeles (90048) ***(P-15385)***
Olaes Design & Marketing, Poway *Also called Olaes Enterprises Inc* ***(P-3111)***
Olaes Enterprises Inc ....E.......858 679-4450
13860 Stowe Dr Poway (92064) ***(P-3111)***
Olam Spices and Vegetables, Woodland *Also called Olam West Coast Inc* ***(P-811)***
Olam Tomato Processors Inc ....F.......559 447-1390
1175 S 19th Ave Lemoore (93245) ***(P-809)***
Olam Tomato Processors Inc (HQ) ....D.......559 447-1390
205 E River Park Cir # 310 Fresno (93720) ***(P-810)***
Olam West Coast Inc ....A.......530 473-4290
1400 Churchill Downs Ave Woodland (95776) ***(P-811)***

Employee Codes: A=Over 500 employees, B=251-500
C=101-250, D=51-100, E=20-50, F=10-19
2020 California
Manfacturers Register
© Mergent Inc. 1-800-342-5647
1189

Olaplex LLC (PA)....F....805 258-7680
1482 E Valley Rd Ste 701 Santa Barbara (93108) ***(P-8550)***
Olark, San Francisco *Also called Habla Incorporated* ***(P-23968)***
Old An Inc....E....949 263-1400
17651 Armstrong Ave Irvine (92614) ***(P-23431)***
Old Bones Co....F....714 641-2800
641 Paularino Ave Costa Mesa (92626) ***(P-4662)***
Old Bones Company, Costa Mesa *Also called Old Bones Co* ***(P-4662)***
Old California Lantern Company, Orange *Also called Contract Illumination* ***(P-17020)***
Old Castle Inclosure Solution, Madera *Also called Oldcastle Infrastructure Inc* ***(P-10615)***
Old Country Bakery, South San Francisco *Also called Bimbo Bakeries Usa Inc* ***(P-1161)***
Old Country Millwork Inc....E....323 234-2940
5855 Hooper Ave Los Angeles (90001) ***(P-14234)***
Old Creek Ranch Winery Inc....F....805 649-4132
10024 Creek Rd Oak View (93022) ***(P-1845)***
Old English Mil & Woodworks, Santa Clarita *Also called Old English Mil & Woodworks* ***(P-4099)***
Old English Mil & Woodworks (PA)....E....661 294-9171
27772 Avenue Scott Santa Clarita (91355) ***(P-4099)***
Old Fashion Lavash, Los Angeles *Also called Lavash Corporation* ***(P-1232)***
Old Guys Rule, Ventura *Also called Streamline Dsign Slkscreen Inc* ***(P-3120)***
Old New York Bagel & Deli Co (PA)....F....805 484-3354
4972 Verdugo Way Camarillo (93012) ***(P-1254)***
Old New York Deli & Bagel Co, Camarillo *Also called Old New York Bagel & Deli Co* ***(P-1254)***
Old Pueblo Ranch Inc....C....323 268-2791
316 N Ford Blvd Los Angeles (90022) ***(P-2575)***
Oldcast Precast (HQ)....E....951 788-9720
2434 Rubidoux Blvd Riverside (92509) ***(P-10609)***
Oldcastle Apg West Inc....E....909 355-6422
10714 Poplar Ave Fontana (92337) ***(P-10427)***
Oldcastle Apg West Inc....F....209 983-1609
4202 Gibralter Ct Stockton (95206) ***(P-9099)***
Oldcastle Buildingenvelope Inc....D....510 651-2292
6850 Stevenson Blvd Fremont (94538) ***(P-10382)***
Oldcastle Buildingenvelope Inc....D....323 722-2007
5631 Ferguson Dr Commerce (90022) ***(P-10383)***
Oldcastle Infrastructure Inc....C....909 428-3700
10650 Hemlock Ave Fontana (92337) ***(P-10610)***
Oldcastle Infrastructure Inc....E....619 390-2251
10441 Vine St Lakeside (92040) ***(P-10611)***
Oldcastle Infrastructure Inc....E....925 846-8183
3786 Valley Ave Pleasanton (94566) ***(P-10612)***
Oldcastle Infrastructure Inc....E....858 578-5336
10050 Black Mountain Rd San Diego (92126) ***(P-10613)***
Oldcastle Infrastructure Inc....E....209 235-1173
2960 S Highway 99 Stockton (95215) ***(P-10614)***
Oldcastle Infrastructure Inc....E....559 674-8093
801 S Pine St Madera (93637) ***(P-13536)***
Oldcastle Infrastructure Inc....F....559 675-1813
801 S Pine St Madera (93637) ***(P-10615)***
Oldcastle Infrastructure Inc....E....530 742-8368
5236 Arboga Rd Marysville (95901) ***(P-10616)***
Oldcastle Infrastructure Inc....E....951 683-8200
2512 Harmony Grove Rd Escondido (92029) ***(P-10617)***
Olde World Corporation....E....209 384-1337
360 Grogan Ave Merced (95341) ***(P-4926)***
Olea Kiosks Inc....D....562 924-2644
13845 Artesia Blvd Cerritos (90703) ***(P-15298)***
Oleumtech Corporation....D....949 305-9009
19762 Pauling Foothill Ranch (92610) ***(P-20912)***
Olin Chlor Alkali Logistics....C....562 692-0510
11600 Pike St Santa Fe Springs (90670) ***(P-7391)***
Olio Devices Inc....E....650 918-6546
1100 La Avenida St Ste A Mountain View (94043) ***(P-22482)***
Oliphant Tool Company....E....714 903-6336
15652 Chemical Ln Huntington Beach (92649) ***(P-14087)***
Oliso, Richmond *Also called Unovo LLC* ***(P-16846)***
Oliso Inc....F....415 864-7600
1200 Harbour Way S 215 Richmond (94804) ***(P-16836)***
Olive Bari Oil Company....F....559 595-9260
40063 Road 56 Dinuba (93618) ***(P-1479)***
Olive Bariani Oil LLC....F....415 864-1917
1330 Waller St San Francisco (94117) ***(P-1480)***
Olive Corto L P....F....209 888-8100
10201 Live Oak Rd Stockton (95212) ***(P-1481)***
Olive Musco Products Inc (PA)....B....209 836-4600
17950 Via Nicolo Tracy (95377) ***(P-812)***
Olive Musco Products Inc....E....530 865-4111
Swift & 5th St # 5 Orland (95963) ***(P-892)***
Olive Press LLC (PA)....F....707 939-8900
24724 Arnold Dr Sonoma (95476) ***(P-1482)***
Oliver De Silva Inc (PA)....E....925 829-9220
11555 Dublin Blvd Dublin (94568) ***(P-317)***
Olivera Egg Ranch LLC....D....408 258-8074
3315 Sierra Rd San Jose (95132) ***(P-523)***
Olivera Foods, San Jose *Also called Olivera Egg Ranch LLC* ***(P-523)***
Olli Salumeria Americana LLC....F....804 427-7866
1301 Rocky Point Dr Oceanside (92056) ***(P-420)***
Ols Controls....F....408 353-6564
15215 Old Ranch Rd Los Gatos (95033) ***(P-20802)***
Olson and Co Steel....D....559 224-7811
3488 W Ashlan Ave Fresno (93722) ***(P-11855)***
Olson and Co Steel (PA)....C....510 489-4680
1941 Davis St San Leandro (94577) ***(P-12502)***
Olson Industrial Systems, Santee *Also called Olson Irrigation Systems* ***(P-13654)***
Olson Irrigation Systems....E....619 562-3100
10910 Wheatlands Ave A Santee (92071) ***(P-13654)***
Olt Solar, San Jose *Also called Orbotech Lt Solar LLC* ***(P-18458)***
Oly, Berkeley *Also called Art of Muse LLC* ***(P-4548)***
Olympia Trading, Los Angeles *Also called Silver Textile Incorporated* ***(P-2761)***
Olympic Cascade Publishing (HQ)....E....916 321-1000
2100 Q St Sacramento (95816) ***(P-5788)***
Olympic Coatings....E....760 745-3322
2200 Micro Pl Escondido (92029) ***(P-13214)***
Olympic Press Inc....F....408 496-6222
461 Nelo St Santa Clara (95054) ***(P-7154)***
Omana Group LLC....F....714 891-9488
11562 Knott St Ste 5 Garden Grove (92841) ***(P-613)***
Omega 2000 Group Corp....D....951 775-5815
160 S Carmalita St Hemet (92543) ***(P-16837)***
Omega Case Company Inc....E....818 238-9263
2231 N Hollywood Way Burbank (91505) ***(P-4423)***
Omega Diamond Inc....F....916 652-8122
10125 Ophir Rd Newcastle (95658) ***(P-14179)***
Omega Extruding, Rancho Cucamonga *Also called Omega Plastics Corp* ***(P-5408)***
Omega Fire Inc....F....818 404-6212
441 W Allen Ave Ste 109 San Dimas (91773) ***(P-9202)***
Omega Graphics, Eastvale *Also called Rivas Industries Inc* ***(P-6844)***
Omega Graphics Printing Hollyw....F....213 784-5200
6000 Fountain Ave Los Angeles (90028) ***(P-6758)***
Omega Graphics Printing Inc....F....818 374-9189
7710 Kester Ave Van Nuys (91405) ***(P-7155)***
Omega Industrial Supply Inc....E....707 864-8164
101 Grobric Ct Fairfield (94534) ***(P-8401)***
Omega Interconnect Inc....F....909 986-1933
1207 Brooks St Ontario (91762) ***(P-16257)***
Omega Leads Inc....E....310 394-6786
1509 Colorado Ave Santa Monica (90404) ***(P-19037)***
Omega Plastics Corp....C....909 987-8716
9614 Lucas Ranch Rd Ste D Rancho Cucamonga (91730) ***(P-5408)***
Omega Precision....E....562 946-2491
13040 Telegraph Rd Santa Fe Springs (90670) ***(P-16258)***
Omega Precision Machine....F....209 833-6502
320 W Larch Rd Ste 15 Tracy (95304) ***(P-16259)***
Omega Products Corp (HQ)....D....916 635-3335
8111 Fruitridge Rd Sacramento (95826) ***(P-11015)***
Omega Products Corp....E....714 935-0900
282 S Anita Dr Fl 3 Orange (92868) ***(P-11016)***
Omega Products International, Sacramento *Also called Omega Products Corp* ***(P-11015)***
Omega Technologies Inc....F....818 264-7970
31125 Via Colinas Ste 905 Westlake Village (91362) ***(P-11538)***
Omega Tool Die & Machine, San Bernardino *Also called McIntire Tool Die & Machine* ***(P-12842)***
Omega Turnstiles, Benicia *Also called Gunnebo Entrance Control Inc* ***(P-21481)***
Omenkastore.com, Inglewood *Also called Omenkausa LLC* ***(P-2101)***
Omenkausa LLC....F....877 415-6590
720 N La Brea Ave Inglewood (90302) ***(P-2101)***
Omf Performance Products....F....951 354-8272
8199 Mar Vista Ct Riverside (92504) ***(P-20517)***
OMI, Yuba City *Also called Organic Mattresses Inc* ***(P-4734)***
Omicron Engineering Inc....F....310 328-4017
1513 Plaza Del Amo Torrance (90501) ***(P-16260)***
Omics Group Inc....B....650 268-9744
731 Gull Ave Foster City (94404) ***(P-5994)***
Oml Inc....F....408 779-2698
300 Digital Dr Morgan Hill (95037) ***(P-21095)***
Omneon Inc (HQ)....C....408 585-5000
4300 N 1st St San Jose (95134) ***(P-17608)***
Omni Connection Intl Inc....B....951 898-6232
126 Via Trevizio Corona (92879) ***(P-19038)***
Omni Duct Systems, West Sacramento *Also called ECB Corp* ***(P-12191)***
Omni Enclosures Inc....E....619 579-6664
505 Raleigh Ave El Cajon (92020) ***(P-4927)***
Omni Metal Finishing Inc (PA)....D....714 231-3716
11665 Coley River Cir Fountain Valley (92708) ***(P-13064)***
Omni Optical Products Inc (PA)....E....714 634-5700
17282 Eastman Irvine (92614) ***(P-21512)***
Omni Pacific, El Cajon *Also called Omni Enclosures Inc* ***(P-4927)***
Omni Seals, Inc., Rancho Cucamonga *Also called Smith International Inc* ***(P-264)***
Omnia Inc....F....818 843-1620
2831 N San Fernando Blvd Burbank (91504) ***(P-20188)***
Omnia Leather Motion Inc....C....909 393-4400
4950 Edison Ave Chino (91710) ***(P-3629)***
Omnical Inc....F....818 837-7531
557 Jessie St San Fernando (91340) ***(P-22059)***
Omnicell Inc....F....408 907-8868
725 Sycamore Dr Milpitas (95035) ***(P-14957)***
Omnicell Inc (PA)....B....650 251-6100
590 E Middlefield Rd Mountain View (94043) ***(P-14958)***
Omnify Software, Foster City *Also called Arena Solutions Inc* ***(P-23623)***
Omnimax International Inc....C....951 928-1000
28921 Us Highway 74 Sun City (92585) ***(P-11974)***
Omniprint Inc....E....949 833-0080
1923 E Deere Ave Santa Ana (92705) ***(P-15299)***
Omnirax, Sausalito *Also called Sausalito Craftworks Inc* ***(P-22569)***
Omnisil....E....805 644-2514
5401 Everglades St Ventura (93003) ***(P-18449)***
Omnitec Precision Mfg Inc....F....408 437-9056
435 Queens Ln San Jose (95112) ***(P-16261)***
Omnitracs Midco LLC (PA)....E....858 651-5812
9276 Scranton Rd Ste 200 San Diego (92121) ***(P-24224)***
Omnitron Systems Tech Inc....D....949 250-6510
38 Tesla Irvine (92618) ***(P-15300)***
Omnivision Technologies Inc (PA)....C....408 567-3000
4275 Burton Dr Santa Clara (95054) ***(P-18450)***
Omnivore Technologies Inc....E....800 293-4058
1191 B St Hayward (94541) ***(P-24225)***

Mergent e-mail: customerrelations@mergent.com
1190
2020 California
Manufacturers Register
(P-0000) Products & Services Section entry number
(PA)=Parent Co (HQ)=Headquarters (DH)=Div Headquarters

Omniyig Inc ....E....408 988-0843
3350 Scott Blvd Bldg 66 Santa Clara (95054) *(P-19039)*
Omron Adept Technologies, Inc., San Ramon *Also called Omron Robotics Safety Tech Inc (P-13830)*
Omron Delta Tau, Chatsworth *Also called Delta Tau Data Systems Inc Cal (P-14808)*
Omron Robotics Safety Tech Inc (HQ) ....C....925 245-3400
4550 Norris Canyon Rd # 150 San Ramon (94583) *(P-13830)*
Omron Scientific Tech Inc (HQ) ....C....510 608-3400
6550 Dumbarton Cir Fremont (94555) *(P-20913)*
Omstar Environmental Products, Wilmington *Also called D-1280-X Inc (P-9044)*
Omtek Inc ....E....805 687-9629
3722 Calle Cita Santa Barbara (93105) *(P-18451)*
Omxie, Chino *Also called Max Smt Corp (P-14635)*
Omya California Inc ....D....760 248-7306
7299 Crystal Creek Rd Lucerne Valley (92356) *(P-7513)*
On Press Printing Service Inc ....F....909 799-9599
1440 Richardson St San Bernardino (92408) *(P-6759)*
On Semiconductor Connectivity (HQ) ....D....669 209-5500
1704 Automation Pkwy San Jose (95131) *(P-18452)*
On-Gard Metals Inc ....F....562 622-9057
8638 Cleta St Downey (90241) *(P-11206)*
On-Line Power Incorporated (PA) ....E....323 721-5017
14000 S Broadway Los Angeles (90061) *(P-16565)*
On-Line Stampco Inc ....F....800 373-5614
3341 Hancock St San Diego (92110) *(P-22954)*
On24 Inc (PA) ....B....877 202-9599
50 Beale St Ste 800 San Francisco (94105) *(P-24226)*
Onanon Inc ....E....408 262-8990
720 S Milpitas Blvd Milpitas (95035) *(P-18783)*
Onc Holdings Inc ....F....415 243-3343
832 Folsom St Ste 1001 San Francisco (94107) *(P-24227)*
Oncology Care Systems Group, Concord *Also called Siemens Med Solutions USA Inc (P-22309)*
Oncomed Pharmaceuticals Inc ....D....650 995-8200
800 Chesapeake Dr Redwood City (94063) *(P-8052)*
Oncore Manufacturing LLC ....D....510 516-5488
6600 Stevenson Blvd Fremont (94538) *(P-17943)*
Oncore Manufacturing LLC ....C....760 737-6777
237 Via Vera Cruz San Marcos (92078) *(P-17944)*
Oncore Manufacturing Svcs Inc ....C....510 360-2222
9340 Owensmouth Ave Chatsworth (91311) *(P-17945)*
Oncore Velocity, San Marcos *Also called Oncore Manufacturing LLC (P-17944)*
Oncternal Therapeutics Inc (PA) ....E....858 434-1113
12230 El Camino Real San Diego (92130) *(P-8053)*
Ondax Inc ....F....626 357-9600
850 E Duarte Rd Monrovia (91016) *(P-21388)*
One At A Time ....F....805 461-1784
3518 El Camino Real 195 Atascadero (93422) *(P-22651)*
One Bella Casa Inc ....E....707 746-8300
101 Lucas Valley Rd # 130 San Rafael (94903) *(P-3630)*
One Color Communications, Alameda *Also called ONe Color Communications LLC (P-7380)*
ONe Color Communications LLC ....D....510 263-1840
1851 Harbor Bay Pkwy Alameda (94502) *(P-7380)*
One Hat One Hand LLC ....E....415 822-2020
1335 Yosemite Ave San Francisco (94124) *(P-3471)*
One Internet America LLC ....F....951 377-8844
350 S Milliken Ave Ste E Ontario (91761) *(P-6300)*
One Lambda Inc (HQ) ....D....818 702-0042
21001 Kittridge St Canoga Park (91303) *(P-8244)*
One Natural Experience, Monrovia *Also called One World Enterprises LLC (P-2102)*
One Park Place, San Diego *Also called Internet Strategy Inc (P-24029)*
One Stop Label Corporation ....F....909 230-9380
1641 S Baker Ave Ontario (91761) *(P-7156)*
One Stop Systems Inc (PA) ....D....760 745-9883
2235 Entp St Ste 110 Escondido (92029) *(P-15301)*
One Stop Systems Inc ....E....858 530-2511
2235 Entp St Ste 110 Escondido (92029) *(P-15302)*
One Time Utilities Sales, Santa Ana *Also called One Time Utility Sales Inc (P-16952)*
One Time Utility Sales Inc ....E....714 953-5700
501 N Garfield St Santa Ana (92701) *(P-16952)*
One Touch Office Technology, Torrance *Also called One Touch Solutions Inc (P-14333)*
One Touch Solutions Inc ....F....310 320-6868
370 Amapola Ave Ste 106 Torrance (90501) *(P-14333)*
One Up Manufacturing LLC ....E....310 749-8347
2555 E Del Amo Blvd Compton (90221) *(P-5169)*
One Vine Wines, Poway *Also called Martellotto Inc (P-1812)*
One World Enterprises LLC ....E....310 802-4220
1333 S Mayflower Ave # 100 Monrovia (91016) *(P-2102)*
One World Meat Company LLC ....F....800 782-1670
6363 Knott Ave Buena Park (90620) *(P-484)*
One-Way Manufacturing Inc ....E....714 630-8833
1195 N Osprey Cir Anaheim (92807) *(P-13478)*
ONeil Capital Management ....D....310 448-6400
12655 Beatrice St Los Angeles (90066) *(P-6961)*
ONeil Digital Solutions LLC ....C....310 448-6407
12655 Beatrice St Los Angeles (90066) *(P-6760)*
ONeil KG Bags ....F....415 460-0111
124 Belvedere St Ste 12 San Rafael (94901) *(P-10201)*
ONeill Wetsuits LLC (PA) ....D....831 475-7500
1071 41st Ave Santa Cruz (95062) *(P-9347)*
Onesolution Light and Control ....E....714 490-5540
225 S Loara St Anaheim (92802) *(P-17150)*
Onesun LLC ....F....415 230-4277
27 Gate 5 Rd Sausalito (94965) *(P-18453)*
Oneto Manufacturing Company ....F....650 875-1710
146 S Maple Ave South San Francisco (94080) *(P-12318)*
Onex Automation, Duarte *Also called Onex Enterprises Corporation (P-14841)*
Onex Enterprises Corporation ....F....626 358-6639
1824 Flower Ave Duarte (91010) *(P-14841)*
Onex Rf Automation Inc ....F....626 358-6639
1824 Flower Ave Duarte (91010) *(P-14249)*
Onki Corp ....F....510 567-8875
294 Hegenberger Rd Oakland (94621) *(P-19732)*
Only You Rx Skin Care, Valencia *Also called Professional Skin Care Inc (P-8569)*
Onnet Usa Inc ....E....408 457-3992
2870 Zanker Rd Ste 205 San Jose (95134) *(P-6301)*
Onnik Shoe Company Inc ....E....818 506-5353
11443 Chandler Blvd North Hollywood (91601) *(P-10174)*
Onq Solutions Inc (PA) ....E....650 262-4150
24540 Clawiter Rd Hayward (94545) *(P-4993)*
Onset Medical Corporation ....E....949 716-1100
13900 Alton Pkwy Ste 120 Irvine (92618) *(P-21848)*
Onshore Technologies Inc ....E....310 533-4888
2771 Plaza Dl Amo 802-8 Torrance (90503) *(P-19040)*
Onspec Technology Partners Inc ....E....408 654-7627
975 Comstock St Santa Clara (95054) *(P-18454)*
Ontario Binding Company Inc ....D....909 947-7866
15951 Promontory Rd Chino Hills (91709) *(P-7340)*
Ontario Foam Products, Ontario *Also called Androp Packaging Inc (P-5196)*
Ontera Inc ....C....831 222-2193
2161 Delaware Ave Ste B Santa Cruz (95060) *(P-18455)*
Onyx Industries Inc (PA) ....D....310 539-8830
1227 254th St Harbor City (90710) *(P-12643)*
Onyx Industries Inc ....E....310 851-6161
521 W Rosecrans Ave Gardena (90248) *(P-12644)*
Onyx Optics Inc ....F....925 833-1969
6551 Sierra Ln Dublin (94568) *(P-21389)*
Onyx Pharmaceuticals Inc ....A....650 266-0000
1 Amgen Center Dr Newbury Park (91320) *(P-8054)*
Onyx Shutters, City of Industry *Also called Tje Company (P-11986)*
Ooglow ....F....530 899-9927
17250 Margaret Dr Jamestown (95327) *(P-2576)*
Ooshirts Inc (PA) ....D....866 660-8667
41454 Christy St Fremont (94538) *(P-7157)*
Op-Test, Redding *Also called Sof-Tek Integrators Inc (P-21122)*
Opal Moon Winery LLC ....F....707 996-0420
21660 8th St E Ste A Sonoma (95476) *(P-1846)*
Opal Service Inc (PA) ....E....714 935-0900
282 S Anita Dr Orange (92868) *(P-11017)*
Open Dmain Sphinx Sltions Corp ....F....510 420-0846
3871 Piedmont Ave 300 Oakland (94611) *(P-24228)*
Open-Xchange Inc (PA) ....F....914 332-5720
530 Lytton Ave Fl 2 Palo Alto (94301) *(P-6302)*
Openclovis Solutions Inc ....E....707 981-7120
765 Baywood Dr Ste 336 Petaluma (94954) *(P-24229)*
Openpro Erp Software, Fountain Valley *Also called Openpro Inc (P-24230)*
Openpro Inc ....F....714 378-4600
10061 Talbert Ave Ste 228 Fountain Valley (92708) *(P-24230)*
Opentv Inc (HQ) ....C....415 962-5000
275 Sacramento St Ste Sl1 San Francisco (94111) *(P-24231)*
Openwave Mobility Inc (PA) ....E....650 480-7200
400 Seaport Ct Ste 104 Redwood City (94063) *(P-24232)*
Opera Commerce LLC ....F....650 625-1262
1875 S Grant St Ste 800 San Mateo (94402) *(P-24233)*
Opera Patisserie Fines Inc ....E....858 536-5800
8480 Redwood Creek Ln San Diego (92126) *(P-1347)*
Opera Software Americas LLC ....F....650 625-1262
1875 S Grant St Ste 750 San Mateo (94402) *(P-24234)*
Ophir Rf Inc ....E....310 306-5556
5300 Beethoven St Fl 3 Los Angeles (90066) *(P-17609)*
Ophthonix, San Diego *Also called Trex Enterprises Corporation (P-14992)*
Ophthonix Inc ....D....760 842-5600
900 Glenneyre St Laguna Beach (92651) *(P-22378)*
Opiant Pharmaceuticals Inc ....F....310 598-5410
201 Santa Monica Blvd # 500 Santa Monica (90401) *(P-8055)*
Opmp, Tracy *Also called Omega Precision Machine (P-16259)*
Opolo Vineyards Inc (PA) ....E....805 238-9593
7110 Vineyard Dr Paso Robles (93446) *(P-1847)*
Opolo Vineyards Inc ....F....805 238-9593
2801 Townsgate Rd Ste 123 Westlake Village (91361) *(P-1848)*
Opotek Inc ....F....760 929-0770
2233 Faraday Ave Ste E Carlsbad (92008) *(P-22291)*
Opotek LLC ....F....760 929-0770
2233 Faraday Ave Ste E Carlsbad (92008) *(P-21390)*
Oppo Original Corp ....F....909 444-3000
108 Brea Canyon Rd 118 Walnut (91789) *(P-10175)*
Ops Technology, San Francisco *Also called Realpage Inc (P-24344)*
Opsveda Inc ....F....408 628-0461
4030 Moorpark Ave Ste 107 San Jose (95117) *(P-24235)*
Optasense Inc ....F....408 970-3500
3350 Scott Blvd Bldg 1 Santa Clara (95054) *(P-18456)*
Optec, Carlsbad *Also called Optimized Fuel Technologies (P-23432)*
Optec Displays Inc ....D....626 369-7188
1700 S De Soto Pl Ste A Ontario (91761) *(P-23170)*
Optec Laser Systems LLC ....E....858 220-1070
11622 El Camino Real San Diego (92130) *(P-7158)*
Optek Group Inc ....E....949 629-2558
23 Corporate Plaza Dr # 150 Newport Beach (92660) *(P-22292)*
Optel-Matic Inc ....F....626 444-2671
11221 Thienes Ave El Monte (91733) *(P-16262)*
Optex Incorporated ....F....800 966-7839
18730 S Wilmington Ave # 100 Compton (90220) *(P-17751)*
Opti Lite Optical ....E....323 932-6828
5552 W Adams Blvd Los Angeles (90016) *(P-22379)*
Opti-Forms Inc ....D....951 296-1300
42310 Winchester Rd Temecula (92590) *(P-13065)*

ALPHABETIC

Optibase Inc (HQ)...E...800 451-5101
931 Benecia Ave Sunnyvale (94085) ***(P-15303)***
Optic Arts Inc...E...213 250-6069
716 Monterey Pass Rd Monterey Park (91754) ***(P-17061)***
Optical Coating Laboratory LLC (HQ)...B...707 545-6440
2789 Northpoint Pkwy Santa Rosa (95407) ***(P-13215)***
Optical Physics Company...F...818 880-2907
4133 Guardian St G Simi Valley (93063) ***(P-21391)***
Optical Sensor Division, Fremont *Also called Omron Scientific Tech Inc* ***(P-20913)***
Optical Zonu Corporation...F...818 780-9701
7510 Hazeltine Ave Van Nuys (91405) ***(P-17396)***
Opticolor Inc...F...714 893-8839
15281 Graham St Huntington Beach (92649) ***(P-9942)***
Opticomm Corp...E...626 293-3400
2015 Chestnut St Alhambra (91803) ***(P-11313)***
Optim Microwave Inc...E...805 482-7093
4020 Adolfo Rd Camarillo (93012) ***(P-17610)***
Optima Technology Corporation...B...949 253-5768
17062 Murphy Ave Irvine (92614) ***(P-15304)***
Optimedica Corporation...C...408 850-8600
510 Cottonwood Dr Milpitas (95035) ***(P-21849)***
Optimis Services Inc...E...310 230-2780
225 Mantua Rd Pacific Palisades (90272) ***(P-24236)***
Optimization Corporation...F...510 614-5890
14680 Wicks Blvd San Leandro (94577) ***(P-14672)***
Optimized Fuel Technologies...F...760 444-5556
5858 Dryden Pl Ste 238 Carlsbad (92008) ***(P-23432)***
Optimum Bioenergy Intl Corp...F...714 903-8872
2463 Pomona Rd Corona (92880) ***(P-7680)***
Optimum Design Associates Inc (PA)...D...925 401-2004
1075 Serpentine Ln Ste A Pleasanton (94566) ***(P-19041)***
Optimum Solutions Group LLC...C...415 954-7100
419 Ponderosa Ct Lafayette (94549) ***(P-24237)***
Optiscan Biomedical Corp...E...510 342-5800
24590 Clawiter Rd Hayward (94545) ***(P-21850)***
Optiscan Ltd...F...760 777-9595
48290 Vista Calico Ste A La Quinta (92253) ***(P-21392)***
Optivus Proton Therapy Inc...D...909 799-8300
1475 Victoria Ct San Bernardino (92408) ***(P-21513)***
Optiworks Inc (PA)...D...510 438-4560
47211 Bayside Pkwy Fremont (94538) ***(P-10323)***
Opto 22...C...951 695-3000
43044 Business Park Dr Temecula (92590) ***(P-19042)***
Optodyne Incorporation...E...310 635-7481
1180 W Mahalo Pl Rancho Dominguez (90220) ***(P-17611)***
Optoelectronix Inc (PA)...F...408 437-9488
111 W Saint John St # 588 San Jose (95113) ***(P-18457)***
Optoma Technology Inc...C...510 897-8600
47697 Westinghouse Dr # 100 Fremont (94539) ***(P-22445)***
Optoplex Corporation (PA)...D...510 490-9930
48500 Kato Rd Fremont (94538) ***(P-17397)***
Optosigma Corporation...E...949 851-5881
3210 S Croddy Way Santa Ana (92704) ***(P-21393)***
Optovue Inc (PA)...D...510 623-8868
2800 Bayview Dr Fremont (94538) ***(P-21851)***
Optronics, Goleta *Also called Karl Storz Imaging Inc* ***(P-21496)***
Opus 12 Incorporated...F...917 349-3740
614 Bancroft Way Ste B Berkeley (94710) ***(P-8759)***
Opus One Winery LLC (PA)...D...707 944-9442
7900 St Helena Hwy Oakville (94562) ***(P-1849)***
or Technology, Chula Vista *Also called Mk Digital Direct Inc* ***(P-21265)***
Oracle, San Mateo *Also called Netsuite Inc* ***(P-24197)***
Oracle America Inc...C...408 276-4300
4220 Network Cir Santa Clara (95054) ***(P-24238)***
Oracle America Inc (HQ)...A...650 506-7000
500 Oracle Pkwy Redwood City (94065) ***(P-14959)***
Oracle America Inc...F...303 272-6473
1001 Sunset Blvd Rocklin (95765) ***(P-24239)***
Oracle America Inc...D...415 908-3609
475 Sansome St Fl 15 San Francisco (94111) ***(P-24240)***
Oracle America Inc...F...408 702-5945
600 Oracle Pkwy Redwood City (94065) ***(P-24241)***
Oracle America Inc...C...408 276-3331
4120 Network Cir Santa Clara (95054) ***(P-24242)***
Oracle America Inc...D...925 694-3314
5815 Owens Dr Pleasanton (94588) ***(P-24243)***
Oracle America Inc...E...818 905-0200
15821 Ventura Blvd # 270 Encino (91436) ***(P-24244)***
Oracle America Inc...D...858 625-5044
9540 Towne Centre Dr San Diego (92121) ***(P-24245)***
Oracle America Inc...F...909 605-0222
3401 Centre Lake Dr # 410 Ontario (91761) ***(P-24246)***
Oracle America Inc...C...408 276-7534
4230 Leonard Stocking Dr Santa Clara (95054) ***(P-24247)***
Oracle Corporation...C...713 654-0919
279 Barnes Rd Tustin (92782) ***(P-24248)***
Oracle Corporation...E...415 834-9731
475 Sansome St Fl 15 San Francisco (94111) ***(P-24249)***
Oracle Corporation...B...650 607-5402
214 Clarence Ave Sunnyvale (94086) ***(P-24250)***
Oracle Corporation...B...650 678-3612
1408 Antigua Ln Foster City (94404) ***(P-24251)***
Oracle Corporation...B...408 421-2890
1490 Newhall St Santa Clara (95050) ***(P-24252)***
Oracle Corporation...B...408 276-5552
231 Kerry Dr Santa Clara (95050) ***(P-24253)***
Oracle Corporation...B...408 276-3822
3084 Thurman Dr San Jose (95148) ***(P-24254)***
Oracle Corporation...C...858 202-0648
9890 Towne Centre Dr # 150 San Diego (92121) ***(P-24255)***
Oracle Corporation...B...650 506-9864
3532 Eastin Pl Santa Clara (95051) ***(P-24256)***
Oracle Corporation...B...408 390-8623
372 Calero Ave San Jose (95123) ***(P-24257)***
Oracle Corporation...C...415 402-7200
525 Market St San Francisco (94105) ***(P-24258)***
Oracle Corporation...B...916 435-8342
6224 Hummingbird Ln Rocklin (95765) ***(P-24259)***
Oracle Corporation...B...877 767-2253
5805 Owens Dr Pleasanton (94588) ***(P-24260)***
Oracle Corporation...B...925 694-6258
3925 Emerald Isle Ln San Jose (95135) ***(P-24261)***
Oracle Corporation...B...510 471-6971
5863 Carmel Way Union City (94587) ***(P-24262)***
Oracle Corporation...B...310 258-7500
200 Crprate Pinte Ste 200 Culver City (90230) ***(P-24263)***
Oracle Corporation...B...310 343-7405
200 N Pacific Coast Hwy # 400 El Segundo (90245) ***(P-24264)***
Oracle Corporation...B...916 315-3500
1001 Sunset Blvd Rocklin (95765) ***(P-24265)***
Oracle Corporation...E...650 506-7000
475 Sansome St Fl 15 San Francisco (94111) ***(P-24266)***
Oracle Systems Corporation...D...818 817-2900
200 Crprate Pinte Ste 200 Culver City (90230) ***(P-24267)***
Oracle Systems Corporation...D...650 506-8648
102 Santa Barbara Ave Daly City (94014) ***(P-24268)***
Oracle Systems Corporation...B...650 654-7606
301 Island Pkwy Belmont (94002) ***(P-24269)***
Oracle Systems Corporation...C...650 506-6780
500 Oracle Pwky San Mateo (94403) ***(P-24270)***
Oracle Systems Corporation...F...650 506-5062
501 Island Pkwy Belmont (94002) ***(P-24271)***
Oracle Systems Corporation...B...650 506-0300
10 Twin Dolphin Dr Redwood City (94065) ***(P-24272)***
Oracle Systems Corporation...F...650 378-1351
1840 Gateway Dr Ste 250 San Mateo (94404) ***(P-24273)***
Oracle Systems Corporation...E...650 506-5887
300 Oracle Pkwy Redwood City (94065) ***(P-24274)***
Oracle Systems Corporation...B...925 694-3000
5840 Owens Dr Pleasanton (94588) ***(P-24275)***
Oracle Systems Corporation...D...949 224-1000
2010 Main St Ste 450 Irvine (92614) ***(P-24276)***
Oracle Systems Corporation...B...949 623-9460
17901 Von Karman Ave # 800 Irvine (92614) ***(P-24277)***
Oracle Taleo LLC...A...925 452-3000
4140 Dublin Blvd Ste 400 Dublin (94568) ***(P-24278)***
Oral Essentials Inc...F...888 773-5273
436 N Roxbury Dr Beverly Hills (90210) ***(P-8551)***
Orange Bang Inc...E...818 833-1000
13115 Telfair Ave Sylmar (91342) ***(P-2103)***
Orange Circle Studio Corp...D...949 727-0800
8687 Research Dr Ste 150 Irvine (92618) ***(P-7159)***
Orange Cnty Mlt-Hsing Svc Corp...F...714 245-9500
525 Cabrillo Park Dr # 125 Santa Ana (92701) ***(P-5995)***
Orange Cnty Name Plate Co Inc...D...714 522-7693
13201 Arctic Cir Santa Fe Springs (90670) ***(P-23171)***
Orange Cnty Prtg Graphics Inc...F...949 464-9898
303 Broadway St Ste 108 Laguna Beach (92651) ***(P-7160)***
Orange Coast Kommunications...E...949 862-1133
1124 Main St Ste A Irvine (92614) ***(P-5996)***
Orange Coast Magazine, Irvine *Also called Orange Coast Kommunications* ***(P-5996)***
Orange Coast Reprographics Inc...E...949 548-5571
659 W 19th St Costa Mesa (92627) ***(P-6761)***
Orange Container Inc...D...714 547-9617
1984 E Mcfadden Ave Santa Ana (92705) ***(P-5249)***
Orange Corporation...F...323 266-0700
1430 S Grande Vista Ave Los Angeles (90023) ***(P-3457)***
Orange County Business Journal, Irvine *Also called Cbj LP* ***(P-5901)***
Orange County Erectors Inc...E...714 502-8455
517 E La Palma Ave Anaheim (92801) ***(P-12568)***
Orange County Label Co Inc...F...714 437-1010
301 W Dyer Rd Ste D Santa Ana (92707) ***(P-7161)***
Orange County Plating Coinc...E...714 532-4610
940 N Parker St 960 Orange (92867) ***(P-13066)***
Orange County Printing, Irvine *Also called Kelmscott Communications LLC* ***(P-6674)***
Orange County Register, El Toro *Also called Freedom Communications Inc* ***(P-5635)***
Orange County Register, The, Santa Ana *Also called Digital First Media LLC* ***(P-5615)***
Orange County Sandbagger, Orange *Also called Sandwood Enterprises* ***(P-13745)***
Orange County Screw Products...E...714 630-7433
2993 E La Palma Ave Anaheim (92806) ***(P-16263)***
Orange Cove Mountain Times, Reedley *Also called Midvalley Publishing Inc* ***(P-5754)***
Orange Metal Spinning and Stam...F...714 754-0770
2601 Orange Ave Santa Ana (92707) ***(P-12851)***
ORANGE PACK SOLUTION, San Diego *Also called Hwa In America Inc* ***(P-18939)***
Orange Woodworks Inc...E...714 997-2600
1215 N Parker St Orange (92867) ***(P-4100)***
Orangegrid LLC...E...657 220-1519
145 S State College Blvd # 350 Brea (92821) ***(P-24279)***
Oratec Interventions Inc (HQ)...F...901 396-2121
3696 Haven Ave Redwood City (94063) ***(P-22293)***
Orb Media Broadcasting Inc...F...323 246-4524
3125 W Beverly Blvd Montebello (90640) ***(P-6303)***
Orban, San Leandro *Also called Crl Systems Inc* ***(P-17497)***
Orbit Industries, Grass Valley *Also called Countis Industries Inc* ***(P-10476)***
Orbit Systems, Laguna Hills *Also called Aot Electronics Inc* ***(P-15157)***
Orbita Corp (PA)...F...213 746-4783
1136 Crocker St Los Angeles (90021) ***(P-3503)***
Orbital Sciences Corporation...D...703 406-5000
20 Ryan Ranch Rd Ste 214 Monterey (93940) ***(P-20670)***

Orbital Sciences Corporation ....F....818 887-8345
1151 W Reeves Ave Ridgecrest (93555) ***(P-20468)***
Orbital Sciences Corporation ....D....805 734-5400
Talo Rd Bldg 1555 Lompoc (93437) ***(P-20453)***
Orbits Lightwave Inc ....F....626 513-7400
41 S Chester Ave Pasadena (91106) ***(P-10324)***
Orbo Corporation ....E....562 806-6171
1000 S Euclid St La Habra (90631) ***(P-4867)***
Orbot ....F....760 295-2100
3275 Corporate Vw Vista (92081) ***(P-13739)***
Orbotech Lt Solar LLC ....E....408 414-3777
5970 Optical Ct San Jose (95138) ***(P-18458)***
Orca Systems Inc ....E....858 679-9295
3990 Old Town Ave San Diego (92110) ***(P-17946)***
Orchard Harvest, Yuba City *Also called Orchard Machinery Corporation* ***(P-13655)***
Orchard Machinery Corporation (PA) ....D....530 673-2822
2700 Colusa Hwy Yuba City (95993) ***(P-13655)***
Orchard Printing ....F....510 490-1736
325 Aleut Ct Fremont (94539) ***(P-6762)***
Orchard's Metal Fabrication, Riverside *Also called Omf Performance Products* ***(P-20517)***
Orco Block & Hardscape (PA) ....D....714 527-2239
11100 Beach Blvd Stanton (90680) ***(P-10511)***
Orco Block & Hardscape ....E....760 757-1780
3501 Oceanside Blvd Oceanside (92056) ***(P-10512)***
Orco Block & Hardscape ....E....951 928-3619
26380 Palomar Rd Romoland (92585) ***(P-10513)***
Orcon Aerospace, Union City *Also called Lamart Corporation* ***(P-10963)***
Orcon Aerospace ....C....510 489-8100
2600 Central Ave Ste E Union City (94587) ***(P-20189)***
Ordway Metal Polishing ....E....323 225-3373
1901 N San Fernando Rd Los Angeles (90065) ***(P-13067)***
OReilly Media Inc (PA) ....C....707 827-7000
1005 Gravenstein Hwy N Sebastopol (95472) ***(P-6131)***
Orexigen Therapeutics Inc ....D....858 875-8600
3344 N Torrey Pines Ct # 200 La Jolla (92037) ***(P-8056)***
Orfila Vineyards & Winery, Escondido *Also called Orfila Vineyards Inc* ***(P-1850)***
Orfila Vineyards Inc (PA) ....E....760 738-6500
13455 San Pasqual Rd Escondido (92025) ***(P-1850)***
Orfium, Santa Monica *Also called Hexacorp Ltd* ***(P-23981)***
Orgain Inc ....F....949 930-0039
16631 Millikan Ave Irvine (92606) ***(P-2104)***
Organ-O-Sil Fiber Co Inc ....E....714 847-8310
17616 Gothard St Ste B Huntington Beach (92647) ***(P-19733)***
Organic Bottle Dctg Co LLC ....E....951 335-4600
575 Alcoa Cir Ste B Corona (92880) ***(P-5170)***
Organic Horseradish Co ....E....530 664-3862
7890 County Road 120 Tulelake (96134) ***(P-893)***
Organic Infusions Inc (PA) ....F....805 419-4118
2390 Las Posas Rd Camarillo (93010) ***(P-9056)***
Organic Mattresses Inc ....E....530 790-6723
1335 Harter Pkwy Yuba City (95993) ***(P-4734)***
Organic Milling Inc ....D....800 638-8686
505 W Allen Ave San Dimas (91773) ***(P-1031)***
Organic Milling Corporation (PA) ....C....909 599-0961
505 W Allen Ave San Dimas (91773) ***(P-1032)***
Organic Milling Corporation ....F....909 305-0185
305 S Acacia St Ste A San Dimas (91773) ***(P-1033)***
Organic Spices (PA) ....E....510 440-1044
4180 Business Center Dr Fremont (94538) ***(P-2577)***
Organicgirl LLC ....A....831 758-7800
900 Work St Salinas (93901) ***(P-2578)***
Organicsorb LLC ....F....310 795-4011
630 S Los Angeles St Los Angeles (90014) ***(P-393)***
Organosil Fiber Co, Huntington Beach *Also called Organ-O-Sil Fiber Co Inc* ***(P-19733)***
Organovo Inc ....C....858 224-1000
6275 Ncny Rdge Dr Ste 110 San Diego (92121) ***(P-8319)***
Orgatech Omegalux, Orange *Also called Western Lighting Inds Inc* ***(P-17085)***
Oric Pharmaceuticals Inc ....E....650 918-8818
240 E Grand Ave South San Francisco (94080) ***(P-8057)***
Orient & Flume Art Glass Co ....E....530 893-0373
2161 Park Ave Chico (95928) ***(P-10325)***
Oriental Odysseys Inc ....E....510 357-6100
14557 Griffith St San Leandro (94577) ***(P-23433)***
Orientex, Pittsburg *Also called Ramar International Corp* ***(P-422)***
Orientex Foods, Pittsburg *Also called Ramar International Corp* ***(P-664)***
Origin LLC (HQ) ....E....818 848-1648
119 E Graham Pl Burbank (91502) ***(P-23434)***
Original Distributor Exchange ....F....323 583-8707
2538 E 52nd St Huntington Park (90255) ***(P-19198)***
Original Glass Design, San Jose *Also called Beveled Edge Inc* ***(P-10342)***
Original Letterman Jacket Co, Paramount *Also called Logos Plus Inc* ***(P-3797)***
Original Pattern Inc ....F....510 844-4833
292 4th St Oakland (94607) ***(P-1554)***
Original Pattern Beer, Oakland *Also called Original Pattern Inc* ***(P-1554)***
Original Watermen Inc ....F....760 599-0990
1198 Joshua Way Vista (92081) ***(P-2973)***
Originals 22 Inc ....F....909 993-5050
13889 Pipeline Ave Chino (91710) ***(P-16983)***
Originclear Inc (PA) ....E....323 939-6645
525 S Hewitt St Los Angeles (90013) ***(P-15553)***
Orion Chandelier Inc ....F....714 668-9668
2202 S Wright St Santa Ana (92705) ***(P-16984)***
Orion Group, The, Kensington *Also called Sempervirens Group* ***(P-8839)***
Orion Manufacturing Inc ....C....408 955-9001
5550 Hellyer Ave San Jose (95138) ***(P-17947)***
Orion Ornamental Iron Inc ....E....818 752-0688
6918 Tujunga Ave North Hollywood (91605) ***(P-11617)***
Orion Plastics Corporation ....D....310 223-0370
700 W Carob St Compton (90220) ***(P-7589)***
Orion Tech, City of Industry *Also called Compucase Corporation* ***(P-15018)***
Orion Woodcraft, San Diego *Also called T L Clark Co Inc* ***(P-4252)***
Orlando Spring Corp ....E....562 594-8411
5341 Argosy Ave Huntington Beach (92649) ***(P-13383)***
Orly International Inc ....D....818 994-1001
7710 Haskell Ave Van Nuys (91406) ***(P-8552)***
Ormco Corporation (HQ) ....D....714 516-7400
1717 W Collins Ave Orange (92867) ***(P-22176)***
Ormet Circuits Inc ....E....858 831-0010
6555 Ncny Rdge Dr Ste 200 San Diego (92121) ***(P-19043)***
Orora Visual LLC ....D....714 879-2400
1600 E Valencia Dr Fullerton (92831) ***(P-7162)***
Orora Visual TX LLC ....D....323 258-4111
3116 W Avenue 32 Los Angeles (90065) ***(P-7163)***
Oroweat, Sacramento *Also called Bimbo Bakeries Usa Inc* ***(P-1164)***
Oroweat Foods, San Diego *Also called Bimbo Bakeries Usa Inc* ***(P-1154)***
Oroweat Foods, Anaheim *Also called Bimbo Bakeries Usa Inc* ***(P-1158)***
Ortech Inc ....E....916 549-9696
6760 Folsom Blvd 100 Sacramento (95819) ***(P-10448)***
Ortech Advanced Ceramics, Sacramento *Also called Ortech Inc* ***(P-10448)***
Ortega Manufacturing Inc ....F....951 766-9363
3960 Industrial Ave Hemet (92545) ***(P-23435)***
Ortel A Division Emcore Co (HQ) ....F....626 293-3400
2015 Chestnut St Alhambra (91803) ***(P-18459)***
Orthaheel, San Rafael *Also called Vionic Group LLC* ***(P-10164)***
Orthera, San Diego *Also called Biom LLC* ***(P-21986)***
Ortho Engineering Inc (PA) ....E....310 559-5996
5759 Uplander Way Culver City (90230) ***(P-22060)***
Ortho Organizers Inc ....C....760 448-8600
1822 Aston Ave Carlsbad (92008) ***(P-22177)***
Ortho-Clinical Diagnostics Inc ....E....908 704-5910
1401 Red Hawk Cir E307 Fremont (94538) ***(P-8245)***
Ortho-Clinical Diagnostics Inc ....E....714 639-2323
612 W Katella Ave Ste B Orange (92867) ***(P-8246)***
Orthodental International Inc ....D....760 357-8070
280 Campillo St Ste J Calexico (92231) ***(P-22178)***
Ortronics Inc ....C....714 776-5420
1443 S Sunkist St Anaheim (92806) ***(P-12319)***
Oryx Advanced Materials Inc (PA) ....E....510 249-1158
46458 Fremont Blvd Fremont (94538) ***(P-15069)***
Osca-Arcosa, San Diego *Also called O & S California Inc* ***(P-19371)***
Oscar Printing, San Francisco *Also called La Brothers Enterprise Inc* ***(P-6689)***
Ose Usa Inc (HQ) ....F....408 452-9080
1737 N 1st St Ste 350 San Jose (95112) ***(P-18460)***
OSI Electronics Inc (HQ) ....C....310 978-0516
12533 Chadron Ave Hawthorne (90250) ***(P-17948)***
OSI Industries LLC ....E....951 684-4500
1155 Mt Vernon Ave Riverside (92507) ***(P-23436)***
OSI Optoelectronics Inc ....E....805 987-0146
1240 Avenida Acaso Camarillo (93012) ***(P-18461)***
OSI Subsidiary Inc ....B....310 978-0516
12525 Chadron Ave Hawthorne (90250) ***(P-19373)***
OSI Systems Inc (PA) ....B....310 978-0516
12525 Chadron Ave Hawthorne (90250) ***(P-18462)***
Osio International Inc ....F....714 935-9700
2550 E Cerritos Ave Anaheim (92806) ***(P-5333)***
Osmosis Technology Inc ....E....714 670-9303
6900 Hermosa Cir Buena Park (90620) ***(P-15554)***
Osmotik, Buena Park *Also called Osmosis Technology Inc* ***(P-15554)***
Osr Enterprises Inc ....E....805 925-1831
1910 E Stowell Rd Santa Maria (93454) ***(P-24280)***
Osram Sylvania Inc ....B....858 748-5077
13350 Gregg St Ste 101 Poway (92064) ***(P-16868)***
Osram Sylvania Inc ....E....408 922-7200
651 River Oaks Pkwy San Jose (95134) ***(P-18463)***
Oss, Escondido *Also called One Stop Systems Inc* ***(P-15301)***
Osseon LLC ....F....707 636-5940
2301 Circadian Way # 300 Santa Rosa (95407) ***(P-21852)***
Ossur Americas Inc (HQ) ....B....949 362-3883
27051 Towne Centre Dr # 100 Foothill Ranch (92610) ***(P-22061)***
Ossur Americas Inc ....F....949 382-3883
19762 Pauling Foothill Ranch (92610) ***(P-22062)***
Ossur Americas Inc ....E....805 484-2600
27051 Towne Centre Dr # 100 Foothill Ranch (92610) ***(P-22063)***
Ossur North America, Foothill Ranch *Also called Ossur Americas Inc* ***(P-22063)***
Ostoich Diesel Service ....F....909 885-0590
1690 Ashley Way Colton (92324) ***(P-15631)***
Osumo Inc ....F....510 346-6888
1933 Republic Ave San Leandro (94577) ***(P-3805)***
OT Precision Inc ....E....408 435-8818
1450 Seareel Ln San Jose (95131) ***(P-16264)***
Otanez New Creations ....F....951 808-9663
7179 E Columbus Dr Anaheim (92807) ***(P-4928)***
Oti Engineering Cons Inc ....E....209 586-1022
24926 State Highway 108 Ml Wuk Village (95346) ***(P-17612)***
Otis Eyewear, Carlsbad *Also called Leisure Collective Inc* ***(P-22367)***
Otonomy Inc ....D....619 323-2200
4796 Executive Dr San Diego (92121) ***(P-8058)***
Otsuka America Inc (HQ) ....F....415 986-5300
1 Embarcadero Ctr # 2020 San Francisco (94111) ***(P-21514)***
Otsuka America Foods Inc (HQ) ....F....424 219-9425
1 Embarcadero Ctr # 2020 San Francisco (94111) ***(P-2579)***
Ottano Inc ....F....805 547-2088
11555 Los Osos Valley Rd # 201 San Luis Obispo (93405) ***(P-1555)***
Otto ARC Systems Inc ....F....916 939-3400
3921 Sandstone Dr Ste 1 El Dorado Hills (95762) ***(P-24654)***
Otto Instrument Service Inc (PA) ....E....909 930-5800
1441 Valencia Pl Ontario (91761) ***(P-20190)***

Employee Codes: A=Over 500 employees, B=251-500
C=101-250, D=51-100, E=20-50, F=10-19
2020 California
Manfacturers Register
© Mergent Inc. 1-800-342-5647
1193

Ottos Pizza Stix Inc......F......562 519-5304
9040 Sunland Blvd Sun Valley (91352) ***(P-970)***
Oudimentary LLC......F......510 501-5057
43170 Osgood Rd Fremont (94539) ***(P-9013)***
Our Powder Coating Inc......F......562 946-0525
10103 Freeman Ave Santa Fe Springs (90670) ***(P-13216)***
Oussoren Eppel Corporation......F......858 483-6770
12232 Thatcher Ct Poway (92064) ***(P-23172)***
Ouster Inc......D......415 949-0108
350 Treat Ave Ste 1 San Francisco (94110) ***(P-21515)***
Outdoor Creations Inc......F......530 365-6106
2270 Barney Rd Anderson (96007) ***(P-10618)***
Outdoor Dimensions LLC......C......714 578-9555
5325 E Hunter Ave Anaheim (92807) ***(P-4519)***
Outdoor Galore Inc......F......661 831-8662
5010 Young St Bakersfield (93311) ***(P-15386)***
Outdoor Lfstyle Collective LLC......F......858 336-5580
829 Windcrest Dr Carlsbad (92011) ***(P-3188)***
Outdoor Products, View Park *Also called Outdoor Recreation Group* ***(P-3662)***
Outdoor Recreation Group (PA)......E......323 226-0830
3450 Mount Vernon Dr View Park (90008) ***(P-3662)***
Outdoor Sign System Inc (PA)......F......714 692-2052
22603 La Palma Ave # 309 Yorba Linda (92887) ***(P-23173)***
Outlaw Beverage Inc......F......310 424-5077
405 14th St Ste 1000 Oakland (94612) ***(P-1556)***
Outlook Resources Inc......D......714 522-2452
14930 Alondra Blvd La Mirada (90638) ***(P-3751)***
Output Inc......F......310 795-6099
1418 N Spring St Ste 102 Los Angeles (90012) ***(P-24281)***
Outreach Slutions As A Svc LLC......F......800 824-8573
980 9th St Fl 16 Sacramento (95814) ***(P-6304)***
Outsol Inc......F......760 415-8060
5910 Sea Lion Pl Ste 120 Carlsbad (92010) ***(P-9593)***
Outsystems Inc......F......925 804-6189
2603 Camino Ramon Ste 210 San Ramon (94583) ***(P-24282)***
Outword News Magazine......E......916 329-9280
1 Ebbtide Ct Sacramento (95831) ***(P-5789)***
Outword Newsmagazine, Sacramento *Also called Outword News Magazine* ***(P-5789)***
Ovation R&G LLC (PA)......E......310 430-7575
2850 Ocean Park Blvd # 225 Santa Monica (90405) ***(P-17613)***
Oven Fresh Bakery Incorporated......F......650 366-9201
23188 Foley St Hayward (94545) ***(P-1255)***
Over & Over Ready Mix Inc......D......818 983-1588
8216 Tujunga Ave Sun Valley (91352) ***(P-10619)***
Overbeck Machine......E......831 425-5912
2620 Mission St Santa Cruz (95060) ***(P-16265)***
Overhill Farms Inc......C......323 587-5985
431 Isis Ave Inglewood (90301) ***(P-971)***
Overhill Farms Inc (HQ)......E......323 582-9977
2727 E Vernon Ave Vernon (90058) ***(P-972)***
Overhill Farms Inc......C......323 584-4375
3055 E 44th St Vernon (90058) ***(P-973)***
Overland Storage Inc (HQ)......D......858 571-5555
4542 Ruffner St Ste 250 San Diego (92111) ***(P-15070)***
Overlook Vineyards LLC (HQ)......E......707 833-0053
101 Adobe Canyon Rd Kenwood (95452) ***(P-1851)***
Overlook Vineyards LLC......F......707 433-6491
58 W North St Ste 101 Healdsburg (95448) ***(P-1852)***
Owen Magic Supreme Inc......F......626 969-4519
734 N Mckeever Ave Azusa (91702) ***(P-23437)***
Owen Oil Tools Inc......E......661 637-1380
5001 Standard St Bakersfield (93308) ***(P-8906)***
Owen Trailers Inc......E......951 361-4557
9020 Jurupa Rd Riverside (92509) ***(P-19827)***
Owens Corning Sales LLC......C......310 631-1062
1501 N Tamarind Ave Compton (90222) ***(P-9123)***
Owens Design Incorporated......E......510 659-1800
47427 Fremont Blvd Fremont (94538) ***(P-16266)***
Owens-Brockway Glass Cont Inc......D......510 436-2000
3600 Alameda Ave Oakland (94601) ***(P-10290)***
Owens-Illinois Inc......C......209 652-1311
14700 W Schulte Rd Tracy (95377) ***(P-10291)***
Owl Territory Inc......F......800 607-0677
227 Broadway Ste 303 Santa Monica (90401) ***(P-24283)***
Oxbo International Corporation......F......559 897-7012
10825 W Goshen Ave Visalia (93291) ***(P-13656)***
Oxbow Activated Carbon LLC......E......760 630-5724
2535 Jason Ct Oceanside (92056) ***(P-7514)***
Oxford Instrs Asylum RES Inc (HQ)......D......805 696-6466
6310 Hollister Ave Santa Barbara (93117) ***(P-21273)***
Oxford Instruments X-Ray Tech......D......831 439-9729
360 El Pueblo Rd Scotts Valley (95066) ***(P-19044)***
Oxnard Lemon Company......F......805 483-1173
2001 Sunkist Cir Oxnard (93033) ***(P-921)***
Oxnard Pallet Company, Oxnard *Also called E Vasquez Distributors Inc* ***(P-4364)***
Oxnard Prcsion Fabrication Inc......E......805 985-0447
2200 Teal Club Rd Oxnard (93030) ***(P-12320)***
OXY USA Inc......C......661 869-8000
9600 Ming Ave Ste 300 Bakersfield (93311) ***(P-60)***
Ozeki Sake U S A Inc (HQ)......E......831 637-9217
249 Hillcrest Rd Hollister (95023) ***(P-1853)***
Ozmo Inc......E......650 515-3524
1600 Technology Dr San Jose (95110) ***(P-15071)***
Ozmo Devices, San Jose *Also called Ozmo Inc* ***(P-15071)***
Ozone Safe Food Inc......F......951 228-2151
31500 Grape St Lake Elsinore (92532) ***(P-14510)***
Ozotech Inc (PA)......E......530 842-4189
2401 E Oberlin Rd Yreka (96097) ***(P-15555)***
P & E Rubber Processing Inc......E......760 241-2643
15380 Lyons Valley Rd Jamul (91935) ***(P-9348)***
P & F Machine Inc......F......209 667-2515
301 S Broadway Turlock (95380) ***(P-16267)***
P & L Concrete Products Inc......E......209 838-1448
1900 Roosevelt Ave Escalon (95320) ***(P-10812)***
P & L Development LLC......C......323 567-2482
11865 Alameda St Lynwood (90262) ***(P-8346)***
P & L Development LLC......E......310 763-1377
11840 Alameda St Lynwood (90262) ***(P-8059)***
P & L Specialties......F......707 573-3141
1650 Almar Pkwy Santa Rosa (95403) ***(P-14511)***
P & R Pallets Inc......E......213 327-1104
2301 Porter St Los Angeles (90021) ***(P-4382)***
P & R Paper Supply Co Inc......F......619 671-2400
1350 Piper Ranch Rd San Diego (92154) ***(P-5517)***
P & S Sales Inc......F......510 732-2628
20943 Cabot Blvd Hayward (94545) ***(P-19734)***
P A C, San Rafael *Also called Packaging Aids Corporation* ***(P-14721)***
P A P, Anaheim *Also called Precision Anodizing & Pltg Inc* ***(P-13075)***
P A S U Inc......C......619 421-1151
1891 Nirvana Ave Chula Vista (91911) ***(P-12321)***
P A X Industries, Costa Mesa *Also called Tk Pax Inc* ***(P-9209)***
P C I Manufacturing Division......F......714 543-3496
2103 N Ross St Santa Ana (92706) ***(P-17614)***
P C S, Hollister *Also called Pride Conveyance Systems Inc* ***(P-13831)***
P C S C, Torrance *Also called Proprietary Controls Systems* ***(P-21523)***
P C Teas, Burlingame *Also called Prestige Chinese Teas Co* ***(P-2588)***
P E N Inc......E......818 954-0775
215 Allen Ave Glendale (91201) ***(P-7164)***
P G Molinari & Sons Inc......E......415 822-5555
1401 Yosemite Ave San Francisco (94124) ***(P-485)***
P H Machining Inc......F......408 627-4222
1099 N 5th St San Jose (95112) ***(P-17615)***
P J Machining Co Inc......F......760 948-2722
17056 Hercules St Ste 101 Hesperia (92345) ***(P-16268)***
P J Milligan & Associates, Santa Barbara *Also called P J Milligan Company LLC* ***(P-4601)***
P J Milligan Company LLC (PA)......F......805 963-4038
436 E Gutierrez St Santa Barbara (93101) ***(P-4601)***
P K C, Santa Ana *Also called Mustard Seed Technologies Inc* ***(P-19023)***
P K Engineering & Mfg Co Inc......F......805 628-9556
200 E Shell Rd 2b Ventura (93001) ***(P-21853)***
P K Metal, Los Angeles *Also called P Kay Metal Inc* ***(P-11279)***
P K Selective Metal Pltg Inc......F......408 988-1910
415 Mathew St Santa Clara (95050) ***(P-13068)***
P Kay Metal Inc (PA)......E......323 585-5058
2448 E 25th St Los Angeles (90058) ***(P-11279)***
P L D S, Milpitas *Also called Philips & Lite-On Digital* ***(P-15073)***
P L M, Los Angeles *Also called Prudential Lighting Corp* ***(P-17066)***
P M I, San Diego *Also called Pacific Maritime Inds Corp* ***(P-11859)***
P M S D Inc (PA)......D......408 988-5235
950 George St Santa Clara (95054) ***(P-16269)***
P M S D Inc......E......408 727-5322
3411 Leonard Ct Santa Clara (95054) ***(P-16270)***
P P I, Corona *Also called Preproduction Plastics Inc* ***(P-9991)***
P P Mfg Co Inc......F......562 921-3640
13130 Arctic Cir Santa Fe Springs (90670) ***(P-12852)***
P P T, Rancho Cucamonga *Also called Pacific Plastic Technology Inc* ***(P-9445)***
P R P Multisource Inc......E......951 681-6100
3836 Wacker Dr Jurupa Valley (91752) ***(P-14720)***
P S C Manufacturing Inc......E......408 988-5115
3424 De La Cruz Blvd Santa Clara (95054) ***(P-9943)***
P S E Boilers, Santa Fe Springs *Also called Pacific Steam Equipment Inc* ***(P-12036)***
P S I, Beaumont *Also called Precision Stampings Inc* ***(P-16921)***
P S R Iron Works......F......626 442-3360
10819 Michael Hunt Dr El Monte (91733) ***(P-11856)***
P T I, Torrance *Also called Plasma Technology Incorporated* ***(P-13226)***
P T I, Bloomington *Also called Products/Techniques Inc* ***(P-8673)***
P T I, Santa Ana *Also called Parpro Technologies Inc* ***(P-17954)***
P T Industries Inc......F......562 961-3431
3220 Industry Dr Signal Hill (90755) ***(P-12322)***
P T M Inc......F......559 673-1552
10842 Road 28 1/2 Madera (93637) ***(P-4383)***
P T P, Carson *Also called Pacific Toll Processing Inc* ***(P-11059)***
P V I, Oxnard *Also called Poole Ventura Inc* ***(P-14638)***
P V T Supply, Paramount *Also called Wagner Plate Works West Inc* ***(P-12068)***
P W Pipe, Perris *Also called Pw Eagle Inc* ***(P-9475)***
P W Pipe, Shingle Springs *Also called Pw Eagle Inc* ***(P-9476)***
P W Wiring Systems LLC......E......562 463-9055
9415 Kruse Rd Pico Rivera (90660) ***(P-18784)***
P&P Enterprises......F......213 802-0890
1246 W 7th St Los Angeles (90017) ***(P-23174)***
P&Y T-Shrts Silk Screening Inc......D......323 585-4604
2126 E 52nd St Vernon (90058) ***(P-14290)***
P-Americas LLC......E......510 732-9500
3586 Arden Rd Hayward (94545) ***(P-2105)***
P-Americas LLC......C......805 641-4200
4375 N Ventura Ave Ventura (93001) ***(P-2106)***
P-W Western Inc......D......562 463-9055
9415 Kruse Rd Pico Rivera (90660) ***(P-12035)***
Pabco Building Products LLC......D......510 792-9555
37851 Cherry St Newark (94560) ***(P-10881)***
Pabco Building Products LLC......E......510 792-1577
37849 Cherry St Newark (94560) ***(P-10882)***
Pabco Building Products LLC (HQ)......E......510 792-1577
10600 White Rock Rd # 100 Rancho Cordova (95670) ***(P-10883)***
Pabco Building Products LLC......D......323 581-6113
4460 Pacific Blvd Vernon (90058) ***(P-10884)***

Mergent e-mail: customerrelations@mergent.com
1194
2020 California
Manufacturers Register
(P-0000) Products & Services Section entry number
(PA)=Parent Co (HQ)=Headquarters (DH)=Div Headquarters

Pabco Building Products LLC .....D.....916 645-3341
601 7th St Lincoln (95648) ***(P-10464)***
Pabco Clay Products LLC .....C.....916 645-3341
601 7th St Lincoln (95648) ***(P-10435)***
Pabco Clay Products LLC .....D.....916 859-6320
4875 Bradshaw Rd Sacramento (95827) ***(P-10436)***
Pabco Gypsum, Newark *Also called Pabco Building Products LLC* ***(P-10881)***
Pabco Paper, Vernon *Also called Pabco Building Products LLC* ***(P-10884)***
Pabst Brewing Company LLC (PA) .....B.....310 470-0962
10635 Santa Monica Blvd Los Angeles (90025) ***(P-1557)***
Pac 21 .....F.....714 891-7000
11888 Western Ave Stanton (90680) ***(P-20914)***
Pac Fill Inc .....E.....818 409-0117
5471 W San Fernando Rd Los Angeles (90039) ***(P-706)***
Pac Foundries Inc .....C.....805 986-1308
705 Industrial Way Port Hueneme (93041) ***(P-11387)***
Pac Powder Inc .....F.....707 826-1630
148 S G St Ste 9 Arcata (95521) ***(P-13217)***
Pac Tech USA Packg Tech Inc .....F.....408 588-1925
328 Martin Ave Santa Clara (95050) ***(P-18464)***
Pac Trim, Rocklin *Also called Pacific Mdf Products Inc* ***(P-4104)***
Pac-Com International .....F.....562 903-3900
13564 Larwin Cir Santa Fe Springs (90670) ***(P-10952)***
Pac-Rancho Inc (HQ) .....C.....909 987-4721
11000 Jersey Blvd Rancho Cucamonga (91730) ***(P-11165)***
Pac-West Rubber Products LLC .....F.....760 891-0911
120 Venture St San Marcos (92078) ***(P-9267)***
Pace Americas Inc .....E.....310 606-8300
887 N Douglas St 200 El Segundo (90245) ***(P-17616)***
Pace International LLC .....E.....559 651-4877
1104 N Nevada St Visalia (93291) ***(P-8402)***
Pace Punches Inc .....D.....949 428-2750
297 Goddard Irvine (92618) ***(P-14088)***
Pace Sportswear Inc .....F.....714 891-8716
12781 Monarch St Garden Grove (92841) ***(P-3381)***
Pacer Technology (HQ) .....C.....909 987-0550
3281 E Guasti Rd Ste 260 Ontario (91761) ***(P-8883)***
Pacer Technology .....D.....909 987-0550
11201 Jersey Blvd Rancho Cucamonga (91730) ***(P-8884)***
Pacesetter Inc .....F.....925 730-4171
6035 Stoneridge Dr Pleasanton (94588) ***(P-22294)***
Pacesetter Inc (HQ) .....A.....818 362-6822
15900 Valley View Ct Sylmar (91342) ***(P-22295)***
Pacesetter Fabrics LLC (HQ) .....F.....213 741-9999
11450 Sheldon St Sun Valley (91352) ***(P-2948)***
Pacful Inc (PA) .....D.....916 233-1488
11311 White Rock Rd # 100 Rancho Cordova (95742) ***(P-6763)***
Pacful Inc .....D.....650 200-4252
131 Glenn Way Ste 4 San Carlos (94070) ***(P-6764)***
Pachunga Gas Station .....F.....951 506-4575
45000 Pechanga Pkwy Temecula (92592) ***(P-241)***
Pacific Accent Incorporated .....F.....909 563-1600
623 S Doubleday Ave Ontario (91761) ***(P-16838)***
Pacific Accesory, Ontario *Also called Clarke Pb & Associates Inc* ***(P-17212)***
Pacific Adhesive, Sacramento *Also called Applied Products Inc* ***(P-8854)***
Pacific Aero Components Inc (PA) .....F.....818 841-9258
28887 Industry Dr Valencia (91355) ***(P-20191)***
Pacific Aerodynamic Inc .....F.....714 450-9140
889 N Main St Orange (92868) ***(P-19973)***
Pacific Aerospace Machine Inc .....E.....714 534-1444
3002 S Rosewood Ave Santa Ana (92707) ***(P-16271)***
Pacific Aggregates Inc .....D.....951 245-2460
28251 Lake St Lake Elsinore (92530) ***(P-10813)***
Pacific Air Industries Inc .....E.....310 829-4345
9650 De Soto Ave Chatsworth (91311) ***(P-20192)***
Pacific Alliance Capital Inc .....F.....949 360-1796
27141 Aliso Creek Rd # 225 Aliso Viejo (92656) ***(P-15072)***
Pacific Analogix Semiconductor, Santa Clara *Also called Analogix Semiconductor Inc* ***(P-18101)***
Pacific Archtectural Mllwk Inc .....F.....714 525-2059
1031 S Leslie St La Habra (90631) ***(P-4101)***
Pacific Archtectural Mllwk Inc (PA) .....D.....562 905-3200
1435 Pioneer St Brea (92821) ***(P-4102)***
Pacific Artglass Corporation .....E.....310 516-7828
125 W 157th St Gardena (90248) ***(P-10384)***
Pacific Athletic Wear Inc .....D.....714 751-8006
7340 Lampson Ave Garden Grove (92841) ***(P-3382)***
Pacific Avalon Yacht Charters, Newport Beach *Also called Fantasea Enterprises Inc* ***(P-20329)***
Pacific Award Metals Inc (HQ) .....D.....626 814-4410
1450 Virginia Ave Baldwin Park (91706) ***(P-12323)***
Pacific Award Metals Inc .....E.....626 814-4410
13169 Slover Ave Fontana (92337) ***(P-12324)***
Pacific Barcode Inc .....F.....951 587-8717
27531 Enterprise Cir W 201c Temecula (92590) ***(P-14334)***
Pacific Biosciences Cal Inc (PA) .....C.....650 521-8000
1305 Obrien Dr Menlo Park (94025) ***(P-21274)***
Pacific Biotech Inc .....C.....858 552-1100
10165 Mckellar Ct San Diego (92121) ***(P-8247)***
Pacific Boat Trailers Inc (PA) .....E.....909 902-0094
13643 5th St Chino (91710) ***(P-20518)***
Pacific Boulevard Inc .....F.....323 581-1656
5075 Pacific Blvd Vernon (90058) ***(P-3247)***
Pacific Bridge Packaging Inc .....F.....909 598-1988
103 Exchange Pl Pomona (91768) ***(P-11501)***
Pacific Broach & Engrg Assoc .....F.....714 632-5678
1513 N Kraemer Blvd Anaheim (92806) ***(P-16272)***
Pacific Capacitor Co .....F.....408 778-6670
288 Digital Dr Morgan Hill (95037) ***(P-18684)***

Pacific Cast Fther Cushion LLC (HQ) .....C.....562 801-9995
7600 Industry Ave Pico Rivera (90660) ***(P-3631)***
Pacific Cast Products, Santa Fe Springs *Also called Alumistar Inc* ***(P-11366)***
Pacific Casual LLC .....E.....805 445-8310
1060 Avenida Acaso Camarillo (93012) ***(P-4697)***
Pacific Catch Inc .....E.....415 504-6905
770 Tamalpais Dr Ste 400 Corte Madera (94925) ***(P-1117)***
Pacific Ceramics Inc .....E.....408 747-4600
3524 Bassett St Santa Clara (95054) ***(P-10480)***
Pacific Choice Brands Inc (PA) .....B.....559 892-5365
4667 E Date Ave Fresno (93725) ***(P-894)***
Pacific Clears, Eureka *Also called Schmidbauer Lumber Inc* ***(P-3946)***
Pacific Cnc Machine Co .....F.....760 431-7558
2702 Gateway Rd Carlsbad (92009) ***(P-16273)***
Pacific Coachworks Inc .....C.....951 686-7294
3411 N Perris Blvd Bldg 1 Perris (92571) ***(P-20491)***
Pacific Coast Bach Label Co .....E.....213 612-0314
3015 S Grand Ave Los Angeles (90007) ***(P-2857)***
Pacific Coast Bus Times Inc .....F.....805 560-6950
14 E Carrillo St Ste A Santa Barbara (93101) ***(P-5790)***
Pacific Coast Fabricators Inc .....F.....909 627-3833
14375 Telephone Ave Chino (91710) ***(P-11857)***
Pacific Coast Feather LLC .....C.....562 222-5560
8500 Rex Rd Pico Rivera (90660) ***(P-3632)***
Pacific Coast Graphics Bindery .....E.....562 908-5900
12250 Coast Dr Whittier (90601) ***(P-7341)***
Pacific Coast Home Furn Inc (PA) .....F.....323 838-7808
2424 Saybrook Ave Commerce (90040) ***(P-3633)***
Pacific Coast Ironworks Inc .....F.....323 585-1320
8831 Miner St Los Angeles (90002) ***(P-11858)***
Pacific Coast Laboratories .....F.....510 351-2770
2100 Orchard Ave San Leandro (94577) ***(P-22064)***
Pacific Coast Lighting, Ventura *Also called Lamps Plus Inc* ***(P-17049)***
Pacific Coast Lighting Inc (PA) .....B.....818 886-9751
20238 Plummer St Chatsworth (91311) ***(P-17151)***
Pacific Coast Lighting Group, Chatsworth *Also called Pacific Coast Lighting Inc* ***(P-17151)***
Pacific Coast Mfg Inc .....D.....909 627-7040
5270 Edison Ave Chino (91710) ***(P-16815)***
Pacific Coast Optics Inc .....E.....916 789-0111
10604 Industrial Ave # 100 Roseville (95678) ***(P-21394)***
Pacific Coast Pallets Inc .....E.....626 937-6565
15151 Salt Lake Ave La Puente (91746) ***(P-4384)***
Pacific Coast Producers .....D.....209 334-3352
741 S Stockton St Lodi (95240) ***(P-813)***
Pacific Coast Producers (PA) .....B.....209 367-8800
631 N Cluff Ave Lodi (95240) ***(P-814)***
Pacific Coast Producers .....C.....530 533-4311
1601 Mitchell Ave Oroville (95965) ***(P-815)***
Pacific Coast Producers .....B.....530 662-8661
1376 Lemen Ave Woodland (95776) ***(P-816)***
Pacific Coast Products LLC (PA) .....F.....831 316-7137
170 Technology Cir Scotts Valley (95066) ***(P-2223)***
Pacific Coast Products LLC .....E.....831 316-7137
200 Technology Cir Scotts Valley (95066) ***(P-2224)***
Pacific Coast Sportswear, Fountain Valley *Also called Watt Enterprise Inc* ***(P-3130)***
Pacific Coast Supply LLC .....E.....559 651-2185
30158 Road 68 Visalia (93291) ***(P-10885)***
Pacific Coast Supply LLC .....F.....916 339-8100
5550 Roseville Rd North Highlands (95660) ***(P-4314)***
Pacific Color Graphics Inc .....F.....925 600-3006
6336 Patterson Pass Rd A Livermore (94550) ***(P-7165)***
Pacific Communications, Irvine *Also called Allergan Usa Inc* ***(P-7742)***
Pacific Composites Inc .....F.....949 498-8600
221 Calle Pintoresco San Clemente (92672) ***(P-11166)***
Pacific Computer Products Inc .....E.....714 549-7535
2210 S Huron Dr Santa Ana (92704) ***(P-22970)***
Pacific Consolidated Inds LLC .....D.....951 479-0860
12201 Magnolia Ave Riverside (92503) ***(P-14842)***
Pacific Containerprint Inc .....E.....909 465-0365
5951 Riverside Dr Apt 4 Chino (91710) ***(P-7166)***
Pacific Contntl Textiles Inc (HQ) .....E.....310 604-1100
2880 E Ana St Compton (90221) ***(P-2858)***
Pacific Contntl Textiles Inc .....F.....310 639-1500
2880 E Ana St E Rncho Dmngz (90221) ***(P-2831)***
Pacific Controls E D M, Encino *Also called Pacific Controls Inc* ***(P-19374)***
Pacific Controls Inc .....F.....818 345-1970
4949 Newcastle Ave Encino (91316) ***(P-19374)***
Pacific Corrugated Pipe, Fontana *Also called W E Hall Co* ***(P-12431)***
Pacific Corrugated Pipe Co, Newport Beach *Also called WE Hall Company Inc* ***(P-11122)***
Pacific Corrugated Pipe Co, Sacramento *Also called WE Hall Company Inc* ***(P-10668)***
Pacific Design Tech Inc .....E.....805 961-9110
6300 Lindmar Dr Goleta (93117) ***(P-20671)***
Pacific Die Cast Inc .....F.....562 407-1390
15980 Bloomfield Ave Cerritos (90703) ***(P-14089)***
Pacific Die Casting Corp .....C.....323 725-1308
6155 S Eastern Ave Commerce (90040) ***(P-11343)***
Pacific Die Cut Industries .....D.....510 732-8103
3399 Arden Rd Hayward (94545) ***(P-9244)***
Pacific Die Services Inc .....F.....562 907-4463
7626 Baldwin Pl Whittier (90602) ***(P-14090)***
Pacific Diversified Capital Co .....A.....619 696-2000
101 Ash St San Diego (92101) ***(P-21516)***
Pacific Door & Cabinet Company .....E.....559 439-3822
7050 N Harrison Ave Pinedale (93650) ***(P-4103)***
Pacific Drapery, San Diego *Also called Manzer Corporation* ***(P-3591)***
Pacific Drilling Co., San Diego *Also called Limited Access Unlimited Inc* ***(P-13649)***
Pacific Dry Goods Inc .....F.....925 288-2929
1085 Essex Ave Richmond (94801) ***(P-2747)***

ALPHABETIC

Employee Codes: A=Over 500 employees, B=251-500
C=101-250, D=51-100, E=20-50, F=10-19

2020 California
Manfacturers Register

© Mergent Inc. 1-800-342-5647

1195

Pacific Duct Inc .... E 909 635-1335
5499 Brooks St Montclair (91763) ***(P-12325)***
Pacific Eagle USA Inc .... E 626 455-0033
9707 El Poche St Ste H South El Monte (91733) ***(P-9349)***
Pacific Earthscape, McKinleyville *Also called Ford Logging Inc* ***(P-3882)***
Pacific Energy Resources Ltd (PA) .... F 562 628-1526
111 W Ocean Blvd Ste 1240 Long Beach (90802) ***(P-61)***
Pacific Ethanol Central LLC (HQ) .... D 916 403-2123
400 Capitol Mall Ste 2060 Sacramento (95814) ***(P-8760)***
Pacific Ethanol West LLC .... C 916 403-2123
400 Capitol Mall Ste 2060 Sacramento (95814) ***(P-8761)***
Pacific Fibre & Rope Co Inc .... F 310 834-4567
903 Flint Ave 927 Wilmington (90744) ***(P-2912)***
Pacific Fixture Company Inc .... F 818 362-2130
12860 San Fernando Rd B1 Sylmar (91342) ***(P-4994)***
Pacific Flyway Decoy Assn .... F 925 754-4978
300 Marble Dr Antioch (94509) ***(P-22863)***
Pacific Foam, Ontario *Also called Induspac California Inc* ***(P-7568)***
Pacific Forge Inc .... D 909 390-0701
10641 Etiwanda Ave Fontana (92337) ***(P-12716)***
Pacific Galvanizing Inc .... E 510 261-7331
715 46th Ave Oakland (94601) ***(P-13218)***
Pacific Gaming .... E 510 562-8900
1975 Adams Ave San Leandro (94577) ***(P-22703)***
Pacific Ginning Company LLC .... E 559 829-9446
33370 W Nebraska Ave Cantua Creek (93608) ***(P-14512)***
Pacific Glass, Gardena *Also called Pacific Artglass Corporation* ***(P-10384)***
Pacific Green Trucking Inc .... F 310 830-4528
512 E C St Wilmington (90744) ***(P-20375)***
Pacific Handy Cutter Inc .... E 714 662-1033
17819 Gillette Ave Irvine (92614) ***(P-11539)***
Pacific Hardware Sales, Anaheim *Also called A J Fasteners Inc* ***(P-12664)***
Pacific Hardwood Cabinetry .... E 707 528-8627
2811 Dowd Dr Santa Rosa (95407) ***(P-4229)***
Pacific Hospitality Design Inc .... E 323 587-4289
2620 S Malt Ave Commerce (90040) ***(P-4868)***
Pacific Imaging .... F 858 536-2600
9687 Distribution Ave San Diego (92121) ***(P-6765)***
Pacific Impressions Inc .... F 408 727-4200
3494 Edward Ave Santa Clara (95054) ***(P-2832)***
Pacific Inspection, Arbuckle *Also called National Oilwell Varco Inc* ***(P-235)***
Pacific Instruments Inc .... E 925 827-9010
4080 Pike Ln Concord (94520) ***(P-21517)***
Pacific Integrated Mfg Inc .... C 619 921-3464
4364 Bonita Rd Ste 454 Bonita (91902) ***(P-21854)***
Pacific International Stl Corp .... E 209 931-0900
2889 Navone Rd Stockton (95215) ***(P-12597)***
Pacific Intl Rice Mills, Woodland *Also called Bunge North America Inc* ***(P-1035)***
Pacific Intrlock Pvngstone Inc (PA) .... F 831 637-9163
1895 San Felipe Rd Hollister (95023) ***(P-10620)***
Pacific Jewelry Services .... E 213 627-3337
606 S Olive St Los Angeles (90014) ***(P-22557)***
Pacific Kiln Insulations Inc .... F 951 697-4422
14370 Veterans Way Moreno Valley (92553) ***(P-14772)***
Pacific Label Inc .... D 714 237-1276
1511 E Edinger Ave Santa Ana (92705) ***(P-7167)***
Pacific Lasertec Inc .... E 760 450-4095
3821 Sienna St Oceanside (92056) ***(P-23438)***
Pacific Light Blown Glass, Cudahy *Also called Alamillo Radolfo* ***(P-10295)***
Pacific Lighting & Electrical, Sacramento *Also called Mw McWong International Inc* ***(P-17146)***
Pacific Link Corp .... F 714 897-3525
15865 Chemical Ln Huntington Beach (92649) ***(P-21395)***
Pacific Lock Company (PA) .... E 661 294-3707
25605 Hercules St Valencia (91355) ***(P-11618)***
Pacific Ltg & Standards Co .... E 310 603-9344
2815 Los Flores Blvd Lynwood (90262) ***(P-17062)***
Pacific Magnetics, Chula Vista *Also called Pacmag Inc* ***(P-19045)***
Pacific Manufacturing MGT Inc .... D 323 263-9000
3110 E 12th St Los Angeles (90023) ***(P-4995)***
Pacific Maritime Inds Corp .... C 619 575-8141
1790 Dornoch Ct San Diego (92154) ***(P-11859)***
Pacific Mdf Products Inc (PA) .... E 916 660-1882
4312 Anthony Ct Ste A Rocklin (95677) ***(P-4104)***
Pacific Metal Buildings Inc .... F 530 438-2777
270 Old Highway 99 Maxwell (95955) ***(P-12569)***
Pacific Metal Fab & Design, Madera *Also called Pacific Sheet Metal Inc* ***(P-12327)***
Pacific Metal Finishing Inc .... F 805 237-8886
440 Sherwood Rd Paso Robles (93446) ***(P-13219)***
Pacific Metal Stampings Inc .... E 661 257-7656
28415 Witherspoon Pkwy Valencia (91355) ***(P-12853)***
Pacific Mfg Inc San Diego .... E 619 423-0316
1520 Corporate Center Dr San Diego (92154) ***(P-16274)***
Pacific Millennium US Corp .... F 858 450-1505
12526 High Bluff Dr # 300 San Diego (92130) ***(P-5141)***
Pacific Miniatures, Fullerton *Also called Pacmin Incorporated* ***(P-23441)***
Pacific Modern Homes Inc .... E 916 685-9514
9723 Railroad St Elk Grove (95624) ***(P-12326)***
pacific Molding Inc .... F 951 683-2100
1390 Dodson Way Riverside (92507) ***(P-9944)***
Pacific Natural Spices, Commerce *Also called Pacific Spice Company Inc* ***(P-2580)***
Pacific Naturals, Pacoima *Also called Gscm Ventures Inc* ***(P-8505)***
Pacific Neon .... E 916 927-0527
2939 Academy Way Sacramento (95815) ***(P-23175)***
Pacific Northwest Pubg Co Inc .... B 916 321-1828
2100 Q St Sacramento (95816) ***(P-5791)***
Pacific Operators Inc .... E 805 899-3144
205 E Carrillo St Ste 200 Santa Barbara (93101) ***(P-101)***
Pacific Packaging McHy LLC .... E 951 393-2200
200 River Rd Corona (92880) ***(P-14390)***
Pacific Pallet Co, Glendale *Also called Long Beach Woodworks LLC* ***(P-4377)***
Pacific Pallet Exchange Inc .... E 916 448-5589
3350 51st Ave Sacramento (95823) ***(P-4385)***
Pacific Panel Products Corp .... E 626 851-0444
15601 Arrow Hwy Irwindale (91706) ***(P-4278)***
Pacific Paper Box Company (PA) .... E 323 771-7733
3928 Encino Hills Pl Encino (91436) ***(P-5191)***
Pacific Paper Tube Inc (PA) .... E 510 562-8823
4343 E Fremont St Stockton (95215) ***(P-5299)***
Pacific Perforating Inc .... E 661 768-9224
25090 Highway 33 Fellows (93224) ***(P-242)***
Pacific Pharmascience Inc .... F 949 916-6955
23052 Alcalde Dr Ste A Laguna Hills (92653) ***(P-8060)***
Pacific Pickle Works Inc .... F 805 765-1779
718 Union Ave Snta Brbara Santa Barbara Santa Barbara (93103) ***(P-895)***
Pacific Piston Ring Co Inc .... D 310 836-3322
3620 Eastham Dr Culver City (90232) ***(P-15615)***
Pacific Plas Injection Molding, Vista *Also called Diversified Plastics Inc* ***(P-9761)***
Pacific Plastic Technology Inc .... E 909 987-4200
9555 Hyssop Dr Rancho Cucamonga (91730) ***(P-9445)***
Pacific Plastics Inc .... D 714 990-9050
111 S Berry St Brea (92821) ***(P-9472)***
Pacific Plating, Sun Valley *Also called K V R Investment Group Inc* ***(P-14486)***
Pacific Play Tents Inc .... F 323 269-0431
2801 E 12th St Los Angeles (90023) ***(P-3695)***
Pacific Plaza Imports Inc .... F 925 349-4000
3018 Willow Pass Rd # 102 Concord (94519) ***(P-2248)***
Pacific Powder Coating, Arcata *Also called Pac Powder Inc* ***(P-13217)***
Pacific Powder Coating Inc .... E 916 381-1154
8637 23rd Ave Sacramento (95826) ***(P-13220)***
Pacific Pprbd Converting LLC (PA) .... E 909 476-6466
8865 Utica Ave Ste A Rancho Cucamonga (91730) ***(P-5518)***
Pacific Precision Labs Inc .... E 818 700-8977
9430 Lurline Ave Chatsworth (91311) ***(P-21518)***
Pacific Precision Metals Inc .... C 951 226-1500
1100 E Orangethorpe Ave Anaheim (92801) ***(P-12854)***
Pacific Press, Anaheim *Also called Wasser Filtration Inc* ***(P-14870)***
Pacific Press Corporation .... E 408 292-3422
2350 S 10th St San Jose (95112) ***(P-5792)***
Pacific Printing, San Diego *Also called Pacific Imaging* ***(P-6765)***
Pacific Process Systems Inc (PA) .... D 661 321-9681
7401 Rosedale Hwy Bakersfield (93308) ***(P-243)***
Pacific Quality Packaging Corp .... D 714 257-1234
660 Neptune Ave Brea (92821) ***(P-5250)***
Pacific Quartz Inc .... E 714 546-8133
900 Glenneyre St Laguna Beach (92651) ***(P-21396)***
Pacific Rim Printers & Mailers, Culver City *Also called Econ-O-Plate Inc* ***(P-6558)***
Pacific Rim Publishing, Fremont *Also called T C Media Inc* ***(P-6037)***
Pacific Scientific Company (HQ) .... E 805 526-5700
1785 Voyager Ave Simi Valley (93063) ***(P-20672)***
Pacific Scientific Energetic (HQ) .... B 831 637-3731
3601 Union Rd Hollister (95023) ***(P-9014)***
Pacific Screw Products Inc .... D 650 583-9682
1331 Old County Rd Ste C Belmont (94002) ***(P-12645)***
Pacific Seismic Products Inc .... E 661 942-4499
233 E Avenue H8 Lancaster (93535) ***(P-13317)***
Pacific Sheet Metal Inc .... F 559 661-4044
497 S Pine St Madera (93637) ***(P-12327)***
Pacific Ship Repr Fbrction Inc (PA) .... B 619 232-3200
1625 Rigel St San Diego (92113) ***(P-20298)***
Pacific Shore Holdings Inc .... F 818 998-0996
8236 Remmet Ave Canoga Park (91304) ***(P-8061)***
Pacific Shore Stones Bakersfie .... F 661 335-0100
3775 Buck Owens Blvd Bakersfield (93308) ***(P-2949)***
Pacific Sky Supply Inc .... D 818 768-3700
8230 San Fernando Rd Sun Valley (91352) ***(P-20193)***
Pacific Southwest Cont LLC (PA) .... B 209 526-0444
4530 Leckron Rd Modesto (95357) ***(P-5334)***
Pacific Southwest Cont LLC .... F 209 526-0444
671 Mariposa Rd Modesto (95354) ***(P-5335)***
Pacific Southwest Cont LLC .... D 559 651-5500
9525 W Nicholas Ct Visalia (93291) ***(P-5251)***
Pacific Southwest Molds .... F 562 803-9811
12307 Woodruff Ave Downey (90241) ***(P-14091)***
Pacific Spice Company Inc .... D 323 726-9190
6430 E Slauson Ave Commerce (90040) ***(P-2580)***
Pacific Stainless, Colton *Also called S & S Installations Inc* ***(P-15573)***
Pacific Standard Print, Sacramento *Also called American Lithographers Inc* ***(P-6408)***
Pacific States Felt Mfg Co Inc .... F 510 783-2357
23850 Clawiter Rd Ste 20 Hayward (94545) ***(P-9245)***
Pacific States Treating Inc .... F 530 938-4408
422 Mill St Weed (96094) ***(P-4479)***
Pacific Steam Equipment Inc .... E 562 906-9292
11748 Slauson Ave Santa Fe Springs (90670) ***(P-12036)***
Pacific Steel, National City *Also called Simec USA Corporation* ***(P-11069)***
Pacific Steel Fabricators Inc .... E 209 464-9474
8275 San Leandro St Oakland (94621) ***(P-11860)***
Pacific Steel Group (PA) .... D 858 251-1100
4805 Murphy Canyon Rd San Diego (92123) ***(P-12598)***
Pacific Steel Group .... E 707 669-3136
2301 Napa Vallejo Hwy NAPA (94558) ***(P-12599)***
Pacific Stone Design Inc .... E 714 836-5757
1201 E Wakeham Ave Santa Ana (92705) ***(P-10621)***
Pacific Stones, Bakersfield *Also called Pacific Shore Stones Bakersfie* ***(P-2949)***
Pacific Sun .... F 415 488-8100
847 5th St Santa Rosa (95404) ***(P-5997)***

Mergent e-mail: customerrelations@mergent.com
1196
2020 California
Manufacturers Register
(P-0000) Products & Services Section entry number
(PA)=Parent Co (HQ)=Headquarters (DH)=Div Headquarters

Pacific Sunshine Enterprises........F.......530 673-1888
857 Gray Ave Ste B Yuba City (95991) *(P-23439)*
Pacific Supply, Visalia *Also called Pacific Coast Supply LLC (P-10885)*
Pacific Supply, North Highlands *Also called Pacific Coast Supply LLC (P-4314)*
Pacific Tank & Cnstr Inc........E.......805 237-2929
17995 E Highway 46 Shandon (93461) *(P-12037)*
Pacific Tchnical Eqp Engrg Inc........F.......714 835-3088
1298 N Blue Gum St Anaheim (92806) *(P-14637)*
Pacific Tech Products Ontario, Union City *Also called California Performance Packg (P-9511)*
Pacific Tek, Anaheim *Also called Pacific Tchnical Eqp Engrg Inc (P-14637)*
Pacific Tent and Awning........F.......559 436-8147
7295 N Palm Bluffs Ave Fresno (93711) *(P-3696)*
Pacific Testtronics Inc........F.......323 721-1077
5983 Smithway St Commerce (90040) *(P-23440)*
Pacific Thermography........E.......323 938-3349
9550 Jellico Ave Northridge (91325) *(P-7168)*
Pacific Timber Contracting........F.......707 498-1374
690 Jacobsen Way Ferndale (95536) *(P-3900)*
Pacific Toll Processing Inc........E.......310 952-4992
24724 Wilmington Ave Carson (90745) *(P-11059)*
Pacific Transformer Corp........C.......714 779-0450
5399 E Hunter Ave Anaheim (92807) *(P-16566)*
Pacific Trendz, Ontario *Also called Sunny Products Inc (P-7318)*
Pacific Truck Equipment Inc........D.......562 464-9674
11655 Washington Blvd Whittier (90606) *(P-19549)*
Pacific Truck Tank Inc........E.......916 379-9280
7029 Florin Perkins Rd A Sacramento (95828) *(P-19550)*
Pacific Urethanes LLC........C.......909 390-8400
1671 Champagne Ave Ste A Ontario (91761) *(P-3634)*
Pacific Utility Products Inc........F.......909 923-1800
2950 E Philadelphia St Ontario (91761) *(P-20974)*
Pacific Valves........D.......562 426-2531
3201 Walnut Ave Signal Hill (90755) *(P-13318)*
Pacific Vial Mfg Inc........E.......323 721-7004
2738 Supply Ave Commerce (90040) *(P-10292)*
Pacific Vista Foods Llc........E.......760 908-9840
2380 Back Nine St Oceanside (92056) *(P-8702)*
Pacific Wave Systems Inc........D.......714 893-0152
2525 W 190th St Torrance (90504) *(P-17617)*
Pacific WD Prserving-New Stine........F.......661 617-6385
5601 District Blvd Bakersfield (93313) *(P-4480)*
Pacific Weaving Corporation........E.......650 592-9434
1068 American St San Carlos (94070) *(P-2707)*
Pacific Welding & Fabrication........F.......619 336-1758
1535 Tidelands Ave Ste F National City (91950) *(P-24655)*
Pacific West Forest Products........F.......530 899-7313
13434 Browns Valley Dr Chico (95973) *(P-12600)*
Pacific West Litho Inc........D.......714 579-0868
3291 E Miraloma Ave Anaheim (92806) *(P-6766)*
Pacific Western Container, Santa Ana *Also called Blower-Dempsay Corporation (P-5201)*
Pacific Western Systems Inc (PA)........E.......650 961-8855
505 E Evelyn Ave Mountain View (94041) *(P-21096)*
Pacific Westline Inc........D.......714 956-2442
1536 W Embassy St Anaheim (92802) *(P-4929)*
Pacific Wire Products Inc........E.......818 755-6400
10725 Vanowen St North Hollywood (91605) *(P-13425)*
Pacific Wood Milling Reload, Cottonwood *Also called Plum Valley Inc (P-3941)*
Pacific World Corporation (PA)........D.......949 598-2400
100 Technology Dr Ste 200 Irvine (92618) *(P-8553)*
Pacific Wstn Arostructures Inc........F.......661 607-0100
27771 Avenue Hopkins Valencia (91355) *(P-16275)*
Pacific Wtrprfing Rstrtion Inc........E.......909 444-3052
2845 Pomona Blvd Pomona (91768) *(P-9015)*
Pacific Yacht Towers........F.......760 744-4831
165 Balboa St Ste C10 San Marcos (92069) *(P-20355)*
Pacifica Tribune, Novato *Also called Ang Newspaper Group Inc (P-5551)*
Pacifico Bindery Inc........E.......714 744-1510
544 W Angus Ave Orange (92868) *(P-7342)*
Pacifictech Molded Pdts Inc........F.......714 279-9928
22805 Savi Ranch Pkwy F Yorba Linda (92887) *(P-9350)*
Pacifitek Systems Inc........F.......619 401-1968
344 Coogan Way El Cajon (92020) *(P-17618)*
Paciolan LLC (HQ)........D.......866 722-4652
5291 California Ave # 100 Irvine (92617) *(P-24284)*
Pacira Pharmaceuticals Inc........D.......858 678-3950
10450 Science Center Dr San Diego (92121) *(P-8062)*
Pack West Machinery, Corona *Also called Pacific Packaging McHy LLC (P-14390)*
Pack West Machinery Co, Corona *Also called W J Ellison Co Inc (P-14736)*
Packageone Inc (PA)........E.......650 761-3339
1100 Union St San Francisco (94109) *(P-5252)*
Packaging Aids Corporation (PA)........E.......415 454-4868
25 Tiburon St San Rafael (94901) *(P-14721)*
Packaging America - Sacramento, McClellan *Also called PCA Central Cal Corrugated LLC (P-5257)*
Packaging Corporation America........D.......323 263-7581
4240 Bandini Blvd Vernon (90058) *(P-5253)*
Packaging Corporation America........C.......562 927-7741
9700 E Frontage Rd Ste 20 South Gate (90280) *(P-5254)*
Packaging Dist Assembly Group........F.......661 607-0600
24730 Avenue Rockefeller Valencia (91355) *(P-5171)*
Packaging Plus........E.......209 858-9200
3816 S Willow Ave Ste 102 Fresno (93725) *(P-5255)*
Packaging Resource Group, Sherman Oaks *Also called Hab Enterprises Inc (P-9234)*
Packaging Specialists Inc........F.......530 742-8441
3663 Feather River Blvd Plumas Lake (95961) *(P-4386)*
Packaging Spectrum, Los Angeles *Also called Advance Paper Box Company (P-5194)*
Packaging Systems Inc........E.......661 253-5700
26435 Summit Cir Santa Clarita (91350) *(P-8885)*
Packers Bar M, Los Angeles *Also called Serv-Rite Meat Company Inc (P-424)*
Packers Food Products Inc........E.......913 262-6200
701 W Kimberly Ave # 210 Placentia (92870) *(P-922)*
Packers Manufacturing Inc........E.......559 732-4886
4212 W Hemlock Ave Visalia (93277) *(P-14391)*
Packit LLC........F.......805 496-2999
875 S Westlake Blvd Westlake Village (91361) *(P-5409)*
Packline Technologies Inc........E.......559 591-3150
5929 Avenue 408 Dinuba (93618) *(P-14722)*
Paclights LLC (PA)........E.......888 983-2165
15830 El Prado Rd Ste F Chino (91708) *(P-17063)*
Pacmag Inc........F.......619 872-0343
87 Georgina St Chula Vista (91910) *(P-19045)*
Pacmin Incorporated (PA)........D.......714 447-4478
2021 Raymer Ave Fullerton (92833) *(P-23441)*
Paco Plastics & Engrg Inc........F.......562 698-0916
8540 Dice Rd Santa Fe Springs (90670) *(P-9945)*
Paco Pumps By Grundfos, Hayward *Also called Grundfos CBS Inc (P-14579)*
Pacobond Inc........E.......818 768-5002
9800 Glenoaks Blvd Sun Valley (91352) *(P-5442)*
Pacon Inc........C.......626 814-4654
4249 Puente Ave Baldwin Park (91706) *(P-9946)*
Pacon Mfg Inc........E.......925 961-0445
4777 Bennett Dr Ste H Livermore (94551) *(P-16276)*
Pacord Inc........E.......619 336-2200
240 W 30th St National City (91950) *(P-20299)*
Pactiv Corp, Visalia *Also called Pactiv LLC (P-9949)*
Pactiv Corporation........E.......562 944-0052
9700 Bell Ranch Dr Santa Fe Springs (90670) *(P-5519)*
Pactiv LLC........B.......661 392-4000
2024 Norris Rd Bakersfield (93308) *(P-9947)*
Pactiv LLC........A.......209 983-1930
4545 Qantas Ln Stockton (95206) *(P-5256)*
Pactiv LLC........D.......562 693-1451
12500 Slauson Ave Ste H1 Santa Fe Springs (90670) *(P-9948)*
Pactiv LLC........C.......909 622-1151
8201 W Elowin Ct Visalia (93291) *(P-9949)*
Pactron........D.......408 329-5500
3000 Patrick Henry Dr Santa Clara (95054) *(P-17949)*
Paddack Almond Hlling Shelling, Escalon *Also called Paddack Enterprises (P-1436)*
Paddack Enterprises........E.......209 838-1536
27052 State Highway 120 Escalon (95320) *(P-1436)*
Paderia LLC........F.......949 478-5273
18279 Brookhurst St Ste 1 Fountain Valley (92708) *(P-1323)*
Padilla Jewelers Inc........F.......323 931-1678
6118 Venice Blvd Fl 2 Los Angeles (90034) *(P-22558)*
Padilla Remberto........F.......323 268-1111
3524 Union Pacific Ave Los Angeles (90023) *(P-2833)*
Padywell Corp........E.......626 359-9149
835 Meridian St Duarte (91010) *(P-7169)*
Pagecorp Industries, Santa Ana *Also called P C I Manufacturing Division (P-17614)*
Pagerduty Inc (PA)........C.......844 800-3889
600 Townsend St Ste 200e San Francisco (94103) *(P-24285)*
Pai Enterprises, Los Angeles *Also called Pai Gp Inc (P-10385)*
Pai Gp Inc........D.......323 549-5355
5914 Crenshaw Blvd Los Angeles (90043) *(P-10385)*
Paige LLC (HQ)........C.......310 733-2100
10119 Jefferson Blvd Culver City (90232) *(P-3047)*
Paige Floor Cvg Specialists, National City *Also called Paige Sitta & Associates Inc (P-20300)*
Paige Premium Denim, Culver City *Also called Paige LLC (P-3047)*
Paige Sitta & Associates Inc (PA)........E.......619 233-5912
2050 Wilson Ave Ste B National City (91950) *(P-20300)*
Paiho North America Corp........E.......661 257-6611
16051 El Prado Rd Chino (91708) *(P-23007)*
Paint Chem, Burbank *Also called Slickote (P-13247)*
Paint Specialists Inc........E.......818 771-0552
8629 Bradley Ave Sun Valley (91352) *(P-13221)*
Paint-Chem Inc........F.......213 747-7725
1680 Miller Ave Los Angeles (90063) *(P-8661)*
Painted Rhino Inc........E.......951 656-5524
14310 Veterans Way Moreno Valley (92553) *(P-9594)*
Pair of Thieves, Culver City *Also called Stateside Merchants LLC (P-3000)*
Paisano Publications LLC (PA)........C.......818 889-8740
28210 Dorothy Dr Agoura Hills (91301) *(P-5998)*
Paisano Publications Inc........D.......818 889-8740
28210 Dorothy Dr Agoura Hills (91301) *(P-5999)*
Pak Group LLC........E.......626 316-6555
236 N Chester Ave Ste 200 Pasadena (91106) *(P-1324)*
Pakedge Device & Software Inc........E.......714 880-4511
17011 Beach Blvd Ste 600 Huntington Beach (92647) *(P-24286)*
Palace Press International, San Rafael *Also called Goff Corporation (P-6106)*
Palace Printing & Design LP........E.......415 526-1370
800 A St San Rafael (94901) *(P-6132)*
Palace Textile Inc........D.......323 587-7756
8453 Terradell St Pico Rivera (90660) *(P-14291)*
Palace Textiles, Pico Rivera *Also called Palace Textile Inc (P-14291)*
Paladar Mfg Inc........D.......760 775-4222
53973 Polk St Coachella (92236) *(P-22631)*
Palermo Products LLC........F.......949 201-9066
16935 Saticoy St Van Nuys (91406) *(P-3635)*
Palex Metals Inc........E.......408 496-6111
3601 Thomas Rd Santa Clara (95054) *(P-12328)*
Palihuse Hllway Rsidences Assn........F.......323 656-4100
8465 Holloway Dr West Hollywood (90069) *(P-3248)*
Palisades Beach Club, Los Angeles *Also called Fortune Swimwear LLC (P-2786)*
Pall Corporation........D.......858 455-7264
4116 Sorrento Valley Blvd San Diego (92121) *(P-14843)*

ALPHABETIC

Employee Codes: A=Over 500 employees, B=251-500
C=101-250, D=51-100, E=20-50, F=10-19
2020 California
Manfacturers Register
© Mergent Inc. 1-800-342-5647
1197

Pall Corporation..........B......626 339-7388
1630 W Industrial Park St Covina (91722) *(P-14844)*

Pallet Depot Inc (PA)..........D......916 645-0490
19049 Avenue 242 Lindsay (93247) *(P-4387)*

Pallet Masters Inc..........D......323 758-1713
655 E Florence Ave Los Angeles (90001) *(P-4388)*

Pallet Recovery Service Inc..........F......209 496-5074
3401 Gaffery Rd Tracy (95304) *(P-4389)*

Pallets 4 Less Inc..........F......213 377-7813
750 Ceres Ave Los Angeles (90021) *(P-4390)*

Pallets Unlimited Inc..........F......916 408-1914
2390 Athens Ave Lincoln (95648) *(P-4391)*

Palm Inc (HQ)..........B......408 617-7000
950 W Maude Ave Sunnyvale (94085) *(P-17619)*

Palm Springs Plating, Palm Springs *Also called Ken Hoffmann Inc (P-13036)*

Palmdale Heat Treating Inc..........F......661 274-8604
38834 17th St E Palmdale (93550) *(P-12038)*

Palmdale Rock and Asphalt, Littlerock *Also called Legacy Vulcan LLC (P-10783)*

Palmer Tank & Construction Inc..........E......661 834-1110
2464 S Union Ave Bakersfield (93307) *(P-244)*

Palo Alto Awning Inc..........F......650 968-4270
1381 N 10th St San Jose (95112) *(P-3697)*

Palo Alto Networks Inc (PA)..........B......408 753-4000
3000 Tannery Way Santa Clara (95054) *(P-15305)*

Palomar Casework Inc..........F......760 941-9860
4275 Clearview Dr Carlsbad (92008) *(P-4996)*

Palomar Products Inc..........D......949 858-8836
23042 Arroyo Vis Rcho STA Marg (92688) *(P-17752)*

Palomar Technologies Inc (PA)..........D......760 931-3600
2728 Loker Ave W Carlsbad (92010) *(P-14513)*

Palpilot International Corp..........E......714 460-0718
15991 Red Hill Ave # 102 Tustin (92780) *(P-17950)*

Palpilot International Corp (PA)..........E......408 855-8866
500 Yosemite Dr Milpitas (95035) *(P-17951)*

Pam Dee Publishing..........F......707 542-1528
303 Talbot Ave Santa Rosa (95405) *(P-6133)*

Pamarco Global Graphics Inc..........E......714 739-0700
6907 Marlin Cir La Palma (90623) *(P-14335)*

Pamarco Western, La Palma *Also called Pamarco Global Graphics Inc (P-14335)*

Pamco, Sun Valley *Also called Precision Arcft Machining Inc (P-16308)*

Pamco Machine Works Inc..........E......909 941-7260
9359 Feron Blvd Rancho Cucamonga (91730) *(P-16277)*

Pamelas Products Incorporated..........D......707 462-6605
1 Carousel Ln Ste D Ukiah (95482) *(P-1256)*

Pampanga Foods Company Inc..........F......714 773-0537
1835 N Orngthrp Park A Anaheim (92801) *(P-486)*

Pampanga Foods Incorporated..........E......714 331-7206
1835 N Orngthrp Park A Anaheim (92801) *(P-974)*

Pan Magna Group..........E......707 433-5508
1141 Grant Ave Healdsburg (95448) *(P-1854)*

Pan Pacific Plastics Mfg Inc..........E......510 785-6888
26551 Danti Ct Hayward (94545) *(P-9950)*

Pan Probe Biotech Inc..........F......858 689-9936
7396 Trade St San Diego (92121) *(P-21855)*

Pan-A-Lite Products Inc..........F......714 258-7111
1601 Ritchey St Santa Ana (92705) *(P-17152)*

Pan-O-Rama Baking Inc..........E......415 522-5500
500 Florida St San Francisco (94110) *(P-1257)*

Pana-Pacific Corporation (HQ)..........C......559 457-4700
838 N Laverne Ave Fresno (93727) *(P-19735)*

Panadent Corporation..........E......909 783-1841
580 S Rancho Ave Colton (92324) *(P-22179)*

Panasonic Appliances Ref..........D......619 661-1134
2001 Sanyo Ave San Diego (92154) *(P-16821)*

Panavision Hollywood, Los Angeles *Also called Panavision Inc (P-22446)*

Panavision Inc..........D......323 464-3800
6735 Selma Ave Los Angeles (90028) *(P-22446)*

Panavision International LP (HQ)..........B......818 316-1080
6101 Variel Ave Woodland Hills (91367) *(P-22447)*

Panchos Bakery..........E......323 582-9109
1759 E Florence Ave Los Angeles (90001) *(P-1258)*

Panco Mens Products Inc..........F......760 342-4368
45605 Citrus Ave Indio (92201) *(P-8554)*

Panda Bowl..........F......714 418-0299
11940 Edinger Ave Fountain Valley (92708) *(P-5075)*

Panel Products Inc..........E......310 830-3331
21818 S Wilmington Ave # 411 Long Beach (90810) *(P-20673)*

Panel Shop Inc..........E......951 739-7000
2800 Palisades Dr Corona (92880) *(P-16605)*

Panel Shop, The, San Fernando *Also called Krego Corporation (P-16601)*

Panel Works, Santa Fe Springs *Also called JC Hanscom Inc (P-4275)*

Panelight Components Group LLC..........F......714 258-7111
1601 Ritchey St Santa Ana (92705) *(P-17153)*

Pangea Silkscreen..........E......707 778-0110
110 Howard St Ste A Petaluma (94952) *(P-3806)*

Panic Plastics..........F......909 946-5529
1652 W 11th St Upland (91786) *(P-5410)*

Pankl Aerospace Systems..........D......562 207-6300
16615 Edwards Rd Cerritos (90703) *(P-11419)*

Pannaway, Fremont *Also called Enablence Systems Inc (P-23858)*

Pano Logic Inc..........D......650 743-1773
1100 La Avenida St Ste A Mountain View (94043) *(P-15306)*

Panob Corp..........E......909 947-8008
1531 E Cedar St Ontario (91761) *(P-9951)*

Panolam Industries Intl Inc..........E......909 581-1970
8535 Oakwood Pl Ste A Rancho Cucamonga (91730) *(P-4485)*

Panorama Intl CL Co Inc..........F......415 891-8478
200 Toland St San Francisco (94124) *(P-742)*

Panoramic Software Corporation..........F......877 558-8526
9650 Research Dr Irvine (92618) *(P-24287)*

Panosoft, Irvine *Also called Panoramic Software Corporation (P-24287)*

Panrosa Enterprises Inc..........D......951 339-5888
550 Monica Cir Ste 101 Corona (92880) *(P-8347)*

Pantronix Corporation..........C......510 656-5898
2710 Lakeview Ct Fremont (94538) *(P-18465)*

Pantry Retail Inc..........F......415 234-3574
3095 Kerner Blvd Ste N San Rafael (94901) *(P-15401)*

Papa Cantella's Sausage Plant, Vernon *Also called Papa Cantellas Incorporated (P-487)*

Papa Cantellas Incorporated..........D......323 584-7272
3341 E 50th St Vernon (90058) *(P-487)*

Papadatos Enterprises Inc..........F......408 299-0190
2015 Stone Ave San Jose (95125) *(P-16278)*

Papco Parts, Chatsworth *Also called Papco Screw Products Inc (P-13938)*

Papco Screw Products Inc..........F......818 341-2266
9410 De Soto Ave Ste A Chatsworth (91311) *(P-13938)*

Pape Material Handling Inc..........D......562 692-9311
2600 Peck Rd City of Industry (90601) *(P-13887)*

Paper Pulp & Film..........E......559 233-1151
2822 S Maple Ave Fresno (93725) *(P-5520)*

Paper Group Company LLC..........E......714 566-0025
15201 Woodlawn Ave # 200 Tustin (92780) *(P-5142)*

Paper Surce Converting Mfg Inc..........E......323 583-3800
4800 S Santa Fe Ave Vernon (90058) *(P-5143)*

Paper-Pak Industries, La Verne *Also called Novipax Inc (P-5516)*

Papercon Packaging Division, City of Industry *Also called Bagcraftpapercon I LLC (P-5433)*

Papercutters Inc..........E......323 888-1330
6023 Bandini Blvd Los Angeles (90040) *(P-5336)*

Pappalecco..........F......619 906-5566
3650 5th Ave Ste 104 San Diego (92103) *(P-13537)*

Pappy's Fine Foods, Fresno *Also called Pappys Meat Company Inc (P-2581)*

Pappys Meat Company Inc..........E......559 291-0218
5663 E Fountain Way Fresno (93727) *(P-2581)*

Paprsa, San Diego *Also called Panasonic Appliances Ref (P-16821)*

Par Global Resources Inc..........F......408 982-5515
2005 De La Cruz Blvd # 111 Santa Clara (95050) *(P-6767)*

Par Orthodontic Laboratory..........E......949 472-4788
23141 La Cadena Dr Ste K Laguna Hills (92653) *(P-22180)*

Para Plate & Plastics Co Inc..........E......562 404-3434
15910 Shoemaker Ave Cerritos (90703) *(P-14336)*

Para Tech Coating, Laguna Hills *Also called Metal Improvement Company LLC (P-11458)*

Parabilis Space Tech Inc..........F......855 727-2245
1195 Linda Vista Dr Ste F San Marcos (92078) *(P-20454)*

Paracor Medical Inc..........E......408 207-1050
19200 Stevns Crk Blvd # 200 Cupertino (95014) *(P-22296)*

Paradigm Contract Mfg LLC..........F......714 889-7074
5531 Belle Ave Cypress (90630) *(P-23442)*

Paradigm Label Inc..........F......951 372-9212
10258 Birtcher Dr Jurupa Valley (91752) *(P-5521)*

Paradigm Packaging East LLC..........C......909 985-2750
9177 Center Ave Rancho Cucamonga (91730) *(P-9952)*

Paradigm Packaging West, Rancho Cucamonga *Also called Paradigm Packaging East LLC (P-9952)*

Paradigm Winery..........F......707 944-1683
683 Dwyer Rd Oakville (94562) *(P-1855)*

Paradise Kitchen Doors, Pomona *Also called Gonzalez Feliciano (P-4051)*

Paradise Manufacturing Co Inc..........C......909 477-3460
13364 Aerospace Dr 100 Victorville (92394) *(P-3698)*

Paradise Printing Inc..........E......714 228-9628
13474 Pumice St Norwalk (90650) *(P-6768)*

Paradise Ranch..........F......951 776-7736
2900 Adams St Ste C8 Riverside (92504) *(P-3573)*

Paradise Ridge Winery..........F......707 528-9463
4545 Thomas Lk Harris Dr Santa Rosa (95403) *(P-1856)*

Paradise Road LLC..........E......714 894-1779
5872 Engineer Dr Huntington Beach (92649) *(P-8403)*

Paragon Building Products Inc (PA)..........E......951 549-1155
2191 5th St Ste 111 Norco (92860) *(P-10622)*

Paragon Controls Incorporated..........F......707 579-1424
2371 Circadian Way Santa Rosa (95407) *(P-20803)*

Paragon Label, Petaluma *Also called Mrs Grossmans Paper Company (P-5483)*

Paragon Laboratories, Torrance *Also called Naturalife Eco Vite Labs (P-608)*

Paragon Machine Works Inc..........D......510 232-3223
253 S 25th St Richmond (94804) *(P-16279)*

Paragon Precision Inc..........E......661 257-1380
25620 Rye Canyon Rd Ste A Valencia (91355) *(P-19974)*

Paragon Products LLC (PA)..........E......916 941-9717
4475 Golden Foothill Pkwy El Dorado Hills (95762) *(P-20376)*

Paragon Swiss Inc..........E......408 748-1617
545 Aldo Ave Ste 1 Santa Clara (95054) *(P-16280)*

Paragon Tactical Inc..........F......951 736-9440
1580 Commerce St Corona (92880) *(P-22864)*

Parallax Incorporated..........E......916 624-8333
599 Menlo Dr Ste 100 Rocklin (95765) *(P-14960)*

Parallax Research, Rocklin *Also called Parallax Incorporated (P-14960)*

Parallocity Inc..........E......408 524-1530
440 N Wolfe Rd Sunnyvale (94085) *(P-19229)*

Parametric Manufacturing Inc..........F......408 654-9845
3465 Edward Ave Santa Clara (95054) *(P-16281)*

Paramit Corporation (PA)..........B......408 782-5600
18735 Madrone Pkwy Morgan Hill (95037) *(P-17952)*

Paramont Metal & Supply Co, Paramount *Also called George Jue Mfg Co Inc (P-14221)*

Paramount Asphalt, Paramount *Also called Paramount Petroleum Corp (P-9058)*

Paramount Dairy Inc (PA)..........E......949 265-8077
17801 Cartwright Rd Irvine (92614) *(P-707)*

Paramount Dairy Inc..........E......562 361-1800
15255 Texaco Ave Paramount (90723) *(P-708)*

Paramount Extrusions Company (PA)..........E......562 634-3291
6833 Rosecrans Ave Paramount (90723) *(P-11242)*

Paramount Extrusions Company ....E....562 634-3291
6833 Rosecrans Ave Ste A Paramount (90723) ***(P-11243)***
Paramount Fabricators, Rancho Cucamonga *Also called Paramunt Plstic Fbricators Inc* ***(P-9954)***
Paramount Farms, Los Angeles *Also called Wonderful Pstchios Almonds LLC* ***(P-1442)***
Paramount Food Processing, Del Rey *Also called Del Rey Juice Co* ***(P-909)***
Paramount Grinding Service....F....562 630-6940
7311 Madison St Ste C Paramount (90723) ***(P-16282)***
Paramount Laminates Inc ....F....562 531-7580
15527 Vermont Ave Paramount (90723) ***(P-9446)***
Paramount Laminates & Cabinets, Paramount *Also called Paramount Laminates Inc* ***(P-9446)***
Paramount Machine Co Inc....E....909 484-3600
10824 Edison Ct Rancho Cucamonga (91730) ***(P-16283)***
Paramount Mattress Inc ....F....323 264-3451
2900 E Olympic Blvd Los Angeles (90023) ***(P-4735)***
Paramount Panels Inc (PA) ....E....909 947-8008
1531 E Cedar St Ontario (91761) ***(P-9953)***
Paramount Panels Inc ....E....909 947-5168
1531 E Cedar St Ontario (91761) ***(P-20194)***
Paramount Petroleum Corp ....F....562 633-4332
8835 Somerset Blvd Paramount (90723) ***(P-9057)***
Paramount Petroleum Corp ....F....916 685-9253
10090 Waterman Rd Elk Grove (95624) ***(P-9100)***
Paramount Petroleum Corp (HQ) ....C....562 531-2060
14700 Downey Ave Paramount (90723) ***(P-9058)***
Paramount Petroleum Corp ....F....661 392-3630
1201 China Grade Loop Bakersfield (93308) ***(P-9059)***
Paramount Roll Forming Co Inc....E....562 944-6151
12120 Florence Ave Santa Fe Springs (90670) ***(P-11861)***
Paramount Tool & Machine Co, Redwood City *Also called Talos Corporation* ***(P-16442)***
Paramount Window & Doors, San Bernardino *Also called Paramount Windows & Doors* ***(P-4105)***
Paramount Windows & Doors....F....909 888-4688
723 W Mill St San Bernardino (92410) ***(P-4105)***
Paramunt Plstic Fbricators Inc ....F....909 987-4757
11251 Jersey Blvd Rancho Cucamonga (91730) ***(P-9954)***
Parasound Products Inc....F....415 397-7100
2250 Mckinnon Ave San Francisco (94124) ***(P-17268)***
Paratech Inc....E....562 633-2045
15940 Minnesota Ave Paramount (90723) ***(P-10975)***
Parco LLC (PA)....C....909 947-2200
1801 S Archibald Ave Ontario (91761) ***(P-9246)***
Parcor, Garden Grove *Also called Ken-Wor Corp* ***(P-11053)***
Parducci Wine Estates LLC ....E....707 463-5350
501 Parducci Rd Ukiah (95482) ***(P-1857)***
Parent Is Sas Ltries H Trbllat, Sonoma *Also called Laura Chenels Chevre Inc* ***(P-562)***
Parex Usa Inc (HQ)....E....714 778-2266
4125 E La Palma Ave # 250 Anaheim (92807) ***(P-11018)***
Parex Usa Inc ....E....209 983-8002
11290 Vallejo Ct French Camp (95231) ***(P-11019)***
Parisa Lingerie & Swim Wear, Northridge *Also called Afr Apparel International Inc* ***(P-3439)***
Park Electrochemical Corp ....E....714 459-4400
1100 E Kimberly Ave Anaheim (92801) ***(P-17953)***
Park Engineering and Mfg Co....E....714 521-4660
6430 Roland St Buena Park (90621) ***(P-16284)***
Park Pets and Boulders, Paso Robles *Also called Sport Rock International Inc* ***(P-22896)***
Park Steel Co Inc....F....310 638-6101
515 E Pine St Compton (90222) ***(P-11862)***
Park West Enterprises ....E....909 383-8341
2586 Shenandoah Way San Bernardino (92407) ***(P-1464)***
Park's Prtg & Lithographic Co, Modesto *Also called Village Instant Printing Inc* ***(P-6923)***
Park-Rand Enterprises Inc ....F....818 362-2565
39630 Fairway Dr Apt 218 Palmdale (93551) ***(P-8404)***
Parker Aerospace, Irvine *Also called Parker-Hannifin Corporation* ***(P-20196)***
Parker Boiler Co, Commerce *Also called Sid E Parker Boiler Mfg Co Inc* ***(P-12051)***
Parker House International, Eastvale *Also called Parker House Mfg Co Inc* ***(P-4754)***
Parker House Mfg Co Inc ....E....800 628-1319
6300 Providence Way Eastvale (92880) ***(P-4754)***
Parker Medical Systems, San Diego *Also called Parker-Hannifin Corporation* ***(P-15637)***
Parker Plastics Inc....E....707 994-6363
12762 Highway 29 Lower Lake (95457) ***(P-9955)***
Parker Powis Inc....D....510 848-2463
2929 5th St Berkeley (94710) ***(P-15387)***
Parker Printing Inc ....F....714 444-4550
11240 Young River Ave Fountain Valley (92708) ***(P-6769)***
Parker Pumper Helmet Co, Mira Loma *Also called Racing Plus Inc* ***(P-22075)***
Parker Service Center, Fremont *Also called Parker-Hannifin Corporation* ***(P-15632)***
Parker Service Center, Buena Park *Also called Parker-Hannifin Corporation* ***(P-9203)***
Parker-Hannifin Corporation....E....714 522-8840
8460 Kass Dr Buena Park (90621) ***(P-9203)***
Parker-Hannifin Corporation ....C....408 592-6480
5650 Stewart Ave Fremont (94538) ***(P-15632)***
Parker-Hannifin Corporation ....D....310 308-0389
13850 Van Ness Ave Gardena (90249) ***(P-16285)***
Parker-Hannifin Corporation ....C....619 661-7000
7664 Panasonic Way San Diego (92154) ***(P-15633)***
Parker-Hannifin Corporation....B....949 833-3000
16666 Von Karman Ave Irvine (92606) ***(P-19975)***
Parker-Hannifin Corporation ....D....510 235-9590
250 Canal Blvd Richmond (94804) ***(P-20915)***
Parker-Hannifin Corporation ....D....216 896-2663
16666 Von Karman Ave Irvine (92606) ***(P-20195)***
Parker-Hannifin Corporation....D....949 833-3000
1666 Don Carmen Irvine (92618) ***(P-20196)***
Parker-Hannifin Corporation....E....951 280-3800
221 Helicopter Cir Corona (92880) ***(P-15634)***
Parker-Hannifin Corporation ....C....949 833-3000
16666 Von Karman Ave Irvine (92606) ***(P-15635)***
Parker-Hannifin Corporation ....C....310 608-5600
19610 S Rancho Way Rancho Dominguez (90220) ***(P-18729)***
Parker-Hannifin Corporation....F....805 658-2984
3007 Bunsen Ave Ste K Ventura (93003) ***(P-15636)***
Parker-Hannifin Corporation ....C....707 584-7558
5500 Business Park Dr Rohnert Park (94928) ***(P-16736)***
Parker-Hannifin Corporation....A....949 833-3000
14300 Alton Pkwy Irvine (92618) ***(P-20197)***
Parker-Hannifin Corporation....E....562 404-1938
14087 Borate St Santa Fe Springs (90670) ***(P-12039)***
Parker-Hannifin Corporation....A....209 521-7860
3400 Finch Rd Modesto (95354) ***(P-14845)***
Parker-Hannifin Corporation ....C....805 604-3400
2340 Eastman Ave Oxnard (93030) ***(P-14846)***
Parker-Hannifin Corporation ....C....310 608-5600
2630 E El Presidio St Carson (90810) ***(P-14514)***
Parker-Hannifin Corporation ....C....805 484-8533
3800 Calle Tecate Camarillo (93012) ***(P-20198)***
Parker-Hannifin Corporation ....C....714 632-6512
7664 Panasonic Way San Diego (92154) ***(P-15637)***
Parks and Open Space, San Rafael *Also called County of Marin* ***(P-4855)***
Parks Optical Inc....E....805 522-6722
80 W Easy St Ste 3 Simi Valley (93065) ***(P-21397)***
Parmatech Corporation....D....707 778-2266
2221 Pine View Way Petaluma (94954) ***(P-11482)***
Parpro Technologies Inc....C....714 545-8886
2700 S Fairview St Santa Ana (92704) ***(P-17954)***
Parquet By Dian Inc....D....310 527-3779
16601 S Main St Gardena (90248) ***(P-3981)***
Parrot Communications Intl Inc....E....818 567-4700
26321 Ferry Ct Santa Clarita (91350) ***(P-6305)***
Parrot Media Network, Santa Clarita *Also called Parrot Communications Intl Inc* ***(P-6305)***
Pars Publishing Corp ....D....818 280-0540
4485 Runway St Simi Valley (93063) ***(P-6770)***
Part Handling Engrg & Dev Corp....F....951 308-4450
42175 Zevo Dr Temecula (92590) ***(P-22297)***
Parter Medical Products Inc ....C....310 327-4417
17015 Kingsview Ave Carson (90746) ***(P-20769)***
Partnership Of Paramount Petro, Long Beach *Also called Tidelands Oil Production Inc* ***(P-69)***
Parts Expediting and Dist Co....E....562 944-3199
10805 Artesia Blvd # 112 Cerritos (90703) ***(P-19736)***
Parts Out Inc (PA)....F....626 560-1540
1875 Century Park E # 2200 Los Angeles (90067) ***(P-19199)***
Partsearch Technologies Inc (HQ) ....E....800 289-0300
27460 Avenue Scott D Valencia (91355) ***(P-19046)***
Partsflex Inc....E....408 677-7121
6700 Brem Ln Ste 4 Gilroy (95020) ***(P-3807)***
Party Time Ice Inc....F....310 833-0187
983 N Pacific Ave San Pedro (90731) ***(P-2359)***
Parylene USA Inc ....F....949 452-0770
23 Spectrum Pointe Dr # 201 Lake Forest (92630) ***(P-23443)***
Pasadena Bio Cllbrtive Incbtor....F....626 507-8487
2265 E Foothill Blvd Pasadena (91107) ***(P-20770)***
PASADENA BIOSCIENCE COLLOBORAT, Pasadena *Also called Pasadena Bio Cllbrtive Incbtor* ***(P-20770)***
Pasadena Newspapers Inc (PA) ....C....626 578-6300
2 N Lake Ave Ste 150 Pasadena (91101) ***(P-5793)***
Pasadena Newspapers Inc....C....707 442-1711
930 6th St Eureka (95501) ***(P-5794)***
Pasadena Star-News, Pasadena *Also called Pasadena Newspapers Inc* ***(P-5793)***
Pascal Systems, West Sacramento *Also called Heco Inc* ***(P-14741)***
Pasco, Buena Park *Also called Yeager Enterprises Corp* ***(P-10960)***
Pasco Corporation of America....E....503 289-6500
19191 S Vt Ave Ste 420 Torrance (90502) ***(P-975)***
Pasco Industries Inc....F....714 992-2051
2040 Redondo Pl Fullerton (92835) ***(P-23030)***
Paso Robles Press, Paso Robles *Also called News Media Inc* ***(P-5778)***
Pasport Communications, Sausalito *Also called Pasport Software Programs Inc* ***(P-24288)***
Pasport Software Programs Inc....F....415 331-2606
307 Bridgeway Sausalito (94965) ***(P-24288)***
Pass, Orange *Also called Prototype & Short-Run Svcs Inc* ***(P-12864)***
Pass & Seymour Inc ....A....562 505-4072
9415 Kruse Rd Pico Rivera (90660) ***(P-16919)***
Pass Laboratories Inc....F....530 878-5350
13395 New Arprt Rd Ste G Auburn (95602) ***(P-17269)***
Passport Food Group LLC (PA)....C....909 627-7312
2539 E Philadelphia St Ontario (91761) ***(P-2582)***
Passy-Muir Inc....F....949 833-8255
1212 Mcgaw Ave Irvine (92614) ***(P-22065)***
Passy-Muir Inc (PA) ....E....949 833-8255
17992 Mitchell S Ste 200 Irvine (92614) ***(P-22066)***
Pasta Mia, Fullerton *Also called Nina Mia Inc* ***(P-2569)***
Pasta Prima, Benicia *Also called Valley Fine Foods Company Inc* ***(P-1011)***
Pasta Sonoma LLC ....F....707 584-0800
640 Martin Ave Ste 1 Rohnert Park (94928) ***(P-2378)***
Pastries By Edie Inc....E....818 340-0203
7226 Topanga Canyon Blvd Canoga Park (91303) ***(P-1259)***
Patch Place....E....909 947-3023
1724 S Grove Ave Ste A Ontario (91761) ***(P-3852)***
Patientpop Inc....D....844 487-8399
214 Wilshire Blvd Santa Monica (90401) ***(P-24289)***
Patina Products, Arroyo Grande *Also called Layne Laboratories Inc* ***(P-2942)***
Patio & Door Outlet Inc (PA) ....E....714 974-9900
410 W Fletcher Ave Orange (92865) ***(P-4769)***
Patio Outlet, Orange *Also called Patio & Door Outlet Inc* ***(P-4769)***

ALPHABETIC

Employee Codes: A=Over 500 employees, B=251-500
C=101-250, D=51-100, E=20-50, F=10-19
2020 California
Manfacturers Register
© Mergent Inc. 1-800-342-5647
1199

Patio Paradise Inc ....F....626 715-4869
444 Athol St San Bernardino (92401) *(P-16985)*
Patricia Edwards, Commerce *Also called Superb Chair Corporation (P-4673)*
Patricks Cabinets ....F....909 823-2524
10160 Redwood Ave Fontana (92335) *(P-4230)*
Patriot Lighting Inc ....F....213 741-9757
2305 S Main St Los Angeles (90007) *(P-17064)*
Patriot Memory LLC (PA) ....C....510 979-1021
47027 Benicia St Fremont (94538) *(P-18466)*
Patriot Mritime Compliance LLC ....F....925 296-2000
1320 Willow Pass Rd # 485 Concord (94520) *(P-20301)*
Patriot Polishing Company ....F....310 903-7409
47260 Wrangler Rd Aguanga (92536) *(P-8405)*
Patriot Products, Irwindale *Also called Pertronix Inc (P-19200)*
Patron Solutions LLC ....C....949 823-1700
5171 California Ave # 200 Irvine (92617) *(P-24290)*
Pats Decorating Service Inc ....F....323 585-5073
2532 Strozier Ave South El Monte (91733) *(P-3594)*
Patsons Media Group, Santa Clara *Also called Patsons Press (P-6771)*
Patsons Press ....E....408 567-0911
3000 Scott Blvd Ste 101 Santa Clara (95054) *(P-6771)*
Patten Systems Inc ....F....714 799-5656
15598 Producer Ln Huntington Beach (92649) *(P-20916)*
Patterson Frozen Foods Inc ....F....209 892-5060
10 S 3rd St Patterson (95363) *(P-923)*
Patterson Kincaid LLC ....F....323 584-3559
5175 S Soto St Vernon (90058) *(P-3383)*
Patton Door and Gate, Palm Springs *Also called Door Service Company (P-11092)*
Pau Hana Group LLC ....F....530 993-6800
94601 State Rte 70 Chilcoot (96105) *(P-11619)*
Paul A Evans Inc ....F....530 859-2505
1215 Audubon Rd Mount Shasta (96067) *(P-13740)*
Paul Baker Printing Inc ....E....916 969-8317
220 Riverside Ave Roseville (95678) *(P-6772)*
Paul Brown Hawaii, Sun Valley *Also called Pbh Marketing Inc (P-8555)*
Paul Crist Studios Inc ....F....562 696-9992
8317 Secura Way Santa Fe Springs (90670) *(P-10386)*
Paul Dosier Associates Inc ....F....714 556-7075
913 Chicago Ave Placentia (92870) *(P-13939)*
Paul Graham Drilling & Svc Co ....C....707 374-5123
2500 Airport Rd Rio Vista (94571) *(P-102)*
Paul Hobbs Winery LP ....F....707 824-9879
3355 Gravenstein Hwy N Sebastopol (95472) *(P-1858)*
Paul Hubbs Construction Inc (PA) ....F....951 360-3990
542 W C St Colton (92324) *(P-318)*
Paul Merrill Company Inc ....F....562 691-1871
350 W Central Ave # 141 Brea (92821) *(P-10918)*
Paul Silver Enterprises Inc ....F....818 998-9900
9155 Alabama Ave Ste F Chatsworth (91311) *(P-6773)*
Paula Keller ....F....310 833-1894
1044 S Gaffey St San Pedro (90731) *(P-4106)*
Paulco Precision Inc ....F....310 679-4900
13916 Cordary Ave Hawthorne (90250) *(P-16286)*
Pauli Systems Inc ....E....707 429-2434
1820 Walters Ct Fairfield (94533) *(P-16287)*
Paulsen White Oak LP ....F....530 656-2201
3976 Garden Hwy Nicolaus (95659) *(P-8838)*
Paulson Manufacturing Corp (PA) ....D....951 676-2451
46752 Rainbow Canyon Rd Temecula (92592) *(P-22067)*
Paulsson Inc ....F....310 780-2219
16543 Arminta St Van Nuys (91406) *(P-133)*
Pavement Recycling Systems Inc ....F....661 948-5599
46205 Division St Lancaster (93535) *(P-9101)*
Pavestone LLC ....E....530 795-4400
27600 County Road 90 Winters (95694) *(P-10919)*
Pavex Construction Co, Seaside *Also called Granite Rock Co (P-10765)*
Pavilion Integration Corp ....F....408 453-8801
2528 Qume Dr Ste 1 San Jose (95131) *(P-21519)*
Paw Prints Inc ....F....650 365-4077
3166 Bay Rd Redwood City (94063) *(P-7170)*
Pax Tag & Label Inc ....E....626 579-2000
9528 Rush St Ste C El Monte (91733) *(P-7171)*
Paxata Inc ....D....650 542-7897
1800 Seaport Blvd 1 Redwood City (94063) *(P-24291)*
Paylocity Holding Corporation ....B....847 956-4850
2107 Livingston St Oakland (94606) *(P-24292)*
Paymentmax Processing Inc ....D....805 557-1692
600 Hampshire Rd Ste 120 Westlake Village (91361) *(P-15376)*
Payne Magnetics Inc ....D....626 332-6207
854 W Front St Covina (91722) *(P-18730)*
Paysonic, Union City *Also called Spacesonics Incorporated (P-12383)*
Payton Technology Corporation ....C....714 885-8000
17665 Newhope St Ste B Fountain Valley (92708) *(P-18467)*
Pazzulla Plastics Inc ....E....714 847-2541
165 Emilia Ln Fallbrook (92028) *(P-4930)*
Pb Fasteners, Gardena *Also called SPS Technologies LLC (P-12693)*
Pbf Energy Inc ....F....310 212-2800
3700 W 190th St Torrance (90504) *(P-9060)*
Pbf Energy Western Region LLC (HQ) ....B....973 455-7500
111 W Ocean Blvd Ste 1500 Long Beach (90802) *(P-9061)*
Pbh Marketing Inc ....F....818 374-9000
9960 Glenoaks Blvd Ste C Sun Valley (91352) *(P-8555)*
Pby Plastics Inc ....F....909 930-6700
2571 Lindsey Privado Dr Ontario (91761) *(P-9956)*
PC Mechanical Inc ....E....805 925-2888
2803 Industrial Pkwy Santa Maria (93455) *(P-245)*
PC Recycle, Newbury Park *Also called Fc Management Services (P-14466)*
PC Vaughan Mfg Corp ....C....805 278-2555
1278 Mercantile St Oxnard (93030) *(P-14847)*

PC World Online, San Francisco *Also called Idg Consumer & Smb Inc (P-5959)*
PCA, Santa Clara *Also called Polishing Corporation America (P-18474)*
PCA Aerospace Inc (PA) ....D....714 841-1750
17800 Gothard St Huntington Beach (92647) *(P-20199)*
PCA Central Cal Corrugated LLC ....C....916 614-0580
4841 Urbani Ave McClellan (95652) *(P-5257)*
PCA Electronics Inc ....E....818 892-0761
16799 Schoenborn St North Hills (91343) *(P-18731)*
PCA Summit Service, Escondido *Also called Summit Services Inc (P-10521)*
PCA/Los Angeles 349, Vernon *Also called Packaging Corporation America (P-5253)*
PCA/South Gate 378, South Gate *Also called Packaging Corporation America (P-5254)*
Pcb Fabrication Facility, San Marcos *Also called Hughes Circuits Inc (P-17896)*
PCC Rollmet Inc ....D....949 221-5333
1822 Deere Ave Irvine (92606) *(P-11194)*
PCC Structurals Inc ....C....510 568-6400
414 Hester St San Leandro (94577) *(P-11420)*
PCC Structurals-San Leandro, San Leandro *Also called PCC Structurals Inc (P-11420)*
Pch International USA Inc ....E....415 643-5463
135 Mississippi St Fl 1 San Francisco (94107) *(P-19047)*
Pch Lime Lab, San Francisco *Also called Pch International USA Inc (P-19047)*
PCI, Riverside *Also called Pacific Consolidated Inds LLC (P-14842)*
PCI, Santa Rosa *Also called Paragon Controls Incorporated (P-20803)*
PCI Holding Company Inc (PA) ....C....951 479-0860
12201 Magnolia Ave Riverside (92503) *(P-14848)*
PCI Industries Inc ....D....323 728-0004
6501 Potello St Commerce (90040) *(P-12329)*
PCL Communications, San Leandro *Also called Pacific Coast Laboratories (P-22064)*
Pcs Company, Sunnyvale *Also called Pcs Machining Service Inc (P-16288)*
Pcs Machining Service Inc ....F....408 735-9974
784 Edale Dr Sunnyvale (94087) *(P-16288)*
Pct, Compton *Also called Pacific Contntl Textiles Inc (P-2858)*
Pct, Fremont *Also called Printed Circuit Technology (P-17963)*
Pct-Gw Carbide Tools Usa Inc ....E....562 921-7898
13701 Excelsior Dr Santa Fe Springs (90670) *(P-7515)*
Pd Group ....E....760 674-3028
41945 Boardwalk Ste L Palm Desert (92211) *(P-23176)*
Pd Products LLC ....F....818 772-0100
21350 Lassen St Chatsworth (91311) *(P-2950)*
Pda Group, Valencia *Also called Packaging Dist Assembly Group (P-5171)*
Pdc LLC ....E....626 334-5000
4675 Vinita Ct Chino (91710) *(P-14092)*
Pdc-Identicard, Valencia *Also called Precision Dynamics Corporation (P-5371)*
Pdf Print Communications Inc (PA) ....D....562 426-6978
2630 E 28th St Long Beach (90755) *(P-6774)*
Pdi, Silverado *Also called Program Data Incorporated (P-21103)*
Pdi, San Carlos *Also called Precision Design Inc (P-17961)*
Pdl Biopharma Inc ....E....650 454-1000
1500 Seaport Blvd Redwood City (94063) *(P-8320)*
PDM Solutions Inc ....E....858 348-1000
8451 Miralani Dr Ste J San Diego (92126) *(P-17955)*
Pdma Ventures Inc ....E....714 777-8770
22951 La Palma Ave Yorba Linda (92887) *(P-23444)*
PDQ Engineering Inc ....E....805 482-1334
1199 Avenida Acaso Ste F Camarillo (93012) *(P-16289)*
Pdr-America, Shingle Springs *Also called White Industrial Corporation (P-14259)*
PDT, Goleta *Also called Pacific Design Tech Inc (P-20671)*
Peabody Engineering & Sup Inc ....E....951 734-7711
13435 Estelle St Corona (92879) *(P-14515)*
Peachpit Press ....E....415 336-6831
1301 Sansome St San Francisco (94111) *(P-6306)*
Peak Seasons, Riverside *Also called Tom Leonard Investment Co Inc (P-23506)*
Peak Servo Corp / Eltrol, Carlsbad *Also called Peak Servo Corporation (P-16737)*
Peak Servo Corporation ....F....760 438-4986
5931 Sea Lion Pl Ste 108 Carlsbad (92010) *(P-16737)*
Peanut Shell, Union City *Also called Farallon Brands Inc (P-3616)*
Pear Valley Vineyard Inc ....F....805 237-2861
4900 Union Rd Paso Robles (93446) *(P-1859)*
Pear Valley Vineyard & Winery, Paso Robles *Also called Pear Valley Vineyard Inc (P-1859)*
Pearl Crop Inc ....E....209 887-3731
8452 Demartini Ln Linden (95236) *(P-2583)*
Pearl Crop Inc ....E....209 982-9933
17641 French Camp Rd Ripon (95366) *(P-1449)*
Pearl Management Group Inc ....E....818 217-0218
14950 Delano St Van Nuys (91411) *(P-8063)*
Pearl Rove Inc ....F....858 869-1827
9570 Ridgehaven Ct Ste B San Diego (92123) *(P-22992)*
Pearlman Enterprises Inc (HQ) ....C....800 969-5561
6210 Garfield Ave Commerce (90040) *(P-10953)*
Pearpoint Inc ....E....760 343-7350
39740 Garand Ln Ste B Palm Desert (92211) *(P-17620)*
Pearson Education Inc ....F....800 653-1918
3700 Inland Empire Blvd Ontario (91764) *(P-6134)*
Pearson Education Inc ....E....415 402-2500
1301 Sansome St San Francisco (94111) *(P-6135)*
Pearson Electronics Inc ....F....650 494-6444
4009 Transport St Palo Alto (94303) *(P-18732)*
Pearson Engineering Corp ....F....626 442-7436
2505 Loma Ave South El Monte (91733) *(P-13222)*
Peay Vineyards LLC ....F....707 894-8720
207a N Cloverdale Blvd Cloverdale (95425) *(P-1860)*
Pebble Technology Corp ....E....888 224-5820
900 Middlefield Rd Ste 5 Redwood City (94063) *(P-22483)*
PEC Manufacturing Inc ....F....408 577-1839
675 Sycamore Dr Milpitas (95035) *(P-19375)*
PEC Tool, Torrance *Also called Products Engineering Corp (P-11541)*
Peca Corporation ....E....626 452-8873
9707 El Poche St Ste H El Monte (91733) *(P-9351)*

Pacific Grinding, Fullerton *Also called Kryler Corp (P-13037)*
Peck Road Gravel Pit...E.......626 574-7570
128 Live Oak Ave Monrovia (91016) *(P-356)*
Peco Controls Corporation...F.......209 576-3345
1616 Culpepper Ave Ste A Modesto (95351) *(P-16738)*
Peco Inspx, Modesto *Also called Peco Controls Corporation (P-16738)*
Pecofacet (us) Inc...F.......916 689-2328
8314 Tiogawoods Dr Sacramento (95828) *(P-14849)*
Pecowood Inc...F.......562 633-2538
7707 Alondra Blvd Paramount (90723) *(P-11620)*
Pedavena Mould and Die Co Inc...E.......310 327-2814
12464 Mccann Dr Santa Fe Springs (90670) *(P-16290)*
Pedco, Cerritos *Also called Parts Expediting and Dist Co (P-19736)*
Pedi, Carlsbad *Also called Providien Injction Molding Inc (P-10001)*
Pednar Products Inc (PA)...F.......626 960-9883
1823 Enterprise Way Monrovia (91016) *(P-9560)*
Pedro Pallan...F.......310 638-1763
344 W Rosecrans Ave Compton (90222) *(P-1260)*
Peei, Los Angeles *Also called Playboy Enterprises Intl Inc (P-6311)*
Peek Arent You Curious Inc (PA)...D.......415 512-7335
425 2nd St Ste 405 San Francisco (94107) *(P-3486)*
Peen-Rite Inc...F.......818 767-3676
11662 Sheldon St Sun Valley (91352) *(P-11465)*
Peep Inc...E.......213 748-5500
720 Towne Ave Los Angeles (90021) *(P-3384)*
Peep Studio, Los Angeles *Also called Peep Inc (P-3384)*
Peerles Coffee and Tea, Oakland *Also called Peerless Coffee Company Inc (P-2307)*
Peerless Coffee Company Inc...D.......510 763-1763
260 Oak St Oakland (94607) *(P-2307)*
Peerless Injection Molding LLC...E.......714 689-1920
14321 Corp Dr Garden Grove (92843) *(P-9957)*
Peerless Materials Company (PA)...E.......323 266-0313
4442 E 26th St Vernon (90058) *(P-8406)*
Peets Coffee & Tea LLC (HQ)...B.......510 594-2100
1400 Park Ave Emeryville (94608) *(P-2308)*
Pega Precision Inc...E.......408 776-3700
18800 Adams Ct Morgan Hill (95037) *(P-12330)*
Pegasus Foods, Los Angeles *Also called Astrochef LLC (P-944)*
Pegasus Med Services/Renalab...F.......805 226-8350
3570 Sibley Ln Templeton (93465) *(P-8064)*
Peggy S Lane Inc...D.......510 483-1202
2701 Merced St San Leandro (94577) *(P-9595)*
Peking Noodle Co Inc...E.......323 223-0897
1514 N San Fernando Rd Los Angeles (90065) *(P-2379)*
Pelagic Pressure Systems Corp...D.......510 569-3100
2002 Davis St San Leandro (94577) *(P-14180)*
Pelican Products Inc (PA)...B.......310 326-4700
23215 Early Ave Torrance (90505) *(P-17154)*
Pelican Rope Works...F.......714 545-0116
1600 E Mcfadden Ave Santa Ana (92705) *(P-2913)*
Pelican Sign Service Inc...F.......408 246-3833
1565 Lafayette St Santa Clara (95050) *(P-23177)*
Pelican Woodworks...E.......951 674-7821
560 Birch St Ste 2 Lake Elsinore (92530) *(P-4231)*
Pellegrine Wine Company, Santa Rosa *Also called Pellegrini Ranches (P-1861)*
Pellegrini Ranches...F.......707 545-8680
4055 W Olivet Rd Santa Rosa (95401) *(P-1861)*
Pellenc America Inc (HQ)...E.......707 568-7286
3171 Guerneville Rd Santa Rosa (95401) *(P-13657)*
Pelton-Shepherd Industries Inc (PA)...E.......209 460-0893
812 W Luce St Ste B Stockton (95203) *(P-2360)*
Pem, Buena Park *Also called Park Engineering and Mfg Co (P-16284)*
Pencil Grip Inc (PA)...F.......310 315-3545
21200 Superior St Ste A Chatsworth (91311) *(P-5484)*
Pencom Accuracy Inc...D.......510 785-5022
1300 Industrial Rd Ste 21 San Carlos (94070) *(P-12646)*
Pendarvis Manufacturing Inc...E.......714 992-0950
1808 N American St Anaheim (92801) *(P-16291)*
Pendragon Costumes, Castaic *Also called Nicole Fullerton (P-3572)*
Penfield Products Inc...E.......916 635-0231
11300 Trade Center Dr A Rancho Cordova (95742) *(P-12331)*
Penguin Pumps Incorporated...E.......818 504-2391
7932 Ajay Dr Sun Valley (91352) *(P-14593)*
Penhall Diamond Products Inc...D.......714 776-0937
1345 S Acacia Ave Fullerton (92831) *(P-14181)*
Penhouse Media Group Inc...E.......310 575-4835
11601 Wilshire Blvd Fl 5 Los Angeles (90025) *(P-6000)*
Peninsula Engrg Solutions Inc...F.......925 837-2243
288 Love Ln Danville (94526) *(P-17621)*
Peninsula Light Metals LLC (HQ)...F.......626 765-4856
875 W 8th St Azusa (91702) *(P-11344)*
Peninsula Metal Fabrication, San Jose *Also called I & A Inc (P-12242)*
Peninsula Metal Fabrication, San Jose *Also called Hardcraft Industries Inc (P-12233)*
Peninsula Packaging LLC (HQ)...D.......559 594-6813
1030 N Anderson Rd Exeter (93221) *(P-23445)*
Peninsula Packaging LLC...C.......831 634-0940
2401 Bert Dr Ste A Hollister (95023) *(P-9958)*
Peninsula Packaging Company, Exeter *Also called Peninsula Packaging LLC (P-23445)*
Peninsula Publishing, Newport Beach *Also called Builder & Developer Magazines (P-5894)*
Peninsula Publishing Inc...E.......949 631-1307
1602 Monrovia Ave Newport Beach (92663) *(P-6001)*
Peninsula Spring Corporation...F.......408 848-3361
6750 Silacci Way Gilroy (95020) *(P-13384)*
Pennoyer-Dodge Co...E.......818 547-2100
6650 San Fernando Rd Glendale (91201) *(P-14182)*
Penny & Giles Drive Technology, Brea *Also called Curtiss-Wright Controls (P-21996)*
Pennysaver, Arcadia *Also called Harte Hanks Inc (P-5654)*
Pennysaver...E.......909 467-8500
1520 N Mountain Ave # 121 Ontario (91762) *(P-5795)*
Penrose Coping Company, Sun Valley *Also called Precision Tile Co (P-10629)*
Penrose Studios Inc...F.......703 354-1801
223 Mississippi St Ste 3 San Francisco (94107) *(P-6307)*
Pensando Systems Inc...F.......408 451-9012
1730 Technology Dr San Jose (95110) *(P-20917)*
Penta Biotech Inc...F.......650 598-9328
1100 Industrial Rd Ste 4 San Carlos (94070) *(P-8762)*
Penta Financial Inc...E.......818 882-3872
2359 Knoll Dr Ventura (93003) *(P-17792)*
Penta Laboratories, Ventura *Also called Penta Financial Inc (P-17792)*
Penta Laboratories LLC...F.......818 882-3872
7868 Deering Ave Canoga Park (91304) *(P-17793)*
Pentair Aquatic Systems, Chino *Also called Pentair Water Pool and Spa Inc (P-15557)*
Pentair Flow Technologies LLC...C.......559 266-0516
2445 S Gearhart Ave Fresno (93725) *(P-15556)*
Pentair Pool Products, Moorpark *Also called Pentair Water Pool and Spa Inc (P-15558)*
Pentair Technical Products, San Diego *Also called Pep West Inc (P-14594)*
Pentair Water Group, Fresno *Also called Pentair Flow Technologies LLC (P-15556)*
Pentair Water Pool and Spa Inc...E.......909 287-7800
13950 Mountain Ave Chino (91710) *(P-15557)*
Pentair Water Pool and Spa Inc...E.......805 553-5003
10951 W Los Angeles Ave Moorpark (93021) *(P-15558)*
Pentrate Metal Processing...E.......323 269-2121
3517 E Olympic Blvd Los Angeles (90023) *(P-13069)*
Penumbra Inc (PA)...B.......510 748-3200
1 Penumbra Alameda (94502) *(P-21856)*
Penumbra Brands Inc...F.......385 336-6120
1010 S Coast Highway 101 Encinitas (92024) *(P-19048)*
People Center Inc...E.......781 864-1232
2443 Fillmore St 380-7 San Francisco (94115) *(P-24293)*
People For Peace, Los Angeles *Also called 2016 Montgomery Inc (P-2662)*
People Trend Inc...F.......213 995-5555
4801 Staunton Ave Vernon (90058) *(P-3112)*
Peoples Sausage Company...F.......213 627-8633
1132 E Pico Blvd Los Angeles (90021) *(P-488)*
PeopleSoft, San Mateo *Also called Oracle Systems Corporation (P-24273)*
Pep West Inc...A.......800 525-4682
7328 Trade St San Diego (92121) *(P-14594)*
Pepper Plant, The, Gilroy *Also called Blossom Valley Foods Inc (P-2194)*
Pepsi Bottling Group...F.......714 522-9742
6230 Descanso Ave Buena Park (90620) *(P-2107)*
Pepsi Co, Oakland *Also called Svc Mfg Inc A Corp (P-2175)*
Pepsi Cola Btlg of Bkersfield...C.......661 327-9992
215 E 21st St Bakersfield (93305) *(P-2108)*
Pepsi-Cola, Fresno *Also called Roger Enrico (P-2162)*
Pepsi-Cola Bottling Group...C.......661 635-1100
215 E 21st St Bakersfield (93305) *(P-2109)*
Pepsi-Cola Btlg Co Mt Shasta, Mount Shasta *Also called Mt Shasta Btlg Distrg Co Inc (P-2095)*
Pepsi-Cola Metro Btlg Co Inc...D.......805 739-2160
2345 Thompson Way Santa Maria (93455) *(P-2110)*
Pepsi-Cola Metro Btlg Co Inc...B.......714 522-9635
6261 Caballero Blvd Buena Park (90620) *(P-2111)*
Pepsi-Cola Metro Btlg Co Inc...C.......408 617-2200
4699 Old Ironsides Dr # 150 Santa Clara (95054) *(P-2112)*
Pepsi-Cola Metro Btlg Co Inc...A.......310 327-4222
19700 Figueroa St Carson (90745) *(P-2113)*
Pepsi-Cola Metro Btlg Co Inc...B.......916 423-1000
7550 Reese Rd Sacramento (95828) *(P-2114)*
Pepsi-Cola Metro Btlg Co Inc...E.......209 367-7140
4225 Pepsi Pl Stockton (95215) *(P-2115)*
Pepsi-Cola Metro Btlg Co Inc...B.......909 885-0741
6659 Sycamore Canyon Blvd Riverside (92507) *(P-2116)*
Pepsi-Cola Metro Btlg Co Inc...C.......707 746-5404
4701 Park Rd Benicia (94510) *(P-2117)*
Pepsi-Cola Metro Btlg Co Inc...B.......858 560-6735
7995 Armour St San Diego (92111) *(P-2118)*
Pepsi-Cola Metro Btlg Co Inc...C.......831 796-2000
135 Martella St Salinas (93901) *(P-2119)*
Pepsi-Cola Metro Btlg Co Inc...C.......626 338-5531
4416 Azusa Canyon Rd Baldwin Park (91706) *(P-2120)*
Pepsi-Cola Metro Btlg Co Inc...C.......818 898-3829
1200 Arroyo St San Fernando (91340) *(P-2121)*
Pepsi-Cola Metro Btlg Co Inc...D.......415 206-7400
200 Jennings St San Francisco (94124) *(P-2122)*
Pepsi-Cola Metro Btlg Co Inc...D.......661 824-2051
2471 Nadeau St Mojave (93501) *(P-2123)*
Pepsi-Cola Metro Btlg Co Inc...F.......760 775-2660
83801 Citrus Ave Indio (92201) *(P-2124)*
Pepsi-Cola Metro Btlg Co Inc...B.......510 781-3600
29000 Hesperian Blvd Hayward (94545) *(P-2125)*
Pepsi-Cola Metro Btlg Co Inc...C.......949 643-5700
27717 Aliso Creek Rd Aliso Viejo (92656) *(P-2126)*
Pepsico, Santa Maria *Also called Pepsi-Cola Metro Btlg Co Inc (P-2110)*
Pepsico, Hayward *Also called P-Americas LLC (P-2105)*
Pepsico, Redding *Also called John Fitzpatrick & Sons (P-2082)*
Pepsico, Buena Park *Also called Pepsi Bottling Group (P-2107)*
Pepsico, Stockton *Also called Pepsi-Cola Metro Btlg Co Inc (P-2115)*
Pepsico, San Diego *Also called Pepsi-Cola Metro Btlg Co Inc (P-2118)*
Pepsico, Bakersfield *Also called Pepsi-Cola Bottling Group (P-2109)*
Pepsico, Ventura *Also called P-Americas LLC (P-2106)*
Pepsico, Aliso Viejo *Also called Pepsi-Cola Metro Btlg Co Inc (P-2126)*
Pepsico, Riverside *Also called Bottling Group LLC (P-2046)*
Pepsico Inc...C.......626 338-5531
4416 Azusa Canyon Rd Baldwin Park (91706) *(P-2127)*

ALPHABETIC

Employee Codes: A=Over 500 employees, B=251-500
C=101-250, D=51-100, E=20-50, F=10-19
2020 California
Manfacturers Register
© Mergent Inc. 1-800-342-5647
1201

Perazza Prints LLC (PA) ....F....925 681-2458
25 Crescent Dr Ste A349 Pleasant Hill (94523) *(P-6775)*

Perazza Prints LLC ....E....925 567-3395
2495 Estand Way Pleasant Hill (94523) *(P-6776)*

Perceptimed Inc ....E....650 941-7000
365 San Antonio Rd Mountain View (94040) *(P-14516)*

Peregrine Mobile Bottling LLC ....F....707 637-7584
20590 Pueblo Ave Sonoma (95476) *(P-2128)*

Perez Severino ....F....818 701-1522
9710 Owensmouth Ave Lbby Chatsworth (91311) *(P-13538)*

Perez Bros Ornamental Iron, Northridge *Also called Perez Brothers (P-4698)*

Perez Brothers ....F....818 780-8482
19607 Prairie St Northridge (91324) *(P-4698)*

Perez Distributing Fresno Inc (PA) ....E....800 638-3512
103 S Academy Ave Sanger (93657) *(P-8065)*

Perez Machine Inc ....F....310 217-9090
1501 W 134th St Gardena (90249) *(P-16292)*

Perfect Image Printing Inc ....F....916 631-8350
3223 Monier Cir Rancho Cordova (95742) *(P-6777)*

Perfect Plank Co ....F....530 533-7606
2850 S 5th Ave Oroville (95965) *(P-4107)*

Perfect Puree of NAPA Vly LLC ....F....707 261-5100
2700 Napa Valley Corp Dr NAPA (94558) *(P-924)*

Perfection Machine & Tl Works, Los Angeles *Also called Perfection Machine and Tl Work (P-16293)*

Perfection Machine and Tl Work ....E....213 749-5095
1568 E 22nd St Los Angeles (90011) *(P-16293)*

Perfection Pet Brands, Visalia *Also called Perfection Pet Foods LLC (P-1080)*

Perfection Pet Foods LLC (HQ) ....E....559 302-4880
1111 N Miller Park Ct Visalia (93291) *(P-1080)*

Perfectvips Inc (PA) ....F....408 912-2316
2099 Gateway Pl Ste 240 San Jose (95110) *(P-18468)*

Performance AG, Kerman *Also called Pinnacle Agriculture Dist Inc (P-13659)*

Performance Aluminum Products ....E....909 391-4131
520 S Palmetto Ave Ontario (91762) *(P-11345)*

Performance Apparel Corp ....F....805 541-0989
174 Suburban Rd Ste 100 San Luis Obispo (93401) *(P-3385)*

Performance Cnc Inc ....F....760 722-1129
3210 Production Ave Ste A Oceanside (92058) *(P-16294)*

Performance Coatings Inc ....E....707 462-3023
360 Lake Mendocino Dr Ukiah (95482) *(P-8662)*

Performance Composites Inc ....D....310 328-6661
1418 S Alameda St Compton (90221) *(P-10326)*

Performance Forged Products ....E....323 722-3460
7401 Telegraph Rd Montebello (90640) *(P-12717)*

Performance Label Intl Inc ....F....619 429-6870
6825 Gateway Park Dr # 1 San Diego (92154) *(P-7172)*

Performance Machine Tech Inc ....E....661 294-8617
25141 Avenue Stanford Valencia (91355) *(P-16295)*

Performance Materials Corp (PA) ....D....805 482-1722
1150 Calle Suerte Camarillo (93012) *(P-7590)*

Performance Pipe Div, San Ramon *Also called Chevron Phillips Chem Co LP (P-9465)*

Performance Plastics Inc ....D....619 482-5031
7919 Saint Andrews Ave San Diego (92154) *(P-20200)*

Performance Plus Laboratories ....C....805 383-7871
3609 Vista Mercado Camarillo (93012) *(P-20771)*

Performance Polymer Tech LLC ....E....916 677-1414
8801 Washington Blvd # 109 Roseville (95678) *(P-9268)*

Performance Powder Inc ....E....714 632-0600
2940 E La Jolla St Ste A Anaheim (92806) *(P-13223)*

Performance Printing Center ....E....415 485-5878
4380 Redwood Hwy Ste B8 San Rafael (94903) *(P-6778)*

Performance Sealing Inc ....F....714 662-5918
1821 Langley Ave Irvine (92614) *(P-9247)*

Performance Trailers Inc ....E....559 673-6300
2901 Falcon Dr Madera (93637) *(P-19828)*

Performance Truck and Trlr LLC ....F....909 605-0323
2429 Peck Rd Whittier (90601) *(P-19829)*

Performance Tube Bending Inc ....F....626 939-9000
5462 Diaz St Baldwin Park (91706) *(P-13479)*

Performance Welding ....F....559 233-0042
2540 S Sarah St Fresno (93706) *(P-24656)*

Performex Machining Inc ....E....650 595-2228
963 Terminal Way San Carlos (94070) *(P-16296)*

Performmediacom Inc Which ....F....858 336-8121
4500 Great America Pkwy Santa Clara (95054) *(P-6308)*

Perfumer's Apprentice, Scotts Valley *Also called Pacific Coast Products LLC (P-2223)*

Perfumer's Apprentice, Scotts Valley *Also called Pacific Coast Products LLC (P-2224)*

Peri Formwork Systems Inc ....E....909 356-5797
15369 Valencia Ave Fontana (92335) *(P-12332)*

Peric Oil Tool, Bakersfield *Also called Weatherford Completion Systems (P-282)*

Pericom Semiconductor Corp (HQ) ....E....408 232-9100
1545 Barber Ln Milpitas (95035) *(P-21097)*

Peridot Corporation ....D....925 461-8830
1072 Serpentine Ln Pleasanton (94566) *(P-12855)*

Perimeter Solutions LP ....E....909 983-0772
10667 Jersey Blvd Rancho Cucamonga (91730) *(P-7516)*

Periodico El Vida ....E....805 483-1008
130 Palm Dr Oxnard (93030) *(P-5796)*

Perkins ....E....818 764-9293
7312 Varna Ave Ste A North Hollywood (91605) *(P-14250)*

Perkins Family Restaurant, North Hollywood *Also called Perkins (P-14250)*

Perkins Market, Descanso *Also called Yaldo Enterprises Inc (P-2366)*

Permacel-Automotive, Fremont *Also called Nitto Americas Inc (P-5370)*

Permalite Plastics Corp ....E....310 669-9492
3121 E Ana St Compton (90221) *(P-8703)*

Permaswage USA, Gardena *Also called Designed Metal Connections Inc (P-12629)*

Permeco ....F....909 599-9600
1970 Walker St La Verne (91750) *(P-10920)*

Pernod Ricard Usa LLC ....D....707 833-5891
9592 Sonoma Hwy Kenwood (95452) *(P-1862)*

Pernod Ricard Usa LLC ....D....707 967-7770
8445 Silverado Trl Rutherford (94573) *(P-1863)*

Pernstner Sons Fabrication Inc ....F....209 345-2430
712 W Harding Rd Turlock (95380) *(P-13480)*

Perpetual Motion Group Inc ....D....818 982-4300
11939 Sherman Rd North Hollywood (91605) *(P-11863)*

Perrault Corporation ....F....760 466-1024
30640 N River Rd Bonsall (92003) *(P-357)*

Perricone Juices, Beaumont *Also called Beaumont Juice Inc (P-755)*

Perrin Craft, City of Industry *Also called Dispensing Dynamics Intl Inc (P-9758)*

Perrins Registration Office ....F....818 832-1332
17727 Chatsworth St Granada Hills (91344) *(P-12856)*

Perris Skyventure ....F....951 940-4290
2093 Goetz Rd Perris (92570) *(P-12040)*

Perris Wind Tunnel, Perris *Also called Perris Skyventure (P-12040)*

Perry Creek Winery ....F....530 620-5175
7400 Perry Creek Rd Somerset (95684) *(P-1864)*

Perry Tool & Research Inc ....E....510 782-9226
3415 Enterprise Ave Hayward (94545) *(P-11483)*

Perrys Custom Chopping ....F....209 667-8777
21365 Williams Ave Hilmar (95324) *(P-13658)*

Perseption, Vernon *Also called W & W Concept Inc (P-3433)*

Person & Covey Inc ....E....818 937-5000
616 Allen Ave Glendale (91201) *(P-8556)*

Persona International, Sausalito *Also called Personal Awareness Systems (P-6309)*

Personal Awareness Systems ....F....415 331-3900
767 Bridgeway Ste 3b Sausalito (94965) *(P-6309)*

Persys Engineering Inc ....E....831 471-9300
815 Swift St Santa Cruz (95060) *(P-14517)*

Pertronix Inc (PA) ....E....909 599-5955
440 E Arrow Hwy San Dimas (91773) *(P-20804)*

Pertronix Inc ....E....909 599-5955
15601 Cypress Ave Unit B Irwindale (91706) *(P-19200)*

Pesenti Winery, Saint Helena *Also called Turley Wine Cellars Inc (P-1975)*

Pet Carousel Inc ....E....316 291-2500
2350 Academy Ave Sanger (93657) *(P-1081)*

Pet Partners Inc (PA) ....C....951 279-9888
450 N Sheridan St Corona (92880) *(P-23446)*

Pet Product News, Irvine *Also called Bowtie Inc (P-5891)*

Petalumaidence Opco LLC ....C....707 763-4109
101 Monroe St Petaluma (94954) *(P-1865)*

Petcube Inc (PA) ....E....424 302-6107
555 De Haro St Ste 280a San Francisco (94107) *(P-17270)*

Peter Cohen Companies, Los Angeles *Also called Piet Retief Inc (P-3389)*

Peter K Inc (PA) ....E....323 585-5343
5175 S Soto St Vernon (90058) *(P-3386)*

Peter Michael Winery, Calistoga *Also called Sugarloaf Farming Corporation (P-1940)*

Peter Pugger Manufacturing ....F....707 463-1333
3661 Christy Ln Ukiah (95482) *(P-13741)*

Petersen Precision Engrg LLC ....C....650 365-4373
611 Broadway St Redwood City (94063) *(P-16297)*

Peterson Sheet Metal Inc ....F....925 830-1766
12925 Alcosta Blvd Ste 2 San Ramon (94583) *(P-12333)*

Peterson Sheetmetal, San Ramon *Also called Peterson Sheet Metal Inc (P-12333)*

Peterson's Spices, Pico Rivera *Also called GPde Slva Spces Incrporation (P-2475)*

Petit Pot Inc ....E....650 488-7432
4221 Horton St Emeryville (94608) *(P-2584)*

Petite Porcelain By Barbara, Modesto *Also called Phoenix Custom Promotions (P-22652)*

Petits Pains & Co LP ....F....650 692-6000
1730 Gilbreth Rd Burlingame (94010) *(P-1261)*

Petra-1 LP ....F....866 334-3702
12386 Osborne Pl Pacoima (91331) *(P-8557)*

Petro-Lud Inc ....F....661 747-4779
12625 Jomani Dr Ste 104 Bakersfield (93312) *(P-103)*

Petrochem Marketing ....F....323 526-4084
3033 E Washington Blvd Los Angeles (90023) *(P-9102)*

Petroil Americas Limited ....F....323 931-3720
5651 W Pico Blvd Ste 102 Los Angeles (90019) *(P-9062)*

Petroleum Sales Inc ....D....415 256-1600
2066 Redwood Hwy Greenbrae (94904) *(P-62)*

Petroleum Solids Control Inc (PA) ....F....562 424-0254
1320 E Hill St Signal Hill (90755) *(P-246)*

Petsport Usa Inc ....F....925 439-9243
1160 Railroad Ave Pittsburg (94565) *(P-23447)*

Pettigrew & Sons Casket Co ....E....916 383-0777
6151 Power Inn Rd Sacramento (95824) *(P-23251)*

Petunia Pickle Bottom Corp ....F....805 643-6697
3567 Old Conejo Rd Newbury Park (91320) *(P-2708)*

Pezeme, Los Angeles *Also called Choon Inc (P-3223)*

Pf Candle Co, Commerce *Also called Pommes Frites Candle Co (P-23450)*

Pf Plastics Inc ....F....909 392-4488
2044 Wright Ave La Verne (91750) *(P-4770)*

Pfanner Communications Inc ....F....714 227-3579
3334 E Coast Hwy Ste 162 Corona Del Mar (92625) *(P-6002)*

Pfanstiel Printing, Long Beach *Also called Pfanstiel Publishers & Prtrs (P-6779)*

Pfanstiel Publishers & Prtrs ....F....562 438-5641
3010 E Anaheim St Long Beach (90804) *(P-6779)*

Pfenex Inc ....D....858 352-4400
10790 Roselle St San Diego (92121) *(P-8066)*

Pfister Faucets, Foothill Ranch *Also called Price Pfister Inc (P-11677)*

Pfizer Health Solutions Inc ....F....310 586-2550
2400 Broadway Ste 500 Santa Monica (90404) *(P-8067)*

Pfizer Inc ....C....858 622-7325
11095 Torreyana Rd San Diego (92121) *(P-8068)*

Pfizer Inc ....A....858 622-3001
10646 Science Center Dr San Diego (92121) *(P-8069)*

Pfp, Milpitas *Also called Precision Fiber Products Inc (P-11314)*

Pfs, Sylmar *Also called Professional Finishing Systems (P-12861)*

PG Emminger Inc .... E.....925 313-5830
4036 Pacheco Blvd A Martinez (94553) *(P-4931)*

Pg Imtech of California LLC .... F.....562 945-8943
8424 Secura Way Santa Fe Springs (90670) *(P-13070)*

Pgac Corp (PA) .... D.....858 560-8213
9630 Ridgehaven Ct Ste B San Diego (92123) *(P-5337)*

Pgi Pacific Graphics Intl .... E.....626 336-7707
14938 Nelson Ave City of Industry (91744) *(P-6780)*

Pgm Metal Finishing .... F.....714 282-9193
409 W Blueridge Ave Orange (92865) *(P-13224)*

Pgp International Inc (HQ) .... C.....530 662-5056
351 Hanson Way Woodland (95776) *(P-2585)*

PH Design, Commerce *Also called Pacific Hospitality Design Inc (P-4868)*

PH Labs Advanced Nutrition .... F.....619 240-3263
9760 Via De La Amistad San Diego (92154) *(P-8070)*

Phantom, Beverly Hills *Also called Melamed International Inc (P-3107)*

Phantom Carriage Brewery .... E.....310 538-5834
18525 S Main St Gardena (90248) *(P-14392)*

Phantom Cyber Corporation .... E.....650 208-5151
2479 E Byshore Rd Ste 185 Palo Alto (94303) *(P-24294)*

Phantom Tool & Die Co .... F.....760 240-4249
23535 Us Highway 18 Apple Valley (92307) *(P-13989)*

Phaostron Instr Electronic Co, Azusa *Also called Phaostron Instr Electronic Co (P-16606)*

Phaostron Instr Electronic Co .... D.....626 969-6801
717 N Coney Ave Azusa (91702) *(P-16606)*

Pharma Alliance Group Inc .... F.....661 294-7955
28518 Constellation Rd Valencia (91355) *(P-8071)*

Pharma Pac, Grover Beach *Also called H J Harkins Company Inc (P-7930)*

Pharmaceutic Litho Label Inc .... D.....805 285-5162
3990 Royal Ave Simi Valley (93063) *(P-8072)*

Pharmachem Laboratories LLC .... F.....714 630-6000
2929 E White Star Ave Anaheim (92806) *(P-614)*

Pharmaco-Kinesis Corporation .... E.....310 641-2700
6053 W Century Blvd # 600 Los Angeles (90045) *(P-21857)*

Pharmacyclics LLC (HQ) .... C.....408 215-3000
995 E Arques Ave Sunnyvale (94085) *(P-8073)*

Pharmapack North America Corp .... F.....909 390-1888
5095 E Airport Dr Ontario (91761) *(P-7591)*

Pharmavite LLC (HQ) .... C.....818 221-6200
8531 Fallbrook Ave West Hills (91304) *(P-7681)*

Pharmavite LLC .... B.....818 221-6200
1150 Aviation Pl San Fernando (91340) *(P-7682)*

Pharr-Palomar Inc .... A.....714 522-4811
6781 8th St Buena Park (90620) *(P-2884)*

Phase II Products Inc (PA) .... E.....619 236-9699
501 W Broadway Ste 2090 San Diego (92101) *(P-5033)*

Phase Research, Costa Mesa *Also called Fire & Safety Electronics Inc (P-16716)*

Phase-A-Matic Inc .... F.....661 947-8485
39360 3rd St E Ste C301 Palmdale (93550) *(P-19376)*

Phasespace Inc (PA) .... F.....925 945-6533
1937 Oak Park Blvd Ste A Pleasant Hill (94523) *(P-22448)*

Phat N Jicy Burgers Brands LLC .... E.....310 420-7983
25876 The Old Rd 305 Stevenson Ranch (91381) *(P-2586)*

Phat N Juicy Brands, Stevenson Ranch *Also called Phat N Jicy Burgers Brands LLC (P-2586)*

Phathom Pharmaceuticals Inc .... F.....650 325-5156
70 Willow Rd Ste 200 Menlo Park (94025) *(P-8074)*

PHC, Irvine *Also called Pacific Handy Cutter Inc (P-11539)*

Phenix Enterprises Inc (PA) .... E.....909 469-0411
1785 Mount Vernon Ave Pomona (91768) *(P-19551)*

Phenix Truck Bodies and Eqp, Pomona *Also called Phenix Enterprises Inc (P-19551)*

Phenomenex Inc (HQ) .... C.....310 212-0555
411 Madrid Ave Torrance (90501) *(P-21275)*

Pheonicia Inc .... F.....951 268-5180
710 E Parkridge Ave # 105 Corona (92879) *(P-7173)*

PHI .... E.....626 968-9680
14955 Salt Lake Ave E City of Industry (91746) *(P-13990)*

PHI Hydraulics, City of Industry *Also called PHI (P-13990)*

Phiaro Incorporated .... E.....949 727-1261
9016 Research Dr Irvine (92618) *(P-23448)*

Phibro Animal Health Corp .... E.....562 698-8036
8851 Dice Rd Santa Fe Springs (90670) *(P-9016)*

Phibro-Tech Inc .... E.....562 698-8036
8851 Dice Rd Santa Fe Springs (90670) *(P-7517)*

Phifer Incorporated .... F.....626 968-0438
14408 Nelson Ave City of Industry (91744) *(P-13426)*

Phifer Western, City of Industry *Also called Phifer Incorporated (P-13426)*

Phil Blazer Enterprises Inc .... F.....818 786-4000
15315 Magnolia Blvd # 101 Sherman Oaks (91403) *(P-5797)*

Philadelphia Gear, Santa Fe Springs *Also called Timken Gears & Services Inc (P-12723)*

Philatron International (PA) .... C.....562 802-0452
15315 Cornet St Santa Fe Springs (90670) *(P-19377)*

Philbrick Inc .... E.....707 964-2277
32180 Airport Rd Fort Bragg (95437) *(P-3901)*

Philbrick Logging & Trucking, Fort Bragg *Also called Philbrick Inc (P-3901)*

Philip A Stitt Agency .... F.....916 451-2801
3900 Stockton Blvd Sacramento (95820) *(P-3699)*

Philip Morris USA Inc .... D.....949 453-3500
185 Technology Dr Irvine (92618) *(P-2654)*

Philippe Charriol USA, San Diego *Also called Alor International Ltd (P-22491)*

Philips & Lite-On Digital (HQ) .... E.....510 687-1800
726 S Hillview Dr Milpitas (95035) *(P-15073)*

Philips Elec N Amer Corp .... C.....626 480-0755
13700 Live Oak Ave Baldwin Park (91706) *(P-21398)*

Philips North America LLC .... E.....909 574-1800
11201 Iberia St Ste A Jurupa Valley (91752) *(P-16986)*

Philips Semiconductors, Sunnyvale *Also called Nxp Usa Inc (P-18443)*

Phillips 66 Co Carbon Group .... F.....805 489-4050
2555 Willow Rd Arroyo Grande (93420) *(P-14518)*

Phillips 66 Spectrum Corp .... F.....707 745-6100
6100 Egret Ct Benicia (94510) *(P-9153)*

Phillips Bros Plastics Inc .... E.....310 532-8020
17831 S Western Ave Gardena (90248) *(P-9447)*

Phillips Lobue & Wilson Mllwk .... F.....951 331-5714
300 E Santa Ana St Anaheim (92805) *(P-4108)*

Phillips Machine & Wldg Co Inc .... E.....626 855-4600
16125 Gale Ave City of Industry (91745) *(P-24657)*

Phillips-Medisize .... C.....949 477-9495
3545 Harbor Blvd Costa Mesa (92626) *(P-21858)*

Phin, San Jose *Also called Connectedyard Inc (P-21208)*

Phl Associates Inc .... F.....530 753-5881
24711 County Road 100a Davis (95616) *(P-8321)*

Phoenix Aerial Systems Inc .... F.....323 577-3366
10131 National Blvd Los Angeles (90034) *(P-21520)*

Phoenix Arms .... E.....909 937-6900
4231 E Brickell St Ontario (91761) *(P-13276)*

Phoenix Audio Technologies, Irvine *Also called Midas Technology Inc (P-17262)*

Phoenix Cars LLC .... F.....909 987-0815
401 S Doubleday Ave Ontario (91761) *(P-19493)*

Phoenix Custom Promotions .... F.....209 579-1557
2005 Casa Grande Ct Modesto (95355) *(P-22652)*

Phoenix Day Co Inc .... F.....415 822-4414
3431 Regatta Blvd Richmond (94804) *(P-16987)*

Phoenix Deventures Inc .... E.....408 782-6240
18655 Madrone Pkwy # 180 Morgan Hill (95037) *(P-9352)*

Phoenix Engineering, Orange *Also called His Industries Inc (P-14711)*

Phoenix Footwear Group Inc (PA) .... D.....760 602-9688
2236 Rutherford Rd # 113 Carlsbad (92008) *(P-10160)*

Phoenix Improving Life LLC .... F.....650 248-0655
148 Farley St Mountain View (94043) *(P-22068)*

Phoenix Marine Corporation (PA) .... D.....415 464-8116
700 Larkspur Landing Cir # 175 Larkspur (94939) *(P-21098)*

Phoenix Motorcars, Ontario *Also called Phoenix Cars LLC (P-19493)*

Phoenix Pharmaceuticals Inc .... E.....650 558-8898
330 Beach Rd Burlingame (94010) *(P-8075)*

Phoenix Technologies Ltd (HQ) .... E.....408 570-1000
150 S Los Robles Ave # 500 Pasadena (91101) *(P-24295)*

Phonak LLC .... F.....510 743-3939
47257 Fremont Blvd Fremont (94538) *(P-22069)*

Phonesuit Inc .... E.....310 774-0282
1431 7th St Ste 201 Santa Monica (90401) *(P-17622)*

Phorus LLC .... F.....310 995-2521
16255 Ventura Blvd # 310 Encino (91436) *(P-17271)*

Photo Fabricators Inc .... D.....818 781-1010
7648 Burnet Ave Van Nuys (91405) *(P-17956)*

Photo Sciences Incorporated (PA) .... E.....310 634-1500
2542 W 237th St Torrance (90505) *(P-15307)*

Photobacks LLC .... F.....760 582-2550
40 Paseo Montecillo Palm Desert (92260) *(P-24296)*

Photoflex Inc .... F.....831 786-1370
1800 Green Hills Rd # 104 Scotts Valley (95066) *(P-22449)*

Photographer's Forum, Santa Barbara *Also called Serbin Communications Inc (P-6026)*

Photon Inc .... F.....408 226-1000
1671 Dell Ave Ste 208 Campbell (95008) *(P-20918)*

Photon Dynamics Inc (HQ) .... C.....408 226-9900
5970 Optical Ct San Jose (95138) *(P-21099)*

Photonic Corp .... F.....310 642-7975
5800 Uplander Way Ste 100 Culver City (90230) *(P-6781)*

Photonics Division, Carlsbad *Also called L3 Technologies Inc (P-17741)*

Photostone LLC .... F.....858 274-3400
8495 Redwood Creek Ln San Diego (92126) *(P-14337)*

Photronics California, Burbank *Also called Photronics Inc (P-22450)*

Photronics Inc (HQ) .... B.....203 740-5653
2428 N Ontario St Burbank (91504) *(P-22450)*

Phu Huong Foods Co Inc .... F.....626 280-8607
9008 Garvey Ave Ste I Rosemead (91770) *(P-524)*

Phyn LLC .... F.....310 400-4001
1855 Del Amo Blvd Torrance (90501) *(P-20919)*

Phynexus, San Jose *Also called Biotage LLC (P-21199)*

Physicans Formula Holdings Inc (HQ) .... E.....626 334-3395
22067 Ferrero Walnut (91789) *(P-8558)*

Physicians Formula Inc (HQ) .... D.....626 334-3395
22067 Ferrero City of Industry (91789) *(P-8559)*

Physicians Formula Inc .... D.....626 334-3395
250 S 9th Ave City of Industry (91746) *(P-8560)*

Physicians Formula Inc .... D.....626 334-3395
753 Arrow Grand Cir Covina (91722) *(P-8561)*

Physicians Formula Cosmt Inc .... C.....626 334-3395
22067 Ferrero City of Industry (91789) *(P-8562)*

Physicians Trust, San Clemente *Also called Srsb Inc (P-24447)*

Phyto Animal Health LLC .... E.....888 871-4505
550 W C St Ste 2040 San Diego (92101) *(P-615)*

Phyto Tech Corp .... E.....949 635-1990
30111 Tomas Rcho STA Marg (92688) *(P-8076)*

Pi-Coral Inc .... D.....408 516-5150
600 California St Fl 6 San Francisco (94108) *(P-15074)*

Piano Exchange, San Diego *Also called Gulbransen Inc (P-22624)*

Pic Flick, Glendale *Also called Dion Rostamian (P-22413)*

Pic Manufacturing Inc .... F.....805 238-5451
410 Sherwood Rd Paso Robles (93446) *(P-14338)*

Picarro Inc (PA) .... E.....408 962-3900
3105 Patrick Henry Dr Santa Clara (95054) *(P-21276)*

Piccone Apparel Corp .... E.....310 559-6702
6444 Fleet St Commerce (90040) *(P-3387)*

Employee Codes: A=Over 500 employees, B=251-500
C=101-250, D=51-100, E=20-50, F=10-19

2020 California
Manfacturers Register

© Mergent Inc. 1-800-342-5647

1203

Pickering Laboratories Inc .... E 650 694-6700
  1280 Space Park Way Mountain View (94043) *(P-7518)*
Picnic At Ascot Inc .... E 310 674-3098
  3237 W 131st St Hawthorne (90250) *(P-4424)*
Pico Corporation, Camarillo Also called Pico Crimping Tools Co *(P-14183)*
Pico Crimping Tools Co .... F 805 388-5510
  444 Constitution Ave Camarillo (93012) *(P-14183)*
Pico Pica Foods, Wilmington Also called Juanitas Foods *(P-732)*
Picotrack .... F 408 988-7000
  309 Laurelwood Rd Ste 21 Santa Clara (95054) *(P-14519)*
Pictron Inc .... F 408 725-8888
  1250 Oakmead Pkwy Ste 210 Sunnyvale (94085) *(P-24297)*
Pictsweet Company .... B 805 928-4414
  732 Hanson Way Santa Maria (93458) *(P-976)*
PICTURE SOURCE OF CALIFORNIA, El Monte Also called Sybman Inc *(P-4538)*
Picture This Framing Inc .... F 714 447-8749
  631 S State College Blvd Fullerton (92831) *(P-4520)*
Piedras Machine Corporation .... F 562 602-1500
  15154 Downey Ave Ste B Paramount (90723) *(P-20201)*
Piercan Usa Inc .... F 760 599-4543
  160 Bosstick Blvd San Marcos (92069) *(P-9353)*
Pierco, Eastvale Also called Cal-Mold Incorporated *(P-9683)*
Pierco Incorporated .... F 909 251-7100
  680 Main St Riverside (92501) *(P-23449)*
Pierre Mitri (PA) .... F 213 747-1838
  1138 Wall St Los Angeles (90015) *(P-3388)*
Pierry Inc (PA) .... F 800 860-7953
  557 Grand St Redwood City (94062) *(P-24298)*
Piet Retief Inc .... F 323 732-8312
  1914 6th Ave Los Angeles (90018) *(P-3389)*
Pietri Bersage Store Design, Anaheim Also called Emporium Di Sanarrey Corp *(P-10905)*
Piezo-Metrics Inc (PA) .... E 805 522-4676
  4509 Runway St Simi Valley (93063) *(P-18469)*
Pigs Tail USA LLC .... F 714 566-0011
  925 W Lambert Rd Brea (92821) *(P-9959)*
Pillow Pets, Oceanside Also called CJ Products Inc *(P-3607)*
Pillsbury Company .... D 818 522-3952
  220 S Kenwood St Ste 202 Glendale (91205) *(P-1008)*
Pilot Software Inc .... F 650 230-2830
  3410 Hillview Ave Palo Alto (94304) *(P-24299)*
Pin Concepts, Sun Valley Also called Pin Craft Inc *(P-22993)*
Pin Craft Inc .... E 818 248-0077
  7933 Ajay Dr Sun Valley (91352) *(P-22993)*
Pin Hsiao & Associates LLC .... E 209 665-4176
  1316 Dupont Ct Manteca (95336) *(P-1262)*
Pina Cellars, NAPA Also called John Pina Jr & Sons *(P-1775)*
Pine Grove Group Inc .... E 209 295-7733
  25500 State Highway 88 Pioneer (95666) *(P-19378)*
Pine Grove Industries Inc .... E 805 485-3700
  2001 Cabot Pl Oxnard (93030) *(P-6782)*
Pine Ridge Vineyards, NAPA Also called Pine Ridge Winery LLC *(P-1866)*
Pine Ridge Winery LLC .... D 707 253-7500
  5901 Silverado Trl NAPA (94558) *(P-1866)*
Pinecone Press, Costa Mesa Also called Jennis Group LLC *(P-6259)*
Pinecraft Custom Shutters Inc .... E 949 642-9317
  946 W 17th St Costa Mesa (92627) *(P-4109)*
Pinky Los Angeles, Burbank Also called Vesture Group Incorporated *(P-3497)*
Pinnacle, La Puente Also called Tristar Global Inc *(P-19788)*
Pinnacle Agriculture Dist Inc .... F 559 842-4601
  1100 S Madera Ave Kerman (93630) *(P-13659)*
Pinnacle Diversified Inc .... F 510 400-7929
  1248 San Luis Obispo St Hayward (94544) *(P-6783)*
Pinnacle Manufacturing Corp .... E 408 778-6100
  17680 Butterfield Blvd # 100 Morgan Hill (95037) *(P-12334)*
Pinnacle Precision Shtmtl Corp (PA) .... C 714 777-3129
  5410 E La Palma Ave Anaheim (92807) *(P-12335)*
Pinnacle Precision Shtmtl Corp .... D 714 777-3129
  5410 E La Palma Ave Anaheim (92807) *(P-12336)*
Pinnacle Press, Hayward Also called Pinnacle Diversified Inc *(P-6783)*
Pinnacle Systems Inc .... F 650 237-1900
  280 Bernardo Ave Mountain View (94043) *(P-17623)*
Pinnacle Worldwide Inc .... F 909 628-2200
  315 S Las Palmas Ave Los Angeles (90020) *(P-16793)*
Pinpoint Media Group Inc .... F 714 545-5640
  3188 Airway Ave Ste L Costa Mesa (92626) *(P-6003)*
Pioneer Automotive Tech Inc .... F 937 746-6600
  8701 Siempre Viva Rd San Diego (92154) *(P-17624)*
Pioneer Balloon Co, West Covina Also called Continental American Corp *(P-9295)*
Pioneer Broach Company (PA) .... D 323 728-1263
  6434 Telegraph Rd Commerce (90040) *(P-14184)*
Pioneer Circuits Inc .... B 714 641-3132
  3000 S Shannon St Santa Ana (92704) *(P-17957)*
Pioneer Custom Elec Pdts Corp .... F 562 944-0626
  10640 Springdale Ave Santa Fe Springs (90670) *(P-16567)*
Pioneer Diecasters Inc .... F 323 245-6561
  4209 Chevy Chase Dr Los Angeles (90039) *(P-11346)*
Pioneer French Bakery, Oxnard Also called Wholesome Harvest Baking LLC *(P-1297)*
Pioneer Materials Inc .... E 650 357-7130
  548 Trinidad Ln Foster City (94404) *(P-21399)*
Pioneer Photo Albums Inc (PA) .... C 818 882-2161
  9801 Deering Ave Chatsworth (91311) *(P-7314)*
Pioneer Sands LLC .... E 661 746-5789
  9952 Enos Ln Bakersfield (93314) *(P-373)*
Pioneer Sands LLC .... D 949 728-0171
  31302 Ortega Hwy San Juan Capistrano (92675) *(P-374)*
Pioneer Speakers Inc (HQ) .... E 310 952-2000
  2050 W 190th St Ste 100 Torrance (90504) *(P-17272)*

Pionetics Corporation .... F 650 551-0250
  151 Old County Rd Ste H San Carlos (94070) *(P-9960)*
Pionite, Rancho Cucamonga Also called Panolam Industries Intl Inc *(P-4485)*
Pionyr Immunotherapeutics Inc .... F 415 226-7503
  953 Indiana St San Francisco (94107) *(P-8077)*
PIP Printing, Mission Viejo Also called Postal Instant Press Inc *(P-6788)*
PIP Printing, Downey Also called Jeb-PHI Inc *(P-6664)*
PIP Printing, Van Nuys Also called Blueberry Enterprises Inc *(P-6452)*
PIP Printing, Hemet Also called J S M Productions Inc *(P-6657)*
PIP Printing, Sacramento Also called Colormarx Corporation *(P-6500)*
PIP Printing Palo Alto Inc .... F 650 323-8388
  2233 El Camino Real Palo Alto (94306) *(P-6784)*
Pipe Dream Products, Chatsworth Also called Pd Products LLC *(P-2950)*
Pipe Fabricating & Supply Co (PA) .... D 714 630-5200
  1235 N Kraemer Blvd Anaheim (92806) *(P-13481)*
Pipe Fabricators International, El Cajon Also called Al & Krla Pipe Fabricators Inc *(P-13456)*
Pipe Guard Inc .... E 818 765-2424
  10723 Sherman Way Sun Valley (91352) *(P-11675)*
Pipeline, Compton Also called Graphic Prints Inc *(P-3791)*
Pipeline Products Inc .... F 760 744-8907
  1650 Linda Vista Dr # 110 San Marcos (92078) *(P-14850)*
Pipeliner Crm .... E 424 280-6445
  15243 La Cruz Dr Unit 492 Pacific Palisades (90272) *(P-24300)*
Piranha Ems Inc .... E 408 520-3963
  2681 Zanker Rd San Jose (95134) *(P-14961)*
Piranha Pipe & Precast Inc .... E 559 665-7473
  16000 Avenue 25 Chowchilla (93610) *(P-10623)*
Piranha Propeller, Jackson Also called Bradford Canning Stahl Inc *(P-15797)*
Pirates Press Inc .... F 415 738-2268
  1260 Powell St Emeryville (94608) *(P-17333)*
Pisani Printing II, Santa Clara Also called Theater Publications Inc *(P-6040)*
Pisor Industries Inc .... E 916 944-2851
  7201 32nd St North Highlands (95660) *(P-16298)*
Piston Hydraulic System Inc .... F 626 350-0100
  11614 Mcbean Dr El Monte (91732) *(P-14851)*
Pitbull Energy Bar, Los Angeles Also called Energy Lane Inc *(P-7638)*
Pitbull Gym Incorporated .... F 909 980-7960
  10782 Edison Ct Rancho Cucamonga (91730) *(P-9961)*
Pitman Family Farms .... D 559 585-3330
  10365 Iona Ave Hanford (93230) *(P-1118)* .
Pitney Bowes Inc .... D 949 855-7844
  25151 Commercentre Dr # 110 Lake Forest (92630) *(P-15388)*
Pitney Bowes Inc .... E 415 330-9423
  71 Park Ln Brisbane (94005) *(P-15389)*
Pitney Bowes Inc .... E 310 312-4288
  11355 W Olympic Blvd Fl 2 Los Angeles (90064) *(P-15390)*
Pittman Outdoors, Placentia Also called Pittman Products International *(P-9962)*
Pittman Products International .... F 562 926-6660
  650 S Jefferson St Ste D Placentia (92870) *(P-9962)*
Pivotal Systems Corporation .... E 510 770-9125
  48389 Fremont Blvd # 100 Fremont (94538) *(P-16739)*
Pixelworks Inc (PA) .... E 408 200-9200
  226 Airport Pkwy Ste 595 San Jose (95110) *(P-18470)*
Pixley Construction Inc .... F 510 783-3020
  27607 Industrial Blvd Hayward (94545) *(P-247)*
Pixon Imaging Inc .... E 858 352-0100
  4930 Longford St San Diego (92117) *(P-21277)*
Pixonimaging, San Diego Also called Pixon Imaging Inc *(P-21277)*
Pixscan .... E 510 595-2222
  1259 Park Ave Emeryville (94608) *(P-7174)*
Pjk Winery LLC .... E 707 431-8333
  4900 W Dry Creek Rd Healdsburg (95448) *(P-1867)*
Pjy Inc .... E 323 583-7737
  3251 Leonis Blvd Vernon (90058) *(P-2709)*
Pk Industries Inc .... F 619 428-6382
  1533 Olivella Way San Diego (92154) *(P-10202)*
Pk1 Inc (HQ) .... D 916 858-1300
  4225 Pell Dr Sacramento (95838) *(P-5258)*
Pl Development, Lynwood Also called P & L Development LLC *(P-8346)*
Pl Development, Lynwood Also called P & L Development LLC *(P-8059)*
Pla-Cor Incorporated .... F 619 478-2139
  10207 Buena Vista Ave D Santee (92071) *(P-9963)*
Placer Waterworks Inc .... E 530 742-9675
  1325 Furneaux Rd Plumas Lake (95961) *(P-11864)*
Planar Monolithics Inds Inc .... E 916 542-1401
  4921 Robert J Mathews El Dorado Hills (95762) *(P-19049)*
Planet Green Cartridges Inc .... D 818 725-2596
  20724 Lassen St Chatsworth (91311) *(P-22971)*
Planet Inc .... F 250 478-8171
  15791 Coleman Valley Rd Occidental (95465) *(P-8407)*
Planet One Products Inc (PA) .... E 707 794-8000
  1445 N Mcdowell Blvd Petaluma (94954) *(P-4932)*
Planet Plexi Corp .... F 949 206-1183
  2872 Walnut Ave Ste A Tustin (92780) *(P-9964)*
Planet Products, Occidental Also called Planet Inc *(P-8407)*
Planet Star, Northridge Also called 5 Star Redemption Inc *(P-23258)*
Planetart LLC (PA) .... E 818 436-3600
  23801 Calabasas Rd # 2005 Calabasas (91302) *(P-5798)*
Planetary Machine and Engrg .... F 760 489-5571
  976 S Andreasen Dr Ste A Escondido (92029) *(P-16299)*
Plangrid Inc (HQ) .... D 800 646-0796
  2111 Mission St 400 San Francisco (94110) *(P-24301)*
Planit Solutions .... F 530 666-6647
  1240 Commerce Ave Woodland (95776) *(P-24302)*
Planned Parenthood Los Angeles .... E 323 256-1717
  1578 Colorado Blvd Ste 13 Los Angeles (90041) *(P-6310)*
Plant 1, North Highlands Also called Livingstons Concrete Svc Inc *(P-10796)*

Plant 3, Lincoln *Also called Livingstons Concrete Svc Inc* ***(P-10797)***
Plantronics Inc (PA) B 831 426-5858
345 Encinal St Santa Cruz (95060) ***(P-17398)***
Plantronics Inc F 831 458-7089
1470 Expo Way Ste 130 San Diego (92154) ***(P-17399)***
Plantronics Inc E 831 426-5858
345 Encinal St Santa Cruz (95060) ***(P-17400)***
Plantronics BV, San Diego *Also called Plantronics Inc* ***(P-17399)***
Plantronics BV, Santa Cruz *Also called Plantronics Inc* ***(P-17400)***
Plas-Tal Manufacturing Co, Santa Fe Springs *Also called Brunton Enterprises Inc* ***(P-11752)***
Plas-Tech Sealing Tech LLC E 951 737-2228
252 Mariah Cir Fl 2 Corona (92879) ***(P-8886)***
Plascene Inc F 562 695-0240
1600 Pacific Ave Oxnard (93033) ***(P-9965)***
Plascor Inc C 951 328-1010
972 Columbia Ave Riverside (92507) ***(P-9490)***
Plasidyne Engineering & Mfg E 562 531-0510
3230 E 59th St Long Beach (90805) ***(P-9966)***
Plaskolite West LLC E 310 637-2103
2225 E Del Amo Blvd Compton (90220) ***(P-7592)***
Plaskolite West, Inc., Compton *Also called Plaskolite West LLC* ***(P-7592)***
Plasma Coating Corporation E 310 532-1951
13309 S Western Ave Gardena (90249) ***(P-16300)***
Plasma Control Technologies, San Jose *Also called Comet Technologies USA Inc* ***(P-21452)***
Plasma Division, Corona *Also called PVA Tepla America Inc* ***(P-16321)***
Plasma Rggedized Solutions Inc E 714 893-6063
5452 Business Dr Huntington Beach (92649) ***(P-13071)***
Plasma Rggedized Solutions Inc (PA) D 408 954-8405
2284 Ringwood Ave Ste A San Jose (95131) ***(P-13225)***
Plasma Technology Incorporated (PA) D 310 320-3373
1754 Crenshaw Blvd Torrance (90501) ***(P-13226)***
Plasmetex Industries F 760 744-8300
1425 Linda Vista Dr San Marcos (92078) ***(P-9967)***
Plastech Specialties Company (PA) F 626 357-6839
4645 Portofino Cir Cypress (90630) ***(P-3808)***
Plasthec Molding Inc D 909 947-4267
1945 S Grove Ave Ontario (91761) ***(P-9968)***
Plasti-Print Inc F 650 652-4950
1620 Gilbreth Rd Burlingame (94010) ***(P-7175)***
Plastic and Metal Center Inc E 949 770-0610
23162 La Cadena Dr Laguna Hills (92653) ***(P-9969)***
Plastic Color Technology F 909 597-9230
3010 Spyglass Ct Chino Hills (91709) ***(P-7460)***
Plastic Dress-Up Company D 626 442-7711
11077 Rush St South El Monte (91733) ***(P-9970)***
Plastic Fabrication Tech LLC D 773 509-1700
2320 E Cherry Indus Cir Long Beach (90805) ***(P-9971)***
Plastic Innovations Inc F 951 361-0251
10513 San Sevaine Way Jurupa Valley (91752) ***(P-9448)***
Plastic Mart Inc E 310 268-1404
43535 Gadsden Ave Ste F Lancaster (93534) ***(P-7593)***
Plastic Molding Shop, The, Oroville *Also called Jess Howard* ***(P-9854)***
Plastic Processing Co, Gardena *Also called Narayan Corporation* ***(P-9489)***
Plastic Processing Corp E 310 719-7330
13432 Estrella Ave Gardena (90248) ***(P-9972)***
Plastic Service Center, Santa Clara *Also called P S C Manufacturing Inc* ***(P-9943)***
Plastic Tops Inc F 714 738-8128
521 E Jamie Ave La Habra (90631) ***(P-4997)***
Plastic View Atc Inc F 805 520-9390
4585 Runway St Ste B Simi Valley (93063) ***(P-5034)***
Plastics Development Corp E 949 492-0217
960 Calle Negocio San Clemente (92673) ***(P-9973)***
Plastics Plus Technology Inc E 909 747-0555
1495 Research Dr Redlands (92374) ***(P-9974)***
Plastics Research Corporation D 909 391-9050
1400 S Campus Ave Ontario (91761) ***(P-9449)***
Plastifab Inc E 909 596-1927
1425 Palomares St La Verne (91750) ***(P-9450)***
Plastifab San Diego F 858 679-6600
12145 Paine St Poway (92064) ***(P-9451)***
Plastifab/Leed Plastics, La Verne *Also called Plastifab Inc* ***(P-9450)***
Plastiject LLC F 562 926-6705
14811 Spring Ave Santa Fe Springs (90670) ***(P-9975)***
Plastikon Industries Inc (PA) B 510 400-1010
688 Sandoval Way Hayward (94544) ***(P-14093)***
Plastique Unique Inc E 310 839-3968
3383 Livonia Ave Los Angeles (90034) ***(P-9976)***
Plasto Tech International Inc E 949 458-1880
4 Autry Irvine (92618) ***(P-9977)***
Plastopan Industries Inc (PA) E 323 231-2225
812 E 59th St Los Angeles (90001) ***(P-5300)***
Plastpro 2000 Inc (PA) C 310 693-8600
5200 W Century Blvd Fl 9 Los Angeles (90045) ***(P-9978)***
Plastpro Doors, Los Angeles *Also called Plastpro 2000 Inc* ***(P-9978)***
Plastruct Inc D 626 912-7017
1020 Wallace Way City of Industry (91748) ***(P-9979)***
Plasvacc USA Inc F 805 434-0321
1535 Templeton Rd Templeton (93465) ***(P-8322)***
Plateronics Processing Inc E 818 341-2191
9164 Independence Ave Chatsworth (91311) ***(P-13072)***
Platescan Inc E 949 851-1600
20101 Sw Birch St Ste 250 Newport Beach (92660) ***(P-12857)***
Plating, Chatsworth *Also called Electro Adapter Inc* ***(P-16896)***
Platinum Distribution, Yorba Linda *Also called Nasco Gourmet Foods Inc* ***(P-801)***
Plato Pet Treats, Fresno *Also called Kdr Pet Treats LLC* ***(P-23379)***
Platron Company West F 510 781-5588
26260 Eden Landing Rd Hayward (94545) ***(P-13073)***
Platt Medical Center, Rancho Mirage *Also called Tfx International* ***(P-8160)***
Plaxicon Co, Rancho Cucamonga *Also called Plaxicon Holding Corporation* ***(P-9491)***
Plaxicon Holding Corporation C 909 944-6868
10660 Acacia St Rancho Cucamonga (91730) ***(P-9491)***
Playa Tool & Marine Inc F 714 972-2722
1746 E Borchard Ave Santa Ana (92705) ***(P-16301)***
Playboy Enterprises Inc D 310 424-1800
10960 Wilshire Blvd # 2200 Los Angeles (90024) ***(P-6004)***
Playboy Enterprises Intl Inc D 310 424-1800
10960 Wilshire Blvd # 2200 Los Angeles (90024) ***(P-6311)***
Playboy Japan Inc F 310 424-1800
9346 Civic Center Dr # 200 Beverly Hills (90210) ***(P-6005)***
Players Circle Barbershop, San Leandro *Also called My World Styles LLC* ***(P-8543)***
Players International Publ, Los Angeles *Also called Bentley Management Corporation* ***(P-5889)***
Players Music Accessories, San Jose *Also called Thunder Products Inc* ***(P-22641)***
Players Music Accessories, Portola *Also called Thunder Products Inc* ***(P-22642)***
Players Press Inc E 818 789-4980
Fulton Ave Studio City (91604) ***(P-6136)***
Playhut Inc E 909 869-8083
18560 San Jose Ave City of Industry (91748) ***(P-22704)***
Plaze De Caviar, Concord *Also called Pacific Plaza Imports Inc* ***(P-2248)***
Plc LLC F 707 462-2423
2350 Mcnab Ranch Rd Ukiah (95482) ***(P-1868)***
Pleasant Mattress Inc F 415 874-7540
1687 Market St San Francisco (94103) ***(P-4736)***
Pleasant Mattress Inc (PA) D 559 268-6446
375 S West Ave Fresno (93706) ***(P-4737)***
Pleasant Valley Farms (PA) D 209 886-1000
30636 E Carter Rd Farmington (95230) ***(P-525)***
Pleasanton Main St Brewry Inc F 925 462-8218
830 Main St Ste Frnt Pleasanton (94566) ***(P-1558)***
Pleasanton Ready Mix Concrete F 925 846-3226
3400 Boulder St Pleasanton (94566) ***(P-10814)***
Pleasanton Readymix Concrete, Pleasanton *Also called Pleasanton Ready Mix Concrete* ***(P-10814)***
Pleasanton Steel Supply, Livermore *Also called Stretch-Run Inc* ***(P-11888)***
Pleasanton Tool & Mfg Inc E 925 426-0500
1181 Quarry Ln Ste 450 Pleasanton (94566) ***(P-16302)***
Pleros LLC F 442 275-6764
2825 E Tahquitz Cyn W Palm Springs (92262) ***(P-8563)***
Plexi Fab Inc F 714 447-8494
1142 E Elm Ave Fullerton (92831) ***(P-9980)***
Plexus Corp C 510 668-9000
431 Kato Ter Fremont (94539) ***(P-17958)***
Plexus Optix Inc E 800 852-7600
3333 Quality Dr Rancho Cordova (95670) ***(P-10327)***
Plexxikon Inc E 510 647-4000
91 Bolivar Dr Berkeley (94710) ***(P-8078)***
Plh Products Inc E 714 739-6622
6655 Knott Ave Buena Park (90620) ***(P-4465)***
Pls Diabetic Shoe Company Inc E 818 734-7080
21500 Osborne St Canoga Park (91304) ***(P-9178)***
Plt Enterprises Inc D 805 389-5335
809 Calle Plano Camarillo (93012) ***(P-16920)***
Plugg ME LNc E 949 705-4472
18100 Von Karman Ave # 850 Irvine (92612) ***(P-24303)***
Plum Creek Timberlands LP C 909 949-2255
615 N Benson Ave Upland (91786) ***(P-3940)***
Plum Valley Inc E 530 262-6262
3308 Cyclone Ct Cottonwood (96022) ***(P-3941)***
Plumbing Products Inc F 760 343-3306
77551 El Duna Ct Ste I Palm Desert (92211) ***(P-11676)***
Plumjack Winery, NAPA *Also called Villa Encinal Partners LP* ***(P-1985)***
Pluot Communications Inc F 202 258-9223
1925 48th Ave San Francisco (94116) ***(P-17273)***
Plural Publishing Inc F 858 492-1555
5521 Ruffin Rd San Diego (92123) ***(P-6137)***
Plush Home Inc E 323 852-1912
6507 Lindenhurst Ave Los Angeles (90048) ***(P-4602)***
Plush Printing, Fullerton *Also called Sticker Hub Inc* ***(P-7229)***
Plusrite, Montclair *Also called Fanlight Corporation Inc* ***(P-16862)***
Plusrite and Ledirect, Ontario *Also called Fanlight Corporation Inc* ***(P-16863)***
Plustek Technology Inc F 562 777-1888
9830 Norwalk Blvd Ste 155 Santa Fe Springs (90670) ***(P-15308)***
Plx Technology Inc C 408 435-7400
1320 Ridder Park Dr San Jose (95131) ***(P-24304)***
Plycraft Industries Inc C 323 587-8101
2100 E Slauson Ave Huntington Park (90255) ***(P-4279)***
PM Corporate Group Inc C 619 498-9199
2285 Michael Faraday Dr San Diego (92154) ***(P-6785)***
PM Lithographers Inc F 818 704-2626
7600 Linley Ln Canoga Park (91304) ***(P-6786)***
PM Packaging, San Diego *Also called PM Corporate Group Inc* ***(P-6785)***
Pmc Inc (HQ) E 818 896-1101
12243 Branford St Sun Valley (91352) ***(P-20202)***
PMC Global Inc (PA) A 818 896-1101
12243 Branford St Sun Valley (91352) ***(P-9561)***
PMC-Sierra Us Inc F 408 239-8000
1380 Bordeaux Dr Sunnyvale (94089) ***(P-18471)***
PMD INC., Santa Fe Springs *Also called Pedavena Mould and Die Co Inc* ***(P-16290)***
Pmdt, San Jose *Also called Power Mntring Dagnstc Tech Ltd* ***(P-21100)***
Pmic, Los Angeles *Also called Practice Management Info Corp* ***(P-6138)***
Pmp Products Inc F 310 549-5122
19827 Hamilton Ave Torrance (90502) ***(P-10203)***
Pmr Precision Mfg & Rbr Co Inc E 909 605-7525
1330 Etiwanda Ave Ontario (91761) ***(P-9354)***
Pmrca Inc (PA) F 661 822-6760
20437 Brian Way Ste B Tehachapi (93561) ***(P-6787)***

Employee Codes: A=Over 500 employees, B=251-500
C=101-250, D=51-100, E=20-50, F=10-19
2020 California
Manfacturers Register
© Mergent Inc. 1-800-342-5647
1205

PMS Systems Corporation.....F.....310 450-2566
31355 Oak Crest Dr # 100 Westlake Village (91361) ***(P-24305)***
PNa Construction Tech Inc.....E.....661 326-1700
301 Espee St Ste E Bakersfield (93301) ***(P-12337)***
PNC Proactive Nthrn Cont LLC.....E.....909 390-5624
602 S Rockefeller Ave A Ontario (91761) ***(P-5259)***
Pneudraulics Inc.....B.....909 980-5366
8575 Helms Ave Rancho Cucamonga (91730) ***(P-20674)***
Pneumatic Scale Angelus, Ontario *Also called Pneumatic Scale Corporation* ***(P-14723)***
Pneumatic Scale Corporation.....F.....909 527-7600
2811 E Philadelphia St B Ontario (91761) ***(P-14723)***
Pneumatic Tube Carrier, Duarte *Also called Lee Machine Products* ***(P-14070)***
Pneumrx Inc.....E.....650 625-4440
4255 Burton Dr Santa Clara (95054) ***(P-21859)***
Pnm Company.....E.....559 291-1986
2547 N Business Park Ave Fresno (93727) ***(P-16303)***
Pny Technologies Inc.....E.....408 392-4100
2099 Gateway Pl Ste 220 San Jose (95110) ***(P-18472)***
Pocino Foods Company.....D.....626 968-8000
14250 Lomitas Ave City of Industry (91746) ***(P-489)***
Pocket, San Francisco *Also called Read It Later Inc* ***(P-24340)***
Pocket Gems Inc (PA).....D.....415 371-1333
220 Montgomery St Ste 750 San Francisco (94104) ***(P-22705)***
Poetry Corporation (PA).....E.....213 765-8957
2111 Long Beach Ave Los Angeles (90058) ***(P-3272)***
Point Blanks Inc.....F.....805 643-8616
43 S Olive St Ventura (93001) ***(P-2016)***
Point Conception Inc.....E.....949 589-6890
23121 Arroyo Vis Ste A Rcho STA Marg (92688) ***(P-3390)***
Point Lakeview Rock & Redi-Mix, Lower Lake *Also called Clearlake Lava Inc* ***(P-10745)***
Point Nine Technologies Inc (PA).....F.....805 375-6600
2697 Lavery Ct Ste 8 Newbury Park (91320) ***(P-18473)***
Pointech.....E.....415 822-8704
Hunters Point Shpyd San Francisco (94124) ***(P-11405)***
Pokka Beverages, American Canyon *Also called Amcan Beverages Inc* ***(P-2023)***
Pol Tech Precision Co, Fremont *Also called Pol-Tech Precision Inc* ***(P-16304)***
Pol-Tech Precision Inc.....F.....510 656-6832
4447 Enterprise St Fremont (94538) ***(P-16304)***
Polargy Inc.....E.....408 752-0186
1148 Sonora Ct Sunnyvale (94086) ***(P-12041)***
Polarion Software Inc.....D.....877 572-4005
1001 Marina Village Pkwy # 403 Alameda (94501) ***(P-24306)***
Polaris E-Commerce Inc.....E.....714 907-0582
1941 E Occidental St Santa Ana (92705) ***(P-14595)***
Polaris Pharmaceuticals Inc.....E.....858 452-6688
9373 Towne Centre Dr # 150 San Diego (92121) ***(P-8079)***
Pole Danzer.....F.....760 419-9514
3777 Paseo De Olivos Fallbrook (92028) ***(P-10624)***
Polerax USA.....F.....323 477-1866
909 S Greenwood Ave Ste K Montebello (90640) ***(P-3574)***
Polishing Corporation America.....E.....888 892-3377
442 Martin Ave Santa Clara (95050) ***(P-18474)***
Polit Farms Inc.....F.....530 438-2759
4334 Old Hwy 99w 99 W Maxwell (95955) ***(P-1049)***
Politezer Newspaers Inc.....F.....805 929-3864
260 Station Way Ste F Arroyo Grande (93420) ***(P-5799)***
Polk Audio LLC.....E.....888 267-5495
1 Viper Way Ste 3 Vista (92081) ***(P-17274)***
Polley Inc (PA).....E.....562 868-9861
11936 Front St Norwalk (90650) ***(P-14852)***
Pollstar LLC (PA).....D.....559 271-7900
1100 Glendon Ave Ste 2100 Los Angeles (90024) ***(P-6006)***
Pollstar.com, Los Angeles *Also called Pollstar LLC* ***(P-6006)***
Pollution Control Specialists.....E.....949 474-0137
1354 Ritchey St Santa Ana (92705) ***(P-14673)***
Polly's Tasty Foods & Pies, Orange *Also called E D D Investment Co* ***(P-1195)***
Pollybyrd Publications Limited, Beverly Hills *Also called Ppl Entertainment Group Inc* ***(P-6315)***
Poly Processing Company LLC.....B.....209 982-4904
8055 Ash St French Camp (95231) ***(P-7594)***
Poly-Fiber Inc (PA).....E.....951 684-4280
4343 Fort Dr Riverside (92509) ***(P-8663)***
Poly-Seal Industries.....F.....510 843-9722
725 Channing Way Berkeley (94710) ***(P-9355)***
Poly-Tainer Inc (PA).....B.....805 526-3424
450 W Los Angeles Ave Simi Valley (93065) ***(P-9492)***
Polyair Inter Pack Inc.....D.....951 737-7125
1692 Jenks Dr Ste 102 Corona (92880) ***(P-3700)***
Polyalloys Injected Metals Inc.....D.....310 715-9800
14000 Avalon Blvd Los Angeles (90061) ***(P-13759)***
Polycom Inc.....E.....209 830-5083
25212 S Schulte Rd Tracy (95377) ***(P-17401)***
Polycom Inc.....E.....408 526-9000
3553 N 1st St San Jose (95134) ***(P-17402)***
Polycom Inc (HQ).....B.....831 426-5858
345 Encinal St Santa Cruz (95060) ***(P-17403)***
Polycraft Inc.....E.....951 296-0860
42075 Avenida Alvarado Temecula (92590) ***(P-7176)***
Polyfet Rf Devices Inc.....E.....805 484-9582
1110 Avenida Acaso Camarillo (93012) ***(P-18475)***
Polymer Concepts Technologies.....F.....760 240-4999
13522 Manhasset Rd Apple Valley (92308) ***(P-9248)***
Polymer Logistics Inc.....E.....951 567-2900
1725 Sierra Ridge Dr Riverside (92507) ***(P-9981)***
Polymerex Medical Corp.....F.....858 695-0765
7358 Trade St San Diego (92121) ***(P-9433)***
Polymeric Technology Inc.....E.....510 895-6001
1900 Marina Blvd San Leandro (94577) ***(P-9356)***
Polymond Dk Inc.....E.....213 327-0771
777 E 10th St Ste 110 Los Angeles (90021) ***(P-3391)***
Polynesian Exploration Inc.....F.....540 808-7538
2210 Otoole Ave Ste 240 San Jose (95131) ***(P-20675)***
Polynetics, Corona *Also called Duonetics* ***(P-14569)***
Polynt Composites USA Inc.....F.....310 886-1070
2801 Lynwood Rd Lynwood (90262) ***(P-7595)***
Polyone Corporation.....D.....310 513-7100
2104 E 223rd St Carson (90810) ***(P-7596)***
Polyone Corporation.....E.....909 987-0253
11400 Newport Dr Ste A Rancho Cucamonga (91730) ***(P-7597)***
Polypure, Los Angeles *Also called Snf Holding Company* ***(P-9025)***
Polystak Inc.....F.....408 441-1400
1159 Sonora Ct 109 Sunnyvale (94086) ***(P-18476)***
Polytec Products Corporation.....E.....650 322-7555
1190 Obrien Dr Menlo Park (94025) ***(P-16305)***
Polytech Color & Compounding.....F.....909 923-7008
847 S Wanamaker Ave Ontario (91761) ***(P-9982)***
Polytex Manufacturing Inc (PA).....F.....323 726-0140
1140 S Hope St Los Angeles (90015) ***(P-2893)***
Polywell Company Inc.....E.....650 583-7222
1461 San Mateo Ave Ste 1 South San Francisco (94080) ***(P-14962)***
Polywell Computers, South San Francisco *Also called Polywell Company Inc* ***(P-14962)***
Poma GL Specialty Windows Inc.....D.....951 321-0116
813 Palmyrita Ave Riverside (92507) ***(P-10273)***
Pomar Junction Cellars LLC.....E.....805 238-9940
5036 S El Pomar Rd Templeton (93465) ***(P-1869)***
Pometta's, Sonoma *Also called Sonoma Gourmet Inc* ***(P-900)***
Pommes Frites Candle Co.....E.....213 488-2016
7300 E Slauson Ave Commerce (90040) ***(P-23450)***
Pomona Quality Foam LLC.....D.....909 628-7844
1279 Philadelphia St Pomona (91766) ***(P-9562)***
Pong Research Corporation.....F.....858 914-5299
1010 S Coast Highway 101 # 105 Encinitas (92024) ***(P-22070)***
Poole Ventura Inc.....F.....805 981-1784
321 Bernoulli Cir Oxnard (93030) ***(P-14638)***
Poolmaster Inc.....D.....916 567-9800
770 Del Paso Rd Sacramento (95834) ***(P-22706)***
Poor Richard's Press, San Luis Obispo *Also called Prpco* ***(P-6816)***
Poor Richards Press, San Luis Obispo *Also called Ws Packaging-Blake Printery* ***(P-6944)***
Pop 82 Inc.....F.....714 523-8500
8211 Orangethorpe Ave Buena Park (90621) ***(P-2731)***
Pop Chips, E Rncho Dmngz *Also called Sonora Mills Foods Inc* ***(P-1329)***
Pop Plastics Acrylic Disp Inc.....E.....714 523-8500
8211 Orangethorpe Ave Buena Park (90621) ***(P-9983)***
Popcorn Tree, Glendora *Also called Tom Clark Confections* ***(P-1405)***
Pope, Canoga Park *Also called Jake Stehelin Etienne* ***(P-9849)***
Pope Plastics Inc.....E.....818 701-1850
9134 Independence Ave Chatsworth (91311) ***(P-14094)***
Popkoff's, City of Industry *Also called Whittier Enterprise LLC* ***(P-984)***
Popla International Inc.....E.....909 923-6899
1740 S Sacramento Ave Ontario (91761) ***(P-1059)***
Popsalot Gourmet Popcorn, Paramount *Also called Popsalot LLC* ***(P-2339)***
Popsalot LLC.....E.....213 761-0156
7723 Somerset Blvd Paramount (90723) ***(P-2339)***
Popsugar Inc.....F.....310 562-8049
3523 Eastham Dr Culver City (90232) ***(P-6312)***
Popsugar Inc (PA).....C.....415 391-7576
111 Sutter St Fl 16 San Francisco (94104) ***(P-6313)***
Popular Printers Inc.....F.....626 307-4281
3210 San Gabriel Blvd Rosemead (91770) ***(P-7177)***
Popular TV Networks LLC.....F.....323 822-3324
8307 Rugby Pl Los Angeles (90046) ***(P-5800)***
Porifera Inc.....F.....510 695-2775
1575 Alvarado St San Leandro (94577) ***(P-15559)***
Port 80 Software Inc.....E.....858 274-4497
2105 Garnet Ave Ste E San Diego (92109) ***(P-24307)***
Port Brewing LLC.....E.....800 918-6816
155 Mata Way Ste 104 San Marcos (92069) ***(P-1559)***
Porta-Bote International, Mountain View *Also called Kaye Sandy Enterprises Inc* ***(P-20342)***
Portable Spndle Repr Spcialist.....F.....909 591-7220
10803 Fremont Ave Ste A Ontario (91762) ***(P-14292)***
Portapaint, Ventura *Also called Wombat Products Inc* ***(P-10129)***
Portellus Inc.....D.....949 250-9600
2522 Chambers Rd Ste 100 Tustin (92780) ***(P-24308)***
Porter Powder Coating Inc.....F.....714 956-2010
510 S Rose St Anaheim (92805) ***(P-13227)***
Porterville Concrete Pipe Inc.....F.....559 784-6187
474 S Main St Porterville (93257) ***(P-10625)***
Porterville Recorder, Porterville *Also called Noticiero Semanal Advertising* ***(P-5785)***
Portocork America Inc.....F.....707 258-3930
164 Gateway Rd E NAPA (94558) ***(P-4521)***
Portola Pharmaceuticals Inc (PA).....C.....650 246-7300
270 E Grand Ave South San Francisco (94080) ***(P-8080)***
Portos Food Product Inc.....D.....323 480-8400
2085 Garfield Ave Commerce (90040) ***(P-1263)***
Pos Portal Inc (HQ).....E.....530 695-3005
180 Promenade Cir Ste 215 Sacramento (95834) ***(P-15377)***
Positano, Los Angeles *Also called Alona Apparel Inc* ***(P-3064)***
Positex Inc.....F.....307 201-0601
2569 Mccabe Way Ste 210 Irvine (92614) ***(P-19923)***
Positive Concepts Inc (PA).....E.....714 685-5800
2021 N Glassell St Orange (92865) ***(P-5522)***
Positive Publishing Inc.....F.....858 551-0889
449 Nautilus St La Jolla (92037) ***(P-6314)***
Positron Access Solutions Inc.....F.....951 272-9100
1640 2nd St Ste 207 Norco (92860) ***(P-17625)***

Mergent e-mail: customerrelations@mergent.com
1206
2020 California
Manufacturers Register
(P-0000) Products & Services Section entry number
(PA)=Parent Co (HQ)=Headquarters (DH)=Div Headquarters

Positronics Incorporated............F.......925 931-0211
173 Spring St Ste 120 Pleasanton (94566) *(P-14277)*
Post Montgomery Center, San Francisco *Also called Sas Institute Inc (P-24383)*
Post Newspaper Group............F.......510 287-8200
360 14th St Ste B05 Oakland (94612) *(P-5801)*
Post-Srgcal Rhab Spcalists LLC............F.......562 236-5600
12774 Florence Ave Santa Fe Springs (90670) *(P-21860)*
Postal Instant Press Inc (HQ)............E.......949 348-5000
26722 Plaza Mission Viejo (92691) *(P-6788)*
Postcard Press Inc (PA)............E.......310 747-3800
8000 Haskell Ave Van Nuys (91406) *(P-7178)*
Poster Compliance Center, Lafayette *Also called Employerware LLC (P-6229)*
Postvision Inc............F.......818 840-0777
2120 Foothill Blvd # 111 La Verne (91750) *(P-15075)*
Potentia Labs Inc............F.......951 603-3531
2870 4th Ave Apt 212 San Diego (92103) *(P-24309)*
Potential Design Inc............F.......559 834-5361
4185 E Jefferson Ave Fresno (93725) *(P-14393)*
Potnetwork Holdings Inc............F.......800 915-3060
3278 Wilshire Blvd Los Angeles (90010) *(P-7683)*
Potrero Medical Inc............D.......888 635-7280
26142 Eden Landing Rd Hayward (94545) *(P-21861)*
Powder Coating Plus, Valencia *Also called Canay Manufacturing Inc (P-13156)*
Powder Coating Usa Inc............F.......805 237-8886
440 Sherwood Rd Paso Robles (93446) *(P-13228)*
Powder Painting By Sundial, Sun Valley *Also called Sundial Industries Inc (P-13256)*
Powdercoat Services LLC............E.......714 533-2251
1747 W Lincoln Ave Ste K Anaheim (92801) *(P-13229)*
Power - Trim Co............F.......714 523-8560
6060 Phyllis Dr Cypress (90630) *(P-13692)*
Power Aire Inc............E.......800 526-7661
8055 E Crystal Dr Anaheim (92807) *(P-16607)*
Power Automation Systems, Lathrop *Also called California Natural Products (P-2418)*
Power Brake Exchange Inc............F.......562 806-6661
6853 Suva St Bell (90201) *(P-19737)*
Power Brands Consulting LLC............E.......818 989-9646
5805 Sepulveda Blvd # 501 Van Nuys (91411) *(P-1560)*
Power Circuits Inc............B.......714 327-3000
2630 S Harbor Blvd Santa Ana (92704) *(P-17959)*
Power Distribution Inc............F.......714 513-1500
4011 W Carriage Dr Santa Ana (92704) *(P-18733)*
Power Efficiency Corporation............F.......858 750-3875
5744 Pcf Ctr Blvd Ste 311 San Diego (92121) *(P-16668)*
Power Fasteners Inc............E.......323 232-4362
650 E 60th St Los Angeles (90001) *(P-12690)*
Power Integrations Inc (PA)............C.......408 414-9200
5245 Hellyer Ave San Jose (95138) *(P-18477)*
Power Integrations Internation............B.......408 414-8528
5245 Hellyer Ave San Jose (95138) *(P-18478)*
Power Knot LLC............F.......408 480-2758
2290 Ringwood Ave Ste A San Jose (95131) *(P-15560)*
Power Magnetics, Gardena *Also called Power Paragon Inc (P-16569)*
Power Mntring Dagnstc Tech Ltd............F.......408 972-5588
6840 Via Del Oro Ste 150 San Jose (95119) *(P-21100)*
Power One, Santa Clara *Also called Bel Power Solutions Inc (P-18703)*
Power Paragon Inc (HQ)............A.......714 956-9200
901 E Ball Rd Anaheim (92805) *(P-16568)*
Power Paragon Inc............B.......714 956-9200
901 E Ball Rd Anaheim (92805) *(P-19379)*
Power Paragon Inc............F.......310 523-4443
711 W Knox St Gardena (90248) *(P-16569)*
Power Printing, La Mesa *Also called Josef Mendelovitz (P-6668)*
Power Pros Exhaust Systems, Placentia *Also called Power Pros Racg Exhust Systems (P-19738)*
Power Pros Racg Exhust Systems............F.......714 777-3278
817 S Lakeview Ave Ste J Placentia (92870) *(P-19738)*
Power Pt Inc............F.......714 826-7407
9292 Nancy St Cypress (90630) *(P-13888)*
Power Services, Los Angeles *Also called On-Line Power Incorporated (P-16565)*
Power Standards Lab Inc............E.......510 522-4400
980 Atlantic Ave Ste 100 Alameda (94501) *(P-21101)*
Power Systems Group, Anaheim *Also called Power Paragon Inc (P-16568)*
Power Systems Group, Anaheim *Also called Power Paragon Inc (P-19379)*
Powercords, Santa Clara *Also called Volex Inc (P-10113)*
Powercube, Chatsworth *Also called Natel Engineering Company Inc (P-17934)*
Powerflare Corporation............F.......650 208-2580
37 Ringwood Ave Atherton (94027) *(P-19380)*
Powerlift Dumbwaiters Inc............E.......800 409-5438
2444 Georgia Slide Rd Georgetown (95634) *(P-13807)*
Powerlux Corporation............F.......760 727-2360
1260 Liberty Way Ste E Vista (92081) *(P-17155)*
Powers Bros Machine Inc............F.......323 728-2010
8100 Slauson Ave Montebello (90640) *(P-16306)*
Powerschool Group LLC (HQ)............C.......916 288-1636
150 Parkshore Dr Folsom (95630) *(P-24310)*
Powerstorm Ess, Rancho Palos Verdes *Also called Powerstorm Holdings Inc (P-19171)*
Powerstorm Holdings Inc............F.......424 327-2991
31244 Palos Verdes Dr W # 245 Rancho Palos Verdes (90275) *(P-19171)*
Powertronix Corporation............E.......650 345-6800
1120 Chess Dr Foster City (94404) *(P-16570)*
Powertye Manufacturing............F.......714 993-7400
1640 E Miraloma Ave Placentia (92870) *(P-16608)*
Powerware, San Diego *Also called B T E Deltec Inc (P-18828)*
Powwow Inc............E.......877 800-4381
71 Stevenson St Ste 400 San Francisco (94105) *(P-24311)*
PPG 9721, Lancaster *Also called PPG Industries Inc (P-8667)*
PPG 9722, Palm Desert *Also called PPG Industries Inc (P-8668)*
PPG 9726, Los Angeles *Also called PPG Industries Inc (P-8666)*
PPG Aerospace, Valencia *Also called PRC - Desoto International Inc (P-8887)*
PPG Aerospace, Sylmar *Also called Sierracin/Sylmar Corporation (P-10056)*
PPG Aerospace, Mojave *Also called PRC - Desoto International Inc (P-8888)*
PPG Industries Inc............F.......925 798-0539
5750 Imhoff Dr Ste A Concord (94520) *(P-8664)*
PPG Industries Inc............F.......562 692-4010
10060 Mission Mill Rd City of Industry (90601) *(P-8665)*
PPG Industries Inc............E.......310 559-2335
1128 N Highland Ave Los Angeles (90038) *(P-8666)*
PPG Industries Inc............E.......661 945-7871
43639 10th St W Lancaster (93534) *(P-8667)*
PPG Industries Inc............E.......760 340-1762
74240 Highway 111 Palm Desert (92260) *(P-8668)*
PPG Industries Inc............E.......714 894-5252
15541 Commerce Ln Huntington Beach (92649) *(P-8669)*
PPG Industries Inc............E.......661 824-4532
11601 United St Mojave (93501) *(P-8670)*
Ppl Entertainment Group Inc (PA)............E.......310 860-7499
468 N Camden Dr Beverly Hills (90210) *(P-6315)*
Ppm Products Inc............F.......408 946-4710
1538 Gladding Ct Milpitas (95035) *(P-16307)*
Ppp LLC............F.......323 581-6058
5991 Alcoa Ave Vernon (90058) *(P-7598)*
Ppp LLC............E.......323 832-9627
601 W Olympic Blvd Montebello (90640) *(P-9984)*
Pps Packaging Company............D.......559 834-1641
3189 E Manning Ave Fowler (93625) *(P-5144)*
Ppst Inc (PA)............E.......800 421-1921
17692 Fitch Irvine (92614) *(P-19050)*
PQ Corporation............F.......323 326-1100
8401 Quartz Ave South Gate (90280) *(P-7519)*
Practice Management Info Corp (PA)............E.......323 954-0224
4727 Wilshire Blvd # 302 Los Angeles (90010) *(P-6138)*
Pranalytica Inc............F.......310 458-3345
1101 Colorado Ave Santa Monica (90401) *(P-21862)*
Pratt Industries Inc............E.......805 348-1097
2643 Industrial Pkwy Ofc Santa Maria (93455) *(P-5145)*
Pratt Industries Inc............E.......760 966-9170
3931 Oceanic Dr Oceanside (92056) *(P-5146)*
Pratt Industries Inc............C.......770 922-0117
2131 E Louise Ave Lathrop (95330) *(P-5147)*
Praxair Inc............F.......925 866-6800
2430 Camino Ramon Ste 310 San Ramon (94583) *(P-7427)*
Praxair Inc............D.......925 427-1051
2000 Loveridge Rd Pittsburg (94565) *(P-7428)*
Praxair Inc............E.......310 816-1066
2006 E 223rd St Long Beach (90810) *(P-7429)*
Praxair Inc............E.......619 596-4558
10728 Prospect Ave Ste A Santee (92071) *(P-7430)*
Praxair Inc............E.......559 674-7306
112 W Olive Ave Madera (93637) *(P-7431)*
Praxair Inc............E.......510 223-9593
2995 Atlas Rd San Pablo (94806) *(P-7432)*
Praxair Inc............F.......805 966-0829
305 E Haley St Ste A Santa Barbara (93101) *(P-7433)*
Praxair Inc............E.......925 427-1950
1950 Loveridge Rd Pittsburg (94565) *(P-14251)*
Praxair Inc............F.......323 562-5200
8300 Atlantic Ave Cudahy (90201) *(P-7434)*
Praxair Inc............E.......661 861-6421
3331 Buck Owens Blvd Bakersfield (93308) *(P-7435)*
Praxair Inc............E.......661 327-5336
3505 Buck Owens Blvd Bakersfield (93308) *(P-7436)*
Praxair Inc............E.......415 657-9880
3994 Bayshore Blvd Brisbane (94005) *(P-7437)*
Praxair Inc............D.......909 390-0283
5705 E Airport Dr Ontario (91761) *(P-7438)*
Praxair Inc............F.......916 786-3900
7501 Foothills Blvd Roseville (95747) *(P-7439)*
Praxair Inc............E.......707 745-5328
331 E Channel Rd Benicia (94510) *(P-7440)*
Praxair Distribution Inc............E.......559 237-5521
2771 S Maple Ave Fresno (93725) *(P-7441)*
Praxair Distribution Inc............E.......951 736-8113
500 Harrington St Ste G Corona (92880) *(P-7442)*
Praxair Distribution Inc............E.......805 966-0829
305 E Haley St Santa Barbara (93101) *(P-7443)*
Praxair Distribution Inc............F.......818 760-2011
5508 Vineland Ave North Hollywood (91601) *(P-7444)*
Praxair Distribution Inc............F.......805 487-2742
455 E Wooley Rd Oxnard (93030) *(P-7445)*
Praxair Distribution Inc............F.......408 995-6089
215 San Jose Ave San Jose (95125) *(P-7446)*
Praxair Distribution Inc............E.......714 547-6684
1545 E Edinger Ave Santa Ana (92705) *(P-7447)*
Praxair Distribution Inc............E.......408 748-1722
2020 De La Cruz Blvd Santa Clara (95050) *(P-7448)*
Praxair Distribution Inc............D.......310 371-1254
19200 Hawthorne Blvd Torrance (90503) *(P-7449)*
Praxis Musical Instrument Inc............F.......714 532-6655
19122 S Vermont Ave Gardena (90248) *(P-13385)*
PRC, Ontario *Also called Plastics Research Corporation (P-9449)*
PRC - Desoto International Inc (HQ)............B.......661 678-4209
24811 Ave Rockefeller Valencia (91355) *(P-8887)*
PRC - Desoto International Inc............C.......661 824-4532
11601 United St Mojave (93501) *(P-8888)*
PRC Composites LLC............D.......909 391-2006
1400 S Campus Ave Ontario (91761) *(P-4771)*

Pre-Insulated Metal Tech Inc (HQ)....E....707 359-2280
929 Aldridge Rd Vacaville (95688) ***(P-12570)***
Pre-Peeled Potato Co Inc....F....209 469-6911
1585 S Union St Stockton (95206) ***(P-2587)***
Pre-Press International....E....415 216-0031
20 S Linden Ave Ste 4a South San Francisco (94080) ***(P-6789)***
Pre/Plastics Inc....E....530 823-1820
12600 Locksley Ln Ste 100 Auburn (95602) ***(P-9985)***
Precast Con Tech Unlimited LLC....D....530 749-6501
1260 Furneaux Rd Olivehurst (95961) ***(P-10626)***
Precast Innovations Inc....E....714 921-4060
1670 N Main St Orange (92867) ***(P-10627)***
Precast Repair....E....909 627-5477
5494 Morgan St Ontario (91762) ***(P-10628)***
Precinct Reporter....F....909 889-0597
357 W 2nd St Ste 1a San Bernardino (92401) ***(P-5802)***
Precinct Reporter Newsprs, San Bernardino *Also called Precinct Reporter* ***(P-5802)***
Precious Metals Plating Co Inc....F....714 546-6271
2635 Orange Ave Santa Ana (92707) ***(P-13074)***
Precise Aero Products Inc....F....951 340-4554
4120 Indus Way Riverside (92503) ***(P-20203)***
Precise Aerospace Mfg Inc....E....951 898-0500
224 Glider Cir Corona (92880) ***(P-9986)***
Precise Industries Inc....C....714 482-2333
610 Neptune Ave Brea (92821) ***(P-12338)***
Precise Iron Doors Inc....E....818 338-6269
12331 Foothill Blvd Sylmar (91342) ***(P-11975)***
Precise Media Services Inc....E....909 481-3305
888 Vintage Ave Ontario (91764) ***(P-17334)***
Precise Plastic Products, Corona *Also called Precise Aerospace Mfg Inc* ***(P-9986)***
Precise-Full Service Media, Ontario *Also called Precise Media Services Inc* ***(P-17334)***
Precision Aeroform Corporation....F....714 725-6611
12619 Hoover St Garden Grove (92841) ***(P-19924)***
Precision Aerospace & Tech Inc....E....714 656-1620
2320 E Orangethorpe Ave A Anaheim (92806) ***(P-14185)***
Precision Aerospace Corp....D....909 945-9604
11155 Jersey Blvd Ste A Rancho Cucamonga (91730) ***(P-20204)***
Precision Anodizing & Pltg Inc....D....714 996-1601
1601 N Miller St Anaheim (92806) ***(P-13075)***
Precision Arcft Machining Inc....E....818 768-5900
10640 Elkwood St Sun Valley (91352) ***(P-16308)***
Precision Babbitt Co Inc....F....562 531-9173
1007 S Whitemarsh Ave Compton (90220) ***(P-14789)***
Precision Circuits San Diego, Carlsbad *Also called First Circuit Inc* ***(P-17877)***
Precision Circuits West Inc....F....714 435-9670
3310 W Harvard St Santa Ana (92704) ***(P-17960)***
Precision Cnc Mil & Turning, Scotts Valley *Also called Larkin Precision Machining* ***(P-16137)***
Precision Coatings Inc....F....510 525-3600
1220 4th St Berkeley (94710) ***(P-8671)***
Precision Coil Spring Company....D....626 444-0561
10107 Rose Ave El Monte (91731) ***(P-13386)***
Precision Companies Inc....F....909 548-2700
15088 La Palma Dr Chino (91710) ***(P-4110)***
Precision Contacts Inc....E....916 939-4147
990 Suncast Ln El Dorado Hills (95762) ***(P-17626)***
Precision Corepins, Santa Ana *Also called West Coast Form Grinding* ***(P-16517)***
Precision Cutting Tools Inc....E....562 921-7898
13701 Excelsior Dr Santa Fe Springs (90670) ***(P-14186)***
Precision Deburring Services....D....562 944-4497
4440 Manning Rd Pico Rivera (90660) ***(P-13940)***
Precision Design Inc....E....650 508-8041
1160 Industrial Rd Ste 16 San Carlos (94070) ***(P-17961)***
Precision Designed Products, Pacoima *Also called Excess Trading Inc* ***(P-21469)***
Precision Die Cutting Inc....E....510 636-9654
150 Doolittle Dr San Leandro (94577) ***(P-19739)***
Precision Diecut, Chino *Also called Pdc LLC* ***(P-14092)***
Precision Doors & Millwork, Chino *Also called Precision Companies Inc* ***(P-4110)***
Precision Dynamics Corporation (HQ)....C....818 897-1111
25124 Sprngfeld Ct Ste 20 Valencia (91355) ***(P-5371)***
Precision Energy Efficient Ltg, Yorba Linda *Also called Precision Fluorescent West Inc* ***(P-17065)***
Precision Engineered Products, Sunland *Also called Engineered Products By Lee Ltd* ***(P-15933)***
Precision Engineering Inds....F....818 767-8590
11627 Cantara St North Hollywood (91605) ***(P-19051)***
Precision Engineering Industry, North Hollywood *Also called Precision Engineering Inds* ***(P-19051)***
Precision Enterprises, Stanton *Also called CJ Enterprises* ***(P-14033)***
Precision European Inc....F....714 241-9657
11594 Coley River Cir Fountain Valley (92708) ***(P-14520)***
Precision Fastener Tooling....F....714 898-8558
11530 Western Ave Stanton (90680) ***(P-13991)***
Precision Fiber Products Inc....F....408 946-4040
142 N Milpitas Blvd # 298 Milpitas (95035) ***(P-11314)***
Precision Fiberglass Products....E....310 539-7470
3105 Kashiwa St Torrance (90505) ***(P-16953)***
Precision Film & Tape, San Leandro *Also called Precision Die Cutting Inc* ***(P-19739)***
Precision Flight Controls....F....916 414-1310
2747 Merc Dr Ste 100 Rancho Cordova (95742) ***(P-19381)***
Precision Fluorescent West Inc (HQ)....D....352 692-5900
23281 La Palma Ave Yorba Linda (92887) ***(P-17065)***
Precision Forging Dies Inc....E....562 861-1878
10710 Sessler St South Gate (90280) ***(P-14095)***
Precision Forklift....F....559 805-5487
15389 Avenue 288 Visalia (93292) ***(P-13889)***
Precision Forming Group LLC....F....562 501-1985
511 Commercial Way La Habra (90631) ***(P-13992)***

Precision Frrites Ceramics Inc....D....714 901-7622
5432 Production Dr Huntington Beach (92649) ***(P-10481)***
Precision Glass & Optics, Santa Ana *Also called Buk Optics Inc* ***(P-21336)***
Precision Glass Bevelling Inc....E....818 989-2727
15201 Keswick St Ste A Van Nuys (91405) ***(P-10328)***
Precision Granite Company, Azusa *Also called Precision Granite USA Inc* ***(P-10921)***
Precision Granite USA Inc....E....562 696-8328
174 N Aspan Ave Azusa (91702) ***(P-10921)***
Precision Graphics, Redwood City *Also called Tilley Manufacturing Co Inc* ***(P-9258)***
Precision Hermetic Tech Inc....D....909 381-6011
1940 W Park Ave Redlands (92373) ***(P-19052)***
Precision Identity Corporation....E....408 374-2346
804 Camden Ave Campbell (95008) ***(P-16309)***
Precision Jewelry Tools & Sups....E....408 251-7990
1555 Alum Rock Ave San Jose (95116) ***(P-11540)***
Precision Label Inc....E....760 757-7533
659 Benet Rd Oceanside (92058) ***(P-5338)***
Precision Laser Tek....E....530 661-3580
285 Industrial Way Woodland (95776) ***(P-11865)***
Precision Litho Inc....E....760 727-9400
1185 Joshua Way Vista (92081) ***(P-6790)***
Precision Machining, Glendale *Also called Premac Inc* ***(P-16312)***
Precision Metal Crafts....F....562 468-7080
16920 Gridley Pl Cerritos (90703) ***(P-11866)***
Precision Metal Products Inc (HQ)....C....619 448-2711
850 W Bradley Ave El Cajon (92020) ***(P-12718)***
Precision Milling, Burbank *Also called BMC East LLC* ***(P-4004)***
Precision Millwork LLC....F....661 402-5021
14300 Davenport Rd Ste 4a Agua Dulce (91390) ***(P-4111)***
Precision Molded Plastics Inc....F....909 981-9662
880 W 9th St Upland (91786) ***(P-9987)***
Precision Offset Inc....D....949 752-1714
15201 Woodlawn Ave Tustin (92780) ***(P-6791)***
Precision One Medical Inc....D....760 945-7966
3923 Oceanic Dr Ste 200 Oceanside (92056) ***(P-22181)***
Precision Optical, Costa Mesa *Also called Sellers Optical Inc* ***(P-21407)***
Precision Plastic LLC....C....510 324-8676
555 Twin Dolphin Dr Redwood City (94065) ***(P-9988)***
Precision Plastics Printing, Anaheim *Also called Interlink Inc* ***(P-6650)***
Precision Printers, Grass Valley *Also called Igraphics* ***(P-7093)***
Precision Pwdred Met Parts Inc....E....909 595-5656
145 Atlantic St Pomona (91768) ***(P-11484)***
Precision Resource Inc....B....714 891-4439
5803 Engineer Dr Huntington Beach (92649) ***(P-12858)***
Precision Resource Cal Div, Huntington Beach *Also called Precision Resource Inc* ***(P-12858)***
Precision Resources, Hawthorne *Also called Paulco Precision Inc* ***(P-16286)***
Precision Services Group, Tustin *Also called Precision Offset Inc* ***(P-6791)***
Precision Sheet Metal, Gardena *Also called Artistic Welding Inc* ***(P-12116)***
Precision Silicones, Chino *Also called Wacker Chemical Corporation* ***(P-8784)***
Precision Sports Inc....D....951 674-1665
29910 Ohana Cir Lake Elsinore (92532) ***(P-22865)***
Precision Stampg Solutions Inc....E....951 845-1174
500 Egan Ave Beaumont (92223) ***(P-12859)***
Precision Stampings Inc (PA)....E....951 845-1174
500 Egan Ave Beaumont (92223) ***(P-16921)***
Precision Steel Products Inc....E....310 523-2002
13124 Avalon Blvd Los Angeles (90061) ***(P-12339)***
Precision Technology and Mfg....E....951 788-0252
3147 Durahart St Riverside (92507) ***(P-12647)***
Precision Tile Co....F....818 767-7673
11140 Penrose St Sun Valley (91352) ***(P-10629)***
Precision Tube Bending....D....562 921-6723
13626 Talc St Santa Fe Springs (90670) ***(P-13482)***
Precision Waterjet, Placentia *Also called Jbb Inc* ***(P-19333)***
Precision Waterjet Inc....E....888 538-9287
880 W Crowther Ave Placentia (92870) ***(P-16310)***
Precision Welding Inc....E....661 729-3436
241 Enterprise Pkwy Lancaster (93534) ***(P-11867)***
Precision Wire Products Inc (PA)....C....323 890-9100
6150 Sheila St Commerce (90040) ***(P-13427)***
Precision Wire Products Inc....E....323 569-8165
11215 Wilmington Ave Los Angeles (90059) ***(P-11060)***
Preco Aircraft Motors Inc....E....626 799-3549
1133 Mission St South Pasadena (91030) ***(P-19201)***
Preco Manufacturing Co, Chino *Also called M E Hodge Inc* ***(P-16160)***
Precon Gage, Anaheim *Also called Precon Inc* ***(P-13941)***
Precon Inc....E....714 630-7632
3131 E La Palma Ave Anaheim (92806) ***(P-13941)***
Pred Technologies USA Inc....D....858 999-2114
7855 Fay Ave Ste 310 La Jolla (92037) ***(P-19053)***
Predator Motorsports Inc....F....760 734-1749
1250 Distribution Way Vista (92081) ***(P-9989)***
Predpol Inc....F....831 331-4550
920 41st Ave Ste D Santa Cruz (95062) ***(P-24312)***
Preferred Mfg Svcs Inc (PA)....D....530 677-2675
4261 Business Dr Cameron Park (95682) ***(P-16311)***
Preferred Pallets Inc....F....909 875-7540
288 E Santa Ana Ave Bloomington (92316) ***(P-4392)***
Preferred Pharmaceuticals Inc....F....714 777-3729
1250 N Lakeview Ave Ste O Anaheim (92807) ***(P-8081)***
Preferred Wire Products Inc....F....559 324-0140
401 N Minnewawa Ave Clovis (93611) ***(P-13428)***
Pregis....E....909 469-8100
159 N San Antonio Ave Pomona (91767) ***(P-9563)***
Pregnancy Magazine, San Francisco *Also called Greatdad LLC* ***(P-5946)***
Premac Inc....F....818 241-8370
625 Thompson Ave Glendale (91201) ***(P-16312)***

Premco Forge Inc....F....323 564-6666
5200 Tweedy Blvd South Gate (90280) *(P-12719)*
Premier Barricades....F....877 345-9700
28441 Felix Valdez Ave Temecula (92590) *(P-13539)*
Premier Coatings Inc....D....209 982-5585
7910 Longe St Stockton (95206) *(P-13230)*
Premier Finishing, Stockton *Also called Premier Coatings Inc (P-13230)*
Premier Fuel Distributors Inc....F....562 602-1000
7213 Rosecrans Ave Ste B Paramount (90723) *(P-8763)*
Premier Gear & Machining Inc....E....951 278-5505
2360 Pomona Rd Corona (92880) *(P-12720)*
Premier Magnetics Inc....E....949 452-0511
20381 Barents Sea Cir Lake Forest (92630) *(P-18734)*
Premier Media Inc....F....562 802-9720
13353 Alondra Blvd # 115 Santa Fe Springs (90670) *(P-5803)*
Premier Metal Processing Inc....F....760 415-9027
971 Vernon Way El Cajon (92020) *(P-13076)*
Premier Mop & Broom, Corona *Also called Northwestern Converting Co (P-3628)*
Premier Plastics Inc....E....213 725-0502
6070 Peachtree St Commerce (90040) *(P-5411)*
Premier Steel Structures Inc....E....951 356-6655
13345 Estelle St Corona (92879) *(P-11868)*
Premier Tank Service Inc....E....661 833-2960
34933 Imperial St Bakersfield (93308) *(P-20499)*
Premier Trailer Manufacturing....E....559 651-2212
30517 Ivy Rd Visalia (93291) *(P-20519)*
Premiere Recycle Co....E....408 297-7910
348 Phelan Ave San Jose (95112) *(P-12042)*
Premio Inc (PA)....C....626 839-3100
918 Radecki Ct City of Industry (91748) *(P-14963)*
Premium Herbal USA LLC....F....800 567-7878
10517 Garden Grove Blvd Garden Grove (92843) *(P-616)*
Premium Pallet Inc....F....909 868-9621
2000 Pomona Blvd Pomona (91768) *(P-4393)*
Premium Pet Foods, Irwindale *Also called J & R Taylor Bros Assoc Inc (P-1076)*
Premium Plastics Machine Inc....F....323 979-3889
15956 Downey Ave Paramount (90723) *(P-9990)*
Premium Windows, Paramount *Also called Mediland Corporation (P-10272)*
Prenav Inc....F....650 264-7279
121 Beech St Redwood City (94063) *(P-20676)*
Preplastics, Auburn *Also called Pre/Plastics Inc (P-9985)*
Preproduction Plastics Inc....E....951 340-9680
210 Teller St Corona (92879) *(P-9991)*
Pres-Tek Plastics Inc (PA)....E....909 360-1600
11060 Tacoma Dr Rancho Cucamonga (91730) *(P-9992)*
Presbia, Aliso Viejo *Also called Presbibio LLC (P-22380)*
Presbibio LLC....E....949 502-7010
36 Plateau Aliso Viejo (92656) *(P-22380)*
Presentation Folder Inc....E....714 289-7000
1130 N Main St Orange (92867) *(P-5451)*
Presentation Systems, Richmond *Also called Coin Gllery of San Frncsco Inc (P-4970)*
Preserved, Turlock *Also called Neogen Corporation (P-8399)*
President Enterprise Inc....E....714 671-9577
700 Columbia St Brea (92821) *(P-7179)*
President Global Corporation (HQ)....F....714 994-2990
6965 Aragon Cir Buena Park (90620) *(P-1325)*
Presidio Pharmaceuticals Inc....F....415 655-7560
1700 Owens St Ste 585 San Francisco (94158) *(P-8082)*
Presquile Winery....F....805 937-8110
5391 Presquile Dr Santa Maria (93455) *(P-1870)*
Press Brothers Juicery LLC....E....213 389-3645
2551 Beverly Blvd Ste A Los Angeles (90057) *(P-817)*
Press Colorcom, Santa Fe Springs *Also called Ace Commercial Inc (P-6392)*
Press Democrat, The, Santa Rosa *Also called Santa Rosa Press Democrat Inc (P-5822)*
Press Forge Company....D....562 531-4962
7700 Jackson St Paramount (90723) *(P-12721)*
Press-Enterprise Company (PA)....A....951 684-1200
3450 14th St Riverside (92501) *(P-5804)*
Press-Enterprise Company....F....951 684-1200
3450 14th St Riverside (92501) *(P-5805)*
Pressed Right LLC....F....866 257-5774
23615 El Toro Rd Lake Forest (92630) *(P-11517)*
Pressnet Express Inc....F....858 694-0070
7283 Engineer Rd Ste Ab San Diego (92111) *(P-6792)*
Presstime, Anaheim *Also called B K Harris Inc (P-6430)*
Pressure Cast Products Corp....E....510 532-7310
4210 E 12th St Oakland (94601) *(P-11359)*
Pressure Profile Systems Inc....F....310 641-8100
5757 W Century Blvd # 600 Los Angeles (90045) *(P-20920)*
Prestale USA LP....E....818 818-0976
3255 Saco St Vernon (90058) *(P-1009)*
Prestige Chinese Teas Co....F....650 697-8989
882 Mahler Rd Burlingame (94010) *(P-2588)*
Prestige Cosmetics Inc....F....714 375-0395
17780 Gothard St Huntington Beach (92647) *(P-8564)*
Prestige Flag & Banner Co....D....619 497-2220
591 Camino Dela Reina 917 San Diego (92108) *(P-3853)*
Prestige Foil Inc....F....714 556-1431
13531 Fairmont Way Tustin (92780) *(P-7180)*
Prestige Limousine, Stockton *Also called Ramon Lopez (P-19496)*
Prestige Mold Incorporated....D....909 980-6600
11040 Tacoma Dr Rancho Cucamonga (91730) *(P-14096)*
Prestige Printing, San Ramon *Also called Sorenson Publishing Inc (P-6863)*
Prestige Printing & Graphics, San Ramon *Also called Trinity Marketing LLC (P-6902)*
Preston Cinema Systems Inc....F....310 453-1852
1659 11th St Ste 100 Santa Monica (90404) *(P-22451)*
Preston Vineyards & Winery, Healdsburg *Also called Preston Vineyards Inc (P-1871)*
Preston Vineyards Inc....F....707 433-3372
9282 W Dry Creek Rd Healdsburg (95448) *(P-1871)*
Prestone Products Corporation....E....424 271-4836
19500 Mariner Ave Torrance (90503) *(P-9017)*
Pretika Corporation....E....949 481-8818
16 Salermo Laguna Niguel (92677) *(P-8565)*
Pretium Packaging LLC....C....760 737-7995
946 S Andreasen Dr Escondido (92029) *(P-9493)*
Pretzelmaker, Santa Paula *Also called Fowlie Enterprises Inc (P-1315)*
Prevail Wines, Healdsburg *Also called Ferrar-Crano Vnyrds Winery LLC (P-1699)*
Prezant Company....F....650 342-7413
940 S Amphlett Blvd San Mateo (94402) *(P-14312)*
Prezi Inc (PA)....E....415 398-8012
450 Bryant St San Francisco (94107) *(P-24313)*
Price Industries Inc....D....858 673-4451
10883 Thornmint Rd San Diego (92127) *(P-11061)*
Price Manufacturing Co Inc....E....951 371-5660
372 N Smith Ave Corona (92880) *(P-12648)*
Price Pfister Inc....E....949 672-4003
19701 Da Vinci Foothill Ranch (92610) *(P-11677)*
Price Pfister Inc (HQ)....A....949 672-4000
19701 Da Vinci Lake Forest (92610) *(P-11678)*
Price Pfister Brass Mfg, Lake Forest *Also called Price Pfister Inc (P-11678)*
Price Rubber Company Inc....F....209 239-7478
17760 Ideal Pkwy Manteca (95336) *(P-9204)*
Price-Leho Co Inc....F....805 482-8967
3841 Mission Oaks Blvd Camarillo (93012) *(P-12860)*
Price/Costco Optical Lab, National City *Also called Costco Wholesale Corporation (P-21346)*
Pride Conveyance Systems Inc....D....831 637-1787
1781 Shelton Dr Hollister (95023) *(P-13831)*
Pride Industries One Inc....A....916 788-2100
10030 Foothills Blvd Roseville (95747) *(P-23451)*
Pride Line Products, Stockton *Also called Value Products Inc (P-8355)*
Pride Metal Polishing Inc....F....626 350-1326
10822 Saint Louis Dr El Monte (91731) *(P-13077)*
Pride Sash, Hawthorne *Also called Computerized Fashion Svcs Inc (P-3548)*
Prieto Sports, Temple City *Also called Zeeni Inc (P-3131)*
Prima Fleur Botanicals Inc....F....415 455-0957
84 Galli Dr Novato (94949) *(P-8566)*
Prima Games Inc....C....916 787-7000
2990 Lava Ridge Ct # 120 Roseville (95661) *(P-6139)*
Prima Publishing, Roseville *Also called Prima Games Inc (P-6139)*
Prima-Tex Industries Cal Inc....D....714 521-6104
6237 Descanso Cir Buena Park (90620) *(P-2834)*
Primal Essence Inc....F....805 981-2409
1351 Maulhardt Ave Oxnard (93030) *(P-2225)*
Primal Pet Foods Inc....F....415 642-7400
535 Watt Dr Ste B Fairfield (94534) *(P-1082)*
Primapharma Inc....E....858 259-0969
3443 Tripp Ct San Diego (92121) *(P-8083)*
Primarch Manufacturing Inc....F....760 730-8572
1211 Liberty Way Vista (92081) *(P-23452)*
Primary Color Systems Corp (PA)....B....949 660-7080
11130 Holder St Cypress (90630) *(P-6793)*
Primary Color Systems Corp....D....310 841-0250
401 Coral Cir El Segundo (90245) *(P-7181)*
Primary Concepts Inc....F....510 559-5545
1338 7th St Berkeley (94710) *(P-22707)*
Prime Alliance LLC....E....310 764-1000
360 W Victoria St Compton (90220) *(P-2814)*
Prime Alloy Steel Casting, Port Hueneme *Also called Pac Foundries Inc (P-11387)*
Prime Alloy Steel Castings Inc....C....805 488-6451
717 Industrial Way Port Hueneme (93041) *(P-11421)*
Prime Building Material Inc (PA)....E....818 765-6767
6900 Lankershim Blvd North Hollywood (91605) *(P-10630)*
Prime Building Material Inc....F....818 503-4242
7811 Lankershim Blvd North Hollywood (91605) *(P-10631)*
Prime Compliance Solutions....F....310 748-8103
4010 Watson Plaza Dr # 245 Lakewood (90712) *(P-248)*
Prime Conduit Inc....E....530 669-0160
1776 E Beamer St Woodland (95776) *(P-7599)*
Prime Converting Corporation....E....909 476-9500
9121 Pttsbrgh Ave Ste 100 Rancho Cucamonga (91730) *(P-5523)*
Prime Engineering, Fresno *Also called Axiom Industries Inc (P-21983)*
Prime Forming & Cnstr Sups....E....714 547-6710
1500a E Chestnut Ave Santa Ana (92701) *(P-10632)*
Prime Heat Incorporated....F....619 449-6623
1844 Friendship Dr Ste A El Cajon (92020) *(P-14773)*
Prime Plating, Sun Valley *Also called Schmidt Industries Inc (P-13098)*
Prime Plating Aerospace Inc....F....818 768-9100
11321 Goss St Sun Valley (91352) *(P-13078)*
Prime Solutions Inc....F....510 490-2255
4261 Business Center Dr Fremont (94538) *(P-18479)*
Prime Surfaces Inc....F....310 448-2292
25111 Normandie Ave Harbor City (90710) *(P-10922)*
Prime Wheel Corporation....B....310 326-5080
23920 Vermont Ave Harbor City (90710) *(P-19740)*
Prime Wheel Corporation....E....310 516-9126
250 W Apra St Compton (90220) *(P-19741)*
Prime Wheel Corporation....E....310 819-4123
17680 S Figueroa St Gardena (90248) *(P-19742)*
Prime Wheel Corporation (PA)....A....310 516-9126
17705 S Main St Gardena (90248) *(P-19743)*
Prime Wheel of Figueroa, Gardena *Also called Prime Wheel Corporation (P-19742)*
Prime Wire & Cable Inc (HQ)....E....888 445-9955
280 Machlin Ct Fl 2 Walnut (91789) *(P-11315)*
Primebore Directional Boring....F....909 821-4643
10822 Vernon Ave Ontario (91762) *(P-104)*

ALPHABETIC

Employee Codes: A=Over 500 employees, B=251-500
C=101-250, D=51-100, E=20-50, F=10-19
2020 California
Manfacturers Register
© Mergent Inc. 1-800-342-5647
1209

Primed Productions Inc....F....626 216-5822
1443 E Washington Blvd Pasadena (91104) ***(P-4869)***
Primetech Silicones Inc....F....951 509-6655
6655 Doolittle Ave Riverside (92503) ***(P-8764)***
Primex, Vacaville *Also called SJ Electro Systems Inc* ***(P-15578)***
Primex, Vacaville *Also called McC Controls LLC* ***(P-15540)***
Primex Farms LLC (PA)....E....661 758-7790
16070 Wildwood Rd Wasco (93280) ***(P-1437)***
Primo Powder Coating & Sndblst....F....714 596-4242
17592 Gothard St Huntington Beach (92647) ***(P-13231)***
Primo Sandblasting, Huntington Beach *Also called Norm Harboldt* ***(P-13212)***
Primus Inc....D....714 527-2261
17901 Jamestown Ln Huntington Beach (92647) ***(P-23178)***
Primus Lighting Inc....F....626 442-4600
3570 Lexington Ave El Monte (91731) ***(P-17156)***
Primus Pipe and Tube Inc (HQ)....D....562 808-8000
5855 Obispo Ave Long Beach (90805) ***(P-11133)***
Primus Power Corporation....E....510 342-7600
3967 Trust Way Hayward (94545) ***(P-19180)***
Prince Development LLC....F....866 774-6234
23302 Oxnard St Woodland Hills (91367) ***(P-8567)***
Prince Lionheart Inc (PA)....E....805 922-2250
2421 Westgate Rd Santa Maria (93455) ***(P-9993)***
Prince Reigns, Woodland Hills *Also called Prince Development LLC* ***(P-8567)***
Princess Brandy Corp (PA)....F....619 563-9722
3161 Adams Ave San Diego (92116) ***(P-1264)***
Princess Paper Inc....E....323 588-4777
4455 Fruitland Ave Vernon (90058) ***(P-5464)***
Princeton Case West Inc....E....805 928-8840
1444 W Mccoy Ln Santa Maria (93455) ***(P-9994)***
Princeton Technology Inc....E....949 851-7776
1691 Browning Irvine (92606) ***(P-15309)***
Principia Biopharma Inc....D....650 416-7700
220 E Grand Ave South San Francisco (94080) ***(P-8084)***
Principle Plastics....E....310 532-3411
1136 W 135th St Gardena (90247) ***(P-9179)***
Pringle's Draperies, Garden Grove *Also called L C Pringle Sales Inc* ***(P-5029)***
Prinsco Inc....E....559 485-5542
2839 S Cherry Ave Fresno (93706) ***(P-9473)***
Print & Mail Solutions Inc....F....916 782-5489
1322 Blue Oaks Blvd # 100 Roseville (95678) ***(P-6794)***
Print Ink Inc....E....925 829-3950
6918 Sierra Ct Dublin (94568) ***(P-7182)***
Print N Save Inc....F....714 634-1133
2120 E Howell Ave Ste 414 Anaheim (92806) ***(P-6795)***
Print Shop, San Bernardino *Also called San Brnrdino Cmnty College Dst* ***(P-7207)***
Print Shop, The, La Mirada *Also called Wintflash Inc* ***(P-7273)***
Print Smith Inc....F....831 688-1538
8047 Soquel Dr Aptos (95003) ***(P-6796)***
Print-N-Stuff Inc....F....925 798-3212
1300 Galaxy Way Ste 3 Concord (94520) ***(P-6797)***
Printcom Inc....F....818 891-8282
14675 Titus St Van Nuys (91402) ***(P-6798)***
Printec Ht Electronics LLC....E....714 484-7597
501 Sally Pl Fullerton (92831) ***(P-18480)***
Printech, Fullerton *Also called High Five Inc* ***(P-6614)***
Printed Circuit Solutions Inc....F....714 825-1090
2040 S Yale St Santa Ana (92704) ***(P-17962)***
Printed Circuit Technology....D....510 659-1866
44081 Old Warm Sprng Blvd Fremont (94538) ***(P-17963)***
Printed Image, The, Chico *Also called Srl Apparel Inc* ***(P-2838)***
Printefex Inc....F....818 240-2400
401 W Los Feliz Rd Ste C Glendale (91204) ***(P-6799)***
Printegra Corp....E....925 373-6368
379 Earhart Way Livermore (94551) ***(P-7283)***
Printer Cartridge USA....F....858 538-7630
14276 Barrymore St San Diego (92129) ***(P-22452)***
Printerprezz Inc....F....510 225-8412
4026 Clipper Ct Fremont (94538) ***(P-6800)***
Printery Inc....F....949 757-1930
1762 Kaiser Ave Irvine (92614) ***(P-6801)***
Printfirm Inc....F....818 992-1005
21352 Nordhoff St Ste 104 Chatsworth (91311) ***(P-6802)***
Printing 4him, Ontario *Also called Ultimate Print Source Inc* ***(P-6906)***
Printing and Marketing Inc....F....510 931-7000
33200 Transit Ave Union City (94587) ***(P-7183)***
Printing Connection , The, Newbury Park *Also called H J S Graphics* ***(P-6601)***
Printing Division Inc....F....714 685-0111
1933 N Main St Orange (92865) ***(P-6803)***
Printing Impressions, Goleta *Also called JD Business Solutions Inc* ***(P-6663)***
Printing Island Corporation....F....714 668-1000
11535 Martens River Cir Fountain Valley (92708) ***(P-6804)***
Printing Management Associates....F....562 407-9977
17128 Edwards Rd Cerritos (90703) ***(P-6805)***
Printing Manufacturer, San Diego *Also called Kyung In Printing Inc* ***(P-6685)***
Printing Palace Inc (PA)....E....310 451-5151
2300 Lincoln Blvd Santa Monica (90405) ***(P-6806)***
Printing Place, The, Palm Desert *Also called Wanda Matranga* ***(P-6926)***
Printing Rsources Southern Cal, Upland *Also called Helens Place Inc* ***(P-6607)***
Printing Safari Co....F....818 709-3752
9855 Topanga Canyon Blvd Chatsworth (91311) ***(P-6807)***
Printing Shoppe, The, San Diego *Also called Wissings Inc* ***(P-6942)***
Printing Solutions, Escondido *Also called LL Baker Inc* ***(P-6706)***
Printivity (PA)....F....877 649-5463
8840 Kenamar Dr Ste 405 San Diego (92121) ***(P-6808)***
Printograph Inc....F....818 252-3000
7625 N San Fernando Rd Burbank (91505) ***(P-6809)***
Printpack Inc....C....925 469-0601
5870 Stoneridge Mall Rd # 200 Pleasanton (94588) ***(P-5412)***
Printronix LLC (PA)....C....714 368-2300
6440 Oak Cyn Ste 200 Irvine (92618) ***(P-15310)***
Printronix Holding Corp....C....714 368-2300
6440 Oak Cyn Ste 200 Irvine (92618) ***(P-15311)***
Printrunner LLC....E....888 296-5760
8000 Haskell Ave Van Nuys (91406) ***(P-6810)***
Prints Charmn Inc (PA)....F....310 312-0904
11560 Tennessee Ave Los Angeles (90064) ***(P-6811)***
Printworx Inc....F....831 722-7147
195 Aviation Way Ste 201 Watsonville (95076) ***(P-15312)***
Priority Pallet Inc....C....951 769-9399
1060 E Third St Beaumont (92223) ***(P-4394)***
Priority Posting and Pubg Inc....E....714 338-2568
17501 Irvine Blvd Ste 1 Tustin (92780) ***(P-6316)***
Priority Tech Systems Inc....F....818 756-5413
14040 Runnymede St Van Nuys (91405) ***(P-19382)***
Prisha Cosmetics Inc....F....818 773-8784
9260 Owensmouth Ave Chatsworth (91311) ***(P-8568)***
Prism Aerospace....E....951 582-2850
3087 12th St Riverside (92507) ***(P-12340)***
Prism Skylabs Inc....F....415 243-0834
799 Market St Fl 8 San Francisco (94103) ***(P-17627)***
Prism Software Corporation....E....949 855-3100
15500 Rockfield Blvd C Irvine (92618) ***(P-24314)***
Prison Ride Share Network....E....314 703-5245
1541 S California Ave Compton (90221) ***(P-6317)***
Prison Rideshare Network, Compton *Also called Prison Ride Share Network* ***(P-6317)***
Private Brand Mdsg Corp....E....213 749-0191
214 W Olympic Blvd Los Angeles (90015) ***(P-3249)***
Private Label By G Inc (PA)....E....562 531-1116
6015 Obispo Ave Long Beach (90805) ***(P-3250)***
Prl Aluminum Inc....D....626 968-7507
14760 Don Julian Rd City of Industry (91746) ***(P-11186)***
Pro American Premium Tools, Baldwin Park *Also called Kal-Cameron Manufacturing* ***(P-11532)***
Pro Cal, South Gate *Also called Productivity California Inc* ***(P-9997)***
Pro Circuit Products Inc....F....951 734-3320
2388 Railroad St Corona (92880) ***(P-20422)***
Pro Coat Powder Coating, Lake Elsinore *Also called Rick Palenshus* ***(P-14529)***
Pro Comp, Chula Vista *Also called Tap Manufacturing LLC* ***(P-19777)***
Pro Design Group Inc....E....310 767-1032
438 E Alondra Blvd Gardena (90248) ***(P-9995)***
Pro Detention Inc....D....714 881-3680
2238 N Glassell St Ste E Orange (92865) ***(P-11104)***
Pro Document Solutions Inc (PA)....D....805 238-6680
1760 Commerce Way Paso Robles (93446) ***(P-6812)***
Pro Fab Manufacturing, Fremont *Also called United Pro Fab Mfg Inc* ***(P-16483)***
Pro Fab Tech LLC....F....626 804-7200
970 W Foothill Blvd Azusa (91702) ***(P-16313)***
Pro Food Inc....F....818 341-4040
19431 Bus Center Dr # 35 Northridge (91324) ***(P-2589)***
Pro Group, Irvine *Also called Professnal Rprgraphic Svcs Inc* ***(P-7185)***
Pro Imaging, Chula Vista *Also called Professional Imaging Svcs Inc* ***(P-21278)***
Pro Line Paint Company....E....619 232-8968
2646 Main St San Diego (92113) ***(P-8672)***
Pro Metal Products....F....760 480-0212
25559 Jesmond Dene Rd Escondido (92026) ***(P-12341)***
Pro Mold Inc....F....951 776-0555
415 Grumman Dr Riverside (92508) ***(P-14097)***
Pro Pack Systems Inc....F....831 771-1300
1354 Dayton St Ste A Salinas (93901) ***(P-14724)***
Pro Power Products Inc....F....818 558-6222
913 S Victory Blvd Burbank (91502) ***(P-16794)***
Pro Systems Fabricators Inc (PA)....F....909 350-9147
14643 Hawthorne Ave Fontana (92335) ***(P-19383)***
Pro Tag Corp....E....213 272-9606
8122 Maie Ave Unit C Los Angeles (90001) ***(P-2800)***
Pro Team Axis LLC....F....833 333-2947
1725 Harding Ave Unit A National City (91950) ***(P-7684)***
Pro Tool Services Inc....E....661 393-9222
1704 Sunnyside Ct Bakersfield (93308) ***(P-14187)***
Pro Tour Memorabilia LLC....E....424 303-7200
700 N San Vicente Blvd G696 West Hollywood (90069) ***(P-4522)***
Pro Vac....F....661 765-7298
26857 Henry Rd Fellows (93224) ***(P-249)***
Pro Wax, Tustin *Also called Baf Industries* ***(P-8366)***
Pro-Action Products, Van Nuys *Also called Neo Pacific Holdings Inc* ***(P-9920)***
Pro-Cision Machining, Morgan Hill *Also called KDF Inc* ***(P-20411)***
Pro-Dex Inc (PA)....D....949 769-3200
2361 Mcgaw Ave Irvine (92614) ***(P-21863)***
Pro-Form Laboratories, Benicia *Also called Pro-Form Manufacturing LLC* ***(P-8085)***
Pro-Form Manufacturing LLC....C....707 752-9010
5001 Industrial Way Benicia (94510) ***(P-8085)***
Pro-Lite Inc....F....714 668-9988
3505 Cadillac Ave Ste D Costa Mesa (92626) ***(P-23179)***
Pro-Mart Industries Inc (PA)....E....949 428-7700
17421 Von Karman Ave Irvine (92614) ***(P-3636)***
Pro-Spot International Inc....F....760 407-1414
5932 Sea Otter Pl Carlsbad (92010) ***(P-19384)***
Pro-Tech Mats Industries Inc....F....760 343-3667
72370 Quarry Trl Ste A Thousand Palms (92276) ***(P-9357)***
Pro-Tek Manufacturing Inc....E....925 454-8100
4849 Southfront Rd Livermore (94551) ***(P-12342)***
Proactive Packg & Display LLC (HQ)....D....909 390-5624
602 S Rockefeller Ave Ontario (91761) ***(P-5260)***
Proair LLC....F....909 930-6224
12151 Madera Way Riverside (92503) ***(P-15448)***

Mergent e-mail: customerrelations@mergent.com
1210
2020 California Manufacturers Register
(P-0000) Products & Services Section entry number
(PA)=Parent Co (HQ)=Headquarters (DH)=Div Headquarters

Probe Racing Components Inc......E......310 784-2977
5022 Onyx St Torrance (90503) ***(P-15616)***
Probe-Logic Inc......D......408 416-0777
1885 Lundy Ave Ste 101 San Jose (95131) ***(P-14964)***
Probe-Rite Corp......E......408 727-0100
600 Mission St Santa Clara (95050) ***(P-21102)***
Procases Inc......F......323 585-4447
4626 E 48th St Vernon (90058) ***(P-4342)***
Procede Software LP......E......858 450-4800
6815 Flanders Dr Ste 200 San Diego (92121) ***(P-24315)***
Proceilingtiles, Bakersfield *Also called Udecor Inc* ***(P-10097)***
Process Advanced Filtration, Oxnard *Also called Parker-Hannifin Corporation* ***(P-14846)***
Process Materials Inc......F......925 245-9626
5625 Brisa St Ste B Livermore (94550) ***(P-11207)***
Process Metrix LLC......F......925 460-0385
6622 Owens Dr Pleasanton (94588) ***(P-21521)***
Process Solutions Inc......E......408 370-6540
1077 Dell Ave Ste A Campbell (95008) ***(P-20921)***
Process Specialties Inc......E......209 832-1344
1660 W Linne Rd Ste A Tracy (95377) ***(P-18481)***
Process Stainless Lab Inc (PA)......E......408 980-0535
1280 Memorex Dr Santa Clara (95050) ***(P-13079)***
Processors Mailing Inc......E......626 358-5075
761 N Dodsworth Ave Covina (91724) ***(P-6813)***
Processors The, Covina *Also called Processors Mailing Inc* ***(P-6813)***
Proco Products Inc (PA)......E......209 943-6088
2431 Wigwam Dr Stockton (95205) ***(P-9358)***
Procoat, San Marcos *Also called Prowest Technologies Inc* ***(P-8674)***
Procolorflex Ink Corp......F......510 293-3033
3588 Arden Rd Hayward (94545) ***(P-8928)***
Procter & Gamble Mfg Co......C......916 383-3800
8201 Fruitridge Rd Sacramento (95826) ***(P-8348)***
Procter & Gamble Mfg Co......B......513 627-4678
18125 Rowland St City of Industry (91748) ***(P-8349)***
Procter & Gamble Paper Pdts Co......B......805 485-8871
800 N Rice Ave Oxnard (93030) ***(P-5465)***
Prodigy Press Inc......F......408 962-0396
1136 W Evelyn Ave Sunnyvale (94086) ***(P-7184)***
Prodigy Surface Tech Inc......E......408 492-9390
807 Aldo Ave Ste 103 Santa Clara (95054) ***(P-13080)***
Produce Apparel Inc......F......949 472-9434
23383 Saint Andrews Mission Viejo (92692) ***(P-3392)***
Produce Available Inc (PA)......D......805 483-5292
910 Commercial Ave Oxnard (93030) ***(P-13660)***
Produce World Inc......D......510 441-1449
30611 San Antonio St Hayward (94544) ***(P-2590)***
Product Design Developments......E......714 898-6895
15611 Container Ln Huntington Beach (92649) ***(P-9996)***
Product Slingshot Inc......D......760 929-9380
2221 Rutherford Rd Carlsbad (92008) ***(P-14098)***
Product Solutions Inc......E......714 545-9757
1182 N Knollwood Cir Anaheim (92801) ***(P-15561)***
Product Virtual Gt, Costa Mesa *Also called E Virtual Corporation* ***(P-17224)***
Production Assmbly Systems Inc......E......858 748-6700
12568 Kirkham Ct Poway (92064) ***(P-14278)***
Production Car Care Products, Stockton *Also called Production Chemical Mfg Inc* ***(P-8408)***
Production Chemical Mfg Inc (PA)......F......209 943-7337
1000 E Channel St Stockton (95205) ***(P-8408)***
Production Data Inc......F......661 327-4776
1210 33rd St Bakersfield (93301) ***(P-250)***
Production Embroidery Inc......F......760 727-7407
1235 Activity Dr Ste D Vista (92081) ***(P-3752)***
Production Engineering & Mch, Fontana *Also called Cavallo & Cavallo Inc* ***(P-15829)***
Production Industries, Brea *Also called Production Systems Group Inc* ***(P-5076)***
Production Lapping Company......E......626 359-0611
124 E Chestnut Ave Monrovia (91016) ***(P-16314)***
Production Saw......F......818 765-6100
9790 Glenoaks Blvd Ste 8 Sun Valley (91352) ***(P-13942)***
Production Specialties, San Francisco *Also called Klein Industries Inc* ***(P-16120)***
Production Specialties, Sacramento *Also called California Pro-Specs Inc* ***(P-3971)***
Production Systems Group Inc......E......714 990-8997
895 Beacon St Brea (92821) ***(P-5076)***
Production Truss Inc......F......619 258-8792
9925 Prospect Ave Ste E Santee (92071) ***(P-4315)***
Productivity California Inc......D......562 923-3100
10533 Sessler St South Gate (90280) ***(P-9997)***
Productplan LLC......E......805 618-2975
10 E Yanonali St Ste 2a Santa Barbara (93101) ***(P-24316)***
Products Engineering Corp (PA)......D......310 787-4500
2645 Maricopa St Torrance (90503) ***(P-11541)***
Products/Techniques Inc......F......909 877-3951
3271 S Riverside Ave Bloomington (92316) ***(P-8673)***
Professional Bearing Svc Inc......E......562 596-5023
3831 Catalina St Ste K Los Alamitos (90720) ***(P-16315)***
Professional Finishing Inc......D......510 233-7629
770 Market Ave Richmond (94801) ***(P-13081)***
Professional Finishing Systems......F......818 365-8888
12341 Gladstone Ave Sylmar (91342) ***(P-12861)***
Professional Imaging Svcs Inc......F......858 565-4217
751 Main St Chula Vista (91911) ***(P-21278)***
Professional McHy Group Inc......F......209 832-0100
1885 N Macarthur Dr Tracy (95376) ***(P-14299)***
Professional Plastics Inc......F......916 374-4580
2940 Ramco St Ste 100 West Sacramento (95691) ***(P-7600)***
Professional Print & Mail Inc......E......559 237-7468
2818 E Hamilton Ave Fresno (93721) ***(P-6814)***
Professional Skin Care Inc (PA)......E......661 257-7771
25028 Avenue Kearny Valencia (91355) ***(P-8569)***
Professnal Rprgraphic Svcs Inc......E......949 748-5400
17731 Cowan Irvine (92614) ***(P-7185)***
Profile Planing Mill, Santa Ana *Also called Strata Forest Products Inc* ***(P-3962)***
Profood Tropical Fruits Inc......F......510 890-0070
33288 Alvarado Niles Rd Union City (94587) ***(P-857)***
Proformance Manufacturing Inc......E......951 279-1230
1922 Elise Cir Corona (92879) ***(P-12862)***
Proformative Inc......F......408 400-3993
99 Almaden Blvd Ste 975 San Jose (95113) ***(P-6318)***
Program Data Incorporated......F......714 649-2122
16291 Jackson Ranch Rd Silverado (92676) ***(P-21103)***
Program Precision Co, San Diego *Also called Fourward Machine Inc* ***(P-15970)***
Programmed Composites Inc......C......951 520-7300
250 Klug Cir Corona (92880) ***(P-20205)***
Prographics Inc......E......626 287-0417
9200 Lower Azusa Rd Rosemead (91770) ***(P-6815)***
Prographics Screenprinting Inc......E......760 744-4555
1975 Diamond St San Marcos (92078) ***(P-7186)***
Progress Group......F......714 630-9017
1600 E Miraloma Ave Placentia (92870) ***(P-19744)***
Progressive Concepts Machining, Pleasanton *Also called Desert Sky Machining Inc* ***(P-15890)***
Progressive Housing Inc......F......916 920-8255
5605 Southfront Rd Livermore (94551) ***(P-19745)***
Progressive Label Inc......E......323 415-9770
2545 Yates Ave Commerce (90040) ***(P-5524)***
Progressive Manufacturing, Anaheim *Also called Progrssive Intgrated Solutions* ***(P-7187)***
Progressive Marketing Pdts Inc......D......714 888-1700
2620 Palisades Dr Corona (92882) ***(P-12571)***
Progressive Packg Group Inc (PA)......E......831 424-2942
18931 Portola Dr Ste C Salinas (93908) ***(P-5261)***
Progressive Products Inc......F......951 784-9930
1650 7th St Riverside (92507) ***(P-2951)***
Progressive Technology Inc......E......916 632-6715
4130 Citrus Ave Ste 17 Rocklin (95677) ***(P-10449)***
Progressive Tool & Die Inc......F......310 327-0569
17016 S Broadway Gardena (90248) ***(P-14188)***
Progressive Woodwork......F......530 343-2211
2255 Ceanothus Ave Chico (95926) ***(P-4232)***
Progrip Cargo Control, Lodi *Also called USA Products Group Inc* ***(P-3864)***
Progrssive Intgrated Solutions......D......714 237-0980
3700 E Miraloma Ave Anaheim (92806) ***(P-7187)***
Prohibition Brewing Co Inc......E......760 295-3525
2004 E Vista Way Vista (92084) ***(P-1561)***
Project 1920 Inc......F......415 529-2245
441 Jackson St San Francisco (94111) ***(P-10225)***
Project Social T LLC......E......323 266-4500
615 S Clarence St Los Angeles (90023) ***(P-3189)***
Projectoris Inc......F......917 972-5553
50 Fremont St Ste 2275 San Francisco (94105) ***(P-24317)***
Projex International Inc......F......661 268-0999
9555 Hierba Rd Santa Clarita (91390) ***(P-23453)***
Prolab Orthotics Inc......E......707 257-4400
575 Airpark Rd NAPA (94558) ***(P-9359)***
Prolacta Bioscience Inc......B......626 599-9260
1800 Highland Ave Duarte (91010) ***(P-617)***
Prolacta Bioscience Inc (PA)......C......626 599-9260
757 Baldwin Park Blvd City of Industry (91746) ***(P-8323)***
Proline Concrete Tools Inc......E......760 758-7240
2664 Vista Pacific Dr Oceanside (92056) ***(P-14521)***
Proline Manufacturing, Banning *Also called DT Mattson Enterprises Inc* ***(P-22672)***
Proma Inc......E......310 327-0035
730 Kingshill Pl Carson (90746) ***(P-22182)***
Promag, South Gate *Also called C&C Metal Form & Tooling Inc* ***(P-12776)***
Promarksvac Corporation......F......909 923-3888
1915 E Acacia St Ontario (91761) ***(P-14725)***
Promart Dazz, Irvine *Also called Pro-Mart Industries Inc* ***(P-3636)***
Promaxo Inc......F......510 982-1202
70 Washington St Ste 407 Oakland (94607) ***(P-21864)***
Promedia Companies......F......714 444-2426
3518 W Lake Center Dr D Santa Ana (92704) ***(P-6007)***
Promedia Printers, Canoga Park *Also called PM Lithographers Inc* ***(P-6786)***
Promega Biosciences LLC......D......805 544-8524
277 Granada Dr San Luis Obispo (93401) ***(P-7685)***
Promega Bsystems Sunnyvale Inc......E......408 636-2400
3945 Freedom Cir Ste 200 Santa Clara (95054) ***(P-21522)***
Prometheus Biosciences Inc......E......858 200-7888
9410 Carroll Park Dr San Diego (92121) ***(P-8086)***
Prometheus Laboratories Inc......B......858 824-0895
9410 Carroll Park Dr San Diego (92121) ***(P-8087)***
Promex Industries Incorporated......E......858 674-4676
10987 Via Frontera San Diego (92127) ***(P-18482)***
Promex Industries Incorporated (PA)......D......408 496-0222
3075 Oakmead Village Dr Santa Clara (95051) ***(P-18483)***
Promex International Plas Inc......E......818 367-5352
12860 San Fernando Rd D Sylmar (91342) ***(P-9998)***
Promises Promises Inc......E......213 749-7725
3121 S Grand Ave Los Angeles (90007) ***(P-3251)***
Promotion West, Glendale *Also called Lin MAI Inc* ***(P-23395)***
Promotion Xpress Prtg Graphics, San Leandro *Also called Akido Printing Inc* ***(P-6399)***
Promotonal Design Concepts Inc......D......626 579-4454
9872 Rush St South El Monte (91733) ***(P-9360)***
Prompt Precision Metals Inc......D......209 531-1210
1649 E Whitmore Ave Ceres (95307) ***(P-12343)***
Prompter People Inc......F......408 353-6000
126 Dillon Ave Campbell (95008) ***(P-17628)***
Pronk Technologies Inc (PA)......F......818 768-5600
8933 Lankershim Blvd Sun Valley (91352) ***(P-21104)***

ALPHABETIC

Employee Codes: A=Over 500 employees, B=251-500
C=101-250, D=51-100, E=20-50, F=10-19
2020 California
Manfacturers Register
© Mergent Inc. 1-800-342-5647
1211

Pronto Drilling Inc (PA) .....E.....562 777-0900
9501 Santa Fe Springs Rd Santa Fe Springs (90670) ***(P-16316)***
Pronto Products Co (PA) .....E.....619 661-6995
9850 Siempre Viva Rd San Diego (92154) ***(P-15562)***
Proof Reading LLC .....F.....650 438-9438
3905 State St Ste 7-516 Santa Barbara (93105) ***(P-6319)***
Propel Biofuels Inc (PA) .....F.....800 871-0773
1815 19th St Sacramento (95811) ***(P-8765)***
Propel Fuels, Sacramento *Also called Propel Biofuels Inc* ***(P-8765)***
Propertyradar.com, Truckee *Also called Acureo Inc* ***(P-23557)***
Prophecy Technology LLC .....E.....909 598-7998
339 Cheryl Ln Walnut (91789) ***(P-15313)***
Proplas Technologies, Garden Grove *Also called Peerless Injection Molding LLC* ***(P-9957)***
Proprietary Controls Systems .....E.....310 303-3600
3541 Challenger St Torrance (90503) ***(P-21523)***
Pros Incorporated .....D.....661 589-5400
3400 Patton Way Bakersfield (93308) ***(P-251)***
Proseries LLC .....F.....213 533-6400
3400 Airport Ave Bldg E Santa Monica (90405) ***(P-22866)***
Proshot Golf, Irvine *Also called Proshot Investors LLC* ***(P-17629)***
Proshot Investors LLC .....F.....949 586-9500
18007 Sky Park Cir Ste F Irvine (92614) ***(P-17629)***
Prosound Communications Inc .....F.....818 367-9593
233 N Maclay Ave Ste 403 San Fernando (91340) ***(P-10152)***
Prospring Inc .....F.....562 726-1800
101 Atlantic Ave Ste 103 Long Beach (90802) ***(P-24318)***
Prostat First Aid LLC (PA) .....E.....661 705-1256
24922 Anza Dr Ste A Valencia (91355) ***(P-22071)***
Prostat First Aid LLC .....E.....888 900-2920
1643 Puddingstone Dr La Verne (91750) ***(P-22072)***
Prosthetic and Orthotic Group (PA) .....F.....562 595-6445
2669 Myrtle Ave Ste 101 Signal Hill (90755) ***(P-22073)***
Prosurg Inc .....E.....408 945-4040
2195 Trade Zone Blvd San Jose (95131) ***(P-21865)***
Protab Laboratories .....D.....949 635-1930
25902 Towne Centre Dr Foothill Ranch (92610) ***(P-8088)***
Protagonist Therapeutics Inc .....D.....510 474-0170
7707 Gateway Blvd Ste 140 Newark (94560) ***(P-8089)***
Protec Arisawa America Inc .....E.....760 599-4800
2455 Ash St Vista (92081) ***(P-12043)***
Protech Design & Manufacturing, San Diego *Also called PDM Solutions Inc* ***(P-17955)***
Protech Materials Inc .....F.....510 887-5870
20919 Cabot Blvd Hayward (94545) ***(P-11360)***
Protech Minerals Inc .....F.....760 245-3441
17092 S D St Victorville (92395) ***(P-10461)***
Protech Systems, Riverside *Also called Alectro Inc* ***(P-16540)***
Protech Thermal Services .....E.....951 272-5808
1954 Tandem Norco (92860) ***(P-11466)***
Protective Industries Inc .....D.....310 537-2300
18704 S Ferris Pl Rancho Dominguez (90220) ***(P-9999)***
Protein Research, Livermore *Also called Berkeley Nutritional Mfg Corp* ***(P-7801)***
Protemach Inc .....F.....310 622-2693
7133 Remmet Ave Canoga Park (91303) ***(P-8766)***
Proterra Inc (PA) .....C.....864 438-0000
1815 Rollins Rd Burlingame (94010) ***(P-19494)***
Proteus Digital Health Inc .....C.....650 632-4031
3956 Point Eden Way Hayward (94545) ***(P-8324)***
Proteus Digital Health Inc (PA) .....C.....650 632-4031
2600 Bridge Pkwy Redwood City (94065) ***(P-8325)***
Proteus Industries Inc .....E.....650 964-4163
340 Pioneer Way Mountain View (94041) ***(P-20922)***
Prothena Corp Pub Ltd Co .....F.....650 837-8550
331 Oyster Point Blvd South San Francisco (94080) ***(P-7686)***
Proto Homes LLC .....E.....310 271-7544
917 W 17th St Los Angeles (90015) ***(P-20492)***
Proto Laminations Inc .....F.....562 926-4777
13666 Bora Dr Santa Fe Springs (90670) ***(P-12863)***
Proto Services Inc .....E.....408 321-8688
1991 Concourse Dr San Jose (95131) ***(P-17753)***
Proto Space Engineering Inc .....E.....626 442-8273
2214 Loma Ave South El Monte (91733) ***(P-16317)***
Protocast, Chatsworth *Also called John List Corporation* ***(P-14233)***
Protonex LLC .....F.....707 566-2260
2331 Circadian Way Santa Rosa (95407) ***(P-18484)***
Protool Co, Tustin *Also called Bernhardt & Bernhardt Inc* ***(P-13904)***
Protoquick Inc .....F.....510 264-0101
3412 Investment Blvd Hayward (94545) ***(P-16318)***
Prototype & Short-Run Svcs Inc .....E.....714 449-9661
1310 W Collins Ave Orange (92867) ***(P-12864)***
Prototype Express LLC .....F.....714 751-3533
3506 W Lake Center Dr D Santa Ana (92704) ***(P-19385)***
Prototype Industries Inc (PA) .....E.....949 680-4890
26035 Acero Ste 100 Mission Viejo (92691) ***(P-6320)***
Prototype Solutions, San Jose *Also called Binh-Nhan D Ngo* ***(P-17838)***
Protrend Ltd (HQ) .....F.....323 832-9323
6001 E Washington Blvd Commerce (90040) ***(P-3252)***
Protype, Orange *Also called G P Manufacturing Inc* ***(P-15981)***
Proulx Manufacturing Inc .....E.....909 980-0662
11433 6th St Rancho Cucamonga (91730) ***(P-10000)***
Provac Sales Inc .....E.....831 462-8900
3131 Soquel Dr Ste A Soquel (95073) ***(P-14596)***
Provasis Therapeutics Inc .....E.....858 712-2101
9177 Sky Park Ct B San Diego (92123) ***(P-21866)***
Provena Foods Inc .....E.....209 858-5555
251 Darcy Pkwy Lathrop (95330) ***(P-490)***
Provenance Vineyards .....F.....707 968-3633
1695 Saint Helena Hwy S Saint Helena (94574) ***(P-1872)***
Provence Stone .....F.....650 631-5600
1040 Varian St San Carlos (94070) ***(P-10923)***
Providence Industries LLC .....D.....562 420-9091
3833 Mcgowen St Long Beach (90808) ***(P-3048)***
Providence Publications LLC .....E.....916 774-4000
1620 Santa Roseville (95661) ***(P-6321)***
Providenet Communications Corp .....E.....408 398-6335
20 Great Oaks Blvd San Jose (95119) ***(P-24319)***
Providien Injction Molding Inc .....D.....760 931-1844
2731 Loker Ave W Carlsbad (92010) ***(P-10001)***
Providien Thermoforming Inc .....E.....858 850-1591
6740 Nancy Ridge Dr San Diego (92121) ***(P-9417)***
Provivi Inc (PA) .....E.....310 828-2307
1701 Colorado Ave Santa Monica (90404) ***(P-8767)***
Prowave Manufacturing, San Marcos *Also called Action Electronic Assembly Inc* ***(P-17804)***
Prowest Technologies Inc .....E.....760 510-9003
2872 S Santa Fe Ave San Marcos (92069) ***(P-8674)***
Proxim Wireless Corporation (PA) .....D.....408 383-7600
2114 Ringwood Ave San Jose (95131) ***(P-17754)***
Proximex Corporation .....F.....408 215-9000
300 Santana Row Ste 200 San Jose (95128) ***(P-24320)***
Prozyme Inc .....E.....510 638-6900
3832 Bay Center Pl Hayward (94545) ***(P-8248)***
Prp Seats, Temecula *Also called Kamm Industries Inc* ***(P-19698)***
Prpco .....E.....805 543-6844
2226 Beebee St San Luis Obispo (93401) ***(P-6816)***
Prs Industries, Ontario *Also called Inland Powder Coating Corp* ***(P-13192)***
Prudential Lighting Corp (PA) .....C.....213 477-1694
1774 E 21st St Los Angeles (90058) ***(P-17066)***
Pryor Products .....E.....760 724-8244
1819 Peacock Blvd Oceanside (92056) ***(P-21867)***
Prysm Inc (PA) .....D.....408 586-1100
180 Baytech Dr Ste 200 San Jose (95134) ***(P-23454)***
PS Intl Inc .....F.....626 333-8168
655 Vineland Ave City of Industry (91746) ***(P-13429)***
PS Print, LLC, Oakland *Also called TYT LLC* ***(P-6905)***
PS Support Inc .....F.....301 351-9366
800 W El Camin Real Mountain View (94040) ***(P-24321)***
PSC, Visalia *Also called Pacific Southwest Cont LLC* ***(P-5251)***
PSC Circuits Inc .....E.....626 373-1728
5160 Rivergrade Rd Baldwin Park (91706) ***(P-19054)***
PSC Industrial Outsourcing LP .....F.....661 833-9991
200 Old Yard Dr Bakersfield (93307) ***(P-252)***
Pscmb Repairs Inc .....E.....626 448-7778
12145 Slauson Ave Santa Fe Springs (90670) ***(P-12601)***
Psemi Corporation (HQ) .....D.....858 731-9400
9369 Carroll Park Dr San Diego (92121) ***(P-18485)***
Psg, San Diego *Also called Pacific Steel Group* ***(P-12598)***
PSI, San Jose *Also called Proto Services Inc* ***(P-17753)***
PSI, Irvine *Also called Performance Sealing Inc* ***(P-9247)***
PSI, El Cajon *Also called Derosa Enterprises Inc* ***(P-12182)***
PSI, Campbell *Also called Process Solutions Inc* ***(P-20921)***
PSI, Plumas Lake *Also called Packaging Specialists Inc* ***(P-4386)***
Psiber Data Systems Inc .....F.....619 287-9970
7075 Mission Gorge Rd K San Diego (92120) ***(P-18486)***
Psitech Inc .....F.....714 964-7818
18368 Bandilier Cir Fountain Valley (92708) ***(P-14965)***
PSM Industries Inc (PA) .....D.....888 663-8256
14000 Avalon Blvd Los Angeles (90061) ***(P-13540)***
Pssc Labs .....F.....949 380-7288
20432 N Sea Cir Lake Forest (92630) ***(P-15076)***
PSW Inc .....F.....951 371-7100
149 Via Trevizio Corona (92879) ***(P-2591)***
Pt Welding Inc .....F.....530 406-0267
1960 E Main St Woodland (95776) ***(P-24658)***
Ptb Sales Inc (PA) .....E.....626 334-0500
1361 Mountain View Cir Azusa (91702) ***(P-14639)***
Ptec Solutions Inc .....D.....510 358-3578
48633 Warm Springs Blvd Fremont (94539) ***(P-16319)***
Pti Technologies Inc (HQ) .....C.....805 604-3700
501 Del Norte Blvd Oxnard (93030) ***(P-20206)***
Ptm & W Industries Inc .....E.....562 946-4511
10640 Painter Ave Santa Fe Springs (90670) ***(P-9452)***
Ptm Images, West Hollywood *Also called Pro Tour Memorabilia LLC* ***(P-4522)***
Ptr Manufacturing Inc .....E.....510 477-9654
33390 Transit Ave Union City (94587) ***(P-16320)***
Ptr Sheet Metal & Fabrication, Union City *Also called Ptr Manufacturing Inc* ***(P-16320)***
Pts Security, Van Nuys *Also called Priority Tech Systems Inc* ***(P-19382)***
Pubinno Inc .....F.....669 251-6538
1040 Mariposa St San Francisco (94107) ***(P-24322)***
Public Utilites Emts, San Diego *Also called City of San Diego* ***(P-21205)***
Public Works, Dept of, La Puente *Also called County of Los Angeles* ***(P-13723)***
Public Works, Dept of, Malibu *Also called County of Los Angeles* ***(P-13724)***
Publishers Development Corp .....E.....858 605-0200
13741 Danielson St Ste A Poway (92064) ***(P-6008)***
Puente Ready Mix Inc (PA) .....E.....626 968-0711
209 N California Ave City of Industry (91744) ***(P-10815)***
Pulitzer Community Newspapers, Hanford *Also called Hanford Sentinel Inc* ***(P-5651)***
Pull-N-Pac, Huntington Park *Also called Crown Poly Inc* ***(P-5393)***
Pulltarps Manufacturing, El Cajon *Also called Transportation Equipment Inc* ***(P-3711)***
Pulmuone Wildwood Inc .....F.....714 361-0806
5755 Rossi Ln Gilroy (95020) ***(P-2592)***
Pulp Story, Orange *Also called Quality Produced LLC* ***(P-926)***
Pulsar Vascular Inc .....F.....408 246-4300
130 Knowles Dr Ste E Los Gatos (95032) ***(P-21868)***
Pulse Electronics Inc (HQ) .....B.....858 674-8100
15255 Innovation Dr # 100 San Diego (92128) ***(P-16571)***
Pulse Electronics Corporation (HQ) .....D.....858 674-8100
15255 Innovation Dr # 100 San Diego (92128) ***(P-19055)***

Pulse Instruments.....E.....310 515-5330
1234 Francisco St Torrance (90502) *(P-21105)*
Pulse Metric Inc.....F.....760 842-8224
2100 Hawley Dr Vista (92084) *(P-21869)*
Pulse Systems LLC.....E.....925 798-4080
4090 Nelson Ave Concord (94520) *(P-22074)*
Pulver Laboratories Inc.....F.....408 399-7000
320 N Santa Cruz Ave Los Gatos (95030) *(P-16740)*
Puma Biotechnology Inc (PA).....D.....424 248-6500
10880 Wilshire Blvd # 2150 Los Angeles (90024) *(P-8090)*
Pump-A-Head, San Diego *Also called Keco Inc (P-15630)*
Pumptop TV, Garden Grove *Also called Adtek Media Inc (P-23043)*
Punch Press Products Inc.....D.....323 581-7151
2035 E 51st St Vernon (90058) *(P-14099)*
Punchh Inc.....F.....415 623-4466
1875 S Grant St Ste 810 San Mateo (94402) *(P-24323)*
Punkpost Inc.....E.....415 818-7677
41 Federal St Unit 4 San Francisco (94107) *(P-7297)*
Pur-Clean Pressure Car Wash, North Highlands *Also called New Wave Industries Ltd (P-15549)*
Pura Naturals Inc (HQ).....F.....949 273-8100
23101 Lake Center Dr # 100 Lake Forest (92630) *(P-8570)*
Pura Naturals Inc.....E.....949 273-8100
3401 Etiwanda Ave Jurupa Valley (91752) *(P-4738)*
Puratos Corporation.....E.....310 632-1361
18831 S Laurel Park Rd Compton (90220) *(P-14394)*
Puratos West Coast, Compton *Also called Puratos Corporation (P-14394)*
Pure Allure Accessories, Oceanside *Also called Pure Allure Inc (P-3393)*
Pure Allure Inc.....D.....760 966-3650
4005 Avenida De La Plata Oceanside (92056) *(P-3393)*
Pure Bioscience Inc (PA).....F.....619 596-8600
1725 Gillespie Way El Cajon (92020) *(P-8409)*
Pure Cotton Incorporated.....D.....213 507-3270
2221 S Main St Fl 2 Los Angeles (90007) *(P-3049)*
Pure Flo Water, Santee *Also called Pure-Flo Water Co (P-2129)*
Pure Forge.....F.....760 201-0951
13011 Kirkham Way Poway (92064) *(P-19746)*
Pure Nature Foods LLC.....E.....530 723-5269
700 Santa Anita Dr Woodland (95776) *(P-2340)*
Pure One Business Svc Group, Santa Ana *Also called Pure One Environmental Inc (P-8768)*
Pure One Environmental Inc.....F.....714 641-1430
3400 W Warner Ave Ste A Santa Ana (92704) *(P-8768)*
Pure Storage Inc (PA).....B.....800 379-7873
650 Castro St Ste 400 Mountain View (94041) *(P-15077)*
Pure Water Centers Inc.....F.....818 316-1250
8860 Corbin Ave Ste 382 Northridge (91324) *(P-15563)*
Pure-Flo Water Co (PA).....D.....619 596-4130
7737 Mission Gorge Rd Santee (92071) *(P-2129)*
Puredepth Inc (PA).....F.....408 394-9146
303 Twin Dolphin Dr Fl 6 Redwood City (94065) *(P-15314)*
Pureformance Cables, Torrance *Also called Lynn Products Inc (P-15279)*
Purelife Dental.....F.....310 587-0783
201 Santa Monica Blvd # 400 Santa Monica (90401) *(P-22183)*
Pureline Oralcare Inc.....F.....831 662-9500
804 Estates Dr Ste 104 Aptos (95003) *(P-22184)*
Puretek Corporation.....C.....818 361-3949
7900 Nelson Rd Unit A Panorama City (91402) *(P-8091)*
Puretek Corporation (PA).....E.....818 361-3316
1145 Arroyo St Ste D San Fernando (91340) *(P-8092)*
Purewave Networks Inc.....E.....650 528-5200
3951 Burton Dr Santa Clara (95054) *(P-17630)*
Purfect Packaging.....F.....909 460-7363
5420 Brooks St Montclair (91763) *(P-5413)*
Puri Tech Inc.....E.....951 360-8380
3167 Progress Cir Mira Loma (91752) *(P-15564)*
Puricle Inc.....E.....909 466-7125
11799 Jersey Blvd Rancho Cucamonga (91730) *(P-8410)*
Purina Animal Nutrition LLC.....E.....209 634-9101
1125 Paulson Rd Turlock (95380) *(P-1119)*
Puritan Bakery Inc.....C.....310 830-5451
1624 E Carson St Carson (90745) *(P-1265)*
Purity Organic LLC.....E.....415 440-7777
405 14th St Ste 1000 Oakland (94612) *(P-925)*
Purity Organics Inc.....E.....559 842-5600
14900 W Belmont Ave Kerman (93630) *(P-818)*
Puroflux Corporation.....F.....805 579-0216
2121 Union Pl Simi Valley (93065) *(P-18735)*
Purolator Advanced Filtration.....E.....916 689-2328
8314 Tiogawoods Dr Sacramento (95828) *(P-14853)*
Purolator Pdts A Filtration Co.....F.....510 785-4800
20671 Corsair Blvd Hayward (94545) *(P-14674)*
Puronics Incorporated (PA).....E.....925 456-7000
5775 Las Positas Rd Livermore (94551) *(P-15565)*
Purosil LLC.....F.....951 271-3900
1660 Leeson Ln Corona (92879) *(P-8769)*
Purosil LLC (HQ).....D.....951 271-3900
708 S Temescal St Ste 102 Corona (92879) *(P-8770)*
Purotecs Inc.....F.....925 215-0380
6678 Owens Dr Ste 104 Pleasanton (94588) *(P-14522)*
Purple Porcupine, Irvine *Also called Oddbox Holdings Inc (P-7151)*
Purple Wine Company LLC.....E.....707 829-6100
9119 Graton Rd Graton (95444) *(P-1873)*
Purus International Inc.....F.....760 775-4500
82860 Avenue 45 Indio (92201) *(P-13082)*
Purveyors Kitchen.....E.....530 823-8527
2043 Airpark Ct Ste 30 Auburn (95602) *(P-819)*
Pushtotest Inc.....F.....408 436-8203
1735 Tech Dr Ste 820 San Jose (95110) *(P-24324)*
Putnam Accessory Group Inc.....E.....323 306-1330
4455 Fruitland Ave Vernon (90058) *(P-3394)*
Puyallup Herald, Sacramento *Also called Olympic Cascade Publishing (P-5788)*
Pv Labels Inc (PA).....F.....760 241-8900
1100 S Linwood Ave Ste B Santa Ana (92705) *(P-23180)*
PVA Tepla America Inc (HQ).....E.....951 371-2500
251 Corporate Terrace St Corona (92879) *(P-16321)*
Pvc Pipe Fttngs Irrgation Pdts, Galt *Also called Galt Pipe Company (P-13355)*
Pvd Coatings II LLC.....F.....714 899-4892
5271 Argosy Ave Huntington Beach (92649) *(P-13232)*
Pvh Neckwear Inc (HQ).....A.....213 688-7970
1735 S Santa Fe Ave Los Angeles (90021) *(P-3001)*
Pvp Advanced Eo Systems Inc.....E.....714 508-2740
14312 Franklin Ave # 100 Tustin (92780) *(P-21400)*
Pw Eagle Inc.....B.....800 621-4404
5200 W Century Blvd Fl 10 Los Angeles (90045) *(P-9474)*
Pw Eagle Inc.....B.....951 657-7400
23711 Rider St Perris (92570) *(P-9475)*
Pw Eagle Inc.....D.....530 677-2286
3500 Robin Ln Shingle Springs (95682) *(P-9476)*
PW Gillibrand Co Inc (PA).....D.....805 526-2195
4537 Ish Dr Simi Valley (93063) *(P-375)*
Pw Wiring Systems, Pico Rivera *Also called P W Wiring Systems LLC (P-18784)*
Pwp Manufacturing LLC.....E.....408 748-0120
1325 Norman Ave Santa Clara (95054) *(P-12344)*
Pyr Preservation Services.....E.....619 338-8395
2393 Newton Ave Ste B San Diego (92113) *(P-20302)*
Pyramid Granite & Metals Inc.....E.....760 745-6309
660 Superior St Escondido (92029) *(P-10924)*
Pyramid Graphics.....F.....650 871-0290
325 Harbor Way South San Francisco (94080) *(P-6817)*
Pyramid Mold & Tool.....E.....909 476-2555
10155 Sharon Cir Rancho Cucamonga (91730) *(P-14100)*
Pyramid Powder Coating Inc.....E.....818 768-5898
12251 Montague St Pacoima (91331) *(P-13233)*
Pyramid Precision Machine Inc.....D.....858 642-0713
6721 Cobra Way San Diego (92121) *(P-16322)*
Pyramid Printing and Graphics, South San Francisco *Also called Pyramid Graphics (P-6817)*
Pyramid Semiconductor Corp.....F.....408 542-9430
1249 Reamwood Ave Sunnyvale (94089) *(P-18487)*
Pyramid Systems Inc.....E.....559 582-9345
10105 8 3/4 Ave Hanford (93230) *(P-4933)*
Pyramids Winery Inc.....E.....707 765-2768
5875 Lakeville Hwy Petaluma (94954) *(P-1874)*
Pyrenees French Bakery Inc.....E.....661 322-7159
717 E 21st St Bakersfield (93305) *(P-1266)*
Pyron Solar III LLC.....F.....760 599-5100
1216 Liberty Way Ste A Vista (92081) *(P-11706)*
Q & B Foods Inc (HQ).....D.....626 334-8090
15547 1st St Irwindale (91706) *(P-896)*
Q C A, San Jose *Also called Quality Circuit Assembly Inc (P-17968)*
Q C M Inc.....E.....714 414-1173
285 Gemini Ave Brea (92821) *(P-16795)*
Q C Poultry, Commerce *Also called Ingenue Inc (P-519)*
Q Corporation.....E.....805 383-8998
4880 Adohr Ln Camarillo (93012) *(P-21279)*
Q I S Inc.....F.....951 244-0500
28005 Oregon Pl Quail Valley (92587) *(P-17755)*
Q M C, Fountain Valley *Also called Quik Mfg Co (P-13742)*
Q Microwave Inc.....D.....619 258-7322
1591 Pioneer Way El Cajon (92020) *(P-19056)*
Q Perfumes, Commerce *Also called Milestones Products Inc (P-8539)*
Q Team.....F.....714 228-4465
6400 Dale St Buena Park (90621) *(P-6818)*
Q Tech Corporation.....C.....310 836-7900
10150 Jefferson Blvd Culver City (90232) *(P-19057)*
Q Technology Inc.....E.....925 373-3456
336 Lindbergh Ave Livermore (94551) *(P-17157)*
Q&A Clothing, Los Angeles *Also called Q&A7 LLC (P-3395)*
Q&A7 LLC.....F.....323 364-4250
2155 E 7th St Ste 150 Los Angeles (90023) *(P-3395)*
Q-Flex Inc.....E.....714 664-0101
1301 E Hunter Ave Santa Ana (92705) *(P-19058)*
Q-Lite Usa LLC.....C.....310 736-2977
3691 Lenawee Ave Los Angeles (90016) *(P-16922)*
Q-Mark Manufacturing Inc.....F.....949 457-1913
30051 Comercio Rcho STA Marg (92688) *(P-20923)*
Q-See, Anaheim *Also called Digital Periph Solutions Inc (P-17218)*
Q1 Test Inc.....E.....909 390-9718
1100 S Grove Ave Ste B2 Ontario (91761) *(P-20207)*
Q3-Cnc Inc.....F.....858 790-0002
9091 Kenamar Dr San Diego (92121) *(P-16323)*
Qad Inc (PA).....C.....805 566-6000
100 Innovation Pl Santa Barbara (93108) *(P-24325)*
Qad Inc.....F.....805 684-6614
6450 Via Real Carpinteria (93013) *(P-24326)*
Qantel Technologies Inc.....E.....510 731-2080
3506 Breakwater Ct Hayward (94545) *(P-14966)*
Qc Manufacturing Inc.....D.....951 325-6340
26040 Ynez Rd Temecula (92591) *(P-14675)*
QED Inc.....E.....714 546-6010
2920 Halladay St Santa Ana (92705) *(P-20924)*
QED Software LLC.....E.....310 214-3118
304 Tejon Pl Palos Verdes Estates (90274) *(P-24327)*
QED Systems Inc.....E.....619 802-0020
1330 30th St Ste C San Diego (92154) *(P-19386)*
Qep, Ontario *Also called QEP Co Inc (P-3982)*

Employee Codes: A=Over 500 employees, B=251-500
C=101-250, D=51-100, E=20-50, F=10-19
2020 California
Manfacturers Register
© Mergent Inc. 1-800-342-5647
1213

QEP Co Inc.....F.....909 622-3537
4200 Santa Ana St Ontario (91761) *(P-3982)*
Qf Liquidation Inc.....E.....949 399-4500
25242 Arctic Ocean Dr Lake Forest (92630) *(P-19747)*
Qf Liquidation Inc (PA).....C.....949 930-3400
25242 Arctic Ocean Dr Lake Forest (92630) *(P-19748)*
Qfi Prv Aerospace, Torrance *Also called Quality Forming LLC (P-20208)*
Qg LLC.....A.....209 384-0444
2201 Cooper Ave Merced (95348) *(P-6819)*
Qg Printing Corp.....C.....951 571-2500
6688 Box Springs Blvd Riverside (92507) *(P-6009)*
Qg Printing II Corp.....A.....951 571-2500
6688 Box Springs Blvd Riverside (92507) *(P-6820)*
Qingmu International Inc.....E.....626 965-7277
1055 Park View Dr Ste 119 Covina (91724) *(P-7188)*
Qjm Corp.....F.....213 622-0264
606 S Olive St Ste 2170 Los Angeles (90014) *(P-22559)*
Qlc Manufacturing LLC.....F.....408 221-8550
462 Vista Way Milpitas (95035) *(P-11267)*
Qlogic LLC (HQ).....C.....949 389-6000
15485 Sand Canyon Ave Irvine (92618) *(P-18488)*
Qmat Inc.....E.....498 228-5858
2424 Walsh Ave Santa Clara (95051) *(P-18489)*
Qmp Inc.....E.....661 294-6860
25070 Avenue Tibbitts Valencia (91355) *(P-15566)*
Qontrol Devices Inc.....F.....626 968-4268
167 Mason Way Ste A7 City of Industry (91746) *(P-14523)*
Qor LLC.....F.....707 658-2539
775 Baywood Dr Ste 312 Petaluma (94954) *(P-3113)*
Qortstone Inc.....F.....877 899-7678
7733 Lemona Ave Van Nuys (91405) *(P-10925)*
Qorvo California Inc.....E.....805 480-5050
950 Lawrence Dr Newbury Park (91320) *(P-19059)*
Qorvo US, Newbury Park *Also called Qorvo California Inc (P-19059)*
Qorvo Us Inc.....E.....805 480-5099
950 Lawrence Dr Newbury Park (91320) *(P-19060)*
Qorvo Us Inc.....E.....408 493-4304
3099 Orchard Dr San Jose (95134) *(P-18490)*
Qostronics Inc.....E.....408 719-1286
2044 Corporate Ct San Jose (95131) *(P-17964)*
Qpc Fiber Optic LLC.....E.....949 361-8855
27612 El Lazo Laguna Niguel (92677) *(P-11316)*
Qpc Laser, Sylmar *Also called Laser Operations LLC (P-18343)*
Qpc Lasers Inc.....F.....818 986-0000
15632 Roxford St Sylmar (91342) *(P-18491)*
Qpe Inc.....F.....949 263-0381
1372 Mcgaw Ave Irvine (92614) *(P-6962)*
Qre Operating LLC.....C.....213 225-5900
707 Wilshire Blvd # 4600 Los Angeles (90017) *(P-134)*
Qrtstone, Van Nuys *Also called Qortstone Inc (P-10925)*
Qsc LLC (PA).....B.....714 754-6175
1675 Macarthur Blvd Costa Mesa (92626) *(P-17275)*
Qsi 2011 Inc (PA).....F.....949 855-6885
2302 Martin Ste 475 Irvine (92612) *(P-24328)*
Qspac Industries Inc (PA).....D.....562 407-3868
15020 Marquardt Ave Santa Fe Springs (90670) *(P-8889)*
Qst Ingredients and Packg Inc.....F.....909 989-4343
9734-40 6th St Rch Rancho Cucamonga (91730) *(P-2593)*
Quad Graphics, Riverside *Also called Qg Printing II Corp (P-6820)*
Quad R Tech, Harbor City *Also called Onyx Industries Inc (P-12643)*
Quad R Tech.....C.....310 851-6161
521 W Rosecrans Ave Gardena (90248) *(P-22560)*
Quad/Graphics Inc.....F.....310 751-3900
17871 Park Plaza Dr # 150 Cerritos (90703) *(P-6821)*
Quad/Graphics Inc.....C.....951 689-1122
7190 Jurupa Ave Riverside (92504) *(P-6822)*
Quad/Graphics Inc.....A.....415 267-3700
350 Rhode Island St # 110 San Francisco (94103) *(P-6823)*
Quad/Graphics Inc.....B.....209 384-0444
2201 Cooper Ave Merced (95348) *(P-6824)*
Quadbase Systems Inc.....F.....408 982-0835
990 Linden Dr Ste 230 Santa Clara (95050) *(P-24329)*
Quadco Printing Inc.....F.....530 894-4061
2535 Zanella Way Chico (95928) *(P-6825)*
Quadrant Solutions Inc.....F.....408 463-9451
561 Monterey Rd Morgan Hill (95037) *(P-13541)*
Quadrant Technology, Morgan Hill *Also called Quadrant Solutions Inc (P-13541)*
Quadriga Americas LLC.....E.....424 634-4900
17800 S Main St Ste 113 Gardena (90248) *(P-6322)*
Quadriga USA Enterprises Inc.....F.....888 669-9994
28410 Witherspoon Pkwy Valencia (91355) *(P-5525)*
Quadrtech Corporation.....C.....310 523-1697
521 W Rosecrans Ave Gardena (90248) *(P-11542)*
Quady LLC (PA).....E.....559 673-8068
13181 Road 24 Madera (93637) *(P-1875)*
Quady Winery Inc.....F.....559 673-8068
13181 Road 24 Madera (93637) *(P-1876)*
Quake Global Inc (PA).....D.....858 277-7290
4711 Vewridge Ave Ste 150 San Diego (92123) *(P-17404)*
Quaker, Whittier *Also called AC Products Inc (P-8851)*
Quaker City Plating.....C.....562 945-3721
11729 Washington Blvd Whittier (90606) *(P-13083)*
Quaker City Plating & Silvrsm, Whittier *Also called Quaker City Plating (P-13083)*
Quaker Oats Company.....C.....510 261-5800
5625 International Blvd Oakland (94621) *(P-2226)*
Qual-Pro Corporation (HQ).....C.....310 329-7535
18510 S Figueroa St Gardena (90248) *(P-17965)*
Qualcomm Atheros Inc (HQ).....A.....408 773-5200
1700 Technology Dr San Jose (95110) *(P-18492)*
Qualcomm Datacenter Tech Inc (HQ).....F.....858 567-1121
5775 Morehouse Dr San Diego (92121) *(P-18493)*
Qualcomm Incorporated.....B.....858 651-8481
2016 Palomar Airport Rd # 100 Carlsbad (92011) *(P-18494)*
Qualcomm Incorporated.....B.....408 216-6797
3135 Kifer Rd Santa Clara (95051) *(P-18495)*
Qualcomm Incorporated (PA).....B.....858 587-1121
5775 Morehouse Dr San Diego (92121) *(P-17631)*
Qualcomm Incorporated.....F.....858 587-1121
3165 Kifer Rd Santa Clara (95051) *(P-17632)*
Qualcomm Incorporated.....B.....858 909-0316
5751 Pacific Center Blvd San Diego (92121) *(P-18496)*
Qualcomm Incorporated.....B.....858 587-1121
9393 Waples St Ste 150 San Diego (92121) *(P-18497)*
Qualcomm Incorporated.....D.....858 587-1121
5525 Morehouse Dr San Diego (92121) *(P-17633)*
Qualcomm Incorporated.....B.....858 587-1121
10160 Pacific Mesa Blvd # 100 San Diego (92121) *(P-18498)*
Qualcomm Innovation Center Inc (HQ).....E.....858 587-1121
4365 Executive Dr # 1100 San Diego (92121) *(P-24330)*
Qualcomm Limited Partner Inc.....E.....858 587-1121
5775 Morehouse Dr San Diego (92121) *(P-18499)*
Qualcomm Mems Technologies Inc.....E.....858 587-1121
5775 Morehouse Dr San Diego (92121) *(P-17756)*
Qualcomm Technologies Inc (HQ).....C.....858 587-1121
5775 Morehouse Dr San Diego (92121) *(P-18500)*
Qualectron Systems Corporation.....F.....408 986-1686
321 E Brokaw Rd San Jose (95112) *(P-21106)*
Quali-Tech Manufacturing, Calexico *Also called Lakim Industries Incorporated (P-23029)*
Quali-Tech Mold.....F.....909 464-8124
5939 Sycamore Ct Chino (91710) *(P-10002)*
Qualigen Inc (PA).....E.....760 918-9165
2042 Corte Del Nogal A Carlsbad (92011) *(P-20772)*
Qualitask Incorporated.....F.....714 237-0900
2840 E Gretta Ln Anaheim (92806) *(P-16324)*
Qualitau Incorporated (PA).....D.....650 282-6226
830 Maude Ave Mountain View (94043) *(P-21107)*
Qualitek Inc (HQ).....D.....408 734-8686
1116 Elko Dr Sunnyvale (94089) *(P-17966)*
Qualitek Inc.....D.....408 752-8422
1272 Forgewood Ave Sunnyvale (94089) *(P-17967)*
Quality Aerostructures Company.....F.....909 987-4888
10291 Trademark St Ste A Rancho Cucamonga (91730) *(P-19976)*
Quality Aluminum Forge LLC (HQ).....D.....714 639-8191
793 N Cypress St Orange (92867) *(P-12735)*
Quality Cabinet and Fixture Co (HQ).....E.....619 266-1011
7955 Saint Andrews Ave San Diego (92154) *(P-4233)*
Quality Car Care Products Inc.....E.....626 359-9174
2734 Huntington Dr Duarte (91010) *(P-7520)*
Quality Circle Institute Inc.....F.....530 893-4095
555 East Ave Chico (95926) *(P-6010)*
Quality Circuit Assembly Inc.....D.....408 441-1001
1709 Junction Ct Ste 380 San Jose (95112) *(P-17968)*
Quality Coating, North Hollywood *Also called Quality Powder Coating LLC (P-13235)*
Quality Components Co, Rcho STA Marg *Also called Q-Mark Manufacturing Inc (P-20923)*
Quality Container Corp.....F.....909 482-1850
866 Towne Center Dr Pomona (91767) *(P-5339)*
Quality Control Plating Inc.....E.....909 605-0206
4425 E Airport Dr Ste 113 Ontario (91761) *(P-13084)*
Quality Control Solutions Inc.....E.....951 676-1616
43339 Bus Pk Dr Ste 101 Temecula (92590) *(P-21524)*
Quality Controlled Mfg Inc.....D.....619 443-3997
9429 Abraham Way Santee (92071) *(P-16325)*
Quality Countertops Inc.....F.....909 597-6888
17853 Santiago Blvd # 107 Villa Park (92861) *(P-4934)*
Quality Craft Cabinets Inc.....F.....626 358-2021
504 E Duarte Rd Monrovia (91016) *(P-4234)*
Quality Craft Mold Inc.....F.....530 873-7790
6424 Woodward Dr Magalia (95954) *(P-11062)*
Quality Digest, Chico *Also called Quality Circle Institute Inc (P-6010)*
Quality Door & Trim, Stockton *Also called J & J Quality Door Inc (P-4060)*
Quality Doors & Trim, Lakeport *Also called Young & Family Inc (P-4158)*
Quality Edm Inc.....F.....714 283-9220
8025 E Crystal Dr Anaheim (92807) *(P-16326)*
Quality Fabrication Inc (PA).....D.....818 407-5015
9631 Irondale Ave Chatsworth (91311) *(P-12345)*
Quality First Woodworks Inc.....C.....714 632-0480
1264 N Lakeview Ave Anaheim (92807) *(P-4523)*
QUALITY FOAM PACKAGING, Lake Elsinore *Also called Aerofoam Industries Inc (P-4851)*
Quality Foam Packaging Inc.....E.....951 245-4429
31855 Corydon St Lake Elsinore (92530) *(P-9564)*
Quality Forming LLC.....D.....310 539-2855
22906 Frampton Ave Torrance (90501) *(P-20208)*
Quality Gears Inc.....F.....562 921-9938
12139 Slauson Ave Santa Fe Springs (90670) *(P-14747)*
Quality Grinding Co Inc.....F.....714 228-2100
6800 Caballero Blvd Buena Park (90620) *(P-14189)*
Quality Heat Treating Inc.....E.....818 840-8212
3305 Burton Ave Burbank (91504) *(P-11467)*
Quality Image Inc.....E.....562 259-9872
15130 Illinois Ave Paramount (90723) *(P-7601)*
Quality Industry Repair, Santa Fe Springs *Also called Pscmb Repairs Inc (P-12601)*
Quality Lift and Equipment Inc.....F.....562 903-2131
10845 Norwalk Blvd Santa Fe Springs (90670) *(P-13890)*
Quality Machine Engrg Inc.....E.....707 528-1900
2559 Grosse Ave Santa Rosa (95404) *(P-16327)*
Quality Machine Shop Inc.....F.....805 653-7944
1676 N Ventura Ave Ventura (93001) *(P-16328)*
Quality Machining, Ramona *Also called Blaha Oldrih (P-14140)*

Mergent e-mail: customerrelations@mergent.com
1214
2020 California
Manufacturers Register
(P-0000) Products & Services Section entry number
(PA)=Parent Co (HQ)=Headquarters (DH)=Div Headquarters

Quality Machining & Design Inc......E......408 224-7976
2857 Aiello Dr San Jose (95111) *(P-14524)*
Quality Magnetics Corporation......F......310 632-1941
18025 Adria Maru Ln Carson (90746) *(P-13542)*
Quality Marble & Granite, Ontario *Also called Regards Enterprises Inc (P-4486)*
Quality Marble & Granite Inc......F......510 635-0228
25 Hegenberger Pl Oakland (94621) *(P-10926)*
Quality Metal Fabrication LLC......E......530 887-7388
2350 Wilbur Way Auburn (95602) *(P-12346)*
Quality Metal Spinning and......E......650 858-2491
4047 Transport St Palo Alto (94303) *(P-12865)*
Quality Packaging and Engrg, Irvine *Also called Qpe Inc (P-6962)*
Quality Painting Co......E......626 964-2529
19136 San Jose Ave Rowland Heights (91748) *(P-13234)*
Quality Plating, San Jose *Also called Sal Rodriguez (P-13093)*
Quality Powder Coating LLC......F......818 982-8322
7373 Atoll Ave Ste B North Hollywood (91605) *(P-13235)*
Quality Produced LLC......F......310 592-8834
987 N Enterprise St Orange (92867) *(P-926)*
Quality Quartz Engineering Inc (PA)......E......510 791-1013
8484 Central Ave Newark (94560) *(P-19061)*
Quality Resources Dist LLC......E......510 378-6861
16254 Beaver Rd Adelanto (92301) *(P-23455)*
Quality Service Pac Industry, Santa Fe Springs *Also called Qspac Industries Inc (P-8889)*
Quality Sheds Inc......F......951 672-6750
33210 Bailey Park Blvd Menifee (92584) *(P-4603)*
Quality Steel Fabricators Inc......E......858 748-8400
13275 Gregg St Poway (92064) *(P-12602)*
Quality Systems Intgrated Corp......B......858 587-9797
6740 Top Gun St San Diego (92121) *(P-17969)*
Quality Tech Machining, Santa Clara *Also called Hung Tung (P-16037)*
Quality Tech Mfg Inc......E......909 465-9565
170 W Mindanao St Bloomington (92316) *(P-19925)*
Quality Transformer & Elec......E......408 935-0231
963 Ames Ave Milpitas (95035) *(P-16572)*
Quality Transformer & Elec Co, Milpitas *Also called Quality Transformer & Elec (P-16572)*
Quality Vessel Engineering Inc......F......562 696-2100
8515 Chetle Ave Santa Fe Springs (90670) *(P-12044)*
Quality Woodworks Inc......E......760 744-4748
261a Redel Rd San Marcos (92078) *(P-4235)*
Quallion LLC......C......818 833-2000
12744 San Fernando Rd # 100 Sylmar (91342) *(P-19181)*
Qualontime Corporation......F......714 523-4751
19 Senisa Irvine (92612) *(P-16329)*
Qualstar Corporation (PA)......E......805 583-7744
1267 Flynn Rd Camarillo (93012) *(P-15078)*
Qualtech Circuits Inc......F......408 727-4125
1101 Comstock St Santa Clara (95054) *(P-17970)*
Quandx Inc......F......650 262-4140
2176 Ringwood Ave San Jose (95131) *(P-8249)*
Quaneco, Woodland Hills *Also called Quantum Energy LLC (P-135)*
Quanergy Systems Inc (PA)......D......408 245-9500
482 Mercury Dr Sunnyvale (94085) *(P-20677)*
Quantal International Inc......E......415 644-0754
455 Market St Ste 1200 San Francisco (94105) *(P-24331)*
Quantam Signs & Graphics, Lake Forest *Also called To Industries Inc (P-23229)*
Quantech Machining Inc......E......661 775-3990
25647 Rye Canyon Rd Valencia (91355) *(P-16330)*
Quanticel Pharmaceuticals Inc......E......858 956-3747
9393 Towne Centre Dr # 110 San Diego (92121) *(P-8093)*
Quantimetrix Corporation......D......310 536-0006
2005 Manhattan Beach Blvd Redondo Beach (90278) *(P-8250)*
Quantum 3d Headquarters......F......408 361-9999
6330 San Ignacio Ave San Jose (95119) *(P-18501)*
Quantum Chromodynamics Inc......F......310 329-5000
3703 W 190th St Torrance (90504) *(P-7189)*
Quantum Clean, San Jose *Also called Quantum Global Tech LLC (P-8411)*
Quantum Concept Inc......F......323 888-8601
5701 S Eastrn Ave Ste 220 Commerce (90040) *(P-3114)*
Quantum Corporation, Irvine *Also called Certance LLC (P-15014)*
Quantum Corporation (PA)......B......408 944-4000
224 Airport Pkwy Ste 550 San Jose (95110) *(P-15079)*
Quantum Corporation......C......213 248-2481
1441 Melanie Ln Arcadia (91007) *(P-15080)*
Quantum Corporation......D......949 856-7800
141 Innovation Dr Irvine (92617) *(P-15081)*
Quantum Design Inc (PA)......C......858 481-4400
10307 Pacific Center Ct San Diego (92121) *(P-21280)*
Quantum Design International, San Diego *Also called Quantum Design Inc (P-21280)*
Quantum Digital Technology Inc......F......310 325-4949
1525 W Alton Ave Santa Ana (92704) *(P-19062)*
Quantum Dynasty......F......347 469-1047
5934 Rancho Mission Rd # 118 San Diego (92108) *(P-15082)*
Quantum Energy LLC......E......800 950-3519
22801 Ventura Blvd # 200 Woodland Hills (91364) *(P-135)*
Quantum Focus Instruments Corp......F......760 599-1122
2385 La Mirada Dr Vista (92081) *(P-21108)*
Quantum Global Tech LLC......E......408 487-1770
1710 Ringwood Ave San Jose (95131) *(P-8411)*
Quantum Global Tech LLC......E......510 687-8000
44010 Fremont Blvd Fremont (94538) *(P-8412)*
Quantum Group Inc......D......858 566-9959
6827 Nancy Ridge Dr San Diego (92121) *(P-21525)*
Quantum Performance Developmen......F......510 870-6381
32537 Jean Dr Union City (94587) *(P-15083)*
Quantum Solar Inc......F......415 924-8140
6 Endeavor Dr Corte Madera (94925) *(P-18502)*
Quantum Technologies, Lake Forest *Also called Qf Liquidation Inc (P-19748)*
Quantum Technologies Inc......C......949 399-4500
25242 Arctic Ocean Dr Lake Forest (92630) *(P-63)*
Quantum-Dynamics Co Inc......F......818 719-0142
6414 Independence Ave Woodland Hills (91367) *(P-20925)*
Quantum3d Inc (PA)......F......408 600-2500
1759 Mccarthy Blvd Milpitas (95035) *(P-20678)*
Quantumclean, Fremont *Also called Quantum Global Tech LLC (P-8412)*
Quantumscape Corporation......C......408 452-2000
1730 Technology Dr San Jose (95110) *(P-18503)*
Quark Pharmaceuticals Inc (HQ)......E......510 402-4020
7999 Gateway Blvd Ste 310 Newark (94560) *(P-8094)*
Quartet Mechanics Inc......F......510 490-1886
4055 Clipper Ct Fremont (94538) *(P-14279)*
Quartic West Technologies......F......909 202-7038
425 W 235th St Carson (90745) *(P-19230)*
Quarton Usa Inc......F......888 532-2221
3230 Fallow Field Dr Diamond Bar (91765) *(P-19387)*
Quashnick Tool Corporation......E......209 334-5283
225 N Guild Ave Lodi (95240) *(P-10003)*
Quatro Composites LLC......E......712 707-9200
13250 Gregg St Ste A1 Poway (92064) *(P-16689)*
Queen Beach Printers Inc......E......562 436-8201
937 Pine Ave Long Beach (90813) *(P-6826)*
Queen Bees, Vernon *Also called Two Guys and One LLC (P-10214)*
Queenship Publishing Company......F......805 692-0043
5951 Encina Rd Ste 100 Goleta (93117) *(P-6140)*
Quellan Inc......E......408 546-3487
1001 Murphy Ranch Rd Milpitas (95035) *(P-18504)*
Quemetco West LLC (HQ)......F......626 330-2294
720 S 7th Ave City of Industry (91746) *(P-11208)*
Quenta Material, Santa Clara *Also called Qmat Inc (P-18489)*
Quest Diagnostics Nichols Inst (HQ)......A......949 728-4000
33608 Ortega Hwy San Juan Capistrano (92675) *(P-21281)*
Quest Inds - Stockton Plant, Stockton *Also called Quest Industries LLC (P-7190)*
Quest Industries LLC......F......209 234-0202
2518 Boeing Way Stockton (95206) *(P-7190)*
Quest Nutrition LLC......E......562 446-3321
2221 Park Pl El Segundo (90245) *(P-2594)*
Quest Software Inc......D......415 373-2222
118 2nd St Fl 6 San Francisco (94105) *(P-24332)*
Quest Software Inc......F......408 899-3823
5450 Great America Pkwy Santa Clara (95054) *(P-24333)*
Quest Software Inc......D......949 754-8000
4 Polaris Way Aliso Viejo (92656) *(P-24334)*
Questivity Inc......F......408 615-1781
1680 Civic Center Dr # 209 Santa Clara (95050) *(P-24335)*
Questys Solutions, Irvine *Also called Qsi 2011 Inc (P-24328)*
Quick Deck Inc......F......704 888-0327
15390 Byron Hwy Byron (94514) *(P-12572)*
Quick Mount Pv, Walnut Creek *Also called Wencon Development Inc (P-12432)*
Quick Silver Prtg & Graphics, Chatsworth *Also called Paul Silver Enterprises Inc (P-6773)*
Quickie Designs, Fresno *Also called Vcp Mobility Holdings Inc (P-22117)*
Quicklogic Corporation (PA)......D......408 990-4000
2220 Lundy Ave San Jose (95131) *(P-18505)*
Quickrete, Corona *Also called Quikrete California LLC (P-10633)*
Quicksilver Aeronautics LLC......F......951 506-0061
40084 Villa Venecia Temecula (92591) *(P-19926)*
Quidel Corporation (PA)......B......858 552-1100
12544 High Bluff Dr # 200 San Diego (92130) *(P-8251)*
Quiel Bros Elc Sign Svc Co Inc......E......909 885-4476
272 S I St San Bernardino (92410) *(P-23181)*
Quiet Ride Solutions LLC......F......209 942-4777
1122 S Wilson Way Ste 1 Stockton (95205) *(P-10004)*
Quik Mfg Co......E......714 754-0337
18071 Mount Washington St Fountain Valley (92708) *(P-13742)*
Quik-Pak, San Diego *Also called Promex Industries Incorporated (P-18482)*
Quikrete California LLC......C......951 277-3155
3940 Temescal Canyon Rd Corona (92883) *(P-10633)*
Quikrete Companies Inc......F......559 781-1949
14200 Road 284 Porterville (93257) *(P-10634)*
Quikrete Companies LLC......E......510 490-4670
7705 Wilbur Way Sacramento (95828) *(P-10635)*
Quikrete Companies LLC......E......858 549-2371
9265 Camino Santa Fe San Diego (92121) *(P-10636)*
Quikrete Companies LLC......D......510 490-4670
6950 Stevenson Blvd Fremont (94538) *(P-10637)*
Quikrete Companies LLC......D......323 875-1367
11145 Tuxford St Sun Valley (91352) *(P-10638)*
Quikrete Northern California, Porterville *Also called Quikrete Companies Inc (P-10634)*
Quikrete of Atlanta, Fremont *Also called Quikrete Companies LLC (P-10637)*
Quikstor, Van Nuys *Also called Cal Star Systems Group Inc (P-19269)*
Quikturn Prof Scrnprinting Inc......F......800 784-5419
567 S Melrose St Placentia (92870) *(P-7191)*
Quilter Laboratories LLC......F......714 519-6114
1700 Sunflower Ave Costa Mesa (92626) *(P-22632)*
Quilting House......E......949 476-7090
16872 Millikan Ave Irvine (92606) *(P-3637)*
Quinn Development Co......F......408 842-9320
5787 Obata Way Gilroy (95020) *(P-10514)*
Quint Graphics, Walnut Creek *Also called Quint Measuring Systems Inc (P-21526)*
Quint Measuring Systems Inc......F......510 351-9405
2922 Saklan Indian Dr Walnut Creek (94595) *(P-21526)*
Quintel Corporation......E......408 776-5190
685 Jarvis Dr Ste A Morgan Hill (95037) *(P-14339)*
Quintessa Vinyards, NAPA *Also called Huneeus Vintners LLC (P-1757)*
Quintron Systems Inc (PA)......D......805 928-4343
2105 S Blosser Rd Santa Maria (93458) *(P-17405)*
Quivira Vineyards, Healdsburg *Also called Pjk Winery LLC (P-1867)*

ALPHABETIC

Qulsar Inc (PA) ....F....408 715-1098
90 Great Oaks Blvd # 204 San Jose (95119) ***(P-16741)***
Qulsar Usa Inc ....F....408 715-1098
90 Great Oaks Blvd # 204 San Jose (95119) ***(P-17634)***
Qumu Inc (HQ) ....D....650 396-8530
1100 Grundy Ln Ste 110 San Bruno (94066) ***(P-24336)***
Quorex Pharm Inc (PA) ....E....760 602-1910
2232 Rutherford Rd Carlsbad (92008) ***(P-8095)***
Quorum Systems Inc ....F....858 546-0895
5960 Cornerstone Ct W # 200 San Diego (92121) ***(P-18506)***
Qve Inc ....E....626 961-0114
7829 Industry Ave Pico Rivera (90660) ***(P-13319)***
Qwilt Inc (PA) ....E....866 824-8009
275 Shoreline Dr Ste 510 Redwood City (94065) ***(P-24337)***
Qxq Inc ....E....510 252-1522
44113 S Grimmer Blvd Fremont (94538) ***(P-21109)***
Qycell Corporation ....E....909 390-6644
600 Etiwanda Ave Ontario (91761) ***(P-9565)***
Qyk Brands LLC ....E....949 312-7119
9 Macarthur Pl Santa Ana (92707) ***(P-16839)***
Qyksonic, Santa Ana *Also called Qyk Brands LLC* ***(P-16839)***
R & B Logging, Montague *Also called Dave Richardson Trucking* ***(P-3880)***
R & B Plastics Inc ....F....714 229-8419
227 E Meats Ave Orange (92865) ***(P-16331)***
R & B Research & Development, Loomis *Also called Hillerich & Bradsby Co* ***(P-22820)***
R & B Wire Products Inc ....E....714 549-3355
2902 W Garry Ave Santa Ana (92704) ***(P-13430)***
R & D Fasteners, Rancho Cucamonga *Also called Doubleco Incorporated* ***(P-12675)***
R & D Mfg Services, San Jose *Also called R Stephenson & D Cram Mfg Inc* ***(P-16336)***
R & D Nova Inc ....F....951 781-7332
833 Marlborough Ave 200 Riverside (92507) ***(P-22298)***
R & D Racing Products USA Inc ....F....562 906-1190
12983 Los Nietos Rd Santa Fe Springs (90670) ***(P-20356)***
R & D Tech, Milpitas *Also called Hytek R&D Inc* ***(P-17897)***
R & I Industries Inc ....E....909 923-7747
2910 S Archibald Ave A Ontario (91761) ***(P-11869)***
R & J Fabricators Inc ....E....951 817-0300
1121 Railroad St Ste 102 Corona (92882) ***(P-5077)***
R & J Leathercraft ....F....951 688-1685
12155 Magnolia Ave Ste 8d Riverside (92503) ***(P-10251)***
R & J Paper Box, La Habra *Also called R & J Rule & Die Inc* ***(P-5452)***
R & J Rule & Die Inc ....F....562 945-7535
701 Sturbridge Dr La Habra (90631) ***(P-5452)***
R & J Wldg Met Fabrication Inc ....F....909 930-2900
2182 Maple Privado Ontario (91761) ***(P-16609)***
R & K Industrial Products Co ....E....510 234-7212
1945 7th St Richmond (94801) ***(P-13543)***
R & L Enterprises Inc ....E....559 233-1608
1955 S Mary St Fresno (93721) ***(P-16332)***
R & M Coils ....F....951 672-9855
27547 Terrytown Rd Sun City (92586) ***(P-18736)***
R & M Energy System, Shafter *Also called National Oilwell Varco Inc* ***(P-234)***
R & R Ductwork LLC ....F....562 944-9660
12820 Lakeland Rd Santa Fe Springs (90670) ***(P-12347)***
R & R Fabrications Inc ....F....562 693-0500
13438 Lambert Rd Whittier (90605) ***(P-11870)***
R & R Industries, San Clemente *Also called Rosen & Rosen Industries Inc* ***(P-22876)***
R & R Industries Inc ....E....323 581-6000
1923 S Santa Fe Ave Los Angeles (90021) ***(P-3753)***
R & R Industries Inc ....E....949 361-9238
204 Avenida Fabricante San Clemente (92672) ***(P-3575)***
R & R Machine Products Inc ....F....909 885-7500
760 W Mill St San Bernardino (92410) ***(P-12649)***
R & R Maintenance Group ....F....707 863-0328
1255 Treat Blvd Ste 300 Walnut Creek (94597) ***(P-13693)***
R & R Metal Fabricators ....F....626 960-6400
14846 Ramona Blvd Baldwin Park (91706) ***(P-11871)***
R & R Pumping Unit Repr & Svc, Ventura *Also called Richard Yarbrough* ***(P-254)***
R & R Rubber Molding Inc ....E....626 575-8105
2444 Loma Ave South El Monte (91733) ***(P-9269)***
R & R Services Corporation ....E....818 889-2562
31119 Via Colinas Ste 502 Westlake Village (91362) ***(P-9361)***
R & R Stamping Four Slide Corp ....D....909 595-6444
2440 Railroad St Corona (92880) ***(P-12866)***
R & S Automation Inc ....F....800 962-3111
283 W Bonita Ave Pomona (91767) ***(P-11976)***
R & S Manufacturing Inc (HQ) ....E....510 429-1788
33955 7th St Union City (94587) ***(P-11977)***
R & S Manufacturing & Sup Inc ....F....909 622-5881
16616 Garfield Ave Paramount (90723) ***(P-8675)***
R & S Mfg, Pomona *Also called R & S Mfg Southern Cal Inc* ***(P-11978)***
R & S Mfg Southern Cal Inc ....F....909 596-2090
283 W Bonita Ave Pomona (91767) ***(P-11978)***
R & S Overhead Door of So Cal ....E....714 680-0600
1617 N Orangethorpe Way Anaheim (92801) ***(P-11979)***
R & S Processing Co Inc ....D....562 531-0738
15712 Illinois Ave Paramount (90723) ***(P-9362)***
R & S Rolling Door Products, Union City *Also called R & S Manufacturing Inc* ***(P-11977)***
R & V Sheet Metal Inc ....F....951 361-9455
3197 Grapevine St Mira Loma (91752) ***(P-12348)***
R & W Inc ....F....323 589-1374
6351 Rege St 100 A & 300 Huntington Park (90255) ***(P-3396)***
R A Jenson Manufacturing Co ....F....415 822-2732
1337 Van Dyke Ave San Francisco (94124) ***(P-4236)***
R A Phillips Industries Inc ....B....562 781-2100
12070 Burke St Santa Fe Springs (90670) ***(P-19830)***
R A Reed Electric Company (PA) ....E....323 587-2284
5503 S Boyle Ave Vernon (90058) ***(P-24694)***
R B I, Burbank *Also called Bargueiras Rene Inc* ***(P-22501)***
R B III Associates Inc ....C....760 471-5370
166 Newport Dr San Marcos (92069) ***(P-3273)***
R B R Meat Company Inc ....D....323 973-4868
5151 Alcoa Ave Vernon (90058) ***(P-421)***
R B S Inc ....F....949 766-2924
31941 La Subida Dr Trabuco Canyon (92679) ***(P-15315)***
R B T Inc ....F....619 781-8802
2240 Encinitas Blvd Encinitas (92024) ***(P-3809)***
R B Welding Inc ....F....310 324-8680
155 E Redondo Beach Blvd Gardena (90248) ***(P-24659)***
R C I, Auburn *Also called Ron & Diana Vanatta* ***(P-4935)***
R C I P Inc ....F....714 630-1239
1476 N Hundley St Anaheim (92806) ***(P-16333)***
R C Industries, Anaheim *Also called R C I P Inc* ***(P-16333)***
R C Products Corp ....D....949 858-8820
22322 Gilberto Rcho STA Marg (92688) ***(P-11621)***
R C S, Rancho Cordova *Also called Residential Ctrl Systems Inc* ***(P-20807)***
R C Westburg Engineering Inc ....F....949 859-4648
23302 Vista Grande Dr Laguna Hills (92653) ***(P-10005)***
R D Mathis Company ....E....562 426-7049
2840 Gundry Ave Signal Hill (90755) ***(P-11083)***
R D Rubber Technology Corp ....E....562 941-4800
12870 Florence Ave Santa Fe Springs (90670) ***(P-9270)***
R E Atckison Co Inc ....F....626 334-0266
1801 W Gladstone St Azusa (91702) ***(P-13743)***
R E Dillard 1 LLC ....D....415 675-1500
300 California St Fl 7 San Francisco (94104) ***(P-11707)***
R E Michel, Long Beach *Also called R E Michel Company LLC* ***(P-15449)***
R E Michel Company LLC ....F....310 885-9820
155 W Victoria St Long Beach (90805) ***(P-15449)***
R F Circuits and Assembly Inc ....F....805 499-7788
3533 Old Conejo Rd # 107 Newbury Park (91320) ***(P-17971)***
R F P & Welding ....F....805 526-3425
310 E Easy St Ste E Simi Valley (93065) ***(P-19749)***
R G B Display Corporation ....F....530 268-2222
22525 Kingston Ln Grass Valley (95949) ***(P-15133)***
R G Hansen Associates (PA) ....F....805 564-3388
5951 Encina Rd Ste 106 Goleta (93117) ***(P-20926)***
R Goodloe & Associates Inc ....F....714 380-3900
25602 Alicia Pkwy Laguna Hills (92653) ***(P-6827)***
R H Barden Inc ....F....714 970-0900
4769 E Wesley Dr Anaheim (92807) ***(P-18737)***
R H Pattern ....E....909 484-9141
10700 Jersey Blvd Ste 590 Rancho Cucamonga (91730) ***(P-14003)***
R I M, Santa Clara *Also called Rimnetics Inc* ***(P-10018)***
R J McGlennon Company Inc (PA) ....E....415 552-0311
198 Utah St San Francisco (94103) ***(P-8676)***
R J R Technologies Inc (PA) ....C....510 638-5901
7875 Edgewater Dr Oakland (94621) ***(P-19388)***
R J Reynolds Tobacco Company ....C....858 625-8453
8380 Miramar Mall Ste 117 San Diego (92121) ***(P-2655)***
R J Vincent Inc ....E....626 448-1509
1030 Abbot Ave San Gabriel (91776) ***(P-4663)***
R K Fabrication Inc ....F....714 630-9654
1283 N Grove St Anaheim (92806) ***(P-7602)***
R K Larrabee Company Inc ....D....925 828-9420
7800 Las Positas Rd Livermore (94551) ***(P-16669)***
R Kern Engineering & Mfg Corp ....D....909 664-2440
13912 Mountain Ave Chino (91710) ***(P-18785)***
R L Anodizing ....F....818 252-3804
11331 Penrose St Sun Valley (91352) ***(P-13085)***
R L Anodizing & Plating, Sun Valley *Also called R L Anodizing* ***(P-13085)***
R L Bennett Engineering Inc ....F....949 367-0700
26945 Cabot Rd Ste 112 Laguna Hills (92653) ***(P-16334)***
R Lang Company ....D....559 651-0701
8240 W Doe Ave Visalia (93291) ***(P-11980)***
R M A Geoscience, Chino *Also called Consolidated Geoscience Inc* ***(P-116)***
R M Baker Machine & Tool Inc ....F....562 697-4007
815 W Front St Covina (91722) ***(P-16335)***
R M I, Van Nuys *Also called Rothlisberger Mfg A Cal Corp* ***(P-16373)***
R M I, Gardena *Also called Rotational Molding Inc* ***(P-10026)***
R M P, San Jose *Also called Rose Metal Products Inc* ***(P-11877)***
R O S, San Diego *Also called Remote Ocean Systems Inc* ***(P-17158)***
R P M, Concord *Also called Renaissance Precision Mfg Inc* ***(P-16353)***
R P M Centerless Grinding, Norco *Also called RPM Grinding Co Inc* ***(P-16376)***
R P M Electric Motors ....F....714 638-4174
11352 Westminster Ave Garden Grove (92843) ***(P-24695)***
R R Donnelley, San Diego *Also called R R Donnelley & Sons Company* ***(P-6829)***
R R Donnelley & Sons Company ....F....310 789-4100
1888 Century Park E # 1650 Los Angeles (90067) ***(P-7192)***
R R Donnelley & Sons Company ....E....415 362-2300
1 Embarcadero Ctr Ste 200 San Francisco (94111) ***(P-6963)***
R R Donnelley & Sons Company ....F....707 446-6195
1050 Aviator Dr Vacaville (95688) ***(P-6828)***
R R Donnelley & Sons Company ....C....619 527-4600
955 Gateway Center Way San Diego (92102) ***(P-6829)***
R R Donnelley & Sons Company ....C....619 527-4600
960 Gateway Center Way San Diego (92102) ***(P-6830)***
R R Donnelley Coml Press Plant, San Diego *Also called R R Donnelley & Sons Company* ***(P-6830)***
R R Donnelley Financial, Los Angeles *Also called R R Donnelley & Sons Company* ***(P-7192)***
R S R Steel Fabrication Inc ....E....760 244-2210
11040 I Ave Hesperia (92345) ***(P-11063)***
R Stephenson & D Cram Mfg Inc ....E....408 452-0882
800 Faulstich Ct San Jose (95112) ***(P-16336)***
R T C Group ....E....949 226-2000
905 Calle Amanecer # 150 San Clemente (92673) ***(P-6011)***
R T I, Morgan Hill *Also called Robson Technologies Inc* ***(P-16366)***

R Torre & Company Inc (PA)........C.......800 775-1925
233 E Harris Ave South San Francisco (94080) ***(P-2227)***
R Torre & Company Inc........E.......650 624-2830
400 Littlefield Ave South San Francisco (94080) ***(P-2228)***
R V Gambler........F.......928 927-5966
6966 Saxon Rd Spc 14 Adelanto (92301) ***(P-19831)***
R W Lyall & Company Inc (HQ)........C.......951 270-1500
2665 Research Dr Corona (92882) ***(P-136)***
R W Swarens Associates Inc........E.......626 579-0943
10768 Lower Azusa Rd El Monte (91731) ***(P-17067)***
R Zamora Inc........E.......760 597-1130
2826 La Mirada Dr Ste D Vista (92081) ***(P-12867)***
R&D Altanova Inc........E.......408 225-7011
6389 San Ignacio Ave San Jose (95119) ***(P-17972)***
R&Js Business Group Inc........F.......714 224-1455
900 S Placentia Ave Ste B Placentia (92870) ***(P-2361)***
R&K Industrial Wheels, Richmond *Also called R & K Industrial Products Co* ***(P-13543)***
R&M Deese Inc........E.......951 734-7342
1875 Sampson Ave Corona (92879) ***(P-23182)***
R-Cold Inc........D.......951 436-5476
1221 S G St Perris (92570) ***(P-15450)***
R-Quest Technologies LLC........F.......530 621-9916
4710 Oak Hill Rd Placerville (95667) ***(P-15316)***
R2 Semiconductor Inc........E.......408 745-7400
1196 Borregas Ave Ste 201 Sunnyvale (94089) ***(P-18507)***
R3 Performance Products Inc........F.......760 364-3001
531 Old Woman Springs Rd Yucca Valley (92284) ***(P-19750)***
RA Industries LLC........E.......714 557-2322
2230 S Anne St Santa Ana (92704) ***(P-16337)***
Ra Medical Systems Inc........C.......760 804-1648
2070 Las Palmas Dr Carlsbad (92011) ***(P-21870)***
Ra-White Inc........F.......661 725-1840
2736 W Industry Rd Delano (93215) ***(P-16338)***
Rabbit Lithographics, Chino *Also called Dare Lithoworks Inc* ***(P-6532)***
Racaar Circuit Industries Inc........E.......818 998-7566
9225 Alabama Ave Ste F Chatsworth (91311) ***(P-17973)***
Race Pak, Rcho STA Marg *Also called Racepak LLC* ***(P-19495)***
Race Technologies LLC........F.......714 438-1118
17422 Murphy Ave Irvine (92614) ***(P-19751)***
Racehorse Supply, Fontana *Also called Michael Hagan* ***(P-22853)***
Racemate Alternators, San Diego *Also called Barrett Engineering Inc* ***(P-19186)***
Racepak LLC........E.......949 709-5555
30402 Esperanza Rcho STA Marg (92688) ***(P-19752)***
Racepak LLC........E.......888 429-4709
30402 Esperanza Rcho STA Marg (92688) ***(P-19495)***
Racer Media & Marketing Inc........F.......949 417-6700
17030 Red Hill Ave Irvine (92614) ***(P-6012)***
Rache Corporation........F.......805 389-6868
1160 Avenida Acaso Camarillo (93012) ***(P-19389)***
Racing Beat Inc........E.......714 779-8677
4789 E Wesley Dr Anaheim (92807) ***(P-13598)***
Racing Plus Inc........F.......951 360-5906
3834 Wacker Dr Mira Loma (91752) ***(P-22075)***
Rack & Riddle, Healdsburg *Also called RB Wine Associates LLC* ***(P-1881)***
Rack Master, Brea *Also called Nycetek Inc* ***(P-4924)***
Raco Manufacturing & Engrg Co........F.......510 658-6713
1400 62nd St Emeryville (94608) ***(P-19390)***
Rada Industry........F.......323 265-3727
1060 S Ditman Ave Los Angeles (90023) ***(P-23456)***
Radarsonics Inc........F.......714 630-7288
1190 N Grove St Anaheim (92806) ***(P-19063)***
Radcal Partners IA California........E.......626 359-4575
426 W Duarte Rd Monrovia (91016) ***(P-21527)***
Radex Stereo Co Inc........F.......310 516-9015
13228 Crenshaw Blvd Gardena (90249) ***(P-22453)***
Radflo Suspension Technology........F.......714 965-7828
11233 Condor Ave Fountain Valley (92708) ***(P-19753)***
Radford Cabinets Inc........D.......661 729-8931
216 E Avenue K8 Lancaster (93535) ***(P-4604)***
Radian Audio Engineering Inc........E.......714 288-8900
600 N Batavia St Orange (92868) ***(P-17635)***
Radian Heat Sinks, Santa Clara *Also called Radian Thermal Products Inc* ***(P-11422)***
Radian Memory Systems Inc........E.......818 222-4080
5010 N Pkwy Ste 205 Calabasas (91302) ***(P-15084)***
Radian Thermal Products Inc........D.......408 988-6200
2160 Walsh Ave Santa Clara (95050) ***(P-11422)***
Radiant Detector Tech LLC........F.......818 709-2468
19355 Bus Center Dr Ste 8 Northridge (91324) ***(P-21528)***
Radiation Protection & Spc Inc........F.......714 771-7702
1531 W Orangewood Ave Orange (92868) ***(P-12349)***
Radiator Specialty Company........E.......707 252-0122
935 Enterprise Way NAPA (94558) ***(P-9018)***
Radicom Research Inc (PA)........F.......408 383-9006
671 E Brokaw Rd San Jose (95112) ***(P-17406)***
Radio Frequency Simulation........E.......714 974-7377
25371 Diana Cir Mission Viejo (92691) ***(P-21110)***
Radio Frequency Systems Inc........F.......408 281-6100
6276 San Ignacio Ave E San Jose (95119) ***(P-17636)***
Radio Frqency Systems Ferrocom, San Jose *Also called Radio Frequency Systems Inc* ***(P-17636)***
Radio Korea USA, Los Angeles *Also called Infokorea Inc* ***(P-5963)***
Radiology Support Devices........E.......310 518-0527
1904 E Dominguez St Long Beach (90810) ***(P-21871)***
Raditek Inc (PA)........D.......408 266-7404
1702 Meridian Ave Ste L San Jose (95125) ***(P-17637)***
Raditek Inc........F.......408 266-7404
44253 Old Warm Sprng Blvd Fremont (94538) ***(P-17638)***
Radius Arospc - San Diego Inc........C.......619 440-2504
203 N Johnson Ave El Cajon (92020) ***(P-20209)***

Radlink Inc........E.......310 643-6900
815 N Nash St El Segundo (90245) ***(P-22299)***
Radtec Engineering Inc........F.......760 510-2715
1780 La Costa Meadows Dr # 102 San Marcos (92078) ***(P-20679)***
Radx Technologies Inc........F.......619 677-1849
10650 Scripps Ranch Blvd # 100 San Diego (92131) ***(P-21111)***
Rae Systems Inc (HQ)........C.......408 952-8200
1349 Moffett Park Dr Sunnyvale (94089) ***(P-21529)***
Rael Inc........E.......800 573-1516
13915 Cerritos Corprt Dr D Cerritos (90703) ***(P-5466)***
Raemica Inc........E.......909 864-1990
7759 Victoria Ave Highland (92346) ***(P-491)***
Rafael Sandoval........E.......209 858-4173
16175 Mckinley Ave Lathrop (95330) ***(P-3942)***
Rafco Products Brickform, Rancho Cucamonga *Also called Rafco-Brickform LLC* ***(P-14190)***
Rafco-Brickform LLC (PA)........D.......909 484-3399
11061 Jersey Blvd Rancho Cucamonga (91730) ***(P-14190)***
Raffaello Research Labs........F.......310 618-8754
120 The Village Unit 109 Redondo Beach (90277) ***(P-8096)***
Rafi Systems Inc........D.......909 861-6574
23453 Golden Springs Dr Diamond Bar (91765) ***(P-22381)***
Rafu Shimpo........E.......213 629-2231
701 E 3rd St Ste 130 Los Angeles (90013) ***(P-5806)***
Rago & Son Inc........D.......510 536-5700
1029 51st Ave Oakland (94601) ***(P-12868)***
Rago Neon Inc........F.......510 537-1903
235 Laurel Ave Hayward (94541) ***(P-23183)***
Rahn Industries Incorporated (PA)........D.......562 908-0680
2630 Pacific Park Dr Whittier (90601) ***(P-15451)***
Raika Inc........E.......818 503-5911
13150 Saticoy St North Hollywood (91605) ***(P-10242)***
Railmakers Inc........F.......949 642-6506
864 W 18th St Costa Mesa (92627) ***(P-11622)***
Rain Bird Corporation (PA)........C.......626 812-3400
970 W Sierra Madre Ave Azusa (91702) ***(P-13362)***
Rain Bird Corporation........E.......626 812-3400
970 W Sierra Madre Ave Azusa (91702) ***(P-11679)***
Rain Bird Golf Division, Azusa *Also called Rain Bird Corporation* ***(P-11679)***
Rain Mstr Irrgtion Systems Inc........E.......805 527-4498
5825 Jasmine St Riverside (92504) ***(P-20927)***
Rainbo Record Mfg Corp (PA)........C.......818 280-1100
8960 Eton Ave Canoga Park (91304) ***(P-17335)***
Rainbo Records & Cassettes, Canoga Park *Also called Rainbo Record Mfg Corp* ***(P-17335)***
Rainbow Fin Company Inc........E.......831 728-2998
677 Beach Dr Watsonville (95076) ***(P-22867)***
Rainbow Magnetics Incorporated........E.......714 540-4777
1 Whatney Irvine (92618) ***(P-6831)***
Rainbow Manufacturing Co Inc........F.......323 778-2093
1504 W 58th St Los Angeles (90062) ***(P-4818)***
Rainbow Novelty Creations Co........E.......323 855-9464
3431 E Olympic Blvd Los Angeles (90023) ***(P-2835)***
Rainbow Orchards........F.......530 644-1594
2569 Larsen Dr Camino (95709) ***(P-2130)***
Rainbow Sublymation Inc........E.......213 489-5001
2438 E 11th St Los Angeles (90021) ***(P-7193)***
Rainbow Symphony Inc........F.......818 708-8400
6860 Canby Ave Ste 120 Reseda (91335) ***(P-5453)***
Raindrip Inc........E.......818 710-4023
2250 Agate Ct Simi Valley (93065) ***(P-13661)***
Rainguard International, Huntington Beach *Also called Weatherman Products Inc* ***(P-8693)***
Rainier Therapeutics Inc........F.......925 413-6140
1040 Davis St Ste 202 San Leandro (94577) ***(P-8326)***
Raintree Business Products........E.......949 859-0801
23101 Terra Dr Laguna Hills (92653) ***(P-6832)***
Raisin Valley Farms LLC........F.......559 846-8138
3678 N Modoc Ave Kerman (93630) ***(P-858)***
Raisin Valley Farms Distrg Inc........F.......559 846-8138
2267 N Lassen Ave Kerman (93630) ***(P-859)***
Raj Manufacturing LLC........F.......714 838-3110
2692 Dow Ave Tustin (92780) ***(P-3397)***
Rakar Incorporated........E.......805 487-2721
1700 Emerson Ave Oxnard (93033) ***(P-10006)***
Rakshak........E.......404 513-5867
2518 Alvin St Mountain View (94043) ***(P-24338)***
Ralc Inc........F.......951 693-0098
42158 Sarah Way Temecula (92590) ***(P-16339)***
Rallio, Irvine *Also called Socialwise Inc* ***(P-6340)***
Ralph E Ames Machine Works........E.......310 328-8523
2301 Dominguez Way Torrance (90501) ***(P-16340)***
Ralph L Florimonte........F.......714 960-4470
517 Alondra Dr Huntington Beach (92648) ***(P-9205)***
Ralphs-Pugh Co Inc........D.......707 745-6222
3931 Oregon St Benicia (94510) ***(P-13832)***
Ram Aerospace Inc........F.......714 853-1703
581 Tamarack Ave Brea (92821) ***(P-20210)***
Ram Centrifical Products, Spring Valley *Also called Euramco Safety Inc* ***(P-14658)***
Ram Centrifugal Products Inc........F.......619 670-9590
2746 Via Orange Way Spring Valley (91978) ***(P-14676)***
Ram Off Road Accessories Inc........E.......323 266-3850
3901 Medford St Los Angeles (90063) ***(P-19754)***
Rama Corporation........E.......951 654-7351
600 W Esplanade Ave San Jacinto (92583) ***(P-14774)***
Rama Food Manufacture Corp (PA)........E.......909 923-5305
1486 E Cedar St Ontario (91761) ***(P-2595)***
Ramar International Corp (PA)........E.......925 439-9009
1101 Railroad Ave Pittsburg (94565) ***(P-664)***
Ramar International Corp........E.......925 432-4267
539 Garcia Ave Ste E Pittsburg (94565) ***(P-422)***
Rambus Inc (PA)........B.......408 462-8000
1050 Entp Way Ste 700 Sunnyvale (94089) ***(P-18508)***

Employee Codes: A=Over 500 employees, B=251-500
C=101-250, D=51-100, E=20-50, F=10-19
2020 California
Manfacturers Register
© Mergent Inc. 1-800-342-5647
1217

Rambus Inc........F......408 462-8000
1050 Enterprise Way # 700 Sunnyvale (94089) ***(P-18509)***
Ramco, Simi Valley *Also called Recycled Aggregate Mtls Co Inc* ***(P-9103)***
Ramda Metal Specialties Inc........E......310 538-2136
13012 Crenshaw Blvd Gardena (90249) ***(P-12350)***
Rami Designs Inc........F......949 588-8288
24 Hammond Ste E Irvine (92618) ***(P-12503)***
Ramko Injection Inc........D......951 652-3510
3500 Tanya Ave Hemet (92545) ***(P-10007)***
Ramon Lopez........F......626 575-3891
9729 Alpaca St South El Monte (91733) ***(P-4664)***
Ramon Lopez........F......209 478-9500
4752 Ijams Rd Stockton (95210) ***(P-19496)***
Ramona Home Journal........F......760 788-8148
726 D St Ramona (92065) ***(P-5807)***
Ramona Mining & Manufacturing........F......760 789-1620
505 Elm St Ramona (92065) ***(P-22599)***
Ramona Research Inc........F......858 679-0717
13741 Danielson St Ste J Poway (92064) ***(P-17639)***
Ramonas Food Group LLC........C......310 323-1950
13633 S Western Ave Gardena (90249) ***(P-743)***
Ramp Engineering Inc........F......562 531-8030
6850 Walthall Way Paramount (90723) ***(P-11872)***
Rampone Industries LLC........E......949 581-8701
14235 Commerce Dr Garden Grove (92843) ***(P-13431)***
Rams Gate Winery LLC........E......707 721-8700
28700 Arnold Dr Sonoma (95476) ***(P-1877)***
Ramsay Highlander Inc........E......831 675-3453
45 Gonzales River Rd Gonzales (93926) ***(P-13662)***
Ramtec Associates Inc........E......714 996-7477
3200 E Birch St Ste B Brea (92821) ***(P-10008)***
Ranboy Sportswear, Chula Vista *Also called Leemax International Inc* ***(P-3102)***
Ranch Systems LLC........F......415 884-2770
37 Commercial Blvd # 101 Novato (94949) ***(P-13663)***
Rancho Bernardo Printing Inc........F......858 486-4540
1519 Industrial Ave Ste D Escondido (92029) ***(P-6833)***
Rancho Cucamonga Division, Rancho Cucamonga *Also called Gasket Specialties Inc* ***(P-9233)***
Rancho Cucamonga Maverick........F......909 466-6445
7349 Milliken Ave Ste 110 Rancho Cucamonga (91730) ***(P-5808)***
Rancho Cucamonga Today, Rancho Cucamonga *Also called Rancho Cucamonga Maverick* ***(P-5808)***
Rancho De Solis Winery Inc........F......408 847-6306
3920 Hecker Pass Rd Gilroy (95020) ***(P-1878)***
Rancho Guejito Corporation........F......800 519-4441
17224 San Pasqual Vly Rd Escondido (92027) ***(P-1879)***
Rancho Ready Mix........E......951 674-0488
28251 Lake St Lake Elsinore (92530) ***(P-10816)***
Rancho Safari, Ramona *Also called Gerald Gentellalli* ***(P-22807)***
Rancho Sisquoc Winery, Santa Maria *Also called Flood Ranch Company* ***(P-1704)***
Rancho Technology Inc........F......909 987-3966
10783 Bell Ct Rancho Cucamonga (91730) ***(P-15317)***
RAND MACHINE WORKS, Fresno *Also called R & L Enterprises Inc* ***(P-16332)***
Randal Optimal Nutrients LLC........E......707 528-1800
1595 Hampton Way Santa Rosa (95407) ***(P-8097)***
Randell Equipment & Mfg, Delano *Also called Randell Equipment & Mfg* ***(P-13664)***
Randell Equipment & Mfg........E......661 725-6380
1408 S Lexington St Delano (93215) ***(P-13664)***
Randolph & Hein........F......323 233-6010
720 E 59th St Los Angeles (90001) ***(P-4605)***
Random Technologies LLC........F......415 255-1267
2325 3rd St Ste 404 San Francisco (94107) ***(P-10329)***
Randtron Antenna Systems, Menlo Park *Also called L3 Technologies Inc* ***(P-17567)***
Randy Nix Cstm Wldg & Mfg Inc........F......559 562-1958
22700 Road 196 Lindsay (93247) ***(P-24660)***
Rang Dong Joint Stock Company........F......707 259-9446
3 Executive Way NAPA (94558) ***(P-1880)***
Rang Dong Winery, NAPA *Also called Rang Dong Joint Stock Company* ***(P-1880)***
Rangefinder Publishing Co Inc........F......310 846-4770
11835 W Olympic Blvd 550e Los Angeles (90064) ***(P-6013)***
Rangeme Inc........F......415 351-9268
665 3rd St Ste 415 San Francisco (94107) ***(P-6323)***
Rani Jewels Inc........F......408 516-6807
1249 Quarry Ln Ste 100 Pleasanton (94566) ***(P-22561)***
Rank Technology Corp........E......408 737-1488
1190 Miraloma Way Ste Q Sunnyvale (94085) ***(P-15085)***
Rankin-Delux Inc (PA)........F......951 685-0081
3245 Corridor Dr Eastvale (91752) ***(P-15567)***
Ranks Big Data........C......510 830-6926
2453 Naglee Rd Tracy (95304) ***(P-3854)***
Ranroy Company........E......858 571-8800
8320 Camino Santa Fe # 200 San Diego (92121) ***(P-6834)***
Ransome Manufacturing, Fresno *Also called Meeder Equipment Company* ***(P-14495)***
Rantec Microwave Systems Inc........E......760 744-1544
2066 Wineridge Pl Escondido (92029) ***(P-19064)***
Rantec Microwave Systems Inc (PA)........D......818 223-5000
31186 La Baya Dr Westlake Village (91362) ***(P-20680)***
Raoul Textiles Inc........F......805 965-1694
110 Los Aguajes Ave Santa Barbara (93101) ***(P-7194)***
Raoul's Hand-Screened Yardage, Santa Barbara *Also called Raoul Textiles Inc* ***(P-7194)***
Raouls Printworks........F......805 965-1694
110 Los Aguajes Ave Santa Barbara (93101) ***(P-2836)***
RAP Security Inc........D......323 560-3493
4630 Cecilia St Cudahy (90201) ***(P-4998)***
Rap4........E......408 434-0434
2345 La Mirada Dr Vista (92081) ***(P-22868)***
Rapco-West Asbestos, Malibu *Also called West Rapco Environmental Svcs* ***(P-14125)***
Raphaels Inc........F......619 670-7999
2780 Sweetwater Spgs Blvd Spring Valley (91977) ***(P-4524)***
Rapid Anodizing LLC........F......323 753-5255
1216 W Slauson Ave Los Angeles (90044) ***(P-14525)***
Rapid Displays Inc........B......510 471-6955
33195 Lewis St Union City (94587) ***(P-23184)***
Rapid Lasergraphics, San Francisco *Also called Rapid Typographers Company* ***(P-7361)***
Rapid Lasergraphics (HQ)........F......415 957-5840
836 Harrison St San Francisco (94107) ***(P-7360)***
Rapid Manufacturing (PA)........F......818 899-4377
9724 Eton Ave Chatsworth (91311) ***(P-23457)***
Rapid Manufacturing A (PA)........C......714 974-2432
8080 E Crystal Dr Anaheim (92807) ***(P-13432)***
Rapid Precision Mfg Inc........E......408 617-0771
1516 Montague Expy San Jose (95131) ***(P-16341)***
Rapid Printers Inc........F......831 373-1822
201 Foam St Monterey (93940) ***(P-6835)***
Rapid Product Solutions Inc........E......805 485-7234
2240 Celsius Ave Ste D Oxnard (93030) ***(P-16342)***
Rapid Ramen Inc........F......916 479-7003
9381 E Stockton Blvd # 230 Elk Grove (95624) ***(P-15568)***
Rapid Typographers Company (PA)........E......415 957-5840
836 Harrison St San Francisco (94107) ***(P-7361)***
Rapidwerks Incorporated........E......925 417-0124
1257 Quarry Ln Ste 140 Pleasanton (94566) ***(P-10009)***
Rapiscan Laboratories Inc (HQ)........D......408 961-9700
3793 Spinnaker Ct Fremont (94538) ***(P-22220)***
Rapiscan Systems Inc (HQ)........C......310 978-1457
2805 Columbia St Torrance (90503) ***(P-22221)***
Rapt Therapeutics Inc........D......650 489-9000
561 Eccles Ave South San Francisco (94080) ***(P-8098)***
Rapt Touch Inc........F......415 994-1537
1875 S Grant St Ste 925 San Mateo (94402) ***(P-14967)***
Raptor Pharmaceuticals Inc........E......415 408-6200
7 Hamilton Landing # 100 Novato (94949) ***(P-8099)***
Rare Breed Distilling LLC (HQ)........E......415 315-8060
55 Francisco St Ste 100 San Francisco (94133) ***(P-2017)***
Rare Elements Hair Care........F......310 277-6524
8950 W Olympic Blvd 641 Beverly Hills (90211) ***(P-23458)***
Rasmussen Iron Works Inc........D......562 696-8718
12028 Philadelphia St Whittier (90601) ***(P-11708)***
Raspadoxpress........F......818 892-6969
8610 Van Nuys Blvd Panorama City (91402) ***(P-6324)***
Rastergraf Inc (PA)........F......510 849-4801
7145 Marlborough Ter Berkeley (94705) ***(P-17974)***
Ratebeer LLC........D......302 476-2337
1381 Velma Ave Santa Rosa (95403) ***(P-6325)***
Ratebeer.com, Santa Rosa *Also called Ratebeer LLC* ***(P-6325)***
Ratermann Manufacturing Inc (PA)........E......800 264-7793
601 Pinnacle Pl Livermore (94550) ***(P-10010)***
Rau Restoration........F......310 445-1128
2027 Pontius Ave Los Angeles (90025) ***(P-4112)***
Rau William Automotive Wdwrk, Los Angeles *Also called Rau Restoration* ***(P-4112)***
Raven's Deli, Armona *Also called Armona Frozen Food Lockers* ***(P-438)***
Ravenswood Winery, Sonoma *Also called Franciscan Vineyards Inc* ***(P-1710)***
Raveon Technologies Corp........E......760 444-5995
2320 Cousteau Ct Vista (92081) ***(P-17640)***
Rawson Custom Cabinets Inc (PA)........E......408 779-9838
16890 Church St Bldg 1a Morgan Hill (95037) ***(P-4237)***
Ray Chinn Construction Inc........E......661 327-2731
424 24th St Bakersfield (93301) ***(P-13993)***
Ray Foster Dental Equipment........F......714 897-7795
5421 Commercial Dr Huntington Beach (92649) ***(P-22185)***
Ray-Bar Engineering Corp........F......626 969-1818
697 W Foothill Blvd Azusa (91702) ***(P-22076)***
Raychem, Fremont *Also called Te Connectivity Corporation* ***(P-9207)***
Raychem Product Division, Redwood City *Also called Te Connectivity Corporation* ***(P-16930)***
Raychem Wire Division, Redwood City *Also called Te Connectivity Corporation* ***(P-16932)***
Rayco B Products, Monrovia *Also called Rayco Burial Products Inc* ***(P-12351)***
Rayco Burial Products Inc........E......626 357-1996
1601 Raymond Ave Monrovia (91016) ***(P-12351)***
Rayco Electronic Mfg Inc........E......310 329-2660
1220 W 130th St Gardena (90247) ***(P-18738)***
Raycon Technology Inc (PA)........F......714 799-4100
5252 Mcfadden Ave Huntington Beach (92649) ***(P-18786)***
Raykorvay Inc........F......714 632-8680
1070 N Kraemer Pl Anaheim (92806) ***(P-22653)***
Raymar Information Tech Inc (PA)........F......916 783-1951
7325 Roseville Rd Sacramento (95842) ***(P-17407)***
Raymonds Little Print Shop Inc........B......510 353-3608
41454 Christy St Fremont (94538) ***(P-6836)***
Raynguard Protective Mtls Inc........F......916 454-2560
8280 14th Ave Sacramento (95826) ***(P-8890)***
Rayotek Scientific Inc........D......858 558-3671
11499 Sorrento Valley Rd San Diego (92121) ***(P-10387)***
Rayotek Sight Windows, San Diego *Also called Rayotek Scientific Inc* ***(P-10387)***
Raypak Inc (HQ)........B......805 278-5300
2151 Eastman Ave Oxnard (93030) ***(P-11709)***
Rayspan Corporation........F......858 259-9596
1493 Poinsettia Ave # 139 Vista (92081) ***(P-17408)***
Raytheon Applied Signal (HQ)........C......408 749-1888
460 W California Ave Sunnyvale (94086) ***(P-17641)***
Raytheon Applied Signal........F......714 917-0255
160 N Rverview Dr Ste 300 Anaheim (92808) ***(P-17757)***
Raytheon Company........C......805 967-5511
6380 Hollister Ave Goleta (93117) ***(P-19391)***
Raytheon Company........F......310 334-0430
14471 Danes Cir Huntington Beach (92647) ***(P-20681)***

ALPHABETIC SECTION Receivd Inc

Raytheon Company...D...310 647-1000
1921 Mariposa St El Segundo (90245) ***(P-20682)***
Raytheon Company...C...626 675-2584
16035 E Bridger St Covina (91722) ***(P-20683)***
Raytheon Company...F...714 446-2584
1801 Hughes Dr Fullerton (92833) ***(P-20684)***
Raytheon Company...D...714 446-3513
1801 Hughes Dr Fullerton (92833) ***(P-20685)***
Raytheon Company...E...760 384-3295
350 E Ridgecrest Blvd # 202 Ridgecrest (93555) ***(P-20686)***
Raytheon Company...C...619 628-3345
8650 Balboa Ave San Diego (92123) ***(P-20687)***
Raytheon Company...D...714 446-2287
1801 Hughes Dr Dd311 Fullerton (92833) ***(P-21530)***
Raytheon Company...C...714 732-0119
1801 Hughes Dr Fullerton (92833) ***(P-20688)***
Raytheon Company...B...310 647-1000
2000 E El Segundo Blvd El Segundo (90245) ***(P-20689)***
Raytheon Company...F...805 562-2730
26 Castilian Dr Goleta (93117) ***(P-14968)***
Raytheon Company...B...310 647-8334
2000 Elsegundo Blvd El Segundo (90245) ***(P-20690)***
Raytheon Company...F...805 985-6851
Bldg 471 North End Port Hueneme (93043) ***(P-20691)***
Raytheon Company...D...310 338-1324
1120 S Vineyard Ave Ontario (91761) ***(P-20692)***
Raytheon Company...A...310 647-9438
2000 E El Segundo Blvd El Segundo (90245) ***(P-20693)***
Raytheon Company...B...310 647-1000
2000 E El Segundo Blvd El Segundo (90245) ***(P-20694)***
Raytheon Company...E...310 647-1000
2000 E El Segundo Blvd El Segundo (90245) ***(P-20695)***
Raytheon Company...C...310 884-1825
9400 Santa Fe Springs Rd Santa Fe Springs (90670) ***(P-19497)***
Raytheon Company...B...714 446-3232
1901 W Malvern Ave 618 Fullerton (92833) ***(P-20696)***
Raytheon Company...D...909 483-4040
10606 7th St Rancho Cucamonga (91730) ***(P-20697)***
Raytheon Company...E...310 334-7675
2175 Park Pl El Segundo (90245) ***(P-20698)***
Raytheon Company...D...805 562-4611
75 Coromar Dr Goleta (93117) ***(P-20699)***
Raytheon Company...A...310 647-9438
2000 E El Segundo Blvd El Segundo (90245) ***(P-20700)***
Raytheon Company...D...858 571-6598
8650 Balboa Ave San Diego (92123) ***(P-20701)***
Raytheon Company...C...805 967-5511
63 Hollister St Goleta (93117) ***(P-20702)***
Raytheon Dgital Force Tech LLC...E...858 546-1244
6779 Mesa Ridge Rd # 150 San Diego (92121) ***(P-20703)***
Rayzist Photomask Inc (PA)...D...760 727-8561
955 Park Center Dr Vista (92081) ***(P-22972)***
RB Design, Escondido *Also called Generation Circuits LLC* ***(P-17889)***
RB Machining Inc...F...661 274-4611
39360 3rd St E Ste B203 Palmdale (93550) ***(P-16343)***
RB Racing...F...310 515-5720
1234 W 134th St Gardena (90247) ***(P-19755)***
RB Wine Associates LLC...D...707 433-8400
499 Moore Ln Healdsburg (95448) ***(P-1881)***
Rbf Group International...F...626 333-5700
1441 W 2nd St Pomona (91766) ***(P-4819)***
Rbf Lifestyle Holdings, Pomona *Also called Rbf Group International* ***(P-4819)***
Rbg Holdings Corp (PA)...E...818 782-6445
7855 Haskell Ave Ste 350 Van Nuys (91406) ***(P-22869)***
Rbm Conveyor Systems Inc...E...909 620-1333
1570 W Mission Blvd Pomona (91766) ***(P-14395)***
Rbs Glass Designs, Van Nuys *Also called Precision Glass Bevelling Inc* ***(P-10328)***
Rbz Vineyards LLC...E...805 542-0133
2324 W Highway 46 Paso Robles (93446) ***(P-1882)***
RC Apparel Inc...F...818 541-1994
3104 Markridge Rd La Crescenta (91214) ***(P-3810)***
RC Furniture Inc...D...626 964-4100
1111 Jellick Ave City of Industry (91748) ***(P-4665)***
RC Readymix Co Inc...E...925 449-7785
1227 Greenville Rd Livermore (94550) ***(P-10817)***
Rcd Engineering Inc...E...530 292-3133
17100 Salmon Mine Rd Nevada City (95959) ***(P-16742)***
Rch Associates Inc...F...510 657-7846
349 Earhart Way Livermore (94551) ***(P-14526)***
RCP Block & Brick Inc (PA)...D...619 460-9101
8240 Broadway Lemon Grove (91945) ***(P-10515)***
RCP Block & Brick Inc...E...619 448-2240
8755 N Magnolia Ave Santee (92071) ***(P-10516)***
RCP Block & Brick Inc...E...619 474-1516
75 N 4th Ave Chula Vista (91910) ***(P-10517)***
RCP Block & Brick Inc...E...760 753-1164
577 N Vulcan Ave Encinitas (92024) ***(P-10518)***
Rcrv Inc...F...323 235-7332
4619 S Alameda St Vernon (90058) ***(P-5414)***
Rcs, Los Angeles *Also called Rider Circulation Services* ***(P-5810)***
Rcs Custom Stoneworks...F...714 309-0620
3280 Vine St Ste 201 Riverside (92507) ***(P-10927)***
Rd Jean, Vernon *Also called California Coast Clothing LLC* ***(P-2675)***
Rd Metal Polishing Inc...E...909 594-8393
244 Pioneer Pl Pomona (91768) ***(P-13086)***
Rdc Machine Inc...E...408 970-0721
384 Laurelwood Rd Santa Clara (95054) ***(P-16344)***
RDD Enterprises Inc...F...213 746-0020
4638 E Washinton Blvd Commerce (90040) ***(P-2974)***
Rdl Machine Inc...E...858 693-3975
7775 Arjons Dr San Diego (92126) ***(P-16345)***
RDm Industrial Products Inc...F...408 945-8400
1652 Watson Ct Milpitas (95035) ***(P-4847)***
RDM Multi-Enterprises Inc...F...562 924-1820
20428 Belshire Ave Lakewood (90715) ***(P-10976)***
RDS Group Inc...F...909 923-8831
1714 E Grevillea Ct Ontario (91761) ***(P-6837)***
RDS Printing and Graphics Ctr, Ontario *Also called RDS Group Inc* ***(P-6837)***
RE Bilt Metalizing Co...F...323 277-8200
2229 E 38th St Vernon (90058) ***(P-16346)***
RE Tranquillity 8 LLC...D...415 675-1500
300 California St Fl 7 San Francisco (94104) ***(P-11710)***
Reach International, Buena Park *Also called Leach International Corp* ***(P-16728)***
Reach Technology, San Jose *Also called Novanta Corporation* ***(P-19031)***
Reaction Technology Inc (PA)...E...408 970-9601
3400 Bassett St Santa Clara (95054) ***(P-18510)***
Read Corp...E...408 705-2123
16012a Flintlock Rd Cupertino (95014) ***(P-24339)***
Read It Later Inc...E...415 692-6111
233 Sansome St Ste 1200 San Francisco (94104) ***(P-24340)***
Reader Magazine...F...909 335-8100
108 Orange St Ste 11 Redlands (92373) ***(P-6014)***
Ready Industries Inc...F...213 749-2041
1520 E 15th St Los Angeles (90021) ***(P-6838)***
Ready Pac Foods Inc (HQ)...A...626 856-8686
4401 Foxdale St Irwindale (91706) ***(P-2596)***
Ready Reproductions, Los Angeles *Also called Ready Industries Inc* ***(P-6838)***
Ready Stamps, San Diego *Also called United Cerebral Palsy Assn San* ***(P-22957)***
Readymix - Delano Rm, Delano *Also called Cemex Cnstr Mtls PCF LLC* ***(P-10722)***
Readymix - Fairfield R/M, Fairfield *Also called Cemex Cnstr Mtls PCF LLC* ***(P-10506)***
Readymix - Old River Rm, Bakersfield *Also called Cemex Cnstr Mtls PCF LLC* ***(P-10725)***
Readymix - Tremont R/M, Dixon *Also called Cemex Cnstr Mtls PCF LLC* ***(P-10507)***
Readymix -Compton Rm, Compton *Also called Cemex Cnstr Mtls PCF LLC* ***(P-10733)***
Readymix -Concord Rm Dual, Concord *Also called Cemex Cnstr Mtls PCF LLC* ***(P-10720)***
Readymix -Elk Grove Rm, Elk Grove *Also called Cemex Cnstr Mtls PCF LLC* ***(P-10724)***
Readymix -Fontana Rm, Fontana *Also called Cemex Cnstr Mtls PCF LLC* ***(P-10730)***
Readymix -Hollywood Rm Dual, West Hollywood *Also called Cemex Cnstr Mtls PCF LLC* ***(P-10735)***
Readymix -Los Angeles Rm Dual, Los Angeles *Also called Cemex Cnstr Mtls PCF LLC* ***(P-10734)***
Readymix -Modesto Rm, Modesto *Also called Cemex Cnstr Mtls PCF LLC* ***(P-10732)***
Readymix -Moorpark Rm, Moorpark *Also called Cemex Cnstr Mtls PCF LLC* ***(P-10731)***
Readymix -Newman Rm, Newman *Also called Cemex Cnstr Mtls PCF LLC* ***(P-10727)***
Readymix -Oakland Rm, Oakland *Also called Cemex Cnstr Mtls PCF LLC* ***(P-10719)***
Readymix -Orange Rm Dual, Orange *Also called Cemex Cnstr Mtls PCF LLC* ***(P-10716)***
Readymix -Redlands Rm Dual, Highland *Also called Cemex Cnstr Mtls PCF LLC* ***(P-10723)***
Readymix -Tracy Rm Dual, Tracy *Also called Cemex Cnstr Mtls PCF LLC* ***(P-10714)***
Readymix -Walnut Rm, Walnut *Also called Cemex Cnstr Mtls PCF LLC* ***(P-10729)***
Readysmart, Mountain View *Also called Phoenix Improving Life LLC* ***(P-22068)***
Readytech Corporation...F...510 834-3344
2201 Broadway Ste 725 Oakland (94612) ***(P-24341)***
Reagent Chemical & RES Inc...E...909 796-4059
1454 S Sunnyside Ave San Bernardino (92408) ***(P-7521)***
Real Action Paintball Inc...F...408 848-2846
2345 La Mirada Dr Vista (92081) ***(P-22870)***
Real Marketing...E...858 847-0335
9955 Black Mountain Rd San Diego (92126) ***(P-6326)***
Real Meat Company, The, Montrose *Also called Flanagan-Gorham Inc* ***(P-409)***
Real Plating Inc...E...909 623-2304
1245 W 2nd St Pomona (91766) ***(P-13087)***
Real Seal, Escondido *Also called REAL Seal Co Inc* ***(P-9249)***
REAL Seal Co Inc...E...760 743-7263
1971 Don Lee Pl Escondido (92029) ***(P-9249)***
Real Software Systems LLC (PA)...D...818 313-8000
21255 Burbank Blvd # 220 Woodland Hills (91367) ***(P-24342)***
Real-Time Radiography Inc...E...925 416-1903
3825 Hopyard Rd Ste 220 Pleasanton (94588) ***(P-22300)***
Realization Technologies Inc...E...408 271-1720
440 N Wolfe Rd 52 Sunnyvale (94085) ***(P-24343)***
Realpage Inc...E...415 222-6996
333 3rd St San Francisco (94107) ***(P-24344)***
Realscout Inc...F...650 397-6500
480 Ellis St Ste 203 Mountain View (94043) ***(P-24345)***
Realtalkla, Los Angeles *Also called Transformationnet Media LLC* ***(P-6044)***
Realtime Technologies Inc...F...408 745-6434
1230 Mtn View Alviso Rd Sunnyvale (94089) ***(P-17975)***
Realware Inc...F...510 382-9045
444 Haas Ave San Leandro (94577) ***(P-24346)***
Realwise Inc...F...661 295-9399
28042 Avenue Stanford E Valencia (91355) ***(P-24347)***
Rebecca International Inc...E...323 973-2602
4587 E 48th St Vernon (90058) ***(P-3754)***
Rebol Technologies Inc...F...707 485-0599
301 S State St Ukiah (95482) ***(P-24348)***
Rebound Therapeutics Corp...E...949 305-8111
13900 Alton Pkwy Ste 120 Irvine (92618) ***(P-21872)***
Rebuilt Metalizing Chrome Pltg, Vernon *Also called RE Bilt Metalizing Co* ***(P-16346)***
Rec Inc...F...760 727-8006
2442 Cades Way Vista (92081) ***(P-14854)***
Rec Solar Commercial Corp...C...844 732-7652
3450 Broad St Ste 105 San Luis Obispo (93401) ***(P-20805)***
Recarbco, Martinez *Also called Noel Burt* ***(P-15614)***
Receivd Inc...F...650 336-5817
655 Castro St Ste 2 Mountain View (94041) ***(P-24349)***

ALPHABETIC

Receptos Inc...E....858 652-5700
3033 Science Park Rd # 300 San Diego (92121) ***(P-8100)***
Recoating-West Inc (PA)...E....916 652-8290
4170 Douglas Blvd Ste 120 Granite Bay (95746) ***(P-12352)***
Recognition Products Mfg, San Jose *Also called Stryker Enterprises Inc* ***(P-13549)***
Recomax Software Inc...F....408 592-0851
706 La Para Ave Palo Alto (94306) ***(P-17642)***
Recommind Inc (HQ)...D....415 394-7899
550 Kearny St Ste 700 San Francisco (94108) ***(P-19231)***
Recon 1 Inc...F....805 388-3911
4045 Via Pescador Camarillo (93012) ***(P-9180)***
Recon Services Inc...F....951 682-1400
2255 Via Cerro Jurupa Valley (92509) ***(P-12045)***
Reconserve Inc (HQ)...E....310 458-1574
2811 Wilshire Blvd # 410 Santa Monica (90403) ***(P-1120)***
Reconserve of Maryland, Santa Monica *Also called Dext Company of Maryland* ***(P-1090)***
Recor Medical Inc (HQ)...F....650 542-7700
1049 Elwell Ct Palo Alto (94303) ***(P-21873)***
Record Technology Inc...E....805 484-2747
486 Dawson Dr Ste 4s Camarillo (93012) ***(P-17336)***
Record The, Stockton *Also called Dow Jones Lmg Stockton Inc* ***(P-5619)***
Recortec Inc...F....408 928-1488
2231 Fortune Dr Ste A San Jose (95131) ***(P-15318)***
Recruitment Services Inc...F....213 364-1960
3600 Wilshire Blvd Ste 15 Los Angeles (90010) ***(P-6015)***
Rectangular Tubing Inc...F....626 333-7884
333 Newquist Pl City of Industry (91745) ***(P-5301)***
Recycled Aggregate Mtls Co Inc (PA)...E....805 522-1646
2655 1st St 210 Simi Valley (93065) ***(P-9103)***
Recycled Paper Products, Santa Fe Springs *Also called Gabriel Container Co* ***(P-5223)***
Recycled Spaces Inc...F....530 587-3394
10191 Donner Pass Rd # 1 Truckee (96161) ***(P-4772)***
Recycler Classified, Sherman Oaks *Also called E Z Buy E Z Sell Recycler Corp* ***(P-5621)***
Red Bluff Daily News, Red Bluff *Also called Medianews Group Inc* ***(P-5748)***
Red Brick Corporation...F....323 549-9444
5364 Venice Blvd Los Angeles (90019) ***(P-6839)***
Red Bull North America Inc...D....310 393-4647
1630 Stewart St Ste A Santa Monica (90404) ***(P-2131)***
Red Caboose of Colorado, Crescent City *Also called William McClung* ***(P-22727)***
Red Digital Cinema Camera Co, Irvine *Also called Redcom LLC* ***(P-22454)***
Red Engine Inc...F....213 742-8858
1850 E 15th St Los Angeles (90021) ***(P-3017)***
Red Engine Jeans, Los Angeles *Also called Red Engine Inc* ***(P-3017)***
Red Gate Software Inc...E....626 993-3949
144 W Colo Blvd Ste 200 Pasadena (91105) ***(P-24350)***
Red Hat Inc...F....650 567-9039
444 Castro St Ste 1200 Mountain View (94041) ***(P-24351)***
Red Line Engineering Inc...F....530 333-2134
4616 Weed Patch Ct Greenwood (95635) ***(P-16347)***
Red Line Synthetic Oil, Benicia *Also called Phillips 66 Spectrum Corp* ***(P-9153)***
Red Mountain Inc...F....949 595-4475
17767 Mitchell N Irvine (92614) ***(P-20806)***
Red River Lumber Co...E....707 963-1251
2959 Saint Helena Hwy N Saint Helena (94574) ***(P-4425)***
Red Robot Labs Inc...F....650 762-8058
1935 Landings Dr Mountain View (94043) ***(P-22708)***
Red Shell Foods Inc...F....626 937-6501
825 Baldwin Park Blvd City of Industry (91746) ***(P-897)***
Red Star Coffee, Goleta *Also called Santa Barbara Coffee LLC* ***(P-2309)***
Red Star Fertilizer Co...D....909 597-4801
17132 Hellman Ave Eastvale (92880) ***(P-8801)***
Red Tricycle Inc...E....415 729-9781
548 Market St San Francisco (94104) ***(P-22709)***
Redart Corporation...F....714 774-9444
2549 Eastbluff Dr Newport Beach (92660) ***(P-4870)***
Redbuilt LLC...E....909 465-1215
5088 Edison Ave Chino (91710) ***(P-4316)***
Redcom LLC (HQ)...D....949 206-7900
34 Parker Irvine (92618) ***(P-22454)***
Redcort Software Inc...F....559 434-8544
619 Woodworth Ave Ste 200 Clovis (93612) ***(P-24352)***
Redding Metal Crafters Inc...F....530 222-4400
3871 Rancho Rd Redding (96002) ***(P-12353)***
Redding Printing Co Inc (PA)...E....530 243-0525
1130 Continental St Redding (96001) ***(P-6840)***
Reddit Inc (PA)...E....415 666-2330
548 Market St San Francisco (94104) ***(P-6327)***
Reddy Ice Corporation...E....760 344-0535
462 N 8th St Brawley (92227) ***(P-2362)***
Redfern Integrated Optics Inc...E....408 970-3500
3350 Scott Blvd Bldg 1 Santa Clara (95054) ***(P-21401)***
Redi Shades, Cotati *Also called Shades Unlimited Inc* ***(P-5037)***
Redlands CCI Inc...E....909 307-6500
721 Nevada St Ste 308 Redlands (92373) ***(P-20423)***
Redlands Daily Facts, Redlands *Also called Califrnia Nwspapers Ltd Partnr* ***(P-5581)***
Redline Detection LLC...F....714 451-1411
828 W Taft Ave Orange (92865) ***(P-14527)***
Redline Prcision Machining Inc...F....909 483-1273
907 E Francis St Ontario (91761) ***(P-11064)***
Redline Solutions Inc...F....408 562-1700
3350 Scott Blvd Bldg 5 Santa Clara (95054) ***(P-15319)***
Redpine Signals Inc (PA)...E....408 748-3385
2107 N 1st St Ste 540 San Jose (95131) ***(P-18511)***
Redseal Inc...D....408 641-2200
1600 Technology Dr Fl 4 San Jose (95110) ***(P-24353)***
Redshark Group Inc...F....925 837-3490
166 Saint Helena Ct Danville (94526) ***(P-6841)***
Redtrac, Bakersfield *Also called Water Associates LLC* ***(P-17703)***
Redwood Apps Inc...F....408 348-3808
805 Veterans Blvd Ste 322 Redwood City (94063) ***(P-24354)***
Redwood Empire Awng & Furn Co...F....707 633-8156
3547 Santa Rosa Ave Santa Rosa (95407) ***(P-3701)***
Redwood Milling Company LLC...E....707 433-1343
12055 Old Redwood Hwy Healdsburg (95448) ***(P-4113)***
Redwood Scientific Tech Inc...E....310 693-5401
11450 Sheldon St Sun Valley (91352) ***(P-8101)***
Redwood Valley Gravel Products...F....707 485-8585
11200 East Rd Redwood Valley (95470) ***(P-10639)***
Redwood Wellness LLC...E....323 843-2676
11814 Jefferson Blvd Culver City (90230) ***(P-2952)***
Redworks Industries LLC...E....949 334-7081
23986 Aliso Creek Rd Laguna Niguel (92677) ***(P-4525)***
Reed LLC...E....909 287-2100
13822 Oaks Ave Chino (91710) ***(P-14597)***
Reed & Graham Inc (PA)...E....408 287-1400
690 Sunol St San Jose (95126) ***(P-9063)***
Reed & Graham Inc...E....888 381-0800
26 Light Sky Ct Sacramento (95828) ***(P-9104)***
Reed Electric & Field Service, Vernon *Also called R A Reed Electric Company* ***(P-24694)***
Reed International (HQ)...E....209 874-2357
13024 Lake Rd Hickman (95323) ***(P-13760)***
Reed Manufacturing, Chino *Also called Reed LLC* ***(P-14597)***
Reed Manufacturing Inc...E....831 637-5641
51 Fallon Rd Hollister (95023) ***(P-11167)***
Reed Mariculture Inc...F....408 377-1065
900 E Hamilton Ave # 100 Campbell (95008) ***(P-1121)***
Reedex Inc...E....714 894-0311
15526 Commerce Ln Huntington Beach (92649) ***(P-19065)***
Reef, Carlsbad *Also called South Cone Inc* ***(P-10176)***
Reel Efx Inc...E....818 762-1710
5539 Riverton Ave North Hollywood (91601) ***(P-23459)***
Reel Picture Productions LLC...D....858 587-0301
5330 Eastgate Mall San Diego (92121) ***(P-19232)***
Reeve Store Equipment Company (PA)...D....562 949-2535
9131 Bermudez St Pico Rivera (90660) ***(P-4999)***
Reeves Enterprises, La Verne *Also called Dennis Reeves Inc* ***(P-4896)***
Reeves Extruded Products Inc...D....661 854-5970
1032 Stockton Ave Arvin (93203) ***(P-9434)***
Refining Technology Division, Orange *Also called Haldor Topsoe Inc* ***(P-7499)***
Refinitiv US LLC...B....415 344-6000
50 California St San Francisco (94111) ***(P-6016)***
Reflectech Inc...F....916 388-7821
5861 88th St Ste 100 Sacramento (95828) ***(P-8413)***
Reflection Technology, Sacramento *Also called Reflectech Inc* ***(P-8413)***
Reflective Images, Novato *Also called Image Star LLC* ***(P-3093)***
Reflex Corporation...E....760 931-9009
1825 Aston Ave Ste A Carlsbad (92008) ***(P-3855)***
Reflex Photonics Inc...E....408 501-8886
1250 Oakmead Pkwy Sunnyvale (94085) ***(P-18512)***
Reflexion Medical Inc...C....650 239-9070
25841 Industrial Blvd # 275 Hayward (94545) ***(P-22301)***
Refresco Beverages US Inc...D....909 915-1400
631 S Waterman Ave San Bernardino (92408) ***(P-2132)***
Refresco Beverages US Inc...E....909 915-1430
499 E Mill St San Bernardino (92408) ***(P-2133)***
Refrigerator Manufacters Inc (PA)...E....562 926-2006
17018 Edwards Rd Cerritos (90703) ***(P-16822)***
Refrigerator Manufacturers LLC...E....562 926-2006
17018 Edwards Rd Cerritos (90703) ***(P-15452)***
Regal Cultured Marble Inc...E....909 802-2388
1239 E Franklin Ave Pomona (91766) ***(P-10928)***
Regal Custom Millwork Inc...F....714 632-2488
301 E Santa Ana St Anaheim (92805) ***(P-3943)***
Regal Electronics Inc (PA)...E....408 988-2288
2029 Otoole Ave San Jose (95131) ***(P-19066)***
Regal Furniture Manufacturing...F....323 971-9185
6007 S St Andrews Pl # 2 Los Angeles (90047) ***(P-4666)***
Regal III LLC...D....707 836-2100
1190 Kittyhawk Blvd Windsor (95492) ***(P-1883)***
Regal Kitchens LLC...C....786 953-6578
3480 Sunset Ln Oxnard (93035) ***(P-4238)***
Regal Machine & Engrg Inc...E....323 773-7462
5200 E 60th St Maywood (90270) ***(P-16348)***
Regal Mfg Co, City of Industry *Also called Creftcon Industries Inc* ***(P-16944)***
Regal Wine Co, Windsor *Also called Regal III LLC* ***(P-1883)***
Regards Enterprises Inc...F....909 983-0655
731 S Taylor Ave Ontario (91761) ***(P-4486)***
Regent Publishing Services...E....760 510-1936
5355 Mira Sorrento Pl # 100 San Diego (92121) ***(P-6328)***
Regina F Barajas...F....760 500-0809
629 Fern St Escondido (92027) ***(P-13744)***
Regional Mtls Recovery Inc...E....760 727-0878
2142 Industrial Ct Ste D Vista (92081) ***(P-293)***
Registrar of Voters Office, Oakland *Also called County of Alameda* ***(P-20963)***
Regulus Intgrted Solutions LLC...E....707 254-4000
860 Latour Ct NAPA (94558) ***(P-6842)***
Regusci Vineyard MGT Inc...E....707 254-0403
5584 Silverado Trl NAPA (94558) ***(P-1884)***
Regusci Winery, NAPA *Also called Regusci Vineyard MGT Inc* ***(P-1884)***
Rehau Constructions, Corona *Also called Rehau Incorporated* ***(P-9477)***
Rehau Incorporated...F....951 549-9017
1250 Corona Pointe Ct # 301 Corona (92879) ***(P-9477)***
Rehrig Pacific Company (HQ)...C....323 262-5145
4010 E 26th St Vernon (90058) ***(P-10011)***
Rehrig Pacific Holdings Inc (PA)...F....323 262-5145
4010 E 26th St Vernon (90058) ***(P-10012)***

Reichert Enterprises Inc..........E.......714 513-9199
2720 S Harbor Blvd Santa Ana (92704) ***(P-23185)***
Reichert's Signs, Santa Ana *Also called Reichert Enterprises Inc* ***(P-23185)***
Reichhold Chemicals, Azusa *Also called Reichhold LLC 2* ***(P-7603)***
Reichhold LLC 2..........F.......626 334-4974
237 S Motor Ave Azusa (91702) ***(P-7603)***
Reid & Clark Screen Arts Co..........F.......619 233-7541
722 33rd St San Diego (92102) ***(P-2846)***
Reid Metal Finishing, Santa Ana *Also called Electrode Technologies Inc* ***(P-12996)***
Reid Plastics, Ontario *Also called Consolidated Container Co LLC* ***(P-9484)***
Reid Plastics Customer Svcs, City of Industry *Also called Consolidated Container Co LLC* ***(P-9719)***
Reid Products Inc..........E.......760 240-1355
21430 Waalew Rd Apple Valley (92307) ***(P-16349)***
Reinhart Oil & Gas Inc..........F.......760 753-3330
1953 San Elijo Ave # 200 Cardiff By The Sea (92007) ***(P-64)***
Reinhold Industries Inc (HQ)..........C.......562 944-3281
12827 Imperial Hwy Santa Fe Springs (90670) ***(P-10013)***
Reisner Enterprises Inc..........F.......951 786-9478
1403 W Linden St Riverside (92507) ***(P-16350)***
Relational Center..........E.......323 935-1807
2717 S Robertson Blvd # 1 Los Angeles (90034) ***(P-24355)***
Relativity Space Inc..........F.......424 393-4309
8701 Aviation Blvd Inglewood (90301) ***(P-11388)***
Relax Medical Systems Inc..........F.......800 405-7677
3260 E Willow St Signal Hill (90755) ***(P-23460)***
Relaxis, San Clemente *Also called Sensory Neurostimulation Inc* ***(P-8124)***
Relcomm Inc..........F.......209 736-0421
4868 Highway 4 Ste G Angels Camp (95222) ***(P-19067)***
Reldom Corporation..........E.......562 498-3346
3241 Industry Dr Signal Hill (90755) ***(P-19392)***
Relectric Inc..........E.......408 467-2222
2390 Zanker Rd San Jose (95131) ***(P-16610)***
Reliable Mill Supply Co..........F.......707 462-1458
1550 Millview Rd Ukiah (95482) ***(P-11065)***
Reliable Packaging Systems Inc..........F.......714 572-1094
1300 N Jefferson St Anaheim (92807) ***(P-8891)***
Reliable Powder Coatings LLC..........F.......510 895-5551
1577 Factor Ave San Leandro (94577) ***(P-13236)***
Reliable Rubber Products Inc..........F.......209 525-9750
2600 Yosemite Blvd Ste B Modesto (95354) ***(P-9363)***
Reliable Sheet Metal Works, Fullerton *Also called Gard Inc* ***(P-12219)***
Reliable Tape Products, Vernon *Also called Chua & Sons Inc* ***(P-2751)***
Reliance Carpet Cushion, Huntington Park *Also called Reliance Upholstery Sup Co Inc* ***(P-3638)***
Reliance Carpet Cushion, Vernon *Also called Reliance Upholstery Supply Inc* ***(P-2953)***
Reliance Computer Corp..........C.......408 492-1915
2451 Mission College Blvd Santa Clara (95054) ***(P-18513)***
Reliance Machine Products Inc..........E.......510 438-6760
4265 Solar Way Fremont (94538) ***(P-16351)***
Reliance Rock, Irwindale *Also called Legacy Vulcan LLC* ***(P-351)***
Reliance Upholstery Sup Co Inc..........D.......323 321-2300
5942 Santa Fe Ave Huntington Park (90255) ***(P-3638)***
Reliance Upholstery Supply Inc..........F.......800 522-5252
4920 S Boyle Ave Vernon (90058) ***(P-2953)***
Reliant Foodservice, Temecula *Also called Canadas Finest Foods Inc* ***(P-906)***
Reloaded Technologies Inc..........F.......949 870-3123
17011 Beach Blvd Ste 320 Huntington Beach (92647) ***(P-24356)***
Rels Foods Inc (PA)..........D.......510 652-2747
1814 Franklin St Ste 310 Oakland (94612) ***(P-2597)***
Relton Corporation..........D.......800 423-1505
317 Rolyn Pl Arcadia (91007) ***(P-9019)***
Relx Inc..........E.......415 908-3200
201 Mission St Fl 26 San Francisco (94105) ***(P-6017)***
Relypsa Inc..........B.......650 421-9500
100 Cardinal Way Redwood City (94063) ***(P-8102)***
Remanfctured Converter MBL LLC..........F.......714 744-8988
582 N Batavia St Orange (92868) ***(P-14790)***
Remanufactured Converter MBL, Orange *Also called Remanfctured Converter MBL LLC* ***(P-14790)***
Remba Partners LLC..........F.......310 858-8495
1419 E Adams Blvd Los Angeles (90011) ***(P-6329)***
Remco, Stockton *Also called Rock Engineered McHy Co Inc* ***(P-9065)***
Remco Mch & Fabrication Inc..........F.......909 877-3530
1966 S Date Ave Bloomington (92316) ***(P-16352)***
Remcor Technical Industries..........E.......619 424-8878
7025 Alamitos Ave San Diego (92154) ***(P-20704)***
Remec Broadband Wire..........C.......858 312-6900
17034 Camino San Bernardo San Diego (92127) ***(P-17643)***
Remec Broadband Wireless LLC (PA)..........C.......858 312-6900
17034 Camino San Bernardo San Diego (92127) ***(P-17644)***
Remedy Blinds Inc..........D.......714 245-0186
220 W Central Ave Santa Ana (92707) ***(P-5035)***
Remington Inc..........E.......661 257-9400
28165 Avenue Crocker Valencia (91355) ***(P-15569)***
Remington Roll Forming Inc..........F.......626 350-5196
2445 Chico Ave El Monte (91733) ***(P-11121)***
Remo Inc (PA)..........B.......661 294-5600
28101 Industry Dr Valencia (91355) ***(P-22633)***
Remote Ocean Systems Inc (PA)..........E.......858 565-8500
5618 Copley Dr San Diego (92111) ***(P-17158)***
Ren Acquisition Inc..........F.......209 245-6979
12225 Steiner Rd Plymouth (95669) ***(P-1885)***
Ren Corporation..........F.......916 739-2000
2201 Francisco Dr El Dorado Hills (95762) ***(P-13665)***
Renaissance Doors & Windows, Rcho STA Marg *Also called Renaissnce Frnch Dors Sash Inc* ***(P-4115)***
Renaissance Food Group LLC (HQ)..........E.......916 638-8825
11020 White Rock Rd Ste 1 Rancho Cordova (95670) ***(P-2598)***
Renaissance Food Inc..........F.......818 778-6230
14540 Friar St Van Nuys (91411) ***(P-1326)***
Renaissance Pastry, Van Nuys *Also called Renaissance Food Inc* ***(P-1326)***
Renaissance Precision Mfg Inc..........F.......925 691-5997
2551 Stanwell Dr Concord Concord (94520) ***(P-16353)***
Renaissance Wdwrk & Design Inc..........F.......818 787-7238
7605 Hazeltine Ave Unit B Van Nuys (91405) ***(P-4114)***
Renaissnce Frnch Dors Sash Inc (PA)..........C.......714 578-0090
38 Segada Rcho STA Marg (92688) ***(P-4115)***
Renau Corporation..........E.......818 341-1994
9309 Deering Ave Chatsworth (91311) ***(P-20928)***
Renau Electronic Laboratories, Chatsworth *Also called Renau Corporation* ***(P-20928)***
Renee C..........F.......213 741-0095
127 E 9th St Ste 506 Los Angeles (90015) ***(P-3274)***
Renee Claire Inc, Los Angeles *Also called Camp Smidgemore Inc* ***(P-3301)***
Renee Rivera Hair Accessories..........F.......415 776-6613
2295 Chestnut St Ste 2 San Francisco (94123) ***(P-9364)***
Renesas Electronics Amer Inc..........A.......408 546-3434
205 Llagas Rd Morgan Hill (95037) ***(P-18514)***
Renesas Electronics Amer Inc (HQ)..........B.......408 432-8888
1001 Murphy Ranch Rd Milpitas (95035) ***(P-19068)***
Renesas Electronics Amer Inc..........A.......858 451-7240
10865 Rancho Bernardo Rd San Diego (92127) ***(P-18515)***
Renkus-Heinz Inc..........D.......949 588-9997
19201 Cook St Foothill Ranch (92610) ***(P-17276)***
Rennovia Inc..........F.......650 804-7400
3040 Oakmead Village Dr Santa Clara (95051) ***(P-8771)***
Reno News & Review, Chico *Also called Chico Community Publishing* ***(P-5586)***
Reno Tenco, Boron *Also called Rio Tinto Minerals Inc* ***(P-19)***
Renos Floor Covering Inc..........F.......415 459-1403
1515 Solano Ave Vallejo (94590) ***(P-23255)***
Renovare International Inc..........F.......510 748-9993
849 Balra Dr El Cerrito (94530) ***(P-15570)***
Rent What, Compton *Also called Sew What Inc* ***(P-3597)***
Rentech Inc (PA)..........D.......310 571-9800
10880 Wilshire Blvd # 1101 Los Angeles (90024) ***(P-9161)***
Rentech Ntrgn Pasadena Spa LLC..........F.......310 571-9805
10877 Wilshire Blvd # 710 Los Angeles (90024) ***(P-8802)***
Renu Chem Inc..........F.......951 736-8072
572 Malloy Ct Corona (92880) ***(P-8414)***
Renwood Winery, NAPA *Also called Rombauer Vineyards Inc* ***(P-1895)***
Reny & Co Inc..........F.......626 962-3078
4505 Littlejohn St Baldwin Park (91706) ***(P-10014)***
Renymed, Baldwin Park *Also called Reny & Co Inc* ***(P-10014)***
Rep-Kote Products Inc..........E.......909 355-1288
10938 Beech Ave Fontana (92337) ***(P-9124)***
Repet Inc..........C.......909 594-5333
14207 Monte Vista Ave Chino (91710) ***(P-9453)***
Replacement Parts Inds Inc..........E.......818 882-8611
625 Cochran St Simi Valley (93065) ***(P-22186)***
Replenish Inc..........F.......626 219-7867
73 N Vinedo Ave Pasadena (91107) ***(P-21874)***
Reporter..........D.......707 448-6401
916 Cotting Ln Vacaville (95688) ***(P-5809)***
Repose Corp..........F.......562 921-9299
16826 Edwards Rd Cerritos (90703) ***(P-16840)***
Repro Magic..........F.......858 277-2488
8585 Miramar Pl San Diego (92121) ***(P-6843)***
Reprodox, Santa Ana *Also called Maria Corporation* ***(P-7131)***
Repsco Inc..........E.......303 294-0364
5300 Claus Rd Ste 3 Modesto (95357) ***(P-10015)***
Republic Bag Inc (PA)..........C.......951 734-9740
580 E Harrison St Corona (92879) ***(P-5415)***
Republic Furniture Mfg Inc..........E.......323 235-2144
2241 E 49th St Vernon (90058) ***(P-4667)***
Republic Iron Works, El Monte *Also called P S R Iron Works* ***(P-11856)***
Republic Machinery Co Inc (PA)..........E.......310 518-1100
800 Sprucelake Dr Harbor City (90710) ***(P-13943)***
Res Med Inc..........E.......858 746-2400
9001 Spectrum Center Blvd San Diego (92123) ***(P-21875)***
Rescue 42 Inc..........F.......530 891-3473
370 Ryan Ave Ste 120 Chico (95973) ***(P-14855)***
Research & Dev GL Pdts &, Berkeley *Also called Research & Dev GL Pdts & Eqp* ***(P-10388)***
Research & Dev GL Pdts & Eqp..........F.......510 547-6464
1808 Harmon St Berkeley (94703) ***(P-10388)***
Research Metal Industries Inc..........E.......310 352-3200
1970 W 139th St Gardena (90249) ***(P-16354)***
Research Way LI LLC..........F.......608 830-6300
1900 Main St Ste 375 Irvine (92614) ***(P-8103)***
Research Way Partners, Irvine *Also called Research Way LI LLC* ***(P-8103)***
Reshape Lifesciences Inc (PA)..........D.......949 429-6680
1001 Calle Amanecer San Clemente (92673) ***(P-22302)***
Residential Ctrl Systems Inc..........E.......916 635-6784
11481 Sunrise Gold Cir # 1 Rancho Cordova (95742) ***(P-20807)***
Resideo Buoy, Santa Cruz *Also called Buoy Labs Inc* ***(P-23703)***
Resina..........F.......951 296-6585
27455 Bostik Ct Temecula (92590) ***(P-15391)***
Resinart Corporation..........E.......949 642-3665
1621 Placentia Ave Costa Mesa (92627) ***(P-10016)***
Resinart Plastics, Costa Mesa *Also called Resinart Corporation* ***(P-10016)***
Resmed Inc (PA)..........B.......858 836-5000
9001 Spectrum Center Blvd San Diego (92123) ***(P-21876)***
Resmed Motor Technologies Inc..........C.......818 428-6400
9540 De Soto Ave Chatsworth (91311) ***(P-16670)***
Resonance Technology Inc..........F.......818 882-1997
18121 Parthenia St Ste A Northridge (91325) ***(P-22303)***

A L P H A B E T I C

Employee Codes: A=Over 500 employees, B=251-500
C=101-250, D=51-100, E=20-50, F=10-19
2020 California
Manfacturers Register
© Mergent Inc. 1-800-342-5647
1221

Resonant Inc (PA)..........D......805 308-9803
175 Cremona Dr Ste 200 Goleta (93117) ***(P-18516)***
Resource Cementing LLC..........F......707 374-3350
2500 Airport Rd Rio Vista (94571) ***(P-253)***
Resource Ctr For Nonviolence, Santa Cruz *Also called Eschaton Foundation* ***(P-6566)***
Resource Label Group LLC..........E......510 477-0707
30803 San Clemente St Hayward (94544) ***(P-7195)***
Respiratory Support Products..........E......619 710-1000
9255 Customhouse Plz N San Diego (92154) ***(P-21877)***
Respironics Inc..........F......562 483-6805
14101 Rosecrans Ave Ste F La Mirada (90638) ***(P-22077)***
Response Envelope Inc (PA)..........C......909 923-5855
1340 S Baker Ave Ontario (91761) ***(P-7196)***
Response Graphics In Print..........F......949 376-8701
1065 La Mirada St Laguna Beach (92651) ***(P-7197)***
Resq Manufacturing..........E......916 638-6786
11365 Sunrise Park Dr # 200 Rancho Cordova (95742) ***(P-23461)***
Resta Mattress, Rancho Cucamonga *Also called Comfort-Pedic Mattress USA* ***(P-4715)***
Restonic/San Francisco, Burlingame *Also called Sleeprite Industries Inc* ***(P-4743)***
Restoration Robotics Inc (PA)..........D......408 457-1280
1972 Hartog Dr San Jose (95131) ***(P-21878)***
Resumemailman, Carlsbad *Also called Edirect Publishing Inc* ***(P-6226)***
Retail Content Service Inc..........E......415 890-2097
440 N Wolfe Rd Sunnyvale (94085) ***(P-6330)***
Retail Print Media Inc..........E......424 488-6950
2355 Crenshaw Blvd # 135 Torrance (90501) ***(P-7198)***
Retail Solutions Incorporated (PA)..........E......650 390-6100
100 Century Center Ct # 800 San Jose (95112) ***(P-24357)***
Retech Systems LLC..........C......707 462-6522
100 Henry Station Rd Ukiah (95482) ***(P-11711)***
Rethink Label Systems, Anaheim *Also called Labeltronix LLC* ***(P-7115)***
Retrophin Inc (PA)..........D......760 260-8600
3721 Vly Cntre Dr Ste 200 San Diego (92130) ***(P-8104)***
Retrospect Inc..........E......888 376-1078
44 Westwind Rd Lafayette (94549) ***(P-24358)***
Rettig Machine Inc..........E......909 793-7811
301 Kansas St Redlands (92373) ***(P-24661)***
Reuland Electric Co (PA)..........C......626 964-6411
17969 Railroad St City of Industry (91748) ***(P-16671)***
Reuser Inc..........F......707 894-4224
370 Santana Dr Cloverdale (95425) ***(P-3944)***
Reuters Television La, Los Angeles *Also called Thomson Reuters Corporation* ***(P-17691)***
Rev Co Spring Mfanufacturing..........F......562 949-1958
9915 Alburtis Ave Santa Fe Springs (90670) ***(P-13387)***
Reva Medical Inc..........D......858 966-3000
5751 Copley Dr Ste B San Diego (92111) ***(P-22078)***
Revance Therapeutics Inc..........C......510 742-3400
7555 Gateway Blvd Newark (94560) ***(P-8105)***
Reveal Imaging Tech Inc..........D......858 826-9909
10260 Campus Point Dr # 6133 San Diego (92121) ***(P-20705)***
Reveal Windows & Doors, Brea *Also called Pacific Archtectural Mllwk Inc* ***(P-4102)***
Revera Incorporated..........E......408 510-7400
3090 Oakmead Village Dr Santa Clara (95051) ***(P-15320)***
Reverie On Diamond Mtn LLC..........F......707 942-6800
4410 Lake County Hwy Calistoga (94515) ***(P-1886)***
Reverie Winery, Calistoga *Also called Reverie On Diamond Mtn LLC* ***(P-1886)***
Reverse Medical Corporation..........F......949 215-0660
13700 Alton Pkwy Ste 167 Irvine (92618) ***(P-21879)***
Reversica Design Inc..........F......831 459-9033
1900 Commercial Way Ste A Santa Cruz (95065) ***(P-11623)***
Review Concierge, Solana Beach *Also called Expert Reputation LLC* ***(P-23885)***
Revivogen, Los Angeles *Also called Advanced Skin & Hair Inc* ***(P-8433)***
Revjet..........C......650 508-2215
981 Industrial Rd Ste F San Carlos (94070) ***(P-24359)***
Revlon Inc..........E......760 599-2900
1125 Joshua Way Ste 12 Vista (92081) ***(P-8571)***
Revolution Enterprises Inc..........F......858 679-5785
12170 Dearborn Pl Poway (92064) ***(P-22871)***
Revolution Screening Inc (PA)..........F......916 604-6865
2523 Evergreen Ave West Sacramento (95691) ***(P-7199)***
Revolutionario, Los Angeles *Also called Susan Zadi* ***(P-2272)***
Rex Creamery, Commerce *Also called Heritage Distributing Company* ***(P-702)***
Rexhall Industries Inc..........E......661 726-5470
26857 Tannahill Ave Canyon Country (91387) ***(P-19843)***
Rexnord Industries LLC..........C......805 583-5514
2175 Union Pl Simi Valley (93065) ***(P-14396)***
Rexnord LLC..........C......909 467-8102
3690 Jurupa St Ontario (91761) ***(P-14748)***
Reyes Coca-Cola Bottling LLC (PA)..........B......213 744-8616
3 Park Plz Ste 600 Irvine (92614) ***(P-2134)***
Reyes Coca-Cola Bottling LLC..........D......661 324-6531
4320 Ride St Bakersfield (93313) ***(P-2135)***
Reyes Coca-Cola Bottling LLC..........D......408 436-3700
1555 Old Bayshore Hwy San Jose (95112) ***(P-2136)***
Reyes Coca-Cola Bottling LLC..........D......562 803-8100
8729 Cleta St Downey (90241) ***(P-2137)***
Reyes Coca-Cola Bottling LLC..........D......510 476-7000
1551 Atlantic St Union City (94587) ***(P-2138)***
Reyes Coca-Cola Bottling LLC..........C......510 667-6300
14655 Wicks Blvd San Leandro (94577) ***(P-2139)***
Reyes Coca-Cola Bottling LLC..........D......559 264-4631
3220 E Malaga Ave Fresno (93725) ***(P-2140)***
Reyes Coca-Cola Bottling LLC..........D......805 644-2211
5335 Walker St Ventura (93003) ***(P-2141)***
Reyes Coca-Cola Bottling LLC..........E......209 466-9501
1467 El Pinal Dr Stockton (95205) ***(P-2142)***
Reyes Coca-Cola Bottling LLC..........D......760 396-4500
86375 Industrial Way Coachella (92236) ***(P-2143)***
Reyes Coca-Cola Bottling LLC..........E......805 925-2629
120 E Jones St Santa Maria (93454) ***(P-2144)***
Reyes Coca-Cola Bottling LLC..........D......831 755-8300
715 Vandenberg St Salinas (93905) ***(P-2145)***
Reyes Coca-Cola Bottling LLC..........C......909 980-3121
10670 6th St Rancho Cucamonga (91730) ***(P-2146)***
Reyes Coca-Cola Bottling LLC..........D......805 614-3702
1000 Fairway Dr Santa Maria (93455) ***(P-2147)***
Reyes Coca-Cola Bottling LLC..........E......530 241-4315
1580 Beltline Rd Redding (96003) ***(P-2148)***
Reyes Coca-Cola Bottling LLC..........E......619 266-6300
1348 47th St San Diego (92102) ***(P-2149)***
Reyes Coca-Cola Bottling LLC..........D......323 278-2600
666 Union St Montebello (90640) ***(P-2150)***
Reyes Coca-Cola Bottling LLC..........E......530 743-6533
1430 Melody Rd Marysville (95901) ***(P-2151)***
Reyes Coca-Cola Bottling LLC..........C......714 974-1901
700 W Grove Ave Orange (92865) ***(P-2152)***
Reyes Coca-Cola Bottling LLC..........C......707 747-2000
530 Getty Ct Benicia (94510) ***(P-2153)***
Reyes Coca-Cola Bottling LLC..........E......213 744-8659
1338 E 14th St Los Angeles (90021) ***(P-2154)***
Reyes Coca-Cola Bottling LLC..........D......925 830-6500
2603 Camino Ramon Ste 550 San Ramon (94583) ***(P-2155)***
Reyes Coca-Cola Bottling LLC..........C......310 965-2653
19875 Pacific Gateway Dr Torrance (90502) ***(P-2156)***
Reyes Coca-Cola Bottling LLC..........E......760 241-2653
15346 Anacapa Rd Victorville (92392) ***(P-2157)***
Reyes Coca-Cola Bottling LLC..........E......760 352-1561
126 S 3rd St El Centro (92243) ***(P-2158)***
Reyes Machining, El Cajon *Also called Kings Crating Inc* ***(P-12833)***
Reyes Machining, El Cajon *Also called Kings Crating Inc* ***(P-19969)***
Reynaldos Mexican Food Co LLC (PA)..........C......562 803-3188
3301 E Vernon Ave Vernon (90058) ***(P-744)***
Reynard Corporation..........E......949 366-8866
1020 Calle Sombra San Clemente (92673) ***(P-21402)***
Reynen Court LLC..........F......917 588-0746
2 Blair Ave Piedmont (94611) ***(P-24360)***
Reynolds Systems Inc..........F......707 928-5244
18649 State Highway 175 Middletown (95461) ***(P-13272)***
Reyrich Plastics Inc..........F......909 484-8444
1734 S Vineyard Ave Ontario (91761) ***(P-10017)***
Rezex Corporation..........E......213 622-2015
1930 E 51st St Vernon (90058) ***(P-2859)***
Rezolute Inc (PA)..........E......303 222-2128
570 El Camino Rd Redwood City (94063) ***(P-8106)***
Rf Communiactions, San Diego *Also called L3harris Technologies Inc* ***(P-20599)***
Rf Digital Corporation..........C......949 610-0008
1601 Pcf Cast Hwy Ste 290 Hermosa Beach (90254) ***(P-18517)***
Rf Industries Ltd (PA)..........D......858 549-6340
7610 Miramar Rd Ste 6000 San Diego (92126) ***(P-18787)***
Rf Precision Cables Inc..........F......714 772-7567
1600 S Anaheim Blvd Ste A Anaheim (92805) ***(P-11317)***
Rf Surgical Systems LLC..........D......855 522-7027
5927 Landau Ct Carlsbad (92008) ***(P-21880)***
Rf Techniques, San Jose *Also called M R F Techniques Inc* ***(P-18998)***
Rf-Lambda Usa LLC..........F......972 767-5998
10509 Vista Sorrento Pkwy # 120 San Diego (92121) ***(P-16743)***
Rfa Medical Solutions..........F......510 583-9500
40874 Calido Pl Fremont (94539) ***(P-22304)***
Rfc Wire Forms Inc..........D......909 467-0559
525 Brooks St Ontario (91762) ***(P-13433)***
Rfid4u, Concord *Also called Esmart Source Inc* ***(P-23875)***
Rfl Global Inc..........F......323 235-2580
732 E Jefferson Blvd Los Angeles (90011) ***(P-24361)***
RG Costumes & Accessories Inc..........E......626 858-9559
726 Arrow Grand Cir Covina (91722) ***(P-3576)***
Rga, Laguna Hills *Also called R Goodloe & Associates Inc* ***(P-6827)***
Rgb Spectrum..........D......510 814-7000
950 Marina Village Pkwy Alameda (94501) ***(P-15321)***
Rgb Systems Inc (PA)..........C......714 491-1500
1025 E Ball Rd Ste 100 Anaheim (92805) ***(P-15322)***
Rgblase LLC..........F......510 585-8449
3984 Washington Blvd # 306 Fremont (94538) ***(P-19393)***
RGF Enterprises Inc..........E......951 734-6922
220 Citation Cir Corona (92880) ***(P-13237)***
Rgm Products Inc..........B......559 499-2222
3301 Navone Rd Stockton (95215) ***(P-9125)***
Rgr Diversified Services Inc..........F......562 522-0028
5635 Panorama Dr Whittier (90601) ***(P-4739)***
Rh Products Inc..........E......510 794-6676
6756 Central Ave Ste E Newark (94560) ***(P-4395)***
RH Strasbaugh (PA)..........D......805 541-6424
825 Buckley Rd San Luis Obispo (93401) ***(P-13944)***
Rh Usa Inc..........E......925 245-7900
455 N Canyons Pkwy Ste B Livermore (94551) ***(P-21881)***
Rh Wood Products, Newark *Also called Rh Products Inc* ***(P-4395)***
Rhapsody Clothing Inc..........D......213 614-8887
810 E Pico Blvd Ste 24 Los Angeles (90021) ***(P-3398)***
Rheetech Sales & Services Inc..........F......213 749-9111
2401 S Main St Los Angeles (90007) ***(P-7200)***
Rhema Net Corp, Walnut *Also called Noodoe Inc* ***(P-16666)***
Rheosense Inc..........F......925 866-3801
2420 Camino Ramon Ste 240 San Ramon (94583) ***(P-21531)***
Rhino Linings Corporation (PA)..........D......858 450-0441
9747 Businesspark Ave San Diego (92131) ***(P-14640)***
Rhino Manufacturing Group Inc..........F......866 624-8844
14440 Meadowrun St San Diego (92129) ***(P-11066)***
Rhino Valve Usa Inc..........F......661 587-0220
5833 Pembroke Ave Bakersfield (93308) ***(P-13320)***

Rhodes Publications Inc ... F ... 213 385-4781
3600 Wilshire Blvd # 1526 Los Angeles (90010) *(P-6018)*
RHS Gas Inc ... F ... 310 710-2331
520 W Pacific Coast Hwy Long Beach (90806) *(P-9064)*
Rhub Communications Inc ... F ... 408 899-2830
4340 Stevens Creek Blvd San Jose (95129) *(P-19394)*
Rhys Vineyards LLC ... F ... 650 419-2050
11715 Skyline Blvd Los Gatos (95033) *(P-1887)*
RI, Santa Clara *Also called Roos Instruments Inc (P-21114)*
Riah Fashion Inc ... F ... 323 325-7308
1820 E 46th St Vernon (90058) *(P-3399)*
Rialto Concrete Products, Rialto *Also called Kti Incorporated (P-10594)*
Rialto Record, San Bernardino *Also called Inland Empire Cmnty Newspapers (P-5673)*
Ricardo Defense Inc (HQ) ... E ... 805 882-1884
175 Cremona Dr Ste 140 Goleta (93117) *(P-19756)*
Ricardo Ochoa ... F ... 530 668-1152
281 N Pioneer Ave Woodland (95776) *(P-5262)*
Ricaurte Precision Inc ... E ... 714 667-0632
1550 E Mcfadden Ave Santa Ana (92705) *(P-16355)*
Rice Field Corporation ... C ... 626 968-6917
14500 Valley Blvd City of Industry (91746) *(P-492)*
Rich Chicks LLC ... E ... 209 879-4104
13771 Gramercy Pl Gardena (90249) *(P-526)*
Rich Chicks LLC (PA) ... E ... 209 879-4104
4276 N Tracy Blvd Tracy (95304) *(P-527)*
Rich Chicks, Rich In Nutrition, Tracy *Also called Rich Chicks LLC (P-527)*
Rich Limited, Oceanside *Also called Britcan Inc (P-4964)*
Rich Products ... F ... 510 234-7547
1041 Broadway Ave San Pablo (94806) *(P-19757)*
Rich Products Corporation ... C ... 559 486-7380
320 O St Fresno (93721) *(P-2268)*
Rich Xiberta Usa Inc ... F ... 707 795-1800
450 Aaron St Cotati (94931) *(P-4526)*
Richandre Inc ... F ... 310 762-1560
1170 Sandhill Ave Carson (90746) *(P-977)*
Richard E Cox Interprizes, Rocklin *Also called Vanishing Vistas (P-6372)*
Richard K Gould Inc ... E ... 916 371-5943
788 Northport Dr West Sacramento (95691) *(P-9020)*
Richard Macdonald Studios Inc (PA) ... F ... 831 655-0424
16 Lower Ragsdale Dr Monterey (93940) *(P-11020)*
Richard Ray Custom Designs ... F ... 323 937-5685
11350 Alethea Dr Sunland (91040) *(P-16988)*
Richard Sanchez ... F ... 805 455-2904
531 Montgomery Ave Oxnard (93036) *(P-12504)*
Richard Tyler, Alhambra *Also called Tyler Trafficante Inc (P-2980)*
Richard Veeck ... F ... 209 667-0872
9966 Golf Link Rd Hilmar (95324) *(P-14528)*
Richard Yarbrough ... E ... 805 643-1021
2493 N Ventura Ave Ventura (93001) *(P-254)*
Richards Label Co Inc ... F ... 714 529-1791
17291 Mount Herrmann St Fountain Valley (92708) *(P-5372)*
Richards Machining Co Inc ... F ... 408 526-9219
2161 Del Franco St San Jose (95131) *(P-16356)*
Richards Neon Shop Inc ... E ... 951 279-6767
4375 Prado Rd Ste 102 Corona (92880) *(P-23186)*
Richardson Steel Inc ... E ... 619 697-5892
9102 Harness St Ste A Spring Valley (91977) *(P-11873)*
Richee Lighting Inc ... F ... 213 814-1638
1600 W Washington Blvd Los Angeles (90007) *(P-17159)*
Richline Group Inc ... C ... 818 848-5555
455 N Moss St Burbank (91502) *(P-22562)*
Richline Group Inc ... C ... 818 848-5555
443 N Varney St Burbank (91502) *(P-22563)*
Richmond Optical Co ... F ... 510 783-1420
923 Berryessa Rd San Jose (95133) *(P-22382)*
Richter Furniture Mfg 2002 ... C ... 323 588-7900
28720 Canwood St Ste 108 Agoura Hills (91301) *(P-5078)*
Richter Furniture Mfr Rfm, Agoura Hills *Also called Richter Furniture Mfg 2002 (P-5078)*
Richview By Tehdex, City of Industry *Also called Ht Window Fashions Corporation (P-5025)*
Richwood Meat Company Inc ... D ... 209 722-8171
2751 N Santa Fe Ave Merced (95348) *(P-423)*
Rick Palenshus ... F ... 951 245-2100
560 3rd St Lake Elsinore (92530) *(P-14529)*
Rick's Hitches & Welding, El Cajon *Also called C L P Inc (P-24620)*
Rickshaw Bagworks Inc ... E ... 415 904-8368
904 22nd St San Francisco (94107) *(P-3663)*
Ricky Reader LLC ... F ... 323 231-4322
6715 Mckinley Ave Unit B Los Angeles (90001) *(P-6141)*
Ricman Mfg Inc ... E ... 510 670-1785
2273 American Ave Ste 1 Hayward (94545) *(P-16357)*
Rico Corporation (HQ) ... E ... 818 394-2700
8484 San Fernando Rd Sun Valley (91352) *(P-22634)*
Rico Holdings Inc ... C ... 818 394-2700
8484 San Fernando Rd Sun Valley (91352) *(P-22635)*
Rico Products, Sun Valley *Also called Rico Corporation (P-22634)*
Ricoh Development California, Tustin *Also called Ricoh Electronics Inc (P-22455)*
Ricoh Electronics Inc (HQ) ... B ... 714 566-2500
1100 Valencia Ave Tustin (92780) *(P-22455)*
Ricoh Electronics Inc ... B ... 714 259-1220
17482 Pullman St Irvine (92614) *(P-15392)*
Ricoh Prtg Systems Amer Inc (HQ) ... B ... 805 578-4000
2390 Ward Ave Ste A Simi Valley (93065) *(P-15323)*
Ricon Corp (HQ) ... C ... 818 267-3000
1135 Aviation Pl San Fernando (91340) *(P-23462)*
Rideau Vineyard LLC ... F ... 805 688-0717
1562 Alamo Pintado Rd Solvang (93463) *(P-1888)*
Rider Circulation Services ... F ... 323 344-1200
1324 Cypress Ave Los Angeles (90065) *(P-5810)*
Ridge Cast Metals, San Leandro *Also called Ridge Foundry Inc (P-11148)*
Ridge Foundry Inc ... E ... 510 352-0551
1554 Doolittle Dr San Leandro (94577) *(P-11148)*
Ridgeline, Stockton *Also called Rgm Products Inc (P-9125)*
Ridgeline Engineering Company, Vista *Also called Rec Inc (P-14854)*
Ridout Plastics Company ... E ... 858 560-1551
5535 Ruffin Rd San Diego (92123) *(P-9418)*
Riedon Inc ... F ... 562 926-2304
13065 Tom White Way Ste F Norwalk (90650) *(P-21112)*
Riedon Inc (PA) ... C ... 626 284-9901
300 Cypress Ave Alhambra (91801) *(P-18691)*
Rieke Corporation ... C ... 707 238-9250
1200 Valley House Dr # 100 Rohnert Park (94928) *(P-12752)*
Riffyn Inc (PA) ... F ... 510 542-9868
484 9th St Oakland (94607) *(P-24362)*
Rigel Pharmaceuticals Inc (PA) ... C ... 650 624-1100
1180 Veterans Blvd South San Francisco (94080) *(P-8107)*
Riggins Engineering Inc ... E ... 818 782-7010
13932 Saticoy St Van Nuys (91402) *(P-16358)*
Right Away Concrete Pmpg Inc ... E ... 510 536-1900
401 Kennedy St Oakland (94606) *(P-10818)*
Right Hand Manufacturing Inc ... C ... 619 819-5056
180 Otay Lakes Rd Ste 205 Bonita (91902) *(P-16744)*
Right Manufacturing LLC ... E ... 858 566-7002
7949 Stromesa Ct Ste G San Diego (92126) *(P-13483)*
Rightway, Vernon *Also called R B R Meat Company Inc (P-421)*
Rigiflex Technology Inc ... E ... 714 688-1500
1166 N Grove St Anaheim (92806) *(P-17976)*
Rignoli Pacific, Monterey Park *Also called Rigoli Enterprises Inc (P-19395)*
Rigoli Enterprises Inc ... F ... 626 573-0242
1983 Potrero Grande Dr Monterey Park (91755) *(P-19395)*
Rigos Equipment Mfg LLC ... E ... 626 813-6621
14501 Joanbridge St Baldwin Park (91706) *(P-12354)*
Rigos Sheet Metal, Baldwin Park *Also called Rigos Equipment Mfg LLC (P-12354)*
Rileys TANKs/D&j Service ... F ... 559 237-1403
3261 S Elm Ave Fresno (93706) *(P-12046)*
Rima Enterprises Inc ... D ... 714 893-4534
5340 Argosy Ave Huntington Beach (92649) *(P-14340)*
Rima-System, Huntington Beach *Also called Rima Enterprises Inc (P-14340)*
Rimnetics Inc ... E ... 650 969-6590
3445 De La Cruz Blvd Santa Clara (95054) *(P-10018)*
Rinat Neuroscience Corp ... F ... 650 615-7300
230 E Grand Ave South San Francisco (94080) *(P-8108)*
Rinco International Inc ... F ... 510 785-1633
31056 Genstar Rd Hayward (94544) *(P-9566)*
Rincon Engineering Corporation ... E ... 805 684-0935
6325 Carpinteria Ave Carpinteria (93013) *(P-16359)*
Rincon Ironworks, Oxnard *Also called Richard Sanchez (P-12504)*
Ring Container Tech LLC ... E ... 209 238-3426
3643 Finch Rd Modesto (95357) *(P-9494)*
Ring Container Tech LLC ... E ... 909 350-8416
8275 Almeria Ave Fontana (92335) *(P-9495)*
Ring LLC (HQ) ... B ... 800 656-1918
1523 26th St Santa Monica (90404) *(P-16573)*
Ring of Fire, Van Nuys *Also called Rof LLC (P-3050)*
Rinsekit, Carlsbad *Also called Outsol Inc (P-9593)*
Rio Pluma Company LLC (HQ) ... E ... 530 846-5200
1900 Highway 99 Gridley (95948) *(P-820)*
Rio Tinto Minerals Inc ... C ... 760 762-7121
14486 Borax Rd Boron (93516) *(P-19)*
Rios-Lovell Estate Winery ... E ... 925 443-0434
6500 Tesla Rd Livermore (94550) *(P-1889)*
Rios-Lovell Winery, Livermore *Also called Rios-Lovell Estate Winery (P-1889)*
Rip Curl Inc (HQ) ... D ... 714 422-3600
3030 Airway Ave Costa Mesa (92626) *(P-22872)*
Rip Curl USA, Costa Mesa *Also called Rip Curl Inc (P-22872)*
Rip-Tie Inc ... F ... 510 577-0200
883 San Leandro Blvd San Leandro (94577) *(P-2914)*
Ripon Mfg Co ... E ... 209 599-2148
652 S Stockton Ave Ripon (95366) *(P-14397)*
Ripon Milling LLC ... E ... 209 599-4269
30636 E Carter Rd Farmington (95230) *(P-1122)*
Ripon Volunteer Firemans Assn ... F ... 209 599-4209
142 S Stockton Ave Ripon (95366) *(P-19498)*
Rippling, San Francisco *Also called People Center Inc (P-24293)*
Risco Inc ... E ... 951 769-2899
390 Risco Cir Beaumont (92223) *(P-12691)*
Rise Bar, Irvine *Also called Divine Foods Inc (P-1363)*
Rising Beverage Company LLC ... D ... 310 556-4500
10351 Santa Monica Blvd Los Angeles (90025) *(P-2159)*
Risvolds Inc ... D ... 323 770-2674
1234 W El Segundo Blvd Gardena (90247) *(P-2599)*
Rita Medical Systems Inc (HQ) ... D ... 510 771-0400
46421 Landing Pkwy Fremont (94538) *(P-22305)*
Ritas Felicita ... F ... 760 975-3302
1875 S Centre City Pkwy Escondido (92025) *(P-665)*
Ritas Fine Food ... F ... 619 698-3925
8900 Grossmont Blvd Ste 5 La Mesa (91941) *(P-2600)*
Ritchey Design Inc (PA) ... F ... 650 368-4018
236 N Santa Cruz Ave # 238 Los Gatos (95030) *(P-20424)*
Rite Screen, Rancho Cucamonga *Also called J T Walker Industries Inc (P-11959)*
Rite Track Equipment Svcs Inc ... F ... 408 432-0131
2151 Otoole Ave Ste 40 San Jose (95131) *(P-14530)*
Ritec, Simi Valley *Also called Rugged Info Tech Eqp Corp (P-15325)*
Ritemp Refrigeration Inc ... F ... 909 941-0444
9155 Archibald Ave # 503 Rancho Cucamonga (91730) *(P-16823)*
Ritescreen Inc ... F ... 800 949-4174
33444 Western Ave Union City (94587) *(P-4116)*

Employee Codes: A=Over 500 employees, B=251-500
C=101-250, D=51-100, E=20-50, F=10-19
2020 California
Manfacturers Register
© Mergent Inc. 1-800-342-5647
1223

Rivas Industries Inc F 951 880-8638
6687 Havenhurst St Eastvale (92880) ***(P-6844)***

River Bench Vineyards F 805 324-4100
137 Anacapa St Santa Barbara (93101) ***(P-1890)***

River City E 707 253-1111
505 Lincoln Ave NAPA (94558) ***(P-5079)***

River City Millwork Inc E 916 364-8981
3045 Fite Cir Sacramento (95827) ***(P-4117)***

River City Print and Mail Inc F 916 638-8400
2431 Mercantile Dr Ste G Rancho Cordova (95742) ***(P-6845)***

River City Printers LLC E 916 638-8400
4251 Gateway Park Blvd Sacramento (95834) ***(P-6846)***

River City Restaurant, NAPA *Also called River City* ***(P-5079)***

River Ready Mix, Forestville *Also called Canyon Rock Co Inc* ***(P-334)***

River Valley Precast Inc E 928 764-3839
14796 Washington Dr Fontana (92335) ***(P-10640)***

Rivera Yarn Products Inc E 619 661-6306
1690 Cactus Rd San Diego (92154) ***(P-2758)***

Riverbend Rice Mill Inc F 530 458-8561
234 Main St Colusa (95932) ***(P-1050)***

Rivermeadow Software Inc F 408 217-6498
2107 N 1st St Ste 660 San Jose (95131) ***(P-24363)***

Riverside Bulletin & Jurupa Th, Riverside *Also called Metropolitan News Company* ***(P-5752)***

Riverside Foundary, Riverside *Also called Oldcast Precast* ***(P-10609)***

Riverside Lamination Corp F 951 682-0100
3016 Kansas Ave Bldg 6 Riverside (92507) ***(P-8892)***

Riverside Machine Works Inc F 951 685-7416
6301 Baldwin Ave Riverside (92509) ***(P-16360)***

Riverside Tent & Awning Co F 951 683-1925
231 E Alcandro Blvd Ste A Riverside (92508) ***(P-3664)***

Riviera Beverages LLC E 714 895-5169
12782 Monarch St Garden Grove (92841) ***(P-2160)***

Rizo-Lopez Foods Inc C 800 626-5587
201 S Mcclure Rd Modesto (95357) ***(P-570)***

RJ Acquisition Corp (PA) C 323 318-1107
3260 E 26th St Vernon (90058) ***(P-7201)***

Rj Boudreau Inc F 209 480-3172
1641 Princeton Ave Ste 6 Modesto (95350) ***(P-13666)***

RJ Jewelry Inc F 213 627-9936
650 S Hill St Ste 414 Los Angeles (90014) ***(P-22564)***

Rj Machine Inc F 858 547-9482
7985 Dunbrook Rd Ste E San Diego (92126) ***(P-16361)***

Rj Media F 510 938-8667
1860 Mowry Ave Ste 200 Fremont (94538) ***(P-5811)***

RJ Mfg F 209 632-9708
1201 S Blaker Rd Turlock (95380) ***(P-2915)***

RJ Singer International Inc D 323 735-1717
4801 W Jefferson Blvd Los Angeles (90016) ***(P-10204)***

RJA Industries Inc E 818 998-5124
9640 Topanga Canyon Pl J Chatsworth (91311) ***(P-19069)***

Rjb, Modesto *Also called Rj Boudreau Inc* ***(P-13666)***

Rjw & Assoc F 818 706-0289
31700 Dunraven Ct Ste 100 Thousand Oaks (91361) ***(P-6331)***

Rk Sport Inc E 951 894-7883
26900 Jefferson Ave Murrieta (92562) ***(P-19758)***

Rkd Engineering Corp Inc F 831 430-9464
316 S Navarra Dr Scotts Valley (95066) ***(P-18518)***

Rks Inc (HQ) F 858 571-4444
1955 Cordell Ct Ste 104 El Cajon (92020) ***(P-19396)***

Rlf Print Shop, Fresno *Also called Dreamteam Business Group LLC* ***(P-7051)***

Rlh Industries Inc (PA) E 714 532-1672
936 N Main St Orange (92867) ***(P-17409)***

Rls Enterprises E 714 493-1735
25072 Wilkes Pl Laguna Hills (92653) ***(P-10019)***

Rlt Seafood Supermarket Inc F 909 888-6520
333 S E St San Bernardino (92401) ***(P-2249)***

Rlv Tuned Exhaust Products E 805 925-5461
2351 Thompson Way Bldg A Santa Maria (93455) ***(P-19759)***

Rm 518 Management LLC E 213 624-6788
719 S Los Angeles St Los Angeles (90014) ***(P-3577)***

Rm Pallets Inc F 209 632-9887
2512 Paulson Rd Turlock (95380) ***(P-4396)***

RMC, Ripon *Also called Ripon Mfg Co* ***(P-14397)***

RMC Engineering Co Inc (PA) E 408 842-2525
255 Mayock Rd Gilroy (95020) ***(P-16362)***

RMC Pacific Materials Inc E 209 835-1454
30350 S Tracy Blvd Tracy (95377) ***(P-10428)***

RMC Pacific Materials Inc (HQ) C 925 426-8787
6601 Koll Center Pkwy Pleasanton (94566) ***(P-10429)***

RMC Pacific Materials Inc E 925 846-2824
1544 Stanley Blvd Pleasanton (94566) ***(P-10819)***

Rmf Salt Holdings LLC F 510 477-9600
2217 S Shore Ctr 200 Alameda (94501) ***(P-8572)***

Rmi, Livermore *Also called Ratermann Manufacturing Inc* ***(P-10010)***

Rmjv LP B 503 526-5752
3285 Corporate Vw Vista (92081) ***(P-14398)***

Rmla Inc D 213 749-4333
1972 E 20th St Vernon (90058) ***(P-3495)***

RMR Products Inc (PA) E 818 890-0896
11011 Glenoaks Blvd Ste 1 Pacoima (91331) ***(P-10641)***

RMS, Signal Hill *Also called Relax Medical Systems Inc* ***(P-23460)***

RMS Monty Crystal, Cardiff By The Sea *Also called Reinhart Oil & Gas Inc* ***(P-64)***

RMS Printing LLC F 818 707-2625
5331 Derry Ave Ste N Agoura Hills (91301) ***(P-6847)***

Rnc, Los Angeles *Also called Rnovate Inc* ***(P-14791)***

Rnd Contractors Inc E 909 429-8500
14796 Jurupa Ave Ste A Fontana (92337) ***(P-11874)***

Rnd Enterprises, Chatsworth *Also called BDR Industries Inc* ***(P-15167)***

Rnj Printing Corporation F 310 638-7768
16005 S Broadway Gardena (90248) ***(P-6848)***

Rnk Industries Co F 323 446-0777
2816 E 11th St Los Angeles (90023) ***(P-2710)***

Rnovate Inc E 213 489-1617
834 S Broadway Los Angeles (90014) ***(P-14791)***

RNS Channel Letters, Corona *Also called Richards Neon Shop Inc* ***(P-23186)***

Ro Gar Mfg, El Centro *Also called Rogar Manufacturing Inc* ***(P-19071)***

Roa Pacific Inc F 619 565-2800
1225 Exposition Way San Diego (92154) ***(P-7604)***

Roach Bros Inc D 707 964-9240
23550 Shady Ln Fort Bragg (95437) ***(P-3902)***

Road Vista, San Diego *Also called Gamma Scientific Inc* ***(P-21478)***

Roadracing World Publishing F 951 245-6411
581 Birch St Ste C Lake Elsinore (92530) ***(P-6019)***

Roadster Wheels Inc F 626 333-3007
14955 Don Julian Rd City of Industry (91746) ***(P-19760)***

Roadwire Distinctive Inds, Santa Fe Springs *Also called Distinctive Inds Texas Inc* ***(P-3513)***

Roan Mills LLC F 818 249-4686
11069 Penrose St Sun Valley (91352) ***(P-1010)***

Roastery, The, Sonoma *Also called Daily Offrngs Cof Roastery LLC* ***(P-2286)***

Rob Inc (PA) D 562 806-5589
6760 Foster Bridge Blvd Bell Gardens (90201) ***(P-3018)***

Robanda International Inc E 619 276-7660
8260 Cmino Santa Fe Ste A San Diego (92121) ***(P-8573)***

Robar Enterprises Inc (PA) C 760 244-5456
17671 Bear Valley Rd Hesperia (92345) ***(P-10820)***

Robb Curtco Media LLC E 310 589-7700
29160 Heathercliff Rd # 200 Malibu (90265) ***(P-6020)***

Robb-Jack Corporation (PA) D 916 645-6045
3300 Nicolaus Rd Ste 1 Lincoln (95648) ***(P-13945)***

Robbins Auto Top LLC D 805 278-8249
321 Todd Ct Oxnard (93030) ***(P-10020)***

Robbins Precast, Corona *Also called Nucast Industries Inc* ***(P-10608)***

Robecks Wldg & Fabrication Inc E 408 287-0202
1150 Mabury Rd Ste 1 San Jose (95133) ***(P-11875)***

Robeks Corporation F 310 642-7800
8905 S Sepulveda Blvd Los Angeles (90045) ***(P-2601)***

Robeks Corporation F 310 838-2332
3891 Overland Ave Culver City (90232) ***(P-821)***

Robeks Juice, Los Angeles *Also called Robeks Corporation* ***(P-2601)***

Robeks Juice, Culver City *Also called Robeks Corporation* ***(P-821)***

Robert A Kerl E 818 341-9281
8930 Quartz Ave Northridge (91324) ***(P-7343)***

Robert Biale Vineyards, NAPA *Also called Biale Estate* ***(P-1599)***

Robert Bosch LLC E 805 966-2000
2030 Alameda Padre Serra Santa Barbara (93103) ***(P-21882)***

Robert Bosch Stiftung GMBH, Palo Alto *Also called Bosch Enrgy Stor Solutions LLC* ***(P-16633)***

Robert Bosch Tool Corporation C 760 357-5603
302 E 3rd St 31-1812 Calexico (92231) ***(P-14226)***

Robert Crowder & Co Inc F 323 248-7737
901 S Greenwood Ave Ste L Montebello (90640) ***(P-9365)***

Robert E Blake Inc F 415 391-2255
135 Clara St San Francisco (94107) ***(P-20303)***

Robert F Chapman Inc D 661 940-9482
43100 Exchange Pl Lancaster (93535) ***(P-12355)***

Robert Grove F 619 562-1268
1860 Joe Crosson Dr El Cajon (92020) ***(P-19927)***

Robert H Oliva Inc E 818 700-1035
19863 Nordhoff St Northridge (91324) ***(P-16363)***

Robert Heely Construction, Bakersfield *Also called Robert Heely Construction LP* ***(P-255)***

Robert Heely Construction LP (PA) B 661 617-1400
5401 Woodmere Dr Bakersfield (93313) ***(P-255)***

Robert J Alandt & Sons E 559 275-1391
4692 N Brawley Ave Fresno (93722) ***(P-11876)***

Robert M Hadley Company Inc D 805 658-7286
4054 Transport St Ventura (93003) ***(P-18739)***

Robert Mann Packaging, Oceanside *Also called Pratt Industries Inc* ***(P-5146)***

Robert Mondavi Corporation (HQ) D 707 967-2100
166 Gateway Rd E NAPA (94558) ***(P-1891)***

Robert Mondavi Corporation E 209 365-2995
770 N Guild Ave Lodi (95240) ***(P-1892)***

Robert P Martin Company F 323 686-2220
2209 Seaman Ave South El Monte (91733) ***(P-11105)***

Robert P Von Zabern F 951 734-7215
4121 Tigris Way Riverside (92503) ***(P-21883)***

Robert R Wix Inc (PA) E 209 537-4561
2140 Pine St Ceres (95307) ***(P-7202)***

Robert Snell Cast Specialist F 530 273-8958
110 Spring Hill Dr Ste 20 Grass Valley (95945) ***(P-22600)***

Robert Talbott Inc (PA) E 831 649-6000
24560 Silver Cloud Ct Monterey (93940) ***(P-2975)***

Robert W Cameron & Co Inc E 707 769-1617
149 Kentucky St Ste 7 Petaluma (94952) ***(P-6142)***

Robert W Wiesmantel F 562 634-0442
15345 Allen St Paramount (90723) ***(P-16364)***

Robert Yick Company Inc E 415 282-9707
261 Bay Shore Blvd San Francisco (94124) ***(P-15571)***

Robert's Engineering, Anaheim *Also called Roberts Precision Engrg Inc* ***(P-16365)***

Roberto Martinez Inc F 800 257-6462
1050 Calle Cordillera # 103 San Clemente (92673) ***(P-22565)***

Roberts Ferry Nut Company Inc F 209 874-3247
20493 Yosemite Blvd Waterford (95386) ***(P-1392)***

Roberts Precision Engrg Inc E 714 635-4485
1345 S Allec St Anaheim (92805) ***(P-16365)***

Roberts Research Laboratory F 310 320-7310
23150 Kashiwa Ct Torrance (90505) ***(P-13284)***

Robertson-Ceco II Corporation .... C 209 727-5504
12101 E Brandt Rd Lockeford (95237) ***(P-12573)***
Robertsons Distributors Inc .... F 951 849-4766
1990 N Hargrave St Banning (92220) ***(P-10821)***
Robertsons Rdy Mix Ltd A Cal .... F 909 337-7577
2975 Hwy 18 Lake Arrowhead (92352) ***(P-10822)***
Robertsons Rdy Mix Ltd A Cal .... F 760 246-4000
12203 Violet Rd Adelanto (92301) ***(P-10823)***
Robertsons Ready Mix Ltd (HQ) .... D 951 493-6500
200 S Main St Ste 200 # 200 Corona (92882) ***(P-10824)***
Robertsons Ready Mix Ltd .... E 909 623-9185
2470 Pomona Blvd Pomona (91768) ***(P-10825)***
Robertsons Ready Mix Ltd .... E 800 834-7557
200 S Main St Ste 200 # 200 Corona (92882) ***(P-10826)***
Robertsons Ready Mix Ltd .... E 909 425-2930
27401 3rd St Highland (92346) ***(P-10827)***
Robeworks, Alhambra *Also called Victoire LLC* ***(P-3505)***
Robin's Jeans, Bell Gardens *Also called Rob Inc* ***(P-3018)***
Robinson Engineering Corp .... F 951 361-8000
3575 Grapevine St Jurupa Valley (91752) ***(P-14235)***
Robinson Family Winery .... F 707 287-8428
5880 Silverado Trl NAPA (94558) ***(P-1893)***
Robinson Farms Feed Company .... F 209 466-7915
7000 S Inland Dr Stockton (95206) ***(P-1123)***
Robinson Helicopter Co Inc .... A 310 539-0508
2901 Airport Dr Torrance (90505) ***(P-19928)***
Robinson Pharma Inc .... D 714 241-0235
3701 W Warner Ave Santa Ana (92704) ***(P-8109)***
Robinson Pharma Inc (PA) .... B 714 241-0235
3330 S Harbor Blvd Santa Ana (92704) ***(P-8110)***
Robinson Pharma Inc .... C 714 241-0235
2811 S Harbor Blvd Santa Ana (92704) ***(P-8111)***
Robinson Printing Inc .... E 951 296-0300
42685 Rio Nedo Temecula (92590) ***(P-7203)***
Robinson Textiles Inc .... E 310 527-8110
24532 Woodward Ave Lomita (90717) ***(P-2976)***
Robles Bros Inc (PA) .... E 408 436-5551
1700 Rogers Ave San Jose (95112) ***(P-2602)***
Roblox Corporation .... B 888 858-2569
970 Park Pl San Mateo (94403) ***(P-24364)***
Roboworm Inc .... F 805 389-1636
764 Calle Plano Camarillo (93012) ***(P-22873)***
Robson Technologies Inc .... E 408 779-8008
135 E Main Ave Ste 130 Morgan Hill (95037) ***(P-16366)***
ROC-Aire Corp .... E 909 784-3385
2198 Pomona Blvd Pomona (91768) ***(P-16367)***
Rocateq North America .... F 925 648-7794
4155 Blackhwk Lasas Cir Danville (94506) ***(P-13434)***
Rochas Cabinets .... F 209 239-2367
108 Industrial Park Dr # 17 Manteca (95337) ***(P-4239)***
Roche Molecular Systems Inc .... C 510 814-2800
1145 Atlantic Ave Ste 100 Alameda (94501) ***(P-8112)***
Roche Molecular Systems Inc (HQ) .... B 925 730-8000
4300 Hacienda Dr Pleasanton (94588) ***(P-8113)***
Roche Pharmaceuticals .... E 908 635-5692
4300 Hacienda Dr Pleasanton (94588) ***(P-8114)***
Rochester Midland Corporation .... E 800 388-4762
7275 Sycamore Canyon Blvd # 101 Riverside (92508) ***(P-5467)***
Rock & Sand Plant, San Diego *Also called Legacy Vulcan LLC* ***(P-303)***
Rock Engineered McHy Co Inc .... F 925 447-0805
1627 Army Ct Ste 1 Stockton (95206) ***(P-9065)***
Rock Rag Inc .... F 818 919-9364
913 N Highland Ave Los Angeles (90038) ***(P-6332)***
Rock Revival, Vernon *Also called Rcrv Inc* ***(P-5414)***
Rock Solid Stone LLC .... F 760 731-6191
308 Industrial Way Ste B Fallbrook (92028) ***(P-10642)***
Rock Wall Wine Company Inc .... E 510 522-5700
2301 Monarch St Alameda (94501) ***(P-1894)***
Rock West Composites Inc (PA) .... E 801 566-3402
1602 Precision Park Ln San Diego (92173) ***(P-9454)***
Rock-Ola Manufacturing Corp .... D 310 328-1306
2335 W 208th St Torrance (90501) ***(P-17277)***
Rocker Industries, Harbor City *Also called Rocker Solenoid Company* ***(P-19070)***
Rocker Solenoid Company .... D 310 534-5660
1500 240th St Harbor City (90710) ***(P-19070)***
Rocket Ems Inc .... C 408 727-3700
2950 Patrick Henry Dr Santa Clara (95054) ***(P-17977)***
Rocket Shop, Folsom *Also called Aerojet Rocketdyne Inc* ***(P-20017)***
Rocketstar Robotics Inc .... F 805 529-7769
177 Estaban Dr Camarillo (93010) ***(P-16672)***
Rockley Photonics Inc (HQ) .... D 626 304-9960
234 E Colo Blvd Ste 600 Pasadena (91101) ***(P-18519)***
Rockley Photonics Inc .... F 408 579-9210
333 W San Carlos St San Jose (95110) ***(P-18520)***
Rockstar Inc .... C 323 785-2820
8530 Wilshire Blvd Fl 3 Beverly Hills (90211) ***(P-2161)***
Rockstar Energy Drink, Beverly Hills *Also called Rockstar Inc* ***(P-2161)***
Rockwell Automation Inc .... D 714 938-9000
2125 E Katella Ave # 250 Anaheim (92806) ***(P-16745)***
Rockwell Automation Inc .... E 714 828-1800
5836 Corporate Ave Cypress (90630) ***(P-16746)***
Rockwell Automation Inc .... D 408 443-5425
111 N Market St Ste 200 San Jose (95113) ***(P-16747)***
Rockwell Automation Inc .... E 925 242-5700
3000 Executive Pkwy # 210 San Ramon (94583) ***(P-16748)***
Rockwell Collins Inc .... D 714 929-3000
1733 Alton Pkwy Irvine (92606) ***(P-20706)***
Rockwell Collins Inc .... E 760 768-4732
1757 Carr Rd Ste 100e Calexico (92231) ***(P-20707)***
Rockwell Collins Optronics Inc .... F 319 295-1000
2752 Loker Ave W Carlsbad (92010) ***(P-20708)***
Rocky Label Mills Inc .... E 323 278-0080
1930 Doreen Ave South El Monte (91733) ***(P-2759)***
Rod L Electronics Inc (PA) .... F 650 322-0711
935 Sierra Vista Ave F Mountain View (94043) ***(P-21113)***
Rodak Plastics Co Inc .... F 510 471-0898
31721 Knapp St Hayward (94544) ***(P-10021)***
Rode Microphones LLC .... C 310 328-7456
2745 Raymond Ave Signal Hill (90755) ***(P-17278)***
Rodon Products Inc .... E 714 898-3528
15481 Electronic Ln Ste A Huntington Beach (92649) ***(P-18740)***
Rodriguez Ismael .... F 805 736-7362
138 N D St Lompoc (93436) ***(P-2341)***
Rods Unfinished Furniture .... E 626 281-9855
1121 S Meridian Ave Alhambra (91803) ***(P-4606)***
Roettele Industries .... F 909 606-8252
15485 Dupont Ave Chino (91710) ***(P-9250)***
Rof LLC .... E 818 933-4000
7800 Arprt Bus Pkwy Ste B Van Nuys (91406) ***(P-3050)***
Rogar Manufacturing Inc .... C 760 335-3700
866 E Ross Ave El Centro (92243) ***(P-19071)***
Roger Enrico .... B 559 485-5050
1150 E North Ave Fresno (93725) ***(P-2162)***
Roger Industry .... F 714 896-0765
11552 Knott St Ste 5 Garden Grove (92841) ***(P-17978)***
Roger R Caruso Enterprises Inc .... E 714 778-6006
2911 Norton Ave Lynwood (90262) ***(P-4397)***
Rogers Corporation .... D 562 404-8942
13937 Rosecrans Ave Santa Fe Springs (90670) ***(P-9366)***
Rogers Holding Company Inc .... E 714 257-4850
1130 Columbia St Brea (92821) ***(P-20211)***
Rogerson Aircraft Corporation (PA) .... D 949 660-0666
2201 Alton Pkwy Irvine (92606) ***(P-20709)***
Rogerson Kratos .... C 626 449-3090
403 S Raymond Ave Pasadena (91105) ***(P-20710)***
Rogue River Rifleworks Inc .... F 805 227-4611
570 Linne Rd Ste 110 Paso Robles (93446) ***(P-22874)***
Rogue River Super Scopes, Paso Robles *Also called Rogue River Rifleworks Inc* ***(P-22874)***
Rohr Inc (HQ) .... A 619 691-4111
850 Lagoon Dr Chula Vista (91910) ***(P-20212)***
Rohrback Cosasco Systems Inc (HQ) .... D 562 949-0123
11841 Smith Ave Santa Fe Springs (90670) ***(P-20929)***
Roi Development Corp .... E 714 751-0488
15272 Newsboy Cir Huntington Beach (92649) ***(P-16796)***
Rojo's, Cypress *Also called Simply Fresh LLC* ***(P-2270)***
Rolenn Manufacturing Inc .... E 951 682-1185
1549 Marlborough Ave Riverside (92507) ***(P-23463)***
Rolenn Manufacturing Inc (PA) .... E 951 682-1185
2065 Roberta St Riverside (92507) ***(P-10022)***
Roll-A-Shade Inc (PA) .... E 951 245-5077
12101 Madera Way Riverside (92503) ***(P-5036)***
Rollapp Inc (PA) .... F 650 617-3372
530 Lytton Ave Fl 2 Palo Alto (94301) ***(P-24365)***
Roller Bones, Santa Barbara *Also called Skate One Corp* ***(P-22887)***
Roller Derby Skate Corp .... F 217 324-3961
3401 Etiwanda Ave 911c Jurupa Valley (91752) ***(P-22875)***
Rollin Industries, San Diego *Also called Yellow Inc* ***(P-22929)***
Rollin J. Lobaugh, Belmont *Also called Pacific Screw Products Inc* ***(P-12645)***
Rolling Dough Corporation .... F 714 884-2801
624 E Holt Blvd Ontario (91761) ***(P-1267)***
Roltec Gasket Manufacturing, Corona *Also called Elastomer Technologies Inc* ***(P-9228)***
Roma Bakery Inc .... D 408 294-0123
655 S Almaden Ave San Jose (95110) ***(P-1268)***
Roma Fabricating Corporation .... E 760 727-8040
2638 S Santa Fe Ave San Marcos (92069) ***(P-10643)***
Roma Marble & Tile, San Marcos *Also called Roma Fabricating Corporation* ***(P-10643)***
Roma Moulding Inc .... E 626 334-2539
6230 N Irwindale Ave Irwindale (91702) ***(P-4527)***
Romac Supply Co Inc .... D 323 721-5810
7400 Bandini Blvd Commerce (90040) ***(P-16611)***
Romakk Engineering, Northridge *Also called Robert H Oliva Inc* ***(P-16363)***
Roman Global Resources Inc .... F 949 276-4100
1027 Calle Trepadora # 2 San Clemente (92673) ***(P-9251)***
Roman Upholstery Manufacturing .... F 310 479-3252
2008 Cotner Ave Los Angeles (90025) ***(P-4668)***
Romance Ring, Moorpark *Also called Star Ring Inc* ***(P-22573)***
Rombauer Vineyards Inc .... F 209 245-6979
851 Napa Vly Corp Way I NAPA (94558) ***(P-1895)***
Rombauer Vineyards Inc (PA) .... D 707 963-5170
3522 Silverado Trl N Saint Helena (94574) ***(P-1896)***
Romeo Packing Company .... E 650 728-3393
106 Princeton Ave Half Moon Bay (94019) ***(P-5443)***
Romeo Power, Vernon *Also called Romeo Systems Inc* ***(P-19397)***
Romeo Systems Inc .... C 323 675-2180
4380 Ayers Ave Vernon (90058) ***(P-19397)***
Romeros Food Products Inc (PA) .... D 562 802-1858
15155 Valley View Ave Santa Fe Springs (90670) ***(P-2603)***
Romeros Food Products Inc .... F 909 884-5531
993 S Waterman Ave San Bernardino (92408) ***(P-2604)***
Romeros Welding & Mar Svcs Inc .... F 925 550-0518
519 Waterfront Ave Vallejo (94592) ***(P-24662)***
Romi Industries Inc .... F 661 294-1142
25443 Rye Canyon Rd Valencia (91355) ***(P-16368)***
Romi Machine Shop, Valencia *Also called Romi Industries Inc* ***(P-16368)***
Romla Co .... E 619 946-1224
9668 Heinrich Hertz Dr D San Diego (92154) ***(P-12356)***
Romla Ventilator Co, San Diego *Also called Romla Co* ***(P-12356)***

ALPHABETIC

Ron & Diana Vanatta ... F ... 530 888-0200
332 Sacramento St Auburn (95603) ***(P-4935)***
Ron Grose Racing Inc ... F ... 209 368-2571
488 E Kettleman Ln Lodi (95240) ***(P-16369)***
Ron Kehl Engineering ... F ... 408 629-6632
384 Umbarger Rd Ste B San Jose (95111) ***(P-13088)***
Ron Nunes Enterprises LLC ... F ... 925 371-0220
7703 Las Positas Rd Livermore (94551) ***(P-12357)***
Ron Teeguarden Enterprises Inc (PA) ... E ... 323 556-8188
5670 Wilshire Blvd # 1500 Los Angeles (90036) ***(P-7687)***
Ron Witherspoon Inc ... D ... 831 633-3568
13525 Blackie Rd Castroville (95012) ***(P-16370)***
Ronald D Teson Inc ... E ... 310 532-5987
13945 Mckinley Ave Los Angeles (90059) ***(P-3983)***
Ronald F Ogletree Inc ... E ... 707 963-3537
935 Vintage Ave Saint Helena (94574) ***(P-12358)***
Ronan Engineering Company (PA) ... D ... 661 702-1344
28209 Avenue Stanford Valencia (91355) ***(P-20930)***
Ronan Engnrng/Rnan Msrment Div, Valencia *Also called Ronan Engineering Company* ***(P-20930)***
Ronatec C2c Inc ... F ... 760 476-1890
5651 Palmer Way Ste H Carlsbad (92010) ***(P-9021)***
Roncelli Plastics Inc ... D ... 800 250-6516
330 W Duarte Rd Monrovia (91016) ***(P-7605)***
Ronco Plastics Incorporated ... E ... 714 259-1385
15022 Parkway Loop Ste B Tustin (92780) ***(P-10023)***
Rondor Music International (PA) ... F ... 310 235-4800
2440 S Sepulveda Blvd # 119 Los Angeles (90064) ***(P-6333)***
Ronford Products Inc ... E ... 909 622-7446
1116 E 2nd St Pomona (91766) ***(P-10024)***
Ronin Content, Culver City *Also called Ronin Content Services Inc* ***(P-24366)***
Ronin Content Services Inc ... F ... 323 445-5945
5900 Smiley Dr Culver City (90232) ***(P-24366)***
Ronlo Engineering Ltd ... E ... 805 388-3227
955 Flynn Rd Camarillo (93012) ***(P-16371)***
Ronpak Inc ... E ... 951 685-3800
10900 San Sevaine Way Jurupa Valley (91752) ***(P-5148)***
Rooke Manufacturing Co ... F ... 714 540-6943
3360 W Harvard St Santa Ana (92704) ***(P-16372)***
Roos Instruments Inc ... E ... 408 748-8589
2285 Martin Ave Santa Clara (95050) ***(P-21114)***
Rootlieb Inc ... F ... 209 632-2203
815 S Soderquist Rd Turlock (95380) ***(P-12747)***
Ropak Corporation (HQ) ... E ... 714 845-2845
10540 Talbert Ave 200w Fountain Valley (92708) ***(P-10025)***
Ropak Packaging, Fountain Valley *Also called Ropak Corporation* ***(P-10025)***
Roplast Industries Inc ... C ... 530 532-9500
3155 S 5th Ave Oroville (95965) ***(P-5416)***
Rosa Brothers Milk Co Inc (PA) ... E ... 559 582-8825
10090 2nd Ave Hanford (93230) ***(P-666)***
Rosa's Cafe & Tortilla Factory, Temecula *Also called Chh Lp* ***(P-2425)***
Rosco Laboratories Inc ... F ... 800 767-2652
9420 Chivers Ave Sun Valley (91352) ***(P-22456)***
Roscoe Moss Company, Los Angeles *Also called Roscoe Moss Manufacturing Co* ***(P-11134)***
Roscoe Moss Manufacturing Co (PA) ... D ... 323 261-4185
4360 Worth St Los Angeles (90063) ***(P-11134)***
Roscoe Moss Manufacturing Co ... D ... 323 263-4111
4360 Worth St Los Angeles (90063) ***(P-11135)***
Rose Business Solutions Inc ... E ... 858 794-9401
875 Chelsea Ln Encinitas (92024) ***(P-24367)***
Rose Chem Intl - USA Corp ... E ... 678 510-8864
25 Rainbow Fls Irvine (92603) ***(P-8115)***
Rose Genuine Inc ... F ... 213 747-4120
834 S Broadway Ste 1100 Los Angeles (90014) ***(P-3487)***
Rose Manufacturing Group Inc ... F ... 760 407-0232
2525 Jason Ct Ste 102 Oceanside (92056) ***(P-13089)***
Rose Metal Products Inc ... D ... 417 865-1676
1754 Tech Dr Ste 100 San Jose (95110) ***(P-11877)***
Rosedale Medical, Fremont *Also called Intuity Medical Inc* ***(P-21756)***
Roselm Industries Inc ... E ... 626 442-6840
2510 Seaman Ave South El Monte (91733) ***(P-17645)***
Rosemead Oil Products Inc ... F ... 562 941-3261
12402 Los Nietos Rd Santa Fe Springs (90670) ***(P-9154)***
Rosen & Rosen Industries Inc ... D ... 949 361-9238
204 Avenida Fabricante San Clemente (92672) ***(P-22876)***
Rosenkranz Enterprises Inc ... F ... 323 583-9021
2447 E 54th St Los Angeles (90058) ***(P-13090)***
Rosetti Gennaro Furniture ... E ... 323 750-7794
6833 Brynhurst Ave Los Angeles (90043) ***(P-4607)***
Rosettis Fine Foods Inc ... F ... 559 323-6450
3 Railroad Ave Clovis (93612) ***(P-1269)***
Rosewill Inc ... E ... 626 271-1420
17708 Rowland St City of Industry (91748) ***(P-14969)***
Ross Bindery Inc ... C ... 562 623-4565
15310 Spring Ave Santa Fe Springs (90670) ***(P-7344)***
Ross Fabrication & Welding Inc ... F ... 661 393-1242
1154 Basta Ave Bakersfield (93308) ***(P-4528)***
Ross Hay, Lincoln *Also called Marybelle Farms Inc* ***(P-1111)***
Ross Name Plate Company ... E ... 323 725-6812
2 Red Plum Cir Monterey Park (91755) ***(P-23187)***
Ross Periodicals, Novato *Also called Excellence Magazine Inc* ***(P-5934)***
Ross Racing Pistons ... D ... 310 536-0100
625 S Douglas St El Segundo (90245) ***(P-15617)***
Rossmoor Pastries MGT Inc ... D ... 562 498-2253
2325 Redondo Ave Signal Hill (90755) ***(P-1270)***
Rostar Filters, Oxnard *Also called PC Vaughan Mfg Corp* ***(P-14847)***
Rotary Club of Ajai West ... E ... 805 646-3794
1129 Maricopa Hwy Ojai (93023) ***(P-1897)***
Rotary Corp ... F ... 559 445-1108
3359 E North Ave Ste 102 Fresno (93725) ***(P-13694)***
Rotating Prcsion McHanisms Inc ... E ... 818 349-9774
8750 Shirley Ave Northridge (91324) ***(P-17646)***
Rotational Molding Inc ... D ... 310 327-5401
17038 S Figueroa St Gardena (90248) ***(P-10026)***
Rotax Incorporated ... E ... 323 589-5999
2940 Leonis Blvd Vernon (90058) ***(P-3400)***
Rotech Engineering Inc ... E ... 714 632-0532
1020 S Melrose St Ste A Placentia (92870) ***(P-19072)***
Roth Wood Products Ltd ... E ... 408 723-8888
2260 Canoas Garden Ave San Jose (95125) ***(P-5080)***
Rothlisberger Mfg A Cal Corp ... F ... 818 786-9462
14718 Arminta St Van Nuys (91402) ***(P-16373)***
Roto Dynamics Inc ... E ... 714 685-0183
1925 N Lime St Orange (92865) ***(P-10027)***
Roto Lite Inc ... E ... 909 923-4353
84701 Avenue 48 Coachella (92236) ***(P-10028)***
Roto Power Inc ... F ... 951 751-9850
191 Granite St Ste A Corona (92879) ***(P-10029)***
Roto West Enterprises Inc ... F ... 714 899-2030
15651 Container Ln Huntington Beach (92649) ***(P-10030)***
Roto-Die Company Inc ... F ... 714 991-8701
712 N Valley St Ste B Anaheim (92801) ***(P-14101)***
Roto-Rooter, Manteca *Also called Sanact Inc* ***(P-8415)***
Rotometrics, Anaheim *Also called Roto-Die Company Inc* ***(P-14101)***
Rotoplas, Merced *Also called Molding Acquisition Corp* ***(P-7582)***
Rotork Controls Inc ... F ... 707 769-4880
419 1st St Petaluma (94952) ***(P-16749)***
Rotron Incorporated ... F ... 619 593-7400
474 Raleigh Ave El Cajon (92020) ***(P-14677)***
Rotta Winery Inc ... F ... 805 237-0510
250 Winery Rd Templeton (93465) ***(P-1898)***
Rouchon Industries Inc ... F ... 310 763-0336
3729 San Gabriel River Pk Pico Rivera (90660) ***(P-15324)***
Roudybush Inc (PA) ... F ... 530 668-6196
340 Hanson Way Woodland (95776) ***(P-1124)***
Rouge & Noir, Petaluma *Also called Marin French Cheese Company* ***(P-568)***
Round Hill Cellars ... D ... 707 968-3200
1680 Silverado Trl S Saint Helena (94574) ***(P-1899)***
Rounds Logging Company ... E ... 530 247-0517
4350 Lynbrook Loop Apt 1 Redding (96003) ***(P-3903)***
Rox Medical Inc (PA) ... E ... 949 276-8968
150 Calle Iglesia Ste A San Clemente (92672) ***(P-22306)***
Roxwood Medical Inc ... F ... 650 779-4555
400 Seaport Ct Ste 103 Redwood City (94063) ***(P-21884)***
Roy & Val Tool Grinding Inc ... F ... 818 341-2434
10131 Canoga Ave Chatsworth (91311) ***(P-16374)***
Roy E Hanson Jr Mfg (PA) ... D ... 213 747-7514
1600 E Washington Blvd Los Angeles (90021) ***(P-12047)***
Royal Adhesives & Sealants LLC ... F ... 949 863-1499
16731 Hale Ave Irvine (92606) ***(P-8893)***
Royal Angelus Macaroni Company ... C ... 909 627-7312
2539 E Philadelphia St Ontario (91761) ***(P-2605)***
Royal Apparel Inc ... D ... 626 579-5168
4331 Baldwin Ave El Monte (91731) ***(P-3401)***
Royal Blue Inc ... E ... 310 888-0156
9025 Wilshire Blvd # 301 Beverly Hills (90211) ***(P-3639)***
Royal Cabinets, Pomona *Also called Royal Industries Inc* ***(P-4241)***
Royal Cabinets Inc ... A ... 909 629-8565
1299 E Phillips Blvd Pomona (91766) ***(P-4240)***
Royal Circuit Solutions Inc (PA) ... E ... 831 636-7789
21 Hamilton Ct Hollister (95023) ***(P-17979)***
Royal Coatings, Simi Valley *Also called Mabel Baas Inc* ***(P-13204)***
Royal Custom Designs Inc ... C ... 909 591-8990
13951 Monte Vista Ave Chino (91710) ***(P-4669)***
Royal Custom Parquet, Santa Fe Springs *Also called Hamar Wood Parquet Company* ***(P-3934)***
Royal Drapery and Interiors, NAPA *Also called Royal Drapery Manufacturing* ***(P-3595)***
Royal Drapery Manufacturing ... F ... 707 226-2022
3149 California Blvd K NAPA (94558) ***(P-3595)***
Royal Flex Circuits Inc ... E ... 562 404-0626
15505 Cornet St Santa Fe Springs (90670) ***(P-17980)***
Royal Industries, Eastvale *Also called Royal Range California Inc* ***(P-16816)***
Royal Industries Inc ... C ... 909 629-8565
1299 E Phillips Blvd Pomona (91766) ***(P-4241)***
Royal Interpack Midwest Inc ... F ... 626 675-0637
475 Palmyrita Ave Riverside (92507) ***(P-10031)***
Royal Interpack North Amer Inc ... E ... 951 787-6925
475 Palmyrita Ave Riverside (92507) ***(P-10032)***
Royal Manufacturing Inds Inc ... F ... 714 668-9199
600 W Warner Ave Santa Ana (92707) ***(P-12359)***
Royal Metal, Santa Ana *Also called Ted Rieck Enterprises Inc* ***(P-12402)***
Royal Mountain King, Copperopolis *Also called Meridian Gold Inc* ***(P-7)***
Royal Paper Box Co California (PA) ... C ... 323 728-7041
1105 S Maple Ave Montebello (90640) ***(P-5314)***
Royal Plasticware, Gardena *Also called La Palm Furnitures & ACC Inc* ***(P-3746)***
Royal Range California Inc ... D ... 951 360-1600
3245 Corridor Dr Eastvale (91752) ***(P-16816)***
Royal Riders ... F ... 408 779-1997
120 Mast St Ste B Morgan Hill (95037) ***(P-3856)***
Royal Stall ... F ... 559 875-8100
1865 Industrial Way Sanger (93657) ***(P-12505)***
Royal Systems Group ... F ... 818 717-5010
18301 Napa St Northridge (91325) ***(P-14280)***
Royal Trim ... E ... 323 583-2121
2529 Chambers St Vernon (90058) ***(P-3811)***
Royal Welding & Fabricating, Fullerton *Also called Cook and Cook Incorporated* ***(P-12013)***

Mergent e-mail: customerrelations@mergent.com
1226
2020 California
Manufacturers Register
(P-0000) Products & Services Section entry number
(PA)=Parent Co (HQ)=Headquarters (DH)=Div Headquarters

Royal Wine Corporation ....E.......805 983-1560
3201 Camino Del Sol Oxnard (93030) *(P-1900)*

Royal-Pedic Mattress Mfg LLC ....E.......310 518-5420
331 N Fries Ave Wilmington (90744) *(P-4740)*

Royale Energy Funds Inc (HQ) ....F.......619 383-6600
1870 Cordell Ct Ste 210 El Cajon (92020) *(P-137)*

Royalite Mfg Inc (PA) ....F.......650 637-1440
1055 Terminal Way San Carlos (94070) *(P-12360)*

Royalpedic Mattress Mfg, Wilmington *Also called Royal-Pedic Mattress Mfg LLC (P-4740)*

Royce Records, Oakland *Also called B-Flat Publishing LLC (P-6197)*

Rozak Engineering Inc ....F.......714 446-8855
556 S State College Blvd Fullerton (92831) *(P-16375)*

Rozendal Associates Inc ....F.......619 562-5596
9530 Pathway St Ste 101 Santee (92071) *(P-20711)*

Rpc Inc ....F.......619 647-9911
9457 Adlai Ter Lakeside (92040) *(P-256)*

RPC Legacy Inc ....D.......818 787-9000
14600 Arminta St Van Nuys (91402) *(P-11624)*

RPI, Simi Valley *Also called Replacement Parts Inds Inc (P-22186)*

RPM, Northridge *Also called Rotating Prcsion McHanisms Inc (P-17646)*

RPM Embroidery Inc ....F.......949 650-0085
1614 Babcock St Costa Mesa (92627) *(P-3755)*

RPM Grinding Co Inc ....F.......951 273-0602
1755 Commerce St Norco (92860) *(P-16376)*

RPM Plastic Molding Inc ....E.......714 630-9300
2821 E Miraloma Ave Anaheim (92806) *(P-10033)*

RPM Products Inc (PA) ....E.......949 888-8543
30065 Comercio Rcho STA Marg (92688) *(P-9252)*

RPS Inc ....E.......818 350-8088
20331 Corisco St Chatsworth (91311) *(P-13435)*

Rpsz Construction LLC ....E.......314 677-5831
1201 W 5th St Ste T340 Los Angeles (90017) *(P-22877)*

RR Donnelley & Sons Company ....B.......209 983-6700
3837 Producers Dr Stockton (95206) *(P-6849)*

RR Donnelley & Sons Company ....E.......949 852-1933
19200 Von Karman Ave # 700 Irvine (92612) *(P-7204)*

RR Donnelley & Sons Company ....A.......310 516-3100
19681 Pacific Gateway Dr Torrance (90502) *(P-7205)*

RR Donnelley & Sons Company ....F.......916 929-8632
1765 Challenge Way # 220 Sacramento (95815) *(P-7284)*

RR Donnelley & Sons Company ....E.......949 476-0505
19200 Von Karman Ave # 700 Irvine (92612) *(P-7285)*

RR Donnelley & Sons Company ....E.......650 845-6600
855 N California Ave A Palo Alto (94303) *(P-7315)*

RR Donnelley Financial, Palo Alto *Also called RR Donnelley & Sons Company (P-7315)*

Rrds Inc (PA) ....F.......949 482-6200
12 Goodyear Ste 100 Irvine (92618) *(P-21403)*

Rs Machining Co Inc ....F.......818 718-0097
9726 Cozycroft Ave Chatsworth (91311) *(P-16377)*

RS Technical Services Inc (PA) ....D.......707 778-1974
1327 Clegg St Petaluma (94954) *(P-21282)*

Rsa Engineered Products LLC ....D.......805 584-4150
110 W Cochran St Ste A Simi Valley (93065) *(P-20213)*

Rsdg International Inc ....E.......626 256-4190
2127 Aralia St Newport Beach (92660) *(P-3488)*

Rsg/Aames Security Inc ....E.......562 529-5100
3300 E 59th St Long Beach (90805) *(P-17758)*

RSI Home Products Inc (HQ) ....A.......714 449-2200
400 E Orangethorpe Ave Anaheim (92801) *(P-4699)*

RSI Home Products Inc ....A.......949 720-1116
620 Newport Center Dr # 1200 Newport Beach (92660) *(P-4700)*

RSI Home Products Mfg Inc ....D.......714 449-2200
400 E Orangethorpe Ave Anaheim (92801) *(P-4701)*

Rsk Tool Incorporated ....E.......310 537-3302
410 W Carob St Compton (90220) *(P-10034)*

RSR Metal Spinning Inc ....F.......626 814-2339
850 E Edna Pl Covina (91723) *(P-12869)*

Rss Manufacturing ....F.......714 361-4800
1261 Logan Ave Costa Mesa (92626) *(P-11680)*

Rta Sales Inc ....F.......661 942-3553
210 E Avenue L Ste A Lancaster (93535) *(P-4118)*

RTC Aerospace, Chatsworth *Also called Cliffdale Manufacturing LLC (P-20473)*

RTC Aerospace, Chatsworth *Also called Logistical Support LLC (P-19970)*

RTC Arspace - Chtswrth Div Inc (PA) ....C.......818 341-3344
20409 Prairie St Chatsworth (91311) *(P-15625)*

Rte Welding, Fontana *Also called Tikos Tanks Inc (P-24674)*

Rtec-Instruments Inc ....E.......408 456-0801
1810 Oakland Rd Ste B San Jose (95131) *(P-21283)*

Rtg Inc ....F.......310 534-3016
4030 Spencer St Ste 108 Torrance (90503) *(P-18521)*

Rtg Investment Group Inc ....F.......310 444-5554
149 S Barrington Ave Los Angeles (90049) *(P-22878)*

Rti, City of Industry *Also called Rectangular Tubing Inc (P-5301)*

Rti, Gardena *Also called D & D Plastics Incorporated (P-9742)*

Rti Los Angeles, Norwalk *Also called New Cntury Mtals Southeast Inc (P-11277)*

Rtie Holdings LLC ....D.......714 765-8200
1800 E Via Burton Anaheim (92806) *(P-19073)*

Rtm Products Inc ....E.......562 926-2400
13120 Arctic Cir Santa Fe Springs (90670) *(P-11067)*

Rtmex Inc ....C.......619 391-9913
1202 Piper Ranch Rd San Diego (92154) *(P-3984)*

Rtr Industries LLC ....E.......714 996-0050
1360 N Jefferson St Anaheim (92807) *(P-15618)*

RTS Packaging LLC ....D.......209 722-2787
1900 Wardrobe Ave Merced (95341) *(P-5526)*

RTS Packaging LLC ....E.......562 356-6550
14103 Borate St Santa Fe Springs (90670) *(P-5263)*

RTS Powder Coating Inc (PA) ....E.......909 393-5404
15121 Sierra Bonita Ln Chino (91710) *(P-13238)*

Rubber Plastic & Metal Pdts, Rcho STA Marg *Also called RPM Products Inc (P-9252)*

Rubber Teck Division, Long Beach *Also called Rubbercraft Corp Cal Ltd (P-9271)*

Rubbercraft Corp Cal Ltd (HQ) ....C.......562 354-2800
3701 E Conant St Long Beach (90808) *(P-9271)*

Rubberite Corp (PA) ....F.......714 546-6464
301 Goetz Ave Santa Ana (92707) *(P-9367)*

Rubberite Cypress Sponge Rubbe, Santa Ana *Also called Rubberite Corp (P-9367)*

Rubberite Cypress Sponge Rubbe, Santa Ana *Also called Cypress Sponge Rubber Products (P-9299)*

Rubel Marguerite Mfg Co ....F.......415 362-2626
27 Pier San Francisco (94111) *(P-3275)*

Ruben and Sharam, Los Angeles *Also called RJ Singer International Inc (P-10204)*

Ruben Ortiz, Sacramento *Also called Capitol Steel Products (P-10942)*

Rubens Jewelry Mfg, Los Angeles *Also called RJ Jewelry Inc (P-22564)*

Rubicon Express (PA) ....F.......916 858-8575
3290 Monier Cir Ste 100 Rancho Cordova (95742) *(P-14531)*

Rubicon Manufacturing, Rancho Cordova *Also called Rubicon Express (P-14531)*

Rubio Fabrics, Sacramento *Also called McCarthys Draperies Inc (P-3593)*

Ruby Rox, Los Angeles *Also called Misyd Corp (P-3485)*

Rucci Inc ....F.......323 778-9000
6700 11th Ave Los Angeles (90043) *(P-23464)*

Rucker & Knolls, Milpitas *Also called Rucker & Kolls Inc (P-14532)*

Rucker & Kolls Inc (HQ) ....E.......408 934-9875
1064 Yosemite Dr Milpitas (95035) *(P-14532)*

Rucker Mill & Cabinet Works ....F.......530 621-0236
5828 Mother Lode Dr Placerville (95667) *(P-4242)*

Ruckus Wireless Inc ....E.......408 235-5500
2450 Walsh Ave Santa Clara (95051) *(P-17647)*

Rudd Winery, Oakville *Also called Rudd Wines Inc (P-1901)*

Rudd Wines Inc (PA) ....E.......707 944-8577
500 Oakville Xrd Oakville (94562) *(P-1901)*

Rudex Broadcasting Ltd Corp ....F.......213 494-3377
12272 Sarazen Pl Granada Hills (91344) *(P-17648)*

Rudolph Foods Company Inc ....D.......909 388-2202
920 W Fourth St Beaumont (92223) *(P-2342)*

Ruffstuff Inc ....F.......916 600-1945
3237 Rippey Rd Ste 200 Loomis (95650) *(P-19761)*

Rugged Info Tech Eqp Corp (PA) ....E.......805 577-9710
25 E Easy St Simi Valley (93065) *(P-15325)*

Rugged Systems Inc ....C.......858 391-1006
13000 Danielson St Ste Q Poway (92064) *(P-14970)*

Ruggeri Marble and Granite Inc ....D.......310 513-2155
16001 S San Pedro St C Gardena (90248) *(P-10929)*

Ruhe Corporation (PA) ....C.......714 777-8321
901 S Leslie St La Habra (90631) *(P-2343)*

Ruiz Flour Tortillas, Riverside *Also called Ruiz Mexican Foods Inc (P-2606)*

Ruiz Food Products Inc (PA) ....A.......559 591-5510
501 S Alta Ave Dinuba (93618) *(P-978)*

Ruiz Industries Inc ....F.......818 582-6882
13027 Telfair Ave Sylmar (91342) *(P-10243)*

Ruiz Mexican Foods Inc (PA) ....C.......909 947-7811
1200 Marlborough Ave A Riverside (92507) *(P-2606)*

Rumble Entertainment Inc ....E.......650 316-8819
2121 S El Cmino Real C1 San Mateo (94403) *(P-22710)*

Rumble Games, San Mateo *Also called Rumble Entertainment Inc (P-22710)*

Rumiano Cheese Co (PA) ....C.......530 934-5438
1629 County Road E Willows (95988) *(P-571)*

Rumiano Cheese Co ....E.......707 465-1535
511 9th St Crescent City (95531) *(P-572)*

Runa Inc ....F.......508 253-5000
2 W 5th Ave Ste 300 San Mateo (94402) *(P-24368)*

Runners World Magazine ....F.......310 615-4567
2101 Rosecrans Ave # 6200 El Segundo (90245) *(P-6021)*

Rupert Gibbon & Spider Inc ....E.......800 442-0455
1147 Healdsburg Ave Healdsburg (95448) *(P-8677)*

Rurisond Inc ....F.......650 395-7136
2725 Ohio Ave Redwood City (94061) *(P-17649)*

Rush Pcb Inc ....F.......408 469-6013
2149 Otoole Ave Ste 20 San Jose (95131) *(P-17981)*

Rush Press Inc ....E.......619 296-7874
955 Gateway Center Way San Diego (92102) *(P-6850)*

Russ Bassett Corp ....C.......562 945-2445
8189 Byron Rd Whittier (90606) *(P-4608)*

Russ International Inc ....E.......310 329-7121
1658 W 132nd St Gardena (90249) *(P-12361)*

Russell Fabrication Corp ....E.......661 861-8495
4940 Gilmore Ave Bakersfield (93308) *(P-13484)*

Russell Kc & Son ....E.......559 686-3236
375 E Paige Ave Tulare (93274) *(P-13667)*

Russell-Stanley ....D.......909 980-7114
9449 Santa Anita Ave Rancho Cucamonga (91730) *(P-10035)*

Russell-Stanley West, Rancho Cucamonga *Also called Russell-Stanley (P-10035)*

Russian River Brewing Co, Santa Rosa *Also called 23 Bottles of Beer LLC (P-1488)*

Russian River Winery Inc ....E.......707 824-2005
2191 Laguna Rd Santa Rosa (95401) *(P-1902)*

Rusty Surfboards, San Diego *Also called Dgb LLC (P-22789)*

Rusty Surfboards Inc (PA) ....E.......858 578-0414
8495 Commerce Ave San Diego (92121) *(P-22879)*

Rusty Surfboards Inc ....F.......858 551-0262
2170 Avenida De La Playa La Jolla (92037) *(P-22880)*

Ruth Training Center Sew Mchs ....F.......213 748-8033
328 E 24th St Los Angeles (90011) *(P-3857)*

Rutherford Wine Company, Saint Helena *Also called Round Hill Cellars (P-1899)*

Ruxco Engineering Inc ....F.......530 622-4122
6051 Entp Dr Ste 105 Diamond Springs (95619) *(P-21885)*

Rvision Inc ....F.......408 437-5777
2365 Paragon Dr Ste D San Jose (95131) *(P-21404)*

Rwi, Granite Bay *Also called Recoating-West Inc (P-12352)*

ALPHABETIC

Employee Codes: A=Over 500 employees, B=251-500
C=101-250, D=51-100, E=20-50, F=10-19

2020 California
Manfacturers Register

© Mergent Inc. 1-800-342-5647

1227

Rwnm Inc..........D.......760 489-1245
1240 Simpson Way Escondido (92029) ***(P-16574)***
Rxd Nova Pharmaceuticals Inc..........F.......610 952-7242
2010 Cessna Dr Vacaville (95688) ***(P-8116)***
Rxsafe LLC..........D.......760 593-7161
2453 Cades Way Bldg A Vista (92081) ***(P-14533)***
Ryan Press, Buena Park *Also called Q Team* ***(P-6818)***
Ryangmw Inc..........F.......530 305-2499
13861 Dry Creek Rd Auburn (95602) ***(P-19552)***
Ryko Plastic Products Inc..........F.......909 773-0050
701 E Francis St Ontario (91761) ***(P-10036)***
Ryko Solutions Inc..........E.......916 372-8815
3939 W Capitol Ave Ste D West Sacramento (95691) ***(P-15572)***
Rypple..........F.......888 479-7753
577 Howard St Fl 3 San Francisco (94105) ***(P-24369)***
Ryss Lab Inc..........F.......510 477-9570
29540 Kohoutek Way Union City (94587) ***(P-20773)***
Rytan Inc..........F.......310 328-6553
1648 W 134th St Gardena (90249) ***(P-13946)***
Ryvec Inc..........E.......714 520-5592
251 E Palais Rd Anaheim (92805) ***(P-7461)***
Ryzer-Rx LLC..........F.......858 454-7477
5575 La Jolla Blvd La Jolla (92037) ***(P-7688)***
S & C Electric Company..........E.......510 864-9300
1135 Atlantic Ave Ste 100 Alameda (94501) ***(P-16750)***
S & C Foods Inc..........E.......323 205-6887
6094 Malburg Way Vernon (90058) ***(P-1393)***
S & H Cabinets and Mfg Inc..........E.......909 357-0551
10860 Mulberry Ave Fontana (92337) ***(P-4820)***
S & H Machine Inc (PA)..........F.......818 846-9847
900 N Lake St Burbank (91502) ***(P-16378)***
S & H Welding Inc..........F.......916 386-8921
8604 Elder Creek Rd Sacramento (95828) ***(P-12048)***
S & J Pro Clean Services, North Hills *Also called S & J Prof Property Svcs* ***(P-80)***
S & J Prof Property Svcs..........F.......818 892-0181
9615 Aqueduct Ave North Hills (91343) ***(P-80)***
S & K Plating Inc..........E.......310 632-7141
2727 N Compton Ave Compton (90222) ***(P-13091)***
S & K Theatrical Drap Inc..........F.......818 503-0596
7313 Varna Ave North Hollywood (91605) ***(P-3596)***
S & L Contracting..........E.......661 371-6379
900 W Kern Ave Ste 900 # 900 Mc Farland (93250) ***(P-12362)***
S & R Cnc Machining, Valencia *Also called Salvador Ramirez* ***(P-19978)***
S & S Bindery Inc..........E.......909 596-2213
2366 1st St La Verne (91750) ***(P-7345)***
S & S Foods LLC..........C.......626 633-1609
1120 W Foothill Blvd Azusa (91702) ***(P-493)***
S & S Installations Inc..........E.......909 370-1730
294 W Olive St Colton (92324) ***(P-15573)***
S & S Numerical Control Inc..........E.......818 341-4141
19841 Nordhoff St Northridge (91324) ***(P-16379)***
S & S Precision Mfg Inc..........E.......714 754-6664
2509 S Broadway Santa Ana (92707) ***(P-16380)***
S & S Precision Sheetmetal, Canoga Park *Also called B S K T Inc* ***(P-15769)***
S & S Printers..........E.......714 535-5592
2100 W Lincoln Ave Ste A Anaheim (92801) ***(P-6851)***
S & S Woodcarver Inc..........E.......714 258-2222
13 San Rafael Pl Laguna Niguel (92677) ***(P-4529)***
S 2 K, Chatsworth *Also called S2k Graphics Inc* ***(P-23188)***
S A C O Your Manufacturing Co, Newbury Park *Also called Saco* ***(P-19398)***
S A Fields Inc..........F.......559 292-1221
3328 N Duke Ave Fresno (93727) ***(P-3702)***
S A Hartman Productions, Sherman Oaks *Also called SA Hartman & Associates Inc* ***(P-22457)***
S and C Precision Inc..........F.......626 338-7149
5045 Calmview Ave Baldwin Park (91706) ***(P-19074)***
S and S Carbide Tool Inc..........E.......619 670-5214
2830 Via Orange Way Ste D Spring Valley (91978) ***(P-14102)***
S B I F Inc..........F.......805 683-1711
873 S Kellogg Ave Goleta (93117) ***(P-13239)***
S Bravo Systems Inc..........E.......323 888-4133
2929 Vail Ave Commerce (90040) ***(P-12049)***
S C Coatings Corporation..........E.......951 461-9777
41745 Elm St Ste 101 Murrieta (92562) ***(P-13240)***
S C P, Berkeley *Also called Spiritual Counterfeits Prj Inc* ***(P-6031)***
S C R Molding Inc..........F.......951 736-5490
2340 Pomona Rd Corona (92880) ***(P-10037)***
S C S, North Highlands *Also called Security Contractor Svcs Inc* ***(P-12508)***
S D Drilling..........F.......760 789-5658
24660 E Old Julian Hwy Ramona (92065) ***(P-257)***
S D I, Visalia *Also called Spraying Devices Inc* ***(P-13697)***
S D I, Camarillo *Also called Structural Diagnostics Inc* ***(P-21129)***
S D M, Chino *Also called Syntech Development & Mfg Inc* ***(P-10077)***
S D M Furniture Co Inc..........F.......323 936-0295
4620 W Jefferson Blvd Los Angeles (90016) ***(P-4609)***
S D S, Ontario *Also called Specialized Dairy Service Inc* ***(P-13672)***
S E M, Fremont *Also called Streamline Electronics Mfg Inc* ***(P-18012)***
S E P E Inc..........E.......714 241-7373
245 Fischer Ave Ste C4 Costa Mesa (92626) ***(P-14971)***
S F Enterprises Incorporated..........F.......650 455-3223
707 Warrington Ave Redwood City (94063) ***(P-16381)***
S F Technology, Cerritos *Also called UFO Designs* ***(P-19792)***
S G S, Baldwin Park *Also called Superior Grounding Systems* ***(P-16927)***
S J Helicopter Service, Delano *Also called San-Joaquin Helicopters Inc* ***(P-19929)***
S J Sterilized Wiping Rags..........F.......408 287-2512
201 San Jose Ave San Jose (95125) ***(P-2954)***
S K Digital Imaging Inc..........F.......858 408-0732
7686 Miramar Rd Ste A San Diego (92126) ***(P-7346)***
S K Laboratories Inc..........D.......714 695-9800
5420 E La Palma Ave Anaheim (92807) ***(P-7689)***
S K Labs, Anaheim *Also called S K Laboratories Inc* ***(P-7689)***
S L Cellars..........F.......707 833-5070
9380 Sonoma Hwy Kenwood (95452) ***(P-1903)***
S L Fusco Inc (PA)..........E.......310 868-1010
1966 E Via Arado Rancho Dominguez (90220) ***(P-13947)***
S M G Custom Cabinets Inc..........E.......916 381-5999
5750 Alder Ave Sacramento (95828) ***(P-4243)***
S M L Industries Inc..........F.......619 258-7941
10965 Hartley Rd Ste P Santee (92071) ***(P-22711)***
S M S Briners Inc..........F.......209 941-8515
17750 E Highway 4 Stockton (95215) ***(P-898)***
S M U, Los Angeles *Also called Rm 518 Management LLC* ***(P-3577)***
S Martinelli & Company (PA)..........C.......831 724-1126
735 W Beach St Watsonville (95076) ***(P-2607)***
S R 3, North Hollywood *Also called Sr3 Solutions LLC* ***(P-5836)***
S R C Devices Inccustomer (PA)..........F.......866 772-8668
6295 Ferris Sq Ste D San Diego (92121) ***(P-16751)***
S R Machining-Properties LLC..........C.......951 520-9486
640 Parkridge Ave Norco (92860) ***(P-16382)***
S R S M Inc..........C.......310 952-9000
945 E Church St Riverside (92507) ***(P-7606)***
S S I, Irvine *Also called Seal Science Inc* ***(P-9254)***
S S Schaffer Co Inc..........F.......323 560-1430
5637 District Blvd Vernon (90058) ***(P-13948)***
S S Sign Electric, Los Angeles *Also called Soteleo Salvadar* ***(P-23213)***
S Sedghi Inc (PA)..........E.......213 745-2019
2416 W 7th St Los Angeles (90057) ***(P-3489)***
S Studio Inc..........D.......213 388-7400
3030 W 6th St Los Angeles (90020) ***(P-3276)***
S T Cycle Wear, El Cajon *Also called St Cyclewear/Gallop LLC* ***(P-3117)***
S T E U Inc..........E.......805 527-0987
1625 Surveyor Ave Simi Valley (93063) ***(P-17160)***
S T I, Corona *Also called Paragon Tactical Inc* ***(P-22864)***
S W C Group Inc..........E.......888 982-1628
2399 Bateman Ave Duarte (91010) ***(P-5309)***
S W G, Union City *Also called Smart Wires Inc* ***(P-18743)***
S&B Development Group LLC..........E.......213 446-2818
1901 Avenue Of The Stars # 200 Los Angeles (90067) ***(P-2732)***
S&B Filters Inc..........D.......909 947-0015
15461 Slover Ave Ste A Fontana (92337) ***(P-19762)***
S&B Industry Inc..........D.......909 569-4155
105 S Puente St Brea (92821) ***(P-10038)***
S&B Pharma Inc..........D.......626 334-2908
405 S Motor Ave Azusa (91702) ***(P-7690)***
S&B Vineyard LLC..........E.......707 963-7194
200 Rutherford Hill Rd Rutherford (94573) ***(P-1904)***
S&H International Inc..........F.......213 626-7112
1240 Palmetto St Los Angeles (90013) ***(P-16989)***
S&H Melkes Inc..........E.......626 448-5062
9928 Hayward Way South El Monte (91733) ***(P-13333)***
S&J Carrera Constructions, Watsonville *Also called Carrera Construction Inc* ***(P-181)***
S&S Flavours, Brea *Also called Scisorek & Son Flavors Inc* ***(P-2229)***
S&S Investment Club (PA)..........F.......707 747-5508
5340 Gateway Plaza Dr Benicia (94510) ***(P-20520)***
S&S Signature Mill Works Inc..........F.......916 652-1046
5951 Jetton Ln Ste C6 Loomis (95650) ***(P-4530)***
S-Energy America Inc (HQ)..........F.......949 281-7897
18022 Cowan Ste 260 Irvine (92614) ***(P-18522)***
S-Matrix Corporation..........F.......707 441-0404
1594 Myrtle Ave Eureka (95501) ***(P-24370)***
S.T. Johnson Company, Fairfield *Also called Innovative Combustion Tech* ***(P-11702)***
S/R Industries Inc (HQ)..........F.......562 968-5800
10652 Bloomfield Ave Santa Fe Springs (90670) ***(P-22881)***
S2e Inc..........F.......626 965-1008
817 Lawson St City of Industry (91748) ***(P-17279)***
S2k Graphics Inc..........E.......818 885-3900
9255 Deering Ave Chatsworth (91311) ***(P-23188)***
S3 Graphics Inc..........C.......510 687-4900
940 Mission Ct Fremont (94539) ***(P-18523)***
S3d Acquisition II Company, San Diego *Also called Overland Storage Inc* ***(P-15070)***
SA Hartman & Associates Inc..........E.......818 907-9681
14570 Benefit St Sherman Oaks (91403) ***(P-22457)***
SA Serving Lines Inc..........F.......714 848-7529
226 W Carleton Ave Orange (92867) ***(P-12363)***
Saab Enterprises Inc..........D.......909 823-2228
1433 Miller Dr Colton (92324) ***(P-494)***
Saags Products LLC..........D.......510 678-3412
1799 Factor Ave San Leandro (94577) ***(P-495)***
Saavy Inc..........F.......323 728-2137
707 W Whittier Blvd Montebello (90640) ***(P-13949)***
Saaz Micro Inc..........F.......805 405-0700
94 W Cochran St Ste A Simi Valley (93065) ***(P-18524)***
Saba Motors Inc..........F.......408 219-8675
521 Charcot Ave Ste 165 San Jose (95131) ***(P-19499)***
Saba Software Inc (PA)..........D.......877 722-2101
4120 Dublin Blvd Ste 200 Dublin (94568) ***(P-24371)***
Sabel, Vista *Also called Surgistar Inc* ***(P-21919)***
Sabert Corporation..........F.......951 342-0240
860 Palmyrita Ave Riverside (92507) ***(P-10039)***
Sabia Incorporated (PA)..........E.......858 217-2200
10919 Technology Pl Ste A San Diego (92127) ***(P-20931)***
Sabre Sciences Inc..........F.......760 448-2750
2233 Faraday Ave Ste K Carlsbad (92008) ***(P-7691)***
Sabred International Packg Inc..........E.......714 996-2800
3740 Prospect Ave Yorba Linda (92886) ***(P-9567)***
Sabrin Corporation..........F.......626 792-3813
2836 E Walnut St Pasadena (91107) ***(P-12364)***

Mergent e-mail: customerrelations@mergent.com
1228
2020 California
Manufacturers Register
(P-0000) Products & Services Section entry number
(PA)=Parent Co (HQ)=Headquarters (DH)=Div Headquarters

Sac EDM & Waterjet, Rancho Cordova *Also called E D M Sacramento Inc* ***(P-15917)***
Sac Valley Ornamental Ir Outl ....F....916 383-6340
8540 Thys Ct Sacramento (95828) ***(P-11106)***
Sac-TEC Labs Inc (PA) ....E....310 375-5295
24301 Wilmington Ave Carson (90745) ***(P-18525)***
Sachs & Associates Inc ....F....310 356-7911
1230 Rosecrans Ave # 408 Manhattan Beach (90266) ***(P-15086)***
Sachs Industries Inc ....F....631 242-9000
801 Kate Ln Woodland (95776) ***(P-5527)***
Saco ....E....805 499-7788
3525 Old Conejo Rd # 107 Newbury Park (91320) ***(P-19398)***
Sacramental Color Coil ....E....916 383-9588
8541 Thys Ct Sacramento (95828) ***(P-7347)***
Sacramento Baking Co Inc ....E....916 361-2000
9221 Beatty Dr Sacramento (95826) ***(P-1271)***
Sacramento Bee, Sacramento *Also called McClatchy Newspapers Inc* ***(P-5728)***
Sacramento Business Journal, Sacramento *Also called American City Bus Journals Inc* ***(P-5548)***
Sacramento Coca-Cola Btlg Inc (HQ) ....B....916 928-2300
4101 Gateway Park Blvd Sacramento (95834) ***(P-2163)***
Sacramento Coca-Cola Btlg Inc ....E....209 541-3200
1733 Morgan Rd Ste 200 Modesto (95358) ***(P-2164)***
Sacramento Envelope Co Inc ....F....916 371-4747
773 Northport Dr Ste C-A West Sacramento (95691) ***(P-6852)***
Sacramento Gazette, The, Sacramento *Also called Gazette Media Co LLC* ***(P-5643)***
Sacramento News & Review, Sacramento *Also called Chico Community Publishing* ***(P-5587)***
Sacramento Rebar Inc (PA) ....E....916 447-9700
5072 Hillsdale Cir # 200 El Dorado Hills (95762) ***(P-12603)***
Sacramento Rendering Co, Sacramento *Also called SRC Milling Co LLC* ***(P-1466)***
Saddleback Educational Inc ....E....714 640-5224
151 Kalmus Dr Ste J1 Costa Mesa (92626) ***(P-6143)***
Saddleback Stair & Millwork ....F....949 460-0384
23291 Peralta Dr Ste B4 Laguna Hills (92653) ***(P-4119)***
Sadie & Sage Inc (PA) ....F....213 234-2188
1900 E 25th St Los Angeles (90058) ***(P-3190)***
Sadra Medical Inc ....E....408 370-1550
160 Knowles Dr Los Gatos (95032) ***(P-21886)***
SAE Engineering Inc ....E....408 492-1784
365 Reed St Santa Clara (95050) ***(P-12365)***
Saehan Electronics America Inc (PA) ....F....858 496-1500
7880 Airway Rd Ste B5g San Diego (92154) ***(P-17982)***
Saeilo Manufacturing Inds, Santa Fe Springs *Also called SMI Ca Inc* ***(P-16407)***
Saeshin America Inc ....E....949 825-6925
216 Technology Dr Ste F Irvine (92618) ***(P-22187)***
Saf West, Redding *Also called Southern Alum Finshg Co Inc* ***(P-11268)***
Saf-T-Cab Inc (PA) ....D....559 268-5541
3241 S Parkway Dr Fresno (93725) ***(P-19553)***
Saf-T-Co Supply ....E....714 547-9975
1300 E Normandy Pl Santa Ana (92705) ***(P-16954)***
Saf-T-Kut LLC ....E....657 210-4426
2652 Dow Ave Tustin (92780) ***(P-13950)***
Safari Books Online, Sebastopol *Also called OReilly Media Inc* ***(P-6131)***
Safari Signs, Chatsworth *Also called Printing Safari Co* ***(P-6807)***
Safariland LLC ....B....909 923-7300
3120 E Mission Blvd Ontario (91761) ***(P-10252)***
Safariland LLC (HQ) ....E....925 219-1097
3120 E Mission Blvd Ontario (91761) ***(P-17759)***
Safc Pharma, Carlsbad *Also called Sigma-Aldrich Corporation* ***(P-9022)***
Safcor Inc ....F....818 392-8437
13455 Ventura Blvd 237a Sherman Oaks (91423) ***(P-10205)***
Safe Catch Inc ....F....415 944-4442
85 Liberty Ship Way Sausalito (94965) ***(P-2250)***
Safe Environment Engineering ....F....661 295-5500
28320 Constellation Rd Valencia (91355) ***(P-19075)***
Safe Plating Inc ....D....626 810-1872
18001 Railroad St City of Industry (91748) ***(P-13092)***
Safe Publishing Company ....D....805 973-1300
5775 Lindero Canyon Rd Westlake Village (91362) ***(P-7206)***
Safeland Industrial Supply Inc (PA) ....F....909 786-1967
10278 Birtcher Dr Jurupa Valley (91752) ***(P-11107)***
Safety America Inc ....F....619 660-6968
2766 Via Orange Way Ste D Spring Valley (91978) ***(P-22383)***
Safety-Kleen Systems Inc ....F....559 486-1960
3561 S Maple Ave Fresno (93725) ***(P-14534)***
Safetychain Software Inc (PA) ....E....415 233-9474
7599 Redwood Blvd Ste 205 Novato (94945) ***(P-24372)***
Safeway Sign Company ....E....760 246-7070
9875 Yucca Rd Adelanto (92301) ***(P-23189)***
Saffola Quality Foods, Ontario *Also called Ventura Foods LLC* ***(P-540)***
Safna A Division of Heateflex, Arcadia *Also called Heateflex Corporation* ***(P-11699)***
Safran Cabin Galleys Us Inc ....E....714 861-7300
14505 Astronautics Ln Huntington Beach (92647) ***(P-20214)***
Safran Cabin Galleys Us Inc (HQ) ....A....714 861-7300
17311 Nichols Ln Huntington Beach (92647) ***(P-20215)***
Safran Cabin Inc ....C....909 652-9700
8595 Milliken Ave Ste 101 Rancho Cucamonga (91730) ***(P-20216)***
Safran Cabin Inc ....C....714 901-2672
12472 Industry St Garden Grove (92841) ***(P-20217)***
Safran Cabin Inc (HQ) ....B....714 934-0000
5701 Bolsa Ave Huntington Beach (92647) ***(P-20218)***
Safran Cabin Inc ....F....805 922-3013
2850 Skyway Dr Santa Maria (93455) ***(P-20219)***
Safran Cabin Inc ....C....562 344-4780
11240 Warland Dr Cypress (90630) ***(P-20220)***
Safran Cabin Inc ....B....714 891-1906
7330 Lincoln Way Garden Grove (92841) ***(P-20221)***
Safran Cabin Inc ....C....619 671-0430
6754 Calle De Linea # 111 San Diego (92154) ***(P-20222)***
Safran Cabin Inc ....B....909 947-2725
1945 S Grove Ave Ontario (91761) ***(P-20223)***
Safran Cabin Materials LLC ....F....909 947-4115
1945 S Grove Ave Ontario (91761) ***(P-20224)***
Safran Elec Def Avnics USA LLC ....C....949 642-2427
3184 Pullman St Costa Mesa (92626) ***(P-20712)***
Safran Pwr Units San Diego LLC ....D....858 223-2228
4255 Ruffin Rd Ste 100 San Diego (92123) ***(P-19977)***
Safran Seats Santa Maria LLC ....A....805 922-5995
2641 Airpark Dr Santa Maria (93455) ***(P-20225)***
Sage (PA) ....E....925 288-4827
1410 Monument Blvd Concord (94520) ***(P-8327)***
Sage Goddess Inc ....E....650 733-6639
3830 Del Amo Blvd Ste 102 Torrance (90503) ***(P-22566)***
Sage Instruments Inc ....D....831 761-1000
240 Airport Blvd Freedom (95019) ***(P-21115)***
Sage Interior Inc ....F....949 654-0184
9 Aspen Tree Ln Irvine (92612) ***(P-4244)***
Sage Machado Inc ....F....323 931-0595
133 N Gramercy Pl Los Angeles (90004) ***(P-22567)***
Sage Metering Inc ....F....831 242-2030
8 Harris Ct Ste D1 Monterey (93940) ***(P-21284)***
Sage Software Inc ....C....650 579-3628
1380 Tatan Trail Rd Burlingame (94010) ***(P-24373)***
Sage Software Holdings Inc (HQ) ....B....866 530-7243
6561 Irvine Center Dr Irvine (92618) ***(P-24374)***
Sage The Label, Los Angeles *Also called Sadie & Sage Inc* ***(P-3190)***
Sager Computers, City of Industry *Also called Midern Computer Inc* ***(P-14948)***
Sago Systems Inc ....F....858 646-5300
10455 Pacific Center Ct San Diego (92121) ***(P-20713)***
SAI Industries ....E....818 842-6144
631 Allen Ave Glendale (91201) ***(P-13277)***
Saigon Nho, Garden Grove *Also called Little Saigon News Inc* ***(P-5699)***
Saigon Times Inc ....F....626 288-2696
9234 Valley Blvd Rosemead (91770) ***(P-5812)***
saint gobain certainteed pipe, Lodi *Also called Certainteed Corporation* ***(P-7547)***
Saint Gobain Containers Inc ....F....707 437-8700
2600 Stanford Ct Fairfield (94533) ***(P-10293)***
Saint Nine America Inc ....E....562 921-5300
10700 Norwalk Blvd Santa Fe Springs (90670) ***(P-22882)***
Saint-Gobain Ceramics Plas Inc ....E....714 701-3900
4905 E Hunter Ave Anaheim (92807) ***(P-8772)***
Saint-Gobain Performance Plas, San Diego *Also called Saint-Gobain Solar Gard LLC* ***(P-9419)***
Saint-Gobain Prfmce Plas Corp ....C....714 893-0470
7301 Orangewood Ave Garden Grove (92841) ***(P-7607)***
Saint-Gobain Solar Gard LLC (HQ) ....D....866 300-2674
4540 Viewridge Ave San Diego (92123) ***(P-9419)***
Saintsbury LLC ....F....707 252-0592
1500 Los Carneros Ave NAPA (94559) ***(P-1905)***
Sake Robotics ....F....650 207-4021
570 El Camino Real 150-3 Redwood City (94063) ***(P-14281)***
Saks Styling Incorporated ....E....818 244-0540
641 W Harvard St Glendale (91204) ***(P-22568)***
Sakura Noodle Inc ....F....213 623-2396
620 E 7th St Los Angeles (90021) ***(P-2380)***
Sal J Acsta Sheetmetal Mfg Inc ....D....408 275-6370
930 Remillard Ct San Jose (95122) ***(P-12366)***
Sal Rodriguez ....F....408 993-8091
1680 Almaden Expy Ste I San Jose (95125) ***(P-13093)***
Saladino Sausage Company, Fresno *Also called Choice Food Products Inc* ***(P-447)***
Salco Dynamic Solutions Inc (PA) ....E....714 374-7500
6248 Surfpoint Cir Huntington Beach (92648) ***(P-9155)***
Salco Oil, Huntington Beach *Also called Salco Dynamic Solutions Inc* ***(P-9155)***
Salco Products, Fontana *Also called Nyx Industries Inc* ***(P-13653)***
Sale 121 Corp (PA) ....D....888 233-7667
1467 68th Ave Sacramento (95822) ***(P-15087)***
Saleen Automotive Inc (PA) ....E....800 888-8945
2735 Wardlow Rd Corona (92882) ***(P-12748)***
Saleen Incorporated (PA) ....B....714 400-2121
2735 Wardlow Rd Corona (92882) ***(P-19500)***
Sales Office, Irwindale *Also called Legacy Vulcan LLC* ***(P-10596)***
Sales Office Accessories Inc ....F....714 896-9600
11562 Knott St Ste 8 Garden Grove (92841) ***(P-23190)***
Salesforcecom Inc ....E....415 323-8685
50 Fremont St Ste 300 San Francisco (94105) ***(P-24375)***
Salesforcecom Inc ....F....703 463-3300
1 Market Ste 300 San Francisco (94105) ***(P-24376)***
Salesforcecom Inc (PA) ....A....415 901-7000
415 Mission St Fl 3 San Francisco (94105) ***(P-24377)***
Salesforcecom Inc ....E....310 752-7000
1442 2nd St Santa Monica (90401) ***(P-24378)***
Salinas Newspapers Inc, Salinas *Also called Salinas Newspapers LLC* ***(P-5813)***
Salinas Newspapers LLC ....C....831 424-2221
1093 S Main St Ste 101 Salinas (93901) ***(P-5813)***
Salinas Tallow Co Inc ....E....831 422-6436
1 Work Cir Salinas (93901) ***(P-1465)***
Salinas Valley Wax Paper Co ....E....831 424-2747
1111 Abbott St Salinas (93901) ***(P-5528)***
Salis International Inc ....E....303 384-3588
3921 Oceanic Dr Ste 802 Oceanside (92056) ***(P-22944)***
Salon Brandy, Compton *Also called California Decor* ***(P-4008)***
Salpy, Encino *Also called International Last Mfg Co* ***(P-9842)***
Salsam Manufacturing Co, Santa Ana *Also called Kalanico Inc* ***(P-4915)***
Salsbury Industries Inc (PA) ....C....323 846-6700
18300 Central Ave Carson (90746) ***(P-5000)***
Salus Enterprises of N Amer, Redwood City *Also called Salus North America Inc* ***(P-20808)***

ALPHABETIC

Salus North America Inc....F....888 387-2587
850 Main St Redwood City (94063) ***(P-20808)***
Salutron Incorporated (PA)....E....510 795-2876
8371 Central Ave Ste A Newark (94560) ***(P-22307)***
Salvador Ramirez....F....661 702-1813
25334 Avenue Stanford B Valencia (91355) ***(P-19978)***
Salwasser Inc....D....559 843-2882
4087 N Howard Ave Kerman (93630) ***(P-860)***
Sam & Lavi, Los Angeles *Also called Valmas Inc* ***(P-3260)***
Sam Machining Inc....F....714 632-7035
1140 N Kraemer Blvd Ste M Anaheim (92806) ***(P-16383)***
Sam Vaziri Vance Inc (PA)....E....323 822-3955
10250 Santa Monica Blvd # 1867 Los Angeles (90067) ***(P-22384)***
Sama Eyewear, Los Angeles *Also called Sam Vaziri Vance Inc* ***(P-22384)***
Samax Precision Inc....E....408 245-9555
926 W Evelyn Ave Sunnyvale (94086) ***(P-16384)***
Sambrailo Packaging, Watsonville *Also called Samco Plastics Inc* ***(P-5340)***
Samco Plastics Inc....F....831 761-1392
1260 W Beach St Watsonville (95076) ***(P-5340)***
Samedan Oil Corporation....B....661 319-5038
1360 Landing Ave Seal Beach (90740) ***(P-65)***
Samil Power US Ltd....A....925 930-3924
3478 Buskirk Ave Ste 1000 Pleasant Hill (94523) ***(P-18526)***
Samis Sports....F....323 965-8093
5215 1/2 W Adams Blvd Los Angeles (90016) ***(P-22883)***
Sammons Equipment Mfg Corp....F....951 340-3419
390 Meyer Cir Ste A Corona (92879) ***(P-5081)***
Sampe, Diamond Bar *Also called Society For The Advancement of* ***(P-6030)***
Sampling International LLC (PA)....F....949 305-5333
2942 Century Pl Costa Mesa (92626) ***(P-3858)***
Sams Crftsman Style Pfab Gzbos, Gardena *Also called Samsgazeboscom Inc* ***(P-3945)***
Sams Tailoring....F....714 963-6776
18120 Brookhurst St Fountain Valley (92708) ***(P-2977)***
Sams Trade Development Corp....E....213 225-0188
818 S Main St Los Angeles (90014) ***(P-22994)***
Samsgazeboscom Inc....F....310 523-3778
132 E 163rd St Gardena (90248) ***(P-3945)***
Samson Pharmaceuticals Inc....E....323 722-3066
2027 Leo Ave Commerce (90040) ***(P-8117)***
Samson Products Inc....B....323 726-9070
6285 Randolph St Commerce (90040) ***(P-5001)***
Samsung Sdi America Inc (HQ)....F....408 544-4470
665 Clyde Ave Mountain View (94043) ***(P-15326)***
Samsung SDS Globl Scl Amer Inc....E....201 263-3000
10509 Vista Sorrento Pkwy San Diego (92121) ***(P-24379)***
Samuel Raoof....E....818 534-3180
20660 Nordhoff St Chatsworth (91311) ***(P-8574)***
Samyang USA Inc....F....562 946-9977
3810 Wilshire Blvd # 1212 Los Angeles (90010) ***(P-2381)***
San Antonio Bakery, Compton *Also called Pedro Pallan* ***(P-1260)***
San Antonio Gift Shop, Los Angeles *Also called San Antonio Winery Inc* ***(P-1906)***
San Antonio Winery Inc (PA)....C....323 223-1401
737 Lamar St Los Angeles (90031) ***(P-1906)***
San Benito Shutter, Hollister *Also called SBS America LLC* ***(P-4121)***
San Benito Supply (PA)....C....831 637-5526
2984 Monterey Hwy San Jose (95111) ***(P-10644)***
San Bernandina Steel, Stockton *Also called Herrick Corporation* ***(P-11807)***
San Bernardino Canning Co., San Bernardino *Also called Refresco Beverages US Inc* ***(P-2133)***
San Bernardino County Sun, The, San Bernardino *Also called Sun Company San Bernardino Cal* ***(P-5842)***
San Brnrdino Cmnty College Dst....C....909 888-6511
701 S Mount Vernon Ave San Bernardino (92410) ***(P-7207)***
San Clemente Times LLC....F....949 388-7700
34932 Calle Del Sol Ste B Capistrano Beach (92624) ***(P-5814)***
San Dego Gographic Info Source....F....858 874-7000
5510 Overland Ave Ste 230 San Diego (92123) ***(P-6334)***
San Dego HM Grdn Lfestyles Mag, San Diego *Also called McKinnon Enterprises* ***(P-5986)***
San Dego Nghborhood Newspapers, Cypress *Also called Community Media Corporation* ***(P-5597)***
San Dego Prcsion Machining Inc....E....858 499-0379
9375 Ruffin Ct San Diego (92123) ***(P-12367)***
San Dego Prtective Coating Inc....F....619 448-7795
9344 Wheatlands Rd Ste A Santee (92071) ***(P-13241)***
San Diegan, San Diego *Also called San Diego Guide Inc* ***(P-6335)***
San Diego Ace Inc....C....619 252-3148
8490 Mathis Pl San Diego (92127) ***(P-10040)***
San Diego Afr Amrcn Gnlogy RSC....E....619 231-5810
5148 Market St San Diego (92114) ***(P-23465)***
San Diego Arcft Interiors Inc....E....619 474-1997
2940 Hoover Ave National City (91950) ***(P-4610)***
San Diego Business Journal, San Diego *Also called Cbj LP* ***(P-5900)***
San Diego Cabinets Inc....E....760 747-3100
2001 Lendee Dr Escondido (92025) ***(P-4245)***
San Diego Cmnty Newsppr Group, San Diego *Also called Mannis Communications Inc* ***(P-5722)***
San Diego Crating & Pkg Inc....F....858 748-0100
12678 Brookprinter Pl Poway (92064) ***(P-5264)***
San Diego Daily Transcript....D....619 232-4381
34 Emerald Gln Laguna Niguel (92677) ***(P-5149)***
San Diego Electric Sign Inc....F....619 258-1775
1890 Cordell Ct Ste 105 El Cajon (92020) ***(P-23191)***
San Diego Family Magazine LLC....F....619 685-6970
1475 6th Ave Ste 500 San Diego (92101) ***(P-6022)***
San Diego Guide Inc....E....858 877-3217
6370 Lusk Blvd Ste F202 San Diego (92121) ***(P-6335)***
San Diego Instruments Inc....F....858 530-2600
9155 Brown Deer Rd Ste 8 San Diego (92121) ***(P-21285)***
San Diego Lgbt Community Ctr, San Diego *Also called Center Health Services* ***(P-21202)***
San Diego Magazine Pubg Co....E....619 230-9292
707 Broadway Ste 1100 San Diego (92101) ***(P-6023)***
San Diego Mirror and Window, Vista *Also called J & B Manufacturing Corp* ***(P-10368)***
San Diego Paper Box Co Inc....E....619 660-9566
10605 Jamacha Blvd Spring Valley (91978) ***(P-5315)***
San Diego Pcb Design LLC....F....858 271-5722
9909 Mira Mesa Blvd # 250 San Diego (92131) ***(P-17983)***
San Diego Powder Coating, El Cajon *Also called BJS&t Enterprises Inc* ***(P-13150)***
San Diego Precast Concrete Inc (HQ)....E....619 240-8000
2735 Cactus Rd San Diego (92154) ***(P-10645)***
San Diego Printers, San Diego *Also called Three Man Corporation* ***(P-7250)***
San Diego Union Tribune, The, San Diego *Also called San Diego Union-Tribune LLC* ***(P-5816)***
San Diego Union-Tribune LLC....D....619 299-3131
600 B St Ste 1201 San Diego (92101) ***(P-5815)***
San Diego Union-Tribune LLC (PA)....A....619 299-3131
600 B St Ste 1201 San Diego (92101) ***(P-5816)***
San Emidio Quarry, Bakersfield *Also called Legacy Vulcan LLC* ***(P-10786)***
San Fernando Valley Bus Jurnl, Woodland Hills *Also called Cbj LP* ***(P-5898)***
San Francisco Bath Salt Co, Alameda *Also called Rmf Salt Holdings LLC* ***(P-8572)***
San Francisco Bay Brand Inc (PA)....E....510 792-7200
8239 Enterprise Dr Newark (94560) ***(P-1125)***
San Francisco Bay Guardian, San Francisco *Also called Bay Guardian Company* ***(P-5564)***
San Francisco Business Time, San Francisco *Also called Business Jrnl Publications Inc* ***(P-5573)***
San Francisco Circuits Inc....F....650 655-7202
1660 S Amphlett Blvd # 200 San Mateo (94402) ***(P-17984)***
San Francisco Daily Journal, San Francisco *Also called Daily Journal Corporation* ***(P-5609)***
San Francisco Elev Svcs Inc....E....925 829-5400
6517 Sierra Ln Dublin (94568) ***(P-13808)***
San Francisco Envelope, Fremont *Also called Cleansmart Solutions Inc* ***(P-5469)***
San Francisco Fine Bakery, Redwood City *Also called Golden Octagon Inc* ***(P-1219)***
San Francisco Foods Inc....D....510 357-7343
14054 Catalina St San Leandro (94577) ***(P-979)***
San Francisco Network....E....415 468-1110
2171 Francisco Blvd E G San Rafael (94901) ***(P-3447)***
San Francisco Offset Printing, San Jose *Also called Southwest Offset Prtg Co Inc* ***(P-7221)***
San Francisco Pipe &....E....510 785-9148
23099 Connecticut St Hayward (94545) ***(P-13485)***
San Francisco Print Media Co (PA)....E....415 487-2594
835 Market St Ste 550 San Francisco (94103) ***(P-6853)***
San Francisco Victoriana Inc....F....415 648-0313
2070 Newcomb Ave San Francisco (94124) ***(P-4120)***
San Franstitchco Inc....F....707 795-6891
624 Portal St Ste A Cotati (94931) ***(P-3756)***
San Joaquin Equipment LLC....E....209 538-3831
2413 Crows Landing Rd Modesto (95358) ***(P-13668)***
San Joaquin Facilities MGT Inc (PA)....F....661 631-8713
4520 California Ave # 300 Bakersfield (93309) ***(P-66)***
San Joaquin Orthtics & Prsthtc....F....209 932-0170
2211 N California St Stockton (95204) ***(P-22079)***
San Joaquin Refining Co Inc....C....661 327-4257
3500 Shell St Bakersfield (93308) ***(P-9066)***
San Joaquin Tomato Growers Inc....F....209 837-4721
22001 E St Crows Landing (95313) ***(P-822)***
San Joaquin Valley Dairymen, Turlock *Also called California Dairies Inc* ***(P-537)***
San Joaquin Vly Concentrates, Fresno *Also called E & J Gallo Winery* ***(P-1680)***
San Joaquin Window Inc (PA)....D....909 946-3697
1455 Columbia Ave Riverside (92507) ***(P-11981)***
San Jose Awning Company Inc....F....408 350-7000
755 Chestnut St Ste E San Jose (95110) ***(P-3703)***
San Jose Business Journal....E....408 295-3800
125 S Market St Ste 1100 San Jose (95113) ***(P-5817)***
San Jose Delta Associates Inc....E....408 727-1448
482 Sapena Ct Santa Clara (95054) ***(P-10482)***
San Jose Die Casting Corp....E....408 262-6500
600 Business Park Dr # 100 Lincoln (95648) ***(P-11347)***
San Jose Mercury-News LLC (HQ)....A....408 920-5000
4 N 2nd St Fl 8 San Jose (95113) ***(P-5818)***
San Juan Specialty Pdts Inc....F....888 342-8262
4149 Avenida De La Plata Oceanside (92056) ***(P-4426)***
San Luis Obispo Rdymx Plant, San Luis Obispo *Also called Calportland Company* ***(P-10403)***
San Luis Tribune, San Luis Obispo *Also called McClatchy Newspapers Inc* ***(P-5736)***
San Marco's Tortilla & Market, Los Angeles *Also called Tortilleria San Marcos* ***(P-2632)***
San Marcos Trading Company, San Marcos *Also called GK Foods Inc* ***(P-1003)***
San Mateo Daily News....E....650 327-9090
255 Constitution Dr Menlo Park (94025) ***(P-5819)***
San Mateo Times, San Mateo *Also called Alameda Newspapers Inc* ***(P-5547)***
San Pedro Garage Door and Repr, San Pedro *Also called Paula Keller* ***(P-4106)***
San Pedro Sign Company....E....310 549-4661
701 Lakme Ave Wilmington (90744) ***(P-23192)***
San Rafael Rock Quarry Inc....E....510 970-7700
961 Western Dr Richmond (94801) ***(P-9105)***
San Rafael Rock Quarry Inc (HQ)....D....415 459-7740
2350 Kerner Blvd Ste 200 San Rafael (94901) ***(P-319)***
San Rfl-Trra Linda Newspointer, Larkspur *Also called Marin Scope Incorporated* ***(P-5724)***
San-I-Pak Pacific Inc....E....209 836-2310
23535 S Bird Rd Tracy (95304) ***(P-12050)***
San-Joaquin Helicopters Inc....F....661 725-6603
1408 S Lexington St Delano (93215) ***(P-19929)***
Sanact Inc (PA)....F....925 464-2761
1274 Dupont Ct Manteca (95336) ***(P-8415)***

Mergent e-mail: customerrelations@mergent.com
1230
2020 California
Manufacturers Register
(P-0000) Products & Services Section entry number
(PA)=Parent Co (HQ)=Headquarters (DH)=Div Headquarters

Sanarus Medical Incorporated ....F....925 460-6080
7068 Koll Center Pkwy # 425 Pleasanton (94566) ***(P-21887)***
Sanctuary Clothing Inc ....E....818 505-0018
3611 N San Fernando Blvd Burbank (91505) ***(P-3191)***
Sandberg Furniture Mfg Co Inc (PA) ....C....323 582-0711
5705 Alcoa Ave Vernon (90058) ***(P-4611)***
Sandee Plastic Extrusions ....E....323 979-4020
14932 Gwenchris Ct Paramount (90723) ***(P-9272)***
Sandel Avionics Inc ....C....760 727-4900
2405 Dogwood Way Vista (92081) ***(P-20714)***
Sandel Avionics Inc (PA) ....E....760 727-4900
2401 Dogwood Way Vista (92081) ***(P-20715)***
Sanders Aircraft Inc ....F....209 274-2955
17149 Lambert Rd Ione (95640) ***(P-20716)***
Sanders Aircraft Technologies, Ione *Also called Sanders Aircraft Inc* ***(P-20716)***
Sanders Candy Factory Inc ....E....626 814-2038
5051 Calmview Ave Baldwin Park (91706) ***(P-1394)***
Sanders Composites Inc (HQ) ....E....562 354-2800
3701 E Conant St Long Beach (90808) ***(P-20226)***
Sanders Composites Industries, Long Beach *Also called Sanders Composites Inc* ***(P-20226)***
Sanders Orthodontic Lab Inc ....F....925 251-0019
5653 Stoneridge Dr # 107 Pleasanton (94588) ***(P-22188)***
Sandi Duty Free, San Diego *Also called Dynamic E-Markets LLC* ***(P-2652)***
Sandia Plastics Inc ....E....714 901-8400
15571 Container Ln Huntington Beach (92649) ***(P-10041)***
Sandisk LLC ....F....408 801-2928
1101 Sandisk Dr Bldg 5 Milpitas (95035) ***(P-15088)***
Sandisk LLC (HQ) ....C....408 801-1000
951 Sandisk Dr Milpitas (95035) ***(P-15089)***
Sandisk LLC ....D....408 321-0320
630 Alder Dr Ste 202 Milpitas (95035) ***(P-15090)***
Sandman Inc (PA) ....E....408 947-0669
1404 S 7th St San Jose (95112) ***(P-10646)***
Sandman Inc ....E....408 947-0159
1510 S 7th St San Jose (95112) ***(P-10647)***
Sandra Sparks & Associates ....F....805 985-2057
2510 Peninsula Rd Oxnard (93035) ***(P-8575)***
Sandstone Designs Inc ....E....818 787-5005
14828 Calvert St Van Nuys (91411) ***(P-10648)***
SANDUSKY LEE CORPORATION, Arvin *Also called Lee Sandusky Corporation* ***(P-4694)***
Sandvik Thermal Process Inc ....D....209 533-1990
19500 Nugget Blvd Sonora (95370) ***(P-14535)***
Sandwood Enterprises ....F....714 637-2000
2424 N Batavia St Orange (92865) ***(P-13745)***
Sanford Metal Processing Co ....F....650 327-5172
990 Obrien Dr Menlo Park (94025) ***(P-13094)***
Sangfor Technologies Inc ....A....408 520-7898
46721 Fremont Blvd Fremont (94538) ***(P-21116)***
Sangis, San Diego *Also called San Dego Gographic Info Source* ***(P-6334)***
Sani-Tech West Inc (PA) ....D....805 389-0400
1020 Flynn Rd Camarillo (93012) ***(P-9206)***
Sanie Manufacturing Company ....F....714 751-7700
2600 S Yale St Santa Ana (92704) ***(P-12506)***
Sanitek Products Inc ....F....323 245-6781
3959 Goodwin Ave Los Angeles (90039) ***(P-8416)***
Sanko Electronics America Inc (HQ) ....F....310 618-1677
20700 Denker Ave Ste A Torrance (90501) ***(P-19763)***
Sanluisina, Ontario *Also called Andrew LLC* ***(P-988)***
Sanmina Corporation ....A....408 244-0266
425 El Camino Real Bldg A Santa Clara (95050) ***(P-17985)***
Sanmina Corporation ....E....408 964-3500
2700 N 1st St San Jose (95134) ***(P-17986)***
Sanmina Corporation ....E....408 964-3500
2701 Zanker Rd San Jose (95134) ***(P-17987)***
Sanmina Corporation ....B....408 964-6400
2050 Bering Dr San Jose (95131) ***(P-17988)***
Sanmina Corporation ....B....408 964-3500
2036 Bering Dr San Jose (95131) ***(P-17989)***
Sanmina Corporation ....B....408 557-7210
60 E Plumeria Dr B2db San Jose (95134) ***(P-17990)***
Sanmina Corporation ....B....510 897-2000
42735 Christy St Fremont (94538) ***(P-17991)***
Sanmina Corporation ....D....408 964-3000
60 E Plumeria Dr San Jose (95134) ***(P-17992)***
Sanmina Corporation ....D....714 371-2800
2945 Airway Ave Costa Mesa (92626) ***(P-17993)***
Sanmina Corporation (PA) ....B....408 964-3500
2700 N 1st St San Jose (95134) ***(P-17994)***
Sanmina Corporation ....C....714 913-2200
2950 Red Hill Ave Costa Mesa (92626) ***(P-17995)***
Sanmina-Sci, San Jose *Also called Sanmina Corporation* ***(P-17989)***
Sanofi US Services Inc ....C....415 856-5000
185 Berry St San Francisco (94107) ***(P-8118)***
Sanovas Inc ....E....415 729-9391
2597 Kerner Blvd San Rafael (94901) ***(P-21888)***
Santa Ana Packaging Inc ....F....714 670-6397
14655 Firestone Blvd La Mirada (90638) ***(P-5172)***
Santa Ana Plating Corp (PA) ....D....310 923-8305
1726 E Rosslynn Ave Fullerton (92831) ***(P-13095)***
Santa Barbara Coffee LLC ....F....805 683-2555
6489 Calle Real Ste G Goleta (93117) ***(P-2309)***
Santa Barbara Control Systems ....F....805 683-8833
5375 Overpass Rd Santa Barbara (93111) ***(P-20932)***
Santa Barbara Design Studio (PA) ....D....805 966-3883
1600 Pacific Ave Oxnard (93033) ***(P-10492)***
Santa Barbara Independent Inc ....E....805 965-5205
12 E Figueroa St Santa Barbara (93101) ***(P-5820)***
Santa Barbara Indus Finshg, Goleta *Also called S B I F Inc* ***(P-13239)***
Santa Barbara Magazine, Santa Barbara *Also called Smith Publishing Inc* ***(P-6028)***
Santa Barbara Music Publishing ....E....805 962-5800
260 Loma Media Rd Santa Barbara (93103) ***(P-6336)***
Santa Barbara News-Press Info, Santa Barbara *Also called Ampersand Publishing LLC* ***(P-5550)***
Santa Barbara Olives Co, Santa Maria *Also called Krinos Foods LLC* ***(P-886)***
Santa Brbara Essntial Fods LLC ....E....805 965-1948
233 E Gutierrez St Santa Barbara (93101) ***(P-1327)***
Santa Clara Facility, Santa Clara *Also called Summit Interconnect Inc* ***(P-18016)***
Santa Clara Imaging ....E....408 296-5555
1825 Civic Center Dr # 1 Santa Clara (95050) ***(P-21532)***
Santa Clara Plating Co Inc ....D....408 727-9315
1773 Grant St Santa Clara (95050) ***(P-13096)***
Santa Clara Valley Brewing Inc ....F....408 288-5181
101 E Alma Ave San Jose (95112) ***(P-1562)***
Santa Clarita Plastic Molding ....F....661 294-2257
24735 Avenue Rockefeller Valencia (91355) ***(P-10042)***
Santa Cruz Biotechnology Inc ....E....831 457-3800
2145 Delaware Ave Santa Cruz (95060) ***(P-8328)***
Santa Cruz Coffee Roasting Co ....E....831 685-0100
19 Rancho Del Mar Ste A Aptos (95003) ***(P-2310)***
Santa Cruz Guitar Corporation ....E....831 425-0999
151 Harvey West Blvd C Santa Cruz (95060) ***(P-22636)***
Santa Cruz Industries Inc ....F....831 423-9211
129 Bulkhead Santa Cruz (95060) ***(P-5002)***
Santa Cruz Nutritionals ....B....831 457-3200
2200 Delaware Ave Santa Cruz (95060) ***(P-8119)***
Santa Cruz Skateboards, Santa Cruz *Also called Nhs Inc* ***(P-22859)***
Santa Fe Aggregates Inc (HQ) ....F....209 358-3303
11650 Shaffer Rd Winton (95388) ***(P-358)***
Santa Fe Enterprises Inc ....E....562 692-7596
11654 Pike St Santa Fe Springs (90670) ***(P-14103)***
Santa Fe Extruders Inc ....D....562 921-8991
15315 Marquardt Ave Santa Fe Springs (90670) ***(P-10043)***
Santa Fe Footwear Corporation ....F....562 941-9689
9988 Santa Fe Springs Rd Santa Fe Springs (90670) ***(P-10182)***
Santa Fe Machine Works Inc ....E....909 350-6877
14578 Rancho Vista Dr Fontana (92335) ***(P-16385)***
Santa Fe Rubber Products Inc ....E....562 693-2776
12306 Washington Blvd Whittier (90606) ***(P-9368)***
Santa Fe Supply Company, Santa Fe Springs *Also called Philatron International* ***(P-19377)***
Santa Fe Textiles Inc ....F....949 251-1960
17370 Mount Herrmann St Fountain Valley (92708) ***(P-2760)***
Santa Maria Enrgy Holdings LLC ....E....805 938-3320
2811 Airpark Dr Santa Maria (93455) ***(P-138)***
Santa Maria Times, Santa Maria *Also called Lee Enterprises Incorporated* ***(P-5697)***
Santa Maria Times Inc ....C....805 925-2691
3200 Skyway Dr Santa Maria (93455) ***(P-5821)***
Santa Monica City of ....F....310 826-6712
1228 S Bundy Dr Los Angeles (90025) ***(P-15574)***
Santa Monica Daily Press, Santa Monica *Also called Newlon Rouge LLC* ***(P-5776)***
Santa Monica Millworks ....E....805 643-0010
2568 Channel Dr Ste C Ventura (93003) ***(P-4246)***
Santa Monica Plastics Llc ....F....310 403-2849
1631 Stanford St Santa Monica (90404) ***(P-10044)***
Santa Monica Propeller Svc Inc ....F....310 390-6233
3135 Dnald Douglas Loop S Santa Monica (90405) ***(P-20227)***
Santa Monica Seafood Company (PA) ....D....310 886-7900
18531 S Broadwick St Rancho Dominguez (90220) ***(P-2251)***
Santa Rosa Lead Products LLC (PA) ....F....800 916-5323
33 S University St Healdsburg (95448) ***(P-13746)***
Santa Rosa Lead Products Inc ....E....707 431-1477
33 S University St Healdsburg (95448) ***(P-11423)***
Santa Rosa Press Democrat Inc (HQ) ....B....707 546-2020
427 Mendocino Ave Santa Rosa (95401) ***(P-5822)***
Santa Rosa Stain ....E....707 544-7777
1400 Airport Blvd Santa Rosa (95403) ***(P-20500)***
Santa Ynez Vineyards, Santa Barbara *Also called Lafond Vineyard Inc* ***(P-1790)***
Santafe Spg PKS&rec Lake Cntr, Santa Fe Springs *Also called City of Santa Fe Springs* ***(P-22782)***
Santan Software Systems Inc ....E....310 836-2802
19504 Ronald Ave Torrance (90503) ***(P-24380)***
Santana Formal Accessories Inc ....C....818 898-3677
707 Arroyo St Ste B San Fernando (91340) ***(P-2978)***
Santarus Inc ....E....858 314-5700
3611 Vly Cntre Dr Ste 400 San Diego (92130) ***(P-8120)***
Santec Inc ....E....310 542-0063
3501 Challenger St Fl 2 Torrance (90503) ***(P-11681)***
Santee Cosmetics USA ....F....310 329-2305
13202 Estrella Ave Gardena (90248) ***(P-8576)***
Santier Inc ....D....858 271-1993
10103 Carroll Canyon Rd San Diego (92131) ***(P-18527)***
Santini Fine Wines, San Lorenzo *Also called Santini Foods Inc* ***(P-618)***
Santini Foods Inc ....C....510 317-8888
16505 Worthley Dr San Lorenzo (94580) ***(P-618)***
Santos Precision Inc ....E....714 957-0299
2220 S Anne St Santa Ana (92704) ***(P-20228)***
Santoshi Corporation ....E....626 444-7118
2439 Seaman Ave El Monte (91733) ***(P-13097)***
Santronics, Sunnyvale *Also called Ahn Enterprises LLC* ***(P-18697)***
Santur Corporation (HQ) ....E....510 933-4100
40931 Encyclopedia Cir Fremont (94538) ***(P-14536)***
Sanyo Foods Corp America (HQ) ....E....714 891-3671
11955 Monarch St Garden Grove (92841) ***(P-2382)***
Sap AG ....C....650 849-4000
3410 Hillview Ave Palo Alto (94304) ***(P-15091)***
Sapa Extrusions Inc ....C....909 947-7682
2821 E Philadelphia St A Ontario (91761) ***(P-11244)***

A L P H A B E T I C

Employee Codes: A=Over 500 employees, B=251-500
C=101-250, D=51-100, E=20-50, F=10-19

2020 California
Manfacturers Register

© Mergent Inc. 1-800-342-5647
1231

Sapar Usa Inc (PA)....E....510 441-9500
1610 Delta Ct Ste 1 Hayward (94544) ***(P-496)***
Saperi Systems Inc....F....858 381-0085
9444 Waples St Ste 300 San Diego (92121) ***(P-24381)***
Sapphire Chandelier LLC....F....714 630-3660
505 Porter Way Placentia (92870) ***(P-17068)***
Sapphire Energy Inc....D....858 768-4700
10996 Torreyana Rd # 280 San Diego (92121) ***(P-7692)***
Sapphire Manufacturing Inc....E....714 401-3117
505 Porter Way Placentia (92870) ***(P-12507)***
Sappi North America Inc....D....714 456-0600
333 S Anita Dr Ste 840 Orange (92868) ***(P-5529)***
Saputo Cheese USA Inc....B....559 687-8411
800 E Paige Ave Tulare (93274) ***(P-573)***
Saputo Cheese USA Inc....C....559 687-9999
901 E Levin Ave Tulare (93274) ***(P-574)***
Saputo Cheese USA Inc....C....562 862-7686
5611 Imperial Hwy South Gate (90280) ***(P-575)***
Saputo Dairy Foods Usa LLC....C....209 854-6461
299 5th Ave Gustine (95322) ***(P-709)***
Saputo Dairy Foods Usa LLC....C....714 772-8861
1901 Via Burton Fullerton (92831) ***(P-710)***
Sara Lee, San Lorenzo *Also called Hillshire Brands Company* ***(P-465)***
Sara Lee Bakery Group, Loomis *Also called Bimbo Bakeries Usa Inc* ***(P-1150)***
Sara Lee Fresh Inc....A....215 347-5500
5200 S Alameda St Vernon (90058) ***(P-1272)***
Saraya Healthcare, Nevada City *Also called Witt Hillard* ***(P-8424)***
Sardee Corporation California....E....209 466-1526
2731 E Myrtle St Stockton (95205) ***(P-13833)***
Sardee Industries Inc....E....209 466-1526
2731 E Myrtle St Stockton (95205) ***(P-14726)***
Sardo Bus & Coach Upholstery, Gardena *Also called Louis Sardo Upholstery Inc* ***(P-4864)***
Sardo Bus & Coach Upholstery....D....800 654-3824
512 W Rosecrans Ave Gardena (90248) ***(P-4821)***
Sargam International Inc....F....310 855-9694
719 Huntley Dr West Hollywood (90069) ***(P-17280)***
Sari Art & Printing Inc....F....626 305-0888
3733 San Gabriel River Pk Pico Rivera (90660) ***(P-6854)***
SARR Industries Inc....F....818 998-7735
8975 Fullbright Ave Chatsworth (91311) ***(P-16386)***
Sarris Interiors, Paramount *Also called Sibyl Shepard Inc* ***(P-3640)***
Sars Software Products Inc....F....415 226-0040
2175 Francisco Blvd E San Rafael (94901) ***(P-24382)***
Sas Institute Inc....E....415 421-2227
50 Post St Ste 50 # 50 San Francisco (94104) ***(P-24383)***
Sas Institute Inc....F....919 677-8000
2121 N 1st St Ste 100 San Jose (95131) ***(P-24384)***
Sas Institute Inc....D....949 250-9999
1148 N Lemon St Orange (92867) ***(P-24385)***
Sas Manufacturing Inc....E....951 734-1808
405 N Smith Ave Corona (92880) ***(P-19076)***
Sas Safety Corporation....D....562 427-2775
3031 Gardenia Ave Long Beach (90807) ***(P-22080)***
Sas Stressteel, Fremont *Also called Stressteel Inc* ***(P-11076)***
Sas Textiles Inc....D....323 277-5555
3100 E 44th St Vernon (90058) ***(P-2819)***
Sass Labs Inc....E....404 731-7284
121 W Washington Ave # 209 Sunnyvale (94086) ***(P-24386)***
Sat, Sacramento *Also called Lpa Insurance Agency Inc* ***(P-24111)***
Satco Inc (PA)....C....310 322-4719
1601 E El Segundo Blvd El Segundo (90245) ***(P-4398)***
Satcom Solutions Corporation....F....818 991-9794
31119 Via Colinas Ste 501 Westlake Village (91362) ***(P-20717)***
Satellite 2000 Systems....F....818 991-9794
741 Lakefield Rd Ste I Westlake Village (91361) ***(P-17650)***
Satellite Telework Centers Inc (PA)....F....831 222-2100
6265 Highway 9 Felton (95018) ***(P-21117)***
Saticoy Rock Asphalt and Rdymx, Oxnard *Also called Legacy Vulcan LLC* ***(P-10782)***
Satori Seal Corporation....F....909 987-8234
8455 Utica Ave Rancho Cucamonga (91730) ***(P-9369)***
Satsuma Pharmaceuticals Inc....F....650 410-3200
400 Oyster Point Blvd # 221 South San Francisco (94080) ***(P-8121)***
Saturn Fasteners Inc....C....818 973-1807
425 S Varney St Burbank (91502) ***(P-11625)***
Sauer Brands Inc....D....805 597-8900
184 Suburban Rd San Luis Obispo (93401) ***(P-2608)***
Saunco Air Technologies, Hickman *Also called Reed International* ***(P-13760)***
Saunders Manufacturing Svcs....F....714 961-8492
15330 Fairfield Ranch Rd G Chino Hills (91709) ***(P-23466)***
Sausalito Craftworks Inc....F....415 331-4031
2342 Marinship Way Sausalito (94965) ***(P-22569)***
Sauvage Inc (PA)....F....858 408-0100
7717 Formula Pl San Diego (92121) ***(P-3115)***
Savannah Chanelle Vineyards....E....408 741-2934
23600 Big Basin Way Saratoga (95070) ***(P-1907)***
Save-Sorb, Los Angeles *Also called Organicsorb LLC* ***(P-393)***
Savensealcom Ltd....F....530 478-0238
15478 Applewood Ln Nevada City (95959) ***(P-5417)***
Savi Technology Holdings Inc (PA)....E....650 316-4950
615 Tasman Dr Sunnyvale (94089) ***(P-17651)***
Savnik & Company Inc....F....510 568-4628
601 Mcclary Ave Oakland (94621) ***(P-2878)***
Savory Creations International....E....510 477-0395
32611 Central Ave Union City (94587) ***(P-497)***
Sawbird Inc (PA)....E....415 861-0644
721 Brannan St San Francisco (94103) ***(P-11555)***
Sawtelle & Rosprim Machine Sp, Corcoran *Also called Corcoran Sawtelle Rosprim Inc* ***(P-11775)***
Saxton Industrial Inc....F....818 265-0702
1736 Standard Ave Glendale (91201) ***(P-12368)***
Saybolt LP....F....310 518-4400
21730 S Wilmington Ave # 203 Carson (90810) ***(P-258)***
Saydel Inc (PA)....F....323 585-2800
2475 E Slauson Ave Huntington Park (90255) ***(P-8577)***
Sazerac Company Inc....E....310 604-8717
2202 E Del Amo Blvd Carson (90749) ***(P-2018)***
SBC, San Francisco *Also called AT&T Corp* ***(P-6193)***
Sbm Dairies Inc (HQ)....D....626 923-3000
17851 Railroad St City of Industry (91748) ***(P-2165)***
Sbnw LLC (PA)....C....213 234-5122
320 W 31st St Los Angeles (90007) ***(P-10226)***
Sbragia Family Vineyards LLC....E....707 473-2992
9990 Dry Creek Rd Geyserville (95441) ***(P-1908)***
SBS, Fremont *Also called South Bay Solutions Inc* ***(P-16411)***
SBS America LLC (PA)....D....831 637-8700
1600 Lana Way Hollister (95023) ***(P-4121)***
SC Beverage Inc....E....562 463-8918
2300 Peck Rd City of Industry (90601) ***(P-14399)***
SC Bluwood Inc....E....909 519-5470
2604 El Camino Real Ste B Carlsbad (92008) ***(P-4481)***
SC Works....F....831 332-5311
1805 Contra Costa St A Seaside (93955) ***(P-23193)***
Scafco Corporation....F....415 852-7974
2177 Jerrold Ave San Francisco (94124) ***(P-23467)***
Scafco Corporation....F....559 256-9911
2443 Foundry Park Ave Fresno (93706) ***(P-11485)***
Scafco Corporation....E....209 670-8053
2525 S Airport Way Stockton (95206) ***(P-23468)***
Scafco Corporation....E....916 624-7700
4301 Jetway Ct North Highlands (95660) ***(P-13669)***
Scafco Steel Stud Mfg, San Francisco *Also called Scafco Corporation* ***(P-23467)***
Scafco Steel Stud Mfg, North Highlands *Also called Scafco Corporation* ***(P-13669)***
Scalable Systems RES Labs Inc....E....650 322-6507
2680 N 1st St Ste 200 San Jose (95134) ***(P-18528)***
Scale Services Inc....F....909 266-0896
3553a N Perris Blvd Ste 8 Perris (92571) ***(P-15642)***
Scaled Composites LLC....B....661 824-4541
1624 Flight Line Mojave (93501) ***(P-19930)***
Scality Inc....E....650 356-8500
555 California St # 3050 San Francisco (94104) ***(P-15092)***
Scanart, Emeryville *Also called Pixscan* ***(P-7174)***
Scantibodies Laboratory Inc (PA)....C....619 258-9300
9336 Abraham Way Santee (92071) ***(P-8252)***
Scapa Tapes North America LLC....E....310 419-0567
540 N Oak St Inglewood (90302) ***(P-5373)***
Scape Goat Ind....F....760 931-1802
6901 Quail Pl Unit E Carlsbad (92009) ***(P-22884)***
Scarlet Saints Softball....F....530 613-1443
304 Grande Ave Davis (95616) ***(P-22885)***
Scarrott Metallurgical Co, Los Angeles *Also called Interntonal Metallurgical Svcs* ***(P-11454)***
Scb Division, Bell Gardens *Also called Cal Southern Braiding Inc* ***(P-18848)***
Scb Division of Dcx-Chol, Bell *Also called Dcx-Chol Enterprises Inc* ***(P-18884)***
SCC Chemical Corporation....F....909 796-8369
32215 Dunlap Blvd Yucaipa (92399) ***(P-7392)***
SCE Gaskets Inc....F....661 728-9200
24927 Avenue Tibbitts F Valencia (91355) ***(P-9253)***
Scene 53 Inc....E....415 404-2461
800 E Charleston Rd Apt 7 Palo Alto (94303) ***(P-24387)***
Scenewise Inc....D....310 466-7692
2201 Park Pl Ste 100 El Segundo (90245) ***(P-19233)***
Sceptre Inc....E....626 369-3698
16800 Gale Ave City of Industry (91745) ***(P-19077)***
Schaefer Systems Intl Inc....E....209 365-6030
1250 Thurman St Lodi (95240) ***(P-10045)***
Schaeffler Group USA Inc....B....949 234-9799
34700 Pacific Coast Hwy # 203 Capistrano Beach (92624) ***(P-14614)***
Schaffer Laboratories Inc....F....714 202-1594
8441 Monroe Ave Stanton (90680) ***(P-9455)***
Schamas Mfg Coinc....F....626 334-6870
6356 N Irwindale Ave Irwindale (91702) ***(P-13747)***
Schawk, San Francisco *Also called Sgk LLC* ***(P-7381)***
Schawk, Los Angeles *Also called Sgk LLC* ***(P-7382)***
Schea Holdings Inc....E....818 888-3818
9812 Independence Ave Chatsworth (91311) ***(P-23194)***
Schecter Guitar Research Inc....E....818 767-1029
10953 Pendleton St Sun Valley (91352) ***(P-22637)***
Schell & Kampeter Inc....E....209 983-4900
250 Roth Rd Lathrop (95330) ***(P-1083)***
Schellinger Spring Inc....F....909 373-0799
8477 Utica Ave Rancho Cucamonga (91730) ***(P-13342)***
Scheu Manufacturing Co (PA)....F....909 982-8933
297 Stowell St Upland (91786) ***(P-11712)***
Schindler Elevator Corporation....E....510 382-2075
555 Mccormick St San Leandro (94577) ***(P-13809)***
Schlage Lock Company LLC....E....619 671-0276
2297 Niels Bohr Ct # 209 San Diego (92154) ***(P-11626)***
Schley Products Inc....F....714 693-7666
5350 E Hunter Ave Anaheim (92807) ***(P-11543)***
Schlumberger Oilfield Services, Ventura *Also called Schlumberger Technology Corp* ***(P-259)***
Schlumberger Technology Corp....E....805 642-8230
1710 Callens Rd Ventura (93003) ***(P-259)***
Schlumberger Technology Corp....D....661 864-4750
2841 Pegasus Dr Bakersfield (93308) ***(P-260)***
Schlumberger Technology Corp....D....714 379-7332
12131 Industry St Garden Grove (92841) ***(P-261)***
Schlumberger Technology Corp....F....805 644-8325
3530 Arundell Cir Ventura (93003) ***(P-262)***

Schlumberger Well Services, Bakersfield *Also called Schlumberger Technology Corp* ***(P-260)***
Schlumberger Well Services, Ventura *Also called Schlumberger Technology Corp* ***(P-262)***
Schmartboard Inc.......F.......510 744-9900
37423 Fremont Blvd Fremont (94536) ***(P-16752)***
Schmeiser Farm Equipment, Fresno *Also called T G Schmeiser Co Inc* ***(P-11635)***
Schmid Thermal Systems Inc.......C.......831 763-0113
200 Westridge Dr Watsonville (95076) ***(P-14775)***
Schmidbauer Lumber Inc (PA).......C.......707 443-7024
1099 W Waterfront Dr Eureka (95501) ***(P-3946)***
Schmidbauer Lumber Inc.......E.......707 822-7607
1017 Samoa Blvd Arcata (95521) ***(P-3947)***
Schmidt Industries Inc.......D.......818 768-9100
11321 Goss St Sun Valley (91352) ***(P-13098)***
Schmitt Superior Classics, Redding *Also called William R Schmitt* ***(P-3919)***
Schneider Elc Systems USA Inc.......F.......949 885-0700
26561 Rancho Pkwy S Lake Forest (92630) ***(P-20933)***
Schneider Electric It Usa.......B.......714 513-7313
1660 Scenic Ave Costa Mesa (92626) ***(P-19078)***
Schneider Electric Usa Inc.......C.......858 385-5040
10805 Thornmint Rd # 140 San Diego (92127) ***(P-16612)***
Schneiders Deisgn Studio Inc.......F.......562 437-0448
245 The Promenade N Fl 2 Long Beach (90802) ***(P-22570)***
Schneiders Manufacturing Inc.......E.......818 771-0082
11122 Penrose St Sun Valley (91352) ***(P-16387)***
Schoenstein & Co.......E.......707 747-5858
4001 Industrial Way Benicia (94510) ***(P-22638)***
Scholastic Inc.......E.......626 337-9996
4821 Charter St Baldwin Park (91706) ***(P-6144)***
Scholastic Sports Inc.......D.......858 496-9221
4878 Ronson Ct Ste Kl San Diego (92111) ***(P-6855)***
Scholle Ipn Corporation.......B.......209 384-3100
2500 Cooper Ave Merced (95348) ***(P-10046)***
Scholle Ipn Packaging Inc.......B.......209 384-3100
2500 Cooper Ave Merced (95348) ***(P-10047)***
Scholten Surgical Instrs Inc.......F.......209 365-1393
170 Commerce St Ste 101 Lodi (95240) ***(P-21889)***
School Apparel Inc (PA).......C.......650 777-4500
838 Mitten Rd Burlingame (94010) ***(P-3277)***
School Innovations Achievement (PA).......D.......916 933-2290
5200 Golden Foothill Pkwy El Dorado Hills (95762) ***(P-24388)***
Schott Magnetics.......F.......619 661-7510
1401 Air Wing Rd San Diego (92154) ***(P-13544)***
Schreiber Foods Inc.......C.......714 490-7360
1901 Via Burton Fullerton (92831) ***(P-576)***
Schrey & Sons Mold Co Inc.......E.......661 294-2260
24735 Avenue Rockefeller Valencia (91355) ***(P-14104)***
Schrillo Company LLC.......E.......818 894-8241
16750 Schoenborn St North Hills (91343) ***(P-12692)***
Schroeder Iron Corporation.......E.......909 428-6471
8417 Beech Ave Fontana (92335) ***(P-11878)***
Schroeder Tool & Die Corp.......E.......818 786-9360
25448 Cumberland Ln Calabasas (91302) ***(P-16388)***
Schuberth North America LLC.......F.......949 215-0893
33 Journey Ste 200 Aliso Viejo (92656) ***(P-12870)***
Schultz Controls Inc.......F.......714 693-2900
565 Draft Horse Pl Norco (92860) ***(P-16613)***
Schulz Engineering, Sylmar *Also called Dg Engineering Corp* ***(P-20570)***
Schulz Industries, Paramount *Also called Schulz Leather Co Inc* ***(P-3704)***
Schulz Leather Co Inc.......E.......562 633-1081
16247 Minnesota Ave Paramount (90723) ***(P-3704)***
Schuman Enterprises Inc.......F.......760 940-1322
1621 Ord Way Oceanside (92056) ***(P-13545)***
Schurman Fine Papers.......C.......951 653-1934
22500 Town Cir Moreno Valley (92553) ***(P-7298)***
Schwarzkopf Inc (HQ).......E.......310 641-0990
600 Corporate Pointe # 400 Culver City (90230) ***(P-23469)***
Schwin and Tran Mill & Bakery, Berkeley *Also called Vital Vittles Bakery Inc* ***(P-1291)***
SCI, Santa Clara *Also called Santa Clara Imaging* ***(P-21532)***
SCI, Santa Ana *Also called Semiconductor Components Inc* ***(P-18533)***
SCI, Pomona *Also called Structural Composites Inds LLC* ***(P-12059)***
SCI, National City *Also called Southern California Insulation* ***(P-20305)***
SCI Instruments Inc (PA).......F.......760 634-3822
6355 Corte Del Abeto C105 Carlsbad (92011) ***(P-21286)***
SCI Publishing Inc.......F.......415 382-0580
42 Digital Dr Ste 5 Novato (94949) ***(P-6024)***
SCI-Tech Glassblowing Inc.......F.......805 523-9790
5555 Tech Cir Moorpark (93021) ***(P-10389)***
Sciabica's, Modesto *Also called Nick Sciabica & Sons A Corp* ***(P-1478)***
Sciambr-Passini French Bky Inc.......E.......707 252-3072
685 S Freeway Dr NAPA (94558) ***(P-1273)***
Sciambra French Bakery, NAPA *Also called Sciambr-Passini French Bky Inc* ***(P-1273)***
Sciclone Pharmaceuticals Inc (HQ).......E.......650 358-3456
950 Tower Ln Ste 900 Foster City (94404) ***(P-8122)***
Science Wiz Summer Camp, Richmond *Also called Norman & Globus Inc* ***(P-6130)***
Scientific Components Systems.......F.......714 554-3960
1514 N Susan St Ste C Santa Ana (92703) ***(P-17069)***
Scientific Cutting Tools Inc.......E.......805 584-9495
110 W Easy St Simi Valley (93065) ***(P-14191)***
Scientific Drilling Intl Inc.......E.......661 831-0636
31101 Coberly Rd Shafter (93263) ***(P-105)***
Scientific Learning Corp.......E.......510 444-3500
300 Frank H Ogawa Plz # 600 Oakland (94612) ***(P-24389)***
Scientific Metal Finishing.......E.......408 970-9011
3180 Molinaro St Santa Clara (95054) ***(P-13242)***
Scientific Molding Corp Ltd.......D.......707 303-3041
3250 Brickway Blvd Santa Rosa (95403) ***(P-10048)***
Scientific Repair Inc.......F.......310 214-5092
20720 Earl St Ste 2 Torrance (90503) ***(P-20934)***
Scientific Specialties Inc.......D.......209 333-2120
1310 Thurman St Lodi (95240) ***(P-9420)***
Scientific Spray Finishes Inc.......E.......714 871-5541
315 S Richman Ave Fullerton (92832) ***(P-13243)***
Scientific Surface Inds Inc.......F.......805 499-5100
855 Rancho Conejo Blvd Newbury Park (91320) ***(P-4936)***
Scientific-Atlanta LLC.......B.......619 679-6000
13112 Evening Creek Dr S San Diego (92128) ***(P-20718)***
Scigen Inc.......F.......310 324-6576
7041 Marcelle St Paramount (90723) ***(P-8773)***
Scigene Corporation.......F.......408 733-7337
1287 Reamwood Ave Sunnyvale (94089) ***(P-21890)***
Scintera Networks Inc.......E.......408 636-2600
160 Rio Robles San Jose (95134) ***(P-18529)***
Scisorek & Son Flavors Inc.......E.......714 524-0550
2951 Enterprise St Brea (92821) ***(P-2229)***
Sciton Inc.......D.......650 493-9155
925 Commercial St Palo Alto (94303) ***(P-21891)***
SCM Accelerators LLC.......F.......415 595-8091
2731 California St San Francisco (94115) ***(P-24390)***
Scodan Systems Inc.......F.......626 444-1020
12373 Barringer St South El Monte (91733) ***(P-12722)***
Scone Henge Inc.......F.......510 845-5168
2787 Shattuck Ave Berkeley (94705) ***(P-1274)***
Sconza Candy Company.......D.......209 845-3700
1 Sconza Candy Ln Oakdale (95361) ***(P-1395)***
Scope City (PA).......E.......805 522-6646
2978 Topaz Ave Simi Valley (93063) ***(P-21405)***
Scope Packaging Inc.......E.......714 998-4411
13400 Nelson Ave City of Industry (91746) ***(P-5265)***
Scopely Inc (PA).......C.......323 400-6618
3530 Hayden Ave Ste A Culver City (90232) ***(P-24391)***
Scor Industries.......F.......909 820-5046
2321 S Willow Ave Bloomington (92316) ***(P-23470)***
Scosche Industries Inc.......C.......805 486-4450
1550 Pacific Ave Oxnard (93033) ***(P-17281)***
Scotch Paint Corporation.......F.......310 329-1259
5928 Garfield Ave Commerce (90040) ***(P-8678)***
Scotland Entry Systems Inc.......F.......818 376-0777
159 S Beverly Dr Beverly Hills (90212) ***(P-10049)***
Scott Architectural, Fairfield *Also called Scott Lamp Company Inc* ***(P-17070)***
Scott Craft Co (PA).......F.......323 560-3949
4601 Cecilia St Cudahy (90201) ***(P-16389)***
Scott Craft Co.......F.......323 560-3949
5 Stallion Rd Rancho Palos Verdes (90275) ***(P-16390)***
Scott Craft Co & STC, Rancho Palos Verdes *Also called Scott Craft Co* ***(P-16390)***
Scott Engineering Inc.......E.......909 594-9637
5051 Edison Ave Chino (91710) ***(P-16797)***
Scott Foresman Pearson Educatn, Ontario *Also called Pearson Education Inc* ***(P-6134)***
Scott Lamp Company Inc.......D.......707 864-2066
355 Watt Dr Fairfield (94534) ***(P-17070)***
Scott Welsher.......F.......949 574-4000
2031 S Lynx Ave Ontario (91761) ***(P-10206)***
Scottex Inc.......F.......310 516-1411
12828 S Broadway Los Angeles (90061) ***(P-3859)***
Scotts Company LLC.......F.......661 387-9555
742 Industrial Way Shafter (93263) ***(P-8803)***
Scotts Food Products Inc.......F.......562 630-8448
7331 Alondra Blvd Paramount (90723) ***(P-899)***
Scotts Temecula Operations LLC (HQ).......E.......951 719-1700
42375 Remington Ave Temecula (92590) ***(P-13695)***
Scotts Valley Magnetics Inc.......E.......831 438-3600
300 El Pueblo Rd Ste 107 Scotts Valley (95066) ***(P-18741)***
Scotts- Hyponex, Chino *Also called Hyponex Corporation* ***(P-8794)***
Scotts- Hyponex, Linden *Also called Hyponex Corporation* ***(P-8795)***
Scrape Certified Welding Inc.......D.......760 728-1308
2525 Old Highway 395 Fallbrook (92028) ***(P-11879)***
Screamin Mimis Inc.......F.......707 823-5902
6902 Sebastopol Ave Sebastopol (95472) ***(P-667)***
Screaming Squeegee, Sacramento *Also called Creo Inc* ***(P-7040)***
Screen Art Inc.......F.......714 891-4185
15162 Triton Ln Huntington Beach (92649) ***(P-7208)***
Screen Machine, San Jose *Also called Lights Fantastic* ***(P-6703)***
Screen Printers Resource Inc.......F.......714 441-1155
1251 Burton St Fullerton (92831) ***(P-7209)***
Screen Shop Inc.......F.......408 295-7384
601 Hamline St San Jose (95110) ***(P-11982)***
Screen Tech Inc.......D.......408 885-9750
4754 Bennett Dr Livermore (94551) ***(P-12369)***
Screening Systems Inc (PA).......E.......949 855-1751
36 Blackbird Ln Aliso Viejo (92656) ***(P-21287)***
Screenmeet.com, San Francisco *Also called Projectoris Inc* ***(P-24317)***
Screenprintit.com, Sacramento *Also called New Direction Silk Screen* ***(P-7148)***
Screenworks Co Tim.......E.......310 532-7239
1705 W 134th St Gardena (90249) ***(P-7210)***
Screw Conveyor Pacific Corp.......E.......559 651-2131
7807 W Doe Ave Visalia (93291) ***(P-13834)***
Screwmatic Inc.......D.......626 334-7831
925 W 1st St Azusa (91702) ***(P-16391)***
Scribble Press Inc.......E.......212 288-2928
1109 Montana Ave Santa Monica (90403) ***(P-6337)***
Scribe Technologies Inc.......F.......415 746-9935
739 Bryant St San Francisco (94107) ***(P-24392)***
Scribner Engineering Inc.......E.......916 638-1515
11455 Hydraulics Dr Rancho Cordova (95742) ***(P-10050)***
Scribner Plastics.......F.......916 638-1515
11455 Hydraulics Dr Rancho Cordova (95742) ***(P-10051)***
Scrimco Inc.......F.......559 237-7442
2377 S Orange Ave Fresno (93725) ***(P-2733)***

A L P H A B E T I C

Employee Codes: A=Over 500 employees, B=251-500
C=101-250, D=51-100, E=20-50, F=10-19
2020 California
Manfacturers Register
© Mergent Inc. 1-800-342-5647
1233

Scripps Laboratories Inc.....E.....858 546-5800
6838 Flanders Dr San Diego (92121) *(P-8329)*
Scripps Media Inc.....C.....805 437-0000
771 E Daily Dr Ste 300 Camarillo (93010) *(P-5823)*
Scripto-Tokai Corporation (HQ).....D.....909 930-5000
2055 S Haven Ave Ontario (91761) *(P-23471)*
Scully Sportswear Inc.....D.....805 483-6339
1701 Pacific Ave Oxnard (93033) *(P-3522)*
Sculptor Body Molding (PA).....F.....818 761-3767
10817 W Stallion Ranch Rd Sunland (91040) *(P-10052)*
SD Desserts LLC.....F.....702 480-9083
1608 India St Ste 104 San Diego (92101) *(P-2609)*
SD Fresh Products, San Diego *Also called Cg Financial LLC (P-722)*
SDC Technologies Inc (HQ).....E.....714 939-8300
45 Parker Ste 100 Irvine (92618) *(P-13244)*
Sdi, Simi Valley *Also called Special Devices Incorporated (P-19771)*
Sdi LLC.....E.....949 351-1866
21 Morgan Ste 150 Irvine (92618) *(P-16392)*
Sdi Industries Inc (PA).....C.....818 890-6002
13000 Pierce St Pacoima (91331) *(P-13835)*
Sdm, Los Angeles *Also called S D M Furniture Co Inc (P-4609)*
Sdo Communications Corp.....D.....408 979-0289
47365 Galindo Dr Fremont (94539) *(P-21406)*
SE Industries Inc.....F.....714 744-3200
300 W Collins Ave Orange (92867) *(P-4247)*
Se-Gl Products Inc.....E.....951 737-8320
20521 Teresita Way Lake Forest (92630) *(P-12370)*
Sea Breeze Technology Inc.....F.....760 727-6366
1160 Joshua Way Vista (92081) *(P-19399)*
Sea Critters, Culver City *Also called Ecoly International Inc (P-8485)*
Sea Magazine, Fountain Valley *Also called Duncan McIntosh Company Inc (P-5926)*
Sea One Seafood, Santa Fe Springs *Also called Long Beach Enterprise Inc (P-2262)*
Sea Shield Marine Products.....E.....909 594-2507
20832 Currier Rd Walnut (91789) *(P-11348)*
Sea Snack Foods Inc (PA).....E.....213 622-2204
914 E 11th St Los Angeles (90021) *(P-2269)*
Sea Tek Spars & Rigging Inc.....F.....310 549-1800
508 E E St Ste B Wilmington (90744) *(P-20304)*
Seaboard Envelope Co Inc.....E.....626 960-4559
15601 Cypress Ave Irwindale (91706) *(P-5474)*
Seaboard International Inc.....D.....661 325-5026
3912 Gilmore Ave Bakersfield (93308) *(P-13790)*
Seaborn Canvas.....E.....310 519-1208
435 N Harbor Blvd Ste B1 San Pedro (90731) *(P-3860)*
Seachrome Corporation.....C.....310 427-8010
1906 E Dominguez St Long Beach (90810) *(P-11650)*
Seaco Technologies Inc.....F.....661 326-1522
280 El Cerrito Dr Bakersfield (93305) *(P-15575)*
Seagate Systems, Fremont *Also called Seagate Technology LLC (P-15096)*
Seagate Systems (us) Inc (HQ).....D.....510 687-5200
46831 Lakeview Blvd Fremont (94538) *(P-15093)*
Seagate Technology LLC.....C.....530 410-6594
10042 Wolf Rd Grass Valley (95949) *(P-15094)*
Seagate Technology LLC (HQ).....A.....408 658-1000
10200 S De Anza Blvd Cupertino (95014) *(P-15095)*
Seagate Technology LLC.....E.....510 624-3728
47488 Kato Rd Fremont (94538) *(P-15096)*
Seagate Technology LLC.....F.....405 324-4799
10200 S De Anza Blvd Cupertino (95014) *(P-15097)*
Seagate US LLC.....F.....408 658-1000
10200 S De Anza Blvd Cupertino (95014) *(P-15098)*
Seagra Technology Inc.....E.....408 230-8706
816 W Ahwanee Ave Sunnyvale (94085) *(P-15327)*
Seagra Technology Inc (PA).....F.....949 419-6796
14252 Culver Dr Irvine (92604) *(P-15328)*
Seagull Solutions Inc.....F.....408 778-1127
15105 Concord Cir Ste 100 Morgan Hill (95037) *(P-21118)*
Seal Innovations Inc.....F.....626 282-7325
820 S Palm Ave Ste 15 Alhambra (91803) *(P-9370)*
Seal Methods Inc (PA).....D.....562 944-0291
11915 Shoemaker Ave Santa Fe Springs (90670) *(P-5374)*
Seal Science Inc (PA).....D.....949 253-3130
17131 Daimler St Irvine (92614) *(P-9254)*
Seal Seat Co.....F.....626 923-2504
9160 Norwalk Blvd Santa Fe Springs (90670) *(P-14252)*
Seal Software Inc (PA).....F.....650 938-7325
1990 N Calif Blvd Ste 500 Walnut Creek (94596) *(P-24393)*
Sealed Air Corporation.....D.....909 594-1791
19440 Arenth Ave City of Industry (91748) *(P-9568)*
Sealed Air Corporation.....E.....201 791-7600
16201 Commerce Way Cerritos (90703) *(P-5418)*
Sealed Air Corporation.....E.....619 421-9003
2311 Boswell Rd Ste 8 Chula Vista (91914) *(P-5419)*
Sealing Corporation.....F.....818 765-7327
7353 Greenbush Ave B North Hollywood (91605) *(P-9255)*
Sealtight Technology, Santa Barbara *Also called B&B Hardware Inc (P-12666)*
Sealy Mattress Mfg Co Inc.....C.....510 235-7171
1130 7th St Richmond (94801) *(P-4741)*
Seamaid Manufacturing Corp.....E.....415 777-9978
960 Mission St San Francisco (94103) *(P-2993)*
Seaman Products of California.....F.....818 361-2012
12329 Gladstone Ave Sylmar (91342) *(P-20229)*
Seaport Stainless, Richmond *Also called Andrus Sheet Metal Inc (P-12109)*
Searing Industries Inc.....C.....909 948-3030
8901 Arrow Rte Rancho Cucamonga (91730) *(P-11068)*
Searles Valley Minerals Inc.....A.....760 372-2259
80201 Trona Rd Trona (93562) *(P-380)*
Seascape Lamps Inc.....F.....831 728-5699
125a Lee Rd Watsonville (95076) *(P-16990)*
Seasonic Electronics Inc.....F.....626 969-9966
301 Aerojet Ave Azusa (91702) *(P-19079)*
Seaspace Corporation.....E.....858 746-1100
13000 Gregg St Ste A Poway (92064) *(P-17652)*
Seaspine Inc.....D.....760 727-8399
5770 Armada Dr Carlsbad (92008) *(P-22081)*
Seaspine Orthopedics Corp (HQ).....E.....866 942-8698
5770 Armada Dr Carlsbad (92008) *(P-22082)*
Seastar Medical Inc.....F.....734 272-4772
2187 Newcastle Ave # 200 Cardiff By The Sea (92007) *(P-21892)*
Seating Component Mfg Inc.....F.....714 693-3376
3951 E Miraloma Ave Anaheim (92806) *(P-4773)*
Seating Concepts LLC.....E.....619 491-3159
4229 Ponderosa Ave Ste B San Diego (92123) *(P-4871)*
Seavey Vineyard Ltd Partnr.....F.....707 963-8339
1310 Conn Valley Rd Saint Helena (94574) *(P-1909)*
Seb, Chino *Also called Specilty Enzymes Btechnologies (P-8776)*
Sebastiani Vineyards Inc.....D.....707 933-3200
389 4th St E Sonoma (95476) *(P-1910)*
Sebastiani Vineyards & Winery, Sonoma *Also called Sebastiani Vineyards Inc (P-1910)*
SEC, Moorpark *Also called Semiconductor Equipment Corp (P-14537)*
Sechrist Industries Inc.....D.....714 579-8400
4225 E La Palma Ave Anaheim (92807) *(P-21893)*
Seco Industries, Commerce *Also called Specialty Enterprises Co (P-9569)*
Seco Manufacturing Company Inc.....C.....530 225-8155
4155 Oasis Rd Redding (96003) *(P-21533)*
Second Generation Inc.....D.....213 743-8700
1950 Naomi Ave Los Angeles (90011) *(P-3402)*
Second Sight Medical Pdts Inc (PA).....C.....818 833-5000
12744 San Fernando Rd Sylmar (91342) *(P-21894)*
Secondwind Products Inc.....E.....805 239-2555
4301 Second Wind Way Paso Robles (93446) *(P-8417)*
Secret Road Music Pubg Inc.....F.....323 464-1234
5850 Foothill Dr Los Angeles (90068) *(P-6145)*
Sector9, San Diego *Also called Bravo Sports (P-22768)*
Secugen Corporation.....E.....408 834-7712
2065 Martin Ave Ste 108 Santa Clara (95050) *(P-15329)*
Secura Inc.....D.....760 804-7313
6965 El Camino Re Ste 105 Oceanside (92054) *(P-3051)*
Secura Key, Chatsworth *Also called Soundcraft Inc (P-19411)*
Secure Comm Systems Inc (HQ).....C.....714 547-1174
1740 E Wilshire Ave Santa Ana (92705) *(P-17653)*
Secure Comm Systems Inc.....F.....714 547-1174
1740 E Wilshire Ave Santa Ana (92705) *(P-17654)*
Secure Computing Corporation (HQ).....E.....408 979-2020
3965 Freedom Cir 4 Santa Clara (95054) *(P-24394)*
Secure Technology, Santa Ana *Also called Secure Comm Systems Inc (P-17653)*
Secured Gold Buyers, Newport Beach *Also called SGB Holdings LLC (P-22571)*
Securedata Inc.....F.....424 363-8529
3255 Chnga Blvd W Ste 301 Los Angeles (90068) *(P-24395)*
Security Contractor Svcs Inc.....E.....916 338-4800
5311 Jackson St North Highlands (95660) *(P-12508)*
Security Door Controls (PA).....E.....805 494-0622
801 Avenida Acaso Camarillo (93012) *(P-11627)*
Security Front Desk, Mc Kittrick *Also called Aera Energy LLC (P-83)*
Security Metal Products Corp (HQ).....E.....310 641-6690
5678 Concours Ontario (91764) *(P-11983)*
Security People Inc.....E.....707 766-6000
9 Willowbrook Ct Petaluma (94954) *(P-19080)*
Security Pro USA.....F.....310 841-5845
10530 Venice Blvd Ste 200 Culver City (90232) *(P-22083)*
Security Sales & Integration, Torrance *Also called E H Publishing Inc (P-5928)*
Security Textile Corporation.....D.....213 747-2673
1457 E Washington Blvd Los Angeles (90021) *(P-3812)*
Securityman, Ontario *Also called Teklink Security Inc (P-19421)*
Sedas Printing Inc.....F.....323 469-1034
5335 Santa Monica Blvd Los Angeles (90029) *(P-6856)*
Sedenquist-Fraser Entps Inc.....E.....562 924-5763
16730 Gridley Rd Cerritos (90703) *(P-19764)*
See's Candies, South San Francisco *Also called Sees Candy Shops Incorporated (P-1397)*
See's Candies, Los Angeles *Also called Sees Candy Shops Incorporated (P-1399)*
Seed Factory Northwest Inc (PA).....E.....209 634-8522
4319 Jessup Rd Ceres (95307) *(P-1126)*
Seedorff Acme, Anaheim *Also called A P Seedorff & Company Inc (P-16692)*
Seeger's Printing, Turlock *Also called Seegers Industries Inc (P-6857)*
Seegers Industries Inc.....F.....209 667-2750
210 N Center St Turlock (95380) *(P-6857)*
Seektech, San Diego *Also called Seescan Inc (P-14227)*
Seelect Inc.....F.....714 744-3700
833 N Elm St Orange (92867) *(P-2230)*
Sees Candies Inc (HQ).....B.....650 761-2490
210 El Camino Real South San Francisco (94080) *(P-1396)*
Sees Candy Shops Incorporated (HQ).....E.....650 761-2490
210 El Camino Real South San Francisco (94080) *(P-1397)*
Sees Candy Shops Incorporated.....F.....562 928-2912
9839 Paramount Blvd Downey (90240) *(P-1398)*
Sees Candy Shops Incorporated.....C.....310 559-4919
3423 S La Cienega Blvd Los Angeles (90016) *(P-1399)*
Seescan Inc (PA).....C.....858 244-3300
3855 Ruffin Rd San Diego (92123) *(P-14227)*
Sega of America Inc (HQ).....E.....949 788-0455
6400 Oak Cyn Ste 100 Irvine (92618) *(P-23472)*
Seghesio Wineries Inc.....E.....707 433-3579
700 Grove St Healdsburg (95448) *(P-1911)*
Seghesio Winery, Healdsburg *Also called Seghesio Wineries Inc (P-1911)*
Segmentio Inc.....F.....844 611-0621
100 California St Ste 700 San Francisco (94111) *(P-15330)*

Seguin Moreau Holdings Inc (PA) ... D ... 707 252-3408
151 Camino Dorado NAPA (94558) ***(P-4427)***

Segundo Metal Products Inc ... D ... 925 667-2009
7855 Southfront Rd Livermore (94551) ***(P-12371)***

Sehanson Inc ... E ... 714 778-1900
2121 E Via Burton Anaheim (92806) ***(P-20230)***

Seiko Epson, Long Beach *Also called Epson America Inc* ***(P-15225)***

Seirus Innovation, Poway *Also called Seirus Innovative ACC Inc* ***(P-3501)***

Seirus Innovative ACC Inc ... D ... 858 513-1212
13975 Danielson St Poway (92064) ***(P-3501)***

Seismic Reservoir 2020 Inc ... E ... 562 697-9711
3 Pointe Dr Ste 212 Brea (92821) ***(P-139)***

Sekai Electronics Inc (PA) ... E ... 949 783-5740
38 Waterworks Way Irvine (92618) ***(P-17655)***

Sekisui America Corporation ... E ... 858 452-3198
6659 Top Gun St San Diego (92121) ***(P-8253)***

Sel-Tech, Chico *Also called Selken Enterprises Inc* ***(P-24663)***

Selane Products Inc (PA) ... D ... 818 998-7460
9129 Lurline Ave Chatsworth (91311) ***(P-22189)***

Selby Inc ... F ... 707 431-1703
498 Moore Ln Ste A Healdsburg (95448) ***(P-1912)***

Selby Winery, Healdsburg *Also called Selby Inc* ***(P-1912)***

Select Circuits ... F ... 714 825-1090
3700 W Segerstrom Ave Santa Ana (92704) ***(P-17996)***

Select Communications Inc ... E ... 650 948-9000
138 Main St Los Altos (94022) ***(P-6025)***

Select Fabrications, Corona *Also called Grand Metals Inc* ***(P-11046)***

Select Graphics ... F ... 714 537-5250
11931 Euclid St Garden Grove (92840) ***(P-6858)***

Select Office Systems Inc ... F ... 818 861-8320
1811 W Magnolia Blvd Burbank (91506) ***(P-8929)***

Select Supplements Inc ... E ... 760 431-7509
2390 Oak Ridge Way Vista (92081) ***(P-7693)***

Select Supplements Inc ... F ... 760 431-7509
2390 Oak Ridge Way Vista (92081) ***(P-619)***

Selectra Industries Corp ... D ... 323 581-8500
5166 Alcoa Ave Vernon (90058) ***(P-3448)***

Self Esteem, Montebello *Also called All Access Apparel Inc* ***(P-3473)***

Selfoptima Inc ... F ... 408 217-8667
1601 S De Anza Blvd # 255 Cupertino (95014) ***(P-6338)***

Selken Enterprises Inc ... F ... 530 891-4200
108 Boeing Ave Chico (95973) ***(P-24663)***

Sell Lumber Corporation ... F ... 530 241-2085
7887 Eastside Rd Redding (96001) ***(P-3948)***

Sellers Optical Inc ... D ... 949 631-6800
320 Kalmus Dr Costa Mesa (92626) ***(P-21407)***

Selma Enterprise, Selma *Also called Lee Central Cal Newspapers* ***(P-5696)***

Selma Pallet Inc ... E ... 559 896-7171
1651 Pacific St Selma (93662) ***(P-4399)***

Seloah Gourmet Food, Tustin *Also called Country House* ***(P-1362)***

Selvage Concrete Products ... F ... 707 542-2762
3309 Sebastopol Rd Santa Rosa (95407) ***(P-10649)***

Semano Inc ... E ... 510 489-2360
31757 Knapp St Hayward (94544) ***(P-13099)***

Semco ... E ... 909 799-9666
1495 S Gage St San Bernardino (92408) ***(P-21534)***

Semco Aerospace ... F ... 818 678-9381
9637 Owensmouth Ave Chatsworth (91311) ***(P-3705)***

Semi Automation & Tech Inc ... E ... 408 374-9549
1510 Dell Ave Ste C Campbell (95008) ***(P-18530)***

Semi-Kinetics Inc ... D ... 949 830-7364
20191 Windrow Dr Ste A Lake Forest (92630) ***(P-17997)***

Semicndctor Cmponents Inds LLC ... C ... 408 542-1000
2975 Stender Way Santa Clara (95054) ***(P-18531)***

Semicoa, Costa Mesa *Also called Falkor Partners LLC* ***(P-18234)***

Semicoa Corporation ... D ... 714 979-1900
333 Mccormick Ave Costa Mesa (92626) ***(P-18532)***

Semiconductor Components Inc ... E ... 714 547-6059
1353 E Edinger Ave Santa Ana (92705) ***(P-18533)***

Semiconductor Equipment Corp ... F ... 805 529-2293
5154 Goldman Ave Moorpark (93021) ***(P-14537)***

Semiconductor Logistics Corp ... F ... 562 921-0399
14409 Iseli Rd Santa Fe Springs (90670) ***(P-18534)***

Semiconductor Process Eqp Corp ... E ... 661 257-0934
27963 Franklin Pkwy Valencia (91355) ***(P-18535)***

Semiconductorstore.com, El Segundo *Also called Symmetry Electronics LLC* ***(P-18598)***

Semiconix Corp (PA) ... F ... 408 986-8026
2968 Scott Blvd Santa Clara (95054) ***(P-18536)***

Semifab Inc ... D ... 408 414-5928
150 Great Oaks Blvd San Jose (95119) ***(P-20935)***

Seminet Inc ... F ... 408 754-8537
150 Great Oaks Blvd San Jose (95119) ***(P-18537)***

Semler Scientific Inc ... E ... 877 774-4211
911 Bern Ct Ste 110 San Jose (95112) ***(P-21895)***

Semore Inc ... F ... 213 746-4122
1437 Santee St Ste 201 Los Angeles (90015) ***(P-3019)***

Semotus Inc ... E ... 408 667-2046
718 University Ave # 110 Los Gatos (95032) ***(P-24396)***

Sempervirens Group ... F ... 510 847-0801
820 Coventry Rd Kensington (94707) ***(P-8839)***

Sempra Global (HQ) ... D ... 619 696-2000
488 8th Ave San Diego (92101) ***(P-16575)***

Semprex Corporation ... F ... 408 379-3230
782 Camden Ave Campbell (95008) ***(P-21408)***

Semtech Corporation (PA) ... C ... 805 498-2111
200 Flynn Rd Camarillo (93012) ***(P-18538)***

Semtech San Diego Corporation ... E ... 858 695-1808
10021 Willow Creek Rd San Diego (92131) ***(P-18539)***

Semtek Innvtive Solutions Corp ... E ... 858 436-2270
12777 High Bludd Dr 225 San Diego (92130) ***(P-15331)***

Sencha Naturals Inc ... F ... 213 353-9908
104 N Union Ave Los Angeles (90026) ***(P-1400)***

Senetrics International, Berkeley *Also called Sensys Networks Inc* ***(P-17760)***

Senetur LLC ... F ... 650 269-1023
399 Lakeside Dr Ste 400 Oakland (94612) ***(P-24397)***

Seng Cheang Mong Co ... F ... 626 442-2899
2661 Merced Ave El Monte (91733) ***(P-2383)***

Seng Cheang Mong Food, El Monte *Also called Seng Cheang Mong Co* ***(P-2383)***

Senga Engineering Inc ... E ... 714 549-8011
1525 E Warner Ave Santa Ana (92705) ***(P-16393)***

Senior Aerospace Jet Pdts Corp (HQ) ... C ... 858 278-8400
9106 Balboa Ave San Diego (92123) ***(P-19979)***

Senior Aerospace Jet Pdts Corp ... F ... 858 278-8400
9150 Balboa Ave San Diego (92123) ***(P-16394)***

Senior Flexonics, San Diego *Also called Senior Operations LLC* ***(P-16395)***

Senior Operations LLC ... B ... 858 278-8400
9106 Balboa Ave San Diego (92123) ***(P-16395)***

Senior Operations LLC ... B ... 818 260-2900
2980 N San Fernando Blvd Burbank (91504) ***(P-20231)***

Senior Operations LLC ... D ... 909 627-2723
790 Greenfield Dr El Cajon (92021) ***(P-16396)***

Senior Operations LLC ... C ... 858 278-8400
9106 Balboa Ave San Diego (92123) ***(P-16397)***

Senju Comtek Corp ... F ... 408 792-3830
1171 N 4th St Ste 80 San Jose (95112) ***(P-11486)***

Senju Comtek Corp (HQ) ... F ... 408 963-5300
2989 San Ysidro Way Santa Clara (95051) ***(P-11487)***

Senju Usa Inc ... F ... 818 719-7190
21700 Oxnard St Ste 1070 Woodland Hills (91367) ***(P-8123)***

Senor Snacks Holdings, Fullerton *Also called Senor Snacks Inc* ***(P-2344)***

Senor Snacks Inc ... F ... 714 739-1073
2325 Raymer Ave Fullerton (92833) ***(P-2344)***

Senor Snacks Manufacturing Ltd ... D ... 714 739-1073
2325 Raymer Ave Fullerton (92833) ***(P-1401)***

Senreve, San Francisco *Also called Project 1920 Inc* ***(P-10225)***

Sensata Technologies Inc ... D ... 805 716-0322
1461 Lawrence Dr Thousand Oaks (91320) ***(P-15332)***

Sensata Technologies Inc ... F ... 805 684-8401
6382 Rose Ln Carpinteria (93013) ***(P-16753)***

Sensbey Inc (PA) ... F ... 650 697-2032
833 Mahler Rd Ste 3 Burlingame (94010) ***(P-14253)***

Sense Fashion Corporation ... E ... 626 454-3381
2415 Merced Ave South El Monte (91733) ***(P-3192)***

Sense Fashions, South El Monte *Also called Sense Fashion Corporation* ***(P-3192)***

Sensient Dehydrated Flavors, Turlock *Also called Sensient Ntral Ingredients LLC* ***(P-862)***

Sensient Ntral Ingredients LLC ... F ... 209 394-7979
7474 Cressey Way Livingston (95334) ***(P-861)***

Sensient Ntral Ingredients LLC (HQ) ... D ... 209 667-2777
151 S Walnut Rd Turlock (95380) ***(P-862)***

Sensient Technologies Corp ... F ... 209 394-7971
9984 W Walnut Ave Livingston (95334) ***(P-2610)***

Sensit Inc ... F ... 909 793-5816
1652 Plum Ln Ste 106 Redlands (92374) ***(P-20809)***

Senso-Metrics Inc ... F ... 805 527-3640
4584 Runway St Simi Valley (93063) ***(P-21535)***

Sensonetics Inc ... F ... 714 799-1616
11164 Young River Ave Fountain Valley (92708) ***(P-18540)***

Sensor Concepts Incorporated ... D ... 925 443-9001
7950 National Dr Livermore (94550) ***(P-20719)***

Sensor Dynamics Inc ... F ... 510 623-1459
4568 Enterprise St Fremont (94538) ***(P-22308)***

Sensor Engineering, Oxnard *Also called Sensortech Systems Inc* ***(P-20936)***

Sensor Systems Inc ... B ... 818 341-5366
8929 Fullbright Ave Chatsworth (91311) ***(P-20720)***

Sensor-Kinesis Corporation (PA) ... F ... 424 331-0900
10604 S La Cienega Blvd Inglewood (90304) ***(P-21288)***

Sensoronix Inc ... F ... 949 528-0906
16181 Scientific Irvine (92618) ***(P-18541)***

Sensortech Systems Inc ... F ... 805 981-3735
341 Bernoulli Cir Oxnard (93030) ***(P-20936)***

Sensory Neurostimulation Inc ... F ... 949 492-0550
1235 Puerta Del Sol # 600 San Clemente (92673) ***(P-8124)***

Sensoscientific Inc ... E ... 800 279-3101
685 Cochran St Ste 200 Simi Valley (93065) ***(P-20937)***

Sensys Networks Inc (HQ) ... D ... 510 548-4620
1608 4th St Ste 200 Berkeley (94710) ***(P-17760)***

Sentient Energy Inc (PA) ... F ... 650 523-6680
880 Mitten Rd Ste 105 Burlingame (94010) ***(P-21119)***

Sentiments Inc (PA) ... F ... 323 843-2080
5635 Smithway St Commerce (90040) ***(P-23473)***

Sentinel Hydrosolutions LLC ... F ... 866 410-1134
1223 Pacific Oaks Pl # 104 Escondido (92029) ***(P-21536)***

Sentinel Offender Services LLC ... F ... 626 336-5150
16046 Amar Rd City of Industry (91744) ***(P-20810)***

Sentinel Printing & Publishing ... F ... 559 591-4632
145 S L St Dinuba (93618) ***(P-5824)***

Sentran L L C (PA) ... F ... 888 545-8988
4355 E Lowell St Ste F Ontario (91761) ***(P-21537)***

Sentry Industries Inc ... F ... 909 986-3642
1245 Brooks St Ontario (91762) ***(P-7608)***

Sentynl Therapeutics Inc ... E ... 888 227-8725
420 Stevens Ave Ste 200 Solana Beach (92075) ***(P-8125)***

Seollem Corporation ... F ... 323 265-3266
2856 E Pico Blvd Los Angeles (90023) ***(P-3052)***

Separation Engineering Inc ... E ... 760 489-0101
931 S Andreasen Dr Ste A Escondido (92029) ***(P-14856)***

Sepasoft Inc ... F ... 916 939-1684
1264 Hawks Flight Ct El Dorado Hills (95762) ***(P-24398)***

ALPHABETIC

Employee Codes: A=Over 500 employees, B=251-500
C=101-250, D=51-100, E=20-50, F=10-19

2020 California
Manfacturers Register

© Mergent Inc. 1-800-342-5647

1235

Sepor Inc....F....310 830-6601
718 N Fries Ave Wilmington (90744) ***(P-20774)***
Sepragen Corporation....E....510 475-0650
1205 San Luis Obispo St Hayward (94544) ***(P-21289)***
Sequent Medical Inc....D....949 830-9600
11 Columbia Ste A Aliso Viejo (92656) ***(P-21896)***
Sequent Software Inc....F....650 419-2713
4699 Old Ironsides Dr # 470 Santa Clara (95054) ***(P-24399)***
Sequenta LLC....D....650 243-3900
329 Oyster Point Blvd South San Francisco (94080) ***(P-8254)***
Sequoia Pure Water Inc....E....310 637-8500
1640 W 134th St Compton (90222) ***(P-2166)***
Seradyn Inc....D....317 610-3800
46360 Fremont Blvd Fremont (94538) ***(P-8255)***
Serbin Communications Inc....F....805 963-0439
813 Reddick St Santa Barbara (93103) ***(P-6026)***
Serco Mold Inc (PA)....E....626 331-0517
2009 Wright Ave La Verne (91750) ***(P-10053)***
Sercomp LLC (PA)....D....805 299-0020
5401 Tech Cir Ste 200 Moorpark (93021) ***(P-22973)***
Sergio Shoes, North Hollywood *Also called Onnik Shoe Company Inc* ***(P-10174)***
Serious Energy Inc (PA)....D....408 541-8000
1250 Elko Dr Sunnyvale (94089) ***(P-4872)***
Serious Windows, Sunnyvale *Also called Serious Energy Inc* ***(P-4872)***
Serpa Packaging Solutions, Visalia *Also called Food Machinery Sales Inc* ***(P-14707)***
Serpac Electronic Enclosures, La Verne *Also called Serco Mold Inc* ***(P-10053)***
Serra Laser and Waterjet Inc....E....714 680-6211
1740 N Orangethorpe Park Anaheim (92801) ***(P-19400)***
Serra Manufacturing Corp (PA)....E....310 537-4560
3039 E Las Hermanas St Compton (90221) ***(P-12871)***
Serra Systems Inc (HQ)....F....707 433-5104
126 Mill St Healdsburg (95448) ***(P-24400)***
Serrano Industries Inc....E....562 777-8180
9922 Tabor Pl Santa Fe Springs (90670) ***(P-16398)***
Serta International, Livermore *Also called National Bedding Company LLC* ***(P-4733)***
Serv-Rite Meat Company Inc....D....323 227-1911
2515 N San Fernando Rd Los Angeles (90065) ***(P-424)***
Servers Direct LLC....C....800 576-7931
20480 Business Pkwy Walnut (91789) ***(P-14972)***
Service Press Inc....F....650 592-3484
935 Tanklage Rd San Carlos (94070) ***(P-6859)***
Service Rock Products Corp....E....760 252-1615
2820 E Main St Barstow (92311) ***(P-10828)***
Service Rock Products Corp....E....760 373-9140
7900 Moss Ave California City (93505) ***(P-10829)***
Service Rock Products Corp....F....760 245-7997
200 S Main St Ste 200 # 200 Corona (92882) ***(P-10830)***
Service Rock Products Corp....D....760 446-2606
2157 W Inyokern Rd Ridgecrest (93555) ***(P-10831)***
Service Rock Products Corp....E....661 533-3443
37790 75th St E Palmdale (93552) ***(P-10832)***
Servicenow Inc....F....858 720-0477
4810 Eastgate Mall San Diego (92121) ***(P-24401)***
Servtech Plastics, Monrovia *Also called Crescent Plastics Inc* ***(P-9734)***
Sesame Software Inc....E....866 474-7575
5201 Great America Pkwy # 320 Santa Clara (95054) ***(P-24402)***
Sessa Manufacturing & Welding....E....805 644-2284
2932 Golf Course Dr Ventura (93003) ***(P-12872)***
Sessions....E....831 461-5080
60 Old El Pueblo Rd Scotts Valley (95066) ***(P-3403)***
Setco LLC....F....812 424-2904
4875 E Hunter Ave Anaheim (92807) ***(P-10054)***
Setco Sales Company....F....714 372-3730
5572 Buckingham Dr Huntington Beach (92649) ***(P-14192)***
Settlers Jerky Inc....E....909 444-3999
307 Paseo Sonrisa Walnut (91789) ***(P-498)***
Setzer Forest Products Inc (PA)....C....916 442-2555
2555 3rd St Ste 200 Sacramento (95818) ***(P-4122)***
Setzer Forest Products Inc....C....530 534-8100
1980 Kusel Rd Oroville (95966) ***(P-3949)***
Sev-Cal Tool Inc....E....714 549-3347
3231 Halladay St Santa Ana (92705) ***(P-14193)***
Seven Up Bottling, Sacramento *Also called Capitol Beverage Packers* ***(P-2051)***
Seven Up Btlg Co San Francisco (HQ)....C....925 938-8777
2875 Prune Ave Fremont (94539) ***(P-2167)***
Seven Up Btlg Co San Francisco....E....831 632-0777
11205 Commercial Pkwy Castroville (95012) ***(P-2168)***
Seven Up Btlg Co San Francisco....D....916 929-7777
2670 Land Ave Sacramento (95815) ***(P-2169)***
Seven Wells LLC....F....213 305-4775
14801 Able Ln Ste 102 Huntington Beach (92647) ***(P-4531)***
Seven-Up Bottling, Fremont *Also called Seven Up Btlg Co San Francisco* ***(P-2167)***
Seven-Up Bottling, Castroville *Also called Seven Up Btlg Co San Francisco* ***(P-2168)***
Seven-Up Bottling, Petaluma *Also called American Bottling Company* ***(P-2025)***
Seven-Up Bottling, Ukiah *Also called American Bottling Company* ***(P-2026)***
Seven-Up Bottling, Sacramento *Also called Seven Up Btlg Co San Francisco* ***(P-2169)***
Seven-Up Btlg Co Marysville, Sacramento *Also called American Bottling Company* ***(P-2034)***
Seven-Up RC of Chico....E....530 893-4501
306 Otterson Dr Ste 10 Chico (95928) ***(P-2170)***
Seventh Heaven Inc....E....408 287-8945
1025 S 5th St San Jose (95112) ***(P-3861)***
Sew Forth Inc....E....323 725-3500
2350 Central Ave Duarte (91010) ***(P-3053)***
Sew Sporty....E....760 599-0585
2215 La Mirada Dr Vista (92081) ***(P-3404)***
Sew What Inc....E....310 639-6000
1978 E Gladwick St Compton (90220) ***(P-3597)***
Sew-Eurodrive Inc....E....510 487-3560
30599 San Antonio St Hayward (94544) ***(P-14749)***
Sewer Rodding Equipment Co (PA)....E....310 301-9009
3217 Carter Ave Marina Del Rey (90292) ***(P-15576)***
Sewing Collection Inc....D....323 264-2223
3113 E 26th St Vernon (90058) ***(P-9256)***
Sewing Experts Inc....E....760 357-8525
227 Lincoln St Calexico (92231) ***(P-3193)***
Sextant Wines, Paso Robles *Also called Rbz Vineyards LLC* ***(P-1882)***
Seychelle Envmtl Tech Inc....F....949 234-1999
32963 Calle Perfecto San Juan Capistrano (92675) ***(P-8126)***
Seymour Duncan, Santa Barbara *Also called Duncan Carter Corporation* ***(P-22614)***
Seymour Levinger & Co....E....909 673-9800
1455 Citrus St Riverside (92507) ***(P-12749)***
SF Global LLC....F....888 536-5593
250 Frank H Ogawa Plz Oakland (94612) ***(P-10055)***
SF Motors Inc (HQ)....C....408 617-7878
3303 Scott Blvd Santa Clara (95054) ***(P-19501)***
SF Tube, Hayward *Also called San Francisco Pipe &* ***(P-13485)***
Sfc, Perris *Also called Stretch Forming Corporation* ***(P-12392)***
Sfc Communications Inc....F....949 553-8566
65 Post Ste 1000 Irvine (92618) ***(P-20811)***
SFE, Santa Fe Springs *Also called Santa Fe Enterprises Inc* ***(P-14103)***
Sffi Company Inc (PA)....D....323 586-0000
4383 Exchange Ave Vernon (90058) ***(P-823)***
Sfo Apparel....C....415 468-8816
41 Park Pl 43 Brisbane (94005) ***(P-3405)***
Sfs, Brea *Also called Kirkhill Inc* ***(P-7631)***
SGB Better Baking Co LLC....D....818 787-9992
14528 Blythe St Van Nuys (91402) ***(P-1275)***
SGB Bubbles Baking Co LLC....D....818 786-1700
15215 Keswick St Van Nuys (91405) ***(P-1276)***
SGB Enterprises Inc....E....661 294-8306
24844 Anza Dr Ste A Valencia (91355) ***(P-15134)***
SGB Holdings LLC....E....949 722-1149
7 Balboa Cvs Newport Beach (92663) ***(P-22571)***
SGC International Inc....F....323 318-2998
6489 Corvette St Commerce (90040) ***(P-10274)***
Sgk LLC....D....415 438-6700
650 Townsend St Ste 160 San Francisco (94103) ***(P-7381)***
Sgk LLC....C....323 258-4111
3116 W Avenue 32 Los Angeles (90065) ***(P-7382)***
Sgl Composites Inc (HQ)....D....424 329-5250
1551 W 139th St Gardena (90249) ***(P-5302)***
Sgl Technic LLC (HQ)....D....661 257-0500
28176 Avenue Stanford Valencia (91355) ***(P-10977)***
Sgps Inc....D....310 538-4175
15823 S Main St Gardena (90248) ***(P-23474)***
Sgt Boardriders Inc....F....714 274-8000
7403 Slater Ave Huntington Beach (92647) ***(P-9371)***
Shades Unlimited Inc....F....707 285-2233
361 Blodgett St Cotati (94931) ***(P-5037)***
Shadow Holdings LLC (PA)....E....661 252-3807
26455 Ruether Ave Santa Clarita (91350) ***(P-8578)***
Shadow Holdings LLC....C....661 252-3807
26421 Ruether Ave Santa Clarita (91350) ***(P-8579)***
Shadow Industries Inc....F....714 995-4353
8941 Electric St Cypress (90630) ***(P-20493)***
Shadow Trailers, Cypress *Also called Shadow Industries Inc* ***(P-20493)***
Shafer Metal Stake (PA)....F....559 674-9487
25176 Avenue 5 1/2 Madera (93637) ***(P-12372)***
Shafer Vineyards....F....707 944-2877
6154 Silverado Trl NAPA (94558) ***(P-1913)***
Shafton Inc....F....818 985-5025
6932 Tujunga Ave North Hollywood (91605) ***(P-3578)***
Shaka Wear, Los Angeles *Also called Gino Corporation* ***(P-2990)***
Shamir Insight Inc....D....858 514-8330
9938 Via Pasar San Diego (92126) ***(P-10330)***
Shammi Industries, Corona *Also called Sammons Equipment Mfg Corp* ***(P-5081)***
Shamrock Die Cutting Company....E....323 266-4556
3020 Meyerloa Ln Pasadena (91107) ***(P-5454)***
Shamrock Fireplace, San Rafael *Also called Shamrock Materials Inc* ***(P-10835)***
Shamrock Manufacturing, Chino *Also called Shamrock Marketing Co Inc* ***(P-22084)***
Shamrock Marketing Co Inc (HQ)....F....909 591-8855
5445 Daniels St Chino (91710) ***(P-22084)***
Shamrock Materials Inc (PA)....E....707 781-9000
181 Lynch Creek Way # 201 Petaluma (94954) ***(P-10833)***
Shamrock Materials Inc....F....707 792-4695
8150 Gravenstein Hwy Cotati (94931) ***(P-10834)***
Shamrock Materials Inc....E....415 455-1575
548 Du Bois St San Rafael (94901) ***(P-10835)***
Shamrock Materials of Cotati, Cotati *Also called Shamrock Materials Inc* ***(P-10834)***
Shamrock Materials of Novato....F....415 892-1571
7552 Redwood Blvd Novato (94945) ***(P-10836)***
Shanghai Anc Electronic Tech, Moorpark *Also called Anc Technology LLC* ***(P-17820)***
Shannon Ridge Inc....E....707 994-9656
13888 Point Lakeview Rd Lower Lake (95457) ***(P-1914)***
Shannon Side Welding Inc....F....415 680-6101
620 Villa St Daly City (94014) ***(P-24664)***
Shape Memory Applications, San Jose *Also called Matthey Johnson Inc* ***(P-21790)***
Shape Memory Medical Inc....F....979 599-5201
807 Aldo Ave Ste 109 Santa Clara (95054) ***(P-22085)***
Shape Products, Oakland *Also called Vulpine Inc* ***(P-9035)***
Shara-Tex Inc....E....323 587-7200
3338 E Slauson Ave Vernon (90058) ***(P-2812)***
Sharcar Enterprises Inc....D....209 531-2200
201 Winmoore Way Modesto (95358) ***(P-10930)***
Sharedata Inc....D....408 490-2500
2465 Augustine Dr Santa Clara (95054) ***(P-24403)***
Sharedta/E Trade Bus Solutions, Santa Clara *Also called Sharedata Inc* ***(P-24403)***

Mergent e-mail: customerrelations@mergent.com
1236
2020 California
Manufacturers Register
(P-0000) Products & Services Section entry number
(PA)=Parent Co (HQ)=Headquarters (DH)=Div Headquarters

Shark Wheel Inc ... F ... 818 216-8001
22600 Lambert St Ste 704 Lake Forest (92630) ***(P-19765)***
Sharkey Technology Group Inc ... F ... 661 267-2118
39450 3rd St E Ste 154 Palmdale (93550) ***(P-16399)***
Sharkninja Operating LLC ... F ... 909 325-4412
16300 Fern Ave Chino (91708) ***(P-16853)***
Sharkrack Inc ... F ... 510 477-7900
23842 Cabot Blvd Hayward (94545) ***(P-15333)***
Sharon Havriluk ... E ... 714 630-1313
1164 N Kraemer Pl Anaheim (92806) ***(P-7316)***
Sharp Dimension Inc ... E ... 510 656-8938
4240 Business Center Dr Fremont (94538) ***(P-16400)***
Sharp Dots.com, Pico Rivera *Also called Sharpdots LLC* ***(P-15334)***
Sharp Industries Inc (PA) ... E ... 310 370-5990
3501 Challenger St Fl 2 Torrance (90503) ***(P-13994)***
Sharp Performance USA Inc (PA) ... F ... 626 888-1190
16029 Arrow Hwy Ste D Baldwin Park (91706) ***(P-22995)***
Sharp Profiles LLC ... F ... 760 246-9446
828 W Cienega Ave San Dimas (91773) ***(P-11544)***
Sharp-Rite Tool Inc ... F ... 909 948-1234
8443 Whirlaway St Alta Loma (91701) ***(P-14194)***
Sharpcast, Los Angeles *Also called Sugarsync Inc* ***(P-24465)***
Sharpdots LLC ... F ... 626 599-9696
3733 San Gabriel Rver Pkw Pico Rivera (90660) ***(P-15334)***
Sharpe Energy Services Inc ... F ... 408 489-3581
5094 Northlawn Dr San Jose (95130) ***(P-140)***
Sharpe Software Inc ... F ... 530 671-6499
925 Market St Yuba City (95991) ***(P-24404)***
Shasta Beverages Inc (HQ) ... D ... 954 581-0922
26901 Indl Blvd Hayward (94545) ***(P-2171)***
Shasta Beverages Inc ... D ... 714 523-2280
14405 Artesia Blvd La Mirada (90638) ***(P-2172)***
Shasta Electronic Mfg Svcs Inc ... E ... 408 436-1267
525 E Brokaw Rd San Jose (95112) ***(P-14973)***
Shasta Ems, San Jose *Also called Shasta Electronic Mfg Svcs Inc* ***(P-14973)***
Shasta Forest Products Inc (PA) ... E ... 530 842-0527
1412 Montague Rd Yreka (96097) ***(P-4532)***
Shasta Forest Products Inc ... E ... 530 842-2787
1423 Montague Rd Yreka (96097) ***(P-4533)***
Shasta Green Inc ... E ... 530 335-4924
35586a State Hwy 299 E Burney (96013) ***(P-3904)***
Shasta Ready Mix, Redding *Also called J F Shea Co Inc* ***(P-10774)***
Shasta Wood Products ... E ... 530 378-6880
19751 Hirsch Ct Anderson (96007) ***(P-4937)***
Shaver Specialty Coinc ... E ... 310 370-6941
20608 Earl St Torrance (90503) ***(P-14400)***
Shaw Industries Group Inc ... C ... 562 430-4445
11411 Valley View St Cypress (90630) ***(P-2879)***
Shawcor Pipe Protection LLC ... F ... 909 357-9002
14000 San Bernardino Ave Fontana (92335) ***(P-13245)***
Shaxon Industries Inc ... D ... 714 779-1140
4852 E La Palma Ave Anaheim (92807) ***(P-15099)***
Shb Instruments Inc ... F ... 818 773-2000
19215 Parthenia St Ste A Northridge (91324) ***(P-21120)***
Shear Tech, Canoga Park *Also called Y Nissim Inc* ***(P-15394)***
Sheathing Technologies Inc ... E ... 408 782-2720
675 Jarvis Dr Ste A Morgan Hill (95037) ***(P-21897)***
Sheedy Drayage Co ... F ... 510 441-7300
34301 7th St Union City (94587) ***(P-13851)***
Sheedy Hoist, Union City *Also called Sheedy Drayage Co* ***(P-13851)***
Sheepskin Specialties, San Diego *Also called Superlamb Inc* ***(P-3523)***
Sheer Design Inc ... D ... 310 306-2121
6309 Esplanade Playa Del Rey (90293) ***(P-8580)***
Sheervision Inc (PA) ... F ... 310 265-8918
4030 Palos Verdes Dr N # 104 Rllng HLS Est (90274) ***(P-21409)***
Sheet Metal Prototype Inc ... F ... 818 772-2715
19420 Londelius St Northridge (91324) ***(P-12373)***
Sheet Metal Service ... F ... 714 446-0196
2310 E Orangethorpe Ave Anaheim (92806) ***(P-12374)***
Sheet Metal Specialist LLC ... E ... 951 351-6828
11698 Warm Springs Rd Riverside (92505) ***(P-12375)***
Sheet Mtal Fabrication Sup Inc ... D ... 916 641-6884
2020 Railroad Dr Sacramento (95815) ***(P-12376)***
Sheetmetal Engineering ... E ... 805 306-0390
1780 Voyager Ave Simi Valley (93063) ***(P-12377)***
Sheffield Manufacturing Inc ... E ... 818 767-4948
13849 Magnolia Ave Chino (91710) ***(P-16401)***
Sheffield Platers Inc ... E ... 858 546-8484
9850 Waples St San Diego (92121) ***(P-13100)***
Shelby Carroll Intl Inc (PA) ... E ... 310 538-2914
19021 S Figueroa St Gardena (90248) ***(P-19502)***
Shelcore Inc (PA) ... F ... 818 883-2400
7811 Lemona Ave Van Nuys (91405) ***(P-22712)***
Shelcore Toys, Van Nuys *Also called Shelcore Inc* ***(P-22712)***
Sheldons Hobby Shop ... F ... 408 943-0220
2135 Oakland Rd San Jose (95131) ***(P-17656)***
Shell Catalysts & Tech LP ... D ... 626 334-1241
1001 N Todd Ave Azusa (91702) ***(P-7522)***
Shell Catalysts & Tech LP ... D ... 925 458-9045
2840 Willow Pass Rd Bay Point (94565) ***(P-7523)***
Shell Chemical LP ... D ... 925 313-8601
10 Mococo Rd Martinez (94553) ***(P-7524)***
Shell Martinez Refinery, Martinez *Also called Shell Martinez Refining Co* ***(P-9067)***
Shell Martinez Refining Co ... A ... 925 313-3000
3485 Pacheco Blvd Martinez (94553) ***(P-9067)***
Shellpro Inc ... E ... 209 334-2081
18378 Atkins Rd Lodi (95240) ***(P-23475)***
Shelter International Inc ... E ... 323 888-8856
6310 Corsair St Commerce (90040) ***(P-4534)***
Shelter Island Boatyard, San Diego *Also called Shelter Island Yachtways Ltd* ***(P-20357)***
Shelter Island Yachtways Ltd ... E ... 619 222-0481
2330 Shelter Island Dr # 1 San Diego (92106) ***(P-20357)***
Shelter Systems ... F ... 650 323-6202
224 Walnut St Menlo Park (94025) ***(P-3706)***
Sheng-Kee Bakery ... D ... 415 468-3800
201 S Hill Dr Brisbane (94005) ***(P-1277)***
Sheng-Kee of California Inc ... E ... 408 865-6000
10961 N Wolfe Rd Cupertino (95014) ***(P-1328)***
Shepard Bros Inc (PA) ... C ... 562 697-1366
503 S Cypress St La Habra (90631) ***(P-15577)***
Shephard Casters ... F ... 909 393-0597
4451 Eucalyptus Ave Chino (91710) ***(P-14615)***
Sherbit Health Inc ... F ... 925 683-8116
2200 Powell St Ste 460 Emeryville (94608) ***(P-24405)***
Shercon Inc ... D ... 800 228-3218
18704 S Ferris Pl Rancho Dominguez (90220) ***(P-9372)***
Sherline Products Incorporated ... E ... 760 727-5181
3235 Executive Rdg Vista (92081) ***(P-13951)***
Sherman Corporation ... E ... 310 671-2117
10803 Los Jardines E Fountain Valley (92708) ***(P-16402)***
Sherry Kline, Commerce *Also called Pacific Coast Home Furn Inc* ***(P-3633)***
Sherwin-Williams Company ... E ... 323 726-7272
5501 E Slauson Ave Commerce (90040) ***(P-2898)***
Shg Holdings Corp (PA) ... D ... 310 410-4907
201 Hindry Ave Inglewood (90301) ***(P-14228)***
Shield CA, Chino *Also called Shield Realty California Inc* ***(P-7450)***
Shield Realty California Inc (PA) ... E ... 909 628-4707
5165 G St Chino (91710) ***(P-7450)***
Shieldnseal, Nevada City *Also called Savensealcom Ltd* ***(P-5417)***
Shift Calendars Inc ... F ... 626 967-5862
809 N Glendora Ave Covina (91724) ***(P-6860)***
Shihs Printing ... F ... 626 281-2989
673 Monterey Pass Rd Monterey Park (91754) ***(P-7211)***
Shikai Products, Santa Rosa *Also called Trans-India Products Inc* ***(P-8595)***
Shim-It Corporation ... F ... 562 467-8600
1691 California Ave Corona (92881) ***(P-20232)***
Shimada Enterprises Inc ... E ... 562 802-8811
14009 Dinard Ave Santa Fe Springs (90670) ***(P-17161)***
Shimmer Fashion ... F ... 619 426-7781
555 Broadway Ste 134 Chula Vista (91910) ***(P-3194)***
Shimtech Industries US Inc (HQ) ... D ... 661 295-8620
29101 The Old Rd Valencia (91355) ***(P-20233)***
Shimtech US, Santa Clarita *Also called Lamsco West Inc* ***(P-20153)***
Shine & Pretty (usa) Corp ... F ... 805 388-8581
456 Constitution Ave Camarillo (93012) ***(P-8581)***
Shine Company Inc ... F ... 909 590-5005
3535 Philadelphia St Chino (91710) ***(P-4535)***
Shine Food Inc (PA) ... E ... 310 329-3829
19216 Normandie Ave Torrance (90502) ***(P-745)***
Shine Food Inc ... E ... 310 533-6010
21100 S Western Ave Torrance (90501) ***(P-980)***
Ship Supply International Inc ... F ... 310 325-3188
1215 255th St Harbor City (90710) ***(P-10483)***
Shiploop, San Francisco *Also called Squamtech Inc* ***(P-24443)***
Shire ... F ... 805 372-3000
1445 Lawrence Dr Newbury Park (91320) ***(P-8127)***
Shire Rgenerative Medicine Inc ... E ... 858 202-0673
10933 N Torrey Pines Rd # 200 La Jolla (92037) ***(P-8128)***
Shire Rgenerative Medicine Inc ... D ... 858 754-3700
10933 N Torrey Pines Rd # 200 La Jolla (92037) ***(P-8129)***
Shire Rgenerative Medicine Inc ... D ... 858 754-5396
11095 Torreyana Rd San Diego (92121) ***(P-8130)***
Shirlee Industries Inc ... F ... 909 590-4120
13985 Sycamore Way Chino (91710) ***(P-12604)***
Shmaze Custom Coatings, Lake Forest *Also called Shmaze Industries Inc* ***(P-13246)***
Shmaze Industries Inc ... E ... 949 583-1448
20792 Canada Rd Lake Forest (92630) ***(P-13246)***
Shock Doctor Inc (PA) ... D ... 800 233-6956
11488 Slater Ave Fountain Valley (92708) ***(P-22886)***
Shock Doctor Sports, Fountain Valley *Also called Shock Doctor Inc* ***(P-22886)***
Shockhound, City of Industry *Also called Hot Topic Inc* ***(P-3036)***
Shocking Technologies Inc ... E ... 831 331-4558
5870 Hellyer Ave San Jose (95138) ***(P-7609)***
Shockwave Medical Inc (PA) ... D ... 510 279-4262
5403 Betsy Ross Dr Santa Clara (95054) ***(P-21898)***
Shoes For Crews Intl Inc ... E ... 561 683-5090
760 Baldwin Park Blvd City of Industry (91746) ***(P-10161)***
Shop -Bradshaw Maintenance Sho, Sacramento *Also called Cemex Cnstr Mtls PCF LLC* ***(P-10718)***
Shop -Ncal Rmx Fixed Maint Sho, Fairfield *Also called Cemex Cnstr Mtls PCF LLC* ***(P-10547)***
Shop4techcom ... E ... 909 248-2725
13745 Seminole Dr Chino (91710) ***(P-15100)***
Shore Western Manufacturing ... E ... 626 357-3251
225 W Duarte Rd Monrovia (91016) ***(P-21290)***
Shoreline Cellars Inc ... F ... 909 322-6816
217 Pine Ave Long Beach (90802) ***(P-1915)***
Shoreline Products Inc ... F ... 949 388-1919
120 Calle Iglesia Ste A San Clemente (92672) ***(P-23008)***
Shorett Printing Inc (PA) ... E ... 714 545-4689
250 W Rialto Ave San Bernardino (92408) ***(P-7212)***
Shorett Printing Inc ... F ... 714 956-9001
250 W Rialto Ave San Bernardino (92408) ***(P-6861)***
Short Run Swiss Inc ... F ... 626 974-9373
714 E Edna Pl Covina (91723) ***(P-16403)***
Shortcuts Software Inc ... E ... 714 622-6600
7711 Center Ave Ste 550 Huntington Beach (92647) ***(P-24406)***

Shotspotter Inc ...D......510 794-3100
7979 Gateway Blvd Ste 210 Newark (94560) *(P-24407)*
Show Group Production Services, Gardena *Also called Sgps Inc (P-23474)*
Show Off Time, Ventura *Also called Fnc Medical Corporation (P-8494)*
Show Offs ...E......909 885-5223
1696 W Mill St Unit 10 Colton (92324) *(P-4938)*
Showcase Components, Santa Fe Springs *Also called Alumafab (P-17010)*
Showdogs Inc ...E......760 603-3269
168 S Pacific St San Marcos (92078) *(P-5038)*
Showerdoordirect LLC ...D......310 327-8060
20100 Normandie Ave Torrance (90502) *(P-12378)*
Showertek Inc ...F......707 224-1480
952 School St 219 NAPA (94559) *(P-10390)*
Shred-Tech Usa LLC ...E......909 923-2783
1100 S Grove Ave Ontario (91761) *(P-13891)*
Shrin Corporation ...C......714 850-0303
900 E Arlee Pl Anaheim (92805) *(P-19766)*
Shrink Wrap Pros LLC ...F......805 207-9050
275 E Hillcrest Dr Ste 16 Thousand Oaks (91360) *(P-14727)*
Shubb Capos ...E......707 876-3001
14471 Hwy 1 Valley Ford (94972) *(P-22639)*
Shugar Soapworks Inc ...F......323 234-2874
5955 Rickenbacker Rd Commerce (90040) *(P-8350)*
Shugart Corporation (PA) ...C......949 488-8779
25 Brookline Aliso Viejo (92656) *(P-14974)*
Shusters Logging Inc ...D......707 459-4131
750 E Valley St Willits (95490) *(P-3905)*
Shuttercraft of California, Santa Fe Springs *Also called Steiner & Mateer Inc (P-4129)*
Shutters By Angel Co, Lancaster *Also called Rta Sales Inc (P-4118)*
Shye West Inc (PA) ...E......949 486-4598
43 Corporate Park Ste 102 Irvine (92606) *(P-23195)*
Si, Fontana *Also called California Steel Inds Inc (P-11032)*
Si Manufacturing Inc ...E......714 956-7110
1440 S Allec St Anaheim (92805) *(P-18742)*
Sibyl Shepard Inc ...E......562 531-8612
8225 Alondra Blvd Paramount (90723) *(P-3640)*
Sid E Parker Boiler Mfg Co Inc ...D......323 727-9800
5930 Bandini Blvd Commerce (90040) *(P-12051)*
Sidco Labelling Systems, Santa Clara *Also called Context Engineering Co (P-12788)*
Sidney Millers Black Radio Ex ...E......818 907-9959
15030 Ventura Blvd # 864 Sherman Oaks (91403) *(P-6027)*
Sidus Solutions LLC (PA) ...F......619 275-5533
7352 Trade St San Diego (92121) *(P-19401)*
Sieena Inc ...E......310 455-6188
1901 Avenue Of The Stars Los Angeles (90067) *(P-24408)*
Siegfried Irvine, Irvine *Also called Alliance Medical Products Inc (P-21591)*
Siegwerk USA Inc ...E......707 469-7648
871 Cotting Ct Ste H Vacaville (95688) *(P-8930)*
Siella Medical, Irvine *Also called IV Support Systems Inc (P-21762)*
Siemens Hlthcare Dgnostics Inc ...D......310 645-8200
5210 Pacific Concourse Dr Los Angeles (90045) *(P-8256)*
Siemens Hlthcare Dgnostics Inc ...F......510 982-4000
725 Potter St Berkeley (94710) *(P-17410)*
Siemens Hlthcare Dgnostics Inc ...E......916 372-1900
2040 Enterprise Blvd West Sacramento (95691) *(P-8257)*
Siemens Industry Inc ...E......323 277-1500
5375 S Boyle Ave Vernon (90058) *(P-14857)*
Siemens Industry Inc ...D......949 448-0600
6 Journey Ste 200 Aliso Viejo (92656) *(P-20812)*
Siemens Industry Inc ...E......724 772-1237
1441 E Washington Blvd Los Angeles (90021) *(P-14858)*
Siemens Industry Inc ...D......510 237-2325
2775 Goodrick Ave Richmond (94801) *(P-20813)*
Siemens Industry Inc ...F......916 553-4444
3650 Industrial Blvd # 100 West Sacramento (95691) *(P-20814)*
Siemens Industry Inc ...C......916 681-3000
7464 French Rd Sacramento (95828) *(P-20815)*
Siemens Industry Inc ...D......714 252-3100
10855 Business Center Dr Cypress (90630) *(P-16614)*
Siemens Med Solutions USA Inc ...B......925 246-8200
4040 Nelson Ave Concord (94520) *(P-22309)*
Siemens Medical Solutions, Los Angeles *Also called Siemens Hlthcare Dgnostics Inc (P-8256)*
Siemens Medical Systems, Berkeley *Also called Siemens Hlthcare Dgnostics Inc (P-17410)*
Siemens PLM Software, San Jose *Also called Siemens Product Life Mgmt Sftw (P-24409)*
Siemens Product Life Mgmt Sftw ...E......408 941-4600
2077 Gateway Pl Ste 400 San Jose (95110) *(P-24409)*
Siemens Rail Automation Corp ...C......909 532-5405
9568 Archibald Ave Rancho Cucamonga (91730) *(P-17761)*
Siena Decor Inc ...F......909 895-8585
1250 Philadelphia St Pomona (91766) *(P-22945)*
Sienna Corporation Inc ...E......510 440-0200
41350 Christy St Fremont (94538) *(P-19402)*
Sientra Inc (PA) ...C......805 562-3500
420 S Fairview Ave # 200 Santa Barbara (93117) *(P-22086)*
Sierra Aerospace LLC ...F......805 526-8669
2263 Ward Ave Simi Valley (93065) *(P-19980)*
Sierra Alloys Company ...D......626 969-6711
5467 Ayon Ave Irwindale (91706) *(P-12736)*
Sierra Aluminum Company (HQ) ...E......951 781-7800
2345 Fleetwood Dr Riverside (92509) *(P-11245)*
Sierra Asset Servicing LLC ...F......530 582-7300
10232 Donner Pass Rd # 4 Truckee (96161) *(P-263)*
Sierra Automated Sys/Eng Corp ...E......818 840-6749
2821 Burton Ave Burbank (91504) *(P-17657)*
Sierra Aviation ...E......760 778-2845
3400 E Tahquitz Canyon Wa Palm Springs (92262) *(P-10207)*
Sierra Cascade Aggregate & Asp ...F......530 258-4555
6600 Old Ski Rd Chester (96020) *(P-359)*
Sierra Chemical Company, West Sacramento *Also called Richard K Gould Inc (P-9020)*
Sierra Circuits Inc ...C......408 735-7137
1108 W Evelyn Ave Sunnyvale (94086) *(P-17998)*
Sierra Design Mfg Inc (PA) ...E......925 443-3140
1113 Greenville Rd Livermore (94550) *(P-17092)*
Sierra Energy, Garden Valley *Also called Toms Sierra Company Inc (P-271)*
Sierra Feeds, Reedley *Also called Mission AG Resources LLC (P-605)*
Sierra Foods Inc ...F......562 802-3500
13352 Imperial Hwy Santa Fe Springs (90670) *(P-11518)*
Sierra Foothills Fudge Factory ...F......530 644-3492
2860 High Hill Rd Placerville (95667) *(P-1402)*
Sierra Hygiene Products LLC ...F......925 371-7173
4749 Bennett Dr Ste B Livermore (94551) *(P-5150)*
Sierra Lumber Manufacturers ...C......209 943-7777
375 W Hazelton Ave Stockton (95203) *(P-4123)*
Sierra Metal Fabricators Inc ...E......530 265-4591
529 Searls Ave Nevada City (95959) *(P-11880)*
Sierra Metalk Fabricators, Nevada City *Also called Sierra Metal Fabricators Inc (P-11880)*
Sierra Monitor Corporation (HQ) ...D......408 262-6611
1991 Tarob Ct Milpitas (95035) *(P-21538)*
Sierra Monolithics Inc ...F......949 269-4400
5141 California Ave # 200 Irvine (92617) *(P-20721)*
Sierra National Corporation ...E......619 258-8200
5140 Alzeda Dr La Mesa (91941) *(P-15378)*
Sierra Natural Science Inc ...F......831 757-1702
538 Brunken Ave Ste 2 Salinas (93901) *(P-8774)*
Sierra Nevada Brewing Co (PA) ...B......530 893-3520
1075 E 20th St Chico (95928) *(P-1563)*
Sierra Nevada Cheese Co Inc ...D......530 934-8660
6505 County Road 39 Willows (95988) *(P-577)*
Sierra Nevada Corporation ...E......510 446-8400
39465 Paseo Padre Pkwy # 2900 Fremont (94538) *(P-17658)*
Sierra Nevada Corporation ...E......916 985-8799
145 Parkshore Dr Folsom (95630) *(P-19403)*
Sierra Office Supply & Prtg, Sacramento *Also called Sierra Office Systems Pdts Inc (P-6862)*
Sierra Office Systems Pdts Inc (PA) ...D......916 369-0491
9950 Horn Rd Ste 5 Sacramento (95827) *(P-6862)*
Sierra Pacific Engrg & Pdts, Long Beach *Also called SPEP Acquisition Corp (P-11630)*
Sierra Pacific Industries ...F......530 226-5181
2771 Bechelli Ln Redding (96002) *(P-3950)*
Sierra Pacific Industries (PA) ...D......530 378-8000
19794 Riverside Ave Anderson (96007) *(P-3951)*
Sierra Pacific Industries ...C......530 378-8301
14980 Camage Ave Sonora (95370) *(P-3952)*
Sierra Pacific Industries ...F......530 378-8301
36336 Highway 299 E Burney (96013) *(P-3953)*
Sierra Pacific Industries ...C......530 532-6630
3025 S 5th Ave Oroville (95965) *(P-3954)*
Sierra Pacific Industries ...C......530 335-3681
Hwy 299 E Burney (96013) *(P-3955)*
Sierra Pacific Industries ...B......530 824-2474
Alameda Rd Corning (96021) *(P-4124)*
Sierra Pacific Industries ...C......530 275-8851
3735 El Cajon Ave Shasta Lake (96019) *(P-3956)*
Sierra Pacific Industries ...B......530 365-3721
19758 Riverside Ave Anderson (96007) *(P-3957)*
Sierra Pacific Industries ...B......530 644-2311
3950 Carson Rd Camino (95709) *(P-3958)*
Sierra Pacific Industries ...B......916 645-1631
1440 Lincoln Blvd Lincoln (95648) *(P-3959)*
Sierra Pacific Industries ...B......530 527-9620
11605 Reading Rd Red Bluff (96080) *(P-3960)*
Sierra Pacific Machining Inc ...F......408 924-0281
530 Parrott St San Jose (95112) *(P-16404)*
Sierra Pacific Packaging, Oroville *Also called Graphic Packaging Intl LLC (P-7075)*
Sierra Pharmacy, Rancho Cucamonga *Also called Akaranta Inc (P-7734)*
Sierra Precast Inc ...D......408 779-1000
1 Live Oak Ave Morgan Hill (95037) *(P-10650)*
Sierra Precision, Anaheim *Also called 3d Instruments LP (P-20824)*
Sierra Precision Optics Inc ...E......530 885-6979
12830 Earhart Ave Auburn (95602) *(P-21410)*
Sierra Proto Express, Sunnyvale *Also called Sierra Circuits Inc (P-17998)*
Sierra Resource Management Inc ...E......209 984-1146
12015 La Grange Rd Jamestown (95327) *(P-3906)*
Sierra Rm / Bm, El Dorado *Also called Cemex Cnstr Mtls PCF LLC (P-10713)*
Sierra Safety Company ...F......916 663-2026
215 Taylor Rd Newcastle (95658) *(P-13546)*
Sierra Sculpture Inc ...F......530 887-1581
13333 New Airport Rd Auburn (95602) *(P-11406)*
Sierra Sun Newspaper, Truckee *Also called Mount Rose Publishing Co Inc (P-5765)*
Sierra Sunrise Vineyard Inc ...E......209 245-6942
20680 Shenandoah Schl Rd Plymouth (95669) *(P-1916)*
Sierra Sunscreens, Rancho Cordova *Also called Hadco Products Inc (P-5022)*
Sierra Swiss & Machine Inc ...F......530 346-1110
12854 Earhart Ave Ste 103 Auburn (95602) *(P-12650)*
Sierra Tech, Chatsworth *Also called A F B Systems Inc (P-19941)*
Sierra Technical Services Inc ...F......661 823-1092
101 Commercial Way Unit D Tehachapi (93561) *(P-11168)*
Sierra Traffic Service Inc ...F......805 388-2474
225 W Loop Dr Camarillo (93010) *(P-17762)*
Sierra View Inc ...E......760 371-4301
109 N Sanders St Ridgecrest (93555) *(P-5825)*
Sierra Woodworking Inc ...E......949 493-4528
960 6th St Ste 101a Norco (92860) *(P-4125)*
Sierra-Tahoe Ready Mix Inc ...E......530 541-1877
1526 Emerald Bay Rd South Lake Tahoe (96150) *(P-10837)*
Sierracin Corporation (HQ) ...A......818 741-1656
12780 San Fernando Rd Sylmar (91342) *(P-8679)*

Mergent e-mail: customerrelations@mergent.com
1238
2020 California
Manufacturers Register
(P-0000) Products & Services Section entry number
(PA)=Parent Co (HQ)=Headquarters (DH)=Div Headquarters

Sierracin/Sylmar Corporation..........A.......818 362-6711
12780 San Fernando Rd Sylmar (91342) *(P-10056)*
Sieva Networks Inc (PA)..........F.......408 475-1953
281 Countrybrook Loop San Ramon (94583) *(P-20722)*
Siftery Inc..........E.......415 484-8211
49 Geary St Ste 530 San Francisco (94108) *(P-24410)*
Sig, San Diego *Also called Strafford Intl Group Inc (P-5004)*
Sight Machine Inc..........D.......888 461-5739
243 Vallejo St San Francisco (94111) *(P-24411)*
Sigma 6 Electronics Inc..........F.......858 279-4300
7030 Alamitos Ave Ste E San Diego (92154) *(P-19404)*
Sigma Circuit Technology LLC..........D.......858 523-0146
4624 Calle Mar De Armonia San Diego (92130) *(P-17999)*
Sigma Mfg & Logistics LLC..........E.......916 781-3052
10050 Fthlls Blvd Ste 100 Roseville (95747) *(P-14975)*
Sigma-Aldrich Corporation..........E.......760 710-6213
6211 El Camino Real Carlsbad (92009) *(P-9022)*
Sigmatex High Tech Fabrics Inc (HQ)..........D.......707 751-0573
6001 Egret Ct Benicia (94510) *(P-16690)*
Sigmatron International Inc..........C.......510 477-5000
30000 Eigenbrodt Way Union City (94587) *(P-18000)*
Sigmatronix Inc..........F.......714 436-1618
2109 S Susan St Santa Ana (92704) *(P-17282)*
Sign Art Co..........F.......626 287-2512
423 S California St San Gabriel (91776) *(P-23196)*
Sign Designs Inc..........E.......209 524-4484
204 Campus Way Modesto (95350) *(P-23197)*
Sign Excellence LLC..........F.......818 308-1044
8515 Telfair Ave Sun Valley (91352) *(P-23198)*
Sign Industries Inc..........E.......909 930-0303
2101 Carrillo Privado Ontario (91761) *(P-23199)*
Sign Mart, Orange *Also called Metal Art of California Inc (P-23160)*
Sign Mart Retail Store, Orange *Also called Metal Art of California Inc (P-23159)*
Sign of Times Inc..........E.......323 826-9766
4950 S Santa Fe Ave Vernon (90058) *(P-5530)*
Sign Post, The, Sacramento *Also called Eggleston Signs (P-23095)*
Sign Solutions Inc..........F.......408 245-7133
532 Mercury Dr Sunnyvale (94085) *(P-23200)*
Sign Source Inc..........F.......714 979-9979
204 W Carleton Ave Ste A Orange (92867) *(P-23201)*
Sign Specialists Corporation..........E.......714 641-0064
111 W Dyer Rd Ste F Santa Ana (92707) *(P-23202)*
Sign Technology Inc..........E.......916 372-1200
1700 Entp Blvd Ste F West Sacramento (95691) *(P-23203)*
Sign-A-Rama, Redding *Also called Jar Ventures Inc (P-23139)*
Sign-A-Rama, Palm Desert *Also called Pd Group (P-23176)*
Signa Chemistry Inc..........E.......212 933-4101
720 Olive Dr Ste Cd Davis (95616) *(P-7525)*
Signage Solutions Corporation..........E.......714 491-0299
2231 S Dupont Dr Anaheim (92806) *(P-23204)*
Signal..........D.......661 259-1234
26330 Diamond Pl Ste 100 Santa Clarita (91350) *(P-5826)*
Signal Hill Petroleum Inc..........E.......562 595-6440
2633 Cherry Ave Signal Hill (90755) *(P-141)*
Signal Newspaper, The, Santa Clarita *Also called Morris Multimedia Inc (P-5761)*
Signal Pharmaceuticals LLC..........C.......858 795-4700
10300 Campus Point Dr # 100 San Diego (92121) *(P-8131)*
Signature Control Systems Inc..........D.......949 580-3640
16485 Laguna Canyon Rd # 130 Irvine (92618) *(P-13670)*
Signature Flexible Packg Inc..........D.......323 887-1997
5519 Jillson St Commerce (90040) *(P-8894)*
Signature Press, Sacramento *Also called Arden & Howe Printing Inc (P-6418)*
Signature Propellers, Santa Ana *Also called Hill Marine Products LLC (P-16030)*
Signature Tech Group Inc..........E.......818 890-7611
11960 Borden Ave San Fernando (91340) *(P-19081)*
Signet Armorlite Inc (HQ)..........B.......760 744-4000
5803 Newton Dr Ste A Carlsbad (92008) *(P-22385)*
Signgroup/Karman, Chatsworth *Also called Schea Holdings Inc (P-23194)*
Signode Industrial Group LLC..........D.......209 931-0917
3901 Navone Rd Stockton (95215) *(P-5531)*
Signquest..........E.......310 355-0528
13040 Cerise Ave Hawthorne (90250) *(P-23205)*
Signs and Services Company..........E.......714 761-8200
10980 Boatman Ave Stanton (90680) *(P-23206)*
Signs of Success Inc..........F.......805 925-7545
2350 Skyway Dr Ste 10 Santa Maria (93455) *(P-23207)*
Signsource, Orange *Also called Sign Source Inc (P-23201)*
Signtech, West Sacramento *Also called Sign Technology Inc (P-23203)*
Signtech Electrical Advg Inc..........C.......619 527-6100
4444 Federal Blvd San Diego (92102) *(P-23208)*
Signum Systems Corporation..........F.......805 383-3682
1211 Flynn Rd Unit 104 Camarillo (93012) *(P-21121)*
Signworks, Seaside *Also called SC Works (P-23193)*
Signworld America Inc (PA)..........F.......844 900-7446
12023 Arrow Rte Rancho Cucamonga (91739) *(P-23209)*
Sigtronics Corporation..........E.......909 305-9399
178 E Arrow Hwy San Dimas (91773) *(P-17763)*
Siho Corporation..........F.......323 721-4000
5750 Grace Pl Commerce (90022) *(P-3406)*
Sii Semiconductor USA Corp..........F.......310 517-7771
21221 S Wstn Ave Ste 250 Torrance (90501) *(P-18542)*
Sika Corporation..........F.......562 941-0231
12767 Imperial Hwy Santa Fe Springs (90670) *(P-9023)*
Sikama International Inc..........F.......805 962-1000
118 E Gutierrez St Santa Barbara (93101) *(P-14254)*
Sil, Santa Maria *Also called Space Information Labs LLC (P-20726)*
Sila Nanotechnologies Inc..........E.......408 475-7452
2450 Mariner Square Loop Alameda (94501) *(P-19172)*
Silao Tortilleria Inc..........E.......626 961-0761
250 N California Ave City of Industry (91744) *(P-2611)*
Silent Servant, Rohnert Park *Also called Miller Manufacturing Inc (P-5031)*
Silenus Vintners..........F.......707 299-3930
5225 Solano Ave NAPA (94558) *(P-1917)*
Silenx Corporation..........F.......562 941-4200
10606 Shoemaker Ave Ste A Santa Fe Springs (90670) *(P-20938)*
Silfine America Inc..........D.......408 823-8663
1750 Cleveland Ave San Jose (95126) *(P-7610)*
Silgan Containers Corporation (HQ)..........D.......818 348-3700
21600 Oxnard St Ste 1600 Woodland Hills (91367) *(P-11502)*
Silgan Containers LLC (HQ)..........D.......818 710-3700
21600 Oxnard St Ste 1600 Woodland Hills (91367) *(P-11503)*
Silgan Containers Mfg Corp..........D.......209 521-6469
4000 Yosemite Blvd Modesto (95357) *(P-11504)*
Silgan Containers Mfg Corp..........E.......925 778-8000
2200 Wilbur Ave Antioch (94509) *(P-11505)*
Silgan Containers Mfg Corp..........E.......209 869-3601
3250 Patterson Rd Riverbank (95367) *(P-11506)*
Silgan Containers Mfg Corp (HQ)..........B.......818 710-3700
21600 Oxnard St Ste 1600 Woodland Hills (91367) *(P-11507)*
Silica Engineering Group, Santa Clara *Also called Superior Quartz Inc (P-11195)*
Silicon 360 LLC..........F.......408 432-1790
801 Buckeye Ct Milpitas (95035) *(P-5444)*
Silicon Electronics (PA)..........E.......408 738-8236
1148 Sonora Ct Sunnyvale (94086) *(P-18543)*
Silicon Energy LLC (PA)..........F.......360 618-6500
9 Cushing Ste 200 Irvine (92618) *(P-11713)*
Silicon Graphics Intl Corp (HQ)..........C.......669 900-8000
940 N Mccarthy Blvd Milpitas (95035) *(P-15335)*
Silicon Image Inc (HQ)..........D.......408 616-4000
2115 Onel Dr San Jose (95131) *(P-18544)*
Silicon Laboratories, San Jose *Also called Silicon Labs Integration Inc (P-18545)*
Silicon Labs Integration Inc (HQ)..........F.......408 702-1400
2708 Orchard Pkwy 30 San Jose (95134) *(P-18545)*
Silicon Light Machines Corp (HQ)..........F.......408 240-4700
820 Kifer Rd Sunnyvale (94086) *(P-18546)*
Silicon Microstructures Inc..........D.......408 473-9700
1701 Mccarthy Blvd Milpitas (95035) *(P-16754)*
Silicon Motion Inc..........D.......408 501-5300
690 N Mccarthy Blvd # 200 Milpitas (95035) *(P-18547)*
Silicon Specialists Inc..........F.......510 732-9796
2487 Industrial Pkwy W Hayward (94545) *(P-18548)*
Silicon Standard Corp..........E.......408 234-6964
4701 Patrick Henry Dr # 16 Santa Clara (95054) *(P-18549)*
Silicon Tech Inc..........C.......949 476-1130
3009 Daimler St Santa Ana (92705) *(P-15101)*
Silicon Turnkey Solutions Inc (HQ)..........F.......408 904-0200
1804 Mccarthy Blvd Milpitas (95035) *(P-18550)*
Silicon Valley Elite Mfg..........F.......408 654-9534
460 Aldo Ave Santa Clara (95054) *(P-16405)*
Silicon Valley Launch, Redwood City *Also called Sposato John (P-17669)*
Silicon Valley Mfg Inc..........E.......510 791-9450
6520 Central Ave Newark (94560) *(P-11108)*
Silicon Valley Precision Mch, San Jose *Also called Hiep Nguyen Corporation (P-16025)*
Silicon Vly Cmnty Newspapers, San Jose *Also called McClatchy Newspapers Inc (P-5735)*
Silicon Vly McRelectronics Inc..........E.......408 844-7100
2985 Kifer Rd Santa Clara (95051) *(P-18551)*
Silicon Vly World Trade Corp..........F.......408 945-6355
1474 Gladding Ct Milpitas (95035) *(P-16615)*
Siliconcore Technology Inc..........E.......408 946-8185
890 Hillview Ct Ste 120 Milpitas (95035) *(P-18552)*
Silicone Hose, Gardena *Also called Flex Technologies Inc (P-7629)*
Siliconix Incorporated (HQ)..........A.......408 988-8000
2585 Junction Ave San Jose (95134) *(P-18553)*
Siliconix Semiconductor Inc..........C.......408 988-8000
2201 Laurelwood Rd Santa Clara (95054) *(P-18554)*
Silicontech, Santa Ana *Also called Silicon Tech Inc (P-15101)*
Silk Road Medical Inc..........C.......408 720-9002
1213 Innsbruck Dr Sunnyvale (94089) *(P-21899)*
Silk Screen Shirts Inc..........E.......760 233-3900
6185 El Camino Real Carlsbad (92009) *(P-2837)*
Silke Communications Inc..........F.......916 245-6555
1050 Riverside Pkwy # 110 West Sacramento (95605) *(P-17659)*
Sillajen Biotherapeutics Inc..........F.......415 281-8886
450 Sansome St Ste 650 San Francisco (94111) *(P-8132)*
Siller Aviation, Yuba City *Also called Siller Brothers Inc (P-3907)*
Siller Brothers Inc (PA)..........D.......530 673-0734
1250 Smith Rd Yuba City (95991) *(P-3907)*
Silmar Division, Hawthorne *Also called Interplastic Corporation (P-7570)*
Silo City Inc..........E.......661 387-0179
1401 S Union Ave Bakersfield (93307) *(P-13748)*
Silpak Inc (PA)..........F.......909 625-0056
470 E Bonita Ave Pomona (91767) *(P-7611)*
Siluria Technologies Inc..........E.......415 978-2170
409 Illinois St San Francisco (94158) *(P-67)*
Silver Eagle Corporation..........E.......916 925-6843
2655 Land Ave Sacramento (95815) *(P-3641)*
Silver Horse Vineyards Inc..........F.......805 467-9463
1205 Beaver Creek Ln Paso Robles (93446) *(P-1918)*
Silver Moon Lighting Inc..........F.......858 613-3600
12225 World Trade Dr F San Diego (92128) *(P-16991)*
Silver Oak Wine Cellars LP (PA)..........F.......707 942-7022
915 Oakville Cross Rd Oakville (94562) *(P-1919)*
Silver Peak Systems Inc (PA)..........C.......408 935-1800
2860 De La Cruz Blvd # 100 Santa Clara (95050) *(P-18555)*
Silver Press Inc..........F.......408 435-0449
940 Rincon Cir San Jose (95131) *(P-7348)*
Silver Ranch and Winery, Paso Robles *Also called Silver Horse Vineyards Inc (P-1918)*

A L P H A B E T I C

Employee Codes: A=Over 500 employees, B=251-500
C=101-250, D=51-100, E=20-50, F=10-19

2020 California
Manfacturers Register

© Mergent Inc. 1-800-342-5647
1239

Silver Textile Incorporated ....F....213 747-2221
2101 S Flower St Los Angeles (90007) ***(P-2761)***
Silverado Brewing Co L L C ....E....707 341-3089
4104 Saint Helena Hwy Calistoga (94515) ***(P-1564)***
Silveron Industries Inc ....F....909 598-4533
182 S Brent Cir City of Industry (91789) ***(P-16755)***
Silverrest, Fullerton *Also called Brentwood Home LLC* ***(P-4713)***
Silvester California, Los Angeles *Also called Silvestri Studio Inc* ***(P-23476)***
Silvestri Studio Inc (PA) ....D....323 277-4420
8125 Beach St Los Angeles (90001) ***(P-23476)***
Silvias Costumes ....E....323 661-2142
4964 Hollywood Blvd Los Angeles (90027) ***(P-3579)***
Silvus Technologies Inc (PA) ....E....310 479-3333
10990 Wilshire Blvd # 1500 Los Angeles (90024) ***(P-17660)***
Simba Recycling, San Marcos *Also called Arna Trading Inc* ***(P-5090)***
Simco-Ion Technology Group (PA) ....C....510 217-0600
1601 Harbor Bay Pkwy # 150 Alameda (94502) ***(P-16798)***
Simec USA Corporation ....E....619 474-7081
1700 Cleveland Ave Ste B National City (91950) ***(P-11069)***
Simex-Iwerks, Santa Clarita *Also called Iwerks Entertainment Inc* ***(P-19330)***
Simi Winery, Healdsburg *Also called Franciscan Vinyards Inc* ***(P-1713)***
Simon Harrison ....E....818 898-1036
551 5th St Ste A San Fernando (91340) ***(P-21539)***
Simon of California (PA) ....F....310 559-4871
9545 Sawyer St Los Angeles (90035) ***(P-10208)***
Simone Fruit Co Inc ....F....559 275-1368
8008 W Shields Ave Fresno (93723) ***(P-863)***
Simons Brick Corporation ....E....951 279-1000
4301 Firestone Blvd South Gate (90280) ***(P-10993)***
Simonton Windows, Vacaville *Also called Fortune Brands Windows Inc* ***(P-9793)***
Simpa Networks Inc ....F....415 216-3204
2595 Mission St Ste 300 San Francisco (94110) ***(P-21540)***
Simplay Labs LLC ....E....408 616-4000
1140 E Arques Ave Sunnyvale (94085) ***(P-21900)***
Simple Container Solutions Inc ....E....310 638-0900
250 W Artesia Blvd Rancho Dominguez (90220) ***(P-5173)***
Simple Green, Huntington Beach *Also called Sunshine Makers Inc* ***(P-8419)***
Simple Orthotic Solutions LLC ....F....951 353-8127
9960 Indiana Ave Ste 15 Riverside (92503) ***(P-10153)***
Simplefeed Inc ....F....650 947-7445
289 S San Antonio Rd # 2 Los Altos (94022) ***(P-24412)***
Simplelegal Inc ....F....415 763-5366
488 Ellis St Mountain View (94043) ***(P-24413)***
Simplex Filler Co, NAPA *Also called Wild Horse Industrial Corp* ***(P-14737)***
Simplex Isolation Systems, Fontana *Also called Simplex Strip Doors LLC* ***(P-9421)***
Simplex Strip Doors LLC (HQ) ....E....800 854-7951
14500 Miller Ave Fontana (92336) ***(P-9421)***
Simpliphi Power Inc ....F....805 640-6700
3100 Camino Del Sol Oxnard (93030) ***(P-19173)***
Simply Automated Inc ....F....760 431-2100
6108 Avd Encinas Ste B Carlsbad (92011) ***(P-16923)***
Simply Country Inc ....F....530 615-0565
10110 Harvest Ln Rough and Ready (95975) ***(P-13671)***
Simply Fresh LLC ....C....714 562-5000
11215 Knott Ave Ste A Cypress (90630) ***(P-2270)***
Simply Fresh Fruit, Vernon *Also called Sffi Company Inc* ***(P-823)***
Simply Smashing Inc ....E....559 658-2367
4790 W Jacquelyn Ave Fresno (93722) ***(P-23210)***
Simpson Coatings Group Inc ....E....650 873-5990
401 S Canal St A South San Francisco (94080) ***(P-8680)***
Simpson Coatings Group, The, South San Francisco *Also called D J Simpson Company* ***(P-8640)***
Simpson Industries Inc ....E....310 605-1224
1093 E Bedmar St Carson (90746) ***(P-8133)***
Simpson Manufacturing Co Inc (PA) ....C....925 560-9000
5956 W Las Positas Blvd Pleasanton (94588) ***(P-11488)***
Simpson Manufacturing Co Inc ....B....209 234-7775
5151 S Airport Way Stockton (95206) ***(P-10954)***
Simpson Performance Pdts Inc ....D....310 325-6035
1407 240th St Harbor City (90710) ***(P-22087)***
Simpson Strong-Tie Company Inc (HQ) ....C....925 560-9000
5956 W Las Positas Blvd Pleasanton (94588) ***(P-12605)***
Simpson Strong-Tie Company Inc ....C....714 871-8373
12246 Holly St Riverside (92509) ***(P-4317)***
Simpson Strong-Tie Company Inc ....D....209 234-7775
5151 S Airport Way Stockton (95206) ***(P-12606)***
Simpson Strong-Tie Intl Inc (HQ) ....D....925 560-9000
5956 W Las Positas Blvd Pleasanton (94588) ***(P-12607)***
Simpson Timber Company ....F....707 668-4566
1165 Maple Creek Rd Korbel (95550) ***(P-3961)***
Simpsonsimpson Industries, Carson *Also called Simpson Industries Inc* ***(P-8133)***
Simso Tex Sublimation (PA) ....D....310 885-9717
3028 E Las Hermanas St Compton (90221) ***(P-3813)***
Simsolve ....F....951 898-6880
310 Elizabeth Ln Corona (92880) ***(P-11070)***
Simwon America Corp ....F....925 276-3412
400 Darcy Pkwy Lathrop (95330) ***(P-19767)***
Sin MA Imports Company ....F....415 285-9369
1425 Minnesota St San Francisco (94107) ***(P-1062)***
Sinbad Foods LLC ....E....559 674-4445
2401 W Almond Ave Madera (93637) ***(P-2612)***
Sincere Food Co, El Monte *Also called Agra-Farm Foods Inc* ***(P-1014)***
Sincere Orient Commercial Corp ....D....626 333-8882
15222 Valley Blvd City of Industry (91746) ***(P-2613)***
Sincere Orient Food Company, City of Industry *Also called Sincere Orient Commercial Corp* ***(P-2613)***
Sinclair & Valentine, Watsonville *Also called Smith & Vandiver Corporation* ***(P-8584)***
Sinclair Companies ....D....559 228-0913
4192 N Fresno St Fresno (93726) ***(P-9068)***
Sinclair Companies ....D....714 826-5886
7760 Crescent Ave Buena Park (90620) ***(P-9069)***
Sinclair Companies ....D....559 997-3617
5792 N Palm Ave Fresno (93704) ***(P-9070)***
Sinclair Companies ....D....559 351-1916
1703 W Olive Ave Fresno (93728) ***(P-9071)***
Sinclair Printing Company, Palmdale *Also called D & J Printing Inc* ***(P-6529)***
Sinclair Systems, Fresno *Also called Atlas Pacific Engineering Co* ***(P-14345)***
Sinclair Systems Intl LLC ....F....559 233-4500
3115 S Willow Ave Fresno (93725) ***(P-7213)***
Sine-Tific Solutions Inc ....F....408 432-3434
1701 Fortune Dr Ste C San Jose (95131) ***(P-7214)***
Sing Tao Daily, Burlingame *Also called Sing Tao Newspapers* ***(P-5827)***
Sing Tao Newspapers (HQ) ....D....650 808-8800
1818 Gilbreth Rd Ste 108 Burlingame (94010) ***(P-5827)***
Sing Tao Newspapers Ltd ....D....626 839-8200
17059 Green Dr City of Industry (91745) ***(P-5828)***
Sing Tao Nwspapers Los Angeles, City of Industry *Also called Sing Tao Newspapers Ltd* ***(P-5828)***
Singha North America Inc ....F....714 206-5097
303 Twin Dolphin Dr # 600 Redwood City (94065) ***(P-1565)***
Singular Bio Inc ....F....415 553-8773
455 Mission Bay Blvd S # 145 San Francisco (94158) ***(P-8258)***
Sinister Mfg Company Inc ....E....916 772-9253
2025 Opportunity Dr Ste 7 Roseville (95678) ***(P-19768)***
Sinkpad LLC ....F....714 660-2944
511 Princeland Ct Corona (92879) ***(P-19082)***
Sinosource Intl Co Inc ....F....650 697-6668
230 Adrian Rd Millbrae (94030) ***(P-10931)***
Sinusys Corporation ....F....650 213-9988
4030 Fabian Way Palo Alto (94303) ***(P-8330)***
Sios Technology Corp (HQ) ....F....650 645-7000
155 Bovet Rd Ste 476 San Mateo (94402) ***(P-24414)***
Sipex Corporation (HQ) ....C....510 668-7000
48720 Kato Rd Fremont (94538) ***(P-18556)***
Sipi Company Inc ....F....650 201-1169
34734 Williams Way Union City (94587) ***(P-22713)***
Sipix Imaging Inc (HQ) ....E....510 743-2928
47428 Fremont Blvd Fremont (94538) ***(P-14976)***
Sir Speedy, Whittier *Also called George Coriaty* ***(P-6590)***
Sirena Incorporated ....F....866 548-5353
22717 S Western Ave Torrance (90501) ***(P-7215)***
Sirf Technology Holdings Inc (HQ) ....D....408 523-6500
1060 Rincon Cir San Jose (95131) ***(P-18557)***
Sirna Therapeutics Inc ....D....415 512-7200
1700 Owens St San Francisco (94158) ***(P-8134)***
Siskiyou County Family Plng R, Mount Shasta *Also called Sousa Ready Mix LLC* ***(P-10838)***
Siskiyou Daily News, Yreka *Also called Gatehouse Media LLC* ***(P-5641)***
Siskiyou Forest Products (PA) ....E....530 378-6980
6275 State Highway 273 Anderson (96007) ***(P-4126)***
Sisneros Inc ....E....562 777-9797
12717 Los Nietos Rd Santa Fe Springs (90670) ***(P-4848)***
Sisneros Office Furntiure, Santa Fe Springs *Also called Sisneros Inc* ***(P-4848)***
Sissell Bros ....F....323 261-0106
4322 E 3rd St Los Angeles (90022) ***(P-10651)***
Sistema US Inc (PA) ....E....707 773-2200
775 Southpoint Blvd Petaluma (94954) ***(P-10057)***
Sistone Inc ....E....818 988-9918
15530 Lanark St Van Nuys (91406) ***(P-4939)***
Sit On It, Buena Park *Also called Exemplis LLC* ***(P-4836)***
Sitek Process Solutions ....F....916 797-9000
233 Technology Way Ste 3 Rocklin (95765) ***(P-18558)***
Sitime Corporation (HQ) ....C....408 328-4400
5451 Patrick Henry Dr Santa Clara (95054) ***(P-18559)***
Sitonit, Cypress *Also called Exemplis LLC* ***(P-4838)***
Situne Corporation ....F....408 324-1711
2216 Ringwood Ave San Jose (95131) ***(P-17661)***
Siui America Inc ....F....408 432-8881
780 Montague Expy Ste 608 San Jose (95131) ***(P-22310)***
Sius Products-Distributor Inc (PA) ....F....510 382-1700
700 Kevin Ct Oakland (94621) ***(P-5420)***
Six Sigma, Milpitas *Also called Winslow Automation Inc* ***(P-18657)***
Six Sigma Precision Inc ....F....707 836-0869
7706 Bell Rd Ste C Windsor (95492) ***(P-16406)***
Sixteen Rivers Press Inc ....F....415 273-1303
1195 Green St San Francisco (94109) ***(P-6339)***
Size Control Plating Co ....F....626 369-3014
13349 Temple Ave La Puente (91746) ***(P-13101)***
Sizto Tech Corporation ....F....650 856-8833
892 Commercial St Palo Alto (94303) ***(P-13321)***
Sizzix, Lake Forest *Also called Ellison Educational Eqp Inc* ***(P-14305)***
SJ Electro Systems Inc ....E....707 449-0341
859 Cotting Ct Ste G Vacaville (95688) ***(P-15578)***
Sj Valley Plating Inc ....F....408 988-5502
491 Perry Ct Santa Clara (95054) ***(P-13102)***
SJ&I Bias Binding & Tex Co Inc ....E....213 747-5271
1950 E 20th St Vernon (90058) ***(P-3814)***
SJcontrols Inc ....F....562 494-1400
2248 Obispo Ave Ste 203 Long Beach (90755) ***(P-20939)***
Sjm Facility, Irvine *Also called St Jude Medical LLC* ***(P-8140)***
Sjt Tech Industries Inc ....F....408 980-9547
1400 Coleman Ave Ste E28 Santa Clara (95050) ***(P-18560)***
Sk Drapes, North Hollywood *Also called S & K Theatrical Drap Inc* ***(P-3596)***
Sk Hynix Memory Solutions Inc ....E....408 514-3500
3103 N 1st St San Jose (95134) ***(P-18561)***

Mergent e-mail: customerrelations@mergent.com
1240
2020 California
Manufacturers Register
(P-0000) Products & Services Section entry number
(PA)=Parent Co (HQ)=Headquarters (DH)=Div Headquarters

Skagfield Corporation ....B....858 635-7777
2225 Avenida Costa Este San Diego (92154) *(P-5039)*
Skalli Vineyards, Rutherford *Also called St Supery Inc (P-1927)*
Skandia Industries, San Diego *Also called Skagfield Corporation (P-5039)*
Skasol Incorporated ....F....510 839-1000
1696 W Grand Ave Oakland (94607) *(P-9024)*
Skat-Trak Inc ....C....909 795-2505
654 Avenue K Calimesa (92320) *(P-9169)*
Skate Group Inc ....F....213 749-6651
830 E 14th Pl Los Angeles (90021) *(P-3580)*
Skate One Corp ....D....805 964-1330
30 S La Patera Ln Ste 9 Santa Barbara (93117) *(P-22887)*
Skateboard, Hacienda Heights *Also called Gravity Boarding Company Inc (P-22813)*
Skaug Truck Body Works ....F....818 365-9123
1404 1st St San Fernando (91340) *(P-19554)*
SKB Corporation (PA) ....B....714 637-1252
434 W Levers Pl Orange (92867) *(P-10058)*
SKB Corporation ....B....714 637-1572
1633 N Leslie Way Orange (92867) *(P-10209)*
Skechers Collection LLC (HQ) ....E....310 318-3100
228 Manhattan Beach Blvd Manhattan Beach (90266) *(P-9181)*
Skechers USA Inc ....E....310 318-3100
330 S Sepulveda Blvd Manhattan Beach (90266) *(P-9182)*
Skechers USA Inc (PA) ....D....310 318-3100
228 Manhattan Beach Blvd # 200 Manhattan Beach (90266) *(P-10183)*
Skechers USA Inc II (HQ) ....E....310 318-3100
225 S Sepulveda Blvd Manhattan Beach (90266) *(P-9183)*
Sketchers, Manhattan Beach *Also called Skechers Collection LLC (P-9181)*
SKF Aptitude Exchange, San Diego *Also called SKF Condition Monitoring Inc (P-21541)*
SKF Condition Monitoring Inc (HQ) ....C....858 496-3400
9444 Balboa Ave Ste 150 San Diego (92123) *(P-21541)*
Skirt Inc ....F....213 553-1134
2600 E 8th St Los Angeles (90023) *(P-3054)*
Skiva Graphics Screen Prtg Inc ....E....760 602-9124
2258 Rutherford Rd Ste A Carlsbad (92008) *(P-7216)*
Skjonberg Controls Inc ....F....805 650-0877
1363 Donlon St Ste 6 Ventura (93003) *(P-16756)*
Skm Industries Inc ....F....661 294-8373
28966 Hancock Pkwy Valencia (91355) *(P-12873)*
Skog Furniture, Pomona *Also called Aw Industries Inc (P-4551)*
Sks Die Cast & Machining Inc (PA) ....E....510 523-2541
1849 Oak St Alameda (94501) *(P-11349)*
Skullduggery Inc ....F....714 777-6425
5433 E La Palma Ave Anaheim (92807) *(P-22714)*
Skurka Aerospace Inc (HQ) ....C....216 706-2939
4600 Calle Bolero Camarillo (93012) *(P-16673)*
Sky Global Services Inc ....F....949 291-5511
23 Corporate Plaza Dr # 100 Newport Beach (92660) *(P-23477)*
Sky Jeans Inc ....E....323 778-2065
6600 Avalon Blvd Ste 102 Los Angeles (90003) *(P-2711)*
Sky Luxury Corp ....E....323 940-0111
3001 Humboldt St Los Angeles (90031) *(P-3407)*
Sky One Inc ....F....909 622-3333
1793 W 2nd St Pomona (91766) *(P-10469)*
Sky Rider Equipment Co Inc ....E....714 632-6890
1180 N Blue Gum St Anaheim (92806) *(P-4742)*
Sky Signs & Graphics ....F....818 898-3802
15340 San Fernnd Missn Bl Mission Hills (91345) *(P-3757)*
Skyco Shading Systems Inc ....E....714 708-3038
3411 W Fordham Ave Santa Ana (92704) *(P-4127)*
Skyco Skylights Inc ....E....949 629-4090
401 Goetz Ave Santa Ana (92707) *(P-10275)*
Skydio Inc ....F....408 203-8497
114 Hazel Ave Redwood City (94061) *(P-20723)*
Skyepharma Inc ....F....858 678-3950
10450 Science Center Dr San Diego (92121) *(P-8135)*
Skyera, San Jose *Also called Hgst Inc (P-15040)*
Skyguard LLC ....E....703 262-0500
2945 Townsgate Rd Ste 200 Westlake Village (91361) *(P-19405)*
Skylight Software Inc ....E....408 858-3933
3792 Bertini Ct Apt 1 San Jose (95117) *(P-24415)*
Skyline Alterations Inc ....E....530 549-4010
6727 Deschutes Rd Anderson (96007) *(P-3908)*
Skyline Cabinet & Millworks, Bakersfield *Also called Spalinger Enterprises Inc (P-4940)*
Skyline Concrete, Sun Valley *Also called Viking Ready Mix Co Inc (P-10865)*
Skyline Concrete, Canoga Park *Also called Viking Ready Mix Co Inc (P-10867)*
Skyline Digital Images Inc ....E....562 944-1677
10420 Pioneer Blvd Santa Fe Springs (90670) *(P-23211)*
Skyline Seating, Westminster *Also called Dang Tha (P-4856)*
Skylock Industries ....D....626 334-2391
1290 W Optical Dr Azusa (91702) *(P-20234)*
Skymicro Inc ....E....805 491-8935
2060 E Ave Arboles 344 Thousand Oaks (91362) *(P-15336)*
Skyway Signs LLC ....F....505 401-5270
2400 W Carson St Ste 115 Torrance (90501) *(P-23212)*
Skyworks Solutions ....F....301 874-6408
1767 Carr Rd Ste 105 Calexico (92231) *(P-16799)*
Skyworks Solutions Inc ....D....805 480-4400
2427 W Hillcrest Dr Newbury Park (91320) *(P-18562)*
Skyworks Solutions Inc ....D....805 480-4227
730 Lawrence Dr Newbury Park (91320) *(P-18563)*
Slack Technologies Inc (PA) ....C....415 902-5526
500 Howard St Ste 100 San Francisco (94105) *(P-24416)*
Slam Specialties LLC (PA) ....F....559 348-9038
5845 E Terrace Ave Fresno (93727) *(P-19769)*
Slawomira Sobczyk, Milpitas *Also called Yuhas Tooling & Machining (P-16536)*
SLC, Livermore *Also called Software Licensing Consultants (P-24428)*
Sld Laser, Goleta *Also called Soraa Laser Diode Inc (P-19409)*
Sleep Therapy, San Marcos *Also called Wickline Bedding Entp Corp (P-4749)*
Sleepow Ltd ....E....646 688-0808
11706 Darlington Ave Los Angeles (90049) *(P-2712)*
Sleeprite Industries Inc ....E....650 344-1980
1492 Rollins Rd Burlingame (94010) *(P-4743)*
Slickote ....F....818 749-3066
730 University Ave Burbank (91504) *(P-13247)*
Sligh Cabinets Inc ....F....805 239-2550
105 Calle Propano Paso Robles (93446) *(P-4248)*
Slimsuit, Bell *Also called Carol Wior Inc (P-3302)*
Sling-Light, Newport Beach *Also called Freeform Research & Dev (P-14160)*
Slivnik Machining Inc ....E....760 744-8692
1070 Linda Vista Dr Ste A San Marcos (92078) *(P-22888)*
Slj Wholesale LLC ....E....323 662-8900
13850 Del Sur St San Fernando (91340) *(P-1278)*
Slo New Times Inc ....E....805 546-8208
1010 Marsh St San Luis Obispo (93401) *(P-5829)*
Sloanled, Ventura *Also called The Sloan Company Inc (P-17168)*
Slp Limited LLC ....F....714 517-1955
2031 E Cerritos Ave Ste H Anaheim (92806) *(P-18001)*
SM Asian Market, San Bernardino *Also called Rlt Seafood Supermarket Inc (P-2249)*
SMA America Production LLC ....C....720 347-6000
6020 West Oaks Blvd # 300 Rocklin (95765) *(P-11714)*
Smac, Carlsbad *Also called Systems Machines Automatio (P-16760)*
Small Paper Co Inc ....F....323 277-0525
2559 E 56th St Huntington Park (90255) *(P-5151)*
Small Precision Tools Inc ....D....707 765-4545
1330 Clegg St Petaluma (94954) *(P-11021)*
Small Wnders Hndcrfted Mntures ....F....818 703-7450
7033 Canoga Ave Ste 5 Canoga Park (91303) *(P-23478)*
Small World Trading Co ....C....415 945-1900
90 Windward Way San Rafael (94901) *(P-8582)*
Smart Action Company LLC ....E....310 776-9200
300 Continental Blvd # 350 El Segundo (90245) *(P-24417)*
Smart Caregiver Corporation ....E....707 781-7450
1229 N Mcdowell Blvd Petaluma (94954) *(P-22311)*
Smart Elec & Assembly Inc ....C....714 772-2651
2000 W Corporate Way Anaheim (92801) *(P-18002)*
Smart Foam Pads, Lake Forest *Also called Innovative R Advanced (P-4723)*
Smart Foods LLC ....E....818 660-2238
3398 Leonis Blvd Vernon Vernon (90058) *(P-1063)*
Smart Global Holdings Inc (PA) ....E....510 623-1231
39870 Eureka Dr Newark (94560) *(P-18564)*
Smart LLC ....E....310 674-8135
14108 S Western Ave Gardena (90249) *(P-10059)*
Smart Machines Inc ....E....510 661-5000
46702 Bayside Pkwy Fremont (94538) *(P-13836)*
Smart Meetings, Sausalito *Also called Bright Business Media LLC (P-5893)*
Smart Modular Tech De Inc (HQ) ....C....510 623-1231
45800 Northport Loop W Fremont (94538) *(P-18565)*
Smart Modular Technologies Inc (HQ) ....C....510 623-1231
39870 Eureka Dr Newark (94560) *(P-18566)*
Smart Storage Systems Inc (HQ) ....F....510 623-1231
39672 Eureka Dr Newark (94560) *(P-15102)*
Smart TV & Sound, Chico *Also called Videomaker Inc (P-6053)*
Smart Wax, Gardena *Also called Smart LLC (P-10059)*
Smart Wireless Computing Inc (HQ) ....F....510 683-9999
39870 Eureka Dr Newark (94560) *(P-19083)*
Smart Wires Inc (PA) ....D....415 800-5555
3292 Whipple Rd Union City (94587) *(P-18743)*
Smart-Tek Automated Svcs Inc (HQ) ....F....858 798-1644
11838 Bernardo Plaza Ct # 250 San Diego (92128) *(P-24418)*
Smartdraw Software LLC ....E....858 225-3300
9909 Mira Mesa Blvd San Diego (92131) *(P-24419)*
Smartlogic Semaphore Inc ....F....408 213-9500
111 N Market St Ste 300 San Jose (95113) *(P-24420)*
Smartqed Inc ....F....925 922-4618
421 37th Ave San Mateo (94403) *(P-24421)*
Smartrunk Systems Inc ....E....619 426-3781
867 Bowsprit Rd Chula Vista (91914) *(P-17662)*
Smartwash Solutions LLC (HQ) ....F....831 676-9750
1129 Harkins Rd Salinas (93901) *(P-7526)*
Smashbox Beauty Cosmetics Inc ....C....310 558-1490
8538 Warner Dr Culver City (90232) *(P-8583)*
Smashbox Cosmetics, Culver City *Also called Smashbox Beauty Cosmetics Inc (P-8583)*
Smb Clothing Inc ....F....213 489-4949
1016 Towne Ave Unit 104 Los Angeles (90021) *(P-3408)*
Smb Industries Inc (PA) ....D....530 534-6266
550 Georgia Pacific Way Oroville (95965) *(P-11881)*
SMD Enterprises Inc ....E....323 235-4151
859 E 60th St Los Angeles (90001) *(P-10450)*
SMI Ca Inc ....E....562 926-9407
14340 Iseli Rd Santa Fe Springs (90670) *(P-16407)*
Smi, Scb, Los Angeles *Also called Dcx-Chol Enterprises Inc (P-17781)*
Smiley Group Inc (PA) ....F....323 290-4690
4434 Crenshaw Blvd Los Angeles (90043) *(P-6146)*
Smith & Company, Los Angeles *Also called A S G Corporation (P-23260)*
Smith & Hook Winery Inc, Soledad *Also called Hahn Estate (P-1742)*
Smith & Nephew Inc ....E....925 681-3300
4085 Nelson Ave Ste E Concord (94520) *(P-22088)*
Smith & Vandiver Corporation ....D....831 722-9526
480 Airport Blvd Watsonville (95076) *(P-8584)*
Smith Bros Cstm Met Fbrication, South El Monte *Also called Smith Bros Strl Stl Pdts Inc (P-11071)*
Smith Bros Strl Stl Pdts Inc ....F....626 350-1872
1535 Potrero Ave South El Monte (91733) *(P-11071)*
Smith Brothers Manufacturing ....F....619 296-3171
5304 Banks St San Diego (92110) *(P-16408)*

ALPHABETIC

Smith International Inc..........C......909 906-7900
11031 Jersey Blvd Ste A Rancho Cucamonga (91730) ***(P-264)***
Smith International Inc..........F......661 589-8304
3101 Steam Ct Bakersfield (93308) ***(P-265)***
Smith Precision Products Co..........E......805 498-6616
1299 Lawrence Dr Newbury Park (91320) ***(P-14598)***
Smith Printing Corporation..........F......949 250-9709
17344 Eastman Irvine (92614) ***(P-7217)***
Smith Publishing Inc..........F......805 965-5999
2064 Alameda Padre Serra # 120 Santa Barbara (93103) ***(P-6028)***
Smith Pumps, Newbury Park *Also called Smith Precision Products Co* ***(P-14598)***
Smithco Plastics Inc (PA)..........F......714 545-9107
3330 W Harvard St Santa Ana (92704) ***(P-10060)***
Smithcorp Inc..........F......888 402-9979
7196 Clairemont Mesa Blvd San Diego (92111) ***(P-5152)***
Smithfield Foods, Vernon *Also called Clougherty Packing LLC* ***(P-404)***
Smithfield Packaged Meats Corp..........C......408 392-0442
1660 Old Bayshore Hwy San Jose (95112) ***(P-425)***
Smiths Action Plastic Inc (PA)..........F......714 836-4141
645 S Santa Fe St Santa Ana (92705) ***(P-9596)***
Smiths Detection LLC..........A......714 258-4400
1251 E Dyer Rd Ste 140 Santa Ana (92705) ***(P-21291)***
Smiths Interconnect Inc..........F......805 267-0100
375 Conejo Ridge Ave Thousand Oaks (91361) ***(P-19084)***
Smiths Intrcnnect Americas Inc..........B......714 371-1100
1550 Scenic Ave Ste 150 Costa Mesa (92626) ***(P-19085)***
Smiths Medical Asd Inc..........E......619 710-1000
9255 Customhouse Plz N San Diego (92154) ***(P-21901)***
Smiths Medical Asd Inc..........C......760 602-4400
2231 Rutherford Rd Carlsbad (92008) ***(P-21902)***
SMK Manufacturing Inc..........E......619 216-6400
1055 Tierra Del Rey Ste H Chula Vista (91910) ***(P-15135)***
Sml Space Maintainers Labs, Chatsworth *Also called Selane Products Inc* ***(P-22189)***
Smooth Operator LLC..........E......619 233-8177
3388 Main St San Diego (92113) ***(P-22889)***
Smooth Run Equine Inc..........F......760 751-8988
11590 W Bernardo Ct # 110 San Diego (92127) ***(P-1127)***
Smoothie Operator Inc..........F......916 773-9541
8690 Sierra College Blvd Roseville (95661) ***(P-927)***
Smoothreads Inc..........E......800 536-5959
13750 Stowe Dr Ste A Poway (92064) ***(P-3815)***
Smp Robotics Systems Corp..........D......415 572-2316
851 Burlway Rd Ste 216 Burlingame (94010) ***(P-13837)***
SMS Fabrications Inc..........E......951 351-6828
11698 Warm Springs Rd Riverside (92505) ***(P-12379)***
SMS Industrial Inc..........F......831 337-4271
1628 N Main St Salinas (93906) ***(P-12052)***
Smt Centre, Fremont *Also called Surface Mount Tech Centre* ***(P-15341)***
Smt Electronics Mfg Inc..........E......714 751-8894
2630 S Shannon St Santa Ana (92704) ***(P-18567)***
SMt Mfg Incorporataed..........E......714 738-9999
970 S Loyola Dr Anaheim (92807) ***(P-19086)***
Smtc Corporation..........D......510 737-0700
431 Kato Ter Fremont (94539) ***(P-18003)***
Smtc Manufacturing Corp Cal..........A......408 934-7100
431 Kato Ter Fremont (94539) ***(P-18004)***
Smtcl Usa Inc..........F......626 667-1192
21127 Commerce Point Dr Walnut (91789) ***(P-14195)***
Smucker Natural Foods Inc (HQ)..........C......530 899-5000
37 Speedway Ave Chico (95928) ***(P-2173)***
Smurfit Kappa North Amer LLC..........B......626 322-2123
440 Baldwin Park Blvd City of Industry (91746) ***(P-5266)***
Smurfit-Stone Container, Milpitas *Also called Westrock Cp LLC* ***(P-5272)***
Smurfit-Stone Container, Santa Fe Springs *Also called Westrock Cp LLC* ***(P-5273)***
Sna Electronics Inc..........E......510 656-3903
3249 Laurelview Ct Fremont (94538) ***(P-18005)***
Snack It Forward LLC..........E......310 242-5517
6080 Center Dr Ste 600 Los Angeles (90045) ***(P-2345)***
Snak Club LLC..........E......323 278-9578
5560 E Slauson Ave Commerce (90040) ***(P-1438)***
Snap, Sunnyvale *Also called Spiracur Inc* ***(P-21913)***
Snap Creative Manufacturing..........F......818 735-3830
3760 Calle Tecate Ste B Camarillo (93012) ***(P-22654)***
Snaplogic Inc (PA)..........C......888 494-1570
1825 S Grant St Ste 550 San Mateo (94402) ***(P-24422)***
Snapmd Inc..........F......310 953-4800
121 W Lexington Dr # 412 Glendale (91203) ***(P-24423)***
Snaptracs Inc..........F......858 587-1121
5775 Morehouse Dr San Diego (92121) ***(P-20724)***
Snapware Corporation..........C......951 361-3100
3900 Hamner Ave Eastvale (91752) ***(P-10061)***
Snf Holding Company..........F......323 266-4435
4690 Worth St Los Angeles (90063) ***(P-9025)***
Snl Group Inc..........F......530 222-5048
9818 Holton Way Redding (96003) ***(P-13749)***
Snowflake Designs..........E......559 291-6234
2893 Larkin Ave Clovis (93612) ***(P-2801)***
Snowline Engineering, Cameron Park *Also called Preferred Mfg Svcs Inc* ***(P-16311)***
Snowpure LLC..........E......949 240-2188
130 Calle Iglesia Ste A San Clemente (92672) ***(P-15579)***
Snowpure Water Technologies, San Clemente *Also called Snowpure LLC* ***(P-15579)***
Snowsound USA, Santa Fe Springs *Also called Atlantic Representations Inc* ***(P-4683)***
Snyder Industries LLC..........D......559 665-7611
800 Commerce Dr Chowchilla (93610) ***(P-10062)***
So Cal Graphics, San Diego *Also called Brett Corp* ***(P-7008)***
So Cal Soft-Pak Incorporated..........E......619 283-2338
8525 Gibbs Dr Ste 300 San Diego (92123) ***(P-24424)***
So Cal Tractor Sales Co Inc..........E......818 252-1900
30517 The Old Rd Castaic (91384) ***(P-24665)***
So California Biodiesel, Bloomington *Also called Southern California Biodiesel* ***(P-9072)***
So-Cal Value Added, Camarillo *Also called Plt Enterprises Inc* ***(P-16920)***
So-Cal Value Added LLC..........E......805 389-5335
809 Calle Plano Camarillo (93012) ***(P-19087)***
Soap & Water LLC..........E......310 639-3990
11450 Sheldon St Sun Valley (91352) ***(P-8585)***
Soaptronic LLC..........E......949 465-8955
20562 Crescent Bay Dr Lake Forest (92630) ***(P-8418)***
Soaring America Corporation..........E......909 270-2628
8354 Kimball Ave F360 Chino (91708) ***(P-19931)***
Soberlink Healthcare LLC..........F......714 975-7200
16787 Beach Blvd 211 Huntington Beach (92647) ***(P-21542)***
Socal Skateshop..........F......949 305-5321
24002 Via Fabricante # 205 Mission Viejo (92691) ***(P-22890)***
Soccer 90..........F......650 599-9900
1235 Veterans Blvd Redwood City (94063) ***(P-22891)***
Soccer Learning Systems Inc..........F......209 858-4300
17610 Murphy Pkwy Lathrop (95330) ***(P-6029)***
Socco Plastic Coating Company..........E......909 987-4753
11251 Jersey Blvd Rancho Cucamonga (91730) ***(P-13248)***
Social Brands LLC..........E......415 728-1761
6575 Simson St Oakland (94605) ***(P-23479)***
Social Media Day San Diego, San Diego *Also called Casual Fridays Inc* ***(P-6211)***
Socialight, The, Campbell *Also called Afn Services LLC* ***(P-5047)***
Socialize Inc..........E......415 529-4019
450 Townsend St 102 San Francisco (94107) ***(P-24425)***
Socialwise Inc..........F......949 861-3900
400 Spectrum Center Dr # 1250 Irvine (92618) ***(P-6340)***
Societe Brewing Company LLC..........F......858 598-5415
8262 Clairemont Mesa Blvd Del Mar (92014) ***(P-1920)***
Society For The Advancement of..........F......626 521-9460
21680 Gateway Center Dr # 300 Diamond Bar (91765) ***(P-6030)***
Society For The Study Ntiv Art..........E......510 549-4270
2526 Mrtin Lther King Jr Berkeley (94704) ***(P-6147)***
Socket Mobile Inc..........D......510 933-3000
39700 Eureka Dr Newark (94560) ***(P-17663)***
Socksmith Design Inc (PA)..........E......831 426-6416
1515 Pacific Ave Santa Cruz (95060) ***(P-2767)***
Sodamail LLC..........F......707 794-1289
1300 Valley House Dr # 100 Rohnert Park (94928) ***(P-6341)***
Soderberg Manufacturing Co Inc..........D......909 595-1291
20821 Currier Rd Walnut (91789) ***(P-17093)***
Sof-Tek Integrators Inc..........F......530 242-0527
4712 Mtn Lakes Blvd # 200 Redding (96003) ***(P-21122)***
Sofa U Love (PA)..........E......323 464-3397
1207 N Western Ave Los Angeles (90029) ***(P-4670)***
Sofi Clothing, Los Angeles *Also called Skirt Inc* ***(P-3054)***
Sofie Biosciences Inc (PA)..........E......310 215-3159
160 Briston Pkwy Ste 200 Culver City (90230) ***(P-8259)***
Soft Flex Co..........E......707 938-3539
22678 Broadway Sonoma (95476) ***(P-11109)***
Soft Gel Technologies Inc (HQ)..........D......323 726-0700
6982 Bandini Blvd Commerce (90040) ***(P-8136)***
Soft Pak, San Diego *Also called So Cal Soft-Pak Incorporated* ***(P-24424)***
Soft Touch Inc..........F......714 524-3382
1830 E Miraloma Ave Ste C Placentia (92870) ***(P-7218)***
Soft-Touch Tissue, Vernon *Also called Paper Surce Converting Mfg Inc* ***(P-5143)***
Softmax Inc..........F......213 718-2100
2341 E 49th St Fl 2 Vernon (90058) ***(P-3458)***
Softsell Business Systems, Sausalito *Also called Ascert LLC* ***(P-23627)***
Softub Inc (PA)..........D......858 602-1920
24700 Avenue Rockefeller Valencia (91355) ***(P-23480)***
Software Ag Inc..........C......408 490-5300
2901 Tasman Dr Ste 219 Santa Clara (95054) ***(P-24426)***
Software AG of Virginia, Santa Clara *Also called Software Ag Inc* ***(P-24426)***
Software Development Inc..........E......925 847-8823
5000 Hopyard Rd Ste 160 Pleasanton (94588) ***(P-24427)***
Software Licensing Consultants..........E......925 371-1277
1001 Shannon Ct Ste B Livermore (94550) ***(P-24428)***
Software Motor Company..........F......408 601-7781
1295 Forgewood Ave Sunnyvale (94089) ***(P-16674)***
Software Partners LLC..........E......760 944-8436
906 2nd St Encinitas (92024) ***(P-24429)***
Soho Carpet & Rugs, Santa Ana *Also called Ohno America Inc* ***(P-2877)***
Soil Retention Products Inc (PA)..........F......951 928-8477
1265 Carlsbad Village Dr # 100 Carlsbad (92008) ***(P-10519)***
Soil Retention Products Inc..........F......951 928-8477
1765 Watson Rd Romoland (92585) ***(P-10520)***
Soilmoisture Equipment Corp..........E......805 964-3525
801 S Kellogg Ave Goleta (93117) ***(P-21543)***
Sola Products, San Clemente *Also called Shoreline Products Inc* ***(P-23008)***
Soladigm, Milpitas *Also called View Inc* ***(P-10400)***
Solaicx..........D......408 988-5000
600 Clipper Dr Belmont (94002) ***(P-18568)***
Solano County Water Agency..........F......707 455-1105
810 Vaca Valley Pkwy # 203 Vacaville (95688) ***(P-2174)***
Solano Diagnostics Imaging..........F......707 646-4646
1101 B Gale Wilson Blvd # 100 Fairfield (94533) ***(P-21544)***
Solar Art, Irvine *Also called Budget Enterprises Inc* ***(P-10260)***
Solar Atmospheres Inc..........E......909 217-7400
8606 Live Oak Ave Fontana (92335) ***(P-11468)***
Solar Electronics Company, North Hollywood *Also called A T Parker Inc* ***(P-19245)***
Solar Industries Inc..........E......916 567-9650
731 N Market Blvd Ste J Sacramento (95834) ***(P-11715)***
Solar Region Inc..........F......909 595-8500
1314 John Reed Ct City of Industry (91745) ***(P-14977)***
Solar Turbines Incorporated (HQ)..........A......619 544-5000
2200 Pacific Hwy San Diego (92101) ***(P-13575)***

Solar Turbines Incorporated E 619 544-5352
2200 Pacific Hwy San Diego (92101) ***(P-14750)***

Solar Turbines Incorporated C 858 715-2060
9250a Sky Park Ct San Diego (92123) ***(P-13576)***

Solar Turbines Incorporated F 949 450-0870
18 Morgan Ste 100 Irvine (92618) ***(P-13577)***

Solar Turbines Intl Co (HQ) E 619 544-5000
2200 Pacific Hwy San Diego (92101) ***(P-13578)***

Solar Turbines Intl Co E 858 694-1616
9330 Sky Park Ct San Diego (92123) ***(P-13579)***

Solara Engineering, Sun Valley *Also called Excelity* ***(P-11415)***

Solarbos (HQ) D 925 456-7744
310 Stealth Ct Livermore (94551) ***(P-16616)***

Solaredge Technologies Inc (PA) C 510 498-3200
47505 Seabridge Dr Fremont (94538) ***(P-16800)***

Solarflare Communications Inc (PA) D 949 581-6830
7505 Irvine Center Dr Irvine (92618) ***(P-14978)***

Solarius Development Inc F 408 541-0151
2390 Bering Dr San Jose (95131) ***(P-21123)***

Solaron Pool Heating Inc (PA) F 916 858-8146
3460 Business Dr Ste 100 Sacramento (95820) ***(P-14859)***

Solarreserve LLC (PA) E 310 315-2200
520 Broadway Fl 6 Santa Monica (90401) ***(P-11716)***

Solarroofscom Inc F 916 481-7200
5840 Gibbons Dr Ste H Carmichael (95608) ***(P-11717)***

Solartech Power Inc F 909 673-0178
901 E Cedar St Ontario (91761) ***(P-18569)***

Solatron Enterprises, Torrance *Also called Mahmood Izadi Inc* ***(P-14836)***

Solatube International Inc (PA) D 888 765-2882
2210 Oak Ridge Way Vista (92081) ***(P-11984)***

Soldermask Inc F 714 842-1987
17905 Metzler Ln Huntington Beach (92647) ***(P-18006)***

Soldo Capital Inc (HQ) E 800 659-6745
4695 Macarthur Ct # 1200 Newport Beach (92660) ***(P-7527)***

SOLE Designs Inc F 626 452-8642
11685 Mcbean Dr El Monte (91732) ***(P-4671)***

Sole Society Group Inc C 310 220-0808
8511 Steller Dr Culver City (90232) ***(P-10154)***

Sole Survivor Corporation C 818 338-3760
28632 Roadside Dr Ste 200 Agoura Hills (91301) ***(P-3409)***

Sole Technology Inc (PA) C 949 460-2020
26921 Fuerte Lake Forest (92630) ***(P-10184)***

Sole Technology Inc F 949 460-2020
17300 Slover Ave Fontana (92337) ***(P-10185)***

Solecta Inc (PA) E 760 630-9643
4113 Avenida De La Plata Oceanside (92056) ***(P-2899)***

Solectek Corporation E 858 450-1220
8375 Cmino Santa Fe Ste A San Diego (92121) ***(P-17664)***

Soledad Bee, King City *Also called South County Newspapers LLC* ***(P-5833)***

Soleno Therapeutics Inc (PA) F 650 213-8444
1235 Radio Rd Ste 110 Redwood City (94065) ***(P-8137)***

Solflower Computer Inc F 408 733-8100
3337 Kifer Rd Santa Clara (95051) ***(P-15337)***

Solher Iron F 415 822-9900
1555 Galvez Ave Ste 400 San Francisco (94124) ***(P-12608)***

Soli-Bond Inc E 661 631-1633
4230 Foster Ave Bakersfield (93308) ***(P-266)***

Soliant Energy Inc E 626 396-9500
1100 La Avenida St Ste A Mountain View (94043) ***(P-19406)***

Solid 21 Incorporated F 213 688-0900
22287 Mulholland Hwy # 82 Calabasas (91302) ***(P-22572)***

Solid Data Systems Inc F 408 845-5700
3542 Bassett St Santa Clara (95054) ***(P-15103)***

Solid State Battery Inc F 310 753-6769
7825 Industry Ave Pico Rivera (90660) ***(P-19182)***

Solid State Devices Inc C 562 404-4474
14701 Firestone Blvd La Mirada (90638) ***(P-18570)***

Solid-Scope Machining Co Inc F 310 523-2366
17925 Adria Maru Ln Carson (90746) ***(P-11628)***

Soligen 2006, Northridge *Also called DC Partners Inc* ***(P-11376)***

Soligen 2006, Northridge *Also called DC Partners Inc* ***(P-11377)***

Solimar Energy LLC F 805 643-4100
121 N Fir St Ste H Ventura (93001) ***(P-142)***

Solmetric Corporation E 707 823-4600
117 Morris St Ste 100 Sebastopol (95472) ***(P-21545)***

Solo Enterprise Corp E 626 961-3591
220 N California Ave City of Industry (91744) ***(P-16409)***

Solo Golf, City of Industry *Also called Solo Enterprise Corp* ***(P-16409)***

Solo Steel Erectors Inc F 530 893-2293
762 Portal Dr Chico (95973) ***(P-12574)***

Solomon Colors Inc E 909 484-9156
1371 Laurel Ave Rialto (92376) ***(P-7462)***

Solonics Inc (PA) F 650 589-9798
31082 San Antonio St Hayward (94544) ***(P-17411)***

Solta Medical Inc (HQ) F 510 786-6946
7031 Koll Center Pkwy # 260 Pleasanton (94566) ***(P-21903)***

Solta Medical Inc C 510 782-2286
25901 Industrial Blvd Hayward (94545) ***(P-22312)***

Soltech Solar Inc F 909 890-2282
1836 Commercenter Cir San Bernardino (92408) ***(P-13580)***

Solution Box Inc F 949 387-3223
1923 Avenida Plaza Real Oceanside (92056) ***(P-6964)***

Solutions Unlimited, Fullerton *Also called Wilsons Art Studio Inc* ***(P-7272)***

Solutionsoft Systems Inc E 408 346-1491
2350 Mission College Blvd Santa Clara (95054) ***(P-24430)***

Solv Inc C 858 622-4040
16798 W Bernardo Dr San Diego (92127) ***(P-24431)***

Solvay USA Inc F 310 669-5300
20851 S Santa Fe Ave Long Beach (90810) ***(P-7528)***

Soma Magnetics Corporation E 714 447-0782
585 S State College Blvd Fullerton (92831) ***(P-16576)***

Somacis Inc C 858 513-2200
13500 Danielson St Poway (92064) ***(P-18007)***

Somar Corporation F 310 329-1446
13006 Halldale Ave Gardena (90249) ***(P-12380)***

Some Crust Bakery, Claremont *Also called Feemster Co Inc* ***(P-1202)***

Somerset Printing, Belmont *Also called Somerset Traveller Inc* ***(P-7349)***

Somerset Traveller Inc F 650 593-7350
2765 Comstock Cir Belmont (94002) ***(P-7349)***

Sonance, San Clemente *Also called Dana Innovations* ***(P-17216)***

Sonant Corporation F 858 623-8180
6215 Ferris Sq Ste 220 San Diego (92121) ***(P-17412)***

Sonasoft Corp (PA) E 408 583-1600
1735 N 1st St Ste 110 San Jose (95112) ***(P-24432)***

Sonatech Division, Santa Barbara *Also called Alta Properties Inc* ***(P-19255)***

Soncell North America Inc (HQ) E 619 795-4600
10729 Whelt Lands Ave C San Diego (92107) ***(P-20725)***

Sonendo Inc (PA) E 949 766-3636
26061 Merit Cir Ste 102 Laguna Hills (92653) ***(P-22190)***

Sonfarrel Aerospace LLC D 714 630-7280
3010 E La Jolla St Anaheim (92806) ***(P-11389)***

Song Beoung F 510 670-8788
501 Murphy Ranch Rd # 148 Milpitas (95035) ***(P-7317)***

Songbird Ocarinas LLC F 323 269-2524
2751 E 11th St Los Angeles (90023) ***(P-22640)***

Songs Music Publishing LLC F 323 939-3511
7656 W Sunset Blvd Los Angeles (90046) ***(P-6342)***

Sonic Air Systems Inc E 714 255-0124
1050 Beacon St Brea (92821) ***(P-14678)***

Sonic Dry Clean, Ramona *Also called Hockin Diversfd Holdings Inc* ***(P-14662)***

Sonic Manufacturing Tech Inc B 510 580-8500
47951 Westinghouse Dr Fremont (94539) ***(P-18008)***

Sonic Plating Company, Gardena *Also called Granath & Granath Inc* ***(P-13016)***

Sonic Solutions Holdings Inc D 408 562-8400
2830 De La Cruz Blvd Santa Clara (95050) ***(P-24433)***

Sonic Studio LLC F 415 944-7642
93 Madrone Rd Fairfax (94930) ***(P-24434)***

Sonic Technology Products Inc E 530 272-4607
108 Boulder St Nevada City (95959) ***(P-18571)***

Sonic Vr LLC F 206 227-8585
225 Broadway Ste 650 San Diego (92101) ***(P-24435)***

Sonicsensory Inc (PA) F 213 336-3747
1163 Logan St Los Angeles (90026) ***(P-9184)***

Sonix, Torrance *Also called Lenntek Corporation* ***(P-17571)***

Sonnet Technologies Inc E 949 587-3500
8 Autry Irvine (92618) ***(P-19407)***

Sonoco Corrflex LLC F 818 507-7477
1225 Grand Central Ave Glendale (91201) ***(P-5267)***

Sonoco Industrial Products Div, City of Industry *Also called Sonoco Products Company* ***(P-5174)***

Sonoco Products Company D 626 369-6611
166 Baldwin Park Blvd City of Industry (91746) ***(P-5174)***

Sonoco Products Company D 562 921-0881
12851 Leyva St Norwalk (90650) ***(P-5175)***

Sonoco Prtective Solutions Inc D 510 785-0220
3466 Enterprise Ave Hayward (94545) ***(P-5268)***

Sonoma Access Ctrl Systems Inc E 707 935-3458
21600 8th St E Sonoma (95476) ***(P-12509)***

Sonoma Beverage Company LLC (PA) E 707 431-1099
2710 Giffen Ave Santa Rosa (95407) ***(P-928)***

Sonoma Business Magazine, Santa Rosa *Also called Gammon LLC* ***(P-5942)***

Sonoma Cast Stone Corporation E 877 283-2400
133 Copeland St Ste A Petaluma (94952) ***(P-10652)***

Sonoma Creek Winery, Sonoma *Also called Larson Family Winery Inc* ***(P-1797)***

Sonoma Foods, Santa Rosa *Also called MS Intertrade Inc* ***(P-2265)***

Sonoma Gourmet Inc E 707 939-3700
21684 8th St E Ste 100 Sonoma (95476) ***(P-900)***

Sonoma Index-Tribune D 707 938-2111
117 W Napa St Ste A Sonoma (95476) ***(P-5830)***

Sonoma International Inc E 707 935-0710
462 W Napa St Fl 2 Sonoma (95476) ***(P-22715)***

Sonoma Metal Products Inc D 707 484-9876
601 Aviation Blvd Santa Rosa (95403) ***(P-12381)***

Sonoma Orthopedic Products Inc F 847 807-4378
50 W San Fernando St Fl 5 San Jose (95113) ***(P-21904)***

Sonoma Pacific Company, Sonoma *Also called El Pelado LLC* ***(P-4365)***

Sonoma Pacific Company LLC D 707 938-2877
1180 Fremont Dr Sonoma (95476) ***(P-4400)***

Sonoma Pharmaceuticals Inc D 707 283-0550
1129 N Mcdowell Blvd Petaluma (94954) ***(P-21905)***

Sonoma Photonics Inc E 707 568-1202
1750 Northpoint Pkwy C Santa Rosa (95407) ***(P-18744)***

Sonoma Pins Etc Corporation D 707 996-9956
841 W Napa St Sonoma (95476) ***(P-7219)***

Sonoma Plant Works Inc F 707 588-8002
235 Classic Ct Rohnert Park (94928) ***(P-13696)***

Sonoma Promotional Solutions, Sonoma *Also called Sonoma Pins Etc Corporation* ***(P-7219)***

Sonoma Tilemakers Inc (HQ) D 707 837-8177
7750 Bell Rd Windsor (95492) ***(P-10451)***

Sonoma Valley Foods Inc E 707 585-2200
3645 Standish Ave Santa Rosa (95407) ***(P-746)***

Sonoma Valley Publishing, Sonoma *Also called Sonoma Index-Tribune* ***(P-5830)***

Sonoma West Publishers Inc (PA) F 707 823-7845
135 S Main St Sebastopol (95472) ***(P-5831)***

Sonoma West Times & News, Sebastopol *Also called Sonoma West Publishers Inc* ***(P-5831)***

Sonoma Wine Company LLC C 707 829-6100
9119 Graton Rd Graton (95444) ***(P-1921)***

ALPHABETIC

Employee Codes: A=Over 500 employees, B=251-500
C=101-250, D=51-100, E=20-50, F=10-19
2020 California
Manfacturers Register
© Mergent Inc. 1-800-342-5647
1243

Sonoma Wine Hardware Inc......E......650 866-3020
360 Swift Ave Ste 34 South San Francisco (94080) ***(P-1922)***
Sonora Face Co......E......323 560-8188
5233 Randolph St Maywood (90270) ***(P-4280)***
Sonora Mills Foods Inc (PA)......D......310 639-5333
3064 E Maria St E Rncho Dmngz (90221) ***(P-1329)***
Sonos Inc (PA)......D......805 965-3001
614 Chapala St Santa Barbara (93101) ***(P-17283)***
Sonosim Inc......F......323 473-3800
1738 Berkeley St Ste A Santa Monica (90404) ***(P-24436)***
Sony Biotechnology Inc......D......800 275-5963
1730 N 1st St Fl 2 San Jose (95112) ***(P-19408)***
Sony Broadcast Products, San Jose *Also called Sony Electronics Inc* ***(P-15338)***
Sony Corporation of America (PA)......E......212 833-8000
16530 Via Esprillo Mz7190 San Diego (92127) ***(P-14979)***
Sony Dadc US Inc......E......310 760-8500
4499 Glencoe Ave Marina Del Rey (90292) ***(P-19234)***
Sony Electronics Inc (HQ)......A......858 942-2400
16535 Via Esprillo Bldg 1 San Diego (92127) ***(P-17284)***
Sony Electronics Inc......E......408 352-4000
1730 N 1st St San Jose (95112) ***(P-15338)***
Sony Electronics Inc......C......858 942-2400
16530 Via Esprillo San Diego (92127) ***(P-17285)***
Sony Electronics Inc......E......858 824-6960
5510 Morehouse Dr Ste 100 San Diego (92121) ***(P-17337)***
Sony Mobile Communications USA......C......866 766-9374
2207 Bridgepoint Pkwy San Mateo (94404) ***(P-17665)***
Sony Network Studios Division, San Diego *Also called Sony Electronics Inc* ***(P-17337)***
Sony Style, San Diego *Also called Sony Electronics Inc* ***(P-17285)***
Sony/Atv Music Publishing LLC......E......310 441-1300
10635 Santa Monica Blvd # 300 Los Angeles (90025) ***(P-6343)***
Soojians Inc......E......559 875-5511
89 Academy Ave Sanger (93657) ***(P-1330)***
Sooraksan Soojebi......F......213 389-2818
4003 Wilshire Blvd Ste I Los Angeles (90010) ***(P-11519)***
Soper-Wheeler Company LLC (PA)......E......530 675-2343
19855 Barton Hill Rd Strawberry Valley (95981) ***(P-3909)***
Soprano, Los Angeles *Also called SSC Apparel Inc* ***(P-3411)***
Sora Power Inc (PA)......F......951 479-9880
1141 Olympic Dr Corona (92881) ***(P-19088)***
Soraa Inc (PA)......D......510 456-2200
6500 Kaiser Dr Ste 110 Fremont (94555) ***(P-18572)***
Soraa Laser Diode Inc (PA)......E......805 696-6999
485 Pine Ave Goleta (93117) ***(P-19409)***
Soraa Laser Diode Inc......E......805 696-6999
6500 Kaiser Dr Fremont (94555) ***(P-19410)***
Sorenson Engineering Inc (PA)......C......909 795-2434
32032 Dunlap Blvd Yucaipa (92399) ***(P-12651)***
Sorenson Publishing Inc......F......925 866-1514
12925 Alcosta Blvd Ste 6 San Ramon (94583) ***(P-6863)***
Sorma USA LLC......B......559 651-1269
9810 W Ferguson Ave Visalia (93291) ***(P-5421)***
Sorrento Networks Corporation (HQ)......F......510 577-1400
7195 Oakport St Oakland (94621) ***(P-17413)***
Sotcher Measurement Inc......F......408 574-0112
115 Phelan Ave Ste 10 San Jose (95112) ***(P-21124)***
Soteleo Salvadar......E......213 621-2040
620 Imperial St Los Angeles (90021) ***(P-23213)***
Sotera Wireless Inc......C......858 427-4620
10020 Huennekens St San Diego (92121) ***(P-22313)***
Sound Imaging Inc......F......858 622-0082
7580 Trade St Ste A San Diego (92121) ***(P-22314)***
Sound Storm Laboratory LLC......E......805 983-8008
3451 Lunar Ct Oxnard (93030) ***(P-17286)***
Sound United, Carlsbad *Also called Dei Headquarters Inc* ***(P-17724)***
Sound Waves Insullation Inc......E......714 556-2110
1406 Ritchey St Ste D Santa Ana (92705) ***(P-20940)***
Soundcoat Company Inc......E......631 242-2200
16901 Armstrong Ave Irvine (92606) ***(P-16757)***
Soundcraft Inc......E......818 882-0020
20301 Nordhoff St Chatsworth (91311) ***(P-19411)***
Soundview Applications Inc......F......530 888-7593
2390 Lindbergh St Ste 101 Auburn (95602) ***(P-17287)***
Soup Bases Loaded Inc......E......909 230-6890
2355 E Francis St Ontario (91761) ***(P-2614)***
Source Bio Inc......F......951 676-1000
43379 Bus Pk Dr Ste 100 Temecula (92590) ***(P-8260)***
Source of Health Inc......E......619 409-9500
1055 Bay Blvd Ste A Chula Vista (91911) ***(P-620)***
Source Print Media Solutions......F......661 263-1880
29108 Summer Oak Ct Santa Clarita (91390) ***(P-6864)***
Source Superfoods LLC......F......760 884-6575
15615 Vista Vicente Dr # 200 Ramona (92065) ***(P-621)***
Source Surgical Inc......F......415 861-7040
3130 20th St Ste 200 San Francisco (94110) ***(P-21906)***
Sourcing Group LLC......E......510 471-4749
1672 Delta Ct Hayward (94544) ***(P-6865)***
Souriau Usa Inc (HQ)......E......805 238-2840
1750 Commerce Way Paso Robles (93446) ***(P-16924)***
Sousa Ready Mix LLC......F......530 926-4485
100 Upton Rd Mount Shasta (96067) ***(P-10838)***
South Alliance Industrial Mch......F......626 442-3744
2423 Troy Ave South El Monte (91733) ***(P-16410)***
South Amrcn Imging Sltions Inc......F......805 824-4036
2360 Eastman Ave Ste 110 Oxnard (93030) ***(P-16675)***
South Bay Cable Corp (PA)......D......951 659-2183
54125 Maranatha Dr Idyllwild (92549) ***(P-11318)***
South Bay Cable Corp......F......951 296-9900
42033 Rio Nedo Temecula (92590) ***(P-11319)***
South Bay Chrme/Chrome Effects, Huntington Beach *Also called Classic Components Inc* ***(P-12969)***
South Bay Chrome, Santa Ana *Also called Classic Components Inc* ***(P-12968)***
South Bay Circuits Inc......C......408 978-8992
210 Hillsdale Ave San Jose (95136) ***(P-19089)***
South Bay Corporation......F......310 532-5353
1335 W 134th St Gardena (90247) ***(P-9373)***
South Bay Cstm Plstic Extrders......E......619 544-0808
2554 Commercial St San Diego (92113) ***(P-10063)***
South Bay Diversfd Systems Inc......F......510 784-3094
1841 National Ave Hayward (94545) ***(P-12382)***
South Bay International Inc......E......909 718-5000
8570 Hickory Ave Rancho Cucamonga (91739) ***(P-4744)***
South Bay Marble Inc (PA)......F......650 594-4251
15745 E Alta Vista Way San Jose (95127) ***(P-10932)***
South Bay Neon, San Diego *Also called Carreon Development Inc* ***(P-23073)***
South Bay Salt Works, Chula Vista *Also called Ggtw LLC* ***(P-8971)***
South Bay Solutions Inc (PA)......E......650 843-1800
37399 Centralmont Pl Fremont (94536) ***(P-16411)***
South Bay Solutions Texas LLC......E......936 494-0180
37399 Centralmont Pl Fremont (94536) ***(P-16801)***
South Bay Welding, El Cajon *Also called M W Reid Welding Inc* ***(P-11831)***
South Coast Baking LLC (HQ)......D......949 851-9654
1722 Kettering Irvine (92614) ***(P-1331)***
South Coast Baking Co., Irvine *Also called South Coast Baking LLC* ***(P-1331)***
South Coast Circuits Inc......D......714 966-2108
3506 W Lake Center Dr A Santa Ana (92704) ***(P-18009)***
South Coast Materials Co, San Diego *Also called Forterra Pipe & Precast LLC* ***(P-10578)***
South Coast Mold Inc......F......949 253-2000
1852 Mcgaw Ave Irvine (92614) ***(P-14105)***
South Coast Publishing Inc......F......562 988-1222
2599 E 28th St Ste 212 Long Beach (90755) ***(P-5832)***
South Coast Screen and Casing......F......310 632-3200
19112 S Santa Fe Ave Compton (90221) ***(P-13791)***
South Coast Stairs Inc......E......949 858-1685
30251 Tomas Rcho STA Marg (92688) ***(P-4128)***
South Coast Water, Santa Ana *Also called Hannah Industries Inc* ***(P-15519)***
South Coast Winery Inc......E......951 587-9463
34843 Rancho Cal Rd Temecula (92591) ***(P-1923)***
South Coast Winery Resort Spa, Temecula *Also called South Coast Winery Inc* ***(P-1923)***
South Cone Inc......C......760 431-2300
5935 Darwin Ct Carlsbad (92008) ***(P-10176)***
South County Newspapers LLC......F......831 385-4880
522 Broadway St Ste B King City (93930) ***(P-5833)***
South Gate Engineering LLC......C......909 628-2779
13477 Yorba Ave Chino (91710) ***(P-12053)***
South Orange County Ww Auth......F......949 234-5400
34156 Del Obispo St Dana Point (92629) ***(P-9026)***
South Pacific Tuna Corporation......F......619 233-2060
501 W Broadway San Diego (92101) ***(P-2252)***
South Street Inc......F......562 984-6240
2231 E Curry St Long Beach (90805) ***(P-22892)***
South Swell Screen Arts......F......858 566-3095
8440 Production Ave San Diego (92121) ***(P-7220)***
South Valley Materials Inc (HQ)......D......559 277-7060
7673 N Ingram Ave Ste 101 Fresno (93711) ***(P-10839)***
South Valley Materials Inc......E......559 582-0532
7761 Hanford Armona Rd Hanford (93230) ***(P-10840)***
South West Lubricants Inc......F......619 449-5000
9266 Abraham Way Santee (92071) ***(P-9156)***
South Western Paving Company......F......714 577-5750
2250 E Orangethorpe Ave Fullerton (92831) ***(P-9106)***
Southcoast Cabinet Inc (PA)......E......909 594-3089
755 Pinefalls Ave Walnut (91789) ***(P-4249)***
Southcoast Welding & Mfg LLC......B......619 429-1337
2591 Faivre St Ste 1 Chula Vista (91911) ***(P-24666)***
Southeast Kern Weekender, Tehachapi *Also called Tehachapi News Inc* ***(P-5847)***
Souther Archtctural Cast Stone, Oceanside *Also called Ms Cast Stone Inc* ***(P-10604)***
Souther Cast Stone Inc......E......760 754-9697
235 Via Del Monte Oceanside (92058) ***(P-10653)***
Southern Alum Finshg Co Inc......D......530 244-7518
4356 Caterpillar Rd Redding (96003) ***(P-11268)***
Southern Cal Bndery Miling Inc......D......909 829-1949
10661 Business Dr Fontana (92337) ***(P-7350)***
Southern Cal Gold Pdts Inc......F......805 988-0777
2350 Santiago Ct Oxnard (93030) ***(P-11072)***
Southern Cal Tchnical Arts Inc......E......714 524-2626
370 E Crowther Ave Placentia (92870) ***(P-16412)***
Southern Cal Trck Bdies Sls In......F......909 469-1132
1131 E 2nd St Pomona (91766) ***(P-19555)***
Southern Cal Valve MGT Co Inc......F......562 404-2246
13209 Barton Cir Ste C Whittier (90605) ***(P-13322)***
Southern California Biodiesel......F......951 377-4007
18760 6th St Ste C Bloomington (92316) ***(P-9072)***
Southern California Carbide......E......858 513-7777
12216 Thatcher Ct Poway (92064) ***(P-13952)***
Southern California Components......D......760 949-5144
9927 C Ave Hesperia (92345) ***(P-4318)***
Southern California Ice Co......F......310 325-1040
22921 Lockness Ave Torrance (90501) ***(P-2363)***
Southern California Insulation......E......619 477-1303
2050 Wilson Ave Ste C National City (91950) ***(P-20305)***
Southern California Mtl Hdlg......E......714 773-9630
168 E Freedom Ave Anaheim (92801) ***(P-13892)***
Southern California Mulch Inc......F......951 352-5355
30141 Antelope Rd 116 Menifee (92584) ***(P-4536)***
Southern California Plas Inc......D......714 751-7084
3122 Maple St Santa Ana (92707) ***(P-7612)***

Mergent e-mail: customerrelations@mergent.com
1244
2020 California
Manufacturers Register
(P-0000) Products & Services Section entry number
(PA)=Parent Co (HQ)=Headquarters (DH)=Div Headquarters

Southern California Soap Co .... F.....323 888-1332
2700 Tanager Ave Commerce (90040) *(P-8351)*
Southern California Tow Eqp, Anaheim *Also called Moda Enterprises Inc (P-19488)*
Southern California Trane, Brea *Also called Trane US Inc (P-15458)*
Southern Electronics, Pomona *Also called Electrocube Inc (P-18900)*
Southern International Packg, Rancho Palos Verdes *Also called Western Summit Mfg Corp (P-9426)*
Southern Valley Chemical Co .... F.....661 366-3308
S Derby & Sycamore Rd Arvin (93203) *(P-8840)*
Southland Clutch Inc .... F.....619 477-2105
101 E 18th St National City (91950) *(P-19770)*
Southland Container Corp .... F.....909 937-9781
1600 Champagne Ave Ontario (91761) *(P-5269)*
Southland Enterprises, Escondido *Also called Southland Manufacturing Inc (P-14196)*
Southland Envelope Company Inc .... C.....619 449-3553
10111 Riverford Rd Lakeside (92040) *(P-5475)*
Southland Manufacturing Inc .... F.....760 745-7913
210 Market Pl Escondido (92029) *(P-14196)*
Southland Mixer Service .... F.....760 246-6080
12231 Hibiscus Rd Adelanto (92301) *(P-19556)*
Southland Publishing Inc (PA) .... F.....626 584-1500
50 S Delacey Ave Ste 200 Pasadena (91105) *(P-5834)*
Southland Ready Mix Concrete, Escondido *Also called Superior Ready Mix Concrete LP (P-10852)*
Southland Tool Mfg Inc .... F.....714 632-8198
1430 N Hundley St Anaheim (92806) *(P-14197)*
Southwall Technologies (HQ) .... E.....650 798-1285
3788 Fabian Way Palo Alto (94303) *(P-7613)*
Southwest Concrete Products .... E.....909 983-9789
519 S Benson Ave Ontario (91762) *(P-10654)*
Southwest Data Products, San Bernardino *Also called Innovative Metal Inds Inc (P-12592)*
Southwest Greene Intl Inc .... C.....760 639-4960
4055 Calle Platino # 200 Oceanside (92056) *(P-12874)*
Southwest Machine & Plastic Co .... E.....626 963-6919
620 W Foothill Blvd Glendora (91741) *(P-20235)*
Southwest Offset Prtg Co Inc (PA) .... B.....310 965-9154
13650 Gramercy Pl Gardena (90249) *(P-6866)*
Southwest Offset Prtg Co Inc .... D.....408 232-5160
587 Charcot Ave San Jose (95131) *(P-7221)*
Southwest Plastics Co, Glendora *Also called Southwest Machine & Plastic Co (P-20235)*
Southwest Plating Co Inc .... F.....323 753-3781
1344 W Slauson Ave Los Angeles (90044) *(P-13103)*
Southwest Processors Inc .... F.....323 269-9876
4120 Bandini Blvd Vernon (90058) *(P-1128)*
Southwest Products Corporation .... F.....360 887-7400
2875 Cherry Ave Signal Hill (90755) *(P-13599)*
Southwest Products LLC .... C.....619 263-8000
8441 Siempre Viva Rd San Diego (92154) *(P-2615)*
Southwest Shutter Shaque, Orange *Also called Bayside Shutters (P-11935)*
Southwest Sign Company, Corona *Also called Fovell Enterprises Inc (P-23115)*
Southwest Sign Systems, El Centro *Also called Western Electrical Advg Co (P-23241)*
Southwest Trade Bindery, Northridge *Also called Robert A Kerl (P-7343)*
Southwest Treatment Systems, Vernon *Also called Southwest Processors Inc (P-1128)*
Southwestern Industries Inc (PA) .... D.....310 608-4422
2615 Homestead Pl Rancho Dominguez (90220) *(P-13953)*
Southwire Inc (HQ) .... F.....310 884-8500
11695 Pacific Ave Fontana (92337) *(P-11223)*
Sova Pharmaceuticals Inc .... F.....858 750-4700
11099 N Torrey Pines Rd La Jolla (92037) *(P-8138)*
Sovereign Packaging Inc .... E.....714 670-6811
8420 Kass Dr Buena Park (90621) *(P-5270)*
Soyfoods of America .... E.....626 358-3836
1091 Hamilton Rd Duarte (91010) *(P-1446)*
Sp, City of Industry *Also called Scope Packaging Inc (P-5265)*
Sp Controls Inc .... F.....650 392-7880
930 Linden Ave South San Francisco (94080) *(P-15339)*
Sp3 Diamond Technologies Inc .... F.....877 773-9940
1605 Wyatt Dr Santa Clara (95054) *(P-14860)*
Spa Girl Corporation .... E.....714 444-1040
3100 W Warner Ave Ste 11 Santa Ana (92704) *(P-8586)*
Spa La La Inc .... F.....605 321-1276
21430 Strathern St Unit I Canoga Park (91304) *(P-23481)*
Space Components, Commerce *Also called Atk Space Systems Inc (P-20541)*
Space Exploration Tech Corp (PA) .... A.....310 363-6000
1 Rocket Rd Hawthorne (90250) *(P-20455)*
Space Information Labs LLC .... E.....805 925-9010
2260 Meredith Ln Ste A Santa Maria (93455) *(P-20726)*
Space Jam Juice LLC .... D.....714 660-7467
1041 Calle Trepadora San Clemente (92673) *(P-2656)*
Space Micro Inc .... D.....858 332-0700
15378 Ave Of Science # 200 San Diego (92128) *(P-17666)*
Space Propulsions Div, San Jose *Also called United Technologies Corp (P-19988)*
Space Systems Division, Monterey *Also called Orbital Sciences Corporation (P-20670)*
Space Systems/Loral LLC .... E.....916 605-5448
5130 Rbert J Mathews Pkwy El Dorado Hills (95762) *(P-17667)*
Space Time Insight Inc (HQ) .... E.....650 513-8550
1850 Gateway Dr Ste 125 San Mateo (94404) *(P-24437)*
Space-Lok Inc .... C.....310 527-6150
13306 Halldale Ave Gardena (90249) *(P-20236)*
Spaceship Company, The, Mojave *Also called Tsc LLC (P-20459)*
Spacesonics Incorporated .... D.....650 610-0999
30300 Union City Blvd Union City (94587) *(P-12383)*
Spacesystems Holdings LLC .... C.....714 226-1400
4398 Corporate Center Dr Los Alamitos (90720) *(P-16691)*
Spacetron Metal Billows Corp .... F.....818 633-1075
15303 Ventura Blvd # 900 Sherman Oaks (91403) *(P-16413)*

Spacewall Inc .... F.....714 961-1300
350 E Crowther Ave Placentia (92870) *(P-4281)*
Spacewall West Slotwall Mfg, Placentia *Also called Spacewall (P-4281)*
Spacex, Hawthorne *Also called Space Exploration Tech Corp (P-20455)*
Spadia Inc .... F.....562 206-2505
10440 Pioneer Blvd Ste 1 Santa Fe Springs (90670) *(P-16992)*
Spalinger Enterprises Inc .... F.....661 834-4550
800 S Mount Vernon Ave Bakersfield (93307) *(P-4940)*
Span-O-Matic Inc .... E.....714 256-4700
825 Columbia St Brea (92821) *(P-12384)*
Spanish Castle Inc .... F.....818 222-4496
22201 Camay Ct Calabasas (91302) *(P-1924)*
Spansion Inc (HQ) .... F.....408 962-2500
198 Champion Ct San Jose (95134) *(P-18573)*
Spansion LLC (HQ) .... D.....512 691-8500
198 Champion Ct San Jose (95134) *(P-18574)*
Spar Sausage Co .... F.....510 614-8100
688 Williams St San Leandro (94577) *(P-499)*
Sparitual, Van Nuys *Also called Orly International Inc (P-8552)*
Spark Compass, Los Angeles *Also called Total Cmmnication Solutions Inc (P-24521)*
Spark Stone LLC .... F.....714 772-7575
2300 E Winston Rd Anaheim (92806) *(P-294)*
Sparkcentral Inc (PA) .... F.....866 559-6229
535 Mission St Fl 14 San Francisco (94105) *(P-6344)*
Sparkletts Water, Los Angeles *Also called Ds Services of America Inc (P-2073)*
Sparling Instruments LLC .... E.....626 444-0571
4097 Temple City Blvd El Monte (91731) *(P-20941)*
Sparqtron Corporation .... D.....510 657-7198
5079 Brandin Ct Fremont (94538) *(P-16802)*
Spartak Enterprises Inc .... E.....951 360-0610
11186 Venture Dr Mira Loma (91752) *(P-4755)*
Spartan .... E.....800 743-6950
444 E Taylor St San Jose (95112) *(P-7222)*
Spartan Inc .... E.....661 327-1205
3030 M St Bakersfield (93301) *(P-11882)*
Spartan Manufacturing Co .... E.....714 894-1955
7081 Patterson Dr Garden Grove (92841) *(P-16414)*
Spartan Truck Company Inc .... E.....818 899-1111
12266 Branford St Sun Valley (91352) *(P-19557)*
Spartech LLC .... F.....714 523-2260
14263 Gannet St La Mirada (90638) *(P-9456)*
Sparton Irvine LLC .... D.....949 855-6625
2802 Kelvin Ave Ste 100 Irvine (92614) *(P-19090)*
Spates Fabricators Inc .... D.....760 397-4122
85435 Middleton Thermal (92274) *(P-4319)*
Spatial Photonics Inc .... E.....408 940-8800
930 Hamlin Ct Sunnyvale (94089) *(P-18575)*
Spatial Wave Inc .... F.....949 540-6400
23461 S Pointe Dr Ste 300 Laguna Hills (92653) *(P-24438)*
Spatz Corporation .... C.....805 487-2122
1600 Westar Dr Oxnard (93033) *(P-8587)*
Spatz Laboratories, Oxnard *Also called Spatz Corporation (P-8587)*
Spaulding Crusher Parts, Perris *Also called Spaulding Equipment Company (P-13761)*
Spaulding Equipment Company (PA) .... E.....951 943-4531
75 Paseo Adelanto Perris (92570) *(P-13761)*
Spawn Mate Inc .... E.....805 473-7250
4000 Huasna Rd Arroyo Grande (93420) *(P-8804)*
SPD Manufacturing Inc .... F.....985 302-1902
1101 E Truslow Ave Fullerton (92831) *(P-2734)*
Speakeasy Ales & Lagers, San Francisco *Also called Brewmaster Inc (P-1506)*
Spec, Valencia *Also called Semiconductor Process Eqp Corp (P-18535)*
Spec Engineering Co Inc .... E.....818 780-3045
13754 Saticoy St Van Nuys (91402) *(P-16415)*
Spec Formliners Inc .... F.....714 429-9500
1038 E 4th St Santa Ana (92701) *(P-10655)*
Spec Iron Inc .... F.....818 765-4070
7244 Varna Ave North Hollywood (91605) *(P-11883)*
Spec Tool Company .... E.....323 723-9533
11805 Wakeman St Santa Fe Springs (90670) *(P-20727)*
Spec-Built Systems Inc .... D.....619 661-8100
2150 Michael Faraday Dr San Diego (92154) *(P-12385)*
Specfoam LLC .... F.....951 685-3626
13215 Marlay Ave Fontana (92337) *(P-4745)*
Special Devices Incorporated .... A.....805 387-1000
2655 1st St Ste 300 Simi Valley (93065) *(P-19771)*
Special Forces Custom Gear Inc .... E.....619 241-5453
2949 Hoover Ave National City (91950) *(P-3665)*
Special Iron Security Systems .... F.....626 443-7877
2030 Rosemead Blvd El Monte (91733) *(P-12510)*
Special Products Group, Chula Vista *Also called Sealed Air Corporation (P-5419)*
Special-T, North Hollywood *Also called Specialty Coatings & Chem Inc (P-8682)*
Specialist Media Group, Carlsbad *Also called L & L Printers Carlsbad LLC (P-6686)*
Specialists In Cstm Sftwr Inc .... E.....310 315-9660
2574 Wellesley Ave Los Angeles (90064) *(P-24439)*
Speciality Labs, Fullerton *Also called Magtech & Power Conversion Inc (P-18725)*
Specialized Coating, Huntington Beach *Also called Specilized Crmic Powdr Coating (P-13250)*
Specialized Coating Services .... D.....510 226-8700
42680 Christy St Fremont (94538) *(P-18010)*
Specialized Dairy Service Inc .... E.....909 923-3420
1710 E Philadelphia St Ontario (91761) *(P-13672)*
Specialized Graphics Inc .... E.....925 680-0265
3951 Industrial Way Ste A Concord (94520) *(P-23214)*
Specialized Milling Corp .... F.....909 357-7890
10330 Elm Ave Fontana (92337) *(P-8681)*
Specialized Products & Design .... F.....714 289-1428
1428 N Manzanita St Orange (92867) *(P-8775)*

Employee Codes: A=Over 500 employees, B=251-500
C=101-250, D=51-100, E=20-50, F=10-19

2020 California
Manfacturers Register

© Mergent Inc. 1-800-342-5647

1245

Specialized Screen Printing ....E......714 964-1230
  18435 Bandilier Cir Fountain Valley (92708) (P-7223)
Specialteam Medical Svc Inc ....F......714 694-0348
  22445 La Palma Ave Ste F Yorba Linda (92887) (P-21907)
Specialty Apartment Supply Inc ....F......714 630-2275
  3991 E Miraloma Ave Anaheim (92806) (P-11629)
Specialty Car Wash System ....F......909 869-6300
  146 Mercury Cir Pomona (91768) (P-15580)
Specialty Co Pack LLC ....F......909 673-0439
  1651 Fremont Ct Ontario (91761) (P-824)
Specialty Coating Systems Inc ....E......909 390-8818
  4435 E Airport Dr Ste 100 Ontario (91761) (P-13249)
Specialty Coatings & Chem Inc ....E......818 983-0055
  7360 Varna Ave North Hollywood (91605) (P-8682)
Specialty Division, Santa Fe Springs Also called Distinctive Industries (P-3784)
Specialty Enterprises Co ....D......323 726-9721
  6858 E Acco St Commerce (90040) (P-9569)
Specialty Equipment Co ....E......714 258-1622
  1921 E Pomona St Santa Ana (92705) (P-19558)
Specialty Fabrications Inc ....E......805 579-9730
  2674 Westhills Ct Simi Valley (93065) (P-12386)
Specialty Finance Inc ....E......951 735-5200
  1230 Quarry St Corona (92879) (P-12875)
Specialty Finishes, Fontana Also called Specialized Milling Corp (P-8681)
Specialty Granules LLC ....E......209 274-5323
  1900 State Hwy 104 Ione (95640) (P-10978)
Specialty Graphics Inc ....F......510 351-7705
  1998 Republic Ave San Leandro (94577) (P-7351)
Specialty International Inc ....D......818 768-8810
  11144 Penrose St Ste 11 Sun Valley (91352) (P-12876)
Specialty Manufacturing, Inc., San Diego Also called Providien Thermoforming Inc (P-9417)
Specialty Metal Fabrication, Goleta Also called Tan Set Corporation (P-11896)
Specialty Minerals Inc ....C......760 248-5300
  6565 Meridian Rd Lucerne Valley (92356) (P-304)
Specialty Motions Inc ....E......951 735-8722
  5480 Smokey Mountain Way Yorba Linda (92887) (P-14616)
Specialty Products Design Inc ....F......916 635-8108
  11252 Sunco Dr Rancho Cordova (95742) (P-19772)
Specialty Rock Inc ....F......909 334-2265
  5405 Alton Pkwy Irvine Irvine (92604) (P-360)
Specialty Science Counter Tops, Newbury Park Also called H and M Industries LLC (P-4908)
Specialty Steel Products Inc ....F......619 671-0720
  1202 Piper Ranch Rd San Diego (92154) (P-13436)
Specialty Surface Grinding ....F......310 538-4352
  345 W 131st St Los Angeles (90061) (P-16416)
Specific Diagnostics Inc ....E......561 655-5588
  855 Maude Ave Mountain View (94043) (P-21908)
Specilized Crmic Powdr Coating ....F......714 901-2628
  5862 Research Dr Huntington Beach (92649) (P-13250)
Specilized Packg Solutions Inc ....E......510 494-5670
  38505 Cherry St Ste H Newark (94560) (P-4428)
Specilty Enzymes Btechnologies, Chino Also called Cal-India Foods International (P-8725)
Specilty Enzymes Btechnologies ....F......909 613-1660
  13591 Yorba Ave Chino (91710) (P-8776)
Specilty Mtals Fabrication Inc ....F......619 937-6100
  11222 Woodside Ave N Santee (92071) (P-2900)
Specilized Packg Solutions-Wood, Newark Also called Specilized Packg Solutions Inc (P-4428)
Speck Products, San Mateo Also called Speculative Product Design LLC (P-10211)
Spectra Color Inc ....E......951 277-0200
  9116 Stellar Ct Corona (92883) (P-7463)
Spectra USA, Chino Also called Isiqalo LLC (P-2791)
Spectra Watermakers, Petaluma Also called Katadyn Desalination LLC (P-16831)
Spectra Watermakers Inc (HQ) ....F......415 526-2780
  2220 S Mcdowell Blvd Ext Petaluma (94954) (P-15581)
Spectra-Physics Inc ....A......650 961-2550
  3635 Peterson Way Santa Clara (95054) (P-19412)
Spectra-Physics Laser Div, Santa Clara Also called Newport Corporation (P-19367)
Spectral Dynamics Inc (PA) ....E......760 761-0440
  2199 Zanker Rd San Jose (95131) (P-21546)
Spectral Labs Incorporated ....E......858 451-0540
  15920 Bernardo Center Dr San Diego (92127) (P-21547)
Spectranetics ....F......408 592-2111
  6531 Dumbarton Cir Fremont (94555) (P-22315)
Spectranetics Corporation ....D......510 933-7964
  5055 Brandin Ct Fremont (94538) (P-21909)
Spectraprint Inc ....F......415 460-1228
  24 Moody Ct San Rafael (94901) (P-7224)
Spectrasensors Inc ....E......909 980-4238
  11027 Arrow Rte Rancho Cucamonga (91730) (P-21292)
Spectraswitch Inc ....E......707 568-7000
  445 Tesconi Cir Santa Rosa (95401) (P-17414)
Spectratek Technologies Inc (PA) ....E......310 822-2400
  9834 Jordan Cir Santa Fe Springs (90670) (P-6867)
Spectre Performance, Riverside Also called Seymour Levinger & Co (P-12749)
Spectrolab Inc ....B......818 365-4611
  12500 Gladstone Ave Sylmar (91342) (P-18576)
Spectrum Accessory Distrs ....C......858 653-6470
  9770 Carroll Centre Rd San Diego (92126) (P-19773)
Spectrum Assembly Inc ....D......760 930-4000
  6300 Yarrow Dr Ste 100 Carlsbad (92011) (P-18011)
Spectrum Bags, Cerritos Also called Ips Industries Inc (P-9844)
Spectrum Brands Inc ....C......805 222-3611
  5144 N Commerce Ave Ste A Moorpark (93021) (P-23482)
Spectrum Electronics, Carlsbad Also called Spectrum Assembly Inc (P-18011)
Spectrum Grafix Inc ....F......415 648-2400
  141 10th St San Francisco (94103) (P-6868)

Spectrum Instruments Inc ....F......909 971-9710
  570 E Arrow Hwy Ste D San Dimas (91773) (P-21125)
Spectrum Label, Hayward Also called Resource Label Group LLC (P-7195)
Spectrum Lithograph Inc ....E......510 438-9192
  4300 Business Center Dr Fremont (94538) (P-6869)
Spectrum Naturals, Petaluma Also called Spectrum Organic Products LLC (P-1483)
Spectrum Organic Products LLC ....D......888 343-6637
  2201 S Mcdowell Blvd Ext Petaluma (94954) (P-1483)
Spectrum Plating Company Inc ....E......310 533-0748
  202 W 140th St Los Angeles (90061) (P-13104)
Spectrum Prosthetics/Orthotics ....F......530 243-4500
  1844 South St Redding (96001) (P-22089)
Spectrum Scientific Inc 949 260-9900
  16692 Hale Ave Ste A Irvine (92606) (P-21411)
Speculative Product Design LLC 650 462-9086
  303 Bryant St Mountain View (94041) (P-10210)
Speculative Product Design LLC (HQ) ....D......650 462-2040
  177 Bovet Rd Ste 200 San Mateo (94402) (P-10211)
Speed-O-Pin International ....F......562 433-4911
  1401 Freeman Ave Long Beach (90804) (P-5040)
Speedplay Inc ....E......858 453-4707
  10151 Pacific Mesa Blvd # 107 San Diego (92121) (P-22893)
Speedpress Sign Supply, Carlsbad Also called Coplan & Coplan Inc (P-14151)
Speedskins Inc ....F......760 439-3119
  2919 San Luis Rey Rd Oceanside (92058) (P-22894)
Speedwear.com, Huntington Beach Also called Gachupin Enterprises LLC (P-7072)
Speedy Bindery Inc ....E......619 275-0261
  4386 Jutland Dr San Diego (92117) (P-7352)
Speedy Circuits, Huntington Beach Also called Coast To Coast Circuits Inc (P-17854)
Spellbound Development Group ....F......949 474-8577
  17192 Gillette Ave Irvine (92614) (P-22386)
Spellbound Entertainment, Irvine Also called Spellbound Development Group (P-22386)
Spencer Home Decor, City of Industry Also called Spencer N Enterprises LLC (P-3642)
Spencer N Enterprises LLC (HQ) ....E......909 895-8495
  425 S Lemon Ave City of Industry (91789) (P-3642)
Spenco Machine & Manufacturing ....F......951 699-5566
  27556 Commerce Center Dr Temecula (92590) (P-16417)
Spenuzza Inc (PA) ....C......951 281-1830
  1128 Sherborn St Corona (92879) (P-15582)
Spenuzza Inc ....E......626 358-8063
  913 Oak Ave Duarte (91010) (P-15583)
SPEP Acquisition Corp (PA) ....D......310 608-0693
  4041 Via Oro Ave Long Beach (90810) (P-11630)
Sperry West Inc ....F......858 551-2000
  5575 Magnatron Blvd Ste J San Diego (92111) (P-17668)
Sphere Alliance Inc ....E......951 352-2400
  3051 Myers St Riverside (92503) (P-7614)
SPI Solar Inc (PA) ....F......408 919-8000
  4677 Old Ironsides Dr Santa Clara (95054) (P-11718)
Spices Unlimited Inc ....F......831 636-3596
  2339 Tech Pkwy Ste J Hollister (95023) (P-2616)
Spidell Publishing Inc ....E......714 776-7850
  1134 N Gilbert St Anaheim (92801) (P-6345)
Spike Chunsoft Inc ....F......562 786-5080
  5000 Airport Plaza Dr # 230 Long Beach (90815) (P-24440)
Spikey Wear, Monterey Park Also called Miholin Inc (P-3108)
Spill Magic Inc ....E......714 557-2001
  630 Young St Santa Ana (92705) (P-5153)
Spin Memory Inc ....E......510 933-8200
  45500 Northport Loop W Fremont (94538) (P-18577)
Spin Products Inc ....E......909 590-7000
  13878 Yorba Ave Chino (91710) (P-10064)
Spin Shades Corporation ....E......805 650-4849
  3115 Breaker Dr Ventura (93003) (P-17162)
Spin Tek Machining Inc ....F......408 298-8223
  540 Parrott St Ste A San Jose (95112) (P-16418)
Spinal and Orthopedic Devices ....F......818 908-9000
  5920 Noble Ave Van Nuys (91411) (P-22090)
Spinalmotion Inc ....F......650 947-3472
  201 San Antonio Cir # 115 Mountain View (94040) (P-21910)
Spine View Inc ....D......510 490-1753
  110 Pioneer Way Ste A Mountain View (94041) (P-21911)
Spineex Inc ....E......510 573-1093
  4046 Clipper Ct Fremont (94538) (P-21912)
Spinelli Graphic Inc ....F......562 431-3232
  10621 Bloomfield St Ste 2 Los Alamitos (90720) (P-7225)
Spinergy Inc ....D......760 496-2121
  1914 Palomar Oaks Way # 100 Carlsbad (92008) (P-20425)
Spinner Toys & Gifts, San Diego Also called Beejay LLC (P-22662)
Spintek Filtration Inc ....F......714 236-9190
  10863 Portal Dr Los Alamitos (90720) (P-14861)
Spira Manufacturing Corp ....F......818 764-8222
  650 Jessie St San Fernando (91340) (P-9257)
Spiracle Technology LLC ....F......714 418-1091
  10601 Calle Lee Ste 190 Los Alamitos (90720) (P-21548)
Spiracur Inc (PA) ....D......650 364-1544
  1180 Bordeaux Dr Sunnyvale (94089) (P-21913)
Spiral Ppr Tube & Core Co Inc ....E......562 801-9705
  5200 Industry Ave Pico Rivera (90660) (P-5303)
Spire Manufacturing Inc ....E......510 226-1070
  49016 Milmont Dr Fremont (94538) (P-16925)
Spirent Calabasas, Calabasas Also called Spirent Communications Inc (P-21127)
Spirent Communications Inc ....C......408 752-7100
  2708 Orchard Pkwy Ste 20 San Jose (95134) (P-21126)
Spirent Communications Inc (HQ) ....B......818 676-2300
  27439 Agoura Rd Calabasas (91301) (P-21127)
Spirit Activewear, Vernon Also called Spirit Clothing Company (P-3410)
Spirit Clothing Company ....E......213 784-0251
  2211 E 37th St Vernon (90058) (P-3410)

Mergent e-mail: customerrelations@mergent.com
1246
2020 California
Manufacturers Register
(P-0000) Products & Services Section entry number
(PA)=Parent Co (HQ)=Headquarters (DH)=Div Headquarters

Spirit Throws, Roseville *Also called Hudson & Company LLC (P-3618)*
Spirit West Coast, Campbell *Also called Christian Music Today Inc (P-5589)*
Spiritual Counterfeits Prj Inc....F....510 540-0300
2606 Dwight Way Berkeley (94704) **(P-6031)**
Spitzlift, San Diego *Also called Hirok Inc (P-13736)*
Splunk Inc (PA)....C....415 848-8400
270 Brannan St San Francisco (94107) **(P-24441)**
Spm, Anaheim *Also called Bace Manufacturing Inc (P-9650)*
Spn Investments Inc....E....562 777-1140
6481 Orangethorpe Ave # 12 Buena Park (90620) **(P-22895)**
Spoety Cuts Corporation....F....310 908-1512
6510 Wooster Ave Los Angeles (90056) **(P-8777)**
Spooners Woodworks Inc....D....858 679-9086
12460 Kirkham Ct Poway (92064) **(P-4941)**
Sport Boat Trailers Inc....F....209 892-5388
430 C St Patterson (95363) **(P-20521)**
Sport Kites Inc....F....714 998-6359
500 W Blueridge Ave Orange (92865) **(P-19932)**
Sport Pins International Inc....F....909 985-4549
888 Berry Ct Ste A Upland (91786) **(P-22996)**
Sport Rock International Inc....F....805 434-5474
450 Marquita Ave Paso Robles (93446) **(P-22896)**
Sportifeye Optics Inc....E....626 521-5600
1231 Mountain View Cir Azusa (91702) **(P-22387)**
Sportrx Inc....E....858 571-0240
5070 Santa Fe St Ste C San Diego (92109) **(P-22388)**
Sports Hoop Inc....F....626 387-6027
12669 Beryl Way Jurupa Valley (92509) **(P-22897)**
Sports Medicine Info Network....F....310 659-6889
8737 Beverly Blvd Ste 303 West Hollywood (90048) **(P-5835)**
Sports Publications Inc (PA)....F....310 607-9956
228 Nevada St El Segundo (90245) **(P-6032)**
Sports Rack Vehicle Outfitters, Sacramento *Also called Bauer Industries (P-11572)*
Sportscar, Corona Del Mar *Also called Pfanner Communications Inc (P-6002)*
Sportscar International, Novato *Also called SCI Publishing Inc (P-6024)*
Sportsco, San Bernardino *Also called All Sports Services Inc (P-6980)*
Sportsman Steel Gun Safe, Long Beach *Also called Sportsmen Steel Safe Fabg Co (P-13547)*
Sportsmen Steel Safe Fabg Co (PA)....E....562 984-0244
6311 N Paramount Blvd Long Beach (90805) **(P-13547)**
Sportsrobe Inc....E....310 559-3999
8654 Hayden Pl Culver City (90232) **(P-3116)**
Sposato John....F....408 215-8727
257 Vera Ave Redwood City (94061) **(P-17669)**
Spotless Water Systems LLC....F....858 530-9993
372 Coogan Way El Cajon (92020) **(P-15584)**
Spotlite America Corporation (PA)....E....310 829-0200
9937 Jefferson Blvd # 110 Culver City (90232) **(P-10331)**
Spotlite Power Corporation....E....310 838-2367
9937 Jefferson Blvd # 110 Culver City (90232) **(P-17071)**
Spoton Computing Inc....E....650 293-7464
209 9th St Fl 3 San Francisco (94103) **(P-24442)**
Spragg Industries Inc....F....661 424-9673
20049 Crestview Dr Canyon Country (91351) **(P-23483)**
Spragues Ready Mix, Irwindale *Also called Spragues Rock and Sand Company (P-10841)*
Spragues Ready Mix Concrete, Simi Valley *Also called Spragues Rock and Sand Company (P-10842)*
Spragues Rock and Sand Company (PA)....E....626 445-2125
230 Longden Ave Irwindale (91706) **(P-10841)**
Spragues Rock and Sand Company....F....805 522-7010
5400 Bennett Rd Simi Valley (93063) **(P-10842)**
Spray Enclosure Technologies....E....909 419-7011
1427 N Linden Ave Rialto (92376) **(P-12387)**
Spray Tech, Rialto *Also called Spray Enclosure Technologies (P-12387)*
Spraying Devices Inc....F....559 734-5555
447 E Caldwell Ave Visalia (93277) **(P-13697)**
Sprayline Enterprises Inc....E....909 627-8411
10774 Grand Ave Ontario (91762) **(P-13251)**
Sprayline Manufacturing....F....562 941-5313
10110 Greenleaf Ave Santa Fe Springs (90670) **(P-14641)**
Spraytronics Inc....E....408 988-3636
6001 Butler Ln Ste 204 Scotts Valley (95066) **(P-13252)**
Spread Effect LLC....E....888 705-1127
7580 Fay Ave Ste 304 La Jolla (92037) **(P-7226)**
Spreadco Inc....E....760 351-0747
803 Us Highway 78 Brawley (92227) **(P-2847)**
Spreckels Sugar, Brawley *Also called Imperial Sugar Company (P-1351)*
Spreckels Sugar Company Inc....B....760 344-3110
395 W Keystone Rd Brawley (92227) **(P-1352)**
Spring Bioscience Corp....A....925 474-8463
4300 Hacienda Dr Pleasanton (94588) **(P-8261)**
Spring Delgau Inc....F....951 371-1000
322 N Garfield Ave Corona (92882) **(P-13388)**
Spring Industries, Ventura *Also called Juengermann Inc (P-13338)*
Spring Mountain Vineyards Inc....E....707 967-4188
2805 Spring Mountain Rd Saint Helena (94574) **(P-1925)**
Springpudic, Los Angeles *Also called Cuevas Mattress Inc (P-4717)*
Springs Window Fashions LLC....F....877 792-0002
6754 Calle De Linea San Diego (92154) **(P-5041)**
Sprint Copy Center Inc....F....707 823-3900
175 N Main St Sebastopol (95472) **(P-6870)**
Sprite Industries Incorporated....E....951 735-1015
1791 Railroad St Corona (92880) **(P-21293)**
Sprite Showers, Corona *Also called Sprite Industries Incorporated (P-21293)*
Sprout Inc....F....415 894-9629
475 Brannan St Ste 410 San Francisco (94107) **(P-6346)**
Sproutling Inc....F....415 323-3270
8 California St Ste 300 San Francisco (94111) **(P-17415)**

Spruce Biosciences Inc....F....415 655-3803
1700 Montgomery St # 212 San Francisco (94111) **(P-7694)**
SPS Studios Inc....E....858 456-2336
7917 Ivanhoe Ave La Jolla (92037) **(P-7299)**
SPS Technologies LLC....B....714 545-9311
1224 E Warner Ave Santa Ana (92705) **(P-23009)**
SPS Technologies LLC....B....310 323-6222
1700 W 132nd St Gardena (90249) **(P-12693)**
SPS Technologies LLC....E....714 892-5571
12570 Knott St Garden Grove (92841) **(P-12694)**
SPS Technologies LLC....B....714 371-1925
1224 E Warner Ave Santa Ana (92705) **(P-23010)**
SPS Technologies LLC....D....562 426-9411
14800 S Figueroa St Gardena (90248) **(P-13363)**
Spt Microtechnologies....F....408 571-1400
1755 Junction Ave San Jose (95112) **(P-18578)**
Spt Microtechnologies USA Inc....E....408 571-1400
1150 Ringwood Ct San Jose (95131) **(P-14538)**
Spun Products, Long Beach *Also called M L Z Inc (P-12840)*
SPX Cooling Technologies Inc....E....714 529-6080
550 Mercury Ln Brea (92821) **(P-12054)**
SPX Corporation....D....714 434-2576
17815 Newhope St Ste M Fountain Valley (92708) **(P-12055)**
SPX Corporation....F....714 634-3855
1515 S Harris Ct Anaheim (92806) **(P-12056)**
SPX Flow Us LLC....D....949 455-8150
26561 Rancho Pkwy S Lake Forest (92630) **(P-14401)**
Spy Inc (PA)....D....760 804-8420
1896 Rutherford Rd Carlsbad (92008) **(P-22389)**
Spyder Manufacturing Inc....F....714 528-8010
545 Porter Way Placentia (92870) **(P-13698)**
Spyke Inc....E....562 803-1700
12155 Pangborn Ave Downey (90241) **(P-20426)**
Spyrus Inc (PA)....E....408 392-9131
103 Bonaventura Dr San Jose (95134) **(P-15340)**
Squaglia Manufacturing (PA)....E....650 965-9644
275 Polaris Ave Mountain View (94043) **(P-16419)**
Squamtech Inc....F....415 867-8300
2023 22nd St San Francisco (94107) **(P-24443)**
Square Inc (PA)....E....415 375-3176
1455 Market St Ste 600 San Francisco (94103) **(P-24444)**
Square Deal Mat Fctry & Uphl, Chico *Also called Square Deal Mattress Factory (P-4746)*
Square Deal Mattress Factory....E....530 342-2510
1354 Humboldt Ave Chico (95928) **(P-4746)**
Square H Brands Inc....C....323 267-4600
2731 S Soto St Vernon (90058) **(P-500)**
Squarebar Inc....F....530 412-0209
1035 22nd Ave Unit 8 Oakland (94606) **(P-8139)**
Squelch Inc....E....650 241-2700
555 Twin Dolphin Dr # 170 Redwood City (94065) **(P-24445)**
Sr Plastics Company LLC (PA)....F....951 520-9486
640 Parkridge Ave Norco (92860) **(P-10065)**
Sr Plastics Company LLC....E....951 479-5394
692 Parkridge Ave Norco (92860) **(P-10066)**
Sr3 Solutions LLC....F....818 255-3131
13136 Saticoy St North Hollywood (91605) **(P-5836)**
Sra Oss Inc....C....408 855-8200
5201 Great America Pkwy # 419 Santa Clara (95054) **(P-24446)**
SRC, Linden *Also called Stockton Rubber Mfgcoinc (P-9374)*
SRC Milling Co LLC....E....916 363-4821
11350 Kiefer Blvd Sacramento (95830) **(P-1466)**
Srco Inc....F....626 350-8321
2305 Merced Ave El Monte (91733) **(P-16420)**
Sream Inc....E....951 245-6999
12869 Temescal Canyon Rd A Corona (92883) **(P-10391)**
SRI Instruments, Torrance *Also called Scientific Repair Inc (P-20934)*
Srl Apparel Inc....E....530 898-9525
2209 Park Ave Chico (95928) **(P-2838)**
Srm Contracting & Paving, San Diego *Also called Superior Ready Mix Concrete LP (P-10847)*
SRS, Sunnyvale *Also called Stanford Research Systems Inc (P-21294)*
Srsb Inc....F....949 234-1881
5004 Cmino Escllo Ste 200 San Clemente (92673) **(P-24447)**
Srss LLC....F....707 544-7777
1400 Airport Blvd Santa Rosa (95403) **(P-12609)**
Ss Brewtech, Tustin *Also called CM Brewing Technologies LLC (P-15502)*
Ss Metal Fabricators....F....949 631-4272
2501 S Birch St Santa Ana (92707) **(P-11884)**
Ssb Manufacturing Company....C....770 512-7700
20100 S Alameda St Compton (90221) **(P-4747)**
SSC, Santa Clara *Also called Silicon Standard Corp (P-18549)*
SSC Apparel Inc....E....213 746-0200
2025 Long Beach Ave Los Angeles (90058) **(P-3411)**
SSC Racing, Palm Desert *Also called Karbz Inc (P-19699)*
Ssco Manufacturing Inc....E....619 628-1022
1245 30th St San Diego (92154) **(P-14255)**
Sscor Inc....F....818 504-4054
11064 Randall St Sun Valley (91352) **(P-21914)**
Ssdi, La Mirada *Also called Solid State Devices Inc (P-18570)*
Ssg Alliance LLC (PA)....F....925 526-6050
2550 Somersville Rd # 55 Antioch (94509) **(P-19413)**
Ssi, Lodi *Also called Scientific Specialties Inc (P-9420)*
Ssi G Debbas Chocolatier LLC....E....559 294-2071
2794 N Larkin Ave Fresno (93727) **(P-1413)**
Ssi Surfaces, Newbury Park *Also called Scientific Surface Inds Inc (P-4936)*
SSS, Carlsbad *Also called Silk Screen Shirts Inc (P-2837)*
SST, Newark *Also called Shotspotter Inc (P-24407)*

ALPHABETIC

Employee Codes: A=Over 500 employees, B=251-500
C=101-250, D=51-100, E=20-50, F=10-19
2020 California
Manfacturers Register
© Mergent Inc. 1-800-342-5647
1247

Sst Technologies ... E ... 562 803-3361
9801 Everest St Downey (90242) ***(P-20942)***
Sst Vacuum Reflow Systems, Downey *Also called Sst Technologies* ***(P-20942)***
St Cyclewear/Gallop LLC ... F ... 619 449-9191
1200 Billy Mitchell Dr D El Cajon (92020) ***(P-3117)***
St George Spirits Inc ... E ... 510 769-1601
2601 Monarch St Alameda (94501) ***(P-1926)***
St John Knits, Irvine *Also called St John Knits Intl Inc* ***(P-3413)***
St John Knits Inc (HQ) ... C ... 949 863-1171
17522 Armstrong Ave Irvine (92614) ***(P-3412)***
St John Knits Intl Inc (HQ) ... C ... 949 863-1171
17522 Armstrong Ave Irvine (92614) ***(P-3413)***
St John Knits Intl Inc ... B ... 949 399-8200
17622 Armstrong Ave Irvine (92614) ***(P-2802)***
ST Johnson Company LLC ... E ... 510 652-6000
5160 Fulton Dr Fairfield (94534) ***(P-11719)***
St Jude Medical LLC ... E ... 949 769-5000
2375 Morse Ave Irvine (92614) ***(P-8140)***
St Jude Medical LLC ... B ... 408 738-4883
645 Almanor Ave Sunnyvale (94085) ***(P-21915)***
St Louis Post-Dispatch LLC ... E ... 415 892-1516
1068 Machin Ave Novato (94945) ***(P-5837)***
St Louis Post-Dispatch LLC ... E ... 707 762-4541
830 Petaluma Blvd N Petaluma (94952) ***(P-5838)***
St Louis Post-Dispatch LLC ... F ... 661 763-3171
800 Center St Taft (93268) ***(P-5839)***
St Paul Brands Inc ... E ... 714 903-1000
11555 Monarch St Ste B Garden Grove (92841) ***(P-7641)***
St Pierre Gonzalez Enterprises ... E ... 714 491-2191
419 E La Palma Ave Anaheim (92801) ***(P-13253)***
St Supertec, Paramount *Also called Supertec Machinery Inc* ***(P-13954)***
St Supery Inc (HQ) ... E ... 707 963-4507
8440 St Helena Hwy Rutherford (94573) ***(P-1927)***
STA Pharmaceutical US LLC ... E ... 609 606-6499
6114 Nancy Ridge Dr San Diego (92121) ***(P-8141)***
STA-Slim Products Inc ... F ... 310 514-1155
600 N Pacific Ave San Pedro (90731) ***(P-22898)***
Staar Surgical Company (PA) ... C ... 626 303-7902
1911 Walker Ave Monrovia (91016) ***(P-22390)***
Staar Surgical Company ... F ... 626 303-7902
15102 Redhiill Ave Tustin (92780) ***(P-22391)***
Stabile Plating Company Inc ... E ... 626 339-9091
1150 E Edna Pl Covina (91724) ***(P-13105)***
Stablcor Technology Inc ... F ... 714 375-6644
17011 Beach Blvd Ste 900 Huntington Beach (92647) ***(P-5304)***
Staccato, Vernon *Also called Atrevete Inc* ***(P-3138)***
Stack Labs Inc ... E ... 503 453-5172
10052 Pasadena Ave Ste A Cupertino (95014) ***(P-17072)***
Stack Lighting, Cupertino *Also called Stack Labs Inc* ***(P-17072)***
Stack Plastics Inc ... E ... 650 361-8600
3525 Haven Ave Menlo Park (94025) ***(P-10067)***
Stackla Inc ... D ... 415 789-3304
33 New Mont San Francisco (94105) ***(P-24448)***
Stackrox Inc (PA) ... E ... 650 489-6769
700 E El Camino Real # 200 Mountain View (94040) ***(P-24449)***
Staco Switch, Irvine *Also called Staco Systems Inc* ***(P-16617)***
Staco Systems Inc (HQ) ... D ... 949 297-8700
7 Morgan Irvine (92618) ***(P-16617)***
Stadco (PA) ... C ... 323 227-8888
107 S Avenue 20 Los Angeles (90031) ***(P-14198)***
Staffing Industry Analysts Inc ... E ... 650 390-6200
1975 W El Cmno Rl 304 Mountain View (94040) ***(P-6347)***
Staffing Industry Report, Mountain View *Also called Staffing Industry Analysts Inc* ***(P-6347)***
Stags Leap Wine Cellars ... C ... 707 944-2020
5766 Silverado Trl NAPA (94558) ***(P-1928)***
Stailess Polishing Co., Oakland *Also called General Grinding Inc* ***(P-15990)***
Stainless Fixtures Inc ... E ... 909 622-1615
1250 E Franklin Ave Pomona (91766) ***(P-5082)***
Stainless Industrial Companies ... D ... 310 575-9400
11111 Santa Monica Blvd # 1120 Los Angeles (90025) ***(P-14106)***
Stainless Micro-Polish Inc ... F ... 714 632-8903
1286 N Grove St Anaheim (92806) ***(P-13106)***
Stainless Process Systems Inc ... F ... 805 483-7100
1650 Beacon Pl Oxnard (93033) ***(P-11885)***
Stainless Technologies LLC ... F ... 559 651-0460
19425 W Grove Ave Visalia (93291) ***(P-24667)***
Stainless Works Inc ... F ... 559 688-4310
201 E Owens Ave Tulare (93274) ***(P-24668)***
Stainless Works Mfg Inc ... E ... 831 728-5097
225 Salinas Rd Bldg 5a Royal Oaks (95076) ***(P-14402)***
Stake Fastener, Chino *Also called Dupree Inc* ***(P-12676)***
Stalfab ... F ... 831 786-1600
131 Algen Ln Watsonville (95076) ***(P-14403)***
Stalker Software Inc ... E ... 415 569-2280
125 Park Pl Ste 210 Richmond (94801) ***(P-24450)***
Stamats Communications Inc ... E ... 800 358-0388
550 Montgomery St Ste 750 San Francisco (94111) ***(P-6148)***
Stamats Travel Group, San Francisco *Also called Stamats Communications Inc* ***(P-6148)***
Standard Armament, Glendale *Also called SAI Industries* ***(P-13277)***
Standard Bias Binding Co Inc ... E ... 323 277-9763
4621 Pacific Blvd Vernon (90058) ***(P-3816)***
Standard Cognition Corp (PA) ... E ... 201 707-7782
965 Mission St Fl 7 San Francisco (94103) ***(P-24451)***
Standard Concrete Products (HQ) ... E ... 310 829-4537
13550 Live Oak Ln Baldwin Park (91706) ***(P-10843)***
Standard Crystal Corp ... F ... 626 443-2121
17626 Barber Ave Artesia (90701) ***(P-19091)***
Standard Fiber LLC (PA) ... E ... 650 872-6528
577 Airport Blvd Ste 200 Burlingame (94010) ***(P-3643)***
Standard Filter Corporation (PA) ... E ... 866 443-3615
5928 Balfour Ct Carlsbad (92008) ***(P-14679)***
Standard Homeopathic Co (PA) ... D ... 310 768-0700
204 W 131st St Los Angeles (90061) ***(P-8142)***
Standard Homeopathic Co ... E ... 424 224-4127
108 W Walnut St Fl 1 Gardena (90248) ***(P-8143)***
Standard Industries Inc ... C ... 951 360-4274
11800 Industry Ave Fontana (92337) ***(P-4487)***
Standard Lumber Company Inc (HQ) ... E ... 559 651-2037
8009 W Doe Ave Visalia (93291) ***(P-4401)***
Standard Metal Products Inc ... E ... 310 532-9861
1541 W 132nd St Gardena (90249) ***(P-13107)***
Standard Tool & Die Co, Los Angeles *Also called Stadco* ***(P-14198)***
Standard Wire & Cable Co (PA) ... E ... 310 609-1811
2050 E Vista Bella Way Rancho Dominguez (90220) ***(P-11320)***
Standardvision LLC ... E ... 323 222-3630
3370 N San Fernando Rd # 206 Los Angeles (90065) ***(P-23215)***
Standish Precision Products, Fallbrook *Also called Fallbrook Industries Inc* ***(P-12803)***
Standridge Granite Corporation ... E ... 562 946-6334
9437 Santa Fe Springs Rd Santa Fe Springs (90670) ***(P-10933)***
Staness Jonekos Entps Inc ... E ... 818 606-2710
4000 W Magnolia Blvd D Burbank (91505) ***(P-2617)***
Stanford Advanced Materials, Lake Forest *Also called Oceania International LLC* ***(P-11278)***
Stanford Daily Publishing Corp ... E ... 650 723-2555
456 Panama Mall Stanford (94305) ***(P-5840)***
STANFORD DAILY, THE, Stanford *Also called Stanford Daily Publishing Corp* ***(P-5840)***
Stanford Furniture Mfg Inc ... E ... 916 387-5300
5851 Alder Ave Ste A Sacramento (95828) ***(P-5083)***
Stanford Humanities Review, Stanford *Also called Leland Stanford Junior Univ* ***(P-6272)***
Stanford Materials Corporation ... F ... 949 380-7362
23661 Birtcher Dr Lake Forest (92630) ***(P-7464)***
Stanford Mu Corporation ... E ... 310 605-2888
20725 Annalee Ave Carson (90746) ***(P-20480)***
Stanford Research Systems Inc ... C ... 408 744-9040
1290 Reamwood Ave Ste D Sunnyvale (94089) ***(P-21294)***
Stanford Sign & Awning Inc (PA) ... D ... 619 423-6200
2556 Faivre St Chula Vista (91911) ***(P-23216)***
Stanford University Libraries, Stanford *Also called Leland Stanford Junior Univ* ***(P-6271)***
Stanford University Press, Redwood City *Also called Leland Stanford Junior Univ* ***(P-5698)***
Stang Industrial Products, Corona *Also called Stang Industries Inc* ***(P-23484)***
Stang Industries Inc ... F ... 714 556-0222
2616 Research Dr Ste B Corona (92882) ***(P-23484)***
Stangenes Industries Inc (PA) ... C ... 650 855-9926
1052 E Meadow Cir Palo Alto (94303) ***(P-18745)***
Stanislaus Distributing Co, Modesto *Also called Varni Brothers Corporation* ***(P-2180)***
Stanislaus Food Products Co (PA) ... C ... 209 548-3537
1202 D St Modesto (95354) ***(P-825)***
Stanley Access Tech LLC ... C ... 909 628-9272
4230 E Airport Dr Ste 107 Ontario (91761) ***(P-11545)***
Stanley Access Tech LLC ... C ... 209 221-4066
1312 Dupont Ct Manteca (95336) ***(P-11546)***
Stanley Electric Motor Co Inc ... E ... 209 464-7321
1520 E Miner Ave Stockton (95205) ***(P-24696)***
Stantec Consulting Svcs Inc ... F ... 916 434-5062
1245 Fiddyment Rd Lincoln (95648) ***(P-15585)***
Stanton Carpet Corp ... E ... 562 945-8711
2209 Pine Ave Manhattan Beach (90266) ***(P-2880)***
Stanza, San Francisco *Also called Spoton Computing Inc* ***(P-24442)***
Stanzino Inc ... C ... 818 602-5171
17937 Santa Rita St Encino (91316) ***(P-2713)***
Stanzino Inc (PA) ... F ... 213 746-8822
16325 S Avalon Blvd Gardena (90248) ***(P-2714)***
Staples Inc ... F ... 213 623-4395
731 S Spring St Ste 300 Los Angeles (90014) ***(P-3414)***
Star Ave ... E ... 213 623-5799
514 E 8th St Ste 500 Los Angeles (90014) ***(P-3415)***
Star Building Products, Fresno *Also called E-Z Haul Ready Mix Inc* ***(P-10754)***
Star Building Systems, Lockeford *Also called Robertson-Ceco II Corporation* ***(P-12573)***
Star Concrete, San Jose *Also called Sandman Inc* ***(P-10646)***
Star Die Casting Inc ... D ... 562 698-0627
12209 Slauson Ave Santa Fe Springs (90670) ***(P-11631)***
Star Finishes Inc ... F ... 559 261-1076
40429 Brickyard Dr Madera (93636) ***(P-13108)***
Star Fish Inc ... F ... 415 468-6688
410 Talbert St Daly City (94014) ***(P-3817)***
Star Lion, Los Angeles *Also called Starlion Inc* ***(P-2994)***
Star Milling Co ... C ... 951 657-3143
24067 Water Ave Perris (92570) ***(P-1129)***
Star One Investments LLC ... F ... 916 858-1178
1304 Buttercup Ct Roseville (95661) ***(P-11632)***
Star Pacific Inc ... E ... 510 471-6555
27462 Sunrise Farm Rd Los Altos Hills (94022) ***(P-8352)***
Star Plastic Design ... D ... 310 530-7119
25914 President Ave Harbor City (90710) ***(P-10068)***
Star Products ... E ... 408 727-8421
312 Brokaw Rd Santa Clara (95050) ***(P-16421)***
Star Racecars, Pacoima *Also called Valley Motor Center Inc* ***(P-19510)***
Star Ring Inc ... D ... 818 773-4900
4429 Summerglen Ct Moorpark (93021) ***(P-22573)***
Star Route LLC ... F ... 805 405-8510
4522 Henley Ct Westlake Village (91361) ***(P-7300)***
Star Sanitation Services ... F ... 831 754-6794
4 Harris Rd Salinas (93908) ***(P-10069)***
Star Shield Solutions LLC ... D ... 866 662-4477
4315 Santa Ana St Ontario (91761) ***(P-10070)***
Star Stainless Screw Co ... F ... 510 489-6569
30150 Ahern Ave Union City (94587) ***(P-11073)***

Mergent e-mail: customerrelations@mergent.com
1248
2020 California
Manufacturers Register
(P-0000) Products & Services Section entry number
(PA)=Parent Co (HQ)=Headquarters (DH)=Div Headquarters

ALPHABETIC SECTION **Steven Varrati**

Star Tool & Engineering Co Inc — E 510 742-0500
49235 Milmont Dr Fremont (94538) ***(P-16422)***

Star-Kist, Carson *Also called Big Heart Pet Brands* ***(P-759)***

Star-Luck Enterprise Inc — F 661 665-9999
11807 Harrington St Bakersfield (93311) ***(P-20943)***

Starco Enterprises Inc (PA) — D 323 266-7111
3137 E 26th St Vernon (90058) ***(P-14539)***

Stardust Diamond Corp — F 213 239-9999
550 S Hill St Ste 1420 Los Angeles (90013) ***(P-22601)***

Starix Technology Inc — E 949 387-8120
9120 Irvine Center Dr # 200 Irvine (92618) ***(P-17670)***

Stark Awning & Canvas, Chula Vista *Also called Stark Mfg Co* ***(P-3707)***

Stark Mfg Co — E 619 425-5880
76 Broadway Chula Vista (91910) ***(P-3707)***

Starled Inc — F 310 603-0403
2059 E Del Amo Blvd Rancho Dominguez (90220) ***(P-19092)***

Starlineoem Inc — F 949 342-8889
3183 Airway Ave Ste 112f Costa Mesa (92626) ***(P-16577)***

Starlion Inc — E 323 233-8823
706 E 32nd St Los Angeles (90011) ***(P-2994)***

Starmont Winery, Saint Helena *Also called Merryvale Vineyards LLC* ***(P-1817)***

Starr Design Fabrics Inc — F 530 467-5121
440 Pig Aly Etna (96027) ***(P-2860)***

Starscroll, Los Angeles *Also called Twelve Signs Inc* ***(P-6045)***

Starview Inc — E 406 890-5910
2841 Junction Ave Ste 110 San Jose (95134) ***(P-24452)***

Stason Pharmaceuticals Inc (PA) — E 949 380-0752
11 Morgan Irvine (92618) ***(P-8144)***

Stat Clinical Systems Inc — F 510 705-8700
2560 9th St Ste 317 Berkeley (94710) ***(P-24453)***

Stat Systems, Berkeley *Also called Stat Clinical Systems Inc* ***(P-24453)***

State Hornet — D 916 278-6583
6000 J St Sacramento (95819) ***(P-5841)***

State Pipe & Supply Inc — E 909 356-5670
2180 N Locust Ave Rialto (92377) ***(P-11074)***

State Ready Mix Inc — E 805 647-2817
3127 Los Angeles Ave Oxnard (93036) ***(P-10844)***

State Ready Mix Inc (PA) — E 805 647-2817
1011 Azahar St Ste 1 Ventura (93004) ***(P-10845)***

Statek Corporation (HQ) — D 714 639-7810
512 N Main St Orange (92868) ***(P-19093)***

Stateside Merchants LLC — F 424 251-5190
5813 Washington Blvd Culver City (90232) ***(P-3000)***

Statewide Distributors, Ontario *Also called USA Sales Inc* ***(P-2657)***

Statewide Safety & Signs Inc — E 707 825-6927
40 S G St Arcata (95521) ***(P-23217)***

Statewide Safety and Signs I — B 714 468-1919
522 Lindon Ln Nipomo (93444) ***(P-17764)***

Stats Chippac Inc (HQ) — E 510 979-8000
46429 Landing Pkwy Fremont (94538) ***(P-18579)***

Stats Chippac Test Svcs Inc — E 858 228-4084
9710 Scranton Rd Ste 360 San Diego (92121) ***(P-18580)***

Stats Chippac Test Svcs Inc (HQ) — F 510 979-8000
46429 Landing Pkwy Fremont (94538) ***(P-18581)***

Status Collection & Co Inc — F 310 432-7788
8383 Wilshire Blvd # 112 Beverly Hills (90211) ***(P-22574)***

Stauber Prfmce Ingredients (HQ) — C 714 441-3900
4120 N Palm St Fullerton (92835) ***(P-7695)***

Stavatti Industries Ltd — D 651 238-5369
1443 S Gage St San Bernardino (92408) ***(P-8)***

Stci, Rancho Cucamonga *Also called Superior Tank Co Inc* ***(P-12061)***

Steady Clothing Inc — F 714 444-2058
1711 Newport Cir Santa Ana (92705) ***(P-3118)***

Steadymed Therapeutics Inc — F 925 361-7111
2603 Camino Ramon Ste 350 San Ramon (94583) ***(P-8145)***

Stealth Security Inc — F 844 978-3258
100 S Murphy Ave Ste 300 Sunnyvale (94086) ***(P-24454)***

Stearns Corporation — E 805 582-2710
2130 Ward Ave Simi Valley (93065) ***(P-8588)***

Stearns Park — E 562 570-1685
4520 E 23rd St Long Beach (90815) ***(P-4873)***

Stearns Product Dev Corp (PA) — D 951 657-0379
20281 Harvill Ave Perris (92570) ***(P-14862)***

Stec Inc (HQ) — B 415 222-9996
3355 Michelson Dr Ste 100 Irvine (92612) ***(P-15104)***

Stecher Enterprises Inc — F 714 484-6900
8536 Central Ave Stanton (90680) ***(P-13389)***

Steecon Inc — F 714 895-5313
5362 Indl Dr Huntington Beach (92649) ***(P-20237)***

Steel Products International, Los Angeles *Also called Precision Steel Products Inc* ***(P-12339)***

Steel Services Co, Vernon *Also called S S Schaffer Co Inc* ***(P-13948)***

Steel Structures Inc — E 559 673-8021
28777 Avenue 15 1/2 Madera (93638) ***(P-12057)***

Steel Unlimited Inc — D 909 873-1222
3200 Myers St Riverside (92503) ***(P-12058)***

Steel Works Etc, Newbury Park *Also called Millworks Etc Inc* ***(P-11972)***

Steelcase Inc — B 415 865-0261
111 Rhode Island St San Francisco (94103) ***(P-4849)***

Steelclad Inc — E 714 529-0277
2664 Saturn St Ste A Brea (92821) ***(P-267)***

Steelco USA, Chino *Also called West Coast Steel & Proc LLC* ***(P-11175)***

Steelcraft West — F 909 548-2696
14575 Yorba Ave Chino (91710) ***(P-22590)***

Steeldeck Inc — E 323 290-2100
13147 S Western Ave Gardena (90249) ***(P-23485)***

Steeldyne Industries — E 714 630-6200
2871 E La Cresta Ave Anaheim (92806) ***(P-12388)***

Steele Wines Inc — E 707 279-9475
4350 Thomas Dr Kelseyville (95451) ***(P-1929)***

Steeler Inc — F 916 483-3600
2901 Orange Grove Ave North Highlands (95660) ***(P-12389)***

Steelscape Inc — F 909 987-4711
11200 Arrow Rte Rancho Cucamonga (91730) ***(P-13254)***

Steico Industries Inc — C 760 438-8015
1814 Ord Way Oceanside (92056) ***(P-12877)***

Stein Industries Inc (PA) — E 714 522-4560
4005 Artesia Ave Fullerton (92833) ***(P-12390)***

Steinbeck Brewing Company — D 510 888-0695
1082 B St Hayward (94541) ***(P-1566)***

Steiner & Mateer Inc — E 562 464-9082
8333 Secura Way Santa Fe Springs (90670) ***(P-4129)***

Steinhausen Inc — F 661 702-1400
28478 Westinghouse Pl Valencia (91355) ***(P-22602)***

Steiny & Company, Corona *Also called Computer Service Company* ***(P-17721)***

Stell Industries Inc — E 951 369-8777
1477 Davril Cir Corona (92880) ***(P-12575)***

Stella Carakasi, Berkeley *Also called Two Star Dog Inc* ***(P-3257)***

Stella Cheese, Tulare *Also called Saputo Cheese USA Inc* ***(P-574)***

Stella Fashions Inc — E 213 746-6889
1015 Crocker St Ste Q04 Los Angeles (90021) ***(P-3416)***

Stellar Biotechnologies Inc — F 805 488-2147
332 E Scott St Port Hueneme (93041) ***(P-8146)***

Stellar Exploration Inc — F 805 459-1425
835 Airport Dr San Luis Obispo (93401) ***(P-20456)***

Stellarvue — F 530 823-7796
11820 Kemper Rd Auburn (95603) ***(P-21412)***

Stem Inc (PA) — D 415 937-7836
100 Rollins Rd Millbrae (94030) ***(P-21128)***

Stem Consultants Inc — F 612 987-8008
651 W Terrylynn Pl Long Beach (90807) ***(P-20975)***

Stemrad Inc — F 650 933-3377
228 Hamilton Ave Fl 3 Palo Alto (94301) ***(P-22091)***

Stencil Master Inc — F 408 428-9695
780 Charcot Ave San Jose (95131) ***(P-22955)***

Step Mobile Inc — F 203 913-9229
2765 Sand Hill Rd Ste 201 Menlo Park (94025) ***(P-24455)***

Step Tools Unlimited Inc — F 408 988-8898
3233 De La Cruz Blvd C Santa Clara (95054) ***(P-14199)***

Stepan Company — E 714 776-9870
1208 N Patt St Anaheim (92801) ***(P-7615)***

Steps Mobile Inc — F 408 806-5178
231 3rd St 1 Davis (95616) ***(P-24456)***

Stepstone Inc (PA) — E 310 327-7474
17025 S Main St Gardena (90248) ***(P-10656)***

Stepstone Inc — E 310 327-7474
13238 S Figueroa St Los Angeles (90061) ***(P-10657)***

Steril-Aire Inc — E 818 565-1128
2840 N Lima St Burbank (91504) ***(P-17163)***

Steripax Inc — E 714 892-8811
5412 Research Dr Huntington Beach (92649) ***(P-5341)***

Steris Corporation — F 800 614-6789
324 Martin Ave Santa Clara (95050) ***(P-22092)***

Steris Corporation — D 858 586-1166
9020 Activity Rd Ste D San Diego (92126) ***(P-19414)***

Sterisyn Inc — E 805 991-9694
11969 Challenger Ct Moorpark (93021) ***(P-8147)***

Sterling Foods, Union City *Also called Caravan Trading Company* ***(P-1175)***

Sterling Pacific Meat Co., Commerce *Also called Interstate Meat Co Inc* ***(P-14375)***

Sterling Shutters, Costa Mesa *Also called Pinecraft Custom Shutters Inc* ***(P-4109)***

Sterling Vineyards Inc (PA) — E 707 942-3300
1111 Dunaweal Ln Calistoga (94515) ***(P-1930)***

Sterling Vineyards Inc — E 707 252-7410
1105 Oak Knoll Ave NAPA (94558) ***(P-1931)***

Sterling Vineyards Inc — F 707 942-9602
3690 Santa Lina Hwy Calistoga (94515) ***(P-1932)***

Sterno Candle Lamp, Corona *Also called Sterno Group Companies LLC* ***(P-15586)***

Sterno Group Companies LLC (HQ) — E 951 682-9600
1880 Compton Ave Ste 101 Corona (92881) ***(P-15586)***

Sterno Group LLC (HQ) — E 800 669-6699
1880 Compton Ave Ste 101 Corona (92881) ***(P-15587)***

Steve and Cynthia Kizanis — F 510 352-2832
2483 Washington Ave San Leandro (94577) ***(P-4250)***

Steve Bruner — E 707 744-1103
81 Hwy 175 Hopland (95449) ***(P-4130)***

Steve Leshner Clear Systems — F 818 764-9223
13438 Wyandotte St North Hollywood (91605) ***(P-10071)***

Steve Morris — F 707 822-8537
1500 Glendale Dr McKinleyville (95519) ***(P-3910)***

Steve Morris Logging & Contg, McKinleyville *Also called Steve Morris* ***(P-3910)***

Steve Rock & Ready Mix — F 916 966-1600
5044 Osgood Way Fair Oaks (95628) ***(P-10846)***

Steve Zappetini & Son Inc — E 415 454-2511
885 Penny Royal Ln San Rafael (94903) ***(P-12511)***

Steven Handelman Studios (PA) — E 805 884-9070
716 N Milpas St Santa Barbara (93103) ***(P-11151)***

Steven Kent LLC — E 925 243-6442
5443 Tesla Rd Livermore (94550) ***(P-1933)***

Steven Label Corporation — F 562 906-2612
9046 Sorensen Ave Santa Fe Springs (90670) ***(P-7227)***

Steven Label Corporation — F 562 698-9971
11926 Burke St Santa Fe Springs (90670) ***(P-7228)***

Steven Madden Ltd — D 909 393-7575
6725 Kimball Ave Chino (91708) ***(P-10162)***

Steven Rhoades Ceramic Designs — F 949 250-1076
17595 Harvard Ave Ste C Irvine (92614) ***(P-10493)***

Steven Varrati — F 209 545-0107
5237 American Ave Modesto (95356) ***(P-16423)***

ALPHABETIC

Employee Codes: A=Over 500 employees, B=251-500
C=101-250, D=51-100, E=20-50, F=10-19

2020 California
Manfacturers Register

© Mergent Inc. 1-800-342-5647
1249

Stevens, M Dancewear & Design, Los Angeles *Also called M Stevens Inc (P-3365)*
Steves Plating Corporation..........C.......818 842-2184
3111 N San Fernando Blvd Burbank (91504) **(P-5003)**
Steward Terra Inc..........E.......619 713-0028
4323 Palm Ave La Mesa (91941) **(P-16578)**
Stewart & Jasper Marketing Inc (PA)..........C.......209 862-9600
3500 Shiells Rd Newman (95360) **(P-1439)**
Stewart & Jasper Orchards, Newman *Also called Stewart & Jasper Marketing Inc (P-1439)*
Stewart Audio (HQ)..........F.......209 588-8111
100 W El Camino Real # 72 Mountain View (94040) **(P-19094)**
Stewart Filmscreen Corp (PA)..........C.......310 326-1422
1161 Sepulveda Blvd Torrance (90502) **(P-22458)**
Stewart Tool Company..........D.......916 635-8321
3647 Omec Cir Rancho Cordova (95742) **(P-14200)**
Stewart/Walker Company, Tracy *Also called Consolidated Container Co LLC (P-9721)*
Stg Machine, Santa Clara *Also called James Stout (P-16076)*
Stic-Adhesive Products Co Inc..........C.......323 268-2956
3950 Medford St Los Angeles (90063) **(P-8895)**
Sticker City, Sherman Oaks *Also called Vpro Inc (P-23240)*
Sticker Hub Inc..........F.......714 912-8457
1452 Manhattan Ave Fullerton (92831) **(P-7229)**
Stiers Rv Centers LLC..........F.......661 254-6000
25410 The Old Rd Santa Clarita (91381) **(P-20522)**
Stigtec Manufacturing LLC..........F.......760 744-7239
1125 Linda Vista Dr # 110 San Marcos (92078) **(P-16424)**
Stiles Custom Metal Inc..........D.......209 538-3667
1885 Kinser Rd Ceres (95307) **(P-11985)**
Stiles Paint Manufacturing Inc..........F.......510 887-8868
21595 Curtis St Hayward (94545) **(P-8683)**
Stines Machine Inc..........E.......760 599-9955
2481 Coral St Vista (92081) **(P-16425)**
Stinger Solar Kits, San Diego *Also called Maddox Defense Inc (P-3848)*
Stingray Shields Corporation..........F.......619 325-9003
850 Beech St Unit 302 San Diego (92101) **(P-22093)**
Stir..........F.......626 657-0918
2210 Lincoln Ave Pasadena (91103) **(P-19415)**
Stir Foods LLC..........E.......714 871-9231
1820 E Walnut Ave Fullerton (92831) **(P-981)**
Stir Foods LLC (HQ)..........C.......714 637-6050
1581 N Main St Orange (92867) **(P-982)**
Stirworks Inc..........E.......800 657-2427
2010 Lincoln Ave Pasadena (91103) **(P-10253)**
Stitch and Hide LLC..........F.......310 377-6912
4 Bowie Rd Rolling Hills (90274) **(P-10143)**
Stitch City Industries Inc (PA)..........F.......562 408-6144
11823 Slauson Ave Ste 31 Santa Fe Springs (90670) **(P-14293)**
Stitch Factory..........F.......310 523-3337
120 W 131st St Los Angeles (90061) **(P-3758)**
Stitch Industries Inc..........E.......888 282-0842
6055 E Wash Blvd Ste 900 Commerce (90040) **(P-4672)**
Stitch Service, Los Angeles *Also called Stitch Factory (P-3758)*
Stj Orthotic Services Inc..........E.......951 279-5650
225 Benjamin Dr Ste 103 Corona (92879) **(P-22094)**
Stl Fabrication Inc..........F.......909 823-5033
10207 Elm Ave Fontana (92335) **(P-11886)**
Stm Networks Inc..........E.......949 273-6800
2 Faraday Irvine (92618) **(P-17671)**
Stm Wireless, Irvine *Also called Stm Networks Inc (P-17671)*
Stmicroelectronics Inc..........E.......949 347-0717
85 Enterprise Ste 300 Aliso Viejo (92656) **(P-18582)**
Sto-Kar Enterprises..........E.......818 886-5600
1112 Arroyo St Ste 2 San Fernando (91340) **(P-11887)**
Stockon Mailing & Printing..........F.......209 466-6741
4133 Postal Ave Stockton (95204) **(P-6871)**
Stockton Propeller Inc..........F.......209 982-4000
2478 Wilcox Rd Stockton (95215) **(P-20238)**
Stockton Rubber Mfgcoinc..........E.......209 887-1172
5023 N Flood Rd Linden (95236) **(P-9374)**
Stockton Tri-Industries Inc..........D.......209 948-9701
2141 E Anderson St Stockton (95205) **(P-13838)**
Stokes Ladders Inc..........F.......707 279-4306
4545 Renfro Dr Kelseyville (95451) **(P-13548)**
Stoll Metalcraft Inc..........C.......661 295-0401
24808 Anza Dr Valencia (91355) **(P-12391)**
Stolo Cabinets Inc (PA)..........E.......714 529-7303
860 Challenger St Brea (92821) **(P-4822)**
Stolo Custom Cabinets, Brea *Also called Stolo Cabinets Inc (P-4822)*
Stolpman Vineyards LLC (PA)..........F.......805 736-5000
2434 Alamo Pintado Rd Los Olivos (93441) **(P-1934)**
Stolpman Vineyards LLC..........E.......805 736-5000
1700 Industrial Way B Lompoc (93436) **(P-1935)**
Stone Boat Yard Inc..........F.......510 523-3030
2517 Blanding Ave Alameda (94501) **(P-20358)**
Stone Bridge Cellars Inc (PA)..........D.......707 963-2745
200 Taplin Rd Saint Helena (94574) **(P-1936)**
Stone Candles, Santa Monica *Also called Ecolight Inc (P-23321)*
Stone Canyon Industries LLC (PA)..........D.......310 570-4869
1875 Century Park E # 320 Los Angeles (90067) **(P-10072)**
Stone Edge Farm, Sonoma *Also called Stone Edge Winery LLC (P-1937)*
Stone Edge Winery LLC..........F.......707 935-6520
19330 Carriger Rd Sonoma (95476) **(P-1937)**
Stone Impressions, San Diego *Also called Photostone LLC (P-14337)*
Stone Manufacturing Company, Gardena *Also called Tomorrows Heirlooms Inc (P-11636)*
Stone Merchants LLC..........D.......310 471-1815
889 Linda Flora Dr Los Angeles (90049) **(P-10934)**
Stone Publishing Inc (PA)..........C.......408 450-7910
2549 Scott Blvd Santa Clara (95050) **(P-7230)**
Stone Truss Inc (PA)..........F.......760 967-6171
507 Jones Rd Oceanside (92058) **(P-4320)**
Stone Valley Materials LLC..........F.......951 681-7830
3500b Pyrite St Riverside (92509) **(P-361)**
Stone Yard Inc..........E.......858 586-1580
6056 Corte Del Cedro Carlsbad (92011) **(P-4774)**
Stonecrop Technologies LLC..........E.......781 659-0007
103 H St Ste B Petaluma (94952) **(P-17672)**
Stonecushion Inc (PA)..........E.......707 433-1911
1400 Lytton Springs Rd Healdsburg (95448) **(P-1938)**
Stoneware Design Co..........F.......562 432-8145
5332 Polis Dr La Palma (90623) **(P-10494)**
Stoneybrook Publishing Inc..........E.......858 674-4600
10815 Rncho Brnrdo Rd Ste San Diego (92127) **(P-6149)**
Stony Apparel Corp (PA)..........C.......323 981-9080
1500 S Evergreen Ave Los Angeles (90023) **(P-3417)**
Stony Point Rock Quarry Inc (PA)..........F.......707 795-1775
7171 Stony Point Rd Cotati (94931) **(P-362)**
Stop Look Plastics Inc, La Habra *Also called Stop-Look Sign Co Intl Inc (P-23218)*
Stop Staring Designs..........E.......213 627-1480
1151 Goodrick Dr Tehachapi (93561) **(P-3253)**
Stop-Look Sign Co Intl Inc..........F.......562 690-7576
401 Commercial Way La Habra (90631) **(P-23218)**
Storm Industries Inc (PA)..........D.......310 534-5232
23223 Normandie Ave Torrance (90501) **(P-13673)**
Storm Manufacturing, Torrance *Also called FCkingston Co (P-13305)*
Storm Manufacturing Group Inc..........D.......310 326-8287
23201 Normandie Ave Torrance (90501) **(P-13323)**
Storm8 Inc..........F.......650 596-8600
2400 Bridge Pkwy 2 Redwood City (94065) **(P-24457)**
Storm8 Entertainment, Redwood City *Also called Storm8 Inc (P-24457)*
Stormpath, San Mateo *Also called Okta Inc (P-24223)*
Storopack Inc..........E.......408 435-1537
2210 Junction Ave San Jose (95131) **(P-9422)**
Storus Corporation (PA)..........F.......925 322-8700
3266 Buskirk Ave Pleasant Hill (94523) **(P-11633)**
Stoughton Printing Co..........E.......626 961-3678
130 N Sunset Ave City of Industry (91744) **(P-6872)**
Stracon Inc..........F.......949 851-2288
1672 Kaiser Ave Ste 1 Irvine (92614) **(P-19416)**
Strada Wheels Inc..........F.......626 336-1634
560 S Magnolia Ave Ontario (91762) **(P-11075)**
Strafford Intl Group Inc..........F.......619 446-6960
877 Island Ave Unit 704 San Diego (92101) **(P-5004)**
Strahmcolor..........F.......415 459-5409
3000 Kerner Blvd San Rafael (94901) **(P-6873)**
Straight Down Clothing Co, San Luis Obispo *Also called Straight Down Sportswear (P-3119)*
Straight Down Sportswear (PA)..........E.......805 543-3086
625 Clarion Ct San Luis Obispo (93401) **(P-3119)**
Straightline Mechanical Inc..........F.......714 204-0940
1051 E 6th St Santa Ana (92701) **(P-13364)**
Strand Art Company Inc..........E.......714 777-0444
4700 E Hunter Ave Anaheim (92807) **(P-10073)**
Strand Products Inc..........E.......805 568-0304
721 E Yanonali St Santa Barbara (93103) **(P-2916)**
Strand Products Inc (PA)..........E.......805 568-0304
725 E Yanonali St Santa Barbara (93103) **(P-22316)**
Strat Edge, Santee *Also called Stratedge Corporation (P-18584)*
Strata Forest Products Inc (PA)..........D.......714 751-0800
2600 S Susan St Santa Ana (92704) **(P-3962)**
Strata Technologies..........E.......714 368-9785
1800 Irvine Blvd Ste 205 Tustin (92780) **(P-16803)**
Stratamet Inc..........E.......510 651-7176
46009 Hotchkiss St Fremont (94539) **(P-18583)**
Stratamet Advanced Mtls Corp..........F.......510 440-1697
2718 Prune Ave Fremont (94539) **(P-10452)**
Stratasys Direct Inc (HQ)..........C.......661 295-4400
28309 Avenue Crocker Valencia (91355) **(P-10074)**
Stratasys Direct Manufacturing, Valencia *Also called Stratasys Direct Inc (P-10074)*
Stratedge Corporation..........E.......866 424-4962
9424 Abraham Way Ste A Santee (92071) **(P-18584)**
Strategic Distribution L P..........C.......818 671-2100
9800 De Soto Ave Chatsworth (91311) **(P-3055)**
Strategic Info Group Inc..........E.......760 697-1050
1953 San Elijo Ave # 201 Cardiff By The Sea (92007) **(P-24458)**
Strategic Insights Inc..........D.......858 452-7500
9191 Towne Centre Dr # 401 San Diego (92122) **(P-24459)**
Strategic Medical Ventures LLC (PA)..........E.......949 355-5212
280 Newport Center Dr Newport Beach (92660) **(P-22222)**
Strategic Partners Inc (PA)..........C.......818 671-2100
9800 De Soto Ave Chatsworth (91311) **(P-10163)**
Strategic Prtg Solution Inc..........F.......562 242-5880
3731 San Gabriel River Pk Pico Rivera (90660) **(P-7231)**
Strategy Companion Corp..........D.......714 460-8398
3240 El Camino Real # 120 Irvine (92602) **(P-24460)**
Strathmore Ladder, Strathmore *Also called Michael D Wilson Inc (P-13534)*
Stratoflex Product Division, Camarillo *Also called Parker-Hannifin Corporation (P-20198)*
Stratoflight (HQ)..........D.......949 622-0700
25540 Rye Canyon Rd Valencia (91355) **(P-20239)**
Stratos Renewables Corporation..........E.......310 402-5901
9440 Santa Monica Blvd Beverly Hills (90210) **(P-8778)**
Stratus Coml Cooking Eqp Inc..........F.......626 969-7041
1760 W 1st St Irwindale (91702) **(P-12878)**
Straus Family Creamery Inc..........D.......707 776-2887
1105 Industrial Ave # 200 Petaluma (94952) **(P-539)**
Strauss Karl Brewery and Rest..........E.......858 551-2739
1044 Wall St Ste C La Jolla (92037) **(P-1567)**
Streak Technology Inc..........F.......408 206-2373
43575 Mission Blvd 614 Fremont (94539) **(P-22716)**
Streamline Avionics Inc..........E.......949 861-8151
17672 Armstrong Ave Irvine (92614) **(P-16579)**

Streamline Development LLC ....E 415 499-3355
100 Smith Ranch Rd # 124 San Rafael (94903) ***(P-24461)***

Streamline Dsign Slkscreen Inc ....F 805 884-1025
1328 N Ventura Ave Ventura (93001) ***(P-7232)***

Streamline Dsign Slkscreen Inc (PA) ....D 805 884-1025
1299 S Wells Rd Ventura (93004) ***(P-3120)***

Streamline Electronics Mfg Inc ....E 408 263-3600
4285 Technology Dr Fremont (94538) ***(P-18012)***

Streamline Solutions, San Rafael *Also called Streamline Development LLC* ***(P-24461)***

Street Glow Inc ....D 310 631-1881
2710 E El Presidio St Carson (90810) ***(P-17094)***

Street Graphics Inc ....E 209 948-1713
1834 W Euclid Ave Stockton (95204) ***(P-23219)***

Streeter Printing ....E 858 278-6611
13865 Sagewood Dr Ste C Poway (92064) ***(P-6874)***

Streeter Printing Inc ....F 858 566-0866
9880 Via Pasar Ste C San Diego (92126) ***(P-6875)***

Streets Ahead Inc ....E 323 277-0860
5510 S Soto St Unit B Vernon (90058) ***(P-3533)***

Streetwise Reports LLC ....E 707 981-8999
755 Baywood Dr Fl 2 Petaluma (94954) ***(P-6348)***

Streivor Inc ....F 925 960-9090
2150 Kitty Hawk Rd Livermore (94551) ***(P-22591)***

Streivor Air Systems, Livermore *Also called Streivor Inc* ***(P-22591)***

Stremicks Heritage Foods LLC (HQ) ....B 714 775-5000
4002 Westminster Ave Santa Ana (92703) ***(P-711)***

Stremicks Heritage Foods LLC ....D 951 352-1344
11503 Pierce St Riverside (92505) ***(P-668)***

Strenumed Inc ....F 805 477-1000
4864 Market St Ste D Ventura (93003) ***(P-22095)***

Stressteel Inc ....F 888 284-8752
47375 Fremont Blvd Fremont (94538) ***(P-11076)***

Stretch Inc ....D 408 543-2700
48720 Kato Rd Fremont (94538) ***(P-18585)***

Stretch Art, Gardena *Also called AR-Ce Inc* ***(P-22939)***

Stretch Film Center, Santa Fe Springs *Also called Our Powder Coating Inc* ***(P-13216)***

Stretch Forming Corporation ....C 951 443-0911
804 S Redlands Ave Perris (92570) ***(P-12392)***

Stretch-Run Inc ....F 925 606-1599
6621 Brisa St Livermore (94550) ***(P-11888)***

Streuter Technologies ....E 949 369-7630
208 Avenida Fabricante # 200 San Clemente (92672) ***(P-10658)***

Strevus Inc ....D 415 704-8182
455 Market St Ste 1670 San Francisco (94105) ***(P-24462)***

Strike Technology Inc ....E 562 437-3428
24311 Wilmington Ave Carson (90745) ***(P-19095)***

String Letter Publishing Inc ....E 510 215-0010
941 Marina Way S Ste E Richmond (94804) ***(P-6349)***

Stroppini Enterprises ....F 916 635-8181
2546 Mercantile Dr Ste A Rancho Cordova (95742) ***(P-13893)***

Structural Composites Inds LLC (HQ) ....E 909 594-7777
336 Enterprise Pl Pomona (91768) ***(P-12059)***

Structural Diagnostics Inc ....E 805 987-7755
650 Via Alondra Camarillo (93012) ***(P-21129)***

Structural Wood Systems ....F 760 375-2772
505 San Bernardino Blvd Ridgecrest (93555) ***(P-4321)***

Structurecast ....D 661 833-4490
8261 Mccutchen Rd Bakersfield (93311) ***(P-10659)***

Structures Unlimited ....F 951 688-6300
7671 Arlington Ave Riverside (92503) ***(P-11682)***

Stryder Corp (PA) ....E 415 981-8400
225 Bush St Fl 12 San Francisco (94104) ***(P-24463)***

Stryker Corporation ....E 510 413-2500
47900 Bayside Pkwy Fremont (94538) ***(P-21916)***

Stryker Corporation ....E 714 764-1700
3407 E La Palma Ave Anaheim (92806) ***(P-21917)***

Stryker Enterprises Inc ....E 408 295-6300
1358 E San Fernando St San Jose (95116) ***(P-13549)***

Stryker Neurovascular, Fremont *Also called Stryker Corporation* ***(P-21916)***

STS, Tehachapi *Also called Sierra Technical Services Inc* ***(P-11168)***

STS Instruments Inc ....F 580 223-4773
17711 Mitchell N Irvine (92614) ***(P-21130)***

Stuart Cellars LLC ....F 951 676-6414
41006 Simi Ct Temecula (92591) ***(P-1939)***

Stuart David Inc (PA) ....E 209 537-7449
3419 Railroad Ave Ceres (95307) ***(P-4612)***

Stuart's Fine Furniture, Ceres *Also called Stuart David Inc* ***(P-4612)***

Stuart-Dean Co Inc ....F 714 544-4460
14731 Franklin Ave Ste L Tustin (92780) ***(P-13109)***

Stud Welding Systems Inc ....E 626 330-7434
15306 Proctor Ave City of Industry (91745) ***(P-12695)***

Student Sports ....F 310 791-1142
23954 Madison St Torrance (90505) ***(P-2881)***

Studer Creative Packaging Inc ....F 818 344-1665
5652 Mountain View Ave Yorba Linda (92886) ***(P-10075)***

Studex, Gardena *Also called Quadrtech Corporation* ***(P-11542)***

Studio 311 Inc ....F 707 795-6599
466 Primero Ct Ste E Cotati (94931) ***(P-22575)***

Studio Krp LLC ....F 310 589-5777
6133 Bonsall Dr Malibu (90265) ***(P-3254)***

Studio OH, Irvine *Also called Orange Circle Studio Corp* ***(P-7159)***

Studio Systems Inc (PA) ....E 323 634-3400
5700 Wilshire Blvd # 600 Los Angeles (90036) ***(P-6350)***

Studio Two Black Diamond Prtg, Laguna Hills *Also called Benjamin Lewis Inc* ***(P-6441)***

Studio Two Graphics and Prtg, Laguna Hills *Also called Studio Two Printing Inc* ***(P-6876)***

Studio Two Printing Inc ....E 949 859-5119
23042 Alcalde Dr Ste C Laguna Hills (92653) ***(P-6876)***

Studio9d8 Inc ....E 626 350-0832
9743 Alesia St South El Monte (91733) ***(P-2803)***

Stumbleupon Inc (HQ) ....E 415 979-0640
535 Mission St Fl 11 San Francisco (94105) ***(P-24464)***

Sturdy Gun Safe Manufactruing ....F 559 485-8361
2030 S Sarah St Fresno (93721) ***(P-13550)***

Sturdy Safe, Fresno *Also called Sturdy Gun Safe Manufactruing* ***(P-13550)***

Stutz Packing Company ....F 760 342-1666
82689 Avenue 45 Indio (92201) ***(P-864)***

Stutzman Plating, Los Angeles *Also called Virgil M Stutzman Inc* ***(P-13128)***

Style Knits Inc ....D 323 890-9080
1745 Chapin Rd Montebello (90640) ***(P-2804)***

Style Media Group Inc ....E 916 988-9888
120 Blue Ravine Rd Ste 5 Folsom (95630) ***(P-6033)***

Style Plus Inc (PA) ....F 213 205-8408
2807 S Olive St Los Angeles (90007) ***(P-3195)***

Style Up America Inc ....F 213 553-1134
2600 E 8th St Los Angeles (90023) ***(P-22899)***

Styrotek Inc ....C 661 725-4957
345 Road 176 Delano (93215) ***(P-9570)***

Su Mano Inc ....F 562 529-8835
536 Milton Dr San Gabriel (91775) ***(P-10144)***

Sub-One Technology Inc ....F 925 924-1020
161 S Vasco Rd Ste L Livermore (94551) ***(P-13255)***

Suba Mfg Inc ....E 707 745-0358
921 Bayshore Rd Benicia (94510) ***(P-4942)***

Suba Technology Inc ....E 408 434-6500
46501 Landing Pkwy Fremont (94538) ***(P-18013)***

Subco, Fresno *Also called Subdirect LLC* ***(P-6034)***

Subdirect LLC (PA) ....F 559 321-0449
653 W Fallbrook Ave # 101 Fresno (93711) ***(P-6034)***

Sublime Machining Inc ....E 858 349-2445
2537 Willow St Oakland (94607) ***(P-23486)***

Submersible Systems Inc ....F 714 842-6566
7413 Slater Ave Huntington Beach (92647) ***(P-22900)***

Subsidy of Be Aerospace, Fullerton *Also called ADB Industries* ***(P-11429)***

Substance Abuse Program ....E 951 791-3350
1370 S State St Ste A Hemet (92543) ***(P-18586)***

Suburban Steel Inc (PA) ....E 559 268-6281
706 W California Ave Fresno (93706) ***(P-11889)***

Sue Wong, Los Angeles *Also called S Studio Inc* ***(P-3276)***

Suez Wts Services Usa Inc ....C 408 360-5900
5900 Silver Creek Vly Rd San Jose (95138) ***(P-15588)***

Suez Wts Services Usa Inc ....D 562 942-2200
7777 Industry Ave Pico Rivera (90660) ***(P-15589)***

Suez Wts Services Usa Inc ....F 951 681-5555
11689 Pacific Ave Fontana (92337) ***(P-15590)***

Suez Wts Usa Inc ....E 661 393-3035
3050 Pegasus Dr Bakersfield (93308) ***(P-9027)***

Sugar Bowl Bakery, Hayward *Also called Ly Brothers Corporation* ***(P-1238)***

Sugar Bowl Bakery, Hayward *Also called Ly Brothers Corporation* ***(P-1239)***

Sugar Foods Corporation ....D 323 727-8290
6190 E Slauson Ave Commerce (90040) ***(P-1279)***

Sugared + Bronzed LLC ....D 747 264-0477
13033 Ventura Blvd Studio City (91604) ***(P-3459)***

Sugarloaf Farming Corporation ....E 707 942-4459
12400 Ida Clayton Rd Calistoga (94515) ***(P-1940)***

Sugarsync Inc ....E 650 571-5105
6922 Hollywood Blvd # 500 Los Angeles (90028) ***(P-24465)***

Suheung-America Corporation (HQ) ....F 714 854-9882
428 Saturn St Brea (92821) ***(P-8148)***

Sui Companies, Riverside *Also called Steel Unlimited Inc* ***(P-12058)***

Suitable Technologies Inc (PA) ....F 650 294-3170
921 E Charleston Rd Palo Alto (94303) ***(P-14282)***

Sukarne, City of Industry *Also called Viz Cattle Corporation* ***(P-430)***

Sullins Connector Solutions, San Marcos *Also called Sullins Electronics Corp* ***(P-16926)***

Sullins Electronics Corp (PA) ....E 760 744-0125
801 E Mission Rd B San Marcos (92069) ***(P-16926)***

Sullivan & Brampton, San Leandro *Also called Brampton Mthesen Fabr Pdts Inc* ***(P-3674)***

Sullivan Counter Tops Inc ....E 510 652-2337
1189 65th St Oakland (94608) ***(P-4943)***

Sulzer Bingham Pumps, Santa Fe Springs *Also called Sulzer Pump Services (us) Inc* ***(P-24669)***

Sulzer Electro-Mechanical Serv ....E 909 825-7971
620 S Rancho Ave Colton (92324) ***(P-24697)***

Sulzer Pump Services (us) Inc ....E 562 903-1000
9856 Jordan Cir Santa Fe Springs (90670) ***(P-24669)***

Sulzer Pump Solutions US Inc ....E 916 925-8508
1650 Bell Ave Ste 140 Sacramento (95838) ***(P-14599)***

Sumas Media, City of Industry *Also called Solar Region Inc* ***(P-14977)***

Sumbody Union Street LLC ....E 707 823-4043
118 N Main St Sebastopol (95472) ***(P-8589)***

Sumco Phoenix Corporation ....D 408 352-3880
2099 Gateway Pl Ste 400 San Jose (95110) ***(P-18587)***

Sumi Office Services, Carson *Also called Sumi Printing & Binding Inc* ***(P-6877)***

Sumi Printing & Binding Inc ....F 310 769-1600
1139 E Janis St Carson (90746) ***(P-6877)***

Sumicom-Usa ....F 408 385-2046
1729 Little Orchard St San Jose (95125) ***(P-14980)***

Sumitomo Electric Interconn ....D 760 761-0600
915 Armorlite Dr San Marcos (92069) ***(P-9375)***

Sumitronics USA Inc ....E 619 661-0450
9335 Airway Rd Ste 203c San Diego (92154) ***(P-18014)***

Summer Rio Corp (PA) ....E 626 854-1498
17501 Rowland St City of Industry (91748) ***(P-9185)***

Summertree Interiors Inc ....F 951 549-0590
4111 Buchanan St Riverside (92503) ***(P-4613)***

Summit Electric & Data Inc ....E 661 775-9901
28338 Constellation Rd # 920 Valencia (91355) ***(P-19417)***

Summit Forest Products, Cerritos *Also called J Summitt Inc* ***(P-4062)***

ALPHABETIC

Employee Codes: A=Over 500 employees, B=251-500
C=101-250, D=51-100, E=20-50, F=10-19
2020 California
Manfacturers Register
© Mergent Inc. 1-800-342-5647
1251

Summit Furniture Inc (PA).....F.....831 375-7811
5 Harris Ct Bldg W Monterey (93940) ***(P-4614)***
Summit Industries Inc.....E.....951 739-5900
1280 Graphite Dr Corona (92881) ***(P-11890)***
Summit Interconnect Inc (PA).....C.....714 239-2433
220 N Crescent Way Ste B Anaheim (92801) ***(P-18015)***
Summit Interconnect Inc.....C.....408 727-1418
1401 Martin Ave Santa Clara (95050) ***(P-18016)***
Summit Interconnect - Anaheim, Anaheim *Also called Kca Electronics Inc* ***(P-17910)***
Summit Interconnect Orange, Orange *Also called Fabricated Components Corp* ***(P-17873)***
Summit International Packg Inc.....D.....626 333-3333
30200 Cartier Dr Rancho Palos Verdes (90275) ***(P-5342)***
Summit Machine LLC.....C.....909 923-2744
2880 E Philadelphia St Ontario (91761) ***(P-16426)***
Summit Services Inc.....F.....760 737-7630
1430 Valle Grande Escondido (92025) ***(P-10521)***
Summit Window Products Inc.....D.....408 526-1600
6336 Patterson Pass Rd F Livermore (94550) ***(P-4131)***
Summit Wireless Tech Inc.....E.....408 627-4716
6840 Via Del Oro Ste 280 San Jose (95119) ***(P-18588)***
Sumopti.....F.....650 331-1126
742 Moreno Ave Palo Alto (94303) ***(P-24466)***
Sun & Sun Industries Inc.....D.....714 210-5141
2101 S Yale St Santa Ana (92704) ***(P-17073)***
Sun Badge Co.....E.....909 930-1444
2248 S Baker Ave Ontario (91761) ***(P-23487)***
Sun Basket Inc.....D.....408 669-4418
1 Clarence Pl Unit 14 San Francisco (94107) ***(P-2618)***
Sun Chemical Corporation.....F.....925 695-2601
120 Mason Cir Concord (94520) ***(P-8931)***
Sun Chemical Corporation.....E.....562 946-2327
12963 Park St Santa Fe Springs (90670) ***(P-8932)***
Sun Chemical Corporation.....E.....510 618-1302
1599 Factor Ave San Leandro (94577) ***(P-8933)***
Sun Coast Calamari Inc.....C.....805 385-0056
928 E 3rd St Oxnard (93030) ***(P-2271)***
Sun Company San Bernardino Cal (PA).....B.....909 889-9666
4030 Georgia Blvd San Bernardino (92407) ***(P-5842)***
Sun Company San Bernardino Cal.....C.....909 889-9666
290 N D St Ste 100 San Bernardino (92401) ***(P-9073)***
Sun Dairy, Los Angeles *Also called Pac Fill Inc* ***(P-706)***
Sun Deep Cosmetics, Hayward *Also called Sun Deep Inc* ***(P-8590)***
Sun Deep Inc.....E.....510 441-2525
31285 San Clemente St B Hayward (94544) ***(P-8590)***
Sun Dog International, Fullerton *Also called Sun Trade Group Inc* ***(P-2806)***
Sun Dyeing and Finishing Co.....F.....310 329-0844
15621 Broadway Center St Gardena (90248) ***(P-2805)***
Sun Frost, Arcata *Also called Larry Schlussler* ***(P-16820)***
Sun Glo Foods, Fullerton *Also called Khyber Foods Incorporated* ***(P-2498)***
Sun Ice USA, Riverside *Also called Mackie International Inc* ***(P-655)***
Sun Marble Inc.....E.....510 783-9900
1300 Norman Ave Santa Clara (95054) ***(P-10935)***
Sun Marble/Home Express, Santa Clara *Also called Sun Marble Inc* ***(P-10935)***
Sun Microsystems, Santa Clara *Also called Oracle America Inc* ***(P-24238)***
Sun Microsystems, Redwood City *Also called Oracle America Inc* ***(P-14959)***
Sun Microsystems, Rocklin *Also called Oracle America Inc* ***(P-24239)***
Sun Microsystems, Pleasanton *Also called Oracle America Inc* ***(P-24243)***
Sun Microsystems, Encino *Also called Oracle America Inc* ***(P-24244)***
Sun Microsystems, San Diego *Also called Oracle America Inc* ***(P-24245)***
Sun Microsystems, Ontario *Also called Oracle America Inc* ***(P-24246)***
Sun Microsystems, Santa Clara *Also called Oracle America Inc* ***(P-24247)***
Sun Microsystems Tech Ltd.....E.....650 960-1300
4150 Network Cir Santa Clara (95054) ***(P-24467)***
Sun Mountain Inc.....E.....415 852-2320
2 Henry Adams St Ste 150 San Francisco (94103) ***(P-4132)***
Sun Plastics Inc.....E.....323 888-6999
7140 E Slauson Ave Commerce (90040) ***(P-5422)***
Sun Power Security Gates Inc.....F.....209 722-3990
438 Tyler Rd Merced (95341) ***(P-11110)***
Sun Power Source (PA).....F.....805 644-2520
1650 Palma Dr Ventura (93003) ***(P-17164)***
Sun Precision Machining Inc.....F.....951 817-0056
1651 Market St Ste A Corona (92880) ***(P-16427)***
Sun Reporter Newspaper, San Francisco *Also called Sun Reporter Publishing Inc* ***(P-5843)***
Sun Reporter Publishing Inc.....F.....415 671-1000
1286 Fillmore St San Francisco (94115) ***(P-5843)***
Sun Rich Foods Intl Corp.....F.....714 632-7577
1240 N Barsten Way Anaheim (92806) ***(P-2619)***
Sun Sheet Metal, San Diego *Also called Monaco Sheet Metal* ***(P-12309)***
Sun Sheetmetal Solutions Inc.....E.....408 445-8047
3565 Charter Park Dr San Jose (95136) ***(P-12393)***
Sun Stone Sales, Temecula *Also called Sunstone Components Group Inc* ***(P-12879)***
Sun Trade Group Inc (PA).....F.....714 525-4888
1251 Burton St Fullerton (92831) ***(P-2806)***
Sun Tropics Inc.....F.....925 202-2221
2420 Camino Ramon Ste 101 San Ramon (94583) ***(P-929)***
Sun Valley Extrusion, Los Angeles *Also called Sun Valley Products Inc* ***(P-11246)***
Sun Valley Floral Group LLC.....A.....707 826-8700
3160 Upper Bay Rd Arcata (95521) ***(P-23488)***
Sun Valley Ltg Standards Inc.....B.....661 233-2000
660 W Avenue O Palmdale (93551) ***(P-17074)***
Sun Valley Products Inc.....E.....818 247-8350
4640 Sperry St Los Angeles (90039) ***(P-11246)***
Sun Valley Products Inc (HQ).....D.....818 247-8350
4626 Sperry St Los Angeles (90039) ***(P-11247)***
Sun Valley Rice Company LLC.....D.....530 476-3000
7050 Eddy Rd Arbuckle (95912) ***(P-1051)***
Sun Valley Rock and Asphalt, Sun Valley *Also called Legacy Vulcan LLC* ***(P-10792)***
Sun Valley Skylights Inc.....F.....818 686-0032
12884 Pierce St Pacoima (91331) ***(P-10276)***
Sun Vlley Rsins Inc A Cal Corp.....F.....559 233-8070
9595 S Hughes Ave Fresno (93706) ***(P-865)***
Sun Vlly Skylghts Plus Windws, Pacoima *Also called Sun Valley Skylights Inc* ***(P-10276)***
Sun, The, San Bernardino *Also called Sun Company San Bernardino Cal* ***(P-9073)***
Sun-Gro Commodities Inc (PA).....E.....661 393-2612
34575 Famoso Rd Bakersfield (93308) ***(P-1130)***
Sun-Mate Corp.....F.....818 700-0572
19730 Ventura Blvd Ste 18 Woodland Hills (91364) ***(P-22717)***
Sunar Rf Motion Inc.....F.....925 833-9936
6780 Sierra Ct Ste R Dublin (94568) ***(P-17673)***
Sunbeam Trailer Products Inc.....E.....714 373-5000
5312 Production Dr Huntington Beach (92649) ***(P-17095)***
Sunbio Inc.....E.....925 876-0439
57 Claremont Ave Orinda (94563) ***(P-8149)***
Sunbritetv LLC.....E.....805 214-7250
2630 Townsgate Rd Ste F Westlake Village (91361) ***(P-17674)***
Sunburst Products Inc.....E.....949 722-0158
1570 Corporate Dr Ste F Costa Mesa (92626) ***(P-22484)***
Suncore Inc.....E.....949 450-0054
3200 El Camino Real # 100 Irvine (92602) ***(P-18589)***
Sundance Spas, Chino Hills *Also called Jacuzzi Brands LLC* ***(P-23370)***
Sundance Spas Inc (HQ).....D.....909 606-7733
13925 City Center Dr # 200 Chino Hills (91709) ***(P-23489)***
Sundance Uniform & Embroidery.....F.....530 676-6900
4050 Durock Rd Ste 13 Shingle Springs (95682) ***(P-3759)***
Sundance Uniforms & Embroidery, Shingle Springs *Also called Sundance Uniform & Embroidery* ***(P-3759)***
Sunday Brunch, San Rafael *Also called San Francisco Network* ***(P-3447)***
Sunderstorm LLC.....F.....818 605-6682
1146 N Central Ave Glendale (91202) ***(P-23490)***
Sundial Industries Inc.....E.....818 767-4477
8421 Telfair Ave Sun Valley (91352) ***(P-13256)***
Sundial Orchrds Hulling Drying.....E.....530 846-6155
1500 Kirk Rd Gridley (95948) ***(P-1440)***
Sundial Powder Coatings Inc.....E.....818 767-4477
8421 Telfair Ave Sun Valley (91352) ***(P-13257)***
Sundown Foods USA Inc.....E.....909 606-6797
10891 Business Dr Fontana (92337) ***(P-826)***
Sundown Liquidating Corp (PA).....C.....714 540-8950
401 Goetz Ave Santa Ana (92707) ***(P-10277)***
Sundry Clothing, Los Angeles *Also called Sunnyside Llc* ***(P-3449)***
Sunearth Inc.....E.....909 434-3100
8425 Almeria Ave Fontana (92335) ***(P-11720)***
Sunesis Pharmaceuticals Inc (PA).....E.....650 266-3500
395 Oyster Point Blvd # 400 South San Francisco (94080) ***(P-8150)***
Suneva Medical Inc (PA).....E.....858 550-9999
5870 Pacific Center Blvd San Diego (92121) ***(P-8591)***
Sunex Inc.....F.....760 597-2966
3160 Lionshead Ave Ste 2 Carlsbad (92010) ***(P-21413)***
Suneye, Sebastopol *Also called Solmetric Corporation* ***(P-21545)***
Sunflower Imports Inc.....F.....213 748-3444
412 W Pico Blvd Los Angeles (90015) ***(P-3121)***
Sunfoods LLC.....F.....530 661-1923
194 W Main St Ste 200 Woodland (95695) ***(P-1052)***
Sunfusion Energy Systems Inc.....E.....800 544-0282
9020 Kenamar Dr Ste 204 San Diego (92121) ***(P-23491)***
Sungear Inc.....E.....858 549-3166
8535 Arjons Dr Ste G San Diego (92126) ***(P-20240)***
Sunland Aerospace Fasteners.....F.....818 485-8929
12920 Pierce St Pacoima (91331) ***(P-12696)***
Sunland Tool Inc.....F.....714 974-6500
1819 N Case St Orange (92865) ***(P-16428)***
Sunline Energy Inc.....E.....858 997-2408
7546 Trade St San Diego (92121) ***(P-18590)***
Sunny America & Global Autotec.....D.....714 544-0400
2681 Dow Ave Ste A Tustin (92780) ***(P-19774)***
Sunny Delight Beverages Co.....C.....714 630-6251
1230 N Tustin Ave Anaheim (92807) ***(P-827)***
Sunny Products Inc.....F.....909 923-4128
1989 S Campus Ave Ontario (91761) ***(P-7318)***
Sunnygem LLC.....B.....661 758-0491
500 N F St Wasco (93280) ***(P-828)***
Sunnyside Llc.....F.....213 745-3070
3763 S Hill St Los Angeles (90007) ***(P-3449)***
Sunnytech.....F.....408 943-8100
2243 Ringwood Ave San Jose (95131) ***(P-18017)***
Sunnyvalley Smoked Meats Inc.....C.....209 825-0288
2475 W Yosemite Ave Manteca (95337) ***(P-501)***
Sunon Inc (PA).....E.....714 255-0208
1075 W Lambert Rd Ste A Brea (92821) ***(P-14680)***
Sunopta Food Solutions, Scotts Valley *Also called Sunopta Glbal Orgnic Ing Inc* ***(P-901)***
Sunopta Glbal Orgnic Ing Inc (HQ).....E.....831 685-6506
100 Enterprise Way Ste B1 Scotts Valley (95066) ***(P-901)***
Sunopta Grains and Foods Inc.....D.....323 774-6000
12128 Center St South Gate (90280) ***(P-2620)***
Sunoptics Prismatic Skylights, Sacramento *Also called Washoe Equipment Inc* ***(P-17000)***
Sunpower Corporation (HQ).....A.....408 240-5500
51 Rio Robles San Jose (95134) ***(P-18591)***
Sunpower USA, Union City *Also called Aei Electech Corp* ***(P-18811)***
Sunpreme Inc.....E.....408 419-9281
4701 Patrick Henry Dr # 25 Santa Clara (95054) ***(P-18592)***
Sunrise Bakery.....F.....209 632-9400
1561 Geer Rd Turlock (95380) ***(P-1280)***
Sunrise Bakery and Cafe, Turlock *Also called Sunrise Bakery* ***(P-1280)***
Sunrise Fresh Dried Fruit Co, Stockton *Also called Sunrise Fresh LLC* ***(P-866)***

Sunrise Fresh LLC ....E....209 932-0192
2716 E Miner Ave Stockton (95205) *(P-866)*
Sunrise Imaging Inc ....F....949 252-3003
1813 E Dyer Rd Ste 410 Santa Ana (92705) *(P-22459)*
Sunrise Jewelry Mfg Corp ....B....619 270-5624
4425 Convoy St Ste 226 San Diego (92111) *(P-22576)*
Sunrise Med HM Hlth Care Group, Chula Vista *Also called Vcp Mobility Holdings Inc (P-22116)*
Sunrise Medical (us) LLC ....D....559 292-2171
2842 N Business Park Ave Fresno (93727) *(P-22096)*
Sunrise Mfg Inc (PA) ....E....916 635-6262
2665 Mercantile Dr Rancho Cordova (95742) *(P-5532)*
Sunrise Pillow Co Inc ....F....626 401-9283
2215 Merced Ave El Monte (91733) *(P-3644)*
Sunrise Shutters, Los Angeles *Also called Sunrise Wood Products Inc (P-4133)*
Sunrise Specialty Company ....F....510 729-7277
61 Skyway Ln Oakland (94619) *(P-11683)*
Sunrise Wood Products Inc ....E....323 971-6540
6701 11th Ave Los Angeles (90043) *(P-4133)*
Suns Out Inc ....F....714 556-2314
2915 Red Hill Ave A210c Costa Mesa (92626) *(P-22718)*
Sunsation Inc ....E....909 542-0280
100 S Cambridge Ave Claremont (91711) *(P-930)*
Sunset Islandwear ....F....310 372-7960
601 Mary Ann Dr Redondo Beach (90278) *(P-2839)*
Sunset Leather Group ....E....310 388-4898
8527 Melrose Ave West Hollywood (90069) *(P-10254)*
Sunset Magazine, Oakland *Also called Sunset Publishing Corporation (P-6035)*
Sunset Moulding Co (PA) ....E....530 790-2700
2231 Paseo Rd Live Oak (95953) *(P-3963)*
Sunset Printing, Gardena *Also called Coast Color Printing Inc (P-6492)*
Sunset Publishing Corporation (HQ) ....C....800 777-0117
55 Harrison St Ste 150 Oakland (94607) *(P-6035)*
Sunset Signs and Printing ....F....714 255-9104
2981 E White Star Ave Anaheim (92806) *(P-23220)*
Sunshine Enterprises, Monterey Park *Also called DHm International Corp (P-3318)*
Sunshine Makers Inc (PA) ....D....562 795-6000
15922 Pacific Coast Hwy Huntington Beach (92649) *(P-8419)*
Sunshine Raisin Corporation (PA) ....C....559 834-5981
626 S 5th St Fowler (93625) *(P-1403)*
Sunsil Inc (PA) ....F....925 648-7779
3174 Danville Blvd Ste 1 Alamo (94507) *(P-18593)*
Sunsports LP ....C....949 273-6202
7 Holland Irvine (92618) *(P-10155)*
Sunstar Spa Covers Inc (HQ) ....E....858 602-1950
26074 Avenue Hall Ste 13 Valencia (91355) *(P-23492)*
Sunstone Components Group Inc (HQ) ....E....951 296-5010
42136 Avenida Alvarado Temecula (92590) *(P-12879)*
Sunstream Technology Inc ....D....720 502-4446
749 Azure Hills Dr Simi Valley (93065) *(P-11721)*
Sunsweet Dryers ....F....530 824-5854
23760 Loleta Ave Corning (96021) *(P-867)*
Sunsweet Dryers ....D....530 846-5578
26 E Evans Reimer Rd Gridley (95948) *(P-868)*
Sunsweet Dryers Inc ....F....559 673-4140
28390 Avenue 12 Madera (93637) *(P-869)*
Sunsweet Growers Inc (PA) ....A....800 417-2253
901 N Walton Ave Yuba City (95993) *(P-870)*
Sunsystem Technology LLC ....B....510 984-2027
2802 10th St Berkeley (94710) *(P-18594)*
Suntech America Inc (PA) ....F....415 882-9922
2721 Shattuck Ave Berkeley (94705) *(P-11722)*
Suntech Power, Berkeley *Also called Suntech America Inc (P-11722)*
Suntile Inc ....F....949 489-8990
32951 Calle Perfecto San Juan Capistrano (92675) *(P-10453)*
Suntsu Electronics Inc ....E....949 783-7300
142 Technology Dr Ste 150 Irvine (92618) *(P-19096)*
Sunvair Inc (HQ) ....D....661 294-3777
29145 The Old Rd Valencia (91355) *(P-16429)*
Sunvair Overhaul Inc ....E....661 257-6123
29145 The Old Rd Valencia (91355) *(P-20241)*
Sunwater Solar Inc ....F....650 739-5297
865 Marina Bay Pkwy # 39 Richmond (94804) *(P-11723)*
Sunway Mechanical & Elec Tech ....F....909 673-7959
1650 S Grove Ave Ste A Ontario (91761) *(P-19832)*
Sunwest Printing Inc ....F....909 890-3898
118 E Airport Dr Ste 209 San Bernardino (92408) *(P-7233)*
Sunwood Doors Inc ....E....562 951-9401
21176 S Alameda St Long Beach (90810) *(P-4134)*
Sunworks Inc (PA) ....D....916 409-6900
1030 Winding Creek Rd # 100 Roseville (95678) *(P-18595)*
Sunyeah Group Corp ....E....909 218-8490
930 S Wanamaker Ave Ontario (91761) *(P-10392)*
Super Binge Media Inc ....F....714 688-6231
530 Bush St Ste 600 San Francisco (94108) *(P-24468)*
Super Chef, Redwood City *Also called American Production Co Inc (P-11492)*
Super Color Digital LLC (PA) ....E....949 622-0010
16761 Hale Ave Irvine (92606) *(P-7234)*
Super Glue Corporation, Ontario *Also called Pacer Technology (P-8883)*
Super Glue Corporation ....F....909 987-0550
4970 Vanderbilt St Ontario (91761) *(P-8896)*
Super Micro Computer Inc (PA) ....A....408 503-8000
980 Rock Ave San Jose (95131) *(P-14981)*
Super Store Industries ....D....209 668-2100
2600 Spengler Way Turlock (95380) *(P-669)*
Super Vias & Trim ....F....323 233-2556
3651 S Main St E Los Angeles (90007) *(P-3818)*
Super Welding Southern Cal Inc ....E....619 239-8003
609 Anita St Chula Vista (91911) *(P-14256)*
Super-Fit Inc ....F....657 218-4827
1031 S Linwood Ave Santa Ana (92705) *(P-22097)*
Super73 Inc ....E....949 313-6340
16591 Noyes Ave Irvine (92606) *(P-20427)*
Superb Chair Corporation ....E....562 776-1771
6861 Watcher St Commerce (90040) *(P-4673)*
Supercloset ....E....831 588-7829
3555 Airway Dr Santa Rosa (95403) *(P-11547)*
Superfish Inc ....F....650 752-6564
2595 E Byshore Rd Ste 150 Palo Alto (94303) *(P-20944)*
Superform USA Incorporated ....E....951 351-4100
6825 Jurupa Ave Riverside (92504) *(P-12737)*
Superheat Fgh Services Inc ....F....925 808-6711
1333 Willow Pass Rd Concord (94520) *(P-11469)*
Superior Automation Inc ....F....408 227-4898
47770 Westinghouse Dr Fremont (94539) *(P-14540)*
Superior Awning Inc ....E....818 780-7200
14555 Titus St Panorama City (91402) *(P-3708)*
Superior Bias Trims, Vernon *Also called SJ&I Bias Binding & Tex Co Inc (P-3814)*
Superior Coffee & Foods, Santa Fe Springs *Also called Hillshire Brands Company (P-466)*
Superior Connector Plating Inc ....E....714 774-1174
1901 E Cerritos Ave Anaheim (92805) *(P-13110)*
Superior Dairy Products Co ....E....559 582-0481
325 N Douty St Hanford (93230) *(P-670)*
Superior Duct Fabrication Inc ....C....909 620-8565
1683 Mount Vernon Ave Pomona (91768) *(P-12394)*
Superior Electric Mtr Svc Inc ....F....323 583-1040
4622 Alcoa Ave Vernon (90058) *(P-24698)*
Superior Electrical Advg (PA) ....D....562 495-3808
1700 W Anaheim St Long Beach (90813) *(P-23221)*
Superior Electrical Advg ....F....209 334-3337
125 Houston Ln Lodi (95240) *(P-23222)*
Superior Emblem & Embroidery ....E....213 747-4103
2601 S Hill St Los Angeles (90007) *(P-3760)*
Superior Equipment Solutions ....D....323 722-7900
1085 Bixby Dr Hacienda Heights (91745) *(P-16817)*
Superior Essex Inc ....F....909 481-4804
5250 Ontario Mills Pkwy # 300 Ontario (91764) *(P-11321)*
Superior Farms, Vernon *Also called Transhumance Holding Co Inc (P-504)*
Superior Farms, Dixon *Also called Transhumance Holding Co Inc (P-426)*
Superior Farms, Sacramento *Also called Ellensburg Lamb Company Inc (P-407)*
Superior Filtration Pdts LLC ....F....951 681-1700
3401 Etiwanda Ave 811b Jurupa Valley (91752) *(P-14681)*
Superior Foam Products Inc ....F....760 722-1585
394 Via El Centro Oceanside (92058) *(P-22901)*
Superior Food Machinery Inc ....E....562 949-0396
8311 Sorensen Ave Santa Fe Springs (90670) *(P-14404)*
Superior Graphic Packaging Inc ....D....323 263-8400
3055 Bandini Blvd Vernon (90058) *(P-6878)*
Superior Grounding Systems ....E....626 814-1981
16021 Arrow Hwy Ste A Baldwin Park (91706) *(P-16927)*
Superior Honey Company, San Bernardino *Also called Millers American Honey Inc (P-2551)*
Superior Inds Intl Hldings LLC (HQ) ....E....818 781-4973
7800 Woodley Ave Van Nuys (91406) *(P-19775)*
Superior Jig Inc ....E....714 525-4777
1540 N Orangethorpe Way Anaheim (92801) *(P-14107)*
Superior Lithographics, Vernon *Also called Superior Graphic Packaging Inc (P-6878)*
Superior Manufacturing, Bell *Also called Alfred Picon (P-4962)*
Superior Metal Fabricators ....F....951 360-2474
4768 Felspar St Riverside (92509) *(P-12395)*
Superior Metal Finishing Inc ....F....310 464-8010
1733 W 134th St Gardena (90249) *(P-13111)*
Superior Metal Shapes Inc ....E....909 947-3455
4730 Eucalyptus Ave Chino (91710) *(P-11248)*
Superior Metals Inc ....F....408 938-3488
838 Jury Ct Ste B San Jose (95112) *(P-12396)*
Superior Millwork of Sb Inc ....E....805 685-1744
7330 Hollister Ave Ste B Goleta (93117) *(P-4251)*
Superior Mold Co Inc ....E....909 947-7028
1927 E Francis St Ontario (91761) *(P-10076)*
Superior Packing Co, Dixon *Also called Ellensburg Lamb Company Inc (P-406)*
Superior Pipe Fabricators Inc ....F....323 569-6500
10211 S Alameda St Los Angeles (90002) *(P-11891)*
Superior Plating, Anaheim *Also called Superior Connector Plating Inc (P-13110)*
Superior Plating Inc ....E....818 252-1088
9001 Glenoaks Blvd Sun Valley (91352) *(P-13112)*
Superior Press, Santa Fe Springs *Also called Superior Printing Inc (P-7235)*
Superior Printing Inc ....D....888 590-7998
9440 Norwalk Blvd Santa Fe Springs (90670) *(P-7235)*
Superior Processing ....F....714 524-8525
1115 Las Brisas Pl Placentia (92870) *(P-13113)*
Superior Quartz Inc ....F....408 844-9663
3370 Edward Ave Santa Clara (95054) *(P-11195)*
Superior Radiant Insul Inc ....F....909 305-1450
175 Principia Ct Claremont (91711) *(P-5533)*
Superior Ready Mix Concrete LP ....E....619 265-0955
7192 Mission Gorge Rd San Diego (92120) *(P-10847)*
Superior Ready Mix Concrete LP ....E....619 265-0296
7500 Mission Gorge Rd San Diego (92120) *(P-10848)*
Superior Ready Mix Concrete LP ....E....760 352-4341
802 E Main St El Centro (92243) *(P-10849)*
Superior Ready Mix Concrete LP ....F....760 728-1128
1508 W Mission St Escondido (92029) *(P-10850)*
Superior Ready Mix Concrete LP ....E....951 277-3553
24635 Temescal Canyon Rd Corona (92883) *(P-10851)*
Superior Ready Mix Concrete LP (PA) ....E....760 745-0556
1508 Mission Rd Escondido (92029) *(P-10852)*
Superior Ready Mix Concrete LP ....E....951 658-9225
1130 N State St Hemet (92543) *(P-10853)*

ALPHABETIC

Employee Codes: A=Over 500 employees, B=251-500
C=101-250, D=51-100, E=20-50, F=10-19
2020 California
Manfacturers Register
© Mergent Inc. 1-800-342-5647
1253

Superior Ready Mix Concrete LP ....E.....619 443-7510
12494 Highway 67 Lakeside (92040) ***(P-10854)***
Superior Ready Mix Concrete LP ....E.....760 343-3418
72270 Varner Rd Thousand Palms (92276) ***(P-10855)***
Superior Sheet Metal, Anaheim *Also called Campbell & Loftin Inc* ***(P-12149)***
Superior Sndblst & Coating ....F.....909 428-9994
8315 Beech Ave Fontana (92335) ***(P-8684)***
Superior Software Inc ....F.....818 990-1135
16055 Ventura Blvd # 650 Encino (91436) ***(P-24469)***
Superior Sound Technology LLC ....F.....707 863-7431
707 Vintage Ave Suisun City (94534) ***(P-22098)***
Superior Spring Company ....E.....714 490-0881
1260 S Talt Ave Anaheim (92806) ***(P-13390)***
Superior Stone Products Inc ....F.....714 635-7775
923 E Arlee Pl Anaheim (92805) ***(P-10936)***
Superior Storage Tank Inc ....F.....714 226-1914
14700 Industry Cir La Mirada (90638) ***(P-12060)***
Superior Tank Co Inc (PA) ....E.....909 912-0580
9500 Lucas Ranch Rd Rancho Cucamonga (91730) ***(P-12061)***
Superior Tbeppe Bnding Fbrctn, Hayward *Also called Superior Tube Pipe Bnding Fbco* ***(P-13486)***
Superior Tech Inc ....F.....909 364-2300
13850 Benson Ave Chino (91710) ***(P-11136)***
Superior Technologies, Chino *Also called Superior Tech Inc* ***(P-11136)***
Superior Trailer Works ....E.....909 350-0185
13700 Slover Ave Fontana (92337) ***(P-13894)***
Superior Tube Pipe Bnding Fbco ....E.....510 782-9311
2407 Industrial Pkwy W Hayward (94545) ***(P-13486)***
Superior Window Coverings Inc ....E.....818 762-6685
7683 N San Fernando Rd Burbank (91505) ***(P-3598)***
Superior-Studio Spc Inc ....E.....323 278-0100
2239 Yates Ave Commerce (90040) ***(P-23493)***
Superlamb Inc ....F.....858 566-2031
8026 Miramar Rd San Diego (92126) ***(P-3523)***
Supermedia LLC ....B.....209 472-6011
1215 W Center St Ste 102 Manteca (95337) ***(P-6351)***
Supermedia LLC ....B.....909 390-5000
3401 Centre Lake Dr # 500 Ontario (91761) ***(P-6352)***
Supermedia LLC ....B.....626 331-9440
1270 E Garvey St Covina (91724) ***(P-6353)***
Supermedia LLC ....B.....562 594-5101
3131 Katella Ave Los Alamitos (90720) ***(P-6354)***
Supermedia LLC ....B.....916 782-6866
1200 Melody Ln Ste 100 Roseville (95678) ***(P-6355)***
Supernova Spirits Inc ....E.....415 819-3154
10288 Richwood Dr Cupertino (95014) ***(P-2019)***
Supernutrition, Pacifica *Also called Forever Young* ***(P-2462)***
Supernutrition ....E.....510 446-7980
3034 Jordan Rd Oakland (94602) ***(P-8151)***
Superprint Lithographics Inc ....F.....562 698-8001
8332 Secura Way Santa Fe Springs (90670) ***(P-6879)***
Supersonic ADS Inc ....E.....650 825-6010
17 Bluxome St San Francisco (94107) ***(P-23223)***
Supersprings International ....F.....805 745-5553
505 Maple St Carpinteria (93013) ***(P-13343)***
Supertec Machinery Inc ....F.....562 220-1675
6435 Alondra Blvd Paramount (90723) ***(P-13954)***
Supertex Inc (HQ) ....D.....408 222-8888
1235 Bordeaux Dr Sunnyvale (94089) ***(P-18596)***
Supervision Eyewear Suppliers, Beverly Hills *Also called H Silani & Associates Inc* ***(P-21358)***
Supplier Diversity Program, Carlsbad *Also called Life Technologies Corporation* ***(P-8313)***
Support Equipment, Escondido *Also called C & H Machine Inc* ***(P-15620)***
Support Systems Intl Corp ....D.....510 234-9090
136 S 2nd St Dept B Richmond (94804) ***(P-19097)***
Support Technologies Inc ....F.....949 442-2957
1939 Deere Ave Irvine (92606) ***(P-24470)***
Supportcom Inc ....F.....516 393-6759
1200 Crossman Ave Ste 240 Sunnyvale (94089) ***(P-24471)***
Supportpay, Sacramento *Also called Ittavi Inc* ***(P-24051)***
Suppress Fire Atmtc Sprinklers ....F.....714 671-5939
363 Cliffwood Park St G Brea (92821) ***(P-14863)***
Supreme Abrasives ....F.....949 250-8644
1021 Fuller St Santa Ana (92701) ***(P-10955)***
Supreme Bindery, Gardena *Also called Investment Land Appraisers* ***(P-7334)***
Supreme Corporation ....C.....951 656-6101
22135 Alessandro Blvd Moreno Valley (92553) ***(P-19559)***
Supreme Enterprise, Santa Fe Springs *Also called Kingsolver Inc* ***(P-23028)***
Supreme Graphics Inc ....F.....310 531-8300
3403 Jack Northrop Ave Hawthorne (90250) ***(P-6880)***
Supreme Machine Products Inc ....F.....909 974-0349
302 Sequoia Ave Ontario (91761) ***(P-16430)***
Supreme Steel Treating Inc ....E.....626 350-5865
2466 Seaman Ave El Monte (91733) ***(P-11470)***
Supreme Truck Body, Moreno Valley *Also called Supreme Corporation* ***(P-19559)***
Surco Products Inc ....F.....310 323-2520
14001 S Main St Los Angeles (90061) ***(P-12512)***
Sure Guard Socal ....F.....714 556-5497
11702 Anabel Ave Garden Grove (92843) ***(P-4135)***
Sure Guard Windows, Garden Grove *Also called Sure Guard Socal* ***(P-4135)***
Sure Inc ....F.....833 787-3462
1404 Granvia Altamira Palos Verdes Estates (90274) ***(P-21918)***
Sure Power Inc ....E.....310 542-8561
1111 Knox St Torrance (90502) ***(P-19098)***
Surecall, Fremont *Also called Cellphone-Mate Inc* ***(P-17484)***
Surefire LLC ....D.....714 545-9444
17680 Newhope St Ste B Fountain Valley (92708) ***(P-22099)***
Surefire LLC ....E.....714 545-9444
17760 Newhope St Ste A Fountain Valley (92708) ***(P-22100)***
Surefire LLC ....E.....714 641-0483
2110 S Anne St Santa Ana (92704) ***(P-22101)***
Surefire LLC ....E.....714 545-9444
18300 Mount Baldy Cir Fountain Valley (92708) ***(P-17165)***
Surefire LLC ....E.....714 545-9444
2121 S Yale St Santa Ana (92704) ***(P-22102)***
Surefire LLC ....D.....714 641-0483
2300 S Yale St Santa Ana (92704) ***(P-22103)***
Surefire LLC (PA) ....C.....714 545-9444
18300 Mount Baldy Cir Fountain Valley (92708) ***(P-22104)***
Suregrip International Co ....D.....562 923-0724
5519 Rawlings Ave South Gate (90280) ***(P-22902)***
Suretouch, Palos Verdes Estates *Also called Sure Inc* ***(P-21918)***
Surf City Garage ....E.....714 894-1707
5872 Engineer Dr Huntington Beach (92649) ***(P-8420)***
Surf More Products Inc ....E.....949 492-0753
250 Calle Pintoresco San Clemente (92672) ***(P-22903)***
Surf Ride ....F.....760 433-4020
1609 Ord Way Oceanside (92056) ***(P-3122)***
Surf To Summit Inc ....F.....805 964-1896
7234 Hollister Ave Goleta (93117) ***(P-22904)***
Surface Art Engineering Inc ....E.....408 433-4700
81 Bonaventura Dr San Jose (95134) ***(P-18597)***
Surface Engineering Spc ....E.....408 734-8810
919 Hamlin Ct Sunnyvale (94089) ***(P-14294)***
Surface Manufacturing Inc ....F.....530 885-0700
2025 Airpark Ct Ste 10 Auburn (95602) ***(P-16431)***
Surface Mdfication Systems Inc ....F.....562 946-7472
12917 Park St Santa Fe Springs (90670) ***(P-13258)***
Surface Mount Tech Centre ....B.....408 935-9548
431 Kato Ter Fremont (94539) ***(P-15341)***
Surface Optics Corp ....E.....858 675-7404
11555 Rancho Bernardo Rd San Diego (92127) ***(P-21131)***
Surface Techniques Corporation (PA) ....E.....510 887-6000
25673 Nickel Pl Hayward (94545) ***(P-4944)***
Surface Technologies Corp ....E.....619 564-8320
3170 Commercial St San Diego (92113) ***(P-16758)***
Surface Technology, Hayward *Also called Surface Techniques Corporation* ***(P-4944)***
Surfaces Tile Craft Inc ....F.....818 609-0719
7900 Andasol Ave Northridge (91325) ***(P-10454)***
Surfacing Solutions Inc ....F.....951 699-0035
27637 Commerce Center Dr Temecula (92590) ***(P-13114)***
Surfside News, Malibu *Also called Malibu Enterprises Inc* ***(P-5718)***
Surfside Prints Inc ....F.....805 620-0052
2686 Johnson Dr Ste D Ventura (93003) ***(P-3819)***
Surfy Surfy ....F.....760 452-7687
974 N Coast Highway 101 Encinitas (92024) ***(P-22905)***
Surgeon Worldwide Inc ....E.....707 501-7962
4000 Broadway Pl Los Angeles (90037) ***(P-10177)***
Surgistar Inc (PA) ....E.....760 598-2480
2310 La Mirada Dr Vista (92081) ***(P-21919)***
Suri Steel Inc ....F.....323 224-3166
5851 Towne Ave Los Angeles (90003) ***(P-11892)***
Surplus Ctys Fbrction Mfg Wldg, Oroville *Also called Direct Surplus Sales Inc* ***(P-12185)***
Surprisesilkcom ....F.....626 568-9889
628 Madre St Pasadena (91107) ***(P-2735)***
Surrounding Elements LLC ....E.....949 582-9000
33051 Calle Aviador Ste A San Juan Capistrano (92675) ***(P-4702)***
Surtec Inc ....E.....209 820-3700
1880 N Macarthur Dr Tracy (95376) ***(P-8421)***
Surtec System , The, Tracy *Also called Surtec Inc* ***(P-8421)***
Survey Stake and Marker Inc ....F.....626 960-4802
13470 Dalewood St Baldwin Park (91706) ***(P-4537)***
Susan Zadi ....F.....424 223-3526
4220 Beverly Blvd Los Angeles (90004) ***(P-2272)***
Suspender Factory Inc ....E.....510 547-5400
1425 63rd St Emeryville (94608) ***(P-3581)***
Suspender Factory of S F, Emeryville *Also called Suspender Factory Inc* ***(P-3581)***
Suss McRtec Phtnic Systems Inc ....D.....951 817-3700
220 Klug Cir Corona (92880) ***(P-19418)***
Suss McRtec Prcision Photomask ....E.....415 494-3113
821 San Antonio Rd Palo Alto (94303) ***(P-22460)***
Suss Microtec Inc (HQ) ....C.....408 940-0300
220 Klug Cir Corona (92880) ***(P-14541)***
Sust Manufacturing Company ....F.....209 931-9571
2380 Wilcox Rd Stockton (95215) ***(P-16432)***
Sustain Technologies Inc (PA) ....F.....213 229-5300
915 E 1st St Los Angeles (90012) ***(P-19235)***
Sustainable Fibr Solutions LLC (PA) ....F.....949 265-8287
30950 Rancho Viejo Rd San Juan Capistrano (92675) ***(P-5343)***
Susy Clothing Co ....E.....818 500-7879
2256 Hollister Ter Glendale (91206) ***(P-3418)***
Sutherland Presses ....F.....310 453-6981
22561 Carbon Mesa Rd Malibu (90265) ***(P-13995)***
Sutro Biopharma Inc (PA) ....C.....650 392-8412
310 Utah Ave Ste 150 South San Francisco (94080) ***(P-8331)***
Sutter Buttes Olive Oil, Yuba City *Also called California Olive and Vine LLC* ***(P-1467)***
Sutter Gold Mining Company, Sutter Creek *Also called Usecb Joint Venture Inc* ***(P-9)***
Sutter Home Winery Inc (PA) ....C.....707 963-3104
100 Saint Helena Hwy S Saint Helena (94574) ***(P-1941)***
Sutter Home Winery Inc ....C.....707 963-5928
18655 Jacob Brack Rd Lodi (95242) ***(P-1942)***
Sutter Home Winery Inc ....E.....707 963-3104
560 Gateway Dr NAPA (94558) ***(P-1943)***
Sutter P Dahlglen Entps Inc ....F.....408 727-4640
1650 Grant St Santa Clara (95050) ***(P-16433)***
Sutter Printing, Sacramento *Also called Baise Enterprises Inc* ***(P-6434)***

Mergent e-mail: customerrelations@mergent.com
1254
2020 California
Manufacturers Register
(P-0000) Products & Services Section entry number
(PA)=Parent Co (HQ)=Headquarters (DH)=Div Headquarters

Suttini, Oceanside *Also called Secura Inc (P-3051)*
Suttons Forest Products ....F....530 741-2747
8222 Hallwood Blvd Marysville (95901) *(P-23494)*
Sutura Inc ....E....714 427-0398
17080 Newhope St Fountain Valley (92708) *(P-22105)*
Suvolta Inc ....E....408 866-4125
130 Knowles Dr Ste D Los Gatos (95032) *(P-14542)*
Suzhou South ....B....626 322-0101
18351 Colima Rd Ste 82 Rowland Heights (91748) *(P-15379)*
Suzuki Musical Instruments, Santee *Also called Hpf Corporation (P-22626)*
Sv Probe Inc ....D....480 635-4700
6680 Via Del Oro San Jose (95119) *(P-21132)*
Sv Probe Inc ....F....408 653-2387
535 E Brokaw Rd San Jose (95112) *(P-21133)*
Svc Mfg Inc A Corp ....F....510 261-5800
5625 International Blvd Oakland (94621) *(P-2175)*
Sven Design Handbag Outlet, Berkeley *Also called Sven Design Inc (P-10227)*
Sven Design Inc ....F....510 848-7836
2301 4th St Berkeley (94710) *(P-10227)*
Svetwheel LLC ....F....650 245-6080
121 Arundel Rd San Carlos (94070) *(P-21414)*
Svevia Usa Inc ....F....909 559-4134
14567 Rancho Vista Dr Fontana (92335) *(P-22956)*
Svm Machining Inc ....E....510 791-9450
6520 Central Ave Newark (94560) *(P-11893)*
Svp Winery LLC ....F....805 237-8693
111 Clark Rd Shandon (93461) *(P-1944)*
SW Fixtures Inc ....F....909 595-2506
3940 Valley Blvd Ste C Walnut (91789) *(P-4945)*
SW Safety Solutions Inc ....E....510 429-8692
33278 Central Ave Ste 102 Union City (94587) *(P-2820)*
Swa Mountain Gate ....F....530 221-3406
20285 Radcliffe Redding (96003) *(P-363)*
Swaner Hardwood Co Inc (PA) ....D....818 953-5350
5 W Magnolia Blvd Burbank (91502) *(P-4282)*
Swanky Prints LLC ....F....760 407-9265
42309 Winchester Rd Ste D Temecula (92590) *(P-6881)*
Swedcom Corporation ....F....650 348-1190
851 Burlway Rd Ste 300 Burlingame (94010) *(P-17416)*
Sweeneys Ale House, Encino *Also called Lord Leviason Enterprises LLC (P-1544)*
Sweet Earth Inc ....D....831 375-8673
3080 Hilltop Rd Moss Landing (95039) *(P-2621)*
Sweet Earth Natural Foods, Moss Landing *Also called Sweet Earth Inc (P-2621)*
Sweet Girl, Los Angeles *Also called Bd Impotex LLC (P-3218)*
Sweet Inspirations Inc ....E....310 886-9010
17770 Ridgeway Rd Granada Hills (91344) *(P-3255)*
Sweet Lady Jane, San Fernando *Also called Slj Wholesale LLC (P-1278)*
Sweetie Pies LLC ....F....707 257-7280
520 Main St NAPA (94559) *(P-1281)*
Sweetwater Technologies, Temecula *Also called National Sweetwater Inc (P-9008)*
Sweety Novelty Inc ....F....310 533-6010
633 Monterey Pass Rd Monterey Park (91754) *(P-671)*
Swenson Group ....F....650 655-4990
1620 S Amphlett Blvd San Mateo (94402) *(P-22461)*
Swenson Group Inc Xerox, San Mateo *Also called Swenson Group (P-22461)*
Swift Beef Company ....C....951 571-2237
15555 Meridian Pkwy Riverside (92518) *(P-502)*
Swift Fab ....F....310 366-7295
515 E Alondra Blvd Gardena (90248) *(P-12397)*
Swift Health Systems Inc ....E....877 258-8677
111 Academy Ste 150 Irvine (92617) *(P-22191)*
Swift Metal Finishing, Santa Clara *Also called Montoya & Jaramillo Inc (P-13054)*
Swift Navigation Inc (PA) ....E....415 484-9026
650 Townsend St Ste 410 San Francisco (94103) *(P-17675)*
Swift-Cor Precision Inc ....D....310 354-1207
344 W 157th St Gardena (90248) *(P-12398)*
Swiftech, Pico Rivera *Also called Rouchon Industries Inc (P-15324)*
Swiftstack Inc (PA) ....E....415 625-0293
660 Market St Ste 500 San Francisco (94104) *(P-24472)*
Swiftstack Inc ....E....408 642-1865
1054 S De Anza Blvd San Jose (95129) *(P-24473)*
Swim Cap Company , The, Chula Vista *Also called Next Day Printed Tees (P-3803)*
Swimming World Magazine, El Segundo *Also called Sports Publications Inc (P-6032)*
Swimwear ....E....323 584-7536
1961 Hawkins Cir Los Angeles (90001) *(P-3419)*
Swinerton Builders, San Diego *Also called Solv Inc (P-24431)*
Swiss Dairy, City of Industry *Also called Dean Socal LLC (P-697)*
Swiss House, Glendora *Also called Grico Precision Inc (P-16004)*
Swiss Machine Products, Anaheim *Also called Farrell Brothers Holding Corp (P-15952)*
Swiss Pattern Corp ....F....714 545-8040
2611 S Yale St Santa Ana (92704) *(P-14004)*
Swiss Productions Inc ....E....805 654-8379
2801 Golf Course Dr Ventura (93003) *(P-9457)*
Swiss Screw Products Inc ....E....408 748-8400
339 Mathew St Santa Clara (95050) *(P-16434)*
Swiss Wire EDM ....F....714 540-2903
3505 Cadillac Ave Ste J1 Costa Mesa (92626) *(P-16435)*
Swiss-Micron Inc ....D....949 589-0430
22361 Gilberto Ste A Rcho STA Marg (92688) *(P-12652)*
Swiss-Tech Machining LLC ....E....916 797-6010
10564 Industrial Ave Roseville (95678) *(P-12653)*
Swissdigital USA Co Ltd ....F....626 351-1999
11533 Slater Ave Ste H Fountain Valley (92708) *(P-23495)*
Swisstrax LLC ....F....760 347-3330
82579 Fleming Way Ste A Indio (92201) *(P-10455)*
Swm, El Cajon *Also called Delstar Technologies Inc (P-9401)*
Sworn Virgins, Vernon *Also called Ema Textiles Inc (P-2783)*
Syagen Technology LLC ....E....714 258-4400
1251 E Dyer Rd Ste 140 Santa Ana (92705) *(P-21295)*
Syapse Inc ....C....650 924-1461
303 2nd St Ste N500 San Francisco (94107) *(P-24474)*
Syar Industries Inc ....D....707 643-3261
885 Lake Herman Rd Vallejo (94591) *(P-305)*
Sybman Inc ....F....626 579-9911
9911 Gidley St El Monte (91731) *(P-4538)*
Sybron Dental Specialties Inc ....A....650 340-0393
824 Cowan Rd Burlingame (94010) *(P-22192)*
Sybron Dental Specialties Inc ....A....909 596-0276
1332 S Lone Hill Ave Glendora (91740) *(P-22193)*
Sybron Dental Specialties Inc (HQ) ....C....714 516-7400
1717 W Collins Ave Orange (92867) *(P-22194)*
Sybron Endo, Orange *Also called Ormco Corporation (P-22176)*
Sygma Inc ....F....562 906-8880
13168 Flores St Santa Fe Springs (90670) *(P-14201)*
Sylvester Winery Inc ....E....805 227-4000
5115 Buena Vista Dr Paso Robles (93446) *(P-1945)*
Symbol Technologies LLC ....C....510 684-2974
208 Channing Way Alameda (94502) *(P-15342)*
Symbolic Displays Inc ....D....714 258-2811
1917 E Saint Andrew Pl Santa Ana (92705) *(P-20242)*
Symcoat Metal Processing Inc ....E....858 451-3313
7887 Dunbrook Rd Ste C San Diego (92126) *(P-13115)*
Symmetricom Inc ....E....408 433-0910
3870 N 1st St San Jose (95134) *(P-17417)*
Symmetry Electronics LLC (HQ) ....E....310 536-6190
222 N Pacific Coast Hwy El Segundo (90245) *(P-18598)*
Symphonix Devices Inc ....F....408 323-8218
1735 N 1st St San Jose (95112) *(P-22106)*
Symphonyrm Inc ....F....650 336-8430
530 University Ave Palo Alto (94301) *(P-24475)*
Symprotek Co ....E....408 956-0700
950 Yosemite Dr Milpitas (95035) *(P-18018)*
Symrise Inc ....F....949 276-4600
332 Forest Ave Laguna Beach (92651) *(P-2231)*
Synapsense Corporation ....F....916 294-0110
340 Palladio Pkwy Ste 530 Folsom (95630) *(P-15105)*
Synaptics Incorporated ....F....408 904-1100
1109 Mckay Dr San Jose (95131) *(P-15343)*
Synaptics Incorporated (PA) ....B....408 904-1100
1251 Mckay Dr San Jose (95131) *(P-15344)*
Synbiotics LLC ....E....858 451-3771
16420 Via Esprillo San Diego (92127) *(P-8262)*
Synchronized Technologies Inc ....F....213 368-3760
7536 Tyrone Ave Van Nuys (91405) *(P-15345)*
Synchrotech, Van Nuys *Also called Synchronized Technologies Inc (P-15345)*
Synder Inc (PA) ....E....707 451-6060
4941 Allison Pkwy Vacaville (95688) *(P-18746)*
Synder California Container, Chowchilla *Also called Central California Cont Mfg (P-9701)*
Synder Filtration, Vacaville *Also called Synder Inc (P-18746)*
Synectic Packaging Inc ....F....650 474-0132
1201 San Luis Obispo St Hayward (94544) *(P-7236)*
Synergetic Tech Group Inc ....F....909 305-4711
1712 Earhart La Verne (91750) *(P-11634)*
Synergex International Corp ....D....916 635-7300
2355 Gold Meadow Way # 200 Gold River (95670) *(P-24476)*
Synergeyes Inc (PA) ....D....760 476-9410
2236 Rutherford Rd # 115 Carlsbad (92008) *(P-22392)*
Synergistic Research Inc ....F....949 642-2800
1736 E Borchard Ave Santa Ana (92705) *(P-13437)*
Synergy Beverages, Vernon *Also called Gts Living Foods LLC (P-2079)*
Synergy Direct Response, Santa Ana *Also called Cowboy Direct Response (P-23082)*
Synergy Global Inc ....F....415 766-3540
4 Embarcadero Ctr # 1400 San Francisco (94111) *(P-24477)*
Synergy Microsystems Inc (HQ) ....D....858 452-0020
28965 Avenue Penn Valencia (91355) *(P-14982)*
Synergy Oil LLC ....E....888 333-1933
1201 Dove St Ste 475 Newport Beach (92660) *(P-14864)*
Synergy Prosthetics, San Diego *Also called Norell Prsthtics Orthotics Inc (P-22055)*
Syneron Inc (HQ) ....D....866 259-6661
3 Goodyear Ste A Irvine (92618) *(P-22317)*
Syneron Candela, Irvine *Also called Syneron Inc (P-22317)*
Synertech PM Inc ....F....714 898-9151
11711 Monarch St Garden Grove (92841) *(P-11424)*
Synfonia Floors Inc ....F....714 300-0770
1550 S Anaheim Blvd Ste A Anaheim (92805) *(P-3985)*
Synnex Corporation ....F....510 656-3333
6551 W Schulte Rd Ste 100 Tracy (95377) *(P-14983)*
Synopsys Inc (PA) ....B....650 584-5000
690 E Middlefield Rd Mountain View (94043) *(P-24478)*
Synopsys Inc ....D....626 795-9101
199 S Los Robles Ave # 400 Pasadena (91101) *(P-24479)*
Synplicity Inc (HQ) ....C....650 584-5000
690 E Middlefield Rd Mountain View (94043) *(P-24480)*
Syntech Development & Mfg Inc ....E....909 465-5554
13948 Mountain Ave Chino (91710) *(P-10077)*
Syntest Technologies Inc ....F....408 720-9956
4320 Stevens Creek Blvd # 100 San Jose (95129) *(P-24481)*
Synthesis ....E....530 899-7708
210 W 6th St Chico (95928) *(P-6036)*
Synthesys Research Inc (HQ) ....D....408 753-1630
4250 Burton Dr Santa Clara (95054) *(P-21134)*
Synthorx Inc ....E....858 750-4700
11099 N Torrey Pines Rd La Jolla (92037) *(P-8152)*
Syntiant Corp ....F....948 774-4887
7555 Irvine Center Dr Irvine (92618) *(P-18599)*
Syntron Bioresearch Inc ....B....760 930-2200
2774 Loker Ave W Carlsbad (92010) *(P-8263)*

Employee Codes: A=Over 500 employees, B=251-500
C=101-250, D=51-100, E=20-50, F=10-19
2020 California
Manfacturers Register
© Mergent Inc. 1-800-342-5647
1255

Synvasive Technology Inc ... E ... 916 939-3913
4925 R J Mathews Park 1 El Dorado Hills (95762) ***(P-21920)***
Sypris Data Systems Inc (HQ) ... E ... 909 962-9400
160 Via Verde San Dimas (91773) ***(P-15106)***
Sysop Tools Inc ... F ... 310 598-3885
815 Moraga Dr Los Angeles (90049) ***(P-24482)***
Sysparc, Van Nuys *Also called Bijan Rad Inc* ***(P-14434)***
Systech Corporation ... E ... 858 674-6500
10908 Technology Pl San Diego (92127) ***(P-17765)***
System Studies Incorporated (PA) ... E ... 831 475-5777
21340 E Cliff Dr Santa Cruz (95062) ***(P-17418)***
System Studies Incorporated ... E ... 831 475-5777
2900 Research Park Dr Soquel (95073) ***(P-17419)***
System Technical Support Corp ... E ... 310 845-9400
960 Knox St Bldg B Torrance (90502) ***(P-16759)***
Systems Machines Automatio (PA) ... C ... 760 929-7575
5807 Van Allen Way Carlsbad (92008) ***(P-16760)***
Systems Integrated LLC ... E ... 714 998-0900
2200 N Glassell St Ste A Orange (92865) ***(P-21549)***
Systems L C Womack ... F ... 909 593-7304
1615 Yeager Ave La Verne (91750) ***(P-21550)***
Systems Plus Lumber, Anderson *Also called Haisch Construction Co Inc* ***(P-4303)***
Systems Printing Inc ... F ... 714 832-4677
14311 Chambers Rd Tustin (92780) ***(P-7362)***
Systems Technology Inc ... D ... 909 799-9950
1350 Riverview Dr San Bernardino (92408) ***(P-14728)***
Systems Upgrade Inc ... F ... 949 429-8900
806 Avenida Pico Ste I San Clemente (92673) ***(P-15107)***
Systems Wire & Cable Limited ... F ... 310 532-7870
1165 N Stanford Ave Los Angeles (90059) ***(P-13438)***
Systron Donner Inertial, Walnut Creek *Also called Carros Sensors Systems Co LLC* ***(P-18852)***
Systron Donner Inertial Inc ... C ... 925 979-4400
2700 Systron Dr Concord (94518) ***(P-19099)***
T & D Services Inc ... F ... 951 304-1190
42363 Guava St Murrieta (92562) ***(P-106)***
T & F Sheet Metals Fab ... E ... 310 516-8548
15607 New Century Dr Gardena (90248) ***(P-12399)***
T & H Store Fixtures, Commerce *Also called Teichman Enterprises Inc* ***(P-5006)***
T & J Sausage Kitchen, Anaheim *Also called T&J Sausage Kitchen Inc* ***(P-503)***
T & M Machining Inc ... E ... 805 983-6716
331 Irving Dr Oxnard (93030) ***(P-16436)***
T & R Lumber Company (PA) ... D ... 909 899-2383
8685 Etiwanda Ave Rancho Cucamonga (91739) ***(P-4429)***
T & S Die Cutting ... F ... 562 802-1731
13301 Alondra Blvd Ste A Santa Fe Springs (90670) ***(P-14108)***
T & T Box Company Inc ... E ... 909 465-0848
1353 Philadelphia St Pomona (91766) ***(P-5316)***
T & T Foods Inc ... E ... 323 588-2158
3080 E 50th St Vernon (90058) ***(P-747)***
T & V Printing Inc ... F ... 951 353-8470
7101 Jurupa Ave Ste 3 Riverside (92504) ***(P-6882)***
T and T Industries Inc (PA) ... D ... 714 284-6555
1835 Dawns Way Ste A Fullerton (92831) ***(P-13439)***
T B C, Santa Rosa *Also called Barricade Co & Traffic Sup Inc* ***(P-13501)***
T C I, San Diego *Also called Turbine Components Inc* ***(P-19986)***
T C Media Inc ... F ... 510 656-5100
40748 Encyclopedia Cir Fremont (94538) ***(P-6037)***
T C Quality Machining Inc ... F ... 951 509-4633
12155 Magnolia Ave 10d Riverside (92503) ***(P-16437)***
T D I Signs ... E ... 562 436-5188
1419 Seabright Ave Long Beach (90813) ***(P-23224)***
T E B Inc ... F ... 909 941-8100
8754 Lion St Rancho Cucamonga (91730) ***(P-16438)***
T E M P, Gardena *Also called Thermally Engineered Manufactu* ***(P-12064)***
T E R, Santa Clara *Also called Ter Inc* ***(P-16452)***
T F S, Camarillo *Also called Technical Film Systems Inc* ***(P-22462)***
T F X, Oxnard *Also called Trans Fx Inc* ***(P-23509)***
T G Schmeiser Co Inc ... E ... 559 486-4569
3160 E California Ave Fresno (93702) ***(P-11635)***
T Hasegawa USA Inc (HQ) ... E ... 714 522-1900
14017 183rd St Cerritos (90703) ***(P-2232)***
T I B Inc ... F ... 619 562-3071
9525 Pathway St Santee (92071) ***(P-14109)***
T L Care Inc ... F ... 650 589-3659
1459 San Mateo Ave South San Francisco (94080) ***(P-3450)***
T L Clark Co Inc ... F ... 619 230-1400
3430 Kurtz St San Diego (92110) ***(P-4252)***
T L Machine Inc ... D ... 714 554-4154
14272 Commerce Dr Garden Grove (92843) ***(P-12654)***
T L Timmerman Construction ... E ... 760 244-2532
9845 Santa Fe Ave E Hesperia (92345) ***(P-4322)***
T M C, Berkeley *Also called Terminal Manufacturing Co LLC* ***(P-11898)***
T M Cobb Company (PA) ... E ... 951 248-2400
500 Palmyrita Ave Riverside (92507) ***(P-4136)***
T M Cobb Company ... D ... 209 948-5358
2651 E Roosevelt St Stockton (95205) ***(P-4137)***
T M Cobb Company ... C ... 909 796-6969
1592 E San Bernardino Ave San Bernardino (92408) ***(P-4946)***
T M Cobb Company ... E ... 714 670-2112
6291 Orangethorpe Ave Buena Park (90620) ***(P-4138)***
T M I, Santa Clara *Also called Tool Makers International Inc* ***(P-13958)***
T M I, Gardena *Also called Timbucktoo Manufacturing Inc* ***(P-15592)***
T M Industries Incorporated ... F ... 408 736-5202
1085 Di Giulio Ave Santa Clara (95050) ***(P-11894)***
T M O, Rancho Cucamonga *Also called Thermostatic Industries Inc* ***(P-10964)***
T M P Services Inc (PA) ... E ... 951 213-3900
2929 Kansas Ave Riverside (92507) ***(P-12576)***
T M W Engineering Inc ... F ... 310 768-8211
14810 S San Pedro St Gardena (90248) ***(P-20243)***
T McGee Electric Inc ... F ... 909 591-6461
12375 Mills Ave Ste 2 Chino (91710) ***(P-16928)***
T N T Auto Inc ... D ... 310 715-1117
535 Patrice Pl Gardena (90248) ***(P-10145)***
T P S, Colfax *Also called Transworld Printing Svcs Inc* ***(P-6896)***
T Q M Apparel Group, Los Angeles *Also called High-End Knitwear Inc* ***(P-2790)***
T R I, Yucaipa *Also called Technical Resource Industries* ***(P-16933)***
T S M, Los Angeles *Also called Tubular Specialties Mfg Inc* ***(P-10468)***
T S Microtech Inc ... F ... 626 839-8998
17109 Gale Ave City of Industry (91745) ***(P-15346)***
T T E Products Inc ... F ... 408 955-0100
1701 Fortune Dr Ste N San Jose (95131) ***(P-16439)***
T Ultra Equipment Company Inc ... F ... 510 440-3900
41980 Christy St Fremont (94538) ***(P-14543)***
T W I, Sunnyvale *Also called Thomas West Inc* ***(P-3645)***
T&D Trenchless, Murrieta *Also called T & D Services Inc* ***(P-106)***
T&J Sausage Kitchen Inc ... E ... 714 632-8350
2831 E Miraloma Ave Anaheim (92806) ***(P-503)***
T&L Air Conditioning Inc ... F ... 626 294-9888
164 W Live Oak Ave Arcadia (91007) ***(P-20816)***
T&S Manufacturing Tech LLC ... E ... 408 441-0285
1530 Oakland Rd Ste 120 San Jose (95112) ***(P-11895)***
T&T Precision Machining ... F ... 323 583-0064
9812 Atlantic Ave South Gate (90280) ***(P-16440)***
T-1 Lighting Inc ... F ... 626 234-2328
9929 Pioneer Blvd Santa Fe Springs (90670) ***(P-17075)***
T-Bags LLC ... F ... 323 225-9525
1530 E 25th St Los Angeles (90011) ***(P-3420)***
T-Ram Semiconductor Inc ... E ... 408 597-3670
2109 Landings Dr Mountain View (94043) ***(P-18600)***
T-Rex Grilles, Corona *Also called T-Rex Truck Products Inc* ***(P-12750)***
T-Rex Products Incorporated ... F ... 619 482-4424
7920 Airway Rd Ste A6 San Diego (92154) ***(P-23496)***
T-Rex Truck Products Inc ... D ... 800 287-5900
2365 Railroad St Corona (92880) ***(P-12750)***
T. H. E. Swimwear, Los Angeles *Also called Swimwear* ***(P-3419)***
T/Q Systems Inc ... E ... 949 455-0478
25131 Arctic Ocean Dr Lake Forest (92630) ***(P-16441)***
T3 Micro Inc (PA) ... E ... 310 452-2888
228 Main St Ste 12 Venice (90291) ***(P-23497)***
T3 Motion Inc ... E ... 951 737-7300
425 Klug Cir Corona (92880) ***(P-20428)***
Ta Aerospace Co (HQ) ... C ... 661 775-1100
28065 Franklin Pkwy Valencia (91355) ***(P-9376)***
Ta Aerospace Co ... C ... 661 702-0448
28065 Franklin Pkwy Valencia (91355) ***(P-7616)***
Ta Division, Valencia *Also called Ta Aerospace Co* ***(P-7616)***
Tab Label Inc ... F ... 510 638-4411
21 Hegenberger Ct Oakland (94621) ***(P-5534)***
Tabc Inc (HQ) ... C ... 562 984-3305
6375 N Paramount Blvd Long Beach (90805) ***(P-19776)***
Tabco Precision, Fallbrook *Also called Workman Holdings Inc* ***(P-21964)***
Tablas Creek Vineyard LLC ... F ... 805 237-1231
9339 Adelaida Rd Paso Robles (93446) ***(P-1946)***
Table Bluff Brewing Inc (PA) ... E ... 707 445-4480
617 4th St Eureka (95501) ***(P-1568)***
Table De France Inc ... F ... 909 923-5205
2020 S Haven Ave Ontario (91761) ***(P-1282)***
Table Mountain Quarry, Oroville *Also called Vulcan Materials Company* ***(P-307)***
Tabor Communications Inc ... E ... 858 625-0070
8445 Camino Santa Fe # 101 San Diego (92121) ***(P-6356)***
Tachyon Networks Incorporated ... D ... 858 882-8100
9339 Carroll Park Dr # 150 San Diego (92121) ***(P-17676)***
Tackett Volume Press Inc ... E ... 916 374-8991
1348 Terminal St West Sacramento (95691) ***(P-7237)***
Taco Works Inc ... E ... 805 541-1556
3424 Sacramento Dr San Luis Obispo (93401) ***(P-2346)***
Tacoma News Inc (HQ) ... B ... 916 321-1846
2100 Q St Sacramento (95816) ***(P-5844)***
Tacsense Inc ... F ... 530 797-0008
10 N East St Ste 108 Woodland (95776) ***(P-21921)***
Tactical Communications Corp ... E ... 805 987-4100
473 Post St Camarillo (93010) ***(P-17766)***
Tacticombat Inc ... F ... 626 315-4433
11640 Mcbean Dr El Monte (91732) ***(P-13278)***
Tactx Medical Inc (HQ) ... C ... 408 364-7100
1353 Dell Ave Campbell (95008) ***(P-21922)***
Tacupeto Chips & Salsa Inc ... F ... 760 597-9400
1330 Distribution Way A Vista (92081) ***(P-2347)***
Tae Gwang Inc ... F ... 323 233-2882
4922 S Figueroa St Los Angeles (90037) ***(P-23225)***
Tae Life Sciences LLC ... F ... 310 633-5042
1756 Cloverfield Blvd Santa Monica (90404) ***(P-22318)***
Taft Production Company ... D ... 661 765-7194
950 Petroleum Club Rd Taft (93268) ***(P-20)***
Taft Street Inc ... E ... 707 823-2049
2030 Barlow Ln Sebastopol (95472) ***(P-1947)***
Taft Street Winery, Sebastopol *Also called Taft Street Inc* ***(P-1947)***
Tag Rag, Los Angeles *Also called Fetish Group Inc* ***(P-3081)***
Tag Toys Inc ... D ... 310 639-4566
1810 S Acacia Ave Compton (90220) ***(P-23498)***
Tag-Connect LLC ... F ... 877 244-4156
433 Airport Blvd Ste 425 Burlingame (94010) ***(P-11322)***
Tag-It Pacific Inc ... E ... 818 444-4100
21900 Burbank Blvd # 270 Woodland Hills (91367) ***(P-2861)***
Tags & Labels ... E ... 510 465-1125
290 27th St Oakland (94612) ***(P-6883)***

Mergent e-mail: customerrelations@mergent.com
1256
2020 California
Manufacturers Register
(P-0000) Products & Services Section entry number
(PA)=Parent Co (HQ)=Headquarters (DH)=Div Headquarters

Tagtime U S A Inc....B....323 587-1555
4601 District Blvd Vernon (90058) ***(P-5535)***
Tahiti Cabinets Inc....D....714 693-0618
5419 E La Palma Ave Anaheim (92807) ***(P-5084)***
Tahiti Trading Company, Riverside *Also called Tropical Functional Labs LLC* ***(P-622)***
Tahoe House Inc....F....530 583-1377
625 W Lake Blvd Tahoe City (96145) ***(P-1283)***
Tahoe Rf Semiconductor Inc....F....530 823-9786
12834 Earhart Ave Auburn (95602) ***(P-18601)***
Tahoe World, Tahoe City *Also called Mount Rose Publishing Co Inc* ***(P-5766)***
Taicom International Inc....F....510 656-9200
4241 Business Center Dr A Fremont (94538) ***(P-15136)***
Taiga Embroidery Inc....F....626 448-4812
12368 Valley Blvd Ste 114 El Monte (91732) ***(P-3761)***
Tailgate Printing Inc....C....714 966-3035
2930 S Fairview St Santa Ana (92704) ***(P-7238)***
Tailgater Inc....F....831 424-7710
881 Vertin Ave Salinas (93901) ***(P-20494)***
Tait & Associates Inc....D....714 560-8222
2131 S Dupont Dr Anaheim (92806) ***(P-12062)***
Tait Cabinetry Woodworks....F....951 776-1192
6572 Whitman Ct Riverside (92506) ***(P-4139)***
Tajen Graphics Inc....E....714 527-3122
2100 W Lincoln Ave Ste B Anaheim (92801) ***(P-6884)***
Tajima /Crl, Vernon *Also called Tajima USA Dissolving Corp* ***(P-12513)***
Tajima USA Dissolving Corp....F....323 588-1281
2503 E Vernon Ave Vernon (90058) ***(P-12513)***
Tajima USA Inc....E....310 604-8200
19925 S Susana Rd Compton (90221) ***(P-14295)***
Takane USA Inc (HQ)....E....310 212-1411
369 Van Ness Way Ste 715 Torrance (90501) ***(P-22485)***
Takara Sake USA Inc (HQ)....E....510 540-8250
708 Addison St Berkeley (94710) ***(P-2020)***
Take A Break Paper....E....323 333-7773
263 W Olive Ave 307 Burbank (91502) ***(P-5845)***
Take It For Granite Inc....E....408 790-2812
345 Phelan Ave San Jose (95112) ***(P-295)***
Takex America Inc....E....877 371-2727
151 San Zeno Way Sunnyvale (94086) ***(P-18602)***
Takipi Inc....F....408 203-9585
797 Bryant St San Francisco (94107) ***(P-24483)***
Takt Manufacturing Inc....F....408 250-4975
1300 E Victor Rd Lodi (95240) ***(P-23499)***
Talbott Ties, Monterey *Also called Robert Talbott Inc* ***(P-2975)***
Talco Foam Inc (PA)....F....916 492-8840
1631 Entp Blvd Ste 30 West Sacramento (95691) ***(P-9377)***
Talco Foam Products, West Sacramento *Also called Talco Foam Inc* ***(P-9377)***
Talco Plastics Inc....E....562 630-1224
3270 E 70th St Long Beach (90805) ***(P-10078)***
Tali Pak Lumber Milling, Hopland *Also called Steve Bruner* ***(P-4130)***
Talimar Systems Inc....E....714 557-4884
3105 W Alpine St Santa Ana (92704) ***(P-4874)***
Talins Company....F....310 378-3715
17800 S Main St Ste 121 Gardena (90248) ***(P-12400)***
Talis Biomedical Corporation....E....650 433-3000
230 Constitution Dr Menlo Park (94025) ***(P-21296)***
Talisman Systems Group Inc....F....415 357-1751
1111 Oak St San Francisco (94117) ***(P-24484)***
Talix Inc....D....628 220-3885
660 3rd St Ste 302 San Francisco (94107) ***(P-24485)***
Talkdesk Inc (PA)....E....888 743-3044
535 Mission St Fl 12 San Francisco (94105) ***(P-24486)***
Talladium Inc (PA)....E....661 295-0900
27360 Muirfield Ln Valencia (91355) ***(P-22195)***
Talley Metal Fabrication, San Jacinto *Also called J Talley Corporation* ***(P-12484)***
Tallygo Inc (PA)....F....510 858-1969
4133 Redwood Ave # 1015 Los Angeles (90066) ***(P-24487)***
Talon Therapeutics Inc....C....949 788-6700
157 Technology Dr Irvine (92618) ***(P-8153)***
Talos Corporation....E....650 364-7364
512 2nd Ave Redwood City (94063) ***(P-16442)***
Talsco, Garden Grove *Also called Jvr Sheetmetal Fabrication Inc* ***(P-19908)***
Talyarps Corporation....E....310 559-2335
3465 S La Cienega Blvd Los Angeles (90016) ***(P-8685)***
Tam Printing Inc....F....714 224-4488
2961 E White Star Ave Anaheim (92806) ***(P-6885)***
Tamaki Rice Corporation....E....530 473-2862
1701 Abel Rd Williams (95987) ***(P-1053)***
Tamalpais Coml Cabinetry Inc....E....510 231-6800
200 9th St Richmond (94801) ***(P-4947)***
Tamarco Contractor Specialties, San Diego *Also called Tomarco Contractor Spc Inc* ***(P-23012)***
Tamco (HQ)....D....909 899-0660
12459 Arrow Rte Rancho Cucamonga (91739) ***(P-11077)***
Tammy Taylor Nails Inc....E....949 250-9287
2001 E Deere Ave Santa Ana (92705) ***(P-7617)***
Tampico Spice Co Incorporated....E....323 235-3154
5901 S Central Ave 5941 Los Angeles (90001) ***(P-2622)***
Tampico Spice Company, Los Angeles *Also called Tampico Spice Co Incorporated* ***(P-2622)***
Tamshell Corp....D....951 272-9395
237 Glider Cir Corona (92880) ***(P-10079)***
Tan Set Corporation....F....805 967-4567
1 S Fairview Ave Goleta (93117) ***(P-11896)***
Tanbil Bakery Inc....F....626 280-2638
8150 Garvey Ave Ste 104 Rosemead (91770) ***(P-1284)***
Tanbit Bakery, Rosemead *Also called Tanbil Bakery Inc* ***(P-1284)***
Tandem Design Inc....E....714 978-7272
1846 W Sequoia Ave Orange (92868) ***(P-23500)***
Tandem Diabetes Care Inc (PA)....B....858 366-6900
11075 Roselle St San Diego (92121) ***(P-21923)***
Tandem Exhibit, Orange *Also called Tandem Design Inc* ***(P-23500)***
Tandem Wines LLC....F....707 395-3902
4900 W Dry Creek Rd Healdsburg (95448) ***(P-1948)***
Tanfield Engrg Systems US Inc....F....559 443-6602
2686 S Maple Ave Fresno (93725) ***(P-13750)***
Tangent Computer Inc....D....650 342-9388
45800 Northport Loop W Fremont (94538) ***(P-14984)***
Tangent Computer Inc (PA)....D....888 683-2881
191 Airport Blvd Burlingame (94010) ***(P-14985)***
Tanget Fastnet, Burlingame *Also called Tangent Computer Inc* ***(P-14985)***
Tangle Inc....E....650 616-7900
385 Oyster Point Blvd 8b South San Francisco (94080) ***(P-22719)***
Tangle Creations, South San Francisco *Also called Tangle Inc* ***(P-22719)***
Tango Systems Inc....D....408 526-2330
1980 Concourse Dr San Jose (95131) ***(P-19100)***
Tangoe Us Inc....D....858 452-6800
9920 Pcf Hts Blvd Ste 200 San Diego (92121) ***(P-24488)***
Tangome Inc (PA)....E....650 375-2620
615 National Ave Sunnyvale (94085) ***(P-17677)***
Tanko Streetlighting Inc....E....415 254-7579
220 Bay Shore Blvd San Francisco (94124) ***(P-17076)***
Tanko Streetlighting Services, San Francisco *Also called Tanko Streetlighting Inc* ***(P-17076)***
Tanox Inc (HQ)....C....650 851-1607
1 Dna Way South San Francisco (94080) ***(P-8154)***
Taokaenoi Usa Inc....F....562 404-9888
13767 Milroy Pl Santa Fe Springs (90670) ***(P-2253)***
Tap Manufacturing LLC....F....619 216-1444
2360 Boswell Rd Chula Vista (91914) ***(P-19777)***
Tap Plastics Inc A Cal Corp (PA)....F....510 357-3755
3011 Alvarado St Ste A San Leandro (94577) ***(P-7618)***
Tapatio Foods LLC....F....323 587-8933
4685 District Blvd Vernon (90058) ***(P-829)***
Tapatio Hot Sauce, Vernon *Also called Tapatio Foods LLC* ***(P-829)***
Tapclicks, San Jose *Also called Taponix Inc* ***(P-24490)***
Tape & Label Converters Inc....E....562 945-3486
8231 Allport Ave Santa Fe Springs (90670) ***(P-5375)***
Tape Factory Inc....E....714 979-7742
11899 Lotus Ave Fountain Valley (92708) ***(P-5376)***
Tape Service Ltd....F....909 627-8811
4510 Carter Ct Chino (91710) ***(P-9378)***
Tapemation Machining Inc (PA)....F....831 438-3069
13 Janis Way Scotts Valley (95066) ***(P-16443)***
Tapemation Machining Inc....F....831 438-3069
15 Janis Way Scotts Valley (95066) ***(P-16444)***
Tapestry Inc....F....323 725-6792
100 Citadel Dr Ste 709 Commerce (90040) ***(P-10228)***
Tapestry Inc....F....909 337-5207
28200 Highway 189 Lake Arrowhead (92352) ***(P-10229)***
Tapingo Inc (HQ)....E....415 283-5222
39 Stillman St San Francisco (94107) ***(P-24489)***
Tapioca Express....F....408 999-0128
81 Curtner Ave San Jose (95125) ***(P-1064)***
Tapioca Express....F....619 286-0484
6145 El Cajon Blvd Ste G San Diego (92115) ***(P-1065)***
Taponix Inc....F....408 725-2942
5300 Stevens Creek Blvd San Jose (95129) ***(P-24490)***
Tapp Label Inc (HQ)....F....707 252-8300
161 S Vasco Rd L Livermore (94551) ***(P-5536)***
Tara Enterprises Inc....F....661 510-2206
27023 Mack Bean Pkwy Valencia (91355) ***(P-4253)***
Tara Materials Inc....E....619 671-1018
7615 Siempre Viva Rd San Diego (92154) ***(P-22946)***
Taracom Corporation....F....408 691-6655
1220 Memorex Dr Santa Clara (95050) ***(P-14986)***
Taral Plastics....F....510 972-6300
34343 Zwissig Way Union City (94587) ***(P-10080)***
Tarana Wireless Inc (PA)....F....408 365-8483
590 Alder Dr Milpitas (95035) ***(P-17678)***
Tarazi Specialty Foods LLC....F....909 628-3601
13727 Seminole Dr Chino (91710) ***(P-2623)***
Tardif Sheet Metal & AC....F....714 547-7135
412 N Santa Fe St Santa Ana (92701) ***(P-11897)***
Tardio Enterprises Inc....E....650 877-7200
457 S Canal St South San Francisco (94080) ***(P-2273)***
Target Mdia Prtners Intractive, North Hollywood *Also called Target Media Partners* ***(P-7239)***
Target Media Partners (HQ)....F....323 930-3123
5200 Lankershim Blvd North Hollywood (91601) ***(P-7239)***
Target Media Partners Oper LLC....E....323 930-3123
5900 Wilshire Blvd # 550 Los Angeles (90036) ***(P-5846)***
Target Technology Company LLC....E....949 788-0909
564 Wald Irvine (92618) ***(P-19236)***
Targus US LLC....F....714 765-5555
1211 N Miller St Anaheim (92806) ***(P-10212)***
Tarina Tarantino Designs LLC....F....213 533-8070
910 S Broadway Fl 6 Los Angeles (90015) ***(P-22577)***
Tarpin Corporation....E....714 891-6944
5361 Business Dr Huntington Beach (92649) ***(P-14110)***
Tarps & Tie-Downs Inc (PA)....F....510 782-8772
24967 Huntwood Ave Hayward (94544) ***(P-3709)***
Tarrica Wine Cellars, Shandon *Also called Svp Winery LLC* ***(P-1944)***
Tarsal Pharmaceuticals Inc....E....818 919-9723
3909 Oceanic Dr Ste 401 Oceanside (92056) ***(P-8155)***
Tartan Fashion Inc....E....626 575-2828
4357 Rowland Ave El Monte (91731) ***(P-3123)***
Tartine LP....E....415 487-2600
600 Guerrero St San Francisco (94110) ***(P-1285)***
Tartine Bakery & Cafe, San Francisco *Also called Tartine LP* ***(P-1285)***

ALPHABETIC

Employee Codes: A=Over 500 employees, B=251-500
C=101-250, D=51-100, E=20-50, F=10-19
2020 California
Manfacturers Register
© Mergent Inc. 1-800-342-5647
1257

TAS Group Inc ... F ... 925 551-3700
2333 San Ramon Vly Blvd San Ramon (94583) ***(P-7363)***

Tascent Inc ... F ... 650 799-4611
475 Alberto Way Ste 200 Los Gatos (95032) ***(P-19419)***

Taschen America LLC (PA) ... F ... 323 463-4441
6671 W Sunset Blvd Los Angeles (90028) ***(P-6150)***

Tasco Molds Inc ... F ... 909 613-1926
6260 Prescott Ct Chino (91710) ***(P-14111)***

Taseon Inc ... D ... 408 240-7800
515 S Flower St Fl 25 Los Angeles (90071) ***(P-21135)***

Tasker Metal Products Inc ... F ... 213 765-5400
1823 S Hope St Los Angeles (90015) ***(P-19778)***

Taste Adventure, Ontario *Also called Will Pak Foods Inc* ***(P-877)***

Taste Nirvana International, Corona *Also called PSW Inc* ***(P-2591)***

Tate Shoes, Sun Valley *Also called Tatiossian Bros Inc* ***(P-10178)***

Tatiossian Bros Inc ... D ... 818 768-3200
11144 Penrose St Ste 11 Sun Valley (91352) ***(P-10178)***

Tatung Company America Inc (HQ) ... D ... 310 637-2105
2850 E El Presidio St Long Beach (90810) ***(P-17679)***

Tatung Telecom Corporation ... D ... 650 961-2288
2660 Marine Way Mountain View (94043) ***(P-17420)***

Taurus Products Inc ... E ... 805 584-1555
67 W Easy St Ste 118 Simi Valley (93065) ***(P-13955)***

Tay Ho, Santa Ana *Also called West Lake Food Corporation* ***(P-431)***

Tay Ho Food Corporation ... E ... 714 973-2286
2430 Cape Cod Way Santa Ana (92703) ***(P-748)***

Tayco Engineering Inc ... C ... 714 952-2240
10874 Hope St Cypress (90630) ***(P-20457)***

Taylor Coml Foodservice Inc ... E ... 714 255-7200
221 S Berry St Brea (92821) ***(P-15453)***

Taylor Communications Inc ... E ... 951 203-9011
8972 Cuyamaca St Corona (92883) ***(P-7286)***

Taylor Communications Inc ... F ... 916 927-1891
1300 Ethan Way Ste 675 Sacramento (95825) ***(P-7287)***

Taylor Communications Inc ... F ... 866 541-0937
5151 Murphy Canyon Rd # 100 San Diego (92123) ***(P-7288)***

Taylor Communications Inc ... D ... 916 340-0200
3885 Seaport Blvd Ste 40 West Sacramento (95691) ***(P-7289)***

Taylor Communications Inc ... E ... 714 708-2005
535 Anton Blvd Ste 530 Costa Mesa (92626) ***(P-7290)***

Taylor Communications Inc ... E ... 714 664-8865
400 N Tustin Ave Ste 275 Santa Ana (92705) ***(P-7291)***

Taylor Communications Inc ... F ... 916 368-1200
10390 Coloma Rd Ste 7 Rancho Cordova (95670) ***(P-7292)***

Taylor Communications Inc ... F ... 866 541-0937
330 E Lambert Rd Ste 100 Brea (92821) ***(P-6965)***

Taylor Graphics Inc ... E ... 949 752-5200
1582 Browning Irvine (92606) ***(P-7240)***

Taylor Investments LLC ... E ... 530 273-4135
13355 Nevada City Ave Grass Valley (95945) ***(P-14642)***

Taylor Made Golf Company Inc (HQ) ... B ... 877 860-8624
5545 Fermi Ct Carlsbad (92008) ***(P-22906)***

Taylor Maid Farms LLC ... E ... 707 824-9110
6790 Mckinley Ave Sebastopol (95472) ***(P-2311)***

Taylor Wings Inc ... E ... 916 851-9464
3720 Omec Cir Rancho Cordova (95742) ***(P-12401)***

Taylor-Dunn Manufacturing Co (HQ) ... D ... 714 956-4040
2114 W Ball Rd Anaheim (92804) ***(P-13895)***

Tazi Designs ... F ... 415 503-0013
2660 Bridgeway Sausalito (94965) ***(P-4775)***

Tb Kawashima Usa Inc ... F ... 714 389-5310
19200 Von Karman Ave # 870 Irvine (92612) ***(P-3862)***

TBs Irrigation Products Inc ... E ... 619 579-0520
8787 Olive Ln Bldg 3 Santee (92071) ***(P-11684)***

Tbyci LLC ... F ... 805 985-6800
3615 Victoria Ave Oxnard (93035) ***(P-20359)***

Tc Communications Inc ... E ... 949 852-1972
17881 Cartwright Rd Irvine (92614) ***(P-17767)***

Tc Cosmotronic Inc ... D ... 949 660-0740
4663 E Guasti Rd Ste A Ontario (91761) ***(P-18019)***

TC Steel ... E ... 707 773-2150
464 Sonoma Mountain Rd Petaluma (94954) ***(P-24670)***

Tca Precision Products LLC ... F ... 714 257-4850
1130 Columbia St Brea (92821) ***(P-20244)***

Tcho Ventures Inc ... F ... 415 981-0189
1900 Powell St Ste 600 Emeryville (94608) ***(P-1414)***

Tcho Ventures Inc (HQ) ... E ... 510 210-8445
3100 San Pablo Ave Berkeley (94702) ***(P-1415)***

TCI Engineering Inc ... D ... 909 984-1773
1416 Brooks St Ontario (91762) ***(P-19503)***

TCI International Inc (HQ) ... C ... 510 687-6100
3541 Gateway Blvd Fremont (94538) ***(P-17680)***

TCI Texarkana Inc (HQ) ... F ... 562 808-8000
5855 Obispo Ave Long Beach (90805) ***(P-11224)***

Tcj Manufacturing LLC ... E ... 213 488-8400
2744 E 11th St Los Angeles (90023) ***(P-3421)***

Tck Membrane America Inc ... F ... 714 678-8832
3390 E Miraloma Ave Anaheim (92806) ***(P-9028)***

Tck USA Corporation ... F ... 323 269-2969
2580 Corp Pl Ste F101 Monterey Park (91754) ***(P-8897)***

Tcomt Inc ... D ... 408 351-3340
111 N Market St Ste 670 San Jose (95113) ***(P-17681)***

TCS, Chatsworth *Also called Telemtry Cmmnctons Systems Inc* ***(P-17685)***

Tct Advanced Machining Inc ... F ... 714 871-9371
2454 Fender Ave Ste C Fullerton (92831) ***(P-16445)***

Tcth Screenworks, Gardena *Also called Screenworks Co Tim* ***(P-7210)***

Tcw Trends Inc ... F ... 310 533-5177
2886 Columbia St Torrance (90503) ***(P-3422)***

Tda Magnetics LLC ... F ... 424 213-1585
1175 W Victoria St Rancho Dominguez (90220) ***(P-13551)***

Tdc Medical California, Sunnyvale *Also called Nordson Med Design & Dev Inc* ***(P-21840)***

Tdg Aerospace Inc ... F ... 760 466-1040
2180 Chablis Ct Ste 106 Escondido (92029) ***(P-20245)***

Tdg Operations LLC ... D ... 559 781-4116
600 S E St Porterville (93257) ***(P-2885)***

Tdg Operations LLC ... D ... 323 724-9000
340 S Avenue 17 Los Angeles (90031) ***(P-2882)***

Tdg Operations LLC ... F ... 323 724-9000
6433 Gayhart St Commerce (90040) ***(P-2883)***

Tdi2 Custom Packaging Inc ... F ... 714 751-6782
3400 W Fordham Ave Santa Ana (92704) ***(P-5423)***

Tdk Machining ... F ... 714 554-4166
10772 Capital Ave Ste 7n Garden Grove (92843) ***(P-20246)***

Tdl Aero Enterprises ... F ... 209 722-7300
44 Macready Dr Merced (95341) ***(P-19933)***

Tdo Software Inc ... E ... 858 558-3696
6235 Lusk Blvd San Diego (92121) ***(P-24491)***

Te Circuit Protection, Fremont *Also called Te Connectivity Ltd* ***(P-19101)***

Te Connectivity, Grass Valley *Also called Measurement Specialties Inc* ***(P-21077)***

Te Connectivity ... F ... 951 765-2200
5733 W Whittier Ave Hemet (92545) ***(P-18788)***

Te Connectivity Corporation ... E ... 650 361-3333
6900 Paseo Padre Pkwy Fremont (94555) ***(P-18789)***

Te Connectivity Corporation ... B ... 650 361-3333
300 Constitution Dr Menlo Park (94025) ***(P-18790)***

Te Connectivity Corporation ... A ... 650 361-3333
301 Constitution Dr Menlo Park (94025) ***(P-16929)***

Te Connectivity Corporation ... F ... 650 361-2495
501 Oakside Ave Side Redwood City (94063) ***(P-16930)***

Te Connectivity Corporation ... B ... 650 361-3333
308 Constitution Dr Menlo Park (94025) ***(P-16618)***

Te Connectivity Corporation ... C ... 805 684-4560
550 Linden Ave Carpinteria (93013) ***(P-16761)***

Te Connectivity Corporation ... E ... 650 361-3306
307 Constitution Dr Menlo Park (94025) ***(P-16931)***

Te Connectivity Corporation ... B ... 951 929-3323
700 S Hathaway St Banning (92220) ***(P-18791)***

Te Connectivity Corporation ... D ... 951 765-2250
5733 W Whittier Ave Hemet (92545) ***(P-18792)***

Te Connectivity Corporation ... A ... 760 757-7500
3390 Alex Rd Oceanside (92058) ***(P-18793)***

Te Connectivity Corporation ... C ... 650 361-3302
1455 Adams Dr Menlo Park (94025) ***(P-18794)***

Te Connectivity Corporation ... B ... 650 361-3333
6900 Paseo Padre Pkwy Fremont (94555) ***(P-9207)***

Te Connectivity Corporation ... B ... 408 624-3000
5300 Hellyer Ave San Jose (95138) ***(P-18795)***

Te Connectivity Corporation ... F ... 650 361-3333
501 Oakside Ave Side Redwood City (94063) ***(P-11323)***

Te Connectivity Corporation ... B ... 650 361-2495
501 Oakside Ave Side Redwood City (94063) ***(P-16932)***

Te Connectivity Corporation ... E ... 619 454-5176
9543 Henrich Dr Ste 7 San Diego (92154) ***(P-18796)***

Te Connectivity Corporation ... A ... 650 361-3615
6900 Paseo Padre Pkwy Fremont (94555) ***(P-18797)***

Te Connectivity Corporation ... B ... 951 765-2200
5733 W Whittier Ave Hemet (92545) ***(P-18798)***

Te Connectivity Ltd ... E ... 650 361-4923
6900 Paseo Padre Pkwy Fremont (94555) ***(P-19101)***

Te Connectivity MOG, El Cajon *Also called Brantner and Associates Inc* ***(P-18752)***

Teacher Created Materials Inc ... C ... 714 891-2273
5301 Oceanus Dr Huntington Beach (92649) ***(P-6151)***

Teacher Created Resources Inc ... D ... 714 230-7060
12621 Western Ave Garden Grove (92841) ***(P-6152)***

Teachers Curriculum Inst LLC (PA) ... E ... 800 497-6138
2440 W El Cam Mountain View (94040) ***(P-6153)***

Teal Electronics Corporation (PA) ... D ... 858 558-9000
10350 Sorrento Valley Rd San Diego (92121) ***(P-16762)***

Team Inc ... D ... 310 514-2312
2580 W 237th St Torrance (90505) ***(P-11471)***

Team Air Inc (PA) ... E ... 909 823-1957
12771 Brown Ave Riverside (92509) ***(P-15454)***

Team Air Conditioning Eqp, Riverside *Also called Team Air Inc* ***(P-15454)***

Team Casing ... F ... 530 743-5424
5073 Arboga Rd Marysville (95901) ***(P-268)***

Team China California LLC ... F ... 714 424-9999
3138 Madeira Ave Costa Mesa (92626) ***(P-21297)***

Team Color Inc ... E ... 949 646-6486
837 W 18th St Costa Mesa (92627) ***(P-3820)***

Team Color Screen Printing, Costa Mesa *Also called Team Color Inc* ***(P-3820)***

Team Econolite ... F ... 408 577-1733
4120 Business Center Dr Fremont (94538) ***(P-17768)***

Team Fashion ... F ... 323 589-3388
2303 E 55th St Vernon (90058) ***(P-3196)***

Team Industrial Services, Torrance *Also called Team Inc* ***(P-11471)***

Team Manufacturing Inc ... E ... 310 639-0251
2625 Homestead Pl Rancho Dominguez (90220) ***(P-12880)***

Team Simpson Racing, Harbor City *Also called Simpson Performance Pdts Inc* ***(P-22087)***

Teamifier Inc ... F ... 408 591-9872
514 Live Oak Ln Emerald Hills (94062) ***(P-24492)***

Teammate Builders Inc ... F ... 408 377-9000
281 E Mcglincy Ln Frnt Campbell (95008) ***(P-5005)***

Teamwork Athletic Apparel, San Marcos *Also called R B III Associates Inc* ***(P-3273)***

Teamwork Packaging, San Bernardino *Also called Ocean Blue Inc* ***(P-9559)***

Tearlab Corporation (PA) ... F ... 858 455-6006
150 La Terraza Blvd # 101 Escondido (92025) ***(P-21924)***

Teasdale Foods Inc (PA) ... B ... 209 358-5616
901 Packers St Atwater (95301) ***(P-749)***

Teasdale Latin Foods, Atwater *Also called Teasdale Foods Inc* ***(P-749)***

Mergent e-mail: customerrelations@mergent.com
1258
2020 California
Manufacturers Register
(P-0000) Products & Services Section entry number
(PA)=Parent Co (HQ)=Headquarters (DH)=Div Headquarters

TEC, Compton *Also called Thermal Equipment Corporation* ***(P-12063)***
TEC Color Craft (PA).....E.....909 392-9000
1860 Wright Ave La Verne (91750) ***(P-7241)***
TEC Color Craft Products, La Verne *Also called TEC Color Craft* ***(P-7241)***
TEC Lighting Inc.....F.....714 529-5068
115 Arovista Cir Brea (92821) ***(P-17166)***
Tecan Systems Inc.....D.....408 953-3100
2450 Zanker Rd San Jose (95131) ***(P-20775)***
Tecfar Manufacturing Inc.....F.....818 767-0677
8525 Telfair Ave Sun Valley (91352) ***(P-16446)***
Tech 22, Vista *Also called Sea Breeze Technology Inc* ***(P-19399)***
Tech Air Northern Cal LLC.....F.....408 293-9353
140 S Montgomery St San Jose (95110) ***(P-7451)***
Tech Air Northern Cal LLC.....F.....925 449-9353
800 Greenville Rd Livermore (94550) ***(P-7452)***
Tech Air Northern Cal LLC.....F.....510 524-9353
1224 6th St Berkeley (94710) ***(P-7453)***
Tech Air Northern Cal LLC.....F.....925 568-9353
1135 Erickson Rd Concord (94520) ***(P-7454)***
Tech Air Northern Cal LLC.....F.....650 593-9353
820 Industrial Rd San Carlos (94070) ***(P-7455)***
Tech Air Northern Cal LLC.....F.....510 533-9353
4445 Jensen St Oakland (94601) ***(P-7456)***
Tech Electronic Systems Inc.....F.....909 986-4395
404 S Euclid Ave Ontario (91762) ***(P-19102)***
Tech Powers, Santa Fe Springs *Also called Turbine Eng Cmpnents Tech Corp* ***(P-12738)***
Tech West Vacuum Inc.....E.....559 291-1650
2625 N Argyle Ave Fresno (93727) ***(P-22196)***
Tech-Semi Inc.....F.....408 451-9588
2355 Paragon Dr Ste A San Jose (95131) ***(P-18603)***
Tech-Star Industries Inc.....F.....650 369-7214
1171 Sonora Ct Sunnyvale (94086) ***(P-16447)***
Tech4learning Inc (PA).....F.....619 563-5348
6160 Mission San Diego (92120) ***(P-24493)***
Techcomp (usa) Inc.....E.....510 683-4300
3500 W Warren Ave Fremont (94538) ***(P-21298)***
Techflex Packaging LLC.....D.....424 266-9400
13771 Gramercy Pl Gardena (90249) ***(P-5344)***
Techko Inc.....A.....949 486-0678
27301 Calle De La Rosa San Juan Capistrano (92675) ***(P-19420)***
Techko Kobot Inc.....F.....949 380-7300
11 Marconi Ste A Irvine (92618) ***(P-16845)***
Techko Maid, Irvine *Also called Techko Kobot Inc* ***(P-16845)***
Techmer Pm Inc.....B.....310 632-9211
18420 S Laurel Park Rd Compton (90220) ***(P-7619)***
Techmo Entertainment Inc.....F.....408 309-3039
3191 17 Mile Dr Pebble Beach (93953) ***(P-24494)***
Techni-Cast Corp.....D.....562 923-4585
11220 Garfield Ave South Gate (90280) ***(P-11425)***
Technibuilders Iron Inc.....E.....408 287-8797
1049 Felipe Ave San Jose (95122) ***(P-12514)***
Technic Inc.....E.....714 632-0200
1170 N Hawk Cir Anaheim (92807) ***(P-13116)***
Technical Anodize.....F.....909 865-9034
1142 Price Ave Pomona (91767) ***(P-11225)***
Technical Devices, Torrance *Also called Winther Technologies Inc* ***(P-14260)***
Technical Devices Company.....E.....310 618-8437
560 Alaska Ave Torrance (90503) ***(P-14257)***
Technical Film Systems Inc.....F.....805 384-9470
4650 Calle Quetzal Camarillo (93012) ***(P-22462)***
Technical Heaters Inc.....F.....818 361-7185
10959 Tuxford St Sun Valley (91352) ***(P-9208)***
Technical Manufacturing W LLC.....E.....661 295-7226
24820 Avenue Tibbitts Valencia (91355) ***(P-23501)***
Technical Resource Industries (PA).....E.....909 446-1109
12854 Daisy Ct Yucaipa (92399) ***(P-16933)***
Technical Sales Intl LLC (HQ).....F.....866 493-6337
910 Pleasant Grove Blvd # 120 Roseville (95678) ***(P-24495)***
Technical Screen Printing Inc.....E.....714 541-8590
677 N Hariton St Orange (92868) ***(P-7242)***
Technical Trouble Shooting Inc.....E.....661 257-1202
27822 Fremont Ct B Valencia (91355) ***(P-16448)***
Techniche International, Vista *Also called Techniche Solutions* ***(P-3056)***
Techniche Solutions.....E.....619 818-0071
2575 Pioneer Ave Ste 101 Vista (92081) ***(P-3056)***
Technicolor Connected USA, Lebec *Also called Technicolor Usa Inc* ***(P-17289)***
Technicolor Content Services, Glendale *Also called Technicolor Usa Inc* ***(P-17291)***
Technicolor Disc Services Corp (HQ).....C.....805 445-1122
3233 Mission Oaks Blvd Camarillo (93012) ***(P-19237)***
Technicolor Thomson Group.....A.....805 445-7652
3233 Mission Oaks Blvd Camarillo (93012) ***(P-17288)***
Technicolor Usa Inc.....C.....661 496-1309
4049 Industrial Pkwy Dr Lebec (93243) ***(P-17289)***
Technicolor Usa Inc.....C.....818 500-9090
1507 Railroad St Glendale (91204) ***(P-17290)***
Technicolor Usa Inc.....C.....818 260-3651
440 W Los Feliz Rd Glendale (91204) ***(P-17291)***
Technicolor Usa Inc.....A.....530 478-3000
400 Providence Mine Rd Nevada City (95959) ***(P-17682)***
Technicote Inc.....E.....951 372-0627
1141 California Ave Corona (92881) ***(P-8898)***
Technifex Products LLC.....E.....661 294-3800
25261 Rye Canyon Rd Valencia (91355) ***(P-10956)***
Techniglove International Inc.....F.....951 582-0890
3750 Pierce St Riverside (92503) ***(P-22107)***
Technipfmc US Holdings Inc.....F.....661 283-1069
5200 Northspur Ct Bakersfield (93308) ***(P-13792)***
Technipfmc US Holdings Inc.....F.....310 328-1236
810 Manley Dr San Gabriel (91776) ***(P-13793)***
Technipfmc US Holdings Inc.....E.....530 753-6718
260 Cousteau Pl Davis (95618) ***(P-13794)***
Technique Designs Inc.....F.....760 904-6223
63665 19th Ave North Palm Springs (92258) ***(P-4948)***
Technisoil Global Inc.....F.....530 605-4881
5660 Westside Rd Redding (96001) ***(P-8841)***
Technlogy Knwldgable Machining.....F.....310 608-7756
1920 Kona Dr Compton (90220) ***(P-12881)***
Technology Training Corp.....D.....310 644-7777
3238 W 131st St Hawthorne (90250) ***(P-6886)***
Technoprobe America Inc.....E.....408 573-9911
2526 Qume Dr Ste 27 San Jose (95131) ***(P-18604)***
Technotronix Inc.....E.....714 630-9200
1381 N Hundley St Anaheim (92806) ***(P-18020)***
Techpro Sales & Service Inc.....F.....562 594-7878
3429 Cerritos Ave Los Alamitos (90720) ***(P-8899)***
Techserve Industries Inc.....E.....714 505-2755
6032 E West View Dr Orange (92869) ***(P-18021)***
Techshop San Jose LLC.....F.....408 916-4144
300 S 2nd St San Jose (95113) ***(P-14005)***
Techtron Products Inc.....E.....510 293-3500
2694 W Winton Ave Hayward (94545) ***(P-16993)***
Teck Advanced Materials Inc (HQ).....F.....858 391-2935
13670 Danielson St Ste H Poway (92064) ***(P-18605)***
Tecnadyne, San Diego *Also called Tecnova Advanced Systems Inc* ***(P-20728)***
Tecnico Corporation.....E.....619 426-7385
1670 Brandywine Ave Ste D Chula Vista (91911) ***(P-20306)***
Tecno Industrial Engineering.....E.....562 623-4517
13528 Pumice St Norwalk (90650) ***(P-16449)***
Tecnova Advanced Systems Inc.....E.....858 586-9660
9770 Carroll Centre Rd San Diego (92126) ***(P-20728)***
Teco Diagnostics.....D.....714 693-7788
1268 N Lakeview Ave Anaheim (92807) ***(P-8264)***
Tecomet Inc.....A.....626 334-1519
503 S Vincent Ave Azusa (91702) ***(P-21925)***
Tecxel, Vista *Also called R Zamora Inc* ***(P-12867)***
Ted Rieck Enterprises Inc.....F.....714 542-4763
1228 S Wright St Santa Ana (92705) ***(P-12402)***
Tedco, Livermore *Also called Thomas E Davis Inc* ***(P-12407)***
Tee -N -Jay Manufacturing Inc.....E.....818 504-2961
9145 Glenoaks Blvd Sun Valley (91352) ***(P-12403)***
Teeco Products Inc.....E.....916 688-3535
7471 Reese Rd Sacramento (95828) ***(P-19779)***
Teefor 2 Inc.....F.....909 613-0055
5460 Vine St Ontario (91710) ***(P-6887)***
Teen Bell, Los Angeles *Also called Touch ME Fashion Inc* ***(P-3426)***
Tegerstrand Orthtics Prsthtics, Redding *Also called Donn & Doff Inc* ***(P-21999)***
Teh-Pari International.....E.....707 829-9116
334 Ohair Ct Ste B Santa Rosa (95407) ***(P-9029)***
Tehachapi News Inc (PA).....F.....661 822-6828
411 N Mill St Tehachapi (93561) ***(P-5847)***
Teichert Inc (PA).....C.....916 484-3011
3500 American River Dr Sacramento (95864) ***(P-10856)***
Teichert Aggregates, Truckee *Also called A Teichert & Son Inc* ***(P-321)***
Teichert Aggregates, Tracy *Also called A Teichert & Son Inc* ***(P-322)***
Teichert Aggregates, Woodland *Also called A Teichert & Son Inc* ***(P-323)***
Teichert Aggregates, Cool *Also called A Teichert & Son Inc* ***(P-324)***
Teichert Aggregates, Marysville *Also called A Teichert & Son Inc* ***(P-325)***
Teichert Aggregates, Marysville *Also called A Teichert & Son Inc* ***(P-326)***
Teichert Aggregates, Rancho Cordova *Also called A Teichert & Son Inc* ***(P-327)***
Teichert Aggregates, Sacramento *Also called A Teichert & Son Inc* ***(P-328)***
Teichert Readymix, Pleasant Grove *Also called A Teichert & Son Inc* ***(P-10680)***
Teichert Readymix, Sacramento *Also called A Teichert & Son Inc* ***(P-10681)***
Teichert Readymix, Roseville *Also called A Teichert & Son Inc* ***(P-10682)***
Teichman Enterprises Inc.....E.....323 278-9000
6100 Bandini Blvd Commerce (90040) ***(P-5006)***
Teikoku Pharma Usa Inc (HQ).....D.....408 501-1800
1718 Ringwood Ave San Jose (95131) ***(P-8156)***
Tek Enterprises Inc.....E.....818 785-5971
7730 Airport Bus Pkwy Van Nuys (91406) ***(P-19103)***
Tek Labels and Printing Inc.....E.....408 586-8107
472 Vista Way Milpitas (95035) ***(P-6888)***
Tek84 Inc.....E.....858 676-5382
13495 Gregg St Poway (92064) ***(P-21551)***
Teka Illumination Inc.....F.....559 438-5800
40429 Brickyard Dr Madera (93636) ***(P-17167)***
Tekever Corporation.....D.....408 730-2617
5201 Great America Pkwy Santa Clara (95054) ***(P-24496)***
Tekia Inc.....E.....949 699-1300
17 Hammond Ste 414 Irvine (92618) ***(P-22393)***
Teklam Corporation, Corona *Also called B/E Aerospace Inc* ***(P-20052)***
Teklink Security Inc.....E.....909 230-6668
4601 E Airport Dr Ontario (91761) ***(P-19421)***
Tekma, Compton *Also called Technlogy Knwldgable Machining* ***(P-12881)***
Tekni-Plex Inc.....C.....909 589-4366
19555 Arenth Ave City of Industry (91748) ***(P-5537)***
Teknor Apex Company.....C.....626 968-4656
420 S 6th Ave City of Industry (91746) ***(P-7620)***
Tekram Usa Inc.....F.....714 961-0800
14228 Albers Way Chino (91710) ***(P-15108)***
Teksun Inc.....F.....310 479-0794
1549 N Poinsettia Pl # 1 Los Angeles (90046) ***(P-10081)***
Tektest Inc.....E.....626 446-6175
225 N 2nd Ave Arcadia (91006) ***(P-18799)***
Tektronix Inc.....E.....408 496-0800
2368 Walsh Ave Santa Clara (95051) ***(P-21136)***
Tekvisions Inc (PA).....F.....951 506-9709
40970 Anza Rd Temecula (92592) ***(P-21552)***

ALPHABETIC

Employee Codes: A=Over 500 employees, B=251-500
C=101-250, D=51-100, E=20-50, F=10-19
2020 California
Manfacturers Register
© Mergent Inc. 1-800-342-5647
1259

Tekvisons Tuchscreen Solutions, Temecula *Also called Tekvisions Inc* ***(P-21552)***
Tela Innovations Inc........E.......408 558-6300
475 Alberto Way Ste 120 Los Gatos (95032) ***(P-18606)***
Telatemp Corporation........F.......714 414-0343
2910 E La Palma Ave Ste C Anaheim (92806) ***(P-21553)***
Telco Food, Colton *Also called HC Brill* ***(P-1342)***
Telecard LLC........F.......760 752-1700
220 Bingham Dr Ste 101 San Marcos (92069) ***(P-7243)***
Telechem International Inc (HQ)........E.......408 744-1331
927 Thompson Pl Sunnyvale (94085) ***(P-22720)***
Telecommunications Engrg Assoc........F.......650 590-1801
1160 Industrial Rd Ste 15 San Carlos (94070) ***(P-17683)***
Teledesign Systems........F.......408 941-1808
1729 S Main St Milpitas (95035) ***(P-17684)***
Teledyne Analytical Instrs, City of Industry *Also called Teledyne Instruments Inc* ***(P-20945)***
Teledyne API, San Diego *Also called Teledyne Instruments Inc* ***(P-21555)***
Teledyne Battery Products, Redlands *Also called Teledyne Technologies Inc* ***(P-19174)***
Teledyne Blueview, Poway *Also called Teledyne Instruments Inc* ***(P-19422)***
Teledyne Controls, El Segundo *Also called Teledyne Technologies Inc* ***(P-19109)***
Teledyne Controls LLC........A.......310 765-3600
501 Continental Blvd El Segundo (90245) ***(P-20729)***
Teledyne Cougar, Sunnyvale *Also called Teledyne Technologies Inc* ***(P-18610)***
Teledyne Defense Elec LLC........C.......323 777-0077
12525 Daphne Ave Hawthorne (90250) ***(P-19104)***
Teledyne Defense Elec LLC........F.......310 823-5491
1001 Knox St Torrance (90502) ***(P-19105)***
Teledyne Defense Elec LLC........C.......408 737-0992
765 Sycamore Dr Milpitas (95035) ***(P-18607)***
Teledyne Defense Elec LLC........C.......310 823-5491
1001 Knox St Torrance (90502) ***(P-19106)***
Teledyne Defense Elec LLC........C.......916 638-3344
11361 Sunrise Park Dr Rancho Cordova (95742) ***(P-19107)***
Teledyne Defense Elec LLC (HQ)........E.......650 691-9800
1274 Terra Bella Ave Mountain View (94043) ***(P-19108)***
Teledyne Dgital Imaging US Inc........F.......408 736-6000
765 Sycamore Dr Milpitas (95035) ***(P-21554)***
Teledyne E2v Hirel Electronics, Milpitas *Also called Teledyne Defense Elec LLC* ***(P-18607)***
Teledyne E2v, Inc.........E.......408 737-0992
765 Sycamore Dr Milpitas (95035) ***(P-18608)***
Teledyne Elctronic Safety Pdts, Chatsworth *Also called Teledyne Risi Inc* ***(P-19981)***
Teledyne Hirel Electronics, Milpitas *Also called Teledyne E2v, Inc.* ***(P-18608)***
Teledyne Impulse, San Diego *Also called Impulse Enterprise* ***(P-16905)***
Teledyne Impulse, San Diego *Also called Impulse Enterprise* ***(P-16906)***
Teledyne Impulse, San Diego *Also called Teledyne Instruments Inc* ***(P-16934)***
Teledyne Instruments Inc........D.......619 239-5959
9970 Carroll Canyon Rd A San Diego (92131) ***(P-21555)***
Teledyne Instruments Inc........E.......858 842-3127
9855 Carroll Canyon Rd San Diego (92131) ***(P-18609)***
Teledyne Instruments Inc........C.......626 934-1500
16830 Chestnut St City of Industry (91748) ***(P-20945)***
Teledyne Instruments Inc........E.......760 754-2400
2245 Camino Vida Roble Carlsbad (92011) ***(P-20946)***
Teledyne Instruments Inc........C.......858 842-2600
14020 Stowe Dr Poway (92064) ***(P-20730)***
Teledyne Instruments Inc........E.......425 492-7400
14020 Stowe Dr Poway (92064) ***(P-19422)***
Teledyne Instruments Inc........D.......619 239-5959
14020 Stowe Dr Poway (92064) ***(P-14283)***
Teledyne Instruments Inc........E.......818 882-7266
9810 Variel Ave Chatsworth (91311) ***(P-21299)***
Teledyne Instruments Inc........D.......858 565-7050
9855 Carroll Canyon Rd San Diego (92131) ***(P-16934)***
Teledyne Lecroy Inc........E.......408 727-6600
765 Sycamore Dr Milpitas (95035) ***(P-21137)***
Teledyne Microwave, Santa Clara *Also called Teledyne Wireless Inc* ***(P-16818)***
Teledyne Microwave Solutions, Mountain View *Also called Teledyne Wireless LLC* ***(P-19113)***
Teledyne Microwave Solutions, Rancho Cordova *Also called Teledyne Defense Elec LLC* ***(P-19107)***
Teledyne Microwave Solutions, Mountain View *Also called Teledyne Defense Elec LLC* ***(P-19108)***
Teledyne Oceanscience, Carlsbad *Also called Teledyne Instruments Inc* ***(P-20946)***
Teledyne RAD-Icon Imaging, Milpitas *Also called Teledyne Dgital Imaging US Inc* ***(P-21554)***
Teledyne Rd Instruments, Poway *Also called Teledyne Instruments Inc* ***(P-20730)***
Teledyne Redlake Masd LLC........E.......805 373-4545
1049 Camino Dos Rios Thousand Oaks (91360) ***(P-21300)***
Teledyne Reynolds, Torrance *Also called Teledyne Defense Elec LLC* ***(P-19105)***
Teledyne Reynolds, Torrance *Also called Teledyne Defense Elec LLC* ***(P-19106)***
Teledyne Risi Inc (HQ)........E.......925 456-9700
32727 W Corral Hollow Rd Tracy (95376) ***(P-8907)***
Teledyne Risi Inc........F.......818 718-6640
19735 Dearborn St Chatsworth (91311) ***(P-19981)***
Teledyne Seabotix, Poway *Also called Teledyne Instruments Inc* ***(P-14283)***
Teledyne Technologies Inc........B.......310 765-3600
501 Continental Blvd El Segundo (90245) ***(P-19109)***
Teledyne Technologies Inc........B.......310 820-4616
3350 Moore St Los Angeles (90066) ***(P-19110)***
Teledyne Technologies Inc (PA)........C.......805 373-4545
1049 Camino Dos Rios Thousand Oaks (91360) ***(P-19111)***
Teledyne Technologies Inc........B.......310 822-8229
12964 Panama St Los Angeles (90066) ***(P-19112)***
Teledyne Technologies Inc........D.......909 793-3131
840 W Brockton Ave Redlands (92374) ***(P-19174)***
Teledyne Technologies Inc........B.......408 773-8814
290 Santa Ana Ct Sunnyvale (94085) ***(P-18610)***
Teledyne Wireless LLC........C.......650 691-9800
1274 Terra Bella Ave Mountain View (94043) ***(P-19113)***
Teledyne Wireless LLC........C.......916 638-3344
11361 Sunrise Park Dr Rancho Cordova (95742) ***(P-19114)***
Teledyne Wireless Inc........C.......408 986-5060
3236 Scott Blvd Santa Clara (95054) ***(P-16818)***
Telefunken Semiconductors Amer, Roseville *Also called Tsi Semiconductors America LLC* ***(P-18625)***
Telegent Systems Usa Inc........E.......408 523-2800
10180 Telesis Ct Ste 500 San Diego (92121) ***(P-18611)***
Telemetria Telephony Tech Inc........F.......408 428-0101
2635 N 1st St Ste 205 San Jose (95134) ***(P-19202)***
Telemtry Cmmnctons Systems Inc........E.......818 718-6248
10020 Remmet Ave Chatsworth (91311) ***(P-17685)***
Telenav Inc (PA)........C.......408 245-3800
4655 Great America Pkwy # 300 Santa Clara (95054) ***(P-20731)***
Telepathy Inc........E.......408 306-8421
1202 Kifer Rd Sunnyvale (94086) ***(P-15347)***
Telesign Holdings Inc (HQ)........E.......310 740-9700
13274 Fiji Way Ste 600 Marina Del Rey (90292) ***(P-24497)***
Telesynergy Research USA Inc........F.......408 200-9879
40101 Spady St Fremont (94538) ***(P-15348)***
Televic Us Corp........F.......916 920-0900
4620 Northgate Blvd # 120 Sacramento (95834) ***(P-17292)***
Telewave Inc........E.......408 929-4400
660 Giguere Ct San Jose (95133) ***(P-17686)***
Telexca Inc........F.......760 247-4277
13463 Nomwaket Rd Apple Valley (92308) ***(P-19934)***
Telirite Technical Svcs Inc........E.......510 440-3888
2857 Lakeview Ct Fremont (94538) ***(P-18022)***
Tellme Networks Inc........B.......650 693-1009
1065 La Avenida St Mountain View (94043) ***(P-6357)***
Tellus Solutions Inc........E.......408 850-2942
3350 Scott Blvd Bldg 34a Santa Clara (95054) ***(P-24498)***
Telsor Corporation........F.......951 296-3066
42181 Avenida Alvarado B Temecula (92590) ***(P-21138)***
Temblor Brewing LLC........E.......661 489-4855
3200 Buck Owens Blvd Bakersfield (93308) ***(P-1569)***
Temecula Precision Mfg, Temecula *Also called Temecula Precison Fabrication* ***(P-16450)***
Temecula Precison Fabrication........F.......951 699-4066
42201 Sarah Way Temecula (92590) ***(P-16450)***
Temecula Quality Plating Inc........F.......951 296-9875
43095 Black Deer Loop Temecula (92590) ***(P-14544)***
Temecula T-Shirt Printers Inc........F.......951 296-0184
41607 Enterprise Cir N A Temecula (92590) ***(P-7244)***
Temecula Valley Winery MGT LLC........D.......951 699-8896
27495 Diaz Rd Temecula (92590) ***(P-1949)***
Temeka Advertising Inc........D.......951 277-2525
9073 Pulsar Ct Corona (92883) ***(P-4949)***
Temeka Group, Corona *Also called Temeka Advertising Inc* ***(P-4949)***
Tempco Engineering Inc........C.......818 767-2326
8866 Laurel Canyon Blvd A Sun Valley (91352) ***(P-16451)***
Tempest Technology Corporation........E.......559 277-7577
4708 N Blythe Ave Fresno (93722) ***(P-14682)***
Templock Enterprises LLC........F.......805 962-3100
1 N Calle Cesar Chavez # 170 Santa Barbara (93103) ***(P-9571)***
Tempo Automation Inc........E.......415 320-1261
2460 Alameda St San Francisco (94103) ***(P-18023)***
Tempo Industries, Irvine *Also called Tempo Lighting Inc* ***(P-17077)***
Tempo Lighting Inc........E.......949 442-1601
1961 Mcgaw Ave Irvine (92614) ***(P-17077)***
Tempo Plastic Co........F.......559 651-7711
1227 N Miller Park Ct Visalia (93291) ***(P-9572)***
Tempted Apparel Corp........E.......323 859-2480
4516 Loma Vista Ave Vernon (90058) ***(P-3423)***
Temptrol Industries Inc........F.......916 344-4457
3909 Onawa Ct Antelope (95843) ***(P-3710)***
Temptron Engineering Inc........E.......818 346-4900
7823 Deering Ave Canoga Park (91304) ***(P-21556)***
Ten Enthusiast Network LLC........C.......760 722-7777
2052 Corte Del Nogal # 100 Carlsbad (92011) ***(P-6038)***
Ten Fu Company Limited, El Monte *Also called Uncle Lees Tea Inc* ***(P-2641)***
Tenacore Holdings Inc........D.......714 444-4643
1525 E Edinger Ave Santa Ana (92705) ***(P-21926)***
Tencate Advanced Armor USA Inc (HQ)........E.......805 845-4085
120 Cremona Dr Ste 130 Goleta (93117) ***(P-13279)***
Tencate Performance Composite, Camarillo *Also called Performance Materials Corp* ***(P-7590)***
Tender Corporation........E.......510 261-7414
1141 Harbor Bay Pkwy # 103 Alameda (94502) ***(P-22108)***
Tender Loving Things Inc........E.......510 300-1260
26203 Prod Ave Ste 4 Hayward (94545) ***(P-8592)***
Tenenblatt Corporation........C.......323 232-2061
3750 Broadway Pl Los Angeles (90007) ***(P-2813)***
Tenergy Corporation........D.......510 687-0388
436 Kato Ter Fremont (94539) ***(P-19175)***
Tenex Health Inc........D.......949 454-7500
26902 Vista Ter Lake Forest (92630) ***(P-21927)***
Tenneco Automotive Oper Co Inc........D.......562 630-0700
6925 Atlantic Ave Long Beach (90805) ***(P-19780)***
Tennis Media Co LLC........F.......310 966-8182
814 S Westgate Ave # 100 Los Angeles (90049) ***(P-6039)***
Tensorcom Inc........E.......760 496-3264
3530 John Hopkins Ct San Diego (92121) ***(P-18612)***
Tensys Medical Inc........E.......858 552-1941
12625 High Bluff Dr # 213 San Diego (92130) ***(P-22319)***
Tent City Canvas House, Fresno *Also called S A Fields Inc* ***(P-3702)***
Teohc California Inc........B.......209 234-1600
1320 Performance Dr Stockton (95206) ***(P-12404)***

Mergent e-mail: customerrelations@mergent.com
1260
2020 California
Manufacturers Register
(P-0000) Products & Services Section entry number
(PA)=Parent Co (HQ)=Headquarters (DH)=Div Headquarters

Tequilas Premium Inc .... F 415 399-0496
470 Columbus Ave Ste 210 San Francisco (94133) ***(P-2021)***
Ter Inc .... E 408 986-9920
306 Mathew St Santa Clara (95050) ***(P-16452)***
Ter Precision Machining Inc .... E 408 986-9920
306 Mathew St Santa Clara (95050) ***(P-16453)***
Terabit Radios Inc .... F 408 431-6032
1551 Mccarthy Blvd # 210 Milpitas (95035) ***(P-17687)***
Teradata Corporation (PA) .... B 866 548-8348
17095 Via Del Campo San Diego (92127) ***(P-15109)***
Teradata Operations Inc (HQ) .... D 937 242-4030
17095 Via Del Campo San Diego (92127) ***(P-14987)***
Teradyne Inc .... C 818 991-9700
30801 Agoura Rd Agoura Hills (91301) ***(P-21139)***
Teradyne Inc .... B 818 991-2900
30701 Agoura Rd Agoura Hills (91301) ***(P-19115)***
Teradyne Inc .... D 949 453-0900
5251 California Ave # 100 Irvine (92617) ***(P-21140)***
Teradyne Inc .... C 408 960-2400
875 Embedded Way San Jose (95138) ***(P-21141)***
Terarecon Inc (PA) .... D 650 372-1100
4000 E 3rd Ave Ste 200 Foster City (94404) ***(P-15349)***
Teridian Semiconductor Corp (HQ) .... D 714 508-8800
6440 Oak Cyn Ste 100 Irvine (92618) ***(P-18613)***
Terminal Freezers, Oxnard *Also called Fresh Innovations LLC* ***(P-2354)***
Terminal Manufacturing Co LLC .... E 510 526-3071
707 Gilman St Berkeley (94710) ***(P-11898)***
Termo Company .... E 562 595-7401
3275 Cherry Ave Long Beach (90807) ***(P-68)***
Tern, Davis *Also called Electronic Resources Network* ***(P-15223)***
Tern Design Ltd .... E 760 754-2400
14020 Stowe Dr Poway (92064) ***(P-20947)***
Terra Furniture Inc .... E 626 912-8523
549 E Edna Pl Covina (91723) ***(P-4674)***
Terra Nova Technologies Inc .... D 619 596-7400
10770 Rockvill St Santee (92071) ***(P-13839)***
Terra Nova Technologies, Inc., Santee *Also called Wood Minerals Conveyors Inc* ***(P-13842)***
Terra Tech Corp (PA) .... E 855 447-6967
2040 Main St Ste 225 Irvine (92614) ***(P-13674)***
Terra Universal Inc .... C 714 526-0100
800 S Raymond Ave Fullerton (92831) ***(P-14683)***
Terralink Communications Inc .... F 916 439-4367
5145 Golden Foothill Pkwy El Dorado Hills (95762) ***(P-17688)***
Terramar Graphics Inc .... F 805 529-8845
5345 Townsgate Rd Ste 330 Westlake Village (91361) ***(P-7245)***
Terran Orbital Corporation (PA) .... E 212 496-2300
15330 Barranca Pkwy Irvine (92618) ***(P-20458)***
Terrasat Communications Inc .... E 408 782-5911
315 Digital Dr Morgan Hill (95037) ***(P-17689)***
Terravant Wine Company LLC (PA) .... E 805 688-4245
70 Industrial Way Buellton (93427) ***(P-1950)***
Terre Rouge Winery, Plymouth *Also called Domaine De La Terre Rouge* ***(P-1670)***
Terri Bell .... F 530 541-4180
2152 Ruth Ave Ste 4 South Lake Tahoe (96150) ***(P-24671)***
Terry B Lowe .... F 510 651-7350
42430 Blacow Rd Fremont (94539) ***(P-14729)***
Terry Hinge & Hardware, Van Nuys *Also called RPC Legacy Inc* ***(P-11624)***
Terry Town Corporation .... F 619 421-5354
8851 Kerns St Ste 100 San Diego (92154) ***(P-3504)***
Terryberry Company LLC .... D 661 257-9971
25600 Rye Canyon Rd # 109 Santa Clarita (91355) ***(P-22578)***
Terumo Americas Holding Inc .... C 714 258-8001
1311 Valencia Ave Tustin (92780) ***(P-21301)***
Tesco Products .... F 661 257-0153
25601 Avenue Stanford Santa Clarita (91355) ***(P-13956)***
Teseda Corporation .... F 650 320-8188
160 Rio Robles Bldg D San Jose (95134) ***(P-21142)***
Teselagen Biotechnology Inc .... F 650 387-5932
1501 Mariposa St Ste 312 San Francisco (94107) ***(P-24499)***
Tesla Inc .... F 310 219-4652
3203 Jack Northrop Ave Hawthorne (90250) ***(P-19781)***
Tesla Inc .... F 209 647-7037
18260 S Harlan Rd Lathrop (95330) ***(P-19504)***
Tesla Inc .... A 510 896-6400
38503 Cherry St Ste I Newark (94560) ***(P-19505)***
Tesla Inc .... E 707 373-4035
1055 Page Ave Fremont (94538) ***(P-19506)***
Tesla Inc (PA) .... C 650 681-5000
3500 Deer Creek Rd Palo Alto (94304) ***(P-19507)***
Tesla Motors Inc., Lathrop *Also called Tesla Inc* ***(P-19504)***
Tesla Solar, Fremont *Also called Tesla Inc* ***(P-19506)***
Tesla Vineyards Lp .... F 925 456-2500
4590 Tesla Rd Livermore (94550) ***(P-1951)***
Tesoro, Carson *Also called Andeavor* ***(P-21)***
Tesoro Refining & Mktg Co LLC .... B 562 728-2215
5905 N Paramount Blvd Long Beach (90805) ***(P-9074)***
Tesorx Pharma LLC .... F 909 595-0500
3670 W Temple Ave Pomona (91768) ***(P-8157)***
Tessenderlo Kerley Inc .... F 559 582-9200
10724 Energy St Hanford (93230) ***(P-8815)***
Tessenderlo Kerley Inc .... E 559 485-0114
5247 E Central Ave Fresno (93725) ***(P-7529)***
Tessera Inc (HQ) .... F 408 321-6000
3025 Orchard Pkwy San Jose (95134) ***(P-18614)***
Tessera Intellectual Prpts Inc .... D 408 321-6000
3025 Orchard Pkwy San Jose (95134) ***(P-18615)***
Tessera Intllctual Prprty Corp .... E 408 321-6000
3025 Orchard Pkwy San Jose (95134) ***(P-18616)***
Tessera Technologies Inc (HQ) .... E 408 321-6000
3025 Orchard Pkwy San Jose (95134) ***(P-18617)***

Test Connections Inc .... F 909 981-1810
1146 W 9th St Upland (91786) ***(P-21143)***
Test Electronics .... E 831 763-2000
821 Smith Rd Watsonville (95076) ***(P-21144)***
Test Enterprises Inc (PA) .... E 408 542-5900
1288 Reamwood Ave Sunnyvale (94089) ***(P-20948)***
Test Enterprises Inc .... E 408 778-0234
1288 Reamwood Ave Sunnyvale (94089) ***(P-21145)***
Test Laboratories Inc (PA) .... F 818 881-4251
7121 Canby Ave Reseda (91335) ***(P-2624)***
Test-Um Inc .... F 818 464-5021
430 N Mccarthy Blvd Milpitas (95035) ***(P-21146)***
Testarossa Vineyards LLC .... E 408 354-6150
300 College Ave Ste A Los Gatos (95030) ***(P-1952)***
Testmetrix Inc .... E 408 730-5511
426 S Hillview Dr Milpitas (95035) ***(P-21147)***
Tetra Pak Processing Equip .... D 209 599-4634
1408 W Main St Ste E Ripon (95366) ***(P-14405)***
Tetra Tech Ec Inc .... E 949 809-5000
17885 Von Karman Ave # 500 Irvine (92614) ***(P-21302)***
Tetracam Inc .... F 818 718-2119
21601 Devonshire St # 310 Chatsworth (91311) ***(P-22463)***
Tetrad Services Inc .... F 530 527-5889
960 Diamond Ave Red Bluff (96080) ***(P-16454)***
Teva Foods Inc .... E 323 267-8110
4401 S Downey Rd Vernon (90058) ***(P-2625)***
Teva Parenteral Medicines Inc .... A 949 455-4700
19 Hughes Irvine (92618) ***(P-8158)***
Teva Pharmaceuticals Usa Inc .... E 949 457-2828
19 Hughes Irvine (92618) ***(P-8159)***
Tex Shoemaker & Son Inc .... F 909 592-2071
19034 E Donington St Glendora (91741) ***(P-3524)***
Tex-Coat LLC .... E 323 233-3111
5950 Avalon Blvd Los Angeles (90003) ***(P-8686)***
Texas Boom Company Inc .... F 281 441-2002
2433 Sagebrush Ct La Jolla (92037) ***(P-13795)***
Texas Instruments Incorporated .... E 408 541-9900
165 Gibraltar Ct Sunnyvale (94089) ***(P-18618)***
Texas Instruments Incorporated .... E 669 721-5000
2900 Semiconductor Dr Santa Clara (95051) ***(P-18619)***
Texas Instruments Incorporated .... C 714 731-7110
14351 Myford Rd Tustin (92780) ***(P-18620)***
Texas Tst Inc .... E 951 685-2155
13428 Benson Ave Chino (91710) ***(P-11209)***
Texchem Chemical, Sacramento *Also called Kds Nail Products* ***(P-23380)***
Texollini Inc .... C 310 537-3400
2575 E El Presidio St Long Beach (90810) ***(P-2904)***
Texon USA Inc .... F 510 256-7210
48438 Milmont Dr Fremont (94538) ***(P-14545)***
Textile 2000 Screen Printing .... E 858 735-8521
8675 Miralani Dr San Diego (92126) ***(P-7246)***
Textile Products Inc .... E 714 761-0401
2512-2520 W Woodland Dr Anaheim (92801) ***(P-2736)***
Texture Design, Anaheim *Also called Textured Design Furniture* ***(P-4615)***
Textured Design Furniture .... E 714 502-9121
1303 S Claudina St Anaheim (92805) ***(P-4615)***
TFC Manufacturing Inc .... D 562 426-9559
4001 Watson Plaza Dr Lakewood (90712) ***(P-12405)***
Tfd Incorporated .... E 714 630-7127
1180 N Tustin Ave Anaheim (92807) ***(P-21415)***
Tfn Architectural Signage Inc (PA) .... E 714 556-0990
3411 W Lake Center Dr Santa Ana (92704) ***(P-23226)***
Tfx International .... F 760 836-3232
72785 Frank Sinatra Dr Rancho Mirage (92270) ***(P-8160)***
Tge Distribution, Vista *Also called Glorious Empire LLC* ***(P-19673)***
Tgs Molding LLC .... F 909 890-1707
425 E Parkcenter Cir S San Bernardino (92408) ***(P-10082)***
Tgs Plastic, San Bernardino *Also called Tgs Molding LLC* ***(P-10082)***
Thai Silks, Mountain View *Also called Exotic Silks Inc* ***(P-2686)***
Thai Union North America Inc (HQ) .... F 424 397-8556
9330 Scranton Rd Ste 500 El Segundo (90245) ***(P-2254)***
Thales Alenia Space North Amer .... F 408 973-9845
20400 Stevens Creek Blvd # 245 Cupertino (95014) ***(P-20469)***
Thales Avionics Inc .... F 949 381-3033
48 Discovery Irvine (92618) ***(P-20247)***
Thales Avionics Inc .... C 949 790-2500
51 Discovery Irvine (92618) ***(P-20248)***
Thales Transport & SEC Inc (HQ) .... E 949 790-2500
51 Discovery Irvine (92618) ***(P-17421)***
That Casting Place Inc .... F 323 258-5691
6229 Outlook Ave Los Angeles (90042) ***(P-22603)***
Thats It Nutrition LLC .... F 818 782-1701
834 S Broadway Ste 800 Los Angeles (90014) ***(P-1404)***
Thawte Inc .... E 650 426-7400
487 E Middlefield Rd Mountain View (94043) ***(P-17690)***
Thawte Consulting USA, Mountain View *Also called Thawte Inc* ***(P-17690)***
Thc Design LLC .... F 562 980-0056
1346 Elwood St Los Angeles (90021) ***(P-23502)***
The Badge Company, Huntington Beach *Also called Badge Co* ***(P-23283)***
The Beacon, San Diego *Also called Mannis Communications Inc* ***(P-5721)***
The Black & Decker Inc .... B 949 672-4000
19701 Da Vinci El Toro (92610) ***(P-14229)***
The Bristol Group, San Rafael *Also called Bgl Development Inc* ***(P-23664)***
The China Press, San Gabriel *Also called Asia Pacific California Inc* ***(P-5555)***
The Clearwater Company, Rancho Cordova *Also called Nca Laboratories Inc* ***(P-17265)***
The French Patisserie Inc .... D 650 738-4990
1080 Palmetto Ave Pacifica (94044) ***(P-1286)***
The Hispanic News, La Puente *Also called Total Media Enterprises Inc* ***(P-6360)***

Employee Codes: A=Over 500 employees, B=251-500
C=101-250, D=51-100, E=20-50, F=10-19
2020 California
Manfacturers Register
© Mergent Inc. 1-800-342-5647
1261

The Ligature Inc (HQ) ....E....323 585-6000
4909 Alcoa Ave Vernon (90058) ***(P-6889)***
The Ligature Inc ....E....510 526-5181
750 Gilmore St Berkeley (94710) ***(P-7247)***
The Mayflower Group, Santa Barbara *Also called Maysoft Inc* ***(P-24133)***
The Microfilm Company of Cal ....F....310 354-2610
14214 S Figueroa St Los Angeles (90061) ***(P-6154)***
The Orange County Printing Co, Irvine *Also called Ocpc Inc* ***(P-6756)***
The Orgnal Los Angeles APT Mag, Costa Mesa *Also called Pinpoint Media Group Inc* ***(P-6003)***
The Rupp Butler Studio, Cotati *Also called Lili Butler Studio Inc* ***(P-3175)***
The Rutter Group, Los Angeles *Also called West Publishing Corporation* ***(P-6161)***
The Sloan Company Inc (PA) ....C....805 676-3200
5725 Olivas Park Dr Ventura (93003) ***(P-17168)***
The Valley Business Jurnl Inc ....F....951 461-0400
40335 Winchester Rd # 128 Temecula (92591) ***(P-5848)***
The Vitamin Barn, Canoga Park *Also called California Natural Vitamins* ***(P-7820)***
The Wave, Los Angeles *Also called Wave Community Newspapers Inc* ***(P-5862)***
The White Sheet, Palm Desert *Also called Associated Desert Shoppers* ***(P-6191)***
Theater Publications Inc ....F....408 748-1600
3485 Victor St Santa Clara (95054) ***(P-6040)***
Theboom Headsets, Petaluma *Also called Ume Voice Inc* ***(P-17298)***
Thebrain Technologies LP ....F....310 751-5000
11522 W Washington Blvd Los Angeles (90066) ***(P-24500)***
Thehomemag Bay Area, Brentwood *Also called Nyabenga Llc* ***(P-6299)***
Theranos Inc (PA) ....D....650 838-9292
7373 Gateway Blvd Newark (94560) ***(P-21928)***
Therapeutic Industries Inc ....F....760 343-2502
72096 Dunham Way Ste E Thousand Palms (92276) ***(P-21929)***
Therapeutic RES Faculty LLC ....C....209 472-2240
3120 W March Ln Stockton (95219) ***(P-7248)***
Therasense Inc ....F....510 749-5400
1360 S Loop Rd Alameda (94502) ***(P-21930)***
Theravance Biopharma Us Inc ....C....650 808-6000
901 Gateway Blvd South San Francisco (94080) ***(P-8161)***
Theravnce Bphrma Antbotics Inc ....C....877 275-6930
901 Gateway Blvd South San Francisco (94080) ***(P-8162)***
Therm-O-Namel Inc ....F....310 631-7866
2780 M L King Jr Blvd Lynwood (90262) ***(P-13259)***
Therm-X of California Inc (PA) ....C....510 441-7566
3200 Investment Blvd Hayward (94545) ***(P-21557)***
Therma LLC ....A....408 347-3400
1601 Las Plumas Ave San Jose (95133) ***(P-12406)***
Therma-Tek Range Corp ....E....570 455-9491
9121 Atlanta Ave Ste 331 Huntington Beach (92646) ***(P-16854)***
Thermal Bags By Ingrid Inc ....F....847 836-4400
5801 Skylab Rd Huntington Beach (92647) ***(P-5317)***
Thermal Dynamics, Ontario *Also called Yinlun Tdi LLC* ***(P-19810)***
Thermal Dynamics, Ontario *Also called Yinlun Tdi LLC* ***(P-19811)***
Thermal Electronics Inc ....F....951 674-3555
403 W Minthorn St Lake Elsinore (92530) ***(P-19116)***
Thermal Equipment Corporation ....E....310 328-6600
2030 E University Dr Compton (90220) ***(P-12063)***
THERMAL SOLUTIONS MANUFACTURING INC., San Bernardino *Also called Thermal Solutions Mfg Inc* ***(P-19782)***
Thermal Solutions Mfg Inc ....E....909 796-0754
1390 S Tippecanoe Ave B San Bernardino (92408) ***(P-19782)***
Thermal Structures Inc (HQ) ....B....951 736-9911
2362 Railroad St Corona (92880) ***(P-19982)***
Thermal-Vac Technology Inc ....E....714 997-2601
1221 W Struck Ave Orange (92867) ***(P-11472)***
Thermally Engineered Manufactu ....E....310 523-9934
543 W 135th St Gardena (90248) ***(P-12064)***
Thermalrite, Rancho Cucamonga *Also called Everidge Inc* ***(P-15432)***
Thermalsun Glass Products Inc ....E....707 579-9534
3950 Brickway Blvd Santa Rosa (95403) ***(P-10393)***
Thermaprint Corp ....E....949 583-0800
11 Autry Ste B Irvine (92618) ***(P-22464)***
Thermcore, Grass Valley *Also called Thermo Products Inc* ***(P-11473)***
Thermcraft Inc ....F....916 363-9411
3762 Bradview Dr Sacramento (95827) ***(P-7249)***
Thermech Corporation ....E....714 533-3183
1773 W Lincoln Ave Ste I Anaheim (92801) ***(P-5345)***
Thermech Engineering, Anaheim *Also called Thermech Corporation* ***(P-5345)***
Thermeon Corporation (PA) ....F....714 731-9191
1175 Warner Ave Tustin (92780) ***(P-24501)***
Thermionics Laboratory Inc ....D....510 786-0680
3118 Depot Rd Hayward (94545) ***(P-13117)***
Thermo Finnigan LLC (HQ) ....B....408 965-6000
355 River Oaks Pkwy San Jose (95134) ***(P-21303)***
Thermo Fisher, Sunnyvale *Also called Dionex Corporation* ***(P-21217)***
Thermo Fisher Scientific, Fremont *Also called Lab Vision Corporation* ***(P-21252)***
Thermo Fisher Scientific, Santa Clara *Also called Fiberlite Centrifuge LLC* ***(P-21228)***
Thermo Fisher Scientific ....B....408 894-9835
355 River Oaks Pkwy San Jose (95134) ***(P-21304)***
Thermo Fisher Scientific Inc ....B....909 393-3205
15982 San Antonio Ave Chino (91708) ***(P-21305)***
Thermo Fisher Scientific Inc ....B....858 481-6386
675 S Sierra Ave Solana Beach (92075) ***(P-21306)***
Thermo Fisher Scientific Inc ....D....650 876-1949
200 Oyster Point Blvd South San Francisco (94080) ***(P-21307)***
Thermo Fisher Scientific Inc ....E....510 979-5000
3400 W Warren Ave Fremont (94538) ***(P-21308)***
Thermo Fisher Scientific Inc ....F....650 246-5265
180 Oyster Point Blvd South San Francisco (94080) ***(P-21309)***
Thermo Fisher Scientific Inc ....D....858 453-7551
9389 Waples St San Diego (92121) ***(P-21310)***
Thermo Fisher Scientific Inc ....C....650 638-6409
7000 Shoreline Ct South San Francisco (94080) ***(P-21311)***
Thermo Fisher Scientific Inc ....F....317 490-5809
46500 Kato Rd Fremont (94538) ***(P-21312)***
Thermo Fisher Scientific Inc ....E....408 731-5056
3380 Central Expy Santa Clara (95051) ***(P-21313)***
Thermo Fisher Scientific Inc ....F....747 494-1413
22801 Roscoe Blvd West Hills (91304) ***(P-21314)***
Thermo Fisher Scientific Inc ....F....858 882-1286
10010 Mesa Rim Rd San Diego (92121) ***(P-21315)***
Thermo Gamma-Metrics LLC (HQ) ....E....858 450-9811
10010 Mesa Rim Rd San Diego (92121) ***(P-20976)***
Thermo Kevex X-Ray Inc ....E....831 438-5940
320 El Pueblo Rd Scotts Valley (95066) ***(P-17794)***
Thermo Products Inc ....D....909 888-2882
13185 Nevada City Ave Grass Valley (95945) ***(P-11473)***
Thermo Trilogy, Wasco *Also called Certis USA LLC* ***(P-8822)***
Thermobile, Santa Ana *Also called Hood Manufacturing Inc* ***(P-9827)***
Thermodyne International Ltd ....C....909 923-9945
1841 S Business Pkwy Ontario (91761) ***(P-10083)***
Thermofinnegan, San Jose *Also called Thermo Fisher Scientific* ***(P-21304)***
Thermogenesis Holdings Inc (PA) ....D....916 858-5100
2711 Citrus Rd Rancho Cordova (95742) ***(P-20776)***
Thermolab, Sun Valley *Also called Technical Heaters Inc* ***(P-9208)***
Thermometrics Corporation (PA) ....E....818 886-3755
18714 Parthenia St Northridge (91324) ***(P-20949)***
Thermonics, Sunnyvale *Also called Test Enterprises Inc* ***(P-20948)***
Thermoplaque Company Inc ....F....818 988-1080
14928 Calvert St Van Nuys (91411) ***(P-23503)***
Thermoquest Corporation ....A....408 965-6000
355 River Oaks Pkwy San Jose (95134) ***(P-21316)***
Thermostatic Industries, Rancho Cucamonga *Also called Newtex Industries Inc* ***(P-23426)***
Thermostatic Industries Inc ....E....323 277-0900
9654 Hermosa Ave Rancho Cucamonga (91730) ***(P-10964)***
Thermtronix Corporation (PA) ....E....760 246-4500
17129 Muskrat Ave Adelanto (92301) ***(P-14776)***
Thermx Southwest, San Diego *Also called Thermx Temperature Tech* ***(P-20950)***
Thermx Temperature Tech ....F....858 573-0983
7370 Opportunity Rd Ste S San Diego (92111) ***(P-20950)***
Theta Digital Corporation ....E....818 572-4300
1749 Chapin Rd Montebello (90640) ***(P-17293)***
Thibiant International Inc ....B....818 709-1345
20320 Prairie St Chatsworth (91311) ***(P-8593)***
Thiele Technologies Inc ....B....559 638-8484
1949 E Manning Ave Reedley (93654) ***(P-14730)***
Thienes Apparel Inc ....C....626 575-2818
1811 Floradale Ave South El Monte (91733) ***(P-2807)***
Thiessen Products Inc ....C....805 482-6913
555 Dawson Dr Ste A Camarillo (93012) ***(P-16455)***
Thin Film Devices, Anaheim *Also called Tfd Incorporated* ***(P-21415)***
Thin Film Electronics Inc ....D....408 503-7300
2581 Junction Ave San Jose (95134) ***(P-19117)***
Thin-Lite Corporation ....E....805 987-5021
530 Constitution Ave Camarillo (93012) ***(P-17169)***
Thinci Inc (PA) ....F....916 235-8466
4659 Gldn Fthl Pkwy # 201 El Dorado Hills (95762) ***(P-18621)***
Thingap LLC ....E....805 477-9741
4035 Via Pescador Camarillo (93012) ***(P-16676)***
Thingap Holdings LLC ....F....805 477-9741
4035 Via Pescador Camarillo (93012) ***(P-16677)***
Thingap.com, Camarillo *Also called Thingap Holdings LLC* ***(P-16677)***
Think Surgical Inc ....C....510 249-2300
47201 Lakeview Blvd Fremont (94538) ***(P-22109)***
Thinkcp Technologies, Irvine *Also called H Co Computer Products* ***(P-15036)***
Thinksmart LLC ....F....888 489-4284
530 Jackson St Fl 3 San Francisco (94133) ***(P-24502)***
Thinkwave Inc ....F....707 824-6200
7959 Covert Ln Sebastopol (95472) ***(P-19238)***
Third Floor North Company, Santa Ana *Also called Tfn Architectural Signage Inc* ***(P-23226)***
Thirdmotion Inc ....F....415 848-2724
795 Folsom St Fl 1 San Francisco (94107) ***(P-24503)***
Thirdrock Software ....F....408 777-2910
7098 Chiala Ln San Jose (95129) ***(P-24504)***
Thirsty Bear Brewing Co LLC ....D....415 974-0905
661 Howard St San Francisco (94105) ***(P-1570)***
Thirty Three Threads Inc ....E....877 486-3769
1330 Park Center Dr Vista (92081) ***(P-2768)***
Thistle Roller Co Inc ....E....323 685-5322
209 Van Norman Rd Montebello (90640) ***(P-14341)***
Thomas Cnc Machining ....F....714 692-9373
23650 Via Del Rio Yorba Linda (92887) ***(P-16456)***
Thomas Container & Packaging, Pomona *Also called T & T Box Company Inc* ***(P-5316)***
Thomas Craven Wood Finishers ....F....805 341-7713
15746 W Arminta St Simi Valley (93065) ***(P-5085)***
Thomas Dehlinger ....F....707 823-2378
4101 Ginehill Rd Sebastopol (95472) ***(P-1953)***
Thomas E Davis Inc ....F....925 373-1373
6736 Preston Ave Ste A Livermore (94551) ***(P-12407)***
Thomas Fogarty Winery LLC (PA) ....E....650 851-6777
3130 Alpine Rd Portola Valley (94028) ***(P-1954)***
Thomas Lavin, West Hollywood *Also called Lavinder Inc* ***(P-2940)***
Thomas Leonardini ....F....707 963-9454
1563 Saint Helena Hwy S Saint Helena (94574) ***(P-1955)***
Thomas Lundberg ....F....415 695-0110
2620 3rd St San Francisco (94107) ***(P-4703)***
Thomas Manufacturing Co LLC ....E....530 893-8940
1308 W 8th Ave Chico (95926) ***(P-24672)***
Thomas Products, Madera *Also called Nutra Blend LLC* ***(P-1114)***

Mergent e-mail: customerrelations@mergent.com
1262
2020 California
Manufacturers Register
(P-0000) Products & Services Section entry number
(PA)=Parent Co (HQ)=Headquarters (DH)=Div Headquarters

Thomas T Bernstein ....E....626 351-0570
1160 Daveric Dr Pasadena (91107) *(P-12655)*
Thomas Tellez ....E....707 668-1825
100 Taylor Way Blue Lake (95525) *(P-4140)*
Thomas Welding & Mch Sp Inc....E....530 893-8940
1308 W 8th Ave Chico (95926) *(P-24673)*
Thomas West Inc (PA)....E....408 481-3850
470 Mercury Dr Sunnyvale (94085) *(P-3645)*
Thomas-Swan Sign Company Inc ....E....415 621-1511
2717 Goodrick Ave Richmond (94801) *(P-23227)*
Thomes Creek Rock Co Inc....F....530 824-0191
6069 99w Corning (96021) *(P-364)*
Thompson ADB Industries, Westminster *Also called Thompson Industries Ltd (P-20249)*
Thompson Aerospace Inc (PA)....F....949 264-1600
8687 Research Dr Ste 250 Irvine (92618) *(P-19983)*
Thompson Building Materials, Fontana *Also called Edessa Inc (P-10565)*
Thompson Gundrilling Inc....E....323 873-4045
13840 Saticoy St Van Nuys (91402) *(P-11149)*
Thompson Industries Ltd....E....310 679-9193
7155 Fenwick Ln Westminster (92683) *(P-20249)*
Thompson Magnetics Inc....F....951 676-0243
42255 Baldaray Cir Ste C Temecula (92590) *(P-19118)*
Thompson Multimedia, Camarillo *Also called Technicolor Thomson Group (P-17288)*
Thompson Tank Inc ....F....562 869-7711
8029 Phlox St Downey (90241) *(P-12065)*
Thompson Type Inc....E....619 224-3137
3687 Voltaire St San Diego (92106) *(P-7364)*
Thomson Reuters Corporation....B....949 400-7782
163 Albert Pl Costa Mesa (92627) *(P-6358)*
Thomson Reuters Corporation....F....877 518-2761
633 W 5th St Ste 2300 Los Angeles (90071) *(P-17691)*
Thor Electronics of California, Salinas *Also called Abrams Electronics Inc (P-16872)*
Thor Fiber, Torrance *Also called Digi Group LLC (P-17501)*
Thoratec LLC (HQ)....C....925 847-8600
6035 Stoneridge Dr Pleasanton (94588) *(P-22320)*
Thoreen Designs Inc....E....949 645-0981
930 W 16th St Ste C1 Costa Mesa (92627) *(P-3646)*
Thornton Steel & Ir Works Inc ....E....714 491-8800
1323 S State College Pkwy Anaheim (92806) *(P-12515)*
Thornton Winery....D....951 699-0099
32575 Rancho Cal Rd Temecula (92591) *(P-1956)*
Thorock Metals Inc ....E....310 537-1597
1213 S Pacific Coast Hwy Redondo Beach (90277) *(P-11210)*
Thorx Laboratories Inc ....F....510 240-6000
30831 Huntwood Ave Hayward (94544) *(P-8163)*
Thoughtspot Inc....B....800 508-7008
910 Hermosa Ct Sunnyvale (94085) *(P-24505)*
Thousand LLC....F....310 745-0110
915 Mateo St Ste 302 Los Angeles (90021) *(P-22907)*
Thousandeyes Inc (PA)....D....415 513-4526
201 Mission St Ste 1700 San Francisco (94105) *(P-24506)*
Thousands Oaks Hand Wash....F....805 379-2732
2725 E Thousand Oaks Blvd Thousand Oaks (91362) *(P-15591)*
Thousandshores Inc....F....510 477-0249
37707 Cherry St Newark (94560) *(P-14988)*
Three Brothers Cutting....F....323 564-4774
8416 Otis St South Gate (90280) *(P-3197)*
Three Dots LLC....D....714 799-6333
7340 Lampson Ave Garden Grove (92841) *(P-3198)*
Three Man Corporation ....E....858 684-5200
10025 Huennekens St San Diego (92121) *(P-7250)*
Three Plus One Inc....F....213 623-3070
3007 Fruitland Ave Vernon (90058) *(P-3199)*
Three Sisters Design Inc ....F....760 230-2813
967 S Coast Highway 101 Encinitas (92024) *(P-22579)*
Three Sisters Jewelry Design, Encinitas *Also called Three Sisters Design Inc (P-22579)*
Three Star Rfrgn Engrg Inc ....E....310 327-9090
21720 S Wilmington Ave # 309 Long Beach (90810) *(P-15455)*
Three Sticks Wines LLC ....E....707 996-3328
21692 8th St E Ste 280 Sonoma (95476) *(P-1957)*
Three Twins Organic Ice Cream, Petaluma *Also called Three Twins Organic Inc (P-672)*
Three Twins Organic Inc (PA)....E....707 763-8946
419 1st St Petaluma (94952) *(P-672)*
Three-D Plastics Inc....F....323 849-1316
424 N Varney St Burbank (91502) *(P-10084)*
Three-D Plastics Inc (PA)....E....323 849-1316
430 N Varney St Burbank (91502) *(P-10085)*
Three-D Traffic Works, Burbank *Also called Three-D Plastics Inc (P-10084)*
Three-D Traffics Works, Burbank *Also called Three-D Plastics Inc (P-10085)*
Threshold Enterprises Ltd ....F....831 425-3955
165 Technology Dr Watsonville (95076) *(P-7696)*
Threshold Enterprises Ltd (PA)....B....831 438-6851
23 Janis Way Scotts Valley (95066) *(P-7697)*
Threshold Enterprises Ltd....D....831 461-6413
11 Janis Way Scotts Valley (95066) *(P-7698)*
Threshold Enterprises Ltd....E....831 461-6343
19 Janis Way Scotts Vly Scotts Valle Scotts Valley (95066) *(P-7699)*
Threshold Enterprises Ltd ....E....831 466-4014
2280 Delaware Ave Santa Cruz (95060) *(P-7700)*
Thrift Town, Sacramento *Also called Norquist Salvage Corp Inc (P-3109)*
Thrift Town, Sacramento *Also called Norquist Salvage Corp Inc (P-3110)*
Thrifty Corporation ....F....818 571-0122
9200 Telstar Ave El Monte (91731) *(P-673)*
Thrio Inc....E....747 258-4201
5230 Las Virgenes Rd Calabasas (91302) *(P-24507)*
Thrun Mfg Inc....E....949 677-2461
31947 Corydon St Ste 170 Lake Elsinore (92530) *(P-19984)*
Thuasne North America Inc (HQ) ....B....800 432-3466
4615 Shepard St Bakersfield (93313) *(P-22110)*
Thunder Products Inc....F....408 270-7800
2469 Klein Rd San Jose (95148) *(P-22641)*
Thunder Products Inc....F....480 833-2500
127 Escondido Way Portola (96122) *(P-22642)*
Thunderbird Industries Inc ....E....909 394-1633
695 W Terrace Dr San Dimas (91773) *(P-14112)*
Thunderbolt Manufacturing Inc....E....714 632-0397
641 S State College Blvd Fullerton (92831) *(P-16457)*
Thunderbolt Sales Inc ....E....209 869-4561
3400 Patterson Rd Riverbank (95367) *(P-4482)*
Thunderworks Division, Santee *Also called Decatur Electronics Inc (P-20569)*
Thyssenkrupp Bilstein Amer Inc....E....858 386-5900
14102 Stowe Dr Poway (92064) *(P-19783)*
TI Gotham Inc....E....415 434-5244
2 Embarcadero Ctr San Francisco (94111) *(P-6041)*
TI Inc....F....559 972-1475
13802 Avenue 352 Visalia (93292) *(P-8805)*
TI Limited LLC (PA)....D....323 877-5991
20335 Ventura Blvd Woodland Hills (91364) *(P-24508)*
TI Wire, Walnut *Also called Tree Island Wire (usa) Inc (P-11078)*
Tianello Inc....C....323 231-0599
138 W 38th St Los Angeles (90037) *(P-3200)*
Tianello By Steve Barraza, Los Angeles *Also called Tianello Inc (P-3200)*
Tibban Manufacturing Inc ....F....760 961-1160
12593 Highline Dr Apple Valley (92308) *(P-23504)*
Tibbetts Newport Corporation ....F....714 546-6662
2337 S Birch St Santa Ana (92707) *(P-8687)*
Tibco Software Inc....F....415 344-0339
575 Market St Fl 15 San Francisco (94105) *(P-24509)*
Ticketswest, Irvine *Also called Paciolan LLC (P-24284)*
Tidelands Oil Production Inc (HQ) ....E....562 436-9918
301 E Ocean Blvd Ste 300 Long Beach (90802) *(P-69)*
Tidelands Oil Production Inc ....E....562 436-2836
705 Pico Ave Long Beach (90813) *(P-70)*
Tidings....E....213 637-7360
3424 Wilshire Blvd Los Angeles (90010) *(P-5849)*
Tien-Hu Knitting Co (us) Inc ....D....510 268-8833
18935 Sydney Cir Castro Valley (94546) *(P-2808)*
Tiffany Coach Builders, Perris *Also called Warlock Industries (P-19511)*
Tiffany Coachworks, Perris *Also called Limos By Tiffany Inc (P-19541)*
Tiffany Coachworks Inc ....C....951 657-2680
420 N Mckinley St 111-465 Corona (92879) *(P-19508)*
Tiffany Structures....E....619 905-9684
13162 Hwy 8 Bus Spc 205 El Cajon (92021) *(P-12577)*
Tig/M LLC....E....818 709-8500
9160 Jordan Ave Chatsworth (91311) *(P-13840)*
Tiger Beat Magazine, Glendale *Also called Laufer Media Inc (P-5976)*
Tiger Cased Hole Services Inc....F....562 426-4044
2828 Junipero Ave Signal Hill (90755) *(P-269)*
Tiger Tanks Inc....E....661 363-8335
3397 Edison Hwy Bakersfield (93307) *(P-20501)*
Tiger-Sul Products LLC....F....209 451-2725
61 Stork Rd Stockton (95203) *(P-7530)*
Tigers Plastics Inc....F....818 901-9393
14721 Lull St Van Nuys (91405) *(P-10086)*
Tikos Tanks Inc ....E....951 757-8014
14561 Hawthorne Ave Fontana (92335) *(P-24674)*
Tile Artisans Inc....F....800 601-4199
4288 State Highway 70 Oroville (95965) *(P-10456)*
Tile Guild Inc....F....323 581-3770
2424 E 55th St Vernon (90058) *(P-10457)*
Tilley Manufacturing Co Inc (PA)....E....650 365-3598
2734 Spring St Redwood City (94063) *(P-9258)*
Tilton Engineering Inc ....E....805 688-2353
25 Easy St Buellton (93427) *(P-19784)*
Tim Guzzy Services Inc ....F....626 813-0626
5136 Calmview Ave Baldwin Park (91706) *(P-16458)*
Tim Hoover Enterprises....D....951 237-9210
8532 Yarrow Ln Riverside (92508) *(P-17692)*
Timber Products Co Ltd Partnr ....C....530 842-2310
130 N Phillipe Ln Yreka (96097) *(P-4283)*
Timberline Molding, San Marcos *Also called Doors Unlimited (P-4189)*
Timbucktoo Manufacturing Inc....E....310 323-1134
1633 W 134th St Gardena (90249) *(P-15592)*
Timbuk2 Designs Inc....E....800 865-2513
2031 Cessna Dr Vacaville (95688) *(P-3666)*
Timbuk2 Designs Inc (PA)....D....415 252-4300
583 Shotwell St San Francisco (94110) *(P-3667)*
Timco, Hesperia *Also called T L Timmerman Construction (P-4322)*
Timco/Cal Rf Inc....E....805 582-1777
3910 Royal Ave Ste A Simi Valley (93063) *(P-18800)*
Time Masters, Los Angeles *Also called AMG Employee Management Inc (P-22476)*
Time Prtg Solutions Provider....F....916 446-6152
1614 D St Sacramento (95814) *(P-6890)*
Timely Data Resources Inc ....F....831 462-2510
107 Washburn Ave Capitola (95010) *(P-24510)*
Timemed Labeling Systems Inc (HQ) ....D....818 897-1111
27770 N Entrmt Dr Ste 200 Valencia (91355) *(P-9379)*
Times Herald, Hayward *Also called Alameda Newspapers Inc (P-5546)*
Times Litho Inc....E....503 359-0300
300 S Grand Ave Ste 1200 Los Angeles (90071) *(P-6891)*
Times Media Inc ....F....408 494-7000
1900 Camden Ave San Jose (95124) *(P-5850)*
Times Publishing, Torrance *Also called National Law Digest Inc (P-6126)*
Times-Standard, Eureka *Also called Humboldt Newspaper Inc (P-5669)*
Timet, Vallejo *Also called Titanium Metals Corporation (P-11280)*
Timevalue Software ....E....949 727-1800
22 Mauchly Irvine (92618) *(P-24511)*

ALPHABETIC

Employee Codes: A=Over 500 employees, B=251-500
C=101-250, D=51-100, E=20-50, F=10-19
2020 California
Manfacturers Register
© Mergent Inc. 1-800-342-5647
1263

Timken Company ....B 714 484-2400
4422 Corporate Center Dr Los Alamitos (90720) ***(P-14617)***
Timken Gears & Services Inc ....E 310 605-2600
12935 Imperial Hwy Santa Fe Springs (90670) ***(P-12723)***
Timkev International Inc ....F 562 232-1691
9050 Rosecrans Ave Bellflower (90706) ***(P-1332)***
Timlin Industries Inc ....E 541 947-6771
6777 Nancy Ridge Dr San Diego (92121) ***(P-23228)***
Timmons Wood Products Inc ....F 951 940-4700
4675 Wade Ave Perris (92571) ***(P-4539)***
Tini Aerospace Inc ....E 415 524-2124
2505 Kerner Blvd San Rafael (94901) ***(P-17693)***
Tink Inc ....E 530 895-0897
2361 Durham Dayton Hwy Durham (95938) ***(P-13751)***
Tiny Hero, San Francisco *Also called Northern Quinoa Prod Corp* ***(P-1030)***
Tinyinklingcom LLC ....F 877 777-6287
6303 Owensmouth Ave Fl 10 Woodland Hills (91367) ***(P-9380)***
Tiodize Co Inc (PA) ....D 714 898-4377
5858 Engineer Dr Huntington Beach (92649) ***(P-13260)***
Tiodize Co Inc ....F 248 348-6050
5858 Engineer Dr Huntington Beach (92649) ***(P-13261)***
Tipestry Inc ....F 650 421-1344
940 Stewart Dr 203 Sunnyvale (94085) ***(P-24512)***
Titan Frozen Fruit LLC (PA) ....E 831 540-4110
585 Auto Center Dr Ste A Watsonville (95076) ***(P-931)***
Titan Medical Dme Inc ....F 818 889-9998
803 Camarillo Springs Rd A Camarillo (93012) ***(P-21931)***
Titan Medical Enterprises Inc ....F 562 903-7236
11100 Greenstone Ave Santa Fe Springs (90670) ***(P-8164)***
Titan Metal Fabricators Inc (PA) ....D 805 487-5050
352 Balboa Cir Camarillo (93012) ***(P-11899)***
Titan Metal Products, Sacramento *Also called Tmp LLC* ***(P-11987)***
Titan Oilfield Services Inc ....F 661 861-1630
21535 Kratzmeyer Rd Bakersfield (93314) ***(P-270)***
Titan Pharmaceuticals Inc (PA) ....F 650 244-4990
400 Oyster Point Blvd # 505 South San Francisco (94080) ***(P-8165)***
Titan Photonics Inc ....E 510 687-0488
1241 Quarry Ln Ste 140 Pleasanton (94566) ***(P-17422)***
Titan Steel Fabricators Inc ....F 619 449-1271
1069 E Bradley Ave El Cajon (92021) ***(P-24675)***
Titanium Metals Corporation ....D 707 552-4850
403 Ryder St Vallejo (94590) ***(P-11280)***
Titleist, Carlsbad *Also called Acushnet Company* ***(P-22732)***
Tivix Inc (PA) ....F 415 680-1299
2845 California St San Francisco (94115) ***(P-24513)***
Tivoli LLC ....E 714 957-6101
15602 Mosher Ave Tustin (92780) ***(P-16869)***
Tivoli Industries Inc ....E 714 957-6101
1550 E Saint Gertrude Pl Santa Ana (92705) ***(P-17170)***
Tj Aerospace Inc ....E 714 891-3564
12601 Monarch St Garden Grove (92841) ***(P-13957)***
Tj Composites Inc ....E 951 928-8713
7231 Boulder Ave Highland (92346) ***(P-12408)***
Tj Giant Llc ....A 562 906-1060
12623 Cisneros Ln Santa Fe Springs (90670) ***(P-7251)***
Tje Company ....F 909 869-7777
18343 Gale Ave City of Industry (91748) ***(P-11986)***
Tjs Metal Manufacturing Inc ....E 310 604-1545
10847 Drury Ln Lynwood (90262) ***(P-12516)***
Tk and Company Watches ....F 213 545-1971
5827 W Pico Blvd Los Angeles (90019) ***(P-22580)***
Tk Classics LLC ....E 916 209-5500
3771 Channel Dr 100 West Sacramento (95691) ***(P-4704)***
Tk Pax Inc ....E 714 850-1330
1561 Macarthur Blvd Costa Mesa (92626) ***(P-9209)***
Tl Enterprises LLC (HQ) ....E 805 981-8393
2750 Park View Ct Ste 240 Oxnard (93036) ***(P-6042)***
TL Shield & Associates Inc ....E 818 509-8228
1030 Arroyo St San Fernando (91340) ***(P-13810)***
TLC Logistics Inc ....F 323 665-0474
3109 Casitas Ave Los Angeles (90039) ***(P-5538)***
TLC Machining Incorporated ....E 408 321-9002
2571 Chant Ct San Jose (95122) ***(P-14202)***
Tli Enterprises Inc (PA) ....E 510 538-3304
3118 Depot Rd Hayward (94545) ***(P-20777)***
Tlk Industries Inc ....F 714 692-9373
23650 Via Del Rio Yorba Linda (92887) ***(P-23505)***
Tlm International Inc ....F 650 952-2257
860 Mahler Rd Burlingame (94010) ***(P-16855)***
Tm Noodle ....F 916 486-2579
4110 Manzanita Ave Carmichael (95608) ***(P-2384)***
Tma Laser Group Inc ....F 310 421-0550
41656 Big Bear Blvd Ste 4 Big Bear City (92314) ***(P-8934)***
Tmarzetti Company ....C 408 263-7540
876 Yosemite Dr Milpitas (95035) ***(P-902)***
TMC Aero, Murrieta *Also called TMC Ice Protection Systems LLC* ***(P-20732)***
TMC Aerospace Inc ....E 949 250-4999
2865 Pullman St Santa Ana (92705) ***(P-20250)***
TMC Ice Protection Systems LLC ....E 951 677-6934
25775 Jefferson Ave Murrieta (92562) ***(P-20732)***
TMI, San Marcos *Also called Trade Marker International* ***(P-2918)***
TMJ Concepts, Ventura *Also called TMJ Solutions Inc* ***(P-21932)***
TMJ Products Inc ....F 626 576-4063
515 S Palm Ave Ste 6 Alhambra (91803) ***(P-19985)***
TMJ Solutions Inc ....F 805 650-3391
2233 Knoll Dr Ventura (93003) ***(P-21932)***
Tmk Manufacturing ....D 408 732-3200
2110 Oakland Rd San Jose (95131) ***(P-14113)***
Tmk Manufacturing Inc ....E 408 844-8289
386 Laurelwood Rd Santa Clara (95054) ***(P-14203)***

Tmp LLC ....E 916 920-2555
3011 Academy Way Sacramento (95815) ***(P-11987)***
Tmr Executive Interiors Inc ....F 559 346-0631
1287 W Nielsen Ave Fresno (93706) ***(P-4141)***
Tmr Wine Company ....F 707 944-8100
1677 Sage Canyon Rd Saint Helena (94574) ***(P-1958)***
TMW Corporation ....E 818 374-1074
14647 Arminta St Panorama City (91402) ***(P-13118)***
Tmx ....E 657 325-1756
5882 Fullerton Ave Apt 3 Buena Park (90621) ***(P-24514)***
Tmx Engineering and Mfg Corp ....D 714 641-5884
2141 S Standard Ave Santa Ana (92707) ***(P-16459)***
TN Sheet Metal Inc ....F 714 593-0100
18385 Bandilier Cir Fountain Valley (92708) ***(P-12409)***
Tncoopers, Sonoma *Also called Toneleria Nacional Usa Inc* ***(P-3987)***
Tnp Instruments Inc ....F 310 532-2222
119 Star Of India Ln Carson (90746) ***(P-19119)***
TNT Assembly LLC ....E 760 410-1750
1331 Specialty Dr Vista (92081) ***(P-2917)***
TNT Cable Industries, Vista *Also called TNT Assembly LLC* ***(P-2917)***
TNT Electric Signs Co, Long Beach *Also called Dynamite Sign Group Inc* ***(P-23091)***
TNT Industrial Contractors Inc (PA) ....E 916 395-8400
3800 Happy Ln Sacramento (95827) ***(P-13752)***
TNT Plastic Molding Inc (PA) ....C 951 808-9700
725 E Harrison St Corona (92879) ***(P-10087)***
To Die For, Ontario *Also called Scott Welsher* ***(P-10206)***
To Industries Inc ....F 949 454-6078
23180 Del Lago Dr Lake Forest (92630) ***(P-23229)***
Toad & Co International Inc (PA) ....E 805 957-1474
2020 Alameda Padre Serra Santa Barbara (93103) ***(P-3424)***
Toad Hollow Vineyards Inc ....F 707 431-1441
4024 Westside Rd Healdsburg (95448) ***(P-1959)***
Tobar Industries ....D 408 494-3530
912 Olinder Ct San Jose (95122) ***(P-16935)***
Tobin Steel Company Inc ....D 714 541-2268
817 E Santa Ana Blvd Santa Ana (92701) ***(P-11900)***
Tocabi America Corporation ....E 619 661-6136
333 H St Ste 5007 Chula Vista (91910) ***(P-4756)***
Tocagen Inc ....D 858 412-8400
4242 Campus Point Ct # 500 San Diego (92121) ***(P-8166)***
Today Pvc Bending Inc ....F 714 953-5707
501 N Garfield St Santa Ana (92701) ***(P-16955)***
Toffee Tops, San Francisco *Also called Cjs Toffee & Toppings LLC* ***(P-1361)***
Tofu Shop Specialty Foods Inc ....E 707 822-7401
65 Frank Martin Ct Arcata (95521) ***(P-2626)***
Tognazzini Beverage Service ....F 805 928-1144
241 Roemer Way Santa Maria (93454) ***(P-2176)***
Tok America, Milpitas *Also called Tokyo Ohka Kogyo America Inc* ***(P-7531)***
Tokbox Inc (HQ) ....F 415 284-4688
501 2nd St Ste 310 San Francisco (94107) ***(P-24515)***
Tokyo Ohka Kogyo America Inc ....F 408 956-9901
190 Topaz St Milpitas (95035) ***(P-7531)***
Tokyopop Inc ....D 323 920-5967
5200 W Century Blvd Fl 7 Los Angeles (90045) ***(P-6155)***
Tolar Manufacturing Co Inc ....E 951 808-0081
258 Mariah Cir Corona (92879) ***(P-11901)***
Tolco Incorporated ....E 951 656-3111
6480 Box Springs Blvd Riverside (92507) ***(P-12578)***
Toleeto Fastener International ....E 619 662-1355
1580 Jayken Way Chula Vista (91911) ***(P-23011)***
Tolemar Inc ....E 714 362-8166
5221 Oceanus Dr Huntington Beach (92649) ***(P-20429)***
Tolemar Manufacturing, Huntington Beach *Also called Tolemar Inc* ***(P-20429)***
Tolerance Technology Inc ....F 408 586-8811
1756 Junction Ave Ste C San Jose (95112) ***(P-22936)***
Tolosa Winery, San Luis Obispo *Also called Courtside Cellars LLC* ***(P-1653)***
Tom Clark Confections ....E 909 599-4700
1193 Nicole Ct Glendora (91740) ***(P-1405)***
Tom Garcia Inc ....F 619 232-4881
2777 Newton Ave San Diego (92113) ***(P-24699)***
Tom Harris Inc ....D 951 352-5700
5821 Wilderness Ave Riverside (92504) ***(P-2627)***
Tom Leonard Investment Co Inc ....E 951 351-7778
7240 Sycamore Canyon Blvd Riverside (92508) ***(P-23506)***
Tom York Enterprises Inc ....E 323 581-6194
2050 E 48th St Vernon (90058) ***(P-10088)***
Toma Tek, Firebaugh *Also called Neil Jones Food Company* ***(P-803)***
Tomahawk Power LLC ....F 866 577-4476
501 W Broadway Ste 2020 San Diego (92101) ***(P-16804)***
Tomarco Contractor Spc Inc ....F 858 547-0700
9372 Cabot Dr San Diego (92126) ***(P-23012)***
Tomasini Inc ....E 323 231-2349
1001 E 60th St Los Angeles (90001) ***(P-2737)***
Tomi Engineering Inc ....D 714 556-1474
414 E Alton Ave Santa Ana (92707) ***(P-16460)***
Tomiko Inc ....F 925 754-5694
1615 W 10th St Antioch (94509) ***(P-14600)***
Tomorrows Heirlooms Inc ....E 310 323-6720
1636 W 135th St Gardena (90249) ***(P-11636)***
Tomorrows Look Inc ....D 949 596-8400
17462 Von Karman Ave Irvine (92614) ***(P-2840)***
Tomra Sorting Inc (HQ) ....D 720 870-2240
875 Embarcadero Dr West Sacramento (95605) ***(P-14406)***
Toms Metal Specialists Inc ....E 415 822-7971
1416 Wallace Ave San Francisco (94124) ***(P-24676)***
Toms Printing Inc ....F 916 444-7788
1819 E St Sacramento (95811) ***(P-6892)***
Toms Sierra Company Inc ....F 530 333-4620
4710 Marshall Rd Garden Valley (95633) ***(P-271)***

Mergent e-mail: customerrelations@mergent.com
1264
2020 California
Manufacturers Register
(P-0000) Products & Services Section entry number
(PA)=Parent Co (HQ)=Headquarters (DH)=Div Headquarters

Toms Welding & Fabrication, San Francisco *Also called Toms Metal Specialists Inc* ***(P-24676)***
Toneleria Nacional Usa Inc ....F........707 501-8728
21481 8th St E Ste 20c Sonoma (95476) ***(P-3987)***
Toner2print Inc ....F........909 972-9656
9450 7th St Ste J Rancho Cucamonga (91730) ***(P-15350)***
Tonnellerie Francaise French C ....F........707 942-9301
1401 Tubbs Ln Calistoga (94515) ***(P-4430)***
Tonnellerie Radoux Usa Inc ....F........707 284-2888
480 Aviation Blvd Santa Rosa (95403) ***(P-4431)***
Tonusa LLC ....F........626 961-8700
16770 E Johnson Dr City of Industry (91745) ***(P-4254)***
Tony Borges ....E........310 962-8700
8685 Bowers Ave South Gate (90280) ***(P-12579)***
Tony Glazing Specialties Co ....F........323 770-8400
13011 S Normandie Ave Gardena (90249) ***(P-4950)***
Tony Hawk Inc ....F........760 477-2477
1161-A S Melrose Dr 362 Vista (92081) ***(P-22908)***
Tony Marterie & Associates ....E........415 331-7150
28 Liberty Ship Way Fl 2 Sausalito (94965) ***(P-3256)***
Tool & Jig Plating Co, Whittier *Also called Aguilar Williams Inc* ***(P-12910)***
Tool Makers International Inc ....F........408 980-8888
3390 Woodward Ave Santa Clara (95054) ***(P-13958)***
Toolander Engineering Inc ....F........949 498-8339
1110 Via Callejon San Clemente (92673) ***(P-12882)***
Toolbox Medical Innovations, Carlsbad *Also called Foundry Med Innovations Inc* ***(P-21717)***
Tools & Production Inc ....E........626 286-0213
466 W Arrow Hwy Ste C San Dimas (91773) ***(P-14114)***
Toomey Racing USA ....F........805 239-8870
5050 Wing Way Paso Robles (93446) ***(P-20430)***
Top Art LLC ....F........858 554-0102
8830 Rehco Rd Ste G San Diego (92121) ***(P-6359)***
Top Brands Distribution Inc ....F........858 578-0319
9675 Distribution Ave San Diego (92121) ***(P-578)***
Top Heavy Clothing Company Inc (PA) ....C........951 442-8839
28381 Vincent Moraga Dr Temecula (92590) ***(P-2995)***
Top It Off Bottling LLC ....F........707 252-0331
2747 Napa Valley Corp Dr NAPA (94558) ***(P-1960)***
Top Line Mfg Inc ....E........562 633-0605
7032 Alondra Blvd Paramount (90723) ***(P-11637)***
Top Notch Manufacturing Inc ....F........619 588-2033
1488 Pioneer Way Ste 17 El Cajon (92020) ***(P-12883)***
Top Printing & Graphic Inc ....F........714 484-9200
1210 N Knollwood Cir Anaheim (92801) ***(P-7252)***
Top Quest Inc ....F........626 839-8618
13872 Magnolia Ave Chino (91710) ***(P-21933)***
Top Shelf Manufacturing LLC ....F........209 834-8185
1851 Paradise Rd Ste B Tracy (95304) ***(P-21934)***
Top Ten, Los Angeles *Also called Smb Clothing Inc* ***(P-3408)***
Top-Shelf Fixtures LLC ....D........909 627-7423
5263 Schaefer Ave Chino (91710) ***(P-13440)***
Topaz Systems Inc (PA) ....E........805 520-8282
875 Patriot Dr Ste A Moorpark (93021) ***(P-15351)***
Topcon Med Laser Systems Inc ....E........888 760-8657
606 Enterprise Ct Livermore (94550) ***(P-22321)***
Topcon Positioning Systems Inc (HQ) ....C........925 245-8300
7400 National Dr Livermore (94550) ***(P-21558)***
Topguest Inc ....E........646 415-9402
601 Montgomery St Fl 17 San Francisco (94111) ***(P-24516)***
Topi Systems Inc ....F........408 807-5124
20650 4th St Apt 2 Saratoga (95070) ***(P-24517)***
Topline Game Labs LLC ....F........310 461-0350
10351 Santa Monica Blvd # 410 Los Angeles (90025) ***(P-24518)***
Topnotch Foods Inc ....F........323 586-2007
1988 E 57th St Vernon (90058) ***(P-2628)***
Topnotch Quality Works Inc ....F........818 897-7679
12455 Branford St Ste 8 Pacoima (91331) ***(P-20251)***
Toppage Inc ....F........510 471-6366
3101 Whipple Rd Ste 28 Union City (94587) ***(P-24519)***
Topper Manufacturing Corp ....F........310 375-5000
23880 Madison St Torrance (90505) ***(P-15593)***
Topper Plastics Inc ....F........626 331-0561
461 E Front St Covina (91723) ***(P-9573)***
Tops Slt Inc ....C........562 968-2000
8550 Chetle Ave Ste B Whittier (90606) ***(P-5455)***
Topslide International, Huntington Beach *Also called European Services Group* ***(P-11589)***
Topson Downs California Inc ....E........310 558-0300
3545 Motor Ave Los Angeles (90034) ***(P-3278)***
Topstar International Inc ....F........909 595-8807
13668 Valley Blvd Unit D2 City of Industry (91746) ***(P-16870)***
Tor C A M Industries Inc ....E........562 531-8463
2160 E Cherry Indus Cir Long Beach (90805) ***(P-15619)***
Torah-Aura Productions Inc ....F........323 585-1847
2710 Supply Ave Commerce (90040) ***(P-6156)***
Torani Syrups & Flavors, South San Francisco *Also called R Torre & Company Inc* ***(P-2227)***
Toray Membrane Usa Inc ....F........714 678-8832
13400 Danielson St Poway (92064) ***(P-15594)***
Toray Membrane Usa Inc (HQ) ....D........858 218-2360
13435 Danielson St Poway (92064) ***(P-9030)***
Torcano Industries Inc ....E........855 359-3339
20381 Lk Frest Dr Ste B10 Lake Forest (92630) ***(P-20431)***
Torco International Corp ....F........909 980-1495
1720 S Carlos Ave Ontario (91761) ***(P-9075)***
Torero Specialty Products LLC ....F........415 520-3481
222 E Huntington Dr # 225 Monrovia (91016) ***(P-22909)***
Torian Group Inc ....F........559 733-1940
519 W Center Ave Visalia (93291) ***(P-24520)***
Torn Ranch Inc (PA) ....D........415 506-3000
2198 S Mcdowell Blvd Ext Petaluma (94954) ***(P-2629)***
Toro Company ....D........619 562-2950
1588 N Marshall Ave El Cajon (92020) ***(P-13675)***
Toro Company ....D........951 688-9221
5825 Jasmine St Riverside (92504) ***(P-13676)***
Toro Company ....D........760 321-8396
70221 Dinah Shore Dr Rancho Mirage (92270) ***(P-13677)***
Torrance Manufacturing, Chatsworth *Also called Torrance Precision Machining* ***(P-16461)***
Torrance Precision Machining ....F........818 709-7838
9530 Owensmouth Ave Ste 8 Chatsworth (91311) ***(P-16461)***
Torrance Refinery, Torrance *Also called Pbf Energy Inc* ***(P-9060)***
Torrance Refining Company LLC ....A........310 483-6900
3700 W 190th St Torrance (90504) ***(P-9076)***
Torrance Steel Window Co Inc ....E........310 328-9181
1819 Abalone Ave Torrance (90501) ***(P-11988)***
Torrence Trading Inc ....E........310 649-1188
21041 S Wstn Ave Ste 200 Torrance (90501) ***(P-22721)***
Torrey Pines Scientific Inc ....F........760 930-9400
2713 Loker Ave W Carlsbad (92010) ***(P-20778)***
Tortilla Land, San Diego *Also called Southwest Products LLC* ***(P-2615)***
Tortilleria La California Inc ....E........323 221-8940
2241 Cypress Ave Los Angeles (90065) ***(P-2630)***
Tortilleria La Mejor ....D........559 747-0739
684 S Farmersville Blvd Farmersville (93223) ***(P-2631)***
Tortilleria San Marcos ....E........323 263-0208
1927 E 1st St Los Angeles (90033) ***(P-2632)***
Tortilleria Santa Fe ....E........619 585-0350
387 Zenith St Chula Vista (91911) ***(P-2633)***
Tortilleria Temecula ....F........951 676-5272
28780 Old Town Front St A7 Temecula (92590) ***(P-2634)***
Tortolani Inc ....F........323 268-1488
1313 Mirasol St Los Angeles (90023) ***(P-23230)***
Tosco - Tool Specialty Company ....E........323 232-3561
1011 E Slauson Ave Los Angeles (90011) ***(P-14204)***
Toshiba Amer Info Systems Inc ....D........949 587-6378
2 Musick Irvine (92618) ***(P-14989)***
Toshiba America Electronic (HQ) ....B........949 462-7700
5231 California Ave Irvine (92617) ***(P-17294)***
Toska Inc ....F........213 746-0088
1100 S San Pedro St I06 Los Angeles (90015) ***(P-3425)***
Total Brand Delivery, Camarillo *Also called Corprint Incorporated* ***(P-7036)***
Total Cmmnicator Solutions Inc ....D........619 277-1488
11150 Santa Monica Blvd # 600 Los Angeles (90025) ***(P-24521)***
Total Cost Involved, Ontario *Also called TCI Engineering Inc* ***(P-19503)***
Total Media Enterprises Inc ....F........626 961-7887
16235 Montbrook St La Puente (91744) ***(P-6360)***
Total Paper and Packaging Inc ....F........818 885-1072
2175 Agate Ct Unit A Simi Valley (93065) ***(P-5539)***
Total Phase Inc ....F........408 850-6500
2350 Mission College Blvd # 1100 Santa Clara (95054) ***(P-15110)***
Total Process Solutions LLC ....E........661 829-7910
1400 Norris Rd Bakersfield (93308) ***(P-14601)***
Total Resources Intl Inc (PA) ....D........909 594-1220
420 S Lemon Ave Walnut (91789) ***(P-22111)***
Total Source Manufacturing ....A........760 598-2146
1445 Engineer St Vista (92081) ***(P-20779)***
Total Source Manufacturing Co, Vista *Also called Total Source Manufacturing* ***(P-20779)***
Total Structures Inc ....E........805 676-3322
1696 Walter St Ventura (93003) ***(P-17171)***
Total Technologies, Irvine *Also called Turn-Luckily International Inc* ***(P-15356)***
Total-Western Inc (HQ) ....E........562 220-1450
8049 Somerset Blvd Paramount (90723) ***(P-272)***
Totally Bamboo, San Marcos *Also called Hollywood Chairs* ***(P-4575)***
Totally Radical Associates Inc ....F........714 630-2740
1025 Ortega Way Ste A Placentia (92870) ***(P-14115)***
Totalthermalimagingcom ....F........619 303-5884
8341 La Mesa Blvd La Mesa (91942) ***(P-15352)***
Totex Manufacturing Inc ....D........310 326-2028
3050 Lomita Blvd Torrance (90505) ***(P-10089)***
Totty Printing ....F........714 633-7081
18946 Spectacular Bid Ln Yorba Linda (92886) ***(P-7253)***
Toucaned Inc ....F........831 464-0508
1716 Brommer St Santa Cruz (95062) ***(P-6361)***
Touch Coffee & Beverages LLC ....F........626 968-0300
15312 Valley Blvd City of Industry (91746) ***(P-16841)***
Touch Litho Company ....F........562 927-8899
7215 E Gage Ave Commerce (90040) ***(P-6893)***
Touch ME Fashion Inc ....E........323 234-9200
906 E 60th St Los Angeles (90001) ***(P-3426)***
Touchdown Technologies Inc ....C........626 472-6732
5188 Commerce Dr Baldwin Park (91706) ***(P-18622)***
Touchmark, Hayward *Also called Delphon Industries LLC* ***(P-9750)***
Touchpint Elctrnic Sltions LLC ....F........951 734-8083
38372 Innovation Ct # 306 Murrieta (92563) ***(P-14990)***
Touchpoint Solutions ....F........714 740-7242
18426 Brookhurst St # 207 Fountain Valley (92708) ***(P-24522)***
Touchsport Footwear LLC ....F........310 763-0208
2969 E Pcf Commerce Dr E Rncho Dmngz (90221) ***(P-9186)***
Toufic Inc ....F........209 478-4780
2324 Grand Canal Blvd # 1 Stockton (95207) ***(P-1287)***
Toughbuilt Industries Inc (PA) ....F........949 528-3100
25371 Cmmrcntre Dr Dte 20 200 Dte Lake Forest (92630) ***(P-11548)***
Tourism Development Corp (PA) ....F........310 280-2880
3679 Motor Ave Ste 300 Los Angeles (90034) ***(P-6043)***
Toutapp Inc ....F........866 548-1927
901 Mariners Island Blvd # 500 San Mateo (94404) ***(P-24523)***
Tow Industries, West Covina *Also called Baatz Enterprises Inc* ***(P-19458)***
Tower Industries Inc ....C........909 947-2723
1720 S Bon View Ave Ontario (91761) ***(P-16462)***

Employee Codes: A=Over 500 employees, B=251-500
C=101-250, D=51-100, E=20-50, F=10-19

2020 California
Manfacturers Register

© Mergent Inc. 1-800-342-5647

1265

Tower Mechanical Products Inc ....C....714 947-2723
1720 S Bon View Ave Ontario (91761) ***(P-20733)***
Tower Semiconductor Usa Inc ....F....408 770-1320
2570 N 1st St Ste 480 San Jose (95131) ***(P-18623)***
Towerjazz, Newport Beach *Also called Jazz Semiconductor Inc* ***(P-18329)***
Towerjazz Texas Inc (HQ) ....D....949 435-8000
4321 Jamboree Rd Newport Beach (92660) ***(P-19120)***
Towne Park Brew Inc ....E....714 844-2492
1566 W Lincoln Ave Anaheim (92801) ***(P-1571)***
Toye Corporation ....F....818 882-4000
9230 Deering Ave Chatsworth (91311) ***(P-15353)***
Toykidz Inc ....F....213 688-2999
100 S Doheny Dr Ph 10 Los Angeles (90048) ***(P-23507)***
Toyo Automotive Parts USA Inc ....D....714 229-6125
5665 Plaza Dr Ste 200 Cypress (90630) ***(P-19785)***
Toyo Ink International Corp ....E....714 899-2377
11190 Valley View St Cypress (90630) ***(P-8935)***
Toyo Ink North America, Cypress *Also called Toyo Ink International Corp* ***(P-8935)***
Toyo Tire Hldings Americas Inc (HQ) ....E....562 431-6502
5900 Katella Ave Ste 200a Cypress (90630) ***(P-9170)***
TP Products, San Fernando *Also called Triumph Precision Products* ***(P-12656)***
TP Solar Inc ....E....562 808-2171
16310 Downey Ave Paramount (90723) ***(P-14777)***
TPC Advance Technology Inc ....F....626 810-4337
18519 Gale Ave City of Industry (91748) ***(P-22197)***
TPC Industries LLC ....E....310 849-9574
5920 W Birch Ave Fresno (93722) ***(P-23508)***
Tpg Growth, San Francisco *Also called Tpg Partners III LP* ***(P-71)***
Tpg Partners III LP (HQ) ....E....415 743-1500
345 California St # 3300 San Francisco (94104) ***(P-71)***
Tpi, Covina *Also called Topper Plastics Inc* ***(P-9573)***
Tpi Marketing LLC ....F....302 703-0283
14985 Hilton Dr Fontana (92336) ***(P-14407)***
Tpl Communications, Panorama City *Also called D X Communications Inc* ***(P-17499)***
Tpsi, Paramount *Also called TP Solar Inc* ***(P-14777)***
Tr Engineering Inc ....F....831 430-9920
1350 Green Hills Rd 10 Scotts Valley (95066) ***(P-14602)***
Tr Manufacturing LLC (HQ) ....C....510 657-3850
33210 Central Ave Union City (94587) ***(P-19121)***
Tr Theater Research Inc (PA) ....F....714 894-5888
11150 Hope St Cypress (90630) ***(P-17295)***
Tra Medical, Placentia *Also called Totally Radical Associates Inc* ***(P-14115)***
Tracet Manufacturing Inc ....F....408 779-8846
40 Kirby Ave Morgan Hill (95037) ***(P-16463)***
Trackonomy Systems Inc ....F....833 872-2566
2350 Mission College Blvd # 490 Santa Clara (95054) ***(P-17694)***
Trackstar Printing Inc ....F....310 216-1275
1140 W Mahalo Pl Compton (90220) ***(P-6894)***
Tracon Pharmaceuticals Inc (PA) ....E....858 550-0780
4350 La Jolla Village Dr # 800 San Diego (92122) ***(P-8167)***
Tracy Industries Inc ....C....562 692-9034
3200 E Guasti Rd Ste 100 Ontario (91761) ***(P-13600)***
Tracy Press Inc ....E....209 835-3030
145 W 10th St Tracy (95376) ***(P-5851)***
Trade Lithography, Richmond *Also called John Lompa* ***(P-7104)***
Trade Marker International ....F....760 602-4864
445 Ryan Dr Ste 101 San Marcos (92078) ***(P-2918)***
Trade Only Screen Printing Inc ....E....510 887-2020
23482 Foley St Hayward (94545) ***(P-7254)***
Trade Printing Services LLC ....E....760 496-0230
2080 Las Palmas Dr Carlsbad (92011) ***(P-6895)***
Trademark Construction Co Inc (PA) ....D....760 489-5647
15916 Bernardo Center Dr San Diego (92127) ***(P-19203)***
Trademark Cosmetic Inc ....E....951 683-2631
545 Columbia Ave Riverside (92507) ***(P-8594)***
Trademark Hoist Inc ....E....909 455-0801
1369 Ridgeway St Pomona (91768) ***(P-13852)***
Trademark Hoist & Crane, Pomona *Also called Trademark Hoist Inc* ***(P-13852)***
Trademark Plastics Inc ....C....909 941-8810
807 Palmyrita Ave Riverside (92507) ***(P-14546)***
Tradenet Enterprise Inc ....D....888 595-3956
1580 Magnolia Ave Corona (92879) ***(P-23231)***
Tradesman Trucktops, Winters *Also called Access Mfg Inc* ***(P-19515)***
Tradewinds, Monrovia *Also called Headwinds* ***(P-20406)***
Traditional Baking Inc ....D....909 877-8471
2575 S Willow Ave Bloomington (92316) ***(P-1333)***
Traditional Medicinals Inc (PA) ....C....707 823-8911
4515 Ross Rd Sebastopol (95472) ***(P-2635)***
Traffic Control & Safety Corp ....F....858 679-7292
13755 Blaisdell Pl Poway (92064) ***(P-23232)***
Traffic Works Inc ....E....323 582-0616
5720 Soto St Huntington Park (90255) ***(P-9423)***
Traffix Devices Inc ....E....760 246-7171
12128 Yucca Rd Adelanto (92301) ***(P-9381)***
Traffix Devices Inc (PA) ....F....949 361-5663
160 Avenida La Pata San Clemente (92673) ***(P-17769)***
Tragara Pharmaceuticals Inc ....F....760 208-6900
12481 High Bluff Dr # 150 San Diego (92130) ***(P-8168)***
Train Reaction, Huntington Beach *Also called West Coast Trends Inc* ***(P-22923)***
Trams International, Bell Gardens *Also called Bus Services Corporation* ***(P-19601)***
Trane US Inc ....F....408 257-5212
1601 S De Anza Blvd 235 Cupertino (95014) ***(P-15456)***
Trane US Inc ....C....408 481-3600
310 Soquel Way Sunnyvale (94085) ***(P-15457)***
Trane US Inc ....D....626 913-7123
3253 E Imperial Hwy Brea (92821) ***(P-15458)***
Trane US Inc ....E....626 913-7913
20450 E Walnut Dr N Walnut (91789) ***(P-15459)***
Trane US Inc ....D....951 801-6020
2222 Kansas Ave Ste C Riverside (92507) ***(P-15460)***
Trane US Inc ....D....408 437-0390
890 Service St Ste A San Jose (95112) ***(P-15461)***
Trane US Inc ....D....310 971-4555
1930 E Carson St Ste 101 Carson (90810) ***(P-15462)***
Trane US Inc ....E....858 292-0833
3565 Corporate Ct Fl 1 San Diego (92123) ***(P-15463)***
Trane US Inc ....E....559 271-4625
3026 N Bus Park Ave # 104 Fresno (93727) ***(P-15464)***
Tranpak Inc ....E....800 827-2474
2860 S East Ave Fresno (93725) ***(P-10090)***
Trans Bay Steel Corporation (PA) ....E....510 277-3756
2801 Giant Rd Ste H San Pablo (94806) ***(P-11902)***
Trans Fx Inc ....F....805 485-6110
2361 Eastman Ave Oxnard (93030) ***(P-23509)***
Trans Western Polymers Inc ....B....925 449-7800
7539 Las Positas Rd Livermore (94551) ***(P-5424)***
Trans-India Products Inc ....E....707 544-0298
3330 Coffey Ln Ste A&B Santa Rosa (95403) ***(P-8595)***
Transcend Medical Inc ....F....650 325-2050
127 Independence Dr Menlo Park (94025) ***(P-21935)***
Transcendent Imaging LLC ....F....805 964-1400
5765 Thornwood Dr Goleta (93117) ***(P-22465)***
Transchem Coatings, Los Angeles *Also called Paint-Chem Inc* ***(P-8661)***
Transco, El Monte *Also called Transgo* ***(P-19786)***
Transcontinental Nrthern CA 20 ....C....510 580-7700
47540 Kato Rd Fremont (94538) ***(P-7255)***
Transcontinental US LLC ....C....559 585-2040
10801 Iona Ave Hanford (93230) ***(P-5425)***
Transcontinental US LLC ....E....909 390-8866
5601 Santa Ana St Ontario (91761) ***(P-5426)***
Transdesign Inc ....F....661 631-1062
440 19th St Bakersfield (93301) ***(P-4142)***
Transdigm Inc ....E....323 269-9181
5000 Triggs St Commerce (90022) ***(P-20252)***
Transdigm Inc ....C....323 269-9181
5000 Triggs St Commerce (90022) ***(P-20253)***
Transdigm Inc ....C....323 269-9181
5000 Triggs St Commerce (90022) ***(P-20254)***
Transducer Techniques LLC ....E....951 719-3965
42480 Rio Nedo Temecula (92590) ***(P-19122)***
Transfer Engineering & Mfg Inc ....E....510 651-3000
1100 La Avenida St Ste A Mountain View (94043) ***(P-14731)***
Transfirst Corporation ....E....831 424-2911
900 E Blanco Rd Salinas (93901) ***(P-20817)***
Transformationnet Media LLC ....E....310 476-5259
1640 N Spring St Los Angeles (90012) ***(P-6044)***
Transglobal Apparel Group Inc ....F....714 890-9200
12362 Knott St Garden Grove (92841) ***(P-3427)***
Transgo ....E....626 443-7456
2621 Merced Ave El Monte (91733) ***(P-19786)***
Transhumance Holding Co Inc ....F....323 583-5503
2851 E 44th St Vernon (90058) ***(P-504)***
Transhumance Holding Co Inc ....C....707 693-2303
7390 Rio Dixon Rd Dixon (95620) ***(P-426)***
Transit Care Inc ....F....818 267-3002
7900 Nelson Rd Panorama City (91402) ***(P-10278)***
Transko Electronics Inc ....F....714 528-8000
3981 E Miraloma Ave Anaheim (92806) ***(P-19123)***
Translarity Inc ....F....510 371-7900
46575 Fremont Blvd Fremont (94538) ***(P-21148)***
Translattice Inc (PA) ....E....408 749-8478
3398 Londonderry Dr Santa Clara (95050) ***(P-14991)***
Transline Technology Inc ....E....714 533-8300
1106 S Technology Cir Anaheim (92805) ***(P-18024)***
Translogic Incorporated ....E....714 890-0058
5641 Engineer Dr Huntington Beach (92649) ***(P-20951)***
Transonic Combustion Inc ....E....805 465-5145
461 Calle San Pablo Camarillo (93012) ***(P-13601)***
Transparent Devices Inc ....E....805 499-5000
853 Lawrence Dr Newbury Park (91320) ***(P-15354)***
Transparent Products Inc ....E....661 294-9787
28064 Avenue Stanford E Valencia (91355) ***(P-15137)***
Transplant Connect Inc ....E....310 392-1400
2701 Ocean Park Blvd # 222 Santa Monica (90405) ***(P-24524)***
Transportation Equipment Inc (PA) ....E....619 449-8860
1404 N Marshall Ave El Cajon (92020) ***(P-3711)***
Transportation Power Inc ....E....858 248-4255
2415 Auto Park Way Escondido (92029) ***(P-19787)***
Transpower, Escondido *Also called Transportation Power Inc* ***(P-19787)***
Transworld Printing Svcs Inc ....F....209 982-1511
152 Whitcomb Ave Colfax (95713) ***(P-6896)***
Trantronics Inc ....E....949 553-1234
1822 Langley Ave Irvine (92614) ***(P-18025)***
Trashy Lingerie, West Hollywood *Also called 402 Shoes Inc* ***(P-3437)***
Trattoria Amici/Americana LLC ....F....818 502-1220
783 Americana Way Glendale (91210) ***(P-5086)***
Travcom, Los Angeles *Also called Travel Computer Systems Inc* ***(P-24525)***
Travel Computer Systems Inc ....F....310 558-3130
1990 Westwood Blvd # 310 Los Angeles (90025) ***(P-24525)***
Travelers Choice Travelware ....D....909 529-7688
2805 S Reservoir St Pomona (91766) ***(P-10213)***
Travis American Group LLC ....C....714 258-1200
11450 Sheldon St Sun Valley (91352) ***(P-4143)***
Travis Industries, Sun Valley *Also called Travis American Group LLC* ***(P-4143)***
Travis Mike Inc ....F....805 201-3363
2420 Celsius Ave Ste D Oxnard (93030) ***(P-12884)***
Travismathew LLC ....F....562 799-6900
15202 Graham St Huntington Beach (92649) ***(P-3124)***

Mergent e-mail: customerrelations@mergent.com
1266
2020 California
Manufacturers Register
(P-0000) Products & Services Section entry number
(PA)=Parent Co (HQ)=Headquarters (DH)=Div Headquarters

Traxx Corporation.................................D....909 623-8032
1201 E Lexington Ave Pomona (91766) *(P-23510)*

Trayer Engineering Corporation.................D....415 285-7770
1569 Alvarado St San Leandro (94577) *(P-16619)*

Traylor Management Inc (PA)...................F....858 486-7700
12120 Tech Center Dr B Poway (92064) *(P-6362)*

TRC Cocoa LLC..................................F....916 847-2390
3721 Douglas Blvd Ste 375 Roseville (95661) *(P-1416)*

TRC Operating Company Inc......................F....661 763-0081
805 Blackgold Ct Taft (93268) *(P-72)*

Treana Winery LLC..............................E....805 237-2932
4280 Second Wind Way Paso Robles (93446) *(P-1961)*

Treasury Chateau & Estates.....................F....707 996-5870
1700 Moon Mountain Rd Sonoma (95476) *(P-1962)*

Treasury Wine Estates Americas (HQ)............B....707 259-4500
555 Gateway Dr NAPA (94558) *(P-1963)*

Treasury Wine Estates Americas.................C....707 259-4500
600 Airpark Rd NAPA (94558) *(P-1964)*

Treasury Wine Estates Americas.................D....707 963-7115
2000 Main St Saint Helena (94574) *(P-1965)*

Treasury Wine Estates Americas.................B....707 963-4812
1000 Pratt Ave Saint Helena (94574) *(P-1966)*

Treasury Wine Estates Americas.................E....707 833-4134
8555 Sonoma Hwy Kenwood (95452) *(P-1967)*

Treasury Wine Estates Americas.................E....707 894-2541
26150 Asti Rd Cloverdale (95425) *(P-1968)*

Treasury Wine Estates Americas.................D....707 963-7115
2000 Saint Helena Hwy N Saint Helena (94574) *(P-1969)*

Treat Manufacturing Inc........................F....209 532-2220
19401 Rawhide Rd Sonora (95370) *(P-13959)*

Tree House Pad & Paper Inc.....................D....800 213-4184
2341 Pomona Rd Ste 108 Corona (92880) *(P-5485)*

Tree Island Wire (usa) Inc (HQ)................C....909 594-7511
3880 Valley Blvd Walnut (91789) *(P-11078)*

Tree Island Wire (usa) Inc.....................D....909 594-7511
13470 Philadelphia Ave Fontana (92337) *(P-11111)*

Tree Island Wire (usa) Inc.....................B....909 595-6617
3880 W Valley Blvd Pomona (91769) *(P-11112)*

Tree Island Wire (usa) Inc.....................D....800 255-6974
12459 Arrow Rte Rancho Cucamonga (91739) *(P-11113)*

Tree Top Inc...................................C....509 697-7251
1250 E 3rd St Oxnard (93030) *(P-830)*

Trefethen Family Vineyards, NAPA *Also called Trefethen Vineyards Winery Inc (P-1970)*

Trefethen Vineyards Winery Inc.................E....707 255-7700
1160 Oak Knoll Ave NAPA (94558) *(P-1970)*

Trek Armor Incorporated........................F....951 319-4008
41795 Elm St Ste 401 Murrieta (92562) *(P-23511)*

Trekell & Co Inc...............................F....800 378-3867
17459 Lilac St Ste B Hesperia (92345) *(P-22947)*

Trelleborg Sealing Solutions (HQ)..............C....714 415-0280
2761 Walnut Ave Tustin (92780) *(P-21936)*

Tremco Incorporated............................F....323 587-3014
3060 E 44th St Vernon (90058) *(P-9126)*

Trend Chasers LLC..............................E....213 749-2661
2311 S Santa Fe Ave Vernon (90058) *(P-10255)*

Trend Frames, San Diego *Also called Trend Marketing Corporation (P-4540)*

Trend Manor Furn Mfg Co Inc....................E....626 964-6493
17047 Gale Ave City of Industry (91745) *(P-4616)*

Trend Marketing Corporation....................D....800 468-7363
3025 Beyer Blvd Ste 102 San Diego (92154) *(P-4540)*

Trend Offset Printing Svcs Inc.................C....859 449-2900
3701 Catalina St Los Alamitos (90720) *(P-6897)*

Trend Offset Printing Svcs Inc (PA)............A....562 598-2446
3701 Catalina St Los Alamitos (90720) *(P-6898)*

Trend Offset Printing Svcs Inc.................B....562 598-2446
3791 Catalina St Los Alamitos (90720) *(P-6899)*

Trend Technologies LLC (HQ)....................C....909 597-7861
4626 Eucalyptus Ave Chino (91710) *(P-12410)*

Trendpoint Systems Inc.........................F....925 855-0600
283 Winfield Cir Corona (92880) *(P-21149)*

Trent Beverage Company LLC.....................F....310 384-6776
47230 Golden Bush Ct Palm Desert (92260) *(P-2177)*

Trepanning Spcialty A Cal Corp.................E....562 408-0044
16201 Illinois Ave Paramount (90723) *(P-16464)*

Trepanning Specialties, Paramount *Also called Trepanning Spcialty A Cal Corp (P-16464)*

Tres Bien Inc (PA).............................F....213 747-3366
1016 Towne Ave Unit 113 Los Angeles (90021) *(P-3428)*

Tresco Paint Co................................F....510 887-7254
21595 Curtis St Hayward (94545) *(P-8688)*

Trex Enterprises Corporation (PA)..............D....858 646-5300
10455 Pacific Center Ct San Diego (92121) *(P-14992)*

Tri A Machine Inc..............................F....714 408-8907
7221 Garden Grove Blvd Ab Garden Grove (92841) *(P-13996)*

Tri All, San Clemente *Also called Try All 3 Sports (P-20433)*

Tri C Machine Shop, West Sacramento *Also called Tri-C Machine Corporation (P-16466)*

Tri City Voice, Fremont *Also called Whats Happening Tri City (P-7271)*

Tri County Spring & Stamping, Ventura *Also called Tricoss Inc (P-13391)*

Tri Dental Innovators Corp.....................F....714 554-1170
13902 West St Garden Grove (92843) *(P-22198)*

Tri Fab Associates Inc.........................D....510 651-7628
48351 Lakeview Blvd Fremont (94538) *(P-12411)*

Tri Map International Inc......................F....209 234-0100
119 Val Dervin Pkwy Ste 5 Stockton (95206) *(P-14993)*

Tri Models Inc.................................D....714 896-0823
5191 Oceanus Dr Huntington Beach (92649) *(P-19935)*

Tri Power Electric Inc.........................F....714 630-6445
1211 N La Loma Cir Anaheim (92806) *(P-19423)*

Tri Precision Sheetmetal Inc...................E....714 632-8838
845 N Elm St Orange (92867) *(P-12412)*

Tri Print LLC.................................F....714 847-1400
7573 Slater Ave Ste C Huntington Beach (92647) *(P-6900)*

Tri Quality Inc................................E....916 388-5939
5840 S Watt Ave Ste A Sacramento (95829) *(P-22112)*

Tri Service Co Inc.............................F....626 442-3270
2465 Loma Ave South El Monte (91733) *(P-9031)*

Tri Star Metals Inc............................F....707 678-1140
8749 Pedrick Rd Dixon (95620) *(P-12610)*

Tri State Manufacturing Inc....................F....949 855-9121
27212 Burbank El Toro (92610) *(P-16465)*

Tri State Truss Corporation....................F....760 326-3868
600 River Rd Needles (92363) *(P-4323)*

Tri Tek Electronics Inc........................E....661 295-0020
25358 Avenue Stanford Valencia (91355) *(P-19124)*

Tri-C Machine Corporation (PA).................F....916 371-8090
520 Harbor Blvd West Sacramento (95691) *(P-16466)*

Tri-C Manufacturing Inc........................F....916 371-1700
517 Houston St West Sacramento (95691) *(P-14547)*

Tri-City Print & Mail, West Sacramento *Also called Tri-City Technologies Inc (P-7256)*

Tri-City Technologies Inc......................F....916 503-5300
2615 Del Monte St West Sacramento (95691) *(P-7256)*

Tri-Co Building Supply Inc.....................D....805 343-2555
695 Obispo St Guadalupe (93434) *(P-4324)*

Tri-Continent Scientific Inc...................D....530 273-8888
12740 Earhart Ave Auburn (95602) *(P-20977)*

Tri-Dim Filter Corporation.....................F....626 333-9428
15271 Fairfield Ranch Rd # 150 Chino Hills (91709) *(P-14684)*

Tri-Dim Filter Corporation.....................E....626 826-5893
15271 Fairfield Ranch Rd # 150 Chino Hills (91709) *(P-14685)*

Tri-Fitting Mfg Company........................F....626 442-2000
10414 Rush St South El Monte (91733) *(P-20255)*

Tri-J Metal Heat Treating Co (PA)..............F....909 622-9999
327 E Commercial St Pomona (91767) *(P-11474)*

Tri-K Truss Company............................F....559 784-8511
453 S Main St Porterville (93257) *(P-4325)*

Tri-Mag Inc....................................E....559 651-2222
1601 Clancy Ct Visalia (93291) *(P-19125)*

Tri-Net Inc....................................F....909 483-3555
14721 Hilton Dr Fontana (92336) *(P-21150)*

Tri-Net Technology Inc.........................D....909 598-8818
21709 Ferrero Walnut (91789) *(P-15355)*

Tri-Phase Inc..................................C....408 284-7700
6190 San Ignacio Ave San Jose (95119) *(P-18026)*

Tri-Star Dyeing & Finshg Inc...................D....562 483-0123
15125 Marquardt Ave Santa Fe Springs (90670) *(P-2748)*

Tri-Star Electronics Intl Inc (HQ).............B....310 536-0444
2201 Rosecrans Ave El Segundo (90245) *(P-16936)*

Tri-Star Laminates Inc.........................E....949 587-3200
20322 Windrow Dr Ste 100 Lake Forest (92630) *(P-18027)*

Tri-Star Technologies Inc......................F....310 567-9243
1111 E El Segundo Blvd El Segundo (90245) *(P-22322)*

Tri-State Manufacturing, Lake Forest *Also called June Precision Mfg Inc (P-12637)*

Tri-State Stairway Corp........................E....559 268-0875
706 W California Ave Fresno (93706) *(P-12517)*

Tri-Tech Precision Inc.........................F....714 970-1363
1863 N Case St Orange (92865) *(P-20256)*

Triactive America Inc..........................F....805 595-1005
1244 Trail View Pl Nipomo (93444) *(P-22910)*

Triad Bellows Design & Mfg Inc.................E....714 204-4444
2897 E La Cresta Ave Anaheim (92806) *(P-16467)*

Triad Energy Resources Inc.....................E....209 527-0607
204 Kerr Ave Modesto (95354) *(P-8816)*

Triad Tool & Engineering Inc...................E....408 436-8411
1750 Rogers Ave San Jose (95112) *(P-10091)*

Triad Waste Management, Modesto *Also called Triad Energy Resources Inc (P-8816)*

Triangle Brass Mfg Co Inc (PA).................D....323 262-4191
1351 Rocky Point Dr Oceanside (92056) *(P-11638)*

Triangle Rock Products, Sacramento *Also called Legacy Vulcan LLC (P-10789)*

Triangle Rock Products LLC.....................E....818 553-8820
500 N Brand Blvd Ste 500 # 500 Glendale (91203) *(P-320)*

Triangle Tool & Die Corp.......................F....562 944-2117
13189 Flores St Santa Fe Springs (90670) *(P-16468)*

Tribal Print Source............................F....760 597-2650
36146 Pala Temecula Rd Pala (92059) *(P-6901)*

Tribe Media Corp...............................E....213 368-1661
3250 Wilshire Blvd Los Angeles (90010) *(P-5852)*

Tribeworx LLC..................................D....800 949-3432
4 San Joaquin Plz Ste 150 Newport Beach (92660) *(P-24526)*

Tribune Los Angeles Inc........................F....213 237-5000
202 W 1st St Ste 500 Los Angeles (90012) *(P-5853)*

Tribune Studios, Los Angeles *Also called 5800 Sunset Productions Inc (P-5543)*

Tribune, The, Oakland *Also called Oakland Tribune Inc (P-5786)*

Trical Inc.....................................F....559 651-0736
28679 Rd 68 Visalia (93277) *(P-8842)*

Trical Inc (PA)................................E....831 637-0195
8100 Arroyo Cir Gilroy (95020) *(P-8843)*

Trical Inc.....................................D....831 637-0195
8770 Hwy 25 Hollister (95023) *(P-8844)*

Trical Inc.....................................F....951 737-6960
1029 Railroad St Corona (92882) *(P-8845)*

Trical Inc.....................................E....661 824-2494
1667 Purdy Rd Mojave (93501) *(P-8846)*

Tricida Inc....................................D....415 429-7800
7000 Shoreline Ct Ste 201 South San Francisco (94080) *(P-8169)*

Tricir Technologies, City of Industry *Also called Lanstreetcom (P-15128)*

Trico Sports Inc...............................D....818 899-7705
13541 Desmond St Pacoima (91331) *(P-20432)*

Tricom Research Inc............................D....949 250-6024
17791 Sky Park Cir Ste J Irvine (92614) *(P-17695)*

Triconex, Lake Forest *Also called Schneider Elc Systems USA Inc (P-20933)*

Employee Codes: A=Over 500 employees, B=251-500
C=101-250, D=51-100, E=20-50, F=10-19

2020 California
Manfacturers Register

© Mergent Inc. 1-800-342-5647
1267

ALPHABETIC

Tricor Refining LLC......E......661 393-7110
1134 Manor St Bakersfield (93308) ***(P-9077)***
Tricoss Inc......F......805 644-4107
4450 Dupont Ct Ste A Ventura (93003) ***(P-13391)***
Tridecs Corporation......E......510 785-2620
3513 Arden Rd Hayward (94545) ***(P-16469)***
Trident Diving Equipment......E......818 998-7518
9616 Owensmouth Ave Chatsworth (91311) ***(P-22911)***
Trident Plating Inc......E......562 906-2556
10046 Romandel Ave Santa Fe Springs (90670) ***(P-13119)***
Trident Products Inc......D......760 510-1160
1370 W San Marcos Blvd # 120 San Marcos (92078) ***(P-10092)***
Trident Technologies, San Diego *Also called Chemtreat Inc* ***(P-8948)***
Tridus International Inc......F......310 884-3200
1145 W Victoria St Compton (90220) ***(P-13552)***
Tridus Magnetics and Assenblie, Compton *Also called Tridus International Inc* ***(P-13552)***
Trifoil Imaging, Chatsworth *Also called Northrdge Tr-Mdlity Imging Inc* ***(P-20768)***
Trigon Components Inc......F......714 990-1367
935 Mariner St Brea (92821) ***(P-18685)***
Trigon Electronics Inc......F......714 633-7442
22865 Savi Ranch Pkwy A Yorba Linda (92887) ***(P-19424)***
Trijicon Electro Optics, Auburn *Also called IRD Acquisitions LLC* ***(P-22363)***
Trilibis Inc (PA)......F......650 646-2400
66 Bovet Rd Ste 285 San Mateo (94402) ***(P-24527)***
Trilibis Mobile, San Mateo *Also called Trilibis Inc* ***(P-24527)***
Trillium Pumps Usa Inc (HQ)......C......559 442-4000
2494 S Railroad Ave Fresno (93706) ***(P-14603)***
Trilogy Glass and Packg Inc......E......707 521-1300
975 Corporate Cntr Pkwy # 120 Santa Rosa (95407) ***(P-10394)***
Trilore Technologies Inc......E......925 295-0734
3000 Danville Blvd 525f Alamo (94507) ***(P-11390)***
Trim Quick, Corona *Also called Vinylvisions Company LLC* ***(P-8691)***
Trim Quick Co, Norco *Also called Halle-Hopper LLC* ***(P-4053)***
Trim To Trade, Palm Desert *Also called Plumbing Products Inc* ***(P-11676)***
Trim-Lok Inc (PA)......C......714 562-0500
6855 Hermosa Cir Buena Park (90620) ***(P-10093)***
Trimatic, Pasadena *Also called C & D Precision Components* ***(P-15807)***
Trimble Inc......F......408 481-8490
945 Stewart Dr Ste 100 Sunnyvale (94085) ***(P-20734)***
Trimble Inc (PA)......A......408 481-8000
935 Stewart Dr Sunnyvale (94085) ***(P-21559)***
Trimble Inc......E......916 294-2000
1720 Prairie City Rd Folsom (95630) ***(P-20735)***
Trimble Inc......F......408 481-8000
510 Deguigne Dr Sunnyvale (94085) ***(P-20736)***
Trimble Military & Advnced Sys......D......408 481-8000
510 De Guigne Dr Sunnyvale (94085) ***(P-20737)***
Trimco, Oceanside *Also called Triangle Brass Mfg Co Inc* ***(P-11638)***
Trimedyne Inc (PA)......E......949 951-3800
530 Technology Dr Ste 275 Irvine (92618) ***(P-22323)***
Trimknit Inc......E......818 768-7878
7542 San Fernando Rd Sun Valley (91352) ***(P-2762)***
Trinchero Family Estates, Saint Helena *Also called Sutter Home Winery Inc* ***(P-1941)***
Trinchero Family Estates, Lodi *Also called Sutter Home Winery Inc* ***(P-1942)***
Trinchero Family Estates Inc......F......707 963-1160
3070 Saint Helena Hwy N Saint Helena (94574) ***(P-1971)***
Trinet Construction Inc......F......415 695-7814
3934 Geary Blvd San Francisco (94118) ***(P-14865)***
Tringen Corporation......F......661 393-3039
238 E Norris Rd Bakersfield (93308) ***(P-273)***
Trinidad Benham Holding Co......E......909 627-7535
5177 Chino Ave Chino (91710) ***(P-2636)***
Trinity - 4, Paramount *Also called International Trend - 3 Corp* ***(P-3094)***
Trinity Engineering......E......707 585-2959
583 Martin Ave Rohnert Park (94928) ***(P-5007)***
Trinity Lighweight, Frazier Park *Also called Trnlwb LLC* ***(P-23512)***
Trinity Marketing LLC......F......925 866-1514
12925 Alcosta Blvd Ste 6 San Ramon (94583) ***(P-6902)***
Trinity Office Furniture Inc......D......909 888-5551
1050 W Rialto Ave San Bernardino (92410) ***(P-4823)***
Trinity Process Solutions Inc......E......714 701-1112
4740 E Bryson St Anaheim (92807) ***(P-13487)***
Trinity River Lumber Company (PA)......C......530 623-5561
1375 Main St Weaverville (96093) ***(P-3964)***
Trinity Steel Corporation......F......805 648-3486
918 Mission Rock Rd B1 Santa Paula (93060) ***(P-11903)***
Trinium Technologies, Palos Verdes Estates *Also called QED Software LLC* ***(P-24327)***
Trio Engineered Products Inc (HQ)......E......626 851-3966
505 W Foothill Blvd Azusa (91702) ***(P-13753)***
Trio Manufacturing Inc......D......310 640-6123
601 Lairport St El Segundo (90245) ***(P-20257)***
Trio Metal Stamping Inc......D......626 336-1228
15318 Proctor Ave City of Industry (91745) ***(P-12413)***
Trio Tool & Die Co (PA)......F......310 644-4431
3340 W El Segundo Blvd Hawthorne (90250) ***(P-14116)***
Trio-Tech International (PA)......F......818 787-7000
16139 Wyandotte St Van Nuys (91406) ***(P-14548)***
Triple A Pallets Inc......F......559 313-7636
3555 S Academy Ave Sanger (93657) ***(P-4402)***
Triple C Foods Inc......D......510 357-8880
1465 Factor Ave San Leandro (94577) ***(P-1334)***
Triple DOT Corp......E......714 241-0888
3302 S Susan St Santa Ana (92704) ***(P-9496)***
Triple E Manufacturing Inc......E......661 831-7553
2121 S Union Ave Bakersfield (93307) ***(P-14408)***
Triple H Food Processors LLC......D......951 352-5700
5821 Wilderness Ave Riverside (92504) ***(P-2637)***
Triplett Harps......F......805 544-2777
220 Suburban Rd Ste C San Luis Obispo (93401) ***(P-22643)***
Tripos Industries Inc......E......323 669-0488
2448 Glendower Ave Los Angeles (90027) ***(P-11685)***
Triprism Inc......F......858 675-7552
15950 Bernardo Center Dr B San Diego (92127) ***(P-22466)***
Tripus Industries, Los Angeles *Also called Tripos Industries Inc* ***(P-11685)***
Triquint Wj Inc......D......408 577-6200
3099 Orchard Dr San Jose (95134) ***(P-17696)***
Trireme Medical LLC......D......925 931-1300
7060 Koll Center Pkwy Pleasanton (94566) ***(P-21937)***
Trisar Inc......E......714 972-2626
2200 W Orangewood Ave # 235 Orange (92868) ***(P-7257)***
Trisep Corporation, Goleta *Also called Microdyn-Nadir Us Inc* ***(P-15543)***
Tristar Global Inc......F......626 363-6978
526 Coralridge Pl La Puente (91746) ***(P-19788)***
Triton Chandelier Inc......E......714 957-9600
1301 Dove St Ste 900 Newport Beach (92660) ***(P-17078)***
Triumph Actuation Systms-Valen......C......661 295-1015
28150 Harrison Pkwy Valencia (91355) ***(P-20258)***
Triumph Aerostructures LLC......A......310 322-1000
3901 Jack Northrop Ave Hawthorne (90250) ***(P-20259)***
Triumph Arstrctres - Vght Coml, Hawthorne *Also called Triumph Aerostructures LLC* ***(P-20259)***
Triumph Equipment Inc......E......909 947-5983
13434 S Ontario Ave Ontario (91761) ***(P-20260)***
Triumph Group, Calexico *Also called Triumph Insulation Systems LLC* ***(P-20262)***
Triumph Group Inc......B......714 546-9842
2136 S Hathaway St Santa Ana (92705) ***(P-11475)***
Triumph Group Inc......F......760 768-1700
2401 Portico Blvd Calexico (92231) ***(P-20261)***
Triumph Insulation Systems LLC......A......949 250-4999
1754 Carr Rd Ste 103 Calexico (92231) ***(P-20262)***
Triumph Precision Products......F......818 897-4700
13636 Vaughn St Ste A San Fernando (91340) ***(P-12656)***
Triumph Processing Inc......C......323 563-1338
2605 Industry Way Lynwood (90262) ***(P-13120)***
Triune Enterprises Inc......E......310 719-1600
13711 S Normandie Ave Gardena (90249) ***(P-5346)***
Triune Enterprises Mfg, Gardena *Also called Triune Enterprises Inc* ***(P-5346)***
Trius Therapeutics LLC......D......858 452-0370
4747 Executive Dr # 1100 San Diego (92121) ***(P-8170)***
Trivascular Inc (HQ)......E......707 543-8800
3910 Brickway Blvd Santa Rosa (95403) ***(P-21938)***
Trivascular Technologies Inc (HQ)......F......707 543-8800
3910 Brickway Blvd Santa Rosa (95403) ***(P-21939)***
Trivec-Avant Corporation, Huntington Beach *Also called Cobham Trivec-Avant Inc* ***(P-17488)***
Triview Glass Industries LLC......D......626 363-7980
711 S Stimson Ave City of Industry (91745) ***(P-10395)***
Trixxi Clothing Company Inc (PA)......E......323 585-4200
6817 E Acco St Commerce (90040) ***(P-3201)***
Triyar Capital California LLC (PA)......F......310 441-5654
10850 Wilshire Blvd Los Angeles (90024) ***(P-20263)***
Trizic Inc......E......415 366-6583
60 E Sir Francis Drake Bl Larkspur (94939) ***(P-24528)***
Trlg Intermediate Holdings LLC (PA)......F......323 266-3072
1888 Rosecrans Ave Manhattan Beach (90266) ***(P-3496)***
TRM Manufacturing Inc......C......951 256-8550
375 Trm Cir Corona (92879) ***(P-9424)***
Trmc Sale Corporation......D......800 290-7073
4215 E Airport Dr Ontario (91761) ***(P-15465)***
Trnlwb LLC......A......661 245-3736
17410 Lockwood Valley Rd Frazier Park (93225) ***(P-23512)***
Troesh Readymix Inc......D......805 928-3764
2280 Hutton Rd Nipomo (93444) ***(P-10857)***
Trojan Battery Company LLC (HQ)......B......562 236-3000
10375 Slusher Dr Santa Fe Springs (90670) ***(P-19183)***
Tronex Technology Incorporated......E......707 426-2550
2860 Cordelia Rd Ste 230 Fairfield (94534) ***(P-11549)***
Tronson Manufacturing Inc......E......408 533-0369
3421 Yale Way Fremont (94538) ***(P-16470)***
Tropian Inc......D......408 865-1300
20813 Stevens Creek Blvd Cupertino (95014) ***(P-18624)***
Tropical Asphalt LLC (PA)......F......714 739-1408
14435 Macaw St La Mirada (90638) ***(P-9127)***
Tropical Functional Labs LLC......F......951 688-2619
7111 Arlington Ave Ste F Riverside (92503) ***(P-622)***
Tropical Preserving Co Inc......E......213 748-5108
1711 E 15th St Los Angeles (90021) ***(P-831)***
Tropical Roofing Products CA, La Mirada *Also called Tropical Asphalt LLC* ***(P-9127)***
Tropicale Foods Inc......E......909 635-0390
1237 W State St Ontario (91762) ***(P-674)***
Tropicana Products Inc......C......626 968-1299
240 N Orange Ave City of Industry (91744) ***(P-832)***
Tropitone Furniture Co Inc (HQ)......B......949 595-2000
5 Marconi Irvine (92618) ***(P-4705)***
Trosak Cabinets Inc......F......760 744-9042
1478 Alpine Pl San Marcos (92078) ***(P-4951)***
Trouble At The Mill, Huntington Park *Also called Cotton Generation Inc* ***(P-3476)***
Trov Inc (PA)......E......925 478-5500
347 Hartz Ave Danville (94526) ***(P-24529)***
Trovagene Inc......F......858 952-7570
11055 Flintkote Ave Ste A San Diego (92121) ***(P-8265)***
Troy Metal Products, Goleta *Also called Neal Feay Company* ***(P-11241)***
Troy Products, Montebello *Also called Troy Sheet Metal Works Inc* ***(P-12751)***
Troy Sheet Metal Works Inc......E......323 720-4100
1024 S Vail Ave Montebello (90640) ***(P-12751)***
Troy-Csl Lighting Inc......D......626 336-4511
14508 Nelson Ave City of Industry (91744) ***(P-16994)***

Mergent e-mail: customerrelations@mergent.com
1268
2020 California
Manufacturers Register
(P-0000) Products & Services Section entry number
(PA)=Parent Co (HQ)=Headquarters (DH)=Div Headquarters

Trs International Mfg Inc....F....949 855-0673
27152 Burbank Foothill Ranch (92610) ***(P-16937)***
TRT Bsness Ntwrk Solutions Inc....F....714 380-3888
15551 Red Hill Ave Ste A Tustin (92780) ***(P-21151)***
Tru Form Industries, Santa Fe Springs *Also called Tru-Form Industries Inc* ***(P-12885)***
Tru Machining....F....510 573-3408
45979 Warm Springs Blvd Fremont (94539) ***(P-16471)***
Tru-Cut Inc....E....310 630-0422
141 E 157th St Gardena (90248) ***(P-13699)***
Tru-Duct Inc....E....619 660-3858
2500 Swetwater Sprng Blvd Spring Valley (91978) ***(P-12414)***
Tru-Fit Manufacturing, Lathrop *Also called Accurate Heating & Cooling Inc* ***(P-12084)***
Tru-Form Industries Inc (PA)....D....562 802-2041
14511 Anson Ave Santa Fe Springs (90670) ***(P-12885)***
Tru-Form Plastics Inc....E....310 327-9444
14600 Hoover St Westminster (92683) ***(P-10094)***
Tru-Trailers Inc....F....559 251-7591
4444 E Lincoln Ave Fresno (93725) ***(P-19833)***
Tru-Trailers Manufacturing, Fresno *Also called Tru-Trailers Inc* ***(P-19833)***
Tru-Wood Products, Azusa *Also called McMurtrie & Mcmurtrie Inc* ***(P-3978)***
Truabutment Inc....D....714 956-1488
17742 Cowan Irvine (92614) ***(P-22199)***
Truck Accessories Group LLC....C....530 666-0176
1686 E Beamer St Woodland (95776) ***(P-20495)***
Truck Club Publishing Inc....E....323 726-8620
7807 Telegraph Rd Ste H Montebello (90640) ***(P-6157)***
True Cast Concrete Products, Sun Valley *Also called Gibbel Bros Inc* ***(P-10762)***
True Cast Concrete Products, Sun Valley *Also called Quikrete Companies LLC* ***(P-10638)***
True Circuits Inc....F....650 949-3400
4300 El Camino Real # 200 Los Altos (94022) ***(P-19126)***
True Design Inc....F....562 699-2001
9427 Norwalk Blvd Santa Fe Springs (90670) ***(P-4255)***
True Fresh Hpp LLC....F....949 629-7645
6535 Caballero Blvd B Buena Park (90620) ***(P-20818)***
True Grit, Newport Beach *Also called Calor Apparel Group Intl Corp* ***(P-3440)***
True Leaf Farms LLC....B....831 623-4667
1275 San Justo Rd San Juan Bautista (95045) ***(P-871)***
True Leaf Technologies, Cotati *Also called Biotherm Hydronic Inc* ***(P-11691)***
True Organic Products Inc....F....559 866-3001
20225 W Kamm Ave Helm (93627) ***(P-8817)***
True Position Technologies LLC....D....661 294-0030
24900 Avenue Stanford Valencia (91355) ***(P-16472)***
True Precision Machining Inc....E....805 964-4545
175 Indstrial Way Bellton Buellton Buellton (93427) ***(P-16473)***
True Protein, Vista *Also called Myosci Technologies Inc* ***(P-607)***
True Religion Apparel Inc (HQ)....B....323 266-3072
1888 Rosecrans Ave # 1000 Manhattan Beach (90266) ***(P-3020)***
True Religion Brand Jeans, Manhattan Beach *Also called True Religion Apparel Inc* ***(P-3020)***
True Temper Sports Inc....E....858 404-0405
9401 Waples St Ste 140 San Diego (92121) ***(P-22912)***
True Vision Displays Inc....F....562 407-0630
16402 Berwyn Rd Cerritos (90703) ***(P-19127)***
True Warrior LLC....E....661 237-6588
21226 Lone Star Way Santa Clarita (91390) ***(P-3582)***
Truer Medical Inc....F....714 628-9785
1050 N Batavia St Ste C Orange (92867) ***(P-21940)***
Truett-Hurst Inc (PA)....E....707 431-4423
125 Foss Creek Cir Healdsburg (95448) ***(P-1972)***
Truevision 3d Surgical, Goleta *Also called Truevision Systems Inc* ***(P-21941)***
Truevision Systems Inc....E....805 963-9700
315 Bollay Dr Ste 101 Goleta (93117) ***(P-21941)***
Trufocus Corporation....F....831 761-9981
468 Westridge Dr Watsonville (95076) ***(P-22223)***
Truframe, Visalia *Also called R Lang Company* ***(P-11980)***
Trulite GL Alum Solutions LLC....F....800 877-8439
19430 San Jose Ave City of Industry (91748) ***(P-11249)***
Truly Green Solutions LLC....E....818 206-4404
9601 Variel Ave Chatsworth (91311) ***(P-17172)***
Trumaker Inc....E....415 662-3836
228 Grant Ave Fl 2 San Francisco (94108) ***(P-2979)***
Trumaker & Co., San Francisco *Also called Trumaker Inc* ***(P-2979)***
Trumed Systems Incorporated....E....844 878-6331
4350 Executive Dr Ste 120 San Diego (92121) ***(P-15466)***
Trumer Brauerei, Berkeley *Also called Comeback Brewing II Inc* ***(P-1513)***
Trupart Manufacturing Inc....F....805 644-4107
4450 Dupont Ct Ste A Ventura (93003) ***(P-16474)***
Trupart Mfg, Ventura *Also called Trupart Manufacturing Inc* ***(P-16474)***
Truroots Inc (HQ)....E....925 218-2205
6999 Southfront Rd Livermore (94551) ***(P-2638)***
Truroots Inc....F....925 218-2205
37 Speedway Ave Chico (95928) ***(P-2639)***
Trus Joist Macmillan, Chino *Also called Redbuilt LLC* ***(P-4316)***
Truspro, Guadalupe *Also called Tri-Co Building Supply Inc* ***(P-4324)***
Truss Engineering Inc....E....209 527-6387
477 Zeff Rd Modesto (95351) ***(P-4326)***
Trussworks International Inc....D....714 630-2772
2850 E Coronado St Anaheim (92806) ***(P-11904)***
Trusted Energy LLC....F....818 646-3137
5478 Wilshire Blvd # 303 Los Angeles (90036) ***(P-73)***
Trutouch Technologies Inc....F....909 703-5963
2020 Iowa Ave Ste 102 Riverside (92507) ***(P-21560)***
Truwest Inc....E....714 895-2444
5592 Engineer Dr Huntington Beach (92649) ***(P-3125)***
Try All 3 Sports....F....949 492-2255
931 Calle Negocio Ste O San Clemente (92673) ***(P-20433)***
Tryad Service Corporation....D....661 391-1524
5900 E Lerdo Hwy Shafter (93263) ***(P-274)***
Trymax....F....661 391-1572
5900 E Lerdo Hwy Shafter (93263) ***(P-13488)***
TS Logging....F....707 895-3751
18121 Rays Rd Philo (95466) ***(P-3911)***
Tsc LLC (HQ)....A....661 824-6600
16555 Speship Landing Wa Mojave (93501) ***(P-20459)***
TSC Precision Machining Inc....F....714 542-3182
1311 E Saint Gertrude Pl A Santa Ana (92705) ***(P-16475)***
Tschida Engineering....F....707 224-4482
1812 Yajome St NAPA (94559) ***(P-16476)***
TSE Worldwide Press Inc....E....909 989-8282
9830 6th St Ste 101 Rancho Cucamonga (91730) ***(P-6363)***
Tsf Construction Services Inc....F....619 202-7615
4805 Mercury St Ste E San Diego (92111) ***(P-2919)***
Tsi Semiconductors America LLC (PA)....C....916 786-3900
7501 Foothills Blvd Roseville (95747) ***(P-18625)***
Tsi/Protherm, Orange *Also called Allen Morgan* ***(P-14752)***
Tsmc Technology Inc....D....408 382-8052
2585 Junction Ave San Jose (95134) ***(P-18626)***
TSS Embroidery Inc....F....909 590-1383
3432 Royal Ridge Rd Chino Hills (91709) ***(P-3762)***
Tst Inc....E....951 727-3169
13428 Benson Ave Chino (91710) ***(P-11211)***
Tst Inc (PA)....B....951 737-3169
13428 Benson Ave Chino (91710) ***(P-11212)***
TST Molding LLC....E....951 296-6200
42322 Avenida Alvarado Temecula (92590) ***(P-10095)***
TST Water LLC....F....951 541-9517
42188 Rio Nedo Ste B Temecula (92590) ***(P-15595)***
Tst/Impreso California Inc....F....909 357-7190
10589 Business Dr Fontana (92337) ***(P-7293)***
TT Machine Corp....E....714 534-5288
11651 Anabel Ave Garden Grove (92843) ***(P-14205)***
TTI Floor Care North Amer Inc....B....440 996-2802
13055 Valley Blvd Fontana (92335) ***(P-9210)***
TTI Performance Exhaust, Corona *Also called Tube Technologies Inc* ***(P-19789)***
Ttl Holdings LLC (HQ)....F....909 597-7861
4626 Eucalyptus Ave Chino (91710) ***(P-10096)***
Ttm Printed Circuit Group Inc....C....408 486-3100
407 Mathew St Santa Clara (95050) ***(P-18028)***
Ttm Printed Circuit Group Inc (HQ)....D....714 327-3000
2630 S Harbor Blvd Santa Ana (92704) ***(P-18029)***
Ttm Technologies Inc....B....408 486-3100
407 Mathew St Santa Clara (95050) ***(P-18030)***
Ttm Technologies Inc (PA)....B....714 327-3000
200 Sandpointe Ave # 400 Santa Ana (92707) ***(P-18031)***
Ttm Technologies Inc....B....714 688-7200
3140 E Coronado St Anaheim (92806) ***(P-18032)***
Ttm Technologies Inc....D....858 874-2701
5037 Ruffner St San Diego (92111) ***(P-18033)***
Ttm Technologies Inc....B....714 327-3000
2630 S Harbor Blvd Santa Ana (92704) ***(P-18034)***
Ttm Technologies Inc....C....408 280-0422
355 Turtle Creek Ct San Jose (95125) ***(P-18035)***
Ttm Technologies N Amer LLC....C....408 719-4000
355 Turtle Creek Ct San Jose (95125) ***(P-18036)***
Ttn Machining Inc....F....619 303-4573
9105 Olive Dr Spring Valley (91977) ***(P-16477)***
Tts Products, Los Angeles *Also called Tvs Distributors Inc* ***(P-23013)***
TTT Concrete, Lakeside *Also called Superior Ready Mix Concrete LP* ***(P-10854)***
Tu-K Industries Inc....E....562 927-3365
5702 Firestone Pl South Gate (90280) ***(P-8596)***
Tua Fashion Inc (PA)....F....213 422-2384
8936 Appian Way Los Angeles (90046) ***(P-2715)***
Tua USA, Los Angeles *Also called Tua Fashion Inc* ***(P-2715)***
Tube Bending Llc....F....562 692-5829
4747 Citrus Dr Pico Rivera (90660) ***(P-13489)***
Tube Form Solutions LLC....F....760 599-5001
43218 Bus Pk Dr Ste 202 Temecula (92590) ***(P-14284)***
Tube Lighting Products, El Cajon *Also called Tujayar Enterprises Inc* ***(P-17079)***
Tube One Industries Inc....F....951 300-2998
4055 Garner Rd Riverside (92501) ***(P-11137)***
Tube Rags....F....323 264-7770
4382 Bandini Blvd Vernon (90058) ***(P-2815)***
Tube Technologies Inc....E....951 371-4878
1555 Consumer Cir Corona (92880) ***(P-19789)***
Tube-Tainer Inc....E....562 945-3711
8174 Byron Rd Whittier (90606) ***(P-5305)***
Tubemogul Inc....D....510 653-0126
1250 53rd St Ste 1 Emeryville (94608) ***(P-24530)***
Tubing Seal Cap Co, Anaheim *Also called Pacific Precision Metals Inc* ***(P-12854)***
Tubit Enterprises Inc....E....530 335-5085
21640 S Vallejo St Burney (96013) ***(P-3912)***
Tuboscope Nat Oilwell Varco, Bakersfield *Also called Tuboscope Pipeline Svcs Inc* ***(P-275)***
Tuboscope Pipeline Svcs Inc....E....661 321-3400
4621 Burr St Bakersfield (93308) ***(P-275)***
Tubular Specialties Mfg Inc....D....310 515-4801
13011 S Spring St Los Angeles (90061) ***(P-10468)***
Tuesday Review, The, Newman *Also called Index Printing Inc* ***(P-7095)***
Tuff - Toe Inc....F....714 997-9585
5443 E La Palma Ave Anaheim (92807) ***(P-8900)***
Tuff Boy Holding Inc....E....209 239-1361
5151 Almondwood Rd Manteca (95337) ***(P-19834)***
Tuff Boy Trailers, Manteca *Also called Tuff Boy Holding Inc* ***(P-19834)***
Tuff Kote Systems Inc....F....714 522-7341
7033 Orangethorpe Ave B Buena Park (90621) ***(P-8689)***
Tuff Shed Inc....F....408 935-8833
931 Cadillac Ct Milpitas (95035) ***(P-4466)***

ALPHABETIC

Employee Codes: A=Over 500 employees, B=251-500
C=101-250, D=51-100, E=20-50, F=10-19
2020 California
Manfacturers Register
© Mergent Inc. 1-800-342-5647
1269

Tuff Shed Inc...F...925 681-3492
1401 Franquette Ave Concord (94520) ***(P-4467)***
Tuff Stuff Products...B...559 535-5778
9600 Road 256 Terra Bella (93270) ***(P-7621)***
Tuffer Manufacturing Co Inc...E...714 526-3077
163 E Liberty Ave Anaheim (92801) ***(P-20738)***
Tuffstuff Fitness Intl Inc...C...909 629-1600
13971 Norton Ave Chino (91710) ***(P-22913)***
Tujayar Enterprises Inc...E...619 442-0577
1346 Pioneer Way El Cajon (92020) ***(P-17079)***
Tukko Group LLC...E...408 598-1251
530 Alameda Del Prado Novato (94949) ***(P-24531)***
Tukko Labs, Novato *Also called Tukko Group LLC* ***(P-24531)***
Tul Inc...D...909 444-0577
663 Brea Canyon Rd Ste 6 Walnut (91789) ***(P-11639)***
Tulare Advance Register, Tulare *Also called Gannett Co Inc* ***(P-5637)***
Tulip Pubg & Graphics Inc...E...510 898-0000
1003 Canal Blvd Richmond (94804) ***(P-6903)***
Tulkoff Food Products West Inc...E...925 427-5157
705 Bliss Ave Pittsburg (94565) ***(P-2640)***
Tullys Coffee Co Inc (HQ)...E...415 929-8808
2455 Fillmore St San Francisco (94115) ***(P-2312)***
Tullys Coffee Co Inc...F...415 213-8791
1509 Sloat Blvd San Francisco (94132) ***(P-2313)***
Tulocay Winery...F...707 255-4064
1426 Coombsville Rd NAPA (94558) ***(P-1973)***
Tumelo Inc...E...707 523-4411
420 Tesconi Cir Ste B Santa Rosa (95401) ***(P-9032)***
Tung Fei Plastic Inc...F...510 783-9688
1859 Sabre St Hayward (94545) ***(P-5427)***
Tung Tai Group...F...408 573-8681
1726 Rogers Ave San Jose (95112) ***(P-12886)***
Tungsten Heavy Powder Inc (PA)...D...858 693-6100
6170 Cornerstone Ct E # 310 San Diego (92121) ***(P-11084)***
Tungsten Heavy Powder & Parts, San Diego *Also called Tungsten Heavy Powder Inc* ***(P-11084)***
Tur-Bo Jet Products Co Inc...D...626 285-1294
5025 Earle Ave Rosemead (91770) ***(P-18747)***
Turbine Components Inc...E...858 678-8568
8985 Crestmar Pt San Diego (92121) ***(P-19986)***
Turbine Eng Cmpnents Tech Corp...C...562 908-0200
8839 Pioneer Blvd Santa Fe Springs (90670) ***(P-12738)***
Turbo Coil Inc...F...626 644-6254
1532 Sinaloa Ave Pasadena (91104) ***(P-15467)***
Turbo International...F...760 476-1444
2151 Las Palmas Dr Ste E Carlsbad (92011) ***(P-12724)***
Turbo Refrigeration Systems...E...626 599-9777
1740 Evergreen St Duarte (91010) ***(P-15468)***
Turbonetics Holdings Inc...E...805 581-0333
14399 Princeton Ave Moorpark (93021) ***(P-19790)***
Turbosand, Anderson *Also called Voorwood Company* ***(P-14300)***
Turbotax, San Diego *Also called Intuit Inc* ***(P-24041)***
Turbotools Corporation...F...415 759-5599
2190 31st Ave San Francisco (94116) ***(P-24532)***
Turkey Processing Plant, Fresno *Also called Zacky & Sons Poultry LLC* ***(P-533)***
Turkhan Nuts, Ripon *Also called Pearl Crop Inc* ***(P-1449)***
Turley Wine Cellars...F...805 434-1030
2900 Vineyard Dr Templeton (93465) ***(P-1974)***
Turley Wine Cellars Inc...F...707 968-2700
3358 Saint Helena Hwy N Saint Helena (94574) ***(P-1975)***
Turlock Cabinet Shop Inc...F...209 632-1311
1475 West Ave S Turlock (95380) ***(P-4256)***
Turlock Journal...F...209 634-9141
138 S Center St Turlock (95380) ***(P-5854)***
Turn-Luckily International Inc...F...949 465-0200
9710 Research Dr Irvine (92618) ***(P-15356)***
Turnbull Wine Cellars...F...707 963-5839
8210 St Helena Hwy Oakville (94562) ***(P-1976)***
Turner Designs Inc...E...408 749-0994
1995 N 1st St San Jose (95112) ***(P-21317)***
Turner Designs Hydrocarbon Ins...E...559 253-1414
2027 N Gateway Blvd # 109 Fresno (93727) ***(P-19425)***
Turner Fiberfill Inc...E...323 724-7957
1600 Date St Montebello (90640) ***(P-7642)***
Turner Group Publications Inc...F...408 297-3299
27788 Klaus Ct Hayward (94542) ***(P-7258)***
Turner Precision, Gardena *Also called Aldo Fragale* ***(P-15716)***
Turnham Corporation (PA)...F...626 330-0415
15312 Proctor Ave City of Industry (91745) ***(P-14206)***
Turnham Corporation...F...626 968-6481
15310 Proctor Ave City of Industry (91745) ***(P-14207)***
Turning Point Therapeutics Inc...E...858 926-5251
10628 Science Center Dr # 200 San Diego (92121) ***(P-8171)***
Turnkey Technologies Inc...E...707 745-9520
4650 E 2nd St Ste C Benicia (94510) ***(P-16478)***
Turret Lathe Specialists Inc...F...714 520-0058
875 S Rose Pl Anaheim (92805) ***(P-16479)***
Turret Punch Co Inc...F...909 587-1820
7780 Edison Ave Fontana (92336) ***(P-9458)***
Turtle Beach Corporation (PA)...E...914 345-2255
11011 Via Frontera Ste A San Diego (92127) ***(P-19128)***
Turtle Storage Ltd...E...805 933-3688
401 S Beckwith Rd Santa Paula (93060) ***(P-5008)***
Turtleback Case, Sylmar *Also called Leather Pro Inc* ***(P-10237)***
Tuscany Pavers Inc...F...866 596-4092
241 S Twin Oaks Valley Rd San Marcos (92078) ***(P-13754)***
Tusco Casting Corporation...E...209 368-5137
934 E Victor Rd Lodi (95240) ***(P-11173)***
Tutti, Los Angeles *Also called Adwear Inc* ***(P-3022)***
Tuula Inc...F...858 761-6045
26019 Jefferson Ave Ste D Murrieta (92562) ***(P-8353)***
Tvs Distributors Inc...F...323 268-1347
2822 E Olympic Blvd Los Angeles (90023) ***(P-23013)***
Twed-Dells Inc...E...714 754-6900
1900 S Susan St Santa Ana (92704) ***(P-10396)***
Twelve Signs Inc...D...310 553-8000
3369 S Robertson Blvd Los Angeles (90034) ***(P-6045)***
Twelve Strike, Long Beach *Also called South Street Inc* ***(P-22892)***
Twenty Niners Club, Vernon *Also called Twenty-Niners Provisions Inc* ***(P-528)***
Twenty-Niners Provisions Inc...E...323 233-7864
1784 E Vernon Ave Vernon (90058) ***(P-528)***
Twilight Technology Inc (PA)...E...714 257-2257
325 N Shepard St Anaheim (92806) ***(P-18627)***
Twin Coast Metrology Inc (PA)...F...310 709-2308
333 Wshngton Blvd Ste 362 Marina Del Rey (90292) ***(P-21416)***
Twin Creeks Technologies Inc (PA)...F...408 368-3733
3930 N 1st St Ste 10 San Jose (95134) ***(P-18628)***
Twin Design Co LLC...F...510 329-4991
18458 Carlwyn Dr Castro Valley (94546) ***(P-14866)***
Twin Eagles Inc...D...562 802-3488
13259 166th St Cerritos (90703) ***(P-16819)***
Twin Glass Industries Inc...F...408 779-8801
16880 Joleen Way Ste 2 Morgan Hill (95037) ***(P-10397)***
Twin Industries, San Ramon *Also called Gemini Consultants Inc* ***(P-17887)***
Twin Industries Inc...D...925 866-8946
2303 Camino Ramon Ste 106 San Ramon (94583) ***(P-18037)***
Twin Peak Industries Inc...E...800 259-5906
12420 Montague St Ste E Pacoima (91331) ***(P-22914)***
Twin Peaks Ingrdients, Fontana *Also called Tpi Marketing LLC* ***(P-14407)***
Twin Peaks Winery Inc...F...707 945-0855
1473 Yountville Cross Rd Yountville (94599) ***(P-1977)***
Twindom, Berkeley *Also called Machinables Inc* ***(P-15280)***
Twist Frozen Yogurt, Los Angeles *Also called Venture Capital Entps LLC* ***(P-676)***
Twist Tite Mfg Inc...E...562 229-0990
13344 Cambridge St Santa Fe Springs (90670) ***(P-12697)***
Twisted Oak Winery LLC (PA)...E...209 728-3000
4280 Red Hill Rd Vallecito (95251) ***(P-1978)***
Twitch Interactive Inc...A...415 919-5000
350 Bush St Ste 2 San Francisco (94104) ***(P-6364)***
Two Bears Metal Products...E...310 326-2533
723 N Meyler St San Pedro (90731) ***(P-16480)***
Two Blind Mice LLC...F...714 279-0600
5016 E Crescent Dr Anaheim (92807) ***(P-1979)***
Two Brothers Racing Inc...F...714 550-6070
167 Via Trevizio Corona (92879) ***(P-20434)***
Two Guys and One LLC...F...213 239-0310
4433 Pacific Blvd Vernon (90058) ***(P-10214)***
Two Hands, Los Angeles *Also called Lialee Inc* ***(P-2794)***
Two Lads Inc (PA)...E...323 584-0064
5001 Hampton St Vernon (90058) ***(P-23014)***
Two Star Dog Inc...F...510 525-1100
1329 9th St Berkeley (94710) ***(P-3257)***
Two Star Dog Inc (PA)...E...510 525-1100
1329 9th St Berkeley (94710) ***(P-3202)***
Two Thirty Two Productins Inc...E...714 317-5317
7108 Katella Ave Ste 440 Stanton (90680) ***(P-22467)***
Twpm Inc...F...714 522-8881
15320 Valley View Ave La Mirada (90638) ***(P-5318)***
Txc Technology Inc (HQ)...F...714 990-5510
451 W Lambert Rd Ste 201 Brea (92821) ***(P-19129)***
Txd International Usa Inc...F...909 947-6568
2336 S Vineyard Ave A Ontario (91761) ***(P-5855)***
Tyco Electronics, San Diego *Also called Te Connectivity Corporation* ***(P-18796)***
Tyco Fire Products LP...C...925 687-6957
6952 Preston Ave Livermore (94551) ***(P-14867)***
Tyco Fire Protection Products, Livermore *Also called Tyco Fire Products LP* ***(P-14867)***
Tyco International MGT Co LLC...B...650 361-3333
300 Constitution Dr Menlo Park (94025) ***(P-11324)***
Tyco Simplexgrinnell...E...707 578-3212
3077 Wiljan Ct Ste B Santa Rosa (95407) ***(P-14868)***
Tyflong International Inc...F...530 746-3001
606 Pena Dr Davis (95618) ***(P-10957)***
Tyler Camera Systems, Van Nuys *Also called Tyler Technologies Inc* ***(P-24533)***
Tyler Technologies Inc...F...818 989-4420
14218 Aetna St Van Nuys (91401) ***(P-24533)***
Tyler Trafficante Inc (PA)...D...323 869-9299
700 S Palm Ave Alhambra (91803) ***(P-2980)***
Tylerco Inc...E...949 769-3991
17831 Sky Park Cir Ste A Irvine (92614) ***(P-16995)***
Tyloon Media Corporation...F...626 330-5838
6168 Fielding St Chino (91710) ***(P-6365)***
Typecraft Inc...E...626 795-8093
2040 E Walnut St Pasadena (91107) ***(P-6904)***
Typecraft Wood & Jones, Pasadena *Also called Typecraft Inc* ***(P-6904)***
Typehaus Inc...F...760 334-3555
2262 Rutherford Rd # 103 Carlsbad (92008) ***(P-15111)***
Tyson Fresh Meats Inc...F...714 528-5543
500 S Kraemer Blvd # 380 Brea (92821) ***(P-427)***
TYT LLC (HQ)...C...510 444-3933
2861 Mandela Pkwy Oakland (94608) ***(P-6905)***
Tyte Jeans, Commerce *Also called 4 What Its Worth Inc* ***(P-3133)***
Tyvak Nn-Satellite Systems Inc...D...949 753-1020
15330 Barranca Pkwy Irvine (92618) ***(P-20460)***
Tz, Los Angeles *Also called Toska Inc* ***(P-3425)***
Tz Holdings LP...A...949 719-2200
567 San Nicolas Dr # 120 Newport Beach (92660) ***(P-24534)***
U M S Inc...E...661 324-5454
317 Mount Vernon Ave Bakersfield (93307) ***(P-13121)***

Mergent e-mail: customerrelations@mergent.com
1270
2020 California
Manufacturers Register
(P-0000) Products & Services Section entry number
(PA)=Parent Co (HQ)=Headquarters (DH)=Div Headquarters

U P C, Huntington Beach *Also called Urethane Products Corporation* **(P-10102)**

U R M, Vista *Also called United Research & Mfg* **(P-19794)**

U R U, Escondido *Also called URu By Kristine St Rrik Inc* **(P-3259)**

U S Air Filtration Inc (PA)..........F.......951 491-7282
23811 Washington Ave C110176 Murrieta (92562) **(P-20952)**

U S Architectural Lighting, Palmdale *Also called US Pole Company Inc* **(P-17173)**

U S Bearings..........E.......626 358-0181
5001b Commerce Dr Baldwin Park (91706) **(P-14618)**

U S Bowling Corporation..........F.......909 548-0644
5480 Schaefer Ave Chino (91710) **(P-22915)**

U S Chrome Corp California..........F.......562 437-2825
1480 Canal Ave Long Beach (90813) **(P-13122)**

U S Circuit Inc..........D.......760 489-1413
2071 Wineridge Pl Escondido (92029) **(P-19130)**

U S Cold Storage, Bakersfield *Also called United States Cold Storage Inc* **(P-2365)**

U S Divers Co Inc..........C.......760 597-5000
2340 Cousteau Ct Vista (92081) **(P-22916)**

U S Enterprise Corporation..........E.......510 487-8877
30560 San Antonio St Hayward (94544) **(P-903)**

U S Fabrications, Hayward *Also called South Bay Diversfd Systems Inc* **(P-12382)**

U S I, Saratoga *Also called United Supertek Inc* **(P-18038)**

U S L, San Luis Obispo *Also called Ultra-Stereo Labs Inc* **(P-19426)**

U S Medical Instruments Inc (PA)..........D.......619 661-5500
888 Prospect St Ste 100 La Jolla (92037) **(P-21942)**

U S Precision Manufacturing, Riverside *Also called US Precision Sheet Metal Inc* **(P-12419)**

U S Saw & Blades, Santa Ana *Also called US Saws Inc* **(P-13755)**

U S Technical Institute, Placentia *Also called US Computers Inc* **(P-15359)**

U S Weatherford L P..........D.......661 589-9483
2815 Fruitvale Ave Bakersfield (93308) **(P-276)**

U S Weatherford L P..........E.......661 746-3415
19608 Broken Ct Shafter (93263) **(P-143)**

U S Weatherford L P..........F.......661 746-1391
19468 Creek Rd Bakersfield (93314) **(P-13490)**

U S Wheel Corporation..........F.......714 892-0021
15702 Producer Ln Huntington Beach (92649) **(P-19791)**

U-Blox San Diego Inc..........F.......858 847-9611
12626 High Bluff Dr San Diego (92130) **(P-17423)**

U-C Components Inc (PA)..........E.......408 782-1929
18700 Adams Ct Morgan Hill (95037) **(P-12698)**

U-Nited Printing and Copy Ctr, Van Nuys *Also called Printrunner LLC* **(P-6810)**

U.S. Concrete Precast Group, Morgan Hill *Also called Sierra Precast Inc* **(P-10650)**

U.S. Horizon Mfg, Valencia *Also called US Horizon Manufacturing Inc* **(P-10279)**

U.S. Patriot Lite, Los Angeles *Also called Patriot Lighting Inc* **(P-17064)**

U.S. Specialty Vehicles, Rancho Cucamonga *Also called American HX Auto Trade Inc* **(P-19453)**

Ubi Energy Corporation..........C.......310 283-6978
9465 Wilshire Blvd # 300 Beverly Hills (90212) **(P-9078)**

Ubicom Inc..........D.......408 433-3330
195 Baypointe Pkwy San Jose (95134) **(P-18629)**

Ubm Canon LLC (HQ)..........C.......310 445-4200
2901 28th St Ste 100 Santa Monica (90405) **(P-6046)**

Ubm LLC..........D.......415 947-6770
18301 Von Karman Ave # 920 Irvine (92612) **(P-6047)**

Ubm LLC..........C.......415 947-6488
303 2nd St Ste 900s San Francisco (94107) **(P-6048)**

Ubm Techweb (HQ)..........F.......415 947-6000
303 Secon St Tower Fl 9 9 Stower San Francisco (94107) **(P-6049)**

Ubst Inc..........F.......424 222-9908
373 Van Ness Ave Torrance (90501) **(P-3203)**

Ubtech Robotics Corp..........E.......213 261-7153
767 S Alameda St Los Angeles (90021) **(P-14285)**

UC Plastic Manufacture Inc..........E.......510 785-6777
3202 Diablo Ave Hayward (94545) **(P-5428)**

Uc2, San Diego *Also called Biota Technology Inc* **(P-23670)**

Ucan Zippers, Los Angeles *Also called Catame Inc* **(P-22999)**

Ucsf School of Pharmacy..........F.......415 476-1444
3333 California St San Francisco (94118) **(P-8172)**

Uct, Hayward *Also called Ultra Clean Technology Systems* **(P-20953)**

Ucview, Northridge *Also called ATI Solutions Inc* **(P-17714)**

Udecor Inc (PA)..........F.......877 550-0600
8302 Espresso Dr Ste 130 Bakersfield (93312) **(P-10097)**

UFO Designs (PA)..........F.......714 892-4420
5812 Machine Dr Huntington Beach (92649) **(P-10098)**

UFO Designs..........E.......562 924-5763
16730 Gridley Rd Cerritos (90703) **(P-19792)**

UFO Inc..........E.......323 588-5450
2110 Belgrave Ave Huntington Park (90255) **(P-10099)**

Ufp Technologies Inc..........E.......714 662-0277
20211 S Susana Rd Compton (90221) **(P-9574)**

Uhv Sputtering Inc..........F.......408 779-2826
275 Digital Dr Morgan Hill (95037) **(P-18630)**

Ukiah Brewing Co LLC..........E.......707 468-5898
551 Cypress Ave Ukiah (95482) **(P-1572)**

Ullman Sails Inc (PA)..........F.......714 432-1860
2710 S Croddy Way Santa Ana (92704) **(P-3712)**

Ultera Systems Inc..........F.......949 367-8800
28241 Crown Valley Pkwy F115 Laguna Niguel (92677) **(P-15357)**

Ulti-Mate Connector Inc..........E.......714 637-7099
1872 N Case St Orange (92865) **(P-18801)**

Ultimate Ears Consumer LLC..........E.......949 502-8340
3 Jenner Ste 180 Irvine (92618) **(P-22113)**

Ultimate Game Chair Inc..........E.......925 756-6944
5089 Lone Tree Way Antioch (94531) **(P-17296)**

Ultimate Jumpers Inc..........F.......626 337-3086
14924 Arrow Hwy Ste A Baldwin Park (91706) **(P-5087)**

Ultimate Metal Finishing Corp..........F.......323 890-9100
6150 Sheila St Commerce (90040) **(P-13262)**

Ultimate Paper Box Company, City of Industry *Also called Boxes R Us Inc* **(P-5311)**

Ultimate Print Source Inc..........E.......909 947-5292
2070 S Hellman Ave Ontario (91761) **(P-6906)**

Ultimate Rail Equipment Inc..........F.......510 324-5000
30914 San Antonio St Hayward (94544) **(P-20377)**

Ultimate Software Group Inc..........E.......949 214-2710
5 Hutton Centre Dr # 130 Santa Ana (92707) **(P-24535)**

Ultimate Solutions, Huntington Beach *Also called Sandia Plastics Inc* **(P-10041)**

Ultimate Sound Inc..........B.......909 861-6200
1200 S Diamond Bar Blvd # 200 Diamond Bar (91765) **(P-17297)**

Ultimatte Corporation..........E.......818 993-8007
5828 Calvin Ave Tarzana (91356) **(P-17697)**

Ultra Built Kitchens Inc..........E.......323 232-3362
1814 E 43rd St Los Angeles (90058) **(P-4257)**

Ultra Chem Labs Corp..........F.......909 605-1640
4581 Brickell Privado St Ontario (91761) **(P-8422)**

Ultra Clean Technology Systems (HQ)..........C.......510 576-4400
26462 Corporate Ave Hayward (94545) **(P-20953)**

Ultra Glass..........F.......916 338-3911
4001 Vista Park Ct Ste 1 Sacramento (95834) **(P-10398)**

Ultra Gro LLC..........E.......559 661-0977
1043 S Granada Dr Madera (93637) **(P-8806)**

Ultra H2 LP..........F.......657 999-5188
1601 Dove St Ste 126 Newport Beach (92660) **(P-623)**

Ultra Pro Acquisition LLC..........C.......323 725-1975
6049 E Slauson Ave Commerce (90040) **(P-7319)**

Ultra Pro International LLC (PA)..........D.......323 890-2100
6049 E Slauson Ave Commerce (90040) **(P-7320)**

Ultra TEC Manufacturing Inc..........F.......714 542-0608
1025 E Chestnut Ave Santa Ana (92701) **(P-14549)**

Ultra-Pure Metal Finishing..........F.......714 637-3150
1764 N Case St Orange (92865) **(P-13123)**

Ultra-Stereo Labs Inc..........E.......805 549-0161
181 Bonetti Dr San Luis Obispo (93401) **(P-19426)**

Ultragenyx Pharmaceutical Inc (PA)..........C.......415 483-8800
60 Leveroni Ct Novato (94949) **(P-8173)**

Ultramar Inc..........F.......530 345-7901
2233 Esplanade Chico (95926) **(P-9079)**

Ultramar Inc..........F.......661 944-2496
9508 E Palmdale Blvd Palmdale (93591) **(P-9080)**

Ultramar Inc..........E.......310 834-7254
961 S La Paloma Ave Wilmington (90744) **(P-277)**

Ultramet..........D.......818 899-0236
12173 Montague St Pacoima (91331) **(P-13124)**

Ultraneon Sign Company, San Diego *Also called Ultraneon Sign Corp* **(P-23233)**

Ultraneon Sign Corp..........E.......858 569-6716
5458 Complex St Ste 401 San Diego (92123) **(P-23233)**

Ultrasil LLC..........E.......510 266-3700
3527 Breakwater Ave Hayward (94545) **(P-18631)**

Ultratech Inc (HQ)..........C.......408 321-8835
3050 Zanker Rd San Jose (95134) **(P-14550)**

Ultratype & Graphics..........F.......858 541-1894
1929 Hancock St Ste D San Diego (92110) **(P-7365)**

Ultron Systems Inc..........F.......805 529-1485
5105 Maureen Ln Moorpark (93021) **(P-14551)**

Ulysses Press, Berkeley *Also called Bookpack Inc* **(P-6204)**

Umc Acquisition Corp (PA)..........E.......562 940-0300
9151 Imperial Hwy Downey (90242) **(P-11281)**

Umc Group(usa)..........D.......408 523-7800
488 De Guigne Dr Sunnyvale (94085) **(P-18632)**

Ume Voice Inc..........F.......707 939-8607
1435 Technology Ln Ste B4 Petaluma (94954) **(P-17298)**

Umec, Union City *Also called United Mech Met Fbricators Inc* **(P-12417)**

Umex, Downey *Also called Universal Mlding Extrusion Inc* **(P-11251)**

Umeya Inc..........E.......213 626-8341
414 Crocker St Los Angeles (90013) **(P-1335)**

Umeya Rice Cake Co, Los Angeles *Also called Umeya Inc* **(P-1335)**

Umgee USA Inc..........F.......323 526-9138
1565 E 23rd St Los Angeles (90011) **(P-3204)**

Umo Steel, Union City *Also called United Misc & Orna Stl Inc* **(P-12611)**

Ump, Corona *Also called United Metal Products Inc* **(P-11489)**

Umpco Inc..........D.......714 897-3531
7100 Lampson Ave Garden Grove (92841) **(P-11640)**

Umx, Walnut *Also called Universal Mercantile Exchange* **(P-23235)**

Uncks Unique Plastics Inc..........F.......909 983-5181
1215 Brooks St Ontario (91762) **(P-10100)**

Uncle Ben's, Los Angeles *Also called Mars Food Us LLC* **(P-1048)**

Uncle Bum's Gourmet Sauces, Riverside *Also called Tom Harris Inc* **(P-2627)**

Uncle Lees Tea Inc..........E.......626 350-3309
11020 Rush St El Monte (91733) **(P-2641)**

Undercar Express Inc..........F.......626 683-2787
57 N Altadena Dr Pasadena (91107) **(P-19509)**

Underground Autowerks Inc (PA)..........F.......619 336-9000
106 E 17th St National City (91950) **(P-11550)**

Underground Games Inc..........F.......310 379-0100
2356 253rd St Lomita (90717) **(P-22722)**

Underground Labs Inc..........F.......925 297-5333
1114 Oakwood Cir Clayton (94517) **(P-24536)**

Undersea Systems Intl Inc..........D.......714 754-7848
3133 W Harvard St Santa Ana (92704) **(P-19427)**

Underwraps Costume Corporation..........F.......818 349-5300
9600 Irondale Ave Chatsworth (91311) **(P-3583)**

Underwraps Costumes Inc., Chatsworth *Also called Underwraps Costume Corporation* **(P-3583)**

Unger Fabrik LLC (PA)..........C.......626 469-8080
18525 Railroad St City of Industry (91748) **(P-3205)**

UNI Filter Inc..........D.......714 535-6933
1468 Manhattan Ave Fullerton (92831) **(P-19793)**

Employee Codes: A=Over 500 employees, B=251-500
C=101-250, D=51-100, E=20-50, F=10-19
2020 California
Manfacturers Register
© Mergent Inc. 1-800-342-5647
1271

UNI Sport Inc.....E.....310 217-4587
16933 Gramercy Pl Gardena (90247) *(P-6907)*
UNI-Caps LLC.....E.....714 529-8400
540 Lambert Rd Brea (92821) *(P-7701)*
UNI-Poly Inc.....F.....510 357-9898
2040 Williams St San Leandro (94577) *(P-5429)*
Unichem, Bakersfield *Also called Baker Hughes A GE Company LLC (P-165)*
Unichem Enterprises, Ontario *Also called Imp International Inc (P-7669)*
Unico Incorporated.....F.....619 209-6124
8880 Rio San Diego Dr # 8 San Diego (92108) *(P-13)*
Unicom Electric Inc.....E.....626 964-7873
565 Brea Canyon Rd Ste A Walnut (91789) *(P-17770)*
Unicor, Lompoc *Also called Federal Prison Industries (P-23113)*
Unicor, Lompoc *Also called Federal Prison Industries (P-4570)*
Unicorn Group, Novato *Also called Forest Investment Group Inc (P-6580)*
Unifi Software Inc.....E.....732 614-9522
1810 Gateway Dr Ste 380 San Mateo (94404) *(P-24537)*
Unifyid Inc.....F.....650 561-2202
603 Jefferson Ave Redwood City (94063) *(P-24538)*
Unilabel, Santa Fe Springs *Also called Universal Label Printers Inc (P-7260)*
Unilete Inc.....F.....714 557-1271
18774 Ashford Ln Huntington Beach (92648) *(P-3126)*
Unimark, Gardena *Also called Matsui International Co Inc (P-8995)*
Unimark International Inc.....F.....949 497-1235
22601 Allview Ter Laguna Beach (92651) *(P-14409)*
Union Carbide Corporation.....D.....310 214-5300
19206 Hawthorne Blvd Torrance (90503) *(P-5176)*
Union Electric Motor Service, San Diego *Also called Tom Garcia Inc (P-24699)*
Union Flavors Inc.....F.....626 333-1612
14145 Proctor Ave Ste 15 City of Industry (91746) *(P-2233)*
Union Ice Company.....F.....323 277-1000
2970 E 50th St Vernon (90058) *(P-2364)*
Union Publications Inc.....F.....510 525-6300
653 Wellesley Ave Kensington (94708) *(P-6050)*
Union Solutions Inc.....F.....510 483-1222
15355 Bittern Ct San Leandro (94579) *(P-24539)*
Union Swiss Manufacturing Co, Glendale *Also called Irl-Mex Manufacturing Company (P-12636)*
Union Tank Car Company.....C.....312 431-3111
175 W Jackson Blvd Bakersfield (93311) *(P-20378)*
Union Tribune, San Marcos *Also called Copley Press Inc (P-5603)*
Union Wine Company, Calabasas *Also called Spanish Castle Inc (P-1924)*
Union, The, Grass Valley *Also called Nevada County Publishing Co (P-5774)*
Uniproducts, North Highlands *Also called Mikes Sheet Metal Products (P-12302)*
Uniq Vision Inc.....C.....408 330-0818
2924 Scott Blvd Santa Clara (95054) *(P-22468)*
Unique Apparel Inc.....D.....213 321-8192
3777 S Main St Los Angeles (90007) *(P-3429)*
Unique Drawer Boxes Inc.....F.....619 873-4240
9435 Bond Ave El Cajon (92021) *(P-4343)*
Unique Functional Products, San Marcos *Also called Dexter Axle Company (P-19819)*
Unique Image Inc.....F.....818 727-7785
19365 Bus Center Dr Ste 4 Northridge (91324) *(P-6908)*
Unique Media Inc.....F.....408 733-9999
2991 Corvin Dr Santa Clara (95051) *(P-17338)*
Unique Sales, Vernon *Also called Zk Enterprises Inc (P-3132)*
Unique Screen Printing Inc.....E.....626 575-2725
2115 Central Ave South El Monte (91733) *(P-3821)*
Uniquify Inc.....E.....408 235-8810
2030 Fortune Dr Ste 200 San Jose (95131) *(P-19131)*
Unirex Corp.....F.....323 589-4000
2288 E 27th St Vernon (90058) *(P-18633)*
Unirex Technology, Vernon *Also called Unirex Corp (P-18633)*
Unisem (sunnvale) Inc (PA).....F.....408 734-3222
2241 Calle De Luna Santa Clara (95054) *(P-18634)*
Unisoft Corporation.....F.....650 259-1290
10 Rollins Rd Ste 118 Millbrae (94030) *(P-24540)*
Unisorb Inc.....F.....626 793-1000
101 N Indian Hill Blvd C2-201 Claremont (91711) *(P-13553)*
Unistrut International Corp.....F.....510 476-1200
1679 Atlantic St Union City (94587) *(P-11905)*
Unisun Multinational, Chino *Also called Ht Multinational Inc (P-19685)*
Unit Industries Inc (PA).....E.....714 871-4161
3122 Maple St Santa Ana (92707) *(P-18802)*
Unitech Deco Inc.....E.....818 700-1373
19731 Bahama St Northridge (91324) *(P-7259)*
Unitech Industries, Northridge *Also called Unitech Deco Inc (P-7259)*
Unitech Tool & Machine Inc.....E.....408 566-0333
3025 Stender Way Santa Clara (95054) *(P-16481)*
United Advg Publications Inc.....E.....916 746-2300
3017 Douglas Blvd Roseville (95661) *(P-6051)*
United Audio Video Group Inc.....E.....818 980-6700
6855 Vineland Ave North Hollywood (91605) *(P-19239)*
United Bakery Equipment Co Inc (PA).....D.....310 635-8121
19216 S Laurel Park Rd Rancho Dominguez (90220) *(P-14732)*
United Bakery Equipment Co Inc.....E.....310 635-8121
19216 S Laurel Park Rd Compton (90220) *(P-14410)*
United Bakery Inc.....E.....818 843-1892
727 S Flower St Burbank (91502) *(P-1288)*
United Brands Company Inc.....E.....619 461-5220
5930 Cornerstone Ct W # 170 San Diego (92121) *(P-2234)*
United Cabinet Company Inc.....E.....909 796-3015
1510 S Mountain View Ave San Bernardino (92408) *(P-4258)*
United California, Downey *Also called United Drill Bushing Corp (P-14208)*
United California Corporation.....C.....562 803-1521
12200 Woodruff Ave Downey (90241) *(P-14117)*
United Carports LLC.....F.....800 757-6742
7280 Sycamore Canyon Blvd # 1 Riverside (92508) *(P-12580)*
United Castings Inc.....F.....909 627-7645
5154 F St Chino (91710) *(P-11426)*
United Cerebral Palsy Assn San.....F.....619 282-8790
10405 Sn Dgo Mssn Rd 10 San Diego (92108) *(P-22957)*
United Craftsmen Priniting.....E.....408 224-6464
6660 Via Del Oro San Jose (95119) *(P-6909)*
United Distlrs Vintners N Amer, San Francisco *Also called Diageo North America Inc (P-1665)*
United Drill Bushing Corp.....C.....562 803-1521
12200 Woodruff Ave Downey (90241) *(P-14208)*
United Drilling Co.....E.....562 945-8833
11807 Slauson Ave Santa Fe Springs (90670) *(P-16482)*
United Duralume Products Inc.....F.....714 773-4011
350 S Raymond Ave Fullerton (92831) *(P-12415)*
United Fabrication Inc.....F.....805 482-2354
1250 Avenida Acaso Ste C Camarillo (93012) *(P-12416)*
United Foods Intl USA Inc (HQ).....E.....510 264-5850
23447 Cabot Blvd Hayward (94545) *(P-2642)*
United Granite & Cabinets LLC.....F.....510 558-8999
5225 Central Ave Richmond (94804) *(P-4259)*
United Launch Alliance LLC.....D.....303 269-5876
1579 Utah Ave Bldg 7525 Vandenberg Afb (93437) *(P-20461)*
United Mech Met Fbricators Inc.....E.....510 537-4744
33353 Lewis St Union City (94587) *(P-12417)*
United Memorial Products Inc.....D.....562 699-3578
4845 Pioneer Blvd Whittier (90601) *(P-10660)*
United Memorial/Matthews Intl, Whittier *Also called United Memorial Products Inc (P-10660)*
United Metal Products Inc.....F.....951 739-9535
234 N Sherman Ave Corona (92882) *(P-11489)*
United Misc & Orna Stl Inc.....E.....510 429-8755
4700 Horner St Union City (94587) *(P-12611)*
United Optronics Inc.....F.....408 503-8900
1323 Great Mall Dr Milpitas (95035) *(P-17424)*
United Orthopedic Group LLC.....F.....760 729-8585
2885 Loker Ave E Carlsbad (92010) *(P-21943)*
United Pacific Designs, Vernon *Also called UPD INC (P-22655)*
United Pallet Services Inc.....C.....209 538-5844
4043 Crows Landing Rd Modesto (95358) *(P-4403)*
United Paper Box Inc.....E.....714 777-8383
1530 Lakeview Loop Anaheim (92807) *(P-5319)*
United Partition Systems Inc.....F.....909 947-1077
2180 S Hellman Ave Ontario (91761) *(P-4468)*
United Pet Group, Moorpark *Also called Spectrum Brands Inc (P-23482)*
United Pharma LLC.....C.....714 738-8999
2317 Moore Ave Fullerton (92833) *(P-9033)*
United Precision Corp.....F.....818 576-9540
20810 Plummer St Chatsworth (91311) *(P-13392)*
United Pro Fab Mfg Inc.....F.....510 651-5570
45300 Industrial Pl Ste 5 Fremont (94538) *(P-16483)*
United Reporting Pubg Corp.....E.....916 542-7501
1835 Iron Point Rd # 100 Folsom (95630) *(P-6366)*
United Research & Mfg.....F.....760 727-4320
2630 Progress St Vista (92081) *(P-19794)*
United Rotary Brush Corp.....E.....909 629-9117
688 New York Dr Pomona (91768) *(P-23031)*
United Rotary Brush Corp.....E.....913 888-8450
160 Enterprise Ct Ste B Galt (95632) *(P-23032)*
United Security Products Inc.....E.....800 227-1592
13250 Gregg St Ste B Poway (92064) *(P-19428)*
United Sheetmetal Inc.....F.....510 257-1858
44153 S Grimmer Blvd Fremont (94538) *(P-12418)*
United Sign Systems, Modesto *Also called Johnson United Inc (P-23142)*
United States Ball Corporation.....F.....714 521-6500
15919 Phoebe Ave La Mirada (90638) *(P-14619)*
United States Cold Storage Inc.....E.....661 834-2371
4701 Stine Rd Bakersfield (93313) *(P-2365)*
United States Dept of Navy.....E.....805 989-5402
672 13th St Ste 1 Port Hueneme (93042) *(P-20264)*
United States Dept of Navy.....A.....559 998-2488
Vfa 122 Hanger 5 Lemoore (93246) *(P-13602)*
United States Gypsum Company.....B.....760 358-3200
3810 Evan Hewes Hwy Imperial (92251) *(P-10886)*
United States Logistics Group.....E.....562 989-9555
2700 Rose Ave Ste A Signal Hill (90755) *(P-19835)*
United States Mineral Pdts Co.....D.....909 473-6993
4062 Georgia Blvd San Bernardino (92407) *(P-10989)*
United States Pumice Company (PA).....F.....818 882-0300
20219 Bahama St Chatsworth (91311) *(P-394)*
United States Thermoelectric.....E.....530 345-8000
13267 Contractors Dr Chico (95973) *(P-21318)*
United Supertek Inc.....E.....408 922-0730
14930 Vintner Ct Saratoga (95070) *(P-18038)*
United Technologies Corp.....A.....408 779-9121
600 Metcalf Rd San Jose (95138) *(P-19987)*
United Technologies Corp.....A.....408 779-9121
600 Metcalf Rd San Jose (95138) *(P-19988)*
United Technologies Corp.....B.....510 438-1300
4384 Enterprise Pl Fremont (94538) *(P-19989)*
United Technologies Corp.....F.....562 944-6244
11120 Norwalk Blvd Santa Fe Springs (90670) *(P-20265)*
United Testing Systems Inc.....D.....714 638-2322
1375 S Acacia Ave Fullerton (92831) *(P-21561)*
United Tote Company.....E.....858 279-4250
4205 Ponderosa Ave San Diego (92123) *(P-15358)*
United Traffic Services & Sup, La Puente *Also called Blue Sky Remediation Svcs Inc (P-17717)*
United Uniform Mfrs Inc.....F.....909 381-2682
1096 W Rialto Ave San Bernardino (92410) *(P-2996)*

United Wealth Control, Bakersfield *Also called B & L Casing Service LLC* ***(P-156)***
United Western Enterprises Inc....E....805 389-1077
850 Flynn Rd Ste 200 Camarillo (93012) ***(P-13263)***
United Western Industries Inc....E....559 226-7236
3515 N Hazel Ave Fresno (93722) ***(P-16484)***
United Wholesale Lumber Co, Visalia *Also called Standard Lumber Company Inc* ***(P-4401)***
United Yearbook Printing Svcs, Rancho Cucamonga *Also called TSE Worldwide Press Inc* ***(P-6363)***
Unitek Technology Inc....F....909 930-5700
10211 Bellegrave Ave Mira Loma (91752) ***(P-14994)***
Unitex International, Vernon *Also called Destiney Group Inc* ***(P-2682)***
Unity Clothing Company, El Monte *Also called Unity Clothing Inc* ***(P-22917)***
Unity Clothing Inc....F....626 579-5588
3788 Rockwell Ave El Monte (91731) ***(P-22917)***
Unity Digital, Costa Mesa *Also called Unity Sales International Inc* ***(P-22469)***
Unity Forest Products Inc....E....530 671-7152
1162 Putman Ave Yuba City (95991) ***(P-4144)***
Unity Sales International Inc....F....714 800-1700
2950 Airway Ave Ste A12 Costa Mesa (92626) ***(P-22469)***
Universal Alloy Corporation....B....714 630-7200
2871 E John Ball Way Anaheim (92806) ***(P-11250)***
Universal Cell Site Svcs Inc....E....925 447-4500
2428 Research Dr Livermore (94550) ***(P-11906)***
Universal Ctrl Solutions Corp....F....818 898-3380
19770 Bahama St Northridge (91324) ***(P-16763)***
Universal Cushion Company Inc (PA)....E....323 887-8000
3121 Fujita St Torrance (90505) ***(P-3647)***
Universal Custom Design, Elk Grove *Also called Universal Custom Display* ***(P-23234)***
Universal Custom Display....C....916 714-2505
9104 Elkmont Dr Ste 100 Elk Grove (95624) ***(P-23234)***
Universal Defense....E....909 626-4178
412 Cucamonga Ave Claremont (91711) ***(P-12066)***
Universal Directory Publishing....E....714 994-6025
2995 E White Star Ave Anaheim (92806) ***(P-6367)***
Universal Dyeing & Printing....D....213 746-0818
2303 E 11th St Los Angeles (90021) ***(P-2848)***
Universal Dynamics Inc....F....626 480-0035
5313 3rd St Irwindale (91706) ***(P-144)***
Universal Electronics Inc....F....760 431-8804
2055 Corte Del Miguel Carlsbad (92008) ***(P-19429)***
Universal Filtration Inc....F....626 308-1832
914 Westminster Ave Alhambra (91803) ***(P-15596)***
Universal Forest Products, Ontario *Also called Idx Los Angeles LLC* ***(P-4059)***
Universal Hosiery Inc....D....661 702-8444
28337 Constellation Rd Valencia (91355) ***(P-2769)***
Universal Imaging Tech Inc....F....310 961-2098
4733 Torrance Blvd 997 Torrance (90503) ***(P-22974)***
Universal Interior Industries....F....951 743-5446
4111 Buchanan St Riverside (92503) ***(P-4617)***
Universal Label Printers Inc....E....562 944-0234
13003 Los Nietos Rd Santa Fe Springs (90670) ***(P-7260)***
Universal Maritime, Harbor City *Also called Ship Supply International Inc* ***(P-10483)***
Universal McLoud USA Corp....F....613 222-5904
580 California St San Francisco (94104) ***(P-24541)***
Universal Meat Company, Rancho Cucamonga *Also called Formosa Meat Company Inc* ***(P-456)***
Universal Medical Press Inc....F....415 436-9790
2443 Fillmore St San Francisco (94115) ***(P-6052)***
Universal Meditech Inc....E....559 366-7798
1320 E Fortune Ave # 102 Fresno (93725) ***(P-23252)***
Universal Mercantile Exchange....F....909 839-0556
21128 Commerce Point Dr Walnut (91789) ***(P-23235)***
Universal Merchandise Inc....F....818 344-2044
5422 Aura Ave Tarzana (91356) ***(P-2981)***
Universal Metal Plating....F....626 969-7932
704 S Taylor Ave Montebello (90640) ***(P-13125)***
Universal Metal Spinning Inc....F....510 782-0980
2543 W Winton Ave Ste 5j Hayward (94545) ***(P-17080)***
Universal Mlding Extrusion Inc (HQ)....E....562 401-1015
9151 Imperial Hwy Downey (90242) ***(P-11251)***
Universal Molding Company, Downey *Also called Umc Acquisition Corp* ***(P-11281)***
Universal Molding Company (HQ)....C....310 886-1750
9151 Imperial Hwy Downey (90242) ***(P-11282)***
Universal Music Publishing Inc....F....310 235-4700
2100 Colorado Ave Santa Monica (90404) ***(P-6368)***
Universal Orthodontic Lab Inc....E....562 908-2929
11917 Front St Norwalk (90650) ***(P-22200)***
Universal Plant Services Cal (HQ)....F....310 618-1600
20545a Belshaw Ave Carson (90746) ***(P-16485)***
Universal Plastic Bags Mfg Inc....F....909 218-2247
1309 S Wanamaker Ave Ontario (91761) ***(P-5430)***
Universal Plastic Mold, Baldwin Park *Also called Upm Inc* ***(P-14118)***
Universal Precast Concrete Inc....F....530 243-6477
16538 Clear Creek Rd Redding (96001) ***(P-10661)***
Universal Printing Services....F....951 788-1500
26012 Atlantic Ocean Dr Lake Forest (92630) ***(P-6910)***
Universal Products, Rancho Cucamonga *Also called Proulx Manufacturing Inc* ***(P-10000)***
Universal Punch Corp....D....714 556-4488
4001 W Macarthur Blvd Santa Ana (92704) ***(P-13997)***
Universal Screw Products Inc....E....310 371-1170
20421 Earl St Torrance (90503) ***(P-12657)***
Universal Specialty Vehicles....F....951 943-7747
7879 Pine Crest Dr Riverside (92506) ***(P-19844)***
Universal Steel Services Inc....F....626 960-1455
5034 Heintz St Baldwin Park (91706) ***(P-11907)***
Universal Surface Techlgy Inc....E....310 352-6969
13023 S Main St Los Angeles (90061) ***(P-8354)***
Universal Trailers Inc....F....951 784-0543
2750 Mulberry St Riverside (92501) ***(P-20523)***
Universal Turbo Technology....D....714 600-9585
1120 E Elm Ave Fullerton (92831) ***(P-13581)***
Universal Wire Inc....F....626 285-2288
1705 S Campus Ave Ontario (91761) ***(P-13441)***
Universe Industries, Anaheim *Also called American Industrial Corp* ***(P-14014)***
University Blanket & Flag Corp (PA)....F....619 435-4100
1111 Orange Ave Ste C Coronado (92118) ***(P-3863)***
University Cal Press Fundation (PA)....D....510 642-4247
155 Grand Ave Ste 400 Oakland (94612) ***(P-6158)***
University Cal Press Fundation....E....510 642-4247
2000 Center St Ste 303 Berkeley (94704) ***(P-6159)***
University California Berkeley....E....510 642-4247
155 Grand Ave Ste 400 Oakland (94612) ***(P-6160)***
University Frames Inc....E....714 575-5100
3060 E Miraloma Ave Anaheim (92806) ***(P-4541)***
University of California Press, Oakland *Also called University California Berkeley* ***(P-6160)***
University Plating Co, San Jose *Also called Hane & Hane Inc* ***(P-13021)***
University Printing, Loma Linda *Also called Loma Linda University* ***(P-6707)***
University Readers, San Diego *Also called Cognella Inc* ***(P-6090)***
Univocity Media Inc....F....760 904-5200
2901 E Alejo Rd Bldg 4 Palm Springs (92262) ***(P-6369)***
Uniweb Inc (PA)....D....951 279-7999
222 S Promenade Ave Corona (92879) ***(P-5009)***
Unix Packaging Inc....C....213 627-5050
9 Minson Way Montebello (90640) ***(P-2178)***
Unlimited Trck Trlr Maint Inc....E....323 727-2500
825 S Maple Ave Ste D Montebello (90640) ***(P-19836)***
Unmanned Innovation Inc (PA)....D....877 714-4828
2625 Franklin St Apt 301 San Francisco (94123) ***(P-19936)***
Unocal, Lompoc *Also called Chevron Corporation* ***(P-43)***
Unorth, San Jose *Also called Mota Group Inc* ***(P-19225)***
Unovo LLC....F....415 864-7600
1200 Hrbour Way S Ste 215 Richmond (94804) ***(P-16846)***
Unshackled, Palo Alto *Also called Level Labs LP* ***(P-24100)***
Untangle Holdings Inc....E....408 598-4299
100 W San Fernando St # 565 San Jose (95113) ***(P-24542)***
UOP LLC....E....714 870-7590
2100 E Orangethorpe Ave Anaheim (92806) ***(P-5347)***
UPD INC....D....323 588-8811
4507 S Maywood Ave Vernon (90058) ***(P-22655)***
UPF Corporation....E....661 323-8227
3747 Standard St Bakersfield (93308) ***(P-10990)***
Upguard Inc (PA)....E....888 882-3223
723 N Shoreline Blvd Mountain View (94043) ***(P-24543)***
Upholstery By Wayne Stoec....F....559 233-1960
3316 E Annadale Ave Fresno (93725) ***(P-2716)***
Upholstery Factory Inc (PA)....F....760 341-6865
74757 Joni Dr Ste 1 Palm Desert (92260) ***(P-4675)***
Upholstery Workroom, Los Angeles *Also called Custom Upholstered Furn Inc* ***(P-4635)***
Upland Fab Inc....E....909 933-9185
1445 Brooks St Ste L Ontario (91762) ***(P-10101)***
Upm Inc....B....626 962-4001
13245 Los Angeles St Baldwin Park (91706) ***(P-14118)***
Upm Raflatac Inc....E....909 390-4657
1105 Auto Center Dr Ontario (91761) ***(P-5377)***
Upper Crust, San Rafael *Also called Christine Milne* ***(P-1339)***
Upper Crust Enterprises Inc....E....213 625-0038
411 Center St Los Angeles (90012) ***(P-2643)***
Upper Deck Company....C....800 873-7332
5830 El Camino Real Carlsbad (92008) ***(P-6370)***
Upper Deck Company LLC....B....800 873-7332
5830 El Camino Real Carlsbad (92008) ***(P-6911)***
Upright, Fresno *Also called Tanfield Engrg Systems US Inc* ***(P-13750)***
Upstanding LLC....C....949 788-9900
440 Exchange Ste 100 Irvine (92602) ***(P-24544)***
Upton Engineering & Mfg Co, South El Monte *Also called BCI Inc* ***(P-15780)***
Uptown, Los Angeles *Also called Lets Go Apparel Inc* ***(P-3565)***
Urban Decal LLC (HQ)....E....949 574-9712
833 W 16th St Newport Beach (92663) ***(P-8597)***
Urban Decay Cosmetics, Newport Beach *Also called Urban Decal LLC* ***(P-8597)***
Urban Empire, San Diego *Also called Quantum Dynasty* ***(P-15082)***
Urban Expressions Inc....E....310 593-4574
5500 Union Pacific Ave Commerce (90022) ***(P-10230)***
Urban Outfitters Inc....E....626 449-1818
139 W Colorado Blvd Pasadena (91105) ***(P-3258)***
Urban Outfitters Store 18, Pasadena *Also called Urban Outfitters Inc* ***(P-3258)***
Urban Steel Designs Inc....F....415 305-2570
4679 18th St Unit A San Francisco (94114) ***(P-4706)***
Urban Trading Software Inc....E....877 633-6171
21227 Foothill Blvd Hayward (94541) ***(P-24545)***
Urbanista, South Gate *Also called YH Texpert Corporation* ***(P-3435)***
Uremet Corporation....E....714 641-8813
3026 Orange Ave Santa Ana (92707) ***(P-7622)***
Urethane Masters Inc....F....651 829-1032
455 54th St Ste 102 San Diego (92114) ***(P-9575)***
Urethane Masters Incorporated....F....651 357-8821
455 54th St San Diego (92114) ***(P-23513)***
Urethane Products Corporation....F....800 913-0062
17842 Sampson Ln Huntington Beach (92647) ***(P-10102)***
Urethane Science Inc....F....714 828-3210
8357 Standustrial St Stanton (90680) ***(P-10103)***
Urgent Upfits, Rancho Cordova *Also called Form & Fusion Mfg Inc* ***(P-12805)***
Uri Tech Inc....F....408 456-0115
1340 Norman Ave Santa Clara (95054) ***(P-18039)***
Uriman Inc (HQ)....C....714 257-2080
650 N Puente St Brea (92821) ***(P-19204)***
Urocare Products Inc....F....909 621-6013
2735 Melbourne Ave Pomona (91767) ***(P-9382)***

Employee Codes: A=Over 500 employees, B=251-500
C=101-250, D=51-100, E=20-50, F=10-19
2020 California
Manfacturers Register
© Mergent Inc. 1-800-342-5647
1273

Urolift, Pleasanton *Also called Neotract Inc* ***(P-21832)***
Urovant Sciences Inc (HQ)....E....949 226-6029
5281 California Ave # 100 Irvine (92617) ***(P-8174)***
URu By Kristine St Rrik Inc....F....760 745-1800
622 Aero Way Escondido (92029) ***(P-3259)***
Uruhu Highlands Ltd....F....424 213-9725
14360 Valerio St Apt 311 Van Nuys (91405) ***(P-13273)***
US Apothecary Crown Labs, Santa Fe Springs *Also called Titan Medical Enterprises Inc* ***(P-8164)***
US Architectural Lighting, Palmdale *Also called Sun Valley Ltg Standards Inc* ***(P-17074)***
US Armor Corporation....E....562 207-4240
10715 Bloomfield Ave Santa Fe Springs (90670) ***(P-22114)***
US Bioservices (PA)....E....800 801-1140
5100 E Hunter Ave Anaheim (92807) ***(P-8690)***
US Blanks LLC (PA)....E....310 225-6774
14700 S San Pedro St Gardena (90248) ***(P-7623)***
US Borax Inc....A....760 762-7000
14486 Borax Rd Boron (93516) ***(P-7532)***
US Borax Inc....C....310 522-5300
300 Falcon St Wilmington (90744) ***(P-7533)***
US Composite Pipe South, Rialto *Also called Uscps* ***(P-23515)***
US Computers Inc....F....714 528-0514
181 W Orangethorpe Ave C Placentia (92870) ***(P-15359)***
US Concrete Inc....E....408 779-1000
1 Live Oak Ave Morgan Hill (95037) ***(P-10662)***
US Concrete Inc....F....408 947-8606
755 Stockton Ave San Jose (95126) ***(P-10858)***
US Concrete Precast, San Diego *Also called San Diego Precast Concrete Inc* ***(P-10645)***
US Container and Housing Co....E....844 762-8242
22320 Fthill Blvd Ste 450 Hayward (94541) ***(P-4469)***
US Continental Marketing Inc (PA)....D....951 808-8888
310 Reed Cir Corona (92879) ***(P-8423)***
US Cotton LLC....B....559 651-3015
7100 W Sunnyview Ave Visalia (93291) ***(P-8598)***
US Critical, Lake Forest *Also called US Critical LLC* ***(P-15112)***
US Critical LLC (PA)....E....949 916-9326
6 Orchard Ste 150 Lake Forest (92630) ***(P-15112)***
US Critical LLC....E....800 884-8945
25422 Trabuco Rd 320 Lake Forest (92630) ***(P-15113)***
US Dental Inc....E....562 404-3500
13043 166th St Cerritos (90703) ***(P-22201)***
US Dies Inc (PA)....E....209 664-1402
1992 Rockefeller Dr # 300 Ceres (95307) ***(P-14119)***
US Door and Fence LLC....F....951 300-0010
3880 Garner Rd Riverside (92501) ***(P-3913)***
US Duty Gear Inc....E....909 391-8800
1616 E Francis St Unit Qr Ontario (91761) ***(P-10256)***
US Environmental....F....951 359-9002
7085 Jurupa Ave Ste 1 Riverside (92504) ***(P-9034)***
US Eta Inc....F....408 778-2793
16170 Vineyard Blvd # 180 Morgan Hill (95037) ***(P-19132)***
US Garment LLC....E....323 415-6464
4440 E 26th St Vernon (90058) ***(P-3057)***
US Gear & Pumps....E....909 525-3026
1249 S Diamond Bar Blvd # 325 Diamond Bar (91765) ***(P-14751)***
US Gold Trading Inc (PA)....F....818 558-7766
117 E Providencia Ave Burbank (91502) ***(P-22581)***
US Gov GA Aeronautical Uav, Poway *Also called General Atomic Aeron* ***(P-19901)***
US Hanger Company LLC....E....310 323-8030
17501 S Denver Ave Gardena (90248) ***(P-11114)***
US Horizon Manufacturing Inc....E....661 775-1675
28539 Industry Dr Valencia (91355) ***(P-10279)***
US Hybrid Corporation (PA)....E....310 212-1200
445 Maple Ave Torrance (90503) ***(P-19795)***
US Industrial Tool & Sup Co....E....310 464-8400
14083 S Normandie Ave Gardena (90249) ***(P-13998)***
US Logistics, Signal Hill *Also called United States Logistics Group* ***(P-19835)***
US Machining, San Jose *Also called TLC Machining Incorporated* ***(P-14202)***
US Motor Works LLC (PA)....C....562 404-0488
14722 Anson Ave Santa Fe Springs (90670) ***(P-19796)***
US Nuclear Corp (PA)....F....818 296-0746
7051 Eton Ave Canoga Park (91303) ***(P-21562)***
US Packagers Inc....E....310 327-7721
13620 Crenshaw Blvd Gardena (90249) ***(P-7321)***
US Pipe Fabrication LLC....E....530 742-5171
3387 Plumas Arboga Rd Marysville (95901) ***(P-9478)***
US Plastic Inc....E....951 300-9360
1561 Estridge Ave Ste 102 Riverside (92507) ***(P-9497)***
US Pole Company Inc (PA)....C....800 877-6537
660 W Avenue O Palmdale (93551) ***(P-17173)***
US Polymers Inc....E....323 727-6888
5910 Bandini Blvd Commerce (90040) ***(P-11252)***
US Polymers Inc (PA)....D....323 728-3023
1057 S Vail Ave Montebello (90640) ***(P-10104)***
US Precision Sheet Metal Inc....D....951 276-2611
4020 Garner Rd Riverside (92501) ***(P-12419)***
US Premier Inc....F....323 267-4463
624 S Clarence St Los Angeles (90023) ***(P-3206)***
US Print & Toner Inc....E....619 562-6995
1990 Friendship Dr El Cajon (92020) ***(P-22975)***
US Radiator Corporation (PA)....E....323 826-0965
4423 District Blvd Vernon (90058) ***(P-19797)***
US Rigging Supply Corp....E....714 545-7444
1600 E Mcfadden Ave Santa Ana (92705) ***(P-13442)***
US Rockets....F....707 267-3393
Munsey Rd Mile 11 Cantil (93519) ***(P-20462)***
US Rubber Recycling Inc....E....909 825-1200
1231 Lincoln St Colton (92324) ***(P-9383)***
US Rubber Roller Company Inc....F....951 682-2221
1516 7th St Riverside (92507) ***(P-9384)***

US Saws Inc (PA)....F....860 668-2402
3702 W Central Ave Santa Ana (92704) ***(P-13755)***
US Sensor Corp....D....714 639-1000
1832 W Collins Ave Orange (92867) ***(P-18635)***
US Steel Rule Dies Inc....E....562 921-0690
40 E Verdugo Ave Burbank (91502) ***(P-14120)***
US Tower Corp....D....559 564-6000
1099 W Ropes Ave Woodlake (93286) ***(P-11908)***
US Toyo Fan Corporation (HQ)....F....626 338-1111
16025 Arrow Hwy Ste F Irwindale (91706) ***(P-14686)***
US Union Tool Inc (HQ)....E....714 521-6242
1260 N Fee Ana St Anaheim (92807) ***(P-13960)***
US Wheel, Huntington Beach *Also called U S Wheel Corporation* ***(P-19791)***
US Wholesale Drug Corp....F....323 227-4258
2611 N San Fernando Rd Los Angeles (90065) ***(P-8175)***
Us-Vn-Mynmar Rare Erth Mtls Gr....F....949 262-3673
4000 Barranca Pkwy # 250 Irvine (92604) ***(P-14)***
Us1com Inc....F....707 781-2560
715 Southpoint Blvd Ste D Petaluma (94954) ***(P-7261)***
USA Extruded Plastics Inc....F....714 991-6061
965 E Discovery Ln Anaheim (92801) ***(P-10105)***
USA Fire Glass....F....949 302-7728
6789 Quail Hill Pkwy # 613 Irvine (92603) ***(P-10399)***
USA Printer Company LLC....F....800 279-7768
41571 Corning Pl Ste 115 Murrieta (92562) ***(P-6912)***
USA Printer Guy, Murrieta *Also called USA Printer Company LLC* ***(P-6912)***
USA Printing, West Hollywood *Also called A & J Enterprises Inc* ***(P-6389)***
USA Products Group Inc (PA)....E....209 334-1460
1300 E Vine St Lodi (95240) ***(P-3864)***
USA Sales Inc....E....909 390-9606
1560 S Archibald Ave Ontario (91761) ***(P-2657)***
USA Solar Technology Inc....F....714 356-8360
28381 Vincent Moraga Dr Temecula (92590) ***(P-23514)***
USA Topdon LLC....F....833 233-5535
18351 Colima Rd Unit 255 Rowland Heights (91748) ***(P-19430)***
USA Vision Systems Inc (HQ)....E....949 583-1519
9301 Irvine Blvd Irvine (92618) ***(P-19431)***
USAopoly Inc....E....760 431-5910
5607 Palmer Way Carlsbad (92010) ***(P-22723)***
Uscps....D....909 434-1888
3009 N Laurel Ave Rialto (92377) ***(P-23515)***
Usecb Joint Venture Inc....F....209 267-5594
11500 String Bean Aly Sutter Creek (95685) ***(P-9)***
Used Pellet Co, Fresno *Also called Charles Jj Inc* ***(P-4474)***
Usglobalsat Inc....F....909 597-8525
14740 Yorba Ct Chino (91710) ***(P-17698)***
Ushio America Inc....E....714 236-8600
14 Mason Irvine (92618) ***(P-17081)***
USI Manufacturing Services Inc....D....408 636-9600
1255 E Arques Ave Sunnyvale (94085) ***(P-15360)***
Usit Co, Gardena *Also called US Industrial Tool & Sup Co* ***(P-13998)***
Usiwater LLC....F....626 600-5156
1433 W San Bernardino Rd Covina (91722) ***(P-2179)***
Usk Manufacturing Inc....E....510 471-7555
720 Zwissig Way Union City (94587) ***(P-12420)***
Usl Parallel Products Cal....E....909 980-1200
12281 Arrow Rte Rancho Cucamonga (91739) ***(P-8779)***
USP Inc....D....760 842-7700
1818 Ord Way Oceanside (92056) ***(P-8599)***
Uspar Enterprises Inc....E....909 591-7506
2037 S Vineyard Ave Ontario (91761) ***(P-16996)***
USS-Psco Inds A Cal Jint Ventr (PA)....A....800 877-7672
900 Loveridge Rd Pittsburg (94565) ***(P-11079)***
UST, Los Angeles *Also called Universal Surface Techlgy Inc* ***(P-8354)***
Ustc, Chico *Also called United States Thermoelectric* ***(P-21318)***
Utak Laboratories Inc....E....661 294-3935
25020 Avenue Tibbitts Valencia (91355) ***(P-8780)***
Utap Printing Co Inc....F....650 588-2818
1423 San Mateo Ave South San Francisco (94080) ***(P-6913)***
Utbbb Inc....C....562 594-4411
10711 Bloomfield St Los Alamitos (90720) ***(P-1336)***
UTC Aerospace Systems, Santa Fe Springs *Also called United Technologies Corp* ***(P-20265)***
UTC Aerospace Systems, Fairfield *Also called Goodrich Corporation* ***(P-20475)***
Utility Composite Solutions In (PA)....F....858 442-3187
4600 Pavlov Ave Unit 221 San Diego (92122) ***(P-10663)***
Utility Refrigerator....F....818 764-6200
12160 Sherman Way North Hollywood (91605) ***(P-15469)***
Utility Trailer Mfg Co....B....909 594-6026
17295 Railroad St Ste A City of Industry (91748) ***(P-19837)***
Utility Trailer Mfg Co....E....909 428-8300
15567 Valley Blvd Fontana (92335) ***(P-19838)***
Utility Trlr Sls Southern Cal, Fontana *Also called Utility Trailer Mfg Co* ***(P-19838)***
Utility Vault, Fontana *Also called Oldcastle Infrastructure Inc* ***(P-10610)***
Utility Vault, Pleasanton *Also called Oldcastle Infrastructure Inc* ***(P-10612)***
Utility Vault, San Diego *Also called Oldcastle Infrastructure Inc* ***(P-10613)***
Utility Vault, Madera *Also called Oldcastle Infrastructure Inc* ***(P-13536)***
Utility Vault, Escondido *Also called Oldcastle Infrastructure Inc* ***(P-10617)***
Utopia Lighting....F....310 327-7711
2329 E Pacifica Pl Compton (90220) ***(P-16580)***
Utstarcom Inc (HQ)....C....510 749-1503
1732 N 1st St Ste 200 San Jose (95112) ***(P-17425)***
Uv Landscaping LLC....F....831 275-5296
477 Old Natividad Rd Salinas (93906) ***(P-10522)***
Uv Skinz Inc (PA)....F....209 536-9200
13775 Mono Way Ste A Sonora (95370) ***(P-3127)***
Uvexs Incorporated....F....408 734-4402
1287 Hammerwood Ave Sunnyvale (94089) ***(P-8936)***

Mergent e-mail: customerrelations@mergent.com
1274
2020 California
Manufacturers Register
(P-0000) Products & Services Section entry number
(PA)=Parent Co (HQ)=Headquarters (DH)=Div Headquarters

Uvify Inc ....F....628 200-4469
1 Market Ste 3600 San Francisco (94105) *(P-20739)*
Uwe, Camarillo *Also called United Western Enterprises Inc (P-13263)*
V & F Fabrication Company Inc ....E....714 265-0630
13902 Seaboard Cir Garden Grove (92843) *(P-11909)*
V & M Plating Co ....F....310 532-5633
14024 Avalon Blvd Los Angeles (90061) *(P-13126)*
V & M Precision Grinding Co., Brea *Also called Rogers Holding Company Inc (P-20211)*
V & P Scientific Inc ....F....858 455-0643
9823 Pacific Heights Blvd San Diego (92121) *(P-21319)*
V & S Engineering Company Ltd ....F....714 898-7869
5766 Research Dr Huntington Beach (92649) *(P-16486)*
V & V Manufacturing Inc ....F....626 330-0641
15320 Proctor Ave City of Industry (91745) *(P-22997)*
V 3, Oxnard *Also called V3 Printing Corporation (P-6914)*
V Fly, El Monte *Also called Vfly Corporation (P-3763)*
V H Paris Co, La Habra Heights *Also called Viet Hung Paris Inc (P-506)*
V Himark (usa) Inc ....F....626 305-5766
16019 E Foothill Blvd Irwindale (91702) *(P-8901)*
V I P Ironworks Inc ....F....310 216-2890
8319 Hindry Ave Los Angeles (90045) *(P-12518)*
V J Provision Inc ....F....818 843-3945
410 S Varney St Burbank (91502) *(P-428)*
V M P Inc ....F....661 294-9934
24830 Avenue Tibbitts Valencia (91355) *(P-12658)*
V M I, Visalia *Also called Voltage Multipliers Inc (P-18649)*
V Manufacturing Logistics Inc ....E....909 869-6200
20501 Earlgate St Walnut (91789) *(P-8600)*
V Q Orthocare, Irvine *Also called Vision Quest Industries Inc (P-22119)*
V Tech, Sunnyvale *Also called V-Tech Manufacturing Inc (P-16487)*
V Twest Inc ....F....714 521-2167
16222 Phoebe Ave La Mirada (90638) *(P-4952)*
V Twin Magazine, Agoura Hills *Also called Paisano Publications LLC (P-5998)*
V&H Performance LLC ....D....562 921-7461
13861 Rosecrans Ave Santa Fe Springs (90670) *(P-20435)*
V&M Prcsion Machining Grinding, Brea *Also called Tca Precision Products LLC (P-20244)*
V-A Optical Company Inc ....F....415 459-1919
60 Red Hill Ave San Anselmo (94960) *(P-21417)*
V-Silicon Inc ....F....510 897-0168
47467 Fremont Blvd Fremont (94538) *(P-18636)*
V-T Industries Inc ....F....714 521-2008
16222 Phoebe Ave La Mirada (90638) *(P-10106)*
V-Tech Manufacturing Inc ....F....408 730-9200
1140 W Evelyn Ave Sunnyvale (94086) *(P-16487)*
V/ Twins, Agoura Hills *Also called Paisano Publications Inc (P-5999)*
V2 Lighting Group Inc ....F....707 383-4600
276 E Gish Rd San Jose (95112) *(P-17174)*
V3, Oxnard *Also called Ventura Printing Inc (P-7262)*
V3 Printing Corporation ....D....805 981-2600
200 N Elevar St Oxnard (93030) *(P-6914)*
Va-Tran Systems Inc ....F....619 423-4555
677 Anita St Ste A Chula Vista (91911) *(P-14552)*
Vaca Energy LLC ....F....310 385-3684
4407 Sturgis Rd Oxnard (93030) *(P-145)*
Vacaville Fruit Co Inc ....E....707 448-5292
2055 Cessna Dr Vacaville (95688) *(P-872)*
Vacco Industries (HQ) ....C....626 443-7121
10350 Vacco St South El Monte (91733) *(P-13365)*
Vacmet Inc ....E....909 948-9344
8740 Hellman Ave Rancho Cucamonga (91730) *(P-13264)*
Vacumed, Ventura *Also called Vacumetrics Inc (P-21944)*
Vacumetrics Inc ....F....805 644-7461
4538 Wstnghouse St Unit A Ventura (93003) *(P-21944)*
Vacuum Engrg & Mtls Co Inc ....E....408 871-9900
390 Reed St Santa Clara (95050) *(P-7534)*
Vacuum Tube Logic of America ....F....909 627-5944
4774 Murietta St Ste 10 Chino (91710) *(P-17795)*
Vaga Industries, South El Monte *Also called Pearson Engineering Corp (P-13222)*
Vagrant Records Inc ....E....323 302-0100
6351 Wilshire Blvd # 101 Los Angeles (90048) *(P-7322)*
Vahe Enterprises Inc ....D....323 235-6657
750 E Slauson Ave Los Angeles (90011) *(P-19560)*
Vaider Inc ....F....707 584-3655
553 Martin Ave Ste 1 Rohnert Park (94928) *(P-13265)*
Vaider Manufacturing, Rohnert Park *Also called Vaider Inc (P-13265)*
Val Pak Products ....F....661 252-0115
20731 Centre Pointe Pkwy Santa Clarita (91350) *(P-9385)*
Val Plastic USA L L C ....F....909 390-9600
4570 Eucalyptus Ave Ste C Chino (91710) *(P-13678)*
Val-Aero Industries Inc ....F....661 295-8645
25319 Rye Canyon Rd Valencia (91355) *(P-16488)*
Valadons Plumbing Service Inc ....F....661 201-1460
315 Coleshill St Bakersfield (93312) *(P-11686)*
Valco Boats, Fresno *Also called Henderson Services Inc (P-20336)*
Valco Planer Works Inc ....E....323 582-6355
6131 Maywood Ave Huntington Park (90255) *(P-14121)*
Valco Precision Works, Huntington Park *Also called Valco Planer Works Inc (P-14121)*
Valdor Fiber Optics Inc (PA) ....E....510 293-1212
1838 D St Hayward (94541) *(P-21152)*
Valence Lynwood, Lynwood *Also called Triumph Processing Inc (P-13120)*
Valence Surface Tech LLC ....E....323 770-0240
1000 Commercial St San Carlos (94070) *(P-20740)*
Valencia Mold ....F....661 257-0066
25611 Hercules St Santa Clarita (91355) *(P-10107)*
Valencia Pipe Company ....E....661 257-3923
28839 Industry Dr Valencia (91355) *(P-9479)*
Valent Dublin Laboratories, Dublin *Also called Valent USA LLC (P-8847)*
Valent USA LLC ....E....925 256-2700
6560 Trinity Ct Dublin (94568) *(P-8847)*
Valerie Trading Inc ....E....323 231-4255
870 E 59th St Los Angeles (90001) *(P-2862)*
Valero, Wilmington *Also called Ultramar Inc (P-277)*
Valero Energy Corporation ....E....760 946-3322
17928 Us Highway 18 Apple Valley (92307) *(P-9081)*
Valero Ref Company-California ....B....707 745-7011
3400 E 2nd St Benicia (94510) *(P-9082)*
Valero Ref Company-California ....B....562 491-6754
2401 E Anaheim St Wilmington (90744) *(P-9083)*
Valet Cstm Cabinets & Closets ....F....408 374-4407
1190 Dell Ave Ste J Campbell (95008) *(P-4260)*
Valew Welding & Fabrication, Adelanto *Also called Hayes Welding Inc (P-24639)*
Valew Welding & Fabrication, Hesperia *Also called Hayes Welding Inc (P-24640)*
Valiantica Inc (PA) ....F....408 694-3803
940 Saratoga Ave Ste 108 San Jose (95129) *(P-24546)*
Validant, San Francisco *Also called Kinsale Holdings Inc (P-9325)*
Valimet Inc (PA) ....D....209 444-1600
431 Sperry Rd Stockton (95206) *(P-11490)*
Vallejo Electric Motor Inc ....F....707 552-7488
925 Maine St Vallejo (94590) *(P-24700)*
Valley Business Printers Inc ....D....818 362-7771
16230 Filbert St Sylmar (91342) *(P-6915)*
Valley Cabinet, El Cajon *Also called Vcsd Inc (P-4262)*
Valley Casework Inc ....D....619 579-6886
1112 Cleghorn Way Alpine (91901) *(P-4261)*
Valley Chrome Plating Inc ....D....559 298-8094
1028 Hoblitt Ave Clovis (93612) *(P-13127)*
Valley Circuits ....F....661 294-0077
24940 Avenue Tibbitts Valencia (91355) *(P-18040)*
Valley Community Newspaper ....F....916 429-9901
1109 Markham Way Sacramento (95818) *(P-5856)*
Valley Controls Inc ....F....559 638-5115
583 E Dinuba Ave Reedley (93654) *(P-20954)*
Valley Cutting System Inc ....E....559 684-1229
1455 N Belmont Rd Exeter (93221) *(P-13961)*
Valley Decorating Company ....E....559 495-1100
2829 E Hamilton Ave Fresno (93721) *(P-10108)*
Valley Drapery Inc ....D....818 892-7744
16616 Schoenborn St North Hills (91343) *(P-2738)*
Valley Drapery and Upholstery, North Hills *Also called Valley Drapery Inc (P-2738)*
Valley Engravers, Santa Clarita *Also called Valley Precision Metal Product (P-12421)*
Valley Fabrication Inc ....D....831 757-5151
1056 Pellet Ave Salinas (93901) *(P-13679)*
Valley Fine Foods Company Inc ....D....530 671-7200
300 Epley Dr Yuba City (95991) *(P-2644)*
Valley Fine Foods Company Inc (PA) ....D....707 746-6888
3909 Park Rd Ste H Benicia (94510) *(P-1011)*
Valley Forge Acquisition Corp ....F....626 969-8701
444 S Motor Ave Azusa (91702) *(P-12725)*
Valley Fresh Inc (HQ) ....E....209 943-5411
1404 S Fresno Ave Stockton (95206) *(P-529)*
Valley Garlic Inc ....E....559 934-1763
500 Enterprise Pkwy Coalinga (93210) *(P-904)*
Valley Images ....F....408 279-6777
1925 Kyle Park Ct San Jose (95125) *(P-3822)*
Valley Lahvosh Baking Co Inc ....E....559 485-2700
502 M St Fresno (93721) *(P-1289)*
Valley Metal Treating Inc ....E....909 623-6316
355 S East End Ave Pomona (91766) *(P-11476)*
Valley Metals LLC ....E....858 513-1300
13125 Gregg St Poway (92064) *(P-11138)*
Valley Mfg & Engrg Inc ....F....818 504-6085
9105 De Garmo Ave Sun Valley (91352) *(P-14122)*
Valley Motor Center Inc ....F....818 686-3350
10639 Glenoaks Blvd Pacoima (91331) *(P-19510)*
Valley News Gardens, Gardena *Also called Gardena Valley News Inc (P-5639)*
Valley Oak Cabinets, Santa Ynez *Also called Valley Oaks Industries (P-4824)*
Valley Oaks Industries ....F....805 688-2754
3550 E Highway 246 Ste Ae Santa Ynez (93460) *(P-4824)*
Valley of Moon Winery ....E....707 939-4500
777 Madrone Rd Glen Ellen (95442) *(P-1980)*
Valley Packline Solutions ....E....559 638-7821
5259 Avenue 408 Reedley (93654) *(P-14411)*
Valley Perforating LLC ....D....661 324-4964
3201 Gulf St Bakersfield (93308) *(P-16489)*
Valley Pipe & Supply Inc ....E....559 233-0321
1801 Santa Clara St Fresno (93721) *(P-13366)*
Valley Post, Anderson *Also called North Valley Newspapers Inc (P-5784)*
Valley Power Services Inc ....E....909 969-9345
425 S Hacienda Blvd City of Industry (91745) *(P-16678)*
Valley Power Systems Inc (PA) ....D....626 333-1243
425 S Hacienda Blvd City of Industry (91745) *(P-13603)*
Valley Precision Inc ....F....209 847-1758
536 Hi Tech Pkwy Oakdale (95361) *(P-16490)*
Valley Precision Metal Product ....E....661 607-0100
27771 Avenue Hopkins Santa Clarita (91355) *(P-12421)*
Valley Printers, Sylmar *Also called Valley Business Printers Inc (P-6915)*
Valley Printing, Ceres *Also called Robert R Wix Inc (P-7202)*
Valley Protein LLC ....D....559 498-7115
1828 E Hedges Ave Fresno (93703) *(P-505)*
Valley Publications ....F....661 298-5330
27259 One Half Camp Plnty Canyon Country (91351) *(P-6371)*
Valley Rock Lndscpe Material ....E....916 652-7209
4018 Taylor Rd Loomis (95650) *(P-10523)*
Valley Rubber & Gasket, Stockton *Also called Lewis-Goetz and Company Inc (P-9199)*
Valley Sailboards, Oxnard *Also called Advantage Engineering Corp (P-22733)*

ALPHABETIC

Employee Codes: A=Over 500 employees, B=251-500
C=101-250, D=51-100, E=20-50, F=10-19
2020 California
Manfacturers Register
© Mergent Inc. 1-800-342-5647
1275

Valley Services Electronics, San Jose *Also called Tri-Phase Inc* ***(P-18026)***
Valley Sleurry Seal Co, Redding *Also called Vss Emultech Inc* ***(P-9107)***
Valley Spuds of Oxnard, Oxnard *Also called Produce Available Inc* ***(P-13660)***
Valley Stairway Inc..........F.......559 299-0151
5684 E Shields Ave Fresno (93727) ***(P-12519)***
Valley Syncom Circuits, Valencia *Also called Valley Circuits* ***(P-18040)***
Valley Tool & Mfg Co Inc..........E.......209 883-4093
2507 Tully Rd Hughson (95326) ***(P-16491)***
Valley Tool and Machine Co Inc..........E.......909 595-2205
111 Explorer St Pomona (91768) ***(P-16492)***
Valley View Foods Inc..........D.......530 673-7356
7547 Sawtelle Ave Yuba City (95991) ***(P-833)***
Valley View Packing Co Inc..........E.......408 289-8300
1764 The Alameda San Jose (95126) ***(P-873)***
Valley Water Management Co..........F.......661 410-7500
7500 Meany Ave Bakersfield (93308) ***(P-278)***
Valley Welding & Machine Works, Fresno *Also called Garabedian Bros Inc* ***(P-15985)***
Valley Yellow Pages, Fresno *Also called Agi Publishing Inc* ***(P-6175)***
Valley Yellow Pages, Fresno *Also called Agi Publishing Inc* ***(P-6176)***
Valley-Todeco Inc (HQ)..........E.......800 992-4444
12975 Bradley Ave Sylmar (91342) ***(P-12699)***
Valma Properties, San Francisco *Also called James P McNair Co Inc* ***(P-11600)***
Valmas Inc..........E.......323 677-2211
1233 S Boyle Ave Los Angeles (90023) ***(P-3260)***
Valmont Industries Inc..........D.......323 264-6660
4116 Whiteside St Los Angeles (90063) ***(P-11910)***
Valmont Industries Inc..........F.......760 253-3070
3970 Lenwood Rd Barstow (92311) ***(P-11911)***
Valmont Newmark, Barstow *Also called Valmont Industries Inc* ***(P-11911)***
Valprint, Fresno *Also called Zip Print Inc* ***(P-6949)***
Valterra Products LLC (PA)..........E.......818 898-1671
15230 San Fernando Mission Hills (91345) ***(P-13367)***
Value Products Inc..........E.......209 345-3817
2128 Industrial Dr Stockton (95206) ***(P-8355)***
Valvex Enterprises Inc..........E.......408 928-2510
885 Jarvis Dr Morgan Hill (95037) ***(P-16493)***
Vampire Penguin LLC (PA)..........F.......916 553-4197
907 K St Sacramento (95814) ***(P-675)***
Van Brunt Foundry Inc..........F.......323 569-2832
5136 Chakemco St South Gate (90280) ***(P-11391)***
Van Grace Quality Injection..........F.......323 931-5255
9164 Appleby St Downey (90240) ***(P-10109)***
Van Heusen Factory Outlet..........F.......951 674-1190
17600 Collier Ave D134 Lake Elsinore (92530) ***(P-2997)***
Van Howd Studios, Auburn *Also called Sierra Sculpture Inc* ***(P-11406)***
Van R Dental Products Inc..........F.......805 488-1122
600 E Hueneme Rd Oxnard (93033) ***(P-22202)***
Van Sark Inc (PA)..........E.......510 635-1111
888 Doolittle Dr San Leandro (94577) ***(P-4676)***
Van Tisse Inc..........F.......415 543-2404
2565 3rd St Ste 319 San Francisco (94107) ***(P-2810)***
Vanard Lithographers Inc..........E.......619 291-5571
3220 Kurtz St San Diego (92110) ***(P-6916)***
Vance & Hines, Santa Fe Springs *Also called V&H Performance LLC* ***(P-20435)***
Vander-Bend Manufacturing Inc (PA)..........B.......408 245-5150
2701 Orchard Pkwy San Jose (95134) ***(P-19133)***
Vander-Bend Manufacturing Inc..........C.......916 631-6375
3510 Luyung Dr Rancho Cordova (95742) ***(P-16494)***
Vanderhulst Associates Inc..........E.......408 727-1313
3300 Victor Ct Santa Clara (95054) ***(P-16495)***
Vanderlans & Sons Inc (PA)..........E.......209 334-4115
1320 S Sacramento St Lodi (95240) ***(P-15597)***
Vandersteen Audio Inc..........E.......559 582-0324
116 W 4th St Hanford (93230) ***(P-17299)***
Vanderveer Industrial Plas LLC..........E.......714 579-7700
515 S Melrose St Placentia (92870) ***(P-10110)***
Vandorn Plastering..........F.......530 671-2748
657 Lincoln Rd Ste D Yuba City (95991) ***(P-11022)***
Vangie L Cortes..........E.......858 578-6807
9466 Black Mountain Rd San Diego (92126) ***(P-5857)***
Vanguard Fabrication Corp..........F.......909 355-0832
14578 Hawthorne Ave Fontana (92335) ***(P-12422)***
Vanguard Industries East Inc..........D.......800 433-1334
2440 Impala Dr Carlsbad (92010) ***(P-3865)***
Vanguard Industries West Inc (PA)..........C.......760 438-4437
2440 Impala Dr Carlsbad (92010) ***(P-3866)***
Vanguard Instruments, Ontario *Also called Doble Engineering Company* ***(P-16595)***
Vanguard Marketing, Scotts Valley *Also called Threshold Enterprises Ltd* ***(P-7697)***
Vanguard Printing, Oxnard *Also called DBC Printing Incorporated* ***(P-6534)***
Vanguard Tool & Manufacturing, Rancho Cucamonga *Also called Vanguard Tool & Mfg Co Inc* ***(P-12887)***
Vanguard Tool & Mfg Co Inc..........E.......909 980-9392
8388 Utica Ave Rancho Cucamonga (91730) ***(P-12887)***
Vaniman Manufacturing, Murrieta *Also called Vmc International LLC* ***(P-22204)***
Vanishing Vistas..........E.......916 624-1237
5043 Midas Ave Rocklin (95677) ***(P-6372)***
Vannelli Brands LLC..........F.......916 824-1717
4031 Alvis Ct Rocklin (95677) ***(P-834)***
Vans Inc..........F.......831 444-0158
796 Northridge Shopg Ctr Salinas (93906) ***(P-9187)***
Vans Inc..........F.......310 390-7548
6000 Sepulveda Blvd # 2155 Culver City (90230) ***(P-9188)***
Vans Inc..........F.......818 990-1098
14006 Riverside Dr Sherman Oaks (91423) ***(P-9189)***
Vans Inc..........F.......650 401-3542
1354 Burlingame Ave Burlingame (94010) ***(P-9190)***
Vans Inc..........F.......562 856-1695
5232 E 2nd St Long Beach (90803) ***(P-9191)***
Vans Inc..........F.......415 566-3762
3251 20th Ave Ste 237 San Francisco (94132) ***(P-9192)***
Vans Inc..........F.......909 517-3141
13920 Cy Ctr Dr Ste 4035 Chino Hills (91709) ***(P-9193)***
Vans Inc (HQ)..........B.......855 909-8267
1588 S Coast Dr Costa Mesa (92626) ***(P-9194)***
Vans Inc..........F.......415 479-1284
5800 Northgate Dr Ste 44 San Rafael (94903) ***(P-9195)***
Vans Instant Printers Inc..........F.......626 966-1708
221 E San Bernardino Rd Covina (91723) ***(P-6917)***
Vans Manufacturing Inc..........F.......805 522-6267
330 E Easy St Ste C Simi Valley (93065) ***(P-16496)***
Vans Shoes, Costa Mesa *Also called Vans Inc* ***(P-9194)***
Vantage Associates Inc..........E.......619 477-6940
900 Civic Center Dr National City (91950) ***(P-20266)***
Vantage Associates Inc (PA)..........E.......619 477-6940
900 Civic Center Dr National City (91950) ***(P-20481)***
Vantage Associates Inc..........D.......562 968-1400
12333 Los Nietos Rd Santa Fe Springs (90670) ***(P-10111)***
Vantage Led, Corona *Also called Tradenet Enterprise Inc* ***(P-23231)***
Vantage Master Machine Company, National City *Also called Vantage Associates Inc* ***(P-20266)***
Vantage Point Products Corp (PA)..........D.......562 946-1718
9115 Dice Rd Ste 18 Santa Fe Springs (90670) ***(P-17300)***
Vantage Vehicle Group, Corona *Also called Vantage Vehicle Intl Inc* ***(P-19205)***
Vantage Vehicle Intl Inc..........E.......951 735-1200
1740 N Delilah St Corona (92879) ***(P-19205)***
Vantiq Inc..........F.......303 377-2882
1990 N Calif Blvd Ste 400 Walnut Creek (94596) ***(P-24547)***
Vape Craft LLC..........E.......760 295-7484
2100 Palomar Airpt Rd # 210 Carlsbad (92011) ***(P-22582)***
Vapex-Genex-Precision, Gardena *Also called Electrical Rebuilders Sls Inc* ***(P-19190)***
Vapor Delux Inc (PA)..........F.......818 856-3750
5221 Lankershim Blvd North Hollywood (91601) ***(P-7323)***
Vaporbrothers Inc..........F.......310 618-1188
2908 Oregon Ct Ste I9 Torrance (90503) ***(P-16842)***
Vaquero Energy Inc..........E.......661 616-0600
5060 California Ave Bakersfield (93309) ***(P-279)***
Vaquero Energy Incorporated..........E.......661 363-7240
15545 Hermosa Rd Bakersfield (93307) ***(P-74)***
Varco Heat Treating, Garden Grove *Also called Diversfied Mtllrgical Svcs Inc* ***(P-11450)***
Varedan Technologies LLC..........F.......310 542-2320
3860 Del Amo Blvd Ste 401 Torrance (90503) ***(P-16764)***
Variable Image Printing..........F.......949 296-1444
16540 Aston Ste A Irvine (92606) ***(P-6918)***
Variable Image Printing..........E.......858 530-2443
9020 Kenamar Dr Ste 204 San Diego (92121) ***(P-6919)***
Varian Associates Limited..........E.......650 493-4000
3100 Hansen Way Palo Alto (94304) ***(P-21945)***
Varian Medical Systems Inc (PA)..........A.......650 493-4000
3100 Hansen Way Palo Alto (94304) ***(P-22224)***
Varian Medical Systems Inc..........E.......408 321-4468
3120 Hansen Way Palo Alto (94304) ***(P-21946)***
Varian Medical Systems Inc..........F.......650 493-4000
3175 Hanover St Palo Alto (94304) ***(P-17796)***
Varian Medical Systems Inc..........C.......408 321-9400
660 N Mccarthy Blvd Milpitas (95035) ***(P-21947)***
Varian Medical Systems Inc..........C.......650 493-4000
3045 Hanover St Palo Alto (94304) ***(P-21948)***
Varian Thin Film Systems, Palo Alto *Also called Varian Medical Systems Inc* ***(P-17796)***
Variant Technology Inc..........F.......626 278-4343
635 Hampton Rd Arcadia (91006) ***(P-17175)***
Various Technologies Inc..........E.......408 972-4460
2720 Aiello Dr Ste C San Jose (95111) ***(P-16765)***
Varmour Networks Inc (PA)..........E.......650 564-5100
270 3rd St Los Altos (94022) ***(P-24548)***
Varni Brothers Corporation (PA)..........D.......209 521-1777
400 Hosmer Ave Modesto (95351) ***(P-2180)***
Varni Brothers Corporation..........E.......209 464-7778
1109 W Anderson St Stockton (95206) ***(P-2181)***
Varni Lite, Hayward *Also called Varni-Lite Coatings Associates* ***(P-8902)***
Varni-Lite Coatings Associates..........F.......510 887-8997
21595 Curtis St Hayward (94545) ***(P-8902)***
Vas Engineering Inc..........E.......858 569-1601
4750 Viewridge Ave San Diego (92123) ***(P-19134)***
Vascular Imaging Professionals (PA)..........F.......949 278-5622
1340 N Dynamics St Ste A Anaheim (92806) ***(P-21949)***
Vascular Therapies, Irvine *Also called Covidien LP* ***(P-21674)***
Vast Enterprises..........F.......562 633-3224
7739 Monroe St Paramount (90723) ***(P-9157)***
Vast National Inc..........F.......951 788-7030
4480 Main St A Riverside (92501) ***(P-11491)***
Vastcircuits & Mfg LLC..........F.......805 421-4299
2226 Goodyear Ave Unit B Ventura (93003) ***(P-19135)***
Vat Incorporated..........E.......408 813-2700
655 River Oaks Pkwy San Jose (95134) ***(P-13324)***
Vave Health Inc..........F.......650 387-7059
2350 Mission College Blvd Santa Clara (95054) ***(P-22324)***
Vaxart Inc (PA)..........E.......650 550-3500
290 Utah Ave Ste 200 South San Francisco (94080) ***(P-8176)***
Vclad Laminates Inc..........E.......626 442-2100
2103 Seaman Ave South El Monte (91733) ***(P-9459)***
Vcp Mobility Inc..........B.......559 292-2171
2842 N Business Park Ave Fresno (93727) ***(P-22115)***
Vcp Mobility Holdings Inc..........B.......619 213-6500
745 Design Ct Ste 602 Chula Vista (91911) ***(P-22116)***
Vcp Mobility Holdings Inc..........B.......303 218-4500
2842 N Business Park Ave Fresno (93727) ***(P-22117)***

ALPHABETIC SECTION

Verseon Corporation (PA)

Vcsd Inc........E.......619 579-6886
585 Vernon Way El Cajon (92020) *(P-4262)*

Vdi Motor Sports, Lake Elsinore *Also called Vertical Doors Inc (P-5042)*

Vdp Direct LLC (PA)........E.......858 300-4510
5520 Ruffin Rd Ste 111 San Diego (92123) *(P-6920)*

Vector Electronics & Tech Inc........E.......818 985-8208
11115 Vanowen St North Hollywood (91605) *(P-18041)*

Vector Fabrication Inc (PA)........E.......408 942-9800
1629 Watson Ct Milpitas (95035) *(P-18042)*

Vector Laboratories Inc (PA)........D.......650 697-3600
30 Ingold Rd Burlingame (94010) *(P-8332)*

Vector Launch Inc........C.......888 346-7778
100 Century Center Ct # 400 San Jose (95112) *(P-13285)*

Veeco C V C, Santa Clara *Also called Veeco Instruments Inc (P-18637)*

Veeco Electro Fab Inc........E.......714 630-8020
1176 N Osprey Cir Anaheim (92807) *(P-18043)*

Veeco Instruments Inc........E.......510 657-8523
3100 Laurelview Ct Santa Clara (95054) *(P-18637)*

Veeco Process Equipment Inc........C.......805 967-1400
112 Robin Hill Rd Goleta (93117) *(P-21320)*

Veeco Process Equipment Inc........D.......805 967-2700
112 Robin Hill Rd Goleta (93117) *(P-16497)*

Veeva Systems Inc (PA)........C.......925 452-6500
4280 Hacienda Dr Pleasanton (94588) *(P-24549)*

Veex Inc........F.......510 651-0500
2827 Lakeview Ct Fremont (94538) *(P-20955)*

Veezee Inc........E.......949 265-0800
121 Waterworks Way Irvine (92618) *(P-3207)*

Vefo Inc........E.......909 598-3856
3202 Factory Dr Pomona (91768) *(P-9576)*

Vega Textile Inc........F.......323 923-0600
2751 S Alameda St Los Angeles (90058) *(P-2763)*

Vege - Kurl Inc........D.......818 956-5582
412 W Cypress St Glendale (91204) *(P-8601)*

Vege-Mist Inc........E.......310 353-2300
407 E Redondo Beach Blvd Gardena (90248) *(P-15470)*

Vege-Tech Company, Glendale *Also called Vege - Kurl Inc (P-8601)*

Velco Tool & Die Inc........F.......949 855-6638
20431 Barents Sea Cir Lake Forest (92630) *(P-14123)*

Vellios Automotive Machine Sp, Lawndale *Also called Vellios Machine Shop Inc (P-16498)*

Vellios Machine Shop Inc........F.......310 643-8540
4625 29th Mnhattan Bch Bl Lawndale (90260) *(P-16498)*

Vello Systems Inc........D.......650 324-7688
1530 Obrien Dr Menlo Park (94025) *(P-17426)*

Velo3d Inc........C.......408 666-5309
511 Division St Campbell (95008) *(P-6921)*

Velocity Imaging Products Inc........F.......619 433-8000
8139 Center St La Mesa (91942) *(P-22470)*

Velodyne Acoustics Inc........D.......408 465-2800
345 Digital Dr Morgan Hill (95037) *(P-17301)*

Velodyne Lidar Inc........B.......408 465-2800
345 Digital Dr Morgan Hill (95037) *(P-20741)*

Velox Cnc, Orange *Also called Liboon Group Inc (P-13931)*

Velti Inc (HQ)........E.......415 362-2077
150 California St Fl 10 San Francisco (94111) *(P-24550)*

Velti USA, San Francisco *Also called Velti Inc (P-24550)*

Velvet Heart, Los Angeles *Also called Tcj Manufacturing LLC (P-3421)*

Venator Americas LLC........D.......323 269-7311
3700 E Olympic Blvd Los Angeles (90023) *(P-7465)*

Vending Security Products........F.......949 646-1474
770 Newton Way Costa Mesa (92627) *(P-12067)*

Venice Baking Co........E.......310 322-7357
134 Main St El Segundo (90245) *(P-1290)*

Venoco Inc........E.......805 644-1400
4483 Mcgrath St Ste 101 Ventura (93003) *(P-75)*

Venoco Inc........E.......805 961-2305
7979 Hollister Ave Goleta (93117) *(P-9084)*

Venolia Pistons, Long Beach *Also called Tor C A M Industries Inc (P-15619)*

Venstar Inc (PA)........F.......818 341-8760
9250 Owensmouth Ave Chatsworth (91311) *(P-15471)*

Venta Medical Inc........E.......510 429-9300
1971 Milmont Dr Milpitas (95035) *(P-21950)*

Ventek International, Petaluma *Also called Caracal Enterprises LLC (P-15397)*

Ventritex, Sylmar *Also called Pacesetter Inc (P-22295)*

Ventsam Sash & Door Mfg Co, Sun Valley *Also called Monty Ventsam Inc (P-4090)*

Ventura Aerospace Inc........F.......818 540-3130
31355 Agoura Rd Westlake Village (91361) *(P-20267)*

Ventura Coastal LLC (PA)........D.......805 653-7000
2325 Vista Del Mar Dr Ventura (93001) *(P-932)*

Ventura Coastal LLC........F.......559 737-9836
12310 Avenue 368 Visalia (93291) *(P-933)*

Ventura County Reporter, Pasadena *Also called Southland Publishing Inc (P-5834)*

Ventura County Star, Camarillo *Also called Scripps Media Inc (P-5823)*

Ventura County Star........F.......805 437-0138
771 E Daily Dr Ste 300 Camarillo (93010) *(P-5858)*

Ventura Foods LLC........C.......714 257-3700
2900 Jurupa St Ontario (91761) *(P-1484)*

Ventura Foods LLC........C.......323 262-9157
2900 Jurupa St Ontario (91761) *(P-540)*

Ventura Foods LLC (PA)........C.......714 257-3700
40 Pointe Dr Brea (92821) *(P-1485)*

Ventura GL Inc........F.......818 890-1886
12595 Foothill Blvd Sylmar (91342) *(P-10937)*

Ventura Harbor Boatyard Inc........E.......805 654-1433
1415 Spinnaker Dr Ventura (93001) *(P-20360)*

Ventura Hydrulic Mch Works Inc........E.......805 656-1760
1555 Callens Rd Ventura (93003) *(P-16499)*

Ventura Printing Inc (PA)........D.......805 981-2600
200 N Elevar St Oxnard (93030) *(P-7262)*

Ventura Technology Group........E.......805 581-0800
855 E Easy St Ste 104 Simi Valley (93065) *(P-18638)*

Venture Capital Entps LLC........F.......914 275-7305
10669 Wellworth Ave Los Angeles (90024) *(P-676)*

Venture Electronics Intl Inc........F.......510 744-3720
6701 Mowry Ave Newark (94560) *(P-18044)*

Venturedyne Ltd........D.......909 793-2788
1320 W Colton Ave Redlands (92374) *(P-14687)*

Ventus Medical Inc........E.......408 200-5299
1100 La Avenida St Ste A Mountain View (94043) *(P-21951)*

Venus Alloys Inc (PA)........E.......714 635-8800
1415 S Allec St Anaheim (92805) *(P-11350)*

Venus Bridal Gowns, San Gabriel *Also called Lotus Orient Corp (P-3243)*

Venus Foods Inc........E.......626 369-5188
770 S Stimson Ave City of Industry (91745) *(P-429)*

Venus Laboratories Inc........D.......714 891-3100
11150 Hope St Cypress (90630) *(P-7535)*

Vera Security Inc........E.......844 438-8372
777 California Ave Palo Alto (94304) *(P-24551)*

Verb Surgical Inc........D.......408 438-3363
2450 Bayshore Pkwy Mountain View (94043) *(P-21952)*

Verb Technology Company Inc (PA)........F.......855 250-2300
2210 Newport Blvd Ste 200 Newport Beach (92663) *(P-24552)*

Verbio Inc........E.......650 862-8935
2225 E Byshore Rd Ste 200 Palo Alto (94303) *(P-24553)*

Verco Decking Inc........F.......909 822-8079
8333 Lime Ave Fontana (92335) *(P-12423)*

Verco Decking Inc........F.......925 778-2102
607 Wilbur Ave Antioch (94509) *(P-12424)*

Verde, Vernon *Also called Pacific Boulevard Inc (P-3247)*

Verde Cosmetic Labs LLC........F.......818 284-4080
19845 Nordhokk St Northridge (91324) *(P-8602)*

Verdugo Tool & Engrg Co Inc........F.......818 998-1101
20600 Superior St Chatsworth (91311) *(P-12888)*

Veredatech LLC........F.......858 342-6468
4645 Vereda Mar Del Sol San Diego (92130) *(P-6373)*

Vericool Inc........E.......925 337-0808
7066 Las Positas Rd Ste C Livermore (94551) *(P-14733)*

Veridiam Inc (HQ)........C.......619 448-1000
1717 N Cuyamaca St El Cajon (92020) *(P-14258)*

Verifone Inc........C.......808 623-2911
1400 W Stanford Ranch Rd Rocklin (95765) *(P-17699)*

Verifone Inc (HQ)........C.......408 232-7800
88 W Plumeria Dr San Jose (95134) *(P-15380)*

Verifone Inc........C.......408 232-7800
2455 Augustine Dr Santa Clara (95054) *(P-15381)*

Verifone Inc........E.......858 436-2270
10590 W Ocean Air Dr # 250 San Diego (92130) *(P-15361)*

Verifone Systems Inc (HQ)........D.......408 232-7800
88 W Plumeria Dr San Jose (95134) *(P-15382)*

Verilogix Inc........F.......310 527-5100
960 Knox St Bldg A Torrance (90502) *(P-24554)*

Verint, Santa Clara *Also called Kana Software Inc (P-24070)*

Veripic, San Jose *Also called Kwan Software Engineering Inc (P-24088)*

Veris Manufacturing, Brea *Also called Q C M Inc (P-16795)*

Verisilicon Inc (HQ)........F.......408 844-8560
2150 Gold St Ste 200 San Jose (95002) *(P-18639)*

Veritas Software Global LLC........F.......650 335-8000
1600 Plymouth St Mountain View (94043) *(P-24555)*

Verizon, Los Alamitos *Also called Supermedia LLC (P-6354)*

Verizon, Santa Ana *Also called Cellco Partnership (P-17483)*

Verizon, Roseville *Also called Supermedia LLC (P-6355)*

Verlo Industries Inc........E.......714 236-2191
10762 Chestnut Ave Stanton (90680) *(P-5010)*

Vermillions Environmental........E.......760 777-8035
78900 Avenue 47 Ste 106 La Quinta (92253) *(P-20819)*

Vern Lackey, Armona *Also called Central Valley Cabinet Mfg (P-4180)*

Vernon Machine and Foundry........F.......323 277-0550
5420 S Santa Fe Ave Vernon (90058) *(P-23516)*

Veronica Foods Company........E.......510 535-6833
1991 Dennison St Oakland (94606) *(P-1486)*

Veros Software Inc........E.......714 415-6300
2333 N Broadway Ste 350 Santa Ana (92706) *(P-24556)*

Verrix LLC........F.......949 668-1234
1330 Calle Avanzado # 200 San Clemente (92673) *(P-21953)*

Versa Networks Inc (PA)........E.......408 385-7660
6001 America Center Dr # 400 San Jose (95002) *(P-24557)*

Versa Stage, Torrance *Also called Forrester Eastland Corporation (P-23335)*

Versacall Technologies Inc........F.......858 677-6766
7047 Carroll Rd San Diego (92121) *(P-17771)*

Versacheck, San Diego *Also called G7 Productivity Systems (P-23925)*

Versaclimber, Santa Ana *Also called Heart Rate Inc (P-22819)*

Versaco Manufacturing Inc........F.......408 848-2880
550 E Luchessa Ave Gilroy (95020) *(P-14412)*

Versafab Corp (PA)........E.......800 421-1822
15919 S Broadway Gardena (90248) *(P-12425)*

Versaform Corporation........D.......760 599-0961
1377 Specialty Dr Vista (92081) *(P-12426)*

Versant Corporation (HQ)........F.......650 232-2400
500 Arguello St Ste 200 Redwood City (94063) *(P-24558)*

Versarack, Salinas *Also called Tailgater Inc (P-20494)*

Versatile Power Inc........F.......408 341-4600
743 Camden Ave B Campbell (95008) *(P-21954)*

Versatraction Inc........F.......714 973-4589
1424 Ritchey St Ste C Santa Ana (92705) *(P-5378)*

Verseon Corporation........F.......510 255-9000
47071 Bayside Pkwy Fremont (94538) *(P-8177)*

Verseon Corporation (PA)........E.......510 668-1622
48820 Kato Rd Ste 100b Fremont (94538) *(P-8178)*

ALPHABETIC

Employee Codes: A=Over 500 employees, B=251-500
C=101-250, D=51-100, E=20-50, F=10-19

2020 California
Manfacturers Register

© Mergent Inc. 1-800-342-5647
1277

Versicolor Inc.....F.....949 361-9698
934 Calle Negocio Ste E San Clemente (92673) ***(P-14296)***
Versicolor Screenprinting, San Clemente *Also called Versicolor Inc* ***(P-14296)***
Vertechs Enterprises Inc (PA).....D.....858 578-3900
1071 Industrial Pl El Cajon (92020) ***(P-11361)***
Vertek, Grass Valley *Also called Guy G Veralrud* ***(P-17234)***
Vertex China, Pomona *Also called Sky One Inc* ***(P-10469)***
Vertex Diamond Tool Company.....D.....909 599-1129
940 W Cienega Ave San Dimas (91773) ***(P-14209)***
Vertex Industrial Inc.....F.....909 626-2100
5138 Brooks St Montclair (91763) ***(P-14869)***
Vertex Lcd Inc.....E.....714 223-7111
600 S Jefferson St Ste K Placentia (92870) ***(P-19136)***
Vertex Water Products, Montclair *Also called Vertex Industrial Inc* ***(P-14869)***
Vertical Collective LLC.....F.....310 567-6200
116 S Catalina Ave # 119 Redondo Beach (90277) ***(P-2998)***
Vertical Doors Inc.....F.....951 273-1069
542 3rd St Lake Elsinore (92530) ***(P-5042)***
Vertical Fiber Technologies, Montebello *Also called Vft Inc* ***(P-3648)***
Vertical Printing & Graphics.....F.....760 334-2004
2240 Encinitas Blvd Ste F Encinitas (92024) ***(P-6922)***
Vertiflex Inc.....E.....442 325-5900
2714 Loker Ave W Ste 100 Carlsbad (92010) ***(P-22325)***
Vertimass LLC.....F.....949 417-1396
2 Park Plz Ste 700 Irvine (92614) ***(P-8781)***
Vertiv Corporation.....B.....925 734-8660
6960 Koll Center Pkwy # 300 Pleasanton (94566) ***(P-16620)***
Vertiv Corporation.....F.....760 768-7522
325 Weakley St 4 Calexico (92231) ***(P-16621)***
Vertiv Corporation.....E.....949 457-3600
35 Parker Irvine (92618) ***(P-20956)***
Vertiv JV Holdings LLC (PA).....E.....310 712-1195
360 N Crescent Dr Beverly Hills (90210) ***(P-19137)***
Vertos Medical Inc.....D.....949 349-0008
95 Enterprise Ste 325 Aliso Viejo (92656) ***(P-21955)***
Vertox Company.....F.....714 530-4541
11752 Garden Grove Blvd # 113 Garden Grove (92843) ***(P-21153)***
Verus Pharmaceuticals Inc.....F.....858 436-1600
11455 El Camino Real # 460 San Diego (92130) ***(P-8179)***
Very Special Chocolats Inc.....C.....626 334-7838
760 N Mckeever Ave Azusa (91702) ***(P-1417)***
Vescio Manufacturing Intl, Santa Fe Springs *Also called Vescio Threading Co* ***(P-16500)***
Vescio Threading Co.....D.....562 802-1868
14002 Anson Ave Santa Fe Springs (90670) ***(P-16500)***
Vest Inc.....D.....800 421-6370
6023 Alcoa Ave Vernon (90058) ***(P-11139)***
Vesta, Corona *Also called Extrumed Inc* ***(P-9784)***
Vesta Medical LLC.....F.....949 660-8648
3750 Torrey View Ct San Diego (92130) ***(P-21956)***
Vesta Solutions Inc (HQ).....B.....951 719-2100
42555 Rio Nedo Temecula (92590) ***(P-17427)***
Vesta Technology Inc.....F.....408 519-5800
3973 Soutirage Ln San Jose (95135) ***(P-18640)***
Vestara, San Diego *Also called Vesta Medical LLC* ***(P-21956)***
Vesture Group Incorporated.....E.....818 842-0200
3405 W Pacific Ave Burbank (91505) ***(P-3497)***
Veteran Company, Los Angeles *Also called Veteran Enterprise Inc* ***(P-2717)***
Veteran Enterprise Inc.....F.....323 937-2233
620 Gladys Ave Los Angeles (90021) ***(P-2717)***
Veterans Employment Agency Inc.....F.....650 245-0599
3906 Ginko Way Sacramento (95834) ***(P-10938)***
Vetpowered LLC.....F.....619 269-7116
2970 Main St San Diego (92113) ***(P-24677)***
Vf Contemporary Brands Inc.....F.....213 747-7002
777 S Alameda St Bldg 1 Los Angeles (90021) ***(P-3021)***
Vf Engineering USA, Anaheim *Also called Zurich Engineering Inc* ***(P-19992)***
Vf Outdoor LLC (HQ).....C.....510 618-3500
2701 Harbor Bay Pkwy Alameda (94502) ***(P-3128)***
Vf Outdoor LLC.....E.....415 433-3223
180 Post St San Francisco (94108) ***(P-22918)***
Vfa 122 Power Plants, Lemoore *Also called United States Dept of Navy* ***(P-13602)***
Vfly Corporation.....F.....626 575-3115
4137 Peck Rd El Monte (91732) ***(P-3763)***
Vft Inc.....E.....323 728-2280
1040 S Vail Ave Montebello (90640) ***(P-3648)***
Vgw Us Inc.....F.....415 240-0498
442 Post St Fl 9 San Francisco (94102) ***(P-24559)***
VI Aesthetics, Los Angeles *Also called Vitality Inst Med Pdts Inc* ***(P-8605)***
Vi-Star Gear Co Inc.....E.....323 774-3750
7312 Jefferson St Paramount (90723) ***(P-12726)***
Vi-TEC Manufacturing Inc.....F.....925 447-8200
288 Boeing Ct Livermore (94551) ***(P-16501)***
Via Mechanics (usa) Inc (HQ).....F.....408 392-9650
150 Charcot Ave Ste C San Jose (95131) ***(P-15362)***
Via Telecom Inc.....C.....858 350-5560
3390 Carmel Mountain Rd # 100 San Diego (92121) ***(P-18641)***
Viade Products Inc.....E.....805 484-2114
354 Dawson Dr Camarillo (93012) ***(P-22203)***
Viader Vineyard & Winery, Deer Park *Also called Viader Vineyards* ***(P-1981)***
Viader Vineyards.....F.....707 963-3816
1120 Deer Park Rd Deer Park (94576) ***(P-1981)***
Vianh Company Inc.....E.....714 590-9808
13841 A Better Way 10c Garden Grove (92843) ***(P-16502)***
Viant Medical LLC.....F.....510 657-5800
45581 Northport Loop W Fremont (94538) ***(P-10112)***
Viasat Inc.....D.....619 438-6000
1935 Cordell Ct El Cajon (92020) ***(P-20742)***
Viasat Inc (PA).....B.....760 476-2200
6155 El Camino Real Carlsbad (92009) ***(P-17700)***
Viasys Respiratory Care Inc.....C.....714 283-2228
22745 Savi Ranch Pkwy Yorba Linda (92887) ***(P-21957)***
Viatech Pubg Solutions Inc.....D.....323 721-3629
5668 E 61st St Commerce (90040) ***(P-7324)***
Viavi Solutions Inc.....C.....408 577-1478
80 Rose Orchard Way San Jose (95134) ***(P-18642)***
Viavi Solutions Inc (PA).....B.....408 404-3600
6001 America Center Dr # 6 San Jose (95002) ***(P-21321)***
Viavi Solutions Inc.....C.....707 545-6440
2789 Northpoint Pkwy Santa Rosa (95407) ***(P-19432)***
Viavi Solutions Inc.....D.....805 465-1875
3601 Calle Tecate Camarillo (93012) ***(P-17428)***
Viavi Solutions Inc.....C.....408 546-5000
430 N Mccarthy Blvd Milpitas (95035) ***(P-21322)***
Viavi Solutions Inc.....C.....408 546-5000
1750 Automation Pkwy San Jose (95131) ***(P-19433)***
Vibes Audio LLC.....F.....866 866-8484
36 Argonaut Ste 140 Aliso Viejo (92656) ***(P-17302)***
Vibes Modular, Aliso Viejo *Also called Vibes Audio LLC* ***(P-17302)***
Vibra Finish Co (PA).....E.....805 578-0033
2220 Shasta Way Simi Valley (93065) ***(P-10958)***
Vibrahone, Simi Valley *Also called Vibra Finish Co* ***(P-10958)***
Vibrant Care Pharmacy Inc.....F.....510 638-9851
7400 Macarthur Blvd Ste B Oakland (94605) ***(P-8180)***
Vibration Impact & Pres.....F.....949 429-3558
32242 Paseo Adelanto C San Juan Capistrano (92675) ***(P-21563)***
Vibrex, Valencia *Also called MWsausse & Co Inc* ***(P-16734)***
Vibrynt Inc.....E.....650 362-6100
2570 W El Camino Real # 310 Mountain View (94040) ***(P-22326)***
Vic Company, Santa Fe Springs *Also called Victor Wieteski* ***(P-19138)***
Vic Cosmetics LLC.....F.....949 330-7668
3420 Bristol St Ste 517 Costa Mesa (92626) ***(P-8603)***
Vicki Marsha Uniforms, Huntington Beach *Also called Marsha Vicki Originals Inc* ***(P-2969)***
Vicolo Pizza, Hayward *Also called Vicolo Wholesale* ***(P-1012)***
Vicolo Wholesale (PA).....E.....510 475-6019
31112 San Clemente St Hayward (94544) ***(P-1012)***
Victoire LLC.....F.....323 225-0101
955 S Meridian Ave Alhambra (91803) ***(P-3505)***
Victor Martin Inc.....C.....323 587-3101
1640 W 132nd St Gardena (90249) ***(P-4707)***
Victor Packing Inc.....E.....559 673-5908
11687 Road 27 1/2 Madera (93637) ***(P-874)***
Victor Wieteski.....F.....562 946-9715
9427 Santa Fe Springs Rd Santa Fe Springs (90670) ***(P-19138)***
Victor Wire & Cable, Los Angeles *Also called Dacon Systems Inc* ***(P-11300)***
Victor Wire and Cable LLC.....F.....310 842-9933
12915 S Spring St Los Angeles (90061) ***(P-11325)***
Victoria Skimboards.....E.....949 494-0059
2955 Laguna Canyon Rd # 1 Laguna Beach (92651) ***(P-22919)***
Victorian Shutters Inc (PA).....F.....707 678-1776
305 Industrial Way Frnt Dixon (95620) ***(P-4145)***
Victory Custom Athletics.....D.....818 349-8476
2001 Anchor Ct Ste A Newbury Park (91320) ***(P-3430)***
Victory Koredrry, Huntington Beach *Also called Victory Professional Products* ***(P-3431)***
Victory Oil Company.....E.....310 519-9500
461 W 6th St Ste 300 San Pedro (90731) ***(P-76)***
Victory Professional Products.....E.....714 887-0621
5601 Engineer Dr Huntington Beach (92649) ***(P-3431)***
Victory Sportswear Inc.....E.....626 359-5400
2381 Buena Vista St Duarte (91010) ***(P-2739)***
Victory Studio.....F.....818 972-0737
1840 Victory Blvd Glendale (91201) ***(P-22471)***
Vida Corporation.....E.....626 839-4912
17807 Maclaren St Ste A City of Industry (91744) ***(P-19240)***
Vida Newspaper, Oxnard *Also called Periodico El Vida* ***(P-5796)***
VIDA NUEVA, Los Angeles *Also called Tidings* ***(P-5849)***
Video Simplex Inc.....F.....858 467-9762
5160 Mercury Pt Ste C San Diego (92111) ***(P-19434)***
Videoamp Inc (PA).....F.....949 294-0351
2229 S Carmelina Ave Los Angeles (90064) ***(P-24560)***
Videomaker Inc.....E.....530 891-8410
645 Mangrove Ave Chico (95926) ***(P-6053)***
Videssence LLC (PA).....E.....626 579-0943
10768 Lower Azusa Rd El Monte (91731) ***(P-16997)***
Videssence LLC.....E.....626 579-0943
10768 Lower Azusa Rd El Monte (91731) ***(P-17176)***
Vie Products Inc.....E.....310 684-3566
9663 Santa Monica Blvd Beverly Hills (90210) ***(P-8604)***
Vie-Del Company (PA).....D.....559 834-2525
11903 S Chestnut Ave Fresno (93725) ***(P-835)***
Vie-Del Company.....E.....559 896-3065
13363 S Indianola Ave Kingsburg (93631) ***(P-1982)***
Vien Dong Daily News, Westminster *Also called Vietnmese Amrcn Mdia Corp Vamc* ***(P-5859)***
Vierra Bros Dairy, Oakdale *Also called Vierra Bros Farms LLC* ***(P-13680)***
Vierra Bros Farms LLC.....F.....209 247-3468
6960 Crane Rd Oakdale (95361) ***(P-13680)***
Viet Hung Paris Inc.....F.....562 944-4919
1975 Chota Rd La Habra Heights (90631) ***(P-506)***
Viet Nam Daily Newspaper, San Jose *Also called Pacific Press Corporation* ***(P-5792)***
Vietnmese Amrcn Mdia Corp Vamc.....F.....714 379-2851
14891 Moran St Westminster (92683) ***(P-5859)***
View Inc (PA).....D.....408 263-9200
195 S Milpitas Blvd Milpitas (95035) ***(P-10400)***
View Rite Manufacturing.....E.....415 468-3856
455 Allan St Daly City (94014) ***(P-4953)***
Vigilant Ballistics Inc.....F.....213 212-3232
1055 W 7th St Ph 33 Los Angeles (90017) ***(P-10524)***
Vigilant Marine Systems LLC.....F.....909 597-9508
2045 S Baker Ave Ontario (91761) ***(P-19798)***

Mergent e-mail: customerrelations@mergent.com
1278
2020 California
Manufacturers Register
(P-0000) Products & Services Section entry number
(PA)=Parent Co (HQ)=Headquarters (DH)=Div Headquarters

Vigilent Corporation (PA) ...... E 888 305-4451
1111 Broadway Fl 3 Oakland (94607) *(P-20820)*
Vigitron Inc ...... F 858 484-5209
7810 Trade St 100 San Diego (92121) *(P-19435)*
Vignette Winery LLC ...... F 707 637-8821
45 Enterprise Ct Ste 3 NAPA (94558) *(P-1983)*
Vigor Systems Inc ...... E 866 748-4467
4660 La Jolla Village Dr # 500 San Diego (92122) *(P-17701)*
Viking Access Systems LLC ...... E 949 753-1280
631 Wald Irvine (92618) *(P-19436)*
Viking Fabrication, Riverside Also called Tolco Incorporated *(P-12578)*
Viking Products, Orange Also called Pro Detention Inc *(P-11104)*
Viking Products Inc ...... E 949 379-5100
20 Doppler Irvine (92618) *(P-14210)*
Viking Ready Mix Co Inc ...... E 818 243-4243
4549 Brazil St Los Angeles (90039) *(P-10859)*
Viking Ready Mix Co Inc ...... E 323 564-1866
4988 Firestone Blvd South Gate (90280) *(P-10860)*
Viking Ready Mix Co Inc ...... E 559 225-3667
1641 Tollhouse Clovis (93611) *(P-10861)*
Viking Ready Mix Co Inc ...... F 559 344-7931
12100 11th Ave Hanford (93230) *(P-10862)*
Viking Ready Mix Co Inc ...... E 562 865-6211
11725 Artesia Blvd Artesia (90701) *(P-10863)*
Viking Ready Mix Co Inc ...... E 818 786-2210
15203 Oxnard St Van Nuys (91411) *(P-10864)*
Viking Ready Mix Co Inc ...... E 818 768-0050
9010 Norris Ave Sun Valley (91352) *(P-10865)*
Viking Ready Mix Co Inc ...... E 626 303-7755
2620 Buena Vista St Duarte (91010) *(P-10866)*
Viking Ready Mix Co Inc ...... E 818 884-0893
6969 Deering Ave Canoga Park (91303) *(P-10867)*
Viking Rubber Products Inc ...... D 310 868-5200
2600 Homestead Pl Compton (90220) *(P-9386)*
Viking Therapeutics Inc ...... F 858 704-4660
12340 El Cmino Real Ste 2 San Diego (92130) *(P-8181)*
Viko Test Labs, Santa Clara Also called Integra Technologies LLC *(P-18301)*
Villa Amorosa ...... D 707 942-8200
4045 Saint Helena Hwy Calistoga (94515) *(P-1984)*
Villa Dolce Gelato, Van Nuys Also called Dolce Dolci LLC *(P-639)*
Villa Encinal Partners LP ...... F 707 945-1220
620 Oakville Cross Rd NAPA (94558) *(P-1985)*
Villa Firenze, Studio City Also called F R Industries Inc *(P-2933)*
Villa Furniture Mfg Co ...... C 714 535-7272
13760 Midway St Cerritos (90703) *(P-4875)*
Villa International, Cerritos Also called Villa Furniture Mfg Co *(P-4875)*
Villa Pallet LLC ...... F 510 794-6676
6756 Central Ave Hayward (94544) *(P-4404)*
Villa Toscano Winery ...... E 209 245-3800
10600 Shenandoah Rd Plymouth (95669) *(P-1986)*
Village Center Ultramar, Palmdale Also called Ultramar Inc *(P-9080)*
Village Collection Inc ...... F 650 594-1635
1303 Elmer St A Belmont (94002) *(P-4263)*
Village Instant Printing Inc ...... E 209 576-2568
1515 10th St Modesto (95354) *(P-6923)*
Village Voice Media ...... D 510 879-3700
318 Harrison St Ste 302 Oakland (94607) *(P-5860)*
Villanueva Plastic Company Inc ...... F 909 581-3870
372 W Tullock St Rialto (92376) *(P-9460)*
Villlage News Inc ...... E 760 451-3488
41740 Enterprise Cir S Temecula (92590) *(P-5861)*
Vim Tools, La Verne Also called Durston Manufacturing Company *(P-11527)*
Vimco, Santa Rosa Also called Randal Optimal Nutrients LLC *(P-8097)*
Vin-Max, San Leandro Also called MArs Engineering Company Inc *(P-12640)*
Vinaco Engineering Company, Chatsworth Also called Le Hung Tuan *(P-16142)*
Vinatronic Inc ...... E 714 845-3480
15571 Industry Ln Huntington Beach (92649) *(P-18045)*
Vincent Electic Motor Company, Oakland Also called Vincent Electric Company *(P-24701)*
Vincent Electric Company (PA) ...... E 510 639-4500
8383 Baldwin St Oakland (94621) *(P-24701)*
Vindicia Inc ...... C 650 264-4700
2988 Campus Dr Ste 300 San Mateo (94403) *(P-24561)*
Vineburg Wine Company Inc (PA) ...... E 707 938-5277
2000 Denmark St Sonoma (95476) *(P-1987)*
Vineyard 29 LLC ...... F 707 963-9292
2929 Saint Helena Hwy N Saint Helena (94574) *(P-1988)*
Vineyard 7 & 8, Saint Helena Also called 7 & 8 LLC *(P-1575)*
Vineyard Post Acute, Petaluma Also called Petalumaidence Opco LLC *(P-1865)*
Vineyards of Monterey, Santa Rosa Also called Jackson Family Wines Inc *(P-1766)*
Vinotemp International Corp (PA) ...... D 310 886-3332
16782 Von Karman Ave # 15 Irvine (92606) *(P-4776)*
Vinotheque Wine Cellars ...... F 209 466-9463
1738 E Alpine Ave Stockton (95205) *(P-15472)*
Vintage 99 Label Mfg Inc ...... E 925 294-5270
611 Enterprise Ct Livermore (94550) *(P-5379)*
Vintage Aero Engines ...... F 661 822-4107
1582 Goodrick Dr Ste 8a Tehachapi (93561) *(P-20361)*
Vintage Point LLC ...... E 707 939-6766
564 Broadway Sonoma (95476) *(P-1989)*
Vintage Production California, Bakersfield Also called California Resources Prod Corp *(P-41)*
Vintage Transport Inc ...... F 530 622-3046
161 Fair Ln Placerville (95667) *(P-19839)*
Vintage Wine Estates Inc ...... F 707 942-4981
1060 Dunaweal Ln Calistoga (94515) *(P-1990)*
Vintage Wine Estates Inc ...... E 707 933-9675
15000 Hwy 12 Glen Ellen (95442) *(P-1991)*

Vintage Wine Estates Inc (PA) ...... C 877 289-9463
205 Concourse Blvd Santa Rosa (95403) *(P-1992)*
Vintellus Inc ...... F 510 972-4710
19918 Wellington Ct Saratoga (95070) *(P-24562)*
Vintique Inc ...... E 714 634-1932
1828 W Sequoia Ave Orange (92868) *(P-19799)*
Vinyl Fabrications Inc ...... F 530 532-1236
2690 5th Ave Oroville (95965) *(P-3713)*
Vinyl Specialties, Fresno Also called Millerton Builders Inc *(P-5032)*
Vinyl Technology Inc ...... C 626 443-5257
200 Railroad Ave Monrovia (91016) *(P-5348)*
Vinylvisions Company LLC ...... E 800 321-8746
1233 Enterprise Ct Corona (92882) *(P-8691)*
Violin Mmory Fdral Systems Inc ...... F 650 396-1500
4555 Great America Pkwy Santa Clara (95054) *(P-18643)*
Vionic Group LLC ...... D 415 526-6932
4040 Civic Center Dr # 430 San Rafael (94903) *(P-10164)*
Vioski Inc ...... F 626 359-4571
1625 S Magnolia Ave Monrovia (91016) *(P-4677)*
VIP Manufacturing & Engrg ...... F 408 727-6545
1084 Martin Ave Santa Clara (95050) *(P-19990)*
VIP Mfg & Engr, Santa Clara Also called VIP Manufacturing & Engrg *(P-19990)*
VIP Rubber Company Inc (PA) ...... C 714 774-7635
540 S Cypress St La Habra (90631) *(P-9387)*
VIP Sensors, San Juan Capistrano Also called Vibration Impact & Pres *(P-21563)*
Vipology Inc ...... F 626 502-8661
1278 Center Court Dr Covina (91724) *(P-6374)*
Virage Logic Corporation (HQ) ...... B 650 584-5000
700 E Middlefield Rd Mountain View (94043) *(P-18644)*
Virco Mfg Corporation (PA) ...... B 310 533-0474
2027 Harpers Way Torrance (90501) *(P-4876)*
Virgil M Stutzman Inc ...... E 323 732-9146
5045 Exposition Blvd Los Angeles (90016) *(P-13128)*
Virgil Walker Inc ...... F 661 797-4101
24856 Avenue Rockefeller Valencia (91355) *(P-11912)*
Virgil Walker Inc ...... F 661 294-9142
29102 Hancock Pkwy Valencia (91355) *(P-18686)*
Virgin Orbit LLC (PA) ...... C 562 384-4400
4022 E Conant St Long Beach (90808) *(P-20463)*
Virginia Park LLC ...... F 816 592-0776
2225 Via Cerro Ste A Riverside (92509) *(P-2645)*
Virginia Park Foods, Riverside Also called Virginia Park LLC *(P-2645)*
Virsec Systems Inc ...... F 978 274-7260
226 Airport Pkwy Ste 350 San Jose (95110) *(P-24563)*
Virtual Composites Co Inc ...... F 714 256-8850
584 Explorer St Brea (92821) *(P-7624)*
Virtus Nutrition LLC ...... F 559 992-5033
520 Industrial Ave Corcoran (93212) *(P-1131)*
Vis Tech, Modesto Also called Vistech Mfg Solutions LLC *(P-14734)*
Visage Ladies Fashions, Los Angeles Also called D & R Brothers Inc *(P-3153)*
Visage Software Inc ...... F 949 614-0759
5151 California Ave # 230 Irvine (92617) *(P-24564)*
Visalia Cams, Visalia Also called Visalia Ctr 4 Ambltry Med & Sv *(P-22118)*
Visalia Ctr 4 Ambltry Med & Sv ...... E 559 740-4094
842 S Akers St Visalia (93277) *(P-22118)*
Visalia Electric Motor Service, Visalia Also called Visalia Electric Motor Sp Inc *(P-24702)*
Visalia Electric Motor Sp Inc ...... F 559 651-0606
7515 W Sunnyview Ave Visalia (93291) *(P-24702)*
Viscon California LLC ...... F 661 327-7061
3121 Standard St Bakersfield (93308) *(P-8782)*
Visger Precision Inc ...... F 408 988-0184
1815 Russell Ave Santa Clara (95054) *(P-16503)*
Vishay Siliconix LLC ...... A 408 988-8000
2585 Junction Ave San Jose (95134) *(P-8783)*
Vishay Spectoral Electronics, Ontario Also called Vishay Thin Film LLC *(P-18645)*
Vishay Spectro, Ontario Also called Vishay Techno Components LLC *(P-16766)*
Vishay Spectrol, Ontario Also called Vishay Thin Film LLC *(P-18692)*
Vishay Techno Components LLC ...... D 909 923-3313
4051 Greystone Dr Ontario (91761) *(P-16766)*
Vishay Thin Film LLC ...... D 909 923-3313
4051 Greystone Dr Ontario (91761) *(P-18645)*
Vishay Thin Film LLC ...... E 909 923-3313
4051 Greystone Dr Ontario (91761) *(P-18692)*
Vishay Transducers Ltd ...... E 626 363-7500
2930 Inland Empire Blvd # 100 Ontario (91764) *(P-18646)*
Visibility Solutions Inc ...... F 714 434-7040
320 E Dyer Rd Santa Ana (92707) *(P-5088)*
Visible Graphics Inc ...... F 818 787-0477
9736 Eton Ave Chatsworth (91311) *(P-23236)*
Visier Inc (PA) ...... F 888 277-9331
550 S Wnchester Blvd # 620 San Jose (95128) *(P-24565)*
Vision Aquatics Inc ...... F 818 749-2178
4542 Skidmore Ct Moorpark (93021) *(P-22920)*
Vision Design Studio, Long Beach Also called Vision Publications Inc *(P-6375)*
Vision Engrg Met Stamping Inc ...... D 661 575-0933
114 Grand Cypress Ave Palmdale (93551) *(P-17082)*
Vision Envelope & Prtg Co Inc (PA) ...... E 310 324-7062
13707 S Figueroa St Los Angeles (90061) *(P-5476)*
Vision Imaging Supplies Inc ...... E 818 710-7200
9540 Cozycroft Ave Chatsworth (91311) *(P-22976)*
Vision Plastics Mfg Inc ...... F 855 476-2767
283 Meadowood Ln Sonoma (95476) *(P-22724)*
Vision Press, San Ramon Also called TAS Group Inc *(P-7363)*
Vision Publications ...... E 562 597-4000
3745 Long Beach Blvd Long Beach (90807) *(P-6375)*
Vision Quest Industries Inc (PA) ...... D 949 261-6382
18011 Mitchell S Ste A Irvine (92614) *(P-22119)*
Vision Quest Industries Inc ...... D 760 734-1550
1390 Decision St Ste A Vista (92081) *(P-22120)*

Employee Codes: A=Over 500 employees, B=251-500
C=101-250, D=51-100, E=20-50, F=10-19

2020 California
Manfacturers Register

© Mergent Inc. 1-800-342-5647
1279

A
L
P
H
A
B
E
T
I
C

Vision Smart Center Inc....F....213 625-1740
123 Astronaut E S Onizuka Los Angeles (90012) *(P-7702)*
Vision Systems Inc....D....619 258-7300
11322 Woodside Ave N Santee (92071) *(P-11253)*
Visionaire Lighting LLC....A....310 512-6480
19645 S Rancho Way Rancho Dominguez (90220) *(P-17083)*
Visionary Electronics Inc....D....415 751-8811
141 Parker Ave San Francisco (94118) *(P-18647)*
Visionary Inc....E....714 237-1900
2940 E Miraloma Ave Anaheim (92806) *(P-22394)*
Visionary Sleep LLC....D....909 605-2010
2060 S Wineville Ave A Ontario (91761) *(P-4748)*
Visionary Solutions Inc....F....805 845-8900
2060 Alameda Padre Serra Santa Barbara (93103) *(P-19437)*
Visioneer Inc (HQ)....E....925 251-6300
5673 Gibraltar Dr Ste 150 Pleasanton (94588) *(P-15363)*
Visioneered Image Systems Inc....F....818 613-7600
444 W Ocean Blvd Ste 1400 Long Beach (90802) *(P-23237)*
Visionmax Inc....F....626 839-1602
17232 Railroad St City of Industry (91748) *(P-3432)*
Visoy Food Products & Mfg Inc....F....323 221-4079
111 W Elmyra St Los Angeles (90012) *(P-1447)*
Vista Coatings Inc....E....310 635-7697
1440 6th St Manhattan Beach (90266) *(P-13266)*
Vista Landscape Lighting, Simi Valley *Also called S T E U Inc (P-17160)*
Vista Metals Corp (PA)....C....909 823-4278
13425 Whittram Ave Fontana (92335) *(P-11254)*
Vista Outdoor Inc....D....831 461-7500
5550 Scotts Valley Dr Scotts Valley (95066) *(P-22921)*
Vista Point Technologies Inc....D....408 576-7000
847 Gibraltar Dr Milpitas (95035) *(P-17702)*
Vista Powder Coatings, Manhattan Beach *Also called Vista Coatings Inc (P-13266)*
Vista Prime Management LLC....F....858 256-9221
7895 Convoy Ct Ste 17 San Diego (92111) *(P-23517)*
Vista Steel Co Inc (PA)....E....805 964-4732
6100 Francis Botello Rd C Goleta (93117) *(P-12612)*
Vistan Corporation....F....510 351-0560
855 Montague St San Leandro (94577) *(P-14413)*
Vistanomics Inc....F....818 249-1236
3450 Ocean View Blvd Frnt Glendale (91208) *(P-6054)*
Vistech Mfg Solutions LLC (PA)....E....209 544-9333
1156 Scenic Dr Ste 120 Modesto (95350) *(P-14734)*
Visualon Inc....C....408 645-6618
2590 N 1st St Ste 100 San Jose (95131) *(P-24566)*
Vit Best, Tustin *Also called Vitabest Nutrition Inc (P-8182)*
VIT Products Inc....E....760 480-6702
2063 Wineridge Pl Escondido (92029) *(P-11641)*
Vita Science Health Products, Long Beach *Also called Get (P-15516)*
Vita-Pakt Citrus Products Co (PA)....E....626 332-1101
203 E Badillo St Covina (91723) *(P-836)*
Vitabest Nutrition Inc....B....714 832-9700
2802 Dow Ave Tustin (92780) *(P-8182)*
Vitachrome Graphics Inc....E....818 957-0900
3710 Park Pl Montrose (91020) *(P-7263)*
Vitacig Inc....D....310 402-6937
433 N Camden Dr Fl 6 Beverly Hills (90210) *(P-2658)*
Vitafoods America LLC....F....800 695-4750
680 E Colo Blvd Ste 180 Pasadena (91101) *(P-712)*
Vitagen Acquisition Corp....F....858 673-6840
15222 Avenue Of Science B San Diego (92128) *(P-8183)*
Vitajoy USA Inc....F....626 965-8830
14165 Ramona Ave Chino (91710) *(P-7703)*
Vital Connect Inc....E....408 963-4600
224 Airport Pkwy Ste 300 San Jose (95110) *(P-22327)*
Vital Vittles Bakery Inc....F....510 644-2022
2810 San Pablo Ave Berkeley (94702) *(P-1291)*
Vitale Home Designs Inc....F....818 888-2481
24425 Woolsey Canyon Rd # 46 Canoga Park (91304) *(P-22486)*
Vitalhue....F....323 646-8775
2036 Nevada City Hwy # 188 Grass Valley (95945) *(P-23518)*
Vitality Extracts LLC....F....844 429-6580
1350 Columbia St Unit 701 San Diego (92101) *(P-8333)*
Vitality Inst Med Pdts Inc....F....310 587-1910
6121 Santa Monica Blvd Los Angeles (90038) *(P-8605)*
Vitamer Laboratories, Irvine *Also called Anabolic Incorporated (P-7756)*
Vitamin Friends LLC....E....310 356-9018
17120 S Figueroa St Ste B Gardena (90248) *(P-624)*
Vitavet Labs Inc....E....818 865-2600
5717 Corsa Ave Westlake Village (91362) *(P-23519)*
Vitek Indus Video Pdts Inc....E....661 294-8043
28492 Constellation Rd Valencia (91355) *(P-22472)*
Vitesse Manufacturing & Dev....C....805 388-3700
11861 Western Ave Garden Grove (92841) *(P-18648)*
Vitesse Semiconductor, Garden Grove *Also called Vitesse Manufacturing & Dev (P-18648)*
Vitrek LLC....F....858 689-2755
12169 Kirkham Rd Ste C Poway (92064) *(P-21154)*
Vitrico Corp....F....510 652-6731
2181 Williams St San Leandro (94577) *(P-10332)*
Vitro Flat Glass LLC....C....559 485-4660
3333 S Peach Ave Fresno (93725) *(P-10280)*
Vitron Electronic Services Inc....D....408 251-1600
5400 Hellyer Ave San Jose (95138) *(P-18046)*
Vitron Electronics Mfg & Svcs, San Jose *Also called Vitron Electronic Services Inc (P-18046)*
Viv Labs Inc....F....650 268-9837
60 S Market St Ste 900 San Jose (95113) *(P-24567)*
Viva Concepts, Glendale *Also called Viva Holdings LLC (P-5486)*
Viva Holdings LLC (PA)....F....818 243-1363
700 N Central Ave Ste 220 Glendale (91203) *(P-5486)*
Viva Photo Albums Company, Milpitas *Also called Song Beoung (P-7317)*
Viva Print LLC (HQ)....F....818 243-1363
1025 N Brand Blvd Ste 300 Glendale (91202) *(P-5487)*
Vivax-Metrotech, Santa Clara *Also called Metrotech Corporation (P-20630)*
Viver Co Inc....F....310 327-4578
1934 W 144th St Gardena (90249) *(P-12427)*
Viver Sheet Metal, Gardena *Also called Viver Co Inc (P-12427)*
Vivid Inc....D....408 982-9101
1250 Memorex Dr Santa Clara (95050) *(P-12428)*
Viviglo Technologies Inc....E....949 933-9738
620 Lunar Ave Ste B Brea (92821) *(P-23520)*
Vivometrics Inc....E....805 667-2225
16030 Ventura Blvd # 470 Encino (91436) *(P-22328)*
Vivus Inc (PA)....E....650 934-5200
900 E Hamilton Ave # 550 Campbell (95008) *(P-8184)*
Viz Cattle Corporation....E....310 884-5260
17890 Castleton St # 350 City of Industry (91748) *(P-430)*
Viz Media LLC....C....415 546-7073
1355 Market St Ste 200 San Francisco (94103) *(P-6055)*
Viz Media Music, San Francisco *Also called Viz Media LLC (P-6055)*
Vizio Inc (PA)....C....855 833-3221
39 Tesla Irvine (92618) *(P-17303)*
Vizualogic LLC....C....407 509-3421
1493 E Bentley Dr Corona (92879) *(P-14553)*
Vline Industries, Simi Valley *Also called Computer Metal Products Corp (P-12160)*
Vlsi Standards Inc....E....408 428-1800
5 Technology Dr Milpitas (95035) *(P-21155)*
Vm Discovery Inc....F....510 818-1018
45535 Northport Loop E Fremont (94538) *(P-8185)*
Vm International, Riverside *Also called S R S M Inc (P-7606)*
Vm Provider Inc (PA)....F....800 674-3233
1135 1/2 N Berendo St Los Angeles (90029) *(P-2770)*
Vmc Holdings Group Corp....E....818 993-1466
9667 Owensmouth Ave # 202 Chatsworth (91311) *(P-14995)*
Vmc International LLC....F....760 723-1498
25799 Jefferson Ave Murrieta (92562) *(P-22204)*
VME Acquisition Corp (PA)....E....805 384-2748
820 Flynn Rd Camarillo (93012) *(P-22121)*
Vmg Engineering Inc....F....818 837-6320
1046 Griswold Ave San Fernando (91340) *(P-16504)*
Vml Winery, Healdsburg *Also called HDD LLC (P-1750)*
Vmware Inc (HQ)....C....650 427-5000
3401 Hillview Ave Palo Alto (94304) *(P-24568)*
Vnomic Inc....F....408 890-2220
1250 Oakmead Pkwy Ste 210 Sunnyvale (94085) *(P-24569)*
Vnu Business, San Juan Capistrano *Also called Emerald Expositions LLC (P-5930)*
Vnus Medical Technologies Inc....C....408 360-7200
5799 Fontanoso Way San Jose (95138) *(P-21958)*
Vocera Communications Inc (PA)....C....408 882-5100
525 Race St Ste 150 San Jose (95126) *(P-17772)*
Vode Lighting LLC....F....707 996-9898
21684 8th St E Ste 700 Sonoma (95476) *(P-16998)*
Voelker Sensors Inc....F....650 361-0570
3790 El Camino Real Palo Alto (94306) *(P-3823)*
Vogt Western Silver Ltd....F....530 669-6840
1210 Commerce Ave Ste 1 Woodland (95776) *(P-22583)*
Vogue Sign Inc....F....805 487-7222
715 Commercial Ave Oxnard (93030) *(P-23238)*
Voice Assist Inc....F....949 655-1611
15 Enterprise Ste 350 Aliso Viejo (92656) *(P-19139)*
Voiceboard Corporation....F....805 389-3100
473 Post St Camarillo (93010) *(P-14996)*
Volcano Corporation (HQ)....B....800 228-4728
3721 Vly Cntre Dr Ste 500 San Diego (92130) *(P-22329)*
Volcano Corporation....B....916 281-2932
2451 Merc Dr Ste 200 Rancho Cordova (95742) *(P-22330)*
Volcano Corporation....B....650 938-5300
1931 Old Middlefield Way Mountain View (94043) *(P-22331)*
Volcano Corporation....B....916 638-8008
2870 Kilgore Rd Rancho Cordova (95670) *(P-22332)*
Volcano Therapeutics, Rancho Cordova *Also called Volcano Corporation (P-22330)*
Volex Inc (HQ)....E....669 444-1740
3110 Coronado Dr Santa Clara (95054) *(P-10113)*
Volex Inc....E....619 205-4900
511 E San Ysidro Blvd San Ysidro (92173) *(P-10114)*
Volk Enterprises Inc....D....209 632-3826
618 S Kilroy Rd Turlock (95380) *(P-13443)*
Volta Industries LLC (PA)....F....917 838-3590
144 King St San Francisco (94107) *(P-23521)*
Voltage Multipliers Inc (PA)....C....559 651-1402
8711 W Roosevelt Ave Visalia (93291) *(P-18649)*
Voltage Valet Division, Santa Rosa *Also called Hybrinetics Inc (P-16557)*
Voltedge LLC....F....949 877-8900
1701 Quail St Ste 600 Newport Beach (92660) *(P-14997)*
Volterra Semiconductor Corp, San Jose *Also called Volterra Semiconductor LLC (P-18650)*
Volterra Semiconductor LLC (HQ)....E....408 601-1000
160 Rio Robles San Jose (95134) *(P-18650)*
Voltus Inc....E....415 617-9602
2442 Fillmore St San Francisco (94115) *(P-20821)*
Voluspa, Irvine *Also called Flame & Wax Inc (P-23332)*
Volvo Construction Eqp & Svcs....E....951 277-7620
22099 Knabe Rd Corona (92883) *(P-13756)*
Vomar Products Inc....E....818 610-5115
7800 Deering Ave Canoga Park (91304) *(P-7264)*
Vomela Specialty Company....E....562 944-3853
9810 Bell Ranch Dr Santa Fe Springs (90670) *(P-6924)*
Vomela Specialty Company....E....650 877-8000
1342 San Mateo Ave South San Francisco (94080) *(P-23239)*
Von Hoppen Ice Cream (HQ)....F....805 965-2009
1525 State St Ste 203 Santa Barbara (93101) *(P-677)*

Von Hoppen Ice Cream F 858 695-9111
8221 Arjons Dr Ste A San Diego (92126) *(P-678)*
Vonnic Inc E 626 964-2345
16610 Gale Ave City of Industry (91745) *(P-22473)*
Voorwood Company E 530 365-3311
2350 Barney Rd Anderson (96007) *(P-14300)*
Vortech Engineering Inc E 805 247-0226
1650 Pacific Ave Oxnard (93033) *(P-14688)*
Vortex Engineering LLC F 619 258-9660
9425 Wheatlands Ct Santee (92071) *(P-11913)*
Vortex Enterprise, Santa Fe Springs *Also called Spadia Inc (P-16992)*
Vortex Whirlpool Systems Inc D 951 940-4556
26035 Jefferson Ave Murrieta (92562) *(P-9597)*
Vortran Laser Technology Inc F 916 283-8208
21 Golden Land Ct Ste 200 Sacramento (95834) *(P-19438)*
Vortran Medical Technology 1 (PA) E 916 648-8460
21 Golden Land Ct Ste 100 Sacramento (95834) *(P-21959)*
Vossloh Signaling Usa Inc E 530 272-8194
12799 Loma Rica Dr Grass Valley (95945) *(P-12727)*
Votaw Precision Tech Inc F 562 944-0661
13153 Lakeland Rd Santa Fe Springs (90670) *(P-20743)*
Voteblast Inc E 650 387-9147
8478 Hollywood Blvd Los Angeles (90069) *(P-6376)*
Voxara LLC F 844 869-2721
5737 Kanan Rd Ste 700 Agoura Hills (91301) *(P-6377)*
Voyage Medical Inc E 650 503-7500
610 Galveston Dr Redwood City (94063) *(P-21960)*
Voyager Learning Company F 909 923-3120
2060 Lynx Pl Unit G Ontario (91761) *(P-6378)*
Voyant Aviation Broadband, Mountain View *Also called Voyant International Corp (P-24570)*
Voyant International Corp F 800 710-6637
444 Castro St Ste 318 Mountain View (94041) *(P-24570)*
Voyomotive LLC F 888 321-4633
2443 Fillmore St Ste 157 San Francisco (94115) *(P-19800)*
Vp Footwear Inc F 626 443-2186
2536 Loma Ave South El Monte (91733) *(P-9196)*
Vpro Inc F 818 905-5678
4638 Van Nuys Blvd Sherman Oaks (91403) *(P-23240)*
Vpt Direct, Santa Fe Springs *Also called Vantage Point Products Corp (P-17300)*
Vq Orthocare, Vista *Also called Vision Quest Industries Inc (P-22120)*
Vra Manufacturing, Cameron Park *Also called Vultures Row Aviation LLC (P-16505)*
Vrtcal Markets Inc F 228 313-3327
10 E Yanonali St Santa Barbara (93101) *(P-6379)*
Vs Vincenzo Ltd Inc F 949 388-8791
34700 Pacific Coast Hwy Capistrano Beach (92624) *(P-8606)*
Vsc Incorporated (PA) F 909 877-0975
2038 S Sycamore Ave Bloomington (92316) *(P-11914)*
Vsmpo Tirus US E 909 230-9020
2850 E Cedar St Ontario (91761) *(P-11283)*
Vsmpo-Tirus US Inc E 909 230-9020
2850 E Cedar St Ontario (91761) *(P-11284)*
Vsp Labs Inc (PA) E 866 569-8800
3333 Quality Dr Rancho Cordova (95670) *(P-21418)*
Vsp Products Inc D 209 862-1200
3324 Orestimba Rd Newman (95360) *(P-875)*
Vspone, Rancho Cordova *Also called Vsp Labs Inc (P-21418)*
VSR Network Technologies LLC E 530 889-1500
11760 Atwood Rd Ste 8 Auburn (95603) *(P-17429)*
Vss Emultech Inc (HQ) F 530 243-0111
7200 Pit Rd Redding (96001) *(P-9107)*
Vss Emultech Inc F 916 371-8480
3785 Channel Dr West Sacramento (95691) *(P-9108)*
Vti Instruments Corporation (HQ) E 949 955-1894
2031 Main St Irvine (92614) *(P-19439)*
Vtl Amplifiers Inc E 909 627-5944
4774 Murietta St Ste 10 Chino (91710) *(P-17304)*
Vts Medical Systems, Santa Clara *Also called Steris Corporation (P-22092)*
Vts Sheetmetal Specialist Co E 714 237-1420
1041 N Grove St Anaheim (92806) *(P-12429)*
Vue-Temp Inc (PA) D 209 634-2914
618 S Kilroy Rd Turlock (95380) *(P-530)*
Vulcan Aggregates Company LLC F 408 354-7904
18500 Limekiln Canyon Rd Los Gatos (95033) *(P-365)*
Vulcan Construction Mtls LLC F 408 213-4270
346 Mathew St Santa Clara (95050) *(P-366)*
Vulcan Materials, Glendale *Also called Calmat Co (P-9088)*
Vulcan Materials Co E 760 737-3486
849 W Washington Ave Escondido (92025) *(P-10868)*
Vulcan Materials Company F 619 661-1088
7522 Pso De La Fnte Nrte San Diego (92154) *(P-10869)*
Vulcan Materials Company F 619 440-2363
3605 Dehesa Rd El Cajon (92019) *(P-306)*
Vulcan Materials Company F 626 334-4913
16005 E Foothill Blvd Irwindale (91702) *(P-10870)*
Vulcan Materials Company F 818 241-7356
500 N Brand Blvd Ste 500 # 500 Glendale (91203) *(P-10871)*
Vulcan Materials Company F 530 534-4517
2216 Table Mountain Blvd Oroville (95965) *(P-307)*
VULCAN STEEL COMPANY, Bloomington *Also called Vsc Incorporated (P-11914)*
Vulpine Inc F 510 534-1186
1127 57th Ave Oakland (94621) *(P-9035)*
Vultures Row Aviation LLC F 530 676-9245
3152 Cameron Park Dr Cameron Park (95682) *(P-16505)*
Vuze Inc E 650 963-4750
489 S El Camino Real San Mateo (94402) *(P-15364)*
Vyaire Medical Inc E 714 919-3265
22745 Savi Ranch Pkwy Yorba Linda (92887) *(P-21961)*
Vyakar Inc F 844 321-5323
830 Stewart Dr Ste 228 Sunnyvale (94085) *(P-24571)*
Vybion Inc F 607 227-2502
584 Oak St Monterey (93940) *(P-7643)*
Vycom America Inc E 800 235-9195
39252 Winchester Rd 107-3 Murrieta (92563) *(P-18047)*
Vycon Inc D 562 282-5500
16323 Shoemaker Ave # 600 Cerritos (90703) *(P-19176)*
W & J Dairy, Oakdale *Also called Willie Bylsma (P-14415)*
W & M Textile, Vernon *Also called Jml Textile Inc (P-2700)*
W & W Concept Inc D 323 233-9202
4890 S Alameda St Vernon (90058) *(P-3433)*
W A Call Manufacturing Co Inc F 408 436-1450
1710 Rogers Ave San Jose (95112) *(P-12430)*
W A Murphy Inc F 760 245-8711
26550 National Trails Hwy Helendale (92342) *(P-8908)*
W B Powell Inc E 951 270-0095
630 Parkridge Ave Norco (92860) *(P-4146)*
W C Q, Fremont *Also called West Coast Quartz Corporation (P-10333)*
W E Hall Co F 909 829-4235
13680 Slover Ave Fontana (92337) *(P-12431)*
W E Plemons McHy Svcs Inc E 559 646-6630
13479 E Industrial Dr Parlier (93648) *(P-14735)*
W G Holt Inc D 949 859-8800
23351 Madero Mission Viejo (92691) *(P-18651)*
W J Ellison Co Inc E 626 814-4766
200 River Rd Corona (92880) *(P-14736)*
W L Gore & Associates Inc C 928 864-2705
2890 De La Cruz Blvd Santa Clara (95050) *(P-21962)*
W L Rubottom Co D 805 648-6943
320 W Lewis St Ventura (93001) *(P-4264)*
W Machine Works Inc E 818 890-8049
13814 Del Sur St San Fernando (91340) *(P-16506)*
W P Keith Co Inc E 562 948-3636
8323 Loch Lomond Dr Pico Rivera (90660) *(P-14778)*
W Plastics Inc E 800 442-9727
2543 41573 Dendy Pkwy Temecula (92590) *(P-9425)*
W R E Colortech, Berkeley *Also called Western Roto Engravers Inc (P-7269)*
W R Grace & Co F 562 927-8513
7237 E Gage Ave Commerce (90040) *(P-7536)*
W R Grace & Co C 209 839-2800
252 W Larch Rd Ste H Tracy (95304) *(P-7537)*
W R Grace & Co-Conn D 760 244-6107
17434 Mojave St Hesperia (92345) *(P-21323)*
W R Grace Construction Pdts, Commerce *Also called W R Grace & Co (P-7536)*
W R Meadows Inc E 909 469-2606
2300 Valley Blvd Pomona (91768) *(P-10664)*
W S Dodge Oil Co Inc F 323 583-3478
3710 Fruitland Ave Maywood (90270) *(P-9158)*
W S West, Fresno *Also called Gea Farm Technologies Inc (P-8384)*
W T E, Ontario *Also called Wallner Expac Inc (P-14286)*
W Three Co E 760 344-5841
1679 River Dr D Brawley (92227) *(P-13681)*
W. R. Meadows Southern Cal, Pomona *Also called W R Meadows Inc (P-10664)*
W2 Optronics Inc F 510 220-2796
39523 Pardee Ct Fremont (94538) *(P-18652)*
W5 Concepts Inc E 323 231-2415
2049 E 38th St Vernon (90058) *(P-3208)*
Waag, Van Nuys *Also called Wsw Corp (P-19809)*
WAbenjamin Electric Co E 213 749-7731
1615 Staunton Ave Los Angeles (90021) *(P-16622)*
Wac Lighting, Ontario *Also called Wangs Alliance Corporation (P-16999)*
Wacker Chemical Corporation E 909 590-8822
13910 Oaks Ave Chino (91710) *(P-8784)*
Wacker Development Inc F 408 356-0208
36 Hollywood Ave Los Gatos (95030) *(P-16507)*
Waco Products, Santa Ana *Also called Ackley Metal Products Inc (P-15682)*
Wadco Industries Inc E 909 874-7800
2625 S Willow Ave Bloomington (92316) *(P-11915)*
Wadco Steel Sales, Bloomington *Also called Wadco Industries Inc (P-11915)*
Waddington North America Inc C 626 913-4022
1135 Samuelson St City of Industry (91748) *(P-10115)*
Wade Metal Products F 559 237-9233
1818 Los Angeles St Fresno (93721) *(P-11916)*
Wafer Process Systems Inc F 408 445-3010
3641 Charter Park Dr San Jose (95136) *(P-18653)*
Wafernet Inc F 408 437-9747
2142 Paragon Dr San Jose (95131) *(P-18654)*
Waggl Inc (PA) F 415 399-9949
3 Harbor Dr Ste 200 Sausalito (94965) *(P-24572)*
Wagner Die Supply (PA) E 909 947-3044
2041 Elm Ct Ontario (91761) *(P-14124)*
Wagner Plate Works West Inc (PA) E 562 531-6050
14015 Garfield Ave Paramount (90723) *(P-12068)*
Wagonmasters Corporation F 909 823-6188
11060 Cherry Ave Fontana (92337) *(P-20524)*
Wah Fung Noodles Inc F 626 442-0588
4443 Rowland Ave El Monte (91731) *(P-2385)*
Wah Hung Group Inc (PA) E 626 571-8700
1000 E Garvey Ave Monterey Park (91755) *(P-19801)*
Wah Hung Group Inc E 626 571-8700
283 E Garvey Ave Monterey Park (91755) *(P-19802)*
Wahlco Inc C 714 979-7300
15 Marconi Ste B Irvine (92618) *(P-16508)*
Waiakea Inc F 855 924-2532
5800 Hannum Ave Ste A135 Culver City (90230) *(P-2182)*
Waiakea Investments LLC (PA) F 805 450-0981
736 Cima Linda Ln Santa Barbara (93108) *(P-2183)*
Wain Industries F 805 581-5900
5688 Via Bonita Newbury Park (91320) *(P-19140)*
Wako Life Sciences, Inc., Mountain View *Also called Fujifilm Wako Diagnostics US (P-8222)*

ALPHABETIC

Wakunaga of America Co Ltd (HQ) ....D....949 855-2776
23501 Madero Mission Viejo (92691) **(P-625)**
Walashek Industrial & Mar Inc ....F....206 624-2880
2826 Eighth St Berkeley (94710) **(P-20307)**
Walashek Industrial & Mar Inc ....E....619 498-1711
1428 Mckinley Ave National City (91950) **(P-20308)**
Walco Inc ....E....909 483-3333
9017 Arrow Rte Rancho Cucamonga (91730) **(P-14554)**
Walden Structures Inc ....D....909 389-9100
1000 Bristol St N 126 Newport Beach (92660) **(P-4470)**
Walker Bags, San Francisco *Also called Walker/Dunham Corp* **(P-10215)**
Walker Corporation ....E....909 390-4300
1555 S Vintage Ave Ontario (91761) **(P-13444)**
Walker Creations ....F....805 349-0755
907 Vista Del Rio Santa Maria (93458) **(P-22122)**
Walker Design Inc ....E....818 252-7788
9255 San Fernando Rd Sun Valley (91352) **(P-20309)**
Walker Engineering Enterprises, Sun Valley *Also called Walker Design Inc* **(P-20309)**
Walker Foods Inc ....D....323 268-5191
237 N Mission Rd Los Angeles (90033) **(P-837)**
Walker Lithograph ....F....530 527-2142
20869 Walnut St Red Bluff (96080) **(P-6925)**
Walker Printing, Red Bluff *Also called Walker Lithograph* **(P-6925)**
Walker Products (PA) ....E....714 554-5151
14291 Commerce Dr Garden Grove (92843) **(P-19803)**
Walker Spring & Stamping Corp ....C....909 390-4300
1555 S Vintage Ave Ontario (91761) **(P-12889)**
Walker Street Pallets LLC ....F....831 724-6088
801 Ohlone Pkwy Watsonville (95076) **(P-4405)**
Walker/Dunham Corp ....F....415 821-3070
445 Barneveld Ave San Francisco (94124) **(P-10215)**
Wallace, Blue Lake *Also called Thomas Tellez* **(P-4140)**
Wallace E Miller Inc ....F....818 998-0444
9155 Alabama Ave Ste B Chatsworth (91311) **(P-16509)**
Wallace Wood Products ....F....951 654-9311
1247 S Buena Vista St C San Jacinto (92583) **(P-4954)**
Wallarm Inc (PA) ....F....415 940-7077
415 Brannan St 2 San Francisco (94107) **(P-19440)**
Wallner Expac Inc (PA) ....D....909 481-8800
1274 S Slater Cir Ontario (91761) **(P-14286)**
Wally International Inc (PA) ....C....805 444-7764
20520 E Walnut Dr N Walnut (91789) **(P-5177)**
Walmsley Design ....F....310 836-0772
3825 Willat Ave Bldg A Culver City (90232) **(P-4618)**
Walt Disney Imagineering ....C....714 781-3152
1200 N Miller St Unit D Anaheim (92806) **(P-3584)**
Waltco Lift Corp ....D....323 321-4131
227 E Compton Blvd Gardena (90248) **(P-13896)**
Walter N Coffman Inc ....D....619 266-2642
5180 Naranja St San Diego (92114) **(P-9577)**
Walters & Wolf Glass Company ....D....510 226-9800
41450 Cowbell Rd Fremont (94538) **(P-10665)**
Walters & Wolf Precast ....C....510 226-9800
41450 Boscell Rd Fremont (94538) **(P-10666)**
Walton Company Inc ....F....714 847-8800
17900 Sampson Ln Huntington Beach (92647) **(P-4542)**
Walton Industries Inc ....F....559 233-6300
1220 E North Ave Fresno (93725) **(P-8692)**
Walz Caps Inc ....E....760 683-9259
2215 La Mirada Dr Vista (92081) **(P-3525)**
Wan Ll Industrial Dev Inc ....F....909 594-1818
1967 W Holt Ave Pomona (91768) **(P-19206)**
Wanada Investments LLC ....E....818 292-8627
2010 Fox Hills Dr Los Angeles (90025) **(P-24573)**
Wanda Matranga ....F....760 773-4701
41651 Corporate Way Ste 5 Palm Desert (92260) **(P-6926)**
Waneshear Technologies LLC ....E....707 462-4761
3471 N State St Ukiah (95482) **(P-14301)**
Wangs Alliance Corporation ....E....909 230-9401
1750 S Archibald Ave Ontario (91761) **(P-16999)**
Wanna B, Los Angeles *Also called Style Plus Inc* **(P-3195)**
Warco, Orange *Also called West American Rubber Co LLC* **(P-9388)**
Warco, Orange *Also called West American Rubber Co LLC* **(P-9389)**
Ward Automatic Machine Pdts ....F....661 822-7543
1265 Goodrick Dr Ste E Tehachapi (93561) **(P-12659)**
Ward E Waldo & Son Inc ....F....626 355-1218
273 E Highland Ave Sierra Madre (91024) **(P-838)**
Ward E Waldo & Son Marmalades, Sierra Madre *Also called Ward E Waldo & Son Inc* **(P-838)**
Ward Enterprises ....F....661 251-4890
10332 Trumbull St California City (93505) **(P-16510)**
Wardley Industrial Inc ....E....209 932-1088
907 Stokes Ave Stockton (95215) **(P-9578)**
Wardrobe Specialties Ltd ....F....209 523-2094
607 Glass Ln Modesto (95356) **(P-10401)**
Warlock Industries ....E....951 657-2680
23129 Cajalco Rd Ste A Perris (92570) **(P-19511)**
Warmboard Inc ....E....831 685-9276
8035 Soquel Dr Ste 41a Aptos (95003) **(P-14779)**
Warmelin Precision Pdts LLC ....D....323 777-5003
12705 Daphne Ave Hawthorne (90250) **(P-16511)**
Warnaco Swimwear Inc (HQ) ....E....323 837-6000
1201 W 5th St Ste 1200 Los Angeles (90017) **(P-3129)**
Warnaco Swimwear Products, Los Angeles *Also called Warnaco Swimwear Inc* **(P-3129)**
Warner Enterprises Inc ....E....530 241-4000
1577 Beltline Rd Redding (96003) **(P-3914)**
Warner Music Group Corp ....F....818 846-9090
3300 Warner Blvd Burbank (91505) **(P-17339)**
Warner Music Inc ....D....818 953-2600
3400 W Riverside Dr # 900 Burbank (91505) **(P-17340)**
Warner/Chappell Music Inc (HQ) ....C....310 441-8600
10585 Santa Monica Blvd # 200 Los Angeles (90025) **(P-6380)**
Warnock Food Products Inc ....D....559 661-4845
20237 Masa St Madera (93638) **(P-2348)**
Warren & Baerg Mfg Inc ....E....559 591-6790
39950 Road 108 Dinuba (93618) **(P-13682)**
Warren Packaging Inc ....F....909 923-0613
1722 E Grevillea Ct Ontario (91761) **(P-7265)**
Warren Printing & Mailing Inc ....F....323 258-2621
5000 Eagle Rock Blvd Los Angeles (90041) **(P-6927)**
Warrens Department Store Inc ....E....888 577-2735
9800 De Soto Ave Chatsworth (91311) **(P-2982)**
Wartsila Dynmc Positioning Inc (HQ) ....E....858 679-5500
12131 Community Rd Ste A Poway (92064) **(P-16767)**
Wasabi Mint, Los Angeles *Also called Ammiel Enterprise Inc* **(P-3213)**
Wasatch Co ....F....310 637-6160
11000 Wright Rd Lynwood (90262) **(P-3649)**
Wasatch Import, Lynwood *Also called Wasatch Co* **(P-3649)**
Wasco Hardfacing Co ....D....559 485-5860
2660 S East Ave Fresno (93706) **(P-13683)**
Wasco Sales & Marketing Inc ....E....805 739-2747
2245 A St Santa Maria (93455) **(P-16938)**
Wash System and Dry Wall Works, Sacramento *Also called Delta Lath & Plaster Inc* **(P-13912)**
Washburn Grove Management Inc ....E....909 322-4690
27781 Fairview Ave Hemet (92544) **(P-3915)**
Washington Garment Dyeing (PA) ....D....213 747-1111
1341 E Washington Blvd Los Angeles (90021) **(P-2849)**
Washington Garment Dyeing ....E....213 747-1111
1332 E 18th St Los Angeles (90021) **(P-2841)**
Washington Orna Ir Works Inc ....E....310 327-8660
17913 S Main St Gardena (90248) **(P-12520)**
Washoe Equipment Inc ....E....916 395-4700
6201 27th St Sacramento (95822) **(P-17000)**
Wask Engineering Inc ....F....530 672-2795
3905 Dividend Dr Cameron Park (95682) **(P-20470)**
Wasser Filtration Inc (PA) ....D....714 982-5600
1215 N Fee Ana St Anaheim (92807) **(P-14870)**
Wastweet Studio Inc ....F....206 369-9060
962 Adams St Albany (94706) **(P-11023)**
Watch L.A., Los Angeles *Also called Pierre Mitri* **(P-3388)**
Water Associates LLC ....E....661 281-6077
34929 Flyover Ct Bakersfield (93308) **(P-17703)**
Water Filter Exchange Inc ....F....818 808-2541
980 Kirkton Pl Glendale (91207) **(P-14871)**
Water Heater Warehouse LLC ....F....714 244-8562
1853 W Commonwealth Ave Fullerton (92833) **(P-20822)**
Water One Industries Inc ....F....707 747-4300
2913 Pattern St Unit D Brea (92821) **(P-15598)**
Water One Industries Inc (PA) ....E....707 747-4300
5410 Gateway Plaza Dr Benicia (94510) **(P-15599)**
Water Planet Engineering LLC ....F....424 331-7700
8915 S La Cienega Blvd C Inglewood (90301) **(P-15600)**
Water Purification, Rancho Dominguez *Also called Parker-Hannifin Corporation* **(P-18729)**
Water Resources Cal Dept ....D....916 651-9203
901 P St Lbby Sacramento (95814) **(P-20957)**
Water Studio Inc ....F....310 313-5553
5681 Selmaraine Dr Culver City (90230) **(P-13554)**
Water Treatment Plant, Riverside *Also called City of Riverside* **(P-15498)**
Water Works Manufacturing, Marysville *Also called US Pipe Fabrication LLC* **(P-9478)**
Wateranywhere, Vista *Also called Applied Membranes Inc* **(P-15482)**
Watercrest Inc ....D....909 390-3944
4850 E Airport Dr Ontario (91761) **(P-12069)**
Waterdog Products Inc ....F....619 441-9688
1148 Pioneer Way El Cajon (92020) **(P-10116)**
Waterfountainscom Inc ....F....760 946-0525
13870 Riverside Dr Apple Valley (92307) **(P-13555)**
Waterguru Inc ....F....415 269-5480
2 Embarcadero Ctr Fl 8 San Francisco (94111) **(P-15601)**
Watergush Inc ....E....408 524-3074
440 N Wolfe Rd Ste E252 Sunnyvale (94085) **(P-10667)**
Waterhealth International Inc ....C....949 716-5790
9601 Irvine Center Dr Irvine (92618) **(P-15602)**
Waterless Co Inc ....F....760 727-7723
1050 Joshua Way Vista (92081) **(P-11687)**
Waterman Valve LLC (HQ) ....C....559 562-4000
25500 Road 204 Exeter (93221) **(P-15603)**
Watermans Guild ....F....714 751-0603
260 E Dyer Rd Ste L Santa Ana (92707) **(P-22922)**
Watermark, Riverside *Also called Irrometer Company Inc* **(P-21491)**
Waters Edge Wineries Inc ....F....909 468-9463
8560 Vineyard Ave Ste 408 Rancho Cucamonga (91730) **(P-1993)**
Waters Edge Winery, Rancho Cucamonga *Also called Waters Edge Wineries Inc* **(P-1993)**
Waters Edge Winery - Long Bch, Long Beach *Also called Shoreline Cellars Inc* **(P-1915)**
Waters Technologies Corp ....F....949 474-4320
18271 Mcdurmott St Irvine (92614) **(P-21324)**
Watersentinel, Temecula *Also called TST Water LLC* **(P-15595)**
Waterstone Faucets, Murrieta *Also called Waterstone LLC* **(P-11688)**
Waterstone LLC ....C....951 304-0520
41180 Raintree Ct Murrieta (92562) **(P-11688)**
Waterway Plastics, Oxnard *Also called B & S Plastics Inc* **(P-9648)**
Watkins Manufacturing Corp (HQ) ....B....760 598-6464
1280 Park Center Dr Vista (92081) **(P-23522)**
Watkins Manufacturing Corp ....F....760 598-6464
1325 Hot Springs Way Vista (92081) **(P-9598)**
Watkins Wellness, Vista *Also called Watkins Manufacturing Corp* **(P-23522)**

Mergent e-mail: customerrelations@mergent.com
1282
2020 California
Manufacturers Register
(P-0000) Products & Services Section entry number
(PA)=Parent Co (HQ)=Headquarters (DH)=Div Headquarters

Watkins, Luis, Los Angeles *Also called Luis Wtkins Cstm Wrught Ir LLC* ***(P-4695)***
Watson ME Inc (PA).....F.....661 763-5254
801 Kern St Taft (93268) ***(P-280)***
Watsons Profiling Corp.....F.....909 923-5500
1460 S Balboa Ave Ontario (91761) ***(P-16512)***
Watsonvlle Register-Pajaronian, Watsonville *Also called News Media Corporation* ***(P-5777)***
Watt Enterprise Inc.....F.....714 963-0781
10575 Bechler River Ave Fountain Valley (92708) ***(P-3130)***
Watt Stopper Inc (HQ).....E.....408 988-5331
2700 Zanker Rd Ste 168 San Jose (95134) ***(P-16939)***
Watt Stopper Inc.....F.....760 804-9701
2234 Rutherford Rd Carlsbad (92008) ***(P-16940)***
Watt Stopper Le Grand, San Jose *Also called Watt Stopper Inc* ***(P-16939)***
Watts Liquidation Corporation.....F.....310 328-5999
555 Van Ness Ave Torrance (90501) ***(P-2863)***
Watts Machining Inc.....E.....408 654-9300
2339 Calle Del Mundo Santa Clara (95054) ***(P-16513)***
Wave 80 Biosciences Inc.....F.....415 487-7976
1100 26th St San Francisco (94107) ***(P-21963)***
Wave Community Newspapers Inc (PA).....E.....323 290-3000
3731 Wilshire Blvd # 840 Los Angeles (90010) ***(P-5862)***
Wave Precision Inc.....D.....805 529-3324
5390 Kazuko Ct Moorpark (93021) ***(P-21419)***
Wavenet Inc (PA).....E.....310 885-4200
707 E Sepulveda Blvd Carson (90745) ***(P-11115)***
Wavestream Corporation (HQ).....C.....909 599-9080
545 W Terrace Dr San Dimas (91773) ***(P-19141)***
Wavexing Inc.....F.....408 896-1982
3200 Scott Blvd Santa Clara (95054) ***(P-18655)***
Wawa, Cupertino *Also called Sheng-Kee of California Inc* ***(P-1328)***
Wawona Frozen Foods (PA).....A.....559 299-2901
100 W Alluvial Ave Clovis (93611) ***(P-934)***
Wax Box Firelog Corporation.....E.....530 846-2200
1791 State Highway 99 Gridley (95948) ***(P-11724)***
Wax Research Inc.....F.....760 607-0850
1212 Distribution Way Vista (92081) ***(P-9162)***
Way of The World Inc.....F.....408 616-7700
170 Commercial St Sunnyvale (94086) ***(P-7266)***
Way Out West Inc.....E.....310 769-6937
15760 Ventura Blvd # 1730 Encino (91436) ***(P-3058)***
Wayfarers, Alamo *Also called Edner Corporation* ***(P-1197)***
Wayne - Dalton Sacramento, Sacramento *Also called Hrh Door Corp* ***(P-11958)***
Wayne J Sand & Gravel Inc.....F.....805 529-1323
9455 Buena Vista St Moorpark (93021) ***(P-367)***
Wayne Tool & Die Co.....E.....818 364-1611
15853 Olden St Sylmar (91342) ***(P-11080)***
Wbp Associates Inc.....F.....626 575-0747
2017 Seaman Ave South El Monte (91733) ***(P-5011)***
Wbt Group LLC.....E.....323 735-1201
1401 S Shamrock Ave Monrovia (91016) ***(P-23523)***
Wbt Industries, Monrovia *Also called Wbt Group LLC* ***(P-23523)***
WBwalton Enterprises Inc.....E.....951 683-0930
4185 Hallmark Pkwy San Bernardino (92407) ***(P-17704)***
Wc, Fairfield *Also called West-Com Nrse Call Systems Inc* ***(P-17705)***
Wcbm Company (PA).....E.....323 262-3274
1812 W 135th St Gardena (90249) ***(P-23015)***
Wce Products Inc.....F.....714 895-4381
7542 Santa Rita Cir Stanton (90680) ***(P-7633)***
WCI, Santa Ana *Also called Wright Capacitors Inc* ***(P-18687)***
Wcitiescom Inc.....F.....415 495-8090
1212 Broadway Ste 500 Oakland (94612) ***(P-6381)***
WCP Inc.....D.....562 653-9797
17730 Crusader Ave Cerritos (90703) ***(P-10117)***
Wct, Garden Grove *Also called Broncs Inc* ***(P-2672)***
Wct/Pac Data, Aliso Viejo *Also called Pacific Alliance Capital Inc* ***(P-15072)***
WD, San Jose *Also called Western Digital Tech Inc* ***(P-15115)***
WD Media LLC.....B.....408 576-2000
1710 Automation Pkwy San Jose (95131) ***(P-19241)***
WD-40 Company (PA).....B.....619 275-1400
9715 Businesspark Ave San Diego (92131) ***(P-9159)***
Wd-40 Company.....C.....619 275-1400
9715 Businesspark Ave San Diego (92131) ***(P-9085)***
We Can Foundation, Los Angeles *Also called West E Cmnty Access Netwrk Inc* ***(P-19937)***
We Do Graphics Inc.....E.....714 997-7390
1150 N Main St Orange (92867) ***(P-6928)***
We Five-R Corporation.....F.....323 263-6757
1507 S Sunol Dr Los Angeles (90023) ***(P-13129)***
WE Hall Company Inc (PA).....F.....949 650-4555
471 Old Newport Blvd # 205 Newport Beach (92663) ***(P-11122)***
WE Hall Company Inc.....F.....916 383-4891
5999 Power Inn Rd Sacramento (95824) ***(P-10668)***
We Imagine Inc.....D.....818 709-0064
9371 Canoga Ave Chatsworth (91311) ***(P-18048)***
We The Pie People LLC.....E.....818 349-1880
9909 Topanga Canyon Blvd # 159 Chatsworth (91311) ***(P-679)***
We-Cel Creations, San Fernando *Also called Jay Gee Sales* ***(P-10491)***
Wearable Integrity Inc.....E.....213 748-6044
1360 E 17th St Los Angeles (90021) ***(P-3434)***
Weartech International Inc (HQ).....E.....714 683-2430
1177 N Grove St Anaheim (92806) ***(P-14620)***
Weather TEC Corp.....F.....559 291-5555
5645 E Clinton Ave Fresno (93727) ***(P-13684)***
Weatherford Artificia.....E.....661 654-8120
21728 Rosedale Hwy Bakersfield (93314) ***(P-281)***
Weatherford Completion Systems.....E.....661 746-1391
19468 Creek Rd Bakersfield (93314) ***(P-282)***
Weatherford International LLC.....E.....805 933-0242
201 Hallock Dr Santa Paula (93060) ***(P-283)***
Weatherford International LLC.....D.....805 781-3580
1880 Santa Barbara Ave # 220 San Luis Obispo (93401) ***(P-284)***
Weatherford International LLC.....D.....661 587-9753
21728 Rosedale Hwy Bakersfield (93314) ***(P-285)***
Weatherford International LLC.....E.....661 589-2146
3701 Enterprise St Shafter (93263) ***(P-286)***
Weatherford International LLC.....D.....805 933-0200
201 Hallock Dr Santa Paula (93060) ***(P-13491)***
Weatherford International LLC.....F.....562 595-0931
3356 Lime Ave Long Beach (90755) ***(P-13796)***
Weatherford International LLC.....F.....805 643-1279
250 W Stanley Ave Ventura (93001) ***(P-287)***
Weatherman Products Inc (PA).....F.....949 515-8800
21622 Surveyor Cir Huntington Beach (92646) ***(P-8693)***
Web CAM, Riverside *Also called Web CAM Inc* ***(P-19804)***
Web CAM Inc.....F.....951 369-5144
1815 Massachusetts Ave Riverside (92507) ***(P-19804)***
Webalo Inc.....F.....310 828-7335
1990 S Bundy Dr Ste 540 Los Angeles (90025) ***(P-19242)***
Webb Designs Inc.....F.....559 641-5400
40300 Greenwood Way Oakhurst (93644) ***(P-5043)***
Webb Massey Co Inc.....E.....714 639-6012
201 W Carleton Ave Orange (92867) ***(P-4757)***
Webb-Stotler Engineering.....F.....951 735-2040
1701 Commerce St Corona (92880) ***(P-16514)***
Webber EMI, Ontario *Also called Emission Methods Inc* ***(P-21466)***
Webbshade, Oakhurst *Also called Webb Designs Inc* ***(P-5043)***
Webcloak LLC.....F.....949 417-9940
2 Park Plz Ste 700 Irvine (92614) ***(P-24574)***
Webedoctor Inc.....E.....714 990-3999
231 Imperial Hwy Ste 104a Fullerton (92835) ***(P-24575)***
Weber Drilling Co Inc.....E.....310 670-7708
401 Hindry Ave Inglewood (90301) ***(P-13762)***
Weber Orthopedic Inc (PA).....E.....805 525-8474
1185 E Main St Santa Paula (93060) ***(P-22123)***
Weber Precision Graphics, Santa Ana *Also called Artisan Nameplate Awards Corp* ***(P-6993)***
Weber Printing Company Inc.....E.....310 639-5064
1124 E Del Amo Blvd Carson (90746) ***(P-6929)***
Webers Auto Parts, Montebello *Also called Eagle Enterprises Inc* ***(P-19643)***
Weddingchannelcom Inc.....C.....213 599-4100
5757 Wilshire Blvd # 504 Los Angeles (90036) ***(P-6382)***
Wedemeyer Bakery, South San Francisco *Also called Windmill Corporation* ***(P-1298)***
Weekend Balita, La Crescenta *Also called Balita Media Inc* ***(P-5562)***
Wefea Inc.....E.....925 218-1839
4695 Chabot Dr Ste 200 Pleasanton (94588) ***(P-19243)***
Wehah Farm Inc.....B.....530 538-3500
5311 Midway Richvale (95974) ***(P-1054)***
WEI Laboratories Inc.....E.....408 970-8700
3002 Scott Blvd Santa Clara (95054) ***(P-750)***
Weibel Champagne Vineyards, Lodi *Also called Weibel Incorporated* ***(P-1994)***
Weibel Incorporated.....E.....209 365-9463
1 Winemaster Way Ste D Lodi (95240) ***(P-1994)***
Weider Health and Fitness.....B.....818 884-6800
21100 Erwin St Woodland Hills (91367) ***(P-2235)***
Weider Leasing Inc.....D.....818 884-6800
21100 Erwin St Woodland Hills (91367) ***(P-6056)***
WEIDNERCA, Sacramento *Also called Architectural S Weidner* ***(P-23052)***
Weir Seaboard, Bakersfield *Also called Seaboard International Inc* ***(P-13790)***
Weis/Robart Partitions Inc.....F.....714 666-0822
3501 E La Palma Ave Anaheim (92806) ***(P-12521)***
Weiser Iron Inc.....E.....909 429-4600
64 Sundance Dr Pomona (91766) ***(P-11081)***
Weiss-Mcnair LLC (HQ).....D.....530 891-6214
100 Loren Ave Chico (95928) ***(P-13685)***
Welaco, Bakersfield *Also called Well Analysis Corporation Inc* ***(P-3916)***
Weld Design, Santa Ana *Also called Dave Annala* ***(P-12174)***
Weld-On Adhesives, Compton *Also called Ips Corporation* ***(P-8878)***
Weldcraft Industries.....F.....559 784-4322
18794 Avenue 96 Terra Bella (93270) ***(P-13686)***
Weldex Corporation (PA).....E.....714 761-2100
6751 Katella Ave Cypress (90630) ***(P-18656)***
Weldlogic Inc.....D.....805 375-1670
2651 Lavery Ct Newbury Park (91320) ***(P-24678)***
Weldmac Manufacturing Company.....C.....619 440-2300
1451 N Johnson Ave El Cajon (92020) ***(P-16515)***
Weldon Company, Gardena *Also called Ips Corporation* ***(P-8879)***
Weldstone Portable Welders, Anaheim *Also called Lodestone LLC* ***(P-14244)***
Weldway Inc.....E.....209 847-8083
521 Hi Tech Pkwy Oakdale (95361) ***(P-11917)***
Well Analysis Corporation Inc (PA).....E.....661 283-9510
5500 Woodmere Dr Bakersfield (93313) ***(P-3916)***
Welland Industries LLC.....F.....714 528-9900
3860 Prospect Ave Yorba Linda (92886) ***(P-23524)***
Wellbore Navigation Inc (PA).....F.....714 259-7760
1240 N Jefferson St Ste M Anaheim (92807) ***(P-21564)***
Wellex Corporation (PA).....C.....510 743-1818
551 Brown Rd Fremont (94539) ***(P-19142)***
Wellington Foods Inc.....E.....562 989-0111
1930 California Ave Corona (92881) ***(P-751)***
Wellprint Inc.....F.....714 838-3962
380 E 1st St Ste B Tustin (92780) ***(P-6930)***
Wells Dental Inc.....F.....707 937-0521
5860 Flynn Creek Rd Comptche (95427) ***(P-22205)***
Wells Media Group Inc (PA).....E.....619 584-1100
3570 Camino Delrio N 20 San Diego (92108) ***(P-6057)***
Wells Mfg USA Inc.....F.....626 575-2886
9698 Telstar Ave Ste 312 El Monte (91731) ***(P-19207)***
Wells Precision Machining, Comptche *Also called Wells Dental Inc* ***(P-22205)***

A L P H A B E T I C

Employee Codes: A=Over 500 employees, B=251-500
C=101-250, D=51-100, E=20-50, F=10-19
2020 California
Manfacturers Register
© Mergent Inc. 1-800-342-5647
1283

Welmark Textile Inc.......F.......310 516-7289
14824 S Main St Gardena (90248) ***(P-2955)***
Welnav, Anaheim *Also called Wellbore Navigation Inc* ***(P-21564)***
Welovefine, Los Angeles *Also called Mf Inc* ***(P-3180)***
Wemo Media Inc.......F.......310 399-8058
550 Rose Ave Venice (90291) ***(P-24576)***
Wems Electronics, Hawthorne *Also called Wems Inc* ***(P-14689)***
Wems Inc (PA).......D.......310 644-0251
4650 W Rosecrans Ave Hawthorne (90250) ***(P-14689)***
Wems Inc.......E.......310 644-0255
4652 W Rosecrans Ave Hawthorne (90250) ***(P-16768)***
Wencon Development Inc.......D.......925 478-8269
2700 Mitchell Dr Ste 2 Walnut Creek (94598) ***(P-12432)***
Wente Bros (PA).......D.......925 456-2300
5565 Tesla Rd Livermore (94550) ***(P-1995)***
Wente Bros.......E.......831 674-5642
37995 Elm Ave Greenfield (93927) ***(P-1996)***
Wente Brothers Winery, Greenfield *Also called Wente Bros* ***(P-1996)***
Wente Vineyards, Livermore *Also called Wente Bros* ***(P-1995)***
Wep Transport Holdings LLC.......F.......858 756-1010
16909 Via De Santa Fe Rancho Santa Fe (92067) ***(P-146)***
Wepower LLC.......F.......866 385-9463
32 Journey Ste 250 Aliso Viejo (92656) ***(P-13582)***
Werner Co.......F.......209 383-3989
1810 Grogan Ave Merced (95341) ***(P-13556)***
Werner Corporation.......F.......951 277-4586
25050 Maitri Rd Corona (92883) ***(P-10872)***
Werner Systems Inc.......E.......714 838-4444
14321 Myford Rd Tustin (92780) ***(P-11269)***
Wes Go Inc.......E.......818 504-1200
8211 Lankershim Blvd North Hollywood (91605) ***(P-7267)***
Wes Manufacturing Inc.......E.......408 727-0750
3241 Keller St Santa Clara (95054) ***(P-16516)***
Wesanco Inc.......E.......714 739-4989
14870 Desman Rd La Mirada (90638) ***(P-20268)***
Wescam Sonoma Operations, Santa Rosa *Also called L-3 Cmmnications Sonoma Eo Inc* ***(P-22437)***
Wescam Usa Inc (HQ).......F.......707 236-1077
424 Aviation Blvd Santa Rosa (95403) ***(P-20744)***
Wesco Enterprises Inc.......F.......562 944-3100
12681 Corral Pl Santa Fe Springs (90670) ***(P-10118)***
Wesco Mounting & Finishing Inc.......E.......714 562-0122
5450 Dodds Ave Buena Park (90621) ***(P-7353)***
Wesco Sign, Torrance *Also called Skyway Signs LLC* ***(P-23212)***
Wesfac Inc (HQ).......D.......562 861-2160
9300 Hall Rd Downey (90241) ***(P-15604)***
Weslan Systems Inc.......F.......530 668-3304
1244 Commerce Ave Woodland (95776) ***(P-14555)***
Wesley Allen Inc (PA).......C.......323 231-4275
1001 E 60th St Los Angeles (90001) ***(P-4708)***
Wespac, Downey *Also called Wesfac Inc* ***(P-15604)***
Wessco International Ltd A C (PA).......E.......310 477-4272
11400 W Olympic Blvd # 450 Los Angeles (90064) ***(P-3668)***
Wessex Industries Inc.......E.......562 944-5760
8619 Red Oak St Rancho Cucamonga (91730) ***(P-13492)***
West American Energy Corp.......F.......661 747-7732
4949 Buckley Way Ste 207 Bakersfield (93309) ***(P-107)***
West American Rubber Co LLC (PA).......B.......714 532-3355
1337 W Braden Ct Orange (92868) ***(P-9388)***
West American Rubber Co LLC.......C.......714 532-3355
750 N Main St Orange (92868) ***(P-9389)***
WEST AREA OPPORTUNITY CENTER, Los Angeles *Also called Casa De Hermandad* ***(P-22777)***
West Bent Bolt Division, Santa Fe Springs *Also called Mid-West Fabricating Co* ***(P-19720)***
West Bond Inc (PA).......E.......714 978-1551
1551 S Harris Ct Anaheim (92806) ***(P-14872)***
West Bsin Wtr Rclamation Plant, El Segundo *Also called N A Suez* ***(P-20908)***
West Cast Architectural Shtmtl.......F.......408 776-2700
2215 Oakland Rd San Jose (95131) ***(P-12522)***
West Coast Aerospace Inc (PA).......D.......310 518-3167
220 W E St Wilmington (90744) ***(P-23016)***
West Coast Aerospace Inc.......F.......310 632-2064
3017 E Las Hermanas St Compton (90221) ***(P-23017)***
West Coast Aggregate Supply.......E.......760 342-7598
92500 Airport Blvd Thermal (92274) ***(P-368)***
West Coast Airlines, Riverside *Also called West Coast Unlimited* ***(P-19512)***
West Coast Asm, San Jose *Also called West Cast Architectural Shtmtl* ***(P-12522)***
West Coast Binders, Gardena *Also called US Packagers Inc* ***(P-7321)***
West Coast Business Prtrs Inc.......F.......818 709-4980
9822 Independence Ave Chatsworth (91311) ***(P-6931)***
West Coast Button Mfg Co, Gardena *Also called Wcbm Company* ***(P-23015)***
West Coast Canvas (PA).......F.......209 333-0243
1242 W Fremont St Stockton (95203) ***(P-3714)***
West Coast Catrg Trcks Mfg Inc.......F.......323 278-1279
1217 Goodrich Blvd Commerce (90022) ***(P-4619)***
West Coast Chain Mfg Co.......E.......909 923-7800
4245 Pacific Privado Ontario (91761) ***(P-19441)***
West Coast Consulting LLC.......C.......949 250-4102
9233 Research Dr Ste 200 Irvine (92618) ***(P-24577)***
West Coast Cryogenics Inc.......E.......800 657-0545
503 W Larch Rd Ste K Tracy (95304) ***(P-14556)***
West Coast Cryogenics Services, Tracy *Also called West Coast Cryogenics Inc* ***(P-14556)***
West Coast Custom Sheet Metal.......F.......818 252-7500
9045 Glenoaks Blvd Sun Valley (91352) ***(P-12433)***
West Coast Digital, Chatsworth *Also called West Coast Business Prtrs Inc* ***(P-6931)***
West Coast Enterprizes, Stanton *Also called Wce Products Inc* ***(P-7633)***
West Coast Fab Inc.......F.......510 529-0177
700 S 32nd St Richmond (94804) ***(P-12434)***
West Coast Fixtures Inc (PA).......E.......707 752-6373
511 Stone Rd Benicia (94510) ***(P-4955)***
West Coast Form Grinding.......F.......714 540-5621
2548 S Fairview St Santa Ana (92704) ***(P-16517)***
West Coast Foundry LLC (HQ).......E.......323 583-1421
2450 E 53rd St Huntington Park (90255) ***(P-11174)***
West Coast Garment Mfg.......E.......415 896-1772
70 Elmira St San Francisco (94124) ***(P-3059)***
West Coast Gasket Co.......D.......714 869-0123
300 Ranger Ave Brea (92821) ***(P-9259)***
West Coast Growers Inc.......E.......559 843-2294
1849 N Helm Ave Ste 110 Fresno (93727) ***(P-876)***
West Coast Labels, Placentia *Also called Cinton* ***(P-5359)***
West Coast Laboratories Inc.......E.......310 527-6163
156 E 162nd St Gardena (90248) ***(P-8186)***
West Coast Laboratories Inc (PA).......F.......323 321-4774
116 E Alondra Blvd Gardena (90248) ***(P-8187)***
West Coast Machining Inc.......F.......562 229-1087
14560 Marquardt Ave Santa Fe Springs (90670) ***(P-16518)***
West Coast Magnetics, Stockton *Also called Wjlp Company Inc* ***(P-18748)***
West Coast Manufacturing Inc.......E.......714 897-4221
1822 Western Ave Stanton (90680) ***(P-12890)***
West Coast Metal Stamping Inc.......E.......714 792-0322
550 W Crowther Ave Placentia (92870) ***(P-12891)***
West Coast Microwave, Artesia *Also called M G Watanabe Inc* ***(P-17578)***
West Coast Milling, Lancaster *Also called Pavement Recycling Systems Inc* ***(P-9101)***
West Coast Orthotic/Prosthetic.......F.......209 942-4166
3215 N California St # 2 Stockton (95204) ***(P-22124)***
West Coast Pallets Inc.......F.......209 524-3587
680 Janopaul Ave Modesto (95351) ***(P-4406)***
West Coast Plastics Inc.......F.......562 777-8024
10025 Shoemaker Ave Santa Fe Springs (90670) ***(P-10119)***
West Coast Porcelain Inc.......E.......951 278-8680
133 N Sherman Ave Corona (92882) ***(P-10495)***
West Coast Products, Orland *Also called Decamilla Brothers LLC* ***(P-1471)***
West Coast Quartz Corporation (HQ).......D.......510 249-2160
1000 Corporate Way Fremont (94539) ***(P-10333)***
West Coast Sand Gravel.......E.......559 625-9426
7715 Avenue 296 Visalia (93291) ***(P-369)***
West Coast Service Center, Ontario *Also called Vsmpo-Tirus US Inc* ***(P-11284)***
West Coast Sheepskin Import.......F.......562 945-5151
14056 Whittier Blvd Whittier (90605) ***(P-3867)***
West Coast Steel & Proc LLC (PA).......D.......909 393-8405
3534 Philadelphia St Chino (91710) ***(P-11175)***
West Coast Switchgear (HQ).......D.......562 802-3441
13837 Bettencourt St Cerritos (90703) ***(P-16623)***
West Coast Timber Corp.......F.......714 893-4374
6221 Apache Rd Westminster (92683) ***(P-3917)***
West Coast Trends Inc.......E.......714 843-9288
17811 Jamestown Ln Huntington Beach (92647) ***(P-22923)***
West Coast Unlimited.......F.......951 352-1234
11161 Pierce St Riverside (92505) ***(P-19512)***
West Coast Venture Capital LLC (PA).......A.......408 725-0700
10050 Bandley Dr Cupertino (95014) ***(P-17430)***
West Coast Vinyl Windows, Cerritos *Also called WCP Inc* ***(P-10117)***
West Coast Welding & Cnstr.......F.......805 604-1222
390 S Del Norte Blvd Oxnard (93030) ***(P-24679)***
West Coast Windows & Doors Inc.......F.......925 681-1776
1112 Willow Pass Ct Concord (94520) ***(P-10120)***
West Coast-Accudyne Inc.......E.......562 927-2546
7180 Scout Ave Bell (90201) ***(P-13999)***
West E Cmnty Access Netwrk Inc.......D.......323 967-0520
646 W 60th St Los Angeles (90044) ***(P-19937)***
West Lake Food Corporation.......D.......714 973-2286
2430 Cape Cod Way Santa Ana (92703) ***(P-431)***
West Newport Oil Company.......F.......949 631-1100
1080 W 17th St Costa Mesa (92627) ***(P-77)***
West Pacific Cabinet Mfg.......F.......916 652-6840
3121 Swetzer Rd Ste A Loomis (95650) ***(P-4265)***
West Publishing Corporation.......E.......800 747-3161
633 W 5th St Ste 2300 Los Angeles (90071) ***(P-6161)***
West Rapco Environmental Svcs.......E.......310 450-3335
23852 Pacific Coast Hwy # 941 Malibu (90265) ***(P-14125)***
West Rock, Milpitas *Also called Westrock Cp LLC* ***(P-5276)***
West Star Industries, Stockton *Also called Hackett Industries Inc* ***(P-14370)***
West Trend, Santa Ana *Also called Memory Threads* ***(P-2730)***
West Valley Plating Inc.......F.......818 709-1684
21061 Superior St Ste A Chatsworth (91311) ***(P-13130)***
West World Manufacturing Inc.......F.......619 287-4403
6420 Federal Blvd Ste F Lemon Grove (91945) ***(P-4620)***
West-Bag Inc.......E.......323 264-0750
1161 Monterey Pass Rd Monterey Park (91754) ***(P-10121)***
West-Com Nrse Call Systems Inc (PA).......E.......707 428-5900
2200 Cordelia Rd Fairfield (94534) ***(P-17705)***
West-Mark, Ceres *Also called Certified Stainless Svc Inc* ***(P-12003)***
West-Mark, Atwater *Also called Certified Stainless Svc Inc* ***(P-12004)***
West-World Co, Lemon Grove *Also called West World Manufacturing Inc* ***(P-4620)***
Westaire Engineering Inc.......F.......323 587-3347
5820 S Alameda St Vernon (90058) ***(P-15473)***
Westak, Sunnyvale *Also called Qualitek Inc* ***(P-17967)***
Westak Inc (PA).......D.......408 734-8686
1116 Elko Dr Sunnyvale (94089) ***(P-18049)***
Westak International Sales Inc (HQ).......C.......408 734-8686
1116 Elko Dr Sunnyvale (94089) ***(P-18050)***
Westamerica Bancorporation.......F.......707 863-6000
4550 Mangels Blvd Fairfield (94534) ***(P-22725)***

Mergent e-mail: customerrelations@mergent.com 2020 California (P-0000) Products & Services Section entry number
1284 Manufacturers Register (PA)=Parent Co (HQ)=Headquarters (DH)=Div Headquarters

Westar Metal Fabrication Inc ....F....626 350-0718
1926 Potrero Ave South El Monte (91733) *(P-11918)*
Westar Nutrition Corp ....C....949 645-6100
350 Paularino Ave Costa Mesa (92626) *(P-7704)*
Westbase Inc (PA) ....F....626 969-6801
717 N Coney Ave Azusa (91702) *(P-16624)*
Westbridge Agricultural Pdts ....F....760 599-8855
1260 Avenida Chelsea Vista (92081) *(P-8848)*
Westbridge Research Group (PA) ....F....760 599-8855
1260 Avenida Chelsea Vista (92081) *(P-8849)*
Westco Industries Inc ....E....909 874-8700
2625 S Willow Ave Bloomington (92316) *(P-12613)*
Westco Iron Works Inc (PA) ....D....925 961-9152
5828 S Naylor Rd Livermore (94551) *(P-11919)*
Westcoast Brush Mfg Inc ....E....909 627-7170
1330 Philadelphia St Pomona (91766) *(P-23033)*
Westcoast Business Solutions, Agoura Hills *Also called Jamaco Enterprises Inc (P-5189)*
Westcoast Companies Inc ....F....626 794-9330
725-729 E Washington Blvd Pasadena (91104) *(P-3715)*
Westcoast Elevator Pads, Pasadena *Also called Westcoast Companies Inc (P-3715)*
Westcoast Grinding Corporation ....F....818 890-1841
10517 San Fernando Rd Pacoima (91331) *(P-16519)*
Westcoast Inksolutions LLC ....F....323 726-8100
5928 Garfield Ave Commerce (90040) *(P-8937)*
Westcoast Precision Inc ....E....408 943-9998
2091 Fortune Dr San Jose (95131) *(P-16520)*
Westcoast Rotor Inc ....E....310 327-5050
119 W 154th St Gardena (90248) *(P-14604)*
Westcorp Engineering, Riverside *Also called Reisner Enterprises Inc (P-16350)*
Westcott Press Inc ....F....626 794-7716
1121 W Isabel St Burbank (91506) *(P-6932)*
Westech Inv Advisors LLC (PA) ....E....650 234-4300
104 La Mesa Dr 102 Portola Valley (94028) *(P-983)*
Westech Metal Fabrication Inc ....F....619 702-9353
3420 E St San Diego (92102) *(P-11920)*
Westek Electronics Inc ....E....831 740-6300
185 Westridge Dr Watsonville (95076) *(P-17773)*
Westend Software Inc (PA) ....F....310 370-0367
1905 Speyer Ln Redondo Beach (90278) *(P-24578)*
Westerly Marine Inc ....E....714 966-8550
3535 W Garry Ave Santa Ana (92704) *(P-20362)*
Western Abrasives Inc ....F....323 588-1245
4383 Fruitland Ave Vernon (90058) *(P-10959)*
Western Bagel Baking Corp (PA) ....C....818 786-5847
7814 Sepulveda Blvd Van Nuys (91405) *(P-1292)*
Western Bagel Baking Corp ....E....818 887-5451
21749 Ventura Blvd Woodland Hills (91364) *(P-1293)*
Western Bagel Baking Corp ....E....310 479-4823
11628 Santa Monica Blvd # 12 Los Angeles (90025) *(P-1294)*
Western Bagel Too, Los Angeles *Also called Western Bagel Baking Corp (P-1294)*
Western Bay Sheet Metal Inc ....E....619 233-1753
1410 Hill St El Cajon (92020) *(P-11921)*
Western Cactus Growers Inc ....E....760 726-1710
1860 Monte Vista Dr Vista (92084) *(P-13700)*
Western Case Incorporated (PA) ....D....951 214-6380
6400 Sycam Canyo Blvd Ste Riverside (92507) *(P-10122)*
Western Cnc Inc ....D....760 597-7000
1001 Park Center Dr Vista (92081) *(P-16521)*
Western Combustion Engrg Inc ....F....310 834-9389
640 E Realty St Carson (90745) *(P-12070)*
Western Concrete Products, Pleasanton *Also called Central Precast Concrete Inc (P-10548)*
Western Die & Printing Corp ....F....323 665-0474
3109 Casitas Ave Los Angeles (90039) *(P-7268)*
Western Die Cutting and Prtg, Los Angeles *Also called TLC Logistics Inc (P-5538)*
Western Digital, Milpitas *Also called Sandisk LLC (P-15089)*
Western Digital Corporation (PA) ....A....408 717-6000
5601 Great Oaks Pkwy San Jose (95119) *(P-15114)*
Western Digital Tech Inc (HQ) ....A....949 672-7000
5601 Great Oaks Pkwy San Jose (95119) *(P-15115)*
Western Division, Morgan Hill *Also called Greif Inc (P-5295)*
Western Division, Tehachapi *Also called Legacy Vulcan LLC (P-301)*
Western Division, Rialto *Also called Legacy Vulcan LLC (P-10785)*
Western Dning - Schneider Cafe ....E....559 292-1981
3500 Never Forget Ln Clovis (93612) *(P-19442)*
Western Dovetail Incorporated ....E....707 556-3683
1101 Nimitz Ave Ste 209 Vallejo (94592) *(P-4621)*
Western Edge Inc ....F....661 947-3900
37957 Sierra Hwy Palmdale (93550) *(P-13267)*
Western Electrical Advg Co ....E....760 352-0471
853 Dogwood Ave El Centro (92243) *(P-23241)*
Western Energy Production LLC ....F....858 756-1010
16909 Via De Santa Fe Rancho Santa Fe (92067) *(P-147)*
Western Equipment Mfg, Corona *Also called Western Equipment Mfg Inc (P-13757)*
Western Equipment Mfg Inc ....F....951 284-2000
1160 Olympic Dr Corona (92881) *(P-13757)*
Western Fab Inc ....F....760 949-1441
9823 E Ave Hesperia (92345) *(P-13557)*
Western Fabrication & Eqp, Bakersfield *Also called F E W Inc (P-15948)*
WESTERN FABRICATORS, Hesperia *Also called Western Fab Inc (P-13557)*
Western Fiber Co Inc ....E....661 854-5556
4234a Sandrini Rd Arvin (93203) *(P-13962)*
Western Foam, Hayward *Also called Induspac California Inc (P-7569)*
Western Foods LLC (PA) ....E....530 601-5991
420 N Pioneer Ave Woodland (95776) *(P-1013)*
Western Forge Die, Huntington Beach *Also called Tarpin Corporation (P-14110)*
Western Gage Corporation ....E....805 445-1410
3316 Maya Linda Ste A Camarillo (93012) *(P-14211)*
Western Glass Co, Pomona *Also called Da-Ly Glass Corp (P-10352)*
Western Glove Mfg Inc ....D....562 903-1339
10747 Norwalk Blvd Santa Fe Springs (90670) *(P-22125)*
Western Golf Inc ....F....800 448-4409
1340 N Jefferson St Anaheim (92807) *(P-22924)*
Western Golf Car Mfg Inc ....D....760 671-6691
69391 Dillon Rd Desert Hot Springs (92241) *(P-22925)*
Western Golf Car Sales Co, Desert Hot Springs *Also called Western Golf Car Mfg Inc (P-22925)*
Western Grinding Service Inc ....E....650 591-2635
2375 De La Cruz Blvd Santa Clara (95050) *(P-16522)*
Western Hardware Company, Walnut *Also called Hardware Imports Inc (P-19538)*
Western Hardware Company ....F....909 595-6201
161 Commerce Way Walnut (91789) *(P-11642)*
Western Hellenic Journal Inc ....E....925 939-3900
1839 Ygnacio Valley Rd Walnut Creek (94598) *(P-5863)*
Western Highway Products, Huntington Beach *Also called Primus Inc (P-23178)*
Western Hose & Gasket, National City *Also called Westflex Inc (P-9211)*
Western Hydrostatics Inc (PA) ....E....951 784-2133
1956 Keats Dr Riverside (92501) *(P-15638)*
Western Illuminated Plas Inc ....F....714 895-3067
14451 Edwards St Westminster (92683) *(P-17084)*
Western Imperial Trading Inc ....F....818 907-0768
13946 Ventura Blvd Sherman Oaks (91423) *(P-22584)*
Western Integrated Mtls Inc (PA) ....E....562 634-2823
3310 E 59th St Long Beach (90805) *(P-4147)*
Western Lighting Inds Inc ....E....626 969-6820
205 W Blueridge Ave Orange (92865) *(P-17085)*
Western Lithographics, Costa Mesa *Also called Batida Inc (P-6438)*
Western Mesquite Mines Inc ....E....928 341-4653
6502 E Us Highway 78 Brawley (92227) *(P-11196)*
Western Metal Dctg Co Coil Div ....F....909 987-2506
8875 Industrial Ln Rancho Cucamonga (91730) *(P-6933)*
Western Metal Spinning & Mfg ....F....951 657-0711
5055 Western Way Perris (92571) *(P-12892)*
Western Metal Spinning Farming, Perris *Also called Western Metal Spinning & Mfg (P-12892)*
Western Metal Supply Co Inc ....F....760 233-7800
2115 E Valley Pkwy Ste E Escondido (92027) *(P-12581)*
Western Methods, Valencia *Also called Stratoflight (P-20239)*
Western Methods Machinery Corp ....C....949 252-6600
2344 Pullman St Santa Ana (92705) *(P-20269)*
Western Mfg & Distrg LLC ....E....805 988-1010
835 Flynn Rd Camarillo (93012) *(P-20436)*
Western Mill Fabricators Inc ....E....714 993-3667
615 Fee Ana St Placentia (92870) *(P-5089)*
Western Motor Works Inc ....F....310 382-6896
8332 Osage Ave Los Angeles (90045) *(P-14302)*
Western Mountaineering, San Jose *Also called Seventh Heaven Inc (P-3861)*
Western Nutrients Corporation ....E....661 327-9604
245 Industrial St Bakersfield (93307) *(P-8807)*
Western Organics Inc ....E....209 982-4936
4343 Mckinley Ave Stockton (95206) *(P-8808)*
Western Outdoor News, San Clemente *Also called Western Outdoors Publications (P-5864)*
Western Outdoors Publications (PA) ....E....949 366-0030
1211 Puerta Del Sol # 270 San Clemente (92673) *(P-5864)*
Western Pacific Pulp and Paper (HQ) ....D....562 803-4401
9400 Hall Rd Downey (90241) *(P-5095)*
Western Pacific Signal LLC ....F....510 276-6400
15890 Foothill Blvd San Leandro (94578) *(P-17774)*
Western PCF Stor Solutions Inc (PA) ....D....909 451-0303
300 E Arrow Hwy San Dimas (91773) *(P-5012)*
Western Plastic Products, Stanton *Also called Schaffer Laboratories Inc (P-9455)*
Western Plastics Temecula, Temecula *Also called W Plastics Inc (P-9425)*
Western Pllet Sup Lgistics LLC ....F....209 836-1968
7675 W 11th St Tracy (95304) *(P-4407)*
Western Precision Aero LLC ....E....714 893-7999
11600 Monarch St Garden Grove (92841) *(P-16523)*
Western Printing and Label, Irvine *Also called Western Prtg & Graphics LLC (P-6934)*
Western Prtg & Graphics LLC (PA) ....E....714 532-3946
17931 Sky Park Cir Irvine (92614) *(P-6934)*
Western Ready Mix Concrete Co (PA) ....E....530 934-2185
Gyle Rd Willows (95988) *(P-10873)*
Western Real Estate News, South San Francisco *Also called Business Extension Bureau (P-5895)*
Western Roto Engravers Inc ....F....510 525-2950
1225 6th St Berkeley (94710) *(P-7269)*
Western Saw Manufacturers Inc ....E....805 981-0999
3200 Camino Del Sol Oxnard (93030) *(P-11556)*
Western Screw Products Inc ....E....562 698-5793
11770 Slauson Ave Santa Fe Springs (90670) *(P-12660)*
Western Sheet Metals Inc ....F....951 272-3600
190 E Harrison St Ste B Corona (92879) *(P-12435)*
Western Sheld Acquisitions LLC ....E....310 527-6212
2146 E Gladwick St Rancho Dominguez (90220) *(P-6966)*
Western Shield Label, Rancho Dominguez *Also called Western Sheld Acquisitions LLC (P-6966)*
Western Sign Company Inc ....E....916 933-3765
6221a Enterprise Dr Ste A Diamond Springs (95619) *(P-23242)*
Western Sign Systems Inc ....E....760 736-6070
261 S Pacific St San Marcos (92078) *(P-23243)*
Western Square Industries Inc ....E....209 944-0921
1621 N Brdwy Stockton (95205) *(P-12523)*
Western Stabilization, Dixon *Also called J & A Jeffery Inc (P-23368)*
Western States Envelope Corp ....D....714 449-0909
2301 Raymer Ave Fullerton (92833) *(P-5477)*
Western States Glass, Sacramento *Also called Wsglass Holdings Inc (P-21422)*
Western States Glass, Fremont *Also called Wsglass Holdings Inc (P-10281)*

ALPHABETIC

Employee Codes: A=Over 500 employees, B=251-500
C=101-250, D=51-100, E=20-50, F=10-19
2020 California
Manfacturers Register
© Mergent Inc. 1-800-342-5647
1285

Western States Packaging Inc..........E......818 686-6045
13276 Paxton St Pacoima (91331) ***(P-5431)***
Western States Weeklies Inc..........F......619 280-2988
6312 Riverdale St San Diego (92120) ***(P-5865)***
Western States Wholesale Inc (PA)..........C......909 947-0028
1420 S Bon View Ave Ontario (91761) ***(P-10525)***
Western Summit Manufacturing, Rancho Palos Verdes *Also called Summit International Packg Inc* ***(P-5342)***
Western Summit Mfg Corp..........D......626 333-3333
30200 Cartier Dr Rancho Palos Verdes (90275) ***(P-9426)***
Western Supreme Inc..........C......213 627-3861
865 Produce Ct Los Angeles (90021) ***(P-531)***
Western Telematic Inc..........E......949 586-9950
5 Sterling Irvine (92618) ***(P-15365)***
Western Trade Printing Inc..........F......559 251-8595
5695 E Shields Ave Fresno (93727) ***(P-6935)***
Western Tube & Conduit Corp (HQ)..........C......310 537-6300
2001 E Dominguez St Long Beach (90810) ***(P-16956)***
Western Web Inc..........E......707 444-6236
1900 Bendixsen St Ste 2 Samoa (95564) ***(P-6936)***
Western Widgets Cnc Inc..........F......408 436-1230
915 Commercial St San Jose (95112) ***(P-16524)***
Western Wire Works Inc..........F......909 483-1186
7923 Cartilla Ave Rancho Cucamonga (91730) ***(P-13445)***
Western Wood, Lake Elsinore *Also called Faith Industries Inc* ***(P-4501)***
Western Wood Treating, Woodland *Also called California Cascade-Woodland* ***(P-4473)***
Western Yankee Inc..........E......562 944-6889
13233 Barton Cir Whittier (90605) ***(P-7270)***
Western Yarn Dyeing Inc..........E......714 578-9500
2011 Raymer Ave Fullerton (92833) ***(P-2864)***
Westfab Manufacturing Inc..........E......408 727-0550
3370 Keller St Santa Clara (95054) ***(P-12436)***
Westfield Hydraulics Inc..........F......818 896-6414
13834 Del Sur St San Fernando (91340) ***(P-13334)***
Westflex Inc (PA)..........E......619 474-7400
325 W 30th St National City (91950) ***(P-9211)***
Westgate Hardwoods Inc (PA)..........E......530 892-0300
9296 Midway Durham (95938) ***(P-4148)***
Westgate Mfg Inc..........F......877 805-2252
2462 E 28th St Vernon (90058) ***(P-19443)***
Westlake Bakery Inc..........F......650 994-7741
7099 Mission St Daly City (94014) ***(P-1295)***
Westlake Engrg Roto Form..........E......805 525-8800
1041 E Santa Barbara St Santa Paula (93060) ***(P-10123)***
Westlam Foods, Chino *Also called Trinidad Benham Holding Co* ***(P-2636)***
Westland Technologies Inc..........D......800 877-7734
107 S Riverside Dr Modesto (95354) ***(P-9273)***
Westmark, Atwater *Also called Certified Stainless Svc Inc* ***(P-12002)***
Westminster Press Inc..........E......714 210-2881
4906 W 1st St Santa Ana (92703) ***(P-6937)***
Westmont Industries (PA)..........D......562 944-6137
10805 Painter Ave Uppr Santa Fe Springs (90670) ***(P-13853)***
Westpak Usa Inc..........F......714 530-6995
1235 N Red Gum St Anaheim (92806) ***(P-19444)***
Westport Scandinavia, Watsonville *Also called Nordic Naturals Inc* ***(P-1462)***
Westridge Laboratories Inc..........E......714 259-9400
1671 E Saint Andrew Pl Santa Ana (92705) ***(P-8607)***
Westrock Converting Company..........F......951 601-4164
16110 Cosmos St Moreno Valley (92551) ***(P-5271)***
Westrock Cp LLC..........C......408 946-3600
201 S Hillview Dr Milpitas (95035) ***(P-5272)***
Westrock Cp LLC..........C......714 523-3550
13833 Freeway Dr Santa Fe Springs (90670) ***(P-5273)***
Westrock Cp LLC..........C......831 424-1831
1078 Merrill St Salinas (93901) ***(P-5274)***
Westrock Cp LLC..........C......951 734-1870
185 N Smith Ave Corona (92880) ***(P-5275)***
Westrock Cp LLC..........F......661 327-3841
2710 O St Bakersfield (93301) ***(P-5178)***
Westrock Cp LLC..........E......770 448-2193
205 E Alma Ave San Jose (95112) ***(P-5179)***
Westrock Cp LLC..........D......951 273-7900
2577 Research Dr Corona (92882) ***(P-6938)***
Westrock Cp LLC..........C......408 946-3600
201 S Hillview Dr Milpitas (95035) ***(P-5276)***
Westrock Cp LLC..........E......818 557-1500
3003 N San Fernando Blvd Burbank (91504) ***(P-5180)***
Westrock Cp LLC..........F......559 441-1166
24 S Thorne Ave Fresno (93706) ***(P-5181)***
Westrock Cp LLC..........D......559 685-1102
701 E Continental Ave Tulare (93274) ***(P-5277)***
Westrock Cp LLC..........E......916 379-2200
4800 Florin Perkins Rd Sacramento (95826) ***(P-5182)***
Westrock Cp LLC..........E......714 641-8891
2540 S Main St Santa Ana (92707) ***(P-5183)***
Westrock Cp LLC..........C......559 519-7240
3366 E Muscat Ave Fresno (93725) ***(P-5278)***
Westrock Cp LLC..........D......714 523-3550
15300 Marquardt Ave Santa Fe Springs (90670) ***(P-5184)***
Westrock Cp LLC..........D......925 946-0842
2363 Boulevard Cir Ste 4 Walnut Creek (94595) ***(P-5380)***
Westrock Mwv LLC..........B......909 597-2197
15750 Mountain Ave Chino (91708) ***(P-5185)***
Westrock Rkt LLC..........F......559 441-1181
1854 E Home Ave Fresno (93703) ***(P-5192)***
Westrock Rkt Company..........C......714 978-2895
749 N Poplar St Orange (92868) ***(P-5279)***
Westrock Rkt Company..........C......559 497-1662
3366 E Muscat Ave Fresno (93725) ***(P-5280)***
Westrock Rkt Company..........E......818 729-0610
100 E Tujunga Ave Ste 102 Burbank (91502) ***(P-5281)***
Westrock Rkt Company..........C......626 859-7633
536 S 2nd Ave Covina (91723) ***(P-5282)***
Westrock Usc Inc..........F......562 282-0000
13820 Mica St Santa Fe Springs (90670) ***(P-5283)***
Westrock Usc Inc..........F......562 282-4200
13833 Freeway Dr Santa Fe Springs (90670) ***(P-5284)***
Westside Accessories Inc (PA)..........E......626 858-5452
8920 Vernon Ave Ste 128 Montclair (91763) ***(P-3534)***
Westside Building Materials, San Jose *Also called Central Concrete Supply Coinc* ***(P-10743)***
Westside Concrete Materials, San Jose *Also called US Concrete Inc* ***(P-10858)***
Westside Pallet Inc..........D......209 862-3941
2138 L St Newman (95360) ***(P-4408)***
Westside Research Inc..........F......530 330-0085
4293 County Road 99w Orland (95963) ***(P-3824)***
Westside Resources Inc..........E......800 944-3939
8850 Research Dr Irvine (92618) ***(P-22206)***
Westway Feed Products LLC..........F......209 466-4391
2130 W Washington St Stockton (95203) ***(P-1132)***
Westway Magazine, Costa Mesa *Also called Auto Club Enterprises* ***(P-5884)***
Westwood Laboratories, Azusa *Also called Cardinal Laboratories Inc* ***(P-8456)***
Westwood Laboratories Inc (PA)..........E......626 969-3305
710 S Ayon Ave Azusa (91702) ***(P-8608)***
Wetmore Cutting Tools, Chino *Also called Wetmore Tool and Engrg Co* ***(P-14212)***
Wetmore Tool and Engrg Co..........D......909 364-1000
5091 G St Chino (91710) ***(P-14212)***
Wetzels Pretzels LLC (HQ)..........F......626 432-6900
35 Hugus Aly Ste 300 Pasadena (91103) ***(P-1337)***
Weyerhaeuser Company..........C......800 238-3676
543 Country Club Dr Simi Valley (93065) ***(P-5285)***
Weyerhaeuser Company..........E......661 250-3500
27027 Weyerhauser Way Santa Clarita (91351) ***(P-3965)***
Weyerhaeuser Company..........F......209 942-1825
2700 S California St Stockton (95206) ***(P-3966)***
Wg, Santa Fe Springs *Also called Ethosenergy Field Services LLC* ***(P-195)***
WG Best Weinkellerei Inc..........F......858 627-1747
8929 Aero Dr Ste C San Diego (92123) ***(P-1997)***
Wg Security Products Inc..........E......408 241-8000
591 W Hamilton Ave # 260 Campbell (95008) ***(P-19445)***
Whalen Furniture Manufacturing, San Diego *Also called Whalen LLC* ***(P-4622)***
Whalen LLC (HQ)..........C......619 423-9948
1578 Air Wing Rd San Diego (92154) ***(P-4622)***
Whaley, Kevin Enterprises, Santee *Also called Kevin Whaley* ***(P-13421)***
Whamcloud Inc..........E......925 452-7599
696 San Ramon Valley Blvd Danville (94526) ***(P-24579)***
What Kids Want Inc..........F......818 775-0375
19428 Londelius St Northridge (91324) ***(P-22726)***
Whatever Publishing Inc..........F......415 884-2100
14 Pamaron Way Ste 1 Novato (94949) ***(P-6162)***
Whats Happening Tri City..........E......510 494-1999
39120 Argonaut Way # 335 Fremont (94538) ***(P-7271)***
Wheaton International, Hayward *Also called Tung Fei Plastic Inc* ***(P-5427)***
Wheel and Tire Club Inc..........E......714 422-3505
1301 Burton St Fullerton (92831) ***(P-11082)***
Wheeler & Reeder Inc..........F......323 268-4163
3334 Montrose Ave La Crescenta (91214) ***(P-13841)***
Wheeler Deeler, North Hollywood *Also called Mid Michigan Trading Post Ltd* ***(P-6281)***
Wheeler Lumber Co Inc..........F......707 943-3424
2407 Cathy Rd Miranda (95553) ***(P-3918)***
Wheeler Optical Lab..........F......714 891-2016
8200 Katella Ave Ste A Stanton (90680) ***(P-22395)***
Wheeler Winery Inc..........E......415 979-0630
849 Zinfandel Ln Saint Helena (94574) ***(P-1998)***
Wheels and Deals, Redding *Also called Great Northern Wheels Deals* ***(P-5649)***
Wheels Magazine Inc..........E......310 402-9013
1409 Centinela Ave Inglewood (90302) ***(P-20363)***
Wheelskins Inc..........F......510 841-2128
2821 10th St Berkeley (94710) ***(P-10257)***
Where Orange County Magazine, Los Angeles *Also called Tourism Development Corp* ***(P-6043)***
Whill Inc (PA)..........F......844 699-4455
951 Mariners Island Blvd # 300 San Mateo (94404) ***(P-20525)***
Whipple Industries Inc..........F......559 442-1261
3292 N Weber Ave Fresno (93722) ***(P-14690)***
Whisperkoll, Stockton *Also called Whisperkool Corporation* ***(P-1999)***
Whisperkool Corporation..........F......800 343-9463
1738 E Alpine Ave Stockton (95205) ***(P-1999)***
Whistle Labs Inc..........E......623 337-3679
1355 Market St Fl 2 San Francisco (94103) ***(P-19446)***
White Fire Tagets, San Bernardino *Also called Reagent Chemical & RES Inc* ***(P-7521)***
White Industrial Corporation..........F......530 676-6262
3869 Dividend Dr Ste 1 Shingle Springs (95682) ***(P-14259)***
White Labs Inc (PA)..........F......858 693-3441
9495 Candida St San Diego (92126) ***(P-2646)***
White Wave Foods, City of Industry *Also called Wwf Operating Company* ***(P-714)***
Whitefish Enterprises Inc..........F......510 357-6100
14557 Griffith St San Leandro (94577) ***(P-23525)***
Whitehall Lane Winery, Saint Helena *Also called Thomas Leonardini* ***(P-1955)***
Whitehall Manufacturing Inc..........A......626 336-4561
15125 Proctor Ave City of Industry (91746) ***(P-22126)***
Whites Hvac Services Inc..........F......805 801-0167
131 E Knotts St Nipomo (93444) ***(P-15474)***
Whitestone Industries Inc..........F......888 567-2234
2076 White Ln Spc 283 Bakersfield (93304) ***(P-23526)***
Whitmor Plstic Wire Cable Corp (PA)..........D......661 257-2400
27737 Avenue Hopkins Santa Clarita (91355) ***(P-13446)***

Mergent e-mail: customerrelations@mergent.com
1286
2020 California
Manufacturers Register
(P-0000) Products & Services Section entry number
(PA)=Parent Co (HQ)=Headquarters (DH)=Div Headquarters

Whitmor Plstic Wire Cable Corp....E....661 257-2400
28420 Stanford Ave Valencia (91355) *(P-13447)*
Whitmor Wire and Cable, Santa Clarita *Also called Whitmor Plstic Wire Cable Corp (P-13446)*
Whitmor Wirenetics, Valencia *Also called Whitmor Plstic Wire Cable Corp (P-13447)*
Whittaker Corporation....E....805 526-5700
1955 Surveyor Ave Fl 2 Simi Valley (93063) *(P-20270)*
Whitten Machine Shop....F....559 686-3428
4770 S K St Tulare (93274) *(P-16525)*
Whittier Enterprise LLC....E....844 767-5633
18901 Railroad St City of Industry (91748) *(P-984)*
Whittier Fertilizer Company....D....562 699-3461
9441 Kruse Rd Pico Rivera (90660) *(P-8809)*
Whittier Filtration Inc (HQ)....E....714 986-5300
120 S State College Blvd Brea (92821) *(P-15605)*
Whittier Mailing Products Inc (PA)....E....562 464-3000
13019 Park St Santa Fe Springs (90670) *(P-15393)*
Whizz Systems Inc....E....408 207-0400
3240 Scott Blvd Santa Clara (95054) *(P-18051)*
Who What Wear, West Hollywood *Also called Clique Brands Inc (P-5905)*
Wholesale Shade, San Marcos *Also called Showdogs Inc (P-5038)*
Wholesale Shutter Company Inc....F....951 845-8786
411 Olive Ave Beaumont (92223) *(P-4149)*
Wholesales Shutter Specialist, Spring Valley *Also called French Custom Shutters Inc (P-4045)*
Wholesome Harvest Baking Inc....F....916 967-1633
7840 Madison Ave Ste 135 Fair Oaks (95628) *(P-432)*
Wholesome Harvest Baking LLC....C....510 231-7200
3200 Regatta Blvd Ste G Richmond (94804) *(P-1296)*
Wholesome Harvest Baking LLC....C....805 487-5191
2701 Statham Blvd Oxnard (93033) *(P-1297)*
Wholesome Valley Foods (PA)....F....858 480-1543
1746 Berkeley St Unit B Santa Monica (90404) *(P-2647)*
Wholesome Yo Curd....F....909 859-8758
19755 Colima Rd Rowland Heights (91748) *(P-680)*
Wi2wi Inc (PA)....E....408 416-4200
1879 Lundy Ave Ste 218 San Jose (95131) *(P-17706)*
Wiakea Springs, Culver City *Also called Waiakea Inc (P-2182)*
Wick Communications Co....E....760 379-3667
6404 Lake Isabella Blvd Lake Isabella (93240) *(P-5866)*
Wick Communications Co....E....650 726-4424
714 Kelly St Half Moon Bay (94019) *(P-5867)*
Wickland Pipelines LLC (PA)....F....916 978-2432
8950 Cal Center Dr # 125 Sacramento (95826) *(P-148)*
Wickline Bedding Entp Corp....E....760 747-7761
1199 Elfin Forest Rd E San Marcos (92078) *(P-4749)*
Wide Open Industries LLC....E....949 635-2292
21088 Bake Pkwy Ste 100 Lake Forest (92630) *(P-19513)*
Wide USA Corporation....E....714 300-0540
2210 E Winston Rd Anaheim (92806) *(P-15138)*
Widescreen Review, Temecula *Also called Wsr Publishing Inc (P-6061)*
Wiegmann & Rose, Livermore *Also called Xchanger Manufacturing Corp (P-12072)*
Wiens Cellars LLC....E....951 694-9892
35055 Via Del Ponte Temecula (92592) *(P-2000)*
Wiggins Lift Co Inc....E....805 485-7821
2571 Cortez St Oxnard (93036) *(P-13897)*
Wikoff Color Corporation....F....916 928-6965
1329 N Market Blvd # 160 Sacramento (95834) *(P-8938)*
Wilbur Curtis Co Inc....B....323 837-2300
6913 W Acco St Montebello (90640) *(P-15606)*
Wilbur Manufacturing, Hayward *Also called Nova Tool Co (P-22953)*
Wilbur-Ellis Company LLC....D....559 442-1220
2903 S Cedar Ave Fresno (93725) *(P-13687)*
Wilco Building Corporation....F....805 765-4188
2005 Palma Dr Ste A Ventura (93003) *(P-4150)*
Wilcox AG Products, Walnut Grove *Also called Wilcox Brothers Inc (P-13688)*
Wilcox Brothers Inc....D....916 776-1784
14180 State Highway 160 Walnut Grove (95690) *(P-13688)*
Wilcox Machine Co....D....562 927-5353
7180 Scout Ave Bell Gardens (90201) *(P-16526)*
Wild Horse Industrial Corp....F....707 265-6801
640 Airpark Rd Ste A NAPA (94558) *(P-14737)*
Wild Lizard, Los Angeles *Also called Bb Co Inc (P-3293)*
Wild Side West....E....213 388-9792
1543 Truman St San Fernando (91340) *(P-22958)*
Wild Turkey Distillery, San Francisco *Also called Rare Breed Distilling LLC (P-2017)*
Wild Wood Designs Inc....F....714 543-6549
1607 E Edinger Ave Ste P Santa Ana (92705) *(P-4623)*
Wildbrine LLC (PA)....E....707 657-7607
322 Bellevue Ave Santa Rosa (95407) *(P-839)*
Wilden Pump and Engrg LLC (HQ)....B....909 422-1700
22069 Van Buren St Grand Terrace (92313) *(P-14605)*
Wilderness Trail Bikes Inc (PA)....F....415 389-5040
475 Miller Ave Mill Valley (94941) *(P-20437)*
Wildflower Linen Inc (PA)....E....714 522-2777
2655 Napa Valley Corp Dr NAPA (94558) *(P-2956)*
Wildlife Fur Dressing Inc....F....209 538-2901
3415 Harold St Ceres (95307) *(P-10146)*
Wildlife In Wood Inc....F....714 773-5816
165 E Liberty Ave Anaheim (92801) *(P-4543)*
Wildthings Snap-Ons Inc....F....415 457-0112
4 De Luca Pl San Rafael (94901) *(P-3490)*
Wildwood Designs, Santa Ana *Also called Wild Wood Designs Inc (P-4623)*
Wiley X Eyewear, Livermore *Also called X Wiley Inc (P-22396)*
Wilkinson Mfg Inc....F....408 988-3588
332 Piercy Rd San Jose (95138) *(P-16527)*
Will Pak Foods Inc....F....800 874-0883
4471 Santa Ana St Ste C Ontario (91761) *(P-877)*
Will's Fresh Foods, San Leandro *Also called Woolery Enterprises Inc (P-2648)*
Will-Mann Inc....E....714 870-0350
225 E Santa Fe Ave Fullerton (92832) *(P-12437)*
Willard Marine Inc....D....714 630-4018
1250 N Grove St Anaheim (92806) *(P-20364)*
Willey Printing Company Inc (PA)....E....209 524-4811
1405 10th St Modesto (95354) *(P-6939)*
William A Shubeck....E....909 795-6970
10961 Desert Lawn Dr # 102 Calimesa (92320) *(P-23256)*
William Bounds Ltd....E....310 375-0505
23625 Madison St Torrance (90505) *(P-14414)*
William Getz Corp....E....714 516-2050
539 W Walnut Ave Orange (92868) *(P-22926)*
William Ho....F....510 226-9089
40760 Encyclopedia Cir Fremont (94538) *(P-15366)*
William J Hammett Inc....F....626 966-1708
221 E San Bernardino Rd Covina (91723) *(P-6940)*
William Kreysler & Assoc Inc....E....707 552-3500
501 Green Island Rd American Canyon (94503) *(P-10124)*
William McClung....F....970 535-4601
987 Keller Ave Crescent City (95531) *(P-22727)*
William R Schmitt....E....530 243-3069
18135 Clear Creek Rd Redding (96001) *(P-3919)*
Williams & Selyem Winery....F....707 433-6425
7227 Westside Rd Healdsburg (95448) *(P-2001)*
Williams Cabinets Inc....F....530 365-8421
2011 Frontier Trl Anderson (96007) *(P-4266)*
Williams Comfort Products, Colton *Also called Williams Furnace Co (P-15475)*
Williams Foam Inc....F....818 833-4343
12961 San Fernando Rd Sylmar (91342) *(P-4750)*
Williams Furnace Co (HQ)....C....562 450-3602
250 W Laurel St Colton (92324) *(P-15475)*
Williams Manufacturing Company....F....818 898-2272
12727 Foothill Blvd Sylmar (91342) *(P-13368)*
Williams Metal Blanking Dies....F....562 634-4592
16222 Minnesota Ave Paramount (90723) *(P-12893)*
Williams Selyem, Healdsburg *Also called Williams & Selyem Winery (P-2001)*
Williams Sign Co....F....909 622-5304
111 S Huntington St Pomona (91766) *(P-23244)*
Willick Engineering Co Inc....F....562 946-4242
12516 Lakeland Rd Santa Fe Springs (90670) *(P-22225)*
Willie Bylsma....F....209 847-3362
10217 Atlas Ct Oakdale (95361) *(P-14415)*
Willis Construction Co Inc....C....831 623-2900
2261 San Juan Hwy San Juan Bautista (95045) *(P-10669)*
Willis Machine Inc....E....805 604-4500
200 Kinetic Dr Oxnard (93030) *(P-16528)*
Willits News, Willits *Also called Media News Group (P-5739)*
Willits Redwood Company Inc....E....707 459-4549
220 Franklin Ave Willits (95490) *(P-3967)*
Willow, Mountain View *Also called Exploramed Nc7 Inc (P-22255)*
Willow & Clay, Vernon *Also called Complete Clothing Company (P-3224)*
Willow Technology Inc (PA)....E....360 393-4962
215 Cummins Ln McKinleyville (95519) *(P-24580)*
Willpower Labs Inc....F....415 805-1518
3318 California St Apt 4 San Francisco (94118) *(P-8188)*
Wills Wing, Orange *Also called Sport Kites Inc (P-19932)*
Wilmanco....F....805 523-2390
5350 Kazuko Ct Moorpark (93021) *(P-17707)*
Wilmar Oils Fats Stockton LLC....E....925 627-1600
2008 Port Road B Stockton (95203) *(P-1450)*
Wilmington Ironworks, Wilmington *Also called Wilmington Machine Inc (P-16529)*
Wilmington Machine Inc....F....310 518-3213
432 W C St Wilmington (90744) *(P-16529)*
Wilmington Woodworks Inc....E....310 834-1015
318 E C St Wilmington (90744) *(P-4409)*
Wilorco, Carson *Also called Strike Technology Inc (P-19095)*
Wilsenergy LLC....F....951 676-7700
42440 Winchester Rd Temecula (92590) *(P-13268)*
Wilsey Foods Inc....A....714 257-3700
40 Pointe Dr Brea (92821) *(P-1487)*
Wilshire Book Company Inc....E....818 700-1522
22647 Ventura Blvd Woodland Hills (91364) *(P-6163)*
Wilshire Precision Pdts Inc....E....818 765-4571
7353 Hinds Ave North Hollywood (91605) *(P-16530)*
Wilson Artisan Wineries, Healdsburg *Also called Stonecushion Inc (P-1938)*
Wilson Creek Wnery Vnyards Inc....C....951 699-9463
35960 Rancho Cal Rd Temecula (92591) *(P-2002)*
Wilson Imaging and Publishing....F....909 931-1818
305 N 2nd Ave Pmb 324 Upland (91786) *(P-6383)*
Wilsons Art Studio Inc....D....714 870-7030
501 S Acacia Ave Fullerton (92831) *(P-7272)*
Wilsted & Taylor Pubg Svcs....F....510 428-9087
430 40th St Oakland (94609) *(P-7366)*
Wilwood Engineering....C....805 388-1188
4700 Calle Bolero Camarillo (93012) *(P-19805)*
Win Fat Food LLC....E....323 261-1869
700 Monterey Pass Rd A Monterey Park (91754) *(P-532)*
Win Soon Inc....E....323 564-5070
4569 Firestone Blvd South Gate (90280) *(P-713)*
Win-Glo Window Coverings, San Jose *Also called Hunter Douglas Fabrications (P-5026)*
Win-Holt Equipment Corp....F....909 625-2624
2717 N Towne Ave Pomona (91767) *(P-13898)*
Winbo Usa Inc....E....951 738-9978
2120 California Ave Ste 2 Corona (92881) *(P-12438)*
Winc Inc....F....855 282-5829
5340 Alla Rd Ste 105 Los Angeles (90066) *(P-2003)*
Winchester Electronics Div, Sacramento *Also called L3 Technologies Inc (P-14936)*
Wind & Shade Screens Inc....F....760 761-4994
1223 Linda Vista Dr San Marcos (92078) *(P-2740)*

Wind River Systems Inc (HQ) ....C.......510 748-4100
500 Wind River Way Alameda (94501) ***(P-24581)***
Wind River Systems Inc ....D.......858 824-3100
10505 Sorrento Valley Rd San Diego (92121) ***(P-24582)***
Windline Marine ....C.......310 516-9812
14601 S Broadway Gardena (90248) ***(P-11643)***
Windmill Corporation ....E.......650 873-1000
314 Harbor Way South San Francisco (94080) ***(P-1298)***
Window & Door Shop Inc (PA) ....F.......415 282-6192
185 Industrial St San Francisco (94124) ***(P-4151)***
Window Hardware Supply ....F.......510 463-0301
1717 Kirkham St Oakland (94607) ***(P-10125)***
Window Products Management Inc ....F.......805 677-6800
5917 Olivas Park Dr Ste F Ventura (93003) ***(P-4152)***
Windshield Pros Incorporated ....E.......951 272-2867
4501 E Airport Dr Ontario (91761) ***(P-19806)***
Windsor Foods, Hayward *Also called Ajinomoto Foods North Amer Inc* ***(P-936)***
Windsor Foods, Ontario *Also called Ajinomoto Foods North Amer Inc* ***(P-937)***
Windsor Foods, Ontario *Also called Windsor Quality Food Co Ltd* ***(P-985)***
Windsor House Investments Inc ....E.......323 261-0231
12250 Coast Dr Whittier (90601) ***(P-5456)***
Windsor Mill, Cotati *Also called Windsor Willits Company* ***(P-4153)***
Windsor Mill, Willits *Also called Windsor Willits Company* ***(P-4154)***
Windsor Oaks Vineyards LLP ....E.......707 433-4050
10810 Hillview Rd Windsor (95492) ***(P-2004)***
Windsor Quality Food Co Ltd ....A.......713 843-5200
4200 Concours Ste 100 Ontario (91764) ***(P-985)***
Windsor Textile Corporation ....F.......310 323-3997
13122 S Normandie Ave Gardena (90249) ***(P-2886)***
Windsor Vineyards, Santa Rosa *Also called Mildara Blass Inc* ***(P-1819)***
Windsor Willits Company (PA) ....E.......707 665-9663
7950 Redwood Dr Ste 4 Cotati (94931) ***(P-4153)***
Windsor Willits Company ....E.......707 459-8568
661 Railroad Ave Willits (95490) ***(P-4154)***
Windtamer Tarps ....F.......559 584-2080
13704 Hanford Armona Rd B2 Hanford (93230) ***(P-3716)***
Windward Yacht & Repair Inc ....F.......310 823-4581
13645 Fiji Way Venice (90292) ***(P-20365)***
Windward Yacht Center, Venice *Also called Windward Yacht & Repair Inc* ***(P-20365)***
Windy Balloon Company, Gardena *Also called South Bay Corporation* ***(P-9373)***
Wine Business Monthly, Sonoma *Also called Wine Communications Group* ***(P-6058)***
Wine Cellar Impressions Inc ....F.......408 277-0100
2013 Stone Ave San Jose (95125) ***(P-2005)***
Wine Communications Group ....F.......707 939-0822
35 Maple St Sonoma (95476) ***(P-6058)***
Wine Company of San Francisco ....F.......650 851-0965
231 Ware Rd Ste 823 Woodside (94062) ***(P-2006)***
Wine Country Cases Inc ....D.......707 967-4805
621 Airpark Rd NAPA (94558) ***(P-4432)***
Wine Foundry, NAPA *Also called Vignette Winery LLC* ***(P-1983)***
Wine Group Inc (HQ) ....C.......209 599-4111
17000 E State Highway 120 Ripon (95366) ***(P-2007)***
Winery Direct Distributors, Lodi *Also called Ah Wines Inc* ***(P-1578)***
Winery Services Group, Salinas *Also called SMS Industrial Inc* ***(P-12052)***
Wing Hing Noodle Company, Ontario *Also called Passport Food Group LLC* ***(P-2582)***
Wing Inflatables Inc (HQ) ....C.......707 826-2887
1220 5th St Arcata (95521) ***(P-10126)***
Wing Master, Clovis *Also called Valley Chrome Plating Inc* ***(P-13127)***
Wing Nien Company, Hayward *Also called U S Enterprise Corporation* ***(P-903)***
Winner Industrial Chemicals ....E.......909 887-6228
154 W Foothill Blvd Ste A Upland (91786) ***(P-8785)***
Winning Laboratories Inc ....F.......562 921-6880
16218 Arthur St Cerritos (90703) ***(P-7705)***
Winning Team Inc ....F.......661 295-1428
24922 Anza Dr Ste E Valencia (91355) ***(P-3764)***
Winnov Inc ....F.......888 315-9460
3945 Freedom Cir Ste 560 Santa Clara (95054) ***(P-17305)***
Winonics Inc ....C.......714 626-3755
1257 S State College Blvd Fullerton (92831) ***(P-18052)***
Winslow Automation Inc ....D.......408 262-9004
905 Montague Expy Milpitas (95035) ***(P-18657)***
Winstar Textile Inc ....E.......626 357-1133
16815 E Johnson Dr City of Industry (91745) ***(P-3491)***
Winstronics, Fremont *Also called Wintronics International Inc* ***(P-11326)***
Wint Corporation ....C.......408 816-4818
2880 Zanker Rd Ste 203 San Jose (95134) ***(P-21420)***
Wintec Industries Inc (PA) ....D.......510 953-7440
8674 Thornton Ave Newark (94560) ***(P-15367)***
Winter & Bain Manufacturing (PA) ....F.......213 749-3568
1417 Elwood St Los Angeles (90021) ***(P-13811)***
Winter & Bain Manufacturing ....F.......213 749-3561
1410 Elwood St Los Angeles (90021) ***(P-13812)***
Wintflash Inc ....F.......562 944-6548
13720 De Alcala Dr La Mirada (90638) ***(P-7273)***
Winther Technologies Inc (PA) ....E.......310 618-8437
560 Alaska Ave Torrance (90503) ***(P-14260)***
Winton Times ....E.......209 358-5311
6950 Gerard Ave Winton (95388) ***(P-5868)***
Wintriss Engineering Corp ....E.......858 550-7300
9010 Kenamar Dr Ste 101 San Diego (92121) ***(P-21421)***
Wintronics International Inc ....E.......510 226-7588
3817 Spinnaker Ct Fremont (94538) ***(P-11326)***
Winway Usa Inc ....E.......203 775-9311
1800 Wyatt Dr Ste 2 Santa Clara (95054) ***(P-18658)***
Wire Bonding Tools, Petaluma *Also called Small Precision Tools Inc* ***(P-11021)***
Wire Cut Company Inc ....E.......714 994-1170
6750 Caballero Blvd Buena Park (90620) ***(P-16531)***
Wire Guard Systems Inc ....F.......323 588-2166
2050 E Slauson Ave Huntington Park (90255) ***(P-16957)***
Wire Harness & Cable Assembly, Santa Monica *Also called Omega Leads Inc* ***(P-19037)***
Wire Technology Corporation ....E.......310 635-6935
9527 Laurel St Los Angeles (90002) ***(P-11327)***
Wired Ventures Inc ....C.......415 276-8400
520 3rd St Ste 305 San Francisco (94107) ***(P-6059)***
Wireless Glue Networks Inc ....F.......925 310-4561
4185 Blackhawk Plaza Cir # 220 Danville (94506) ***(P-24583)***
Wireless Innovation Inc ....F.......916 357-6700
1024 Iron Point Rd Folsom (95630) ***(P-19143)***
Wireless Systems Segment, San Jose *Also called Te Connectivity Corporation* ***(P-18795)***
Wireless Technology Inc ....E.......805 339-9696
2064 Eastman Ave Ste 113 Ventura (93003) ***(P-17306)***
Wireman Fence Products, Rancho Cordova *Also called Fencer Enterprises LLC* ***(P-11093)***
Wirenetics Co, Valencia *Also called Circle W Enterprises Inc* ***(P-13404)***
Wiretech Inc (PA) ....D.......323 722-4933
6440 Canning St Commerce (90040) ***(P-11116)***
Wirewright Inc ....F.......805 499-9194
3563 Old Conejo Rd Newbury Park (91320) ***(P-10127)***
Wirta Logging Inc ....E.......928 440-3446
970 Kandy Ln Portola (96122) ***(P-3920)***
Wirz & Co ....F.......909 825-6970
444 Colton Ave Colton (92324) ***(P-6941)***
Wise Living Inc ....E.......323 541-0410
2001 W 60th St Los Angeles (90047) ***(P-4777)***
Wise Solar Inc ....F.......888 406-7879
4401 Atlantic Ave Ste 200 Long Beach (90807) ***(P-11725)***
Wissings Inc ....F.......858 625-4111
9906 Mesa Rim Rd San Diego (92121) ***(P-6942)***
Wit Group ....E.......530 243-4447
1822 Buenaventura Blvd # 101 Redding (96001) ***(P-2184)***
Witt Hillard ....E.......530 510-0756
310 Providence Mine Rd Nevada City (95959) ***(P-8424)***
Witten Logging ....F.......760 378-3640
4600 Kelso Creek Rd Weldon (93283) ***(P-3921)***
Witts Everything For Office, Tehachapi *Also called Pmrca Inc* ***(P-6787)***
Wixen Music Publishing Inc ....F.......818 591-7355
24025 Park Sorrento # 130 Calabasas (91302) ***(P-6164)***
Wizard Enterprise ....F.......323 756-8430
12605 Daphne Ave Hawthorne (90250) ***(P-10458)***
Wizard Graphics Inc ....F.......530 893-3636
411 Otterson Dr Ste 20 Chico (95928) ***(P-7274)***
Wizard Manufacturing Inc ....F.......530 342-1861
2244 Ivy St Chico (95928) ***(P-1441)***
Wizeline Inc (PA) ....E.......415 373-6365
456 Montgomery St # 2200 San Francisco (94104) ***(P-14998)***
Wjb Bearings Inc ....E.......909 598-6238
535 Brea Canyon Rd City of Industry (91789) ***(P-12739)***
Wjlp Company Inc ....D.......800 628-1123
4848 Frontier Way Ste 100 Stockton (95215) ***(P-18748)***
Wkf (friedman Enterprises Inc (PA) ....F.......925 673-9100
2334 Stagecoach Rd Ste B Stockton (95215) ***(P-19991)***
Wls Coatings Inc ....F.......310 538-2155
1680 Miller Ave Los Angeles (90063) ***(P-8694)***
Wm J Clark Trucking Svc Inc ....F.......831 385-4000
319 Division St King City (93930) ***(P-370)***
Wm J Matson Company ....F.......805 684-9410
213 N Olive St Ventura (93001) ***(P-13269)***
WMC Precision Machining ....F.......714 773-0059
1234 E Ash Ave Ste A Fullerton (92831) ***(P-16532)***
Wme Bi LLC ....D.......877 592-2472
17075 Camino San Diego (92127) ***(P-24584)***
Wna City of Industry, City of Industry *Also called Wna Comet West Inc* ***(P-10128)***
Wna City of Industry, City of Industry *Also called Waddington North America Inc* ***(P-10115)***
Wna Comet West Inc ....C.......626 913-0724
1135 Samuelson St City of Industry (91748) ***(P-10128)***
Wohler Technologies Inc ....E.......510 870-0810
1280 San Luis Obispo St Hayward (94544) ***(P-17708)***
Wolfe Engineering, Inc., San Jose *Also called Jabil Silver Creek Inc* ***(P-24644)***
Wolfpack Inc ....E.......760 736-4500
2440 Grand Ave Ste B Vista (92081) ***(P-23245)***
Wolfpack Gear Inc ....F.......805 439-1911
3765 S Higuera St Ste 150 San Luis Obispo (93401) ***(P-5445)***
Wolfpack Sign Group, Vista *Also called Wolfpack Inc* ***(P-23245)***
Wolfram Inc ....F.......209 238-9610
1309 Doker Dr Ste B Modesto (95351) ***(P-10334)***
Wolfs Precision Works Inc ....F.......650 364-1341
3549 Haven Ave Ste F Menlo Park (94025) ***(P-16533)***
Wolfson Knitting Mills Inc ....F.......213 627-8746
2124 Sacramento St Los Angeles (90021) ***(P-2718)***
Wolverine World Wide Inc ....F.......800 253-2184
1020 Prosperity Way Beaumont (92223) ***(P-10165)***
Womack International Inc ....E.......707 763-1800
3855 Cypress Dr Ste H Petaluma (94954) ***(P-14873)***
Wombat Products Inc ....E.......805 794-1767
1384 Callens Rd Ste B Ventura (93003) ***(P-10129)***
Wonder Grip USA Inc ....F.......404 290-2015
3070 Bristol St Ste 440 Costa Mesa (92626) ***(P-10130)***
Wonder Marketing Inc ....E.......310 235-1469
11601 Wilshire Blvd # 2150 Los Angeles (90025) ***(P-8695)***
Wonder Metals Corporation ....F.......530 241-3251
4351 Caterpillar Rd Redding (96003) ***(P-11989)***
Wonderful Pstchios Almonds LLC (HQ) ....E.......310 966-4650
11444 W Olympic Blvd Los Angeles (90064) ***(P-1442)***
Wondergrove LLC ....F.......800 889-7249
17563 Ventura Blvd Fl 1 Encino (91316) ***(P-24585)***
Wood Box Specialties Inc ....F.......510 786-1600
23308 Kidder St Hayward (94545) ***(P-4433)***

Wood Connection Inc ....E....209 577-1044
4701 N Star Way Modesto (95356) *(P-4155)*
Wood Minerals Conveyors Inc ....D....619 596-7400
10770 Rockville St Ste A Santee (92071) *(P-13842)*
Wood Tech Inc ....D....510 534-4930
4611 Malat St Oakland (94601) *(P-4624)*
Wood-N-Wood Products Cal, Fresno *Also called Wood-N-Wood Products Inc (P-4436)*
Wood-N-Wood Products Cal Inc (PA) ....E....559 896-3636
2247 W Birch Ave Fresno (93711) *(P-4434)*
Wood-N-Wood Products Cal Inc ....E....559 896-3636
13598 S Golden State Blvd Selma (93662) *(P-4435)*
Wood-N-Wood Products Inc ....F....559 896-3636
2247 W Birch Ave Fresno (93711) *(P-4436)*
Woodbridge Glass, Tustin *Also called Werner Systems Inc (P-11269)*
Woodbridge Winery, Acampo *Also called Franciscan Vineyards Inc (P-1711)*
Woodcrafters International ....F....949 498-0739
946 Calle Amanecer Ste C San Clemente (92673) *(P-4956)*
Wooden Bridge Inc ....F....408 436-9663
483 Reynolds Cir San Jose (95112) *(P-4267)*
Wooden Wick Co ....F....714 594-7790
1440 S Coast Hwy Ste A Laguna Beach (92651) *(P-23527)*
Woodford Wicks LLC ....F....614 554-8474
302 Williams Way Hayward (94541) *(P-23528)*
Woodford Wicks Candle Company, Hayward *Also called Woodford Wicks LLC (P-23528)*
Woodie Woodpeckers Woodworks ....E....818 999-2090
21268 Deering Ct Canoga Park (91304) *(P-4268)*
Woodland Bedrooms Inc ....D....562 408-1558
3423 Merced St Los Angeles (90065) *(P-4625)*
Woodland Products Co Inc ....F....909 622-3456
10825 7th St Ste C Rancho Cucamonga (91730) *(P-4957)*
Woodland Welding Works ....F....530 666-5531
1955 E Main St Woodland (95776) *(P-11922)*
Woodline Cabinets, Fairfield *Also called Woodline Partners Inc (P-4269)*
Woodline Partners Inc ....E....707 864-5445
5165 Fulton Dr Fairfield (94534) *(P-4269)*
Woodmark Manufacturing, Sacramento *Also called Silver Eagle Corporation (P-3641)*
Woodpecker Cabinet Inc ....E....310 404-4805
21512 Nordhoff St Chatsworth (91311) *(P-4270)*
Woodruff Corporation ....E....310 378-1611
109 Calle Mayor Redondo Beach (90277) *(P-16534)*
Woodside Investment Inc ....D....209 787-8040
12405 E Brandt Rd Lockeford (95237) *(P-13558)*
Woodsmiths Architectural Casew ....F....916 456-8871
2709 Del Monte St West Sacramento (95691) *(P-4958)*
Woodsource International ....F....310 328-9663
2201 Dominguez St Torrance (90501) *(P-4284)*
Woodtech Industries, Santa Clara *Also called Wti Jkb Inc (P-4157)*
Woodward Drilling Company ....E....707 374-4300
550 River Rd Rio Vista (94571) *(P-108)*
Woodward Duarte, Duarte *Also called Woodward Hrt Inc (P-20271)*
Woodward Hrt Inc (HQ) ....A....661 294-6000
25200 Rye Canyon Rd Santa Clarita (91355) *(P-16769)*
Woodward Hrt Inc ....D....661 702-5552
25200 Rye Canyon Rd Santa Clarita (91355) *(P-16770)*
Woodward Hrt Inc ....C....626 359-9211
1700 Business Center Dr Duarte (91010) *(P-20271)*
Woodwork Pioneers Corp ....E....714 991-1017
1757 S Claudina Way Anaheim (92805) *(P-4156)*
Woodworks ....F....831 688-8420
107 Nunes Rd Watsonville (95076) *(P-4626)*
Woof & Poof Inc ....E....530 895-0693
388 Orange St Chico (95928) *(P-3650)*
Woojin Is America Inc ....F....626 386-0101
5108 Azusa Canyon Rd Irwindale (91706) *(P-20379)*
Woolery Enterprises Inc ....E....510 357-5700
1991 Republic Ave San Leandro (94577) *(P-2648)*
Wordsmart Corporation ....D....858 565-8068
10025 Mesa Rim Rd San Diego (92121) *(P-24586)*
Workbook Inc ....E....323 856-0008
110 N Doheny Dr Beverly Hills (90211) *(P-6165)*
Working Nurse, Los Angeles *Also called Recruitment Services Inc (P-6015)*
Working World, Los Angeles *Also called Rhodes Publications Inc (P-6018)*
Workman Holdings Inc ....F....760 723-5283
525 Industrial Way Fallbrook (92028) *(P-21964)*
Works Connection ....F....530 642-9488
4130 Product Dr Cameron Park (95682) *(P-20438)*
Works Performance Products Inc ....E....818 701-1010
21045 Osborne St Canoga Park (91304) *(P-19807)*
Works, The, Eureka *Also called Eureka Record Works Inc (P-17229)*
Workshare Technology Inc ....C....415 590-7700
650 California St Fl 7 San Francisco (94108) *(P-24587)*
Workspot Inc (PA) ....F....888 426-8113
1901 S Bascom Ave Ste 900 Campbell (95008) *(P-24588)*
World Amenities, San Diego *Also called Robanda International Inc (P-8573)*
World Centric ....F....707 241-9190
1400 Valley House Dr # 220 Rohnert Park (94928) *(P-5540)*
World Harmony Organization ....F....415 246-6886
514 Arballo Dr San Francisco (94132) *(P-6166)*
World Journal Inc (PA) ....D....650 692-9936
231 Adrian Rd Millbrae (94030) *(P-5869)*
World Journal La LLC (HQ) ....C....323 268-4982
1588 Corporate Center Dr Monterey Park (91754) *(P-5870)*
World Manufacturing Inc (PA) ....F....714 662-3539
350 Fischer Ave Ste B Costa Mesa (92626) *(P-9461)*
World Oil Corp ....E....562 928-0100
9302 Garfield Ave South Gate (90280) *(P-78)*
World Peas Brand, Los Angeles *Also called Snack It Forward LLC (P-2345)*
World Service Office, Chatsworth *Also called Narcotics Anonymous World Serv (P-6124)*
World Tariff Limited ....E....415 391-7501
220 Montgomery St Ste 448 San Francisco (94104) *(P-6060)*
World Textile and Bag Inc ....E....916 922-9222
4680 Pell Dr Ste B Sacramento (95838) *(P-3669)*
World Trade Printing Company, Garden Grove *Also called Wtpc Inc (P-6945)*
World Traditions Inc ....E....951 990-6346
332 Camino De La Luna Perris (92571) *(P-10496)*
World Trend Inc (PA) ....F....909 620-9945
1920 W Holt Ave Pomona (91768) *(P-23034)*
World Upholstery & Trim Inc ....F....805 921-0100
1320 E Main St Santa Paula (93060) *(P-3825)*
World Wine Bottles LLC ....E....707 339-2102
1370 Trancas St Ste 411 NAPA (94558) *(P-10294)*
World Wine Bottles & Packaging, NAPA *Also called World Wine Bottles LLC (P-10294)*
Worldflash Software Inc ....E....310 745-0632
3853 Marcasel Ave Ste 101 Los Angeles (90066) *(P-24589)*
Worldlink Media ....F....415 561-2141
38 Keyes Ave Ste 17 San Francisco (94129) *(P-24590)*
Worldtariff, San Francisco *Also called World Tariff Limited (P-6060)*
Worldview Project ....F....858 964-0709
2445 Morena Blvd Ste 210 San Diego (92110) *(P-6167)*
Worldwide Aeros Corp ....D....818 344-3999
1734 Aeros Way Montebello (90640) *(P-19938)*
Worldwide Energy & Mfg USA Inc (PA) ....E....650 692-7788
1675 Rollins Rd Ste F Burlingame (94010) *(P-18659)*
Worldwide Envmtl Pdts Inc (PA) ....D....714 990-2700
1100 Beacon St Brea (92821) *(P-20958)*
Worldwide Gaming Systems Corp ....E....818 678-9150
9205 Alabama Ave Ste E Chatsworth (91311) *(P-22728)*
Worldwide Specialties Inc ....C....323 587-2200
2420 Modoc St Los Angeles (90021) *(P-2649)*
Worthington Cylinder Corp ....C....909 594-7777
336 Enterprise Pl Pomona (91768) *(P-12071)*
Wpi Salem Division, Camarillo *Also called Cooper Crouse-Hinds LLC (P-9297)*
Wpm, Ventura *Also called Window Products Management Inc (P-4152)*
Wrenchware Inc ....F....951 784-2717
2751 Reche Canyon Rd # 104 Colton (92324) *(P-10472)*
Wrex Products Inc Chico ....D....530 895-3838
25 Wrex Ct Chico (95928) *(P-10131)*
Wright Business Forms Inc ....E....909 614-6700
13602 12th St Ste A Chino (91710) *(P-7294)*
Wright Business Graphics Calif, Chino *Also called Wright Business Forms Inc (P-7294)*
Wright Capacitors Inc ....F....714 546-2490
2610 Oak St Santa Ana (92707) *(P-18687)*
Wright Engineered Plastics Inc ....D....707 575-1218
3681 N Laughlin Rd Santa Rosa (95403) *(P-14126)*
Wright Pharma Inc ....E....209 549-9771
700 Kiernan Ave Ste A Modesto (95356) *(P-8189)*
Wright Technologies Inc ....F....916 773-4424
1352 Blue Oaks Blvd # 140 Roseville (95678) *(P-19144)*
Wrightspeed Inc ....E....866 960-9482
650 W Tower Ave Alameda (94501) *(P-19808)*
Wrought Iron Fencing & Supply ....E....760 591-3110
1370 La Mirada Dr San Marcos (92078) *(P-12524)*
Ws Packaging-Blake Printery (HQ) ....F....805 543-6843
2222 Beebee St San Luis Obispo (93401) *(P-6943)*
Ws Packaging-Blake Printery ....E....805 543-6844
2224 Beebee St San Luis Obispo (93401) *(P-6944)*
Wsglass Holdings Inc ....F....916 388-5885
180 Main Ave Sacramento (95838) *(P-21422)*
Wsglass Holdings Inc (HQ) ....E....510 623-5000
3241 Darby Cmn Fremont (94539) *(P-10281)*
Wsr Publishing Inc (PA) ....F....951 676-4914
27645 Commerce Center Dr Temecula (92590) *(P-6061)*
Wsw Corp (PA) ....E....818 989-5008
16000 Strathern St Van Nuys (91406) *(P-19809)*
Wti, Ventura *Also called Wireless Technology Inc (P-17306)*
Wti Jkb Inc (PA) ....F....408 297-8579
405 Aldo Ave Santa Clara (95054) *(P-4157)*
Wtpc Inc ....E....714 903-2500
12082 Western Ave Garden Grove (92841) *(P-6945)*
Wunder-Mold Inc ....E....707 448-2349
790 Eubanks Dr Vacaville (95688) *(P-10132)*
WV Communications Inc ....E....805 376-1820
1125 Bus Ctr Cir Ste A Newbury Park (91320) *(P-17709)*
Wwf Operating Company ....C....626 810-1775
18275 Arenth Ave Bldg 1 City of Industry (91748) *(P-714)*
Wwt International Inc ....F....714 632-0810
1150 N Tustin Ave Anaheim (92807) *(P-13797)*
Www.asbworkshop.com, San Francisco *Also called A S Batle Company (P-10994)*
Www.b-Dazzle.com, Redondo Beach *Also called B Dazzle Inc (P-22660)*
Www.masterlocks.com, San Diego *Also called Hodge Products Inc (P-11596)*
Www.slp-Formx.com, Anaheim *Also called Slp Limited LLC (P-18001)*
Www.zerran.com, Pacoima *Also called Zerran International Corp (P-8611)*
Wyatt Precision Machine Inc ....E....562 634-0524
3301 E 59th St Long Beach (90805) *(P-12661)*
Wyatt Technology Corporation (PA) ....C....805 681-9009
6330 Hollister Ave Goleta (93117) *(P-21325)*
Wycen Foods Inc (PA) ....F....510 351-1987
560 Estabrook St San Leandro (94577) *(P-507)*
Wylatti Resource MGT Inc ....E....707 983-8135
23601 Cemetery Ln Covelo (95428) *(P-3922)*
Wymore Inc ....E....760 352-2045
697 S Dogwood Rd El Centro (92243) *(P-24680)*
Wyndham Collection LLC ....E....888 522-8476
1175 Aviation Pl San Fernando (91340) *(P-4271)*
Wypo, Long Beach *Also called Maitlen & Benson Inc (P-14247)*
Wyred 4 Sound LLC ....F....805 466-9973
4235 Traffic Way Atascadero (93422) *(P-17307)*

Employee Codes: A=Over 500 employees, B=251-500
C=101-250, D=51-100, E=20-50, F=10-19
2020 California
Manfacturers Register
© Mergent Inc. 1-800-342-5647
1289

Wyrefab Inc ....E 310 523-2147
15711 S Broadway Gardena (90248) ***(P-13448)***

Wyroc Inc (PA) ....F 760 727-0878
2142 Industrial Ct Ste D Vista (92081) ***(P-296)***

Wyroc Materials, Vista *Also called Regional Mtls Recovery Inc* ***(P-293)***

Wyvern Technologies Inc ....E 714 966-0710
1205 E Warner Ave Santa Ana (92705) ***(P-19145)***

X Cell Tool & Manufacturing Co, Gardena *Also called Parker-Hannifin Corporation* ***(P-16285)***

X Controls Inc ....F 858 717-0004
6640 Lusk Blvd Ste A101 San Diego (92121) ***(P-20823)***

X Sublimation Inc ....F 213 700-1024
2837 S Olive St Los Angeles (90007) ***(P-3585)***

X Tri Inc ....F 805 286-4544
8787 Plata Ln Ste 7 Atascadero (93422) ***(P-8939)***

X Wiley Inc (PA) ....D 925 243-9810
7800 Patterson Pass Rd Livermore (94550) ***(P-22396)***

X-Igent Printing Inc ....F 323 837-9779
1001 Goodrich Blvd Commerce (90022) ***(P-6946)***

X-Ray Technology Group, Scotts Valley *Also called Oxford Instruments X-Ray Tech* ***(P-19044)***

Xandex Inc ....D 707 763-7799
1360 Redwood Way Ste A Petaluma (94954) ***(P-21156)***

Xavient Digital LLC ....A 805 955-4111
21700 Oxnard St Ste 1700 Woodland Hills (91367) ***(P-24591)***

Xavient Info Systems Inc, Woodland Hills *Also called Xavient Digital LLC* ***(P-24591)***

Xceive Corporation ....E 408 486-5610
3900 Freedom Cir Ste 200 Santa Clara (95054) ***(P-19146)***

Xcelaero Corporation ....F 805 547-2660
4540 Broad St Ste 120 San Luis Obispo (93401) ***(P-14691)***

Xceliron Corp ....F 818 700-8404
9540 Vassar Ave Chatsworth (91311) ***(P-14213)***

Xcelmobility Inc ....D 650 320-1728
2225 E Byshore Rd Ste 200 Palo Alto (94303) ***(P-24592)***

Xchanger Manufacturing Corp ....E 510 632-8828
263 S Vasco Rd Livermore (94551) ***(P-12072)***

Xcom Wireless Inc ....F 562 981-0077
2700 Rose Ave Ste E Signal Hill (90755) ***(P-17710)***

Xcvi LLC (PA) ....C 213 749-2661
2311 S Santa Fe Ave Los Angeles (90058) ***(P-2719)***

Xdr Radiology, Los Angeles *Also called Cyber Medical Imaging Inc* ***(P-22140)***

XEL Group, Aliso Viejo *Also called XEL USA Inc* ***(P-18660)***

XEL USA Inc ....E 949 425-8686
21 Argonaut Ste B Aliso Viejo (92656) ***(P-18660)***

Xeltek, Sunnyvale *Also called Exp Computer* ***(P-21470)***

Xencor Inc ....C 626 305-5900
111 W Lemon Ave Monrovia (91016) ***(P-8190)***

Xenonics Inc ....F 760 477-8900
3186 Lionshead Ave # 100 Carlsbad (92010) ***(P-19447)***

Xenonics Holdings Inc ....F 760 477-8900
3186 Lionshead Ave # 100 Carlsbad (92010) ***(P-17177)***

Xentric Drapery Hardware Inc ....F 818 897-0444
11001 Sutter Ave Pacoima (91331) ***(P-5044)***

Xerox Corporation ....F 909 605-7900
2980 Inland Empire Blvd # 105 Ontario (91764) ***(P-22474)***

Xerox International Partners (HQ) ....E 408 953-2700
3174 Porter Dr Palo Alto (94304) ***(P-14342)***

Xerxes Corporation ....D 714 630-0012
1210 N Tustin Ave Anaheim (92807) ***(P-7625)***

Xfit Brands Inc ....F 949 916-9680
25731 Commercentre Dr Lake Forest (92630) ***(P-22927)***

Xgrass Turf Direct, Anaheim *Also called Leonards Carpet Service Inc* ***(P-4921)***

Xhale Distributors ....F 888 942-5355
464 E 4th St Los Angeles (90013) ***(P-626)***

Xia LLC ....F 510 494-9020
31057 Genstar Rd Hayward (94544) ***(P-21565)***

Xicato Inc (PA) ....E 408 829-4758
101 Daggett Dr San Jose (95134) ***(P-17001)***

Xilinx Inc ....D 510 770-9449
42063 Benbow Dr Fremont (94539) ***(P-18661)***

Xilinx Inc (PA) ....A 408 559-7778
2100 All Programable San Jose (95124) ***(P-18053)***

Xilinx Inc ....F 408 879-6563
2050 All Programable # 4 San Jose (95124) ***(P-18662)***

Xilinx Development Corporation (HQ) ....F 408 559-7778
2100 All Programable San Jose (95124) ***(P-18663)***

Ximed Medical Systems, San Jose *Also called Prosurg Inc* ***(P-21865)***

Ximenez Icons ....F 310 344-6670
1107 Fair Oaks Ave Ste 11 South Pasadena (91030) ***(P-3651)***

Xintec Corporation (PA) ....E 510 832-2130
1660 S Loop Rd Alameda (94502) ***(P-22333)***

Xirgo Technologies LLC ....E 805 319-4079
188 Camino Ruiz Fl 2 Camarillo (93012) ***(P-19448)***

Xirrus Inc ....C 805 262-1600
2101 Corporate Center Dr A Thousand Oaks (91320) ***(P-20959)***

Xl Dynamics Inc ....E 562 916-1402
18303 Gridley Rd Cerritos (90703) ***(P-24593)***

Xlsoft Corporation (PA) ....F 949 453-2781
12 Mauchly Ste K Irvine (92618) ***(P-24594)***

Xmultiple Technologies (PA) ....F 805 579-1100
543 Country Club Dr B-128 Simi Valley (93065) ***(P-14999)***

Xmultiple/Xrjax, Simi Valley *Also called Xmultiple Technologies* ***(P-14999)***

Xolar Corporation ....E 916 983-6301
1012 E Bidwell St Ste 600 Folsom (95630) ***(P-23529)***

Xoma Corporation (PA) ....F 510 204-7200
2200 Powell St Ste 310 Emeryville (94608) ***(P-8191)***

Xomv Media Corporation ....E 424 284-4024
9465 Wilshire Blvd Beverly Hills (90212) ***(P-6384)***

Xotic Guitars & Effects, San Fernando *Also called Prosound Communications Inc* ***(P-10152)***

Xpansiv Data Systems Inc ....E 415 915-5124
2 Bryant St San Francisco (94105) ***(P-24595)***

Xperi Corporation (PA) ....D 408 321-6000
3025 Orchard Pkwy San Jose (95134) ***(P-18664)***

Xpert Marketing Group Inc ....E 949 309-6300
32 Alicante Trabuco Canyon (92679) ***(P-23246)***

Xplain Corporation ....F 805 494-9797
705 Lakefield Rd Ste I Westlake Village (91361) ***(P-6062)***

Xr LLC ....E 714 847-9292
15251 Pipeline Ln Huntington Beach (92649) ***(P-22127)***

Xs Scuba Inc (PA) ....E 714 424-0434
4040 W Chandler Ave Santa Ana (92704) ***(P-22928)***

Xsential, Gardena *Also called Techflex Packaging LLC* ***(P-5344)***

Xtandi, San Francisco *Also called Medivation Inc* ***(P-8007)***

Xtime Inc ....E 650 508-4300
1400 Bridge Pkwy Ste 200 Redwood City (94065) ***(P-10133)***

Xtreme Manufacturing LLC ....E 559 891-2978
1775 Park St Ste 82 Selma (93662) ***(P-12073)***

Xy Corp Inc ....F 760 323-0333
1258 Montalvo Way Ste A Palm Springs (92262) ***(P-14000)***

Xylem Inc ....F 559 265-4731
3878 S Willow Ave Fresno (93725) ***(P-14606)***

Xyratex, Fremont *Also called Seagate Systems (us) Inc* ***(P-15093)***

XYZ Graphics Inc (PA) ....E 415 227-9972
190 Lombard St San Francisco (94111) ***(P-7275)***

XYZ Text Book, San Luis Obispo *Also called McKeague Patpatrick* ***(P-6121)***

Xzavier, Vernon *Also called Mjck Corporation* ***(P-2799)***

Y & D Rubber Corporation ....F 909 517-1683
1451 S Carlos Ave Ontario (91761) ***(P-9390)***

Y B S Enterprises Inc ....F 818 848-7790
3116 W Vanowen St Burbank (91505) ***(P-17431)***

Y I C, Carson *Also called Yun Industrial Co Ltd* ***(P-18055)***

Y K K U S A, Anaheim *Also called YKK (usa) Inc* ***(P-23018)***

Y Nissim Inc ....F 818 718-9024
23509 Spires St Canoga Park (91304) ***(P-15394)***

Y Y K Inc ....F 213 622-0741
411 W 7th St Ste 710 Los Angeles (90014) ***(P-22585)***

Y-Change Inc ....F 510 573-2205
43575 Mission Blvd 416 Fremont (94539) ***(P-24596)***

Y2k Precision Sheetmetal Inc ....F 714 632-3901
3831 E La Palma Ave Anaheim (92807) ***(P-12439)***

Yadav Technology Inc ....F 510 438-0148
48371 Fremont Blvd # 101 Fremont (94538) ***(P-18665)***

Yaesu Usa Inc ....E 714 827-7600
6125 Phyllis Dr Cypress (90630) ***(P-17711)***

Yageo America Corporation ....E 408 240-6200
2550 N 1st St Ste 480 San Jose (95131) ***(P-18693)***

Yagi Brothers Produce LLC, Livingston *Also called Ybp Holdings LLC* ***(P-2650)***

Yaldo Enterprises Inc ....F 619 445-2578
24680 Viejas Grade Rd B Descanso (91916) ***(P-2366)***

Yamachan Ramen, San Jose *Also called Nippon Trends Food Service Inc* ***(P-2571)***

Yamagata America Inc ....F 858 751-1010
3760 Convoy St Ste 219 San Diego (92111) ***(P-6385)***

Yamaha Guitar Group Inc (HQ) ....C 818 575-3600
26580 Agoura Rd Calabasas (91302) ***(P-22644)***

Yamamoto Manufacturing USA Inc (HQ) ....F 408 387-5250
2025 Gateway Pl Ste 450 San Jose (95110) ***(P-18054)***

Yamamoto of Orient Inc ....F 909 591-7654
12475 Mills Ave Chino (91710) ***(P-3670)***

Yamamotoyama of America, Chino *Also called Yamamoto of Orient Inc* ***(P-3670)***

Yamasa Enterprises ....E 213 626-2211
515 Stanford Ave Los Angeles (90013) ***(P-2255)***

Yamasa Fish Cake, Los Angeles *Also called Yamasa Enterprises* ***(P-2255)***

Yanfeng US Automotive ....E 616 886-3622
30559 San Antonio St Hayward (94544) ***(P-4877)***

Yang's Screen Printing, South El Monte *Also called Unique Screen Printing Inc* ***(P-3821)***

Yankon Industries Inc ....E 909 591-2345
13445 12th St Chino (91710) ***(P-17086)***

Yara North America Inc ....E 916 375-1109
3961 Channel Dr West Sacramento (95691) ***(P-8850)***

Yardney Water MGT Systems, Riverside *Also called Yardney Water MGT Systems Inc* ***(P-15607)***

Yardney Water MGT Systems Inc (PA) ....E 951 656-6716
6666 Box Springs Blvd Riverside (92507) ***(P-15607)***

Yaskawa America Inc ....F 949 263-2640
1701 Kaiser Ave Irvine (92614) ***(P-14874)***

Yates Gear Inc ....D 530 222-4606
2608 Hartnell Ave Ste 6 Redding (96002) ***(P-10258)***

Yavar Manufacturing Co Inc ....E 323 722-2040
1900 S Tubeway Ave Commerce (90040) ***(P-5320)***

Yawitz Inc ....E 909 865-5599
1379 Ridgeway St Pomona (91768) ***(P-17002)***

Yayyo Inc ....F 310 926-2643
433 N Camden Dr Ste 600 Beverly Hills (90210) ***(P-24597)***

Yb Media LLC ....E 310 467-5804
1534 Plaza Ln 146 Burlingame (94010) ***(P-6386)***

Ybcc Inc ....E 626 213-3945
17800 Castleton St # 386 City of Industry (91748) ***(P-627)***

Ybp Holdings LLC ....E 209 394-7311
5614 Lincoln Blvd Livingston (95334) ***(P-2650)***

Yeager Enterprises Corp ....D 714 994-2040
7100 Village Dr Buena Park (90621) ***(P-10960)***

Yeager Manufacturing Corp (PA) ....E 714 879-2800
2320 E Orangethorpe Ave Anaheim (92806) ***(P-20272)***

Yellow Inc ....E 858 689-4851
9350 Trade Pl Ste C San Diego (92126) ***(P-22929)***

Yellow Letters Inc ....F 661 864-7860
5908 Dartmoor Wood Ave Bakersfield (93314) ***(P-7276)***

Mergent e-mail: customerrelations@mergent.com
1290
2020 California
Manufacturers Register
(P-0000) Products & Services Section entry number
(PA)=Parent Co (HQ)=Headquarters (DH)=Div Headquarters

Yellow Magic Incorporated......F.....951 506-4005
41571 Date St Murrieta (92562) *(P-24598)*
Yellow Pages Inc......E.....714 776-0534
24931 Nellie Gail Rd Laguna Hills (92653) *(P-6387)*
Yellow Springs Instruments, San Diego *Also called Ysi Incorporated* *(P-21326)*
Yen-Nhai Inc......E.....323 584-1315
4940 District Blvd Vernon (90058) *(P-4678)*
Yenor Inc......F.....310 410-1573
5640 W 63rd St Los Angeles (90056) *(P-7277)*
Yerma Jewelry Mfg Inc......E.....818 551-0690
671 W Broadway Glendale (91204) *(P-22586)*
Yes To Carrots, Pasadena *Also called Yes To Inc* *(P-8609)*
Yes To Inc......E.....626 365-1976
177 E Colo Blvd Ste 110 Pasadena (91105) *(P-8609)*
Yes-Tek, San Jose *Also called Yield Enhancement Services Inc* *(P-18667)*
Yesco, Sacramento *Also called Young Electric Sign Company* *(P-23247)*
Yesco, Jurupa Valley *Also called Young Electric Sign Company* *(P-23248)*
Yesco, Fremont *Also called Young Electric Sign Company* *(P-23249)*
Yf Manufacture Inc......F.....626 768-0029
2455 Maple Ave Pomona (91767) *(P-10497)*
YH Texpert Corporation......F.....323 562-8800
5052 Cecelia St South Gate (90280) *(P-3435)*
Yield Engineering Systems Inc......E.....925 373-8353
203 Lawrence Dr Ste A Livermore (94551) *(P-18666)*
Yield Enhancement Services Inc......F.....408 410-5825
364 Sunpark Ct San Jose (95136) *(P-18667)*
Yillik Precision Industries......D.....909 947-2785
1621 S Cucamonga Ave Ontario (91761) *(P-14214)*
Yinlun Tdi LLC......F.....800 266-5645
760 S Milliken Ave Ste A Ontario (91761) *(P-19810)*
Yinlun Tdi LLC (HQ)......D.....909 390-3944
4850 E Airport Dr Ontario (91761) *(P-19811)*
YKK (usa) Inc......C.....714 701-1200
5001 E La Palma Ave Anaheim (92807) *(P-23018)*
YMI Jeanswear Inc (PA)......F.....323 581-7700
1155 S Boyle Ave Los Angeles (90023) *(P-3261)*
YMi Jeanswear Inc......D.....213 746-6681
1015 Wall St Ste 115 Los Angeles (90015) *(P-3436)*
Ynez Corporation......F.....805 688-5522
432 2nd St Solvang (93463) *(P-5871)*
Yocup Company......F.....310 884-9888
13711 S Main St Los Angeles (90061) *(P-5310)*
Yogi Investments Inc......F.....909 984-5703
419 Capron Ave West Covina (91792) *(P-10134)*
Yonekyu USA Inc......D.....323 581-4194
3615 E Vernon Ave Vernon (90058) *(P-508)*
Yong Kee Rice Noodle Co......F.....415 986-3759
946 Stockton St Apt 10c San Francisco (94108) *(P-2386)*
Yoplait U S A Inc......E.....310 632-9502
1055 Sandhill Ave Carson (90746) *(P-715)*
Yorba Linda Country Club, Garden Grove *Also called Sanyo Foods Corp America* *(P-2382)*
York Engineering......F.....323 256-0439
7575 Jurupa Ave Riverside (92504) *(P-14127)*
York Label, El Dorado Hills *Also called Cameo Crafts* *(P-7015)*
Yosemite Association, El Portal *Also called Yosemite Natural History Assn* *(P-6168)*
Yosemite Natural History Assn......D.....209 379-2646
5020 El Portal Rd El Portal (95318) *(P-6168)*
Yosemite Vly Beef Pkg Co Inc......E.....626 435-0170
970 E Sandy Mush Rd Merced (95341) *(P-433)*
Yoshimasa Display Case Inc......E.....213 637-9999
108 Pico St Pomona (91766) *(P-4959)*
You Are Loved Foods LLC......F.....818 578-8288
1282 Newbury Rd Newbury Park (91320) *(P-1299)*
Youcare Pharma (usa) Inc......D.....951 258-3114
132 Business Center Dr Corona (92880) *(P-8192)*
Young & Family Inc......F.....707 263-8877
64 Soda Bay Rd Lakeport (95453) *(P-4158)*
Young Angels Children's Wear, Los Angeles *Also called Angels Young Inc* *(P-2959)*
Young Dental, Cerritos *Also called US Dental Inc* *(P-22201)*
Young Electric Sign Company......E.....916 419-8101
875 National Dr Ste 107 Sacramento (95834) *(P-23247)*
Young Electric Sign Company......D.....909 923-7668
10235 Bellegrave Ave Jurupa Valley (91752) *(P-23248)*
Young Electric Sign Company......E.....510 877-7815
46750 Fremont Blvd # 101 Fremont (94538) *(P-23249)*
Young Engineering & Mfg Inc (PA)......E.....909 394-3225
560 W Terrace Dr San Dimas (91773) *(P-20960)*
Young Engineers Inc......D.....949 581-9411
25841 Commercentre Dr Lake Forest (92630) *(P-11644)*
Young Kee, San Francisco *Also called Yong Kee Rice Noodle Co* *(P-2386)*
Young Knitting Mills......E.....323 980-8677
3499 E 15th St Los Angeles (90023) *(P-2809)*
Young Machine Inc......F.....909 464-0405
12282 Colony Ave Chino (91710) *(P-16535)*
Young Nails Inc......F.....714 992-1400
1149 N Patt St Anaheim (92801) *(P-8610)*
Young Sung USA Inc......F.....213 427-2580
1122 S Alvarado St Los Angeles (90006) *(P-3868)*
Youngdale Manufacturing Corp......E.....760 727-0644
1216 Liberty Way Ste B Vista (92081) *(P-11645)*
Younger Mfg Co (PA)......B.....310 783-1533
2925 California St Torrance (90503) *(P-22397)*
Younger Optics, Torrance *Also called Younger Mfg Co* *(P-22397)*
Youngs Custom Cabinet Inc......F.....415 822-8313
1760 Yosemite Ave San Francisco (94124) *(P-4272)*
Youngs Evergreen Nursery Co, Fountain Valley *Also called California Clock Co* *(P-22478)*
Youngstown Grape Distrs Inc......C.....559 638-2271
1625 G St Reedley (93654) *(P-935)*

Yourpeople Inc......A.....888 249-3263
50 Beale St San Francisco (94105) *(P-24599)*
Yreka Division, Yreka *Also called Timber Products Co Ltd Partnr* *(P-4283)*
Yreka Transit Mix Concrete......F.....530 842-4351
126 Schantz Rd Yreka (96097) *(P-10874)*
Ys Controls LLC......E.....714 641-0727
3041 S Shannon St Santa Ana (92704) *(P-21566)*
Ysi Incorporated......E.....858 546-8327
9940 Summers Ridge Rd San Diego (92121) *(P-21326)*
Yti Enterprises Inc......F.....714 632-8696
1260 S State College Pkwy Anaheim (92806) *(P-4544)*
Yuba City Steel Products Co......E.....530 673-4554
532 Crestmont Ave Yuba City (95991) *(P-11923)*
Yuba Cy Wste Wtr Trtmnt Fcilty......E.....530 822-7698
302 Burns Dr Yuba City (95991) *(P-15608)*
Yuba River Moulding Mlwk Inc (PA)......E.....530 742-2168
3757 Feather River Blvd Olivehurst (95961) *(P-4159)*
Yucatan Foods LLC......F.....310 342-5363
9841 Arprt Blvd Ste 1578 Los Angeles (90045) *(P-752)*
Yuciapa & Calimesa News Mirror, Yucaipa *Also called Hi-Desert Publishing Company* *(P-5663)*
Yuhas Tooling & Machining......F.....408 934-9196
1031 Pecten Ct Milpitas (95035) *(P-16536)*
Yuja Inc......C.....888 257-2278
84 W Santa Clara St # 690 San Jose (95113) *(P-24600)*
Yukon Trail Inc......F.....909 218-5286
1175 Woodlawn St Ontario (91761) *(P-20439)*
Yuku.com, San Francisco *Also called Ezboard Inc* *(P-23888)*
Yumi, Los Angeles *Also called Caer Inc* *(P-721)*
Yun Industrial Co Ltd......E.....310 715-1898
161 Selandia Ln Carson (90746) *(P-18055)*
Yutaka Electric Intl Inc......F.....626 962-7770
5116 Azusa Canyon Rd Baldwin Park (91706) *(P-16805)*
Ywd Cartoners, Fresno *Also called Kodiak Cartoners Inc* *(P-14714)*
Z B P Inc......F.....323 266-3363
2871 E Pico Blvd Los Angeles (90023) *(P-5541)*
Z B Wire Works Inc......F.....909 391-0995
1139 Brooks St Ontario (91762) *(P-13449)*
Z C & R Coating For Optics Inc......E.....310 381-3060
1401 Abalone Ave Torrance (90501) *(P-21423)*
Z Industries, Los Angeles *Also called Active Window Products* *(P-11927)*
Z-Barten Productions, Los Angeles *Also called Z B P Inc* *(P-5541)*
Z-Communications Inc......F.....858 621-2700
6779 Mesa Ridge Rd # 150 San Diego (92121) *(P-19147)*
Z-Line Designs Inc (PA)......D.....925 743-4000
2410 San Ramon Valley Blv San Ramon (94583) *(P-4850)*
Z-Tronix Inc......E.....562 808-0800
6327 Alondra Blvd Paramount (90723) *(P-19148)*
Zacharon Pharmaceuticals Inc......F.....415 506-6700
105 Digital Dr Novato (94949) *(P-8193)*
Zacky & Sons Poultry LLC......B.....559 443-2750
2222 S East Ave Fresno (93721) *(P-533)*
Zacky & Sons Poultry LLC (PA)......C.....559 443-2700
2020 S East Ave Fresno (93721) *(P-534)*
Zacky & Sons Poultry LLC......B.....209 948-0129
1111 Navy Dr Stockton (95206) *(P-535)*
Zacky Farms, Fresno *Also called Zacky & Sons Poultry LLC* *(P-534)*
Zada Graphics Inc......F.....323 321-8940
11180 Lewis Hill Dr Santa Clarita (91390) *(P-6947)*
Zada International Printing, Chatsworth *Also called Havana Graphic Center Inc* *(P-6606)*
Zadara Storage Inc......E.....949 251-0360
9245 Research Drv Irvine Irvine (92618) *(P-15116)*
Zadro Products Inc......E.....714 892-9200
14462 Astronautics Ln # 101 Huntington Beach (92647) *(P-10402)*
Zalemark Holding Company Inc......F.....888 682-6885
15260 Ventura Blvd # 120 Sherman Oaks (91403) *(P-22587)*
Zaolla......E.....714 736-9270
6650 Caballero Blvd Buena Park (90620) *(P-17308)*
Zap Printing and Graphics, Corona *Also called Zap Printing Incorporated* *(P-6948)*
Zap Printing Incorporated......F.....951 734-8181
127 Radio Rd Corona (92879) *(P-6948)*
Zapp Packaging Inc......D.....909 930-1500
1921 S Business Pkwy Ontario (91761) *(P-5186)*
Zarif Companies......F.....805 318-1800
4187 Carpinteria Ave # 3 Carpinteria (93013) *(P-2008)*
Zazzie Foods Inc......F.....510 526-7664
1398 University Ave Berkeley (94702) *(P-23530)*
Zbe Inc......E.....805 576-1600
1035 Cindy Ln Carpinteria (93013) *(P-16771)*
Zebra Technologies Corporation......B.....619 661-5465
1440 Innovative Dr # 100 San Diego (92154) *(P-15368)*
Zebra Technologies Corporation......B.....805 579-1800
30601 Agoura Rd Agoura Hills (91301) *(P-15369)*
Zebra Technologies Intl LLC......F.....408 473-8500
2940 N 1st St San Jose (95134) *(P-15370)*
Zed Audio Corporation......F.....805 499-5559
2624 Lavery Ct Ste 203 Newbury Park (91320) *(P-17309)*
Zee Consulting, Bakersfield *Also called Contraband Control Specialists* *(P-8951)*
Zeeni Inc......F.....626 350-1024
9536 Gidley St Temple City (91780) *(P-3131)*
Zelco Cabinet Mfg Inc......F.....707 584-1121
298 W Robles Ave Santa Rosa (95407) *(P-4758)*
Zeltiq Aesthetics Inc......F.....925 474-2519
6723 Sierra Ct Dublin (94568) *(P-21965)*
Zeltiq Aesthetics Inc (HQ)......B.....925 474-2500
4410 Rosewood Dr Pleasanton (94588) *(P-21966)*
Zelzah Pharmacy Inc (PA)......F.....818 609-0692
17911 Ventura Blvd Encino (91316) *(P-8194)*

Employee Codes: A=Over 500 employees, B=251-500
C=101-250, D=51-100, E=20-50, F=10-19

2020 California
Manfacturers Register

© Mergent Inc. 1-800-342-5647
1291

A
L
P
H
A
B
E
T
I
C

Zen Monkey LLC ....F....310 504-2899
655 N Central Ave Fl 1700 Glendale (91203) ***(P-986)***
Zenana, Los Angeles *Also called Kc Exclusive Inc* ***(P-3353)***
Zenbooth Inc ....E....510 646-8368
650 University Ave # 10 Berkeley (94710) ***(P-4825)***
Zendesk Inc (PA) ....C....415 418-7506
1019 Market St San Francisco (94103) ***(P-24601)***
Zenefits, San Francisco *Also called Yourpeople Inc* ***(P-24599)***
Zenith Manufacturing Inc ....E....818 767-2106
3087 12th St Riverside (92507) ***(P-20273)***
Zenith Screw Products Inc ....E....562 941-0281
10910 Painter Ave Santa Fe Springs (90670) ***(P-12662)***
Zenner Performance Meters Inc ....E....951 849-8822
1910 E Westward Ave Banning (92220) ***(P-20978)***
Zenpayroll Inc (PA) ....C....800 936-0383
525 20th St San Francisco (94107) ***(P-24602)***
Zense-Life Inc ....F....858 888-5289
2218 Faraday Ave Ste 120 Carlsbad (92008) ***(P-22334)***
Zentec Group ....F....949 586-3609
26190 Entp Way Ste 200 Lake Forest (92630) ***(P-19149)***
Zentera Systems Inc ....F....408 436-4811
97 E Brokaw Rd Ste 360 San Jose (95112) ***(P-24603)***
Zentis North America LLC ....D....310 719-2600
16911 S Normandie Ave Gardena (90247) ***(P-8786)***
Zenverge Inc ....D....408 350-5052
2680 Zanker Rd Ste 200 San Jose (95134) ***(P-18668)***
Zenyx Inc ....F....415 741-0170
2870 Zanker Rd Ste 210 San Jose (95134) ***(P-24604)***
Zeons Inc ....B....323 302-8299
291 S Cienega Blvd 102 Beverly Hills (90211) ***(P-10335)***
Zep Solar Llc (HQ) ....E....415 479-6900
161 Mitchell Blvd Ste 104 San Rafael (94903) ***(P-18669)***
Zepco ....F....818 848-0880
1047 E Palm Ave Burbank (91501) ***(P-10135)***
Zephyr Manufacturing Co Inc ....D....310 410-4907
201 Hindry Ave Inglewood (90301) ***(P-14230)***
Zephyr Tool Group, Inglewood *Also called Zephyr Manufacturing Co Inc* ***(P-14230)***
Zephyr Tool Group, Inglewood *Also called Shg Holdings Corp* ***(P-14228)***
Zepp Labs Inc ....E....314 662-2145
75 E Santa Clara St # 93 San Jose (95113) ***(P-22930)***
Zero Base, Fremont *Also called Zerobase Energy LLC* ***(P-19177)***
Zero Gravity Corporation ....E....805 388-8803
912 Pancho Rd Ste A Camarillo (93012) ***(P-20440)***
Zero Gravity Group, Camarillo *Also called Zero Gravity Corporation* ***(P-20440)***
Zerobase Energy LLC ....E....888 530-9376
46609 Fremont Blvd Fremont (94538) ***(P-19177)***
Zerouv ....F....714 584-0015
16792 Burke Ln Huntington Beach (92647) ***(P-22398)***
Zerran International Corp ....F....818 897-5494
12880 Pierce St Pacoima (91331) ***(P-8611)***
Zest Labs Inc (HQ) ....E....408 200-6500
2349 Bering Dr San Jose (95131) ***(P-18670)***
Zet-Tek Machining, Yorba Linda *Also called Zet-Tek Precision Machining* ***(P-16537)***
Zet-Tek Precision Machining (PA) ....F....714 777-8770
22951 La Palma Ave Yorba Linda (92887) ***(P-16537)***
Zeth Engineering Inc ....F....310 930-9100
11929 Pepperwood St Victorville (92392) ***(P-11924)***
Zettler Magnetics Inc ....E....949 831-5000
75 Columbia Aliso Viejo (92656) ***(P-16581)***
Zev Technologies Inc (PA) ....F....805 486-5800
1051 Yarnell Pl Oxnard (93033) ***(P-13280)***
Zevia LLC ....D....310 202-7000
15821 Ventura Blvd # 145 Encino (91436) ***(P-2185)***
ZF Array Technology Inc ....D....408 433-9920
2302 Trade Zone Blvd San Jose (95131) ***(P-18688)***
ZF Micro Solutions Inc ....F....650 846-6500
1000 Elwell Ct Ste 134 Palo Alto (94303) ***(P-18671)***
Zl Chemicals ....F....818 827-1301
8605 Santa Monica Blvd Los Angeles (90069) ***(P-7538)***
Zi Machine Manufacturing, El Dorado Hills *Also called 478826 Limited* ***(P-15647)***
Zico Beverages LLC (HQ) ....E....866 729-9426
2101 E El Segundo Blvd # 403 El Segundo (90245) ***(P-2186)***
Ziegenfelder Company ....E....909 590-0493
12290 Colony Ave Chino (91710) ***(P-681)***
Ziehm Instrumentarium ....E....407 615-8560
4181 Latham St Riverside (92501) ***(P-22226)***
Zigzagzoom, Glendale *Also called Jtea Inc* ***(P-24062)***
Zilift Inc ....F....661 369-8579
3600 Pegasus Dr Unit 7 Bakersfield (93308) ***(P-14607)***
Zilog Inc (HQ) ....E....408 513-1500
1590 Buckeye Dr Milpitas (95035) ***(P-18672)***
Zimmer Intermed Inc ....E....909 392-0882
1647 Yeager Ave La Verne (91750) ***(P-22128)***
Zing Racing Products ....F....760 219-4700
27430 Bostik Ct Ste 101 Temecula (92590) ***(P-20441)***
Zinio Systems Inc ....D....415 494-2700
114 Sansome St Fl 4 San Francisco (94104) ***(P-24605)***
Zinsser Na Inc (HQ) ....F....818 341-2906
19145 Parthenia St Ste C Northridge (91324) ***(P-21327)***
Zinus Inc (HQ) ....D....925 417-2100
1951 Fairway Dr Ste A San Leandro (94577) ***(P-4751)***
Zion Health Inc ....F....650 520-4313
430 E Grand Ave South San Francisco (94080) ***(P-8612)***
Zion Packaging, Corona *Also called Organic Bottle Dctg Co LLC* ***(P-5170)***
Zip Notes LLC ....F....415 931-8020
2822 Van Ness Ave San Francisco (94109) ***(P-5154)***
Zip Print Inc (PA) ....E....559 486-3112
1257 G St Fresno (93706) ***(P-6949)***
Zip-Chem Products, Morgan Hill *Also called Mitann Inc* ***(P-9001)***
Zipco, Riverside *Also called Zenith Manufacturing Inc* ***(P-20273)***
Zipline Medical Inc ....F....408 412-7228
747 Camden Ave Ste A Campbell (95008) ***(P-21967)***
Zircon Corporation (PA) ....E....408 866-8600
1580 Dell Ave Campbell (95008) ***(P-14231)***
Zk Enterprises Inc ....E....213 622-7012
4368 District Blvd Vernon (90058) ***(P-3132)***
Zmb Industries LLC ....F....858 842-1000
12925 Brookprinter Pl # 400 Poway (92064) ***(P-23531)***
Zmp Aquisition Corporation ....C....714 278-6500
4141 N Palm St Fullerton (92835) ***(P-16772)***
Zo Skin Health Inc (PA) ....D....949 988-7524
9685 Research Dr Irvine (92618) ***(P-8613)***
Zoasis Corporation ....E....800 745-4725
1960 E Grand Ave Ste 555 El Segundo (90245) ***(P-6063)***
Zodiac Aerospace, Carson *Also called Monogram Systems* ***(P-20182)***
Zodiac Aerospace ....F....909 652-9700
11340 Jersey Blvd Rancho Cucamonga (91730) ***(P-19939)***
Zodiac Electrical Inserts USA, Huntington Beach *Also called Safran Cabin Galleys Us Inc* ***(P-20214)***
Zodiac Pool Solutions LLC (HQ) ....B....760 599-9600
2882 Whiptail Loop # 100 Carlsbad (92010) ***(P-15609)***
Zodiac Pool Systems LLC (HQ) ....C....760 599-9600
2882 Whiptail Loop # 100 Carlsbad (92010) ***(P-15610)***
Zodiac Seat Shells U.S. LLC, Santa Maria *Also called Safran Seats Santa Maria LLC* ***(P-20225)***
Zodiac Wtr Waste Aero Systems ....E....310 884-7000
1500 Glenn Curtiss St Carson (90746) ***(P-20274)***
Zodiak Services America ....D....310 884-7200
6734 Valjean Ave Van Nuys (91406) ***(P-20275)***
Zogenix Inc (PA) ....E....510 550-8300
5959 Horton St Ste 500 Emeryville (94608) ***(P-8195)***
Zoho Corporation (HQ) ....F....925 924-9500
4141 Hacienda Dr Pleasanton (94588) ***(P-24606)***
Zola Acai, San Francisco *Also called Amazon Prsrvation Partners Inc* ***(P-754)***
Zoll Circulation Inc ....C....408 541-2140
2000 Ringwood Ave San Jose (95131) ***(P-22335)***
Zoll Medical Corporation ....F....408 419-2929
2000 Ringwood Ave San Jose (95131) ***(P-22336)***
Zollner Electronics Inc ....E....408 434-5400
575 Cottonwood Dr Milpitas (95035) ***(P-18056)***
Zombie Industries, Poway *Also called Zmb Industries LLC* ***(P-23531)***
Zonex Systems, Huntington Beach *Also called California Economizer* ***(P-16704)***
Zonson Company Inc ....E....760 597-0338
3197 Lionshead Ave Carlsbad (92010) ***(P-22931)***
Zoo Printing Inc (PA) ....D....310 253-7751
25152 Springfield Ct # 280 Valencia (91355) ***(P-6950)***
Zoo Printing Trade Printer, Valencia *Also called Zoo Printing Inc* ***(P-6950)***
Zoo Zoo Wham Whams Blip Blops ....F....213 248-9591
645 W Rosecrans Ave Compton (90222) ***(P-2957)***
Zoom Bookz LLC ....F....800 662-9982
10000 Fairway Dr Ste 140 Roseville (95678) ***(P-6169)***
Zoox Inc (PA) ....C....650 733-9669
1149 Chess Dr Foster City (94404) ***(P-19514)***
Zoox Labs, Foster City *Also called Zoox Inc* ***(P-19514)***
Zoran Corporation (HQ) ....E....972 673-1600
1060 Rincon Cir San Jose (95131) ***(P-18673)***
Zosano Pharma Corporation (PA) ....E....510 745-1200
34790 Ardentech Ct Fremont (94555) ***(P-8196)***
Zotos International Inc ....E....626 321-4100
488 E Santa Clara St # 301 Arcadia (91006) ***(P-8614)***
Zpower LLC ....C....805 445-7789
4765 Calle Quetzal Camarillo (93012) ***(P-16806)***
Zs Pharma Inc ....F....650 753-1823
1100 Park Pl Fl 3 San Mateo (94403) ***(P-8197)***
Zt Plus ....F....626 208-3440
1321 Mountain View Cir Azusa (91702) ***(P-18674)***
Ztech ....F....916 635-6784
11481 Sunrise Gold Cir # 1 Rancho Cordova (95742) ***(P-15476)***
Zuca Inc ....E....408 377-9822
320 S Milpitas Blvd Milpitas (95035) ***(P-10216)***
Zulip Inc ....F....617 945-7653
185 Berry St Ste 400 San Francisco (94107) ***(P-24607)***
Zumar Industries Inc ....D....562 941-4633
9719 Santa Fe Springs Rd Santa Fe Springs (90670) ***(P-23250)***
Zuo Modern Contemporary Inc (PA) ....E....510 777-1030
80 Swan Way Ste 300 Oakland (94621) ***(P-4826)***
Zurich Engineering Inc ....F....714 528-0066
1365 N Dynamics St Ste E Anaheim (92806) ***(P-19992)***
Zuza ....E....760 438-9411
2304 Faraday Ave Carlsbad (92008) ***(P-7278)***
Zye Labs LLC ....F....904 800-9935
310 S Twin Oaks Valley Rd San Marcos (92078) ***(P-24608)***
Zygo Corporation ....E....714 918-7433
2031 Main St Irvine (92614) ***(P-21424)***
Zygo Corporation ....E....408 434-1000
3350 Scott Blvd Santa Clara (95054) ***(P-21328)***
Zygo Epo ....F....510 243-7592
3900 Lakeside Dr Richmond (94806) ***(P-21425)***
Zygo Optical Systems, Irvine *Also called Zygo Corporation* ***(P-21424)***
Zymed Laboratories ....E....650 952-0110
458 Carlton Ct South San Francisco (94080) ***(P-23532)***
Zynga Inc ....F....415 621-2391
650 Townsend St San Francisco (94103) ***(P-24609)***
Zypcom Inc ....F....510 324-2501
29400 Kohoutek Way # 170 Union City (94587) ***(P-17712)***
Zyrel Inc ....F....707 995-2551
15322 Lkeshore Dr Ste 301 Clearlake (95422) ***(P-18057)***

Mergent e-mail: customerrelations@mergent.com
1292
2020 California
Manufacturers Register
(P-0000) Products & Services Section entry number
(PA)=Parent Co (HQ)=Headquarters (DH)=Div Headquarters

Zyrion Inc..D......408 524-7424
  440 N Wolfe Rd Sunnyvale (94085) *(P-24610)*
Zytek Corp...E......408 520-4287
  1755 Mccarthy Blvd Milpitas (95035) *(P-18058)*

Zytek Ems, Milpitas *Also called Zytek Corp* *(P-18058)*

Employee Codes: A=Over 500 employees, B=251-500
C=101-250, D=51-100, E=20-50, F=10-19

2020 California
Manfacturers Register

© Mergent Inc. 1-800-342-5647
1293

COUNTY/CITY CROSS-REFERENCE INDEX

Alameda
Alameda
Albany
Berkeley
Castro Valley
Dublin
Emeryville
Fremont
Hayward
Kensington
Livermore
Newark
Oakland
Piedmont
Pleasanton
San Leandro
San Lorenzo
Sunol
Union City

Amador
Ione
Jackson
Pioneer
Plymouth
Sutter Creek

Butte
Biggs
Chico
Durham
Gridley
Magalia
Nelson
Oroville
Paradise
Richvale

Calaveras
Angels Camp
Copperopolis
Murphys
San Andreas
Vallecito
West Point

Colusa
Arbuckle
Colusa
Maxwell
Princeton
Williams

Contra Costa
Alamo
Antioch
Bay Point
Brentwood
Byron
Clayton
Concord
Crockett
Danville
El Cerrito
Hercules
Lafayette
Martinez
Moraga
Orinda
Pacheco

Pinole
Pittsburg
Pleasant Hill
Richmond
Rodeo
San Pablo
San Ramon
Walnut Creek

Del Norte
Crescent City

El Dorado
Cameron Park
Camino
Cool
Diamond Springs
El Dorado
El Dorado Hills
Garden Valley
Georgetown
Greenwood
Pilot Hill
Placerville
Pollock Pines
Shingle Springs
Somerset
South Lake Tahoe

Fresno
Auberry
Cantua Creek
Caruthers
Clovis
Coalinga
Del Rey
Firebaugh
Fowler
Fresno
Helm
Kerman
Kingsburg
Parlier
Pinedale
Reedley
Riverdale
Sanger
Selma
Tranquillity

Glenn
Orland
Willows

Humboldt
Arcata
Blue Lake
Eureka
Ferndale
Fields Landing
Fortuna
Hoopa
Kneeland
Korbel
Loleta
McKinleyville
Miranda
Samoa

Imperial
Brawley

Calexico
Calipatria
El Centro
Heber
Imperial

Inyo
Bishop
Little Lake
Olancha

Kern
Arvin
Bakersfield
Boron
Buttonwillow
California City
Cantil
Delano
Di Giorgio
Edwards
Fellows
Frazier Park
Inyokern
Lake Isabella
Lamont
Lebec
Maricopa
Mc Farland
Mc Kittrick
Mojave
Ridgecrest
Rosamond
Shafter
Taft
Tehachapi
Wasco
Weldon

Kings
Armona
Corcoran
Hanford
Lemoore

Lake
Clearlake
Glenhaven
Hidden Valley Lake
Kelseyville
Lakeport
Lower Lake
Middletown
Nice

Lassen
Bieber
Susanville

Los Angeles
Agoura Hills
Agua Dulce
Alhambra
Altadena
Arcadia
Arleta
Artesia
Azusa
Baldwin Park
Bell
Bell Gardens

Bellflower
Beverly Hills
Burbank
Calabasas
Canoga Park
Canyon Country
Carson
Castaic
Cerritos
Chatsworth
City of Industry
Claremont
Commerce
Compton
Covina
Cudahy
Culver City
Diamond Bar
Downey
Duarte
E Rncho Dmngz
El Monte
El Segundo
Encino
Gardena
Glendale
Glendora
Granada Hills
Hacienda Heights
Harbor City
Hawaiian Gardens
Hawthorne
Hermosa Beach
Hollywood
Huntington Park
Inglewood
Irwindale
La Canada
La Canada Flintridge
La Crescenta
La Mirada
La Puente
La Verne
Lakewood
Lancaster
Lawndale
Littlerock
Lomita
Long Beach
Los Angeles
Lynwood
Malibu
Manhattan Beach
Marina Del Rey
Maywood
Mission Hills
Monrovia
Montebello
Monterey Park
Montrose
Newhall
North Hills
North Hollywood
Northridge
Norwalk
Pacific Palisades
Pacoima

Palmdale
Palos Verdes Estates
Panorama City
Paramount
Pasadena
Pearblossom
Pico Rivera
Playa Del Rey
Playa Vista
Pls Vrds Pnsl
Pomona
Porter Ranch
Rancho Dominguez
Rancho Palos Verdes
Redondo Beach
Reseda
Rllng HLS Est
Rolling Hills
Rosemead
Rowland Heights
San Dimas
San Fernando
San Gabriel
San Marino
San Pedro
Santa Clarita
Santa Fe Springs
Santa Monica
Sherman Oaks
Sierra Madre
Signal Hill
South El Monte
South Gate
South Pasadena
Stevenson Ranch
Studio City
Sun Valley
Sunland
Sylmar
Tarzana
Temple City
Toluca Lake
Topanga
Torrance
Tujunga
Valencia
Valley Village
Van Nuys
Venice
Vernon
View Park
Walnut
West Covina
West Hills
West Hollywood
Whittier
Wilmington
Winnetka
Woodland Hills

Madera
Chowchilla
Madera
North Fork
Oakhurst
Raymond

Marin

Belvedere Tiburon
Corte Madera
Fairfax
Greenbrae
Larkspur
Mill Valley
Novato
San Anselmo
San Quentin
San Rafael
Sausalito
Tomales

Mariposa

El Portal
Mariposa

Mendocino

Boonville
Comptche
Covelo
Fort Bragg
Gualala
Hopland
Mendocino
Philo
Potter Valley
Redwood Valley
Ukiah
Willits

Merced

Atwater
Delhi
Dos Palos
Gustine
Hilmar
Le Grand
Livingston
Los Banos
Merced
South Dos Palos
Winton

Mono

Mammoth Lakes

Monterey

Aromas
Carmel
Carmel Valley
Castroville
Gonzales
Greenfield
King City
Marina
Monterey
Moss Landing
Pacific Grove
Pebble Beach
Salinas
Seaside
Soledad

Napa

American Canyon
Angwin
Calistoga
Deer Park
NAPA
Oakville
Rutherford

Saint Helena
Vallejo
Yountville

Nevada

Grass Valley
Nevada City
Penn Valley
Rough and Ready
Truckee

Orange

Aliso Viejo
Anaheim
Brea
Buena Park
Capistrano Beach
Corona Del Mar
Costa Mesa
Cypress
Dana Point
El Toro
Foothill Ranch
Fountain Valley
Fullerton
Garden Grove
Huntington Beach
Irvine
La Habra
La Habra Heights
La Palma
Ladera Ranch
Laguna Beach
Laguna Hills
Laguna Niguel
Lake Forest
Los Alamitos
Midway City
Mission Viejo
Newport Beach
Newport Coast
Orange
Placentia
Rancho Santa Margari
Rcho STA Marg
San Clemente
San Juan Capistrano
Santa Ana
Seal Beach
Silverado
Stanton
Sunset Beach
Trabuco Canyon
Tustin
Villa Park
Westminster
Yorba Linda

Placer

Alpine Meadows
Auburn
Colfax
Granite Bay
Lincoln
Loomis
Newcastle
Penryn
Rocklin
Roseville
Sheridan
Tahoe City

Plumas

Chester
Chilcoot
Greenville
Portola
Quincy

Riverside

Aguanga
Banning
Beaumont
Blythe
Calimesa
Canyon Lake
Cathedral City
Cherry Valley
Coachella
Corona
Desert Hot Springs
Eastvale
Hemet
Idyllwild
Indian Wells
Indio
Jurupa Valley
La Quinta
Lake Elsinore
March ARB
Mecca
Menifee
Mira Loma
Moreno Valley
Murrieta
Norco
North Palm Springs
Palm Desert
Palm Springs
Perris
Quail Valley
Rancho Mirage
Riverside
Romoland
San Jacinto
Sun City
Temecula
Thermal
Thousand Palms
Wildomar

Sacramento

Antelope
Carmichael
Citrus Heights
Elk Grove
Fair Oaks
Folsom
Galt
Gold River
Isleton
Mather
McClellan
North Highlands
Orangevale
Rancho Cordova
Sacramento
Walnut Grove
Wilton

San Benito

Hollister
San Juan Bautista

San Bernardino

Adelanto
Alta Loma
Apple Valley
Barstow
Big Bear City
Bloomington
Chino
Chino Hills
Colton
Etiwanda
Fontana
Grand Terrace
Helendale
Hesperia
Highland
Lake Arrowhead
Loma Linda
Lucerne Valley
Mentone
Montclair
Mountain Pass
Needles
Newberry Springs
Nipton
Ontario
Oro Grande
Rancho Cucamonga
Redlands
Rialto
San Bernardino
Trona
Upland
Victorville
Yucaipa
Yucca Valley

San Diego

Alpine
Bonita
Bonsall
Cardiff
Cardiff By The Sea
Carlsbad
Chula Vista
Coronado
Del Mar
Descanso
El Cajon
Encinitas
Escondido
Fallbrook
Jamul
La Jolla
La Mesa
Lakeside
Lemon Grove
National City
Oceanside
Pala
Poway
Ramona
Rancho Santa Fe
San Diego
San Marcos
San Ysidro
Santee
Solana Beach
Spring Valley
Tecate

Valley Center
Vista

San Francisco

San Francisco

San Joaquin

Acampo
Escalon
Farmington
French Camp
Lathrop
Linden
Lockeford
Lodi
Manteca
Ripon
Stockton
Tracy

San Luis Obispo

Arroyo Grande
Atascadero
Avila Beach
Cholame
Grover Beach
Harmony
Los Osos
Morro Bay
Nipomo
Paso Robles
Pismo Beach
San Luis Obispo
San Miguel
Shandon
Templeton

San Mateo

Atherton
Belmont
Brisbane
Burlingame
Colma
Daly City
El Granada
Emerald Hills
Foster City
Half Moon Bay
La Honda
Menlo Park
Millbrae
Moss Beach
Pacifica
Pescadero
Portola Valley
Redwood City
San Bruno
San Carlos
San Gregorio
San Mateo
South San Francisco
Woodside

Santa Barbara

Buellton
Carpinteria
Goleta
Guadalupe
Lompoc
Los Alamos
Los Olivos
New Cuyama
Orcutt

Santa Barbara
Santa Maria
Santa Ynez
Solvang
Vandenberg Afb

Santa Clara

Alviso
Campbell
Cupertino
East Palo Alto
Gilroy
Los Altos
Los Altos Hills
Los Gatos
Milpitas
Moffett Field
Morgan Hill
Mountain View
Palo Alto
San Jose
San Martin
Santa Clara
Saratoga
Stanford
Sunnyvale

Santa Cruz

Aptos
Capitola
Davenport
Felton
Freedom
Los Gatos
Royal Oaks

Santa Cruz
Scotts Valley
Soquel
Watsonville

Shasta

Anderson
Burney
Cottonwood
Redding
Shasta Lake

Siskiyou

Etna
Fort Jones
Happy Camp
Mccloud
Montague
Mount Shasta
Seiad Valley
Tulelake
Weed
Yreka

Solano

Benicia
Dixon
Fairfield
Rio Vista
Suisun City
Travis Afb
Vacaville
Vallejo

Sonoma

Cazadero

Cloverdale
Cotati
Forestville
Geyserville
Glen Ellen
Graton
Guerneville
Healdsburg
Kenwood
Occidental
Petaluma
Rohnert Park
Santa Rosa
Sebastopol
Sonoma
Valley Ford
Windsor

Stanislaus

Ceres
Crows Landing
Denair
Hickman
Hughson
Modesto
Newman
Oakdale
Patterson
Riverbank
Salida
Turlock
Waterford

Sutter

Live Oak

Nicolaus
Pleasant Grove
Sutter
Yuba City

Tehama

Corning
Red Bluff

Trinity

Junction City
Lewiston
Weaverville

Tulare

Calif Hot Spg
Dinuba
Exeter
Farmersville
Lindsay
Orosi
Pixley
Porterville
Springville
Strathmore
Terra Bella
Three Rivers
Tipton
Traver
Tulare
Visalia
Woodlake

Tuolumne

Columbia
Jamestown

MI Wuk Village
Sonora

Ventura

Camarillo
Fillmore
Moorpark
Newbury Park
Oak Park
Oak View
Ojai
Oxnard
Port Hueneme
Santa Paula
Simi Valley
Somis
Thousand Oaks
Ventura
Westlake Village

Yolo

Broderick
Clarksburg
Davis
Madison
West Sacramento
Winters
Woodland
Zamora

Yuba

Marysville
Olivehurst
Plumas Lake
Strawberry Valley

GEOGRAPHIC SECTION

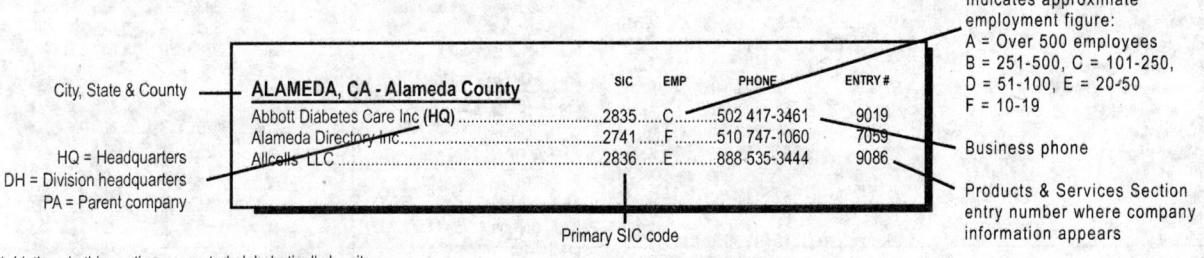

City, State & County → **ALAMEDA, CA - Alameda County**

	SIC	EMP	PHONE	ENTRY #
Abbott Diabetes Care Inc **(HQ)**	2835	C	502 417-3461	9019
Alameda Directory Inc	2741	F	510 747-1060	7059
Allcells LLC	2836	E	888 535-3444	9086

HQ = Headquarters
DH = Division headquarters
PA = Parent company

Primary SIC code

Indicates approximate employment figure:
A = Over 500 employees
B = 251-500, C = 101-250,
D = 51-100, E = 20-50
F = 10-19

Business phone

Products & Services Section entry number where company information appears

* Listings in this section are sorted alphabetically by city.
* Listings within each city are sorted alphabetically by company name.

	SIC	EMP	PHONE	ENTRY #
ACAMPO, CA - San Joaquin County				
AG Ray Inc	3523	F	209 334-1999	13604
California Concentrate Company	2037	E	209 334-9112	905
Calva Products Co Inc	2048	E	209 339-1516	1087
Franciscan Vineyards Inc	2084	B	209 369-5861	1711
Langetwins Wine Company Inc	2084	E	209 334-9780	1796
Macchia Inc	2084	F	209 333-2600	1807
ADELANTO, CA - San Bernardino County				
Adelanto Elementary School Dst	2099	E	760 530-7680	2388
Andersen Industries Inc	3715	E	760 246-8766	19813
Barker-Canoga Inc	3545	F	760 246-4777	14136
California Silica Products LLC	2819	F	909 947-0028	7476
Carberry LLC **(HQ)**	3999	E	800 564-0842	23299
Continental Fiberglass Inc **(PA)**	3949	F	760 246-6480	22785
Dar-Ken Inc	3053	F	760 246-4010	9227
Diversitech Corporation	3272	E	760 246-4200	10561
Ducommun Aerostructures Inc	3728	E	760 246-4191	20092
Fiber Care Baths Inc	3088	B	760 246-0019	9586
Flavor House Inc	2087	E	760 246-9131	2209
Furniture Technologies Inc	2426	E	760 246-9180	3974
General Atomic Aeron	3721	C	760 246-3660	19897
General Atomic Aeron	3721	E	760 388-8208	19900
Hayes Welding Inc **(PA)**	7692	D	760 246-4878	24639
Hayward Gordon Us Inc	3556	F	760 246-3430	14371
McElroy Metal Mill Inc	3448	E	760 246-5545	12558
Mk Magnetics Inc	3315	D	760 246-6373	11102
Molded Fiber GL Companies - W	3089	D	760 246-4042	9906
National Filter Media Corp	3569	D	760 246-4551	14840
Northwest Pipe Company	3317	B	760 246-3191	11132
Quality Resources Dist LLC	3999	E	510 378-6861	23455
R V Gambler	3715	F	928 927-5966	19831
Robertsons Rdy Mix Ltd A Cal	3273	F	760 246-4000	10823
Safeway Sign Company	3993	F	760 246-7070	23189
Southland Mixer Service	3713	F	760 246-6080	19556
Thermtronix Corp **(PA)**	3567	E	760 246-4500	14776
Traffix Devices Inc	3069	E	760 246-7171	9381
AGOURA HILLS, CA - Los Angeles County				
Acorn Newspaper Inc	2711	E	818 706-0266	5544
Caldera Medical Inc	3841	D	818 879-6555	21647
Candu Graphics	2752	F	310 822-1620	6472
Chatsworth Products Inc **(PA)**	3499	E	818 735-6100	13509
Cheesecake Factory Bakery Inc **(HQ)**	2051	B	818 880-9323	1178
Integrated Business Network	2759	F	818 879-0670	7099
Internet Machines Corporation **(PA)**	3577	D	818 575-2100	15258
Jamaco Enterprises Inc	2652	F	818 991-2050	5189
Millpledge North America Inc	2835	F	310 215-0400	8239
Novastor Corporation **(PA)**	7372	E	805 579-6700	24212
Paisano Publications LLC **(PA)**	2721	C	818 889-8740	5998
Paisano Publications Inc	2721	C	818 889-8740	5999
Richter Furniture Mfg 2002	2599	C	323 588-7900	5078
RMS Printing LLC	2752	F	818 707-2625	6847
Sole Survivor Corporation	2339	C	818 338-3760	3409
Teradyne Inc	3825	C	818 991-9700	21139
Teradyne Inc	3679	B	818 991-2900	19115
Voxara LLC	2741	F	844 869-2721	6377
Zebra Technologies Corporation	3577	B	805 579-1800	15369
AGUA DULCE, CA - Los Angeles County				
Agua Dulce Vineyards LLC	2084	E	661 268-7402	1577
Precision Millwork LLC	2431	F	661 402-5021	4111
AGUANGA, CA - Riverside County				
Patriot Polishing Company	2842	F	310 903-7409	8405

	SIC	EMP	PHONE	ENTRY #
ALAMEDA, CA - Alameda County				
ABB Enterprise Software Inc	3612	D	510 987-7111	16538
Abbott Diabetes Care Inc **(HQ)**	2835	C	510 749-5400	8198
Alameda Directory Inc	2741	F	510 747-1060	6179
Allergy Research Group LLC	2834	E	510 263-2000	7743
Bay Ship & Yacht Co **(PA)**	3731	C	510 337-9122	20280
Center For Cllbrtive Classroom	2731	D	510 533-0213	6084
Clear-Com LLC	3663	A	510 337-6600	17486
Comstock Press	2752	E	510 522-4115	6506
Contra Costa Newspapers Inc	2711	B	510 748-1683	5599
Edutone Corporation **(PA)**	7372	F	888 904-9773	23845
Ettore Products Co	3999	E	510 748-4100	23327
Exelixis Inc	3824	D	650 837-7000	20969
Exelixis Inc	2834	C	650 837-7000	7886
Exelixis Inc **(PA)**	2834	D	650 837-7000	7887
Fleenor Company Inc **(PA)**	2679	E	800 433-2531	5508
Fluxion Biosciences Inc	3841	E	650 241-4777	21715
Golden West Envelope Corp	2677	E	510 452-5419	5470
Heliotrope Technologies Inc	3211	E	510 871-3980	10269
Jansport Inc **(HQ)**	2393	F	510 814-7400	3660
Lens C-C Inc **(PA)**	3851	F	800 772-3911	22368
Motorola Solutions Inc	3663	C	510 217-7400	17595
Natel Energy Inc	3511	F	510 342-5269	13574
Novx Corporation	3825	E	408 998-5555	21094
ONe Color Communications LLC	2796	D	510 263-1640	7380
Penumbra Inc **(PA)**	3841	B	510 748-3200	21856
Polarion Software Inc	7372	D	877 572-4005	24306
Power Standards Lab Inc	3825	E	510 522-4400	21101
Rgb Spectrum	3577	D	510 814-7000	15321
Rmf Salt Holdings LLC	2844	F	510 477-9600	8572
Roche Molecular Systems Inc	2834	C	510 814-2800	8112
Rock Wall Wine Company Inc	2084	E	510 522-5700	1894
S & C Electric Company	3625	E	510 864-9300	16750
Sila Nanotechnologies Inc	3691	E	408 475-7452	19172
Simco-Ion Technology Group **(PA)**	3629	C	510 217-0600	16798
Sks Die Cast & Machining Inc **(PA)**	3363	E	510 523-2541	11349
St George Spirits Inc	2084	E	510 769-1601	1926
Stone Boat Yard Inc	3732	E	510 523-3030	20358
Symbol Technologies LLC	3577	C	510 684-2974	15342
Tender Corporation	3842	E	510 261-7414	22108
Therasense Inc	3841	F	510 749-5400	21930
Vf Outdoor LLC **(HQ)**	2329	C	510 618-3500	3128
Wind River Systems Inc **(HQ)**	7372	C	510 748-4100	24581
Wrightspeed Inc	3714	E	866 960-9482	19808
Xintec Corporation **(PA)**	3845	E	510 832-2130	22333
ALAMO, CA - Contra Costa County				
Edner Corporation	2051	E	925 831-1248	1197
Feedstuffs Processing Co	2048	F	925 820-5454	1093
Heirloom Computing Inc	7372	F	510 709-7245	23976
Sunsil Inc	3674	F	925 648-7779	18593
Trilore Technologies Inc	3365	E	925 295-0734	11390
ALBANY, CA - Alameda County				
Albany Swimming Pool	3949	E	510 559-6640	22736
Mingo Enterprises Inc	2721	F	510 528-3044	5989
Multimetrixs LLC	3629	F	510 527-6769	16792
Wastweet Studio Inc	3299	F	206 369-9060	11023
ALHAMBRA, CA - Los Angeles County				
Active Knitwear Resources Inc	2331	F	626 308-1328	3134
Air Blast Inc	3564	F	626 576-0144	14645
Alhambra Foundry Company Ltd	3321	E	626 289-4294	11140
Amertex International Inc	2331	E	626 570-9409	3137

Employment Codes: A=Over 500 employees, B=251-500,
C=101-250, D=51-100, E=20-50, F=10-19

2020 California
Manufacturers Register

© Mergent Inc. 1-800-342-5647

1299

GEOGRAPHIC

	SIC	EMP	PHONE	ENTRY #
Century Sewing Co	2335	E	626 289-0533	3222
China Press	2711	F	626 281-8500	5588
Coast To Coast Met Finshg Corp	3471	E	626 282-2122	12972
Comprhnsive Crdvsclar Spcalist (PA)	2834	E	626 281-8663	7847
Copy Solutions Inc	2752	E	323 307-0900	6513
E-Freight Technology Inc	7372	E	626 943-8418	23838
EDM International Logistics	3086	F	626 588-2299	9525
Ember Acquisition Sub Inc (HQ)	3679	C	626 293-3400	18903
Emcore Corporation (PA)	3674	C	626 293-3400	18213
Emcore Corporation	3674	C	626 293-3400	18214
Global Ocean Trading LLC	2091	F	626 281-0800	2244
Gluesmith Industries	2891	F	626 282-9390	8870
Green Dining Table	2013	F	626 782-7916	462
Home Paradise LLC	3469	F	626 284-9999	12816
Just Saying Inc	2389	F	888 512-5007	3560
K Live	3674	F	626 289-2885	18331
Kelly Tool & Mfgcoinc	3469	F	626 289-7962	12831
Lusida Rubber Products	3069	F	323 446-0280	9330
Makeit Inc	3577	F	626 470-7938	15282
N Z Pump Co Inc	3561	F	626 458-8023	14592
Opticomm Corp	3357	F	626 293-3400	11313
Ortel A Division Emcore Co (HQ)	3674	F	626 293-3400	18459
Riedon Inc (PA)	3676	C	626 284-9901	18691
Rods Unfinished Furniture	2511	F	626 281-9855	4606
Seal Innovations Inc	3069	F	626 282-7325	9370
TMJ Products Inc	3724	F	626 576-4063	19985
Tyler Trafficante Inc (PA)	2311	D	323 869-9299	2980
Universal Filtration Inc	3589	F	626 308-1832	15596
Victoire LLC	2384	F	323 225-0101	3505

ALISO VIEJO, CA - Orange County

	SIC	EMP	PHONE	ENTRY #
Adaptive Inc (PA)	7372	F	888 399-4621	23559
Agile Technologies Inc	3674	F	949 454-8030	18072
Appware Inc	7372	E	415 732-9298	23617
Astronic	3672	C	949 454-1180	17828
Avanir Pharmaceuticals Inc (HQ)	2834	E	949 389-6700	7781
AZ Displays Inc	3679	E	949 831-5000	18826
Biovail Technologies Ltd	2834	C	703 995-2400	7813
Brainchip Inc (HQ)	7372	E	949 330-6750	23693
Bridgeport Products Inc	3161	D	949 348-8800	10190
Catalina Lifesciences Inc	2834	E	800 898-6888	7834
Centon Electronics Inc (PA)	3572	D	949 855-9111	15013
Cianna Medical Inc	3061	F	949 360-0059	9260
Cove20 LLC	3674	F	949 297-4930	18184
Eeye Inc (HQ)	7372	E	949 333-1900	23846
Fuel Injection Engineering Co	3714	F	949 360-0909	19665
Global Wave Group LLC	7372	F	949 916-9800	23945
HD Carry Inc	3086	F	949 831-6022	9550
Hilborn Manufacturing Corp	3714	F	949 360-0909	19681
Indie Semiconductor	2211	D	949 608-0854	2693
Interactive Entertainment Inc	3944	F	714 460-2343	22684
Ipayables Inc (PA)	7372	D	949 215-9122	24044
Ixys Intgrtd Crcts Div AV Inc	3674	E	949 831-4621	18326
Liquid Bioscience Inc	2834	F	949 432-9559	7997
Microsemi Corporation (HQ)	3674	F	949 380-6100	18405
Microsoft Corporation	7372	E	949 680-3000	24154
Microvention Inc (DH)	3841	B	714 258-8000	21820
Modernpro LLC	2741	F	949 232-2148	6284
Nuvasive Spclzed Orthpdics Inc	3841	F	949 837-3600	21844
Pacific Alliance Capital Inc	3572	F	949 360-1796	15072
Pepsi-Cola Metro Btlg Co Inc	2086	C	949 643-5700	2126
Presbibio LLC	3851	E	949 502-7010	22380
Quest Software Inc	7372	D	949 754-8000	24334
Schuberth North America LLC	3469	F	949 215-0893	12870
Screening Systems Inc (PA)	3826	E	949 855-1751	21287
Sequent Medical Inc	3841	D	949 830-9600	21896
Shugart Corporation (PA)	3571	C	949 488-8779	14974
Siemens Industry Inc	3822	E	949 448-0600	20812
Stmicroelectronics Inc	3674	E	949 347-0717	18582
Vertos Medical Inc	3841	E	949 349-0008	21955
Vibes Audio LLC	3651	F	866 866-8484	17302
Voice Assist Inc	3679	F	949 655-1611	19139
Wepower LLC	3511	F	866 385-9463	13582
XEL USA Inc	3674	E	949 425-8686	18660
Zettler Magnetics Inc	3612	E	949 831-5000	16581

ALPINE, CA - San Diego County

	SIC	EMP	PHONE	ENTRY #
Custom Installations	2434	F	619 445-0692	4185
Valley Casework Inc	2434	D	619 579-6886	4261

ALPINE MEADOWS, CA - Placer County

	SIC	EMP	PHONE	ENTRY #
Arcade Belts Inc (PA)	2387	E	530 580-8089	3526

ALTA LOMA, CA - San Bernardino County

	SIC	EMP	PHONE	ENTRY #
Sharp-Rite Tool Inc	3545	F	909 948-1234	14194

ALTADENA, CA - Los Angeles County

	SIC	EMP	PHONE	ENTRY #
3becom Inc (PA)	7372	F	818 726-0007	23536
Acton Inc	3621	F	323 250-0685	16627
Dockum Research Laboratory	3843	F	626 794-1821	22150
Hdkaraoke Llc	3651	F	626 296-6200	17239
My Fruity Faces LLC	2079	F	877 358-9210	1477

ALVISO, CA - Santa Clara County

	SIC	EMP	PHONE	ENTRY #
Esilicon Corporation (PA)	3674	C	408 635-6300	18225
Flextronics Corporation (DH)	3679	B	803 936-5200	18917

AMERICAN CANYON, CA - Napa County

	SIC	EMP	PHONE	ENTRY #
Amcan Beverages Inc	2086	C	707 557-0500	2023
Amcor Flexibles LLC	2671	C	707 257-6481	5321
Barry Callebaut USA LLC	2066	F	707 642-8200	1406
Envirocare International Inc	3564	E	707 638-6800	14657
G L Mezzetta Inc	2033	D	707 648-1050	770
Midwestern Pipeline Svcs Inc (PA)	2952	F	707 557-6633	9122
William Kreysler & Assoc Inc	3089	E	707 552-3500	10124

ANAHEIM, CA - Orange County

	SIC	EMP	PHONE	ENTRY #
180 Snacks (PA)	2068	E	714 238-1192	1418
3d Instruments LP (DH)	3823	E	714 399-9200	20824
3d Machine Co Inc	3599	E	714 777-8985	15645
A & D Precision Mfg Inc	3599	E	714 779-2714	15652
A & G Instr Svc & Calibration	3491	F	714 630-7400	13286
A & R Powder Coating Inc	3479	F	714 630-0709	13131
A and G Inc	2231	C	714 756-0400	2741
A D S Gold Inc	3339	F	714 632-1888	11187
A J Fasteners Inc	3452	E	714 630-1556	12664
A P Seedorff & Company Inc	3625	F	714 252-5330	16692
A-L-L Magnetics	3499	F	714 632-1754	13493
Aaron Dutt Enterprises Inc	3469	E	714 632-7035	12758
Acrylic Designs Inc	3089	F	714 630-1370	9608
Action Enterprises Inc	3089	F	714 978-0333	9609
Action Innovations Inc	3089	E	714 978-0333	9610
Adcraft Products Co Inc	2759	F	714 776-1230	6974
Advanced Global Tech Group	3678	E	714 281-8020	18749
Advanced Manufacturing Tech	3699	C	714 238-1488	19248
Advanced Tech Plating	3471	F	714 630-7093	12907
Advanced Thermal Sciences	3674	F	714 688-4200	18068
Adwest Technologies Inc (HQ)	3564	E	714 632-8595	14644
Aerofab Corporation	3441	F	714 635-0902	11737
Aerospace Parts Holdings Inc	3728	A	949 877-3630	20023
Affluent Target Marketing Inc	2721	E	714 446-6280	5877
Airworthy Cabin Solutions LLC	3429	F	714 901-0660	11559
Allbrite Car Care Products	2842	F	714 666-8683	8360
Alstyle AP & Activewear MGT Co	2253	F	714 765-0400	2771
Alstyle Apparel LLC	2211	A	714 765-0400	2665
Alvarez Refinishing Inc	2262	E	714 780-0171	2842
American Circuit Tech Inc (PA)	3672	E	714 777-2480	17817
American Crcuit Card Retainers	3571	F	714 738-6194	14887
American Fabrication Corp (PA)	3714	C	714 632-1709	19579
American Index and Files LLC	2679	F	714 630-3360	5492
American Industrial Corp	3544	F	714 680-4763	14014
American Ingredients Inc	2833	F	714 630-6000	7644
American Sheet Metal Inc	3444	F	714 780-0155	12108
Anacom General Corporation	3651	E	714 774-8484	17188
Anaheim Automation Inc	3625	F	714 992-6990	16698
Anaheim Custom Extruders Inc	3089	E	714 693-8508	9630
Anaheim Embroidery Inc	2395	E	714 563-5220	3723
Anaheim Wire Products Inc (PA)	3496	E	714 563-8300	13395
Animal Nutrition Inds Inc	2833	F	949 583-2920	7645
Annmar Industries Inc	3089	F	714 630-5443	9632
Anvil Arts Inc	2514	F	714 630-2870	4682
Apex Technology Holdings Inc	3812	C	714 688-7188	20535
Apple Paper Converting Inc	2679	E	714 632-3195	5493
Applied Manufacturing Tech Inc	3555	E	714 630-9530	14315
APT Electronics Inc	3672	C	714 687-6760	17822
Aquarian Accessories Corp	3931	E	714 632-0230	22606
Aquarian Coatings Corp	3471	E	714 632-0230	12932
Aquatic Co	3088	E	714 993-1220	9580
Aquatic Industries Inc	3088	C	800 877-2005	9582
Arch-Rite Inc	2431	F	714 630-9305	3996
Arden Engineering Inc (DH)	3728	E	949 877-3642	20040
Arista Foods Corporation	2038	F	714 666-1001	942
Artistic Pltg & Met Finshg Inc	3471	D	619 661-1691	12934
Ascent Manufacturing LLC	3469	E	714 540-6414	12767
Asdak International	3269	F	714 447-0733	10484
Aseptic Innovations Inc	3221	F	714 584-2110	10284
Assa Abloy Entrance Systems US	3699	D	714 578-0526	19262
Astro-Tek Industries LLC	3728	D	714 238-0022	20045
Atlas Magnetics Inc	3679	F	714 632-9718	18823
Automatic Switch Company	3491	F	714 283-4000	13290
B & B Specialties Inc (PA)	3429	E	714 985-3000	11568
B & Cawnings Inc	3444	E	714 632-3303	12124

Mergent email: customerrelations@mergent.com
1300　　　　　　　　　　　　　2020 California
　　　　　　　　　　　　　　　Manufacturers Register　　　　　(P-0000) Products & Services Section entry number
　　　　　　　　　　　　　　　　　　　　　　　　　　　　　(PA)=Parent Co (HQ)=Headquarters (DH)=Div Headquarters

Name	SIC	EMP	PHONE	ENTRY #
B & E Enterprises	3751	F	714 630-3731	20382
B K Harris Inc	2752	F	714 630-8780	6430
B/E Aerospace Inc	3728	B	714 688-4200	20054
Bace Manufacturing Inc (HQ)	3089	A	714 630-6002	9650
Bananafish Productions Inc	3231	F	714 956-2129	10340
Barbee Valve & Supply Inc (HQ)	3491	F	619 585-8484	13294
Bassani Manufacturing	3498	F	714 630-1821	13461
Bechler Cams Inc	3829	F	714 774-5150	21443
Berry Global Inc	3089	F	714 777-5200	9660
Bimbo Bakeries Usa Inc	2051	D	714 634-8068	1158
Bimbo Bakeries Usa Inc	2099	F	714 533-9436	2405
Birchwood Lighting Inc	3648	E	714 550-7118	17105
Black Oxide Industries Inc	3471	E	714 870-9610	12943
Block Tops Inc (PA)	2541	F	714 978-5080	4884
Botanx LLC	2844	E	714 854-1601	8451
Bowers & Kelly Products Inc	3086	E	714 630-1285	9509
Bpo Management Services Inc (HQ)	7372	F	714 974-2670	23690
Bracton Sosafe Inc	2842	F	714 632-8499	8369
Bradfield Manufacturing Inc	3446	F	714 543-8348	12457
Brice Tool & Stamping	3469	F	714 630-6400	12775
Bridgford Foods Corporation (HQ)	2045	B	714 526-5533	1056
British American Tl & Die LLC	3423	C	714 776-8995	11522
Bud Wil Inc	3086	F	714 630-1242	9510
Buds Cotton Inc	2844	E	714 223-7800	8452
Buds Polishing & Metal Finshg	3471	F	714 632-0121	12952
C & S Assembly Inc	3679	F	866 779-8939	18844
C B S Fasteners Inc	3452	E	714 779-6368	12671
C T L Printing Inds Inc	2759	E	714 635-2980	7011
Cadence Aerospace LLC (PA)	3728	F	949 877-3630	20062
Cal Tech Precision Inc	3728	D	714 992-4130	20063
Campbell & Loftin Inc	3444	F	714 871-1950	12149
Canyon Composites Incorporated	3728	E	714 991-8181	20065
Ccda Waters LLC	3221	D	714 991-7031	10286
Ceco Environmental Corp	3089	E	760 530-1409	9700
Ced Anaheim 018	3699	F	714 956-5156	19271
Cemtrol Inc	3571	F	714 666-6606	14895
Certifix Inc	3999	F	714 496-3850	23302
Chad Industries Incorporated	3569	E	714 938-0080	14802
Champions Choice Inc	2992	F	714 635-4491	9135
Cheek Machine Corp	3599	E	714 279-9466	15843
Ciscos Shop	3432	F	657 230-9158	11664
Clean Cut Technologies LLC	3086	D	714 864-3500	9514
Cns Aviation Inc	3721	F	714 901-7072	19889
Coast 2 Coast Cables LLC	3357	F	714 666-1062	11298
Coast Sign Incorporated	3993	C	714 520-9144	23078
Cobra Systems	2741	E	714 688-7992	6216
Coca-Cola Company	2086	E	714 991-7031	2062
Colortech Label Inc	2679	F	714 999-5545	5501
Commercial Furniture	2521	E	714 350-7045	4792
Community Close-Up Westminster	2711	D	714 704-5811	5595
Computed Tool & Engineering	3544	F	714 630-3911	14036
Craftech EDM Corporation	3089	C	714 630-8117	9732
Crafters Companion	3944	E	714 630-2444	22668
Craftsman Cutting Dies Inc (PA)	3423	E	714 776-8995	11526
Creative Press LLC	2752	D	714 774-5060	6522
Crescent Inc	2752	E	714 992-6030	6523
Cresco Manufacturing Inc	3599	E	714 525-2326	15870
Crest Coating Inc	3479	D	714 635-7090	13162
Cristek Interconnects Inc (PA)	3678	C	714 696-5200	18762
Crystal Cal Lab Inc	3679	E	714 991-1580	18878
Custom Industries Inc	3231	E	714 779-9101	10349
Custom Tooling & Stamping of O	3544	F	714 979-6782	14039
Cytec Engineered Materials Inc	2821	E	714 632-8444	7552
Cytec Engineered Materials Inc	3365	C	714 632-1174	11375
Cyvex Nutrition Inc	2023	F	949 622-9030	584
D & B Supply Corp	3535	E	714 632-3020	13820
D & D Gear Incorporated	3728	C	714 692-6570	20080
D & S Industries Inc	3728	F	714 779-8074	20081
D-Mac Inc	2451	E	714 808-3918	4443
Daisy Scout Publishing	2741	F	714 630-6611	6219
Danville Materials LLC	3843	E	714 399-0334	22141
Delta Coast Beer LLC	2082	F	213 604-2428	1519
DG Performance Spc Inc	3799	D	714 961-8850	20506
Diamodent Inc	3843	F	888 281-8850	22149
Digital Periph Solutions Inc	3651	F	714 998-3440	17218
Disney Enterprises Inc	2389	D	407 397-6000	3553
Display Fabrication Group Inc	2399	E	714 373-2100	3836
Dretloh Aircraft Supply Inc (PA)	3728	E	714 634-6982	20090
Dust Collector Services Inc	3499	E	714 237-1690	13518
Dynaflex International	3949	E	714 630-0909	22793
E-Solution Inc	3535	E	714 589-2012	13823
Eagle Ridge Paper Ltd (HQ)	2621	E	714 780-1799	5103
Eastman Performance Films LLC	2821	E	714 634-0900	7557
Econolite Control Products Inc (PA)	3669	C	714 630-3700	17727
Econotek Inc (PA)	3843	F	714 238-1131	22151
Edco Plastics Inc	3089	F	714 772-1986	9772
Electro Metal Finishing Corp (PA)	3479	F	714 630-8940	13171
Electron Beam Engineering Inc	7692	F	714 491-5990	24633
Elegance Entries Inc	3442	F	714 632-3667	11951
Elysium Mosaics Inc	3253	F	714 991-7885	10440
Emazing Lights LLC	3648	F	626 628-6482	17122
Emitcon Inc	3824	F	714 632-8595	20968
Emporium Di Sanarrey Corp	3281	F	714 780-5474	10905
Endress & Hauser Conducta Inc	3826	E	800 835-5474	21225
Endress + Hauser Inc	3821	F	714 577-5600	20756
Energy Reconnaissance Inc	3567	F	714 630-4491	14761
Ennis Inc	3544	C	714 765-0400	14049
Euramax Holdings Inc	3353	F	714 563-8260	11216
Evert Hancock Incorporated	3444	F	714 870-0376	12202
Excelsior Nutrition Inc	2833	E	657 999-5188	7659
Executive Tool Inc	3444	F	714 996-1276	12204
Expert Coatings & Graphics LLC	3479	F	714 476-2086	13177
Expo Dyeing & Finishing Inc	2269	C	714 220-9583	2853
Fab Tron	3444	F	714 996-4270	12208
Fabrication Network Inc	3444	D	714 393-5282	12209
Fantasia Distribution Inc	2131	E	714 817-8300	2660
Farrell Brothers Holding Corp	3599	F	714 630-3417	15952
Federal Signal Corporation	3711	D	714 871-3336	19469
Filtronics	3589	F	714 630-5040	15514
Firmenich	2869	C	714 535-2871	8738
Foam Concepts Inc	3086	E	714 693-1037	9530
Foam Plastics & Rbr Pdts Corp	3086	F	714 779-0990	9535
Foreseeson Custom Displays Inc (PA)	3577	E	714 300-0540	15230
Friedl Corporation	3714	F	714 443-0122	19662
Fulcrum International Inc	2261	E	310 763-6823	2825
Gear Manufacturing Inc	3728	E	714 792-2895	20113
Gemini Mfg & Engrg Inc	3544	E	714 999-0010	14058
Genesis Computer Systems Inc	3571	F	714 632-3648	14915
Gentry Golf Maintenance	3949	E	714 630-3541	22806
Ges US (new England) Inc	3679	C	978 459-4434	18924
Gforce Corporation	2051	F	714 630-0909	1215
Gledhill/Lyons Inc	3728	F	714 502-0274	20115
Global Enterprise Mfg Inc	3999	E	657 234-1150	23344
Global Paper Solutions Inc	2621	F	714 687-6102	5106
Globalscale Technologies Inc	3572	F	714 632-9239	15032
Gmp Laboratories America Inc	2834	D	714 630-2467	7925
Golden Coast Sportswear Inc	2339	E	714 704-4655	3330
Greenfields Outdoor Fitnes Inc	3949	F	888 315-9037	22814
Griffiths Services Inc	2752	E	714 685-7700	6598
Guptill Gear Corporation	3599	F	714 956-2170	16009
Haddads Fine Arts Inc	2893	F	714 996-2100	8919
Harrys Dye and Wash Inc	2261	E	714 446-0300	2826
Heidens Inc	2033	F	714 525-3414	773
Hestan Commercial Corporation	3639	C	714 869-2380	16851
High Energy Sports Inc	2399	F	714 632-3323	3845
Hitech Metal Fabrication Corp	3441	D	714 635-3505	11808
Hollinger Metal Edge Inc	2653	E	323 721-7800	5236
I M B Electronic Products	3675	D	714 523-2110	18678
ICM Installations Inc	3499	E	714 751-4026	13525
Ideal Fasteners Inc	3452	E	714 630-7840	12682
Ideal Graphics Inc	2752	E	714 632-3398	6625
Inland Litho LLC	2752	E	714 993-6000	6641
Innovative Manufacturing Inc	3599	F	714 524-5246	16048
Innovative Organics Inc	2869	E	714 701-3900	8744
Intense Lighting LLC	3646	E	714 630-9877	17045
Interlink Inc	2752	E	714 905-7700	6650
Interlog Corporation	3679	E	714 529-7808	18951
International Abrasive Mfg Co	2844	E	714 779-9970	8517
International Paper Company	2653	C	714 776-6060	5237
International West Inc	3444	D	714 632-9190	12249
Interstate Electronics Corp (DH)	3825	B	714 758-0500	21056
Interstate Electronics Corp	3663	E	714 758-3395	17543
Ironwood Electric Inc	3699	E	714 630-2350	19329
J&S Goodwin Inc (HQ)	3537	D	714 956-4040	13877
Jabil Inc	3672	E	714 938-0080	17906
Jaco Engineering	3599	E	714 991-1680	16072
Jaguar Litho Incorporated	2796	F	714 978-1821	7378
Janus International Group LLC	3442	F	714 503-6120	11960
Jasper Electronics	3679	E	714 917-0749	18960
JDC Development Group Inc	2449	E	714 575-1108	4417
Jeico Security Inc	3699	F	-	19335
Jellco Container Inc	2653	D	714 666-2728	5240
Jenson Custom Furniture Inc	2512	D	714 634-8145	4648
Joint Technologies Limited	3571	F	949 361-1158	14931
K & J Wire Products Corp	3446	E	714 816-0360	12488
Kanstul Musical Instrs Inc	3931	E	714 563-1000	22628
Kca Electronics Inc	3672	C	714 239-2433	17910
Kehoe Custom Wood Designs	2511	F	714 993-0444	4581
Kempton Machine Works Inc	3545	F	714 990-0596	14167
Kiva Container Corporation	3086	F	714 630-3850	9554

Employment Codes: A=Over 500 employees, B=251-500,
C=101-250, D=51-100, E=20-50, F=10-19

2020 California
Manufacturers Register

© Mergent Inc. 1-800-342-5647

1301

GEOGRAPHIC

	SIC	EMP	PHONE	ENTRY #		SIC	EMP	PHONE	ENTRY #
L & H Industries	2037	F	714 635-1555	919	Rapid Manufacturing A (PA)	3496	C	714 974-2432	13432
L3 Technologies Inc	3663	C	714 758-4222	17562	Raykorvay Inc	3942	F	714 632-8680	22653
Labeltronix LLC	2759	D	800 429-4321	7115	Raytheon Applied Signal	3669	F	714 917-0255	17757
Leonards Carpet Service Inc (PA)	2541	D	714 630-1930	4921	Regal Custom Millwork Inc	2421	F	714 632-2488	3943
Lester Lithograph Inc	2752	E	714 491-3981	6699	Reliable Packaging Systems Inc	2891	F	714 572-1094	8891
Link4 Corporation	3822	F	714 524-0004	20797	Rf Precision Cables Inc	3357	F	714 772-7567	11317
Lodestone LLC	3548	F	714 970-0900	14244	Rgb Systems Inc (PA)	3577	C	714 491-1500	15322
Magnetic Metals Corporation	3542	E	714 828-4625	13982	Rigiflex Technology Inc	3672	E	714 688-1500	17976
Magnetic Sensors Corp	3679	D	714 630-8380	19003	Roberts Precision Engrg Inc	3599	E	714 635-4485	16365
Mako Industries SC Inc	3826	E	714 632-1400	21255	Rockwell Automation Inc	3625	D	714 938-9000	16745
Mako Overhead Door Inc	3442	F	714 998-0122	11968	Roto-Die Company Inc	3544	F	714 991-8701	14101
Man-Grove Industries Inc	2752	D	714 630-3020	6713	RPM Plastic Molding Inc	3089	E	714 630-9300	10033
Master Arts Inc	2796	F	714 240-4550	7379	RSI Home Products Inc (HQ)	2514	A	714 449-2200	4699
Maverick Abrasives Corporation	3291	D	714 854-9531	10950	RSI Home Products Mfg Inc	2514	A	714 449-2200	4701
Maxlite Inc	3646	E	714 678-5000	17059	Rtie Holdings LLC	3679	D	714 765-8200	19073
McCormick & Company Inc	2099	D	714 685-0934	2546	Rtr Industries LLC	3592	E	714 996-0050	15618
McLeod Racing LLC	3714	F	714 630-2764	19716	Ryvec Inc	2816	E	714 520-5592	7461
Mechanized Enterprises Inc	3599	F	714 630-5512	16187	S & S Printers	2752	F	714 535-5592	6851
Medivision Inc	3845	F	714 563-2772	22279	S K Laboratories Inc	2833	D	714 695-9800	7689
Metal-Fab Services Industries	3444	E	714 630-7771	12296	Saint-Gobain Ceramics Plas Inc	2869	E	714 701-3900	8772
Mettler Electronics Corp	3841	E	714 533-2221	21818	Sam Machining Inc	3599	F	714 632-7035	16383
Micrometals Inc (PA)	3679	D	714 970-9400	19016	Schley Products Inc	3423	F	714 693-7666	11543
Micrometals/Texas Inc	3679	C	325 677-8753	19017	Seating Component Mfg Inc	2519	E	714 693-3376	4773
Mid-West Wholesale Hardware Co	3429	E	714 630-4751	11611	Sechrist Industries Inc	3841	D	714 579-8400	21893
Millcraft Inc	2431	D	714 632-9621	4085	Sehanson Inc	3728	E	714 778-1900	20230
Mobile Wireless Tech Llc	3669	F	714 239-1535	17747	Serra Laser and Waterjet Inc	3699	E	714 680-6211	19400
Moda Enterprises Inc	3711	F	714 484-0076	19488	Setco LLC	3089	E	812 424-2904	10054
Modern Manufacturing Inc	3599	F	714 254-0156	16218	Sharon Havriluk	2782	E	714 630-1313	7316
Moeller Mfg & Sup LLC	3429	E	714 999-5551	11612	Shaxon Industries Inc	3572	D	714 779-1140	15099
Mondelez Global LLC	2051	E	714 634-2773	1245	Sheet Metal Service	3444	F	714 446-0196	12374
Moreno Industries Inc	3714	F	714 229-9696	19723	Shrin Corporation	3714	C	714 850-0303	19766
Nbty Manufacturing LLC	2834	C	714 765-8323	8027	Si Manufacturing Inc	3677	E	714 956-7110	18742
Nelco Products Inc (HQ)	3083	C	714 879-4293	9444	Signage Solutions Corporation	3993	E	714 491-0299	23204
Nellson Nutraceutical Inc (PA)	2064	B	626 812-6522	1390	Skullduggery Inc	3944	F	714 777-6425	22714
Nellson Nutraceutical LLC (PA)	2064	B	714 765-7000	1391	Sky Rider Equipment Co Inc	2515	F	714 632-6890	4742
Neutron Plating Inc	3471	D	714 632-9241	13059	Slp Limited LLC	3672	F	714 517-1955	18001
Nu TEC Powdercoating	3479	F	714 632-5045	13213	Smart Elec & Assembly Inc	3672	C	714 772-2651	18002
Nylok LLC	3452	E	714 635-3993	12689	SMt Mfg Incorporataed	3679	E	714 738-9999	19086
Oasis Alloy Wheels Inc	3365	F	714 533-3286	11386	Sonfarrel Aerospace LLC	3365	D	714 630-7230	11389
One-Way Manufacturing Inc	3498	E	714 630-8833	13478	Southern California Mtl Hdlg	3537	E	714 773-9630	13892
Onesolution Light and Control	3648	E	714 490-5540	17150	Southland Tool Mfg Inc	3545	F	714 632-8198	14197
Orange County Erectors Inc	3448	E	714 502-8455	12568	Spark Stone LLC	1411	F	714 772-7575	294
Orange County Screw Products	3599	E	714 630-7433	16263	Specialty Apartment Supply Inc	3429	E	714 630-2275	11629
Ortronics Inc	3444	C	714 776-5420	12319	Spidell Publishing Inc	2741	E	714 776-7850	6345
Osio International Inc	2671	F	714 935-9700	5333	SPX Corporation	3443	F	714 634-3855	12056
Otanez New Creations	2541	F	951 808-9663	4928	St Pierre Gonzalez Enterprises	3479	E	714 491-2191	13253
Outdoor Dimensions LLC	2499	C	714 578-9555	4519	Stainless Micro-Polish Inc	3471	F	714 632-8903	13106
Pacific Broach & Engrg Assoc	3599	F	714 632-5678	16272	Steeldyne Industries	3444	E	714 630-6200	12388
Pacific Precision Metals Inc	3469	C	951 226-1500	12854	Stepan Company	2821	E	714 776-9870	7615
Pacific Tchnical Eqp Engrg Inc	3563	F	714 835-3088	14637	Strand Art Company Inc	3089	E	714 777-0444	10073
Pacific Transformer Corp	3612	C	714 779-0450	16566	Stryker Corporation	3841	E	714 764-1700	21917
Pacific West Litho Inc	2752	E	714 779-0868	6766	Summit Interconnect Inc (PA)	3672	C	714 239-2433	18015
Pacific Westline Inc	2541	F	714 956-2442	4929	Sun Rich Foods Intl Corp	2099	E	714 632-7577	2619
Pampanga Foods Company Inc	2013	F	714 773-0537	486	Sunny Delight Beverages Co	2033	C	714 630-6251	827
Pampanga Foods Incorporated	2038	E	714 331-7206	974	Sunset Signs and Printing	3993	F	714 255-9104	23220
Parex Usa Inc (DH)	3299	E	714 774-2266	11018	Superior Connector Plating Inc	3471	E	714 774-1101	13110
Park Electrochemical Corp	3672	E	714 459-4400	17953	Superior Jig Inc	3544	F	714 525-4777	14107
Pendarvis Manufacturing Inc	3599	E	714 992-0950	16291	Superior Spring Company	3495	E	714 490-0881	13390
Performance Powder Inc	3479	E	714 632-0600	13223	Superior Stone Products Inc	3281	F	714 635-7775	10936
Pharmachem Laboratories LLC	2023	F	714 630-6000	614	Synfonia Floors Inc	2426	F	714 300-0770	3985
Phillips Lobue & Wilson Mllwk	2431	F	951 331-5714	4108	T&J Sausage Kitchen Inc	2013	E	714 632-8350	503
Pinnacle Precision Shtmtl Corp (PA)	3444	C	714 777-3129	12335	Tahiti Cabinets Inc	2599	D	714 693-0618	5084
Pinnacle Precision Shtmtl Corp	3444	D	714 777-3129	12336	Tait & Associates Inc	3443	E	714 560-8222	12062
Pipe Fabricating & Supply Co (PA)	3498	D	714 630-5200	13481	Tajen Graphics Inc	2752	F	714 527-3122	6884
Porter Powder Coating Inc	3479	F	714 956-2001	13227	Tam Printing Inc	2752	F	714 224-1486	6885
Powdercoat Services LLC	3479	E	714 533-2251	13229	Targus US LLC	3161	F	714 765-5555	10212
Power Aire Inc	3613	E	800 526-7661	16607	Taylor-Dunn Manufacturing Co (DH)	3537	D	714 956-4040	13895
Power Paragon Inc (DH)	3612	A	714 956-9200	16568	Tck Membrane America Inc	2899	F	714 678-8832	9028
Power Paragon Inc	3699	B	714 956-9200	19379	Technic Inc	3471	E	714 632-0200	13116
Precision Aerospace & Tech Inc	3545	E	714 656-1620	14185	Technotronix Inc	3672	E	714 630-9200	18020
Precision Anodizing & Pltg Inc	3471	D	714 996-1601	13075	Teco Diagnostics	2835	E	714 693-7788	8264
Precon Inc	3541	E	714 630-7632	13941	Telatemp Corporation	3829	F	714 414-0343	21553
Preferred Pharmaceuticals Inc	2834	F	714 777-3729	8081	Textile Products Inc	2221	E	714 761-0401	2736
Print N Save Inc	2752	F	714 634-1133	6795	Textured Design Furniture	2511	E	714 502-9121	4615
Product Solutions Inc	3589	E	714 545-9757	15561	Tfd Incorporated	3827	E	714 630-7127	21415
Progrssive Intgrated Solutions	2759	D	714 237-0980	7187	Thermech Corporation	2671	F	714 533-3183	5345
Qualitask Incorporated	3599	F	714 237-0900	16324	Thornton Steel & Ir Works Inc	3446	E	714 491-8800	12515
Quality Edm Inc	3599	F	714 283-9220	16326	Top Printing & Graphic Inc	2759	E	714 484-9200	7252
Quality First Woodworks Inc	2499	C	714 632-0480	4523	Towne Park Brew Inc	2082	E	714 844-2492	1571
R & S Overhead Door of So Cal	3442	E	714 680-0600	11979	Transko Electronics Inc	3679	E	714 528-8000	19123
R C I P Inc	3599	F	714 630-1239	16333	Transline Technology Inc	3672	E	714 533-8300	18024
R H Barden Inc	3677	F	714 970-0900	18737	Tri Power Electric Inc	3699	F	714 630-6445	19423
R K Fabrication Inc	2821	F	714 630-9654	7602	Triad Bellows Design & Mfg Inc	3599	E	714 204-4444	16467
Racing Beat Inc	3519	E	714 779-8677	13598	Trinity Process Solutions Inc	3498	E	714 701-1112	13487
Radarsonics Inc	3679	F	714 630-7288	19063	Trussworks International Inc	3441	D	714 630-2772	11904

Mergent email: customerrelations@mergent.com
1302

2020 California
Manufacturers Register

(P-0000) Products & Services Section entry number
(PA)=Parent Co (HQ)=Headquarters (DH)=Div Headquarters

	SIC	EMP	PHONE	ENTRY #
Ttm Technologies Inc	3672	B	714 688-7200	18032
Tuff - Toe Inc	2891	E	714 997-9585	8900
Tuffer Manufacturing Co Inc	3812	E	714 526-3077	20738
Turret Lathe Specialists Inc	3599	F	714 520-0058	16479
Twilight Technology Inc (PA)	3674	E	714 257-2257	18627
Two Blind Mice LLC	2084	F	714 279-0600	1979
United Paper Box Inc	2657	F	714 777-8383	5319
Universal Alloy Corporation	3354	B	714 630-7200	11250
Universal Directory Publishing	2741	E	714 994-6025	6367
University Frames Inc	2499	E	714 575-5100	4541
UOP LLC	2671	E	714 870-7590	5347
US Bioservices (PA)	2851	E	800 801-1140	8690
US Union Tool Inc (HQ)	3541	E	714 521-6242	13960
USA Extruded Plastics Inc	3089	F	714 991-6061	10105
Vascular Imaging Professionals (PA)	3841	F	949 278-5622	21949
Veeco Electro Fab Inc	3672	E	714 630-8020	18043
Venus Alloys Inc (PA)	3363	F	714 635-8800	11350
Visionary Inc	3851	E	714 237-1900	22394
Vts Sheetmetal Specialist Co	3444	E	714 237-1420	12429
Walt Disney Imagineering	2389	C	714 781-3152	3584
Wasser Filtration Inc (PA)	3569	D	714 982-5600	14870
Weartech International Inc (HQ)	3562	F	714 683-2430	14620
Weis/Robart Partitions Inc	3446	F	714 666-0822	12521
Wellbore Navigation Inc (PA)	3829	F	714 259-7760	21564
West Bond Inc (PA)	3569	F	714 978-1551	14872
Western Golf Inc	3949	F	800 448-4409	22924
Westpak Usa Inc	3699	F	714 530-6995	19444
Wide USA Corporation	3575	E	714 300-0540	15138
Wildlife In Wood Inc	2499	F	714 773-5816	4543
Willard Marine Inc	3732	D	714 630-4018	20364
Woodwork Pioneers Corp	2431	F	714 991-1017	4156
Wwt International Inc	3533	F	714 632-0810	13797
Xerxes Corporation	2821	D	714 630-0012	7625
Y2k Precision Sheetmetal Inc	3444	F	714 632-3901	12439
Yeager Manufacturing Corp (PA)	3728	E	714 879-2800	20272
YKK (usa) Inc	3965	C	714 701-1200	23018
Young Nails Inc	2844	F	714 992-1400	8610
Yti Enterprises Inc	2499	F	714 632-8696	4544
Zurich Engineering Inc	3724	F	714 528-0066	19992

ANDERSON, CA - Shasta County

	SIC	EMP	PHONE	ENTRY #
B & B Rv Inc	3716	E	530 365-7043	19840
Blue Lake Roundstock Co LLC	2491	F	530 515-7007	4471
Checchi Enterprises Inc	2752	F	530 378-1207	6481
Dpm Inc	3599	F	530 378-3420	15907
Folsom Ready Mix Inc	3273	F	530 365-0191	10758
Haisch Construction Co Inc	2439	F	530 378-6800	4303
James A Headrick Ii/Elizabeth	2411	D	530 247-8000	3890
North Valley Newspapers Inc	2711	F	530 365-2797	5784
Outdoor Creations Inc	3272	F	530 365-6106	10618
Shasta Wood Products	2541	F	530 378-6880	4937
Sierra Pacific Industries (PA)	2421	D	530 378-8000	3951
Sierra Pacific Industries	2421	E	530 365-3721	3957
Siskiyou Forest Products (PA)	2431	E	530 378-6980	4126
Skyline Alterations Inc	2411	F	530 549-4010	3908
Voorwood Company	3553	F	530 365-3311	14300
Williams Cabinets Inc	2434	F	530 365-8421	4266

ANGELS CAMP, CA - Calaveras County

	SIC	EMP	PHONE	ENTRY #
Angels Sheet Metal Inc	3444	F	209 736-0911	12110
California Electric Steel	3325	E	209 736-0465	11169
Foothill Pritnig & Graphics/ C (PA)	2752	F	209 736-4332	6579
Relcomm Inc	3679	F	209 736-0421	19067

ANGWIN, CA - Napa County

	SIC	EMP	PHONE	ENTRY #
Gina Designs	3911	F	707 967-1041	22521
Neal Family Vineyards LLC	2084	F	707 965-2800	1837

ANTELOPE, CA - Sacramento County

	SIC	EMP	PHONE	ENTRY #
Temptrol Industries Inc	2394	F	916 344-4457	3710

ANTIOCH, CA - Contra Costa County

	SIC	EMP	PHONE	ENTRY #
Allied Container Systems Inc	3448	C	925 944-7600	12527
Bond Manufacturing Co Inc (PA)	3272	D	925 252-1135	10538
Chep (usa) Inc	2448	D	925 234-4970	4356
Contra Costa Newspapers Inc	2711	F	925 634-2125	5602
Georgia-Pacific LLC	3275	C	925 757-2870	10877
K I O Kables Inc	3496	F	925 778-7500	13419
Marine & Industrial Services	3498	F	925 757-8791	13476
Pacific Flyway Decoy Assn	3949	F	925 754-4978	22863
Silgan Containers Mfg Corp	3411	C	925 778-8000	11505
Ssg Alliance LLC (PA)	3699	F	925 526-6050	19413
Tomiko Inc	3561	F	925 754-5694	14600
Ultimate Game Chair Inc	3651	E	925 756-6944	17296
Verco Decking Inc	3444	F	925 778-2102	12424

APPLE VALLEY, CA - San Bernardino County

	SIC	EMP	PHONE	ENTRY #
EE Pauley Plastic Extrusion	3089	F	760 240-3737	9775
Global Pumice LLC	1499	F	760 240-3544	388
Induction Technology Corp	3567	F	760 246-7333	14764
Land N Top Cleaning Services	2273	E	760 624-8845	2871
Phantom Tool & Die Co	3542	F	760 240-4249	13989
Polymer Concepts Technologies	3053	F	760 240-4999	9248
Reid Products Inc	3599	F	760 240-1355	16349
Telexca Inc	3721	F	760 247-4277	19934
Tibban Manufacturing Inc	3999	F	760 961-1160	23504
Valero Energy Corporation	2911	E	760 946-3322	9081
Waterfountainscom Inc	3499	F	760 946-0525	13555

APTOS, CA - Santa Cruz County

	SIC	EMP	PHONE	ENTRY #
Engage Communication Inc (PA)	3661	E	831 688-1021	17365
Farr West Fashions	2341	F	831 661-5039	3441
Mariannes Ice Cream LLC	2024	F	831 713-4746	656
Print Smith Inc	2752	F	831 688-1538	6796
Pureline Oralcare Inc	3843	F	831 662-9500	22184
Santa Cruz Coffee Roasting Co	2095	E	831 685-0100	2310
Warmboard Inc	3567	E	831 685-9276	14779

ARBUCKLE, CA - Colusa County

	SIC	EMP	PHONE	ENTRY #
ADM Milling Co	2041	D	530 476-2662	987
Cal Vsta Erosion Ctrl Pdts LLC	3531	E	530 476-0706	13713
California Family Foods LLC	2044	D	530 476-3326	1036
Conrad Wood Preserving Co	2491	F	530 476-2894	4476
National Oilwell Varco Inc	1389	F	530 682-0571	235
Sun Valley Rice Company LLC	2044	D	530 476-3000	1051

ARCADIA, CA - Los Angeles County

	SIC	EMP	PHONE	ENTRY #
Airsoft Zone Corporation (PA)	3949	E	818 495-6502	22735
Bendick Precision Inc	3599	F	626 445-0217	15786
Butane Propane News Inc	2721	F	626 357-2168	5897
Cardenas Enterprises Inc	2542	F	323 588-0137	4968
Cremax U S A Corporation	3429	F	626 956-8800	11582
Danco Anodizing Inc (PA)	3471	F	626 445-3303	12982
Dear John Denim Inc	2211	F	626 350-5100	2680
Dimad Enterprises Inc (PA)	3471	F	626 445-3303	12986
Enas Media Inc	3652	E	626 962-1115	17318
Harte Hanks Inc	2711	F	626 251-4500	5654
Heateflex Corporation	3433	F	626 599-8566	11699
J&M Analytik AG	3826	E	626 297-2930	21250
Joico Laboratories Inc	2844	C	626 321-4100	8524
Kustomer Kinetics Inc	2844	E	626 445-6161	8529
Quantum Corporation	3572	C	213 248-2481	15080
Relton Corporation	2899	D	800 423-1505	9019
T&L Air Conditioning Inc	3822	F	626 294-9888	20816
Tektest Inc	3678	E	626 446-6115	18799
Variant Technology Inc	3648	F	626 278-4343	17175
Zotos International Inc	2844	E	626 321-4100	8614

ARCATA, CA - Humboldt County

	SIC	EMP	PHONE	ENTRY #
Crestmark Architractural Mill	2431	E	707 822-4034	4024
Cummins Pacific LLC	3519	F	707 822-7392	13585
Cypress Grove Chevre Inc	2022	D	707 825-1100	545
Desserts On US Inc	2051	F	707 822-0160	1186
Fire and Light Originals LP	3231	F	707 825-7500	10359
Holly Yashi Inc	3911	D	707 822-0389	22528
JR Stephens Company	2434	E	707 825-0100	4213
Kokatat Inc	2329	D	707 822-7621	3098
Larry Schlussler	3632	F	707 822-9095	16820
Lindgren Lumber Co	2421	F	707 822-6519	3938
Living Waters Logging Inc	2411	F	707 822-3955	3893
Pac Powder Inc	3479	F	707 826-1630	13217
Schmidbauer Lumber Inc	2421	F	707 822-7607	3947
Statewide Safety & Signs Inc	3993	E	707 825-6927	23217
Sun Valley Floral Group LLC	3999	A	707 826-8700	23488
Tofu Shop Specialty Foods Inc	2099	E	707 822-7401	2626
Wing Inflatables Inc (HQ)	3089	F	707 826-2887	10126

ARLETA, CA - Los Angeles County

	SIC	EMP	PHONE	ENTRY #
Juicy Couture Inc	2221	C	888 824-8826	2729
M & R Plating Corporation	3471	F	818 896-2700	13044

ARMONA, CA - Kings County

	SIC	EMP	PHONE	ENTRY #
Armona Frozen Food Lockers	2013	F	559 584-3948	438
Central Valley Cabinet Mfg	2434	F	559 584-8441	4180

AROMAS, CA - Monterey County

	SIC	EMP	PHONE	ENTRY #
Granite Rock Co	1442	D	831 768-2300	342

ARROYO GRANDE, CA - San Luis Obispo County

	SIC	EMP	PHONE	ENTRY #
Alliance Ready Mix Inc (PA)	3273	E	805 343-0360	10683
Coastal Vineyard Services LLC	2084	F	805 441-4465	1642
Corbett Canyon Vineyards	2084	F	805 782-9463	1650
Crosno Construction Inc	3443	E	805 343-7437	12014
Laetitia Vineyard & Winery Inc	2084	D	805 481-1772	1789

Employment Codes: A=Over 500 employees, B=251-500,
C=101-250, D=51-100, E=20-50, F=10-19

2020 California
Manufacturers Register

© Mergent Inc. 1-800-342-5647

1303

GEOGRAPHIC

	SIC	EMP	PHONE	ENTRY #
Layne Laboratories Inc	2299	F	805 242-7918	2942
Lopez Water Treatment Plant	3589	F	805 473-7152	15537
M29 Technology and Design	7372	F	805 489-9402	24118
Phillips 66 Co Carbon Group	3559	F	805 489-4050	14518
Politezer Newspaers Inc	2711	F	805 929-3864	5799
Spawn Mate Inc	2873	E	805 473-7250	8804

ARTESIA, CA - Los Angeles County

	SIC	EMP	PHONE	ENTRY #
Applied Liquid Polymer	3271	F	562 402-6300	10501
Cal Plate (PA)	3555	D	562 403-3000	14318
California Dairies Inc	2026	D	562 809-2595	690
M G Watanabe Inc	3663	F	562 402-8989	17578
National Ready Mixed Con Co	3273	F	562 865-6211	10809
Standard Crystal Corp	3679	F	626 443-2121	19091
Viking Ready Mix Co Inc	3273	E	562 865-6211	10863

ARVIN, CA - Kern County

	SIC	EMP	PHONE	ENTRY #
Lee Sandusky Corporation	2514	E	661 854-5551	4694
Moore Farms Inc	2099	F	661 854-5588	2556
Reeves Extruded Products Inc	3082	D	661 854-5970	9434
Southern Valley Chemical Co	2879	F	661 366-3308	8840
Western Fiber Co Inc	3541	E	661 854-5556	13962

ATASCADERO, CA - San Luis Obispo County

	SIC	EMP	PHONE	ENTRY #
Drymax Technologies Inc	2252	F	805 239-2555	2765
Fence Factory	3496	F	805 462-1362	13413
Ground Control Systems Inc	3663	F	805 783-4600	17528
One At A Time	3942	F	805 461-1784	22651
Wyred 4 Sound LLC	3651	F	805 466-9973	17307
X Tri Inc	2893	F	805 286-4544	8939

ATHERTON, CA - San Mateo County

	SIC	EMP	PHONE	ENTRY #
Novatorque Inc	3621	E	510 933-2700	16667
Powerflare Corporation	3699	F	650 208-2580	19380

ATWATER, CA - Merced County

	SIC	EMP	PHONE	ENTRY #
Certified Stainless Svc Inc	3443	F	209 356-3300	12002
Certified Stainless Svc Inc	3443	E	209 537-4747	12004
Five Keys Inc	2329	E	209 358-7971	3083
Gallo Global Nutrition LLC	2022	C	209 394-7984	551
Hansens Oak Inc (PA)	2511	F	209 357-3424	4574
Keney Manufacturing Co (PA)	2434	F	209 358-6474	4215
MB Sports Inc	3732	E	209 357-4153	20350
Nci Group Inc	3448	C	209 357-1000	12567
Teasdale Foods Inc (PA)	2032	B	209 358-5616	749

AUBERRY, CA - Fresno County

	SIC	EMP	PHONE	ENTRY #
Auberry Forest Products Inc	2411	F	559 855-6255	3874
Messer Logging Inc	2411	E	559 855-3160	3898

AUBURN, CA - Placer County

	SIC	EMP	PHONE	ENTRY #
Absinthe Group Inc	2033	E	530 823-8527	753
API Marketing	2752	F	916 632-1946	6417
Armstrong Technology Inc	3599	F	530 888-6262	15748
Auburn Journal Inc (HQ)	2711	E	530 885-5656	5559
Auburn Journal Inc	2711	D	530 346-2232	5560
Audio Partners Publishing	3652	F	530 888-7803	17310
Broach Masters Inc	3545	E	530 885-1939	14141
Dimaxx Technologies LLC	3827	F	530 888-1942	21350
Gara Inc	3646	F	530 887-1110	17038
Interior Wood Design Inc	2511	F	530 888-7707	4577
IRD Acquisitions LLC	3851	F	530 210-2966	22363
Magorian Mine Services (PA)	1442	F	530 269-1960	352
Mitchell-Duckett Corporation	3599	F	530 268-2112	16214
Morgan Advanced Ceramics Inc	2819	C	530 823-3401	7509
Mydax Inc	3585	F	530 888-6662	15447
Nor Cal Food Solutions LLC	2035	F	530 823-8527	891
Pass Laboratories Inc	3651	F	530 878-5350	17269
Pre/Plastics Inc	3089	F	530 823-1820	9985
Purveyors Kitchen	2033	E	530 823-8527	819
Quality Metal Fabrication LLC	3444	E	530 887-7388	12346
Ron & Diana Vanatta	2541	F	530 888-0200	4935
Ryangmw Inc	3713	F	530 305-2499	19552
Sierra Precision Optics Inc	3827	E	530 885-6979	21410
Sierra Sculpture Inc	3366	F	530 887-1581	11406
Sierra Swiss & Machine Inc	3451	F	530 346-1110	12650
Soundview Applications Inc	3651	F	530 888-7593	17287
Stellarvue	3827	F	530 823-7796	21412
Surface Manufacturing Inc	3599	F	530 885-0700	16431
Tahoe Rf Semiconductor Inc	3674	F	530 823-9786	18601
Tri-Continent Scientific Inc	3824	D	530 273-8888	20977
VSR Network Technologies LLC	3661	E	530 889-1500	17429

AVILA BEACH, CA - San Luis Obispo County

	SIC	EMP	PHONE	ENTRY #
Gander Publishing Inc	2731	F	805 541-5523	6105

AZUSA, CA - Los Angeles County

	SIC	EMP	PHONE	ENTRY #
A & B Aerospace Inc	3599	E	626 334-2976	15650

	SIC	EMP	PHONE	ENTRY #
Able Card LLC	2759	E	626 969-1888	6972
Acme Portable Machines Inc	3571	E	626 610-1888	14879
American International Racing	3714	F	626 969-7733	19580
Ancra International LLC (HQ)	3537	C	626 765-4800	13856
Arminak Solutions LLC	2844	E	626 385-5858	8439
Artisan Screen Printing Inc	2759	E	626 815-2700	6994
Avery Dennison Corporation	2672	C	626 938-7239	5351
Azusa Rock LLC (DH)	1422	F	858 530-9444	297
BK Signs Inc	3993	F	626 334-5600	23060
Bojer Inc	2392	F	626 334-1711	3603
Bolcof Plstic Mtls Stheast Inc	2821	F	800 621-2681	7546
Buchanans Spoke & Rim	3751	E	626 969-4655	20387
California Amforge Corporation	3312	D	626 334-4931	11031
California Master Printers	2752	E	626 812-8930	6467
Calportland Company	3273	F	626 334-3226	10703
Cardinal Laboratories Inc	2844	D	626 610-1200	8456
Casella Aluminum Extrusions	3354	E	714 961-8322	11227
Cee -Jay Research & Sales LLC	2759	E	626 815-1530	7019
Chipmasters Manufacturing Inc (PA)	3599	E	626 804-8178	15845
D & L Moulding and Lumber Co	2431	F	626 444-0134	4028
D W Mack Co Inc	3089	F	626 969-1817	9744
Dependble Incontinence Sup Inc	2676	F	626 812-0044	5460
Digital Printing Systems Inc (PA)	2752	D	626 815-1888	6542
Dolphin Spas Inc	3999	F	626 334-0099	23317
Ducommun Incorporated	3677	C	626 812-9666	18713
Gale Banks Engineering	3519	C	626 969-9600	13596
Hallett Boats	3732	F	626 969-8844	20335
Hannemann Fiberglass Inc	3714	F	626 969-7317	19678
I/O Controls Corporation (PA)	3625	D	626 812-5353	16721
Illinois Tool Works Inc	2992	C	847 724-7500	9146
Innovative Designs & Mfg Inc	2514	F	626 812-4422	4691
Intertex LLC	3564	E	626 385-3300	14664
Inwesco Incorporated (PA)	3315	D	626 334-7115	11098
Lindsey Manufacturing Co	3463	C	626 969-3471	12733
Magparts (DH)	3365	F	626 334-7897	11385
Mat Cactus Mfg Co	2273	E	626 969-0444	2873
Mc William & Son Inc	3469	F	626 969-1821	12841
McKeever Danlee Confectionary	2064	F	626 334-8964	1389
McMurtrie & Mcmurtrie Inc	2426	D	626 815-0177	3978
Melco Steel Inc	3443	E	626 334-7875	12030
Metal Engineering & Mfg	3444	F	626 334-5271	12292
Mortech Manufacturing Co Inc	2531	E	626 334-1471	4865
National Stabilizers Inc	2099	F	626 969-5700	2563
Ncla Inc	2679	F	562 926-6252	5515
Nicks Doors Inc	2431	F	626 812-6491	4095
Norac Inc (PA)	2869	B	626 334-2907	8758
Northrop Grumman Systems Corp	3812	C	626 812-1000	20662
Northrop Grumman Systems Corp	3812	B	626 812-1464	20666
Owen Magic Supreme Inc	3999	F	626 969-4519	23437
Peninsula Light Metals LLC (HQ)	3363	F	626 765-4856	11344
Phaostron Instr Electronic Co	3613	D	626 969-6401	16606
Precision Granite USA Inc	3281	E	562 696-8328	10921
Pro Fab Tech LLC	3599	F	626 804-7200	16313
Ptb Sales Inc (PA)	3563	F	626 334-0500	14639
R E Atckison Co Inc	3531	F	626 334-0266	13743
Rain Bird Corporation (PA)	3494	F	626 812-3400	13362
Rain Bird Corporation	3432	F	626 812-3400	11679
Ray-Bar Engineering Corp	3842	F	626 969-1818	22076
Reichhold LLC 2	2821	F	626 334-4974	7603
S & S Foods LLC	2013	C	626 633-1609	493
S&B Pharma Inc	2833	D	626 334-2908	7690
Screwmatic Inc	3599	D	626 334-7831	16391
Seasonic Electronics Inc	3679	F	626 969-9966	19079
Shell Catalysts & Tech LP	2819	D	626 334-1241	7522
Skylock Industries	3728	E	626 334-2391	20234
Sportifeye Optics Inc	3851	E	626 521-5600	22387
Tecomet Inc	3841	A	626 334-1519	21925
Trio Engineered Products Inc (HQ)	3531	E	626 851-3966	13753
Valley Forge Acquisition Corp	3462	F	626 969-8701	12725
Very Special Chocolats Inc	2066	C	626 334-7838	1417
Westbase Inc (PA)	3613	F	626 969-6801	16624
Westwood Laboratories Inc (PA)	2844	E	626 969-3305	8608
Zt Plus	3674	F	626 208-3440	18674

BAKERSFIELD, CA - Kern County

	SIC	EMP	PHONE	ENTRY #
3g Rebar Inc	3449	F	661 588-0294	12582
Acco Engineered Systems Inc	3585	F	661 631-1975	15406
Advanced Technologies	7372	F	661 872-4807	23571
Aera Energy LLC (HQ)	1381	A	661 665-5000	82
Airgas Usa LLC	2813	E	661 201-8107	7410
Alder & Co LLC	2511	F	661 326-0320	4545
Ally Enterprises	1389	E	661 412-9933	152
Alon Usa LP	2911	F	661 392-3630	9037
American Bottling Company	2086	F	661 323-7921	2027
American Yeast Corporation	2099	F	661 834-1050	2391
Ampligraphix	2752	F	661 321-3150	6413

2020 California
Manufacturers Register

(P-0000) Products & Services Section entry number
(PA)=Parent Co (HQ)=Headquarters (DH)=Div Headquarters

	SIC	EMP	PHONE	ENTRY #
Anatesco Inc	1389	F	661 399-6990	154
Archrock Inc	1389	F	661 321-0271	155
B & B Pipe and Tool Co	3599	F	661 323-8208	15763
B & L Casing Service LLC	1389	F	661 589-9080	156
Baker Hghes Olfld Oprtions LLC	1389	F	661 831-5200	157
Baker Hughes A GE Company LLC	1389	D	661 387-1010	163
Baker Hughes A GE Company LLC	1389	D	800 229-7447	164
Baker Hughes A GE Company LLC	3533	D	661 834-9654	13767
Baker Hughes A GE Company LLC	1389	F	661 391-0794	165
Baker Petrolite LLC	1389	F	661 325-4138	167
Bakersfield Elc Mtr Repr Inc	7694	F	661 327-3583	24685
Bakersfield Machine Company	3599	D	661 709-1992	15773
Bakersfield Well Casing LLC	1381	F	661 399-2976	88
Bakersfield Woodworks Inc	2431	E	661 282-8492	4002
Basic Energy Services Inc	1389	E	661 588-3800	171
Becs Pacific Ltd	3465	F	661 397-9400	12742
Berry Petroleum Company LLC (HQ)	1311	D	661 616-3900	26
Boyd & Boyd Industries (PA)	3565	F	661 831-8400	14701
Brocks Trailers Inc	3523	E	661 363-5038	13616
C & H Testing Service Inc (PA)	1389	E	661 589-4030	174
C Pallets From Bkersfield Call	2448	F	661 833-2801	4353
Califia Farms LLC	2086	A	661 679-1000	2048
California Mini Truck Inc	3714	F	661 398-9585	19605
California Resources Corp	1311	E	661 395-8000	35
California Resources Corp	1382	F	661 412-5222	112
California Resources Prod Corp (HQ)	1311	C	661 869-8000	41
Califrnia Rsrces Elk Hills LLC	1382	B	661 412-5000	115
Calmini Products Inc	3714	F	661 398-9500	19606
Calpi Inc	1389	F	661 589-5648	179
Cameron International Corp	3533	F	661 323-8183	13768
Carlos Shower Doors Inc	3231	F	661 327-5594	10347
Cemex Cnstr Mtls PCF LLC	3273	C	661 396-0510	10725
Central California Cnstr Inc	1389	F	661 978-8230	182
Century Rubber Company Inc	3069	F	661 366-7009	9294
Child Evngelism Fellowship Inc	2752	E	661 837-9032	6482
CL Knox Inc	1389	D	661 837-0477	184
Coastal Products Company Inc	3561	E	661 323-0487	14564
Computational Systems Inc	3829	E	661 832-5306	21453
Consolidated Fibrgls Pdts Co	3296	D	661 323-6026	10982
Containment Solutions Inc	3443	D	661 399-9556	12011
Contraband Control Specialists	2899	F	661 322-3363	8951
Core Laboratories LP	1389	E	661 325-5657	186
Core Tech Products Inc	2844	F	661 833-1572	8465
Coretex Products Inc (PA)	2844	F	661 834-6805	8466
Crimson Resource MGT Corp	1311	E	303 892-8878	48
Crystal Geyser Water Company	2086	E	661 323-6296	2068
Crystal Geyser Water Company	2086	F	661 321-0896	2069
Cummins Pacific LLC	3519	E	661 325-9404	13591
Delaney Manufacturing Inc	3444	F	661 587-6681	12179
Delta Trading LP	2951	E	661 834-5560	9089
Domino Plastics Mfg Inc	3089	F	661 396-3744	9763
Douglass Truck Bodies Inc	3713	E	661 327-0258	19529
Downhole Stabilization Inc	3533	E	661 631-1044	13774
Dunbar Electric Sign Company	3993	E	661 323-2600	23089
E & B Ntral Resources Mgt Corp (PA)	1311	D	661 679-1714	49
E and B Natural Resources	1382	D	661 679-1700	121
Eaton Corporation	3625	C	661 396-2557	16714
El Popular Spanish Newspaper	2711	F	661 325-7725	5629
Electric Motor Works Inc	7694	E	661 327-4271	24688
Elysium Jennings LLC	1381	C	661 679-1700	91
Energy Link Indus Svcs Inc	3599	E	661 765-4444	15931
Engineered Well Svc Intl Inc	1389	C	866 913-6283	193
Ennis-Flint Inc	2851	E	661 328-0503	8645
Enova Solutions Inc	2899	F	661 327-2405	8963
Ensign US Drlg Cal Inc (HQ)	3541	D	661 589-0111	13920
Excalibur Well Services Corp (PA)	1381	E	661 589-5338	92
F E W Inc	3599	F	661 323-8319	15948
Farley Machine Inc	3533	F	661 397-4987	13775
Farmer Bros Co	2095	F	661 663-9908	2291
First Energy Services Inc	1389	E	661 387-1972	198
Freeport-Mcmoran Oil & Gas LLC	1311	D	661 322-7600	52
Frito-Lay North America Inc	2096	A	661 328-6000	2331
Genesis Mch & Fabrication Inc	3599	F	661 324-4366	15993
Georg Fischer Harvel LLC	3084	D	661 396-0653	9466
Glam and Glits Nail Design Inc	2844	D	661 393-4800	8499
Global Elastomeric Pdts Inc	3533	D	661 831-5380	13778
Golden Empire Concrete Co	3273	F	661 325-6833	10764
Golden Empire Dental Lab Inc	3843	F	661 327-1888	22157
Golden State Drilling Inc	1381	F	661 589-0730	93
Grayson Service Inc	1389	C	661 589-5444	202
Hall Letter Shop Inc	2752	F	661 327-3228	6603
Halliburton Company	1389	D	661 393-8111	204
Hancor Inc	3084	E	661 366-1520	9467
Harbison-Fischer Inc	3561	E	661 387-0166	14580
Harrell Holdings (PA)	2711	C	661 322-5627	5652

	SIC	EMP	PHONE	ENTRY #
Hathaway LLC	1311	E	661 393-2004	55
Hills Wldg & Engrg Contr Inc	1389	D	661 746-5400	207
Hudson Valve Co Inc	3491	E	661 831-6208	13307
Hunting Energy Services Inc	1389	D	661 633-4272	210
HWF Construction Inc	2721	E	661 587-3590	5958
Hydril Company	3533	B	661 588-9332	13780
Hydril USA Distribution LLC	3533	F	661 588-9332	13781
Ironclad Tool and Machine Inc	3599	F	661 833-9990	16055
J Flying Manufacturing	3061	E	805 839-9229	9265
James L Craft Inc	3599	E	661 323-8251	16075
JC Pallet Co	2448	F	661 393-2229	4376
Johasee Rebar Inc	3441	E	661 589-0972	11821
John M Phillips LLC	1389	F	661 327-3118	215
Jts Modular Inc	3448	E	661 835-9270	12552
Kba Engineering LLC	3533	D	661 323-0487	13782
Kba Ltd of Kern County LLP	1389	F	661 323-0487	217
Kern River Holding Inc	1382	F	661 589-2507	127
Key Energy Services Inc	1389	D	661 334-8100	218
Konecranes Inc	3536	F	661 397-9700	13848
Kw Plastics Recycling Division	3081	D	661 392-0500	9407
Legacy Vulcan LLC	3273	D	661 835-4800	10784
Legacy Vulcan LLC	3273	E	661 858-2673	10786
Lengthwise Brewing Company	2082	E	661 836-2537	1543
Lightspeed Software	7372	F	661 716-7600	24101
Linnco LLC	1311	A	661 616-3900	57
LMS Reinforcing Steel Usa LP (PA)	3449	F	604 598-9930	12594
Lortz & Son Mfg Co	3471	C	281 241-9418	13042
Macpherson Oil Company	1382	F	661 556-6096	129
Mark Sheffield Construction	1389	E	661 589-8520	221
Material Control Inc	3499	E	661 617-6033	13532
Mazzei Injector Company LLC	3589	E	661 363-6500	15539
Mc Cain & Mc Cain Inc	3599	F	661 322-7764	16181
MD Manufacturing Inc	3589	E	661 283-7550	15541
Metro Ready Mix	3273	F	661 829-7851	10802
Millwood Cabinet Co Inc	2434	E	661 327-0371	4225
MJM Expert Pipe Fbrcation Wldg	3441	E	661 330-8698	11847
Mmi Services Inc	1389	C	661 589-9366	224
Mobile Equipment Company	3536	E	661 327-8476	13850
MTS Stimulation Services Inc (PA)	1389	E	661 589-5804	226
Nabors Well Services Co	1389	C	661 588-6140	228
Nabors Well Services Co	1389	B	661 589-3970	229
Nabors Well Services Co	1389	D	661 392-7668	231
Nalco Company LLC	2899	F	661 864-7955	9004
Nalco Company LLC	2819	F	661 834-0454	7510
Nations Petroleum Cal LLC	1382	D	661 387-6402	131
Nestle Dreyers Ice Cream Co	2024	F	661 398-5448	662
Newby Rubber Inc	3069	E	661 327-5137	9343
Norman Wireline Service Inc	1389	F	661 399-5697	237
Nusil Technology LLC	3069	D	661 391-4750	9345
Outdoor Galore Inc	3579	E	661 831-8662	15386
Owen Oil Tools Inc	2892	F	661 637-1380	8906
OXY USA Inc	1311	C	661 869-8000	60
Pacific Process Systems Inc (PA)	1389	E	661 321-9681	243
Pacific Shore Stones Bakersfie	2299	E	661 335-0100	2949
Pacific WD Prserving-New Stine	2491	F	661 617-6385	4480
Pactiv LLC	3089	B	661 392-4000	9947
Palmer Tank & Construction Inc	1389	E	661 834-1110	244
Paramount Petroleum Corp	2911	F	661 392-3630	9059
Pepsi Cola Btlg of Bkersfield	2086	C	661 327-9992	2108
Pepsi-Cola Bottling Group	2086	F	661 635-1100	2109
Petro-Lud Inc	1381	F	661 747-4779	103
Pioneer Sands LLC	1446	E	661 746-5789	373
PNa Construction Tech Inc	3444	E	661 326-1700	12337
Praxair Inc	2813	E	661 861-6421	7435
Praxair Inc	2813	E	661 327-5336	7436
Premier Tank Service Inc	3795	E	661 833-2960	20499
Pro Tool Services Inc	3545	E	661 393-9222	14187
Production Data Inc	1389	F	661 327-4776	250
Pros Incorporated	1389	D	661 589-5400	251
PSC Industrial Outsourcing LP	1389	E	661 833-9991	252
Pyrenees French Bakery Inc	2051	E	661 322-7159	1266
Ray Chinn Construction Inc	3542	E	661 327-2731	13993
Reyes Coca-Cola Bottling LLC	2086	D	661 324-6531	2135
Rhino Valve Usa Inc	3491	F	661 587-0220	13320
Robert Heely Construction LP (PA)	1389	B	661 617-1400	255
Ross Fabrication & Welding Inc	2499	F	661 393-1242	4528
Russell Fabrication Corp	3498	F	661 861-8495	13484
San Joaquin Facilities MGT Inc (PA)	1311	A	661 631-8713	66
San Joaquin Refining Co Inc	2911	C	661 327-4257	9066
Schlumberger Technology Corp	1389	D	661 864-4750	260
Seaboard International Inc	3533	D	661 325-5026	13790
Seaco Technologies Inc	3589	F	661 326-1522	15575
Silo City Inc	3531	E	661 387-0179	13748
Smith International Inc	1389	F	661 589-8304	265
Soli-Bond Inc	1389	E	661 631-1633	266

Employment Codes: A=Over 500 employees, B=251-500,
C=101-250, D=51-100, E=20-50, F=10-19

2020 California
Manufacturers Register

© Mergent Inc. 1-800-342-5647

1305

	SIC	EMP	PHONE	ENTRY #
Spalinger Enterprises Inc	2541	F	661 834-4550	4940
Spartan Inc	3441	D	661 327-1205	11882
Star-Luck Enterprise Inc	3823	F	661 665-9999	20943
Structurecast	3272	D	661 833-4490	10659
Suez Wts Usa Inc	2899	E	661 393-3035	9027
Sun-Gro Commodities Inc (PA)	2048	E	661 393-2612	1130
Technipfmc US Holdings Inc	3533	F	661 283-1069	13792
Temblor Brewing LLC	2082	E	661 489-4855	1569
Thuasne North America Inc (DH)	3842	B	800 432-3466	22110
Tiger Tanks Inc	3795	F	661 363-8335	20501
Titan Oilfield Services Inc	1389	F	661 861-1630	270
Total Process Solutions LLC	3561	E	661 829-7910	14601
Transdesign Inc	2431	F	661 631-1062	4142
Tricor Refining LLC	2911	E	661 393-7110	9077
Tringen Corporation	1389	F	661 393-3039	273
Triple E Manufacturing Inc	3556	F	661 831-7553	14408
Tuboscope Pipeline Svcs Inc	1389	E	661 321-3400	275
U M S Inc	3471	E	661 324-5454	13121
U S Weatherford L P	1389	D	661 589-9483	276
U S Weatherford L P	3498	F	661 746-1391	13490
Udecor Inc (PA)	3089	F	877 550-0600	10097
Union Tank Car Company	3743	C	312 431-3111	20378
United States Cold Storage Inc	2097	E	661 834-2371	2365
UPF Corporation	3296	E	661 323-8227	10990
Valadons Plumbing Service Inc	3432	F	661 201-1460	11686
Valley Perforating LLC	3599	D	661 324-4964	16489
Valley Water Management Co	1389	F	661 410-7500	278
Vaquero Energy Inc	1389	F	661 616-0600	279
Vaquero Energy Incorporated	1311	F	661 363-7240	74
Viscon California LLC	2869	F	661 327-7061	8782
Water Associates LLC	3663	E	661 281-6077	17703
Weatherford Artificia	1389	E	661 654-8120	281
Weatherford Completion Systems	1389	E	661 746-1391	282
Weatherford International LLC	1389	D	661 587-9753	285
Well Analysis Corporation Inc (PA)	2411	E	661 283-9510	3916
West American Energy Corp	1381	F	661 747-7732	107
Western Nutrients Corporation	2873	E	661 327-9604	8807
Westrock Cp LLC	2631	E	661 327-3841	5178
Whitestone Industries Inc	3999	F	888 567-2234	23526
Yellow Letters Inc	2759	F	661 864-7860	7276
Zilift Inc	3561	F	661 369-8579	14607

BALDWIN PARK, CA - Los Angeles County

	SIC	EMP	PHONE	ENTRY #
Above All Co Forearm Forklift	3537	E	626 962-2990	13854
Alphena Technologies	3089	F	626 961-6098	9619
American Reliance Inc	3571	E	626 443-6818	14888
Ametek Ameron LLC	3812	E	626 337-4640	20533
Ametek Ameron LLC (HQ)	3823	D	626 856-0101	20832
Anura Plastic Engineerign	3089	D	626 814-9684	9633
B & B Red-I-Mix Concrete Inc	3273	E	626 359-8371	10695
Cal Bind	2789	E	626 338-3699	7328
Cera Inc	3821	E	626 814-2688	20748
Checkworks Inc	2782	D	626 333-1444	7307
Color Sky Inc	3281	F	626 338-8565	10900
Condor Outdoor Products Inc (PA)	3949	E	626 358-3270	22784
Denovo Dental Inc	3843	E	626 480-0182	22144
Distinct Indulgence Inc	2051	F	818 546-1700	1188
Dreams Closets	2434	F	626 641-5070	4190
Exquisite Corporation	2844	E	626 856-0200	8491
EZ Inflatables Inc	3069	E	626 480-9100	9308
Fabtronic Inc	3444	F	626 962-3293	12211
Falcon Electric Inc	3612	F	626 962-7770	16549
Fellyr International Inc	2339	F	626 960-5111	3327
Freudenberg Medical LLC	3842	C	626 814-9684	22017
Front Edge Technology Inc	3691	E	626 856-8979	19167
G & I Islas Industries Inc (PA)	3556	F	626 960-5020	14366
Hanson Aggregates LLC	1442	F	626 856-6700	345
Hemosure Inc	2899	E	888 436-6787	8973
Inflatable Enterprises Inc	3069	F	818 482-6509	9321
Ipp Plastics Products Inc	2821	F	626 357-1178	7572
Kal-Cameron Manufacturing (HQ)	3423	D	626 338-7308	11532
Lawrence Roll Up Doors Inc (PA)	3442	E	626 962-4163	11964
Lawrence Roll Up Doors Inc	3442	F	626 338-6041	11966
Little Digger Mining & Sup LLC	1041	E	626 856-3366	5
Macdonald Carbide Co	3544	E	626 960-4034	14073
Meritek Electronics Corp (PA)	3559	D	626 373-1728	14497
Mission Kleensweep Prod Inc	2841	D	323 223-1405	8344
Miyako Oriental Foods Inc	2075	F	626 962-9633	1444
Motek Industries	3599	F	626 960-6005	16228
My Machine Inc	3599	F	626 214-9223	16235
New York Frozen Foods Inc	2051	E	626 338-3000	1248
Nsd Industries Inc	3599	F	626 813-2001	16251
Pacific Award Metals Inc (HQ)	3444	D	626 814-4410	12323
Pacon Inc	3089	C	626 814-4654	9946
Pepsi-Cola Metro Btlg Co Inc	2086	C	626 338-5531	2120
Pepsico Inc	2086	C	626 338-5531	2127

	SIC	EMP	PHONE	ENTRY #
Performance Tube Bending Inc	3498	F	626 939-9000	13479
Philips Elec N Amer Corp	3827	C	626 480-0755	21398
PSC Circuits Inc	3679	E	626 373-1728	19054
R & R Metal Fabricators	3441	F	626 960-6400	11871
Reny & Co Inc	3089	F	626 962-3078	10014
Rigos Equipment Mfg LLC	3444	F	626 813-6621	12354
S and C Precision Inc	3679	F	626 338-7149	19074
Sanders Candy Factory Inc	2064	E	626 814-2038	1394
Scholastic Inc	2731	E	626 337-9996	6144
Sharp Performance USA Inc (PA)	3961	E	626 888-1190	22995
Standard Concrete Products (HQ)	3273	E	310 829-4537	10843
Superior Grounding Systems	3643	E	626 814-1981	16927
Survey Stake and Marker Inc	2499	F	626 960-4802	4537
Tim Guzzy Services Inc	3599	F	626 813-0626	16458
Touchdown Technologies Inc	3674	C	626 472-6732	18622
U S Bearings	3562	E	626 358-0181	14618
Ultimate Jumpers Inc	2599	F	626 337-3086	5087
Universal Steel Services Inc	3441	F	626 960-1455	11907
Upm Inc	3544	B	626 962-4001	14118
Yutaka Electric Intl Inc	3629	F	626 962-7770	16805

BANNING, CA - Riverside County

	SIC	EMP	PHONE	ENTRY #
Allen Industrial Inc	3471	F	951 849-4966	12916
Belovac LLC	3559	F	951 427-4299	14432
Century Publishing	2759	F	951 849-4586	7020
DT Mattson Enterprises Inc	3944	E	951 849-9781	22672
KSD Inc	3599	F	951 849-7669	16127
Robertsons Distributors Inc	3273	F	951 849-4766	10821
Te Connectivity Corporation	3678	B	951 929-3323	18791
Zenner Performance Meters Inc	3824	F	951 849-8822	20978

BARSTOW, CA - San Bernardino County

	SIC	EMP	PHONE	ENTRY #
Five Star Food Containers Inc	3086	D	626 437-6219	9529
Green Valley Foods Product	2022	F	760 964-1105	553
Kar Ice Service Inc (PA)	2097	F	760 256-2648	2358
Service Rock Products Corp	3273	E	760 252-1615	10828
Valmont Industries Inc	3441	F	760 253-3070	11911

BAY POINT, CA - Contra Costa County

	SIC	EMP	PHONE	ENTRY #
Chemtrade Chemicals US LLC	2819	E	925 458-7300	7481
Shell Catalysts & Tech LP	2819	D	925 458-9045	7523

BEAUMONT, CA - Riverside County

	SIC	EMP	PHONE	ENTRY #
Beaumont Juice Inc	2033	D	951 769-7171	755
Big Tex Trailer Mfg Inc	3523	F	951 845-5344	13613
Dura Plastic Products Inc (PA)	3089	F	951 845-3161	9767
Katchall Filtration Systems LLC	3589	F	866 528-2425	15533
Precision Stampg Solutions Inc	3469	E	951 845-1174	12859
Precision Stampings Inc (PA)	3643	E	951 845-1174	16921
Priority Pallet Inc	2448	C	951 769-9399	4394
Risco Inc	3452	E	951 769-2899	12691
Rudolph Foods Company Inc	2096	D	909 388-2202	2342
Wholesale Shutter Company Inc	2431	F	951 845-8786	4149
Wolverine World Wide Inc	3143	F	800 253-2184	10165

BELL, CA - Los Angeles County

	SIC	EMP	PHONE	ENTRY #
A&R Lighting Co	3648	F	562 927-8617	17096
Alfred Picon	2542	F	562 928-2561	4962
Bluprint Clothing Corp	2331	D	323 780-4347	3142
Carol Wior Inc	2339	D	562 927-0052	3302
Custom Building Products Inc	2891	D	323 582-0846	8865
Dcx-Chol Enterprises Inc	3679	D	562 927-5531	18884
Flores Brothers Inc	2099	E	562 806-9128	2460
Hain Celestial Group Inc	2844	C	323 859-0553	8507
J P Turgeon & Sons Inc	3471	F	323 773-3105	13033
Lynco Grinding Company Inc	3599	F	562 927-2631	16155
Marika LLC	2339	D	323 888-7755	3370
Power Brake Exchange Inc	3714	F	562 806-6661	19737
West Coast-Accudyne Inc	3542	E	562 927-2546	13999

BELL GARDENS, CA - Los Angeles County

	SIC	EMP	PHONE	ENTRY #
Bus Services Corporation	3714	E	562 231-1770	19601
Cal Southern Braiding Inc	3679	D	562 927-5545	18848
Carnevale & Lohr Inc	3281	D	562 927-8311	10895
Construction TI & Threading Co	3452	F	562 927-1326	12674
Eurocraft Archtectural Met Inc	3446	E	323 771-1323	12472
Flexco Inc	3728	F	562 927-2525	20105
G R J Fashions	2284	F	323 537-5814	2890
Infinity Kitchen Products Inc	3444	F	562 806-5771	12244
Mc Lane Manufacturing Inc	3524	D	562 633-8158	13691
Metal Surfaces Inc	3471	C	562 927-1331	13051
Rob Inc (PA)	2325	D	562 806-5589	3018
Wilcox Machine Co	3599	D	562 927-5353	16526

BELLFLOWER, CA - Los Angeles County

	SIC	EMP	PHONE	ENTRY #
Black & Decker (us) Inc	3546	F	562 925-7551	14215
Bryant Rubber Corp	3053	D	310 530-2530	9220
Express Sheet Metal Product	3444	F	562 925-9340	12206

Mergent email: customerrelations@mergent.com
1306

2020 California
Manufacturers Register

(P-0000) Products & Services Section entry number
(PA)=Parent Co (HQ)=Headquarters (DH)=Div Headquarters

	SIC	EMP	PHONE	ENTRY #
Ice Man Inc	2097	F	562 633-4423	2357
Ivoprop Corporation	3728	F	562 602-1451	20144
Kamashian Engineering Inc	3544	F	562 920-9692	14066
Timkev International Inc	2052	F	562 232-1691	1332

BELMONT, CA - San Mateo County

	SIC	EMP	PHONE	ENTRY #
Aco Pacific Inc	3829	F	650 595-8588	21428
Cutting Edge Machining Inc (PA)	3451	E	408 738-8677	12628
Fineline Carpentry Inc	2434	F	650 592-2442	4196
Intex Forms Inc	3229	E	650 654-7855	10313
Js Trade Bindery Services Inc	2789	D	650 486-1475	7337
Megaprint Digital Prtg Corp	2752	F	650 517-0200	6721
Moquin Press Inc	2752	D	650 592-0575	6739
Nikon Research Corp America	3825	F	800 446-4566	21091
Oracle Systems Corporation	7372	B	650 654-7606	24269
Oracle Systems Corporation	7372	F	650 506-5062	24271
Pacific Screw Products Inc	3451	F	650 583-9682	12645
Solaicx	3674	D	408 988-5000	18568
Somerset Traveller Inc	2789	F	650 593-7350	7349
Village Collection Inc	2434	F	650 594-1635	4263

BELVEDERE TIBURON, CA - Marin County

	SIC	EMP	PHONE	ENTRY #
Ammi Publishing Inc	2711	F	415 435-2652	5549
Mila Usa Inc	3634	E	415 734-8540	16834

BENICIA, CA - Solano County

	SIC	EMP	PHONE	ENTRY #
Applied Sewing Resources Inc	2211	E	707 748-1614	2667
Barrys Cultured Marble Inc	3281	F	707 745-3444	10891
Bay Area Coffee Inc	2095	E	707 745-1320	2276
Bay Valve Service & Engrg LLC	2599	E	707 748-7166	5050
Benicia Fabrication & Mch Inc	3443	C	707 745-8111	11996
Bio-RAD Laboratories Inc	3826	F	510 741-5790	21193
Bolttech Mannings Inc	3546	D	707 751-0157	14218
Bulls-Eye Marketing Inc	3714	F	707 745-5278	19598
California Motor Controls Inco	3625	F	707 746-6255	16705
Cameron International Corp	3533	F	707 752-8800	13769
Crane Co	3679	F	707 748-7166	18876
Custom Coils Inc	3677	F	707 752-8633	18710
Dunlop Manufacturing Inc (PA)	3931	D	707 745-2722	22615
Dunlop Manufacturing Inc	3931	E	707 745-2709	22616
Dusouth Industries	3823	E	707 745-5117	20861
Flowserve Corporation	3561	F	707 745-4710	14574
Frontline Environmental TEC	3823	F	707 745-1116	20873
Frontline Instrs & Contrls	3829	F	707 747-9766	21477
Gibbs Plastic & Rubber Co	3069	F	707 746-7300	9311
Gibson Printing & Publishing	2711	F	707 745-0733	5645
Gold Rush Kettle Korn Llc	2064	E	707 747-6773	1369
Gunnebo Entrance Control Inc (HQ)	3829	F	707 748-0885	21481
Instrument & Valve Services Co	3823	E	707 745-4664	20891
Interhealth Nutraceuticals Inc	2833	E	800 783-4636	7670
J R Schneider Co Inc	3569	F	707 745-0404	14831
Johansing Iron Works Inc	3443	E	707 361-8190	12023
Larson-Juhl US LLC	2499	E	707 747-0555	4513
Metlsaw Systems Inc	3541	E	707 746-6200	13934
Molecule Labs Inc	2869	E	925 473-8200	8753
Nor Cal Truck Sales & Mfg	3537	F	925 787-9735	13885
Pepsi-Cola Metro Btlg Co Inc	2086	C	707 746-5404	2117
Phillips 66 Spectrum Corp	2992	F	707 745-6100	9153
Praxair Inc	2813	F	707 745-5328	7440
Pro-Form Manufacturing LLC	2834	F	707 752-9010	8085
Ralphs-Pugh Co Inc	3535	D	707 746-6222	13832
Reyes Coca-Cola Bottling LLC	2086	C	707 747-2000	2153
S&S Investment Club (PA)	3799	F	707 747-5508	20520
Schoenstein & Co	3931	E	707 747-5858	22638
Sigmatex High Tech Fabrics Inc (HQ)	3624	D	707 751-0573	16690
Suba Mfg Inc	2541	E	707 745-0358	4942
Turnkey Technologies Inc	3599	E	707 745-9520	16478
Valero Ref Company-California	2911	B	707 745-7011	9082
Valley Fine Foods Company Inc (PA)	2041	D	707 746-6888	1011
Water One Industries Inc (PA)	3589	F	707 747-4300	15599
West Coast Fixtures Inc (PA)	2541	E	707 752-6373	4955

BERKELEY, CA - Alameda County

	SIC	EMP	PHONE	ENTRY #
3d Robotics Inc (PA)	3699	D	415 599-1404	19244
Aduro Biotech Inc (PA)	2834	D	510 848-4400	7728
Annies Inc (HQ)	2099	D	510 558-7500	2393
Annies Baking LLC (DH)	2051	F	510 558-7500	1137
Anto Offset Printing	2752	F	510 843-8454	6415
Apress L P	2721	F	510 549-5930	5882
Art of Muse LLC	2511	E	510 644-1870	4548
Assoc Students University CA	2741	E	510 590-7874	6190
Autumn Press Inc (PA)	2752	E	510 654-4545	6422
Avid Technology Inc	3861	B	510 486-8302	22403
Barra LLC (HQ)	7372	B	510 548-5442	23652
Bayer Corporation	3841	B	510 705-5000	21621
Bayer Healthcare LLC	2834	C	510 705-7545	7793
Bayer Healthcare LLC	2834	B	510 705-7539	7794

	SIC	EMP	PHONE	ENTRY #
Bayer Healthcare LLC	2834	C	510 705-4421	7795
Bayer Healthcare LLC	2834	C	510 705-4914	7796
Bebop Sensors Inc	2296	E	510 848-3231	2901
Berkeley Forge & Tool Inc	3462	D	510 525-5117	12705
Berkeley Mllwk & Furn Co Inc	2511	E	510 549-2854	4555
Bonsai Ai Inc	7372	E	510 900-1112	23686
Bookpack Inc	2741	F	510 601-8301	6204
Cadence Design Systems Inc	7372	F	510 647-2800	23710
California Gold Bars Inc (PA)	2066	F	510 848-9292	1408
Checkerspot Inc	2836	F	510 239-7921	8288
Cheese Cake City Inc	2051	F	510 524-9404	1177
Clp Apg LLC	2731	D	510 528-1444	6089
Comeback Brewing II Inc	2082	F	510 526-1160	1513
Consolidated Printers Inc	2732	F	510 843-8524	6170
Data Agent LLC	7372	F	800 772-8314	23800
Doughtronics Inc (PA)	2051	E	510 524-1327	1191
Doughtronics Inc	2051	E	510 841-0690	1192
Ed Jones Company	3999	F	510 704-0704	23322
Edition One Group	2752	F	510 705-1930	6562
Edward Koehn Co Inc	3451	F	510 843-0821	12630
Eko Devices Inc	3845	F	844 356-3384	22252
Fantasy Inc	3652	D	510 486-2038	17321
Four D Imaging	3829	F	510 290-3533	21476
Fra Mani LLC	2013	F	510 526-7000	457
George M Martin Co	3554	F	510 652-2200	14310
Gradescope Inc	7372	F	702 985-7442	23951
Graysix Company	3444	E	510 845-5936	12226
Gu	2834	C	510 527-4664	7928
Hesperian Health Guides (PA)	2731	E	510 845-1447	6108
Heyday	2731	F	510 549-3564	6109
Indepndent Brkley Stdnt Pubg I	2711	D	510 548-8300	5671
Ingram Publisher Services LLC	2741	D	510 528-1444	6256
Ironies LLC	2521	E	510 644-2100	4804
Janco Chemical Corporation	2851	F	510 527-9770	8648
John L Staton Inc	2431	F	510 527-3114	4066
Kirsen Technologies Inc	3663	F	510 540-5383	17553
Le Barbocce Inc	2043	E	510 526-7664	1029
Libby Laboratories Inc	2844	E	510 527-5400	8533
Living Tree Community Foods	2099	F	510 526-7106	2530
Luxfer-GTM Technologies LLC (PA)	3443	E	415 856-0570	12027
Machinables Inc	3577	F	415 216-9467	15280
Mango Materials Inc	2821	F	650 440-0430	7580
Meyer Sound Laboratories Inc (PA)	3651	C	510 486-1166	17260
Mulholland Brothers (PA)	2512	F	415 824-5995	4661
Nabolom Bakery	2051	F	510 845-2253	1247
NAPA Valley Kitchens Inc	2099	D	510 558-7500	2562
Nolo	2731	C	510 549-1976	6129
Opus 12 Incorporated	2869	F	917 349-3740	8759
Parker Powis Inc	3579	D	510 848-2463	15387
Plexxikon Inc	2834	E	510 647-4000	8078
Poly-Seal Industries	3069	F	510 843-9722	9355
Precision Coatings Inc	2851	F	510 525-3600	8671
Primary Concepts Inc	3944	F	510 559-5545	22707
Rastergraf Inc (PA)	3672	F	510 849-4801	17974
Research & Dev GL Pdts & Eqp	3231	F	510 547-6464	10388
Scone Henge Inc	2051	F	510 845-5168	1274
Sensys Networks Inc (HQ)	3669	D	510 548-4620	17760
Siemens Hlthcare Dgnostics Inc	3661	F	510 982-4000	17410
Society For The Study Ntiv Art	2731	E	510 549-4270	6147
Spiritual Counterfeits Prj Inc	2721	F	510 540-0300	6031
Stat Clinical Systems Inc	7372	F	510 705-8700	24453
Sunsystem Technology LLC	3674	B	510 984-2027	18594
Suntech America Inc (PA)	3433	F	415 882-9922	11722
Sven Design Inc	3171	F	510 848-7836	10227
Takara Sake USA Inc (DH)	2085	E	510 540-8250	2020
Tcho Ventures Inc (HQ)	2066	E	510 210-8445	1415
Tech Air Northern Cal LLC	2813	E	510 524-9353	7453
Terminal Manufacturing Co LLC	3441	E	510 526-3071	11898
The Ligature Inc	2759	F	510 526-5181	7247
Two Star Dog Inc	2335	F	510 525-1100	3257
Two Star Dog Inc (PA)	2331	F	510 525-1100	3202
University Cal Press Fundation	2731	E	510 642-4247	6159
Vital Vittles Bakery Inc	2051	F	510 644-2022	1291
Walashek Industrial & Mar Inc	3731	F	206 624-2880	20307
Western Roto Engravers Inc	2759	F	510 525-2950	7269
Wheelskins Inc	3199	F	510 841-2128	10257
Zazzie Foods Inc	3999	F	510 526-7664	23530
Zenbooth Inc	2521	E	510 646-8368	4825

BEVERLY HILLS, CA - Los Angeles County

	SIC	EMP	PHONE	ENTRY #
Beverly Hills Courier Inc	2711	E	310 278-1322	5566
Building Components	3089	F	310 274-6516	9675
Capricor Therapeutics Inc (PA)	2834	F	310 358-3200	7828
Cerner Corporation	7372	F	310 247-7700	23728
Dermanew LLC (PA)	2844	F	626 442-2813	8482
Dermanew LLC	3841	F	310 276-0457	21680

Employment Codes: A=Over 500 employees, B=251-500,
C=101-250, D=51-100, E=20-50, F=10-19

2020 California
Manufacturers Register

© Mergent Inc. 1-800-342-5647

1307

GEOGRAPHIC

	SIC	EMP	PHONE	ENTRY #
Drywired Defense LLC	3479	E	310 684-3891	13166
ERA Products Inc	2531	F	310 324-4908	4859
Gibson Brands Inc	3931	C	310 300-2369	22622
Goomby LLC	3949	F	323 556-0637	22811
H Silani & Associates Inc	3827	E	310 623-4848	21358
Instant Tuck Inc	2392	E	310 955-8824	3619
Ira Gold Group LLC	3339	F	800 984-6008	11191
Irene Kasmer Inc	2335	F	310 553-8986	3231
Jeffrey Rudes LLC	2329	F	310 281-0800	3096
Jivago Inc (PA)	2844	E	310 205-5535	8521
Kate Somerville Skincare LLC (HQ)	2834	D	323 655-7546	7975
Klooma Holdings Inc	7372	E	305 747-3315	24080
L F P Inc (PA)	2721	D	323 651-3525	5971
Larry B LLC	2371	F	310 652-3877	3500
Leaner Creamer LLC	2023	F	818 621-5274	601
Levi Strauss & Co	2325	F	310 246-9044	3013
Lorber Industries California	2261	B	310 275-1568	2828
Mastini Designs	3911	A	800 979-4848	22547
Matchless LLC	3663	E	310 473-5100	17580
Melamed International Inc (PA)	2329	E	310 271-8585	3107
Nooshin Inc	2339	E	310 559-5766	3378
Oral Essentials Inc	2844	E	888 773-5273	8551
Playboy Japan Inc	2721	F	310 424-1800	6005
Ppl Entertainment Group Inc (PA)	2741	E	310 860-7499	6315
Rare Elements Hair Care	3999	F	310 277-6524	23458
Rockstar Inc	2086	C	323 785-2820	2161
Royal Blue Inc	2392	E	310 888-0156	3639
Scotland Entry Systems Inc	3089	F	818 376-0777	10049
Status Collection & Co Inc	3911	F	310 432-7788	22574
Stratos Renewables Corporation	2869	E	310 402-5901	8778
Ubi Energy Corporation	2911	C	310 283-6978	9078
Vertiv JV Holdings LLC (PA)	3679	E	310 712-1195	19137
Vie Products Inc	2844	E	310 684-3566	8604
Vitacig Inc	2111	D	310 402-6937	2658
Workbook Inc	2731	E	323 856-0008	6165
Xomv Media Corporation	2741	F	424 284-4024	6384
Yayyo Inc	7372	F	310 926-2643	24597
Zeons Inc	3229	B	323 302-8299	10335

BIEBER, CA - Lassen County

	SIC	EMP	PHONE	ENTRY #
Del Logging Inc	2411	E	530 294-5492	3881

BIG BEAR CITY, CA - San Bernardino County

	SIC	EMP	PHONE	ENTRY #
Tma Laser Group Inc	2893	E	310 421-0550	8934

BIGGS, CA - Butte County

	SIC	EMP	PHONE	ENTRY #
Bayliss Botanicals LLC	2834	F	530 868-5466	7799

BISHOP, CA - Inyo County

	SIC	EMP	PHONE	ENTRY #
Cal-Tron Corporation	3089	E	760 873-8491	9684
High Sierra Plastics	3089	F	760 873-5600	9824
Horizon Publications Inc	2711	F	760 873-3535	5667

BLOOMINGTON, CA - San Bernardino County

	SIC	EMP	PHONE	ENTRY #
Cooper Lighting LLC	3648	E	909 605-6615	17113
Cummins Pacific LLC	3519	E	909 877-0433	13589
Dayton Superior Corporation	3315	E	909 820-0112	11090
Dura Technologies Inc	2851	C	909 877-8477	8642
E-Z Mix Inc	2674	E	909 874-7686	5436
Frito-Lay North America Inc	2096	D	909 877-0902	2329
G & F Horse Trailer Repair	3799	E	909 820-4600	20510
Heater Designs Inc	3567	F	909 421-0971	14763
Hogan Co Inc	3315	E	909 421-0245	11097
Hydraulic Shop Inc	3537	E	909 875-9336	13875
Menasha Packaging Company LLC	2653	E	951 374-5281	5245
Mitco Industries Inc (PA)	3599	E	909 877-0800	16215
Preferred Pallets Inc	2448	F	909 875-7540	4392
Products/Techniques Inc	2851	F	909 877-3951	8673
Quality Tech Mfg Inc	3721	E	909 465-9565	19925
Remco Mch & Fabrication Inc	3599	F	909 877-3530	16352
Scor Industries	3999	F	909 820-5046	23470
Southern California Biodiesel	2911	F	951 377-4007	9072
Traditional Baking Inc	2052	D	909 877-8471	1333
Vsc Incorporated (PA)	3441	F	909 877-0975	11914
Wadco Industries Inc	3441	E	909 874-7800	11915
Westco Industries Inc	3449	E	909 874-8700	12613

BLUE LAKE, CA - Humboldt County

	SIC	EMP	PHONE	ENTRY #
Calgon Carbon Corporation	2819	F	707 668-5637	7474
Thomas Tellez	2431	E	707 668-1825	4140

BLYTHE, CA - Riverside County

	SIC	EMP	PHONE	ENTRY #
Blythe Energy Inc	1321	F	760 922-9950	79

BONITA, CA - San Diego County

	SIC	EMP	PHONE	ENTRY #
Pacific Integrated Mfg Inc	3841	C	619 921-3464	21854
Right Hand Manufacturing Inc	3625	C	619 819-5056	16744

BONSALL, CA - San Diego County

	SIC	EMP	PHONE	ENTRY #
Perrault Corporation	1442	F	760 466-1024	357

BOONVILLE, CA - Mendocino County

	SIC	EMP	PHONE	ENTRY #
Anderson Valley Brewing Inc	2082	E	707 895-2337	1490

BORON, CA - Kern County

	SIC	EMP	PHONE	ENTRY #
Rio Tinto Minerals Inc	1241	C	760 762-7121	19
US Borax Inc	2819	A	760 762-7000	7532

BRAWLEY, CA - Imperial County

	SIC	EMP	PHONE	ENTRY #
Alger Alternative Energy LLC	3295	F	317 493-5289	10967
Border Precast Inc	3272	F	760 351-1233	10543
Crown Citrus Company Inc	2037	F	760 344-1930	908
Fiesta Mexican Foods Inc	2051	E	760 344-3580	1203
Imperial Compost LLC	2879	F	760 351-1900	8832
Imperial Sugar Company	2063	C	760 344-3110	1351
Reddy Ice Corporation	2097	E	760 344-0535	2362
Spreadco Inc	2262	E	760 351-0747	2847
Spreckels Sugar Company Inc	2063	B	760 344-3110	1352
W Three Co	3523	E	760 344-5841	13681
Western Mesquite Mines Inc	3339	E	928 341-4653	11196

BREA, CA - Orange County

	SIC	EMP	PHONE	ENTRY #
Able Wire EDM Inc	3599	F	714 255-1967	15671
Absolute Screenprint Inc	2396	C	714 529-2120	3766
Aci Supplies LLC	3955	E	714 989-1821	22959
Advanced Mold Technology Inc	3544	F	714 990-0144	14010
Aerospace Engineering Corp	3728	D	714 996-8178	20022
American Induction Tech Inc	3567	F	714 456-1122	14754
Ameron International Corp	3851	E	714 256-7755	22339
Applied Cmpsite Structures Inc (HQ)	3728	E	714 990-6300	20038
AST Sportswear Inc (PA)	2361	D	714 223-2030	3474
Avery Dennison Corporation	2672	B	714 674-8500	5350
Avery Products Corporation (DH)	2678	E	714 675-8500	5479
B & W Precision Inc	3599	F	714 447-0971	15767
B O A Inc	2329	E	714 256-8960	3070
Baker Furnace Inc	3567	F	714 223-7262	14756
Bamberger Polymers Inc	2821	E	714 672-4740	7543
Beckman Coulter Inc	3841	C	818 970-2161	21622
Bedard Machine Inc	3599	F	714 990-4846	15781
Belt Drives Ltd	3751	E	714 693-1313	20384
Blower Drive Service Co	3714	E	562 693-4302	19594
California Cocktails Inc	2087	F	714 990-0982	2197
Caran Precision Engrg Mfg Corp	3469	D	714 447-5400	12781
Carolina Lquid Chmistries Corp	3841	E	336 722-8910	21659
Cks Solution Incorporated	3679	E	714 292-6307	18867
Clean America Inc	3699	E	562 694-5990	19273
Cnp Industries Inc	3639	F	714 482-2320	16849
Coyle Reproductions Inc (PA)	2752	C	866 269-5373	6517
Crossroads Software Inc	7372	F	714 990-6433	23782
Curtiss-Wright Controls	3842	F	714 982-1860	21996
Cybortronics Incorporated	3826	F	949 855-2814	21213
D G Industries	3541	F	714 990-3787	13909
Darbo Manufacturing Company	2339	E	714 529-7693	3312
Database Works Inc	7372	F	714 203-8800	23802
DOT Haizol Com	3549	F	657 258-9027	14265
Ecmm Services Inc	3955	C	714 988-9388	22963
Educational Ideas Incorporated	2731	E	714 990-4332	6099
Electronic Precision Spc Inc	3471	E	714 256-8950	13004
Energy Cnvrsion Applctions Inc	3612	F	714 256-2166	16548
Envista Holdings Corporation	3843	A	714 817-7000	22154
Esmart Massage Inc	3634	F	657 341-0360	16827
Fineline Circuits & Technology	3672	E	714 529-2942	17876
Fixtures By Design LLC	2541	F	714 572-5406	4904
Flint Group US LLC	2893	E	626 369-6900	8915
Foxlink International Inc (HQ)	3643	E	714 256-1777	16899
Foxlink World Circuit Tech	3672	E	714 256-0877	17883
Goodrich Corporation	3728	C	714 984-1461	20121
Hand & Nail Harmony Inc	2844	D	714 773-9758	8509
Harbor Truck Bodies Inc	3713	D	714 996-0411	19537
Harte Hanks Inc	2711	E	714 577-4462	5653
Herrick Retail Corporation Th	2752	E	714 256-9543	6612
IAC Industries	2599	E	714 990-8997	5066
Iddea California LLC	3714	F	714 257-7389	19686
Imperial Cal Products Inc	3469	E	714 990-9100	12820
Instrument Design Eng Assoc I	3679	E	714 525-3302	18946
ITS Group Inc	3625	F	714 256-4100	16712
Jade Range LLC	3631	C	714 961-2400	16812
Kanex	3699	E	714 332-1681	19337
Kingson Mold & Machine Inc	3544	E	714 871-0221	14068
Kirkhill Inc (HQ)	2822	E	714 529-4901	7631
Kirkhill Inc	3053	A	714 529-4901	9240
Kirkhill Inc	3053	A	714 529-4901	9241
Kworld (usa) Computer Inc	3663	E	626 581-0867	17556
La Paz Products Inc	2087	F	714 990-0982	2219

Mergent email: customerrelations@mergent.com
1308

2020 California
Manufacturers Register

(P-0000) Products & Services Section entry number
(PA)=Parent Co (HQ)=Headquarters (DH)=Div Headquarters

	SIC	EMP	PHONE	ENTRY #
Ledconn Corp	3674	F	714 256-2111	18346
Life Science Outsourcing Inc	3841	D	714 672-1090	21774
Lifebloom Corporation	2834	E	562 944-6800	7992
Lite Line Frame Bags	3172	E	562 905-3150	10238
Lucky Devil LLC	2759	F	714 990-2237	7126
M3 Products Inc	2542	E	626 371-1900	4988
Media Blast & Abrasive Inc	3589	F	714 257-0484	15542
Metals USA Building Pdts LP (DH)	3355	A	713 946-9000	11263
Metals USA Building Pdts LP	3355	F	714 529-0407	11266
Mfg Packaging Products	3565	F	714 984-2300	14718
Mike Kenney Tool Inc	3599	E	714 577-9262	16201
Mildef Inc (PA)	3571	F	703 224-8835	14949
Mkt Innovations	3599	D	714 524-7668	16216
Mobility Specialists Inc	3999	F	714 674-0480	23414
Moravek Biochemicals Inc (PA)	2819	E	714 990-2018	7508
Moxa Americas Inc	3577	E	714 528-6777	15293
MPS Medical Inc	3841	E	714 672-1090	21829
MR Mold & Engineering Corp	3544	E	714 996-5511	14082
Muirsis Inc	3432	E	714 579-1555	11674
Mullen Technologies Inc (PA)	3711	E	714 613-1900	19489
Nycetek Inc	2541	E	714 671-3860	4924
Orangegrid LLC	7372	E	657 220-1519	24279
Pacific Archtectural Mllwk Inc (PA)	2431	D	562 905-3200	4102
Pacific Plastics Inc	3084	D	714 990-9050	9472
Pacific Quality Packaging Corp	2653	D	714 257-1234	5250
Paul Merrill Company Inc	3281	F	562 691-1871	10918
Pigs Tail USA LLC	3089	F	714 566-0011	9959
Precise Industries Inc	3444	C	714 482-2333	12338
President Enterprise Inc	2759	E	714 671-9577	7179
Production Systems Group Inc	2599	E	714 990-8997	5076
Q C M Inc	3629	E	714 414-1173	16795
Ram Aerospace Inc	3728	F	714 853-1703	20210
Ramtec Associates Inc	3089	E	714 996-7477	10008
Rogers Holding Company Inc	3728	E	714 257-4850	20211
S&B Industry Inc	3089	D	909 569-4155	10038
Scisorek & Son Flavors Inc	2087	E	714 524-0550	2229
Seismic Reservoir 2020 Inc	1382	E	562 697-9711	139
Sonic Air Systems Inc	3564	E	714 255-0124	14678
Span-O-Matic Inc	3444	E	714 256-4700	12384
SPX Cooling Technologies Inc	3443	E	714 529-6080	12054
Steelclad Inc	1389	E	714 529-0277	267
Stolo Cabinets Inc (PA)	2521	E	714 529-7303	4822
Suheung-America Corporation (HQ)	2834	F	714 854-9882	8148
Sunon Inc (PA)	3564	E	714 255-0208	14680
Suppress Fire Atmtc Sprinklers	3569	F	714 671-5939	14863
Taylor Coml Foodservice Inc	3585	E	714 255-7200	15453
Taylor Communications Inc	2754	F	866 541-0937	6965
Tca Precision Products LLC	3728	F	714 257-4850	20244
TEC Lighting Inc	3648	F	714 529-5068	17166
Trane US Inc	3585	D	626 913-7123	15458
Trigon Components Inc	3675	F	714 990-1367	18685
Txc Technology Inc (HQ)	3679	F	714 990-5510	19129
Tyson Fresh Meats Inc	2011	F	714 528-5543	427
UNI-Caps LLC	2833	E	714 529-8400	7701
Uriman Inc (HQ)	3694	C	714 257-2080	19204
Ventura Foods LLC (PA)	2079	C	714 257-3700	1485
Virtual Composites Co Inc	2821	F	714 256-8850	7624
Viviglo Technologies Inc	3999	E	949 933-9738	23520
Water One Industries Inc	3589	F	707 747-4300	15598
West Coast Gasket Co	3053	D	714 869-0123	9259
Whittier Filtration Inc (DH)	3589	E	714 986-5300	15605
Wilsey Foods Inc	2079	A	714 257-3700	1487
Worldwide Envmtl Pdts Inc (PA)	3823	D	714 990-2700	20958

BRENTWOOD, CA - Contra Costa County

	SIC	EMP	PHONE	ENTRY #
Antioch Building Materials Co	3273	E	925 634-3541	10690
Bay Standard Manufacturing Inc (PA)	3452	E	925 634-1181	12667
Bluewater Publishing LLC	2741	E	925 634-0880	6203
Brentwood Press & Pubg LLC	2711	E	925 516-4757	5569
Nyabenga Llc	2741	F	925 418-4221	6299

BRISBANE, CA - San Mateo County

	SIC	EMP	PHONE	ENTRY #
Aimmune Therapeutics Inc	2834	C	650 614-5220	7733
Aircraft Technical Publishers (PA)	2741	D	415 330-9500	6178
Cutera Inc (PA)	3845	C	415 657-5500	22246
Dolby Laboratories Inc	3663	D	415 715-2500	17505
Florian Industries Inc	3441	F	415 330-9000	11795
Fong Brothers Printing Inc (PA)	2752	C	415 467-1050	6577
G Pucci & Sons Inc	3949	F	415 468-0452	22805
Innoviva Inc (PA)	2834	F	650 238-9600	7950
Leemah Corporation (PA)	3671	C	415 394-1288	17788
Macrogenics West Inc	2834	F	650 624-2600	8001
Pitney Bowes Inc	3579	E	415 330-9423	15389
Praxair Inc	2813	E	415 657-9880	7437
Sfo Apparel	2339	C	415 468-8816	3405
Sheng-Kee Bakery	2051	D	415 468-3800	1277

BRODERICK, CA - Yolo County

	SIC	EMP	PHONE	ENTRY #
Gemini Bio Products	3568	F	916 471-3540	14783

BUELLTON, CA - Santa Barbara County

	SIC	EMP	PHONE	ENTRY #
Aero Industries LLC	3599	E	805 688-6734	15704
Alma Rosa Winery Vineyards LLC (PA)	2084	F	805 688-9090	1580
Equestrian Designs LLC	2339	E	805 686-4455	3321
Firestone Walker Inc	2082	E	805 254-4205	1527
Gavial Holdings Inc	3679	E	805 688-6734	18922
Global Silicones Inc	2869	F	805 686-4500	8741
GP Machining Inc	3599	E	805 686-0852	16001
Infraredvision Technology Corp	3823	E	805 686-8848	20888
Lockheed Martin Corporation	3812	B	805 686-4069	20609
Terravant Wine Company LLC (PA)	2084	E	805 688-4245	1950
Tilton Engineering Inc	3714	E	805 688-2353	19784
True Precision Machining Inc	3599	E	805 964-4545	16473

BUENA PARK, CA - Orange County

	SIC	EMP	PHONE	ENTRY #
Abad Foam Inc	3086	E	714 994-2223	9498
ABN Industrial Co Inc (PA)	3599	F	714 521-9211	15672
Advertising Services	2752	E	714 522-2781	6398
Alloy Die Casting Co	3363	B	714 521-9800	11330
Ameripec Inc	2086	C	714 690-9191	2038
Aqua Products Inc	3581	E	714 670-0691	15395
Awesome Products Inc (PA)	2842	C	714 562-8873	8365
Blasted Wood Products Inc	2421	E	714 237-1600	3927
Creative Impressions Inc	3081	E	714 521-4441	9399
Cyu Lithographics Inc	2752	E	888 878-9898	6528
Dean Foods Company Cal Inc	2026	E	714 684-2160	696
Dream International Usa Inc	3942	F	714 521-6007	22647
Elwin Inc	2591	E	714 752-6962	5021
Erika Records Inc	3652	E	714 228-5420	17319
Evantec Corporation	3069	F	949 632-2811	9307
Exemplis LLC	2522	E	714 995-4800	4836
Exemplis LLC	2522	B	714 898-5500	4837
General Container	2653	D	714 562-8700	5225
Guest Chex Inc	2752	F	714 522-1860	6600
H Q Machine Tech Inc	3599	E	714 956-3388	16013
Haley Bros Inc (HQ)	2431	C	714 670-2112	4052
Hi-Tech Labels Incorporated (PA)	3599	E	714 670-2150	16021
Hq Machine Tech LLC	3728	E	714 956-3388	20127
International Paper Company	2621	C	714 736-0296	5114
International Paper Company	2621	D	562 868-2246	5127
Interntional Color Posters Inc	2759	E	949 768-1005	7101
Island Snacks Inc	2064	E	714 994-1228	1375
J & H Drilling Co Inc	1381	F	714 994-0402	95
Jaz Distribution Inc	3462	F	714 521-3888	12711
Knotts Berry Farm LLC (HQ)	2099	B	714 827-1776	2499
Leach International Corp (DH)	3679	B	714 736-7537	18986
Leach International Corp	3625	B	714 739-0770	16728
Mar Cor Purification Inc	3589	E	800 633-3080	15538
Mashindustries Inc	2599	E	714 736-9600	5073
Metals USA Building Pdts LP	3441	E	714 522-7852	11843
Mondelez Global LLC	2013	A	714 690-7428	482
Nectave Inc	2099	F	714 393-0144	2565
Norwich Aero Products Inc (DH)	3812	E	607 336-7636	20668
One World Meat Company LLC	2013	F	800 782-1670	484
Osmosis Technology Inc	3589	E	714 670-9303	15554
Park Engineering and Mfg Co	3599	E	714 521-4660	16284
Parker-Hannifin Corporation	3052	E	714 522-8840	9203
Pepsi Bottling Group	2086	F	714 522-9742	2107
Pepsi-Cola Metro Btlg Co Inc	2086	E	714 522-9635	2111
Pharr-Palomar Inc	2281	A	714 522-4811	2884
Plh Products Inc	2452	E	714 739-6622	4465
Pop 82 Inc	2221	F	714 523-8500	2731
Pop Plastics Acrylic Disp Inc	3089	E	714 523-8500	9983
President Global Corporation (HQ)	2052	F	714 994-2990	1325
Prima-Tex Industries Cal Inc	2261	D	714 521-6104	2834
Q Team	2752	F	714 228-4465	6818
Quality Grinding Co Inc	3545	F	714 228-2100	14189
Sinclair Companies	2911	D	714 826-5886	9069
Sovereign Packaging Inc	2653	E	714 670-6811	5270
Spn Investments Inc	3949	E	562 777-1140	22895
T M Cobb Company	2431	E	714 670-2112	4138
Tmx	7372	C	657 325-1756	24514
Trim-Lok Inc (PA)	3089	C	714 562-0500	10093
True Fresh Hpp LLC	3822	F	949 629-7645	20818
Tuff Kote Systems Inc	2851	F	714 522-7341	8689
Wesco Mounting & Finishing Inc	2789	E	714 562-0122	7353
Wire Cut Company Inc	3599	E	714 994-1170	16531
Yeager Enterprises Corp	3291	D	714 994-2040	10960
Zaolla	3651	E	714 736-9270	17308

BURBANK, CA - Los Angeles County

	SIC	EMP	PHONE	ENTRY #
24/7 Studio Equipment Inc	3663	D	818 840-8247	17432
Accratronics Seals Corporation	3679	D	818 843-1500	18806

Employment Codes: A=Over 500 employees, B=251-500,
C=101-250, D=51-100, E=20-50, F=10-19

2020 California
Manufacturers Register

© Mergent Inc. 1-800-342-5647

1309

GEOGRAPHIC

Company	SIC	EMP	PHONE	ENTRY #
Acsco Products Inc	3714	E	818 953-2240	19564
Advanced Publishing Tech Inc	2741	F	818 557-3035	6174
Advanced Publishing Tech Inc (PA)	7372	E	818 557-3035	23570
American Fine Arts Foundry LLC	3366	E	818 848-7593	11393
Aphex Systems Ltd	3663	E	818 767-2929	17454
Arte De Mexico Inc (PA)	2522	D	818 753-4559	4829
Astra Communications Inc	3663	F	818 859-7305	17461
Avid Technology Inc	3861	E	818 557-2520	22404
Bandmerch LLC	2396	E	818 736-4800	3773
Bandy Manufacturing LLC	3728	D	818 846-9020	20056
Bargueiras Rene Inc	3911	F	818 500-8288	22501
Bico Inc	3821	F	818 842-7179	20747
BMC East LLC	2431	F	818 842-8139	4004
Brady Sheet Metal Inc	3444	F	818 846-4043	12136
Bravo Design Inc	2759	F	818 563-1385	7006
Bucy Die Casting	3544	E	818 843-5044	14024
Buildit Engineering Co Inc	3354	E	818 244-6666	11226
Burbank Steel Treating Inc	3398	E	818 842-0975	11442
California Insulated Wire &	3357	D	818 569-4930	11292
Cardona Manufacturing Corp	3728	E	818 841-8358	20068
Carter Plating Inc	3471	F	818 842-1325	12963
Centerpoint Mfg Co Inc	3599	E	818 842-2147	15833
Chulada Inc	2833	E	818 841-6536	7649
Cinemills Corporation (PA)	3648	F	818 843-4560	17110
Color Service Inc	2752	E	323 283-4793	6495
Comco Inc	3589	E	818 333-8500	15503
Computer Prompting Service	3861	E	818 563-3465	22410
Connell Processing Inc	3471	E	818 845-7661	12978
Corona Pathology	2869	E	818 566-1891	8733
Crane Aerospace Inc	3812	D	818 526-2600	20562
Cydwoq Inc	3131	E	818 848-8307	10150
Delray Lighting Inc	3648	E	818 767-3793	17117
Disney Book Group LLC (DH)	2731	F	818 560-1000	6098
Disney Publishing Worldwide (DH)	2721	D	212 633-4400	5920
Divine Pasta Company	2099	E	213 542-3300	2447
Dji Technology Inc	3861	E	818 235-0789	22414
Dolby Laboratories Inc	3651	E	818 562-1101	17220
Doremi Cinema LLC	3861	E	818 562-1101	22415
Doves Jewelry Corporation	3911	E	818 955-8886	22512
Eastwest Clothing Inc (PA)	2331	E	323 980-1177	3157
Eaton Aerospace LLC	3812	E	818 550-4200	20571
Eckert Zegler Isotope Pdts Inc	3829	E	661 309-1010	21463
Eckert Zegler Isotope Pdts Inc	3829	E	661 309-1010	21465
Effective Graphics Inc	2796	D	310 323-2223	7370
Electronic Theatre Contrls Inc	3648	F	323 461-0216	17119
ESM Aerospace Inc	3444	E	818 841-3653	12199
Excelline Food Products LLC	2038	C	818 701-7710	957
Excelline Foods Inc	2038	F	818 701-7710	958
Gary Schroeder Enterprises	3714	E	818 565-1133	19667
Gerhardt Gear Co Inc	3714	E	818 842-6700	19670
Gilderfluke & Company Inc	3651	F	818 840-9484	17232
Golden Fleece Designs Inc	2394	F	323 849-1901	3684
Granite Software Inc	7372	E	818 252-1950	23952
Hair By Couture Inc	3999	F	310 848-7676	23351
Haskel International LLC (HQ)	3561	E	818 843-4000	14581
Hollywood Records Inc	3652	E	818 560-5670	17327
Hutchinson Arospc & Indust Inc	3728	E	818 843-1000	20129
Hutchinson Arospc & Indust Inc	3069	C	818 843-1000	9320
Hydra-Electric Company (PA)	3613	C	818 843-6211	16600
Hydro-Aire Inc (DH)	3728	E	818 526-2600	20132
Insomniac Games Inc (PA)	3944	D	818 729-2400	22683
J L Fisher Inc	3861	D	818 846-8366	22433
Kadi Enterprises Inc	2013	E	818 556-3400	471
Keystone Cabinetry Inc	2434	E	818 565-3330	4216
Kh9100 LLC	3851	F	818 972-2580	22366
Klinky Manufacturing Co	3429	F	818 766-6256	11604
Kotonica Inc	3089	E	818 898-0978	9869
Linde Gas North America LLC	2813	F	626 855-8344	7414
Little Einsteins LLC	2731	F	818 560-1000	6118
Luminar Creations	3911	E	818 843-0010	22542
Makse Inc	3911	F	213 622-5030	22544
Matthews Studio Equipment Inc	3861	E	818 843-6715	22439
Matz Rubber Co Inc	3069	E	323 849-5170	9331
McMillin Mfg Corp	3444	D	323 981-8585	12287
Melrose Mac Inc	3571	F	818 840-8466	14944
Multi Packaging Solutions Inc	2752	E	818 638-0216	6740
Musclepharm Corporation (PA)	2023	D	303 396-6100	606
Mvp Rv Inc	3792	E	951 848-4288	20490
My Eye Media LLC	7372	E	818 559-7200	24185
Natural Balance Pet Foods Inc (DH)	2048	E	800 829-4493	1113
Nerdist Channel LLC	3663	E	818 333-2705	17601
New Gold Manufacturing Inc	3911	D	818 847-1020	22555
No Static Pro Audio Inc	3651	F	818 729-8554	17266
Omega Case Company Inc	2449	E	818 238-9263	4423
Omnia Inc	3728	F	818 843-1620	20188

Company	SIC	EMP	PHONE	ENTRY #
Origin LLC (HQ)	3999	E	818 848-1648	23434
Photronics Inc (DH)	3861	B	203 740-5653	22450
Printograph Inc	2752	F	818 252-3000	6809
Pro Power Products Inc	3629	F	818 558-6222	16794
Quality Heat Treating Inc	3398	E	818 840-8212	11467
Richline Group Inc	3911	C	818 848-5555	22562
Richline Group Inc	3911	C	818 848-5555	22563
S & H Machine Inc (PA)	3599	F	818 846-9847	16378
Sanctuary Clothing Inc	2331	E	818 505-0018	3191
Saturn Fasteners Inc	3429	C	818 973-1807	11625
Select Office Systems Inc	2893	E	818 861-8320	8929
Senior Operations LLC	3728	B	818 260-2900	20231
Sierra Automated Sys/Eng Corp	3663	E	818 840-6749	17657
Slickote	3479	E	818 749-3066	13247
Staness Jonekos Entps Inc	2099	E	818 606-2710	2617
Steril-Aire Inc	3648	E	818 565-1128	17163
Steves Plating Corporation	2542	C	818 842-2184	5003
Superior Window Coverings Inc	2391	E	818 762-6685	3598
Swaner Hardwood Co Inc (PA)	2435	D	818 953-5350	4282
Take A Break Paper	2711	E	323 333-7773	5845
Three-D Plastics Inc	3089	F	323 849-1316	10084
Three-D Plastics Inc (PA)	3089	F	323 849-1316	10085
United Bakery Inc	2051	E	818 843-1892	1288
US Gold Trading Inc (PA)	3911	E	818 558-7766	22581
US Steel Rule Dies Inc	3544	F	562 921-0690	14120
V J Provision Inc	2011	E	818 843-3945	428
Vesture Group Incorporated	2369	E	818 842-0200	3497
Warner Music Group Corp	3652	F	818 846-9090	17339
Warner Music Inc	3652	D	818 953-2600	17340
Westcott Press Inc	2752	F	626 794-7716	6932
Westrock Cp LLC	2631	F	818 557-1500	5180
Westrock Rkt Company	2653	F	818 729-0610	5281
Y B S Enterprises Inc	3661	F	818 848-7790	17431
Zepco	3089	F	818 848-0880	10135

BURLINGAME, CA - San Mateo County

Company	SIC	EMP	PHONE	ENTRY #
A & C Trade Consultants Inc	3432	F	650 375-7000	11651
Advanced Chemblocks Inc	2834	F	650 692-2368	7729
Advanced Components Mfg	3599	E	650 344-6272	15693
Aldran Chemical Inc	2842	E	650 347-8242	8359
Aperia Technologies Inc	3559	E	415 494-9624	14423
Asia America Enterprise Inc	2752	E	650 348-2333	6421
Asia Pacific California Inc (PA)	2711	F	650 513-6189	5554
Burlingame Htg Ventilation Inc	3444	F	650 697-9142	12138
Caban Systems Inc	3691	E	650 270-0113	19153
Cal Signal Corp	3669	F	650 343-6100	17719
Clic LLC	2752	F	415 421-2900	6488
Collabrative DRG Discovery Inc	7372	F	650 204-3084	23758
Colorprint	2752	F	650 697-7611	6501
Corvus Pharmaceuticals Inc	2834	D	650 900-4520	7854
Devincenzi Metal Products Inc	3444	F	650 692-5800	12183
Devincnzi Archtctural Pdts Inc	3446	F	650 692-5800	12470
Garratt-Callahan Company (PA)	2899	E	650 697-5811	8969
Guittard Chocolate Co	2066	C	650 697-4427	1411
Hanergy Holding (america) LLC (HQ)	3674	F	650 288-3722	18265
Hysterical Software Inc	7372	F	415 793-5785	23992
Igenica Inc	2834	E	650 231-4320	7939
Imply Data Inc	7372	F	415 685-8187	24004
Ingenuity Foods Inc	2043	F	650 562-7483	1023
July Systems Inc (PA)	3695	E	650 685-2460	19221
Kindred Biosciences Inc (PA)	2834	E	650 701-7901	7980
Lahlouh Inc	2752	C	650 692-6600	6691
Lithiumstart Inc	3679	E	800 520-8864	18993
Loma Vista Medical Inc	3841	E	650 490-4747	21780
Mentzer Electronics	3845	E	650 697-2642	22282
Merrills Packaging Inc	3081	D	650 259-5959	9410
Middle East Baking Co	2051	E	650 348-7200	1241
Mixed Bag Designs Inc	2673	D	650 239-5358	5405
Motorola Mobility LLC	3663	D	206 383-7785	17593
Petits Pains & Co LP	2051	E	650 692-6000	1261
Phoenix Pharmaceuticals Inc	2834	E	650 558-8898	8075
Plasti-Print Inc	2759	F	650 652-4950	7175
Prestige Chinese Teas Co	2099	F	650 697-8989	2588
Proterra Inc (PA)	3711	C	864 438-0000	19494
Sage Software Inc	7372	C	650 579-3628	24373
School Apparel Inc (PA)	2337	C	650 777-4500	3277
Sensbey Inc (PA)	3548	F	650 697-2032	14253
Sentient Energy Inc (PA)	3825	F	650 523-6680	21119
Sing Tao Newspapers (HQ)	2711	D	650 808-8800	5827
Sleeprite Industries Inc	2515	E	650 344-1980	4743
Smp Robotics Systems Corp	3535	D	415 572-2316	13837
Standard Fiber LLC (PA)	2392	E	650 872-6528	3643
Swedcom Corporation	3661	F	650 348-1190	17416
Sybron Dental Specialties Inc	3843	A	650 340-0393	22192
Tag-Connect LLC	3357	F	877 244-4156	11322
Tangent Computer Inc (PA)	3571	D	888 683-2881	14985

Mergent email: customerrelations@mergent.com
1310

2020 California
Manufacturers Register

(P-0000) Products & Services Section entry number
(PA)=Parent Co (HQ)=Headquarters (DH)=Div Headquarters

	SIC	EMP	PHONE	ENTRY #
Tlm International Inc	3639	F	650 952-2257	16855
Vans Inc	3021	F	650 401-3542	9190
Vector Laboratories Inc (PA)	2836	D	650 697-3600	8332
Worldwide Energy & Mfg USA Inc (PA)	3674	E	650 692-7788	18659
Yb Media LLC	2741	E	310 467-5804	6386

BURNEY, CA - Shasta County

	SIC	EMP	PHONE	ENTRY #
Shasta Green Inc	2411	E	530 335-4924	3904
Sierra Pacific Industries	2421	F	530 378-8301	3953
Sierra Pacific Industries	2421	C	530 335-3681	3955
Tubit Enterprises Inc	2411	E	530 335-5085	3912

BUTTONWILLOW, CA - Kern County

	SIC	EMP	PHONE	ENTRY #
Albert Goyenetche Dairy	2026	F	661 764-6176	682
B W Implement Co	3523	E	661 764-5254	13612
JG Boswell Tomato - Kern LLC	2033	F	661 764-9000	779

BYRON, CA - Contra Costa County

	SIC	EMP	PHONE	ENTRY #
Covia Holdings Corporation	1446	E	925 634-3575	372
Marin Food Specialties Inc	2032	E	925 634-6126	738
Quick Deck Inc	3448	F	704 888-0327	12572

CALABASAS, CA - Los Angeles County

	SIC	EMP	PHONE	ENTRY #
Alcatel-Lucent USA Inc	3661	E	818 880-3500	17344
Ale USA Inc	3663	A	818 878-4816	17445
Apex Precision Tech Inc	3714	E	317 821-1000	19583
Art Impressions Inc	2741	E	818 591-0105	6189
Catapult Communications Corp (DH)	7372	E	818 871-1800	23724
Counterpoint Software Inc	7372	F	818 222-7777	23780
Dts LLC	3651	D	818 436-1000	17222
Fulcrum Microsystems Inc	3674	F	818 871-8100	18245
Global Edge LLC	7372	E	888 315-2692	23942
Ixia (HQ)	3825	B	818 871-1800	21057
Ixia	3825	F	818 871-1800	21058
Melco Engineering Corporation	3841	F	818 591-1000	21815
Netsol Technologies Inc (PA)	7372	E	818 222-9197	24196
Nia Energy LLC	3641	F	818 422-8000	16867
Nova-One Diagnostics LLC	2835	D	818 348-1543	8242
Planetart LLC (DH)	2711	E	818 436-3600	5798
Radian Memory Systems Inc	3572	F	818 222-4080	15084
Schroeder Tool & Die Corp	3599	F	818 786-9360	16388
Solid 21 Incorporated	3911	F	213 688-0900	22572
Spanish Castle Inc	2084	E	818 222-4496	1924
Spirent Communications Inc (HQ)	3825	B	818 676-2300	21127
Thrio Inc	7372	E	747 258-4201	24507
Wixen Music Publishing Inc	2731	F	818 591-7355	6164
Yamaha Guitar Group Inc (HQ)	3931	C	818 575-3600	22644

CALEXICO, CA - Imperial County

	SIC	EMP	PHONE	ENTRY #
Bi Technologies Corporation	3679	E	714 447-2402	18838
Celestica LLC	3643	B	760 357-4880	16883
Clover Technologies Group LLC	3861	E	760 357-9277	22409
Creation Tech Calexico Inc (HQ)	3672	C	760 336-8543	17856
Cs Manfacturing Indus Svcs Inc (PA)	3678	F	760 890-7746	18763
Honeywell International Inc	3724	A	760 312-5300	19964
Imperial Valley Foods Inc	2037	B	760 203-1896	915
Lakim Industries Incorporated (PA)	3991	E	310 637-8900	23029
Lorenz Inc	3699	B	760 427-1815	19348
National Oilwell Varco Inc	3533	C	760 357-0970	13786
Orthodental International Inc	3843	D	760 357-8070	22178
Robert Bosch Tool Corporation	3546	C	760 357-5603	14226
Rockwell Collins Inc	3812	E	760 768-4732	20707
Sewing Experts Inc	2331	E	760 357-8525	3193
Skyworks Solutions	3629	F	301 874-6408	16799
Triumph Group Inc	3728	F	760 768-1700	20261
Triumph Insulation Systems LLC	3728	A	949 250-4999	20262
Vertiv Corporation	3613	F	760 768-7522	16621

CALIF HOT SPG, CA - Tulare County

	SIC	EMP	PHONE	ENTRY #
California Hot Springs Water	2086	F	661 548-6582	2050

CALIFORNIA CITY, CA - Kern County

	SIC	EMP	PHONE	ENTRY #
Fabricor Products Inc	3446	F	760 373-8292	12474
Service Rock Products Corp	3273	E	760 373-9140	10829
Ward Enterprises	3599	F	661 251-4890	16510

CALIMESA, CA - Riverside County

	SIC	EMP	PHONE	ENTRY #
B & Y Machine Co	3592	F	909 795-8588	15611
Calimesa News Mirror	2711	E	909 795-8145	5583
Skat-Trak Inc	3011	C	909 795-2505	9169
William A Shubeck	3996	E	909 795-6970	23256

CALIPATRIA, CA - Imperial County

	SIC	EMP	PHONE	ENTRY #
Earthrise Nutritionals LLC	2099	F	760 348-5027	2449

CALISTOGA, CA - Napa County

	SIC	EMP	PHONE	ENTRY #
Bailey Essel William Jr	2084	F	707 341-3391	1589
Chateau Montelena Winery	2084	E	707 942-5105	1632
Clos Pegase Winery Inc	2084	E	707 942-4981	1641

	SIC	EMP	PHONE	ENTRY #
Coffee Guys Inc (PA)	2095	E	707 942-5747	2284
Diamond Creek Vineyard	2084	F	707 942-6926	1667
Envy Wines LLC	2084	F	707 942-4670	1689
Jack McMahon Landscape	2421	F	707 942-1122	3937
Lane Bennett Winery	2084	F	707 942-6684	1795
Madrigal Vineyard Management	2084	E	707 942-8691	1808
Reverie On Diamond Mtn LLC	2084	F	707 942-6800	1886
Silverado Brewing Co L L C	2082	E	707 341-3089	1564
Sterling Vineyards Inc (PA)	2084	E	707 942-3300	1930
Sterling Vineyards	2084	E	707 942-9602	1932
Sugarloaf Farming Corporation	2084	E	707 942-4459	1940
Tonnellerie Francaise French C	2449	F	707 942-9301	4430
Villa Amorosa	2084	D	707 942-8200	1984
Vintage Wine Estates Inc	2084	F	707 942-4981	1990

CAMARILLO, CA - Ventura County

	SIC	EMP	PHONE	ENTRY #
3dcd	3695	F	805 383-3837	19208
Abel Automatics Inc	3451	E	805 484-8789	12614
Airborne Technologies Inc	3728	D	805 389-3700	20025
Americon	2521	F	805 987-0412	4780
Amh International Inc	3599	F	805 388-2082	15741
Applied Wireless Inc	3674	F	805 383-9600	18118
Artisan Vehicle Systems Inc	3711	D	805 512-9955	19454
Askgene Pharma Inc	2834	F	805 807-9868	7771
Astrofoam Molding Company Inc	3086	F	805 482-7276	9506
August Hat Company Inc (PA)	2353	E	805 983-4651	3461
Barta-Schoenewald Inc (PA)	3621	C	805 389-1935	16632
Battery-Biz Inc	3694	D	805 437-7777	19187
Belport Company Inc (PA)	3843	E	805 484-1051	22136
Bestforms Inc	2761	E	805 388-0503	7280
Bimbo Bakeries Usa Inc	2051	E	805 384-1059	1162
Bnk Petroleum (us) Inc	1382	E	805 484-3613	110
Cal-Sensors Inc (PA)	3812	E	707 303-3837	20552
California Designers Choice	2434	E	805 987-5820	4177
California Pharmaceuticals LLC	2834	F	805 482-3737	7821
California St UNI Channel Isla	3612	E	805 437-2670	16543
Calram LLC	3499	F	805 987-6205	13507
Camland Inc	7692	F	805 485-9242	24624
Chargetek Inc	3629	E	805 444-7792	16782
Chauhan Industries Inc	3089	F	805 484-1616	9705
Ciao Wireless Inc	3679	D	805 389-3224	18860
CK Technologies Inc (PA)	3823	E	805 987-4801	20849
Coastal Embroidery Inc	2395	F	805 383-5593	3733
Coherus Biosciences Inc	2836	D	805 445-7051	8291
Cooper Crouse-Hinds Inc	3678	C	805 484-0543	18759
Cooper Crouse-Hinds LLC	3069	C	805 484-0543	9296
Cooper Crouse-Hinds LLC	3069	C	805 484-0543	9297
Cooper Interconnect Inc (DH)	3643	C	805 484-0543	16888
Cooper Interconnect Inc	3678	C	805 553-9632	18760
Cooper Interconnect Inc	3644	E	805 553-9632	16943
Corprint Incorporated	2759	F	818 839-5316	7036
CPI Malibu Division	3663	D	805 383-1829	17495
Crockett Graphics Inc (PA)	2653	F	805 987-8577	5215
Enterprise Services LLC	7372	F	805 388-8000	23865
Evergreen Avionics Inc (PA)	3674	E	805 445-6492	18229
Futureflite Inc	2531	F	818 653-2145	4860
Galtech Computer Corporation	2521	E	805 376-1060	4798
Gc International Inc (PA)	3652	E	805 389-4631	17323
Gc International Inc	3652	E	805 389-4631	17324
GKN Aerospace Camarillo Inc	3444	F	805 383-6684	12224
Gms Landscapes Inc	3432	D	805 402-3925	11670
Gtran Inc (PA)	3679	E	805 445-4500	18928
Hanson Lab Furniture Inc	3821	E	805 498-3121	20760
Hi-Temp Insulation Inc	3469	B	805 484-2774	12815
Hte Acquisition LLC	3599	F	805 987-5449	16036
Hygiena LLC (PA)	2835	C	805 388-2383	8228
IL Helth Buty Natural Oils Inc	2899	F	805 384-0473	8977
Illinois Tool Works Inc	3674	F	805 499-0335	18279
Infab Corporation	3842	D	805 987-5255	22030
Innovative Integration Inc	3823	E	805 520-3300	20889
Insulfab Inc	3296	D	805 482-2751	10983
Interconnect Systems Inc (DH)	3674	D	805 482-2870	18313
Interglobal Waste Management	3826	D	805 388-1588	21248
International Paper Company	2621	F	805 933-4347	5116
J C Industries Inc	3999	F	805 389-4040	23369
Johanson Dielectrics Inc (HQ)	3675	C	805 389-1166	18681
Johanson Technology Inc	3675	C	805 389-1166	18682
Jolly Jumps Inc	3599	E	805 484-0026	16092
K9 Ballistics Inc	3999	F	805 233-8103	23377
Kinamed Inc	3842	E	805 384-2748	22040
Koltov Inc (PA)	3172	E	805 764-0280	10236
Linabond Inc	3479	E	805 484-7373	13201
Livewire Test Labs Inc	3825	F	801 293-8300	21067
Lucix Corporation (HQ)	3679	D	805 987-6645	18997
Lundberg Survey Inc	2721	E	805 383-2400	5980
Maddiebrit Products LLC	2851	F	818 483-0096	8655

Employment Codes: A=Over 500 employees, B=251-500, C=101-250, D=51-100, E=20-50, F=10-19

2020 California
Manufacturers Register

© Mergent Inc. 1-800-342-5647

1311

GEOGRAPHIC

Name	SIC	EMP	PHONE	ENTRY #
Magicall Inc	3621	E	805 484-4300	16661
Mediapointe Inc	3651	F	805 480-3700	17258
Medical Packaging Corporation	3842	D	805 388-2383	22045
Mercury Systems Inc	3672	C	805 388-1345	17922
Merex Inc	3825	F	805 446-2700	21078
Meyers Publishing Inc	2721	F	805 445-8881	5987
Microsemi Communications Inc (DH)	3674	E	805 388-3700	18399
Microsemi Frequency Time Corp	3674	E	805 465-1700	18410
Microvoice Corporation	3663	E	805 389-2922	17586
Mintronix Inc	3571	F	805 482-1298	14950
Mosaic Distributors LLC	2844	F	805 383-7711	8541
Mosaic Marketing Partners LLC	2844	F	805 383-7711	8542
Nanoprecision Products Inc	3469	E	310 597-4991	12848
Nevion Usa Inc	3663	D	805 247-8575	17602
Old New York Bagel & Deli Co (PA)	2051	F	805 484-3354	1254
Optim Microwave Inc	3663	E	805 482-7093	17610
Organic Infusions Inc (PA)	2911	F	805 419-4118	9056
OSI Optoelectronics Inc	3674	E	805 987-0146	18461
Pacific Casual LLC	2514	E	805 445-8310	4697
Parker-Hannifin Corporation	3728	C	805 484-8533	20198
PDQ Engineering Inc	3599	E	805 482-1334	16289
Performance Materials Corp (PA)	2821	D	805 482-1722	7590
Performance Plus Laboratories	3821	C	805 383-7871	20771
Pico Crimping Tools Co	3545	F	805 388-5510	14183
Plt Enterprises Inc	3643	D	805 389-5335	16920
Polyfet Rf Devices Inc	3674	E	805 484-4210	18475
Price-Leho Co Inc	3469	F	805 482-8967	12860
Q Corporation	3826	E	805 383-8998	21279
Qualstar Corporation (PA)	3572	E	805 583-7744	15078
Rache Corporation	3699	E	805 389-6868	19389
Recon 1 Inc	3021	E	805 388-3911	9180
Record Technology Inc	3652	F	805 484-2747	17336
Roboworm Inc	3949	F	805 389-1636	22873
Rocketstar Robotics Inc	3621	E	805 529-7769	16672
Ronlo Engineering Ltd	3599	E	805 389-3227	16371
Sani-Tech West Inc (PA)	3052	D	805 389-0400	9206
Scripps Media Inc	2711	C	805 437-0000	5823
Security Door Controls (PA)	3429	E	805 494-0622	11627
Semtech Corporation (PA)	3674	C	805 498-2111	18538
Shine & Pretty (usa) Corp	2844	F	805 388-8581	8581
Sierra Traffic Service Inc	3669	F	805 388-2474	17762
Signum Systems Corporation	3825	F	805 383-3682	21121
Skurka Aerospace Inc (DH)	3621	C	216 706-2939	16673
Snap Creative Manufacturing	3942	F	818 735-3830	22654
So-Cal Value Added LLC	3679	E	805 389-5335	19087
Structural Diagnostics Inc	3825	E	805 987-7755	21129
Tactical Communications Corp	3669	E	805 987-4100	17766
Technical Film Systems Inc	3861	F	805 384-9470	22462
Technicolor Disc Services Corp (HQ)	3695	C	805 445-1122	19237
Technicolor Thomson Group	3651	A	805 445-7652	17288
Thiessen Products Inc	3599	F	805 482-6913	16455
Thin-Lite Corporation	3648	E	805 987-5021	17169
Thingap LLC	3621	F	805 477-9741	16676
Thingap Holdings LLC	3621	F	805 477-9741	16677
Titan Medical Dme Inc	3841	F	818 889-9998	21931
Titan Metal Fabricators Inc (PA)	3441	D	805 487-5050	11899
Transonic Combustion Inc	3519	E	805 465-5145	13601
United Fabrication Inc	3444	F	805 482-2354	12416
United Western Enterprises Inc	3479	E	805 389-1077	13263
Ventura County Star	2711	F	805 437-0138	5858
Viade Products Inc	3843	E	805 484-2114	22203
Viavi Solutions Inc	3661	D	805 465-1875	17428
VME Acquisition Corp (PA)	3842	E	805 384-2748	22121
Voiceboard Corporation	3571	E	805 389-3100	14996
Western Gage Corporation	3545	E	805 445-1410	14211
Western Mfg & Distrg LLC	3751	E	805 988-1010	20436
Wilwood Engineering	3714	C	805 388-1188	19805
Xirgo Technologies LLC	3699	E	805 319-4079	19448
Zero Gravity Corporation	3751	E	805 388-8803	20440
Zpower LLC	3629	C	805 445-7789	16806

CAMERON PARK, CA - El Dorado County

Name	SIC	EMP	PHONE	ENTRY #
Artisan Moss LLC	2077	F	833 667-7278	1451
First Gold Corp	1041	F	530 677-5974	3
Preferred Mfg Svcs Inc (PA)	3599	D	530 677-2675	16311
Vultures Row Aviation LLC	3599	F	530 676-9245	16505
Wask Engineering Inc	3764	F	530 672-2795	20470
Works Connection	3751	E	530 642-9488	20438

CAMINO, CA - El Dorado County

Name	SIC	EMP	PHONE	ENTRY #
Rainbow Orchards	2086	F	530 644-1594	2130
Sierra Pacific Industries	2421	B	530 644-2311	3958

CAMPBELL, CA - Santa Clara County

Name	SIC	EMP	PHONE	ENTRY #
Activewire Inc	3577	F	650 465-4000	15144
Afn Services LLC	2599	E	408 364-1564	5047
Allergan Sales LLC	2834	E	408 376-3001	7738
Alternators Starters Etc	3694	F	408 559-3540	19184
Aoptix Technologies Inc	3699	D	408 558-3300	19258
Apama Medical Inc	3841	F	408 903-4094	21600
Arteris Inc	3674	E	408 470-7300	18126
Arteris Holdings Inc	3674	E	408 470-7300	18127
Barracuda Networks Inc (HQ)	7372	C	408 342-5400	23653
Bering Technology Inc	3577	E	408 364-6500	15168
Bluestack Systems Inc	7372	E	408 412-9439	23684
Brilliant Instruments Inc	3823	F	408 866-0426	20841
Bruker Corporation	3577	F	408 376-4040	15179
C T V Inc	2752	F	408 378-1606	6464
Campbell Graphics Inc	2752	E	408 371-6411	6470
Carmel Instruments LLC	3823	F	408 866-0426	20846
Chargepoint Inc (PA)	3629	B	408 841-4500	16781
Christian Music Today Inc	2711	F	408 377-9232	5589
Collimated Holes Inc	3827	E	408 374-5080	21344
Condeco Software Inc (HQ)	7372	E	917 677-7600	23768
Consoldted Hnge Mnfctured Pdts	3599	F	408 379-6550	15864
Deluxe Corporation	2782	D	408 370-8801	7309
Dynalinear Technologies Inc	3559	F	408 376-5090	14454
Eos Software Inc	7372	F	855 900-4876	23868
Etched Media Corporation	3471	E	408 374-6895	13007
Firetide Inc (DH)	3577	E	408 399-7771	15228
Harris Precision	3444	F	408 866-4160	12234
Hotronic Inc	3661	E	408 378-3883	17378
Imperative Care Inc	3842	E	669 228-3814	22028
Iwatt Inc (DH)	3674	E	408 374-4200	18324
Jessee Brothers Machine Sp Inc	3599	E	408 866-1755	16082
Kalila Medical Inc	3829	E	408 819-5175	21494
Kerrock Countertops Inc (PA)	2511	E	510 441-2300	4582
Keyssa Inc (PA)	3674	E	408 637-2300	18332
Keyssa Systems Inc	3559	E	408 637-2300	14487
List Biological Labs Inc	2836	E	408 866-6363	8315
Medleycom Incorporated	2711	F	408 745-5418	5749
Metric Design & Manufacturing	3544	F	408 378-4544	14077
Mips Tech Inc (HQ)	3674	D	408 530-5000	18418
Photon Inc	3823	F	408 226-1000	20918
Precision Identity Corporation	3599	E	408 374-2346	16309
Process Solutions Inc	3823	E	408 370-6540	20921
Prompter People Inc	3663	F	408 353-6000	17628
Reed Mariculture Inc	2048	F	408 377-1065	1121
Semi Automation & Tech Inc	3674	E	408 374-9549	18530
Semprex Corporation	3827	F	408 379-3230	21408
Tactx Medical Inc (DH)	3841	C	408 364-7100	21922
Teammate Builders Inc	2542	F	408 377-9000	5005
Valet Cstm Cabinets & Closets	2434	F	408 374-4407	4260
Velo3d Inc	2752	C	408 666-5309	6921
Versatile Power Inc	3841	F	408 341-4600	21954
Vivus Inc (PA)	2834	E	650 934-5200	8184
Wg Security Products Inc	3699	E	408 241-8000	19445
Workspot Inc (PA)	7372	F	888 426-8113	24588
Zipline Medical Inc	3841	F	408 412-7228	21967
Zircon Corporation (PA)	3546	E	408 866-8600	14231

CANOGA PARK, CA - Los Angeles County

Name	SIC	EMP	PHONE	ENTRY #
3M Company	3613	F	818 882-0606	16582
Advanced Safety Devices LLC	3825	F	818 701-9200	20983
Aerojet Rocketdyne De Inc (HQ)	2869	C	818 586-1000	8706
Alexander Business Supplies	2752	F	818 346-1820	6401
Allman Products Inc	3086	E	818 715-0093	9502
American Activated Carbon Corp	3624	F	310 491-2842	16681
American Mfg Netwrk Inc	3599	F	818 786-1113	15739
B & R Accessories Inc	3961	F	213 688-8727	22978
B S K T Inc	3599	E	818 349-1566	15769
Barrys Printing Inc	2752	E	818 998-8600	6436
Best Data Products Inc	3577	D	818 534-1414	15169
Boeing Company	3721	A	818 428-1154	19881
California Natural Vitamins	2834	E	818 772-8441	7820
Casmari Inc	2253	F	818 727-1856	2778
Cg Manufacturing Inc	3444	F	818 886-1191	12155
Cicon Engineering Inc	3679	F	818 909-6060	18861
Cicon Engineering Inc	3679	F	818 882-6508	18862
Darrell Zbrowski	3537	D	818 324-5961	13870
Den-Mat Corporation	2844	E	800 445-0345	8479
Eastman Performance Films LLC	2821	E	818 882-5744	7558
Eca Medical Instruments	3841	E	818 998-7284	21695
Elite Generators Inc	3621	F	818 718-0200	16641
Emac Assembly Corp	3679	F	818 882-2999	18902
Glastar Corporation	3559	E	818 341-0301	14472
Holsum Bakery Inc	2051	E	818 884-6562	1225
Infinity Precision Inc	3599	F	818 447-3008	16044
Infinity Stamps Inc	3469	F	818 576-1188	12821
International Beauty Pdts LLC (PA)	2844	F	818 999-1222	8518
Interntnal Hmeopathic Mfg Dist	2834	F	818 884-8040	7959
Interntnal Virtual PDT MGT Inc	3661	F	818 812-9500	17382

Mergent email: customerrelations@mergent.com
1312

2020 California
Manufacturers Register

(P-0000) Products & Services Section entry number
(PA)=Parent Co (HQ)=Headquarters (DH)=Div Headquarters

	SIC	EMP	PHONE	ENTRY #
Jake Stehelin Etienne	3089	D	818 998-4250	9849
Jot Engineering Inc	3599	F	818 727-7572	16093
Kama Interconnect Inc	3679	F	818 713-9810	18971
Micro Steel Inc	3769	E	818 348-8701	20479
Mir Printing & Graphics	2752	F	818 313-9333	6731
Mixed Chicks LLC	2844	F	818 888-4008	8540
Mooney Industries	3599	F	818 998-0199	16225
Mww Inc	2499	E	800 575-3475	4518
National Ready Mixed Con Co	3273	F	818 884-0893	10807
Natural Wonders Ca Inc	2833	F	818 593-2001	7675
Odette Christiane LLC	2339	F	818 803-0410	3380
One Lambda Inc (HQ)	2835	D	818 702-0042	8244
Pacific Shore Holdings Inc	2834	F	818 998-0996	8061
Pastries By Edie Inc	2051	E	818 340-0203	1259
Penta Laboratories Inc	3671	E	818 882-3872	17793
Pls Diabetic Shoe Company Inc.	3021	E	818 734-7080	9178
PM Lithographers Inc	2752	F	818 704-2626	6786
Protemach Inc	2869	F	310 622-2693	8766
Rainbo Record Mfg Corp (PA)	3652	C	818 280-1100	17335
Small Wnders Hndcrfted Mntures	3999	F	818 703-7450	23478
Spa La La Inc	3999	F	605 321-1276	23481
Temptron Engineering Inc	3829	F	818 346-4900	21556
US Nuclear Corp (PA)	3829	F	818 296-0746	21562
Viking Ready Mix Co Inc	3273	E	818 884-0893	10867
Vitale Home Designs Inc	3873	F	818 888-2481	22486
Vomar Products Inc	2759	E	818 610-5115	7264
Woodie Woodpeckers Woodworks	2434	E	818 999-2090	4268
Works Performance Products Inc	3714	E	818 701-1010	19807
Y Nissim Inc	3579	F	818 718-9024	15394

CANTIL, CA - Kern County

	SIC	EMP	PHONE	ENTRY #
US Rockets	3761	F	707 267-3393	20462

CANTUA CREEK, CA - Fresno County

	SIC	EMP	PHONE	ENTRY #
Pacific Ginning Company LLC	3559	E	559 829-9446	14512

CANYON COUNTRY, CA - Los Angeles County

	SIC	EMP	PHONE	ENTRY #
American Garment Finishing	2221	E	310 962-1929	2722
Box Master	3469	E	661 298-2666	12773
California Compactor Svc Inc	3499	F	661 298-5556	13506
Candlelight Press Inc	2752	E	323 299-3798	6471
Commercial Display Systems LLC	3585	E	818 361-8160	15419
Continental Security Inds	3669	F	661 251-8800	17722
Ilona Draperies Inc	2391	E	818 840-8811	3589
Legacy Vulcan LLC	3273	E	661 252-1010	10788
Next System Inc	2273	E	661 257-1600	2876
Rexhall Industries Inc	3716	E	661 726-5470	19843
Spragg Industries Inc	3999	F	661 424-9673	23483
Valley Publications	2741	F	661 298-5330	6371

CANYON LAKE, CA - Riverside County

	SIC	EMP	PHONE	ENTRY #
Golding Publications	2791	F	951 244-1966	7358

CAPISTRANO BEACH, CA - Orange County

	SIC	EMP	PHONE	ENTRY #
San Clemente Times LLC	2711	F	949 388-7700	5814
Schaeffler Group USA Inc	3562	B	949 234-9799	14614
Vs Vincenzo Ltd Inc	2844	F	949 388-8791	8606

CAPITOLA, CA - Santa Cruz County

	SIC	EMP	PHONE	ENTRY #
Alpha Machine Company Inc	3599	F	831 462-7400	15728
Timely Data Resources Inc	7372	F	831 462-2510	24510

CARDIFF, CA - San Diego County

	SIC	EMP	PHONE	ENTRY #
Alliance Multimedia LLC	2759	F	760 522-3455	6982

CARDIFF BY THE SEA, CA - San Diego County

	SIC	EMP	PHONE	ENTRY #
Accurate Solutions Inc	3671	F	760 753-6524	17775
Biomet San Diego LLC	3842	F	760 942-2786	21988
Igrad Inc	7372	E	858 705-2917	23999
L&H Enterprises	3577	F	760 230-2275	15269
Nutrition Resource Connection	3652	F	760 803-8234	17332
Reinhart Oil & Gas Inc	1311	F	760 753-3330	64
Seastar Medical Inc	3841	F	734 272-4772	21892
Strategic Info Group Inc	7372	E	760 697-1050	24458

CARLSBAD, CA - San Diego County

	SIC	EMP	PHONE	ENTRY #
800total Gym Commercial LLC	3949	F	858 586-6080	22729
Acushnet Company	3949	B	760 804-6500	22732
Acutus Medical Inc	3842	F	858 673-1621	21968
Aea Technology Inc	3825	F	760 931-8979	20984
Aethercomm Inc	3663	C	760 208-6002	17439
Aih LLC (DH)	3621	F	760 930-4600	16629
Air Products and Chemicals Inc	2813	C	760 931-9555	7398
Aldila Inc (HQ)	3949	D	858 513-1801	22737
Aldila Golf Corp (DH)	3949	D	858 513-1801	22740
Alphatec Holdings Inc	3842	E	760 431-9286	21976
Alphatec Holdings Inc (PA)	3841	E	760 431-9286	21592
Alphatec Spine Inc (HQ)	3842	C	760 494-6610	21977

	SIC	EMP	PHONE	ENTRY #
American Lithium Energy Corp	2819	F	760 599-7388	7469
American Rim Supply Inc	3714	E	760 431-3666	19581
Amigo Custom Screen Prints LLC	2759	E	760 525-5593	6988
Anchor Audio Inc	3651	D	760 827-7100	17189
Arrk Product Dev Group USA Inc	3444	C	858 552-1587	12114
Astura Medical	3841	F	760 814-8047	21612
Avid Lyfe Inc	2339	F	888 510-2517	3289
Beckman Coulter Inc	3826	C	760 438-9151	21182
Biosource International Inc	2835	C	805 659-5759	8208
Bitchin Inc	2099	E	760 224-7447	2406
Borsos Engineering Inc	3571	E	760 930-0296	14893
Breg Inc (HQ)	3841	C	760 599-3000	21643
Brendan Technologies Inc	7372	E	760 929-7500	23696
Cabo International Inc	2211	F	760 597-9199	2674
Cal-Comp USA (san Diego) Inc	3672	C	858 587-6900	17839
Calamp Corp	3663	F	760 438-9010	17477
Caleb Enterprises Inc	7372	F	760 683-8787	23713
California Sensor Corporation	3829	E	760 438-0525	21447
Callaway Golf Company	3949	A	760 804-4502	22772
Callaway Golf Company (PA)	3949	B	760 931-1771	22774
Canary Medical USA LLC	3841	F	760 448-5066	21649
Carlsbad Technology Inc (DH)	2834	D	760 431-8284	7832
Carlsbad Technology Inc	2834	E	760 431-8284	7833
Chromacode Inc	3821	E	442 244-4369	20750
Continuous Cartridge	3861	E	760 929-4808	22411
Coola LLC	2844	E	760 940-2125	8464
Coplan & Coplan Inc	3545	E	760 268-0583	14151
Covidien Holding Inc	3841	E	760 603-5020	21672
CPS Printing	2752	D	760 494-9000	6519
Crown Circuits Inc	3672	D	949 922-0144	17858
Custopharm Inc	3559	F	760 683-0901	14450
Danville Materials LLC (HQ)	3843	E	760 743-7744	22142
Dei Headquarters Inc	3669	B	760 598-6200	17724
Denso International Amer Inc	3714	F	760 597-7400	19636
Designer Drinks	2086	E	760 444-2355	2071
Designline Windows & Doors Inc	3442	F	760 931-9422	11946
Dexters Deli	2047	E	760 720-7507	1072
Diligent Solutions Inc	3599	F	760 814-8960	15898
Drs Own Inc (PA)	3842	F	760 804-0751	22000
Eagle Creek Inc (DH)	3161	D	760 431-6400	10193
Ecolink Intelligent Tech Inc	3651	F	855 432-6546	17225
Edirect Publishing Inc	2741	E	760 602-8300	6226
Eevelle LLC	2399	E	760 434-2231	3839
Ef Composite Technologies LP	3949	F	800 433-6723	22795
Eklin Medical Systems Inc	3841	D	760 918-9626	21698
Electro Surface Tech Inc	3672	D	760 431-8306	17866
Entropic Communications LLC (HQ)	3674	E	858 768-3600	18221
Ezoic Inc (PA)	7372	E	760 444-4995	23889
Fc Global Realty Incorporated	3841	E	760 602-3300	21712
Finishing Touch Moulding Inc	2434	D	760 444-1019	4197
First Circuit Inc	3672	E	760 560-0530	17877
Fish On Rice LLC	2082	F	619 696-6262	1530
Foundry Med Innovations Inc	3841	F	888 445-2333	21717
Fujikura Composite America Inc	3949	E	760 598-6060	22804
Funktion USA	3444	F	760 473-4171	12217
Genmark Diagnostics Inc (PA)	3841	C	760 448-4300	21723
Gold Couture 22 K	3911	F	760 602-0690	22523
Graphics Ink Lithography LLC	2759	E	760 438-9052	7079
Great Lakes Data Systems Inc	7372	F	760 602-1900	23954
Greenwich Biosciences Inc (HQ)	2834	E	760 795-2200	7927
Gtr Enterprises Incorporated	3599	E	760 931-1192	16007
Gunnar Optiks LLC	3851	E	858 769-2500	22359
Heat Factory Inc	2673	E	760 734-5300	5399
Hudson Printing Inc	2759	E	760 602-1260	7087
Hygeia II Medical Group Inc	3845	F	714 515-7571	22262
Idex Health & Science LLC	3827	C	760 438-2131	21362
Impedimed Inc (HQ)	3841	E	760 585-2100	21741
Industrial Zinc Plating Corp	3471	E	760 918-6877	13029
International Mercantile	3714	F	760 438-2205	19692
International Stem Cell Corp (PA)	2834	E	760 940-6383	7956
Intevac Photonics Inc	3827	E	760 476-0339	21368
Ionis Pharmaceuticals Inc	2834	E	760 603-3567	7961
Ionis Pharmaceuticals Inc (PA)	2834	B	760 931-9200	7962
Ipitek Group Inc	3663	C	760 438-8362	17544
Iris Group Inc	2759	C	760 431-1103	7103
Jones Glyn Productions Inc	2741	F	760 431-8955	6261
Joseph McCrink	3312	F	760 489-1500	11052
Kayo Corp (PA)	3949	F	760 918-0405	22836
L & L Printers Carlsbad LLC	2752	E	760 477-0321	6686
L & L Printers Inc	2752	F	858 278-4300	6687
L3 Technologies Inc	3669	C	760 431-6800	17741
Laird R & F Products Inc (DH)	3812	F	760 916-9410	20600
Laurelwood Industries Inc	3599	E	760 705-1649	16141
Lawinfocom Inc	7372	D	800 397-3743	24094
Leading Biosciences Inc	2834	F	858 395-6099	7987

Employment Codes: A=Over 500 employees, B=251-500,
C=101-250, D=51-100, E=20-50, F=10-19

2020 California
Manufacturers Register

© Mergent Inc. 1-800-342-5647
1313

G E O G R A P H I C

Company	SIC	EMP	PHONE	ENTRY #
Leisure Collective Inc	3851	F	760 814-2840	22367
LF Industries Inc	3599	F	760 438-5711	16145
Life Technologies Corporation (HQ)	2835	C	760 603-7200	8234
Life Technologies Corporation	2836	D	760 918-4259	8313
Lineage Cell Therapeutics Inc (PA)	2836	D	510 521-3390	8314
Liquid Force Wakeboards	3949	E	760 943-8364	22842
Lite Machines Corporation	3812	F	765 463-0959	20601
Lithographix Inc	2759	D	760 438-3456	7122
Living Wellness Partners LLC (PA)	2099	E	800 642-3754	2531
Lucite Intl Prtnr Holdings Inc	3949	E	760 929-0001	22845
Lumistar Inc (DH)	3672	F	760 431-2181	17916
Luxtera LLC	3674	C	760 448-3520	18364
Machinetek LLC	3728	E	760 438-6644	20162
Maxlinear Inc (PA)	3674	E	760 692-0711	18377
Means Engineering Inc	3826	D	760 931-9452	21260
Mellace Family Brands Inc	2068	C	760 448-1940	1433
Melles Griot Inc	3827	F	760 438-2131	21381
Meps Real-Time Inc	3829	E	760 448-9500	21505
Mercotac Inc	3643	F	760 431-7723	16916
Metric Systems Corporation	3663	F	760 560-0348	17584
Microvision Development Inc	7372	F	760 438-7781	24165
Mikroscan Technologies Inc	3841	F	760 893-8095	21822
Miltons Baking Company LLC	2051	E	858 350-9696	1243
Mizu Inc (PA)	3069	F	307 690-3219	9337
Myron L Company	3823	D	760 438-2021	20907
Natural Alternatives Intl Inc (PA)	2834	E	760 736-7700	8025
Naturemaker Inc	3999	E	760 438-4244	23422
Neurohacker Collective LLC	2023	F	855 281-2328	611
New Dimension One Spas Inc (DH)	3999	C	800 345-7727	23424
Nordson Asymtek Inc (HQ)	3823	C	760 431-1919	20911
Nordson California Inc	3695	D	760 918-8490	19228
Nordson Dage Inc	3844	E	440 985-4496	22217
Nordson Yestech Inc	3827	E	949 361-2714	21386
Nova Mobile Systems Inc	3678	F	800 734-9885	18782
NTN Buzztime Inc (PA)	7372	C	760 438-7400	24214
Obalon Therapeutics Inc	3841	C	760 795-6558	21845
Oceanside Glasstile Company (PA)	3253	B	760 929-4000	10447
Ogio International Inc	3161	D	801 619-4100	10200
OH Juice Inc	2033	F	619 318-0207	808
Opotek Inc	3845	F	760 929-0770	22291
Opotek LLC	3827	F	760 929-0770	21390
Optimized Fuel Technologies	3999	F	760 444-5556	23432
Ortho Organizers Inc	3843	C	760 448-8600	22177
Outdoor Lfstyle Collective LLC	2331	F	858 336-5580	3188
Outsol Inc	3088	F	760 415-8060	9593
Pacific Cnc Machine Co	3599	F	760 431-7558	16273
Palomar Casework Inc	2542	F	760 941-9860	4996
Palomar Technologies Inc (PA)	3559	D	760 931-3600	14513
Peak Servo Corporation	3625	F	760 438-4986	16737
Phoenix Footwear Group Inc (PA)	3143	D	760 602-9688	10160
Pro-Spot International Inc	3699	F	760 407-1414	19384
Product Slingshot Inc	3544	D	760 929-9380	14098
Providien Injction Molding Inc	3089	F	760 931-1844	10001
Qualcomm Incorporated	3674	B	858 651-8481	18494
Qualigen Inc (PA)	3821	E	760 918-9165	20772
Quorex Pharm Inc (PA)	2834	E	760 602-1910	8095
Ra Medical Systems Inc	3841	C	760 804-1648	21870
Reflex Corporation	2399	E	760 931-9009	3855
Rf Surgical Systems LLC	3841	D	855 522-7027	21880
Rockwell Collins Optronics Inc	3812	F	319 295-1000	20708
Ronatec C2c Inc	2899	F	760 476-1890	9021
Sabre Sciences Inc	2833	F	760 448-2750	7691
SC Bluwood Inc	2491	E	909 519-5470	4481
Scape Goat Ind	3949	F	760 931-1802	22884
SCI Instruments Inc (PA)	3826	F	760 634-3822	21286
Seaspine Inc	3842	D	760 727-8399	22081
Seaspine Orthopedics Corp (HQ)	3842	E	866 942-8698	22082
Sigma-Aldrich Corporation	2899	F	760 710-6213	9022
Signet Armorlite Inc (DH)	3851	B	760 744-4000	22385
Silk Screen Shirts Inc	2261	F	760 233-3900	2837
Simply Automated Inc	3643	F	760 431-2100	16923
Skiva Graphics Screen Prtg Inc	2759	E	760 602-9124	7216
Smiths Medical Asd Inc	3841	C	760 602-4400	21902
Soil Retention Products Inc (PA)	3271	E	951 928-8477	10519
South Cone Inc	3144	C	760 431-2300	10176
Spectrum Assembly Inc	3672	D	760 930-4000	18011
Spinergy Inc	3751	D	760 496-2121	20425
Spy Inc (PA)	3851	D	760 804-8420	22389
Standard Filter Corporation (PA)	3564	E	866 443-3615	14679
Stone Yard Inc	2519	E	858 586-1580	4774
Sunex Inc	3827	F	760 597-2966	21413
Synergeyes Inc (PA)	3851	D	760 476-9410	22283
Syntron Bioresearch Inc	2835	B	760 930-2200	8263
Systems Machines Automatio (PA)	3625	C	760 929-7575	16760
Taylor Made Golf Company Inc (HQ)	3949	B	877 860-8624	22906
Teledyne Instruments Inc	3823	E	760 754-2400	20946
Ten Enthusiast Network LLC	2721	C	760 722-7777	6038
Torrey Pines Scientific Inc	3821	F	760 930-9400	20778
Trade Printing Services LLC	2752	E	760 496-0230	6895
Turbo International	3462	F	760 476-1444	12724
Typehaus Inc	3572	F	760 334-3555	15111
United Orthopedic Group LLC	3841	F	760 729-8585	21943
Universal Electronics Inc	3699	F	760 431-8804	19429
Upper Deck Company	2741	C	800 873-7332	6370
Upper Deck Company LLC	2752	B	800 873-7332	6911
USAopoly Inc	3944	E	760 431-5910	22723
Vanguard Industries East Inc	2399	D	800 433-1334	3865
Vanguard Industries West Inc (PA)	2399	C	760 438-4437	3866
Vape Craft LLC	3911	F	760 295-7484	22582
Vertiflex Inc	3845	E	442 325-5900	22325
Viasat Inc (PA)	3663	B	760 476-2200	17700
Watt Stopper Inc	3643	F	760 804-9701	16940
Xenonics Inc	3699	F	760 477-8900	19447
Xenonics Holdings Inc	3648	F	760 477-8900	17177
Zense-Life Inc	3845	F	858 888-5289	22334
Zodiac Pool Solutions LLC (DH)	3589	B	760 599-9600	15609
Zodiac Pool Systems LLC (DH)	3589	C	760 599-9600	15610
Zonson Company Inc	3949	E	760 597-0338	22931
Zuza	2759	E	760 438-9411	7278

CARMEL, CA - Monterey County

Company	SIC	EMP	PHONE	ENTRY #
Caffe Cardinale Cof Roasting	2095	F	831 626-2095	2281
Fresco Plastics Inc	3089	E	831 625-9877	9794

CARMEL VALLEY, CA - Monterey County

Company	SIC	EMP	PHONE	ENTRY #
Bernardus LLC (PA)	2084	E	831 659-1900	1596
Durney Winery Corporation	2084	F	831 659-2690	1677
Georis Winery	2084	F	831 659-1050	1721
Holman Ranch Corporation	2084	F	831 659-2640	1753

CARMICHAEL, CA - Sacramento County

Company	SIC	EMP	PHONE	ENTRY #
Maxit Designs Inc	2253	F	916 489-1023	2796
Solarroofscom Inc	3433	F	916 481-7200	11717
Tm Noodle	2098	F	916 486-2579	2384

CARPINTERIA, CA - Santa Barbara County

Company	SIC	EMP	PHONE	ENTRY #
32 Bar Blues LLC	2389	F	805 962-6665	3535
Agilent Technologies Inc	3825	F	805 566-6655	20989
Applied Silicone Company LLC	2869	D	805 525-5657	8715
Bega/Us Inc	3648	D	805 684-0533	17104
Channel Islands Surfboards Inc	3949	E	805 745-2823	22780
Clipper Windpower PLC	3511	A	805 690-3275	13565
Dac International Inc (PA)	3541	E	805 684-8307	13910
Development Assoc Contrls	3541	E	805 684-8307	13913
Ditec Co	3841	F	805 566-7800	21689
Dsy Educational Corporation	2399	F	805 684-8111	3838
Essex Electronics Inc	3674	E	805 684-7601	18227
Freudenberg Medical LLC (DH)	3842	B	805 684-3304	22018
H S N Consultants Inc	2721	F	805 684-8800	5947
Inhealth Technologies	3842	F	800 477-5969	22031
Island Brewing Co	2082	F	805 745-8272	1539
Lufft Usa Inc	3829	F	805 335-8500	21501
Nusil Technology LLC	2821	D	805 684-8780	7588
Nusil Technology LLC	3069	D	805 684-8780	9346
Qad Inc	7372	F	805 684-6614	24326
Rincon Engineering Corporation	3599	E	805 684-0935	16359
Sensata Technologies Inc	3625	F	805 684-8401	16753
Supersprings International	3493	F	805 745-5553	13343
Te Connectivity Corporation	3625	C	805 684-4560	16761
Zarif Companies	2084	F	805 318-1800	2008
Zbe Inc	3625	E	805 576-1600	16771

CARSON, CA - Los Angeles County

Company	SIC	EMP	PHONE	ENTRY #
A & R Engineering Co Inc	3599	E	310 603-9060	15656
Air Products and Chemicals Inc	2813	F	310 847-7300	7395
Alpha Wire Corporation	3357	A	310 639-9475	11285
Andeavor	1311	A	310 847-5705	21
Arctic Glacier USA Inc	2097	C	310 638-0321	2350
Avalon Glass & Mirror Company	3231	D	323 321-8806	10339
Big Heart Pet Brands	2033	F	310 519-3791	759
Big Time Digital	2752	F	714 752-5959	6449
Bolttech Mannings Inc	3546	D	310 604-9500	14217
BP West Coast Products LLC	1311	B	310 816-8787	29
Brentwood Originals Inc (PA)	2392	A	310 637-6804	3604
C Preme Limited LLC	3949	F	310 355-0498	22771
Cal-Coast Pkg & Crating Inc	2441	E	310 518-7215	4333
Cali-Fame Los Angeles Inc	2353	D	310 747-5263	3462
Calwest Galvanizing Corp	3479	C	310 549-2200	13155
Cardic Machine Products Inc	3599	C	310 884-3400	15824
CCL Tube Inc (HQ)	3089	C	310 635-4444	9699
Cedarlane Natural Foods Inc (PA)	2099	C	310 886-7720	2420
Cedarlane Natural Foods Inc	2038	A	310 527-7833	951

Mergent email: customerrelations@mergent.com
1314

2020 California
Manufacturers Register

(P-0000) Products & Services Section entry number
(PA)=Parent Co (HQ)=Headquarters (DH)=Div Headquarters

	SIC	EMP	PHONE	ENTRY #
Chagall Design Limited	2389	F	310 537-9530	3546
Cmp Display Systems Inc	3089	D	805 499-3642	9711
Consolidated Container Co LLC	3085	D	310 952-8736	9483
Cosway Company Inc (PA)	2844	E	310 900-4100	8474
Crate Modular Inc	3448	D	310 405-0829	12541
Dan-Loc Group LLC	3053	E	310 538-2822	9226
Dermalogica LLC (HQ)	2844	C	310 900-4000	8481
DMC Power Inc (PA)	3643	D	310 323-1616	16894
Ducommun Aerostructures Inc	3724	E	310 513-7200	19950
Ducommun Labarge Tech Inc (HQ)	3728	C	310 513-7200	20094
Duro-Sense Corp	3823	F	310 533-6877	20860
Dynamex Corporation	2298	F	310 329-0399	2911
Elite 4 Print Inc	2752	E	310 366-1344	6563
Elite Color Technologies Inc	2759	F	310 324-3040	7057
Empire Container Corporation	2653	D	310 537-8190	5219
First Lithium LLC	3691	F	310 489-6266	19165
General Mills Inc	2026	E	310 605-6108	700
Generation Alpha Inc (PA)	3645	F	888 998-8881	16970
Giuliano-Pagano Corporation	2051	E	310 537-7700	1217
Global Billiard Mfg Co Inc	3949	E	310 764-5000	22809
Gms Molds (PA)	3544	F	310 684-1168	14059
Gordon Laboratories Inc	2844	C	310 527-5240	8501
Huck International Inc	3452	F	310 830-8200	12681
Hydroform USA Incorporated	3728	C	310 632-6353	20133
I & I Sports Supply Company (PA)	3949	E	310 715-6800	22825
International Paper Company	2621	E	310 549-5525	5126
Jarden Corporation	3089	D	800 755-9520	9850
Jnj Operations LLC	3999	E	855 525-6545	23371
Johnson Laminating Coating Inc	3083	D	310 635-4929	9441
Js Apparel Inc	2329	D	310 631-6333	3097
Jvic Catalyst Services LLC	2819	E	310 327-0991	7501
Kts Kitchens Inc	2099	C	310 764-0850	2502
Letterhead Factory Inc	2752	F	310 538-3321	6700
Lpj Aerospace LLC	3728	F	310 834-5700	20160
Mag Aerospace Industries Inc	3431	B	310 631-3800	11649
Magtek Inc	3674	F	562 631-8602	18369
Mars Medical Ride Corp	3711	F	310 518-1024	19485
Mechanized Engineering Systems	3537	F	310 830-9763	13884
Mestek Inc	3585	C	310 835-7500	15445
Monogram Systems	3728	F	801 400-7944	20182
Moreau Wetzel Engineering Co	3544	F	310 830-5479	14081
Natures Bounty Co	2833	F	310 952-7107	7676
Northrop Grumman Corporation	3812	A	310 764-3000	20646
Nu-Health California LLC	2033	F	800 806-0519	804
O W I Inc	3651	F	310 515-1900	17267
Oak-It Inc	2541	E	310 719-3999	4925
Off Dock USA Inc	3537	E	310 522-4400	13886
Pacific Toll Processing Inc	3312	E	310 952-4992	11059
Parker-Hannifin Corporation	3559	C	310 608-5600	14514
Parter Medical Products Inc	3821	C	310 327-4417	20769
Pepsi-Cola Metro Btlg Co Inc	2086	A	310 327-4222	2113
Polyone Corporation	2821	D	310 513-7100	7596
Proma Inc	3843	E	310 327-0035	22182
Puritan Bakery Inc	2051	C	310 830-5451	1265
Quality Magnetics Corporation	3499	F	310 632-1941	13542
Quartic West Technologies	3695	F	909 202-7038	19230
Richandre Inc	2038	F	310 762-1560	977
Sac-TEC Labs Inc (PA)	3674	E	310 375-5295	18525
Salsbury Industries Inc (PA)	2542	C	323 846-6700	5000
Saybolt LP	1389	F	310 518-4400	258
Sazerac Company Inc	2085	E	310 604-8717	2018
Simpson Industries Inc	2834	E	310 605-1224	8133
Solid-Scope Machining Co Inc	3429	F	310 523-2366	11628
Stanford Mu Corporation	3769	E	310 605-2888	20480
Street Glow Inc	3647	D	310 631-1881	17094
Strike Technology Inc	3679	E	562 437-3428	19095
Sumi Printing & Binding Inc	2752	F	310 769-1600	6877
Tnp Instruments Inc	3679	F	310 532-2222	19119
Trane US Inc	3585	D	310 971-4555	15462
Universal Plant Services Cal (HQ)	3599	F	310 618-1600	16485
Wavenet Inc (PA)	3315	E	310 885-4200	11115
Weber Printing Company Inc	2752	E	310 639-5064	6929
Western Combustion Engrg Inc	3443	F	310 834-9389	12070
Yoplait U S A Inc	2026	E	310 632-9502	715
Yun Industrial Co Ltd	3672	E	310 715-1898	18055
Zodiac Wtr Waste Aero Systems	3728	E	310 884-7000	20274

CARUTHERS, CA - Fresno County

	SIC	EMP	PHONE	ENTRY #
Batth Dehydrator LLC	2034	E	559 864-3501	844
Caruthers Raisin Pkg Co Inc (PA)	2034	D	559 864-9448	847
Mid Valley Mfg Inc	3599	F	559 864-9441	16200

CASTAIC, CA - Los Angeles County

	SIC	EMP	PHONE	ENTRY #
Castaic Clay Products LLC	3251	D	661 259-3066	10433
Castaic Lake R V Park Inc	2451	F	661 257-3340	4439
Castaic Truck Stop Inc	2911	E	661 295-1374	9040

	SIC	EMP	PHONE	ENTRY #
Clay Castaic Manufacturing Co	3251	D	661 259-3066	10434
Nicole Fullerton	2389	F	661 257-0406	3572
So Cal Tractor Sales Co Inc	7692	E	818 252-1900	24665

CASTRO VALLEY, CA - Alameda County

	SIC	EMP	PHONE	ENTRY #
Community Media Corporation	2711	D	657 337-0200	5596
Jack Brain and Associates Inc	2741	F	510 889-1360	6258
Tien-Hu Knitting Co (us) Inc	2253	D	510 268-8833	2808
Twin Design Co LLC	3569	F	510 329-4991	14866

CASTROVILLE, CA - Monterey County

	SIC	EMP	PHONE	ENTRY #
American Bottling Company	2086	D	831 632-0777	2036
California New Foods LLC	2099	E	831 444-1872	2419
Corbin Pacific Inc	3751	E	408 633-2500	20390
Fujifilm Ultra Pure Sltons Inc (DH)	2899	E	831 632-2120	8968
Ron Witherspoon Inc	3599	E	831 633-3568	16370
Seven Up Btlg Co San Francisco	2086	E	831 632-0777	2168

CATHEDRAL CITY, CA - Riverside County

	SIC	EMP	PHONE	ENTRY #
Cushion Works	2392	F	760 321-7808	3610

CAZADERO, CA - Sonoma County

	SIC	EMP	PHONE	ENTRY #
Dharma Mudranalaya (PA)	2731	E	707 847-3380	6097
Flowers Vineyard & Winery LLC	2084	F	707 847-3661	1706
Hagist Welding	7692	F	707 847-3362	24637

CERES, CA - Stanislaus County

	SIC	EMP	PHONE	ENTRY #
Aemetis Advnced Fels Keyes Inc	2869	D	209 632-4511	8705
B & H Manufacturing Co Inc (PA)	3565	C	209 537-5785	14697
Barrel Ten Qarter Cir Land Inc (HQ)	2084	E	707 258-0550	1591
Certified Stainless Svc Inc (PA)	3443	C	209 537-4747	12003
Classic Wine Vinegar Co Inc	2099	E	209 538-7600	2429
Enova Engineering LLC (PA)	3644	F	209 538-3313	16947
Prompt Precision Metals Inc	3444	D	209 531-1210	12343
Robert R Wix Inc (PA)	2759	E	209 537-4561	7202
Seed Factory Northwest Inc (PA)	2048	E	209 634-8522	1126
Stiles Custom Metal Inc	3442	D	209 538-3667	11985
Stuart David Inc (PA)	2511	E	209 537-7449	4612
US Dies Inc (PA)	3544	E	209 664-1402	14119
Wildlife Fur Dressing Inc	3111	F	209 538-2901	10146

CERRITOS, CA - Los Angeles County

	SIC	EMP	PHONE	ENTRY #
A & H Engineering & Mfg Inc	3599	E	562 623-9717	15653
AB Mauri Food Inc	2099	F	562 483-4619	2387
Advanced Uv Inc	3589	E	562 407-0299	15480
Alpha Dental of Utah Inc	3843	F	562 467-7759	22132
Alumflam North America	3471	E	562 926-9520	12922
American Garment Company	2389	F	562 483-8300	3540
American Non Stop Label Corp	2759	F	562 921-9437	6986
Apperson Inc (PA)	2761	D	562 356-3333	7279
ARI Industries Inc	3585	D	714 993-3700	15413
Artistic Coverings Inc	3086	E	562 404-9343	9505
Award Packaging Spc Corp	2653	E	323 727-1200	5197
Bermingham Controls Inc A (PA)	3491	E	562 860-0463	13295
Better Beverages Inc (PA)	2087	E	562 924-8321	2192
Big 5 Electronics Inc	3651	E	562 941-4669	17205
Blairs Metal Polsg Pltg Co Inc	3471	F	562 860-7106	12945
Blc Wc Inc (PA)	2759	C	562 926-1452	7002
Calnetix Technologies LLC	3621	E	562 293-1660	16634
Captek Softgel Intl Inc (DH)	2834	B	562 921-9511	7829
Clio Inc	3495	E	562 926-3724	13379
Compressed Air Concepts	3563	E	310 537-1350	14626
Dec Fabricators Inc	3499	F	562 403-3626	13513
Dji Service LLC	3728	F	818 235-0788	20086
Docupak Inc	2782	E	714 670-7944	7312
Dool Fna Inc	2221	C	562 483-4100	2725
Dr J Skinclinic Inc	2834	F	562 474-8861	7873
Eide Industries Inc	2394	E	562 402-8335	3682
Foam Molders and Specialties (PA)	3086	E	562 924-7757	9533
Foam Molders and Specialties	3086	E	562 924-7757	9534
Ftg Inc (PA)	3714	E	562 865-9200	19663
Funtastic Factory Inc	3599	E	562 777-1140	15977
G & P Group Inc	2068	F	323 268-2686	1426
International Coatings Co Inc (PA)	2891	E	562 926-1010	8877
International Paper Company	2621	E	562 404-1856	5119
IPC Cal Flex Inc	3672	E	714 952-0373	17902
Ips Industries Inc	3089	E	562 623-2555	9844
J Summitt Inc	2431	E	562 236-5744	4062
Kaltec Electronics Inc (PA)	3861	F	813 888-9555	22435
LA Triumph Inc	2326	E	562 404-7657	3042
Lees Precision Tooling	3599	E	562 926-1302	16143
Madison Inc of Oklahoma	3441	D	918 224-6990	11832
Madison Industries (HQ)	3448	C	323 583-4061	12557
Madison Industries Inc Arizona	3441	D	602 252-3083	11833
Molino Company	2752	D	323 726-1000	6734
Mpd Holdings Inc	3577	E	562 777-1051	15294
Nippon Carbide Inds USA Inc	2819	F	562 777-1810	7512

Employment Codes: A=Over 500 employees, B=251-500,
C=101-250, D=51-100, E=20-50, F=10-19

2020 California
Manufacturers Register

© Mergent Inc. 1-800-342-5647

1315

GEOGRAPHIC

	SIC	EMP	PHONE	ENTRY #
North America Pwr & Infra	3241	E	562 403-4337	10426
NSK Precision America Inc	3562	F	562 968-1000	14613
Olea Kiosks Inc	3577	D	562 924-2644	15298
Pacific Die Cast Inc	3544	F	562 407-1390	14089
Pankl Aerospace Systems	3369	D	562 207-6300	11419
Para Plate & Plastics Co Inc	3555	F	562 404-3434	14336
Parts Expediting and Dist Co	3714	F	562 944-3199	19736
Precision Metal Crafts	3441	F	562 468-7080	11866
Printing Management Associates	2752	F	562 407-9977	6805
Quad/Graphics Inc	2752	F	310 751-3900	6821
Rael Inc	2676	E	800 573-1516	5466
Refrigerator Manufacters Inc (PA)	3632	E	562 926-2006	16822
Refrigerator Manufacturers LLC	3585	E	562 926-2006	15452
Repose Corp	3634	F	562 921-9299	16840
Sealed Air Corporation	2673	E	201 791-7600	5418
Sedenquist-Fraser Entps Inc	3714	F	562 924-5763	19764
T Hasegawa USA Inc (HQ)	2087	E	714 522-1900	2232
True Vision Displays Inc	3679	E	562 407-0630	19127
Twin Eagles Inc	3631	D	562 802-3488	16819
UFO Designs	3714	E	562 924-5763	19792
US Dental Inc	3843	E	562 404-3500	22201
Villa Furniture Mfg Co	2531	C	714 535-7272	4875
Vycon Inc	3691	D	562 282-5500	19176
WCP Inc	3089	D	562 653-9797	10117
West Coast Switchgear (HQ)	3613	D	562 802-3441	16623
Winning Laboratories Inc	2833	F	562 921-6880	7705
Xl Dynamics Inc	7372	E	562 916-1402	24593

CHATSWORTH, CA - Los Angeles County

	SIC	EMP	PHONE	ENTRY #
A & S Mold & Die Corp	3089	D	818 341-5393	9599
A B C Plastics Inc	3083	F	818 775-0065	9435
A F B Systems Inc	3724	F	818 775-0151	19941
A H Systems Inc	3825	F	818 998-0223	20980
Absolute Machining	3441	F	818 709-7367	11731
Academic Ch Choir Gwns Mfg Inc	2389	F	818 886-8697	3536
Advanced Cosmetic RES Labs Inc	3999	E	818 709-9945	23264
Aei Manufacturing Inc	3643	F	818 407-5400	16873
Aero Mechanism Precision Inc	3599	F	818 886-1855	15705
Aeroantenna Technology Inc	3812	C	818 993-3842	20530
Aerojet Rocketdyne De Inc	2869	C	818 586-1000	8708
Aitech Defense Systems Inc	3699	E	818 700-2000	19251
Aitech Rugged Group Inc (PA)	3699	E	818 700-2000	19252
Alan Hamilton Industries	2752	D	818 885-5121	6400
Alatus Aerosystems	3728	D	626 498-7376	20030
Aleratec Inc	3571	E	818 678-6900	14884
Align Aerospace Holding Inc (DH)	3324	F	818 727-7800	11152
Align Aerospace LLC (DH)	3728	C	818 727-7800	20031
Alliance Metal Products Inc	3444	C	818 709-1204	12100
Almack Liners Inc	2335	E	818 718-5878	3211
Andrews Powder Coating Inc	3479	E	818 700-1030	13142
Ansell Sndel Med Solutions LLC	3842	E	818 534-2500	21981
Apparel Prod Svcs Globl LLC	2339	E	818 700-3700	3287
Aquasyn LLC	3491	F	818 350-0423	13288
Aram Precision Tool Die Inc	3599	F	818 998-1000	15744
Audionics System Inc	3651	F	818 345-9599	17196
Automoco LLC	3714	D	707 544-4761	19586
Avet Industries Inc	3949	F	818 576-9895	22752
Avn Media Network Inc	2731	E	818 718-5788	6073
Aware Products Inc	2844	E	818 206-6700	8440
Aware Products LLC	2844	C	818 206-6700	8441
Axess Products Corp	3651	F	818 785-4000	17199
BDR Industries Inc	3577	E	818 341-2112	15167
Bey-Berk International (PA)	3499	F	818 773-7534	13502
Bio-Nutraceuticals Inc	2834	D	818 727-0246	7803
Bizinkcom LLC	2759	F	818 676-0766	6999
Botanicalabs Inc	2844	E	818 466-5639	8450
Breakaway Press Inc	2759	F	818 727-7388	7007
Bvp Designs Inc	3581	F	818 280-2900	15396
Cac Fabrication Inc	3441	F	818 882-2626	11755
California Deluxe Window Indus (PA)	2431	E	818 349-5566	4009
Canoga Perkins Corporation (HQ)	3669	D	818 718-6300	17720
Cdc Data LLC	3577	F	818 350-5070	15188
Celesco Transducer Products	3679	E	818 701-2701	18855
Celltron Inc	3679	F	620 783-1333	18857
Challenge Publications Inc	2721	E	818 700-6868	5902
Chatsworth Products Inc	3499	C	818 882-8595	13510
Cicon Engineering Inc	3679	F	818 909-6060	18864
Cine Mechanics Inc	3861	F	818 701-7944	22408
Ciphertex LLC	3577	F	818 773-8989	15189
Circuit Services Llc	3672	F	818 701-5391	17849
Classic Cosmetics Inc	2844	F	818 773-9042	8457
Classic Cosmetics Inc (PA)	2844	C	818 773-9042	8458
Cliffdale LLC	3761	F	818 885-0300	20445
Cliffdale Manufacturing LLC	3769	C	818 341-3344	20473
Colbrit Manufacturing Co Inc	3544	E	818 709-3608	14035
Commercial Clear Print Inc	2752	F	818 709-1220	6503

	SIC	EMP	PHONE	ENTRY #
Container Components Inc (PA)	3089	E	818 882-4300	9723
Cosmojet Inc	2754	F	818 773-6544	6952
CRC Services LLC	1311	F	888 848-4754	47
Custom Control Sensors LLC (PA)	3613	C	818 341-4610	16592
Custom Design Iron Works Inc	3364	F	818 700-9182	11354
Cyron Inc	3648	F	818 772-1900	17114
Datadirect Networks Inc (PA)	3572	C	818 700-7600	15020
Delta Fabrication Inc	3444	D	818 407-4000	12180
Delta Hi-Tech	3599	C	818 407-4000	15886
Delta Tau Data Systems Inc Cal (HQ)	3569	C	818 998-2095	14808
Delta Tau International Inc	3569	E	818 998-2095	14809
DOT Copy Inc	2752	E	818 341-6666	6549
Double K Industries Inc	3523	E	818 772-2887	13627
Dream Products Incorporated	3171	E	818 773-4233	10220
Dwa Alminum Composites USA Inc	3365	F	818 998-1504	11379
Dynamic Sciences Intl Inc	3663	E	818 226-6262	17507
Dytran Instruments Inc	3679	C	818 700-7818	18894
Electro Adapter Inc	3643	D	818 998-1198	16896
Enormarel Inc	2844	E	818 882-4666	8489
Envy Medical Inc (HQ)	2834	F	818 874-2700	7880
Epic Technologies LLC (HQ)	3661	C	701 426-2192	17366
Erbaviva Inc	2833	E	818 998-7112	7656
Euro Machine Inc	3599	E	818 998-5198	15937
Exact Cnc Industries Inc	3469	F	818 527-1908	12801
Excel Manufacturing Inc	3599	E	661 257-1900	15941
Excellence Opto Inc	3669	F	818 674-1921	17728
Execuprint Inc	2759	F	818 993-8184	7061
Executive Bus Solutions Inc	3555	E	805 499-3290	14320
Exhart Envmtl Systems Inc	3999	F	818 576-9628	23329
Featherock Inc (PA)	1499	F	818 882-3888	387
Federal Manufacturing Corp	3452	E	818 341-9825	12678
Firan Tech Group USA Corp (HQ)	3812	D	818 407-4024	20577
Flowmetrics Inc	3823	E	818 407-3420	20868
Fluid Line Technology Corp	3841	E	818 998-8848	21714
Ftg Aerospace Inc (DH)	3364	E	818 407-4024	11358
Ftg Circuits Inc (DH)	3672	D	818 407-4024	17884
Gadia Polythylene Supplies Inc	3089	E	818 775-0096	9799
Ganesh Industries LLC	3549	F	818 349-9166	14267
General Ribbon Corp	3955	B	818 709-1234	22964
Globalvision Systems Inc	3572	F	888 227-7967	15033
Golden Bolt LLC	3452	F	818 626-8261	12679
Graphic Research Inc	3672	F	818 886-7340	17892
Graphics Factory Inc	2759	F	818 727-9040	7078
Gsp Acquisition Corporation	3471	E	310 532-9430	13018
Hallmark Lighting LLC	3646	C	818 885-5010	17040
Hart Electronic Assembly Inc	3679	D	818 709-2761	18931
Havana Graphic Center Inc	2752	E	818 841-3774	6606
Heritage Cabinet Co Inc	2541	E	818 786-4900	4910
Hitachi High-Technologies	3826	E	818 280-0745	21238
Huntco Industries LLC	3999	F	818 700-1600	23359
Hydraulics International Inc (PA)	3728	B	818 998-1231	20130
Hydraulics International Inc	3728	E	818 998-1236	20131
Hydromach Inc	3769	E	818 341-0915	20476
Imatte Inc	3651	E	818 993-8007	17245
Imperial Enterprises Inc	3229	E	818 886-5028	10312
Impress Communications Inc	2752	D	818 701-8800	6633
Innovative Cosmetic Labs Inc	2844	F	818 349-1121	8516
Intelligent Cmpt Solutions Inc (PA)	3825	E	818 998-5805	21053
International Precision Inc	3599	E	818 882-3933	16053
Invelop Inc	3523	E	818 772-2887	13636
log Products LLC	3674	F	818 350-5070	18321
J & J Products Inc	3499	F	818 998-4250	13527
Jim James Enterprises Inc	3444	F	818 772-8595	12255
Jmr Electronics Inc	3572	F	818 993-4801	15051
John List Corporation	3547	E	818 882-7848	14233
Just Cellular Inc	3663	F	818 701-3039	17548
K Tech Telecommunications Inc	3663	F	818 773-0333	17550
Keene Engineering Inc (PA)	3561	F	818 485-2681	14588
Keith E Archambeau Sr Inc	3444	F	818 718-6110	12262
Kerning Data Systems Inc	3555	F	818 882-8712	14329
Key Item Sales Inc	3961	F	818 885-0928	22986
Labeling Hurst Systems LLC	2759	F	818 701-0710	7114
Lasalle Intl Hldings Group Inc	3533	E	818 233-8000	13784
Lca Promotions Inc	2759	E	818 773-9170	7118
Le Hung Tuan	3599	F	818 700-1008	16142
Lehrer Brllnprfktion Werks Inc (PA)	3089	E	818 407-1890	9875
Lf Illumination LLC	3646	D	818 885-1335	17051
Lightcraft Otdoor Environments	3645	E	818 349-2663	16975
Lighting Control & Design Inc	3648	E	323 226-0000	17140
Line One Laboratories Inc USA	3069	E	818 886-2288	9329
Litepanels Inc	3641	F	818 752-7009	16866
Logicube Inc (PA)	3577	E	888 494-8832	15276
Logistical Support LLC	3724	C	818 341-3344	19970
Loungefly LLC	3961	E	818 718-5600	22989
Machineworks Manufacturing	3728	F	818 527-1327	20163

Mergent email: customerrelations@mergent.com
1316

2020 California
Manufacturers Register

(P-0000) Products & Services Section entry number
(PA)=Parent Co (HQ)=Headquarters (DH)=Div Headquarters

Company	SIC	EMP	PHONE	ENTRY #
Magic Gumball International	2064	E	818 716-1888	1385
Mat Mat	3411	F	818 678-9392	11498
Materials Development Corp (PA)	3825	F	818 700-8290	21075
Maxwell Alarm Screen Mfg Inc	3993	E	818 773-5533	23155
MBK Enterprises Inc	3842	E	818 998-1477	22043
Measurement Specialties Inc	3829	D	818 701-2750	21502
Mercury Magnetics Inc	3677	E	818 998-7791	18726
Metal Chem Inc	3471	E	818 727-9951	13049
Metal Improvement Company LLC	3398	D	818 407-6280	11459
Micro Plastics Inc	3643	E	818 882-0244	16917
Mist Incorporated	3545	E	818 678-5619	14174
Mono Engineering Corp	3599	E	818 772-4998	16221
Moog Inc	3812	C	818 341-5156	20633
Narcotics Anonymous World Serv	2731	C	818 773-9999	6124
Natel Engineering Company LLC (PA)	3674	C	818 495-8617	18426
Natel Engineering Company Inc	3672	E	818 734-6552	17934
Natrol LLC (DH)	2834	C	818 739-6000	8023
Networks Electronic Co LLC	3489	E	818 341-0440	13283
Neutraderm Inc	2844	E	818 534-3190	8546
Newage Pavilions LLC	3699	F	818 701-9600	19366
Newvac LLC (HQ)	3643	C	310 525-1205	16918
Newvac LLC	3671	C	310 990-0401	17789
Newvac LLC	3671	E	310 990-0401	17790
Newvac LLC	3671	D	310 516-1692	17791
Newvac LLC	3679	E	310 525-1205	19027
Norsal Printing Inc	2752	F	818 886-4164	6753
Northrdge Tr-Mdlity Imging Inc	3821	F	818 709-2468	20768
Northrop Grumman Corporation	3812	A	818 715-3264	20641
Nydr Holdings Inc	2099	F	818 626-8174	2573
Oncore Manufacturing Svcs Inc	3672	C	510 360-2222	17945
Pacific Air Industries Inc	3728	E	310 829-4345	20192
Pacific Coast Lighting Inc (PA)	3648	B	818 886-9751	17151
Pacific Precision Labs Inc	3829	E	818 700-8977	21518
Papco Screw Products Inc	3541	F	818 341-2266	13938
Paul Silver Enterprises Inc	2752	F	818 998-9900	6773
Pd Products LLC	2299	F	818 772-0100	2950
Pencil Grip Inc (PA)	2678	F	310 315-3545	5484
Perez Severino	3499	F	818 701-1522	13538
Pioneer Photo Albums Inc (PA)	2782	C	818 882-2161	7314
Planet Green Cartridges Inc	3955	D	818 725-2596	22971
Plateronics Processing Inc	3471	E	818 341-2191	13072
Pope Plastics Inc	3544	E	818 701-1850	14094
Printfirm Inc	2752	F	818 992-1005	6802
Printing Safari Co	2752	F	818 709-3752	6807
Prisha Cosmetics Inc	2844	F	818 773-8784	8568
Quality Fabrication Inc (PA)	3444	D	818 407-5015	12345
Racaar Circuit Industries Inc	3672	E	818 998-7566	17973
Rapid Manufacturing (PA)	3999	F	818 899-4377	23457
Renau Corporation	3823	E	818 341-1994	20928
Resmed Motor Technologies Inc	3621	C	818 428-6400	16670
RJA Industries Inc	3679	E	818 998-5124	19069
Roy & Val Tool Grinding Inc	3599	F	818 341-2434	16374
RPS Inc	3496	E	818 350-8088	13435
Rs Machining Co Inc	3599	F	818 718-0097	16377
RTC Arspace - Chtswrth Div Inc (PA)	3593	C	818 341-3344	15625
S2k Graphics Inc	3993	E	818 885-3900	23188
Samuel Raoof	2844	F	818 534-3180	8574
SARR Industries Inc	3599	F	818 998-7735	16386
Schea Holdings Inc	3993	E	818 888-3818	23194
Selane Products Inc (PA)	3843	D	818 998-7460	22189
Semco Aerospace	2394	F	818 678-9381	3705
Sensor Systems Inc	3812	B	818 341-5366	20720
Soundcraft Inc	3699	E	818 882-0020	19411
Strategic Distribution L P	2326	C	818 671-2100	3055
Strategic Partners Inc (PA)	3143	C	818 671-2100	10163
Teledyne Instruments Inc	3826	E	818 882-7266	21299
Teledyne Risi Inc	3724	F	818 718-6640	19981
Telemtry Cmmnctons Systems Inc	3663	E	818 718-6248	17685
Tetracam Inc	3861	F	818 718-2119	22463
Thibiant International Inc	2844	B	818 709-1345	8593
Tig/M LLC	3535	F	818 709-8500	13840
Torrance Precision Machining	3599	F	818 709-7838	16461
Toye Corporation	3577	F	818 882-4000	15353
Trident Diving Equipment	3949	E	818 998-7518	22911
Truly Green Solutions LLC	3648	E	818 206-4404	17172
Underwraps Costume Corporation	2389	F	818 349-5300	3583
United Precision Corp	3495	F	818 576-9540	13392
United States Pumice Company (PA)	1499	F	818 882-0300	394
Venstar Inc (PA)	3585	F	818 341-8760	15471
Verdugo Tool & Engrg Co Inc	3469	F	818 998-1101	12888
Visible Graphics Inc	3993	E	818 787-0477	23236
Vision Imaging Supplies Inc	3955	F	818 710-7200	22976
Vmc Holdings Group Corp	3571	E	818 993-1466	14995
Wallace E Miller Inc	3599	F	818 998-0444	16509
Warrens Department Store Inc	2311	E	888 577-2735	2982

Company	SIC	EMP	PHONE	ENTRY #
We Imagine Inc	3672	D	818 709-0064	18048
We The Pie People LLC	2024	E	818 349-1880	679
West Coast Business Prtrs Inc	2752	F	818 709-4980	6931
West Valley Plating Inc	3471	F	818 709-1684	13130
Woodpecker Cabinet Inc	2434	E	310 404-4805	4270
Worldwide Gaming Systems Corp	3944	E	818 678-9150	22728
Xceliron Corp	3545	F	818 700-8404	14213

CHERRY VALLEY, CA - Riverside County

Company	SIC	EMP	PHONE	ENTRY #
Cherry Valley Sheet Metal	3523	F	951 845-1578	13619

CHESTER, CA - Plumas County

Company	SIC	EMP	PHONE	ENTRY #
Collins Pine Company	2421	B	530 258-2111	3930
Sierra Cascade Aggregate & Asp	1442	F	530 258-4555	359

CHICO, CA - Butte County

Company	SIC	EMP	PHONE	ENTRY #
2xwireless Inc	3663	D	877 581-8002	17434
A & A Ready Mixed Concrete Inc	3273	E	530 342-5989	10674
Agra Trading LLC	2873	E	530 894-1782	8788
Bertagna Orchards Inc	2084	F	530 343-8014	1597
Boards On Nord Inc	3949	E	530 513-3922	22765
Cal Traders	2068	F	530 566-1405	1423
California Olive Ranch Inc (PA)	2079	F	530 846-8000	1468
Chico Community Publishing (PA)	2711	E	530 894-2300	5586
Chico Custom Counter	2541	F	530 894-8123	4891
Chicoeco Inc	2393	E	530 342-4426	3654
Dan M Swofford	2721	F	530 343-9994	5916
Enviro-Commercial Sweeping	3991	F	408 920-0274	23025
Fafco Inc (PA)	3433	E	530 332-2100	11696
Fanno Saw Works	3425	F	530 895-1762	11552
Farmer Bros Co	2095	F	530 343-3165	2292
Gatehouse Media LLC	2711	D	530 891-1234	5642
Graphic Fox Inc	2752	F	530 895-1359	6595
Haemonetics Corporation	3841	B	530 774-2081	21728
Hcp Industries Inc	3261	F	530 899-5591	10466
Hupp Signs & Lighting Inc	3993	F	530 345-7078	23129
Industrial Power Products	3599	E	530 893-0584	16042
Infofax Inc	2721	F	530 895-0431	5962
Johnson Controls	3669	F	530 893-0110	17737
Joy Signal Technology LLC	3643	E	530 891-3551	16909
Keurig Dr Pepper Inc	2086	E	530 893-4501	2084
Klean Kanteen Inc	3411	D	530 592-4552	11497
Lares Research	3843	E	530 345-1767	22171
Lifetouch Nat Schl Studios Inc	2782	D	530 345-3993	7313
Mabrey Products Inc	2431	F	530 895-3799	4079
Mathews Readymix Inc	3273	F	530 893-8856	10801
Matrix Logic Corporation	7372	F	415 893-9897	24130
Mtech Inc	3089	F	530 894-5091	9915
Nature Zone Pet Products	3999	F	530 343-5199	23421
Nor-Cal Vans Inc	3713	F	530 892-0150	19547
North Valley Rain Gutters	3444	F	530 894-3347	12316
Orient & Flume Art Glass Co	3229	F	530 893-0373	10325
Pacific West Forest Products	3449	F	530 899-7313	12600
Progressive Woodwork	2434	F	530 343-2211	4232
Quadco Printing Inc	2752	F	530 894-4061	6825
Quality Circle Institute Inc	2721	F	530 893-4095	6010
Rescue 42 Inc	3569	F	530 891-3473	14855
Selken Enterprises Inc	7692	F	530 891-4200	24663
Seven-Up RC of Chico	2086	E	530 893-4501	2170
Sierra Nevada Brewing Co (PA)	2082	B	530 893-3520	1563
Smucker Natural Foods Inc (HQ)	2086	C	530 899-5000	2173
Solo Steel Erectors Inc	3448	F	530 893-2293	12574
Square Deal Mattress Factory	2515	E	530 342-2510	4746
Srl Apparel Inc	2261	E	530 898-9525	2838
Synthesis	2721	E	530 899-7708	6036
Thomas Manufacturing Co LLC	7692	E	530 893-8940	24672
Thomas Welding & Mch Sp Inc	7692	E	530 893-8940	24673
Truroots Inc	2099	F	925 218-2205	2639
Ultramar Inc	2911	F	530 345-7901	9079
United States Thermoelectric	3826	E	530 345-8000	21318
Videomaker Inc	2721	F	530 891-8410	6053
Weiss-Mcnair LLC (DH)	3523	E	530 891-6214	13685
Wizard Graphics Inc	2759	F	530 893-3636	7274
Wizard Manufacturing Inc	2068	F	530 342-1861	1441
Woof & Poof Inc	2392	F	530 895-0693	3650
Wrex Products Inc Chico	3089	D	530 895-3838	10131

CHILCOOT, CA - Plumas County

Company	SIC	EMP	PHONE	ENTRY #
Pau Hana Group LLC	3429	F	530 993-6800	11619

CHINO, CA - San Bernardino County

Company	SIC	EMP	PHONE	ENTRY #
AC Air Technology Inc	3465	F	855 884-7222	12740
Acorn Plastics Inc (HQ)	3089	D	909 591-8461	9606
Acorn-Gencon Plastics LLC	3089	E	909 591-8461	9607
Acornvac Inc	3432	E	909 902-1141	11652
Action Graphic Arts Inc	2796	F	626 443-3113	7367
Air Craftors Engineering Inc	3599	F	909 900-0635	15714

Employment Codes: A=Over 500 employees, B=251-500,
C=101-250, D=51-100, E=20-50, F=10-19

2020 California
Manufacturers Register

© Mergent Inc. 1-800-342-5647

1317

GEOGRAPHIC

	SIC	EMP	PHONE	ENTRY #
Alaco Ladder Company	2499	E	909 591-7561	4489
Albers Mfg Co Inc (PA)	3523	E	909 597-5537	13607
All Stars Packaging Inc	2631	F	626 664-3797	5155
Alston Tascom Inc	3661	E	909 517-3660	17345
Alvarado Manufacturing Co Inc	3829	D	909 591-8431	21432
Amcor Rigid Packaging Usa LLC	3089	F	520 746-0737	9621
Amcor Rigid Packaging Usa LLC	3085	C	909 517-2700	9480
American Pride Inc	3161	E	909 591-7688	10187
American SD Power Inc	3621	F	909 947-0673	16630
Anthony California Inc (PA)	3645	E	909 627-0351	16960
Apex Digital Inc	3645	F	909 366-2028	16961
Aranda Tooling Inc	3599	D	714 379-6565	15745
Arnold-Gonsalves Engrg Inc	3599	E	909 465-1579	15749
Artiva USA Inc (PA)	3645	E	909 628-1388	16964
Asrock America Inc	3672	E	909 590-8308	17825
B E & P Enterprises LLC (PA)	2499	E	909 591-7561	4492
Balaji Trading Inc	3661	D	909 444-7999	17349
Base Lite Corporation	3645	E	909 444-2776	16966
Beckman Coulter Inc	3826	E	909 597-3967	21180
Berry Global Inc	3089	C	909 465-9055	9661
Berry Global Films LLC	3081	C	909 517-2872	9395
Bill Wood Lathing	3496	E	909 628-1733	13397
Brad Barry Company Ltd	2095	E	909 591-9493	2278
Bright Shark Powder Coating	3479	F	909 591-1385	13151
Brooks Millwork Company	2431	F	562 920-3000	4005
Bti Aerospace & Electronics	3599	E	909 465-1569	15800
C & M Spring & Engineering Co	3495	E	909 597-2030	13378
C B Machine Products Inc	3599	F	909 517-1828	15809
Cal-India Foods International	2869	F	909 613-1660	8725
CG Motor Sports Inc	3089	F	909 628-1440	9704
Champion Pblications Chino Inc	2711	E	909 628-5501	5585
Chemcor Chemical Corporation	2842	F	909 590-7234	8372
Chino Ice Service LLC	2097	E	909 628-2105	2351
Churchill Aerospace LLC	3546	C	909 266-3116	14219
Clariant Plas Coatings USA LLC	2869	E	909 606-1325	8732
Closetmaid LLC	3496	F	909 590-4444	13405
Consolidated Container Co LP	3089	E	909 590-7334	9722
Consolidated Geoscience	1382	F	909 393-9700	116
Corona Millworks Company (PA)	2434	D	909 606-3288	4183
CPI Advanced Inc	3612	C	909 597-5533	16545
Craneveyor Corp	3446	E	909 627-6801	12465
Custom Source Design Inc	3441	F	909 597-5221	11777
Dare Lithoworks Inc	2752	F	213 250-9062	6532
Delta Manufacturing Inc	3599	E	909 590-4563	15887
Diamond Wipes Intl Inc (PA)	2844	D	909 230-9888	8483
Dick Farrell Industries Inc	3567	F	909 613-9424	14759
Dupree Inc	3452	F	909 597-4889	12676
Dvtech Solution Corp	3613	F	909 308-0358	16596
E S M Plastics Inc	3599	F	909 591-7658	15918
E W Smith Chemical Co	2899	F	909 590-9717	8961
Eep Holdings LLC (PA)	3089	E	909 597-7861	9776
El & El Wood Products Corp (PA)	2431	C	909 591-0339	4042
Enersys	3691	D	909 464-8251	19160
Esslinger Engineering Inc	3714	E	909 539-0544	19650
Exhaust Gas Technologies Inc	3714	E	909 548-8100	19652
Factory Reproductions	3714	F	909 590-5252	19654
Fenchem Inc (PA)	2844	E	909 597-8880	8492
Ferco Color & Compounding Inc	2821	E	909 930-0773	7563
Flexcon Company Inc	3081	E	909 465-0408	9404
Fonegear LLC	3661	F	909 627-7999	17322
Fsp Group USA Corp	3677	F	909 606-0960	18718
General Photonics Corp	3661	E	909 590-5473	17374
Gianno Co Ltd	2331	F	909 628-6928	3160
Globe Plastics Inc	3089	E	909 464-1520	9808
Gluten Free Foods Mfg LLC (PA)	2099	F	909 823-8230	2469
Gmp Global Nutrition Inc	2834	F	909 628-8889	7924
Golden Gate Hosiery Inc	2252	E	909 464-0805	2766
Gro-Power Inc	2873	E	909 393-3744	8793
H P Group	3999	F	909 364-1069	23350
H2 Environmental	3292	E	909 628-0369	10962
Hanson Truss Inc	2439	B	909 591-9256	4304
Hasbro Inc	3944	B	909 393-3248	22680
Hasco Fabrication Inc	3565	F	909 627-0326	14710
Hi-Lite Manufacturing Co Inc	3646	E	909 465-1999	17043
HSG Manufacturing Inc	3469	F	909 902-5915	12818
Ht Multinational Inc	3714	E	626 964-2686	19685
Hua Rong International Corp	3799	F	909 591-8800	20513
Hussmann Corporation	3585	B	909 590-4910	15434
Hyponex Corporation	2873	E	909 597-2811	8794
Hyx Tech Corp	2759	F	951 907-3386	7088
Imaginary Fiber Glass Inc	2221	F	909 597-4110	2728
Impact Printing & Graphics	2752	F	909 614-1678	6631
Imperial Rubber Products Inc	3555	E	909 393-0528	14327
Ingrersoll Rand Indus Refrig	3131	F	909 477-2037	10151
Inter Packing Inc	3086	E	909 465-5555	9552
ISC Engineering LLC	3629	D	909 596-3315	16790
Isiqalo LLC	2253	B	714 683-2820	2791
Jacuzzi Inc (DH)	3589	C	909 606-7733	15530
Jacuzzi Products Co	3088	B	909 548-7732	9590
Kanetic Ltd LLC	3471	F	505 228-5692	13035
Kemper Enterprises Inc	3423	E	909 627-6191	11533
KVP International Inc	3842	E	888 411-7387	22042
Larin Corp	3423	E	909 464-0605	11534
Level Trek Corp	3089	F	626 689-4829	9876
Lifemed of California	3841	E	800 543-3633	21775
Liner Technologies Inc	3089	E	909 594-6610	9878
Liquid Technologies Inc	2844	E	909 393-9475	8534
Lollicup USA Inc (HQ)	2656	E	626 965-8882	5308
M & M Printed Bag Inc	2673	E	909 393-5537	5402
M and M Sports	2395	F	909 548-3371	3748
M and M Stamping Corp	3441	F	909 590-2704	11830
M C O Inc	3714	F	909 627-3574	19709
M E Hodge Inc	3599	F	909 393-0675	16160
Manley Laboratories Inc	3651	E	909 627-4256	17256
Maplegrove Gluten Free Foods	2099	E	909 334-7828	2540
Max Smt Corp	3563	E	877 589-9422	14635
Maxon Auto Corporation	2631	F	626 400-6464	5168
Mikhail Darafeev Inc (PA)	2511	E	909 613-1818	4593
Morehouse-Cowles LLC	3559	E	909 627-7222	14501
Myers & Sons Hi-Way Safety Inc (PA)	3669	C	909 591-1781	17749
Myojo USA Inc	2098	F	909 464-1411	2372
National Sign & Marketing Corp	3993	D	909 591-4742	23165
Natura-Genics Inc	2834	F	909 597-6676	8024
Newport Thin Film Lab Inc	3089	F	909 591-0276	9927
Norco Injection Molding Inc	3089	D	909 393-4000	9929
Norco Plastics Inc	3089	E	909 393-4000	9930
North Pacific International	3497	E	909 628-2224	13453
Oak Design Corporation	2521	E	909 628-9597	4814
Omnia Leather Motion Inc	2392	C	909 393-4400	3629
Originals 22 Inc	3645	F	909 993-5050	16983
Pacific Boat Trailers Inc (PA)	3799	E	909 902-0094	20518
Pacific Coast Fabricators Inc	3441	F	909 627-3833	11857
Pacific Coast Mfg Inc	3631	D	909 627-7040	16815
Pacific Containerprint Inc	2759	E	909 465-0365	7166
Paclights LLC (PA)	3646	E	888 983-2165	17063
Paiho North America Corp	3965	E	661 257-6611	23007
Pdc LLC	3544	E	626 334-5000	14092
Pentair Water Pool and Spa Inc	3589	E	909 287-7800	15557
Precision Companies Inc	2431	F	909 548-2700	4110
Quali-Tech Mold	3089	F	909 464-8124	10002
R Kern Engineering & Mfg Corp	3678	D	909 664-2440	18785
Redbuilt LLC	2439	E	909 465-1215	4316
Reed LLC	3561	E	909 287-2100	14597
Repet Inc	3083	C	909 594-5333	9453
Roettele Industries	3053	F	909 606-8252	9250
Royal Custom Designs Inc	2512	C	909 591-8990	4669
RTS Powder Coating Inc (PA)	3479	E	909 393-5404	13238
Scott Engineering Inc	3629	E	909 594-9637	16797
Shamrock Marketing Co Inc (HQ)	3842	E	909 591-8855	22084
Sharkninja Operating LLC	3639	F	909 325-4412	16853
Sheffield Manufacturing Inc	3599	E	818 767-4948	16401
Shephard Casters	3562	E	909 393-0597	14615
Shield Realty California Inc (PA)	2813	E	909 628-4707	7450
Shine Company Inc	2499	F	909 590-5005	4535
Shirlee Industries Inc	3449	F	909 590-1204	12604
Shop4techcom	3572	E	909 248-2725	15100
Soaring America Corporation	3721	E	909 270-2628	19931
South Gate Engineering LLC	3443	C	909 628-2779	12053
Specilty Enzymes Btechnologies	2869	F	909 613-1660	8776
Spin Products Inc	3089	E	909 590-7000	10064
Steelcraft West	3914	F	909 548-2696	22590
Steven Madden Ltd	3143	D	909 393-7575	10162
Superior Metal Shapes Inc	3354	E	909 947-3455	11248
Superior Tech Inc	3317	F	909 364-2300	11136
Syntech Development & Mfg Inc	3089	E	909 465-5554	10077
T McGee Electric Inc	3643	F	909 591-6461	16928
Tape Service Ltd	3069	F	909 627-8811	9378
Tarazi Specialty Foods LLC	2099	F	909 628-3601	2623
Tasco Molds Inc	3544	F	909 613-1926	14111
Tekram Usa Inc	3572	F	714 961-0800	15108
Texas Tst Inc	3341	E	951 685-2155	11209
Thermo Fisher Scientific Inc	3826	B	909 393-3205	21305
Top Quest Inc	3841	E	626 839-8618	21933
Top-Shelf Fixtures LLC	3496	D	909 627-7423	13440
Trend Technologies LLC (DH)	3444	C	909 597-7861	12410
Trinidad Benham Holding Co	2099	E	909 627-7535	2636
Tst Inc	3341	E	951 727-3169	11211
Tst Inc (PA)	3341	B	951 737-3169	11212
Ttl Holdings LLC (HQ)	3089	E	909 597-7861	10096
Tuffstuff Fitness Intl Inc	3949	C	909 629-1600	22913

Mergent email: customerrelations@mergent.com

1318

2020 California
Manufacturers Register

(P-0000) Products & Services Section entry number
(PA)=Parent Co (HQ)=Headquarters (DH)=Div Headquarters

	SIC	EMP	PHONE	ENTRY #
Tyloon Media Corporation	2741	F	626 330-5838	6365
U S Bowling Corporation	3949	F	909 548-0644	22915
United Castings Inc	3369	F	909 627-7645	11426
Usglobalsat Inc	3663	F	909 597-8525	17698
Vacuum Tube Logic of America	3671	F	909 627-5944	17795
Val Plastic USA L L C	3523	F	909 390-9600	13678
Vitajoy USA Inc	2833	F	626 965-8830	7703
Vtl Amplifiers Inc	3651	E	909 627-5944	17304
Wacker Chemical Corporation	2869	E	909 590-8822	8784
West Coast Steel & Proc LLC (PA)	3325	D	909 393-8405	11175
Westrock Mwv LLC	2631	B	909 597-2197	5185
Wetmore Tool and Engrg Co	3545	E	909 364-1000	14212
Wright Business Forms Inc	2761	E	909 614-6700	7294
Yamamoto of Orient Inc	2393	F	909 591-7654	3670
Yankon Industries Inc	3646	E	909 591-2345	17086
Young Machine Inc	3599	F	909 464-0405	16535
Ziegenfelder Company	2024	E	909 590-0493	681

CHINO HILLS, CA - San Bernardino County

	SIC	EMP	PHONE	ENTRY #
Ad Industries LLC (PA)	2782	F	818 765-4200	7302
Cal Stitch Embroidery Inc	2395	F	909 465-5448	3728
Hoya Surgical Optics Inc	3841	E	909 680-3900	21735
Jacuzzi Brands LLC (DH)	3842	E	909 606-1416	22035
Jacuzzi Brands LLC	3999	E	909 606-1416	23370
Jacuzzi Inc	3088	E	909 606-1416	9588
Jacuzzi Products Co (DH)	3088	C	909 606-1416	9589
Ontario Binding Company Inc	2789	D	909 947-7866	7340
Plastic Color Technology	2816	F	909 597-9230	7460
Saunders Manufacturing Svcs	3999	F	714 961-8492	23466
Sundance Spas Inc (DH)	3999	D	909 606-7733	23489
Tri-Dim Filter Corporation	3564	F	626 333-9428	14684
Tri-Dim Filter Corporation	3564	F	626 826-5893	14685
TSS Embroidery Inc	2395	F	909 590-1383	3762
Vans Inc	3021	F	909 517-3141	9193

CHOLAME, CA - San Luis Obispo County

	SIC	EMP	PHONE	ENTRY #
Central Coast Water Authority	3589	F	805 463-2122	15494

CHOWCHILLA, CA - Madera County

	SIC	EMP	PHONE	ENTRY #
Almond Company	2068	D	559 665-4405	1419
Blacks Irrigations Systems	3272	F	559 665-4891	10537
Central California Cont Mfg	3089	E	559 665-7611	9701
Certainteed Corporation	3296	B	559 665-4831	10981
Global Diversified Inds Inc (PA)	2452	E	559 665-5800	4460
Global Modular Inc (HQ)	2452	E	559 665-5800	4461
Piranha Pipe & Precast Inc	3272	E	559 665-7473	10623
Snyder Industries LLC	3089	D	559 665-7611	10062

CHULA VISTA, CA - San Diego County

	SIC	EMP	PHONE	ENTRY #
Ace Industries Inc	3599	E	619 482-2700	15680
Advanced McHning Solutions Inc	3599	E	619 671-3055	15698
Aker International Inc	3199	E	619 423-5182	10244
Allied Dvbe Inc	2321	F	619 690-4900	2984
American Design Inc	3089	F	619 429-1995	9623
American Metal Filter Company	3564	F	619 628-1917	14648
Astor Manufacturing	3728	E	661 645-5585	20044
Bastan Corporation	2032	F	619 424-3416	718
Bellama Cstm Met Fbrcators Inc	3444	F	619 585-3351	12130
Boochery Inc	2085	F	619 738-1008	2010
Califrnia Furn Collections Inc	2519	C	619 621-2455	4764
Canvas Concepts Inc	2394	F	619 424-3428	3676
Career Cap Corporation	2353	E	619 575-2277	3464
Curbell Plastics Inc	3089	E	619 575-4633	9736
DStyle Inc	3499	F	619 662-0560	13517
Flagcrafters Inc	2399	E	619 585-1044	3842
Flexible Metal Inc (HQ)	3498	D	678 280-0127	13470
Ggtw LLC	2899	E	619 423-3388	8971
Glaxosmithkline LLC	2834	E	619 863-0399	7921
Gold Belt Line Inc	2326	F	619 424-5544	3034
Goodrich Corporation	3728	D	619 691-4111	20120
H & M Wrought Iron Factory	3446	F	619 912-0054	12479
Hitachi Home Elec Amer Inc (DH)	3651	C	619 591-5200	17243
Husks Unlimited (PA)	2037	F	619 476-8301	914
Hyspan Precision Products Inc (PA)	3568	D	619 421-1355	14784
Hyspan Precision Products Inc	3499	D	619 421-1355	13524
Ichia Usa Inc	3674	C	619 482-2222	18276
Integrated Marine Services Inc	3731	D	619 429-0300	20289
Jack West Cnc Inc	3599	F	619 421-1695	16071
Kama-Tech Corporation	3827	E	619 421-7858	21372
Kinetic Electric Corporation	3699	E	619 654-1157	19340
Lamb Fuels Inc	2869	E	619 216-6940	8750
Laprensa San Diego	2711	F	619 425-7400	5694
Latina & Associates Inc (PA)	2711	E	619 426-1491	5695
Leemax International Inc	2329	E	619 208-2355	3102
Legacy Graphics LLC	2759	F	619 585-1044	7119
Marine Group Boat Works LLC	3732	C	619 427-6767	20346
Marshall Genuine Products LLC	3545	F	619 754-4099	14170

	SIC	EMP	PHONE	ENTRY #
Mask U S Inc	2389	F	619 476-9041	3568
McMahon Steel Company Inc	3429	C	619 671-9700	11610
Mgb Industries Inc	3728	F	619 247-9284	20177
Mk Digital Direct Inc	3826	F	619 661-0628	21265
Mya International Inc	2834	F	619 429-6012	8018
Next Day Printed Tees	2396	F	619 420-8618	3803
Nypro Inc	3089	D	619 498-9250	9938
Nypro San Diego Inc	3089	D	619 482-7033	9939
Oak Land Furniture	2514	F	619 424-8758	4696
P A S U Inc	3444	C	619 421-1151	12321
Pacmag Inc	3679	F	619 872-0343	19045
Professional Imaging Svcs Inc	3826	F	858 565-4217	21278
RCP Block & Brick Inc	3271	E	619 474-1516	10517
Rohr Inc (HQ)	3728	A	619 691-4111	20212
Sealed Air Corporation	2673	E	619 421-9003	5419
Shimmer Fashion	2331	F	619 426-7781	3194
Smartrunk Systems Inc	3663	E	619 426-3781	17662
SMK Manufacturing Inc	3575	E	619 216-6400	15135
Source of Health Inc	2023	E	619 409-9500	620
Southcoast Welding & Mfg LLC	7692	B	619 429-1337	24666
Stanford Sign & Awning Inc (PA)	3993	D	619 423-6200	23216
Stark Mfg Co	2394	E	619 425-5880	3707
Super Welding Southern Cal Inc	3548	E	619 239-8003	14256
Tap Manufacturing LLC	3714	F	619 216-1444	19777
Tecnico Corporation	3731	E	619 426-7385	20306
Tocabi America Corporation	2517	E	619 661-6136	4756
Toleeto Fastener International	3965	E	619 662-1355	23011
Tortilleria Santa Fe	2099	E	619 585-0350	2633
Va-Tran Systems Inc	3559	E	619 423-4555	14552
Vcp Mobility Holdings Inc	3842	B	619 213-6500	22116

CITRUS HEIGHTS, CA - Sacramento County

	SIC	EMP	PHONE	ENTRY #
American Amplifier Tech LLC	3825	F	530 574-3474	21000
Hearst Communications Inc	2711	B	916 725-8694	5655
Mline Transportation Company	2075	E	916 729-1053	1445
Nvision Laser Eye Centers Inc	3851	F	916 723-7400	22374

CITY OF INDUSTRY, CA - Los Angeles County

	SIC	EMP	PHONE	ENTRY #
Abis Signs Inc	3993	F	626 818-4329	23039
Abrasive Wheels Inc	3291	F	626 935-8800	10939
Acorn Engineering Company (PA)	3448	A	800 488-8999	12525
Acromil LLC (HQ)	3728	C	626 964-2522	20001
Acromil Corporation (PA)	3728	C	626 964-2522	20003
Adams-Campbell Company Ltd	3444	E	626 330-3425	12085
Addice Inc (PA)	3577	F	626 617-7779	15147
Adtech Photonics Inc	3827	E	626 956-1000	21331
Alatus Aerosystems (PA)	3728	C	610 251-1000	20029
All Label Inc	2679	F	626 964-6744	5490
Alta-Dena Certified Dairy LLC	2026	A	800 395-7004	684
Alta-Dena Certified Dairy LLC (DH)	2026	B	626 964-6401	685
American Foam Fiber & Sups Inc	2299	D	626 969-7268	2923
American Steel Masters Inc	3441	E	626 333-3375	11743
Aremac Heat Treating	3398	C	626 333-3898	11432
Astrophysics Inc (PA)	3844	C	909 598-5488	22209
Avant Enterprises Inc (PA)	3423	C	866 300-3311	11521
Bagcraftpapercon I LLC	2674	D	626 961-6766	5433
Battery Technology Inc (PA)	3691	C	626 336-6878	19152
Bentley Mills Inc	2273	F	800 423-4709	2866
Bentley Mills Inc (PA)	2273	C	626 333-4585	2867
Best Formulations Inc	2099	C	626 912-9998	2403
Beyond Ultimate LLC	2611	F	626 330-9777	5091
Blackseries Campers Inc	3715	E	626 579-1069	19814
Blue PCF Flvors Fragrances Inc	2087	E	626 934-0099	2195
Boss Litho Inc	2752	D	626 820-5410	5311
Boxes R Us Inc	2657	D	626 961-9257	6460
Bryan Press Inc	2752	F	626 961-7221	6454
Burton James Inc	2512	D	626 723-1000	4630
C & F Foods Inc (PA)	2099	D	626 369-3564	2412
California Expanded Met Pdts (PA)	3444	D	626 912-0036	12144
California Hydroforming Co Inc	3444	F	909 354-8962	12145
Cambro Manufacturing Company	3999	F	626 937-6767	23295
Cardinal Paint and Powder Inc	2851	C	626 937-3444	8631
Cast Parts Inc	3324	C	626 330-3182	11155
Central Blower Co	3564	E	626 961-5775	14652
Centric Parts Inc	3711	F	626 336-6063	19463
CH Image Inc	2752	F	626 435-0077	6479
Charades LLC (PA)	2389	C	626 810-9372	3547
China Master USA Entrmt Co	3299	F	310 534-2300	11005
Chronomite Laboratories Inc	3822	E	800 959-2100	20787
Circle Racing Wheels Inc (PA)	3714	F	626 330-0631	19615
Clay Laguna Co (HQ)	3295	C	626 443-9381	10969
Clayton Manufacturing Company (PA)	3569	C	626 443-9381	14803
Clayton Manufacturing Inc (HQ)	3569	D	626 939-4226	14804
Clo Systems LLC	3621	F	562 699-9945	16635
Closets By Design Inc	2541	C	626 855-4440	4892
Coca-Cola Company	2086	E		2060

Employment Codes: A=Over 500 employees, B=251-500,
C=101-250, D=51-100, E=20-50, F=10-19

2020 California
Manufacturers Register

© Mergent Inc. 1-800-342-5647
1319

G E O G R A P H I C

Company	SIC	EMP	PHONE	ENTRY #
Coi Rubber Products Inc	2822	B	626 965-9966	7627
Collection Development	3674	F	909 595-8588	18168
Colorwen International Corp	2816	F	626 363-8855	7457
Commercial Lbr & Pallet Co Inc (PA)	2448	C	626 968-0631	4357
Compucase Corporation	3572	A	626 336-6588	15018
Consolidated Cont Holdings LLC	3089	E	626 964-9657	9717
Consolidated Container Co LLC	3089	E	888 425-7343	9719
Continental Marketing Svc Inc	2393	F	626 626-8888	3655
Cosmos Food Co Inc	2099	E	323 221-9142	2433
Cpp Ind	3812	F	909 595-2252	20561
Creftcon Industries Inc	3644	C	203 377-5944	16944
Custom Alloy Sales Inc (PA)	3341	D	626 369-3641	11198
D-Tech Optoelectronics Inc (DH)	3669	E	626 956-1100	17723
Dacor	3631	F	626 799-1000	16808
Dacor	3631	F	626 799-1000	16809
Darnell Corporation	3429	D	626 912-1688	11585
Dean Socal LLC	2026	C	951 734-3950	697
Define Toys Inc	3942	F	626 330-8800	22646
Delori Products Inc	2099	F	626 965-3006	2443
Dennison Inc	3446	E	626 965-8917	12469
Derek and Constance Lee Corp (PA)	2013	F	909 595-8831	453
Diamond Collection LLC	2389	F	626 435-0077	3551
Dispensing Dynamics Intl Inc (PA)	3089	D	626 961-3691	9758
Duro Corporation	3631	F	626 839-6541	16810
Dxg Technology USA Inc	3861	B	626 820-0687	22416
Ecolab Inc	2841	F	626 935-1212	8338
El Burrito Mxican Fd Pdts Corp	2033	F	626 369-7828	767
Engineering Model Associates (PA)	3089	F	626 912-7011	9780
Environmental Ltg For Arch Inc	3646	F	626 965-0821	17030
Evans Industries Inc	3499	C	626 912-1688	13521
Express It Delivers	2741	E	626 855-1294	6233
Exxel Outdoors Inc	2399	B	626 369-7278	3840
Foot Imprint Inc	3555	B	626 991-4430	14322
Fremarc Industries Inc (PA)	2511	D	626 965-0802	4571
General Sealants Inc	2891	C	626 961-0211	8869
Geo A Diack Inc	3355	E	626 961-2491	11260
Gff Inc	2035	D	323 232-6255	882
Globalux Lighting LLC	3645	F	909 591-7506	16971
Golden State Foods Corp	2038	B	626 465-7500	960
Goldencorr Sheets LLC	2653	C	626 369-6446	5231
Gordon Brush Mfg Co Inc (PA)	3991	D	323 724-7777	23027
Goulds Pumps	3561	E	562 949-2113	14576
H & H Specialties Inc	3999	E	626 575-0776	23349
H&N Brothers Co Ltd	3651	F	626 465-3383	17236
Harbor Green Grain LP	2048	E	310 991-8089	1099
Harvard Label LLC	2621	C	626 333-8881	5108
Henkel US Operations Corp	2891	E	626 968-6511	8873
Herbal Science International	2833	F	626 333-9998	7668
Heritage Distributing Company	2023	E	626 333-9526	595
Hexpol Compounding CA Inc	3069	D	626 961-0311	9315
Hill Brothers Chemical Company	2812	F	626 333-2251	7389
Hitex Dyeing & Finishing Inc	2399	E	626 363-0160	3846
Hot Topic Inc (DH)	2326	A	626 839-4681	3036
Ht Window Fashions Corporation (PA)	2591	D	626 839-8866	5025
Hydro Extruder LLC	3354	B	626 964-3411	11233
Ideal Printing Co Inc	2752	E	626 964-2019	6626
Ilos Corp	3648	F	213 255-2060	17134
Integral Engrg Fabrication Inc	3441	E	626 369-0958	11812
Invenlux Corporation	3674	E	626 277-4163	18319
ITT LLC	3625	D	562 908-4144	16724
Jada Group Inc	3944	E	626 810-8382	22685
JC USA Trading Inc	2211	F	626 333-9990	2698
Jishan Usa Inc	3646	F	408 609-3286	17046
Johnson Wilshire Inc	3842	E	562 777-0088	22038
Jon Brooks Inc (PA)	3295	C	626 330-0631	10974
K-1 Packaging Group (PA)	2752	D	626 964-9384	6673
K-Tops Plastic Mfg Inc	3999	E	626 575-9679	23376
Kandi Inc	3711	E	909 941-4588	19481
Kontech USA LLC	3646	F	626 622-1325	17047
Krallcast Inc	3324	F	626 333-0678	11159
La Indiana Tamales Inc	2032	E	323 262-4682	737
Lanstreetcom	3575	E	626 964-2000	15128
Lee Kum Kee (usa) Foods Inc	2099	D	626 709-1888	2525
Lhoist North America Ariz Inc	3274	F	626 336-4578	10875
Likom Caseworks USA Inc (DH)	3575	E	210 587-7824	15129
Linde Gas North America LLC	2813	E	626 780-3104	7415
Lt Security Inc	3699	E	626 435-2838	19350
Magnell Associate Inc	3571	F	626 271-1320	14939
Marrs Printing Inc	2752	D	909 594-9459	6715
Material Sciences Corporation	3353	E	562 699-4550	11221
Maverick Aerospace Inc	3728	E	714 578-1700	20170
Maverick Aerospace LLC	3728	E	714 578-1700	20171
Maxim Lighting Intl Inc (PA)	3645	C	626 956-4200	16979
Maxim Lighting Intl Inc	3645	D	626 956-4200	16980
Mercury Plastics Inc (PA)	2673	B	626 961-0165	5403
Messer LLC	2813	D	626 855-8366	7426
Microprint Inc	2752	E	626 369-1950	6727
Midern Computer Inc	3571	E	626 964-8682	14948
Miracle Bedding Corporation	2515	E	562 500-2370	4732
Modem Graphic Inc	2752	D	626 912-7088	6732
Monadnock Company	3429	C	626 964-6581	11613
Morehouse Foods Inc	2035	E	626 854-1655	890
Morris Group International (PA)	3448	D	626 336-4561	12565
Nefful USA Inc	2341	F	626 839-6657	3446
Newton Heat Treating Company	3398	D	626 964-6528	11464
Nuset Inc	3429	E	626 246-1668	11616
Pape Material Handling Inc	3537	D	562 692-9311	13887
Pgi Pacific Graphics Intl	2752	E	626 336-7707	6780
PHI	3542	E	626 968-9680	13990
Phifer Incorporated	3496	F	626 968-0438	13426
Phillips Machine & Wldg Co Inc	7692	E	626 855-4600	24657
Physicians Formula Inc (DH)	2844	D	626 334-3395	8559
Physicians Formula Inc	2844	D	626 334-3395	8560
Physicians Formula Cosmt Inc	2844	D	626 334-3395	8562
Plastruct Inc	3089	D	626 912-7017	9979
Playhut Inc	3944	F	909 869-8083	22704
Pocino Foods Company	2013	D	626 968-8000	489
PPG Industries Inc	2851	F	562 692-4010	8665
Premio Inc (PA)	3571	C	626 839-3100	14963
Prl Aluminum Inc	3334	D	626 968-7507	11186
Procter & Gamble Mfg Co	2841	B	513 627-4678	8349
Prolacta Bioscience Inc (PA)	2836	C	626 599-9260	8323
PS Intl Inc	3496	F	626 333-8168	13429
Puente Ready Mix Inc (PA)	3273	E	626 968-0711	10815
Qontrol Devices Inc	3559	F	626 912-1688	14523
Quemetco West LLC (DH)	3341	E	626 330-2294	11208
RC Furniture Inc	2512	D	626 964-4100	4665
Rectangular Tubing Inc	2655	F	626 333-7884	5301
Red Shell Foods Inc	2035	F	626 937-6501	897
Reuland Electric Co (PA)	3621	C	626 964-6411	16671
Rice Field Corporation	2013	D	626 968-6917	492
Roadster Wheels Inc	3714	F	626 333-3007	19760
Rosewill Inc	3571	F	626 271-1420	14969
S2e Inc	3651	F	626 965-1008	17279
Safe Plating Inc	3471	D	626 810-1872	13092
Sbm Dairies Inc (HQ)	2086	D	626 923-3000	2165
SC Beverage Inc	3556	F	562 463-8918	14399
Sceptre Inc	3679	E	626 369-3698	19077
Scope Packaging Inc	2653	E	714 998-4411	5265
Sealed Air Corporation	3086	D	909 594-1791	9568
Sentinel Offender Services LLC	3822	F	626 336-5150	20810
Shoes For Crews Intl Inc	3143	F	561 683-5090	10161
Silao Tortilleria Inc	2099	E	626 961-0761	2611
Silveron Industries Inc	3625	F	909 598-4533	16755
Sincere Orient Commercial Corp	2099	D	626 333-8882	2613
Sing Tao Newspapers Ltd	2711	D	626 839-8200	5828
Smurfit Kappa North Amer LLC	2653	B	626 322-2123	5266
Solar Region Inc	3571	F	909 595-8500	14977
Solo Enterprise Corp	3599	E	626 961-3591	16409
Sonoco Products Company	2631	D	626 369-6611	5174
Spencer N Enterprises LLC (DH)	2392	C	909 895-8495	3642
Stoughton Printing Co	2752	E	626 961-3678	6872
Stud Welding Systems Inc	3452	E	626 330-7434	12695
Summer Rio Corp (PA)	3021	E	626 854-1498	9185
T S Microtech Inc	3577	E	626 839-8998	15346
Tekni-Plex Inc	2679	C	909 589-4366	5537
Teknor Apex Company	2821	C	626 968-4656	7620
Teledyne Instruments Inc	3823	C	626 934-1500	20945
Tje Company	3442	F	909 869-7773	11986
Tonusa LLC	2434	F	626 961-8700	4254
Topstar International Inc	3641	F	909 595-8807	16870
Touch Coffee & Beverages LLC	3634	F	626 968-0300	16841
TPC Advance Technology Inc	3843	F	626 810-4337	22197
Trend Manor Furn Mfg Co Inc	2511	E	626 964-6493	4616
Trio Metal Stamping Inc	3444	D	626 336-1228	12413
Triview Glass Industries LLC	3231	D	626 363-7980	10395
Tropicana Products Inc	2033	C	626 968-1299	832
Troy-Csl Lighting Inc	3645	D	626 336-4511	16994
Trulite GL Alum Solutions LLC	3354	F	800 877-8439	11249
Turnham Corporation (PA)	3545	F	626 330-0415	14206
Turnham Corporation	3545	F	626 968-6481	14207
Unger Fabrik LLC (PA)	2331	C	626 469-8080	3205
Union Flavors Inc	2087	E	626 333-1612	2233
Utility Trailer Mfg Co	3715	B	909 594-6026	19837
V & V Manufacturing Inc	3961	E	626 330-0641	22997
Valley Power Services Inc	3621	E	909 969-9345	16678
Valley Power Systems Inc (PA)	3519	D	626 333-1243	13603
Venus Foods Inc	2011	E	626 369-5188	429
Vida Corporation	3695	D	626 839-4912	19240
Visionmax Inc	2339	F	626 839-1602	3432

	SIC	EMP	PHONE	ENTRY #
Viz Cattle Corporation	2011	E	310 884-5260	430
Vonnic Inc	3861	E	626 964-2345	22473
Waddington North America Inc	3089	C	626 913-4022	10115
Whitehall Manufacturing Inc	3842	A	626 336-4561	22126
Whittier Enterprise LLC	2038	E	844 767-5633	984
Winstar Textile Inc	2361	E	626 357-1133	3491
Wjb Bearings Inc	3463	E	909 598-6238	12739
Wna Comet West Inc	3089	C	626 913-0724	10128
Wwf Operating Company	2026	C	626 810-1775	714
Ybcc Inc	2023	E	626 213-3945	627

CLAREMONT, CA - Los Angeles County

	SIC	EMP	PHONE	ENTRY #
Baumann Engineering Inc	3599	D	909 621-4181	15775
Bert & Rockys Cream Co Inc	2024	F	909 625-1852	631
Claremont Courier	2711	E	909 621-4761	5593
Conveyor Mfg & Svc Inc	3535	F	909 621-0406	13819
Feemster Co Inc	2051	E	909 621-9772	1202
Green Spot Packaging Inc	2086	E	909 625-8771	2078
HI Rel Connectors Inc	3643	B	909 626-1820	16902
Micro Matrix Systems (PA)	3469	E	909 626-8544	12847
National Scientific Sup Co Inc	3089	F	909 621-4585	9919
New Bedford Panoramex Corp	3648	E	909 982-9806	17148
Sunsation Inc	2037	E	909 542-0280	930
Superior Radiant Insul Inc	2679	F	909 305-1450	5533
Unisorb Inc	3499	F	626 793-1000	13553
Universal Defense	3443	E	909 626-4178	12066

CLARKSBURG, CA - Yolo County

	SIC	EMP	PHONE	ENTRY #
Carvalho Family Winery LLC	2084	F	916 744-1615	1621

CLAYTON, CA - Contra Costa County

	SIC	EMP	PHONE	ENTRY #
Comco Sheet Metal Company	3444	F	510 832-6433	12159
Hanson Aggrgtes Md-Pacific Inc	3281	F	925 672-4955	10910
Underground Labs Inc	7372	E	925 297-5333	24536

CLEARLAKE, CA - Lake County

	SIC	EMP	PHONE	ENTRY #
Medianews Group Inc	2711	C	707 994-6656	5747
Zyrel Inc	3672	F	707 995-2551	18057

CLOVERDALE, CA - Sonoma County

	SIC	EMP	PHONE	ENTRY #
Bear Republic Brewing Co Inc (PA)	2082	C	707 894-2722	1501
Centersource Systems LLC	2731	F	707 838-1061	6085
Charlois Cooperage USA	2429	F	707 224-2377	3986
Classic Mill & Cabinet	2434	E	707 894-9800	4182
Dyna-King Inc	3949	F	707 894-5566	22792
Indian Head Industries Inc	3714	D	707 894-3333	19689
MGM Brakes	3714	D	707 894-3333	19719
New World Manufacturing Inc	3069	F	707 894-5257	9342
Peay Vineyards LLC	2084	F	707 894-8720	1860
Reuser Inc	2421	F	707 894-4224	3944
Treasury Wine Estates Americas	2084	E	707 894-2541	1968

CLOVIS, CA - Fresno County

	SIC	EMP	PHONE	ENTRY #
Anlin Industries	2431	C	800 287-7996	3993
Atmf Inc	3471	E	559 299-6836	12938
Excelsior Machine Inc	3599	F	559 291-7710	15942
Fresno Precision Plastics Inc (PA)	3089	F	559 323-9595	9795
Kw Automotive North Amer Inc	3714	E	800 445-3767	19703
Machine Exprnce & Design Inc	3599	E	559 291-7710	16164
Mb2 Raceway Clovis Inc (PA)	3644	F	559 298-7223	16951
MI Rancho Tortilla Inc	2099	D	559 299-3183	2550
Preferred Wire Products Inc	3496	F	559 324-0140	13428
Redcort Software Inc	7372	F	559 434-8544	24352
Rosettis Fine Foods Inc	2051	F	559 323-6450	1269
Snowflake Designs	2253	E	559 291-6234	2801
Valley Chrome Plating Inc	3471	D	559 298-8094	13127
Viking Ready Mix Co Inc	3273	E	559 225-3667	10861
Wawona Frozen Foods (PA)	2037	A	559 299-2901	934
Western Dning - Schneider Cafe	3699	E	559 292-1981	19442

COACHELLA, CA - Riverside County

	SIC	EMP	PHONE	ENTRY #
Armtec Countermeasures Co (DH)	3812	F	760 398-0143	20537
Armtec Defense Products Co (DH)	3489	B	760 398-0143	13281
Ernie Ball Inc	3931	D	800 543-2255	22619
Paladar Mfg Inc	3931	D	760 775-4222	22631
Reyes Coca-Cola Bottling LLC	2086	D	760 396-4500	2143
Roto Lite Inc	3089	E	909 923-4353	10028

COALINGA, CA - Fresno County

	SIC	EMP	PHONE	ENTRY #
Aera Energy LLC	3533	E	559 935-7418	13763
Valley Garlic Inc	2035	E	559 934-1763	904

COLFAX, CA - Placer County

	SIC	EMP	PHONE	ENTRY #
Crispinian Inc	2082	E	530 346-8411	1515
Fox Barrel Cider Company Inc	2084	E	530 346-9699	1708
M B I Ready-Mix L L C	3273	E	530 346-2432	10799
Transworld Printing Svcs Inc	2752	F	209 982-1511	6896

COLMA, CA - San Mateo County

	SIC	EMP	PHONE	ENTRY #
Christy Vault Company (PA)	3272	E	650 994-1378	10550

COLTON, CA - San Bernardino County

	SIC	EMP	PHONE	ENTRY #
Alfonso Jaramillo	3495	F	951 276-2777	13372
Als Garden Art Inc (PA)	3299	B	909 424-0221	10995
Archer-Daniels-Midland Company	2041	F	909 783-7574	989
Ardent Mills LLC	2041	E	951 201-1170	994
Black Diamond Blade Company (PA)	3531	F	800 949-9014	13710
Boyd Specialties LLC	2013	D	909 219-5120	442
C and R Sales Inc	3441	F	951 686-6864	11754
Cal Portland Cement Co	3273	E	909 423-0436	10701
California Churros Corporation	2051	C	909 370-4777	1172
Calportland Company	3241	E	909 825-4260	10405
Cemex Materials LLC	3273	E	909 825-1500	10741
Clariant Corporation	2672	E	909 825-1793	5360
Computerized Embroidery Co	2395	F	909 825-3841	3735
Coronado Equipment Sales	3537	F	877 830-7447	13862
County of San Bernardino	3821	E	909 580-0015	20752
Darnell-Rose Inc	3429	F	626 912-1688	11586
E-Z Up Directcom	2394	F	909 426-0060	3681
Elizabeth Shutters Inc	3442	E	909 825-1531	11952
Erf Enterprises Inc	3713	F	909 825-4080	19532
Hawa Corporation	2013	E	909 825-8882	463
HC Brill	2053	B	909 825-7343	1342
Hydro Conduit of Texas LP	3272	F	909 825-1500	10587
La Carreta Food Products	2099	E	909 825-0737	2504
Leemco Inc (PA)	3491	F	909 422-0088	13310
Lrb Millwork & Casework Inc	2431	F	951 328-0105	4077
Masterbrand Cabinets Inc	2434	E	951 686-3614	4223
McNeilus Truck and Mfg Inc	3713	E	909 370-2100	19545
Microdyne Plastics Inc	3089	D	909 503-4010	9895
Mrs Redds Pie Co Inc	2051	E	909 825-4800	1246
Ostoich Diesel Service	3594	F	909 885-0590	15631
Panadent Corporation	3843	E	909 783-1841	22179
Paul Hubbs Construction Inc (PA)	1429	F	951 360-3990	318
S & S Installations Inc	3589	E	909 370-1730	15573
Saab Enterprises Inc	2013	D	909 823-2228	494
Show Offs	2541	E	909 885-5223	4938
Sulzer Electro-Mechanical Serv	7694	E	909 825-7971	24697
US Rubber Recycling Inc	3069	E	909 825-1200	9383
Williams Furnace Co (HQ)	3585	C	562 450-3602	15475
Wirz & Co	2752	F	909 825-6970	6941
Wrenchware Inc	3263	F	951 784-2717	10472

COLUMBIA, CA - Tuolumne County

	SIC	EMP	PHONE	ENTRY #
Columbia Communications Inc	3663	F	203 533-0252	17489
Gerard H Tanzi Inc	3556	F	209 532-0855	14368

COLUSA, CA - Colusa County

	SIC	EMP	PHONE	ENTRY #
American Carports Inc (PA)	3448	F	866 730-9865	12530
Riverbend Rice Mill Inc	2044	F	530 458-8561	1050

COMMERCE, CA - Los Angeles County

	SIC	EMP	PHONE	ENTRY #
4 What Its Worth Inc (PA)	2331	F	323 728-4503	3133
A-1 Metal Products Inc	3444	E	323 721-3334	12082
Aahs Enterprises Inc	3993	F	323 838-9130	23037
AB&r Inc	2339	E	323 727-0007	3280
Abisco Products Co	2782	E	562 906-9330	7301
Acclaim Lighting LLC	3646	F	323 213-4626	17006
Advance Screen Graphic	2759	F	323 724-9910	6975
Advanced Process Services Inc	3491	E	323 278-6530	13287
Ajg Inc	2386	E	323 346-0171	3506
Alarin Aircraft Hinge Inc	3429	E	323 725-1666	11560
Alcast Mfg Inc (PA)	3365	E	310 542-3581	11365
Allegro Pacific Corporation	3172	F	323 724-0101	10231
Alliance Apparel Inc	2331	E	323 888-8900	3136
Alloy Machining and Honing Inc	3599	F	323 726-8248	15723
Alloy Machining Services Inc	3599	F	323 725-2545	15724
AM Retail Group Inc	2335	E	323 728-8996	3212
Amcor Flexibles LLC	2671	C	323 721-6777	5322
American & Efird LLC	2284	D	323 724-6884	2889
American Brass & Alum Fndry Co	3432	E	800 545-9988	11654
American Graphic Board Inc	2679	E	323 721-0585	5491
American Intl Inds Inc	2844	A	323 728-2999	8435
American Scale Co Inc	3596	F	323 269-0305	15639
Apex Drum Company Inc	2449	F	323 721-8994	4411
Arbo Box Inc	2441	E	562 404-2726	4328
Architectural Enterprises Inc	3446	E	323 268-4000	12452
Ardent Mills LLC	2041	F	323 725-0771	995
Arevalo Tortilleria Inc	2099	E	323 888-1711	2395
Arthurmade Plastics Inc	3089	D	323 721-7325	9641
Asco Sintering Co	3429	E	323 725-3550	11564
Atk Space Systems Inc (DH)	3812	E	323 722-0222	20541
Avery Dennison Corporation	2672	C	323 728-8888	5355
B & B Battery (usa) Inc (PA)	3692	E	323 278-1900	19178

GEOGRAPHIC

Company	SIC	EMP	PHONE	ENTRY #
Ball of Cotton Inc	2253	E	323 888-9448	2773
Biorx Pharmaceuticals Inc	2834	E	323 725-3100	7812
Blisterpak Inc	3089	E	323 728-5555	9666
Bonded Fiberloft Inc	2211	B	323 726-7820	2671
Bottlemate Inc	3089	E	323 887-9009	9671
Bridge Publications Inc (PA)	2731	E	323 888-6200	6081
C-Quest Inc	2331	D	323 980-1400	3147
Canvas Specialty Inc	2394	E	323 722-1156	3677
Capitol Steel Fabricators Inc	3441	E	323 721-5460	11761
Cappac Plastic Products	3086	E	323 721-7542	9512
Carmi Flvr & Fragrance Co Inc (PA)	2087	E	323 888-9240	2199
Cee Sportswear	2339	E	323 726-8158	3303
Century Wire & Cable Inc	3357	D	213 236-8879	11296
Chameleon Beverage Company Inc (PA)	2086	D	323 724-8223	2055
Colorcom Inc	2752	F	323 246-4640	6497
Commercial Intr Resources Inc	2512	D	562 926-5885	4633
Connected Apparel Company LLC (PA)	2339	E	323 890-8000	3308
Crystolon Inc	2542	F	323 725-3482	4971
Ctd Machines Inc	3541	E	213 689-4455	13908
Cure Apparel LLC	2331	F	562 927-7460	3151
Datapage Inc	2759	E	323 725-7500	7043
Deamco Corporation	3535	D	323 890-1190	13822
Deco Enterprises Inc	3646	D	323 726-2575	17023
Deskmakers Inc	2521	E	323 264-2260	4795
Dynaflex Products (PA)	3713	E	323 724-1555	19530
E & J Gallo Winery	2084	B	323 720-6400	1685
E-Z Plastic Packaging Corp	2673	E	323 887-0123	5395
El Clasificado	2741	D	323 278-5310	6227
Elation Lighting Inc	3646	D	323 582-3322	17026
Elite Comfort Solutions LLC	3086	C	323 266-0422	9526
Elite Lighting	3648	C	323 888-1973	17121
Evy of California Inc (HQ)	2361	E	213 746-4647	3478
Fairway Trading Inc	2241	F	323 582-8111	2752
Fast Sportswear Inc	2339	E	323 720-1078	3326
Faustinos Chair Factory Inc	2521	F	323 724-8055	4796
Fleming Metal Fabricators	3713	E	323 723-8203	19533
Floride Products LLC (PA)	2819	E	323 201-4363	7497
Fungs Village Inc	2098	E	323 881-1600	2369
Furniture Technics Inc	2511	F	562 802-0261	4573
Galaxy Enterprises Inc	3999	E	323 728-3980	23339
Gehr Industries Inc (HQ)	3357	C	323 728-5558	11305
General Industrial Repair	3599	F	323 278-0873	15991
Ginger Golden Products Inc	2035	E	323 838-1070	883
Globe Iron Foundry Inc	3321	D	323 723-8983	11143
Gold Coast Ingredients Inc	2099	D	323 724-8935	2471
Guardian Survival Gear Inc	3842	F	760 519-5643	22019
Haley Indus Ctings Linings Inc	3479	F	323 588-8086	13189
Hangers Randy West Coast Ctr	3315	F	323 728-2253	11096
Heeger Inc	3621	F	323 728-5108	16653
Heritage Distributing Company (PA)	2026	E	323 838-1225	702
Hollywood Bed Spring Mfg Inc	3429	D	323 887-9500	11597
Hospitality Wood Products Inc	2431	F	562 806-5564	4056
Hse Usa Inc (PA)	3999	F	323 278-0888	23357
Huhtamaki Inc	3086	B	323 269-0151	9551
Hurley International LLC	2329	F	323 728-1821	3089
Image Micro Spare Parts Inc	3621	F	562 776-9808	16656
In Pro Car Wear Inc	3648	F	323 724-0568	17135
Indio Products Inc	2899	E	323 720-9117	8979
Ingenue Inc	2015	D	323 726-8084	519
Ink Makers Inc	2893	F	323 728-7500	8921
Interstate Meat Co Inc	3556	F	323 838-9400	14375
J & F Design Inc	2339	D	323 526-4444	3340
JC Window Fashions Inc	2591	E	909 364-8888	5027
JP Products LLC	2511	E	310 237-6237	4579
Jr Grease Services	2077	E	323 318-2096	1461
Jsl Foods Inc	2099	D	323 727-9999	2494
Just For Wraps Inc (PA)	2339	C	213 239-0503	3351
Kaiser Aluminum Corporation	3354	E	323 726-8011	11234
Kaiser Aluminum Fab Pdts LLC	3354	C	323 722-7151	11235
Kirk API Containers	3089	E	323 278-5400	9867
La Bath Vanity Inc	2434	F	909 303-3323	4220
La Xpress Air & Heating Svcs	2741	D	310 856-9678	6267
LCI Laundry Inc	2335	C	323 767-1900	3241
Liberty Packg & Extruding Inc	2673	E	323 722-5124	5401
Lion Tank Line Inc	2911	E	323 726-1966	9050
Los Angeles Board Mills Inc	2631	C	323 685-8900	5166
Lucky Star Silkscreen LLC	2759	E	323 728-4071	7127
Maidenform LLC	2341	C	323 724-9558	3444
Martin Sprocket & Gear Inc	3566	F	323 728-8117	14746
Mascorro Leather Inc	3172	D	323 724-6759	10240
Mastertaste Inc	2087	D	323 727-2100	2220
Matthew Warren Inc	3493	D	800 237-5225	13340
Mega Sign Inc	3993	E	888 315-7446	23158
MGM Transformer Co	3612	D	323 726-0888	16562
Milestones Products Inc	2844	F	323 728-3434	8539
Mojave Foods Corporation	2099	C	323 890-8900	2555
Monogram Aerospace Fas Inc (HQ)	3429	C	323 722-4760	11614
Motorshield LLC	2851	F	323 396-9200	8659
MSE Media Solutions Inc	3695	E	323 721-1656	19226
Nanoflowx LLC	3479	E	323 396-9200	13210
Ni Industries Inc	3449	E	309 283-3355	12596
Nico Nat Mfg Corp	2541	E	323 721-1900	4922
Norstar Office Products Inc (PA)	2521	E	323 262-1919	4812
Nova Lifestyle Inc (PA)	2511	E	323 888-9999	4599
Oakhurst Industries Inc (PA)	2051	C	323 724-3000	1252
Oldcastle Buildingenvelope Inc	3231	D	323 722-2007	10383
Pacific Coast Home Furn Inc (PA)	2392	F	323 838-7808	3633
Pacific Die Casting Corp	3363	C	323 725-1308	11343
Pacific Hospitality Design Inc	2531	E	323 587-4289	4868
Pacific Spice Company Inc	2099	D	323 726-9190	2580
Pacific Testtronics Inc	3999	D	323 721-1077	23440
Pacific Vial Mfg Inc	3221	E	323 721-7004	10292
PCI Industries Inc	3444	D	323 728-0004	12329
Pearlman Enterprises Inc (DH)	3291	C	800 969-5561	10953
Piccone Apparel Corp	2339	E	310 559-6702	3387
Pioneer Broach Company (PA)	3545	D	323 728-1263	14184
Pommes Frites Candle Co	3999	E	213 488-2016	23450
Portos Food Product Inc	2051	D	323 480-8400	1263
Precision Wire Products Inc (PA)	3496	C	323 890-9100	13427
Premier Plastics Inc	2673	E	213 725-0502	5411
Progressive Label Inc	2679	E	323 415-9770	5524
Protrend Ltd (HQ)	2335	F	323 832-9323	3252
Quantum Concept Inc	2329	F	323 888-8601	3114
RDD Enterprises Inc	2311	F	213 746-0020	2974
Romac Supply Co Inc	3613	D	323 721-5810	16611
S Bravo Systems Inc	3443	E	323 888-4133	12049
Samson Pharmaceuticals Inc	2834	E	323 722-3066	8117
Samson Products Inc	2542	B	323 726-9070	5001
Scotch Paint Corporation	2851	E	310 329-1259	8678
Sentiments Inc (PA)	3999	F	323 843-2080	23473
SGC International Inc	3211	E	323 318-2998	10274
Shelter International Inc	2499	E	323 888-8856	4534
Sherwin-Williams Company	2295	E	323 726-7272	2898
Shugar Soapworks Inc	2841	F	323 234-2874	8350
Sid E Parker Boiler Mfg Co Inc	3443	D	323 727-9800	12051
Signature Flexible Packg Inc	2891	D	323 887-1997	8894
Siho Corporation	2339	F	323 721-4000	3406
Snak Club LLC	2068	E	323 278-9578	1438
Soft Gel Technologies Inc (HQ)	2834	D	323 726-0700	8136
Southern California Soap Co	2841	F	323 888-1332	8351
Specialty Enterprises Co	3086	D	323 726-9721	9569
Stitch Industries Inc	2512	E	888 282-0842	4672
Sugar Foods Corporation	2051	D	323 727-8290	1279
Sun Plastics Inc	2673	E	323 888-6999	5422
Superb Chair Corporation	2512	E	562 776-1771	4673
Superior-Studio Spc Inc	3999	E	323 278-0100	23493
Tapestry Inc	3171	E	323 725-6792	10228
Tdg Operations LLC	2273	E	323 724-9000	2883
Teichman Enterprises Inc	2542	E	323 278-9000	5006
Torah-Aura Productions Inc	2731	F	323 585-1847	6156
Touch Litho Company	2752	F	562 927-8899	6893
Transdigm Inc	3728	C	323 269-9181	20252
Transdigm Inc	3728	C	323 269-9181	20253
Transdigm Inc	3728	C	323 269-9181	20254
Trixxi Clothing Company Inc (PA)	2331	E	323 585-4200	3201
Ultimate Metal Finishing Corp	3479	F	323 890-9100	13262
Ultra Pro Acquisition LLC	2782	C	323 725-1975	7319
Ultra Pro International LLC (PA)	2782	D	323 890-2100	7320
Urban Expressions Inc	3171	E	310 593-4574	10230
US Polymers Inc	3354	C	323 727-6888	11252
Viatech Pubg Solutions Inc	2782	D	323 721-3629	7324
W R Grace & Co	2819	F	562 927-8513	7536
West Coast Catrg Trcks Mfg Inc	2511	F	323 278-1279	4619
Westcoast Inksolutions LLC	2893	F	323 726-8100	8937
Wiretech Inc (PA)	3315	D	323 722-4933	11116
X-Igent Printing Inc	2752	F	323 837-9779	6946
Yavar Manufacturing Co Inc	2657	E	323 722-2040	5320

COMPTCHE, CA - Mendocino County

Company	SIC	EMP	PHONE	ENTRY #
Wells Dental Inc	3843	F	707 937-0521	22205

COMPTON, CA - Los Angeles County

Company	SIC	EMP	PHONE	ENTRY #
A & V Engineering Inc	3599	F	310 637-9906	15657
AAA Plating & Inspection Inc	3471	D	323 979-8930	12898
Accurate Anodizing Inc	3471	D	310 637-0349	12901
Ace Clearwater Enterprises Inc	3544	F	310 538-5380	14007
Advanced Materials Inc (HQ)	3086	F	310 537-5444	9500
Alameda Construction Svcs Inc	1442	E	310 635-3277	329
Allan Kidd	3643	E	310 762-1600	16875
American Dawn Inc (PA)	2299	D	310 223-2000	2922
Andrew Alexander Inc	3111	D	323 752-0066	10136

2020 California
Manufacturers Register

(P-0000) Products & Services Section entry number
(PA)=Parent Co (HQ)=Headquarters (DH)=Div Headquarters

Company	SIC	EMP	PHONE	ENTRY #
Anoroc Precision Shtmtl Inc	3444	E	310 515-6015	12112
Audio Video Color Corporation **(PA)**	2671	D	424 213-7500	5324
Barkens Hardchrome Inc	3559	F	310 632-2000	14431
Bay Cities Italian Bakery Inc	2051	F	310 608-1881	1143
Bestway Hydraulics Co Inc	3561	E	310 639-2507	14561
BHC Industries Inc	3471	E	310 632-2000	12942
Bodycote Thermal Proc Inc	3398	E	310 604-8000	11436
Bowman Plating Co Inc	3471	C	310 639-4343	12949
Bruce Iversen	2448	E	310 537-4168	4352
Cal Pipe Manufacturing Inc **(PA)**	3498	E	562 803-4388	13462
California Decor	2431	E	310 603-9944	4008
California Metal Group Inc	3444	F	310 609-1400	12146
California Pak Intl Inc	3612	E	310 223-2500	16542
Cemex Cnstr Mtls PCF LLC	3273	F	310 603-9122	10733
Chem-Tainer Industries Inc	3089	E	310 635-5400	9707
Chemtex Print USA Inc	2759	E	310 900-1818	7021
Circle Industrial Mfg Corp **(PA)**	3567	E	310 638-5101	14757
Circle Industrial Mfg Corp.	3542	E	310 638-5101	13974
CK Steel Inc	3441	F	310 638-0855	11767
Complete Truck Body Repair Inc	3713	F	323 445-2675	19523
Concrete Mold Corporation	3544	E	310 537-5171	14038
Continental Forge Company **(PA)**	3463	D	310 603-1014	12731
Cotton Knits Trading	2259	E	310 884-9600	2817
Cri Sub 1 **(DH)**	2521	F	310 537-1657	4794
Crossfield Products Corp **(PA)**	2821	E	310 886-9100	7551
De Menno-Kerdoon Trading Co **(HQ)**	2911	C	310 537-7100	9045
Demenno Kerdoon	1382	C	310 537-7100	119
E M E Inc.	3471	E	310 639-1621	12991
Edmund Kim International Inc **(PA)**	2329	E	310 604-1100	3078
Electronic Stamping Corp	3613	E	310 639-2120	16599
Epsilon Plastics Inc	2673	D	310 609-1320	5396
ESP Corp	3679	E	310 639-2535	18907
Essilor Laboratories Amer Inc	3851	E	310 604-8668	22354
Excellon Acquisition LLC **(HQ)**	3559	E	310 668-7700	14463
Fastener Innovation Tech Inc	3451	D	310 538-1111	12631
First Choice International	3841	F	310 537-1500	21713
Fleetwood Continental Inc	3366	D	310 609-1477	11397
Flowserve Corporation	3561	E	310 667-4220	14573
Fmf Racing	3751	C	310 631-4363	20401
Foam Fabricators Inc	3089	F	310 537-5760	9790
Foam Factory Inc	3086	E	310 603-9808	9532
Forming Specialties Inc.	3728	E	310 639-1122	20108
Foster Poultry Farms	2015	B	310 223-1499	517
Fs - Precision Tech Co LLC	3369	E	310 638-0595	11417
GP Design Inc	2396	E	310 638-8737	3790
Graphic Prints Inc.	2396	E	310 768-0474	3791
Hammond Power Solutions Inc	3612	E	310 537-4690	16554
Henkel US Operations Corp.	2843	C	310 764-4600	8428
Hf Group Inc **(PA)**	3861	E	310 605-0755	22424
Idemia America Corp.	3089	C	310 884-7900	9835
Ilco Industries Inc	3498	E	310 631-8655	13472
Innovative Stamping Inc.	3469	E	310 537-6996	12822
International Paper Company	2621	F	310 639-2310	5117
Ips Corporation **(HQ)**	2891	C	310 898-3300	8878
J&T Designs LLC	2599	E	310 868-5190	5067
James Kim Young	2339	E	310 605-5328	3341
Jaubin Sales & Mfg Corp	3444	F	310 631-8647	12252
Jbi LLC	2514	E	310 537-2910	4692
Jimway Inc	3648	D	310 886-3718	17137
Kens Spray Equipment Inc **(DH)**	3479	D	310 635-9995	13197
Kim & Roy Co Inc	2326	F	310 762-1896	3040
Kizure Product Co Inc	3634	E	310 604-0058	16832
Kmr Label LLC	2754	E	310 603-8910	6957
Lamons Gasket Company	3053	F	310 886-1133	9242
Lekos Dye & Finishing Inc	2231	D	310 763-0900	2746
LMC Enterprises	2842	E	310 632-7124	8394
Los Angles Tmes Cmmnctions LLC	2711	F	310 638-9414	5715
Lynwood Pattern Service Inc	3365	F	310 631-2225	11384
M N M Manufacturing Inc	3442	D	310 898-1099	11967
Magnesium Alloy Pdts Co Inc	3366	E	310 605-1440	11401
Magnesium Alloy Products Co LP	3363	E	323 636-2276	11342
Mainetti USA Inc.	2759	F	562 741-2920	7129
McCormick Fresh Herbs LLC	2099	D	323 278-9750	2549
Mercado Latino Inc	3999	E	310 537-1062	23408
Morrells Electro Plating Inc	3471	E	310 639-1024	13055
Nabors Well Services Co	1389	C	310 639-7074	230
One Up Manufacturing LLC	2631	E	310 749-8347	5169
Optex Incorporated	3669	F	800 966-7839	17751
Orion Plastics Corporation	2821	E	310 223-0370	7589
Owens Corning Sales LLC	2952	C	310 631-1062	9123
Pacific Contntl Textiles Inc **(HQ)**	2269	E	310 604-1100	2858
Park Steel Co Inc	3441	F	310 638-6101	11862
Pedro Pallan	2051	F	310 638-1763	1260
Performance Composites Inc.	3229	D	310 328-6661	10326
Permalite Plastics Corp	2865	E	310 669-9492	8703
Plaskolite West LLC	2821	E	310 637-2103	7592
Precision Babbitt Co Inc	3568	F	562 531-9173	14789
Prime Alliance LLC	2258	E	310 764-1000	2814
Prime Wheel Corporation	3714	E	310 516-9126	19741
Prison Ride Share Network	2741	E	314 703-5245	6317
Puratos Corporation	3556	E	310 632-1361	14394
Rsk Tool Incorporated	3089	E	310 537-3302	10034
S & K Plating Inc	3471	E	310 632-7141	13091
Sequoia Pure Water Inc	2086	E	310 637-8500	2166
Serra Manufacturing Corp **(PA)**	3469	E	310 537-4560	12871
Sew What Inc	2391	E	310 639-6000	3597
Simso Tex Sublimation **(PA)**	2396	D	310 885-9717	3813
South Coast Screen and Casing	3533	F	310 632-3200	13791
Ssb Manufacturing Company	2515	C	770 512-7700	4747
Tag Toys Inc	3999	D	310 639-4566	23498
Tajima USA Inc.	3552	E	310 604-8200	14295
Techmer Pm Inc	2821	B	310 632-9211	7619
Technlogy Knwldgable Machining	3469	E	310 608-7756	12881
Thermal Equipment Corporation	3443	F	310 328-6600	12063
Trackstar Printing Inc.	2752	F	310 216-1275	6894
Tridus International Inc.	3499	F	310 884-3200	13552
Ufp Technologies	3086	E	714 662-0277	9574
United Bakery Equipment Co Inc	3556	E	310 635-8121	14410
Utopia Lighting	3612	F	310 327-7711	16580
Viking Rubber Products Inc.	3069	D	310 868-5200	9386
West Coast Aerospace Inc	3965	F	310 632-2064	23017
Zoo Zoo Wham Whams Blip Blops	2299	F	213 248-9591	2957

CONCORD, CA - Contra Costa County

Company	SIC	EMP	PHONE	ENTRY #
Acme Press Inc	2752	D	925 682-1111	6394
Airgas Usa LLC	2813	F	925 969-0419	7405
Alvellan Inc	3599	E	925 689-2421	15734
Baker Petrolite LLC	1389	F	925 682-3313	166
Bcg/Management Resources	7372	F	800 456-8474	23655
Beko Radiator Cores Inc	3714	E	925 671-2975	19591
Benchmark Electronics Inc.	3672	B	925 363-1151	17837
Biomicrolab Inc	3596	E	925 689-1200	15640
C&T Publishing Inc.	2741	E	925 677-0377	6210
Cable Manufacturing Tech	2298	E	925 687-3700	2908
Cache Phlow Enterprise	2782	F	925 609-8649	7305
Caffe Classico Foods Inc	2095	F	925 602-5400	2283
Calex Mfg Co Inc.	3679	E	925 687-4411	18849
Carols Roman Shades Inc	2591	E	925 674-9622	5018
Cemex Cnstr Mtls PCF LLC	3273	E	925 688-1025	10720
Cerus Corporation **(PA)**	2836	C	925 288-6000	8287
Clearwater Paper Corporation	2621	A	925 947-4700	5100
Cole Print & Marketing	2752	F	925 276-2344	6493
Contra Costa Newspapers Inc.	2711	C	925 977-8520	5601
Coolsystems Inc **(HQ)**	3845	C	888 426-3732	22244
Cubic Trnsp Systems Inc	3829	C	925 348-9163	21456
D & D Security Resources Inc **(PA)**	3699	F	800 453-4195	19287
Delta Rebar Services Inc	3441	F	925 798-4220	11784
Delta Turnstiles LLC	3699	F	925 969-1498	19289
Dresser-Rand Company	3563	E	925 356-5700	14629
Eagle Iron Fabrication Inc	3441	F	925 686-9510	11787
Energy Steel Corporation	3599	E	925 685-5300	15932
Epidemic Ales	2082	F	925 566-8850	1525
Erg Transit Systems (usa) Inc	3589	C	925 686-8233	15511
Esmart Source Inc.	7372	F	408 739-3500	23875
Fresenius Usa Inc **(DH)**	2834	C	925 288-4218	7898
Frito-Lay North America Inc	2096	E	925 689-4260	2326
G Hartzell & Son Inc	3843	F	925 798-2206	22156
Gagne-Mulford Enterprises	3069	F	925 671-7434	9310
Ggf Marble & Supply Inc	3281	F	925 676-8385	10907
GM Marble & Granite Inc	1429	F	925 676-8385	314
Hnc Printing Services LLC	2752	F	925 771-2080	6615
Hyde Printing and Graphics	2752	F	925 686-4933	6620
I3 Nanotec LLC	3559	E	510 594-2299	14476
Indepndnt Flr Tstg Insptn Inc	3272	F	925 676-7682	10588
Laserbeam Software LLC	7372	E	925 459-2595	24090
Lehigh Southwest Cement Co **(DH)**	3241	F	972 653-5500	10422
Marketing Bus Advantage Inc	3559	F	925 933-3637	14494
Marvac Scientific Mfg Co	3821	F	925 825-4636	20765
Monterey Mechanical Co	3444	F	925 689-6670	12310
Nalco Company LLC	2899	F	800 798-2247	9005
New Logic Research Inc	3559	D	510 655-7305	14507
Pacific Instruments Inc.	3829	F	925 827-9010	21517
Pacific Plaza Imports Inc.	2091	F	925 349-4000	2248
Patriot Mritime Compliance LLC	3731	F	925 296-2000	20301
PPG Industries Inc	2851	F	925 708-0539	8664
Print-N-Stuff Inc.	2752	F	925 798-3212	6797
Pulse Systems LLC	3842	F	925 798-4080	22074
Renaissance Precision Mfg Inc	3599	F	925 691-5997	16353
Sage **(PA)**	2836	C	925 288-4827	8327
Siemens Med Solutions USA Inc	3845	B	925 246-8200	22309
Smith & Nephew Inc.	3842	E	925 681-3300	22088

Employment Codes: A=Over 500 employees, B=251-500,
C=101-250, D=51-100, E=20-50, F=10-19

2020 California
Manufacturers Register

© Mergent Inc. 1-800-342-5647

1323

GEOGRAPHIC

	SIC	EMP	PHONE	ENTRY #
Specialized Graphics Inc	3993	E	925 680-0265	23214
Sun Chemical Corporation	2893	F	925 695-2601	8931
Superheat Fgh Services Inc	3398	F	925 808-6711	11469
Systron Donner Inertial Inc	3679	C	925 979-4400	19099
Tech Air Northern Cal LLC	2813	F	925 568-9353	7454
Tuff Shed Inc	2452	F	925 681-3492	4467
West Coast Windows & Doors Inc	3089	F	925 681-1776	10120

COOL, CA - El Dorado County

	SIC	EMP	PHONE	ENTRY #
A Teichert & Son Inc	1442	F	530 885-4244	324

COPPEROPOLIS, CA - Calaveras County

	SIC	EMP	PHONE	ENTRY #
Custom Equipment Coinc	3523	F	209 785-9891	13621
Meridian Gold Inc	1041	C	209 785-3222	7

CORCORAN, CA - Kings County

	SIC	EMP	PHONE	ENTRY #
Camfil USA Inc	3564	D	559 992-5118	14651
Clougherty Packing LLC	2013	F	559 992-8421	448
Corcoran Sawtelle Rosprim Inc	3441	F	559 992-2117	11775
Crookshanks Sales Co Inc	3273	E	559 992-5077	10751
Mar Vista Resources LLC	2873	F	559 992-4535	8797
Virtus Nutrition LLC	2048	F	559 992-5033	1131

CORNING, CA - Tehama County

	SIC	EMP	PHONE	ENTRY #
Barns By Harrahs	3448	F	530 824-4611	12534
Bell-Carter Foods Inc	2035	B	530 528-4820	879
Eco-Shell Inc	3999	F	530 824-8794	23320
Sierra Pacific Industries	2431	B	530 824-2474	4124
Sunsweet Dryers	2034	F	530 824-5854	867
Thomes Creek Rock Co Inc	1442	F	530 824-0191	364

CORONA, CA - Riverside County

	SIC	EMP	PHONE	ENTRY #
2nd Gen Productions Inc	2842	F	800 877-6282	8356
3-V Fastener Co Inc	3452	D	951 734-4391	12663
3M Company	3295	C	951 737-3441	10965
A and M Ornamental Iron & Wldg	3446	F	951 734-6730	12440
Absolute Graphic Tech USA Inc	3625	E	909 597-1133	16693
Accent Plastics Inc (PA)	3089	D	951 273-7777	9601
Accent Plastics Inc	3089	E	951 273-7777	9602
Accurate Grinding and Mfg Corp	3724	F	951 479-0909	19943
Ace Heaters LLC	3585	E	951 738-2230	15407
Acker Stone Industries Inc (HQ)	3272	E	951 674-0047	10526
Acromil LLC	3728	D	951 808-9929	20002
Actavis LLC	2834	F	951 493-5582	7722
Actavis LLC	2834	F	909 270-1400	7723
Actron Manufacturing Inc	3429	F	951 371-0885	11558
Adomani Inc	3714	F	951 407-9860	19565
Adura Led Solutions LLC	3672	F	714 660-2944	17806
Advanced Flow Engineering Inc (PA)	3714	F	951 493-7155	19569
Aero-Craft Hydraulics Inc	3728	F	951 736-4690	20015
Aerospace Seals & Gaskets	3053	F	951 256-8380	9216
Aggregate Mining Products LLC	3561	F	951 277-1267	14558
Airspace Seal and Gasket Corp	3053	F	951 256-8380	9217
All Manufacturers Inc	3841	E	951 280-4200	21590
Alpha Laser	3699	F	951 582-0285	19254
American National Mfg Inc	2515	C	951 273-7888	4710
American Solar Advantage Inc	3674	E	951 496-1075	18093
Ameriflex Inc	3498	F	951 737-5557	13457
AMF Support Surfaces Inc (DH)	2515	C	951 549-6800	4711
Amrapur Overseas Incorporated (PA)	2299	E	714 893-8808	2924
Amron Manufacturing Inc	3728	F	714 278-9204	20035
Anaco Inc	3568	C	951 372-2732	14780
Anatomic Global Inc	2392	C	800 874-7237	3600
Anderson Bros Artistic Iron Co	3499	F	951 898-6880	13498
Approved Aeronautics LLC	3728	F	951 200-3730	20039
Aqua Mix Inc	2842	D	951 256-3040	8363
Aquatic Co (HQ)	3088	D	714 993-1220	9581
Aqueous Technologies Corp	3589	E	909 944-7771	15485
Architectural Design Signs Inc (PA)	3993	D	951 278-0680	23051
Arms Precision Inc	3599	E	951 273-1800	15747
Artistic Plastics Inc	3089	F	951 808-9700	9642
Arvinyl Laminates LP	3081	E	951 371-7800	9393
Aseptic Sitons USA Vntures LLC	2086	C	951 736-9230	2040
Asturies Manufacturing Co Inc	3728	E	951 270-1766	20046
Avalon Mfg Co Incoirporated	3556	F	951 340-0280	14347
B & G Aerospace Metals	3369	E	951 738-8133	11410
B/E Aerospace Inc	3728	D	951 278-4563	20052
Band-It Rubber Company Inc	3069	F	951 735-5072	9287
Best- In- West	2395	E	909 947-6507	3725
Big Gun Inc	3714	F	714 970-0423	19593
Bills Pipes Inc	3751	F	951 371-1329	20385
Bimbo Bakeries Usa Inc	2051	F	951 280-9044	1148
Blue Desert International Inc	3589	D	951 273-7575	15493
Brasscraft Manufacturing Co	3494	D	951 735-4375	13349
Bu LLC	2082	E	951 277-7470	1507
C S America Inc (HQ)	2282	E	323 583-7627	2887
Cadence Gourmet LLC	2099	E	951 272-5949	2415

	SIC	EMP	PHONE	ENTRY #
Cal Precision Inc	3599	F	951 273-9901	15817
Caliber Sealing Solutions Inc (PA)	3053	F	949 461-0555	9221
California Wire Products Corp	3496	E	951 371-7730	13401
Carr Management Inc	3089	D	951 277-4800	9697
Carter Holt Harvey Holdings	3312	D	951 272-8180	11036
Case Automation Corporation	3535	F	951 493-6666	13817
Century Blinds Inc	2591	D	951 734-3762	5019
Certainteed Corona Inc	3089	C	951 272-1300	9702
Chandler Aggregates Inc (PA)	1411	E	951 277-1341	290
Circor Aerospace Inc	3728	A	951 270-6200	20071
Circor Aerospace Inc (HQ)	3491	C	951 270-6200	13298
Circor Aerospace Pdts Group	3324	B	951 270-6200	11156
Clarcor Air Filtration Pdts	3564	F	951 272-1850	14653
Clear Path Technologies Inc	3699	F	951 278-3520	19274
Club Speed LLC	7372	E	951 817-7073	23755
Columbia Aluminum Products LLC	3354	D	323 728-7361	11228
Computer Service Company	3669	F	951 738-1444	17721
Computrus Inc	3443	E	951 245-9103	12008
Corona Magnetics Inc	3677	C	951 735-7558	18709
Cramer Engineering Inc	3599	E	562 903-5556	15868
Creative Color Printing Inc	2752	F	951 737-4551	6521
Cremach Tech Inc (PA)	3541	D	951 735-3194	13906
Cremach Tech Inc	3541	F	951 735-3194	13907
Crescent Woodworking Co Ltd	2511	F	909 673-9955	4562
CTA Manufacturing Inc	2393	E	951 280-2400	3656
Currie Enterprises	3714	E	714 528-6957	19626
Custom Quality Door & Trim Inc	2431	F	951 278-0066	4026
Dacon Systems Inc	3357	F	951 735-2100	11299
Dairy Farmers America Inc	2026	F	951 493-4900	693
Dart Container Corp California (PA)	3086	B	951 735-8115	9521
Data Physics Corporation	3559	E	408 216-8443	14451
Decra Roofing Systems Inc (DH)	3444	D	951 272-8180	12177
Della Robbia Inc	2515	E	951 372-9199	4718
Developlus Inc	3999	D	951 738-8595	23314
Dietzgen Corporation	2679	E	951 278-3259	5505
Dita Inc (PA)	3851	E	949 599-2700	22348
Do It American Mfg Company LLC	3499	F	951 254-9204	13515
Duonetics	3561	F	951 808-4903	14569
Duralum Products Inc	3355	F	951 736-4500	11259
Eclypse International Corp (PA)	3825	E	951 371-8008	21025
Eibach Springs Inc	3493	D	951 256-8300	13337
Elastomer Technologies Inc	3053	F	951 272-5820	9228
Electrasem Corp	3822	F	951 371-6140	20793
Engineered Food Systems	3589	E	714 921-9913	15510
Ergonomnic Comfort Design Inc	2522	E	951 277-1558	4835
Esl Power Systems Inc	3643	D	800 922-4188	16898
Excel Cabinets Inc	2434	E	951 279-4545	4193
Exide Technologies	3691	E	951 520-0677	19164
Extrumed Inc (DH)	3089	E	951 547-7400	9784
F & L Tools Corporation	3728	F	951 279-1555	20101
Fender Musical Instrs Corp	3931	A	480 596-9690	22620
Fiore Stone Inc	3272	E	909 424-0221	10573
Fireblast Global Inc	3569	F	951 277-8319	14815
Fischer Mold Incorporated	3089	D	951 279-1140	9787
Fischler Investments Inc (DH)	2087	F	951 479-4682	2208
Fleetwood Enterprises Inc (DH)	3799	C	951 354-3000	20509
Fleetwood Enterprises Inc	2451	B	951 750-1971	4446
Fleetwood Homes of Kentucky (DH)	2451	F	800 688-1745	4450
Fletcher Bldg Holdings USA Inc (DH)	3444	D	951 272-8180	12212
Fmk Labs Inc	2844	E	951 736-1212	8493
Four Seasons Restaurant Eqp	3444	E	951 278-9100	12216
Fovell Enterprises Inc	3993	E	951 734-6275	23115
Frutarom	2087	F	951 734-6620	2213
G & N Rubicon Gear Inc	3462	D	951 356-3800	12710
Gail Materials Inc	1442	E	951 667-6106	340
Galleys Plus Custom Cabinets	2434	F	951 278-4596	4201
Gibson Performance Corporation	3714	D	951 372-1220	19672
Glasman Shim & Stamping Inc	3569	F	951 278-8197	14822
Grand Metals Inc	3312	F	310 327-5554	11046
Grand Pacific Fire Protection	3524	F	951 226-8304	13689
Growest Inc (PA)	2084	F	951 638-1000	1739
H & N Tool & Die Co Inc	3542	F	951 372-9071	13976
Handbill Printers LP	2752	F	951 547-5910	6604
Hannan Products Corp (PA)	3565	F	951 735-1587	14709
Hanson Aggregates LLC	3241	E	951 371-7625	10414
Hardy Frames Inc	3312	D	951 245-9525	11047
Harrington Hoists Inc	3536	F	717 665-2000	13847
Hi-Line Industrial Saw and Sup	3425	F	714 921-1600	11553
His Company Inc	2672	F	951 493-0200	5363
Hoosier Plstic Fabrication Inc	3089	C	951 272-3070	9828
Icsn Inc	3363	F	951 687-2305	11339
Imperial Manufacturing Co	3589	C	951 281-1830	15524
Industrial Eqp Solutions Inc	3569	F	951 272-9540	14828
International Wind Inc (PA)	3724	E	562 240-3963	19966
Interstate Cabinet Inc	3999	E	951 736-0777	23366

Mergent email: customerrelations@mergent.com
1324

2020 California
Manufacturers Register

(P-0000) Products & Services Section entry number
(PA)=Parent Co (HQ)=Headquarters (DH)=Div Headquarters

Company	SIC	EMP	PHONE	ENTRY #
Irwin Aviation Inc	3728	E	951 372-9555	20141
J & L Metal Products	3444	F	951 278-0100	12251
Janda Company Inc	3548	E	951 734-1935	14242
Jayco Interface Technology Inc	3679	E	951 738-2000	18963
Jayco Mmi Inc	3679	E	951 738-2000	18964
Jhawar Industries LLC	3567	E	951 340-4646	14767
Johnson Caldraul Inc	3728	E	951 340-1067	20147
K & W Manufacturing Co Inc	3429	F	951 277-3300	11602
K S Printing Inc	2759	F	951 268-5180	7105
Kap Medical	3829	E	951 340-4360	21495
Kobelco Compressors Amer Inc	3563	D	951 739-3030	14633
Kobelco Compressors Amer Inc (DH)	3563	B	951 739-3030	14634
Laticrete International Inc	3241	F	951 277-1776	10419
Lavey Craft Prfmce Boats Inc	3732	F	951 273-9690	20343
Le Elegant Bath Inc	3088	C	951 734-0238	9591
Leepers Wood Turning Co Inc (PA)	2431	D	562 422-6525	4074
Legacy Vulcan LLC	1422	E	714 737-2922	300
Lejon of California Inc	2387	E	951 736-1229	3531
Lock America Inc	3429	F	951 277-5180	11606
Lucas Oil Products Inc (PA)	2992	C	951 270-0154	9151
M & O Perry Industries Inc	3565	E	951 734-9838	14716
Machine Control Tech Inc	3825	F	951 808-0973	21070
Maruhachi Ceramics America Inc	3259	E	800 736-6221	10463
Master Fab Inc	3444	F	951 277-4772	12281
MBC Mattress Co Inc	2515	E	951 371-8044	4731
MCP Industries Inc (PA)	3069	E	951 736-1881	9332
MCP Industries Inc	3432	E	951 736-1313	11673
MD Engineering Inc.	3599	F	951 736-5390	16185
Mec Corona Summit III LLC	2086	C	951 739-6200	2092
Meggitt Airdynamics Inc (DH)	3564	C	951 734-0070	14671
Merit Aluminum Inc (PA)	3354	D	951 335-1770	11238
Merrick Engineering Inc (PA)	3089	C	951 737-6040	9894
Millworx Prcsion Machining Inc	3599	F	951 371-2683	16209
Monson Machine Inc	3599	F	951 736-6615	16222
Monster Beverage Company	2086	A	866 322-4466	2093
Monster Beverage Corporation (PA)	2086	D	951 739-6200	2094
Motor Technology Inc	3621	E	951 270-6200	16663
Multimedia Led Inc (PA)	3679	F	951 280-7500	19022
Nafm LLC	3565	F	951 738-1114	14719
National Certified Fabricators	3677	E	951 278-8992	18728
Navcom Defense Electronics Inc (PA)	3812	D	951 268-9205	20638
Neutronic Stamping & Plating	3471	E	714 964-8900	13060
Nibco Inc	3499	C	951 737-5599	13535
Northrop Grumman Innovation	3764	D	951 520-7300	20467
Northwestern Converting Co	2392	F	800 959-3402	3628
Nucast Industries Inc.	3272	F	951 277-8888	10608
Oak-It Inc.	2431	E	951 735-5973	4098
Omni Connection Intl Inc	3679	B	951 898-6232	19038
Optimum Bioenergy Intl Corp	2833	E	714 903-8872	7680
Organic Bottle Dctg Co LLC	2631	E	951 335-4600	5170
Pacific Packaging McHy LLC	3556	F	951 393-2200	14390
Panel Shop Inc	3613	F	951 739-7000	16605
Panrosa Enterprises Inc.	2841	D	951 339-5888	8347
Paragon Tactical Inc.	3949	F	951 736-9440	22864
Parker-Hannifin Corporation	3594	E	951 280-3800	15634
Peabody Engineering & Sup Inc	3559	E	951 734-7711	14515
Pet Partners Inc (PA)	3999	C	951 279-9888	23446
Pheonicia Inc.	2759	F	951 268-5180	7173
Plas-Tech Sealing Tech LLC	2891	E	951 737-2228	8886
Polyair Inter Pack Inc	2394	D	951 737-7125	3700
Praxair Distribution Inc	2813	E	951 736-8113	7442
Precise Aerospace Mfg Inc	3089	E	951 898-0500	9986
Premier Gear & Machining Inc	3462	E	951 278-5505	12720
Premier Steel Structures Inc	3441	E	951 356-6655	11868
Preproduction Plastics Inc	3089	E	951 340-9680	9991
Price Manufacturing Co Inc.	3451	E	951 371-5660	12648
Pro Circuit Products Inc	3751	F	951 734-3320	20422
Proformance Manufacturing Inc	3469	F	951 279-1230	12862
Programmed Composites Inc.	3728	C	951 520-7300	20205
Progressive Marketing Pdts Inc	3448	D	714 888-1700	12571
PSW Inc	2099	F	951 371-7100	2591
Purosil LLC	2869	F	951 271-3900	8769
Purosil LLC (HQ)	2869	D	951 271-3900	8770
PVA Tepla America Inc (HQ)	3599	F	951 371-2500	16321
Quikrete California LLC	3272	C	951 277-3155	10633
R & J Fabricators Inc.	2599	E	951 817-0300	5077
R & R Stamping Four Slide Corp	3469	D	909 595-6444	12866
R W Lyall & Company Inc (DH)	1382	C	951 270-1500	136
R&M Deese Inc	3993	E	951 734-7342	23182
Rehau Incorporated	3084	F	951 549-9017	9477
Renu Chem Inc	2842	F	951 736-8072	8414
Republic Bag Inc (PA)	2673	C	951 734-9740	5415
RGF Enterprises Inc.	3479	E	951 734-6922	13237
Richards Neon Shop Inc	3993	E	951 279-6767	23186
Robertsons Ready Mix Ltd (HQ)	3273	D	951 493-6500	10824

Company	SIC	EMP	PHONE	ENTRY #
Robertsons Ready Mix Ltd	3273	E	800 834-7557	10826
Roto Power Inc	3089	F	951 751-9850	10029
S C R Molding Inc	3089	F	951 736-5490	10037
Saleen Automotive Inc (PA)	3465	E	800 888-8945	12748
Saleen Incorporated (PA)	3711	B	714 400-2121	19500
Sammons Equipment Mfg Corp	2599	F	951 340-3419	5081
Sas Manufacturing Inc	3679	E	951 734-1808	19076
Service Rock Products Corp	3273	F	760 245-7997	10830
Shim-It Corporation	3728	F	562 467-8600	20232
Simsolve	3312	F	951 898-6880	11070
Sinkpad LLC	3679	F	714 660-2944	19082
Sora Power Inc (PA)	3679	F	951 479-9880	19088
Specialty Finance Inc	3469	E	951 735-5200	12875
Spectra Color Inc	2816	E	951 277-0200	7463
Spenuzza Inc (PA)	3589	C	951 281-1830	15582
Spring Delgau Inc	3495	E	951 371-1000	13388
Sprite Industries Incorporated	3826	E	951 735-1015	21293
Sream Inc.	3231	E	951 245-6999	10391
Stang Industries Inc	3999	F	714 556-0222	23484
Stell Industries Inc.	3448	E	951 369-8777	12575
Sterno Group Companies LLC (HQ)	3589	E	951 682-9600	15586
Sterno Group LLC (DH)	3589	D	800 669-6699	15587
Stj Orthotic Services Inc.	3842	E	951 279-5650	22094
Summit Industries Inc.	3441	E	951 739-5900	11890
Sun Precision Machining Inc.	3599	F	951 817-0056	16427
Superior Ready Mix Concrete LP	3273	E	951 277-3553	10851
Suss McRtec Phtnic Systems Inc	3699	D	951 817-3700	19418
Suss Microtec Inc (HQ)	3559	C	408 940-0300	14541
T-Rex Truck Products Inc	3465	D	800 287-5900	12750
T3 Motion Inc	3751	E	951 737-7300	20428
Tamshell Corp	3089	E	951 272-9395	10079
Taylor Communications Inc	2761	E	951 203-9011	7286
Technicote Inc	2891	E	951 372-0627	8898
Temeka Advertising Inc	2541	F	951 277-2525	4949
Thermal Structures Inc (DH)	3724	B	951 736-9911	19982
Tiffany Coachworks Inc	3711	C	951 657-2680	19508
TNT Plastic Molding Inc (PA)	3089	C	951 808-9700	10087
Tolar Manufacturing Co Inc	3441	D	951 808-0081	11901
Tradenet Enterprise Inc	3993	D	888 595-3956	23231
Tree House Pad & Paper Inc	2678	D	800 213-4184	5485
Trendpoint Systems Inc.	3825	F	925 855-0600	21149
Trical Inc.	2879	F	951 737-6960	8845
TRM Manufacturing Inc.	3081	C	951 256-8550	9424
Tube Technologies Inc	3714	F	951 371-4878	19789
Two Brothers Racing Inc	3751	F	714 550-6070	20434
United Metal Products Inc.	3399	F	951 739-9535	11489
Uniweb Inc (PA)	2542	D	951 279-7999	5009
US Continental Marketing Inc (PA)	2842	C	951 808-8888	8423
Vantage Vehicle Intl Inc.	3694	D	951 735-1200	19205
Vinylvisions Company LLC	2851	E	800 321-8746	8691
Vizualogic LLC	3559	C	407 509-3421	14553
Volvo Construction Eqp & Svcs	3531	C	951 277-7620	13756
W J Ellison Co Inc	3565	F	626 814-4766	14736
Webb-Stotler Engineering	3599	F	951 735-2040	16514
Wellington Foods Inc.	2032	E	562 989-0111	751
Werner Corporation	3273	E	951 277-4586	10872
West Coast Porcelain Inc.	3269	F	951 278-8680	10495
Western Equipment Mfg Inc	3531	F	951 284-2000	13757
Western Sheet Metals Inc.	3444	F	951 272-3600	12435
Westrock Cp LLC	2653	C	951 734-1870	5275
Westrock Cp LLC	2752	D	951 273-7900	6938
Winbo Usa Inc.	3444	F	951 738-9978	12438
Youcare Pharma (usa) Inc.	2834	D	951 258-3114	8192
Zap Printing Incorporated	2752	F	951 734-8181	6948

CORONA DEL MAR, CA - Orange County

Company	SIC	EMP	PHONE	ENTRY #
Duron Incorporated	3559	F	949 721-0900	14453
Pfanner Communications Inc	2721	F	714 227-3579	6002

CORONADO, CA - San Diego County

Company	SIC	EMP	PHONE	ENTRY #
Eagle Newspapers LLC	2711	E	619 437-8800	5622
Earthologytech LLC	3523	E	619 435-5296	13631
Intercom Energy Inc	3612	F	619 863-9644	16558
Makerplace Inc.	3944	F	619 435-1279	22690
Northrop Grumman Systems Corp.	3812	E	619 437-4231	20659
University Blanket & Flag Corp (PA)	2399	F	619 435-4100	3863

CORTE MADERA, CA - Marin County

Company	SIC	EMP	PHONE	ENTRY #
Michaels Furniture Company Inc.	2511	B	916 381-9086	4591
Micromega Systems Inc.	7372	F	415 924-4700	24152
Pacific Catch Inc	2048	F	415 504-6905	1117
Quantum Solar Inc	3674	F	415 924-8140	18502

COSTA MESA, CA - Orange County

Company	SIC	EMP	PHONE	ENTRY #
Adaptive Shelters LLC	2452	F	949 923-5444	4453
Advanced Conservation Technolo	3433	F	714 668-1200	11689
Advanced Micro Instruments Inc	3826	E	714 848-5533	21161

GEOGRAPHIC

CORONA, CA

Company	SIC	EMP	PHONE	ENTRY#
Advanced Prcsion Machining Inc	3599	F	949 650-6113	15700
Agility Fuel Systems LLC	3519	F	256 831-6155	13583
Akzo Nobel Inc	2869	E	714 966-0934	8709
Allura Printing Inc	2752	F	714 433-0200	6405
Analog Devices Inc	3674	E	714 641-9391	18100
Armite Laboratories Inc	2992	F	949 646-9035	9133
Armstrong Petroleum Corp (PA)	1311	E	949 650-4000	22
Associated Microbreweries Inc	2082	D	714 546-2739	1496
Astro Haven Enterprises Inc	3829	F	949 215-3777	21437
Atomic Aquatics Inc (PA)	3949	F	714 375-1433	22751
Auto Club Enterprises	2721	B	714 885-2376	5884
Baier Marine Company Inc	3429	E	800 455-3917	11569
Balboa Water Group LLC (PA)	3625	C	714 384-0384	16702
Batida Inc	2752	F	714 557-4597	6438
Bay Ornamental Iron Inc	3446	E	949 548-1015	12455
Bdfco Inc	3669	D	714 228-2900	17715
Bio Creative Enterprises	2844	F	714 352-3600	8444
Burns Stainless LLC	3714	F	949 631-5120	19600
C-Fab	3429	E	949 646-2616	11575
California Blimps	3721	F	949 650-1183	19886
Caperon Designs Inc	3944	E	714 552-3201	22667
CCI Industries Inc (PA)	3089	E	714 662-3879	9698
Cevians LLC	3211	D	714 619-5135	10262
Chet Cooper	2721	F	949 854-8700	5903
Chup Corporation	2752	F	949 455-0676	6485
Cisco Systems Inc	3577	F	714 434-2100	15193
Coach Inc	3171	F	949 365-0771	10218
Coast Sheet Metal Inc	3444	E	949 645-2224	12158
Concept Studio Inc	3253	F	949 759-0606	10438
Contech Engnered Solutions Inc	3317	A	714 281-7883	11125
Cosmic Fog Vapors	2111	D	949 266-1730	2651
CRP Sports LLC	3999	F	949 395-7759	23307
Crystaliner Corp	3732	E	949 548-0292	20319
Cytec Aerospace Mtls CA Inc	2295	C	714 899-0400	2896
Darcy AK Corporation	3599	F	949 650-5566	15879
Dee Engineering Inc (PA)	3714	F	714 979-4990	19632
Delphi Display Systems Inc	3577	D	714 825-3400	15214
Djh Enterprises	3663	E	714 424-6500	17503
Duffield Marine Inc (PA)	3732	E	760 246-1211	20326
Dynamic Cooking Systems Inc	3589	A	714 372-7000	15508
E Virtual Corporation	3651	F	949 515-3670	17224
Eba Design Inc	2844	F	714 417-9222	8484
Ebanista Inc (PA)	2512	E	949 650-6397	4639
El Metate Foods Inc	2051	F	949 646-9362	1199
Endural LLC	3083	F	714 434-6533	9438
Eq Technologic Inc	7372	E	215 891-9010	23872
Eventure Interactive Inc	7372	F	855 986-5669	23878
Eye Care Network of Cal Inc (PA)	3841	F	714 619-4660	21710
Eyebrain Medical Inc	3851	F	949 339-5157	22356
Falkor Partners LLC	3674	D	714 721-8772	18234
Fineline Woodworking Inc	2431	F	714 540-5468	4044
Fire & Safety Electronics Inc	3625	F	714 850-1320	16716
Fisher & Paykel Appliances Inc (DH)	3639	C	949 790-8900	16850
Fisker Auto & Tech Group LLC	3711	C	714 723-3247	19470
Flare Group	3728	E	714 850-2080	20104
Fxc Corporation	2399	D	714 557-8032	3844
Fxc Corporation (PA)	3429	E	714 556-7400	11590
Gs Manufacturing	3563	F	949 642-1500	14631
Gsp Precision Inc	3599	F	818 845-2212	16006
Hamax America Inc (PA)	3826	F	714 641-7528	21234
Handcraft Mattress Company	2515	F	714 241-8316	4721
Hartley Company	3951	E	949 646-9643	22934
Haze Bert and Assossiates	1389	F	714 557-1567	206
Hurley International LLC (HQ)	2329	C	949 548-9375	3091
Husky Injection Molding	3089	F	714 545-8200	9832
Hw Holdco LLC	2721	E	714 540-8500	5957
Impac Technologies Inc	3663	D	714 427-2000	17541
Indian Ink Screen Print	2759	E	714 437-0882	7096
International Bus Mchs Corp	3571	A	714 472-2237	14927
Irvine Sensors Corporation	3674	E	714 444-8700	18323
Jennis Group LLC	2741	F	714 227-7972	6259
JG Plastics Group LLC	3089	F	714 751-4266	9856
Kelly Pneumatics Inc	3699	F	800 704-7552	19338
Kingsley Mfg Co (PA)	3842	F	949 645-4401	22041
L & L Custom Shutters Inc	2431	C	714 996-9539	4071
L & S Machine Inc	3451	F	562 924-9007	12638
Labworks Inc	3679	F	714 549-1981	18982
Lambda Research Optics Inc	3826	D	714 327-0600	21253
Lava Products Inc	2752	E	949 951-7191	6692
Lexmark International Inc	3577	E	714 641-1007	15274
Livetime Software Inc	7372	F	415 905-4009	24105
Lynx Studio Technology Inc	3651	F	714 545-4700	17253
Macgregor Yacht Corporation	3732	D	310 621-2206	20345
Maurer Marine Inc	3732	F	949 645-7673	20349
Membrane Switch and Panel Inc	3679	F	714 957-6905	19011
Metal X Direct Inc	3446	F	949 336-0055	12499
Mina Product Development Inc	3089	F	714 966-2150	9898
Minute Man Envmtl Systems Inc	2752	E	949 637-5446	6730
Mirth Corporation	7372	E	714 389-1200	24170
Moleculum	2911	F	714 619-5139	9053
Mpc Networkcom Inc	2741	F	949 873-1002	6287
National Appraisal Guides Inc	2741	E	714 556-8511	6291
Newport Medical Instrs Inc	3841	D	949 642-3910	21838
Newport Mesa Usd Campus C	2752	F	714 424-8939	6746
Nils Inc (PA)	2339	F	714 755-1600	3377
Npi Services Inc	3672	F	714 850-0550	17942
Nwp Services Corporation (HQ)	7372	C	949 253-2500	24219
Old Bones Co	2512	F	714 641-2800	4662
Orange Coast Reprographics Inc	2752	E	949 548-5571	6761
Phillips-Medisize	3841	C	949 477-9495	21858
Pinecraft Custom Shutters Inc	2431	E	949 642-9317	4109
Pinpoint Media Group Inc	2721	F	714 545-5640	6003
Pro-Lite Inc	3993	F	714 668-9988	23179
Qsc LLC (PA)	3651	B	714 754-6175	17275
Quilter Laboratories LLC	3931	F	714 519-6114	22632
Railmakers Inc	3429	F	949 642-6506	11622
Resinart Corporation	3089	E	949 642-3665	10016
Rip Curl Inc (DH)	3949	D	714 422-3600	22872
RPM Embroidery Inc	2395	F	949 650-0085	3755
Rss Manufacturing	3432	F	714 361-4800	11680
S E P E Inc	3571	E	714 241-7373	14971
Saddleback Educational Inc	2731	E	714 640-5224	6143
Safran Elec Def Avnics USA LLC	3812	C	949 642-2427	20712
Sampling International LLC (PA)	2399	F	949 305-5333	3858
Sanmina Corporation	3672	D	714 371-2800	17993
Sanmina Corporation	3672	C	714 913-2200	17995
Schneider Electric It Usa	3679	B	714 513-7313	19078
Sellers Optical Inc	3827	D	949 631-6800	21407
Semicoa Corporation	3674	D	714 979-1900	18532
Smiths Intrcnnect Americas Inc	3679	B	714 371-1100	19085
Starlineoem Inc	3612	F	949 342-8889	16577
Sunburst Products Inc	3873	E	949 722-0158	22484
Suns Out Inc	3944	F	714 556-2314	22718
Swiss Wire EDM	3599	F	714 540-2903	16435
Taylor Communications Inc	2761	E	714 708-2005	7290
Team China California LLC	3826	F	714 424-9999	21297
Team Color Inc	2396	F	949 646-6486	3820
Thomson Reuters Corporation	2741	B	949 400-7782	6358
Thoreen Designs Inc	2392	F	949 645-0981	3646
Tk Pax Inc	3052	E	714 850-1330	9209
Unity Sales International Inc	3861	F	714 800-1700	22469
Vans Inc (DH)	3021	B	855 909-8267	9194
Vending Security Products	3443	F	949 646-1474	12067
Vic Cosmetics LLC	2844	F	949 330-7668	8603
West Newport Oil Company	1311	F	949 631-1100	77
Westar Nutrition Corp	2833	C	949 645-6100	7704
Wonder Grip USA Inc	3089	F	404 290-2015	10130
World Manufacturing Inc (PA)	3083	F	714 662-3539	9461

COTATI, CA - Sonoma County

Company	SIC	EMP	PHONE	ENTRY#
Barlow and Sons Printing Inc	2752	F	707 664-9773	6435
Biotherm Hydronic Inc	3433	E	707 794-9660	11691
J&M Manufacturing Inc	3679	E	707 795-8223	18958
Liberty Valley Doors Inc	2431	F	707 795-8040	4075
Lili Butler Studio Inc	2331	F	707 793-0222	3175
Rich Xiberta Usa Inc	2499	F	707 795-1800	4526
San Franstitchco Inc	2395	F	707 795-6891	3756
Shades Unlimited Inc	2591	F	707 285-2233	5037
Shamrock Materials Inc	3273	F	707 792-4695	10834
Stony Point Rock Quarry Inc (PA)	1442	F	707 795-1775	362
Studio 311 Inc	3911	F	707 795-6599	22575
Windsor Willits Company (PA)	2431	F	707 665-9663	4153

COTTONWOOD, CA - Shasta County

Company	SIC	EMP	PHONE	ENTRY#
Borden Manufacturing	3542	E	530 347-6642	13970
Plum Valley Inc	2421	E	530 262-6262	3941

COVELO, CA - Mendocino County

Company	SIC	EMP	PHONE	ENTRY#
Wylatti Resource MGT Inc	2411	E	707 983-8135	3922

COVINA, CA - Los Angeles County

Company	SIC	EMP	PHONE	ENTRY#
Amity Rubberized Pen Company	3951	E	626 969-0863	22932
Anvil Cases Inc	3161	C	626 968-4100	10188
Apricot Designs Inc	3841	E	626 966-3299	21607
Azusa Engineering Inc	3714	F	626 966-4071	19588
Cabinet Master & Son Inc	2434	F	626 332-0300	4173
Caco-Pacific Corporation (PA)	3544	C	626 331-3361	14027
Chemeor Inc	2843	E	626 966-3808	8427
Cobel Technologies Inc	3613	E	626 332-2100	16590
Composites Horizons LLC (HQ)	3728	C	626 331-0861	20074
Covina Welding & Shtmtl Inc	3441	E	626 332-6293	11776
Cozzia USA LLC	3699	E	626 667-2272	19281

(P-0000) Products & Services Section entry number
(PA)=Parent Co (HQ)=Headquarters (DH)=Div Headquarters

	SIC	EMP	PHONE	ENTRY #
Data Label Products Inc	2679	F	626 915-6478	5504
Dauntless Industries Inc	3544	E	626 966-4494	14040
Decorative Construction	2434	F	626 862-6814	4188
Dexin International Inc **(PA)**	3646	C	626 859-7475	17024
Edgewell Per Care Brands LLC	3421	B	949 466-0131	11514
Excelitas Technologies Corp	3829	C	626 967-6021	21468
G & D Industries Inc	3089	F	626 331-1250	9797
Haemonetics Manufacturing Inc **(HQ)**	3841	E	626 339-7388	21729
Hydro Fitting Mfg Corp	3494	E	626 967-5151	13357
K C Photo Engraving Company	3555	F	626 795-4127	14328
Matrix Document Imaging Inc	2759	D	626 966-9959	7132
Monterey Machine Products	3599	F	626 967-2242	16224
Moores Ideal Products LLC	3944	F	626 339-9007	22696
Pall Corporation	3569	B	626 339-7388	14844
Payne Magnetics Inc	3677	D	626 332-6207	18730
Physicians Formula Inc	2844	D	626 334-3395	8561
Processors Mailing Inc	2752	E	626 358-5075	6813
Qingmu International Inc	2759	E	626 965-7277	7188
R M Baker Machine & Tool Inc	3599	F	562 697-4007	16335
Raytheon Company	3812	C	626 675-2584	20683
RG Costumes & Accessories Inc	2389	E	626 858-9559	3576
RSR Metal Spinning Inc	3469	F	626 814-2339	12869
Shift Calendars Inc	2752	F	626 967-5862	6860
Short Run Swiss Inc	3599	F	626 974-9373	16403
Stabile Plating Company Inc	3471	E	626 339-9091	13105
Supermedia LLC	2741	B	626 331-9440	6353
Terra Furniture Inc	2512	F	626 912-8523	4674
Topper Plastics Inc	3086	F	626 331-0561	9573
Usiwater LLC	2086	F	626 600-5156	2179
Vans Instant Printers Inc	2752	F	626 966-1708	6917
Vipology Inc	2741	F	626 502-8661	6374
Vita-Pakt Citrus Products Co **(PA)**	2033	E	626 332-1101	836
Westrock Rkt Company	2653	C	626 859-7633	5282
William J Hammett Inc	2752	F	626 966-1708	6940

CRESCENT CITY, CA - Del Norte County

	SIC	EMP	PHONE	ENTRY #
Fashion Blacksmith Inc	3732	F	707 464-9219	20330
Rumiano Cheese Co	2022	E	707 465-1535	572
William McClung	3944	F	970 535-4601	22727

CROCKETT, CA - Contra Costa County

	SIC	EMP	PHONE	ENTRY #
American Sugar Refining Inc	2062	B	510 787-6763	1349
C&H Sugar Company Inc	2063	A	510 787-2121	1350

CROWS LANDING, CA - Stanislaus County

	SIC	EMP	PHONE	ENTRY #
Darling International Inc	2077	E	209 667-9153	1460
San Joaquin Tomato Growers Inc	2033	F	209 837-4721	822

CUDAHY, CA - Los Angeles County

	SIC	EMP	PHONE	ENTRY #
Alamillo Radolfo	3229	F	323 773-9614	10295
All American Frame & Bedg Corp	2514	F	323 773-7415	4681
Consoldted Precision Pdts Corp	3365	C	323 773-2363	11371
Day-Glo Color Corp	2816	F	323 560-2000	7458
Dur-Red Products	3444	F	323 771-9000	12187
G E Shell Core Co	3544	E	323 773-4242	14057
Grace Machine Co Inc	3599	E	323 771-6215	16002
Mfb Worldwide Inc **(PA)**	2299	F	323 562-2339	2945
Myers Mixers LLC	3569	F	323 560-4723	14839
Praxair Inc	2813	F	323 562-5200	7434
RAP Security Inc	2542	D	323 560-3493	4998
Scott Craft Co **(PA)**	3599	F	323 560-3949	16389

CULVER CITY, CA - Los Angeles County

	SIC	EMP	PHONE	ENTRY #
Apic Corporation	3674	D	310 642-7975	18103
Beats Electronics LLC **(PA)**	3679	F	424 268-3055	18832
Beats Electronics LLC **(HQ)**	3651	D	424 326-4679	17201
Borin Manufacturing Inc	3561	E	310 822-1000	14562
Bull Hn Info Systems Inc	3571	E	310 337-3600	14894
Cal Southern Graphics Corp	2752	D	310 559-3600	6466
Clay Designs Inc	3269	E	562 432-3991	10486
Dogeared Inc	3961	D	310 846-4444	22980
Ecoly International Inc	2844	F	818 718-6982	8485
Econ-O-Plate Inc	2752	F	310 342-5900	6558
Farchitecture Bb LLC	2024	E	917 701-2777	642
Fortune Casuals **(PA)**	2331	C	310 733-2100	3159
Fulltone Musical Products Inc	3931	F	310 204-0155	22621
Genius Products Nt Inc	2086	C	510 671-0219	2077
Given Imaging Los Angeles LLC	3845	F	310 641-8492	22257
Grand Casino On Main Inc	2051	F	310 253-9066	1222
Hain Celestial Group Inc	2676	F	310 945-4300	5462
Indi Molecular Inc	2835	F	310 417-4999	8230
Integrated Magnetics Inc	3621	E	310 391-7213	16657
Interconnect Solutions Gr	3643	F	323 691-5485	16907
La Siciliana Inc	2335	E	323 870-4155	3239
Liveoffice LLC	7372	D	877 253-2793	24104
Loaded Boards Inc	3751	F	310 839-1800	20415
M Group Inc	3161	E	843 221-7830	10199

	SIC	EMP	PHONE	ENTRY #
Magnet Sales & Mfg Co Inc **(HQ)**	3264	D	310 391-7213	10479
Metric Products Inc **(PA)**	2342	E	310 815-9000	3454
Minton-Spidell Inc **(PA)**	2511	F	310 836-0403	4595
Miracle Greens Inc	2023	C	800 521-5867	604
Moldex-Metric Inc	3842	A	310 837-6500	22050
Nantkwest Inc	2836	F	858 633-0300	8316
Nike Inc	3021	E	310 736-3800	9176
Nutrition Without Borders LLC	3581	F	310 845-7745	15399
Oracle Corporation	7372	B	310 258-7500	24263
Oracle Systems Corporation	7372	D	818 817-2900	24267
Ortho Engineering Inc **(PA)**	3842	E	310 559-5996	22060
Pacific Piston Ring Co Inc	3592	D	310 836-3322	15615
Paige LLC **(HQ)**	2326	C	310 733-2100	3047
Photonic Corp	2752	F	310 642-7975	6781
Popsugar Inc	2741	F	310 562-8049	6312
Q Tech Corporation	3679	C	310 836-7900	19057
Redwood Wellness LLC	2299	E	323 843-2676	2952
Robeks Corporation	2033	F	310 838-2332	821
Ronin Content Services Inc	7372	F	323 445-5945	24366
Schwarzkopf Inc **(DH)**	3999	D	310 641-0990	23469
Scopely Inc **(PA)**	7372	C	323 400-6618	24391
Security Pro USA	3842	E	310 841-5845	22083
Smashbox Beauty Cosmetics Inc	2844	C	310 558-1490	8583
Sofie Biosciences Inc **(PA)**	2835	E	310 215-3159	8259
Sole Society Group Inc	3131	C	310 220-0808	10154
Sportsrobe Inc	2329	E	310 559-3999	3116
Spotlite America Corporation **(PA)**	3229	E	310 829-0200	10331
Spotlite Power Corporation	3646	E	310 838-2367	17071
Stateside Merchants LLC	2322	F	424 251-5190	3000
Vans Inc	3021	F	310 390-7548	9188
Waiakea Inc	2086	F	855 924-2532	2182
Walmsley Design	2511	F	310 836-0772	4618
Water Studio Inc	3499	F	310 313-5553	13554

CUPERTINO, CA - Santa Clara County

	SIC	EMP	PHONE	ENTRY #
Advin Systems Inc	3674	F	408 243-7000	18071
Altia Systems Inc	3861	E	408 996-9710	22401
America Techcode Semicdtr Inc	3674	F	408 910-2028	18091
Amino Technologies (us) LLC **(HQ)**	3663	D	408 861-1400	17448
Apple Inc **(PA)**	3663	A	408 996-1010	17455
Cloudpic Inc	7372	F	408 786-1098	23753
Cmos Sensor Inc	3674	F	408 366-2898	18166
Codefast Inc	7372	F	408 687-4700	23757
Crystal Mining Corporation	1041	F	386 479-5823	2
Dlive Inc	2741	E	650 491-9555	6223
Do-Nut Wheel Inc	2051	F	408 252-8193	1189
Durect Corporation **(PA)**	2834	D	408 777-1417	7874
Durect Corporation	2834	D	408 777-1417	7875
E-Transactions Software Tech	7372	F	408 873-9100	23839
Ecrio Inc	7372	F	408 973-7290	23841
Esq Business Services Inc **(PA)**	7372	D	925 734-9800	23876
Foresite Systems Limited **(PA)**	7372	F	408 855-8600	23910
Fortemedia Inc	3572	D	408 716-8028	15030
Fortune Denim Inc	2086	F	408 805-9526	2076
Greenvolts Inc	3433	D	415 963-4030	11698
Gregory Associates Inc	3825	E	408 446-5725	21047
Hanson Aggregates LLC	1442	F	408 996-4000	344
Hantronix Inc	3559	E	408 252-1100	14475
Kelly Network Solutions Inc	3825	F	650 364-7201	21060
Lehigh Southwest Cement Co	3241	F	408 996-4271	10421
Mockingbird Networks	3571	D	408 342-5300	14953
Nix Mouthwash	2844	E	888 909-9088	8548
Paracor Medical Inc	3845	E	408 207-1050	22296
Read Corp	7372	E	408 705-2123	24339
Seagate Technology LLC **(DH)**	3572	A	408 658-1000	15095
Seagate Technology LLC	3572	F	405 324-4799	15097
Seagate US LLC	3572	F	408 658-1000	15098
Selfoptima Inc	2741	F	408 217-8667	6338
Sheng-Kee of California Inc	2052	E	408 865-6000	1328
Stack Labs Inc	3646	E	503 453-5172	17072
Supernova Spirits Inc	2085	E	415 819-3154	2019
Thales Alenia Space North Amer	3764	F	408 973-9845	20469
Trane US Inc	3585	F	408 257-5212	15456
Tropian Inc	3674	D	408 865-1300	18624
West Coast Venture Capital LLC **(PA)**	3661	A	408 725-0700	17430

CYPRESS, CA - Orange County

	SIC	EMP	PHONE	ENTRY #
Advanex Americas Inc **(HQ)**	3495	D	714 995-4519	13371
Awake Inc	2335	D	818 365-9361	3215
Boeing Company	3721	A	714 952-1509	19862
Buena Park Anaheim Independent	2711	E	714 952-8505	5570
Cavotec Dabico US Inc	3728	E	714 947-0005	20069
Cavotec Inet US Inc	3531	D	714 947-0005	13721
Cenic Ntwrk Operations Website	3761	F	714 220-3494	20444
Christie Digital Systems Inc **(HQ)**	3861	E	714 236-8610	22407
Community Media Corporation **(PA)**	2711	F	714 220-0292	5597

Employment Codes: A=Over 500 employees, B=251-500,
C=101-250, D=51-100, E=20-50, F=10-19

2020 California
Manufacturers Register

© Mergent Inc. 1-800-342-5647

1327

GEOGRAPHIC

	SIC	EMP	PHONE	ENTRY #
Creative Teaching Press Inc (PA)	2731	D	714 799-2100	6094
Dameron Alloy Foundries (PA)	3325	D	310 631-5165	11170
Dentium USA (HQ)	3843	F	714 226-0229	22145
Diasorin Molecular LLC	2835	C	562 240-6500	8220
Dmg Mori Usa Inc	3541	F	562 430-3800	13915
Drs Advanced Isr LLC	3674	C	714 220-3800	18199
Drs Ntwork Imaging Systems LLC	3674	D	714 220-3800	18200
Exemplis LLC (PA)	2522	E	714 995-4800	4838
Hitachi Automotive Systems	3621	D	310 212-0200	16655
International Paper Company	2621	F	714 889-4900	5120
J & F Machine Inc	3599	E	714 527-3499	16057
Johnson Controls Inc	2531	C	562 799-8882	4862
Lady Jayne LP	2678	F	-	5481
Lt Foods Americas Inc (HQ)	2041	E	562 340-4040	1006
Luma Comfort LLC	3634	E	855 963-9247	16833
Magna Tool Inc	3599	F	714 826-2500	16168
Manhattan Beachwear Inc (DH)	2339	C	714 892-7354	3366
Manhattan Beachwear Inc	2339	D	714 892-7354	3367
Manhattan Components Inc	3089	F	714 761-7249	9885
Mitsubishi Electric Visual	3679	C	800 553-7278	19021
Ocean Protecta Incorporated	3732	E	714 891-2628	20353
Paradigm Contract Mfg LLC	3999	F	714 889-7074	23442
Plastech Specialties Company (PA)	2396	F	626 357-6839	3808
Power - Trim Co	3524	F	714 523-8560	13692
Power Pt Inc	3537	F	714 826-7407	13888
Primary Color Systems Corp (PA)	2752	B	949 660-7080	6793
Rockwell Automation Inc	3625	E	714 828-1800	16746
Safran Cabin Inc	3728	C	562 344-4780	20220
Shadow Industries Inc	3792	F	714 995-4353	20493
Shaw Industries Group Inc	2273	C	562 430-4445	2879
Siemens Industry Inc	3613	D	714 252-3100	16614
Simply Fresh LLC	2092	C	714 562-5000	2270
Tayco Engineering Inc	3761	C	714 952-2240	20457
Toyo Automotive Parts USA Inc	3714	C	714 229-6125	19785
Toyo Ink International Corp	2893	E	714 899-2377	8935
Toyo Tire Hldings Americas Inc (HQ)	3011	E	562 431-6502	9170
Tr Theater Research Inc (PA)	3651	F	714 894-5888	17295
Venus Laboratories Inc	2819	D	714 891-3100	7535
Weldex Corporation (PA)	3674	E	714 761-2100	18656
Yaesu Usa Inc	3663	E	714 827-7600	17711

DALY CITY, CA - San Mateo County

	SIC	EMP	PHONE	ENTRY #
Genesys Telecom Labs Inc (HQ)	7372	B	650 466-1100	23934
Irvine & Jachens Inc	3999	F	650 755-4715	23367
Mah Kuo	3441	F	805 766-2309	11835
Oracle Systems Corporation	7372	D	650 506-8648	24268
Shannon Side Welding Inc	7692	F	415 680-6101	24664
Star Fish Inc	2396	F	415 468-6688	3817
View Rite Manufacturing	2541	F	415 468-3856	4953
Westlake Bakery Inc	2051	F	650 994-7741	1295

DANA POINT, CA - Orange County

	SIC	EMP	PHONE	ENTRY #
Captive Ocean Reef Enterprises	3569	F	949 581-8888	14801
Desert Shutters Inc	2426	E	949 388-8344	3972
South Orange County Ww Auth	2899	F	949 234-5400	9026

DANVILLE, CA - Contra Costa County

	SIC	EMP	PHONE	ENTRY #
A Lot To Say Inc (PA)	2399	F	877 366-8448	3827
Advertiser Perceptions	2711	E	925 648-3902	5545
Aqueous Vets	3589	F	951 764-9384	15486
Choice Foodservices Inc	3365	D	925 837-0104	11370
Container Decorating Inc	2396	F	510 489-9212	3781
Eatyourmealscom LLC	3999	F	925 984-5452	23319
Morrison Mar & Intermodal Inc	3731	E	925 362-4599	20294
Peninsula Engrg Solutions Inc	3663	F	925 837-2243	17621
Redshark Group Inc	2752	F	925 837-3490	6841
Rocateq North America	3496	F	925 648-7794	13434
Trov Inc (PA)	7372	F	925 478-5500	24529
Whamcloud Inc	7372	F	925 452-7599	24579
Wireless Glue Networks Inc	7372	F	925 310-4561	24583

DAVENPORT, CA - Santa Cruz County

	SIC	EMP	PHONE	ENTRY #
Lundberg Studios Inc	3231	E	831 423-2532	10375

DAVIS, CA - Yolo County

	SIC	EMP	PHONE	ENTRY #
Antibodies Incorporated	2835	F	800 824-8540	8204
Digital Technology Lab Corp	3545	D	530 746-7400	14155
Dmg Mori Manufacturing USA Inc (HQ)	3541	E	530 746-7400	13914
Electronic Resources Network	3577	E	530 758-0180	15223
Expression Systems LLC (PA)	2836	E	877 877-7421	8299
FMC Corporation	2812	D	530 753-6718	7387
Frontier AG Co Inc (PA)	2048	F	530 297-1020	1097
Marrone Bio Innovations Inc (PA)	2879	C	530 750-2800	8833
McNaughton Newspapers	2711	F	530 756-0800	5737
Phl Associates Inc	2836	F	530 753-5881	8321
Scarlet Saints Softball	3949	F	530 613-1443	22885
Signa Chemistry Inc	2819	E	212 933-4101	7525

	SIC	EMP	PHONE	ENTRY #
Steps Mobile Inc	7372	F	408 806-5178	24456
Technipfmc US Holdings Inc	3533	E	530 753-6718	13794
Tyflong International Inc	3291	F	530 746-3001	10957

DEER PARK, CA - Napa County

	SIC	EMP	PHONE	ENTRY #
Viader Vineyards	2084	F	707 963-3816	1981

DEL MAR, CA - San Diego County

	SIC	EMP	PHONE	ENTRY #
Aztech Products International	3699	E	858 481-8412	19264
Fairmont Global LLC (PA)	2541	F	415 320-2929	4903
Interntional Thermal Instr Inc	3826	F	858 755-4436	21249
Knorr Beeswax Products Inc	3999	F	760 431-2007	23384
Societe Brewing Company LLC	2084	F	858 598-5415	1920

DEL REY, CA - Fresno County

	SIC	EMP	PHONE	ENTRY #
Choojlian & Sons Inc	3556	D	559 888-2031	14355
Cy Truss	2439	E	559 888-2160	4298
Del Rey Enterprises Inc	2034	F	559 233-4452	849
Del Rey Juice Co	2037	D	559 888-8533	909
Economy Stock Feed Company	2048	F	559 888-2187	1091

DELANO, CA - Kern County

	SIC	EMP	PHONE	ENTRY #
Agri Cel Inc	3086	D	661 792-2107	9501
Anthony Welded Products Inc (PA)	3537	E	661 721-7211	13858
Asv Wines Inc (PA)	2084	F	661 792-3159	1585
Cemex Cnstr Mtls PCF LLC	3273	E	661 725-1819	10722
City of Delano	3589	E	661 721-3352	15497
Delano Growers Grape Products	2087	D	661 725-3255	2202
Ra-White Inc	3599	F	661 725-1840	16338
Randell Equiptment & Mfg	3523	E	661 725-6380	13664
San-Joaquin Helicopters Inc	3721	F	661 725-6603	19929
Styrolek Inc	3086	C	661 725-4957	9570

DELHI, CA - Merced County

	SIC	EMP	PHONE	ENTRY #
Glenn Engineering Inc	3715	F	209 667-4555	19822

DENAIR, CA - Stanislaus County

	SIC	EMP	PHONE	ENTRY #
Almond Valley Nut Co	2068	E	209 480-7300	1420

DESCANSO, CA - San Diego County

	SIC	EMP	PHONE	ENTRY #
Yaldo Enterprises Inc	2097	F	619 445-2578	2366

DESERT HOT SPRINGS, CA - Riverside County

	SIC	EMP	PHONE	ENTRY #
Back Support Systems Inc	3086	F	760 329-1472	9508
Western Golf Car Mfg Inc	3949	D	760 671-6691	22925

DI GIORGIO, CA - Kern County

	SIC	EMP	PHONE	ENTRY #
F Korbel & Bros	2084	E	661 854-6120	1695

DIAMOND BAR, CA - Los Angeles County

	SIC	EMP	PHONE	ENTRY #
Evensphere Incorporation	3678	E	909 247-3030	18767
Garden Pals Inc	3423	E	909 605-0200	11530
Gohz Inc	3621	E	800 603-1219	16651
Impro Industries Usa Inc (DH)	3369	E	909 396-6525	11418
Jentex Co Ltd	2211	F	909 273-1088	2699
Niagara Bottling LLC (PA)	2086	E	909 230-5000	2098
Quarton Usa Inc	3699	F	888 532-2221	19387
Rafi Systems Inc	3851	D	909 861-6574	22381
Society For The Advancement of	2721	F	626 521-9460	6030
Ultimate Sound Inc	3651	B	909 861-6200	17297
US Gear & Pumps	3566	F	909 525-3026	14751

DIAMOND SPRINGS, CA - El Dorado County

	SIC	EMP	PHONE	ENTRY #
Adept Med International Inc (PA)	3841	F	530 621-1220	21581
Airpoint Precision Inc	3599	F	530 622-0510	15715
California Integration Coordin	3672	F	530 626-6168	17840
Demtech Services Inc	3089	F	530 621-3200	9752
Fastener Depot Inc	3452	F	530 621-3070	12677
McDaniel Manufacturing Inc	3429	F	530 626-6336	11609
Ruxco Engineering Inc	3841	F	530 622-4122	21885
Western Sign Company Inc	3993	E	916 933-3765	23242

DINUBA, CA - Tulare County

	SIC	EMP	PHONE	ENTRY #
Kobus Business Systems LLC	3578	F	559 595-1915	15375
Olive Bari Oil Company	2079	F	559 595-9260	1479
Packline Technologies Inc	3565	F	559 591-3150	14722
Ruiz Food Products Inc (PA)	2038	A	559 591-5510	978
Sentinel Printing & Publishing	2711	F	559 591-4632	5824
Warren & Baerg Mfg Inc	3523	E	559 591-6790	13682

DIXON, CA - Solano County

	SIC	EMP	PHONE	ENTRY #
Alpha Alarm & Audio Inc	3651	F	707 452-8334	17186
Altec Industries Inc	3531	F	707 678-0800	13703
Altec Industries Inc	3531	D	707 678-0800	13704
California Pipe Fabricators	3498	E	707 678-3069	13463
Castlelite Block LLC	3271	E	707 678-3465	10505
Cemex Cnstr Mtls PCF LLC	3271	D	707 580-3138	10507
Cemex Materials LLC	3273	C	707 678-4311	10736
Dixon Tribune	2711	F	707 678-5594	5617
Ellensburg Lamb Company Inc	2011	C	707 678-3091	406

Mergent email: customerrelations@mergent.com
1328

2020 California
Manufacturers Register

(P-0000) Products & Services Section entry number
(PA)=Parent Co (HQ)=Headquarters (DH)=Div Headquarters

	SIC	EMP	PHONE	ENTRY #
Gibson Printing & Publishing	2711	F	707 678-5594	5647
Hemostat Laboratories Inc (PA)	2836	E	707 678-9594	8308
INX International Ink Co	2893	F	707 693-2990	8925
J & A Jeffery Inc	3999	E	707 678-0369	23368
Moller International	3721	F	530 756-5086	19916
Transhumance Holding Co Inc	2011	C	707 693-2303	426
Tri Star Metals Inc	3449	F	707 678-1140	12610
Victorian Shutters Inc (PA)	2431	F	707 678-1776	4145

DOS PALOS, CA - Merced County

	SIC	EMP	PHONE	ENTRY #
C&S Global Foods Inc	2099	F	209 392-2223	2413

DOWNEY, CA - Los Angeles County

	SIC	EMP	PHONE	ENTRY #
A & A Ready Mixed Concrete Inc	3273	F	562 923-7281	10676
A-1 Engraving Co Inc	3479	F	562 861-2216	13132
Ad-De-Pro Inc	3451	F	562 862-1915	12616
Advanced Building Systems Inc	3999	E	818 652-4252	23263
Advanced Lgs LLC	3441	F	818 652-4252	11735
Alpha Grinding Inc	3599	F	562 803-1509	15727
American Security Educators	2741	F	562 928-1847	6183
Arrow Abrasive Company Inc	3291	F	562 869-2282	10940
Bradley Manufacturing Co Inc	3089	F	562 923-5556	9672
Can Lines Engineering Inc (PA)	3565	D	562 861-2996	14702
Classic Graphix	2395	F	562 940-0806	3731
Cummins Pacific LLC	3519	F	866 934-4373	13588
Detroit Diesel Corporation	3519	F	562 929-7016	13595
Downey Grinding Co	3541	E	562 803-5556	13918
Downey Manufacturing Inc	3728	F	562 862-3311	20088
Downey Patriot	2711	E	562 904-3668	5620
Ebus Inc	3713	E	562 904-3474	19531
EJ Lauren LLC	2512	E	562 803-1113	4640
Engine Electronics Inc	3694	E	562 803-1700	19191
Gann Products Company Inc	3052	F	562 862-2337	9198
Hartwick Combustion Tech Inc	3569	F	562 922-8300	14824
Hutchinson Seal Corporation (DH)	3053	B	248 375-4190	9236
Instant Web LLC	2752	C	562 658-2020	6643
J F Duncan Industries Inc (PA)	3589	D	562 862-4269	15528
Jeb-PHI Inc	2752	F	562 861-0863	6664
Jewels By Angelo Inc	3911	F	562 862-6293	22532
Kf Fiberglass Inc (PA)	3714	E	562 869-1536	19701
Kirkhill Inc	3069	D	562 803-1117	9326
Lynx Grills Inc (HQ)	3631	F	323 722-4324	16813
MD Stainless Services	3498	E	562 904-7022	13477
On-Gard Metals Inc	3341	F	562 622-9057	11206
Pacific Southwest Molds	3544	F	562 803-9811	14091
Reyes Coca-Cola Bottling LLC	2086	D	562 803-8100	2137
Sees Candy Shops Incorporated	2064	C	562 928-2912	1398
Spyke Inc	3751	E	562 803-1700	20426
Sst Technologies	3823	E	562 803-3361	20942
Thompson Tank Inc	3443	F	562 869-7711	12065
Umc Acquisition Corp (PA)	3356	E	562 940-0300	11281
United California Corporation	3544	C	562 803-1521	14117
United Drill Bushing Corp	3545	C	562 803-1521	14208
Universal Mlding Extrusion Inc (DH)	3354	E	562 401-1015	11251
Universal Molding Company (HQ)	3356	C	310 886-1750	11282
Van Grace Quality Injection	3089	F	323 931-5255	10109
Wesfac Inc (HQ)	3589	D	562 861-2160	15604
Western Pacific Pulp and Paper (HQ)	2611	D	562 803-4401	5095

DUARTE, CA - Los Angeles County

	SIC	EMP	PHONE	ENTRY #
A & B Brush Mfg Corp	3991	F	626 303-8856	23019
Accu-Sembly Inc	3672	D	626 357-3447	17801
Assembly Automation Industries	3549	E	626 303-2777	14263
Cosmo Fiber Corporation (PA)	2759	E	626 256-6098	7037
Delafield Corporation (PA)	3599	C	626 303-0740	15884
Dynametric Inc	3661	F	626 358-2559	17362
Endodent Inc	3843	E	626 359-5715	22153
Jetco Torque Tools LLC	3566	F	626 359-2881	14743
Justice Bros Dist Co Inc	2843	F	626 359-9174	8429
Lee Machine Products	3544	F	626 301-4105	14070
Micro-OHM Corporation	3676	E	626 357-5377	18690
Onex Enterprises Corporation	3569	F	626 358-6639	14841
Onex Rf Automation Inc	3548	E	626 358-6639	14249
Padywell Corp	2759	E	626 359-9149	7169
Prolacta Bioscience Inc	2023	B	626 599-9260	617
Quality Car Care Products Inc	2819	E	626 359-9174	7520
S W C Group Inc	2656	E	888 982-1628	5309
Sew Forth Inc	2326	E	323 725-3500	3053
Soyfoods of America	2075	E	626 358-3836	1446
Spenuzza Inc	3589	E	626 358-8063	15583
Turbo Refrigeration Systems	3585	E	626 599-9777	15468
Victory Sportswear Inc	2221	F	626 359-5400	2739
Viking Ready Mix Co Inc	3273	E	626 303-7755	10866
Woodward Hrt Inc	3728	C	626 359-9211	20271

DUBLIN, CA - Alameda County

	SIC	EMP	PHONE	ENTRY #
A A Label Inc (PA)	2679	E	925 803-5709	5488

	SIC	EMP	PHONE	ENTRY #
Advantec Mfs Inc	3564	F	925 479-0625	14643
Allyn James Inc	2752	F	925 828-5530	6406
Azure Biosystems Inc	2836	E	925 307-7127	8278
Carl Zeiss Inc	3827	E	925 557-4100	21337
Carl Zeiss Meditec Inc (DH)	3827	B	925 557-4100	21338
Carl Zeiss Meditec Inc	3827	E	858 716-0661	21339
Carl Zeiss Ophthalmic Systems	3841	C	925 557-4100	21658
Eg Systems LLC (PA)	3674	E	510 324-0126	18209
Epicor Software Corporation	7372	C	925 361-9900	23869
Giga-Tronics Incorporated (PA)	3825	E	925 328-4650	21043
Glaxosmithkline LLC	2834	D	925 833-1551	7920
Hexcel Corporation	2821	D	925 551-4900	7565
ICEE Company	2087	F	925 828-5807	2216
Immunoscience LLC	2835	F	925 400-6055	8229
International Petroleum Produc	2992	F	925 556-5530	9147
Ipac Inc	2992	F	925 556-5530	9148
Kensington Laboratories LLC (PA)	3625	F	510 324-0126	16727
Lockheed Martin Corporation	3812	B	925 756-4594	20607
Microsource Inc	3825	D	925 328-4650	21080
Nexfon Corporation	3229	F	925 200-2233	10322
Oliver De Silva Inc (PA)	1429	E	925 829-9220	317
Onyx Optics Inc	3827	E	925 833-1969	21389
Oracle Taleo LLC	7372	A	925 452-3000	24278
Print Ink Inc	2759	F	925 829-3950	7182
Saba Software Inc (PA)	7372	D	877 722-2101	24371
San Francisco Elev Svcs Inc	3534	E	925 829-5400	13808
Sunar Rf Motion Inc	3663	F	925 833-9936	17673
Valent USA LLC	2879	F	925 256-2700	8847
Zeltiq Aesthetics Inc	3841	F	925 474-2519	21965

DURHAM, CA - Butte County

	SIC	EMP	PHONE	ENTRY #
Tink Inc	3531	E	530 895-0897	13751
Westgate Hardwoods Inc (PA)	2431	E	530 892-0300	4148

E RNCHO DMNGZ, CA - Los Angeles County

	SIC	EMP	PHONE	ENTRY #
Beu Industries Inc	2671	E	310 885-9626	5325
Coy Industries Inc	3444	D	310 603-2970	12165
Industrial Tctnics Brings Corp (DH)	3562	D	310 537-3750	14610
Modern Concepts Inc	3089	D	310 637-0013	9902
Pacific Contntl Textiles Inc	2261	F	310 639-1500	2831
Sonora Mills Foods Inc (PA)	2052	D	310 639-5333	1329
Touchsport Footwear LLC	3021	F	310 763-0208	9186

EAST PALO ALTO, CA - Santa Clara County

	SIC	EMP	PHONE	ENTRY #
Calspray Inc	3479	F	650 325-0096	13154
La Estrellita Tizapan Mercado	2099	F	650 328-0799	2507

EASTVALE, CA - Riverside County

	SIC	EMP	PHONE	ENTRY #
Cal-Mold Incorporated	3089	C	951 361-6400	9683
Herff Jones LLC	3911	F	951 541-3938	22527
Jim Perry	2789	F	909 947-0747	7336
Led One Corporation (PA)	3674	F	510 770-1189	18345
Lennox	3585	F	800 953-6669	15439
Medtronic Inc	3841	F	951 332-3600	21810
Nortek Security & Control LLC	3699	F	760 438-7000	19369
Parker House Mfg Co Inc	2517	E	800 628-1319	4754
Rankin-Delux Inc (PA)	3589	F	951 685-0081	15567
Red Star Fertilizer Co.	2873	D	909 597-4801	8801
Rivas Industries Inc	2752	F	951 880-8638	6844
Royal Range California Inc	3631	D	951 360-1600	16816
Snapware Corporation	3089	C	951 361-3100	10061

EDWARDS, CA - Kern County

	SIC	EMP	PHONE	ENTRY #
Boeing Company	3721	A	661 810-4686	19864
Jacobs Technology Inc	3761	E	661 275-6100	20447
Lockheed Martin Corporation	3812	A	661 277-0691	20614

EL CAJON, CA - San Diego County

	SIC	EMP	PHONE	ENTRY #
A-1 Plastics Incorporated	3553	F	619 444-9442	14297
Access Professional Inc	3446	F	858 571-4444	12444
Aerowind Corporation	3769	F	619 569-1960	20471
Al & Krla Pipe Fabricators Inc	3498	F	619 448-0060	13456
Alturdyne Power Systems Inc	3511	E	619 343-3204	13559
American Metal Processing	3444	E	619 444-6171	12106
Arctic Zero Inc	2024	E	619 342-1423	629
Asm Construction Inc	3444	E	619 449-1966	12118
Azusa Rock Inc	1422	F	619 440-2363	298
BJS&t Enterprises Inc	3479	F	619 448-7795	13150
Bowen Printing Inc	2679	F	619 440-8605	5496
Brantner and Associates Inc (DH)	3678	C	619 562-7070	18752
Burning Beard Brewing Company	2082	F	619 456-9185	1508
C L P Inc (PA)	7692	F	619 444-3105	24620
C W McGrath Inc	1423	F	619 443-3811	308
Calbiotech Inc	3841	E	619 660-6162	21646
California Panel Systems LLP	3444	E	619 562-7010	12147
Certified Metal Craft Inc	3398	E	619 593-3636	11445
Combustion Parts Inc	3511	E	858 759-3320	13566

Employment Codes: A=Over 500 employees, B=251-500,
C=101-250, D=51-100, E=20-50, F=10-19

2020 California
Manufacturers Register

© Mergent Inc. 1-800-342-5647

1329

GEOGRAPHIC

	SIC	EMP	PHONE	ENTRY #
Cummins Pacific LLC	3519	E	619 593-3093	13593
Dave Whipple Sheet Metal Inc	3444	E	619 562-6962	12175
Daymar Corporation	2095	F	619 444-1155	2287
Decco Castings Inc	3369	E	619 444-9437	11413
Delstar Technologies Inc	3081	E	619 258-1503	9401
Derosa Enterprises Inc	3444	E	760 743-5500	12182
Dn Tanks Inc (PA)	3795	C	619 440-8181	20497
Doctors Signature Sales	2833	E	800 531-4877	7653
Dyk Incorporated (HQ)	3795	E	619 440-8181	20498
East County Gazette	2711	E	619 444-5774	5623
Ecp Powder Coating	3479	E	619 448-3932	13169
Eddy Pump Corporation (PA)	3594	E	619 258-7020	15629
Emberton Machine & Tool Inc	3599	E	619 401-1870	15929
Entra Health Systems LLC	3841	E	877 458-2646	21704
Ethos Natural Medicine LLC	2833	E	858 267-7599	7657
First Class Packaging Inc	2631	E	619 579-7166	5161
Flexsystems Usa Inc	2399	E	619 401-1858	3843
Fox Factory Holding Corp	3714	F	619 768-1800	19660
Fuzetron Inc	3559	F	619 244-5141	14469
Gear Vendors Inc	3714	E	619 562-0060	19668
Get Engineering Corp	3823	E	619 443-8295	20880
GKN Aerospace Chem-Tronics Inc	3724	C	619 258-5012	19952
GKN Aerospace Chem-Tronics Inc (DH)	3724	A	619 448-2320	19953
Greenbroz Inc	3523	E	844 379-8746	13634
Hi-Tech Welding & Forming Inc	3599	E	619 562-5929	16023
High Precision Grinding	3599	E	619 440-0303	16026
Hollands Custom Cabinets Inc	2434	E	619 443-6081	4206
Inflatable Design Group Inc	3993	F	619 596-6100	23134
Integrated Sign Associates	3993	E	619 579-2229	23136
J P Gunite Inc	3273	E	619 938-0228	10775
Jerames Industries Inc	3599	E	619 334-2204	16080
Jet Air Fbo LLC	3728	E	619 448-5991	20145
Johnson Outdoors Inc	3949	E	619 402-1023	22834
Js Plastics Inc (PA)	3089	E	619 672-5972	9859
Kings Crating Inc (PA)	3724	E	619 590-1664	19969
Kings Crating Inc	3469	E	619 590-2631	12833
Life Line Packaging Inc	2671	E	619 444-2737	5330
Lorimar Group Inc	3663	F	619 954-9300	17576
M W Reid Welding Inc	3441	D	619 401-5880	11831
Micro-Mode Products Inc	3663	C	619 449-3844	17585
Mmix Technologies	3444	F	619 631-6644	12305
New Brunswick Industries Inc	3672	E	619 448-4900	17938
Norberg Crushing Inc	1429	F	619 390-4200	316
Omni Enclosures Inc	2541	E	619 579-6664	4927
Pacifitek Systems Inc	3663	F	619 401-1968	17618
Precision Metal Products Inc (HQ)	3462	C	619 448-2711	12718
Premier Metal Processing Inc	3471	E	760 415-9027	13076
Prime Heat Incorporated	3567	F	619 449-6623	14773
Pure Bioscience Inc (PA)	2842	F	619 596-8600	8409
Q Microwave Inc	3679	D	619 258-7322	19056
Radius Arospc - San Diego Inc	3728	C	619 440-2504	20209
Rks Inc (HQ)	3699	F	858 571-4444	19396
Robert Grove	3721	F	619 562-1268	19927
Rotron Incorporated	3564	E	619 593-7400	14677
Royale Energy Funds Inc (HQ)	1382	F	619 383-6600	137
San Diego Electric Sign Inc	3993	F	619 258-1775	23191
Senior Operations LLC	3599	D	909 627-2723	16396
Spotless Water Systems LLC	3589	F	858 530-9993	15584
St Cyclewear/Gallop LLC	2329	F	619 449-9191	3117
Tiffany Structures	3448	E	619 905-9684	12577
Titan Steel Fabricators Inc	7692	F	619 449-1271	24675
Top Notch Manufacturing Inc	3469	F	619 588-2033	12883
Toro Company	3523	D	619 562-2950	13675
Transportation Equipment Inc (PA)	2394	E	619 449-8860	3711
Tujayar Enterprises Inc	3646	E	619 442-0577	17079
Unique Drawer Boxes Inc	2441	F	619 873-4240	4343
US Print & Toner Inc	3955	E	619 562-6995	22975
Vcsd Inc	2434	E	619 579-6886	4262
Veridiam Inc (DH)	3548	C	619 448-1000	14258
Vertechs Enterprises Inc (PA)	3364	D	858 578-3900	11361
Viasat Inc	3812	D	619 438-6000	20742
Vulcan Materials Company	1422	F	619 440-2363	306
Waterdog Products Inc	3089	F	619 441-9688	10116
Weldmac Manufacturing Company	3599	C	619 440-2300	16515
Western Bay Sheet Metal Inc	3441	E	619 233-1753	11921

EL CENTRO, CA - Imperial County

	SIC	EMP	PHONE	ENTRY #
Associated Desert Newspaper (DH)	2711	E	760 337-3400	5557
Caliber Screenprinting Inc	2396	F	760 353-3499	3777
Complete Metal Fabrication Inc	3441	F	760 353-0260	11771
Ew Corprtion Indus Fabricators (PA)	3441	D	760 337-0020	11789
Imperial Printers Inc (PA)	2752	F	760 352-4374	6632
IV Welding & Mechanical Inc	7692	F	760 482-9353	24642
K C Welding Inc	7692	F	760 352-3832	24647
Mulherin Monumental Inc	3281	F	760 353-7717	10917
Reyes Coca-Cola Bottling LLC	2086	E	760 352-1561	2158

	SIC	EMP	PHONE	ENTRY #
Rogar Manufacturing Inc	3679	C	760 335-3700	19071
Superior Ready Mix Concrete LP	3273	E	760 352-4341	10849
Western Electrical Advg Co	3993	E	760 352-0471	23241
Wymore Inc	7692	E	760 352-2045	24680

EL CERRITO, CA - Contra Costa County

	SIC	EMP	PHONE	ENTRY #
Renovare International Inc	3589	F	510 748-9993	15570

EL DORADO, CA - El Dorado County

	SIC	EMP	PHONE	ENTRY #
Cemex Cnstr Mtls PCF LLC	3273	E	530 626-3590	10713
Hearthco Inc	3429	F	530 622-3877	11594

EL DORADO HILLS, CA - El Dorado County

	SIC	EMP	PHONE	ENTRY #
478826 Limited	3599	E	916 933-5280	15647
Access Systems Inc	3826	F	916 941-8099	21159
Aerometals Inc (PA)	3728	D	916 939-6888	20018
All Sales Manufacturing Inc	3714	E	916 933-0236	19575
Alpha Research & Tech Inc	3571	D	916 431-9340	14886
Ampac Fine Chemicals LLC	2834	D	916 245-6500	7753
Bar Manufacturing Inc	3674	D	916 939-0551	18144
Bruder Industry	3599	E	916 939-6888	15799
Bulletproof Brands Co Inc	2086	E	916 635-3718	2047
Cameo Crafts	2759	E	513 381-1480	7015
Cason Engineering Inc	3599	E	916 939-9311	15828
Cemex (PA)	3273	E	916 941-2800	10706
Clear Image Inc (PA)	2673	E	916 933-4700	5390
Filtration Development Co LLC	3677	E	415 884-0555	18715
Illinois Tool Works Inc	3674	D	916 939-4332	18280
Otto ARC Systems Inc	7692	E	916 939-3400	24654
Paragon Products LLC (PA)	3743	E	916 941-9717	20376
Planar Monolithics Inds Inc	3679	E	916 542-1401	19049
Precision Contacts Inc	3663	E	916 939-4147	17626
Ren Corporation	3523	E	916 739-2000	13665
Sacramento Rebar Inc (PA)	3449	E	916 447-9700	12603
School Innovations Achievement (PA)	7372	D	916 933-2290	24388
Sepasoft Inc	7372	E	916 939-1684	24398
Space Systems/Loral LLC	3663	E	916 605-5448	17667
Synvasive Technology Inc	3841	E	916 939-3913	21920
Terralink Communications Inc	3663	E	916 439-4367	17688
Thinci Inc (PA)	3674	F	916 235-8466	18621

EL GRANADA, CA - San Mateo County

	SIC	EMP	PHONE	ENTRY #
Acoustical Interiors Inc (PA)	3296	F	650 728-9441	10979

EL MONTE, CA - Los Angeles County

	SIC	EMP	PHONE	ENTRY #
Aero-k Inc	3599	E	626 350-5125	15706
Agra-Farm Foods Inc	2043	F	626 443-2335	1014
Air Dreams Mattresses	2515	F	626 573-5733	4709
All New Stamping Co	3469	C	626 443-8813	12763
American Apparel ACC Inc (PA)	3089	E	626 350-3828	9622
Andari Fashion Inc	2329	C	626 575-2759	3066
Applied Coatings & Linings	3479	E	626 280-6354	13143
Cal Coil Magnetics Inc	3677	E	626 455-0011	18705
California Treats Inc	2033	D	626 454-4099	760
Craneveyor Corp (PA)	3536	E	626 442-1524	13845
Dianas Mexican Food Pdts Inc	2099	D	626 444-0555	2446
Dos Fashions	2211	E	626 454-4558	2683
E E Systems Group Inc	3699	F	626 452-8988	19298
Eco World USA LLC	3646	E	626 433-1333	17025
El Gallito Market Inc	2099	E	626 442-1190	2450
El Monte Plating Company	3471	F	626 448-3607	12992
Fanboys Window Factory Inc (PA)	3442	E	626 280-8787	11954
Fay and Qrtrmine McHining Corp	3545	F	323 686-0224	14159
Flexfirm Holdings LLC	2295	F	323 283-1173	2897
GAI Manufacturing Co LLC	3534	F	626 443-8616	13800
Georg Fischer Signet LLC	3823	D	626 571-2770	20879
George Fischer Inc (HQ)	3599	F	626 571-2770	15995
Gill Corporation (PA)	3089	C	626 443-6094	9805
Gsl Tech Inc	2023	F	626 572-9617	593
Industrial Machine & Mfg Co	3441	F	626 444-0181	11810
Jansen Ornamental Supply Co	3446	E	626 442-0271	12485
Jisoncase (usa) Limited	3111	F	888 233-8880	10139
Justin Inc	3612	E	626 444-4516	16559
Keck & Schmidt Tool & Die Inc	3544	F	626 579-3890	14067
L & N Fixtures Inc	2541	E	323 686-0041	4918
La Chapalita Inc (PA)	2099	E	626 443-8556	2505
Lanty Inc	2099	C	626 582-8001	2519
LAweb Offset Printing Inc	2759	C	626 454-2469	7117
Lawrence Equipment Inc (PA)	3556	C	626 442-2894	14382
Leyvas Mexican Food	2051	E	626 350-6328	1234
Liberty Industries	3599	F	626 575-3206	16146
Lith-O-Roll Corporation	3555	E	626 579-0340	14330
Lithotech International LLC	2759	E	626 443-4210	7123
Lithotechs Inc	2759	E	626 433-1333	7124
Los Angeles Ltg Mfg Co Inc	3646	D	626 454-8300	17053
Mercury Broach Company Inc	3545	F	626 443-5904	14171
Micro Gage Inc	3674	E	626 443-1741	18391

Mergent email: customerrelations@mergent.com
1330

2020 California
Manufacturers Register

(P-0000) Products & Services Section entry number
(PA)=Parent Co (HQ)=Headquarters (DH)=Div Headquarters

	SIC	EMP	PHONE	ENTRY #
Newhouse Upholstery	2531	E	626 444-1370	4866
Optel-Matic Inc	3599	F	626 444-2671	16262
P S R Iron Works	3441	F	626 442-3360	11856
Pax Tag & Label Inc	2759	E	626 579-2000	7171
Peca Corporation	3069	E	626 452-8873	9351
Piston Hydraulic System Inc	3569	F	626 350-0100	14851
Precision Coil Spring Company	3495	D	626 444-0561	13386
Pride Metal Polishing Inc	3471	F	626 350-1326	13077
Primus Lighting Inc	3648	F	626 442-4600	17156
R W Swarens Associates Inc	3646	E	626 579-0943	17067
Remington Roll Forming Inc	3316	F	626 350-5196	11121
Royal Apparel Inc	2339	D	626 579-5168	3401
Santoshi Corporation	3471	E	626 444-7118	13097
Seng Cheang Mong Co	2098	F	626 442-2899	2383
SOLE Designs Inc	2512	F	626 452-8642	4671
Sparling Instruments LLC	3823	E	626 444-0571	20941
Special Iron Security Systems	3446	F	626 443-7877	12510
Srco Inc	3599	F	626 350-8321	16420
Sunrise Pillow Co Inc	2392	F	626 401-9283	3644
Supreme Steel Treating Inc	3398	E	626 350-5865	11470
Sybman Inc	2499	F	626 579-9911	4538
Tacticombat Inc	3484	F	626 315-4443	13278
Taiga Embroidery Inc	2395	E	626 448-4812	3761
Tartan Fashion Inc	2329	E	626 575-2828	3123
Thrifty Corporation	2024	F	818 571-0122	673
Transgo	3714	E	626 443-7456	19786
Uncle Lees Tea Inc	2099	F	626 350-3309	2641
Unity Clothing Inc	3949	F	626 579-5588	22917
Vfly Corporation	2395	F	626 575-3115	3763
Videssence LLC (PA)	3645	E	626 579-0943	16997
Videssence LLC	3648	F	626 579-0943	17176
Wah Fung Noodles Inc	2098	F	626 442-0588	2385
Wells Mfg USA Inc	3694	F	626 575-2886	19207

EL PORTAL, CA - Mariposa County

	SIC	EMP	PHONE	ENTRY #
Yosemite Natural History Assn	2731	D	209 379-2646	6168

EL SEGUNDO, CA - Los Angeles County

	SIC	EMP	PHONE	ENTRY #
A Alpha Wave Guide Co (PA)	2211	F	310 322-3487	2663
Abl Space Systems Company	3812	F	650 996-8214	20527
Active Interest Media Inc (PA)	2721	D	310 356-4100	5874
Aerojet Rcketdyne Holdings Inc (PA)	3812	F	310 252-8100	20531
Alcatel-Lucent USA Inc	3577	E	310 297-2620	15149
Aptean Inc	7372	F	310 536-6080	23619
Artissimo Designs LLC (HQ)	2679	E	310 906-3700	5494
Atk Space Systems Inc	3812	A	310 343-3799	20543
Bandai America Incorporated (DH)	3944	D	714 816-9751	22661
Beyond Meat Inc (PA)	2038	E	866 756-4112	947
Beyond Meat Inc	2038	E	310 567-3323	948
Boeing Company	3663	E	310 662-9000	17471
Boeing Company	3721	D	310 426-4100	19871
Boeing Company	3721	A	310 416-9319	19880
Boeing Satellite Systems	3812	D	310 364-5088	20551
Boeing Satellite Systems Inc	3721	E	310 568-2735	19884
Boeing Satellite Systems Inc	3721	E	310 364-6444	19885
Boeing Satellite Systems Inc (HQ)	3663	E	310 791-7450	17473
Browntrout Publishers Inc (PA)	2741	E	424 290-6122	6206
Bundy Manufacturing Inc	3599	E	323 772-3273	15803
Continental Graphics Corp	2752	E	310 662-2307	6510
Craig Tools Inc	3545	F	310 322-0614	14152
Diane Markin Inc	3231	F	310 322-0200	10354
Dkp Designs Inc	3999	F	310 322-6000	23315
El Segundo Bread Bar LLC	2051	E	310 615-9898	1200
Epirus Inc	7372	F	310 487-5016	23871
Federal Aviation ADM	3728	E	310 640-9640	20103
Federal Industries Inc	3494	F	310 297-4040	13353
Flight Microwave Corporation	3559	F	310 607-9819	14467
Glentek Inc	3621	D	310 322-3026	16648
Governmentjobscom Inc	7372	C	310 426-6304	23950
Haydenshapes Surfboards	3949	F	310 648-8268	22818
Hco Holding II Corporation	2952	D	310 955-9200	9114
Henry Company LLC (HQ)	2952	A	310 955-9200	9115
Hnc Parent Inc (PA)	2952	A	310 955-9200	9116
Hr Cloud Inc	7372	E	510 909-1993	23990
Infineon Tech Americas Corp (HQ)	3674	A	310 726-8000	18282
Infineon Tech Americas Corp	3674	A	310 726-8000	18283
Infineon Tech Americas Corp	3674	C	310 252-7116	18285
Integra Technologies Inc	3674	E	310 606-0855	18300
J L Cooper Electronics Inc	3679	E	310 322-9990	18956
James Hunkins	3724	F	310 640-8243	19967
Karl Storz Endscpy-America Inc	3841	E	508 248-9011	21767
Karl Storz Endscpy-America Inc (HQ)	3841	B	424 218-8100	21768
Kinkisharyo International LLC (HQ)	3743	F	424 276-1803	20371
Konami Digital Entrmt Inc (DH)	7372	D	310 220-8100	24083
Kore Infrastructure LLC	2869	F	310 367-1003	8749
Lambs & Ivy Inc	2392	D	310 322-3800	3623

	SIC	EMP	PHONE	ENTRY #
Los Angles Tmes Cmmnctions LLC (PA)	2711	C	213 237-5000	5704
M Nexon Inc	7372	E	213 858-5930	24117
Mattel Inc (PA)	3942	A	310 252-2000	22650
Mattel Direct Import Inc (HQ)	3944	F	310 252-2000	22693
Metalore Inc	3599	E	310 643-0360	16197
Millennium Space Systems Inc (HQ)	3812	E	310 683-5840	20631
Mod Electronics Inc	3873	E	310 322-2136	22481
MTI Laboratory Inc	3663	E	310 955-3700	17599
Murad LLC (HQ)	2834	C	310 726-0600	8017
N A Suez	3823	E	310 414-0183	20908
Northrop Grumman Corporation	3812	C	310 332-1000	20642
Northrop Grumman Systems Corp	3812	B	310 632-1846	20655
Northrop Grumman Systems Corp	3721	C	310 332-1000	19919
Oracle Corporation	7372	A	310 343-7405	24264
Pace Americas Inc	3663	E	310 606-8300	17616
Primary Color Systems Corp	2759	D	310 841-0250	7181
Quest Nutrition LLC	2099	E	562 446-3321	2594
Radlink	3845	E	310 643-6900	22299
Raytheon Company	3812	D	310 647-1000	20682
Raytheon Company	3812	E	310 647-1000	20689
Raytheon Company	3812	B	310 647-8334	20690
Raytheon Company	3812	A	310 647-9438	20693
Raytheon Company	3812	E	310 647-1000	20694
Raytheon Company	3812	E	310 647-1000	20695
Raytheon Company	3812	E	310 334-7675	20698
Raytheon Company	3812	A	310 647-9438	20700
Ross Racing Pistons	3592	F	310 536-0100	15617
Runners World Magazine	2721	F	310 615-4567	6021
Satco Inc (PA)	2448	C	310 322-4719	4398
Scenewise	3695	D	310 466-7692	19233
Smart Action Company LLC	7372	F	310 776-9200	24417
Sports Publications Inc (PA)	2721	F	310 607-9956	6032
Symmetry Electronics LLC (DH)	3674	E	310 536-6190	18598
Teledyne Controls LLC	3812	A	310 765-3600	20729
Teledyne Technologies Inc	3679	E	310 765-3600	19109
Thai Union North America Inc (HQ)	2091	F	424 397-8556	2254
Tri-Star Electronics Intl Inc (HQ)	3643	B	310 536-0444	16936
Tri-Star Technologies Inc	3845	F	310 567-9243	22322
Trio Manufacturing Inc	3728	D	310 640-6123	20257
Venice Baking Co	2051	E	310 322-7357	1290
Zico Beverages LLC (HQ)	2086	D	866 729-9426	2186
Zoasis Corporation	2721	E	800 745-4725	6063

EL TORO, CA - Orange County

	SIC	EMP	PHONE	ENTRY #
Amtec Human Capital Inc	3544	E	949 472-0396	14016
Beverly Hillcrest Oil Corp	1311	F	949 598-7300	28
Dynamic Services Inc	2759	F	949 458-2553	7052
Freedom Communications Inc	2711	E	949 454-7300	5635
Kott Inc	2851	F	949 770-5055	8652
Mission Flavors Fragrances Inc	2087	F	949 461-3344	2221
Oakley Sales Corp	3851	F	949 951-0991	22376
The Black & Decker Inc	3546	B	949 672-4000	14229
Tri State Manufacturing Inc	3599	F	949 855-9121	16465

ELK GROVE, CA - Sacramento County

	SIC	EMP	PHONE	ENTRY #
Alldata LLC	7372	D	916 684-5200	23595
Assa Abloy Entrance Sys US Inc	3699	F	916 686-4116	19261
Boris Bs Frms Vtrnary Svcs Inc	2048	D	916 730-4225	1085
Cal-Asia Truss Inc	2439	E	916 685-5648	4291
Cemex Cnstr Mtls PCF LLC	3273	D	916 686-8310	10724
Champion Installs Inc	2434	F	916 627-0929	4181
Concrete Inc	3273	F	209 933-6999	10747
Decore-Ative Specialties	2431	C	916 686-4700	4034
Elk Grove Milling Inc	2048	E	916 684-2056	1092
Glacier Valley Ice Company LP (PA)	2097	E	916 394-2939	2355
GNB Corporation	3541	D	916 233-3543	13922
Hanford Ready-Mix Inc	3273	E	916 405-1918	10766
Hanford Sand & Gravel Inc	3273	F	916 782-9150	10767
Herburger Publications Inc	2711	F	916 685-3945	5661
International Paper Company	2621	D	916 685-9000	5113
Iparis LLC	3571	F	866 293-2872	14928
Jmgj Group Inc	3961	F	866 293-2872	22985
Pacific Modern Homes Inc	3444	E	916 685-9514	12326
Paramount Petroleum Corp	2951	F	916 685-9253	9100
Rapid Ramen Inc	3589	F	916 479-7003	15568
Universal Custom Display	3993	C	916 714-2505	23234

EMERALD HILLS, CA - San Mateo County

	SIC	EMP	PHONE	ENTRY #
Davtron	3812	F	650 369-1188	20566
Mongabayorg Corporation	2741	E	209 315-5573	6285
Teamifier Inc	7372	F	408 591-9872	24492

EMERYVILLE, CA - Alameda County

	SIC	EMP	PHONE	ENTRY #
Adamas Pharmaceuticals Inc (PA)	2834	D	510 450-3500	7725
Alive & Radiant Foods Inc	2096	E	510 238-0128	2316
Amyris Inc (PA)	2869	B	510 450-0761	8714
Bacchus Press Inc (PA)	2752	E	510 420-5800	6432

	SIC	EMP	PHONE	ENTRY #
Bayer Healthcare LLC	2834	C	510 597-6150	7792
Biospacific Inc (DH)	2835	F	510 652-6155	8209
Cleaire Advanced Emission (PA)	2911	F	510 347-6103	9043
Coco Delice	2066	F	510 601-1394	1409
Coulter Forge Technology Inc	3462	F	510 420-3500	12706
Credence Id LLC	3663	E	888 243-5452	17496
Daniel Loria Novartis	2834	E	510 655-8729	7863
Dynavax Technologies Corp (PA)	2836	C	510 848-5100	8294
Elaine Gill Inc	2731	F	510 559-1600	6100
Elemental Led LLC (PA)	3648	E	877 564-5051	17120
Engine World LLC	3714	E	510 653-4444	19649
Feasible Inc	3679	F	310 702-5803	18912
First American Building Svcs	3822	F	415 299-7597	20794
Folkmanis Inc	3999	F	510 658-7677	23334
FReal Foods LLC	2023	D	800 483-3218	591
Geo M Martin Company (PA)	3554	D	510 652-2200	14309
Gritstone Oncology Inc (PA)	2836	C	510 871-6100	8306
Intelligrated Systems Inc	3535	B	510 263-2300	13827
Jayco Hawaii California	3355	E	510 601-9916	11262
Leapfrog Enterprises Inc (HQ)	3944	E	510 420-5000	22689
Lucira Health Inc	3841	F	510 360-8071	21782
Lumigrow Inc	3646	E	800 514-0487	17055
Medtronic Inc	3841	C	510 985-9670	21804
Motorola Solutions Inc	3575	E	510 420-7400	15130
Novabay Pharmaceuticals Inc	2834	E	510 899-8800	8041
Novartis Corporation	2879	D	510 879-9500	8837
Novartis Inst For Biomedical R	2834	E	510 923-4248	8043
Novvi LLC (PA)	2911	E	281 488-0833	9054
Nugeneration Technologies LLC (PA)	2899	F	707 820-4080	9011
Nugentec Oilfield Chem LLC	2841	E	707 891-3012	8345
Peets Coffee & Tea LLC (HQ)	2095	E	510 594-2100	2308
Petit Pot Inc	2099	F	650 488-7432	2584
Pirates Press Inc	3652	F	415 738-2268	17333
Pixscan	2759	F	510 595-2222	7174
Raco Manufacturing & Engrg Co	3699	F	510 658-6713	19390
Sherbit Health Inc	7372	F	925 683-8116	24405
Suspender Factory Inc	2389	E	510 547-5400	3581
Tcho Ventures Inc	2066	F	415 981-0189	1414
Tubemogul Inc	7372	D	510 653-0126	24530
Xoma Corporation (PA)	2834	E	510 204-7200	8191
Zogenix Inc (PA)	2834	E	510 550-8300	8195

ENCINITAS, CA - San Diego County

	SIC	EMP	PHONE	ENTRY #
Access Scientific Inc	3841	E	858 354-8761	21576
Bahne and Company Inc	3949	F	760 753-8847	22754
Cable Builders Inc	2298	F	760 308-0042	2907
Coast News	2711	E	760 436-9737	5594
Cratex Manufacturing Co Inc	3291	D	760 942-2877	10945
Encinitas Oggis Inc	2082	F	760 579-3211	1523
Ideas In Motion	3861	F	760 635-1181	22428
Lees Fashions Inc	2335	F	760 753-2408	3242
Mako Labs LLC	7372	E	619 786-3618	24124
Nphase Inc	7372	E	805 750-8580	24213
Penumbra Brands Inc	3679	F	385 336-6120	19048
Pong Research Corporation	3842	F	858 914-5299	22070
R B T Inc	2396	F	619 781-8802	3809
RCP Block & Brick Inc	3271	E	760 753-1164	10518
Rose Business Solutions Inc	7372	F	858 794-9401	24367
Software Partners LLC	7372	F	760 944-8436	24429
Surfy Surfy	3949	F	760 452-7687	22905
Three Sisters Design Inc	3911	F	760 230-2813	22579
Vertical Printing & Graphics	2752	F	760 334-2004	6922

ENCINO, CA - Los Angeles County

	SIC	EMP	PHONE	ENTRY #
Astraeus Aerospace LLC	3721	F	310 907-9205	19858
Builders Concrete Inc Npp	3273	F	559 229-6643	10699
California Respiratory Care	2899	D	818 379-9999	8945
Caulipower LLC	2038	E	844 422-8544	950
Columbia Fabricating Co Inc	3446	E	818 247-4220	12463
Contempo Window Fashions	2211	F	818 768-1773	2677
D3publisher of America Inc	7372	D	310 268-0820	23796
Ect News Network Inc	2741	F	818 461-9700	6225
Facefirst Inc	7372	F	805 482-8428	23890
Graypay LLC	7372	D	818 387-6735	23953
International Last Mfg Co	3089	F	818 767-2045	9842
Ipressroom Inc	7372	F	310 499-0544	24046
Lord Leviason Enterprises LLC	2082	E	818 453-8245	1544
Mach Oil Corp	2992	F	818 783-3567	9152
Manning Holoff Co Inc	3823	E	818 407-2500	20901
Minestone	1411	F	818 775-5999	292
MSA West LLC	2342	E	213 536-9880	3455
Music Connection Inc	2721	F	818 995-0101	5992
National Cement Co Cal Inc (DH)	3273	E	818 728-5200	10805
National Cement Company Inc (HQ)	3241	E	818 728-5200	10425
National Ready Mixed Con Co (DH)	3273	E	818 728-5200	10808
Oracle America Inc	7372	E	818 905-0200	24244

	SIC	EMP	PHONE	ENTRY #
Pacific Controls Inc	3699	F	818 345-1970	19374
Pacific Paper Box Company (PA)	2652	E	323 771-7733	5191
Phorus LLC	3651	F	310 995-2521	17271
Stanzino Inc	2211	C	818 602-5171	2713
Superior Software Inc	7372	E	818 990-1135	24469
Vivometrics Inc	3845	E	805 667-2225	22328
Way Out West Inc	2326	E	310 769-6937	3058
Wondergrove LLC	7372	E	800 889-7249	24585
Zelzah Pharmacy Inc (PA)	2834	F	818 609-0692	8194
Zevia LLC	2086	E	310 202-7000	2185

ESCALON, CA - San Joaquin County

	SIC	EMP	PHONE	ENTRY #
Caron Compactor Co	3531	E	800 448-8236	13717
Hogan Mfg Inc (PA)	3999	B	209 838-7323	23353
Hogan Mfg Inc	3999	C	209 838-2400	23354
Kraft Heinz Foods Company	2033	B	209 552-6021	787
Lagier Ranches Inc	2824	F	209 982-5618	7640
Morrill Industries Inc	3494	D	209 838-2550	13360
P & L Concrete Products Inc	3273	E	209 838-1448	10812
Paddack Enterprises	2068	F	209 838-1536	1436

ESCONDIDO, CA - San Diego County

	SIC	EMP	PHONE	ENTRY #
A & D Plating Inc	3471	F	760 480-4580	12894
A C Manufacturing Inc	3599	F	760 745-3717	15659
Adti Media LLC	3993	E	951 795-4446	23044
Akzo Nobel Inc	2869	F	760 743-7374	8710
Arcmate Manufacturing Corp	3429	F	760 489-1140	11563
Avr Global Technologies Inc (PA)	3679	F	949 391-1180	18825
Aztec Perlite Company Inc	3295	F	760 741-1733	10968
Bimbo Bakeries Usa Inc	2051	F	760 737-7700	1153
Bliss Holdings LLC	3648	E	626 506-8696	17106
Brainstormproducts LLC	3944	F	760 871-1135	22664
Broken Token	3944	E	760 294-1923	22665
C & H Machine Inc	3593	D	760 746-6459	15620
California Cstm Furn & Uphl Co	2396	E	760 727-1444	3778
Capstone Fire Management Inc (PA)	3569	E	760 839-2290	14800
Clorox Sales Company	2812	E	760 432-8362	7386
Continental Components LLC	2499	F	760 480-4420	4497
Davis Stone Inc	3281	F	760 745-7881	10902
Dcc General Engrg Contrs Inc	3272	D	760 480-7400	10559
Decratek Inc	3442	F	760 747-1706	11945
Escondido Sand & Gravel LLC	2951	F	760 432-4690	9092
Esperanzas Tortilleria Inc	2099	E	760 743-5908	2452
Estco Enterprises Inc	3069	E	760 489-8745	9306
Frans Manufacturing Inc	3841	E	760 741-9135	21718
Freeberg Indus Fbrication Corp	3441	D	760 737-7614	11797
Gem Enterprises LLC	3471	E	760 746-6616	13013
Generation Circuits LLC	3672	E	760 743-7459	17889
Gmj Woodworking	2431	E	760 294-7428	4050
Goddard Rotary Tool Co Inc	3541	E	760 743-6717	13923
Heatshield Products Inc	3297	E	760 751-0441	10992
Hometex Corporation	2392	E	619 661-0400	3617
Hydrabrush Inc	2844	F	760 743-5160	8513
Imerys Perlite Usa Inc	3569	F	760 745-5900	14827
J Flying Machine Inc	3599	F	760 504-0323	16066
Lisi Medical Jeropa Inc (DH)	3541	D	760 432-9785	13932
LL Baker Inc	2752	F	760 741-9899	6706
Lormac Plastics Inc (PA)	3089	F	760 745-9115	9880
Maas-Rowe Carillons Inc	3699	E	760 743-1311	19351
Manufacturing & Prod Svcs Corp	3714	F	760 796-4300	19713
Meziere Enterprises Inc	3599	E	800 208-1755	16198
Myers & Sons Hi-Way Safety Inc	3669	E	909 591-1781	17748
Natel Engineering Company Inc	3672	C	760 737-6777	17936
Nexsan Technologies Inc	3572	E	760 745-3550	15063
North County Polishing	3471	E	760 480-0847	13063
Oldcastle Infrastructure Inc	3272	E	951 683-8200	10617
Olympic Coatings Inc	3479	E	760 745-3322	13214
One Stop Systems Inc (PA)	3577	D	760 745-9883	15301
One Stop Systems Inc	3577	E	858 530-2511	15302
Orfila Vineyards Inc (PA)	2084	E	760 738-6500	1850
Planetary Machine and Engrg	3599	F	760 489-5571	16299
Pretium Packaging LLC	3085	C	760 737-7995	9493
Pro Metal Products	3444	F	760 480-0212	12341
Pyramid Granite & Metals Inc	3281	E	760 745-6309	10924
Rancho Bernardo Printing Inc	2752	E	858 486-4540	6833
Rancho Guejito Corporation	2084	F	800 519-4441	1879
Rantec Microwave Systems Inc	3679	E	760 744-1544	19064
REAL Seal Co Inc	3053	F	760 743-7263	9249
Regina F Barajas	3531	F	760 500-0809	13744
Ritas Felicita	2024	F	760 975-3302	665
Rwnm Inc	3612	D	760 489-1245	16574
San Diego Cabinets Inc	2434	E	760 747-3100	4245
Sentinel Hydrosolutions LLC	3829	F	866 410-1134	21536
Separation Engineering Inc	3569	E	760 489-0101	14856
Southland Manufacturing Inc	3545	F	760 745-7913	14196
Summit Services Inc	3271	F	760 737-7630	10521

2020 California
Manufacturers Register

(P-0000) Products & Services Section entry number
(PA)=Parent Co (HQ)=Headquarters (DH)=Div Headquarters

	SIC	EMP	PHONE	ENTRY #
Superior Ready Mix Concrete LP	3273	F	760 728-1128	10850
Superior Ready Mix Concrete LP **(PA)**	3273	E	760 745-0556	10852
Tdg Aerospace Inc	3728	F	760 466-1040	20245
Tearlab Corporation **(PA)**	3841	F	858 455-6006	21924
Transportation Power Inc	3714	E	858 248-4255	19787
U S Circuit Inc	3679	D	760 489-1413	19130
URu By Kristine St Rrik Inc	2335	E	760 745-1800	3259
VIT Products Inc	3429	E	760 480-6702	11641
Vulcan Materials Co	3273	E	760 737-3486	10868
Western Metal Supply Co Inc	3448	F	760 233-7800	12581

ETIWANDA, CA - San Bernardino County

	SIC	EMP	PHONE	ENTRY #
Commercial Metals Company	3312	F	909 899-9993	11040

ETNA, CA - Siskiyou County

	SIC	EMP	PHONE	ENTRY #
Starr Design Fabrics Inc	2269	F	530 467-5121	2860

EUREKA, CA - Humboldt County

	SIC	EMP	PHONE	ENTRY #
Bien Padre Foods Inc	2032	E	707 442-4585	719
Carlson Wireless Tech Inc	3663	F	707 443-0100	17481
Cdh Painting Inc	2851	F	707 443-4429	8634
Coast Seafoods Company	2091	E	707 442-2947	2243
Coca Cola Btlg of Eureka Cal	2086	F	707 442-2796	2058
Eureka Record Works Inc **(PA)**	3651	F	707 442-8121	17229
Hanah Silk Inc	2241	F	707 442-0886	2753
Hilfiker Pipe Co	3272	E	707 443-5091	10585
Humboldt Newspaper Inc	2711	A	707 442-1711	5669
Jo Sonjas Folk Art Studio	2731	F	707 445-9306	6115
Marine Spill Response Corp	3826	E	707 442-6087	21258
Natural Decadence LLC	2053	F	707 444-2629	1346
North Coast Journal Inc	2711	F	707 442-1400	5781
Pasadena Newspapers Inc	2711	C	707 442-1711	5794
S-Matrix Corporation	7372	F	707 441-0404	24370
Schmidbauer Lumber Inc **(PA)**	2421	C	707 443-7024	3946
Table Bluff Brewing Inc **(PA)**	2082	E	707 445-4480	1568

EXETER, CA - Tulare County

	SIC	EMP	PHONE	ENTRY #
Amarillo Wind Machine LLC	3523	F	559 592-4256	13608
Exeter Mercantile Company	3523	F	559 592-2121	13632
Foothills Sun-Gazette	2711	E	559 592-3171	5634
Fruit Growers Supply Company	2653	F	559 592-6550	5222
International Paper Company	2621	D	559 592-7279	5112
Peninsula Packaging LLC **(DH)**	3999	D	559 594-6813	23445
Valley Cutting System Inc	3541	E	559 684-1229	13961
Waterman Valve LLC **(HQ)**	3589	C	559 562-4000	15603

FAIR OAKS, CA - Sacramento County

	SIC	EMP	PHONE	ENTRY #
Modern Metal Installations	3446	F	916 316-0997	12500
Steve Rock & Ready Mix	3273	F	916 966-1600	10846
Wholesome Harvest Baking Inc	2011	F	916 967-1633	432

FAIRFAX, CA - Marin County

	SIC	EMP	PHONE	ENTRY #
Sonic Studio LLC	7372	F	415 944-7642	24434

FAIRFIELD, CA - Solano County

	SIC	EMP	PHONE	ENTRY #
Abbott Nutrition	2834	F	707 399-1100	7711
Abbott Nutrition Mfg Inc **(HQ)**	2834	C	707 399-1100	7712
Abco Laboratories Inc **(PA)**	2834	D	707 427-1818	7714
Ball Metal Beverage Cont Corp	3411	C	707 437-7516	11494
Cemex Cnstr Mtls PCF LLC	3272	E	707 422-2520	10547
Cemex Cnstr Mtls PCF LLC	3271	E	707 422-2520	10506
Cemex Materials LLC	3273	F	707 448-7121	10738
Clorox Products Mfg Co	2842	D	707 437-1051	8379
Compu Tech Lumber Products	2439	D	707 437-6683	4297
Courage Production LLC	2013	A	707 422-6300	451
Crystal Geyser Water Company	2086	E	707 647-4410	2067
Dependable Plas & Pattern Inc	3086	E	707 863-4900	9523
Drake Enterprises Incorporated	2399	D	707 864-3077	3837
Duo Pane Industries	3231	F	707 426-9696	10355
Ethosenergy Field Services LLC	1389	F	707 399-0420	194
Fabricated Glass Spc Inc	3231	F	707 429-6160	10358
Goodrich Corporation	3769	E	707 422-1880	20475
Halabi Inc **(PA)**	3281	C	707 402-1600	10909
IL Fiorello Olive Oil Co	2079	F	707 864-1529	1473
Innovative Combustion Tech **(PA)**	3433	F	510 652-6000	11702
ITT Water & Wastewater USA Inc	3561	E	707 422-9894	14587
Jelly Belly Candy Company **(PA)**	2064	B	707 428-2800	1376
Jelly Belly Candy Company	2064	E	707 428-2800	1377
Jsj Electrical Display Corp	3993	F	707 747-5595	23143
Lin Frank Distillers	2085	F	707 437-1092	2015
Macro Plastics **(DH)**	3089	E	707 437-1200	9883
McNaughton Newspapers Inc **(PA)**	2711	D	707 425-4646	5738
Nippon Industries Inc	2038	E	707 427-3127	969
OHara Metal Products	3493	E	707 863-9090	13341
Omega Industrial Supply Inc	2842	E	707 864-8164	8401
Pauli Systems Inc	3599	E	707 429-2434	16287
Primal Pet Foods Inc	2047	F	415 642-7400	1082
Saint Gobain Containers Inc	3221	F	707 437-8700	10293

	SIC	EMP	PHONE	ENTRY #
Scott Lamp Company Inc	3646	D	707 864-2066	17070
Solano Diagnostics Imaging	3829	F	707 646-4646	21544
ST Johnson Company LLC	3433	E	510 652-6000	11719
Tronex Technology Incorporated	3423	E	707 426-2550	11549
West-Com Nrse Call Systems Inc **(PA)**	3663	E	707 428-5900	17705
Westamerica Bancorporation	3944	F	707 863-6000	22725
Woodline Partners Inc	2434	E	707 864-5445	4269

FALLBROOK, CA - San Diego County

	SIC	EMP	PHONE	ENTRY #
Accurate Wire & Display Inc	3496	E	310 532-7821	13393
AVI	3679	F	760 451-9379	18824
Axelgaard Manufacturing Co Ltd **(PA)**	3845	D	760 723-7554	22229
Axelgaard Manufacturing Co Ltd	3845	E	760 723-7554	22230
Cord Industries Inc	3089	F	760 728-4590	9727
Don Conibear	3089	F	760 728-4590	9764
Fallbrook Industries Inc	3469	E	760 728-7229	12803
Fallbrook Printing Corp	2752	F	760 731-2020	6568
Med-Fit Systems Inc	3949	C	760 723-3618	22851
Pazzulla Plastics Inc	2541	E	714 847-2541	4930
Pole Danzer	3272	F	760 419-9514	10624
Rock Solid Stone LLC	3272	F	760 731-6191	10642
Scrape Certified Welding Inc	3441	D	760 728-1308	11879
Workman Holdings Inc	3841	F	760 723-5283	21964

FARMERSVILLE, CA - Tulare County

	SIC	EMP	PHONE	ENTRY #
Tortilleria La Mejor	2099	D	559 747-0739	2631

FARMINGTON, CA - San Joaquin County

	SIC	EMP	PHONE	ENTRY #
Pleasant Valley Farms **(PA)**	2015	D	209 886-1000	525
Ripon Milling LLC	2048	E	209 599-4269	1122

FELLOWS, CA - Kern County

	SIC	EMP	PHONE	ENTRY #
Freeport-Mcmoran Oil & Gas LLC	1311	E	661 768-4831	51
Pacific Perforating Inc	1389	E	661 768-9224	242
Pro Vac	1389	F	661 765-7298	249

FELTON, CA - Santa Cruz County

	SIC	EMP	PHONE	ENTRY #
Hudson Industries Inc	3999	E	831 335-4431	23358
Satellite Telework Centers Inc **(PA)**	3825	F	831 222-2100	21117

FERNDALE, CA - Humboldt County

	SIC	EMP	PHONE	ENTRY #
Pacific Timber Contracting	2411	F	707 498-1374	3900

FIELDS LANDING, CA - Humboldt County

	SIC	EMP	PHONE	ENTRY #
Environmental Technology Inc	2821	E	707 443-9323	7562

FILLMORE, CA - Ventura County

	SIC	EMP	PHONE	ENTRY #
Ameron International Corp	3272	C	425 258-2616	10528
Ameron International Corp	3272	D	805 524-0223	10529
Honey Bennetts Farm Inc	2099	E	805 521-1375	2480

FIREBAUGH, CA - Fresno County

	SIC	EMP	PHONE	ENTRY #
Eagle Valley Ginning LLC	3559	E	209 826-5002	14455
Hiller Aircraft Corporation	3728	E	559 659-5959	20126
Neil Jones Food Company	2033	E	559 659-5100	803

FOLSOM, CA - Sacramento County

	SIC	EMP	PHONE	ENTRY #
Aerojet Rocketdyne Inc	3728	F	916 355-4000	20017
Agilent Technologies Inc	3825	C	916 985-7888	20988
Altergy Systems	3629	E	916 458-8590	16774
AMO Corporation	3545	F	916 791-2001	14130
Brehm Communications Inc	2711	F	916 985-2581	5568
Care Innovations LLC	3845	E	800 450-0970	22236
Gekkeikan Sake USAinC	2084	E	916 985-3111	1720
General Dynmics Ots Ncvlle Inc	3812	D	916 355-7700	20582
Intel Corporation	3674	D	916 943-6809	18305
Intel Corporation	3674	D	916 356-8080	18308
L3 Technologies Inc	3663	C	916 351-4556	17563
Micron Technology Inc	3674	A	916 458-3003	18396
Microsemi Corp- Rf Integrated **(DH)**	3674	C	916 850-8640	18401
Military Aircraft Parts **(PA)**	3599	E	916 635-8010	16205
Powerschool Group LLC **(HQ)**	7372	C	916 288-1636	24310
Sierra Nevada Corporation	3699	E	916 985-8799	19403
Style Media Group Inc	2721	E	916 988-9888	6033
Synapsense Corporation	3572	F	916 294-0110	15105
Trimble Inc	3812	E	916 294-2000	20735
United Reporting Pubg Corp	2741	E	916 542-7501	6366
Wireless Innovation Inc	3679	F	916 357-6700	19143
Xolar Corporation	3999	E	916 983-6301	23529

FONTANA, CA - San Bernardino County

	SIC	EMP	PHONE	ENTRY #
101 Vertical Fabrication Inc	3441	E	909 428-6000	11726
Advanti Racing Usa LLC **(DH)**	3714	E	951 272-5930	19570
Alabama Metal Industries Corp	3446	E	909 350-9280	12448
Allied West Paper Corp	2676	D	909 349-0710	5457
American Die Casting Inc	3364	E	909 356-7768	11352
American Security Products Co	3499	C	951 685-9680	13496
American Truck Dismantling	1389	F	909 429-2166	153
Apple Tree International Corp	3571	F	626 679-7025	14891

Employment Codes: A=Over 500 employees, B=251-500,
C=101-250, D=51-100, E=20-50, F=10-19

2020 California
Manufacturers Register

© Mergent Inc. 1-800-342-5647
1333

GEOGRAPHIC

	SIC	EMP	PHONE	ENTRY #
Arrow Steel Products Inc	3316	F	909 349-1032	11117
Arrow Truck Sales Incorporated	3713	F	909 829-2365	19520
ASC Profiles LLC	3441	C	909 823-0401	11744
Assisvis Inc	3084	E	909 628-2031	9463
Avery Dennison Corporation	2672	C	909 428-4238	5353
Avilas Garden Art (PA)	3272	C	909 350-4546	10533
Aztec Technology Corporation	2448	F	909 350-8830	4349
B & M Machine Inc	3599	F	909 355-0998	15766
Bab Steering Hydraulics (PA)	3714	E	208 573-4502	19590
Becker Specialty Corporation	3677	F	909 356-1095	18702
Betts Company	3495	F	909 427-9988	13377
Bluefield Associates Inc	2844	E	909 476-6027	8447
Buildmat Plus Investments Inc	3272	F	909 823-7663	10544
Bway Corporation	3411	E	951 361-4100	11495
California Steel Inds Inc (PA)	3312	B	909 350-6300	11032
California Steel Inds Inc	3312	A	909 350-6300	11033
California Turbo Inc	3564	F	909 854-2800	14650
Cameron West Coast (PA)	3533	F	909 355-8995	13771
Cannon Gasket Inc	3053	F	909 355-1547	9222
Canyon Steel Fabricators Inc	3441	E	951 683-2352	11759
Carlstar Group LLC	3714	F	909 829-1703	19611
Castle Importing Inc	2022	F	909 428-9200	543
Cavallo & Cavallo Inc	3599	F	909 428-6994	15829
Cemex Cnstr Mtls PCF LLC	3273	F	909 355-8754	10730
Chemicals Incorporated	2899	F	951 681-9697	8947
Clark - Pacific Corporation	3272	C	909 823-1433	10552
Colonial Enterprises Inc	2844	E	909 822-8700	8459
Continental Coatings Inc	2851	F	909 355-1200	8637
Creative Stone Mfg Inc (PA)	3272	C	909 357-8295	10557
Crown Technical Systems	3613	F	951 332-4170	16591
Custom Fabricated Metals LLC	3449	F	909 822-8828	12588
Cvc Technologies Inc	3565	E	909 355-0311	14705
Dayton Superior Corporation	3721	E	909 957-7271	19891
Dennie Manning Concrete Inc	3273	F	909 823-7521	10752
Door Components Inc	3442	C	909 770-5700	11948
Dorel Juvenile Group Inc	3089	C	909 428-0295	9765
DSM&t Co Inc	3694	C	909 357-7960	19189
Duro Dyne West Corp	3585	B	562 926-1774	15426
Ecoplast Corporation Inc	3089	D	909 346-0450	9771
Edessa Inc	3272	E	909 823-1377	10565
Everett Charles Tech LLC (DH)	3825	D	909 625-5551	21033
Everett Charles Tech LLC	3825	F	909 625-5551	21034
Fabco Steel Fabrication Inc	3441	F	909 350-1535	11790
Fontana Foundry Corporation	3365	E	909 822-6128	11381
Fontana Paper Mills Inc	2952	D	909 823-4100	9112
Forged Metals Inc	3462	C	909 350-9260	12709
G O Pallets Inc	2448	E	909 823-4663	4368
Gator Machinery Company	3531	F	909 823-1688	13729
General Mills Inc	2043	D	951 685-7030	1022
Great Northern Corporation	2671	E	951 361-4770	5329
Greif Inc	3412	E	909 350-2112	11509
Harvest Asia Inc	3944	F	888 800-3133	22679
High Tech Machine Shop S-Corp	3519	F	909 356-5437	13597
Ifco Systems North America Inc	2448	F	909 356-0697	4372
Indigo Designs	2434	F	909 997-0854	4209
Industrial Insulations Inc (PA)	3644	E	909 574-7433	16950
Iparts Inc	3089	F	909 587-6059	9843
J-M Manufacturing Company Inc	2821	D	909 822-3009	7576
JE Thomson & Company LLC	3537	F	626 334-7190	13878
Jensen Enterprises Inc	3272	B	909 357-7264	10592
Jeti Inc (PA)	7692	F	909 357-2966	24645
Kemira Water Solutions Inc	2819	E	909 350-5678	7502
Kemira Water Solutions Inc	2899	E	909 350-5678	8984
Kymera Industries Inc	3999	F	909 228-7194	23387
Lamer Street Kreations Corp	3499	F	909 305-4824	13529
Lopez Pallets Inc	2448	F	909 823-0865	4378
Luster Cote Inc	3479	F	909 355-9995	13203
Lynam Industries Inc	3444	D	951 360-1919	12270
Material Supply Inc (PA)	3444	C	951 801-5004	12283
Metal Sales Manufacturing Corp	3444	F	909 829-8618	12295
Metal Tek Engineering Inc	2431	E	909 821-4158	4084
Meza Pallet Inc	2441	F	909 829-0223	4339
Michael Hagan	3949	F	909 213-5916	22853
Michaels Stores Inc	3999	E	909 646-9656	23411
Mission Custom Extrusion Inc	3089	E	909 822-1581	9899
Mohawk Industries Inc	2273	D	909 357-1064	2874
Morin Corp	3448	E	909 428-3747	12564
New Greenscreen Incorporated	3444	E	951 685-9660	12313
Northrop Grumman Corporation	3812	A	626 812-2842	20640
Nyx Industries Inc	3523	F	909 937-3923	13653
Oldcastle Apg West Inc	3241	F	909 355-6422	10427
Oldcastle Infrastructure Inc	3272	A	909 428-3700	10610
Pacific Award Metals Inc	3444	E	626 814-4410	12324
Pacific Forge Inc	3462	D	909 390-0701	12716
Patricks Cabinets	2434	F	909 823-2524	4230

	SIC	EMP	PHONE	ENTRY #
Peri Formwork Systems Inc	3444	E	909 356-5797	12332
Pro Systems Fabricators Inc (PA)	3699	F	909 350-9147	19383
Rep-Kote Products Inc	2952	E	909 355-1288	9124
Ring Container Tech LLC	3085	E	909 350-8416	9495
River Valley Precast Inc	3272	E	928 764-3839	10640
Rnd Contractors Inc	3441	E	909 429-8500	11874
S & H Cabinets and Mfg Inc	2521	E	909 357-0551	4820
S&B Filters Inc	3714	D	909 947-0015	19762
Santa Fe Machine Works Inc	3599	E	909 350-6877	16385
Schroeder Iron Corporation	3441	E	909 428-6471	11878
Shawcor Pipe Protection LLC	3479	F	909 357-9002	13245
Simplex Strip Doors LLC (DH)	3081	E	800 854-7951	9421
Solar Atmospheres Inc	3398	E	909 217-7400	11468
Sole Technology Inc	3149	F	949 460-2020	10185
Southern Cal Bndery Miling Inc	2789	D	909 829-1949	7350
Southwire Inc (HQ)	3353	F	310 884-8500	11223
Specfoam LLC	2515	F	951 685-3626	4745
Specialized Milling Corp	2851	F	909 357-7890	8681
Standard Industries Inc	2493	C	951 360-4274	4487
Stl Fabrication Inc	3441	F	909 823-5033	11886
Suez Wts Services Usa Inc	3589	F	951 681-5555	15590
Sundown Foods USA Inc	2033	E	909 606-6797	826
Sunearth Inc	3433	E	909 434-3100	11720
Superior Sndblst & Coating	2851	E	909 428-9994	8684
Superior Trailer Works	3537	E	909 350-0185	13894
Svevia Usa Inc	3953	F	909 559-4134	22956
Tikos Tanks Inc	7692	E	951 757-8014	24674
Tpi Marketing LLC	3556	F	302 703-0283	14407
Tree Island Wire (usa) Inc	3315	D	909 594-7511	11111
Tri-Net Inc	3825	F	909 483-3555	21150
Tst/Impreso California Inc	2761	F	909 357-7190	7293
TTI Floor Care North Amer Inc	3052	B	440 996-2802	9210
Turret Punch Co Inc	3083	F	909 587-1820	9458
Utility Trailer Mfg Co	3715	F	909 428-8300	19838
Vanguard Fabrication Corp	3444	F	909 355-0832	12422
Verco Decking Inc	3444	F	909 822-8079	12423
Vista Metals Corp (PA)	3354	C	909 823-4278	11254
W E Hall Co	3444	F	909 829-4235	12431
Wagonmasters Corporation	3799	F	909 823-6188	20524

FOOTHILL RANCH, CA - Orange County

	SIC	EMP	PHONE	ENTRY #
A & A Ready Mixed Concrete Inc	3273	F	949 580-1844	10678
A & J Manufacturing Company	3469	E	714 544-9570	12755
Allied Components Intl	3677	E	949 356-1780	18698
Avion Graphics Inc	2752	E	949 472-0438	6423
Azure Microdynamics Inc	3599	D	949 699-3344	15760
Bal Seal Engineering Inc (PA)	3495	B	949 460-2100	13375
Baldwin Hardware Corporation (DH)	3429	A	949 672-4000	11570
Carr Manufacturing Company Inc	3643	F	949 215-7952	16882
Chroma Systems Solutions Inc (HQ)	3825	D	949 297-4848	21016
Elite Global Solutions Inc	2821	F	949 709-4872	7561
Exhibit Works Inc	3993	F	949 470-0850	23103
Fredi & Sons Inc	3142	F	818 881-1170	10156
Gatekeeper Systems Inc (PA)	3699	E	949 268-1414	19316
Kaiser Aluminum Corporation (PA)	3334	D	949 614-1740	11184
Kaiser Aluminum Fab Pdts LLC (HQ)	3353	A	949 614-1740	11219
Kaiser Aluminum Investments Co (HQ)	3353	C	949 614-1740	11220
Lantic Inc	3089	F	949 830-9951	9874
Leoch Battery Corporation (PA)	3621	E	949 588-5853	16659
Nike Inc	2353	F	949 768-4000	3470
Oakley Inc	3851	D	949 672-6849	22375
Oakley Inc (DH)	2331	A	949 951-0991	3187
Oleumtech Corporation	3823	F	949 305-9009	20912
Ossur Americas Inc (HQ)	3842	B	949 362-3883	22061
Ossur Americas Inc	3842	F	949 382-3883	22062
Ossur Americas Inc	3842	E	805 484-2600	22063
Price Pfister Inc	3432	E	949 672-4003	11677
Protab Laboratories	2834	D	949 635-1930	8088
Renkus-Heinz Inc	3651	D	949 588-9997	17276
Trs International Mfg Inc	3643	F	949 855-0673	16937

FORESTVILLE, CA - Sonoma County

	SIC	EMP	PHONE	ENTRY #
Canyon Rock Co Inc	1442	E	707 887-2207	334
Hartford Jackson LLC	2084	F	707 887-1756	1749
Kozlowski Farms A Corporation	2033	E	707 887-1587	783

FORT BRAGG, CA - Mendocino County

	SIC	EMP	PHONE	ENTRY #
Anderson Logging Inc	2411	D	707 964-2770	3872
Gatehouse Media LLC	2711	F	707 964-5642	5640
Goodall Guitars Inc	3931	F	707 962-1620	22623
H&M Logging	2411	F	707 964-2340	3885
Mendocino Lithographers	2752	F	707 964-0062	6723
North Coast Brewing Co Inc (PA)	2082	D	707 964-2739	1550
Ocean Fresh LLC (PA)	2091	F	707 964-1389	2247
Philbrick Inc	2411	F	707 964-2277	3901
Roach Bros Inc	2411	D	707 964-9240	3902

Mergent email: customerrelations@mergent.com
1334

2020 California
Manufacturers Register

(P-0000) Products & Services Section entry number
(PA)=Parent Co (HQ)=Headquarters (DH)=Div Headquarters

FORT JONES, CA - Siskiyou County

Name	SIC	EMP	PHONE	ENTRY #
Eggtooth Originals Consulting	3944	F	530 468-5131	22673

FORTUNA, CA - Humboldt County

Name	SIC	EMP	PHONE	ENTRY #
Foster Dairy Farms	2023	C	707 725-6182	590
Huffman Logging Co Inc	2411	E	707 725-4335	3887

FOSTER CITY, CA - San Mateo County

Name	SIC	EMP	PHONE	ENTRY #
American Precision Gear Co	3566	E	650 627-8060	14739
Arena Solutions Inc	7372	E	978 988-3800	23623
Central Business Forms Inc	2752	F	650 548-0918	6477
Getgoing Inc	7372	E	415 608-7474	23937
Gilead Colorado Inc	2834	C	650 574-3000	7913
Gilead Palo Alto Inc (HQ)	2834	D	650 384-8500	7915
Gilead Sciences Inc (PA)	2834	B	650 574-3000	7916
Gridgain Systems Inc (PA)	7372	D	650 241-2281	23958
Iar Systems Software Inc (HQ)	7372	E	650 287-4250	23996
Illumina Inc	3826	E	510 670-9300	21244
Inbenta Technologies Inc (PA)	7372	E	408 213-8771	24006
Life Technologies Corporation	3826	C	760 603-7200	21254
Louis Roesch Company	2752	F	650 212-2052	6709
Mirum Pharmaceuticals Inc	2834	E	650 667-4085	8015
Omics Group Inc	2721	B	650 268-9744	5994
Oracle Corporation	7372	B	650 678-3612	24251
Pioneer Materials Inc	3827	E	650 357-7130	21399
Powertronix Corporation	3612	E	650 345-6800	16570
Sciclone Pharmaceuticals Inc (HQ)	2834	E	650 358-3456	8122
Terarecon Inc (PA)	3577	D	650 372-1100	15349
Zoox Inc (PA)	3711	C	650 733-9669	19514

FOUNTAIN VALLEY, CA - Orange County

Name	SIC	EMP	PHONE	ENTRY #
Action Bag & Cover Inc	2393	D	714 965-7777	3652
Adrienne Designs LLC	3911	E	714 558-1209	22488
Advanced Architectural Frames	3442	E	424 209-6018	11929
Avatar Machine LLC	3599	E	949 817-7728	15756
California Clock Co (PA)	3873	F	714 545-4321	22478
Coast To Coast Label Inc (PA)	2679	F	657 203-2583	5500
Compuvac Industries Inc	3563	F	949 574-5085	14627
Custom Enamelers Inc	3479	E	714 540-7884	13163
D & D Gold Product Corp	2041	F	714 550-0372	999
Duncan McIntosh Company Inc (PA)	2721	E	949 660-6150	5926
Epe Industries Usa Inc	3086	F	800 315-0336	9527
Epe Industries Usa Inc (HQ)	3086	F	800 315-0336	9528
Express Lens Lab Inc	3851	E	714 545-1024	22355
Fntech	3648	F	714 429-1686	17125
Freightgate Inc	7372	F	714 799-2833	23921
Gaffoglio Fmly Mtlcrafters Inc (PA)	3231	C	714 444-2000	10361
Genesis Group Sftwr Developers	7372	F	714 630-4297	23933
Gfmi Aerospace & Defense Inc	3728	E	714 361-4444	20114
Gigamem LLC	3572	F	949 461-9999	15031
Intercity Centerless Grinding	3599	F	714 546-5644	16052
Joy Products California Inc	3953	F	714 437-7250	22952
KB Sheetmetal Fabrication Inc	3444	E	714 979-1780	12261
Kingston Digital Inc (DH)	3577	F	714 435-2600	15266
Kingston Technology Corp (PA)	3577	B	714 445-3495	15267
Lakin Industries Inc (PA)	3471	F	714 968-6438	13040
Los Angles Tmes Cmmnctions LLC	2711	B	714 966-5600	5707
Makino Inc	3545	E	714 444-4334	14169
Meyco Machine and Tool Inc	3545	E	714 435-1546	14172
Microscale Industries Inc	2752	F	714 593-1422	6728
Microtech LLC	3843	E	714 966-1645	22173
Mobis Parts America LLC	3714	B	949 450-0014	19722
Moving Image Technologies LLC	3861	E	714 751-7998	22442
Northrop Grumman Corporation	3812	A	310 332-6653	20645
Omni Metal Finishing Inc (PA)	3471	D	714 231-3716	13064
Openpro Inc	7372	F	714 378-4600	24230
Paderia LLC	2052	F	949 478-5273	1323
Panda Bowl	2599	F	714 418-0299	5075
Parker Printing Inc	2752	F	714 444-4550	6769
Payton Technology Corporation	3674	C	714 885-8000	18467
Precision European Inc	3559	F	714 241-9657	14520
Printing Island Corporation	2752	F	714 668-1000	6804
Psitech Inc	3571	F	714 964-7818	14965
Quik Mfg Co	3531	E	714 754-0337	13742
Radflo Suspension Technology	3714	F	714 965-7828	19753
Richards Label Co Inc	2672	E	714 529-1791	5372
Ropak Corporation (DH)	3089	E	714 845-2845	10025
Sams Tailoring	2311	F	714 963-6776	2977
Santa Fe Textiles Inc	2241	F	949 251-1960	2760
Sensonetics Inc	3674	F	714 799-1616	18540
Sherman Corporation	3599	E	310 671-2117	16402
Shock Doctor Inc (PA)	3949	D	800 233-6956	22886
Specialized Screen Printing	2759	F	714 964-1230	7223
SPX Corporation	3443	D	714 434-2576	12055
Surefire LLC	3842	D	714 545-9444	22099
Surefire LLC	3842	E	714 545-9444	22100
Surefire LLC	3648	E	714 545-9444	17165
Surefire LLC (PA)	3842	C	714 545-9444	22104
Sutura Inc	3842	E	714 427-0398	22105
Swissdigital USA Co Ltd	3999	F	626 351-1999	23495
Tape Factory Inc	2672	E	714 979-7742	5376
TN Sheet Metal Inc	3444	F	714 593-0100	12409
Touchpoint Solutions	7372	F	714 740-7242	24522
Watt Enterprise Inc	2329	F	714 963-0781	3130

FOWLER, CA - Fresno County

Name	SIC	EMP	PHONE	ENTRY #
Bobby Slzars Mxcan Fd Pdts Inc (PA)	2032	E	559 834-4787	720
Borga Stl Bldngs Cmponents Inc	3444	E	559 834-5375	12134
Dale Brisco Inc	3444	F	559 834-5926	12172
Jacobsen Trailer Inc	3715	E	559 834-5971	19825
Pps Packaging Company	2621	D	559 834-1641	5144
Sunshine Raisin Corporation (PA)	2064	C	559 834-5981	1403

FRAZIER PARK, CA - Kern County

Name	SIC	EMP	PHONE	ENTRY #
Trnlwb LLC	3999	A	661 245-3736	23512

FREEDOM, CA - Santa Cruz County

Name	SIC	EMP	PHONE	ENTRY #
Sage Instruments Inc	3825	D	831 761-1000	21115

FREMONT, CA - Alameda County

Name	SIC	EMP	PHONE	ENTRY #
3dconnexion Inc	3577	D	510 713-6000	15139
3par Inc (HQ)	3571	C	510 445-1046	14876
A & D Precision Machining Inc	3599	E	510 657-6781	15651
ABC Assembly Inc	3672	F	408 293-3560	17799
Abd El & Larson Holdings LLC (PA)	3613	E	510 656-1600	16583
Acm Research Inc	3589	C	510 445-3700	15478
Acrometrix Corporation	2835	E	707 746-8888	8199
Adtec Technology Inc	3677	F	510 226-5766	18694
Advance Electronic Service	3672	F	510 490-1065	17807
Advanced Enterprises LLC	3663	F	408 923-5000	17438
Aehr Test Systems (PA)	3825	D	510 623-9400	20985
Air Liquide Electronics US LP	2819	E	510 624-4338	7467
Airgas Usa LLC	2813	E	510 624-4000	7408
Alertenterprise Inc	7372	C	510 440-0840	23591
All Quality & Services Inc	3672	D	510 249-5800	17809
All West Fabricators Inc	3441	E	510 623-1200	11741
All-Tech Machine & Engrg Inc	3599	E	510 353-2000	15721
Alpha Ems Corporation	3672	C	510 498-8788	17812
Alta Manufacturing Inc	3672	E	510 668-1870	17813
Altair Technologies Inc	3559	E	650 508-8700	14421
Alterg Inc	3949	D	510 270-5900	22741
American Air Liquide Inc (DH)	2813	D	510 624-4000	7412
Ampro Systems Inc	3672	E	510 624-9000	17818
Antec Inc	3577	E	510 770-1200	15156
Applied Ceramics Inc (PA)	3674	E	510 249-9700	18105
Applied Materials Inc	3674	E	510 687-8018	18114
Applied Thin-Film Products (PA)	3679	C	510 661-4287	18818
Applied Thin-Film Products	3679	F	510 661-4287	18819
Ardelyx Inc	2834	D	510 745-1700	7763
Areesys Corporation	3699	E	510 979-9601	19259
Aries Research Inc	3577	F	925 818-1078	15159
Aruba Networks Inc	3663	E	408 227-4500	17459
Asante Technologies Inc	3577	E	408 435-8388	15163
Asteelflash USA Corp (HQ)	3672	C	510 440-2840	17827
Atlas Copco Compressors LLC	3563	E	510 413-5200	14622
Atlas Copco Compressors LLC	3563	F	510 413-5200	14624
Avalanche Technology Inc	3674	E	510 438-0148	18136
Avermedia Technologies Inc	3577	E	510 403-0006	15164
Avp Technology LLC	3565	E	510 683-0157	14696
Axp Technology Inc	3646	E	510 683-1180	17013
Axt Inc	3674	E	510 683-5900	18140
Axt Inc (PA)	3674	E	510 438-4700	18141
Ayantra Inc	3661	F	510 623-7526	17348
B & G Precision Inc	3599	F	510 438-9785	15764
Bace Manufacturing Inc	3089	D	510 657-5800	9651
Ball Screws & Actuators Co Inc (HQ)	3568	D	510 770-5932	14782
Bart Manufacturing Inc (PA)	3999	D	408 320-4373	23285
BASF Catalysts LLC	2869	F	510 490-2150	8716
BASF Venture Capital Amer Inc	2869	F	510 445-6140	8720
Bay AR Yellow Pages	2741	F	650 558-8888	6198
Bay Area Circuits Inc	3672	F	510 933-9000	17831
Bay Associates Wire Tech Corp (DH)	2298	D	510 988-3800	2906
Bay Equipment Co Inc	3462	D	510 226-8800	12704
Bayview Plastic Solutions Inc	3089	E	510 360-0001	9655
Belden Inc	3357	F	510 438-9071	11288
Bema Electronic Mfg Inc	3679	D	510 490-7770	18834
Benchmark Electronics Inc	3672	D	510 360-2800	17836
Berkeley Design Automation Inc	3674	E	408 496-6600	18146
Biogenex Laboratories (PA)	3841	E	510 824-1400	21634
Biokey Inc	2834	E	510 668-0881	7806
Biometric Solutions LLC	3577	F	408 625-7763	15171
Biotium Inc	2865	F	510 265-1027	8697
Bipolarics Inc	3674	E	408 372-7574	18147

GEOGRAPHIC

Name	SIC	EMP	PHONE	ENTRY #
Bitmicro Networks Inc (PA)	3572	F	510 743-3124	15008
Bizlink Technology Inc (HQ)	3643	D	510 252-0786	16878
Blazer Exhibits & Graphics Inc	3993	F	408 263-7000	23064
Bo-Sherrel Corporation	3577	F	510 744-3525	15176
Bodycote Thermal Proc Inc	3398	E	510 492-4200	11439
Bold Data Technology Inc	3571	F	510 490-8296	14892
Bridgelux Inc	3674	D	925 583-8400	18150
Brooks Automation Inc	3585	D	510 498-8745	15417
C3-Ilex LLC (PA)	3822	E	510 659-8300	20785
Cable Connection Inc	3643	D	510 249-9000	16879
Cae Automation and Test LLC	3599	F	408 204-0006	15816
Cal-Weld Inc	3499	C	510 226-0100	13505
California Stone Coating	3531	F	510 284-2554	13715
Calogic LLC (PA)	3825	F	510 656-2900	21015
Cambridge Laser Laboratories	3231	F	510 651-0110	10345
Camtek Usa Inc	3674	E	510 624-9905	18156
Celestica LLC	3679	C	510 770-5100	18856
Celestica Prcsion McHining Ltd	3599	F	510 252-2100	15831
Cellphone-Mate Inc	3663	D	510 770-0469	17484
Cenergy Solutions Inc	3714	F	510 474-7593	19612
Ceramic Tech Inc	3599	E	510 252-8500	15837
Certainteed Corporation	2952	D	510 490-0890	9111
Ceterix Orthopaedics Inc	3841	E	650 241-1748	21662
Cha Industries Inc	3559	E	510 683-8554	14438
Chart Inc	3443	E	408 371-3303	12005
China Custom Manufacturing Ltd	3089	A	510 979-1920	9708
China Loco Szhou Precise Indus	3678	E	510 429-3700	18753
Chinese Overseas Mktg Svc Corp	2741	E	626 280-8588	6214
Cirrus Logic Inc	3674	D	510 226-1204	18162
Citragen Pharmaceuticals Inc	2834	F	510 249-9066	7842
Clean Sciences Inc	3471	F	510 440-8660	12970
Cleansmart Solutions Inc	2677	E	650 871-9123	5469
Cli Liquidating Corporation	3845	D	510 354-0300	22240
Colleen & Herb Enterprises Inc	3599	C	510 226-6083	15858
Comcore Technologies Inc	3827	E	510 498-8858	21345
Commercial Casework Inc (PA)	2431	D	510 657-7933	4018
Compass Components Inc (PA)	3679	C	510 656-4700	18873
Compugraphics USA Inc (HQ)	3674	D	510 249-2600	18171
Concentric Medical Inc	3841	E	650 938-2100	21670
Confluent Medical Tech Inc (PA)	3841	B	510 683-2000	21671
Content Management Corporation	2759	F	510 505-1100	7034
Contract Metal Products Inc	3444	E	510 979-4811	12162
Coorstek Inc	3264	D	510 492-6600	10475
Corsair Components Inc (PA)	3577	C	510 657-8747	15208
Corsair Memory Inc	3674	C	510 657-8747	18181
Creative Shower Door Corp	3088	F	510 623-9000	9583
Crossing Automation Inc (HQ)	3559	E	510 661-5000	14444
Custom Micro Machining Inc	3599	E	510 651-9434	15873
Custom Microwave Components	3679	F	510 651-3434	18881
Cytek Biosciences Inc (PA)	3845	D	510 657-0110	22247
Cytek Development Inc	3826	F	510 657-0102	21214
D&H Manufacturing Company	3999	F	510 770-5100	23309
Dataguise Inc	7372	E	510 824-1036	23805
Dawn VME Products	3679	E	510 657-4444	18883
Digital Power Corporation (HQ)	3679	E	510 657-2635	18888
Discopylabs (PA)	3652	F	510 651-5100	17316
Document Capture Tech Inc (PA)	3577	F	408 436-9888	15217
Du-All Safety LLC	3599	F	510 651-8289	15908
Duke Scientific Corporation	3821	E	650 424-1177	20755
Edc-Biosystems Inc (PA)	3823	E	510 257-1500	20863
Electronics For Imaging Inc (HQ)	2759	F	650 357-3500	7056
Ellex Iscience	3841	F	510 291-1300	21701
Elma Electronic Inc (HQ)	3571	C	510 656-3400	14907
Enablence Systems Inc (HQ)	7372	E	510 226-8900	23858
Enablence USA Components Inc	3661	D	510 226-8900	17364
Enphase Energy Inc (PA)	3674	C	707 774-7000	18219
Envizio Inc	7372	E	650 814-4302	23867
Epoch International Entps Inc	3559	C	510 556-1225	14461
Essai Inc (PA)	3825	C	510 580-1700	21031
Evolve Manufacturing Tech Inc	3841	D	650 968-9292	21709
Exar Corporation	3674	B	408 927-9975	18231
Excelitas Technologies Corp	3648	D	510 979-6500	17124
Fabri-Tech Components Inc	3679	F	510 249-2000	18909
Famsoft Corp	7372	F	408 452-1550	23893
Famsoft Corporation	7372	F	510 683-3940	23894
Fancy Models Corp	3999	F	510 683-0819	23331
Fei Efa Inc (DH)	3678	D	510 897-6800	18768
Finisar Corporation	3674	B	408 548-1000	18235
FM Industries Inc	3599	C	510 673-0192	15963
FM Industries Inc (DH)	3599	C	510 668-1900	15964
Fremont Amgen Inc (HQ)	2834	B	510 284-6500	7897
Fujikin of America Inc (HQ)	3492	E	408 980-8269	13330
Genoa Corporation	3674	E	510 979-3000	18247
Gigamat Technologies Inc	3674	F	510 770-8008	18249
Global Plating Inc	3471	E	510 659-8764	13015
Golden State Assembly Inc	3353	C	510 226-8155	11217
Gooch & Housego Palo Alto LLC (HQ)	3679	D	650 856-7911	18926
Gupshup Inc	7372	F	415 506-9095	23966
Hayward Quartz Technology	3674	C	510 657-9605	18267
Helitek Company Ltd	3674	F	510 933-7688	18268
Henry Plastic Molding Inc	3089	C	510 490-7993	9821
Hi/Fn Inc (DH)	3674	F	408 778-2944	18271
Highpoint Technologies Inc	3572	F	408 942-5800	15043
Hpe Government Llc	3575	D	916 435-9200	15123
I-Tech Company Ltd Lblty Co	3572	F	510 226-9226	15045
I2a Technologies Inc	3674	E	510 770-0322	18274
Ic Sensors Inc	3674	D	510 498-1570	18275
Ichor Systems Inc (HQ)	3674	E	510 897-5200	18277
Identiv Inc (PA)	3577	B	949 250-8888	15240
Igolping Inc	3949	F	866 507-4440	22826
Imtec Acculine LLC	3559	E	510 770-1800	14477
Incal Technology Inc	3577	E	510 657-8405	15243
Innodisk Usa Corporation	3674	E	510 770-9421	18291
Inspur Systems Inc (HQ)	3571	E	800 697-5893	14925
Integrated Mfg Tech Inc (DH)	3471	F	408 934-5879	13031
INTEL Corporation	3674	E	510 651-9841	18307
International Paper Company	2621	E	510 490-5887	5110
Intest Corporation	3674	E	408 678-9123	18316
Intest Silicon Valley Corp	3674	E	408 678-9123	18317
Intuity Medical Inc	3841	D	408 530-1700	21756
Iscience Interventional Corp	3841	D	650 421-2700	21760
Isomedia LLC	3652	E	510 668-1656	17330
Ituner Networks Corporation	3577	F	510 226-6033	15260
Jaf International Inc	3571	F	510 656-1718	14929
Jaton Corporation	3672	B	510 933-8888	17908
Jem America Corp	3825	F	510 683-9234	21059
Johnson & Johnson	2676	D	650 237-4878	5463
Just Light Technology Inc	7372	F	510 585-5652	24065
Kaser Corporation	3571	F	510 657-9002	14932
Kashiyama USA Inc	3823	F	510 979-0070	20893
Kelly-Moore Paint Company Inc	2851	F	510 505-9834	8650
KLA Corporation	3825	D	510 456-2490	21064
Kln Precision Machining Corp	3599	D	510 770-5001	16121
Kmt International Inc	3533	E	510 713-1400	13783
Knightsbridge Plastics Inc	3089	D	510 249-9722	9868
Lab Vision Corporation (DH)	3826	F	510 979-5000	21252
Lam Research Corporation (PA)	3674	D	510 572-0200	18340
Lam Research Corporation	3559	C	510 572-3200	14489
Lam Research Corporation	3674	D	510 572-0200	18342
Lam Research Intl Holdg Co (HQ)	3559	F	510 572-0200	14490
Lees Imperial Welding Inc	3441	C	510 657-4900	11826
Legacy Systems Incorporated	3559	F	510 651-2312	14491
Linear Integrated Systems Inc	3674	F	510 490-9160	18350
Loginext Solutions Inc	7372	D	339 244-0380	24108
Luca International Group LLC (PA)	1382	F	510 498-8829	128
Lucio Family Enterprises Inc	3444	E	510 623-2323	12268
Lumens Integration Inc	3861	F	510 657-8367	22438
Lyncean Technologies Inc	3844	F	650 320-8300	22215
Magellan International Corp	3354	F	510 656-6661	11237
Mahindra Tractor Assembly Inc (DH)	3751	E	650 779-5180	20416
Martinek Manufacturing	3599	E	510 438-0357	16175
Mass Precision Inc	3444	C	408 954-0200	12278
Materion Brush Inc	3497	C	510 623-1500	13452
Mattson Technology Inc (HQ)	3674	C	510 657-5900	18374
Mean Well Usa Inc	3679	F	510 683-8886	19010
Mecoptron Inc	3599	E	510 226-9966	16188
Medical Analysis Systems Inc (DH)	2835	C	510 979-5000	8236
Medika Therapeutics Inc	3841	F	510 377-0898	21801
Medplast Group Inc	3089	C	510 657-5800	9890
Melrose Metal Products Inc	3444	C	510 657-8771	12289
Mens Wearhouse	2326	E	510 657-9821	3044
Mercury Systems - Trsted Mssio (HQ)	3571	D	510 252-0870	14945
Micro Lambda Wireless Inc	3679	E	510 770-9221	19014
Microbar Inc	3559	B	510 657-9498	14498
Micron Consumer Pdts Group Inc (HQ)	3572	F	669 226-3000	15058
Microwave Technology Inc (DH)	3679	E	510 651-6700	19019
Millennium Automation	3569	F	510 683-5942	14838
Millennium Metalcraft Inc	3444	E	510 657-4700	12304
Minitouch Inc	3841	F	510 651-5000	21824
Mission Valley Regional Occu	2899	E	510 657-1865	9000
Mitac Usa Inc (DH)	3571	E	510 661-2800	14951
Mitxpc Inc	3571	F	510 226-6883	14952
Mobile Mini Inc	3448	F	510 252-9326	12560
Mohawk Industries Inc	2273	C	510 440-8790	2875
Mt Systems Inc	3559	F	510 651-5277	14503
Multi Power Products Inc	3699	F	415 883-6300	19360
Myntahl Corporation	3661	E	510 413-0002	17387
Nationwide Boiler Incorporated (PA)	3443	D	510 490-7100	12033
Ncoup Inc	7372	E	510 739-4010	24190
Neophotonics Corporation	3674	F	408 232-9200	18430

2020 California
Manufacturers Register

(P-0000) Products & Services Section entry number
(PA)=Parent Co (HQ)=Headquarters (DH)=Div Headquarters

Company	SIC	EMP	PHONE	ENTRY #
Neptec Optical Solutions Inc	3229	E	510 687-1101	10321
Neptec Os Inc	3357	E	510 687-1101	11310
New England Interconnect Syste	3357	B	603 355-3515	11311
New Iem LLC	3613	D	510 656-1600	16604
New Wave Research Incorporated (DH)	3699	C	510 249-1550	19365
Nitinol Development Corp	3851	A	510 683-2000	22373
Nitto Americas Inc (HQ)	2672	C	510 445-5400	5370
Nova Measuring Instruments Inc	3825	E	408 200-4344	21092
Novanta Corporation	3679	E	510 770-1417	19030
NRC Manufacturing Inc	3679	F	510 438-9400	19032
Oldcastle Buildingenvelope Inc	3231	C	510 651-2292	10382
Omron Scientific Tech Inc (DH)	3823	C	510 608-3400	20913
Oncore Manufacturing LLC	3672	D	510 516-5488	17943
Ooshirts Inc (PA)	2759	D	866 660-8667	7157
Optiworks Inc (PA)	3229	E	510 438-4560	10323
Optoma Technology Inc	3861	C	510 897-8600	22445
Optoplex Corporation (PA)	3661	D	510 490-9930	17397
Optovue Inc (PA)	3841	D	510 623-8868	21851
Orchard Printing	2752	F	510 490-1736	6762
Organic Spices (PA)	2099	E	510 440-1044	2577
Ortho-Clinical Diagnostics Inc	2835	E	908 704-5910	8245
Oryx Advanced Materials Inc (PA)	3572	E	510 249-1158	15069
Oudimentary LLC	2899	F	510 501-5057	9013
Owens Design Incorporated	3599	F	510 659-1800	16266
Pantronix Corporation	3674	C	510 656-5898	18465
Parker-Hannifin Corporation	3594	C	408 592-6480	15632
Patriot Memory LLC (PA)	3674	C	510 979-1021	18466
Phonak LLC	3842	F	510 743-3939	22069
Pivotal Systems Corporation	3625	E	510 770-9125	16739
Plexus Corp	3672	C	510 668-9000	17958
Pol-Tech Precision Inc	3599	F	510 656-6832	16304
Prime Solutions Inc	3674	F	510 490-2255	18479
Printed Circuit Technology	3672	D	510 659-1866	17963
Printerprezz Inc	2752	F	510 225-8412	6800
Ptec Solutions Inc	3599	D	510 358-3578	16319
Quantum Global Tech LLC	2842	C	510 687-8000	8412
Quartet Mechanics Inc	3549	F	510 490-1886	14279
Quikrete Companies LLC	3272	D	510 490-4670	10637
Qxq Inc	3825	E	510 252-1522	21109
Raditek Inc	3663	F	408 266-7404	17638
Rapiscan Laboratories Inc (HQ)	3844	D	408 961-9700	22220
Raymonds Little Print Shop Inc	2752	B	510 353-3608	6836
Reliance Machine Products Inc	3599	E	510 438-6760	16351
Rfa Medical Solutions	3845	E	510 583-9500	22304
Rgblase LLC	3699	E	510 585-8449	19393
Rita Medical Systems Inc (HQ)	3845	D	510 771-0400	22305
Rj Media	2711	F	510 938-8667	5811
S3 Graphics Inc	3674	C	510 687-4900	18523
Sangfor Technologies Inc	3825	A	408 520-7898	21116
Sanmina Corporation	3672	B	510 897-2000	17991
Santur Corporation (HQ)	3559	E	510 933-4100	14536
Schmartboard Inc	3625	F	510 744-9900	16752
Sdo Communications Corp	3827	D	408 979-0289	21406
Seagate Systems (us) Inc (DH)	3572	E	510 687-5200	15093
Seagate Technology LLC	3572	E	510 624-3728	15096
Sensor Dynamics Inc	3845	F	510 623-1459	22308
Seradyn Inc	2835	E	317 610-3800	8255
Seven Up Btlg Co San Francisco (HQ)	2086	C	925 938-8777	2167
Sharp Dimension Inc	3599	E	510 656-8938	16400
Sienna Corporation Inc	3699	E	510 440-0200	19402
Sierra Nevada Corporation	3663	E	510 446-8400	17658
Sipex Corporation (DH)	3674	C	510 668-7000	18556
Sipix Imaging Inc (DH)	3571	E	510 743-2928	14976
Smart Machines Inc	3535	E	510 661-5000	13836
Smart Modular Tech De Inc (HQ)	3674	C	510 623-1231	18565
Smtc Corporation	3672	D	510 737-0700	18003
Smtc Manufacturing Corp Cal	3672	A	408 934-7100	18004
Sna Electronics Inc	3672	E	510 656-3903	18005
Solaredge Technologies Inc (PA)	3629	C	510 498-3200	16800
Sonic Manufacturing Tech Inc	3672	B	510 580-8500	18008
Soraa Inc (PA)	3674	D	510 456-2200	18572
Soraa Laser Diode Inc	3699	E	805 696-6999	19410
South Bay Solutions Inc (PA)	3599	E	650 843-1800	16411
South Bay Solutions Texas LLC	3629	E	936 494-0180	16801
Sparqtron Corporation	3629	E	510 657-7198	16802
Specialized Coating Services	3672	D	510 226-8700	18010
Spectranetics	3845	F	408 592-2111	22315
Spectranetics Corporation	3841	D	510 933-7964	21909
Spectrum Lithograph Inc	2752	F	510 438-9192	6869
Spin Memory Inc	3674	E	510 933-8200	18577
Spineex Inc	3841	F	510 573-1093	21912
Spire Manufacturing Inc	3643	E	510 226-1070	16925
Star Tool & Engineering Co Inc	3599	F	510 742-0500	16422
Stats Chippac Inc (DH)	3674	E	510 979-8000	18579
Stats Chippac Test Svcs Inc (DH)	3674	F	510 979-8000	18581
Stratamet Inc	3674	E	510 651-7176	18583
Stratamet Advanced Mtls Corp	3253	F	510 440-1697	10452
Streak Technology Inc	3944	F	408 206-2373	22716
Streamline Electronics Mfg Inc	3672	E	408 263-3600	18012
Stressteel Inc	3312	F	888 284-8752	11076
Stretch Inc	3674	D	408 543-2700	18585
Stryker Corporation	3841	E	510 413-2500	21916
Suba Technology Inc	3672	E	408 434-6500	18013
Superior Automation Inc	3559	F	408 227-4898	14540
Surface Mount Tech Centre	3577	B	408 935-9548	15341
T C Media Inc	2721	F	510 656-5100	6037
T Ultra Equipment Company Inc	3559	F	510 440-3900	14543
Taicom International Inc	3575	F	510 656-9200	15136
Tangent Computer Inc	3571	D	650 342-9388	14984
TCI International Inc (HQ)	3663	C	510 687-6100	17680
Te Connectivity Corporation	3678	E	650 361-3333	18789
Te Connectivity Corporation	3052	B	650 361-3333	9207
Te Connectivity Corporation	3678	A	650 361-3615	18797
Te Connectivity Ltd	3679	F	650 361-4923	19101
Team Econolite	3669	F	408 577-1733	17768
Techcomp (usa) Inc	3826	E	510 683-4300	21298
Telesynergy Research USA Inc	3577	F	408 200-9879	15348
Telirite Technical Svcs Inc	3672	E	510 440-3888	18022
Tenergy Corporation	3691	D	510 687-0388	19175
Terry B Lowe	3565	F	510 651-7350	14729
Tesla Inc	3711	E	707 373-4035	19506
Texon USA Inc	3559	F	510 256-7210	14545
Thermo Fisher Scientific Inc	3826	E	510 979-5000	21308
Thermo Fisher Scientific Inc	3826	F	317 490-5809	21312
Think Surgical Inc	3842	C	510 249-2300	22109
Transcontinental Nrthern CA 20	2759	C	510 580-7700	7255
Translarity Inc	3825	F	510 371-7900	21148
Tri Fab Associates Inc	3444	D	510 651-7628	12411
Tronson Manufacturing Inc	3599	F	408 533-0369	16470
Tru Machining	3599	F	510 573-3408	16471
United Pro Fab Mfg Inc	3599	F	510 651-5570	16483
United Sheetmetal Inc	3444	F	510 257-1858	12418
United Technologies Corp	3724	B	510 438-1300	19989
V-Silicon Inc	3674	F	510 897-0168	18636
Veex Inc	3823	F	510 651-0500	20955
Verseon Corporation	2834	F	510 255-9000	8177
Verseon Corporation (PA)	2834	E	510 668-1622	8178
Viant Medical LLC	3089	F	510 657-5800	10112
Vm Discovery Inc	2834	F	510 818-1018	8185
W2 Optronics Inc	3674	F	510 220-2796	18652
Walters & Wolf Glass Company	3272	D	510 226-9800	10665
Walters & Wolf Precast	3272	C	510 226-9800	10666
Wellex Corporation (PA)	3679	C	510 743-1818	19142
West Coast Quartz Corporation (HQ)	3229	D	510 249-2160	10333
Whats Happening Tri City	2759	E	510 494-1999	7271
William Ho	3577	E	510 226-9089	15366
Wintronics International Inc	3357	E	510 226-7588	11326
Wsglass Holdings Inc (HQ)	3211	E	510 623-5000	10281
Xilinx Inc	3674	D	510 770-9449	18661
Y-Change Inc	7372	F	510 573-2205	24596
Yadav Technology Inc	3674	F	510 438-0148	18665
Young Electric Sign Company	3993	E	510 877-7815	23249
Zerobase Energy LLC	3691	E	888 530-9376	19177
Zosano Pharma Corporation (PA)	2834	E	510 745-1200	8196

FRENCH CAMP, CA - San Joaquin County

Company	SIC	EMP	PHONE	ENTRY #
Boral Roofing LLC	3272	E	209 982-1473	10540
Parex Usa Inc	3299	E	209 983-8002	11019
Poly Processing Company LLC	2821	B	209 982-4904	7594

FRESNO, CA - Fresno County

Company	SIC	EMP	PHONE	ENTRY #
3 Ink Productions Inc	2221	F	559 275-4565	2720
A Plus Signs Inc	3993	E	559 275-0700	23036
A-1 Ornamental Ironworks Inc	3462	F	559 251-1447	12700
Ace Trailer Co	3715	E	559 442-1500	19812
Actagro LLC (PA)	2875	C	559 369-2222	8810
Advanced Metal Works Inc	3444	F	559 237-2332	12087
Agi Publishing Inc (PA)	2741	E	559 251-8888	6175
Agi Publishing Inc	2741	C	559 251-8888	6176
Agricultural Manufacturing	3531	F	559 485-1662	13702
Agrifim Irrigation Pdts Inc	3523	F	559 443-6680	13605
Allied Electric Motor Svc Inc	7694	F	559 486-4222	24681
American Bottling Company	2086	D	559 442-1553	2028
American Carrier Systems	3711	F	559 442-1500	19452
Ampersand Ice Cream LLC	2024	F	559 264-8000	628
Ansons Transportation Inc	3537	F	559 892-1867	13857
Architectural Wood Design Inc	2434	E	559 292-9104	4165
Arrow Electric Motor Service	7694	F	559 266-0104	24683
Atlas Pacific Engineering Co	3556	F	559 233-4500	14345
Auernheimer Labs Inc	3651	F	559 442-1048	17197
Automated Bldg Components Inc	2439	F	559 485-8232	4288

GEOGRAPHIC

	SIC	EMP	PHONE	ENTRY #
Automotive Electronics Svcs	3496	F	559 292-7851	13396
Aweta-Autoline Inc (PA)	3523	E	559 244-8340	13611
Axiom Industries Inc	3842	E	559 276-1310	21983
Bailey Valve Inc	3491	E	559 434-2838	13293
Barney & Co California LLC	2099	F	559 442-1752	2399
Bermad Inc (PA)	3494	E	877 577-4283	13348
Better World Manufacturing Inc (PA)	3089	F	559 291-4276	9663
Betts Company (PA)	3495	D	559 498-3304	13376
Betts Company	3713	E	559 498-8624	19521
Beynon Sports Surfaces Inc	3949	E	559 237-2590	22761
Big3d	2752	E	559 233-3380	6450
Bimbo Bakeries Usa Inc	2051	F	559 498-3632	1155
Bimbo Bakeries Usa Inc	2051	E	650 291-3213	1166
Bimbo Bakeries Usa Inc	2051	C	559 489-0980	1167
Blue Eagle Stucco Products	3299	F	559 485-4100	10998
Bottling Group LLC	2086	F	559 485-5050	2045
Brandt Consolidated Inc	2875	F	559 499-2100	8811
Broadway Knitting Mills Corp	2253	E	559 456-0955	2774
Brownie Baker Inc	2052	D	559 277-7070	1310
Builders Concrete Inc (DH)	3273	E	559 225-3667	10698
Business Journal	2721	E	559 490-3400	5896
Busseto Foods Inc (PA)	2013	C	559 485-9882	444
Cal West Construction Inc	3544	F	559 217-3306	14029
California Bedrooms Inc	2511	E	559 233-7050	4559
California Dairies Inc	2026	D	559 233-5154	689
California Dried Fruit Inc	2034	E	559 233-0970	845
Candies Tolteca	2064	E	559 266-9193	1359
Cargill Meat Solutions Corp	2011	C	559 268-5586	400
Caro Nut Company	2034	E	559 439-2365	846
Cemex Materials LLC	3273	E	559 275-2241	10740
Central Valley Machining Inc	3441	E	559 291-7749	11764
Central Valley Tank of Cal	3443	F	559 456-3500	12001
Central Vly Assembly Packg Inc	3432	E	559 486-4260	11662
Certified Meat Products Inc	2011	E	559 256-1433	402
Ch Industrial Technology Inc	3441	F	559 485-8011	11765
Charles Jj Inc	2491	E	559 264-6664	4474
Choice Food Products Inc	2013	E	559 266-1674	447
Clay Mix LLC	3273	F	559 485-0065	10744
CMr Marketing and RES Inc	2879	E	559 499-2100	8824
Cold Spring Granite Company	3281	E	559 438-2100	10899
Commercial Manufacturing	3556	F	559 237-1855	14356
Concept Vehicle Technologies	3715	F	559 233-1313	19817
Crown Equipment Corporation	3537	E	559 585-8000	13864
Cummins Pacific LLC	3519	D	559 277-6760	13590
Custom AG Formulators Inc (PA)	2879	F	559 435-1052	8825
D & M Manufacturing	3523	F	559 834-4668	13622
Dantel Inc	3661	E	559 292-1111	17357
Darling Ingredients Inc	2077	E	559 268-5325	1457
Diamond Weld Industries Inc	3548	E	559 268-9999	14241
Digital Prototype Systems Inc	3663	E	559 454-1600	17502
Display Advertising Inc	2759	F	559 266-0231	7048
Dkp Inc	3523	E	559 266-2695	13625
Dreamteam Business Group LLC	2759	F	559 430-7676	7051
Dumont Printing Inc	2752	E	559 485-6311	6553
Duncan Enterprises (HQ)	2851	C	559 291-4444	8641
Duracite	2542	F	559 346-1181	4974
DV Kap Inc	2392	E	559 435-5575	3614
E & J Gallo Winery	2084	C	559 458-0807	1679
E & J Gallo Winery	2084	D	559 458-2500	1680
E-Z Haul Ready Mix Inc	3273	E	559 233-6603	10754
Eezer Products Inc	2821	E	559 255-4140	7559
Element Materials LLC	2819	E	559 304-1008	7489
Elite Fashion Accessories Inc	2387	F	559 435-0225	3530
Elliott Manufacturing Company	3599	F	559 233-6235	15927
Emerzian Woodworking Inc	2541	E	559 292-2448	4900
Envelope Products Co	2621	E	925 939-5173	5104
Ernest Packaging Solutions (PA)	2819	E	800 757-4968	7494
Evans Electric Service (PA)	7694	E	559 268-4704	24690
Fiore Di Pasta Inc	2099	D	559 457-0431	2458
Five Star Trailers Inc	3715	F	559 498-0337	19821
Foster Poultry Farms	2015	A	559 265-2000	515
Fresno Distributing Co	3651	E	559 442-8800	17230
Fresno French Bread Bakery Inc	2051	E	559 268-7088	1207
Fresno Gem & Mineral Society	3915	F	559 486-7280	22595
Fresno Neon Sign Co Inc	3993	E	559 292-2944	23116
Fruit Fillings Inc	2033	E	559 237-4715	768
Gallery Cabinet Connection	2434	F	559 294-7007	4200
Garabedian Bros Inc (PA)	3599	E	559 268-5014	15985
Gea Farm Technologies Inc	2842	E	559 497-5074	8384
General Coatings Mfg Corp	3479	F	559 495-4004	13185
Generitech Corporation	2844	F	559 346-0233	8497
Georgia-Pacific LLC	2656	C	559 485-4900	5307
Ghazarian Wldg Fabrication Inc	7692	F	559 233-1210	24635
Glaxosmithkline Consumer	2834	D	559 650-1550	7919
Glovefit International Corp	3089	F	559 243-1110	9809
GNA Industries Inc	3625	E	559 276-0953	16719
Golden Gate Freightliner Inc	3537	C	559 486-4310	13873
Gregor Inc	3732	F	559 441-7703	20334
Gruma Corporation	2096	D	559 498-7820	2333
Gusmer Enterprises Inc	3569	D	908 301-1811	14823
Helados La Tapatia Inc	2024	F	559 441-1105	650
Helados Vallarta Inc	2024	F	559 709-1177	651
Henderson Services Inc	3732	E	559 435-8874	20336
Hershey Company	2098	C	559 485-8110	2370
Holcomb Products Inc	2395	F	559 822-2067	3745
HP Water Systems Inc	3561	F	559 268-4751	14583
Innovation Alley LLC	3441	F	559 453-6974	11811
Irritec Usa Inc	3523	F	559 275-8825	13637
ITT LLC	3561	F	559 265-4730	14586
J & L Irrigation Company Inc	3523	F	559 237-2181	13638
J P Lamborn Co (PA)	3585	C	559 650-2120	15435
Jain Irrigation Inc	3523	C	559 485-7171	13640
James Clark	2789	E	559 456-3893	7335
JR Simplot Company	2037	D	559 439-3900	917
Kasco Fab Inc	3441	D	559 442-1018	11823
Kdr Pet Treats LLC	3999	F	559 485-4316	23379
Kearneys Aluminum Foundry Inc (PA)	3363	E	559 233-2591	11340
Keiser Corporation	3949	D	559 256-8000	22837
Klippenstein Corporation	3565	F	559 834-4258	14713
Kodiak Cartoners Inc	3565	F	559 266-4844	14714
Kraft Heinz Foods Company	2033	B	559 441-8515	785
Kraft Heinz Foods Company	2068	D	559 237-9206	1431
La Boulangerie French Bky Cafe	2051	F	559 222-0555	1228
La Tapatia Tortilleria Inc	2099	C	559 441-1030	2514
Label Masters Inc	2759	F	559 445-1208	7111
Larson Brothers	2741	E	559 292-8161	6268
Legacy Vulcan LLC	3273	D	559 434-1202	10787
Lehmans Manufacturing Co Inc	3441	F	559 486-1700	11828
Lidestri Foods Inc	2033	E	559 251-1000	789
Lily Pond Products	3559	F	559 431-5203	14492
LLC Lyons Magnus (PA)	2033	B	559 268-5966	790
Los Gatos Tomato Products LLC (PA)	2033	F	559 945-2700	791
Louie Foods International	2099	F	559 264-2745	2533
Lyons Magnus Inc	2033	B	559 268-5966	793
M2 Antenna Systems Inc	3679	F	559 221-2271	19000
Manna Pro Products LLC	2048	E	559 486-1810	1110
Mbtechnology	2952	E	559 233-2181	9120
McClatchy Newspapers Inc	2711	B	559 441-6111	5729
McGrayel Company Inc	2899	E	559 299-7660	8997
Meeder Equipment Company (PA)	3559	E	559 485-0979	14495
Michelsen Packaging Co Cal	2671	E	559 237-3819	5331
Mike Murach & Associates	2731	F	559 440-9071	6123
Miller Milling Company LLC	2041	E	559 441-8133	1007
Millerton Builders Inc	2591	E	559 252-0490	5032
Mineral King Minerals Inc (PA)	2873	F	559 582-9228	8798
Modern Custom Fabrication	3443	E	559 264-4741	12031
Moles Farm	2034	D	559 444-0324	856
Monster City Studios	3086	E	559 498-0540	9556
Neclec	3471	E	559 797-0103	13058
Nestle Dreyers Ice Cream Co	2024	F	559 834-2554	663
Nestle Usa Inc	2023	E	559 834-2554	609
Nevocal Enterprises Inc	1442	D	559 277-0700	353
New Age Metal Finishing LLC	3471	E	559 498-8585	13061
Ohanyans Inc (PA)	2013	F	559 225-4290	483
Olam Tomato Processors Inc (DH)	2033	F	559 447-1390	810
Olson and Co Steel	3441	F	559 224-7811	11855
Pacific Choice Brands Inc (PA)	2035	B	559 892-5365	894
Pacific Tent and Awning	2394	F	559 436-8147	3696
Packaging Plus	2653	E	209 858-9200	5255
Pana-Pacific Corporation (HQ)	3714	C	559 457-4700	19735
Paper Pulp & Film	2679	E	559 233-1151	5520
Pappys Meat Company Inc	2099	E	559 291-0218	2581
Pentair Flow Technologies LLC	3589	C	559 266-0516	15556
Performance Welding	7692	F	559 233-0042	24656
Pleasant Mattress Inc (PA)	2515	D	559 268-6446	4737
Pnm Company	3599	F	559 291-1986	16303
Potential Design Inc	3556	F	559 834-5361	14393
Praxair Distribution Inc	2813	C	559 237-5521	7441
Prinsco Inc	3084	C	559 485-5542	9473
Professional Print & Mail Inc	2752	E	559 237-7468	6814
R & L Enterprises Inc	3599	E	559 233-1608	16332
Reyes Coca-Cola Bottling LLC	2086	D	559 264-4631	2140
Rich Products Corporation	2092	C	559 486-7380	2268
Rileys TANks/D&j Service	3443	E	559 237-1403	12046
Robert J Alandt & Sons	3441	E	559 275-1391	11876
Roger Enrico	2086	B	559 485-5050	2162
Rotary Corp	3524	E	559 485-1315	13694
S A Fields Inc	2394	F	559 292-1221	3702
Saf-T-Cab Inc (PA)	3713	D	559 268-5541	19553
Safety-Kleen Systems Inc	3559	F	559 486-1960	14534

Mergent email: customerrelations@mergent.com
1338

2020 California
Manufacturers Register

(P-0000) Products & Services Section entry number
(PA)=Parent Co (HQ)=Headquarters (DH)=Div Headquarters

	SIC	EMP	PHONE	ENTRY #
Scafco Corporation	3399	F	559 256-9911	11485
Scrimco Inc	2221	F	559 237-7442	2733
Simone Fruit Co Inc	2034	F	559 275-1368	863
Simply Smashing Inc	3993	E	559 658-2367	23210
Sinclair Companies	2911	D	559 228-0913	9068
Sinclair Companies	2911	F	559 997-3617	9070
Sinclair Companies	2911	D	559 351-1916	9071
Sinclair Systems Intl LLC	2759	F	559 233-4500	7213
Slam Specialties LLC (PA)	3714	F	559 348-9038	19769
South Valley Materials Inc (DH)	3273	D	559 277-7060	10839
Ssi G Debbas Chocolatier LLC	2066	F	559 294-2071	1413
Sturdy Gun Safe Manufacruing	3499	F	559 485-8361	13550
Subdirect LLC (PA)	2721	F	559 321-0449	6034
Suburban Steel Inc (PA)	3441	F	559 268-6281	11889
Sun Vlley Rsins Inc A Cal Corp	2034	F	559 233-8070	865
Sunrise Medical (us) LLC	3842	D	559 292-2171	22096
T G Schmeiser Co Inc	3429	E	559 486-4569	11635
Tanfield Engrg Systems US Inc	3531	F	559 443-6602	13750
Tech West Vacuum Inc	3843	E	559 291-1650	22196
Tempest Technology Corporation	3564	E	559 277-7577	14682
Tessenderlo Kerley Inc	2819	C	559 485-0114	7529
Tmr Executive Interiors Inc	2431	F	559 346-0631	4141
TPC Industries LLC	3999	E	310 849-9574	23508
Trane US Inc	3585	E	559 271-4625	15464
Tranpak Inc	3089	E	800 827-2474	10090
Tri-State Stairway Corp	3446	E	559 268-0875	12517
Trillium Pumps Usa Inc (DH)	3561	C	559 442-4000	14603
Tru-Trailers Inc	3715	F	559 251-7591	19833
Turner Designs Hydrocarbon Ins	3699	E	559 253-1414	19425
United Western Industries Inc	3599	E	559 226-7236	16484
Universal Meditech Inc	3995	E	559 366-7798	23252
Upholstery By Wayne Stoec	2211	F	559 233-1960	2716
Valley Decorating Company	3089	E	559 495-1100	10108
Valley Lahvosh Baking Co Inc	2051	E	559 485-2700	1289
Valley Pipe & Supply Inc	3494	F	559 233-0321	13366
Valley Protein LLC	2013	D	559 498-7115	505
Valley Stairway Inc	3446	F	559 299-0151	12519
Vcp Mobility Inc	3842	B	559 292-2171	22115
Vcp Mobility Holdings Inc	3842	B	303 218-4500	22117
Vie-Del Company (PA)	2033	C	559 834-2525	835
Vitro Flat Glass LLC	3211	C	559 485-4660	10280
Wade Metal Products	3441	F	559 237-9233	11916
Walton Industries Inc	2851	F	559 233-6300	8692
Wasco Hardfacing Co	3523	D	559 485-5860	13683
Weather TEC Corp	3523	F	559 291-5555	13684
West Coast Growers Inc	2034	E	559 843-2294	876
Western Trade Printing Inc	2752	F	559 251-8595	6935
Westrock Cp LLC	2631	F	559 441-1166	5181
Westrock Cp LLC	2653	C	559 519-7240	5278
Westrock Rkt LLC	2652	F	559 441-1181	5192
Westrock Rkt Company	2653	C	559 497-1662	5280
Whipple Industries Inc	3564	E	559 442-1261	14690
Wilbur-Ellis Company LLC	3523	D	559 442-1220	13687
Wood-N-Wood Products Cal Inc (PA)	2449	E	559 896-3636	4434
Wood-N-Wood Products Inc	2449	F	559 896-3636	4436
Xylem Inc	3561	F	559 265-4731	14606
Zacky & Sons Poultry LLC	2015	B	559 443-2750	533
Zacky & Sons Poultry LLC (PA)	2015	C	559 443-2700	534
Zip Print Inc (PA)	2752	E	559 486-3112	6949

FULLERTON, CA - Orange County

	SIC	EMP	PHONE	ENTRY #
Accurate Laminated Pdts Inc	2542	E	714 632-2773	4960
Adams Rite Aerospace Inc (DH)	3728	C	714 278-6500	20005
ADB Industries	3398	D	310 679-9193	11429
Advanced Equipment Corporation (PA)	2542	E	714 635-5350	4961
Aero Engineering Inc	3599	F	714 879-6200	15703
Aerofit LLC	3498	C	714 521-5060	13455
Ampertech Inc	3545	E	714 523-4068	14132
Amtrend Corporation	2541	D	714 630-2070	4880
Anderco Inc	2431	E	714 446-9508	3992
Arconic Global Fas & Rings Inc	3324	C	714 871-1550	11153
Arconic Inc	3334	B	714 871-1550	11179
Arconic Inc	3334	B	714 278-8981	11180
Aurident Inc	3843	E	714 870-1851	22135
Axceleon Inc	7372	F	714 960-5200	23645
Bbe Sound Inc (PA)	3931	E	714 897-6766	22609
Beckman Instruments Inc	2835	E	714 871-4848	8206
Bench-Craft Inc	2599	F	714 523-3322	5051
Betterline Products Inc	3599	E	760 535-5030	15790
Biomed Instruments Inc	3845	E	714 459-5716	22233
Braiform Enterprises Inc	3089	D	714 526-0257	9673
Brentwood Home LLC (PA)	2515	C	562 949-3759	4713
Bushnell Ribbon Corporation	3955	D	562 948-1410	22960
Byrnes & Kiefer Co	2087	E	714 554-4000	2196
Cargill Incorporated	2833	D	714 449-6708	7647
Cargill Incorporated	2079	E	323 588-2274	1469

	SIC	EMP	PHONE	ENTRY #
Centerline Manufacturing Inc	3679	F	714 525-9890	18858
Chefmaster	2099	E	714 554-4000	2424
CJ Foods Manufacturing Corp	2099	E	714 888-3500	2426
Coast Cutters Co Inc	3312	F	626 444-2965	11039
Comant Industries Incorporated (DH)	3812	E	714 870-2420	20556
Concreteaccessoriescom	3452	F	714 871-9434	12672
Consolidated Aerospace Mfg LLC (PA)	3812	F	714 989-2797	20559
Cook and Cook Incorporated	3443	E	714 680-6669	12013
Corru-Kraft IV	2653	F	714 773-0124	5212
Cove Four-Slide Stamping Corp (PA)	3496	C	516 379-4232	13406
Cove Four-Slide Stamping Corp	3496	F	714 525-2930	13407
Cura Medical Technologies LLC	3844	F	949 939-4406	22212
Dae Shin Usa Inc	2221	D	714 578-8900	2724
Delta Pacific Activewear Inc	2253	F	714 871-9281	2781
Delta Sportswear Inc	2331	F	714 568-1102	3154
Delta Stag Manufacturing	3713	D	562 904-6444	19526
Demes Gourmet Corporation	2013	E	714 870-6040	452
Direct Drive Systems Inc	3621	D	714 872-5500	16638
Dr Smoothie Brands Inc	2087	E	714 449-9787	2204
Dr Smoothie Enterprises	2087	E	714 449-9787	2205
Ejays Machine Co Inc	3599	F	714 879-0558	15923
Ellingson Inc	3599	F	714 773-1923	15926
Evo Manufacturing Inc	3999	F	714 879-8913	23328
Faac	3699	F	800 221-8278	19309
Fibco Composites Inc	3812	F	714 269-1118	20576
Fluid Power Ctrl Systems Inc	3823	E	714 525-3727	20870
FMC Technologies Inc	3533	F	714 872-5574	13776
Foam-Craft Inc	3086	C	714 459-9971	9536
Fuller Laboratories	2835	F	714 525-7660	8223
Fullerton Printing Inc	2752	F	714 870-7500	6588
Future Foam Inc	3086	E	714 871-2344	9540
Future Foam Inc	3086	C	714 459-9971	9542
Future Foam Inc	3086	E	714 459-9971	9543
Gard Inc	3444	E	714 738-5891	12219
Gaylords HRI Meats	2011	F	714 526-2278	410
General Linear Systems	7694	F	714 994-4822	24692
GLC General Inc	2499	F	714 870-9825	4505
Global Infovision Inc	7372	F	714 738-4465	23943
Global Mfg Solutions LLC	3357	C	562 356-3222	11306
Gold Venture Inc	3086	C	909 623-1810	9547
Golden Pacific Seafoods Inc	3556	C	714 589-8888	14369
Golden West Technology	3672	D	714 738-3775	17890
High Five Inc	2752	F	714 847-2200	6614
Interntnal Cnnctors Cable Corp	3661	C	888 275-4422	17381
Jmu Dental Inc	3843	F	909 676-0000	22164
Jonel Engineering	3596	E	714 879-2360	15641
Khyber Foods Incorporated	2099	E	714 879-0900	2498
Kimberly-Clark Corporation	2621	B	714 578-0705	5128
Kims Welding and Iron Works	3462	E	714 680-7700	12712
Kip Steel Inc	3316	E	714 461-1051	11119
KMW USA Inc (HQ)	3679	E	714 515-1100	18978
Kraft Heinz Foods Company	2099	B	714 870-8235	2501
Kryler Corp	3471	E	714 871-9611	13037
Labl Holding Corporation	2679	D	714 992-2574	5512
Lange Precision Inc	3599	E	714 870-5420	16134
Laser Industries Inc	3599	D	714 532-3271	16138
Magtech & Power Conversion Inc	3677	E	714 451-0106	18725
Marton Precision Mfg LLC	3724	E	714 808-6523	19972
McKenna Labs Inc (PA)	2834	E	714 687-6888	8003
Mozaik LLC	2652	F	562 207-1900	5190
Mytrex Inc	3523	F	949 800-9725	13651
National Signal Inc	3799	E	714 441-7707	20516
Nicholas Michael Designs Inc	2519	C	714 562-8101	4768
Nina Mia Inc	2099	D	714 773-5588	2569
Orora Visual LLC	2759	D	714 879-2400	7162
Pacmin Incorporated (PA)	3999	E	714 447-4478	23441
Pasco Industries Inc	3991	F	714 992-2051	23030
Penhall Diamond Products Inc	3545	D	714 776-0937	14181
Picture This Framing Inc	2499	F	714 447-8749	4520
Plexi Fab Inc	3089	F	714 447-8494	9980
Printec Ht Electronics LLC	3674	E	714 484-7597	18480
Raytheon Company	3812	F	714 446-2584	20684
Raytheon Company	3812	D	714 446-3513	20685
Raytheon Company	3829	E	714 446-2287	21530
Raytheon Company	3812	C	714 732-0119	20688
Raytheon Company	3812	B	714 446-3232	20696
Rozak Engineering Inc	3599	F	714 446-8855	16375
Santa Ana Plating Corp (PA)	3471	D	310 923-8305	13095
Saputo Dairy Foods Usa LLC	2026	C	714 772-8861	710
Schreiber Foods Inc	2022	C	714 490-7360	576
Scientific Spray Finishes Inc	3479	E	714 871-5541	13243
Screen Printers Resource Inc	2759	F	714 441-1155	7209
Senor Snacks Inc	2096	F	714 739-1073	2344
Senor Snacks Manufacturing Ltd	2064	D	714 739-1073	1401
Soma Magnetics Corporation	3612	E	714 447-0782	16576

GEOGRAPHIC

	SIC	EMP	PHONE	ENTRY #
South Western Paving Company	2951	F	714 577-5750	9106
SPD Manufacturing Inc	2221	F	985 302-1902	2734
Stauber Prfmce Ingredients (HQ)	2833	C	714 441-3900	7695
Stein Industries Inc (PA)	3444	E	714 522-4560	12390
Sticker Hub Inc	2759	F	714 912-8457	7229
Stir Foods LLC	2038	E	714 871-9231	981
Sun Trade Group Inc (PA)	2253	F	714 525-4888	2806
T and T Industries Inc (PA)	3496	D	714 284-6555	13439
Tct Advanced Machining Inc	3599	F	714 871-9371	16445
Terra Universal Inc	3564	C	714 526-0100	14683
Thunderbolt Manufacturing Inc	3599	E	714 632-0397	16457
UNI Filter Inc	3714	D	714 535-6933	19793
United Duralume Products Inc	3444	F	714 773-4011	12415
United Pharma LLC	2899	C	714 738-8999	9033
United Testing Systems Inc	3829	D	714 638-2322	21561
Universal Turbo Technology	3511	D	714 600-9585	13581
Water Heater Warehouse LLC	3822	F	714 244-8562	20822
Webedoctor Inc	7372	C	714 990-3999	24575
Western States Envelope Corp	2677	D	714 449-0909	5477
Western Yarn Dyeing Inc	2269	E	714 578-9500	2864
Wheel and Tire Club Inc	3312	C	714 422-3505	11082
Will-Mann Inc	3444	F	714 870-0350	12437
Wilsons Art Studio Inc	2759	D	714 870-7030	7272
Winonics Inc	3672	C	714 626-3755	18052
WMC Precision Machining	3599	F	221 773-0059	16532
Zmp Aquisition Corporation	3625	C	714 278-6500	16772

GALT, CA - Sacramento County

	SIC	EMP	PHONE	ENTRY #
All American Modular LLC	2452	F	209 744-0400	4455
Berger Modular	2451	F	209 329-9368	4438
Calstone Company	3271	E	209 745-2981	10504
Carsons Inc	3469	E	209 745-2387	12782
Consolidated Fabricators Corp	3469	D	209 745-4604	12787
Galt Pipe Company	3494	E	209 745-2936	13355
Herburger Publications Inc (PA)	2711	D	916 685-5533	5660
Lodi Iron Works Inc	3321	F	209 368-5395	11146
United Rotary Brush Corp	3991	E	913 888-8450	23032

GARDEN GROVE, CA - Orange County

	SIC	EMP	PHONE	ENTRY #
A Q Pharmaceuticals Inc	2834	E	714 903-1000	7708
Acco Brands USA LLC	3089	E	562 941-0505	9603
Adtek Media Inc	3993	E	949 680-4200	23043
Advanced Aerospace	3585	C	714 265-6200	15408
Advanced Chemistry & Tech Inc (HQ)	2891	E	714 373-8118	8852
Aero Dynamic Machining Inc	3728	D	714 379-1073	20009
Aero Pacific Corporation	3728	E	714 961-9200	20012
Airflex5d LLC	2514	F	855 574-0158	4680
American Metal Bearing Company	3562	E	714 892-5527	14608
Assault Industries Inc	3799	F	714 799-6711	20503
B & E Manufacturing Co Inc	3728	E	714 898-2269	20051
Banh MI & Che Cali	2051	E	714 534-6987	1142
Basic Electronics Inc	3679	E	714 530-2400	18831
Basic Energy Services Inc	1389	E	714 530-0855	170
Baton Lock & Hardware Co Inc	3429	E	714 265-3636	11571
Beauty & Health International (PA)	2834	E	714 903-9730	7800
Broncs Inc	2211	C	714 705-4377	2672
C & A Transducers Inc	3679	E	714 554-9188	18843
Cali Chem Inc	2844	E	714 265-3740	8454
Carmen Abato Enterprises	3357	F	714 895-1887	11294
Catalina Cylinders Inc (PA)	3443	E	714 890-0999	12000
Chemical Methods Assoc LLC (DH)	3589	D	714 898-8781	15495
Coastline High Prfmce Coatings	3663	F	714 372-3263	17487
Coastline Metal Finishing Corp	3471	D	714 895-9099	12973
Commercial Cstm Sting Uphl Inc	2599	D	714 850-0520	5053
Criterion Composites Inc	3751	E	714 554-2717	20392
CTS Cement Manufacturing Corp (PA)	2891	C	714 379-8260	8862
Custom Pack Inc	3221	F	714 534-2201	10287
D & S Custom Plating Inc	3714	F	714 537-5411	19629
Diversfied Mtllrgical Svcs Inc	3398	E	714 895-7777	11450
East West Printing	2752	F	714 899-7885	6556
Easyflex Inc	3312	E	888 577-8999	11043
Elasco Inc	2821	D	714 373-4767	7560
Electron Plating III Inc	3471	E	714 554-2210	13002
Essence Water Inc	2086	F	855 738-7426	2074
Esys Energy Control Company	3823	E	714 372-3322	20867
Evans Manufacturing Inc (PA)	3993	C	714 379-6100	23100
Expo-3 International Inc	3993	E	714 379-8383	23104
F T B & Son Inc	3444	E	714 891-8003	12207
Fei-Zyfer Inc (HQ)	3663	E	714 933-4000	17519
Fleet Management Solutions Inc	3663	E	800 500-6009	17520
Fourbro Inc	2329	F	714 277-3858	3084
Full Spectrum Omega Inc	2844	F	714 866-0039	8495
GKN Arspace Trnsprncy Systems (DH)	3089	C	714 893-7531	9807
Golden Stone Group LLC	3253	F	714 723-1505	10443
Goodwin Ammonia Company (PA)	2842	F	714 894-0531	8385
House Foods America Corp (HQ)	2099	C	714 901-4350	2481

	SIC	EMP	PHONE	ENTRY #
Houston Bazz Co	3469	D	714 898-2666	12817
Hv Industries Inc	2426	F	651 233-5676	3976
Hyatt Die Cast Engrg Corp - S	3363	E	714 622-2131	11337
Hycor Biomedical LLC	3841	C	714 933-3000	21736
Inductor Supply Inc	3677	F	714 894-9050	18720
Infinite Engineering Inc	3599	F	714 534-4688	16043
Informer Computer Systems	3575	F	714 899-2049	15125
Innovative Casework Mfg Inc	3999	F	714 890-9100	23362
ITW Plymers Salants N Amer Inc	2821	E	714 898-0025	7573
J L Wingert Company	3589	D	714 379-5519	15529
Jason Tool & Engineering Inc	3089	E	714 895-5067	9851
Joong-Ang Daily News Cal Inc	2711	F	714 638-2341	5679
Jvr Sheetmetal Fabrication Inc	3721	E	714 841-2464	19908
Ken-Wor Corp	3312	E	714 554-6210	11053
Kimberly Machine Inc	3599	E	714 539-0151	16117
King Instrument Company Inc	3823	E	714 891-0008	20895
King Shock Technology Inc	3714	D	714 530-8701	19702
Korea Times Los Angeles Inc	2711	F	714 530-6001	5686
Kpi Services Inc	3398	E	714 895-5024	11455
L C Pringle Sales Inc (PA)	2591	E	714 892-1524	5029
Lear Baylor Inc	3732	E	714 799-9396	20344
Leiner Health Products Inc	2834	B	714 898-9936	7988
Little Saigon News Inc	2711	F	714 265-0800	5699
Lnt P/M Inc	3999	F	714 552-7245	23398
Luxe Laboratory	3851	F	714 221-2330	22370
Microsemi Communications Inc	3674	E	805 388-3700	18398
Microsemi Corp-Analog (DH)	3674	D	714 898-8121	18403
Microsemi Corp-Power MGT Group	3625	C	714 994-6500	16732
Microsemi Corporation	3674	B	714 898-7112	18404
Mitchell Dean Collins	2434	F	714 894-6767	4227
Monco Products Inc	3089	E	714 891-2788	9910
Nails 2000 International Inc	3999	F	714 265-1983	23418
Natures Bounty Co	2833	F	714 898-9936	7677
Nelson Engineering Llc	3599	E	714 893-7999	16240
Nu Engineering	3599	E	714 894-1206	16253
Omana Group LLC	2023	F	714 891-9488	613
Pace Sportswear Inc	2339	F	714 891-8716	3381
Pacific Athletic Wear Inc	2339	D	714 751-8006	3382
Peerless Injection Molding LLC	3089	E	714 689-1920	9957
Precision Aeroform Corporation	3721	E	714 725-6611	19924
Premium Herbal USA LLC	2023	F	800 567-7878	616
R P M Electric Motors	7694	F	714 638-4174	24695
Rampone Industries LLC	3496	E	949 581-8701	13431
Riviera Beverages LLC	2086	F	714 895-5169	2160
Roger Industry	3672	F	714 896-0765	17978
Safran Cabin Inc	3728	C	714 901-2672	20217
Safran Cabin Inc	3728	B	714 891-1906	20221
Saint-Gobain Prfmce Plas Corp	2821	C	714 893-0470	7607
Sales Office Accessories Inc	3993	E	714 896-9600	23190
Sanyo Foods Corp America (HQ)	2098	E	714 891-3671	2382
Schlumberger Technology Corp	1389	D	714 379-7332	261
Select Graphics	2752	F	714 537-5250	6858
Spartan Manufacturing Co	3599	F	714 894-1955	16414
SPS Technologies LLC	3452	E	714 892-5571	12694
St Paul Brands Inc	2824	E	714 903-1000	7641
Sure Guard Socal	2431	F	714 556-5497	4135
Synertech PM Inc	3369	F	714 898-9151	11424
T L Machine Inc	3451	D	714 554-4154	12654
Tdk Machining	3728	F	714 554-4166	20246
Teacher Created Resources Inc	2731	D	714 230-7060	6152
Three Dots LLC	2331	E	714 799-6333	3198
Tj Aerospace Inc	3541	E	714 891-3564	13957
Transglobal Apparel Group Inc	2339	E	714 890-9200	3427
Tri A Machine Inc	3542	F	714 408-8007	13996
Tri Dental Innovators Corp	3843	F	714 554-1170	22198
TT Machine Corp	3545	E	714 534-5288	14205
Umpco Inc	3429	D	714 897-3531	11640
V & F Fabrication Company Inc	3441	E	714 265-0630	11909
Vertox Company	3825	F	714 530-4541	21153
Vianh Company Inc	3599	E	714 590-9808	16502
Vitesse Manufacturing & Dev	3674	C	805 388-3700	18648
Walker Products (PA)	3714	E	714 554-5151	19803
Western Precision Aero LLC	3599	E	714 893-7999	16523
Wtpc Inc	2752	E	714 903-2500	6945

GARDEN VALLEY, CA - El Dorado County

	SIC	EMP	PHONE	ENTRY #
Toms Sierra Company Inc	1389	F	530 333-4620	271

GARDENA, CA - Los Angeles County

	SIC	EMP	PHONE	ENTRY #
3-D Polymers	3069	F	310 324-7694	9274
3deo Inc	3542	F	844 496-3825	13963
4-D Engineering Inc	3599	E	310 532-2384	15646
A & A Machine & Dev Co Inc	3599	F	310 532-7706	15649
A & A Ready Mixed Concrete Inc	3273	E	310 515-0933	10671
A & M Welding Inc	7692	F	310 329-2700	24611
A M Cabinets Inc (PA)	2521	D	310 532-1919	4778

Mergent email: customerrelations@mergent.com
1340

2020 California
Manufacturers Register

(P-0000) Products & Services Section entry number
(PA)=Parent Co (HQ)=Headquarters (DH)=Div Headquarters

Name	SIC	EMP	PHONE	ENTRY #
A&W Precision Machining Inc	3599	F	310 527-7242	15666
AAA Air Support	3728	F	310 538-1377	19996
Abrasive Finishing Co	3398	E	310 323-7175	11427
Accucrome Plating Co Inc	3471	F	310 327-8268	12900
Ace Air Manufacturing	3728	F	310 323-7246	19998
Acrylicore Inc	3083	F	310 515-4846	9436
Adtech Tool Engrg Corporations	3545	F	310 515-1717	14128
Advanced Foam Inc	3086	E	310 515-0728	9499
Aerodynamic Plating Co	3471	D	310 329-7959	12909
Ahf-Ducommun Incorporated (HQ)	3728	C	310 380-5390	20024
Alan Pre-Fab Building Corp	2452	E	310 538-0333	4454
Aldo Fragale	3599	F	310 324-0050	15716
All-Ways Metal Inc	3444	E	310 217-1177	12099
American Aircraft Products Inc	3444	D	310 532-7434	12104
American Maple Inc	3949	F	310 515-8881	22742
Americhip Inc (PA)	2752	D	310 323-3697	6412
Angelus Plating Works	3714	F	310 516-1883	19582
AR-Ce Inc	3952	F	310 771-1960	22939
Arandas Woodcraft Inc	2434	F	310 538-9945	4164
Arktura LLC (PA)	2519	E	310 532-1050	4762
Artemis Pet Food Company Inc	2048	F	818 771-0700	1084
Artistic Welding Inc	3444	D	310 515-4922	12116
Arto Brick Veneer Mfgco	3251	E	310 768-8500	10430
Ashford Textiles LLC	2299	E	310 327-4670	2925
Autoflow Products Co	3823	F	310 515-2866	20837
Avcorp Cmpsite Fabrication Inc	3728	B	310 970-5658	20047
Avcorp Cmpstes Fabrication Inc	3728	F	310 527-0700	20048
Bake R Us Inc	2051	F	310 630-5873	1140
Barco Uniforms Inc	2311	C	310 323-7315	2960
Barnes Plastics Inc	3089	E	310 329-6301	9654
Bath Petals Inc	2844	F	310 532-4532	8442
Baxstra Inc	2426	D	323 770-4171	3968
Bay Cities Tin Shop Inc	3444	E	310 660-0351	12129
BDS Natural Products Inc (PA)	2099	D	310 518-2227	2401
Bega Supply Inc	3651	F	310 719-1252	17202
Better Nutritionals LLC	2023	D	310 502-2277	580
Binder Metal Products Inc	3469	D	626 602-3824	12771
Binders Express Inc	2782	F	310 329-4811	7303
Bixolon America Inc	3577	F	858 764-4580	15172
Bob Lewis Machine Company Inc	3599	F	310 538-9406	15795
Boinca Inc (PA)	2844	F	714 809-6313	8448
Bradley Tchnologies-California	2891	E	310 538-0714	8861
Briles Aerospace Inc	3452	F	310 701-2087	12669
Butler Inc	3452	F	310 323-3114	12670
C&J Fab Center Inc	3444	F	310 323-0970	12141
Cabletek Inc	3643	F	310 523-5000	16880
Caitac Garment Processing Inc	2261	B	310 217-9888	2823
Cal Pacific Dyeing & Finishing	2269	D	310 327-3792	2851
California Glass Bending Corp	3231	D	310 549-5255	10344
Capstan California Inc (PA)	3499	B	310 366-5999	13508
Capstan Permaflow	3599	F	310 366-5999	15823
Cast-Rite Corporation	3544	D	310 532-2080	14030
Cast-Rite International Inc (PA)	3369	D	310 532-2080	11411
Centron Industries Inc	3663	F	310 324-6443	17485
Century Precision Engrg Inc	3599	E	310 538-0015	15835
CH Laboratories Inc (PA)	2834	E	310 516-8273	7839
Chief Neon Sign Co Inc	3993	F	310 327-1317	23076
Cilajet LLC	2842	E	310 320-8000	8373
Clegg Industries Inc	3993	C	310 225-3800	23077
Cliff Digital	2759	F	310 323-5600	7025
Coast Color Printing Inc	2752	F	310 352-3560	6492
Coast Plating Inc	3471	F	323 770-0240	12971
Columbia Holding Corp	3442	B	310 327-4107	11942
Continental Bdr Specialty Corp (PA)	2782	C	310 324-8227	7308
Coral Head Inc (PA)	2329	F	310 366-7712	3073
Cosway Company Inc	2844	E	310 527-9135	8473
CR Laurence Co Inc	3442	F	310 327-9300	11943
Crisol Metal Finishing	3471	F	310 516-1165	12980
CST Power and Construction Inc (HQ)	3355	D	310 523-2322	11257
Custom Displays Inc	2541	E	323 770-8074	4895
Custom Metal Finishing Corp	3559	F	310 532-5075	14449
Cytydel Plastics Inc	3089	E	310 523-2884	9741
D & D Plastics Incorporated	3089	F	310 515-1934	9742
D and J Marketing Inc	2396	F	310 538-1583	3782
Dasol Inc	3641	C	310 327-6700	16859
Davis Gear & Machine Co	3599	F	310 337-9881	15883
Decore Plating Company Inc	3471	F	310 324-6755	12984
Del Mar Industries (PA)	3364	D	323 321-0600	11355
Del Mar Industries	3364	F	310 327-2634	11356
Designed Metal Connections Inc (DH)	3451	B	310 323-6200	12629
Doringer Manufacturing Co Inc	3541	F	310 366-7766	13917
Dr DBurr	3541	F	310 323-6900	13919
Ducommun Aerostructures Inc (HQ)	3724	B	310 380-5390	19948
Dynamic Solutions	3829	F	253 273-7936	21461
El Camino Wood Products	2441	F	310 768-3447	4335
Electrical Rebuilders Sls Inc (PA)	3694	D	323 249-7545	19190
Elro Manufacturing Company (PA)	3993	E	310 380-7444	23096
Eptronics Inc	3646	F	310 536-0700	17031
Estar Limited	3641	E	310 989-6265	16861
Eternal Star Corporation	2678	E	310 768-1945	5480
Evergreen Oil Inc (HQ)	2992	F	949 757-7770	9142
Ew Trading Inc	3089	F	310 515-9898	9782
Faber Enterprises Inc	3492	C	310 323-6200	13329
Finntech Inc	3599	F	310 323-0790	15959
Flex Technologies Inc	2822	F	310 323-1801	7629
Flight Metals LLC	3812	F	800 838-9047	20578
Fluid Lubrication & Chem Co	2992	F	800 826-2415	9144
French Tradition (PA)	2511	F	310 719-9977	4572
Gage Wafco Co Inc	3545	F	310 532-3106	14162
Ganar Industries Inc	2299	F	310 515-5683	2935
Gardena Valley News Inc	2711	E	310 329-6351	5639
Gasket Manufacturing Co	3053	E	310 217-5600	9232
Geiger Plastics Inc	3089	E	310 327-9926	9801
German Machined Products Inc	3599	F	310 532-4480	15996
Global Casuals Inc	2329	F	310 817-2828	3086
Gloria Lance Inc (PA)	2331	D	310 767-4400	3161
Gramercy Aerospace Mfg LLC	3812	F	310 515-0576	20586
Granath & Granath Inc	3471	E	310 327-5740	13016
Grow More Inc	2879	D	310 515-1700	8830
Gsp Metal Finishing Inc	3471	E	818 744-1328	13019
GT Precision Inc	3451	C	310 323-4374	12633
Hamilton Technology Corp	3646	F	310 217-1191	17041
Hammer Collection Inc	2512	E	310 515-0276	4645
Hannahmax Baking Inc	2051	C	310 380-6778	1223
Hansens Welding Inc	7692	E	310 329-6888	24638
Hasala Engineering Inc	3599	F	310 538-4268	16017
Hawaiian Host Candies La Inc	2064	D	310 532-0543	1370
HI Tech Heat Treating Inc	3398	F	310 532-3705	11453
Hi-Craft Metal Products	3444	E	310 323-6949	12236
His Life Woodworks	2431	F	310 756-0170	4055
HUD Industries	3556	F	310 327-7110	14373
Impresa Aerospace LLC (PA)	3728	F	310 354-1200	20136
Impresa Aerospace LLC	3728	F	843 553-2021	20137
Inca One Corporation	3675	E	310 808-0001	18679
Independent Ink Inc	2899	E	310 323-4657	8978
Integrated Communications Inc	2752	E	310 851-8066	6645
Investment Land Appraisers	2789	F	310 819-8831	7334
Ips Corporation	2891	D	310 516-7013	8879
J & S Inc	3599	E	310 719-7144	16060
J&L Press Inc (PA)	2752	F	818 549-8344	6658
Jonathan Louis Intl Ltd (PA)	2512	C	323 770-3330	4650
Joy Active	2339	D	310 660-0022	3349
Juno Graphics	2752	F	310 329-0126	6671
K C Hilites Inc	3647	E	928 635-2607	17091
Karrior Electric Vehicles Inc	3537	F	310 515-7600	13879
Keller Engineering	3599	F	310 532-0554	16111
Ken Mason Tile Inc	3253	E	562 432-7574	10445
Keyline Lithography Inc	2752	E	310 538-8618	6675
Kingdom Mattress Inc	2515	E	562 630-5531	4726
Knk Apparel Inc	2326	C	310 768-3333	3041
Koam Knitech Inc	2253	E	310 515-1121	2793
Kumi Kookoon	2392	F	310 515-8811	3622
L J R Grinding Corp	3599	F	310 532-7232	16131
L&F Wood LLC	2431	F	310 400-5569	4073
La Palm Furnitures & ACC Inc (PA)	2395	D	310 217-2700	3746
Learning Resources Inc	3999	E	800 995-4436	23393
Leo Molds	3544	F	562 714-4807	14071
Lets Do Lunch	2099	D	310 523-3664	2528
Lite Extrusions Manufacturing	3083	E	323 770-4298	9443
Little Brothers Bakery LLC	2051	E	310 225-3790	1236
Lni Custom Manufacturing Inc	3446	E	310 978-2000	12494
Louis Sardo Upholstery Inc (PA)	2531	D	310 327-0532	4864
M M Book Bindery	2789	F	310 532-0780	7339
Maneri Sign Co Inc	3993	E	310 327-6261	23151
Mars Air Systems LLC	3564	D	310 532-1555	14670
Martin-Chandler Inc	3599	F	323 321-5119	16174
Martin/Brattrud Inc	2512	D	323 770-4171	4658
Matsuda House Printing Inc	2752	D	310 532-1533	6719
Matsui International Co Inc	2899	C	310 767-7812	8995
Matterhorn Filter Corporation	2819	F	310 329-8073	7504
Maya Steels Fabrication Inc	3441	D	310 532-8830	11838
Meadows Sheet Metal and AC Inc	3444	E	310 615-1125	12288
Megiddo Global LLC	3999	F	818 267-6686	23406
Melling Tool Rush Metals LLC	3399	D	580 725-3295	11480
Metco Manufacturing Inc	3469	E	310 516-6547	12844
Mills Iron Works	3494	D	323 321-6520	13359
Mod Shop	2511	E	310 523-1008	4596
Monte Allen Interiors Inc	2512	E	310 380-4640	4659
Moveel Fuel LLC	2869	F	213 748-1444	8754
MPS Industries Incorporated (PA)	3612	E	310 325-1043	16563

	SIC	EMP	PHONE	ENTRY #
Narayan Corporation	3085	E	310 719-7330	9489
Nasco Aircraft Brake Inc	3728	D	310 532-4430	20185
Nationwide Plastic Products	3081	E	310 366-7585	9414
NC Engineering Inc	3599	F	310 532-4810	16238
New Maverick Desk Inc	2521	C	310 217-1554	4811
Nike Inc	3021	E	310 670-6770	9177
Nissin Foods USA Company Inc (HQ)	2098	C	310 327-8478	2376
Noma Bearing Corporation	3562	F	310 329-1800	14612
Norberts Athletic Products	3949	E	310 830-6672	22861
Nugier Press Company Inc	3542	F	310 515-6025	13988
O Industries Corporation	2426	F	310 719-2289	3980
Ocean Direct LLC (PA)	2092	E	424 266-9300	2267
Onyx Industries Inc	3451	E	310 851-6161	12644
Pacific Artglass Corporation	3231	E	310 516-7828	10384
Parker-Hannifin Corporation	3599	D	310 308-0389	16285
Parquet By Dian Inc	2426	D	310 527-3779	3981
Perez Machine Inc	3599	F	310 217-9090	16292
Phantom Carriage Brewery	3556	E	310 538-5834	14392
Phillips Bros Plastics Inc	3083	E	310 532-8020	9447
Plasma Coating Corporation	3599	E	310 532-1951	16300
Plastic Processing Corp	3089	E	310 719-7330	9972
Power Paragon Inc	3612	E	310 523-4443	16569
Praxis Musical Instrument Inc	3495	F	714 532-6655	13385
Prime Wheel Corporation	3714	E	310 819-4123	19742
Prime Wheel Corporation (PA)	3714	A	310 516-9126	19743
Principle Plastics	3021	E	310 532-3411	9179
Pro Design Group Inc	3089	E	310 767-1032	9995
Progressive Tool & Die Inc	3545	F	310 327-0569	14188
Quad R Tech	3911	C	310 851-6161	22560
Quadriga Americas LLC	2741	E	424 634-4900	6322
Quadrtech Corporation	3423	E	310 523-1697	11542
Qual-Pro Corporation (HQ)	3672	C	310 329-7535	17965
R B Welding Inc	7692	F	310 324-8680	24659
Radex Stereo Co Inc	3861	E	310 516-9015	22453
Ramda Metal Specialties Inc	3444	E	310 538-2136	12350
Ramonas Food Group LLC	2032	C	310 323-1950	743
Rayco Electronic Mfg Inc	3677	E	310 329-2660	18738
RB Racing	3714	E	310 515-5720	19755
Research Metal Industries Inc	3599	E	310 352-3200	16354
Rich Chicks LLC	2015	E	209 879-4104	526
Risvolds Inc	2099	D	323 770-2674	2599
Rnj Printing Corporation	2752	F	310 638-7768	6848
Rotational Molding Inc	3089	D	310 327-5401	10026
Ruggeri Marble and Granite Inc	3281	D	310 513-2155	10929
Russ International Inc	3444	E	310 329-7121	12361
Rytan Inc	3541	E	310 328-6553	13946
Samsgazeboscom Inc	2421	E	310 523-3778	3945
Santee Cosmetics USA	2844	F	310 329-2305	8576
Sardo Bus & Coach Upholstery	2521	D	800 654-3824	4821
Screenworks Co Tim	2759	E	310 532-7239	7210
Sgl Composites Inc (DH)	2655	D	424 329-5250	5302
Sgps Inc	3999	D	310 538-4175	23474
Shelby Carroll Intl Inc (PA)	3711	E	310 538-2914	19502
Smart LLC	3089	E	310 674-8135	10059
Somar Corporation	3444	F	310 329-1446	12380
South Bay Corporation	3069	F	310 532-5353	9373
Southwest Offset Prtg Co Inc (PA)	2752	B	310 965-9154	6866
Space-Lok Inc	3728	C	310 527-6150	20236
SPS Technologies LLC	3452	B	310 323-6222	12693
SPS Technologies LLC	3494	D	562 426-9411	13363
Standard Homeopathic Co	2834	E	424 224-4127	8143
Standard Metal Products Inc	3471	E	310 532-9861	13107
Stanzino Inc (PA)	2211	F	213 746-8822	2714
Steeldeck Inc	3999	E	323 290-2100	23485
Stepstone Inc (PA)	3272	E	310 327-7474	10656
Sun Dyeing and Finishing Co	2253	F	310 329-0844	2805
Superior Metal Finishing Inc	3471	E	310 464-8010	13111
Swift Fab	3444	F	310 366-7295	12397
Swift-Cor Precision Inc	3444	D	310 354-1207	12398
T & F Sheet Metals Fab	3444	E	310 516-8548	12399
T M W Engineering Inc	3728	F	310 768-8211	20243
T N T Auto Inc	3111	D	310 715-1117	10145
Talins Company	3444	E	310 378-3715	12400
Techflex Packaging LLC	2671	D	424 266-9400	5344
Thermally Engineered Manufactu	3443	E	310 523-9934	12064
Timbucktoo Manufacturing Inc	3589	E	310 323-1134	15592
Tomorrows Heirlooms Inc	3429	E	310 323-6720	11636
Tony Glazing Specialties Co	2541	F	323 770-8400	4950
Triune Enterprises Inc	2671	E	310 719-1600	5346
Tru-Cut Inc	3524	E	310 630-0422	13699
UNI Sport Inc	2752	E	310 217-4587	6907
US Blanks LLC (PA)	2821	E	310 225-6774	7623
US Hanger Company LLC	3315	E	310 323-8030	11114
US Industrial Tool & Sup Co	3542	E	310 464-8400	13998
US Packagers Inc	2782	E	310 327-7721	7321
Vege-Mist Inc	3585	E	310 353-2300	15470
Versafab Corp (PA)	3444	E	800 421-1822	12425
Victor Martin Inc	2514	C	323 587-3101	4707
Vitamin Friends LLC	2023	E	310 356-9018	624
Viver Co Inc	3444	E	310 327-4578	12427
Waltco Lift Corp	3537	D	323 321-4131	13896
Washington Orna Ir Works Inc	3446	E	310 327-8660	12520
Wcbm Company (PA)	3965	E	323 262-3274	23015
Welmark Textile Inc	2299	F	310 516-7289	2955
West Coast Laboratories Inc	2834	E	310 527-6163	8186
West Coast Laboratories Inc (PA)	2834	E	323 321-4774	8187
Westcoast Rotor Inc	3561	E	310 327-5050	14604
Windline Marine	3429	C	310 516-9812	11643
Windsor Textile Corporation	2281	E	310 323-3997	2886
Wyrefab Inc	3496	E	310 523-2147	13448
Zentis North America LLC	2869	D	310 719-2600	8786

GEORGETOWN, CA - El Dorado County

	SIC	EMP	PHONE	ENTRY #
Georgetown Precast Inc	3272	F	530 333-4404	10581
Powerlift Dumbwaiters Inc	3534	E	800 409-5438	13807

GEYSERVILLE, CA - Sonoma County

	SIC	EMP	PHONE	ENTRY #
Clos Du Bois Wines Inc	2084	E	707 857-1651	1638
Francis Ford Cppola Prsnts LLC	2084	E	707 251-3200	1709
J Pedroncelli Winery	2084	E	707 857-3531	1761
Marietta Cellars Incorporated	2084	F	707 433-2747	1810
Mosaic Vineyards & Winery Inc	2084	E	707 857-2000	1826
Munselle Vineyards LLC	2084	F	707 857-9988	1829
Sbragia Family Vineyards LLC	2084	E	707 473-2992	1908

GILROY, CA - Santa Clara County

	SIC	EMP	PHONE	ENTRY #
Accent Manufacturing Inc	2599	E	408 846-9993	5046
American Steel & Stairways Inc	3446	E	408 848-2992	12449
Architctural Facades Unlimited	3272	D	408 846-5350	10531
B & R Vinyards Inc	2084	F	408 842-5649	1588
Blossom Valley Foods Inc	2087	E	408 848-5520	2194
Boulder Creek Guitars Inc	3931	F	408 842-0222	22610
Chalgren Enterprises	3845	E	408 847-3994	22238
Chameleon Like Inc	2782	E	408 847-3661	7306
Containment Consultants Inc	3443	F	408 848-6998	12010
Germains Seed Technology Inc	3999	E	408 848-8120	23343
Guess Inc	2329	E	408 847-3400	3087
Heart Wood Manufacturing Inc	2434	D	408 848-9750	4203
Instant Asphalt Inc	2891	F	408 280-7733	8875
International Paper Company	2621	D	408 846-2060	5115
International Paper Company	2621	D	408 847-6400	5123
Lloyd E Hennessey Jr	3599	E	408 842-8437	16147
Lucas/Signatone Corporation (PA)	3825	E	408 848-2851	21068
Mainstreet Media Group LLC	2711	C	408 842-6400	5717
Makplate LLC	3471	F	408 842-7572	13047
Metech Recycling Inc	3341	E	408 848-3050	11205
Morgan Hill Plastics Inc	3089	E	408 779-2118	9911
Nice Rack Tower Accessories	3714	F	408 846-1919	19728
Northern California Stair	2431	E	408 847-0106	4097
Partsflex Inc	2396	E	408 677-7121	3807
Peninsula Spring Corporation	3495	F	408 848-3361	13384
Pulmuone Wildwood Inc	2099	F	714 361-0806	2592
Quinn Development Co	3271	F	408 842-9320	10514
Rancho De Solis Winery Inc	2084	F	408 847-6306	1878
RMC Engineering Co Inc (PA)	3599	E	408 842-2525	16362
Trical Inc (PA)	2879	C	831 637-0195	8843
Versaco Manufacturing Inc	3556	F	408 848-2880	14412

GLEN ELLEN, CA - Sonoma County

	SIC	EMP	PHONE	ENTRY #
Bfw Associates LLC (HQ)	2084	E	707 935-3000	1598
Deerfield Ranch Winery LLC	2084	F	707 833-5215	1658
Valley of Moon Winery	2084	E	707 939-4500	1980
Vintage Wine Estates Inc	2084	E	707 933-9675	1991

GLENDALE, CA - Los Angeles County

	SIC	EMP	PHONE	ENTRY #
4 Over LLC (HQ)	2759	B	818 246-1170	6967
4 Over LLC	2759	F	818 246-1170	6968
Accurate Dial & Nameplate Inc (PA)	3479	F	323 245-9181	13134
Aero Manufacturing & Pltg Co	3471	E	818 241-2844	12908
Alcotrevi Inc	3841	F	818 244-0400	21588
Ambrit Industries Inc	3542	E	818 243-1224	13966
Arecont Vision Costar LLC	3629	D	818 937-0700	16777
Art & Sign Production Inc	3993	E	818 245-6945	23055
Automation Plating Corporation	3471	E	323 245-4951	12939
Avery Dennison Corporation (PA)	2672	B	626 304-2000	5349
Btrade LLC	7372	E	818 334-4433	23701
California Paper Bag Inc	2674	F	818 240-6717	5434
Calmat Co (DH)	2951	C	818 553-8821	9088
Challenger Ornamental Ir Works	3446	F	818 507-7030	12461
Chromatic Inc Lithographers	2752	E	818 242-5785	6484
Coda Energy Holdings LLC	3699	E	626 775-3900	19275
Color Inc	2752	E	818 240-1350	6494

Mergent email: customerrelations@mergent.com
1342

2020 California
Manufacturers Register

(P-0000) Products & Services Section entry number
(PA)=Parent Co (HQ)=Headquarters (DH)=Div Headquarters

	SIC	EMP	PHONE	ENTRY #
Color Depot Inc	2759	F	818 500-9033	7031
Cryst Mark Inc A Swan Techno C	3559	F	818 240-7520	14448
Custom Characters Inc	2389	F	818 507-5940	3549
Cygnet Stampng & Fabrictng Inc	3469	F	818 240-7574	12790
Cygnet Stampng & Fabrictng Inc (PA)	3469	F	818 240-7574	12791
Daily Computing Solutions Inc	2711	E	818 240-5400	5605
De Novo Software	7372	F	213 814-1240	23809
Denttio Inc	3843	F	323 254-1000	22147
Dion Rostamian	3861	F	877 633-0293	22413
Dwa Nova LLC	7372	D	818 695-5000	23837
Fortner Eng & Mfg Inc	3599	F	818 240-7740	15969
G Printing Inc	2759	F	818 246-1156	7070
Garlic Research Labs Inc	2879	F	800 424-7990	8829
Garlic Valley Farms Inc	2035	F	818 247-9600	881
Gcg Corporation	3471	F	818 247-8508	13012
General Mills Inc	2043	D	818 553-6777	1021
Hi-Temp Forming Co Inc	3599	D	714 529-6556	16024
Hub Construction Spc Inc	3444	D	909 379-2100	12241
Huntmix Inc	2951	C	818 548-5200	9095
Information Integration Group	7372	E	818 956-3744	24018
Irl-Mex Manufacturing Company	3451	F	818 246-7211	12636
J P Weaver & Company Inc	3299	F	818 500-1740	11008
Joar Labs Inc	2844	E	818 243-0700	8522
Jtea Inc	7372	E	847 878-2226	24062
K K Molds Inc	3442	F	818 548-8988	11962
Kadbanou LLC	2033	F	368 409-0118	781
Laufer Media Inc	2721	E	818 291-8408	5976
Le Chef Costumier Inc	2389	E	818 242-0868	3564
Learners Digest Intl LLC	3999	C	818 240-7500	23392
Lin MAI Inc	3999	E	818 890-1220	23395
Long Beach Woodworks LLC	2448	F	562 437-2293	4377
Los Angles Tmes Cmmnctions LLC	2711	D	818 637-3203	5708
Malakan Inc (PA)	2435	F	310 910-9270	4277
Manufacturing USA Enterprises	3911	E	818 409-3070	22546
McCoppin Enterprises	3599	E	818 240-4840	16183
Mid Valley Grinding Co Inc	3999	F	818 764-1086	23412
Mini Vac Inc	3635	F	818 244-6777	16844
Modern Engine Inc	3599	E	818 409-9494	16217
Mold Masters Inc	3544	F	323 999-2599	14079
N J P Sports Inc	2394	F	818 247-3914	3692
N2 Development Inc	3728	F	323 210-3251	20184
Nadin Company	2834	E	818 500-8908	8022
Nestle Purina Petcare Company	2047	C	314 982-1000	1079
Nestle Refrigerated Food Co	2098	B	818 549-6000	2374
North American Textile Co LLC (PA)	2396	E	818 409-0019	3804
Notron Manufacturing Inc	3599	F	818 247-7739	16249
P E N Inc	2759	E	818 954-0775	7164
Pennoyer-Dodge Co	3545	E	818 547-2100	14182
Person & Covey Inc	2844	E	818 937-5000	8556
Pillsbury Company LLC	2041	D	818 522-3952	1008
Premac Inc	3599	F	818 241-8370	16312
Printefex Inc	2752	F	818 240-2400	6799
SAI Industries	3484	E	818 842-6144	13277
Saks Styling Incorporated	3911	E	818 244-0540	22568
Saxton Industrial Inc	3444	F	818 265-0702	12368
Snapmd Inc	7372	F	310 953-4800	24423
Sonoco Corrflex LLC	2653	F	818 507-7477	5267
Sunderstorm LLC	3999	F	818 605-6682	23490
Susy Clothing Co	2339	E	818 500-7879	3418
Technicolor Usa Inc	3651	C	818 500-9090	17290
Technicolor Usa Inc	3651	E	818 260-3651	17291
Trattoria Amici/Americana LLC	2599	F	818 502-1220	5086
Triangle Rock Products LLC	1429	E	818 553-8820	320
Vege - Kurl Inc	2844	D	818 956-5582	8601
Victory Studio	3861	F	818 972-0737	22471
Vistanomics Inc	2721	F	818 249-1236	6054
Viva Holdings LLC (PA)	2678	F	818 243-1363	5486
Viva Print LLC (HQ)	2678	F	818 243-1363	5487
Vulcan Materials Company	3273	F	818 241-7356	10871
Water Filter Exchange Inc	3569	F	818 808-2541	14871
Yerma Jewelry Mfg Inc	3911	E	818 551-0690	22586
Zen Monkey LLC	2038	F	310 504-2899	986

GLENDORA, CA - Los Angeles County

	SIC	EMP	PHONE	ENTRY #
Action Stamping Inc	3469	E	626 914-7466	12760
Americana Sports Inc	3949	E	626 914-0238	22745
Bashoura Inc	3911	F	626 963-7600	22503
Calportland	1442	F	760 343-3403	332
Calportland Company (DH)	3241	D	626 852-6200	10408
Cjd Construction Services Inc	1389	E	626 335-1116	183
Complete Metal Design	3599	E	626 335-3636	15859
Deccofelt Corporation	2299	E	626 963-8511	2931
Electro-Tech Products Inc	3679	E	909 592-1434	18899
Eshields LLC	2671	E	909 305-8848	5327
Ever-Glory Intl Group Inc	2339	F	626 859-6638	3323
Grico Precision Inc	3599	F	626 963-0368	16004

	SIC	EMP	PHONE	ENTRY #
Hallmark Metals Inc	3444	E	626 335-1263	12231
Mackenzie Laboratories Inc	3674	E	909 394-9007	18366
Mariba Corporation	2449	F	626 963-6775	4421
Metrex Valve Corp	3491	E	626 335-4027	13315
Millipart Inc (PA)	3599	F	626 963-4101	16208
National Hot Rod Association	2711	E	626 250-2300	5771
Oasis Medical Inc (PA)	3851	D	909 305-5400	22377
Southwest Machine & Plastic Co	3728	E	626 963-6919	20235
Sybron Dental Specialties Inc	3843	A	909 596-0276	22193
Tex Shoemaker & Son Inc	2386	F	909 592-2071	3524
Tom Clark Confections	2064	E	909 599-4700	1405

GLENHAVEN, CA - Lake County

	SIC	EMP	PHONE	ENTRY #
Cvps Inc	7372	E	707 998-9364	23788

GOLD RIVER, CA - Sacramento County

	SIC	EMP	PHONE	ENTRY #
Cleanworld	3949	F	916 635-7300	22783
CTS Fabrication USA Inc	3351	F	916 852-6303	11214
Kirk A Schliger	3564	F	916 638-8433	14667
Levac Specialties Inc	3743	F	916 362-3795	20373
Markes International Inc	3826	D	513 745-0241	21259
Synergex International Corp	7372	D	916 635-7300	24476

GOLETA, CA - Santa Barbara County

	SIC	EMP	PHONE	ENTRY #
A B C-Clio Inc (PA)	2731	C	805 968-1911	6065
A&A Engineering Inc	3599	F	805 685-4882	15663
ABC - Clio LLC	2731	F	800 368-6868	6066
Acra Enterprises Inc	3599	F	805 964-4757	15685
Acroamatics Inc	3663	E	805 967-9909	17436
Advanced Vision Science Inc	3851	E	805 683-3851	22338
Alta-Dena Certified Dairy LLC	2026	C	805 685-8328	683
Appfolio Inc (PA)	7372	C	805 364-6093	23608
Arguello Inc	1382	E	805 567-1632	109
Atk Space Systems Inc	3812	D	805 685-2262	20542
Biopac Systems Inc	3826	E	805 685-0066	21197
Boone Printing & Graphics Inc	2759	D	805 683-2349	7003
Burnet Machining Inc	3599	F	805 964-6321	15804
C N C Machining Inc	3599	F	805 681-8855	15814
Calient Technologies Inc (PA)	3661	F	805 562-5500	17351
Caribbean Coffee Company Inc	2043	E	805 692-2200	1016
Carriercomm Inc	3663	E	805 968-9621	17482
Cbrite Inc	3823	F	805 722-1121	20847
Check Yourself Inc	3599	F	805 967-6190	15842
Deckers Outdoor Corporation (PA)	2389	B	805 967-7611	3550
Digital Surgery Systems Inc	3841	D	805 308-6909	21687
DR Radon Boatbuilding Inc (PA)	3732	F	805 692-2170	20322
Electro Optical Industries	3827	E	805 964-6701	21351
Electromatic Inc (PA)	3471	F	805 964-9880	13000
Far West Technology Inc	3829	F	805 964-3615	21472
Flir Motion Ctrl Systems Inc	3559	E	650 692-3900	14468
Flir Systems Inc	3812	E	805 964-9797	20579
Grind Food Company Inc	3599	F	805 964-8344	16005
Hollister Brewing Company LLC	2082	E	805 968-2810	1535
Innovative Micro Tech Inc	3674	C	805 681-2807	18293
Innovative Technology Inc	3479	F	805 571-8384	13193
Inogen Inc (PA)	3841	C	805 562-0500	21744
Intouch Technologies Inc (PA)	7372	C	805 562-8686	24033
Intri-Plex Technologies Inc (HQ)	3469	C	805 683-3414	12824
JD Business Solutions Inc	2752	E	805 962-8193	6663
Karl Storz Imaging Inc (HQ)	3829	B	805 968-5563	21496
Lastline Inc	7372	C	805 456-7075	24091
Launchpoint Technologies Inc	3568	F	805 683-9659	14788
Linvatec Corporation	3841	D	805 571-8100	21779
Lockheed Martin Corporation	3812	D	805 571-2346	20620
Madera Concepts	2499	F	805 692-0033	4514
Medtronic Inc	3845	F	805 571-3769	22280
Medtronic PS Medical Inc (DH)	3841	C	805 571-3769	21812
Memory Glass LLC	3229	F	805 682-6469	10319
Microdyn-Nadir Us Inc (DH)	3589	D	805 964-8003	15543
Mission Research Corporation (DH)	3721	F	805 690-2447	19915
Moog Inc	3812	B	805 618-3900	20634
Moseley Associates Inc (HQ)	3663	C	805 968-9621	17592
Neal Feay Company	3354	D	805 967-4521	11241
Northrop Grumman Innovation	3812	D	805 961-8600	20652
Pacific Design Tech Inc	3812	C	805 961-9110	20671
Queenship Publishing Company	2731	F	805 692-0043	6140
R G Hansen Associates (PA)	3823	F	805 564-3388	20926
Raytheon Company	3699	C	805 967-5511	19391
Raytheon Company	3571	F	805 562-2730	14968
Raytheon Company	3812	D	805 562-4611	20699
Raytheon Company	3812	C	805 967-5511	20702
Resonant Inc (PA)	3674	D	805 308-9803	18516
Ricardo Defense Inc (DH)	3714	D	805 477-1902	19756
S B I F Inc	3479	F	805 683-1711	13239
Santa Barbara Coffee LLC	2095	F	805 683-2555	2309
Soilmoisture Equipment Corp	3829	E	805 964-3525	21543

Employment Codes: A=Over 500 employees, B=251-500,
C=101-250, D=51-100, E=20-50, F=10-19

2020 California
Manufacturers Register

© Mergent Inc. 1-800-342-5647

1343

GEOGRAPHIC

	SIC	EMP	PHONE	ENTRY #
Soraa Laser Diode Inc (PA)	3699	E	805 696-6999	19409
Superior Millwork of Sb Inc	2434	E	805 685-1744	4251
Surf To Summit Inc	3949	F	805 964-1896	22904
Tan Set Corporation	3441	F	805 967-4567	11896
Tencate Advanced Armor USA Inc (DH)	3484	F	805 845-4085	13279
Transcendent Imaging LLC	3861	F	805 964-1400	22465
Truevision Systems Inc	3841	E	805 963-9700	21941
Veeco Process Equipment Inc	3826	C	805 967-1400	21320
Veeco Process Equipment Inc	3599	D	805 967-2700	16497
Venoco Inc	2911	E	805 961-2305	9084
Vista Steel Co Inc (PA)	3449	E	805 964-4732	12612
Wyatt Technology Corporation (PA)	3826	C	805 681-9009	21325

GONZALES, CA - Monterey County

	SIC	EMP	PHONE	ENTRY #
Ramsay Highlander Inc	3523	E	831 675-3453	13662

GRANADA HILLS, CA - Los Angeles County

	SIC	EMP	PHONE	ENTRY #
Akupara Games LLC	7372	F	747 998-2193	23588
Almac Fixture & Supply Co	2299	E	818 360-1706	2921
Brite-Lite Neon Corp	3993	F	818 763-4798	23067
Carpod Inc	3089	F	818 395-8676	9696
Garys Leather Creations Inc	3172	D	818 831-9977	10234
How 2 Save Fuel LLC	2869	F	818 882-1189	8743
Kouzouians Fine Custom Furn	2599	F	818 772-1212	5070
Perrins Registration Office	3469	F	818 832-1332	12856
Rudex Broadcasting Ltd Corp	3663	F	213 494-3377	17648
Sweet Inspirations Inc	2335	E	310 886-9010	3255

GRAND TERRACE, CA - San Bernardino County

	SIC	EMP	PHONE	ENTRY #
Griswold Pump Company	3561	E	909 422-1700	14577
Wilden Pump and Engrg LLC (DH)	3561	B	909 422-1700	14605

GRANITE BAY, CA - Placer County

	SIC	EMP	PHONE	ENTRY #
Cal Nor Embroidery & Spc	2395	F	916 786-3131	3727
New Cal Metals Inc	3444	F	916 652-7424	12312
Recoating-West Inc (PA)	3444	E	916 652-8290	12352

GRASS VALLEY, CA - Nevada County

	SIC	EMP	PHONE	ENTRY #
Aja Video Systems Inc (PA)	3663	E	530 274-2048	17443
Applied Science Inc (PA)	3841	F	530 273-8299	21606
Autometrix Inc	3552	F	530 477-5065	14287
Barger & Associates	3069	E	530 271-5424	9289
Benchmark Thermal Corporation	3433	D	530 477-5011	11690
Cabinet Company Inc	2541	F	530 273-7533	4887
Cake Cafe Bar LLC	2051	F	530 615-4126	1171
Countis Industries Inc	3264	E	530 272-8334	10476
Datum Precision Inc	3728	F	530 272-8415	20084
Diamond Truss	2439	F	530 477-1477	4299
Ei Corp	3651	E	530 274-1240	17226
Farlows Scntfc Glssblwing Inc	3229	E	530 477-5513	10305
Grass Valley Inc	3663	A	530 478-3000	17526
Grass Valley Inc (HQ)	3663	D	530 265-1000	17527
Grass Valley Usa LLC (HQ)	3661	B	800 547-8949	17375
Guy G Veralrud	3651	F	530 477-7323	17234
Hansen Bros Enterprises (PA)	1442	D	530 273-3100	343
High Sierra Electronics Inc	3826	E	530 273-2080	21237
House of Print & Copy	2752	F	530 273-1000	6617
Huntington Mechanical Labs Inc	3563	E	530 273-9533	14632
Igraphics (PA)	2759	E	530 273-2200	7093
Lifekind Products Inc	2841	E	530 477-5395	8343
Maier Manufacturing Inc	3751	E	530 272-2936	20417
Manufacturers Coml Fin LLC	3433	E	530 477-5011	11705
Measurement Specialties Inc	3825	D	530 273-4608	21077
Naggiar Vineyards LLC	2084	F	530 268-9059	1833
National Directory Services	2731	E	530 268-8636	6125
Nevada County Publishing Co	2711	A	530 273-9561	5774
R G B Display Corporation	3575	F	530 268-2222	15133
Robert Snell Cast Specialist	3915	F	530 273-8958	22600
Seagate Technology LLC	3572	C	530 410-6594	15094
Taylor Investments LLC	3563	E	530 273-4135	14642
Thermo Products Inc	3398	D	909 888-2882	11473
Vitalhue	3999	F	323 646-8775	23518
Vossloh Signaling Usa Inc	3462	E	530 272-8194	12727

GRATON, CA - Sonoma County

	SIC	EMP	PHONE	ENTRY #
Empire West Inc	3089	E	707 823-1190	9778
Purple Wine Company LLC	2084	E	707 829-6100	1873
Sonoma Wine Company LLC	2084	C	707 829-6100	1921

GREENBRAE, CA - Marin County

	SIC	EMP	PHONE	ENTRY #
Petroleum Sales Inc	1311	D	415 256-1600	62

GREENFIELD, CA - Monterey County

	SIC	EMP	PHONE	ENTRY #
Wente Bros	2084	E	831 674-5642	1996

GREENVILLE, CA - Plumas County

	SIC	EMP	PHONE	ENTRY #
D L Stoy Logging Co	2411	F	530 283-3292	3878

GREENWOOD, CA - El Dorado County

	SIC	EMP	PHONE	ENTRY #
Red Line Engineering Inc	3599	F	530 333-2134	16347

GRIDLEY, CA - Butte County

	SIC	EMP	PHONE	ENTRY #
California Industiral Mfg LLC (PA)	3999	F	530 846-9960	23294
E D Kilby Mfg & Farming	3523	E	530 846-5625	13630
Rio Pluma Company LLC (HQ)	2033	E	530 846-5200	820
Sundial Orchrds Hulling Drying	2068	E	530 846-6155	1440
Sunsweet Dryers	2034	D	530 846-5578	868
Wax Box Firelog Corporation	3433	E	530 846-2200	11724

GROVER BEACH, CA - San Luis Obispo County

	SIC	EMP	PHONE	ENTRY #
C F W Research & Dev Co	3351	F	805 489-8750	11213
David B Anderson	2752	E	805 489-0661	6533
H J Harkins Company Inc	2834	E	805 929-1333	7930
Hotlix (PA)	2064	E	805 473-0596	1372

GUADALUPE, CA - Santa Barbara County

	SIC	EMP	PHONE	ENTRY #
Tri-Co Building Supply Inc	2439	D	805 343-2555	4324

GUALALA, CA - Mendocino County

	SIC	EMP	PHONE	ENTRY #
Independent Coast Observer	2711	F	707 884-3501	5670

GUERNEVILLE, CA - Sonoma County

	SIC	EMP	PHONE	ENTRY #
F Korbel & Bros (PA)	2084	B	707 824-7000	1694

GUSTINE, CA - Merced County

	SIC	EMP	PHONE	ENTRY #
John B Sanfilippo & Son Inc	2068	B	209 854-2455	1428
Legacy Vulcan LLC	3272	F	209 854-3088	10597
Saputo Dairy Foods Usa LLC	2026	C	209 854-6461	709

HACIENDA HEIGHTS, CA - Los Angeles County

	SIC	EMP	PHONE	ENTRY #
Adamant Enterprise Inc	2673	E	626 934-3399	5381
Barhena Inc	3589	E	888 383-8800	15491
Cotton Tale Designs Inc	2392	E	714 435-9558	3609
Easterncctv (usa) LLC	3699	D	626 961-8810	19300
Gravity Boarding Company Inc	3949	E	760 591-4144	22813
Superior Equipment Solutions	3631	D	323 722-7900	16817

HALF MOON BAY, CA - San Mateo County

	SIC	EMP	PHONE	ENTRY #
Accurate Always Inc	3571	E	650 728-9428	14878
Romeo Packing Company	2674	E	650 728-3393	5443
Wick Communications Inc	2711	E	650 726-4424	5867

HANFORD, CA - Kings County

	SIC	EMP	PHONE	ENTRY #
Baker Commodities Inc	2077	E	559 686-4797	1454
Britz Fertilizers Inc	3523	E	559 582-0942	13615
California Bio-Productex Inc	2869	E	559 582-5308	8727
Central Valley Meat Co Inc (PA)	2011	C	559 583-9624	401
Clw Foods LLC (PA)	2099	E	559 639-6661	2430
Del Monte Foods Inc	2033	C	559 639-6160	763
Hanford Sentinel Inc	2711	D	559 582-0471	5651
Helena Agri-Enterprises LLC	2879	E	559 582-0291	8831
Jack B Martin	3993	F	559 583-1175	23138
Kings Cabinet Systems	2521	E	559 584-9662	4806
Lacey Milling Company Inc	2041	F	559 584-6634	1005
McLellan Equipment Inc	3713	D	559 582-8100	19543
McLellan Industries Inc	3713	D	650 873-8100	19544
Nichols Pistachio	2068	C	559 584-6811	1435
Norwesco Inc	3089	E	559 585-1668	9933
Pitman Family Farms	2048	D	559 585-3330	1118
Pyramid Systems Inc	2541	E	559 582-9345	4933
Rosa Brothers Milk Co Inc (PA)	2024	E	559 582-8825	666
South Valley Materials Inc	3273	E	559 582-0532	10840
Superior Dairy Products Co	2024	E	559 582-0481	670
Tessenderlo Kerley Inc	2875	F	559 582-9200	8815
Transcontinental US LLC	2673	C	559 585-2040	5425
Vandersteen Audio Inc	3651	E	559 582-0324	17299
Viking Ready Mix Co Inc	3273	E	559 344-7931	10862
Windtamer Tarps	2394	F	559 584-2080	3716

HAPPY CAMP, CA - Siskiyou County

	SIC	EMP	PHONE	ENTRY #
Northwest Skyline Logging Inc	2411	F	530 493-5150	3899

HARBOR CITY, CA - Los Angeles County

	SIC	EMP	PHONE	ENTRY #
A & J Industries Inc	2441	F	310 216-2170	4327
Adegbesan Adefemi	3571	E	310 663-0789	14880
Aerostar Engineering & Mfg Inc	3599	F	310 326-5098	15711
Basmat Inc (PA)	3444	D	310 325-2063	12128
Bjc	2121	F	310 977-6068	2659
Brea Canon Oil Co Inc	1311	F	310 326-4002	31
Bryant Rubber Corp (PA)	3053	E	310 530-2530	9219
Cal Partitions Inc	2542	F	310 539-1911	4966
City Industrial Tool & Die (PA)	3312	F	310 530-1234	11038
Corn Maiden Foods Inc	2032	D	310 784-0400	723
Decco Graphics Inc	3469	E	310 534-2861	12792
Joanka Inc	3442	F	310 326-8940	11961
La Espanola Meats Inc	2013	E	310 539-0455	476
Lumination Lighting & Tech Inc	3646	C	855 283-1100	17056

Mergent email: customerrelations@mergent.com
1344

2020 California
Manufacturers Register

(P-0000) Products & Services Section entry number
(PA)=Parent Co (HQ)=Headquarters (DH)=Div Headquarters

	SIC	EMP	PHONE	ENTRY #
Miller Woodworking Inc	2431	E	310 257-6806	4086
Monographx Inc	3993	F	310 325-6780	23162
Onyx Industries Inc (PA)	3451	D	310 539-8830	12643
Prime Surfaces Inc	3281	F	310 448-2292	10922
Prime Wheel Corporation	3714	B	310 326-5080	19740
Republic Machinery Co Inc (PA)	3541	C	310 518-1100	13943
Rocker Solenoid Company	3679	D	310 534-5660	19070
Ship Supply International Inc	3264	F	310 325-3188	10483
Simpson Performance Pdts Inc	3842	D	310 325-6035	22087
Star Plastic Design	3089	D	310 530-7119	10068

HARMONY, CA - San Luis Obispo County

	SIC	EMP	PHONE	ENTRY #
Harmony Cellars	2084	E	805 927-1625	1748

HAWAIIAN GARDENS, CA - Los Angeles County

	SIC	EMP	PHONE	ENTRY #
Consolidated Color Corporation	2851	E	562 420-7714	8636

HAWTHORNE, CA - Los Angeles County

	SIC	EMP	PHONE	ENTRY #
Acuna Dionisio Able	3599	F	310 978-4741	15689
Advanced Engine Management Inc (PA)	3714	C	310 484-2322	19568
Astro Machine Co Inc	3599	F	310 679-8291	15753
Computerized Fashion Svcs Inc	2389	F	310 973-0106	3548
Cxc Simulations LLC	3699	F	888 918-2010	19284
D3 Inc (PA)	2522	C	310 223-2200	4831
Dolphin Medical Inc (HQ)	3845	D	800 448-6506	22249
Firstclass Foods - Trojan Inc	2011	C	310 676-2500	408
Fulham Co Inc	3612	E	323 779-2980	16552
Glen-Mac Swiss Co	3678	F	310 978-4555	18770
Greenform LLC	3531	F	310 331-1665	13732
Heinz Weber Incorporated	2796	E	310 477-3561	7376
Interplastic Corporation	2821	E	323 757-1801	7570
K & E Inc	3728	F	310 675-3309	20148
Katch Precision Machining Inc	3599	F	310 676-4989	16108
Lithographix Inc (PA)	2752	F	323 770-1000	6704
Local Neon Co Inc	3993	E	310 978-2000	23149
Los Angeles Ale Works LLC	2082	F	213 422-6569	1545
Marco Fine Arts	2759	D	310 615-1818	7130
Marleon Inc	7692	E	310 679-1242	24650
Maxon Crs LLC	3731	E	424 236-4660	20292
Medical Tactile Inc	3841	E	310 641-8228	21799
OSI Electronics Inc (HQ)	3672	C	310 978-0516	17948
OSI Subsidiary Inc	3699	B	310 978-0516	19373
OSI Systems Inc (PA)	3674	B	310 978-0516	18462
Paulco Precision Inc	3599	F	310 679-4900	16286
Picnic At Ascot Inc	2449	E	310 674-3098	4424
Signquest	3993	E	310 355-0528	23205
Space Exploration Tech Corp (PA)	3761	A	310 363-6000	20455
Supreme Graphics Inc	2752	F	310 531-8300	6880
Technology Training Corp	2752	D	310 644-7777	6886
Teledyne Defense Elec LLC	3679	C	323 777-0077	19104
Tesla Inc	3714	F	310 219-4652	19781
Trio Tool & Die Co (PA)	3544	F	310 644-4431	14116
Triumph Aerostructures LLC	3728	A	310 322-1000	20259
Warmelin Precision Pdts LLC	3599	D	323 777-5003	16511
Wems Inc (PA)	3564	E	310 644-0251	14689
Wems Inc	3625	E	310 644-0255	16768
Wizard Enterprise	3253	F	323 756-8430	10458

HAYWARD, CA - Alameda County

	SIC	EMP	PHONE	ENTRY #
ABB Motors and Mechanical Inc	3621	F	510 785-9900	16625
Acologix Inc	2834	E	510 512-7200	7720
Action Laminates LLC	2521	F	510 259-6217	4779
Admail-Express Inc	2752	E	510 471-6200	6396
Advance Carbon Products Inc	3624	E	510 293-5930	16679
Ajinomoto Foods North Amer Inc	2038	F	510 293-1838	936
Akas Manufacturing Corporation	3444	E	510 786-3200	12095
Alameda Newspapers Inc (DH)	2711	C	510 783-6111	5546
Alcatel-Lucent USA Inc	3661	E	510 475-5000	17343
All Bay Pallet Company Inc (PA)	2448	E	510 636-4131	4345
Allstate Plastics LLC	2673	F	510 783-9600	5383
Allure Labs Inc	2844	E	510 489-8896	8434
Alpha Magnetics Inc	3499	F	510 732-6698	13495
Amaral Industries Common Law	2499	D	510 569-8669	4490
Amedica Biotech Inc	3841	F	510 785-5980	21596
American Blinds and Drap Inc	2391	E	510 487-3500	3586
American Poly-Foam Company Inc	3086	E	510 786-3626	9503
Ampex Data Systems Corporation (HQ)	3572	D	650 367-2011	15004
Annabelle Candy Inc	2064	E	510 783-2900	1356
Applied Photon Technology Inc	3641	E	510 780-9500	16856
Applied Silver Inc	2499	F	888 939-4747	4491
Arch Foods Inc (PA)	3421	E	510 331-8352	11512
Archer-Daniels-Midland Company	2041	C	510 346-3309	991
Armanino Foods Distinction Inc	2038	E	510 441-9300	943
Automatic Control Engrg Corp	3829	E	510 293-6040	21439
Axl Musical Instruments Ltd	3931	C	415 508-1398	22608
Azuma Foods Intl Inc USA (HQ)	2092	D	510 782-1112	2256
B C Song International Inc	2911	D	510 785-8383	9039

	SIC	EMP	PHONE	ENTRY #
Baxter International Inc	2834	E	510 723-2000	7790
Bay Tech Manufacturing Inc	3599	F	510 783-0660	15778
Beeline Group LLC	3993	D	510 477-5400	23059
Berkeley Farms LLC (DH)	2026	B	510 265-8600	687
Best Express Foods Inc	2051	E	510 782-5338	1145
Bimbo Bakeries Usa Inc	2051	C	510 436-5350	1165
Biolog Inc	3826	E	510 785-2564	21195
Buffalo Distribution Inc	3613	E	510 324-3800	16587
C NC Noodle Co	2098	F	510 732-1318	2367
CEC Print Solutions Inc	2752	E	510 670-0160	6476
Chawk Technology Intl Inc (PA)	3089	D	510 330-5299	9706
Chiquita Brands Intl Inc	2037	F	510 732-9500	907
Clarmil Manufacturing Corp (PA)	2099	D	510 476-0700	2427
Columbus Foods LLC	2011	B	510 921-3400	405
Columbus Manufacturing Inc (HQ)	2013	D	510 921-3423	449
Commercial Patterns Inc	3089	F	510 784-1014	9715
Commex Corporation	3081	F	510 887-4000	9397
Computer Plastics	3544	E	510 785-3600	14037
Conxtech Inc	3441	C	510 264-9112	11773
Corefact Corporation	2732	F	866 777-3986	6171
Corrugated Packaging Pdts Inc	2653	E	650 615-9180	5214
Crafton Carton	2657	C	510 441-5985	5312
Crown Equipment Corporation	3537	E	510 471-7272	13867
Custom Label and Decal LLC	2759	F	510 876-0000	7041
Cypress Furniture Inc	2511	C	510 723-4890	4563
Daily Review	2711	E	510 783-6111	5611
Danworth Manufacturing Co	3599	F	510 487-8290	15878
Davis Instruments Corporation	3812	D	510 732-9229	20565
Delphon Industries LLC (PA)	3089	C	510 576-2220	9750
Detention Device Systems	3599	E	510 783-0771	15891
Die & Tool Products Co Inc	3599	F	415 822-2888	15896
Dielectric Coating Industries	3827	E	510 487-5980	21348
Do Dine Inc	7372	F	510 583-7546	23820
Dow Chemical Company	2821	C	510 786-0100	7556
Dupont De Nemours Inc	2879	F	510 784-9105	8828
E-Z Mix Inc	2674	E	510 782-8010	5438
EDS Wrap and Roll Foods LLC	2032	E	510 266-0888	726
Ekc Technology Inc (DH)	2899	C	510 784-9105	8962
Electro Plating Specialties	3471	E	510 786-1881	12993
EMD Millipore Corporation	3826	E	510 576-1367	21222
Fante Inc (PA)	2096	E	650 697-7525	2322
Farasis Energy Usa Inc	3621	D	510 732-6600	16645
Farmer Bros Co	2095	E	510 638-1660	2290
First Impressions Printing	2752	F	510 784-0811	6573
Flo Stor Engineering Inc (PA)	3535	E	510 887-7179	13824
Florence & New Itln Art Co Inc	3272	E	510 785-9674	10574
Fmw Machine Shop	3599	F	650 363-1313	15965
Folgergraphics Inc	2791	E	510 293-2294	7357
Forderer Cornice Works	3442	F	415 431-4100	11955
Four Dimensions Inc	3825	F	510 782-1843	21040
Glazier Steel Inc	3441	D	510 471-5300	11804
Goorin Brosinc	2353	F		3466
Grundfos CBS Inc	3561	E	510 512-1300	14579
Haigs Delicacies LLC	2099	E	510 782-6285	2476
Hantel Technologies Inc	3841	E	510 400-1164	21732
Impax Laboratories Inc	2834	D	510 240-6000	7944
Impax Laboratories LLC (DH)	2834	A	510 240-6000	7945
Impax Laboratories LLC	2834	F	510 240-6000	7946
Impax Laboratories LLC	2834	F	510 476-2000	7947
Impax Laboratories Usa LLC	2834	F	510 240-6000	7948
IMT Precision Inc	3599	E	510 324-8926	16040
Induspac California Inc (HQ)	2821	E	510 324-3626	7569
Infrared Industries Inc	3826	F	510 782-8100	21245
Inland Marine Industries Inc	3444	C	510 785-8555	12245
Integrity Technology Corp	3679	E	270 812-8867	18948
Ironridge Inc (HQ)	3433	C	800 227-9523	11703
Iwen Naturals	2844	F	510 589-8019	8519
J S Hackl Archi Signa Inc	3993	F	510 940-2608	23137
J W Floor Covering Inc	2099	D	858 444-1214	2485
Jupiter Systems LLC	3575	C	510 675-1000	15126
Justipher Inc	3993	F	510 918-6800	23144
Keen-Kut Products Inc	3545	F	510 785-5168	14166
Kinestral Technologies Inc (PA)	3231	C	650 416-5200	10372
King Abrasives Inc	2672	F	510 785-8100	5364
Kinwai USA Inc	2511	E	510 780-9388	4583
KLA Tencor	3568	E	510 887-2647	14787
Kore Print Solutions Inc	2752	F	510 445-1638	6680
Kosan Biosciences Incorporated	2834	D	650 995-7356	7982
Krisalis Inc (PA)	3599	E	510 786-0858	16126
La Tapatia - Norcal Inc	2099	C	510 783-2045	2513
Legend Silicon Corp	3663	E	408 735-9888	17570
Longevity Global Inc	3548	E	877 566-4462	14245
Ly Brothers Corporation (PA)	2051	E	510 782-2118	1238
Ly Brothers Corporation	2051	C	510 782-2118	1239
Lyrical Foods Inc	2099	C	510 784-0955	2535

Employment Codes: A=Over 500 employees, B=251-500,
C=101-250, D=51-100, E=20-50, F=10-19

2020 California
Manufacturers Register

© Mergent Inc. 1-800-342-5647

1345

GEOGRAPHIC

Company	SIC	EMP	PHONE	ENTRY #
M&L Metals Inc	3444	F	510 732-1745	12273
Magico LLC	3651	E	510 649-9700	17255
Maier Racing Enterprises Inc	3714	F	510 581-7600	19712
Mdc Vacuum Products LLC (PA)	3674	D	510 265-3500	18378
Mdc Vacuum Products LLC	3491	D	510 265-3500	13313
Melrose Nameplate Label Co Inc (PA)	3479	E	510 732-3100	13205
Menches Tool & Die Inc	3599	E	650 592-2328	16195
Micro Connectors Inc	3577	E	510 266-0299	15289
Mission Tool and Mfg Co Inc	3599	E	510 782-8383	16213
Montague Company	3589	C	510 785-8822	15544
Morgan Technical Ceramics Inc	3299	F	510 491-1100	11013
National Metal Fabricators	3441	F	510 887-6231	11853
Norton Packaging Inc (PA)	3089	C	510 786-1922	9931
Nova Tool Co	3953	F	925 828-7172	22953
Octillion Power Systems Inc	3714	E	510 397-5952	19730
Oki Doki Signs	3993	F	510 940-7446	23169
Omnivore Technologies Inc	7372	E	800 293-4058	24225
Onq Solutions Inc (PA)	2542	E	650 262-4150	4993
Optiscan Biomedical Corp	3841	E	510 342-5800	21850
Oven Fresh Bakery Incorporated	2051	F	650 366-9201	1255
P & S Sales Inc	3714	F	510 732-2628	19734
P-Americas LLC	2086	E	510 732-9500	2105
Pacific Die Cut Industries	3053	D	510 732-8103	9244
Pacific States Felt Mfg Co Inc	3053	E	510 783-2357	9245
Pan Pacific Plastics Mfg Inc	3089	E	510 785-6888	9950
Pepsi-Cola Metro Btlg Co Inc	2086	E	510 781-3600	2125
Perry Tool & Research Inc	3399	E	510 782-9226	11483
Pinnacle Diversified Inc	2752	F	510 400-7929	6783
Pixley Construction Inc	1389	F	510 783-3020	247
Plastikon Industries Inc (PA)	3544	B	510 400-1010	14093
Platron Company West	3471	F	510 781-5588	13073
Potrero Medical Inc	3841	D	888 635-7280	21861
Primus Power Corporation	3692	E	510 342-7600	19180
Procolorflex Ink Corp	2893	F	510 293-3033	8928
Produce World Inc	2099	D	510 441-1449	2590
Protech Materials Inc	3364	F	510 887-5870	11360
Proteus Digital Health Inc	2836	C	650 632-4031	8324
Protoquick Inc	3599	F	510 264-0101	16318
Prozyme Inc	2835	E	510 638-6900	8248
Purolator Pdts A Filtration Co	3564	E	510 785-4800	14674
Qantel Technologies Inc	3571	E	510 731-2080	14966
Rago Neon Inc	3993	F	510 537-1903	23183
Reflexion Medical Inc	3845	C	650 239-9070	22301
Resource Label Group LLC	2759	E	510 477-0707	7195
Ricman Mfg Inc	3599	E	510 670-1785	16357
Rinco International Inc	3086	F	510 785-1633	9566
Rodak Plastics Co Inc	3089	F	510 471-0898	10021
San Francisco Pipe &	3498	E	510 785-9148	13485
Sapar Usa Inc (PA)	2013	E	510 441-9500	496
Semano Inc	3471	E	510 489-2360	13099
Sepragen Corporation	3826	E	510 475-0650	21289
Sew-Eurodrive Inc	3566	E	510 487-3560	14749
Sharkrack Inc	3577	F	510 477-7900	15333
Shasta Beverages Inc (DH)	2086	D	954 581-0922	2171
Silicon Specialists Inc	3674	E	510 732-9796	18548
Solonics Inc (PA)	3661	E	650 589-9798	17411
Solta Medical Inc	3845	C	510 782-2286	22312
Sonoco Prtective Solutions Inc	2653	D	510 785-0220	5268
Sourcing Group LLC	2752	E	510 471-4749	6865
South Bay Diversfd Systems Inc	3444	F	510 784-3094	12382
Steinbeck Brewing Company	2082	D	510 888-0695	1566
Stiles Paint Manufacturing Inc	2851	F	510 887-8868	8683
Sun Deep Inc	2844	E	510 441-2525	8590
Superior Tube Pipe Bnding Fbco	3498	E	510 782-9311	13486
Surface Techniques Corporation (PA)	2541	E	510 887-6000	4944
Synectic Packaging Inc	2759	F	650 474-0132	7236
Tarps & Tie-Downs Inc (PA)	2394	F	510 782-8772	3709
Techtron Products Inc	3645	E	510 293-3500	16993
Tender Loving Things Inc	2844	E	510 300-1260	8592
Therm-X of California Inc (PA)	3829	C	510 441-7566	21557
Thermionics Laboratory Inc	3471	D	510 786-0680	13117
Thorx Laboratories Inc	2834	F	510 240-6000	8163
Tli Enterprises Inc (PA)	3821	F	510 538-3304	20777
Trade Only Screen Printing Inc	2759	F	510 887-2020	7254
Tresco Paint Co	2851	F	510 887-7254	8688
Tridecs Corporation	3599	E	510 785-2620	16469
Tung Fei Plastic Inc	2673	E	510 783-9688	5427
Turner Group Publications Inc	2759	F	408 297-3299	7258
U S Enterprise Corporation	2035	E	510 487-8877	903
UC Plastic Manufacture Inc	2673	E	510 785-6777	5428
Ultimate Rail Equipment Inc	3743	F	510 324-5000	20377
Ultra Clean Technology Systems (HQ)	3823	C	510 576-4400	20953
Ultrasil LLC	3674	E	510 266-3700	18631
United Foods Intl USA Inc (HQ)	2099	E	510 264-5850	2642
Universal Metal Spinning Inc	3646	F	510 782-0980	17080
Urban Trading Software Inc	7372	E	877 633-6171	24545
US Container and Housing Co	2452	E	844 762-8242	4469
Valdor Fiber Optics Inc (PA)	3825	E	510 293-1212	21152
Varni-Lite Coatings Associates	2891	F	510 887-8997	8902
Vicolo Wholesale (PA)	2041	E	510 475-6019	1012
Villa Pallet LLC	2448	F	510 794-6676	4404
Wohler Technologies Inc	3663	F	510 870-0810	17708
Wood Box Specialties Inc	2449	F	510 786-1600	4433
Woodford Wicks LLC	3999	F	614 544-9307	23528
Xia LLC	3829	F	510 494-9020	21565
Yanfeng US Automotive	2531	F	616 886-3622	4877

HEALDSBURG, CA - Sonoma County

Company	SIC	EMP	PHONE	ENTRY #
Alexander Valley Gourmet LLC	2099	E	707 473-0116	2389
AVV Winery Co LLC	2084	E	707 433-7209	1586
Bear Republic Brewing Co Inc	2082	F	707 433-2337	1502
Bella Vineyards LLC	2084	F	707 473-9171	1594
Cable Car Classics Inc	3743	E	707 433-6810	20368
Chateau Diana LLC (PA)	2084	F	707 433-6992	1630
Constellation Brands US Oprs	2084	A	707 433-8268	1648
Cooling Tower Resources Inc (PA)	2499	E	707 433-3900	4498
Copain Wine Cellars LLC	2084	E	707 836-8822	1649
Criveller California Corp	3556	F	707 431-2211	14357
DJ Grey Company Inc	3679	F	707 431-2779	18891
Dry Creek Vineyard Inc	2084	E	707 433-1000	1672
Duff Bevill Vineyard Managment	2084	E	707 433-6691	1676
E & J Gallo Winery	2084	E	707 431-1946	1681
Ferrar-Crano Vnyrds Winery LLC (PA)	2084	C	707 433-6700	1699
Field Stone Winery & Vineyard	2084	F	707 433-7266	1702
Franciscan Vinyards Inc	2084	D	707 433-6981	1713
General Dynmics Ots Ncvlle Inc	3593	D	707 473-9200	15622
Geyser Peak Winery	2084	E	707 857-9463	1722
Hanna Winery Inc (PA)	2084	F	707 431-4310	1746
HDD LLC	2084	F	707 433-9545	1750
Jackson Family Wines Inc	2084	F	707 433-9463	1768
Jordan Vineyard & Winery LP	2084	E	707 431-5250	1776
Jvw Corporation	2084	D	707 431-5250	1778
L Foppiano Wine Co	2084	E	707 433-2736	1788
Lambert Bridge Winery Inc	2084	F	707 431-9600	1793
Michel-Schlmberger Partners LP	2084	E	707 433-7427	1818
Mill Creek Vneyards Winery Inc	2084	F	707 433-4788	1820
Mix Garden Inc	3273	F	707 433-4327	10803
Overlook Vineyards LLC	2084	E	707 433-6491	1852
Pan Magna Group	2084	E	707 433-5508	1854
Pjk Winery LLC	2084	E	707 431-8333	1867
Preston Vineyards Inc	2084	F	707 433-3372	1871
RB Wine Associates LLC	2084	D	707 433-8400	1881
Redwood Milling Company LLC	2431	E	707 433-1343	4113
Rupert Gibbon & Spider Inc	2851	E	800 442-0455	8677
Santa Rosa Lead Products LLC (PA)	3531	F	800 916-5323	13746
Santa Rosa Lead Products Inc	3369	E	707 431-1477	11423
Seghesio Wineries Inc	2084	F	707 433-3579	1911
Selby Inc	2084	F	707 431-1703	1912
Serra Systems Inc (HQ)	7372	F	707 433-5104	24400
Stonecushion Inc (PA)	2084	F	707 433-1911	1938
Tandem Wines LLC	2084	F	707 395-3902	1948
Toad Hollow Vineyards Inc	2084	F	707 431-1441	1959
Truett-Hurst Inc (PA)	2084	F	707 431-4423	1972
Williams & Selyem Winery	2084	F	707 433-6425	2001

HEBER, CA - Imperial County

Company	SIC	EMP	PHONE	ENTRY #
Gibson and Schaefer Inc (PA)	3273	E	619 352-3535	10763

HELENDALE, CA - San Bernardino County

Company	SIC	EMP	PHONE	ENTRY #
W A Murphy Inc	2892	F	760 245-8711	8908

HELM, CA - Fresno County

Company	SIC	EMP	PHONE	ENTRY #
JR Simplot Company	2099	E	559 866-5681	2492
True Organic Products Inc	2875	F	559 866-3001	8817

HEMET, CA - Riverside County

Company	SIC	EMP	PHONE	ENTRY #
Brazeau Thoroughbred Farms LP	3523	F	951 925-8957	13614
Danaher Corporation	3824	C	951 652-6811	20965
Easy Ad Incorporated	2711	E	951 658-2244	5624
EZ Lube LLC	2992	A	951 766-1996	9143
J S M Productions Inc	2752	E	951 929-5771	6657
McCrometer Inc	3824	C	951 652-6811	20972
Medi Kid Company	3842	F	951 925-8800	22044
Omega 2000 Group Corp	3634	D	951 775-5815	16837
Ortega Manufacturing Inc	3999	F	951 766-9363	23435
Ramko Injection Inc	3089	D	951 652-3510	10007
Substance Abuse Program	3674	E	951 791-3350	18586
Superior Ready Mix Concrete LP	3273	E	951 658-9225	10853
Te Connectivity	3678	F	951 765-2200	18788
Te Connectivity Corporation	3678	D	951 765-2250	18792
Te Connectivity Corporation	3678	B	951 765-2200	18798
Washburn Grove Management Inc	2411	E	909 322-4690	3915

HERCULES, CA - Contra Costa County

	SIC	EMP	PHONE	ENTRY#
A & B Die Casting Co Inc	3363	E	877 708-0009	11328
Benda Tool & Model Works Inc	3544	E	510 741-3170	14022
Bio-RAD Laboratories Inc (PA)	3845	B	510 724-7000	22232
Bio-RAD Laboratories Inc	3826	A	510 741-6916	21185
Bio-RAD Laboratories Inc	3826	C	510 741-1000	21187
Bio-RAD Laboratories Inc	3826	C	510 741-6709	21188
Bio-RAD Laboratories Inc	3826	A	510 232-7000	21189
Bio-RAD Laboratories Inc	3826	B	510 741-6715	21190
Bio-RAD Laboratories Inc	3826	B	510 741-6999	21191
Naia Inc	2024	E	510 724-2479	661

HERMOSA BEACH, CA - Los Angeles County

	SIC	EMP	PHONE	ENTRY#
Becker Surfboards Inc	3949	F	310 372-6554	22758
Easy Reader Inc	2711	E	310 372-4611	5625
Hammitt Inc	3161	F	310 293-3787	10196
National Media Inc	2711	E	310 372-0388	5773
Rf Digital Corporation	3674	C	949 610-0008	18517

HESPERIA, CA - San Bernardino County

	SIC	EMP	PHONE	ENTRY#
A Terrycable California Corp.	3714	E	760 244-9351	19562
Apex Specialty Cnstr Entps	2431	F	714 334-1118	3995
Brown & Honeycutt Truss Systms	2439	E	760 244-8887	4290
C & M Wood Industries	2591	C	760 949-3292	5017
CAr Enterprises Inc	3578	F	760 947-6411	15373
Daytec Center LLC	3751	E	760 995-3515	20397
Dial Precision Inc	3599	D	760 947-3557	15894
Dyell Machine	3599	F	760 244-3333	15912
E R Metals Inc	3366	F	760 948-2309	11396
Geeriraj Inc	3672	F	760 246-6149	17886
Hayes Welding Inc	7692	F	760 246-4878	24640
Hesperia Resorter	2711	E	760 244-0021	5662
Hesperia Unified School Dst	2099	F	760 948-1051	2479
High Tech Etch (PA)	3599	F	760 244-8916	16028
Jim Ellis	2439	F	760 244-8566	4311
Leadmasters	3949	F	760 949-6566	22841
Maurice & Maurice Engrg Inc	3334	F	760 949-5151	11185
Moore Tool Co	3429	F	760 949-4142	11615
P J Machining Co Inc	3599	F	760 948-2722	16268
R S R Steel Fabrication Inc	3312	F	760 244-2210	11063
Robar Enterprises Inc (PA)	3273	C	760 244-5456	10820
Southern California Components	2439	D	760 949-5144	4318
T L Timmerman Construction	2439	E	760 244-2532	4322
Trekell & Co Inc	3952	F	800 378-3867	22947
W R Grace & Co-Conn	3826	D	760 244-6107	21323
Western Fab Inc	3499	F	760 949-1441	13557

HICKMAN, CA - Stanislaus County

	SIC	EMP	PHONE	ENTRY#
Reed International (HQ)	3532	E	209 874-2357	13760

HIDDEN VALLEY LAKE, CA - Lake County

	SIC	EMP	PHONE	ENTRY#
Jensen Graphics & Printing	2752	F	707 987-8966	6665

HIGHLAND, CA - San Bernardino County

	SIC	EMP	PHONE	ENTRY#
Alpha I Publishing Inc	2741	F	909 862-9572	6180
Boudoir Spirits Inc	2085	F	909 714-6644	2011
Cemex Cnstr Mtls PCF LLC	3273	E	909 335-3105	10723
Master-Halco Inc	3315	E	909 350-4740	11100
Raemica Inc	2013	E	909 864-1990	491
Robertsons Ready Mix Ltd	3273	E	909 425-2930	10827
Tj Composites Inc	3444	E	951 928-8713	12408

HILMAR, CA - Merced County

	SIC	EMP	PHONE	ENTRY#
Americore Inc	3448	E	209 632-5679	12531
Hilmar Cheese Company Inc (PA)	2022	B	209 667-6076	555
Hilmar Whey Protein Inc (PA)	2023	B	209 667-6076	596
Hilmar Whey Protein Inc	2023	B	209 667-6076	597
Perrys Custom Chopping	3523	F	209 667-8777	13658
Richard Veeck	3559	F	209 667-0872	14528

HOLLISTER, CA - San Benito County

	SIC	EMP	PHONE	ENTRY#
A & R Doors Inc	2431	F	831 637-8139	3988
Advantage Truss Company LLC	2439	E	831 635-0377	4285
B & R Farms LLC	2034	E	831 637-9168	842
C & C Built-In Inc	2434	E	831 635-5880	4171
Corbin Pacific Inc (PA)	3751	D	831 634-1100	20391
Diablo Precision Inc	3599	E	831 634-0136	15893
Food Equipment Mfg Co	3556	F	831 637-1624	14361
Gabilan Welding Inc	3599	F	831 637-3360	15983
Gimelli Vineyards	2084	E	831 637-5445	1724
Gregory Patterson	3446	E	831 636-1015	12478
Kmg Chemicals Inc	2899	E	800 956-7467	8986
Kmg Electronic Chemicals Inc	2899	E	831 636-5151	8987
Kopin Corporation	3674	E	831 636-5556	18335
Mandego Inc	2261	F	831 637-5241	2830
Marich Confectionery Co Inc	2064	C	831 634-4700	1386
Mc Electronics LLC	3679	B	831 637-1651	19009

	SIC	EMP	PHONE	ENTRY#
Nanotronics Imaging Inc	3699	F	831 630-0700	19362
Neil Jones Food Company	2033	D	831 637-0573	802
Ozeki Sake U S A Inc (HQ)	2084	E	831 637-9217	1853
Pacific Intrlock Pvngstone Inc (PA)	3272	F	831 637-9163	10620
Pacific Scientific Energetic (HQ)	2899	E	831 637-3731	9014
Peninsula Packaging LLC	3089	C	831 634-0940	9958
Pride Conveyance Systems Inc	3535	D	831 637-1787	13831
Reed Manufacturing Inc	3324	E	831 637-5641	11167
Royal Circuit Solutions Inc (PA)	3672	E	831 636-7789	17979
SBS America LLC (PA)	2431	D	831 637-8700	4121
Spices Unlimited Inc	2099	F	831 636-3596	2616
Trical Inc	2879	F	831 637-0195	8844

HOLLYWOOD, CA - Los Angeles County

	SIC	EMP	PHONE	ENTRY#
Aftermaster Inc (PA)	3861	F	310 657-4886	22400
Body Glove International LLC	2329	F	310 374-3441	3072

HOOPA, CA - Humboldt County

	SIC	EMP	PHONE	ENTRY#
Hoopa Forest Industries	2411	E	530 625-4281	3886

HOPLAND, CA - Mendocino County

	SIC	EMP	PHONE	ENTRY#
Brutocao Cellars (PA)	2084	F	707 744-1066	1609
Brutocao Vineyards	2084	E	707 744-1320	1610
Duckhorn Wine Company	2084	E	707 744-2800	1673
Fetzer Vineyards (HQ)	2084	C	707 744-1250	1700
Mendocino Brewing Company Inc	2082	E	707 744-1015	1548
Steve Bruner	2431	E	707 744-1103	4130

HUGHSON, CA - Stanislaus County

	SIC	EMP	PHONE	ENTRY#
Assali Hulling & Shelling	2068	F	209 883-4263	1421
Calaveras Materials Inc (DH)	3273	E	209 883-0448	10702
Calaveras Materials Inc.	3272	F	209 883-0448	10545
California Truss Company	2439	E	209 883-8000	4295
Grossi Fabrication Inc	3496	E	209 883-2817	13415
Hughson Nut Inc (HQ)	2068	D	209 883-0403	1427
Nuwest Milling LLC	2048	F	209 883-1163	1116
Valley Tool & Mfg Co Inc	3599	E	209 883-4093	16491

HUNTINGTON BEACH, CA - Orange County

	SIC	EMP	PHONE	ENTRY#
A G Artwear Inc	3961	F	714 898-3636	22977
ADS LLC	3823	E	714 379-9778	20827
Advanced Cmpsite Pdts Tech Inc	3089	F	714 895-5544	9611
Advanced Cutting Tools Inc	3423	F	714 842-9376	11520
Advanced Packaging & Crating	2449	F	714 892-1702	4410
Aero-Mechanical Engrg Inc	3599	F	714 891-2423	15707
Aerodynamic Engineering Inc	3599	E	714 891-2651	15708
Aerodyne Prcsion Machining Inc	3599	F	714 891-1311	15709
Airtech International Inc (PA)	3728	C	714 899-8100	20028
All Forms Express	2759	F	714 596-8641	6979
All West Plastics Inc	3082	E	714 894-9922	9427
Alphalogix Inc	3695	D	714 901-1456	19209
American Automated Engrg Inc	3769	D	714 898-9951	20472
American Battery Charging LLC	3629	E	401 231-5227	16775
American Blast Systems Inc	3312	E	949 244-6859	11025
American Metal Enterprises Inc	3842	E	714 894-6810	21979
American Precision Hydraulics	3542	E	714 903-8610	13968
AMG Torrance LLC (DH)	3728	E	310 515-2584	20032
Asea Power Systems	3679	E	714 896-9695	18821
B & B Enameling Inc	3479	F	714 848-0044	13146
Badge Co	3999	F	714 842-3037	23283
Baker Hghes Olfld Oprtions LLC	1389	D	714 893-8511	158
Baker Hghes Olfld Oprtions LLC	1389	F	714 891-8544	159
Baker Hughes A GE Company LLC	1389	D	714 893-8511	161
Bare Nothings Inc (PA)	2339	E	714 848-8532	3292
Beekee Corp	7372	F	949 275-5861	23657
Bent Manufacturing Co Bdaa Inc	3089	F	714 842-0600	9657
Blue Iron Network Inc	7372	E	714 901-1456	23681
Blue-White Industries Ltd (PA)	3824	D	714 893-8529	20961
Boardriders Inc (DH)	2329	C	714 889-2200	3071
Boeing Company	3761	B	714 896-3311	20443
Boeing Company	3721	A	714 934-9801	19870
Boeing Company	3721	A	714 896-3311	19872
Boeing Company	3721	E	714 896-1301	19874
Boeing Company	3721	E	714 896-1670	19876
Boeing Company	3721	E	714 896-1839	19878
Boeing Company	3721	E	714 896-3311	19879
Boeing Intellectual	3721	F	562 797-2020	19880
Buena Park Tool & Engineering	3599	F	714 843-6215	15801
Cable Harness Systems Inc	3679	E	714 841-9650	18846
Cal-Aurum Industries	3471	E	714 898-0996	12959
California Economizer	3625	E	714 898-9963	16704
California Faucets Inc	3432	F	657 400-1639	11660
California Faucets Inc (PA)	3432	D	714 890-0450	11661
Calmoseptine Inc	2834	E	714 848-2949	7825
Cambro Manufacturing Company (PA)	3089	B	714 848-1555	9689
Cambro Manufacturing Company	3089	B	714 848-1555	9690
Cambro Manufacturing Company	3089	B	714 848-1555	9691

Employment Codes: A=Over 500 employees, B=251-500,
C=101-250, D=51-100, E=20-50, F=10-19

2020 California
Manufacturers Register

© Mergent Inc. 1-800-342-5647
1347

GEOGRAPHIC

Company	SIC	EMP	PHONE	ENTRY #
Chase Corporation	3644	F	714 964-6268	16942
Circuit Automation Inc	3679	F	714 763-4180	18866
Classic Components Inc	3471	E	714 619-5690	12969
CMS Engineering Inc	3599	F	714 896-6900	15851
Coast To Coast Circuits Inc (PA)	3672	F	714 891-9441	17854
Cobham Trivec-Avant Inc	3663	F	714 841-4976	17488
Conversion Devices Inc	3845	E	714 898-6551	22243
Creative Costuming Designs Inc	2211	E	714 895-0982	2679
Creative Sign Inc	3993	F	714 842-4343	23083
Crenshaw Die and Mfg Corp	3469	D	949 475-5505	12789
Curlin Healthcare Products Inc	3599	D	714 893-2200	15872
Curlin Medical Inc (HQ)	3561	F	714 897-9301	14567
Custom Building Products Inc (DH)	2891	D	800 272-8786	8864
D & D Technologies (usa) Inc	3429	F	714 677-1300	11584
D & D Technologies USA Inc	3315	E	949 852-5140	11087
Dairy Conveyor Corp	3535	E	714 891-0883	13821
DC Shoes (DH)	2329	D	714 889-4206	3074
Delfin Design & Mfg Inc	3089	E	949 888-4644	9749
Dime Research and Development	3711	E	714 969-7879	19466
Donoco Industries Inc	3229	E	714 893-7889	10304
Dynamet Incorporated	3356	F	714 375-3150	11270
Dynatrac Products Co Inc	3714	E	714 596-4461	19642
Ebs Products	3559	F	714 896-6700	14456
Electronic Waveform Lab Inc	3841	E	714 843-0463	21699
Encore Interiors Inc (HQ)	3728	C	949 559-0930	20097
Encore Interiors Inc	3728	C	562 344-1700	20098
Encore International	3724	C	949 559-0930	19951
Encore Seats Inc	3728	C	949 559-0930	20099
Enhanced Vision Systems Inc (HQ)	3827	D	800 440-9476	21352
European Services Group	3429	F	714 898-0055	11589
Fibreform Electronics Inc	3599	E	714 898-9641	15955
Fiolas Development LLC	3272	F	714 893-7559	10572
Fotis and Son Imports Inc	3556	E	714 894-9022	14364
Fox Hills Industries	3321	E	714 893-1940	11142
Fox Hills Machining Inc	3599	F	714 899-2211	15972
Frequency Management Intl (PA)	3679	E	714 373-8100	18918
Gachupin Enterprises LLC	2759	E	714 375-4111	7072
Glacier Design Systems Inc (PA)	2082	F	714 897-2337	1532
Global Tech Instruments Inc	3812	F	714 375-1811	20584
Harris Industries Inc (PA)	2672	D	714 898-8048	5362
HB Products LLC	2759	E	714 799-6967	7086
Home & Body Company (PA)	2842	E	714 842-8000	8389
Honeywell International Inc	3724	A	310 512-4237	19955
Hytron Mfg Co Inc	3599	E	714 903-6701	16038
ID Supply	2759	F	714 728-6478	7092
Ideal Pallet System Inc	2448	F	714 847-9657	4371
Initium Eyewear Inc	3851	F	714 444-0866	22362
Inkwright LLC	2752	F	714 892-3300	6640
Innovative Plastics Inc	3083	F	714 891-8800	9440
Intertrade Aviation Corp	3728	E	714 895-3335	20140
Itech Medical Inc	3841	F	714 841-2670	21761
JCM Industries Inc (PA)	2542	F	714 902-9000	4985
Jet Performance Products Inc	3694	E	714 848-5500	19194
JGM Automotive Tooling Inc	3559	E	714 895-7001	14484
Johnson Manufacturing Inc	3599	E	714 903-0393	16090
Jolyn Clothing Company LLC	2339	E	714 794-2149	3348
Kadan Consultants Incorporated	3599	F	562 988-1165	16103
Kaged Muscle LLC	2023	E	844 445-2433	599
Karls Custom Sash and Doors	2431	E	714 842-7877	4067
Kastle Stair Inc (PA)	2431	E	714 596-2600	4068
Kennedy Hills Enterprises LLC	1221	F	714 596-7444	17
Kettenbach LP	3843	F	877 532-2123	22167
Laird Coatings Corporation	2851	E	714 894-5252	8653
Leda Corporation	3769	E	714 847-7821	20478
License Frame Inc	3479	E	714 903-7550	13200
Lightning Dversion Systems LLC	3643	F	714 841-1080	16913
Logi Graphics Incorporated	3672	E	714 841-3686	17915
M I T Inc	3544	F	714 899-6066	14072
Madsen Products Incorporated	3599	E	714 894-1816	16167
Marsha Vicki Originals Inc	2311	E	714 895-6371	2969
Mechanized Science Seals Inc	3829	E	714 898-5602	21503
Mgfso LLC	2834	F	949 500-7645	8013
Milco Wire Edm Inc	3599	F	714 373-0098	16203
Miracle Cover (PA)	2851	F	714 842-8863	8657
Mission Crtical Composites LLC	3728	F	714 831-2100	20180
Mjc Engineering and Tech Inc	3542	F	714 890-0618	13985
Momeni Engineering LLC	3599	F	714 897-9301	16220
NDT Systems Inc	3829	E	714 893-2438	21511
Newlight Technologies Inc	3089	E	714 556-4500	9923
Nordson Medical (ca) LLC	3841	D	657 215-4200	21841
Norm Harboldt	3479	E	714 596-4242	13212
Ocg Inc	3679	D	714 375-4024	19036
Ofs Brands Holdings Inc	2521	F	714 903-2257	4816
Oliphant Tool Company	3544	E	714 903-6336	14087
Opticolor Inc	3089	F	714 893-8839	9942
Organ-O-Sil Fiber Co Inc	3714	E	714 847-8310	19733
Orlando Spring Corp	3495	E	562 594-8411	13383
Pacific Link Corp	3827	F	714 897-3525	21395
Pakedge Device & Software Inc	7372	E	714 880-4511	24286
Paradise Road LLC	2842	F	714 894-1779	8403
Patten Systems Inc	3823	F	714 799-5656	20916
PCA Aerospace Inc (PA)	3728	D	714 841-1750	20199
Plasma Rggedized Solutions Inc	3471	E	714 893-6063	13071
PPG Industries Inc	2851	E	714 894-5252	8669
Precision Frrites Ceramics Inc	3264	E	714 901-7622	10481
Precision Resource Inc	3469	B	714 891-4439	12858
Prestige Cosmetics Inc	2844	E	714 375-0395	8564
Primo Powder Coating & Sndblst	3479	F	714 596-4242	13231
Primus Inc	3993	D	714 527-2261	23178
Product Design Developments	3089	E	714 898-6895	9996
Pvd Coatings II LLC	3479	F	714 899-4892	13232
Ralph L Florimonte	3052	F	760 460-4470	9205
Ray Foster Dental Equipment	3843	F	714 897-7795	22185
Raycon Technology Inc (PA)	3678	F	714 799-4100	18786
Raytheon Company	3812	F	310 334-0430	20681
Reedex Inc	3679	E	714 894-0311	19065
Reloaded Technologies Inc	7372	F	949 870-3123	24356
Rima Enterprises Inc	3555	D	714 893-4534	14340
Rodon Products Inc	3677	E	714 898-3528	18740
Roi Development Corp	3629	E	714 751-0488	16796
Roto West Enterprises Inc	3089	F	714 899-2030	10030
Safran Cabin Galleys Us Inc	3728	E	714 861-7300	20214
Safran Cabin Galleys Us Inc (HQ)	3728	A	714 861-7300	20215
Safran Cabin Inc (HQ)	3728	B	714 934-0000	20218
Salco Dynamic Solutions Inc (PA)	2992	E	714 374-7500	9155
Sandia Plastics Inc	3089	E	714 901-8400	10041
Screen Art Inc	2759	F	714 891-4185	7208
Setco Sales Company	3545	F	714 372-3730	14192
Seven Wells LLC	2499	F	213 305-4775	4531
Sgt Boardriders Inc	3069	F	714 274-8000	9371
Shortcuts Software Inc	7372	F	714 622-6600	24406
Soberlink Healthcare LLC	3829	F	714 975-7200	21542
Soldermask Inc	3672	F	714 842-1987	18006
Specilized Crmic Powdr Coating	3479	F	714 901-2628	13250
Stablcor Technology Inc	2655	F	714 375-6644	5304
Steecon Inc	3728	F	714 895-5313	20237
Steripax Inc	2671	E	714 892-8811	5341
Submersible Systems Inc	3949	F	714 842-6566	22900
Sunbeam Trailer Products Inc	3647	E	714 373-5000	17095
Sunshine Makers Inc (PA)	2842	D	562 795-6000	8419
Surf City Garage	2842	E	714 894-1707	8420
Tarpin Corporation	3544	E	714 891-6944	14110
Teacher Created Materials Inc	2731	C	714 891-2273	6151
Therma-Tek Range Corp	3639	E	570 455-9491	16854
Thermal Bags By Ingrid Inc	2657	F	847 836-4400	5317
Tiodize Co Inc (PA)	3479	D	714 898-4377	13260
Tiodize Co Inc	3479	F	248 348-6050	13261
Tolemar Inc	3751	E	714 362-8166	20429
Translogic Incorporated	3823	E	714 890-0058	20951
Travismathew LLC	2329	F	562 799-6900	3124
Tri Models Inc	3721	D	714 896-0823	19935
Tri Print LLC	2752	F	714 847-1400	6900
Truwest Inc	2329	E	714 895-2444	3125
U S Wheel Corporation	3714	F	714 892-0021	19791
UFO Designs (PA)	3089	F	714 892-4420	10098
Unilete Inc	2329	F	714 557-1271	3126
Urethane Products Corporation	3089	F	800 913-0062	10102
V & S Engineering Company Ltd	3599	F	714 898-7869	16486
Victory Professional Products	2339	F	714 887-0621	3431
Vinatronic Inc	3672	E	714 845-3480	18045
Walton Company Inc	2499	F	714 847-8800	4542
Weatherman Products Inc (PA)	2851	F	949 515-8800	8693
West Coast Trends Inc	3949	E	714 843-9288	22923
Xr LLC	3842	F	714 847-9292	22127
Zadro Products Inc	3231	E	714 892-9200	10402
Zerouv	3851	F	714 584-0015	22398

HUNTINGTON PARK, CA - Los Angeles County

Company	SIC	EMP	PHONE	ENTRY #
Acme Castings Inc	3366	E	323 583-3129	11392
Acme Screw Products Inc	3449	E	323 581-8611	12583
Aircraft Foundry Co Inc	3365	F	323 587-3171	11364
B F Mc Gilla Inc	3498	E	323 581-8288	13459
Bodycote Thermal Proc Inc	3471	D	323 583-1231	12947
Cal-Pac Chemical Co Inc	2819	F	323 585-2178	7473
Canterbury Designs Inc	3446	E	323 936-7111	12460
Citizens of Humanity LLC (PA)	2339	D	323 923-1240	3304
Coh-Fb LLC	2326	E	323 923-1240	3030
Cotton Generation Inc	2361	E	323 581-8555	3476
Covert Iron Works	3322	F	323 560-2792	11150
Crown Poly Inc	2673	C	323 268-1298	5393
Dynamic Machine Inc	3599	F	323 585-0710	15915

2020 California
Manufacturers Register

(P-0000) Products & Services Section entry number
(PA)=Parent Co (HQ)=Headquarters (DH)=Div Headquarters

Company	SIC	EMP	PHONE	ENTRY #
Eti Sound Systems Inc	3651	E	323 835-6660	17228
J Heyri Inc	2331	E	323 588-1234	3168
Los Angeles Galvanizing Co	3479	D	323 583-2263	13202
Los Angles Pump Valve Pdts Inc	3561	E	323 277-7788	14589
NL&a Collections Inc	3645	E	323 277-6266	16982
Oheck LLC	2386	C	323 923-2700	3521
Original Distributor Exchange	3694	F	323 583-8707	19198
Plycraft Industries Inc	2435	C	323 587-8101	4279
R & W Inc	2339	F	323 589-1374	3396
Reliance Upholstery Sup Co Inc	2392	D	323 321-2300	3638
Saydel Inc (PA)	2844	E	323 585-2800	8577
Small Paper Co Inc	2621	F	323 277-0525	5151
Traffic Works Inc	3081	E	323 582-0616	9423
UFO Inc	3089	E	323 588-5450	10099
Valco Planer Works Inc	3544	E	323 582-6355	14121
West Coast Foundry LLC (HQ)	3325	E	323 583-1421	11174
Wire Guard Systems Inc	3644	F	323 588-2166	16957

IDYLLWILD, CA - Riverside County

Company	SIC	EMP	PHONE	ENTRY #
South Bay Cable Corp (PA)	3357	D	951 659-2183	11318

IMPERIAL, CA - Imperial County

Company	SIC	EMP	PHONE	ENTRY #
Franklin Lee Enterprises LLC	2759	F	760 355-1500	7069
Honeywell International Inc	3714	E	760 355-3420	19682
United States Gypsum Company	3275	B	760 358-3200	10886

INDIAN WELLS, CA - Riverside County

Company	SIC	EMP	PHONE	ENTRY #
Callaway Golf Company	3949	A	760 345-4653	22773
Kenny Giannini Putters LLC	3949	F	760 851-9475	22838

INDIO, CA - Riverside County

Company	SIC	EMP	PHONE	ENTRY #
A Plus Cabinets Inc	2434	F	760 322-5262	4160
Coachelle Valley Ice Co	2097	E	760 347-3529	2352
Coronet Concrete Products (PA)	3273	E	760 398-2441	10750
Cortima Co	3281	E	760 347-5535	10901
Cv Ice Company Inc	2097	E	760 347-3529	2353
Dejagers Inc	3281	E	760 775-4755	10903
Latino Americanos Revista	2721	F	760 342-2312	5974
Lindsey Doors Inc	3083	E	760 775-1959	9442
M F G Eurotec Inc	2511	F	760 863-0033	4588
Master Washer Stamping Svc Co	3544	F	323 722-0969	14075
MTI De Baja Inc	3812	E	951 654-2333	20637
Panco Mens Products Inc	2844	F	760 342-4368	8554
Pepsi-Cola Metro Btlg Co Inc	2086	F	760 775-2660	2124
Purus International Inc	3471	F	760 775-4500	13082
Stutz Packing Company	2034	F	760 342-1666	864
Swisstrax LLC	3253	F	760 347-3330	10455

INGLEWOOD, CA - Los Angeles County

Company	SIC	EMP	PHONE	ENTRY #
A H Machine Inc	3599	F	310 672-0016	15661
Acutek Adhesive Specialties	3069	E	310 419-0190	9279
AF Machine & Tool Co Inc	3599	F	310 674-1919	15712
All-Star Mktg & Promotions Inc	2395	F	323 582-4880	3721
Antique Designs Ltd Inc	2521	E	310 671-5400	4784
C C M D Inc	3471	F	310 673-5532	12956
Creamer Printing Co	2752	F	310 671-9491	6520
Doorking Inc (PA)	3699	C	310 645-0023	19293
Empower Rf Systems Inc (PA)	3663	D	310 412-8100	17511
Engineered Magnetics Inc	3629	E	310 649-9000	16785
Farrar Grinding Company	3728	F	323 678-4879	20102
Glp Designs Inc	2599	F	310 652-6800	5062
Golf Apparel Brands Inc	2339	C	310 327-5188	3331
Goodman Food Products Inc (PA)	2099	C	310 674-3180	2474
Industrious Software Solution	7372	F	310 672-8700	24010
Kazmere Entertainment	3651	E	323 448-9009	17249
Leads360 LLC	7372	E	888 843-1777	24097
Line Publications Inc	2721	F	310 234-9501	5978
Marvin Engineering Co Inc (PA)	3728	A	310 674-5030	20166
Marvin Land Systems Inc	3711	E	310 674-5030	19486
Minus K Technology Inc	3674	C	310 348-9656	18417
Multichrome Company Inc (PA)	3471	E	310 216-1086	13056
N/S Corporation (PA)	3589	D	310 412-7074	15546
Odwalla Inc	2033	E	310 342-3920	806
Omenkausa LLC	2086	F	877 415-6590	2101
Overhill Farms Inc	2038	C	323 587-5985	971
Relativity Space Inc	3365	F	424 393-4309	11388
Scapa Tapes North America LLC	2672	E	310 419-0567	5373
Sensor-Kinesis Corporation (PA)	3826	F	424 331-0900	21288
Shg Holdings Corp (PA)	3546	D	310 410-4907	14228
Water Planet Engineering LLC	3589	F	424 331-7700	15600
Weber Drilling Co Inc	3532	E	310 670-7708	13762
Wheels Magazine Inc	3732	F	310 402-9013	20363
Zephyr Manufacturing Co Inc	3546	D	310 410-4907	14230

INYOKERN, CA - Kern County

Company	SIC	EMP	PHONE	ENTRY #
Firequick Products Inc	3569	F	760 371-4279	14816
Indian Wells Companies	2082	E	760 377-4290	1538

Company	SIC	EMP	PHONE	ENTRY #
Intelligence Support Group Ltd	3699	E	800 504-3341	19326

IONE, CA - Amador County

Company	SIC	EMP	PHONE	ENTRY #
Isp Granule Products Inc	3295	D	209 274-2930	10972
Mp Associates Inc	2892	C	209 274-4715	8905
Sanders Aircraft Inc	3812	F	209 274-2955	20716
Specialty Granules LLC	3295	E	209 274-5323	10978

IRVINE, CA - Orange County

Company	SIC	EMP	PHONE	ENTRY #
1891 Alton A California Co	3643	F	949 261-6402	16871
3 Point Distribution LLC	2329	E	949 266-2700	3060
3h Communication Systems Inc	3812	E	949 529-1583	20526
3M Company	3843	F	949 863-1360	22129
3y Power Technology Inc	3679	F	949 450-0152	18804
A S A Engineering Inc	3571	E	949 460-9911	14877
A-Info Inc	3728	E	949 346-7326	19995
ABC Imaging of Washington	2759	F	949 419-3728	6971
Acclarent Inc	3841	B	650 687-5888	21577
Acti Corporation Inc	3651	E	949 753-0352	17181
Activision Blizzard Inc	7372	D	949 955-1380	23554
Adenna LLC	3842	F	909 510-6999	21969
Adex Electronics Inc	3674	F	949 597-1772	18062
Advanced Biocatalytics Corp	2841	F	949 442-0880	8334
Advanced Sterlization (HQ)	3841	F	800 595-0200	21584
Advanced Vsual Image Dsign LLC	2759	C	951 279-2138	6976
Advantest Test Solutions Inc	3674	E	949 523-6900	18070
Advisys Inc	7372	E	949 752-4927	23574
Agents West Inc	3699	E	949 614-0293	19250
Alcon Lensx Inc (DH)	3841	D	949 753-1393	21586
Alcon Manufacturing Ltd (PA)	2834	F	949 753-1393	7735
Alcon Vision LLC	3841	A	949 753-6488	21587
Aleks Corporation (PA)	7372	E	714 245-7191	23590
Allergan Sales LLC	2834	E	714 246-2288	7739
Allergan Sales LLC (DH)	2834	A	862 261-7000	7740
Allergan Spclty Thrpeutics Inc	2834	E	714 246-4500	7741
Allergan Usa Inc	2834	A	714 427-1900	7742
Alliance Medical Products Inc	3841	C	949 768-4690	21591
Altaviz LLC (PA)	2834	F	949 656-4003	7744
Aluratek Inc	3651	E	949 468-2046	17187
American Arium Inc	3674	E	949 623-7090	18092
American Audio Component Inc	3679	E	909 596-3788	18814
American Foil & Embosing Inc	2759	F	949 580-0080	6985
American Indus Systems Inc	3679	E	888 485-6688	18815
American PCF Prtrs College Inc	2752	E	949 250-3212	6409
American Scence Tech As T Corp	3721	D	310 773-1978	19856
Ametek Inc	3621	D	949 642-2400	16631
Amkor Technology Inc	3674	E	949 724-9370	18096
Anabolic Incorporated	2834	E	949 863-0340	7756
Anchen Pharmaceuticals Inc	2834	F	949 639-8100	7759
Apollo Instruments Inc	3827	E	949 756-3111	21334
Applied Cardiac Systems Inc	3841	E	949 855-9366	21602
Aptiv Services 3 (us) LLC (HQ)	3714	E	949 458-3100	19584
Aquatec International Inc	3561	E	949 225-2200	14560
Arrive-Ai Inc	3999	E	949 221-0166	23277
Aspect Software Inc	7372	E	408 595-5002	23628
Aspen Medical Products LLC	3841	D	949 681-0200	21610
Astea International Inc	7372	E	949 784-5000	23631
Astron Corporation	3677	E	949 458-7277	18701
Astronics Test Systems Inc (HQ)	3825	C	800 722-2528	21007
Atlas Sheet Metal Inc	3444	F	949 600-8787	12120
Axcelis Technologies Inc	3829	B	949 477-5160	21440
Axent Corporation Limited	2676	E	949 900-4349	5458
B Braun Medical Inc	3841	A	610 691-5400	21617
B Gone Bird Inc (PA)	3082	F	949 387-5662	9428
Barrot Corporation	3544	F	949 852-1640	14021
Barton Perreira LLC (PA)	3851	E	949 305-5360	22340
Bauer International Corp	3589	F	714 259-9800	15492
Bausch & Lomb Incorporated	2834	D	949 788-6000	7784
Bausch & Lomb Incorporated	3851	E	949 788-6000	22341
Bausch Health Americas Inc	2834	F	800 548-5100	7785
Baxter Healthcare Corporation	3841	C	949 474-6301	21619
Baxter Healthcare Corporation	3841	C	949 250-2500	21620
Baywa RE Solar Projects LLC	3674	E	949 398-3915	18145
Bear Industrial Holdings Inc	3084	E	562 926-3000	9464
Bi-Search International Inc	3679	E	714 258-4500	18839
Bien Air Usa Inc	3843	E	949 477-6050	22137
Bio-Medical Devices Inc	3841	E	949 752-9642	21628
Bio-Medical Devices Intl Inc	3841	F	800 443-3842	21629
Bio-Nutritional RES Group Inc (PA)	2023	D	714 427-6990	582
Bio-RAD Laboratories Inc	3826	B	949 789-0685	21186
Bio-RAD Laboratories Inc	2833	C	949 598-1200	7646
Biodot Inc (PA)	3823	E	949 440-3685	20840
Biolase Inc (PA)	3843	C	949 361-1200	22138
Biomerica Inc (PA)	3841	E	949 645-2111	21636
Biorad Inc	3826	E	949 598-1200	21198

Employment Codes: A=Over 500 employees, B=251-500,
C=101-250, D=51-100, E=20-50, F=10-19

2020 California
Manufacturers Register

© Mergent Inc. 1-800-342-5647
1349

GEOGRAPHIC

Company	SIC	EMP	PHONE	ENTRY #
Biosense Webster Inc (HQ)	3845	C	909 839-8500	22235
Biosynthetic Technologies LLC (HQ)	3556	F	949 390-5910	14350
Bivar Inc	3679	E	949 951-8808	18840
Bk Sems Usa Inc	2499	F	949 390-7120	4493
Blazar Communications Corp	2782	F	949 336-7115	7304
Blitzz Technology Inc	3663	E	949 380-7709	17469
Blizzard Entertainment Inc (HQ)	7372	D	949 955-1380	23678
Bonnier Corporation	2721	D	760 707-0100	5890
Boscogen Inc	2834	D	949 380-4317	7816
Bowtie Inc	2721	D	949 855-8822	5891
Braille Signs Inc	3993	F	949 797-1570	23065
Breathe Technologies Inc	3842	E	949 988-7700	21993
Brent Engineering Inc	3531	F	949 679-5630	13712
Brewer Irvine Inc	3089	D	949 474-7000	9674
Broadley-James-Corporation	3823	D	949 829-5555	20842
Bsh Home Appliances Corp (DH)	3639	C	949 440-7100	16848
Budget Enterprises Inc	3211	E	949 697-9544	10260
Buy Insta Slim Inc	2326	F	949 263-2301	3028
Cadence Design Systems Inc	7372	E	949 788-6080	23708
Calamp Corp (PA)	3663	C	949 600-5600	17476
Cardlogix	3577	E	949 380-1312	15186
Cartel Industries LLC	3444	E	949 474-3200	12154
Carttronics LLC	3699	E	888 696-2278	19270
Cbj LP	2721	E	949 833-8373	5901
Central Admxture Phrm Svcs Inc (DH)	2834	F	949 660-2000	7836
Ceradyne (HQ)	3299	B	949 862-9600	11003
Ceradyne Inc	3299	F	949 756-0642	11004
Cercacor Laboratories Inc	3829	F	949 679-6100	21451
Certance LLC (HQ)	3572	B	949 856-7800	15014
Cheek Engineering & Stamping	3469	F	714 832-9480	12783
Chen-Tech Industries Inc (DH)	3841	F	949 855-6716	21663
Chromadex Corporation (PA)	2833	D	949 419-0288	7648
Circuit Assembly Corp (PA)	3678	E	949 855-7887	18754
Cisco Systems Inc	3577	A	408 526-4000	15194
Clariphy Communications Inc (HQ)	3674	D	949 861-3074	18164
Clearflow Inc (PA)	3841	E	714 916-5010	21666
Clr Analytics Inc	3799	F	949 864-6696	20504
CMS Products Inc	3572	E	714 424-5520	15017
Coast Composites LLC	3599	E	949 455-0665	15855
Coast Composites LLC (DH)	3599	D	949 455-0665	15856
Coastal Cocktails Inc (PA)	2086	E	949 250-3129	2057
Coca-Cola Company	2086	C	949 250-5961	2061
Coda Automotive Inc	3714	D	949 830-7000	19620
Colimatic Usa Inc	3565	F	949 600-6440	14703
Columbia Sanitary Products	3432	E	949 474-0777	11666
Combimatrix Corporation (HQ)	3826	E	949 753-0624	21207
Commerce Velocity LLC	7372	F	949 756-8950	23761
Compugroup Medical Inc	7372	F	949 789-0500	23764
Computer Asssted Mfg Tech Corp	3599	D	949 263-8911	15860
Concept Development Llc	3672	E	949 623-8000	17855
Conexant Systems Inc (HQ)	3674	E	949 483-4600	18175
Connectec Company Inc (PA)	3643	D	949 252-1077	16885
Connective Solutions LLC	3229	E	800 241-2792	10302
Control Systems Intl Inc	3533	E	949 238-4150	13772
Cooper Microelectronics Inc	3674	E	949 553-8352	18179
Corsair Elec Connectors Inc	3678	C	949 833-0273	18761
Cosemi Technologies Inc (PA)	3674	F	949 623-9816	18183
Covidien LP	3841	B	949 837-3700	21674
Cp-Carrillo Inc	3592	E	949 567-9000	15612
Cp-Carrillo Inc (DH)	3592	C	949 567-9000	15613
Creaform USA Inc	3577	F	855 939-4446	15210
Critical Io LLC	3577	F	949 553-2200	15211
Cryogenic Inds Svc Cmpanies LLC (DH)	3561	F	949 261-7533	14565
Cryoport Systems Inc (HQ)	3559	F	949 540-7204	14446
Crystal Tips Holdings	3061	E	800 944-3939	9262
Cs Systems Inc	3577	E	949 475-9100	15212
Ctc Global Corporation (PA)	3643	C	949 428-8500	16889
Cummins Pacific LLC (HQ)	3519	D	949 253-6000	13592
Curtiss-Wright Flow Control	3491	D	949 271-7500	13302
Cybernet Manufacturing Inc	3571	A	949 600-8000	14902
Cycle News Inc (PA)	2711	E	949 863-7082	5604
Cylance Inc (DH)	7372	C	949 375-3380	23793
Dannier Chemical Inc	2899	E	949 221-8660	8957
Danone Us LLC	2024	B	949 474-9670	638
Data Circle Inc	3674	F	949 260-6569	18192
Daz Inc	3613	F	949 724-8800	16593
Db Studios Inc	3999	E	949 833-0100	23312
De Vries International Inc (PA)	1389	E	949 252-1212	189
Decisioninsite Ltd Lblty Co	7372	E	877 204-1392	23810
Delafoil Holdings Inc (PA)	3444	B	949 752-4580	12178
Dellarobbia Inc	2512	E	949 251-9532	4638
Diamon Fusion Intl Inc	2899	F	949 388-8000	8958
Digi Print Plus	2752	F	949 770-5000	6539
Dinsmore & Associates Inc	3081	F	714 641-7111	9403
Diversitycomm Inc	2721	F	949 825-5777	5922
Divine Foods Inc	2064	E	800 440-6476	1363
DOT Printer Inc (PA)	2752	C	949 474-1100	6551
Double-Take Software Inc (HQ)	7372	E	949 253-6500	23827
Dti Holdings Inc	3724	F	949 485-1725	19947
Duraled Ltg Technolgies Corp	3641	F	949 753-0162	16860
Duramar Floor Inc	3253	F	949 724-8800	10439
Dyln Lifestyle LLC	3914	F	949 209-9401	22589
Dynalloy Inc	3679	E	714 436-1206	18893
Eaglemetric Corp	3829	F	949 288-3363	21462
Earthwise Packaging Inc	3643	F	714 602-2169	16895
Easydial Inc	3841	D	949 916-5851	21693
Eaton Aerospace LLC	3812	E	949 452-9500	20572
Eaton Industrial Corporation	3728	B	949 425-9700	20096
Eco-Gen Distributors Inc	3621	F	760 712-7460	16639
Edwards Lfsciences Cardiaq LLC	3841	F	949 387-2615	21696
Edwards Lifescience Fing LLC	3999	F	949 250-3480	23324
Edwards Lifesciences Corp.	3842	F	949 250-2500	22004
Edwards Lifesciences Corp.	3841	F	949 250-3783	21697
Edwards Lifesciences Corp (PA)	3842	A	949 250-2500	22005
Edwards Lifesciences Corp.	3842	E	949 553-0611	22006
Edwards Lifesciences US Inc.	3845	E	949 250-2500	22251
Ei-Lo Inc	2321	F	949 200-6626	2988
Elafree Inc	3999	F	949 724-9390	23326
Electrolurgy Inc (PA)	3471	E	949 250-4494	12998
Elephant Filmz & Music Inc	3861	F	310 925-8712	22420
Elite Aviation Products Inc.	3812	E	949 536-7199	20574
Ellsworth Corporation	2891	F	949 341-9329	8867
EMC Corporation	3571	D	949 794-9999	14908
Emcor Group Inc	3824	E	949 475-6020	20967
EMI Solutions Inc	3679	F	949 206-9960	18904
Endologix Inc (PA)	3841	C	949 595-7200	21703
Energy Management Group Inc (PA)	3648	F	949 296-0764	17123
Enevate Corporation	3691	E	949 243-0399	19162
Entrepreneur Media Inc (PA)	2721	D	949 261-2325	5933
Epicor Software Corporation	3577	D	949 585-4000	15224
Equus Products Inc	3825	E	714 424-6779	21029
Ethicon Inc	3842	B	949 581-5799	22011
Evergreen Holdings Inc (PA)	2992	E	949 757-7770	9141
Evolve Dental Technologies Inc	3843	F	949 713-0909	22155
Eyeonics Inc	3851	E	949 788-6000	22358
Ezaki Glico USA Corp	2064	F	949 251-0144	1366
Farstone Technology Inc	3695	C	949 336-4321	19218
Federal Custom Cable LLC	3679	E	949 851-3114	18913
Fema Electronics Corporation	3679	E	714 825-0140	18914
Fieldcentrix Inc	7372	E	949 784-5000	23895
Flame & Wax Inc	3999	E	949 752-4000	23332
Flow Control LLC	3561	F	949 608-3900	14571
Fmh Aerospace Corp	3728	D	714 751-1000	20107
Foampro Mfg Inc	3991	D	949 252-0112	23026
Focus Point of Sale	7372	C	949 336-7500	23907
Franklin Covey Co.	2741	F	949 788-8102	6239
Freedom Innovations LLC (HQ)	3842	E	949 672-0032	22016
Fringe Studio LLC	3999	F	949 387-9680	23338
Futek Advanced Sensor Tech Inc	3823	C	949 465-0900	20876
Gary Bale Redi-Mix Con Inc	3273	D	949 786-9441	10761
Gas Recovery Systems LLC	1389	F	949 718-1430	200
Gateway Inc (DH)	3571	C	949 471-7000	14912
Gateway US Retail Inc	3571	C	949 471-7000	14913
GE Nutrients Inc	2833	F	949 502-5760	7663
Genovation Incorporated	3577	F	949 833-3355	15234
Gensia Sicor Inc (HQ)	2834	A	949 455-4700	7910
Gillette Company	3421	F	949 851-2222	11515
Git America Inc	2835	F	714 433-2180	8225
Global Future City Holding Inc	2834	F	949 769-3550	7923
Global Pcci (gpc) (PA)	3469	C	757 637-9000	12808
Golden State Foods Corp (PA)	2087	E	949 247-8000	2214
Grand Fusion Housewares Inc (PA)	3089	F	888 614-7263	9815
Graphic Packaging Intl LLC	2631	C	949 250-0900	5162
Graphtec America Inc (DH)	3823	E	949 770-6010	20881
Griswold Controls LLC (PA)	3494	C	949 559-6000	13356
H Co Computer Products (PA)	3572	F	949 833-3222	15036
Hancock Jaffe Laboratories Inc.	3841	F	949 261-2900	21730
Hanger Inc	3842	F	949 408-3320	22022
Hanger Prsthetcs & Ortho Inc	3842	D	949 863-1951	22024
Hanwha Q Cells America Inc	3674	F	949 748-5996	18266
Haymarket Worldwide Inc	2721	F	949 417-6700	5949
Health Naturals Inc.	2834	F	714 259-1821	7936
Hearst Corporation	2721	D	760 707-0100	5951
Henkel Electronic Mtls LLC	2891	C	888 943-6535	8872
HIC Corporation (PA)	2721	F	949 261-1636	5954
Homefacts Management LLC	2741	F	949 502-8300	6252
Horiba Instruments Inc (DH)	3826	C	949 250-4811	21240
Hormel Foods Corp Svcs LLC	2013	E	949 753-5350	467
I Amira Grand Foods Inc (PA)	2044	F	949 852-4468	1045
I Source Technical Svcs Inc	3679	F	949 453-1500	18941

Mergent email: customerrelations@mergent.com
1350

2020 California
Manufacturers Register

(P-0000) Products & Services Section entry number
(PA)=Parent Co (HQ)=Headquarters (DH)=Div Headquarters

Name	SIC	EMP	PHONE	ENTRY #
I-Flow LLC	3841	A	800 448-3569	21737
Iconn Inc	3678	E	949 297-8448	18774
Igo Inc (PA)	3663	F	888 205-0093	17539
Illuminate Education Inc (PA)	7372	D	949 656-3133	24000
Image Distribution Services (PA)	2752	E	949 754-9000	6628
Immport Therapeutics Inc	3844	F	949 679-4068	22214
Inari Medical Inc	3841	E	949 600-8433	21742
Incipio Technologies Inc (PA)	3577	D	949 250-4929	15244
Infinite Electronics Inc (HQ)	3679	E	949 261-1920	18945
Infinite Electronics Intl Inc (DH)	3678	C	949 261-1920	18775
Informa Business Media Inc	2741	E	949 252-1146	6255
Innova Electronics Corporation	3714	E	714 241-6800	19691
Innovative Tech & Engrg Inc	3577	F	949 955-2501	15247
Integrated Polymer Inds Inc	2891	E	949 788-1050	8876
Intel Corporation	3674	F	408 765-8080	18306
Interctive Dsplay Slutions Inc	3679	F	949 727-9493	18949
International Rectifier Corp (PA)	3674	F	949 453-1008	18315
International Sensor Tech	3829	E	949 452-9000	21490
International Vitamin Corp (PA)	2834	B	949 664-5500	7958
Interntnal Plymr Solutions Inc	3491	E	949 458-3731	13308
Interpore Cross Intl Inc (DH)	3842	D	949 453-3200	22033
INX Prints Inc	2262	D	949 660-9190	2845
Iomic Inc	3069	F	714 564-1600	9324
Irvine Electronics Inc	3672	D	949 250-0315	17903
Island Color Inc	2752	F	714 352-5888	6653
ITT Corporation	3625	B	714 547-4700	16723
IV Support Systems Inc	3841	F	888 688-6822	21762
J F Fong Inc	3841	F	949 553-8885	21764
Janteq Corp (PA)	3663	E	949 215-2603	17547
Jeremywell International Inc	3569	F	949 588-6888	14832
Jim Beam Brands Co	2085	F	949 200-7200	2014
Jonathan Engnred Slutions Corp (PA)	3429	E	714 665-4400	11601
Joseph Company International	3411	E	949 474-2200	11496
Jsn Industries Inc	3089	D	949 458-0050	9860
Jsn Packaging Products Inc	3082	D	949 458-0050	9429
Ju-Ju-Be Intl LLC (PA)	2393	E	877 258-5823	3661
Jump Start Juice Bar	2037	F	949 754-3120	918
Justenough Software Corp Inc (HQ)	7372	E	949 706-5400	24066
Karma Automotive LLC	3711	F	949 722-7121	19482
Karma Automotive LLC (DH)	3711	B	714 723-3247	19483
Kelley Blue Book Co Inc (DH)	2721	D	949 770-7704	5969
Kelmscott Communications LLC	2752	F	949 475-1900	6674
Keystone Dental Inc	3843	E	781 328-3382	22168
Knight LLC (HQ)	3569	D	949 595-4800	14834
Kofax Limited (DH)	7372	C	949 783-1000	24082
Kor Water	3069	F	714 708-7567	9327
Kraft Heinz Foods Company	2032	C	949 250-4080	735
Kratos Instruments LLC	3812	F	949 660-0666	20594
Kronos Incorporated	7372	D	800 580-7374	24087
Kuraray America Inc	2821	F	949 476-9600	7579
L A Supply Co	2759	F	949 470-9900	7108
L T Litho & Printing Co	2752	F	949 466-8584	6688
Lantronix Inc (PA)	3577	C	949 453-3990	15270
Lasergraphics Inc	3577	F	949 753-8282	15271
Lens Technology I LLC	3827	F	714 690-6470	21374
Lg-Ericsson USA Inc	3661	E	877 828-2673	17384
Lifetime Memory Products Inc	3672	E	949 794-9000	17914
Lilly Ming International Inc	2834	F	949 266-4836	7996
Links Medical Products Inc (PA)	3841	E	949 753-0001	21778
Linmarr Associates Inc	3562	F	949 215-5466	14611
Logitech Inc	3577	E	510 795-8500	15277
Lombard Medical Tech Inc (PA)	3841	F	949 379-3750	21781
Lost International LLC	2329	F	949 600-6950	3105
Lps Agency Sales and Posting	2759	E	714 247-7500	7125
LSI Corporation	3674	E	800 372-2447	18361
Lspace America LLC	2331	E	949 596-8726	3177
Lubrication Scientifics Inc	3491	F	714 557-0664	13312
Lubrication Scientifics LLC	3569	F	714 557-0664	14835
Luna Sciences Corporation	3645	F	949 225-0000	16978
M K Products Inc	3548	D	949 798-1425	14246
M P C Industrial Products Inc	3471	E	949 863-0106	13045
Mahivr	2674	F	949 559-5470	5441
Mangia Inc	2033	F	949 581-1274	794
Manta Instruments Inc	3826	F	844 633-2500	21256
Marelli North America Inc	3585	C	949 855-8050	15442
Marko Foam Products Inc (PA)	3086	E	800 862-7561	9555
Maruchan Inc (HQ)	2099	B	949 789-2300	2543
Maruchan Inc	2098	C	949 789-2300	2371
Marukome USA Inc	2099	F	949 863-0110	2545
Marvell Semiconductor Inc	3674	F	949 614-7700	18371
Marvin Test Solutions Inc	3825	D	949 263-2222	21074
Masimo Americas Inc	3841	F	949 297-7000	21188
Masimo Corporation	3845	E	949 297-7000	22275
Masimo Corporation (PA)	3845	B	949 297-7000	22276
Masimo Semiconductor Inc	3674	E	603 595-8900	18373
Meade Instruments Corp	3827	D	949 451-1450	21380
Medata Inc (PA)	7372	D	714 918-1310	24139
Medennium Inc (PA)	3851	E	949 789-9000	22372
Media Nation Enterprises LLC	3993	E	714 371-9494	23157
Mediatek USA Inc	3571	F	408 526-1899	14943
Medical Data Recovery Inc	7372	F	949 251-0073	24141
Medifarm So Cal Inc	3523	E	855 447-6967	13650
Medtronic Inc	3841	E	949 837-3700	21806
Meggitt (orange County) Inc (HQ)	3829	C	949 493-8181	21504
Meggitt Defense Systems Inc	3728	B	949 465-7700	20174
Meguiars Inc (HQ)	2842	E	949 752-8000	8396
Menlo Microsystems Inc	3674	F	949 771-0277	18383
Mentor Graphics Corporation	7372	F	949 790-3200	24118
Mentor Worldwide LLC (DH)	3842	C	800 636-8678	22048
Micro Therapeutics Inc (HQ)	3841	F	949 837-3700	21819
Microsoft Corporation	7372	C	949 263-3000	24160
Microwave Dynamics	3663	F	949 679-7788	17587
Midas Technology Inc	3651	E	818 937-4774	17262
Min-E-Con LLC	3678	E	949 250-0087	18779
Mino Industry USA Inc (PA)	3999	F	949 943-8070	23413
Mission Hockey Company (PA)	3949	F	949 585-9390	22855
Mitsubishi Chemical Crbn Fbr	2891	C	800 929-5471	8881
Mophie Inc (HQ)	3663	E	888 866-7443	17591
Mplus Motors Corp	3751	F	510 259-8435	20421
Mri Interventions Inc	3841	E	949 900-6833	21830
Multi-Fineline Electronix Inc (HQ)	3672	A	949 453-6800	17928
N H Research Incorporated	3825	E	949 474-3900	21084
Nanovea Inc (PA)	3826	F	949 461-9292	21271
National Medical Products Inc	3089	F	949 768-1147	9918
Neomend Inc	3841	D	949 783-3300	21831
Netaphor Software Inc	7372	F	949 470-7955	24193
Netlist Inc (PA)	3674	D	949 435-0025	18433
Netwrix Corporation (PA)	7372	E	888 638-9749	24200
Neurostructures Inc	3842	F	800 352-6103	22053
Newmatic Engineering Inc (PA)	3822	F	415 824-2664	20800
Newport Corporation (HQ)	3821	B	949 863-3144	20767
Newport Energy LLC	1382	E	408 230-7545	132
Nexgen Pharma Inc (PA)	2834	C	949 863-0340	8033
Nexgen Pharma Inc	2834	E	949 260-3702	8034
Nexgen Pharma Inc	2834	E	949 863-0340	8035
Nextgen Healthcare Inc (PA)	7372	C	949 255-2600	24206
Ngd Systems Inc	3572	E	949 870-9148	15065
NGK Spark Plugs (usa) Inc	3694	E	949 580-2639	19197
Nihon Kohden Orangemed Inc	3845	F	949 502-6448	22289
Nimbus Data Inc	3572	E	650 276-4500	15067
Nixsys Inc	3571	F	714 435-9610	14956
Novus Therapeutics Inc	2834	F	949 238-8090	8044
Ntrust Infotech Inc	7372	D	562 207-1600	24215
Numecent Inc	7372	E	949 833-2800	24216
Nutrawise Health & Beauty Corp (PA)	2834	D	949 900-2400	8045
Nxp Usa Inc	3674	F	949 399-4000	18445
Ocpc Inc	2752	E	949 475-1900	6756
Oct Medical Imaging Inc	3841	E	949 701-6656	21846
Oddbox Holdings Inc	2759	F	949 474-9222	7151
Old An Inc	3999	E	949 263-1400	23431
Omni Optical Products Inc (PA)	3829	E	714 634-5700	21512
Omnitron Systems Tech Inc	3577	D	949 250-6510	15300
Onset Medical Corporation	3841	E	949 716-1100	21848
Optima Technology Corporation	3577	B	949 253-5768	15304
Oracle Systems Corporation	7372	D	949 224-1000	24276
Oracle Systems Corporation	7372	B	949 623-9460	24277
Orange Circle Studio Corp	2759	D	949 727-0800	7159
Orange Coast Kommunications	2721	E	949 862-1133	5996
Orgain Inc	2086	F	949 930-0039	2104
Pace Punches Inc	3544	D	949 428-2750	14088
Pacific Handy Cutter Inc	3423	E	714 662-1033	11539
Pacific World Corporation (PA)	2844	D	949 598-2400	8553
Paciolan LLC (DH)	7372	D	866 722-4652	24284
Panoramic Software Corporation	7372	F	877 558-8526	24287
Paramount Dairy Inc (PA)	2026	E	949 265-8077	707
Parker-Hannifin Corporation	3724	B	949 833-3000	19975
Parker-Hannifin Corporation	3728	D	216 896-2663	20195
Parker-Hannifin Corporation	3728	D	949 833-3000	20196
Parker-Hannifin Corporation	3594	C	949 833-3000	15635
Parker-Hannifin Corporation	3728	A	949 833-3000	20197
Passy-Muir Inc	3842	E	949 833-8255	22065
Passy-Muir Inc (PA)	3842	E	949 833-8255	22066
Patron Solutions LLC	7372	C	949 823-1700	24290
PCC Rollmet Inc	3339	D	949 221-5333	11194
Performance Sealing Inc	3053	F	714 662-5918	9247
Phiaro Incorporated	3999	E	949 727-1261	23448
Philip Morris USA Inc	2111	D	949 458-3500	2654
Plasto Tech International Inc	3089	E	949 458-1880	9977
Plugg ME LNc	7372	E	949 705-4472	24303
Positex Inc	3721	F	307 201-0601	19923

Employment Codes: A=Over 500 employees, B=251-500,
C=101-250, D=51-100, E=20-50, F=10-19

2020 California
Manufacturers Register

© Mergent Inc. 1-800-342-5647
1351

GEOGRAPHIC

Name	SIC	EMP	PHONE	ENTRY #
Ppst Inc (PA)	3679	E	800 421-1921	19050
Princeton Technology Inc	3577	E	949 851-7776	15309
Printery Inc	2752	F	949 757-1930	6801
Printronix LLC (PA)	3577	C	714 368-2300	15310
Printronix Holding Corp	3577	C	714 368-2300	15311
Prism Software Corporation	7372	E	949 855-3100	24314
Pro-Dex Inc (PA)	3841	D	949 769-3200	21863
Pro-Mart Industries Inc (PA)	2392	E	949 428-7700	3636
Professnal Rprgraphic Svcs Inc	2759	E	949 748-5400	7185
Proshot Investors LLC	3663	E	949 586-9500	17629
Qlogic LLC (DH)	3674	C	949 389-6000	18488
Qpe Inc	2754	F	949 263-0381	6962
Qsi 2011 Inc (PA)	7372	F	949 855-6885	24328
Qualontime Corporation	3599	C	714 523-4751	16329
Quantum Corporation	3572	D	949 856-7800	15081
Quilting House	2392	E	949 476-7090	3637
Race Technologies LLC	3714	F	714 438-1118	19751
Racer Media & Marketing Inc	2721	F	949 417-6700	6012
Rainbow Magnetics Incorporated	2752	F	714 540-4777	6831
Rami Designs Inc	3446	F	949 588-8288	12503
Rebound Therapeutics Corp	3841	E	949 305-8111	21872
Red Mountain Inc	3822	F	949 595-4475	20806
Redcom LLC (HQ)	3861	D	949 206-7900	22454
Research Way LI LLC	2834	F	608 830-6300	8103
Reverse Medical Corporation	3841	F	949 215-0660	21879
Reyes Coca-Cola Bottling LLC (PA)	2086	B	213 744-8616	2134
Ricoh Electronics Inc	3579	E	714 259-1220	15392
Rockwell Collins Inc	3812	D	714 929-3000	20706
Rogerson Aircraft Corporation (PA)	3812	D	949 660-0666	20709
Rose Chem Intl - USA Corp	2834	E	678 510-8864	8115
Royal Adhesives & Sealants LLC	2891	F	949 863-1499	8893
RR Donnelley & Sons Company	2759	E	949 852-1933	7204
RR Donnelley & Sons Company	2761	E	949 476-0505	7285
Rrds Inc (PA)	3827	F	949 482-6200	21403
S-Energy America Inc (HQ)	3674	F	949 281-7897	18522
Saeshin America Inc	3843	E	949 825-6925	22187
Sage Interior Inc	2434	F	949 654-0184	4244
Sage Software Holdings Inc (HQ)	7372	B	866 530-7243	24374
SDC Technologies Inc (DH)	3479	E	714 939-8300	13244
Sdi LLC	3599	F	949 351-1866	16392
Seagra Technology Inc (PA)	3577	F	949 419-6796	15328
Seal Science Inc (PA)	3053	D	949 253-3130	9254
Sega of America Inc (DH)	3999	E	949 788-0455	23472
Sekai Electronics Inc (PA)	3663	E	949 783-5740	17655
Sensoronix Inc	3674	F	949 528-0906	18541
Sfc Communications Inc	3822	F	949 553-8566	20811
Shye West Inc (PA)	3993	E	949 486-4598	23195
Sierra Monolithics Inc	3812	F	949 269-4400	20721
Signature Control Systems Inc	3523	D	949 580-3640	13670
Silicon Energy LLC (PA)	3433	F	360 618-6500	11713
Smith Printing Corporation	2759	F	949 250-9709	7217
Socialwise Inc	2741	F	949 861-3900	6340
Solar Turbines Incorporated	3511	F	949 450-0870	13577
Solarflare Communications Inc (PA)	3571	D	949 581-6830	14978
Sonnet Technologies Inc	3699	E	949 587-3500	19407
Soundcoat Company Inc	3625	E	631 242-2200	16757
South Coast Baking LLC (HQ)	2052	D	949 851-9654	1331
South Coast Mold Inc	3544	F	949 253-2000	14105
Sparton Irvine LLC	3679	D	949 855-6625	19090
Specialty Rock Inc	1442	F	909 334-2265	360
Spectrum Scientific Inc	3827	F	949 260-9900	21411
Spellbound Development Group	3851	F	949 474-8577	22386
St John Knits Inc (DH)	2339	C	949 863-1171	3412
St John Knits Intl Inc (HQ)	2339	C	949 863-1171	3413
St John Knits Intl Inc	2253	B	949 399-8200	2802
St Jude Medical LLC	2834	C	949 769-5000	8140
Staco Systems Inc (HQ)	3613	D	949 297-8700	16617
Starix Technology Inc	3663	E	949 387-8120	17670
Stason Pharmaceuticals Inc (PA)	2834	E	949 380-0752	8144
Stec Inc (HQ)	3572	B	415 222-9996	15104
Steven Rhoades Ceramic Designs	3269	F	949 250-1076	10493
Stm Networks Inc	3663	E	949 273-6800	17671
Stracon Inc	3699	E	714 351-2288	19416
Strategy Companion Corp	7372	D	714 460-8398	24460
Streamline Avionics Inc	3612	F	949 861-8151	16579
STS Instruments Inc	3825	F	580 223-4773	21130
Suncore Inc	3674	E	949 450-0054	18589
Sunsports LP	3131	C	949 273-6202	10155
Suntsu Electronics Inc	3679	E	949 783-7300	19096
Super Color Digital LLC (PA)	2759	E	949 622-0010	7234
Super73 Inc	3751	E	949 313-6340	20427
Support Technologies Inc	7372	F	949 442-2957	24470
Swift Health Systems Inc	3843	E	877 258-8677	22191
Syneron Inc (DH)	3845	D	866 259-6661	22317
Syntiant Corp	3674	F	948 774-4887	18599
Talon Therapeutics Inc	2834	C	949 788-6700	8153
Target Technology Company LLC	3695	E	949 788-0909	19236
Taylor Graphics Inc	2759	E	949 752-5200	7240
Tb Kawashima Usa Inc	2399	F	714 389-5310	3862
Tc Communications Inc	3669	E	949 852-1972	17767
Techko Kobot Inc	3635	F	949 380-7300	16845
Tekia Inc	3851	E	949 699-1300	22393
Tempo Lighting Inc	3646	E	949 442-1601	17077
Teradyne Inc	3825	D	949 453-0900	21140
Teridian Semiconductor Corp (DH)	3674	E	714 508-8800	18613
Terra Tech Corp (PA)	3523	E	855 447-6967	13674
Terran Orbital Corporation (PA)	3761	E	212 496-2300	20458
Tetra Tech Ec Inc	3826	E	949 809-5000	21302
Teva Parenteral Medicines Inc	2834	A	949 455-4700	8158
Teva Pharmaceuticals Usa Inc	2834	E	949 457-2828	8159
Thales Avionics Inc	3728	F	949 381-3033	20247
Thales Avionics Inc	3728	C	949 790-2500	20248
Thales Transport & SEC Inc (HQ)	3661	E	949 790-2500	17421
Thermaprint Corp	3861	E	949 583-0800	22464
Thompson Aerospace Inc (PA)	3724	F	949 264-1600	19983
Timevalue Software	7372	E	949 727-1800	24511
Tomorrows Look Inc	2261	D	949 596-8400	2840
Toshiba Amer Info Systems Inc	3571	D	949 587-6378	14989
Toshiba America Electronic (DH)	3651	B	949 462-7700	17294
Trantronics Inc	3672	E	949 553-1234	18025
Tricom Research Inc	3663	D	949 250-6024	17695
Trimedyne Inc (PA)	3845	E	949 951-3800	22323
Tropitone Furniture Co Inc (HQ)	2514	B	949 595-2000	4705
Truabutment Inc	3843	E	714 956-1488	22199
Turn-Luckily International Inc	3577	F	949 465-0200	15356
Tylerco Inc	3645	E	949 769-3991	16995
Tyvak Nn-Satellite Systems Inc	3761	D	949 753-1020	20460
Ubm LLC	2721	D	415 947-6770	6047
Ultimate Ears Consumer LLC	3842	E	949 502-8340	22113
Upstanding LLC	7372	C	949 788-9900	24544
Urovant Sciences Inc (HQ)	2834	E	949 226-6029	8174
Us-Vn-Mynmar Rare Erth Mtls Gr	1099	F	949 262-3673	14
USA Fire Glass	3231	F	949 302-7728	10399
USA Vision Systems Inc (HQ)	3699	E	949 583-1519	19431
Ushio America Inc	3646	E	714 236-8600	17081
Variable Image Printing	2752	F	949 296-1444	6918
Veezee Inc	2331	E	949 265-0800	3207
Vertimass LLC	2869	F	949 417-1396	8781
Vertiv Corporation	3823	E	949 457-3600	20956
Viking Access Systems LLC	3699	E	949 753-1280	19436
Viking Products Inc	3545	E	949 379-5100	14210
Vinotemp International Corp (PA)	2519	D	310 886-3332	4776
Visage Software Inc	7372	F	949 614-0759	24564
Vision Quest Industries Inc (PA)	3842	D	949 261-6382	22119
Vizio Inc (PA)	3651	C	855 833-3221	17303
Vti Instruments Corporation (HQ)	3699	E	949 955-1894	19439
Wahlco Inc	3599	C	714 979-7300	16508
Waterhealth International Inc	3589	C	949 716-5790	15602
Waters Technologies Corp	3826	F	949 474-4320	21324
Webcloak LLC	7372	F	949 417-9940	24574
West Coast Consulting LLC	7372	C	949 250-4102	24577
Western Prtg & Graphics LLC (PA)	2752	E	714 532-3946	6934
Western Telematic Inc	3577	E	949 586-9950	15365
Westside Resources Inc	3843	E	800 944-3939	22206
Xlsoft Corporation (PA)	7372	F	949 453-2781	24594
Yaskawa America Inc	3569	F	949 263-2640	14874
Zadara Storage Inc	3572	E	949 251-0360	15116
Zo Skin Health Inc (PA)	2844	D	949 988-7524	8613
Zygo Corporation	3827	E	714 918-7433	21424

IRWINDALE, CA - Los Angeles County

Name	SIC	EMP	PHONE	ENTRY #
A & M Engineering Inc	3599	D	626 813-2020	15655
Alpha Printing & Graphics Inc	2752	E	626 851-9800	6407
American Capacitor Corporation	3675	E	626 814-4444	18675
Arrow Engineering	3599	E	626 960-2806	15750
Bimeda Inc	2834	F	626 815-1680	7802
Bsst LLC	3714	F	626 593-4500	19597
Cal Springs LLC	2759	D	562 943-5599	7012
California Community News LLC (HQ)	2711	B	626 472-5297	5576
California Custom Fruits (PA)	2087	D	626 736-4130	2198
Calportland Company	3273	D	626 691-2596	10704
Chem Arrow Corp	2992	E	626 358-2255	9136
Clark - Pacific Corporation	3272	D	626 962-8751	10551
Cni Mfg Inc	3599	E	626 962-6646	15854
Connor J Inc	3825	F	626 358-3820	21021
Consolidated Container Co LLC	3089	D	626 856-2100	9720
Contour Energy Systems Inc	3691	E	626 610-0660	19156
Davis Wire Corporation (HQ)	3315	D	626 969-7651	11088
Decore-Ative Specialties	2431	C	626 960-7731	4033
Emdin International Corp	3843	F	626 813-3740	22152
Entreprise Arms Inc	3484	E	626 962-4692	13275

Mergent email: customerrelations@mergent.com

1352

2020 California
Manufacturers Register

(P-0000) Products & Services Section entry number
(PA)=Parent Co (HQ)=Headquarters (DH)=Div Headquarters

	SIC	EMP	PHONE	ENTRY #
Fine Ptch Elctrnic Assmbly LLC	3672	E	626 337-2800	17875
Food Makers Bakery Eqp Inc	3556	E	626 358-1343	14362
Gentherm Incorporated	3714	F	626 593-4500	19669
Halcyon Microelectronics Inc	3674	F	626 814-4688	18263
Hanson Aggregates LLC	3273	E	626 358-1811	10768
Huy Fong Foods Inc	2033	E	626 286-8328	776
J & R Taylor Bros Assoc Inc	2047	D	626 334-9301	1076
J C S Volks Machine	3714	F	626 338-6003	19693
Johnson & Johnson	3842	B	909 839-8650	22037
Jonell Oil Corporation	2992	F	626 303-4691	9149
Kifuki USA Co Inc (HQ)	2015	D	626 334-8090	520
Km Printing Production Inc	2752	F	626 821-0008	6679
Kong Veterinary Products	3841	F	626 633-0077	21771
Legacy Vulcan LLC	3273	E	626 856-6150	10781
Legacy Vulcan LLC	1442	F	626 856-6153	349
Legacy Vulcan LLC	2951	E	626 633-4258	9096
Legacy Vulcan LLC	3272	F	626 856-6148	10596
Legacy Vulcan LLC	1442	E	626 856-6143	351
Martin Engineering Inc	3556	F	626 960-5153	14384
Matheson Tri-Gas Inc	2813	E	626 334-2905	7416
Mee Industries Inc (PA)	3585	F	626 359-4550	15444
Millercoors LLC	2082	D	626 969-6811	1549
Million Corporation	2759	D	626 969-1888	7143
Nkok Inc	3944	F	626 330-1988	22702
Pacific Panel Products Corp	2435	E	626 851-0444	4278
Pertronix Inc	3694	E	909 599-5955	19200
Q & B Foods Inc (DH)	2035	D	626 334-8090	896
Ready Pac Foods Inc (HQ)	2099	A	626 856-8686	2596
Roma Moulding Inc	2499	E	626 334-2539	4527
Schamas Mfg Coinc	3531	F	626 334-6870	13747
Seaboard Envelope Co Inc	2677	E	626 960-4559	5474
Sierra Alloys Company	3463	D	626 969-6711	12736
Spragues Rock and Sand Company (PA)	3273	E	626 445-2125	10841
Stratus Coml Cooking Eqp Inc	3469	F	626 969-7041	12878
Universal Dynamics Inc	1382	F	626 480-0035	144
US Toyo Fan Corporation (HQ)	3564	F	626 338-1111	14686
V Himark (usa) Inc	2891	F	626 305-5766	8901
Vulcan Materials Company	3273	F	626 334-4913	10870
Woojin Is America Inc	3743	F	626 386-0101	20379

ISLETON, CA - Sacramento County

	SIC	EMP	PHONE	ENTRY #
Ethanol Energy Systems LLC	2869	F	916 777-5654	8737

JACKSON, CA - Amador County

	SIC	EMP	PHONE	ENTRY #
Bradford Canning Stahl Inc	3599	F	209 257-1535	15797
Buy and Sell Press Inc	2741	F	209 223-3333	6208

JAMESTOWN, CA - Tuolumne County

	SIC	EMP	PHONE	ENTRY #
Fray Logging Inc	2411	E	209 984-5968	3884
M & M Sportswear Manufacturing	2253	F	209 984-5632	2795
Ooglow	2099	F	530 899-9927	2576
Sierra Resource Management Inc	2411	E	209 984-1146	3906

JAMUL, CA - San Diego County

	SIC	EMP	PHONE	ENTRY #
Mikes Metal Works Inc	3312	F	619 440-8804	11057
P & E Rubber Processing Inc	3069	E	760 241-2643	9348

JUNCTION CITY, CA - Trinity County

	SIC	EMP	PHONE	ENTRY #
Eagle Rock Incorporated	3531	F	530 623-4444	13727

JURUPA VALLEY, CA - Riverside County

	SIC	EMP	PHONE	ENTRY #
A and G Inc (HQ)	2329	A	714 765-0400	3061
Activeapparel Inc (PA)	2329	A	951 361-0060	3062
Aftermarket Parts Company LLC	3711	B	951 681-2751	19449
Aluminum Die Casting Co Inc	3363	D	951 681-3900	11332
Brothers Machine & Tool Inc	3542	E	951 361-9454	13971
Brothers Machine & Tool Inc (PA)	3542	E	951 361-2909	13972
C & H Molding Incorporated	3544	E	951 361-5030	14025
Calpaco Papers Inc (PA)	2679	C	323 767-2800	5498
Calstrip Industries Inc (PA)	3316	E	323 726-1345	11118
Calstrip Steel Corporation (HQ)	3398	D	323 838-2097	11444
Del Real LLC (PA)	2038	C	951 681-0395	954
Eaton Corporation	3699	F	951 685-5788	19301
Enhance America Inc	3993	E	951 361-3000	23099
Galleano Enterprises Inc	2084	D	951 685-5376	1718
Highland Plastics Inc	3089	C	951 360-9587	9825
Ideal Products Inc	2541	F	951 727-8600	4911
Innovative R Advanced	2515	E	949 273-8100	4724
Koch Filter Corporation	3585	F	951 361-9017	15437
Langlois Company	2045	E	951 360-3900	1058
Levecke LLC	2084	D	951 681-8600	1801
Los Angles Tmes Cmmnctns LLC	2711	E	951 683-6066	5712
Luce Communications LLC	2752	E	951 361-7404	6711
Luxco Holdings LLC	3089	F	626 888-7688	9881
McGrath Rentcorp	3448	C	951 360-6600	12559
Metal Container Corporation	3411	D	951 360-4500	11500
Milestone AV Technologies LLC	3444	F	800 266-7225	12303

	SIC	EMP	PHONE	ENTRY #
Mitchell Rubber Products LLC (PA)	3069	C	951 681-5655	9335
Mitchell Rubber Products LLC	3069	D	951 681-5655	9336
Nestle Usa Inc	2038	F	951 360-7200	968
Nfi Industries	3999	F	951 681-6455	23427
P R P Multisource Inc	3565	F	951 681-6100	14720
Paradigm Label Inc	2679	F	951 372-9212	5521
Philips North America LLC	3645	E	909 574-1800	16986
Plastic Innovations Inc	3083	F	951 361-0251	9448
Pura Naturals Inc	2515	E	949 273-8100	4738
Recon Services Inc	3443	F	951 682-1400	12045
Robinson Engineering Corp	3547	F	951 361-8000	14235
Roller Derby Skate Corp	3949	F	217 324-3961	22875
Ronpak Inc	2621	E	951 685-3800	5148
Safeland Industrial Supply Inc (PA)	3315	F	909 786-1967	11107
Sports Hoop Inc	3949	F	626 387-6027	22897
Superior Filtration Pdts LLC	3564	F	951 681-1700	14681
Young Electric Sign Company	3993	D	909 923-7668	23248

KELSEYVILLE, CA - Lake County

	SIC	EMP	PHONE	ENTRY #
Lake County Walnut Inc	2068	F	707 279-1200	1432
Naptech Test Equipment Inc	3825	F	707 995-7145	21085
Steele Wines Inc	2084	F	707 279-9475	1929
Stokes Ladders Inc	3499	F	707 279-4306	13548

KENSINGTON, CA - Alameda County

	SIC	EMP	PHONE	ENTRY #
Berkeley Scientific	3679	F	510 525-1945	18837
Sempervirens Group	2879	F	510 847-0801	8839
Union Publications Inc	2721	F	510 525-6300	6050

KENWOOD, CA - Sonoma County

	SIC	EMP	PHONE	ENTRY #
Kunde Enterprises Inc	2084	D	707 833-5501	1786
Muscardini Cellars LLC	2084	F	707 933-9305	1830
Overlook Vineyards LLC (DH)	2084	E	707 833-0053	1851
Pernod Ricard Usa LLC	2084	D	707 833-5891	1862
S L Cellars	2084	F	707 833-5070	1903
Treasury Wine Estates Americas	2084	E	707 833-4134	1967

KERMAN, CA - Fresno County

	SIC	EMP	PHONE	ENTRY #
Baker Commodities Inc	2077	E	559 237-4320	1453
California Mfg & Engrg Co LLC	3531	C	559 842-1500	13714
Central Grease Company Inc	2843	F	559 846-9607	8426
Pinnacle Agriculture Dist Inc	3523	F	559 842-4601	13659
Purity Organics Inc	2033	E	559 842-5600	818
Raisin Valley Farms LLC	2034	E	559 846-8138	858
Raisin Valley Farms Distrg Inc	2034	F	559 846-8138	859
Salwasser Inc	2034	D	559 843-2882	860

KING CITY, CA - Monterey County

	SIC	EMP	PHONE	ENTRY #
Casey Printing Inc	2752	E	831 385-3221	6474
Delicato Vineyards	2084	F	831 385-7587	1662
King Rustler	2711	F	831 385-4880	5682
Montery Wine Company LLC	2084	F	831 386-1100	1823
South County Newspapers LLC	2711	F	831 385-4880	5833
Wm J Clark Trucking Svc Inc	1442	F	831 385-4000	370

KINGSBURG, CA - Fresno County

	SIC	EMP	PHONE	ENTRY #
Cencal Cnc Inc	3599	E	559 897-8706	15832
Del Monte Foods Inc	2033	D	559 419-9214	762
Foster Commodities	2048	E	559 897-1081	1094
Foster Farms LLC	2048	E	559 897-1081	1095
Guardian Industries LLC	3211	B	559 891-8867	10265
Guardian Industries Corp	3211	D	559 891-8867	10266
Guardian Industries Corp	3211	D	559 638-3588	10267
Kingsburg Cultivator Inc	3523	F	559 897-3662	13643
Nutrius LLC	2048	E	559 897-5862	1115
Vie-Del Company	2084	E	559 896-3065	1982

KNEELAND, CA - Humboldt County

	SIC	EMP	PHONE	ENTRY #
J & S Stakes Inc	2499	F	707 668-5647	4507

KORBEL, CA - Humboldt County

	SIC	EMP	PHONE	ENTRY #
Simpson Timber Company	2421	F	707 668-4566	3961

LA CANADA, CA - Los Angeles County

	SIC	EMP	PHONE	ENTRY #
Foothill Instruments LLC	3829	F	818 952-5600	21475
Majestic Garlic Inc	2035	F	951 677-0555	889

LA CANADA FLINTRIDGE, CA - Los Angeles County

	SIC	EMP	PHONE	ENTRY #
Data Storm Inc	3699	F	818 352-4994	19288
Los Angles Tmes Cmmnctns LLC	2711	E	818 790-8774	5711

LA CRESCENTA, CA - Los Angeles County

	SIC	EMP	PHONE	ENTRY #
Accurate Screen Processing	2396	F	818 957-3965	3767
Air Transport Manufacturing	3444	F	818 504-3300	12092
Balita Media Inc	2711	E	818 552-4503	5562
Brains Out Media Inc	7372	F	818 296-1036	23694
Casa Mexico Enterprises Inc	2759	F	888 411-9530	7016
Faith Knight Inc	3911	F	213 488-1569	22518
RC Apparel Inc	2396	F	818 541-1994	3810

Employment Codes: A=Over 500 employees, B=251-500,
C=101-250, D=51-100, E=20-50, F=10-19

2020 California
Manufacturers Register

© Mergent Inc. 1-800-342-5647

1353

GEOGRAPHIC

	SIC	EMP	PHONE	ENTRY #
Wheeler & Reeder Inc	3535	F	323 268-4163	13841

LA HABRA, CA - Orange County

	SIC	EMP	PHONE	ENTRY #
American Acrylic Display Inc	3993	F	714 738-7990	23047
Auro Pharmaceuticals Inc	2834	F	562 352-9630	7778
Auro Pharmacies Inc	2834	E	562 352-9630	7779
B&W Custom Restaurant Eqp	3589	F	714 578-0332	15489
Candamar Designs Inc	3999	F	714 871-6190	23296
Castor Engineering Inc	3491	F	562 690-4036	13296
Ckd Industries Inc	3469	F	714 871-5600	12785
Cryopacific Incorporated	3999	F	562 697-7904	23308
Dp Print Services Inc	2269	F	310 600-5250	2852
J C Ford Company	3556	D	714 871-7361	14376
JB Industries Corp	3469	F	562 691-2105	12827
Jcr Aircraft Deburring LLC	3541	E	714 870-4427	13926
K&K World Inc	2599	F	714 234-6237	5069
Keyin Inc	3695	F	562 690-3888	19222
La Habra Plating Co Inc	3471	F	562 694-2704	13039
Marsal Packaging & Rfrgn	3585	F	714 812-6775	15443
Mmp Sheet Metal Inc	3444	F	562 691-1055	12306
Orbo Corporation	2531	F	562 806-6171	4867
Pacific Archtectural Mllwk Inc	2431	F	714 525-2059	4101
Plastic Tops Inc	2542	F	714 738-8128	4997
Precision Forming Group LLC	3542	F	562 501-1985	13992
R & J Rule & Die Inc	2675	F	562 945-7535	5452
Ruhe Corporation (PA)	2096	C	714 777-8321	2343
Shepard Bros Inc (PA)	3589	C	562 697-1366	15577
Stop-Look Sign Co Intl Inc	3993	F	562 690-7576	23218
VIP Rubber Company Inc (PA)	3069	C	714 774-7635	9387

LA HABRA HEIGHTS, CA - Orange County

	SIC	EMP	PHONE	ENTRY #
Flexo-Technologies Inc	2893	E	626 444-2595	8914
Viet Hung Paris Inc	2013	F	562 944-4919	506

LA HONDA, CA - San Mateo County

	SIC	EMP	PHONE	ENTRY #
Brodhead Steel Products Co (PA)	3446	E	650 871-8251	12459

LA JOLLA, CA - San Diego County

	SIC	EMP	PHONE	ENTRY #
Agilent Technologies Inc	3825	B	858 373-6300	20991
Agilent Technologies Inc	3825	B	858 373-6300	20997
Aira Tech Corp	7372	E	619 271-9152	23584
Altium LLC	7372	D	800 544-4186	23597
Ambrx Inc	2834	D	858 875-2400	7747
Aristamd Inc	7372	F	858 750-4777	23625
Auspex Pharmaceuticals Inc	2834	E	858 558-2400	7780
Berenice 2 AM Corp	2024	F	858 255-8693	630
Carbon Recycling Incorporated	2869	C	619 491-9200	8730
Commnexus San Diego	3674	F	888 926-3987	18169
Dm Luxury LLC	2759	C	858 366-9721	7050
Dow Theory Letters Inc	2721	F	858 454-0481	5923
Equillium Inc	2836	F	858 412-5302	8297
Flexaust Company Inc (HQ)	3599	F	619 232-8429	15962
Froglanders La Jolla	2026	F	858 459-3764	699
Howardsoft	7372	F	858 454-0121	23988
International RES Dev Corp Nev (PA)	3694	F	858 488-9900	19192
Kyowa Kirin Phrm RES Inc (HQ)	2834	E	858 952-7000	7983
Metabasis Therapeutics Inc	2834	E	858 550-7500	8012
Muller Company	3842	F	858 587-9955	22051
Nucleus Enterprises LLC	3089	D	619 517-8747	9935
Orexigen Therapeutics Inc	2834	D	858 875-8600	8056
Positive Publishing Inc	2741	F	858 551-0889	6314
Pred Technologies USA Inc	3679	D	858 999-2114	19053
Rusty Surfboards Inc	3949	F	858 551-0262	22880
Ryzer-Rx LLC	2833	F	858 454-7477	7688
Shire Rgenerative Medicine Inc	2834	E	858 202-0673	8128
Shire Rgenerative Medicine Inc	2834	D	858 754-3700	8129
Sova Pharmaceuticals Inc	2834	F	858 750-4700	8138
Spread Effect LLC	2759	E	888 705-1127	7226
SPS Studios Inc	2771	F	858 456-2336	7299
Strauss Karl Brewery and Rest	2082	E	858 551-2739	1567
Synthorx Inc	2834	E	858 750-4700	8152
Texas Boom Company Inc	3533	F	281 441-2002	13795
U S Medical Instruments Inc (PA)	3841	D	619 661-5500	21942

LA MESA, CA - San Diego County

	SIC	EMP	PHONE	ENTRY #
California Countertop Inc (PA)	2542	E	619 460-0205	4967
Circlemaster Inc	3444	F	858 578-3900	12156
In To Ink	2752	F	858 271-6363	6634
Josef Mendelovitz	2752	F	619 231-3555	6668
Logic Beach Inc (PA)	3823	F	619 698-3300	20900
Ritas Fine Food	2099	F	619 698-3925	2600
Sierra National Corporation	3578	E	619 258-8200	15378
Steward Terra Inc	3612	E	619 713-0028	16578
Totalthermalimagingcom	3577	F	619 303-5884	15352
Velocity Imaging Products Inc	3861	F	619 433-8000	22470

LA MIRADA, CA - Los Angeles County

	SIC	EMP	PHONE	ENTRY #
365 Printing Inc	2752	F	714 752-6990	6388
Advanced Charging Tech Inc	3629	E	877 228-5922	16773
Airgas Inc	2873	F	714 521-4789	8789
American Power Solutions Inc	3648	E	714 626-0300	17101
Apparel Unified LLC	2759	F	562 639-7233	6989
Beemak Plastics LLC	3089	D	310 886-5880	9656
Bonsal American Inc	3272	F	714 523-1530	10539
Caravan Canopy Intl Inc	2394	F	714 367-3000	3678
Cook King Inc	3589	F	714 739-0502	15505
Dbv Inc	2834	F	562 404-9714	7865
Dow Chemical Company	2819	C	714 228-4700	7486
Frito-Lay North America Inc	2096	C	714 562-7260	2324
G A Doors Inc	2431	D	714 739-1144	4046
Gallagher Rental Inc	3648	F	714 690-1559	17129
Garfield Commercial Entps	2521	F	714 690-5959	4799
Gemsa Enterprises LLC	2079	F	714 521-1736	1472
General Grinding & Mfg Co LLC	3593	E	562 921-7033	15623
Golden Kraft Inc	2679	D	562 926-8888	5510
Hager Mfg Inc	3728	E	714 522-8870	20124
Head First Productions Inc	3546	F	714 522-3311	14223
Headwaters Construction Inc	3241	F	714 523-1530	10416
Iqair North America Inc	3564	E	877 715-4247	14665
Jdh Pacific Inc (PA)	3321	E	562 926-8088	11144
Jmg Machine Inc	3599	E	714 522-6221	16086
Korea Aerospace Industries Ltd	3721	F	714 868-8560	19910
Lequios Japan Co Ltd	2099	F	410 629-8694	2527
Lindblade Metalworks Inc	3446	E	714 670-7172	12493
Meese Inc	3089	E	714 739-4005	9892
Monaero Engineering Inc	3728	F	714 994-5463	20181
Montebello Container Co LLC	2653	D	714 994-2351	5247
Nutri Granulations Inc	2023	D	714 994-7855	612
Oceania Inc	3081	E	562 926-8886	9416
Outlook Resources Inc	2395	D	714 522-2452	3751
Respironics Inc	3842	F	562 483-6805	22077
Santa Ana Packaging Inc	2631	F	714 670-6397	5172
Shasta Beverages Inc	2086	D	714 523-2280	2172
Solid State Devices Inc	3674	C	562 404-4474	18570
Spartech LLC	3083	F	714 523-2260	9456
Superior Storage Tank Inc	3443	F	714 226-1914	12060
Tropical Asphalt LLC (PA)	2952	F	714 739-1408	9127
Twpm Inc	2657	F	714 522-8881	5318
United States Ball Corporation	3562	F	714 521-6500	14619
V Twest Inc	2541	F	714 521-2167	4952
V-T Industries Inc	3089	F	714 521-2008	10106
Wesanco Inc	3728	E	714 739-4989	20268
Wintflash Inc	2759	F	562 944-6548	7273

LA PALMA, CA - Orange County

	SIC	EMP	PHONE	ENTRY #
Encore Seating Inc	2522	D	562 926-1969	4833
Filbur Manufacturing LLC	3569	E	714 228-6000	14814
Greif Inc	2655	D	714 523-9580	5296
Honeywell International Inc	3724	C	714 562-3000	19954
Honeywell International Inc	3724	D	714 562-3016	19963
Keebler Company	2052	D	714 228-1555	1318
Pamarco Global Graphics Inc	3555	E	714 739-0700	14335
Stoneware Design Co	3269	F	562 432-8145	10494

LA PUENTE, CA - Los Angeles County

	SIC	EMP	PHONE	ENTRY #
Blue Sky Remediation Svcs Inc	3669	F	626 961-5736	17717
Bomark Inc	2893	F	626 968-1666	8910
Cad Works Inc	3599	E	626 336-5491	15815
California Fashion Club Inc (PA)	2337	F	626 575-1838	3263
Cott Technologies Inc	3498	F	626 961-3399	13464
County of Los Angeles	3531	F	626 968-3312	13723
Craftsman Lighting	3645	F	626 330-8512	16968
Crown Pallet Company Inc	2448	E	626 937-6565	4359
Genesis Tc Inc	2512	F	626 968-4455	4642
Goharddrive Inc	3572	E	626 593-9927	15034
Jona Global Trading Inc	2515	F	626 855-2588	4725
Ld Smart Inc	3571	F	626 581-8887	14937
Ley Grand Foods Corporation	2051	E	626 336-2244	1233
Mymichelle Company LLC (HQ)	2331	B	626 934-4166	3183
Pacific Coast Pallets Inc	2448	E	626 937-6565	4384
Size Control Plating Co	3471	F	626 369-3014	13101
Total Media Enterprises Inc	2741	F	626 961-7887	6360
Tristar Global Inc	3714	F	626 363-6978	19788

LA QUINTA, CA - Riverside County

	SIC	EMP	PHONE	ENTRY #
CT Oldenkamp LLC	3991	F	760 200-9510	23024
Donnashi Enterprises Inc	3823	E	760 200-3402	20859
LLC Marsh Perkins	2389	F	760 880-4558	3566
Optiscan Ltd	3827	F	760 777-9595	21392
Vermillions Environmental	3822	E	760 777-8035	20819

Mergent email: customerrelations@mergent.com
1354

2020 California
Manufacturers Register

(P-0000) Products & Services Section entry number
(PA)=Parent Co (HQ)=Headquarters (DH)=Div Headquarters

LA VERNE, CA - Los Angeles County

	SIC	EMP	PHONE	ENTRY #
Aero-Clas Heat Tran Prod Inc	3443	F	909 596-1630	11991
American Thermoform Corp (PA)	3555	F	909 593-6711	14313
Attends Healthcare Pdts Inc	2621	C	909 392-1200	5098
Beonca Machine Inc	3599	F	909 392-9991	15787
Biocalth International Inc	2834	F	909 267-3988	7804
Crown Equipment Corporation	3537	D	626 968-0556	13865
Dennis Reeves Inc	2541	F	909 392-9999	4896
Dhl Wire Products	3315	F	909 596-2909	11091
Dow Hydraulic Systems Inc (PA)	3599	D	909 596-6602	15906
DPI Labs Inc	3728	E	909 392-5777	20089
Durston Manufacturing Company	3423	F	909 593-1506	11527
Expression In Wood	2434	F	909 596-8496	4194
Farbotech Color Inc	2893	F	909 596-9330	8913
Fortress Inc	2521	F	909 593-8600	4797
Gainey Ceramics Inc	3269	C	909 596-4464	10488
Inseat Solutions LLC	3634	F	562 447-1780	16829
Joann Lammens	3999	F	909 593-8478	23372
Juicy Whip Inc	3556	E	909 392-7500	14381
Layton Printing & Mailing	2752	F	909 592-4419	6693
Micro Analog Inc	3674	C	909 392-8277	18390
Mohawk Western Plastics Inc	2673	E	909 593-7547	5406
Novipax Inc (DH)	2679	D	909 392-1750	5516
Permeco	3281	F	909 599-9600	10920
Pf Plastics Inc	2519	F	909 392-4488	4770
Plastifab Inc	3083	E	909 596-1927	9450
Postvision Inc	3572	F	818 840-0777	15075
Prostat First Aid LLC	3842	E	888 900-2920	22072
S & S Bindery Inc	2789	F	909 596-2213	7345
Serco Mold Inc (PA)	3089	E	626 331-0517	10053
Synergetic Tech Group Inc	3429	F	909 305-4711	11634
Systems L C Womack	3829	F	909 593-7304	21550
TEC Color Craft (PA)	2759	E	909 392-9000	7241
Zimmer Intermed Inc	3842	E	909 392-0882	22128

LADERA RANCH, CA - Orange County

	SIC	EMP	PHONE	ENTRY #
Emisense Technologies LLC (DH)	3674	F	949 502-8440	18215
Juicebot & Co LLC	3556	F	651 270-8860	14380
Ksu Corporation	3441	F	951 409-7055	11825

LAFAYETTE, CA - Contra Costa County

	SIC	EMP	PHONE	ENTRY #
Acp Ventures	2752	F	925 297-0100	6395
Clickscanshare Inc	3577	E	925 283-1400	15204
Econoday Inc	2741	F	925 299-5350	6224
Employerware LLC	2741	E	925 283-9735	6229
Frances Mary Accessories Inc	3171	A	925 962-2111	10221
Gildedtree Inc	7372	F	925 246-5624	23939
Legacy Vulcan LLC	1422	A	925 284-4686	302
Optimum Solutions Group LLC	7372	C	415 954-7100	24237
Retrospect Inc	7372	E	888 376-1078	24358

LAGUNA BEACH, CA - Orange County

	SIC	EMP	PHONE	ENTRY #
American Historic Inns Inc	2741	F	949 499-8070	6182
Atlantis Computing Inc (PA)	7372	E	650 917-9471	23635
Awcc Corporation	2386	F	949 497-6313	3507
Blick Industries LLC	3565	E	949 499-5026	14700
Chantilly	2024	E	949 494-7702	634
Ear Charms Inc	3911	F	949 494-4147	22513
Firebrand Media LLC	2752	F	949 715-4410	6572
Laguna Beach Ales & Lagers LLC	2711	F	949 228-4496	5692
Lasertron Inc	3599	E	954 846-8600	16139
Myotek Industries Incorporated (PA)	3694	D	949 502-3776	19196
Ocean Avenue Brewing Co	2082	E	949 497-3381	1552
Ophthonix Inc	3851	D	760 842-5600	22378
Orange Cnty Prtg Graphics Inc	2759	F	949 464-9898	7160
Pacific Quartz Inc	3827	E	714 546-8133	21396
Response Graphics In Print	2759	F	949 376-8701	7197
Symrise Inc	2087	F	949 276-4600	2231
Unimark International Inc	3556	F	949 497-1235	14409
Victoria Skimboards	3949	E	949 494-0059	22919
Wooden Wick Co	3999	F	714 594-7790	23527

LAGUNA HILLS, CA - Orange County

	SIC	EMP	PHONE	ENTRY #
Adco Products Inc	3679	D	937 339-6267	18808
Anterra Group Inc	2843	F	949 215-0658	8425
Aot Electronics Inc	3577	F	949 600-6335	15157
Autotechbizcom Inc	3559	F	949 245-7033	14429
Benjamin Lewis Inc	2752	F	949 859-5119	6441
Bingo Publishers Incorporated	2741	E	949 581-5410	6199
Chavers Gasket Corporation	3053	F	949 472-8118	9223
Cmt Sheet Metal	3443	F	949 679-9868	12007
Epicuren Discovery	2835	D	949 588-5807	8221
Eurotech Showers Inc	3088	E	949 716-4099	9585
Garrett Precision Inc	3599	F	949 855-9710	15986
Gregory M Fink	3993	F	949 305-4242	23125
Hka Elevator Consulting Inc	3534	F	949 348-9711	13802

	SIC	EMP	PHONE	ENTRY #
In Sync Computer Solutions Inc	7372	F	949 837-5000	24005
Magic Software Enterprises Inc	7372	E	949 250-1718	24121
Medelita LLC	2311	F	949 542-4100	2970
Metal Improvement Company LLC	3398	E	949 855-8010	11458
Metrolaser Inc	3826	F	949 553-0688	21263
Metronome Software LLC	7372	F	949 273-5190	24150
Neuroptics Inc	3841	F	949 250-9792	21834
Nflash Inc	3572	F	949 678-9411	15064
Pacific Pharmascience Inc	2834	F	949 916-6955	8060
Par Orthodontic Laboratory	3843	F	949 472-4788	22180
Plastic and Metal Center Inc	3089	F	949 770-0610	9969
R C Westburg Engineering Inc	3089	E	949 859-4648	10005
R Goodloe & Associates	2752	F	714 380-3900	6827
R L Bennett Engineering Inc	3599	F	949 367-0700	16334
Raintree Business Products	2752	F	949 859-0801	6832
Rls Enterprises	3089	E	714 493-1735	10019
Saddleback Stair & Millwork	2431	F	949 460-0384	4119
Sonendo Inc (PA)	3843	E	949 766-3636	22190
Spatial Wave Inc	7372	E	949 540-6400	24438
Studio Two Printing Inc	2752	E	949 859-5119	6876
Yellow Pages Inc	2741	E	714 776-0534	6387

LAGUNA NIGUEL, CA - Orange County

	SIC	EMP	PHONE	ENTRY #
Agricultural Data Systems Inc	7372	F	949 363-5353	23582
American Pacific Truss	2439	E	949 363-1691	4287
Apnea Sciences Corporation	3069	F	949 226-4421	9282
Bau Furniture Manufacturing (PA)	2511	E	949 643-2729	4552
Burke Display Systems Inc	2542	F	949 248-0091	4965
Ener-Core Inc (PA)	3621	F	949 732-4400	16642
Ener-Core Power Inc (HQ)	3511	E	949 428-3300	13567
Murrey International Inc	3949	E	310 532-6091	22856
N-Synch Technologies	3575	F	949 218-7761	15131
Neways Inc	3679	E	949 264-1542	19026
Pretika Corporation	2844	E	949 481-8818	8565
Qpc Fiber Optic LLC	3357	F	949 361-8855	11316
Redworks Industries LLC	2499	E	949 334-7081	4525
S & S Woodcarver Inc	2499	E	714 258-2222	4529
San Diego Daily Transcript	2621	D	619 232-4381	5149
Ultera Systems Inc	3577	F	949 367-8800	15357

LAKE ARROWHEAD, CA - San Bernardino County

	SIC	EMP	PHONE	ENTRY #
Hi-Desert Publishing Company	2711	E	909 336-3555	5664
Robertsons Rdy Mix Ltd A Cal	3273	F	909 337-7577	10822
Tapestry Inc	3171	F	909 337-5207	10229

LAKE ELSINORE, CA - Riverside County

	SIC	EMP	PHONE	ENTRY #
Aerofoam Industries Inc	2531	D	951 245-4429	4851
Afakori Inc	3441	E	949 859-4277	11738
American Compaction Eqp Inc	3531	E	949 661-2921	13705
Boozak Inc	3444	E	951 245-6045	12133
California Cart Builder LLC	3715	F	951 245-1114	19815
Camsoft Corporation	3695	E	951 674-8100	19211
Castle & Cooke Inc	3531	D	951 245-2460	13718
Discount Blind Center	2591	F	951 678-3980	5020
Dura-Chem Inc	2899	F	951 245-7778	8960
Empire Pre Cast	3272	E	909 600-1590	10569
Faith Industries Inc	2499	F	951 351-1486	4501
Flour Fusion	2051	F	951 245-1166	1204
Golden Office Trailers Inc	3792	E	951 678-2177	20487
Hilz Cable Assemblies Inc	3829	F	951 245-0499	21485
Levi Strauss & Co	2325	F	951 674-2694	3014
Mercury Metal Die & Letter Co (PA)	3479	F	951 674-8717	13206
Mold Vision Inc	3599	F	951 245-8020	16219
Ozone Safe Food Inc	3559	F	951 228-2151	14510
Pacific Aggregates Inc	3273	D	951 245-2460	10813
Pelican Woodworks	2434	E	951 674-7821	4231
Precision Sports Inc	3949	D	951 674-1665	22865
Quality Foam Packaging Inc	3086	E	951 245-4429	9564
Rancho Ready Mix	3273	F	951 674-0488	10816
Rick Palenshus	3559	F	951 245-2100	14529
Roadracing World Publishing	2721	F	951 245-6411	6019
Thermal Electronics Inc	3679	F	951 674-3555	19116
Thrun Mfg Inc	3724	F	949 677-2461	19984
Van Heusen Factory Outlet	2321	F	951 674-1190	2997
Vertical Doors Inc	2591	F	951 273-1069	5042

LAKE FOREST, CA - Orange County

	SIC	EMP	PHONE	ENTRY #
ABC Custom Wood Shutters Inc	2431	E	949 595-0300	3991
AC&a Enterprises LLC (HQ)	3724	D	949 716-3511	19942
American Deburring Inc	3599	E	949 457-9790	15738
Aminco International USA Inc (PA)	3911	E	949 457-3261	22494
Anabolic Laboratories Inc	2834	F	949 863-0340	7757
Approved Networks Inc (PA)	3299	D	800 590-9535	10996
Associated Electrics Inc	3944	E	949 544-7500	22659
Beyond Green LLC	3089	F	800 983-7221	9664
BNP Enterprises LLC	3714	F	949 770-5438	19596
Cac Inc	3679	F	949 587-3328	18847

Employment Codes: A=Over 500 employees, B=251-500,
C=101-250, D=51-100, E=20-50, F=10-19

2020 California
Manufacturers Register

© Mergent Inc. 1-800-342-5647

1355

GEOGRAPHIC

	SIC	EMP	PHONE	ENTRY #
Camisasca Automotive Mfg Inc	3469	E	949 452-0195	12779
Camisasca Automotive Mfg Inc (PA)	3469	E	949 452-0195	12780
Campbell Engineering Inc	3545	E	949 859-3306	14144
Cod USA Inc	2531	E	949 381-7367	4854
Cyber Mdia Solutions Ltd Lblty	7372	F	877 480-8255	23789
Dss Networks Inc	3577	F	949 981-3473	15219
Dynacast LLC	3364	C	949 707-1211	11357
Ellison Educational Eqp Inc (PA)	3554	D	949 598-8822	14305
Equimine	7372	F	877 437-8464	23873
Fanuc America Corporation	3559	E	949 595-2700	14465
Focus Industries Inc	3646	D	949 830-1350	17037
Formtran Inc	7372	F	949 829-5822	23914
General Monitors Inc (DH)	3669	C	949 581-4464	17732
Global Power Tech Group Inc	3674	F	949 273-4373	18253
Greenshine New Energy LLC	3648	D	949 609-9636	17130
Herbalife Manufacturing LLC	2087	D	949 457-0951	2215
Hexagon Metrology Inc	3545	E	949 916-4400	14165
I Source Technical Svcs Inc (PA)	3679	E	949 453-1500	18942
I/Omagic Corporation (PA)	3572	E	949 707-4800	15046
IMC Networks Corp (PA)	3575	E	949 465-3000	15124
Infor (us) Inc	7372	C	678 319-8000	24012
Innovative Control Systems Inc	3589	E	610 881-8061	15525
Innovative R Advanced (PA)	2515	E	949 273-8100	4723
June Precision Mfg Inc	3451	E	949 855-9121	12637
L J Smith Inc	2431	E	949 609-0544	4072
Laminating Company of America	3672	E	949 587-3300	17912
Liquidmetal Technologies Inc (PA)	3325	E	949 635-2100	11171
Markap Inc	2387	E	949 240-1418	3532
Monobind Inc (PA)	3841	E	949 951-2665	21827
Movement Products Inc	3751	E	949 206-0000	20420
Oceania International LLC	3356	F	949 407-8904	11278
Parylene USA Inc	3999	F	949 452-0770	23443
Pitney Bowes Inc	3579	D	949 855-7844	15388
Premier Magnetics Inc	3677	E	949 452-0511	18734
Pressed Right LLC	3421	F	866 257-5774	11517
Price Pfister Inc (DH)	3432	A	949 672-4000	11678
Pssc Labs	3572	F	949 380-7288	15076
Pura Naturals Inc (HQ)	2844	F	949 273-8100	8570
Qf Liquidation Inc	3714	E	949 399-4500	19747
Qf Liquidation Inc (PA)	3714	C	949 930-3400	19748
Quantum Technologies Inc	1311	C	949 399-4500	63
Schneider Elc Systems USA Inc	3823	F	949 885-0700	20933
Se-GI Products Inc	3444	E	951 737-8320	12370
Semi-Kinetics Inc	3672	D	949 830-7364	17997
Shark Wheel Inc	3714	F	818 216-8001	19765
Shmaze Industries Inc	3479	E	949 583-1448	13246
Soaptronic LLC	2842	E	949 465-8955	8418
Sole Technology Inc (PA)	3149	C	949 460-2020	10184
SPX Flow Us LLC	3556	D	949 455-8150	14401
Stanford Materials Corporation	2816	F	949 380-7362	7464
T/Q Systems Inc	3599	E	949 455-0478	16441
Tenex Health Inc	3841	D	949 454-7500	21927
To Industries Inc	3993	E	949 454-6078	23229
Torcano Industries Inc	3751	E	855 359-3339	20431
Toughbuilt Industries Inc (PA)	3423	F	949 528-3100	11548
Tri-Star Laminates Inc	3672	E	949 587-3200	18027
Universal Printing Services	2752	F	951 788-1500	6910
US Critical LLC (PA)	3572	E	949 916-9326	15112
US Critical LLC	3572	E	800 884-8945	15113
Velco Tool & Die Inc	3544	F	949 855-6638	14123
Wide Open Industries LLC	3711	E	949 635-2292	19513
Xfit Brands Inc	3949	E	949 916-9680	22927
Young Engineers Inc	3429	D	949 581-9411	11644
Zentec Group	3679	F	949 586-3609	19149

LAKE ISABELLA, CA - Kern County

	SIC	EMP	PHONE	ENTRY #
Wick Communications Co	2711	E	760 379-3667	5866

LAKEPORT, CA - Lake County

	SIC	EMP	PHONE	ENTRY #
Lake County Publishing Co (DH)	2711	D	707 263-5636	5693
Mountain Lake Labs	3812	F	707 331-3297	20636
Nutrition Resource Inc (PA)	2834	E	707 263-0411	8046
Young & Family Inc	2431	E	707 263-8877	4158

LAKESIDE, CA - San Diego County

	SIC	EMP	PHONE	ENTRY #
Clark Steel Fabricators Inc	3446	E	619 390-1502	12462
Coating Services Group LLC	3479	F	619 596-7444	13159
Conductive Science Inc	2851	F	858 699-1837	8635
Dixietruss Inc	3272	F	619 873-0440	10562
Enniss Inc	1442	E	619 561-1101	338
Hanson Aggregates LLC	2951	F	858 715-5600	9094
Inland PCF Resource Recovery	2611	E	619 390-1418	5093
Lite Stone Concrete LLC	3272	F	619 596-9151	10600
M DAmico Inc	2599	E	619 390-5858	5071
Mardian Equipment Co Inc	3537	F	619 938-8071	13883
Masterpiece Leaded Windows	3231	E	858 391-3344	10379

	SIC	EMP	PHONE	ENTRY #
McQuaide Brothers Corporation	3715	F	619 444-9932	19826
Oldcastle Infrastructure Inc	3272	E	619 390-2251	10611
Rpc Inc	1389	F	619 647-9911	256
Southland Envelope Company Inc	2677	C	619 449-3553	5475
Superior Ready Mix Concrete LP	3273	E	619 443-7510	10854

LAKEWOOD, CA - Los Angeles County

	SIC	EMP	PHONE	ENTRY #
Bates Industries Inc	2386	F	562 426-8668	3509
Custom Aircraft Interiors Inc	3728	F	562 426-5098	20078
Long Beach Seafoods Co	2092	E	562 432-7300	2263
Magma Products Inc	3631	D	562 627-0500	16814
Prime Compliance Solutions	1389	F	310 748-8103	248
RDM Multi-Enterprises Inc	3295	F	562 924-1820	10976
TFC Manufacturing Inc	3444	D	562 426-9559	12405

LAMONT, CA - Kern County

	SIC	EMP	PHONE	ENTRY #
Franks Cabinet Shop Inc	2434	F	661 845-0781	4199

LANCASTER, CA - Los Angeles County

	SIC	EMP	PHONE	ENTRY #
A V Poles and Lighting Inc	3646	E	661 945-2731	17005
Advanced Clutch Technology Inc	3714	E	661 940-7555	19567
Aerotech News and Review Inc (PA)	2721	E	520 623-9321	5876
Antelope Valley Newspapers Inc	2711	E	661 940-1000	5552
Arrow Transit Mix	3273	E	661 945-7600	10691
Block Alternatives	3949	E	661 729-2800	22764
Bohns Printing	2752	F	661 948-8081	6453
Ccbcc Operations LLC	2086	C	661 723-0714	2052
Deluxe Corporation	2782	B	661 942-1144	7311
Do It Right Products LLC (PA)	3272	E	661 722-9664	10563
Geographic Data Mgt Solutions	7372	F	661 949-1025	23935
Griff Industries Inc	3089	F	661 728-0111	9818
Harvest Farms Inc	2038	D	661 945-3636	961
J & R Machine Works	3599	F	661 945-8826	16058
McWhirter Steel Inc	3441	F	661 951-8998	11840
Mobile Mini Inc	3448	E	909 356-1690	12562
Morton Grinding	3965	C	661 298-0895	23006
National Band Saw Company	3556	C	661 294-9552	14388
National Metal Stampings Inc	3469	D	661 945-1157	12849
Pacific Seismic Products Inc	3491	E	661 942-4499	13317
Pavement Recycling Systems Inc	2951	F	661 948-5599	9101
Plastic Mart Inc	2821	E	310 268-1404	7593
PPG Industries Inc	2851	E	661 945-7871	8667
Precision Welding Inc	3441	E	661 729-3436	11867
Radford Cabinets Inc	2511	D	661 729-8931	4604
Robert F Chapman Inc	3444	D	661 940-9482	12355
Rta Sales Inc	2431	F	661 942-3553	4118

LARKSPUR, CA - Marin County

	SIC	EMP	PHONE	ENTRY #
Evolva Inc	2836	F	415 448-5451	8298
Kavi Skin Solutions Inc (PA)	2834	E	415 839-5156	7976
Marin Scope Incorporated	2711	E	415 892-1516	5724
Myway Learning Company Inc	7372	F	415 937-1722	24187
Phoenix Marine Corporation (PA)	3825	D	415 464-8116	21098
Trizic Inc	7372	E	415 366-6583	24528

LATHROP, CA - San Joaquin County

	SIC	EMP	PHONE	ENTRY #
Accurate Heating & Cooling Inc	3444	E	209 858-4125	12084
Big Heart Pet Brands	2033	F	209 547-7200	758
Boise Cascade Company	2621	E	209 983-4114	5099
Boral Roofing LLC	3272	D	209 983-1600	10541
California Natural Products	2099	C	209 858-2525	2418
Captive Plastics LLC	3089	D	209 858-9188	9694
Cbc Steel Buildings LLC	3448	C	209 858-2425	12539
Clorox Company	2842	F	209 234-1094	8376
Con-Fab California Corporation (PA)	3272	E	209 249-4700	10554
Diamond Pet Food Processors O	2047	E	209 983-4900	1073
Heritage Paper Co	2752	F	925 449-1148	6611
Horizon Snack Foods Inc	2053	D	925 373-7700	1343
Mobile Mini Inc	3448	E	209 858-9300	12561
Pratt Industries Inc	2621	C	770 922-0117	5147
Provena Foods Inc	2013	E	209 858-5555	490
Rafael Sandoval	2421	F	209 858-4173	3942
Schell & Kampeter Inc	2047	E	209 983-4900	1083
Simwon America Corp	3714	F	925 276-3412	19767
Soccer Learning Systems Inc	2721	F	209 858-4300	6029
Tesla Inc	3711	F	209 647-7037	19504

LAWNDALE, CA - Los Angeles County

	SIC	EMP	PHONE	ENTRY #
Anthonys Rdymx & Bldg Sups Inc (PA)	3273	F	310 542-9400	10689
Carbro Corporation	3545	F	310 643-8400	14145
Vellios Machine Shop Inc	3599	F	310 643-8540	16498

LE GRAND, CA - Merced County

	SIC	EMP	PHONE	ENTRY #
Oasis Foods Inc	2033	E	209 382-0263	805

LEBEC, CA - Kern County

	SIC	EMP	PHONE	ENTRY #
National Cement Co Cal Inc	3273	F	661 248-6733	10804
Technicolor Usa Inc	3651	C	661 496-1309	17289

Mergent email: customerrelations@mergent.com
1356

2020 California
Manufacturers Register

(P-0000) Products & Services Section entry number
(PA)=Parent Co (HQ)=Headquarters (DH)=Div Headquarters

	SIC	EMP	PHONE	ENTRY #
LEMON GROVE, CA - San Diego County				
Custom Wire Products	3496	F	619 469-2328	13408
Imperial Custom Cabinet Inc	2511	F	619 461-4093	4576
Jci Metal Products (PA)	3441	D	619 229-8206	11819
Micro Tool & Manufacturing Inc	3545	E	619 582-2884	14173
RCP Block & Brick Inc (PA)	3271	D	619 460-9101	10515
West World Manufacturing Inc	2511	F	619 287-4403	4620
LEMOORE, CA - Kings County				
Agusa	2034	E	559 924-4785	840
Boeing Company	3721	E	559 998-8260	19859
Boeing Company	3812	E	559 998-8214	20548
Kay and Associates Inc	3721	E	559 410-0917	19909
Leprino Foods Company	2022	B	559 924-7722	564
Leprino Foods Company	2022	C	559 924-7939	565
Northland Process Piping Inc	3312	D	559 925-9724	11058
Olam Tomato Processors Inc	2033	F	559 447-1390	809
United States Dept of Navy	3519	A	559 998-2488	13602
LEWISTON, CA - Trinity County				
EH Suda Inc	3599	E	530 778-9830	15922
LINCOLN, CA - Placer County				
Earth & Vine Provisions Inc	2033	F	916 434-8399	766
Far West Equipment Rentals	3273	F	916 645-2929	10756
Gc Products Inc	3272	E	916 645-3870	10579
Gdas-Lincoln Inc	3721	D	916 645-8961	19894
Jbr Inc (PA)	2099	C	916 258-8000	2487
Livingstons Concrete Svc Inc	3273	E	916 334-4313	10797
Marybelle Farms Inc	2048	E	916 645-8568	1111
Pabco Building Products LLC	3259	D	916 645-3341	10464
Pabco Clay Products LLC	3251	C	916 645-3341	10435
Pallets Unlimited Inc	2448	E	916 408-1914	4391
Robb-Jack Corporation (PA)	3541	D	916 645-6045	13945
San Jose Die Casting Corp	3363	E	408 262-6500	11347
Sierra Pacific Industries	2421	B	916 645-1631	3959
Stantec Consulting Svcs Inc	3589	F	916 434-5062	15585
LINDEN, CA - San Joaquin County				
Hyponex Corporation	2873	E	209 887-3845	8795
Pearl Crop Inc	2099	E	209 887-3731	2583
Stockton Rubber Mfgcoinc	3069	E	209 887-1172	9374
LINDSAY, CA - Tulare County				
Arts Custom Cabinets Inc	2511	F	559 562-2766	4549
Doug Deleo Welding Inc	7692	F	559 562-3700	24632
Harvest Container Company	2653	E	559 562-1394	5233
Pallet Depot Inc (PA)	2448	D	916 645-0490	4387
Randy Nix Cstm Wldg & Mfg Inc	7692	E	559 562-1958	24660
LITTLE LAKE, CA - Inyo County				
Kiewit Corporation	1423	E	760 377-3117	309
LITTLEROCK, CA - Los Angeles County				
Hi-Grade Materials Co	3273	E	661 533-3100	10771
Legacy Vulcan LLC	3273	E	661 533-2127	10783
Legacy Vulcan LLC	3273	E	661 533-2125	10791
LIVE OAK, CA - Sutter County				
Coe Orchard Equipment Inc	3523	D	530 695-5121	13620
Sunset Moulding Co (PA)	2421	E	530 790-2700	3963
LIVERMORE, CA - Alameda County				
Adams Label Company LLC (PA)	2759	F	925 371-5393	6973
Aero Precision Industries LLC (PA)	3728	C	925 455-9900	20013
Aerospace Composite Products (PA)	3728	E	925 443-5900	20020
Air Factors Inc	3564	F	925 579-0040	14646
Akira Seiki U S A Inc	3541	F	925 443-1200	13903
Aiere Inc	2835	B	510 732-7200	8201
Altamont Manufacturing Inc	3599	F	925 371-5401	15730
Amerimade Technology Inc	3089	E	925 243-9090	9628
Aria Technologies Inc	3357	E	925 292-1616	11286
Bartolini Guitars	3679	F	386 517-6823	18830
Baycorr Packaging LLC (PA)	2653	C	925 449-1148	5199
Berkeley Nutritional Mfg Corp	2834	D	925 243-6300	7801
Bonner Metal Processing LLC	3449	E	925 455-3833	12586
Bonner Processing Inc	3471	E	925 455-3833	12948
Byer California	2331	D	925 245-0184	3146
C D International Tech Inc	3679	F	408 986-0725	18845
Cedar Mountain Winery Inc	2084	F	925 373-6636	1623
Cemex	3273	C	925 606-2200	10707
Cooling Source Inc	3363	C	925 292-1293	11334
Country Floral Supply Inc	3999	D	925 960-9823	23306
Covan Systems Inc	3651	F	510 226-9886	17215
Curtis Instruments Inc	3824	D	925 961-1088	20964
Daa Draexlmaier Auto Amer LLC	3714	D	864 485-1000	19630
Eklavya LLC	3569	F	925 443-3296	14812
Exacta-Technology Inc	3599	F	925 443-6200	15939

	SIC	EMP	PHONE	ENTRY #
Fabco Holdings Inc	3714	A	925 454-9500	19653
Ferrotec (usa) Corporation	3053	E	925 371-4170	9229
Fitpro USA LLC	2833	F	877 645-5776	7660
Formfactor Inc	3674	F	925 290-4000	18239
Formfactor Inc (PA)	3674	C	925 290-4000	18240
Fred Matter Inc	3599	E	925 371-1234	15975
Fusion Coatings Inc	3479	F	925 443-8083	13180
G2 Metal Fab	3441	E	925 443-7903	11799
Gdca Inc	3577	E	925 456-9900	15233
Gillig LLC	3713	B	510 785-1500	19536
Goalsr Inc	7372	E	650 453-5844	23946
Gpo Display	3993	E	510 659-9855	23123
GS Cosmeceutical Usa Inc	2844	E	925 371-5000	8504
Hanger Prsthetcs & Ortho Inc	3842	F	925 371-5081	22026
IMG Companies LLC	3599	C	925 273-1100	16039
Individual Software Inc	7372	E	925 734-6767	24009
Inland Valley Publising Co	2711	F	925 243-8000	5675
Inphenix Inc	3674	E	925 606-8809	18295
Internationally Delicious Inc (PA)	2053	F	925 426-6155	1344
Jifco Inc (PA)	3498	D	925 449-4665	13473
Johnson Controls	3669	C	925 273-0100	17736
Johnson Controls Inc	3714	A	925 447-9200	19697
Konecranes Inc	3536	F	925 273-0140	13849
Lam Research Corporation	3674	E	510 572-8400	18341
Lazestar	7692	E	925 443-5293	24649
Legacy Vulcan LLC	3273	E	925 373-1802	10790
Maranti Networks Inc	3572	D	408 834-4000	15054
Marpo Kinetics Inc	3949	F	925 606-6919	22847
Medical Device Resource Corp	3841	F	510 732-9950	21797
Meritor Specialty Products LLC (HQ)	3714	A	248 435-1000	19717
Messer LLC	2813	E	925 371-4170	7425
Metal Improvement Company LLC	3398	E	925 960-1090	11460
Modus Advanced Inc	3069	E	925 962-5943	9338
National Bedding Company LLC	2515	C	925 373-1350	4733
Nuprodx Inc	3842	F	925 292-0866	22057
Pacific Color Graphics Inc	2759	F	925 600-3006	7165
Pacon Mfg Inc	3599	F	925 961-0445	16276
Printegra Corp	2761	F	925 373-6368	7283
Pro-Tek Manufacturing Inc	3444	F	925 454-8100	12342
Process Materials Inc	3341	F	925 245-9626	11207
Progressive Housing Inc	3714	F	916 920-8255	19745
Puronics Incorporated (PA)	3589	E	925 456-7000	15565
Q Technology Inc	3648	E	925 373-3456	17157
R K Larrabee Company Inc	3621	D	925 828-9420	16669
Ratermann Manufacturing Inc (PA)	3089	E	800 264-7793	10010
RC Readymix Co Inc	3273	E	925 449-7855	10817
Rch Associates Inc	3559	F	510 657-7846	14526
Rh Usa Inc	3841	E	925 245-7900	21881
Rios-Lovell Estate Winery	2084	E	925 443-0434	1889
Ron Nunes Enterprises LLC	3444	F	925 371-0220	12357
Screen Tech Inc	3444	D	408 885-9750	12369
Segundo Metal Products Inc	3444	D	925 667-2009	12371
Sensor Concepts Incorporated	3812	D	925 443-9001	20719
Sierra Design Mfg Inc (PA)	3647	E	925 443-3140	17092
Sierra Hygiene Products LLC	2621	E	925 371-7173	5150
Software Licensing Consultants	7372	E	925 371-1277	24428
Solarbos (HQ)	3613	D	925 456-7744	16616
Steven Kent LLC	2084	E	925 243-6442	1933
Streivor Inc	3914	E	925 960-9090	22591
Stretch-Run Inc	3441	E	925 606-1599	11888
Sub-One Technology Inc	3479	F	925 924-1020	13255
Summit Window Products Inc	2431	D	408 526-1600	4131
Tapp Label Inc (HQ)	2679	F	707 252-8300	5536
Tech Air Northern Cal LLC	2813	E	925 449-9353	7452
Tesla Vineyards Lp	2084	F	925 456-2500	1951
Thomas E Davis Inc	3444	F	925 373-1373	12407
Topcon Med Laser Systems Inc	3845	E	888 760-8657	22321
Topcon Positioning Systems Inc (DH)	3829	C	925 245-8300	21558
Trans Western Polymers Inc	2673	B	925 449-7800	5424
Truroots Inc (HQ)	2099	E	925 218-2205	2638
Tyco Fire Products LP	3569	C	925 687-6957	14867
Universal Cell Site Svcs Inc	3441	D	925 447-4500	11906
Vericool Inc	3565	E	925 337-0808	14733
Vi-TEC Manufacturing Inc	3599	F	925 447-8200	16501
Vintage 99 Label Mfg Inc	2672	E	925 294-5270	5379
Wente Bros Inc	2084	A	925 456-2300	1995
Westco Iron Works Inc (PA)	3441	D	925 961-9152	11919
X Wiley Inc (PA)	3851	D	925 243-9810	22396
Xchanger Manufacturing Corp	3443	C	510 632-8828	12072
Yield Engineering Systems Inc	3674	E	925 373-8353	18666
LIVINGSTON, CA - Merced County				
E & J Gallo Winery	2084	C	209 394-6215	1683
Fortuna Tortilla Factory	2099	F	209 394-3028	2463
Foster Poultry Farms (PA)	2015	C	209 394-6914	511
Foster Poultry Farms	2015	C	209 394-7901	513

Employment Codes: A=Over 500 employees, B=251-500,
C=101-250, D=51-100, E=20-50, F=10-19

2020 California
Manufacturers Register

© Mergent Inc. 1-800-342-5647

1357

G E O G R A P H I C

	SIC	EMP	PHONE	ENTRY #
Foster Poultry Farms	2048	E	209 394-7950	1096
Menezes Hay Co	2048	F	209 394-3111	1112
Sensient Ntral Ingredients LLC	2034	F	209 394-7979	861
Sensient Technologies Corp	2099	F	209 394-7971	2610
Ybp Holdings LLC	2099	E	209 394-7311	2650

LOCKEFORD, CA - San Joaquin County

	SIC	EMP	PHONE	ENTRY #
Elements By Grapevine Inc	2511	E	209 727-3711	4567
John Hewitt	2434	F	209 727-9534	4212
Kellogg Supply Inc	2873	E	209 727-3130	8796
Lomelis Statuary Inc (PA)	3299	F	209 367-1131	11009
Robertson-Ceco II Corporation	3448	C	209 727-5504	12573
Woodside Investment Inc	3499	D	209 787-8040	13558

LODI, CA - San Joaquin County

	SIC	EMP	PHONE	ENTRY #
Ah Wines Inc	2084	F	209 625-8170	1578
Allied Disc Grinding	3599	F	209 339-0333	15722
American Mstr Tech Scntfic Inc	3841	C	209 368-4031	21598
Archer-Daniels-Midland Company	2041	C	209 339-1252	993
Armorstruxx LLC	3728	E	209 365-9400	20042
Basalite Building Products LLC	3272	E	209 333-6161	10535
Baywood Cellars Inc	2084	E	415 606-4640	1592
Belco Cabinets Inc	3442	F	209 334-5437	11936
Bullzeye Mfg	3315	F	209 482-5626	11085
Campbell Grinding Inc	3599	F	209 339-8838	15821
Certainteed Corporation	2821	C	209 365-7500	7547
Dart Container Corp California	3086	C	209 333-8088	9522
Del Castillo Foods Inc	2099	E	209 369-2877	2441
Dependable Precision Mfg Inc	3444	E	209 369-1055	12181
Doors Plus Inc	2431	F	209 463-3667	4037
Duncan Press Inc	2752	F	209 462-5245	6554
Fairmont Sign Company	3993	E	209 365-6490	23106
Garys Signs and Screen Prtg	3993	F	209 369-8592	23120
General Mills Inc	2043	E	209 334-7061	1020
Goldstone Land Company LLC	2084	E	209 368-3113	1731
Holz Rubber Company Inc	3069	C	209 368-7171	9318
Honeywell International Inc	3724	A	209 323-8520	19959
Ipex USA LLC	3084	E	209 368-7131	9469
Jessies Grove Winery	2084	F	209 368-0880	1773
Kubota Tractor Corporation	3523	F	209 334-9910	13646
Larry Mthvin Installations Inc	3231	E	209 368-2105	10374
Lodi Iron Works Inc (PA)	3321	F	209 368-5395	11145
Lodi News Sentinel	2711	D	209 369-2761	5702
Lustre-Cal Nameplate Corp	3449	D	209 370-1600	12595
Mepco Label Systems	2759	C	209 946-0201	7133
Miller Packing Company	2013	E	209 339-2310	481
North Amrcn Specialty Pdts LLC	2821	C	209 365-7500	7587
Oak Ridge Winery LLC	2084	E	209 369-4768	1844
Pacific Coast Producers	2033	D	209 334-3352	813
Pacific Coast Producers (PA)	2033	F	209 367-8800	814
Quashnick Tool Corporation	3089	E	209 334-5283	10003
Robert Mondavi Corporation	2084	E	209 365-2995	1892
Ron Grose Racing Inc	3599	F	209 368-2571	16369
Schaefer Systems Intl Inc	3089	E	209 365-6030	10045
Scholten Surgical Instrs Inc	3841	E	209 365-1393	21889
Scientific Specialties Inc	3081	D	209 333-2120	9420
Shellpro Inc	3999	F	209 334-2081	23475
Superior Electrical Advg	3993	F	209 334-3337	23222
Sutter Home Winery Inc	2084	C	707 963-5928	1942
Takt Manufacturing Inc	3999	F	408 250-4975	23499
Tusco Casting Corporation	3325	E	209 368-5137	11173
USA Products Group Inc (PA)	2399	E	209 334-1460	3864
Vanderlans & Sons Inc (PA)	3589	E	209 334-4115	15597
Weibel Incorporated	2084	E	209 365-9463	1994

LOLETA, CA - Humboldt County

	SIC	EMP	PHONE	ENTRY #
Loleta Cheese Company Inc	2022	F	707 733-5470	567

LOMA LINDA, CA - San Bernardino County

	SIC	EMP	PHONE	ENTRY #
Dvele Inc	2451	E	909 796-2561	4444
Dvele Omega Corporation	2451	D	909 796-2561	4445
Loma Linda University	2752	E	909 558-4552	6707

LOMITA, CA - Los Angeles County

	SIC	EMP	PHONE	ENTRY #
Aab Garage Door Inc	2431	F	310 530-3637	3990
Anacrown Inc	3499	F	310 530-1165	13497
Coin Dealer Newsletter Inc	2721	F	310 515-7369	5906
Robinson Textiles Inc	2311	E	310 527-8110	2976
Underground Games Inc	3944	F	310 379-0100	22722

LOMPOC, CA - Santa Barbara County

	SIC	EMP	PHONE	ENTRY #
Alliance Technical Svcs Inc	3731	F	805 606-3020	20276
Celite Corporation	1499	F	805 736-1221	384
Chevron Corporation	1311	F	805 733-5174	43
Den-Mat Holdings LLC (HQ)	3843	F	805 346-3700	22143
Federal Prison Industries	3993	E	805 735-2771	23113
Federal Prison Industries	2511	C	805 736-4154	4570

	SIC	EMP	PHONE	ENTRY #
Henry L Hudson (PA)	2752	F	805 736-2737	6608
Horizon Well Logging Inc	1389	F	805 733-0972	209
Imerys Clays Inc	1455	F	805 737-2445	376
Imerys Minerals California Inc	1481	B	805 736-1221	382
Imerys Minerals California Inc (DH)	1499	D	805 736-1221	391
Lockheed Martin Corporation	3663	B	805 606-4860	17574
Melville Winery LLC	2084	F	805 735-7030	1816
Orbital Sciences Corporation	3761	D	805 734-5400	20453
Rodriguez Ismael	2096	F	805 736-7362	2341
Stolpman Vineyards LLC	2084	E	805 736-5000	1935

LONG BEACH, CA - Los Angeles County

	SIC	EMP	PHONE	ENTRY #
A & A Aerospace Inc	3728	F	562 901-6803	19993
A & A Aerospace Inc	3728	F	562 901-6803	19994
Acme Headlining Co	3714	D	562 432-0281	19563
Air Marketing	2741	F	562 208-3990	6177
Air Products and Chemicals Inc	2813	E	562 437-0462	7396
Air Source Industries	2813	E	562 426-4017	7400
Altasens Inc (HQ)	3674	E	818 338-9400	18085
American Plant Services Inc (PA)	3312	D	562 630-1773	11026
Anivive Lifesciences Inc	2834	F	714 931-7810	7760
APR Engineering Inc	3731	E	562 983-3800	20277
Arias Industries Inc	3714	E	310 532-9737	19585
Asphalt Products Oil Corp (HQ)	2952	E	562 423-6471	9109
B & B Pipe and Tool Co (PA)	3599	E	562 424-0704	15762
Backflow Apparatus & Valve	3494	E	310 639-5231	13347
Bandag Licensing Corporation	3069	D	562 531-3880	9288
Berg-Nelson Company Inc	3052	F	562 432-3491	9197
Berns Bros Inc	3599	F	562 437-0471	15788
Big Studio Inc	2261	F	562 989-2444	2822
Bill Williams Welding Co	3441	E	562 432-5421	11749
Boeing Company	3721	A	714 317-1070	19865
Boeing Company	3721	A	562 593-6668	19866
Boeing Company	3721	A	562 425-3613	19868
Boeing Company	3812	E	562 593-5511	20549
Boeing Company	3721	A	562 496-1000	19873
Boeing Company	3721	A	562 593-5511	19876
Cablestrand Corp	3496	F	562 595-4527	13400
California Jig Grinding Co	3599	F	323 723-4017	15819
California Plastic Cntrs Inc	3089	F	562 423-3900	9686
California Resources Corp	1311	D	562 624-3400	37
Califrnia Rsurces Long Bch Inc	1389	C	562 624-3204	178
Canam Technology Inc	3663	F	562 856-0178	17479
Canzone and Company	3993	E	714 537-8175	23071
Cavanaugh Machine Works Inc	3599	F	562 437-1126	15830
Cemex Cnstr Mtls PCF LLC	3273	F	562 435-0195	10710
Clariant Corporation	2869	E	661 763-5192	8731
Coastal Marine Maint Co LLC (PA)	3731	F	562 432-8066	20283
Compulink Management Ctr Inc	7372	C	562 988-1688	23766
Continental Graphics Corp	2752	A	714 827-1752	6508
Control Switches Inc (PA)	3625	E	562 498-7331	16707
Control Switches Intl Inc	3625	E	562 498-7331	16708
Corazonas Foods Inc	2096	F	800 388-8998	2320
CRC Marketing Inc	1311	F	562 624-3400	46
Crestec Usa Inc	2752	E	310 327-9000	6524
Crown Equipment Corporation	3537	D	310 952-6600	13869
Custom Fibreglass Mfg Co	3792	C	562 432-5454	20483
Cw Industries	3441	F	562 432-5421	11779
CW Welding Service Inc (PA)	7692	E	562 432-5421	24628
D&S Brewing Solutions Inc	2082	E	650 207-4524	1518
Diamond-U Products Inc	3492	F	562 436-8245	13327
Diecraft Corporation	3599	E	323 728-2601	15897
Dynamite Sign Group Inc	3993	F	562 595-7725	23091
Eco Services Operations Corp	2819	D	310 885-6719	7488
Edgington Oil Company LLC	2951	D	562 423-1465	9091
Ej Usa Inc	3321	F	562 528-0258	11141
Ellegra Print & Imaging	2752	F	562 432-2931	6564
Engineering Materials Co Inc	3965	E	562 436-0063	23000
Epson America Inc (DH)	3577	A	800 463-7766	15225
Everson Spice Company Inc	2099	E	562 595-4785	2453
F-J-E Inc	2541	F	562 437-7466	4902
Ferraco Inc (HQ)	3842	E	562 988-2414	22012
Fine Quality Metal Finshg Inc	3471	E	562 983-7425	13009
Flynn Signs and Graphics Inc	3993	F	562 498-6655	23114
Forty-Niners Publication	2721	F	562 985-5568	5937
Foss Maritime Company	3441	E	562 437-6098	11796
Frontier Engrg & Mfg Tech Inc	3599	E	562 606-2655	15976
Fundamental Tech Intl Inc	3823	E	562 595-0661	20874
G B Remanufacturing Inc	3089	D	562 272-7333	9798
Gambol Industries Inc	3732	E	562 901-2470	20332
Gazette Newspapers	2711	E	562 433-2000	5644
Georgia-Pacific LLC	3275	E	562 435-7094	10878
Get	3589	F	562 989-5400	15516
Ginza Collection Design Inc	2335	E	562 531-1116	3228
Glencore Ltd	2911	E	562 427-6611	9046
Gulf Streams	3721	F	562 420-1818	19904

2020 California
Manufacturers Register

(P-0000) Products & Services Section entry number
(PA)=Parent Co (HQ)=Headquarters (DH)=Div Headquarters

	SIC	EMP	PHONE	ENTRY #
H Roberts Construction	3448	D	562 590-4825	12549
Harbor Custom Canvas	2394	F	562 436-7708	3686
Harding Containers Intl Inc	2448	E	310 549-7272	4370
Harsco Corporation	3443	F	909 444-2527	12019
Hearts For Long Beach Inc	2711	E	562 433-2000	5659
Hi-Flo Corp	3561	F	562 468-0800	14582
Howell Dick Hole Drilling Svc	1381	F	562 633-9898	94
Hufcor California Inc (HQ)	2542	D	562 634-3116	4981
Indel Engineering Inc	3732	E	562 594-0995	20338
Integrted Polymr Solutions Inc (HQ)	2824	E	562 354-2920	7639
Ix Medical (PA)	3842	F	877 902-6446	22034
Ixys Long Beach Inc (DH)	3674	E	562 296-6584	18327
Jacobson Plastics Inc	3089	D	562 433-4911	9848
Jbi LLC (PA)	2599	C	310 886-8034	5068
Jeteffect Inc (PA)	3721	F	562 989-8800	19907
Joy Processed Foods Inc	2099	E	562 435-1106	2491
Katana Software Inc	7372	F	562 495-1366	24071
Kbr Inc	3624	E	562 436-9281	16686
Keystone Engineering Company (HQ)	3599	E	562 497-3200	16114
Kuster Co Oil Well Services	1381	E	562 595-0661	97
La Rutan	3999	E	310 940-7956	23389
Lester Box Inc	2449	F	562 437-5123	4420
Leviton Manufacturing Co Inc	3643	F	631 812-6041	16911
Long Beach Creamery LLC	2024	F	562 252-2730	654
Lubeco Inc	2992	E	562 602-1791	9150
M L Z Inc	3469	F	562 436-3540	12840
Macs Lift Gate Inc (PA)	3999	E	562 634-5962	23401
Macs Lift Gate Inc	3537	E	562 634-5962	13882
Maitlen & Benson Inc	3548	E	562 597-2200	14247
Malibu Ceramic Works	3253	E	310 455-2485	10446
Marisa Foods Inc	2013	F	562 437-7775	477
Maruhide Marine Products Inc	2092	D	562 435-6509	2264
Medianews Group Inc	2711	D	562 435-1161	5740
Medway Plastics Corporation	3089	C	562 630-1175	9891
Mercury Security Products LLC	3699	F	562 986-9105	19356
Metal Preparations	3471	E	213 628-5176	13050
Metra Electronics Corporation	3714	F	562 470-6601	19718
Midonna Inc	2759	F	562 983-5140	7142
Mill 42 Inc	2253	F	714 979-4200	2797
Morton Salt Inc	1479	F	562 437-0071	379
National Emblem Inc (PA)	2395	C	310 515-5055	3750
NC Dynamics Incorporated	3728	C	562 634-7392	20186
NC Dynamics LLC	3599	C	562 634-7392	16237
Neill Aircraft Co	3728	B	562 432-7981	20187
Neurosmith LLC	3944	E	562 296-1100	22698
New Ngc Inc	3275	C	562 435-4465	10880
Obagi Cosmeceuticals LLC (PA)	2834	D	800 636-7546	8048
Pacific Energy Resources Ltd (PA)	1311	F	562 628-1526	61
Panel Products LLC	3812	E	310 830-3331	20673
Pbf Energy Western Region LLC (DH)	2911	B	973 455-7500	9061
Pdf Print Communications Inc (PA)	2752	D	562 426-6978	6774
Pfanstiel Publishers & Prtrs	2752	F	562 438-5641	6779
Plasidyne Engineering & Mfg	3089	E	562 531-0510	9966
Plastic Fabrication Tech LLC	3089	D	773 509-1700	9971
Praxair Inc	2813	E	310 816-1066	7429
Primus Pipe and Tube Inc (DH)	3317	D	562 808-8000	11133
Private Label By G Inc (PA)	2335	F	562 531-1116	3250
Prospring Inc	7372	F	562 726-1800	24318
Providence Industries LLC	2326	D	562 420-9091	3048
Queen Beach Printers Inc	2752	E	562 436-8201	6826
R E Michel Company LLC	3585	F	310 885-9820	15449
Radiology Support Devices	3841	F	310 518-0527	21871
RHS Gas Inc	2911	F	310 710-2331	9064
Rsg/Aames Security Inc	3669	E	562 529-5100	17758
Rubbercraft Corp Cal Ltd (DH)	3061	C	562 354-2800	9271
Sanders Composites Inc (DH)	3728	C	562 354-2800	20226
Sas Safety Corporation	3842	D	562 427-2775	22080
Schneiders Deisgn Studio Inc	3911	F	562 437-0448	22570
Seachrome Corporation	3431	C	310 427-8010	11650
Shoreline Cellars Inc	2084	F	909 322-6816	1915
SJcontrols Inc	3823	F	562 494-1400	20939
Solvay USA Inc	2819	F	310 669-5300	7528
South Coast Publishing Inc	2711	F	562 988-1222	5832
South Street Inc	3949	F	562 984-6240	22892
Speed-O-Pin International	2591	F	562 433-4911	5040
SPEP Acquisition Corp (PA)	3429	D	310 608-0693	11630
Spike Chunsoft Inc	7372	F	562 786-5080	24440
Sportsmen Steel Safe Fabg Co (PA)	3499	E	562 984-0244	13547
Stearns Park	2531	F	562 570-1685	4873
Stem Consultants Inc	3824	F	612 987-8008	20975
Sunwood Doors Inc	2431	E	562 951-9401	4134
Superior Electrical Advg (PA)	3993	D	562 495-3808	23221
T D I Signs	3993	E	562 436-5188	23224
Tabc Inc (DH)	3714	C	562 984-3305	19776
Talco Plastics Inc	3089	E	562 630-1224	10078

	SIC	EMP	PHONE	ENTRY #
Tatung Company America Inc (HQ)	3663	D	310 637-2105	17679
TCI Texarkana Inc (DH)	3353	F	562 808-8000	11224
Tenneco Automotive Oper Co Inc	3714	D	562 630-0700	19780
Termo Company	1311	E	562 595-7401	68
Tesoro Refining & Mktg Co LLC	2911	B	562 728-2215	9074
Texollini Inc	2297	C	310 537-3400	2904
Three Star Rfrgn Engrg Inc	3585	E	310 327-9090	15455
Tidelands Oil Production Inc (DH)	1311	E	562 436-9918	69
Tidelands Oil Production Inc	1311	E	562 436-2836	70
Tor C A M Industries Inc	3592	E	562 531-8463	15619
U S Chrome Corp California	3471	E	562 437-2825	13122
Vans Inc	3021	F	562 856-1695	9191
Virgin Orbit LLC (PA)	3761	C	562 384-4400	20463
Vision Publications	2741	E	562 597-4000	6375
Visioneered Image Systems Inc	3993	F	818 613-7600	23237
Weatherford International LLC	3533	F	562 595-0931	13796
Western Integrated Mtls Inc (PA)	2431	E	562 634-2823	4147
Western Tube & Conduit Corp (HQ)	3644	C	310 537-6300	16956
Wise Solar Inc	3433	E	888 406-7879	11725
Wyatt Precision Machine Inc	3451	E	562 634-0524	12661

LOOMIS, CA - Placer County

	SIC	EMP	PHONE	ENTRY #
American Die & Rollforming	3544	F	916 652-7667	14013
Apex Brewing Supply	3556	F	916 250-7950	14344
Bimbo Bakeries Usa Inc	2051	F	916 456-3863	1150
Gary Doupnik Manufacturing Inc	2452	D	916 652-9291	4459
Hillerich & Bradsby Co	3949	E	916 652-4267	22820
Ruffstuff Inc	3714	F	916 600-1945	19761
S&S Signature Mill Works Inc	2499	F	916 652-1046	4530
Valley Rock Lndscpe Material	3271	E	916 652-7209	10523
West Pacific Cabinet Mfg	2434	F	916 652-6840	4265

LOS ALAMITOS, CA - Orange County

	SIC	EMP	PHONE	ENTRY #
Absolute Sign Inc	3993	F	562 592-5838	23040
Aero Corporation	3721	E	562 598-2281	19847
Alliance Spacesystems LLC	3624	C	714 226-1400	16680
Arrowhead Products Corporation	3728	A	714 828-7770	20043
Bloomfield Bakers	2052	A	626 610-2253	1308
Blue Sphere Inc	2311	E	714 953-7555	2961
Brodhead Grating Products LLC	3446	F	562 598-4314	12458
Caravan Manufacturing Co Inc	3089	F	714 220-9722	9695
Dwi Enterprises	3651	E	714 842-2236	17223
Flowline Inc	3829	E	562 598-3015	21474
Golf Design Inc	3949	D	714 899-4040	22810
Grating Pacific Inc (PA)	3441	E	562 598-4314	11806
Haus of Grey LLC	2326	F	562 270-4739	3035
Institute of Electrical and El	2754	D	714 821-8380	6956
James Jackson	3599	F	562 493-1402	16074
Katlan Industries Inc	3469	F	562 618-0940	12829
Lab-Clean LLC	2842	E	714 689-0063	8392
Merrill Corporation	2759	D	714 690-2200	7135
North American Petroleum	2899	C	562 598-6671	9010
Professional Bearing Svc Inc	3599	E	562 596-5023	16315
Spacesystems Holdings LLC	3624	C	714 226-1400	16691
Spinelli Graphic Inc	2759	F	562 431-3232	7225
Spintek Filtration Inc	3569	F	714 236-9190	14861
Spiracle Technology LLC	3829	F	714 418-1091	21548
Supermedia LLC	2741	B	562 594-5101	6354
Techpro Sales & Service Inc	2891	F	562 594-7878	8899
Timken Company	3562	A	714 484-2400	14617
Trend Offset Printing Svcs Inc	2752	C	859 449-2900	6897
Trend Offset Printing Svcs Inc (PA)	2752	A	562 598-2446	6898
Trend Offset Printing Svcs Inc	2752	B	562 598-2446	6899
Utbbb Inc	2052	C	562 594-4411	1336

LOS ALAMOS, CA - Santa Barbara County

	SIC	EMP	PHONE	ENTRY #
Bedford Winery	2084	F	805 344-2107	1593

LOS ALTOS, CA - Santa Clara County

	SIC	EMP	PHONE	ENTRY #
Anova Microsystems Inc	3577	F	408 941-1888	15155
Antypas & Associates Inc	3663	F	650 961-4311	17453
April Instrument	3825	F	650 964-8379	21005
Eurodesign Ltd (PA)	2511	F	650 948-5160	4569
Hambly Studios Inc	2396	E	408 496-1100	3792
Jemstep Inc	7372	F	650 966-6500	24058
Netcube Systems Inc	7372	D	650 862-7858	24194
Select Communications Inc	2721	E	650 948-9000	6025
Simplefeed Inc	7372	F	650 947-7445	24412
True Circuits Inc	3679	F	650 949-3400	19126
Varmour Networks Inc (PA)	7372	E	650 564-5100	24548

LOS ALTOS HILLS, CA - Santa Clara County

	SIC	EMP	PHONE	ENTRY #
Apton Biosystems Inc	3826	F	650 284-6992	21174
Fabri-Corp	3599	E	650 941-2076	15949
Lw Consulting Services LLC	7372	F	650 919-3001	24113
Star Pacific Inc	2841	E	510 471-6555	8352

GEOGRAPHIC

LOS ANGELES, CA - Los Angeles County

Company	SIC	EMP	PHONE	ENTRY #
10100 Holdings Inc (PA)	2451	F	310 552-0705	4437
2016 Montgomery Inc	2211	F	323 316-6886	2662
2bb Unlimited Inc	2311	E	213 253-9810	2958
515 W Seventh LLC	3646	F	323 278-8116	17004
55 Degree Wine	2084	F	323 662-5556	1574
5800 Sunset Productions Inc	2711	F	323 460-3987	5543
6f Resolution Inc	3714	D	209 467-0490	19561
A & A Jewelry Tools Findings	3999	F	213 627-8004	23259
A & M Sculptured Metals LLC	3444	E	323 263-2221	12079
A A Cater Truck Mfg Co Inc	2514	D	323 233-2343	4679
A S G Corporation	3999	F	213 748-6361	23260
A-1 Estrn-Home-Made Pickle Inc	2035	E	323 223-1141	878
AAA Flag & Banner Mfg Co Inc	2399	C	310 836-3341	3828
Able Sheet Metal Inc (PA)	3444	F	323 269-2181	12083
Abraxis Bioscience LLC (DH)	2834	C	800 564-0216	7716
ABS By Allen Schwartz LLC (HQ)	2339	E	213 895-4400	3281
ABs Clothing Collection Inc	2339	F	213 895-4400	3282
Absolute Usa Inc	3651	E	213 744-0044	17180
Acapulco Mexican Deli Inc	2096	F	323 266-0267	2315
Accepted Co	2741	F	310 815-9553	6173
Accurate Plating Company	3471	E	323 268-8567	12902
Accurate Staging Mfg Inc (PA)	3999	F	310 324-1040	23262
Ace Holdings Inc	3911	C	213 972-2100	22487
Active Window Products	3442	D	323 245-5185	11927
Acuant (HQ)	3577	E	213 867-2621	15145
Ad Hoc Labs Inc	7372	F	323 800-4927	23558
Adexa Inc (PA)	7372	E	310 642-2100	23563
Adfa Incorporated	3479	E	213 627-8004	13135
Adrienne Dresses Inc	2335	F	213 622-8557	3210
Advance Engineering & Tech Co	3821	F	213 250-8338	20745
Advance Finishing	3479	F	323 754-2889	13136
Advance Paper Box Company	2653	C	323 750-2550	5194
Advanced Skin & Hair Inc	2844	F	310 442-9700	8433
Adwear Inc	2326	F	213 629-2535	3022
Aercap US Global Aviation LLC (HQ)	3721	E	310 788-1999	19846
Aero Precision Engineering Inc	3444	E	310 642-9747	12090
Aerospace Welding Inc	7692	F	310 914-0324	24613
Agencycom LLC	7372	B	415 817-3800	23578
Agoura Music	3931	F	818 991-8316	22604
Agron Inc	2353	D	310 473-7223	3460
Ahr Signs Incorporated	3993	F	323 255-1102	23045
Aircoat Inc	3479	F	310 527-2258	13139
Ajinomoto Windsor Inc	2038	C	323 277-7000	939
Akn Holdings LLC (PA)	2721	F	310 432-7100	5878
Alan Lem & Co Inc	3231	E	310 538-4282	10336
Albion Knitting Mills Inc	2339	E	213 624-7740	3283
Alco Plating Corp (PA)	3471	C	213 749-7561	12912
Alex Velvet Inc	3911	E	323 255-6900	22489
Alger-Triton Inc	3645	E	310 229-9500	16958
All American Label	2241	E	213 622-2222	2749
Allhealth Inc	3571	C	213 538-0762	14885
Allied Pressroom Products Inc	3952	F	323 266-6250	22938
Alna Envelope Company Inc	2754	E	323 235-3161	6951
Alona Apparel Inc	2329	F	323 232-1548	3064
Alpha Impressions Inc	2396	F	323 234-8221	3769
Alpha Polishing Corporation (PA)	3471	D	323 263-7593	12920
Alpha Productions Incorporated	3444	E	310 559-1364	12101
Alpha Technologies Group Inc (PA)	3443	B	310 566-4005	11992
Alphacast Foundry Inc	3363	F	213 624-7156	11331
Altmans Products LLC (HQ)	3431	E	310 559-4093	11646
Aluminum Pros Inc	3556	F	310 366-7696	14343
Alvarado Alta Calidad LLC	2519	F	323 222-0038	4760
Amays Bakery & Noodle Co Inc (PA)	2052	D	213 626-2713	1300
Ambassador Industries	2591	F	213 383-1171	5015
Ambiance USA Inc (PA)	2339	D	323 587-0007	3284
America Wood Finishes Inc	2851	F	323 232-8256	8618
American AP Dyg & Finshg Inc	2231	D	310 644-4001	2742
American Apparel (usa) Inc	2389	F	213 488-0226	3538
American Apparel Retail Inc (DH)	2211	F	213 488-0226	2666
American Fashion Group Inc (PA)	2329	F	213 748-2100	3065
American Fruits & Flavors LLC	2087	E	323 264-7791	2190
American Furniture Systems Inc	2522	F	626 457-9900	4827
American Israel Public Affairs	7372	F	323 937-1184	23598
American Marble & Granite Co (PA)	3281	F	323 268-7979	10887
American Marble & Onyx Coinc	3281	E	323 776-0900	10888
American Medical Sales Inc	3844	E	310 471-8900	22207
American Quilting Company Inc	2395	E	323 233-2500	3722
American Society of Composers	2741	E	323 883-1000	6184
American Spring Inc	3493	F	310 324-2181	13335
American Straw Company LLC	3999	F	213 304-1095	23273
American System Publications	2741	F	323 259-1867	6185
American Zabin Intl Inc	2759	E	213 746-3770	6987
Americas Gold Inc	3911	E	213 688-4904	22493
Ames Rubber Mfg Co Inc	3069	E	818 240-9313	9281
AMG Employee Management Inc	3873	F	323 254-7448	22476
AMI/Coast Magnetics Inc	3677	E	323 936-6188	18699
Amko Restaurant Furniture Inc	2599	E	323 234-0388	5049
Ammiel Enterprise Inc	2335	F	213 973-5032	3213
Amtex California Inc	2391	E	323 859-2200	3587
Amzart Inc	2099	F	323 404-9372	2392
Analytic and Computational Res	7372	F	310 471-3023	23599
Angell & Giroux Inc	2522	D	323 269-8596	4828
Angels Garments	2329	F	213 748-0581	3067
Angels Young Inc	2311	E	213 614-0742	2959
Angelus Aluminum Foundry Co	3365	F	323 268-0145	11367
Angelus Sheet Metal Mfg Co	3444	F	323 221-4191	12111
Anki Inc (PA)	3944	E	877 721-2654	22657
Anodizing Industries Inc	3471	E	323 227-4916	12929
Anschutz Film Group LLC (HQ)	3861	F	310 887-1000	22402
Anthem Music & Media Fund LLC	2731	F	310 286-6600	6072
App Winndown LLC (HQ)	2389	E	213 488-0226	3541
Apparel Limited Inc	2339	D	323 859-2430	3286
Apparel News Group	2721	E	213 327-1002	5880
Appetize Technologies Inc	7372	C	877 559-4225	23607
Aptan Corp	2211	F	213 748-5271	2668
Aq Transportation	3743	F	626 143-4552	20366
Aquahydrate Inc	2086	D	310 559-5058	2039
Aquarius Rags LLC (PA)	2335	F	213 895-4400	3214
Archer-Daniels-Midland Company	2041	E	323 266-2750	990
Archer-Daniels-Midland Company	2041	E	323 269-8175	992
Argonaut	2711	E	310 822-1629	5553
Aries 33 LLC	2329	E	310 355-8330	3069
Arnies Supply Service Ltd (PA)	2448	E	323 263-1696	4347
Arrow Diecasting Inc	3363	F	323 245-8439	11333
Arrowhead Brass & Plumbing LLC	3432	D	323 221-9137	11657
Arsenic Inc	2721	E	310 701-7559	5883
Arteffex Conceptioneering	3999	F	818 506-5358	23278
Arthur Dogswell LLC (PA)	2047	E	888 559-8833	1068
Artisan Crust	2051	E	323 759-7000	1138
Artistic Concepts	2521	F	323 257-8101	4785
Aryzta Holdings IV LLC (HQ)	2052	C	310 417-4700	1302
Aryzta LLC (DH)	2052	C	310 417-4700	1305
Arzy Company Inc	3911	F	213 627-7844	22498
Ashka Print LLC	2759	E	323 980-6008	6995
Associated Students UCLA	2711	C	310 825-2787	5558
Assoluto Inc	2339	F	213 748-1116	3288
Astourian Jewelry Mfg Inc	3911	F	213 683-0436	22499
Astrochef Inc	2038	D	213 627-9860	944
Ata Boy Inc	3999	E	323 644-0117	23281
Atelier Luxury Group LLC	2396	E	310 751-2444	3771
Atlas Spring Mfgcorp	3495	C	310 532-6200	13374
Audience Inc	2741	E	323 413-2370	6194
Automation Printing Co (PA)	2791	E	213 488-1230	7354
Avalon Apparel LLC (PA)	2361	C	323 581-3511	3475
Avanzato Technology Corp	3559	E	312 509-0506	14430
Avis Roto Die Co	3544	E	323 255-7070	14019
Ax II Inc	2241	E	310 292-6523	2750
Azitex Trading Corp	2259	D	213 745-7072	2816
Azpire Print & Mediaworks LLC	2752	F	310 736-5952	6426
Azteca Jeans Inc	2339	E	323 758-7721	3290
B & C Plating Co	3471	E	323 263-6757	12940
B & Y Global Sourcing LLC	2335	F	213 891-1112	3217
B H Tank Works Inc	3443	F	323 221-1579	11994
B&F Fedelini Inc (PA)	2299	E	213 628-3901	2926
B&F Fedelini Inc	2299	E	213 628-3901	2927
B2 Apparel Inc	2389	F	323 233-0044	3542
Baby Box Company Inc (PA)	2676	F	844 422-2926	5459
Baby Guess Inc	2369	E	213 765-3100	3492
Backstage West	2721	E	323 525-2356	5885
Bae Systems Controls Inc	3511	C	323 642-5000	13562
Bandel Mfg Inc	3469	E	818 246-7493	12769
Barber-Webb Company Inc (PA)	3089	E	541 488-4821	9653
Barkevs Inc	3911	E	800 227-7321	22502
Barry Avenue Plating Co Inc	3471	D	310 478-0078	12941
Baxalta Incorporated	2834	A	818 240-5600	7786
Bb Co Inc	2339	E	213 747-4701	3293
Bd Impotex LLC	2335	F	323 521-1500	3218
Becker Woodworking	2426	F	323 564-2441	3969
Bee Darlin Inc (PA)	2335	D	213 749-2116	3219
Belagio Enterprises Inc	2211	E	323 731-6934	2670
Beningna	2321	F	323 262-2484	2985
Bentley Management Corporation	2721	E	323 653-8060	5889
Bereshith Inc (PA)	2331	E	213 749-7304	3140
Best Box Company Inc	2653	F	323 589-6088	5200
Best-Way Marble & Tile Co Inc	3281	E	323 266-6794	10893
Beta Box Inc	3651	F	323 383-9820	17204
Better Instant Copy	2752	F	323 782-6934	6446
Bez Ambar Inc	3911	E	213 629-9191	22504
Bhaktivedanta Book Tr Intl Inc	2731	F	310 837-5284	6078

Mergent email: customerrelations@mergent.com
1360

2020 California
Manufacturers Register

(P-0000) Products & Services Section entry number
(PA)=Parent Co (HQ)=Headquarters (DH)=Div Headquarters

Company	SIC	EMP	PHONE	ENTRY #
Bidu Inc	2339	F	213 748-4433	3295
Bimbo Bakeries Usa Inc	2051	E	323 913-7214	1160
Biosig Technologies Inc	3841	E	310 620-9320	21638
Bitmax LLC (PA)	3669	E	323 978-7878	17716
Blocks Wearables Inc	3873	E	650 307-9557	22477
Bombardier Transportation	3743	D	323 224-3461	20367
Boulevard Style Inc	2331	F	213 749-1551	3143
Boulevard Style Inc (PA)	2331	F	213 749-1551	3144
Breitburn Energy Partners I LP	1311	E	213 225-5900	32
Breitburn GP LLC	1311	A	213 225-5900	33
Brent-Wood Products Inc	2499	E	800 400-7335	4494
Brentwood Home LLC	2515	F	213 457-7626	4714
Brighton Collectibles LLC	2387	E	626 961-9381	3528
Brite Lite Enterprises	3651	F	310 363-7120	17210
Brite Plating Co Inc	3471	D	323 263-7593	12950
Bromwell Company (PA)	3263	F	800 683-2626	10470
Bronze-Way Plating Corporation (PA)	3471	E	323 266-6933	12951
Bruce Eicher Inc (PA)	3645	F	310 657-4630	16967
Bruck Braid Company	2396	E	213 627-7611	3775
Brud Inc	2741	E	310 806-2283	6207
Bruin Biometrics LLC	3841	F	310 268-9494	21645
Brunettes Printing Service	2752	F	213 749-7441	6459
Brush Research Mfg Co	3991	C	323 261-2193	23022
Bulthaup Corp	2514	F	310 288-3875	4686
Bunkerhill Indus Group Inc	2326	F	323 227-4222	3027
Burning Torch Inc	2339	E	323 733-7700	3298
Byd Energy LLC	3694	E	661 949-2918	19188
Byd Motors LLC (HQ)	3714	E	213 748-3980	19602
Byer California	2253	B	323 780-7615	2775
C & Y Investment Inc	2339	F	323 267-9000	3299
C Gonshor Fine Jewelry Inc	3911	F	213 629-1075	22505
C M H Records LLC	3652	D	323 663-8098	17311
C P Auto Products Inc	3471	E	323 266-3850	12957
Caer Inc	2032	E	415 879-9864	721
Cal Fiber Inc	2299	F	323 268-0191	2929
Cal Quake Construction Inc	1389	F	323 931-2969	177
Calhoun & Poxon Company Inc	3613	F	323 225-2328	16588
California Broach Company	3599	F	323 260-4812	15818
California Dynamics Corp (PA)	3829	E	323 223-3882	21446
California Heavy Oil Inc	1382	E	888 848-4754	111
California Metal Processing Co	3471	E	323 753-2247	12961
California Potteries Inc	3253	E	323 235-4151	10437
California Stay Co Inc	3131	F	310 839-7236	10147
California Swatch Dyers Inc	2262	E	213 748-8425	2843
California Webbing Mills Inc	2299	F	323 753-0260	2930
Califrnia Cstume Cllctions Inc (PA)	2389	E	323 262-8383	3544
Camp Smidgemore Inc (DH)	2339	E	323 634-0333	3301
Cancer Genetics Inc	2835	C	323 224-3900	8211
Candella Lighting Co Inc	3646	E	323 798-1091	17019
Capsa Solutions LLC	3572	E	800 437-6633	15011
Cardigan Road Productions	3679	E	310 289-1442	18850
Cardinal Glass Industries Inc	3231	E	323 319-0070	10346
Casa De Hermandad	3949	F	310 477-8272	22777
Caspian Research & Tech LLC	7372	F	310 474-3244	23721
Catalina Tempering Inc (PA)	3423	E	323 789-7800	11525
Catame Inc (PA)	3965	E	213 749-2610	22999
Cbj LP	2721	E	323 549-5225	5899
Cdr Graphics Inc (PA)	2752	E	310 474-7600	6475
Cds California LLC	3861	F	818 766-5000	22406
Celerinos Pallets	2448	F	626 923-4182	4354
Cemcoat Inc	3471	E	323 733-0125	12964
Cemex Cnstr Mtls PCF LLC	3273	E	323 221-1828	10734
Center Thtre Group Los Angeles	2389	E	213 972-3751	3545
Cenveo Worldwide Limited	2677	D	323 261-7171	5468
Certified Enameling Inc	3479	D	323 264-4403	13157
Cha Bio & Diostech Co Ltd	2834	D	213 487-3211	7840
Champion-Arrowhead LLC	3432	D	323 221-9137	11663
Charles Gemeiner Cabinets	2431	E	323 299-8696	4017
Charles Ligeti Co	3911	E	213 612-0831	22506
Chinecherem Eze Inc	3144	F	310 806-1807	10167
Chol Enterprises Inc	3728	E	310 516-1328	20070
Choon Inc (PA)	2335	E	213 225-2500	3223
Christian Today Inc	2711	F	323 931-0505	5591
Christine Alexander Inc	2395	E	213 488-1114	3730
Chromal Plating Company	3471	E	323 222-0119	12967
Chrome Hearts LLC (PA)	2386	E	323 957-7544	3510
Church Scientology Intl	2759	D	323 960-3500	7022
Cisco Bros Corp	2512	F	323 778-8612	4631
Cisco Bros Corp (PA)	2512	C	323 778-8612	4632
Citrix Systems Inc	7372	F	800 424-8749	23742
City Paper Box Co	2653	F	323 231-5990	5207
Civic Center News Inc	2711	E	213 481-1448	5592
Ckcc Inc	2396	E	213 629-0939	3780
Clean Water Technology Inc (HQ)	3589	D	310 380-4648	15500
Cleanlogic LLC	2842	E	310 261-3001	8374
Clothing By Frenzii Inc	2331	F	213 670-0265	3149
Clothing Illustrated Inc (PA)	2339	E	213 403-9950	3306
Coast Heat Treating Co	3398	E	323 263-6944	11447
Coating Specialties Inc	3728	F	310 639-6900	20072
Coda Automotive Inc	3714	E	310 820-3611	19618
Colon Manufacturing Inc (PA)	2331	E	213 749-6149	3150
Color Image Apparel Inc	2253	E	855 793-3100	2779
Colormax Industries Inc (PA)	2211	E	213 748-6600	2676
Coltrin Inc	3317	F	323 266-6872	11124
Commercial Sheet Metal Works	3441	E	213 748-7321	11770
Concepts By J Inc	2511	E	323 564-9988	4561
Concord Music Group Inc (PA)	2731	D	310 385-4455	6091
Connector Plating Corp	3471	F	310 323-1622	12977
Consolidated Graphics Inc	2759	D	323 460-4115	7033
Coral Reef Aquarium	3231	E	310 538-4282	10348
Cortez Furniture Mfg Inc	2512	F	323 581-5935	4634
Cougar Biotechnology Inc	2834	D	310 943-8040	7855
Cprint Holdings LLC	2752	F	213 488-0456	6518
CR & A Custom Apparel Inc	2759	E	213 749-4440	7039
Crave Foods Inc	2038	E	562 900-7272	952
Crellin Machine Company	3451	E	323 225-8101	12626
Crew Knitwear LLC (PA)	2339	D	323 526-3888	3309
Cristal Materials Inc	2515	E	323 855-1688	4716
Crucial Power Products	3679	F	323 721-5017	18877
CTS Cement Manufacturing Corp	2891	F	310 472-4004	8863
Cuadra Associates Inc (PA)	7372	E	310 591-2490	23785
Cuahutemoc Tortilleria	2099	F	323 262-0410	2435
Cubic Zee Jewelry Inc	3911	F	213 614-9800	22509
Cuddly Toys	3942	F	323 980-0572	22645
Cuevas Mattress Inc	2515	E	310 631-8382	4717
Custom Lithograph	2752	E	323 778-7751	6527
Custom Upholstered Furn Inc	2512	F	323 731-3033	4635
Cvr Nitrogen LP (DH)	2873	E	310 571-9800	8791
Cyber Medical Imaging Inc	3843	E	888 937-9729	22140
Cybrex Consulting Inc	7372	D	513 999-2109	23792
Cytrx Corporation (PA)	2836	E	310 826-5648	8292
D & R Brothers Inc	2331	E	213 747-4309	3153
D Hauptman Co Inc	3949	E	323 734-2507	22788
Dacon Systems Inc	3357	F	310 842-9933	11300
Daily Graphs Inc	2721	E	310 448-6843	5914
Daily Journal Corporation (PA)	2711	C	213 229-5300	5608
Daily Sports Seoul Usa Inc	2711	E	213 487-9331	5612
Dal-Tile Corporation	2824	F	323 257-7553	7637
Danbee Inc	2335	F	323 780-0077	3225
Darling Ingredients Inc	2077	D	323 583-6311	1458
Dash Sportswear	2339	E	323 846-2640	3313
David H Fell & Co Inc (PA)	3341	E	323 722-9992	11199
David Haid	2599	E	323 752-8096	5054
David Kordansky Gallery Inc (PA)	2731	E	323 935-3030	6095
David Pirrotta Dist Inc	2844	F	323 645-7456	8476
Dbg Subsidiary Inc	2337	C	323 837-3700	3265
Dcx-Chol Enterprises Inc (PA)	3671	D	310 516-1692	17781
Dcx-Chol Enterprises Inc	3671	E	310 516-1692	17782
Dcx-Chol Enterprises Inc	3671	F	310 516-1692	17783
Dcx-Chol Enterprises Inc	3671	E	310 525-1205	17784
Dda Holdings Inc	2339	F	213 624-5200	3314
Decor Auto Inc	2396	F	323 733-9025	3783
Decor Fabrics Inc	2512	E	323 752-2200	4637
Deist Engineering Inc	2326	E	818 240-7866	3033
Delco Operating Co LP	1382	F	310 525-3535	118
Delgado Brothers LLC	2499	E	323 233-9793	4500
Delivery Zone LLC	2099	D	323 780-0888	2442
Demetrius Pohl	1481	F	323 735-1027	381
Desert Shades Inc	3999	F	323 731-5000	23313
Design Todays Inc (PA)	2339	D	213 745-9091	3317
Designed By Scorpio Inc	3911	F	213 612-4440	22510
Designs By Batya Inc	2311	F	213 746-7844	2963
Diaring Inc	3911	F	213 489-3894	22511
Didi of California Inc	2331	E	323 256-4514	3155
Dimufidra Usa Inc	2051	D	323 651-3822	1187
Discount Instant Printing	2752	F	213 622-4347	6544
DJ Safety Inc	2396	E	323 221-0000	3785
Dmbm LLC	2339	E	714 321-6032	3319
Dolores Canning Coinc	2032	E	323 263-9155	725
Dosa Inc	2339	E	213 627-3672	3320
Doval Industries Inc	3429	D	323 226-0335	11587
Dreamplay Toys LLC	3944	F	424 208-7010	22671
Dry Aged Denim LLC (PA)	2325	F	323 780-6206	3003
Ds Services of America Inc	2086	D	323 551-5724	2073
Dubon & Sons Inc	2038	F	213 923-1182	956
Dynamation Research Inc	3728	F	909 864-2310	20095
Dynamics Orthotics & Prostheti	3842	E	213 383-9212	22001
E J Y Corporation	2395	F	213 748-1700	3739
E8 Denim House LLC	2329	F	310 386-4413	3077
Earth Lab Inc	2842	F	888 835-2276	8382

G
E
O
G
R
A
P
H
I
C

Employment Codes: A=Over 500 employees, B=251-500,
C=101-250, D=51-100, E=20-50, F=10-19

2020 California
Manufacturers Register

© Mergent Inc. 1-800-342-5647

1361

Company	SIC	EMP	PHONE	ENTRY #
East La Lamination Inc	3089	F	323 881-9838	9770
East West Tea Company LLC	2043	F	310 275-9891	1018
Ebsco Productions Inc	3469	E	323 960-2599	12798
Eden Creamery LLC (PA)	2024	F	855 425-6867	640
Eden Equipment Company Inc	3569	F	909 629-2217	14811
Edey Manufacturing Co Inc	3442	E	323 566-6151	11950
Edmons Unque Furn Stone Gllery (PA)	2511	F	323 462-5787	4566
Edmund A Gray Co (PA)	3498	D	213 625-0376	13467
Eema Industries Inc	3648	E	323 904-0200	17118
Efaxcom (DH)	3577	D	323 817-3207	15221
Ej Diamonds Inc	3911	F	213 623-2329	22514
El Paraiso No 2	2024	E	323 587-2073	641
Electrolizing Inc	3471	E	213 749-7876	12997
Electronic Arts Inc	7372	F	310 754-7000	23851
Electronic Systems Innovation	3571	F	310 645-8400	14906
Element Technica LLC	3861	F	323 993-5329	22419
Elephant Flowers LLC	3089	D	213 327-6323	9777
Elevator Research & Mfg Co	3534	D	213 746-1914	13799
Embroidertex West Ltd (PA)	2395	F	213 749-4319	3740
Embroidery One Corp	2395	F	213 572-0280	3742
Emerald Expositions LLC	2721	D	323 525-2000	5931
Energy Lane Inc	2824	F	323 962-5020	7638
Eqh Limited Inc	3423	E	310 736-4130	11528
Ergo Baby Carrier Inc (HQ)	3944	E	213 283-2090	22674
Eska Inc	2339	E	323 268-2134	3322
ET Balancing Inc	3599	F	310 538-9738	15936
Euro Bello USA	2386	E	213 446-2818	3514
Everbrands Inc	2844	F	855 595-2999	8490
Everspring Chemical Inc	2899	D	310 707-1600	8965
Exactuals LLC	7372	F	310 689-7491	23882
Exploding Kittens LLC	3944	E	310 788-8699	22675
Express Sign and Neon	3993	F	323 291-3333	23105
EZ 2000 Inc	7372	E	800 273-5033	23887
F Conrad Furlong Inc	3911	F	213 623-4191	22517
Fabritex Inc	2221	F	213 747-1417	2726
Factory One Studio Inc	2211	D	323 752-1670	2687
Falcon Waterfree Tech LLC (HQ)	3069	E	310 209-7250	9309
Family Industries LLC	3999	F	619 306-1035	23330
Farsi Jewelry Mfg Co Inc	3911	F	213 624-0043	22519
Fashion Queen Mania Inc	2337	F	213 788-7310	3266
Fashion Today Inc	2339	F	213 744-1636	3324
Fashion Today Inc (PA)	2339	F	213 744-1636	3325
Fear of God LLC	2329	E	310 466-9751	3079
Felbro Inc	2542	C	323 263-8686	4976
Felbro Food Products Inc	2087	E	323 936-5266	2207
Fetish Group Inc (PA)	2329	E	323 587-7873	3081
Fierra Design Inc	2329	E	213 622-2426	3082
Filet Menu Inc	2754	E	310 202-8000	6954
Fisher Printing & Stamping Co	2759	F	323 933-9193	7064
Flame Gard Inc	3569	D	323 888-8707	14819
Flame Out Inc	3999	E	323 221-0000	23333
Flap Happy Inc	2369	F	310 453-3527	3493
Flash Code Solutions LLC	7372	F	800 633-7467	23902
Flaunt Magazine	2721	F	323 836-1044	5935
Flo-Mac Inc	3498	E	323 583-8751	13471
Flyer Defense LLC	3711	E	310 674-5030	19471
Foh Group Inc (PA)	2342	E	323 466-5151	3452
Food-O-Mex Corporation	2099	D	323 225-1737	2461
Foote Axle & Forge LLC	3714	E	323 268-4151	19658
Formsolver Inc	2499	E	323 664-7888	4502
Fortune Swimwear LLC (HQ)	2253	E	310 733-2130	2786
Foster Planing Mill Co	2499	F	323 759-9156	4503
Freedom Wood Finishing Inc	2269	D	213 534-6620	2854
Freeport-Mcmoran Oil & Gas LLC	1311	E	323 298-2200	53
Fresh Jive Manufacturing Inc	2321	E	213 748-0129	2989
Frisco Baking Company Inc	2051	C	323 225-6111	1208
Frm USA LLC	3497	E	323 469-9006	13451
Frontiers Media LLC	2741	E	323 930-3220	6240
Fun o Cake	2051	F	323 213-8684	1210
G&A Apparel Group	2396	F	323 234-1746	3789
Gabels Cosmetics Inc	2844	F	323 221-2430	8496
Galdaza Food Corporation	2051	E	213 747-4025	1213
Gali Corporation	3728	F	310 477-1224	20111
Gannett Co Inc	2711	E	310 444-2120	5636
Gans Ink and Supply Co Inc (PA)	2893	E	323 264-2200	8917
Gardena Textile Inc	2253	F	310 327-5060	2788
Gaze USA Inc	2339	E	213 622-0022	3328
Gaze USA Inc	2335	E	213 622-0022	3227
Gebe Electronic Services Inc	3479	E	323 731-2439	13183
Gem Box of West	2653	E	213 748-4875	5224
Gemini - G E L	2796	F	323 651-0513	7372
General Carbon Company	2816	F	323 588-9291	7459
Genesis Printing	2752	F	323 965-7935	6589
George Industries	3471	B	323 264-6660	13014
Gilli Inc	2389	F	213 744-9808	3554
Gino Corporation	2321	F	323 234-7979	2990
Giving Keys Inc	3911	D	213 935-8791	22522
Gleason Corporation (PA)	2393	F	310 470-6001	3658
Glendale Iron	3446	F	818 247-1098	12476
Global Doors Corp	2431	E	213 622-2003	4049
Global Sales Inc	2844	E	310 474-7700	8500
Global Unlimited Export LLC	3171	F	213 365-7051	10223
Gold Craft Jewelry Corp (PA)	3911	F	213 623-8673	22524
Gold Craft Jewelry Corp	3911	E	213 623-8673	22525
Gold Leaf & Metallic Powders	3999	E	323 769-4888	23347
Golden Textile Inc	2211	E	323 620-2612	2689
Good Time Usa Inc	2389	E	213 741-0100	3555
Good Worldwide LLC	2741	E	323 206-6495	6246
Gores Radio Holdings LLC	3699	A	310 209-3010	19320
Gourmet Coffee Warehouse Inc (PA)	2095	E	323 871-8930	2296
Grace Communications Inc (PA)	2711	E	213 628-4384	5648
Grain Craft Inc	2041	E	323 585-0131	1004
Grand West Inc (PA)	2253	F	323 235-2700	2789
Graphic Film Group LLC (PA)	2721	F	310 887-6330	5945
Grau Design Inc	2331	F	323 461-4462	3162
Greek Marble Inc	3281	F	323 221-6624	10908
Green Mattress Inc	2269	F	323 752-2026	2855
Green Mochi LLC	2335	F	213 225-2250	3229
Greneker Furniture	2541	E	323 263-9000	4906
Grenfield Consulting	1382	E	310 286-0200	126
Grey Studio Inc	2211	E	323 780-8111	2690
Grifols Biologicals LLC (DH)	2836	B	323 225-2221	8305
Group Martin LLC Johnathon	2331	F	323 235-1555	3163
Grover Products Co (PA)	3714	E	323 263-9981	19675
Grover Products Co	3714	D	323 263-9981	19676
Gtx Corp	3663	F	213 489-3019	17530
Guess Inc (PA)	2325	A	213 765-3100	3004
Guru Knits Inc	2331	D	323 235-9424	3164
GUSB Inc	2331	F	323 233-0044	3165
Gypsy 05 Inc	2339	E	323 265-2700	3332
H Starlet LLC	2339	F	323 235-8777	3333
H2 Wellness Incorporated	7372	D	310 362-1888	23967
Hanger Prsthetcs & Ortho Inc	3842	D	323 866-2555	22023
Harkham Industries Inc	2331	E	323 586-4600	3167
Hbc Solutions Holdings LLC	3663	A	321 727-9100	17534
Hd Window Fashions Inc (DH)	2591	B	213 749-6333	5024
Helicopter Tech Co Ltd Partnr	3728	E	310 523-2750	20125
Hidden Jeans Inc (PA)	2211	F	213 746-4223	2691
High-End Knitwear Inc	2253	E	323 582-6061	2790
Hip & Hip Inc (PA)	2339	F	310 494-6742	3337
Hirsh Inc	1389	E	213 622-9441	208
Hits Magazine Inc (PA)	2721	F	323 946-7600	5956
Hive Lighting Inc	3645	F	310 773-4362	16972
Holloway House Publishing Co	2731	F	323 653-8060	6110
Hollywood Engineering Inc	3429	F	310 516-8600	11598
Home Portal LLC	3612	F	310 559-6100	16556
Honey Punch Inc (PA)	2339	F	323 800-3812	3338
Honeywell International Inc	3724	B	310 410-9605	19962
Housewares International Inc	3089	F	323 581-3000	9830
HP Core Co Inc	3543	F	323 582-1688	14002
Hq Brands LLC	2389	F	213 627-7922	3556
Huge Usa Inc	2211	F	213 741-1707	2692
Hunter Digital Ltd	3577	F	310 471-5852	15239
Hunter/Gratzner Industries	3999	F	310 578-9929	23360
Huntsman Advanced Materials AM	2821	C	818 265-7221	7567
I Color Printing & Mailing Inc (PA)	2752	F	310 997-1452	6622
I Joah (PA)	2339	F	213 742-0500	3339
I T I Electro-Optic Corp (PA)	3823	E	310 445-8900	20886
I T I Electro-Optic Corp	3823	E	310 312-4526	20887
IaMplus LLC	3629	D	323 210-0852	16788
Ibisworld Inc	2741	E	212 626-6794	6254
ICI Architectural Millwork Inc	2431	F	323 759-4993	4058
Idea Tooling & Engineering Inc	3544	D	310 608-7488	14063
Impak Corporation	3081	F	323 277-4700	9406
Imperial Shade Venetian Blind	2542	F	323 233-4391	4983
Indie Source Inc	2326	F	424 200-2027	3039
Industrial Glass Products Inc	3231	F	323 526-7125	10365
Infiniti Plastic Technologies	3089	F	310 618-8288	9838
Inflatable Advertising Co Inc	3993	F	213 387-6839	23133
Infokorea Inc	2721	F	213 487-1580	5963
Informa Media Inc	2721	D	301 755-0162	5965
Ink & Color Inc	2752	E	310 280-6060	6637
International Bus Mchs Corp	3571	A	310 412-8699	14926
Interntonal Metallurgical Svcs	3398	F	310 645-7300	11454
Interstate Steel Center Co	3355	E	323 583-0855	11261
Investors Business Daily Inc (HQ)	2711	C	310 448-6000	5677
IOu International Inc	2297	E	323 846-0056	2903
Iq Textile Ind Inc	2299	E	213 745-2290	2937
Izurieta Fence Company Inc	3315	F	323 661-4759	11099
J & C Apparel	2325	E	323 490-8260	3009

Company	SIC	EMP	PHONE	ENTRY #
J Brand Inc	2211	D	213 749-3500	2695
J C Trimming Company Inc	2335	E	323 235-4458	3232
J Hellman Frozen Foods Inc (PA)	2037	E	213 243-9105	916
J K Star Corp	2329	D	310 538-0185	3095
J P B Jewelry Box Co (PA)	2541	F	323 225-0500	4913
J-M Manufacturing Company Inc (PA)	3084	C	800 621-4404	9470
James Stewart	2834	E	323 778-1687	7967
James West Inc (PA)	2325	F	310 380-1510	3010
Jamm Industries Corp	2339	E	213 622-0555	3342
Jan-Al Innerprizes Inc	2441	E	323 260-7212	4337
Janel Glass Company Inc	3231	E	323 661-8621	10369
Jason Markk Inc	2842	E	213 687-7060	8390
Jay-Cee Blouse Co Inc	2335	C	213 622-0116	3234
Jd/Cmc Inc	2339	E	818 767-2260	3345
Jerry Solomon Enterprises Inc	2499	E	323 556-2265	4508
Jet Plastics (PA)	3089	D	323 268-6706	9855
Jewelry Club House Inc	3911	F	213 362-7888	22531
Jimo Enterprises	2499	E	323 469-0805	4509
Jinx Inc	2339	E	818 399-4544	3346
JM Kitchen Cabinets	2434	F	323 752-6520	4211
Jml Connection Inc	7372	F	213 519-2000	24061
Jodi Kristopher LLC (PA)	2335	C	323 890-8000	3235
Joes Custom Furn & Frames	2511	E	323 721-1881	4578
Johnny Was Collection Inc (PA)	2335	E	323 231-8222	3236
Johnson & Johnson Consumer Inc	2844	E	310 642-1150	8523
Jonathan Louis Intl Ltd	2512	B	213 622-6114	4649
Jones Iron Works	3446	F	323 386-2368	12487
Joong-Ang Daily News Cal Inc (HQ)	2711	C	213 368-2500	5678
Jose Martinez	2064	F	323 263-6230	1379
Journal of Bocommunication Inc	2711	F	310 475-4708	5680
Jsl Foods Inc (PA)	2099	C	323 223-2484	2493
JT Design Studio Inc (PA)	2339	F	213 891-1500	3350
Juan Brambila Sr	2511	F	323 939-8312	4580
Judson Studios Inc	3231	F	323 255-0131	10371
Judy O Productions Inc	2731	E	323 938-8513	6117
K Too	2331	E	213 747-7766	3169
K-Swiss Inc (HQ)	3021	C	323 675-2700	9174
Kalypsys Inc	2834	C	858 552-0674	7973
Kamiran Inc	2331	F	213 746-9161	3170
Kan Group Corp	2741	F	213 383-1236	6265
Kareem Corporation	3949	E	323 234-0724	22835
Karoun Dairies Inc	2022	F	323 666-6222	557
Kathryn M Ireland Inc (PA)	2211	E	323 965-9888	2701
Katz Millennium Sls & Mktg Inc	3663	D	323 966-5066	17552
Kayo of California (PA)	2337	E	323 233-6107	3267
Kc Exclusive Inc (PA)	2339	D	213 749-0088	3353
Keepcup Ltd	3089	F	310 957-2070	9862
Keller Entertainment Group Inc	3577	F	310 443-2226	15263
Kenneth Miller Clothing Inc	2339	E	213 746-8866	3354
Kesmor Associates	3911	F	213 629-2300	22534
Kim Seng Jewelry Inc	3915	F	213 628-8566	22597
Kitsch LLC (PA)	3911	F	424 240-5551	22535
Klk Forte Industry Inc (PA)	2339	E	323 415-9181	3356
Knight Publishing Corp	2721	E	323 653-8060	5970
Knit Fit Inc	2396	F	213 673-4731	3795
Knoll Inc	2521	E	310 289-5800	4807
Kobi Katz Inc	3911	D	213 689-9505	22536
Komarov Enterprises Inc	2337	D	213 244-7000	3269
Komex International Inc	2331	E	323 233-9005	3172
Krissy Op Shins USA Inc	2329	D	213 747-2591	3100
Kritech Manufacturing (PA)	3679	F	310 538-9940	18979
Kt Industries Inc	3613	E	323 255-7143	16602
Kwdz Manufacturing LLC (PA)	2361	D	323 526-3526	3481
Kymsta Corp	2339	E	213 380-8118	3358
Kyocharo USA LLC	2711	F	213 383-1236	5687
L Y A Group Inc	2339	F	213 683-1123	3359
La Aloe LLC	2037	E	888 968-2563	920
La Barca Tortilleria Inc	2099	E	323 268-1744	2503
LA Cabinet & Millwork Inc	2541	E	323 227-5000	4919
La Famosa Manufacture Inc	2512	F	323 241-3100	4652
La Fortaleza Inc	2099	D	323 261-1211	2508
LA Gem and Jwly Design Inc	3911	D	213 488-1290	22537
La Gloria Foods Corp (PA)	2099	D	323 262-0410	2509
La Gloria Foods Corp	2099	D	323 263-6755	2510
La La Land Production & Design	3111	E	323 267-8485	10140
La Mamba LLC	2331	E	323 526-3526	3173
La Mousse	2038	D	310 478-6051	965
La Opinion LP (HQ)	2711	D	213 896-2196	5688
La Opinion LP	2711	D	213 896-2222	5689
La Princesita Tortilleria (PA)	2099	E	323 267-0673	2512
LA Printing & Graphics Inc	2752	E	310 527-4526	6690
La Times	2711	F	213 237-2279	5690
La Weekly	2711	C	310 574-7100	5691
La Zamorana Candy	2064	F	323 583-7100	1381
Labeltex Mills Inc (PA)	3965	C	323 582-0228	23005
Larry Spun Products Inc	3469	E	323 881-6300	12837
Lasani-Felt Co	2299	E	323 233-5278	2939
Lasercare Technologies Inc (PA)	3955	E	310 202-4200	22968
Lauras French Baking Co Inc	2051	E	323 585-5144	1230
Lavash Corporation	2051	E	323 663-5249	1232
Lavish Clothing Inc	2335	F	213 745-5400	3240
Lawrence O Lawrence Ltd	2299	F	323 935-1100	2941
Lee & Fields Publishing Inc	2741	F	213 380-5858	6270
Lee Thomas Inc (PA)	2339	F	310 532-7560	3362
Lefton Technologies Inc	3625	F	818 986-1728	16729
Lefty Production Co LLC	2339	F	323 515-9266	3363
Legal Vision Group LLC	2752	F	310 945-5550	6697
Legion Creative Group	2759	E	323 498-1100	7120
Lemor Trims Inc	2396	F	213 741-1646	3796
Lets Go Apparel Inc (PA)	2389	F	213 863-1767	3565
Lf Sportswear Inc (PA)	2331	E	310 437-4100	3174
Lialee Inc	2253	F	213 765-7788	2794
Line Euro-Americas Corp	7372	E	323 591-0380	24102
Lito	2341	E	323 260-4692	3443
Lito Childrens Wear Inc	2311	E	323 260-4692	2968
Livingstone Jewelry Co Inc	3911	F	213 683-1040	22541
Los Angeles Bus Jurnl Assoc	2721	E	323 549-5225	5979
Los Angeles Mills Inc	2211	E	424 307-0075	2702
Los Angeles Poultry Co Inc	2015	D	323 232-1619	521
Los Angeles Sentinel Inc	2711	D	323 299-3800	5703
Los Angles Tmes Cmmnctions LLC	2711	C	213 237-7203	5706
Los Angles Tmes Cmmnctions LLC	2711	C	213 237-7987	5713
Los Angles Tmes Cmmnctions LLC	2711	C	213 237-5691	5714
Lost Art Liquids LLC	3999	F	213 816-2988	23399
Louise Green Millinery Co Inc	2353	F	310 479-1881	3469
Low Voltage Architecture Inc	3699	D	310 573-7588	19349
Lucky Brand Dungarees LLC (PA)	2325	D	213 443-5700	3015
Luis Wtkins Cstm Wrught Ir LLC	2514	E	310 836-5655	4695
Lumenton Inc	3648	E	323 904-0202	17141
Luna Imaging Inc	7372	F	323 908-1400	24112
Luna Mora LLC	2396	F	310 550-6979	3798
Lupitas Bakery Inc (PA)	2051	F	323 752-2391	1237
Lyric Culture LLC	2331	F	323 581-3511	3178
M & H Creative Design Inc	3911	F	213 627-8860	22543
M C Woodwork	2448	F	323 233-0954	4379
M Stevens Inc	2339	F	323 661-2147	3365
M-5 Steel Mfg Inc (PA)	3443	E	323 263-9383	12028
Machine Building Specialties	3556	F	323 666-8289	14383
Makerskit LLC	3944	E	213 973-7019	22691
March Vision Care Inc	3851	E	310 665-0975	22371
Margus Automotive Elc Exch	3714	D	323 232-5281	19714
Marina Sportswear Inc	2339	D	323 232-2012	3371
Marna Ro LLC	2361	F	310 801-5788	3484
Mars Food Us LLC	2044	B	662 616-7347	1048
Marshall & Swift/Boeckh LLC	2731	F	213 683-9000	6119
Martin Aerospace Corporation	3492	F	310 231-0055	13332
Martin Sports Inc	3949	F	509 529-2554	22848
Matchmaster Dyg & Finshg Inc (PA)	2269	C	323 232-2061	2856
Matchmaster Dyg & Finshg Inc	2257	D	323 232-2061	2811
Matteo LLC	2392	E	213 617-2813	3625
Matthews Manufacturing Inc	3444	E	323 980-4373	12284
Max Fischer & Sons Inc	2392	E	213 624-8756	3626
McKenna Boiler Works Inc	3443	F	323 221-1171	12029
Mdc Interior Solutions LLC	2389	D	800 621-4006	3570
ME & ME Costumes Inc	3861	F	323 876-4432	22440
Meadow Farms Sausage Co Inc	2013	F	323 752-2300	479
Meat Packers Butchers Sup Inc	3556	F	323 268-8514	14385
Mededge Inc	3841	F	310 745-2290	21794
Media Gobbler Inc	7372	F	323 203-3222	24140
Mercury Plastics Inc	3081	D	323 264-2400	9409
Merelex Corporation	2819	E	310 208-0551	7505
Merit Printing Ink Company	2893	F	323 268-1807	8927
Merle Norman Cosmetics Inc (PA)	2844	B	310 641-3000	8538
Merrill Corporation	2759	D	213 253-5900	7134
Merrill Corporation	2759	F	949 252-9449	7139
Merrill Corporation Inc	2759	E	310 552-5288	7140
Metal Fabrication and Art LLC	3441	F	323 980-9595	11841
Metro Novelty & Pleating Co	2396	D	213 748-1201	3800
Mf Inc	2331	C	213 627-2498	3180
MGM Data Inc	3572	F	213 747-3282	15057
MGT Industries Inc (PA)	2339	C	310 516-5900	3373
Micro Surface Engr Inc (PA)	3399	E	323 582-7348	11481
Midthrust Imports Inc	2259	E	213 749-6651	2818
Mighty Networks Inc	2741	F	323 464-1050	6282
Mighty Soy Inc	3556	F	323 266-6969	14386
Millennial Brands LLC	3144	E	925 230-0617	10173
Mimi Chica (PA)	2339	F	323 264-9278	3374
Minachee Inc	2326	E	213 745-8100	3046
Miss Kim Inc	2335	F	213 747-4011	3244
Misyd Corp (PA)	2361	D	213 742-1800	3485

Company	SIC	EMP	PHONE	ENTRY #	Company	SIC	EMP	PHONE	ENTRY #
Mitratech Holdings Inc	7372	F	323 964-0000	24171	Paint-Chem Inc	2851	F	213 747-7725	8661
Mixmor Inc	3531	F	323 664-1941	13738	Pallet Masters Inc	2448	D	323 758-1713	4388
Mj Blanks Inc	2253	E	213 629-0006	2798	Pallets 4 Less Inc	2448	F	213 377-7813	4390
Mjw Inc	3561	D	323 778-8900	14591	Panavision Inc	3861	D	323 464-3800	22446
Mk Tool and Abrasive Inc	3291	F	562 776-8818	10951	Panchos Bakery	2051	E	323 582-9109	1258
Mnm Corporation (PA)	2721	E	213 627-3737	5990	Papercutters Inc	2671	E	323 888-1330	5336
Mobile Tone Inc	3663	F	323 939-6928	17589	Paramount Mattress Inc	2515	F	323 264-3451	4735
Mod2 Inc	7372	F	213 747-8424	24176	Parts Out Inc (PA)	3694	F	626 560-1540	19199
Modern Gold Design Inc	3911	E	213 614-1818	22550	Patriot Lighting Inc	3646	F	213 741-9757	17064
Modern Metals Industries Inc	3841	E	800 437-6633	21826	Peep Inc	2339	E	213 748-5500	3384
Modular Communications Systems	3663	E	818 764-1333	17590	Peking Noodle Co Inc	2098	E	323 223-0897	2379
Monarchy Diamond Inc	1499	B	213 924-1161	392	Penhouse Media Group Inc	2721	E	310 575-4835	6000
Monopole Inc	2851	F	818 500-8585	8658	Pentrate Metal Processing	3471	E	323 269-2121	13069
Monrow Inc	2331	F	213 741-6007	3181	Peoples Sausage Company	2013	E	213 627-8633	488
Monterey Canyon LLC (PA)	2339	D	213 741-0209	3375	Perfection Machine and TI Work	3599	F	213 749-5095	16293
Morris Kitchen Inc	2099	F	646 413-5186	2558	Petrochem Marketing	2951	F	323 526-4084	9102
Morrissey Bros Printers Inc	2759	E	323 233-7197	7145	Petroil Americas Limited	2911	F	323 931-3720	9062
Mother Plucker Feather Co Inc	3999	F	213 637-0411	23416	Pharmaco-Kinesis Corporation	3841	E	310 641-2700	21857
Motorola Solutions Inc	3663	E	213 362-6706	17596	Phoenix Aerial Systems Inc	3829	F	323 577-3366	21520
Motorola Solutions Inc	3663	C	954 723-4730	17597	Pierre Mitri (PA)	2339	F	213 747-1838	3388
MSP Group Inc	2211	E	310 660-0022	2704	Piet Retief Inc	2339	E	323 732-8312	3389
MXF Designs Inc	2331	D	323 266-1451	3182	Pinnacle Worldwide Inc	3629	E	909 628-2200	16793
Naftex Westside Partners Limit	1311	E	310 277-9004	58	Pioneer Diecasters Inc	3363	F	323 245-6561	11346
Naked Princess Worldwide LLC (PA)	2844	F	310 271-1199	8544	Pitney Bowes Inc	3579	E	310 312-4288	15390
NAPA Industries Inc	3999	F	310 293-1209	23419	Planned Parenthood Los Angeles	2741	E	323 256-1717	6310
Nareg Jewelry Inc	3911	E	213 683-1660	22552	Plastique Unique Inc	3089	E	310 839-3968	9976
Nathan Kimmel Company LLC	2394	F	213 627-8556	3693	Plastopan Industries Inc (PA)	2655	E	323 231-2225	5300
National Diamond Lab Cal	3545	F	818 240-5770	14177	Plastpro 2000 Inc (PA)	3089	C	310 693-8600	9978
National Ready Mixed Con Co	3273	F	323 245-5539	10806	Playboy Enterprises Inc	2721	D	310 424-1800	6004
Nationwide Jewelry Mfrs Inc	3911	F	213 489-1215	22553	Playboy Enterprises Intl Inc	2741	D	310 424-1800	6311
Native American Media	2721	E	310 475-6845	5993	Plush Home Inc	2511	E	323 852-1912	4602
Nelson Jewellery (usa) Inc	3915	E	213 489-3323	22598	Poetry Corporation (PA)	2337	E	213 765-8957	3272
Nelson Name Plate Company (PA)	2759	C	323 663-3971	7147	Pollstar LLC (PA)	2721	D	559 271-7900	6006
Netmarble Us Inc	2741	F	714 276-1196	6295	Polyalloys Injected Metals Inc	3532	D	310 715-9800	13759
Network Automation Inc	7372	E	213 738-1700	24198	Polymond Dk Inc	2339	E	213 327-0771	3391
Neural Analytics Inc	3841	F	818 317-4999	21833	Polytex Manufacturing Inc (PA)	2284	E	323 726-0140	2893
New Fragrance Continental	2844	F	323 766-0060	8547	Popular TV Networks LLC	2711	F	323 822-3324	5800
New Green Day LLC	2611	E	323 566-7603	5094	Potnetwork Holdings Inc	2833	F	800 915-3060	7683
New Rise Brand Holdings LLC	2325	E	323 233-9005	3016	Power Fasteners Inc	3452	E	323 232-4362	12690
Nexsun Corp	2869	E	213 382-2220	8757	PPG Industries Inc	2851	E	310 559-2335	8666
Nexxen Apparel Inc (PA)	2339	F	323 267-9900	3376	Practice Management Info Corp (PA)	2731	E	323 954-0224	6138
Night Fashion Inc	2335	E	213 747-8740	3245	Precision Steel Products Inc	3444	E	310 523-2002	12339
Ninja Jump Inc	3944	D	323 255-5418	22701	Precision Wire Products Inc	3312	E	323 569-8165	11060
Noahs Ark International Inc	2331	F	714 521-1235	3184	Press Brothers Juicery LLC	2033	E	213 389-3645	817
Nonstop Printing Inc	2752	E	323 464-1640	6751	Pressure Profile Systems Inc	3823	E	310 641-8100	20920
Norchem Corporation (PA)	3559	D	323 221-0221	14508	Prints Charmn Inc (PA)	2752	F	310 312-0904	6811
Normandie Country Bakery Inc (PA)	2051	E	323 939-5528	1249	Private Brand Mdsg Corp	2335	E	213 749-0191	3249
Not Only Jeans LLC	2211	E	213 765-9725	2705	Pro Tag Corp	2253	E	213 272-9606	2800
Novela Designs Inc	3961	F	213 505-4092	22991	Project Social T LLC	2331	E	323 266-4500	3189
NRC USA Inc	3639	F	213 325-2780	16852	Promises Promises Inc	2335	E	213 749-7725	3251
Nuorder Inc	7372	E	310 954-1313	24217	Proto Homes LLC	3792	E	310 271-7544	20492
Oak Apparel Inc	2339	F	213 489-9766	3379	Prudential Lighting Corp (PA)	3646	C	213 477-1694	17066
Ocean Beauty Seafoods LLC	2091	C	213 624-2101	2246	PSM Industries Inc (PA)	3499	D	888 663-8256	13540
Off Price Network LLC	2337	E	213 477-8205	3271	Puma Biotechnology Inc (PA)	2834	D	424 248-6500	8090
Offenhauser Sales Corp	3714	F	323 225-1307	19731	Pure Cotton Incorporated	2326	D	213 507-3270	3049
Offline Inc	2342	F	213 742-9001	3456	Pvh Neckwear Inc (HQ)	2323	A	213 688-7970	3001
Ola Corporate Services Inc	3579	F	323 655-1005	15385	Pw Eagle Inc	3084	B	800 621-4404	9474
Old Country Millwork Inc	3547	E	323 234-2940	14234	Q&A7 LLC	2339	F	323 364-4250	3395
Old Pueblo Ranch Inc	2099	C	323 268-2791	2575	Q-Lite Usa LLC	3643	C	310 736-2977	16922
Omega Graphics Printing Hollyw	2752	F	213 784-5200	6758	Qjm Inc	3911	F	213 622-0264	22559
On-Line Power Incorporated (PA)	3612	E	323 721-5017	16565	Qre Operating LLC	1382	C	213 225-5900	134
ONeil Capital Management	2754	D	310 448-6400	6961	R & R Industries Inc	2395	E	323 581-6000	3753
ONeil Digital Solutions LLC	2752	C	310 448-6407	6760	R R Donnelley & Sons Company	2759	F	310 789-4100	7192
Ophir Rf Inc	3663	E	310 306-5556	17609	Rada Industry	3999	F	323 265-3727	23456
Opti Lite Optical	3851	F	323 932-6828	22379	Rafu Shimpo	2711	E	213 629-2231	5806
Orange Corporation	2342	F	323 266-0700	3457	Rainbow Manufacturing Co Inc	2521	E	323 778-2093	4818
Orbita Corp (PA)	2381	F	213 746-4783	3503	Rainbow Novelty Creations Co	2261	E	323 855-9464	2835
Ordway Metal Polishing	3471	E	323 225-3373	13067	Rainbow Sublymation Inc	2759	E	213 489-5001	7193
Organicsorb LLC	1499	F	310 795-4011	393	Ram Off Road Accessories Inc	3714	E	323 266-3850	19754
Originclear Inc (PA)	3589	F	323 939-6645	15553	Randolph & Hein	2511	E	323 233-6010	4605
Orora Visual TX LLC	2759	D	323 258-4111	7163	Rangefinder Publishing Co Inc	2721	F	310 846-4770	6013
Output Inc	7372	F	310 795-6099	24281	Rapid Anodizing LLC	3559	F	323 753-5255	14525
P & R Pallets Inc	2448	E	213 327-1104	4382	Rau Restoration	2431	F	310 445-1128	4112
P Kay Metal Inc (PA)	3356	F	323 585-5058	11279	Ready Industries Inc	2752	F	213 749-2041	6838
P&P Enterprises	3993	F	213 802-0890	23174	Recruitment Services Inc	2721	F	213 364-1960	6015
Pabst Brewing Company LLC (PA)	2082	B	310 470-0962	1557	Red Brick Corporation	2752	F	323 549-9444	6839
Pac Fill Inc	2026	E	818 409-0117	706	Red Engine Inc	2325	F	213 742-8858	3017
Pacific Coast Bach Label Co	2269	F	213 612-0314	2857	Regal Furniture Manufacturing	2512	F	323 971-9185	4666
Pacific Coast Ironworks Inc	3441	F	323 585-1320	11858	Relational Center	7372	E	323 935-1807	24355
Pacific Jewelry Services	3911	E	213 627-3337	22557	Remba Partners LLC	2741	F	310 858-8495	6329
Pacific Manufacturing MGT Inc	2542	D	323 263-9000	4995	Renee C	2337	F	213 741-0095	3274
Pacific Play Tents Inc	2394	E	323 269-0431	3695	Rentech Inc	2999	D	310 571-9800	9161
Padilla Jewelers Inc	3911	F	323 931-1678	22558	Rentech Ntrgn Pasadena Spa LLC	2873	F	310 571-9805	8802
Padilla Remberto	2261	F	323 268-1111	2833	Reyes Coca-Cola Bottling LLC	2086	E	213 744-8659	2154
Pai Gp Inc	3231	D	323 549-5355	10385	Rfl Global Inc	7372	F	323 235-2580	24361

Company	SIC	EMP	PHONE	ENTRY #
Rhapsody Clothing Inc	2339	D	213 614-8887	3398
Rheetech Sales & Services Inc	2759	F	213 749-9111	7200
Rhodes Publications Inc	2721	F	213 385-4781	6018
Richee Lighting Inc	3648	F	213 814-1638	17159
Ricky Reader LLC	2731	F	323 231-4322	6141
Rider Circulation Services	2711	F	213 344-1200	5810
Rising Beverage Company LLC	2086	D	310 556-4500	2159
RJ Jewelry Inc	3911	F	213 627-9936	22564
RJ Singer International Inc	3161	D	323 735-1717	10204
Rm 518 Management LLC	2389	F	213 624-6788	3577
Rnk Industries Co	2211	F	323 446-0777	2710
Rnovate Inc	3568	E	213 489-1617	14791
Robeks Corporation	2099	F	310 642-7800	2601
Rock Rag Inc	2741	F	818 919-9364	6332
Roman Upholstery Manufacturing	2512	F	310 479-3252	4668
Ron Teeguarden Enterprises Inc (PA)	2833	E	323 556-8188	7687
Ronald D Teson Inc	2426	E	310 532-5987	3983
Rondor Music International (PA)	2741	D	310 235-4800	6333
Roscoe Moss Manufacturing Co (PA)	3317	D	323 261-4185	11134
Roscoe Moss Manufacturing Co	3317	D	323 263-4111	11135
Rose Genuine Inc	2361	F	213 747-4120	3487
Rosenkranz Enterprises Inc	3471	F	323 583-9021	13090
Rosetti Gennaro Furniture	2511	E	323 750-7794	4607
Roy E Hanson Jr Mfg (PA)	3443	D	213 747-7514	12047
Rpsz Construction LLC	3949	E	314 677-5831	22877
Rtg Investment Group Inc	3949	F	310 444-5554	22878
Rucci Inc	3999	F	323 778-9000	23464
Ruth Training Center Sew Mchs	2399	F	213 748-8033	3857
S D M Furniture Co Inc	2511	F	323 936-0295	4609
S Sedghi Inc (PA)	2361	E	213 745-2019	3489
S Studio Inc	2337	D	213 388-7400	3276
S&B Development Group LLC	2221	E	213 446-2818	2732
S&H International Inc	3645	F	213 626-7112	16989
Sadie & Sage Inc (PA)	2331	F	213 234-2188	3190
Sage Machado Inc	3911	F	323 931-0595	22567
Sakura Noodle Inc	2098	F	213 623-2396	2380
Sam Vaziri Vance Inc (PA)	3851	E	323 822-3955	22384
Samis Sports	3949	F	323 965-8093	22883
Sams Trade Development Corp	3961	F	213 225-0188	22994
Samyang USA Inc	2098	F	562 946-9977	2381
San Antonio Winery Inc (PA)	2084	C	323 223-1401	1906
Sanitek Products Inc	2842	F	323 245-6781	8416
Santa Monica City of	3589	F	310 826-6712	15574
Sbnw LLC (PA)	3171	C	213 234-5122	10226
Scottex Inc	2399	F	310 516-1411	3859
Sea Snack Foods Inc (PA)	2092	E	213 622-2204	2269
Second Generation Inc	2339	D	213 743-8700	3402
Secret Road Music Pubg Inc	2731	F	323 464-1234	6145
Securedata Inc	7372	F	424 363-8529	24395
Security Textile Corporation	2396	D	213 747-2673	3812
Sedas Printing Inc	2752	F	323 469-1034	6856
Sees Candy Shops Incorporated	2064	C	310 559-4919	1399
Semore Inc	2325	F	213 746-4122	3019
Sencha Naturals Inc	2064	F	213 353-9908	1400
Seollem Corporation	2326	F	323 265-3266	3052
Serv-Rite Meat Company Inc	2011	D	323 227-1911	424
Sgk LLC	2796	C	323 258-4111	7382
Sieena Inc	7372	E	310 455-6188	24408
Siemens Hlthcare Dgnostics Inc	2835	D	310 645-8200	8256
Siemens Industry Inc	3569	E	724 772-1237	14858
Silver Textile Incorporated	2241	F	213 747-2221	2761
Silvestri Studio Inc (PA)	3999	D	323 277-4420	23476
Silvias Costumes	2389	E	323 661-2142	3579
Silvus Technologies Inc (PA)	3663	E	310 479-3333	17660
Simon of California (PA)	3161	F	310 559-4871	10208
Sissell Bros	3272	F	323 261-0106	10651
Skate Group Inc	2389	F	213 749-6651	3580
Skirt Inc	2326	F	213 553-1134	3054
Sky Jeans Inc	2211	F	323 778-2065	2711
Sky Luxury Corp	2339	E	323 940-0111	3407
Sleepow Ltd	2211	E	646 688-0808	2712
Smb Clothing Inc	2339	F	213 489-4949	3408
SMD Enterprises Inc	3253	E	323 235-4151	10450
Smiley Group Inc (PA)	2731	F	323 290-4690	6146
Snack It Forward LLC	2096	E	310 242-5517	2345
Snf Holding Company	2899	F	323 266-4435	9025
Sofa U Love (PA)	2512	E	323 464-3397	4670
Songbird Ocarinas Inc	3931	F	323 269-2524	22640
Songs Music Publishing LLC	2741	F	323 939-3511	6342
Sonicsensory Inc (PA)	3021	F	213 336-3747	9184
Sony/Atv Music Publishing LLC	2741	E	310 441-1300	6343
Sooraksan Soojebi	3421	F	213 389-2818	11519
Soteleo Salvadar	3993	E	213 621-2040	23213
Southwest Plating Co Inc	3471	F	323 753-3781	13103
Specialists In Cstm Sftwr Inc	7372	E	310 315-9660	24439
Specialty Surface Grinding	3599	F	310 538-4352	16416
Spectrum Plating Company Inc	3471	E	310 533-0748	13104
Spoety Cuts Corporation	2869	F	310 908-1512	8777
SSC Apparel Inc	2339	E	213 746-0200	3411
Stadco (PA)	3545	C	323 227-8888	14198
Stainless Industrial Companies	3544	D	310 575-9400	14106
Standard Homeopathic Co (PA)	2834	D	310 768-0700	8142
Standardvision LLC	3993	E	323 222-3630	23215
Staples Inc	2339	F	213 623-4395	3414
Star Ave	2339	E	213 623-5799	3415
Stardust Diamond Corp	3915	F	213 239-9999	22601
Starlion Inc	2321	E	323 233-8823	2994
Stella Fashions Inc	2339	E	213 746-6889	3416
Stepstone Inc	3272	E	310 327-7474	10657
Stic-Adhesive Products Co Inc	2891	C	323 268-2956	8895
Stitch Factory	2395	F	310 523-3337	3758
Stone Canyon Industries LLC (PA)	3089	D	310 570-4869	10072
Stone Merchants LLC	3281	F	310 471-1815	10934
Stony Apparel Corp (PA)	2339	C	323 981-9080	3417
Studio Systems Inc (PA)	2741	E	323 634-3400	6350
Style Plus Inc (PA)	2331	F	213 205-8408	3195
Style Up America Inc	3949	F	213 553-1134	22899
Sugarsync Inc	7372	F	650 571-5105	24465
Sun Valley Products Inc	3354	E	818 247-8350	11246
Sun Valley Products Inc (HQ)	3354	D	818 247-8350	11247
Sunflower Imports Inc	2329	F	213 748-3444	3121
Sunnyside Llc	2341	F	213 745-3070	3449
Sunrise Wood Products Inc	2431	E	323 971-6540	4133
Super Vias & Trim	2396	F	323 233-2556	3818
Superior Emblem & Embroidery	2395	E	213 747-4103	3760
Superior Pipe Fabricators Inc	3441	F	323 569-6500	11891
Surco Products Inc	3446	F	310 323-2520	12512
Surgeon Worldwide Inc	3144	E	707 501-7962	10177
Suri Steel Inc	3441	F	323 224-1166	11892
Susan Zadi	2092	F	424 223-3526	2272
Sustain Technologies Inc (PA)	3695	F	213 229-5300	19235
Swimwear	2339	E	323 584-7536	3419
Sysop Tools Inc	7372	F	310 598-3885	24482
Systems Wire & Cable Limited	3496	D	310 532-7870	13438
T-Bags LLC	2339	F	323 225-9525	3420
Tae Gwang Inc	3993	F	323 233-2882	23225
Tallygo Inc (PA)	7372	F	510 858-1969	24487
Talyarps Corporation	2851	E	310 559-2335	8685
Tampico Spice Co Incorporated	2099	F	323 235-3154	2622
Target Media Partners Oper LLC	2711	E	323 930-3123	5846
Tarina Tarantino Designs LLC	3911	F	213 533-8070	22577
Taschen America LLC (PA)	2731	F	323 463-4441	6150
Taseon Inc	3825	D	408 240-7800	21135
Tasker Metal Products Inc	3714	F	213 765-5400	19778
Tcj Manufacturing LLC	2339	E	213 488-8400	3421
Tdg Operations LLC	2273	D	323 724-9000	2882
Teksun Inc	3089	F	310 479-0794	10081
Teledyne Technologies Inc	3679	B	310 820-4616	19110
Teledyne Technologies Inc	3679	B	310 822-8229	19112
Tenenblatt Corporation	2257	C	323 232-2061	2813
Tennis Media Co LLC	2721	F	310 966-8182	6039
Tex-Coat LLC	2851	E	323 233-3111	8686
That Casting Place Inc	3915	F	323 258-5691	22603
Thats It Nutrition LLC	2064	F	818 782-1701	1404
Thc Design LLC	3999	F	562 980-0056	23502
The Microfilm Company of Cal	2731	F	310 354-2610	6154
Thebrain Technologies LP	7372	F	310 751-5000	24500
Thomson Reuters Corporation	3663	F	877 518-2761	17691
Thousand LLC	3949	F	310 745-0110	22907
Tianello Inc	2331	C	323 231-0599	3200
Tidings	2711	F	213 637-7360	5849
Times Litho Inc	2752	E	503 359-0300	6891
Tk and Company Watches	3911	F	213 545-1971	22580
TLC Logistics Inc	2679	F	323 665-0474	5538
Tokyopop Inc	2731	D	323 920-5967	6155
Tomasini Inc	2221	E	323 231-2349	2737
Topline Game Labs LLC	7372	F	310 461-0350	24518
Topson Downs California Inc	2337	E	310 558-0300	3278
Tortilleria La California Inc	2099	E	323 221-8940	2630
Tortilleria San Marcos	2099	E	323 263-0208	2632
Tortolani Inc	3993	F	323 268-1488	23230
Tosco - Tool Specialty Company	3545	E	323 232-3561	14204
Toska Inc	2339	F	213 746-0088	3425
Total Cmmnicator Solutions Inc	7372	D	619 277-1488	24521
Touch ME Fashion Inc	2339	E	323 234-9200	3426
Tourism Development Corp (PA)	2721	F	310 280-2860	6043
Toykidz Inc	3999	F	213 688-2999	23507
Transformationnet Media LLC	2721	F	310 476-5259	6044
Travel Computer Systems Inc	7372	F	310 558-3130	24525
Tres Bien Inc (PA)	2339	F	213 747-3366	3428

Employment Codes: A=Over 500 employees, B=251-500,
C=101-250, D=51-100, E=20-50, F=10-19

2020 California
Manufacturers Register

© Mergent Inc. 1-800-342-5647

1365

GEOGRAPHIC

	SIC	EMP	PHONE	ENTRY #
Tribe Media Corp	2711	E	213 368-1661	5852
Tribune Los Angeles Inc	2711	F	213 237-5000	5853
Tripos Industries Inc	3432	E	323 669-0488	11685
Triyar Capital California LLC **(PA)**	3728	F	310 441-5654	20263
Tropical Preserving Co Inc	2033	F	213 748-5108	831
Trusted Energy LLC	1311	F	818 646-3137	73
Tua Fashion Inc **(PA)**	2211	F	213 422-2384	2715
Tubular Specialties Mfg Inc	3261	D	310 515-4801	10468
Tvs Distributors Inc	3965	F	323 268-1347	23013
Twelve Signs Inc	2721	D	310 553-8000	6045
Ubtech Robotics Corp	3549	E	213 261-7153	14285
Ultra Built Kitchens Inc	2434	E	323 232-3362	4257
Umeya Inc	2052	F	213 626-8341	1335
Umgee USA Inc	2331	F	323 526-9138	3204
Unique Apparel Inc	2339	D	213 321-8192	3429
Universal Dyeing & Printing	2262	F	213 746-0818	2848
Universal Surface Techlgy Inc	2841	E	310 352-6969	8354
Upper Crust Enterprises Inc	2099	F	213 625-0038	2643
US Premier Inc	2331	F	323 267-4463	3206
US Wholesale Drug Corp	2834	F	323 227-4258	8175
V & M Plating Co	3471	F	310 532-5633	13126
V I P Ironworks Inc	3446	F	310 216-2890	12518
Vagrant Records Inc	2782	F	323 302-0100	7322
Vahe Enterprises Inc	3713	D	323 235-6657	19560
Valerie Trading Inc	2269	E	323 231-4255	2862
Valmas Inc	2335	F	323 677-2211	3260
Valmont Industries Inc	3441	D	323 264-6660	11910
Vega Textile Inc	2241	F	323 923-0600	2763
Venator Americas LLC	2816	D	323 269-7311	7465
Venture Capital Entps LLC	2024	F	914 275-7305	676
Veteran Enterprise Inc	2211	F	323 937-2233	2717
Vf Contemporary Brands Inc	2325	F	213 747-7002	3021
Victor Wire and Cable LLC	3357	F	310 842-9933	11325
Videoamp Inc **(PA)**	7372	F	949 294-0351	24560
Vigilant Ballistics Inc	3271	F	213 212-3232	10524
Viking Ready Mix Co Inc	3273	E	818 243-4243	10859
Virgil M Stutzman Inc	3471	F	323 732-9146	13128
Vision Envelope & Prtg Co Inc **(PA)**	2677	E	310 324-7062	5476
Vision Smart Center Inc	2833	F	213 625-1740	7702
Visoy Food Products & Mfg Inc	2075	F	323 221-4079	1447
Vitality Inst Med Pdts Inc	2844	F	310 587-1910	8605
Vm Provider LLC **(PA)**	2252	F	800 674-3233	2770
Voteblast Inc	2741	E	650 387-9147	6376
WAbenjamin Electric Co	3613	E	213 749-7731	16622
Walker Foods Inc	2033	D	323 268-5191	837
Wanada Investments LLC	7372	E	818 292-8627	24573
Warnaco Swimwear Inc **(DH)**	2329	E	323 837-6000	3129
Warner/Chappell Music Inc **(DH)**	2741	C	310 441-8600	6380
Warren Printing & Mailing Inc	2752	F	323 258-2621	6927
Washington Garment Dyeing **(PA)**	2262	D	213 747-1111	2849
Washington Garment Dyeing	2261	E	213 747-1111	2841
Wave Community Newspapers Inc **(PA)**	2711	E	323 290-3000	5862
We Five-R Corporation	3471	E	323 263-6757	13129
Wearable Integrity Inc	2339	E	213 748-6044	3434
Webalo Inc	3695	F	310 828-7335	19242
Weddingchannelcom Inc	2741	C	213 599-4100	6382
Wesley Allen Inc **(PA)**	2514	C	323 231-4275	4708
Wessco International Ltd A C **(PA)**	2393	E	310 477-4272	3668
West E Cmnty Access Netwrk Inc	3721	D	323 967-0520	19937
West Publishing Corporation	2731	E	800 747-3161	6161
Western Bagel Baking Corp	2051	D	310 479-4823	1294
Western Die & Printing Corp	2759	F	323 665-0474	7268
Western Motor Works Inc	3553	F	310 382-6896	14302
Western Supreme Inc	2015	C	213 627-3861	531
Winc Inc	2084	F	855 282-5829	2003
Winter & Bain Manufacturing **(PA)**	3534	F	213 749-3568	13811
Winter & Bain Manufacturing	3534	F	213 749-3561	13812
Wire Technology Corporation	3357	E	310 635-6935	11327
Wise Living Inc	2519	F	323 541-0410	4777
Wls Coatings Inc	2851	F	310 538-2155	8694
Wolfson Knitting Mills Inc	2211	F	213 627-8746	2718
Wonder Marketing Inc	2851	E	310 235-1469	8695
Wonderful Pstchios Almonds LLC **(HQ)**	2068	E	310 966-4650	1442
Woodland Bedrooms Inc	2511	D	562 408-1558	4625
Worldflash Software Inc	7372	E	310 745-0632	24589
Worldwide Specialties Inc	2099	C	323 587-2200	2649
X Sublimation Inc	2389	F	213 700-1024	3585
Xcvi LLC **(PA)**	2211	F	213 749-2661	2719
Xhale Distributors	2023	F	888 942-5355	626
Y Y K Inc	3911	F	213 622-0741	22585
Yamasa Enterprises	2091	E	213 626-2211	2255
Yenor Inc	2759	F	310 410-1573	7277
YMI Jeanswear Inc **(PA)**	2335	F	323 581-7700	3261
YMi Jeanswear Inc	2339	D	213 746-6681	3436
Yocup Company	2656	F	310 884-9888	5310

	SIC	EMP	PHONE	ENTRY #
Young Knitting Mills	2253	E	323 980-8677	2809
Young Sung USA Inc	2399	F	213 427-2580	3868
Yucatan Foods LLC	2032	F	310 342-5363	752
Z B P Inc	2679	F	323 266-3363	5541
ZI Chemicals	2819	F	818 827-1301	7538

LOS BANOS, CA - Merced County

	SIC	EMP	PHONE	ENTRY #
Azusa Rock Inc	3273	E	209 826-5066	10694
Cheese Administrative Corp Inc	2022	E	209 826-3744	544
Ingomar Packing Company LLC **(PA)**	2033	D	209 826-9494	777
Kagome Inc **(HQ)**	2033	C	209 826-8850	782
Los Banos Abattoir Co Inc	2011	E	209 826-2212	416
McClatchy Newspapers Inc	2711	D	209 826-3831	5732
Morning Star Company	2033	D	209 827-2724	797
Morning Star Packing Co LP	2033	E	209 826-8000	798

LOS GATOS, CA - Santa Clara County

	SIC	EMP	PHONE	ENTRY #
Accurite Technologies Inc	3577	F	408 395-7100	15141
Acquis Inc	7372	F	408 402-5367	23551
Adara Power Inc	3691	F	844 223-2969	19151
Atomera Incorporated	3674	F	408 442-5248	18131
Brightsign LLC	3993	D	408 852-9263	23066
C B Concrete Construction	3273	F	408 354-3484	10700
Chemical & Material Technology	3827	F	408 354-2656	21343
Cirtec Medical LLC	3841	D	408 395-0443	21665
Cryptic Studios Inc	3944	F	408 399-1969	22669
Depuy Synthes Products Inc	3841	F	408 246-4300	21679
E-Fuel Corporation	3699	F	408 267-2667	19299
Einstein Noah Rest Group Inc	2022	F	408 358-5895	548
Facilitron Inc **(PA)**	7372	F	800 272-2962	23891
Foodlink Online LLC	7372	F	408 395-7280	23908
Healthywealthyhack Inc	7372	F	669 225-3745	23973
Highwire Press Inc **(PA)**	2741	E	650 721-6388	6251
McCarthy Ranch	2452	E	408 356-2300	4464
Netflix Inc **(PA)**	2741	C	408 540-3700	6294
Pulsar Vascular Inc	3841	F	408 246-4300	21868
Pulver Laboratories Inc	3625	F	408 399-7000	16740
Ritchey Design Inc **(PA)**	3751	F	650 368-4018	20424
Sadra Medical Inc	3841	F	408 370-1550	21886
Semotus Inc	7372	F	408 667-2046	24396
Suvolta Inc	3559	F	408 866-4125	14542
Tascent Inc	3699	F	650 799-4611	19419
Tela Innovations Inc	3674	F	408 558-6300	18606
Testarossa Vineyards LLC	2084	E	408 354-6150	1952
Wacker Development Inc	3599	F	408 356-0208	16507
Automation & Entertainment Inc **(PA)**	3491	F	408 353-4223	13291
David Bruce Winery Inc	2084	F	408 354-4214	1657
Ols Controls	3822	F	408 353-6564	20802
Rhys Vineyards LLC	2084	F	650 419-2050	1887
Vulcan Aggregates Company LLC	1442	F	408 354-7904	365

LOS OLIVOS, CA - Santa Barbara County

	SIC	EMP	PHONE	ENTRY #
Escalera-Boulet LLC	2084	F	805 691-1020	1691
Firestone Vineyard LP	2084	D	805 688-3940	1703
Stolpman Vineyards LLC **(PA)**	2084	F	805 736-5000	1934

LOS OSOS, CA - San Luis Obispo County

	SIC	EMP	PHONE	ENTRY #
California Resources Corp	1311	E	661 763-6107	34
Cygnet Aerospace Corp	3365	F	805 528-2376	11374

LOWER LAKE, CA - Lake County

	SIC	EMP	PHONE	ENTRY #
Aloha Bay	3999	E	707 994-3267	23271
Barrick Gold Corporation	1041	D	707 995-6070	1
Clearlake Lava Inc	3273	F	707 995-1515	10745
Parker Plastics Inc	3089	E	707 994-6363	9955
Shannon Ridge Inc	2084	E	707 994-9656	1914

LUCERNE VALLEY, CA - San Bernardino County

	SIC	EMP	PHONE	ENTRY #
Mitsubishi Cement Corporation	3241	C	760 248-7373	10423
Omya California Inc	2819	D	760 248-7306	7513
Specialty Minerals Inc	1422	C	760 248-5300	304

LYNWOOD, CA - Los Angeles County

	SIC	EMP	PHONE	ENTRY #
Ace Machine Shop Inc	3599	D	310 608-2277	15681
Amerasia Furniture Components	2512	E	310 638-0570	4628
California Steel Products	3449	F	310 603-5645	12587
D & D Motorcycle Service Inc	3751	E	323 567-9480	20396
Ermm Corporation	3715	E	310 635-0524	19820
First Finish Inc	2211	E	310 631-6717	2688
Gomen Furniture Mfg Inc	2512	E	310 635-4894	4643
Hgc Holdings Inc	2064	C	323 567-2226	1371
Kayo of California	2339	E	310 605-2693	3352
La Candelaria Manufacturing	2511	F	310 763-0112	4585
Leos Metal Polishing	3471	F	310 635-5257	13041
Linens Exchange Inc	2299	F	310 638-5507	2944
Metal Improvement Company LLC	3398	E	323 585-2168	11456
Metal Improvement Company LLC	3398	F	323 563-1533	11462
Next Day Frame Inc	2519	D	310 886-0851	4767

2020 California
Manufacturers Register

(P-0000) Products & Services Section entry number
(PA)=Parent Co (HQ)=Headquarters (DH)=Div Headquarters

	SIC	EMP	PHONE	ENTRY #
P & L Development LLC	2841	C	323 567-2482	8346
P & L Development LLC	2834	E	310 763-1377	8059
Pacific Ltg & Standards Co	3646	E	310 603-9344	17062
Polynt Composites USA Inc	2821	F	310 886-1070	7595
Roger R Caruso Enterprises Inc	2448	E	714 778-6006	4397
Therm-O-Namel Inc	3479	F	310 631-7866	13259
Tjs Metal Manufacturing Inc	3446	E	310 604-1545	12516
Triumph Processing Inc	3471	C	323 563-1338	13120
Wasatch Co	2392	F	310 637-6160	3649

MADERA, CA - Madera County

	SIC	EMP	PHONE	ENTRY #
Advanced Drainage Systems Inc	3084	E	559 674-4989	9462
Ardagh Glass Inc	3221	E	559 675-4700	10283
B-K Lighting Inc	3645	D	559 438-5800	16965
Baltimore Aircoil Company Inc	3585	C	559 673-9231	15415
Better Cleaning Systems Inc	3635	E	559 673-5700	16843
Canandaigua Wine Company Inc	2084	A	559 673-7071	1619
Carris Reels California Inc (HQ)	2499	E	559 674-0804	4496
Church & Dwight Co Inc	2812	E	559 661-2790	7384
Color-Box LLC	2653	E	559 674-1049	5209
Constellation Brands US Oprs	2084	A	559 485-0141	1647
Design Industries Inc	3272	E	559 675-3535	10560
Domries Enterprises Inc	3523	E	559 485-4306	13626
Encore Fine Cabinetry Inc	2434	F	559 822-4333	4191
Evapco Inc	3585	C	559 673-2207	15431
Florestone Products Co (PA)	3088	E	559 661-4171	9587
Gardner Family Ltd Partnership	3429	E	559 675-8149	11591
Georgia-Pacific LLC	2653	C	559 674-4685	5228
Golden Vly Grape Jice Wine LLC (PA)	2084	F	559 661-4657	1730
Hastings Irrigation Pipe Co	3354	F	559 675-1200	11232
Horn Machine Tools Inc	3542	E	559 431-4131	13977
Innovtive Rttional Molding Inc	3089	F	559 673-4764	9841
John Bean Technologies Corp	3556	C	559 661-3200	14377
La Viena Ranch	2034	E	559 674-6725	851
Lees Concrete Materials Inc	3273	F	559 486-2440	10780
Madera Carports Inc	3448	F	559 662-1815	12556
Madera Printing & Pubg Co Inc	2711	E	559 674-2424	5716
Moore Quality Galvanizing Inc	3479	E	559 673-2822	13208
Moore Quality Galvanizing LP	3479	E	559 673-2822	13209
Muscle Road Inc	3714	F	559 499-6888	19725
Nutra Blend LLC	2048	D	559 661-6161	1114
Oldcastle Infrastructure Inc	3499	E	559 674-8093	13536
Oldcastle Infrastructure Inc	3272	E	559 675-1813	10615
P T M Inc	2448	F	559 673-1552	4383
Pacific Sheet Metal Inc	3444	F	559 661-4044	12327
Performance Trailers Inc	3715	E	559 673-6300	19828
Praxair Inc	2813	E	559 674-7306	7431
Quady LLC (PA)	2084	F	559 673-8068	1875
Quady Winery Inc	2084	F	559 673-8068	1876
Shafer Metal Stake (PA)	3444	F	559 674-9487	12372
Sinbad Foods LLC	2099	E	559 674-4445	2612
Star Finishes Inc	3471	F	559 261-1076	13108
Steel Structures Inc	3443	E	559 673-8021	12057
Sunsweet Dryers Inc	2034	F	559 673-4140	869
Teka Illumination Inc	3648	F	559 438-5800	17167
Ultra Gro LLC	2873	E	559 661-0977	8806
Victor Packing Inc	2034	E	559 673-5908	874
Warnock Food Products Inc	2096	D	559 661-4845	2348

MADISON, CA - Yolo County

	SIC	EMP	PHONE	ENTRY #
Cemex Cnstr Mtls PCF LLC	3273	E	530 666-2137	10728

MAGALIA, CA - Butte County

	SIC	EMP	PHONE	ENTRY #
Quality Craft Mold Inc	3312	F	530 873-7790	11062

MALIBU, CA - Los Angeles County

	SIC	EMP	PHONE	ENTRY #
Cafecito Organico Oc LLC	2095	F	213 537-8367	2280
County of Los Angeles	3531	F	310 456-8014	13724
Curtco Media Group LLC	2721	E	310 589-7700	5913
Edgy Soul	3961	F	310 800-2861	22981
Games Production Company LLC	3944	F	310 456-0099	22677
Malibu Enterprises Inc	2711	E	310 457-2112	5718
Malibu Times Inc	2711	F	310 456-5507	5719
Marys Country Kitchen	2053	F	310 456-7845	1345
Robb Curtco Media LLC	2721	E	310 589-7700	6020
Studio Krp LLC	2335	F	310 589-5777	3254
Sutherland Presses	3542	F	310 453-6981	13995
West Rapco Environmental Svcs	3544	F	310 450-3335	14125

MAMMOTH LAKES, CA - Mono County

	SIC	EMP	PHONE	ENTRY #
Fluidix Inc (PA)	3567	F	760 935-2016	14762
Horizon Cal Publications	2711	F	760 934-3929	5666
Nato LLC	3999	E	760 934-8677	23420

MANHATTAN BEACH, CA - Los Angeles County

	SIC	EMP	PHONE	ENTRY #
Applecore	2396	F	310 567-6768	3770
Autumn Milling Co Inc	2421	E	310 635-0703	3925

	SIC	EMP	PHONE	ENTRY #
De Nora Water Technologies Inc	3589	D	310 618-9700	15506
Dhy Inc	2329	E	310 376-7512	3075
Gasser-Olds Inc	3366	E	323 583-9031	11400
Joe Montana Footwear	3021	D	310 318-3100	9173
Sachs & Associates Inc	3572	E	310 356-7911	15086
Skechers Collection LLC (HQ)	3021	E	310 318-3100	9181
Skechers USA Inc	3021	E	310 318-3100	9182
Skechers USA Inc (PA)	3149	D	310 318-3100	10183
Skechers USA Inc II (HQ)	3021	E	310 318-3100	9183
Stanton Carpet Corp	2273	E	562 945-8711	2880
Trlg Intermediate Holdings LLC (PA)	2369	F	323 266-3072	3496
True Religion Apparel Inc (HQ)	2325	B	323 266-3072	3020
Vista Coatings Inc	3479	E	310 635-7697	13266

MANTECA, CA - San Joaquin County

	SIC	EMP	PHONE	ENTRY #
American Modular Systems Inc	2452	D	209 825-1921	4456
California Stl Stair Rail Mfr	3312	E	209 824-1785	11034
Delicato Vineyards (PA)	2084	C	209 824-3600	1659
Dkw Precision Machining Inc	3599	E	209 824-7899	15901
E-M Manufacturing Inc	3444	F	209 825-1800	12190
Frito-Lay North America Inc	2096	C	209 824-3700	2325
Gb Industrial Spray Inc	3479	F	209 825-7176	13182
Golnex Inc	3549	E	510 490-6003	14269
H Lima Company Inc	1499	E	209 239-6787	389
Lockheed Martin Corporation	3812	B	408 756-1400	20604
Morris Newspaper Corp Cal (HQ)	2711	D	209 249-3500	5762
Pin Hsiao & Associates LLC	2051	E	209 665-4176	1262
Price Rubber Company Inc	3052	F	209 239-7478	9204
Rochas Cabinets	2434	F	209 239-2367	4239
Sanact Inc (PA)	2842	F	925 464-2761	8415
Stanley Access Tech LLC	3423	C	209 221-4066	11546
Sunnyvalley Smoked Meats Inc	2013	C	209 825-0288	501
Supermedia LLC	2741	B	209 472-6011	6351
Tuff Boy Holding Inc	3715	E	209 239-1361	19834

MARCH ARB, CA - Riverside County

	SIC	EMP	PHONE	ENTRY #
Boeing Company	3721	A	951 571-0122	19882

MARICOPA, CA - Kern County

	SIC	EMP	PHONE	ENTRY #
Aera Energy LLC	1381	D	661 665-3200	84
Calmat Co	1422	E	661 858-2673	299
Nestle Purina Petcare Company	3999	D	661 769-8261	23423

MARINA, CA - Monterey County

	SIC	EMP	PHONE	ENTRY #
Eldridge Products Inc	3823	E	831 648-7777	20864
English Ales Brewers Inc	2082	F	831 883-3000	1524
Fort Ord Works Inc	3812	E	831 275-1294	20580
Fox Thermal Instruments Inc	3823	E	831 384-4300	20872
Hearst Corporation	2711	C	831 582-9605	5657
Indtec Corporation	3672	E	831 582-9388	17899
Lifeline Food Co Inc	2022	F	831 899-5040	566
Light & Motion Industries	3648	D	831 645-1525	17139

MARINA DEL REY, CA - Los Angeles County

	SIC	EMP	PHONE	ENTRY #
Ace Iron Inc	3446	C	510 324-3300	12445
Arbor Snowboards Inc	3949	E	310 577-1120	22749
Armata Pharmaceuticals Inc (PA)	2836	D	310 655-2928	8272
Dollar Shave Club Inc (HQ)	3541	E	310 975-8528	13916
Excavo LLC	2426	E	310 823-7670	3973
Sewer Rodding Equipment Co (PA)	3589	E	310 301-9009	15576
Sony Dadc US Inc	3695	E	310 760-8500	19234
Telesign Holdings Inc (DH)	7372	E	310 740-9700	24497
Twin Coast Metrology Inc (PA)	3827	F	310 709-2308	21416

MARIPOSA, CA - Mariposa County

	SIC	EMP	PHONE	ENTRY #
Haztech Systems Inc	2865	E	209 966-8088	8701
Mariposa Gazette & Miner	2711	F	209 966-2500	5725

MARTINEZ, CA - Contra Costa County

	SIC	EMP	PHONE	ENTRY #
Document Proc Solutions Inc	2621	E	925 839-1182	5102
Eco Services Operations Corp	2819	E	925 313-8224	7487
Euv Tech Inc	3826	F	925 229-4388	21227
Gibson Printing & Publishing	2711	E	925 228-6400	5646
Independent Printing Co Inc (PA)	2752	E	925 229-5050	6635
McCormacks Guides Inc	2741	F	925 229-1869	6279
Noel Burt	3592	E	925 439-7030	15614
PG Emminger Inc	2541	E	925 313-5830	4931
Shell Chemical LP	2819	D	925 313-8601	7524
Shell Martinez Refining Co	2911	A	925 313-3000	9067

MARYSVILLE, CA - Yuba County

	SIC	EMP	PHONE	ENTRY #
A Teichert & Son Inc	1442	E	530 749-1230	325
A Teichert & Son Inc	1442	E	530 743-6111	326
American Wood Fibers Inc	2421	F	530 741-3700	3923
Homewood Components Inc	2439	D	530 743-8855	4307
Mariani Packing Co Inc	2034	E	530 749-6565	853
Oldcastle Infrastructure Inc	3272	E	530 742-8368	10616
Reyes Coca-Cola Bottling LLC	2086	E	530 743-6533	2151

Employment Codes: A=Over 500 employees, B=251-500,
C=101-250, D=51-100, E=20-50, F=10-19

2020 California
Manufacturers Register

© Mergent Inc. 1-800-342-5647
1367

GEOGRAPHIC

	SIC	EMP	PHONE	ENTRY #
Suttons Forest Products	3999	F	530 741-2747	23494
Team Casing	1389	F	530 743-5424	268
US Pipe Fabrication LLC	3084	E	530 742-5171	9478

MATHER, CA - Sacramento County

	SIC	EMP	PHONE	ENTRY #
Construction Innovations LLC	3699	C	855 725-9555	19278

MAXWELL, CA - Colusa County

	SIC	EMP	PHONE	ENTRY #
American Rice Inc	2044	D	530 438-2265	1034
California Heritage Mills Inc	2044	E	530 438-2100	1037
Pacific Metal Buildings Inc	3448	F	530 438-2777	12569
Polit Farms Inc	2044	F	530 438-2759	1049

MAYWOOD, CA - Los Angeles County

	SIC	EMP	PHONE	ENTRY #
Cook Induction Heating Co Inc	3398	E	323 560-1327	11449
Gemini Film & Bag Inc (PA)	3089	E	323 582-0901	9802
Heritage Leather Company Inc	3111	E	323 983-0420	10138
Kitchen Cuts LLC	2013	E	323 560-7415	472
Regal Machine & Engrg Inc	3599	E	323 773-7462	16348
Sonora Face Co	2435	E	323 560-8188	4280
W S Dodge Oil Co Inc	2992	F	323 583-3478	9158

MC FARLAND, CA - Kern County

	SIC	EMP	PHONE	ENTRY #
Amaretto Orchards LLC	3999	E	661 399-9697	23272
Aptco LLC (PA)	2821	E	661 792-2107	7542
S & L Contracting	3444	F	661 371-6379	12362

MC KITTRICK, CA - Kern County

	SIC	EMP	PHONE	ENTRY #
Aera Energy LLC	1381	E	661 665-4400	83
Dwaynes Engineering & Cnstr	1389	D	661 762-7261	191

MCCLELLAN, CA - Sacramento County

	SIC	EMP	PHONE	ENTRY #
ASC Profiles LLC	3448	E	916 376-2899	12532
Aviate Enterprises Inc	3585	E	916 993-4000	15414
Dmea MSC	3728	E	916 568-4087	20087
Le Vu	3679	E	916 231-1594	18985
Meriliz Incorporated (PA)	2752	C	916 923-3663	6725
Northrop Grumman Systems Corp	3812	E	916 570-4454	20664
PCA Central Cal Corrugated LLC	2653	C	916 614-0580	5257

MCCLOUD, CA - Siskiyou County

	SIC	EMP	PHONE	ENTRY #
Hearst Corporation	2721	E	530 964-3131	5952

MCKINLEYVILLE, CA - Humboldt County

	SIC	EMP	PHONE	ENTRY #
American Bottling Company	2086	F	707 840-9727	2029
Cabinets By Andy Inc	2434	F	707 839-0220	4176
Ford Logging Inc	2411	F	707 840-9442	3882
Oasis Structures & Water Works	3589	F	707 839-1683	15552
Steve Morris	2411	F	707 822-8537	3910
Willow Technology Inc (PA)	7372	E	360 393-4962	24580

MECCA, CA - Riverside County

	SIC	EMP	PHONE	ENTRY #
Kerry Inc	2023	D	760 396-2116	600

MENDOCINO, CA - Mendocino County

	SIC	EMP	PHONE	ENTRY #
Iverson & Logging Inc	2411	F	707 937-0028	3888

MENIFEE, CA - Riverside County

	SIC	EMP	PHONE	ENTRY #
Blitzers Premium Frozen Yogurt	2024	F	951 679-7709	632
Datatronics Romoland Inc	3612	D	951 928-7700	16546
Quality Sheds Inc	2511	F	951 672-6750	4603
Southern California Mulch Inc	2499	F	951 352-5355	4536

MENLO PARK, CA - San Mateo County

	SIC	EMP	PHONE	ENTRY #
18 Media Inc (PA)	2721	F	650 324-1818	5872
Adverum Biotechnologies Inc	2836	D	650 272-6269	8267
Aha Labs Inc	7372	F	650 575-1425	23583
American Printing & Copy Inc	2752	F	650 325-2322	6410
Artifact Puzzles	3944	F	650 283-0589	22658
Bluerun Ventures LP	7372	F	650 462-7250	23682
C S Bio Co (PA)	2834	F	650 322-1111	7818
Calysta Inc (PA)	2869	C	650 492-6880	8728
Cfkba Inc (PA)	3357	D	650 847-3900	11297
Cohbar Inc	2834	F	650 446-7888	7844
Colby Pharmaceutical Company (PA)	2834	F	650 333-3150	7845
Corcept Therapeutics Inc	2834	C	650 327-3270	7850
Corium Inc (HQ)	2834	C	650 298-8255	7852
Countryman Associates Inc	3651	F	650 364-9988	17214
Coyne & Blanchard Inc	2721	E	650 326-6040	5911
Delmar Pharmaceutical Inc	2834	F	650 269-1984	7866
Dermira Inc	2834	B	650 421-7200	7869
Dssd Inc	3572	F	775 773-8665	15021
Earlens Corporation	3842	F	650 366-9000	22003
Evalve Inc	3494	D	650 330-8100	13352
Forty Seven Inc	2834	D	650 352-4150	7896
GE Ventures Inc	3841	E	650 233-3900	21721
Geron Corporation (PA)	2834	E	650 473-7700	7912
Infoimage of California Inc (PA)	2759	D	650 473-6388	7097
Intersect Ent Inc (PA)	3841	C	650 641-2100	21749

	SIC	EMP	PHONE	ENTRY #
Intuit Inc	7372	C	650 944-6000	24040
Iowa Approach Inc	3841	F	650 422-3633	21759
Jomar Machining Inc	3679	F	650 324-2143	18969
Katerra Inc (PA)	1389	D	650 422-3572	216
L3 Technologies Inc	3663	C	650 326-9500	17567
Lattice Data Inc	7372	C	650 800-7262	24093
Legacy Us LLC	3229	F	650 714-9750	10316
Medianews Group Inc	2711	C	650 391-1000	5744
Medical Aesthetics Menlo Park	3841	F	650 336-3358	21796
Memry Corporation	3841	C	650 463-3400	21816
Merchandising Systems Inc	2542	E	510 477-9100	4990
Monster Route Inc	3441	F	650 368-1628	11848
Motherly Inc	2741	F	917 860-9926	6286
Pacific Biosciences Cal Inc (PA)	3826	C	650 521-8000	21274
Phathom Pharmaceuticals Inc	2834	F	650 325-5156	8074
Polytec Products Corporation	3599	E	650 322-7555	16305
San Mateo Daily News	2711	E	650 327-9090	5819
Sanford Metal Processing Co	3471	F	650 327-5172	13094
Shelter Systems	2394	F	650 323-6202	3706
Stack Plastics Inc	3089	E	650 361-8600	10067
Step Mobile Inc	7372	F	203 510-3229	24455
Talis Biomedical Corporation	3826	E	650 433-3000	21296
Te Connectivity Corporation	3678	B	650 361-3333	18790
Te Connectivity Corporation	3643	A	650 361-3333	16929
Te Connectivity Corporation	3613	B	650 361-3333	16618
Te Connectivity Corporation	3643	B	650 361-3306	16931
Te Connectivity Corporation	3678	C	650 361-3302	18794
Transcend Medical Inc	3841	F	650 325-2050	21935
Tyco International MGT Co LLC	3357	B	650 361-3333	11324
Vello Systems Inc	3661	D	650 324-7688	17426
Wolfs Precision Works Inc	3599	F	650 364-1341	16533

MENTONE, CA - San Bernardino County

	SIC	EMP	PHONE	ENTRY #
Bausman and Company Inc (PA)	2521	C	909 947-0139	4786
Bps Tactical Inc	2321	F	909 794-2435	2986
Bristol Omega Inc	2541	E	909 794-6862	4886
Hovey Tile Art	3996	E	909 794-3815	23254
Marwell Corporation	3613	F	909 794-4192	16603

MERCED, CA - Merced County

	SIC	EMP	PHONE	ENTRY #
American Probe & Tech Inc	3825	F	408 263-3356	21001
Calif Frut and Tmto Ktchn LLC	2099	F	530 666-6600	2417
Fineline Industries Inc (PA)	3732	C	209 384-0255	20331
Greif Inc	2655	D	209 383-4396	5294
International Inboard Mar Inc	3732	E	209 384-2566	20340
Kirby Manufacturing Inc (PA)	3523	D	209 723-0778	13644
Laird Mfg LLC (PA)	3523	E	209 722-4145	13647
Laird Mfg LLC	3523	E	209 349-8918	13648
McClatchy Newspapers Inc	2711	C	209 722-1511	5733
Merced Screw Products Inc	3451	E	209 723-7706	12641
Mid Valley Publication	2711	E	209 383-0433	5753
Molding Acquisition Corp	2821	E	209 723-5000	7582
Olde World Corporation	2541	E	209 384-1337	4926
Qg LLC	2752	A	209 384-0444	6819
Quad/Graphics Inc	2752	B	209 384-0444	6824
Richwood Meat Company Inc	2011	D	209 722-8171	423
RTS Packaging LLC	2679	D	209 722-2787	5526
Scholle Ipn Corporation	3089	B	209 384-3100	10046
Scholle Ipn Packaging Inc	3089	B	209 384-3100	10047
Sun Power Security Gates Inc	3315	F	209 722-3990	11110
Tdl Aero Enterprises	3721	F	209 722-7300	19933
Werner Co	3499	F	209 383-3989	13556
Yosemite Vly Beef Pkg Co Inc	2011	E	626 435-0170	433

MI WUK VILLAGE, CA - Tuolumne County

	SIC	EMP	PHONE	ENTRY #
Oti Engineering Cons Inc	3663	E	209 586-1022	17612

MIDDLETOWN, CA - Lake County

	SIC	EMP	PHONE	ENTRY #
Morris Welding Co Inc	7692	F	707 987-1114	24652
Reynolds Systems Inc	3483	F	707 928-5244	13272

MIDWAY CITY, CA - Orange County

	SIC	EMP	PHONE	ENTRY #
Lin Consulting LLC	3792	F	714 650-8595	20489

MILL VALLEY, CA - Marin County

	SIC	EMP	PHONE	ENTRY #
Endurance Ptc	3751	F	415 445-9155	20400
Eyvo Inc	7372	F	888 237-9801	23886
Latitude 38 Publishing Company	2721	F	415 383-8200	5975
Liz Palacios Designs Ltd	3961	E	628 444-3339	22988
Wilderness Trail Bikes Inc (PA)	3751	F	415 389-5040	20437

MILLBRAE, CA - San Mateo County

	SIC	EMP	PHONE	ENTRY #
Aei Communications Corp	3661	E	650 552-9416	17342
American Ornamental Studio	3272	F	650 589-0561	10527
Brighton Collectibles LLC	3171	F	650 838-0086	10217
Cargo Chief Inc	7372	F	650 560-5001	23718
Cycle Shack Inc	3751	D	650 583-7014	20395
Sinosource Intl Co Inc	3281	F	650 697-6668	10931

(P-0000) Products & Services Section entry number
(PA)=Parent Co (HQ)=Headquarters (DH)=Div Headquarters

	SIC	EMP	PHONE	ENTRY #
Stem Inc (PA)	3825	D	415 937-7836	21128
Unisoft Corporation	7372	F	650 259-1290	24540
World Journal Inc (PA)	2711	D	650 692-9936	5869

MILPITAS, CA - Santa Clara County

	SIC	EMP	PHONE	ENTRY #
ABC Printing Inc	2752	F	408 263-1118	6391
Adcotech Corporation	3559	D	408 943-9999	14419
Advanced Microtechnology Inc	3825	F	408 945-9191	20982
Airgard Inc (PA)	3564	E	408 573-0701	14647
Alliance Analytical Inc	2836	E	800 916-5600	8268
Allied Telesis Inc	3577	D	408 519-6700	15151
Altigen Communications Inc	3661	C	408 597-9000	17346
Ambios Technology Inc (PA)	3826	E	831 427-1160	21170
Analog Devices Inc	3674	B	408 727-9222	18099
Applied Materials Inc	3674	E	408 727-5555	18110
Appointy Software Inc	7372	E	408 634-4141	23614
Aras Power Technologies (PA)	3677	F	408 935-8877	18700
Asante Technologies Inc	3577	F	408 435-8388	15162
Aviat Networks Inc (PA)	3663	C	408 941-7100	17463
Aviat US Inc (HQ)	3663	B	408 941-7100	17464
Bar-S Foods Co	2013	E	408 941-9958	439
Barco Inc	3575	F	510 490-1005	15120
Bestek Manufacturing Inc	3577	E	408 321-8834	15170
Blue Sky Research Incorporated (PA)	3827	E	408 941-6068	21335
Bmi Products Northern Cal Inc	3299	D	408 293-4008	10999
Brandt Electronics Inc	3679	E	408 240-0014	18841
Builders Drapery Service Inc	2211	E	408 263-3300	2673
Circuit Check Inc	3825	D	408 263-7444	21017
Cisco Systems Inc	3577	A	408 570-9149	15191
Cisco Systems Inc	3577	A	408 526-4000	15196
Commercial Mtl & Door Sup Inc	2431	F	408 432-3383	4019
Composite Software LLC (HQ)	7372	D	800 553-6387	23763
Continuum Electro-Optics Inc	3826	D	408 727-3240	21209
Corasia Corp	3565	C	408 321-8508	14704
Crain Cutter Company Inc	3429	D	408 946-6100	11580
Cummins Electrified Power NA (HQ)	3714	F	408 624-1231	19625
Daystar Technologies Inc	3674	D	408 582-7100	18194
Eico Inc (PA)	3825	D	408 945-9898	21026
Elixir Medical Corporation (PA)	3841	F	408 636-2000	21700
Ess Technology Inc (HQ)	3674	C	408 643-8818	18226
Evoqua Water Technologies	3589	F	408 586-9745	15512
Extron Contract Mfg Inc	3944	C	510 353-0177	22676
Fireeye Inc (PA)	7372	C	408 321-6300	23899
Flex Interconnect Tech Inc	3679	E	408 956-8204	18916
Flextronics International Usa	3672	A	408 576-7000	17879
Flextronics Intl PA Inc	3444	F	408 577-2489	12213
Flextronics Intl USA Inc	3577	F	510 814-7000	15229
Flextronics Intl USA Inc	3672	F	408 678-3268	17880
Flextronics Intl USA Inc	3672	A	408 576-7000	17882
Fluid Industrial Mfg Inc	3585	E	408 782-9900	15433
Frontier Semiconductor (PA)	3674	E	408 432-8338	18244
Globe Motors Inc	3621	C	408 935-8989	16649
Golden Altos Corporation	3825	E	408 956-1010	21044
Gyrfalcon Technology Inc	3674	E	408 944-9219	18261
Headway Technologies Inc	3572	F	408 935-1020	15037
Headway Technologies Inc (HQ)	3572	C	408 934-5300	15038
Headway Technologies Inc	3572	C	408 934-5300	15039
Hgst Inc	3572	F	408 801-2394	15041
HI Relblity McRelectronics Inc	3674	E	408 764-5500	18270
Honeywell International Inc	3674	C	408 954-1100	18272
Hoya Corporation USA	3812	F	408 654-2200	20587
Hoya Corporation USA (DH)	3827	F	408 492-1069	21359
Hoya Holdings Inc (HQ)	3861	C	408 654-2300	22427
HP Inc	3571	A	650 857-1501	14917
Hunter Technology Corporation (DH)	3679	C	408 957-1300	18938
Huntford Printing	2752	E	408 957-5000	6619
Hytek R&D Inc (PA)	3672	E	408 761-5271	17897
Infineon Tech Americas Corp	3674	A	866 951-9519	18284
Infineon Tech N Amer Corp (DH)	3674	B	408 503-2642	18286
Infineon Tech US Holdco Inc (HQ)	3674	D	866 951-9519	18287
Innovative Machining Inc	3599	E	408 262-2270	16047
Integra Tech Silicon Vly LLC (DH)	3674	C	408 618-8700	18299
Integrated Mfg Tech Inc	3599	E	510 366-8793	16050
Integrted Silicon Solution Inc (PA)	3674	D	408 969-6600	18304
Isolink Inc	3679	E	408 946-1968	18954
Ixys LLC (HQ)	3674	D	408 457-9000	18325
JIC Industrial Co Inc	3679	F	408 935-9880	18967
Johnson & Johnson	3841	E	408 273-4100	21765
Jt Manufacturing Inc (PA)	3999	F	408 674-4338	23374
K A Tool & Technology Inc	3599	E	408 957-9600	16099
Kelytech Corporation	3679	E	408 935-0888	18975
Khuus Inc	3599	D	408 522-8000	16115
KLA Corporation (PA)	3827	B	408 875-3000	21373
KLA-Tencor Asia-Pac Dist Corp	3674	E	408 875-4144	18334
Larson Packaging Company LLC	2441	E	408 946-4971	4338
Lifescan Products LLC (HQ)	3841	D	408 719-8443	21776

	SIC	EMP	PHONE	ENTRY #
Linear Technology Corporation	3674	F	408 428-2050	18351
Linear Technology Corporation	3674	D	408 434-6237	18352
Linear Technology LLC (HQ)	3674	A	408 432-1900	18353
Lite On Technology Intl Inc (HQ)	3577	E	408 945-0222	15275
Lumentum Holdings Inc (PA)	3669	C	408 546-5483	17744
Lumentum Operations LLC (HQ)	3669	C	408 546-5483	17745
Manutronics Inc	3679	F	408 262-6579	19005
Marburg Technology Inc	3577	E	408 262-8400	15283
Marketshare Inc (PA)	3993	D	408 262-0677	23153
Medtronic Inc	3841	E	408 548-6618	21809
Meridian Technical Sales Inc	2731	E	408 526-2000	6122
Meritronics Inc (PA)	3672	E	408 969-0888	17924
Meritronics Materials Inc	3672	F	408 390-5642	17925
Micron Technology Inc	3674	D	408 855-4000	18395
Milpitas Post Newspapers Inc	2711	F	408 262-2454	5756
Mobiveil Inc	3674	F	408 791-2977	18419
Modulus Inc	3672	F	408 457-3712	17927
Nanosys Inc	3674	C	408 240-6700	18425
Nichols Manufacturing Inc	3599	F	408 945-0911	16244
Nortra Cables Inc	3679	D	408 942-1106	19029
Nova Drilling Services Inc	3672	E	408 732-6682	17941
Oclaro Inc (HQ)	3674	D	408 383-1400	18446
Oclaro Fiber Optics Inc (DH)	3674	E	408 383-1400	18447
Oclaro Photonics Inc (DH)	3827	D	408 383-1400	21387
Oclaro Subsystems Inc	3661	C	408 383-1400	17394
Oclaro Technology Inc (DH)	3661	E	408 383-1400	17395
Omnicell Inc	3571	F	408 907-8868	14957
Onanon Inc	3678	E	408 262-8990	18783
Optimedica Corporation	3841	C	408 850-8600	21849
Palpilot International Corp (PA)	3672	E	408 855-8866	17951
PEC Manufacturing Inc	3699	F	408 577-1839	19375
Pericom Semiconductor Corp (HQ)	3825	E	408 232-9100	21097
Philips & Lite-On Digital (DH)	3572	E	510 687-1800	15073
Ppm Products Inc	3599	F	408 946-4710	16307
Precision Fiber Products Inc	3357	F	408 946-4040	11314
Qlc Manufacturing LLC	3355	F	408 221-8550	11267
Quality Transformer & Elec	3612	E	408 935-0231	16572
Quantum3d Inc (PA)	3812	F	408 600-2500	20678
Quellan Inc	3674	E	408 546-3487	18504
RDm Industrial Products Inc	2522	E	408 945-8400	4847
Renesas Electronics Amer Inc (HQ)	3679	B	408 432-8888	19068
Rucker & Kolls Inc (HQ)	3559	E	408 934-9875	14532
Sandisk LLC	3572	F	408 801-2928	15088
Sandisk LLC (DH)	3572	C	408 801-1000	15089
Sandisk LLC	3572	D	408 321-0320	15090
Sierra Monitor Corporation (HQ)	3829	D	408 262-6611	21538
Silicon 360 LLC	2674	F	408 432-1790	5444
Silicon Graphics Intl Corp (HQ)	3577	C	669 900-8000	15335
Silicon Microstructures Inc	3625	D	408 473-9700	16754
Silicon Motion Inc	3674	E	408 501-5300	18547
Silicon Turnkey Solutions Inc (HQ)	3674	F	408 904-0200	18550
Silicon Vly World Trade Corp	3613	E	408 945-6355	16615
Siliconcore Technology Inc	3674	E	408 945-8185	18552
Song Beoung	2782	F	510 670-8788	7317
Symprotek Co	3672	E	408 956-0700	18018
Tarana Wireless Inc (PA)	3663	F	408 365-8483	17678
Tek Labels and Printing Inc	2752	E	408 586-8107	6888
Teledesign Systems Inc	3663	F	408 941-1808	17684
Teledyne Defense Elec LLC	3674	C	408 737-0992	18607
Teledyne Dgital Imaging US Inc	3829	F	408 736-6000	21554
Teledyne E2v, Inc.	3674	F	408 737-0992	18608
Teledyne Lecroy Inc	3825	E	408 727-6600	22137
Terabit Radios Inc	3663	F	408 431-6032	17687
Test-Um Inc	3825	F	818 464-5021	21146
Testmetrix Inc	3825	E	408 730-5511	21147
Tmarzetti Company	2035	C	408 263-7540	902
Tokyo Ohka Kogyo America Inc	2819	F	408 956-9901	7531
Tuff Shed Inc	2452	F	408 935-8833	4466
United Optronics Inc	3661	F	408 503-8900	17424
Varian Medical Systems Inc	3841	C	408 321-9400	21947
Vector Fabrication Inc (PA)	3672	E	408 942-9800	18042
Venta Medical Inc	3841	F	510 429-9300	21950
Viavi Solutions Inc	3826	C	408 546-5000	21322
View Inc (PA)	3231	D	408 263-9200	10400
Vista Point Technologies Inc	3663	D	408 576-7000	17702
Vlsi Standards Inc	3825	E	408 428-1800	21155
Westrock Cp LLC	2653	C	408 946-3600	5272
Westrock Cp LLC	2653	C	408 946-3600	5276
Winslow Automation Inc	3674	D	408 262-9004	18657
Yuhas Tooling & Machining	3599	F	408 934-9196	16536
Zilog Inc (DH)	3674	E	408 513-1500	18672
Zollner Electronics Inc	3672	E	408 434-5400	18056
Zuca Inc	3161	E	408 377-9822	10216
Zytek Corp	3672	E	408 520-4287	18058

Employment Codes: A=Over 500 employees, B=251-500,
C=101-250, D=51-100, E=20-50, F=10-19

2020 California
Manufacturers Register

© Mergent Inc. 1-800-342-5647
1369

GEOGRAPHIC

	SIC	EMP	PHONE	ENTRY #

MIRA LOMA, CA - Riverside County

	SIC	EMP	PHONE	ENTRY #
Califrnia Indus Rfrgn Mchs Inc	3585	F	951 361-0040	15418
Cryoworks Inc	3498	E	951 360-0920	13465
General Electric Company	3646	E	951 360-2400	17039
International Vitamin Corp	2834	C	951 361-1120	7957
Puri Tech Inc	3589	E	951 360-8380	15564
R & V Sheet Metal Inc	3444	F	951 361-9455	12348
Racing Plus Inc	3842	F	951 360-5906	22075
Spartak Enterprises Inc	2517	E	951 360-0610	4755
Unitek Technology Inc	3571	E	909 930-5700	14994

MIRANDA, CA - Humboldt County

	SIC	EMP	PHONE	ENTRY #
Wheeler Lumber Co Inc	2411	F	707 943-3424	3918

MISSION HILLS, CA - Los Angeles County

	SIC	EMP	PHONE	ENTRY #
Electric Gate Store Inc	3699	C	818 361-6872	19303
Lawrence Roll Up Doors Inc	3442	F	818 837-1963	11965
Sky Signs & Graphics	2395	F	818 898-3802	3757
Valterra Products LLC (PA)	3494	E	818 898-1671	13367

MISSION VIEJO, CA - Orange County

	SIC	EMP	PHONE	ENTRY #
Bailey Industries Inc	3728	F	949 461-0807	20055
Boeing Company	3721	A	949 452-0259	19863
Community Merch Solutions LLC	3578	E	877 956-9258	15374
Elixir Industries	3469	F	949 860-5000	12799
Foundstone Inc (PA)	7372	D	949 297-5600	23917
Franchise Services Inc (PA)	2752	E	949 348-5400	6584
Gregg Hammork Enterprizes Inc	1311	F	949 586-7902	54
Honeywell International Inc	3724	A	949 425-3992	19958
James Hardie Building Pdts Inc	3241	D	949 348-1800	10417
James Hardie Trading Co Inc	2952	C	949 582-2378	9118
Jorlind Enterprises Inc	2752	F	949 364-2309	6667
Nasco Petroleum LLC	1389	E	949 461-5212	232
Postal Instant Press Inc (HQ)	2752	E	949 348-5000	6788
Produce Apparel Inc	2339	E	949 472-9434	3392
Prototype Industries Inc (PA)	2741	E	949 680-4890	6320
Radio Frequency Simulation	3825	E	714 974-7377	21110
Socal Skateshop	3949	F	949 305-5321	22890
W G Holt Inc	3674	D	949 859-8800	18651
Wakunaga of America Co Ltd (HQ)	2023	D	949 855-2776	625

MODESTO, CA - Stanislaus County

	SIC	EMP	PHONE	ENTRY #
1le California Inc	3646	E	209 846-7541	17003
A B Boyd Co (PA)	3069	E	209 236-1111	9276
Accelerated Cnstr & Met LLC	3441	E	209 846-7998	11732
Allied Concrete & Supply Co	3273	E	209 524-3177	10684
Amcor Manufacturing	2819	E	209 581-9687	7468
Arctic Glacier California Inc	2097	D	209 524-3128	2349
Atlas Pacific Engineering Co	3556	E	209 574-9884	14346
Bambacigno Steel Company	3312	E	209 524-9681	11029
Batchlder Bus Cmmnications Inc	2752	F	209 577-2222	6437
Bell-Carter Foods Inc	2033	E	209 549-5939	756
Billington Welding & Mfg Inc	3556	E	209 526-0846	14349
Bimbo Bakeries Usa Inc	2051	B	209 538-6170	1146
Boyd Corporation	2891	C	888 244-6931	8860
Bunge Oils Inc	2076	D	209 574-9981	1448
Cal-Sign Wholesale Inc	3993	F	209 523-7446	23068
Cemex Cnstr Mtls PCF LLC	3273	E	209 524-6322	10732
Concentric Components Inc	3621	F	209 529-4840	16637
Consolidated Container Co LLC	3085	D	209 531-9180	9485
Container Graphics Corp	3555	D	209 577-0181	14319
Dawn Food Products Inc	2052	F	517 789-4400	1312
Dayton Superior Corporation	3537	E	209 869-1201	13871
Del Monte Foods Inc	2033	B	209 548-5509	764
Deltatrak Inc	3829	E	209 579-5343	21459
Dry Creek Nutrition Inc	2087	F	209 341-5696	2206
E & J Gallo Winery (PA)	2084	A	209 341-3111	1678
E & J Gallo Winery	2084	F	209 341-3111	1682
E & J Gallo Winery	2084	F	209 341-7862	1687
E & S Precision Machine Inc	3599	F	209 545-6161	15916
Fabricated Extrusion Co LLC (PA)	3089	E	209 529-9200	9785
Fabritec Precision Inc (PA)	3444	F	209 529-8504	12210
First Taçtical	2311	A	855 665-3410	2964
Fisher Graphic Inds A Cal Corp	3555	B	209 577-0181	14321
Fisher Nut Company	2099	F	209 527-0108	2459
Flowers Baking Co Modesto LLC	2051	D	209 857-4600	1205
Foam Fabricators Inc	3086	F	209 523-7002	9531
Fowlers Machine Works Inc	3599	F	209 522-5146	15971
Frito-Lay North America Inc	2096	B	209 544-5400	2330
Gallo Glass Company (HQ)	3221	A	209 341-3710	10288
Georgia-Pacific LLC	2653	C	209 522-5201	5226
Gilwin Company	3442	F	209 522-9775	11956
Golden Valley & Associates Inc	3537	E	209 549-1549	13874
Golden Valley Industries Inc	2011	E	209 939-3370	411
Graham Packaging Company LP	3089	D	209 578-1112	9814
Grand Packaging Pet Tech	3089	D	209 578-1112	9817

	SIC	EMP	PHONE	ENTRY #
Hess Precision Laser Inc	3699	F	209 575-1634	19321
Honeywell International Inc	3724	A	951 500-6086	19957
Hoya Optical Inc (PA)	3851	D	209 579-7739	22361
Hsi Mechanical Inc	3444	E	209 408-0183	12240
International Paper Company	2631	C	209 526-4700	5163
Iron Works Enterprises Inc	3715	E	209 572-7450	19824
J S West Milling Co Inc	2048	E	209 529-4232	1103
Jims Optical	3827	F	209 549-2517	21371
Johnson United Inc (PA)	3993	E	209 543-1320	23142
JR Daniels Commercial Bldrs	3449	D	209 545-6040	12593
Kingspan Insulated Panels Inc	3448	D	209 531-9091	12553
Lamar Tool and Die Casting Inc	3312	E	209 545-5525	11054
LTI Boyd	3549	A	800 554-0200	14275
LTI Holdings Inc (HQ)	2822	F	209 236-1111	7632
Martinez Pallet Services LLC	2448	F	209 968-1393	4380
McClatchy Newspapers Inc	2711	F	305 740-8440	5730
McClatchy Newspapers Inc	2711	B	209 238-4636	5731
McClatchy Newspapers Inc	2711	B	209 587-2250	5734
Mercer Foods LLC	2034	F	209 529-0150	855
Modesto Pltg & Powdr Coating	3471	E	209 526-2696	13053
Modesto Tent and Awning Inc	2394	E	209 545-1607	3691
Nestle Usa Inc	2023	D	209 574-2000	610
Newly Weds Foods Inc	2099	E	209 491-7777	2568
Nick Sciabica & Sons A Corp	2079	E	209 577-5067	1478
Noahs Bottled Water	2086	E	209 526-2945	2099
Nutrien AG Solutions Inc	2875	E	209 551-1424	8814
Pacific Southwest Cont LLC (PA)	2671	B	209 526-0444	5334
Pacific Southwest Cont LLC	2671	F	209 526-0444	5335
Parker-Hannifin Corporation	3569	A	209 521-7860	14845
Peco Controls Corporation	3625	F	209 576-3345	16738
Phoenix Custom Promotions	3942	F	209 579-1557	22652
Reliable Rubber Products Inc	3069	F	209 525-9750	9363
Repsco Inc	3089	E	303 294-0364	10015
Ring Container Tech LLC	3085	E	209 238-3426	9494
Rizo-Lopez Foods Inc	2022	C	800 626-5587	570
Rj Boudreau Inc	3523	F	209 480-3172	13666
Sacramento Coca-Cola Btlg Inc	2086	E	209 541-3200	2164
San Joaquin Equipment LLC	3523	E	209 538-3831	13668
Sharcar Enterprises Inc	3281	D	209 531-2200	10930
Sign Designs Inc	3993	E	209 524-4484	23197
Silgan Containers Mfg Corp	3411	D	209 521-6469	11504
Stanislaus Food Products Co (PA)	2033	C	209 548-3537	825
Steven Varrati	3599	F	209 545-0107	16423
Triad Energy Resources Inc	2875	E	209 527-0607	8816
Truss Engineering Inc	2439	E	209 527-6387	4326
United Pallet Services Inc	2448	C	209 538-5844	4403
Varni Brothers Corporation (PA)	2086	D	209 521-1777	2180
Village Instant Printing Inc	2752	E	209 576-2568	6923
Vistech Mfg Solutions LLC (PA)	3565	E	209 544-9333	14734
Wardrobe Specialties Ltd	3231	F	209 523-2094	10401
West Coast Pallets Inc	2448	F	209 534-3587	4406
Westland Technologies Inc	3061	D	800 877-7734	9273
Willey Printing Company Inc (PA)	2752	E	209 524-4811	6939
Wolfram Inc	3229	F	209 238-9610	10334
Wood Connection Inc	2431	E	209 577-1044	4155
Wright Pharma Inc	2834	E	209 549-9771	8189

MOFFETT FIELD, CA - Santa Clara County

	SIC	EMP	PHONE	ENTRY #
Aquila Space Inc	3663	F	650 224-8559	17457

MOJAVE, CA - Kern County

	SIC	EMP	PHONE	ENTRY #
Alpha Dyno Nobel	2892	F	661 824-1356	8903
Calportland Company	3241	C	661 824-2401	10404
Commodity Resource Envmtl Inc	3339	E	661 824-2416	11189
Golden Queen Mining Co LLC	1041	C	661 824-4300	4
Interorbital Systems	3365	F	661 824-1662	11383
Masten Space Systems Inc	3761	F	661 824-3423	20452
Mustang Hills LLC	2282	E	661 888-5810	2888
Pepsi-Cola Metro Btlg Co Inc	2086	D	661 824-2051	2123
PPG Industries Inc	2851	E	661 824-4532	8670
PRC - Desoto International Inc	2891	C	661 824-4532	8888
Scaled Composites LLC	3721	E	661 824-4541	19930
Trical Inc	2879	E	661 824-2494	8846
Tsc LLC (DH)	3761	A	661 824-6600	20459

MONROVIA, CA - Los Angeles County

	SIC	EMP	PHONE	ENTRY #
3M Company	3069	E	626 358-0136	9275
3M Unitek Corporation	3843	B	626 445-7960	22130
Aerovironment Inc	3721	D	626 357-9983	19849
Aerovironment Inc	3721	E	626 357-9983	19851
Aerovironment Inc	3721	E	626 357-9983	19852
Aerovironment Inc	3721	E	626 357-9983	19854
Age Logistics Corporation	3536	F	626 243-5253	13843
Air Logistics Corporation (PA)	3089	E	626 633-0294	9614
Amada Miyachi America Inc (HQ)	3548	C	626 303-5676	14236
Amada Miyachi America Inc	3841	E	626 303-5676	21595

Mergent email: customerrelations@mergent.com
1370

2020 California
Manufacturers Register

(P-0000) Products & Services Section entry number
(PA)=Parent Co (HQ)=Headquarters (DH)=Div Headquarters

	SIC	EMP	PHONE	ENTRY #
Aremac Associates Inc	3599	E	626 303-8795	15746
Arrowhead Press Inc	2752	E	626 358-1168	6419
Atlas Sponge Rubber Company	3069	F	626 359-5391	9284
B & H Signs Inc	3993	D	626 359-6643	23058
Beacon Mktg Inc	2711	F	626 301-1010	5565
Belco Packaging Systems Inc	3565	E	626 357-9566	14698
Bond Furs Inc	2371	F	626 471-9912	3498
Burnett & Son Meat Co Inc	2011	D	626 357-2165	396
Cacique Inc (PA)	2022	C	626 961-3399	542
Califrnia Nwspapers Ltd Partnr (DH)	2711	B	626 962-8811	5579
Chromologic LLC	3841	E	626 381-9974	21664
Clary Corporation	3679	F	626 359-4486	18868
Consilio - A First Advantage	7372	E	626 921-1600	23771
CPS Gem Corporation	3911	F	213 627-4019	22508
Crescent Plastics Inc	3089	F	626 359-9248	9734
D & M Draperies Inc	2391	F	626 256-1993	3588
Decco US Post-Harvest Inc (HQ)	2879	E	800 221-0925	8827
Decore-Ative Specialties (PA)	2431	A	626 254-9191	4032
Ducommun Aerostructures Inc	3728	E	626 358-3211	20091
Duracold Refrigeration Mfg LLC	3448	E	626 358-1710	12542
Genzyme Corporation	2834	D	800 255-1616	7911
Global Compliance	2741	E	626 303-6855	6243
Harbor Seal Incorporated	3053	E	626 305-5754	9235
Headwinds	3751	F	626 359-8044	20406
Hoya Holdings Inc	3827	D	626 739-5200	21360
Imagerlabs	3674	F	949 310-9560	18281
Innovyze Inc (DH)	7372	E	626 568-6868	24025
ITT LLC	3625	F	626 305-6100	16725
K Short Inc	3441	F	626 358-8511	11822
Koncept Technologies Inc	3645	F	323 261-8999	16974
Kruse and Son Inc	2013	E	626 358-4536	475
Mask-Off Company Inc	2891	F	626 303-8015	8880
Micile Inc	3571	F	626 381-9974	14946
Mulgrew Arcft Components Inc	3728	D	626 256-1375	20183
Ondax Inc	3827	F	626 357-9600	21388
One World Enterprises LLC	2086	E	310 802-4220	2102
Peck Road Gravel Pit	1442	E	626 574-7570	356
Pednar Products Inc (PA)	3086	F	626 960-9883	9560
Production Lapping Company	3599	F	626 359-0611	16314
Quality Craft Cabinets Inc	2434	F	626 358-2021	4234
Radcal Partners IA California	3829	E	626 359-4575	21527
Rayco Burial Products Inc	3444	F	626 357-1996	12351
Roncelli Plastics Inc	2821	D	800 250-6516	7605
Shore Western Manufacturing	3826	F	626 357-3251	21290
Staar Surgical Company (PA)	3851	C	626 303-7902	22390
Torero Specialty Products LLC	3949	F	415 520-3481	22909
Vinyl Technology Inc	2671	C	626 443-5257	5348
Vioski Inc	2512	E	626 359-4571	4677
Wbt Group LLC	3999	E	323 735-1201	23523
Xencor Inc	2834	C	626 305-5900	8190

MONTAGUE, CA - Siskiyou County

	SIC	EMP	PHONE	ENTRY #
Chuck L Logging Inc	2411	E	530 459-3842	3877
Dave Richardson Trucking	2411	F	530 459-5088	3880

MONTCLAIR, CA - San Bernardino County

	SIC	EMP	PHONE	ENTRY #
Amazing Steel Company	3441	E	909 590-0393	11742
American Nail Plate Ltg Inc	3645	D	909 982-1807	16959
Brooks Street Companies	2051	C	909 983-6090	1170
Califoam Products Inc	3069	F	909 364-1600	9292
Carboline Company	2851	E	909 459-1090	8628
Cnc Industries Inc	3599	F	909 445-0300	15852
Cobra Performance Boats Inc	3732	F	909 482-0047	20318
Cpd Industries	3086	E	909 465-5596	9519
E & R Glass Contractors Inc	3231	E	909 624-1763	10356
Elements Food Group Inc	2052	D	909 983-2011	1314
Evk Inc	2891	F	617 335-3180	8868
Falcon Abrasive Manufacturing	3291	F	909 598-3078	10946
Fanlight Corporation Inc	3641	F	909 868-6538	16862
Fittings That Fit Inc	3496	F	909 248-2808	13414
Gang Yan Diamond Products Inc	3545	E	909 590-2255	14163
Ingredients By Nature LLC	2099	E	909 230-6200	2484
Jlp Manufacturing Inc	3441	F	909 931-7797	11820
John L Conley Inc	3448	D	909 627-0981	12551
Kois & Ponds Inc	2048	F	800 936-3638	1106
McDaniel Inc	3324	F	909 591-8353	11161
Mechanical and Mch Repr Svcs	3599	F	909 625-8705	16186
Mitchell Fabrication	3441	E	909 590-0393	11846
Montclair Bronze Inc (PA)	3366	F	909 986-2664	11404
Montclair Machine Shop Inc	3599	F	909 986-2664	16223
National Ewp Inc	1081	E	909 931-4014	12
Nef Tech Inc	3589	F	909 548-4900	15548
Pacific Duct Inc	3444	F	909 635-1335	12325
Purfect Packaging	2673	F	909 460-7363	5413
Vertex Industrial Inc	3569	F	909 626-2100	14869
Westside Accessories Inc (PA)	2387	E	626 858-5452	3534

MONTEBELLO, CA - Los Angeles County

	SIC	EMP	PHONE	ENTRY #
Academy Awning Inc	2395	E	800 422-9646	3719
All Access Apparel Inc (PA)	2361	C	323 889-4300	3473
Allied Feather & Down Corp (PA)	3999	E	323 581-5677	23270
Amplifier Technologies Inc	3663	E	323 278-0001	17449
Arevalo Tortilleria Inc (PA)	2099	C	323 888-1711	2396
Atlas Survival Shelters LLC	2514	E	323 727-7084	4684
Beacon Concrete Inc	3273	E	323 889-7775	10696
Big Sleep Futon Inc	2515	E	800 647-2671	4712
Big Tree Furniture & Inds Inc (PA)	2511	E	310 894-7500	4556
Bimbo Bakeries Usa Inc	2051	F	323 720-6099	1149
Bltee LLC	2331	E	213 802-1736	3141
Bread Los Angeles	2052	E	323 201-3953	1309
Cavern Club LLC	2331	F	323 837-9800	3148
Cee Baileys Aircraft Plas Inc	3751	E	323 721-4900	20389
Conroy & Knowlton Inc	3089	F	323 665-5288	9716
Craig Manufacturing Company (PA)	3714	D	323 726-7355	19623
Crawford Products Company Inc	2851	F	323 721-6429	8639
Delamo Manufacturing Inc	3089	D	323 936-3566	9748
Desert Brothers Craft	2082	F	323 530-0015	1520
Dony Corp	3161	F	323 725-7697	10192
Dow-Elco Inc	3612	E	323 723-1288	16547
Eagle Enterprises Inc	3714	E	323 721-4741	19643
General Truck Body Inc	3713	D	323 276-1933	19535
Graphicpak Corporation	2653	F	323 306-3054	5232
Grover Smith Mfg Corp	3561	E	323 724-3444	14578
H & L Tooth Company (PA)	3531	D	323 721-5146	13735
Icsh Parent Inc	2655	D	323 724-8507	5298
Ingalls Conveyors Inc	3535	E	323 837-9900	13826
Jade Apparel Inc	2335	E	323 867-9800	3233
Katzkin Leather Interiors Inc	3172	F	323 725-1243	10235
La Bottleworks Inc	2086	E	323 724-4076	2088
LA Envelope Incorporated	2677	E	323 838-9300	5473
Monarch Litho Inc (PA)	2752	E	323 727-0300	6735
Montebello Plastics LLC	3081	E	323 726-6814	9413
National Cnstr Rentals Inc	1389	F	323 838-1800	233
Orb Media Broadcasting Inc	2741	F	323 246-4524	6303
Performance Forged Products	3462	E	323 722-3460	12717
Polerax USA	2389	F	323 477-1866	3574
Powers Bros Machine Inc	3599	F	323 728-2010	16306
Ppp LLC	3089	E	323 832-9627	9984
Reyes Coca-Cola Bottling LLC	2086	D	323 278-2600	2150
Robert Crowder & Co Inc	3069	E	323 248-7737	9365
Royal Paper Box Co California (PA)	2657	C	323 728-7041	5314
Saavy Inc	3541	F	323 728-2137	13949
Style Knits Inc	2253	D	323 890-9080	2804
Theta Digital Corporation	3651	E	818 572-4300	17293
Thistle Roller Co Inc	3555	E	323 685-5322	14341
Troy Sheet Metal Works Inc	3465	E	323 720-4100	12751
Truck Club Publishing Inc	2731	E	323 726-8620	6157
Turner Fiberfill Inc	2824	F	323 724-7957	7642
Universal Metal Plating	3471	F	626 969-7932	13125
Unix Packaging Inc	2086	C	213 627-5050	2178
Unlimited Trck Trlr Maint Inc	3715	E	323 727-2500	19836
US Polymers Inc (PA)	3089	D	323 728-3023	10104
Vft Inc	2392	E	323 728-2280	3648
Wilbur Curtis Co Inc	3589	B	323 837-2300	15606
Worldwide Aeros Corp	3721	D	818 344-3999	19938

MONTEREY, CA - Monterey County

	SIC	EMP	PHONE	ENTRY #
Acecad Inc	3577	F	831 655-1900	15142
China Circuit Tech Corp N Amer	3672	F	831 646-2194	17845
Cyberdata Corporation	3577	E	831 373-2601	15213
Dole Fresh Vegetables Inc (HQ)	2099	C	831 422-8871	2448
Evan-Moor Corporation (HQ)	2731	E	831 649-5901	6101
Great American Wineries Inc	2084	E	831 920-4736	1735
Hampton-Brown Company LLC	2732	F	831 620-6001	6172
Lockwood Vineyard (PA)	2084	F	831 642-9566	1803
Monterey County Herald Company (DH)	2711	E	831 372-3311	5758
Montero Printing Inc	2752	F	831 655-5511	6738
Nor-Cal Smokeshop	3949	E	831 645-9021	22860
North Bay Rhblitation Svcs Inc	2331	E	831 372-4094	3185
Orbital Sciences Corporation	3812	D	703 406-5000	20670
Rapid Printers Inc	2752	F	831 373-1822	6835
Richard Macdonald Studios Inc (PA)	3299	F	831 655-0424	11020
Robert Talbott Inc (PA)	2311	E	831 649-6000	2975
Sage Metering Inc	3826	F	831 242-2030	21284
Summit Furniture Inc (PA)	2511	F	831 375-7811	4614
Vybion Inc	2824	F	607 227-2502	7643

MONTEREY PARK, CA - Los Angeles County

	SIC	EMP	PHONE	ENTRY #
Aero Powder Coating Inc	3479	E	323 264-6405	13138
Architectural Woodworking Co	2541	D	626 570-4125	4881
Asia Food Inc	2011	F	626 284-1328	395
CHI-AM Comics Daily Inc	2741	F	626 281-2989	6212
Derik Plastics Industries Inc	2631	A	626 371-7799	5160

Employment Codes: A=Over 500 employees, B=251-500,
C=101-250, D=51-100, E=20-50, F=10-19

2020 California
Manufacturers Register

© Mergent Inc. 1-800-342-5647
1371

GEOGRAPHIC

	SIC	EMP	PHONE	ENTRY #
Dermacare Neuroscience Inst.	2844	F	323 780-2981	8480
DHm International Corp	2339	D	323 263-3888	3318
Elle Boutique	2335	F	626 307-9882	3226
Franco American Corporation	3292	F	323 268-2345	10961
Graphic Color Systems Inc	2752	D	323 283-3000	6594
Inertech Supply Inc	3053	D	626 282-2000	9238
International Daily News Inc (PA)	2711	E	323 265-1317	5676
J E J Print Inc	2752	F	626 281-8989	6655
K-Cal Group Inc	2024	F	626 922-1103	652
L C Miller Company	3567	E	323 268-3611	14768
La Colonial Tortilla Pdts Inc	2099	C	626 289-3647	2506
Lightcross	3679	E	626 236-4500	18991
Los Olivos Packaging Inc (PA)	2033	C	323 261-2218	792
Mako Inc	2241	E	323 262-2168	2756
Miholin Inc	2329	F	213 820-8225	3108
Optic Arts Inc	3646	F	213 250-6069	17061
Rigoli Enterprises Inc	3699	F	626 573-0242	19395
Ross Name Plate Company	3993	F	323 725-6812	23187
Shihs Printing	2759	F	626 281-2989	7211
Sweety Novelty Inc	2024	F	310 533-6010	671
Tck USA Corporation	2891	F	323 269-2969	8897
Wah Hung Group Inc (PA)	3714	E	626 571-8700	19801
Wah Hung Group Inc.	3714	E	626 571-8700	19802
West-Bag Inc	3089	F	323 264-0750	10121
Win Fat Food LLC	2015	E	323 261-1869	532
World Journal La LLC (HQ)	2711	C	323 268-4982	5870

MONTROSE, CA - Los Angeles County

	SIC	EMP	PHONE	ENTRY #
Avalco Inc	3491	F	310 676-3057	13292
Flanagan-Gorham Inc (PA)	2011	F	818 279-2473	409
Flow N Control Inc.	3491	F	818 330-7425	13306
Micro/Sys Inc.	3571	E	818 244-4600	14947
Northrop Grumman Systems Corp.	3812	F	818 249-5252	20660
Vitachrome Graphics Inc.	2759	E	818 957-0900	7263

MOORPARK, CA - Ventura County

	SIC	EMP	PHONE	ENTRY #
Ace Graphics Inc	2752	F	213 746-5100	6393
AG Machining Inc	3441	D	805 531-9555	11739
American Board Assembly Inc	3672	C	805 523-0274	17816
Amphenol Corporation	3678	E	805 378-6464	18751
Anc Technology LLC	3672	D	805 530-3958	17820
AVC Specialists Inc	3822	E	513 458-2600	20784
Benchmark Elec Mfg Sol Moorpk	3679	A	805 532-2800	18835
Cemex Cement Inc	3273	E	805 529-1355	10709
Cemex Cnstr Mtls PCF LLC	3273	E	805 529-1544	10731
Conversion Technology Co Inc (PA)	3952	E	805 378-0033	22940
Corporate Graphics & Printing	2752	E	805 529-5333	6515
Ensign-Bickford Arospc Def Co	3812	E	805 292-4000	20575
Erp Power LLC (PA)	3825	F	805 517-1300	21030
G T Water Products Inc	3432	F	805 529-2900	11669
Garage Equipment Supply Inc	3559	F	805 530-0027	14470
Global Uxe Inc	3999	E	805 583-4600	23345
Globaluxe Inc	3999	E	805 583-4600	23346
Gooch and Housego Cal LLC	3827	D	805 529-3324	21356
H&F Technologies Inc	3651	F	805 523-2759	17235
Koros USA Inc	3841	E	805 529-0825	21772
Laritech Inc	3672	C	805 529-5000	17913
Martronic Engineering Inc (PA)	3699	F	805 583-0808	19353
Mc Cully Mac M Corporation	3621	E	805 529-0661	16662
Mpo Videotronics Inc (PA)	3861	D	805 499-8513	22443
Nea Electronics Inc	3678	E	805 292-4010	18781
Pentair Water Pool and Spa Inc	3589	E	805 553-5003	15558
SCI-Tech Glassblowing Inc	3231	F	805 523-9790	10389
Semiconductor Equipment Corp	3559	F	805 529-2293	14537
Sercomp LLC (PA)	3955	D	805 299-0020	22973
Spectrum Brands Inc.	3999	C	805 222-3611	23482
Star Ring Inc	3911	D	818 773-4900	22573
Sterisyn Inc	2834	E	805 991-9694	8147
Topaz Systems Inc (PA)	3577	E	805 520-8282	15351
Turbonetics Holdings Inc	3714	E	805 581-0333	19790
Ultron Systems Inc	3559	F	805 529-1485	14551
Vision Aquatics Inc	3949	F	818 749-2178	22920
Wave Precision Inc	3827	E	805 529-3324	21419
Wayne J Sand & Gravel Inc	1442	F	805 529-1323	367
Wilmanco	3663	F	805 523-2390	17707

MORAGA, CA - Contra Costa County

	SIC	EMP	PHONE	ENTRY #
J F K & Associates Inc	7372	E	925 388-0255	24055

MORENO VALLEY, CA - Riverside County

	SIC	EMP	PHONE	ENTRY #
Accuturn Corporation	3812	E	951 656-6621	20528
Amro Fabricating Corporation	3728	E	951 842-6140	20033
BAS Recycling Inc	3011	E	951 214-6590	9164
California Supertrucks Inc	3713	E	951 656-2903	19522
Cardinal Glass Industries Inc.	3211	D	951 485-9007	10261
Cimc Reefer Trailer Inc (PA)	3537	F	951 218-1414	13861
Envirnmntal Mlding Cncepts LLC	3069	F	951 214-6596	9305

	SIC	EMP	PHONE	ENTRY #
Forest Laboratories LLC	2834	D	951 941-0024	7892
Harman Professional Inc	3651	B	951 242-2927	17237
Masonite Entry Door Corp	2431	F	951 243-2261	4081
Modular Metal Fabricators Inc	3444	C	951 242-3154	12308
Nursesbond Inc	7372	F	951 286-8537	24218
Pacific Kiln Insulations Inc	3567	F	951 697-4422	14772
Painted Rhino Inc	3088	E	951 656-5524	9594
Schurman Fine Papers	2771	C	951 653-1934	7298
Supreme Corporation	3713	C	951 656-6101	19559
Westrock Converting Company	2653	C	951 601-4164	5271

MORGAN HILL, CA - Santa Clara County

	SIC	EMP	PHONE	ENTRY #
A & J Machining Inc.	3599	F	903 566-0304	15654
A H K Electronic Shtmtl Inc	3444	E	408 778-3901	12080
Admi Inc	7372	E	408 776-0060	23564
Advanced McHning Tchniques Inc	3599	F	408 778-4500	15699
Aircraft Covers Inc	2211	D	408 738-3959	2664
Airtronics Metal Products Inc (PA)	3444	C	408 977-7800	12094
Al Fresco Concepts Inc	3674	F	408 497-1579	18076
All Sensors Corporation	3674	E	408 776-9434	18079
AMP III LLC.	3545	D	408 779-2927	14131
Amtech Microelectronics Inc	3672	E	408 612-8888	17819
Anritsu Company (DH)	3663	B	800 267-4878	17451
Anritsu Instruments Company	3229	E	315 797-4449	10299
Anritsu US Holding Inc (HQ)	3825	B	408 778-2000	21003
Art Brand Studios LLC (PA)	2741	E	408 201-5000	6188
California Kit Cab Door Corp (PA)	2434	D	408 782-5700	4178
Collaris LLC	3679	D	510 825-9995	18871
Coretest Systems Inc (PA)	3826	E	408 778-3771	21210
Creative Mfg Solutions	3444	E	408 327-0600	12167
Custom Chrome Manufacturing	3751	C	408 825-5000	20394
Custom Labeling & Btlg Corp	2086	E	408 371-6171	2070
Digital View Inc	3679	F	408 782-7773	18889
Elmech Inc	3679	F	408 782-2990	18901
Emtec Engineering	3444	F	408 779-5800	12196
Flextronics Intl USA Inc	3672	B	408 577-2262	17881
Global Motorsport Parts Inc	3751	C	408 778-0500	20404
Greif Inc.	2655	D	408 779-2161	5295
Hanaps Enterprises	3577	D	669 235-3810	15238
Italix Company Inc.	3479	F	408 988-2487	13195
Kal Machining Inc.	3599	F	408 782-8989	16104
Kalman Manufacturing Inc	3599	E	408 776-7664	16105
KDF Inc	3751	E	408 779-3731	20411
Koco Motion Us LLC	3823	F	408 612-4970	20897
Lara Manufacturing Inc	3444	E	408 778-0811	12265
Lin Engineering Inc	3621	C	408 919-0200	16660
Lynex Company Inc.	2844	F	408 778-7884	8536
M & L Precision Machining Inc (PA)	3599	E	408 436-3955	16157
Marki Microwave Inc	3679	E	408 778-4200	19006
Metrophones Unlimited Inc	3661	E	650 630-5400	17386
Mitann Inc (HQ)	2899	E	408 782-2500	9001
Morgan Hill Precision Inc	3599	F	408 778-7895	16226
New Product Integration Solutn	3315	D	408 944-9178	11103
Newera Software Inc.	7372	F	408 520-7100	24205
Oml Inc	3825	F	408 779-2698	21095
Pacific Capacitor Co.	3675	F	408 778-6670	18684
Paramit Corporation (PA)	3672	B	408 782-5600	17952
Pega Precision Inc	3444	E	408 776-3700	12330
Phoenix Deventures Inc	3069	E	408 782-6240	9352
Pinnacle Manufacturing Corp	3444	E	408 778-6100	12334
Quadrant Solutions Inc.	3499	F	408 463-9451	13541
Quintel Corporation	3555	E	408 776-5190	14339
Rawson Custom Cabinets Inc (PA)	2434	E	408 779-9838	4237
Renesas Electronics Amer Inc	3674	A	408 546-3434	18514
Robson Technologies Inc	3599	E	408 779-8008	16366
Royal Riders	2399	F	408 779-1997	3856
Seagull Solutions Inc.	3825	F	408 778-1127	21118
Sheathing Technologies Inc	3841	E	408 782-2720	21897
Sierra Precast Inc.	3272	D	408 779-1000	10650
Terrasat Communications Inc.	3663	E	408 782-5911	17689
Tracet Manufacturing Inc.	3599	E	408 779-8846	16463
Twin Glass Industries Inc	3231	F	408 779-8801	10397
U-C Components Inc (PA)	3452	E	408 782-1929	12698
Uhv Sputtering Inc.	3674	E	408 779-2826	18630
US Concrete Inc.	3272	E	408 779-1000	10662
US Eta Inc	3679	F	408 778-2793	19132
Valvex Enterprises Inc.	3599	E	408 928-2510	16493
Velodyne Acoustics Inc	3651	D	408 465-2800	17301
Velodyne Lidar Inc.	3812	B	408 465-2800	20741

MORRO BAY, CA - San Luis Obispo County

	SIC	EMP	PHONE	ENTRY #
Hanson Aggrgtes Md-Pacific Inc	3273	F	805 928-3764	10769
Mills ASAP Reprographics (PA)	2678	F	805 772-2019	5482

MOSS BEACH, CA - San Mateo County

	SIC	EMP	PHONE	ENTRY #
Biz Performance Solutions Inc	7372	F	408 844-4284	23673

Mergent email: customerrelations@mergent.com
1372

2020 California
Manufacturers Register

(P-0000) Products & Services Section entry number
(PA)=Parent Co (HQ)=Headquarters (DH)=Div Headquarters

	SIC	EMP	PHONE	ENTRY #

MOSS LANDING, CA - Monterey County

	SIC	EMP	PHONE	ENTRY #
Calera Corporation	2869	E	831 731-6000	8726
Moss Landing Cement Co LLC	3241	F	831 731-6000	10424
Sweet Earth Inc	2099	D	831 375-8673	2621

MOUNT SHASTA, CA - Siskiyou County

	SIC	EMP	PHONE	ENTRY #
Alpine Industries	3469	F	530 926-2460	12764
Mt Shasta Btlg Distrg Co Inc	2086	F	530 926-3121	2095
Paul A Evans Inc	3531	F	530 859-2505	13740
Sousa Ready Mix LLC	3273	F	530 926-4485	10838

MOUNTAIN PASS, CA - San Bernardino County

	SIC	EMP	PHONE	ENTRY #
Chevron Mining Inc	1221	F	760 856-7625	15
Mp Mine Operations LLC	1481	C	702 277-0848	383

MOUNTAIN VIEW, CA - Santa Clara County

	SIC	EMP	PHONE	ENTRY #
Advanced Materials Analysis	3081	F	650 391-4190	9391
Agilepoint Inc (PA)	7372	E	650 968-6789	23580
Alcatel-Lucent USA Inc	3674	B	408 878-6500	18077
Alivecor Inc (PA)	7372	E	650 396-8650	23594
Alza Corporation	3826	A	650 564-5000	21168
Anda Networks Inc (PA)	3661	F	408 519-4900	17347
Applied Physics Systems Inc (PA)	3829	D	650 965-0500	21434
Apteligent Inc	7372	D	415 371-1402	23620
Ardian Inc	3841	F	650 417-6500	21608
Aromyx Corporation	3822	F	650 430-8100	20783
Asrc Aerospace Corp	3812	E	650 604-5946	20539
Audience Inc (HQ)	3674	D	650 254-2800	18132
Avid Systems Inc (HQ)	3663	C	650 526-1600	17465
Bioelectron Technology Corp (PA)	2834	E	650 641-9200	7805
Blue Coat LLC	7372	A	408 220-2200	23679
Blue Coat Systems LLC (HQ)	7372	D	650 527-8000	23680
Boosted Inc (PA)	3949	E	650 933-5151	22767
C K Tool Company Inc	3599	F	650 968-0261	15811
Cadence Design Systems Inc	7372	E	408 943-1234	23707
Cal Moto	3751	F	650 966-1183	20388
Cathera	3841	F	650 388-5088	21660
Celeros Corp	3572	E	650 325-6900	15012
Chemocentryx Inc (PA)	2834	D	650 210-2900	7841
Cisc Semiconductor Corp	3674	F	847 553-4204	18163
Clearwell Systems Inc	7372	C	877 253-2793	23746
Codar Ocean Sensors Ltd (PA)	3812	E	408 773-8240	20555
Cumulus Networks Inc (PA)	7372	C	650 383-6700	23787
Digital Video Systems Inc (PA)	3651	E	650 938-8815	17219
Driveai Inc	7372	C	408 693-0765	23832
Edcast Inc (PA)	7372	F	650 823-3511	23842
Enervault Corporation	3691	F	408 636-7519	19161
Ericsson Inc	3663	E	972 583-0000	17513
Euphonix Inc (HQ)	3663	D	650 526-1600	17517
Everest Networks Inc	3577	E	408 300-9236	15227
Exotic Silks Inc	2211	F	650 948-8611	2686
Exploramed Nc7 Inc	3845	E	650 559-5805	22255
Eyefluence Inc	3851	E	408 586-8632	22357
Fernqvist Retail Systems Inc (HQ)	2754	F	650 428-0330	6953
Fortanix Inc (PA)	7372	E	628 400-2043	23915
FTC - Forward Threat Control	3669	F	650 906-7917	17729
Fujifilm Wako Diagnostics US	2835	E	650 210-9153	8222
Future Fibre Tech US Inc (HQ)	3699	F	650 903-2222	19315
Guardian Analytics Inc	7372	E	650 383-9200	23960
Guidant Sales LLC	3841	E	650 965-2634	21727
Guy Chaddock & Company (PA)	2512	C	408 907-9200	4644
Guzik Technical Enterprises	3825	D	650 625-8000	21049
Hansen Medical Inc	3841	E	650 404-5800	21731
Hitachi Chem Diagnostics Inc	3821	C	650 961-5501	20761
Hytrust Inc (PA)	7372	E	650 681-8100	23993
Igm Biosciences Inc	2834	D	650 965-7873	7940
Impeva Labs Inc (PA)	3699	F	650 559-0103	19323
Inmage Systems Inc	7372	E	408 200-3840	24022
Intuit Inc (PA)	7372	D	650 944-6000	24035
Intuit Inc	7372	C	650 944-6000	24036
Intuit Inc	7372	F	650 944-6000	24037
Intuit Inc	7372	F	650 944-6000	24038
Iridex Corporation (PA)	3845	C	650 940-4700	22267
Iris Medical Instruments Inc	3845	C	650 940-4700	22268
J G Torres Company of Hawaii (PA)	3272	E	650 967-7293	10590
Jumio Software & Dev LLC	7372	E	650 388-0264	24063
Kaye Sandy Enterprises Inc	3732	E	650 961-5334	20342
Kelly Computer Systems Inc	3577	E	650 960-1010	15264
Khan Academy Inc	7372	D	650 336-5426	24074
Knightscope Inc	3699	F	650 924-1025	19341
Lenz Precision Technology Inc	3599	F	650 966-1784	16144
Lifescience Plus Inc	3841	F	650 565-8172	21777
Matternet Inc (PA)	3728	E	650 260-2727	20169
Medimmune Inc	2834	B	650 603-2000	8006
Microsemi Soc Corp	3674	A	650 318-4200	18413
Microsoft Corporation	7372	D	650 964-7200	24156

	SIC	EMP	PHONE	ENTRY #
Mint Software Inc	7372	F	650 944-6000	24169
Mobileiron Inc (PA)	7372	C	650 919-8100	24174
Mobius Photonics Inc	3699	F	408 496-1084	19358
Monterey Design Systems Inc	3695	C	408 747-7370	19224
Motorola Solutions Inc	3663	D	650 318-3200	17598
Nextinput Inc (PA)	3625	F	408 770-9293	16735
Nokia Slutions Networks US LLC	3661	F	650 623-2767	17391
Nuro Inc	3559	F	650 476-2687	14509
Olio Devices Inc	3873	E	650 918-6546	22482
Omnicell Inc (PA)	3571	B	650 251-6100	14958
Pacific Western Systems Inc (PA)	3825	E	650 961-8855	21096
Pano Logic Inc	3577	D	650 743-1773	15306
Perceptimed Inc	3559	F	650 941-7000	14516
Phoenix Improving Life LLC	3842	F	650 248-0655	22068
Pickering Laboratories Inc	2819	E	650 694-6700	7518
Pinnacle Systems Inc	3663	F	650 237-1900	17623
Proteus Industries Inc	3823	E	650 964-4163	20922
PS Support Inc	7372	F	301 351-9366	24321
Pure Storage Inc (PA)	3572	B	800 379-7873	15077
Qualitau Incorporated (PA)	3825	D	650 282-6226	21107
Rakshak	7372	E	404 513-5867	24338
Realscout Inc	7372	F	650 397-6500	24345
Receivd Inc	7372	F	650 336-5817	24349
Red Hat Inc	7372	F	650 567-9039	24351
Red Robot Labs Inc	3944	F	650 762-8058	22708
Rod L Electronics Inc (PA)	3825	F	650 322-0711	21113
Samsung Sdi America Inc (HQ)	3577	F	408 544-4470	15326
Simplelegal Inc	7372	F	415 763-5366	24413
Soliant Energy Inc	3699	E	626 396-9500	19406
Specific Diagnostics Inc	3841	E	561 655-5588	21908
Speculative Product Design LLC	3161	C	650 462-9086	10210
Spinalmotion Inc	3841	F	650 947-3472	21910
Spine View Inc	3841	D	510 490-1753	21911
Squaglia Manufacturing (PA)	3599	E	650 965-9644	16419
Stackrox Inc (PA)	7372	E	650 489-6769	24449
Staffing Industry Analysts Inc	2741	E	650 390-6200	6347
Stewart Audio (HQ)	3679	F	209 588-8111	19094
Synopsys Inc (PA)	7372	B	650 584-5000	24478
Synplicity Inc (HQ)	7372	C	650 584-5000	24480
T-Ram Semiconductor Inc	3674	E	408 597-3670	18600
Tatung Telecom Corporation	3661	D	650 961-2288	17420
Teachers Curriculum Inst LLC (PA)	2731	E	800 497-6138	6153
Teledyne Defense Elec LLC (HQ)	3679	E	650 691-9800	19108
Teledyne Wireless LLC	3679	C	650 691-9800	19113
Tellme Networks Inc	2741	B	650 693-1009	6357
Thawte Inc	3663	E	650 426-7400	17690
Transfer Engineering & Mfg Inc	3565	E	510 651-3000	14731
Upguard Inc (PA)	7372	E	888 882-3223	24543
Ventus Medical Inc	3841	E	408 200-5299	21951
Verb Surgical Inc	3841	D	408 438-3363	21952
Veritas Software Global LLC	7372	F	650 335-8000	24555
Vibrynt Inc	3845	E	650 362-6100	22326
Virage Logic Corporation (HQ)	3674	B	650 584-5000	18644
Volcano Corporation	3845	B	650 938-5300	22331
Voyant International Corp	7372	F	800 710-6637	24570

MURPHYS, CA - Calaveras County

	SIC	EMP	PHONE	ENTRY #
Blastronix Inc	3577	F	209 795-0738	15174
Kaiser Enterprises Inc	3498	D	209 728-2091	13474

MURRIETA, CA - Riverside County

	SIC	EMP	PHONE	ENTRY #
Abbott Vascular Inc	3841	C	408 845-3186	21574
Apex Conveyor Corp	3535	E	951 304-7808	13815
Apex Conveyor Systems Inc	3535	F	951 304-7808	13816
Art Signworks Inc	3993	F	951 698-8484	23056
Artifcial Grass Recyclers Corp	3999	E	714 635-7000	23279
Aviator Systems Inc	3728	F	949 677-2461	20049
B P John Recycle Inc	2421	E	951 696-1144	3926
California Trusframe LLC (PA)	2439	C	951 350-4880	4294
CMS Circuit Solutions Inc	3672	E	951 698-4452	17853
Coldstone Creamery 256	2024	F	951 304-9777	636
Cryoquip LLC (DH)	3559	F	951 677-2060	14447
Custom Wheels and ACC Inc	3714	F	714 827-5200	19627
Denso Pdts & Svcs Americas Inc	3714	C	951 698-3379	19637
Elite Cabinetry Inc	2599	F	951 698-5050	5057
Express Systems & Engrg Inc	3089	F	951 461-1500	9783
Gamecloud Studios Inc	7372	E	951 677-2345	23926
Glassplax	3231	E	951 677-4800	10362
Global Link Sourcing Inc	2671	D	951 698-1977	5328
Gold Prospectors Assn of Amer	2721	E	951 699-4749	5944
Guano Records LLC	2759	F	714 263-5398	7083
H & M Four-Slide Inc	3599	F	951 461-8244	16011
Ikhana Group Inc	3728	C	951 600-0009	20135
International Immunology Corp	2835	E	951 677-5629	8233
J P Specialties Inc	3089	F	951 763-7077	9847
Jeluz Electric Ltd LLC	3699	E	800 216-8307	19336

Employment Codes: A=Over 500 employees, B=251-500,
C=101-250, D=51-100, E=20-50, F=10-19

2020 California
Manufacturers Register

© Mergent Inc. 1-800-342-5647

1373

GEOGRAPHIC

Company	SIC	EMP	PHONE	ENTRY #
Kingman Industries Inc	2841	E	951 698-1812	8342
Lobue Laser & Eye Medical Ctrs	3845	E	951 696-1135	22272
Logo Joes Inc	2395	F	951 461-0388	3747
Martin Brass Foundry	3366	D	951 698-7041	11402
McCalls Country Canning Inc (PA)	3999	F	951 461-2277	23403
Medical Extrusion Tech Inc (PA)	3082	E	951 698-4346	9432
Muhlhauser Enterprises Inc (PA)	3441	E	909 877-2792	11850
Muhlhauser Steel Inc	3441	E	909 877-2792	11851
Nittobo America Inc	2836	D	951 677-5629	8318
Nuphoton Technologies Inc	3699	E	951 696-8366	19370
Rk Sport Inc	3714	E	951 894-7883	19758
S C Coatings Corporation	3479	E	951 461-9777	13240
T & D Services Inc	1381	F	951 304-1190	106
TMC Ice Protection Systems LLC	3812	E	951 677-6934	20732
Touchpint Elctrnic Sltions LLC	3571	F	951 734-8083	14990
Trek Armor Incorporated	3999	F	951 319-4008	23511
Tuula Inc	2841	F	858 761-6045	8353
U S Air Filtration Inc (PA)	3823	F	951 491-7282	20952
USA Printer Company LLC	2752	F	800 279-7768	6912
Vmc International LLC	3843	F	760 723-1498	22204
Vortex Whirlpool Systems Inc	3088	D	951 940-4556	9597
Vycom America Inc	3672	E	800 235-9195	18047
Waterstone LLC	3432	C	951 304-0520	11688
Yellow Magic Incorporated	7372	F	951 506-4005	24598

NAPA, CA - Napa County

Company	SIC	EMP	PHONE	ENTRY #
Advanced Pressure Technology	3823	D	707 259-0102	20829
Antinori California	2084	E	707 265-8866	1583
Archangel Investments LLC	2084	F	707 944-9261	1584
At Mobile Bottling Line LLC	2086	F	707 257-3757	2041
AUL Corp (PA)	7694	F	707 257-9700	24684
Awg Ltd Inc	2084	F	707 259-6777	1587
Babcock & Wilcox Company	3511	E	707 259-1122	13561
Barbour Vineyards LLC	2084	F	707 257-1829	1590
Bergin Glass Impressions Inc	3231	E	707 224-0111	10341
Biale Estate	2084	F	707 257-7555	1599
Black Stallion Winery LLC	2084	F	707 253-1400	1600
Blacktalon Industries Inc	3496	F	707 256-1812	13398
Bottlers Unlimited Inc	2086	E	707 255-0595	2044
Bouchaine Vineyards Inc	2084	E	707 252-9065	1605
California Etching Inc	3479	F	707 224-9966	13153
Carneros Ranching Inc	2084	E	707 253-9464	1620
Cemex Materials LLC	3273	E	707 255-3035	10739
Chateau Potelle Inc	2084	E	707 255-9440	1633
Cliff Vine Winery Inc	2084	F	707 944-2388	1636
Clos Du Val Wine Company Ltd	2084	E	707 259-2200	1639
Codorniu Napa Inc	2084	D	707 254-2148	1643
Collotype Labels USA Inc (HQ)	2759	D	707 603-2500	7028
County of NAPA	3823	F	707 259-8620	20852
Cultured Stone Corporation (DH)	3272	A	707 255-1727	10558
Darioush Khaledi Winery LLC	2084	F	707 257-2345	1656
Decor Shower Door and Glass Co	3231	F	707 253-0622	10353
Decrevel Incorporated	3544	F	707 258-8065	14041
Delicato Vineyards	2084	E	707 265-1700	1660
Delicato Vineyards	2084	E	707 253-1400	1661
Demptos NAPA Cooperage (HQ)	2449	E	707 257-2628	4415
Dexta Corporation	3843	D	707 255-2454	22148
Diageo North America Inc	2084	D	707 299-2600	1666
Distinctive Prpts NAPA Vly	2721	E	707 256-2251	5921
Eco Global Solutions Inc	3822	F	707 254-9844	20792
Etude Wines Inc	2084	F	707 257-5300	1693
Eurostampa North America Inc	2759	F	707 927-4848	7059
Feather Farm Inc	3496	F	707 255-8833	13411
Golden State Vintners	2084	E	707 254-1985	1727
Hagafen Cellars Inc	2084	F	707 252-0781	1741
Hayward Enterprises Inc	2037	F	707 261-5100	913
Hedgeside Vintners	2084	F	707 963-2134	1751
Hess Collection Winery (DH)	2084	E	707 255-1144	1752
Huneeus Vintners LLC (PA)	2084	E	707 286-2724	1757
Hurleys LP	2599	D	707 944-2345	5065
Jarvis	2084	F	707 255-5280	1772
John Pina Jr & Sons	2084	F	707 944-2229	1775
Krupp Brothers LLC	2084	F	707 226-2215	1784
Laird Family Estate LLC (PA)	2084	F	707 257-0360	1792
Le Belge Chocolatier Inc	2064	E	707 258-9200	1383
Lixit Corporation (PA)	3999	D	800 358-8254	23397
Luna Vineyards Inc	2084	E	707 255-2474	1806
Mello Sales Group Inc	3999	F	707 257-6451	23407
Mont St John Cellars Inc	2084	F	707 255-8864	1821
Monticello Cellars Inc	2084	D	707 253-2802	1824
Myers Wine Cntry Kitchens LLC	3221	F	707 252-9463	10289
NAPA Beaucanon Estate	2084	F	707 254-1460	1834
NAPA Printing & Graphics Ctr (PA)	2752	F	707 257-6555	6743
NAPA Valley Coffee Roasting Co (PA)	2095	F	707 224-2233	2305
NAPA Valley Publishing Co	2711	D	707 226-3711	5769
NAPA Valley Publishing Co (PA)	2711	E	707 226-3711	5770

Company	SIC	EMP	PHONE	ENTRY #
North Bay Plywood Inc	2431	E	707 224-7849	4096
Pacific Steel Group	3449	E	707 669-3136	12599
Perfect Puree of NAPA Vly LLC	2037	F	707 261-5100	924
Pine Ridge Winery LLC	2084	D	707 253-7500	1866
Portocork America Inc	2499	F	707 258-3930	4521
Prolab Orthotics Inc	3069	F	707 257-4400	9359
Radiator Specialty Company	2899	E	707 252-0122	9018
Rang Dong Joint Stock Company	2084	F	707 259-9446	1880
Regulus Intgrted Solutions LLC	2752	E	707 254-4000	6842
Regusci Vineyard MGT Inc	2084	E	707 254-0403	1884
River City	2599	E	707 253-1111	5079
Robert Mondavi Corporation (HQ)	2084	D	707 967-2100	1891
Robinson Family Winery	2084	F	707 287-8428	1893
Rombauer Vineyards Inc	2084	F	209 245-6979	1895
Royal Drapery Manufacturing	2391	E	707 226-2022	3595
Saintsbury LLC	2084	E	707 252-0592	1905
Sciambr-Passini French Bky Inc	2051	E	707 252-3072	1273
Seguin Moreau Holdings Inc (PA)	2449	D	707 252-3408	4427
Shafer Vineyards	2084	F	707 944-2877	1913
Showertek Inc	3231	F	707 224-1480	10390
Silenus Vintners	2084	F	707 299-3930	1917
Stags Leap Wine Cellars	2084	C	707 944-2020	1928
Sterling Vineyards Inc	2084	E	707 252-7410	1931
Sutter Home Winery Inc	2084	E	707 963-3104	1943
Sweetie Pies LLC	2051	F	707 257-7280	1281
Top It Off Bottling LLC	2084	F	707 252-0331	1960
Treasury Wine Estates Americas (HQ)	2084	B	707 259-4500	1963
Treasury Wine Estates Americas	2084	C	707 259-4500	1964
Trefethen Vineyards Winery Inc	2084	E	707 255-7700	1970
Tschida Engineering	3599	F	707 224-4482	16476
Tulocay Winery	2084	F	707 255-4064	1973
Vignette Winery LLC	2084	F	707 637-8821	1983
Villa Encinal Partners LP	2084	E	707 945-1220	1985
Wild Horse Industrial Corp	3565	F	707 265-6001	14737
Wildflower Linen Inc (PA)	2299	E	714 522-2777	2956
Wine Country Cases Inc	2449	D	707 967-4805	4432
World Wine Bottles LLC	3221	E	707 339-2102	10294

NATIONAL CITY, CA - San Diego County

Company	SIC	EMP	PHONE	ENTRY #
Adelaide Marine Services LLC	2992	F	619 852-8722	9128
Adept Process Services Inc	3732	E	619 434-3194	20310
Apparel Enterprises Co Inc	2339	E	619 474-6916	3285
B and P Plastics Inc	3089	E	619 477-1893	9649
Bay City Marine Inc (PA)	3441	E	619 477-3991	11747
Bay City Marine Inc	3731	E	619 477-3991	20279
Carroll Metal Works Inc	3441	D	619 477-9125	11763
Coastal Decking Inc	3731	E	619 477-0567	20282
Costco Wholesale Corporation	3827	B	619 336-3360	21346
Craft Labor & Support Svcs LLC	3731	D	619 336-9977	20286
Dav Termite & Pest Inc	2879	F	619 828-8901	8826
Fabrication Tech Inds Inc	3441	D	619 477-4141	11791
Family Loompya Corporation	2099	E	619 477-2125	2455
G V Industries Inc	3599	E	619 474-3013	15982
Gary Manufacturing Inc	3089	E	619 429-4479	9800
Ghazal & Sons Inc (PA)	2673	D	619 474-6677	5397
Hyperbaric Technologies Inc	3845	D	619 336-2022	22263
Indu Fashions	2325	E	619 336-4638	3008
Jaann Inc	3441	F	619 336-0584	11815
Navigational Services Inc	3731	F	619 477-1564	20296
Pacific Welding & Fabrication	7692	F	619 336-1758	24655
Pacord Inc	3731	E	619 336-2200	20299
Paige Sitta & Associates Inc (PA)	3731	E	619 233-5912	20300
Pro Team Axis LLC	2833	F	833 333-2947	7684
San Diego Arcft Interiors Inc	2511	E	619 474-1997	4610
Simec USA Corporation	3312	E	619 474-7081	11069
Southern California Insulation	3731	E	619 477-1303	20305
Southland Clutch Inc	3714	E	619 477-2105	19770
Special Forces Custom Gear Inc	2393	E	619 241-5453	3665
Underground Autowerks Inc (PA)	3423	F	619 336-9000	11550
Vantage Associates Inc	3728	E	619 477-6940	20266
Vantage Associates Inc (PA)	3769	E	619 477-6940	20481
Walashek Industrial & Mar Inc	3731	E	619 498-1711	20308
Westflex Inc (PA)	3052	E	619 474-7400	9211

NEEDLES, CA - San Bernardino County

Company	SIC	EMP	PHONE	ENTRY #
Tri State Truss Corporation	2439	F	760 326-3868	4323

NELSON, CA - Butte County

Company	SIC	EMP	PHONE	ENTRY #
Far West Rice Inc	2044	E	530 891-1339	1039

NEVADA CITY, CA - Nevada County

Company	SIC	EMP	PHONE	ENTRY #
Barry Costello	2386	F	530 265-3300	3508
Best Sanitizers Inc	2842	D	530 265-1800	8367
Dylern Incorporated	3599	E	530 470-8785	15913
N C W G Inc	2084	F	530 265-9463	1832
Rcd Engineering Inc	3625	F	530 292-3133	16742
Savensealcom Ltd	2673	F	530 478-0238	5417

Company	SIC	EMP	PHONE	ENTRY #
Sierra Metal Fabricators Inc	3441	E	530 265-4591	11880
Sonic Technology Products Inc	3674	E	530 272-4607	18571
Technicolor Usa Inc	3663	A	530 478-3000	17682
Witt Hillard	2842	E	530 510-0756	8424

NEW CUYAMA, CA - Santa Barbara County

Company	SIC	EMP	PHONE	ENTRY #
E & B Ntral Resources MGT Corp	1382	E	661 766-2501	120

NEWARK, CA - Alameda County

Company	SIC	EMP	PHONE	ENTRY #
Accurate Tube Bending Inc	3498	E	510 790-6500	13454
Agilent Technologies Inc	3825	B	510 794-1234	20987
Air Solutions LLC	3585	E	510 573-6474	15409
Aradigm Corporation (PA)	2834	E	510 265-9000	7762
Atieva Usa Inc (HQ)	3711	B	510 648-3553	19455
BASF Corporation	2869	F	510 796-9911	8718
Caliente Systems Inc	3443	D	510 790-0300	11999
Cellotape Inc (HQ)	3993	C	510 651-5551	23074
Crown Mfg Co Inc	3089	E	510 742-8800	9735
Cymabay Therapeutics Inc (PA)	2834	E	510 293-8800	7860
Dow Chemical Company	2819	C	510 797-2281	7485
Dwell Home Inc	2519	E	877 864-5752	4765
Emcore Corporation	3674	F	510 896-2139	18212
Envia Systems Inc	3699	E	510 509-1367	19305
Etm—Electromatic Inc (PA)	3663	D	510 471-1100	17516
Five Star Lumber Company LLC (PA)	2448	E	510 795-7204	4367
Foot Locker Retail Inc	3149	F	510 797-5750	10179
Fullbloom Baking Company Inc	2051	B	510 456-3638	1209
Futuris Automotive (ca) LLC	2396	B	510 771-2300	3788
Incarda Therapeutics Inc	2834	E	510 422-5522	7949
Jri Inc	3444	E	510 494-5300	12257
Kateeva Inc	3663	B	510 953-7600	17551
Knt Inc	3599	C	510 651-7163	16122
Knt Manufacturing Inc	3999	E	510 896-1699	23385
Kwj Engineering Inc (PA)	3829	E	510 794-4296	21498
Landmark Label Manufacturing	2759	E	510 651-5551	7116
Lifetrak Incorporated	3845	F	510 413-9030	22271
Logitech Inc (HQ)	3577	B	510 795-8500	15278
Logitech Streaming Media Inc	3679	E	510 795-8500	18994
Matheson Tri-Gas Inc	2813	F	510 714-3026	7417
Matheson Tri-Gas Inc	2813	D	510 793-2559	7419
Medina Medical Inc	3841	F	650 396-7756	21802
Mitac Information Systems	3577	D	510 668-3679	15291
Mitac Information Systems Corp (DH)	3572	C	510 284-3000	15059
Morton Salt Inc	2899	F	510 797-2281	9003
Nakagawa Manufacturing USA Inc	2621	E	510 782-0197	5133
Neato Robotics Inc (HQ)	3549	D	510 795-1351	14276
Nefab Packaging Inc	2441	D	408 678-2500	4340
Nevada Heat Treating LLC (PA)	7692	E	510 790-2300	24653
Novaray Medical Inc	3844	F	510 619-9200	22219
Oatey Co	2891	F	800 321-9532	8882
Pabco Building Products LLC	3275	D	510 792-9555	10881
Pabco Building Products LLC	3275	E	510 792-1577	10882
Protagonist Therapeutics Inc	2834	D	510 474-0170	8089
Quality Quartz Engineering Inc (PA)	3679	E	510 791-1013	19061
Quark Pharmaceuticals Inc (DH)	2834	E	510 402-4020	8094
Revance Therapeutics Inc	2834	C	510 742-3400	8105
Rh Products Inc	2448	E	510 794-6676	4395
Salutron Incorporated (PA)	3845	E	510 795-2876	22307
San Francisco Bay Brand Inc (PA)	2048	E	510 792-7200	1125
Shotspotter Inc	7372	D	510 794-3100	24407
Silicon Valley Mfg Inc	3315	E	510 791-9450	11108
Smart Global Holdings Inc	3674	E	510 623-1231	18564
Smart Modular Technologies Inc (HQ)	3674	C	510 623-1231	18566
Smart Storage Systems Inc (DH)	3572	F	510 623-1231	15102
Smart Wireless Computing Inc (HQ)	3679	F	510 683-9999	19083
Socket Mobile Inc	3663	D	510 933-3000	17663
Specilized Packg Solutions Inc	2449	E	510 494-5670	4428
Svm Machining Inc	3441	E	510 791-9450	11893
Tesla Inc	3711	A	510 896-6400	19505
Theranos Inc (PA)	3841	D	650 838-9292	21928
Thousandshores Inc	3571	F	510 477-0249	14988
Venture Electronics Intl Inc	3672	F	510 744-3720	18044
Wintec Industries Inc (PA)	3577	D	510 953-7440	15367

NEWBERRY SPRINGS, CA - San Bernardino County

Company	SIC	EMP	PHONE	ENTRY #
Elementis Specialties Inc	1459	E	760 257-9112	378

NEWBURY PARK, CA - Ventura County

Company	SIC	EMP	PHONE	ENTRY #
360 Systems	3651	F	818 991-0360	17178
Amgen Inc	2834	F	805 499-0512	7749
Amgen Inc	2834	D	805 447-1000	7751
Amgen Manufacturing Limited	3999	F	787 656-2000	23274
Aqua Man Inc (PA)	3589	F	805 499-5707	15483
Arconic Inc	3334	B	805 262-4230	11178
Atara Biotherapeutics Inc	2834	F	805 623-4211	7775
Boostpower USA Inc	3519	F	805 376-6077	13584
CHE Precision Inc	3599	F	805 499-8885	15841

Company	SIC	EMP	PHONE	ENTRY #
Colorful Products Corporation	2844	F	805 498-2195	8461
Componetics Inc	3677	F	805 498-0939	18708
Compulink Business Systems Inc (PA)	7372	D	805 446-2050	23765
Condor Pacific Inds Cal Inc	3728	E	818 889-2150	20076
Diamond Ground Products Inc	3548	E	805 498-3837	14240
Eca Medical Instruments (DH)	3841	E	805 376-2509	21694
Electronic Sensor Tech Inc	3826	F	805 480-1994	21221
Eli Lilly and Company	2834	C	805 499-5475	7877
Envel Design Corporation	3646	F	805 376-8111	17029
Excaliber Systems Inc	2759	F	805 376-1366	7060
Fc Management Services	3559	E	805 499-0050	14466
Filthy Grill Inc	3631	F	818 282-2017	16811
Follmer Development Inc	2813	E	805 498-4531	7413
Grateful Naturals Corp	2844	F	323 379-4553	8503
H and M Industries LLC	2541	F	805 499-5100	4908
H J S Graphics	2752	F	818 782-5490	6601
H K Lighting Group Inc	3648	F	805 480-4881	17131
Isolutecom Inc (PA)	7372	E	805 498-6259	24048
JBW Precision Inc	3444	E	805 499-1973	12253
JW Molding Inc	3544	F	805 499-2682	14065
Ltd Tech Inc	3549	F	805 480-1886	14274
Meisei Corporation	3546	F	805 497-2626	14224
Millworks Etc Inc	3442	F	805 499-3400	11972
Multilayer Prototypes Inc	3672	F	805 498-9390	17929
Odcombe Press (nashville)	2752	E	615 793-5414	6757
Onyx Pharmaceuticals Inc	2834	A	650 266-0000	8054
Petunia Pickle Bottom Corp	2211	F	805 643-6697	2708
Point Nine Technologies Inc (PA)	3674	F	805 375-6600	18473
Qorvo California Inc	3679	E	805 480-5050	19059
Qorvo Us Inc	3679	F	805 480-5099	19060
R F Circuits and Assembly Inc	3672	F	805 499-7788	17971
Saco	3699	E	805 499-7788	19398
Scientific Surface Inds Inc	2541	F	805 499-5100	4936
Shire	2834	F	805 372-3000	8127
Skyworks Solutions Inc	3674	D	805 480-4400	18562
Skyworks Solutions Inc	3674	D	805 480-4227	18563
Smith Precision Products Co	3561	F	805 498-6616	14598
Transparent Devices Inc	3577	F	805 499-5000	15354
Victory Custom Athletics	2339	D	818 349-8476	3430
Wain Industries	3679	F	805 581-5900	19140
Weldlogic Inc	7692	D	805 375-1670	24678
Wirewright Inc	3089	F	805 499-9194	10127
WV Communications Inc	3663	F	805 376-1820	17709
You Are Loved Foods LLC	2051	F	818 578-8288	1299
Zed Audio Corporation	3651	F	805 499-5559	17309

NEWCASTLE, CA - Placer County

Company	SIC	EMP	PHONE	ENTRY #
Omega Diamond Inc	3545	F	916 652-8122	14179
Sierra Safety Company	3499	F	916 663-2026	13546

NEWHALL, CA - Los Angeles County

Company	SIC	EMP	PHONE	ENTRY #
Berry Petroleum Company LLC	1311	F	661 255-6066	24

NEWMAN, CA - Stanislaus County

Company	SIC	EMP	PHONE	ENTRY #
Cemex Cnstr Mtls PCF LLC	3273	E	209 862-0182	10727
Index Printing Inc	2759	E	209 862-2222	7095
Newman Flange & Fitting Co	3462	D	209 862-2977	12715
Stewart & Jasper Marketing Inc (PA)	2068	C	209 862-9600	1439
Vsp Products Inc	2034	D	209 862-1200	875
Westside Pallet Inc	2448	D	209 862-3941	4408

NEWPORT BEACH, CA - Orange County

Company	SIC	EMP	PHONE	ENTRY #
260 Resource Management LLC	1389	F	866 700-1031	149
A & A Ready Mixed Concrete Inc (PA)	3273	E	949 253-2800	10672
Able Software Inc	7372	E	949 274-8321	23544
Adaptive Digital Systems Inc	3663	E	949 955-3116	17437
Air Products and Chemicals Inc	2813	F	949 474-1860	7397
American Vanguard Corporation (PA)	2879	D	949 260-1200	8818
AMS Drilling	1381	F	949 232-1149	86
Amvac Chemical Corporation (HQ)	2879	E	323 264-3910	8819
Amvac Chemical Corporation	2879	F	949 260-1212	8820
Anacapa Marine Services (PA)	3732	F	805 985-1818	20312
Applied Materials Inc	3674	E	949 244-1600	18108
Associated Ready Mix Con Inc (PA)	3273	E	949 253-2800	10692
Balboa Boat Yard Inc	3732	F	949 673-6834	20313
Basin Marine Inc	3732	F	949 673-0360	20314
Builder & Developer Magazines	2721	F	949 631-0308	5894
C & H Hydraulics Inc	3728	F	949 646-6230	20060
Calor Apparel Group Intl Corp	2341	E	949 548-9095	3440
CDM Company Inc	3999	E	949 644-2820	23301
Center Line Wheel Corporation	3714	D	562 921-9637	19613
Churm Publishing Inc (PA)	2721	E	714 796-7000	5904
Clinical Formula LLC	2834	F	949 631-0149	7843
Comac America Corporation	3721	F	760 616-9614	19890
Conexant Holdings Inc	3674	A	415 983-2706	18174
Conexant Systems Worldwide Inc	3674	D	949 483-4600	18176
Conversionpoint Holdings Inc	7372	D	888 706-6764	23774

GEOGRAPHIC

	SIC	EMP	PHONE	ENTRY #
Crm Co LLC (PA)	3061	E	949 263-9100	9261
Crossport Mocean	2311	F	949 646-1701	2962
Cure Medical LLC (PA)	3841	F	800 570-1778	21676
Duffield Marine Inc	3732	E	949 645-6812	20327
Electric Bike Company LLC	3751	F	949 264-4080	20399
Ericsson Inc	3577	D	949 721-6604	15226
Evolus Inc (DH)	2834	D	949 284-4555	7884
Fantasea Enterprises Inc	3732	F	949 673-8465	20329
Firstelement Fuel Inc	2869	F	949 274-5701	8739
Freeform Research & Dev	3545	F	949 646-3217	14160
Fruselva Usa LLC	2033	F	949 798-0061	769
Fusion Diet Systems Inc (PA)	2023	F	801 783-1194	592
Gst Inc	3572	D	949 510-1142	15035
Hacker Industries Inc (PA)	3275	F	949 729-3101	10879
Hixson Metal Finishing	3471	D	800 900-9798	13025
Hmr Building Systems LLC	2421	F	951 749-4700	3935
Image Magazine Inc	2721	E	949 608-5188	5961
Jazz Semiconductor Inc (DH)	3674	A	949 435-8000	18329
Lebata Inc	3273	E	949 253-2800	10779
Lewis Barricade Inc	2951	E	661 363-0912	9097
Lumens Audio Visual Inc	3669	F	970 988-6268	17743
M L Interiors Inc	2391	F	949 723-5001	3590
Macom Technology Solutions Inc	3663	F	310 320-6160	17579
Mfi Inc	3999	F	949 887-8691	23409
Microtelematics Inc	7372	F	949 537-3636	24164
Mindspeed Technologies LLC (HQ)	3674	D	949 579-3000	18416
Morris Roberts LLC	3993	E	800 672-3974	23163
Mscsoftware Corporation (HQ)	7372	C	714 540-8900	24180
Newport Fab LLC	3674	D	949 435-8000	18434
Optek Group Inc	3845	E	949 629-2558	22292
Peninsula Publishing Inc	2721	E	949 631-1307	6001
Platescan Inc	3469	E	949 851-1600	12857
Redart Corporation	2531	F	714 774-9444	4870
Rsdg International Inc	2361	E	626 256-4190	3488
RSI Home Products Inc	2514	A	949 720-1116	4700
SGB Holdings LLC	3911	E	949 722-1149	22571
Sky Global Services Inc	3999	F	949 291-5511	23477
Soldo Capital Inc (DH)	2819	E	800 659-6745	7527
Strategic Medical Ventures LLC (PA)	3844	E	949 355-5212	22222
Synergy Oil LLC	3569	F	888 333-1933	14864
Towerjazz Texas Inc (DH)	3679	D	949 435-8000	19120
Tribeworx LLC	7372	D	800 949-3432	24526
Triton Chandelier Inc	3646	E	714 957-9600	17078
Tz Holdings LP	7372	A	949 719-2200	24534
Ultra H2 LP	2023	F	657 999-5188	623
Urban Decal LLC (HQ)	2844	E	949 574-9712	8597
Verb Technology Company Inc (PA)	7372	F	855 250-2300	24552
Voltedge LLC	3571	F	949 877-8900	14997
Walden Structures Inc	2452	D	909 389-9100	4470
WE Hall Company Inc (PA)	3316	F	949 650-4555	11122

NEWPORT COAST, CA - Orange County

	SIC	EMP	PHONE	ENTRY #
AST Power LLC	3694	E	949 226-2275	19185

NICE, CA - Lake County

	SIC	EMP	PHONE	ENTRY #
Bent Fir Company	2511	F	707 274-6628	4554

NICOLAUS, CA - Sutter County

	SIC	EMP	PHONE	ENTRY #
Paulsen White Oak LP	2879	F	530 656-2201	8838

NIPOMO, CA - San Luis Obispo County

	SIC	EMP	PHONE	ENTRY #
LR Baggs Corporation	3931	E	805 929-3545	22629
Malcolm Demille Inc	3911	F	805 929-4353	22545
Statewide Safety and Signs I	3669	B	714 468-1919	17764
Triactive America Inc	3949	F	805 595-1005	22910
Troesh Readymix Inc	3273	D	805 928-3764	10857
Whites Hvac Services Inc	3585	F	805 801-0167	15474

NIPTON, CA - San Bernardino County

	SIC	EMP	PHONE	ENTRY #
NRG Energy Services LLC	3612	D	702 815-2023	16564

NORCO, CA - Riverside County

	SIC	EMP	PHONE	ENTRY #
Avid Idntification Systems Inc (PA)	3674	D	951 371-7505	18137
Canidae Corporation	2047	F	909 599-5190	1070
Gentle Giants Products Inc	2047	F	951 818-2512	1074
Halle-Hopper LLC	2431	E	951 284-7373	4053
Husk-ITT Distributors Corp	2992	F	951 340-4000	9145
Industrial Process Eqp Inc	3567	F	714 447-0171	14766
Inland Artfl Limb & Brace Inc (PA)	3842	F	951 734-1805	22032
Inland Color Graphics	2796	F	951 493-2999	7377
International E-Z Up Inc (PA)	2394	D	800 457-4233	3687
Jeffrey Court Inc	3253	D	951 340-3383	10444
Paragon Building Products Inc (PA)	3272	E	951 549-1155	10622
Positron Access Solutions Inc	3663	F	951 272-9100	17625
Protech Thermal Services	3398	F	951 272-5808	11466
RPM Grinding Co Inc	3599	F	951 273-0602	16376
S R Machining-Properties LLC	3599	C	951 520-9486	16382

	SIC	EMP	PHONE	ENTRY #
Schultz Controls Inc	3613	F	714 693-2900	16613
Sierra Woodworking Inc	2431	E	949 493-4528	4125
Sr Plastics Company LLC (PA)	3089	F	951 520-9486	10065
Sr Plastics Company LLC	3089	F	951 479-5394	10066
W B Powell Inc	2431	E	951 270-0095	4146

NORTH FORK, CA - Madera County

	SIC	EMP	PHONE	ENTRY #
Crossroads Recycled Lumber LLC	2421	F	559 877-3645	3931

NORTH HIGHLANDS, CA - Sacramento County

	SIC	EMP	PHONE	ENTRY #
ACS Controls Corporation	3822	F	916 640-8800	20780
Kacee Company	3599	F	916 348-3204	16102
Livingstons Concrete Svc Inc (PA)	3273	E	916 334-4313	10795
Livingstons Concrete Svc Inc	3273	E	916 334-4313	10796
Mikes Sheet Metal Products	3444	E	916 348-3800	12302
New Wave Industries Ltd (PA)	3589	F	800 882-8854	15549
Pacific Coast Supply LLC	2439	F	916 339-8100	4314
Pisor Industries Inc	3599	F	916 944-2851	16298
Scafco Corporation	3523	E	916 642-7700	13669
Security Contractor Svcs Inc	3446	F	916 338-4800	12508
Steeler Inc	3444	F	916 483-3600	12389

NORTH HILLS, CA - Los Angeles County

	SIC	EMP	PHONE	ENTRY #
Alpha Aviation Components Inc (PA)	3599	E	818 894-8801	15725
Alpha Aviation Components Inc	3599	F	818 894-8468	15726
Challenge Graphics Inc	2752	E	818 892-0123	6480
Graphics Bindery	2789	F	818 886-2463	7332
Imperial Toy LLC (PA)	3944	C	818 536-6500	22682
Morris Enterprises Inc	3089	E	818 894-9103	9912
PCA Electronics Inc	3677	E	818 892-0761	18731
S & J Prof Property Svcs	1321	E	818 892-0181	80
Schrillo Company LLC	3452	E	818 894-8241	12692
Valley Drapery Inc	2221	D	818 892-7744	2738

NORTH HOLLYWOOD, CA - Los Angeles County

	SIC	EMP	PHONE	ENTRY #
6480 Corporation	2759	E	818 765-9670	6969
A T Parker Inc (PA)	3699	E	818 755-1700	19245
ABC Sun Control LLC	2394	F	818 982-6989	3672
Advanced Inst of Skin Care	2844	F	818 765-2606	8432
Advanced Semiconductor Inc (PA)	3674	D	818 982-1200	18067
Airgas Usa LLC	2813	F	818 787-6010	7407
Alco Tech Inc	3469	F	818 503-9209	12762
Allan Aircraft Supply Co LLC	3494	F	818 765-4992	13344
Almore Dye House Inc	2269	E	818 506-5444	2850
Alpena Sausage Inc	2013	F	818 505-9482	435
American Costume Corp	2389	F	818 432-4350	3539
Americh Corporation (PA)	3842	C	818 982-1711	21980
Anmar Precision Components	3728	F	818 764-0901	20036
Applica Inc	3663	E	818 565-0011	17456
AR Casting Inc	3911	E	818 765-1202	22496
Architectural Plywood Inc	2435	E	818 255-1900	4273
Armenco Catrg Trck Mfg Co Inc	3713	E	818 768-0400	19518
Armored Group Inc	2441	E	818 767-3030	4329
Artcrafters Cabinets Inc	2434	E	818 752-8960	4166
Arte De Mexico Inc	3646	E	818 753-4510	17012
Artisan House Inc	3499	E	818 767-7476	13499
Asi Semiconductor Inc	3674	E	818 982-1200	18129
Astro Chrome and Polsg Corp	3471	E	818 781-1463	12937
Ave Jewelry Inc	3911	E	213 488-0097	22500
Avibank Mfg Inc (DH)	3728	C	818 392-2100	20050
Backstage Equipment Inc	3449	E	818 504-6026	12585
Basaw Manufacturing Inc (PA)	2441	E	818 765-6650	4330
Basaw Services Inc	2441	E	818 765-6650	4331
Basaw Services Inc	2441	E	818 765-6650	4332
Bauers & Collins	3842	E	818 983-1281	21984
Black Phoenix Inc	2844	F	818 506-9404	8445
Bogner Amplification	3651	E	818 765-8929	17207
Cal-June Inc (PA)	3429	E	323 877-4164	11576
Capco/Psa	3089	E	818 762-4276	9693
Carl Nersesian	2431	F	818 888-0111	4015
Cecilias Designs Inc	2395	E	323 584-6151	3729
Cheerpak	2043	F	818 922-5451	1017
Clarke Engineering Inc	3566	E	818 768-0690	14740
Corporate Impressions La Inc	2759	E	818 761-9295	7035
Cosmo - Pharm Inc	2833	E	818 764-0246	7650
Crabtree Glass Company Inc	3446	E	818 765-1840	12464
Crane Co	3492	E	310 403-2820	13326
Cryogenic Machinery Corp	3559	F	818 765-6688	14445
Custom Plastic Form Inc	3089	E	818 765-2229	9738
Daily Doses LLC	2711	E	858 220-0076	5606
Dakotahouse Industries Inc	1499	E	310 596-1100	385
Datagenics Software Inc	7372	E	818 487-3900	23804
Davenport International Corp	3651	E	818 765-6400	17217
Dennis Bolton Enterprises Inc	2752	E	818 982-1800	6535
Deux Lux Inc (PA)	3172	E	213 746-7040	10233
Dowell Aluminum Foundry Inc	3365	F	323 877-9645	11378
Electromatic Inc	3471	F	818 765-3236	12999

Mergent email: customerrelations@mergent.com
1376

2020 California
Manufacturers Register

(P-0000) Products & Services Section entry number
(PA)=Parent Co (HQ)=Headquarters (DH)=Div Headquarters

Company	SIC	EMP	PHONE	ENTRY #
Empire Optical of California	3851	E	818 997-6474	22352
Enviro-Intercept Inc	3585	F	818 982-6063	15430
F & H Plating LLC	3471	F	818 765-1221	13008
Fastener Technology Corp	3965	D	818 764-6467	23001
Fayes Foods Inc	2099	E	818 508-8392	2456
G & H Precision Inc	3599	F	818 982-3873	15979
G2 Graphic Service Inc	2759	D	818 623-3100	7071
Gahh LLC (HQ)	3714	F	800 722-2292	19666
General Wax Co Inc (PA)	3999	D	818 765-5800	23342
Glima Inc	2339	F	818 980-9686	3329
Gourmet Coffee Warehouse Inc	2095	D	818 423-2626	2295
Graphic Visions Inc	2752	E	818 845-8393	6596
Groundwork Coffee Roasters LLC	2095	C	818 506-6020	2297
Harman Press	2752	F	818 432-0570	6605
Hope Plastic Co Inc	3089	E	818 769-5560	9829
Hughes Price & Sharp Inc	2711	E	865 675-6278	5668
Infinity Access Plus Inc	3446	F	818 270-8172	12481
Inter Color Plus Inter	2759	E	818 764-5034	7100
Jack C Drees Grinding Co Inc	3599	F	818 764-8301	16070
Jam Design Inc	3961	F	818 505-1680	22984
Jay Manufacturing Corp	3469	F	818 255-0500	12826
John A Thomson PHD	2833	E	323 877-5186	7673
Johnson doc Enterprises	3089	F	818 764-1543	9858
Johnson Marble Machinery Inc	3559	F	818 764-6186	14485
Karapet Engineering Inc	3599	F	818 255-0838	16107
Kk Audio Inc	3861	E	818 765-2921	22436
Klune Industries Inc (DH)	3728	B	818 503-8100	20149
Kobis Windows & Doors Mfg Inc	2434	F	818 764-6400	4219
Lepera Enterprises Inc	3751	E	818 767-5110	20414
Lob-Ster Inc (PA)	3949	F	818 764-6000	22843
Lookout Enterprises Inc	2096	F	323 969-0178	2337
Mar Engineering Company	3599	E	818 765-4805	16170
Mave Enterprises Inc	2064	E	818 767-4533	1388
Meco-Nag Corporation	3144	D	818 764-2020	10172
Meggitt North Hollywood Inc (HQ)	3491	C	818 764-3800	13314
Metal Improvement Company LLC	3398	D	818 983-1952	11457
Mid Century Imports Inc	2511	F	818 509-3050	4592
Mid Michigan Trading Post Ltd	2741	D	517 323-9020	6281
Modern Studio Equipment Inc	3861	F	818 764-8574	22441
Modern-Aire Ventilating Inc	3444	F	818 765-9870	12307
My Sign Design LLC	2752	F	818 384-0800	6741
Nelson Thread Grinding Inc	3599	F	818 768-2578	16241
North Hollywood Uniform Inc	2337	F	818 503-5931	3270
Norths Bakery California Inc	2051	F	818 761-2892	1250
Onnik Shoe Company Inc	3144	E	818 506-5353	10174
Orion Ornamental Iron Inc	3429	E	818 752-0688	11617
Pacific Wire Products Inc	3496	E	818 755-6400	13425
Perkins	3548	F	818 764-9293	14250
Perpetual Motion Group Inc	3441	D	818 982-4300	11863
Praxair Distribution Inc	2813	F	818 760-2011	7444
Precision Engineering Inds	3679	F	818 767-8590	19051
Prime Building Material Inc (PA)	3272	E	818 765-6767	10630
Prime Building Material Inc	3272	F	818 503-4242	10631
Quality Powder Coating LLC	3479	F	818 982-8322	13235
Raika Inc	3172	E	818 503-5911	10242
Reel Efx Inc	3999	E	818 762-1710	23459
S & K Theatrical Drap Inc	2391	F	818 503-0596	3596
Sealing Corporation	3053	F	818 765-7327	9255
Shafton Inc	2389	F	818 985-5025	3578
Spec Iron Inc	3441	F	818 765-4070	11883
Specialty Coatings & Chem Inc	2851	F	818 983-0055	8682
Sr3 Solutions LLC	2711	F	818 255-3131	5836
Steve Leshner Clear Systems	3089	F	818 764-9223	10071
Target Media Partners (HQ)	2759	F	323 930-3123	7239
United Audio Video Group Inc	3695	E	818 980-6700	19239
Utility Refrigerator	3585	F	818 764-6200	15469
Vapor Delux Inc (PA)	2782	F	818 856-3750	7323
Vector Electronics & Tech Inc	3672	E	818 985-8208	18041
Wes Go Inc	2759	E	818 504-1200	7267
Wilshire Precision Pdts Inc	3599	F	818 765-4571	16530

NORTH PALM SPRINGS, CA - Riverside County

Company	SIC	EMP	PHONE	ENTRY #
E & S Precision Sheetmetal Mfg	3444	F	760 329-1607	12189
Technique Designs Inc	2541	F	760 904-6223	4948

NORTHRIDGE, CA - Los Angeles County

Company	SIC	EMP	PHONE	ENTRY #
3M Company	2834	B	818 341-1300	7706
5 Star Redemption Inc	3999	E	818 709-0875	23258
A and C Electronics	3672	E	818 886-8900	17798
Afr Apparel International Inc	2341	D	818 773-5000	3439
Alliant Tchsystems Oprtons LLC	3812	F	818 887-8195	20532
Artistry In Motion Inc	2679	E	818 994-7388	5495
ATI Solutions Inc (PA)	3669	F	818 772-7900	17714
Catalina Industries Inc	2851	E	818 772-8888	8633
Chemat Technology Inc	3821	E	818 727-9786	20749
Color Design Laboratory	2844	E	818 341-5100	8460

Company	SIC	EMP	PHONE	ENTRY #
DC Partners Inc (PA)	3365	E	714 558-9444	11376
DC Partners Inc	3365	E	818 718-1221	11377
Dealzer Com	2865	F	818 429-1155	8700
Dukes Research and Mfg Inc	3714	E	818 998-9811	19641
Emanuel Morez Inc	2511	E	818 780-2787	4568
First Responder Fire	3569	F	562 842-6602	14817
Germanex Imports Inc	3714	F	818 700-0441	19671
Giannelli Cabinet Mfg Co	2542	F	818 882-9787	4978
Gst Industries Inc	3728	E	818 350-1900	20123
Harman Professional Inc (DH)	3651	B	818 893-8411	17238
Infinity Aerospace Inc (PA)	3724	D	818 998-9811	19965
Ink 2000 Corp	2893	F	818 882-0168	8920
Instrument Bearing Factory USA	3452	F	818 989-5052	12683
Instrumentation Tech Systems	3577	F	818 886-2034	15249
Laboratorios Camacho Inc	2834	F	818 764-2748	7986
Lloyd Design Corporation	3714	D	818 768-6001	19705
Mansoor Amarna Corp	3952	F	818 894-8937	22943
Maroney Company	3599	F	818 882-2722	16173
Medtronic Inc	3841	C	300 646-4633	21805
Medtronic Minimed Inc (DH)	3845	A	800 646-4633	22281
Micro Matic Usa Inc	3585	E	818 701-9765	15446
Micro Matic Usa Inc	3491	E	818 882-8012	13316
N M H Inc	2752	F	818 843-8522	6742
Numotech Inc	3841	D	818 772-1579	21842
Pacific Thermography	2759	E	323 938-3349	7168
Perez Brothers	2514	F	818 780-8482	4698
Pro Food Inc	2099	F	818 341-4040	2589
Pure Water Centers Inc	3589	F	818 316-1250	15563
Radiant Detector Tech LLC	3829	F	818 709-2468	21528
Resonance Technology Inc	3845	F	818 882-1997	22303
Robert A Kerl	2789	E	818 341-9281	7343
Robert H Oliva Inc	3599	F	818 700-1035	16363
Rotating Prcsion McHanisms Inc	3663	E	818 349-9774	17646
Royal Systems Group	3549	F	818 717-5010	14280
S & S Numerical Control Inc	3599	F	818 341-4141	16379
Shb Instruments Inc	3825	F	818 773-2000	21120
Sheet Metal Prototype Inc	3444	F	818 772-2715	12373
Surfaces Tile Craft Inc	3253	F	818 609-0719	10454
Thermometrics Corporation (PA)	3823	E	818 886-3755	20949
Unique Image Inc	2752	F	818 727-7785	6908
Unitech Deco Inc	2759	E	818 700-1373	7259
Universal Ctrl Solutions Corp	3625	F	818 898-3380	16763
Verde Cosmetic Labs LLC	2844	F	818 284-4080	8602
What Kids Want Inc	3944	E	818 775-0375	22726
Zinsser Na Inc (DH)	3826	F	818 341-2906	21327

NORWALK, CA - Los Angeles County

Company	SIC	EMP	PHONE	ENTRY #
Ace Precision Mold Co Inc	3089	F	562 921-8999	9605
Advanced Sealing (DH)	3053	D	562 802-7782	9215
Aerospace Tool Grinding	3541	F	562 802-3339	13902
Aerotec Alloys Inc	3363	E	562 809-1378	11329
AG Global Products LLC	3634	E	323 334-2900	16824
American Relays Inc	3625	F	562 926-2837	16696
ARC Plastics Inc	3089	E	562 802-3299	9635
Architectural Cathode Lighting	3648	F	323 581-8800	17103
Argo Spring Mfg Co Inc	3493	D	800 252-2740	13336
Cabinets 2000 LLC	2434	C	562 868-0909	4175
Century Pattern Co Inc	3543	F	562 402-1707	14001
Dianas Mexican Food Pdts Inc (PA)	2099	E	562 926-5802	2445
Dragon Valves Inc (PA)	3494	F	562 921-6605	13351
G & L Tooling Inc	3541	F	562 802-2857	13921
Golden Specialty Foods LLC	2099	F	562 802-2537	2472
I & I Deburring Inc	3541	F	562 802-0058	13924
International Paper Company	2621	F	562 483-6680	5121
Jmt Inc	3599	F	562 404-2014	16087
Master Research & Mfg Inc	3728	D	562 483-8789	20168
McDowell & Craig Off Systems	2522	D	562 921-4441	4844
New Cntury Mtals Southeast Inc	3356	F	562 356-6804	11277
New Incorporation Now	2711	F	562 484-3020	5775
Paradise Printing Inc	2752	E	714 228-9628	6768
Polley Inc (PA)	3569	F	562 868-9861	14852
Riedon Inc	3825	F	562 926-2304	21112
Sonoco Products Company	2631	D	562 921-0881	5175
Tecno Industrial Engineering	3599	E	562 623-4517	16449
Universal Orthodontic Lab Inc	3843	E	562 908-2929	22200

NOVATO, CA - Marin County

Company	SIC	EMP	PHONE	ENTRY #
Activision Blizzard Inc	7372	C	415 881-9100	23552
ADS Solutions	7372	F	415 897-3700	23569
Ang Newspaper Group Inc (DH)	2711	F	650 359-6666	5551
Arena Press	2741	F	415 883-3314	6187
Bella Notte Linens Inc	2221	E	415 883-3434	2723
Biomarin Pharmaceutical Inc	2834	A	415 506-3258	7808
Biomarin Pharmaceutical Inc	2834	F	415 218-7386	7809
California Newspapers Inc	2711	A	415 883-8600	5577
Celamark Corp	3823	E	415 883-3386	20848

Employment Codes: A=Over 500 employees, B=251-500,
C=101-250, D=51-100, E=20-50, F=10-19

2020 California
Manufacturers Register

© Mergent Inc. 1-800-342-5647
1377

GEOGRAPHIC

Name	SIC	EMP	PHONE	ENTRY #
Cork Pops	3499	F	415 884-6000	13511
CRGsynergy	3822	E	415 497-0182	20790
Cricket Company LLC	3069	E	415 475-4150	9298
Crittenden Publishing Inc (HQ)	2741	F	415 475-1522	6217
Diamics Inc	3841	E	415 883-0414	21685
Dickinson Corporation	3821	E	415 883-7147	20754
Et Water Systems LLC	3829	E	415 945-9383	21467
Excellence Magazine Inc	2721	E	415 382-0582	5934
Forest Investment Group Inc	2752	E	415 459-2330	6580
Image Star LLC	2329	F	415 883-5815	3093
Integrity Support Services Inc	2899	F	415 898-0044	8981
Keys Cabinetry Inc	2541	F	415 382-1466	4916
Marin Scope Incorporated	2711	E	415 892-1516	5723
Marin USA	3429	F	415 382-6000	11608
Northbay Stone Wrks Cntertops	2541	F	415 898-0200	4923
Prima Fleur Botanicals Inc	2844	E	415 455-0957	8566
Ranch Systems LLC	3523	F	415 884-2770	13663
Raptor Pharmaceuticals Inc	2834	F	415 408-6200	8099
Safetychain Software Inc (PA)	7372	E	415 233-9474	24372
SCI Publishing Inc	2721	F	415 382-0580	6024
Shamrock Materials of Novato	3273	F	415 892-1571	10836
St Louis Post-Dispatch LLC	2711	F	415 892-1516	5837
Tukko Group LLC	7372	F	408 598-1251	24531
Ultragenyx Pharmaceutical Inc (PA)	2834	C	415 483-8800	8173
Whatever Publishing Inc	2731	F	415 884-2100	6162
Zacharon Pharmaceuticals Inc	2834	F	415 506-6700	8193

OAK PARK, CA - Ventura County

Name	SIC	EMP	PHONE	ENTRY #
Audio Impressions Inc	3931	F	818 532-7360	22607
Foldimate Inc	3634	E	805 876-4418	16828

OAK VIEW, CA - Ventura County

Name	SIC	EMP	PHONE	ENTRY #
Old Creek Ranch Winery Inc	2084	F	805 649-4132	1845

OAKDALE, CA - Stanislaus County

Name	SIC	EMP	PHONE	ENTRY #
Accu-Swiss Inc (PA)	3451	F	209 847-1016	12615
Ball Corporation	3411	B	209 848-6500	11493
Central Valley AG Grinding Inc (PA)	2041	E	209 869-1721	998
Central Valley Professional SE	2673	F	209 847-7832	5388
Conagra Brands Inc	2099	A	209 847-0321	2432
D & B Precision Shtmtl Inc	3444	F	209 848-3030	12169
Falcon Iron	3441	F	209 845-8229	11792
Falton Custom Cabinets Inc	2434	F	209 845-9823	4195
Fisher Sand & Gravel Co	1442	F	602 619-0325	339
Formulation Technology Inc	2834	F	209 847-0331	7894
Haeger Incorporated (DH)	3549	F	209 848-4000	14271
Heighten America Inc	3599	E	209 845-0455	16018
Inter Mountain Truss & Girder	2439	F	209 847-9184	4310
Morris Publications (PA)	2711	F	209 847-3021	5763
Norsco Inc	3451	F	209 845-2327	12642
Oakdale Cheese & Specialties	2022	F	209 848-3139	569
Sconza Candy Company	2064	D	209 845-3700	1395
Valley Precision Inc	3599	F	209 847-1758	16490
Vierra Bros Farms LLC	3523	F	209 247-3468	13680
Weldway Inc	3441	E	209 847-8083	11917
Willie Bylsma	3556	F	209 847-3362	14415

OAKHURST, CA - Madera County

Name	SIC	EMP	PHONE	ENTRY #
Control Enterprises Inc	3492	F	559 683-2044	13325
Frost Magnetics Incorporated	3677	E	559 642-2536	18717
Webb Designs Inc	2591	F	559 641-5400	5043

OAKLAND, CA - Alameda County

Name	SIC	EMP	PHONE	ENTRY #
3 D Studios	3441	F	510 535-1809	11727
A Taste of Denmark	2051	E	510 420-8889	1133
A&M Products Manufacturing Co (HQ)	3295	E	510 271-7000	10966
Able Metal Plating Inc	3471	E	510 569-6539	12899
Acuity Brands Lighting Inc	3646	E	510 845-2760	17007
Agribag Inc	2299	E	510 533-2388	2920
Agriculture Bag Mfg USA Inc (PA)	2221	E	510 632-5637	2721
AJW Construction	2951	E	510 568-2300	9086
Alumatherm Incorporated	3442	F	510 832-2819	11930
American Cylinder Head Inc	3714	F	510 261-1590	19577
American Cylndr Hd RPR/Excg	3714	F	510 536-1764	19578
Americas Best Beverage Inc	2095	E	800 723-8808	2274
Anoto Incorporated	3951	F	510 777-0071	22933
Arbo Inc	2052	E	510 658-3700	1301
Arch Foods Inc	3421	E	510 868-6000	11511
Arrow Sign Co (PA)	3993	E	209 931-5522	23053
Art Craft Staturary Inc	3281	F	510 633-1411	10890
Avoy Corp (PA)	2752	F	510 832-7746	6425
B C H Manufacturing Co Inc	3531	F	510 569-6586	13707
B-Flat Publishing LLC	2741	F	510 639-7170	6197
Babette	2339	F	510 625-8500	3291
Bay Area Indus Filtration Inc	3569	E	510 562-6373	14797
Bay Classifieds Inc	3555	E	510 636-1867	14317
Berrett-Koehler Publishers Inc (PA)	2731	E	510 817-2277	6074

Name	SIC	EMP	PHONE	ENTRY #
Binti Inc	7372	E	844 424-6844	23669
Black Hills Nanosystems Corp	3674	F	605 341-3641	18148
Blank and Cables Inc	2511	F	415 648-3842	4557
Bobs Iron Inc	3441	E	510 567-8983	11750
Brand X Hurarches	3143	E	510 658-9006	10158
Brite Industries Inc	3999	D	510 250-9330	23289
Broadly Inc	7372	E	510 400-6039	23699
Building Robotics Inc	7372	E	510 761-6482	23702
Bulldog Reporter	2711	F	510 596-9300	5571
C H K Manufacturing Inc	2673	E	510 632-5637	5385
Cable Moore Inc (PA)	3496	E	510 436-8000	13399
Cellscope Inc	3661	F	510 282-0674	17353
Cemex Cnstr Mtls PCF LLC	3273	E	925 858-4344	10719
Channel Systems Inc	3272	E	510 568-7170	10549
CHI Fung Plastics Inc	3085	F	510 532-4835	9481
Chiodo Candy Co	2064	D	510 464-2977	1360
Chris French Metal Inc	3441	E	510 238-9339	11766
Clamp Swing Pricing Co Inc	3999	E	510 567-1600	23304
Clorox Company (PA)	2842	B	510 271-7000	8375
Clorox Company Voluntary	2812	C	510 271-7000	7385
Clorox International Company (HQ)	2879	C	510 271-7000	8823
Clorox Manufacturing Company (HQ)	2842	C	510 271-7000	8378
Cnc Noodle Corporation	2099	F	510 835-2269	2431
Commercial Energy Montana Inc	1311	E	510 567-2700	44
County of Alameda	3824	E	510 272-6964	20963
Creative Wood Products Inc	2521	C	510 635-5399	4793
Custom Mechanical Systems LLC	3585	C	510 347-5500	15422
Dasan Zhone Solutions Inc (HQ)	3661	C	510 777-7000	17359
Deluxe Corporation	2782	B	651 483-7100	7310
Design Workshops	2541	F	510 434-0727	4897
Diamond Tool and Die Inc	3599	E	510 534-7050	15895
Digicom Electronics Inc	3672	E	510 639-7003	17864
Dorado Network Systems Corp	7372	C	650 227-7300	23826
East Bay Fixture Company	2491	E	510 652-4421	4477
East Bay Glass Company Inc	3442	E	510 834-2535	11949
ELF Beauty Inc (PA)	2844	E	510 210-8602	8488
Emerald Steel Inc	3441	E	510 553-1386	11788
Erg Aerospace Corporation	2819	D	510 658-9785	7493
Everett Graphics Inc	2657	D	510 567-6777	5313
Exo Systems Inc	3845	E	510 655-5033	22254
Fargo Choice Foods LLC	2051	E	510 774-0064	1201
Feeney Inc	3496	E	510 893-9473	13412
Five Flavors Herbs	2023	F	510 923-0178	588
Flipcause Inc	7372	E	800 523-1950	23904
Forem Manufacturing Inc	3339	F	510 577-9500	11190
Forward Printing & Design	2759	F	510 535-2222	7068
Foss Lampshade Studios Inc (PA)	3999	F	510 534-4133	23336
Franz Inc	7372	E	510 452-2000	23919
Garner Heat Treat Inc	3398	F	510 568-0587	11451
General Graphic Chemicals Co	2899	F	510 832-4404	8970
General Grinding Inc	3599	E	510 261-5557	15990
Glad Products Company (HQ)	3081	C	510 271-7000	9405
Global Steel Products Corp	2542	F	510 652-2060	4979
GM Associates Inc	3679	D	510 430-0806	18925
Golden Gate Litho	2752	F	510 568-5335	6593
Golden Plastics Corporation	3089	F	510 569-6465	9810
H V Food Products Company	2035	C	510 271-7612	884
Higher One Payments Inc	7372	E	510 769-9888	23982
Holo Inc	3999	E	510 221-4177	23356
Hydrapak Inc	3949	E	510 652-8800	22824
Idg Games Media Group Inc	2721	E	510 768-2700	5960
Industrial Wiper & Supply Inc	2241	E	408 286-4752	2755
Inter-City Printing Co Inc	2752	F	510 451-4775	6649
Jiminys LLC	2048	F	415 939-6314	1104
Kay Chesterfield Inc	2512	F	510 533-5565	4651
Kemeera Incorporated	3577	F	510 281-9000	15265
Key Source International (PA)	3575	F	510 562-5000	15127
Kingsford Products Company LLC (HQ)	2861	D	510 271-7000	8696
Kitanica Manufacturing	3999	F	707 272-7286	23383
Korea Daily News & Korea Times	2711	E	510 777-1111	5684
Korea Times Los Angeles Inc	2711	E	510 777-1111	5685
Kyoho Manufacturing California	3465	C	209 941-6200	12745
La Cascada Inc	2032	F	510 452-3663	736
Label Art-Easy Stik Labels	2759	F	510 465-1125	7109
Learners Guild Ltd	7372	F	415 448-7054	24098
Leons Powder Coating	3479	F	510 437-9224	13199
Lewis John Glass Studio	3229	F	510 635-4607	10317
Lignum Vitae Cabinet	2521	F	510 444-2030	4808
Linoleum Sales Co Inc (PA)	3211	D	661 327-4053	10271
Live Journal Inc	2711	E	415 230-3600	5700
Log(n) LLC	2741	F	323 839-4538	6274
Mack & Reiss Inc	2369	D	510 434-9122	3494
McWane Inc (PA)	3321	C	510 632-3467	11147
Meditab Software Inc	7372	C	510 632-2021	24144
Meridian Jewelry & Design Inc	3911	F	510 428-2095	22548

Mergent email: customerrelations@mergent.com
1378

2020 California
Manufacturers Register

(P-0000) Products & Services Section entry number
(PA)=Parent Co (HQ)=Headquarters (DH)=Div Headquarters

Company	SIC	EMP	PHONE	ENTRY #
Mettler-Toledo Rainin LLC (HQ)	3829	C	510 564-1600	21506
Miwa Inc	3496	E	510 261-5999	13424
Modern Bamboo Incorporated	2511	F	925 820-2804	4597
Moz Designs Inc	3446	E	510 632-0853	12501
National Recycling Corporation	2679	F	510 268-1022	5514
Nestle Pizza Company Inc	2038	F	510 261-8001	967
New Harbinger Publications Inc (PA)	2731	E	510 652-0215	6128
Nextsport Inc	3944	F	510 601-8802	22700
Noodle Theory	2098	F	510 595-6988	2377
Nor-Cal Metal Fabricators	3444	D	510 350-0121	12315
Oakland Tribune Inc	2711	A	510 208-6300	5786
Onki Corp	3714	C	510 567-8875	19732
Open Dmain Sphinx Sltions Corp	7372	F	510 420-0846	24228
Original Pattern Inc	2082	F	510 844-4833	1554
Outlaw Beverage Inc	2082	F	310 424-5077	1556
Owens-Brockway Glass Cont Inc	3221	D	510 436-2000	10290
Pacific Galvanizing Inc	3479	E	510 261-7331	13218
Pacific Steel Fabricators Inc	3441	D	209 464-9474	11860
Paylocity Holding Corporation	7372	B	847 956-4850	24292
Peerless Coffee Company Inc	2095	D	510 763-1763	2307
Post Newspaper Group	2711	F	510 287-8200	5801
Pressure Cast Products Corp	3364	C	510 532-7310	11359
Promaxo Inc	3841	F	510 982-1202	21864
Purity Organic LLC	2037	E	415 440-7777	925
Quaker Oats Company	2087	C	510 261-5800	2226
Quality Marble & Granite Inc	3281	F	510 635-0228	10926
R J R Technologies Inc (PA)	3699	C	510 638-5901	19388
Rago & Son Inc	3469	D	510 536-5700	12868
Readytech Corporation	7372	F	510 834-3344	24341
Rels Foods Inc (PA)	2099	D	510 652-2747	2597
Riffyn Inc (PA)	7372	F	510 542-9868	24362
Right Away Concrete Pmpg Inc	3273	E	510 536-1900	10818
Savnik & Company Inc	2273	F	510 568-4628	2878
Scientific Learning Corp	7372	F	510 444-3500	24389
Senetur LLC	7372	E	650 269-1023	24397
SF Global LLC	3089	F	888 536-5593	10055
Sius Products-Distributor Inc (PA)	2673	F	510 382-1700	5420
Skasol Incorporated	2899	F	510 839-1000	9024
Social Brands LLC	3999	E	415 728-1761	23479
Sorrento Networks Corporation (DH)	3661	F	510 577-1400	17413
Squarebar Inc	2834	F	530 412-0209	8139
Sublime Machining Inc	3999	E	858 349-2445	23486
Sullivan Counter Tops Inc	2541	F	510 652-2337	4943
Sunrise Specialty Company	3432	F	510 729-7277	11683
Sunset Publishing Corporation (HQ)	2721	C	800 777-0117	6035
Supernutrition	2834	E	510 446-7980	8151
Svc Mfg Inc A Corp	2086	F	510 261-5800	2175
Tab Label Inc	2679	F	510 638-4411	5534
Tags & Labels	2752	F	510 465-1125	6883
Tech Air Northern Cal LLC	2813	F	510 533-9353	7456
TYT LLC (HQ)	2752	C	510 444-3933	6905
University Cal Press Fundation (PA)	2731	D	510 642-4247	6158
University California Berkeley	2731	F	510 642-4247	6160
Veronica Foods Company	2079	E	510 535-6833	1486
Vibrant Care Pharmacy Inc	2834	F	510 638-9851	8180
Vigilent Corporation (PA)	3822	E	888 305-4451	20820
Village Voice Media	2711	E	510 879-3700	5860
Vincent Electric Company (PA)	7694	E	510 639-4500	24701
Vulpine Inc	2899	F	510 534-1186	9035
Wcitiescom Inc	2741	F	415 495-8090	6381
Wilsted & Taylor Pubg Svcs	2791	F	510 428-9087	7366
Window Hardware Supply	3089	F	510 463-0301	10125
Wood Tech Inc	2511	D	510 534-4930	4624
Zuo Modern Contemporary Inc (PA)	2521	E	510 777-1030	4826

OAKVILLE, CA - Napa County

Company	SIC	EMP	PHONE	ENTRY #
Far Niente Winery Inc	2084	D	707 944-2861	1698
Jackson Family Wines Inc	2084	E	707 948-2643	1764
NAPA Wine Company LLC	2084	E	707 944-8669	1835
Opus One Winery LLC (PA)	2084	D	707 944-9442	1849
Paradigm Winery	2084	F	707 944-1683	1855
Rudd Wines LLC (PA)	2084	F	707 944-8577	1901
Silver Oak Wine Cellars LP (PA)	2084	F	707 942-7022	1919
Turnbull Wine Cellars	2084	F	707 963-5839	1976

OCCIDENTAL, CA - Sonoma County

Company	SIC	EMP	PHONE	ENTRY #
Planet Inc	2842	F	250 478-8171	8407

OCEANSIDE, CA - San Diego County

Company	SIC	EMP	PHONE	ENTRY #
2 S 2 Inc	3679	F	760 599-9225	18803
Absolute Board Co Inc	3949	E	760 295-2201	22730
Ace Aviation Service Inc	3728	F	760 721-2804	19999
Advanced Oxygen Therapy Inc (HQ)	3841	F	760 431-4700	21582
Advanced Thrmlforming Entp Inc	3089	F	760 722-4400	9613
Alpha Sensors Inc	3823	E	949 250-6578	20830
Alpha Technics Inc	3823	C	949 250-6578	20831

Company	SIC	EMP	PHONE	ENTRY #
American Food Ingredients Inc	2034	E	760 967-6287	841
American Innotek Inc (PA)	3089	D	760 741-6600	9625
Amerillum LLC	3648	D	760 727-7675	17102
Amflex Plastics Incorporated	3089	F	760 643-1756	9629
Apollo Med Extrusion Tech Inc	3841	E	760 453-2944	21601
Asigma Corporation	3599	F	760 966-3103	15752
Balda HK Plastics Inc	3451	D	760 757-1100	12623
BMW Precision Machining Inc	3599	E	760 439-6813	15794
Brand Ink Inc	2759	E	760 721-4465	7005
Britcan Inc	2542	E	760 722-2300	4964
Cal-Mil Plastic Products Inc (PA)	3089	E	800 321-9069	9682
Campbell Certified Inc (PA)	3441	E	760 722-9353	11758
Car Sound Exhaust System Inc (PA)	3714	E	949 858-5900	19608
Car Sound Exhaust System Inc	2819	E	949 888-1625	7478
CJ Products Inc	2392	F	760 444-4217	3607
Coca-Cola Refreshments USA Inc	2086	D	760 435-7111	2065
Component Concepts LLC	3691	F	760 722-9559	19155
Core Supplement Technology	2834	F	760 452-7364	7851
Custom Converting Inc	3086	F	760 724-0664	9520
Custom Window Design Inc	2431	F	760 439-6213	4027
Dupaco Inc	3841	E	760 758-4550	21692
Envirnmental Catalyst Tech LLC	2819	E	949 459-3870	7492
Federal Heath Sign Company LLC	3993	C	760 941-0715	23111
Federal Heath Sign Company LLC	3993	F	760 901-7447	23112
Foxfury LLC	3648	F	760 945-4231	17127
Genentech Inc	2834	B	760 231-2440	7904
Gilead Sciences Inc	2836	F	760 945-7701	8304
Hexagon Metrology Inc	3825	D	760 994-1401	21050
Hobie Cat Company	3732	C	760 758-9100	20337
Horstman Manufacturing Co Inc	3714	E	760 598-2100	19683
Hts-Engineering Inc	3451	F	760 631-2070	12635
Hydranautics (DH)	2899	B	760 901-2597	8975
International Sales Inc	3949	F	760 722-1455	22829
Isis Pharmaceuticals	2834	F	760 603-2631	7965
J B L Enterprises Inc	3949	F	760 754-2727	22832
Kainalu Blue Inc	3296	F	760 806-6400	10986
Kapan - Kent Company Inc	2396	E	760 631-1716	3794
Kds Ingredients LLC	2099	F	760 310-5245	2497
Kellermyer Bergensons Svcs LLC (PA)	3589	F	760 631-5111	15534
Lab Surf Company	3949	F	760 757-1975	22840
Landmark Mfg Inc	3599	E	760 941-6626	16133
Lb Manufacturing LLC	3999	F	413 222-2857	23391
Legacy Vulcan LLC	3272	F	760 439-0624	10598
Lexstar Inc (PA)	3646	E	845 947-1415	17050
Mary Matava	2879	F	760 439-9920	8834
Metrotile Manufacturing LLC	2952	E	760 435-9842	9121
Miller Machine Inc	3599	E	814 723-5700	16206
Ms Cast Stone Inc	3272	E	760 754-9697	10604
Mtm Industrial Inc	3599	E	760 967-1346	16232
Nelgo Industries Inc	3599	E	760 433-6434	16239
Oceanside Marine Center Inc (PA)	3732	F	760 722-1833	20354
Oceanside Plastic Enterprises	3544	F	760 433-0779	14086
Olli Salumeria Americana LLC	2011	F	804 427-7866	420
Orco Block & Hardscape	3271	E	760 757-1780	10512
Oxbow Activated Carbon LLC	2819	E	760 630-5724	7514
Pacific Lasertec Inc	3999	E	760 450-4095	23438
Pacific Vista Foods Llc	2865	E	760 908-9840	8702
Performance Cnc Inc	3599	F	760 722-1129	16294
Pratt Industries Inc	2621	E	760 966-9170	5146
Precision Label Inc	2671	E	760 757-7533	5338
Precision One Medical Inc	3843	D	760 945-7966	22181
Proline Concrete Tools Inc	3559	E	760 758-7240	14521
Pryor Products	3841	E	760 724-8244	21867
Pure Allure Inc	2339	D	760 966-3650	3393
Rose Manufacturing Group Inc	3471	F	760 407-0232	13089
Salis International Inc	3952	E	303 384-3588	22944
San Juan Specialty Pdts Inc	2449	F	888 342-8262	4426
Schuman Enterprises Inc	3499	F	760 940-1322	13545
Secura Inc	2326	D	760 804-7313	3051
Solecta Inc (PA)	2295	E	760 630-9643	2899
Solution Box Inc	2754	F	949 387-3223	6964
Souther Cast Stone Inc	3272	E	760 754-9697	10653
Southwest Greene Intl Inc	3469	C	760 639-4960	12874
Speedskins Inc	3949	F	760 439-3119	22894
Steico Industries Inc	3469	C	760 438-8015	12877
Stone Truss Inc (PA)	2439	F	760 967-6171	4320
Superior Foam Products Inc	3949	F	760 722-1585	22901
Surf Ride	2329	F	760 433-4020	3122
Tarsal Pharmaceuticals Inc	2834	F	818 919-9723	8155
Te Connectivity Corporation	3678	A	760 757-7500	18793
Triangle Brass Mfg Co Inc (PA)	3429	D	323 262-4191	11638
USP Inc	2844	D	760 842-7700	8599

OJAI, CA - Ventura County

Company	SIC	EMP	PHONE	ENTRY #
Ellen Lark Farm	2043	F	805 272-8448	1019
Fermented Sciences Inc	2082	F	805 798-2790	1526

GEOGRAPHIC

	SIC	EMP	PHONE	ENTRY #
Mastering Lab Inc	3652	F	805 640-2900	17331
Rotary Club of Ajai West	2084	E	805 646-3794	1897

OLANCHA, CA - Inyo County

	SIC	EMP	PHONE	ENTRY #
Cg Roxane LLC (PA)	2086	D	760 764-2885	2054

OLIVEHURST, CA - Yuba County

	SIC	EMP	PHONE	ENTRY #
Ace Composites Inc	3089	D	530 743-1885	9604
D & D Cbnets - Svage Dsgns Inc	2434	E	530 634-9713	4186
Hanson Truss Components Inc	2439	D	530 740-7750	4305
Precast Con Tech Unlimited LLC	3272	D	530 749-6501	10626
Yuba River Moulding Mllwk Inc (PA)	2431	E	530 742-2168	4159

ONTARIO, CA - San Bernardino County

	SIC	EMP	PHONE	ENTRY #
A Lot To Say Inc	2399	F	925 964-5079	3826
AAA Stamping Inc	3469	E	909 947-4151	12757
Aamp of America	3699	E	805 338-6800	19246
Aaren Scientific Inc (DH)	3827	D	909 937-1033	21329
Abba Roller LLC (DH)	3069	E	909 947-1244	9277
Able Industrial Products Inc (PA)	3053	E	909 930-1585	9214
Absolute Screen Graphics Inc	2396	F	909 923-1227	3765
Accracutt Cabinets	2434	F	951 685-7322	4161
Accufab Inc	3599	F	909 930-1751	15677
Ace Calendering Enterprises (PA)	3069	F	909 937-1901	9278
Action Embroidery Corp (PA)	2399	C	909 983-1359	3829
Adesa International LLC	2032	E	909 321-8240	716
Advanced Color Graphics	2752	D	909 930-1500	6397
Advanced Pattern & Mold	3334	F	909 930-3444	11177
Advanced Refreshment LLC (HQ)	2086	F	425 746-8100	2022
Aerospace and Coml Tooling Inc	3541	F	909 930-5780	13901
Ajinomoto Foods North Amer Inc	2038	C	909 477-4700	937
Ajinomoto Foods North Amer Inc (DH)	2038	D	909 477-4700	938
Akra Plastic Products Inc	3089	E	909 930-1999	9616
Alger Precision Machining LLC	3451	C	909 986-4591	12617
All Time Machine Inc	3599	F	909 673-1899	15720
Alpha Publishing Corporation	2731	E	909 464-0500	6069
Alta Advanced Technologies Inc	2836	E	909 983-2973	8269
Alum-Alloy Coinc	3463	E	909 986-0410	12728
Alumin-Art Plating Co Inc	3471	E	909 983-1866	12923
Am-Tek Engineering Inc	3599	F	909 673-1633	15736
AMD International Tech LLC	3444	E	909 985-8300	12102
American Fleet & Ret Graphics	3993	E	909 937-7570	23048
American Premier Corp	3949	E	909 923-7070	22743
American Publishing Corp	2731	E	909 390-7548	6071
AMF Pharma LLC	2834	E	909 930-9599	7748
Amish Country Gazebos Inc	2511	F	800 700-1777	4547
Amrep Inc (DH)	2842	C	909 923-0430	8361
An Environmental Inks	2893	F	909 930-9656	8909
Andrew LLC	2041	E	909 270-9356	988
Androp Packaging Inc	2653	E	909 605-8842	5196
Anvil International LLC	3498	F	909 418-3233	13458
Armorcast Products Company Inc	3089	E	909 390-1365	9639
Arrow Truck Bodies & Equipment	3713	E	909 947-3991	19519
Artesia Sawdust Products Inc	2421	E	909 947-5983	3924
Aryzta LLC	2052	C	909 472-3500	1303
Ashtel Studios Inc	3844	E	909 434-0911	22208
Astro Display Company Inc	3993	E	909 605-2875	23057
Athanor Group Inc	3451	C	909 467-1205	12621
Auburn Tile Inc	3272	F	909 984-2841	10532
Axium Plastics LLC	3089	D	909 969-0766	9646
B & D Litho Group Inc	2752	E	909 390-0903	6427
B Stephen Cooperage Inc	3412	F	909 591-2929	11508
Balda C Brewer Inc (DH)	3089	C	714 630-6810	9652
Barzillai Manufacturing Co	3444	F	909 947-4200	12127
Baxter Healthcare Corporation	2834	C	303 222-6837	7789
Bee Wire & Cable Inc	3357	E	909 923-5800	11287
Bericap LLC	3089	D	909 390-5518	9658
Bernman Mold and Engineering	3544	F	909 930-3844	14023
Bert-Co Industries Inc	2759	F	323 669-5700	6998
Bert-Co Industries Inc (PA)	2752	C	323 669-5700	6445
Best Quality Furniture Mfg Inc	2512	F	909 230-6440	4629
Bhk Inc	3641	E	909 983-2973	16857
Bishamon Industries Corp	3537	E	909 390-0055	13860
Black & Decker Corporation	3546	F	909 390-5548	14216
Blue Sky Home & ACC Inc	1459	E	909 930-6200	377
Bmci Inc	3549	E	951 361-8000	14264
Bock Machine Company Inc	3599	F	909 947-7250	15796
Bomatic Inc	3089	E	909 947-3900	9670
Bradley Corp	3432	F	909 481-7255	11658
C & S Products CA Inc (PA)	2842	F	909 218-8971	8371
Calidad Inc	3365	E	909 947-3937	11369
California Die Casting Inc	3364	E	909 947-9947	11353
California Exotic Novlt LLC	3999	D	909 606-1950	23293
California Mfg Cabinetry Inc	2541	F	909 930-3632	4888
California Quality Plas Inc	3089	E	909 930-5667	9688
Canvas Awning Co Inc	2394	F	909 447-5100	3675

	SIC	EMP	PHONE	ENTRY #
Caraustar Industries Inc	2655	E	951 685-5544	5289
Carl Zeiss Meditec Prod LLC	3841	D	877 644-4657	21657
Carlstar Group LLC	3011	C	310 816-1015	9166
Carlyle Glasgow Wldg Svcs Inc	3441	F	909 902-1814	11762
Case Hardigg Center	2441	F	413 665-2163	4334
Case World Co	3172	F	626 330-1000	10232
Castillo Maritess	2394	F	949 216-0468	3679
Caterpillar Inc	3531	B	909 390-9035	13720
Celestica Aerospace Tech Corp	3672	C	512 310-7540	17843
Cemex Inc	3273	E	909 974-5500	10708
Champion Discs Incorporated	3949	E	800 408-8449	22779
Chenbro Micom (usa) Inc	3572	F	909 937-0100	15015
Chladni & Jariwala Inc	3491	E	909 947-5227	13297
Clarke Pb & Associates Inc	3651	E	714 835-3022	17212
Classic Containers Inc	3085	B	909 930-3610	9482
Clearchem Diagnostics Inc	2819	F	714 734-8041	7483
Coca-Cola Company	2086	C	909 975-5200	2059
Coca-Cola Company	2087	D	909 975-5200	2200
Coco Products LLC	2842	F	909 218-8971	8381
Commander Packaging West Inc	2653	E	714 921-9350	5210
Consolidated Container Co LLC	3085	F	909 390-6637	9484
Creative Image Systems Inc	2844	E	909 947-8588	8475
Crown Equipment Corporation	3537	C	909 923-8357	13866
Crown Paper Converting Inc	2679	E	909 923-5226	5503
Cspc Healthcare Inc	2834	F	909 395-5272	7859
CTA Fixtures Inc	2541	D	909 390-6744	4894
Custom Plastics LLC (PA)	3089	F	909 984-0200	9739
Daaze Inc	3444	F	626 442-4961	12171
Danco Anodizing Inc	3471	C	909 923-0562	12983
DB Building Fasteners Inc (PA)	3449	E	909 581-6740	12589
Dee Engineering Inc	3714	E	909 947-5616	19633
Defoe Furniture For Kids Inc	2531	F	909 947-4459	4857
Delta Tech Industries LLC	3647	F	909 673-1900	17088
Diagnostic Solutions Intl LLC	3728	F	909 930-3600	20085
Diamond Injection Molds Inc	3544	F	909 390-2260	14042
Discopylabs	3652	D	909 390-3800	17317
Diversified Litho Services	2752	F	714 558-2995	6545
Doble Engineering Company	3613	F	909 923-9390	16595
Dorel Juvenile Group Inc	3089	C	909 390-5705	9766
Dspm Inc	3677	E	714 970-2304	18712
Dura Micro Inc	3572	E	909 947-4590	15023
Eagle Products - Plast Indust	3089	E	909 465-1548	9769
Eagle Signs Inc	3993	E	909 923-3034	23092
Ecko Products Group LLC	2653	E	909 628-5678	5218
Eclipse Prtg & Graphics LLC	2752	E	909 390-2452	6557
Edelmann Usa Inc (DH)	3993	E	323 669-5700	23093
Edison Opto USA Corporation	3674	F	909 284-9710	18208
Egr Incorporated (DH)	3714	C	909 923-7075	19647
Elegance Upholstery Inc	2599	F	562 698-2584	5056
Elite Comfort Solutions LLC	3069	F	909 390-6800	9304
Emission Methods Inc	3829	E	909 605-6800	21466
Empire Sheet Metal Inc	3444	F	909 923-2927	12195
Encore Image Inc	3993	E	909 986-4632	23097
Envirokinetics Inc (PA)	3559	F	909 621-7599	14460
Eubanks Engineering Co (PA)	3549	E	909 483-2456	14266
Eugenios Sheet Metal Inc	3444	F	909 923-2002	12201
Evans Food West Inc (PA)	2096	F	909 947-3001	2321
Everest Group Usa Inc	2299	E	909 923-1818	2932
Excel Industries Inc	3469	E	909 947-4867	12802
F & D Flores Enterprises Inc	3829	F	909 975-4853	21471
Fan Fave Inc	3993	E	909 975-4999	23107
Fanlight Corporation Inc (PA)	3641	E	909 930-6868	16863
Ferrari Intrcnnect Sltions Inc	3679	F	951 684-8034	18915
Five Star Gourmet Foods Inc	2038	A	909 390-0032	959
Flor De California	2024	E	909 673-1968	644
Flow Dynamics Inc	3312	F	909 930-5522	11044
Forbes Industries Div	2599	C	909 923-4559	5061
Foundry Service & Supplies Inc	3299	E	909 284-5000	11007
Freeland Exceed Inc	3648	E	626 695-8031	17128
Fuji Natural Foods Inc (HQ)	2099	D	909 947-1008	2466
Genius Tools Americas Corp (PA)	3545	E	909 230-9588	14164
Geo Labels Inc	2759	F	909 923-6832	7073
George Verhoeven Grain Inc (PA)	2048	C	909 605-1531	1098
Glenco Manufacturing Company	3451	E	909 984-3348	12632
Gold Crest Industries Inc	2393	E	909 930-9069	3659
Graphic Sciences Inc	2893	F	909 947-3366	8918
Guess Inc	2325	E	909 987-7776	3007
Gund Company Inc	3644	E	909 890-9300	16949
H Fam Engineering Inc	3599	F	909 930-5678	16012
Haldex Brake Products Corp	3714	F	909 974-1200	19677
Halex Corporation (HQ)	3423	E	909 629-6219	11531
Hallmark Floors Inc (PA)	2426	E	909 947-7736	3975
Halsteel Inc (DH)	3315	F	909 937-1001	11094
Hannibal Lafayette	2448	F	909 322-0600	4369
Hchd	3711	F	909 923-8889	19478

Mergent email: customerrelations@mergent.com
1380

2020 California
Manufacturers Register

(P-0000) Products & Services Section entry number
(PA)=Parent Co (HQ)=Headquarters (DH)=Div Headquarters

	SIC	EMP	PHONE	ENTRY #
Hco Holding I Corporation	2952	F	310 684-5320	9113
Heitman Brooks II LLC (PA)	3272	F	909 947-7470	10584
Herman Engineering & Mfg Inc	3089	F	909 483-1631	9822
HI Performance Electric Vehicl	3621	F	909 923-1973	16654
Hillerich & Bradsby Co	3949	D	800 282-2287	22821
Horizon Hobby LLC	3944	C	909 390-9595	22681
Hubbell Incorporated	3643	F	909 390-8002	16903
ICEE Company (HQ)	2038	D	800 426-4233	962
ICEE Company	2038	F	909 974-3518	963
IDB Holdings Inc (DH)	2022	F	909 390-5624	556
Idx Los Angeles LLC	2431	C	909 212-8333	4059
Imp International Inc (PA)	2833	F	909 321-1000	7669
Inca Plastics Molding Co Inc	3089	D	909 923-3235	9837
Induspac California Inc	2821	F	909 390-4422	7568
Industrial Furnace & Insul Inc	3567	F	909 947-2449	14765
Ink Fx Corporation	2759	E	909 673-1950	7098
Inland Empire Drive Line Svc (PA)	3714	F	909 390-3030	19690
Inland Powder Coating Corp	3479	C	909 947-1122	13192
Inland Signs Inc	3993	F	909 581-0699	23135
Inline Plastics Inc	3089	E	909 923-1033	9839
International Paper Company	2631	D	909 605-2540	5164
Ivars Cabinet Shop Inc (PA)	2541	C	909 923-2761	4912
IVEX Protective Packaging Inc	2821	F	909 390-4422	7574
J R Rapid Print Inc	2752	F	909 947-4868	6656
Jamac Steel Inc	3441	E	909 983-7592	11816
James Jones Company	3491	C	909 418-2558	13309
Jasper Engine Exchange Inc	3714	F	800 827-7455	19694
Jns Industries Inc	3599	F	909 923-8334	16089
K & Z Cabinet Co Inc	2434	D	909 947-3567	4214
Kik Pool Additives Inc	2899	C	909 390-9912	8985
Kingfa Global Inc	3452	F	909 212-5413	12685
Kitchen Equipment Mfg Co Inc	3469	E	909 923-3153	12834
Kls Doors LLC	2431	E	909 605-6468	4070
Korden Inc	2522	F	909 988-8979	4841
Kraft Heinz Foods Company	2033	F	909 605-7201	784
Kushwood Chair Inc	2511	C	909 930-2100	4584
Lanpar Inc	2511	B	541 484-1962	4586
Larry Mthvin Installations Inc (HQ)	3231	C	909 563-1700	10373
Lassonde Pappas and Co Inc	2099	D	909 923-4041	2523
Leggett & Platt Incorporated	2515	F	909 937-1010	4727
Levco Fab Inc	3498	F	909 465-0840	13475
Lieder Development Inc	3679	F	909 947-7722	18990
Linpeng International Inc	3999	F	909 923-9881	23396
Liqui-Box Corporation	3085	E	909 390-4646	9487
M and W Glass	3231	F	909 517-3585	10376
Mag Instrument Inc (PA)	3648	B	909 947-1006	17144
Magnussen Home Furnishings Inc	2511	F	336 841-4424	4589
Maney Aircraft Inc	3728	E	909 390-2500	20164
Marlee Manufacturing Inc	3841	E	909 390-3222	21787
Matsun America Corp	2326	F	909 930-0779	3043
Maury Microwave Inc	3679	C	909 987-4715	19008
Maximum Quality Metal Pdts Inc	3444	E	909 902-5018	12285
Meadow Decor Inc	2519	F	909 923-2558	4766
Medegen LLC (DH)	3089	E	909 390-9080	9889
Medrano Raymundo	2284	E	909 947-5507	2892
Melmarc Products Inc	2395	B	714 549-2170	3749
Metal Engineering Inc	3444	E	626 334-1819	12291
Metals USA Building Pdts LP	3355	E	800 325-1305	11264
Mid Ohio Field Services LLC	1389	F	614 755-5067	223
Mikron Products Inc	3061	D	909 545-8600	9266
Minsley Inc	2099	E	909 458-1100	2552
Mission Plastics Inc	3089	C	909 947-7287	9900
Moldings Plus Inc	2431	E	909 947-3310	4089
N S Ceramic Molding Co	3544	E	909 947-3231	14083
Nac Mfg Inc	2873	E	909 472-3033	8799
Naturestar Bio Tech Inc	2834	F	909 930-1878	8026
Neptune Trading Inc	3421	F	909 923-0236	11516
Net Shapes Inc	3324	C	909 947-3231	11164
New Greenscreen Incorporated	2542	F	800 767-9378	4992
New-Indy Containerboard LLC (DH)	2621	D	909 296-3400	5136
New-Indy Ontario LLC	2621	C	909 390-1055	5137
Newfield Technology Corp (PA)	3711	E	909 931-4405	19491
Nexus California Inc	3081	F	909 937-1000	9415
North American Composites Co	2821	E	909 605-8977	7586
Office Master Inc	2522	D	909 392-5678	4846
Omega Interconnect Inc	3599	F	909 986-1933	16257
One Internet America LLC	2741	F	951 377-8844	6300
One Stop Label Corporation	2759	F	909 230-9380	7156
Optec Displays Inc	3993	D	626 369-7188	23170
Oracle America Inc	7372	F	909 605-0222	24246
Otto Instrument Service Inc (PA)	3728	E	909 930-5800	20190
Pacer Technology (HQ)	2891	C	909 987-0550	8883
Pacific Accent Incorporated	3634	C	909 563-1600	16838
Pacific Urethanes LLC	2392	C	909 390-8400	3634
Pacific Utility Products Inc	3824	F	909 923-1800	20974

	SIC	EMP	PHONE	ENTRY #
Panob Corp	3089	E	909 947-8008	9951
Paramount Panels Inc (PA)	3089	E	909 947-8008	9953
Paramount Panels Inc	3728	E	909 947-5168	20194
Parco LLC (PA)	3053	C	909 947-2200	9246
Passport Food Group LLC (PA)	2099	C	909 627-7312	2582
Patch Place	2399	E	909 947-3023	3852
Pby Plastics Inc	3089	F	909 930-6700	9956
Pearson Education Inc	2731	F	800 653-1918	6134
Pennysaver	2711	E	909 467-8500	5795
Performance Aluminum Products	3363	E	909 391-4131	11345
Pharmapack North America Corp	2821	F	909 390-1888	7591
Phoenix Arms	3484	E	909 937-6900	13276
Phoenix Cars LLC	3711	F	909 987-0815	19493
Plasthec Molding Inc	3089	D	909 947-4267	9968
Plastics Research Corporation	3083	D	909 391-9050	9449
Pmr Precision Mfg & Rbr Co Inc	3069	F	909 605-7525	9354
PNC Proactive Nthrn Cont LLC	2653	E	909 390-5624	5259
Pneumatic Scale Corporation	3565	F	909 527-7600	14723
Polytech Color & Compounding	3089	F	909 923-7008	9982
Popla International Inc	2045	F	909 923-6899	1059
Portable Spndle Repr Spcialist	3552	F	909 591-7220	14292
Praxair Inc	2813	D	909 390-0283	7438
PRC Composites LLC	2519	D	909 391-2006	4771
Precast Repair	3272	E	909 627-5477	10628
Precise Media Services Inc	3652	E	909 481-3305	17334
Primebore Directional Boring	1381	F	909 821-4643	104
Proactive Packg & Display LLC (DH)	2653	E	909 390-5624	5260
Promarksvac Corporation	3565	F	909 923-3888	14725
Q1 Test Inc	3728	E	909 390-9718	20207
QEP Co Inc	2426	F	909 622-3537	3982
Quality Control Plating Inc	3471	E	909 605-0206	13084
Qycell Corporation	3086	E	909 390-6644	9565
R & I Industries Inc	3441	E	909 923-7747	11869
R & J Wldg Met Fabrication Inc	3613	F	909 930-2900	16609
Rama Food Manufacture Corp (PA)	2099	C	909 923-5305	2595
Raytheon Company	3812	D	310 338-1324	20692
RDS Group Inc	2752	F	909 923-8831	6837
Redline Prcision Machining Inc	3312	F	909 483-1273	11064
Regards Enterprises Inc	2493	D	909 821-0655	4486
Response Envelope Inc (PA)	2759	C	909 923-5855	7196
Rexnord LLC	3566	C	909 467-8102	14748
Reyrich Plastics Inc	3089	F	909 484-8444	10017
Rfc Wire Forms Inc	3496	D	909 467-0559	13433
Rolling Dough Corporation	2051	F	714 884-2801	1267
Royal Angelus Macaroni Company	2099	C	909 627-7312	2605
Ryko Plastic Products Inc	3089	F	909 773-0050	10036
Safariland LLC	3199	B	909 923-7300	10252
Safariland LLC (DH)	3669	E	925 219-1097	17759
Safran Cabin Inc	3728	B	909 947-2725	20223
Safran Cabin Materials LLC	3728	F	909 947-4115	20224
Sapa Extrusions Inc	3354	C	909 947-7682	11244
Scott Welsher	3161	F	949 574-4000	10206
Scripto-Tokai Corporation (DH)	3999	D	909 930-5000	23471
Security Metal Products Corp (DH)	3442	E	310 641-6690	11983
Sentran L L C (PA)	3829	F	888 545-8988	21537
Sentry Industries Inc	2821	E	909 986-3642	7608
Shred-Tech Usa LLC	3537	E	909 923-2783	13891
Sign Industries Inc	3993	E	909 930-0303	23199
Solartech Power Inc	3674	F	909 673-0178	18569
Soup Bases Loaded Inc	2099	E	909 230-6890	2614
Southland Container Corp	2653	E	909 937-9781	5269
Southwest Concrete Products	3272	E	909 983-9789	10654
Specialized Dairy Service Inc	3523	E	909 923-3420	13672
Specialty Co Pack LLC	2033	F	909 673-0439	824
Specialty Coating Systems Inc	3479	E	909 390-8818	13249
Sprayline Enterprises Inc	3479	E	909 627-8411	13251
Stanley Access Tech LLC	3423	C	909 628-9272	11545
Star Shield Solutions LLC	3089	D	866 662-4477	10070
Strada Wheels Inc	3312	F	626 336-1634	11075
Summit Machine LLC	3599	C	909 923-2744	16426
Sun Badge Co	3999	E	909 930-1444	23487
Sunny Products Inc	2782	F	909 923-4128	7318
Sunway Mechanical & Elec Tech	3715	F	909 673-7959	19832
Sunyeah Group Corp	3231	E	909 218-8490	10392
Super Glue Corporation	2891	F	909 987-0550	8896
Superior Essex Inc	3357	F	909 481-4804	11321
Superior Mold Co Inc	3089	E	909 947-7028	10076
Supermedia LLC	2741	B	909 390-5000	6352
Supreme Machine Products Inc	3599	F	909 974-0349	16430
Table De France Inc	2051	F	909 923-5205	1282
Tc Cosmotronic Inc	3672	D	949 660-0740	18019
TCI Engineering Inc	3711	F	909 984-1773	19503
Tech Electronic Systems Inc	3679	F	909 986-4395	19102
Teefor 2 Inc	2752	F	909 613-0055	6887
Teklink Security Inc	3699	E	909 230-6668	19421

Employment Codes: A=Over 500 employees, B=251-500, C=101-250, D=51-100, E=20-50, F=10-19

2020 California
Manufacturers Register

© Mergent Inc. 1-800-342-5647

1381

GEOGRAPHIC

Company	SIC	EMP	PHONE	ENTRY #
Thermodyne International Ltd	3089	C	909 923-9945	10083
Torco International Corp	2911	F	909 980-1495	9075
Tower Industries Inc	3599	C	909 947-2723	16462
Tower Mechanical Products Inc	3812	C	714 947-2723	20733
Tracy Industries Inc	3519	C	562 692-9034	13600
Transcontinental US LLC	2673	E	909 390-8866	5426
Triumph Equipment Inc	3728	E	909 947-5983	20260
Trmc Sale Corporation	3585	D	800 290-7073	15465
Tropicale Foods Inc	2024	F	909 635-0390	674
Txd International Usa Inc	2711	F	909 947-6568	5855
Ultimate Print Source Inc	2752	E	909 947-5292	6906
Ultra Chem Labs Corp	2842	F	909 605-1640	8422
Uncks Unique Plastics Inc	3089	F	909 983-5181	10100
United Partition Systems Inc	2452	F	909 947-1077	4468
Universal Plastic Bags Mfg Inc	2673	F	909 218-2247	5430
Universal Wire Inc	3496	F	626 285-2288	13441
Upland Fab Inc	3089	E	909 933-9185	10101
Upm Raflatac Inc	2672	E	909 390-4657	5377
US Duty Gear Inc	3199	C	909 391-8800	10256
USA Sales Inc	2111	C	909 390-9606	2657
Uspar Enterprises Inc	3645	E	909 591-7506	16996
Ventura Foods LLC	2079	C	714 257-3700	1484
Ventura Foods LLC	2021	C	323 262-9157	540
Vigilant Marine Systems LLC	3714	F	909 597-9508	19798
Vishay Techno Components LLC	3625	D	909 923-3313	16766
Vishay Thin Film LLC	3674	E	909 923-3313	18645
Vishay Thin Film LLC	3676	E	909 923-3313	18692
Vishay Transducers Ltd	3674	F	626 363-7500	18646
Visionary Sleep LLC	2515	D	909 605-2010	4748
Voyager Learning Company	2741	F	909 923-3120	6378
Vsmpo Tirus US	3356	E	909 230-9020	11283
Vsmpo-Tirus US Inc	3356	E	909 230-9020	11284
Wagner Die Supply (PA)	3544	E	909 947-3044	14124
Walker Corporation	3496	E	909 390-4300	13444
Walker Spring & Stamping Corp	3469	C	909 390-4300	12889
Wallner Expac Inc (PA)	3549	D	909 481-8800	14286
Wangs Alliance Corporation	3645	E	909 230-9401	16999
Warren Packaging Inc	2759	F	909 923-0613	7265
Watercrest Inc	3443	F	909 390-3944	12069
Watsons Profiling Corp	3599	F	909 923-5500	16512
West Coast Chain Mfg Co	3699	E	909 923-7800	19441
Western States Wholesale Inc (PA)	3271	C	909 947-0028	10525
Will Pak Foods Inc	2034	F	800 874-0883	877
Windshield Pros Incorporated	3714	E	951 272-2867	19806
Windsor Quality Food Co Ltd	2038	A	713 843-5200	985
Xerox Corporation	3861	F	909 605-7900	22474
Y & D Rubber Corporation	3069	F	909 517-1683	9390
Yillik Precision Industries	3545	D	909 947-2785	14214
Yinlun Tdi LLC	3714	F	800 266-5645	19810
Yinlun Tdi LLC (HQ)	3714	D	909 390-3944	19811
Yukon Trail Inc	3751	F	909 218-5286	20439
Z B Wire Works Inc	3496	F	909 391-0995	13449
Zapp Packaging Inc	2631	D	909 930-1500	5186

ORANGE, CA - Orange County

Company	SIC	EMP	PHONE	ENTRY #
101 Apparel Inc	2321	F	714 454-8988	2983
5h Sheet Metal Fabrication Inc	3444	F	714 633-7544	12076
7 U P RC Bottling Company	3565	D	714 974-8560	14692
A&D Fire Sprinklers Inc	3569	F	714 634-3923	14792
ADC Enterprises Inc	3599	F	714 538-3102	15690
Advanced Ceramic Technology	3599	F	714 538-2524	15692
Aerosysng Inc	3721	F	714 633-1901	19848
Air Tube Transfer Systems Inc	3535	F	714 363-0700	13813
All Diameter Grinding Inc	3599	E	714 744-1200	15718
Allen Mold Inc	3089	F	714 538-6517	9617
Allen Morgan	3567	F	714 538-7492	14752
Alliance Hose & Extrusions Inc	2869	F	714 202-8500	8711
Allied Mdular Bldg Systems Inc (PA)	3448	E	714 516-1188	12528
Altemp Alloys Inc	3312	F	714 279-0249	11024
Amscan Inc	2656	D	714 972-2626	5306
Anchored Prints Inc	2752	F	714 929-9317	6414
Angelus Block Co Inc	3271	D	714 637-8594	10500
Anillo Industries Inc (PA)	3452	E	714 637-7000	12665
APM Manufacturing (HQ)	3721	C	714 453-0100	19857
Arden Engineering Inc	3728	E	714 998-6410	20041
Arz Tech Inc	3089	F	714 642-9954	9643
Asco Automatic Switch	3491	F	714 937-0811	13289
Autobahn Construction Inc	3531	F	714 769-7025	13706
Avantec Manufacturing Inc	3672	E	714 532-6197	17830
B-J Machine Inc	3469	F	714 685-0712	12768
BASF Corporation	2869	E	714 921-1430	8717
Bayside Shutters	3442	F	714 628-9994	11935
Brothers Optical Laboratory	3851	D	714 639-9852	22342
Bryan Edwards Publishing Co.	2731	F	714 634-0264	6082
Burlington Engineering Inc	3471	F	714 921-4045	12954
C W Moss Auto Parts Inc	3465	F	714 639-3083	12743

Company	SIC	EMP	PHONE	ENTRY #
Cadillac Plating Inc	3471	F	714 639-0342	12958
Cal-West Machining Inc	3593	F	714 637-4161	15621
California Gasket and Rbr Corp (PA)	3069	E	310 323-4250	9293
Califrnia Anlytical Instrs Inc	3823	D	714 974-5560	20843
Cemex Cnstr Mtls PCF LLC	3273	F	714 637-9470	10716
Century Precision Machine Inc	3599	F	714 637-3691	15836
CF&b Manufacturing Inc	2673	E	714 744-8361	5389
City Steel Heat Treating Inc	3398	F	562 789-7373	11446
Cleatech LLC	3821	F	714 754-6668	20751
Coastal Component Inds Inc	3679	F	714 685-6677	18869
Coastal Enterprises	2821	F	714 771-4969	7549
Coatings By Sandberg Inc	3479	F	714 538-0888	13160
Coil Winding Specialist	3677	F	714 279-9010	18707
Commercial Metal Forming Inc	3469	F	714 532-6321	12786
Continuous Coating Corp (PA)	3471	D	714 637-4642	12979
Contract Illumination	3646	E	714 771-5223	17020
Convergint Technologies LLC	3699	F	714 546-2780	19280
Counterpart Automotive Inc	3714	F	714 771-1732	19622
Crd Mfg Inc	3429	F	714 871-3300	11581
Cytec Engineered Materials Inc	2821	C	714 630-9400	7553
Data Aire Inc (HQ)	3585	C	800 347-2473	15423
Daves Interiors Inc	2512	E	714 998-5554	4636
Dilco Industrial Inc	3552	F	714 998-5266	14288
Direct Edge Screenworks Inc	2759	F	714 579-3686	7047
Do It Right Products LLC	3999	F	714 998-8152	23316
Don Miguel Mexican Foods Inc (HQ)	2038	C	714 385-4500	955
Ducommun Aerostructures Inc	3724	F	714 637-4401	19949
Dunham Metal Processing Co	3471	F	714 532-5551	12989
E D D Investment Co	2051	E	714 637-3040	1195
Edgewood Press Inc	2752	F	714 516-2455	6561
El Metate Foods Inc	2051	E	714 542-3913	1198
Fabricated Components Corp	3672	C	714 974-8590	17873
Fabtex Inc	2221	C	714 538-0877	2727
Fat Performance Inc	3714	F	714 637-2889	19655
Fieldpiece Instruments Inc	3825	E	714 634-1844	21037
Fisher Printing Inc (PA)	2752	C	714 998-9200	6574
Fletcher Coating Co	3479	F	714 637-4763	13179
Fur Accents LLC	2371	F	714 403-5286	3499
Fxi Inc	3086	C	714 637-0110	9545
G A Systems Inc	3589	F	714 848-7529	15515
G P Manufacturing Inc	3599	F	714 974-0288	15981
George L Kovacs	3547	E	714 538-8026	14232
Grand Meadows Inc	2834	F	714 628-1690	7926
Greenberg Teleprmpt	3661	F	714 633-1111	17376
Haldor Topsoe Inc	2819	F	714 621-3800	7499
Hand Piece Parts and Products	3843	E	714 997-4331	22158
Harpers Pharmacy Inc	2834	C	877 778-3773	7934
Hexion Inc	2869	F	714 971-0180	8742
Hightower Metal Products	3599	D	714 637-7000	16029
Hightower Plating & Mfg Co	3471	F	714 637-9110	13024
His Industries Inc	3565	E	562 407-0512	14711
Hoke Outdoor Advertising Inc	3993	E	714 637-3610	23128
Howmedica Osteonics Corp.	3841	E	714 557-5010	21734
Ice Link LLC	3556	F	714 771-6580	14374
Icon Screening Inc	2759	F	714 630-4266	7091
Independent Forge Company	3463	E	714 997-7337	12732
Integrated Marketing Group LLC	2211	F	714 771-2401	2694
Intellipower Inc	3677	D	714 921-1580	18721
ISI Detention Contg Group Inc	3599	D	714 288-1770	16056
J G Hernandez Company	3851	E	800 242-2020	22364
J J Foil Company Inc	2675	E	714 998-9920	5449
Jeneric/Pentron Incorporated (HQ)	3843	C	203 265-7397	22163
John Bishop Design Inc	3993	E	714 744-2300	23141
Jtb Supply Company Inc	3669	F	714 639-9558	17739
K & D Graphics	2675	E	714 639-8900	5450
Kerr Corporation (DH)	3843	C	714 516-7400	22166
King Plastics Inc	3089	D	714 997-7540	9866
Label Impressions Inc	2759	E	714 634-3466	7110
Lcptracker Inc	7372	C	714 669-0052	24095
Liboon Group Inc	3541	F	714 639-3639	13931
Lido Industries Inc	3089	F	714 633-3731	9877
Lmm Enterprises	3599	F	714 543-8044	16148
Lochaber Cornwall Inc (PA)	3567	F	714 935-0302	14769
M & R Engineering Co	3451	F	714 991-8480	12639
Magcomp Inc	3612	E	714 532-3584	16561
Marbil Industries Inc	3826	E	714 974-4032	21257
Marcel Electronics Inc	3672	E	714 974-8590	17917
Marcel Electronics Inc	3672	E	714 974-8590	17918
Marimix Company Inc	2064	E	714 633-7300	1387
Merlex Stucco Inc	3299	E	877 547-8822	11011
Mesa Safe Company Inc	3499	E	714 202-8000	13533
Metal Art of California Inc	3993	D	714 532-7100	23159
Metal Art of California Inc (PA)	3993	E	714 532-7100	23160
Microflex Technologies LLC	3674	F	714 937-1507	18394
Mufich Engineering Inc	3599	E	714 283-0599	16233

Mergent email: customerrelations@mergent.com
1382

2020 California
Manufacturers Register

(P-0000) Products & Services Section entry number
(PA)=Parent Co (HQ)=Headquarters (DH)=Div Headquarters

	SIC	EMP	PHONE	ENTRY #
National Oilwell Varco Inc	3533	E	714 978-1900	13785
National Oilwell Varco Inc	3533	E	714 978-1900	13787
National Oilwell Varco Inc	1381	F	714 456-1244	100
National Oilwell Varco Inc	3533	E	714 978-1900	13788
Newport Flavors & Fragrances	2087	E	714 771-2200	2222
Next Level Elevator Inc	3534	F	888 959-6010	13805
Niedwick Corporation	3599	E	714 771-9999	16246
Nursery Supplies Inc	3089	E	714 538-0251	9937
Oc Baking Company	2051	D	714 998-2253	1253
Oc Waterjet	3441	F	714 685-0851	11854
Omega Products Corp	3299	E	714 935-0900	11016
Opal Service Inc (PA)	3299	E	714 935-0900	11017
Orange County Plating Coinc	3471	E	714 532-4610	13066
Orange Woodworks Inc	2431	E	714 997-2600	4100
Ormco Corporation (DH)	3843	D	714 516-7400	22176
Ortho-Clinical Diagnostics Inc	2835	E	714 639-2323	8246
Pacific Aerodynamic Inc	3724	F	714 450-9140	19973
Pacifico Bindery Inc	2789	E	714 744-1510	7342
Patio & Door Outlet Inc (PA)	2519	E	714 974-9900	4769
Pgm Metal Finishing	3479	F	714 282-9193	13224
Positive Concepts Inc (PA)	2679	E	714 685-5800	5522
Precast Innovations Inc	3272	E	714 921-4060	10627
Presentation Folder Inc	2675	E	714 289-7000	5451
Printing Division Inc	2752	F	714 685-0111	6803
Pro Detention Inc	3315	D	714 881-3680	11104
Prototype & Short-Run Svcs Inc	3469	E	714 449-9661	12864
Quality Aluminum Forge LLC (HQ)	3463	D	714 639-8191	12735
Quality Produced LLC	2037	F	310 592-8834	926
R & B Plastics Inc	3599	F	714 229-8419	16331
Radian Audio Engineering Inc	3663	E	714 288-8900	17635
Radiation Protection & Spc Inc	3444	F	714 771-7702	12349
Redline Detection LLC	3559	F	714 451-1411	14527
Remanfctured Converter MBL LLC	3568	F	714 744-8988	14790
Reyes Coca-Cola Bottling LLC	2086	C	714 974-1901	2152
Rlh Industries Inc (PA)	3661	E	714 532-1672	17409
Roto Dynamics Inc	3089	E	714 685-0183	10027
SA Serving Lines Inc	3444	F	714 848-7529	12363
Sandwood Enterprises	3531	F	714 637-2000	13745
Sappi North America Inc	2679	D	714 456-0600	5529
Sas Institute Inc	7372	E	949 250-9999	24385
SE Industries Inc	2434	F	714 744-3200	4247
Seelect Inc	2087	F	714 744-3700	2230
Sign Source Inc	3993	F	714 979-9979	23201
SKB Corporation (PA)	3089	B	714 637-1252	10058
SKB Corporation	3161	B	714 637-1572	10209
Specialized Products & Design	2869	F	714 289-1428	8775
Sport Kites Inc	3721	F	714 998-6359	19932
Statek Corporation (HQ)	3679	D	714 639-7810	19093
Stir Foods LLC (HQ)	2038	C	714 637-6050	982
Sunland Tool Inc	3599	F	714 974-6500	16428
Sybron Dental Specialties Inc (HQ)	3843	C	714 516-7400	22194
Systems Integrated LLC	3829	E	714 998-0900	21549
Tandem Design Inc	3999	E	714 978-7272	23500
Technical Screen Printing Inc	2759	E	714 541-8590	7242
Techserve Industries Inc	3672	E	714 505-2755	18021
Thermal-Vac Technology Inc	3398	E	714 997-2601	11472
Tri Precision Sheetmetal Inc	3444	E	714 632-8838	12412
Tri-Tech Precision Inc	3728	F	714 970-1363	20256
Trisar Inc	2759	E	714 972-2626	7257
Truer Medical Inc	3841	F	714 628-9785	21940
Ulti-Mate Connector Inc	3678	E	714 637-7099	18801
Ultra-Pure Metal Finishing	3471	F	714 637-3150	13123
US Sensor Corp	3674	D	714 639-1000	18635
Vintique Inc	3714	E	714 634-1932	19799
We Do Graphics Inc	2752	E	714 997-7390	6928
Webb Massey Co Inc	2517	E	714 639-6012	4757
West American Rubber Co LLC (PA)	3069	B	714 532-3355	9388
West American Rubber Co LLC	3069	C	714 532-3355	9389
Western Lighting Inds Inc	3646	E	626 969-6820	17085
Westrock Rkt Company	2653	C	714 978-2895	5279
William Getz Corp	3949	E	714 516-2050	22926

ORANGEVALE, CA - Sacramento County

	SIC	EMP	PHONE	ENTRY #
Brand Identity Inc	2752	F	916 553-0000	6457
Natural Pest Controls & Firewd (PA)	2879	F	916 726-0855	8836

ORCUTT, CA - Santa Barbara County

	SIC	EMP	PHONE	ENTRY #
Den-Mat Corporation (DH)	2844	B	805 922-8491	8478

ORINDA, CA - Contra Costa County

	SIC	EMP	PHONE	ENTRY #
Bay Leaf Spice Company	2099	E	925 330-1918	2400
Sunbio Inc	2834	E	925 876-0439	8149

ORLAND, CA - Glenn County

	SIC	EMP	PHONE	ENTRY #
Decamilla Brothers LLC	2079	F	530 865-3379	1471
Jensen Enterprises Inc	3272	F	530 865-4277	10591
Kraemer & Co Mfg Inc	3448	F	530 865-7982	12554

	SIC	EMP	PHONE	ENTRY #
Land OLakes Inc	2022	E	530 865-7626	561
Olive Musco Products Inc	2035	E	530 865-4111	892
Westside Research Inc	2396	F	530 330-0085	3824

ORO GRANDE, CA - San Bernardino County

	SIC	EMP	PHONE	ENTRY #
Calportland Company	3241	F	760 245-5321	10406

OROSI, CA - Tulare County

	SIC	EMP	PHONE	ENTRY #
Lochirco Fruit and Produce Inc	2064	E	559 528-4194	1384

OROVILLE, CA - Butte County

	SIC	EMP	PHONE	ENTRY #
Afc Finishing Systems	3448	E	530 533-8907	12526
Apex Enterprises Inc	2411	F	530 871-0732	3873
Chico Metal Finishing Inc	3471	F	530 534-7308	12966
Conners Oro-Cal Mfg Co	3911	F	530 533-5065	22507
Direct Surplus Sales Inc	3444	F	530 533-9999	12185
Endeavor Homes Inc	3531	E	530 534-0300	13728
Feather River Concrete Product	3273	F	530 532-7915	10757
George Delallo Company Inc	2033	E	530 533-3303	771
Graphic Packaging Intl LLC	2759	C	530 533-1058	7075
J W Bamford Inc	2411	F	530 533-0732	3889
Jess Howard	3089	F	530 533-3888	9854
Night Optics Usa Inc	3669	F	714 899-4475	17750
North State Rendering Co Inc	2077	E	530 343-6076	1463
Pacific Coast Producers	2033	C	530 533-4311	815
Perfect Plank Co	2431	F	530 533-7606	4107
Roplast Industries Inc	2673	C	530 532-9500	5416
Setzer Forest Products Inc	2421	C	530 534-8100	3949
Sierra Pacific Industries	2421	C	530 532-6630	3954
Smb Industries Inc (PA)	3441	D	530 534-6266	11881
Tile Artisans Inc	3253	F	800 601-4199	10456
Vinyl Fabrications Inc	2394	F	530 532-1236	3713
Vulcan Materials Company	1422	F	530 534-4517	307

OXNARD, CA - Ventura County

	SIC	EMP	PHONE	ENTRY #
ACC Precision Inc	3599	F	805 278-9801	15674
Acme Cryogenics Inc	3559	E	805 981-4500	14417
Advanced Structural Tech Inc	3462	C	805 204-9133	12701
Advantage Engineering Corp	3949	E	805 216-9920	22733
Alliance Chemical & Envmtl	3471	F	805 385-3330	12917
Alpha Products Inc	3678	E	805 981-8666	18750
Aluminum Precision Pdts Inc	3463	C	805 488-4401	12729
American Alupack Inds LLC	3353	E	805 485-1500	11215
American Tooth Industries	3843	D	805 487-9868	22133
Amiad USA Inc	3589	F	805 988-3323	15481
Angelus Block Co Inc	3271	E	805 485-1137	10499
Applied Powdercoat Inc	3479	E	805 981-1991	13144
Astro Aerospace	3812	C	805 684-6641	20540
B & S Plastics Inc	3089	A	805 981-0262	9648
Basic Business Forms Inc	2759	E	805 278-4551	6997
Becker Automotive Designs Inc	3711	E	805 487-5227	19459
Beckman Industries	3965	F	805 375-3003	22998
Berry Petroleum Company LLC	1311	F	805 984-0053	27
Cal Simba Inc (PA)	3914	E	805 240-1177	22588
California Plastics Inc	3089	F	805 483-8188	9687
California Resources Prod Corp	1311	D	805 483-8017	39
California Woodworking Inc	2434	E	805 982-9090	4179
Casa Agria	2082	F	805 485-1454	1510
Casualway Usa LLC	2514	D	805 660-7408	4687
Catalytic Solutions Inc (HQ)	3822	E	805 486-4649	20786
Cdti Advanced Materials Inc (PA)	2819	E	805 639-9458	7480
Clamshell Structures Inc	3448	F	805 988-1340	12540
Cloudburst Inc	3564	E	805 986-4125	14654
Coastal Cnting Indus Scale Inc	3545	F	805 486-5754	14147
Complyright Distribution Svcs	2761	E	805 981-0992	7281
Component Equipment Coinc	3678	D	805 988-8004	18755
Cool-Pak LLC	3089	C	805 981-2434	9726
Cosmetic Specialties Intl LLC	3089	C	805 487-6698	9729
Dabmar Lighting Inc (PA)	3648	E	805 604-9090	17115
DBC Printing Incorporated	2752	F	805 988-8855	6534
Diversified Minerals Inc	3273	E	805 247-1069	10753
Diversified Panels Systems Inc	3585	F	805 487-9241	15424
Drum Workshop Inc (PA)	3931	D	805 485-6999	22613
E Vasquez Distributors Inc	2448	E	805 487-8458	4364
Eagle Dominion Energy Corp	1382	E	805 272-9557	122
Elite Metal Finishing LLC (PA)	3471	D	805 983-4320	13005
Elite Metal Finishing LLC	3471	D	805 983-4320	13006
Ergonom Corporation	2599	D	805 981-9978	5059
Ets Express Inc (PA)	3479	E	805 278-7771	13175
Force Fabrication Inc	3444	F	805 754-2235	12214
Frank Stubbs Co Inc	3842	E	805 278-4300	22014
Freeport-Mcmoran Oil & Gas LLC	1382	E	805 567-1601	123
Fresh Innovations LLC	2097	E	805 483-2265	2354
Gold Coast Ironworks	3446	F	805 485-6921	12477
Gramberg Machine Inc	3599	F	805 278-4500	16003
Granatelli Motor Sports Inc	3714	E	805 486-6644	19674
Hanson Aggregates LLC	3241	D	805 485-3101	10411

Employment Codes: A=Over 500 employees, B=251-500,
C=101-250, D=51-100, E=20-50, F=10-19

2020 California
Manufacturers Register

© Mergent Inc. 1-800-342-5647

1383

GEOGRAPHIC

	SIC	EMP	PHONE	ENTRY #
Harwil Precision Products	3679	E	805 988-6800	18932
Henry J Perez DDS	3843	F	805 983-6768	22159
Hypress Technologies Inc	3542	F	805 485-4060	13978
Illah Sports Inc A Corporation	3949	E	805 240-7790	22827
Industrial Tools Inc	3559	E	805 483-1111	14479
Infratab	2836	E	805 986-8880	8311
International Forming Tech Inc	3542	E	805 278-8060	13979
J M Smucker Company	2033	E	805 487-5483	778
John L Perry Studio Inc	3089	E	805 981-9665	9857
Kevita Inc (HQ)	2086	D	805 200-2250	2086
Kim Laube & Company Inc	2844	E	805 240-1300	8527
KI-Megla America LLC	3429	E	818 334-5311	11603
Legacy Vulcan LLC	3273	C	805 647-1161	10782
Lennox Industries Inc	3585	C	805 288-8200	15440
Little Castle Furniture Co Inc	2512	E	805 278-4646	4653
Lotw Light of World	3679	F	805 278-4806	18995
Masters In Metal Inc	3263	E	805 988-1992	10471
Mgr Design International Inc	3999	C	805 981-6400	23410
Mirage Sprtfshng & Commrcl	3949	E	805 983-0975	22854
Mist & Cool LLC	3634	E	805 986-4125	16835
Mjolnir Industries LLC	3544	F	805 488-3550	14078
New-Indy Oxnard LLC	2621	C	805 986-3881	5138
Northrop Grumman Systems Corp	3812	A	805 278-2074	20656
Noushig Inc	2051	E	805 983-2903	1251
Nu Venture Diving Co	3563	E	805 815-4044	14636
Nutrien AG Solutions Inc	2873	F	805 488-3646	8800
Oxnard Lemon Company	2037	F	805 483-1173	921
Oxnard Prcsion Fabrication Inc	3444	E	805 985-0447	12320
Parker-Hannifin Corporation	3569	C	805 604-3400	14846
PC Vaughan Mfg Corp	3569	C	805 278-2555	14847
Periodico El Vida	2711	E	805 483-1008	5796
Pine Grove Industries Inc	2752	E	805 485-3700	6782
Plascene Inc	3089	F	562 695-0240	9965
Poole Ventura Inc	3563	F	805 981-1784	14638
Praxair Distribution Inc	2813	F	805 487-2742	7445
Primal Essence Inc	2087	E	805 981-2409	2225
Procter & Gamble Paper Pdts Co	2676	B	805 485-8871	5465
Produce Available Inc (PA)	3523	D	805 483-5292	13660
Pti Technologies Inc (DH)	3728	C	805 604-3700	20206
Rakar Incorporated	3089	E	805 487-2721	10006
Rapid Product Solutions Inc	3599	E	805 485-7234	16342
Raypak Inc (DH)	3433	C	805 278-5300	11709
Regal Kitchens LLC	2434	C	786 953-6578	4238
Richard Sanchez	3446	F	805 455-2904	12504
Robbins Auto Top LLC	3089	D	805 278-8249	10020
Royal Wine Corporation	2084	E	805 983-1560	1900
Sandra Sparks & Associates	2844	F	805 985-2057	8575
Santa Barbara Design Studio (PA)	3269	D	805 966-3883	10492
Scosche Industries Inc	3651	C	805 486-4450	17281
Scully Sportswear Inc	2386	D	805 483-6339	3522
Sensortech Systems Inc	3823	F	805 981-3735	20936
Simpliphi Power Inc	3691	F	805 640-6700	19173
Sound Storm Laboratory LLC	3651	E	805 983-8008	17286
South Amrcn Imging Sltions Inc	3621	F	805 824-4036	16675
Southern Cal Gold Pdts Inc	3312	F	805 988-0777	11072
Spatz Corporation	2844	C	805 487-2122	8587
Stainless Process Systems Inc	3441	F	805 483-7100	11885
State Ready Mix Inc	3273	E	805 647-2817	10844
Sun Coast Calamari Inc	2092	C	805 385-0056	2271
T & M Machining Inc	3599	E	805 983-6716	16436
Tbyci LLC	3732	E	805 985-6800	20359
TI Enterprises LLC (DH)	2721	E	805 981-8393	6042
Trans Fx Inc	3999	E	805 485-6110	23509
Travis Mike Inc	3469	F	805 201-3363	12884
Tree Top Inc	2033	C	509 697-7251	830
V3 Printing Corporation	2752	D	805 981-2600	6914
Vaca Energy LLC	1382	F	310 385-3684	145
Van R Dental Products Inc	3843	F	805 488-1122	22202
Ventura Printing Inc (PA)	2759	D	805 981-2600	7262
Vogue Sign Inc	3993	F	805 487-7222	23238
Vortech Engineering Inc	3564	E	805 247-0226	14688
West Coast Welding & Cnstr	7692	E	805 604-1222	24679
Western Saw Manufacturers Inc	3425	E	805 981-0999	11556
Wholesome Harvest Baking LLC	2051	C	805 487-5191	1297
Wiggins Lift Co Inc	3537	E	805 485-7821	13897
Willis Machine Inc	3599	E	805 604-4500	16528
Zev Technologies Inc (PA)	3484	F	805 486-5800	13280

PACHECO, CA - Contra Costa County

	SIC	EMP	PHONE	ENTRY #
Biocare Medical LLC	3841	C	925 603-8000	21630

PACIFIC GROVE, CA - Monterey County

	SIC	EMP	PHONE	ENTRY #
Carmel Communications Inc	2711	F	831 274-8593	5584
Happy Girl Kitchen Co	2033	F	831 373-4475	772
Manutech Mfg & Dist	3524	F	831 655-8794	13690

PACIFIC PALISADES, CA - Los Angeles County

	SIC	EMP	PHONE	ENTRY #
Brickstone Group Inc	2099	F	310 991-4747	2410
Optimis Services Inc	7372	E	310 230-2780	24236
Pipeliner Crm	7372	E	424 280-6445	24300

PACIFICA, CA - San Mateo County

	SIC	EMP	PHONE	ENTRY #
Forever Young	2099	E	650 355-5481	2462
Jodel Enterprises	3651	F	650 343-4510	17248
Kibblwhite Precision Machining	3751	E	650 359-4704	20412
Maurice Landstrass	3825	E	650 355-5532	21076
The French Patisserie Inc	2051	D	650 738-4990	1286

PACOIMA, CA - Los Angeles County

	SIC	EMP	PHONE	ENTRY #
A & A Custom Shutters	3442	F	818 383-1819	11925
American Cnc Inc	3599	F	818 890-3400	15737
American Etching & Mfg	3479	E	323 875-3910	13141
American Fruits & Flavors LLC (HQ)	2087	C	818 899-9574	2189
American Range Corporation	3444	C	818 897-0808	12107
Anwright Corporation	3451	E	818 896-2465	12620
APT Metal Fabricators Inc	3469	E	818 896-7478	12766
Brice Manufacturing Co Inc	3728	E	818 896-2938	20059
Burbank Plating Service Corp	3471	F	818 899-1157	12953
Cabrac Inc	3469	E	818 834-0177	12777
California Signs Inc	3993	E	818 899-1888	23070
California Trade Converters	2631	E	818 899-1455	5159
Color TEC Industrial Finishing	3479	E	818 897-2669	13161
Cosmetic Enterprises Ltd	2844	F	818 896-5355	8468
D & M Steel Inc	3441	E	818 896-2070	11780
Excess Trading Inc	3829	E	310 212-0020	21469
Flamemaster Corporation	2899	E	818 890-1401	8967
Gscm Ventures Inc	2844	F	818 303-2600	8505
Hanmar LLC (PA)	3469	E	818 240-0170	12811
Hrk Pet Food Products Inc	2048	F	818 897-2521	1100
Imagemover Inc	2752	F	818 485-8840	6629
JKL Components Corporation	3647	E	818 896-0019	17090
Kdl Precision Molding Corp	3769	E	818 896-9899	20477
Kitch Engineering Inc	3599	E	818 897-7133	16519
LA Hardwood Flooring Inc (PA)	2426	F	818 361-0099	3977
Legacy Bands Inc	3911	E	818 890-2527	22538
Lex Products LLC	3829	E	818 768-4474	21499
Mayoni Enterprises	3444	D	818 896-0026	12286
Metalite Manufacturing Company	3469	E	818 890-2802	12843
Moc Products Company Inc (PA)	2899	D	818 794-3500	9002
Molding Corporation America	3089	E	818 890-7877	9907
Nu-Hope Laboratories Inc	3842	E	818 899-7711	22056
Petra-1 LP	2844	F	866 334-3702	8557
Pyramid Powder Coating Inc	3479	E	818 768-5898	13233
RMR Products Inc (PA)	3272	E	818 890-0896	10641
Sdi Industries Inc (PA)	3535	C	818 890-6002	13835
Sun Valley Skylights Inc	3211	F	818 686-0032	10276
Sunland Aerospace Fasteners	3452	F	818 485-8929	12696
Topnotch Quality Works Inc	3728	F	818 897-7679	20251
Trico Sports Inc	3751	D	818 899-7705	20432
Twin Peak Industries Inc	3949	E	800 259-5906	22914
Ultramet	3471	D	818 899-0236	13124
Valley Motor Center Inc	3711	F	818 686-3350	19510
Westcoast Grinding Corporation	3599	F	818 890-1841	16519
Western States Packaging Inc	2673	E	818 686-6045	5431
Xentric Drapery Hardware Inc	2591	F	818 897-0444	5044
Zerran International Corp	2844	F	818 897-5494	8611

PALA, CA - San Diego County

	SIC	EMP	PHONE	ENTRY #
Tribal Print Source	2752	F	760 597-2650	6901

PALM DESERT, CA - Riverside County

	SIC	EMP	PHONE	ENTRY #
Associated Desert Shoppers (DH)	2741	D	760 346-1729	6191
Daniels Inc (PA)	2741	E	801 621-3355	6220
Equipment De Sport Usa Inc	2395	F	760 772-5544	3744
Farley Paving Stone Co Inc	3272	D	760 773-3960	10570
Karbz Inc	3714	E	760 567-9953	19699
Lf Visuals Inc	2299	F	760 345-5571	2943
Pd Group	3993	E	760 674-3028	23176
Pearpoint Inc	3663	E	760 343-7350	17620
Photobacks LLC	7372	E	760 582-2550	24296
Plumbing Products Inc	3432	E	760 343-3306	11676
PPG Industries Inc	2851	E	760 340-1762	8668
Trent Beverage Company LLC	2086	E	310 384-6776	2177
Upholstery Factory Inc (PA)	2512	F	760 341-6865	4675
Wanda Matranga	2752	F	760 773-4701	6926

PALM SPRINGS, CA - Riverside County

	SIC	EMP	PHONE	ENTRY #
Adams Trade Press LP (PA)	2721	E	760 318-7000	5875
Bear Brothers Enterprises Ltd	2721	E	914 588-6685	5887
Carefusion 207 Inc	3841	B	760 778-7200	21653
Carefusion Corporation	2834	F	760 778-7200	7831
Desert Publications Inc (PA)	2721	E	760 325-2333	5917
Desert Sun Publishing Co (HQ)	2711	C	760 322-8889	5614

Mergent email: customerrelations@mergent.com
1384

2020 California
Manufacturers Register

(P-0000) Products & Services Section entry number
(PA)=Parent Co (HQ)=Headquarters (DH)=Div Headquarters

	SIC	EMP	PHONE	ENTRY #
Dimora Enterprises	3711	F	760 832-9070	19467
Door Service Company	3315	F	760 320-0788	11092
Galaxy Energy Systems Inc	3511	F	760 778-4254	13569
Gannett Co Inc	2711	D	760 322-8889	5638
Iqd Frequency Products Inc	3679	E	760 318-2824	18953
Joe Blasco Enterprises Inc	3999	D	323 467-4949	23373
Just Off Melrose Inc	2052	E	714 533-4566	1317
Ken Hoffmann Inc	3471	E	760 325-6012	13036
Pleros LLC	2844	F	442 275-6764	8563
Sierra Aviation	3161	F	760 778-2845	10207
Univocity Media Inc	2741	F	760 904-5200	6369
Xy Corp Inc	3542	F	760 323-0333	14000

PALMDALE, CA - Los Angeles County

	SIC	EMP	PHONE	ENTRY #
Aamstamp Machine Company LLC	3497	F	661 272-0500	13450
Aero Bending Company	3444	E	661 948-2363	12089
Azachorok Contract Svcs LLC	3444	F	661 951-6566	12123
Bimbo Bakeries Usa Inc	2099	F	661 274-8458	2404
Boeing Company	3812	B	661 212-0024	20550
D & J Printing Inc	2752	D	661 775-4586	6529
Ectec Inc	3812	F	661 451-1098	20573
Instathreads LLC	2284	F	661 470-7841	2891
Kennedy Engineered Products	3714	F	661 272-1147	19700
Lockheed Martin Corporation	3812	F	661 572-2974	20605
Lockheed Martin Corporation	3812	A	661 572-7428	20618
Lucky Luke Brewing Company	2082	F	661 270-5588	1546
Lusk Quality Machine Products	3599	E	661 272-0630	16154
Northrop Grumman Systems Corp	3721	B	661 272-7000	19918
Northrop Grumman Systems Corp	3812	B	661 540-0446	20663
Palmdale Heat Treating Inc	3443	F	661 274-8604	12038
Park-Rand Enterprises Inc	2842	F	818 362-2565	8404
Phase-A-Matic Inc	3699	F	661 947-8485	19376
RB Machining Inc	3599	F	661 274-4611	16343
Service Rock Products Corp	3273	E	661 533-3443	10832
Sharkey Technology Group Inc	3599	F	661 267-2118	16399
Sun Valley Ltg Standards Inc	3646	B	661 233-2000	17074
Ultramar Inc	2911	F	661 944-2496	9080
US Pole Company Inc (PA)	3648	C	800 877-6537	17173
Vision Engrg Met Stamping Inc	3646	F	661 575-0933	17082
Western Edge Inc	3479	F	661 947-3900	13267

PALO ALTO, CA - Santa Clara County

	SIC	EMP	PHONE	ENTRY #
Abaqus Inc	7372	F	415 496-9436	23540
Adaptive Insghts LLC A Workday (HQ)	7372	C	650 528-7500	23560
Agilent Technologies Inc	3825	D	877 424-4536	20992
Alro Cstm Drapery Installation	2591	F	650 847-4343	5014
Anacor Pharmaceuticals Inc	2834	E	650 543-7500	7758
Appbackr Inc	7372	F	650 272-6129	23604
Applied Expert Systems Inc	7372	E	650 617-2400	23612
Apporto Corporation	7372	E	650 326-0920	23615
Ariba Inc (DH)	7372	C	650 849-4000	23624
Ascendis Pharma Inc	2834	F	650 352-8389	7769
Astro Technology Inc	7372	E	650 533-5087	23633
Avail Medsystems Inc	3841	E	650 772-1529	21614
Billcom Inc	7372	C	650 353-3301	23667
Birdcage Press LLC	2741	F	650 462-6300	6200
Birdeye Inc (PA)	2741	E	800 561-3357	6201
Bosch Enrgy Stor Solutions LLC	3621	E	650 320-2933	16633
Bridgebio Pharma Inc	2834	C	650 391-9740	7817
Calmar Optcom Inc	3661	E	408 733-7800	17352
Clariant Corporation	2821	C	650 494-1749	7548
Cobalt Robotics Inc	3571	D	650 781-3626	14898
Communications & Pwr Inds LLC	3671	E	650 846-3494	17777
Communications & Pwr Inds LLC	3663	A	650 846-3729	17491
Communications & Pwr Inds LLC (HQ)	3671	A	650 846-2900	17778
Communications & Pwr Inds LLC	3671	C	650 846-2900	17779
Condor Electronics Inc	3823	E	408 745-7141	20850
Confluent Inc (PA)	7372	E	650 453-5860	23770
CPI International Inc (PA)	3671	F	650 846-2801	17780
CPI International Holding Corp	3679	F	650 846-2900	18875
Cymmetria Inc	7372	E	415 568-6870	23794
Danisco US Inc (DH)	2835	C	650 846-7500	8218
Duda Mobile Inc	7372	E	855 790-0003	23836
Eiger Biopharmaceuticals Inc (PA)	2836	F	650 272-6138	8295
Embarcadero Publishing Company (PA)	2711	C	650 964-6300	5630
Endepo Inc	3433	F	707 428-3245	11695
Eton Corporation	3699	E	650 903-3866	19308
Fiorano Software Inc	7372	D	650 326-1136	23898
Fono Unlimited Inc (PA)	2024	E	650 322-4664	645
Hammon Plating Corporation	3471	E	650 494-2691	13020
Hp Inc (PA)	3571	A	650 857-1501	14916
HP Inc	3571	A	650 857-4946	14918
HP Inc	3571	D	650 857-1501	14919
HP Inc	3571	E	650 857-1501	14920
Hpi Federal LLC (HQ)	3571	F	650 857-1501	14922
Inscopix Inc	3827	F	650 600-3886	21366

	SIC	EMP	PHONE	ENTRY #
Integral Development Corp (PA)	7372	C	650 424-4500	24028
Ivydoctors Inc	7372	F	415 890-3937	24053
Jazz Pharmaceuticals Inc (HQ)	2834	C	650 496-3777	7971
Kodiak Sciences Inc (PA)	2834	E	650 281-0850	7981
KUDos&co Inc	2741	E	650 799-9104	6266
Level Labs LP	7372	E	408 499-6839	24100
Liveaction Inc (PA)	7372	E	415 837-3303	24103
Lockheed Martin Corporation	3812	A	650 424-2000	20610
Magnet Systems Inc	7372	E	650 329-5904	24123
Matician Inc	3569	F	650 504-9181	14837
Maximus Holdings Inc	7372	A	650 935-9500	24131
Mda Cmmunications Holdings LLC	3663	A	650 852-4000	17582
Merck & Co Inc	2834	D	650 496-6400	8010
Merrill Corporation	2759	C	650 493-1400	7136
Metricstream Inc (PA)	7372	C	650 620-2900	24149
Mountain View Voice	2711	E	650 326-8210	5767
Network Chemistry Inc	3699	F	650 858-3120	19363
Nevro Corp	3841	E	650 251-0005	21835
Nyansa Inc	7372	E	650 446-7818	24220
Open-Xchange Inc (PA)	2741	F	914 332-5720	6302
Pearson Electronics Inc	3677	E	650 494-6444	18732
Phantom Cyber Corporation	7372	E	650 208-5151	24294
Pilot Software Inc	7372	F	650 230-2830	24299
PIP Printing Palo Alto Inc	2752	F	650 323-8388	6784
Quality Metal Spinning and	3469	E	650 858-2491	12865
Recomax Software Inc	3663	E	408 592-0851	17642
Recor Medical Inc (HQ)	3841	E	650 542-7700	21873
Rollapp Inc (PA)	7372	F	650 617-3372	24365
RR Donnelley & Sons Company	2782	C	650 845-6600	7315
Sap AG	3572	C	650 849-4000	15091
Scene 53 Inc	7372	F	415 404-2461	24387
Sciton Inc	3841	D	650 493-9155	21891
Sinusys Corporation	2836	F	650 213-9988	8330
Sizto Tech Corporation	3491	F	650 856-8833	13321
Southwall Technologies Inc (DH)	2821	E	650 798-1285	7613
Stangenes Industries Inc (PA)	3677	C	650 855-9926	18745
Stemrad Inc	3842	F	650 933-3377	22091
Suitable Technologies Inc (PA)	3549	F	650 294-3190	14282
Sumopti	7372	F	650 331-1126	24466
Superfish Inc	3823	F	650 752-6564	20944
Suss McRtec Prcision Photomask	3861	F	415 494-3113	22460
Symphonyrm Inc	7372	E	650 336-8430	24475
Tesla Inc (PA)	3711	C	650 681-5000	19507
Varian Associates Limited	3841	E	650 493-4000	21945
Varian Medical Systems Inc (PA)	3844	A	650 493-4000	22224
Varian Medical Systems Inc	3841	E	408 321-4468	21946
Varian Medical Systems Inc	3671	F	650 493-4000	17796
Varian Medical Systems Inc	3841	C	650 493-4000	21948
Vera Security Inc	7372	E	844 438-8372	24551
Verbio Inc	7372	E	650 862-8935	24553
Vmware Inc (DH)	7372	C	650 427-5000	24568
Voelker Sensors Inc	2396	F	650 361-0570	3823
Xcelmobility Inc	7372	D	650 320-1728	24592
Xerox International Partners (DH)	3555	E	408 953-2700	14342
ZF Micro Solutions Inc	3674	F	650 846-6500	18671

PALOS VERDES ESTATES, CA - Los Angeles County

	SIC	EMP	PHONE	ENTRY #
QED Software LLC	7372	F	310 214-3118	24327
Sure Inc	3841	F	833 787-3462	21918

PANORAMA CITY, CA - Los Angeles County

	SIC	EMP	PHONE	ENTRY #
ARC Machines Inc (HQ)	3548	D	818 896-9556	14238
D X Communications Inc	3663	E	323 256-3000	17499
Mag High Tech	3444	F	818 786-8366	12276
Puretek Corporation	2834	C	818 361-3949	8091
Raspadoxpress	2741	F	818 892-6969	6324
Superior Awning Inc	2394	E	818 780-7200	3708
TMW Corporation	3471	E	818 374-1074	13118
Transit Care Inc	3211	F	818 267-3002	10278

PARADISE, CA - Butte County

	SIC	EMP	PHONE	ENTRY #
B C Yellow Pages	2741	F	530 876-8616	6196
Califrnia Nwspapers Ltd Partnr	2711	C	530 877-4413	5582

PARAMOUNT, CA - Los Angeles County

	SIC	EMP	PHONE	ENTRY #
Aerocraft Heat Treating Co Inc	3398	D	562 674-2400	11430
After Hours	3651	F	562 925-5737	17184
Air Frame Forming Inc	3542	F	562 663-1662	13965
Amrex-Zetron Inc	3699	E	310 527-6868	19257
Amsco US Inc	3679	C	562 630-0333	18816
Anaplex Corporation	3471	E	714 522-4481	12927
Apollo Metal Spinning Co Inc	3465	F	562 634-5141	12741
Ariza Cheese Co Inc	2022	E	562 630-4144	541
ARS Enterprises (PA)	3842	F	562 946-3505	21982
Bison Engineering Company	3599	F	562 408-1525	15791
Bkon Interior Soution	2521	F	562 408-1655	4787
Blue Circle Corp	3452	F	562 531-2711	12668

Employment Codes: A=Over 500 employees, B=251-500,
C=101-250, D=51-100, E=20-50, F=10-19

2020 California
Manufacturers Register

© Mergent Inc. 1-800-342-5647
1385

GEOGRAPHIC

	SIC	EMP	PHONE	ENTRY #
Bluegate Surface Works Inc	2434	F	562 630-9005	4170
C & J Metal Products Inc	3444	E	562 634-3101	12140
C S Dash Cover Inc	2396	F	562 790-8300	3776
Cad Manufacturing Inc	3728	F	562 408-1113	20061
California Screw Products Corp	3429	C	562 633-6626	11577
Danrich Welding Coinc	3444	F	562 634-4811	12173
Demaria Electric Inc	7694	E	310 549-4980	24686
Denmac Industries Inc	3479	E	562 634-2714	13164
Die Shop	3544	E	562 630-4400	14044
Dlc Laboratories Inc	2834	F	562 602-2184	7872
Drees Wood Products Inc	2431	E	562 633-7337	4039
Drees Wood Products Inc (PA)	2431	E	562 633-7337	4040
Exodust Collectors LLC	3564	F	562 808-0842	14659
Extrude Hone Deburring Service	3599	F	562 531-2976	15947
Fenico Precision Castings Inc	3369	D	562 634-5000	11416
Gammell Industries Inc	3441	F	562 634-6653	11800
George Jue Mfg Co Inc	3546	D	562 634-8181	14221
Golden State Engineering Inc	3549	C	562 634-3125	14268
Graphic Trends Incorporated	2759	E	562 531-2339	7077
Harbor Products Inc	3069	E	562 633-8184	9314
Hoffman Plastic Compounds Inc	2821	D	323 636-3346	7566
Instrument & Valve Services Co	3823	F	562 633-0179	20890
International Trend - 3 Corp	2329	F	562 360-5185	3094
Iron Works & Custom Racks	7692	F	323 581-2222	24641
Jade Spec LLC	2211	F	310 933-4338	2697
Jayone Foods Inc	2099	F	562 633-7400	2486
Jeffrey Fabrication LLC	3444	E	562 634-3101	12254
Jimenes Food Inc	2099	E	562 602-2505	2489
Kum Kang Trading USAinC	2844	F	562 531-6111	8528
LMC Enterprises (PA)	2842	D	562 602-2116	8393
Logos Plus Inc	2396	F	562 634-3009	3797
Marukan Vinegar U S A Inc (HQ)	2099	C	562 630-6060	2544
Mattco Forge Inc (PA)	3462	D	562 634-8635	12714
Mediland Corporation	3211	D	562 630-9696	10272
Merlin-Alltec Mold Making Inc	3089	F	562 529-5050	9893
Millbrook Kitchens Inc	2434	F	310 684-3366	4224
Mr T Transport	1389	F	562 602-5536	225
New Century Industries Inc	3714	E	562 634-9551	19727
Paramount Dairy Inc	2026	F	562 361-1800	708
Paramount Extrusions Company (PA)	3354	F	562 634-3291	11242
Paramount Extrusions Company	3354	F	562 634-3291	11243
Paramount Grinding Service	3599	F	562 630-6940	16282
Paramount Laminates Inc	3083	F	562 531-7580	9446
Paramount Petroleum Corp	2911	F	562 633-4332	9057
Paramount Petroleum Corp (DH)	2911	C	562 531-2060	9058
Paratech Inc	3295	E	562 633-2045	10975
Pecowood Inc	3429	F	562 633-2538	11620
Piedras Machine Corporation	3728	F	562 602-1500	20201
Popsalot LLC	2096	E	213 761-0156	2339
Premier Fuel Distributors Inc	2869	F	562 602-1000	8763
Premium Plastics Machine Inc	3089	F	323 979-3889	9990
Press Forge Company	3462	F	562 531-4962	12721
Quality Image Inc	2821	E	562 259-9872	7601
R & S Manufacturing & Sup Inc	2851	F	909 622-5881	8675
R & S Processing Co Inc	3069	D	562 531-0738	9362
Ramp Engineering Inc	3441	F	562 531-8030	11872
Robert W Wiesmantel	3599	F	562 634-0442	16364
Sandee Plastic Extrusions	3061	E	323 979-4020	9272
Schulz Leather Co Inc	2394	E	562 633-1081	3704
Scigen Inc	2869	F	310 324-6576	8773
Scotts Food Products Inc	2035	F	562 630-8448	899
Sibyl Shepard Inc	2392	F	562 531-8612	3640
Supertec Machinery Inc	3541	F	562 220-1675	13954
Top Line Mfg Inc	3429	F	562 633-0605	11637
Total-Western Inc (HQ)	1389	E	562 220-1450	272
TP Solar Inc	3567	E	562 808-2171	14777
Trepanning Spcialty A Cal Corp	3599	F	562 408-0044	16464
Vast Enterprises	2992	F	562 633-3224	9157
Vi-Star Gear Co Inc	3462	E	323 774-3750	12726
Wagner Plate Works West Inc (PA)	3443	E	562 531-6050	12068
Williams Metal Blanking Dies	3469	F	562 634-4592	12893
Z-Tronix Inc	3679	E	562 808-0800	19148

PARLIER, CA - Fresno County

	SIC	EMP	PHONE	ENTRY #
John Daniel Gonzalez	2449	E	559 646-6621	4418
W E Plemons McHy Svcs Inc	3565	E	559 646-6630	14735

PASADENA, CA - Los Angeles County

	SIC	EMP	PHONE	ENTRY #
A N Tool & Die Inc	3599	F	626 795-3238	15662
Accu-Gage & Thread Grinding Co	3823	F	626 568-2932	20825
ADS Water Inc	3589	F	415 448-6266	15479
Advanced Mtls Joining Corp (PA)	3728	E	626 449-2696	20007
Aea Ribbon Mics	3651	F	626 798-9128	17183
All Metal Fabrication	3444	F	626 449-6191	12097
American Craftsmen Corporation	2511	F	626 793-3329	4546
Arrowhead Pharmaceuticals Inc (PA)	2834	F	626 304-3400	7768

	SIC	EMP	PHONE	ENTRY #
Arts Elegance Inc	3911	E	626 793-4794	22497
At Systems Technologies Inc	3578	E	317 591-2616	15372
Auritec Pharmaceuticals Inc	2834	F	424 272-9501	7777
Avery Dennison Corporation	2672	C	626 304-2000	5354
Branch Messenger Inc	7372	F	323 300-4063	23695
C & D Precision Components	3599	F	626 799-7109	15807
Calimmune Inc	2834	F	310 806-6240	7822
Calimmune Inc (DH)	2834	F	310 806-6240	7823
Camtek LLC	2834	F	626 508-1700	7826
Chase Corporation	3644	E	626 395-7706	16941
Estephanian Originals Inc	2261	E	626 358-7265	2824
Evolution Design Lab Inc	3144	E	626 960-8388	10169
Evolution Robotics Inc	7372	E	626 993-3300	23880
Floor Covering Soft	7372	E	626 683-9188	23905
Fvo Solutions Inc	3479	D	626 449-0218	13181
George L Throop Co	3272	E	626 796-0285	10580
Get Ahead Learning LLC	7372	F	626 796-8500	23936
Gmto Corporation	3827	D	626 204-0500	21355
Guidance Software Inc (HQ)	7372	C	626 229-9191	23963
Guidance Software Inc	7372	E	626 229-9199	23964
Hamilton Metalcraft Inc	3444	E	626 795-4811	12232
Hemodialysis Inc	3841	E	626 792-0548	21733
Honeybee Robotics Ltd	3569	F	510 207-4555	14825
House of Printing Inc	2752	E	626 793-7034	6618
Hybrid Kinetic Motors Corp	3711	F	626 683-7330	19479
Innovate Labs LLC	7372	E	917 753-2673	24024
Integrated Design Tools Inc (PA)	3861	E	850 222-5939	22430
L A Steel Craft Products (PA)	3949	E	626 798-7401	22839
Licher Direct Mail Inc	2752	E	626 795-3333	6702
Lida Childrens Wear Inc	2361	E	626 967-8868	3483
Lifesource Water Systems Inc (PA)	3589	E	626 792-9996	15536
Materia Inc (PA)	2819	C	626 584-8400	7503
Max Leon Inc (PA)	2339	D	626 797-6886	3372
Meridian Rapid Def Group LLC	3444	E	720 616-7795	12290
Myricom Inc	3571	E	626 821-5555	14955
Normandy Refinishers Inc	3471	E	626 792-9202	13062
Nutraceutical Brews For Lf Inc	2082	F	310 273-8339	1551
Orbits Lightwave Inc	3229	F	626 513-7400	10324
Pak Group LLC	2052	F	626 316-6555	1324
Pasadena Bio Cllbrtive Incbtor	3821	F	626 507-8487	20770
Pasadena Newspapers Inc (PA)	2711	C	626 578-6300	5793
Phoenix Technologies Ltd (HQ)	7372	E	408 570-1000	24295
Primed Productions Inc	2531	F	626 216-5822	4869
Red Gate Software Inc	7372	F	626 993-3949	24350
Replenish Inc	3841	F	626 219-7867	21874
Rockley Photonics Inc (HQ)	3674	D	626 304-9960	18519
Rogerson Kratos	3812	C	626 449-3090	20710
Sabrin Corporation	3444	E	626 792-3813	12364
Shamrock Die Cutting Company	2675	E	323 266-4556	5454
Southland Publishing Inc (PA)	2711	E	626 584-1500	5834
Stir	3699	F	626 657-0918	19415
Stirworks Inc	3199	F	800 657-2427	10253
Surprisesilkcom	2221	F	626 568-9889	2735
Synopsys Inc	7372	D	626 795-9101	24479
Thomas T Bernstein	3451	F	626 351-0570	12655
Turbo Coil Inc	3585	F	626 644-6254	15467
Typecraft Inc	2752	E	626 795-8093	6904
Undercar Express Inc	3711	E	626 683-2787	19509
Urban Outfitters Inc	2335	E	626 449-1818	3258
Vitafoods America LLC	2026	F	800 695-4750	712
Westcoast Companies Inc	2394	F	626 794-9330	3715
Wetzels Pretzels LLC (HQ)	2052	F	626 432-6900	1337
Yes To Inc	2844	E	626 365-1976	8609

PASO ROBLES, CA - San Luis Obispo County

	SIC	EMP	PHONE	ENTRY #
A B G Instruments & Engrg	3544	F	805 238-6262	14006
Acme Vial & Glass Co	3221	E	805 239-2666	10282
Advance Adapters Inc	3714	E	805 238-7000	19566
Advanced Keyboard Tech Inc	3571	F	805 237-2055	14881
Air Dry Co of America LLC	3822	E	805 238-2840	20781
AMC Machining	3449	E	805 238-5452	12584
Applied Technologies Assoc Inc (HQ)	3829	C	805 239-9100	21435
Arbiter Systems Incorporated (PA)	3825	E	805 237-3831	21006
Broken Earth Winery	2084	E	805 239-2562	1607
Calipaso Winery LLC	2084	E	805 226-9296	1617
Casa Grande Woodworks	2431	E	805 226-2040	4016
Cornucopia Tool & Plastics Inc	3089	E	805 238-7660	9728
Cws Beverage	2082	F	805 286-2735	1516
Davis Boats	3732	E	805 227-1170	20320
Diversified Hangar Company	3441	E	805 239-8229	11785
Ennis Inc	2761	C	805 238-1144	7282
Eos Estate Winery	2084	E	805 239-2562	1690
Fetzer Vineyards	2084	F	805 467-0192	1701
Firestone Walker Inc (PA)	2082	C	805 225-5911	1528
Flight Environments Inc	3728	E	805 226-2912	20106
Foley Family Wines Inc (HQ)	2084	D	707 708-7600	1707

(P-0000) Products & Services Section entry number
(PA)=Parent Co (HQ)=Headquarters (DH)=Div Headquarters

Company	SIC	EMP	PHONE	ENTRY #
GP Industries Inc	3949	F	805 227-6565	22812
Halter Winery LLC	2084	E	805 226-9455	1744
Hope Family Wines (PA)	2084	E	805 238-4112	1755
Iqms (HQ)	7372	C	805 227-1122	24047
James Tobin Cellars Inc	2084	E	805 239-2204	1771
Joslyn Sunbank Company LLC	3678	B	805 238-2840	18777
Justin Vineyards & Winery LLC (DH)	2084	E	805 238-6932	1777
Los Angles Tmes Cmmnctions LLC	2711	E	805 238-2720	5709
Lubrizol Advanced Mtls Inc	2899	D	805 239-1550	8991
Minatronic Inc	3679	F	805 239-8864	19020
Nanometer Technologies Inc	3661	F	805 226-7332	17388
Navajo Concrete Inc	3273	F	805 238-0955	10810
News Media Inc	2711	E	805 237-6060	5778
Niner Wine Estates LLC	2084	E	805 239-2233	1843
Opolo Vineyards Inc (PA)	2084	E	805 238-9593	1847
Pacific Metal Finishing Inc	3479	F	805 237-8886	13219
Pear Valley Vineyard Inc	2084	F	805 237-2861	1859
Pic Manufacturing Inc	3555	F	805 238-5451	14338
Powder Coating Usa Inc	3479	F	805 237-8886.	13228
Pro Document Solutions Inc (PA)	2752	D	805 238-6680	6812
Rbz Vineyards LLC	2084	E	805 542-0133	1882
Rogue River Rifleworks Inc	3949	F	805 227-4611	22874
Secondwind Products Inc	2842	F	805 239-2555	8417
Silver Horse Vineyards Inc	2084	F	805 467-9463	1918
Sligh Cabinets Inc	2434	F	805 239-2550	4248
Souriau Usa Inc (DH)	3643	E	805 238-2840	16924
Sport Rock International Inc	3949	F	805 434-5474	22896
Sylvester Winery Inc	2084	E	805 227-4000	1945
Tablas Creek Vineyard LLC	2084	E	805 237-1231	1946
Toomey Racing USA	3751	E	805 239-8870	20430
Treana Winery LLC	2084	E	805 237-2932	1961

PATTERSON, CA - Stanislaus County

Company	SIC	EMP	PHONE	ENTRY #
Bay Area Ems Solutions LLC	3672	F	408 753-3651	17832
Hpl Contract Inc	2521	F	209 892-1717	4802
Patterson Frozen Foods Inc	2037	F	209 892-5060	923
Sport Boat Trailers Inc	3799	F	209 892-5388	20521

PEARBLOSSOM, CA - Los Angeles County

Company	SIC	EMP	PHONE	ENTRY #
Doug Trim Sub Contractor	3479	F	661 944-2884	13165

PEBBLE BEACH, CA - Monterey County

Company	SIC	EMP	PHONE	ENTRY #
Aquest Inc	3432	E	831 622-9296	11656
Techmo Entertainment Inc	7372	F	408 309-3039	24494

PENN VALLEY, CA - Nevada County

Company	SIC	EMP	PHONE	ENTRY #
Firestone Walker LLC	2082	D	805 225-5911	1529
Ijot Development Inc	2531	A	925 258-9909	4861

PENRYN, CA - Placer County

Company	SIC	EMP	PHONE	ENTRY #
K S Telecom Inc	3661	F	916 652-4735	17383

PERRIS, CA - Riverside County

Company	SIC	EMP	PHONE	ENTRY #
AAA Pallet Recycling & Mfg Inc	2448	E	951 681-7748	4344
Accu-Blend Corporation	2911	F	626 334-7744	9036
Alpha Corporation of Tennessee	2821	D	951 657-5161	7540
American Coffee Urn Mfg Co Inc	3444	F	951 943-1495	12105
Aoc LLC	2295	D	951 657-5161	2894
Avalon Shutters Inc	2431	C	909 937-4900	4000
Axxis Corporation	3599	E	951 436-9921	15758
California Composite Cont Corp	2655	E	951 940-9343	5287
California Trusframe LLC	2439	C	951 657-7491	4293
Clayton Homes Inc	2451	C	951 657-1611	4442
Coreslab Structures La Inc	3272	C	951 943-9119	10556
Craftech Metal Forming Inc	3365	E	951 940-6444	11373
Genesis Supreme Rv Inc	3799	E	951 337-0254	20511
Green Products Packaging Corp	2655	F	951 940-9343	5293
Inland Truss Inc (PA)	2439	D	951 300-1758	4308
J & R Concrete Products Inc	3272	E	951 943-5855	10589
J F Christopher Inc	3949	F	951 943-1166	22833
J-M Manufacturing Company Inc	2821	D	951 657-7400	7575
Limos By Tiffany Inc	3713	C	951 657-2680	19541
Navigator Yachts and Pdts Inc	3732	C	951 657-2117	20352
Npg Inc (PA)	2951	D	951 940-0200	9098
Pacific Coachworks Inc	3792	C	951 686-7294	20491
Perris Skyventure	3443	F	951 940-4290	12040
Pw Eagle Inc	3084	B	951 657-7400	9475
R-Cold Inc	3585	D	951 436-5476	15450
Scale Services Inc	3596	F	909 266-0896	15642
Spaulding Equipment Company (PA)	3532	E	951 943-4531	13761
Star Milling Co	2048	C	951 657-3143	1129
Stearns Product Dev Corp (PA)	3569	D	951 657-0379	14862
Stretch Forming Corporation	3444	C	951 443-0911	12392
Timmons Wood Products Inc	2499	E	951 940-4700	4539
Warlock Industries	3711	E	951 657-2680	19511
Western Metal Spinning & Mfg	3469	F	951 657-0711	12892
World Traditions Inc	3269	E	951 990-6346	10496

PESCADERO, CA - San Mateo County

Company	SIC	EMP	PHONE	ENTRY #
Atmos Engineering Inc	3829	F	650 879-1674	21438

PETALUMA, CA - Sonoma County

Company	SIC	EMP	PHONE	ENTRY #
Accountmate Software Corp (PA)	7372	E	707 774-7500	23548
Ace Products Enterprises Inc	3161	E	707 765-1500	10186
American Bottling Company	2086	E	707 766-9750	2025
Amys Kitchen Inc	2038	E	707 568-4500	940
Andalou Naturals	2844	F	415 446-9470	8437
Architectural Plastics Inc	3089	E	707 765-9898	9636
Arcturus Uav Inc	3761	F	707 206-9372	20442
Bausch Health Americas Inc	3826	C	707 793-2600	21178
Bechhold & Son Flasher & Lure	3949	F	530 367-6650	22757
Berkley Integrated Audio Softw	3695	E	707 782-1866	19210
Bibbero Systems Inc (HQ)	2752	E	800 242-2376	6447
Biosearch Technologies Inc (DH)	2836	C	415 883-8400	8284
Camelbak Acquisition Corp	3949	E	707 792-9700	22775
Camelbak Products LLC (HQ)	3949	D	707 792-9700	22776
Caracal Enterprises LLC	3581	E	707 773-3373	15397
Chad Empey	3211	F	707 762-1900	10263
Collidion Inc (PA)	2834	F	707 668-7600	7846
Colvin-Friedman LLC	3089	E	707 769-4488	9714
Curation Foods Inc	2099	F	707 766-7511	2439
Dairymens Feed & Sup Coop Assn	2048	F	707 763-1585	1089
Deweyl Tool Co Inc	3545	E	707 765-5779	14153
Donal Machine Inc	3599	E	707 763-6625	15904
Eclipse Design Inc	3446	E	707 763-3104	12471
Empire Shower Doors Inc	3231	E	707 773-2898	10357
Field To Family Natural Foods	2015	F	707 765-6756	510
Fulton Acres Inc	2396	F	707 762-2280	3787
G M P C LLC	3993	F	707 766-9504	23118
Gefen LLC	3699	E	818 772-9100	19317
Gmpc LLC	3993	F	707 766-7600	23122
Hain Celestial Group Inc	2844	D	707 347-1200	8508
Hydrofarm LLC (PA)	3648	E	707 765-9990	17133
Hydropoint Data Systems Inc	3523	E	707 769-9696	13635
Illinois Tool Works Inc	3589	D	800 762-7600	15523
John N Hansen Co Inc	3944	E	650 652-9833	22688
Katadyn Desalination LLC	3634	E	415 526-2780	16831
Kval Inc	3553	C	707 762-4363	14298
Labcon North America	3089	C	707 766-2100	9873
Lagunitas Brewing Company (DH)	2082	C	707 322-4651	1541
Leslies Organics LLC	2869	F	415 383-9800	8751
Lind Marine Inc (PA)	2048	E	707 762-7251	1108
Marin French Cheese Company	2022	F	707 762-6001	568
McEvoy of Marin LLC	2079	D	707 778-2307	1475
McGunagle William H & Sons Mfg (PA)	2511	F	707 762-7900	4590
Mesa/Boogie Limited (PA)	3651	D	707 765-1805	17259
Miyokos Kitchen	2021	D	415 521-5313	538
Molecular Bioproducts Inc	3826	C	707 763-6884	21267
Morgan Manufacturing Inc	3423	F	707 763-6848	11536
MPS Lansing Inc	2672	E	707 778-1250	5369
Mrs Grossmans Paper Company	2678	D	707 763-1700	5483
Openclovis Solutions Inc	7372	E	707 981-7120	24229
Pangea Silkscreen	2396	F	707 778-0110	3806
Parmatech Corporation	3399	D	707 778-2266	11482
Petalumaidence Opco LLC	2084	C	707 763-4109	1865
Planet One Products Inc (PA)	2541	E	707 794-8000	4932
Pyramids Winery Inc	2084	E	707 765-2768	1874
Qor LLC	2329	F	707 658-2539	3113
Robert W Cameron & Co Inc	2731	E	707 769-1617	6142
Rotork Controls Inc	3625	F	707 769-4880	16749
RS Technical Services Inc (PA)	3826	D	707 778-1974	21282
Security People Inc	3679	E	707 766-6000	19080
Shamrock Materials Inc (PA)	3273	E	707 781-9000	10833
Sistema US Inc (PA)	3089	E	707 773-2200	10057
Small Precision Tools Inc	3299	D	707 765-4545	11021
Smart Caregiver Corporation	3845	E	707 781-7450	22311
Sonoma Cast Stone Corporation	3272	E	877 283-2400	10652
Sonoma Pharmaceuticals Inc	3841	D	707 283-0550	21905
Spectra Watermakers (HQ)	3589	E	415 526-2780	15581
Spectrum Organic Products LLC	2079	D	888 343-6637	1483
St Louis Post-Dispatch LLC	2711	E	707 762-4541	5838
Stonecrop Technologies LLC	3663	E	781 659-0007	17672
Straus Family Creamery Inc	2021	D	707 776-2887	539
Streetwise Reports LLC	2741	E	707 981-8999	6348
TC Steel	7692	E	707 773-2150	24670
Three Twins Organic Inc (PA)	2024	E	707 763-8946	672
Torn Ranch Inc (PA)	2099	D	415 506-3000	2629
Ume Voice Inc	3651	E	707 939-8607	17298
Us1com Inc	2759	F	707 781-2560	7261
Womack International Inc	3569	E	707 763-1800	14873
Xandex Inc	3825	D	707 763-7799	21156

PHILO, CA - Mendocino County

Company	SIC	EMP	PHONE	ENTRY #
Duckhorn Wine Company	2084	F	707 895-3202	1675

Employment Codes: A=Over 500 employees, B=251-500,
C=101-250, D=51-100, E=20-50, F=10-19

2020 California
Manufacturers Register

© Mergent Inc. 1-800-342-5647

1387

Company	SIC	EMP	PHONE	ENTRY #
Handley Cellars Ltd	2084	F	707 895-3876	1745
Husch Vineyards Inc (PA)	2084	E	707 895-3216	1758
I & E Lath Mill Inc	2421	E	707 895-3380	3936
Navarro Winery	2084	D	707 895-3686	1836
TS Logging	2411	E	707 895-3751	3911

PICO RIVERA, CA - Los Angeles County

Company	SIC	EMP	PHONE	ENTRY #
Advanced Laser Dies Inc	3554	F	562 949-0081	14303
Aoclsc Inc	2992	C	813 248-1988	9130
ATI Flat Rlled Pdts Hldngs LLC	3312	F	562 654-3900	11028
Bakemark USA LLC (PA)	2045	B	562 949-1054	1055
Bay Cities Container Corp (PA)	2653	C	562 948-3751	5198
Brk Group LLC	2299	E	562 949-4394	2928
C&O Manufacturing Company Inc	3444	D	562 692-7525	12142
CD Container Inc	2653	D	562 948-1910	5206
Coastal Container Inc	2653	E	562 801-4595	5208
Coastwide Tag & Label Co	2759	E	323 721-1501	7027
Cordovan & Grey Ltd	2325	E	562 699-8300	3002
Dodge - Wasmund Mfg Inc	3089	F	562 692-8104	9762
Endpak Packaging Inc	2674	E	562 801-0281	5439
Feit Electric Company Inc (PA)	3645	C	562 463-2852	16969
Genesis Foods Corporation (DH)	2064	D	323 890-5890	1368
GPde Slva Spces Incrporation	2099	E	562 407-2643	2475
Kater-Crafts Incorporated	2789	E	562 692-0665	7338
Lombard Enterprises Inc	2752	E	562 692-7070	6708
Madrid Inc	2435	F	562 404-9941	4276
Mannings Beef LLC	2011	D	562 908-1089	417
Metal Tite Products (PA)	3442	E	562 695-0645	11970
Mixed Nuts Inc	2068	E	323 587-6887	1434
Noels Lighting Inc	3646	E	562 908-6181	17060
P W Wiring Systems LLC	3678	E	562 463-9055	18784
P-W Western Inc	3443	D	562 463-9055	12035
Pacific Cast Fther Cushion LLC (DH)	2392	C	562 801-9995	3631
Pacific Coast Feather LLC	2392	C	562 222-5560	3632
Palace Textile Inc	3552	D	323 587-7756	14291
Pass & Seymour Inc	3643	A	562 505-4072	16919
Precision Deburring Services	3541	E	562 944-4497	13940
Qve Inc	3491	E	626 961-0114	13319
Reeve Store Equipment Company (PA)	2542	D	562 949-2535	4999
Rouchon Industries Inc	3577	E	310 763-0336	15324
Sari Art & Printing Inc	2752	F	626 305-0888	6854
Sharpdots LLC	3577	F	626 599-9696	15334
Solid State Battery Inc	3692	F	310 753-6769	19182
Spiral Ppr Tube & Core Co Inc	2655	F	562 801-9705	5303
Strategic Prtg Solution Inc	2759	F	562 242-5880	7231
Suez Wts Services Usa Inc	3589	D	562 942-2200	15589
Tube Bending Llc	3498	F	562 692-5829	13489
W P Keith Co Inc	3567	E	562 948-3636	14778
Whittier Fertilizer Company	2873	D	562 699-3461	8809

PIEDMONT, CA - Alameda County

Company	SIC	EMP	PHONE	ENTRY #
Avoy Corp	2752	F	510 295-8055	6424
Reynen Court LLC	7372	F	917 588-0746	24360

PILOT HILL, CA - El Dorado County

Company	SIC	EMP	PHONE	ENTRY #
Ao Sky Corporation	3812	F	415 717-9901	20534

PINEDALE, CA - Fresno County

Company	SIC	EMP	PHONE	ENTRY #
Pacific Door & Cabinet Company	2431	E	559 439-3822	4103

PINOLE, CA - Contra Costa County

Company	SIC	EMP	PHONE	ENTRY #
Cameron International Corp	1389	D	510 928-1480	180

PIONEER, CA - Amador County

Company	SIC	EMP	PHONE	ENTRY #
Pine Grove Group Inc	3699	E	209 295-7733	19378

PISMO BEACH, CA - San Luis Obispo County

Company	SIC	EMP	PHONE	ENTRY #
Entropy Enterprises LLC	3841	F	805 305-1400	21705
Hotlix	2064	F	805 773-1942	1373

PITTSBURG, CA - Contra Costa County

Company	SIC	EMP	PHONE	ENTRY #
All Spec Sheet Metal Inc	3444	F	925 427-4900	12098
Atlas Pallet Corp	2448	F	925 432-6261	4348
Baker Filtration	3589	E	925 252-2400	15490
Bay Area Drilling Inc	1442	F	925 427-7574	330
Biozone Laboratories Inc (DH)	2834	F	925 473-1000	7814
Biozone Laboratories Inc	2834	F	925 431-1010	7815
Bishop-Wisecarver Corporation (PA)	3499	D	925 439-8272	13503
Black Diamond Manufacturing Co	3599	F	925 439-9160	15792
California Expanded Met Pdts	3448	D	925 473-9340	12537
Creative Concepts Holdings LLC (HQ)	2087	F	949 705-6584	2201
Dow Chemical Company	2821	D	925 432-3165	7555
Frase Enterprises	3644	E	510 856-3600	16948
Generon Igs Inc	3569	F	925 431-1030	14821
Granberg Pump and Meter Ltd	3546	F	707 562-2099	14222
Hammond Enterprises Inc	3599	F	925 432-3537	16015
Hasa Inc	2812	F	661 259-5848	7388
Hospital Systems Inc	3845	D	925 427-7800	22261

Company	SIC	EMP	PHONE	ENTRY #
K2 Pure Solutions LP	3589	D	925 203-1196	15532
K2 Pure Solutions Nocal LP	2899	E	647 776-0273	8982
Levmar Inc	3444	F	925 680-8723	12266
LLC Baker Cummins	2844	D	925 732-9338	8535
Marble Shop Inc (PA)	3281	E	925 439-6910	10915
Nustar Logistics LP	1311	F	925 427-6880	59
Petsport Usa Inc	3999	F	925 439-9243	23447
Praxair Inc	2813	D	925 427-1051	7428
Praxair Inc	3548	E	925 427-1950	14251
Ramar International Corp (PA)	2024	E	925 439-9009	664
Ramar International Corp	2011	E	925 432-4267	422
Tulkoff Food Products West Inc	2099	E	925 427-5157	2640
USS-Psco Inds A Cal Jint Ventr (PA)	3312	A	800 877-7672	11079

PIXLEY, CA - Tulare County

Company	SIC	EMP	PHONE	ENTRY #
Cacciatore Fine Wns & Olv Oil (PA)	2084	F	559 757-9463	1614
Correa Pallet Inc (PA)	2448	E	559 757-1790	4358
Gfp Ethanol LLC	2869	E	559 757-3850	8740
J D Heiskell Holdings LLC	2048	D	559 757-3135	1102

PLACENTIA, CA - Orange County

Company	SIC	EMP	PHONE	ENTRY #
Aero Pacific Corporation (PA)	3728	D	714 961-9200	20011
Altinex Inc	3663	F	714 990-0877	17447
Alva Manufacturing Inc	3451	E	714 237-0925	12619
Anderson Bat Company LLC	3949	D	714 524-7500	22747
Arlon Graphics LLC	3081	C	714 985-6300	9392
Arnold Electronics Inc	3672	F	714 646-8343	17824
Atlas Match LLC	3999	D	714 993-3328	23282
Auger Industries Inc	3599	E	714 577-9350	15754
Bentley Prtg & Graphics Inc	2752	F	714 636-1622	6444
Bestest International	3823	F	714 974-8837	20839
Bioseal	3841	E	714 528-4695	21637
Btm-Beartech Manufacturing	3451	F	714 550-1700	12624
Caldigit Inc	3572	E	714 572-6668	15010
Cardinal Health 414 LLC	2834	C	714 572-9900	7830
Cinton	2672	E	714 961-8808	5359
CMi Precision Machining LLC	3599	F	714 528-3000	15849
CMi Precision Machining LLC	3599	F	714 528-3000	15850
Coast Aerospace Mfg Inc	3441	E	714 893-8066	11768
Diversified Mfg Tech Inc	3544	F	714 577-7000	14045
Eisel Enterprises Inc	3272	E	714 993-1706	10566
Excello Circuits Inc	3672	E	714 993-0560	17871
Foremost Precision Pdts Inc	3599	E	714 961-0165	15967
Gerard Roof Products LLC (DH)	3444	E	714 529-0407	12223
Gryphon Mobile Electronics LLC	3663	F	626 810-7770	17529
Hai Advnced Mtl Spcialists Inc	3399	F	714 414-0575	11478
Handy Service Corporation	2822	F	714 632-7832	7630
Hartwell Corporation (DH)	3429	C	714 993-4200	11593
Heritage Carbide Inc	3599	F	714 524-0222	16020
HI Tech Solder	3356	F	714 572-1200	11273
Industrial Metal Finishing	3471	F	714 628-8808	13028
J B Tool Inc	3599	F	714 993-7173	16063
Jbb Inc	3699	F	888 538-9287	19333
Jet Abrasives Inc	3291	E	323 588-1245	10948
Keesee Tank Company	3443	D	714 528-1814	12024
Kipe Molds Inc	3544	F	714 572-9576	14069
L & M Machining Corporation	3678	D	714 414-0923	18778
Label Specialties Inc	2759	F	714 961-8074	7113
Las Colinas	3589	F	714 528-8100	15535
Marie Joann Designs Inc	2399	F	714 996-0550	3849
Microplex Inc	3674	F	714 630-8220	18397
Nalco Wtr Prtrtment Sltons LLC	3589	E	714 792-0708	15547
Nelson Case Corporation	2441	E	714 528-2215	4341
Packers Food Products Inc	2037	E	913 262-6200	922
Paul Dosier Associates Inc	3541	E	714 556-7075	13939
Pittman Products International	3089	F	562 926-6660	9962
Power Pros Racg Exhust Systems	3714	F	714 777-3278	19738
Powertye Manufacturing	3613	F	714 993-7400	16608
Precision Waterjet Inc	3599	E	888 538-9287	16310
Progress Group	3714	F	714 630-9017	19744
Quikturn Prof Scrnprinting Inc	2759	F	800 784-5419	7191
R&Js Business Group Inc	2097	F	714 224-1455	2361
Rotech Engineering Inc	3679	F	714 632-0532	19072
Sapphire Chandelier LLC	3646	F	714 630-3660	17068
Sapphire Manufacturing Inc	3446	E	714 401-3117	12507
Soft Touch Inc	2759	F	714 524-3382	7218
Southern Cal Tchnical Arts Inc	3599	F	714 524-2626	16412
Spacewall Inc	2435	F	714 961-1300	4281
Spyder Manufacturing Inc	3524	F	714 528-8010	13698
Superior Processing	3471	F	714 524-8525	13113
Totally Radical Associates Inc	3544	F	714 630-2740	14115
US Computers Inc	3577	F	714 528-0514	15359
Vanderveer Industrial Plas LLC	3089	E	714 579-7700	10110
Vertex Lcd Inc	3679	E	714 223-7111	19136
West Coast Metal Stamping Inc	3469	E	714 792-0322	12891
Western Mill Fabricators Inc	2599	E	714 993-3667	5089

	SIC	EMP	PHONE	ENTRY #

PLACERVILLE, CA - El Dorado County

	SIC	EMP	PHONE	ENTRY #
Applied Control Electronics	3625	F	530 626-5181	16699
Boeger Winery Inc	2084	E	530 622-8094	1601
Chili Bar LLC	1429	E	530 622-3325	313
Coastal PVA Opco LLC	3571	F	530 406-3303	14897
Dillon Precision Incorporated	3599	E	530 672-6794	15899
El Dorado Gold Panner Inc	2711	F	530 626-5057	5626
El Dorado Truss Coinc	2439	E	530 622-1264	4300
Gist Inc	3965	D	530 644-8000	23002
Lava Springs Inc	2084	E	530 621-0175	1799
Mother Lode Printing & Pubg Co	2711	D	530 344-5030	5764
Norden Millimeter Inc	3663	E	530 642-9123	17605
R-Quest Technologies LLC	3577	F	530 621-9916	15316
Rucker Mill & Cabinet Works	2434	F	530 621-0236	4242
Sierra Foothills Fudge Factory	2064	F	530 644-3492	1402
Vintage Transport Inc	3715	F	530 622-3046	19839

PLAYA DEL REY, CA - Los Angeles County

	SIC	EMP	PHONE	ENTRY #
Chipton-Ross Inc	3721	D	310 414-7800	19887
Keith Nichols	2084	E	310 305-0397	1780
L-Nutra Inc	2834	F	310 245-1724	7985
Mold USA	3544	G	310 823-6653	14080
Sheer Design Inc	2844	D	310 306-2121	8580

PLAYA VISTA, CA - Los Angeles County

	SIC	EMP	PHONE	ENTRY #
1on1 LLC	7372	E	310 448-5376	23534
Belkin Inc	3651	C	800 223-5546	17203
Chownow Inc	7372	D	888 707-2469	23735
Dimensional Plastics Corp	3089	E	305 691-5961	9757
Honest Company Inc (PA)	2341	C	310 917-9199	3442
Microsoft Corporation	7372	D	213 806-7300	24161

PLEASANT GROVE, CA - Sutter County

	SIC	EMP	PHONE	ENTRY #
A Teichert & Son Inc	3273	E	916 991-8170	10680

PLEASANT HILL, CA - Contra Costa County

	SIC	EMP	PHONE	ENTRY #
Castle Hill Holdings Inc	3842	F	925 943-1119	21994
Chemsw Inc	7372	F	707 864-0845	23734
Clark - Pacific Corporation	3272	D	925 746-7176	10553
Color Tone Inc	2752	E	925 680-2695	6496
Mosaic Brands Inc	3999	E	925 322-8700	23415
Nady Systems Inc	3651	E	510 652-2411	17264
Perazza Prints LLC (PA)	2752	F	925 681-2458	6775
Perazza Prints LLC	2752	F	925 567-3395	6776
Phasespace Inc (PA)	3861	F	925 945-6533	22448
Samil Power US Ltd	3674	A	925 930-3924	18526
Storus Corporation (PA)	3429	F	925 322-8700	11633

PLEASANTON, CA - Alameda County

	SIC	EMP	PHONE	ENTRY #
10x Genomics Inc (PA)	3826	C	925 401-7300	21157
Accsys Technology Inc	3699	E	925 462-6949	19247
Accusplit (PA)	3873	E	925 290-1900	22475
American Bottling Company	2086	D	925 251-3001	2037
Archeyy & Friends LLC	2047	E	703 579-7649	1066
Astex Pharmaceuticals Inc (DH)	2834	D	925 560-0100	7773
Avatier Corporation (PA)	7372	E	925 217-5170	23643
Axcelis Technologies Inc	3829	B	510 979-1970	21441
Biomer Technology LLC	2836	F	925 426-0787	8283
Blanco Basura Beverage Inc	2082	C	888 705-7225	1503
Boresha International Inc	2095	E	925 676-1400	2277
Boyd Corporation (DH)	2891	E	209 236-1111	8859
Cadence Design Systems Inc	7372	F	925 895-3202	23711
Carl Ziss X-Ray Microscopy Inc	3844	D	925 701-3600	22210
Cemex Cnstr Mtls PCF LLC	3273	E	925 846-2824	10712
Central Precast Concrete Inc	3272	E	925 417-6854	10548
Cerebrotech Medical Systems (PA)	3841	F	925 399-5392	21661
Cisco Systems Inc	3577	A	925 223-1006	15198
Clorox Company	2842	F	925 368-6000	8377
Compserv Inc	3679	F	415 331-4571	18874
Contra Costa Newspapers Inc	2711	D	925 847-2123	5600
Conxtech Inc (PA)	3441	E	510 264-9111	11774
Cooper Bussmann LLC	3629	F	925 924-8500	16783
Cooper Companies Inc (PA)	3851	C	925 460-3600	22346
Coopervision Inc	3851	D	925 251-6600	22347
Custom Blenders Corporation	2841	F	510 635-4352	8337
Deltatrak (PA)	3829	E	925 249-2250	21460
Desert Sky Machining Inc	3599	E	925 426-0400	15890
Diablo Molding & Trim Company	3442	E	925 417-0663	11947
E2e Mfg LLC	3469	E	925 862-2057	12796
Eclipse Data Technologies Inc	3695	F	925 224-8880	19214
Ellie Mae Inc (HQ)	7372	C	855 224-8572	23854
EMC Corporation	3572	D	925 948-9000	15024
EMC Corporation	3572	D	925 600-6800	15026
Full Spectrum Group LLC (PA)	3826	F	925 485-9000	21232
Gitacloud Inc	7372	E	925 519-5965	23940
Handcraft Tile Inc	3255	F	408 262-1140	10460
Imagex Inc	2752	F	925 474-8100	6630

	SIC	EMP	PHONE	ENTRY #
Inneos LLC	3827	E	925 226-0138	21365
Integenx Inc (HQ)	3826	D	925 701-3400	21247
Interson Corp	3845	E	925 462-4948	22264
Inverse Solutions Inc	3599	E	925 931-9500	16054
It Concepts LLC	3827	F	925 401-0010	21370
Kapsch Trafficcom Usa Inc	3625	F	925 225-1600	16726
Leaf Healthcare Inc	3845	E	925 621-1800	22270
Leo Lam Inc	2752	E	925 484-3690	6698
Lucerne Foods Inc	2099	E	925 951-4724	2534
Matchpoint Solutions (PA)	7372	F	925 829-4455	24129
Metamaterial Tech USA Inc	3827	F	650 993-9223	21382
Micros Systems Inc	7372	E	443 285-8000	24153
Millennium Graphics Inc	2754	E	925 602-0635	6959
Natus Medical Incorporated (PA)	3845	B	925 223-6700	22286
Neotract Inc (DH)	3841	F	925 401-0700	21832
New Source Technology LLC	3845	F	925 462-6888	22287
Oculeve Inc	2834	F	415 745-3784	8049
Oldcastle Infrastructure Inc	3272	E	925 846-8183	10612
Optimum Design Associates Inc (PA)	3679	D	925 401-2004	19041
Oracle America Inc	7372	D	925 694-3314	24243
Oracle Corporation	7372	B	877 767-2253	24260
Oracle Systems Corporation	7372	E	925 694-3000	24275
Pacesetter Inc	3845	F	925 730-4171	22294
Peridot Corporation	3469	D	925 461-8830	12855
Pleasanton Main St Brewry Inc	2082	F	925 462-8218	1558
Pleasanton Ready Mix Concrete	3273	F	925 846-3226	10814
Pleasanton Tool & Mfg Inc	3599	F	925 426-0500	16302
Positronics Incorporated	3549	F	925 931-0211	14277
Printpack Inc	2673	C	925 469-0601	5412
Process Metrix LLC	3829	F	925 460-0385	21521
Purotecs Inc	3559	F	925 215-0380	14522
Rani Jewels Inc	3911	F	408 516-6807	22561
Rapidwerks Incorporated	3089	E	925 417-0124	10009
Real-Time Radiography Inc	3845	F	925 416-1903	22300
RMC Pacific Materials Inc (DH)	3241	C	925 426-8787	10429
RMC Pacific Materials Inc	3273	E	925 846-2824	10819
Roche Molecular Systems Inc (DH)	2834	B	925 730-8000	8113
Roche Pharmaceuticals	2834	A	908 635-5692	8114
Sanarus Medical Incorporated	3841	F	925 460-6080	21887
Sanders Orthodontic Lab Inc	3843	F	925 251-0019	22188
Simpson Manufacturing Co Inc (PA)	3399	C	925 560-9000	11488
Simpson Strong-Tie Company Inc (HQ)	3449	C	925 560-9000	12605
Simpson Strong-Tie Intl Inc (DH)	3449	D	925 560-9000	12607
Software Development Inc	7372	E	925 847-8823	24427
Solta Medical Inc (DH)	3841	F	510 786-6946	21903
Spring Bioscience Corp	2835	A	925 474-8463	8261
Thoratec LLC (HQ)	3845	C	925 847-8600	22320
Titan Photonics Inc	3661	E	510 687-0488	17422
Trireme Medical LLC	3841	D	925 931-1300	21937
Veeva Systems Inc (PA)	7372	C	925 452-6500	24549
Vertiv Corporation	3613	B	925 734-8660	16620
Visioneer Inc (HQ)	3577	E	925 251-6300	15363
Wefea Inc	3695	E	925 218-1839	19243
Zeltiq Aesthetics Inc (DH)	3841	B	925 474-2500	21966
Zoho Corporation (HQ)	7372	F	925 924-9500	24606

PLS VRDS PNSL, CA - Los Angeles County

	SIC	EMP	PHONE	ENTRY #
Converging Systems Inc	3577	F	310 544-2628	15207

PLUMAS LAKE, CA - Yuba County

	SIC	EMP	PHONE	ENTRY #
Packaging Specialists Inc	2448	F	530 742-8441	4386
Placer Waterworks Inc	3441	F	530 742-9675	11864

PLYMOUTH, CA - Amador County

	SIC	EMP	PHONE	ENTRY #
Acm Machining Inc	3599	E	916 804-9489	15683
Domaine De La Terre Rouge	2084	F	209 245-4277	1670
Ren Acquisition Inc	2084	F	209 245-6979	1885
Sierra Sunrise Vineyard Inc	2084	E	209 245-6942	1916
Villa Toscano Winery	2084	E	209 245-3800	1986

POLLOCK PINES, CA - El Dorado County

	SIC	EMP	PHONE	ENTRY #
Dan Arens and Son Inc	2411	F	530 644-6307	3879

POMONA, CA - Los Angeles County

	SIC	EMP	PHONE	ENTRY #
A E T C O Inc	2499	E	909 593-2521	4488
A/C Folding Gates	3446	F	909 629-3026	12441
Able Iron Works	3446	E	909 397-5300	12442
American Rotary Broom Co Inc	3991	E	909 629-9117	23021
Analytical Industries Inc	3823	E	909 392-6900	20834
Anheuser-Busch LLC	2082	C	800 622-2667	1493
Atr Technologies Incorporated	3446	F	909 399-9724	12453
Avery Dennison Corporation	2672	C	626 304-2000	5356
Aw Industries Inc	2511	D	909 629-1500	4551
Baughn Engineering Inc	3825	F	909 392-0933	21011
Bio Cybernetics International	3842	F	909 447-7050	21985
Boom Industrial Inc	3559	D	909 495-3555	14435
Bragel International Inc	2342	E	909 598-8808	3451

Employment Codes: A=Over 500 employees, B=251-500,
C=101-250, D=51-100, E=20-50, F=10-19

2020 California
Manufacturers Register

© Mergent Inc. 1-800-342-5647

1389

GEOGRAPHIC

Company	SIC	EMP	PHONE	ENTRY #
Bright Glow Candle Company Inc (PA)	3999	E	909 469-0119	23288
Ca-WA Corp	3069	E	909 868-0630	9291
Cabinets & Doors Direct Inc	2434	F	909 629-3388	4174
California Acrylic Inds Inc (HQ)	3999	E	909 623-8781	23292
California Plastix Inc	2673	E	909 629-8288	5386
Camlever Inc	3531	F	909 629-9669	13716
Casa Herrera Inc (PA)	3556	C	909 392-3930	14354
Complete Cutng & Wldg Sups Inc (PA)	7692	F	909 868-9292	24626
Consolidated Foundries Inc	3324	E	909 595-2252	11157
Consolidated Laundry LLC	3582	E	323 232-2417	15403
Cooltec Refrigeration Corp	3585	E	909 865-2229	15421
Copp Industrial Mfg Inc	3444	E	909 593-7448	12163
CPS Wood Works Inc	2431	F	909 326-1102	4022
D G U Trading Corporation	3231	E	909 469-1288	10351
Da-Ly Glass Corp	3231	E	323 589-5461	10352
De Larshe Cabinetry LLC	2431	E	909 627-2757	4031
Deers Merchandise Inc	3269	F	909 869-8619	10487
Delphi Control Systems Inc	3823	F	909 593-8099	20855
Desiccare Inc	3295	E	909 444-8272	10970
Diagnostixx California Corp	3841	E	909 482-0840	21684
DOT Blue Safes Corporation	3499	E	909 445-8888	13516
Dow Hydraulic Systems Inc	3594	F	909 596-6602	15628
Ekko Material Hdlg Eqp Mfg Inc	3799	F	909 212-1962	20508
Electrocube Inc (PA)	3679	D	909 595-1821	18900
Epic Printing Ink Corp	2893	F	909 598-6771	8912
Equipment Design & Mfg Inc	3444	D	909 594-2229	12198
Essential Pharmaceutical Corp	2834	E	909 623-4565	7882
Everbrite West LLC	3993	D	909 592-0870	23101
FDS Manufacturing Company (PA)	2679	C	909 591-1733	5507
G Powell Electric	7694	E	909 865-2291	24691
Gemini Aluminum Corporation	3354	E	909 595-7403	11230
General Nucleonics Inc	3829	F	909 593-4985	21479
Gonzalez Feliciano	2431	F	909 236-1372	4051
Gould & Bass Company Inc	3825	E	909 623-6793	21045
Gutierrez Grading	2759	F	909 397-8717	7084
Headwaters Incorporated	3272	F	909 627-9066	10583
Holland & Herring Mfg Inc	3599	E	909 469-4700	16033
Honor Plastics & Molding Inc	3089	E	909 594-7487	9826
Image Distribution Services	2752	E	909 599-7680	6627
In House Custom Decals	2759	F	909 613-1403	7094
Inca Pallets Supply Inc	2448	E	909 622-1414	4374
Industrial Design Products	3537	F	909 468-0693	13876
Inland Envelope Company	2677	D	909 622-2016	5471
J E S Disc Grinding Inc	3599	F	909 596-3823	16065
Jacks Technologies & Inds Inc	3559	F	909 865-2595	14482
Juell Machine Coinc	3599	F	909 594-8164	16096
K-1 Packaging Group	2752	E	626 964-9384	6672
K-Max Health Products Internat	2023	F	909 455-0158	598
Kc Pharmaceuticals Inc (PA)	2834	D	909 598-9499	7977
Kc Pharmaceuticals Inc.	2834	E	909 598-9499	7978
Kelly & Thome	3599	E	909 623-2559	16113
Kensington Protective Products	2394	E	909 469-1240	3689
Kerber Industries Inc	3999	E	909 319-0877	23381
Kittrich Corporation (PA)	2591	C	714 736-1000	5028
L & H Mold & Engineering Inc (PA)	3089	E	909 930-1547	9872
Lightwave Pdl Inc	3645	F	909 548-3677	16977
Lock-Ridge Tool Company Inc	3469	D	909 865-8309	12838
Los Pericos Food Products LLC	2099	F	909 623-5625	2532
Lur Inc	3446	F	909 623-4999	12495
Luxor Industries International	2431	E	909 469-4757	4078
Marge Carson Inc (PA)	2512	E	626 571-1111	4656
Martin Purefoods Corporation	2013	F	909 865-4440	478
McPrint Corp	2752	F	714 632-9966	6720
Med-Pharmex Inc	2834	F	909 593-7875	8004
Mil-Spec Magnetics Inc	3677	E	909 598-8116	18727
Mitchell Processing LLC	3069	E	909 519-5759	9334
Nancys Tortilleria & Mini Mkt	2099	E	909 629-5889	2561
Natural Envrntl Protection Co	2821	E	909 620-8003	7583
Numatech West (kmp) LLC	2653	E	909 706-3627	5248
Pacific Bridge Packaging Inc	3411	F	909 598-1988	11501
Pacific Wtrprfing Rstrtion Inc	2899	E	909 444-3052	9015
Phenix Enterprises Inc (PA)	3713	E	909 469-0411	19551
Pomona Quality Foam LLC	3086	D	909 628-7844	9562
Precision Pwdred Met Parts Inc	3399	E	909 595-5656	11484
Pregis	3086	E	909 469-8100	9563
Premium Pallet Inc	2448	F	909 868-9621	4393
Quality Container Corp	2671	F	909 482-1850	5339
R & S Automation Inc	3442	F	800 962-3111	11976
R & S Mfg Southern Cal Inc	3442	F	909 596-2090	11978
Rbf Group International	2521	F	626 333-5700	4819
Rbm Conveyor Systems Inc.	3556	F	909 620-1333	14395
Rd Metal Polishing Inc	3471	E	909 594-8393	13086
Real Plating Inc	3471	E	909 623-2304	13087
Regal Cultured Marble Inc	3281	E	909 802-2388	10928
Robertsons Ready Mix Ltd	3273	E	909 623-9185	10825

Company	SIC	EMP	PHONE	ENTRY #
ROC-Aire Corp	3599	E	909 784-3385	16367
Ronford Products Inc	3089	E	909 622-7446	10024
Royal Cabinets Inc	2434	A	909 629-8565	4240
Royal Industries Inc	2434	C	909 629-8565	4241
Siena Decor Inc	3952	E	909 895-8585	22945
Silpak Inc (PA)	2821	F	909 625-0056	7611
Sky One Inc	3262	F	909 622-3333	10469
Southern Cal Trck Bdies Sls In	3713	F	909 469-1132	19555
Specialty Car Wash System	3589	F	909 869-6300	15580
Stainless Fixtures Inc	2599	E	909 622-1615	5082
Structural Composites Inds LLC (DH)	3443	E	909 594-7777	12059
Superior Duct Fabrication Inc	3444	C	909 620-8565	12394
T & T Box Company Inc	2657	E	909 465-0848	5316
Technical Anodize	3353	F	909 865-9034	11225
Tesorx Pharma LLC	2834	F	909 595-0500	8157
Trademark Hoist Inc	3536	E	909 455-0801	13852
Travelers Choice Travelware	3161	D	909 529-7688	10213
Traxx Corporation	3999	D	909 623-8032	23510
Tree Island Wire (usa) Inc	3315	B	909 595-6617	11112
Tri-J Metal Heat Treating Co (PA)	3398	F	909 622-9999	11474
United Rotary Brush Corp	3991	E	909 629-9117	23031
Urocare Products Inc	3069	F	909 621-6013	9382
Valley Metal Treating Inc	3398	E	909 623-6316	11476
Valley Tool and Machine Co Inc	3599	F	909 595-2205	16492
Vefo Inc	3086	E	909 598-3856	9576
W R Meadows Inc	3272	E	909 469-2606	10664
Wan LI Industrial Dev Inc	3694	F	909 594-1818	19206
Weiser Iron Inc	3312	E	909 429-4600	11081
Westcoast Brush Mfg Inc	3991	F	909 627-7170	23033
Williams Sign Co	3993	F	909 622-5304	23244
Win-Holt Equipment Corp	3537	F	909 625-2624	13898
World Trend Inc (PA)	3991	F	909 620-9945	23034
Worthington Cylinder Corp	3443	C	909 594-7777	12071
Yawitz Inc	3645	E	909 865-5599	17002
Yf Manufacture Inc	3269	F	626 768-0029	10497
Yoshimasa Display Case Inc	2541	E	213 637-9999	4959

PORT HUENEME, CA - Ventura County

Company	SIC	EMP	PHONE	ENTRY #
Consoldted Precision Pdts Corp	3365	C	805 488-6451	11372
Cpp-Port Hueneme	3369	C	805 488-6451	11412
Dla Document Services	2752	E	805 982-4310	6546
Pac Foundries Inc	3365	C	805 986-1308	11387
Prime Alloy Steel Castings Inc	3369	C	805 488-6451	11421
Raytheon Company	3812	F	805 985-6851	20691
Stellar Biotechnologies Inc	2834	F	805 488-2147	8146
United States Dept of Navy	3728	F	805 989-5402	20264

PORTER RANCH, CA - Los Angeles County

Company	SIC	EMP	PHONE	ENTRY #
Jevin Enterprises Inc	3021	E	818 408-0488	9172

PORTERVILLE, CA - Tulare County

Company	SIC	EMP	PHONE	ENTRY #
Beckman Coulter Inc	3826	C	559 784-0800	21181
Chiapa Welding Inc (PA)	7692	F	559 784-3400	24625
Distributors Processing Inc	2087	F	559 781-0297	2203
Endurequest Corporation	3089	E	559 783-9220	9779
Foster Poultry Farms	2015	B	559 793-5501	516
Greenpower Motor Company Inc	3711	F	604 563-4144	19475
Horizon International Ltd	3589	F	559 781-4640	15520
Hubbell Incorporated	3643	E	559 783-0470	16904
Noticiero Semanal Advertising	2711	D	559 784-5000	5785
Porterville Concrete Pipe Inc	3272	F	559 784-6187	10625
Quikrete Companies Inc.	3272	F	559 781-1949	10634
Tdg Operations LLC	2281	D	559 781-4116	2885
Tri-K Truss Company	2439	F	559 784-8511	4325

PORTOLA, CA - Plumas County

Company	SIC	EMP	PHONE	ENTRY #
Coates Incorporated	3714	F	530 832-1533	19616
Thunder Products Inc	3931	F	480 833-2500	22642
Wirta Logging Inc	2411	E	928 440-3446	3920

PORTOLA VALLEY, CA - San Mateo County

Company	SIC	EMP	PHONE	ENTRY #
Intuit Inc.	7372	C	650 944-2840	24039
Ladera Foods Inc	2043	F	650 823-7186	1028
Thomas Fogarty Winery LLC (PA)	2084	F	650 851-6777	1954
Westech Inv Advisors LLC (PA)	2038	E	650 234-4300	983

POTTER VALLEY, CA - Mendocino County

Company	SIC	EMP	PHONE	ENTRY #
Matthews Skyline Logging Inc	2411	E	707 743-2890	3897

POWAY, CA - San Diego County

Company	SIC	EMP	PHONE	ENTRY #
Advanced Engineering & EDM Inc	3599	F	858 679-6800	15694
Advanced Enginering and EDM Inc	3599	F	858 679-6800	15695
Advanced Machining Tooling Inc	3544	E	858 486-9050	14009
Aldila Inc	3949	C	858 513-1801	22738
Aldila Golf Corp	3949	C	858 513-1801	22739
Aldila Materials Technology (DH)	2895	E	858 513-1801	8940
Alfa Scientific Designs Inc	2835	D	858 513-3888	8203
Alta Solutions Inc	3825	F	858 668-5200	20999

2020 California
Manufacturers Register

(P-0000) Products & Services Section entry number
(PA)=Parent Co (HQ)=Headquarters (DH)=Div Headquarters

Company	SIC	EMP	PHONE	ENTRY #
American Ceramic Technology (PA)	3842	F	619 992-3104	21978
Apricorn	3577	E	858 513-2000	15158
Broadcast Microwave Services (PA)	3663	C	858 391-3050	17474
Brooks Automation Inc	3559	F	858 527-7000	14436
Cohu Inc (PA)	3825	C	858 848-8100	21018
Component Surfaces Inc	3471	F	858 513-3656	12976
Connectpv Inc	3829	F	858 246-6140	21454
Creative Foods LLC	2099	E	858 748-0070	2434
Darmark Corporation	3599	D	858 679-3970	15881
Data Device Corporation	3769	E	858 503-3300	20474
Decision Sciences Med Co LLC	3845	E	858 602-1600	22248
Delta Design Inc (HQ)	3569	E	858 848-8000	14807
Delta Design Littleton Inc (HQ)	3825	F	858 848-8100	21022
Df Grafix Inc	2752	E	858 866-0858	6537
Digital One Printing Inc	2752	F	858 278-2228	6541
Digitalpro Inc	2759	D	858 874-7750	7046
Disguise Inc (HQ)	2389	E	858 391-3600	3552
Eagle Mold Technologies Inc	3089	E	858 530-0888	9768
Economy Printing	2752	E	858 679-8630	6560
Eidon Inc	2834	F	800 700-1169	7876
Electron Imaging Incorporated	3826	F	858 679-1569	21220
EPC Power Corp	3629	E	858 748-5590	16786
Franklins Inds San Diego Inc	3599	E	858 486-9399	15974
Gaines Manufacturing Inc	3444	E	858 486-7100	12218
General Atomic Aeron	3721	F	858 455-4560	19895
General Atomic Aeron (DH)	3721	B	858 312-2810	19901
General Atomic Aeron	3721	F	858 312-2543	19902
Granite Gold Inc	2842	F	858 499-8933	8386
Hanger Prsthetcs & Ortho Inc	3842	F	858 487-4516	22025
Harmonic Design Inc	3621	E	858 391-9085	16652
Hoist Fitness Systems Inc	3949	F	858 578-7676	22822
Honeywell International Inc	3823	A	858 848-3187	20884
Horizon Engineering Inc	3599	F	858 679-0785	16034
Imagine That Unlimited	3993	F	858 566-8868	23131
Integrity Municpl Systems LLC	3589	E	858 486-1620	15527
Jds Technologies	3679	F	858 486-8787	18966
K-Tube Corporation	3317	D	858 513-9229	11129
Kia Incorporated (PA)	3149	E	858 824-2999	10180
L & T Precision Corporation	3444	C	858 513-7874	12263
Liberty Diversified Intl Inc	2653	C	858 391-7302	5244
Martellotto Inc	2084	F	619 567-9244	1812
Mesa Label Express Inc	2759	F	858 668-2820	7141
Micron Machine Company	3599	E	858 486-5900	16199
Mitchell Repair Info Co LLC (HQ)	2741	E	858 391-5000	6283
Mobile Mini Inc	3448	E	858 578-9222	12563
Mytee Products Inc	3589	E	858 679-1191	15545
Network Printing & Copy Center	2752	F	858 695-8221	6745
Niterider Technical Lighting &	3648	E	858 268-9316	17149
Oasis Materials Company LP	3679	E	858 486-8846	19034
Olaes Enterprises Inc	2329	E	858 679-4450	3111
Osram Sylvania Inc	3641	B	858 748-5077	16868
Oussoren Eppel Corporation	3993	F	858 483-6770	23172
Plastifab San Diego	3083	E	858 679-6600	9451
Production Assmbly Systems Inc	3549	E	858 748-6700	14278
Publishers Development Corp	2721	E	858 605-0200	6008
Pure Forge	3714	F	760 201-0951	19746
Quality Steel Fabricators Inc	3449	E	858 748-8400	12602
Quatro Composites LLC	3624	E	712 707-9200	16689
Ramona Research Inc	3663	F	858 679-0717	17639
Revolution Enterprises Inc	3949	F	858 679-5785	22871
Rugged Systems Inc	3571	C	858 391-1006	14970
San Diego Crating & Pkg Inc	2653	F	858 748-0100	5264
Seaspace Corporation	3663	E	858 746-1100	17652
Seirus Innovative ACC Inc	2371	D	858 513-1212	3501
Smoothreads Inc	2396	E	800 536-5959	3815
Somacis Inc	3672	C	858 513-2200	18007
Southern California Carbide	3541	E	858 513-7777	13952
Spooners Woodworks Inc	2541	D	858 679-9086	4941
Streeter Printing	2752	E	858 278-6611	6874
Teck Advanced Materials Inc (DH)	3674	E	858 391-2935	18605
Tek84 Inc	3829	E	858 676-5382	21551
Teledyne Instruments Inc	3812	C	858 842-2600	20730
Teledyne Instruments Inc	3699	E	425 492-7400	19422
Teledyne Instruments Inc	3549	D	619 239-5959	14283
Tern Design Ltd	3823	E	760 754-2400	20947
Thyssenkrupp Bilstein Amer Inc	3714	E	858 386-5900	19783
Toray Membrane Usa Inc	3589	F	714 678-8832	15594
Toray Membrane Usa Inc (DH)	2899	D	858 218-2360	9030
Traffic Control & Safety Corp	3993	F	858 679-7292	23232
Traylor Management Inc (PA)	2741	F	858 486-7700	6362
United Security Products Inc	3699	E	800 227-1592	19428
Valley Metals LLC	3317	E	858 513-1300	11138
Vitrek LLC	3825	F	858 689-2755	21154
Wartsila Dynmc Positioning Inc (DH)	3625	E	858 679-5500	16767
Zmb Industries LLC	3999	F	858 842-1000	23531

PRINCETON, CA - Colusa County

Company	SIC	EMP	PHONE	ENTRY #
AA Production Services Inc	1381	E	530 982-0123	81

QUAIL VALLEY, CA - Riverside County

Company	SIC	EMP	PHONE	ENTRY #
Q I S Inc	3669	F	951 244-0500	17755

QUINCY, CA - Plumas County

Company	SIC	EMP	PHONE	ENTRY #
Feather Publishing Company Inc (PA)	2711	E	530 283-0800	5632

RAMONA, CA - San Diego County

Company	SIC	EMP	PHONE	ENTRY #
Blaha Oldrih	3545	F	760 789-9791	14140
EMD Millipore Corporation	3826	F	760 788-9692	21223
Gerald Gentellalli	3949	F	760 789-2094	22807
Hockin Diversfd Holdings Inc	3564	F	760 787-0510	14662
Millwork Co	2431	F	760 788-1533	4087
Ramona Home Journal	2711	F	760 788-8148	5807
Ramona Mining & Manufacturing	3915	F	760 789-1620	22599
S D Drilling	1389	F	760 789-5658	257
Source Superfoods LLC	2023	F	760 884-6575	621

RANCHO CORDOVA, CA - Sacramento County

Company	SIC	EMP	PHONE	ENTRY #
A Teichert & Son Inc	1442	F	916 351-0123	327
Acm Machining Inc (PA)	3599	E	916 852-8600	15684
Aerojet Rocketdyne Inc (HQ)	3728	A	916 355-4000	20016
Ampac Fine Chemicals LLC (HQ)	2834	B	916 357-6880	7752
Arteez	2759	F	916 631-0473	6992
Atlas Granite & Stone	2541	F	916 638-7100	4883
Aztec Machine Co Inc	3599	F	916 638-4894	15759
Bmb Metal Products Corporation	3444	E	916 631-9120	12132
Chemical Technologies Intl Inc	3589	E	916 638-1315	15496
Custom Furniture Design Inc	2434	E	916 631-6300	4184
D3 Led LLC (PA)	3993	F	916 669-7408	23086
E D M Sacramento Inc	3599	E	916 851-9285	15917
Elmco & Assoc (PA)	3088	F	916 383-0110	9584
Energy Operations Management	1311	E	916 859-4700	50
Fencer Enterprises LLC	3315	E	916 635-1700	11093
Folsom Ready Mix Inc (PA)	3272	E	916 851-8300	10576
Foremost Interiors Inc	3281	E	916 635-1423	10906
Form & Fusion Mfg Inc	3469	E	916 638-8576	12804
Form & Fusion Mfg Inc (PA)	3469	E	916 638-8576	12805
Group Manufacturing Services	3444	E	916 858-3270	12228
Guided Wave Inc	3827	E	916 638-4944	21357
Hadco Products Inc	2591	F	916 966-2409	5022
Infor (us) Inc	7372	C	916 921-0883	24013
Infor Public Sector Inc (DH)	7372	C	916 921-0883	24014
Intercontinental N Mas	3999	E	916 631-1674	23364
J & C Custom Cabinets Inc	2521	E	916 638-3400	4805
JL Haley Enterprises Inc	3599	C	916 631-6375	16085
Kargo Master Inc	3444	E	916 638-8703	12260
Lakeview Innovations Inc	2389	F	212 502-6702	3563
Metals USA Building Pdts LP	3355	E	916 635-2245	11265
Military Aircraft Parts	3599	E	916 635-8010	16204
Motivational Systems Inc	3993	E	916 635-0234	23164
Nca Laboratories Inc	3651	F	916 852-7029	17265
Nidec Motor Corporation	3534	B	916 463-9200	13806
Nightingale Vantagemed Corp (HQ)	7372	D	916 638-4744	24208
Pabco Building Products LLC (HQ)	3275	F	510 792-1577	10883
Pacful Inc (PA)	2752	D	916 233-1488	6763
Penfield Products Inc	3444	E	916 635-0231	12331
Perfect Image Printing Inc	2752	F	916 631-8350	6777
Plexus Optix Inc	3229	E	800 852-7600	10327
Precision Flight Controls	3699	F	916 414-1310	19381
Renaissance Food Group LLC (HQ)	2099	E	916 638-8825	2598
Residential Ctrl Systems Inc	3822	E	916 635-6784	20807
Resq Manufacturing	3999	E	916 638-6786	23461
River City Print and Mail Inc	2752	F	916 638-8400	6845
Rubicon Express (PA)	3559	E	916 858-8575	14531
Scribner Engineering Inc	3089	E	916 638-1515	10050
Scribner Plastics	3089	F	916 638-1515	10051
Specialty Products Design Inc	3714	F	916 635-8108	19772
Stewart Tool Company	3545	D	916 635-8321	14200
Stroppini Enterprises	3537	F	916 635-8181	13893
Sunrise Mfg Inc (PA)	2679	E	916 635-6262	5532
Taylor Communications Inc	2761	F	916 368-1200	7292
Taylor Wings Inc	3444	E	916 851-9464	12401
Teledyne Defense Elec LLC	3679	C	916 638-3344	19107
Teledyne Wireless LLC	3679	C	916 638-3344	19114
Thermogenesis Holdings Inc (PA)	3821	D	916 858-5100	20776
Vander-Bend Manufacturing Inc	3599	C	916 631-6375	16494
Volcano Corporation	3845	B	916 281-2932	22330
Volcano Corporation	3845	B	916 638-8008	22332
Vsp Labs Inc (PA)	3827	E	866 569-8800	21418
Ztech	3585	F	916 635-6784	15476

RANCHO CUCAMONGA, CA - San Bernardino County

Company	SIC	EMP	PHONE	ENTRY #
Advanced Chemical Tech Inc	2819	E	800 527-9607	7466
Advantage Adhesives Inc	2891	E	909 204-4990	8853

	SIC	EMP	PHONE	ENTRY #
Air Liquid Healthcare	2813	E	909 899-4633	7393
Airgas Usa LLC	2813	F	909 899-4670	7411
Akaranta Inc	2834	F	909 989-9800	7734
All Star Precision	3599	E	909 944-8373	15719
American Furniture Aliance Inc	2519	F	323 804-5242	4761
American HX Auto Trade Inc	3711	D	909 484-1010	19453
Amphastar Pharmaceuticals Inc (PA)	2834	C	909 980-9484	7754
Aqua Measure Instrument Co	3829	F	909 941-7776	21436
Aquamar Inc	2091	C	909 481-4700	2236
AR Square	3161	F	909 985-5995	10189
Arga Controls Inc	3823	F	626 799-3314	20836
Avery Dennison Corporation	2672	C	909 987-4631	5352
B & G Electronic Assembly Inc	3679	F	909 608-2077	18827
Bellasposa Wedding Center	2335	F	909 758-0176	3220
Bernell Hydraulics Inc (PA)	3594	E	909 899-1751	15626
Butler Home Products LLC	3991	F	909 476-3884	23023
California Box II	2653	E	909 944-9202	5204
Califrnia Nwspapers Ltd Partnr	2711	B	909 987-6397	5580
Cargill Meat Solutions Corp	2011	E	909 476-3120	399
Carpenter Technology Corp	3312	E	909 476-4000	11035
Charlies Beer Company USA LLC	2082	F	909 980-0436	1511
Chick Publications Inc	2731	F	909 987-0771	6087
Ciuti International Inc	2079	F	909 484-1414	1470
Cold Jet LLC	3559	F	513 831-3211	14441
Comfort-Pedic Mattress USA	2515	F	909 810-2600	4715
Continental Graphics Corp	2752	E	909 758-9800	6509
Criticalpoint Capital LLC	2822	D	909 987-9533	7628
Cypress Magnetics Inc	3677	F	909 987-3570	18711
Davidson Optronics Inc	3829	E	626 962-5181	21458
Dicarlo Concrete Inc	3652	F	909 261-4294	17314
Digital Check Technologies Inc	3577	E	909 204-4638	15215
Diverse Optics Inc	3089	E	909 593-9330	9760
Doubleco Incorporated	3452	D	909 481-0799	12675
Dow Chemical Co Foundation	2821	E	909 476-4127	7554
Ds Cypress Magnetics Inc	3678	F	909 987-3570	18765
Eagle Labs LLC	3851	D	909 481-0011	22350
Eddie Motorsports	3429	E	909 581-7398	11588
Electro Switch Corp	3613	C	909 581-0855	16597
Electro Switch Corp	3679	E	909 581-0855	18897
EMD Specialty Materials LLC	3672	F	909 987-9533	17869
ES Kluft & Company Inc (PA)	2515	C	909 373-4211	4719
Everidge Inc	3585	E	909 605-6419	15432
Executive Safe and SEC Corp	3499	E	909 947-7020	13522
Faust Printing Inc	2752	F	909 980-1577	6569
Firth Rixson Inc	3462	E	909 483-2200	12708
Fluorescent Supply Co Inc	3646	E	909 948-8878	17036
Formosa Meat Company Inc	2013	E	909 987-0470	456
Fresh Peaches Incorporated (PA)	2253	E	909 980-0172	2787
Frito-Lay North America Inc	2096	B	909 941-6214	2323
Frozen Bean Inc	2087	E	855 837-6936	2212
Future Molds Inc	3544	F	909 989-7398	14055
Gasket Specialties Inc	3053	F	909 987-4724	9233
Gcn Supply LLC	3448	E	909 643-4603	12547
Global Aerostructures	3728	E	909 987-4888	20117
GME Mfg Inc	3728	F	909 989-4478	20118
Golden Island Jerky Co Inc (DH)	2013	E	844 362-3222	460
Golden Island Jerky Co Inc	2013	F	844 362-3222	461
Golden Vantage LLC	2499	F	626 255-3362	4506
Good-West Rubber Corp (PA)	3069	D	909 987-1774	9312
Goodwest Rubber Linings Inc	3069	E	888 499-0085	9313
Graham Packaging Co Europe LLC	3085	C	909 989-5367	9486
Graham Packaging Company LP	3089	E	909 484-2900	9813
Gruma Corporation	2096	C	909 980-3566	2334
Gw Partners International	3229	F	909 989-1010	10308
Hartwell Corporation	3469	D	909 987-4616	12812
Heritage Bag Company	2673	F	909 899-5554	5400
Highball Signal Inc	3669	F	909 341-5367	17733
Hillo America Inc	3651	F	626 570-0899	17242
Hillshire Brands Company	2013	B	909 481-0760	464
Hotech Corporation	3674	E	909 987-8828	18273
Ifco Systems Us LLC	2448	E	909 484-4332	4373
Inland Tek Inc	7372	F	909 900-8457	24021
Intermetro Industries Corp	3496	E	909 987-4731	13418
Intra Aerospace LLC	3566	E	909 476-0343	14742
J T Walker Industries Inc	3442	F	909 481-1909	11959
JCPM Inc	3599	F	909 484-9040	16078
Jet Cutting Solutions Inc	2452	F	909 948-2424	4463
Jixing (usa) Inc	3494	F	626 261-9539	13358
Jsj Inc Corrugated	2653	F	909 987-4746	5241
Kindred Litho Incorporated	2752	F	909 944-4015	6676
Kitchen Post Inc	2434	F	909 468-6768	4217
Klatch Coffee Inc (PA)	2095	E	909 981-4031	2304
Lanic Engineering Inc (PA)	3728	E	877 763-0411	20154
Lee Augustyn Inc	2752	F	909 483-0688	6694
Lee Maxton Inc	2752	F	909 483-0688	6695
Mape Engineering Inc	3724	F	626 338-7964	19971
Marino Enterprises Inc	3728	E	909 476-0343	20165
Master Builders LLC	2899	E	909 987-1758	8994
Matheson Tri-Gas Inc	2813	E	909 758-5464	7418
Mercury United Electronics Inc	3679	E	909 466-0427	19012
Metal Coaters California Inc	3479	D	909 987-4681	13207
Milcomm Inc	3728	F	626 523-8305	20179
Milky Mama LLC	2051	F	877 886-4559	1242
Mindrum Precision Inc	3824	F	909 989-1728	20973
Mizkan Americas Inc	2099	E	909 484-8743	2554
Modular Office Solutions Inc	2522	D	909 476-4200	4845
Molex LLC	3678	E	909 803-1362	18780
Nci Group Inc	3448	D	909 987-4681	12566
New World Medical Incorporated	3841	D	909 466-4304	21837
New York Toy Exchange Inc	3944	F	626 327-4547	22699
Newtex Industries Inc	3999	D	323 277-0900	23426
Norm Tessier Cabinets Inc	2434	F	909 987-8955	4228
Ohadi Management Corporation	3841	F	909 625-2000	21847
Omega Plastics Corp	2673	C	909 987-8716	5408
Pac-Rancho Inc (DH)	3324	C	909 987-4721	11165
Pacer Technology	2891	D	909 987-0550	8884
Pacific Plastic Technology Inc	3083	E	909 987-4200	9445
Pacific Pprbd Converting LLC (PA)	2679	C	909 476-6466	5518
Pamco Machine Works Inc	3599	E	909 941-7260	16277
Panolam Industries Intl Inc	2493	E	909 581-1970	4485
Paradigm Packaging East LLC	3089	C	909 985-2750	9952
Paramount Machine Co Inc	3599	E	909 484-3600	16283
Paramunt Plstic Fbricators Inc	3089	F	909 987-4757	9954
Perimeter Solutions LP	2819	E	909 983-0772	7516
Pitbull Gym Incorporated	3089	F	909 980-7960	9961
Plaxicon Holding Corporation	3085	C	909 944-6868	9491
Pneudraulics Inc	3812	B	909 980-5366	20674
Polyone Corporation	2821	E	909 987-0253	7597
Precision Aerospace Corp	3728	D	909 945-9604	20204
Pres-Tek Plastics Inc (PA)	3089	F	909 360-1600	9992
Prestige Mold Incorporated	3544	E	909 980-6600	14096
Prime Converting Corporation	2679	E	909 476-9500	5523
Proulx Manufacturing Inc	3089	E	909 980-0662	10000
Puricle Inc	2842	E	909 466-7125	8410
Pyramid Mold & Tool	3544	E	909 476-2555	14100
Qst Ingredients and Packg Inc	2099	F	909 989-4343	2593
Quality Aerostructures Company	3724	F	909 987-4888	19976
R H Pattern	3543	F	909 484-9141	14003
Rafco-Brickform LLC (PA)	3545	D	909 484-3399	14190
Rancho Cucamonga Maverick	2711	F	909 466-6445	5808
Rancho Technology Inc	3577	F	909 987-3966	15317
Raytheon Company	3812	D	909 483-4040	20697
Reyes Coca-Cola Bottling LLC	2086	C	909 980-3121	2146
Ritemp Refrigeration Inc	3632	F	909 941-0444	16823
Russell-Stanley	3089	D	909 980-7114	10035
Safran Cabin Inc	3728	C	909 652-9700	20216
Satori Seal Corporation	3069	E	909 987-8234	9369
Schellinger Spring Inc	3493	F	909 373-0799	13342
Searing Industries Inc	3312	E	909 948-3030	11068
Siemens Rail Automation Corp	3669	C	909 532-5405	17761
Signworld America Inc (PA)	3993	F	844 900-7446	23209
Smith International Inc	1389	C	909 906-7900	264
Socco Plastic Coating Company	3479	E	909 987-4753	13248
South Bay International Inc	2515	E	909 718-5000	4744
Spectrasensors Inc	3826	E	909 980-4238	21292
Steelscape Inc	3479	F	909 987-4711	13254
Superior Tank Co Inc (PA)	3443	E	909 912-0580	12061
T & R Lumber Company (PA)	2449	D	909 899-2383	4429
T E B Inc	3599	F	909 941-8100	16438
Tamco (DH)	3312	D	909 899-0660	11077
Thermostatic Industries Inc	3292	E	323 277-0900	10964
Toner2print Inc	3577	F	909 972-9656	15350
Tree Island Wire (usa) Inc	3315	D	800 255-6974	11113
TSE Worldwide Press Inc	2741	E	909 989-8282	6363
Usl Parallel Products Cal	2869	E	909 980-1200	8779
Vacmet Inc	3479	E	909 948-9344	13264
Vanguard Tool & Mfg Co Inc	3469	F	909 980-9392	12887
Walco Inc	3559	F	909 483-3333	14554
Waters Edge Wineries Inc	2084	F	909 468-9463	1993
Wessex Industries Inc	3498	F	562 944-5760	13492
Western Metal Dctg Co Coil Div	2752	F	909 987-2506	6933
Western Wire Works Inc	3496	F	909 483-1186	13445
Woodland Products Co Inc	2541	F	909 622-3456	4957
Zodiac Aerospace	3721	F	909 652-9700	19939

RANCHO DOMINGUEZ, CA - Los Angeles County

	SIC	EMP	PHONE	ENTRY #
Adf Incorporated	3446	E	310 669-9700	12447
Aerol Co Inc (PA)	3365	E	310 762-2660	11363
Bi Nutraceuticals Inc (HQ)	2087	E	310 669-2100	2193
Buff and Shine Mfg Inc	3291	E	310 886-5111	10941
Carol Anderson Inc (PA)	2335	E	310 638-3333	3221

2020 California
Manufacturers Register

(P-0000) Products & Services Section entry number
(PA)=Parent Co (HQ)=Headquarters (DH)=Div Headquarters

Company	SIC	EMP	PHONE	ENTRY #
Ceratizit Los Angeles LLC	3541	D	310 464-8050	13905
Dresser-Rand Company	3563	E	310 223-0600	14628
Enlink Geoenergy Services Inc	3585	E	424 242-1200	15429
Fairway Import-Export Inc	3949	E	310 637-6162	22799
Giovanni Cosmetics Inc	2844	D	310 952-9960	8498
Grand General Accessories LLC	3612	E	310 631-2589	16553
KT Engineering Corporation	3599	F	310 537-3818	16128
Laclede Inc	3843	E	310 605-4280	22169
Mars Food Us LLC (HQ)	2099	B	310 933-0670	2542
Masco Corporation	3432	D	313 274-7400	11672
Optodyne Incorporation	3663	E	310 635-7481	17611
Parker-Hannifin Corporation	3677	C	310 608-5600	18729
Protective Industries Inc	3089	D	310 537-2300	9999
S L Fusco Inc (PA)	3541	E	310 868-1010	13947
Santa Monica Seafood Company (PA)	2091	D	310 886-7900	2251
Shercon Inc	3069	D	800 228-3218	9372
Simple Container Solutions Inc	2631	E	310 638-0900	5173
Southwestern Industries Inc (PA)	3541	D	310 608-4422	13953
Standard Wire & Cable Co (PA)	3357	D	310 609-1811	11320
Starled Inc	3679	F	310 603-0403	19092
Tda Magnetics LLC	3499	F	424 213-1585	13551
Team Manufacturing Inc	3469	E	310 639-0251	12880
United Bakery Equipment Co Inc (PA)	3565	D	310 635-8121	14732
Visionaire Lighting LLC	3646	A	310 512-6480	17083
Western Sheld Acquisitions LLC	2754	E	310 527-6212	6966

RANCHO MIRAGE, CA - Riverside County

Company	SIC	EMP	PHONE	ENTRY #
Fujisawa Bristol Corporation	2833	D	760 324-1488	7661
Kathy Ireland Worldwide	2331	F	310 557-2700	3171
Natures Baby Products Inc	2844	F	818 521-5054	8545
Tfx International	2834	F	760 836-3232	8160
Toro Company	3523	D	760 321-8396	13677

RANCHO PALOS VERDES, CA - Los Angeles County

Company	SIC	EMP	PHONE	ENTRY #
Powerstorm Holdings Inc	3691	F	424 327-2991	19171
Scott Craft Co	3599	F	323 560-3949	16390
Summit International Packg Inc	2671	D	626 333-3333	5342
Western Summit Mfg Corp	3081	D	626 333-3333	9426

RANCHO SANTA FE, CA - San Diego County

Company	SIC	EMP	PHONE	ENTRY #
Black Silver Enterprises Inc (PA)	2339	F	858 623-9220	3297
Wep Transport Holdings LLC	1382	F	858 756-1010	146
Western Energy Production LLC	1382	F	858 756-1010	147

RANCHO SANTA MARGARI, CA - Orange County

Company	SIC	EMP	PHONE	ENTRY #
Allstar Microelectronics Inc	3572	F	949 546-0888	15002
Foundation 9 Entertainment Inc (PA)	7372	C	949 698-1500	23916
Jacksam Corporation	3565	E	800 605-3580	14712
Lubrizol Corporation	2899	F	949 212-1863	8993

RAYMOND, CA - Madera County

Company	SIC	EMP	PHONE	ENTRY #
Cold Spring Granite Company	3281	E	559 689-3257	10898

RCHO STA MARG, CA - Orange County

Company	SIC	EMP	PHONE	ENTRY #
Amest Corporation	3674	F	949 766-9692	18094
Applied Manufacturing LLC	3841	A	949 713-8000	21603
Applied Medical Corporation (PA)	3841	C	949 713-8000	21604
Applied Medical Resources Corp (HQ)	3841	B	949 713-8000	21605
Ats Tool Inc	3544	E	949 888-1744	14018
Ats Workholding Inc	3545	D	800 321-1833	14135
Car Sound Exhaust System Inc	3714	D	949 858-5900	19607
Car Sound Exhaust System Inc	3714	D	949 858-5900	19609
Car Sound Exhaust System Inc	3714	D	949 858-5900	19610
Chapmn-Wlters Introcoastal Corp	3949	E	949 448-9940	22781
Control Components Inc (DH)	3491	B	949 858-1877	13300
Desco Manufacturing Company (PA)	3599	F	949 858-7400	15889
Eastman Kodak Company	3861	D	949 306-9034	22418
Ep Holdings Inc	3572	E	949 713-4600	15027
Extreme Precision LLC	3599	F	949 459-1062	15946
Form Grind Corporation	3599	E	949 858-7000	15968
Fortron/Source Corporation (PA)	3612	E	949 766-9240	16551
Glas Werk Inc	3229	F	949 766-1296	10307
Grandis Metals Intl Corp	3356	F	949 459-2621	11272
Impact LLC	3679	E	714 546-6000	18944
Inform Decisions	7372	F	949 709-5838	24015
Light Composite Corporation	3429	D	949 858-8820	11605
Mc Products Inc	2899	F	949 888-7100	8996
Multicoat Products Inc	2851	F	949 888-7100	8660
Palomar Products Inc	3669	D	949 858-8836	17752
Phyto Tech Corp	2834	F	949 635-1990	8076
Point Conception Inc	2339	F	949 589-6890	3390
Q-Mark Manufacturing Inc	3823	F	949 457-1913	20923
R C Products Corp	3429	D	949 858-8820	11621
Racepak LLC	3714	E	949 709-5555	19752
Racepak LLC	3711	E	888 429-4709	19495
Renaissnce Frnch Dors Sash Inc (PA)	2431	C	714 578-0090	4115
RPM Products Inc (PA)	3053	E	949 888-8543	9252

Company	SIC	EMP	PHONE	ENTRY #
South Coast Stairs Inc	2431	E	949 858-1685	4128
Swiss-Micron Inc	3451	D	949 589-0430	12652

RED BLUFF, CA - Tehama County

Company	SIC	EMP	PHONE	ENTRY #
Amundson Tom Tmber Flling Cntr	2411	F	530 529-0504	3871
Electro Star Indus Coating Inc	3479	F	530 527-5400	13172
Foothill Ready Mix Inc	3273	E	530 527-2565	10759
John Wheeler Logging Inc	2411	C	530 527-2993	3891
Lassen Forest Products Inc	2439	E	530 527-7677	4313
Medianews Group Inc	2711	E	530 527-2151	5748
Sierra Pacific Industries	2421	B	530 527-9620	3960
Tetrad Services Inc	3599	F	530 527-5889	16454
Walker Lithograph	2752	F	530 527-2142	6925

REDDING, CA - Shasta County

Company	SIC	EMP	PHONE	ENTRY #
A&M Timber Inc	2411	F	530 515-1740	3869
AB Medical Technologies Inc	3841	F	530 605-2522	21569
Absolute Machine	3599	E	530 242-6840	15673
Best Value Textbooks LLC	2731	E	530 222-5980	6076
Bundy and Sons Inc	2411	E	530 246-3868	3876
Cameron International Corp	3533	D	530 242-6965	13770
Captive-Aire Systems Inc	3444	C	530 351-7150	12151
Cdg Technology LLC	3624	F	530 243-4451	16684
Contech Engnered Solutions LLC	3443	F	530 243-1207	12012
Cook Concrete Products Inc	3272	F	530 243-2562	10555
Cummins Pacific LLC	3519	F	530 244-6898	13586
Dataray Incorporated	3826	F	530 472-1717	21215
David Beard	2434	E	530 244-1248	4187
Donn & Doff Inc (PA)	3842	F	530 241-4040	21999
Ferrosaur Inc	3441	F	530 246-7843	11793
Fife Metal Fabricating Inc	3441	E	530 243-4696	11794
Franklin Logging Inc	2411	E	530 549-4924	3883
Gerlinger Fndry Mch Works Inc (PA)	3441	D	530 243-1053	11803
Great Northern Wheels Deals	2711	E	530 533-2134	5649
Heritage Woodworking Co Inc	2434	E	530 243-7215	4204
Innespace Productions	3732	E	530 241-2800	20339
J F Shea Co Inc	3273	E	530 246-2200	10774
Jar Ventures Inc	3993	E	530 224-9655	23139
John Fitzpatrick & Sons	2086	F	530 241-3216	2082
Kings Way Sales and Mktg LLC	3569	F	530 722-0272	14833
Lehigh Southwest Cement Co	3273	C	530 275-1581	10793
Mc Clellan Bottling Group	2086	F	530 241-2600	2091
McHale Sign Company Inc	3993	F	530 223-2030	23156
Metals Direct Inc	3444	E	530 605-1931	12298
Miniature Precision Inc	3599	F	530 244-4131	16212
Mobile Designs Inc	3354	E	530 244-1050	11240
Morts Custom Sheetmetal	3444	E	530 241-7013	12311
Norcal Respiratory Inc	3845	E	530 246-1200	22290
North Valley Candle Molds	3999	E	530 247-0447	23429
Redding Metal Crafters Inc	3444	E	530 222-4400	12353
Redding Printing Co Inc (PA)	2752	E	530 243-0525	6840
Reyes Coca-Cola Bottling LLC	2086	E	530 241-4315	2148
Rounds Logging Company	2411	E	530 247-0517	3903
Seco Manufacturing Company Inc	3829	C	530 225-8155	21533
Sell Lumber Corporation	2421	E	530 241-2085	3948
Sierra Pacific Industries	2421	F	530 226-5181	3950
Snl Group Inc	3531	F	530 222-5048	13749
Sof-Tek Integrators Inc	3825	F	530 242-0527	21122
Southern Alum Finshg Co Inc	3355	D	530 244-7518	11268
Spectrum Prosthetics/Orthotics	3842	F	530 243-4500	22089
Swa Mountain Gate	1442	F	530 221-3406	363
Technisoil Global Inc	2879	F	530 605-4881	8841
Universal Precast Concrete Inc	3272	F	530 243-6477	10661
Vss Emultech Inc (HQ)	2951	F	530 243-0111	9107
Warner Enterprises Inc	2411	E	530 241-4000	3914
William R Schmitt	2411	E	530 243-3069	3919
Wit Group	2086	E	530 243-4447	2184
Wonder Metals Corporation	3442	F	530 241-3251	11989
Yates Gear Inc	3199	D	530 222-4606	10258

REDLANDS, CA - San Bernardino County

Company	SIC	EMP	PHONE	ENTRY #
American Custom Coach Inc	3713	F	909 796-4747	19516
California Prtg Solutions Inc	2759	E	909 307-2032	7014
Califrnia Nwspapers Ltd Partnr	2711	E	909 793-3221	5581
Caseworx Inc	2521	E	909 799-8550	4789
Cemex USA Inc	3273	C	909 798-1144	10742
Clorox Products Mfg Co	2842	D	909 307-2756	8380
Coast To Coast Mfg LLC	3089	F	909 798-5024	9712
Continental Datalabel Inc	2679	F	909 307-3600	5502
Daryls Pet Shop	3999	F	909 793-1788	23311
Duden Enterprises Inc	2395	F	909 795-0160	3738
Engineered Pnt Applications LLC	2851	F	626 737-7400	8644
Express Container Inc	2653	E	909 798-5024	5220
Fast Access Inc	3272	F	909 748-1245	10571
Garner Holt Productions Inc	3571	E	909 799-3030	14911
Loran Inc	3612	E	405 340-0660	16560

Employment Codes: A=Over 500 employees, B=251-500,
C=101-250, D=51-100, E=20-50, F=10-19

2020 California
Manufacturers Register

© Mergent Inc. 1-800-342-5647

1393

GEOGRAPHIC

	SIC	EMP	PHONE	ENTRY #
Plastics Plus Technology Inc	3089	E	909 747-0555	9974
Precision Hermetic Tech Inc	3679	D	909 381-6011	19052
Reader Magazine	2721	F	909 335-8100	6014
Redlands CCI Inc	3751	E	909 307-6500	20423
Rettig Machine Inc	7692	E	909 793-7811	24661
Sensit Inc	3822	F	909 793-5816	20809
Teledyne Technologies Inc	3691	D	909 793-3131	19174
Venturedyne Ltd	3564	D	909 793-2788	14687

REDONDO BEACH, CA - Los Angeles County

	SIC	EMP	PHONE	ENTRY #
Advanced Arm Dynamics (PA)	3842	E	310 372-3050	21971
Alcast Mfg Inc	3364	E	310 542-3581	11351
B Dazzle Inc	3944	F	310 374-3000	22660
Calpak Usa Inc	3672	E	310 937-7335	17841
Funktion Technologies Inc	3823	E	310 937-7335	20875
H3 High Security Solutions LLC	3482	E	310 373-2319	13270
Jariet Technologies Inc	3812	E	310 698-1001	20592
Mass Group	2752	E	310 214-2000	6717
Northrop Grumman Corporation	3812	E	310 812-4321	20649
Northrop Grumman Systems Corp	3663	C	310 812-5149	17606
Northrop Grumman Systems Corp	3812	B	310 812-4321	20665
Northrop Grumman Systems Corp	3721	E	310 812-1089	19921
Northrop Grumman Systems Corp	3721	E	310 812-4321	19922
Quantimetrix Corporation	2835	D	310 536-0006	8250
Raffaello Research Labs	2834	F	310 618-8754	8096
Sunset Islandwear	2261	F	310 372-7960	2839
Thorock Metals Inc	3341	E	310 537-1597	11210
Vertical Collective LLC	2321	F	310 567-6200	2998
Westend Software Inc (PA)	7372	F	310 370-0367	24578
Woodruff Corporation	3599	E	310 378-1611	16534

REDWOOD CITY, CA - San Mateo County

	SIC	EMP	PHONE	ENTRY #
AB Sciex LLC (HQ)	3826	D	877 740-2129	21158
Acelrx Pharmaceuticals Inc	2834	D	650 216-3500	7718
Actiance Inc	3446	E	650 631-6300	12446
Advanced Circuits Inc	3672	D	415 602-6834	17808
Agiloft Inc	7372	E	650 587-8615	23581
Ai Industries LLC (PA)	3471	D	650 366-4099	12911
Alation Inc (PA)	7372	E	650 779-4440	23589
Allakos Inc	2834	E	650 597-5002	7736
American Production Co Inc	3411	E	650 368-5334	11492
Apical Instruments Inc	3829	F	650 967-1030	21433
Applied Process Equipment	3599	F	650 365-6895	15743
Armo Biosciences Inc	2834	E	650 779-5075	7767
Astrazeneca Pharmaceuticals LP	2834	E	650 305-2600	7774
Atreca Inc	2836	E	650 595-2595	8275
Auris Health Inc (DH)	3841	C	650 610-0750	21613
Avast Software Inc (PA)	7372	F	844 340-9251	23642
Avinger Inc	3841	D	650 241-7900	21616
Badgeville Inc	7372	F	650 323-6668	23649
Balsam Hill LLC	3999	F	888 552-2572	23284
Banjo Inc (PA)	7372	F	650 425-6376	23651
Bay Precision Machining Inc	3599	E	650 365-3010	15777
Betterworks Systems Inc	7372	F	650 656-9013	23663
Biocentury Publications Inc (PA)	2711	E	650 595-5333	5567
Bioware Austin LLC	7372	F	650 628-1500	23671
Box Inc (PA)	7372	C	877 729-4269	23689
Brava Home Inc	3634	E	408 675-2569	16826
Broadvision Inc (PA)	7372	D	650 331-1000	23700
Broadvision Rcao Broadvisi	2741	F	650 261-5100	6205
C3ai Inc (PA)	7372	C	650 503-2200	23704
Carbon Inc	3577	C	650 285-6307	15185
Ci Management LLC	3131	F	650 654-8900	10148
Coalign Innovations Inc	3841	E	888 714-4440	21667
Codexis Inc (PA)	2819	C	650 421-8100	7484
Coraid Inc (PA)	3572	D	650 517-9300	15019
Crystal Dynamics Inc (DH)	7372	C	650 421-7600	23784
D N G Cummings Inc	3993	E	650 593-8974	23085
Delphix Corp (PA)	7372	E	650 494-1645	23814
Douce De France	2051	F	650 369-9644	1190
Eclipse Metal Fabrication Inc	3444	E	650 298-8731	12192
Electronic Arts Inc (PA)	7372	B	650 628-1500	23850
Electronic Arts Redwood Inc (HQ)	3695	D	650 628-1500	19215
Flywheel Software Inc	7372	E	650 260-1700	23906
Galen Robotics Inc	3841	F	408 502-5960	21720
Geneforge Inc	3825	F	650 219-9335	21042
Genelabs Technologies Inc (HQ)	2834	F	415 297-2901	7900
Genentech Inc	2834	E	650 216-2900	7905
Glasslab Inc	7372	F	415 244-5584	23941
Golden Octagon Inc	2051	F	650 369-8573	1219
Granite Rock Co	2951	E	650 482-3800	9093
Grass Manufacturing Co Inc	3469	E	650 366-2556	12809
H N Lockwood Inc	3089	E	650 366-9557	9819
Holt Tool & Machine Inc	3312	E	650 364-2547	11049
Host Analytics Inc (HQ)	7372	E	650 249-7100	23987
Impossible Foods Inc (PA)	2099	D	650 461-4385	2483

	SIC	EMP	PHONE	ENTRY #
Inevit Inc	3691	D	650 298-6001	19169
Informatica LLC (PA)	7372	C	650 385-5000	24017
Internet Systems Cnsortium Inc (PA)	7372	F	650 423-1300	24030
Invoice2go Inc (PA)	7372	E	650 300-5180	24042
Larson Electronic Glass Inc	3229	E	650 369-6734	10315
Lastline Inc (PA)	7372	D	805 456-7075	24092
Leland Stanford Junior Univ	2711	E	650 723-9434	5698
Light Labs Inc	3827	E	650 272-6942	21375
Mad Apparel Inc	2329	E	800 714-9697	3106
Menlo Therapeutics Inc	2834	E	650 486-1416	8009
Minerva Surgical Inc	3841	E	650 399-1770	21823
Monolith Materials Inc	2819	E	650 933-4957	7507
Mr Gears Inc	3599	E	650 364-7793	16231
Neural Id LLC	3695	F	650 394-8800	19227
Nevro Corp (PA)	3841	C	650 251-0005	21836
Nextag Inc (PA)	2741	D	650 645-4700	6296
Nvent Thermal LLC (DH)	3822	B	650 474-7414	20801
Oncomed Pharmaceuticals Inc	2834	D	650 995-8200	8052
Openwave Mobility Inc (PA)	7372	E	650 480-7200	24232
Oracle America Inc (HQ)	3571	A	650 506-7000	14959
Oracle America Inc	7372	F	408 702-5945	24241
Oracle Systems Corporation	7372	B	650 506-0300	24272
Oracle Systems Corporation	7372	F	650 506-5887	24274
Oratec Interventions Inc (DH)	3845	F	901 396-2121	22293
Paw Prints Inc	2759	F	650 365-4077	7170
Paxata Inc	7372	D	650 542-7897	24291
Pdl Biopharma Inc	2836	C	650 454-1000	8320
Pebble Technology Corp	3873	E	888 224-5820	22483
Petersen Precision Engrg LLC	3599	C	650 365-4373	16297
Pierry Inc (PA)	7372	F	800 860-7953	24298
Precision Plastic LLC	3089	C	510 324-8676	9988
Prenav Inc	3812	E	650 264-7279	20676
Proteus Digital Health Inc (PA)	2836	C	650 632-4031	8325
Puredepth Inc (PA)	3577	F	408 394-9146	15314
Qwilt Inc (PA)	7372	E	866 824-8009	24337
Redwood Apps Inc	7372	F	408 348-3808	24354
Relypsa Inc	2834	B	650 421-9500	8102
Rezolute Inc (PA)	2834	E	303 222-2128	8106
Roxwood Medical Inc	3841	E	650 779-4555	21884
Rurisond Inc	3663	E	650 395-7136	17649
S F Enterprises Incorporated	3599	E	650 455-3223	16381
Sake Robotics	3549	E	650 207-4021	14281
Salus North America Inc	3822	E	888 387-2587	20808
Singha North America Inc	2082	F	714 206-5097	1565
Skydio Inc	3812	F	408 203-8497	20723
Soccer 90	3949	F	650 599-9900	22891
Soleno Therapeutics Inc (PA)	2834	E	650 213-8444	8137
Sposato John	3663	F	408 215-8727	17669
Squelch Inc	7372	E	650 241-2700	24445
Storm8 Inc	7372	F	650 596-8600	24457
Talos Corporation	3599	E	650 364-7364	16442
Te Connectivity Corporation	3643	C	650 361-2495	16930
Te Connectivity Corporation	3357	E	650 361-3333	11323
Te Connectivity Corporation	3643	B	650 361-2495	16932
Tilley Manufacturing Co Inc (PA)	3053	E	650 365-3598	9258
Unifyid Inc	7372	E	650 561-2202	24538
Versant Corporation (HQ)	7372	E	650 232-2400	24558
Voyage Medical Inc	3841	E	650 503-7500	21960
Xtime Inc	3089	E	650 508-4300	10133

REDWOOD VALLEY, CA - Mendocino County

	SIC	EMP	PHONE	ENTRY #
Gregory Graziano	2084	F	707 485-9463	1736
Redwood Valley Gravel Products	3272	F	707 485-8585	10639

REEDLEY, CA - Fresno County

	SIC	EMP	PHONE	ENTRY #
Air-O Fan Products Corporation (PA)	3523	F	559 638-6546	13606
Durand-Wayland Machinery Inc (PA)	3523	E	559 591-6904	13629
Maxco Supply Inc	2631	D	559 638-8449	5167
Midvalley Publishing Inc	2711	E	559 638-2244	5754
Mission AG Resources LLC	2023	E	559 591-3333	605
Thiele Technologies Inc	3565	B	559 638-8484	14730
Valley Controls Inc	3823	F	559 638-5115	20954
Valley Packline Solutions	3556	E	559 638-7821	14411
Youngstown Grape Distrs Inc	2037	C	559 638-2271	935

RESEDA, CA - Los Angeles County

	SIC	EMP	PHONE	ENTRY #
Alumatec Inc	1381	D	818 609-7460	85
Hill Products Inc	3651	F	818 877-9256	17241
Rainbow Symphony Inc	2675	F	818 708-8400	5453
Test Laboratories Inc (PA)	2099	F	818 881-4251	2624

RIALTO, CA - San Bernardino County

	SIC	EMP	PHONE	ENTRY #
Advantage Business Forms Inc	2759	F	909 875-7163	6978
Biscomerica Corp	2052	C	909 877-5997	1307
Boral Roofing LLC	3272	D	909 822-4407	10542
Burlingame Industries Inc	3299	C	909 355-7000	11001
Calcraft Corporation	3441	F	909 879-2900	11757

2020 California
Manufacturers Register

(P-0000) Products & Services Section entry number
(PA)=Parent Co (HQ)=Headquarters (DH)=Div Headquarters

Company	SIC	EMP	PHONE	ENTRY #
Cemex Cnstr Mtls PCF LLC	3273	F	951 377-9657	10711
Columbia Steel Inc	3441	D	909 874-8840	11769
Dyell Machine (PA)	3599	E	909 350-4101	15911
Eagle Roofing Products Fla LLC	3259	E	909 822-6000	10462
Forest River Inc	3792	E	909 873-3777	20485
H Wayne Lewis Inc	3449	E	909 874-2213	12591
Kti Incorporated	3272	D	909 434-1888	10594
Legacy Vulcan LLC	3273	E	909 875-5180	10785
Lippert Components Inc	3711	D	909 873-0061	19484
Martinez and Turek Inc	3599	C	909 820-6800	16176
Meerkat Inc	3599	F	909 877-0093	16191
Niagara Bottling LLC	2086	F	909 230-5000	2096
Solomon Colors Inc	2816	E	909 484-9156	7462
Spray Enclosure Technologies	3444	E	909 419-7011	12387
State Pipe & Supply Inc	3312	E	909 356-5670	11074
Uscps	3999	D	909 434-1888	23515
Villanueva Plastic Company Inc	3083	F	909 581-3870	9460

RICHMOND, CA - Contra Costa County

Company	SIC	EMP	PHONE	ENTRY #
A M T Metal Fabricators Inc	3441	E	510 236-1414	11729
AA Portable Power Corporation	3691	F	510 525-2328	19150
ACS Instrumentation Valves Inc	3823	D	510 262-1880	20826
Alion Energy Inc	3674	F	510 965-0868	18078
Amtecol Inc	2992	E	510 235-7979	9129
Andrus Sheet Metal Inc	3444	E	510 232-8687	12109
Ats Products Inc (PA)	3089	E	510 234-3173	9644
Bay Area Mch & Mar Repr Inc	3599	F	510 815-2339	15776
Bay Marine Boatworks Inc	3732	E	510 237-0140	20315
Bio-RAD Laboratories Inc	3826	B	510 232-7000	21192
Bio-RAD Laboratories Inc	3826	B	510 724-7000	21194
Black Diamond Video Inc	3577	D	510 439-4500	15173
Black Point Products Inc	3661	E	510 232-7723	17350
BP Lubricants USA Inc	2992	E	510 236-6312	9134
BP West Coast Products LLC	1311	B	510 231-4724	30
Cemex Materials LLC	3273	E	510 234-3616	10737
Chemtrade Chemicals US LLC	2819	E	510 232-7193	7482
Chimes Printing Incorporated	2752	F	510 235-2388	6483
Coin Gllery of San Frncsco Inc	2542	F	510 236-8882	4970
Dicon Fiberoptics Inc (PA)	3679	C	510 620-5000	18887
Douglas & Sturgess Inc	3299	F	510 235-8411	11006
Eagle Systems Inc	3743	F	510 231-2686	20369
East Bay Brass Foundry Inc	3363	E	510 233-7171	11335
Ekso Bionics Inc (PA)	3559	D	510 984-1761	14457
Ekso Bionics Holdings Inc	3842	D	510 984-1761	22007
Foamordercom Inc	3086	F	415 503-1188	9539
Galaxy Desserts	2053	C	510 439-3160	1341
GK Welding Inc	7692	F	510 233-0133	24636
Hauser & Sons Inc	2591	F	510 234-8850	5023
Hero Arts Rubber Stamps Inc	3953	D	510 232-4200	22951
Hoefer Inc	3826	E	415 282-2307	21239
International Group Inc	2911	F	510 232-8704	9048
International Group Inc	2911	D	510 232-8704	9049
John Lompa	2759	E	510 965-6501	7104
Kodiak Precision Inc (PA)	3599	F	510 234-4165	16123
Living Apothecary LLC	2086	F	917 951-2810	2090
Messer LLC	2813	F	510 233-8911	7423
Metalset Inc	3441	E	510 233-9998	11844
Mom Enterprises Inc	2834	F	415 526-2710	8016
My True Image Mfg Inc	3842	D	510 970-7990	22052
National Ewp Inc	1081	F	510 236-6282	11
Norman & Globus Inc	2731	F	510 222-2638	6130
Novacart	2621	D	510 215-8999	5139
Nutiva	2099	D	510 255-2700	2572
Oliso Inc	3634	F	415 864-7600	16836
Pacific Dry Goods Inc	2231	F	925 288-2929	2747
Paragon Machine Works Inc	3599	D	510 232-3223	16279
Parker-Hannifin Corporation	3823	D	510 235-9590	20915
Phoenix Day Co Inc	3645	F	415 822-4414	16987
Professional Finishing Inc	3471	D	510 233-7629	13081
R & K Industrial Products Co	3499	E	510 234-7212	13543
San Rafael Rock Quarry Inc	2951	E	510 970-7700	9105
Sealy Mattress Mfg Co Inc	2515	C	510 235-7171	4741
Siemens Industry Inc	3822	D	510 237-2325	20813
Stalker Software Inc	7372	E	415 569-2280	24450
String Letter Publishing Inc	2741	E	510 215-0010	6349
Sunwater Solar Inc	3433	F	650 739-5297	11723
Support Systems Intl Corp	3679	D	510 234-9090	19097
Tamalpais Coml Cabinetry Inc	2541	E	510 231-6800	4947
Thomas-Swan Sign Company Inc	3993	F	415 621-1511	23227
Tulip Pubg & Graphics Inc	2752	E	510 898-0000	6903
United Granite & Cabinets LLC	2434	F	510 558-8999	4259
Unovo LLC	3635	F	415 864-7600	16846
West Coast Fab Inc	3444	F	510 529-0177	12434
Wholesome Harvest Baking LLC	2051	C	510 231-7200	1296
Zygo Epo	3827	F	510 243-7592	21425

RICHVALE, CA - Butte County

Company	SIC	EMP	PHONE	ENTRY #
Wehah Farm Inc	2044	B	530 538-3500	1054

RIDGECREST, CA - Kern County

Company	SIC	EMP	PHONE	ENTRY #
American Ready Mix Inc	3273	F	760 446-4556	10688
Lockheed Martin Corporation	3812	C	760 446-1700	20626
Mpb Furniture Corporation	2512	E	760 375-4800	4660
Orbital Sciences Corporation	3764	F	818 887-8345	20468
Raytheon Company	3812	E	760 384-3295	20686
Service Rock Products Corp	3273	D	760 446-2606	10831
Sierra View Inc	2711	F	760 371-4301	5825
Structural Wood Systems	2439	F	760 375-2772	4321

RIO VISTA, CA - Solano County

Company	SIC	EMP	PHONE	ENTRY #
Asta Construction Co Inc (PA)	1381	E	707 374-6472	87
California Resources Corp	1382	F	707 374-4109	113
Coughran Mechanical Services	3599	F	707 374-2100	15865
Dick Brown Technical Services	1381	F	707 374-2133	90
Dry Vac Environmental Inc (PA)	3826	E	707 374-7500	21218
I DES Inc	3823	F	707 374-7500	20885
Jim Graham Inc	1389	E	707 374-5114	214
Lindsay Trnsp Solutions Inc (HQ)	3272	D	707 374-6800	10599
Paul Graham Drilling & Svc Co	1381	C	707 374-5123	102
Resource Cementing LLC	1389	F	707 374-3350	253
Woodward Drilling Company	1381	F	707 374-4300	108

RIPON, CA - San Joaquin County

Company	SIC	EMP	PHONE	ENTRY #
Better Built Truss Inc	2439	E	209 869-4545	4289
California Nuggets Inc	2096	E	209 599-7131	2319
Franzia/Sanger Winery	2084	C	209 599-4111	1714
Gate-Or-Door Inc	7372	E	209 751-4881	23928
Guntert Zmmerman Const Div Inc	3531	E	209 599-0066	13734
Jackrabbit (PA)	3523	D	209 599-6118	13639
Kamper Fabrication Inc	3523	E	209 599-7137	13642
Ken Anderson	3273	E	209 604-8579	10776
Pearl Crop Inc	2076	E	209 982-9933	1449
Ripon Mfg Co	3556	F	209 599-2148	14397
Ripon Volunteer Firemans Assn	3711	F	209 599-4209	19498
Tetra Pak Processing Equip	3556	D	209 599-4634	14405
Wine Group Inc (HQ)	2084	C	209 599-4111	2007

RIVERBANK, CA - Stanislaus County

Company	SIC	EMP	PHONE	ENTRY #
Silgan Containers Mfg Corp	3411	E	209 869-3601	11506
Thunderbolt Sales Inc	2491	E	209 869-4561	4482

RIVERDALE, CA - Fresno County

Company	SIC	EMP	PHONE	ENTRY #
C Case Company Inc	1389	E	559 867-3912	175

RIVERSIDE, CA - Riverside County

Company	SIC	EMP	PHONE	ENTRY #
220 Laboratories Inc	2844	C	951 683-2912	8430
220 Laboratories Inc (PA)	2844	C	951 683-2912	8431
Aarons Signs & Printing	3993	E	951 352-7303	23038
Aatech	3589	E	909 854-3200	15477
Accurate Metal Products Inc	3441	E	951 360-3594	11733
Acm Student Chapter At Ucr	7372	F	951 389-0713	23549
Acro-Spec Grinding Co Inc	3599	F	951 736-1199	15686
Adex Medical Inc	3842	E	951 653-9122	21970
Advanced Orthotic Designs	3842	F	951 710-1640	21975
Alectro Inc	3612	F	909 590-9521	16540
Aleph Group Inc	3711	E	951 213-4815	19451
Aleph Group Inc	3841	F	951 213-4815	21589
Alpha Materials Inc	3273	E	951 788-5150	10686
Alstom Signaling Operation LLC	3669	C	951 343-9699	17713
AM Castenada Inc	3915	E	951 686-3966	22592
AMA Plastics (PA)	3089	B	951 734-5600	9620
Amazon Environmental Inc (PA)	2851	E	951 588-0206	8617
American Bottling Company	2086	C	951 341-7500	2024
American Quality Tools Inc	3545	E	951 280-4700	14129
AP Plastics	3089	F	951 782-0705	9634
Applied Systems LLC	3443	F	951 842-6300	11993
Aqua Backflow and Chlorination	3671	F	909 598-7251	17776
Artech Industries Inc	3679	E	951 276-3331	18820
Arturo Campos	3471	F	951 300-2111	12935
Astro Seal Inc	3679	E	951 787-6670	18822
BA Holdings (DH)	3443	E	951 684-5110	11995
Better Bar Manufacturing	2023	E	951 525-3111	579
Blacoh Fluid Controls Inc (PA)	3443	E	951 342-3100	11997
Blanchard Signs	3993	F	951 354-5050	23063
Blow Molded Products Inc	3089	E	951 360-6055	9667
Bottling Group LLC	2086	E	951 697-3200	2046
Bourns (PA)	3677	C	951 781-5500	18704
Bourns Inc	3825	C	951 781-5690	21013
Brenner-Fiedler & Associates (PA)	3829	E	562 404-2721	21444
Brookhurst Mill	2048	F	951 688-3511	1086
C W Enterprises Inc	3648	F	951 786-9999	17108
California Interfill Inc	2844	F	951 351-2619	8455
Canine Caviar Pet Foods Inc	2048	E	714 223-1800	1088

Employment Codes: A=Over 500 employees, B=251-500,
C=101-250, D=51-100, E=20-50, F=10-19

2020 California
Manufacturers Register

© Mergent Inc. 1-800-342-5647
1395

GEOGRAPHIC

	SIC	EMP	PHONE	ENTRY #
Canine Caviar Pet Foods De Inc	2047	F	714 223-1800	1071
Captive-Aire Systems Inc	3444	F	951 231-5102	12150
Carbon Solutions Inc	3624	F	909 234-2738	16683
Cardinal Sheet Metal Inc	3444	F	951 788-8800	12152
Carlisle Interconnect Tech Inc	3315	E	951 788-0252	11086
Carpenter Co	3086	B	951 354-7550	9513
Cavco Industries Inc	2451	C	951 688-5353	4440
Champion Laboratories Inc	3714	F	951 275-0715	19614
City of Riverside	3589	D	951 351-6140	15498
Clarkwestern Dietrich Building	3444	F	951 360-3500	12157
Club Car LLC	3799	E	951 735-4675	20505
Cnc Machining Solutions Inc	3845	F	951 688-4267	22241
Coachworks Holdings Inc	3711	B	951 684-9585	19464
Cody Cylinder Services	3599	F	951 786-3650	15857
Connection Enterprises Inc	3643	F	951 688-8133	16887
Connector Kings Corporation	3678	F	951 710-1180	18758
Consolidated Cont Holdings LLC	3089	E	951 340-9390	9718
Criterion Automation Inc	3317	F	951 683-2400	11126
CT Coachworks LLC	3716	F	951 343-8787	19841
Cummings Resources LLC	3993	E	951 248-1130	23084
CV Wndows Dors Riverside Inc	3231	F	951 784-8766	10350
D L B Pallets (PA)	2448	F	951 360-9896	4361
D Mills Grnding Machining Inc	3599	F	951 697-6847	15876
D S McGee Enterprises Inc	2431	E	951 378-8473	4029
Dayton Superior Corporation	3315	D	951 782-9517	11089
Denali Water Solutions LLC	3089	F	714 799-0801	9753
Desert Microsystems Inc	3823	F	951 682-3867	20856
DGA Machine Shop Inc	3599	F	951 354-2113	15892
Doka USA Ltd	3444	F	951 509-0023	12186
Dura Coat Products Inc (PA)	3479	D	951 341-6500	13167
E & R Pallets Inc	2448	F	951 790-1212	4363
Edge Plastics Inc (PA)	3089	F	951 786-4750	9773
Ejay Filtration Inc	3496	F	951 683-0805	13410
Eldorado National Cal Inc (HQ)	3711	B	951 727-9300	19468
Elisid Magazine	2721	F	619 990-9999	5929
Embroidery Outlet	2395	F	951 687-1750	3743
Esco Industries Inc	3462	F	951 782-2130	12707
Evans Walker Enterprises	3714	E	951 784-7223	19651
Everpac	3552	D	951 774-3274	14289
Fleetwood Homes California Inc (DH)	2451	E	951 351-2494	4447
Fleetwood Homes of Florida (DH)	2451	E	909 261-4274	4448
Fleetwood Homes of Idaho Inc	2451	C	951 354-3000	4449
Fleetwood Homes of Virginia	2451	C	951 351-3500	4451
Fleetwood Motor Homes-Califinc (DH)	3716	E	951 354-3000	19842
Fleetwood Travel Trlrs Ind Inc (DH)	3792	C	951 354-3000	20484
Foot In Motion Inc	3842	F	312 752-0990	22013
Fpc Graphics Inc	2752	E	951 686-0232	6583
Fusion Sign & Design Inc (PA)	3993	C	877 477-8777	23117
Future Tech Metals Inc	3599	E	951 781-4801	15978
Glengarry Manufacturing Inc	3599	F	951 248-1111	15997
Grech Motors LLC (PA)	7694	E	951 688-8347	24693
Greenscape Solutions Inc	3271	E	909 714-8333	10509
Harber All Natural Products	2844	F	347 921-1004	8510
Harber Foods LLC (PA)	2844	F	347 921-1004	8511
Heritage Container Inc	2653	D	951 360-1900	5234
Hi-Rel Plastics & Molding Corp	3089	E	951 354-0258	9823
Hydraforce Incorporated	3561	E	951 689-3987	14584
Imperial Pipe Services LLC	3317	E	951 682-3307	11128
IMS Products Inc	3751	F	951 653-7720	20408
Inland Empire Foods Inc (PA)	2034	E	951 682-8222	850
Inland Empire Media Group Inc	2721	E	951 682-3026	5967
Innovative Design and Sheet ME	3444	F	951 222-2270	12246
Irrometer Company Inc	3829	F	951 682-9505	21491
It Retail Inc	7372	F	951 683-4950	24049
J & A Pallet Accessory Inc	2448	F	951 785-1594	4375
J&C Tapocik Inc	2389	F	951 351-4333	3559
Jaffa Precision Engrg Inc	3599	F	951 278-8797	16073
Jimenez Mexican Foods Inc	2032	E	951 351-0102	731
Joa Corporation (PA)	3842	F	951 785-4411	22036
John Bean Technologies Corp	3556	E	951 222-2300	14378
K & N Engineering Inc (PA)	3751	A	951 826-4000	20410
Keurig Dr Pepper Inc	2086	D	951 341-7500	2083
L & L Louvers Inc	3442	E	951 735-9300	11963
L T Seroge Inc	3699	F	951 354-7141	19343
LSI Products Inc	3714	D	951 343-9270	19707
Luxfer Inc (DH)	3728	D	951 684-5110	20161
Luxfer Inc	3354	C	951 684-5110	11236
Luxfer Inc	3463	C	951 351-4100	12734
M G Deanza Acquisition Inc	3599	F	951 683-3080	16161
Mackie International Inc (PA)	2024	E	951 346-0530	655
Magnotek Manufacturing Inc	3677	D	951 653-8461	18724
Main Steel Ltd	3471	D	951 789-3010	13046
Marlin Machine Products	3599	F	951 275-0050	16172
Martin Marietta Materials Inc	1423	E	951 682-0918	310
Maskell Rigging & Equipment (PA)	3317	F	951 900-7460	11131
Masonry Fireplace Inds LLC	3272	F	714 542-5397	10601
Mdi East Inc (HQ)	3089	E	951 509-6918	9888
Mega Machinery Inc	3559	F	951 300-9300	14496
Merchants Metals LLC	3315	F	951 686-1888	11101
Metal Container Corporation	3411	C	951 354-0444	11499
Metric Machining (PA)	3541	E	909 947-9222	13935
Metropolitan News Company	2711	E	951 369-5890	5752
Micromold Inc	3089	E	951 684-7130	9896
Millers Fab & Weld Corp	3441	E	951 359-3100	11845
Molded Devices Inc (PA)	3089	E	480 785-9100	9905
Mortan Industries Inc	3069	E	951 682-2215	9340
Neoplast Inc	3089	E	951 300-9300	9921
Nevada Window Supply Inc	2431	F	951 300-0100	4093
Newbasis West LLC	3272	C	951 787-0600	10606
Newman Bros California Inc (PA)	2431	E	951 782-0102	4094
ODonnell Manufacturing Inc	3599	F	562 944-9671	16255
Oldcast Precast (DH)	3272	F	951 788-9720	10609
Omf Performance Products	3799	F	951 354-8222	20517
OSI Industries LLC	3999	E	951 684-4500	23436
Owen Trailers Inc	3715	E	951 361-4557	19827
Pacific Consolidated Inds LLC	3569	D	951 479-0860	14842
pacific Molding Inc	3089	F	951 683-2100	9944
Paradise Ranch	2389	F	951 776-7736	3573
PCI Holding Company Inc (PA)	3569	C	951 479-0860	14848
Pepsi-Cola Metro Btlg Co Inc	2086	B	909 885-0741	2116
Pierco Incorporated	3999	F	909 251-7100	23449
Plascor Inc	3085	C	951 328-1010	9490
Poly-Fiber Inc (PA)	2851	E	951 684-4280	8663
Polymer Logistics Inc	3089	E	951 567-2900	9981
Poma GL Specialty Windows Inc	3211	D	951 321-0116	10273
Precise Aero Products Inc	3728	F	951 340-4554	20203
Precision Technology and Mfg	3451	E	951 788-0252	12647
Press-Enterprise Company (PA)	2711	A	951 684-1200	5804
Press-Enterprise Company	2711	F	951 684-1200	5805
Primetech Silicones Inc	2869	F	951 509-6655	8764
Prism Aerospace	3444	F	951 582-2850	12340
Pro Mold Inc	3544	E	951 776-0555	14097
Proair LLC	3585	F	909 930-6224	15448
Progressive Products Inc	2299	F	951 784-9930	2951
Qg Printing Corp	2721	C	951 571-2500	6009
Qg Printing II Corp	2752	A	951 571-2500	6820
Quad/Graphics Inc	2752	C	951 689-1122	6822
R & D Nova Inc	3845	F	951 781-7332	22298
R & J Leathercraft	3199	F	951 688-1685	10251
Rain Mstr Irrgtion Systems Inc	3823	F	805 527-4498	20927
Rcs Custom Stoneworks	3281	F	714 309-0620	10927
Reisner Enterprises Inc	3599	F	951 786-9478	16350
Riverside Lamination Corp	2891	F	951 682-0100	8892
Riverside Machine Works Inc	3599	F	951 685-7416	16360
Riverside Tent & Awning Co	2393	F	951 683-1925	3664
Robert P Von Zabern	3841	F	951 734-7215	21883
Rochester Midland Corporation	2676	F	800 388-4762	5467
Rolenn Manufacturing Inc	3999	F	951 682-1185	23463
Rolenn Manufacturing Inc (PA)	3089	F	951 682-1185	10022
Roll-A-Shade Inc (PA)	2591	F	951 245-5077	5036
Royal Interpack Midwest Inc	3089	F	626 675-0637	10031
Royal Interpack North Amer Inc	3089	F	951 787-6925	10032
Ruiz Mexican Foods Inc (PA)	2099	C	909 947-7811	2606
S R S M Inc	2821	C	310 952-9000	7606
Sabert Corporation	3089	F	951 342-0240	10039
San Joaquin Window Inc (PA)	3442	D	909 946-3697	11981
Seymour Levinger & Co	3465	E	909 673-9800	12749
Sheet Metal Specialist LLC	3444	F	951 351-6828	12375
Sierra Aluminum Company (HQ)	3354	E	951 781-7800	11245
Simple Orthotic Solutions LLC	3131	F	951 353-8127	10153
Simpson Strong-Tie Company Inc	2439	C	714 871-8373	4317
SMS Fabrications Inc	3444	F	951 351-6828	12379
Sphere Alliance Inc	2821	E	951 352-2400	7614
Steel Unlimited Inc	3443	D	909 873-1222	12058
Stone Valley Materials LLC	1442	F	951 681-7830	361
Stremicks Heritage Foods LLC	2024	D	951 352-1344	668
Structures Unlimited	3432	F	951 688-6300	11682
Summertree Interiors Inc	2511	E	951 549-0590	4613
Superform USA Incorporated	3463	E	951 351-4100	12737
Superior Metal Fabricators	3444	F	951 360-2474	12395
Swift Beef Company	2013	C	951 571-2237	502
T & V Printing Inc	2752	F	951 353-8470	6882
T C Quality Machining Inc	3599	F	951 509-4663	16437
T M Cobb Company (PA)	2431	F	951 248-2400	4136
T M P Services Inc (PA)	3448	E	951 213-3900	12576
Tait Cabinetry Woodworks	2431	F	951 776-1192	4139
Team Air Inc	3585	E	909 823-1957	15454
Techniglove International Inc	3842	F	951 582-0890	22107
Tim Hoover Enterprises	3663	D	951 237-9210	17692
Tolco Incorporated	3448	E	951 656-3111	12578

Mergent email: customerrelations@mergent.com
1396

2020 California
Manufacturers Register

(P-0000) Products & Services Section entry number
(PA)=Parent Co (HQ)=Headquarters (DH)=Div Headquarters

	SIC	EMP	PHONE	ENTRY #
Tom Harris Inc	2099	D	951 352-5700	2627
Tom Leonard Investment Co Inc	3999	D	951 351-7778	23506
Toro Company	3523	D	951 688-9221	13676
Trademark Cosmetic Inc	2844	E	951 683-2631	8594
Trademark Plastics Inc	3559	C	909 941-8810	14546
Trane US Inc	3585	E	951 801-6020	15460
Triple H Food Processors LLC	2099	D	951 352-5700	2637
Tropical Functional Labs LLC	2023	F	951 688-2619	622
Trutouch Technologies Inc	3829	F	909 703-5963	21560
Tube One Industries Inc	3317	F	951 300-2998	11137
United Carports LLC	3448	F	800 757-6742	12580
Universal Interior Industries	2511	F	951 743-5446	4617
Universal Specialty Vehicles	3716	F	951 943-7747	19844
Universal Trailers	3799	F	951 784-0543	20523
US Door and Fence LLC	2411	F	951 300-0010	3913
US Environmental	2899	F	951 359-9002	9034
US Plastic Inc	3085	E	951 300-9360	9497
US Precision Sheet Metal Inc	3444	D	951 276-2611	12419
US Rubber Roller Company Inc	3069	F	951 682-2221	9384
Vast National Inc	3399	F	951 788-7030	11491
Virginia Park LLC	2099	F	816 592-0776	2645
Web CAM Inc	3714	F	951 369-5144	19804
West Coast Unlimited	3711	F	951 352-1234	19512
Western Case Incorporated (PA)	3089	D	951 214-6380	10122
Western Hydrostatics Inc (PA)	3594	E	951 784-2133	15638
Yardney Water MGT Systems Inc (PA)	3589	F	951 656-6716	15607
York Engineering	3544	F	323 256-0439	14127
Zenith Manufacturing Inc	3728	E	818 767-2106	20273
Ziehm Instrumentarium	3844	E	407 615-8560	22226

RLLNG HLS EST, CA - Los Angeles County

	SIC	EMP	PHONE	ENTRY #
Cade Corporation	2899	D	310 539-2508	8944
Dincloud Inc	7372	D	310 929-1101	23817
Ecw Technology Inc	3564	D	310 373-0082	14655
Flipagram Inc	7372	F	415 827-8373	23903
National Media Inc (HQ)	2711	E	310 377-6877	5772
Sheervision Inc (PA)	3827	F	310 265-8918	21409

ROCKLIN, CA - Placer County

	SIC	EMP	PHONE	ENTRY #
Advantage Pharmaceuticals	2834	F	916 630-4960	7730
Asa Corporation	3826	F	530 305-3720	21176
Backyard Unlimited (PA)	2449	F	916 630-7433	4412
Cell Marque Corporation	2835	E	916 746-8900	8212
Cosmedica Skincare	2844	F	800 922-5280	8467
Diamond Tech Incorporated	3546	F	916 624-1118	14220
Diverse McHning Fbrication LLC	3499	F	916 672-6591	13514
Energy Absorption Systems Inc	3499	C	916 645-8181	13520
Galil Motion Control Inc	3823	E	800 377-6329	20877
Greenheck Fan Corporation	3564	C	916 626-3400	14661
Hugin Components Inc	3469	F	916 652-1070	12819
Hydraulic Technology Inc	3561	F	916 645-3317	14585
Jeld-Wen Inc	2431	C	916 782-4900	4064
Logan Smith Machine Co	3599	F	916 632-2692	16149
Oracle America Inc	7372	F	303 272-6473	24239
Oracle Corporation	7372	B	916 435-8342	24259
Oracle Corporation	7372	B	916 315-3500	24265
Pacific Mdf Products Inc (PA)	2431	E	916 660-1882	4104
Parallax Incorporated	3571	F	916 624-8333	14960
Progressive Technology Inc	3253	E	916 632-6715	10449
Sitek Process Solutions	3674	F	916 797-9000	18558
SMA America Production LLC	3433	C	720 347-6000	11714
Vanishing Vistas	2741	E	916 624-1237	6372
Vannelli Brands LLC	2033	F	916 824-1717	834
Verifone Inc	3663	C	808 623-2911	17699

RODEO, CA - Contra Costa County

	SIC	EMP	PHONE	ENTRY #
Asbury Graphite Inc California	2911	F	510 799-3636	9038

ROHNERT PARK, CA - Sonoma County

	SIC	EMP	PHONE	ENTRY #
Arcturus Marine Systems	3511	D	707 586-3155	13560
Asm Precision Inc	3444	F	707 584-7950	12119
Driven Raceway and Family Ente	3644	F	707 585-3748	16946
Green Sheet Inc	2759	F	707 284-1684	7082
Idex Health & Science LLC (HQ)	3821	D	707 588-2000	20762
Innovative Molding (HQ)	3089	D	707 238-9250	9840
KG Technologies Inc	3679	F	888 513-1874	18977
Miller Manufacturing Inc	2591	F	707 584-9528	5031
Nelson Banner Inc	2673	E	707 585-9942	5407
North Bay Rhblitation Svcs Inc (PA)	2399	C	707 585-1991	3851
Parker-Hannifin Corporation	3625	C	707 584-7558	16736
Pasta Sonoma LLC	2098	F	707 584-0800	2378
Rieke Corporation	3466	C	707 238-9250	12752
Sodamail LLC	2741	F	707 794-1289	6341
Sonoma Plant Works Inc	3524	F	707 588-8002	13696
Trinity Engineering	2542	F	707 585-2959	5007
Vaider Inc	3479	F	707 584-3655	13265
World Centric	2679	F	707 241-9190	5540

ROLLING HILLS, CA - Los Angeles County

	SIC	EMP	PHONE	ENTRY #
California Digital Inc (PA)	3577	D	310 217-0500	15182
Stitch and Hide LLC	3111	F	310 377-6912	10143

ROMOLAND, CA - Riverside County

	SIC	EMP	PHONE	ENTRY #
General Electric Company	3511	B	951 928-2829	13571
Orco Block & Hardscape	3271	E	951 928-3619	10513
Soil Retention Products Inc	3271	F	951 928-8477	10520

ROSAMOND, CA - Kern County

	SIC	EMP	PHONE	ENTRY #
American Performance Engi	3751	F	661 256-7309	20381

ROSEMEAD, CA - Los Angeles County

	SIC	EMP	PHONE	ENTRY #
Azteca Ornamental Metals	3446	F	626 280-2822	12454
C & R Extrusions Inc	3081	F	626 642-0244	9396
Carryout Bags Inc (PA)	2671	F	626 279-7000	5326
Chinese Overseas Mktg Svc Corp (PA)	2741	D	626 280-8588	6215
Fongs Graphics & Printing Inc	2754	E	626 307-1898	6955
HCC Industries Inc (HQ)	3678	F	626 443-8933	18771
Hermetic Seal Corporation (DH)	3679	C	626 443-8931	18935
Interior Corner Usa Inc	2542	F	626 452-8833	4984
J F McCaughin Co	3952	E	626 573-3000	22942
Ldvc Inc	2064	E	626 448-4611	1382
Lee Fasteners Inc	3399	F	626 287-6848	11479
Lonix Pharmaceutical Inc	2023	F	626 287-4700	602
Lotus Beverages	2084	F	213 216-1434	1804
M Argeso & Co Inc	2911	F	626 573-3000	9052
Phu Huong Foods Co Inc	2015	F	626 280-8607	524
Popular Printers Inc	2759	F	626 307-4281	7177
Prographics Inc	2752	F	626 287-0417	6815
Saigon Times Inc	2711	F	626 288-2696	5812
Tanbil Bakery Inc	2051	F	626 280-2638	1284
Tur-Bo Jet Products Co Inc	3677	D	626 285-1294	18747

ROSEVILLE, CA - Placer County

	SIC	EMP	PHONE	ENTRY #
A Teichert & Son Inc	3273	C	916 783-7132	10682
Advanced Metal Finishing LLC	3471	E	530 888-7772	12905
Amazing Facts International	2731	D	916 434-3880	6070
Applied Materials Inc	3559	F	916 786-3900	14425
Arm Electronics Inc	3699	E	916 787-1100	19260
Arrive Technologies Inc (PA)	3674	F	888 864-6959	18124
Basalite Building Products LLC (HQ)	3272	E	707 678-1901	10534
Bead Shoppe	3999	F	916 782-8642	23286
Bioinitiatives Inc	3841	E	916 780-9100	21635
Brookshire Innovations LLC	3751	E	916 786-7601	20386
Ca Inc	7372	E	800 405-5540	23706
California Bottling Company	2086	E	916 772-1000	2049
Cmd Products	3086	F	916 434-0228	9515
Cooks Truck Body Mfg Inc	3713	F	916 784-3220	19524
Cooltouch Corporation	3845	F	916 677-1975	22245
Coors Brewing Company	2082	E	916 786-2666	1514
David Corporation	7372	E	916 762-8688	23807
Energy Exemplar LLC (DH)	7372	F	916 722-1484	23859
Garner Products Inc	3812	F	916 784-0200	20581
Gutterglove Inc	3444	D	916 624-5000	12229
Harris & Bruno Machine Co Inc (PA)	3555	D	916 781-7676	14324
HB Fuller Company	2891	D	916 787-6000	8871
Hudson & Company LLC	2392	F	916 774-6465	3618
Intelligrated Systems Inc	3535	B	916 772-6800	13828
Iosafe Inc	3572	F	888 984-6723	15050
Kellogg Sales Company	2043	E	916 787-0414	1027
Kenco Engineering Inc	3531	E	916 782-8494	13737
Kyles Rock & Redi-Mix Inc	3273	E	916 681-4848	10777
Microsemi Stor Solutions Inc	3674	F	916 788-3300	18415
Nates Fine Foods LLC	2038	E	310 897-2690	966
New Star Lasers Inc	3845	E	916 677-1900	22288
New Vision Display Inc (DH)	3679	E	916 786-8111	19025
Pacific Coast Optics Inc	3827	E	916 789-0111	21394
Paul Baker Printing Inc	2752	E	916 969-8317	6772
Performance Polymer Tech LLC	3061	F	916 677-1414	9268
Praxair Inc	2813	C	916 786-3900	7439
Pride Industries One Inc	3999	A	916 788-2100	23451
Prima Games Inc	2731	C	916 787-7000	6139
Print & Mail Solutions Inc	2752	F	916 782-5489	6794
Providence Publications LLC	2741	E	916 774-4000	6321
Sigma Mfg & Logistics LLC	3571	E	916 781-3052	14975
Sinister Mfg Company Inc	3714	E	916 772-9253	19768
Smoothie Operator Inc	2037	F	916 773-9541	927
Star One Investments LLC	3429	E	916 858-1178	11632
Sunworks Inc (PA)	3674	D	916 409-6900	18595
Supermedia LLC	2741	B	916 782-6866	6355
Swiss-Tech Machining LLC	3451	E	916 797-6010	12653
Technical Sales Intl LLC (HQ)	7372	F	866 493-6337	24495
TRC Cocoa LLC	2066	F	916 847-2390	1416
Tsi Semiconductors America LLC (PA)	3674	C	916 786-3900	18625
United Advg Publications Inc	2721	E	916 746-2300	6051

Employment Codes: A=Over 500 employees, B=251-500,
C=101-250, D=51-100, E=20-50, F=10-19

2020 California
Manufacturers Register

© Mergent Inc. 1-800-342-5647

1397

GEOGRAPHIC

	SIC	EMP	PHONE	ENTRY #
Wright Technologies Inc	3679	F	916 773-4424	19144
Zoom Bookz LLC	2731	F	800 662-9982	6169

ROUGH AND READY, CA - Nevada County

	SIC	EMP	PHONE	ENTRY #
Gro-Tech Systems Inc	3448	F	530 432-7012	12548
Simply Country Inc	3523	F	530 615-0565	13671

ROWLAND HEIGHTS, CA - Los Angeles County

	SIC	EMP	PHONE	ENTRY #
Hubbell Lighting Inc	3646	D	714 386-5550	17044
Lip Hing Metal Inc	3542	F	714 871-9220	13980
Lip Hing Metal Mfg Amer Inc	3549	F	626 810-8204	14273
Quality Painting Co	3479	E	626 964-2529	13234
Suzhou South	3578	B	626 322-0101	15379
USA Topdon LLC	3699	F	833 233-5535	19430
Wholesome Yo Curd	2024	F	909 859-8758	680

ROYAL OAKS, CA - Santa Cruz County

	SIC	EMP	PHONE	ENTRY #
Classic Salads LLC	2099	E	928 726-6196	2428
Farmhouse Culture Inc (PA)	2834	E	831 466-0499	7889
Kristich-Monterey Pipe Co Inc	3272	F	831 724-4186	10593
Stainless Works Mfg Inc	3556	E	831 728-5097	14402

RUTHERFORD, CA - Napa County

	SIC	EMP	PHONE	ENTRY #
Cakebread Cellars	2084	D	707 963-5221	1616
Diageo North America Inc	2085	D	707 967-5200	2013
Frogs Leap Winery	2084	F	707 963-4704	1717
Grgich Hills Cellar	2084	E	707 963-2784	1737
Inglenook	2084	F	707 968-1100	1759
Niebam-Cppola Estate Winery LP (PA)	2084	C	707 968-1100	1842
Pernod Ricard Usa LLC	2084	D	707 967-7770	1863
S&B Vineyard LLC	2084	E	707 963-7194	1904
St Supery Inc (DH)	2084	E	707 963-4507	1927

SACRAMENTO, CA - Sacramento County

	SIC	EMP	PHONE	ENTRY #
A & A Ready Mixed Concrete Inc	3273	E	916 383-3756	10679
A Teichert & Son Inc	3273	E	916 386-6974	10681
A Teichert & Son Inc	1442	E	916 386-6900	328
A&A Metal Finishing Entps LLC	3471	E	916 442-1063	12896
AAA Garments & Lettering Inc	2395	F	916 363-4590	3717
Admail West Inc	2655	D	916 554-5755	5286
Affordable Goods	3571	E	916 514-1049	14883
Ainor Signs Inc	3993	F	916 348-4370	23046
Alder Creek Millwork	2434	E	916 379-9831	4162
Aldetec Inc	3663	E	916 453-3382	17444
Alex Design Inc	2434	F	916 386-8020	4163
All Weather Inc	3829	D	916 928-1000	21430
Allied Printing Company	2752	F	916 442-1373	6404
Aluminum Coating Tech Inc	3471	E	916 442-1063	12924
American Bottling Company	2086	F	916 929-3575	2034
American Bottling Company	2086	D	916 929-7777	2035
American City Bus Journals Inc	2711	F	916 447-7661	5548
American Lithographers Inc	2752	D	916 441-5392	6408
Applied Products Inc	2891	F	800 274-9801	8854
Architectural Blomberg LLC	3442	F	916 428-8060	11932
Architectural S Weidner	3993	E	800 561-7446	23052
Arden & Howe Printing Inc	2752	F	916 444-7154	6418
Atlas Specialties Corporation (PA)	3231	E	503 636-8182	10338
Audio Fx LLC	3651	F	916 929-2100	17195
Baise Enterprises Inc	2752	F	916 446-0167	6434
Bauer Industries (PA)	3429	F	916 648-9200	11572
Beauty Craft Furniture Corp	2511	E	916 428-2238	4553
Bellaterra Home LLC	2434	F	916 896-3188	4168
Bennetts Baking Company	2053	F	916 481-3349	1338
Berkeley Farms LLC	2026	E	916 689-7613	686
Bimbo Bakeries Usa Inc	2051	E	916 681-8069	1151
Bimbo Bakeries Usa Inc	2051	A	916 732-4733	1152
Bimbo Bakeries Usa Inc	2051	E	916 922-1307	1164
Blomberg Building Materials (PA)	3442	D	916 428-8060	11938
Blomberg Windows Systems	3231	C	916 428-8060	10343
Blue Diamond Growers	2099	C	916 446-8464	2407
C & Gtool Inc	3545	F	916 614-9114	14142
California Cab & Store Fix	2431	E	916 386-1340	4007
California Cascade Industries	2491	C	916 736-3353	4472
California Pro-Specs Inc	2426	F	916 455-9890	3971
California Surveying & Draftin (PA)	3577	E	916 344-0232	15184
Califrnia Mantel Fireplace Inc (PA)	2431	F	916 925-5775	4012
Camelia City Millwork Inc	2431	F	916 451-2454	4013
Capital Corrugated LLC	2653	D	916 388-7848	5205
Capitol Beverage Packers	2086	D	916 929-7777	2051
Capitol Iron Works Inc	3441	F	916 381-1554	11760
Capitol Neon	3993	F	916 349-1800	23072
Capitol Steel Products	3291	F	916 383-3368	10942
Capitol Store Fixtures	2521	E	916 646-9096	4788
Carbonyte Systems Incorporated	2851	F	916 387-0316	8629
Cemex Cnstr Mtls PCF LLC	3273	E	916 364-2470	10718
Cemex Cnstr Mtls PCF LLC	3273	F	916 383-0526	10721
Chico Community Publishing	2711	D	916 498-1234	5587

	SIC	EMP	PHONE	ENTRY #
Clarus Lighting LLC	3648	F	916 363-2888	17111
Class A Powdercoat Inc	3479	E	916 681-7474	13158
Clayton Homes Inc	2451	F	916 363-2681	4441
Coffee Works Inc	2095	F	916 452-1086	2285
Colormarx Corporation	2752	F	916 334-0334	6500
Composite Technology Intl Inc	2431	E	916 551-1850	4020
Comstock Publishing Inc	2721	F	916 364-1000	5909
Creo Inc	2759	F	530 756-1477	7040
Crystal Bottling Company Inc	2086	D	916 568-3300	2066
Crystal Cream & Butter Co (HQ)	2026	F	916 444-7200	692
D & T Fiberglass Inc	3089	F	916 383-9012	9743
Daily Recorder	2711	F	916 444-2355	5610
Danoc Manufacturing Corp Inc	2337	F	916 455-2876	3264
Davison Iron Works Inc	3441	E	916 381-2121	11783
Delta Lath & Plaster Inc	3541	E	916 383-6756	13912
Dhm Enterprises Inc	3799	E	916 688-7767	20507
Dorris Lumber and Moulding Co (PA)	2431	C	916 452-7531	4038
Duralum Products Inc (PA)	3355	F	916 452-7021	11258
Ebara Technologies Inc (DH)	3563	E	916 920-5451	14630
Eg Wear Inc	3999	F	916 361-1508	23325
Eggleston Signs	3993	F	916 920-1750	23095
El Dorado Newspapers Inc (DH)	2711	C	916 321-1826	5627
Elevator Industries Inc	3534	F	916 921-1495	13798
Elite Ready-Mix LLC	3273	E	916 366-4627	10755
Elite Service Experts Inc (PA)	3559	F	916 275-3956	14458
Ellensburg Lamb Company Inc (HQ)	2011	F	530 758-3091	407
Elliott Company	3561	D	916 920-5451	14570
Ernest Packaging Solutions	2819	E	800 486-7222	7495
Ethosenergy Pwr Plant Svcs LLC	1389	E	916 391-2993	196
Evoqua Water Technologies LLC	3589	F	916 564-1222	15513
Farmers Rice Cooperative (PA)	2044	E	916 923-5100	1040
Farmers Rice Cooperative	2044	E	916 373-5549	1041
Fong Fong Prtrs Lthgrphers Inc	2752	E	916 739-1313	6578
Forterra Pipe & Precast LLC	3272	D	916 379-9695	10577
Freeport Bakery Inc	2051	E	916 442-4256	1206
Fremont Package Express	3537	F	916 541-1812	13872
Fresno Precision Plastics Inc	3089	E	916 689-5284	9796
Fruitridge Prtg Lithograph Inc (PA)	2752	E	916 452-9213	6586
Full Color Business	2752	F	916 218-7845	6587
Gazette Media Co LLC	2711	F	916 567-9654	5643
General Dynmics Mssion Systems	3571	C	916 339-3852	14914
Geo Drilling Fluids Inc	3295	E	916 383-2811	10971
Gh Foods Ca LLC (DH)	2099	B	916 844-1140	2467
Golden State Fire Appratus Inc	3711	E	916 330-1638	19473
Golden West Packg Group LLC (PA)	2653	B	404 345-8365	5230
Gsl Fine Lithographers	2752	E	916 231-1410	6599
Gunthers Quality Ice Cream	2024	F	916 457-3339	647
Hand Biomechanics Lab Inc	3842	F	916 923-5073	22020
Hansen Haulers Inc	3599	F	916 443-7755	16016
Helen Noble	2721	F	916 457-8990	5953
Hni Corporation	2522	B	916 927-0400	4840
HP Hood LLC	2026	B	916 379-9266	703
Hrh Door Corp	3442	F	916 928-0600	11958
Huhtamaki Inc	2655	F	916 688-4938	5297
Illuminated Creations Inc	3993	E	916 924-1936	23130
Immuno Concepts Inc	3841	E	916 363-2649	21740
Imperial Die Cutting Inc	2675	F	916 443-6142	5448
Intake Screens Inc	3496	F	916 665-2727	13417
Intelmail USA Inc	3579	F	916 361-9300	15383
Intermag Inc	3695	C	916 568-6744	19220
Interpress Technologies Inc (HQ)	2631	E	916 929-9771	5165
Ips Printing Inc	2752	E	916 442-8961	6652
Ittavi Inc	7372	E	866 246-4408	24051
ITW Blding Cmponents Group Inc	3443	E	916 387-0116	12022
James Frasinetti & Sons	2084	E	916 383-2447	1770
Jampro Antennas Inc	3663	D	916 383-1177	17546
Jenkins Beverage Inc	3585	F	916 686-1800	15436
John Boyd Enterprises Inc	3714	C	916 504-3622	19695
John Boyd Enterprises Inc (PA)	3714	C	916 504-3622	19696
Johnson Controls	3669	D	916 283-0300	17738
Johnson Industrial Sheet Metal	3444	F	916 927-8244	12256
Katz & Klein	3851	E	916 444-2024	22365
Kds Nail Products	3999	F	916 381-9358	23380
Kitchens Now Inc	2434	F	916 229-8222	4218
Kratos Unmanned Aerial Systems	3089	B	916 431-7977	9870
L3 Technologies Inc	3571	D	916 363-6581	14936
Langills General Machine Inc	3599	E	916 452-0167	16135
Laser Recharge Inc (PA)	3955	F	916 737-6360	22966
Legacy Vulcan LLC	3273	F	916 682-0850	10789
Lifeline SEC & Automtn Inc	3699	D	916 285-9078	19346
Lpa Insurance Agency Inc	7372	D	916 286-7850	24111
Mailrite Print & Mail Inc	2752	E	916 927-6245	6712
Martin Sprocket & Gear Inc	3566	E	916 441-7172	14745
Mary Anns Baking Co Inc	2051	C	916 681-7444	1240
Matterhorn Ice Cream Inc	2024	D	208 287-8916	658

Mergent email: customerrelations@mergent.com
1398

2020 California
Manufacturers Register

(P-0000) Products & Services Section entry number
(PA)=Parent Co (HQ)=Headquarters (DH)=Div Headquarters

Company	SIC	EMP	PHONE	ENTRY #
McCarthys Draperies Inc	2391	E	916 422-0155	3593
McClatchy Company (PA)	2711	C	916 321-1844	5727
McClatchy Newspapers Inc (HQ)	2711	A	916 321-1855	5728
Meditab Software Inc	7372	F	510 673-1838	24143
Mencarini & Jarwin Inc	3471	F	916 383-1660	13048
Merchants Metals LLC	3496	E	916 381-8243	13422
Mesotech International Inc	3826	F	916 368-2020	21261
Messer LLC	2813	E	916 381-1606	7424
Metal Manufacturing Co Inc	3442	E	916 922-3484	11969
Microform Precision LLC	3444	D	916 419-0580	12301
Microsoft Corporation	7372	E	916 369-3600	24158
Milgard Manufacturing Inc	3442	C	916 387-0700	11971
Mitsubishi Chemical Crbn Fbr (DH)	3624	C	916 386-1733	16688
MNC Bliss Enterprises Inc	3648	F	916 483-1167	17145
Mova Stone Inc	3281	E	916 922-2080	10916
Mpj Recycling LLC	3559	F	916 761-5740	14502
Mw McWong International Inc	3648	F	916 371-8080	17146
New Direction Silk Screen	2759	F	916 971-3939	7148
New Generation Software Inc	7372	F	916 920-2200	24203
New Image Foam Products LLC	3086	E	916 388-0741	9558
Newbold Cleaners	3582	F	916 481-1130	15405
Next Level Warehouse Solutions	3535	F	916 922-7225	13829
Nivagen Pharmaceuticals Inc	2834	E	916 364-1662	8040
Norquist Salvage Corp Inc	2329	E	916 454-0435	3109
Norquist Salvage Corp Inc	2329	E	916 922-9942	3110
North Area News (PA)	2711	F	916 486-1248	5780
Northern Cal Pet Imaging Ctr	3844	F	916 737-3211	22218
Olympic Cascade Publishing (DH)	2711	F	916 321-1000	5788
Omega Products Corp (HQ)	3299	D	916 635-3335	11015
Ortech Inc	3253	E	916 549-9696	10448
Outreach Slutions As A Svc LLC	2741	F	800 824-8573	6304
Outword News Magazine	2711	E	916 329-9280	5789
Pabco Clay Products LLC	3251	D	916 859-6320	10436
Pacific Ethanol Central LLC (HQ)	2869	D	916 403-2123	8760
Pacific Ethanol West LLC	2869	C	916 403-2123	8761
Pacific Neon	3993	E	916 927-0527	23175
Pacific Northwest Pubg Co Inc	2711	B	916 321-1828	5791
Pacific Pallet Exchange Inc	2448	E	916 448-5589	4385
Pacific Powder Coating Inc	3479	E	916 381-1154	13220
Pacific Truck Tank Inc	3713	E	916 379-9280	19550
Pecofacet (us) Inc	3569	F	916 689-2328	14849
Pepsi-Cola Metro Btlg Co Inc	2086	B	916 423-1000	2114
Pettigrew & Sons Casket Co	3995	E	916 383-0777	23251
Philip A Stitt Agency	2394	F	916 451-2801	3699
Pk1 Inc (HQ)	2653	D	916 858-1300	5258
Poolmaster Inc	3944	D	916 567-9800	22706
Pos Portal Inc (HQ)	3578	E	530 695-3005	15377
Procter & Gamble Mfg Co	2841	C	916 383-3800	8348
Propel Biofuels Inc (PA)	2869	F	800 871-0773	8765
Purolator Advanced Filtration	3569	E	916 689-2328	14853
Quikrete Companies LLC	3272	E	510 490-4670	10635
Raymar Information Tech Inc (PA)	3661	F	916 783-1951	17407
Raynguard Protective Mtls Inc	2891	F	916 454-2560	8890
Reed & Graham Inc	2951	E	888 381-0800	9104
Reflectech Inc	2842	F	916 388-7821	8413
River City Millwork Inc	2431	E	916 364-8981	4117
River City Printers Inc	2752	E	916 638-8400	6846
RR Donnelley & Sons Company	2761	F	916 929-8632	7284
S & H Welding Inc	3443	F	916 386-8921	12048
S M G Custom Cabinets Inc	2434	F	916 381-5999	4243
Sac Valley Ornamental Ir Outl	3315	F	916 383-6340	11106
Sacramental Color Coil	2789	E	916 383-9588	7347
Sacramento Baking Co Inc	2051	E	916 361-2000	1271
Sacramento Coca-Cola Btlg Inc (HQ)	2086	B	916 928-2300	2163
Sale 121 Corp (PA)	3572	D	888 233-7667	15087
Setzer Forest Products Inc (PA)	2431	C	916 442-2555	4122
Seven Up Btlg Co San Francisco	2086	D	916 929-7777	2169
Sheet Mtl Fabrication Sup Inc	3444	D	916 641-6884	12376
Siemens Industry Inc	3822	C	916 681-3000	20815
Sierra Office Systems Pdts Inc (PA)	2752	D	916 369-0491	6862
Silver Eagle Corporation	2392	E	916 925-6843	3641
Solar Industries Inc	3433	E	916 567-9650	11715
Solaron Pool Heating Inc (PA)	3569	F	916 858-8146	14859
SRC Milling Co LLC	2077	E	916 363-4821	1466
Stanford Furniture Mfg Inc	2599	E	916 387-5300	5083
State Hornet	2711	D	916 278-6583	5841
Sulzer Pump Solutions US Inc	3561	E	916 925-8508	14599
Tacoma News Inc (DH)	2711	B	916 321-1846	5844
Taylor Communications Inc	2761	F	916 927-1891	7287
Teeco Products Inc	3714	E	916 688-3535	19779
Teichert Inc (PA)	3273	C	916 484-3011	10856
Televic Us Corp	3651	F	916 920-0900	17292
Thermcraft Inc	2759	F	916 363-9411	7249
Time Prtg Solutions Provider	2752	F	916 446-6152	6890
Tmp LLC	3442	E	916 920-2555	11987
TNT Industrial Contractors Inc (PA)	3531	E	916 395-8400	13752
Toms Printing Inc	2752	F	916 444-7788	6892
Tri Quality Inc	3842	E	916 388-5939	22112
Ultra Glass	3231	F	916 338-3911	10398
Valley Community Newspaper	2711	F	916 429-9901	5856
Vampire Penguin LLC (PA)	2024	F	916 553-4197	675
Veterans Employment Agency Inc	3281	F	650 245-0599	10938
Vortran Laser Technology Inc	3699	F	916 283-8208	19438
Vortran Medical Technology 1 (PA)	3841	E	916 648-8460	21959
Washoe Equipment Inc	3645	E	916 395-4700	17000
Water Resources Cal Dept	3823	D	916 651-9203	20957
WE Hall Company Inc	3272	F	916 383-4891	10668
Westrock Cp LLC	2631	E	916 379-2200	5182
Wickland Pipelines LLC (PA)	1382	F	916 978-2432	148
Wikoff Color Corporation	2893	F	916 928-6965	8938
World Textile and Bag Inc	2393	E	916 922-9222	3669
Wsglass Holdings Inc	3827	F	916 388-5885	21422
Young Electric Sign Company	3993	E	916 419-8101	23247

SAINT HELENA, CA - Napa County

Company	SIC	EMP	PHONE	ENTRY #
7 & 8 LLC	2084	F	707 963-9425	1575
Alpha Omega Winery LLC	2084	F	707 963-9999	1581
Brown Estate Vineyard LLC	2084	F	707 963-2435	1608
Burgess Cellars Inc	2084	F	707 963-4766	1611
C Mondavi & Family (PA)	2084	D	707 967-2200	1613
Cain Cellars Inc	2084	F	707 963-1616	1615
Chappellet Vineyard	2084	F	707 286-4219	1628
Chappellet Winery Inc (PA)	2084	F	707 286-4268	1629
Chateau Potelle Holdings LLC	2084	F	707 255-9440	1634
Duckhorn Wine Company (HQ)	2084	F	707 963-7108	1674
E & J Gallo Winery	2084	F	707 963-2736	1686
Fanuccicharter Oak Winery	2084	F	707 963-2298	1697
Flora Springs Wine Company	2084	F	707 963-5711	1705
Franciscan Vineyards Inc (PA)	2084	D	707 963-7111	1712
Freemark Abbey Wnery Ltd Prtnr	2084	F	707 963-9694	1715
Gandona Inc A California Corp	2084	F	707 967-5550	1719
Hall Wines LLC	2084	F	707 967-2626	1743
Herdell Printing & Lithography	2752	F	707 963-3634	6610
Merryvale Vineyards LLC	2084	F	707 963-2225	1817
Newton Vineyard LLC (DH)	2084	F	707 963-9000	1839
Provenance Vineyards	2084	F	707 968-3633	1872
Red River Lumber Co	2449	E	707 963-1251	4425
Rombauer Vineyards Inc (PA)	2084	D	707 963-5170	1896
Ronald F Ogletree Inc	3444	E	707 963-3537	12358
Round Hill Cellars	2084	D	707 968-3200	1899
Seavey Vineyard Ltd Partnr	2084	F	707 963-8339	1909
Spring Mountain Vineyards Inc	2084	F	707 967-4188	1925
Stone Bridge Cellars Inc (PA)	2084	D	707 963-2745	1936
Sutter Home Winery Inc (PA)	2084	C	707 963-3104	1941
Thomas Leonardini	2084	F	707 963-9454	1955
Tmr Wine Company	2084	F	707 944-8100	1958
Treasury Wine Estates Americas	2084	D	707 963-7115	1965
Treasury Wine Estates Americas	2084	B	707 963-4812	1966
Treasury Wine Estates Americas	2084	D	707 963-7115	1969
Trinchero Family Estates Inc	2084	F	707 963-1160	1971
Turley Wine Cellars Inc	2084	F	707 968-2700	1975
Vineyard 29 LLC	2084	F	707 963-9292	1988
Wheeler Winery Inc	2084	E	415 979-0630	1998

SALIDA, CA - Stanislaus County

Company	SIC	EMP	PHONE	ENTRY #
Flory Industries	3523	D	209 545-1167	13633
Inventive Resources Inc	3444	F	209 545-1663	12250

SALINAS, CA - Monterey County

Company	SIC	EMP	PHONE	ENTRY #
A&G Machine Shop Inc	3599	F	831 759-2261	15664
Abrams Electronics Inc	3643	F	831 758-6400	16872
Aggrigator Inc	7372	F	650 245-5117	23579
All American Fabrication	3999	F	831 676-3490	23268
Alsop Pump	7694	F	831 424-3946	24682
Associated Rebar Inc	3441	E	831 758-1820	11745
Bindel Bros Grading &	3531	F	831 754-1490	13709
Bookette Software Co Inc	7372	F	831 484-9250	23687
California Kit Cab Door Corp	2431	C	831 784-5142	4010
Copymat Salinas LLC	2752	F	831 753-0471	6514
County of Monterey	2759	F	831 755-4790	7038
Cyberware Laboratory Inc	3823	F	831 484-1064	20854
Dales Welding Inc	3523	F	831 424-6583	13623
Delta Ironworks Inc	3446	F	831 663-1190	12468
El Camino Machine & Wldg LLC (PA)	3599	F	831 758-8309	15924
Five Star Lumber Company LLC	2448	E	831 422-4493	4366
Fresh Express Incorporated	2099	E	831 424-2921	2465
Green Rubber-Kennedy Ag LP (PA)	3086	E	831 753-6100	9548
Growers Ice Co	2097	E	831 424-5781	2356
Hollister Landscape Supply Inc (HQ)	3273	F	831 443-8644	10773
International Paper Company	2621	F	831 755-2100	5122
Lifeline Systems Company	3669	C	831 755-0788	17742

Employment Codes: A=Over 500 employees, B=251-500,
C=101-250, D=51-100, E=20-50, F=10-19

2020 California
Manufacturers Register

© Mergent Inc. 1-800-342-5647
1399

GEOGRAPHIC

	SIC	EMP	PHONE	ENTRY #
Magnetic Circuit Elements Inc	3679	E	831 757-8752	19001
McCormick & Company Inc	2099	D	831 775-3350	2547
McCormick & Company Inc	2099	C	831 758-2411	2548
Merrill Corporation	2759	F	831 759-9300	7138
Monterey Coast Brewing LLC	3556	F	831 758-2337	14387
Morgan Winery Inc (PA)	2084	F	831 751-7777	1825
Next Pharmaceuticals Inc	2834	E	831 621-8712	8036
Organicgirl LLC	2099	A	831 758-7800	2578
Pepsi-Cola Metro Btlg Co Inc	2086	C	831 796-2000	2119
Pro Pack Systems Inc	3565	F	831 771-1300	14724
Progressive Packg Group Inc (PA)	2653	E	831 424-2942	5261
Reyes Coca-Cola Bottling LLC	2086	D	831 755-8300	2145
Salinas Newspapers LLC	2711	C	831 424-2221	5813
Salinas Tallow Co Inc	2077	E	831 422-6436	1465
Salinas Valley Wax Paper Co	2679	E	831 424-2747	5528
Sierra Natural Science Inc	2869	F	831 757-1702	8774
Smartwash Solutions LLC (HQ)	2819	F	831 676-9750	7526
SMS Industrial Inc	3443	F	831 337-4271	12052
Star Sanitation Services	3089	F	831 754-6794	10069
Tailgater Inc	3792	F	831 424-7710	20494
Transfirst Corporation	3822	E	831 424-2911	20817
Uv Landscaping LLC	3271	F	831 275-5296	10522
Valley Fabrication Inc	3523	D	831 757-5151	13679
Vans Inc	3021	F	831 444-0158	9187
Westrock Cp LLC	2653	C	831 424-1831	5274

SAMOA, CA - Humboldt County

	SIC	EMP	PHONE	ENTRY #
Western Web Inc	2752	E	707 444-6236	6936

SAN ANDREAS, CA - Calaveras County

	SIC	EMP	PHONE	ENTRY #
Calaveras First Co Inc	2711	E	209 754-3861	5574
Krisalis Inc	3599	F	209 286-1637	16125

SAN ANSELMO, CA - Marin County

	SIC	EMP	PHONE	ENTRY #
V-A Optical Company Inc	3827	F	415 459-1919	21417

SAN BERNARDINO, CA - San Bernardino County

	SIC	EMP	PHONE	ENTRY #
Adams and Brooks Inc	2064	D	213 392-8700	1354
Alexanders Textile Pdts Inc	2389	F	951 276-2500	3537
All Sports Services Inc	2759	F	909 885-4626	6980
Aluminum Seating Inc	2531	F	909 884-9449	4853
American Wire Inc	3496	F	909 884-9990	13394
Anco International Inc	3494	E	909 887-2521	13346
Anitas Mexican Foods Corp (PA)	2096	C	909 884-8706	2317
Ardent Mills LLC	2041	E	909 887-3407	996
Blackcoffee Fabricators Inc	3993	F	909 974-4499	23061
Blacklion Enterprises Inc (PA)	3446	F	951 328-0400	12456
C-Pak Industries Inc	3089	F	909 880-6017	9681
Caesar Hardware Intl Ltd	3999	F	800 306-3829	23291
Container Options Inc	3089	F	909 478-0045	9724
D&W Fine Pack LLC	3089	C	206 767-7777	9745
Dateline Products LLC	2511	F	909 888-9785	4564
Dean Distributors Inc	2099	E	323 587-8147	2440
Die-Namic Fabrication Inc	3469	F	909 350-2870	12794
Dynamic Bindery Inc	2789	F	909 884-1296	7330
Farmdale Creamery Inc	2026	D	909 888-4938	698
Fenix Space Inc	3761	F	909 382-5677	20446
Foamex LP	3086	F	909 824-8981	9538
Global Environmental Pdts Inc	3711	D	909 713-1600	19472
Ground Hog Inc	3531	F	909 478-5700	13733
Hayden Products LLC	3443	D	951 736-2600	12020
Hospitality Sleep Systems Inc	2515	F	909 387-9779	4722
Inland Empire Cmnty Newspapers	2711	E	909 381-9898	5673
Innocor West LLC	3069	E	909 307-3737	9322
Innovative Metal Inds Inc	3449	D	909 796-6200	12592
Jon Steel Erectors Inc	7692	E	909 799-0005	24646
Juice Heads Inc	2033	F	909 386-7933	780
Kav America Ag Inc	2095	E	855 528-8721	2302
Kendra Group Inc	3669	F	909 473-7206	17740
Kmb Foods Inc (PA)	2013	E	626 447-0545	473
Kohler Co	3431	E	909 890-4291	11648
Lane Winpak Inc (HQ)	3565	D	909 386-1762	14715
Las Cuatros Milpas	2051	F	909 885-3344	1229
Legacy Vulcan LLC	1442	E	909 875-1150	348
Legend Pump & Well Service Inc	1381	E	909 384-1000	98
Leitz Tooling Systems LP	3541	E	909 799-8494	13930
Lifetime Camper Shells Inc	3792	E	909 885-2814	20488
M & L Pharmaceuticals Inc	2834	F	909 890-0078	7999
M D Software Inc	7372	F	909 881-7599	24116
Macroair Technologies Inc (PA)	3564	E	909 890-2270	14669
Magnum Abrasives Inc	3291	E	909 890-1100	10949
Mapei Corporation	2821	E	909 475-4100	7581
Mars Petcare Us Inc	2047	E	909 887-8131	1077
Mattel Inc	3944	F	909 382-3780	22692
McIntire Tool Die & Machine (PA)	3469	F	909 888-0440	12842
Millers American Honey Inc	2099	E	909 825-1722	2551
Mkkr Inc	3545	F	909 890-5994	14175

	SIC	EMP	PHONE	ENTRY #
Nagles Veal Inc	2011	E	909 383-7075	419
Nitro 2 Go Inc	2833	E	909 864-4886	7678
Ocean Blue Inc	3086	E	909 478-9910	9559
On Press Printing Service Inc	2752	F	909 799-9599	6759
Optivus Proton Therapy Inc	3829	D	909 799-8300	21513
Paramount Windows & Doors	2431	F	909 888-4688	4105
Park West Enterprises	2077	E	909 383-8341	1464
Patio Paradise Inc	3645	F	626 715-4869	16985
Precinct Reporter	2711	F	909 889-0597	5802
Quiel Bros Elc Sign Svc Co Inc	3993	E	909 885-4476	23181
R & R Machine Products Inc	3451	F	909 885-7500	12649
Reagent Chemical & RES Inc	2819	E	909 796-4059	7521
Refresco Beverages US Inc	2086	D	909 915-1400	2132
Refresco Beverages US Inc	2086	E	909 915-1430	2133
Rlt Seafood Supermarket Inc	2091	E	909 888-6520	2249
Romeros Food Products Inc	2099	E	909 884-5531	2604
San Brnrdino Cmnty College Dst	2759	C	909 888-6511	7207
Semco	3829	E	909 799-9666	21534
Shorett Printing Inc (PA)	2759	E	714 545-4689	7212
Shorett Printing Inc	2752	F	714 956-9001	6861
Soltech Solar Inc	3511	F	909 890-2282	13580
Stavatti Industries Ltd	1041	D	651 238-5369	8
Sun Company San Bernardino Cal (PA)	2711	B	909 889-9666	5842
Sun Company San Bernardino Cal	2911	C	909 889-9666	9073
Sunwest Printing Inc	2759	F	909 890-3898	7233
Systems Technology Inc	3565	D	909 799-9950	14728
T M Cobb Company	2541	C	909 796-6969	4946
Tgs Molding LLC	3089	F	909 890-1707	10082
Thermal Solutions Mfg Inc	3714	E	909 796-0754	19782
Trinity Office Furniture Inc	2521	F	909 888-5551	4823
United Cabinet Company Inc	2434	E	909 796-3015	4258
United States Mineral Pdts Co	3296	D	909 473-6993	10989
United Uniform Mfrs Inc	2321	F	909 381-2682	2996
WBwalton Enterprises Inc	3663	E	951 683-0930	17704

SAN BRUNO, CA - San Mateo County

	SIC	EMP	PHONE	ENTRY #
Infrastructureworld LLC	3826	E	650 871-3950	21246
Kuna Systems Corporation	3571	F	650 263-8257	14935
Locix Inc	3625	F	650 231-2180	16731
Qumu Inc (HQ)	7372	D	650 396-8530	24336

SAN CARLOS, CA - San Mateo County

	SIC	EMP	PHONE	ENTRY #
Advanced Adbag Packaging Inc	2673	F	650 591-1625	5382
Alliance Memory Inc	3674	F	650 610-6800	18080
Alpine Biomed Corp	3841	C	650 802-0400	21593
Apex Die Corporation	2675	D	650 592-6350	5446
Apexigen Inc	2834	E	650 931-6236	7761
Ardax Systems Inc	3663	F	650 591-2656	17458
B & H Technical Ceramics Inc	3599	F	650 637-1171	15765
Begovic Industries Inc	3599	F	650 594-2861	15782
Brew4u LLC	2082	F	415 516-8211	1505
Brown Wood Products Inc	2449	E	650 593-9875	4413
Carevault Corporation	7372	F	714 333-0556	23717
Check Point Software Tech Inc (HQ)	7372	C	650 628-2000	23733
Concepts & Methods Co Inc	3567	F	650 593-1064	14758
Dishcraft Robotics Inc	3559	F	415 595-9671	14452
Education Elements Inc	7372	F	650 336-0660	23844
EH Suda Inc (PA)	3599	F	650 622-9700	15921
Ergodirect Inc	2522	F	650 654-4300	4834
Fable Inc	3446	F	650 598-9616	12473
Fabtron	3599	F	650 622-9700	15950
House of Bagels Inc (PA)	2051	F	650 595-4700	1226
Hy-Tech Plating Inc	3471	E	650 593-4566	13027
Incelldx Inc	3841	F	650 777-7630	21743
Iovance Biotherapeutics Inc (PA)	2834	E	650 260-7120	7963
J & L Digital Precision Inc	3679	E	650 592-0170	18955
Jerry Carroll Machinery Inc	3599	F	650 591-3302	16081
Kelly-Moore Paint Company Inc (PA)	2851	C	650 592-8337	8649
Kelly-Moore Paint Company Inc	2851	E	650 595-0333	8651
Kinetic Farm Inc	7372	F	650 503-3279	24077
L & M Electronics	3674	F	650 341-1608	18338
Lumascape USA Inc	3646	F	650 595-5862	17054
M S F Inc	2542	F	650 592-0239	4987
Magnitude Electronics LLC	3679	F	650 551-1850	19004
Marble City Company Inc	3281	F	650 802-8189	10914
Meskin Khosrow Kay	3172	F	650 595-3090	10241
Mylan Pharmaceuticals Inc	2834	D	650 631-3100	8019
Natus Medical Incorporated	3845	C	303 962-1800	22284
Nektar Therapeutics	2834	E	650 622-1790	8029
Nxedge San Carlos LLC	3674	F	650 422-2269	18440
Pacful Inc	2752	D	650 200-4252	6764
Pacific Weaving Corporation	2211	E	650 592-9434	2707
Pencom Accuracy Inc	3451	D	510 785-5022	12646
Penta Biotech Inc	2869	F	650 598-9328	8762
Performex Machining Inc	3599	E	650 595-2228	16296
Pionetics Corporation	3089	F	650 551-0250	9960

2020 California
Manufacturers Register

(P-0000) Products & Services Section entry number
(PA)=Parent Co (HQ)=Headquarters (DH)=Div Headquarters

	SIC	EMP	PHONE	ENTRY #
Precision Design Inc	3672	E	650 508-8041	17961
Provence Stone	3281	F	650 631-5600	10923
Revjet	7372	C	650 508-2215	24359
Royalite Mfg Inc (PA)	3444	F	650 637-1440	12360
Service Press Inc	2752	F	650 592-3484	6859
Svetwheel LLC	3827	F	650 245-6080	21414
Tech Air Northern Cal LLC	2813	E	650 593-9353	7455
Telecommunications Engrg Assoc	3663	F	650 590-1801	17683
Valence Surface Tech LLC	3812	E	323 770-0240	20740

SAN CLEMENTE, CA - Orange County

	SIC	EMP	PHONE	ENTRY #
American Chain & Gear Company	3566	F	323 581-9131	14738
American Qualex Inc	3229	F	949 492-8298	10297
American Qualex International	2899	F	949 492-8298	8942
Atomic Monkey Industries Inc	2396	F	949 415-8846	3772
Azimuth Electronics Inc	3825	F	949 492-6481	21008
Bionorica LLC	2834	F	949 361-4900	7810
BT Sheet Metal Inc	3444	F	949 481-5715	12137
Buldoor LLC	3429	F	877 388-1366	11574
Bunker Corp (PA)	3714	D	949 361-3935	19599
Capistrano Labs Inc	3841	E	949 492-0390	21650
Catch Surfboard Co LLC	3949	F	949 218-0428	22778
Clean Wave Management Inc	3721	E	949 488-2922	19888
Clean Wave Management Inc	3562	E	949 361-5356	14609
Code-In-Motion LLC	3569	F	949 361-2633	14806
Composite Manufacturing Inc	3841	E	949 361-7580	21669
Dana Innovations	3651	D	949 492-7777	17216
Dose Medical Corporation	3841	F	949 367-9600	21690
Dragon Alliance Inc	3851	E	760 931-4900	22349
Electric Visual Evolution LLC (PA)	3851	E	949 940-9125	22351
Elevate Inc	7372	E	949 276-5428	23853
Epica Medical Innovations LLC	3841	E	949 238-6323	21706
Flavorchem Corporation	2087	E	949 369-7900	2210
Flow Sports Inc (PA)	3949	E	949 361-5260	22802
Four Star Distribution	3021	D	949 369-4420	9171
Glaukos Corporation (PA)	3841	C	949 367-9600	21724
Gps Logic LLC	3663	F	949 812-6942	17525
H I S C Inc	3229	F	949 492-8968	10309
Hot Shoppe Designs Inc	2329	F	949 487-2828	3088
Icu Medical Inc (PA)	3841	B	949 366-2183	21738
Icu Medical Sales Inc (HQ)	3841	F	949 366-2183	21739
Innovative Earth Products	3949	F	888 588-5955	22828
Innovative Rv Technologies	1389	E	949 559-5372	212
International Rubber Pdts Inc (PA)	3069	D	909 947-1244	9323
Kelcourt Plastics Inc (DH)	3082	D	949 361-0774	9430
Kui Co Inc	2621	E	949 369-7949	5130
Left Coast Brewing Company	2082	F	949 218-3961	1542
Model Match Inc	7372	E	949 525-9405	24178
Mvm Products LLC	3861	D	949 366-1470	22444
Nationwide Printing Svcs Inc	2759	F	714 258-7899	7146
Pacific Composites Inc	3324	F	949 498-8600	11166
Plastics Development Corp	3089	E	949 492-0217	9973
R & R Industries Inc	2389	F	949 361-9238	3575
R T C Group	2721	E	949 226-2000	6011
Reshape Lifesciences Inc (PA)	3845	D	949 429-6680	22302
Reynard Corporation	3827	F	949 366-8866	21402
Roberto Martinez Inc	3911	F	800 257-6462	22565
Roman Global Resources Inc	3053	F	949 276-4100	9251
Rosen & Rosen Industries Inc	3949	D	949 361-9238	22876
Rox Medical Inc (PA)	3845	E	949 276-8968	22306
Sensory Neurostimulation Inc	2834	F	949 492-0550	8124
Shoreline Products Inc	3965	F	949 388-1919	23008
Snowpure LLC	3589	E	949 240-2188	15579
Space Jam Juice LLC	2111	D	714 660-7467	2656
Srsb Inc	7372	F	949 234-1881	24447
Streuter Technologies	3272	E	949 369-7630	10658
Surf More Products Inc	3949	E	949 492-0753	22903
Systems Upgrade Inc	3572	F	949 429-8900	15107
Toolander Engineering Inc	3469	F	949 498-8339	12882
Traffix Devices Inc (PA)	3669	F	949 361-5663	17769
Try All 3 Sports	3751	F	949 492-2255	20433
Verrix LLC	3841	F	949 668-1234	21953
Versicolor Inc	3552	F	949 361-9698	14296
Western Outdoors Publications (PA)	2711	E	949 366-0030	5864
Woodcrafters International	2541	F	949 498-0739	4956

SAN DIEGO, CA - San Diego County

	SIC	EMP	PHONE	ENTRY #
2j Antennas USA	3663	F	858 866-1072	17433
3d Systems Inc	3571	F	803 280-7777	14875
5 I Sciences Inc	3841	F	858 943-4566	21568
5th Axis Inc	3599	D	858 505-0432	15648
A Thanks Million Inc	2361	F	858 432-7744	3472
Abzena (san Diego) Inc	2836	F	858 550-4094	8266
Acadia Pharmaceuticals Inc (PA)	2834	B	858 558-2871	7717
Accel-Rf Corporation	3825	F	858 278-2074	20981
Acces I/O Products Inc	3577	F	858 550-9559	15140

	SIC	EMP	PHONE	ENTRY #
Accriva Dgnostics Holdings Inc (DH)	3841	B	858 404-8203	21578
Actavalon Inc	2834	F	949 244-5684	7721
Activeon Inc (PA)	3651	F	858 798-3300	17182
Aculon Inc	2869	F	858 350-9474	8704
Adamis Pharmaceuticals Corp (PA)	2834	F	858 997-2400	7726
Adhara Inc	3471	F	619 661-9901	12904
Advanced Electromagnetics Inc	3823	F	619 449-9492	20828
Advanced Hpc Inc	3572	F	858 716-8262	15001
Advanced Intl Tech LLC	3599	F	858 566-2945	15696
Advanced Lighting Concepts Inc	3646	F	888 880-1880	17008
Advanced Metal Forming Inc	3441	F	619 239-9437	11736
Advanced Refractive Tech	3841	F	949 940-1300	21583
Aem (holdings) Inc	3613	D	858 481-0210	16584
Aem Electronics (usa) Inc	3677	E	858 481-0210	18696
Affymetrix Inc	3826	C	858 642-2058	21163
Agouron Pharmaceuticals Inc (HQ)	2834	E	858 622-3000	7731
Air & Gas Tech Inc	3732	E	619 557-8373	20311
Air-Trak	3663	F	858 677-9950	17441
Airgain Inc (PA)	3663	C	760 579-0200	17442
Al Shellco LLC (HQ)	3651	C	570 296-6444	17185
Alere Connect LLC	3845	E	888 876-3327	22227
Alere San Diego Inc	2835	A	858 455-4808	8202
All Energy Inc	3648	F	619 988-7030	17099
All Source Coatings Inc	3479	F	858 586-0903	13140
Alliance Air Products Llc	3585	C	619 428-9688	15410
Alliance Tags	2759	E	858 549-7297	6983
Alor International Ltd	3911	E	858 454-0011	22491
Alphacoat Finishing LLC	3471	E	949 748-7796	12921
Althea Ajinomoto Inc	3841	C	858 882-0123	21594
Ambit Biosciences Corporation	2834	D	858 334-2100	7746
Amcan Usa LLC	3572	F	858 587-1032	15003
Ameditech Inc	3841	C	858 535-1968	21597
American Garage Decor Inc	3089	F	760 975-9148	9624
Ametek Programmable Power Inc (HQ)	3825	C	858 450-0085	21002
Amex Manufacturing Inc	3446	F	619 391-7412	12450
Amkor Technology Inc	3674	D	858 320-6280	18095
Amobee Inc	3823	F	858 638-1515	20833
Amylin Pharmaceuticals LLC	2834	D	858 552-2200	7755
Ana Global LLC	2517	A	619 482-9990	4752
Anderson Desk Inc	2521	B	619 671-1040	4783
Anheuser-Busch LLC	2082	A	858 581-7000	1492
Anocote	3471	F	858 566-1015	12928
Anokiwave Inc (PA)	3674	E	858 792-9910	18102
Any Budget Printing & Mailing	2752	F	858 278-3151	6416
AP Precision Metals Inc	3444	F	619 628-0003	12113
Apollo Manufacturing Services	3629	F	858 271-8009	16776
Appfolio Inc	7372	A	866 648-1536	23609
Apta Group Inc (PA)	3674	E	619 710-8170	18119
Aqua Logic Inc	3585	E	858 292-4773	15412
Aquadyne Computer Corporation	3625	F	858 495-1040	16700
Aquaneering Inc	3523	E	858 578-2028	13610
Arena Pharmaceuticals Inc (PA)	2834	D	858 453-7200	7764
Argen Corporation	3843	E	858 455-7900	22134
Argen Corporation (PA)	3339	C	858 455-7900	11188
Arm Inc	3674	C	858 453-1900	18123
Asias Finest	3421	F	619 297-0800	11513
Asset General Inc	7372	E	800 753-2556	23629
Asset Science LLC	7372	E	858 255-7982	23630
Associated Microbreweries Inc	2082	D	858 587-2739	1495
Associated Microbreweries Inc (PA)	2082	C	858 273-2739	1497
Associated Microbreweries Inc	2082	C	619 234-2739	1498
Asteres Inc (PA)	3578	E	858 777-8600	15371
AT&T Corp	2741	C	619 521-6100	6192
Atm Plus Inc	3069	F	619 575-3278	9285
Atx Networks (san Diego) Corp (DH)	3663	D	858 546-5050	17462
Atxco Inc	2834	E	650 334-2079	7776
Atyr Pharma Inc	2836	E	858 731-8389	8276
Audatex North America Inc (DH)	7372	C	858 946-1900	23638
Aurum Assembly Plus Inc	3672	E	858 578-8710	17829
Autoanything Inc	3711	C	858 569-8111	19456
Autoliv Safety Technology Inc	2399	A	619 662-8000	3833
Automation Technical Svcs Inc	3559	F	619 302-6970	14428
Automotive Engineered Pdts Inc	3542	D	619 229-7797	13969
Automotive Exch & Sup of Cal (PA)	3714	E	619 282-3207	19587
Autosplice Inc	3643	C	858 535-0077	16877
Avery Plastics Inc	3089	D	619 696-1230	9645
Avery Products Corporation	2678	E	619 671-1022	5478
Aviva Biosciences Corporation	3699	E	858 552-0888	19263
AVX Antenna Inc (DH)	3663	E	858 550-3820	17466
Azaa Investments Inc (PA)	3711	F	858 569-8111	19457
Azumex Corp	2061	E	619 710-8855	1348
B & I Fender Trims Inc	3714	D	718 326-4323	19589
B D Pharmingen Inc (HQ)	2835	C	858 812-8800	8205
B T E Deltec Inc	3679	C	619 291-4211	18828
B-Efficient Inc	3646	E	209 663-9199	17014

Employment Codes: A=Over 500 employees, B=251-500,
C=101-250, D=51-100, E=20-50, F=10-19

2020 California
Manufacturers Register

© Mergent Inc. 1-800-342-5647

1401

GEOGRAPHIC

	SIC	EMP	PHONE	ENTRY #
Bae Systems Info & Elec Sys	3825	C	858 592-5000	21010
Bae Systems San Diego	3731	A	619 238-1000	20278
Bae Systems Tech Sol Srvc Inc	3812	F	858 278-3042	20545
Bajasys LLC	3577	F	619 661-0748	15165
Balboa Manufacturing Co LLC (PA)	2253	C	858 715-0060	2772
Ballast Point Spirits LLC	2082	C	858 695-2739	1499
Barrett Engineering Inc	3694	F	858 256-9194	19186
BASF Enzymes LLC (DH)	2869	F	858 431-8520	8719
Becton Dickinson and Company	3841	B	858 812-8800	21623
Becton Dickinson and Company	3841	F	888 876-4287	21625
Beejay LLC	3944	F	619 220-8697	22662
Before Butcher Inc	2013	F	858 265-9511	441
Beme International LLC	2392	E	858 751-0580	3602
Benchmark Elec Phoenix Inc	3672	F	619 397-2402	17835
Bernardo Winery Inc (PA)	2084	E	858 487-1866	1595
Bh-Tech Inc	3089	A	858 694-0900	9665
Bimbo Bakeries Usa Inc	2051	D	858 677-0573	1154
Biogeneral Inc	3841	F	858 453-4451	21633
Biolegend Inc (PA)	2836	C	858 455-9588	8282
Biom LLC	3842	F	858 717-2995	21986
Bionano Genomics Inc (PA)	3826	D	858 888-7600	21196
Bioserv Corporation	2835	E	917 817-1326	8207
Biospherical Instruments Inc	3812	F	619 686-1888	20547
Biota Technology Inc	7372	E	650 888-6512	23670
Biotix Inc (HQ)	2869	E	858 875-7696	8724
Bit Group Usa Inc (PA)	3841	D	858 613-1200	21639
Blastrac NA	3531	E	800 256-3440	13711
Blue Book Publishers Inc (PA)	2741	D	858 454-7939	6202
Blue Nalu Inc	3556	F	858 703-8703	14352
Blue Squirrel Inc	3669	D	858 268-0717	17718
Bonded Window Coverings Inc	2591	E	858 974-7700	5016
Bonelli Fine Food Inc	2021	F	650 906-9896	536
Bourns Inc	3825	F	951 781-5360	21014
Box Co Inc	2752	F	619 661-8090	6456
Branan Medical Corporation (PA)	3841	E	949 598-7166	21642
Bravo Sports	3949	E	858 408-0083	22768
Breezaire Products Co	3443	F	858 566-7465	11998
Brehm Communications Inc (PA)	2752	E	858 451-6200	6458
Brett Corp	2759	E	858 292-4919	7008
Bridgewave Communications Inc	3357	E	408 567-6900	11290
Broadcom Corporation	3674	A	858 385-8800	18153
Brothers Enterprises Inc	7692	F	619 229-8003	24619
Bumble Bee Capital Corp	2091	C	858 715-4000	2237
Bumble Bee Foods LLC (DH)	2091	B	858 715-4000	2238
Bumble Bee Holdings Inc (HQ)	2013	B	858 715-4000	443
Bumble Bee Seafoods LP	2091	D	858 715-4000	2239
Bumble Bee Seafoods Inc	2091	E	858 715-4000	2240
Bumble Bee Seafoods Inc	2091	A	858 715-4068	2241
Bumbleride Inc	3944	F	619 615-0475	22666
Bumjin America Inc (PA)	3089	F	619 671-0386	9677
C & L Tool and Die Inc	3544	F	619 270-8385	14026
C A Botana International Inc (PA)	2844	E	858 450-1717	8453
CA Skyhook Inc	2431	E	619 229-2169	4006
Cabinets Galore Orange County	2421	E	858 586-0555	3928
Cafe Virtuoso	2095	F	619 550-1830	2279
Caffe Clabria Cof Roasters LLC	2095	E	619 683-7787	2282
California Commercial Asp Corp (PA)	2951	F	858 513-0611	9087
California Industrial Fabrics	2231	E	619 661-7166	2743
California Neon Products	3993	D	619 283-2191	23069
California Precision Pdts Inc	3444	D	858 638-7300	12148
California Scene Publishing	2752	F	858 635-9400	6468
Camino Neurocare	3841	D	858 455-1115	21648
Cannalink Inc	3823	F	310 921-1955	20845
Canyon Graphics Inc	2431	D	858 646-0444	4014
Caps & Tabs Inc	2023	F	619 285-5400	583
Carbomer Inc	2819	D	858 552-0992	7479
Care Fusion	3841	A	858 617-2000	21652
Carefusion 213 LLC (DH)	3841	B	800 523-0502	21655
Carefusion Corporation (HQ)	3845	B	858 617-2000	22237
Carl Zeiss Vision Inc (DH)	3851	C	858 790-7700	22344
Carlson & Beauloye Air Pwr Inc	3599	F	619 232-5719	15825
Carlson & Beauloye Mach Sp Inc	3599	F	619 232-5719	15826
Carreon Development Inc	3993	F	619 690-4973	23073
Carturner Inc (PA)	3829	F	760 598-7448	21449
Casual Fridays Inc	2741	F	858 433-1442	6211
Caterpillar Pwr Gnrtn Sys	3511	E	858 694-6629	13564
Cbj LP	2721	E	858 277-6359	5900
CBS Scientific Co Inc (PA)	3829	E	858 755-4959	21450
CCM Assembly & Mfg Inc	3679	E	760 560-1310	18854
Cellesta Inc	2835	F	858 552-0888	8213
Center Health Services	3826	F	619 692-2077	21202
Central Admxture Phrm Svcs Inc	2834	E	858 578-1380	7838
Central Marble Supply Inc	3281	F	619 595-1800	10896
Centurm Information Tech Inc	3357	E	619 224-1100	11295
Cg Financial LLC	2032	F	619 656-2919	722

	SIC	EMP	PHONE	ENTRY #
Chantilly Bakery Inc	2051	F	858 693-3300	1176
Chemdiv Inc	2899	E	858 794-4860	8946
Chemtreat Inc	2899	E	804 935-2000	8948
Chosen Foods LLC (PA)	2899	F	877 674-2244	8950
Chrontrol Corporation (PA)	3613	E	619 282-8686	16589
Cidara Therapeutics Inc (PA)	2836	D	858 752-6170	8289
Cimmaron Software Inc	7372	E	858 385-1291	23736
Cimrmaan Ivo	3469	F	858 693-1536	12784
City of San Diego	3826	E	619 758-2310	21205
Clarify Medical Inc	3845	E	877 738-6041	22239
Classy Inc	7372	E	619 961-1892	23744
Clear Blue Energy Corp	3648	D	858 451-1549	17112
Clickscanshare Inc (PA)	3577	F	619 461-5880	15205
Clint Precision Mfg Inc	3599	F	858 271-4041	15848
Coastal Die Cutting Inc	3542	F	619 677-3180	13975
Coastline International	3845	C	888 748-7177	22242
Cobham Adv Elec Sol Inc	3812	C	858 560-1301	20553
Coda Automotive Inc	3714	D	619 291-2040	19619
Cognella Inc	2731	E	858 552-1120	6090
Cohuhd Costar LLC	3651	D	858 391-1800	17213
Coi Ceramics Inc	3728	E	858 621-5700	20073
Cold Pack System Inc	3086	F	858 586-0800	9516
Coldstone Mira Mesa 114	2024	E	858 695-9771	637
Colmol Inc	2759	E	858 693-7575	7030
Colonnas Shipyard West LLC	3731	E	619 557-8373	20284
Colorcards 960	3471	E	858 535-9915	12974
Commaai Inc	7372	E	415 712-8205	23760
Commercial Truss Co	2439	E	858 693-1771	4296
Commsystems LLC	3663	F	858 824-0056	17490
Companion Medical Inc	3841	D	858 522-0252	21668
Competitor Group Inc (HQ)	2721	C	858 450-6510	5907
Competitor Magazine	2721	E	858 768-6800	5908
Compliance Products Usa Inc	3825	F	619 878-9696	21019
Concise Fabricators Inc	3444	E	520 746-3226	12161
Concisys Inc	3825	E	858 292-5888	21020
Confident Technologies Inc	7372	E	858 345-5640	23769
Continental Controls Corp	3823	E	858 453-9880	20851
Continental Feature/ News Svc	2721	E	858 492-8696	5910
Continental Graphics Corp	2752	B	858 552-6520	6507
Continental Maritime Inds Inc	3731	B	619 234-8851	20285
Continuous Computing Corp	3571	E	858 882-8800	14901
Contrctor Cmpliance Monitoring	3822	E	619 472-9065	20789
Cool Jams Inc	2326	F	858 566-6165	3031
Coretex USA Inc	3812	E	877 247-8725	20560
Coronado Leather Co Inc	2386	F	619 238-0265	3511
Corrugados De Baja California	2653	A	619 662-8672	5213
Corrugated Technologies Inc	7372	E	858 578-3550	23778
Covidien Holding Inc	3841	A	619 690-8500	21673
CP Kelco Us Inc	2899	E	858 467-6542	8953
CP Kelco US Inc	2899	E	858 292-4900	8954
CP Kelco US Inc	2899	F	858 292-4900	8955
CP Manufacturing Inc (HQ)	3559	C	619 477-3175	14443
Crazy Industries	3949	F	619 270-9090	22786
Creative Computer Products	3089	F	858 458-1965	9733
Creative Design Industries	2321	C	619 710-2525	2987
Crest Beverage LLC	2026	B	858 452-2300	691
Cri 2000 LP (PA)	2499	D	619 542-1975	4499
Crinetics Pharmaceuticals Inc	2834	E	858 450-6464	7857
Crisi Medical Systems Inc	2834	F	858 754-8640	7858
Crower Engrg & Sls Co Inc	3714	C	619 690-7810	19624
Crydom Inc (DH)	3625	B	619 210-1590	16709
Cubic Corporation (PA)	3812	A	858 277-6780	20564
Cubic Defense Applications Inc	3699	C	858 505-2870	19282
Cubic Defense Applications Inc (HQ)	3699	A	858 277-6780	19283
Cubic Trnsp Systems Inc (HQ)	3829	A	858 268-3100	21455
Cue Health Inc	2835	E	256 651-1656	8217
Curtis Technology Inc	3679	F	858 453-5797	18880
Custom Engineering Plastics LP	3089	F	858 452-0961	9737
Cutwater Spirits LLC	2899	E	858 672-3848	8956
Cv Sciences Inc (PA)	2833	E	866 290-2157	7652
Cydea Inc	2082	E	800 710-9939	1517
Cymer LLC (HQ)	3699	A	858 385-7300	19286
Cynergy3 Components Corp (PA)	3625	F	858 715-7200	16711
D A M Bindery Inc	2789	F	858 621-7000	7329
Dal-Tile Corporation	2824	F	858 565-7767	7635
Dangerous Coffee Co LLC	3999	F	619 405-8291	23310
Dare Bioscience Inc	2834	F	858 926-7655	7864
Dassault Systemes Biovia Corp	7372	E	858 799-5000	23797
Dassault Systemes Biovia Corp (DH)	7372	E	858 799-5000	23798
Dawn Sign Press Inc	2731	E	858 625-0600	6096
Daylight Solutions Inc (DH)	3674	C	858 432-7500	18193
De Soto Clothing Inc	2339	F	858 578-6672	3315
Decatur Electronics Inc (HQ)	3812	D	888 428-4315	20568
Decisionlogic LLC	7372	E	858 586-0202	23811
Del Mar Datatrac Inc	7372	E	858 550-8810	23813

Company	SIC	EMP	PHONE	ENTRY #
Delphi Connection Systems LLC	3714	F	949 458-3155	19635
Delta Group Electronics Inc	3679	D	858 569-1681	18886
Dexcom Inc (PA)	3841	B	858 200-0200	21682
Dgb LLC	3949	E	858 578-0414	22789
Diego & Son Printing Inc	2752	E	619 233-5373	6538
Diggimac Inc DBA Ltg Element	3643	F	858 322-6000	16893
Digivision Inc	3823	F	858 530-0100	20858
Dih Technologies Co	3841	F	858 768-9816	21688
Dinner On A Dollar Inc	2741	F	858 693-3939	6221
Diversfied Nano Solutions Corp	2893	E	858 924-1017	8911
Diversified Nano Corporation (PA)	3577	E	858 673-0387	15216
Diving Unlimited International	3949	D	619 236-1203	22791
Dove Tree Canyon Software Inc	7372	F	619 236-8895	23829
Dream Communications Inc	2721	F	619 275-9100	5924
Driscoll Inc	3732	E	619 226-2500	20323
Driscoll Mission Bay LLC	3732	F	619 223-5191	20324
Dynamic E-Markets LLC	2111	F	619 327-4777	2652
E Phocus Inc	3861	F	858 646-5462	22417
E Seek Inc	3577	F	714 832-7980	15220
E-Band Communications LLC	3663	E	858 408-0660	17508
Eclipse Chocolate Bar & Bistro	2066	F	619 578-2984	1410
Ecoatm LLC (HQ)	3671	C	858 999-3200	17785
Economy Print & Image Inc	2752	F	619 295-4455	6559
Ecr4kids LP	2531	E	619 323-2005	4858
Ectron Corporation	3663	E	858 278-0600	17509
Edgate Correlation Svcs LLC	3999	E	858 712-9341	23323
El Chavito Inc	2064	E	844 424-2848	1364
El Super Leon Pnchin Sncks Inc	2064	E	619 426-2968	1365
Elco Rfrgn Solutions LLC	3585	A	619 255-5251	15427
Eldema Products	3647	F	619 661-5113	17089
Eleanor Rigby Leather Co	3199	E	619 356-5590	10247
Electronic Prtg Solutions LLC	2759	E	858 576-3000	7055
Electronic Surfc Mounted Inds	3672	E	858 455-1710	17868
Elm System Inc	3695	F	408 694-2750	19216
Elsevier Inc	2741	D	619 231-6616	6228
Embedded Designs Inc	3823	E	858 673-6050	20865
Emerson Process Management	3823	E	858 492-1069	20866
Endura Technologies LLC	3674	F	858 412-2135	18217
Energy Labs Inc (DH)	3585	B	619 671-0100	15428
Enfora Inc	3679	D	972 234-1689	18906
Enterprise Informatics Inc	7372	E	858 625-3000	23864
Epicson Inc	2759	F	858 558-5757	7058
Equity Ford Research	2741	F	858 755-1327	6230
Ereplacements LLC	3691	E	714 361-2652	19163
Es3 Prime Logistics Group Inc (PA)	3721	F	619 338-0380	19892
Escient Pharmaceuticals Inc	2834	F	858 617-8236	7881
Eurus Energy America Corp (DH)	3621	F	858 638-7115	16644
Evofem Inc	3841	F	858 550-1900	21708
Evofem Biosciences Inc (PA)	2834	E	858 550-1900	7883
Express Business Systems Inc	2759	E	858 549-9828	7062
Factory Direct Dist Corp	2842	F	619 435-3437	8383
Farmer Bros Co	2095	E	858 292-7578	2289
Fastec Imaging Corporation	3861	E	858 592-2342	22422
Fate Therapeutics Inc	2836	F	858 875-1800	8300
Filmetrics Inc (PA)	3826	E	858 573-9300	21229
Fine Electronic Assembly Inc	3672	E	858 573-0887	17874
Finest Food Inc	2099	F	858 699-4746	2457
Fitness Warehouse LLC (PA)	3949	F	858 578-7676	22801
Flame-Spray Inc	3479	E	619 283-2007	13178
Flo TV Incorporated	3663	F	858 651-1645	17521
Flydive Inc (PA)	3949	F	844 359-3483	22803
FM Plastics	3089	F	619 661-5929	9789
Fondo De Cultura Economica	2731	F	619 429-0455	6102
Formex LLC	2834	E	858 529-6600	7893
Forterra Pipe & Precast LLC	3272	F	858 715-5600	10578
Found Image Press Inc	2771	F	619 282-3452	7295
Four Seasons Design Inc (PA)	2396	C	619 761-5151	3786
Fourward Machine Inc	3599	F	858 272-0601	15970
Fragmob LLC	7372	F	858 587-6659	23918
Franklin Wireless Corp	3661	D	858 623-0000	17373
Frito-Lay North America Inc	2096	E	858 576-3300	2328
Fusion Food Factory	2051	E	858 578-8001	1211
Fyfe Co LLC (HQ)	3449	F	858 444-2970	12590
G7 Productivity Systems	7372	D	858 675-1095	23925
Gamma Scientific Inc	3829	E	858 635-9008	21478
Ganpac Distribution LLC	2051	E	858 586-1868	1214
Gantner Instruments Inc	3825	E	858 537-2060	21041
GE Healthcare Inc	2833	E	858 279-9382	7662
Gen-Probe Incorporated	2835	D	858 410-8000	8224
Genalyte Inc	3841	F	858 956-1200	21722
General Atomic Aeron	3721	B	858 964-6700	19896
General Atomic Aeron	3721	B	858 455-2810	19898
General Atomic Aeron	3721	B	858 455-4309	19899
General Dynamics Corporation	3731	E	619 544-3400	20287
General Dynamics Mission	3625	D	619 671-5400	16717
General Dynmics Mtion Ctrl LLC	3625	F	619 671-5400	16718
General Media Systems LLC	7372	F	818 210-4236	23932
Genetronics Inc	3821	E	858 597-6006	20759
Genopis Inc	2834	E	858 875-4700	7909
Geodetics Inc	3812	E	858 729-0872	20583
Gfbc Inc	2082	E	858 622-0085	1531
Gilbert Martin Wdwkg Co Inc (PA)	2517	E	800 268-5669	4753
Glimmer Gear	3949	F	619 399-9211	22808
Global Marine Group Inc	3732	F	800 729-1665	20333
Global Packaging Solutions Inc	2653	B	619 710-2661	5229
Global Polishing Solutions LLC (HQ)	3531	F	619 295-5505	13730
Glysens Incorporated	3841	E	858 638-7708	21725
Gnosis International Inc	2835	E	858 254-6369	8226
Goto California Inc (HQ)	3651	C	619 691-8722	17233
Gpr Stabilizer LLC	3751	F	619 661-0101	20405
Gps Metals Lab Inc	3341	E	858 433-6125	11202
Grand Fusion Housewares Inc	3089	F	909 292-5776	9816
Greathouse Screen Printing	2759	F	858 279-4939	7081
Greenlee Textron Inc	3825	D	858 530-3100	21046
Groundmetrics Inc	1389	F	619 786-8023	203
Gruma Corporation	2096	F	858 673-5780	2332
Guardian Corporate Services	2394	F	619 295-2646	3685
Guardion Health Sciences Inc (PA)	2834	F	858 605-9055	7929
Gulbransen Inc	3931	F	619 296-5760	22624
Gyt San Diego Inc	3599	F	619 661-2568	16010
Halozyme Therapeutics Inc (PA)	2836	D	858 794-8889	8307
Hanson Aggregates LLC	3241	F	619 299-8640	10412
Hanson Aggregates LLC	3241	F	858 577-2727	10413
Harbor Biosciences Inc (PA)	2834	F	858 587-9333	7933
Hardy Process Solutions	3823	F	858 278-2900	20882
Harrow Health Inc (PA)	2834	F	858 704-4040	7935
Healthline Systems LLC (HQ)	7372	E	858 673-1700	23971
Healthstream Inc	7372	C	800 733-8737	23972
Healthy Times	2099	F	858 513-1550	2478
Hemosense Inc	3845	D	408 719-1393	22259
Herley Industries Inc	3679	D	858 812-7300	18934
Heron Therapeutics Inc (PA)	2834	C	858 251-4400	7937
HI Tech Honeycomb Inc	3469	C	858 974-1600	12814
Hi-Q Environmental Pdts Co Inc	3826	F	858 549-2818	21236
Hi-Tech Electronic Mfg Corp	3672	D	858 657-0908	17894
Hi-Z Technology Inc	3629	E	858 695-6660	16787
Hii San Diego Shipyard Inc	3731	B	619 234-8851	20288
Hire Elegance	2599	F	858 740-7862	5064
Hirok Inc	3531	E	619 713-5066	13736
His Company Inc	3612	E	858 513-7748	16555
HK Enterprise Group Inc	2899	F	858 652-4400	8974
Hodge Products Inc	3429	E	619 444-3147	11596
Holiday Foliage Inc	3999	F	619 661-9094	23355
Hologic Inc	3845	E	858 410-8000	22260
Home Brew Mart Inc	2082	E	858 695-2739	1536
Home Brew Mart Inc (HQ)	2082	E	858 790-6900	1537
Honeywell International Inc	3822	C	619 671-5612	20796
Honeywell Safety Pdts USA Inc	3842	C	619 661-8383	22027
Hot Can Inc	2095	E	707 601-6013	2299
Houghton Mifflin Harcourt Pubg	2731	F	617 351-5000	6111
Howco Inc	3714	F	619 275-1663	19684
Hoya Corporation	3851	C	858 309-6050	22360
Hughes Network Systems LLC	3663	E	858 455-9550	17538
Hwa In America Inc (PA)	3679	F	619 567-4539	18939
Hy Jo Mfg Imports Corp	3499	E	619 671-1018	13523
Hyundai Translead (HQ)	3443	D	619 574-1500	12021
I/O Select Inc	3829	F	858 537-2060	21487
Ikanos Communications Inc (DH)	3674	C	858 587-1121	18278
Ikegami Mold Corp America	3089	F	619 858-6855	9836
Illumina Inc	3826	E	800 809-4566	21242
Illumina Inc (PA)	3826	B	858 202-4500	21243
Imageware Systems Inc (PA)	7372	D	858 673-8600	24001
Imaging Technologies	3577	F	858 487-8944	15241
Immunic Inc	2834	F	858 673-6840	7943
Impulse Enterprise	3643	E	858 565-7050	16905
Impulse Enterprise	3643	D	858 565-7050	16906
Incharacter Costumes LLC	2389	E	858 552-3600	3557
Industrial Fire Sprnklr Co Inc	3569	E	619 266-6030	14829
Industrial SEC Allianc Ptnrs (PA)	3861	F	619 232-7041	22429
Informa Media Inc	2721	E	619 295-7685	5964
Ingenu Inc (PA)	3663	E	858 201-6000	17542
Initium Aerospace Inc	3324	F	818 324-3864	11158
Innfinity Software Systems LLC	7372	F	619 798-3915	24023
Inno Tech Manufacturing Inc	3599	F	858 565-4556	16046
Innominata	2835	F	858 592-9300	8231
Innophase Inc	3674	D	619 541-8280	18292
Innovacon Inc	2835	D	858 805-8900	8232
Innovive LLC (PA)	3496	C	858 309-6620	13416
Inovio Pharmaceuticals Inc	2834	E	267 440-4200	7951
Instant Imprints Franchising	2752	E	858 642-4848	6642

Company	SIC	EMP	PHONE	ENTRY #
Integer Holdings Corporation	3841	F	619 498-9448	21745
Integra Lfscnces Holdings Corp	3841	E	609 529-9748	21746
Integrated Dna Tech Inc	2836	F	858 410-6677	8312
Integrated Microwave Corp	3679	D	858 259-2600	18947
Intel Network Systems Inc	3577	E	858 877-4652	15256
Intelicare Direct Inc	2752	F	702 765-0867	6648
Intelligent Blends LP	2043	E	858 888-7937	1024
Intelligent Technologies LLC	3629	C	858 458-1500	16789
Intercept Pharmaceuticals Inc	2834	F	646 747-1005	7954
Intercontinental Cof Trdg LLC	2095	F	619 338-8335	2300
Interior Wood of San Diego	2521	E	619 295-6469	4803
Internacional De Elevadores SA	3534	F	619 955-6180	13803
International Mfg Tech Inc (DH)	3312	E	619 544-7741	11050
International Technidyne Corp (DH)	3841	C	858 263-2300	21748
Internet Strategy Inc	7372	F	858 673-6022	24029
Interocean Industries Inc	3812	A	858 292-0808	20589
Interocean Systems LLC	3812	E	858 565-8400	20590
Intuit Inc	7372	A	858 215-8726	24034
Intuit Inc	7372	B	858 215-8000	24041
Iq-Analog Corporation	3674	F	858 200-0388	18322
Irisys LLC	2834	E	858 623-1520	7964
Isec Incorporated	3821	C	858 279-9085	20763
Ivera Medical LLC	3841	D	888 861-8228	21763
J M Mills Communications Inc (HQ)	3663	E	613 321-2100	17545
JA Ferrari Print Imaging LLC	2752	F	619 295-8307	6659
James Gang Company	2396	F	619 225-1283	3793
James Gang Custom Printing	2752	F	619 225-1283	6660
Jamis Software Corporation	7372	F	858 300-5542	24056
Janssen Research & Dev LLC	2834	C	858 450-2000	7969
Jay Brewer	2752	F	858 488-4871	6662
Jeld-Wen Inc	2431	E	800 468-3667	4063
Jem-Hd Co Inc	3089	D	619 710-1443	9853
Jensen Meat Company Inc	2013	D	619 754-6400	469
JImachine Company Inc	3599	E	858 695-1787	16084
Jjs Truck Equipment LLC	3713	E	858 566-1155	19539
Joaos A Tin Fish Bar & Eatery	3356	E	619 794-2192	11275
John B Campbell MD A Prof Corp	2869	F	858 576-9960	8747
Johnson Controls	3669	C	858 633-9100	17735
Jumper Media LLC	2741	D	831 333-6202	6264
Juneshine Inc	2099	F	619 501-8311	2495
K & B Foam Inc	3086	F	619 661-1870	9553
Kaar Drect Mail Flfillment LLC	2711	E	619 382-3670	5681
Kahoots Inc	3999	F	619 337-0825	23378
Kai Os Technologies Sftwr Inc	7372	E	858 547-3940	24069
Karl Strauss Brewing Company (PA)	2082	D	858 273-2739	1540
Katolec Development Inc	3679	E	619 710-0075	18972
Kavlico Corporation	3679	E	805 523-2000	18974
Kazuhm Inc	7372	E	858 771-3861	24072
Keco Inc	3594	F	619 546-9533	15630
Kelco Bio Polymers	2899	E	619 595-5000	8983
Kelpac Medical	3082	D	619 710-2550	9431
Kenjitsu USA Corp	3679	E	619 734-5862	18976
Kieran Label Corp	2759	E	619 449-4457	7106
Kings Printing Corp	2752	E	619 297-6000	6677
Kintera Inc (HQ)	7372	D	858 795-3000	24079
Kjm Enterprises Inc	2759	E	858 537-2490	7107
Kontron America Inc	3571	D	800 822-7522	14933
Kontron America Incorporated (DH)	3571	C	858 677-0877	14934
Kovin Corporation Inc	2752	E	858 558-0100	6681
Krasnes Inc	2386	D	619 232-2066	3519
Kratos Def & SEC Solutions Inc (PA)	3663	B	858 812-7300	17555
Kratos Tech Trning Sltions Inc (HQ)	7372	C	858 812-7300	24086
KS Industries	3999	F	858 344-1146	23386
Ksc Industries Inc	3651	E	619 671-0110	17251
Kuantum Brands LLC	2086	C	760 412-2432	2087
Kyocera International Inc (HQ)	3674	C	858 492-1456	18337
Kyriba Corp (PA)	7372	E	858 210-3560	24089
Kyung In Printing Inc	2752	C	619 662-3920	6685
L-3 Communications Corporation	3663	F	858 694-7500	17557
L3 Applied Technologies Inc (DH)	3663	D	858 404-7824	17558
L3 Applied Technologies Inc	3663	C	858 404-7824	17559
L3 Technologies Inc	3663	B	858 279-0411	17560
L3 Technologies Inc	3663	D	858 552-9716	17564
L3 Technologies Inc	3663	D	858 552-9500	17566
L3harris Technologies Inc	3812	E	619 684-7511	20599
L3harris Technologies Inc	3823	C	619 296-6900	20898
Lamart California Inc	3728	C	510 489-8100	20152
Lansing Industries Inc	3999	F	858 523-0719	23390
Lauras Original Boston	2051	E	619 855-3258	1231
Leatherock International Inc	3111	E	619 299-7625	10141
Ledpac LLC	3993	D	760 489-8067	23146
Legacy Vulcan LLC	1422	E	858 566-2730	303
Legendary Holdings Inc	2353	E	619 872-6100	3468
Leidos Inc	3577	E	619 524-2581	15273
Lenus Handcrafted	2844	F	619 200-4266	8532
Leon Assembly Solutions Inc	3264	D	858 397-2826	10478
Leviton Manufacturing Co Inc	3643	B	619 205-8600	16912
Lifeome Biolabs Inc	2835	F	619 302-0129	8235
Ligand Pharmaceuticals Inc	2834	E	858 550-7500	7993
Ligand Pharmaceuticals Inc (PA)	2834	D	858 550-7500	7994
Light Mobile Inc	3843	F	858 278-1750	22172
Lilly Biotechnology Center	2834	F	858 597-4990	7995
Lilly Tortilleria	2099	E	619 281-2890	2529
Limited Access Unlimited Inc	3523	F	619 294-3682	13649
Linear Technology LLC	3674	D	408 432-1900	18355
Litel Instruments Inc	3825	F	858 546-3788	21066
Loanhero Inc	7372	F	888 912-4376	24106
Lockheed Martin Corporation	3812	F	619 542-3273	20603
Lockheed Martin Corporation	3812	C	858 740-5100	20616
Lockheed Martin Corporation	3812	C	858 740-5100	20622
Lockheed Martin Corporation	3721	B	619 298-8453	19914
Logico LLC	3357	F	619 600-5198	11308
Logisterra Inc	3161	E	619 280-9992	10198
Loud Mouth Inc	3949	E	619 743-0370	22844
Lrad Corporation (PA)	3651	E	858 676-1112	17252
Lytx Inc (PA)	3812	B	858 430-4000	20627
M B C Reprographics Inc	2759	E	858 541-1500	7128
Mabvax Thrpeutics Holdings Inc (PA)	2834	F	858 259-9405	8000
Machine Craft of San Diego	3599	E	858 642-0509	16163
Mad Engine LLC (PA)	2261	E	858 558-5270	2829
Madcap Software Inc (PA)	7372	F	858 320-0387	24119
Maddox Defense Inc	2399	F	818 378-8246	3848
Magic-Flight General Mfg Inc	2499	C	619 288-4638	4515
Magnabiosciences LLC	3841	D	858 481-4400	21784
Magnebit Holding Corporation (PA)	3825	E	858 573-0727	21071
Mamma Linas Incorporated	2099	F	858 535-0620	2538
Mannis Communications Inc	2711	E	858 270-3103	5721
Mannis Communications Inc	2711	E	858 270-3103	5722
Manzer Corporation	2391	E	619 295-6031	3591
Marathon Machine Inc	3599	F	858 578-8670	16171
Marcoa Media LLC (PA)	2741	E	858 635-9627	6277
Marcoa Quality Publishing LLC	2741	D	858 695-9600	6278
Marine & Rest Fabricators Inc	3444	E	619 232-7267	12277
Marine Tech	3732	C	619 225-0448	20347
Marinesync Corporation	3823	F	619 578-2953	20902
Maritime Solutions LLC	3732	E	619 234-2676	20348
Marketing Pro Consulting Inc	7372	F	619 233-8591	24127
Mast Biosurgery USA Inc	3841	E	858 550-8050	21789
Master Productions Inc	2752	F	858 677-0037	6718
Masterpiece Artist Canvas LLC	2211	E	619 710-2500	2703
Matthey Johnson Inc	3341	C	858 716-2400	11204
Maxwell Technologies Inc (HQ)	3694	B	858 503-3300	19195
Mbf Interiors Inc	2391	E	858 565-2944	3592
McAfee Inc	7372	D	858 967-2342	24134
McKinnon Enterprises	2721	E	858 571-1818	5986
McV Technologies Inc	3663	F	858 450-0468	17581
Med-Safe Systems Inc	3841	C	855 236-2772	21792
Medical Transcription Billing	7372	A	800 869-3700	24142
Medtronic Inc	3841	B	949 798-3934	21803
Medwaves Inc	3841	E	858 946-0015	21814
Meggitt (san Diego) Inc (DH)	3728	C	858 824-8976	20173
MEI Pharma Inc	2834	E	858 369-7100	8008
Memjet Labels Inc (DH)	3577	F	858 673-3300	15286
Memjet Labels Inc	3577	E	858 798-3061	15287
Mentor Graphics Corporation	7372	E	858 523-2600	24147
Merck Sharp & Dohme Corp	2834	D	619 292-4900	8011
Merrill Corporation	2759	D	858 623-0300	7137
Metal Master Inc	3444	E	858 292-8880	12294
MI Technologies Inc	3672	C	619 710-2637	17926
Microbiotic Health Foods Inc	2052	F	858 273-5775	1321
Microsoft Corporation	7372	E	858 909-3800	24155
Microsoft Corporation	7372	D	619 849-5872	24157
Miller Machine Works LLC	3599	F	619 501-9866	16207
Miller Marine	3731	E	619 791-1500	20293
Mirati Therapeutics Inc	2834	F	858 332-3410	8014
Mission Hills Radio/Tv Inc	3496	F	858 277-1100	13423
Mlim LLC	2711	A	619 299-3131	5757
Mohammad Khan	3089	F	619 231-1664	9904
Molecular Bioproducts Inc (DH)	3826	C	858 453-7551	21266
Monaco Sheet Metal	3444	E	858 272-0297	12309
Montbleau & Associates Inc (PA)	2521	D	619 263-5550	4809
Morgan Polymer Seals LLC (PA)	3053	E	858 679-4946	9243
Motorlamb International Acc	2399	F	858 569-8111	3850
Motorola Solutions Inc	3674	E	858 541-2163	18422
Motsenbocker Advanced Developm (PA)	2842	F	858 581-0222	8398
Mrv Systems LLC	3825	E	800 645-7114	21082
Musicmatch Inc	7372	C	858 485-4300	24184
Mv Excel	3949	F	619 223-7493	22858
Mygrant Glass Company Inc	3714	E	858 455-8022	19726
Nadolife Inc	2024	D	619 522-6890	660

Mergent email: customerrelations@mergent.com
1404

2020 California
Manufacturers Register

(P-0000) Products & Services Section entry number
(PA)=Parent Co (HQ)=Headquarters (DH)=Div Headquarters

Company	SIC	EMP	PHONE	ENTRY #
Nankai Enviro-Tech Corporation	3089	C	619 754-2250	9916
Nanoimaging Services Inc	3826	F	888 675-8261	21270
Nantkwest Inc (HQ)	2836	E	805 633-0300	8317
National Pen Co LLC (DH)	3951	C	866 388-9850	22935
National Stl & Shipbuilding Co (HQ)	3731	B	619 544-3400	20295
Natus Medical Incorporated	3845	D	858 260-2590	22285
Neil A Kjos Music Company (PA)	2741	E	858 270-9800	6292
Neil Patel Digital LLC	2741	E	619 356-8119	6293
Neo Tech Aqua Solutions Inc	2899	F	858 571-6590	9009
Neology Inc (HQ)	3825	E	858 391-0260	21088
Nerveda Inc	2834	D	858 705-2365	8031
Network Vigilance LLC	7372	F	858 695-8676	24199
Neurocrine Biosciences Inc (PA)	2834	C	858 617-7600	8032
Nevwest Inc	3812	E	619 420-8100	20639
New Bi US Gaming LLC	7372	E	858 592-2472	24201
Nextivity Inc (PA)	3663	D	858 485-9442	17604
Nextpharma Tech USA Inc	2834	E	858 450-3123	8037
Nexus Dx Inc	3841	E	858 410-4600	21839
Neyenesch Printers Inc	2752	D	619 297-2281	6747
Nishiba Industries Corporation	3089	A	619 661-8866	9928
Nip Furniture Industries Inc	2599	C	619 661-5170	5074
No Boundaries Inc	2752	E	619 266-2349	6750
No Second Thoughts Inc	2311	D	619 428-5992	2972
Non-Linear Systems	3823	F	619 521-2161	20909
Norell Prsthtics Orthotics Inc (PA)	3842	F	510 770-9010	22055
North County Times (DH)	2711	C	800 533-8830	5782
North Sails Group LLC	2394	D	619 226-1415	3694
Northrop Grumman Corporation	3812	A	858 967-1221	20643
Northrop Grumman Corporation	3812	A	858 618-7617	20647
Northrop Grumman Corporation	3812	A	858 514-9259	20648
Northrop Grumman Innovation	3764	B	858 621-5700	20466
Northrop Grumman Systems Corp	3812	F	858 514-9020	20657
Northrop Grumman Systems Corp	3812	A	858 618-4349	20661
Northrop Grumman Systems Corp	3812	C	858 514-9000	20667
Northwest Circuits Corp	3672	D	619 661-1701	17940
Novartis Corporation	2834	C	858 812-1741	8042
Nu Visions De Mexico SA De Cv	3999	C	619 987-0518	23430
Nuvasive Inc (PA)	3841	D	858 909-1800	21843
O & S California Inc	3699	B	619 661-1800	19371
Oberon Fuels Inc (PA)	2911	F	619 255-9361	9055
Ocean Aero Inc	3812	E	858 945-3768	20669
OCP Group Inc	3575	E	858 279-7400	15132
Ocunexus Therapeutics Inc	2834	F	858 480-2403	8050
Odonate Therapeutics Inc	2834	C	858 731-8180	8051
Oggis Pizza & Brewing Co	2082	E	858 481-7883	1553
Oldcastle Infrastructure Inc	3272	E	858 578-5336	10613
Omnitracs Midco LLC (PA)	7372	E	858 651-5812	24224
On-Line Stampco Inc	3953	F	800 373-5614	22954
Oncternal Therapeutics Inc (PA)	2834	E	858 434-1113	8053
Opera Patisserie Fines Inc	2053	E	858 536-5800	1347
Optec Laser Systems LLC	2759	E	858 220-1070	7158
Oracle America Inc	7372	D	858 625-5044	24245
Oracle Corporation	7372	C	858 202-0648	24255
Orca Systems Inc	3672	E	858 679-9295	17946
Organovo Inc	2836	C	858 224-1000	8319
Ormet Circuits Inc	2834	D	858 831-0010	19043
Otonomy Inc	2834	D	619 323-2200	8058
Overland Storage Inc (HQ)	3572	D	858 571-5555	15070
P & R Paper Supply Co Inc	2679	F	619 671-2400	5517
Pacific Biotech Inc	2835	C	858 552-1100	8247
Pacific Diversified Capital Co	3829	A	619 696-2000	21516
Pacific Imaging	2752	F	858 536-2600	6765
Pacific Maritime Inds Corp	3441	C	619 575-8141	11859
Pacific Mfg Inc San Diego	3599	E	619 423-0316	16274
Pacific Millennium US Corp	2621	E	858 450-1505	5141
Pacific Ship Repr Fbrction Inc (PA)	3731	D	619 232-3200	20298
Pacific Steel Group (PA)	3449	D	858 251-1100	12598
Pacira Pharmaceuticals Inc	2834	D	858 678-3950	8062
Pall Corporation	3569	D	858 455-7264	14843
Pan Probe Biotech Inc	3841	F	858 689-9936	21855
Panasonic Appliances Ref	3632	D	619 661-1134	16821
Pappalecco	3499	F	619 906-5566	13537
Parker-Hannifin Corporation	3594	C	619 661-7000	15633
Parker-Hannifin Corporation	3594	C	714 632-6512	15637
PDM Solutions Inc	3672	E	858 348-1000	17955
Pearl Rove Inc	3961	F	858 869-1827	22992
Pep West Inc	3561	A	800 525-4682	14594
Pepsi-Cola Metro Btlg Co Inc	2086	B	858 560-6735	2118
Performance Label Intl Inc	2759	F	619 429-6870	7172
Performance Plastics Inc	3728	D	619 482-5031	20200
Pfenex Inc	2834	D	858 352-4400	8066
Pfizer Inc	2834	C	858 622-7325	8068
Pfizer Inc	2834	A	858 622-3001	8069
Pgac Corp (PA)	2671	D	858 560-8213	5337
PH Labs Advanced Nutrition	2834	F	619 240-3263	8070
Phase II Products Inc (PA)	2591	E	619 236-9699	5033
Photostone LLC	3555	F	858 274-3400	14337
Phyto Animal Health LLC	2023	E	888 871-4505	615
Pioneer Automotive Tech Inc	3663	F	937 746-6600	17624
Pixon Imaging Inc	3826	E	858 352-0100	21277
Pk Industries Inc	3161	E	619 428-6382	10202
Plantronics Inc	3661	F	831 458-7089	17399
Plural Publishing Inc	2731	F	858 492-1555	6137
PM Corporate Group Inc	2752	C	619 498-9199	6785
Polaris Pharmaceuticals Inc	2834	E	858 452-6688	8079
Polymerex Medical Corp	3082	F	858 695-0765	9433
Port 80 Software Inc	7372	E	858 274-4497	24307
Potentia Labs Inc	7372	F	951 603-3531	24309
Power Efficiency Corporation	3621	F	858 750-3875	16668
Pressnet Express Inc	2752	F	858 694-0070	6792
Prestige Flag & Banner Co	2399	D	619 497-2220	3853
Price Industries Inc	3312	D	858 673-4451	11061
Primapharma Inc	2834	E	858 259-0969	8083
Princess Brandy Corp (PA)	2051	E	619 563-9722	1264
Printer Cartridge USA	3861	F	858 538-7630	22452
Printivity (PA)	2752	F	877 649-5463	6808
Pro Line Paint Company	2851	E	619 232-8968	8672
Procede Software LP	7372	E	858 450-4800	24315
Prometheus Biosciences Inc	2834	E	858 200-7888	8086
Prometheus Laboratories Inc	2834	B	858 824-0895	8087
Promex Industries Incorporated	3674	E	858 674-4676	18482
Pronto Products Co Inc	3589	F	619 661-6995	15562
Provasis Therapeutics Inc	3841	E	858 712-2101	21866
Providien Thermoforming Inc	3081	E	858 850-1591	9417
Psemi Corporation (DH)	3674	D	858 731-9400	18485
Psiber Data Systems Inc	3674	E	619 287-9970	18486
Pulse Electronics Inc (DH)	3612	B	858 674-8100	16571
Pulse Electronics Corporation (HQ)	3679	D	858 674-8100	19055
Pyr Preservation Services	3731	E	619 338-8395	20302
Pyramid Precision Machine Inc	3599	D	858 642-0713	16322
Q3-Cnc Inc	3599	F	858 790-0002	16323
QED Systems Inc	3699	E	619 802-0020	19386
Quake Global Inc (PA)	3661	D	858 277-7290	17404
Qualcomm Datacenter Tech Inc (HQ)	3674	E	858 567-1121	18493
Qualcomm Incorporated (PA)	3663	B	858 587-1121	17631
Qualcomm Incorporated	3674	B	858 909-0316	18496
Qualcomm Incorporated	3674	B	858 587-1121	18497
Qualcomm Incorporated	3663	B	858 587-1121	17633
Qualcomm Incorporated	3674	B	858 587-1121	18498
Qualcomm Innovation Center Inc (HQ)	7372	E	858 587-1121	24330
Qualcomm Limited Partner Inc	3674	E	858 587-1121	18499
Qualcomm Mems Technologies Inc	3669	E	858 587-1121	17756
Qualcomm Technologies Inc (HQ)	3674	C	858 587-1121	18500
Quality Cabinet and Fixture Co (HQ)	2434	E	619 266-1011	4233
Quality Systems Intgrated Corp	3672	B	858 587-9797	17969
Quanticel Pharmaceuticals Inc	2834	E	858 966-3747	8093
Quantum Design Inc (PA)	3826	C	858 481-4400	21280
Quantum Dynasty	3572	F	347 469-1047	15082
Quantum Group Inc	3829	D	858 566-9959	21525
Quidel Corporation (PA)	2835	B	858 552-1100	8251
Quikrete Companies LLC	3272	E	858 549-2371	10636
Quorum Systems Inc	3674	F	858 546-0895	18506
R J Reynolds Tobacco Company	2111	C	858 625-8453	2655
R R Donnelley & Sons Company	2752	C	619 527-4600	6829
R R Donnelley & Sons Company	2752	C	619 527-4600	6830
Radx Technologies Inc	3825	E	619 677-1849	21111
Ranroy Company	2752	E	858 571-8800	6834
Rayotek Scientific Inc	3231	D	858 558-3671	10387
Raytheon Company	3812	C	619 628-3345	20687
Raytheon Company	3812	C	858 571-6598	20701
Raytheon Dgital Force Tech LLC	3812	E	858 546-1244	20703
Rdl Machine Inc	3599	E	858 693-3975	16345
Real Marketing	2741	E	858 847-0335	6326
Receptos Inc	2834	E	858 652-5700	8100
Reel Picture Productions LLC	3695	D	858 587-0301	19232
Regent Publishing Services	2741	E	760 510-1936	6328
Reid & Clark Screen Arts Co	2262	F	619 233-7541	2846
Remcor Technical Industries	3812	E	619 424-8878	20704
Remec Broadband Wire	3663	C	858 312-6900	17643
Remec Broadband Wireless LLC (PA)	3663	C	858 312-6900	17644
Remote Ocean Systems Inc (PA)	3648	E	858 565-8500	17158
Renesas Electronics Amer Inc	3674	A	858 451-7240	18515
Repro Magic	2752	F	858 277-2488	6843
Res Med Inc	3841	E	858 746-2400	21875
Resmed Inc (PA)	3841	B	858 836-5000	21876
Respiratory Support Products	3841	E	619 710-1000	21877
Retrophin Inc	2834	D	760 260-8600	8104
Reva Medical Inc	3842	F	858 966-3000	22078
Reveal Imaging Tech Inc	3812	D	858 826-9909	20705
Reyes Coca-Cola Bottling LLC	2086	E	619 266-6300	2149

Employment Codes: A=Over 500 employees, B=251-500,
C=101-250, D=51-100, E=20-50, F=10-19

2020 California
Manufacturers Register

© Mergent Inc. 1-800-342-5647

1405

GEOGRAPHIC

Company	SIC	EMP	PHONE	ENTRY #
Rf Industries Ltd **(PA)**	3678	D	858 549-6340	18787
Rf-Lambda Usa LLC	3625	F	972 767-5998	16743
Rhino Linings Corporation **(PA)**	3563	D	858 450-0441	14640
Rhino Manufacturing Group Inc	3312	F	866 624-8844	11066
Ridout Plastics Company	3081	E	858 560-1551	9418
Right Manufacturing LLC	3498	E	858 566-7002	13483
Rivera Yarn Products Inc	2241	E	619 661-6306	2758
Rj Machine Inc	3599	F	858 547-9482	16361
Roa Pacific Inc	2821	E	619 565-2800	7604
Robanda International Inc	2844	E	619 276-7660	8573
Rock West Composites Inc **(PA)**	3083	E	801 566-3402	9454
Romla Co	3444	E	619 946-1224	12356
Rtmex Inc	2426	C	619 391-9913	3984
Rush Press Inc	2752	E	619 296-7874	6850
Rusty Surfboards Inc **(PA)**	3949	E	858 578-0414	22879
S K Digital Imaging Inc	2789	F	858 408-0732	7346
S R C Devices Inccustomer **(PA)**	3625	F	866 772-8668	16751
Sabia Incorporated **(PA)**	3823	E	858 217-2200	20931
Saehan Electronics America Inc **(PA)**	3672	F	858 496-1500	17982
Safran Cabin Inc	3728	C	619 671-0430	20222
Safran Pwr Units San Diego LLC	3724	D	858 223-2228	19977
Sago Systems Inc	3812	F	858 646-5300	20713
Saint-Gobain Solar Gard LLC **(DH)**	3081	D	866 300-2674	9419
Samsung SDS Globl Scl Amer Inc	7372	E	201 263-3000	24379
San Dego Gographic Info Source	2741	F	858 874-7000	6334
San Dego Prcsion Machining Inc	3444	E	858 499-0379	12367
San Diego Ace Inc	3089	C	619 252-3148	10040
San Diego Afr Amrcn Gnlogy RSC	3999	E	619 231-5810	23465
San Diego Family Magazine LLC	2721	F	619 685-6970	6022
San Diego Guide Inc	2741	E	858 877-3217	6335
San Diego Instruments Inc	3826	E	858 530-2600	21285
San Diego Magazine Pubg Co	2721	E	619 230-9292	6023
San Diego Pcb Design LLC	3672	F	858 271-5722	17983
San Diego Precast Concrete Inc **(HQ)**	3272	E	619 240-8000	10645
San Diego Union-Tribune LLC	2711	D	619 299-3131	5815
San Diego Union-Tribune LLC **(PA)**	2711	A	619 299-3131	5816
Santarus Inc	2834	E	858 314-5700	8120
Santier Inc	3674	D	858 271-1993	18527
Saperi Systems Inc	7372	F	858 381-0085	24381
Sapphire Energy Inc	2833	D	858 768-4700	7692
Sauvage Inc **(PA)**	2329	F	858 408-0100	3115
Schlage Lock Company LLC	3429	E	619 671-0276	11626
Schneider Electric Usa Inc	3613	C	858 385-5040	16612
Scholastic Sports Inc	2752	D	858 496-9221	6855
Schott Magnetics	3499	F	619 661-7510	13544
Scientific-Atlanta LLC	3812	B	619 679-6000	20718
Scripps Laboratories Inc	2836	E	858 546-5800	8329
SD Desserts LLC	2099	F	702 480-9083	2609
Seating Concepts LLC	2531	E	619 491-3159	4871
Seescan Inc **(PA)**	3546	C	858 244-3300	14227
Sekisui America Corporation	2835	E	858 452-3198	8253
Sempra Global **(HQ)**	3612	D	619 696-2000	16575
Semtech San Diego Corporation	3674	E	858 695-1808	18539
Semtek Innvtive Solutions Corp	3577	E	858 436-2270	15331
Senior Aerospace Jet Pdts Corp **(HQ)**	3724	C	858 278-8400	19979
Senior Aerospace Jet Pdts Corp	3599	F	858 278-8400	16394
Senior Operations LLC	3599	B	858 278-8400	16395
Senior Operations LLC	3599	C	858 278-8400	16397
Servicenow Inc	7372	F	858 720-0477	24401
Shamir Insight Inc	3229	D	858 514-8300	10330
Sheffield Platers Inc	3471	E	858 546-8484	13100
Shelter Island Yachtways Ltd	3732	E	619 222-0481	20357
Shire Rgenerative Medicine Inc	2834	D	858 754-5396	8130
Sidus Solutions LLC **(PA)**	3699	F	619 275-5533	19401
Sigma 6 Electronics Inc	3699	F	858 279-4300	19404
Sigma Circuit Technology LLC	3672	D	858 523-0146	17999
Signal Pharmaceuticals LLC	2834	C	858 795-4700	8131
Signtech Electrical Advg Inc	3993	E	619 527-6100	23208
Silver Moon Lighting Inc	3645	F	858 613-3600	16991
Skagfield Corporation	2591	B	858 635-7777	5039
SKF Condition Monitoring Inc **(DH)**	3829	C	858 496-3400	21541
Skyepharma Inc	2834	F	858 678-3950	8135
Smart-Tek Automated Svcs Inc **(HQ)**	7372	F	858 798-1644	24418
Smartdraw Software LLC	7372	E	858 225-3300	24419
Smith Brothers Manufacturing	3599	F	619 296-3171	16408
Smithcorp Inc	2621	F	888 402-9979	5152
Smiths Medical Asd Inc	3841	E	619 710-1000	21901
Smooth Operator LLC	3949	E	619 233-8177	22889
Smooth Run Equine Inc	2048	F	760 751-8988	1127
Snaptracs Inc	3812	F	858 587-1121	20724
So Cal Soft-Pak Incorporated	7372	E	619 283-2338	24424
Solar Turbines Incorporated **(HQ)**	3511	A	619 544-5000	13575
Solar Turbines Incorporated	3566	E	619 544-5352	14750
Solar Turbines Incorporated	3511	C	858 715-2060	13576
Solar Turbines Intl Co **(DH)**	3511	E	619 544-5000	13578

Company	SIC	EMP	PHONE	ENTRY #
Solar Turbines Intl Co	3511	E	858 694-1616	13579
Solectek Corporation	3663	E	858 450-1220	17664
Solv Inc	7372	C	858 622-4040	24431
Sonant Corporation	3661	F	858 623-8180	17412
Soncell North America Inc **(HQ)**	3812	C	619 795-4600	20725
Sonic Vr LLC	7372	F	206 227-8585	24435
Sony Corporation of America **(PA)**	3571	E	212 833-8000	14979
Sony Electronics Inc **(DH)**	3651	A	858 942-2400	17284
Sony Electronics Inc.	3651	C	858 942-2400	17285
Sony Electronics Inc.	3652	E	858 824-6960	17337
Sotera Wireless Inc	3845	C	858 427-4620	22313
Sound Imaging Inc	3845	F	858 622-0082	22314
South Bay Cstm Plstic Extrders	3089	E	619 544-0808	10063
South Pacific Tuna Corporation	2091	F	619 233-2060	2252
South Swell Screen Arts	2759	F	858 566-3095	7220
Southwest Products LLC	2099	C	619 263-8000	2615
Space Micro Inc	3663	D	858 332-0700	17666
Spec-Built Systems Inc	3444	E	619 661-8100	12385
Specialty Steel Products Inc	3496	F	619 671-0720	13436
Spectral Labs Incorporated	3829	E	858 451-0540	21547
Spectrum Accessory Distrs	3714	C	858 653-6470	19773
Speedplay Inc	3949	E	858 453-4707	22893
Speedy Bindery Inc	2789	E	619 275-0261	7352
Sperry West Inc	3663	F	858 551-2000	17668
Sportrx Inc	3851	E	858 571-0240	22388
Springs Window Fashions LLC	2591	F	877 792-0002	5041
Ssco Manufacturing Inc	3548	E	619 628-1022	14255
STA Pharmaceutical US LLC	2834	E	609 606-6499	8141
Stats Chippac Test Svcs Inc	3674	F	858 228-4084	18580
Steris Corporation	3699	D	858 586-1166	19414
Stingray Shields Corporation	3842	E	619 325-9003	22093
Stoneybrook Publishing Inc.	2731	F	858 674-4600	6149
Strafford Intl Group Inc	2542	F	619 446-6960	5004
Strategic Insights Inc	7372	D	858 452-7500	24459
Streeter Printing Inc	2752	E	858 566-0866	6875
Sumitronics USA Inc	3672	E	619 661-0450	18014
Suneva Medical Inc **(PA)**	2844	E	858 550-9999	8591
Sunfusion Energy Systems Inc	3999	E	800 544-0282	23491
Sungear Inc	3728	E	858 549-3166	20240
Sunline Energy Inc	3674	F	858 997-2408	18590
Sunrise Jewelry Mfg Corp	3911	B	619 270-5624	22576
Superior Ready Mix Concrete LP	3273	E	619 265-0955	10847
Superior Ready Mix Concrete LP	3273	E	619 265-0296	10848
Superlamb Inc	2386	F	858 566-2031	3523
Surface Optics Corp	3825	E	858 675-7404	21131
Surface Technologies Corp	3625	E	619 564-8320	16758
Symcoat Metal Processing Inc	3471	E	858 451-3313	13115
Synbiotics LLC	2835	E	858 451-3771	8262
Systech Corporation	3669	E	858 674-6500	17765
T L Clark Co Inc	2434	F	619 230-1400	4252
T-Rex Products Incorporated	3999	F	619 482-4444	23496
Tabor Communications Inc.	2741	E	858 625-0070	6356
Tachyon Networks Incorporated	3663	D	858 882-8100	17676
Tandem Diabetes Care Inc **(PA)**	3841	B	858 366-6900	21923
Tangoe Us Inc	7372	D	858 452-6800	24488
Tapioca Express	2046	F	619 286-0484	1065
Tara Materials Inc.	3952	F	619 671-1018	22946
Taylor Communications Inc	2761	F	866 541-0937	7288
Tdo Software Inc	7372	E	858 558-3696	24491
Te Connectivity Corporation	3678	E	619 454-5176	18796
Teal Electronics Corporation **(PA)**	3625	D	858 558-9000	16762
Tech4learning Inc **(PA)**	7372	F	619 563-5348	24493
Tecnova Advanced Systems Inc	3812	E	858 586-9660	20728
Teledyne Instruments Inc	3829	D	619 239-5959	21555
Teledyne Instruments Inc	3674	E	858 842-3127	18609
Teledyne Instruments Inc	3643	D	858 565-7050	16934
Telegent Systems Usa Inc.	3674	E	408 523-2800	18611
Tensorcom Inc.	3674	E	760 496-3264	18612
Tensys Medical Inc.	3845	E	858 552-1941	22319
Teradata Corporation **(PA)**	3572	B	866 548-8348	15109
Teradata Operations Inc **(HQ)**	3571	D	937 242-4030	14987
Terry Town Corporation	2384	F	619 421-5354	3504
Textile 2000 Screen Printing	2759	E	858 735-8521	7246
Thermo Fisher Scientific Inc.	3826	D	858 453-7551	21310
Thermo Fisher Scientific Inc.	3826	F	858 882-1286	21315
Thermo Gamma-Metrics LLC **(HQ)**	3824	E	858 450-9811	20976
Thermx Temperature Tech	3823	F	858 573-0983	20950
Thompson Type Inc.	2791	F	619 224-3137	7364
Three Man Corporation	2759	E	858 684-5200	7250
Timlin Industries Inc	3993	E	541 947-6771	23228
Tocagen Inc.	2834	D	858 412-8400	8166
Tom Garcia Inc	7694	E	619 232-4881	24699
Tomahawk Power LLC	3629	F	866 577-4476	16804
Tomarco Contractor Spc Inc.	3965	F	858 547-0700	23012
Top Art LLC	2741	F	858 554-0102	6359

Company	SIC	EMP	PHONE	ENTRY #
Top Brands Distribution Inc	2022	F	858 578-0319	578
Tracon Pharmaceuticals Inc (PA)	2834	E	858 550-0780	8167
Trademark Construction Co Inc (PA)	3694	D	760 489-5647	19203
Tragara Pharmaceuticals Inc	2834	F	760 208-6900	8168
Trane US Inc	3585	E	858 292-0833	15463
Trend Marketing Corporation	2499	D	800 468-7363	4540
Trex Enterprises Corporation (PA)	3571	D	858 646-5300	14992
Triprism Inc	3861	F	858 675-7552	22466
Trius Therapeutics LLC	2834	D	858 452-0370	8170
Trovagene Inc	2835	F	858 952-7570	8265
True Temper Sports Inc	3949	E	858 404-0405	22912
Trumed Systems Incorporated	3585	F	844 878-6331	15466
Tsf Construction Services Inc	2298	E	619 202-7615	2919
Ttm Technologies Inc	3672	D	858 874-2701	18033
Tungsten Heavy Powder Inc (PA)	3313	D	858 693-6100	11084
Turbine Components Inc	3724	E	858 678-8568	19986
Turning Point Therapeutics Inc	2834	E	858 926-5251	8171
Turtle Beach Corporation (PA)	3679	E	914 345-2255	19128
U-Blox San Diego Inc	3661	F	858 847-9611	17423
Ultraneon Sign Corp	3993	E	858 569-6716	23233
Ultratype & Graphics	2791	F	858 541-1894	7365
Unico Incorporated	1081	E	619 209-6124	13
United Brands Company Inc	2087	E	619 461-5220	2234
United Cerebral Palsy Assn San	3953	F	619 282-8790	22957
United Tote Company	3577	E	858 279-4250	15358
Urethane Masters Inc	3086	F	651 829-1032	9575
Urethane Masters Incorporated	3999	F	651 357-8821	23513
Utility Composite Solutions In (PA)	3272	F	858 442-3187	10663
V & P Scientific Inc	3826	F	858 455-0643	21319
Vanard Lithographers Inc	2752	E	619 291-5571	6916
Vangie L Cortes	2711	E	858 578-6807	5857
Variable Image Printing	2752	E	858 530-2443	6919
Vas Engineering Inc	3679	E	858 569-1601	19134
Vdp Direct LLC (PA)	2752	E	858 300-4510	6920
Veredatech LLC	2741	F	858 342-6468	6373
Verifone Inc	3577	E	858 436-2270	15361
Versacall Technologies Inc	3669	F	858 677-6766	17771
Verus Pharmaceuticals Inc	2834	F	858 455-1600	8179
Vesta Medical LLC	3841	F	949 660-8648	21956
Vetpowered LLC	7692	F	619 269-7116	24677
Via Telecom Inc	3674	C	858 350-5560	18641
Video Simplex Inc	3699	F	858 467-9762	19434
Vigitron Inc	3699	F	858 484-5209	19435
Vigor Systems Inc	3663	E	866 748-4467	17701
Viking Therapeutics Inc	2834	F	858 704-4660	8181
Vista Prime Management LLC	3999	F	858 256-9221	23517
Vitagen Acquisition Corp	2834	F	858 673-6840	8183
Vitality Extracts LLC	2836	F	844 429-6580	8333
Volcano Corporation (DH)	3845	B	800 228-4728	22329
Von Hoppen Ice Cream	2024	F	858 695-9111	678
Vulcan Materials Company	3273	F	619 661-1088	10869
Walter N Coffman Inc	3086	D	619 266-2642	9577
WD-40 Company (PA)	2992	B	619 275-1400	9159
Wd-40 Company	2911	C	619 275-1400	9085
Wells Media Group Inc (PA)	2721	E	619 584-1100	6057
Westech Metal Fabrication Inc	3441	F	619 702-9353	11920
Western States Weeklies Inc	2711	F	619 280-2988	5865
WG Best Weinkellerei Inc	2084	F	858 627-1747	1997
Whalen LLC (DH)	2511	C	619 423-9948	4622
White Labs Inc (PA)	2099	F	858 693-3441	2646
Wind River Systems Inc	7372	D	858 824-3100	24582
Wintriss Engineering Corp	3827	E	858 550-7300	21421
Wissings Inc	2752	F	858 625-4111	6942
Wme Bi LLC	7372	D	877 592-2472	24584
Wordsmart Corporation	7372	D	858 565-8068	24586
Worldview Project	2731	F	858 964-0709	6167
X Controls Inc	3822	F	858 717-0004	20823
Yamagata America Inc	2741	F	858 751-1010	6385
Yellow Inc	3949	E	858 689-4851	22929
Ysi Incorporated	3826	E	858 546-8327	21326
Z-Communications Inc	3679	F	858 621-2700	19147
Zebra Technologies Corporation	3577	B	619 661-5465	15368

SAN DIMAS, CA - Los Angeles County

Company	SIC	EMP	PHONE	ENTRY #
AC Propulsion	3621	E	909 592-5399	16626
Act Now Instant Signs Inc	3993	F	909 394-7818	23041
Aircraft Stamping Company Inc	3444	E	323 283-1239	12093
Alfredo Hernandez	3599	F	909 971-9320	15717
Bolide Technology Group Inc	3699	D	909 305-8889	19266
Cabinet Concepts	2434	F	909 599-9191	4172
Co-Color	2752	F	909 394-7888	6491
Cosmobeauti Labs & Mfg Inc	2844	F	909 971-9832	8471
Craic Technologies Inc	3826	F	310 573-8180	21211
Elba Jewelry Inc	3911	F	909 394-5803	22515
Embroidery By P & J Inc	2395	F	909 592-2622	3741
Gei Inc	3559	F	909 592-2234	14471

Company	SIC	EMP	PHONE	ENTRY #
Gilead Palo Alto Inc	2834	B	909 394-4000	7914
Gilead Sciences Inc	2834	F	909 394-4090	7917
Gilead Sciences Inc	2834	C	909 394-4000	7918
Gms Elevator Services Inc	3534	E	909 599-3904	13801
Hagen-Renaker Inc (PA)	3269	C	909 599-2341	10489
Hamilton Sundstrand Corp	3826	A	909 593-5300	21235
Hamilton Sundstrand Spc Systms	3829	D	909 288-5300	21483
J & D Business Forms Inc	2752	F	626 914-1777	6654
Kap Manufacturing Inc	3599	E	909 599-2525	16106
Louis Vuitton US Mfg Inc	3172	F	909 599-2411	10239
Lundia	2511	B	888 989-1370	4587
Magor Mold LLC	3544	F	909 592-5729	14074
Omega Fire Inc	3052	F	818 404-6212	9202
Organic Milling Inc	2043	D	800 638-8686	1031
Organic Milling Corporation (PA)	2043	C	909 599-0961	1032
Organic Milling Corporation	2043	F	909 305-0185	1033
Pertronix Inc (PA)	3822	E	909 599-5955	20804
Sharp Profiles LLC	3423	F	760 246-9446	11544
Sigtronics Corporation	3669	E	909 305-9399	17763
Spectrum Instruments Inc	3825	F	909 971-9710	21125
Sypris Data Systems Inc (HQ)	3572	E	909 962-9400	15106
Thunderbird Industries Inc	3544	E	909 394-1633	14112
Tools & Production Inc	3544	E	626 286-0213	14114
Vertex Diamond Tool Company	3545	D	909 599-1129	14209
Wavestream Corporation (HQ)	3679	C	909 599-9080	19141
Western PCF Stor Solutions Inc (PA)	2542	D	909 451-0303	5012
Young Engineering & Mfg Inc (PA)	3823	F	909 394-3225	20960

SAN FERNANDO, CA - Los Angeles County

Company	SIC	EMP	PHONE	ENTRY #
Abex Display Systems Inc (PA)	2653	C	800 537-0231	5193
Airo Industries Company	2531	E	818 838-1008	4852
American Bottling Company	2086	C	818 898-1471	2031
Araca Merchandise LP	2759	E	818 743-5400	6991
Art Bronze Inc	3366	E	818 897-2222	11394
B & B Doors and Windows Inc	3442	F	818 837-8480	11933
Bellows Mfg & RES Inc	3599	F	818 838-1333	15784
Blue Cross Beauty Products Inc	2844	E	818 896-8681	8446
C A Schroeder Inc (PA)	3296	E	818 365-9561	10980
California Flex Corporation (PA)	3089	F	818 361-1169	9685
California Technical Pltg Corp	3471	E	818 365-8205	12962
Canady Manufacturing Co Inc	3599	F	818 365-9181	15822
Dg Displays LLC	3993	E	877 358-5976	23088
Diasol Inc (PA)	3841	F	818 838-7077	21686
DI Tool and Mfg Co Inc	3544	F	818 837-3451	14046
Electric Gate Store Inc (PA)	3699	C	818 504-2300	19302
Flannery Inc (PA)	3275	F	818 837-7585	10876
Foamation Inc	3086	F	818 837-6613	9537
Frazier Aviation Inc	3728	F	818 898-1998	20110
Fresh & Ready Foods LLC	2099	D	818 837-7600	2464
General Production Services	3599	E	818 365-4211	15992
Graphix Press Inc	2752	E	818 834-8520	6597
Haimetal Duct Inc	3444	F	818 768-2315	12230
International Tents & Supplies	2394	F	818 599-6258	3688
Iron Master	3446	F	818 361-4060	12482
J L Shepherd and Associates	3829	E	818 898-2361	21492
J Miller Co Inc	3053	E	818 837-0181	9239
Jay Gee Sales	3269	F	818 365-1311	10491
Karoun Dairies Inc (PA)	2022	D	818 767-7000	558
Kraft Tech Inc	3751	E	818 837-3520	20413
Krego Corporation	3613	F	818 837-1494	16601
Lehman Foods Inc	2099	E	818 837-7600	2526
Lumenyte International Corp	3648	F	949 279-8687	17142
Mr Tortilla Inc	2099	F	818 307-7414	2559
New Haven Companies Inc	2299	F	213 749-8181	2946
Newco International Inc	2511	B	818 834-7100	4598
Omnical Inc	3842	F	818 837-7531	22059
Pepsi-Cola Metro Btlg Co Inc	2086	C	818 898-3829	2121
Pharmavite LLC	2833	B	818 221-6200	7682
Prosound Communications Inc	3131	E	818 367-9593	10152
Puretek Corporation (PA)	2834	E	818 361-3316	8092
Ricon Corp (HQ)	3999	C	818 267-3000	23462
Santana Formal Accessories Inc	2311	C	818 898-3677	2978
Signature Tech Group Inc	3679	E	818 890-7611	19081
Simon Harrison	3829	E	818 898-1036	21539
Skaug Truck Body Works	3713	F	818 365-9123	19554
Slj Wholesale LLC	2051	E	323 662-8900	1278
Spira Manufacturing Corp	3053	E	818 764-8222	9257
Sto-Kar Enterprises	3441	E	818 886-5600	11887
TL Shield & Associates Inc	3534	E	818 509-8228	13810
Triumph Precision Products	3451	F	818 897-4700	12656
Vmg Engineering Inc	3599	F	818 837-6320	16504
W Machine Works Inc	3599	E	818 890-8049	16506
Westfield Hydraulics Inc	3492	F	818 896-6414	13334
Wild Side West	3953	E	213 388-9792	22958
Wyndham Collection LLC	2434	E	888 522-8476	4271

GEOGRAPHIC

SAN FRANCISCO, CA - San Francisco County

Company	SIC	EMP	PHONE	ENTRY #
101 Roofing & Sheet Metal Co	3444	F	415 695-0101	12074
15five Inc	7372	F	208 816-4225	23533
18 Rabbits Inc (PA)	2064	F	415 922-6006	1353
3dgroundworks LLC	7372	F	415 964-0060	23537
4505 Meats Inc	2096	E	415 255-3094	2314
500friends Inc (DH)	7372	E	800 818-8356	23538
89bio Inc	2834	F	415 500-4614	7707
A S Batle Company	3299	F	415 864-3300	10994
ABB Enterprise Software Inc	7372	C	415 527-2850	23541
Able Health Inc	7372	F	617 529-6264	23543
Ad Art Inc (PA)	3993	D	415 869-6460	23042
Addvocate Inc	7372	F	415 797-7620	23562
Adina For Life Inc	2087	E	415 285-9300	2188
Adobe Inc	7372	A	415 832-2000	23565
Adobe Macromedia Software LLC (HQ)	7372	E	415 832-2000	23568
Aechelon Technology Inc (PA)	3571	E	415 255-0120	14882
Affectlayer Inc	7372	F	650 924-1082	23576
Afresh Technologies Inc	7372	F	805 551-9245	23577
Aktana Inc	7372	E	888 707-3125	23587
Alan Wofsy Fine Arts LLC	2731	F	415 292-6500	6067
All City Printing Inc	2752	F	415 861-8088	6402
Allbirds Inc	3143	C	888 963-8944	10157
Allegra	2752	F	415 824-9610	6403
Allen Sarah &	3577	F	415 242-0906	15150
Allied Concrete Rdymx Svcs LLC	3273	F	415 282-8117	10685
Alm Media Holdings Inc	2721	E	415 490-1054	5879
Amazon Prsrvation Partners Inc	2033	E	415 775-6355	754
American Giant Inc	2326	F	415 529-2429	3025
American Scence Tech As T Corp (PA)	3721	C	415 251-2800	19855
AMR Industries Enterprises Inc	3533	E	415 860-5566	13764
Anchor Distilling Company	2084	E	415 863-8350	1582
Angellist LLC	7372	F	415 857-0840	23601
Appdirect Inc (PA)	7372	D	415 852-3924	23605
Appdynamics Inc (HQ)	7372	C	415 442-8400	23606
Arcline Investment MGT LP (PA)	2824	F	415 801-4570	7634
Ardica Technologies Inc	3674	F	415 568-9270	18121
Arete Therapeutics Inc	2834	F	650 737-4600	7765
Arnold & Egan Manufacturing Co	2541	E	415 822-2700	4882
Asian Week (PA)	2711	F	415 397-0220	5556
AT&T Corp	2741	B	415 542-9000	6193
Atlas Screw Machine Pdts Co	3451	F	415 621-6737	12622
Atlassian Inc (DH)	7372	C	415 701-1110	23636
Attilas Byshore Art Studio LLC	3299	F	415 282-2815	10997
Audentes Therapeutics Inc (PA)	2836	C	415 818-1001	8277
Autodesk Inc	7372	D	415 356-0700	23639
B & M Upholstery	2211	F	415 621-7447	2669
Badger Maps Inc	7372	E	415 592-5909	23648
Baker Interiors Furniture Co	2519	E	415 626-1414	4763
Bar Media Inc	2711	F	415 861-5019	5563
Barebottle Brewing Company Inc	2082	F	415 926-8617	1500
Base Crm	7372	F	773 796-6266	23654
Bay Guardian Company	2711	D	415 255-3100	5564
Bayer Healthcare LLC	2834	B	415 437-5800	7791
Bayer Hlthcare Phrmcticals Inc	2834	B	510 246-3500	7798
Beats Music LLC	7372	D	415 590-5104	23656
Behaviosec Inc	7372	F	833 248-6732	23658
Bento Technologies Inc	7372	F	415 887-2028	23660
Bettercompany Inc	7372	F	415 501-9692	23662
Big Heart Pet Brands Inc (HQ)	2047	B	415 247-3000	1069
Blackthorn Therapeutics Inc	2835	E	415 548-5401	8210
Blue Cedar Networks Inc	3577	E	415 329-0401	15175
Blue Rock Networks LLC	3825	F	415 577-8004	21012
Blurb Inc	2731	D	415 364-6300	6080
Borden Decal Company Inc	2759	F	415 431-1587	7004
Branded Spirits USA Ltd	2085	F	415 813-5045	2012
Brewmaster Inc	2082	E	415 642-3371	1506
Brightidea Incorporated	7372	E	415 814-1387	23697
Brilliant Worldwide Inc	7372	E	650 468-2966	23698
Business Jrnl Publications Inc	2711	E	415 989-2522	5573
Buzzworks Inc	2082	F	415 863-5964	1509
Byer California (PA)	2331	A	415 626-7844	3145
Calco Supply Inc	3648	E	415 760-7793	17109
California Smart Foods	2051	F	415 826-0449	1173
Canary Technologies Corp	7372	E	415 578-1414	23715
Canto Software Inc (PA)	7372	F	415 495-6545	23716
Carpenter Group (PA)	3536	E	415 285-1954	13844
CB Mill Inc	2511	E	415 386-5309	4560
Century Technology Inc	3672	F	650 583-8908	17844
Cenveo Worldwide Limited	2752	D	415 821-7171	6478
Cerego Inc	7372	E	415 518-3926	23727
Certain Inc (PA)	7372	F	415 353-5330	23729
Chronicle Books LLC	2731	C	415 537-4200	6088
Circa 1605 Inc	7372	E	217 899-3512	23738
Cisco Systems Inc	3577	F	415 837-6261	15192
City & County of San Francisco	2759	E	415 557-5251	7023
Cjs Toffee & Toppings LLC	2064	F	415 929-7852	1361
Classdojo Inc	7372	F	650 646-8235	23743
Clearslide (DH)	7372	D	877 360-3366	23745
Cleasby Manufacturing Co Inc (PA)	3531	E	415 822-6565	13722
Clipcall Inc	7372	F	650 285-7597	23747
Clockware	7372	F	650 556-8880	23748
Cloud Engines Inc	3572	E	415 738-8076	15016
Cloudflare Inc (PA)	7372	C	888 993-5273	23751
Cloudnco Inc	7372	F	408 605-8755	23752
Clover Garments Inc	2339	D	415 826-6909	3307
Club Donatello Owners Assn	3873	E	415 474-7333	22480
Cobalt Labs Inc	7372	E	415 651-7028	23756
Colour Drop	2759	E	415 353-5720	7032
Concentric Analgesics Inc	2834	F	415 771-5129	7848
Constellation Brands Inc	2084	E	415 912-3880	1645
Copper Crm Inc (PA)	7372	C	415 231-6360	23775
Copy 1 Inc	2752	F	415 986-0111	6512
Corporatecouch	3674	F	415 312-6078	18180
Council Oak Books LLC	2731	F	415 931-7700	6092
Creative Intl Pastries	2051	F	415 255-1128	1182
Ctg I LLC	2741	F	415 233-9700	6218
Cucina Holdings Inc	2051	F	415 986-8688	1183
Cushion Works Inc	2393	F	415 552-6220	3657
Cut Loose (PA)	2339	D	415 822-2031	3310
Da Global Energy Inc	3641	F	408 916-6303	16858
Daily Journal Corporation	2711	D	415 296-2400	5609
Darling Ingredients Inc	2077	D	415 647-4890	1456
Data Advantage Group Inc	7372	F	415 947-0400	23799
Datafox Intelligence Inc	7372	F	415 969-2144	23803
Davis Shoe Therapeutics	3144	F	415 661-8705	10168
Dcl Productions	2395	F	415 826-2200	3736
Dco Environmental & Recycl LLC	3089	F	573 204-3844	9746
Deem Inc (DH)	7372	D	415 590-8300	23812
Demandbase Inc	7372	B	415 683-2660	23815
Design Imagery	2542	F	650 589-6464	4973
Designer Printing Inc	2752	F	415 989-0008	6536
Diageo North America Inc	2084	D	415 835-7300	1665
Diamond Foods LLC	2068	F	209 467-6000	1425
Digital Mania Inc	2752	E	415 896-0500	6540
Dispatcher Newspaper	2711	E	415 775-0533	5616
Divisadero 500 LLC	2599	F	415 572-6062	5055
Diy Co	3699	F	844 564-6349	19292
Docsend Inc	7372	F	888 258-5951	23821
Doctor On Demand Inc	7372	D	415 935-4447	23822
Docusign Inc (PA)	7372	B	415 489-4940	23823
Dogpatch Wineworks	2084	F	415 525-4440	1668
Dolby Laboratories Inc (PA)	3651	B	415 558-0200	17221
Domino Data Lab Inc (PA)	7372	E	415 570-2425	23825
Doubledutch Inc (PA)	7372	D	800 748-9024	23828
Doughtronics Inc	2051	E	415 288-2978	1193
Dow Jones & Company Inc	2711	E	415 765-6131	5618
Draftday Fantasy Sports Inc	7372	F	310 306-1828	23830
Dreams Duvets & Bed Linens	2392	F	415 543-1800	3613
Dropbox Inc (PA)	7372	C	415 857-6800	23834
Dualcor Technologies Inc	3572	E	831 684-2457	15022
Dwell Life Inc (PA)	2721	E	415 373-5100	5927
Eis Group Inc	7372	C	415 402-2622	23849
Ellipsis Health Inc	7372	F	650 906-6117	23855
EMC Corporation	3572	E	877 636-8589	15025
Emiliomiti LLC	3556	F	415 621-1171	14360
Emx Digital LLC	7372	F	212 792-6810	23857
Epignosis LLC	7372	E	646 797-2799	23870
Eride Inc	7372	E	415 848-7800	23874
Ermico Enterprises Inc	3949	D	415 822-6776	22797
Evergood Sausage Co	2013	D	415 822-4660	455
Evolv Surfaces Inc	2542	C	415 671-0635	4975
Evolv Technology Solutions Inc	7372	E	415 444-9040	23881
Exin LLC	2711	C	415 359-2600	5631
Ezboard Inc	7372	F	415 773-0400	23888
Fabric Walls Inc	2392	F	415 863-2711	3615
Fastsigns	3993	F	415 537-6900	23109
Fat Wreck Chords Inc	3652	F	415 284-1790	17322
Fenix International Inc	3612	B	415 754-9222	16550
Fibrogen Inc (PA)	2834	C	415 978-1200	7890
Finix Payments Inc	7372	F	714 417-2727	23897
First Advantage Talent Managem	7372	F	415 446-3930	23900
First Solar Inc	3674	F	415 935-2500	18236
Fitbit Inc (PA)	3829	B	415 513-1000	21473
Flamestower Inc	3621	D	415 699-8650	16646
FML Inc	3961	F	415 864-5000	22982
Forager Project LLC	2037	D	855 729-5253	912
Forecross Corporation (PA)	7372	F	415 543-1515	23909
Forge Global Inc (PA)	7372	F	415 881-1612	23911
Forgerock US Inc (HQ)	7372	D	415 599-1100	23912

Company	SIC	EMP	PHONE	ENTRY #
Formation Inc	7372	D	650 257-2277	23913
Foundation For Nat Progress	2721	E	415 321-1700	5938
Four M Studios	2731	D	415 249-2362	6103
Freedom of Press Foundation	2721	F	510 995-0780	5940
Frontapp Inc	7372	D	415 680-3048	23922
Fundx Investment Group	2741	F	415 986-7979	6241
Future Us Inc (HQ)	2721	D	650 238-2400	5941
Fuzebox Software Corporation (HQ)	7372	F	415 692-4800	23924
Gatherapp Inc	7372	F	415 409-9476	23929
Gaze Inc	3674	F	415 374-9193	18246
Gb Sport Sf LLC	2386	E	415 863-6171	3515
Gergay and Associates	3469	E	415 431-4163	12807
Glaser Designs Inc	3171	F	415 552-3188	10222
Gobble Inc	2099	C	888 405-7481	2470
Golden Gate Tofu Incorporated	2075	F	415 822-5613	1443
Goodco Inc	7372	F	415 425-1012	23948
Goorin Bros Inc (PA)	2353	E	415 431-9196	3465
Greatdad LLC	2721	F	415 572-8181	5946
Green Acres Cannabis LLC	2833	E	415 657-3484	7664
Guadalupe Associates Inc (PA)	2741	F	415 387-2324	6248
Gum Sun Times Inc (PA)	2711	E	415 379-6788	5650
H&H Imaging Inc	2752	F	415 431-4731	6602
H2 Cards Inc	2759	F	415 788-7888	7085
H2o Plus LLC (PA)	2844	D	312 377-2132	8506
Habla Incorporated	7372	E	703 867-0135	23968
Halo Neuro Inc	3845	F	415 851-3338	22258
Harmless Harvest Inc (PA)	2099	E	347 688-6286	2477
Harpercollins Publishers LLC	2731	E	415 477-4400	6107
Hartle Media Ventures LLC	2721	E	415 362-7797	5948
Healthline Media Inc	2741	B	415 281-3100	6250
Hearsay Social Inc (PA)	7372	D	888 990-3777	23974
Hearst Communications Inc	2711	C	415 537-4200	5656
Hearst Corporation	2711	F	415 777-0600	5658
Heath Ceramics Ltd	3269	D	415 361-5552	10490
Hello Network Inc	7372	F	408 891-4727	23977
Heroku Inc	7372	E	650 704-6107	23978
Highland Technology	3829	E	415 551-1700	21484
Hint Inc	2086	E	415 513-4051	2081
Hitachi Rail Usa Inc (PA)	3743	F	415 397-7010	20370
Ho Tai Printing Co Inc	2752	F	415 421-4218	6616
Homestead Publishing Inc	2741	E	307 733-6248	6253
HP Inc	3571	D	415 979-3700	14921
Humangear Inc	3089	F	415 580-7553	9831
I E P Full Service Printing	2759	F	415 648-6002	7089
Icebreaker Health Inc	7372	F	415 926-5818	23997
Idg Consumer & Smb Inc (DH)	2721	C	415 243-0500	5959
IDO Cabinet Inc	2434	F	415 282-1683	4208
Ifwe Inc (HQ)	7372	D	415 946-1850	23998
Ijk & Co Inc	3699	F	415 826-8899	19322
Incandescent Inc	7372	F	415 464-7975	24007
Infoworld Media Group Inc (DH)	2721	D	415 243-4344	5966
Insideview Technologies Inc	7372	C	415 728-9309	24026
Integrated Digital Media (PA)	2752	E	415 986-4091	6646
Integrated Digital Media	2752	E	415 882-9390	6647
Intelligent Peripherals	3577	F	415 564-4366	15257
Internet Industry Publishing	2721	E	415 733-5400	5968
Internet Science Education Prj	3764	F	415 806-3156	20464
Interntnal Indian Traty Cuncil	3949	F	415 641-4482	22830
Intershop Communications Inc	7372	E	415 844-1500	24031
Invuity Inc	3841	C	415 665-2100	21758
Ionetix Corporation (PA)	3699	E	415 944-1440	19328
Irhythm Technologies Inc (PA)	3845	E	415 632-5700	22266
Isolation Network Inc (PA)	3651	E	415 489-7000	17246
J F Fitzgerald Company Inc	2512	F	415 648-6161	4647
Jaguar Health Inc (PA)	2834	E	415 371-8300	7966
James P McNair Co Inc	3429	E	415 681-2200	11600
JC Metal Specialists Inc (PA)	3441	E	415 822-3878	11818
Jeremiahs Pick Coffee Company	2095	F	415 206-9900	2301
Jessica McClintock Inc (PA)	2361	C	415 553-8200	3479
Jinkosolar (us) Inc	3674	F	415 402-0502	18330
John Wiley & Sons Inc	2731	C	415 433-1740	6116
Johnson Leather Corporation (PA)	2386	F	415 775-7393	3518
JR Watkins LLC	2392	E	415 477-8500	3620
Juniper Square Inc	7372	E	415 841-2722	24064
Just Inc	2035	C	844 423-6637	885
Juul Labs Inc (PA)	3999	B	415 829-2336	23375
K C A Engineered Plastics Inc (PA)	2821	D	415 433-4494	7578
Kaise Perma San Franc Medic Ce	3842	E	415 833-2000	22039
Kba2 Inc	7372	E	415 528-5500	24073
Khn Solutions Inc	3829	F	877 334-6876	21497
Khoros LLC (PA)	7372	E	415 757-3100	24075
Kings Asian Gourmet Inc	2032	E	415 222-6100	733
Kinsale Holdings Inc (PA)	3069	D	415 400-2600	9325
Klein Industries Inc	3599	F	415 695-9117	16120
Kpisoft Inc	7372	D	415 439-5228	24084
L Y Z Ltd (PA)	2335	F	415 445-9505	3238
La Brothers Enterprise Inc	2752	E	415 626-8818	6689
Lcr-Dixon Corporation	7372	F	404 307-1695	24096
Leewood Press Inc	2752	E	415 896-0513	6696
Levi Strauss & Co (PA)	2325	A	415 501-6000	3012
Levi Strauss International (HQ)	2329	F	415 501-6000	3103
Liberty Cafe	2051	E	415 695-8777	1235
Lifi Labs Inc (PA)	3229	F	650 739-5563	10318
Lion Semiconductor Inc	3674	F	415 462-4933	18356
Lois A Valeskie	3829	E	415 641-2570	21500
Los Angles Tmes Cmmnctions LLC	2711	A	415 274-9000	5710
Lowpensky Moulding	2431	E	415 822-7422	4076
Loyyal Corporation	7372	F	415 419-9590	24110
Lyra Corporation	2741	F	415 668-2546	6275
M C Metal Inc	3446	F	415 822-2288	12496
Mac Publishing LLC (HQ)	2721	E	415 243-0505	5982
Magnamosis Inc	3841	F	707 484-8774	21785
Manta Solar Corporation	3433	F	928 853-6216	11704
Mapbox Inc	7372	F	202 250-3633	24126
Marco Fine Furniture Inc	2512	E	415 285-3235	4655
Margaret OLeary Inc (PA)	2339	D	415 354-6663	3369
Mark Resources LLC (PA)	2522	F	415 515-5540	4842
Martinelli Envmtl Graphics	3993	F	415 468-4000	23154
McEvoy Properties LLC	2731	C	415 537-4200	6120
McLean Brewery Inc	2082	E	415 864-7468	1547
Medallia Inc (PA)	7372	C	650 321-3000	24138
Medicines360 (PA)	2834	E	415 951-8700	8005
Medium Entertainment Inc	3944	E	469 951-2688	22694
Medivation Inc (HQ)	2834	C	415 543-3470	8007
Medrio Inc (PA)	7372	F	415 963-3700	24145
Melian Labs Inc (PA)	7372	F	888 423-1944	24146
Menlo Energy LLC	2869	E	415 762-8200	8752
Method Home Products	2621	F	415 568-4600	5132
Metro World Plastics Inc	3081	F	415 255-8515	9411
Micro-Tracers Inc	2899	E	415 822-1100	8999
Microsoft Corporation	7372	C	415 972-6400	24162
Mindjolt	3944	F	415 543-7800	22695
Mindsnacks Inc	7372	E	415 875-9817	24168
Mixamo Inc	7372	F	415 255-7455	24172
Mixonic	2759	F	866 838-5067	7144
Mjus LLC (fka Mindjet Llc)	7372	F	415 229-4344	24173
Mode Analytics Inc	7372	F	415 271-7599	24177
Modern Luxury Media LLC (HQ)	2721	E	404 443-0004	5991
Molekule Inc (PA)	3822	F	352 871-3803	20799
Monitise Inc	7372	F	650 286-1059	24179
Motionloft Inc	3826	E	415 580-7671	21269
Mpl Brands Inc	2084	F	415 515-3536	1828
Mr S Leather	2386	E	415 863-7764	3520
Mulesoft Inc	7372	A	415 229-2009	24181
Munkyfun Inc	7372	E	415 281-3837	24182
Mursion Inc (PA)	7372	D	415 746-9631	24183
Myanimelist LLC	2741	F	714 423-8289	6288
Native Kjalii Foods Inc	2032	E	415 592-8670	740
Naturener Usa LLC (HQ)	3621	E	415 217-5500	16665
Naylor Corp	2066	E	415 421-1789	1412
Nebia Inc	3069	F	203 570-6222	9341
Nektar Therapeutics (PA)	2834	B	415 482-5300	8030
Nektar Therapeutics Al Corp	2869	D	256 512-9200	8755
New Relic Inc (PA)	7372	C	650 777-7600	24204
Nexsys Electronics Inc (PA)	3577	F	415 541-9980	15297
Ng John	2752	F	415 929-7188	6748
Ngmoco Inc	7372	F	415 375-3170	24207
Niebam-Cppola Estate Winery LP	2084	E	415 291-1700	1841
No Starch Press Inc	2741	F	415 863-9900	6298
Norcal Printing Inc	2752	F	415 282-8856	6752
Northern Quinoa Prod Corp	2043	E	806 535-8118	1030
Ohio Inc	2521	F	415 647-6446	4817
Okta Inc (PA)	7372	C	888 722-7871	24222
Olive Bariani Oil LLC	2079	F	415 864-1917	1480
On24 Inc (PA)	7372	B	877 202-9599	24226
Onc Holdings Inc	7372	F	415 243-3343	24227
One Hat One Hand LLC	2353	E	415 822-2020	3471
Opentv Inc (DH)	7372	F	415 962-5000	24231
Oracle America Inc	7372	D	415 908-3609	24240
Oracle Corporation	7372	E	415 834-9731	24249
Oracle Corporation	7372	C	415 402-7200	24258
Oracle Corporation	7372	F	650 506-7000	24266
Otsuka America Inc (HQ)	3829	F	415 986-5300	21514
Otsuka America Foods Inc (HQ)	2099	F	424 219-9425	2579
Ouster Inc	3829	D	415 949-0108	21515
P G Molinari & Sons Inc	2013	E	415 822-5555	485
Packageone Inc (PA)	2653	E	650 761-3339	5252
Pagerduty Inc (PA)	7372	C	844 800-3889	24285
Pan-O-Rama Baking Inc	2051	E	415 522-5500	1257
Panorama Intl CL Co Inc	2032	F	415 891-8478	742

Name	SIC	EMP	PHONE	ENTRY #
Parasound Products Inc	3651	F	415 397-7100	17268
Pch International USA Inc	3679	E	415 643-5463	19047
Peachpit Press	2741	E	415 336-6831	6306
Pearson Education Inc	2731	E	415 402-2500	6135
Peek Arent You Curious Inc (PA)	2361	D	415 512-7335	3486
Penrose Studios Inc	2741	F	703 354-1801	6307
People Center Inc	7372	E	781 864-1232	24293
Pepsi-Cola Metro Btlg Co Inc	2086	D	415 206-7400	2122
Petcube Inc (PA)	3651	E	424 302-6107	17270
Pi-Coral Inc	3572	D	408 516-5150	15074
Pionyr Immunotherapeutics Inc	2834	F	415 226-7503	8077
Plangrid Inc (HQ)	7372	D	800 646-0796	24301
Pleasant Mattress Inc	2515	F	415 874-7540	4736
Pluot Communications Inc	3651	F	202 258-9223	17273
Pocket Gems Inc (PA)	3944	D	415 371-1333	22705
Pointech	3366	E	415 822-8704	11405
Popsugar Inc (PA)	2741	C	415 391-7576	6313
Powwow Inc	7372	F	877 800-4381	24311
Presidio Pharmaceuticals Inc	2834	F	415 655-7560	8082
Prezi Inc (PA)	7372	F	415 398-8012	24313
Prism Skylabs Inc	3663	F	415 243-0834	17627
Project 1920 Inc	3171	F	415 529-2245	10225
Projectoris Inc	7372	F	917 972-5553	24317
Pubinno Inc	7372	F	669 251-6538	24322
Punkpost Inc	2771	E	415 818-7677	7297
Quad/Graphics Inc	2752	A	415 267-3700	6823
Quantal International Inc	7372	E	415 644-0754	24331
Quest Software Inc	7372	D	415 373-2222	24332
R A Jenson Manufacturing Co	2434	F	415 822-2732	4236
R E Dillard 1 LLC	3433	D	415 675-1500	11707
R J McGlennon Company Inc (PA)	2851	E	415 552-0311	8676
R R Donnelley & Sons Company	2754	E	415 362-2300	6963
Random Technologies LLC	3229	F	415 255-1267	10329
Rangeme Inc	2741	F	415 351-9268	6323
Rapid Lasergraphics (HQ)	2791	F	415 957-5840	7360
Rapid Typographers Company (PA)	2791	F	415 957-5840	7361
Rare Breed Distilling LLC (DH)	2085	E	415 315-8060	2017
RE Tranquillity 8 LLC	3433	D	415 675-1500	11710
Read It Later Inc	7372	E	415 692-6111	24340
Realpage Inc	7372	E	415 222-6996	24344
Recommind Inc (HQ)	3695	D	415 394-7899	19231
Red Tricycle Inc	3944	E	415 729-9781	22709
Reddit Inc (PA)	2741	E	415 666-2330	6327
Refinitiv US LLC	2721	B	415 344-6000	6016
Relx Inc	2721	E	415 908-3200	6017
Renee Rivera Hair Accessories	3069	F	415 776-6613	9364
Rickshaw Bagworks Inc	2393	E	415 904-8368	3663
Robert E Blake Inc	3731	F	415 391-2255	20303
Robert Yick Company Inc	3589	E	415 282-9707	15571
Rubel Marguerite Mfg Co	2337	F	415 362-2626	3275
Rypple	7372	F	888 479-7753	24369
Salesforcecom Inc	7372	E	415 323-8685	24375
Salesforcecom Inc	7372	F	703 463-3300	24376
Salesforcecom Inc (PA)	7372	A	415 901-7000	24377
San Francisco Print Media Co (PA)	2752	E	415 487-2594	6853
San Francisco Victoriana Inc	2431	F	415 648-0313	4120
Sanofi US Services Inc	2834	C	415 856-5000	8118
Sas Institute Inc	7372	E	415 421-2227	24383
Sawbird Inc (PA)	3425	E	415 861-0644	11555
Scafco Corporation	3999	E	415 852-7974	23467
Scality Inc	3572	E	650 356-8500	15092
SCM Accelerators LLC	7372	F	415 595-8091	24390
Scribe Technologies Inc	7372	F	415 746-9935	24392
Seamaid Manufacturing Corp	2321	E	415 777-9978	2993
Segmentio Inc	3577	F	844 611-0621	15330
Sgk LLC	2796	D	415 438-6700	7381
Siftery Inc	7372	E	415 484-8211	24410
Sight Machine Inc	7372	D	888 461-5739	24411
Sillajen Biotherapeutics Inc	2834	F	415 281-8886	8132
Siluria Technologies Inc	1311	E	415 978-2170	67
Simpa Networks Inc	3829	F	415 216-3204	21540
Sin MA Imports Company	2046	F	415 285-9369	1062
Singular Bio Inc	2835	F	415 553-8773	8258
Sirna Therapeutics Inc	2834	D	415 512-7200	8134
Sixteen Rivers Press Inc	2741	F	415 273-1303	6339
Slack Technologies Inc (PA)	7372	C	415 902-5526	24416
Socialize Inc	7372	E	415 529-4019	24425
Solher Iron	3449	E	415 822-9900	12608
Source Surgical Inc	3841	F	415 861-7040	21906
Sparkcentral (PA)	2741	F	866 559-6229	6344
Spectrum Grafix Inc	2752	F	415 648-2400	6868
Splunk Inc (PA)	7372	C	415 848-8400	24441
Spoton Computing Inc	7372	E	650 293-7464	24442
Sprout Inc	2741	F	415 894-9629	6346
Sproutling Inc	3661	F	415 323-3270	17415
Spruce Biosciences Inc	2833	F	415 655-3803	7694
Squamtech Inc	7372	F	415 867-8300	24443
Square Inc (PA)	7372	E	415 375-3176	24444
Stackla Inc	7372	D	415 789-3304	24448
Stamats Communications Inc	2731	E	800 358-0388	6148
Standard Cognition Corp (PA)	7372	E	201 707-7782	24451
Steelcase Inc	2522	B	415 865-0261	4849
Strevus Inc	7372	E	415 704-8182	24462
Stryder Corp (PA)	7372	E	415 981-8400	24463
Stumbleupon Inc (HQ)	7372	E	415 979-0640	24464
Sun Basket Inc	2099	D	408 669-4418	2618
Sun Mountain Inc	2431	E	415 852-2320	4132
Sun Reporter Publishing Inc	2711	E	415 671-1000	5843
Super Binge Media Inc	7372	F	714 688-6231	24468
Supersonic ADS Inc	3993	E	650 825-6010	23223
Swift Navigation Inc (PA)	3663	E	415 484-9026	17675
Swiftstack Inc (PA)	7372	E	415 625-0293	24472
Syapse Inc	7372	C	650 924-1461	24474
Synergy Global Inc	7372	F	415 766-3540	24477
Takipi Inc	7372	F	408 203-9585	24483
Talisman Systems Group Inc	7372	F	415 357-1751	24484
Talix Inc	7372	D	628 220-3885	24485
Talkdesk Inc (PA)	7372	F	888 743-3044	24486
Tanko Streetlighting Inc	3646	E	415 254-7579	17076
Tapingo Inc (HQ)	7372	E	415 283-5222	24489
Tartine LP	2051	F	415 487-2600	1285
Tempo Automation Inc	3672	F	415 320-1261	18023
Tequilas Premium Inc	2085	F	415 399-0496	2021
Teselagen Biotechnology Inc	7372	F	650 387-5932	24499
Thinksmart LLC	7372	F	888 489-4284	24502
Thirdmotion Inc	7372	F	415 848-2724	24503
Thirsty Bear Brewing Co LLC	2082	D	415 974-0905	1570
Thomas Lundberg	2514	F	415 695-0110	4703
Thousandeyes Inc (PA)	7372	D	415 513-4526	24506
TI Gotham Inc	2721	E	415 434-5244	6041
Tibco Software Inc	7372	E	415 344-0339	24509
Timbuk2 Designs Inc (PA)	2393	D	415 252-4300	3667
Tivix Inc	7372	F	415 680-1299	24513
Tokbox Inc (DH)	7372	F	415 284-4688	24515
Toms Metal Specialists Inc	7692	E	415 822-7971	24676
Topguest Inc	7372	E	646 415-9402	24516
Tpg Partners III LP (HQ)	1311	E	415 743-1500	71
Trinet Construction Inc	3569	F	415 695-7814	14865
Trumaker Inc	2311	F	415 662-3836	2979
Tullys Coffee Co Inc (HQ)	2095	E	415 929-8808	2312
Tullys Coffee Co Inc	2095	F	415 213-8791	2313
Turbotools Corporation	7372	F	415 759-5599	24532
Twitch Interactive Inc	2741	A	415 919-5000	6364
Ubm LLC	2721	C	415 947-6488	6048
Ubm Techweb (DH)	2721	F	415 947-6000	6049
Ucsf School of Pharmacy	2834	F	415 476-1444	8172
Universal McLoud USA Corp	7372	F	613 222-5904	24541
Universal Medical Press Inc	2721	F	415 436-9790	6052
Unmanned Innovation Inc (PA)	3721	D	877 714-4828	19936
Urban Steel Designs Inc	2514	F	415 305-2570	4706
Uvify Inc	3812	F	628 200-4469	20739
Van Tisse Inc	2254	F	415 543-2404	2810
Vans Inc	3021	F	415 566-3762	9192
Velti Inc (HQ)	7372	E	415 362-2077	24550
Vf Outdoor LLC	3949	E	415 433-3223	22918
Vgw Us Inc	7372	F	415 240-0498	24559
Visionary Electronics Inc	3674	D	415 751-8811	18647
Viz Media LLC	2721	C	415 546-7073	6055
Volta Industries LLC (PA)	3999	F	917 838-3590	23521
Voltus Inc	3822	E	415 617-9602	20821
Voyomotive LLC	3714	F	888 321-4633	19800
Walker/Dunham Corp	3161	F	415 821-3070	10215
Wallarm Inc (PA)	3699	F	415 940-7077	19440
Waterguru Inc	3589	F	415 269-5480	15601
Wave 80 Biosciences Inc	3841	F	415 487-7976	21963
West Coast Garment Mfg	2326	E	415 896-1772	3059
Whistle Labs Inc	3699	F	623 337-3679	19446
Willpower Labs Inc	2834	F	415 805-1518	8188
Window & Door Shop Inc (PA)	2431	F	415 282-6192	4151
Wired Ventures Inc	2721	C	415 276-8400	6059
Wizeline Inc (PA)	3571	E	415 373-6365	14998
Workshare Technology Inc	7372	C	415 590-7700	24587
World Harmony Organization	2731	F	415 246-6886	6166
World Tariff Limited	2721	E	415 391-7501	6060
Worldlink Media	7372	F	415 561-2141	24590
Xpansiv Data Systems Inc	7372	F	415 915-5124	24595
XYZ Graphics Inc (PA)	2759	E	415 227-9972	7275
Yong Kee Rice Noodle Co	2098	F	415 986-3759	2386
Youngs Custom Cabinet Inc	2434	F	415 822-8313	4272
Yourpeople Inc	7372	A	888 249-3263	24599

	SIC	EMP	PHONE	ENTRY #
Zendesk Inc (PA)	7372	C	415 418-7506	24601
Zenpayroll Inc (PA)	7372	C	800 936-0383	24602
Zinio Systems Inc	7372	D	415 494-2700	24605
Zip Notes LLC	2621	F	415 931-8020	5154
Zulip Inc	7372	F	617 945-7653	24607
Zynga Inc	7372	F	415 621-2391	24609

SAN GABRIEL, CA - Los Angeles County

	SIC	EMP	PHONE	ENTRY #
American Prcision Grinding Mch	3599	F	626 357-6610	15740
Asia Pacific California Inc	2711	E	626 281-8500	5555
BF Suma Pharmaceuticals Inc	2023	F	626 285-8366	581
California Shellfish Co Inc (PA)	2092	F	415 923-7400	2257
Cambero Metal Works Inc	7692	F	626 309-5315	24622
Classic Tees Inc	2339	E	626 607-0255	3305
Desais Design Craft	3229	F	626 285-3189	10303
Hsiao & Montano Inc	3161	E	626 588-2528	10197
Jetstream Trading Co	3728	F	818 921-7158	20146
JW Wireless	3663	F	626 532-2511	17549
Lotus Orient Corp (PA)	2335	F	626 285-5796	3243
Man Fon Inc	2099	F	626 287-6043	2539
Marples Gears Inc	3566	E	626 570-1744	14744
Media King Inc	3699	F	626 288-4558	19354
Mueller Gages Company	3545	F	626 287-2911	14176
R J Vincent Inc	2512	E	626 448-1509	4663
Sign Art Co	3993	F	626 287-2512	23196
Su Mano Inc	3111	F	562 529-8835	10144
Technipfmc US Holdings Inc	3533	F	310 328-1236	13793

SAN GREGORIO, CA - San Mateo County

	SIC	EMP	PHONE	ENTRY #
Cybernetic Micro Systems Inc	3575	F	650 726-3000	15121

SAN JACINTO, CA - Riverside County

	SIC	EMP	PHONE	ENTRY #
Amark Industries Inc (PA)	3567	C	951 654-7351	14753
C M Machine Inc	3599	F	951 654-6019	15813
Edelbrock Foundry Corp	3363	A	951 654-6677	11336
Edelbrock Holdings Inc	3714	C	951 654-6677	19645
Hilkers Custom Cabinets Inc	2434	F	951 487-7640	4205
Interstate Carports Corp	3448	F	951 654-1750	12550
J Talley Corporation (PA)	3446	E	951 654-2123	12484
Matthews International Corp	3366	E	951 537-6615	11403
Modern Wall Graphics LLC	3081	F	760 787-0346	9412
Rama Corporation	3567	E	951 654-7351	14774
Wallace Wood Products	2541	F	951 654-9311	4954

SAN JOSE, CA - Santa Clara County

	SIC	EMP	PHONE	ENTRY #
24x7saas Inc	7372	F	408 391-6205	23535
3b Machining Co Inc	3599	F	408 719-9237	15644
A & E Anodizing Inc	3471	F	408 297-5910	12895
A & J Precision Sheetmetal Inc	3444	D	408 885-9134	12078
A R S Mechanical	3444	F	408 288-8822	12081
A&T Precision Machining	3599	F	408 363-1198	15665
A-1 Jays Machining Inc (PA)	3599	D	408 262-1845	15667
AB Manufacturing Inc	3861	F	408 972-5085	22399
ABS Manufacturers Inc	3446	F	408 295-5984	12443
Accordent Technologies Inc	7372	F	310 374-7491	23546
Acer American Holdings Corp (DH)	3577	C	408 533-7700	15143
ACS Co Ltd	3541	C	408 981-7162	13900
Active ID LLC	3537	F	408 782-3900	13855
Adaps Photonics Inc	3661	F	650 521-6390	17341
Adcon Lab Inc	3559	E	408 531-9187	14418
Addison Technology Inc	3672	F	408 749-1000	17805
Adobe Inc	7372	E	408 536-6000	23566
Adobe Inc (PA)	7372	A	408 536-6000	23567
Advance Modular Technology Inc	3577	F	408 453-9880	15148
Advanced Analogic Tech Inc	3674	F	408 330-1400	18063
Advanced Industrial Ceramics	3559	E	408 955-9990	14420
Advanced Precision Spring	3495	F	408 436-6595	13370
Advanced Surface Finishing Inc	3471	F	408 275-9718	12906
Advancedcath Technologies LLC (HQ)	3841	E	408 433-9505	21585
Advantest America Inc (HQ)	3674	D	408 456-3600	18069
AF Gomes Inc	3444	E	408 453-7300	12091
AG Neovo Technology Corp	3575	F	408 321-8210	15119
Ahead Magnetics Inc	3679	D	408 226-9800	18812
Ajile Systems Inc (PA)	3674	E	408 557-0829	18074
Akm Semiconductor Inc	3674	E	408 436-8580	18075
Akon Incorporated	3999	D	408 432-8039	23267
Alien Technology LLC (PA)	3663	E	408 782-3900	17446
Align Technology Inc (PA)	3843	B	408 470-1000	22131
Alliant Tchsystems Oprtons LLC	3484	F	408 513-3271	13274
Allied Telesis Inc	3577	E	408 519-8700	15152
Allied Telesis Inc	3577	E	408 519-8700	15153
Alta Design and Manufacturing	3599	F	408 450-5394	15729
Altera Corporation (HQ)	3674	B	408 544-7000	18086
Altest Corporation	3599	E	408 436-9900	15731
Altierre Corporation	3674	E	408 435-7343	18087
Alumawall Inc	3448	D	408 275-7165	12529
American Gasket & Die Company	3053	F	408 441-6200	9218

	SIC	EMP	PHONE	ENTRY #
Amphenol DC Electronics Inc	3643	B	408 947-4500	16876
Ampro Adlink Technology Inc	3571	D	408 360-0200	14889
Amtek Electronic Inc	3571	E	408 971-8787	14890
Anacom Inc	3663	E	408 519-2062	17450
Andre-Boudin Bakeries Inc	2051	F	408 249-4101	1136
Angular Machining Inc	3599	E	408 954-8326	15742
Ansys Inc	7372	F	408 457-2000	23602
Aplus Flash Technology Inc	3674	F	408 382-1100	18104
Appformix Inc	7372	F	408 899-2240	23610
Applied Anodize Inc	3471	D	408 435-9191	12931
Applied Microstructures Inc	3825	E	408 907-2885	21004
Appro International Inc (DH)	3572	E	408 941-8100	15006
Aptiv Digital LLC	7372	D	818 295-6789	23621
Aquantia Corp (HQ)	3674	D	408 228-8300	18120
Aquatic Av Inc	3651	F	408 559-1668	17191
Ardent Systems Inc	3672	E	408 526-0100	17823
Aridis Pharmaceuticals Inc	2834	E	408 385-1742	7766
Arlo Technologies Inc (PA)	3651	D	408 890-3900	17192
Arm Inc (DH)	3674	B	408 576-1500	18122
Arsh Incorporated	2752	F	408 971-2722	6420
Asante Technologies Inc (PA)	3577	B	408 435-8388	15161
Ascent Technology Inc	3444	E	408 213-1080	12117
Asic Advantage Inc	3674	D	408 541-8686	18130
Atp Electronics Inc	3572	E	408 732-5000	15007
Auxin Solar Inc	3674	E	408 225-4380	18133
Avago Technologies US Inc	3674	F	408 433-4068	18134
Avago Technologies US Inc (HQ)	3674	B	800 433-8778	18135
Avantis Medical Systems Inc	3845	E	408 733-1901	22228
Avogy Inc	3674	E	408 684-5200	18138
Axial Industries Inc	3444	C	408 977-7800	12121
Azazie Inc	2335	F	650 963-9420	3216
B W Padilla Inc	7692	E	408 275-9834	24617
B&Z Manufacturing Company Inc	3599	E	408 943-1117	15770
Babbitt Bearing Co Inc	3599	E	408 298-1101	15772
Babylon Printing Inc	2752	E	408 519-5000	6431
Bae Systems Imging Sltions Inc	3674	C	408 433-2500	18143
Bae Systems Land Armaments LP	3812	A	408 289-0111	20544
Bae Systems Land Armaments LP	3795	D	408 289-0111	20496
Banh An Binh	3679	E	408 935-8950	18829
Barracuda Networks Inc	3577	F	408 342-5400	15166
Bay Elctrnic Spport Trnics Inc	3672	C	408 432-3222	17833
Bayspec Inc	3826	E	408 512-5928	21179
Bd Biscnces Systems Rgents Inc	2819	C	408 518-5024	7471
Becton Dickinson and Company	3841	B	408 432-9475	21624
Benchmark Elec Mfg Sltions Inc (HQ)	3672	C	805 222-1303	17834
Benen Manufacturing LLC	3545	F	408 573-7252	14139
Benjamin Litho Inc	2752	F	408 232-3800	6442
Bentek Corporation	3679	D	408 954-9600	18836
Bestronics Holdings Inc (PA)	3675	E	408 385-7777	18676
Beveled Edge Inc	3231	F	408 467-9900	10342
Bhogart LLC	3556	E	855 553-3887	14348
Big Ink Printing	2752	F	408 624-1204	6448
Billy Beez Usa LLC	3949	F	408 300-9547	22763
Binh-Nhan D Ngo	3672	F	408 641-1721	17838
Bionicsound Inc	3842	F	714 300-4809	21989
Biopharmx Corporation (PA)	2834	E	650 889-5020	7811
Biotage LLC	3826	F	408 267-7214	21199
Bizmatics Inc (PA)	7372	C	408 873-3030	23674
Bloom Energy Corporation (PA)	3674	B	408 543-1500	18149
Blum Construction Co Inc	3442	F	408 629-3740	11939
Bode Concrete LLC	3273	D	415 920-7100	10697
Boston Scientific Corporation	3842	C	408 935-3400	21990
Bravo Communications Inc	3577	E	408 297-8700	15177
Britelab	3824	D	650 961-0671	20962
Broadcom Corporation	3674	E	408 922-7000	18151
Broadcom Corporation (HQ)	3674	B	408 433-8000	18152
Broadcom Inc (PA)	3674	F	408 433-8000	18154
Brocade Cmmnctions Systems LLC (DH)	3577	A	408 333-8000	15178
Bruker Biospin Corporation	3826	E	510 683-4300	21200
Burke Industries Inc (HQ)	3069	C	408 297-3500	9290
Burke Industries Inc	2952	C	408 297-3500	9110
Business Jrnl Publications Inc	2711	E	408 295-3800	5572
C & D Prescision Machining Inc	3599	E	408 383-1888	15808
C & D Semiconductor Svcs Inc (PA)	3559	E	408 383-1888	14437
C L Hann Industries Inc	3599	F	408 293-4800	15812
C8 Medisensors Inc	2834	E	408 623-7281	7819
Cadence Design Systems Inc (PA)	7372	A	408 943-1234	23709
Cadence US Inc (PA)	7372	F	408 943-1234	23712
Cali Today Daily Newspaper	2711	F	408 297-8271	5575
California Newspapers Partnr (PA)	2711	C	408 920-5333	5578
Calix Inc (PA)	3663	B	408 514-3000	17478
Calypto Design Systems Inc	7372	F	408 850-2300	23714
Canary Communications Inc	3663	F	408 365-0609	17480
Cardinal Paint and Powder Inc	2851	E	408 452-8522	8632
Cavium Networks Intl Inc (DH)	3674	F	650 625-7000	18159

Employment Codes: A=Over 500 employees, B=251-500,
C=101-250, D=51-100, E=20-50, F=10-19

2020 California
Manufacturers Register

© Mergent Inc. 1-800-342-5647

1411

GEOGRAPHIC

	SIC	EMP	PHONE	ENTRY #
Ceenee Inc	3651	E	408 890-5018	17211
Celestica LLC	3674	C	408 574-6000	18160
Central Concrete Supply Coinc (HQ)	3273	D	408 293-6272	10743
Central Tech Inc	3699	F	408 955-0919	19272
Cernex Inc	3679	E	408 541-9226	18859
Chavez Welding & Machining	3599	E	408 247-4658	15840
Chemical Safety Technology Inc	3559	E	408 263-0984	14439
Chronix Biomedical Inc (PA)	2835	F	408 960-2306	8215
Chrontel Inc (PA)	3674	C	408 383-9328	18161
Ciphercloud Inc (PA)	7372	D	408 519-6930	23737
Circuit Connections	3672	E	408 955-9505	17847
Circuit Spectrum Inc	3672	F	408 946-8484	17850
Cisco Ironport Systems LLC (HQ)	7372	B	650 989-6500	23740
Cisco Systems Inc	3577	A	408 526-7939	15190
Cisco Systems Inc	3577	A	408 225-5248	15195
Cisco Systems Inc	3577	A	408 526-6698	15197
Cisco Systems Inc (PA)	3577	A	408 526-4000	15199
Cisco Systems Inc	3577	A	408 434-1903	15200
Cisco Systems Inc	3577	A	408 424-4050	15201
Cisco Systems Inc	3577	A	408 526-5999	15202
Cisco Technology Inc (HQ)	3577	F	408 526-4000	15203
City Canvas	2394	F	408 287-2688	3680
Clear View LLC	3442	F	408 271-2734	11941
CM Manufacturing Inc (HQ)	3674	C	408 284-7200	18165
Cnex Labs Inc	3674	E	408 695-1045	18167
Coast Engraving Companies	2796	E	408 297-2555	7369
Cobham Adv Elec Sol Inc	3812	B	408 624-3000	20554
Comet Technologies USA Inc	3829	E	408 325-8770	21452
Communications & Pwr Inds LLC	3663	C	650 846-2900	17492
Communications & Pwr Inds LLC	3679	C	650 846-2900	18872
Concept Part Solutions Inc	3545	E	408 748-1244	14148
Concept Systems Mfg Inc	3674	E	408 855-8595	18172
Concrete Ready Mix Inc	3273	E	408 224-2452	10749
Connectedyard Inc	3826	E	408 686-9466	21208
Construction On Time Inc	1442	F	408 209-1799	336
Continental Intelligent Transp	3011	E	408 391-9008	9167
Cortec Precision Shtmtl Inc (PA)	3444	C	408 278-8540	12164
Cpacket Networks Inc	3577	E	650 969-9500	15209
Cpk Manufacturing Inc	3599	F	408 971-4019	15867
Creative Metal Products Corp	3599	F	408 281-0797	15869
Csr Technology Inc (DH)	3679	C	408 523-6500	18879
CTS Corporation	3672	C	408 955-9001	17859
CTT Inc (PA)	3663	D	408 541-0596	17498
Currie Machinery Co Inc	3556	D	408 727-0422	14358
Cyber Switching Inc	3699	E	408 595-3670	19285
Cyberlinkcom Corp	7372	F	408 217-1850	23791
Cypress Semiconductor Corp	3674	F	408 943-2600	18188
Cypress Semiconductor Corp (PA)	3674	A	408 943-2600	18189
Cypress Semiconductor Intl Inc (PA)	3674	A	408 943-2600	18190
D & F Standler Inc	3599	F	408 226-8188	15874
Dale Grove Corporation	3556	E	408 251-7220	14359
DC Electronics Inc	3643	F	408 947-4531	16891
Dcatalog Inc	7372	E	408 824-5648	23808
Deep Ocean Engineering Inc	3732	F	408 436-1102	20321
Delta Matrix Inc	3599	E	408 955-9140	15888
Demaiz Inc	2032	F	650 518-6268	724
Denali Software Inc (HQ)	7372	E	408 943-1234	23816
Dexerials America Corporation	3824	F	408 441-0846	20966
Dfine Inc (HQ)	3841	D	408 321-9999	21683
Diagnostics For Real World Ltd (PA)	2835	F	408 773-1511	8219
Dialogic Inc	3661	D	800 755-4444	17360
Diamanti Inc	3575	E	408 645-5111	15122
Diamond Multimedia Systems	3672	B	408 868-9613	17863
Dicar Inc	3357	E	408 295-1106	11301
Ditech Networks Inc (HQ)	3661	E	408 883-3636	17361
Dnp America LLC	3674	F	408 616-1200	18196
Dsp Group Inc (PA)	3674	D	408 986-4300	18201
Du-All Anodizing Corporation	3471	F	408 275-6694	12987
Du-All Anodizing Corp	3471	E	408 275-6694	12988
Duel Systems Inc	3678	E	408 453-9500	18766
Dunan Sensing LLC	3699	E	408 613-1015	19295
Dynamic Intgrted Solutions LLC	3674	F	408 727-3400	18203
Eargo Inc (PA)	3842	D	650 996-9508	22002
Eclipse Microwave Inc	3679	F	408 526-1100	18895
El Observador Publications Inc	2711	F	408 938-1700	5628
Elcon Inc	3679	E	408 292-7800	18896
Elcon Precision LLC	3545	E	408 292-7800	14158
Electromax Inc	3672	E	408 428-9474	17867
Electronic Interface Co Inc	3699	D	408 286-2134	19304
Elementcxi	3674	E	408 935-8090	18211
Elite Metal Fabrication Inc	3599	E	408 433-9926	15925
Emsolutions Inc	3672	F	510 668-1118	17870
Encore Industries	3444	E	408 416-0501	12197
Endace USA Limited	3571	F	877 764-5411	14909
Energous Corporation	3663	D	408 963-0200	17512
Energy Sales LLC (PA)	3691	F	503 690-9000	19158
Enpirion	7372	F	408 904-2800	23862
Ensphere Solutions Inc	3674	F	408 598-2441	18220
Enter Music Publishing Inc	2721	F	408 971-9794	5932
Environ-Clean Technology Inc	3674	F	408 487-1770	18222
Eoplex Inc	3699	F	408 638-5100	19306
Eoplex Technologies Inc	3699	F	408 638-5100	19307
Epson Electronics America Inc (DH)	3674	E	408 922-0200	18224
Ericsson Inc	3663	F	408 970-2000	17514
ESP Safety Inc	3842	F	408 886-9746	22010
Espace Enterprises Tech Inc	3559	F	408 844-8176	14462
Etd Precision Ceramics Corp	3674	F	408 577-0405	18228
Eugenus Inc (HQ)	3825	D	669 235-8244	21032
Evissap Inc	3663	A	408 432-7393	17518
Exar Corporation (HQ)	3674	C	669 265-6100	18230
Exatron Inc	3825	E	408 629-7600	21035
Expedite Precision Works Inc	3599	E	408 437-1893	15943
Extreme Networks Inc (PA)	3661	B	408 579-2800	17367
Extreme Precision Inc	3599	F	408 275-8365	15945
Fastrak Manufacturing Svcs Inc	3679	F	408 298-6414	18911
Fibersense & Signals Inc	3661	F	408 941-1900	17370
Filetrail Inc	7372	E	408 289-1300	23896
Flextronics America LLC (DH)	3672	C	408 576-7000	17878
Flextronics Semiconductor (DH)	3674	F	408 576-7000	18237
Foreal Spectrum Inc	3827	E	408 923-1675	21354
Fortrend Engineering Corp	3823	E	408 734-9311	20871
Four Colorcom	2752	F	408 436-7574	6582
Foveon Inc	3674	E	408 855-6800	18242
Foxsemicon Integrated Tech Inc	3674	F	408 383-9880	18243
Franchise Update Inc	2721	F	408 402-5681	5939
Frt of America LLC	3545	F	408 261-2632	14161
G B Mold & Tool Design	3544	F	408 254-3871	14056
G D M Electronic Assembly Inc	3643	D	408 945-4100	16900
Garage Doors Incorporated	2431	D	408 293-7443	4048
Gatsby Inc	3554	F	408 573-8890	14308
Gemfire Corporation	3699	F	408 519-6015	19318
General Dynamics Mission	3669	F	408 908-7300	17730
General Dynmics Stcom Tech Inc	3663	D	408 955-1900	17523
General Elec Assembly Inc	3672	E	408 980-8819	17888
Genetix Usa Inc	3826	F	408 719-6400	21233
Gentec Manufacturing Inc	3599	F	408 432-6220	15994
Geo Semiconductor Inc (PA)	3674	E	408 638-0400	18248
Geometrics Inc	3829	D	408 428-4244	21480
George Hood Inc	3444	E	408 295-6507	12222
Gigpeak Inc (DH)	3674	C	408 546-3316	18250
GM Nameplate Inc	2679	C	408 435-1666	5509
Gold Technologies Inc	3643	E	408 321-9568	16901
Goose Manufacturing Inc	3599	F	408 747-0940	16000
Gordon Biersch Brewing Company	2082	D	408 792-1546	1533
Gorilla Circuits (PA)	3672	C	408 294-9897	17891
Grandesign Decor Inc	3442	E	408 436-9969	11957
Green Circuits Inc	3672	C	408 526-1700	17893
Greenvity Communications Inc (PA)	3559	E	408 935-9358	14474
Gremlin Inc	7372	E	408 214-9885	23956
Grinding & Dicing Services Inc	3674	E	408 451-2000	18256
Group Manufacturing Services (PA)	3444	D	408 436-1040	12227
Guavus Inc (HQ)	7372	D	650 243-3400	23961
H B R Industries Inc	3677	F	408 988-0800	18719
Haig Precision Mfg Corp	3599	D	408 378-4920	16014
Handa Pharmaceuticals LLC	2834	F	510 354-2888	7932
Hane & Hane Inc	3471	E	408 292-2140	13021
Hardcraft Industries Inc	3444	D	408 432-8340	12233
Harmonic Inc (PA)	3663	B	408 542-2500	17531
Heat Software Intermediate Inc	7372	B	408 601-2800	23975
Henry LI	3444	F	408 944-9100	12235
Herman Miller Inc	2521	E	408 432-5730	4801
Hermes-Microvision Inc	3674	E	408 597-8600	18269
Herotek Inc	3663	E	408 941-8399	17535
Hewlett Packard Enterprise Co (PA)	7372	C	650 687-5817	23980
Hgst Inc	3572	C	408 418-4148	15040
Hgst Inc (DH)	3572	F	408 717-6000	15042
Hi-Tech Prcision Machining Inc	3599	F	408 251-1269	16022
Hiep Nguyen Corporation	3599	F	408 451-9042	16025
Hilltron Corporation	3679	F	408 597-4424	18936
Hoojook	7372	F	408 596-9427	23984
Hoopla Software Inc	7372	E	408 498-9600	23985
Hpe Enterprises LLC (HQ)	7372	F	650 857-5817	23989
Hti Turnkey Manufacturing Svcs	3679	E	408 955-0807	18937
Hunter Douglas Fabrications	2591	B	408 435-8844	5026
I & A Inc	3444	E	408 432-8340	12242
Idx Corporation	2542	C	408 270-8094	4982
IL Pastaio Foods Inc	2099	F	408 753-9220	2482
Imagine That Inc	7372	F	408 365-0305	24002
Imerys Filtration Minerals Inc (DH)	1499	E	805 562-0200	390
Immersion Corporation (PA)	3577	D	408 467-1900	15242

Mergent email: customerrelations@mergent.com

1412

2020 California
Manufacturers Register

(P-0000) Products & Services Section entry number
(PA)=Parent Co (HQ)=Headquarters (DH)=Div Headquarters

Company	SIC	EMP	PHONE	ENTRY #
Infinisim Inc	7372	F	408 934-9777	24011
Infiniti Solutions Usa Inc (PA)	3672	D	408 923-7300	17900
Information Storage Dvcs Inc	3674	C	408 943-6666	18289
Ingrasys Technology USA Inc	3825	E	863 271-8266	21052
Initio Corporation	3674	E	408 943-3189	18290
Insieme Networks LLC	3661	F	408 424-1227	17380
Integrated Device Tech Inc (HQ)	3674	B	408 284-8200	18302
Integrated Device Tech Inc	3674	B	408 284-1433	18303
Intel Corporation	3577	A	408 544-7000	15254
Intelligent Energy Inc	3429	C	562 997-3600	11599
Intelligent Storage Solution	3572	C	408 428-0105	15049
Interface Masters Tech Inc	3679	E	408 441-9341	18950
Intermolecular Inc (HQ)	3674	C	408 582-5700	18314
Invensas Corporation	3674	E	408 324-5100	18320
Invensense Inc (HQ)	3812	C	408 501-2200	20591
Iogyn Inc	3845	F	408 996-2517	22265
Isharya Inc	3911	E	415 462-6294	22530
Isign Solutions Inc (PA)	3577	E	650 802-7888	15259
ITW Semisystems Inc	3353	E	408 350-0244	11218
Ixsystems Inc (PA)	7372	D	408 943-4100	24054
J & R Machining Inc	3599	F	408 365-7314	16059
J Lohr Winery Corporation (PA)	2084	E	408 288-5057	1760
J&E Precision Machining Inc	3599	F	408 281-1195	16067
J3 Associates Inc	3599	F	408 281-4412	16069
Ja Solar USA Inc	3674	F	408 586-0000	18328
Jabil Circuit Inc	3672	D	408 361-3200	17905
Jabil Inc	3672	D	408 361-3200	17907
Jabil Silver Creek Inc (HQ)	7692	C	669 255-2900	24644
Jarvis Manufacturing Inc	3599	F	408 226-2600	16077
Javad Ems Inc	3679	D	408 770-1700	18961
Jazz Imaging LLC	3843	F	567 234-5299	22162
Jdi Display America Inc (PA)	3679	E	408 501-3720	18965
Jdsu Photonic Power (HQ)	3699	F	408 546-5000	19334
Jennings Technology Co LLC (DH)	3675	D	408 292-4025	18680
Jessie Steele Inc	2399	F	510 204-0991	3847
Jnc Machining	3599	F	408 920-2520	16088
Jrd Precision Machining Inc	3599	F	408 246-9327	16095
Jumping Cracker Beans LLC	2771	F	408 265-0658	7296
K C Sheetmetal Inc	3444	F	408 441-6620	12259
Kaazing Corporation (PA)	7372	F	650 960-8148	24068
KC Metal Products Inc (PA)	3441	D	408 436-8754	11824
Kellogg Company	2043	C	408 295-8656	1026
Kennerley-Spratling Inc	3089	C	408 944-9407	9864
Keri Systems Inc (PA)	3699	D	408 435-8400	19339
Keystone Coffee Company	2095	E	408 998-2221	2303
Kimball Electronics Indiana	3825	E	669 234-1110	21062
Kion Technology Inc	3479	F	408 435-3008	13198
Kisco Conformal Coating LLC (PA)	3674	E	408 224-6533	18333
Kmic Technology Inc	3663	E	408 240-3600	17554
Komag Incorporated	3264	F	408 576-2150	10477
Kramarz Enterprises	3599	F	408 293-1187	16124
Kranem Corporation	7372	C	650 319-6743	24085
Ksm Corp	3674	B	408 514-2400	18336
Ksm Vacuum Products Inc	3443	F	408 514-2400	12025
Kuprion Inc	2893	E	650 223-1600	8926
Kwan Software Engineering Inc	7372	E	408 496-1200	24088
L & B Laboratories Inc	3999	F	408 251-7888	23388
L & H Iron Inc	3446	F	408 287-8797	12491
L & T Precision Engrg Inc	3599	E	408 441-1890	16130
La Voies of San Jose	2591	F	408 297-1285	5030
Laird Technologies Inc	3823	E	408 544-9500	20899
Lam Research Corporation	3674	A	408 434-6109	18339
Landmark Technology Inc	3679	E	408 435-8890	18984
Laptalo Enterprises Inc	3444	D	408 727-6633	12264
Laser Reference Inc	3821	E	408 361-0220	20764
Lattice Semiconductor Corp	3674	B	408 826-6000	18344
Ledengin Inc (PA)	3674	E	408 922-7200	18347
Lee Brothers Inc	2035	E	650 964-9650	888
Leeyo Software Inc (HQ)	7372	E	408 988-5800	24099
Leiters Enterprises Inc	2834	D	800 292-6772	7990
Lensvector Inc	3851	E	408 542-0300	22369
Leotek Electronics USA LLC	3993	E	408 380-1788	23147
Lg Innotek Usa Inc (HQ)	3679	F	408 955-0364	18987
Lgc Wireless Inc	3663	C	408 952-2400	17572
Lgphilips Lcd Amer Fin Corp	3699	E	408 350-7600	19345
Lights Fantastic	2752	E	408 266-2787	6703
Lobob Laboratories Inc	2834	E	408 324-0381	7998
Lockheed Martin Corporation	3663	A	408 473-3000	17573
Lockheed Martin Corporation	3812	A	408 473-7498	20612
Lockheed Martin Corporation	3761	B	408 747-2626	20450
Lockheed Martin Corporation	3721	B	408 742-5219	19913
LSI Corporation (DH)	3674	A	408 433-8000	18359
LSI Corporation	3674	C	408 436-8379	18362
Lucero Cables Inc	3679	C	408 536-0340	18996
Lumatronix Mfg Inc	3629	F	408 435-7820	16791
Lumenis Inc (DH)	3841	C	408 764-3000	21783
Lumentum Operations LLC	3827	F	408 546-5483	21376
Lumileds LLC (HQ)	3825	E	408 964-2900	21069
Lynx Software Technologies Inc (PA)	7372	D	408 979-3900	24114
Lyris Inc	7372	E	800 768-2929	24115
M C I Manufacturing Inc (PA)	3444	E	408 456-2700	12272
M R F Techniques Inc	3679	F	408 433-1941	18998
M-Pulse Microwave Inc	3674	E	408 432-1480	18365
Mac Cal Company	3444	D	408 441-1435	12275
Macquarie Electronics Inc	3674	F	408 965-3860	18367
Magellan West LLC	7372	E	408 324-0620	24120
Magnum Semiconductor Inc	3674	C	408 934-3700	18368
Mancias Steel Company Inc	3441	E	408 295-5096	11836
Maquet Medical Systems USA LLC	3845	A	408 635-3900	22274
Maskless Lithography Inc	2752	F	408 433-1864	6716
Mass Precision Inc (PA)	3444	B	408 954-0200	12279
Master Metal Products Company	3444	F	408 275-1210	12282
Matthey Johnson Inc	3841	E	408 727-2221	21790
Maui Imaging Inc	3845	F	408 744-1127	22277
Mavens Creamery LLC	2024	E	408 216-9270	659
Max Precision Machine Inc	3599	F	408 956-8986	16180
Maxim Integrated Products Inc (PA)	3674	A	408 601-1000	18375
McCash Manufacturing Inc	3841	E	408 748-8991	21791
McClatchy Newspapers Inc	2711	D	408 200-1000	5735
McNeal Enterprises Inc	3089	D	408 922-7290	9887
McUbe Inc (PA)	3571	E	408 637-5503	14941
Medianews Group Inc	2711	B	408 920-5713	5743
Mediatek USA Inc (PA)	3571	C	408 526-1899	14942
Mega Force Corporation	3577	E	408 956-9989	15285
Megachips Technology Amer Corp (HQ)	3674	E	408 570-0555	18379
Meivac Incorporated	3674	E	408 362-1000	18380
Mercury Systems Inc	3672	F	669 226-5800	17923
Merlin Solar Technologies Inc	3674	E	650 740-1160	18384
Michael T Mingione	2542	F	408 365-1544	4991
Micrel LLC	3674	A	408 944-0800	18387
Micrel LLC	3674	C	408 944-0800	18388
Micrel LLC	3674	C	408 944-0800	18389
Micro-Metric Inc	3829	F	408 452-8505	21507
Micro-Probe Incorporated (HQ)	3825	D	408 457-3900	21079
Microchip Technology Inc	3674	C	408 735-9110	18393
Microlux Inc	3699	F	408 435-1700	19357
Micronas USA Inc	3651	C	408 625-1200	17261
Microsemi Corp-Analog	3674	E	408 643-6000	18402
Microsemi Corporation	3674	E	408 643-6000	18407
Microsemi Corporation	3674	D	650 318-4200	18408
Microsemi Frequency Time Corp	3674	F	408 433-0910	18411
Microsemi Soc Corp (DH)	3674	E	408 643-6000	18412
Micrus Endovascular LLC (HQ)	3841	C	408 433-1400	21821
Mindray Ds Usa Inc	2835	F	650 230-2800	8240
MMR Technologies Inc (PA)	3559	F	650 962-9620	14499
Modern Ceramics Mfg Inc	3229	E	408 383-0554	10320
Modutek Corp	3823	E	408 362-2000	20905
Mohawk Land & Cattle Co Inc	2011	D	408 436-1800	418
Molecular Devices LLC (HQ)	3826	C	408 747-1700	21268
Montage Technology Inc	3674	F	408 982-2788	18420
Monterey Foam Company Inc	3299	F	408 279-6756	11012
MOSplastics Inc	3089	C	408 944-9407	9913
Mosys Inc	3674	D	408 418-7500	18421
Mota Group Inc (PA)	3695	E	408 370-1248	19225
Motiv Design Group Inc	3599	F	408 441-0611	16229
Mountz Inc (PA)	3823	E	408 292-2214	20906
MPS International Ltd	3674	A	408 826-0600	18423
Multis Inc	3999	E	510 441-2653	23417
Multivitamin Direct Inc	2833	E	408 573-7276	7674
Nanosilicon Inc	3674	E	408 263-7341	18424
Naprotek Inc	3672	D	408 830-5000	17932
Natel Engineering Company Inc	3672	C	408 228-5462	17935
Ndsp Delaware Inc	3674	D	408 626-1640	18428
Neoconix Inc	3674	E	408 530-9393	18429
Neodora LLC	3559	E	650 283-3319	14506
Neonode Inc (PA)	3826	D	408 496-6722	21272
Neophotonics Corporation (PA)	3674	B	408 232-9200	18431
Neosem Technology Inc (HQ)	3825	E	408 643-7000	21089
Netgear Inc (PA)	3661	C	408 907-8000	17389
Network Pcb Inc	3672	C	408 943-8760	17937
Networked Energy Services Corp (HQ)	3699	E	408 622-9900	19364
New World Machining Inc	3599	E	408 227-3810	16242
Nexlogic Technologies Inc	3672	D	408 436-8150	17939
Nextest Systems Corporation	3825	C	408 960-2400	21090
Nimble Storage Inc (HQ)	3572	C	408 432-9600	15066
Nio Usa Inc	3711	D	408 518-7000	19492
Nippon Trends Food Service Inc	2099	D	408 214-0511	2571
NM Laser Products Inc	3699	F	408 227-8299	19368
NM Machining Inc	3599	E	408 972-8978	16247
Nok Nok Labs Inc	7372	F	650 433-1300	24210

GEOGRAPHIC

Company	SIC	EMP	PHONE	ENTRY #
Nokia of America Corporation	3661	F	408 363-5906	17390
Novanta Corporation	3679	E	408 754-4176	19031
NTL Precision Machining Inc	3599	F	408 298-6650	16252
Nxp Usa Inc	3674	D	408 518-5500	18441
Nxp Usa Inc	3674	B	408 518-5500	18442
O and Y Precision Inc	3545	F	408 362-1333	14178
O-S Inc	3599	F	408 946-5890	16254
Oberon Co	3679	D	408 227-3730	19035
Oce Dsplay Grphics Systems Inc	3555	D	773 714-8500	14332
Oclaro (north America) Inc (DH)	3661	B	408 383-1400	17393
Odwalla Inc	2033	E	408 254-5800	807
Oki Graphics Inc	2759	F	408 451-9294	7153
Olivera Egg Ranch LLC	2015	D	408 258-8074	523
Omneon Inc (HQ)	3663	C	408 585-5000	17608
Omnitec Precision Mfg Inc	3599	F	408 437-9056	16261
On Semiconductor Connectivity (HQ)	3674	D	669 209-5500	18452
Onnet Inc	2741	E	408 457-3992	6301
Opsveda Inc	7372	F	408 628-0461	24235
Optoelectronix Inc (PA)	3674	F	408 437-9488	18457
Oracle Corporation	7372	B	408 276-3822	24254
Oracle Corporation	7372	B	408 390-8623	24257
Oracle Corporation	7372	B	925 694-6258	24261
Orbotech Lt Solar LLC	3674	E	408 414-3777	18458
Orion Manufacturing Inc	3672	C	408 955-9001	17947
Ose Usa Inc (HQ)	3674	E	408 452-9080	18460
Osram Sylvania Inc	3674	E	408 922-7200	18463
OT Precision Inc	3599	E	408 435-8818	16264
Ozmo Inc	3572	E	650 515-3524	15071
P H Machining Inc	3663	F	408 627-4222	17615
Pacific Press Corporation	2711	E	408 292-3422	5792
Palo Alto Awning Inc	2394	F	650 968-4270	3697
Papadatos Enterprises Inc	3599	F	408 299-0190	16278
Pavilion Integration Corp	3829	F	408 453-8801	21519
Pensando Systems Inc	3823	F	408 451-9012	20917
Perfectvips Inc (PA)	3674	F	408 912-2316	18468
Photon Dynamics Inc (HQ)	3825	C	408 226-9900	21099
Piranha Ems Inc	3571	E	408 520-3963	14961
Pixelworks Inc (PA)	3674	E	408 200-9200	18470
Plasma Rggedized Solutions Inc (PA)	3479	D	408 954-8405	13225
Plx Technology Inc	7372	C	408 435-7400	24304
Pny Technologies Inc	3674	E	408 392-4100	18472
Polycom Inc	3661	E	408 526-9000	17402
Polynesian Exploration Inc	3812	F	540 808-7538	20675
Power Integrations Inc (PA)	3674	C	408 414-9200	18477
Power Integrations Internation	3674	B	408 414-8528	18478
Power Knot LLC	3589	F	408 480-2758	15560
Power Mntring Dagnstc Tech Ltd	3825	F	408 972-5588	21100
Praxair Distribution Inc	2813	F	408 995-6089	7446
Precision Jewelry Tools & Sups	3423	E	408 251-7990	11540
Premiere Recycle Co	3443	E	408 297-7910	12042
Probe-Logic Inc	3571	D	408 416-0777	14964
Proformative Inc	2741	F	408 400-3993	6318
Prosurg Inc	3841	E	408 945-4040	21865
Proto Services Inc	3669	E	408 321-8688	17753
Providenet Communications Corp	7372	E	408 398-6335	24319
Proxim Wireless Corporation (PA)	3669	D	408 383-7600	17754
Proximex Corporation	7372	F	408 215-9000	24320
Prysm Inc (PA)	3999	D	408 586-1100	23454
Pushtotest Inc	7372	F	408 436-8203	24324
Qorvo Us Inc	3674	E	408 493-4304	18490
Qostronics Inc	3672	E	408 719-1286	17964
Qualcomm Atheros Inc (HQ)	3674	A	408 773-5200	18492
Qualectron Systems Corporation	3825	F	408 986-1686	21106
Quality Circuit Assembly Inc	3672	D	408 441-1001	17968
Quality Machining & Design Inc	3559	E	408 224-7976	14524
Quandx Inc	2835	F	650 262-4140	8249
Quantum 3d Headquarters	3674	F	408 361-9999	18501
Quantum Corporation (PA)	3572	B	408 944-4000	15079
Quantum Global Tech LLC	2842	E	408 487-1770	8411
Quantumscape Corporation	3674	C	408 452-2000	18503
Quicklogic Corporation (PA)	3674	D	408 990-4000	18505
Qulsar Inc (PA)	3625	F	408 715-1098	16741
Qulsar Usa Inc	3663	F	408 715-1098	17634
R Stephenson & D Cram Mfg Inc	3599	E	408 452-0882	16336
R&D Altanova Inc	3672	E	408 225-7011	17972
Radicom Research Inc (PA)	3661	F	408 383-9006	17406
Radio Frequency Systems Inc	3663	F	408 281-6100	17636
Raditek Inc (PA)	3663	F	408 266-7404	17637
Rapid Precision Mfg Inc	3599	E	408 617-0771	16341
Recortec Inc	3577	F	408 928-1488	15318
Redpine Signals Inc (PA)	3674	E	408 748-3385	18511
Redseal Inc	7372	D	408 641-2200	24353
Reed & Graham Inc (PA)	2911	E	408 287-1400	9063
Regal Electronics Inc (PA)	3679	E	408 988-2288	19066
Relectric Inc	3613	E	408 467-2222	16610
Restoration Robotics Inc (PA)	3841	D	408 457-1280	21878
Retail Solutions Incorporated (PA)	7372	E	650 390-6100	24357
Reyes Coca-Cola Bottling LLC	2086	D	408 436-3700	2136
Rhub Communications Inc	3699	F	408 899-2830	19394
Richards Machining Co Inc	3599	F	408 526-9219	16356
Richmond Optical Co	3851	F	510 783-1420	22382
Rite Track Equipment Svcs Inc	3559	F	408 432-0131	14530
Rivermeadow Software Inc	7372	F	408 217-6498	24363
Robecks Wldg & Fabrication Inc	3441	E	408 287-0202	11875
Robles Bros Inc (PA)	2099	E	408 436-5551	2602
Rockley Photonics Inc	3674	F	408 579-9210	18520
Rockwell Automation Inc	3625	D	408 443-5425	16747
Roma Bakery Inc	2051	D	408 294-0123	1268
Ron Kehl Engineering	3471	F	408 629-6632	13088
Rose Metal Products Inc	3441	D	417 865-1676	11877
Roth Wood Products Ltd	2599	E	408 723-8888	5080
Rtec-Instruments Inc	3826	E	408 456-0801	21283
Rush Pcb Inc	3672	F	408 469-6013	17981
Rvision Inc	3827	F	408 437-5777	21404
S J Sterilized Wiping Rags	2299	F	408 287-2512	2954
Saba Motors Inc	3711	F	408 219-8675	19499
Sal J Acsta Sheetmetal Mfg Inc	3444	D	408 275-6370	12366
Sal Rodriguez	3471	F	408 993-8091	13093
San Benito Supply (PA)	3272	C	831 637-5526	10644
San Jose Awning Company Inc	2394	F	408 350-7000	3703
San Jose Business Journal	2711	E	408 295-3800	5817
San Jose Mercury-News LLC (DH)	2711	A	408 920-5000	5818
Sandman Inc (PA)	3272	E	408 947-0669	10646
Sandman Inc	3272	E	408 947-0159	10647
Sanmina Corporation	3672	E	408 964-3500	17986
Sanmina Corporation	3672	E	408 964-3500	17987
Sanmina Corporation	3672	E	408 964-6400	17988
Sanmina Corporation	3672	B	408 964-3500	17989
Sanmina Corporation	3672	E	408 557-7210	17990
Sanmina Corporation	3672	E	408 964-3000	17992
Sanmina Corporation (PA)	3672	A	408 964-3500	17994
Santa Clara Valley Brewing Inc	2082	F	408 288-5181	1562
Sas Institute Inc	7372	F	919 677-8000	24384
Scalable Systems RES Labs Inc	3674	E	650 322-6507	18528
Scintera Networks Inc	3674	E	408 636-2600	18529
Screen Shop Inc	3442	F	408 295-7384	11982
Semifab Inc	3823	D	408 414-5928	20935
Seminet Inc	3674	E	408 754-8537	18537
Semler Scientific Inc	3841	E	877 774-4211	21895
Senju Comtek Corp	3399	F	408 792-3830	11486
Seventh Heaven Inc	2399	E	408 287-8945	3861
Sharpe Energy Services Inc	1382	F	408 489-3581	140
Shasta Electronic Mfg Svcs Inc	3571	E	408 436-1267	14973
Sheldons Hobby Shop	3663	F	408 943-0220	17656
Shocking Technologies Inc	2821	E	831 331-4558	7609
Siemens Product Life Mgmt Sftw	7372	E	408 941-4600	24409
Sierra Pacific Machining Inc	3599	F	408 924-0281	16404
Silfine America Inc	2821	D	408 823-8663	7610
Silicon Image Inc (HQ)	3674	D	408 616-4000	18544
Silicon Labs Integration Inc (HQ)	3674	F	408 702-1400	18545
Siliconix Incorporated (HQ)	3674	A	408 988-8000	18553
Silver Press Inc	2789	F	408 435-0449	7348
Sine-Tific Solutions Inc	2759	F	408 432-3434	7214
Sirf Technology Holdings Inc (DH)	3674	D	408 523-6500	18557
Situne Corporation	3663	F	408 324-1711	17661
Siui America Inc	3845	F	408 432-8881	22310
Sk Hynix Memory Solutions Inc	3674	E	408 514-3500	18561
Skylight Software Inc	7372	E	408 858-3933	24415
Smartlogic Semaphore Inc	7372	E	408 213-9500	24420
Smithfield Packaged Meats Corp	2011	C	408 392-0442	425
Solarius Development Inc	3825	E	408 541-0151	21123
Sonasoft Corp (PA)	7372	E	408 583-1600	24432
Sonoma Orthopedic Products Inc	3841	F	847 807-4378	21904
Sony Biotechnology Inc	3699	D	800 275-5963	19408
Sony Electronics Inc	3577	E	408 352-4000	15338
Sotcher Measurement Inc	3825	F	408 574-0112	21124
South Bay Circuits Inc	3679	C	408 978-8992	19089
South Bay Marble Co	3281	F	650 594-4251	10932
Southwest Offset Prtg Co Inc	2759	D	408 232-5160	7221
Spansion Inc (HQ)	3674	F	408 962-2500	18573
Spansion LLC (HQ)	3674	D	512 691-8500	18574
Spartan	2759	F	800 743-6950	7222
Spectral Dynamics Inc (PA)	3829	F	760 761-0440	21546
Spin Tek Machining Inc	3599	F	408 298-8223	16418
Spirent Communications Inc	3825	C	408 752-7100	21126
Spt Microtechnologies	3674	F	408 571-1400	18578
Spt Microtechnologies USA Inc	3559	E	408 571-1400	14538
Spyrus Inc (PA)	3577	E	408 392-9131	15340
Starview Inc	7372	E	406 890-5910	24452
Stencil Master Inc	3953	F	408 428-9695	22955

Mergent email: customerrelations@mergent.com
1414

2020 California
Manufacturers Register

(P-0000) Products & Services Section entry number
(PA)=Parent Co (HQ)=Headquarters (DH)=Div Headquarters

	SIC	EMP	PHONE	ENTRY #
Storopack Inc	3081	E	408 435-1537	9422
Stryker Enterprises Inc	3499	C	408 295-6300	13549
Suez Wts Services Usa Inc	3589	C	408 360-5900	15588
Sumco Phoenix Corporation	3674	D	408 352-3880	18587
Sumicom-Usa	3571	F	408 385-2046	14980
Summit Wireless Tech Inc	3674	E	408 627-4716	18588
Sun Sheetmetal Solutions Inc	3444	E	408 445-8047	12393
Sunnytech	3672	F	408 943-8100	18017
Sunpower Corporation (DH)	3674	A	408 240-5500	18591
Super Micro Computer Inc (PA)	3571	A	408 503-8000	14981
Superior Metals Inc	3444	E	408 938-3488	12396
Surface Art Engineering Inc	3674	E	408 433-4700	18597
Sv Probe Inc	3825	D	480 635-4700	21132
Sv Probe Inc	3825	F	408 653-2387	21133
Swiftstack	7372	E	408 642-1865	24473
Symmetricom Inc	3661	E	408 433-0910	17417
Symphonix Devices Inc	3842	F	408 323-8218	22106
Synaptics Incorporated	3577	F	408 904-1100	15343
Synaptics Incorporated (PA)	3577	B	408 904-1100	15344
Syntest Technologies Inc	7372	F	408 720-9956	24481
T T E Products Inc	3599	F	408 955-0100	16439
T&S Manufacturing Tech LLC	3441	E	408 441-0285	11895
Take It For Granite Inc	1411	E	408 790-2812	295
Tango Systems Inc	3679	D	408 526-2330	19100
Tapioca Express	2046	F	408 999-0128	1064
Taponix Inc	7372	F	408 725-2942	24490
Tcomt Inc	3663	D	408 351-3340	17681
Te Connectivity Corporation	3678	B	408 624-3000	18795
Tecan Systems Inc	3821	C	408 953-3100	20775
Tech Air Northern Cal LLC	2813	F	408 293-9353	7451
Tech-Semi Inc	3674	F	408 451-9588	18603
Technibuilders Iron Inc	3446	E	408 287-8797	12514
Technoprobe America Inc	3674	E	408 573-9911	18604
Techshop San Jose LLC	3543	F	408 916-4144	14005
Teikoku Pharma Usa Inc (HQ)	2834	D	408 501-1800	8156
Telemetria Telephony Tech Inc	3694	F	408 428-0101	19202
Telewave Inc	3663	E	408 929-4400	17686
Teradyne Inc	3825	C	408 960-2400	21141
Teseda Corporation	3825	F	650 320-8188	21142
Tessera Inc (DH)	3674	E	408 321-6000	18614
Tessera Intellectual Prpts Inc	3674	D	408 321-6000	18615
Tessera Intllctual Prprty Corp	3674	E	408 321-6000	18616
Tessera Technologies Inc (HQ)	3674	E	408 321-6000	18617
Therma LLC	3444	A	408 347-3400	12406
Thermo Finnigan LLC (HQ)	3826	B	408 965-6000	21303
Thermo Fisher Scientific	3826	B	408 894-9835	21304
Thermoquest Corporation	3826	A	408 965-6000	21316
Thin Film Electronics Inc	3679	D	408 503-7300	19117
Thirdrock Software	7372	F	408 777-2910	24504
Thunder Products Inc	3931	F	408 270-7800	22641
Times Media Inc	2711	F	408 494-7000	5850
TLC Machining Incorporated	3545	E	408 321-9002	14202
Tmk Manufacturing	3544	D	408 732-3200	14113
Tobar Industries	3643	F	408 494-3530	16935
Tolerance Technology Inc	3951	F	408 586-6811	22936
Tower Semiconductor Usa Inc	3674	F	408 770-1320	18623
Trane US Inc	3585	D	408 437-0390	15461
Tri-Phase Inc	3672	C	408 284-7700	18026
Triad Tool & Engineering Inc	3089	E	408 436-8411	10091
Triquint Wj Inc	3663	D	408 577-6200	17696
Tsmc Technology Inc	3674	D	408 382-8052	18626
Ttm Technologies Inc	3672	C	408 280-0422	18035
Ttm Technologies N Amer LLC	3672	C	408 719-4000	18036
Tung Tai Group	3469	F	408 573-8681	12886
Turner Designs Inc	3826	E	408 749-0994	21317
Twin Creeks Technologies Inc (PA)	3674	F	408 368-3733	18628
Ubicom Inc	3674	D	408 433-3330	18629
Ultratech Inc (HQ)	3559	C	408 321-8835	14550
Uniquify Inc	3679	E	408 235-8810	19131
United Craftsmen Printing	2752	E	408 224-6464	6909
United Technologies Corp	3724	A	408 779-9121	19987
United Technologies Corp	3724	A	408 779-9121	19988
Untangle Holdings Inc	7372	E	408 598-4299	24542
US Concrete Inc	3273	F	408 947-8606	10858
Utstarcom Inc (HQ)	3661	C	510 749-1503	17425
V2 Lighting Group Inc	3648	F	707 383-4600	17174
Valiantica Inc (PA)	7372	F	408 694-3803	24546
Valley Images	2396	F	408 279-6777	3822
Valley View Packing Co Inc	2037	E	408 289-8300	873
Vander-Bend Manufacturing Inc (PA)	3679	B	408 245-5150	19133
Various Technologies Inc	3625	E	408 972-4460	16765
Vat Incorporated	3491	E	408 813-2700	13324
Vector Launch Inc	3489	C	888 346-7778	13285
Verifone Inc (DH)	3578	C	408 232-7800	15380
Verifone Systems Inc (HQ)	3578	D	408 232-7800	15382

	SIC	EMP	PHONE	ENTRY #
Verisilicon Inc (HQ)	3674	F	408 844-8560	18639
Versa Networks Inc (PA)	7372	E	408 385-7660	24557
Vesta Technology Inc	3674	F	408 519-5800	18640
Via Mechanics (usa) Inc (DH)	3577	F	408 392-9650	15362
Viavi Solutions Inc	3674	C	408 577-1478	18642
Viavi Solutions Inc (PA)	3826	B	408 404-3600	21321
Viavi Solutions Inc	3699	C	408 546-5000	19433
Virsec Systems Inc	7372	F	978 274-7260	24563
Vishay Siliconix LLC	2869	A	408 988-8000	8783
Visier Inc (PA)	7372	F	888 277-9331	24565
Visualon Inc	7372	C	408 645-6618	24566
Vital Connect Inc	3845	E	408 963-4600	22327
Vitron Electronic Services Inc	3672	D	408 251-1600	18046
Viv Labs Inc	7372	C	650 268-9837	24567
Vnus Medical Technologies Inc	3841	C	408 360-7200	21958
Vocera Communications Inc (PA)	3669	C	408 882-5100	17772
Volterra Semiconductor LLC (HQ)	3674	E	408 601-1000	18650
W A Call Manufacturing Co Inc	3444	F	408 436-1450	12430
Wafer Process Systems Inc	3674	F	408 445-3010	18653
Wafernet Inc	3674	F	408 437-9747	18654
Watt Stopper Inc (DH)	3643	E	408 988-5331	16939
WD Media LLC	3695	B	408 576-2000	19241
West Cast Architectural Shtmtl	3446	F	408 776-2700	12522
Westcoast Precision Inc	3599	E	408 943-9998	16520
Western Digital Corporation (PA)	3572	A	408 717-6000	15114
Western Digital Tech Inc (HQ)	3572	A	949 672-7000	15115
Western Widgets Cnc Inc	3599	F	408 436-1230	16524
Westrock Cp LLC	2631	E	770 448-2193	5179
Wi2wi Inc (PA)	3663	E	408 416-4200	17706
Wilkinson Mfg Inc	3599	F	408 988-3588	16527
Wine Cellar Impressions Inc	2084	F	408 277-0100	2005
Wint Corporation	3827	C	408 816-4818	21420
Wooden Bridge Inc	2434	F	408 436-9663	4267
Xicato Inc (PA)	3645	E	408 829-4758	17001
Xilinx Inc (PA)	3672	A	408 559-7778	18053
Xilinx Inc	3674	F	408 879-6563	18662
Xilinx Development Corporation (HQ)	3674	F	408 559-7778	18663
Xperi Corporation (PA)	3674	D	408 321-6000	18664
Yageo America Corporation	3676	E	408 240-6200	18693
Yamamoto Manufacturing USA Inc (HQ)	3672	F	408 387-5250	18054
Yield Enhancement Services Inc	3674	F	408 410-5825	18667
Yuja Inc	7372	C	888 257-2278	24600
Zebra Technologies Intl LLC	3577	F	408 473-8500	15370
Zentera Systems Inc	7372	F	408 436-4811	24603
Zenverge Inc	3674	D	408 350-5052	18668
Zenyx Inc	7372	F	415 741-0170	24604
Zepp Labs Inc	3949	E	314 662-2145	22930
Zest Labs Inc (HQ)	3674	E	408 200-6500	18670
ZF Array Technology Inc	3675	D	408 433-9920	18688
Zoll Circulation Inc	3845	C	408 541-2140	22335
Zoll Medical Corporation	3845	F	408 419-2929	22336
Zoran Corporation (DH)	3674	E	972 673-1600	18673

SAN JUAN BAUTISTA, CA - San Benito County

	SIC	EMP	PHONE	ENTRY #
Monsanto Company	2879	C	831 623-7016	8835
True Leaf Farms LLC	2034	B	831 623-4667	871
Willis Construction Co Inc	3272	C	831 623-2900	10669

SAN JUAN CAPISTRANO, CA - Orange County

	SIC	EMP	PHONE	ENTRY #
3 Gen Inc	3841	F	949 481-6384	21567
Activa Global Spt & Entrmt LLC	3949	E	949 265-8260	22731
American Horse Products	2399	F	949 248-5300	3831
Aqua Prieta Tees LLC	2759	F	714 719-2000	6990
Carparts Technologies	7372	C	949 488-8860	23719
CI-One Corporation	2086	D	949 364-2895	2056
Emerald Expositions LLC	2721	D	949 226-5754	5930
Face First Screen Print Inc	2759	F	949 443-9895	7063
Fluidmaster Inc (PA)	3432	B	949 728-2000	11668
Heritage Design	3993	F	949 248-1300	23127
Hirsch Pipe & Supply Co Inc	3432	F	949 487-7009	11671
Iqinvision Inc	3861	D	949 369-8100	22431
Pioneer Sands LLC	1446	C	949 728-0171	374
Quest Diagnostics Nichols Inst (HQ)	3826	A	949 728-4000	21281
Seychelle Envmtl Tech Inc	2834	F	949 234-1999	8126
Suntile Inc	3253	F	949 489-8990	10453
Surrounding Elements LLC	2514	F	949 582-9000	4702
Sustainable Fibr Solutions LLC (PA)	2671	F	949 265-8287	5343
Techko Inc	3699	A	949 486-0678	19420
Vibration Impact & Pres	3829	F	949 429-3558	21563

SAN LEANDRO, CA - Alameda County

	SIC	EMP	PHONE	ENTRY #
1st Choice Fertilizer Inc	2873	F	800 504-5699	8787
Airspace Systems Inc	3829	E	310 704-7155	16694
Akido Printing Inc	2752	C	510 357-0238	6399
American Emperor Inc	3429	F	713 478-5973	11562
American Underwater Products (HQ)	3949	D	800 435-3483	22744

Employment Codes: A=Over 500 employees, B=251-500,
C=101-250, D=51-100, E=20-50, F=10-19

2020 California
Manufacturers Register

© Mergent Inc. 1-800-342-5647

1415

GEOGRAPHIC

	SIC	EMP	PHONE	ENTRY #
Amerisink Inc (PA)	3432	F	510 667-9998	11655
Artisan Brewers LLC	2082	E	510 567-4926	1494
Aryzta US Holdings I Corp	2052	A	800 938-1900	1306
Bargas Bindery	2789	F	510 357-7901	7327
Bayfab Metals Inc	3442	E	510 568-8950	11934
Bens Alternative Foods	2038	F	510 614-6745	946
Berber Food Manufacturing Inc	2099	C	510 553-0444	2402
Best Marble Co	3281	E	510 614-0155	10892
Bimbo Bakeries Usa Inc	2051	F	510 614-4500	1156
Borden Lighting	3646	E	510 357-0171	17015
Botner Manufacturing Inc	3444	F	510 569-2943	12135
Brampton Mthesen Fabr Pdts Inc	2394	F	510 483-7771	3674
Cal Nor Design Inc (PA)	3544	F	925 829-7722	14028
California Coating Lab	3851	F	510 357-1800	22343
Cleophus Quealy Beer Company	2082	F	510 463-4534	1512
Coca-Cola Company	2086	C	510 476-7048	2063
Columbia Cosmetics Mfrs Inc (PA)	2844	D	510 562-5900	8462
Compatible Software Systems	7372	F	510 562-1172	23762
Contech Solutions Incorporated	3674	F	510 357-7900	18177
Coordnted Wire Rope Rgging Inc	2298	F	510 569-6911	2910
Copper Harbor Company Inc	2899	F	510 639-4670	8952
Crl Systems Inc	3663	D	510 351-3500	17497
Custom Paper Products	2652	D	510 352-6880	5187
Dakota Press	2791	F	510 895-1300	7356
Dakota Press Inc	2752	F	510 895-1300	6531
Double V Industries	2395	E	510 347-3764	3737
Edge Electronics Corporation	3443	E	510 614-7988	12018
Electriq Power Inc	3825	F	408 393-7702	21028
Energy Recovery Inc (PA)	3559	C	510 483-7370	14459
Environmental Sampling Sup Inc	3089	F	510 465-4988	9781
Epac Technologies Inc (PA)	2752	C	510 317-7979	6565
Freewire Technologies Inc	3621	E	415 779-5515	16647
Fxi Inc	3086	D	510 357-2600	9544
Gaming Fund Group	3845	F	510 532-8881	22256
General Foundry Service Corp	3365	D	510 297-5040	11382
Hupalo Repasky Pipe Organs LLC	3931	F	510 483-6905	22627
India-West Publications Inc (PA)	2711	E	510 383-1140	5672
INX International Ink Co	2893	C	510 895-8001	8923
Japan Engine Inc	3694	E	510 532-7878	19193
Jetset California Inc	3241	F	510 632-7800	10418
Kennerley-Spratling Inc (PA)	3089	C	510 351-8230	9863
Kp LLC (PA)	2752	D	510 346-0729	6682
Kp LLC	2752	E	510 346-0729	6683
L3 Technologies Inc	3663	C	858 499-0284	17569
Leeway Iron Works Inc	3441	F	510 357-8637	11827
Leitch & Co Inc	3423	F	510 483-2323	11535
Lightech Fiberoptic Inc	3679	E	510 567-8700	18992
Lindsay/Barnett Incorporated	3499	E	510 483-6300	13530
Loco Ventures Inc	2024	E	510 351-0405	653
Lyru Engineering Inc	3599	F	510 357-5951	16156
M-T Metal Fabrications Inc	3444	F	510 357-5262	12274
MArs Engineering Company Inc	3451	E	510 483-0541	12640
Medical Instr Dev Labs Inc	3841	F	510 357-3952	21798
Metro Poly Corporation	2673	E	510 357-9898	5404
My World Styles LLC	2844	F	800 355-4008	8543
Norcal Waste Equipment Co	3713	E	510 568-8336	19548
Norco Printing Inc	2791	F	510 569-2200	7359
Olson and Co Steel (PA)	3446	C	510 489-4680	12502
Optimization Corporation	3564	F	510 614-5890	14672
Oriental Odysseys Inc	3999	E	510 357-6100	23433
Osumo Inc	2396	F	510 346-6888	3805
Pacific Coast Laboratories	3842	F	510 351-2770	22064
Pacific Gaming	3944	E	510 562-8900	22703
PCC Structurals Inc	3369	C	510 568-6400	11420
Peggy S Lane Inc	3088	D	510 483-1202	9595
Pelagic Pressure Systems Corp	3545	E	510 569-3100	14180
Polymeric Technology Inc	3069	E	510 895-6001	9356
Porifera Inc	3589	F	510 695-2775	15559
Precision Die Cutting Inc	3714	E	510 636-9654	19739
Rainier Therapeutics Inc	2836	F	925 413-6140	8326
Realware Inc	7372	F	510 382-9045	24346
Reliable Powder Coatings LLC	3479	F	510 895-5551	13236
Reyes Coca-Cola Bottling LLC	2086	C	510 667-6300	2139
Ridge Foundry Inc	3321	E	510 352-0551	11148
Rip-Tie Inc	2298	F	510 577-0200	2914
Saags Products LLC	2013	D	510 678-3412	495
San Francisco Foods Inc	2038	D	510 357-7343	979
Schindler Elevator Corporation	3534	E	510 382-2075	13809
Spar Sausage Co	2013	F	510 614-8100	499
Specialty Graphics Inc	2789	F	510 351-7705	7351
Steve and Cynthia Kizanis	2434	F	510 352-2832	4250
Sun Chemical Corporation	2893	A	510 618-1302	8933
Tap Plastics Inc A Cal Corp (PA)	2821	F	510 357-3755	7618
Trayer Engineering Corporation	3613	D	415 285-7770	16619
Triple C Foods Inc	2052	D	510 357-8880	1334
UNI-Poly Inc	2673	F	510 357-9898	5429
Union Solutions Inc	7372	F	510 483-1222	24539
Van Sark Inc (PA)	2512	E	510 635-1111	4676
Vistan Corporation	3556	F	510 351-0560	14413
Vitrico Corp	3229	F	510 652-6731	10332
Western Pacific Signal LLC	3669	F	510 276-6400	17774
Whitefish Enterprises Inc	3999	F	510 357-6100	23525
Woolery Enterprises Inc	2099	E	510 357-5700	2648
Wycen Foods Inc (PA)	2013	F	510 351-1987	507
Zinus Inc (HQ)	2515	D	925 417-2100	4751

SAN LORENZO, CA - Alameda County

	SIC	EMP	PHONE	ENTRY #
Aidells Sausage Company Inc	2013	A	510 614-5450	434
Foam Injection Plastics Inc	3089	F	510 317-0218	9791
Golden W Ppr Converting Corp (PA)	3565	C	510 317-0646	14708
Hillshire Brands Company	2013	B	510 276-1300	465
Santini Foods Inc	2023	C	510 317-8888	618

SAN LUIS OBISPO, CA - San Luis Obispo County

	SIC	EMP	PHONE	ENTRY #
Abraham Steel Fabrication Inc	3441	F	805 544-8610	11730
Air-Vol Block Inc	3271	E	805 543-1314	10498
Alfred Domaine	2084	F	805 541-9463	1579
Amrich Energy Inc	2869	F	805 354-0830	8713
Baba Foods Slo LLC	2038	F	805 439-2250	945
Bimbo Bakeries Usa Inc	2051	D	805 544-7687	1147
Calportland Company	3241	D	805 345-3400	10403
Calzyme Laboratories Inc (PA)	2869	F	805 541-5754	8729
Cattaneo Bros Inc	2013	E	805 543-7188	446
Chamisal Vineyards LLC	2084	F	866 808-9463	1627
Cloud Company (PA)	3569	F	805 549-8093	14805
Courtside Cellars LLC (PA)	2084	E	805 782-0500	1653
Crystal Engineering Corp	3823	F	805 595-5477	20853
Del Ozone Holding Company Inc	3589	F	805 541-1601	15507
E & J Gallo Winery	2084	C	805 544-5855	1684
Ednas Inc	2051	F	805 541-3563	1196
Entegris Gp Inc	3569	C	805 541-9299	14813
Ernie Ball Inc (PA)	3931	D	805 544-7726	22618
Flythissim Technologies Inc	3699	F	844 746-2846	19311
Freeport-Mcmoran Oil & Gas LLC	1382	F	805 547-8969	124
Fziomed Inc (PA)	3841	E	805 546-0610	21719
Gateworks Corporation	3823	F	805 781-2000	20878
H2o Engineering Inc	3589	F	805 542-9253	15518
Hanson Aggregates LLC	1442	E	805 543-8100	347
Humidtech Inc	3911	F	805 541-9500	22529
Imdex Technology Usa LLC	3829	E	805 540-2017	21488
ITW Global Tire Repair Inc	3011	D	805 489-0490	9168
J&J Products	3599	F	805 544-4288	16068
Jennings Aeronautics Inc	3812	E	805 544-0932	20593
Johanson Innovations Inc	3829	F	805 544-4697	21493
Kelsey See Canyon Vineyards	2084	F	805 595-9700	1781
M G A Investment Co Inc	2741	F	805 543-9050	6276
McClatchy Newspapers Inc	2711	C	805 781-7800	5736
McKeague Patpatrick	2731	F	805 541-4593	6121
Next Intent Inc	3599	E	805 781-6755	16243
Noll Inc	3542	F	805 543-3602	13987
Oddworld Inhabitants Inc	7372	D	805 503-3000	24221
Ottano Inc	2082	F	805 547-2088	1555
Performance Apparel Corp	2339	F	805 541-0989	3385
Promega Biosciences LLC	2833	D	805 544-8524	7685
Prpco	2752	F	805 543-6844	6816
Rec Solar Commercial Corp	3822	C	844 732-7652	20805
RH Strasbaugh (PA)	3541	D	805 541-6424	13944
Sauer Brands Inc	2099	D	805 597-8900	2608
Slo New Times Inc	2711	E	805 546-8208	5829
Stellar Exploration Inc	3761	F	805 459-1425	20456
Straight Down Sportswear (PA)	2329	E	805 543-3086	3119
Taco Works Inc	2096	E	805 541-1556	2346
Triplett Harps	3931	F	805 544-2777	22643
Ultra-Stereo Labs Inc	3699	E	805 549-0161	19426
Weatherford International LLC	1389	D	805 781-3580	284
Wolfpack Gear Inc	2674	F	805 439-1911	5445
Ws Packaging-Blake Printery (DH)	2752	F	805 543-6843	6943
Ws Packaging-Blake Printery	2752	F	805 543-6844	6944
Xcelaero Corporation	3564	F	805 547-2660	14691

SAN MARCOS, CA - San Diego County

	SIC	EMP	PHONE	ENTRY #
1254 Industries	3999	F	760 798-8531	23257
A & G Industries Inc	3444	F	760 891-0323	12077
Accu-Seal Sencorpwhite Inc	3565	E	760 591-9800	14693
Accu-Tech Laser Processing Inc	3599	F	760 744-6692	15676
Action Electronic Assembly Inc	3672	E	760 510-0003	17804
Advanced Honeycomb Tech	3469	E	760 744-3200	12761
Airgas Usa LLC	2813	C	760 744-2009	7402
Allied Coatings Inc	2851	F	800 630-2375	8616
American Rotary Broom Co Inc (PA)	3991	F	760 591-4025	23020
Arna Trading Inc (PA)	2611	F	760 940-2775	5090

Mergent email: customerrelations@mergent.com

1416

2020 California
Manufacturers Register

(P-0000) Products & Services Section entry number
(PA)=Parent Co (HQ)=Headquarters (DH)=Div Headquarters

	SIC	EMP	PHONE	ENTRY #
Asi Tooling LLC	3545	F	760 744-2520	14134
Avista Technologies Inc	2899	F	760 744-0536	8943
Bbs Manufacturing Inc	3949	F	760 798-8011	22756
Bestop Baja LLC	3714	E	760 560-2252	19592
Biz Launchers Inc	2752	F	760 744-6604	6451
Black Oxide Service Inc	3471	F	760 744-8692	12944
Blisslights Inc	3699	E	888 868-4603	19265
Blisslights LLC	3648	E	888 868-4603	17107
Boinca Inc	2844	F	619 398-7252	8449
Bree Engineering Corp	3679	E	760 510-4950	18842
Byrum Technologies Inc	3699	E	760 744-6692	19267
Cliniqa Corporation (HQ)	2836	D	760 744-1900	8290
Columbia Stone Products	3291	F	760 737-3215	10944
Copley Press Inc	2711	F	760 752-6700	5603
Craneworks Southwest Inc	3537	F	760 735-9793	13863
Creative Electron Inc	3812	F	760 752-1192	20563
Crown Products Inc	3444	E	760 471-1188	12168
Culinary Specialties Inc	2099	D	760 744-8220	2437
David Duley	2652	E	619 449-8556	5188
Dexter Axle Company	3715	C	760 744-1610	19819
Doors Unlimited	2434	F	760 744-5590	4189
Duplan Industries	3599	E	760 744-4047	15910
Eldorado Stone LLC (DH)	3272	E	800 925-1491	10567
Electro Tech Coatings Inc	3479	F	760 746-0292	13173
Enstrom Mold & Engineering Inc	3544	F	760 744-1880	14050
Eriss	3695	F	858 722-2177	19217
Falmat	3357	C	800 848-4257	11302
Fish House Foods Inc	2092	B	760 597-1270	2259
Fluid Components Intl LLC (PA)	3823	C	760 744-6950	20869
GK Foods Inc	2041	E	760 752-5230	1003
GKM International Llc	3089	D	310 791-7092	9806
Gsi Capital Partners LLC	3949	F	760 745-1768	22815
H & M Cabinet Company	2541	F	760 744-0559	4907
Hadley Media Inc	2741	F	800 270-2084	6249
Headline Graphics Inc	2796	E	760 436-0133	7375
Health Breads Inc	2051	E	760 747-7390	1224
Hocking International Labs Inc (PA)	2842	E	760 432-5277	8388
Hollywood Chairs	2511	F	760 471-6600	4575
HP Precision Inc	3444	E	760 752-9377	12239
Hues Metal Finishing Inc	3479	F	760 744-5566	13191
Hughes Circuits Inc (PA)	3672	E	760 744-0300	17895
Hughes Circuits Inc	3672	C	760 744-0300	17896
Hunter Industries Incorporated (PA)	3084	B	760 744-5240	9468
Impact Project Management Inc	3672	E	760 747-6616	17898
Innovative Biosciences Corp	2844	E	760 603-0772	8515
Jensen Door Systems Inc	2431	F	760 736-4036	4065
Judd Wire Inc	3357	F	760 744-7720	11307
K-Tech Machine Inc	3599	C	800 274-9424	16101
L&S Stone LLC (DH)	3281	F	760 736-3232	10913
Macdermid Prtg Solutions LLC	3555	D	760 510-6277	14331
Magic Touch Software Intl	7372	F	800 714-6490	24122
Manchester Feeds Inc (PA)	2048	F	714 637-7062	1109
Metal Etch Services Inc	3826	E	760 510-9476	21262
Microfab Manufacturing Inc	3444	F	760 744-7240	12300
Neighboring LLC	3843	F	818 271-0640	22174
Neville Industries Inc	3544	F	760 471-8949	14084
Oncore Manufacturing LLC	3672	C	760 737-6777	17944
Pac-West Rubber Products LLC	3061	F	760 891-0911	9267
Pacific Yacht Towers	3732	F	760 744-4831	20355
Parabilis Space Tech Inc	3761	F	855 727-2245	20454
Piercan Usa Inc	3069	F	760 599-4543	9353
Pipeline Products Inc	3569	F	760 744-8907	14850
Plasmetex Industries	3089	F	760 744-8300	9967
Port Brewing LLC	2082	E	800 918-6816	1559
Prographics Screenprinting Inc	2759	E	760 744-4555	7186
Prowest Technologies Inc	2851	E	760 510-9003	8674
Quality Woodworks Inc	2434	F	760 744-4748	4235
R B III Associates Inc	2337	C	760 471-5370	3273
Radtec Engineering Inc	3812	F	760 510-2715	20679
Roma Fabricating Corporation	3272	E	760 727-8040	10643
Showdogs Inc	2591	E	760 603-3269	5038
Slivnik Machining Inc	3949	E	760 744-8692	22888
Stigtec Manufacturing LLC	3599	F	760 744-7239	16424
Sullins Electronics Corp (PA)	3643	E	760 744-0125	16926
Sumitomo Electric Interconn	3069	D	760 761-0600	9375
Telecard LLC	2759	F	760 752-1700	7243
Trade Marker International	2298	F	760 602-4864	2918
Trident Products Inc	3089	D	760 510-1160	10092
Trosak Cabinets Inc	2541	F	760 744-9042	4951
Tuscany Pavers Inc	3531	F	866 596-4092	13754
Western Sign Systems Inc	3993	E	760 736-6070	23243
Wickline Bedding Entp Corp	2515	F	760 747-7761	4749
Wind & Shade Screens Inc	2221	F	760 761-4994	2740
Wrought Iron Fencing & Supply	3446	E	760 591-3110	12524
Zye Labs LLC	7372	F	904 800-9935	24608

SAN MARINO, CA - Los Angeles County

	SIC	EMP	PHONE	ENTRY #
A A A Engineering & Mfg Co	3599	E	626 447-5029	15658
America Mountain Wldg Inds Inc	3548	F	626 698-8066	14237
Cosmi Finance LLC	7372	F	310 603-5800	23779
Feihe International Inc (PA)	2023	A	626 757-8885	587
Intelligent Barcode Systems	3829	F	626 576-8938	21489
L & P Button & Trimming Co	3965	F	626 796-0903	23004

SAN MARTIN, CA - Santa Clara County

	SIC	EMP	PHONE	ENTRY #
Calstone Company	3271	F	408 686-9627	10503
Clos La Chance Wines Inc	2084	E	408 686-1050	1640
Newline Rubber Company	3069	F	408 214-0359	9344

SAN MATEO, CA - San Mateo County

	SIC	EMP	PHONE	ENTRY #
Acco Brands USA LLC	3575	D	650 572-2700	15117
Actuate Corporation (HQ)	7372	F	650 645-3000	23556
Akamai Technologies Inc	7372	E	617 444-3000	23585
Akimbo Systems Inc	7372	E	650 292-3330	23586
Alameda Newspapers Inc	2711	D	650 348-4321	5547
Alienvault Inc (HQ)	7372	F	650 713-3333	23592
Alienvault LLC (DH)	7372	D	650 713-3333	23593
Barkerblue Inc	2791	E	650 696-2100	7355
Bears For Humanity Inc	2869	E	866 325-1668	8721
Big Oak Hardwood Floor Co Inc	2426	D	650 591-8651	3970
Borland Software Corporation	7372	D	650 286-1900	23688
Brilliant Home Technology Inc	3613	E	650 539-5320	16586
Celigo Inc (PA)	7372	E	650 579-0210	23725
Cirrent Inc	7372	F	650 569-1135	23739
Coen Company Inc (DH)	3433	E	650 522-2100	11694
Connor Manufacturing Svcs Inc (PA)	3599	D	650 591-2026	15863
Contract Wrangler Inc	7372	F	310 266-3373	23773
Coupa Software Incorporated (PA)	7372	C	650 931-3200	23781
Daily Journal	2711	E	650 344-5200	5607
Drapery Productions Inc	2211	F	650 340-8555	2684
Edmodo Inc	7372	E	310 614-6868	23843
Engagio Inc	7372	E	650 265-2264	23860
Eoply Usa Inc	3674	F	650 225-9400	18223
Fastsigns	3993	F	650 345-0900	23110
Fortasa Memory Systems Inc	3572	E	888 367-8588	15028
Fujisoft America Inc	7372	F	650 235-9422	23923
Good View Future Group Inc	2099	F	408 834-5698	2473
Gopro Inc (PA)	3861	B	650 332-7600	22423
Guidewire Software Inc (PA)	7372	C	650 357-9100	23965
Hazelcast Inc (PA)	7372	E	650 521-5453	23969
Itouchless Housewares Pdts Inc	3089	E	650 578-0578	9845
Jaunt Inc	7372	E	650 618-6579	24057
Jetlore LLC	7372	E	650 485-1822	24060
JH Baxter A Cal Ltd Partnr (PA)	2491	E	650 349-0201	4478
Jigsaw Data Corporation	2741	F	650 235-8400	6260
Matrix Stream Technologies Inc	3651	F	650 292-4982	17257
NC Interactive LLC	7372	D	650 393-2200	24189
Netsuite Inc (DH)	7372	C	650 627-1000	24197
Okta Inc	7372	F	650 348-2620	24223
Opera Commerce LLC	7372	F	650 625-1262	24233
Opera Software Americas LLC	7372	F	650 625-1262	24234
Oracle Systems Corporation	7372	C	650 506-6780	24270
Oracle Systems Corporation	7372	F	650 378-1351	24273
Prezant Company	3554	F	650 342-7413	14312
Punchh Inc	7372	F	415 623-4466	24323
Rapt Touch Inc	3571	F	415 994-1537	14967
Roblox Corporation	7372	B	888 858-2569	24364
Rumble Entertainment Inc	3944	E	650 316-8819	22710
Runa Inc	7372	F	508 253-5000	24368
San Francisco Circuits Inc	3672	E	650 655-7202	17984
Sios Technology Corp (HQ)	7372	F	650 645-7000	24414
Smartqed Inc	7372	F	925 922-4618	24421
Snaplogic Inc (PA)	7372	C	888 494-1570	24422
Sony Mobile Communications USA	3663	C	866 766-9374	17665
Space Time Insight Inc (HQ)	7372	F	650 513-8550	24437
Speculative Product Design LLC (DH)	3161	D	650 462-2040	10211
Swenson Group	3861	F	650 655-4990	22461
Toutapp Inc	7372	F	866 548-1927	24523
Trilibis Inc (PA)	7372	F	650 646-2400	24527
Unifi Software Inc	7372	E	732 614-9522	24537
Vindicia Inc	7372	C	650 264-4700	24561
Vuze Inc	3577	E	650 963-4750	15364
Whill Inc (PA)	3799	F	844 699-4455	20525
Zs Pharma Inc	2834	F	650 753-1823	8197

SAN MIGUEL, CA - San Luis Obispo County

	SIC	EMP	PHONE	ENTRY #
Courtside Cellars LLC	2084	E	805 467-2882	1652

SAN PABLO, CA - Contra Costa County

	SIC	EMP	PHONE	ENTRY #
Analytcal Scentific Instrs Inc	3826	E	510 669-2250	21171
Praxair Inc	2813	E	510 223-9593	7432
Rich Products	3714	F	510 234-7547	19757

Employment Codes: A=Over 500 employees, B=251-500,
C=101-250, D=51-100, E=20-50, F=10-19

2020 California
Manufacturers Register

© Mergent Inc. 1-800-342-5647

1417

GEOGRAPHIC

	SIC	EMP	PHONE	ENTRY #
Trans Bay Steel Corporation **(PA)**	3441	E	510 277-3756	11902

SAN PEDRO, CA - Los Angeles County

	SIC	EMP	PHONE	ENTRY #
Advent Resources Inc	7372	D	310 241-1500	23572
Apartment Directory of L A	2741	F	310 832-0354	6186
Composite Support and Sltns In	2655	F	310 514-3162	5291
Coppa Woodworking Inc	2431	F	310 548-4142	4021
Farlight LLC	3646	E	310 830-0181	17034
Florence Macaroni Company	2098	F	310 548-5942	2368
J Deluca Fish Company Inc **(PA)**	2092	E	310 684-5180	2261
Kesclo Financial Inc	3446	E	800 322-8676	12490
Larson Al Boat Shop	3731	D	310 514-4100	20290
Party Time Ice Inc	2097	F	310 833-0187	2359
Paula Keller	2431	F	310 833-1894	4106
Seaborn Canvas	2399	E	310 519-1208	3860
STA-Slim Products Inc	3949	E	310 514-1155	22898
Two Bears Metal Products	3599	F	310 326-2533	16480
Victory Oil Company	1311	E	310 519-9500	76

SAN QUENTIN, CA - Marin County

	SIC	EMP	PHONE	ENTRY #
Distillery Inc	7372	D	415 505-5446	23818

SAN RAFAEL, CA - Marin County

	SIC	EMP	PHONE	ENTRY #
Ann Lilli Corp **(PA)**	2337	D	415 482-9444	3262
Autodesk Inc **(PA)**	7372	B	415 507-5000	23640
Autodesk Inc	7372	C	415 507-5000	23641
Ben F Davis Company **(PA)**	2326	F	415 382-1000	3026
Bennett Industries Inc	2752	F	415 482-9000	6443
Bgl Development Inc	7372	F	415 256-2525	23664
Biomarin Pharmaceutical Inc **(PA)**	2834	B	415 506-6700	7807
Biotech Energy of America	2869	F	714 904-7844	8723
Bordenaves Marin Baking	2051	D	415 453-2957	1169
Brush Dance Inc	2679	F	415 491-4950	5497
Califrnia Integrated Media Inc **(PA)**	2752	F	415 627-8310	6469
Christine Milne	2053	F	415 485-5658	1339
Continental Graphix	2752	F	415 864-2345	6511
County of Marin	2531	D	415 446-4414	4855
Dostal Studio	3952	E	415 721-7080	22941
Early Bird Alert Inc	3661	F	415 479-7902	17363
Fair Isaac International Corp **(HQ)**	7372	A	415 446-6000	23892
Fiorellos Italian Ice Cream	2024	F	415 459-8004	643
Goff Corporation	2731	E	415 526-1370	6106
Goff Investment Group LLC	2741	F	415 456-2934	6245
Hahnemann Labortories Inc	2834	F	415 451-6978	7931
Insight Editions LP	2731	D	415 526-1370	6112
Jeff Burgess & Associates Inc **(PA)**	3651	E	415 256-2800	17247
Kinematics Research Ltd **(PA)**	3534	F	707 763-9993	13804
L P McNear Brick Co Inc	3271	D	415 453-7702	10510
Laurent Culinary Service	2099	F	415 485-1122	2524
Lpn Wireless Inc	3663	F	707 781-9210	17577
Marcaflex	2672	F	415 472-4423	5367
Marin County Copy Shops Inc	2752	F	415 457-5600	6714
Marin Manufacturing Inc	3441	F	415 453-1825	11837
Megacycle Engineering Inc	3751	F	415 472-3195	20419
One Bella Casa Inc	2392	E	707 746-8300	3630
ONeil KG Bags	3161	F	415 460-0111	10201
Packaging Aids Corporation **(PA)**	3565	E	415 454-4868	14721
Palace Printing & Design LP	2731	E	415 526-1370	6132
Pantry Retail Inc	3581	E	415 234-3574	15401
Performance Printing Center	2752	E	415 485-5878	6778
San Francisco Network	2341	E	415 468-1110	3447
San Rafael Rock Quarry Inc **(HQ)**	1429	D	415 459-7740	319
Sanovas Inc	3841	E	415 729-9391	21888
Sars Software Products Inc	7372	F	415 226-0040	24382
Shamrock Materials Inc	3273	F	415 455-1575	10835
Small World Trading Co	2844	C	415 945-1900	8582
Spectraprint Inc	2759	F	415 460-1228	7224
Steve Zappetini & Son Inc	3446	E	415 454-2511	12511
Strahmcolor	2752	F	415 459-5409	6873
Streamline Development LLC	7372	F	415 499-3355	24461
Tini Aerospace Inc	3663	E	415 524-2124	17693
Vans Inc	3021	E	415 479-1284	9195
Vionic Group LLC	3143	D	415 526-6932	10164
Wildthings Snap-Ons Inc	2361	F	415 457-0112	3490
Zep Solar Llc **(DH)**	3674	E	415 479-6900	18669

SAN RAMON, CA - Contra Costa County

	SIC	EMP	PHONE	ENTRY #
Accela Inc **(PA)**	7372	C	925 659-3200	23545
Acme Data Inc	7372	F	925 913-4591	23550
Allteq Industries Inc	3674	F	925 833-7666	18081
Anozira Incorporated	3272	F	925 771-8400	10530
Ascor Inc **(HQ)**	3625	F	925 328-4650	16701
Athoc Inc **(DH)**	7372	D	925 242-5660	23634
Bass Angler	2721	E	925 362-3190	5886
Blackberry Corporation **(HQ)**	7372	D	972 650-6126	23675
Blossom Apple Moulding & Mllwk	2431	E	925 820-2345	4003
Chevron Captain Company LLC **(HQ)**	2911	C	925 842-1000	9041

	SIC	EMP	PHONE	ENTRY #
Chevron Global Energy Inc **(HQ)**	2911	D	925 842-1000	9042
Chevron Oronite Company LLC **(DH)**	2899	E	713 432-2500	8949
Chevron Phillips Chem Co LP	3084	D	909 420-5500	9465
Cti-Controltech Inc	3625	F	925 208-4250	16710
Cyberinc Corporation **(HQ)**	7372	E	925 242-0777	23790
D Laurence Gates Ltd	2421	F	925 736-8176	3932
Ecolab Inc	2841	D	925 215-8008	8339
Evolphin Software Inc **(PA)**	7372	F	888 386-4114	23879
Fire & Earth Ceramics	3253	F	303 442-0245	10441
Five9 Inc **(PA)**	7372	C	925 201-2000	23901
Flyleaf Windows Inc	3231	E	925 344-1181	10360
GE Digital LLC **(HQ)**	7372	D	925 242-6200	23930
Gemini Consultants Inc	3672	F	925 866-8946	17887
General Electric Company	7372	D	925 242-6200	23931
Greyheller LLC	7372	F	925 415-5053	23957
Hanson Lehigh Inc	3241	E	925 244-6500	10415
Hanson Lehigh Inc	3273	E	972 653-5603	10770
Japonesque LLC	2844	F	925 866-6670	8520
Kraft Heinz Foods Company	2033	F	925 242-4504	786
Leica Geosystems Hds LLC	3577	D	925 790-2300	15272
Longi Solar Technology US Inc	3674	F	925 380-6084	18358
Mic Labs	1389	F	925 822-2847	222
Mirion Technologies Inc **(PA)**	3829	C	925 543-0800	21508
Omron Robotics Safety Tech Inc **(DH)**	3535	C	925 245-3400	13830
Outsystems Inc	7372	F	925 804-6189	24282
Peterson Sheet Metal Inc	3444	F	925 830-1766	12333
Praxair Inc	2813	F	925 866-6800	7427
Reyes Coca-Cola Bottling LLC	2086	D	925 830-6500	2155
Rheosense Inc	3829	F	925 866-3801	21531
Rockwell Automation Inc	3625	F	925 242-5700	16748
Sieva Networks Inc **(PA)**	3812	F	408 475-1953	20722
Sorenson Publishing Inc	2752	F	925 866-1514	6863
Steadymed Therapeutics Inc	2834	F	925 361-7111	8145
Sun Tropics Inc	2037	F	925 202-2221	929
TAS Group Inc	2791	F	925 551-3700	7363
Trinity Marketing LLC	2752	F	925 866-1514	6902
Twin Industries Inc	3672	D	925 866-8946	18037
Z-Line Designs Inc **(PA)**	2522	D	925 743-4000	4850

SAN YSIDRO, CA - San Diego County

	SIC	EMP	PHONE	ENTRY #
Betty Stillwell	3281	D	619 428-2001	10894
Oceans Flavor Foods LLC	2899	F	619 793-5269	9012
Volex Inc	3089	E	619 205-4900	10114

SANGER, CA - Fresno County

	SIC	EMP	PHONE	ENTRY #
Adco Manufacturing	3565	C	559 875-5563	14695
Algonquin Power Sanger LLC	3612	E	559 875-0800	16541
Blue Diamond Growers	2068	C	559 251-4044	1422
California Trusframe LLC	2439	B	951 657-7491	4292
Cargill Meat Solutions Corp	2011	C	559 875-2232	398
Dole Packaged Foods LLC	2037	C	559 875-3354	911
Fresno Fab-Tech Inc	3441	E	559 875-9800	11798
Gibson Wine Company	2084	C	559 875-2505	1723
Hart & Cooley Inc	3446	E	559 875-1212	12480
If Copack LLC	2032	E	559 875-3354	729
Initiative Foods LLC	2032	C	559 875-3354	730
International Paper Company	2621	F	559 875-3311	5118
Kings River Casting Inc	2531	F	559 875-8250	4863
Melkonian Enterprises Inc	2034	E	559 485-6191	854
Midvalley Publishing Inc	2711	E	559 875-2511	5755
Mill At Kings River LLC	2079	E	559 875-7800	1476
Perez Distributing Fresno Inc **(PA)**	2834	E	800 638-3512	8065
Pet Carousel Inc	2047	E	316 291-2500	1081
Royal Stall	3446	E	559 875-8100	12505
Soojians Inc	2052	E	559 875-5511	1330
Triple A Pallets Inc	2448	F	559 313-7636	4402

SANTA ANA, CA - Orange County

	SIC	EMP	PHONE	ENTRY #
2100 Freedom Inc **(HQ)**	2711	D	714 796-7000	5542
A F M Engineering Inc	3599	F	714 547-0194	15660
A Good Sign & Graphics Co	3993	F	714 444-4466	23035
A Plus Label Incorporated	2679	E	714 229-9811	5489
A World of Moulding	2431	E	714 361-9308	3989
A-Z Mfg Inc	3599	E	714 444-4446	15669
Aardvark Clay & Supplies Inc **(PA)**	3952	E	714 541-4157	22937
Accelerated Memory Prod Inc	3674	E	714 460-9800	18059
Accent Industries Inc **(PA)**	3442	E	714 708-1389	11926
Accurate Circuit Engrg Inc	3672	D	714 546-2162	17802
Accurate Prfmce Machining Inc	3599	E	714 434-7811	15678
Acd LLC **(DH)**	3443	C	949 261-7533	11990
Ackley Metal Products Inc	3599	F	714 979-7431	15682
Acme United Corporation	2621	E	714 557-2001	5096
Acp Noxtat Inc	2821	E	714 547-5477	7539
Acrontos Manufacturing Inc	3469	E	714 850-9133	12759
Active Plating Inc	3471	E	714 547-0356	12903
Adapt Automation Inc	3549	E	714 662-4454	14262

Company	SIC	EMP	PHONE	ENTRY #
ADM Works LLC	3365	E	714 245-0536	11362
Advanced Digital Research Inc	3575	F	949 252-1055	15118
Advanced Power & Controls LLC	3621	F	714 540-9010	16628
AEC Group Inc	3714	F	714 444-1395	19571
Aftco Mfg Co Inc	3949	D	949 660-8757	22734
AGA Precision Systems Inc	3599	F	949 540-3163	15713
Agility Fuel Systems LLC (DH)	3714	C	949 236-5520	19573
Airborne Systems N Amer CA Inc	2399	C	714 662-1400	3830
Airparts Express Inc	3728	D	714 308-2764	20027
Alco Engrg & Tooling Corp	3444	E	714 556-6060	12096
Alco Manufacturing Inc	3544	F	714 549-5007	14011
All American Racers Inc	3751	C	714 557-2116	20380
Allied Electronic Services	3672	F	714 245-2500	17810
Alloy Tech Electropolishing	3471	F	714 434-6604	12918
Alm Chrome	3471	F	714 545-3540	12919
Almatron Electronics Inc	3672	E	714 557-6000	17811
Aluminum Precision Pdts Inc	3463	D	714 549-4075	12730
Ambrit Engineering Corporation	3544	D	714 557-1074	14012
American Aerospace Pdts Inc	3444	F	714 662-7620	12103
American Pneumatic Tools Inc	3542	F	562 204-1555	13967
American Sport Bags Inc	2393	E	714 547-8013	3653
AMO Usa Inc	3841	C	714 247-8200	21599
Anodyne Inc	3471	E	714 549-3321	12930
Arlon LLC	3089	C	714 540-2811	9638
Arsys Inc	3559	F	714 654-7681	14427
Art Manufacturers Inc	3645	E	714 540-9125	16962
Artisan Nameplate Awards Corp	2759	E	714 556-6222	6993
Aryzta LLC	2052	C	949 261-7400	1304
Ascent Tooling Group LLC	3812	A	949 455-0665	20538
Aspen Brands Corporation	2511	F	702 946-9430	4550
Assembly Technologies Co LLC	3672	F	714 979-4400	17826
Atlas Carpet Mills Inc	2273	C	323 724-7930	2865
Atr Sales Inc	3568	E	714 432-8411	14781
Audeze LLC (PA)	3651	F	714 581-8010	17193
Audio Dynamix Inc	3651	F	714 549-5100	17194
Automation West Inc	3599	F	714 556-7381	15755
Axiom Materials Inc	2891	E	949 623-4400	8855
Azteca News	2711	F	714 972-9912	5561
B and Z Printing Inc	2752	E	714 892-2000	6428
B J Bindery	2789	D	714 835-7342	7326
Bambeck Systems Inc (PA)	3823	E	949 250-3100	20838
Bdm Engineering Inc	3531	E	714 558-6129	13708
Behr Holdings Corporation (HQ)	2851	A	714 545-7101	8619
Behr Process Corporation	2851	A	714 545-7101	8620
Behr Process Corporation (DH)	2851	A	714 545-7101	8621
Behr Process Corporation	2851	D	714 545-7101	8622
Behr Process Corporation	2851	D	714 545-7101	8623
Behr Process Corporation	2851	A	714 545-7101	8624
Behr Process Corporation	2851	D	714 545-7101	8625
Behr Sales Inc (HQ)	2851	C	714 545-7101	8626
Bel-Air Machining Co	3599	F	714 953-6616	15783
Belmont Publications Inc	2721	F	714 825-1234	5888
Bend Tek Inc	3444	D	714 210-8966	12131
Benmar Marine Electronics Inc	3812	F	714 540-5120	20546
Berry Global Inc	3089	F	714 751-2920	9659
Blackburn Alton Invstments LLC	2759	E	714 731-2000	7001
Blind Squirrel Games Inc	7372	F	714 460-0860	23677
Blinking Owl Distillery	2082	F	949 370-4688	1504
Blower-Dempsay Corporation	2653	D	714 547-9266	5201
Boss Printing Inc	2752	F	714 545-2677	6455
Brasstech Inc (HQ)	3432	C	949 417-5207	11659
Bristol Sounds Electronics	3651	F	714 549-5923	17209
Brixen & Sons Inc	2759	E	714 566-1444	7009
Brothers Intl Desserts	2024	C	949 655-0080	633
Buk Optics Inc	3827	E	714 384-9620	21336
Bullfrog Printing and Graphics	2752	F	714 641-0220	6461
Bush Polishing & Chrome	3471	F	714 537-7440	12955
C & H Letterpress Inc	2759	F	714 438-1350	7010
Cable Devices Incorporated (HQ)	3577	C	714 554-4370	15181
Cal Pac Sheet Metal Inc	3444	E	714 979-2733	12143
Cal Trends Accessories LLC	2399	E	714 708-5115	3835
California Composites MGT Inc	3728	E	714 258-0405	20064
Calmont Engineering & Elec (PA)	3357	E	714 549-0336	11293
Candlebay Co	3999	F	949 307-1807	23297
Cascade Optical Coating Inc	3827	E	714 543-9777	21340
CD Alexander LLC	3577	E	949 250-3306	15187
CD Video Manufacturing Inc	3695	D	714 265-0770	19212
Cellco Partnership	3663	E	714 775-0600	17483
Content Company	3571	F	714 979-6491	14896
Chapman Engineering Corp	3599	E	714 542-1942	15839
Choose Manufacturing Co LLC	3672	E	714 327-1698	17846
Ciasons Industrial Inc	3053	E	714 259-0838	9225
Clama Products Inc	3544	F	714 258-8606	14034
Classic Components Inc (PA)	3471	E	714 619-5690	12968
Classic Quilting	2395	F	714 558-8312	3732
Clear-Ad Inc	3089	E	877 899-1002	9710
Cnc Factory Corporation	3545	F	714 581-5999	14146
Codan US Corporation	3089	C	714 430-1300	9713
Cole Instrument Corp	3621	D	714 556-3100	16636
Color Science Inc	2865	F	714 434-1033	8699
Colorstitch Inc	2395	E	714 754-4220	3734
Columbia Screw Products Inc	3451	F	714 549-1171	12625
Commerce Printers Inc	2752	E	714 549-5002	6502
Connectec Company Inc	3643	F	949 252-1077	16886
Connelly Machine Works	3599	E	714 558-6855	15862
Consolidated Container Co LP	3086	D	714 241-6640	9517
Corbin-Hill Inc	2051	D	714 966-6695	1181
Cowboy Direct Response	3993	E	714 824-3780	23082
CPC Fabrication Inc	3444	E	714 549-2426	12166
Creative Intgrated Systems Inc	3674	F	949 261-6577	18185
Cult Cvlt	3751	F	714 435-2858	20393
Custom Hardware Mfg Inc	3429	E	714 547-7440	11583
Custom Metal Works	3446	F	714 953-5481	12467
Cvc Audio & Video Supply Inc	3695	F	714 526-5725	19213
Cypress Sponge Rubber Products	3069	F	714 546-6464	9299
D F Stauffer Biscuit Co Inc	2052	E	714 546-6855	1311
Da Vita Tustin Dialysis Ctr	3841	E	714 835-2450	21677
Dadee Manufacturing LLC	3713	E	602 276-4390	19525
Dan R Hunt Inc	3599	F	714 850-9383	15877
Dana Creath Designs Ltd	3648	E	714 662-0111	17116
Danchuk Manufacturing Inc	3714	D	714 540-4363	19631
Daniel Voscloo Jr	3728	F	714 751-1401	20082
Data Solder Inc	3643	F	714 429-9866	16890
Davco Enterprises Inc	2891	F	714 432-0600	8866
Dave Annala	3444	F	714 541-8383	12174
Deltronic Corporation	3827	D	714 545-5800	21347
Deschner Corporation	3569	E	714 557-1261	14810
Design Catapult Manufacturing	3841	F	949 522-6789	21681
Diamond Baseball Company Inc	3949	E	800 366-2999	22790
Diamond Gloves	3842	E	714 667-0506	21997
Digital First Media LLC	2711	A	714 796-7000	5615
Diversified Packaging Inc	3086	E	714 850-9316	9524
Dm Software Inc	7372	F	714 953-2653	23819
Documotion Research Inc	2752	F	714 662-3800	6547
DOT Corp	2752	E	714 708-5960	6550
Driven Concepts Inc	2329	F	714 549-2170	3076
Ducommun Incorporated (PA)	3728	C	657 335-3665	20093
Dynamic Fabrication Inc	3699	F	714 662-2440	19287
Dynasty Electronic Company LLC	3672	D	714 550-1197	17865
E F T Fast Quality Service	3471	E	714 751-1487	12990
Ecoolthing Corp	3499	E	714 368-4791	13519
El Indio Tortilleria	2099	F	714 542-3114	2451
Electrode Technologies Inc	3471	E	714 549-3771	12996
Electrolurgy Inc	3498	E	714 641-7488	13468
Energent Corporation	3511	F	949 885-0365	13568
Envita Labs LLC	2833	E	800 500-4376	7655
Express Chipping	2741	F	562 789-8058	6231
Express Manufacturing Inc (PA)	3679	C	714 979-2228	18908
Fabrica International Inc	2273	C	949 261-7181	2869
Falcon Automotive Inc	2399	E	714 569-1085	3841
Fast Ad Inc	3993	D	714 835-9353	23108
Finart Inc (PA)	3599	F	714 957-1757	15958
Fit-Line Inc	3089	E	714 549-9091	9788
Flathers Precision Inc	3599	E	714 966-8505	15961
Flexible Manufacturing LLC	3678	D	714 259-7996	18769
FM Systems Inc	3663	F	714 979-0537	17522
Fntech	3648	E	714 429-7833	17126
Foodbeast Inc	2741	F	949 344-2634	6238
Foster Printing Company Inc	2752	D	714 731-2000	6581
Freudenberg-Nok General Partnr	3053	C	714 834-0602	9230
Frontera Solutions Inc	3624	D	714 368-1631	16685
Fujifilm Irvine Scientific Inc	2836	C	949 261-7800	8302
Funny-Bunny Inc (PA)	2329	D	714 957-1114	3085
G G C Inc (PA)	3554	E	714 835-6530	14306
G G C Inc	3554	E	714 835-0551	14307
Gardner Systems Inc	3821	F	714 668-9018	20758
GBF Enterprises Inc	3599	E	714 979-7131	15988
Gemini Industries Inc	3341	D	949 250-4011	11201
Gemini Industries Inc	3999	F	949 553-4255	23341
Gemtech Inds Good Earth Mfg	3479	E	714 848-2517	13184
Gold Coast Baking Company Inc (PA)	2051	D	714 545-2253	1218
Graham Packaging Company LP	3089	D	714 979-1835	9812
Greenkraft Inc	3711	D	714 545-7777	19474
Growthstock Inc	3679	C	949 660-9473	18927
Hannah Industries Inc	3589	F	714 939-7873	15519
Headmaster Inc (PA)	2353	E	714 556-5244	3467
Heart Rate Inc	3949	E	714 850-9716	22819
Helfer Enterprises	3599	E	714 557-2733	16019
Helica Biosystems Inc	2835	F	714 578-7830	8227
Heritage Paper Co (HQ)	2653	D	714 540-9737	5235

GEOGRAPHIC

Name	SIC	EMP	PHONE	ENTRY #
Hernandez Zeferino	2891	F	714 953-4010	8874
High End Seating Solutions LLC	3751	E	714 259-0177	20407
High-Tech Coatings Inc	3479	F	714 547-2122	13190
Hill Marine Products LLC	3599	F	714 855-2986	16030
Hitt Companies	3069	E	714 979-1405	9317
Hood Manufacturing Inc	3089	D	714 979-7681	9827
Hook It Up	2111	C	714 600-0100	2653
Hpv Technologies Inc	3651	F	949 476-7000	17244
Humberto Murillo Inc	3471	E	714 541-2628	13026
I J Research Inc	3679	E	714 546-8522	18940
I O Interconnect Ltd (PA)	3678	E	714 564-1111	18773
Image Apparel For Business Inc	2326	E	714 541-5247	3037
Impco Technologies Inc (HQ)	3714	C	714 656-1200	19688
Industrial Cpu Systems Intl	3571	E	714 957-2815	14923
Industrial Tool and Die Inc	3544	F	714 549-1686	14064
Infinite Optics Inc	3827	F	714 557-2299	21364
Inserts & Kits Inc	3599	F	714 708-2888	16049
Insultech LLC (PA)	2899	D	714 384-0506	8980
Integral Aerospace LLC	3728	C	949 250-3123	20139
International Disc Mfr Inc	3652	E	714 210-1780	17329
International Electronic Desig (PA)	3679	F	714 662-1018	18952
Iron Grip Barbell Company Inc	3949	D	714 850-6900	22831
Itc Sftware Slutions Group LLC (PA)	7372	E	877 248-2774	24050
Iteris Inc (PA)	3861	C	949 270-9400	22432
J & J Action Inc	3634	F	877 327-5268	16830
J D Industries	3599	F	714 542-5517	16064
J Miller Canvas LLC	2211	F	714 641-0052	2696
J R V Products Inc	3679	F	714 259-9772	18957
JB Plastics Inc	3089	E	714 541-8500	9852
JD Processing Inc	3471	E	714 972-8161	13034
Johnson & Johnson (HQ)	3845	B	714 247-8200	22269
Johnson & Johnson	3841	E	714 247-8200	21766
Johnson Precision Products Inc	3599	F	714 824-6971	16091
Jolo Industries Inc	3679	E	714 554-6840	18968
Jwc Environmental LLC	3589	D	714 662-5829	15531
K-P Engineering Corp	3599	F	714 545-7045	16100
K-V Engineering Inc	3541	E	714 229-9977	13928
Kaga (usa) Inc	3469	E	714 540-2697	12828
Kalanico Inc	2541	E	714 532-5770	4915
Kenlor Industries Inc	3841	E	714 647-0770	21769
Kilgore Machine Company Inc	3599	E	714 540-3659	16116
Kl Electronics Inc	3672	E	714 751-5611	17911
Kulicke Sffa Wedge Bonding Inc	3699	C	949 660-0440	19342
Laguna Cookie Company Inc	2052	D	714 546-6855	1319
Laperla Spice Co Inc	2099	F	714 543-5533	2520
Laszlo J Lak	3599	F	714 850-0141	16140
Laura Scudders Company LLC	2096	E	714 444-3700	2336
Leonard Craft Co LLC	3911	D	714 549-0678	22539
Level 23 Fab	3441	F	714 979-2323	11829
Limpus Prints Inc	2759	F	714 545-5078	7121
Liquid Graphics Inc	2329	C	949 486-3588	3104
Little Firefighter Corporation	3491	F	714 834-0410	13311
Lotus Hygiene Systems Inc	3261	E	714 259-8805	10467
Lynde-Ordway Company Inc	3579	F	714 957-1311	15384
M & W Machine Corporation	3599	F	714 541-2652	16159
M R S Foods Inc (PA)	2099	E	714 554-2791	2537
Machine Arts Incorporated	3599	F	805 965-5344	16162
Magnetic Design Labs Inc	3679	F	714 558-3355	19002
Maria Corporation	2759	F	714 751-2460	7131
Mark Optics Inc	3827	E	714 545-6684	21379
Markland Industries Inc (PA)	3751	D	714 245-2850	20418
Markzware	7372	F	949 756-5100	24128
Marlin Designs LLC	2512	C	949 637-7257	4657
Marteq Process Solutions Inc	3674	F	714 495-4275	18370
Marway Power Systems Inc (PA)	3577	E	714 917-6200	15284
Mask Technology Inc	3679	F	714 557-3383	19007
Master Inds Worldwide LLC	3999	F	949 660-0644	23402
Master Industries Inc	3949	E	949 660-0644	22849
Matrix USA Inc	3672	E	714 825-0404	17919
Maul Mfg Inc (PA)	3599	E	714 641-0727	16179
Maxtrol Corporation	3672	E	714 245-0506	17920
Medtronic Inc	3841	D	949 474-3943	21808
Medtronic Ats Medical Inc	3841	E	949 380-9333	21811
Mega Plus Pcb Incorporated	3672	F	714 550-0265	17921
Mekong Printing Inc	2752	E	714 558-9595	6722
Memory Experts Intl USA Inc (HQ)	3572	E	714 258-3000	15056
Memory Threads	2221	F	818 837-7070	2730
Merit Cables Incorporated	3841	E	714 547-3054	21817
Metal Cast Inc	3325	F	714 285-9792	11172
Metal Improvement Company LLC	3398	F	714 546-4160	11461
Metro Digital Printing Inc	2752	E	714 546-8400	6726
Micro Trim Inc	3354	F	714 241-7046	11239
Miller & Pidskalny Cstm Wdwrk	2511	F	949 250-8508	4594
ML Kishigo Mfg Co LLC	2389	D	949 852-1963	3571
Modified Plastics Inc (PA)	3089	E	714 546-4667	9903
Monarch Precision Deburring	3541	F	714 258-0342	13936
Mustard Seed Technologies Inc	3679	C	714 556-7007	19023
Mx Electronics Mfg Inc	3357	D	714 258-0200	11309
Nazca Solutions Inc	7372	E	612 279-6100	24188
Nest Environments Inc	2431	F	714 979-5500	4092
Newport Laminates Inc	3089	E	714 545-8335	9924
Newport Metal Finishing Inc	3479	D	714 556-8411	13211
Newport Plastic Inc	3089	E	714 549-1955	9925
Newport Plastics LLC (PA)	3089	E	800 854-8402	9926
Nis America Inc	7372	E	714 540-1199	24209
No Lift Nails Inc	2821	E	714 897-0070	7585
Norotos Inc	3599	C	714 662-3113	16248
Nova Print Inc	2335	F	951 525-4040	3246
Nutrade Inc	2211	E	949 477-2300	2706
Oc Metals Inc	3444	E	714 668-0783	12317
OEM Materials & Supplies Inc	2621	E	714 564-9600	5140
Ohno America Inc	2273	A	770 773-3820	2877
Omniprint Inc	3577	E	949 833-0080	15299
One Time Utility Sales Inc	3644	E	714 953-5700	16952
Optosigma Corporation	3827	E	949 851-5881	21393
Orange Cnty Mlt-Hsing Svc Corp	2721	E	714 245-9500	5995
Orange Container Inc	2653	D	714 547-9617	5249
Orange County Label Co Inc	2759	F	714 437-1010	7161
Orange Metal Spinning and Stam	3469	F	714 754-0770	12851
Orion Chandelier Inc	3645	F	714 668-9668	16984
P C I Manufacturing Division	3663	F	714 543-3496	17614
Pacific Aerospace Machine Inc	3599	E	714 534-1444	16271
Pacific Computer Products Inc	3955	E	714 549-7535	22970
Pacific Label Inc	2759	D	714 237-1276	7167
Pacific Stone Design Inc	3272	E	714 836-5757	10621
Pan-A-Lite Products Inc	3648	F	714 258-7111	17152
Panelight Components Group LLC	3648	F	714 258-7111	17153
Parpro Technologies Inc	3672	C	714 545-8886	17954
Pelican Rope Works	2298	F	714 545-0116	2913
Pioneer Circuits Inc	3672	B	714 641-3132	17957
Playa Tool & Marine Inc	3599	F	714 972-2722	16301
Polaris E-Commerce Inc	3561	E	714 907-0582	14595
Pollution Control Specialists	3564	E	949 474-0137	14673
Power Circuits Inc	3672	B	714 327-3000	17959
Power Distribution Inc	3677	E	714 513-1500	18733
Praxair Distribution Inc	2813	E	714 547-6684	7447
Precious Metals Plating Co Inc	3471	F	714 546-6271	13074
Precision Circuits West Inc	3672	F	714 435-9670	17960
Prime Forming & Cnstr Sups	3272	E	714 547-6710	10632
Printed Circuit Solutions Inc	3672	E	714 825-1090	17962
Promedia Companies	2721	F	714 444-2426	6007
Prototype Express LLC	3699	F	714 751-3533	19385
Pure One Environmental Inc	2869	F	714 641-1430	8768
Pv Labels Inc (PA)	3993	F	760 241-8900	23180
Q-Flex Inc	3679	E	714 664-0101	19058
QED Inc	3823	E	714 546-6010	20924
Quantum Digital Technology Inc	3679	F	310 325-4949	19062
Qyk Brands LLC	3634	E	949 312-7119	16839
R & B Wire Products Inc	3496	E	714 549-3355	13430
RA Industries LLC	3599	E	714 557-2322	16337
Reichert Enterprises Inc	3993	E	714 513-9199	23185
Remedy Blinds Inc	2591	D	714 245-0186	5035
Ricaurte Precision Inc	3599	E	714 667-0632	16355
Robinson Pharma Inc	2834	D	714 241-0235	8109
Robinson Pharma Inc (PA)	2834	B	714 241-0235	8110
Robinson Pharma Inc	2834	C	714 241-0235	8111
Rooke Manufacturing Co	3599	F	714 540-6943	16372
Royal Manufacturing Inds Inc	3444	F	714 668-9199	12359
Rubberite Corp (PA)	3069	F	714 546-6464	9367
S & S Precision Mfg Inc	3599	E	714 754-6664	16380
Saf-T-Co Supply	3644	E	714 547-9975	16954
Sanie Manufacturing Company	3446	F	714 751-7700	12506
Santos Precision Inc	3728	E	714 957-0299	20228
Scientific Components Systems	3646	E	714 554-3960	17069
Secure Comm Systems Inc (HQ)	3663	C	714 547-1174	17653
Secure Comm Systems Inc	3663	F	714 547-1174	17654
Select Circuits	3672	F	714 825-1090	17996
Semiconductor Components Inc	3674	E	714 547-6059	18533
Senga Engineering Inc	3599	E	714 549-8011	16393
Sev-Cal Tool Inc	3545	E	714 549-3347	14193
Sigmatronix Inc	3651	F	714 436-1618	17282
Sign Specialists Corporation	3993	E	714 641-0064	23202
Silicon Tech Inc	3572	C	949 476-1130	15101
Skyco Shading Systems Inc	2431	E	714 708-3038	4127
Skyco Skylights Inc	3211	E	949 629-4090	10275
Smithco Plastics Inc (PA)	3089	F	714 545-9107	10060
Smiths Action Plastic Inc (PA)	3088	E	714 836-4141	9596
Smiths Detection LLC	3826	A	714 258-4400	21291
Smt Electronics Mfg Inc	3674	F	714 751-8894	18567
Sound Waves Insulation Inc	3823	E	714 556-2110	20940

Mergent email: customerrelations@mergent.com
1420
2020 California
Manufacturers Register
(P-0000) Products & Services Section entry number
(PA)=Parent Co (HQ)=Headquarters (DH)=Div Headquarters

	SIC	EMP	PHONE	ENTRY #
South Coast Circuits Inc	3672	D	714 966-2108	18009
Southern California Plas Inc	2821	E	714 751-7084	7612
Spa Girl Corporation	2844	E	714 444-1040	8586
Spec Formliners Inc	3272	E	714 429-9500	10655
Specialty Equipment Co	3713	E	714 258-1622	19558
Spill Magic Inc	2621	E	714 557-2001	5153
SPS Technologies LLC	3965	B	714 545-9311	23009
SPS Technologies LLC	3965	B	714 371-1925	23010
Ss Metal Fabricators	3441	F	949 631-4272	11884
Steady Clothing Inc	2329	F	714 444-2058	3118
Straightline Mechanical Inc	3494	E	714 204-0940	13364
Strata Forest Products Inc (PA)	2421	D	714 751-0800	3962
Stremicks Heritage Foods LLC (HQ)	2026	B	714 775-5000	711
Sun & Sun Industries Inc	3646	D	714 210-5141	17073
Sundown Liquidating Corp (PA)	3211	C	714 540-8950	10277
Sunrise Imaging Inc	3861	F	949 252-3003	22459
Super-Fit Inc	3842	F	657 218-4827	22097
Supreme Abrasives	3291	F	949 250-8644	10955
Surefire LLC	3842	E	714 641-0483	22101
Surefire LLC	3842	E	714 545-9444	22102
Surefire LLC	3842	D	714 641-0483	22103
Swiss Pattern Corp	3543	F	714 545-8040	14004
Syagen Technology LLC	3826	E	714 258-4400	21295
Symbolic Displays Inc	3728	D	714 258-2811	20242
Synergistic Research Inc	3496	F	949 642-2800	13437
Tailgate Printing Inc	2759	C	714 966-3035	7238
Talimar Systems Inc	2531	E	714 557-4884	4874
Tammy Taylor Nails Inc	2821	E	949 250-9287	7617
Tardif Sheet Metal & AC	3441	F	714 547-7135	11897
Tay Ho Food Corporation	2032	E	714 973-2286	748
Taylor Communications Inc	2761	E	714 664-8865	7291
Tdi2 Custom Packaging Inc	2673	F	714 751-6782	5423
Ted Rieck Enterprises Inc	3444	F	714 542-4763	12402
Tenacore Holdings Inc	3841	D	714 444-4643	21926
Tfn Architectural Signage Inc (PA)	3993	E	714 556-0990	23226
Tibbetts Newport Corporation	2851	E	714 546-6662	8687
Tivoli Industries Inc	3648	E	714 957-6101	17170
TMC Aerospace Inc	3728	E	949 250-4999	20250
Tmx Engineering and Mfg Corp	3599	D	714 641-5884	16459
Tobin Steel Company Inc	3441	E	714 541-2268	11900
Today Pvc Bending Inc	3644	F	714 953-5707	16955
Tomi Engineering Inc	3599	D	714 556-1474	16460
Triple DOT Corp	3085	E	714 241-0888	9496
Triumph Group Inc	3398	B	714 546-9842	11475
TSC Precision Machining Inc	3599	F	714 542-3182	16475
Ttm Printed Circuit Group Inc (HQ)	3672	D	714 327-3000	18029
Ttm Technologies Inc (PA)	3672	B	714 327-3000	18031
Ttm Technologies Inc	3672	B	714 327-3000	18034
Twed-Dells Inc	3231	E	714 754-6900	10396
Ullman Sails Inc (PA)	2394	F	714 432-1860	3712
Ultimate Software Group Inc	7372	E	949 214-2710	24535
Ultra TEC Manufacturing Inc	3559	F	714 542-0608	14549
Undersea Systems Intl Inc	3699	D	714 754-7848	19427
Unit Industries Inc (PA)	3678	E	714 871-4161	18802
Universal Punch Corp	3542	D	714 556-4488	13997
Uremet Corporation	2821	E	714 641-8813	7622
US Rigging Supply Corp	3496	E	714 545-7444	13442
US Saws Inc (PA)	3531	F	860 668-2402	13755
Veros Software Inc	7372	E	714 415-6300	24556
Versatraction Inc	2672	F	714 973-4589	5378
Visibility Solutions Inc	2599	F	714 434-7040	5088
Watermans Guild	3949	F	714 751-0603	22922
West Coast Form Grinding	3599	F	714 540-5621	16517
West Lake Food Corporation	2011	D	714 973-2286	431
Westerly Marine Inc	3732	E	714 966-8550	20362
Western Methods Machinery Corp	3728	C	949 252-6600	20269
Westminster Press Inc	2752	E	714 210-2881	6937
Westridge Laboratories Inc	2844	E	714 259-9400	8607
Westrock Cp LLC	2631	E	714 641-8891	5183
Wild Wood Designs Inc	2511	F	714 543-6549	4623
Wright Capacitors Inc	3675	F	714 546-2490	18687
Wyvern Technologies Inc	3679	E	714 966-0710	19145
Xs Scuba Inc (PA)	3949	E	714 424-0434	22928
Ys Controls LLC	3829	E	714 641-0727	21566

SANTA BARBARA, CA - Santa Barbara County

	SIC	EMP	PHONE	ENTRY #
Adding Technology (PA)	7372	F	805 252-6971	23561
Alta Properties Inc	3699	B	805 683-1431	19255
Alta Properties Inc	3825	B	805 683-2575	20998
Alta Properties Inc	3699	B	805 690-5382	19256
Alta Properties Inc	3264	B	805 967-0171	10473
Alta Properties Inc (PA)	3264	C	805 967-0171	10474
Ampersand Publishing LLC (PA)	2711	E	805 564-5200	5550
Anasys Instruments Corp	3826	E	805 730-3310	21173
Anthonys Christmas Trees	3999	E	805 966-6668	23276
Aqueos Corporation (PA)	3533	C	805 364-0570	13766

	SIC	EMP	PHONE	ENTRY #
Architctral Mllwk Snta Barbara	2431	E	805 965-7011	3998
Arthrex Inc	3841	D	805 964-8104	21609
Axia Technologies LLC	7372	E	855 376-2942	23646
Axxcelera Brdband Wireless Inc (DH)	3663	F	805 968-9621	17467
B&B Hardware Inc	3452	E	805 683-6700	12666
Benefit Software Incorporated	7372	E	805 679-6200	23659
Biodico Westside LLC	2869	F	805 683-8103	8722
Brandnew Industries Inc	3953	F	805 964-8251	22948
Brickschain Cnstr Blockchain	3251	F	833 274-2572	10431
Bruker Nano Inc	3826	F	805 967-2700	21201
Christian Science Church	2711	E	805 966-6661	5590
Computational Sensors Corp	3812	E	805 962-1175	20557
Container Technology Inc (PA)	3089	F	805 683-5825	9725
Continntal Advnced Ldar Sltons	3714	F	805 318-2072	19621
Dailymedia Inc (PA)	2711	F	541 821-5207	5613
Debbies Delights Inc	2053	E	805 966-3504	1340
Duncan Carter Corporation (PA)	3931	D	805 964-9749	22614
Ebix Inc	7372	E	805 568-0240	23840
Efaxcom	3577	E	805 692-0064	15222
Esperer Holdings Inc (PA)	3341	E	805 880-4220	11200
Esperer Webstores LLC	2023	E	805 880-1900	586
Federal Buyers Guide Inc (PA)	2741	F	805 963-7470	6234
Foodtools Consolidated Inc (PA)	3556	F	805 962-8383	14363
Forester Communications Inc	2721	F	805 682-1300	5936
Freedom Photonics LLC	3699	E	805 967-4900	19313
Fuelbox Inc	3679	F	919 949-9179	18919
Future Fine Foods	2051	F	805 682-9421	1212
Gavial Itc LLC	3679	D	805 614-0060	18923
Graphiq LLC	2741	C	805 335-2433	6247
Green Hills Software LLC (HQ)	7372	C	805 965-6044	23955
Guess Inc	2325	F	805 963-9490	3006
Hispanic Business Inc	2721	F	805 964-4554	5955
Idrive Inc	3714	F	805 308-6094	19687
Inform Solution Incorporated	7372	F	805 879-6000	24016
Integrity Security Svcs LLC	3699	F	805 965-6044	19325
International Tranducer Corp	3825	C	805 683-2575	21055
Invenios LLC	3231	D	805 962-3333	10367
Ircamera LLC	3827	E	805 965-9650	21369
Jeannines Bkg Co Santa Barbara (PA)	2051	F	805 966-1717	1227
Kate Farms Inc	2099	C	805 845-2446	2496
Kollmorgen Corporation	3621	B	805 696-1236	16658
Kunin Wines LLC	2084	F	805 963-9633	1787
Lafond Vineyard Inc	2084	F	805 962-9303	1790
Linear Technology LLC	3674	D	805 965-6400	18354
Marketing Bulletin Board	2711	F	805 455-2255	5726
Maysoft Inc	7372	F	978 635-1700	24133
Medeia Inc	3841	F	800 433-4609	21795
Motion Engineering Inc (HQ)	3577	D	805 696-1200	15292
Nobbe Orthopedics Inc	3842	F	805 687-7508	22054
Observables Inc	3699	F	805 272-9255	19372
Occam Networks Inc (HQ)	3661	C	805 692-2900	17392
Olaplex LLC (PA)	2844	F	805 258-7680	8550
Omtek Inc	3674	E	805 687-9629	18451
Oxford Instrs Asylum RES Inc (HQ)	3826	D	805 696-6466	21273
P J Milligan Company LLC (PA)	2511	F	805 963-4038	4601
Pacific Coast Bus Times Inc	2711	F	805 560-6950	5790
Pacific Operators Inc	1381	C	805 899-3144	101
Pacific Pickle Works Inc	2035	F	805 765-1779	895
Praxair Inc	2813	F	805 966-0829	7433
Praxair Distribution Inc	2813	F	805 966-0829	7443
Productplan LLC	7372	F	805 618-2975	24316
Proof Reading LLC	2741	F	650 438-9438	6319
Qad Inc (PA)	7372	C	805 566-6000	24325
Raoul Textiles Inc	2759	F	805 965-1694	7194
Raouls Printworks	2261	F	805 965-1694	2836
River Bench Vineyards	2084	F	805 324-4100	1890
Robert Bosch LLC	3841	E	805 966-2000	21882
Santa Barbara Control Systems	3823	F	805 683-8833	20932
Santa Barbara Independent Inc	2711	E	805 965-5205	5820
Santa Barbara Music Publishing	2741	F	805 962-5800	6336
Santa Brbara Essntial Fods LLC	2052	F	805 965-1948	1327
Serbin Communications Inc	2721	F	805 963-0439	6026
Sientra Inc (PA)	3842	C	805 562-3500	22086
Sikama International Inc	3548	E	805 962-1000	14254
Skate One Corp	3949	D	805 964-1330	22887
Smith Publishing Inc	2721	F	805 965-5999	6028
Sonos Inc (PA)	3651	D	805 965-3001	17283
Steven Handelman Studios (PA)	3322	E	805 884-9070	11151
Strand Products Inc	2298	F	805 568-0304	2916
Strand Products Inc (PA)	3845	E	805 568-0304	22316
Templock Enterprises LLC	3086	F	805 962-3100	9571
Toad & Co International Inc (PA)	2339	E	805 957-1474	3424
Visionary Solutions Inc	3699	F	805 845-8900	19437
Von Hoppen Ice Cream (HQ)	2024	F	805 965-2009	677
Vrtcal Markets Inc	2741	F	228 313-3327	6379

Employment Codes: A=Over 500 employees, B=251-500,
C=101-250, D=51-100, E=20-50, F=10-19

2020 California
Manufacturers Register

© Mergent Inc. 1-800-342-5647

1421

	SIC	EMP	PHONE	ENTRY #
Waiakea Investments LLC **(PA)**	2086	F	805 450-0981	2183

SANTA CLARA, CA - Santa Clara County

	SIC	EMP	PHONE	ENTRY #
5-Stars Engineering Assoc Inc	3549	E	408 380-4849	14261
A-1 Machine Manufacturing Inc **(PA)**	3599	C	408 727-0880	15668
Abbott Laboratories	3841	B	408 330-0057	21570
Abbott Laboratories	3841	A	408 845-3000	21571
Abbott Vascular Inc **(HQ)**	3841	B	408 845-3000	21572
Absolute Turnkey Services Inc	3672	E	408 850-7530	17800
AC Photonics Inc	3559	E	408 986-9838	14416
Accel Manufacturing Inc	3541	F	408 727-5883	13899
Access Closure Inc	3841	B	408 610-6500	21575
Accu Machine Inc	3599	E	408 855-8835	15675
Achronix Semiconductor Corp	3674	D	408 889-4100	18060
Acroscope LLC	3599	F	408 727-6896	15687
Actsolar Inc	3829	F	408 721-5000	21429
Acu Spec Inc	3599	F	408 748-8600	15688
Adem LLC	3599	E	408 727-8955	15691
Adesto Technologies Corp **(PA)**	3674	D	408 400-0578	18061
Advanced Assemblies Inc	3679	E	408 988-1016	18809
Advanced Component Labs Inc	3674	E	408 327-0200	18064
Advanced Laser Cutting Inc	3599	F	408 486-0700	15697
Advanced Micro Devices Inc **(PA)**	3674	B	408 749-4000	18066
Aella Data Inc	7372	F	408 391-1430	23575
Affymetrix Inc	3826	D	408 731-5000	21162
Affymetrix Inc	3826	D	408 731-5000	21164
Affymetrix Inc **(HQ)**	3826	D	408 731-5000	21165
Affymetrix Anatrace	3826	F	408 731-5756	21166
Agilent Tech World Trade Inc **(HQ)**	3825	F	408 345-8886	20986
Agilent Technologies Inc	3825	A	408 345-8886	20990
Agilent Technologies Inc **(PA)**	3825	A	408 345-8886	20993
Agilent Technologies Inc	3825	A	408 345-8886	20994
Agilent Technologies Inc	3825	A	408 553-7777	20995
Aixtron Inc	3674	C	669 228-3759	18073
Akt America Inc **(HQ)**	3699	B	408 563-5455	19253
All Metals Inc **(PA)**	3341	E	408 200-7000	11197
Altaflex	3672	D	408 727-6614	17814
Ambarella Inc	3674	A	408 734-8888	18088
America Asia Trade Promotion	2392	F	408 970-8868	3599
American Precision Spring	3495	E	408 986-1020	13373
Amex Plating Incorporated	3471	E	408 986-8222	12925
Amimon Inc	2631	F	650 641-3191	5156
Amlogic Inc	3674	E	408 850-9688	18097
Amq Solutions LLC **(HQ)**	2521	F	877 801-0370	4782
Analogix Semiconductor Inc	3674	E	408 988-8848	18101
Apct Inc **(PA)**	3672	D	408 727-6442	17821
Applied Films Corporation	3674	E	408 727-5555	18106
Applied Materials Inc	3674	E	408 727-5555	18107
Applied Materials Inc	3674	E	406 752-2107	18109
Applied Materials Inc **(PA)**	3559	A	408 727-5555	14424
Applied Materials Inc	3674	E	408 727-5555	18111
Applied Materials Inc	3674	F	512 272-3692	18112
Applied Materials Inc	3674	E	408 727-5555	18113
Applied Materials Inc	3674	D	408 727-5555	18115
Applied Materials Inc	2721	F	408 727-5555	5881
Applied Micro Circuits Corp **(HQ)**	3674	C	408 542-8600	18116
Applied Micro Circuits Corp	3674	E	408 542-8600	18117
Appvance Inc	7372	E	408 871-0122	23616
Appzen Inc **(PA)**	7372	E	408 647-5253	23618
Aruba Networks Inc **(HQ)**	3577	B	408 227-4500	15160
Atypon Systems LLC **(PA)**	7372	D	408 988-1240	23637
Avaya Holdings Corp **(PA)**	7372	E	908 953-6000	23644
B P I Corp	3599	F	408 988-7888	15768
B R & F Spray Inc	3479	F	408 988-7582	13148
B-Bridge International Inc	2836	E	408 252-6200	8279
Bachur & Associates	2752	F	408 988-5861	6433
Baffle Inc	7372	F	408 663-6737	23650
Bay Area Canvas Inc	2394	F	408 727-4314	3673
Beam Dynamics Inc	3545	F	408 764-4805	14138
Beam On Technology Corporation	3569	E	408 982-0161	14798
Bel Power Solutions Inc	3677	A	866 513-2839	18703
Bench-Tek Solutions Llc	2522	F	408 653-1100	4830
Berg Manufacturing Inc	3999	F	408 727-2374	23287
Bertolin Engineering Corp	3469	F	408 988-0166	12770
Big Switch Networks Inc **(PA)**	7372	D	650 322-6510	23666
Bimarian Inc	7372	E	408 520-2666	23668
Bitzer Mobile Inc	7372	E	866 603-8392	23672
Blue Danube Systems Inc **(PA)**	3663	F	650 316-5010	17470
Bluesnap Inc	7372	E	866 475-4687	23683
Brightlight Welding & Mfg Inc	7692	F	408 988-0418	24618
Broadlight Inc	3674	F	408 982-4210	18155
Byington Steel Treating Inc **(PA)**	3398	E	408 727-6630	11443
Byton North America Corp	3711	C	408 966-5078	19461
Ca Inc	7372	E	800 225-5224	23705
California Micro Devices Corp **(HQ)**	3676	E	408 542-1051	18689
Calmax Technology Inc **(PA)**	3599	E	408 748-8660	15820

	SIC	EMP	PHONE	ENTRY #
Calperf Inc **(PA)**	2011	F	408 829-7779	397
Calstar Products Inc	3251	D	262 752-9131	10432
Capella Microsystems Inc	3672	E	408 988-8000	17842
Caraustar Industries Inc	2655	C	408 845-7600	5290
Cardiva Medical Inc	3841	C	408 470-7100	21651
Casemaker Inc	7372	F	408 261-8265	23720
Caspio Inc **(PA)**	7372	E	650 691-0900	23722
Cavium LLC **(HQ)**	3674	B	408 222-2500	18158
Centerline Precision Inc	2836	F	408 988-4380	8286
Cirexx Corporation	3672	E	408 988-3980	17851
Cirexx International Inc **(PA)**	3672	E	408 988-3980	17852
Cisco Mfg Inc	3599	F	510 584-9626	15846
Citrix Systems Inc	7372	D	408 790-8000	23741
Cleanpartset Inc	3559	E	408 886-3300	14440
Cloudcar Inc	7372	F	650 946-1236	23750
Cloudminds Technology Inc	3535	F	650 391-6817	13818
Coherent Inc	3699	A	408 764-4000	19276
Coherent Inc **(PA)**	3826	A	408 764-4000	21206
Coherent Asia Inc	3679	D	408 764-4000	18870
Colfax International	3571	E	408 730-2275	14899
Colortokens Inc	7372	E	408 341-6030	23759
Communicart	2752	F	408 970-0922	6504
Compass Innovations Inc	3081	C	408 418-3985	9398
Component Re-Engineering Inc	3674	E	408 562-4000	18170
Computer Access Tech Corp	3571	D	408 727-6600	14900
Comtech Xicom Technology Inc **(HQ)**	3663	C	408 213-3000	17493
Condor Reliability Services	3674	C	408 486-9600	18173
Context Engineering Co	3469	C	408 748-9112	12788
Convergent Manufacturing Tech	3577	F	408 987-2770	15206
Corporate Sign Systems Inc	3993	E	408 292-1600	23081
Cortina Systems Inc **(HQ)**	3674	C	408 481-2300	18182
Coskata Inc	2869	F	630 657-5800	8734
Creation Tech Santa Clara Inc	3672	B	408 235-7500	17857
Crossbar Inc	3674	E	408 884-0281	18186
Csl Operating LLC	3471	D	408 727-0893	12981
Cupertronix Inc	3826	F	408 887-5455	21212
Custom Pad and Partition Inc	2653	D	408 970-9711	5217
Cytobank Inc	7372	F	650 918-7966	23795
D & T Machining Inc	3599	F	408 486-6035	15875
D-Tek Manufacturing	3674	F	408 588-1574	18191
Dahlhauser Manufacturing Co	3496	E	408 988-3717	13409
Darko Precision Inc	3599	D	408 988-6133	15880
Datera Inc	7372	E	650 384-6366	23806
Dell Inc	3571	F	408 206-5466	14903
Delong Manufacturing Co Inc	3599	F	408 727-3348	15885
Dialog Semiconductor Inc **(DH)**	3674	E	408 845-8500	18195
Digital Loggers Inc	3613	E	408 330-5599	16594
Dongbu Electronics Co	3674	F	408 330-0330	18197
Double Precision Mfg	3599	E	408 727-7726	15905
Dpss Lasers Inc	3699	A	408 988-4300	19294
Dynamic Intgrted Solutions LLC **(PA)**	3674	E	408 727-3400	18204
E-Fab Inc	3479	E	408 727-5218	13168
Earthpro Inc	3271	E	408 294-1920	10508
Easic Corporation	3674	E	408 855-9200	18206
Echelon Corporation **(HQ)**	3825	D	408 938-5200	21024
Edge Compute Inc	3674	E	408 209-0368	18207
Electronic Cooling Solutions	3571	F	408 738-8331	14905
Element Six Tech US Corp	2819	E	408 986-8184	7490
Elite E/M Inc	3444	E	408 988-3505	12194
Eme Technologies Inc	3599	E	408 720-8817	15930
End-Effectors Inc	3491	F	408 727-0100	13304
Enki Technology Inc	2819	F	408 383-9034	7491
Erb Investment Company LLC	3599	F	408 727-6908	15935
Excel Cnc Machining Inc	3599	E	408 970-9460	15940
Excel Precision Corp USA	3825	E	408 727-2400	21036
Exclara Inc	3674	E	408 329-9319	18232
Expandable Software Inc **(PA)**	7372	E	408 261-7880	23884
Expol Inc	3599	F	408 567-9020	15944
Fast Turn Machining Inc	3599	F	408 720-6888	15953
Feitian Technologies Us Inc	3699	F	408 352-5553	19310
Fiberlite Centrifuge LLC	3826	D	408 492-1109	21228
Fizzy Color LLC	2752	F	408 623-6705	6576
Fja Industries Inc	3569	F	408 727-0100	14818
Fortemedia Inc **(PA)**	3674	E	408 716-8028	18241
Fortemedia Inc	3572	D	408 716-8011	15029
Forward Integration Technology	3357	F	408 988-3330	11304
Four-D Metal Finishing Inc	3471	E	408 730-5722	13011
Fujifilm Dimatix Inc **(HQ)**	3577	C	408 565-9150	15232
Galaxy Manufacturing Inc	3469	E	408 654-4583	12806
Gateway Precision Inc	3599	F	408 855-8849	15987
Ghs Champion Inc	2051	E	650 326-8485	1216
Gigamon Inc **(HQ)**	7372	C	408 831-4000	23938
Gilbert Spray Coat Inc	3479	F	408 988-0747	13186
Globalfoundries US Inc **(DH)**	3559	B	408 462-3900	14473
Greenliant Systems Inc	3674	C	408 217-7400	18255

2020 California
Manufacturers Register

(P-0000) Products & Services Section entry number
(PA)=Parent Co (HQ)=Headquarters (DH)=Div Headquarters

Name	SIC	EMP	PHONE	ENTRY #
Gsi Technology Inc	3674	D	408 980-8388	18257
Guidetech Inc	3825	E	408 733-6555	21048
H&M Precision Machining	3451	F	408 982-9184	12634
H-Square Corporation	3674	E	408 732-1240	18262
Hana Microelectronics Inc	3674	F	408 452-7474	18264
Harbor Electronics Inc (PA)	3679	C	408 988-6544	18929
Haros Anodizing Specialist	3471	F	408 980-0892	13022
Harvatek International Corp	3646	F	408 844-9698	17042
Heliovolt Corporation	3679	D	512 767-6079	18933
High Speed Cnc	3599	F	408 492-0331	16027
Hill Manufacturing Company LLC	3444	E	408 988-4744	12237
Hitachi Vantara Corporation (DH)	3572	B	408 970-1000	15044
Honeywell International Inc	2819	D	408 962-2000	7500
Hortonworks Inc (HQ)	7372	A	408 916-4121	23986
Hung Tung	3599	F	408 496-1818	16037
Imergy Power Systems Inc	3679	E	510 668-1485	18943
Impakt Holdings LLC	3444	F	650 692-5800	12243
Impossible Aerospace Corp	3721	F	707 293-9367	19906
Information Scan Tech Inc	3825	E	408 988-1908	21051
Innowi Inc	3571	E	408 609-9404	14924
Inolux Corporation (PA)	3674	F	408 844-8734	18294
Inphi Corporation (PA)	3674	C	408 217-7300	18296
Inta Technologies Corporation	3471	E	408 748-9955	13030
Integra Technologies LLC	3674	D	408 923-7300	18301
Integrated Optical Svcs Corp	2851	E	408 982-9510	8647
Intel Americas Inc (HQ)	3577	D	408 765-8080	15250
INTEL Corporation	3577	F	408 765-2508	15251
Intel Corporation (PA)	3577	B	408 765-8080	15252
Intel Corporation	3577	C	408 425-8398	15253
INTEL Corporation	3577	C	503 696-8080	15255
Intel Federal LLC	3674	E	302 644-3756	18309
INTEL International Limited (HQ)	3674	E	408 765-8080	18310
Intel Network Systems Inc	3674	E	408 765-8080	18311
INTEL Puerto Rico Inc	3674	E	408 765-8080	18312
Intevac (PA)	3559	C	408 986-9888	14480
Intevac Inc	3559	E	408 986-9888	14481
Intevac Photonics Inc (HQ)	3827	F	408 986-9888	21367
Intuitive Surgical Inc	3841	B	408 523-2100	21754
Invecas Inc	3674	E	408 758-5636	18318
Invenio Imaging Inc	3841	F	408 753-9147	21757
J & B Refining Inc	3339	F	408 988-7900	11192
James Stout	3599	E	408 988-8582	16076
Jasper Display Corp	3559	E	408 831-5788	14483
Jetnexus LLC	3571	E	800 568-9921	14930
JP Graphics Inc	2752	E	408 235-8821	6669
JWP Manufacturing LLC	3599	E	408 970-0641	16097
Kana Software Inc (HQ)	7372	D	650 614-8300	24070
Keysight Technologies Inc	3825	E	408 553-3290	21061
KLA Corporation	3825	D	408 496-2055	21063
Kno Inc	7372	D	408 844-8120	24081
L P Glassblowing Inc	3679	E	408 988-7561	18981
Landec Corporation (PA)	2033	D	650 306-1650	788
Lockheed Martin Corporation	3812	A	408 734-4980	20606
Logicool Inc	7372	E	408 907-1344	24107
Lor-Van Manufacturing LLC	3444	E	408 980-1045	12267
Lumasense Tech Holdings Inc (HQ)	3845	D	408 727-1600	22273
Lunas Sheet Metal Inc	3444	E	408 492-1260	12269
Mac Engineering & Components	3429	F	408 286-3030	11607
Magnetic Rcrding Solutions Inc	3825	E	408 970-8266	21072
Manufacturers/Hyland Ltd	3231	F	408 748-1806	10378
Marvell Semiconductor Inc	3825	E	408 855-8839	21073
Marvell Semiconductor Inc (HQ)	3674	A	408 222-2500	18372
Marx Digital Mfg Inc (PA)	3599	E	408 748-1783	16177
Master Precision Machining	3599	E	408 727-0185	16178
Matthias Rath Inc (HQ)	2023	F	408 567-5000	603
Maxford Technology LLC	3299	F	408 855-8288	11010
McAfee LLC (HQ)	7372	C	888 847-8766	24135
McAfee Finance 2 LLC	7372	A	888 847-8766	24136
McAfee Security LLC	7372	A	866 622-3911	24137
McKenzie Machining Inc	3599	F	408 748-8885	16184
Mecpro Inc	3599	E	408 727-9757	16189
Medconx Inc	3069	E	408 330-0003	9333
Mercury Networks LLC	3663	F	408 859-1345	17583
Messer LLC	3561	D	408 496-1177	14590
Metal Finishing Solutions Inc	3444	F	408 988-8642	12293
Metra Biosystems Inc (HQ)	2835	E	408 616-4300	8237
Metrotech Corporation (PA)	3812	D	408 734-3880	20630
Miasole	3674	B	408 919-5700	18385
Miasole Hi-Tech Corp (DH)	3674	C	408 919-5700	18386
Micro Focus LLC (DH)	7372	F	801 861-7000	24151
Micro Semicdtr Researches LLC	3674	E	408 492-1369	18392
Micropoint Bioscience Inc	2835	E	408 588-1682	8238
Microsemi Corp - Pwr Prdts Grp	3674	F	408 986-8031	18400
Microsoft Corporation	7372	D	408 987-9608	24163
Miradry Inc	3842	E	408 940-8700	22049
Mission Park Hotel LP	2819	E	408 809-3838	7506
Modular Process Tech Corp	3567	F	408 325-8640	14771
Molding Company	2499	E	408 748-6968	4516
Montblanc North America LLC	3911	F	408 241-5188	22551
Monterey Bay Office Pdts Inc	2754	F	408 727-4627	6960
Montoya & Jaramillo Inc	3471	F	408 727-5776	13054
Multibeam Corporation	3559	E	408 980-1800	14504
Multimek Inc	3672	E	408 653-1300	17930
Multitest Elctrnic Systems Inc (DH)	3825	B	408 988-6544	21083
N D E Inc	3672	E	408 727-3955	17931
Nanoscale Combinatorial	2899	E	408 987-2000	9007
National Instruments Corp	3825	B	408 610-6800	21086
National Semiconductor Corp (HQ)	3674	A	408 721-5000	18427
Net Optics Inc	7372	E	408 737-7777	24192
Nethra Imaging Inc (PA)	3674	F	408 257-5880	18432
Netsarang Inc	7372	F	669 204-3301	24195
Newnex Technology Corp	3577	F	408 986-9988	15295
Newpacket Wireless Corporation	3577	F	408 747-1003	15296
Newport Corporation	3699	A	408 980-4300	19367
Nexgen Power Systems Inc	3674	E	408 230-7698	18435
Nextec Microwave & Rf Inc	3663	E	408 727-1189	17603
Nominum Inc	7372	E	650 381-6000	24211
Nss Enterprises	2752	E	408 970-9200	6754
Nuvora Inc	2844	E	408 856-2200	8549
Nvidia Corporation (PA)	3674	B	408 486-2000	18437
Nvidia Corporation	3674	E	408 566-5364	18438
Nvidia Development Inc	3674	E	408 486-2000	18439
Nvidia US Investment Company	3663	A	408 615-2500	17607
Nwe Technology Inc	3572	C	408 919-6100	15068
Olympic Press Inc	2759	F	408 496-6222	7154
Omnivision Technologies Inc (PA)	3674	C	408 567-3000	18450
Omniyig Inc	3679	E	408 988-0843	19039
Onspec Technology Partners Inc	3674	E	408 654-7627	18454
Optasense Inc	3674	F	408 970-3500	18456
Oracle America Inc	7372	C	408 276-4300	24238
Oracle America Inc	7372	C	408 276-3331	24242
Oracle America Inc	7372	C	408 276-7534	24247
Oracle Corporation	7372	B	408 421-2890	24252
Oracle Corporation	7372	B	408 276-5552	24253
Oracle Corporation	7372	B	650 506-9864	24256
P K Selective Metal Pltg Inc	3471	F	408 988-1910	13068
P M S D Inc (PA)	3599	D	408 988-5235	16269
P M S D Inc	3599	E	408 727-5322	16270
P S C Manufacturing Inc	3089	E	408 988-5115	9943
Pac Tech USA Packg Tech Inc	3674	E	408 588-1925	18464
Pacific Ceramics Inc	3264	E	408 747-4600	10480
Pacific Impressions Inc	2261	F	408 727-4200	2832
Pactron	3672	D	408 329-5500	17949
Palex Metals Inc	3444	E	408 496-6111	12328
Palo Alto Networks Inc (PA)	3577	B	408 753-4000	15305
Par Global Resources Inc	2752	F	408 982-5515	6767
Paragon Swiss Inc	3599	E	408 748-1617	16280
Parametric Manufacturing Inc	3599	F	408 654-9845	16281
Patsons Press	2752	E	408 567-0911	6771
Pelican Sign Service Inc	3993	F	408 246-3833	23177
Pepsi-Cola Metro Btlg Co Inc	2086	C	408 617-2200	2112
Performmediacom Inc Which	2741	F	858 336-8121	6308
Picarro Inc (PA)	3826	E	408 962-3900	21276
Picotrack	3559	F	408 988-7000	14519
Pneumrx Inc	3841	E	650 625-4440	21859
Polishing Corporation America	3674	E	888 892-3377	18474
Praxair Distribution Inc	2813	E	408 748-1722	7448
Probe-Rite Corp	3825	E	408 727-0100	21102
Process Stainless Lab Inc (PA)	3471	E	408 980-0535	13079
Prodigy Surface Tech Inc	3471	E	408 492-9390	13080
Promega Bsystems Sunnyvale Inc	3829	E	408 636-2400	21522
Promex Industries Incorporated (PA)	3674	D	408 496-0222	18483
Purewave Networks Inc	3663	E	650 528-5200	17630
Pwp Manufacturing LLC	3444	E	408 748-0120	12344
Qmat Inc	3674	E	498 228-5858	18489
Quadbase Systems Inc	7372	F	408 982-0835	24329
Qualcomm Incorporated	3674	B	408 216-6797	18495
Qualcomm Incorporated	3663	F	858 587-1121	17632
Qualtech Circuits Inc	3672	E	408 727-4125	17970
Quest Software Inc	7372	F	408 899-3823	24333
Questivity Inc	7372	F	408 615-1781	24335
Radian Thermal Products Inc	3369	D	408 988-6200	11422
Rdc Machine Inc	3599	F	408 970-0721	16344
Reaction Technology Inc (PA)	3674	E	408 970-9601	18510
Redfern Integrated Optics Inc	3827	E	408 970-3500	21401
Redline Solutions Inc	3577	F	408 562-1700	15319
Reliance Computer Corp	3674	C	408 492-1915	18513
Rennovia Inc	2869	F	650 804-7400	8771
Revera Incorporated	3577	E	408 510-7400	15320
Rimnetics Inc	3089	E	650 969-6590	10018

GEOGRAPHIC

Company	SIC	EMP	PHONE	ENTRY #
Rocket Ems Inc	3672	C	408 727-3700	17977
Roos Instruments Inc	3825	E	408 748-8589	21114
Ruckus Wireless Inc	3663	E	408 235-5500	17647
SAE Engineering Inc	3444	E	408 492-1784	12365
San Jose Delta Associates Inc	3264	E	408 727-1448	10482
Sanmina Corporation	3672	A	408 244-0266	17985
Santa Clara Imaging	3829	E	408 296-5555	21532
Santa Clara Plating Co Inc	3471	D	408 727-9315	13096
Scientific Metal Finishing	3479	E	408 970-9011	13242
Secugen Corporation	3577	E	408 834-7712	15329
Secure Computing Corporation (DH)	7372	E	408 979-2020	24394
Semicndctor Cmponents Inds LLC	3674	C	408 542-1000	18531
Semiconix Corp (PA)	3674	F	408 986-8026	18536
Senju Comtek Corp (HQ)	3399	F	408 963-5300	11487
Sequent Software Inc	7372	F	650 419-2713	24399
Sesame Software Inc	7372	E	866 474-7575	24402
SF Motors Inc (DH)	3711	C	408 617-7878	19501
Shape Memory Medical Inc	3842	E	979 599-5201	22085
Sharedata Inc	7372	D	408 490-2500	24403
Shockwave Medical Inc (PA)	3841	D	510 279-4262	21898
Silicon Standard Corp	3674	E	408 234-6964	18549
Silicon Valley Elite Mfg	3599	E	408 654-9534	16405
Silicon Vly McRelectronics Inc	3674	E	408 844-7100	18551
Siliconix Semiconductor Inc	3674	C	408 988-8000	18554
Silver Peak Systems Inc (PA)	3674	C	408 935-1800	18555
Sitime Corporation (HQ)	3674	C	408 328-4400	18559
Sj Valley Plating Inc	3471	F	408 988-5502	13102
Sjt Tech Industries Inc	3674	F	408 980-9547	18560
Software Ag Inc	7372	C	408 490-5300	24426
Solflower Computer Inc	3577	F	408 733-8100	15337
Solid Data Systems Inc	3572	E	408 845-5700	15103
Solutionsoft Systems Inc	7372	E	408 346-1491	24430
Sonic Solutions Holdings Inc	7372	D	408 562-8400	24433
Sp3 Diamond Technologies Inc	3569	F	877 773-9940	14860
Spectra-Physics Inc	3699	A	650 961-2550	19412
SPI Solar Inc (PA)	3433	F	408 919-8000	11718
Sra Oss Inc	7372	C	408 855-8200	24446
Star Products	3599	E	408 727-8421	16421
Step Tools Unlimited Inc	3545	F	408 988-8898	14199
Steris Corporation	3842	F	800 614-6789	22092
Stone Publishing Inc (PA)	2759	C	408 450-7910	7230
Summit Interconnect Inc	3672	C	408 727-1418	18016
Sun Marble Inc	3281	E	510 783-9900	10935
Sun Microsystems Tech Ltd	7372	E	650 960-1300	24467
Sunpreme Inc	3674	E	408 419-9281	18592
Superior Quartz Inc	3339	F	408 844-9663	11195
Sutter P Dahlglen Entps Inc	3599	F	408 727-4640	16433
Swiss Screw Products Inc	3599	E	408 748-8400	16434
Synthesys Research Inc (DH)	3825	D	408 753-1630	21134
T M Industries Incorporated	3441	F	408 736-5202	11894
Taracom Corporation	3571	F	408 691-6655	14986
Tekever Corporation	7372	D	408 730-2617	24496
Tektronix Inc	3825	E	408 496-0800	21136
Teledyne Wireless Inc	3631	C	408 986-5060	16818
Telenav Inc (PA)	3812	C	408 245-3800	20731
Tellus Solutions Inc	7372	E	408 850-2942	24498
Ter Inc	3599	E	408 986-9920	16452
Ter Precision Machining Inc	3599	E	408 986-9920	16453
Texas Instruments Incorporated	3674	E	669 721-5000	18619
Theater Publications Inc	2721	F	408 748-1600	6040
Thermo Fisher Scientific Inc	3826	E	408 731-5056	21313
Tmk Manufacturing Inc	3545	F	408 844-8289	14203
Tool Makers International Inc	3541	F	408 980-8888	13958
Total Phase Inc	3572	F	408 850-6500	15110
Trackonomy Systems Inc	3663	F	833 872-2566	17694
Translattice Inc (PA)	3571	E	408 749-8478	14991
Ttm Printed Circuit Group Inc	3672	C	408 486-3100	18028
Ttm Technologies Inc	3672	B	408 486-3100	18030
Uniq Vision Inc	3861	C	408 330-0818	22468
Unique Media Inc	3652	F	408 733-9999	17338
Unisem (sunnvale) Inc (PA)	3674	F	408 734-3222	18634
Unitech Tool & Machine Inc	3599	E	408 566-0333	16481
Uri Tech Inc	3672	F	408 456-0115	18039
Vacuum Engrg & Mtls Co Inc	2819	E	408 871-9900	7534
Vanderhulst Associates Inc	3599	E	408 727-1313	16495
Vave Health Inc	3845	F	650 387-7059	22324
Veeco Instruments Inc	3674	E	510 657-8523	18637
Verifone Inc	3578	C	408 232-7800	15381
Violin Mmory Fdral Systems Inc	3674	E	650 396-1500	18643
VIP Manufacturing & Engrg	3724	F	408 727-6545	19990
Visger Precision Inc	3599	F	408 988-0184	16503
Vivid Inc	3444	D	408 982-9101	12428
Volex Inc (HQ)	3089	E	669 444-1740	10113
Vulcan Construction Mtls LLC	1442	F	408 213-4270	366
W L Gore & Associates Inc	3841	C	928 864-2705	21962

Company	SIC	EMP	PHONE	ENTRY #
Watts Machining Inc	3599	E	408 654-9300	16513
Wavexing Inc	3674	F	408 896-1982	18655
WEI Laboratories Inc	2032	E	408 970-8700	750
Wes Manufacturing Inc	3599	E	408 727-0750	16516
Western Grinding Service Inc	3599	E	650 591-2635	16522
Westfab Manufacturing Inc	3444	E	408 727-0550	12436
Whizz Systems Inc	3672	E	408 207-0400	18051
Winnov Inc	3651	F	888 315-9460	17305
Winway Usa Inc	3674	E	203 775-9311	18658
Wti Jkb Inc (PA)	2431	F	408 297-8579	4157
Xceive Corporation	3679	E	408 486-5610	19146
Zygo Corporation	3826	E	408 434-1000	21328

SANTA CLARITA, CA - Los Angeles County

Company	SIC	EMP	PHONE	ENTRY #
3d International LLC	2842	E	661 250-2020	8357
3d/International Inc	2842	D	661 250-2020	8358
Aircraft Hinge Inc	3728	E	661 257-3434	20026
Applied Polytech Systems Inc	2452	E	818 504-9261	4457
B & B Manufacturing Co (PA)	3599	C	661 257-2161	15761
Billy Beez Usa LLC	3949	F	661 383-0050	22762
Blue Cross Laboratories Inc (PA)	2842	C	661 255-0955	8368
California Millworks Corp	2431	E	661 294-2345	4011
California Resources Corp (PA)	1311	C	888 848-4754	36
Certified Thermoplastics LLC	3089	E	661 222-3006	9703
Coast Air Supply Co Inc	3643	F	310 472-5612	16884
Curtiss-Wright Corporation	3491	E	661 257-4430	13301
Daisy Publishing Company Inc	2721	D	661 295-1910	5915
Door & Hardware Installers Inc	2431	E	661 298-9383	4036
Dulce Systems Inc	3669	E	818 435-6007	17726
Frametent Inc	2394	F	661 290-3375	3683
Grand-Way Fabri-Graphic Inc	3479	E	818 206-8560	13187
H2w Technologies Inc	3625	F	661 291-1620	16720
Iwerks Entertainment Inc	3699	D	661 678-1800	19330
Lamsco West Inc	3728	D	661 295-8620	20153
Lansair Corporation	3599	F	661 294-9503	16136
Living Way Industries Inc	3993	F	661 298-3200	23148
Lockheed Martin Corporation	3812	B	661 572-7363	20623
Magic Plastics Inc	3089	D	800 369-0303	9884
Manzanita	3931	F	818 785-1111	22630
Metalpro Industries Inc	3444	E	661 294-0764	12297
Mikailian Meat Product Inc	2013	F	661 257-1055	480
Morgan Products Inc	3599	F	661 257-3022	16227
Morris Multimedia Inc	2711	D	661 259-1234	5761
Old English Mil & Woodworks (PA)	2431	E	661 294-9171	4099
Packaging Systems Inc	2891	E	661 253-5700	8885
Parrot Communications Intl Inc	2741	E	818 567-4700	6305
Projex International Inc	3999	F	661 268-0999	23453
Shadow Holdings LLC (PA)	2844	E	661 252-3807	8578
Shadow Holdings LLC	2844	C	661 252-3807	8579
Signal	2711	D	661 259-1234	5826
Source Print Media Solutions	2752	E	661 263-1880	6864
Stiers Rv Centers LLC	3799	F	661 254-6000	20522
Terryberry Company LLC	3911	D	661 257-9971	22578
Tesco Products	3541	F	661 257-0153	13956
True Warrior LLC	2389	E	661 237-6588	3582
Val Pak Products	3069	F	661 252-0115	9385
Valencia Mold	3089	F	661 257-0066	10107
Valley Precision Metal Product	3444	E	661 607-0100	12421
Weyerhaeuser Company	2421	E	661 250-3500	3965
Whitmor Plstic Wire Cable Corp (PA)	3496	D	661 257-2400	13446
Woodward Hrt Inc (HQ)	3625	A	661 294-6000	16769
Woodward Hrt Inc	3625	D	661 702-5552	16770
Zada Graphics Inc	2752	F	323 321-8940	6947

SANTA CRUZ, CA - Santa Cruz County

Company	SIC	EMP	PHONE	ENTRY #
Anatometal Inc	3911	E	831 454-9880	22495
Bagelry Inc (PA)	2051	E	831 429-8049	1139
Beckmanns Old World Bakery Ltd	2051	C	831 423-9242	1144
Bimbo Bakeries Usa Inc	2051	F	831 465-1214	1163
Bonny Doon Vineyard (PA)	2084	D	831 425-3625	1603
Bonny Doon Winery Inc	2084	D	831 425-3625	1604
Buoy Labs Inc	7372	F	855 481-7112	23703
Community Printers Inc	2752	E	831 426-4682	6505
Cool Lumens Inc	3646	F	831 471-8084	17021
Dallas Electronics Inc	3672	F	831 457-3610	17860
Doerksen Precision Products	3599	F	831 476-1843	15902
Duke Empirical Inc	3841	D	831 420-1104	21691
Dynamic Engineering	3674	F	831 457-8891	18202
Elements Manufacturing Inc	2541	F	831 421-9440	4899
Eschaton Foundation (PA)	2752	F	831 423-1626	6566
Eye Medical Group Santa Cruz	3841	F	831 426-2550	21711
Fiber Systems Inc	3661	E	831 430-0700	17369
Global Precision Manufacturing	3531	F	831 239-9469	13731
Herb KAn Company Inc	2833	F	831 438-9450	7667
Hydro-Logic Purification	3569	F	888 426-5644	14826
Inboard Technology Inc	3751	F	844 846-2627	20409

Company	SIC	EMP	PHONE	ENTRY #
Jeff Frank	3993	F	831 469-8208	23140
Jim Beauregard	2084	D	831 423-9453	1774
Journeyworks Publishing	2741	F	831 423-1400	6263
Keyfax Newmedia Inc	3651	F	831 477-1205	17250
King Precision Inc	3469	E	831 426-2704	12832
Lackey Woodworking Inc	2434	F	831 462-0528	4221
Larsens Inc	2394	F	831 476-3009	3690
Las Animas Con & Bldg Sup Inc	3273	E	831 425-4084	10778
Lifeaid Beverage Company LLC	2086	D	888 558-1113	2089
Lockheed Martin Corporation	3812	A	831 425-6000	20602
Lockheed Martin Corporation	3761	D	831 425-6000	20448
Lockheed Martin Corporation	3812	D	831 425-6375	20619
Looker Data Sciences Inc (PA)	3572	D	831 244-0340	15053
Mariannes Ice Cream LLC (PA)	2024	F	831 457-1447	657
Mel & Associates Inc (PA)	3949	F	831 476-2950	22852
Metro Publishing Inc	2711	F	831 457-9000	5750
Mindsai Inc	7372	F	831 239-4644	24167
National Stock Sign Company	3993	F	831 476-2020	23166
Nhs Inc	3949	D	831 459-7800	22859
Obentec Inc	2449	F	831 457-0301	4422
ONeill Wetsuits LLC (PA)	3069	D	831 475-7500	9347
Ontera Inc	3674	C	831 222-2193	18455
Overbeck Machine	3599	E	831 425-5912	16265
Persys Engineering Inc	3559	E	831 471-9300	14517
Plantronics Inc (PA)	3661	B	831 426-5858	17398
Plantronics Inc	3661	B	831 426-5858	17400
Polycom Inc (HQ)	3661	B	831 426-5858	17403
Predpol Inc	7372	F	831 331-4550	24312
Reversica Design Inc	3429	F	831 459-9033	11623
Santa Cruz Biotechnology Inc	2836	E	831 457-3800	8328
Santa Cruz Guitar Corporation	3931	E	831 425-0999	22636
Santa Cruz Industries Inc	2542	F	831 423-9211	5002
Santa Cruz Nutritionals	2834	B	831 457-3200	8119
Socksmith Design Inc (PA)	2252	E	831 426-6416	2767
System Studies Incorporated (PA)	3661	E	831 475-5777	17418
Threshold Enterprises Ltd	2833	E	831 466-4014	7700
Toucaned Inc	2741	F	831 464-0508	6361

SANTA FE SPRINGS, CA - Los Angeles County

Company	SIC	EMP	PHONE	ENTRY #
2m Machine Corporation	3599	F	562 404-4225	15643
A-W Engineering Company Inc	3469	E	562 945-1041	12756
Aberdeen LLC	3572	E	562 903-1500	15000
Accuride International Inc (PA)	3429	E	562 903-0200	11557
Ace Commercial Inc	2752	E	562 946-6664	6392
Advanced Ground Systems (HQ)	3724	E	562 906-9300	19944
Aero Chip Inc	3599	E	562 404-6300	15702
Aero Chip Intgrted Systems Inc	3812	F	310 329-8600	20529
Age Incorporated	3613	E	562 483-7300	16585
Air Products and Chemicals Inc	2813	E	562 944-3873	7394
Airgas Usa LLC	2813	E	562 946-8394	7403
Airgas Usa LLC	2813	E	562 945-1383	7406
Airgas Usa LLC	2813	E	562 906-8700	7409
Alegacy Foodservice Products	2599	D	562 320-3100	5048
All Power Manufacturing Co	3999	F	562 802-2640	23269
All-Star Lettering Inc	2759	E	562 404-5995	6981
Allblack Co Inc	3471	E	562 946-2955	12915
Altro Usa Inc	3996	D	562 944-8292	23253
Alumafab	3646	F	562 630-6440	17010
Alumistar Inc	3365	E	562 633-6673	11366
Amity Washer & Stamping Co	3469	E	562 941-1259	12765
Angelus Shoe Polish Co Inc	2842	F	562 941-4242	8362
Apex Universal Inc (PA)	3993	F	562 944-8878	23050
Apfels Coffee Inc	2095	E	562 309-0400	2275
Artiva USA Inc	3645	E	562 298-8968	16963
Associated Plating Company	3471	E	562 946-5525	12936
Atlantic Representations Inc	2514	E	562 903-9550	4683
Atlas Copco Compressors LLC	3563	E	866 545-4999	14623
Auto Wash Concepts Inc	3589	F	562 948-2575	15487
Automated Packg Systems Inc	3532	F	562 941-1476	13758
B & B Refractories Inc	3255	F	562 946-4535	10459
B & G Millworks	2431	F	562 944-4599	4001
Baker Petrolite LLC	1389	F	562 406-7090	168
BD Classic Enterprizes Inc	2821	F	562 944-6177	7544
Berry Global Inc	3089	E	800 462-3843	9662
Best Living International Inc	2514	F	626 625-2911	4685
Best Roll-Up Door Inc	3442	F	562 802-2233	11937
Better-Way & Lovell Grinding	3599	F	562 693-8722	15789
Blair Adhesive Products	2891	F	562 946-6004	8856
Blue Ribbon Cont & Display Inc	2653	F	562 944-1217	5202
Bodycote Thermal Proc Inc	3398	F	562 693-3135	11438
Bodycote Thermal Proc Inc	3398	E	562 946-1717	11440
Bolero Inds Inc A Cal Corp	3089	E	562 693-3000	9668
Bot N Bot Inc	2096	F	562 906-4873	2318
Bravo Sports (HQ)	3949	D	562 484-5100	22769
Brown-Pacific Inc	3312	E	562 921-3471	11030
Brunton Enterprises Inc	3441	C	562 945-0013	11752

Company	SIC	EMP	PHONE	ENTRY #
Bumble Bee Plastics Inc	3089	F	562 903-0833	9676
Bumble Bee Seafoods LLC	2091	E	562 483-7474	2242
C & C Die Engraving	3599	F	562 944-3399	15806
C B Sheets Inc	2631	E	562 921-1223	5158
Cableco	2298	E	562 942-8076	2909
Cal-Tron Plating Inc	3471	E	562 945-1181	12960
California Reamer Company Inc	3545	F	562 946-6377	14143
Calmex Fireplace Equipment Mfg	3429	F	716 645-2901	11578
Capital Cooking Equipment	3433	E	562 903-1168	11693
Carpenter Group	3496	F	562 942-8076	13403
Cascade Pump Company	3561	D	562 946-1414	14563
Catalina Carpet Mills Inc (PA)	2273	D	562 926-5811	2868
Central Admxture Phrm Svcs Inc	2834	E	562 941-9595	7837
Chapman Designs Inc	2421	E	562 698-4600	3929
Chubby Gorilla Inc (PA)	3089	E	844 365-5218	9709
Chus Packaging Supplies Inc	3053	E	562 944-6411	9224
City of Santa Fe Springs	3949	F	562 868-8761	22782
Cji Process Systems Inc	3443	D	562 777-0614	12006
Clw Plastic Bag Mfg Co Inc	2673	E	562 903-8878	5391
Collicutt Energy Services Inc	3432	E	562 944-4413	11665
Compulocks Brands Inc	3699	F	562 201-2913	19277
Connect Phillips Tech LLC (HQ)	3812	F	800 423-4512	20558
Continental Heat Treating Inc	3398	D	562 944-8808	11448
Contract Transportation Sys Co	2851	D	562 696-3262	8638
Corrpro Companies Inc	3331	E	562 944-1636	11176
Cosmolara Inc	2844	F	562 273-0348	8472
Crystal Lighting Corp	3646	F	562 944-0223	17022
Ctra Industrial Machine	3554	F	562 698-5188	14304
CTS Cement Manufacturing Corp	2674	E	562 802-2660	5435
CTS Printing	2752	F	562 941-8420	6525
Custom Mfg LLC	3451	F	562 944-0245	12627
Custom Steel Fabrication Inc	3441	F	562 907-2777	11778
David A Neal Inc	3599	F	562 941-5626	15882
Day Star Industries	2431	F	562 926-8800	4030
Deca International Corp	3812	E	714 367-5900	20567
Detoronics Corp	3678	F	626 579-7130	18764
Die Craft Engineering & Mfg Co	3544	F	562 777-8809	14043
Die Craft Stamping Inc	3494	E	562 944-2395	13350
Direct Label & Tag LLC	2752	E	562 948-4499	6543
Distinctive Inds Texas Inc	2386	E	323 889-5766	3512
Distinctive Inds Texas Inc	2386	E	512 491-3500	3513
Distinctive Industries	2396	B	800 421-9777	3784
Diversified Spring Tech	3495	F	562 944-4049	13380
Dorco Electronics Inc	2655	F	562 623-1133	5292
Dub Publishing Inc	2721	F	626 336-3821	5925
Dunstan Enterprises Inc	3599	F	562 630-6292	15909
Dunweizer Machine Inc	3443	F	562 698-7787	12017
Duro Flex Rubber Products Inc	3069	F	562 946-5533	9302
Duro Roller Company Inc	3069	F	562 944-8856	9303
Dynamic Enterprises Inc	3599	E	562 944-0271	15914
E & L Electric Inc	7694	F	562 903-9272	24687
E Z Martin Stick Labels Inc	2759	F	562 906-1577	7053
E-Liq Cube Inc (PA)	3999	F	562 537-9454	23318
Eagleware Manufacturing Co Inc	3469	E	562 320-3100	12797
Electromatic Inc	3471	F	562 623-9993	13001
Electronic Chrome Grinding Co	3471	E	562 946-9499	13003
Elektron Technology Corp (HQ)	3674	F	760 343-3650	18210
Elite Mfg Corp	2522	C	888 354-8356	4832
Employee Owned Pacific Cast PR	3365	E	562 633-6673	11380
Endotec Inc	3842	F	714 681-6306	22009
Ethosenergy Field Services LLC (DH)	1389	D	310 639-3523	195
Eurton Electric Company Inc	7694	E	562 946-4477	24689
Excel Sheet Metal Inc (PA)	3444	D	562 944-0701	12203
Field Foundation	1389	E	562 921-3567	197
Final Finish Inc	2262	E	562 777-7774	2844
Flexline Inc	2796	E	562 921-4141	7371
Flint Group US LLC	2893	F	562 903-7976	8916
Food Technology and Design LLC	2064	E	562 944-7821	1367
Foremost Spring Company Inc	3495	F	562 923-0791	13381
FPec Corporation A Cal Corp (PA)	3556	F	562 802-3727	14365
Fruiti Pops Inc	2024	F	562 404-2568	646
Fry Reglet Corporation (PA)	3354	C	800 237-9773	11229
Gabriel Container Co (PA)	2653	C	562 699-1051	5223
Galaxy Brazing Co Inc	7692	F	562 946-9039	24634
Gaylords Inc (PA)	3713	F	562 529-7543	19534
Golden Supreme Inc	3999	E	562 903-1063	23348
Golden West Machine Inc	3599	E	562 903-1111	15999
Golden West Refining Company	2911	E	562 921-3581	9047
Goldilocks Corp California (PA)	2051	E	562 946-9995	1221
Goodrich Corporation	3728	F	562 906-7372	20119
Goodrich Corporation	3728	D	562 944-4441	20122
Gorlitz Sewer & Drain Inc	3589	E	562 944-3060	15517
GP Merger Sub Inc	3231	D	562 946-7722	10364
Grafico Inc	2796	F	562 404-4976	7373
Graphic Dies Inc	2796	F	562 946-1802	7374

Employment Codes: A=Over 500 employees, B=251-500,
C=101-250, D=51-100, E=20-50, F=10-19

2020 California
Manufacturers Register

© Mergent Inc. 1-800-342-5647

1425

GEOGRAPHIC

	SIC	EMP	PHONE	ENTRY #
Grayd-A Prcsion Met Fbricators	3444	E	562 944-8951	12225
Grimco Inc	3469	E	562 449-4964	12810
Gundrill Tech Inc	3599	E	562 946-9355	16008
Hamar Wood Parquet Company	2421	E	562 944-8885	3934
Hamrock Inc	3315	C	562 944-0255	11095
Heraeus Prcous Mtls N Amer LLC (DH)	3341	C	562 921-7464	11203
Hexpol Compounding LLC	3069	E	562 464-4482	9316
Hillshire Brands Company	2013	E	562 903-9260	466
Holzinger Indus Shtmtl Inc	3444	F	562 944-6337	12238
Howies Moulding Inc	2431	F	562 698-0261	4057
Hydraulic Pneumatic Inc	3593	F	562 926-1122	15624
I-Coat Company LLC	3827	E	562 941-9989	21361
Iclavis LLC	2752	E	310 503-6847	6623
Industrial Manufacturing Inc	3433	F	562 941-5888	11700
Industrial Sprockets Gears Inc	3568	E	323 233-7221	14786
Infinity Textile	2299	F	562 777-9770	2936
Ink Spot Inc	2752	E	626 338-4500	6638
Inkovation Inc (PA)	2752	E	800 465-4174	6639
International Paper Company	2653	C	323 946-6100	5238
International Paper Company	2621	E	562 692-9465	5125
INX International Ink Co	2893	F	562 404-5664	8924
J & J Processing Inc	2087	E	562 926-2333	2217
J & S Machine	3599	E	562 945-6419	16061
J C Grinding (PA)	3541	F	562 944-3025	13925
J R C Industries Inc	2677	D	562 698-0171	5472
J S Paluch Co Inc	2731	E	562 692-0484	6114
Jarrow Industries Inc	2834	C	562 906-1919	7970
JC Hanscom Inc	2435	F	562 789-9955	4275
Jj Lithographics Inc	2752	F	562 698-0280	6666
John Crane Inc	3295	C	562 802-2555	10973
JR Machine Company Inc	3599	F	562 903-9477	16094
K Metal Products Inc	3496	C	562 693-5425	13420
K S Designs Inc	3993	E	562 929-3973	23145
Kik-Socal Inc	2842	A	562 946-6427	8391
Kingsolver Inc	3991	E	562 945-7590	23028
KS Engineering Inc	3728	F	562 483-7788	20151
La Habra Welding Inc	7692	F	562 923-2229	24648
Lanshon Inc	2311	E	562 777-1688	2967
Larson-Juhl US LLC	2499	E	562 946-6873	4512
Liberty Vegetable Oil Company	2079	E	562 921-3567	1474
Life Paint Company (PA)	2851	E	562 944-6391	8654
Liquidspring Technologies Inc	3799	F	562 941-4344	20515
LM Scofield Company (DH)	2899	E	323 720-3000	8990
Lmw Enterprises LLC	3585	E	562 944-1969	15441
Lockhart Furniture Mfg Inc	2512	D	562 404-0561	4654
Long Bar Grinding Inc	3599	F	562 921-1983	16150
Long Beach Enterprise Inc (PA)	2092	E	562 944-8945	2262
Los Angeles Sleeve Co Inc	3714	E	562 945-7578	19706
Louis Levin & Son Inc	3542	F	562 802-8066	13981
Lowers Wldg & Fabrication Inc	3599	F	562 946-4521	16152
M C I Foods Inc	2099	C	562 977-4000	2536
M E D Inc	3714	D	562 921-0464	19710
Machine Precision Components	3599	F	562 404-0500	16165
Maruichi American Corporation	3317	D	562 903-8600	11130
Master Powder Coating Inc	2851	E	562 863-4135	8656
Maxon Industries Inc	3714	D	562 464-0099	19715
Mbf Transportation LLC	3743	F	562 282-0540	20374
Mc-Dowell-Craig Mfgco (PA)	2522	F	714 521-7170	4843
McAero LLC	3599	F	310 787-9911	16182
Medlin Ramps	3542	F	562 229-1991	13984
Melfred Borzall Inc	3599	F	562 946-7524	16193
Menasha Packaging Company LLC	2653	D	562 698-3705	5246
Mid-West Fabricating Co	3714	E	562 698-9615	19720
Mission Microwave Tech LLC	3663	F	951 893-4925	17588
Moen Industries	3554	E	562 946-6381	14311
Morgan Gallacher Inc	2842	E	562 695-1232	8397
Multi-Link International Corp	3086	E	562 941-5380	9557
Muscle Dynamics Corporation	3949	F	562 926-3232	22857
Nakamura-Beeman Inc	2521	F	562 696-1400	4810
Nashua Corporation	2621	D	323 583-8828	5134
ND Industries Inc	3452	E	562 926-3321	12687
Nelson Steel Inc	3149	E	562 944-8081	10181
New Century Machine Tools Inc	3541	F	562 906-8455	13937
New Global Food	2099	F	562 404-9953	2566
New Gordon Industries LLC	3469	E	562 483-7378	12850
Nhk Laboratories (PA)	2834	D	562 903-5835	8039
Nikko Enterprise Corporation	2092	F	562 941-6080	2266
Northern California Labels Inc	2759	F	562 802-8528	7150
Nutcase Inc	3949	F	503 243-4570	22862
Ocean Heat Inc	3842	F	951 208-1923	22058
Office Chairs Inc	2521	F	562 802-0464	4815
Oil Well Service Company (PA)	1389	C	562 612-0600	238
Olin Chlor Alkali Logistics	2812	C	562 692-0510	7391
Omega Precision	3599	E	562 946-2491	16258
Orange Cnty Name Plate Co Inc	3993	D	714 522-7693	23171

	SIC	EMP	PHONE	ENTRY #
Our Powder Coating Inc	3479	F	562 946-0525	13216
P P Mfg Co Inc	3469	F	562 921-3640	12852
Pac-Com International	3291	F	562 903-3900	10952
Pacific Steam Equipment Inc	3443	E	562 906-9292	12036
Paco Plastics & Engrg Inc	3089	F	562 698-0916	9945
Pactiv Corporation	2679	E	562 944-0052	5519
Pactiv LLC	3089	D	562 693-1451	9948
Paramount Roll Forming Co Inc	3441	E	562 944-6151	11861
Parker-Hannifin Corporation	3443	F	562 404-1938	12039
Paul Crist Studios Inc	3231	F	562 696-9992	10386
Pct-Gw Carbide Tools Usa Inc	2819	E	562 921-7898	7515
Pedavena Mould and Die Co Inc	3599	F	310 327-2814	16290
Pg Imtech of California LLC	3471	F	562 945-8943	13070
Phibro Animal Health Corp	2899	F	562 698-8036	9016
Phibro-Tech Inc	2819	E	562 698-8036	7517
Philatron International (PA)	3699	C	562 802-0452	19377
Pioneer Custom Elec Pdts Corp	3612	D	562 944-0626	16567
Plastiject LLC	3089	F	562 926-6705	9975
Plustek Technology Inc	3577	F	562 777-1888	15308
Post-Srgcal Rhab Spcalists LLC	3841	F	562 236-5600	21860
Precision Cutting Tools Inc	3545	E	562 921-7898	14186
Precision Tube Bending	3498	D	562 921-6723	13482
Premier Media Inc	2711	E	562 802-9720	5803
Pronto Drilling Inc (PA)	3599	E	562 777-0900	16316
Proto Laminations Inc	3469	E	562 926-4777	12863
Pscmb Repairs Inc	3449	E	626 448-7718	12601
Ptm & W Industries Inc	3083	E	562 946-4511	9452
Qspac Industries Inc (PA)	2891	D	562 407-3868	8889
Quality Gears Inc	3566	F	562 921-9938	14747
Quality Lift and Equipment Inc	3537	F	562 903-2131	13890
Quality Vessel Engineering Inc	3443	E	562 696-2100	12044
R & D Racing Products USA Inc	3732	F	562 906-1190	20356
R & R Ductwork LLC	3444	F	562 944-9660	12347
R A Phillips Industries Inc	3715	B	562 781-2100	19830
R D Rubber Technology Corp	3061	E	562 941-4800	9270
Raytheon Company	3711	C	310 884-1825	19497
Reinhold Industries Inc (DH)	3089	C	562 944-3281	10013
Rev Co Spring Mfanufacturing	3495	F	562 949-1958	13387
Rogers Corporation	3069	D	562 404-8942	9366
Rohrback Cosasco Systems Inc (DH)	3823	D	562 949-0123	20929
Romeros Food Products Inc (PA)	2099	D	562 802-1858	2603
Rosemead Oil Products Inc	2992	F	562 941-3261	9154
Ross Bindery Inc	2789	C	562 623-4565	7344
Royal Flex Circuits Inc	3672	E	562 404-0626	17980
Rtm Products Inc	3312	E	562 926-2400	11067
RTS Packaging LLC	2653	E	562 356-6550	5263
S/R Industries Inc (HQ)	3949	E	562 968-5800	22881
Saint Nine America Inc	3949	E	562 921-5300	22882
Santa Fe Enterprises Inc	3544	E	562 692-7596	14103
Santa Fe Extruders Inc	3089	D	562 921-8991	10043
Santa Fe Footwear Corporation	3149	E	562 941-9689	10182
Seal Methods Inc (PA)	2672	E	562 944-0291	5374
Seal Seat Co	3548	E	626 923-2504	14252
Semiconductor Logistics Corp	3674	F	562 921-0399	18534
Serrano Industries Inc	3599	E	562 777-8180	16398
Shimada Enterprises Inc	3648	E	562 802-8811	17161
Sierra Foods Inc	3421	E	562 802-3500	11518
Sika Corporation	2899	F	562 941-0231	9023
Silenx Corporation	3823	F	562 941-4200	20938
Sisneros Inc	2522	F	562 777-9797	4848
Skyline Digital Images Inc	3993	E	562 944-1677	23211
SMI Ca Inc	3599	E	562 926-9407	16407
Spadia Inc	3645	F	562 206-2505	16992
Spec Tool Company	3812	E	323 723-9533	20727
Spectratek Technologies Inc (PA)	2752	D	310 822-2400	6867
Sprayline Manufacturing	3563	E	562 941-5313	14641
Standridge Granite Corporation	3281	E	562 946-6334	10933
Star Die Casting Inc	3429	D	562 698-0627	11631
Steiner & Mateer Inc	2431	E	562 464-9082	4129
Steven Label Corporation	2759	F	562 906-2612	7227
Steven Label Corporation	2759	F	562 698-9971	7228
Stitch City Industries Inc (PA)	3552	F	562 408-6144	14293
Sulzer Pump Services (us) Inc	7692	E	562 903-1000	24669
Sun Chemical Corporation	2893	E	562 946-2327	8932
Superior Food Machinery Inc	3556	E	562 949-0396	14404
Superior Printing Inc	2759	D	888 590-7998	7235
Superprint Lithographics Inc	2752	F	562 698-8001	6879
Surface Mdfication Systems Inc	3479	E	562 946-7472	13258
Sygma Inc	3545	F	562 906-8880	14201
T & S Die Cutting	3544	F	562 802-1731	14108
T-1 Lighting Inc	3646	F	626 234-2328	17075
Taokaenoi Usa Inc	2091	F	562 404-9888	2253
Tape & Label Converters Inc	2672	E	562 945-3486	5375
Timken Gears & Services Inc	3462	E	310 605-2600	12723
Titan Medical Enterprises Inc	2834	F	562 903-7236	8164

Mergent email: customerrelations@mergent.com

1426

2020 California
Manufacturers Register

(P-0000) Products & Services Section entry number
(PA)=Parent Co (HQ)=Headquarters (DH)=Div Headquarters

	SIC	EMP	PHONE	ENTRY #
Tj Giant Llc	2759	A	562 906-1060	7251
Tri-Star Dyeing & Finshg Inc	2231	D	562 483-0123	2748
Triangle Tool & Die Corp	3599	F	562 944-2117	16468
Trident Plating Inc	3471	E	562 906-2556	13119
Trojan Battery Company LLC (HQ)	3692	B	562 236-3000	19183
Tru-Form Industries Inc (PA)	3469	D	562 802-2041	12885
True Design Inc	2434	E	562 699-2001	4255
Turbine Eng Cmpnents Tech Corp	3463	C	562 908-0200	12738
Twist Tite Mfg Inc	3452	E	562 229-0990	12697
United Drilling Co	3599	E	562 945-8833	16482
United Technologies Corp	3728	F	562 944-6244	20265
Universal Label Printers Inc	2759	E	562 944-0234	7260
US Armor Corporation	3842	E	562 207-4240	22114
US Motor Works LLC (PA)	3714	C	562 404-0488	19796
V&H Performance LLC	3751	D	562 921-7461	20435
Vantage Associates Inc	3089	D	562 968-1400	10111
Vantage Point Products Corp (PA)	3651	D	562 946-1718	17300
Vescio Threading Co	3599	E	562 802-1868	16500
Victor Wieteski	3679	F	562 946-9715	19138
Vomela Specialty Company	2752	E	562 944-3853	6924
Votaw Precision Tech Inc	3812	F	562 944-0661	20743
Wesco Enterprises Inc	3089	F	562 944-3100	10118
West Coast Machining Inc	3599	F	562 229-1087	16518
West Coast Plastics Inc	3089	F	562 777-8024	10119
Western Glove Mfg Inc	3842	D	562 903-1339	22125
Western Screw Products Inc	3451	E	562 698-5793	12660
Westmont Industries (PA)	3536	D	562 944-6137	13853
Westrock Cp LLC	2653	C	714 523-3550	5273
Westrock Cp LLC	2631	D	714 523-3550	5184
Westrock Usc Inc	2653	F	562 282-0000	5283
Westrock Usc Inc	2653	E	562 282-4200	5284
Whittier Mailing Products Inc (PA)	3579	E	562 464-3000	15393
Willick Engineering Co Inc	3844	F	562 946-4242	22225
Zenith Screw Products Inc	3451	E	562 941-0281	12662
Zumar Industries Inc	3993	D	562 941-4633	23250

SANTA MARIA, CA - Santa Barbara County

	SIC	EMP	PHONE	ENTRY #
A & F Metal Products	3469	F	805 346-2040	12754
Aegis Industries Inc	2851	F	805 922-2700	8615
Alan Johnson Prfmce Engrg Inc	3711	E	805 922-1202	19450
Alltec Integrated Mfg Inc	3089	E	805 595-3500	9618
American Bottling Company	2086	E	805 928-1001	2032
American Cleaner and Laundry	3582	E	805 925-1571	15402
Arrow Screw Products Inc	3599	E	805 928-2269	15751
Atlas Copco Mafi-Trench Co LLC (DH)	3564	C	805 352-0112	14649
B & B Label Inc	2759	F	805 922-0332	6996
Bottelsen Dart Co Inc	3944	F	805 922-4519	22663
Cal Coast Acidizing Co	1389	F	805 934-2411	176
Central Coast Wine Warehouse (PA)	2084	E	805 928-9210	1625
Clendenen Lindquist Vintners	2084	E	805 937-9801	1635
Composite Plastic Systems Inc	3792	F	805 354-1391	20482
Curation Foods Inc (HQ)	2099	D	800 454-1355	2438
Engel & Gray Inc	1389	E	805 925-2771	192
Flood Ranch Company	2084	F	805 937-3616	1704
Gavial Engineering & Mfg Inc (HQ)	3672	F	805 614-0060	17885
Gavial Holdings Inc (PA)	3679	F	805 614-0060	18921
Greka Inc	1241	C	805 347-8700	18
Greka Integrated Inc (PA)	1382	C	805 347-8700	125
Hanson Aggregates LLC	1442	F	805 934-4931	346
Hvi Cat Canyon Inc	1389	C	805 621-5800	211
Impo International LLC	3144	E	805 922-7753	10170
Insight Management Corporation (PA)	3652	E	866 787-3588	17328
J and D Stl Fbrication Repr LP	3441	F	805 928-9674	11814
Jackson Family Wines Inc	2084	E	805 938-7300	1767
Krinos Foods LLC	2035	F	805 922-6700	886
Laguna County Sanatation Dist	2899	F	805 934-6282	8988
Lee Enterprises Incorporated	2711	C	805 925-2691	5697
Lindquist Robert N & Assoc (PA)	2084	F	805 937-9801	1802
Lockheed Martin Corporation	3812	A	805 614-3671	20613
Matthew Warren Inc	3493	E	805 928-3851	13339
Melfred Borzall Inc	3541	E	805 614-4344	13933
Mid-State Concrete Products	3272	E	805 928-2855	10602
Myogenix Incorporated	2834	F	800 950-0348	8020
Nicksons Machine Shop Inc	3599	E	805 925-2525	16245
North American Fire Hose Corp	3052	D	805 922-7076	9201
Okonite Company	3357	C	805 922-6682	11312
Osr Enterprises Inc	7372	E	805 925-1831	24280
PC Mechanical Inc	1389	E	805 925-2888	245
Pepsi-Cola Metro Btlg Co Inc	2086	D	805 739-2160	2110
Pictsweet Company	2038	B	805 928-4414	976
Pratt Industries Inc	2621	E	805 348-1097	5145
Presquile Winery	2084	F	805 937-8110	1870
Prince Lionheart Inc (PA)	3089	E	805 922-2250	9993
Princeton Case West Inc	3089	E	805 928-8840	9994
Quintron Systems Inc (PA)	3661	D	805 928-4343	17405
Reyes Coca-Cola Bottling LLC	2086	E	805 925-2629	2144

	SIC	EMP	PHONE	ENTRY #
Reyes Coca-Cola Bottling LLC	2086	D	805 614-3702	2147
Rlv Tuned Exhaust Products	3714	E	805 925-5461	19759
Safran Cabin Inc	3728	F	805 922-3013	20219
Safran Seats Santa Maria LLC	3728	A	805 922-5995	20225
Santa Maria Enrgy Holdings LLC	1382	E	805 938-3320	138
Santa Maria Times Inc	2711	C	805 925-2691	5821
Signs of Success Inc	3993	F	805 925-7545	23207
Space Information Labs LLC	3812	F	805 925-9010	20726
Tognazzini Beverage Service	2086	F	805 928-1144	2176
Walker Creations	3842	F	805 349-0755	22122
Wasco Sales & Marketing Inc	3643	E	805 739-2747	16938

SANTA MONICA, CA - Los Angeles County

	SIC	EMP	PHONE	ENTRY #
7 Generation Games Inc	7372	F	260 402-1172	23539
Abraxis Bioscience Inc	2834	D	310 883-1300	7715
Activision Blizzard Inc (PA)	7372	A	310 255-2000	23553
Activision Publishing Inc (HQ)	7372	A	310 255-2000	23555
Adolf Goldfarb	3944	F	310 451-1211	22656
Aft Corporation	2796	E	310 576-1007	7368
Americas Finest Products	2841	E	310 450-6555	8336
Apogee Electronics Corporation	3651	E	310 584-9394	17190
Automotive Lease Guide Alg Inc	2741	E	424 258-8026	6195
Berri Pro Inc	2087	F	781 929-8288	2191
C Publishing LLC	2741	E	310 393-3800	6209
C R W Distributors Inc	2013	E	310 463-4577	445
Carr Corporation (PA)	3844	E	310 587-1113	22211
Cequal Products Inc	2731	F	310 458-0441	6086
Coast Flagstone Co	3281	D	310 829-4010	10897
Cornerstone Ondemand Inc (PA)	7372	C	310 752-0200	23777
Design Journal Inc	2721	E	310 394-4394	5918
Dext Company of Maryland (DH)	2048	E	310 458-1574	1090
Draftday Fantasy Sports Inc	7372	E	310 306-1828	23831
Dsj Printing Inc	2752	E	310 828-8051	6552
Ecolight Inc	3999	F	310 450-7444	23321
Elkay Interior Systems Inc	2599	F	800 837-8373	5058
Elyptol Inc	2833	F	424 500-8099	7654
Engrade Inc	7372	E	800 305-1367	23861
Event Farm Inc (HQ)	7372	E	888 444-8162	23877
Express Pipe & Supply Co LLC (DH)	3498	E	310 204-7238	13469
Extreme Group Holdings LLC	3652	E	310 899-3200	17320
Form Factory Inc	2023	D	937 572-6126	589
Gayot Publications	2741	E	323 965-3529	6242
Go Green Mobile Power LLC	3621	F	877 800-4467	16650
Goodrx Inc (PA)	7372	F	310 500-6544	23949
Gosub 60	3577	F	310 394-4760	15236
Hearst Corporation	2721	E	310 752-1040	5950
Hexacorp Ltd	7372	E	760 815-0904	23981
Hone & Strop Inc	2844	F	424 262-4474	8512
Hoorsen Buhs LLC	3961	F	888 692-2997	22983
Hugo Boss Usa Inc	2311	C	310 260-0109	2965
Image Square Inc	2621	E	310 586-2333	5109
International Processing Corp (DH)	2048	E	310 458-1574	1101
Jakks Pacific Inc (PA)	3944	C	424 268-9444	22687
Kingcom(us) LLC (HQ)	7372	E	424 744-5697	24078
Kona Bar LLC	2064	F	808 927-1934	1380
Lanza Research International	2844	D	310 393-5227	8530
Lincoln Iron Works	3312	E	310 684-2543	11055
Los Angles Tmes Cmmnctions LLC	2711	D	310 450-6666	5705
Magna-Pole Products Inc (PA)	2542	F	310 453-3806	4989
Mammoth Media Inc	2711	D	310 393-3024	5720
Maui Toys	3949	E	330 747-4333	22850
Newlon Rouge LLC	2711	F	310 458-7707	5776
Observer Newspaper	2711	E	310 452-9900	5787
Omega Leads Inc	3679	E	310 394-6786	19037
Opiant Pharmaceuticals Inc	2834	F	310 598-5410	8055
Ovation R&G LLC (PA)	3663	E	310 430-7575	17613
Owl Territory Inc	7372	F	800 607-0677	24283
Patientpop Inc	7372	D	844 487-8399	24289
Pfizer Health Solutions Inc	2834	F	310 586-2550	8067
Phonesuit Inc	3663	E	310 774-0282	17622
Pranalytica Inc	3841	E	310 458-3345	21862
Preston Cinema Systems Inc	3861	F	310 453-1852	22451
Printing Palace Inc (PA)	2752	E	310 451-5151	6806
Proseries LLC	3949	F	213 533-6400	22866
Provivi Inc (PA)	2869	E	310 828-2307	8767
Purelife Dental	3843	F	310 587-0783	22183
Reconserve Inc (HQ)	2048	E	310 458-1574	1120
Red Bull North America Inc	2086	D	310 393-4647	2131
Ring LLC (HQ)	3612	B	800 656-1918	16573
Salesforcecom Inc	7372	E	310 752-7000	24378
Santa Monica Plastics Llc	3089	E	310 403-2849	10044
Santa Monica Propeller Svc Inc	3728	F	310 390-6233	20227
Scribble Press Inc	2741	E	212 288-2928	6337
Solarreserve LLC (PA)	3433	C	310 315-2200	11716
Sonosim Inc	7372	F	323 473-3800	24436
Tae Life Sciences LLC	3845	F	310 633-5042	22318

Employment Codes: A=Over 500 employees, B=251-500,
C=101-250, D=51-100, E=20-50, F=10-19

2020 California
Manufacturers Register

© Mergent Inc. 1-800-342-5647

1427

	SIC	EMP	PHONE	ENTRY #
Transplant Connect Inc	7372	E	310 392-1400	24524
Ubm Canon LLC **(DH)**	2721	C	310 445-4200	6046
Universal Music Publishing Inc	2741	F	310 235-4700	6368
Wholesome Valley Foods **(PA)**	2099	F	858 480-1543	2647

SANTA PAULA, CA - Ventura County

	SIC	EMP	PHONE	ENTRY #
Abrisa Industrial Glass Inc **(HQ)**	3211	D	805 525-4902	10259
Abrisa Technologies	3827	E	805 525-4902	21330
Aurora Casting & Engrg Inc	3369	D	805 933-2761	11409
Automotive Racing Products Inc	3429	D	805 525-1497	11566
Baker Petrolite LLC	1389	E	805 525-4404	169
Bendpak Inc	3559	C	805 933-9970	14433
Calavo Growers Inc **(PA)**	2099	B	805 525-1245	2416
California Resources Corp	1311	E	310 208-8800	38
Carbon California Company LLC	1311	E	805 933-1901	42
Consol Enterprises	7692	F	805 648-3486	24627
Fowlie Enterprises Inc	2052	F	805 583-2800	1315
Oil Well Service Company	1389	F	805 525-2103	240
Trinity Steel Corporation	3441	F	805 648-3486	11903
Turtle Storage Ltd	2542	F	805 933-3688	5008
Weatherford International LLC	1389	E	805 933-0242	283
Weatherford International LLC	3498	D	805 933-0200	13491
Weber Orthopedic Inc **(PA)**	3842	F	805 525-8474	22123
Westlake Engrg Roto Form	3089	F	805 525-8800	10123
World Upholstery & Trim Inc	2396	F	805 921-0100	3825

SANTA ROSA, CA - Sonoma County

	SIC	EMP	PHONE	ENTRY #
23 Bottles of Beer LLC	2082	E	707 545-2337	1488
AEG Industries Inc	3728	E	707 575-0697	20008
Ahlborn Structural Steel Inc	3441	E	707 573-0742	11740
Air Monitor Corporation **(PA)**	3822	D	707 544-2706	20782
Alembic Inc	3931	F	707 523-2611	22605
Alluxa Inc	3827	E	707 284-1040	21333
Aluma USA Inc	3911	E	707 545-9344	22492
America Asian Trade Assn Prom	3646	D	408 588-0008	17011
Ampac Usa Inc	2844	F	707 571-1754	8436
Amys Kitchen Inc **(PA)**	2038	A	707 578-7188	941
Architectural Foam Products	3086	F	707 544-2779	9504
Barricade Co & Traffic Sup Inc **(PA)**	3499	F	707 523-2350	13501
Bcj Sand and Rock Inc	1446	F	707 544-0303	371
Blentech Corporation	3556	D	707 523-5949	14351
Bo Dean Co Inc **(PA)**	1411	E	707 576-8205	289
Bohan Cnlis - Astin Creek Rdym	1429	E	707 632-5296	312
California Surveying & Draftin	3577	F	707 293-9449	15183
Conetech Custom Services LLC	2084	F	707 823-2404	1644
Creekside Managed Care	2834	F	707 578-0399	7856
Digital Music Corporation	3931	F	707 545-0600	22612
Dr Pepper/Seven Up Inc	2086	D	707 545-7797	2072
Duncan Design Inc	3993	F	707 636-2300	23090
Dynamic Pre-Cast Co Inc	3272	F	707 573-1110	10564
Dynatex International	3545	E	707 542-4227	14157
E M G Inc	3931	D	707 525-9941	22617
Endrun Technologies LLC	3821	F	707 573-8633	20757
Filtration Group LLC	3564	D	707 525-8633	14660
Flashco Manufacturing Inc **(PA)**	3356	E	707 824-4448	11271
Flex Products Inc	3827	C	707 525-6866	21353
Flowmaster Inc **(HQ)**	3714	E	707 544-4761	19657
Flyers Energy LLC	3569	D	707 546-0766	14820
Galvin Precision Machining Inc	3599	F	707 526-5359	15984
Gammon LLC	2721	F	707 575-8282	5942
Grape Links Inc	2084	F	707 524-8000	1734
Green Lake Investors LLC	3953	E	707 577-1301	22950
Gt Advanced Technologies Inc	3674	F	707 571-1911	18259
Gt Sapphire Systems Group LLC	3661	E	707 571-1911	17377
Guenoc Winery Inc	2084	E	707 987-2385	1740
Hybrinetics Inc	3612	D	707 585-0333	16557
Icore International Inc	3089	C	707 535-2700	9834
Iron Dog Fabrication Inc	3441	F	707 579-7831	11813
Itt LLC	3643	C	707 523-2300	16908
J RS Woodworks Inc	2431	F	707 588-8255	4061
Jackson Family Farms LLC **(PA)**	2084	E	707 837-1000	1762
Jackson Family Farms LLC	2084	E	707 836-2047	1763
Jackson Family Wines Inc **(PA)**	2084	D	707 544-4000	1766
James L Hall Co Incorporated **(PA)**	3679	D	707 547-0775	18959
James L Hall Co Incorporated	3677	E	707 544-2436	18722
Johns Formica Shop Inc	2542	F	707 544-8585	4986
Kendall-Jackson Wine Estates **(HQ)**	2084	B	707 544-4000	1782
Keysight Technologies Inc **(PA)**	3823	B	800 829-4444	20894
Kuleto Villa LLC	2084	F	707 967-8577	1785
L-3 Cmmnications Sonoma Eo Inc	3861	C	707 568-3000	22437
L-3 Communications Wescam	3812	E	707 568-3000	20595
La Tortilla Factory Inc	2099	E	707 586-4000	2516
Laguna Oaks Vnyards Winery Inc	2084	E	707 568-2455	1791
Lancaster Vineyards Inc	2084	F	707 433-8178	1794
Light Guard Systems Inc	3625	F	707 542-4547	16730
Macon Industries Inc	3699	F	707 566-2116	19352

	SIC	EMP	PHONE	ENTRY #
Magazine Publishers Svc Inc	2721	D	707 571-7610	5983
Making It Big Inc	2331	E	707 795-1995	3179
Matanzas Creek Winery	2084	E	707 528-6464	1813
Medtronic Inc	3841	D	707 541-3281	22047
Medtronic Inc	3841	E	707 541-3144	21807
Metro Publishing Inc	2711	F	707 527-1200	5751
Microsemi Corporation	3674	C	707 568-5900	18406
Microsemi Frequency Time Corp	3674	D	707 528-1230	18409
Microsemi Semiconductor US Inc	3679	D	707 568-5900	19018
Mildara Blass Inc	2084	C	707 836-5000	1819
Milners Anodizing	3471	E	707 584-1188	13052
Molding Solutions Inc **(PA)**	3089	F	707 575-1218	9909
MS Intertrade Inc **(PA)**	2092	F	707 837-8057	2265
Mutt Lynch Winery Inc	2084	F	707 473-8080	1831
Neilmed Pharmaceuticals Inc	2834	B	707 525-3784	8028
Optical Coating Laboratory LLC **(HQ)**	3479	B	707 545-6440	13215
Osseon LLC	3841	F	707 636-5940	21852
P & L Specialties	3559	F	707 573-3141	14511
Pacific Hardwood Cabinetry	2434	E	707 528-8627	4229
Pacific Sun	2721	F	415 488-8100	5997
Pam Dee Publishing	2731	F	707 542-1528	6133
Paradise Ridge Winery	2084	F	707 528-9463	1856
Paragon Controls Incorporated	3822	E	707 579-1424	20803
Pellegrini Ranches	2084	F	707 545-8680	1861
Pellenc America Inc **(DH)**	3523	F	707 568-7286	13657
Protonex LLC	3674	F	707 566-2260	18484
Quality Machine Engrg Inc	3599	E	707 528-1900	16327
Randal Optimal Nutrients LLC	2834	E	707 528-1800	8097
Ratebeer LLC	2741	D	302 476-2337	6325
Redwood Empire Awng & Furn Co	2394	F	707 633-8156	3701
Russian River Winery Inc	2084	F	707 824-2005	1902
Santa Rosa Press Democrat Inc **(HQ)**	2711	B	707 546-2020	5822
Santa Rosa Stain	3795	E	707 544-7777	20500
Scientific Molding Corp Ltd	3089	D	707 303-3041	10048
Selvage Concrete Products	3272	F	707 542-2762	10649
Sonoma Beverage Company LLC **(PA)**	2037	F	707 431-1099	928
Sonoma Metal Products Inc	3444	D	707 484-9876	12381
Sonoma Photonics Inc	3677	E	707 568-1202	18744
Sonoma Valley Foods Inc	2032	E	707 585-2200	746
Spectraswitch Inc	3661	E	707 568-7000	17414
Srss LLC	3449	E	707 544-7777	12609
Supercloset	3423	E	831 588-7829	11547
Teh-Pari International	2899	E	707 829-9116	9029
Thermalsun Glass Products Inc	3231	E	707 579-9534	10393
Tonnellerie Radoux Usa Inc	2449	F	707 284-2888	4431
Trans-India Products Inc	2844	E	707 544-0298	8595
Trilogy Glass and Packg Inc	3231	E	707 521-1300	10394
Trivascular Inc **(DH)**	3841	E	707 543-8800	21938
Trivascular Technologies Inc **(HQ)**	3841	F	707 543-8800	21939
Tumelo Inc	2899	E	707 523-4411	9032
Tyco Simplexgrinnell	3569	E	707 578-3212	14868
Viavi Solutions Inc	3699	C	707 545-6400	19432
Vintage Wine Estates Inc **(PA)**	2084	C	877 289-9463	1992
Wescam Usa Inc **(DH)**	3812	F	707 236-1077	20744
Wildbrine LLC **(PA)**	2033	E	707 657-7607	839
Wright Engineered Plastics Inc	3544	D	707 575-1218	14126
Zelco Cabinet Mfg Inc	2517	F	707 584-1121	4758

SANTA YNEZ, CA - Santa Barbara County

	SIC	EMP	PHONE	ENTRY #
Bridlewood Winery	2084	E	805 688-9000	1606
Valley Oaks Industries	2521	F	805 688-2754	4824

SANTEE, CA - San Diego County

	SIC	EMP	PHONE	ENTRY #
Aep-California LLC	3714	F	619 596-1925	19572
Alts Tool & Machine Inc **(PA)**	3599	D	619 562-6653	15732
Argee Mfg Co San Diego Inc	3089	D	619 449-5050	9637
Aymar Engineering	3444	F	619 562-1121	12122
Buxcon Sheetmetal Inc	3444	F	619 937-0001	12139
CCM Enterprises	2541	F	619 562-2605	4889
CCM Enterprises **(PA)**	2541	D	619 562-2605	4890
Compucraft Industries Inc	3728	E	619 448-0787	20075
Computer Intgrted McHining Inc	3599	F	619 596-9246	15861
Cozza Inc	3599	F	619 749-5663	15866
Curapharm Inc	3841	F	619 449-7388	21675
Current Ways Inc	3629	F	619 596-3984	16784
D Benham Corporation	2752	F	619 448-8079	6530
Davis Gregg Enterprises Inc	3443	F	619 449-4250	12015
Decatur Electronics Inc	3812	F	619 596-1925	20569
Deco Plastics Inc	3089	F	619 448-6843	9747
Delstar Holding Corp	3081	F	619 258-1503	9400
Discflo Corporation	3561	E	619 596-3181	14568
Ds Fibertech Corp	3567	E	619 562-7001	14760
Eastwood Machine LLC	3599	F	619 873-3660	15919
European Wholesale Counter	2541	C	619 562-0565	4901
Gondola Skate Mvg Systems Inc **(PA)**	3312	F	619 222-6487	11045
Hpf Corporation **(PA)**	3931	F	858 566-9710	22626

2020 California
Manufacturers Register

(P-0000) Products & Services Section entry number
(PA)=Parent Co (HQ)=Headquarters (DH)=Div Headquarters

	SIC	EMP	PHONE	ENTRY #
Kevin Whaley	3496	E	619 596-4000	13421
Lhv Power Corporation **(PA)**	3679	E	619 258-7700	18988
LSI Corporation	3674	E	619 312-0903	18360
Mathy Machine Inc	3542	E	619 448-0404	13983
Novtek Inc	3825	F	408 441-9934	21093
Olson Irrigation Systems	3523	E	619 562-3100	13654
Pla-Cor Incorporated	3089	F	619 478-2139	9963
Praxair Inc	2813	E	619 596-4558	7430
Production Truss Inc	2439	F	619 258-8792	4315
Pure-Flo Water Co **(PA)**	2086	D	619 596-4130	2129
Quality Controlled Mfg Inc	3599	D	619 443-3997	16325
RCP Block & Brick Inc	3271	E	619 448-2240	10516
Rozendal Associates Inc	3812	E	619 562-5596	20711
S M L Industries Inc	3944	F	619 258-7941	22711
San Dego Prtective Coating Inc	3479	F	619 448-7795	13241
Scantibodies Laboratory Inc **(PA)**	2835	C	619 258-9300	8252
South West Lubricants Inc	2992	F	619 449-5000	9156
Specity Mtals Fabrication Inc	2295	F	619 937-6100	2900
Stratedge Corporation	3674	E	866 424-4962	18584
T I B Inc	3544	F	619 562-3071	14109
TBs Irrigation Products Inc	3432	E	619 579-0520	11684
Terra Nova Technologies Inc	3535	D	619 596-7400	13839
Vision Systems Inc	3354	D	619 258-7300	11253
Vortex Engineering LLC	3441	F	619 258-9660	11913
Wood Minerals Conveyors Inc	3535	D	619 596-7400	13842

SARATOGA, CA - Santa Clara County

	SIC	EMP	PHONE	ENTRY #
Advanced Results Company Inc	3561	F	408 986-0123	14557
Chateau Masson LLC	2084	E	408 741-7002	1631
Inficold Inc	3564	E	408 464-8007	14663
Insight Solutions Inc	7372	E	408 725-0213	24027
Landmark Lcds Inc	3679	F	408 386-4257	18983
Lucidport Technology Inc	3643	F	408 720-8800	16914
Savannah Chanelle Vineyards	2084	E	408 741-2934	1907
Topi Systems Inc	7372	E	408 807-5124	24517
United Supertek Inc	3672	E	408 922-0730	18038
Vintellus Inc	7372	F	510 972-4710	24562

SAUSALITO, CA - Marin County

	SIC	EMP	PHONE	ENTRY #
Ascert LLC **(PA)**	7372	F	415 339-8500	23627
Boyd Lighting Fixture Co **(PA)**	3646	E	415 778-4300	17016
Bright Business Media LLC	2721	F	415 339-9355	5893
C P Shades Inc **(PA)**	2339	F	415 331-4581	3300
Humanconcepts LLC	7372	E	650 581-2500	23991
Marin Magazine Inc	2721	F	415 332-4800	5985
Mpl Brands Inc **(PA)**	2084	F	888 513-3022	1827
Onesun LLC	3674	F	415 230-4277	18453
Pasport Software Programs Inc	7372	F	415 331-2606	24288
Personal Awareness Systems	2741	F	415 331-3900	6309
Safe Catch Inc	2091	F	415 944-4442	2250
Sausalito Craftworks Inc	3911	F	415 331-4031	22569
Tazi Designs	2519	F	415 503-0013	4775
Tony Marterie & Associates	2335	E	415 331-7150	3256
Waggl Inc **(PA)**	7372	F	415 399-9949	24572

SCOTTS VALLEY, CA - Santa Cruz County

	SIC	EMP	PHONE	ENTRY #
Armored Mobility Inc	3083	E	831 430-9899	9437
AV Now Inc	3651	E	831 425-2500	17198
Bell Sports Inc **(HQ)**	3949	D	469 417-6600	22760
Business With Pleasure	2752	F	831 430-9711	6463
Dakota Ultrasonics Corporation	3829	F	831 431-9722	21457
Digital Dynamics Inc	3823	E	831 438-4444	20857
Expert Semiconductor Tech Inc	3559	E	831 439-9300	14464
Fox Factory Holding Corp **(PA)**	3751	E	831 274-6500	20402
Fox Factory Inc **(HQ)**	3751	C	831 274-6500	20403
Hcl Labels Inc	2679	F	800 421-6710	5511
Innerstep BSE **(PA)**	3672	D	831 461-5600	17901
Interworking Labs Inc	7372	F	831 460-7010	24032
J A-Co Machine Works LLC	3599	E	877 429-8175	16062
Larkin Precision Machining	3599	F	831 438-2700	16137
Lintelle Engineering Inc	3699	E	831 439-8400	19347
Maxtor Corporation **(DH)**	3572	D	831 438-6550	15055
Microtech Systems Inc	3695	F	650 596-1900	19223
Oxford Instruments X-Ray Tech	3679	D	831 439-9729	19044
Pacific Coast Products LLC **(PA)**	2087	F	831 316-7137	2223
Pacific Coast Products LLC	2087	F	831 316-7137	2224
Photoflex Inc	3861	F	831 786-1370	22449
Rkd Engineering Corp Inc	3674	F	831 430-9464	18518
Scotts Valley Magnetics Inc	3677	E	831 438-3600	18741
Sessions	2339	E	831 461-5080	3403
Spraytronics Inc	3479	E	408 988-3636	13252
Sunopta Glbal Orgnic Ing Inc **(DH)**	2035	E	831 685-6506	901
Tapemation Machining **(PA)**	3599	F	831 438-3069	16443
Tapemation Machining Inc	3599	F	831 438-3069	16444
Thermo Kevex X-Ray Inc	3671	E	831 438-5940	17794
Threshold Enterprises Ltd **(PA)**	2833	B	831 438-6851	7697

	SIC	EMP	PHONE	ENTRY #
Threshold Enterprises Ltd	2833	D	831 461-6413	7698
Threshold Enterprises Ltd	2833	E	831 461-6343	7699
Tr Engineering Inc	3561	F	831 430-9920	14602
Vista Outdoor Inc	3949	D	831 461-7500	22921

SEAL BEACH, CA - Orange County

	SIC	EMP	PHONE	ENTRY #
Boeing Company	3721	A	562 797-5831	19861
Boeing Company	3663	A	714 372-5361	17472
Cosmodyne LLC	3559	E	562 795-5990	14442
Dendreon Pharmaceuticals Inc	2834	F	562 253-3931	7867
Dendreon Pharmaceuticals LLC **(HQ)**	2834	E	562 252-7500	7868
Diversfied Tchncal Systems Inc **(PA)**	3679	E	562 493-0158	18890
Ftt Holdings Inc	3533	F	562 430-6262	13777
Hellman Properties LLC	1311	F	562 431-6022	56
Magtek Inc **(PA)**	3577	C	562 546-6400	15281
Samedan Oil Corporation	1311	B	661 319-5038	65

SEASIDE, CA - Monterey County

	SIC	EMP	PHONE	ENTRY #
Granite Rock Co	3273	E	831 392-3700	10765
Inter City Manufacturing Inc	3599	E	831 899-3636	16051
Lamorenita Tortillera & Mt Mkt.	2099	F	831 394-3770	2518
Monterey County Weekly	2711	E	831 393-3348	5759
Monterey Signs Inc	2752	F	831 632-0490	6737
SC Works	3993	F	831 332-5311	23193

SEBASTOPOL, CA - Sonoma County

	SIC	EMP	PHONE	ENTRY #
Alasco Rubber & Plastics Corp	3069	F	415 265-5270	9280
Devoto-Wade Llc	2084	F	415 265-4461	1663
KB Wines LLC	2084	E	707 823-7430	1779
Kosta Browne Wines LLC	2084	E	707 823-7430	1783
Kurtz Family Corporation	3089	F	707 823-1213	9871
Magito & Company LLC	2084	F	707 567-1521	1809
Make Community LLC	2721	F	707 548-0833	5984
Manzana Products Co Inc	2033	E	707 823-5313	795
Marimar Torres Estate Corp	2084	F	707 823-4365	1811
Maxstraps Inc	2241	D	707 829-3000	2757
Occidental Manufacturing Inc.	3199	E	707 824-2560	10249
OReilly Media Inc **(PA)**	2731	C	707 827-7000	6131
Paul Hobbs Winery LP	2084	F	707 824-9879	1858
Screamin Mimis Inc	2024	F	707 823-5902	667
Solmetric Corporation	3829	E	707 823-4600	21545
Sonoma West Publishers Inc **(PA)**	2711	E	707 823-7845	5831
Sprint Copy Center Inc	2752	F	707 823-3900	6870
Sumbody Union Street LLC	2844	E	707 824-4043	8589
Taft Street Inc	2084	E	707 823-2049	1947
Taylor Maid Farms LLC	2095	E	707 824-9110	2311
Thinkwave Inc	3695	F	707 824-6200	19238
Thomas Dehlinger	2084	F	707 823-2378	1953
Traditional Medicinals Inc **(PA)**	2099	C	707 823-8911	2635

SEIAD VALLEY, CA - Siskiyou County

	SIC	EMP	PHONE	ENTRY #
Mark Crawford Logging Inc	2411	F	530 496-3272	3895

SELMA, CA - Fresno County

	SIC	EMP	PHONE	ENTRY #
Fresno Valves & Castings Inc **(PA)**	3366	C	559 834-2511	11398
Harris Ranch Beef Company	2011	A	559 896-3081	413
Lee Central Cal Newspapers	2711	E	559 896-1976	5696
Lion Raisins Inc **(PA)**	2034	B	559 834-6677	852
Selma Pallet Inc	2448	E	559 896-7171	4399
Wood-N-Wood Products Cal Inc	2449	E	559 896-3636	4435
Xtreme Manufacturing LLC	3443	E	559 891-2978	12073

SHAFTER, CA - Kern County

	SIC	EMP	PHONE	ENTRY #
Baker Hghes Olfld Oprtions LLC	1389	E	661 834-9654	160
Baker Hughes A GE Company LLC	1389	E	661 834-9654	162
Blowout Tools Inc	1389	F	661 746-1700	173
California Farm Equipment Mag	3523	F	661 589-0435	13618
Cemex Cnstr Mtls PCF LLC	3273	E	661 746-3423	10726
Cummings Vacuum Service Inc	1389	D	661 746-1786	187
Elk Corporation of Texas	3272	C	661 391-3900	10568
Forterra Pipe & Precast LLC	3444	F	661 746-3527	12215
Frank Russell Inc	3599	F	661 324-5575	15973
Harbison-Fischer Inc	3533	F	661 399-0628	13779
Lufkin Industries LLC	3462	F	661 746-0792	12713
M-I LLC	1389	E	661 321-5400	220
National Oilwell Varco Inc	1389	F	661 387-9316	234
Nikkel Iron Works Corporation	3523	F	661 746-4904	13652
Oil Well Service Company	1389	E	661 746-4809	239
Scientific Drilling Intl Inc	1381	E	661 831-0636	105
Scotts Company LLC	2873	F	661 387-9555	8803
Tryad Service Corporation	1389	D	661 391-1524	274
Trymax	3498	F	661 391-1572	13488
U S Weatherford L P	1382	F	661 746-3415	143
Weatherford International LLC	1389	E	661 589-2146	286

SHANDON, CA - San Luis Obispo County

	SIC	EMP	PHONE	ENTRY #
Pacific Tank & Cnstr Inc	3443	E	805 237-2929	12037
Svp Winery LLC	2084	F	805 237-8693	1944

Employment Codes: A=Over 500 employees, B=251-500,
C=101-250, D=51-100, E=20-50, F=10-19

2020 California
Manufacturers Register

© Mergent Inc. 1-800-342-5647

1429

GEOGRAPHIC

SHASTA LAKE, CA - Shasta County

Name	SIC	EMP	PHONE	ENTRY#
Heritage Missional Community	2095	F	530 605-1990	2298
Knauf Insulation Inc	3296	C	530 275-9665	10987
Sierra Pacific Industries	2421	C	530 275-8851	3956

SHERIDAN, CA - Placer County

Name	SIC	EMP	PHONE	ENTRY#
Cemex Cnstr Mtls PCF LLC	3273	E	916 645-1949	10715
Entrussed LLC	2439	F	916 753-5406	4301

SHERMAN OAKS, CA - Los Angeles County

Name	SIC	EMP	PHONE	ENTRY#
American Naturals Company LLC	2099	E	323 201-6891	2390
American Printing & Design	2752	E	310 287-0460	6411
Bidchat Inc	7372	F	818 631-6212	23665
Caden Concepts LLC	2395	F	323 651-1190	3726
Chambers & Chambers Inc	2084	F	818 995-6961	1626
Culture AMP Inc (HQ)	7372	F	415 326-8453	23786
Designer Sound SEC Systems	3699	F	818 981-9249	19290
E Z Buy E Z Sell Recycler Corp (DH)	2711	C	310 886-7808	5621
Envion LLC	3564	D	818 217-2500	14656
Hab Enterprises Inc	3053	F	310 628-9000	9234
Hd Garment Solutions Inc	2386	E	323 581-6000	3516
Inspired Properties LLC	2731	F	818 430-9634	6113
Jesta Digital Entrmt Inc (HQ)	7372	F	323 648-4200	24059
Lisa and Lesley Co	2339	F	323 877-9878	3364
Lucky Strike Entertainment Inc (PA)	3949	E	818 933-3752	22846
Monterey Bay Beverage Co Inc	2033	F	818 784-4885	796
Navistar Inc	3711	D	818 907-0129	19490
Normal Centrix Inc	3999	F	310 715-9977	23428
Phil Blazer Enterprises Inc	2711	F	818 786-4000	5797
SA Hartman & Associates Inc	3861	E	818 907-9681	22457
Safcor Inc	3161	F	818 392-8437	10205
Sidney Millers Black Radio Ex	2721	E	818 907-9959	6027
Spacetron Metal Billows Corp	3599	F	818 633-1075	16413
Vans Inc	3021	F	818 990-1098	9189
Vpro Inc	3993	F	818 905-5678	23240
Western Imperial Trading Inc	3911	F	818 907-0768	22584
Zalemark Holding Company Inc	3911	F	888 682-6885	22587

SHINGLE SPRINGS, CA - El Dorado County

Name	SIC	EMP	PHONE	ENTRY#
BBC Corp	2752	E	530 677-4009	6440
Foamtec LLC	3272	F	916 851-8621	10575
M & W Engineering Inc	3599	E	530 676-7185	16158
Pw Eagle Inc	3084	D	530 677-2286	9476
Sundance Uniform & Embroidery	2395	F	530 676-6900	3759
White Industrial Corporation	3548	F	530 676-6262	14259

SIERRA MADRE, CA - Los Angeles County

Name	SIC	EMP	PHONE	ENTRY#
Greg Ian Islands Inc	2541	E	626 355-0019	4905
Ward E Waldo & Son Inc	2033	F	626 355-1218	838

SIGNAL HILL, CA - Los Angeles County

Name	SIC	EMP	PHONE	ENTRY#
4x Development Inc	3469	F	562 424-2225	12753
AC Pumping Unit Repair Inc	1389	E	562 492-1300	151
Applied Business Software Inc	7372	F	562 426-2188	23611
Asphalt Fabric and Engrg Inc	3949	D	562 997-4129	22750
Black Gold Pump & Supply Inc	1389	F	323 298-0077	172
C J Precision Industries Inc	3599	F	562 426-3708	15810
Colt Services LP	1389	F	562 988-2658	185
D&A Unlimited Inc	2339	E	562 336-1528	3311
Dawson Enterprises (PA)	3533	E	562 424-8564	13773
Evolife Scientific Llc	2833	E	888 750-0310	7658
Flex-Mate Inc	3423	F	562 426-7169	11529
Floyd Dennee	2759	F	562 595-6024	7066
Gem Mobile Treatment Svcs Inc (HQ)	3822	E	562 595-7075	20795
Harper & Two Inc (PA)	3679	F	562 424-3030	18930
K & E Manufacturing Inc	3444	F	562 494-7570	12258
P T Industries Inc	3444	F	562 961-3431	12322
Pacific Valves	3491	D	562 426-2531	13318
Petroleum Solids Control Inc (PA)	1389	F	562 424-0254	246
Prosthetic and Orthotic Group (PA)	3842	F	562 595-6445	22073
R D Mathis Company	3313	E	562 426-7049	11083
Relax Medical Systems Inc	3999	F	800 405-7677	23460
Reldom Corporation	3699	E	562 498-3346	19392
Rode Microphones LLC	3651	C	310 328-7456	17278
Rossmoor Pastries MGT Inc	2051	D	562 498-2253	1270
Signal Hill Petroleum Inc	1382	E	562 595-6440	141
Southwest Products Corporation	3519	F	360 887-7400	13599
Tiger Cased Hole Services Inc	1389	F	562 426-4044	269
United States Logistics Group	3715	E	562 989-9555	19835
Xcom Wireless Inc	3663	F	562 981-0077	17710

SILVERADO, CA - Orange County

Name	SIC	EMP	PHONE	ENTRY#
Program Data Incorporated	3825	F	714 649-2122	21103

SIMI VALLEY, CA - Ventura County

Name	SIC	EMP	PHONE	ENTRY#
Advanced Metal Mfg Inc	3444	E	805 322-4161	12086
Advanced Spectral Tech Inc	3827	E	805 527-7657	21332
Aerovironment Inc (PA)	3721	D	805 581-2187	19850
Aerovironment Inc	3721	F	626 357-9983	19853
Arxis Technology Inc	7372	E	805 306-7890	23626
Aveox Inc	3629	E	805 915-0200	16778
B & R Mold Inc	3544	E	805 526-8665	14020
Bemco Inc (PA)	3826	E	805 583-4970	21184
CFS Tax Software	7372	D	805 522-1157	23731
Cinemag Inc	3679	F	818 993-4644	18865
Circuit Express Inc	3672	F	805 581-2172	17848
Components For Automation Inc (PA)	3491	F	805 582-0065	13299
Computer Metal Products Corp	3444	D	805 520-6966	12160
Delt Industries Inc	3369	F	805 579-0213	11414
Dpa Labs Inc	3674	E	805 581-9200	18198
Embedded Systems Inc	3625	E	805 624-6000	16715
Emling LLC	3679	D	805 409-4807	18905
Enderle Fuel Injection	3714	E	805 526-3838	19648
Entech Instruments Inc	3826	D	805 527-5939	21226
Ferminics Opto-Technology Corp	3661	F	805 582-0155	17368
Fiberoptic Systems Inc	3357	E	805 579-6600	11303
Freedom Designs Inc	3842	C	805 582-0077	22015
Frontier Electronics Corp	3677	F	805 522-9998	18716
Gold Coast Solar LLC	3674	F	310 351-7229	18254
Inkjetmadnesscom Inc	2893	F	805 583-7755	8922
Interscan Corporation	3824	E	805 823-8301	20970
Jaxx Manufacturing Inc	3679	E	805 526-4979	18962
JB Britches Inc	2325	D	818 898-4046	3011
Jessop Industries	3599	E	805 581-6976	16083
Jkf Construction Inc	2434	F	805 583-4228	4210
K & M Software Design LLC	7372	E	805 583-0403	24067
Key Material Handling Inc	3537	E	805 520-6007	13880
L3 Technologies Inc	3663	E	805 584-1717	17565
Laser Toner & Computer Supply	3955	F	805 529-3300	22967
Lee Aerospace Products Inc	3728	F	805 527-1811	20156
Luxbright Inc	3646	F	323 871-4120	17058
M Wave Design Corporation	3679	F	805 499-8825	18999
Mabel Baas Inc	3479	E	805 520-8075	13204
Maury Razon	2389	F	818 989-6246	3569
Meggitt	3728	C	877 666-0712	20172
Meggitt Safety Systems Inc	3728	D	805 584-4100	20175
Meggitt Safety Systems Inc (HQ)	3699	C	805 584-4100	19355
Meggitt Safety Systems Inc	3812	C	805 584-4100	20629
Meggitt-Usa Inc (HQ)	3728	C	805 526-5700	20176
Milgard Manufacturing Inc	3231	C	805 581-6325	10380
Miller Electric Mfg Co	3548	E	805 520-7494	14248
Milodon Incorporated	3714	F	805 577-5950	19721
Nalco Company LLC	2899	F	805 584-9950	9006
Newman and Sons Inc (PA)	3272	E	805 522-1646	10607
Optical Physics Company	3827	F	818 880-2907	21391
Pacific Scientific Company (DH)	3812	C	805 526-5700	20672
Parks Optical Inc	3827	E	805 522-6722	21397
Pars Publishing Corp	2752	D	818 280-0540	6770
Pharmaceutic Litho Label Inc	2834	D	805 285-5162	8072
Piezo-Metrics Inc (PA)	3674	E	805 522-4676	18469
Plastic View Atc Inc	2591	F	805 520-9390	5034
Poly-Tainer Inc (PA)	3085	B	805 526-3424	9492
Puroflux Corporation	3677	F	805 579-0216	18735
PW Gillibrand Co Inc (PA)	1446	D	805 526-2195	375
R F P & Welding	3714	F	805 526-3425	19749
Raindrip Inc	3523	E	818 710-4023	13661
Recycled Aggregate Mtls Co Inc (PA)	2951	E	805 522-1646	9103
Replacement Parts Inds Inc	3843	E	818 882-8611	22186
Rexnord Industries LLC	3556	C	805 583-5514	14396
Ricoh Prtg Systems Amer Inc (HQ)	3577	B	805 578-4000	15323
Rsa Engineered Products LLC	3728	D	805 584-4150	20213
Rugged Info Tech Eqp Corp (PA)	3577	E	805 577-9710	15325
S T E U Inc	3648	E	805 527-0987	17160
Saaz Micro Inc	3674	F	805 405-0700	18524
Scientific Cutting Tools Inc	3545	E	805 584-9495	14191
Scope City Inc	3827	E	805 522-6646	21405
Senso-Metrics Inc	3829	F	805 527-3640	21535
Sensoscientific Inc	3823	E	800 279-3101	20937
Sheetmetal Engineering	3444	E	805 306-0390	12377
Sierra Aerospace LLC	3724	F	805 526-8669	19980
Special Devices Incorporated	3714	A	805 387-1000	19771
Specialty Fabrications Inc	3444	E	805 579-9730	12386
Spragues Rock and Sand Company	3273	F	805 522-7010	10842
Stearns Corporation	2844	E	805 582-2710	8588
Sunstream Technology Inc	3433	D	720 502-4446	11721
Taurus Products Inc	3541	F	805 584-1555	13955
Thomas Craven Wood Finishers	2599	F	805 341-7713	5085
Timco/Cal Rf Inc	3678	F	805 582-1777	18800
Total Paper and Packaging Inc	2679	F	818 885-1072	5539
Vans Manufacturing Inc	3599	F	805 522-6267	16496
Ventura Technology Group	3674	E	805 581-0800	18638
Vibra Finish Co (PA)	3291	E	805 578-0033	10958

	SIC	EMP	PHONE	ENTRY #
Weyerhaeuser Company	2653	C	800 238-3676	5285
Whittaker Corporation	3728	E	805 526-5700	20270
Xmultiple Technologies (PA)	3571	F	805 579-1100	14999

SOLANA BEACH, CA - San Diego County

	SIC	EMP	PHONE	ENTRY #
Annona Company LLC	2043	F	858 299-4238	1015
Dare Technologies Inc (HQ)	3661	F	714 634-5900	17358
Expert Reputation LLC	7372	E	866 407-6020	23885
Future Wave Technologies Inc	2095	E	858 481-1112	2294
Hylete Inc	2329	E	858 225-8998	3092
Kween Foods LLC	2045	F	805 895-0003	1057
Mc Allister Industries Inc (PA)	2754	E	858 755-0683	6958
Sentynl Therapeutics Inc	2834	E	888 227-8725	8125
Thermo Fisher Scientific Inc	3826	B	858 481-6386	21306

SOLEDAD, CA - Monterey County

	SIC	EMP	PHONE	ENTRY #
Estancia Estates	2084	D	707 431-1975	1692
Golden State Vintners	2084	E	831 678-3991	1728
Hahn Estate	2084	D	831 678-2132	1742

SOLVANG, CA - Santa Barbara County

	SIC	EMP	PHONE	ENTRY #
Buttonwood Farm Winery Inc	2084	F	805 688-3032	1612
Graphic Systems	2759	F	805 686-0705	7076
Rideau Vineyard LLC	2084	F	805 688-0717	1888
Ynez Corporation	2711	F	805 688-5522	5871

SOMERSET, CA - El Dorado County

	SIC	EMP	PHONE	ENTRY #
Latcham Granite Inc	2084	F	530 620-6642	1798
Perry Creek Winery	2084	F	530 620-5175	1864

SOMIS, CA - Ventura County

	SIC	EMP	PHONE	ENTRY #
Dudes Brewing Company	2082	E	424 271-2915	1522
Hagle Lumber Company Inc	2421	E	805 987-3887	3933

SONOMA, CA - Sonoma County

	SIC	EMP	PHONE	ENTRY #
3 Badge Beverage Corporation	2084	F	707 343-1167	1573
All-Truss Inc	2439	E	707 938-5595	4286
Arbor Fence Inc	3446	E	707 938-3133	12451
Bonneau Wines LLC	2084	F	707 996-0420	1602
Briggs & Sons	2541	F	707 938-4325	4885
CCL Label Inc	3999	F	707 938-7800	23300
Collotype Labels USA Inc	2759	F	707 931-7400	7029
Convergent Mobile Inc	3674	F	707 343-1200	18178
Daily Offrngs Cof Roastery LLC	2095	F	805 423-7410	2286
Diageo North America Inc	2084	D	707 939-6200	1664
El Pelado LLC	2448	F	707 938-2877	4365
Estate Cheese Group LLC (PA)	2022	F	707 996-1000	549
Franciscan Vineyards Inc	2084	C	707 933-2332	1710
Freixenet Sonoma Caves Inc	2084	E	707 996-4981	1716
Groskopf Warehouse & Logistics	2084	F	707 939-3100	1738
Hanzell Vineyards	2084	F	707 996-3860	1747
Hawaii Pacific Teleport LP	3663	F	707 938-7057	17533
Homewood Winery	2084	F	707 996-6353	1754
Innerstave LLC	2449	E	707 996-8781	4416
Jacuzzi Family Vineyards LLC	2084	F	707 931-7500	1769
Krave Pure Foods Inc	2013	D	707 939-9176	474
La Villeta De Sonoma	3443	E	707 939-9392	12026
Larson Family Winery Inc	2084	F	707 938-3031	1797
Laura Chenels Chevre Inc	2022	D	707 996-4477	562
Marinpak	2099	F	707 996-3931	2541
Mike Fellows	2396	E	707 938-0278	3801
Monica Bruce Designs Inc	2396	F	707 938-0277	3802
Nicholson Ranch LLC	2084	F	707 938-8822	1840
Olive Press LLC (PA)	2079	F	707 939-8900	1482
Opal Moon Winery LLC	2084	F	707 996-0420	1846
Peregrine Mobile Bottling LLC	2086	F	707 637-7584	2128
Rams Gate Winery LLC	2084	F	707 721-8700	1877
Sebastiani Vineyards Inc	2084	D	707 933-3200	1910
Soft Flex Co	3315	F	707 938-3539	11109
Sonoma Access Ctrl Systems Inc	3446	E	707 935-3458	12509
Sonoma Gourmet Inc	2035	F	707 939-3700	900
Sonoma Index-Tribune	2711	D	707 938-2111	5830
Sonoma International Inc	3944	E	707 935-0710	22715
Sonoma Pacific Company LLC	2448	D	707 938-2877	4400
Sonoma Pins Etc Corporation	2759	D	707 996-9956	7219
Stone Edge Winery LLC	2084	E	707 935-6520	1937
Three Sticks Wines LLC	2084	E	707 996-3328	1957
Toneleria Nacional Usa Inc	2429	F	707 501-8728	3987
Treasury Chateau & Estates	2084	F	707 996-5870	1962
Vineburg Wine Company Inc (PA)	2084	E	707 938-5277	1987
Vintage Point LLC	2084	E	707 939-6766	1989
Vision Plastics Mfg Inc	3944	F	855 476-2767	22724
Vode Lighting LLC	3645	F	707 996-9898	16998
Wine Communications Group	2721	F	707 939-0822	6058

SONORA, CA - Tuolumne County

	SIC	EMP	PHONE	ENTRY #
Alderman Timber Company Inc	2411	F	209 532-9636	3870
Bimbo Bakeries Usa Inc	2051	D	209 532-5185	1159
Birchwood Cabinets Sonora Inc	2434	F	209 532-1417	4169
Brandelli Arts Inc	3299	E	714 537-0969	11000
Kinematic Automation Inc	3841	D	209 532-3200	21770
L K Lehman Trucking	3272	E	209 532-5586	10595
Leslie Environmental Inds LLC	2411	F	209 840-1664	3892
O M Jones Inc	3679	E	209 532-1008	19033
Sandvik Thermal Process Inc	3559	D	209 533-1990	14535
Sierra Pacific Industries	2421	C	530 378-8301	3952
Treat Manufacturing Inc	3541	F	209 532-2220	13959
Uv Skinz Inc (PA)	2329	F	209 536-9200	3127

SOQUEL, CA - Santa Cruz County

	SIC	EMP	PHONE	ENTRY #
Design Octaves	3089	E	831 464-8500	9754
Junopacific Inc	3089	C	831 462-1141	9861
Messana Inc	3567	F	855 729-6244	14770
Provac Sales Inc	3561	E	831 462-8900	14596
System Studies Incorporated	3661	E	831 475-5777	17419

SOUTH DOS PALOS, CA - Merced County

	SIC	EMP	PHONE	ENTRY #
Koda Farms Inc	2044	E	209 392-2191	1046
Koda Farms Milling Inc	2044	E	209 392-2191	1047

SOUTH EL MONTE, CA - Los Angeles County

	SIC	EMP	PHONE	ENTRY #
Abacus Powder Coating	3479	E	626 443-7556	13133
Al-Mag Heat Treat	3398	F	626 442-8570	11431
Amro Fabricating Corporation (PA)	3728	C	626 579-2200	20034
Antaeus Fashions Group Inc	2329	E	626 452-0797	3068
Asia Plastics Inc	2673	F	626 448-8100	5384
BCI Inc	3599	F	626 579-4234	15780
Best Industrial Supply	3537	F	626 279-5090	13859
Beyond Seating Inc	3429	F	323 633-5359	11573
Bluetone Muffler Mfg Co	3714	E	626 442-1073	19595
Botanas Mexico Inc	2099	F	626 279-1512	2409
C W Cole & Company Inc	3646	E	626 443-2473	17017
Calfabco (PA)	3469	F	323 265-1205	12778
California Custom Caps	2353	E	626 454-1766	3463
California Ribbon Carbn Co Inc	3955	D	323 724-9100	22961
California Snack Foods Inc	2064	E	626 444-4508	1358
Calison Inc	2251	E	626 448-3328	2764
Cardinal Industrial Finishes (PA)	2851	D	626 444-9274	8630
CPC Group Inc	3089	E	626 350-8848	9731
Curve Line Metal Corporation	2514	F	626 448-5956	4689
Design Shapes In Steel Inc	3312	E	626 579-2032	11041
Dtbm Inc	2051	F	626 579-7033	1194
Eemus Manufacturing Corp	3479	F	626 443-8841	13170
Electro-Mech Components Inc (PA)	3613	F	626 442-7180	16598
Electronic Auto Systems Inc	3651	F	626 280-3855	17227
Engineering Design Inds Inc	3599	F	626 443-7741	15934
Fabricast Inc (PA)	3679	F	626 443-3247	18910
Futon Express	2512	F	626 443-8684	4641
General Metal Engraving Inc	3953	E	626 443-8961	22949
Golden Color Printing Inc	2752	E	626 455-0850	6592
Halcore Group Inc	3711	D	626 575-0880	19477
Henrys Metal Polishing Works	3471	E	323 263-9701	13023
Hoefner Corporation	3599	E	626 443-3258	16032
Hong Fat Dye Cutting Co	2789	F	626 452-0382	7333
Instyle Printing Inc	2342	E	626 575-2725	3453
Interntnal Mdction Systems Ltd	2833	F	626 459-5586	7671
Interntnal Mdction Systems Ltd	2834	A	626 442-6757	7960
Island Powder Coating	3479	E	626 279-2460	13194
J & L Cstm Plstic Extrsons Inc	3089	E	626 442-0711	9846
Kanamax International Inc (PA)	2834	F	213 399-3398	7974
Kinary Inc	2389	F	626 575-7873	3562
Kustom Lighting Products Inc	3648	E	626 443-0166	17138
La Mano Tortilleria	2099	F	626 350-4229	2511
Lee Pharmaceuticals	2844	D	626 442-3141	8531
Master Enterprises Inc	3444	E	626 442-1821	12280
Master Metal Works Inc	3446	E	626 444-8818	12498
Melkes Machine Inc	3599	E	626 448-5062	16194
Mikelson Machine Shop Inc	3728	E	626 448-3920	20178
Mikes Micro Parts Inc	3599	E	626 443-0675	16202
Mywi Fabricators Inc	3441	F	626 279-6994	11852
National Bright Lighting Inc	3648	E	909 818-9188	17147
Pacific Eagle USA Inc	3069	E	626 455-0033	9349
Pats Decorating Service Inc	2391	F	323 585-5073	3594
Pearson Engineering Corp	3479	F	626 442-7436	13222
Plastic Dress-Up Company	3089	D	626 442-7711	9970
Promotional Design Concepts Inc	3069	D	626 579-4454	9360
Proto Space Engineering Inc	3599	E	626 442-8273	16317
R & R Rubber Molding Inc	3061	F	626 575-8105	9269
Ramon Lopez	2512	F	626 575-3891	4664
Robert P Martin Company	3315	F	323 686-2220	11105
Rocky Label Mills Inc	2241	E	323 278-0080	2759
Roselm Industries Inc	3663	F	626 442-6840	17645
S&H Melkes Inc	3492	E	626 448-5062	13333
Scodan Systems Inc	3462	F	626 444-1020	12722

GEOGRAPHIC

	SIC	EMP	PHONE	ENTRY #
Sense Fashion Corporation	2331	E	626 454-3381	3192
Smith Bros Strl Stl Pdts Inc	3312	F	626 350-1872	11071
South Alliance Industrial Mch	3599	F	626 442-3744	16410
Studio9d8 Inc	2253	E	626 350-0832	2803
Thienes Apparel Inc	2253	C	626 575-2818	2807
Tri Service Co Inc	2899	F	626 442-3270	9031
Tri-Fitting Mfg Company	3728	F	626 442-2000	20255
Unique Screen Printing Inc	2396	E	626 575-2725	3821
Vacco Industries (DH)	3494	C	626 443-7121	13365
Vclad Laminates Inc	3083	E	626 442-2100	9459
Vp Footwear Inc	3021	F	626 443-2186	9196
Wbp Associates Inc	2542	F	626 575-0747	5011
Westar Metal Fabrication Inc	3441	F	626 350-0718	11918

SOUTH GATE, CA - Los Angeles County

	SIC	EMP	PHONE	ENTRY #
2m Machining & Mfg Co	3825	F	323 564-9388	20979
Accurate Steel Treating Inc	3398	E	562 927-6528	11428
Anadite Cal Restoration Tr	3471	E	562 861-2205	12926
Arcadia Inc	3442	E	310 665-0490	11931
Artsons Manufacturing Company	3312	E	323 773-3469	11027
Astro Aluminum Treating Co Inc	3398	D	562 923-4344	11433
Bakercorp	3624	F	562 904-3680	16682
Bell Foundry Co (PA)	3949	E	323 564-5701	22759
Brookshire Tool & Mfg Co Inc	3599	F	562 861-2567	15798
Buddy Bar Casting Corporation	3365	E	562 861-9664	11368
C&C Metal Form & Tooling Inc	3469	E	562 861-9554	12776
Care Tex Industries Inc (PA)	2253	D	323 567-5074	2777
Caretex Inc	2865	C	323 567-5074	8698
Cimc Intermodal Equipment LLC (DH)	3715	C	562 904-8600	19816
Conair Corporation	3631	D	323 724-0101	16807
Custom Leathercraft Mfg LLC (DH)	3199	C	323 752-2221	10246
Demenno/Kerdoon Holdings (DH)	2992	D	562 231-1550	9140
General Veneer Mfg Co	2435	F	323 564-2661	4274
Glasswerks La Inc (HQ)	3231	B	888 789-7810	10363
Golden Mattress Co Inc	2515	D	323 887-1888	4720
Graham Lee Associates Inc	2521	F	323 581-8203	4800
Granitize Products Inc	2842	D	562 923-5438	8387
Gwla Acquisition Corp (PA)	3211	E	323 789-7800	10268
Harbor Furniture Manufacturing (PA)	2512	F	323 636-1201	4646
Hughes Bros Aircrafters Inc	3544	E	323 773-4541	14062
In-O-Vate Inc	2952	F	562 806-7515	9117
Johns Manville Corporation	3296	D	323 568-2220	10985
K & L Precision Grinding Co	3599	E	323 564-5151	16098
La Mexicana LLC	2038	E	323 277-3660	964
Liberty Container Company	2653	C	323 564-4211	5243
Lunday-Thagard Company (HQ)	2999	C	562 928-7000	9160
Lunday-Thagard Company	2952	E	562 928-6990	9119
M D H Burner & Boiler Co Inc	3564	F	562 630-2875	14668
Marquez Marquez Inc	2096	E	562 408-0960	2338
Mercury Engineering Corp	3599	F	562 861-7816	16196
Metal Supply LLC	3441	D	562 634-9940	11842
Nextrade Inc (PA)	2299	E	562 944-9950	2947
Packaging Corporation America	2653	C	562 927-7741	5254
PQ Corporation	2819	F	323 326-1100	7519
Precision Forging Dies Inc	3544	E	562 861-1878	14095
Premco Forge Inc	3462	F	323 564-6666	12719
Productivity California Inc	3089	D	562 923-3100	9997
Saputo Cheese USA Inc	2022	C	562 862-7686	575
Simons Brick Corporation	3297	E	951 279-1000	10993
Sunopta Grains and Foods Inc	2099	D	323 774-6000	2620
Suregrip International Co	3949	D	562 923-0724	22902
T&T Precision Machining	3599	F	323 583-0064	16440
Techni-Cast Corp	3369	D	562 923-4585	11425
Three Brothers Cutting	2331	F	323 564-4774	3197
Tony Borges	3448	E	310 962-8700	12579
Tu-K Industries Inc	2844	F	562 927-3365	8596
Van Brunt Foundry Inc	3365	F	323 569-2832	11391
Viking Ready Mix Co Inc	3273	E	323 564-1866	10860
Win Soon Inc	2026	E	323 564-5070	713
World Oil Corp	1311	D	562 928-0100	78
YH Texpert Corporation	2339	F	323 562-8800	3435

SOUTH LAKE TAHOE, CA - El Dorado County

	SIC	EMP	PHONE	ENTRY #
Diamond Woodcraft	2431	F	530 541-0866	4035
Sierra-Tahoe Ready Mix Inc	3273	F	530 541-1877	10837
Terri Bell	7692	F	530 541-4180	24671

SOUTH PASADENA, CA - Los Angeles County

	SIC	EMP	PHONE	ENTRY #
Arroyo Seco Racquet Club	3069	F	323 258-4178	9283
Preco Aircraft Motors Inc	3694	E	626 799-3549	19201
Ximenez Icons	2392	F	310 344-6670	3651

SOUTH SAN FRANCISCO, CA - San Mateo County

	SIC	EMP	PHONE	ENTRY #
253 Inc	3444	F	650 737-5670	12075
Achaogen Inc (PA)	2834	C	650 800-3636	7719
Aclara Biosciences Inc	3829	D	800 297-2728	21427
Acme Bread Co	2051	D	650 938-2978	1134

	SIC	EMP	PHONE	ENTRY #
Actelion Phrmaceuticals US Inc (DH)	2834	E	650 624-6900	7724
Airgas Usa LLC	2813	F	650 873-4212	7401
Alvin D Troyer and Associates	3429	F	650 574-0167	11561
Amgen Inc	2834	E	650 244-2000	7750
Assembly Biosciences Inc	2834	E	415 978-2163	7772
Atara Biotherapeutics Inc (PA)	2836	C	650 278-8930	8273
B Metal Fabrication Inc	3444	E	650 615-7705	12126
Barrango (PA)	3599	F	650 737-9206	15774
Berlin Food & Lab Equipment Co	3821	E	650 589-4231	20746
Bimbo Bakeries Usa Inc	2051	E	650 583-5828	1157
Bimbo Bakeries Usa Inc	2051	E	650 583-3259	1161
Biocheck Inc	3841	E	650 573-1968	21631
Bonelli Enterprises	3442	E	650 873-3222	11940
Burton Ching Ltd	2392	F	415 522-5520	3605
Business Extension Bureau	2721	E	650 737-5700	5895
C&C Building Automation Co Inc	3829	E	650 292-7450	21445
Calithera Biosciences Inc	2834	E	650 870-1000	7824
Calpico Inc	3643	E	650 588-2241	16881
Catalyst Biosciences Inc (PA)	2834	E	650 266-8674	7835
Cav Distributing Corporation	3652	F	650 588-2228	17312
Cedarlane Natural Foods North	2099	E	650 742-0444	2421
City Baking Company	2051	D	650 589-8128	1180
Cortexyme Inc (PA)	2834	F	415 910-5717	7853
Cytokinetics Incorporated (PA)	2834	C	650 624-3000	7861
Cytomx Therapeutics Inc	2834	C	650 515-3185	7862
D J Simpson Company (PA)	2851	F	650 225-9404	8640
Denali Therapeutics Inc (PA)	2836	C	650 866-8548	8293
Dolphin Press Inc	2752	F	650 873-9092	6548
Dvs Sciences Inc	3826	E	408 900-7205	21219
Essence Printing Inc (PA)	2752	E	650 952-5072	6567
Eureka Chemical Company (PA)	2899	F	650 873-5374	8964
Exelixis Inc	2834	C	650 837-8254	7885
First Databank Inc (DH)	2741	D	800 633-3453	6237
Five Prime Therapeutics Inc	2834	C	415 365-5600	7891
Fluidigm Corporation (PA)	3826	C	650 266-6000	21231
Frontier Medicines	2834	E	650 457-1005	7899
Garnett Signs LLC	3993	F	650 871-9518	23119
Genentech Inc (DH)	2834	A	650 225-1000	7902
Genentech Inc	2834	A	408 963-8759	7903
Genentech Inc	2834	A	650 225-3214	7906
Genentech Inc	2834	C	650 225-1000	7907
Genentech Usa Inc	2834	A	650 225-1000	7908
Georgia-Pacific LLC	2653	C	650 873-7800	5227
Giannini Garden Ornaments Inc	3272	E	650 873-4493	10582
Giant Horse Printing Inc	2752	F	650 875-7137	6591
Giustos Specialty Foods LLC (PA)	2041	E	650 873-6566	1001
Giustos Specialty Foods LLC	2041	E	650 873-6566	1002
Global Blood Therapeutics Inc (PA)	2834	D	650 741-7700	7922
Homestead Ravioli Company Inc	2032	E	650 615-0750	728
Hsin Tung Yang Foods Company	2013	F	650 589-7689	468
Ideaya Biosciences Inc	2834	D	650 443-6209	7938
Ignyta Inc (PA)	2834	E	858 255-5959	7941
Immune Design Corp	2834	E	650 225-0214	7942
Intermune Inc (DH)	2834	C	415 466-4383	7955
Io2 Technology LLC	3489	F	650 308-4216	13282
Janssen Biopharma Inc	2834	E	650 635-5500	7968
Japanese Weekend Inc (PA)	2339	E	415 621-0555	3343
JC Metal Specialists Inc	3441	E	650 827-1618	11817
Jesus Cabezas	2099	F	650 583-0469	2488
Kezar Life Sciences Inc	2834	E	650 822-5600	7979
Kk Graphics Inc	2752	F	415 468-1057	6678
Lithotype Company Inc (PA)	2752	D	650 871-1750	6705
Magnolia Lane Soft HM Furn Inc	2392	E	650 624-0700	3624
Matsusada Precision Inc	3844	F	650 877-0151	22216
McLellan Equipment Inc (PA)	3713	D	650 873-8100	19542
Meyers Sheet Metal Box Inc	3444	F	650 873-8889	12299
Monogram Biosciences Inc	2835	B	650 635-1100	8241
Myokardia Inc (PA)	2834	D	650 741-0900	8021
New Hong Kong Noodle Co Inc	2098	E	650 588-6425	2375
New Method Fur Dressing Co	3999	F	650 583-9881	23425
Nexsteppe Seeds Inc	2869	E	650 887-5700	8756
Ngm Biopharmaceuticals Inc	2834	C	650 243-5555	8038
Oneto Manufacturing Company	3444	F	650 875-1710	12318
Oric Pharmaceuticals Inc	2834	E	650 918-8818	8057
Polywell Company Inc	3571	E	650 583-7222	14962
Portola Pharmaceuticals Inc (PA)	2834	C	650 246-7300	8080
Pre-Press International	2752	E	415 216-0031	6789
Principia Biopharma Inc	2834	D	650 416-7700	8084
Prothena Corp Pub Ltd Co	2833	C	650 837-8550	7686
Pyramid Graphics	2752	F	650 871-0290	6817
R Torre & Company Inc (PA)	2087	C	800 775-1925	2227
R Torre & Company Inc	2087	E	650 624-2830	2228
Rapt Therapeutics Inc	2834	D	650 489-9000	8098
Rigel Pharmaceuticals Inc (PA)	2834	C	650 624-1100	8107
Rinat Neuroscience Corp	2834	F	650 615-7300	8108

Mergent email: customerrelations@mergent.com
1432

2020 California
Manufacturers Register

(P-0000) Products & Services Section entry number
(PA)=Parent Co (HQ)=Headquarters (DH)=Div Headquarters

Company	SIC	EMP	PHONE	ENTRY #
Satsuma Pharmaceuticals Inc	2834	F	650 410-3200	8121
Sees Candies Inc (DH)	2064	B	650 761-2490	1396
Sees Candy Shops Incorporated (HQ)	2064	E	650 761-2490	1397
Sequenta LLC	2835	D	650 243-3900	8254
Simpson Coatings Group Inc	2851	E	650 873-5990	8680
Sonoma Wine Hardware Inc	2084	E	650 866-3020	1922
Sp Controls Inc	3577	F	650 392-7880	15339
Sunesis Pharmaceuticals Inc (PA)	2834	E	650 266-3500	8150
Sutro Biopharma Inc (PA)	2836	C	650 392-8412	8331
T L Care Inc	2341	F	650 589-3659	3450
Tangle Inc	3944	E	650 616-7900	22719
Tanox Inc (DH)	2834	C	650 851-1607	8154
Tardio Enterprises Inc	2092	F	650 877-7200	2273
Theravance Biopharma Us Inc	2834	C	650 808-6000	8161
Theravnce Bphrma Antbotics Inc	2834	C	877 275-6930	8162
Thermo Fisher Scientific Inc.	3826	D	650 876-1949	21307
Thermo Fisher Scientific Inc.	3826	F	650 246-5265	21309
Thermo Fisher Scientific Inc.	3826	C	650 638-6409	21311
Titan Pharmaceuticals Inc (PA)	2834	D	650 244-4990	8165
Tricida Inc	2834	D	415 429-7800	8169
Utap Printing Co Inc	2752	F	650 588-2818	6913
Vaxart Inc (PA)	2834	E	650 550-3500	8176
Vomela Specialty Company	3993	E	650 877-8000	23239
Windmill Corporation	2051	E	650 873-1000	1298
Zion Health Inc	2844	F	650 520-4313	8612
Zymed Laboratories	3999	E	650 952-0110	23532

SPRING VALLEY, CA - San Diego County

Company	SIC	EMP	PHONE	ENTRY #
Bish Inc	3728	E	619 660-6220	20058
Crafted Metals Inc	3499	E	619 464-1090	13512
Deering Banjo Company Inc	3931	E	619 464-8252	22611
Euramco Safety Inc	3564	F	619 670-9590	14658
Everbrite West LLC	3993	F	619 444-9000	23102
Folex Co	2841	F	619 670-5588	8340
Formalloy Technologies Inc	3555	F	619 377-9101	14323
French Custom Shutters Inc	2431	F	619 667-2636	4045
Hillholder Blocks By Modern	3272	F	619 463-6344	10586
Homestead Sheet Metal	3441	E	619 469-4373	11809
Mailworks Inc	2621	F	619 670-2365	5131
Modern Stairways Inc	3272	F	619 466-1484	10603
Ram Centrifugal Products Inc	3564	F	619 670-9590	14676
Raphaels Inc	2499	F	619 670-7999	4524
Richardson Steel Inc	3441	F	619 697-5892	11873
S and S Carbide Tool Inc	3544	E	619 670-5214	14102
Safety America Inc	3851	F	619 660-6968	22383
San Diego Paper Box Co Inc	2657	E	619 660-9566	5315
Tru-Duct Inc	3444	F	619 660-3858	12414
Ttn Machining Inc	3599	F	619 303-4573	16477

SPRINGVILLE, CA - Tulare County

Company	SIC	EMP	PHONE	ENTRY #
CA-Te LP	3448	F	559 539-1530	12536

STANFORD, CA - Santa Clara County

Company	SIC	EMP	PHONE	ENTRY #
Leland Stanford Junior Univ	2741	C	650 723-5553	6271
Leland Stanford Junior Univ	2741	C	650 723-3052	6272
Leland Stanford Junior Univ	2741	D	650 723-4455	6273
Stanford Daily Publishing Corp	2711	E	650 723-2555	5840

STANTON, CA - Orange County

Company	SIC	EMP	PHONE	ENTRY #
Ace Bindery Inc	2789	F	714 220-0232	7325
Advanced Display Systems Inc	3799	F	714 995-2200	20502
All Metals Proc San Diego Inc	3471	C	714 828-8238	12914
Blaga Precision Inc	3599	F	714 891-9509	15793
Blake Sign Company Inc	3993	F	714 891-5682	23062
Cameron Welding Supply (PA)	7692	E	714 530-9353	24623
CJ Enterprises	3544	E	714 898-8558	14033
Continental Signs Inc	3993	E	714 894-2011	23079
Custom Pipe & Fabrication Inc (HQ)	3498	D	800 553-3058	13466
Cynthia Garcia	3728	E	714 897-4654	20079
Design Form Inc	3443	F	714 952-3700	12016
Field Time Target Training LLC	3483	E	714 677-2841	13271
Inception Homes Inc	2451	F	714 890-1883	4452
M & G Custom Polishing	3471	F	714 995-0261	13043
Manti-Machine Co Inc	3599	F	714 902-1465	16169
Muth Machine Works (HQ)	3599	E	714 527-2239	16234
Newcomb Spring Corp	3495	E	714 995-5341	13382
Newport Glass Works Ltd	3827	F	714 484-8100	21384
Newport Industrial Glass Inc	3231	F	714 484-7500	10381
Newport Optical Industries (PA)	3827	E	714 484-8100	21385
Oc Fleet Service Inc	3731	F	714 460-8069	20297
Orco Block & Hardscape (PA)	3271	D	714 527-2239	10511
Pac 21	3823	E	714 891-7000	20914
Precision Fastener Tooling	3542	F	714 898-8558	13991
Schaffer Laboratories Inc	3083	F	714 202-1594	9455
Signs and Services Company	3993	F	714 761-8200	23206
Stecher Enterprises Inc	3495	E	714 484-6900	13389
Two Thirty Two Productins Inc	3861	E	714 317-5317	22467

Company	SIC	EMP	PHONE	ENTRY #
Urethane Science Inc	3089	F	714 828-3210	10103
Verlo Industries Inc	2542	E	714 236-2191	5010
Wce Products Inc	2822	F	714 895-4381	7633
West Coast Manufacturing Inc	3469	E	714 897-4221	12890
Wheeler Optical Lab	3851	F	714 891-2016	22395

STEVENSON RANCH, CA - Los Angeles County

Company	SIC	EMP	PHONE	ENTRY #
Phat N Jicy Burgers Brands LLC	2099	E	310 420-7983	2586

STOCKTON, CA - San Joaquin County

Company	SIC	EMP	PHONE	ENTRY #
A & A Ready Mixed Concrete Inc	3273	E	209 546-1950	10677
A & D Rubber Products Co Inc (PA)	3053	E	209 941-0100	9212
Advanced Indus Coatings Inc	3479	D	209 234-2700	13137
Aero Turbine Inc	3724	D	209 983-1112	19945
Aguda Wilson Ramos	3663	F	209 942-2446	17440
Aisin Electronics Inc	3625	C	209 983-4988	16695
Al Kramp Specialties	3648	F	209 464-7539	17097
All Good Pallets Inc	2448	F	209 467-7000	4346
Alpine Meats Inc	2013	E	209 477-2691	436
American Biodiesel Inc	2869	F	209 466-4823	8712
American Containers Inc	2653	E	209 460-1127	5195
Anderson Moulds Incorporated	3089	F	209 943-1145	9631
Anderson Signs	3993	F	209 367-0120	23049
Andrea Zee Corporation	3281	F	209 462-1700	10889
Applied Arospc Structures Corp (PA)	3728	C	209 982-0160	20037
Arandas Tortilla Company Inc	2099	E	209 464-8675	2394
Arrow Sign Co	3993	E	209 931-7852	23054
B & C Painting Solutions Inc	3479	E	209 982-0422	13147
Bakakers Specialty Foods Inc	2041	E	209 234-5935	997
Big GZ Pallets	2448	F	209 465-0351	4350
Buzz Converting Inc	2631	E	209 948-1341	5157
Cal Sheets LLC	2653	D	209 234-3300	5203
Calchef Foods LLC	2035	E	888 638-7083	880
California Cedar Products Co (PA)	2499	E	209 932-5002	4495
California Concrete Pipe Corp	3272	F	209 466-4212	10546
Calportland Company	3241	E	209 469-0109	10407
Carando Technologies Inc	3542	E	209 948-6500	13973
Caraustar Industries Inc	2655	C	209 464-6590	5288
Cencal Recycling LLC	2611	F	209 546-8000	5092
Central Pallets	2448	F	209 462-3019	4355
Cmyk Enterprise Inc	2752	F	209 229-7230	6490
Concrete Inc	3273	E	209 830-1962	10746
Concrete Inc (DH)	3273	D	209 933-6999	10748
Conopco Inc	2844	C	209 466-9580	8463
Corn Products Development Inc (HQ)	2046	E	209 982-1920	1060
Cozad Trailer Sales LLC	3715	D	209 931-3000	19818
Custom Building Products Inc	3531	E	209 983-8322	13725
Cutter Lumber Products	2448	E	209 982-4477	4360
Cwi Trading	3644	F	209 981-7023	16945
Deck West Inc	3444	F	209 939-9700	12176
Del Rio West Pallets	2448	E	209 983-8215	4362
Dentonis Welding Works Inc (PA)	7692	E	209 464-4930	24630
Diamond Foods LLC (PA)	2068	A	209 467-6000	1424
Diamond Truck Body Mfg Inc	3713	F	209 943-1655	19528
Dietrich Industries Inc	3312	D	209 547-9066	11042
Dow Jones Lmg Stockton Inc	2711	C	209 943-6397	5619
DTE Stockton LLC	1389	E	209 467-3838	190
Enviroplex Inc	3448	D	209 466-8000	12544
Es West Coast LLC	3621	E	209 870-1900	16643
Exactacator Inc (PA)	3949	E	209 464-8979	22798
Farmer Bros Co	2095	E	209 466-0203	2293
Fleenor Company Inc	2621	F	209 932-0329	5105
Formurex Inc	2834	F	209 931-2040	7895
G & S Process Equipment Inc	3599	F	209 466-3630	15980
Gallien Technology Inc (PA)	3651	D	209 234-7300	17231
Gbm Manufacturing Inc	3253	F	888 862-8397	10442
Geiger Manufacturing Inc	3599	F	209 464-7746	15989
Gnekow Family Winery LLC	2084	F	209 463-0697	1725
Grimaud Farms California Inc (DH)	2015	E	209 466-3200	518
Hackett Industries Inc	3556	F	209 955-8220	14370
Harbor Signs Inc	3993	F	209 463-8686	23126
Harley Murray Inc	3715	D	209 466-0266	19823
Herrick Corporation (PA)	3441	E	209 956-4751	11807
Herrick Corporation	3312	C	209 956-4751	11048
Highland Wholesale Foods Inc	2033	F	209 933-0580	774
IC Ink Image Co Inc	2759	F	209 931-3040	7090
Industrial Design Fabrication	3599	F	209 937-9128	16041
Ingredion Incorporated	2046	D	209 982-1920	1061
Inland Valley Truss Inc	2439	F	209 943-4710	4309
International Paper Company	2653	E	209 931-9005	5239
Interplastic Corporation	2821	F	209 932-0396	7571
J & J Quality Door Inc	2431	E	209 948-5013	4060
J-M Manufacturing Company Inc	2821	C	209 982-1500	7577
Klein Bros Holdings Ltd	2068	E	209 465-5033	1429
Kp LLC	2752	E	209 466-6761	6684
Kraft Heinz Foods Company	2022	C	209 942-0102	559

GEOGRAPHIC

	SIC	EMP	PHONE	ENTRY #
Kraft Heinz Foods Company	2068	E	209 932-5700	1430
Kruger Foods Inc	2035	C	209 941-8518	887
Lam Enterprises Inc	2099	F	209 586-2217	2517
Lawleys Inc	2048	F	209 572-1700	1107
Lehigh Southwest Cement Co	3273	F	209 465-2624	10794
Lewis-Goetz and Company Inc	3052	F	209 944-0791	9199
Liberty Printing Inc	2752	F	209 467-8800	6701
Luus Family Corp	2015	E	209 466-1952	522
M & K Builders Inc	3448	F	209 478-7531	12555
Mark Ease Products Inc	3993	E	209 462-8632	23152
Martha Olsons Great Foods Inc	2052	F	209 234-5935	1320
Masonite International Corp	2431	E	209 948-0637	4082
Miller Products Inc	2672	D	209 467-2470	5368
Mina-Tree Signs Incorporated **(PA)**	3993	F	209 941-2921	23161
Mitsubishi Chemical Advncd Mtr	3089	F	209 464-2701	9901
Murray Biscuit Company LLC	2052	E	209 472-3718	1322
Natural Std RES Collaboration	2731	F	617 591-3300	6127
Nexcoil Steel LLC	3316	F	209 900-1919	11120
Niagara Bottling LLC	2086	F	209 983-8436	2097
Noll/Norwesco LLC	3444	C	209 234-1600	12314
O H I Company	3556	E	209 466-8921	14389
Off Lead Inc	3199	F	209 931-6909	10250
Oldcastle Apg West Inc	2951	E	209 983-1609	9099
Oldcastle Infrastructure Inc	3272	F	209 235-1173	10614
Olive Corto L P	2079	F	209 888-8100	1481
Pacific International Stl Corp	3449	E	209 931-0900	12597
Pacific Paper Tube Inc **(PA)**	2655	E	510 562-8823	5299
Pactiv LLC	2653	A	209 983-1930	5256
Pelton-Shepherd Industries Inc **(PA)**	2097	E	209 460-0893	2360
Pepsi-Cola Metro Btlg Co Inc	2086	E	209 367-7140	2115
Pre-Peeled Potato Co Inc	2099	E	209 469-6911	2587
Premier Coatings Inc	3479	D	209 982-5585	13230
Proco Products Inc **(PA)**	3069	E	209 943-6088	9358
Production Chemical Mfg Inc **(PA)**	2842	F	209 943-7337	8408
Quest Industries LLC	2759	F	209 234-0202	7190
Quiet Ride Solutions LLC	3089	F	209 942-4777	10004
Ramon Lopez	3711	F	209 478-9500	19496
Reyes Coca-Cola Bottling LLC	2086	E	209 466-9501	2142
Rgm Products Inc	2952	B	559 499-2222	9125
Robinson Farms Feed Company	2048	F	209 466-7915	1123
Rock Engineered McHy Co Inc	2911	F	925 447-0805	9065
RR Donnelley & Sons Company	2752	B	209 983-6700	6849
S M S Briners Inc	2035	F	209 941-8515	898
San Joaquin Orthtics & Prsthtc	3842	F	209 932-0170	22079
Sardee Corporation California	3535	F	209 466-1526	13833
Sardee Industries Inc	3565	E	209 466-1526	14726
Scafco Corporation	3999	E	209 670-8053	23468
Sierra Lumber Manufacturers	2431	C	209 943-7777	4123
Signode Industrial Group LLC	2679	D	209 931-0917	5531
Simpson Manufacturing Co Inc	3291	B	209 234-7775	10954
Simpson Strong-Tie Company Inc	3449	D	209 234-7775	12606
Stanley Electric Motor Co Inc	7694	E	209 464-7321	24696
Stockon Mailing & Printing	2752	F	209 466-6741	6871
Stockton Propeller Inc	3728	F	209 982-4000	20238
Stockton Tri-Industries Inc	3535	D	209 948-9701	13838
Street Graphics Inc	3993	E	209 948-1713	23219
Sunrise Fresh LLC	2034	E	209 932-0192	866
Sust Manufacturing Company	3599	F	209 931-9571	16432
T M Cobb Company	2431	D	209 948-5358	4137
Teohc California Inc	3444	B	209 234-1600	12404
Therapeutic RES Faculty LLC	2759	C	209 472-2240	7248
Tiger-Sul Products LLC	2819	F	209 451-2725	7530
Toufic Inc	2051	F	209 478-4780	1287
Tri Map International Inc	3571	F	209 234-0100	14993
Valimet Inc **(PA)**	3399	D	209 444-1600	11490
Valley Fresh Inc **(HQ)**	2015	E	209 943-5411	529
Value Products Inc	2841	E	209 345-3817	8355
Varni Brothers Corporation	2086	E	209 464-7778	2181
Vinotheque Wine Cellars	3585	F	209 466-9463	15472
Wardley Industrial Inc	3086	F	209 932-1088	9578
West Coast Canvas **(PA)**	2394	F	209 333-0243	3714
West Coast Orthotic/Prosthetic	3842	F	209 942-4166	22124
Western Organics Inc	2873	E	209 982-4936	8808
Western Square Industries Inc	3446	E	209 944-0921	12523
Westway Feed Products LLC	2048	F	209 466-4391	1132
Weyerhaeuser Company	2421	F	209 942-1825	3966
Whisperkool Corporation	2084	F	800 343-9463	1999
Wilmar Oils Fats Stockton LLC	2076	L	925 627-1600	1450
Wjlp Company Inc	3677	D	800 628-1123	18748
Wkf (friedman Enterprises Inc **(PA)**	3724	F	925 673-9100	19991
Zacky & Sons Poultry LLC	2015	B	209 948-0129	535

STRATHMORE, CA - Tulare County

	SIC	EMP	PHONE	ENTRY #
Cellu-Con Inc	2879	E	559 568-0190	8821
Michael D Wilson Inc	3499	F	559 568-1115	13534

STRAWBERRY VALLEY, CA - Yuba County

	SIC	EMP	PHONE	ENTRY #
Soper-Wheeler Company LLC **(PA)**	2411	E	530 675-2343	3909

STUDIO CITY, CA - Los Angeles County

	SIC	EMP	PHONE	ENTRY #
Chill Spot Inc	2024	F	818 762-0041	635
F R Industries Inc	2299	F	818 503-9143	2933
Fear of God LLC **(PA)**	2329	F	213 235-7985	3080
Hank Player Inc	2339	F	818 856-6079	3334
Harmony Infinite Inc	2599	F	818 780-4569	5063
Jbs Private Label Inc	2253	F	818 762-3736	2792
Kimdurla Inc	3229	E	818 504-4041	10314
Mesgona Corporation	2741	F	310 926-3238	6280
Michelle Alisa Designs Inc	3911	F	818 501-9300	22549
Midrange Software Inc	7372	F	818 762-8539	24166
Normel Inc	2759	F	818 504-4041	7149
Players Press Inc	2731	F	818 789-4980	6136
Sugared + Bronzed LLC	2342	D	747 264-0477	3459

SUISUN CITY, CA - Solano County

	SIC	EMP	PHONE	ENTRY #
A & A Ready Mixed Concrete Inc	3273	E	707 399-0682	10675
Superior Sound Technology LLC	3842	F	707 863-7431	22098

SUN CITY, CA - Riverside County

	SIC	EMP	PHONE	ENTRY #
North County Sand and Grav Inc	1442	E	951 928-2881	354
Omnimax International Inc	3442	C	951 928-1000	11974
R & M Coils	3677	F	951 672-9855	18736

SUN VALLEY, CA - Los Angeles County

	SIC	EMP	PHONE	ENTRY #
Abbott Technologies Inc	3612	E	818 504-0644	16539
Accurate Engineering Inc	3672	E	818 768-3919	17803
Acrylic Distribution Corp	2519	D	818 767-6448	4759
Alert Plating Company	3471	E	818 771-9304	12913
American Grip Inc	3648	E	818 768-8922	17100
American Plastic Products Inc	3544	D	818 504-1073	14015
Architectural Foamstone Inc	2675	F	818 767-4500	5447
Aries Prepared Beef Company	2047	E	818 771-0181	1067
Art Mold Die Casting Inc	3544	F	818 767-6464	14017
ASC Group Inc	3674	C	818 896-1101	18128
Associated Ready Mix Concrete	3273	E	818 504-3100	10693
AVX Filters Corporation	3569	D	818 767-6770	14795
B Cumming Company A Corp	3069	F	818 504-2571	9286
Ble Inc	1381	F	818 504-9577	89
Blue Can Water **(PA)**	2086	F	818 450-3290	2043
Brian Klaas Inc	2542	F	818 394-9881	4963
C A Buchen Corp	3441	E	818 767-5408	11753
C F Manufacturing	3714	E	818 504-9899	19603
Ca937 Afjrotc	3999	D	818 394-3600	23290
Cal Coast Stucco	3299	F	818 767-0115	11002
California Iron Design	7692	C	818 767-6690	24621
Calportland Company	3241	D	818 767-0508	10409
Cdeq	3229	E	818 767-5143	10301
Clear Water Corporation Inc	3589	F	818 765-8293	15501
Colorfx Inc	2752	E	818 767-7671	6499
Columbia Showcase & Cab Co Inc	2541	C	818 765-9710	4893
Coronado Manufacturing Inc	3728	E	818 768-5010	20077
Cosmetic Group Usa Inc	2844	C	818 767-2889	8469
De Leon Entps Elec Spclist Inc	3672	E	818 252-6690	17861
Desert Block Co Inc	2951	F	661 824-2624	9090
Dillon Aircraft Deburring	3471	E	818 768-0801	12985
Dip Braze Inc	7692	E	818 768-1555	24631
E-Z Mix Inc **(PA)**	2674	E	818 768-0568	5437
Earl Hays Press	2759	E	818 765-0700	7054
Emergent Group Inc **(DH)**	3842	D	818 394-2800	22008
Encore Cases Inc	3161	E	818 768-8803	10194
Excelity	3369	E	818 767-1000	11415
Florence International Company	3471	E	818 767-9650	13010
Forgiato Inc	3714	D	818 771-9779	19659
General Steel Fabricators Inc	3441	F	818 897-1300	11802
Gibbel Bros Inc	3273	E	323 875-1367	10762
Glenoaks Food Inc	2013	E	818 768-7600	459
Hanson Brass Inc	3648	E	818 767-3501	17132
Hey Baby of California	2339	E	818 504-2060	3336
Hollywood Film Company	3861	D	818 683-1130	22426
Industrial Battery Engrg Inc	3691	E	818 767-7067	19168
Insua Graphics Incorporated	2752	E	818 767-7007	6644
Jack J Engel Manufacturing Inc	3699	E	818 767-6220	19331
Jmi Steel Inc	3446	E	818 768-3955	12486
K V R Investment Group Inc	3559	D	818 896-1102	14486
Kenwalt Die Casting Corp	3363	E	818 768-5800	11341
Kitcor Corporation	3469	E	323 875-2820	12835
Kleen Maid Inc	2392	E	323 581-3000	3621
Kuton Welding Inc	3548	F	818 771-0964	14243
L N L Anodizing Inc	3471	E	818 768-9224	13038
LA Gauge Co Inc	3599	D	818 767-7193	16132
La Propoint Inc	3499	E	818 767-6800	13528
Legacy Vulcan LLC	1442	E	818 983-1323	350

Mergent email: customerrelations@mergent.com
1434

2020 California
Manufacturers Register

(P-0000) Products & Services Section entry number
(PA)=Parent Co (HQ)=Headquarters (DH)=Div Headquarters

	SIC	EMP	PHONE	ENTRY #
Legacy Vulcan LLC	3273	E	818 983-0146	10792
Leon Krous Drilling Inc	1381	E	818 833-4654	99
M & A Plastics Inc	3089	E	818 768-0479	9882
Monty Ventsam Inc	2431	F	818 768-6424	4090
Nupla LLC	3423	C	818 768-6800	11537
Ottos Pizza Stix Inc	2038	F	562 519-5304	970
Over & Over Ready Mix Inc	3272	D	818 983-1588	10619
Pacesetter Fabrics LLC (HQ)	2299	F	213 741-9999	2948
Pacific Sky Supply Inc	3728	D	818 768-3700	20193
Pacobond Inc	2674	E	818 768-5002	5442
Paint Specialists Inc	3479	E	818 771-0552	13221
Pbh Marketing Inc	2844	F	818 374-9000	8555
Peen-Rite Inc	3398	F	818 767-3676	11465
Penguin Pumps Incorporated	3561	E	818 504-2391	14593
Pin Craft Inc	3961	E	818 248-0077	22993
Pipe Guard Inc	3432	E	818 765-2424	11675
Pmc Inc (HQ)	3728	E	818 896-1101	20202
PMC Global Inc (PA)	3086	A	818 896-1101	9561
Precision Arcft Machining Inc	3599	E	818 768-5900	16308
Precision Tile Co	3272	F	818 767-7673	10629
Prime Plating Aerospace Inc	3471	F	818 768-9100	13078
Production Saw	3541	F	818 765-6100	13942
Pronk Technologies Inc (PA)	3825	E	818 768-5600	21104
Quikrete Companies LLC	3272	D	323 875-1367	10638
R L Anodizing	3471	F	818 252-3804	13085
Redwood Scientific Tech Inc	2834	E	310 693-5401	8101
Rico Corporation (HQ)	3931	E	818 394-2700	22634
Rico Holdings Inc	3931	C	818 394-2700	22635
Roan Mills LLC	2041	F	818 249-4686	1010
Rosco Laboratories Inc	3861	F	800 767-2652	22456
Schecter Guitar Research Inc	3931	E	818 767-1029	22637
Schmidt Industries Inc	3471	D	818 768-9100	13098
Schneiders Manufacturing Inc	3599	E	818 771-0082	16387
Sign Excellence LLC	3993	F	818 308-1044	23198
Soap & Water LLC	2844	E	310 639-3990	8585
Spartan Truck Company Inc	3713	E	818 899-1111	19557
Specialty International Inc	3469	D	818 768-8810	12876
Sscor Inc	3841	F	818 504-4054	21914
Sundial Industries Inc	3479	E	818 767-4477	13256
Sundial Powder Coatings Inc	3479	E	818 767-4477	13257
Superior Plating Inc	3471	E	818 252-1088	13112
Tatiossian Bros Inc	3144	D	818 768-3200	10178
Tecfar Manufacturing Inc	3599	F	818 767-0677	16446
Technical Heaters Inc	3052	F	818 361-7185	9208
Tee -N -Jay Manufacturing Inc	3444	E	818 504-2961	12403
Tempco Engineering Inc	3599	C	818 767-2326	16451
Travis American Group LLC	2431	C	714 258-1200	4143
Trimknit Inc	2241	F	818 768-7878	2762
Valley Mfg & Engrg Inc	3544	E	818 504-6085	14122
Viking Ready Mix Co Inc	3273	E	818 768-0050	10865
Walker Design Inc	3731	E	818 252-7788	20309
West Coast Custom Sheet Metal	3444	F	818 252-7500	12433

SUNLAND, CA - Los Angeles County

	SIC	EMP	PHONE	ENTRY #
Engineered Products By Lee Ltd	3599	F	818 352-3322	15933
Richard Ray Custom Designs	3645	F	323 937-5685	16988
Sculptor Body Molding (PA)	3089	F	818 761-3767	10052

SUNNYVALE, CA - Santa Clara County

	SIC	EMP	PHONE	ENTRY #
Abekas Inc	3663	F	650 470-0900	17435
Accurate Technology Mfg Inc	3599	D	408 733-4344	15679
Accuray Incorporated (PA)	3841	C	408 716-4600	21579
Adeza Biomedical Corporation	2835	C	408 745-6491	8200
Adiana Inc	2834	E	650 421-2900	7727
Advanced Linear Devices Inc	3674	E	408 747-1155	18065
Advanced Microwave Inc	3679	F	408 739-4214	18810
Advanced Rtrcraft Trining Svcs	3699	E	650 967-6300	19249
Agilone Inc (PA)	3826	E	877 769-3047	21167
Ahn Enterprises LLC	3677	F	408 734-1878	18697
Alliance Fiber Optic Pdts Inc	3229	D	408 736-6900	10296
Allvia Inc	3674	E	408 720-3333	18082
Alpha and Omega Semicdtr Inc (HQ)	3674	C	408 789-0008	18083
Alta Devices Inc	3674	C	408 988-8600	18084
AMD International Sls Svc Ltd (HQ)	3674	E	408 749-4000	18089
AMD Ventures LLC	3674	E	408 749-4000	18090
American Liquid Packaging Syst (PA)	2821	E	408 524-7474	7541
Analog Bits	3674	E	650 279-9323	18098
Applied Materials Inc	3559	E	408 727-5555	14426
Applied Micro Circuits Corp	3572	C	408 543-1000	15005
ARA Technology	3471	E	408 734-8131	12933
Arctic Wolf Networks Inc (PA)	7372	F	408 610-3263	23622
Art Robbins Instruments LLC	3826	E	408 734-8400	21175
Aruba Networks Inc	3663	F	408 227-4500	17460
Arvi Manufacturing Inc	3499	E	408 734-4776	13500
Asthmatx Inc	3841	D	408 419-0100	21611
Avantec Vascular Corporation	3841	E	408 329-5400	21615

	SIC	EMP	PHONE	ENTRY #
Azul Systems Inc (PA)	7372	D	650 230-6500	23647
Barrx Medical Inc	3845	D	408 328-7300	22231
Bayer Healthcare LLC	2834	D	408 499-0606	7797
Better Chinese LLC	2731	F	650 384-0902	6077
Bondline Elctrnic Adhsive Corp	2891	E	408 830-9200	8857
Cal West Spcialty Coatings Inc	2851	F	408 720-7440	8627
Cantabio Pharmaceuticals Inc	2834	E	408 501-8893	7827
Cellfusion Inc	7372	F	650 347-4000	23726
Cepheid	3826	F	408 541-4191	21203
Cepheid	2835	E	408 548-9104	8214
Cepheid (HQ)	3826	B	408 541-4191	21204
Changyoucom (us) LLC	7372	F	408 889-9866	23732
Clearlight Diagnostics LLC	2835	F	928 525-4290	8216
Cloudshield Technologies LLC	7372	E	408 331-6640	23754
Coadna Photonics Inc (HQ)	3661	D	408 736-1100	17355
Contactual Inc	7372	F	650 292-4408	23772
Covalent Metrology Svcs Inc	3821	F	408 498-4611	20753
Crowdstrike Holdings Inc (PA)	7372	C	888 512-8906	23783
De Anza Manufacturing Svcs Inc	3679	E	408 734-2020	18885
Dialact Corporation	3081	F	510 659-8099	9402
Digilens Inc	3827	E	408 734-0219	21349
Dionex Corporation (HQ)	3826	B	408 737-0700	21216
Dionex Corporation	3826	D	408 737-0700	21217
Dolby Laboratories Inc	3663	F	408 730-5543	17504
Drivescale Inc	7372	F	408 849-4651	23833
Druva Inc (HQ)	7372	D	650 241-3501	23835
Ebr Systems Inc (PA)	3845	E	408 720-1906	22250
Egain Corporation (PA)	7372	C	408 636-4500	23847
Egain Corporation	7372	D	408 212-3400	23848
Elekta Inc	7372	E	408 830-8000	23852
Embolx Inc	3841	F	408 990-2949	21702
Engineered Outsource Solutions	3674	E	408 617-2800	18218
Enlighted Inc (PA)	3646	E	650 964-1094	17028
Entco LLC (DH)	7372	B	312 580-9100	23863
Enterprise Signal Inc	7372	D	877 256-8303	23866
ERC Concepts Co Inc	3469	E	408 734-5345	12800
Exp Computer	3829	F	408 530-8080	21470
Fairchild Semicdtr Intl Inc (HQ)	3674	E	408 822-2000	18233
Finisar Corporation (HQ)	3661	E	408 548-1000	17371
Focus Enhancements (DH)	3674	E	650 230-2400	18238
Fortinet Inc (HQ)	3577	B	408 235-7700	15231
Fujitsu Optical Co	3229	F	408 746-6000	10306
Fullfillment Systems Inc	2013	D	408 745-7675	458
Gannett Co Inc	2721	E	800 859-2091	5943
Glo-Usa Inc	3674	D	408 598-4400	18251
Gsi Technology Inc (PA)	3674	D	408 331-8800	18258
Guck Ariba	7372	C	650 390-1445	23962
Gulshan International Corp	3674	F	408 745-2000	18260
Harmonic Inc	3663	F	408 542-2500	17532
Hayes Manufacturing Svcs LLC	3544	E	408 730-5035	14061
Health Gorilla Inc (PA)	7372	F	844 446-7455	23970
Hewlett Packard Enterprise Co	7372	F	312 580-9100	23979
High Connection Density Inc	3678	E	408 743-9700	18772
Hologic Inc	3844	C	408 745-0975	22213
Horiba Instruments Inc	3829	D	408 730-4772	21486
Horvath Precision Machining	3599	F	510 683-0810	16035
Hyatt Die Cast Engrg Corp - S	3363	E	408 523-7000	11338
I T M Software Corp	7372	E	650 864-2500	23994
Icad Inc	3061	D	408 419-2300	9264
Igs Inc	3211	F	408 733-4621	10270
Impac Medical Systems Inc (HQ)	7372	E	408 830-8000	24003
Indium Software Inc	7372	C	408 501-8844	24008
Infinera Corporation (PA)	3661	B	408 572-5200	17379
Infinera Corporation	3674	E	408 572-5200	18288
Inktomi Corporation (HQ)	7372	E	650 653-2800	24020
Innovalight Inc	3648	E	408 419-4400	17136
Insilixa Inc	3674	F	408 809-3000	18298
Intella Interventional Systems	3841	D	650 269-1375	21747
Intergen Inc	3699	F	408 245-2737	19327
Intuitive Srgcal Oprations Inc	3841	E	408 523-2100	21751
Intuitive Srgical Holdings LLC (HQ)	3841	F	408 523-2100	21752
Intuitive Surgical Inc	3841	E	408 523-7314	21753
Intuitive Surgical Inc (PA)	3841	C	408 523-2100	21755
Ipolipo Inc	7372	D	408 916-5290	24045
Ismart Alarm Inc	3669	E	408 245-2551	17734
Ivanti Inc	7372	F	408 343-8181	24052
Jsl Partners Inc	2752	F	408 747-9000	6670
Jsr Micro Inc (HQ)	2869	C	408 543-8800	8748
Juniper Networks Inc (PA)	3577	B	408 745-2000	15261
Juniper Networks (us) Inc	3577	A	408 745-2000	15262
Kiana Analytics Inc	7372	F	650 575-3871	24076
Krytar Inc	3679	E	408 734-5999	18980
Kurdex Corporation	3577	F	408 734-8181	15268
Level 5 Networks Inc	3674	E	408 245-9300	18349
Liquid Robotics Inc (HQ)	3714	D	408 636-4200	19704

GEOGRAPHIC

	SIC	EMP	PHONE	ENTRY #
Liquid Robotics Federal Inc	3825	F	408 636-4200	21065
Lockheed Martin (HQ)	3721	E	408 834-9741	19911
Lockheed Martin Corporation	3812	B	408 756-1868	20608
Lockheed Martin Corporation	3761	D	408 756-5751	20449
Lockheed Martin Corporation	3812	E	408 781-8570	20611
Lockheed Martin Corporation	3812	E	408 742-6688	20615
Lockheed Martin Corporation	3761	A	408 742-4321	20451
Lockheed Martin Corporation	3812	E	408 756-5836	20621
Lockheed Martin Corporation	3812	B	408 756-4386	20624
Lockheed Martin Corporation	3812	E	408 742-4321	20625
Logic Technology Inc (PA)	2672	F	408 530-1007	5366
Lotusflare Inc	7372	F	626 695-5634	24109
Luminus Inc (HQ)	3646	C	408 708-7000	17057
Luminus Devices Inc	3648	F	978 528-8000	17143
Lyten Inc	3559	F	650 400-5635	14493
Maxim-Dallas Direct Inc	3674	F	800 659-5909	18376
Mc Liquidation Inc	3845	E	408 636-1020	22278
Medtronic Spine LLC	3841	C	408 548-6500	21813
Meggitt (orange County) Inc	3812	E	408 739-3533	20628
Mellanox Technologies Inc	3674	E	408 970-3400	18381
Mellanox Technologies Inc (HQ)	3674	B	408 970-3400	18382
Meru Networks Inc (HQ)	3669	D	408 215-5300	17746
Mhb Group Inc	2721	E	408 744-1011	5988
Micro Lithography Inc	3823	C	408 747-1769	20903
Microsemi Stor Solutions Inc (DH)	3674	D	408 239-8000	18414
Microsoft Corporation	7372	C	650 693-1009	24159
Microsoft Corporation	3577	C	650 693-4000	15290
Mobile Crossing Inc	3812	F	916 485-2773	20632
Mobileops Corporation	7372	F	408 203-0243	24175
Motorola Mobility LLC	3663	D	847 576-5000	17594
MRr Moulding Industries Inc	2431	F	510 794-8116	4091
Myenersave Inc	7372	F	408 464-6385	24186
Myers-Briggs Company (PA)	2741	D	650 969-8901	6289
N-Tek Inc	3559	E	408 737-8442	14505
Nanostim Inc	3845	F	408 530-0700	22283
Nch Corporation	2819	F	972 438-0211	7511
Netapp Inc (PA)	3572	A	408 822-6000	15061
Nexyn Corporation	3679	F	408 962-0895	19028
Ngcodec Inc	3674	E	408 766-4382	18436
Nordson Med Design & Dev Inc	3841	F	603 707-8753	21840
Northrop Grumman Systems Corp	3721	B	408 735-2241	19917
Northrop Grumman Systems Corp	3721	A	408 735-3011	19920
Nxp Usa Inc	3674	E	408 991-2000	18443
Nxp Usa Inc	3674	E	408 991-2000	18444
Oakmead Prtg & Reproduction	2752	E	408 734-5505	6755
Oepic Semiconductors Inc	3674	E	408 747-0388	18448
Optibase Inc (HQ)	3577	E	800 451-5101	15303
Oracle Corporation	7372	B	650 607-5402	24250
Palm Inc (HQ)	3663	B	408 617-7000	17619
Parallocity Inc	3695	E	408 524-1530	19229
Pcs Machining Service Inc	3599	F	408 735-9974	16288
Pharmacyclics LLC (HQ)	2834	C	408 215-3000	8073
Pictron Inc	7372	F	408 725-8888	24297
PMC-Sierra Us Inc	3674	F	408 239-8000	18471
Polargy Inc	3443	E	408 752-0186	12041
Polystak Inc	3674	F	408 441-1400	18476
Prodigy Press Inc	2759	F	408 962-0396	7184
Pyramid Semiconductor Corp	3674	F	408 542-9430	18487
Qualitek Inc (HQ)	3672	D	408 734-8686	17966
Qualitek Inc	3672	D	408 752-8422	17967
Quanergy Systems Inc (PA)	3812	D	408 245-9500	20677
R2 Semiconductor Inc	3674	E	408 745-7400	18507
Rae Systems Inc (DH)	3829	C	408 952-8200	21529
Rambus Inc (PA)	3674	B	408 462-8000	18508
Rambus Inc	3674	F	408 462-8000	18509
Rank Technology Corp	3572	E	408 737-1488	15085
Raytheon Applied Signal (HQ)	3663	C	408 749-1888	17641
Realization Technologies Inc	7372	E	408 271-1720	24343
Realtime Technologies Inc	3672	F	408 745-6434	17975
Reflex Photonics Inc	3674	F	408 501-8886	18512
Retail Content Service Inc	2741	E	415 890-2097	6330
Samax Precision Inc	3599	E	408 245-9555	16384
Sass Labs Inc	7372	E	404 731-7284	24386
Savi Technology Holdings Inc (PA)	3663	E	650 316-4950	17651
Scigene Corporation	3841	F	408 733-7337	21890
Seagra Technology Inc	3577	E	408 230-8706	15327
Serious Energy Inc (PA)	2531	D	408 541-8000	4872
Sierra Circuits Inc	3672	C	408 735-7137	17998
Sign Solutions Inc	3993	F	408 245-7133	23200
Silicon Electronics (PA)	3674	E	408 738-8236	18543
Silicon Light Machines Corp (DH)	3674	E	408 240-4700	18546
Silk Road Medical Inc	3841	C	408 720-9002	21899
Simplay Labs LLC	3841	E	408 616-4000	21900
Software Motor Company	3621	F	408 601-7781	16674
Spatial Photonics Inc	3674	E	408 940-8800	18575
Spiracur Inc (PA)	3841	D	650 364-1544	21913
St Jude Medical LLC	3841	B	408 738-4883	21915
Stanford Research Systems Inc	3826	C	408 744-9040	21294
Stealth Security Inc	7372	F	844 978-3258	24454
Supertex Inc (HQ)	3674	D	408 222-8888	18596
Supportcom Inc	7372	F	516 393-6759	24471
Surface Engineering Spc	3552	E	408 734-8810	14294
Takex America Inc	3674	E	877 371-2727	18602
Tangome Inc (PA)	3663	E	650 375-2620	17677
Tech-Star Industries Inc	3599	E	650 369-7214	16447
Telechem International Inc (HQ)	3944	E	408 744-1331	22720
Teledyne Technologies Inc	3674	B	408 773-8814	18610
Telepathy Inc	3577	E	408 306-8421	15347
Test Enterprises Inc (PA)	3823	E	408 542-5900	20948
Test Enterprises Inc	3825	E	408 778-0234	21145
Texas Instruments Incorporated	3674	E	408 541-9900	18618
Thomas West Inc (PA)	2392	E	408 481-3850	3645
Thoughtspot Inc	7372	B	800 508-7008	24505
Tipestry Inc	7372	F	650 421-1344	24512
Trane US Inc	3585	C	408 481-3600	15457
Trimble Inc	3812	F	408 481-8490	20734
Trimble Inc (PA)	3829	A	408 481-8000	21559
Trimble Inc	3812	F	408 481-8000	20736
Trimble Military & Advnced Sys	3812	D	408 481-8000	20737
Umc Group(usa)	3674	D	408 523-7800	18632
USI Manufacturing Services Inc	3577	D	408 636-9600	15360
Uvexs Incorporated	2893	F	408 734-4402	8936
V-Tech Manufacturing Inc	3599	F	408 730-9200	16487
Vnomic Inc	7372	F	408 890-2220	24569
Vyakar Inc	7372	F	844 321-5323	24571
Watergush Inc	3272	E	408 524-3074	10667
Way of The World Inc	2759	F	408 616-7700	7266
Westak Inc (PA)	3672	D	408 734-8686	18049
Westak International Sales Inc (HQ)	3672	C	408 734-8686	18050
Zyrion Inc	7372	F	408 524-7424	24610

SUNOL, CA - Alameda County

	SIC	EMP	PHONE	ENTRY #
Cemex Cnstr Mtls PCF LLC	3241	F	925 862-2201	10410
Elliston Vineyards Inc	2084	D	925 862-2377	1688
Ge-Hitachi Nuclear Energy	2819	D	925 862-4382	7498

SUNSET BEACH, CA - Orange County

	SIC	EMP	PHONE	ENTRY #
Duffield Marine Inc	3732	F	949 650-4633	20325

SUSANVILLE, CA - Lassen County

	SIC	EMP	PHONE	ENTRY #
Feather Publishing Company Inc	2711	F	530 257-5321	5633

SUTTER, CA - Sutter County

	SIC	EMP	PHONE	ENTRY #
Butte Sand and Gravel	1442	E	530 755-0225	331

SUTTER CREEK, CA - Amador County

	SIC	EMP	PHONE	ENTRY #
Amador Transit Mix Inc	3273	E	209 223-0406	10687
Ampine LLC	2521	C	209 223-1690	4781
Fuller Manufacturing Inc	3699	F	209 267-5071	19314
Usecb Joint Venture Inc	1041	F	209 267-5594	9

SYLMAR, CA - Los Angeles County

	SIC	EMP	PHONE	ENTRY #
Abbott Laboratories	2834	E	818 493-2388	7709
Acufast Aircraft Products Inc	3728	E	818 365-7077	20004
Advanced Bionics LLC (HQ)	3842	B	661 362-1400	21972
Anthony Doors Inc	3231	B	818 365-9451	10337
Anthony Doors Inc (DH)	3585	A	818 365-9451	15411
Arconic Inc	3334	B	818 367-2261	11182
Atlas Foam Products	3086	F	818 837-3626	9507
Bobbys Metal Finishing	3471	F	818 837-1928	12946
C & G Plastics	3089	E	818 837-3773	9678
C & S Plastics	3089	F	818 896-2489	9680
Capna Fabrication	3556	E	888 416-6777	14353
Circor Aerospace Inc	3429	D	951 270-6200	11579
Clear Image Printing Inc	2752	E	818 547-4684	6487
Cosa Marble Co	1411	F	818 364-8800	291
Cylinder Head Exchange Inc	3714	E	818 364-2371	19628
Deiny Automotive Inc	3711	F	818 362-5865	19465
Dg Engineering Corp (PA)	3812	E	818 364-9024	20570
Drapes 4 Show Inc	2392	E	818 838-0852	3612
Eagle Access Control Systems	3625	E	818 837-7900	16713
European Elegance Woodwork	2431	F	818 570-9401	4043
Fierrito Metal Stamping	3599	E	818 362-6136	15956
Fierritos Inc	3599	E	818 362-6136	15957
Fontal Controls Inc	3599	F	818 833-1127	15966
Gibraltar Plastic Pdts Corp	3089	E	818 365-9318	9804
Goldak Inc	3812	E	818 240-2666	20585
Houston Rubber Co Inc	3069	F	818 899-1108	9319
International Academy of Fin (PA)	2869	F	818 361-7724	8745
ISU Petasys Corp	3672	D	818 833-5800	17904
JW Manufacturing Inc	3452	D	805 498-4594	12684
Kay & James Inc	3599	D	818 998-0357	16109

2020 California
Manufacturers Register

(P-0000) Products & Services Section entry number
(PA)=Parent Co (HQ)=Headquarters (DH)=Div Headquarters

Name	SIC	EMP	PHONE	ENTRY #
L3 Technologies Inc	3812	C	818 833-2500	20596
L3 Technologies Inc	3663	C	818 367-0111	17568
Laser Operations LLC	3674	E	818 986-0000	18343
Leather Pro Inc	3172	E	818 833-8822	10237
Llamas Plastics Inc	3728	C	818 362-0371	20157
Mason Electric Co	3728	B	818 361-3366	20167
MS Aerospace Inc	3452	B	818 833-9095	12686
Mulfat LLC	3571	E	818 367-0149	14954
Orange Bang Inc	2086	E	818 833-1000	2103
Pacesetter Inc (DH)	3845	A	818 362-6822	22295
Pacific Fixture Company Inc	2542	F	818 362-2130	4994
Precise Iron Doors Inc	3442	F	818 338-6269	11975
Professional Finishing Systems	3469	F	818 365-8888	12861
Promex International Plas Inc	3089	F	818 367-5352	9998
Qpc Lasers Inc	3674	F	818 986-0000	18491
Quallion LLC	3692	C	818 833-2000	19181
Ruiz Industries Inc	3172	E	818 582-6882	10243
Seaman Products of California	3728	A	818 361-2012	20229
Second Sight Medical Pdts Inc (PA)	3841	C	818 833-5000	21894
Sierracin Corporation (HQ)	2851	A	818 741-1656	8679
Sierracin/Sylmar Corporation	3089	A	818 362-6711	10056
Spectrolab Inc	3674	B	818 365-4611	18576
Valley Business Printers Inc	2752	D	818 362-7771	6915
Valley-Todeco Inc (DH)	3452	A	800 992-4444	12699
Ventura GL Inc	3281	F	818 890-1886	10937
Wayne Tool & Die Co	3312	E	818 364-1611	11080
Williams Foam Inc	2515	F	818 833-4343	4750
Williams Manufacturing Company	3494	F	818 898-2272	13368

TAFT, CA - Kern County

Name	SIC	EMP	PHONE	ENTRY #
Berry Petroleum Company LLC	1311	E	661 769-8820	25
Dawson Enterprises	1389	F	661 765-2181	188
Gene Watson Construction A CA	1389	A	661 763-5254	201
Harbison-Fischer Inc	1389	E	661 765-7792	205
Jerry Melton & Sons Cnstr	1389	D	661 765-5546	213
Oil-Dri Corporation America	2842	F	661 765-7194	8400
St Louis Post-Dispatch LLC	2711	F	661 763-3171	5839
Taft Production Company	1241	D	661 765-7194	20
TRC Operating Company Inc	1311	F	661 763-0081	72
Watson ME Inc (PA)	1389	F	661 763-5254	280

TAHOE CITY, CA - Placer County

Name	SIC	EMP	PHONE	ENTRY #
James Betts Enterprises Inc	3732	E	530 581-1331	20341
Mount Rose Publishing Co Inc (PA)	2711	F	530 583-3487	5766
Tahoe House Inc	2051	F	530 583-1377	1283

TARZANA, CA - Los Angeles County

Name	SIC	EMP	PHONE	ENTRY #
Akm Fire Inc	3569	E	818 343-8208	14794
Avita Beverage Company Inc (PA)	2086	F	213 477-1979	2042
Cgm Inc	3915	E	818 609-7088	22594
Ggco Inc	3911	E	213 623-3636	22520
Hoffman Magnetics Inc	3695	E	818 717-5095	19219
Ultimatte Corporation	3663	E	818 993-8007	17697
Universal Merchandise Inc	2311	F	818 344-2044	2981

TECATE, CA - San Diego County

Name	SIC	EMP	PHONE	ENTRY #
Benchpro Inc	2599	C	619 478-9400	5052
Broan-Nutone LLC	3433	C	262 673-8795	11692
Formula Plastics Inc	3089	B	866 307-1362	9792
Fusion Product Mfg Inc	3544	D	619 819-5521	14054

TEHACHAPI, CA - Kern County

Name	SIC	EMP	PHONE	ENTRY #
Adaptive Aerospace Corporation	3728	F	661 822-2850	20006
Chemtool Incorporated	2992	F	661 823-7190	9137
GE Wind Energy LLC	3511	C	661 823-6423	13570
Henway Inc	3965	F	661 822-6873	23003
Keller Classics Inc (PA)	2337	E	805 524-1322	3268
Legacy Vulcan LLC	1422	E	661 822-4158	301
Lehigh Southwest Cement Co	3241	C	661 822-4445	10420
Pmrca Inc (PA)	2752	F	661 822-6760	6787
Sierra Technical Services Inc	3324	F	661 823-1092	11168
Stop Staring Designs	2335	E	213 627-1480	3253
Tehachapi News Inc (PA)	2711	F	661 822-6828	5847
Vintage Aero Engines	3732	F	661 822-4107	20361
Ward Automatic Machine Pdts	3451	F	661 822-7543	12659

TEMECULA, CA - Riverside County

Name	SIC	EMP	PHONE	ENTRY #
3-D Precision Machine Inc	3724	E	951 296-5449	19940
Aard Industries Inc	3495	E	951 296-0844	13369
Abbott Laboratories	2834	A	951 914-3000	7710
Abbott Vascular Inc	2834	B	951 941-2400	7713
Abbott Vascular Inc	3841	A	951 914-2400	21573
Advanced Composites Engrg LLC	3089	F	951 694-3055	9612
Applied Statistics & MGT Inc	7372	E	951 699-4600	23613
Artificial Grass Liquidators	3999	E	951 677-3377	23280
ASPE Inc	3555	F	951 296-2595	14316
Axeon Water Technologies	3589	D	760 723-5417	15488

Name	SIC	EMP	PHONE	ENTRY #
Basic Microcom Inc	3625	F	951 708-1268	16703
Bigfogg Inc (PA)	3585	F	951 587-2460	15416
Bomatic Inc (HQ)	3089	E	909 947-3900	9669
Bostik Inc	2891	D	951 296-6425	8858
Brightwater Medical Inc	3841	F	951 290-3410	21644
Callaway Vineyard & Winery	2084	D	951 676-4001	1618
Canadas Finest Foods Inc	2037	D	951 296-1040	906
Carr Pattern Co Inc	3465	F	951 719-1068	12744
Celebration Cellars LLC	2084	F	951 506-5500	1624
Cengage Learning Inc	2731	E	951 719-1878	6083
Channell Commercial Corp (PA)	3661	E	951 719-2600	17354
Chh Lp	2099	F	951 506-5800	2425
Custom Art Services Corp	2752	F	951 302-9889	6526
Dale Chavez Company Inc	3111	F	951 303-0592	10137
Danza Del Sol Winery Inc	2084	F	951 302-6363	1655
Davids Natural Toothpaste	2844	F	949 933-1185	8477
Deans Certified Welding Inc	7692	F	951 676-0242	24629
Designer Sash and Door Sys Inc	3089	D	951 657-4179	9756
Egads LLC	3993	F	951 695-9050	23094
Electro-Support Systems Corp	3679	E	951 676-2751	18898
EMD Millipore Corporation	3826	C	951 676-8080	21224
EMD Millipore Corporation	2836	F	951 676-8080	8296
Empower Software Tech LLC	7372	F	951 672-6257	23856
Falkner Winery Inc	2084	D	951 676-6741	1696
Flowserve Corporation	3561	C	951 296-2464	14575
Garmon Corporation	3999	C	951 296-6308	23340
Generic Manufacturing Corp	3556	F	951 296-2838	14367
Glasswerks La Inc	3211	E	800 729-1324	10264
Gospel Recordings Inc	3652	E	951 719-1650	17325
Griffin Laboratories	3841	F	951 695-6727	21726
Hydro Flow Filtration Sys LLC	3955	F	951 296-0904	22965
Infineon Tech Americas Corp	3577	A	951 375-6008	15246
IPC Industries Inc (PA)	3799	F	951 695-2720	20514
Jwc Carbide Inc	3541	F	714 540-8870	13927
Kamm Industries Inc	3714	F	800 317-6253	19698
Label Productions of Cal	2759	F	951 296-1881	7112
Leonesse Cellars LLC	2084	E	951 302-7601	1800
Long Machine Inc	3599	F	951 296-0194	16151
Lost Dutchmans Minings Assn (DH)	1041	E	951 699-4749	6
Louidar LLC	2084	E	951 676-5047	1805
M & L Haight LLC	3199	E	951 587-2267	10248
MAC Products Inc	3312	D	951 296-3077	11056
Maurice Carrie Winery	2084	E	951 676-1711	1814
Medline Industries Inc	3842	F	951 296-2600	22046
Micro Grow Greenhouse Systems	3822	F	951 296-3340	20798
Mikes Precision Welding Inc	7692	F	951 676-4744	24651
Milgard Manufacturing Inc	3089	F	480 763-6000	9897
Molding Intl & Engrg Inc	3089	D	951 296-5010	9908
Monte De Oro Winery	2084	F	951 491-6551	1822
N C Industries	3599	F	951 296-9603	16236
National Sweetwater Inc	2899	F	951 303-0999	9008
Nimbus Water Systems	3589	F	951 984-2800	15551
North County Times	2711	F	951 676-4315	5783
Offerman Industries	3599	F	951 676-5016	16256
Opti-Forms Inc	3471	D	951 296-1300	13065
Opto 22	3679	C	951 695-3000	19042
Pachunga Gas Station	1389	F	951 506-4575	241
Pacific Barcode Inc	3555	F	951 587-8717	14334
Part Handling Engrg & Dev Corp	3845	F	951 308-4450	22297
Paulson Manufacturing Corp (PA)	3842	D	951 676-2451	22067
Polycraft Inc	2759	F	951 296-0860	7176
Premier Barricades	3499	F	877 345-9700	13539
Qc Manufacturing Inc	3564	D	951 325-6340	14675
Quality Control Solutions Inc	3829	E	951 676-1616	21524
Quicksilver Aeronautics LLC	3721	F	951 506-0061	19926
Ralc Inc	3599	F	951 693-0098	16339
Resina	3579	F	951 296-6585	15391
Robinson Printing Inc	2759	E	951 296-0300	7203
Scotts Temecula Operations LLC (DH)	3524	E	951 719-1700	13695
Source Bio Inc	2835	F	951 676-1000	8260
South Bay Cable Corp	3357	F	951 296-9900	11319
South Coast Winery Inc	2084	E	951 587-9463	1923
Spenco Machine & Manufacturing	3599	F	951 699-5566	16417
Stuart Cellars LLC	2084	F	951 676-6414	1939
Sunstone Components Group Inc (HQ)	3469	E	951 296-5010	12879
Surfacing Solutions Inc	3471	F	951 699-0035	13114
Swanky Prints LLC	2752	F	760 407-9265	6881
Tekvisions Inc (PA)	3829	F	951 506-9709	21552
Telsor Corporation	3825	F	951 296-3066	21138
Temecula Precison Fabrication	3599	F	951 699-4066	16450
Temecula Quality Plating Inc	3559	F	951 296-9875	14544
Temecula T-Shirt Printers Inc	2759	F	951 296-0184	7244
Temecula Valley Winery MGT LLC	2084	D	951 699-8896	1949
The Valley Business Jurnl Inc	2711	F	951 461-0400	5848
Thompson Magnetics Inc	3679	F	951 676-0243	19118

GEOGRAPHIC

	SIC	EMP	PHONE	ENTRY #
Thornton Winery	2084	D	951 699-0099	1956
Top Heavy Clothing Company Inc (PA)	2321	C	951 442-8839	2995
Tortilleria Temecula	2099	F	951 676-5272	2634
Transducer Techniques LLC	3679	E	951 719-3965	19122
TST Molding LLC	3089	E	951 296-6200	10095
TST Water LLC	3589	F	951 541-9517	15595
Tube Form Solutions LLC	3549	F	760 599-5001	14284
USA Solar Technology Inc	3999	F	714 356-8360	23514
Vesta Solutions Inc (DH)	3661	B	951 719-2100	17427
Villlage News Inc	2711	E	760 451-3488	5861
W Plastics Inc	3081	E	800 442-9727	9425
Wiens Cellars LLC	2084	F	951 694-9892	2000
Wilsenergy LLC	3479	F	951 676-7700	13268
Wilson Creek Wnery Vnyards Inc	2084	C	951 699-9463	2002
Wsr Publishing Inc (PA)	2721	C	951 676-4914	6061
Zing Racing Products	3751	F	760 219-4700	20441

TEMPLE CITY, CA - Los Angeles County

	SIC	EMP	PHONE	ENTRY #
Art Microelectronics Corp	3674	F	626 447-7503	18125
B & G Metal Inc	3444	E	626 444-8566	12125
California Flexrake Corp	3423	E	626 443-4026	11523
D D Wire Co Inc (PA)	3441	E	626 442-0459	11781
D D Wire Co Inc	3441	E	626 285-0298	11782
Huang Qi	2335	F	626 442-6808	3230
Iron Shield Inc	3446	F	626 287-4568	12483
Jantek Electronics Inc	3699	F	626 350-4198	19332
Zeeni Inc	2329	F	626 350-1024	3131

TEMPLETON, CA - San Luis Obispo County

	SIC	EMP	PHONE	ENTRY #
Castoro Cellars (PA)	2084	E	805 467-2002	1622
Flash Back USA	2836	F	805 434-0321	8301
JA Wouters Inc	1381	F	805 221-5333	96
Pegasus Med Services/Renalab	2834	F	805 226-8350	8064
Plasvacc USA Inc	2836	F	805 434-0321	8322
Pomar Junction Cellars LLC	2084	F	805 238-9940	1869
Rotta Winery Inc	2084	F	805 237-0510	1898
Turley Wine Cellars	2084	F	805 434-1030	1974

TERRA BELLA, CA - Tulare County

	SIC	EMP	PHONE	ENTRY #
Tuff Stuff Products	2821	B	559 535-5778	7621
Weldcraft Industries	3523	F	559 784-4322	13686

THERMAL, CA - Riverside County

	SIC	EMP	PHONE	ENTRY #
Aggregate Products Inc (PA)	1429	F	760 395-5312	311
Jewel Date Company Inc	2064	E	760 399-4474	1378
Oasis Date Garden Inc	2099	E	760 399-5665	2574
Spates Fabricators Inc	2439	D	760 397-4122	4319
West Coast Aggregate Supply	1442	E	760 342-7598	368

THOUSAND OAKS, CA - Ventura County

	SIC	EMP	PHONE	ENTRY #
Amgen Inc (PA)	2836	A	805 447-1000	8270
Amgen USA Inc (HQ)	2836	D	805 447-1000	8271
Andromeda Software Inc	7372	F	805 379-4109	23600
Atara Biotherapeutics Inc	2836	F	805 309-9534	8274
Base Hockey LP (PA)	3949	F	805 405-3650	22755
Baxalta US Inc	3841	B	805 498-8664	21618
Baxalta US Inc	2834	F	805 375-6807	7788
BEI North America LLC (DH)	3679	F	805 716-0642	18833
Bonafide Management Systems	7372	F	805 777-7666	23685
Carros Sensors Systems Co LLC (DH)	3679	C	805 968-0782	18853
Coach Inc	3171	F	805 496-9933	10219
Custom Sensors & Tech Inc (HQ)	3679	D	805 716-0322	18882
DC Shades & Shutters Awnings	3442	F	818 597-9705	11944
Instacure Healing Products	2834	E	818 222-9600	7953
Kamsut Incorporated	2844	E	805 495-7479	8525
Kavlico Corporation (DH)	3679	A	805 523-2000	18973
Mallinckrodt Inc	3841	F	805 553-9303	21786
Natren Inc	2099	D	805 371-4737	2564
Nexsan Technologies Inc (DH)	3572	E	408 724-9809	15062
Officelocale Inc	2759	E	805 777-8866	7152
Rjw & Assoc	2741	F	818 706-0289	6331
Sensata Technologies Inc	3577	D	805 716-0322	15332
Shrink Wrap Pros LLC	3565	F	805 207-9050	14727
Skymicro Inc	3577	F	805 491-8935	15336
Smiths Interconnect Inc	3679	F	805 267-0100	19084
Teledyne Redlake Masd LLC	3826	E	805 373-4545	21300
Teledyne Technologies Inc (PA)	3679	C	805 373-4545	19111
Thousands Oaks Hand Wash	3589	E	805 379-2732	15591
Xirrus Inc	3823	C	805 262-1600	20959

THOUSAND PALMS, CA - Riverside County

	SIC	EMP	PHONE	ENTRY #
A R Electronics Inc	3679	E	760 343-1200	18805
Apex Interior Source Inc	2431	E	760 343-1919	3994
Calportland	1442	F	760 343-3126	333
Demille Marble & Granite Inc	3281	E	760 341-7525	10904
Koolfog Inc (PA)	3585	F	760 321-9203	15438
Microcool	3823	F	760 322-1111	20904

	SIC	EMP	PHONE	ENTRY #
Pro-Tech Mats Industries Inc	3069	F	760 343-3667	9357
Superior Ready Mix Concrete LP	3273	E	760 343-3418	10855
Therapeutic Industries Inc	3841	F	760 343-2502	21929

THREE RIVERS, CA - Tulare County

	SIC	EMP	PHONE	ENTRY #
Innovative Structural GL Inc	3231	E	559 561-7000	10366

TIPTON, CA - Tulare County

	SIC	EMP	PHONE	ENTRY #
Agnaldos Welding Inc	7692	F	559 752-4254	24615
Mid Valley Milk Co	2026	F	661 721-8419	705

TOLUCA LAKE, CA - Los Angeles County

	SIC	EMP	PHONE	ENTRY #
Gmm Inc	2741	E	323 874-1600	6244
My Burbankcom Inc	2711	F	818 842-2140	5768

TOMALES, CA - Marin County

	SIC	EMP	PHONE	ENTRY #
Blue Mtn Ctr of Meditation Inc	2731	E	707 878-2369	6079

TOPANGA, CA - Los Angeles County

	SIC	EMP	PHONE	ENTRY #
Crashcam Industries Corp	3861	F	310 283-5379	22412

TORRANCE, CA - Los Angeles County

	SIC	EMP	PHONE	ENTRY #
A-Aztec Rents & Sells Inc (PA)	2394	C	310 347-3010	3671
Absolution Brewing Company (PA)	2082	F	310 787-9563	1489
Ace Clearwater Enterprises Inc (PA)	3728	D	310 323-2140	20000
Advanced Chip Magnetics Inc	3677	F	310 370-8188	18695
Advanced Enviromental	3544	E	310 782-9400	14008
Advanced Orthopaedic Solutions	3842	E	310 533-9966	21974
Advanced Tactics Inc	3721	F	310 701-3659	19845
Aero-Electric Connector Inc (PA)	3643	D	310 618-3737	16874
Aeroliant Manufacturing Inc	3599	F	310 257-1903	15710
All Access Stging Prdctons Inc (PA)	3648	D	310 784-2464	17098
Alliedsignal Arospc Svc Corp (HQ)	3369	F	310 323-9500	11408
Alpinestars USA	2326	F	310 891-0222	3023
Altus Positioning Systems Inc	3829	F	310 541-8139	21431
Amag Technology Inc (DH)	3577	E	310 518-2380	15154
American Ultraviolet West Inc	3535	E	310 784-2930	13814
Americas Styrenics LLC	2819	F	424 488-3757	7470
Antcom Corporation	3663	E	310 782-1076	17452
Arconic Inc	3334	B	212 836-2674	11181
Arkema Inc	2812	C	310 214-5327	7383
Asclemed Usa Inc	2834	E	310 218-4146	7770
Asiana Cuisine Enterprises Inc	2099	A	310 327-2223	2397
Aviation and Indus Dev Corp	3081	F	310 373-6057	9394
Bachem Americas Inc (DH)	2836	C	310 784-4440	8280
Bachem Bioscience Inc	2836	E	310 784-7322	8281
Barranca Holdings Ltd	3545	F	310 523-5867	14137
Bel Aire Bridal Inc	2396	E	310 325-8160	3774
Beranek Inc	3728	E	310 328-9094	20057
Bethebeast Inc	7372	E	424 206-1081	23661
Bnl Technologies Inc	3572	E	310 320-7272	15009
Body Care Resort Inc	3634	F	310 328-8888	16825
Boeing Company	3721	A	310 662-7286	19860
BQE Software Inc	7372	D	310 602-4020	23692
Bradshaw Kirchofer Home Furn	2511	F	310 325-0010	4558
Bridge USA Inc	2721	E	310 532-5921	5892
Broadata Communications Inc	3357	F	310 530-1416	11291
Cable Aml Inc (PA)	3663	E	310 222-5599	17475
Calcon Steel Construction	3441	E	310 768-8094	11756
Caleb Technology Corporation	3691	E	310 257-4780	19154
California Silkscreen	2396	F	310 320-5111	3779
Canoo Inc	3711	C	318 849-6327	19462
Carbide Products Co Inc	3291	E	310 320-7910	10943
Carley Inc (PA)	3229	B	310 325-8474	10300
Catalina Pacific Concrete	3273	E	310 532-4600	10705
Caterpillar Inc	3531	F	310 921-9811	13719
Celestron Acquisition LLC	3827	D	310 328-9560	21341
Celestron LLC	3827	F	310 328-9560	21342
Celprogen Inc	2836	F	310 542-8822	8285
Century Parts Inc	3599	F	310 328-0281	15834
Classic Litho & Design Inc	2752	E	310 224-5200	6486
Coast/Dvnced Chip Mgnetics Inc	3677	F	310 370-8188	18706
Conesys Inc (PA)	3678	D	310 618-3737	18756
Conesys Inc	3678	F	310 212-0065	18757
Convaid Products Inc	3842	D	310 618-0111	21995
Counter	3131	E	310 406-3300	10149
Creative Pathways Inc	3548	E	310 530-1965	14239
D Goldenwest Inc	2051	E	310 564-2641	1184
Dasco Engineering Corp	3728	C	310 326-2277	20083
Data Linkage Software Inc	7372	F	310 781-3056	23801
Diamond K2	3425	E	310 539-6116	11551
Diamotec Inc	3545	F	310 539-4994	14154
Dicaperl Corporation (DH)	1499	D	610 667-6640	386
Digi Group LLC	3663	F	800 521-8467	17501
Donovan Engineering Corp	3714	F	310 320-3772	19639
Doug Mockett & Company Inc	2511	E	310 318-2491	4565
Dreamgear LLC	3944	E	310 222-5522	22670

Mergent email: customerrelations@mergent.com
1438

2020 California
Manufacturers Register

(P-0000) Products & Services Section entry number
(PA)=Parent Co (HQ)=Headquarters (DH)=Div Headquarters

Company	SIC	EMP	PHONE	ENTRY #
E H Publishing Inc	2721	E	310 533-2400	5928
Eai-Jr286 Inc	3949	F	310 297-6400	22794
Edelbrock LLC (HQ)	3751	B	310 781-2222	20398
Edelbrock Holdings Inc	3714	C	310 781-2290	19644
Efi Technology Inc	3714	E	310 793-2505	19646
Elements	3911	E	310 781-1384	22516
Ely Co Inc	3599	E	310 539-5831	15928
EMI Holding Inc (HQ)	2834	F	310 214-0065	7878
Emmaus Medical Inc (DH)	2834	F	310 214-0065	7879
Emp Connectors Inc	3643	E	310 533-6799	16897
Encore Image Group Inc (PA)	3993	D	310 534-7500	23098
Escape Communications Inc	3663	F	310 997-1300	17515
Excelpro Inc (PA)	2022	F	323 415-8544	550
Express Folding	2741	E	310 316-6762	6232
Family Medicine Center Torr	2834	F	310 326-8600	7888
FCkingston Co	3491	D	310 326-8287	13305
Field Manufacturing Corp (PA)	2542	E	310 781-9292	4977
Fischer Cstm Cmmunications Inc (PA)	3825	F	310 303-3300	21038
Five-Star Graphics Inc	2752	F	310 325-6881	6575
Forrester Eastland Corporation	3999	E	310 784-2464	23335
G F Cole Corporation (PA)	3053	F	310 320-0601	9231
Gc Aero Inc	3433	F	310 539-7600	11697
General Dynmics Stcom Tech Inc	3663	D	310 539-6704	17524
General Forming Corporation	3444	E	310 326-0624	12221
George P Johnson Company	3993	D	310 965-4300	23121
Gizmac Accessories LLC	3577	F	310 320-5563	15235
Global Comm Semiconductors LLC (HQ)	3674	F	310 530-7274	18252
Global Micro Solutions Inc	7372	F	310 218-5678	23944
Goeppner Industries Inc	3599	F	310 784-2800	15998
Hall Associates Racg Pdts Inc	3799	F	310 326-4111	20512
Heidelberg Instruments Inc	3555	F	310 212-5071	14325
Hewitt Industries Los Angeles	3823	E	714 891-9300	20883
Hi-Shear Corporation (DH)	3452	A	310 784-4025	12680
HI-Shear Corporation	3429	E	310 326-8110	11595
Honeywell International Inc	3724	A	310 323-9500	19956
Honeywell International Inc	3663	D	310 618-2140	17537
Hugo Engineering Co Inc	3728	F	310 320-0288	20128
I Color Printing & Mailing Inc	2752	F	310 947-1452	6621
Image Apparel Inc	2326	E	310 464-8991	3038
Inaba Foods (usa) Inc	2047	F	310 818-2270	1075
Industrial Dynamics Co Ltd (PA)	3559	C	310 325-5633	14478
Industrial Gasket and Sup Co	3053	E	310 530-1771	9237
Intellisense Systems Inc	3812	C	310 320-1827	20588
Irtronix Inc	3641	F	310 787-1100	16865
J & A Shoe Company Inc	3144	C	310 324-0139	10171
J-T E C H	3678	C	310 533-6700	18776
Japan Graphics Corp	2752	E	310 222-8639	6661
Jci Jones Chemicals Inc	2812	E	310 523-1629	7390
Just For Fun	2321	E	310 320-1327	2992
Kabushiki Kisha Higuchi Shokai	3645	F	310 212-7234	16973
Kakuichi America Inc	3084	D	310 539-1590	9471
KB Delta Inc	3469	E	310 530-1539	12830
Keller Engineering Inc	3599	E	310 326-6291	16112
Kepner Plas Fabricators Inc	3089	E	310 325-3162	9865
Keysource Foods LLC	2091	E	310 879-4888	2245
Kopykake Enterprises Inc (PA)	3469	F	310 373-8906	12836
Koto Inc	3942	F	310 327-7359	22648
L3 Electron Devices Inc (DH)	3671	A	310 517-6000	17787
L3 Technologies Inc	3663	B	650 591-8411	17561
La Ejuice LLC	2131	E	310 531-3888	2661
Label Service Inc	2672	E	310 329-5605	5365
Laserod Technologies LLC	3699	E	310 328-5869	19344
Ledtronics Inc	3674	C	310 534-1505	18348
Lee Brothers Truck Body Inc	3713	F	310 532-7980	19540
Lenntek Corporation	3663	E	310 534-2738	17571
Lg Nanoh2o Inc	2899	E	424 218-4000	8989
Libra Cable Technologies Inc	3679	F	310 618-8182	18989
Lisi Aerospace North Amer Inc	3324	A	310 326-8110	11160
Loma Scientific International	3663	E	310 539-8655	17575
Lshuver Inc	2752	F	310 323-2326	6710
Luminit LLC (PA)	3827	E	310 320-1066	21377
Lyncole Grunding Solutions LLC	3643	E	310 214-4000	16915
Lynn Products Inc	3577	A	310 530-5966	15279
M2 Marketplace Inc	3571	F	310 354-3600	14938
Magnetic Component Engrg Inc (PA)	3499	D	310 784-3100	13531
Magnetron Power Inventions Inc	1382	F	310 462-6970	130
Mahmood Izadi Inc	3569	F	310 325-0463	14836
Marcea Inc	2339	F	213 746-5191	3368
Medianews Group Inc	2711	C	310 540-5511	5742
Medical Chemical Corporation	2899	E	310 787-6800	8998
Medicool Inc	3841	F	310 782-2200	21800
Mega Precision O Rings Inc	3599	F	310 530-1166	16192
Messer LLC	2813	E	310 533-8394	7422
Metro Truck Body Incorporated	3713	F	310 532-5570	19546
Metromedia Technologies Inc	3577	E	818 552-6500	15288
Michael BS LLC	2032	E	310 320-0141	739
Microcosm Inc	3764	E	310 219-2700	20465
Micronova Manufacturing Inc	2392	E	310 784-6990	3627
Milo Machining Inc	3599	F	310 530-0925	16210
Mistras Group Inc	3829	E	310 793-7173	21509
Mk Diamond Products Inc (PA)	3546	C	310 539-5221	14225
Momentum Management LLC	3069	F	310 329-2599	9339
Monterey Graphics Inc	2752	F	310 787-3370	6736
Moog Inc	3625	B	310 533-1178	16733
Moog Inc	3812	B	310 533-1178	20635
Morinaga Nutritional Foods Inc	2099	F	310 787-0200	2557
Motoart LLC	3299	E	310 375-4531	11014
Motorcar Parts of America Inc (PA)	3714	A	310 212-7910	19724
National Law Digest Inc	2731	E	310 791-9975	6126
Naturalife Eco Vite Labs	2023	D	310 370-1563	608
Navcom Technology Inc (HQ)	3663	E	310 381-2000	17600
Nearfield Systems Inc	3825	D	310 525-7000	21087
Neko World Inc	3944	E	301 649-1188	22697
Nothing To Wear Inc (PA)	2331	E	310 328-0408	3186
O K Color America Corporation	3089	F	310 320-9343	9940
Obatake Inc	3911	E	310 782-2730	22556
Omicron Engineering Inc	3599	F	310 328-4017	16260
One Touch Solutions Inc	3555	F	310 320-6868	14333
Onshore Technologies Inc	3679	E	310 533-4888	19040
Pacific Wave Systems Inc	3663	D	714 893-0152	17617
Pasco Corporation of America	2038	E	503 289-6500	975
Pbf Energy Inc	2911	F	310 212-2800	9060
Pelican Products Inc (PA)	3648	B	310 326-4700	17154
Phenomenex Inc (HQ)	3826	C	310 212-0555	21275
Photo Sciences Incorporated (PA)	3577	E	310 634-1500	15307
Phyn LLC	3823	E	310 400-4001	20919
Pioneer Speakers Inc (DH)	3651	E	310 952-2000	17272
Plasma Technology Incorporated (PA)	3479	D	310 320-3373	13226
Pmp Products Inc	3161	E	310 549-5122	10203
Praxair Distribution Inc	2813	D	310 371-1254	7449
Precision Fiberglass Products	3644	E	310 539-7470	16953
Prestone Products Corporation	2899	E	424 271-4836	9017
Probe Racing Components Inc	3592	E	310 784-2977	15616
Products Engineering Corp (PA)	3423	D	310 787-4500	11541
Proprietary Controls Systems	3829	E	310 303-3600	21523
Pulse Instruments	3825	E	310 515-5330	21105
Quality Forming LLC	3728	D	310 539-2855	20208
Quantum Chromodynamics Inc	2759	F	310 329-5000	7189
Ralph E Ames Machine Works	3599	E	310 328-8523	16340
Rapiscan Systems Inc (HQ)	3844	C	310 978-1457	22221
Retail Print Media Inc	2759	E	424 488-6950	7198
Reyes Coca-Cola Bottling LLC	2086	C	310 965-2653	2156
Roberts Research Laboratory	3489	E	310 320-7310	13284
Robinson Helicopter Co Inc	3721	A	310 539-0508	19928
Rock-Ola Manufacturing Corp	3651	D	310 328-1306	17277
RR Donnelley & Sons Company	2759	A	310 516-3100	7205
Rtg Inc	3674	E	310 534-3016	18521
Sage Goddess Inc	3911	E	650 733-6639	22566
Sanko Electronics America Inc (HQ)	3714	F	310 618-1677	19763
Santan Software Systems Inc	7372	E	310 836-2802	24380
Santec Inc	3432	E	310 542-0063	11681
Scientific Repair Inc	3823	F	310 214-5092	20934
Sharp Industries Inc (PA)	3542	E	310 370-5990	13994
Shaver Specialty Coinc	3556	E	310 370-6941	14400
Shine Food Inc (PA)	2032	E	310 329-3829	745
Shine Food Inc	2038	E	310 533-6010	980
Showerdoordirect LLC	3444	D	310 327-8060	12378
Sii Semiconductor USA Corp	3674	F	310 517-7771	18542
Sirena Incorporated	2759	F	866 548-5353	7215
Skyway Signs LLC	3993	F	505 401-5270	23212
Southern California Ice Co	2097	F	310 325-1040	2363
Stewart Filmscreen Corp (PA)	3861	C	310 326-1422	22458
Storm Industries Inc (PA)	3523	D	310 534-5232	13673
Storm Manufacturing Group Inc	3491	D	310 326-8287	13323
Student Sports	2273	F	310 791-1142	2881
Sure Power Inc	3679	E	310 542-8561	19098
System Technical Support Corp	3625	E	310 845-9400	16759
Takane USA Inc (HQ)	3873	E	310 212-1411	22485
Tcw Trends Inc	2339	F	310 533-5177	3422
Team Inc	3398	D	310 514-2312	11471
Technical Devices Company	3548	E	310 618-8437	14257
Teledyne Defense Elec LLC	3679	F	310 823-5491	19105
Teledyne Defense Elec LLC	3679	C	310 823-5491	19106
Topper Manufacturing Corp	3589	F	310 375-5000	15593
Torrance Refining Company LLC	2911	A	310 483-6900	9076
Torrance Steel Window Co Inc	3442	E	310 328-9181	11988
Torrence Trading Inc	3944	E	310 649-1188	22721
Totex Manufacturing Inc	3089	D	310 326-2028	10089
Ubst Inc	2331	F	424 222-9908	3203
Union Carbide Corporation	2631	D	310 214-5300	5176

GEOGRAPHIC

	SIC	EMP	PHONE	ENTRY #
Universal Cushion Company Inc **(PA)**	2392	E	323 887-8000	3647
Universal Imaging Tech Inc	3955	F	310 961-2098	22974
Universal Screw Products Inc	3451	E	310 371-1170	12657
US Hybrid Corporation **(PA)**	3714	E	310 212-1200	19795
Vaporbrothers Inc	3634	F	310 618-1188	16842
Varedan Technologies LLC	3625	F	310 542-2320	16764
Verilogix Inc	7372	F	310 527-5100	24554
Virco Mfg Corporation **(PA)**	2531	B	310 533-0474	4876
Watts Liquidation Corporation	2269	F	310 328-5999	2863
William Bounds Ltd	3556	E	310 375-0505	14414
Winther Technologies Inc **(PA)**	3548	E	310 618-8437	14260
Woodsource International	2435	F	310 328-9663	4284
Younger Mfg Co **(PA)**	3851	B	310 783-1533	22397
Z C & R Coating For Optics Inc	3827	F	310 381-3060	21423

TRABUCO CANYON, CA - Orange County

	SIC	EMP	PHONE	ENTRY #
R B S Inc	3577	F	949 766-2924	15315
Xpert Marketing Group Inc	3993	E	949 309-6300	23246

TRACY, CA - San Joaquin County

	SIC	EMP	PHONE	ENTRY #
A & A Ready Mixed Concrete Inc	3273	F	209 830-5070	10670
A Teichert & Son Inc	1442	E	209 832-4150	322
American Custom Meats LLC	2013	D	209 839-8800	437
American Trck Trlr Bdy Co Inc **(PA)**	3713	E	209 836-8985	19517
Ameron International Corp	3494	C	209 836-5050	13345
Aubin Industries Inc	3087	F	800 324-0051	9579
Barbosa Cabinets Inc	2434	B	209 836-2501	4167
Basalite Building Products LLC	3271	C	209 833-3670	10502
Bescal Inc	3272	E	209 836-3492	10536
C C T Laser Services Inc	3699	F	209 833-1110	19268
Cemex Cnstr Mtls PCF LLC	3273	C	209 835-1454	10714
Clear Skies Solutions Inc	3822	F	925 570-4471	20788
Clonetab Inc	7372	E	209 292-5663	23749
Consolidated Container Co LLC	3089	C	209 820-1700	9721
Dave Humphrey Enterprises Inc	3531	F	209 835-2222	13726
Drilling & Trenching Sup Inc **(PA)**	3545	F	510 895-1650	14156
Dynatect Ro-Lab Inc	3061	F	262 786-1500	9263
Encompass Dist Svcs LLC	3674	F	925 249-0988	18216
Feral Productions LLC	3599	E	510 791-5392	15954
Finis Inc **(PA)**	3949	E	925 454-0111	22800
Fuel Injection Corporation	3714	F	925 371-6551	19664
Future Foam Inc	3086	F	209 832-1886	9541
Gloriann Farms Inc	3086	C	209 221-7121	9546
Golden State Vintners **(PA)**	2084	F	707 254-4900	1726
Green Soap Inc	2841	F	925 240-5546	8341
Hand Crfted Dutchman Doors Inc	2431	E	209 833-7378	4054
Katerra Inc	2439	B	623 236-5322	4312
Kraft Heinz Foods Company	2032	E	209 832-4269	734
Leprino Foods Company	2022	B	209 835-8340	563
Lockheed Martin Corporation	3721	B	408 756-3008	19912
Lynx Enterprises Inc	3444	D	209 833-3400	12271
Madruga Iron Works Inc	3441	F	209 832-7003	11834
Medina Wood Products Inc	2448	F	209 832-4523	4381
Mission Bell Mfg Co Inc	2434	E	209 229-7280	4226
Moore Epitaxial Inc	3559	E	209 833-0100	14500
Mother Lode Plas Molding Inc	3089	F	209 532-5146	9914
Nq Engineering Inc	3599	F	209 836-3255	16250
Nwpc LLC	3443	D	209 836-5050	12034
Olive Musco Products Inc **(PA)**	2033	B	209 836-4600	812
Omega Precision Machine	3599	E	209 833-6502	16259
Owens-Illinois Inc	3221	C	209 652-1311	10291
Pallet Recovery Service Inc	2448	F	209 496-5074	4389
Polycom Inc	3661	A	209 830-5083	17401
Process Specialties Inc	3674	F	209 832-1344	18481
Professional McHy Group Inc	3553	F	209 832-0100	14299
Ranks Big Data	2399	C	510 830-6926	3854
Rich Chicks LLC **(PA)**	2015	E	209 879-4104	527
RMC Pacific Materials Inc	3241	E	209 835-1454	10428
San-I-Pak Pacific Inc	3443	E	209 836-2310	12050
Surtec Inc	2842	E	209 820-3700	8421
Synnex Corporation	3571	F	510 656-3333	14983
Teledyne Risi **(HQ)**	2892	E	925 456-9700	8907
Top Shelf Manufacturing LLC	3841	F	209 834-8185	21934
Tracy Press Inc	2711	F	209 835-3030	5851
W R Grace & Co	2819	C	209 839-2800	7537
West Coast Cryogenics Inc	3559	E	800 657-0545	14556
Western Pllet Sup Lgistics LLC	2448	F	209 836-1968	4407

TRANQUILLITY, CA - Fresno County

	SIC	EMP	PHONE	ENTRY #
AG Spraying	3499	F	559 698-9507	13494

TRAVER, CA - Tulare County

	SIC	EMP	PHONE	ENTRY #
Maf Industries Inc **(HQ)**	3565	D	559 897-2905	14717

TRAVIS AFB, CA - Solano County

	SIC	EMP	PHONE	ENTRY #
Boeing Company	3721	A	707 437-8574	19877

TRONA, CA - San Bernardino County

	SIC	EMP	PHONE	ENTRY #
Searles Valley Minerals Inc	1479	A	760 372-2259	380

TRUCKEE, CA - Nevada County

	SIC	EMP	PHONE	ENTRY #
A Teichert & Son Inc	1442	E	530 587-3811	321
Acureo Inc	7372	F	530 550-8801	23557
Horvath Holdings Inc	2241	F	530 587-4700	2754
Moonshine Ink	2711	E	530 587-3607	5760
Mount Rose Publishing Co Inc	2711	F	530 587-6061	5765
Recycled Spaces Inc	2519	F	530 587-3394	4772
Sierra Asset Servicing LLC	1389	F	530 582-7300	263

TUJUNGA, CA - Los Angeles County

	SIC	EMP	PHONE	ENTRY #
David Kopf Instruments	3841	E	818 352-3274	21678
Kenneth Cronon Inc	2361	F	818 632-4972	3480
Nic Protection Inc	3645	F	818 249-2539	16981

TULARE, CA - Tulare County

	SIC	EMP	PHONE	ENTRY #
Carl & Irving Printers Inc	2752	F	559 686-8354	6473
Dean Foods Company	2026	E	559 687-1927	695
Dowdys Sales and Services	3523	F	559 688-6973	13628
Fisher Manufacturing Co Inc **(PA)**	3432	E	559 685-5200	11667
Gannett Co Inc	2711	C	559 688-0521	5637
Golden Valley Dairy Products	2022	C	559 687-1188	552
High Sierra Truss Company Inc	2439	F	559 688-6611	4306
Kirby Manufacturing Inc	3523	F	559 686-1571	13645
Land OLakes Inc	2022	D	559 687-8287	560
Langston Companies Inc	2674	E	559 688-3839	5440
Russell Kc & Son	3523	F	559 686-3236	13667
Saputo Cheese USA Inc	2022	B	559 687-8411	573
Saputo Cheese USA Inc	2022	C	559 687-9999	574
Stainless Works Inc	7692	F	559 688-4310	24668
Westrock Cp LLC	2653	D	559 685-1102	5277
Whitten Machine Shop	3599	F	559 686-3428	16525

TULELAKE, CA - Siskiyou County

	SIC	EMP	PHONE	ENTRY #
Organic Horseradish Co	2035	E	530 664-3862	893

TURLOCK, CA - Stanislaus County

	SIC	EMP	PHONE	ENTRY #
Adtek Inc	3441	E	209 634-0300	11734
Arthur P Lamarre & Sons Inc	3444	F	209 667-6557	12115
Big Valley Pallet	2448	E	209 632-7687	4351
Blue Diamond Growers	2099	D	209 604-1501	2408
Cal-Coast Dairy Systems Inc	3523	E	209 634-9026	13617
California Dairies Inc	2021	D	209 656-1942	537
Clausen Meat Company Inc	2011	E	209 667-8690	403
Coast Wood Preserving Inc **(PA)**	2491	E	209 632-9931	4475
Dairy Farmers America Inc	2022	D	209 667-9627	546
Darling Ingredients Inc	2077	F	209 620-7267	1459
Donald H Binkley	3441	F	209 664-9792	11786
Formax Technologies Inc	3699	E	209 668-1001	19312
Foster Poultry Farms	2015	D	209 668-5922	514
Fusion 360 Inc	2836	F	209 632-0139	8303
Golden State Mixing Inc	2026	E	209 632-3656	701
Hilmar Cheese Company Inc	2022	D	209 667-6076	554
Honeywell International Inc	3724	A	209 480-6733	19960
Jackson-Mitchell Inc **(PA)**	2026	E	209 667-0786	704
JDM Properties	2869	E	209 632-0616	8746
Kozy Shack Enterprises LLC	2099	D	209 634-2131	2500
Lock-N-Stitch Inc	3545	E	209 632-2345	14168
Neogen Corporation	2842	E	209 664-1683	8399
Nordic Saw & Tool Mfrs	3425	E	209 634-9015	11554
P & F Machine Inc	3599	F	209 667-2515	16267
Pernstner Sons Fabrication Inc	3498	E	209 345-2430	13480
Purina Animal Nutrition LLC	2048	F	209 634-9101	1119
RJ Mfg	2298	F	209 632-9708	2915
Rm Pallets Inc	2448	F	209 632-9887	4396
Rootlieb Inc	3465	F	209 632-2203	12747
Seegers Industries Inc	2752	F	209 667-2750	6857
Sensient Ntral Ingredients LLC **(HQ)**	2034	D	209 667-2777	862
Sunrise Bakery	2051	F	209 632-9400	1280
Super Store Industries	2024	F	209 668-2100	669
Turlock Cabinet Shop Inc	2434	F	209 632-1311	4256
Turlock Journal	2711	F	209 634-9141	5854
Volk Enterprises Inc	3496	D	209 632-3826	13443
Vue-Temp Inc **(PA)**	2015	D	209 634-2914	530

TUSTIN, CA - Orange County

	SIC	EMP	PHONE	ENTRY #
Abcron Corporation	3651	F	714 730-9988	17179
Add-On Computer Peripheral Inc	3577	C	949 546-8200	15146
Adel Park LLC	3531	E	213 321-2030	13701
Aegis Principia LLC	3999	F	714 731-2283	23266
Alldigital Holdings Inc	7372	F	949 250-7340	23596
Alphabet Lighting	3646	F	714 259-0990	17009
Anajet LLC	3555	E	714 662-3200	14314
Apx Technology Corporation	3545	F	714 838-8501	14133
Avid Bioservices Inc **(PA)**	2834	C	714 508-6000	7782

Mergent email: customerrelations@mergent.com
1440

2020 California
Manufacturers Register

(P-0000) Products & Services Section entry number
(PA)=Parent Co (HQ)=Headquarters (DH)=Div Headquarters

Company	SIC	EMP	PHONE	ENTRY #
Baf Industries (PA)	2842	E	714 258-8055	8366
Bar None Inc	2085	F	714 259-8450	2009
Belts By Simon Inc	2387	D	714 573-0303	3527
Bernhardt & Bernhardt Inc	3541	F	714 544-0708	13904
Bjb Enterprises Inc	2821	E	714 734-8450	7545
Braxton Caribbean Mfg Co Inc	3469	D	714 508-3570	12774
Ces Electronics Mfg Inc	3999	F	714 505-3441	23303
CM Brewing Technologies LLC	3589	F	888 391-9990	15502
Compass Water Solutions Inc (PA)	3589	E	949 222-5777	15504
Corcen Data International Inc	7372	F	714 251-6110	23776
Country House	2064	F	714 505-8988	1362
Custom Quilting Inc	2392	E	714 731-7271	3611
Design West Technologies Inc	3089	D	714 731-0201	9755
Distribution Electrnics Vlued	3699	F	714 368-1717	19291
Diversified Printers Inc	2741	D	714 994-3400	6222
Do Well Laboratories Inc	2023	F	949 252-0001	585
Doublesight Displays Inc	3577	F	949 253-1535	15218
Durabag Company Inc	2673	D	714 259-8811	5394
Epinex Diagnostics Inc	3841	E	949 660-7770	21707
Expert Assembly Services Inc	3672	E	714 258-8880	17872
Fashion Camp	2299	E	714 259-0946	2934
Freeze Tag Inc (PA)	7372	F	714 210-3850	23920
GL Woodworking Inc	2499	D	949 515-2192	4504
Hall Research Technologies LLC (PA)	3577	E	714 641-6607	15237
Henrys Adio Vsual Slutions Inc	3651	E	714 258-7238	17240
Ifiber Optix Inc	3229	E	714 665-9796	10311
Ii-VI Optical Systems Inc	3827	D	714 247-7100	21363
Innovative Diversfd Tech Inc	3572	E	949 455-1701	15048
Intepro America LP (PA)	3825	E	714 953-2686	21054
Interplex Nascal Inc	3469	D	714 505-2900	12823
JI Design Enterprises Inc	2321	E	714 479-0240	2991
Jmp Electronics Inc	3672	F	714 730-2086	17909
Keithco Manufacturing Inc	3599	F	714 258-8933	16110
Landscape Communications Inc	2721	E	714 979-5276	5973
LGarde Inc	3572	E	714 259-0771	15052
Lund Motion Products Inc	3714	E	949 221-0023	19708
Make Beverage Holdings LLC	2599	E	949 923-8238	5072
Meridian Graphics Inc	2752	D	949 833-3500	6724
Millenworks	3711	E	949 426-5500	19487
MTI Technology Corporation (PA)	3572	C	949 251-1101	15060
Myvoicecig LLC	2741	F	714 702-6006	6290
Oak Tree Furniture Inc	2511	D	562 944-0754	4600
Oracle Corporation	7372	C	713 654-0919	24248
Palpilot International Corp	3672	E	714 460-0718	17950
Paper Group Company LLC	2621	E	714 566-0025	5142
Planet Plexi Corp	3089	F	949 206-1183	9964
Portellus Inc	7372	D	949 250-9600	24308
Precision Offset Inc	2752	E	949 752-1714	6791
Prestige Foil Inc	2759	F	714 556-1431	7180
Priority Posting and Pubg Inc	2741	E	714 338-2568	6316
Pvp Advanced Eo Systems Inc	3827	E	714 508-2740	21400
Raj Manufacturing LLC	2339	F	714 838-3110	3397
Ricoh Electronics Inc (DH)	3861	B	714 566-2500	22455
Ronco Plastics Incorporated	3089	E	714 259-1385	10023
Saf-T-Kut LLC	3541	E	657 210-4426	13950
Staar Surgical Company	3851	E	626 303-7902	22391
Strata Technologies	3629	E	714 368-9785	16803
Stuart-Dean Co Inc	3471	F	714 544-4460	13109
Sunny America & Global Autotec	3714	D	714 544-0400	19774
Systems Printing Inc	2791	F	714 832-4677	7362
Terumo Americas Holding Inc	3826	C	714 258-8001	21301
Texas Instruments Incorporated	3674	C	714 731-7110	18620
Thermeon Corporation (PA)	7372	F	714 731-9191	24501
Tivoli LLC	3641	F	714 957-6101	16869
Trelleborg Sealing Solutions (DH)	3841	C	714 415-0280	21936
TRT Bsness Ntwrk Solutions Inc	3825	F	714 380-3888	21151
Vitabest Nutrition Inc	2834	B	714 832-9700	8182
Wellprint Inc	2752	F	714 838-3962	6930
Werner Systems Inc	3355	F	714 838-4444	11269

UKIAH, CA - Mendocino County

Company	SIC	EMP	PHONE	ENTRY #
American Bottling Company	2086	F	707 462-8871	2026
B J Embroidery & Screenprint	2395	F	707 463-2767	3724
BJs Ukiah Embroidery	2759	F	707 463-2767	7000
Cal Nor Powder Coating Inc	3479	F	707 462-0217	13152
California Leisure Products	2452	F	707 462-2106	4458
Cold Creek Compost Inc	2875	F	707 485-5966	8812
Constellation Brands Inc	2084	E	707 467-4840	1646
Evden Enterprises Inc	3599	F	707 462-0375	15938
Liqua-Tech Corporation	3824	F	800 659-3556	20971
Maverick Enterprises Inc	3353	C	707 463-5591	11222
McNab Ridge Winery LLC	2084	F	707 462-2423	1815
Nelson & Sons Inc	2084	F	707 463-3755	1838
North Cal Wood Products Inc	2421	F	707 462-0686	3939
Pamelas Products Incorporated	2051	D	707 462-6605	1256
Parducci Wine Estates LLC	2084	E	707 463-5350	1857

Company	SIC	EMP	PHONE	ENTRY #
Performance Coatings Inc	2851	E	707 462-3023	8662
Peter Pugger Manufacturing	3531	F	707 463-1333	13741
Plc LLC	2084	F	707 462-2423	1868
Rebol Technologies Inc	7372	F	707 485-0599	24348
Reliable Mill Supply Co	3312	F	707 462-1458	11065
Retech Systems LLC	3433	C	707 462-6522	11711
Ukiah Brewing Co LLC	2082	E	707 468-5898	1572
Waneshear Technologies LLC	3553	E	707 462-4761	14301

UNION CITY, CA - Alameda County

Company	SIC	EMP	PHONE	ENTRY #
Abaxis Inc (HQ)	3829	C	510 675-6500	21426
Aei Electech Corp	3679	F	510 489-5088	18811
Airgas Usa LLC	2813	D	510 429-4200	7404
Ajax - Untd Pttrns & Molds Inc	3089	C	510 476-8000	9615
Alvarado Dye & Knitting Mill	2326	F	510 324-8892	3024
American Licorice Company	2064	B	510 487-5500	1355
Ariat International Inc (PA)	3199	C	510 477-7000	10245
Ate Micrographics Inc	3826	F	510 475-5882	21177
Axis Group Inc	3674	F	510 487-7393	18139
Axygen Inc (HQ)	3089	E	510 494-8900	9647
Azimuth Industrial Co Inc	3674	E	510 441-6000	18142
Bakemark USA LLC	2099	E	510 487-8188	2398
Bay Central Printing Inc	2752	F	510 429-9111	6439
Blc Wc Inc	3565	E	510 489-5400	14699
Blc Wc Inc	2672	E	510 471-4100	5358
Blommer Chocolate Co Cal Inc	2066	C	510 471-4300	1407
Blommer Chocolate Company	2064	E	510 471-3401	1357
California Performance Packg	3086	B	909 390-4422	9511
Caravan Bakery Inc	2051	E	510 487-2600	1174
Caravan Trading Company	2051	E	510 487-8090	1175
Chinese Overseas Mktg Svc Corp	2741	E	510 476-0880	6213
Cmy Image Corporation	2752	F	510 516-6668	6489
Compro Packaging LLC	2653	E	510 475-0118	5211
Conklin & Conklin Incorporated	3452	E	510 489-5500	12673
Dawn Food Products Inc	2051	E	510 487-9007	1185
Deep Foods Inc	2052	F	510 475-1900	1313
Delta Yimin Technologies Inc	3089	E	510 487-4411	9751
Electrochem Solutions Inc	3471	F	510 476-1840	12994
Electrochem Solutions LLC	3471	D	510 476-1840	12995
Enersys	3691	F	510 887-8080	19159
Farallon Brands Inc (PA)	2392	E	510 550-4299	3616
Finelite Inc (PA)	3646	C	510 441-1100	17035
Fricke-Parks Press Inc	2752	C	510 489-6543	6585
Gcm Medical & Oem Inc	3444	D	510 475-0404	12220
Heco Pacific Manufacturing	3535	E	510 487-1155	13825
Hongene Biotech Corporation	2836	F	650 520-9678	8309
Ichor Systems Inc	3089	C	510 476-8000	9833
Jenson Mechanical Inc	3599	E	510 429-8078	16079
Knorr Brake Company LLC	3743	F	510 475-0770	20372
Korea Central Daily News	2711	F	213 368-2500	5683
La Terra Fina Usa Inc	2099	D	510 404-5888	2515
Lam Research Corporation	3559	D	510 572-2186	14488
Lamart California Inc	3296	E	973 772-6262	10988
Lamart Corporation	3292	C	510 489-8100	10963
Lane International Trading Inc (PA)	3143	D	510 489-7364	10159
M and M Cabinets Inc	2434	F	510 324-4034	4222
Mas Metals Inc	3446	F	510 259-1426	12497
Mizuho Orthopedic Systems Inc (HQ)	3841	B	510 429-1500	21825
New Horizon Foods Inc	2099	E	510 489-8600	2567
Northwood Design Partners Inc	2521	E	510 731-6505	4813
Oracle Corporation	7372	B	510 471-6971	24262
Orcon Aerospace	3728	C	510 489-8100	20189
Printing and Marketing Inc	2759	E	510 931-7000	7183
Profood Tropical Fruits Inc	2034	F	510 890-0070	857
Ptr Manufacturing Inc	3599	E	510 477-9654	16320
Quantum Performance Developmen	3572	F	510 870-6381	15083
R & S Manufacturing Inc (HQ)	3442	F	510 429-1788	11977
Rapid Displays Inc	3993	B	510 471-6955	23184
Reyes Coca-Cola Bottling LLC	2086	D	510 476-7000	2138
Ritescreen Inc	2431	F	800 949-4174	4116
Ryss Lab Inc	3821	F	510 477-9570	20773
Savory Creations International	2013	E	510 477-0395	497
Sheedy Drayage Co	3536	F	510 441-7300	13851
Sigmatron International Inc	3672	C	510 477-5000	18000
Sipi Company Inc	3944	F	650 201-1169	22713
Smart Wires Inc (PA)	3677	D	415 800-5555	18743
Spacesonics Incorporated	3444	D	650 610-0999	12383
Star Stainless Screw Co	3312	F	510 489-6569	11073
SW Safety Solutions Inc	2259	E	510 429-8692	2820
Taral Plastics	3089	F	510 972-6300	10080
Toppage Inc	7372	F	510 471-6366	24519
Tr Manufacturing LLC (HQ)	3679	C	510 657-3850	19121
Unistrut International Corp	3441	F	510 476-1200	11905
United Mech Met Fbricators Inc	3444	E	510 537-4744	12417
United Misc & Orna Stl Inc	3449	E	510 429-8755	12611
Usk Manufacturing Inc	3444	E	510 471-7555	12420

Employment Codes: A=Over 500 employees, B=251-500,
C=101-250, D=51-100, E=20-50, F=10-19

2020 California
Manufacturers Register

© Mergent Inc. 1-800-342-5647
1441

G E O G R A P H I C

	SIC	EMP	PHONE	ENTRY #
Zypcom Inc	3663	F	510 324-2501	17712

UPLAND, CA - San Bernardino County

	SIC	EMP	PHONE	ENTRY #
909 Media Group Inc	2721	F	909 608-7426	5873
American Technical Molding Inc	3089	C	909 982-1025	9627
Analytik Jena US LLC (DH)	3826	D	909 946-3197	21172
Applied Instrument Tech Inc	3823	E	909 204-3700	20835
Build At Home LLC	3949	F	909 949-1601	22770
Cal Best Ceilings Inc	3646	F	909 946-1565	17018
California Ramp Works Inc	3448	E	909 949-1601	12538
CCL Label Inc	2759	E	909 608-2655	7017
CCL Label (delaware) Inc	2759	C	909 608-2260	7018
Charles Meisner Inc	3544	E	909 946-8216	14031
Claremont Institute Statesmans (PA)	2759	E	909 981-2200	7024
Dimic Steel Tech Inc	3444	C	909 946-6767	12184
Edco Die Inc	3599	F	909 985-4417	15920
Exhaust Center Inc	3444	F	951 685-8602	12205
Gar Enterprises	3679	E	909 985-4575	18920
Garhauer Marine Corporation	3429	E	909 985-9993	11592
Hair Syndicut	2899	F	909 946-3200	8972
Helens Place Inc	2752	F	909 981-5715	6607
Herbs Yeh Manufacturing Co	2023	F	909 946-0794	594
Holliday Rock Trucking Inc (PA)	3273	D	909 982-1553	10772
Inland Valley News Inc	2711	F	909 949-3099	5674
Innovativetek Inc	3699	F	909 981-3401	19324
Integrity Sheet Metal Inc	3444	F	909 608-0449	12247
Judith Von Hopf Inc	2541	E	909 481-1884	4914
Mectec Molds Inc	3544	F	909 981-3636	14076
Montclair Wood Corporation	2426	C	909 985-0302	3979
Motu Global LLC	2033	F	801 471-7800	800
Panic Plastics	2673	F	909 946-5529	5410
Plum Creek Timberlands LP	2421	C	909 949-2255	3940
Precision Molded Plastics Inc	3089	F	909 981-9662	9987
Scheu Manufacturing Co (PA)	3433	F	909 982-8933	11712
Sport Pins International Inc	3961	F	909 985-4549	22996
Test Connections Inc	3825	F	909 981-1810	21143
Wilson Imaging and Publishing	2741	F	909 931-1818	6383
Winner Industrial Chemicals	2869	E	909 887-6228	8785

VACAVILLE, CA - Solano County

	SIC	EMP	PHONE	ENTRY #
Ad Special TS EMB Screen Prtg	2396	F	707 452-7272	3768
Adidas North America Inc	2329	E	707 446-1070	3063
Alza Corporation (HQ)	2834	A	707 453-6400	7745
Alza Corporation	3826	A	707 453-6400	21169
Caborca Leather LLC	2387	C	707 463-7607	3529
Cherry Pit	2992	F	707 449-8378	9138
Designerx Pharmaceuticals Inc	2834	F	707 451-0441	7870
Dr Earth Inc	2873	E	707 448-4676	8792
Duravent Inc (DH)	3444	B	800 835-4429	12188
Fortune Brands Windows Inc	3089	C	707 446-7600	9793
Genentech Inc	2834	A	707 454-1000	7901
Golden State Steel & Stair Inc (PA)	3441	E	707 455-0400	11805
Hurley International LLC	2329	C	707 446-6300	3090
Icon Aircraft Inc (PA)	3728	D	707 564-4000	20134
Joseph Charles Whitson	2741	E	707 694-8806	6262
Magellan Gold Corporation	1044	E	707 884-3766	10
Master Plastics Incorporated	3089	E	707 451-3168	9886
McC Controls LLC	3589	E	218 847-1317	15540
Novartis Pharmaceuticals Corp	2835	A	707 452-8081	8243
Pre-Insulated Metal Tech Inc (HQ)	3448	E	707 359-2280	12570
R R Donnelley & Sons Company	2752	F	707 446-6195	6828
Reporter	2711	D	707 448-6401	5809
Rxd Nova Pharmaceuticals Inc	2834	F	610 952-7242	8116
Siegwerk USA Inc	2893	E	707 469-7648	8930
SJ Electro Systems Inc	3589	F	707 449-0341	15578
Solano County Water Agency	2086	F	707 455-1105	2174
Synder Inc (PA)	3677	E	707 451-6060	18746
Timbuk2 Designs Inc	2393	E	800 865-2513	3666
Vacaville Fruit Co Inc	2034	F	707 448-5292	872
Wunder-Mold Inc	3089	E	707 448-2349	10132

VALENCIA, CA - Los Angeles County

	SIC	EMP	PHONE	ENTRY #
A & M Electronics Inc	3672	E	661 257-3680	17797
A-H Plating Inc	3471	D	818 845-6243	12897
Abl Aero Inc	3728	E	661 257-2500	19997
Accu-Glass Products Inc	3679	F	818 365-4215	18807
Advanced Bionics Corporation (HQ)	3842	C	661 362-1400	21973
Advanced Technology Machining	3599	F	661 257-2313	15701
Aero Engineering & Mfg Co Cal	3728	E	661 295-0875	20010
Aero Sense Inc	3728	F	661 257-1608	20014
Aerospace Dynamics Intl Inc	3728	B	661 257-3535	20021
Air Flow Research Heads Inc	3714	E	661 257-8124	19574
Airbolt Industries Inc	3369	F	818 767-5600	11407
Alinabal Inc	3399	E	661 877-9356	11477
Allen Reed Company Inc	2621	F	310 575-8704	5097
Amzr Inc	2399	C	800 541-2326	3832

	SIC	EMP	PHONE	ENTRY #
Aquafine Corporation (HQ)	3589	D	661 257-4770	15484
ASC Process Systems Inc	3567	C	818 833-0088	14755
Avibank Mfg Inc	3429	D	661 257-2329	11567
Avion TI Mfg Machining Ctr Inc	3599	F	661 257-2915	15757
Bayless Engineering Inc	3599	C	661 257-3373	15779
Bbk Specialties Inc	3261	F	661 255-2857	10465
Bertelsmann Inc	2731	B	661 702-2700	6075
Big Shine Los Angeles Inc	3663	F	818 346-0770	17468
Bioness Inc	3845	D	661 362-4850	22234
Bloomers Metal Stampings Inc	3469	E	661 257-2955	12772
Boston Scientific Corporation	3841	B	661 645-6668	21640
Boston Scientific Corporation	3841	E	800 678-2575	21641
Boston Scntfc Nrmdlation Corp	3842	F	661 949-4869	21991
Boston Scntfc Nrmdlation Corp (HQ)	3842	B	661 949-4310	21992
Canay Manufacturing Inc	3479	F	661 295-0205	13156
Canyon Engineering Pdts Inc	3728	D	661 294-0084	20066
Canyon Plastics Inc	3089	B	800 350-2275	9692
Capax Technologies Inc	3629	E	661 257-7666	16780
Circle W Enterprises Inc	3496	E	661 257-2400	13404
Classic Wire Cut Company Inc	3599	C	661 257-0558	15847
Cornerstone Display Group Inc	3993	E	661 705-1700	23080
Cosmic Plastics Inc (PA)	2821	E	661 257-3274	7550
Creations Grdn Natural Fd Mkts	2833	C	661 877-4280	7651
Crissair Inc	3594	C	661 367-3300	15627
Curran Engineering Company Inc	3446	E	800 643-6353	12466
Curtiss-Wright Flow Control	3491	C	626 851-3100	13303
Cypress Manufacturing LLC	3089	F	818 477-2777	9740
Da/Pro Rubber Inc	3069	D	661 775-6290	9300
Del West Engineering Inc (PA)	3714	C	661 295-5700	19634
Diversified Images Inc	2759	F	661 702-0003	7049
Donaldson Company Inc	3714	E	661 295-0800	19638
Eckert Zegler Isotope Pdts Inc (HQ)	3829	E	661 309-1010	21464
Electrofilm Mfg Co LLC	3492	D	661 257-2242	13328
Exclusive Powder Coatings Inc	3479	F	661 294-9812	13176
Fire Mountain Beverage	2086	E	661 362-0716	2075
Foilflex Products Inc	2759	E	661 702-0775	7067
Forrest Machining Inc	3728	C	661 257-0231	20109
Fruit Growers Supply Company (PA)	2653	C	661 290-8704	5221
G-G Distribution & Dev Co Inc	3494	C	661 257-5700	13354
Galaxy Die & Engineering Inc	3366	E	661 775-9301	11399
Gamma Alloys Inc	3334	E	661 294-5291	11183
Global Aerospace Tech Corp	3728	E	818 407-5600	20116
Gruber Systems Inc	3544	E	661 257-0464	14060
H2scan Corporation	3829	E	661 775-9575	21482
Hardcore Racing Components LLC	3944	E	661 294-5032	22678
Hemisphere Design & Mfg LLC	2541	F	661 294-9500	4909
Hydro Systems Inc (PA)	3431	D	661 775-0686	11647
Ibg Holdings Inc	2844	E	661 702-8680	8514
Indu-Electric North Amer Inc (PA)	3568	E	310 578-2144	14785
Industrial Tube Company LLC	3492	D	661 295-4000	13331
Input/Output Technology Inc	3577	E	661 257-1000	15248
ITT Aerospace Controls LLC	3728	E	661 295-4000	20142
ITT Aerospace Controls LLC	3728	E	661 295-4000	20143
J H P & Associates Inc	3511	E	661 799-5888	13572
Kcb Precision	3643	F	661 295-5695	16910
King Henrys Inc	2096	E	661 295-5566	2335
Koito Aviation LLC	3728	F	661 257-2878	20150
LA Turbine (PA)	3511	D	661 294-8290	13573
Lavi Industries (PA)	3446	D	877 275-5284	12492
Lean Manufacturing Group LLC	3541	F	661 702-9400	13929
Leggett & Platt Incorporated	2541	E	661 775-8500	4920
Leiner Health Products Inc	2834	E	661 775-1422	7989
Leonards Molded Products Inc	3069	E	661 253-2227	9328
Lief Organics LLC	2834	E	661 775-2500	7991
Lightway Industries Inc	3646	E	661 257-0286	17052
Lockwood Industries LLC	3674	C	661 702-6999	18357
Luran Inc	3599	F	661 257-6303	16153
Magnum Data Inc	3955	F	800 869-2589	22969
Mastey De Paris Inc	2844	E	661 257-4814	8537
Mechanix Wear LLC (PA)	2381	D	800 222-4296	3502
Medallion Therapeutics Inc	3841	E	661 621-6122	21793
Medianews Group Inc	2711	C	661 257-5200	5746
Medical Breakthrough Massage	3999	E	408 647-7702	23405
MP Tool Inc	3599	E	661 294-7711	16230
MWsausse & Co Inc (PA)	3625	E	661 257-3311	16734
Mye Technologies Inc	3699	E	661 964-0217	19361
Nasmyth Tmf Inc	3471	D	818 954-9504	13057
Nextclientcom Inc	2741	E	661 222-7755	6297
Northrop Grumman Corporation	3812	A	310 332-0412	20644
Pacific Aero Components Inc (PA)	3728	F	818 841-9258	20191
Pacific Lock Company (PA)	3429	E	661 294-3707	11618
Pacific Metal Stampings Inc	3469	E	661 257-7656	12853
Pacific Wstn Arostructures Inc	3599	F	661 607-0100	16275
Packaging Dist Assembly Group	2631	F	661 607-0600	5171
Paragon Precision Inc	3724	E	661 257-1380	19974

2020 California
Manufacturers Register

(P-0000) Products & Services Section entry number
(PA)=Parent Co (HQ)=Headquarters (DH)=Div Headquarters

Company	SIC	EMP	PHONE	ENTRY #
Partsearch Technologies Inc (DH)	3679	E	800 289-0300	19046
Performance Machine Tech Inc	3599	E	661 294-8617	16295
Pharma Alliance Group Inc	2834	F	661 294-7955	8071
PRC - Desoto International Inc (HQ)	2891	B	661 678-4209	8887
Precision Dynamics Corporation (HQ)	2672	C	818 897-1111	5371
Professional Skin Care Inc (PA)	2844	E	661 257-7771	8569
Prostat First Aid LLC (PA)	3842	E	661 705-1256	22071
Qmp Inc	3589	E	661 294-6860	15566
Quadriga USA Enterprises Inc	2679	F	888 669-9994	5525
Quantech Machining Inc	3599	E	661 775-3990	16330
Realwise Inc	7372	F	661 295-9399	24347
Remington Inc	3589	E	661 257-9400	15569
Remo Inc (PA)	3931	B	661 294-5600	22633
Romi Industries Inc	3599	E	661 294-1142	16368
Ronan Engineering Company (PA)	3823	D	661 702-1344	20930
Safe Environment Engineering	3679	F	661 295-5500	19075
Salvador Ramirez	3724	F	661 702-1813	19978
Santa Clarita Plastic Molding	3089	F	661 294-2257	10042
SCE Gaskets Inc	3053	F	661 728-9200	9253
Schrey & Sons Mold Co Inc	3544	E	661 294-2260	14104
Semiconductor Process Eqp Corp	3674	E	661 257-0934	18535
SGB Enterprises Inc	3575	E	661 294-8306	15134
Sgl Technic LLC (DH)	3295	D	661 257-0500	10977
Shimtech Industries US Inc (DH)	3728	D	661 295-8620	20233
Skm Industries Inc	3469	F	661 294-8373	12873
Softub Inc (PA)	3999	D	858 602-1920	23480
Steinhausen Inc	3915	E	661 702-1400	22602
Stoll Metalcraft Inc	3444	C	661 295-0401	12391
Stratasys Direct Inc (HQ)	3089	C	661 295-4400	10074
Stratoflight Inc	3728	D	949 622-0700	20239
Summit Electric & Data Inc	3699	E	661 775-9901	19417
Sunstar Spa Covers Inc (HQ)	3999	E	858 602-1950	23492
Sunvair Inc (HQ)	3599	D	661 294-3777	16429
Sunvair Overhaul Inc	3728	E	661 257-6123	20241
Synergy Microsystems Inc (DH)	3571	D	858 452-0020	14982
Ta Aerospace Co (DH)	3069	C	661 775-1100	9376
Ta Aerospace Co	2821	C	661 702-0448	7616
Talladium Inc (PA)	3843	E	661 295-0900	22195
Tara Enterprises Inc	2434	F	661 510-2206	4253
Technical Manufacturing W LLC	3999	E	661 295-7226	23501
Technical Trouble Shooting Inc	3599	E	661 257-1202	16448
Technifex Products LLC	3291	E	661 294-3800	10956
Timemed Labeling Systems Inc (DH)	3069	D	818 897-1111	9379
Transparent Products Inc	3575	E	661 294-9787	15137
Tri Tek Electronics Inc	3679	E	661 295-0020	19124
Triumph Actuation Systms-Valen	3728	C	661 295-1015	20258
True Position Technologies LLC	3599	D	661 294-0030	16472
Universal Hosiery Inc	2252	F	661 702-8444	2769
US Horizon Manufacturing Inc	3211	E	661 775-1675	10279
Utak Laboratories Inc	2869	E	661 294-3935	8780
V M P Inc	3451	F	661 294-9934	12658
Val-Aero Industries Inc	3599	E	661 295-8645	16488
Valencia Pipe Company	3084	E	661 257-3923	9479
Valley Circuits	3672	F	661 294-0077	18040
Virgil Walker Inc	3441	F	661 797-4101	11912
Virgil Walker Inc	3675	E	661 294-9142	18686
Vitek Indus Video Pdts Inc	3861	E	661 294-8043	22472
Whitmor Plstic Wire Cable Corp	3496	E	661 257-2400	13447
Winning Team Inc	2395	F	661 295-1428	3764
Zoo Printing Inc (PA)	2752	D	310 253-7751	6950

VALLECITO, CA - Calaveras County

Company	SIC	EMP	PHONE	ENTRY #
Twisted Oak Winery LLC (PA)	2084	E	209 728-3000	1978

VALLEJO, CA - Napa County

Company	SIC	EMP	PHONE	ENTRY #
Golden State Vintners	2084	E	707 553-6480	1729
Kolkka John	2514	E	707 554-3660	4693
N V Cast Stone LLC	3272	D	707 261-6615	10605
Arcmatic Welding Systems Inc (PA)	7692	F	707 643-5517	24616
Carpenter Group	3496	F	707 562-3543	13402
Dimensions Unlimited	2541	F	707 552-6800	4898
Dreamctchers Empwerment Netwrk	3679	E	707 558-1775	18892
Ghiringhlli Spcialty Foods Inc	2099	C	707 561-7670	2468
Hestan Smart Cooking Inc	3469	F	773 710-1538	12813
Intermodal Structures Inc	2452	F	415 887-2211	4462
Luther E Gibson Inc	2721	F	707 643-6104	5981
Mare Island Dry Dock LLC	3731	D	707 652-7356	20291
Meyer Cookware Industries Inc	3469	D	707 551-2800	12845
Meyer Corporation. US (HQ)	3469	D	707 551-2800	12846
Moose Boats Inc	3732	F	707 778-9828	20351
NI Industries Inc	3339	E	707 552-4850	11193
Renos Floor Covering Inc	3996	F	415 459-1403	23255
Romeros Welding & Mar Svcs Inc	7692	F	925 550-0518	24662
Syar Industries Inc	1422	D	707 643-3261	305
Titanium Metals Corporation	3356	D	707 552-4850	11280
Vallejo Electric Motor Inc	7694	F	707 552-7488	24700

Company	SIC	EMP	PHONE	ENTRY #
Western Dovetail Incorporated	2511	E	707 556-3683	4621

VALLEY CENTER, CA - San Diego County

Company	SIC	EMP	PHONE	ENTRY #
Controlled Entrances Inc	3699	F	760 749-1212	19279
Htr LLC	2084	F	760 297-4402	1756
International Decoratives Co	3999	E	760 749-2682	23365

VALLEY FORD, CA - Sonoma County

Company	SIC	EMP	PHONE	ENTRY #
Shubb Capos	3931	E	707 876-3001	22639

VALLEY VILLAGE, CA - Los Angeles County

Company	SIC	EMP	PHONE	ENTRY #
Cannalogic	3999	F	619 458-0775	23298
FBproductions Inc	2752	D	818 773-9337	6570

VAN NUYS, CA - Los Angeles County

Company	SIC	EMP	PHONE	ENTRY #
Advance Latex Products Inc	2341	E	310 559-8300	3438
Advance Overhead Door Inc	3442	E	818 781-5590	11928
Advanced Mobility Inc	3999	F	818 780-1788	23265
Aeroshear Aviation Svcs Inc (PA)	3728	E	818 779-1650	20019
Alfred Music Group Inc (PA)	2731	E	818 891-5999	6068
All American Cabinetry Inc	2541	D	818 376-0500	4879
Allison-Kaufman Inc	3911	D	818 373-5100	22490
Alros Label Co Inc	2759	E	818 781-2403	6984
Alyn Industries Inc	3679	D	818 988-7696	18813
Ambay Circuits Inc	3672	F	818 786-8241	17815
Anheuser-Busch LLC	2082	C	818 989-5300	1491
Archwood Mfg Group Inc	1411	F	818 781-7673	288
Auto-Chlor System Wash Inc	2842	F	818 376-0940	8364
Avid Technology Inc	3861	C	818 779-7860	22405
Baxalta US Inc	2834	E	818 947-5600	7787
Bespoke Coachworks Inc	3711	E	818 571-9900	19460
Bijan Rad Inc	3559	F	818 902-1606	14434
Blake Wire & Cable Corp	3357	F	818 781-8300	11289
Bluebarry Enterprises Inc	2752	F	818 956-0912	6452
Burtree Inc	3599	F	818 786-4276	15805
Cal Star Systems Group Inc	3699	F	818 922-2000	19269
Capstone Turbine Corporation (PA)	3511	C	818 734-5300	13563
Chef Merito Inc (PA)	2099	D	818 787-0100	2423
Cicon Engineering Inc (PA)	3679	C	818 909-6060	18863
Coloron Jewelry Inc	3961	F	818 565-1100	22979
Consolidated Fabricators Corp (PA)	3443	C	818 901-1005	12009
Contex Inc	3851	F	818 788-5836	22345
Cpp/Belwin Inc	2731	E	818 891-5999	6093
Creative Age Publications Inc	2721	E	818 782-7328	5912
Csdr International Inc	3674	F	844 330-0664	18187
Custom Muldings Sash Doors Inc	2431	F	818 787-7367	4025
D&A Metal Fabrication Inc	3444	F	818 780-8231	12170
Dal-Tile Corporation	2824	E	818 787-3224	7636
Dee Sign Co	3993	D	818 988-1000	23087
Delta D V H Circuits Inc	3672	F	818 786-8241	17862
Digital Room Holdings Inc (PA)	2759	C	310 575-4440	7045
Dolce Dolci LLC	2024	F	818 343-8400	639
Dress To Kill Inc	2331	F	818 994-3890	3156
E Alko Inc	3955	C	818 587-9700	22962
Eco-Gen Energy Inc	3621	F	818 756-4700	16640
Edwards Sheet Metal Supply Inc	3444	E	818 785-8600	12193
Espana Metal Craft Inc	3444	F	818 988-4988	12200
Exit Sign Warehouse Inc	3646	F	888 953-3948	17033
Experimental Aircraft Assn	3721	F	818 705-2744	19893
Felix Tool & Engineering	3544	F	818 994-9401	14052
Fitucci LLC	2434	F	818 785-3841	4198
Five Corner Conservation Inc	3599	F	818 792-1805	15960
Flannigans Merchandising Inc	2759	F	818 785-7428	7065
Great Western Packaging LLC	2759	D	818 464-3800	7080
Hollywood Software Inc	7372	F	818 205-2121	23983
I and E Cabinets Inc	2434	F	818 933-6480	4207
Industrial Electronic Engineer	3577	D	818 787-0311	15245
International Printing & Typsg	2752	F	818 787-6804	6651
Investment Enterprises Inc (PA)	2759	E	818 464-3800	7102
Ironhead Studios Inc	2389	F	818 901-7561	3558
Jet/Brella Inc	3724	F	818 786-5480	19968
Katzirs Floor & HM Design Inc	2431	F	818 988-9663	4069
Kimball Nelson Inc	3999	F	310 636-0081	23382
Kimberly-Clark Corporation	2621	F	818 986-2430	5129
Kutzin & Kutzin Inc	2499	F	818 994-0242	4511
L3harris Technologies Inc	3812	B	818 901-2523	20597
L3harris Technologies Inc	3812	B	408 201-8000	20598
Lavi Systems Inc	3728	F	818 373-5400	20155
Linea Pelle Inc (PA)	3111	F	310 231-9950	10142
M P M Building Services Inc	2842	D	818 708-9676	8395
Matrix Cab Parts Inc	2431	F	818 782-7022	4083
Microfabrica Inc	3679	E	888 964-2763	19015
Mike Printer Inc	2752	F	818 902-9922	6729
Monarch Art & Frame Inc	2499	E	818 373-6180	4517
Moticont	3699	E	818 785-1800	19359
Munchkin Inc (PA)	3085	C	818 893-5000	9488
Nat Aronson & Associates Inc	3052	F	818 787-5160	9200

Employment Codes: A=Over 500 employees, B=251-500,
C=101-250, D=51-100, E=20-50, F=10-19

2020 California
Manufacturers Register

© Mergent Inc. 1-800-342-5647
1443

GEOGRAPHIC

	SIC	EMP	PHONE	ENTRY #
Neiman/Hoeller Inc	3993	D	818 781-8600	23167
Neo Pacific Holdings Inc	3089	E	818 786-2900	9920
Niknejad Inc	2752	E	310 478-8363	6749
Omega Graphics Printing Inc	2759	F	818 374-9189	7155
Optical Zonu Corporation	3661	F	818 780-9701	17396
Orly International Inc	2844	D	818 994-1001	8552
Palermo Products LLC	2392	F	949 201-9066	3635
Paulsson Inc	1382	F	310 780-2219	133
Pearl Management Group Inc	2834	E	818 217-0218	8063
Photo Fabricators Inc	3672	D	818 781-1010	17956
Postcard Press Inc (PA)	2759	E	310 747-3800	7178
Power Brands Consulting LLC	2082	E	818 989-9646	1560
Precision Glass Bevelling Inc	3229	F	818 989-2727	10328
Printcom Inc	2752	E	818 891-8282	6798
Printrunner LLC	2752	E	888 296-5760	6810
Priority Tech Systems Inc	3699	E	818 756-5413	19382
Qortstone Inc	3281	F	877 899-7678	10925
Rbg Holdings Corp (PA)	3949	F	818 782-6445	22869
Renaissance Food Inc	2052	F	818 778-6230	1326
Renaissance Wdwrk & Design Inc	2431	E	818 787-7238	4114
Riggins Engineering Inc	3599	E	818 782-7010	16358
Rof LLC	2326	E	818 933-4000	3050
Rothlisberger Mfg A Cal Corp	3599	E	818 786-9462	16373
RPC Legacy Inc	3429	D	818 787-9000	11624
Sandstone Designs Inc	3272	E	818 787-5005	10648
SGB Better Baking Co LLC	2051	E	818 787-9992	1275
SGB Bubbles Baking Co LLC	2051	E	818 786-1700	1276
Shelcore Inc (PA)	3944	F	818 883-2400	22712
Sistone Inc	2541	E	818 988-9918	4939
Spec Engineering Co Inc	3599	E	818 780-3045	16415
Spinal and Orthopedic Devices	3842	E	818 908-9000	22090
Superior Inds Intl Hldings LLC (HQ)	3714	E	818 781-4973	19775
Synchronized Technologies Inc	3577	E	213 368-3760	15345
Tek Enterprises Inc	3679	E	818 785-5971	19103
Thermoplaque Company Inc	3999	E	818 988-1080	23503
Thompson Gundrilling Inc	3321	E	323 873-4045	11149
Tigers Plastics Inc	3089	E	818 901-9393	10086
Trio-Tech International (PA)	3559	E	818 787-7000	14548
Tyler Technologies Inc	7372	E	818 989-4420	24533
Uruhu Highlands Ltd	3483	F	424 213-9725	13273
Viking Ready Mix Co Inc	3273	E	818 786-2210	10864
Western Bagel Baking Corp (PA)	2051	C	818 786-5847	1292
Wsw Corp (PA)	3714	E	818 989-5008	19809
Zodiak Services America	3728	D	310 884-7200	20275

VANDENBERG AFB, CA - Santa Barbara County

	SIC	EMP	PHONE	ENTRY #
United Launch Alliance LLC	3761	D	303 269-5876	20461

VENICE, CA - Los Angeles County

	SIC	EMP	PHONE	ENTRY #
Alpargatas Usa Inc	3144	E	646 277-7171	10166
Gamemine LLC	7372	E	310 310-3105	23927
Hall Health and Longevity Cntr	2833	F	310 566-6690	7666
Jody Maronis Italian	2013	E	310 822-5639	470
MA Cher (usa) Inc (DH)	3999	F	310 581-5222	23400
T3 Micro Inc (PA)	3999	F	310 452-2888	23497
Wemo Media Inc	7372	F	310 399-8058	24576
Windward Yacht & Repair Inc	3732	F	310 823-4581	20365

VENTURA, CA - Ventura County

	SIC	EMP	PHONE	ENTRY #
Abbs Vision Systems Inc	3851	F	805 642-0499	22337
Aquastar Pool Products Inc	3561	F	877 768-2717	14559
Aqueos Corporation	3533	D	805 676-4330	13765
Art Glass Etc Inc	2431	E	805 644-4494	3999
Automotive Racing Products Inc (PA)	3429	D	805 339-2200	11565
Barnett Tool & Engineering	3751	D	805 642-9435	20383
Bell Powder Coating Inc	3479	F	805 658-2233	13149
Bentley-Simonson Inc	1311	D	805 650-2794	23
C & R Molds Inc	3089	E	805 658-7098	9679
California Resources Corp	1382	F	805 641-5566	114
Cargo Data Corporation	3829	F	805 650-5922	21448
CCI Mail & Shipping Systems	2542	F	805 658-9123	4969
Channel Isl Opto Mech	3599	F	805 644-2153	15838
Chapala Iron & Manufacturing	3312	F	805 654-9803	11037
Coastal Connections	3661	E	805 644-5051	17356
Coca-Cola Refreshments USA Inc	2086	C	805 644-2211	2064
Connect Systems Inc	3663	E	805 642-7184	17494
Coorstek Inc	3545	D	805 644-5583	14149
Coorstek Inc	3545	E	805 644-5583	14150
Cord Intrnational/Hana Ola Rec	3652	F	805 648-7881	17313
Cummins Pacific LLC	3519	E	805 644-7281	13594
Dairy Farmers America Inc	2026	D	805 653-0042	694
Dcor LLC (PA)	1382	D	805 535-2000	117
Dna Health Institute Llc	2869	F	805 654-9363	8735
Dow-Key Microwave Corporation	3625	C	805 650-0260	16712
Dynatest Consulting Inc	3825	F	805 648-2230	21023
Edwards Assoc Cmmnications Inc (PA)	2672	E	805 658-2626	5361

	SIC	EMP	PHONE	ENTRY #
Exam Room Supply LLC	3845	F	805 298-3631	22253
Fabricmate Systems Inc	3089	F	805 642-7470	9786
Fca LLC	2441	F	805 477-9901	4336
Fcp Inc	3448	E	805 684-1117	12546
Fed Ex Kinkos Ofc & Print Ctr	2752	F	805 604-6000	6571
Fence Factory	3446	F	805 644-5482	12475
Flir Eoc LLC	3826	E	805 642-4645	21230
Fnc Medical Corporation	2844	F	805 644-7576	8494
Frito-Lay North America Inc	2096	E	805 658-1668	2327
Goldenwood Truss Corporation	2439	D	805 659-2520	4302
Guernsey Coating Laboratory	3479	F	805 642-1508	13188
Hackrod Inc	3711	E	347 331-8919	19476
Hammerhead Industries Inc	3089	F	805 658-9922	9820
Hampton Fitness Products Ltd	3949	F	805 339-9733	22816
Hearts Delight	2339	E	805 648-7123	3335
Hennis Enterprises Inc	2821	E	805 977-0257	7564
Herald Printing Ltd (PA)	2752	F	805 647-1870	6609
High Tech Pet Products Inc	3999	F	805 644-1797	23352
HK Canning Inc (PA)	2033	F	805 652-1392	775
HMcompany	3599	F	805 650-2651	16031
Implantech Associates Inc	3842	E	805 289-1665	22029
Interstate Rebar Inc	3312	F	805 643-6892	11051
Jetair Technologies LLC	3564	E	805 654-7000	14666
Jh Biotech Inc (PA)	2875	E	805 650-8933	8813
Juengermann Inc	3493	E	805 644-7165	13338
Key Energy Services Inc	1389	E	805 653-1300	219
Lamps Plus Inc	3646	F	805 642-9007	17049
Lockheed Martin Corporation	3812	F	805 650-4600	20617
Lynch Ready Mix Concrete Co	3273	F	805 647-2817	10798
Magna Charger Inc	2396	D	805 642-8833	3799
Magnuson Products LLC	3714	F	805 642-8833	19711
Mini-Flex Corporation	3599	F	805 644-1474	16211
Motran Industries Inc	3621	F	661 257-4995	16664
Nabors Well Services Co	1389	D	805 648-2731	227
Naso Industries Corporation	3672	E	805 650-1231	17933
National Graphics LLC	2752	F	805 644-9212	6744
Neon Ideas	3993	E	805 648-7681	23168
Oil Country Manufacturing	3533	C	805 643-1200	13789
Omnisil	3674	E	805 644-2514	18449
P K Engineering & Mfg Co Inc	3841	F	805 628-9556	21853
P-Americas LLC	2086	C	805 641-4200	2106
Parker-Hannifin Corporation	3594	F	805 658-2984	15636
Penta Financial Inc	3671	F	818 882-3872	17792
Point Blanks Inc	2085	F	805 643-8616	2016
Quality Machine Shop Inc	3599	F	805 653-7944	16328
Reyes Coca-Cola Bottling LLC	2086	D	805 644-2211	2141
Richard Yarbrough	1389	E	805 643-1021	254
Robert M Hadley Company Inc	3677	D	805 658-7286	18739
Santa Monica Millworks	2434	E	805 643-0010	4246
Schlumberger Technology Corp	1389	E	805 642-8230	259
Schlumberger Technology Corp	1389	F	805 644-8325	262
Sessa Manufacturing & Welding	3469	F	805 644-2284	12872
Skjonberg Controls Inc	3625	F	805 650-0877	16756
Solimar Energy LLC	1382	F	805 643-4100	142
Spin Shades Corporation	3648	E	805 650-4849	17162
State Ready Mix Inc (PA)	3273	F	805 647-2817	10845
Streamline Dsign Slkscreen Inc	2759	F	805 884-1025	7232
Streamline Dsign Slkscreen Inc (PA)	2329	D	805 884-1025	3120
Strenumed Inc	3842	F	805 477-1000	22095
Sun Power Source (PA)	3648	F	805 644-2520	17164
Surfside Prints Inc	2396	F	805 620-0052	3819
Swiss Productions Inc	3083	F	805 654-8379	9457
The Sloan Company Inc (PA)	3648	C	805 676-3200	17168
TMJ Solutions Inc	3841	F	805 650-3391	21932
Total Structures Inc	3648	E	805 676-3322	17171
Tricoss Inc	3495	F	805 644-4107	13391
Trupart Manufacturing Inc	3599	F	805 644-4107	16474
Vacumetrics Inc	3841	F	805 644-7461	21944
Vastcircuits & Mfg LLC	3679	F	805 421-4299	19135
Venoco Inc	1311	E	805 644-1400	75
Ventura Coastal LLC (PA)	2037	D	805 653-7000	932
Ventura Harbor Boatyard Inc	3732	E	805 654-1433	20360
Ventura Hydrulic Mch Works Inc	3599	E	805 656-1760	16499
W L Rubottom Co	2434	D	805 648-6943	4264
Weatherford International LLC	1389	F	805 643-1279	287
Wilco Building Corporation	2431	E	805 765-4188	4150
Window Products Management Inc	2431	E	805 677-6800	4152
Wireless Technology Inc	3651	E	805 339-9696	17306
Wm J Matson Company	3479	F	805 684-9410	13269
Wombat Products Inc	3089	E	805 794-1767	10129

VERNON, CA - Los Angeles County

	SIC	EMP	PHONE	ENTRY #
4 You Apparel Inc	2335	F	323 583-4242	3209
A F C Hydraulic Seals	3053	F	323 585-9110	9213
A Rudin Inc (PA)	2512	D	323 589-5547	4627
A&A Global Imports Inc	3089	E	323 767-5990	9600

2020 California
Manufacturers Register

(P-0000) Products & Services Section entry number
(PA)=Parent Co (HQ)=Headquarters (DH)=Div Headquarters

Company	SIC	EMP	PHONE	ENTRY #
Aaron Corporation	2339	C	323 235-5959	3279
Ace Pleating & Stitching Inc	2395	E	323 582-8213	3720
Ajax Forge Company (PA)	3462	E	323 582-6307	12702
Ajax Forge Company	3462	E	323 582-6307	12703
All Star Clothing Inc	2331	F	323 233-7773	3135
All-American Mfg Co	3432	E	323 581-6293	11653
Amcor Industries Inc	3714	E	323 585-2852	19576
American Bottling Company	2086	B	323 268-7779	2033
American Consumer Products LLC	2899	E	310 443-3330	8941
AMP Plus Inc	3647	D	323 231-2600	17087
Aoclsc Inc	2992	E	562 776-4000	9131
Apparelway Inc	2297	F	323 581-5888	2902
Arcadia Inc (PA)	3355	C	323 269-7300	11256
Archipelago Inc	2844	E	213 743-9200	8438
Art Masterpiece Gallery	2392	F	323 277-9448	3601
AS Match Dyeing Co Inc	2261	C	323 277-0470	2821
Atlas Galvanizing LLC	3479	E	323 587-6247	13145
Atra International Traders Inc	2671	E	562 864-3885	5323
Atrevete Inc	2331	F	323 277-5551	3138
Bailey 44 LLC	2331	E	213 228-1930	3139
Baker Commodities Inc (PA)	2077	C	323 268-2801	1452
Baker Commodities Inc	2077	E	323 318-8260	1455
Baker Coupling Company Inc	3498	E	323 583-3444	13460
Bakery Depot Inc	2051	F	323 261-8388	1141
Bar-S Foods Co	2013	B	323 589-3600	440
Barksdale Inc (DH)	3829	C	323 583-6243	21442
Bcbg Maxazria Entrmt LLC	2339	E	323 277-4713	3294
Bender Ccp Inc	3599	D	707 745-9970	15785
Berney-Karp Inc	3269	D	323 260-7122	10485
Big Bang Clothing Inc (PA)	2339	F	323 233-7773	3296
Bodycote Thermal Proc Inc	3398	F	323 264-0111	11435
Bodycote Usa Inc	3398	F	323 264-0111	11441
Bon Appetit Danish Inc	2051	D	323 584-9500	1168
Brentwood Appliances Inc	3639	F	323 266-4600	16847
C R Laurence Co Inc (HQ)	3714	B	323 588-1281	19604
California Coast Clothing LLC	2211	F	323 923-3870	2675
California Combining Corp	2295	E	323 589-5727	2895
California Feather Inds Inc	2392	F	323 585-5800	3606
Caltex Plastics Inc (PA)	2673	E	800 584-7303	5387
Camino Real Foods Inc (PA)	2038	C	323 526-6599	949
Cenveo Worldwide Limited	2679	C	323 262-6000	5499
Certified Steel Treating Corp	3471	E	323 583-8711	12965
Charman Manufacturing Inc	3317	E	213 489-7000	11123
Chua & Sons Inc	2241	E	323 588-8044	2751
Chunma Usa Inc	3161	F	323 846-0077	10191
Classic Slipcover Inc	2392	E	323 583-0804	3608
Clougherty Packing LLC (DH)	2011	B	323 583-4621	404
Colorfast Dye & Print Hse Inc	2752	C	323 581-1656	6498
Command Packaging LLC	2673	C	323 980-0918	5392
Commercial Sand Blast Company	3471	F	323 581-8672	12975
Complete Clothing Company (PA)	2335	D	323 277-1470	3224
Complete Garment Inc	2253	E	323 846-3731	2780
Continental Vitamin Co Inc	2834	D	323 581-0176	7849
Corporate Graphics Intl Inc	2752	D	323 826-3440	6516
Cottyon Inc	2211	E	323 589-1563	2678
Crestone LLC	2361	E	323 584-8857	3477
Crown Carton Company Inc	2653	E	323 582-3053	5216
Culinary Brands Inc (PA)	2038	D	626 289-3000	953
Culinary International LLC (PA)	2099	E	626 289-3000	2436
D D Office Products Inc	2621	E	323 582-3400	5101
David Garment Cutng Fusing Svc	2326	F	323 583-9885	3032
Demenno/Kerdoon Holdings	2992	D	323 268-3387	9139
Denim-Tech LLC	3582	D	323 277-8998	15404
Deodar Brands LLC	2211	E	323 235-7303	2681
Design Concepts Inc	2339	F	323 277-4771	3316
Destiney Group Inc	2211	E	323 581-4477	2682
Dm Collective Inc	2253	E	323 923-2400	2782
E G Meat and Provision Inc (PA)	2013	F	323 588-5333	454
East Shore Garment Company LLC	2211	E	323 923-4454	2685
Edris Plastics Mfg Inc	3089	E	323 581-7000	9774
Ema Textiles Inc	2253	E	323 589-9800	2783
Engineered Application LLC	3479	E	323 585-2894	13174
Engineered Coating Tech Inc	2851	E	323 306-5800	8643
Erge Designs LLC	2331	F	310 614-9197	3158
Evonik Corporation	2899	E	323 264-0311	8966
F Gavina & Sons Inc	2095	B	323 582-0671	2288
F I O Imports Inc	2099	C	323 263-5100	2454
Fantasy Activewear Inc (PA)	2253	E	213 705-4111	2784
Fantasy Dyeing & Finishing Inc	2253	F	323 983-9988	2785
Fishermans Pride Prcessors Inc	2092	B	323 232-1980	2260
Flowserve Corporation	3561	B	323 584-1890	14572
Fresh Packing Corporation	2032	E	213 612-0136	727
G & G Quality Case Co Inc	3161	D	323 233-2482	10195
Galaxy Press Inc	2731	E	323 399-3433	6104
General Mills Inc	2041	E	323 584-3433	1000
Geo Plastics	3089	E	323 277-8106	9803
Global Truss America LLC	3354	D	323 415-6225	11231
Golden West Food Group Inc (PA)	2011	E	888 807-3663	412
Goldman Global Greenfield Inc	3089	F	323 589-3444	9811
Great American Packaging	2673	E	323 582-2247	5398
Gts Living Foods LLC	2086	A	323 581-7787	2079
H & L Apparel Enterprise Inc	2331	F	323 589-1563	3166
H P Applications	3398	F	323 585-2894	11452
Hanger	3842	F	323 238-7738	22021
Hannibal Industries Inc (PA)	3317	C	323 513-1200	11127
Hannibal Material Handling	2542	C	323 587-4060	4980
Hollywood Lamp & Shade Co	3641	F	323 585-3999	16864
Isabelle Handbags Inc	3171	E	323 277-9888	10224
J & J Snack Foods Corp Cal (HQ)	2052	C	323 581-0171	1316
J H Textiles Inc	2299	C	323 585-4124	2938
Jaya Apparel Group LLC (PA)	2339	D	323 584-3500	3344
Jejomi Designs Inc	2386	E	323 584-4211	3517
Jml Textile Inc	2211	D	323 584-2323	2700
JNJ Apparel Inc	2339	E	323 584-9700	3347
Jobbers Meat Packing Co Inc	2011	F	323 585-6328	414
Js Glass Wholesale	3231	F	213 746-5577	10370
K & M Packing Co Inc	2011	C	323 585-5318	415
Katie K Inc	2389	F	323 589-3030	3561
Kennedy Name Plate Co Inc	3479	E	323 585-0121	13196
Kim & Cami Productions Inc	2339	E	323 584-1300	3355
Koral LLC	2329	E	323 391-1060	3099
Koral Industries LLC (PA)	2339	D	323 585-5343	3357
L A Air Line Inc	2261	E	323 585-1088	2827
L A S A M Inc	2361	F	323 586-8717	3482
La Spec Industries Inc	3646	F	323 588-8746	17048
Lac Bleu Inc	2339	E	213 973-5335	3360
LAT LLC	2339	E	323 233-3017	3361
Latourette Lift Services	3537	F	323 262-9111	13881
Lifoam Industries LLC	3081	E	323 587-1934	9408
Love Marks Inc (PA)	2331	F	323 859-8770	3176
Luppen Holdings Inc (PA)	3469	E	323 581-8121	12839
Mahar Manufacturing Corp (PA)	3942	E	323 581-9988	22649
Makers Usa Inc	2322	F	323 582-1800	2999
Marspring Corporation (PA)	2273	E	323 589-5637	2872
Marspring Corporation	2515	E	800 522-5252	4729
Marspring Corporation	2515	E	310 484-6849	4730
Matheson Tri-Gas Inc	2813	F	323 773-2777	7420
Metal Products Engineering	3398	E	323 581-8121	11463
Mexapparel Inc (PA)	2326	F	323 364-8600	3045
Mjck Corporation	2253	E	888 992-8437	2799
Mochi Ice Cream Company (PA)	2051	E	323 587-5504	1244
Ms2 Technologies LLC	3356	F	310 277-4110	11276
Nanka Seimen Co	2098	E	323 585-9967	2373
National Corset Supply House (PA)	2341	D	323 261-0265	3445
New Chef Fashion Inc	2311	D	323 581-0300	2971
Norman Paper and Foam Co Inc	2671	E	323 582-7132	5332
Norton Packaging Inc	3089	E	323 588-6167	9932
Nuconic Packaging LLC	3089	E	323 588-9033	9936
Oak Manufacturing Company Inc	3581	F	323 581-8087	15400
Overhill Farms Inc (DH)	2038	D	323 582-9977	972
Overhill Farms Inc	2038	C	323 584-4375	973
P&Y T-Shrts Silk Screening Inc	3552	D	323 585-4604	14290
Pabco Building Products LLC	3275	D	323 581-6113	10884
Pacific Boulevard Inc	2335	F	323 581-1656	3247
Packaging Corporation America	2653	D	323 267-7581	5253
Papa Cantellas Incorporated	2013	D	323 584-7272	487
Paper Surce Converting Mfg Inc	2621	E	323 583-3800	5143
Patterson Kincaid LLC	2339	F	323 584-3559	3383
Peerless Materials Company (PA)	2842	E	323 266-0313	8406
People Trend Inc	2329	F	213 995-5555	3112
Peter K Inc (PA)	2339	E	323 585-5343	3386
Pjy Inc	2211	E	323 583-7737	2709
Ppp LLC	2821	F	323 581-6058	7598
Prestale USA LP	2041	E	818 818-0976	1009
Princess Paper Inc	2676	D	323 588-4777	5464
Procases Inc	2441	F	323 585-4447	4342
Punch Press Products Inc	3544	D	323 581-7151	14099
Putnam Accessory Group Inc	2339	E	323 306-1330	3394
R A Reed Electric Company (PA)	7694	E	323 587-2284	24694
R B R Meat Company Inc	2011	D	323 973-4868	421
Rcrv Inc	2673	F	323 235-7332	5414
RE Bilt Metalizing Co	3599	F	323 277-8200	16346
Rebecca International Inc	2395	E	323 973-2602	3754
Rehrig Pacific Company (HQ)	3089	C	323 262-5145	10011
Rehrig Pacific Holdings Inc (PA)	3089	E	323 262-5145	10012
Reliance Upholstery Supply Inc	2299	F	800 522-5252	2953
Republic Furniture Mfg Inc	2512	E	323 235-2144	4667
Reynaldos Mexican Food Co LLC (PA)	2032	C	562 803-3188	744
Rezex Corporation	2269	E	213 622-2015	2859
Riah Fashion Inc	2339	F	323 325-7308	3399

Company	SIC	EMP	PHONE	ENTRY #
RJ Acquisition Corp (PA)	2759	C	323 318-1107	7201
Rmla Inc	2369	D	213 749-4333	3495
Romeo Systems Inc	3699	C	323 675-2180	19397
Rotax Incorporated	2339	E	323 589-5999	3400
Royal Trim	2396	E	323 583-2121	3811
S & C Foods Inc	2064	E	323 205-6887	1393
S S Schaffer Co Inc	3541	F	323 560-1430	13948
Sandberg Furniture Mfg Co Inc (PA)	2511	C	323 582-0711	4611
Sara Lee Fresh Inc	2051	A	215 347-5500	1272
Sas Textiles Inc	2259	D	323 277-5555	2819
Selectra Industries Corp	2341	D	323 581-8500	3448
Sewing Collection Inc	3053	D	323 264-2223	9256
Sffi Company Inc (PA)	2033	D	323 586-0000	823
Shara-Tex Inc	2257	E	323 587-7200	2812
Siemens Industry Inc	3569	E	323 277-1500	14857
Sign of Times Inc	2679	E	323 826-9766	5530
SJ&I Bias Binding & Tex Co Inc	2396	E	213 747-5271	3814
Smart Foods LLC	2046	E	818 660-2238	1063
Softmax Inc	2342	F	213 718-2100	3458
Southwest Processors Inc	2048	F	323 269-9876	1128
Spirit Clothing Company	2339	E	213 784-0251	3410
Square H Brands Inc	2013	C	323 267-4600	500
Standard Bias Binding Co Inc	2396	E	323 277-9763	3816
Starco Enterprises Inc (PA)	3559	D	323 266-7111	14539
Streets Ahead Inc	2387	E	323 277-0860	3533
Superior Electric Mtr Svc Inc	7694	F	323 583-1040	24698
Superior Graphic Packaging Inc	2752	D	323 263-8400	6878
T & T Foods Inc	2032	E	323 588-2158	747
Tagtime U S A Inc	2679	B	323 587-1555	5535
Tajima USA Dissolving Corp	3446	F	323 588-1281	12513
Tapatio Foods LLC	2033	F	323 587-8933	829
Team Fashion	2331	F	323 589-3388	3196
Tempted Apparel Corp	2339	E	323 859-2480	3423
Teva Foods Inc	2099	E	323 267-8110	2625
The Ligature Inc (HQ)	2752	E	323 585-6000	6889
Three Plus One Inc	2331	F	213 623-3070	3199
Tile Guild Inc	3253	F	323 581-3770	10457
Tom York Enterprises Inc	3089	F	323 581-6194	10088
Topnotch Foods Inc	2099	F	323 586-2007	2628
Transhumance Holding Co Inc	2013	E	323 583-5503	504
Tremco Incorporated	2952	E	323 587-3014	9126
Trend Chasers LLC	3199	E	213 749-2661	10255
Tube Rags	2258	F	323 264-7770	2815
Twenty-Niners Provisions Inc	2015	E	323 233-7864	528
Two Guys and One LLC	3161	F	213 239-0310	10214
Two Lads Inc (PA)	3965	E	323 584-0064	23014
Union Ice Company	2097	F	323 277-1000	2364
Unirex Corp	3674	F	323 589-4000	18633
UPD INC	3942	D	323 588-8811	22655
US Garment LLC	2326	E	323 415-6464	3057
US Radiator Corporation (PA)	3714	E	323 826-0965	19797
Vernon Machine and Foundry	3999	F	323 277-0550	23516
Vest Inc	3317	D	800 421-6370	11139
W & W Concept Inc	2339	D	323 233-9202	3433
W5 Concepts Inc	2331	E	323 231-2415	3208
Westaire Engineering Inc	3585	F	323 587-3347	15473
Western Abrasives Inc	3291	F	323 588-1245	10959
Westgate Mfg Inc	3699	F	877 805-2252	19443
Yen-Nhai Inc	2512	E	323 584-1315	4678
Yonekyu USA Inc	2013	D	323 581-4194	508
Zk Enterprises Inc	2329	E	213 622-7012	3132

VICTORVILLE, CA - San Bernardino County

Company	SIC	EMP	PHONE	ENTRY #
B Brays Card Inc	2752	F	760 265-4720	6429
Boeing Company	3721	A	760 246-0273	19869
Customplanetcom Inc	2759	F	760 508-2648	7042
Demag Cranes & Components Corp	3536	F	909 880-8800	13846
Devoll Rubber Mfg Group Inc	3069	F	760 246-0142	9301
Exportech Worldwide LLC	3571	F	909 278-9477	14910
General Electric Company	3721	A	760 530-5200	19903
Johns Incredible Pizza Co	2099	D	760 951-1111	2490
Lmg National Publishing Inc	2711	D	760 241-7744	5701
Mars Petcare Us Inc	2047	E	760 261-7900	1078
Mojave Copy & Printing Inc	2752	F	760 241-7898	6733
Newell Brands Inc	3089	E	760 246-2700	9922
Paradise Manufacturing Co Inc	2394	C	909 477-3460	3698
Protech Minerals Inc	3255	F	760 245-3441	10461
Reyes Coca-Cola Bottling LLC	2086	E	760 241-2653	2157
Zeth Engineering Inc	3441	F	310 930-9100	11924

VIEW PARK, CA - Los Angeles County

Company	SIC	EMP	PHONE	ENTRY #
Outdoor Recreation Group (PA)	2393	E	323 226-0830	3662

VILLA PARK, CA - Orange County

Company	SIC	EMP	PHONE	ENTRY #
Kett	3826	F	714 974-8837	21251
Quality Countertops Inc	2541	F	909 597-6888	4934

VISALIA, CA - Tulare County

Company	SIC	EMP	PHONE	ENTRY #
AFP Advanced Food Products LLC	2032	C	559 627-2070	717
Approved Turbo Components	3724	F	559 627-3600	19946
Arctic Silver Incorporated	2992	F	559 740-0912	9132
Bluescope Buildings N Amer Inc	3448	C	559 651-5300	12535
Bushnell Industries Inc	2842	F	559 651-9039	8370
California Dairies Inc (PA)	2026	D	559 625-2200	688
Chef Brand Foods	2051	E	559 651-1696	1179
Cnc Machining Service Inc	3599	F	559 732-5599	15853
Corwood Containers	2449	E	559 651-0335	4414
Danair Inc (PA)	3541	F	559 734-1961	13911
Diamond Crystal Brands Inc	2099	E	559 651-7782	2444
Diamond Perforated Metals Inc	3469	D	559 651-1889	12793
Edeniq Inc	2869	D	559 302-1777	8736
Essilor Laboratories Amer Inc	3851	E	800 624-6672	22353
Food Machinery Sales Inc	3565	D	559 651-2339	14707
Graphic Packaging Intl LLC	2621	C	559 651-3535	5107
Hellwig Products Company Inc	3714	E	559 734-7451	19680
Hydrite Chemical Co	2899	E	559 651-3450	8976
Idea Printing & Graphics Inc	2752	F	559 733-4149	6624
Information Resources Inc	7372	E	559 732-0324	24019
International Paper Company	2621	C	559 651-1416	5111
John Bean Technologies Corp	3556	C	559 651-8300	14379
Jostens Inc	3911	C	559 622-5200	22533
Kaweah Container Inc (HQ)	2653	D	559 651-7846	5242
Kawneer Company Inc	3446	C	559 651-4000	12489
Kens Stakes & Supplies	2499	F	559 747-1313	4510
Oxbo International Corporation	3523	F	559 897-7012	13656
Pace International LLC	2842	E	559 651-4877	8402
Pacific Coast Supply LLC	3275	E	559 651-2185	10885
Pacific Southwest Cont LLC	2653	D	559 651-5500	5251
Packers Manufacturing Inc	3556	F	559 732-4886	14391
Pactiv LLC	3089	C	909 622-1151	9949
Perfection Pet Foods LLC (DH)	2047	E	559 302-4880	1080
Precision Forklift	3537	F	559 805-5487	13889
Premier Trailer Manufacturing	3799	E	559 651-2212	20519
R Lang Company	3442	D	559 651-0701	11980
Screw Conveyor Pacific Corp	3535	E	559 651-2131	13834
Sorma USA LLC	2673	B	559 651-1269	5421
Spraying Devices Inc	3524	F	559 734-5555	13697
Stainless Technologies LLC	7692	F	559 651-0460	24667
Standard Lumber Company Inc (HQ)	2448	F	559 651-2037	4401
Tempo Plastic Co	3086	F	559 651-7711	9572
TI Inc	2873	F	559 972-1475	8805
Torian Group Inc	7372	F	559 733-1940	24520
Tri-Mag Inc	3679	E	559 651-2222	19125
Trical Inc	2879	F	559 651-0736	8842
US Cotton LLC	2844	B	559 651-3015	8598
Ventura Coastal LLC	2037	E	559 737-9836	933
Visalia Ctr 4 Ambltry Med & Sv	3842	E	559 740-4094	22118
Visalia Electric Motor Sp Inc	7694	F	559 651-0606	24702
Voltage Multipliers Inc (PA)	3674	C	559 651-1402	18649
West Coast Sand Gravel	1442	E	559 625-9426	369

VISTA, CA - San Diego County

Company	SIC	EMP	PHONE	ENTRY #
Accutech LLC	3841	E	760 599-6555	21580
Accutek Packaging Equipment Co (PA)	3565	E	760 734-4177	14694
Acells Corp	3826	F	760 727-6666	21160
Addition Mfg Tech CA Inc	3542	F	760 597-5220	13964
Advanced Web Offset Inc	2759	D	760 727-1700	6977
All One God Faith Inc (PA)	2841	C	844 937-2551	8335
Alvarado Micro Precision Inc	3599	F	760 598-0186	15733
American General Tool Group	3011	E	760 745-7993	9163
Amron International Inc (PA)	3949	D	760 208-6500	22746
Apem Inc	3679	D	760 598-2518	18817
Apollo Sprayers Intl Inc	3563	F	760 727-8300	14621
Applied Membranes Inc	3589	D	760 727-3711	15482
Aqua-Lung America Inc (DH)	3812	C	760 597-5000	20536
Architctral Mllwk Slutions Inc	2431	F	760 510-6440	3997
Aza Industries Inc (PA)	3949	F	760 560-0440	22753
Aztec Technology Corporation (PA)	3441	E	760 727-2300	11746
Bachem Americas Inc	2834	F	888 422-2436	7783
Biofilm Inc	3841	D	760 727-9030	21632
Blue Sky Energy Inc	3629	F	760 597-1642	16779
Boom Movement LLC	3651	D	410 358-3600	17208
C Enterprises Inc	3577	D	760 599-5111	15180
Carbide Company LLC	3423	C	760 477-1000	11524
Carbon By Design LLC	3728	D	760 643-1300	20067
Chandler Signs LLC	3993	D	760 734-1708	23075
Clarity H2o LLC	3589	F	619 993-4780	15499
Conamco SA De CV	3843	D	760 586-4356	22139
Coorstek Vista Inc	3297	C	760 542-7065	10991
Corrugated and Packaging LLC	3086	C	619 559-1564	9518
Csi Technologies Inc	3675	F	760 682-2222	18677
Datron Wrld Communications Inc (PA)	3663	C	760 597-1500	17500

Mergent email: customerrelations@mergent.com
1446

2020 California
Manufacturers Register

(P-0000) Products & Services Section entry number
(PA)=Parent Co (HQ)=Headquarters (DH)=Div Headquarters

	SIC	EMP	PHONE	ENTRY #
Ddh Enterprise Inc (PA)	3643	C	760 599-0171	16892
Dei Holdings Inc (HQ)	3669	C	760 598-6200	17725
Dig Corporation	3523	D	760 727-0914	13624
Distinctive Plastics Inc	3089	D	760 599-9100	9759
Diversified Mfg Cal Inc	3599	F	760 599-9280	15900
Diversified Plastics Inc	3089	D	760 598-5333	9761
Diversified Tool & Die	3469	E	760 598-9100	12795
Djo LLC	3842	F	760 727-1280	21998
Douglas Technologies Group Inc (PA)	3714	E	760 758-5560	19640
DSB Enterprises Inc	2082	E	760 295-3500	1521
Dss-Cctv Inc	3663	F	609 850-9498	17506
Dutek Incorporated	3699	F	760 566-8888	19296
E/G Electro-Graph Inc	3674	D	760 438-9090	18205
Earthlite LLC (DH)	2514	C	760 599-1112	4690
Eden Beauty Concepts Inc	2844	F	760 330-9941	8487
Efgp Inc	3949	F	760 692-3900	22796
Ellison Biner	3565	D	760 598-6500	14706
Enaqua	3589	E	760 599-2644	15509
Enertron Technologies Inc	3646	E	800 537-7649	17027
Epic Boats LLC (PA)	3732	F	760 542-6060	20328
Exit Light Co Inc	3646	F	877 352-3948	17032
Ferro Corporation	2819	E	442 224-6100	7496
Flotron Inc	3544	E	760 727-2700	14053
Flux Power Inc	3825	F	760 741-3589	21039
Flux Power Holdings Inc (PA)	3691	D	877 505-3589	19166
Frontier Concrete Inc	3273	E	760 724-4483	10760
Glorious Empire LLC	3714	F	760 598-5000	19673
Golden Rule Bindery Inc	2789	E	760 471-2013	7331
Gw Services LLC (DH)	3581	E	760 560-1111	15398
H P Solutions Inc	3549	E	760 727-2880	14270
Hatch Outdoors Inc	3949	F	760 734-4343	22817
HI Rez Digital Solutions	2752	F	760 597-2650	6613
Honor Life Medallions	3281	F	760 727-8581	10911
Hruby Orbital Systems Inc	3589	F	760 936-8054	15521
Hydrocomponents & Tech Inc	3589	F	760 598-0189	15522
Imagine Communications Corp	3663	F	760 936-4000	17540
Innovative Metal Products Inc	3499	E	760 734-1010	13526
Integrated Aqua Systems Inc	3589	F	760 745-2201	15526
Integrated Mfg Solutions LLC	3999	E	760 599-4300	23363
Intubrite LLC	3841	F	760 727-1900	21750
J & B Manufacturing Corp	3231	C	760 846-6316	10368
J & D Laboratories Inc	2833	B	844 453-5227	7672
J-Mark Manufacturing Inc	3469	E	760 727-6956	12825
Javo Beverage Company Inc	2087	D	760 560-5286	2218
K & K Laboratories Inc	2834	E	760 758-2352	7972
Kammerer Enterprises Inc	3281	D	760 560-0550	10912
Killion Industries Inc (PA)	2541	D	760 727-5102	4917
L & M Machining Center Inc	3599	E	760 437-3810	16129
Lancer Orthodontics Inc (PA)	3843	E	760 744-5585	22170
Leemarc Industries LLC	2329	D	760 598-0505	3101
Leica Biosystems Imaging Inc	3841	C	760 539-1100	21773
LMI Aerospace Inc	3728	C	760 597-7066	20158
LMI Aerospace Inc	3728	C	760 599-4477	20159
Lovestrength LLC	2389	F	760 481-9951	3567
M Klemme Technology Corp	3651	F	760 727-0593	17254
Machine Vision Products Inc (PA)	3827	D	760 438-1138	21378
McCain Manufacturing Inc	3441	C	760 295-9290	11839
Micro-Tech Scientific Inc	3826	F	760 597-9088	21264
Mitchell Instruments Co Inc	3825	F	760 744-2690	21081
Mitchell Test & Safety Inc	3829	F	760 744-2690	21510
Moran Tools	3542	E	760 801-3570	13986
Myosci Technologies Inc	2023	F	760 433-5376	607
Nology Engineering Inc	3714	F	760 591-0888	19729
Nordson Asymtek Inc	3823	E	760 727-2880	20910
Nubs Plastics Inc	3089	E	760 598-2525	9934
Nutritional Engineering Inc	2834	F	760 599-5200	8047
Nuzee Inc	2095	E	760 295-2408	2306
Ocean Divers USA LLC	3089	F	760 599-6898	9941
Orbot	3531	F	760 295-2100	13739
Original Watermen Inc	2311	F	760 599-0990	2973
Polk Audio LLC	3651	E	888 267-5495	17274
Powerlux Corporation	3648	F	760 727-2360	17155
Precision Litho Inc	2752	F	760 727-9400	6790
Predator Motorsports Inc	3089	F	760 734-1749	9989
Primarch Manufacturing Inc	3999	F	760 730-8572	23452
Production Embroidery Inc	2395	F	760 727-7407	3752
Prohibition Brewing Co Inc	2082	E	760 295-3525	1561
Protec Arisawa America Inc	3443	E	760 599-4800	12043
Pulse Metric Inc	3841	F	760 842-8224	21869
Pyron Solar III LLC	3433	F	760 599-5100	11706
Quantum Focus Instruments Corp	3825	F	760 599-1122	21108
R Zamora Inc	3469	E	760 597-1130	12867
Rap4	3949	E	408 434-0434	22868
Raveon Technologies Corp	3663	E	760 444-5995	17640
Rayspan Corporation	3661	F	858 259-9596	17408

	SIC	EMP	PHONE	ENTRY #
Rayzist Photomask Inc (PA)	3955	D	760 727-8561	22972
Real Action Paintball Inc	3949	F	408 848-2846	22870
Rec Inc	3569	F	760 727-8006	14854
Regional Mtls Recovery Inc	1411	E	760 727-0878	293
Revlon Inc	2844	E	760 599-2900	8571
Rmjv LP	3556	B	503 526-5752	14398
Rxsafe LLC	3559	D	760 593-7161	14533
Sandel Avionics Inc	3812	C	760 727-4900	20714
Sandel Avionics Inc (PA)	3812	C	760 727-4900	20715
Sea Breeze Technology Inc	3699	F	760 727-6366	19399
Select Supplements Inc	2833	E	760 431-7509	7693
Select Supplements Inc	2023	E	760 431-7509	619
Sew Sporty	2339	E	760 599-0585	3404
Sherline Products Incorporated	3541	E	760 727-5181	13951
Solatube International Inc (PA)	3442	D	888 765-2882	11984
Stines Machine Inc	3599	E	760 599-9955	16425
Surgistar Inc (PA)	3841	E	760 598-2480	21919
Tacupeto Chips & Salsa Inc	2096	F	760 597-9400	2347
Techniche Solutions	2326	E	619 818-0071	3056
Thirty Three Threads Inc	2252	E	877 486-3769	2768
TNT Assembly LLC	2298	E	760 410-1750	2917
Tony Hawk Inc	3949	F	760 477-2477	22908
Total Source Manufacturing	3821	A	760 598-2146	20779
U S Divers Co Inc	3949	C	760 597-5000	22916
United Research & Mfg	3714	E	760 727-4320	19794
Versaform Corporation	3444	D	760 599-0961	12426
Vision Quest Industries Inc	3842	D	760 734-1550	22120
Walz Caps Inc	2386	E	760 683-9259	3525
Waterless Co Inc	3432	F	760 727-7723	11687
Watkins Manufacturing Corp (HQ)	3999	B	760 598-6464	23522
Watkins Manufacturing Corp	3088	E	760 598-6464	9598
Wax Research Inc	2999	F	760 607-0850	9162
Westbridge Agricultural Pdts	2879	F	760 599-8855	8848
Westbridge Research Group (PA)	2879	F	760 599-8855	8849
Western Cactus Growers Inc	3524	E	760 726-1710	13700
Western Cnc Inc	3599	D	760 597-7000	16521
Wolfpack Inc	3993	E	760 736-4500	23245
Wyroc Inc (PA)	1411	E	760 727-0878	296
Youngdale Manufacturing Corp	3429	E	760 727-0644	11645

WALNUT, CA - Los Angeles County

	SIC	EMP	PHONE	ENTRY #
1perfectchoice	2599	F	909 594-8855	5045
All Strong Industry (usa) Inc (PA)	2591	E	909 598-6494	5013
Amergence Technology Inc	3559	E	909 859-8400	14422
Anima International Corp	3999	F	626 723-4960	23275
Biomechanical Analysis &	3842	E	714 990-5932	21987
Body Flex Sports Inc (PA)	3949	F	909 598-9876	22766
C M Automotive Systems Inc (PA)	3563	E	909 869-7912	14625
Cast Parts Inc (DH)	3324	C	909 595-2252	11154
Cemex Cnstr Mtls PCF LLC	3273	E	909 594-0105	10729
Color Marble Project Group Inc	1442	E	909 595-8858	335
Crush Master Grinding Corp	3599	E	909 595-2249	15871
Disc Replicator Inc	3652	F	909 385-0118	17315
Edro Engineering Inc (DH)	3544	D	909 594-5751	14047
Edro Specialty Steels Inc	3544	E	800 368-3376	14048
Essence Imaging Inc	3861	F	909 979-2116	22421
Fairway Injection Molds Inc	3544	F	909 595-2201	14051
Golden Applexx Co Inc	2759	F	909 594-9788	7074
Hardware Imports Inc	3713	F	909 595-6201	19538
Harrison Beverage Inc	2024	F	626 757-1159	649
Heritage Products LLC	3083	F	909 839-1866	9439
Hing WA Lee Inc	3915	E	909 595-3500	22596
Hiti Digital America Inc	3861	E	909 594-0099	22425
Hupa International Inc	3949	F	909 598-9876	22823
Ikong E-Commerce Inc	3555	F	888 556-1522	14326
In Win Development USA Inc	3572	E	909 348-0588	15047
Infinity Watch Corporation	3993	F	626 289-9878	23132
Jakks Pacific Inc	3944	E	909 594-7771	22686
Lights of America Inc (PA)	3645	B	909 594-7883	16976
Myc Direct Inc	3821	F	909 287-9919	20766
Myers Container LLC	3412	F	800 406-9377	11510
Naturas Foods California Inc	2032	F	909 594-7838	741
Nelson Stud Welding Inc	3452	F	909 468-2105	12688
New Origins Accessories Inc (PA)	3961	F	909 869-7559	22990
Ninas Mexican Foods Inc	2099	F	909 468-5888	2570
Niron Inc	3544	F	909 598-1526	14085
Noodoe Inc	3621	F	909 468-1118	16666
Nu-Health Products Co	2833	F	909 869-0666	7679
Oppo Original Corp	3144	F	909 444-3000	10175
Physicans Formula Holdings Inc (HQ)	2844	F	626 334-3395	8558
Prime Wire & Cable Inc (HQ)	3357	E	888 445-9955	11315
Prophecy Technology LLC	3577	E	909 598-7998	15313
Sea Shield Marine Products	3363	E	909 594-2507	11348
Servers Direct LLC	3571	C	800 576-7931	14972
Settlers Jerky Inc	2013	F	909 444-3999	498
Smtcl Usa Inc	3545	F	626 667-1192	14195

2020 California
Manufacturers Register

© Mergent Inc. 1-800-342-5647

	SIC	EMP	PHONE	ENTRY #
Soderberg Manufacturing Co Inc	3647	D	909 595-1291	17093
Southcoast Cabinet Inc (PA)	2434	E	909 594-3089	4249
SW Fixtures Inc	2541	F	909 595-2506	4945
Total Resources Intl Inc (PA)	3842	D	909 594-1220	22111
Trane US Inc	3585	E	626 913-7913	15459
Tree Island Wire (usa) Inc (DH)	3312	C	909 594-7511	11078
Tri-Net Technology Inc	3577	D	909 598-8818	15355
Tul Inc	3429	D	909 444-0577	11639
Unicom Electric Inc	3669	D	626 964-7873	17770
Universal Mercantile Exchange	3993	F	909 839-0556	23235
V Manufacturing Logistics Inc	2844	E	909 869-6200	8600
Wally International Inc (PA)	2631	C	805 444-7764	5177
Western Hardware Company	3429	F	909 595-6201	11642

WALNUT CREEK, CA - Contra Costa County

	SIC	EMP	PHONE	ENTRY #
Advisor Software Inc (PA)	7372	E	925 299-7778	23573
American Bottling Company	2086	D	925 938-8777	2030
Andre-Boudin Bakeries Inc	2051	F	925 935-4375	1135
Basic American Inc (PA)	2034	D	925 472-4438	843
Bell-Carter Foods LLC (PA)	2033	B	209 549-5939	757
Bpo Systems Inc (PA)	7372	E	925 478-4299	23691
Brighton Collectibles LLC	2389	F	925 932-1500	3543
C A N Enterprises	2253	D	925 939-9736	2776
Canadian Solar (usa) Inc	3674	F	925 807-7499	18157
Carros Sensors Systems Co LLC	3679	C	925 979-4400	18852
Computers and Structures Inc	7372	F	510 649-2200	23767
Contra Costa Newspapers Inc (DH)	2711	A	925 935-2525	5598
Del Monte Foods Inc (HQ)	2033	C	925 949-2772	765
Diablo Clinical Research Inc	2834	E	925 930-7267	7871
Diablo Country Magazine Inc	2721	E	925 943-1111	5919
Domico Software	7372	F	510 841-4155	23824
Energetix Solutions Inc	2892	F	925 926-6412	8904
Exadel Inc (PA)	7372	D	925 363-9510	23883
Insignia SC Holdings LLC (HQ)	2064	A	925 399-8900	1374
Institutional Real Estate (PA)	2741	E	925 933-4040	6257
Kainos Dental Technologies LLC (PA)	3843	E	800 331-4834	22165
Kellogg Company	2043	B	925 952-8423	1025
Keurig Dr Pepper Inc	2086	E	925 938-8777	2085
Lubrizol Corporation	2899	F	925 352-4843	8992
Main Street Kitchens	2679	F	925 944-0153	5513
Malikco LLC	7372	E	925 974-3555	24125
Nancys Specialty Foods	2099	B	510 494-1100	2560
Quint Measuring Systems Inc	3829	F	510 351-9405	21526
R & R Maintenance Group	3524	F	707 863-0328	13693
Seal Software Inc (PA)	7372	F	650 938-7325	24393
Vantiq Inc	7372	F	303 377-2882	24547
Wencon Development Inc	3444	D	925 478-8269	12432
Western Hellenic Journal Inc	2711	E	925 939-3900	5863
Westrock Cp LLC	2672	D	925 946-0842	5380

WALNUT GROVE, CA - Sacramento County

	SIC	EMP	PHONE	ENTRY #
Wilcox Brothers Inc	3523	D	916 776-1784	13688

WASCO, CA - Kern County

	SIC	EMP	PHONE	ENTRY #
Ag-Weld Inc	7692	F	661 758-3061	24614
Carter Pump & Machine Inc	3599	F	661 393-8620	15827
Certis USA LLC	2879	F	661 758-8471	8822
Eggs West LLC	2015	E	661 758-9700	509
Primex Farms LLC (PA)	2068	E	661 758-7790	1437
Sunnygem LLC	2033	B	661 758-0491	828

WATERFORD, CA - Stanislaus County

	SIC	EMP	PHONE	ENTRY #
Foster Poultry Farms	2015	E	209 394-7901	512
Roberts Ferry Nut Company Inc	2064	F	209 874-3247	1392

WATSONVILLE, CA - Santa Cruz County

	SIC	EMP	PHONE	ENTRY #
Annieglass Inc (PA)	3229	E	831 761-2041	10298
Boyer Inc	2873	E	831 724-0123	8790
Carrera Construction Inc	1389	F	831 728-3299	181
Central Coast Cabinets	2521	F	831 724-2992	4790
Consolidated Training LLC	3999	E	831 768-8888	23305
Corralitos Market & Sausage Co	2013	E	831 722-2633	450
Del Mar Food Products Corp	2033	B	831 722-3516	761
Del Mar Seafoods Inc (PA)	2092	C	831 763-3000	2258
Eagle Tech Manufacturing Inc	3823	E	831 768-7467	20862
Elecraft Incorporated	3825	E	831 763-4211	21027
Fox Factory Inc (HQ)	3714	D	831 274-6500	19661
Golden Sheaf Bread Co Inc	2051	E	831 722-0179	1220
Granite Rock Co (PA)	1442	D	831 768-2000	341
H A Rider & Sons	2086	E	831 722-3882	2080
Heatwave Labs Inc	3671	E	831 722-9081	17786
Hephaestus Innovations	3556	F	831 254-8555	14372
K S Equipment Inc	3679	F	831 722-7173	18970
Larosa Tortilla Factory	2099	E	831 728-5332	2521
Laselva Beach Spice Co Inc	2099	E	831 724-4500	2522
Mizkan Americas Inc	2099	F	831 728-2061	2553
Monterey Bay Rebar Inc (PA)	3441	F	831 724-3013	11849

	SIC	EMP	PHONE	ENTRY #
News Media Corporation	2711	D	831 761-7300	5777
Nordic Naturals Inc (PA)	2077	C	800 662-2544	1462
Printworx Inc	3577	F	831 722-7147	15312
Rainbow Fin Company Inc	3949	E	831 728-2998	22867
S Martinelli & Company (PA)	2099	C	831 724-1126	2607
Samco Plastics Inc	2671	F	831 761-1392	5340
Schmid Thermal Systems Inc	3567	C	831 763-0113	14775
Seascape Lamps Inc	3645	F	831 728-5699	16990
Smith & Vandiver Corporation	2844	D	831 722-9526	8584
Stalfab	3556	F	831 786-1600	14403
Test Electronics	3825	E	831 763-2000	21144
Threshold Enterprises Ltd	2833	E	831 425-3955	7696
Titan Frozen Fruit LLC (PA)	2037	E	831 540-4110	931
Trufocus Corporation	3844	E	831 761-9981	22223
Walker Street Pallets LLC	2448	F	831 724-6088	4405
Westek Electronics Inc	3669	E	831 740-6300	17773
Woodworks	2511	F	831 688-8420	4626

WEAVERVILLE, CA - Trinity County

	SIC	EMP	PHONE	ENTRY #
Emerald Kingdom Greenhouse LLC	3448	E	530 215-5670	12543
Trinity River Lumber Company (PA)	2421	C	530 623-5561	3964

WEED, CA - Siskiyou County

	SIC	EMP	PHONE	ENTRY #
Cg Roxane LLC	2086	D	530 225-1260	2053
M & M Logging Inc	2411	F	530 938-0745	3894
Pacific States Treating Inc	2491	F	530 938-4408	4479

WELDON, CA - Kern County

	SIC	EMP	PHONE	ENTRY #
Witten Logging	2411	F	760 378-3640	3921

WEST COVINA, CA - Los Angeles County

	SIC	EMP	PHONE	ENTRY #
Baatz Enterprises Inc	3711	F	323 660-4866	19458
Bellavuos	2844	F	626 653-0121	8443
Concorde Battery Corp (PA)	3692	E	626 813-1234	19179
Continental American Corp	3069	D	626 964-0164	9295
Graybills Metal Polishing Inc	3471	F	626 967-5742	13017
Guess Inc	2325	E	626 856-5555	3005
Interspace Battery Inc (PA)	3356	F	626 813-1234	11274
Kulayful Silicone Bracelets	3961	E	626 610-3816	22987
Yogi Investments Inc	3089	F	909 984-5703	10134

WEST HILLS, CA - Los Angeles County

	SIC	EMP	PHONE	ENTRY #
Abacus Printing & Graphics Inc	2752	F	818 929-6740	6390
Aerojet Rocketdyne De Inc	2869	C	818 586-9629	8707
Kelly Teegarden Organics LLC	2844	F	818 518-0707	8526
Mitrani USA Corp	3088	F	818 888-9994	9592
Pharmavite LLC (DH)	2833	C	818 221-6200	7681
Thermo Fisher Scientific Inc	3826	F	747 494-1413	21314

WEST HOLLYWOOD, CA - Los Angeles County

	SIC	EMP	PHONE	ENTRY #
402 Shoes Inc	2341	E	323 655-5437	3437
A & J Enterprises Inc	2752	F	323 654-5902	6389
AAA Printing By Wizard	2395	E	310 285-0505	3718
Art Services Melrose	3089	E	310 247-1452	9640
Cemex Cnstr Mtls PCF LLC	3273	E	323 466-4928	10735
Chase-Durer Ltd (PA)	3873	F	310 550-7280	22479
Clique Brands Inc (PA)	2721	E	323 648-5619	5905
Cosmo International Corp	2844	E	310 271-1100	8470
Cycle House LLC	3949	E	310 358-0888	22787
Fountainhead Industries	3999	E	310 248-2444	23337
Grade A Sign LLC	3993	E	310 652-9700	23124
Growdiaries LLC	7372	E	626 354-8935	23959
Halo Top International LLC (PA)	2024	E	434 409-2057	648
Haworth Inc	2522	F	310 854-7633	4839
Holland & Sherry Inc	2273	F	310 657-8550	2870
Iac/Interactivecorp	7372	F	212 314-7300	23995
J R U D E S Holdings LLC	2311	F	310 281-0800	2966
Kathrine Baumann Beverly Hills	2335	E	310 274-7441	3237
Lavinder Inc	2299	F	310 278-2456	2940
Muzik Inc (PA)	3679	E	973 615-1223	19024
Neatpocket LLC	7372	F	323 632-7440	24191
Palihuse Hllway Rsidences Assn	2335	F	323 656-4100	3248
Pro Tour Memorabilia LLC	2499	E	424 303-7200	4522
Sargam International Inc	3651	F	310 855-9694	17280
Sports Medicine Info Network	2711	F	310 659-6889	5835
Sunset Leather Group	3199	E	310 388-4898	10254

WEST POINT, CA - Calaveras County

	SIC	EMP	PHONE	ENTRY #
Martin Fischer Logging Inc	2411	F	209 293-4847	3896

WEST SACRAMENTO, CA - Yolo County

	SIC	EMP	PHONE	ENTRY #
Aerospace Facilities Group Inc	3569	F	702 513-8336	14793
Agraquest Inc (DH)	2834	D	866 992-2937	7732
Arcadia Inc	3355	E	916 375-1478	11255
Beckman Coulter Inc	3826	A	916 374-3511	21183
Big Valley Metals	3441	F	916 372-2383	11748
Bullet Guard Corporation	3499	F	800 233-5632	13504
Bullseye Leak Detection Inc	3599	F	916 760-8944	15802

Mergent email: customerrelations@mergent.com
1448

2020 California
Manufacturers Register

(P-0000) Products & Services Section entry number
(PA)=Parent Co (HQ)=Headquarters (DH)=Div Headquarters

Company	SIC	EMP	PHONE	ENTRY #
Cintas Corporation	2326	F	916 375-8633	3029
Cosmo Import & Export LLC (PA)	2514	E	916 209-5500	4688
Crown Equipment Corporation	3537	E	916 373-8980	13868
Cummins Pacific LLC	3519	E	916 371-0630	13587
Delta Web Printing Inc	2759	F	916 375-0044	7044
East Penn Manufacturing Co	3691	F	916 374-9965	19157
ECB Corp	3444	E	916 492-8900	12191
Farmers Rice Cooperative	2044	C	916 373-5500	1042
Farmers Rice Cooperative	2044	C	916 373-5500	1043
Flowmaster Inc	3714	C	916 371-2345	19656
Grand Cabinets and Stone Inc	2434	F	510 759-3268	4202
Heco Inc	3566	F	916 372-5411	14741
Hydrolynx Systems Inc	3826	F	916 374-1800	21241
Icon Apparel Group LLC	2231	E	916 372-4266	2745
International Paper Company	2621	E	916 371-4634	5124
Mikuni Color USA Inc	3624	F	916 572-0704	16687
National Sales Inc	2621	F	916 912-2894	5135
Nor-Cal Beverage Co Inc	2086	E	916 372-1700	2100
Professional Plastics Inc	2821	F	916 374-4580	7600
Revolution Screening Inc (PA)	2759	F	916 604-6865	7199
Richard K Gould Inc	2899	E	916 371-5943	9020
Ryko Solutions Inc	3589	E	916 372-8815	15572
Sacramento Envelope Co Inc	2752	F	916 371-4747	6852
Siemens Hlthcare Dgnostics Inc	2835	E	916 372-1900	8257
Siemens Industry Inc	3822	F	916 553-4444	20814
Sign Technology Inc	3993	E	916 372-1200	23203
Silke Communications Inc	3663	E	916 245-6555	17659
Tackett Volume Press Inc	2759	E	916 374-8991	7237
Talco Foam Inc (PA)	3069	F	916 492-8840	9377
Taylor Communications Inc	2761	D	916 340-0200	7289
Tk Classics LLC	2514	F	916 209-5500	4704
Tomra Sorting Inc (DH)	3556	D	720 870-2240	14406
Tri-C Machine Corporation (PA)	3599	F	916 371-8090	16466
Tri-C Manufacturing Inc	3559	F	916 371-1700	14547
Tri-City Technologies Inc	2759	F	916 503-5300	7256
Vss Emultech Inc	2951	F	916 371-8480	9108
Woodsmiths Architectural Casew	2541	F	916 456-8871	4958
Yara North America Inc	2879	E	916 375-1109	8850

WESTLAKE VILLAGE, CA - Ventura County

Company	SIC	EMP	PHONE	ENTRY #
ABF Data Systems Inc	7372	F	818 591-8307	23542
Agilent Technologies Inc	3825	A	408 345-8886	20996
American Clubs LLC	2741	F	805 496-1218	6181
Astera Software Corporation	7372	F	805 579-0004	23632
Baltic Ltvian Unvrsal Elec LLC	3651	E	818 879-5200	17200
Beaudry International LLC	3915	F	213 623-5025	22593
Blue Microphones LLC	3651	F	818 879-5200	17206
Boatworks	3732	F	805 374-9455	20316
Borett Automation Technologies	3569	F	818 597-8664	14799
Carros Americas Inc	3679	E	805 267-7176	18851
Cforia Software Inc	7372	E	818 871-9687	23730
Dole Packaged Foods LLC (HQ)	2037	A	805 601-5500	910
Earth Print Inc	2752	F	818 879-6050	6555
Edge Solutions Consulting Inc (PA)	3571	E	818 591-3500	14904
EKA Technologies Inc	3663	E	805 379-8668	17510
General Dynmics Mssion Systems	3669	C	805 497-5042	17731
Global Custom Security Inc	3699	F	818 889-6900	19319
Implant Direct Sybron Mfg LLC	3843	C	818 444-3300	22161
Inphi International Pte Ltd	3674	F	805 719-2300	18297
Inspyr Therapeutics Inc (PA)	2834	F	818 661-6302	7952
Interntional Photo Plates Corp	3471	E	805 496-5031	13032
Invia Robotics Inc (PA)	3569	F	818 597-1680	14830
K-Swiss Sales Corp	3021	C	818 706-5100	9175
Kythera Biopharmaceuticals Inc	2834	C	818 587-4500	7984
Mannkind Corporation (PA)	2834	C	818 661-5000	8002
Millworks By Design Inc	2431	F	818 597-1326	4088
Omega Technologies Inc	3423	F	818 264-7970	11538
Opolo Vineyards Inc	2084	F	805 238-9593	1848
Packit LLC	2673	F	805 496-2999	5409
Paymentmax Processing Inc	3578	D	805 557-1692	15376
PMS Systems Corporation	7372	F	310 450-2566	24305
R & R Services Corporation	3069	E	818 889-2562	9361
Rantec Microwave Systems Inc (PA)	3812	D	818 223-5000	20680
Safe Publishing Company	2759	D	805 973-1300	7206
Satcom Solutions Corporation	3812	F	818 991-9794	20717
Satellite 2000 Systems	3663	E	818 991-9794	17650
Skyguard LLC	3699	E	703 262-0500	19405
Star Route LLC	2771	F	805 405-8510	7300
Sunbritetv LLC	3663	E	805 214-7250	17674
Terramar Graphics Inc	2759	F	805 529-8845	7245
Ventura Aerospace Inc	3728	F	818 540-3130	20267
Vitavet Labs Inc	3999	E	818 865-2600	23519
Xplain Corporation	2721	F	805 494-9797	6062

WESTMINSTER, CA - Orange County

Company	SIC	EMP	PHONE	ENTRY #
AA Laboratory Eggs Inc (PA)	2087	F	714 893-5675	2187

Company	SIC	EMP	PHONE	ENTRY #
Adams Welding Inc	7692	F	714 412-7684	24612
Anthony Jones	3949	F	714 894-3483	22748
B/E Aerospace Inc	3599	D	714 896-9001	15771
B/E Aerospace Inc	3728	C	714 896-9001	20053
Biolargo Inc (PA)	2819	F	949 643-9540	7472
Bodycote Imt Inc	3398	D	714 893-6561	11434
Bodycote Thermal Proc Inc	3398	D	714 893-6561	11437
Cgr/Thompson Industries Inc	3612	D	714 678-4200	16544
Dang Tha	2531	F	714 898-0989	4856
Dolstra Automatic Products	3599	F	714 894-2062	15903
Einstein Noah Rest Group Inc	2022	F	714 847-4609	547
European Woodwork	2434	F	714 892-8831	4192
Finddoctr Inc	2741	F	657 888-2629	6236
Happy2ez Inc	3086	F	714 897-6100	9549
Lavang Tech Prcsion Sheet Mtls	3549	F	714 901-2782	14272
Lexor Inc	3999	D	714 444-4144	23394
Machining Specialist Corp	3599	E	714 847-1214	16166
New CAM Commerce Solutions LLC	7372	D	714 338-0200	24202
New Technology Plastics Inc	2821	E	562 941-6034	7584
Nguoi Vietnamese People Inc (PA)	2711	F	714 892-9414	5779
Thompson Industries Ltd	3728	E	310 679-9193	20249
Tru-Form Plastics Inc	3089	F	310 327-9444	10094
Vietnmese Amrcn Mdia Corp Vamc	2711	F	714 379-2851	5859
West Coast Timber Corp	2411	F	714 893-4374	3917
Western Illuminated Plas Inc	3646	F	714 895-3067	17084

WHITTIER, CA - Los Angeles County

Company	SIC	EMP	PHONE	ENTRY #
A & A Fabrication & Polsg Corp	3441	F	562 696-0441	11728
A F E Industries Inc (PA)	2759	D	562 944-6889	6970
AC Products Inc	2891	F	714 630-7311	8851
Aguilar Williams Inc	3471	F	562 693-2736	12910
Allergan Inc	2834	C	512 527-6688	7737
Boeing Company	3721	A	562 944-6583	19867
Calico Tag & Label Inc	2759	F	562 944-6889	7013
Cameron Technologies Us Inc	3823	D	562 222-8440	20844
Carson Valley Inc	3444	F	562 906-0062	12153
Chip-Makers Tooling Supply Inc	3544	F	562 698-5840	14032
Coastal Tag & Label Inc	2759	D	562 946-4318	7026
Comfort Industries Inc	2231	E	562 692-8288	2744
Compu Aire Inc	3585	C	562 945-8971	15420
Consteel Industrial Inc	3441	E	562 806-4575	11772
Cryostar USA LLC	3561	D	562 903-1290	14566
Cutting Edge Creative LLC	2542	D	562 907-7007	4972
Dukers Appliance Co USA Ltd (DH)	3585	F	562 568-4060	15425
Epmar Corporation	2851	E	562 946-8781	8646
George Coriaty	2752	E	562 698-7513	6590
Georgia Pacific Holdings Inc	2676	A	626 926-1474	5461
Grand Motif Records	3652	F	562 698-8538	17326
Gulfstream Aerospace Corp GA	3721	A	562 907-9300	19905
Harris Organs Inc	3931	E	562 693-3442	22625
Harten Jewelry Co Inc	3911	E	562 652-5006	22526
Hedman Manufacturing (PA)	3714	E	562 204-1031	19679
Industry Color Printing Inc	2752	E	626 961-2403	6636
Jason Incorporated	3291	E	562 921-9821	10947
Leggett & Platt Incorporated	2515	D	562 945-2641	4728
Loren Industries	3993	E	562 699-1122	23150
Mar Vista Wood Products Inc	2431	F	562 698-2024	4080
Medlin and Son Engineering Svc	3599	E	562 464-5889	16190
Messer LLC	2813	F	562 903-1290	7421
Miller Castings Inc (PA)	3324	F	562 695-0461	11162
Miller Castings Inc	3324	F	562 695-0461	11163
Pacific Coast Graphics Bindery	2789	D	562 908-5900	7341
Pacific Die Services Inc	3544	F	562 907-4463	14090
Pacific Truck Equipment Inc	3713	D	562 464-9674	19549
Performance Truck and Trlr LLC	3715	F	909 605-0323	19829
Quaker City Plating	3471	C	562 945-3721	13083
R & R Fabrications Inc	3441	F	562 693-0500	11870
Rahn Industries Incorporated (PA)	3585	D	562 908-0680	15451
Rasmussen Iron Works Inc	3433	D	562 696-8718	11708
Rgr Diversified Services Inc	2515	F	562 522-0028	4739
Russ Bassett Corp	2511	C	562 945-2445	4608
Santa Fe Rubber Products Inc	3069	E	562 693-2776	9368
Southern Cal Valve MGT Co Inc	3491	F	562 404-2246	13322
Tops Slt Inc	2675	C	562 968-2000	5455
Tube-Tainer Inc	2655	F	562 945-3711	5305
United Memorial Products Inc	3272	E	562 699-3578	10660
West Coast Sheepskin Import	2399	F	562 945-5151	3867
Western Yankee Inc	2759	F	562 944-6889	7270
Windsor House Investments Inc	2675	E	323 261-0231	5456

WILDOMAR, CA - Riverside County

Company	SIC	EMP	PHONE	ENTRY #
Barns and Buildings Inc	3448	D	951 678-4571	12533
Fcp Inc	3448	D	951 678-4571	12545

WILLIAMS, CA - Colusa County

Company	SIC	EMP	PHONE	ENTRY #
Morning Star Packing Co LP	2033	E	530 473-3642	799

GEOGRAPHIC

Company	SIC	EMP	PHONE	ENTRY #
Tamaki Rice Corporation	2044	E	530 473-2862	1053

WILLITS, CA - Mendocino County

Company	SIC	EMP	PHONE	ENTRY #
Advanced Mfg & Dev Inc	3444	C	707 459-9451	12088
G and S Milling Co	2431	E	707 459-0294	4047
Magnetic Coils Inc	3677	E	707 459-5994	18723
Media News Group	2711	F	707 459-4643	5739
Norcal Recycled Rock Aggregate (PA)	3273	F	707 459-9636	10811
Northern Aggregates Inc	1442	E	707 459-3929	355
Shusters Logging Inc	2411	D	707 459-4131	3905
Willits Redwood Company Inc	2421	F	707 459-4549	3967
Windsor Willits Company	2431	E	707 459-8568	4154

WILLOWS, CA - Glenn County

Company	SIC	EMP	PHONE	ENTRY #
Calplant I LLC	2493	E	530 570-0542	4483
Calplant I Holdco LLC (PA)	2493	E	530 570-0542	4484
Johns Manville Corporation	3296	B	530 934-6243	10984
Rumiano Cheese Co (PA)	2022	C	530 934-5438	571
Sierra Nevada Cheese Co Inc	2022	D	530 934-8660	577
Western Ready Mix Concrete Co (PA)	3273	E	530 934-2185	10873

WILMINGTON, CA - Los Angeles County

Company	SIC	EMP	PHONE	ENTRY #
5 Ball Inc	2731	F	310 830-0630	6064
Air Products and Chemicals Inc	2813	E	310 952-9172	7399
Associated Wire Rope & Rigging	2298	E	310 448-5444	2905
Bgm Installation Inc	3011	F	310 830-3113	9165
Cal LLC Breakwater Intl	3731	F	310 518-1718	20281
California Carbon Company Inc	2819	F	562 436-1962	7475
California Sulphur Company	2819	E	562 437-0768	7477
Cooper & Brain Inc	1311	F	310 834-4411	45
D-1280-X Inc	2911	E	310 835-6909	9044
Japanese Truck Dismantling	3711	F	310 835-3100	19480
Juanitas Foods	2032	C	310 834-5339	732
Los Angeles Refining Co	2911	F	310 522-6000	9051
Marine Fenders Intl Inc	3465	E	310 834-7037	12746
Pacific Fibre & Rope Co Inc	2298	F	310 834-4567	2912
Pacific Green Trucking Inc	3743	F	310 830-4528	20375
Royal-Pedic Mattress Mfg LLC	2515	F	310 518-5420	4740
San Pedro Sign Company	3993	F	310 549-4661	23192
Sea Tek Spars & Rigging Inc	3731	F	310 549-1800	20304
Sepor Inc	3821	F	310 830-6601	20774
Ultramar Inc	1389	E	310 834-7254	277
US Borax Inc	2819	C	310 522-5300	7533
Valero Ref Company-California	2911	B	562 491-6754	9083
West Coast Aerospace Inc (PA)	3965	D	310 518-3167	23016
Wilmington Machine Inc	3599	F	310 518-3213	16529
Wilmington Woodworks Inc	2448	E	310 834-1015	4409

WILTON, CA - Sacramento County

Company	SIC	EMP	PHONE	ENTRY #
Gaines Well Service Inc (PA)	1389	E	916 687-6751	199

WINDSOR, CA - Sonoma County

Company	SIC	EMP	PHONE	ENTRY #
Advanced Viticulture Inc	2084	F	707 838-3805	1576
Denbeste Manufacturing Inc	3713	F	707 838-1407	19527
Fantasy Manufacturing Inc	3599	F	707 838-7686	15951
Hausenware Koyo LLC	3229	F	412 897-3064	10310
Jackson Family Wines Inc	2084	E	707 528-6278	1765
Micro-Vu Corp California (PA)	3827	D	707 838-6272	21383
Morgan Medesign Inc	3841	F	707 568-2929	21828
Nieco Corporation	3589	D	707 838-3226	15550
Regal III LLC	2084	D	707 836-2100	1883
Six Sigma Precision Inc	3599	F	707 836-0869	16406
Sonoma Tilemakers Inc (DH)	3253	D	707 837-8177	10451
Windsor Oaks Vineyards LLP	2084	E	707 433-4050	2004

WINNETKA, CA - Los Angeles County

Company	SIC	EMP	PHONE	ENTRY #
Green Cures Inc	2833	E	818 773-3929	7665
Life Media Inc	2721	E	800 201-9440	5977

WINTERS, CA - Yolo County

Company	SIC	EMP	PHONE	ENTRY #
Access Mfg Inc	3713	F	530 795-0720	19515
Creative Concepts and Design	2431	F	707 812-9320	4023
J McDowell Wldg Frm Mchy Inc	7692	F	530 661-6006	24643
Pavestone LLC	3281	E	530 795-4400	10919

WINTON, CA - Merced County

Company	SIC	EMP	PHONE	ENTRY #
Koch Feeds Inc	2048	E	209 725-8253	1105
Santa Fe Aggregates Inc (HQ)	1442	F	209 358-3303	358
Winton Times	2711	E	209 358-5311	5868

WOODLAKE, CA - Tulare County

Company	SIC	EMP	PHONE	ENTRY #
Cemex Cnstr Mtls PCF LLC	3273	F	559 597-2397	10717
Country Plastics Inc	3089	F	559 597-2556	9730
Dryvit Systems Inc	2899	E	559 564-3591	8959
Mosier Bros	3443	F	559 564-3304	12032
US Tower Corp	3441	D	559 564-6000	11908

WOODLAND, CA - Yolo County

Company	SIC	EMP	PHONE	ENTRY #
A Teichert & Son Inc	1442	E	530 661-4290	323

Company	SIC	EMP	PHONE	ENTRY #
AA Production Services Inc (PA)	1389	E	530 668-7525	150
Acme Bag Co Inc (PA)	2674	F	530 662-6130	5432
Alemad Inc	2541	E	530 661-1697	4878
American International Mfg Co	3523	E	530 666-2446	13609
Ames Fire Waterworks	3625	D	530 666-2493	16697
Baron Usa LLC	3569	E	931 528-8476	14796
Bentec Medical Opco LLC	3841	E	530 406-3333	21626
Bentec Scientific LLC	3841	E	530 406-3333	21627
Bright People Foods Inc (PA)	2099	E	530 669-6870	2411
Bunge North America Inc	2044	D	530 666-1691	1035
Cache Creek Foods LLC	2099	E	530 662-1764	2414
California Cascade-Woodland	2491	E	530 666-1261	4473
Califrnia PCF Rice Mil A CA LP	2044	C	530 661-1923	1038
Cfarms Inc	2099	E	916 375-3000	2422
Colombaras Cabinet & Mllwk Inc	2521	F	530 662-2665	4791
Culinary Farms Inc	2034	E	916 375-3000	848
Earthsavers Erosion Ctrl LLC	3822	F	530 662-7700	20791
Four Wheel Campers Inc	3792	E	530 666-1442	20486
Gayle Manufacturing Co Inc (PA)	3441	C	530 662-0284	11801
Gold River Mills LLC (PA)	2044	D	530 661-1923	1044
Hygieia Biological Labs (PA)	2836	E	530 661-1443	8310
Interlock Industries Inc	3444	D	530 668-5690	12248
Johnson Farm Machinery Co Inc	3523	E	530 662-1788	13641
Johnstons Trading Post Inc	2449	E	530 661-6152	4419
Jr3 Inc	3823	F	530 661-3677	20892
Kimzey Welding Works Inc	3599	F	530 662-9331	16118
Medianews Group Inc	2711	F	530 662-5421	5745
Noble Methane Inc	1389	F	530 668-7961	236
Olam West Coast Inc	2033	A	530 473-4290	811
Pacific Coast Producers	2033	B	530 662-8661	816
Pgp International Inc (DH)	2099	C	530 662-5056	2585
Planit Solutions	7372	E	530 666-6647	24302
Precision Laser Tek	3441	E	530 661-3580	11865
Prime Conduit Inc	2821	E	530 669-0160	7599
Pt Welding Inc	7692	F	530 406-0267	24658
Pure Nature Foods LLC	2096	E	530 723-5269	2340
Ricardo Ochoa	2653	E	530 668-1152	5262
Roudybush Inc (PA)	2048	E	530 668-6196	1124
Sachs Industries Inc	2679	F	631 242-9000	5527
Sunfoods LLC	2044	E	530 661-1923	1052
Tacsense Inc	3841	F	530 797-0008	21921
Truck Accessories Group LLC	3792	C	530 666-0176	20495
Vogt Western Silver Ltd	3911	E	530 669-6840	22583
Weslan Systems Inc	3559	F	530 668-3304	14555
Western Foods LLC (PA)	2041	E	530 601-5991	1013
Woodland Welding Works	3441	F	530 666-5531	11922

WOODLAND HILLS, CA - Los Angeles County

Company	SIC	EMP	PHONE	ENTRY #
American Plastic Card LLC	3089	C	818 784-4224	9626
Apex Communications Inc (DH)	7372	F	818 379-8400	23603
Asi/Silica Machinery LLC (PA)	3366	E	818 920-1962	11395
Blackline Systems Inc (HQ)	7372	C	877 777-7750	23676
Cabeau Inc	2399	E	877 962-2232	3834
Catalina Yachts Inc (PA)	3732	C	818 884-7700	20317
Cbj LP	2721	F	818 676-1750	5898
Cut & Trim Inc	2331	F	818 264-0101	3152
Eddies Perfume & Cosmtc Co Inc	2844	F	818 341-1717	8486
Final Data Inc	2741	F	818 835-9560	6235
Forsythe Tech Worldwide	3841	F	818 710-8694	21716
Goengineer Inc	7372	F	818 716-1650	23947
Graham Webb International Inc (DH)	2844	D	760 918-3600	8502
Hillside Capital Inc	3663	C	650 367-2011	17536
ICON Line Inc	3999	E	818 709-4266	23361
Invotech Systems Inc	7372	E	818 461-9800	24043
King Nutronics Corporation	3823	E	818 887-5460	20896
La Parent Magazine (PA)	2721	E	818 264-2222	5972
Leadmmatic LLC	2741	E	310 857-4511	6269
Linx Bracelets Inc	3911	E	818 224-4050	22540
Lumio Inc	3674	F	586 861-2408	18363
Lynx Phtnic Ntworks A Del Corp	3661	F	818 878-7500	17385
Medianews Group Inc	2711	A	818 713-3000	5741
Medic Ids	3999	F	818 705-0595	23404
Micro Chips of America Inc	3679	E	818 577-9543	19013
Moki International (usa) Inc	3651	E	205 208-0179	17263
National Diversified Sales Inc (HQ)	3089	C	559 562-9888	9917
New Century Gold LLC	3911	E	818 936-2676	22554
Northrop Grumman Corporation	3812	F	818 715-2383	20650
Northrop Grumman Innovation	3812	B	818 887-8100	20651
Northrop Grumman Intl Trdg Inc	3812	A	818 715-3607	20653
Northrop Grumman Systems Corp	3812	A	818 715-4040	20654
Northrop Grumman Systems Corp	3812	F	818 715-2597	20658
Panavision International LP (HQ)	3861	B	818 316-1080	22447
Prince Development LLC	2844	E	866 774-6234	8567
Quantum Energy LLC	1382	E	800 950-3519	135
Quantum-Dynamics Co Inc	3823	E	818 719-0142	20925
Real Software Systems LLC (PA)	7372	D	818 313-8000	24342

2020 California
Manufacturers Register

(P-0000) Products & Services Section entry number
(PA)=Parent Co (HQ)=Headquarters (DH)=Div Headquarters

	SIC	EMP	PHONE	ENTRY #
Senju Usa Inc	2834	F	818 719-7190	8123
Silgan Containers Corporation (DH)	3411	D	818 348-3700	11502
Silgan Containers LLC (HQ)	3411	D	818 710-3700	11503
Silgan Containers Mfg Corp (DH)	3411	B	818 710-3700	11507
Sun-Mate Corp	3944	F	818 700-0572	22717
Tag-It Pacific Inc	2269	E	818 444-4100	2861
TI Limited LLC (PA)	7372	D	323 877-5991	24508
Tinyinklingcom LLC	3069	F	877 777-6287	9380
Weider Health and Fitness	2087	B	818 884-6800	2235
Weider Leasing Inc	2721	D	818 884-6800	6056
Western Bagel Baking Corp	2051	E	818 887-5451	1293
Wilshire Book Company Inc	2731	E	818 700-1522	6163
Xavient Digital LLC	7372	A	805 955-4111	24591

WOODSIDE, CA - San Mateo County

	SIC	EMP	PHONE	ENTRY #
Clos De La Tech LLC	2084	F	650 722-3038	1637
Langley Hill Quarry	1429	F	650 851-0179	315
Nemco Electronics Corp	3675	C	650 571-1234	18683
Wine Company of San Francisco	2084	F	650 851-0965	2006

YORBA LINDA, CA - Orange County

	SIC	EMP	PHONE	ENTRY #
Aaero Swiss	3599	F	714 692-0558	15670
Alpha Omega Swiss Inc	3451	E	714 692-8009	12618
Aseptic Technology LLC	3221	D	714 694-0168	10285
B&K Precision Corporation (PA)	3825	E	714 921-9095	21009
Beckers Fabrication Inc	2672	E	714 692-1600	5357
Boyd Corporation (PA)	3441	F	714 533-2375	11751
C4 Litho	2752	F	714 259-1073	6465
Carefusion 211 Inc	3841	A	714 283-2228	21654
Carefusion Corporation	3841	E	800 231-2466	21656
Cobra Engineering Inc	3714	D	714 692-8180	19617
Comstar Industries Inc	3625	E	714 556-1400	16706
Dan Copp Crushing Corp	1442	E	714 777-6400	337
Digital Label Solutions Inc	2679	E	714 982-5000	5506
Engineering Jk Aerospace & Def	3728	F	714 414-6722	20100
Euroline Steel Windows	3442	E	877 590-2741	11953
Filter Concepts Incorporated	3677	E	714 545-7003	18714
Fixture Design & Mfg Co	2599	E	714 776-3104	5060
Fpg Oc Inc	2087	D	714 692-2950	2211
GE Aviation Systems LLC	3728	C	714 692-0200	20112
Gramic Enterprises Inc	2082	F	714 329-8627	1534
Honeywell International Inc	3724	A	714 337-6864	19961
Implant Direct Sybron Intl LLC (HQ)	3843	E	818 444-3000	22160
Infinity Systems Inc	3599	F	714 692-1722	16045
Inflight Warning Systems Inc	3728	F	714 993-9394	20138
Infrared Dynamics Inc	3433	E	714 572-4050	11701
Jondo Ltd (PA)	3861	D	714 279-2300	22434
Loritz & Associates Inc	3089	F	714 694-0200	9879
M B S Inc	3691	F	714 693-9952	19170
Maxxess Systems Inc (PA)	7372	F	714 772-1000	24132
Mc2 Sabtech Holdings Inc	3571	E	714 221-5000	14940
Multiquip Industries Corp	3442	F	888 996-7267	11973
Nasco Gourmet Foods Inc	2033	D	714 279-2100	801
Nobel Biocare Usa LLC	3843	B	714 282-4800	22175
Outdoor Sign System Inc (PA)	3993	F	714 692-2052	23173
Pacifictech Molded Pdts Inc	3069	E	714 279-9928	9350
Pdma Ventures Inc	3999	E	714 777-8770	23444
Precision Fluorescent West Inc (DH)	3646	D	352 692-5900	17065
Sabred International Packg Inc	3086	E	714 996-2800	9567
Specialteam Medical Svc Inc	3841	E	714 694-0348	21907
Specialty Motions Inc	3562	E	951 735-8722	14616
Studer Creative Packaging Inc	3089	F	818 344-1665	10075
Thomas Cnc Machining	3599	F	714 692-9373	16456
Tlk Industries Inc	3999	F	714 692-9373	23505
Totty Printing	2759	F	714 633-7081	7253

	SIC	EMP	PHONE	ENTRY #
Trigon Electronics Inc	3699	F	714 633-7442	19424
Viasys Respiratory Care Inc	3841	C	714 283-2228	21957
Vyaire Medical Inc	3841	E	714 919-3265	21961
Welland Industries LLC	3999	F	714 528-9900	23524
Zet-Tek Precision Machining (PA)	3599	F	714 777-8770	16537

YOUNTVILLE, CA - Napa County

	SIC	EMP	PHONE	ENTRY #
Cosentino Signature Wineries	2084	E	707 921-2809	1651
Domaine Chandon Inc (DH)	2084	D	707 944-8844	1669
Dominus Estate Corporation	2084	F	707 944-8954	1671
Goosecross Cellars A Cal Corp	2084	F	707 944-1986	1732
Goosecross Cellars Coorstek	2084	F	707 944-1986	1733
Twin Peaks Winery Inc	2084	F	707 945-0855	1977

YREKA, CA - Siskiyou County

	SIC	EMP	PHONE	ENTRY #
Custom Crushing Industries	1221	F	530 842-5544	16
Gatehouse Media LLC	2711	E	530 842-5777	5641
Madrone Hospice Inc	3231	E	530 842-2547	10377
Nor-Cal Products Inc (DH)	3494	C	530 842-4457	13361
Ozotech Inc (PA)	3589	F	530 842-4189	15555
Shasta Forest Products Inc (PA)	2499	E	530 842-0527	4532
Shasta Forest Products Inc	2499	E	530 842-2787	4533
Timber Products Co Ltd Partnr	2435	C	530 842-2310	4283
Yreka Transit Mix Concrete	3273	F	530 842-4351	10874

YUBA CITY, CA - Sutter County

	SIC	EMP	PHONE	ENTRY #
A & A Ready Mixed Concrete Inc	3273	F	530 671-1220	10673
Am-Par Manufacturing Co Inc	3599	F	530 671-1800	15735
Big Hill Logging & Rd Building (PA)	2411	E	530 673-4155	3875
Business Fulfillment Svcs Inc	2752	E	530 671-7006	6462
California Industrial Rbr Co	2822	E	530 674-2444	7626
California Olive and Vine LLC	2079	E	530 763-7921	1467
California Resources Prod Corp	1311	E	530 671-8201	40
Chipco Manufacturing Co Inc	3599	F	530 751-8150	15844
Eagle Moulding Company 1 (PA)	2431	E	530 673-6517	4041
Mathews Ready Mix LLC	3273	E	530 671-2400	10800
Orchard Machinery Corporation (PA)	3523	D	530 673-2822	13655
Organic Mattresses Inc	2515	E	530 790-6723	4734
Pacific Sunshine Enterprises	3999	F	530 673-1888	23439
Sharpe Software Inc	7372	F	530 671-6499	24404
Siller Brothers Inc (PA)	2411	D	530 673-0734	3907
Sunsweet Growers Inc (PA)	2034	A	800 417-2253	870
Unity Forest Products Inc	2431	E	530 671-7152	4144
Valley Fine Foods Company Inc	2099	D	530 671-7200	2644
Valley View Foods Inc	2033	D	530 673-7356	833
Vandorn Plastering	3299	F	530 671-2748	11022
Yuba City Steel Products Co	3441	E	530 673-4554	11923
Yuba Cy Wste Wtr Trtmnt Fcilty	3589	E	530 822-7698	15608

YUCAIPA, CA - San Bernardino County

	SIC	EMP	PHONE	ENTRY #
Accountants Edge Software Svcs (PA)	7372	F	800 689-6932	23547
Dentsply Sirona Inc	3843	D	909 795-2080	22146
Hi-Desert Publishing Company	2711	E	909 797-9101	5663
SCC Chemical Corporation	2812	F	909 796-8369	7392
Sorenson Engineering Inc (PA)	3451	C	909 795-2434	12651
Technical Resource Industries (PA)	3643	E	909 446-1109	16933

YUCCA VALLEY, CA - San Bernardino County

	SIC	EMP	PHONE	ENTRY #
Catalyst Development Corp	7372	E	760 228-9653	23723
Hi-Desert Publishing Company (HQ)	2711	D	760 365-3315	5665
R3 Performance Products Inc	3714	F	760 364-3001	19750

ZAMORA, CA - Yolo County

	SIC	EMP	PHONE	ENTRY #
Crew Wine Company LLC	2084	F	530 662-1032	1654

Employment Codes: A=Over 500 employees, B=251-500,
C=101-250, D=51-100, E=20-50, F=10-19

2020 California
Manufacturers Register

© Mergent Inc. 1-800-342-5647

1451

GEOGRAPHIC